1995 edition
standard catalog of

WORLD COINS

by Chester L. Krause and Clifford Mishler - Colin R. Bruce II, Editor

Marian S.Moe
Coordinating Editor

Thomas Michael
Market Analyst

Robert Wilhite
U.S. Market Analyst

Fred Borgmann
New Issues Editor

Alan Herbert
Technical Consultant

Samuel Lachman
Ladislav Sin
Special Consultants

Joan Melum
Project Coordinator

UNCIRCULATED VALUATIONS

The uncirculated valuations represented in this edition are for typical quality specimens; for some of the more popularly collected series. Brilliant uncirculated (BU), or superior quality examples may easily command 10% to 50% premiums, or even greater where particularly popular or rare types or dates are concerned. **Exceptions:** The MS-60, MS-63, MS-64 and MS-65 grades are indicated in selected areas of the United States section.

BULLION VALUE (BV) MARKET VALUATIONS

Valuations for all platinum, gold, palladium or silver coins of the more common, basically bullion types, or those possessing only modest numismatic premiums are presented in this edition based on market levels of $395 per ounce for platinum, $375 for gold, $130 for palladium and $5 per ounce for silver. Wherever the letters "BV" – Bullion Value – appear in a value column, that particular issue in the condition indicated generally trades at or near the bullion value of its precious metal content. Further information on using this catalog to evaluate platinum, gold, palladium or silver coins amid fluctuating precious metal market conditions is presented on page 28.

A taste of every sort of knowledge is necessary to form the mind, and is the only way to give the understanding its due improvement to the full extent of its capacity. – Locke.

twenty - second edition
standard catalog of

WORLD COINS

Published in the United States by

700 E. State St., Iola, WI 54990-0001
Phone: 715-445-2214 • FAX: 715-445-4087

Library of Congress Catalog Card Number: 79-640940
International Standard Book Number: 0-87341-281-8

Printed in the United States of America

TABLE OF CONTENTS

ADVERTISING INDEX

INTRODUCTION

More than twenty years have passed since the first 800 page edition of the *Standard Catalog of World Coins* was published — embracing approximately 120 years of coinage listings, from the mid-1800s to 1971 — providing collectors with their first single volume, comprehensive source of world coinage information arranged by dates and mints of issue.

This 22nd edition — numbering 2216 pages and almost embracing two centuries of world coinage, from 1800 through early 1994 — has become the numismatic community's number one reference. Such has been the magnitude of the expansion and enhancement of the listings incorporated through the intervening years, that the present volume has made all previous editions obsolete.

The arrangement of the *Standard Catalog* has been, from the beginning, such that it ably suits the needs of both the novice, seeking basic guidance in the direction of his efforts, and the advanced collectors, requiring detailed coverage differentiating the scarce and rare varieties of coinage types. The detailed instant identifier, monogram and varied index pages, coupled with the liberally illustrated listings, assure its friendliness to even a first time user.

This edition shares with its predecssors the fact that it is, first and foremost, "basically a compilation of the digested knowledge which students of numismatic science have contributed to the coin collecting hobby through the years," as stated in the first edition introduction. Secondarily, however, original contributions incorporated into its page down through the years have also substantially expanded the realm of awareness.

The editors accept, however, as was acknowledged with publication of the first edition, "the unavoidable fact that, like other references, this work will have its errors and shortcomings." While a multitude of corrections and refinements have been incorporated from edition to edition, a call made in the first edition is no less valid today than it was then; "The reach is for perfection, however, and in seeking to attain that end each collector purchasing a copy of this catalog is invited — *make that encouraged* — to offer criticism pointing up errors or omissions."

As the breadth and depth of world coin collecting interests continue to develop, the staff that presents the *Standard Catalog of World Coins* is committed to expanding its scope and detail to meet, lead and serve the evolution which unfolds through the years to come.

We are looking forward to producing many more editions holding forth promises of experiences that will be no less challenging, and will be rewarding in the equal of that realized from those now past.

ACKNOWLEDGEMENTS

Many hundreds of individuals have contributed countless valuable contributions which have been incorporated in this twenty-second edition. While all can not be so acknowledged, special appreciation is extended to the following principal authors, contributors and organizations who have exhibited a special dedication — revising and verifying historical and technical data and coin listings, reviewing market valuations and loaning coins for photographing — for this edition.

Dr. Lawrence A. Adams
Esko Ahlroth
Kevin Akin
Luis Alandy
Stephen Album
Antonio Alessandrini
Burnett Anderson
Jim Anderson
Norman I. Applebaum
Robert Archer
Adrian Ataman
Don Bailey
Paul Baker
Cem Barlock
Yuri Barshay
George M. Beach
Dr. Bernd Becker
Dr. Anton Belcev
Richard Benson
Peter N. Berger
Allan G. Berman
Robert O. Bertelson
Wolfgang Bertsch
C. H. Blackburn
Joseph Boling
Al Boulanger
B.F. Brekke
Irv Brotman
Robert Burg
Davis Burnett, Jr.
Theodore V. Buttrey
Ferrán Calicó
Xavier Calicó
Ralph A. Cannito
Michael D. Carter
Douglas S. Cass
Carlos Castan
Juan R. Cayon
K.H. Chan
Peter A. Chase
Anthony Cole
Scott E. Cordry
Freeman Craig, Jr.
Jerry Crain
Joseph Cribb
Jed Crump
George Cuhaj
Arnaldo J. Cunietti-Ferrando
John S. Davenport
Dolores H. Davis
J.R. DeMey
Robert Diedrich
Jean-Paul Divo
Andrzej Dobrowolski
Yossi Dotan
Kevin L. Doyle
Frederic Droulers
Michael J. Druck
Graham P. Dyer
Dr. Jan M. Dyroff
Stephen D. Eccles
Wilhelm Eglseer
Esko Ekman
Daniel L. Erwin
George Falcke
John Ferm
George A. Fisher, Jr.
Horace P. Flatt
Joe Flores
Luis H. Flores
Arthur Friedberg
Victor Gadoury (deceased)
Tom Galway
Gary Ganguillet
Edward J. Ganister
Morris Geiger
Eng. Lajos Gergely
Dennis Gill
Wojciecm Gogolinski
Lawrence S. Goldberg
Mark Goldberg
Alberto Gomes
Ralph C. Gordan
Bruce Griffith
Dr. G.R. Gruber
Mario Gutierrez Minera
Marcel Häberling
Ray Hackett
Edmond Hakimian
Hakim Hamidi
Brian Hannon
David Harrison
Martin Rodney Hayter
Istvan Hegedus
Leon Hendrickson
Hans Herrli
Anton Holt
Charles R. Hosch
Nicolae Hridan
Serge Huard
Clyde Hubbard
Louis Hudson
Charles L. Huff
Curtis Iverson
Larry Jackson
Prof Norman Jacobs
Ton Jacobs
A.K. Jain
Chester R. Johnson
Robert Johnston
Werner H. Jorg
William M. Judd
Robert W. Julian
William S. Kable
Alex Kaglyan
Henry V. Karolkiewicz
John M. Kleeberg
Jean Koetz
Lawrence C. Korchnak
Peter Kraneveld
Harold Kritzman
Kurt R. Krueger
Russell Kruzell
Prashant P. Kulkarni
Ricardo Kuthe
Joseph E. Lang
Joseph R. Lasser
Peter Last
Lee Shin Song
Dave Liljestrand
George Lill III
Jan Lingen
Richard Lobel
James Lorah
Alan Luedeking
Odd Lund
Ma Tak Wo
Kenneth MacKenzie
Enrico Manara
Ranko Mandic
Steven Mansdorf
Harrington Manville
Richard Margolis
Virg Marshall III
John B. McCaugherty
Robert T. McIntire
Balazs Meekesh (Mikes)
Ulf Mietens
Jurgen Mikeska
Dr. William J.D. Mira
Robert Mish
Lazar Mishev
Dr. Richard Montrey
E.J. Moschetti
R. Paul Nadin-Davis
Hitoshi Nagai
Oen Nelson
N. Douglas Nicol
Andrew Oberbilig
William O'Connor
Alex Oguy-D.PH
Frank Olrog
Krzysztof Panuciak
Gus A. Pappas
Jim Payette
Jens Pilegaard
Rick Ponterio
M. Angel Pratt Mayans
Paul Puckett
Dr. S.K. Punshi
Bill Randel
Tony Raymond
Leo Reich
Nicholas Rhodes
Alistair F. Robb
Dana Roberts
Dr. K.A. Rodgers
Jay Roe
Maurice Rosen
Jon Ross
Jose Luis Rubio
Russell Rulau
Arnaldo Russo
John Sacher
Gerhard Schön
Dr. Wolfgang Schuster
Michael Sedgwick
Frank Sedwick
David E. Seelye
Dale Seppa
Frovin Sieg
Arlie R. Slabaugh
Marian C. Smith
Lester D. Snell
Jorgen Somod
Wm. F. Spengler
Robert Steinberg
Richard Stuart
Dr. Vladimir Suchy
Alim A. Sumana
James O. Sweeny
M. Louis Teller
Guillermo Triana Aguiar
Joaquin Trigo
Antonio M. Trigueiros
David Tucker
Warren Tucker
Jan W. Vandersande
J.J. Van Grover
Erik J. Van Loon
J. Ferraro Vaz
Zdenek Vesely
David Vice
Edmundo F. Vicente
Igor Victorov-Orlov
Justin C.Wang
William B. Warden, Jr.
John Wells
Paul C. Welz
Stewart Westdal
J.H. Witherow
Augusto Wing
Richard Wright
Ertekin Yenisey
Joseph Zaffern
Ran Zander

AUCTION HOUSES

Leu Numismatics Ltd
Bowers & Merena Inc.
Frankfurter Münzhandlung
Giessener Münzhandlung
Glendinings
Adolph Hess Ag
Fritz Rudolf Künker
Münzhandlung Möller
Numismatik Lanz (Munich)
H.D. Rauch
Laurens Schulman
Sotheby's
Spink & Son Ltd.
Spink Noble Numismatics
Stack's
Superior Galleries
Swiss Bank Corp.
Taisei Stamps & Coins
A.G. Van Der Dussen, B.V.
World Wide Coins of CA

SOCIETIES and INSTITUTIONS

American Numismatic Association
American Numismatic Society
British Museum
Johns Hopkins University
Numismatics International
Smithsonian Institution

PUBLICATION

The Statesman's Year-Book, 1993-94, 130th Edition.
by Brian Hunter, editor, The Statesman's Year-Book Office, The Macmillan Press Ltd., Little Essex St., London WC2 R3LF, England. (Statistical and Historical Annual of the States Of The World — used in preparation of emerging republics' introductions).

STANDARD INTERNATIONAL NUMERAL SYSTEMS

PREPARED ESPECIALLY FOR THE STANDARD CATALOG OF WORLD COINS © 1994 BY KRAUSE PUBLICATIONS

WESTERN	0	½	1	2	3	4	5	6	7	8	9	10	50	100	500	1000
ROMAN			I	II	III	IV	V	VI	VII	VIII	IX	X	L	C	D	M
ARABIC-TURKISH	٠	١/٢	١	٢	٣	٤	٥	٦	٧	٨	٩	١٠	٥٠	١٠٠	٥٠٠	١٠٠٠
MALAY—PERSIAN	٠	١/٢	١	٢	٣	۴	۵	٦ or ۶	٧	٨	٩	١٠	۵٠	١٠٠	۵٠٠	١٠٠٠
EASTERN ARABIC	0	½	۱	۲	۳	۴	۵	۶	۷	۸	۹	10	۵0	100	۵00	1000
HYDERABAD ARABIC	0	١/٢	١	٢	٣	۴	۵	۶	۷	۸	۹	10	۵0	100	۵00	1000
INDIAN (Sanskrit)	०	१/२	१	२	३	४	५	६	७	८	९	१०	५०	१००	५००	१०००
ASSAMESE	০	১/২	১	২	৩	৪	৫	৬	৭	৮	৯	১০	৫০	১০০	৫০০	১০০০
BENGALI	০	১/২	১	২	৩	৪	৫	৬	৭	৮	৯	১০	৫০	১০০	৫০০	১০০০
GUJARATI	૦	૧/૨	૧	૨	૩	૪	૫	૬	૭	૮	૯	૧૦	૫૦	૧૦૦	૫૦૦	૧૦૦૦
KUTCH	0	1/२	1	२	३	४	५	६	७	८	९	10	५0	100	५00	1000
DEVAVNAGRI	०	९/२	९	२	३	४	५	६ or ६	७	८	९ or ९	९०	५०	९००	५००	९०००
NEPALESE	०	१/२	१ or १	२	३	४	५ or ५	६	७	८ or ८	९ or ९ or ९	१०	५०	१००	५००	१०००
TIBETAN	༠	༡/༢	༡	༢	༣	༤	༥	༦	༧	༨	༩	༡༠	༥༠	༡༠༠	༥༠༠	༡༠༠༠
MONGOLIAN	᠐	᠑/᠒	᠑	᠒	᠓	᠔	᠕	᠖	᠗	᠘	᠙	᠑᠐	᠕᠐	᠑᠐᠐	᠕᠐᠐	᠑᠐᠐᠐
BURMESE	၀	၁/၂	၁	၂	၃	၄	၅	၆	၇	၈	၉	၁၀	၅၀	၁၀၀	၅၀၀	၁၀၀၀
THAI-LAO	๐	๑/๒	๑	๒	๓	๔	๕	๖	๗	๘	๙	๑๐	๕๐	๑๐๐	๕๐๐	๑๐๐๐
JAVANESE	꧐		꧑	꧒	꧓	꧔	꧕	꧖	꧗	꧘	꧙	꧑꧐	꧕꧐	꧑꧐꧐	꧕꧐꧐	꧑꧐꧐꧐
ORDINARY CHINESE JAPANESE-KOREAN	零	半	一	二	三	四	五	六	七	八	九	十	十五	百	百五	千
OFFICIAL CHINESE			壹	貳	叁	肆	伍	陸	柒	捌	玖	拾	拾伍	佰	佰伍	仟
COMMERCIAL CHINESE			〡	〢	〣	〤	〥	〦	〧	〨	〩	十	〥十	〡百	〥百	〡千
KOREAN		반	일	이	삼	사	오	육	칠	팔	구	십	오십	백	오백	천
GEORGIAN			ა	ბ	გ	დ	ე	ვ	ზ	ჱ	თ	ი	ნ	რ	უ	ჩ
			[11] ია	[20] კ	[30] ლ	[40] მ	[50] ნ	[60] ჲ	[70] ო	[80] პ	[90] ჟ	[100] რ	[200] ს [300] ტ	[400] ჳ	[600] ფ [700] ქ	[800] ღ
ETHIOPIAN	◆		፩	፪	፫	፬	፭	፮	፯	፰	፱	፲	፶	፻	፭፻	፲፻
				[20] ፳	[30] ፴	[40] ፵		[60] ፷	[70] ፸	[80] ፹	[90] ፺					
HEBREW			א	ב	ג	ד	ה	ו	ז	ח	ט	י	נ	ק	תק	
				[20] כ	[30] ל	[40] מ		[60] ס	[70] ע	[80] פ	[90] צ	[200] ר	[300] ש	[400] ת	[600] תר [700] תש	[800] תת
GREEK			Α	Β	Γ	Δ	Ε	ΣΤ	Ζ	Η	Θ	Ι	Ν	Ρ	Φ	Α
				[20] Κ	[30] Λ	[40] Μ	[60] Ξ	[70] Ο	[80] Π		[200] Σ	[300] Τ	[400] Υ	[600] Χ	[700] Ψ	[800] Ω

WANTED CHINA

We BUY CHINA for our retail clientele. As the leading dealer in Taiwan, we are in a position to pay a higher price than dealers who wholesale their purchases overseas. We will meet or beat all legitimate buying prices. As Chinese can be complicated going far beyond Krause, NOT everyone knows the material. We have the ability to place your material to the final customer whether it is a common item or a unique pattern. We also have strong needs for all better Asian material from Japan, Korea, Hong Kong, Straits Settlements, Thailand, and Philippines. Please offer us your better world coins and banknotes. Simply contact us at our New York location by phone, FAX, letter or simply send for our top offer. Please include your phone number so we can discuss your holdings. We also service collector's wantlists, please contact us in New York. When in Taiwan visit us at our location in Taipei or Tainan. Some sample prices:

Please check with us for current and other prices.

Empire Dollar 1907 K212 Ch.BU ..$1500+	Pavilion K676.1 large characters Ch.BU 1500+, K676 Ch.BU ....750.
1932 Birds y344 Ch.BU ....350.	Wedding Y336.1 large characters Ch.BU 1500+, Y336 Ch.BU ....750.
Kiangnan Y145 1898 Ch.BU ....$1500+,	Kwangtung Dollar Y198.1 (1889) pattern BU 50,000, Y198 proof .... 12,000+
Taiwan set 1965 (4) perfect box ....38.	
Kiangnan Y144a 50 cents 1899 ....3000+, 1900 2000+, Y144 Ch.BU ....1200+	

TAIWAN BANK NOTES P938-975, R1001-1043 PAYING UP TO 200% IN CU. Also buying other notes and lower grades. Ship or Call.

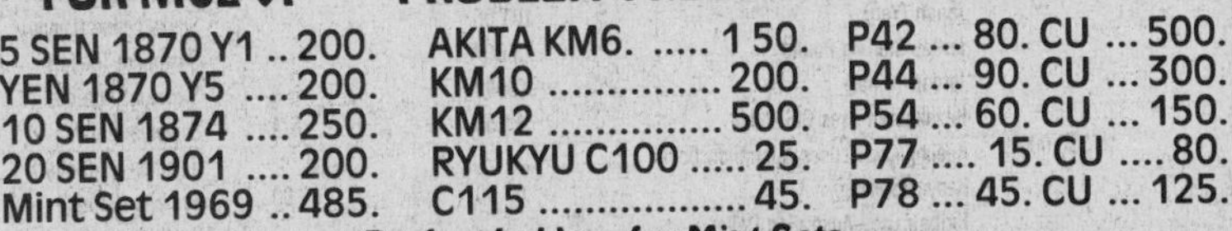

JAPAN PRICES FOR NICE VF	PROVINCIAL COINAGE PROBLEM-FREE FINE	BANK NOTES NICE VF
5 SEN 1870 Y1 .. 200.	AKITA KM6. ..... 1 50.	P42 ... 80. CU ... 500.
YEN 1870 Y5 .... 200.	KM10 .... 200.	P44 ... 90. CU ... 300.
10 SEN 1874 .... 250.	KM12 .... 500.	P54 ... 60. CU ... 150.
20 SEN 1901 .... 200.	RYUKYU C100 ..... 25.	P77 .... 15. CU .... 80.
Mint Set 1969 .. 485.	C115 .... 45.	P78 ... 45. CU ... 125.

Perfect holders for Mint Sets.
Other type and grade wanted. Paid more for better grade and variety.
Buying all better Japanese orders.

KOREA		BANK NOTES
5 Yang VF-EF ....1250.	10 hwan 1959 RED BU ...20.	P41 VF ....300. CU .... 750.
1 WARN Y3 AU ..12,000+	5 WON 1967 GEM BU ....5.	P37 CU .... 1000.
3 CHON VF-EF ....450.		S. KOREA P16 CU .. 50. P18 CU .. 750.
½ WON VF ....90.		P20 CU .... 200. P22 .... 100.

Fu Chin Numistmatic Journal is to be introduced at the ANA convention in Detroit, Michigan. The journal will be edited by Bruce Smith and issued on a bi-monthly basis with an average of 60-70 pages. The format will consist of articles, primarily in English, on Asian numismatics with a concentration on Chinese topics. Every issue will also include a mail bid sale. Please contact us on subscription, advertising and consignment information at Dept FM at our NY location. **A new catalog on Chinese coins will be published in Taiwan by Fu Chin Coins & Stamps and made available in fall 1994.**

Annual Subscription (U.S. only) $35.00

Fu Chin International is at your service. You can meet us at one of the many shows we attend or we can visit you on large holdings. Please contact Michael or Peter Chou at our New York location.

SHOW SCHEDULE 1994-1995

FEB., JUNE, OCTOBER - Long Beach Numismatics Convention
JUNE, DECEMBER - NYIC Sheraton, New York
JUNE - Memphis Paper Convention TN, Baltimore
JULY - Pre-ANA Dearborn, MI, ANA Convention, Detroit, MI
SEPTEMBER - HKIC Hong Kong, Boston International, East Expo NJ
OCTOBER - Coinex London, England, Munich, Germany, Baltimore
NOVEMBER - St. Louis Paper Fair, Michigan State Dearborn, MI
DECEMBER - Tokyo, Japan
JANUARY - Fun Orlando, Florida
FEBRUARY - Singapore
MARCH - Munich Germany, Baltimore
APRIL - Masstrich Paper Fair, Holland, CICF Chicago
MAY - TICC Tokyo, Japan

Contact Or Ship To: **FU CHIN INTERNATIONAL**
P.O. Box 9229, Niskayuna, NY 12309-0229 USA
Phone (518) 382-8888 • FAX (518) 382-1451

Visit Us At: **FU CHIN COINS & STAMPS**
28 Yen Ping S. Road, Taipei, Taiwan ROC (02) 312-1761
80 Lu Ning Road, Tainan, Taiwan ROC (06) 225-0812

Foreign Exchange Table

The latest foreign exchange fixed rates below apply to trade with banks in the country of origin. Courtesy of Monetary Research International, Houston, Texas as of May 5, 1994.

Country	US $	#/$
Abu Dhabi uses U.A.E. Dirham		
Afghanistan (Afghani)	500.00	1,700
Ajman uses U.A.E. Dirham		
Albania (Lek)	110.00	—
Alderney uses British Pound		
Algeria (Dinar)	24.00	100.00
Andorra uses French Franc and Spanish Peseta		
Angola (Novo Kwanza)	120,000	130,000
Anguilla uses E.C. Dollar	2.67	—
Antigua uses E.C. Dollar	2.67	—
Argentina (New Peso)	.99	—
Armenia (Dram)	175.00	180.00
Aruba (Florin)	1.79	—
Australia (Dollar)	1.39	—
Austria (Schilling)	12.08	—
Azerbaijan (Manat)	350.00	—
Azores uses Portuguese Escudo		
Bahamas (Dollar)	1.00	—
Bahrain Is. (Dinar)	.3770	—
Bangladesh (Taka)	40.20	42.50
Barbados (Dollar)	1.98	2.05
Belarus (Ruble)	7,000	—
Belgium (Franc)	35.30	—
Belize (Dollar)	1.98	2.05
Benin uses CFA Franc West	592.00	—
Bermuda (Dollar)	1.00	—
Bhutan (Ngultrum)	31.30	33.00
Bolivia (Boliviano)	4.52	—
Bosnia-Herzegovina, Moslem	N/A	N/A
Serbian (New Dinar)	N/A	N/A
Botswana (Pula)	2.61	—
Brazil (Cruzeiro real)	660.00	—
British Virgin Islands uses U.S. Dollar	1.00	—
Brunei Darussalam (Dollar)	1.58	—
Bulgaria (Lev)	37.30	—
Burkina Faso uses CFA Fr. West	584.00	—
Burundi (Franc)	259.00	330.00
Byelorussia uses CIS Ruble		
Cambodia (Riel)	2,700	—
Cameroon uses CFA Franc Central	584.00	595.00
Canada (Dollar)	1.3882	—
Cape Verde (Escudo)	74.20	80.00
Cayman Is. (Dollar)	.833	—
Central African Rep. (Franc)	584.00	595.00
CFA Franc Central	584.00	595.00
CFA Franc West	584.00	595.00
CFP Franc	106.18	—
Chad uses CFA Franc Central	584.00	595.00
Chile (Peso)	430.00	—
China, P.R. (R. Yuan)	5.80	8.70
Colombia (Peso)	780.00	—
Comm. Indep. State (Ruble)		
Comoros (Franc)	439.09	—
Congo uses Franc CFA Central	584.00	595.00
Cook Islands (Dollar)	1.7343	—
Costa Rica (Colon)	152.00	—
Croatia (Dinar)	6,289	—
Croatia-Krajina/Dinar	N/A	N/A
Cuba (Peso)	7575	132.00
Cyprus (Pound)	5155	—
Czech. (Koruna)	29.90	31.50
Denmark (Krona)	6.73	—
Djibouti (Franc)	178.00	—
Dominica uses E.C. Dollar	2.67	—
Dom. Rep. (Peso)	12.75	—
Dubai uses U.A.E. Dirham		
East Caribbean (Dollar)	2.67	—
Ecuador (Sucre)	2,080	—
Egypt (Pound)	3.39	—
El Salvador (Colon)	8.75	—
Equatorial Guinea uses CFA Fr Central	584.00	595.00
Eritrea, see Ethiopia		
Estonia (Kroon)	13.74	—
Ethiopia (Birr)	5.00	6.50
Falkland Is. (Pound)	.6607	—
Faroe Islands (Krona)	6.73	—
Fiji Islands (Dollar)	1.4848	—
Finland (Markka)	5.56	—
France (Franc)	5.84	—
French Pacific Terr. (Franc)		
French Polynesia uses Franc CFP	107.27	—
Fujairah uses U.A.E. Dirham		
Gabon (Franc)	584.00	595.00
Gambia (Dalasi)	9.45	—
Georgia	140,000	—
Germany (D. Mark)	1.6370	—
Ghana (New Cedi)	900.00	—
Gibraltar (Pound)	.6607	—
Great Britain (Pound)	.6607	—
Greece (Drachma)	249.00	236.00
Greenland uses Denmark		
Grenada uses East Carib. Dollar	2.67	—
Guadeloupe uses French Franc		
Guatemala (Quetzal)	5.70	—
Guernsey uses Sterling Pound	.6607	—
Guinea-Bissau (Peso)	10,000	12,000
Guinea Conakry (Fanc)	976.00	—
Guyana (Dollar)	128.00	—
Haiti (Gourde)	12.50	14.00
Honduras (Lempira)	7.30	7.70
Hong Kong (Dollar)	7.73	—
Hungary (Forint)	104.40	—
Iceland (New Krona)	73.10	—
India (Rupee)	31.30	—
Indonesia (Rupiah)	2,140	—
Iran (Rial)	1,750	2,220
Iraq (Dinar)	.3125	220.00
Ireland (Punt)	1.42	—
Ireland, N. (Pound)		
Isle of Man uses Sterling Pound	.6607	—
Israel (New Shekel)	2.99	—
Italy (Lira)	1,685	—
Ivory Coast uses CFA Franc West	584.00	—
Jamaica (Dollar)	33.25	34.00
Japan (Yen)	101.05	—
Jersey Sterling Pound	.6607	—
Jordan (Dinar)	.6993	—
Kazakhstan uses CIS Ruble	11.50	N/A
Keeling Cocos uses Australian Dollar		
Kenya (Shilling)	67.10	68.00
Kiribati uses Australian Dollar	—	—
Korea-PDR (Won)	2.15	50.00
Korea-Repub. (Won)	808.00	—
Kuwait (Dinar)	.2970	—
Kyrgyzstan (Som)	11.43	12.50
Laos (Kip)	720.00	—
Latvia (Lat)	.58	—
Lebanon (Pound)	1701	—
Lesotho (Maloti)	3.47	4.00
Liberia (Dollar)	1.00	15.00
Libya (Dinar)	.3225	1.20
Liechtenstein uses Swiss Franc		
Lithuania (Litas)	3.90	—
Luxembourg (Franc)	35.30	—
Macao (Pataca)	7.98	—
Macedonia (New Denar)	47.14	—
Madagascar (Franc)	1,880	2,300
Maldives (Rufiya)	11.10	—
Malawi (Kwacha)	6.23	7.00
Malaysia (Ringgit)	2.72	—
Mali uses CFA West Franc	584.00	594.00
Malta (Lira)	.3922	—
Marshall Islands uses U.S. Dollar		
Martinique uses French Franc		
Mauritania (Ouguiya)	120.00	130.00
Mauritius (Rupee)	18.45	—
Mexico (New Peso)	3.26	—
Moldova (Leu)	4.10	—
Monaco uses French Franc		
Mongolia (Tugrik)	360.00	—
Montenegro uses Yugo Super Dinar		
Montserrat uses E.C. Dollar	2.67	—
Morocco (Dirham)	9.42	9.80
Mozambique (Metical)	5,390	6,000
Myanmar (Burma) (Kyat)	6.25	100.00
Nambia (Dollar)	3.47	4.00
Nauru uses Australian Dollar		
Nepal (Rupee)	46.30	—
Netherlands (Gulden)	1.92	—
Netherlands Antilles (Gulden)	1.79	—
New Caledonia uses CFP Franc		
New Zealand (Dollar)	1.734	—
Nicaragua (Cordoba Oro)	6.45	—
Niger uses CFA Franc West	584.00	595.00
Nigeria (Naira)	22.00	41.00
Northern Ireland uses Sterling Pound	1.4850	—
Norway (Krone)	7.45	—
Oman (Rial)	.3850	—
Pakistan (Rupee)	30.50	—
Palau uses U.S. Dollar		
Panama (Balboa) uses U.S. Dollar		
Papua-New Guinea (Kina)	.9550	—
Paraguay (Guarani)	1,793	—
Peru (Nuevo Sol)	2.18	—
Philippines (Piso)	27.70	—
Poland (Zloty)	22,000	—
Portugal (Escudo)	174,50	—
Puerto Rico uses U.S. Dollar		
Qatar (Riyal)	3.63	—
Ras Al Khaima uses U.A.E.Dirham		
Reunion uses French Franc		
Romania (Leu)	1,570	—
Russia (Ruble)	1,635	—
Rwanda (Franc)	145.00	190.00
St. Helena (Pound)	.6607	—
St. Kitts uses E.C. Dollar	2.67	—
St. Lucia uses E.C. Dollar	2.67	—
St. Pierre & Miquelon uses French Franc		
St. Thomas & Prince (Dobra)		
St. Vincent uses E.C.S. Dollar	2.67	—
San Marino uses Italian Lira		
Sao Tome e Principe (Dobra)	240.00	—
Saudi Arabia (Riyal)	3.75	—
Scotland uses Sterling Pound	.6607	—
Senegal uses CFA Franc West	584.00	595.00
Seychelles (Rupee)	5.23	—
Sierra Leone (Leone)	560.00	600.00
Singapore (Dollar)	1.58	—
Slovakia (Koruna)	33.15	34.50
Slovenia (Tolar)	135.00	—
Solomon Is. (Dollar)	3.24	—
Somalia (Somali)	2,620	3,500
South Africa (Rand)	3.47	4.00
Spain (Peseta)	139.75	—
Spanish West Africa uses Spanish Peseta		
Sri Lanka (Rupee)	49.00	—
Sudan (Dinar)	13.00	45.00
Surinam (Gulden)	142.00	165.00
Swaziland (Lilangeni)	3.47	4.00
Sweden (Krona)	7.99	—
Switzerland (Franc)	1.42	—
Syria (Pound)	42.00	50.00
Tahiti (Franc)		
Taiwan (NT Dollar)	26.40	—
Tajikistan uses Russian Ruble		
Tanzania (Shilling)	482.00	490.00
Thailand (Baht)	25.30	—
Togo uses CFA Franc West	584.00	595.00
Tonga (Pa'anga)	1.39	—
Trinidad & Tobago (Dollar)	5.65	—
Tristan Da Cunha uses Great Britain Pound		
Tunisia (Dinar)	1.03	1.10
Turkey (Lira)	19,300	—
Turkmenistan (Manat)	1.97	12.50
Turks & Caicos uses U.S. Dollar		
Tuvalu uses Australian Dollar		
Uganda (Shilling)	1,075	—
Ukraine (Karbovanets)	37,000	100,000
Umm Al Qaiwan uses U.A.E. Dirham		
United Arab Emirates (Dirham)	3.67	—
Uruguay (Peso Uruguayo)	4.56	—
Uzbekistan (Som)	1,200	3,600
Vanuatu (Vatu)	118.00	—
Vatican City uses Italian Lira		
Venezuela (Bolivar)	111.00	—
Vietnam (Dong)	10,840	—
Western Samoa (Tala)	2.61	—
Yemen (North)/Rial	12.00	63.00
Yemen South (Dinar)	.4609	N/A
Yugoslavia (Super Dinar)	1.7180	—
Zaire (New Zaire)	35.00	110.00
Zambia (Kwacha)	648.00	—
Zimbabwe (Dollar)	8.06	—

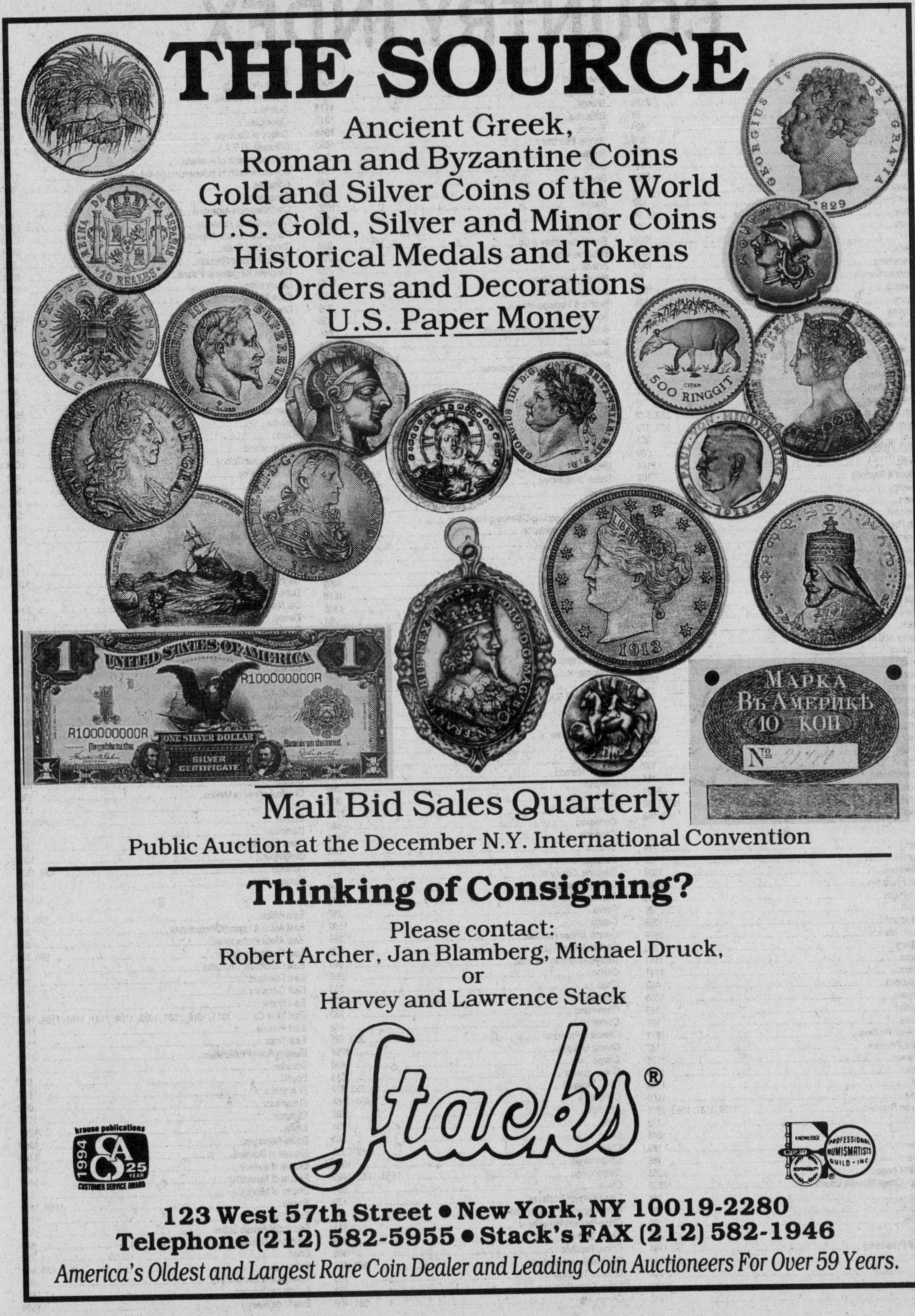

COUNTRY INDEX

T

U

V

W

X

Y

Z

Silver Bullion Chart

Oz.	3.000	3.500	4.000	4.500	5.000	5.500	6.000	6.500	7.000	7.500	8.000	8.500	9.000	9.500	10.000	10.500	Oz.
0.001	0.003	0.004	0.004	0.005	0.005	0.006	0.006	0.007	0.007	0.008	0.008	0.009	0.009	0.010	0.010	0.011	0.001
0.002	0.006	0.007	0.008	0.009	0.010	0.011	0.012	0.013	0.014	0.015	0.016	0.017	0.018	0.019	0.020	0.021	0.002
0.003	0.009	0.011	0.012	0.014	0.015	0.017	0.018	0.020	0.021	0.023	0.024	0.026	0.027	0.029	0.030	0.032	0.003
0.004	0.012	0.014	0.016	0.018	0.020	0.022	0.024	0.026	0.028	0.030	0.032	0.034	0.036	0.038	0.040	0.042	0.004
0.005	0.015	0.018	0.020	0.023	0.025	0.028	0.030	0.033	0.035	0.038	0.040	0.043	0.045	0.048	0.050	0.053	0.005
0.006	0.018	0.021	0.024	0.027	0.030	0.033	0.036	0.039	0.042	0.045	0.048	0.051	0.054	0.057	0.060	0.063	0.006
0.007	0.021	0.025	0.028	0.032	0.035	0.039	0.042	0.046	0.049	0.053	0.056	0.060	0.063	0.067	0.070	0.074	0.007
0.008	0.024	0.028	0.032	0.036	0.040	0.044	0.048	0.052	0.056	0.060	0.064	0.068	0.072	0.076	0.080	0.084	0.008
0.009	0.027	0.032	0.036	0.041	0.045	0.050	0.054	0.059	0.063	0.068	0.072	0.077	0.081	0.086	0.090	0.095	0.009
0.010	0.030	0.035	0.040	0.045	0.050	0.055	0.060	0.065	0.070	0.075	0.080	0.085	0.090	0.095	0.100	0.105	0.010
0.020	0.060	0.070	0.080	0.090	0.100	0.110	0.120	0.130	0.140	0.150	0.160	0.170	0.180	0.190	0.200	0.210	0.020
0.030	0.090	0.105	0.120	0.135	0.150	0.165	0.180	0.195	0.210	0.225	0.240	0.255	0.270	0.285	0.300	0.315	0.030
0.040	0.120	0.140	0.160	0.180	0.200	0.220	0.240	0.260	0.280	0.300	0.320	0.340	0.360	0.380	0.400	0.420	0.040
0.050	0.150	0.175	0.200	0.225	0.250	0.275	0.300	0.325	0.350	0.375	0.400	0.425	0.450	0.475	0.500	0.525	0.050
0.060	0.180	0.210	0.240	0.270	0.300	0.330	0.360	0.390	0.420	0.450	0.480	0.510	0.540	0.570	0.600	0.630	0.060
0.070	0.210	0.245	0.280	0.315	0.350	0.385	0.420	0.455	0.490	0.525	0.560	0.595	0.630	0.665	0.700	0.735	0.070
0.080	0.240	0.280	0.320	0.360	0.400	0.440	0.480	0.520	0.560	0.600	0.640	0.680	0.720	0.760	0.800	0.840	0.080
0.090	0.270	0.315	0.360	0.405	0.450	0.495	0.540	0.585	0.630	0.675	0.720	0.765	0.810	0.855	0.900	0.945	0.090
0.100	0.300	0.350	0.400	0.450	0.500	0.550	0.600	0.650	0.700	0.750	0.800	0.850	0.900	0.950	1.000	1.050	0.100
0.110	0.330	0.385	0.440	0.495	0.550	0.605	0.660	0.715	0.770	0.825	0.880	0.935	0.990	1.045	1.100	1.155	0.110
0.120	0.360	0.420	0.480	0.540	0.600	0.660	0.720	0.780	0.840	0.900	0.960	1.020	1.080	1.140	1.200	1.260	0.120
0.130	0.390	0.455	0.520	0.585	0.650	0.715	0.780	0.845	0.910	0.975	1.040	1.105	1.170	1.235	1.300	1.365	0.130
0.140	0.420	0.490	0.560	0.630	0.700	0.770	0.840	0.910	0.980	1.050	1.120	1.190	1.260	1.330	1.400	1.470	0.140
0.150	0.450	0.525	0.600	0.675	0.750	0.825	0.900	0.975	1.050	1.125	1.200	1.275	1.350	1.425	1.500	1.575	0.150
0.160	0.480	0.560	0.640	0.720	0.800	0.880	0.960	1.040	1.120	1.200	1.280	1.360	1.440	1.520	1.600	1.680	0.160
0.170	0.510	0.595	0.680	0.765	0.850	0.935	1.020	1.105	1.190	1.275	1.360	1.445	1.530	1.615	1.700	1.785	0.170
0.180	0.540	0.630	0.720	0.810	0.900	0.990	1.080	1.170	1.260	1.350	1.440	1.530	1.620	1.710	1.800	1.890	0.180
0.190	0.570	0.665	0.760	0.855	0.950	1.045	1.140	1.235	1.330	1.425	1.520	1.615	1.710	1.805	1.900	1.995	0.190
0.200	0.600	0.700	0.800	0.900	1.000	1.100	1.200	1.300	1.400	1.500	1.600	1.700	1.800	1.900	2.000	2.100	0.200
0.210	0.630	0.735	0.840	0.945	1.050	1.155	1.260	1.365	1.470	1.575	1.680	1.785	1.890	1.995	2.100	2.205	0.210
0.220	0.660	0.770	0.880	0.990	1.100	1.210	1.320	1.430	1.540	1.650	1.760	1.870	1.980	2.090	2.200	2.310	0.220
0.230	0.690	0.805	0.920	1.035	1.150	1.265	1.380	1.495	1.610	1.725	1.840	1.955	2.070	2.185	2.300	2.415	0.230
0.240	0.720	0.840	0.960	1.080	1.200	1.320	1.440	1.560	1.680	1.800	1.920	2.040	2.160	2.280	2.400	2.520	0.240
0.250	0.750	0.875	1.000	1.125	1.250	1.375	1.500	1.625	1.750	1.875	2.000	2.125	2.250	2.375	2.500	2.625	0.250
0.260	0.780	0.910	1.040	1.170	1.300	1.430	1.560	1.690	1.820	1.950	2.080	2.210	2.340	2.470	2.600	2.730	0.260
0.270	0.810	0.945	1.080	1.215	1.350	1.485	1.620	1.755	1.890	2.025	2.160	2.295	2.430	2.565	2.700	2.835	0.270
0.280	0.840	0.980	1.120	1.260	1.400	1.540	1.680	1.820	1.960	2.100	2.240	2.380	2.520	2.660	2.800	2.940	0.280
0.290	0.870	1.015	1.160	1.305	1.450	1.595	1.740	1.885	2.030	2.175	2.320	2.465	2.610	2.755	2.900	3.045	0.290
0.300	0.900	1.050	1.200	1.350	1.500	1.650	1.800	1.950	2.100	2.250	2.400	2.550	2.700	2.850	3.000	3.150	0.300
0.310	0.930	1.085	1.240	1.395	1.550	1.705	1.860	2.015	2.170	2.325	2.480	2.635	2.790	2.945	3.100	3.255	0.310
0.320	0.960	1.120	1.280	1.440	1.600	1.760	1.920	2.080	2.240	2.400	2.560	2.720	2.880	3.040	3.200	3.360	0.320
0.330	0.990	1.155	1.320	1.485	1.650	1.815	1.980	2.145	2.310	2.475	2.640	2.805	2.970	3.135	3.300	3.465	0.330
0.340	1.020	1.190	1.360	1.530	1.700	1.870	2.040	2.210	2.380	2.550	2.720	2.890	3.060	3.230	3.400	3.570	0.340
0.350	1.050	1.225	1.400	1.575	1.750	1.925	2.100	2.275	2.450	2.625	2.800	2.975	3.150	3.325	3.500	3.675	0.350
0.360	1.080	1.260	1.440	1.620	1.800	1.980	2.160	2.340	2.520	2.700	2.880	3.060	3.240	3.420	3.600	3.780	0.360
0.370	1.110	1.295	1.480	1.665	1.850	2.035	2.220	2.405	2.590	2.775	2.960	3.145	3.330	3.515	3.700	3.885	0.370
0.380	1.140	1.330	1.520	1.710	1.900	2.090	2.280	2.470	2.660	2.850	3.040	3.230	3.420	3.610	3.800	3.990	0.380
0.390	1.170	1.365	1.560	1.755	1.950	2.145	2.340	2.535	2.730	2.925	3.120	3.315	3.510	3.705	3.900	4.095	0.390
0.400	1.200	1.400	1.600	1.800	2.000	2.200	2.400	2.600	2.800	3.000	3.200	3.400	3.600	3.800	4.000	4.200	0.400
0.410	1.230	1.435	1.640	1.845	2.050	2.255	2.460	2.665	2.870	3.075	3.280	3.485	3.690	3.895	4.100	4.305	0.410
0.420	1.260	1.470	1.680	1.890	2.100	2.310	2.520	2.730	2.940	3.150	3.360	3.570	3.780	3.990	4.200	4.410	0.420
0.430	1.290	1.505	1.720	1.935	2.150	2.365	2.580	2.795	3.010	3.225	3.440	3.655	3.870	4.085	4.300	4.515	0.430
0.440	1.320	1.540	1.760	1.980	2.200	2.420	2.640	2.860	3.080	3.300	3.520	3.740	3.960	4.180	4.400	4.620	0.440
0.450	1.350	1.575	1.800	2.025	2.250	2.475	2.700	2.925	3.150	3.375	3.600	3.825	4.050	4.275	4.500	4.725	0.450
0.460	1.380	1.610	1.840	2.070	2.300	2.530	2.760	2.990	3.220	3.450	3.680	3.910	4.140	4.370	4.600	4.830	0.460
0.470	1.410	1.645	1.880	2.115	2.350	2.585	2.820	3.055	3.290	3.525	3.760	3.995	4.230	4.465	4.700	4.935	0.470
0.480	1.440	1.680	1.920	2.160	2.400	2.640	2.880	3.120	3.360	3.600	3.840	4.080	4.320	4.560	4.800	5.040	0.480
0.490	1.470	1.715	1.960	2.205	2.450	2.695	2.940	3.185	3.430	3.675	3.920	4.165	4.410	4.655	4.900	5.145	0.490
0.500	1.500	1.750	2.000	2.250	2.500	2.750	3.000	3.250	3.500	3.750	4.000	4.250	4.500	4.750	5.000	5.250	0.500
0.510	1.530	1.785	2.040	2.295	2.550	2.805	3.060	3.315	3.570	3.825	4.080	4.335	4.590	4.845	5.100	5.355	0.510
0.520	1.560	1.820	2.080	2.340	2.600	2.860	3.120	3.380	3.640	3.900	4.160	4.420	4.680	4.940	5.200	5.460	0.520
0.530	1.590	1.855	2.120	2.385	2.650	2.915	3.180	3.445	3.710	3.975	4.240	4.505	4.770	5.035	5.300	5.565	0.530
0.540	1.620	1.890	2.160	2.430	2.700	2.970	3.240	3.510	3.780	4.050	4.320	4.590	4.860	5.130	5.400	5.670	0.540
0.550	1.650	1.925	2.200	2.475	2.750	3.025	3.300	3.575	3.850	4.125	4.400	4.675	4.950	5.225	5.500	5.775	0.550
0.560	1.680	1.960	2.240	2.520	2.800	3.080	3.360	3.640	3.920	4.200	4.480	4.760	5.040	5.320	5.600	5.880	0.560
0.570	1.710	1.995	2.280	2.565	2.850	3.135	3.420	3.705	3.990	4.275	4.560	4.845	5.130	5.415	5.700	5.985	0.570
0.580	1.740	2.030	2.320	2.610	2.900	3.190	3.480	3.770	4.060	4.350	4.640	4.930	5.220	5.510	5.800	6.090	0.580
0.590	1.770	2.065	2.360	2.655	2.950	3.245	3.540	3.835	4.130	4.425	4.720	5.015	5.310	5.605	5.900	6.195	0.590
0.600	1.800	2.100	2.400	2.700	3.000	3.300	3.600	3.900	4.200	4.500	4.800	5.100	5.400	5.700	6.000	6.300	0.600
0.610	1.830	2.135	2.440	2.745	3.050	3.355	3.660	3.965	4.270	4.575	4.880	5.185	5.490	5.795	6.100	6.405	0.610
0.620	1.860	2.170	2.480	2.790	3.100	3.410	3.720	4.030	4.340	4.650	4.960	5.270	5.580	5.890	6.200	6.510	0.620
0.630	1.890	2.205	2.520	2.835	3.150	3.465	3.780	4.095	4.410	4.725	5.040	5.355	5.670	5.985	6.300	6.615	0.630
0.640	1.920	2.240	2.560	2.880	3.200	3.520	3.840	4.160	4.480	4.800	5.120	5.440	5.760	6.080	6.400	6.720	0.640
0.650	1.950	2.275	2.600	2.925	3.250	3.575	3.900	4.225	4.550	4.875	5.200	5.525	5.850	6.175	6.500	6.825	0.650
0.660	1.980	2.310	2.640	2.970	3.300	3.630	3.960	4.290	4.620	4.950	5.280	5.610	5.940	6.270	6.600	6.930	0.660
0.670	2.010	2.345	2.680	3.015	3.350	3.685	4.020	4.355	4.690	5.025	5.360	5.695	6.030	6.365	6.700	7.035	0.670
0.680	2.040	2.380	2.720	3.060	3.400	3.740	4.080	4.420	4.760	5.100	5.440	5.780	6.120	6.460	6.800	7.140	0.680
0.690	2.070	2.415	2.760	3.105	3.450	3.795	4.140	4.485	4.830	5.175	5.520	5.865	6.210	6.555	6.900	7.245	0.690
0.700	2.100	2.450	2.800	3.150	3.500	3.850	4.200	4.550	4.900	5.250	5.600	5.950	6.300	6.650	7.000	7.350	0.700
0.710	2.130	2.485	2.840	3.195	3.550	3.905	4.260	4.615	4.970	5.325	5.680	6.035	6.390	6.745	7.100	7.455	0.710
0.720	2.160	2.520	2.880	3.240	3.600	3.960	4.320	4.680	5.040	5.400	5.760	6.120	6.480	6.840	7.200	7.560	0.720
0.730	2.190	2.555	2.920	3.285	3.650	4.015	4.380	4.745	5.110	5.475	5.840	6.205	6.570	6.935	7.300	7.665	0.730
0.740	2.220	2.590	2.960	3.330	3.700	4.070	4.440	4.810	5.180	5.550	5.920	6.290	6.660	7.030	7.400	7.770	0.740
0.750	2.250	2.625	3.000	3.375	3.750	4.125	4.500	4.875	5.250	5.625	6.000	6.375	6.750	7.125	7.500	7.875	0.750
0.760	2.280	2.660	3.040	3.420	3.800	4.180	4.560	4.940	5.320	5.700	6.080	6.460	6.840	7.220	7.600	7.980	0.760
0.770	2.310	2.695	3.080	3.465	3.850	4.235	4.620	5.005	5.390	5.775	6.160	6.545	6.930	7.315	7.700	8.085	0.770
0.780	2.340	2.730	3.120	3.510	3.900	4.290	4.680	5.070	5.460	5.850	6.240	6.630	7.020	7.410	7.800	8.190	0.780
0.790	2.370	2.765	3.160	3.555	3.950	4.345	4.740	5.135	5.530	5.925	6.320	6.715	7.110	7.505	7.900	8.295	0.790
0.800	2.400	2.800	3.200	3.600	4.000	4.400	4.800	5.200	5.600	6.000	6.400	6.800	7.200	7.600	8.000	8.400	0.800
0.810	2.430	2.835	3.240	3.645	4.050	4.455	4.860	5.265	5.670	6.075	6.480	6.885	7.290	7.695	8.100	8.505	0.810
0.820	2.460	2.870	3.280	3.690	4.100	4.510	4.920	5.330	5.740	6.150	6.560	6.970	7.380	7.790	8.200	8.610	0.820
0.830	2.490	2.905	3.320	3.735	4.150	4.565	4.980	5.395	5.810	6.225	6.640	7.055	7.470	7.885	8.300	8.715	0.830
0.840	2.520	2.940	3.360	3.780	4.200	4.620	5.040	5.460	5.880	6.300	6.720	7.140	7.560	7.980	8.400	8.820	0.840
0.850	2.550	2.975	3.400	3.825	4.250	4.675	5.100	5.525	5.950	6.375	6.800	7.225	7.650	8.075	8.500	8.925	0.850
0.860	2.580	3.010	3.440	3.870	4.300	4.730	5.160	5.590	6.020	6.450	6.880	7.310	7.740	8.170	8.600	9.030	0.860
0.870	2.610	3.045	3.480	3.915	4.350	4.785	5.220	5.655	6.090	6.525	6.960	7.395	7.830	8.265	8.700	9.135	0.870
0.880	2.640	3.080	3.520	3.960	4.400	4.840	5.280	5.720	6.160	6.600	7.040	7.480	7.920	8.360	8.800	9.240	0.880
0.890	2.670	3.115	3.560	4.005	4.450	4.895	5.340	5.785	6.230	6.675	7.120	7.565	8.010	8.455	8.900	9.345	0.890
0.900	2.700	3.150	3.600	4.050	4.500	4.950	5.400	5.850	6.300	6.750	7.200	7.650	8.100	8.550	9.000	9.450	0.900
0.910	2.730	3.185	3.640	4.095	4.550	5.005	5.460	5.915	6.370	6.825	7.280	7.735	8.190	8.645	9.100	9.555	0.910
0.920	2.760	3.220	3.680	4.140	4.600	5.060	5.520	5.980	6.440	6.900	7.360	7.820	8.280	8.740	9.200	9.660	0.920
0.930	2.790	3.255	3.720	4.185	4.650	5.115	5.580	6.045	6.510	6.975	7.440	7.905	8.370	8.835	9.300	9.765	0.930
0.940	2.820	3.290	3.760	4.230	4.700	5.170	5.640	6.110	6.580	7.050	7.520	7.990	8.460	8.930	9.400	9.870	0.940
0.950	2.850	3.325	3.800	4.275	4.750	5.225	5.700	6.175	6.650	7.125	7.600	8.075	8.550	9.025	9.500	9.975	0.950
0.960	2.880	3.360	3.840	4.320	4.800	5.280	5.760	6.240	6.720	7.200	7.680	8.160	8.640	9.120	9.600	10.080	0.960
0.970	2.910	3.395	3.880	4.365	4.850	5.335	5.820	6.305	6.790	7.275	7.760	8.245	8.730	9.215	9.700	10.185	0.970
0.980	2.940	3.430	3.920	4.410	4.900	5.390	5.880	6.370	6.860	7.350	7.840	8.330	8.820	9.310	9.800	10.290	0.980
0.990	2.970	3.465	3.960	4.455	4.950	5.445	5.940	6.435	6.930	7.425	7.920	8.415	8.910	9.405	9.900	10.395	0.990
1.000	3.000	3.500	4.000	4.500	5.000	5.500	6.000	6.500	7.000	7.500	8.000	8.500	9.000	9.500	10.000	10.500	1.000

Gold and Platinum Bullion Chart

oz.	350.00	360.00	370.00	380.00	390.00	400.00	410.00	420.00	430.00	440.00	450.00	460.00	470.00	480.00	490.00	
0.001	0.35	0.36	0.37	0.38	0.39	0.40	0.41	0.42	0.43	0.44	0.45	0.46	0.47	0.48	0.49	0.001
0.002	0.70	0.72	0.74	0.76	0.78	0.80	0.82	0.84	0.86	0.88	0.90	0.92	0.94	0.96	0.98	0.002
0.003	1.05	1.08	1.11	1.14	1.17	1.20	1.23	1.26	1.29	1.32	1.35	1.38	1.41	1.44	1.47	0.003
0.004	1.40	1.44	1.48	1.52	1.56	1.60	1.64	1.68	1.72	1.76	1.80	1.84	1.88	1.92	1.96	0.004
0.005	1.75	1.80	1.85	1.90	1.95	2.00	2.05	2.10	2.15	2.20	2.25	2.30	2.35	2.40	2.45	0.005
0.006	2.10	2.16	2.22	2.28	2.34	2.40	2.46	2.52	2.58	2.64	2.70	2.76	2.82	2.88	2.94	0.006
0.007	2.45	2.52	2.59	2.66	2.73	2.80	2.87	2.94	3.01	3.08	3.15	3.22	3.29	3.36	3.43	0.007
0.008	2.80	2.88	2.96	3.04	3.12	3.20	3.28	3.36	3.44	3.52	3.60	3.68	3.76	3.84	3.92	0.008
0.009	3.15	3.24	3.33	3.42	3.51	3.60	3.69	3.78	3.87	3.96	4.05	4.14	4.23	4.32	4.41	0.009
0.010	3.50	3.60	3.70	3.80	3.90	4.00	4.10	4.20	4.30	4.40	4.50	4.60	4.70	4.80	4.90	0.010
0.020	7.00	7.20	7.40	7.60	7.80	8.00	8.20	8.40	8.60	8.80	9.00	9.20	9.40	9.60	9.80	0.020
0.030	10.50	10.80	11.10	11.40	11.70	12.00	12.30	12.60	12.90	13.20	13.50	13.80	14.10	14.40	14.70	0.030
0.040	14.00	14.40	14.80	15.20	15.60	16.00	16.40	16.80	17.20	17.60	18.00	18.40	18.80	19.20	19.60	0.040
0.050	17.50	18.00	18.50	19.00	19.50	20.00	20.50	21.00	21.50	22.00	22.50	23.00	23.50	24.00	24.50	0.050
0.060	21.00	21.60	22.20	22.80	23.40	24.00	24.60	25.20	25.80	26.40	27.00	27.60	28.20	28.80	29.40	0.060
0.070	24.50	25.20	25.90	26.60	27.30	28.00	28.70	29.40	30.10	30.80	31.50	32.20	32.90	33.60	34.30	0.070
0.080	28.00	28.80	29.60	30.40	31.20	32.00	32.80	33.60	34.40	35.20	36.00	36.80	37.60	38.40	39.20	0.080
0.090	31.50	32.40	33.30	34.20	35.10	36.00	36.90	37.80	38.70	39.60	40.50	41.40	42.30	43.20	44.10	0.090
0.100	35.00	36.00	37.00	38.00	39.00	40.00	41.00	42.00	43.00	44.00	45.00	46.00	47.00	48.00	49.00	0.100
0.110	38.50	39.60	40.70	41.80	42.90	44.00	45.10	46.20	47.30	48.40	49.50	50.60	51.70	52.80	53.90	0.110
0.120	42.00	43.20	44.40	45.60	46.80	48.00	49.20	50.40	51.60	52.80	54.00	55.20	56.40	57.60	58.80	0.120
0.130	45.50	46.80	48.10	49.40	50.70	52.00	53.30	54.60	55.90	57.20	58.50	59.80	61.10	62.40	63.70	0.130
0.140	49.00	50.40	51.80	53.20	54.60	56.00	57.40	58.80	60.20	61.60	63.00	64.40	65.80	67.20	68.60	0.140
0.150	52.50	54.00	55.50	57.00	58.50	60.00	61.50	63.00	64.50	66.00	67.50	69.00	70.50	72.00	73.50	0.150
0.160	56.00	57.60	59.20	60.80	62.40	64.00	65.60	67.20	68.80	70.40	72.00	73.60	75.20	76.80	78.40	0.160
0.170	59.50	61.20	62.90	64.60	66.30	68.00	69.70	71.40	73.10	74.80	76.50	78.20	79.90	81.60	83.30	0.170
0.180	63.00	64.80	66.60	68.40	70.20	72.00	73.80	75.60	77.40	79.20	81.00	82.80	84.60	86.40	88.20	0.180
0.190	66.50	68.40	70.30	72.20	74.10	76.00	77.90	79.80	81.70	83.60	85.50	87.40	89.30	91.20	93.10	0.190
0.200	70.00	72.00	74.00	76.00	78.00	80.00	82.00	84.00	86.00	88.00	90.00	92.00	94.00	96.00	98.00	0.200
0.210	73.50	75.60	77.70	79.80	81.90	84.00	86.10	88.20	90.30	92.40	94.50	96.60	98.70	100.80	102.90	0.210
0.220	77.00	79.20	81.40	83.60	85.80	88.00	90.20	92.40	94.60	96.80	99.00	101.20	103.40	105.60	107.80	0.220
0.230	80.50	82.80	85.10	87.40	89.70	92.00	94.30	96.60	98.90	101.20	103.50	105.80	108.10	110.40	112.70	0.230
0.240	84.00	86.40	88.80	91.20	93.60	96.00	98.40	100.80	103.20	105.60	108.00	110.40	112.80	115.20	117.60	0.240
0.250	87.50	90.00	92.50	95.00	97.50	100.00	102.50	105.00	107.50	110.00	112.50	115.00	117.50	120.00	122.50	0.250
0.260	91.00	93.60	96.20	98.80	101.40	104.00	106.60	109.20	111.80	114.40	117.00	119.60	122.20	124.80	127.40	0.260
0.270	94.50	97.20	99.90	102.60	105.30	108.00	110.70	113.40	116.10	118.80	121.50	124.20	126.90	129.60	132.30	0.270
0.280	98.00	100.80	103.60	106.40	109.20	112.00	114.80	117.60	120.40	123.20	126.00	128.80	131.60	134.40	137.20	0.280
0.290	101.50	104.40	107.30	110.20	113.10	116.00	118.90	121.80	124.70	127.60	130.50	133.40	136.30	139.20	142.10	0.290
0.300	105.00	108.00	111.00	114.00	117.00	120.00	123.00	126.00	129.00	132.00	135.00	138.00	141.00	144.00	147.00	0.300
0.310	108.50	111.60	114.70	117.80	120.90	124.00	127.10	130.20	133.30	136.40	139.50	142.60	145.70	148.80	151.90	0.310
0.320	112.00	115.20	118.40	121.60	124.80	128.00	131.20	134.40	137.60	140.80	144.00	147.20	150.40	153.60	156.80	0.320
0.330	115.50	118.80	122.10	125.40	128.70	132.00	135.30	138.60	141.90	145.20	148.50	151.80	155.10	158.40	161.70	0.330
0.340	119.00	122.40	125.80	129.20	132.60	136.00	139.40	142.80	146.20	149.60	153.00	156.40	159.80	163.20	166.60	0.340
0.350	122.50	126.00	129.50	133.00	136.50	140.00	143.50	147.00	150.50	154.00	157.50	161.00	164.50	168.00	171.50	0.350
0.360	126.00	129.60	133.20	136.80	140.40	144.00	147.60	151.20	154.80	158.40	162.00	165.60	169.20	172.80	176.40	0.360
0.370	129.50	133.20	136.90	140.60	144.30	148.00	151.70	155.40	159.10	162.80	166.50	170.20	173.90	177.60	181.30	0.370
0.380	133.00	136.80	140.60	144.40	148.20	152.00	155.80	159.60	163.40	167.20	171.00	174.80	178.60	182.40	186.20	0.380
0.390	136.50	140.40	144.30	148.20	152.10	156.00	159.90	163.80	167.70	171.60	175.50	179.40	183.30	187.20	191.10	0.390
0.400	140.00	144.00	148.00	152.00	156.00	160.00	164.00	168.00	172.00	176.00	180.00	184.00	188.00	192.00	196.00	0.400
0.410	143.50	147.60	151.70	155.80	159.90	164.00	168.10	172.20	176.30	180.40	184.50	188.60	192.70	196.80	200.90	0.410
0.420	147.00	151.20	155.40	159.60	163.80	168.00	172.20	176.40	180.60	184.80	189.00	193.20	197.40	201.60	205.80	0.420
0.430	150.50	154.80	159.10	163.40	167.70	172.00	176.30	180.60	184.90	189.20	193.50	197.80	202.10	206.40	210.70	0.430
0.440	154.00	158.40	162.80	167.20	171.60	176.00	180.40	184.80	189.20	193.60	198.00	202.40	206.80	211.20	215.60	0.440
0.450	157.50	162.00	166.50	171.00	175.50	180.00	184.50	189.00	193.50	198.00	202.50	207.00	211.50	216.00	220.50	0.450
0.460	161.00	165.60	170.20	174.80	179.40	184.00	188.60	193.20	197.80	202.40	207.00	211.60	216.20	220.80	225.40	0.460
0.470	164.50	169.20	173.90	178.60	183.30	188.00	192.70	197.40	202.10	206.80	211.50	216.20	220.90	225.60	230.30	0.470
0.480	168.00	172.80	177.60	182.40	187.20	192.00	196.80	201.60	206.40	211.20	216.00	220.80	225.60	230.40	235.20	0.480
0.490	171.50	176.40	181.30	186.20	191.10	196.00	200.90	205.80	210.70	215.60	220.50	225.40	230.30	235.20	240.10	0.490
0.500	175.00	180.00	185.00	190.00	195.00	200.00	205.00	210.00	215.00	220.00	225.00	230.00	235.00	240.00	245.00	0.500
0.510	178.50	183.60	188.70	193.80	198.90	204.00	209.10	214.20	219.30	224.40	229.50	234.60	239.70	244.80	249.90	0.510
0.520	182.00	187.20	192.40	197.60	202.80	208.00	213.20	218.40	223.60	228.80	234.00	239.20	244.40	249.60	254.80	0.520
0.530	185.50	190.80	196.10	201.40	206.70	212.00	217.30	222.60	227.90	233.20	238.50	243.80	249.10	254.40	259.70	0.530
0.540	189.00	194.40	199.80	205.20	210.60	216.00	221.40	226.80	232.20	237.60	243.00	248.40	253.80	259.20	264.60	0.540
0.550	192.50	198.00	203.50	209.00	214.50	220.00	225.50	231.00	236.50	242.00	247.50	253.00	258.50	264.00	269.50	0.550
0.560	196.00	201.60	207.20	212.80	218.40	224.00	229.60	235.20	240.80	246.40	252.00	257.60	263.20	268.80	274.40	0.560
0.570	199.50	205.20	210.90	216.60	222.30	228.00	233.70	239.40	245.10	250.80	256.50	262.20	267.90	273.60	279.30	0.570
0.580	203.00	208.80	214.60	220.40	226.20	232.00	237.80	243.60	249.40	255.20	261.00	266.80	272.60	278.40	284.20	0.580
0.590	206.50	212.40	218.30	224.20	230.10	236.00	241.90	247.80	253.70	259.60	265.50	271.40	277.30	283.20	289.10	0.590
0.600	210.00	216.00	222.00	228.00	234.00	240.00	246.00	252.00	258.00	264.00	270.00	276.00	282.00	288.00	294.00	0.600
0.610	213.50	219.60	225.70	231.80	237.90	244.00	250.10	256.20	262.30	268.40	274.50	280.60	286.70	292.80	298.90	0.610
0.620	217.00	223.20	229.40	235.60	241.80	248.00	254.20	260.40	266.60	272.80	279.00	285.20	291.40	297.60	303.80	0.620
0.630	220.50	226.80	233.10	239.40	245.70	252.00	258.30	264.60	270.90	277.20	283.50	289.80	296.10	302.40	308.70	0.630
0.640	224.00	230.40	236.80	243.20	249.60	256.00	262.40	268.80	275.20	281.60	288.00	294.40	300.80	307.20	313.60	0.640
0.650	227.50	234.00	240.50	247.00	253.50	260.00	266.50	273.00	279.50	286.00	292.50	299.00	305.50	312.00	318.50	0.650
0.660	231.00	237.60	244.20	250.80	257.40	264.00	270.60	277.20	283.80	290.40	297.00	303.60	310.20	316.80	323.40	0.660
0.670	234.50	241.20	247.90	254.60	261.30	268.00	274.70	281.40	288.10	294.80	301.50	308.20	314.90	321.60	328.30	0.670
0.680	238.00	244.80	251.60	258.40	265.20	272.00	278.80	285.60	292.40	299.20	306.00	312.80	319.60	326.40	333.20	0.680
0.690	241.50	248.40	255.30	262.20	269.10	276.00	282.90	289.80	296.70	303.60	310.50	317.40	324.30	331.20	338.10	0.690
0.700	245.00	252.00	259.00	266.00	273.00	280.00	287.00	294.00	301.00	308.00	315.00	322.00	329.00	336.00	343.00	0.700
0.710	248.50	255.60	262.70	269.80	276.90	284.00	291.10	298.20	305.30	312.40	319.50	326.60	333.70	340.80	347.90	0.710
0.720	252.00	259.20	266.40	273.60	280.80	288.00	295.20	302.40	309.60	316.80	324.00	331.20	338.40	345.60	352.80	0.720
0.730	255.50	262.80	270.10	277.40	284.70	292.00	299.30	306.60	313.90	321.20	328.50	335.80	343.10	350.40	357.70	0.730
0.740	259.00	266.40	273.80	281.20	288.60	296.00	303.40	310.80	318.20	325.60	333.00	340.40	347.80	355.20	362.60	0.740
0.750	262.50	270.00	277.50	285.00	292.50	300.00	307.50	315.00	322.50	330.00	337.50	345.00	352.50	360.00	367.50	0.750
0.760	266.00	273.60	281.20	288.80	296.40	304.00	311.60	319.20	326.80	334.40	342.00	349.60	357.20	364.80	372.40	0.760
0.770	269.50	277.20	284.90	292.60	300.30	308.00	315.70	323.40	331.10	338.80	346.50	354.20	361.90	369.60	377.30	0.770
0.780	273.00	280.80	288.60	296.40	304.20	312.00	319.80	327.60	335.40	343.20	351.00	358.80	366.60	374.40	382.20	0.780
0.790	276.50	284.40	292.30	300.20	308.10	316.00	323.90	331.80	339.70	347.60	355.50	363.40	371.30	379.20	387.10	0.790
0.800	280.00	288.00	296.00	304.00	312.00	320.00	328.00	336.00	344.00	352.00	360.00	368.00	376.00	384.00	392.00	0.800
0.810	283.50	291.60	299.70	307.80	315.90	324.00	332.10	340.20	348.30	356.40	364.50	372.60	380.70	388.80	396.90	0.810
0.820	287.00	295.20	303.40	311.60	319.80	328.00	336.20	344.40	352.60	360.80	369.00	377.20	385.40	393.60	401.80	0.820
0.830	290.50	298.80	307.10	315.40	323.70	332.00	340.30	348.60	356.90	365.20	373.50	381.80	390.10	398.40	406.70	0.830
0.840	294.00	302.40	310.80	319.20	327.60	336.00	344.40	352.80	361.20	369.60	378.00	386.40	394.80	403.20	411.60	0.840
0.850	297.50	306.00	314.50	323.00	331.50	340.00	348.50	357.00	365.50	374.00	382.50	391.00	399.50	408.00	416.50	0.850
0.860	301.00	309.60	318.20	326.80	335.40	344.00	352.60	361.20	369.80	378.40	387.00	395.60	404.20	412.80	421.40	0.860
0.870	304.50	313.20	321.90	330.60	339.30	348.00	356.70	365.40	374.10	382.80	391.50	400.20	408.90	417.60	426.30	0.870
0.880	308.00	316.80	325.60	334.40	343.20	352.00	360.80	369.60	378.40	387.20	396.00	404.80	413.60	422.40	431.20	0.880
0.890	311.50	320.40	329.30	338.20	347.10	356.00	364.90	373.80	382.70	391.60	400.50	409.40	418.30	427.20	436.10	0.890
0.900	315.00	324.00	333.00	342.00	351.00	360.00	369.00	378.00	387.00	396.00	405.00	414.00	423.00	432.00	441.00	0.900
0.910	318.50	327.60	336.70	345.80	354.90	364.00	373.10	382.20	391.30	400.40	409.50	418.60	427.70	436.80	445.90	0.910
0.920	322.00	331.20	340.40	349.60	358.80	368.00	377.20	386.40	395.60	404.80	414.00	423.20	432.40	441.60	450.80	0.920
0.930	325.50	334.80	344.10	353.40	362.70	372.00	381.30	390.60	399.90	409.20	418.50	427.80	437.10	446.40	455.70	0.930
0.940	329.00	338.40	347.80	357.20	366.60	376.00	385.40	394.80	404.20	413.60	423.00	432.40	441.80	451.20	460.60	0.940
0.950	332.50	342.00	351.50	361.00	370.50	380.00	389.50	399.00	408.50	418.00	427.50	437.00	446.50	456.00	465.50	0.950
0.960	336.00	345.60	355.20	364.80	374.40	384.00	393.60	403.20	412.80	422.40	432.00	441.60	451.20	460.80	470.40	0.960
0.970	339.50	349.20	358.90	368.60	378.30	388.00	397.70	407.40	417.10	426.80	436.50	446.20	455.90	465.60	475.30	0.970
0.980	343.00	352.80	362.60	372.40	382.20	392.00	401.80	411.60	421.40	431.20	441.00	450.80	460.60	470.40	480.20	0.980
0.990	346.50	356.40	366.30	376.20	386.10	396.00	405.90	415.80	425.70	435.60	445.50	455.40	465.30	475.20	485.10	0.990
1.000	350.00	360.00	370.00	380.00	390.00	400.00	410.00	420.00	430.00	440.00	450.00	460.00	470.00	480.00	490.00	1.000

M FÁBRICA NACIONAL DE MONEDA Y TIMBRE DE ESPAÑA

The Fábrica Nacional de Moneda y Timbre has minted a series of four coins in the following denominations: 100, 25, 5 and 1 ECU. The obverse and reverse features classic designs that refer to the life of Miguel de Cervantes and his inmortal work "Don Quixote of the Mancha".

THE SIXTH SPANISH MINTING OF THE ECU

GOLD 10-0 ECU · 3.500 PIECES

OBVERSE

Portrait of bust of Miguel de Cervantes Saavedra (1547-1616)

REVERSE

Allegory of the fantasy wooden horse "Clavileño" on which Don Quixote and Sancho Panza are alleged to have flown to the island of Barataria.

CHARACTERISTICS	
Weight	34,55 gr.
Fineness	900/100
Silver content	31,10 gr.
Diameter	40 mm.
Edge	reeded
Quality	Flor de cuño

SILVER 25 ECU · 15.000 PIECES

OBVERSE

Naval battle of Lepanto between the Armada of the Holy league and the Ottoman fleet, at which Cervantes lost an arm and earned the nickname "Manco de Lepanto".

REVERSE

Building of the University of Alcalá de Henares, Cervantes' home town, an important Plateresque building of the first Spanish Renaissance.

CHARACTERISTICS	
Weight	168,75 gr.
Fineness	925/100
Silver content.	157,25 gr.
Diameter	73 mm.
Edge	plain
Quality	Flor de cuño

SILVER 5 ECU · 75.000 PIECES

OBVERSE

Portrait of bust of Miguel de Cervantes Saavedra (1547-1616)

REVERSE

Allegory of the monument to Cervantes erected at the Plaza de España in Madrid, based on a work by Coullaut Valera.

CHARACTERISTICS	
Weight	33,62 gr.
Fineness	925/100
Silver content	31,10 gr.
Diameter	42 mm.
Edge	reeded
Quality	Flor de cuño

SILVER 5 ECU · 125.000 PIECES

OBVERSE

Allegory of Don Quixote with greyhound, based on a work by Ignacio Zuloaga

REVERSE

Typical landscape of the flat plain of La Mancha. (Campo de Criptana).

CHARACTERISTICS	
Weight	6,72 gr.
Fineness	925/100
Silver content	6,22 gr.
Diameter	24 mm.
Edge	reeded
Quality	Flor de cuño

EARLIER ISSUES

1989: 100, 50, 10 ECU (gold); 5, 1 ECU (silver)
1990: 5 ECU (silver)
1991: 5 ECU (silver)
1992: 100 ECU (gold); 25, 5, 1 ECU (silver)
1993: 100 ECU (gold); 5 ECU (silver)

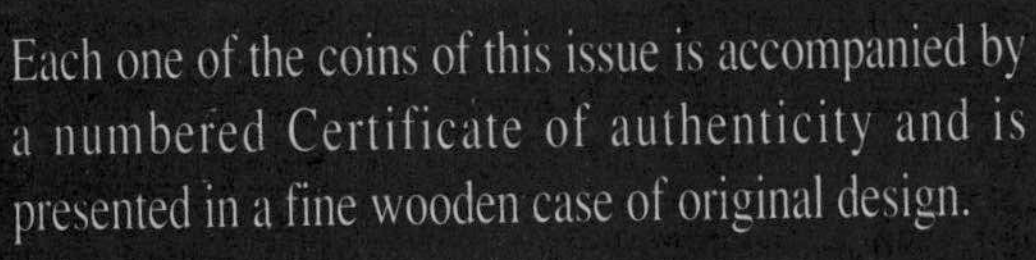

EXCLUSIVE OFFICIAL WORLD DISTRIBUTOR
S.D.F,N. SERVICIOS DOCUMENTALES FILATELICOS Y NUMISMÁTICOS
MADRID (SPAIN)
Telephone: (91) 562 52 77. Fax: (91) 562 70 96
Adviser of the Fábrica Nacional de Moneda y Timbre

HOW TO USE THIS CATALOG

This catalog is designed to serve the needs of both the novice and advanced collectors. It provides a comprehensive guide to over 392 years of world coinage. It is generally arranged so that persons with no more than a basic knowledge of world history after 1800 and a casual acquaintance with coin collecting can consult it with confidence and ease. The following explanations summarize the general practices used in preparing this catalog's listings. However, because of specialized requirements which may vary by country and era, these must not be considered ironclad. Where these standards have been set aside, appropriate notations of the variations are incorporated.

ARRANGEMENT

All coin listings are alphabetically arranged in a historical-geographic approach according to the current identity of the sovereign government concerned. Thus, the coins of Persia can be located by referring to the listings for Iran, or the now defunct Union of Soviet Socialist Republics (U.S.S.R.) by turning to Russia. This approach has also resulted in combining the coin listings for such issuing entities as Annam, French Cochin China, Tonkin, North and South Vietnam as sub-groupings under the identity of Vietnam. Likewise, coins of North and South Korea will be found under Korea, and those of the Congo Free State, Belgian Congo, Congo Democratic Republic, Katanga and Zaire, under the latter identity.

Coins of each country are generally arranged by denomination from lowest to highest, except where arrangement by ruler, mint of issue, type or period makes a series easier to understand. Exceptions which are not readily adaptable to this traditional North American cataloging style are generally found in the more complicated series, most notably those encompassing the early issues of Afghanistan, Mughal issues of India, Indian Princely States, Iran, Nepal and the areas under the influence of the late Ottoman Empire, which are listed by ruler or by mint.

Strict date sequence of listings is also interrupted in a number of countries which have been subjected to major monetary reforms or conversion to decimal or other new currency systems. Where these considerations apply, appropriate headings are incorporated to introduce the change from one standard to another.

IDENTIFICATION

The most important step in the identification of a coin is the determination of the nation of origin. This is generally easily accomplished where English-speaking lands are concerned, however, use of the country index is sometimes required. The coins of Great Britain provide an interesting challenge. For hundreds of years the only indication of the country of origin was in the abbreviated Latin legends. In recent times there have been occasions when there has been no indication of origin. Only through the familiarity of the monarchical portraits, symbols and legends or indication of currency system are they identifiable.

The coins of many countries beyond the English-language realm, such as those of French, Italian or Spanish heritage, are also quite easy to identify through reference to their legends, which appear in the national languages based on Western alphabets. In many instances the name is spelled exactly the same in English as in the national language, such as France; while in other cases it varies only slightly, like Italia for Italy, Belgique or Belgie for Belgium, Brasil for Brazil and Danmark for Denmark.

This is not always the case, however, as in Norge for Norway, Espana for Spain, Sverige for Sweden and Helvetia for Switzerland. Some other examples include:

DEUTSCHES REICH - Germany 1873-1945
BUNDESREPUBLIC DEUTSCHLAND - Federal Republic of Germany.
DEUTSCHE DEMOKRATISCHE REPUBLIK -German Democratic Republic.
EMPIRE CHERIFIEN MAROC - Morocco.
ESTADOS UNIDOS MEXICANOS - United Mexican States (Mexico).
ETAT DU GRAND LIBAN - State of Great Lebanon (Lebanon).

Thus it can be seen there are instances in which a little schooling in the rudiments of foreign languages can be most helpful. In general, colonial possessions of countries using the Western alphabet are similarly identifiable as they often carry portraits of their current rulers, the familiar lettering, sometimes in combination with a companion designation in the local language.

Collectors have the greatest difficulty with coins that do not bear legends or dates in the Western systems. These include coins bearing Cyrillic lettering, attributable to Bulgaria, Russia, the Slavic states and Mongolia, the Greek script peculiar to Greece, Crete and the Ionian Islands; the Amharic characters of Ethiopia, or Hebrew in the case of Israel. Dragons and sunbursts along with the distinctive word characters, attribute a coin to the Oriental countries of China, Japan, Korea, Tibet, Vietnam and their component parts.

The most difficult coins to identify are those bearing only Persian or Arabic script and its derivatives, found on the issues of nations stretching in a wide swath across North Africa and East Asia, from Morocco to Indonesia, and the Indian subcontinent coinages which surely are more confusing in their vast array of Nagari, Sanskrit, Ahom, Assamese and other local dialects found on the local issues of the Indian Princely States. Although the task of identification on the more modern issues of these lands is often eased by the added presence of Western alphabet legends, a feature sometimes adopted as early as the late 19th Century, for the earlier pieces it is often necessary for the uninitiated to laboriously seek and find.

Except for the cruder issues, however, it will be found that certain characteristics and symbols featured in addition to the predominant legends are typical on coins from a given country or group of countries. The toughra monogram, for instance, occurs on some of the coins of Afghanistan, Egypt, the Sudan, Pakistan, Turkey and other areas of the late Ottoman Empire. A predominant design feature on the coins of Nepal is the trident; while neighboring Tibet features a lotus blossom or lion on many of their issues.

To assist in identification of the more difficult coins, we have assembled the *Instant Identifier and Monogram* sections presented on the following pages. They are designed to provide a point of beginning for collectors by allowing them to compare unidentified coins with photographic details from typical issues. We also suggest reference to the *Index of Coin Denominations* presented here and also the comprehensive *Country Index*, where the inscription will be found listed just as it appears on the coin for nations using the Western alphabet.

DATING

Coin dating is the final basic attribution consideration. Here, the problem can be more difficult because the reading of a coin date is subject not only to the vagaries of numeric styling, but to calendar variations caused by the observance of various religious eras or regal periods from country to country, or even within a country. Here again with the exception of the sphere from North Africa through the Orient, it will be found that most countries rely on Western date numerals and Christian (AD) era reckoning, although in a few instances, coin dating has been tied to the year of a reign or government. The Vatican, for example, dates its coinage according to the year of reign of the current pope, in addition to the Christian-era date.

Countries in the Arabic sphere generally date their coins to the Mohammedan era (AH), which commenced on July 16, 622 AD (Julian calendar), when the prophet Mohammed fled from Mecca to Medina. As their calendar is reckoned by the lunar year of 354 days, which is about three percent (precisely 2.98%) shorter than the Christian year, a formula is required to convert AH dating to its Western equivalent. To convert an AH date to the approximate AD date, subtract three percent of the AH date (round to the closest whole number) from the AH date, then add 622. A chart for converting all AH years from 1102 (Oct. 5, 1690) to 1421 (April 6, 2000) is presented on page 2216 of this volume.

The Mohammedan calendar is not always based on the lunar year (AH), however, causing some confusion, particularly in Afghanistan and Iran, where a calendar based on the solar year (SH) was introduced around 1920. These dates can be converted to AD by simply adding 621. In 1976 the government of Iran implemented a new solar calendar based on the foundation of the Iranian monarchy in 559 BC. The first year observed on the new calendar was 2535 (MS), which commenced March 20, 1976. A reversion to the traditional SH dating standards occurred a few years later.

Several different eras of reckoning, including Christian and Mohammedan (AH), have been used to date coins of the Indian subcontinent. The two basic systems are the Vikrama Samvat (VS), which dates from Oct. 18, 58 BC, and the Saka era, the origin of which is reckoned from March 3, 78 AD. Dating according to both eras appears on various coins of the area.

Coins of Thailand (Siam) are found dated by three different eras. The most predominant is the Buddhist era (BE) which originated in 543 BC. Next is the Bangkok or Ratanakosindsok (RS) era, dating from 1781 AD; followed by the Chula-Sakarat (CS) era, dating from 638 AD. The latter era originated in Burma and is used on that country's coins.

Other calendars include that of the Ethiopian era (EE) which commenced seven years, eight months after AD dating; and that of the Jewish people, which commenced on Oct. 7, 3761 BC. Korea claims a legendary dating from 2333 BC, which is acknowledged in some of its coin dating. Some coin issues of the Indonesian area carry dates determined by the Javanese Aji Saka era (AS), a calendar of 354 days (100 Javanese years equal 97 Christian or Gregorian calendar years) which can be matched to AD dating by comparing it to AH dating.

The following table indicates the year dating for the various eras which correspond to 1995 in Christian calendar reckoning, but it must be remembered that there are overlaps between the eras in some instances.

Christian era (AD) —	1995
Mohammedan era (AH) —	AH1416
Solar year (SH) —	SH1374
Monarchic Solar era (MS) —	MS2554
Vikrama Samvat (VS) —	VS2052
Saka era (SE) —	SE1917
Buddhist era (BE) —	BE2538
Bangkok era (RS) —	RS214
Chula-Sakarat era (CS) —	CS1357
Ethiopian era (EE) —	EE1987
Jewish era —	5755
Korean era —	4328
Javanese Aji Saka era (AS) —	AS1928
Fasli era (FE) —	FE1405

Coins of Oriental origin - principally Japan, Korea, China, Turkestan and Tibet and some modern gold issues of Turkey - are generally dated to the year of the government, dynasty, reign or cyclic eras, with the dates indicated in Oriental characters which usually read from right to left. In recent years, however, some dating has been according to the Christian calendar and in Western numerals. In Japan, Oriental character dating was reversed to read from left to right in Showa year 23 (1948 AD).

More detailed guides to less prevalent coin dating systems which are strictly local in nature are presented with the appropriate listings.

Some coins carry dates according to both locally observed and Christian eras. This is particularly true in the Arabic world, where the Hejira date may be indicated in Arabic numerals and the Christian date in Western numerals, or both dates represented in either form.

The date actually carried on a given coin is generally cataloged here in the first column (Date) to the right of the catalog number. If the date is not by AD reckoning, the next column (Year) indicates the date by the conventional calendar which applies, generally Christian. If an AD date appears in either column, the AD is not necessarily indicated. Era abbreviations appearing in the dating table in this section are generally shown in conjunction with the listings of coins dated in those eras.

Dates listed in either column which does not actually appear on a given coin is generally enclosed by parentheses. Undated coins are indicated by the letters ND in the date column and the estimated year of issue in parentheses.

Timing differentials between some era of reckoning particularly the 354-day Mohammedan and 365-day Christian years, cause situations whereby coins which carry dates for both eras exist bearing two year dates from one calendar combined with a single date from another.

NUMBERING SYSTEM

Some catalog numbers assigned in this volume are based on established references. This practice has been observed for two reasons: First, when world coins are listed chronologically they are basically self-cataloging; second, there was no need to confuse collectors with totally new numeric designations where appropriate systems already existed. As time progressed we found many of these established systems incomplete and inadequate and are now replaced with new KM numbers with appropriate cross-referencing.

Some of the coins listed in this catalog are identified or cross referenced by numbers

assigned by R.S. Yeoman (Y#), or slight adaptations thereof, in his *Modern World Coins*, and *Current Coins of the World*. For the pre-Yeoman dated issues, the numbers assigned by William D. Craig (C#) in his *Coins of the World* (1750-1850 period), 3rd edition, have generally been applied.

In some countries, listings are cross-referenced to Robert Friedberg's (FR#) *Gold Coins of the World* or *Coins of the British World*. Major Fred Pridmore's (P#) studies of British colonial coinage are also referenced, as are W.H. Valentine's (V#) references on the *Modern Copper Coins of the Muhammadan States*. Coins issued under the Chinese sphere of influence are assigned numbers from E. Kann's (K#) *Illustrated Catalog of Chinese Coins* and T.K. Hsu's (Su) work of similar title.

DENOMINATIONS

The second basic consideration to be met in the attribution of a coin is the determination of denomination. Since denominations are usually expressed in numeric, rather than word form on a coin, this is usually quite easily accomplished on coins from nations which use Western numerals, except in those instances where issues are devoid of any mention of face value, and denomination must be attributed by size, metallic composition or weight. Coins listed in this volume are generally illustrated in actual size. Where size is critical to proper attribution, the coin's millimeter size is indicated.

The sphere of countries stretching from North Africa through the Orient, on which numeric symbols generally unfamiliar to Westerners are employed, often provide the collector with a much greater challenge. This is particularly true on nearly all pre-20th Century issues. On some of the more modern issues, and increasingly so as the years progress, Western style numerals, usually presented in combination with the local numeric system, are becoming more commonplace on these coins.

Determination of a coin's currency system can also be valuable in attributing the issue to its country of origin. A comprehensive alphabetical index of currency names, applicable to the countries as cataloged in this volume, with all individual nations of use for each, is presented in this section.

The included table of *Standard International Numeral Systems* presents charts of the basic numeric designations found on coins of non-Western origin. Although denomination numerals are generally prominently displayed on coins, it must be remembered that these are general representations of characters which individual coin engravers may have rendered in widely varying styles. Where numeric or script denominations designation forms peculiar to a given coin or country apply, such as the script used on some Persian (Iranian) issues, they are so indicated or illustrated in conjunction with the appropriate listings.

OFF-METAL STRIKES

Off-metal strikes previously designated by "(OMS)" which also included the wide range of error coinage struck in other than their officially authorized compositions have been incorporated into Pattern listings along with special issues which were struck for presentation or other reasons.

Collectors of Germanic coinage may be familiar with the term "Abschlag" which quickly identifies similar types of coinage.

STANDARD INTERNATIONAL GRADING TERMINOLOGY AND ABBREVIATIONS

	PROOF	UNCIRCULATED	EXTREMELY FINE	VERY FINE	FINE	VERY GOOD	GOOD	POOR
U.S. and ENGLISH SPEAKING LANDS	PRF	UNC	EF or XF	VF	F	VG	G	PR
BRAZIL	—	(1)FDC or FC	(3) S	(5) MBC	(7) BC	(8) BC/R	(9) R	UT GeG
DENMARK	M	0	01	1+	1	1÷	2	3
FINLAND	00	0	01	1+	1	1?	2	3
FRANCE	FB Flan Bruni	FDC Fleur de Coin	SUP Superbe	TTB Très très beau	TB Très beau	B Beau	TBC Très Bien Conservée	BC Bien Conservée
GERMANY	PP Polierte Platte	STG Stempelglanz	VZ Vorzüglich	SS Sehr schön	S Schön	S.G.E. Sehr gut erhalten	G.E. Gut erhalten	Gering erhalten
ITALY	FS Fondo Specchio	FDC Fior di Conio	SPL Splendido	BB Bellissimo	MB Molto Bello	B Bello	M	—
JAPAN	—	未使用	極美品	美品	並品	—	—	—
NETHERLANDS	— Proef	FDC Fleur de Coin	Pr. Prachtig	Z.f. Zeer fraai	Fr. Fraai	Z.g. Zeer goed	G	—
NORWAY	M	0	01	1+	1	1÷	2	3
PORTUGAL	—	Soberba	Bela	MBC	BC	MREG	REG	MC
SPAIN	Prueba	SC	EBC	MBC	BC+	BC	RC	MC
SWEDEN	Polerad	0	01	1+	1	1?	2	—

CONDITIONS/GRADING

Wherever possible, coin valuations are given in four grades of preservation. The following standards have been observed to provide continuity in grouping grade ranges in this catalog. However, because they cannot be universally applied, appropriate variations have been incorporated and noted: 1) Good, Very Good, Fine and Very Fine - used for crude "dump" or similar issues: 2) Very Good, Very Fine and Extremely Fine - used for early machine-minted issues of Europe (early 1800s), Latin America (up to the mid-1800s), the present. Listings in three grades of preservation will also be found, usually in cases of modern issues.

There are almost no grading guides for world coins. What follows is an attempt to help bridge that gap until a detailed, illustrated guide becomes available.

In grading world coins, there are two elements to look for: 1) Overall wear, and 2) loss of design details, such as strands of hair, feathers on eagles, designs on coats of arms, etc.

The age, rarity or type of a coin should not be a consideration in grading.

Grade each coin by the weaker of the two sides. This method appears to give results most nearly consistent with conservative American Numismatic Association standards for U.S. coins. Split grades, i.e., F/VF for obverse and reverse, respectively, are normally no more than one grade apart. If the two sides are more than one grade apart, the series of coins probably wears differently on each side and should then be graded by the weaker side alone.

Grade by the amount of overall wear and loss of detail evident in the main design on each side. On coins with a moderately small design element which is prone to early wear, grade by that design alone. For example, the 5-ore (KM#554) of Sweden has a crown above the monogram on which the beads on the arches show wear most clearly. So, grade by the crown alone.

For **Uncirculated** (Unc.) grades there will be no visible signs of wear or handling, even under a 30-power microscope. Bag marks may be present.

For **Almost Uncirculated** (AU), all detail will be visible. There will be wear only on the highest point of the coin. There will often be half or more of the original mint luster present.

On the **Extremely Fine** (XF or EF) coin, there will be about 95% of the original detail visible. Or, on a coin with a design with no inner detail to wear down, there will be a light wear over nearly all the coin. If a small design is used as the grading area, about 90% of the original detail will be visible. This latter rule stems from the logic that a smaller amount of detail needs to be present because a small area is being used to grade the whole coin.

The **Very Fine** (VF) coin will have about 75% of the original detail visible. Or, on a coin with no inner detail, there will be moderate wear over the entire coin. Corners of letters and numbers may be weak. A small grading area will have about 66% of the original detail.

For **Fine** (F), there will be about 50% of the original detail visible. Or, on a coin with no inner detail, there will be fairly heavy wear over all of the coin. Sides of letters will be weak. A typically uncleaned coin will often appear as dirty or dull. A small grading area will have just under 50% of the original detail.

On the **Very Good** (VG) coin, there will be about 25% of the original detail visible. There will be heavy wear on all of the coin.

The **Good** (G) coin's design will be clearly outlined but with substantial wear. Some of the larger detail may be visible. The rim may have a few weak spots of wear.

On the **About Good** (AG) coin, there will typically be only a silhouette of a large design. The rim will be worn down into the letters if any.

Strong or weak strikes, partially weak strikes, damage, corrosion, attractive or unattractive toning, dipping or cleaning should be described along with the above grades. These factors affect the quality of the coin just as do wear and loss of detail, but are easier to describe.

In the case of countermarked/-counterstamped coins, the condition of the host coin will have a bearing on the end valuation. The important factor in determining the grade is the condition, clarity and completeness of the countermark itself. This is in reference to countermarks/counterstamps having a raised design while being struck in a depression.

Incuse countermarks cannot be graded for wear. They are graded by the clarity and completeness including the condition of the host coin which will also have more bearing on the final grade/valuation determined.

VALUATIONS

Values quoted in this catalog represent the current market and are compiled from recommendations provided and verified through various source documents and specialized consultants. **It should be stressed, however, that this book is intended to serve only as an aid for evaluating coins, actual market conditions are constantly changing and additional influences,** such as particularly strong local demand for certain coin series, fluctuation of international exchange rates and worldwide collecting patterns must also be considered. Publication of this catalog is not intended as a solicitation by the publisher, editors or contributors to buy or sell the listed coins at the prices indicated.

All valuations are stated in U.S. dollars, based on careful assessment of the varied international money market. Valuations for coins priced below $1,000.00 are generally stated in full amounts - i.e. 37.50 or 950.00 - while valuations at or above that figure are rounded off in even dollars - i.e., $1250.00 is expressed as 1250. A comma is added to indicate tens of thousands of dollars in value.

For the convenience of overseas collectors and for U.S. collectors doing business with overseas dealers, the base exchange rate for the national currencies of approximately 180 countries are presented in the Foreign Exchange Table.

It should be noted that when particularly select uncirculated or proof-like examples of uncirculated coins become available they can be expected to command proportionately high premiums. Such examples in reference to choice Germanic Thalers are referred to as "erst schlage" or first strikes.

COIN vs. MEDAL ALIGNMENT

Coins are traditionally struck with obverse and reverse aligned at a rotation of 180 degrees from each other. When a coin is held for vertical viewing with the obverse design aligned upright and the index finger and thumb at the top and bottom, upon rotation from left to right for viewing the reverse, the latter will be upside down. Such alignment is called "coin rotation". Some coins are struck with the obverse and reverse designs mated on an alignment of zero or 360 degrees. If such a piece is held and rotated as described, the reverse will appear upright. This is the alignment which is generally observed in the striking of medals, and for that reason coins produced in this manner are termed to have been struck in "medal rotation". In some instances, usually through error, certain coin issues have been struck to both alignment standards, creating interesting collectible varieties which will be found noted in some listings.

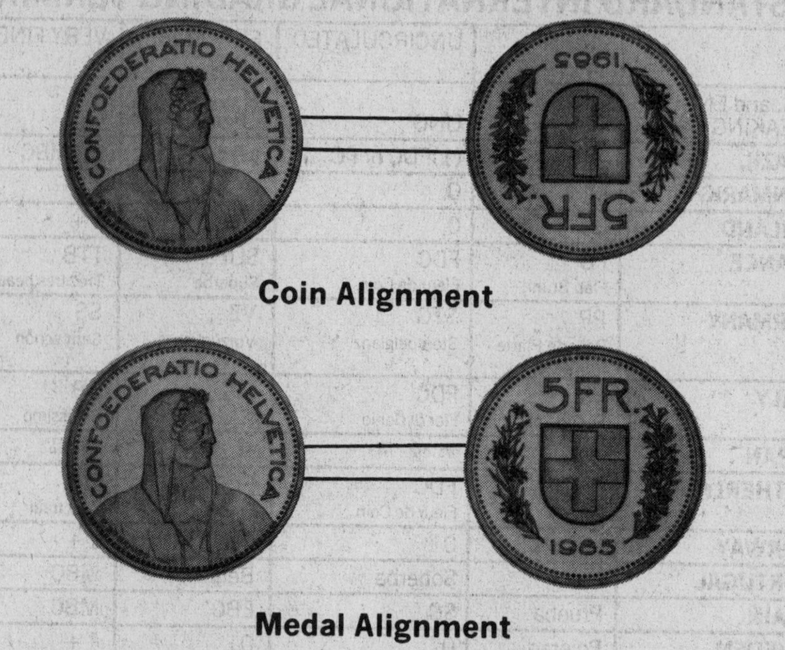

MINTAGES

Quantities minted of each date are indicated where that information is available, generally stated in millions, rounded off to the nearest 10,000 pieces. On quantities of a few thousand or less, actual mintages are generally indicated, a fact that can be determined by the presence of a comma, rather than a decimal point, in the stated figure. The following mintage conversion formulas have been observed:

10,000,000 - 10.000
1,000,000 - 1.000
100,000 - .100
10,000 - .010
9,999 - 9,999
1,000 - 1,000
842 - 842 pcs. (Pieces)
27 - 27 pcs.

The abbreviation "Inc. Ab." or "I.A." means Included Above, while "Inc. Be." or "I.B." means Included Below. An "*" beside a mintage figure indicates the number given is an estimate or mintage limit.

MINT AND PRIVY MARKS

The presence of distinctive, but frequently inconspicuously placed, mint marks indicates the mint of issue for many of the coins listed in this catalog. An appropriate designation in the date listings notes the presence, if any, of a mint mark on a particular coin type by incorporating the letter or letters of the mint mark adjoining the date, i.e., 1950D or 1927R.

The presence of mint and/or mintmaster's privy marks on a coin in non-letter form is indicated by incorporating the mint letter in lower case within parentheses adjoining the date; i.e., 1927(a). The corresponding mark is illustrated or identified in the introduction of the country.

A listing format by mints of issue has been adopted for some countries - including France, Germany, Spain and Mexico - to allow for a more logical arrangement. In these instances, the name of the mint and its mint mark letter or letters is presented at the beginning of each series.

Where listings incorporate mintmaster initials, they are always presented in capital letters separated from the date; i.e., 1850 MF. The different mint mark and mintmaster letters found on the coins of any country, state or city of issue are always shown at the beginning of listings.

TOKEN COINAGE

At times local economic conditions have forced regular coinage from circulation or found mints unable to cope with the demand for coinage, giving rise to privately-issued token coinage substitutes. British tokens of the late 1700s and early 1880s, and the German and French and French Colonial emergency emissions of the World War I era are examples of such tokens being freely accepted in monetary transactions over wide areas. Tokens were likewise introduced to satisfy specific, restricted needs, such as the leper colony issues of Brazil, Colombia and the Philippines.

This catalog includes introductory or detailed listings with "Tn" prefixes of many token coinage issues, particularly those which enjoyed wide circulation and where the series was limited in diversity. More complex series, and those more restricted in scope of circulation are generally not listed, although a representative sample may be illustrated and reference provided to more specialized catalogs.

RESTRIKES, COUNTERFEITS

Deceptive restrike and counterfeit (both contemporary and modern) examples exist of some coin issues. Where possible, the existence of restrikes is noted. Warnings are also incorporated in instances where particularly deceptive counterfeits are known to exist. Collectors who are uncertain about the authenticity of a coin held in their collection, or being offered for sale, should take the precaution of having it authenticated by the American Numismatic Association Certification Service, 818 N. Cascade, Colorado Springs, CO 80903. Their reasonably-priced certification tests are widely accepted by collectors and dealers alike.

NON-CIRCULATING LEGAL TENDER COINS

Coins of non-circulating legal tender (NCLT) origin are individually listed and integrated by denomination into the regular listings for each country. These coins fall outside the customary definitions of coin-of-the-realm issues, but were created and sold by, or under authorization of, agencies of sovereign governments expressly for collectors. These are primarily individual coins and sets of a commemorative nature, marketed at prices substantially in excess of face value, and usually do not have counterparts released for circulation.

HOMELAND TYPES

The era of global empires established by Europe's colonial powers found the homeland coinage types, particularly in the case of Great Britain, of specific dates and denominations being minted exclusively or primarily for circulation in certain overseas possessions. Identical in design and indistinguishable except for the date of issue or less frequently by denomination from the homeland coinages, these issues also circulated freely, if on a somewhat restricted basis, in other colonies, ports of call and even the homeland. A modern example is the French 1 Centime which are used solely in the French Colonies in Africa.

In a departure from established cataloging practice, which incorporated listings of these issues under the designated area of circulation, in this catalog they will be found incorporated under the homelands. Appropriate references note the intended areas of distribution for these somewhat puzzling issues, which range in date from the early 1800s until after World War II.

BULLION VALUE CHARTS

Universal silver, gold, and platinum bullion value charts are provided for use in combination with the ASW, AGW and APW factors to determine approximate intrinsic values of listed coins. By adding the component weights as shown in troy ounces on each chart, the approximate intrinsic value of any silver, gold or platinum coins' precious metal content can be determined.

Again referring to the examples presented in the above section, the intrinsic value of a silver coin with a .6822 ASW would be indicated as $4.43 + based on the application of the silver bullion chart. This result is obtained by moving across the top to the $6.50 column, then moving down to the line indicated .680 in the far left hand corner which reveals a bullion value of $4.420. To determine the value of the remaining .0022 of ASW, return up the same column to the .002 line, the closest factor available, where a $ .0130 value is indicated. The two factors total to $4.433, which would be slightly less than actual value.

The silver bullion chart provides silver values in thousandths from .001 to .009 troy ounce, and in hundredths from .01 to 1.00 in 50¢ value increments from $3.00 to $10.50. If the market value of silver exceeds $10.50, doubling the increments presented will provide valuations in $1 steps from $6.00 to $21.00.

The gold/platinum bullion chart is similarly arranged in $10 increments from $350 to $490, and by doubling the increments presented, $20 steps from $700 to $980 can be determined.

Valuations for most of the silver, gold, platinum and palladium coins listed in this edition are based on assumed market values of $5 per troy ounce for silver, $375 for gold, $395 for platinum, and $130 for palladium. To arrive at accurate current market indications for these issues, increase or decrease the valuations appropriately based on any variations in these indicated levels.

PRECIOUS METAL WEIGHTS

Listings of weight, fineness and actual silver (ASW), gold (AGW), platinum or palladium (APW) content of most machine-struck silver, gold, platinum and palladium coins are provided in this edition. These designations will be found incorporated in the listings immediately beneath illustrations or in conjunction with type changes wherever these factors could be determined.

The ASW, AGW and APW figures were determined by multiplying the gross weight of a given coin by its known or tested fineness and converting the resulting gram or grain weight to troy ounces, rounded to the nearest ten-thousandth of an ounce. A silver coin with a 24.25 gram weight and .875 fineness, for example, would have a fine weight of approximately 21.2188 grams, or a .6822 ASW, a factor that can be used to accurately determine the intrinsic value for multiple examples.

The ASW, AGW or APW figure can be multiplied by the spot price of each precious metal to determine the current intrinsic value of any coin accompanied by these designations.

WEIGHTS AND FINENESSES

Coin weights are indicated in grams (abbreviated "g") along with fineness where the information is of value in differentiating between types. These weights are based on 31.103 grams per troy (scientific) ounce, as opposed to the avoirdupois (commercial) standard of 28.35 grams. Actual coin weights are generally shown in hundredths or thousandths of a gram; i.e., .500 SILVER 2.9200 g.

As the silver and gold bullion markets have advanced and declined sharply in recent years, the fineness and total precious metal content of coins has become especially significant where bullion coins - issues which trade on the basis of their intrinsic metallic content rather than numismatic value - are concerned. In many instances, such issues have become worth more in bullion form than their nominal collector values or denominations indicate.

Establishing the weight of a coin can also be valuable for determining its denomination. Actual weight is also necessary to ascertain the specific gravity of the coin's metallic content, an important factor in determining authenticity.

TROY WEIGHT STANDARDS
24 Grains = 1 Pennyweight
480 Grains = 1 Ounce
31.103 Grams = 1 Ounce

UNIFORM WEIGHTS
15.432 Grains = 1 Gram
0.0648 Gram = 1 Grain

AVOIRDUPOIS STANDARDS
27-11/32 Grains = 1 Dram
437-1/2 Grains = 1 Ounce
28.350 Grams = 1 Ounce

METALS

At the beginning of each date listing, the metallic composition of each coin denomination is listed, and thereafter, whenever a change in metal occurs. The traditional coinage metals and their symbolic chemical abbreviations used in this catalog are:

Platinum - (PT)	Copper - (Cu)
Gold - (Au)	Brass -
Silver - (Ag)	Copper-nickel - (CN)
Billon -	Lead - (Pb)
Nickel - (Ni)	Steel -
Zinc - (Zn)	Tin - (Sn)
Bronze - (Ae)	Aluminum - (Al)

During the 18th and 19th centuries, most of the world's coins were struck of copper or bronze, silver and gold. Commencing in the early years of the 20th century, however, numerous new coinage metals, primarily non-precious metal alloys, were introduced. Gold has not been widely used for circulation coinages since World War I, although silver remained a popular coinage metal in most parts of the world until after World War II. With the disappearance of silver for circulation coinage, numerous additional compositions were introduced to coinage applications.

Most recent is the development of clad or plated planchets in order to maintain circulation life and extend the life of a set of production dies as used in the production of the copper-nickel clad copper 50 centesimos of Panama or in the latter case to reduce production costs of the planchets and yet provide a coin quite similar in appearance to its predecessor as in the case of the copper plated zinc core United States 1983 cent.

COUNTERMARKS/ COUNTERSTAMPS

There is some confusion among collectors over the terms "countermark" and "counterstamp" when applied to a coin bearing an additional mark or change of design and/or denomination.

To clarify, a countermark might be considered similar to the "hall mark" applied to a piece of silverware, by which a silversmith assured the quality of the piece. In the same way, a countermark assures the quality of the coin on which it is placed, as, for example, when the royal crown of England was countermarked (punched into) on segmented Spanish reales, allowing them to circulate in commerce in the British West Indies. An additional countermark indicating the new denomination may also be encounterd on these coins.

Countermarks are generally applied singularly and in most cases indiscriminately on either side of the "host" coin.

Counterstamped coins are more extensively altered. The counterstamping is done with a set of dies, rather than a hand punch. The coin being counterstamped is placed between the new dies and struck as if it were a blank planchet as found with the Manila 8 reales issue of the Philippines. A more unusual application where the counterstamp dies were smaller than the host coin is in the revalidated 50 centimos and 1 colon of Costa Rica issued in 1923.

PHOTOGRAPHS

To assist the reader in coin identification, every effort has been made to present actual size photographs of every coinage type listed. Obverse and reverse are illustrated, except when a change in design is restricted to one side, and the coin has a diameter of 39mm or larger, in which case only the side, required for identification of the type is generally illustrated. All coins up to 60mm are illustrated actual size, to the nearest 1/2mm up to 25mm, and to the nearest 1mm thereafter. Coins larger than 60mm diameter are illustrated in reduced size, with the actual size noted thereunder. Where slight change in size is important to coin type identification, actual millimeter measurements are stated.

NEW ISSUES

All newly released coins that have been physically observed by our staff and those that have been confirmed by press time have been incorporated in this edition. Exceptions exist in some countries where current date coin production lags far behind and !other countries whose fiscal year actually begins in the latter half of the current year.

Collectors and dealers alike are kept up to date with worldwide new issues having newly assigned catalog reference numbers and releases of mintage figures of previous years presented in the weekly feature "World Coin Roundup" in *World Coin News.* Direct ordering instructions from worldwide mints and authorized institutions is also provided through new releases and the "Mint Data" column in *World Coin News.* A free sample copy will be sent upon request. Overseas requests should include 1 international postal reply coupon for surface mail or 2 international postal reply coupons for air mail dispatch: Write to *World Coin News*, 700 East State St., Iola, WI 54990 USA.

MEDALLIC ISSUES

Medallic issues are segregated following the regular issue listings. Grouped there are coin-type issues which can generally be identified as commemoratives produced to the country's established coinage standards but without the usual indicator of denomination. These pieces may or may not feature designs adapted from the country's regular issue or commemorative coinage, and may or may not have been issued in conjunction with related coinage issues.

PROOF SETS (PS)

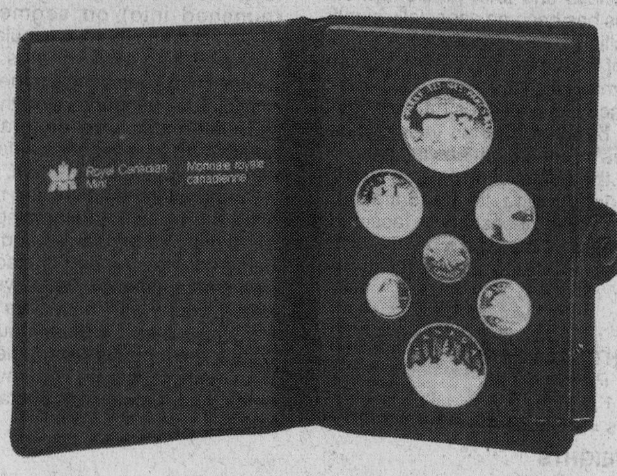

SETS

Listings in this catalog for specimen, proof and mint sets are for official, government-produced sets. In many instances privately packaged sets also exist.

Mint Sets/Fleur de Coin Sets: Specially prepared by worldwide mints to provide banks, collectors and government dignitaries with examples of current coinage. Usuualy subjected to rigorous inspection to insure that top quality specimens of selected business strikes are provided. The most popular mint set is that given out by the monarch of Great Britain each year on Maunday Thursday. This set contains four special coins in denominations of 1, 2, 3 and 4 pence, struck in silver and contained in a little pouch. They have been given away in a special ceremony for the poor for more than two centuries.

The Paris Mint introduced polyvinyl plastic cases packed within a cardboard box for homeland and colonial Fleur de Coin sets of the 1960s. British colonial sets were issued in velvet-lined metal cases similar to those used for proof sets. For its client nations, the Franklin Mint introduced a sealed composition of cardboard and specially-molded hard clear plastic protective container inserted in a soft plastic wallet. Recent discovery that soft polyvinyl packaging has proved hazardous to coins has resulted in a change to the use of hard, inert plastics for virtually all mint sets.

Some of the highest quality mint sets ever produced were those struck by the Franklin Mint during 1972-74. In many cases matte finish dies were used to strike a polished proof planchet. Later on, from 1975, sets contained highly polished, glassy-looking coins similar to those struck by the Bombay Mint for collectors over a period of 12 years.

Specimen Sets: Forerunners of today's proof sets. In most cases the coins were specially struck, perhaps even double struck, to produce a very soft or matte finish on the effigies and fields, along with high, sharp, "wire" rims. The finish is rather dull to the naked eye.

The original purpose of these sets was to provide VIPs, monarchs and mintmasters around the world with samples of the highest quality workmanship of a particular mint. These were usually housed in elaborate velvet-lined leather and metal cases.

Proof-like Sets: A relative late-comer to the field of numismatics. During the mid 1950s the Royal Canadian Mint furnished the hobby with specially selected early business strike coins that exhibited some qualities similar to proof coinage. However, the "proof-like" fields are generally flawed and the edges are rounded. These pieces are not double struck. These are commonly encountered in cardboard holders, later in soft plastic or pliofilm packaging. Of late, the Royal Canadian Mint packages such sets in rigid plastic cases.

Many worldwide officially-issued proof sets would in reality fall into this category upon careful examination of the quality of the coins' finish.

Another term encountered in this category is "Special Select", used to describe the crowns of the Union of South Africa and 100-schilling coins produced for collectors in the late 1970s by the Austrian Mint.

Proof Sets: This is undoubtedly among the most misused terms in the hobby, not only by collectors and dealers, but also by many of the world mints.

A true proof set must be at least double-struck on specially prepared polished planchets and struck using dies (often themselves polished) of the highest quality.

Modern-day proof quality consists of frosted effigies surrounded by absolute mirror-like fields.

Listings for proof sets in this catalog are for officially-issued proof sets so designated by the issuing authority, and may or may not possess what are considered modern proof quality standards.

It is necessary for collectors to acquire the knowledge to allow them to differentiate true proof sets from would-be proof sets and proof-like sets which may be encountered.

TRADE COINS

From approximately 1750-1940, a number of nations, particularly European colonial powers and commercial traders, minted trade coins to facilitate commerce with local populace of Africa, the Arab countries, the Indian subcontinent, Southeast Asia and the Far East. Such coins generally circulated at a value based on the weight and fineness of their silver or gold content, rather than their stated denomination. Examples include the silver trade dollars of Great Britain, Japan and the United States, the Spanish Colonial 8 reales, a very successful world trade coin being very popular in the orient right into the 20th century, the gold ducat issues of Austria, Hungary and the Netherlands, and the Maria Theresa talers of Austria, another of the world's most successful trade coins especially in Africa and the Middle East. Trade coinage will be found listed at the end of the domestic issues.

COIN DENOMINATIONS

A

ABAZI - Russian Caucasia
ABBASI - Afghanistan, Russian Caucasia
ACKEY - Ghana-Gold Coast
ADELAIDE POUND - Australia
ADHIO - India-IPS
ADLI ALTIN - Turkey
AFGHANI - Afghanistan, India-Independent Kingdoms
AGORAH - Israel
AGOROT - Israel
AHMADI RIYAL - Yemen Republic
AKAHI DALA - Hawaii
AKCE - Egypt, Turkey
AKCHEH - Egypt
ALTIN - Turkey
AMANAI - Afghanistan
AMMAN CASH - India-Independent Kingdoms
ANANTARAYA - India-IPS
ANGEL - Isle of Man
ANGSTER - Swiss Cantons
ANNA - India-British, Independent Kingdoms, Republic, IPS; Mombasa; Muscat & Oman; Pakistan; Yemen
ARGENTINO - Argentina
ARIARY - Malagasy Republic
ASARPHI - Nepal
ASHRAFI - Afghanistan, India-IPS
ASHRAPHI - Nepal
ASPER - Algiers, Egypt
ATT - Cambodia, Laos, Thailand
AURAR - Iceland
AUSTRAL - Argentina
AVOS - Indonesia, Macao
AZADI - Iran

B

BAHT - Thailand
BAIOCCHI - Vatican-Papal City States; Papal States
BAIOCCO - Vatican-Papal City States; Papal States
BAISA - Muscat & Oman, Oman
BAIZA - Kuwait, Oman
BALBOA - Panama
BAN - Moldova, Romania
BANI - Moldova, Romania
BANU - Romania
BASTARDO - India-Portuguese
BATZEN - Swiss Cantons, Switzerland
BAZARUCOS - India-Portuguese
BENDUQI - Morocco
BESA - Italian Somaliland
BESE - Italian Somaliland
BIPKWELE - Equatorial Guinea
BIRR - Ethiopia
BISTI - Russian Caucasia
Bit - British Virgin Islands, Danish West Indies, Dominica, Grenada, Guyana, St. Vincent
BLACK DOG - St. Vincent
BOLIVAR - Venezuela
BOLIVIANO - Bolivia
BOLOGNINO - Italian States
BU - Japan
BUDJU - Algiers
BUQSHA - Yemen Arab Republic
BURBE - Tunis
BURBEN - Tunis
BUTUT - Gambia

C

CACHE - India-French
CAGLIARESE - Italian States
CANDAREENS - China
CARLINI - Italian States
CAROLIN - Sweden
CASH - China; India-British, IPS; Vietnam-Annam
CAURIS - Guinea
CAVALLI - Italian States
CEDI - Ghana
CEDID MAHMUDIYE - Turkey
CENT - Aruba, Australia, Bahamas, Barbados, Belize, Bermuda, Botswana, British North Borneo, British Virgin Islands, Brunei, Canada, Cayman Islands, Ceylon, China, Cook Islands, Curacao, Cyprus, Danish West Indies, East Africa, East Caribbean States, Ethiopia, Fiji, French Cochin China, French Indo-China, Guyana, Hawaii, Hong Kong, Indonesia, Jamaica, Kenya, Kiribati, Laos, Liberia, Malaya, Malaya & British Borneo, Malta, Mauritius, Namibia, Netherlands, Netherlands Antilles, New Brunswick, New Zealand, Newfoundland, Nova Scotia, Pahang, Palo Seco, Penang, Prince Edward Island, Rhodesia, Sarawak, Seychelles, Sierra Leone, Singapore, Solomon Islands, Shri Lanka, Straits Settlement, Surinam, Swaziland, Trengganu, Trinidad & Tobago, Tuvalu, Uganda, United States of America, Zanzibar, Zimbabwe
CENTAI - Lithuania
CENTAS - Lithuania
CENTAVO - Angola, Argentina, Bolivia, Brazil, Cape Verde, Chile, Colombia, Costa Rica, Cuba, Culion Island, Dominican Republic, Ecuador, El Salvador, Guatemala, Guinea-Bissau, Honduras, India-Portuguese, Indonesia, Mexico, Mozambique, Nicaragua, Paraguay, Peru, Philippines, Portugal, Puerto Rico, St. Thomas & Prince, Venezuela
CENTECIMO - Bolivia
CENTESIMI - Eritrea, Italian States, Italy, San Marino, Somalia, Vatican-Papal City States, Vatican City
CENTESIMO - Chile, Dominican Republic, Italian States, Italy, Panama, Paraguay, Somalia, Uruguay, Vatican-Papal States
CENTIME - Algeria, Belgian Congo, Belgium, Cambodia, Cameroon, Comoros, Congo Free State, Croatia, Danish West Indies, France, French Colonies, French Equatorial Africa, French Guiana, French Oceania, French Polynesia, French West Africa, German States, Guadeloupe, Haiti, Isle De Bourbon, Luxembourg, Madagascar, Martinique, Monaco, Morocco, New Caledonia, Reunion, Ruanda-Urundi, Swiss Cantons, Togo, Tunisia
CENTIMO - Costa Rica, Guatemala, Mozambique, Paraguay, Peru, Philippines, Puerto Rico, St. Thomas & Prince, Spain, Venezuela
CENTIMS - Andorra
CENTU - Lithuania
CHERVONETZ - Russia
CHETRUM - Bhutan
CHHERTUM - Bhutan
CHIAO - China
CHI'EN - China
CHIFTE RUMI - Egypt
CHITRA RUPEE - India-IPS
CHO GIN - Japan
CHOMSIH - Yemen-Ghurfah, Mukulla, Quati State, Seiyun & Tarim
CHON - Korea, Korea-North
CHRISTIAN D'OR - Denmark
CHUCKRAM - India-IPS
COLON - Costa Rica, El Salvador
COLONES - Costa Rica, El Salvador
CONDOR - Ecuador
CONVENTION THALER - Austrian States
CORDOBA - Nicaragua
CORONA - Austria
CROWN - Austria, Bermuda, Biafra, Gibraltar, Great Britain, Ireland Republic, Isle of Man, Malawi, New Zealand, Rhodesia & Nyasaland, St. Helena-Ascension, Southern Rhodesia, Turks & Caicos Island, Tristan Da Cunha
CRUZADO - Brazil
CRUZEIRO - Brazil
CRUZEIROS REALS - Brazil

D

DALASI - Gambia
DALER - Danish West Indies, Denmark, Norway
DAM - Nepal
DECIME - France, Monaco
DECIMO - Argentina, Chile, Colombia, Ecuador
DENAR - Macedonia
DENARI - Italian States, Macedonia, Swiss Cantons
DENGA - Russia
DENIERS - Haiti, Swiss Cantons
DHABU - India-IPS
DHINGLO - India-IPS
DHOFARI RIYAL - Muscat & Oman
DIME - United States of America
DINAR - Afghanistan, Algeria, Bahrain, Iran, Jordan, Kuwait, Libya, Serbia, Syria, Tunisia, Yemen Republic, Yugoslavia
DINARA - Bosnia & Herzegovina, Yugoslavia-Serbia, Yugoslavia
DINAR HASHIMI - Hejaz
DINER - Andorra
DINERO - Balearic Islands, Peru
DIRHAM - Jordan, Libya, Morocco, United Arab Emirates-Ras Al-Khaima
DIRHEM - Qatar, Qatar & Dubai
DISME - United States of America
DOBRA - St. Thomas & Prince
DODIA PAISA - India-IPS
DOKDA - India-IPS
DOKDO - India-IPS
DOLLAR - Alderney, American Samoa, Anguilla, Antigua & Barbuda, Australia, Bahamas, Barbados, Belize, Bermuda, British Virgin Islands, British West Indies, Brunei, Canada, Cayman Islands, China, Cook Islands, Danish West Indies, Dominica, East Caribbean States, Eritrea, Ethiopia, Fiji, Great Britain, Grenada, Guyana, Hawaii, Hong Kong, Jamaica, Japan, Kiribati, Liberia, Marshall Islands, Mauritius, Montserrat, Namibia, Nauru Island, New Zealand, Newfoundland, Niue, Palau Islands, Panama-Palo Seco, Pitcairn Islands, Puerto Rico, St. Kitts, St. Lucia, St. Vincent, Sierra Leone, Singapore, Solomon Islands, Straits Settlements, Tuvalu, Thailand, Trinidad & Tobago, United States of America, Zimbabwe
DONG - Vietnam, Vietnam-South
DOPPIA - Italian States, Vatican Papal States
DOUBLE - Guernsey
DOUBLE ESCUDO - Ecuador
DOUBLE FANAM - India-British
DOUBLE FLORIN - Great Britain
DOUBLE MOHUR - India-Independent Kingdoms
DOUBLE PAISA - India-Independent Kingdoms, IPS
DOUDOU - India-French
DRACHMA - Greece
DRACHMAI - Greece
DRACHMES - Greece
DREILING - Denmark, German States
DUB - India-British
DUCAT - Austria, Austrian States, Batavian Republic, Czech Republic, German States, Hungary, Indonesia, Kingdom of Holland, Netherlands, Poland, Sweden, Swiss Cantons
DUCAT SPECIE - Denmark
DUCATI - Italian States
DUDU - India-British
DUIT - Indonesia
DUITOLA ASARPHI - Nepal
DUKAT - Bosnia & Herzegovina, Czechoslovakia, Yugoslavia
DUKATA - Yugoslavia
DUKATU - Czechoslovakia
DUKATY - Czechoslovakia
DUPLONE - Swiss Cantons
DURO - Gerona, Tortosa

E

EAGLE - United States of America
ECU - Belgium, Bosnia & Herzegovina, France, Gibraltar, Malta, St. Thomas & Prince
EKUELE - Equatorial Guinea
EKWELE - Equatorial Guinea
EMALANGENI - Swaziland
ESCALIN - Guadeloupe, Haiti, St. Lucia
ESCUDO - Angola, Argentina, Azores, Bolivia, Cape Verde, Central American Republic, Chile, Colombia, Costa Rica, Ecuador, Guatemala, Guinea-Bissau, India-Portuguese, Indonesia, Maderia, Mexico, Mozambique, Peru, Philippines, Portugal, Spain, St. Thomas & Prince
EYRIR - Iceland

F

FALUS - Afghanistan; China; India-Independent Kingdoms, IPS; Iran; Morocco; Russian-Turkestan
FANAM - India-British, IPS
FANO - India-Danish
FANON - India-French
FARTHING - Ceylon, Great Britain, Ireland, Ireland Republic, Isle of Man, Jamaica, Malta, South Africa
FELS - Algeria
FEN - China
FENIG - Poland
FENIGOW - Poland
FIL - Bahrain, Iraq, Jordan, Kuwait, South Arabia, United Arab Emirates, Yemen Republic
FILLER - Hungary
FIORINI - Italian States
FIORINO - Italian States
FLORIN - Aruba, Australia, Austria, East Africa, Fiji, Great Britain, Ireland Republic, Kingdom of Holland, Malawi, New Zealand, South Africa
FORINT - Hungary
FRACTIONAL FALUS - Afghanistan
FRANC - Algeria, Austria, Belgian Congo, Belgium, Benin, Burundi, Cambodia, Cameroon, Cattaro, Central African Republic, Central African States, Chad, Comoros, Congo Dem. Rep., Congo Republic, Croatia, Danish West Indies, Djibouti, France, French Equatorial Africa, French Oceania, French Polynesia, French West Africa, Gabon, Guadeloupe, Guinea, Hungary, Italian States, Ivory Coast, Katanga, Luxembourg, Madagascar, Martinique, Mali, Monaco, Morocco, New Caledonia, New Hebrides, Niger, Reunion, Ruanda-Urundi, Rwanda, Rwanda & Burundi, St. Pierre & Miquelon, Senegal, Sweden, Swiss Cantons, Switzerland, Togo, Tunisia, West African States
FRANCESCONE - Italian States
FRANCHI - Italian States, Swiss Cantons
FRANCO - Dominican Republic, Ecuador, Equatorial Guinea, Italian States, Swiss Cantons
FRANG AR - Albania
FRANK - German States, Liechtenstein, Swiss Cantons
FRANGA AR - Albania
FRANKEN - German States, Germany, Liechtenstein, Swiss Cantons, Switzerland
FREDERIK D'OR - Denmark, German States
FUANG - Cambodia, Thailand
FUN - Japan, Korea

G

GAZETTA - Greece
GAZETTAE - Greece
GERSH - Ethiopia
GHIRSH - Saudi Arabia-Hejaz & Nejd, Nejd, Saudi Arabia, Sudan
GIULIO - Vatican-Papal States
GOLD MISCAL - China
GOLD RUPEE - India-Independent Kingdoms, Indonesia
GOLDE - Sierra Leone
GOLDGULDEN - German States
GORYOBAN - Japan
GOURDE - Haiti
GRAMS - Afghanistan
GRANA - Italian States
GRANI - Italian States
GRANO - Italian States, Mexico
GROAT - Great Britain
GROSCHEL - German States
GROSCHEN - Austria, Danzig, East Prussia, German States, Posen
GROSETTI - Croatia
GROSSO - Vatican-Papal States
GROSZ - Poland
GROSZE - Poland
GROSZY - Poland-Krakow, Zamosc; Poland
GROTE - German States
GROTEN - German States
GUARANI - Paraguay
GUARANIES - Paraguay
GUILDER - Curacao, Guyana, Surinam
GUINEA - Great Britain, Saudi Arabia
GULDEN - Batavian Republic, Curacao, Danzig, German States, Indonesia, Netherlands, Netherlands Antilles, Philippines, Surinam
GUTE GROSHEN - German States

H

HABIBI - Afghanistan
HALALA - Saudi Arabia
HALER - Czechoslovakia
HALERE - Czechoslovakia
HALERU - Bohemia & Moravia, Czech Republic, Czechoslovakia, Slovakia
HALF DOLLAR - United States of America
HALIEROV - Slovakia
HALLER - Swiss Cantons
HAO - Vietnam
HAPA HANERI - Hawaii
HAPAHA - Hawaii
HAPALUA - Hawaii
HAU - Tonga
HAYRIYE ALTIN - Iraq, Turkey
HEAVY AMMAN CASH - India-Independent Kingdoms
HEAVY PAISA - India-Independent Kingdoms
HEAVY RUPEE - Afghanistan, India-IPS
HELLER - Austria, Tanzania-German East Africa, German States
HWAN - Korea-South

I

IMADI RIYAL - Yemen Republic
INTI - Peru

J

JA'U - India-IPS
JIAO - China
JOKOH - Malaysia-Kelantan

K

KALI FANAM - India-IPS
KAROLIN - German States

KAS - India-Danish
KEPING - Indonesia; Malaysia-Kelantan, Malacca, Perak, Selangor, Trengganu
KHARUB - Algeria, Tunis, Tunisia
KHARUBA - Algeria
KINA - Papua New Guinea
KIP - Laos
KOBAN - Japan
KOBO - Nigeria
KOPEJEK - Tannu Tuva
KOPEK - Germany, Poland, Russia
KOPIJOK - Ukraine
KORI - India-IPS
KORONA - Hungary
KORUN - Czech Republic, Czechoslovakia, Slovakia
KORUNA - Bohemia & Moravia, Czech Republic, Czechoslovakia, Slovakia
KORUNY - Czechoslovakia, Slovakia
KOULA - Tonga
KRAJCZAR - Hungary
KRAN - Iran
KREUTZER - German States
KREUZER - Austria, Austrian States, German States, Italian States, Swiss Cantons
KRONA - Iceland, Sweden
KRONE - Austria, Denmark, German States, Greenland, Liechtenstein, Norway
KRONEN - Austria, Liechtenstein
KRONER - Denmark, Greenland, Norway
KRONOR - Sweden
KRONUR - Iceland
KROON - Estonia
KROONI - Estonia
KRUGERRAND - South Africa
KUNA - Croatia
KUNE - Croatia
KUPANG - Thailand
KURUS - Turkey
KURUSH - Turkey
KWACHA - Malawi, Zambia
KWANZA - Angola
KYAT - Myanmar

L

LAARI - Maldive Islands
LANG - Vietnam-Annam
LARI - Maldive Islands
LARIAT - Maldive Islands
LARIN - Maldive Islands
LATI - Latvia
LATS - Latvia
LATU - Latvia
LEI - Moldova, Romania
LEK - Albania
LEKE - Albania
LEKU - Albania
LEMPIRA - Honduras
LEONE - Sierra Leone
LEPTA - Greece
LEPTON - Greece
LEU - Moldova, Romania
LEV - Bulgaria
LEVA - Bulgaria
LI - China
LIANG - China
LIBERTAD - Mexico
LIBRA - Peru
LICENTE - Lesotho
LIGHT PAISA - India-Independent Kingdoms
LIGHT RUPEE - Afghanistan
LIKUTA - Congo Democratic Republic
LILANGENI - Swaziland
LIRA - Eritrea, Italian States, Italy, San Marino, Syria, Turkey, Vatican-Papal States, Vatican City, Yemen Republic
LIRAH - Israel
LIRE - Eritrea; Italian Somaliland; Italian States; Italy; San Marino; Vatican-Papal City States, Papal States
LIROT - Israel
LISENTE - Lesotho
LITAI - Lithuania
LITAS - Lithuania
LITU - Lithuania
LIVRE - Guadeloupe, Isle de France et Bonaparte, Lebanon, Martinique, St. Lucia
LOTI - Lesotho
LOWE - Bophuthatswana
LUHLANGA - Swaziland
LWEI - Angola

M

MACE - China
MACUTA - Angola
MAHALEKI - Ethiopia
MAHALLAK - Ethiopia
MAHBUB - Egypt, Libya-Tripoli, Turkey
MAHMUDI - Mecca
MAHMUDIYE - Turkey
MAKUTA - Congo Democratic Republic, Zaire
MALOTI - Lesotho
MAMEITA GIN - Japan
MANGHIR - Turkey
MANGIR - Libya-Tripoli
MARIEN GROSCHEN - German States
MARK - Estonia, German States, Germany, Papau New Guinea-German New Guinea
MARAVEDI - Navarre, Spain
MARKKA - Finland
MARKKAA - Finland
MAT - Myanmar
MATICAES - Mozambique
MATONA - Ethiopia
MAZUNA - Morocco
MELGAREJO - Bolivia
MEMDUHIYE ALTIN - Turkey
METICA - Mozambique
METICAIS - Mozambique
METICAL - Mozambique
MIL - Cyprus, Hong Kong, Israel, Malta
MILESIMA - Spain
MILLIEME - Egypt, Libya
MILLIM - Sudan, Tunisia
MISCAL - China
MISRIYA - Egypt
MOCO - Dominica
MOHAR - Nepal
MOHUR - Afghanistan; India-British, Independent Kingdoms, IPS, Mughal; Indonesia
MOMME - Japan
MON - Japan, Korea
MONGO - Mongolia
MU - Myanmar, Union of Burma
MUDRA - India-IPS
MULTIPLE PAISAS - India-Independent Kingdoms
MUN - Korea

N

NAN RYO - Japan
NAIRA - Nigeria
NASRI - Tunis
NAYA PAISA - Bhutan, India-Republic
NAYE PAISE - India-Republic
NAZARANA - India-IPS
NAZARANA ANNA - India-IPS
NAZARANA KORI - India-IPS
NAZARANA MOHUR - India-IPS, Mughal
NAZARANA NEW PAISA - India-IPS
NAZARANA OLD PAISA - India-IPS
NAZARANA PAISA - India-IPS
NAZARANA RUPEE - Afghanistan; India-British, French Independent Kingdoms, IPS, Mughal
NAZARANA TAKKA - India-IPS
NEU-GROSCHEN - German States
NEW ALDI ALTIN - Turkey
NEW AGORA - Israel
NEW AGOROT - Israel
NEW ALTIN Turkey
NEW PAISA - India-IPS
NEW PENCE - Gibraltar, Great Britain, Guernsey, Isle of Man, Jersey
NEW PENNY - Great Britain, Guernsey, Isle of Man, Jersey
NEW PESO - Mexico, Uruguay
NEW SHEQALIM - Israel
NEW SHEQEL - Israel
NGULTRUM - Bhutan
NGWEE - Zambia
NICKEL - United States of America
NKWE - Bophuthatswana
NOBLE - Isle of Man
NOVO CRUZADO - Brazil
NUEVO SOL - Peru

O

OBAN - Japan
OBOL - Greece
OBOLI - Greece
OCHAVO - Catalonia
OCTAVO - Philippines
OMANI RIAL - Oman
ONCA - Mozambique
ONCIE - Italian States
ONZA - Bolivia, Chile, Costa Rica, Mexico
ORE - Denmark, Greenland, Norway, Sweden
OUGUIYA - Mauritania
OUNCE - South Africa

P

PA'ANGA - Tonga
PAGODA - India-British, French, IPS
PAHLAVI - Iran
PAI - India-IPS
PAISA - Afghanistan; India-Independent Kingdoms, IPS, Mughal, Republic; Nepal; Pakistan
PAISE - Afghanistan; India-Independent Kingdoms, IPS, Republic
PANA - India-Independent Kingdoms
PANCHIA - India-British
PAOLI - Italian States
PAOLO - Italian States
PARA - Egypt; Hejaz; Iraq; Libya-Tripoli; Turkey; Yugoslavia-Montenegro, Serbia; Yugoslavia
PARAS - Greece
PARDAO - India-Portuguese
PARE - Yugoslavia-Montenegro, Serbia
PATACA - Macao
PAVALI - India-IPS
PAYALO - India-IPS
PE - Cambodia, Myanmar
PECA - Portugal
PENCE - Australia, Belize, Biafra, British Virgin Islands, British West Africa, Ceylon, Danish West Indies, Dominica, Falkland Islands, Gambia, Ghana, Gibraltar, Great Britain, Guernsey, Guyana, Ireland Republic, Isle of Man, Jamaica, Jersey, Malawi, Mozambique, New Guinea, New Zealand, Nigeria, Rhodesia, Rhodesia & Nyasaland, St. Helena & Ascension, St. Kitts & Nevis, South Africa, Southern Rhodesia, Trinidad, Tristan Da Cunha, Zambia
PENCE TOKEN - Ireland
PENGO - Hungary
PENNI - Finland
PENNIA - Finland
PENNY - Australia, Bahamas, British West Africa, Danish West Indies, Falkland Islands, Fiji, Gambia, Ghana, Gibraltar, Great Britain, Guernsey, Ireland, Ireland Republic, Isle of Man, Jamaica, Jersey, Malawi, New Brunswick, New Guinea, New Zealand, Nigeria, Nova Scotia, Rhodesia & Nyasaland, St. Helena & Ascension, South Africa, Southern Rhodesia, Zambia
PENNY FARTHING - South Africa
PERPER - Montenegro
PERPERA - Montenegro
PERPERO - Croatia
PESA - German East Africa
PESETA - Equatorial Guinea; Peru; Spain-Balearic Islands, Barcelona, Catalonia, Tarragona; Spain
PESEWA - Ghana
PESO - Argentina, Cambodia, Chile, Colombia, Costa Rica, Cuba, Dominican Republic, Culion Island, Curacao, El Salvador, Guatemala, Guinea-Bissau, Honduras, Mexico, Paraguay, Peru, Philippines, Puerto Rico, Uruguay.
PESO BOLIVIANO - Bolivia
PESO FUERTES - Paraguay
PESSA - Lahej (Yemen)
PFENNIG - Danzig, German New Guinea, Germany, Swiss Cantons
PFENNIGE - German States
PFENNING - Austrian States, German States
PHAN - Vietnam-Annam
PHOENIX - Greece
PIASTRE - Cambodia, Cyprus, Darfur, Egypt, French Indo China, Hejaz, Iraq, Jordan, Lebanon, Libya, Nejd, Sudan, Syria, Tonkin, Tunis, Tunisia, Turkey
PICE - Bhutan; Ceylon; East Africa; India-British, IPS, Republic; Kenya-Mombasa; Pakistan; Penang
PIE - India-British, IPS; Pakistan
PILON - Mexico
PISO - Philippines
PISTOLE - German States
PIT - Thailand
PITIS - Brunei; Malaysia-Kelantan, Selangor, Trengganu; Thailand
POISHA - Bangladesh
POLTINA - Russia
POLUPOLTINNIK - Russia
POLUSHKA - Russia
POND - South Africa
POUND - Alderney, Australia, Biafra, Cyprus, Egypt, Falkland Islands, Gibraltar, Great Britain, Guernsey, Ireland Republic, Isle of Man, Jersey, Malta, Peru, Rhodesia, St. Helena-Ascension, St. Vincent, South Africa, Sudan, Syria, Tristan da Cunha, Uganda
PROTEA - South Africa
PRUTA - Israel
PRUTAH - Israel
PUL - Afghanistan, Russian Turkestan
PULA - Botswana
PULI - Russian Caucasia
PYA - Myanmar
PYSA - Zanzibar

Q

QAPIK - Azerbaijan
QINDAR AR - Albania
QINDARKA - Albania
QINDAR LEKU - Albania
QIRAN - Afghanistan
QIRSH - Egypt, Jordan
QUAN - Vietnam-Annam
QUART - Gibraltar
QUARTER DOLLAR - United States of America
QUARTO - Philippines; Spain-Barcelona, Catalonia
QUATTRINI - Italian States
QUATTRINO - Italian States, Vatican-Papal States
QUETZAL - Guatemala
QUETZALES - Guatemala

R

RAND - South Africa
RAPPAN - Swiss Cantons
RAPPEN - Swiss Cantons, Switzerland
REAAL - Curacao
REAL - Argentina, Bolivia, Central American Republic, Chile, Colombia, Costa Rica, Dominican Republic, Ecuador, El Salvador, Guatemala, Honduras, Mexico, Paraguay, Peru, Philippines, Spain, Venezuela
REAL BATU - Indonesia
REALE - Italian States
REALES - Argentina, Bolivia, Central American Republic, Chile, Colombia, Costa Rica, Cuba, Danish West Indies, Dominican Republic, Ecuador, El Salvador, Guatemala, Honduras, Indonesia, Mexico, Mozambique, Peru, Philippines, St. Eustatius, Spain, Venezuela
REALES DE VELLON - Valencia
REICHSMARK - Germany
REICHSPFENNING - Germany
REICHSTHALER - German States
REIS - Angola, Azores, Brazil, Danish West Indies, India-Portuguese, Madeira, Mozambique, Portugal, St. Thomas & Prince
RENTENPFENNIG - Germany
RIAL - Iran, Oman, Yemen Republic
RIEL - Cambodia
RIGSBANKDALER - Denmark
RIGSBANKSKILLING - Denmark
RIGSDALER - Denmark
RIGSMONTSKILLING - Denmark
RIJKSDAALER - Netherlands-Batavian Republic; Kingdom of Holland
RIKSDALER - Sweden
RIKSDALER RIKSMYNT Sweden
RIKSDALER SPECIE - Sweden
RIN - Japan
RINGGIT - Malaysia
RIXDOLLAR - Ceylon
RIYAL - Iran; Muscat & Oman; Saudi Arabia-Hejz & Nejd; Saudi Arabia; United Arab Republic-Ajman, Fujairah, Ras Al-Khaima, Sharjah, Umm Al Qaiwain; Yemen Republic
ROUBLE - Russia; Russian Caucasia, Turkestan
ROYAL - Gibraltar
ROYALIN - India-Danish
ROYALINE - India-Danish
RUBLE - Poland
RUFIYAA - Maldive Islands
RUMI ALTIN - Turkey
RUPEE - Afghanistan; Australia; Andaman Islands; Bhutan; India-British, French, Independent Kingdoms, IPS, Mughal, Republic; Indonesia; Mauritius; Mombasa; Mozambique; Nejd; Nepal; Pakistan; Seychelles; Shri Lanka-Ceylon; United Arab Republic-Al Sharjah; Shri Lanka; Tibet; Yemen
RUPEE SIZE - Djibouti
RUPI - Iran
RUPIA - India-Portuguese, Italian Somaliland
RUPIAH - Indonesia
RUPIE - German East Africa
RUPIEN - German East Africa
RUSPONE - Italian States
RYAL - Quaiti State, Yemen, Zanzibar
RYAL SIZE - Djibouti
RYO - Japan
RYO KIN - Japan

S

SAIDI RIYAL - Muscat & Oman
SALUNG - Thailand
SANAR - Afghanistan
SANTIM - Morocco
SANTIMAT - Morocco
SANTIMI - Latvia
SANTIMS - Latvia
SANTIMU - Latvia
SAPEQUE - French Cochin China, French Indo China
SAR - China
SATANG - Thailand
SCELLINO - Somalia
SCHILLING - Danzig, Denmark, German States, East Prussia, Swiss Cantons
SCHILLINGE - German States
SCHWAREN - German States
SCUDI - San Marino, Vatican-Papal States
SCUDO - Bolivia, Italian States, Mexico, San Marino, Vatican-Papal States
SECHSLING - Denmark, German States
SEL - India-Independent Kingdoms
SEN - Brunei, Cambodia, Indonesia, Japan, Malaysia, Thailand
SENE - Western Samoa
SENGI - Congo Dem. Republic
SENITI - Tonga
SENT - Estonia
SENTE - Lesotho
SENTI - Estonia, Somalia, Tanzania
SENTIMO - Philippines
SERTUM - Bhutan
SHAHI - Afghanistan, Iran
SHAHI SEFID - Iran
SHEQEL - Israel
SHEQALIM - Israel
SHILIN - Somalia
SHILINGI - Tanzania
SHILLING - Australia, Austria, Belize, Biafra, British Virgin Islands, British West Africa, Cyprus, Dominica, East Africa, El Salvador, Fiji, Gambia, Ghana, Great Britain, Guernsey, Ireland Republic, Isle of Man, Jamaica, Jersey, Kenya, Malawi, Mozambique, New Guinea, New Zealand, Nigeria, Rhodesia, Rhodesia & Nyasaland, St. Vincent, Somalia, South Africa, Southern Rhodesia, Trinidad, Uganda, Zambia
SHILLINGS TOKEN - Ireland
SHO - Tibet
SHU - Japan
SIK - Thailand
SILBER GROSCHEN - German States
SIO - Thailand
SIXPENCE - Australia, Fiji, Zambia
SKAR - Tibet
SKILLING - Danish West Indies, Denmark, Norway, Sweden
SOL - Argentina, Bolivia, Guadeloupe, Haiti, Peru, Swiss Cantons
SOLDI - Italian States, Swiss Cantons, Vatican-Papal States
SOLDO - Italian States, Vatican-Papal States
SOLES - Argentina, Bolivia, Peru
SOMALO - Somalia
SOU - St. Bartholomew
SOUS - French Guiana, Guadeloupe, Mauritius, St. Lucia
SOVEREIGN - Andorra; Australia; Canada; Gibraltar; Great Britain; India-British, IPS; Isle of Man; South Africa; Yemen Republic
SOVRANO - Italian States
SPECIE DALER - Norway
SRANG - Tibet
STAMPEE - St. Lucia, St. Vincent
STIVER - Ceylon, Guyana, Indonesia, St. Bartholomew
STOTINKA - Bulgaria
STOTINKI - Bulgaria
STOTINOV - Slovenia
STUBER - German States
STUIVER - Curacao, Indonesia-Kingdom of Holland, St. Eustatius, St. Martin
SU - Vietnam-South
SUCRE - Ecuador
SUELDO - Spain-Balearic Islands
SULTANI - Algeria, Tripoli, Tunis
SURRE ALTIN - Turkey
SYLI - Guinea

T

TAEL - China
TAKA - Bangladesh
TAKKA - India-IPS
TALA - Tokelau, Western Samoa
TALAR - Poland
TALARA - Poland
TALER - Djibouti
TALLERO - Eritrea
TAMBALA - Malawi
TAMLUNG - Thailand
TANGA - India-Portuguese
TANGKA - Tibet
TARI - Italian States
TEK RUMI - Egypt
TENE - Cook Islands
TENGA - China, Russian Turkestan
TENNESI - Turkmenistan
THALER - Austria, Austrian States, German States, Hungary, Liechtenstein, Mozambique
THEBE - Botswana
THREEPENCE - Australia, Fiji
TICAL - Cambodia
TIEN - Vietnam-Annam
TILLA - Afghanistan, China, Russian Turkestan
TIMASHA - India-Independent Kingdoms
TLACO - Mexico
TOEA - Papua New Guinea
TOKA CASH - India-IPS
TOLA - Nepal
TOLAR - Slovenia
TOLARJA - Slovenia
TOLARJEV - Slovenia
TOMAN - Afghanistan, Iran, Russian Caucasia
TORNESE - Italian States
TORNESI - Italian States
TOT - Thailand
TRA - Kedah
TRAMBIYO - India-IPS
TRISUL PICE - India-British
TUGRIK - Mongolia

V

VAN - Vietnam-Annam
VATU - Vanuatu
VELLI FANAM - India-IPS
VENEZOLANO - Venezuela
VIRARAYA FANAM - India-IPS

W

WARN - Korea
WERK - Ethiopia
WHAN - Korea
WON - Korea, Korea-North, Korea-South

X

XERAFIM - India-Portuguese
XERAFIN - India-Portuguese
XU - Vietnam-North, Vietnam-South, Vietnam

Y

YANG - Korea
YEN - Japan
YUAN - Cambodia, China
YUZLUK - Turkey

Z

ZAIRE - Congo Democratic Republic, Zaire
ZALAT - Yemen Republic
ZECCHINI - Vatican Papal States
ZECCHINO - Italian States
ZERI MAHBUB - Egypt, Tripoli, Turkey
ZLOTE - Poland
ZLOTY Krakow, Poland, Zamosc
ZLOTYCH - Poland, Russia
ZOLOTA - Turkey

LEGEND ABBREVIATIONS

Following in alphabetical order is a listing of the Latin legends found on World coins. The legend as it appears on the coin is in bold typeface. The translation is followed by issuer.

Common Abbreviations

A.A. - Archidux Austriae. . . . . Archduke of Austria.

Arch. Aust. Dux Burg. Mar. Mor. Co. Tyr - Archidux Austriae Dux Burgundiae Marchio Moraviae Comes Tyrolis. . . . . Archduke of Austria, Duke of Burgundy, Margrave of Moravia, Count of Tyrol.

D.G. - Dei Gratia. . . . .By the grace of God.

Dan. Nor. Van. Got. Rex - Daniae, Norvegiae, Vandalorum Gothorum Rex. . . . . King of Denmark, Norway, Vandalia, Gotland.

Dux Sles. Hol. Stor. Ditm. Com. Old. & Delm. - Dux Slesvivi Holsatiae Stormariae et Ditmarsiae Comes in Oldenburg et Delmenhorst. . . . . Duke of Schleswig-Holstein, Stormarn, and Ditmarsh, Count in Oldenburg and Delmenhorst.

F.D. - Fidei Defensor. . . . . Defender of the Faith.

Ger. Hun. Boh. Rex - Germaniae Hungariae Bohemiae Rex. . . . . King of Germany, Hungary, Bohemia.

P.M. - Pontifex Maximus. . . . . Supreme Pontiff.

Rex Pol. Ma. Dux Lit. Rus. Prus. Mas. Sam. Liv. nec non Svec. Gotor. Vandal. Haere. Rex - Rex Poloniae Magnus Dux Lithuaniae Russiae Prussiae Masoviae Samgitiae Livoniae nec non Svecorum Gothorum Vandalorum Haereditarius Rex. . . . . King of Poland, Grand Duke of Lithuania, Russia, Prussia, Masovia, Semgallia, Livonia, as well as hereditary King of Sweden, Gotland, and Vandalia.

German States Prefaces

Prefaced and numbered below are abbreviations which frequently appear in German States legends. They will be referred to numerous times.

1. ANHALT - F.A.C.A.D.S.B.I. & K. . . . . . Prince of Anhalt, Count of Aschersleben, Lord of Zerbst, Bernburg, Jever, and Knyphausen.

2. BAVARIA - PFALZ - JULICH-BERG - BERG - B.I.C.& M.D.C.V.S.M.R. & M.D.I.R. . . . . . Bavaria, Julich, Cleves, Berg, Count of Veldenz, Sponheim, Mark & Ravensberg & Moers, Lord in Ravenstein.
C.P.R.S.R.I. Archit. & El. D.B. . . . . Count Palatine of the Rhine, Archtreasurer of the H.R.E., Duke of Bavaria. . . . . (as above)

3. BRANDENBURG (Legends are abbreviated in both Latin and German)
Mar. Brand. S.R.I. Arc. & Elec. Magd. Pruss, dux lvl. (Gu.) Cli. & Mont. (Ber.) (Churf. i. Pr. z. Gu. C. & B.). . . . . Margrave of Brandenburg, Archchamberlain and Elector of the H.R.E., Duke of Magdeburg, Prussia, Julich, Cleves, and Berg.
Stet. Pomer. Cas. (der C.) W.a.i.S. zu K. u. I. (Cro. Car. Sile.) Hert. . . . . . Stettin, Pomerania, Cassubia, Vandalia, also Duke in Silesia of Krossen and Jagerndorf.
B.N.P.R.Co. Ma. & Ra. d.i. Rav. (B.z.N.F.z.R.G.z.D.) P.H.M.C. . . . . . Burgrave of Nuremberg, Prince of Rugen, Count of Mark & Ravensberg, Lord in Ravenstein, Prince of Halberstadt, Minden, Cammin.

4. BRUNSWICK - Dux (Hertz.) Bruns. Luneb. . . . . Duke Brunswick and Luneburg.

5. HABSBURG - D.G.R.I.S.A. Germ. Hung. Boh. Rex. . . . . By the grace of God, Roman Emperor always august, King of Germany, Hungary, Bohemia. . . . . **also S.R.I.** . . . . . Holy Roman Empire.

6. MANSFELD - Comes & dn. in Mansf. nob. dm. in Held. Seb. et Schrap. Count and Lord in Mansfeld, noble Lord of Heldrungen, Seeburg, and Schraplau.

7. SAXONY - Saxo. Iul. Cli. B. (Mon.) A. & W. Lan. Thu. Mar. Mis. Pri. Hen. C.M. & R.D.R. . . . . . Saxony, Julich, Cleves, Berg, Angria, and Westphalia, Landgrave of Thuringia, Margrave of Meissen, Prince of Henneberg, Count of Mark & Ravensberg, Lord in Ravenstein.

8. SCHWARZBURG - E. IV. com. imp. com. Schwartz. & Honst. dom. A.S.L.L. et Cl. . . . . . of the four Counts of the Empire, Count of Schwarzburg and Hohnstein, Lord of Arnstein, Sondershausen, Leutenberg, Lohra, and Klettenberg.

9. STOLBERG - Stol. Konig. Rut. (Roch.) Wer. Hon. zu Epst. Mintz. Brev. Eich. Lo. u. Cletten. . . . . . Stolberg, Konigstein, Rochefort, Wernigerode, Hohnstein, Lord of Epstein, Munzenberg, Breuberg, Eichsfeld, Lohra, and Klettenberg.

10. WURTTEMBERG - Dux Wirt. & Tec. (com Montp.) (in Sil. Ols.) (B.). . . . . Duke of Wurttemberg and Teck, Count of Mompelgard, in Silesia-Ols, Bernstadt, or Berolstein.

11. HESSE - Landg. Hass. princ. (admi.) Hersf. C.C.D. Z.E.N.S.Y.B. . . . . . Landgrave of Hesse, Prince (administrator) of Hersfeld, Katzenellenbogen, Cassel, Diez, Ziegenhayn, Nidda, and Schauenburg, Isenburg, Budingen.

A

Ad Norm(am) conv(entionis) According to the convention standard. (Baden, Furstenberg, Hohenzollern-Hechingen, Wurttemberg)
Adolph Georg Furst zu Schaumburg-Lippe Adolph George, Prince of Schaumburg-Lippe. (Schaumburg-Lippe)
Adolph Herzog zu Nassau Adolph, Duke of Nassau. (Nassau)

Agricoltura e Commercio (Agriculture and Commerce. (Italian Republic)
Albert Furst zu Schwarzburg Albert, Prince of Schwarzburg. (Schwarzburg)
Albert Koenig von Sachsen Albert, King of Saxony. (Saxony)
Albert Roi des Belges Albert, King of the Belgians. (Belgium)
Alex(ander) Carl Herzog zu Anhalt Alexander Carl, Duke of Anhalt. (Anhalt)
Alexander I Ces. Ros. Wskrzesiciel Krol Pols. Alexander I, Tsar of all the Russias, King of Poland. (Poland)
Alexander I Cesarz Sa. W. Ros. Krol Polski Alexander I, Tsar of all the Russias, King of Poland. (Poland)
Alexandrine * Ludwig * Friedrich * Wilhelm und Sophie Grosherzogin von Baden Besuchen die Munzstaette den 29 Febr. 1832. Heil Ihnen Alexandrina, Ludwig, Frederick, William, and Sophie, Grand Duchess of Baden visit the mint on February 29, 1832. Prosperity to them. (Baden)
Alexius Friedrich Christian Herzog zu Anhalt Alexius Frederick Christian, Duke of Anhalt. (Anhalt)
Alfonso XII Por La G(racia) de Dios Alfonzo XII, by the grace of God. (Spain)
Alfonzo XII Rey de Espana Alfonzo XII, King of Spain. (Spain)
Alfonzo XIII Por La G(racia) de Dios Alfonzo XIII, by the grace of God. (Spain)
Alfred Herzog von Sachsen Coburg und Gotha Alfred, Duke of Saxe-Coburg-Gotha
Alla Naz(ione) Fran. La Rep(ubblica) Cisal. Riconoscente To the French nation, the grateful Cisalpine Republic. (Cisalpine Republic)
Alleanza Dei Populi Liberi Alliance of the free people. (Venice)
Allgemeine Ausstellung Deutscher Industrie und Gewerbs Erzeugnisse General Exhibition of German industrial and craft products. (Bavaria)
Althingi Vas Sett At Rathi Ulfliots Ok Allra Landsmanna Parliament was established by the Council of Ulfliot and by all the people. (Iceland)
Amadeo I Rey de Espana Amadeus I, King of Spain. (Spain)
Anton Koenig und Friedrich August Mitregent von Sachsen Anton, King and Frederick August, co-regent of Saxony. (Saxony)
Anton Koenig von Sachsen (cross) den 6 Iuni 1836 Anton, King of Saxony (died) on June 6, 1836. (Saxony)
Anton V.G.G. Koenig von Sachsen Anton, by the grace of God, King of Saxony. (Saxony)
Arch. Aust. D. Burg. Loth. M. D. Het. Archduke of Austria, Duke of Burgundy, Lorraine, Grand Duke of Etruria. (Austria)
Arnold Winkelreid. (Switzerland)
Audere Semper Ever to dare. (Albania)
Auxilium de Sancto Aid from the Saint. (Papal States)

B

Bai(y)erischer Kronthaler Bavarian Kronentaler. (Bavaria)
Bayerisch-Wurtembergischer Zollverein, geschlossen 1827 Bavarian-Wurttemberg customs union, formed 1827. (Bavaria)
Bayern Errichteten die H. Ottokapelle zu Kiefersfelden zum Andenken an Koen. Otto's Abschied v. seinem Vaterlande Bavaria, erected the Otto chapel at Kiefersfelden in commemoration of King Otto's departure from his fatherland. (Bavaria)
Bayerns Treue Faithfulness of Bavarians. (Bavaria)
Berathung u. Grundung e. Deutschen Parlaments 31 Marz 1848 Deliberation over the establishment of a German parliament on March 31, 1848. (Frankfurt)
Berg. und Clevische Land Munz Legal coin of Berg and Cleves. (Berg)
Bergische Landmunz Legal coin of Berg. (Berg)
Bergsegen des Harzes Blessings of the Harz mines. (Hannover)
Bernhard Herzog zu Sachsen Meiningen Bernhard, Duke of Saxe-Meiningen. (Saxe-Meiningen)
Besucht zum Erstenmal die von Ihm erbaute Munzstatte zu Wiesbaden den 28 Dec. 1851 Visit for the first time to the mint built by himself at Wiesbaden on December 28, 1851. (Nassau)
Beytritt von Baden zum Teutschen Zollverein Joining of Baden to the German Customs Union. (Bavaria)
Bieberer Silber Silver of the Bieber (mines). (Hesse-Cassel)
Bizalmarn Az Osi Erenyben Affirmed of ancient and good quality. (Hungary)
Bog Cuva Jugoslaviju God guard Yugoslavia. (Yugoslavia)
Bonaparte Premier Consul Bonaparte, First Consul. (France)
Britanniarum Regina Fid. Def. Queen of the Britains, Defender of the Faith. (France)

C

Capit(ulum) Cath(edrale) Monasterien(se) Sede Vacante The Cathedral Chapter, Munster. The seat being vacant. (Munster)
Car. Albertus D.G. Rex Sard. Cyp. et Hier. Charles Albert, D.G., King of Sardinia, Cyprus, and Jerusalem. (Sardinia)
Car. Felix D.G. Rex Sar. Cyp. et Hier. Charles Felix, D.G., King of Sardinia, Cyprus, and Jerusalem. (Sardinia)
Carl Alexander Grossherzog von Sachsen Carl Alexander, Grand Duke of Saxony (Weimar). (Saxony)
Carl Anton Furst zu Hohenzollern Sigmaringen Carl Anton, Prince of Hohenzollern-Sigmaringen. (Hohenzollern-Sigmaringen)
Carl August H.Z.S. Weimar u. Eisenach Carl August, Duke of Saxe-Weimar-Eisenach. (Saxe-Weimar-Eisenach)
Carl Eduard Herzog V. Sachsen Coburg u. Gotha Carl Edward, Duke of Saxe-Coburg, and Gotha. (Saxe-Coburg-Gotha)
Carl Friedr(ich) Grossherzog z(u) Sachsen W(eim.) E(is.) Carl Frederick, Grand Duke of Saxe-Weimar-Eisenach. (Saxe-Weimar-Eisenach)
Carl Friedrich Grosherzog von Baden Carl Frederick, Grand Duke of Baden. (Baden)
Carl Furst Primas (der Rhein Confoed.) Carl, Prince Primate of the Rhine Confederation. (Rhine Confederation)
Carl Furst zu Hohenzollern Sigmaringen Carl, Prince of Hohenzollern-Sigmaringen. (Hohenzollern-Sigmargen)
Carl Furst zu Isenburg Carl, Prince of Isenburg. (Isenburg)
Carl Kronpr. v. Wurttemb. u Olga Grosfurstin v. Russl. verm d. 13 Juli 1846 Carl, Crown Prince of Wurttemberg and Olga, Grand Duchess of Russia, married on July 13, 1846. (Wurttemberg)
Carl Ludwig Erzherzog v. Osterreich Protector D. Osterreichischen Touristen Club Charles Louis, Archduke of Austria, Sponsor of the Austrian Tourist's Club. (Austria)
Carl XIII Sv. Norr. Goth. och V. Konung Charles XIII, King of Sweden, Norway, Gothland, and Vandalia. (Sweden)
Carl XIII Sveriges Goth. och V. Konung Charles XIII, King of Sweden, Gothland, and Vandalia. (Sweden)
Carl XIV Johan, Norges, Sver. G. og V. Konge Charles XIV, John, King of Norway, Sweden, Gothland, and Vandalia. (Norway)
Carl XIV Sveriges Norr. Goth. och V. Konung Charles XIV, King of Sweden, Norway, Gothland, and Vandalia. (Sweden)
Carl XV Norges Sver. G. V. K9nge Charles XV, King of Norway, Sweden, Gothland, Vandalia. (Norway)
Carl XV Sveriges Norr. Goth. och Vend. Konung Charles XIV, King of Sweden, Gothland, and Vandalia. (Sweden)
Carlos I Rei de Portugal Carlos I, King of Portugal. (Portugal)
Carlos I Rei e Amelia Rainha de Portugal Carlos I, King and Amelia, Queen of Portugal. (Portugal)
Carol I Domnul Romaniei Carol I, Prince of Romania. (Romania)
Carol I Rege al Romaniei Carol I, King of Bohemia. (Romania)
Carola Magna Ducissa Feliciter Regnante Grand Duchess Charlotte, happily reigning. (Luxembourg)
Carolus Ioachim D.G. Princ Furstenberg Carl Ioachim, D.G., Prince of Furstenberg. (Furstenberg)
Carolus Lud. D.G. Rex Etr(uriae) & M. Aloysia R(egina) Rectrix I. I. H. H. Charles Louis, D.G., King of Etruria and Maria Luisa, Queen Regent, Prince and Princess of Spain. (Tuscany)
Carolus IIII dei G. Charles IV, D.G. (Spain)
Carolus XIV Ioh. D.G. Rex Svegiae et Norv. An Avril 1821 Charles XIV John, D.G., King of Sweden and Norway, April, 1821. (Sweden)
Cartagena Sitiada Por Los Centralistas Cartagena besieged by the Centralists. (Spain)
Cattaro en Etat de Siege Cattaro in a state of siege. (Cattaro)
Centenaire des Chemins de Fer Belges Centenary of the Belgian railways. (Belgium)
Centenario da Guerra Peninsular Centenary of the Peninsular War. (Portugal)
Charles X Roi de France Charles X, King of France. (France)
Charlotte Grande-Duchesse de Luxembourg Charlotte, Grand Duchess of Luxemburg. (Luxemburg)
Charta Magna Bavariae Magna Carta of Bavaria. (Bavaria)
Christian VIII Konge af Danmark Christian VIII, King of Denmark. (Denmark)
Christian IX Konge af Danmark Christian IX, King of Denmark. (Denmark)
Christianus VII D.G. Dan. Novr. V. G. Rex Christian VII, D.G., King of Denmark, Norway, Vandalia, and Gothland. (Denmark)
Christianus VIII D.G. Daniae V. G. Rex Christian VIII, D.G., King of Denmark, Vandalia, and Gothland. (Denmark)
Christianus IX D.G. Daniae V. G. Rex Christian IX, D.G., King of Denmark, Vandalia, and Gothland. (Denmark)
Cinque Lire Five lire. (Tuscany)
Cinque Lire Italiane Firenze, Marzo 1861 Five Italian lire, Florence, March, 1961. (Italy)
Civitas Lucemborgensis Millesimum Ovans Expletannum Completing the celebration of 1000 years of the city of Luxemburg. (Luxemburg)
Com(es) in Thengen et Sup(remus) Haer(editarius) Prov(inciae) Carn(iolae) Maresch(allus) Count in Thengen and Supreme Hereditary Marshal in the Province of Carniola. (Auersperg)
Concordia patriae Nutrix Peace, the nurse of the fatherland. (Waldeck)
Concordia Res Parvae Crescunt Little things grow through concord. (Batavian Republic)
Confederation Suisse Swiss Confederation. (Swiss Confederation)
Confederaz. Svizzera Swiss Confederation. (Swiss Confederation)
Confoederatio helvetica Helvetian Confederation. (Helvetian Confederation)
Constituirende Versammlung I.D.F. Stadt Frankfurt 18 Mai 1848 Constituting asssembly of the Imperial Diet of Frankfurt, City of Frankfurt, May 18, 1848. (Frankfurt)
Cum Deo et Iure With God and Law. (Wurttemberg)
Custos Regni Deus God the Guardian of the Realm. (Naples & Sicily)

D

D.G. Car. Frid. March. Bad. & H.S.R.I. Elect. C. Pal. Rh. & D.G., Carl Frederick, Margrave of Baden and Elector of S.R.I., Count Palatine of the Rhine. . . . . (Baden)
D.G. Henr. XIII S.L. Ruth S.R.I. Princ. Com. E. Dom. Plav. D.G., Henry XIII, senior line of Reuss, Prince of S.R.I., Count and Lord of Plauen. (Reuss-Greiz)
D.G. Max(im) Ios(eph) C.P.R.U.B.D. S.R.I.A. & El. (D.I.C. & M.) D.G., Maximilian Joseph, Count Palatine of the Rhine and also Duke of Bavaria, Archdapifer and Elector of S.R.I., Duke of Julich, Cleves, and Mark. (Bavaria)
Das Schwert zur Hand in Herzen Gott, So wird D. Schweizer nie z. Spott The sword in hand and God in the heart, so will the Swiss never become a laughing stock. (Swiss)
De Namm des Heeren zy Geloofd The name of the Lord be praised. (Netherlands)
Decus et Tutamen Anno Regni Ornament and safeguard in the year of the reign. (Great Britain)
Dem Bund zum Schutz dem Feind zum Trutz With the League for offense, against the enemy for defense. (Switzerland)
Dem Prinzen Albert Ernst Georg und der Prinzessinn Elisabeth v. Sachs. bei Ihrem Besuche in der Munze zu Dresden im Iahre 1839 For Prince Albert Ernest George and the Princess Elizabeth of Saxony on their visit to the mint at Dresden in the year 1839. (Saxony)
Dem Vaterlande For the fatherland. (Saxe-Weimar)
Dem Verdienste seine Kronen, Reichenbach-Fraunhofer Honor to whom honor is due, Reichenbach and Fraunhofer. (Bavaria)
Den Benediktinern wieder eine Lehranstalt ubergeben On the handing over of another school to the Benedictine Order. (Bavaria)
Den Siegem bei Waterloo gewidmet am 18 Juni 1865 Dedicated to the victors of Waterloo on June 18, 1865. (Hannover)
Den 29 Ianuar 1869 (Died) on January 29, 1869. (Saxe-Coburg-Gotha)
Denkm. der Trennung der Koen. Therese von Ihrem Sohne dem Koen. Otto, Errichtet bei Aibling von Bayerischen Frauen Monument on the separation of Queen Therese from her son, King Otto, erected at Aibling by Bavarian women. (Bavaria)
Denkmahl der Anhaenglichkeit Bayerns an seinen Herrscherstamm, Errichtet zu Oberwittelsbach Monument on the devotion of Bavarians to their ruling house, erected at Oberwittelsbach. (Bavaria)
Denkmahl der Dreyssig Tausend Bayern welche im Russischen Kriege den Tod Fanden Monument for the 30,000 Bavarians who died in the Russian wars. (Bavaria)
Denkmahl des Koenigs Maximilian Joseph, Errichtet von der Hauptstadt Munchen Monument for King Maximilian Joseph, erected by the capital Munich. (Bavaria)
Denkmahl des Konigs Maximilian II in Lindau, Errichtet v.d. Stadten an der Sud-Nord-Bahn Monument for King Maximilian II in Lindau, erected by the cities on the South-North railway. (Monaco)
Deo Juvante With the aid of God. (Monaco)
Der Rhein Deutschlands Strom, nicht Deutschlands Grenze The Rhine, Germany's river, not Germany's frontier. (Germany)
Der St. Michaels-Orden zum Verdienst-Orden bestimmt The Order of St. Michael appointed an order of merit. (Bavaria)
Der Se(e)gen des Bergbaues The blessings of the mines. (Saxony)
Des Bergwerks Wohfahrt ist des Harzes Gluck, Die Grube Bergwerks-Wohlfahrt bei Clausthal kam in Ausbeute 1830 The welfare of the mine is the prosperity of Harz, the pits and the prosperity of the mine at Clausthal came into production in 1830. (Hannover)
Deus et Dies God and the Day. (Parma)
Die Eintheilung d. Konigreichs auf Geschichtl Grundlage zuruckgefuhrt 1838 The divisions of the kingdom restored to their historical foundations. (Bavaria)
Die Koenigin von Bayern Stiftet den Theresien Orden The Queen of Bavaria founds the Order of Therese. (Bavaria)
Dieci Lire Ten lire.
Dieci Paoli. Quattro Fiorini Ten paoli, four florins. (Tuscany)
Dieu Protege La Belgique God protect Belgium. (Belgium)
Dieu Protege La France God protect France. (France)
Dieus Sveti Latviju God guard Latvia. (Latvia)
Dio Benedite L'Italia God bless Italy. (Italy)
Dio Premiera La Costanza God rewards constancy. (Venice)
Dio Protegge (11 Re e) Il Regno God protect the king and the realm. (Naples & Sicily)
Dio Protegge L'Italia God protect Italy. (Sardinia)
Dios Es El Rey de Los Reyes God is the King of Kings. (Spain)
Dirige Me Domine Guide me, Lord. (Parma)
Domine Conserva Nos in Pace Lord, save us in peace. (Zurich)
Domine Salvum Fac Regem Lord, save the king. (France)
Domine Spes Mea A Iuventute Mea Lord, my hope in my youth. (Tuscany)
Dominus Providebit The Lord will provide. (Bern)
Drei(y) Ein Halb Gulden XV Ein Pfund Fein 3-1/2 guldens, 15 to the fine pound. (Bavaria)
Duodecim Lustris 1848, 1908 Gloriose Peractis Twelve lustra (60 years) 1848-1908 gloriously completed. (Austria)

Durch Kampf und Sieg zum Frieden Through struggle and victory to peace. (Bavaria)

Dux Sab. Ianvae (or Genvae) et Montisf. Princ. Ped. Duke of Savoy, Genoa, Montferrat, Prince of Piedmont. (Sardinia)

E

Eala Frya Fresena Frya of all the Frisians. (Hannover)

Eccl. S. Barbarae Patronae Fodin. Kuttenbergensium Duo Flor. Arg. Puri The Church of St. Barbara, Patron of the Kuttenberg Mines, two florins of pure silver. (Austria)

Edwardus VII Dei Gra. Britt. Omn. Rex Fid. Def. Ind. Imp. Edward VII, D.G., King of all the Britains, Defender of the Faith, Emperor of India. (Britains)

Eendragt Maakt Magt Union makes strength. (Netherlands)

Ehre dem Ehre Gebuhrt Honour to whom honour is due. (Bavaria)

Ehre Ist Mein Hoechstes Ziel Honour is my highest goal. (Switzerland)

Eidgen Freischiesen Solothiurn Federal Public Shooting Match in Solothurn. (Switzerland)

Eidgenossisches Frei(y) schiessen Federal Public Shooting Match; in Zurich (KM-S5), in Chur; in Bern (KM-S4); in Glarus (KM-20). (Switzerland)

Eidgenossisches Schutzenfest in Basel (KM-S14) Federal Shooting Festival in Basel; in Bern (KM-S6); in Nidwalden (KM-S6); in St. Gallen (KM-S12); in Schaffhausen (KM-S8); in Schwyz (KM-S9); in Zug (KM-S10); in Zurich (KM-S11). (Switzerland)

Ein Gedenkthaler zu Schiller's Hundertjahriger Geburtsfeier A commemorative taler on the hundredth anniversary of Schiller's birth. (Frankfurt)

Ein Gedenkthaler zum Deutschen Schutzenfeste Juli 1862 A commemorative taler on the German shooting festival July, 1862. (Frankfurt)

Ein Gott-Ein Recht-Eine Wahrheit One God, one justice, one truth. (Oldenburg)

Ein Thaler zu 100 Krzr. - Im Kronen Fuss One taler of 100 kreuzer, on the kronen standard. (Baden)

Ein Vereinsthaler xxx Ein Pfund Fein One convention taler, 30 to the fine pound. (Liechtenstein & German States)

Einigkeit und Recht und Freiheit Unity and right and freedom. (Germany)

Eintracht Macht Stark Union makes strength. (Chur)

Elizabeth II Dei Gratia Britt. Omn. Regina Fidei Defensor Elizabeth II, D.G., Queen of Great Britain, Defender of the Faith. (Great Britain)

Emanuel II Portug. et Algarb. Rex Manuel II, King of Portugal and Algarve. (Portugal)

Emma Furstin Regent c. Vormund. zu Waldeck u. P. Emma, Princess Regent and guardian of Waldeck and Pyrmont. (Waldeck & Pyrmont)

En Barcelona In Barcelona. (Spain)

Entree de Fribourg & Soleure dans La Confederation Suisse Entry of Fribourg and Solothurn into the Swiss Confederation. (Swiss)

Er Saete Gerechtigkeit und Erntete Liebe. Hosea X. 12 He sowed justice and harvested love. (Saxony)

Ernst August Friederike Marie, Marie, Georg Ernest, August, Frederika, Marie, Marie, George. (Hannover)

Ernst August - Viktoria Luise Herzog u. Herzogin zu Braunschweig (u. Luneb.) Ernest August, Victoria Louise, Duke and Duchess of Brunswick-Luneberg. (Brunswick-Luneberg)

Ernst August V.G.G. Koenig von Hannover Ernest August, by the grace of God, King of Hannover. (Hannover)

Ernst August Koenig von Hannover Ernest August, King of Hannover. (Hannover)

Ernst Herzog v. Sachsen Coburg u. Gotha Ernest, Duke of Saxe-Coburg-Gotha. (Saxe-Coburg-Gotha)

Ernst Herzog von Sachsen Altenburg Ernest, Duke of Saxe-Altenburg. (Saxe-Altenburg)

Ernst Herzog z. S. Coburg Saalf. F. z. Lichtenb. Ernest, Duke of Saxe-Coburg-Saalfeld, Prince of Lichtenburg. (Saxe-Coburg-Saalfeld)

Ernst Herzog z. S. Coburg u. Gotha F. z. Lichtenb. Ernest, Duke of Saxe-Coburg and Gotha, Prince of Lichtenburg. (Saxe-Coburg-Gotha)

Ernst Herzog zu Sachsen Coburg-Gotha Ernest, Duke of Saxe-Coburg-Gotha. (Saxe-Coburg-Gotha)

Ernst Herzog zu Sachsen Coburg und Saalfeld Ernest, Duke of Saxe-Coburg and Saalfeld. (Saxe-Coburg-Saalfeld)

Ernst Ludwig Grosherzog von Hessen Ernest Ludwig, Grand Duke of Hesse. (Hesse)

Eroffnung der Neuen Munze Sept. 1840 Opening of the new mint September, 1840. (Frankfurt)

Errichtung der Bayerischen Hypotheken-Bank Establish- ment of the Bavarian Mortgage Bank. (Bavaria)

Erste Eisenbahn in Deutschland mit Dampfwagen von Nurnberg nach Furth First railway in Germany with steam engines from Nuremberg to Furth. (Bavaria)

Erwahlt zum Kaiser der Deutschen d. 28 Marz 1849 Elected the Emperor of the Germans on March 28, 1849. (Frankfurt)

Erwahlt zum Reichsverweser uber Deutschland d 29 Iuni 1849 Elected imperial regent over Germany on June 29, 1849. (Frankfurt)

Erzherzog Johann von Oesterreich Archduke John of Austria. (Frankfurt)

Espana Spain. (Spain)

Et in Minimus Integer Faithful even in the smallest things. (Olmutz)

F

F. Berhard im Bart Prince Berhard the bearded. (Germany)

Feines Silber Fine silver. (Hannover)

Feldherrnhalle Hall of Generals. (Bavaria)

Felice ed Eliza PP. (Principes) de Lucca e Piombino Felix and Elisa, Prince and Princess of Lucca and and Piombino. (Lucca)

Ferd(inandus) D.G. H(ungariae) et B(ohemiae) Reg(ius) Pr(inceps) A. A. S(acri) R(omani) I(mperil) Pr(inceps) El(ector) Salisb(urgensis) Ferdinand, D.G., Royal Prince of Hungary and Bohemia, Archduke of Austria, Prince of S.R.I., Elector of Salzburg. (Salzburg)

Ferd. Hu. et Bo. Reg. Pr. A.A.S.R.I.Pr. El. Salisb. Ferdinand, Royal Prince of Hungary and Bohemia, Archduke of Austria, Prince of S.R.I., Elector of Salzburg. (Salzburg)

Ferd(inandus) I D. G. Aust(riae) Imp(erator) Hung(ariae) B(ohemiae) Rex H(umus) N(ominis) V R(ex) L(ombardiae) I(llyriae) A.A. Ferdinand I, D.G., Emperor of Austria, King of Hungary and Bohemia, Fifth of this name, King of Lombardy, Venice, Dalmatia, Galicia, Lodomeria, Illyria, Archduke of Austria. (Hungary)

Ferd. I D.G. Austr. Imp. Hung. Boh. R(ex) H(etruriae) N(eapolis) V(enetiae) Ferdinand I, D.G., Emperor of Austria, King of Hungary and Bohemia, Fifth of this name, King of Lombardy, Venice, Dalmatia, Galicia, Lodomeria, Illyria, Archduke of Austria. (Austria)

Ferd. I D.G. Regni Sicilarum et Hier Rex Ferdinand I, D.G., King of the Sicilies and Jerusalem. (Naples & Sicily)

Ferd. IV D.G. utr. Sic. et Hier, Rex Ferdinand IV, D.G., King of the Two Sicilies and Jerusalem. (Naples & Sicily)

Ferdin. VII Dei G. Ferdinand VII, D.G. (Spain)

Ferdinan. III D.G. Sicil. et Hier. Rex Ferdinand III, D.G., King of Sicily and Jerusalem. (Naples & Sicily)

Ferdinan. IV D. G. Siciliar, et Hie Rex Ferdinand IV, D.G., King of the Sicilies and Jerusalem. (Naples & Sicily)

Ferdinand Souv. Landgraf z. Hessen Ferdinand, sovereign landgrave of Hesse. (Hesse-Homburg)

Ferdinandus I D.G. Austriae Imperator Ferdinand I, D.G., Emperor of Austria. (Austria)

Ferdinandus II Dei Gratia Rex Ferdinand II, D.G., King. (Naples & Sicily)

Ferdinandus III D.G. P(rinceps) R(egius) H(ungariae) et B(ohemiae) A. A. M(agnus) D(ux) Etrur(iae) Ferdinand III, D.G., Royal Prince of Hungary and Bohemia, Archduke of Austria, Grand Duke of Tuscany. (Tuscany)

Ferdinandus III D.G. Rex Ferdinand III, King, D.G. (Naples & Sicily)

Ferdinandus IV D.G. Rex Ferdinand IV, King, D.G. (Naples & Sicily)

Ferdinandus VII Dei G(ratia) Ferdinand VII, D.G. (Spain)

Ferencz Jozsef I K.A.Cs. Es. M.H.S.D.O. Ap. Kir (Hungary)

Fern. 7 P. La G.D. Dios Y La Const. Ferdinand VII, D.G. and the Constitution. (Spain)

Fern. 7 P.L.G.D. Dios Rey de Espan. E Ynd. Ferdinand VII, D.G., King of Spain and the Indies. (Spain)

Fernando 7 Por La G. De Dios Ferdinand VII, D.G. (Spain)

Fernando 7 Por La Gracia De Dios Y La Constitucion Ferdinand VII, D.G. and the Constitution. (Spain)

Fernando VII Rey de Espana Ferdinand VII, King of Spain. (Spain)

Fert, Fert, Fert (A monogram) (Sardinia & Italy)

Fest Frei Schiessen von Weiner Schutzen Verein Public Shooting Festival of the Vienna Shooting Association. (Austria)

Fid. Def. Ind. Imp. Defender of the Faith, Emperor of India. (Great Britain)

Fideliter et Constanter Faithfully and steadfastly. (Saxe-Coburg-Gotha)

Folkets Karlek Min Beloning The love of the people is my my compensation. (Sweden)

Folkets Kjaerlighed Min Styrke, Dod Den 20 Januar 1848 The love of the people is my strength. (Denmark)

Folkets Val Min Hogsta Lag The welfare of the people is my strength. (Denmark)

Fr. Wilh. III K.V. Preuss Frederick William III, King of Prussia. (Prussia)

Franc. D.G. Ep. Princ Gurc Antiq. Com de Salm Reifferscheid Francis, D.G., Prince-Bishop of Gurk, Count of Reifferscheid. (Gurk)

Franc Ios. I D.G. Austr. Imp. et Hung. Rex Ap. Elisabetha Imp. et Reg. Francis Joseph I, D.G., Emperor of Austria and Apostolic King of Hungary, Elizabeth, Empress and Queen. (Austria)

Franc Ios. I D.G. Austr. Imp. et Hung. Rex Ap. Elisabetha Imp. et Reg. Francis Joseph I, D.G., Emperor of Austria, King of Hungary and Bohemia. (Austria)

Franc. Ios. I D.G. Austrie Imperator Francis Joseph I, D.G., Emperor of Austria. (Austria)

Franc. Ios. I D.G. Imp. Austr. Rex Boh. Gal. Ill. etc. Ap. Rex Hung. Francis Joseph I, D.G., Emperor of Austria, King of Bohemia, Galicia and Illyria and King of Hungary. (Austria)

Franc. I D.G. Aust. Imp. Hung. B.L.V.G.L.II. Rex A.A. Francis I, D.G., Emperor of Austria, King of Hungary and Bohemia, Lombardy, Venice, Galicia, Lodomeria, Illyria, Archduke of Austria. (Hungary)

Franc. II D.G.R.I.S.A. Conservator Castri Francis II, D.G., R.I.S.A., Protector of the city. (Frankfurt)

Francisc. Ios. I D.G. Austriae Imp. et Elisabetha Max. in Bavar. Ducis Fil. Francis Joseph I, D.G., Emperor of Austria and Elizabeth, daughter of Maximilian, Duke of Bavaria. (Austria)

Franciscus I D.G. Austriae Imperator Francis I, D.G., Emperor of Austria. (Austria)

Franciscus I Dei Gratia Rex Francis I, King, D.G. (Naples & Sicily)

Franciscus II D.G. Rom. et Haer. Aust. Imp. Francis II, D.G., Emperor of the Romans and Hereditary Emperor of Austria. (Austria)

Franciscus II D.G. Rom. Imp. Semp. Aug. Francis II, D.G., Emperor of Rome, ever august. (Regensberg)

Franciscus II D.G.R. Imp. S. A. Germ. Hu. Bo. Rex Francis II, D.G., R.I.S.A., King of Germany, Hungary, Bohemia. (Austria)

Franciscus II Dei Gratia Rex Francis II, King, D.G. (Naples & Sicily)

Franz Herzog zu Sachsen Cob. Saalfeld Francis, Duke of Saxe-Coburg-Saalfeld. (Saxe-Coburg-Saalfeld)

Franz Joseph I V.G.G. Kaiser V. Oesterreich Francis Joseph I, D.G., Kaiser of Austria. (Austria)

Fredericus VI D.G. Dan. V.G. Rex Frederick VI, D.G., King of Denmark, Vendalia, and Gothland. (Denmark)

Fredericus VII D.G. Daniae V.G. Rex Frederick VII, D.G., King of Denmark, Vendalia, and Gothland. (Denmark)

Frederick VII Konge af Danmark Frederick VII, King of Denmark. (Denmark)

Frederik IX Konge af Danmark Frederik IX, King of Denmark. (Denmark)

Freie Hansestadt Bremen Free Hanseatic city of Bremen. (Bremen)

Freie Stadt Danzig Free State of Danzig. (Danzig)

Freie Stadt Frankfurt Free city of Frankfurt. (Frankfurt)

Freie und Hansestadt Hamburg Free Hanseatic city of Hamburg. (Hamburg)

Freie und Hansestadt Lubeck Free Hanseatic city of Lubeck. (Lubeck)

Frid. Aug. Rex Sax(oniae) Dux Varsov Frederick August, King of Saxony, Duke of Warsaw. (Poland)

Frid. August D.G. Dux Sax. Elector Frederick August, D.G., Duke and Elector of Saxony. (Saxony)

Frid. August D.G. Rex Saxoniae Frederick August, D.G., King of Saxony. (Saxony)

Friderich I Koenig von Wurttemberg Frederick I, King of Wurttemberg. (Wurttemberg)

Fridericus D.G. Rex Wurt. S.R.I. Ar. Vexill. et Elect Frederick, D.G., King of Wurttemberg, Archmarshal, Standard Bearer, and Elector of the S.R.I. (Wurttemberg)

Fridericus D.G. Rex Wurt(t)emberg(iae) Frederick, D.G., King of Wurttemberg. (Wurttemberg)

Fridericus Pr. Waldecciae Com. Pyr. Frederick, Prince of Waldeck, Count of Pyrmont. (Pyrmont)

Fridericus Wurtembergiae Rex Frederick, King of Wurttemberg. (Wurttemberg)

Fridericus II D.G. Dux Wurt. S.R.I. Ar. Vex. et Elector Frederick II, D.G., Duke of Wurttemberg, Archmarshal, Standard Bearer, and Elector of the S.R.I. (Wurttemberg)

Friedensschluss zu Frankfurt A.M. 10 Mai 1871 Peace of Frankfurt-on-the-Main May 10, 1871. (Bavaria)

Friedr(ich) August Koenig v(on) Sachsen Frederick August, King of Saxony. (Saxony)

Friedr. Franz. I. 1815 - Friedr. Franz. IV. 1915. Grossherzoge v. Mecklenb. Schw. Frederick Francis IV, 1915 - Grand Dukes of Mecklenburg-Schwerin. (Mecklenburg-Schwerin)

Friedr. Gunther Furst zu Schwarzburg Frederick Gunther, Prince of Schwarzburg. (Schwarzburg-Rudolstadt)

Friedr. Wilhelm I Kurfurst v. Hessen Frederick William I, Elector of Hesse. (Hesse-Cassel)

Friedr. Wilhelm III Koenig v(on) Preussen Frederick William III, King of Prussia. (Prussia)

Friedr. Wilhelm IV Koenig v. Preussen Frederick William IV, King of Prussia. (Prussia)

Friedrich August Grossherzog v. Oldenburg Frederick August, Grand Duke of Oldenburg. (Oldenburg)

Friedrich August Herzog zu Nassau Frederick August, Duke of Nassau. (Nassau)

Friedrich August Konig v. Sachsen Frederick August, King of Saxony. (Saxony)

Friedrich August V.G.G. Koenig v. Sachsen Frederick August, D.G., King of Saxony. (Saxony)

Friedrich August II Koenig von Sachsen d. 9 Aug. 1854 Frederick August II, King of Saxony, (died) on August 9, 1854. (Saxony)

Friedrich der Streitbare * Friedrich August * 1409 Universitat Leipzig 1909 Frederick the Valiant, Frederick August, 1409, the University of Leipzig 1909. (Saxony)

Friedrich Deutscher Kaiser Konig v. Preussen Frederick, Emperor of Germany, King of Prussia. (Prussia)

Friedrich Franz - Alexandra Grossherzog u. Grossherzogin v. Mecklenb. Schw. Frederick Francis, Alexandra, Grand Duke and Grand Duchess of MecklenburgSchwerin. (Mecklenburg-Schwerin)

Friedrich Franz Grossh. v. Mecklenb. Schw. Frederick Francis, Grand Duke of Mecklenburg-Schwerin. (Mecklenburg-Schwerin)

Friedrich Franz V.G.G. Grossh. v. Mecklenb. Schw. Frederick Francis, D.G., Grand Duke of Mecklenburg-Schwerin. (Mecklenburg-Schwerin)

Friedrich Furst zu Waldeck und Pyrmont Frederick, Prince of Waldeck and Pyrmont. (Waldeck and Pyrmont)

Friedrich Grosherzog von Vaden Frederick, Grand Duke of Baden. (Baden)

Friedrich Gunther Furst zu Schwarzburg Rudolstadt Frederick Gunther, Prince of SchwarzburgRudolstadt. (Schwarzburg-Rudolstadt)

Friedrich Herzog von Anhalt Frederick, Duke of Anhalt. (Anhalt)

Friedrich Prinz und Regent von Baden Frederick, Prince and Regent of Baden. (Baden)

Friedrich und Luise von Baden Frederick and Louise of Baden. (Baden)

Friedrich W. C. Furst zu Hohenz. Hech. Frederick Wil-

liam Constantine, Prince of Hohenzollern-Hechingen. (Hohenzollern-Hechingen)
Friedrich. Wilh. V.G.G. Grossh. v. Mecklenb. Frederick William, D.G., Grand Duke of Mecklenburg-Strelitz. (Mecklenburg-Strelitz)
Friedrich Wilhelm Furst zu Nassau Frederick William, Prince of Nassau. (Nassau)
Friedrich Wilhelm IV Koenig von Preussen Frederick William IV, King of Prussia. (Prussia)
Friedrich I. 1701. Wilhelm II. 1901 Frederick I, 1701, William II, 1901. (Prussia)
Friedrich II Grossherzog von Baden Frederick II, Grand Duke of Baden. (Baden)
Friedrich II. Marie. Herzog und Herzogin von Anhalt Frederick II, Marie, Duke and Duchess of Anhalt. (Anhalt)
Fur Freiheit und Vaterland For freedom and Fatherland. (Switzerland)
Fur Gott und Vaterland For God and Fatherland. (Bavaria)
Furchtlos und Treu Fearless and true. (Wurttemberg)
Furstentag zu Frankfurt am Main im August 1863 Assembly of Princes in Frankfurt-on-the-Main in August 1863. (Frankfurt)

G

G.N.A. 1808 un Duro Gerona 1808, one duro. (Spain)
Garantie National National Security. (France)
Gaule Subalpine Subalpine Gaul. (Subalpine Republic)
Gedenkthaler zur Eroffnungs Feier der neuen Borse in Bremen am 5 Novemb. 1864 Commemorative taler on the opening celebration of the new Exchange in Bremen on November 5, 1864. (Bremen)
Georg Furst zu Schaumburg-Lippe George, Prince of Schaumburg-Lippe. (Schaumburg-Lippe)
Georg Furst zu Waldeck und Pyrmont & George, Prince of Waldeck and Pyrmont, ... (Waldeck and Pyrmont)
Georg Heinr(ich) Furst z(u) Waldeck u. Pyrmont George Henry, Prince of Waldeck and Pyrmont. (Waldeck and Pyrmont)
Georg Herzog zu Sachsen Altenburg George, Duke of Saxe-Altenburg. (Saxe-Altenburg)
Georg Herzog zu Sachsen Meiningen George, Duke of Saxe-Meiningen. (Saxe-Meiningen)
Georg Koenig von Sachsen George, King of Saxony. (Saxony)
Georg Kronprinz von Hannover, Marie Herzoginn v. S. Altenb. Verm. 18 Febr. 1845 George, Crown Prince of Hannover, Marie, Duchess of Saxe-Altenburg, married Feb. 18, 1845. (Hannover)
Georg Prinz z. Waldeck Furst z. Pyromont George, Prince of Waldeck, Prince of Pyrmont. (Waldeck and Pyrmont)
Georg Victor Furst zu Waldeck u Pyrmont George Victor, Prince of Waldeck and Pyrmont. (Waldeck and Pyrmont)
Georg Wilhelm Furst zu Schaumburg-Lippe George William, Prince of Schaumburg-Lippe. (Schaumburg-Lippe)
Georg II Herzog v(on) Sachsen-Meiningen George II, Duke of Saxe-Meiningen. (Saxe-Meiningen)
Georg III V.G.G. Konig und Churfurst George III, D.G., King and Elector. (Hannover)
Georg IV Konig v. Grosbritan. u. Hannover George IV, King of Great Britain and Hannover. (Hannover)
Georg V V.G.G. Koenig v. Hannover George V, D.G., King of Hannover. (Hannover)
Georgius III D.G. Britanniarum Rex F.D. George III, D.G., King of Great Britain, Defender of the Faith. (Great Britain)
Georgius III Dei Gratia Rex George III, King, D.G. (Great Britain)
Georgius IIII D.G. Britanniar. Rex F.D. George IV, D.G., King of the Britains, Defender of the Faith. (Great Britain)
Georgius V D.G. Britt. Omn. Rex F.D. Ind. Imp. George V, D.G., King of all the Britains, Defender of the Faith, Emperor of India. (Great Britain)
Georgius V Dei Gra. Britt. Omn. Rex George V, D.G., King of all the Britains. (Great Britain)
Georgius VI D.G. Br. Omn. Rex George VI, D.G., King of all the Britains. (Great Britain)
Georgius VI D.G. Br. Omn. Rex F.D. George VI, D.G., King of Great Britain, Defender of the Faith. (Great Britain)
Gepraegt in Gegenwart S.M. des Koenigs. Dresden d. 24 April 1855 Struck in the presence of His Majesty the King, Dresden on April 24, 1855. (Saxony)
Gerecht und Beharrlich Just and firm. (Bavaria)
Germ. Hun. Boh. Rex A.A.D. Loth. Ven. Sal. King of Germnay, Hungary, Bohemia, Archduke of Austria, Duke of Lorraine, Venice, Salzburg. (Austria)
Gerona Ano De 1809 Gerona, Year of 1809. (Spain)
Gioacchino Napol(eone) (Re Delle Due Sicil(ie) Joachim Napoleon, King of the Two Sicilies. (Naples & Sicily)
Glori in Excelsis Deo Glory to God in the highest. (Sweden)
Gluckauf! Clausthal in September 1839 Good luck! Clausthal in September 1839. (Hannover)
God Zy (Zij) Met ons God be with us. (Netherlands)
Goethe Goethe. (Germany)
Gott Beschirme Uns God protect us. (Hesse-Cassel)
Gott Ehre Vaterland God, Honour, Fatherland. (Hesse-Darmstaedt)
Gott Mit Uns (many) God with us. (Germany)
Gott Schirme Mecklenburg God protect Mecklenburg. (Mecklenburg-Strelitz)
Gott Schutze Ihn und den Theuren Erben Seines Throns God protect him and the dear Heir to his Throne. (Prussia)
Gott Segne Anhalt God bless Anhalt. (Anhalt-Bernburg)
Gott Segne Bayern God bless Bavaria. (Bavaria)
Gott Segne Handel u. Schiffahrt God bless business and commerce. (Bremen)
Gott Segne Sachsen God bless Saxony. (Saxony)
Gott und das Vaterland God and the Fatherland. (Bavaria)
Gott und Recht God and right. (Saxe-Weimar)
Gott war mit Uns God was with us. (Bremen)
Gotth. Ephraim Lessing Gotthold Ephraim Lessing. (Germany)
Governo Provvisorio di Lombardia Provisional government of Lombardy. (Lombardy)
Graf Zeppelin Weltflug Graf Zeppelin world flight. (Germany)
Grafl. Schaumburg Lipp. Vormundschaftl. Munze County Schaumburg-Lippe, guardianship coin. (Schaumburg-Lippe)
Grand-Duche de Luxembourg Grand duchy of Luxemburg. (Luxemburg)
Gregorius XVI (Pon(tifex) M(ax)(imus) Gregory XVI, Pope. (Papal States)
Grosherzogthum Baden Grand duchy of Baden. (Papal States)
Grosherzogthum Sachsen Grand duchy of Saxe-Weimar. (Saxe-Weimar)
Gud och Folket God and the people. (Sweden)
Gunth. Fried. Carl Furst z. Schwarzb. Sondersh. Gunther Frederick Carl, Prince of Schwarzburg-Sonderhausen. (Schwarzburg-Sondershausen)
Gunther Fr. C. II Furst z. Schwarzb. Sondersh. Gunther Frederick Carl II, Prince of Schwarzburg-Sondershausen. (Schwarzburg-Sondershausen)
Gustaf IV Adolph Sv. G. och V. Konung Gustav IV, Adolph, King of Sweden, Gothland, and Vendalia. (Sweden)
Gustaf V Sveriges Konung Gustaf V., King of Sweden. (Sweden)
Gustaf VI Adolf Sveriges Konung Gustaf VI, Adolf, King of Sweden. (Sweden)

H

Hac Nitimur Hanc Tuemur With this we strive, this we will defend. (Netherlands)
Hakimiyet Milletindir Sovereignty is of the people. (Turkey)
Handel'sfreiheit durch Eintracht Free trade through agreement. (Wurttemberg)
Handelsvertrag zwischen Bayern, Preussen, Wurttemberg und Hessen Commercial treaty between Bavaria, Prussia, Wurttemberg and Hesse. (Bavaria)
Hans Landwing Retter das Panner Bei Arbedo Hans Landwing saves the standard at Arbedo. (Switzerland)
Harz-Segen Harz blessings. (Hannover)
Heinrich d. Li. lung. Linie Furst Reuss von Ebersdorf Henry of the younger line, line of the princes of Reuss-Ebersdorf. (Reuss-Ebersdorf)
Heinruch Herzog zu Anhalt Henry, Duke of Anhalt. (Anhalt-Cothen)
Heinrich XIV V.G.G. Reg. Furst Reuss I.L. Henry XIV, D.G., ruling Prince of Reuss, Younger Line. (Reuss-Younger Line)
Heinrich XX V.G.G. Aelt. L(in) Souv(erain) Furst Reuss Henry XX, D.G., Older Line, Sovereign Prince of Reuss. (Reuss-Greiz)
Heinrich XXII V.G.G. Alt. L. Souv. Furst Reuss Henry XXII, D.G., Older Line, Sovereign Prince of Reuss. (Reuss-Greiz)
Heinrich LXII lung. Lin. und Stamm. Altest Furst Reuss Henry LXII, Younger Line and oldest branch, Prince of Reuss. (Reuss-Schleiz)
Heinrich LXVII V.G.G. Reg. Furst Reuss I.L. Henry LXVII, D.G., ruling Prince of Reuss, Younger Line. (Reuss-Schleiz)
Heinrich LXXII Jung. Lin. Furst Reuss Henry LXXII, Younger Line, Prince of Reuss. (Reuss-Schleiz)
Helvetia Switzerland. (Switzerland)
Helvetische Republik Swiss Republic. (Swiss Republic)
Herman Frider. Otto D.G. Princ. de Hohenzollern Heching. Herman Frederick Otto, D.G., Prince of Hohenzollern-Hechingen. (Hohenzollern-Hechingen)
Herzogthurn Anhalt, Getheilt 1603 Vereint 1863 Duchy of Anhalt, divided 1603, united 1863. (Anhalt)
Herzogthurn Nassau Duchy of Nassau. (Nassau)
Hieronymus D.G.A. & P.S.A.S.L.N.G. Prim. Jerome, D.G., Archbishop and Prince of Salzburg. (Hieronymus)
Hieronymus Napoleon Jerome Napoleon. (Westphalia)
Hindenburg Reichsprasident Hindenburg, President of Germany. (Germany)
Hispaniar(um) Infans Prince of the Spains. (Spain)
Hispaniarum et Ind. Rex King of the Spains and the Indies. (Spain)
Hispaniarum Rex King of the Spains. (Spain)
Honi Soit Qui Mal Y Pense Evil to him who thinks evil. (Great Britain)
Honore V Prince de Monaco Honore V, Prince of Monaco. (Monaco)
Hun. Boh. Gal. Rex A.A. D. Lo. Sal. Wirc. King of Hungary, Bohemia, Galicia, Archduke of Austria, Dalmatia, Lodomeria, Salzburg, and Wurzburg. (Austria)
Hun. Boh. Gal. Rex A.A. Lo Wi. et in Fr. Dux King of Hungary, Bohemia, Galicia, Archduke of Austria, Lodomeria, Wurzburg, and in Franconia, Duke. (Austria)
Hundert Jahre Bremerhaven Centennial of Bremerhaven. (Germany)
Hundertjahrige Grundung der Hochschule zu Erlangen durch d. Markgr. Friedr. v. Brandenb. Bayr. Centenary of the foundation of the University of Erlangen by the Margrave, Frederick of Brandenburg-Bayreuth. (Bavaria)
Hun(g) Boh. Lomb. et Ven. Gal. Lod. II(I) Rex A.A. King in Hungary, Bohemia, Lombardy, and Venice, Galicia, Lodomeria, Illyria, Archduke of Austria. (Austria)
Hungar. Bohem. Gal. Lod. Ill. Rex. A.A. King in Hungary, Bohemia, Galicia, Lodomeria, Illyria, Archduke of Austria. (Austria)

I

Ich Bau auf Gott I rely on God. (Reuss-Schleiz)
Iedem Das Seinige To each his own. (Appenzell)
In Hoc Signo Vinces In this sign you will conquer. (Portugal)
In Memor. Vindicatae Libert. ac Relig. In memory of the establishment of liberty and religion. (Sweden)
In te Domine Speravi In thee have I hoped, O Lord. (Gurk)
In Terra Pax Peace in the land. (Papal States)
Indipendenza Italiana Italian Independence. (Italian)
Ioachim Grosherzog von Berg Joachim, Grand Duke of Berg. (Berg)
Ioachim Herzog zu Berg u. Cleve Joachim, Duke of Berg and Cleves. (Berg)
Iohann Koenig, Amalie Koenigin v. Sachsen John, King, Amalie, Queen of Saxony. (Saxony)
Iohann V.G.G. Koenig v. Sachsen John, D.G., King of Saxony. (Saxony)
Ioseph Herzog zu Sachsen Altenburg Joseph, Duke of Saxe-Altenburg. (Saxe-Altenburg)
Ioseph Nap. Dei Gratia Joseph Napoleon, D.G. (Spain)
Ioseph Napol. D.G. utr. Sicil. Rex Joseph Napoleon, D.G., King of the Two Sicilies. (Naples & Sicily)
Isabel 2 Por La Gracia De Dios Isabel II, D.G. (Spain)
Isabel 2 Por la Gracia de Dios y La Constitucion Isabel II, D.G., and the Constitution. (Spain)
Isti Sunt Patres Tui Verique Pastores These are your fathers and true shepherds. (Papal States)
Italia Libera Dio Lo Vuole A Free Italy, God wills it. (Lombardy)
Iustitia Regn(orum) Fundamentum Justice, the Foundation for kingdoms. (Austria)

J

Jahrhundertfeier Centennial. (Mecklenburg-Schwerin)
Jahrtausend Feier der Rheinlands Millenary Jubilee of the Rhineland. (Germany)
Jan de Blannen John, the Blind. (Luxembourg)
Joannes D.G. Port. et Alg. P. Regens John, D.G., Prince Regent of Portugal and Algarve. (Portugal)
Joannes D.G. P(rinceps) Portugaliae et Alg(arbiae) John, D.G., Prince of Portugal and Algarve. (Portugal)
Joannes VI D.G. Portug. Brasil et Algarb. Rex John VI, D.G., King of Portugal, Brazil, and Algarve. (Portugal)
Joh. Fried. d. Groszmut Kurf. v. Sachsen, Stifter d. Univ. Jena John Frederick the magnanimous, Elector of Saxony, Founder of the University of Jena. (Saxony)
Johann II Furst zu (or von) Liechtenstein John II, Prince of Liechtenstein. (Liechtenstein)

K

Kanton Schwyz Canton Schwyz. (Schwyz)
Karl Koenig von Wuerttemberg Karl, King of Wurttemberg. (Wurttemberg)
Klar und Fest Clear and firm. (Liechtenstein)
Koenig von Westphalen Fr. Pr. King of Westphalia, Prince of France. (Westphalia)
Koenigl. Wurttemb. Kronen Thaler Kingdom of Wurttemberg crown taler. (Wurttemberg)
Kong Frederik IX Dronning Ingrid af Danmark King Frederik IX, Queen Ingrid of Denmark. (Denmark)
Koningrijk Holland Kingdom of Holland. (Holland)
Kon. Wurttemb. Kingdom of Wurttemberg. (Wurttemberg)
Kur. Hess. Land Munze Electorate of Hesse, legal money. (Hesse-Cassel)
Kurfurstenthurn Hessen Electorate of Hesse. (Hesse-Cassel)

L

L.L. Ph. M.V. Duc de Brabant M.H.A. Duchesse de Brabant 21-22 Aout 1853 Leopold Louis Philippe, Maria Victor, Duke of Brabant, Maria Henrietta, Duchess of Brabant, 21-22 August, 1853. (Belgium)
Land Skal Med Lov Bygges The country shall be built by law. (Norway)
Land Skall Med Lag Byggas The country shall be built by law. (Sweden)
Landtag Provincial legislature. (Bavaria)
Largiente Numine Diety bestowing his bounty. (Regensburg)
Latvijas Republika Latvian Republic. (Latvia)
Lege et Fide By law and faith. (Austria)
Leo XII Pon(tifex) (Max(imus) Leo XII, Pope. (Papal States)
Leopold Friedrich Herzog zu (von) Anhalt Leopold, Grand Duke of Anhalt. (Anhalt-Dessau)
Leopold Grosherzog von Baden Leopold, Grand Duke of Baden. (Baden)
Leopold Premier Roi des Belges Leopold I, King of the Belgians. (Belgians)
Leopold II Roi des Belges Leopold II, King of the Belgians. (Belgians)
Leopoldus D.G. P.I.A. P(rinceps) R(egius) H(ungariae) et B(ohemiae) A.A. Magn(us) Dux

Etr(uriae) Leopold II, D.G., Prince of Imperial Austria, Prince Regent of Hungary and Bohemia, Archduke of Austria, Grand Duke of Tuscany. (Tuscany)
Lerida Ano de 1809 Lerida Year of 1809. (Spain)
Lex Tua Veritas Law is your truth. (Tuscany)
Ley Patria Rey Law, Fatherland, King. (Spain)
Ley 900 Milesimas 40 Piezas en Kilog Law 900/1000, 40 pieces per kilogram. (Spain)
Liberta Eguaglianza Liberty, Equality. (Ligurian Republic)
Libertade Inferme e de' Tiranni Agevol Preda Weak liberty is the easy prey of tyrants. (Switzerland)
Liberte, Egalite, Eridania Liberty, Equality, Eridania. (Subalpine Republic)
Liberte, Egalite, Fraternite Liberty, Equality, Fraternity. (France)
Literatur, Vetenskap, Konst Literature, Science, Art. (Sweden)
Lodew. Nap. Kon. Van Holl Louis Napoleon, King of Holland. (Holland)
Louis Philippe (I) Roi de France Louis Philippe I, King of the French. (France)
Louis XVIII Roi de France Louis XVIII, King of France. (France)
Lucilinburhuc Luxemburg. (Luxemburg)
Ludewig Grosherzog von Hessen Ludwig, Grand Duke of Hesse. (Hesse-Darmstaedt)
Ludovicus I D.G. (Hisp(aniarum) Inf(ans) Rex Etruriae Par(mae) Plac(entiae) and Prince Louis I, D.G., Prince of the Spains, King of Etruria, Prince of Parma and Piacenza. (Tuscany)
Ludovicus II Bavariae Rex Ludwig II, King of Bavaria. (Bavaria)
Ludwig Erbprinz v. B. Geb. 25 August; Ludwig Koen. Prinz v. B. Geb. 7 Januar Ludwig, Crown Prince of Baden, born August 25; Ludwig, Royal Prince of Baden, born January 7. (Baden)
Ludwig Grosherzog von Baden Ludwig, Grand Duke of Baden. (Baden)
Ludwig Loenig von Bayern Ludwig, King of Bavaria. (Bavaria)
Ludwig I Giebt die Krone an seinen Sohn Maximilian am 20 Maerz 1848 Ludwig I, gives his crown to his son Maximilian on March 20, 1848. (Bavaria)
Ludwig I Koenig von Bayern Ludwig I, King of Bavaria. (Bavaria)
Ludwig II Koenig v. Bayern Ludwig II, King of Bavaria. (Bavaria)
Ludwig II Grosherzog von Hessen Ludwig II, Grand Duke of Hesse. (Hesse-Darmstaedt)
Ludwig III Koenig von Bayern Ludwig III, King of Bavaria. (Bavaria)
Ludwig III Grosherzog von Hessen Ludwig III, Grand Duke of Hesse. (Hesse-Darmstaedt)
Ludwig IV Grosherzog von Hessen Ludwig IV, Grand Duke of Hesse. (Hesse-Darmstadt)
Ludwigscanal Ludwig's Canal. (Bavaria)
Luitpold Prinz-Regent v. Bayern Leopold, Prince-Regent of Bavaria. (Bavaria)
Lumen ad Revelationem Gentium Light and revelation for the peoples. (Papal States)
L'Union Fait La Force Union makes strength. (Belgium)

M

Magnus ab Integro Saeclorum Nascitur Ordo The great order of the centuries is born anew. (Bavaria)
Magyar Kiralysag Hungarian Kingdom. (Hungarian)
Magyar Koztarsasag Hungarian Republic. (Hungarian)
Manibus Ne Laedar Avris Lest I be injured by greedy hands. (Sweden)
Maria II D.G. Portug. et Alg. Regina Maria II, D.G., Queen of Portugal and Algarve. (Portugal)
Maria II Portug. et Algarb Regina Maria II, Queen of Portugal and Algarve. (Portugal)
Maria Luigia Princ(ipissa) Imp. Arcid. d'Austria Marie Louise, Imperial Princess Archduchess of Austria. (Parma)
Matrimonio Coniuncti Joined in wedlock. (Austria)
Maximilian Ioseph Churfurst in Baiern Maximilian Joseph, Elector in Bavaria. (Bavaria)
Maximilian Ioseph Churfurst zu Pfalzbaiern Maximilian Joseph, Elector in the Palatinate. (Rhenish Palatinate)
Maximilian Ioseph Konig von Baiern Maximilian Joseph, King of Bavaria. (Bavaria)
Maximilian Kronpr. v. Bayern u. Marie K. Prinz. v. Preuss. verm.d. 12 Octb. 1842 Maximilian, Crown Prince of Bavaria and Marie, Crown Princess of Prussia, married on October 12, 1842. (Bavaria)
Maximilian II Koenig v. Bayern Maximilian II, King of Bavaria. (Bavaria)
Maximilianus Iosephus Bavariae Rex Maximilian Joseph, King of Bavaria. (Bavaria)
Med Folket For Fosterlandet By the people for the fatherland. (Sweden)
Med Gud for Aere og Ret. Dod Den 15 November 1863 With God, for honor and justice, Died on November 15, 1863. (Denmark)
Med Logum Skal Land Byggja By law shall the land be built. (Iceland)
Megkoronaztatasanak Negyvenedik Evfordulojara Fortieth anniversary of the coronation. (Hungary)
Meglio Vivere Un Giorno Da Leone Che Cento Anni Da Pecora Better to live one day as a lion than a hundred years as a sheep. (Italy)
Michael I D.G. Portug. et Algarb. Rex Michael I, D.G., King of Portugal and Algarve. (Portugal)
Mihai I Regele Romanilor Michael I, King of Romania. (Romania)
Mikolay I Ces. Wsz. Rossyi Krol Polski Panuiacy Nicholas I, Tsar of all the Russians and present King of Poland. (Poland)
Mit Gott durch Kampf zu Sieg und Einigung With God through struggle to victory and union. (Wurttemberg)
Mit Gottes Hulfe With God's help. (SchaumburgLippe)
Mit Herz und Hand Fuer's Alpenland With heart and hand for the Alpine land. (Austria)
Mit Vereinten Kraeften With united strength. (Austria)
Mo(neta) Arg(entiae) Ord. Faed. Belg(ii) Holl. Silver money of the Federated Belgian Union - Holland. (Holland)
Mo. Arg. Pro Conf(oederatiae) Belg(ii) D(ucatus) Gel(riae) and C(omitatus) Z(utphaniae) Silver money of the Confederated Belgian Provinces, Duchy of Gelderland and County of Zutphen. (Netherlands)
Mo. No. Arg. Pro. Confoe. Belg. Trai. . . . .Holl. New silver money of the confederated Belgian Provinces - Utrecht or Holland. (Netherlands)
Moldova Lui Stefan in Veci a Romaniei Moldavia, Stefan the Great, his country of Romania forever. (Romania)
Mon. Nov. Castri Imp. Friedberg New money of the free city of Friedberg. (Friedberg)
Munt van Het Koningryk Der Nederlanden Money of the Kingdom of the Netherlands. (Netherlands)
Munzvereinigung Sudteutscher Staaten Monetary union of the South German States. (Bavaria)

N

Nach Funfzig-Jahriger Regierung For the fiftieth anniversary of the reign. (Schaumburg-Lippe)
Nap. Lodew. I Kon. Van Holl. Napoleon Louis I, King of Holland. (Holland)
Napoleone Imperator E Re Napoleon, Emperor and King. (Italy)
Navigare Necesse Est It is necessary to navigate. (Germany)
Nec Aspera Terrent Nor do difficulties terrify. (Brunswick)
Nec Temere Nec Timide Neither rashly nor timidly. (Danzig)
Nicolaus Friedr. Peter Gr. H. v. Oldenburg Nicholas Frederick Peter, Grand Duke of Oldenburg. (Oldenburg)
Non Relinquam Vos Orphanos I shall not leave you as orphans. (Papal States)
Nulla Dolo Via Sub Bono Principe There is no path for guile under a good prince. (Naples & Sicily)

O

Omnia Cum Deo Everything with God. (Reuss-Greiz)
Oscar Norges Sver. G. og V. Konge Oscar, King of Norway, Sweden, Gothland, and Vendalia. (Norway)
Oscar Sveriges Norr. Goth. och Vend. Konung Oscar, King of Sweden, Norway, Gothland, and Vendalia. (Sweden)
Otto Koenig von Bayern Otto, King of Bavaria. (Bavaria)
Otto Prinz v. Bayern Griechenlands Erster Koenig Otto, Prince of Bavaria, first King of Greece. (Bavaria)

P

P.M. Sa. Sc. Cz. nec no. Sv. Go. Va. He. Rex (4336-41) Prussia, Masovia, Semgallia, Czersk as well as hereditary King of Sweden, Gothland, Vandalia. (Poland)
Palma Sub Pondere Crescit The palm grows under its weight. (Waldeck)
Patria Si Dreptul Meu The country and my right. (Romania)
Patrona Bavariae Patroness of Bavaria. (Bavaria)
Paul Alexander Leopold Furst zur Lippe. Paul Alexander Leopold, Prince of hope. (Lippe-Detmold)
Paul Friedr(ich) August Gr(oss)h(erzog) v(on) Oldenburg Paul Frederick August, Grand Duke of Oldenburg. (Oldenburg)
Paul Friedrich Emil Leopold Furst z. Lippe. Paul Friedrich Emil Leopold, Prince of Lippe. (Lippe-Detmold)
Per Aspera - Ad Astra Through difficulties to the stars. (Mecklenburg-Schwerin)
Per La Gr(acia) Di Dio Duch. di Parma Piac. E. Guast D.G., Duchess of Parma, Piacenza, and Guastalla. (Parma)
Peso Grani 1726 Bonta Oncie 10.16 Grain weight 1726, fine ounces 10.16. (Ligurian Republic)
Petrus IV D.G. Portug. Algarb. Rex Peter IV, D.G., King of Portugal and Algarve. (Ligurian Republic)
Philipp. Landgraf z. Hessen. Ernst Ludwig Grossherzog v. Hessen u. B. R. Phillip, Landgrave of Hesse, Ernest Ludwig, Grand Duke of Hesse. (Hesse-Darmstaedt)
Philipp Souv. Landgraf zu Hessen Phillip, Sovereign Landgrave of Hesse. (Hesse-Darmstaedt)
Piece de 5 Francs Piece of 5 francs. (France)
Pius VII Pon(tifex) M(aximus) Pius VII, Pope. (Papal States)
Pius VIII Pont. Max. Pius VIII, Pope. (Papal States)
Pius IX Pont. Max. Pius IX, Pope. (Papal States)
Post Tenebras Lux Light after darkness. (Switzerland)
Pour Etre Forts Soyons Unis Let us be united to be strong. (Switzerland)
Primitiae Fodin Kuttenb. ab Aerari. Iterum Susceptarum First results dug from the Kuttenberg mines in a renewed undertaking. (Austria)
Prin Statornicie La Izbanda Through stability to success. (Romania)
Princ Aichst. Pas. et Ber. S.R.I.P. Elector Prince of Eichstaedt, Passau, and Berchtesgaden, Prince of S.R.I., Elector. (Salzburg)
Princ Aichst. Passau et Berchtolsgad Prince of Eichstaedt, Passau, and Berchtesgaden. (Salzburg)
Princ. Gallic Magn. Elect. Imp. Prince of France, Grand Imperial Elector. (Naples & Sicily)
Principato di Lucca E Piombino Principality of Lucca and Piombino. (Naples & Sicily)
Principe E Grand' Ammiraglio Di Francia Prince and Grand Admiral of France. (Naples & Sicily)
Prinz Jean vu Letzeburg Prince Jean of Luxemburg. (Luxemburg)
Pro Deo et Populo For God and the people. (Bavaria)
Providentia Optimi Principis With the forethought of the wisest leaders. (Naples & Sicily)

Q

Quin Matrimonii Lustrum Celebrant XXIV Aprilis MDCCCLXXIX They celebrate the 25th wedding anniversary April 24, 1879. (Austria)
Quinque Coronae 5 korona. (Austria)

R

Ra(i)n. Farn. Par. et Plac. Dvx IV (4144-47) Ranuccio Farnese, fourth Duke of Parma and Piacenza. (Ronco)
Ran. Far. Par. et Plac. Dvx VI (4122-25) Ranuccio Farnese, sixth Duke of Parma and Piacenza. (Parma)
Ran. Far. Pla. et Par. Dux VI (4130) Ranuccio Farnese, sixth Duke of Parma and Piacenza. (Piacenza)
Ratt och Sanning Justice and truth. (Sweden)
Recta Tueri (or Tveri) Defend the right. (Austria & Hungary)
Regensburg Regensburg (Ratisbon). . . . . (Regensburg)
Regni Vtr. Sic. et Hier. Of the Kingdom of the Two Sicilies and Jerusalem. (Naples & Sicily)
Regno D'Italia Kingdom of Italy. (Italy)
Regno Delle Due Sicilie Kingdom of the Two Sicilies. (Naples & Sicily)
Reitersaule Maximilian's I Churfursten v. Bayern Errichtet v. Konig Ludwig I Equestrian column of Maximilian I, Elector of Bavaria, erected by King Ludwig I. (Bavaria)
Relinquo vos Liberos ab Utroque homine I leave you as children of each man. (San Marino)
Repubblica de S(an) Marino Republic of San Marino. (San Marino)
Repubblica Italiana Italian Republic. (Italian Republic)
Repubblica Ligure Ligurian Republic. (Ligurian Republic)
Repubblica Veneta Venetian Republic. (Venetian Republic)
Republica Bernensis Republic of Bern. (Republic of Bern)
Republica Portuguesa Portugese Republic. (Portugese Republic)
Republica Portuguesa, 5 de Outubro de 1910 Portugese Republic 5 October, 1910. (Portugese)
Republik Osterreich, funfzig schilling Republic of Austria, 50 schilling. (Austria)
Republika Ceskoslovenska Republic of Czechoslovakia. (Czechoslovakia)
Republique et Canton de Geneve Republic and Canton of Geneva. (Geneve)
Respublica S. Marini Republic of San Marino. (San Marino)
Ret og Sandhed Justice and truth. (Norway)
Revolucion - Cinco Pesetas - Cantonal Revolution, 5 pesetas, Cantonal. (Spain)
Rex Lomb. et Ven. Dalm. Gal. Lod. III. A.A. King of Lombardy and Venice, Dalmatia, Galicia, Lodomeria, Illyria, Archduke of Austria. (Austria)
Rey Const. de Espana Constitutional King of Spain. (Spain)
Rey de Espana Y de Las Indias King of Spain and the Indies. (Spain)
Rey de las Espanas King of the Spains. (Spain)
Reyna de Espana Y de Las Indias Queen of Spain and the Indies. (Spain)
Rey(i)na de Las Espanas Queen of the Spains. (Spain)
Roberto I D. DI PAR. PIAC. Ecc. E Luisa M. Di. Borb. Regg. Robert I, Duke of Parma, Piacenza, ... and Luisa Maria of Bourbon, Regent. (Parma)
Royaume de Belgique Kingdom of Belgium. (Belgium)
Rudolph Joan D.G. Case. A.R. Hun. Boh. Princ. A.A. Rudolph John, D.G., Imperial and Royal Prince of Hungary and Bohemia, Archduke of Austria. (Austria)
Rzeczpospolita Polska Polish Republic. (Polish)

S

S. Carolus Magnus Fundator St. Charles the Great, Founder. (Munster)
S. Maria Mater Dei Patrona Hung. Blessed Mary, Mother of God, Patron of Hungary. (Hungary)
S.R.E. Tit. S. Petri in Mont. Aur. Card. Archiep. Olom. Cardinal Archbishop of Olmutz. (Olmutz)
Salus Populi The safety of the people. (Spain)
Salus Reipublicae Suprema Lex Supreme law is the safety of the state. (Poland)
Salvam Fac Rempublicam Tuam Your state safe in union. (San Marino)
Schweizer(tsche) Eidsgenoss(enschaft) Swiss Federal Shooting Match. (Swiss)
Scudo di Lire Sei 27 Pratile Anno VIII Scudo of 6 lire, June 16, 1800. (Cisalpine Republic)
Sede Vacante The chair being vacant. (Papal States)
Segen des Anhalt Bergbaues Blessings of the Anhalt mines. (Anhalt-Bernburg)
Segen des Badischer Bergbaues Blessings of the Baden mines. (Baden)
Segen des Bergbau Blessings of the mines. (Saxony)

Segen des Himmels Blessings of heaven. (Bavaria)
Se(e)gen des Mansfelder Bergbaues Blessings of the Mansfeld mines. (Prussia)
Seinem Vater Carl Friederich dem Gesegneten To his father Caarl Frederick the Victorious. (Bavaria)
Shqipni Albania. (Albania)
Sieges Thaler Victory taler. (Prussia)
Slovenska Republica Slovakian Republic. (Slovakian)
Soberania Nacional National Sovereignty. (Spain)
Sous Le Regne du Roi Leopold III In the reign of King Leopold III. (Belgium)
Standbild A. Durer's Errichtet zu Nurnberg Statue of Albrecht Durer, erected at Nuremberg. (Bavaria)
Standbild des Canzler's Freyherrn v. Kreittmayr, Errichtet in Munchen 1845 Statue of Chancellor Baron von Kreittmayr, erected in Munich, 1845. (Bavaria)
Standbild des Furstbischof's Julius Echter v. Mespelbrunn, Errichtet zu Wurzburg 1847 Statue of Bishop-Elector Julius Echter of Mespelbrunn, erected at Wurzburg, 1847. (Bavaria)
Standbild des Johann Christoph Ritter von Gluck, Errichtet in Munchen v. Konig Ludwig I 1848 Statue of John Christopher, Knight von Gluck, erected at Munich by King Ludwig I, 1848. (Bavaria)
Standbild des Roland de Latre gen. Orlando di Lasso, Errichtet in Munchen v. Konig Ludwig I 1849 Statue of Roland de Latre called Orlando di Lasso, erected in Munich by King Ludwig I, 1849. (Bavaria)
Standbild Jean Paul Friedrich Richter's, Errichtet zu Bayreuth 1841 Statue of Jean Paul Frederick Richter, erected at Bayreuth, 1841. (Bavaria)
Stark im Recht Strong in justice. (Frankfurt)
Stato Pontificio The Papal State. (Papal States)
Stiftung des Ludwigs-Ordens Founding of the Ludwig Order. (Bavaria)
Supra Firmam Petram Upon a firm rock. (Papal States)
Susceptor Noster Deus God is our defense. (Tuscany)
Suum Cuique, Loenungs Thaler To each his own, coronation taler. (Prussia)
Svensk. Odlings Beframjare Promoter of Swedish culture. (Swedish)
Svenska Folkets Lagbundna Frihet Freedom within the law of the Swedish people. (Swedish)
Sveriges Riksdag Swedish Parliament. (Swedish)
Szechenyi, Istvan Stephen Szechenyi. (Hungary)
Szt. Istvan St. Stephen. (Hungary)
Szuletesenek 75 Evfordulojara 75th anniversary of his birth. (Hungary)

T

Tansics, Mihaly Michael Tancsics. (Hungary)
Tausend Jahre Burg und Stadt Meissen A thousand years of the town and city of Meissen. (Germany)
(In) Terra Pax Peace in the land. (Papal States)
Tir Federal a Fribourg Federal Shooting Match at Fribourg. (Switzerland)
Tir Federal a la Chaux-de-Fonds Juillet 1863 Federal Shooting Match at Chaux-de-Fonds, July, 1863. (Switzerland)
Tir Federal de 1876 a Lausanne Federal Shooting Match of 1876 at Lausanne. (Switzerland)
Tiro Federale in Lugano Federal Shooting Match at Lugano. (Switzerland)
Tiroler Freiheit Tyrolean liberty. (Austria)
Trau - Schau - Wem Trust, look, to whom. (Baden)
Treu Der Verfassung Loyal to the constitution. (Germany)
Tritt die Regierung des Landes an am 13 October 1825 Assumes the government of the country on October 13, 1825. (Bavaria)
Tueatur Unita Deus, Anno Dom 1847 May God guard these United (Kingdoms) in the year of our Lord 1847. (Great Britain)
Turkiye Cumhuriyeti Republic of Turkey. (Turkey)

U

Ueb Aug und Hand Fuer's Vaterland Train eye and hand for the fatherland. (Austria)
Umberto I Re D'Italia Humbert I, King of Italy. (Italy)
Union et Force Union and strength. (France)
Unione E Virtu' Union and strength. (Cisalpine Republic)
Unione Italiana Italian Union. (Venice)
Ut sit suo Pondere Tutus That he may be safe by his own weight. (Nassau)
U(V)tr. Sic. Hier. Hisp. Inf(ans) Of the Two Sicilies and Jerusalem, Prince of Spain. (Naples & Sicily)

V

V.G.G. Heinrich d. XIII Aelt. Reuss G.U.H.V.P. Reg. F.z. Greiz D.G., Henry the XIII, eldest line of Reuss, Count and Lord of Plauen, ruling Prince of Greiz. (Reuss-Greiz)
Veni Lumen Cordium Come light of hearts. (Papal States)
Verbum Dni. Manet in Aeternum The word of the Lord abides forever. (Hesse-Darmstaedt)
Vereinsmunze (many) Convention money. (German States)
Vereinten sich mit den Getreuen Staenden zu neuer Verfassung des Staats They united themselves with the faithful supporters in the new composition of the state. (Saxony)
Verfassungssaeule, Errichtet vom Gr. v. Schoenborn, Eingeweiht 1828 Constitution column erected by Count von Schoenborn, dedicated 1828. (Bavaria)
Veritas Lex Tua The truth is your law. (Salzburg)
Verlegung der Ludwig Maximilians Hochschule von Landshut nach Munchen 1826 Removal of the Ludwig Maximilian University from Landshut to Munich, 1826. (Bavaria)
Verni Sebe-Svorne Napred Faithful to ourselves, united forward. (Slovakia)
Vic. Em. D.G. Rex Sar. Cyp. et Ier. Victor Emmanuel, D.G., King of Sardinia, Cyprus, and Jerusalem. (Sardinia)
Victoria Dei Gratia Victoria, D.G. (Great Britain)
Victoria Dei Gratia Britanniar. Reg. F.D. Victoria, D.G., Queen of the Britains, Defender of the Faith. (Great Britain)
Victoria Dei Gra. Britt. Regina Fid. Def. Ind. Imp. Victoria, D.G., Queen of Britain, Defender of the Faith, Empress of India. (Great Britain)
Victoria D.G. Britt. Reg. F.D. Victoria, D.G., Queen of Britain, Defender of the Faith. (Great Britain)
Victorius Emmanuel II D.G. Rex Sard. Cyp. et Hier. Victor Emmanuel II, D.G., King of Sardinia, Cyprus, and Jerusalem. (Great Britain)
Videant Pauperes et Laetentur Let the poor see and rejoice. (Tuscany)
Vierzehn Eine Feine Mark Fourteen to the fine mark. (Prussia)
Viribus Unitis With men united. (Austria)
Virtute et Prudentia With virtue and prudence. (Austria)
Virtute Viam Dimetiar I shall mark the way with valour. (Waldeck)
Vitez Nagybanyai Horthy Miklos Kormanyzosaganak 10 Evfordulojara 10th anniversary of the government of the great hero, Nicholas Horthy. (Hungary)
Vitez Nagybanyai Horthy Miklos Kormanyzorszog Kormanyzoja Hungarian government of the great hero Nicholas Horthy. (Hungary)
Vitt. Em. III Re Victor Emmanuel III, King. (Italy)
Vittorio Emanuele II Victor Emmanuel II; . . . . . **Re d'Italia** King of Italy. (Italy)
Vittorio Emanuele III Victor Emmanuel III; . . . . . **Re** . . . . . King; **d'Italia** . . . . .of Italy; **E Imperator** . . . . . and Emperor. (Italy)
Vollendet den 5 Mai 1827, Psalm 91 V. 14-16 Completed on May 5, 1827, Psalm 91, verses 14-16. (Saxony)
Vollendung der Oesterreichischen Sudbahn Completion of the Austrian Southern Railways. (Austria)

W

W. Setna Rocznice Powstania 100th anniversary of liberation. (Poland)
Waldeckischer Kronthaler Waldeck crown taler. (Waldeck)
Walhalla Valhalla. (Bavaria)
Wiener Munzvertrag 24 Jan. 1857 Vienna monetary convention January 24, 1857. (Schaumburg-Lippe)
Wilh. II Kurf. u. Friedr. Wilh. Kurpr. u. Mitregent William II, Elector, and Frederick William, Elector and Co-Regent. (Hesse-Cassel)
Wilh. II Kurf. u. Friedr. Wilh. Kurprinz-Mitregent William II, Elector, and Frederick William, Electoral Prince and Co-Regent. (Hesse-Cassel)
Wilhalm Ernst - Caroline Groszherzog u. Groszherzogin v. Sachsen William Ernest, Caroline, Grand Duke and Grand Duchess of Saxony (Weimar). (Saxe-Weimar)
Wilhelm Deutscher Kaiser Konig v. Preussen William, Emperor of Germany, King of Prussia. (Prussia)
Wilhelm Herzog z. Braunschweig u. L(un) William, Duke of Brunswick and Luneburg. (Brunswick-Luneburg)
Wilhelm Herzog zu Nassau William, Duke of Nassau. (Nassau)
Wilhelm Koenig. Augusta Koenigin v. Preussen William, King, Augusta, Queen of Prussia. (Prussia)
Wilhelm Koenig von Preussen William, King of Prussia. (Prussia)
Wilhelm Koenig von Wurt(t)em(berg) William, King of Wurttemberg. (Wurttemberg)
Wilhelm Konig v. Wurttemberg William, King of Wurttemberg. (Wurttemberg)
Wilhelm I Kurf. Souv. Landgr. z. Hessen. Gr. H.v. Fulda William I, Elector, Sovereign, Landgrave of Hesse, Grand Duke of Fulda. (Hesse-Cassel)
Wilhelm II Deutscher Kaiser Konig v. Preussen William II, Emperor of Germany, King of Prussia. (Prussia)
Wilhelm II Koenig von Wuerttemberg William II, King of Wurttemberg. (Wurttemberg)
Wilhelm II Kurf. Souv. Langr. z. Hessen Gr. H. v. Fulda William II, Elector, Sovereign, Landgrave of Hesse, Grand Duke of Fulda. (Hesse-Cassel)
Wilhelm IV Koenig v. Gr. Brit. u. Hannover William IV, King of Great Britain and Hannover. (Hannover)
Wilhelmina Koningin der Nederlanden Wilhelmina, Queen of the Netherlands. (Netherlands)
Wilhelmus S(acri) R(omani) I(mperii) Pr(inceps) Auersperg Dux de Gotshee William, Prince of S.R.I. and Auersperg, Duke of Gotschee. (Auersperg)
Wilhelmus I D.G. Elect. Landg. Hass. William I, D.G., Elector and Landgrave of Hesse. (Hesse-Cassel)
Wilhelmus IX D.G. Hass. Landg. Com. Han. William IX, D.G., Landgrave of Hesse, Count of Hanau. (Hesse-Cassel)
Willem Koning der Ned(erlanden) G(root) H(ertog) V(an) L(uxemburg) William, King of the Netherlands, Grand Duke of Luxembourg. (Netherlands)
Willem II Koning der Ned. G.H.V.L. William II, King of the Netherlands. . . . (Netherlands)
Willem III Koning der Ned. G.H.V.L. William III, King of the Netherlands, ... (Netherlands)
Wir Wollen Sein Ein Einig Volk von Brudern We will be a united people of brothers. (Austria)

Y

Ylas Baleares Balearic Islands. (Spain)

Z

Z. Sreba Kraiowego From the nation's silver. (Poland)

Zehen Eine Feine Mark (many). 10 to the fine mark. (German States)
Zehn Eine Feine Mark (many). 10 to the fine mark. (German States)
Zehn Eine Mark Feine (many) 10 to the fine mark. (German States)
Zollverein mit Preussen, Sachsen, Hessen. U. Thuringen Customs union with Prussia, Saxony, Hesse, and Thuringia. (Bavaria)
Zu Gothe's Hundertjahriger Geburtsfeier am 28 August 1849 For the centennial of Goethe's birth on August 28, 1849. (Frankfurt)
Zu Ihrer Voelker Heil To the welfare of the peoples. (Bavaria)
Zur Dritten Sacularfeier des Religions Friedens vom 25 Sept. For the third centenary of the Religious Peace on September 25. (Frankfurt)
Zur Erinnerung an d. Wiederherstellung d. Munsters in Ulm In commemoration of the restoration of the cathedral in Ulm. (Wurttemberg)
Zur Erinnerung an den Glorreich Erkampften Frieden vom 10 Mai 1871 In commemoration of the gloriously fought for peace of May 10, 1871. (Bremen)
Zur Erinnerung an die Feier des 13 Dec. 1865 In commemoration of the celebration of December 13, 1865. (Hannover)
Zur Erinnerung an die Wiederherstellung der Mariensaule in Munchen In commemoration of the restoration of the Madonna column in Munich. (Bavaria)
Zur Erinnerung an Sr. Majestat des Konigs und Ihrer Majestat der Konigin allerhochsten Besuch d. Munze In commemoration of His Majesty the King's and Her Majesty the Queen's most gracious visit to the mint. (Hannover)
Zur Eroffnung des Carl Ludwig Hauses auf der Raxalpe Im September 1877 On the opening of the Carl Ludwig Inn on the Raxalpe in September, 1877. (Austria)
Zur Feier der 25 Jaehrigen Regierung For the of the 25th anniversary of the reign. (Brunswick)
Zur Feier Funf und Zwanzig Jahriger Regierung For the celebration of the 25th anniversary of the reign. (Reuss-Ebersdorf)
Zur Feier 25 Jahriger Regierung am 7 Marz 1867 For the celebration of the 25th anniversary of the reign on March 7, 1867. (Mecklenburg-Schwerin)
Zur Feier 25 Jaehriger Segensreicher Regierung For the celebration of the 25th anniversary of the prosperous reign. (Nassau)
Zur Feier XXV Jaehriger Regierung d. 17 April 1843 For the celebration of the 25th anniversary of the reign on April 17, 1843. (Reuss-Schleiz)
Zur Feier 50 Jaehriger Regierung d. 6 Nov. 1864 For the celebration of the 50th anniversary of the reign on November 6, 1864. (Schwarzburg-Rudolstadt)
Zurich Zurich. (Zurich)
Zur Sicherung des Gewichts On the guarantee of the weight. (Nassau)
Zur v. Sacularfeier des Munz-rechts der Stadt Frankfurt A.M. For the centenary of the minting rights of the city of Frankfurt-on-the-Main. (Frankfurt)
Zur 50 Jahrigen Jubelfeier der Befreiung Deutschlands On the 50th anniversary jubilee of the deliverance of Germany. (Bremen)
Zur 50 Jahrigen Vereinigung Ostfrieslands mit Hannover On the 50th anniversary of the union of East Friesland with Hannover. (Hannover)
Zwei Gulden XLV Ket Forint Two gulden 45 two florins. (Austria)
Zwei Vereinsthaler XV Ein Pfund Fein (many) 2 Vereinstalers, 15 to the fine pound. (German States)
Zweites Deutsches Bundesschiessen in Bremen 1865 Second German Shooting match in Bremen, 1865. (Bremen)

NUMBERS

75/100 Delar Finsilfver 75/100 dollar fine silver. (Sweden)
I Oesterreichisches Bundesschiessen First Austrian Shooting Match. (Austria)
I Thaler Hannoverisch Cassen-Geld One taler Hannoverian Cassa money. (Hannover)
III Deutsches Bundes Schiessen Wien 1869 Third German Shooting Match at Vienna, 1868. (Austria)
4 Centenario da Descoberta da India Fourth centenary of the discovery of India. (Portugal)
IX Olympische Winterspiele Ninth Olympic Winter Games. (Austria)
32 Schillinge Hamburger Courant 32 schilling current Hamburg. (Hamburg)
60 Schilling Schlesw. Holst. Courant 60 schillings current money Schleswig-Holstein. (Schleswig-Holstein)
450 Jahre Universitat Tubingen 450th anniversary of Tubingen University. (Germany)
534 8/9 Troyska Ass Finsilfver 534 8/9 Troy ounces fine silver. (Poland)
600 Jahre Tirol Osterreich 600 years Tyrol Austria. (Austria)
MDCCCLI Civium Industria Floret Civitas By the industry of the people, the state flourishes 1851. (Great Britain)

WE GRADE THE WORLD

NGC GRADES SELECTED INTERNATIONAL COINS

"Strictly the Best"

For years you've trusted the Numismatic Guaranty Corporation of America to grade your coins. Our commitment to **quality,** our **strictest grading practices** and our tradition of **consistency & integrity** is available for all of your coin needs.

Your international coin, encased in the NGC holder, gives you peace of mind and assures potential buyers that the coin has been professionally and accurately graded.

We are currently accepting submissions of the following countries:

Country	Years	Country	Years
Australia	1911-1964	Isle of Man	1786-1860
Austria	1750-1950	Italian Somliland	1909-1925
Belgium (including Austria, Netherlands)	1790-1960	Italy	1750-1947
Bulgaria	1879-1943	Japan	1870-1941
Canada (including Maritimes)	1858-1964	Jersey	1839-1866
Crete	1900-1901	Korea	1892-1910
Cuba	1896-1945	Liechenstein	1750-1961
Cyprus	1879-1960	Luxemberg	1854-1963
Danish West Indies	1859-1913	Mauritius	1877-1951
Denmark	1750-1953	Mexico (Regular issues only)	1732-1964
Fiji	1934-1967	Monaco	1819-1966
Finland	1864-1960	Netherlands/Colonies	1750-1945
France (Post Reform)	1750-1945	New Zealand	1934-1964
French Indo-China	1885-1947	Norway	1750-1959
German East Africa	1890-1916	Panama	1904-1953
German New Guinea	1894-1895	Philippines	1903-1947
German/German States	1700-1940	Poland	1765-1855
Great Britain	1662-1947	Puerto Rico	1895-1896
Greece	1828-1940	Romania	1867-1944
Guernsey	1830-1966	Russia/Provinces	1796-1917
Hong Kong	1863-1950	Sarawak	1796-1917
Hungary	1790-1939	Spain	1801-1949
India (British/East India Co.)	1835-1947	Straits Settlements	1845-1935
India (Portuguese)	1871-1959	Sweden	1750-1962
Ionian Islands	1819-1862	Switzerland	1750-1968
Ireland	1760-1963		

NGC will be adding additional countries in the near future on request.
Please call Ken Krah for details and inquiries, 1-800 NGC COIN.

For the NGC dealer nearest you, contact Numismatic Guaranty Corporation,
P.O. Box 1776, Parsippany, New Jersey 07054, tel. 1-800 NGC COIN.

INSTANT IDENTIFIER

Aachen (German States)

Albania

Austria

Baden (German States)

Bradenburg-Ansbach (German States)

Finland

Jever (German States)

Frankfurt (German States)

Furstenberg (German States)

Geneva (Swiss Cantons)

German Empire

Montenegro (Yugoslavia)

Nurnberg (German States)

Milan (Italian States)

Prussia (German States)

Russia (Czarist) Russian Poland

Schwarzburg-Rudolstadt (German States)

Schwarzburg-Sondershausen (German States)

Serbia (Yugoslavia)

Teutonic Order (German States)

Genoa (Italian States)

Syrian Arab Republic

United Arab Republic (Egypt, Syria)

Arab Republic of Egypt Libya

Yemen Arab Republic

Bulgaria

Burma (Myanmar)

Ethiopia

Finland

Norway

Gorizia (Italian States)

Hannover (German States)

Hesse-Darmstadt (German States)

Hohenlohe-Neuenstein-Oehringen (German States)

Iran (Persia)

Morocco

Siberia

Tibet (China)

Nepal

Morocco (AH1371 = 1951AD)

Manchukuo (China)

Japan

INSTANT IDENTIFIER

Hanau-Munzenberg (German States)

Nassau (German States)

Hesse-Cassel (German States)

Sri Lanka (Ceylon)

Tibet (China)

Utrecht (Netherlands)

Venice (Italian States)

Neuchatel (Swiss Cantons)

China (Empire-Provincial)

China (Empire-Provincial)

Japan

Japan

African States

Bretzenheim (German States)

Hall in Swabia (German States)

Greenland

German New Guinea (Papua New Guinea)

Lithuania

Mongolia

Sudan

Algeria

Lowenstein-Wertheim (German States)

Maldive Islands

Afghanistan

Ireland

Israel

Lebanon

Papal States (Vatican)

Regensburg (German States)

Sweden

North Korea

CCCP-Russia

CCCP-Russia

Yugoslavia

Formosa (Rep. of China)

Mainz (German States)

Solms-Laubach (German States)

Ticino (Swiss Cantons)

Fugger (German States)

Naples & Sicily (Italian States)

Saxe-Saalfield (German States)

Stolberg-Stolberg (German States)

INSTANT IDENTIFIER

French Colonial

French Colonial

French Colonial

Bangladesh

Isle Of Man
Sicily

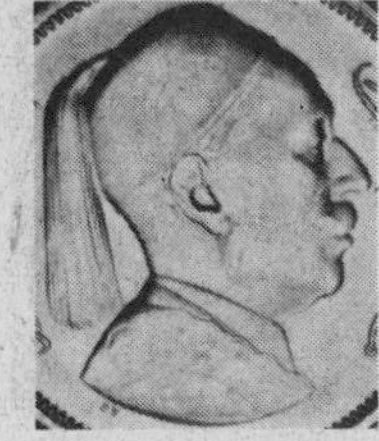
Libya

Anhalt-Bernberg
(German States)

Aargau
(Swiss Cantons)

Augsburg
(German States)

Basel
(Swiss Cantons)

Bavaria
(German States)

Brazil

Bremen
(German States)

Luzern
(Swiss Cantons)

Chur Pfalz
(German States)

Fulda
(German States)

Glarus
(Swiss Cantons)

Grand Duchy
Of Warsaw
(Poland)

Graubunden
(Swiss Cantons)

Hamburg
(German States)

Lucca
(Italian States)

Hesse-Cassel
(German States)

Hesse-Homburg
(German States)

Hildesheim
(German States)

Hohenzollern-
Hechingen
(German States)

Hungary

Julich-Berg
(German States)

Gelderland
(Netherlands)

Lippe-Detmold
(German States)

Lubeck
(German States)

Mecklenburg-
Strelitz
(German States)

Oldenburg
(German States)

Passau
(German States)

Portugal

Vaud
(Swiss Cantons)

Anhalt
(Joint Coinage)
(German States)

Oldenburg
(German States)

Schwarzenberg
(German States)

Schaffhausen
(Swiss Cantons)

Paderborn
(German States)

Thurgau
(Swiss Cantons)

Westfrisia
(Netherlands)

INSTANT IDENTIFIER

Arenberg (German States)

Rhenish Confederation (German States)

Reuss-Greiz (German States)

Sardinia (Italian States)

Saxony (German States)

Schaumburg-Lippe (German States)

Schleswig-Holstein (German States)

St. Gall (Swiss Cantons)

Slovakia

Solothurn (Swiss Cantons)

Unterwalden (Nidwalden) (Swiss Cantons)

Wurttemberg (German States)

Wurzburg (German States)

Zurich (Swiss Cantons)

Waldeck-Pyrmont (German States)

Iraq

Pakistan

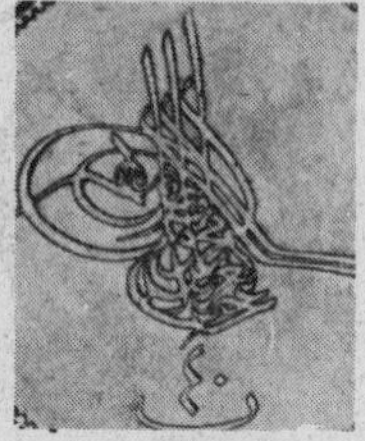
Turkey-Egypt Sudan, Algeria (Ottoman Empire)

Muscat & Oman, Oman

Saudi Arabia

Tunisia

Wismar (German States)

Order of Malta

Bamberg (German States)

Brunswick-Wolfenbuttel (German States)

Brunswick-Luneburg (German States)

Erfurt Mainz (German States)

Hannover (German States)

Eichstadt (German States)

Greece

Serbia

Switzerland

Albania

Thailand (Siam)

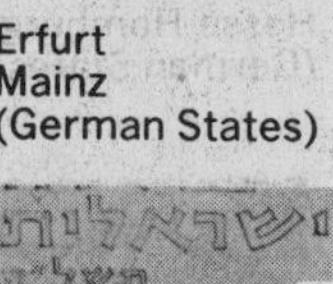
Israel

Japan (Dai Nippon)

South Korea

Sitten (Swiss Cantons)

Rostock (German States)

Saint Alban (German States)

English East India Co. (Sumatra)

China, Japan, Annam, Korea
(All holed 'cash' coins look quite similar.)

Japan

Korea

MONOGRAMS

MJ
Maximilian IV Joseph
Berg

FI
Frederick IX & Ingrid
Denmark

F VI R
Fred. VI Denmark
Tranquebar

FVII
Frederick VII
Denmark

FF8
Frederick VIII
Denmark

F IX R
Frederick IX
Denmark

FVII
Ferdinand VII
Mexico

PI
Paul I
Russia

FVII
Ferdinand VII
Mexico

FW
Friedrich Wilhelm III
Prussia

GA IV
Gustav Adolf IV
Sweden

HI
Nicholas I
Russia

HC
Henri Christophe
Haiti

HVII
Haakon VII
Norway

HN
Hieronymus
Napoleon
Westphalia

J
Joachim (Murat)
Berg

E(K)I II
Katherine II
Russia

L
Ludwig
Hesse-Darmstadt

L
Leopold
Belgium

LL III
Leopold III
Belgium

LL
Louis XVIII
Antwerp

C XIVJ
Carl XIV Johann
Norway

M
Morelos
Revolutionary
Mexico

M 2 R
Margrethe II Regina
Denmark

NII
Nicholas II
Russia

NI
Nicholas I
Russia

NFP
Nicholas Friedrich
Peter
Oldenburg

OII
Oscar II
Norway

E
Ernest I
Saxe-Coburg-Gotha

O V
Olav V
Norway

P I
Paul I
Russia

P III
Peter III
Russia

R
Rainier III
Monaco

WL
Wilhelm Landgraf
Hesse-Cassel

WR
William Rex
Hannover

PFA
Peter Friedrich
August
Oldenburg

OII
Oscar II
Sweden

GR
Georgius Rex
Hannover

FRVI
Frederik VI Rex
Tranquebar

PF
Paul Friedrich
Mecklenburg-
Schwerin

FII
Friedrich II
Wurttemberg

FER VII
Ferdinand VII
(Spain) Gerona

MONOGRAMS

MJ
Maximilian IV Joseph
Berg

CC99
Christian IX
Danish West Indies

V OC
Dutch East India
Co. (Indonesia)

CVII
Christian VII
Danish West Indies

CCX
Christian X
Danish West Indies

G
Georg
Mecklenburg-Strelitz

CWF
Carl Wilhelm
Ferdinand
Brunswick-
Wolfenbuttel

H7
Haakon VII
Norway

A
Albert I
Belgium

GRI
Georgius Rex
Imperator
New Guinea

L
Leopold II
Belgium

EAR
Ernest August Rex
Hannover

FRVI
Frederik VI Rex
Denmark

CX
Christian X
Denmark

A
Albert I
Belgium

AF
Adolph Friederich IV
Mecklenburg-Strelitz

B
Baudouin I
Belgium

C
Cayenne
French Guiana

CL
Carl & Louise
Saxe-Meiningen

CR
Christian VIII (Denmark)
Tranquebar

FW
Friedrich Wilhelm
Mecklenburg-Strelitz

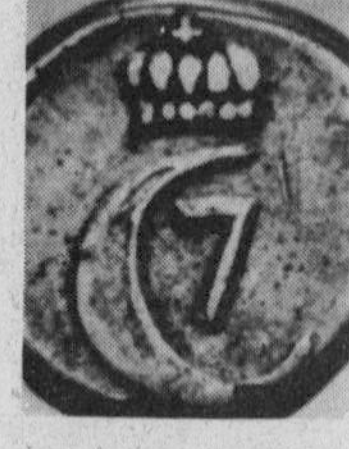
C7
Christian VII
Tranquebar

C7
Christian VII
Denmark

CIX
Christian IX
Denmark

CCX
Christian X
Denmark

CCXIII
Charles XIII
Sweden

CLXIV
Carl XIV Johann
Norway

CXIV
Carl XIV Johann
Sweden

EP
Elizabeth-Philip
Great Britain

ERI
Edward Rex
Imperator
New Guinea

EIIR
Elizabeth II Regina
Cook Isl.

FA
Friedrich August
Lubeck Bishopric

FF
Friedrich Franz
Mecklenburg-
Schwerin

FJI
Franz Joseph I
Austria

O
Oscar I
Sweden

AFC
Alexius Friedrich
Christian
Anhalt-Bernburg

NII
Nicholas II
Russia

FRVII
Frederik VII Rex
Danish West Indies
Denmark

FC
Friedrich Christian
Brandenburg-
Bayreuth

AIII
Alexander III
Russia

W
William I
Netherlands

LLX
Ludwig X
Hesse-Darmstadt

ILLUSTRATED GUIDE TO EASTERN MINT NAMES

PREPARED ESPECIALLY FOR THE **STANDARD CATALOG OF WORLD COINS**

Compiled by Harry S. Scherzer.
Scrip typeset by Ketab Corporation

Eastern mint names are basically composed of the Arabic alphabet which in fact covers a number of languages — Arabic is Semitic: Persian is Indo-European; and Malayan is in the Malayo-Polynesian group. Differences are not just of dialect, they are of basic structure. However, Arabic itself is the really important one, bearing a relationship to other Oriental languages not unlike that of Latin to the languages of Europe. Just as medieval European coins are inscribed in Latin, so are the majority of the coins of North African, Turkish, Persian, and Indian origin inscribed until very recent times in Arabic. A limited knowledge of Persian will also be necessary for unravelling the Persian poetic couplets found on Indian and Persian coins particularly during the seventeenth and eighteenth centuries A.D.

(Courtesy of Richard J. Plant)

ANKARA
Turkey — انقره

AL-'ARAISH
"Larache", Morocco — العرايش

AL-'ARAISHAN
"Larache", Morocco — العرايشة

ABUSHAHR
"Bushire", Iran — ابو شهر

ADRANAH
"Edirne", Turkey — ادرنة

AFGHANISTAN — افغانستان

AHMADABAD
Bombay, India-British — احمد اباد

AHMADNAGAR-FARRUKHABAD
Afghanistan — احمدنكر فرخ اباد

AHMADPUR
See "Bahawalpur", Afghanistan — احمد پور

AHMADSHAHI
See "Ashraf Al-Bilad" and "Qandahar", Afghanistan — احمد شاهی

AJMAN
See "United Arab Emirates" — اجمان

AKSU
China-Sinkiang — اقصو

ALGERIA
See "Al-Jaza 'Iriyat"

BI-ANGLAND
"In England" (Birmingham)
For Morocco — بانكلند

BI-ANGLAND
"In England" (London)
For Morocco — بانكلند

DAULAT ANJAZANCHIYAH
"The State of Anjazanchiyah"
See Comoros — دولة انجزنجية

ANWALA
"Aonla," Afghanistan — انوله

AL-ARABIYAT AS-SA'UDIYAT
"Saudi-Arabian", Saudi Arabia — العربية السعودية

ARDEBIL
Iran — اردبيل

ARKAT
"Arcot", India-French — اركات

ASHRAF AL-BILAD
"Most Noble of Cities"
See "Ahmadshahi", Afghanistan — اشرف البلاد

ILLUSTRATED GUIDE TO EASTERN MINT NAMES

ASTARABAD
Iran
استراباد

ATCHEH
Indonesia
اجه

ATTOCK
Afghanistan
اتك

AZIMABAD
See "Patna", Bengal, India-British
عظيم اباد

BACAIM (no legends)
See "India-Portuguese"

BADAKHSHAN
See Afghanistan
بوخشان

BAGCHIH-SERAI
See "Krim"
باغجه سراي

BAGHDAD
Iraq
بغداد

BAHAWALPUR
See "Ahmadpur" and "Dar Es-Surur", Afghanistan
بهاولپور

BAHRAIN
See "El-Bahrain"
بحرين

EL-BAHRAIN
"Of the Two Seas", Bahrain
البحرين

BALKH
See "Umm Al-Bilad", Afghanistan
بلخ

BANARAS
"Awadh", Bengal, India-British
بنارس

BANDAR ABBAS
Iran
بندر عباس

BANJARMASIN
Indonesia
بنجرمسن

BARELI
Afghanistan
بريلي

BI BARIZ
"In Paris"
For Morocco
بباريز

BEHBEHAN
Iran
بهبهان

BERLIN
For Morocco
برلين

BHAKHAR
Afghanistan
بهكر

BOMBAY
See "Munbai", Bombay, India-British

BORUJERD
Iran
بروجرد

NEGRI BRUNEI
"State of Brunei", Brunei
نكري بروني

BRUSAH
"Bursa", Turkey
بروسة

BUKHARA
See Russian Turkestan
بخارا

BUSHIRE
See "Abushahr", Iran

CALCUTTA
See "Kalkatah", Bengal, India-British
كلكته

COCHIN
See India-Dutch and "V.O.C.", India-Dutch

COMOROS
See "Anjazanchiyah", "The Largest of the Islands", Comoros
كموز

DACCA
See "Jahangirnagar", Bengal, India-British

DAMAO (no legends)
See India-Portuguese

DAR AL-AMAN
"Abode of Security" (honorific)
See "Multan"
دار الامان

DAR AL-ISLAM
See Bahawalpur, India Princely States
دار الاسلام

DAR AL-MULK
"Abode of the King" (honorific)
See "Kabul"
دار لملك

DAR AL-NUSRAT
"Abode of the New (Town?)" (honorific)
See "Herat"
دارالنصرت

DAR AL-KHILAFAT
"Abode of the Caliphate" (honorific)
See "Tehran" and "Yemen"
دار الخلافة

DAR AS-SALAM
"Abode of Peace" (honorific)
See "Ligkeh", Thailand
دار السلام

DAR AS-SULTANAT
"Abode of the Sultanate" (honorific)
See "Herat" and "Kabul", Afghanistan
دارالسلطنة

DAR AS-SURUR
"Abode of Happiness" (honorific)
See "Bahawalpur", Afghanistan
دار السرور

DARBAND
Iran
دربند

ILLUSTRATED GUIDE TO EASTERN MINT NAMES

DARFUR
See "Al-Fasher", Sudan
الفشير

DEHLI
See "Shajahanabad", Afghanistan
دهلي

DELI
Indonesia
دلي

DERA
"Dera Ghazi Khan", Afghanistan
ديره

DERAJAT
"Dera Ishmael Khan", Afghanistan
ديره حات

DEZFUL
Iran
دزفول

DIU (no legends)
See India-Portuguese
—

DJIBOUTI
See "Jaibuti"
—

EDIRNE
See "Adranah", Turkey
—

EGYPT
See "Misr" and "Al-Misriyat"
—

ERAVAN
Iran
ايروان

FARRUKHABAD
Bengal, India-British
فرخ اباد

AL-FASHER
See "Darfur", Sudan
الفشير

FES
"Fez", Morocco
فاس

FERGANA
See "Khoqand",
Russian Turkestan
فرغانة

FILASTIN
"Palestine", Israel
فلسطين

AL-FUJAIRAH
See "United Arab Emirates"
الفجيره

GANJAH
Iran
كنجه

GERMAN EAST AFRICA
See "Sharakat Almaniyah",
Tanzania
شراكة المانيا

GHAZNI
Afghanistan
غزني

GOA (no legends)
See India-Portuguese
—

HAIDARABAD SIND MINT
Afghanistan
حيدرآباد سند

HALEB
"Allepo", Syria
حلب

HAMADAN
Iran
همدان

AL-HARAR
Ethiopia-Eritrea
الهرر

AL-HEJAZ
Saudi Arabia-Hejaz
الحجاز

HERAT
See "Dar Al-Nushat" and "Dar As-Sultanat", Afghanistan
هرات

HERAT
Iran
هرات

ILI
China-Sinkiang
الي

IRAN
ايران

AL-IRAQ
"Iraque"
العراق

AL-IRAQIYAT
"Iraqi," Iraq
العراقية

ISFAHAN
Iran
اصفهان

ISLAMBUL
Turkey
اسلامبول

ITALIAN SOMALILAND
See "Al-Somal Al-Italianiah",
Somalia
الصومال الايطليانية

JAHANGIRNAGAR
See "Dacca", Bengal, India-British
جهانكيرنكر

BI-JAIBUTI
"In Djibouti", Djibouti
بجيبوتي

JAVA
Indonesia
جاوا

JAZA'IR
Algeria-Algiers
جزاير

AL-JAZA'IRIYAT
Algeria-Algiers
الجزايرة

JERING
"Jaring", Thailand
جريج

AL-JOMHURIYAT EL-IRAQIYAT
"The Iraqi Republic" Iraq
الجمهورية العرقية

AL-JOMHURIYAT EL-LUBNANIYAT
"The Lebanese Republic",
Lebanon
الجمهورية البنانية

ILLUSTRATED GUIDE TO EASTERN MINT NAMES

AL-JOMHURIYAT AL-MUTTAHIDAH AL-ARABIYAT
"United Arab Republic"
See "Egypt, Syria, Yemen"
الجمهورية المتحدة العربية

AL-JOMHURIYAT AS-SUDAN
"The Sudanese Republic", Sudan
الجمهورية السودان

AL-JOMHURIYAT AS-SURIYAT
"The Syrian Republic", Syria
الجمهورية السورية

AL-JOMHURIYAT AL-TUNISIAT
"The Tunisian Republic", Tunisia
الجمهورية التونسية

AL-JOMHURIYAT AL-TURKIYAH
"The Turkish Republic", Turkey
الجمهورية توركية

JORDAN
See "Al-Urduniyat" and "Al-Mamlakat, etc.," Jordan
—

KABUL
See "Dar Al-Mulk" > AH1163 and "Dar As-Sultanat" >AH1164, Afghanistan
كابل

KAFFA
Krim, Russian Caucasia
كفه

KALKATAH
"Calcutta", Bengal, India-British
كلكته

KASHAN
Iran
كاشان

KASHMIR
Afghanistan
كشمير

KASHQUAR
China-Sinkiang
كشقر

KEDAH
See "Bilad Kedah" and "Bilad Al-Perlis Kedah", Malaysia
كداه

KELANTAN
See "Khalifat Al-Mu'Minin" and "Negri Kelantin", Malaysia
كلنتن

KEMASIN
Malaysia
كماسن

KERMAN
Iran
كرمان

KERMANSHAHAN
See "Kermanshah", Iran
كرمانشاهان

KHALIFAT AL-MU'MININ
"Commander of the Faithful" (honorific)
See "Kelantin" and "Trengganu"
خليفة المؤمنين

KHALIFAT AL-KARAM
"Noble Caliph" (honorific)
See "Patani"
خليفة الكرم

KHANABAD
Afghanistan
خان اباد

KHOQAND
See Russian Turkestan
خوقند

KHUI
See "Khoy", Iran
خوى

AL-KHURFAH
See "Yemen"
الخرفاه

KHUTAN
China-Sinkiang
خوتن

KHWAREZM
Russian Turkestan-Khiva
خوارزم

KOSOVAH
Turkey
قوصوه

KOTSHA
China-Sinkiang
كوتشر

AL-KUWAIT
Kuwait
الكويت

LADAKH
Afghanistan
لداخ

LAHEJ
See "Yemen"
لحج

LAHIJAN
See "Gilan", Iran
لاهيجان

LAHORE
Afghanistan
لاهور

LEBANON
See "Al-Lubnaniyat" and "Jomhuriyat, etc."
—

AL-LIBIYAT
"Libyan", Libya
الليبية

LIBYA
See "Al-Libyat" and "Mamlakat, etc."
ليبيا

NEGRI LIGKEH
"State of Ligeh (or Ligor)"
See "Dar As-Salam", Thialand
نكري لغكه

ILLUSTRATED GUIDE TO EASTERN MINT NAMES

AL-LUBNANIYAT
"Lebanese", Lebanon
النلنية

MACHHLIPATAN
See "Mazulipatam", India-French
"Masulipatam", India-Madras
مچهلي بتن

MACHHLIPATAN-BANDAR
See "Machhlipatan", India-Madras
مچهلي پتن بندر

AL-MAGHRIBIYAT
"Moroccan", Morocco
المغربية

TANAH MALAYU
"Land of the Malays"
See "Sumatra", Indonesia and
"Malacca", Malaysia
تانه ملايو

PULU MALAYU
"Island of the Malays"
See "Sumatra", Indonesia
فولو ملايو

MALUKA
Indonesia
ملوک

AL-MAMLAKAT AL-ARABIYAT AL-SA'UDIYAT
"The Kingdom of Saudi Arabia"
المملكة العربية السعودية

AL-MAMLAKAT AL-LIBIYAT
"The Kingdom of Libya"
المملكة الليبية

AL-MAMLAKAT AL-MAGHRIBIYAT
"The Kingdom of Morocco"
المملكة المغربية

AL-MAMLAKAT AL-MUTAWAKELIYAT AL-YEMENIAT
"The Mutawakelite Kingdom of Yemen"
المملكة المتوكلية اليمنية

AL-MAMLAKAT AL-MISRIYAT
"The Kingdom of Egypt"
المملكة المصرية

AL-MAMLAKAT AL-URDUNIYAT AL-HASHEMIYAT
"The Hashemite Kingdom of Jordan"
المملكة الاردنية الهاشمية

MANASTIR
Turkey
مناستر

MARAGHEH
Iran
مراغه

MARAKESH
"Marrakech", Morocco
مراكش

AL-MASCARA
Algeria-Algiers
المعسكر

MASH'HAD
Afghanistan
مشهد

MASH'HAD
Iran
مشهد

MASULIPATAM
See "Machhlipatan", India-Madras

MAZANDARAN
Iran
مازندران

MAZULIPATAM
See "Machhlipatan", India-French

MEDEA
Algeria-Algiers
مديه

MEKHA
"Mecca", Saudi-Arabia
مكة

MENANGKABAU
Indonesia
منفكابو

MIKNAS
"Meknes", Morocco
مكناس

MIKNASAH
"Meknes", Morocco
مكناسة

MISR
Egypt
مصر

AL-MISRIYAT
"Egptian", Egypt
المصرية

AL-MOHAMMEDIYAT ASH-SHERIFATE
"The Mohammedan Sherifate" or
"Empire Cherifien" (French), Morocco
المحمدية الشريفة

MOMBASA
Kenya
ممباسه

MOROCCO
See "Al-Maghribyat" and
"Al-Mohammediyat Ash-Sherifate"

MOXOUDABAT
See "Murshidabad", India-French

MUBARAK
"Auspicious" (honorific)
See "Rikab"
مبارک

AL-MAKALA
"Mukalla"
See "Yemen"
المكلا

MULTAN
See "Dar Al-Aman", Afghanistan
ملتان

ILLUSTRATED GUIDE TO EASTERN MINT NAMES

Mint	Description	Legend
MUNBAI	See "Bombay", India-British	منبي
MURADABAD	Afghanistan	مراد اباد
MURSHIDABAD	See "Moxoudabat", India-French	مرشد اباد
MURSHIDABAD	Bengal, India-British	مرشد اباد
MUSCAT	Oman	مسقط
NAJIBABAD	Afghanistan	نجيب اباد
NAKAPATTANAM (Tamil legends)	"Negapatnam", India-Dutch	நாகபட்டணம்
NAKHCHAWAN	Iran	نخجوان
NEGAPATNAM	See "Nakappattanam"	——
NEJD	Saudi Arabia	نجد
NIHAWAND	Iran	نهاوند
NUKHWI	"Sheki", Iran	نخوى
NUKHWI	See "Sheki", Russian Caucasia	نخوي
OMAN		عمان
OMDURMAN	Sudan	ام درمان
PAHANG	"Pahang Company", Malaysia	فاحغ
PAKISTAN		پاکستان
PALEMBANG	Indonesia	فلمبغ
PALESTINE	See "Filastin", Israel	——
PANA'HABAD	"Shusha" See "Karabagh", Russian Caucasia	پناه باد
AL-PATANI	See "Khalifat Al-Karam", "Khalifat Al-Mu'Minin" and "Bilad Al-Patani", Thailand	الفطاني
PATNA	See "Azimabad", Bengal, India-British	پتنه
PULU PENANG	"Prince of Wales Island", Malaysia	فولو فنيغ
NEGRI PERAQ	"State of Perak", Malaysia	نكري فيرق
PULU PERCHA	"Island of Sumatra", Indonesia	فولو فرج
PERLIS	See "Kedah", Malaysia	——
PESHAWAR	Afghanistan	پشاور
PHALICHERY	SEE "Pondichery", India-French	پهلجري
PONDICHERY	See "Phalichery", India-French	——
PONTIANAQ (no legends)	Indonesia	——
PULICAT (no legends)	See "India-Dutch"	——
QANDAHAR	See "Ashraf Al-Bilad" and "Ahmadshahi", Afghanistan	قندهار
QATAR WA DUBAI	"Qatar and Dubai", Qatar	قطرودبي
DAULAT QATAR	"State of Qatar", Qatar	——
QAZWIN	Iran	قزوين
QUAITI	Yemen	قيطي
QUM	Iran	قم
QUSANTINAT	"Constantine", Algeria-Algiers	قسنطينة
QUSTINTINIYAH	"Constantinople", Turkey	قسطنطنية
RA'NASH	Iran	رعنش

ILLUSTRATED GUIDE TO EASTERN MINT NAMES

RABAT
See "Rabat Al-Fath", Morocco
رباط

RABAT AL-FATH
"Rabat", Morocco
رباط الفتح

RAS AL-KHAIMA
See "United Arab Emirates"
راس الخيمه

RASHT
Iran
رشت

REHMAN
Thailand
رحمن

REZA'IYEH
See "Urumi", Iran
رظاعيه

RIKAB
See "Mubarak", Afghanistan
ركاب

RIKAB
Iran
ركاب

SA'UJBALAQ
Iran
ساوج بلاق

SAGAR
Bengal, India-British
ساكر

SAHRIND
Afghanistan
شهرند

AL-SAIWI
See "Bilad Al-Saiwi", "Sai", "Saiburi" and "Teluban", Thailand
السيوي

SAN'A
See "Yemen", Yemen Republic
سنة

SARAKHS
Iran
سرخس

SARHIND
See "Sahrind", Afghanistan

SARI
Iran
ساري

SARI POL
Afghanistan
سربل

SAUDI ARABIA
"See "Al-Hejaz", "Nejd" and "Al-Arabiyat As-Sa'udiya", Saudi Arabia

NEGRI SELANGHUR
"State of Selangor", Malaysia
نكري سلاغور

SELANIK
"Salonika", Turkey
سلانيك

SHAJAHANABAD
See "Dehli", Afghanistan
شاجهان اباد

SHAMAKHI
Russian Caucasia
شماخ

SHAMAKHA
Russian Caucasia
شماخه

SHARAKAT ALMANIYAH
"German Company" or "German East Africa", Tanzania
شراكتة المانيا

ES-SHARJAH
See "United Arab Emirates"
الشارجة

SHIRAZ
Iran
شيراز

SHUSHTAR
Iran
شوشتر

NEGRI SIAK
"State of Siak", Indonesia
نكري سيك

SIMNAN
Iran
سمنان

SIND
Afghanistan
سند

AL-SOMAL AL-ITALIANIYAH
"Italian Somaliland", Somalia
الصومال الايطليانية

SULTANABAD
Iran
سلطاناباد

SUMENEP
Indonesia
سمنف

SURAT
See "Surate", India-French
سورت

SURAT
Bombay, India-British
سورت

AS-SURIYAT
"Syrian", Syria
السورية

AL-SUWAIR
"Essaouira Mogador", Morocco
الصوير

AL-SUWAIRAH
"Essaouira Mogador", Morocco
الصويرة

SYRIA
See "Haleb", As-Suriyat", "Jomhuriyat, etc.", Syria

TABARISTAN
Iran
طبرستان

TABRIZ
Iran
تبريز

ILLUSTRATED GUIDE TO EASTERN MINT NAMES

TANGIER
See "Tanjah", Morocco
———

TANJAH
"Tangier", Morocco
طنجة

TAQIDEMT
Algeria-Algiers
تاقدمت

TARABALUS GHARB
"Tripoli West", Libya
طرابلس غرب

TARIM
See "Yemen"
تريم

NEGRI TARUMON
"State of Tarumon", Indonesia
نكري ترومن

TASHQURGHAN
Afghanistan
تاش قورغان

TATTA
Afghanistan
تته

TEGNAPATAM (no legends)
"Fort St. David", Madras, India-British
———

TEHRAN
See "Dar Al-Khilafat", Iran
طهران

TELLICHERY
Bombay, India-British
تلچري

TETUAN
Morocco
تطوان

TIFLIS
See Russia, Georgia
تفليس

TRANQUEBAR (no legends)
See "India-Danish"
———

TRENGKANU
See "Khalifat Al-Mu'Minin", Malaysia
ترغكانو

TUNIS
Tunisia
تونس

TUNISIA
See "Tunis", "Al-Tunisiyat", "Jomhuriyat, etc."
———

AL-TUNISIYAT
"Tunisian," Tunisia
التونسية

TURKEY
See "Turkiyah", "Jomhuriyat, etc."
———

AL-TURKIYAH
"Turkish", Turkey
التوركية

TUTICORIN (degenerate Nagari legends)
See "India-Dutch"
———

TUYSERKAN
Iran
توى سركان

TANAH UGI
"Land of the Bugis", Indonesia
تانه اغيسى

UMM AL-BILAD
"Mother of Cities"
See "Balkh", Afghanistan
ام البلاد

UMM AL-QAIWAIN
See "United Arab Emirates"
ام القوين

UNITED ARAB EMIRATES
———

UNITED ARAB REPUBLIC
See "Al-Jomhuriyat Al-Arabiyat AL-Muttahidah"
الامارات العربية المتحدة

AL-URDUNIYAT
"Jordanian", Jordan
الاردنية

URUMCHI
China-Sinkiang
ارومجي

URUMI
See "Reza'iyeh", Iran
ارومى

USHI
China-Sinkiang
اوش

WAN
"Van", Turkey
وان

YARKHAND
China-Sinkiang
يارقند

YARKHISSARMARAN
"Yanghissar"
China-Sinkiang
يار كسارمرن

YAZD
Iran
يزد

YEMEN
See "Sana", "Dar Al-Khilafat", Al-Yemeniyat", Mamlakat, etc."
———

AL-YEMENIYAT
"The Yemen"
اليمنية

ZANJAN
Iran
زنجان

ZANJIBARA
"Zanzibar", Tanzania
زنجباراه

MINT INDEX

A

A - Ackroyd & Best (Morley)
A - Alamos (Mexico)
A - Ancona (Italy)
A - Angra (Portugal)
A - Antioquia (Colombia)
A - Beaumont-le-Roger (France)
A - Berlin (Germany)
A - Clausthal (German States)
A - Hall (Austria)
A - Paris (France)
A - Vienna (Austria)
AA - Metz (France)
AARGAU - Swiss Canton
AB - Geneva (Swiss Canton)
AB - Strassburg (France)
ABUSHAHR - Iran
ACKROYD & BEST - East Africa
AD - (Akcionarno Drustvo) Belgrade (Yugoslavia)
A-D - Diu (India-Portuguese)
ADRANAH - Turkey
ADRIANOPLE - Turkey
AE - (Ligate) Aix and Marseilles (France)
AEGINA - Greece
AGRA - India British, India-Mughal, Indian Princely States
AHLUWALIA - India-Independent Kingdom
AHMADABAD - India-British, India-Independent Kingdom, India-Mughal, Indian Princely States
AHMADNAGAR-FARRUKHABAD - Afghanistan, India-Independent Kingdom
AHMADPUR - Afghanistan, Indian Princely States
AHMADSHAHI - Afghanistan
AHMEDABAD - India-Mughal, Indian Princely States
AIX - France
AIZU - Japan
AJMER - India-Independent Kingdom, India-Mughal, Indian Princely States
AKBARABAD - India-British, India-Mughal, Indian Princely States
AKSU - China
ALAMOS - Mexico
ALEPPO - Turkey
ALGIERS - Algeria
ALLAHABAD - India-British, India-Mughal, Indian Princely States
ALLOTE - Indian Princely States
ALMORA - India-Independent Kingdom
ALTONA - Danish West Indies, Denmark, German States, Philippines, Venezuela
AM - Anninsk, Russia
AM - Bogota (Colombia)
AMARAVATI - Indian Princely States
AMBERG - German States
AMID - Turkey
AMIENS - France
AMRELI - Indian Princely States
AMRITSAR - India-Independent Kingdom
AMSTERDAM - Netherlands East Indies
ANANDGARH - India-Independent Kingdom
ANCONA - Papal States, Vatican Papal City States
ANGERS - France
ANGLAND - Morocco
ANHWEI - China
ANNINSK - Russia
ANOLA - Afghanistan, India-Independent Kingdom, IndiaMughal
ANTIOQUIA - Colombia
ANTWERP - Austrian Netherlands
ANUPNAGAR - Indian Princely States
ANWALA - Afghanistan, India-Independent Kingdom, India-Mughal
AP - Goa (India-Portuguese)
AR - Arras (France)
EL'ARAISH - Morocco
EL'ARAISHAN - Morocco
ARCOT - India-British, India-Danish, India-French
ARDABIL - Iran
ARDEBIL - Iran
AREQ - Arequipa, Peru, South Peru
AREQUIPA - Peru, South Peru
AREZZO - Order of Malta, Somalia, Tunis, Tunisia
ARKAT - India-British, India-French, India-Mughal, Indian Princely States
ARRAS - France
AARON - Warsaw (Poland)
ARZI-I-AKDAS - Iran
As - Alamos (Mexico)
ASAFABAD - India-Mughal, Indian Princely States
ASAFNAGAR - India-Independent Kingdom, Indian Princely States
ASCOLI - Vatican Papal City States
ASFI - Morocco
ASHIO - Japan
ASHRAF AL-BILAD - Afghanistan
ASTARABAD - Iran
ATCHEH - Indonesia
ATHANI - Independent Kingdom
ATHENS - Greece
ATTOCK - Afghanistan
AUGSBURG - Austria
AURANGABAD - India-Mughal, Indian Princely States
AURANGNAGAR - India-Independent Kingdom, India-Mughal
AURICH - German States
AVESTA - Sweden
AWADH - India-Mughal, Indian Princely States
AYACUCHO - Peru
AZIMABAD - India-British, India-Mughal, Indian Princely States

B

B - Bacaim (India)
B - Bahia (Brazil)
B - Barcelona (Spain)
B - Basel (Swiss Cantons)
B - Bayreuth (German States)
B - Beaumont-le-Roger (France)
B - Berne (Switzerland)
B - Bogota (Colombia)
B - Bologna (Italy)
B - Bombay (India-British)
B - Breslau (Poland)
B - Brunswick (German States)
B - Brussels (Belgium)
B - Bucharest (Romania)
B - Budapest (Hungary)
B - Buenos Aires (Argentina)
B - Burgos (Spain)
B - Bydgoszcz (Poland)
B - Dieppe (France)
B - Dresden (Germany)
B - Freiburg (Swiss Cantons)
B - Hannover (German States)
B - Kormoczbanya (Czechoslovakia)
B - Kremnitz (Czechslovakia)
B - Luzern (Swiss Cantons)
B - Regensburg (German States)
B - Rouen (France)
B - Schwyz (Swiss Cantons)
B - Vienna-(Germany 1938-45)
B - Zurich (Swiss Cantons)
B and acorn - Bologna (Italy)
BA - Bahia (Brazil)
BA - Barcelona (Spain)
BA - (ligate) Basel (Switzerland)
BA - Buenos Aires (Argentina)
B.AS. - Buenos Aires (Argentina)
Ba - Bogota (Colombia)
BADAKHSHAN - Afghanistan
Bs - Buenos Aires (Argentina)
BAGALKOT - India-Independent Kingdom
BAGCHIH-SERAI - Russia-Krim
BAGHDAD - Mesopotamia-Iraq, Turkey
BAHAWALPUR - Afghanistan, Indian Princely States
BAHIA - Brazil
BAHRAIN - Bahrain
BAIA MARE - German States
BAJRANGGARH - Indian Princely States
BALHARI - India-Independent Kingdom
BALK - Afghanistan, India-Mughal
BALKH - Afghanistan, India-Mughal
BAMBERG - German States
BANARAS - India-British, India-Mughal, Indian Princely States
BANDAR ABBAS - Iran
BANDAR ABU SHAHR - Iran
BANGALORE - Indian Princely States
BANGKO SENTRAL PILIPINAS - Philippines
BANJARMASIN - Indonesia
BARCELONA - Spain
BARELI - Afghanistan, India-Independent Kingdom, India-Mughal, Indian Princely States
bi'BARIZ - Morocco
BAROCH - India-Mughal
BARODA - Indian Princely States
BASEL - Swiss Cantons, Switzerland
BASODA - Indian Princely States
BASRA - Iran, Mesopotamia
BAYERSDORF - German States
BAYONNE - France
BAYREUTH - German States
BB - Strasbourg (France)
BCCR - Philadelphia (USA)
BD - Pau (France)
Be - Berlin (Germany)
BEAUMONT-LE-ROGER - France, French Indo-China
BEHBEHAN - Iran
BEIJING - China
BEL - Basel (Swiss Cantons)
BEL - Freiburg (Swiss Cantons)
BEL - Lausanne (Swiss Cantons)
BELGRADE - Yugoslavia
BENARES - India-British
BENGAL - India-British
BENGALUR - India-Independent Kingdom
BERGA - Spain
BERLIN - Brazil, Bulgaria, Danzig, Dominican Republic, East Prussia, German East Africa, German New Guinea, German States, Germany, Italy, Laos, Morocco, Papua New Guinea, Poland, Posen, Tanzania, Uruguay, Venezuela
BERNE - Botswana, Israel, Liberia, Liechtenstein, Swiss Cantons, Switzerland
BESANCON - France
BGA - Brega (Libya)
B.H. FRANKFURT - German States
B (rosette) H - German States
BHAKKAR - Afghanistan, India-Independent Kingdom, India-Mughal, Iran
BHARATPUR - Indian Princely States
BHILSA - India-Mughal, Indian Princely States
BHINDA - Indian Princely States
BHOPAL - Indian Princely States
BHUJ - Indian Princely States
BI - (ligate) Birmingham (Great Britain)
BICR - Philadelphia (USA)
BIDLIS - Turkey
BIDRUR - India-Mughal
BIKANIR - Indian Princely States
BILBAO - Spain
BINDRABAN - Indian Princely States
BIRMm - Birmingham, Costa Rica, Ecuador
BIRMINGHAM - Ecuador, Italian States
BIRMINGHAM H - Belize, British Honduras, British North Borneo, British West Africa, Bulgaria, Canada, Ceylon, Colombia, Costa Rica, Cyprus, Dominican Republic, East Africa, Ecuador, Egypt, El Salvador, Finland, French Indo-China, Great Britain, Greece, Guatemala, Guernsey, Haiti, Hong Kong, India-British, Italy, Jamaica, Jersey, Kenya, Liberia, Malaya & British Borneo, Mauritius, Mombasa, Morocco, Newfoundland, Nicaragua, Oman, Romania, Sarawak, Serbia, Straits Settlements, Thailand, Uruguay, Venezuela, Yugoslavia, Zaire
BIRMINGHAM K,KN - British West Africa, East Africa, Great Britain, Greece, Hong Kong, Malaya & British Borneo, Romania
BISAULI - India-Independent Kingdom
BITLIS - Turkey
BM - Warsaw (Poland)
BNCR - London (England)
BNCR - San Jose (Costa Rica)
BNT - Turin (Italy)
Bo - Bilbao (Spain)
BOARD OF PUBLIC WORKS - China
BOARD OF REVENUE - China
BOGOTA - Colombia, Estados Unidos De Nueva Granada, Granadine Confederation, Lazareto, Republic of Colombia, Republic of Nueva Granada, United Provinces of Nueva Granada
BOLOGNA - Italian States, Italy, Papal States, Vatican Papal City States, Vatican Papal States
BOLSHAYA KAZNA - Russia
BOMBAY - Australia, Ceylon, East Africa, India, India-British, Iraq, Malaya, Straits Settlements
BOMBAY B - India-Republic
BOMBAY I - Great Britain, India
BOMBAY (Mumbai) - India-British
BON - Bologna
BON DOCET - Bologna
BONON DOCET - Bologna
BORDEAUX - France, French Cochin China, Greece, Vietnam-French Cochin China
BORUJERD - Iran
BOURGES - France
BP - Budapest (Hungary)
BRAJ INDRAPUR - Indian Princely States
BREGA - Libya
BRESLAU - Austria, German States, Posen
BRIEG - Austria
BROACH - Indian Princely States
BRUGES - Austrian Netherlands
BRUNSWICK - German States
BRUSAH - Turkey
BRUSSELS - Austria, Austrian Netherlands, Belgium, Brazil, Burundi, Congo Democratic Republic, France, Luxembourg, Netherlands, Peru, Philippines, Romania, Russia, Rwanda, Spain, Switzerland, Venezuela
BSP - Bangko Sentral Pilipinas
BUCHAREST - Romania
BUDAPEST - Bulgaria, Egypt, Hungary, Serbia, Yugoslavia
BUENOS AIRES - Argentina
BUKHARA - Russian Turkestan
BUNDI - Indian Princely States
BURHANABAD - Indian Princely State
BURHANPUR - India-Mughal, Indian Princely States
BURGOS - Spain
BURSA - Turkey
BURUJERD - Iran
BUSHIRE - Iran

C

C - Bucharest (Romania)
C - Caen (France)
C - Calcutta (India)
C - Calcutta (India-British)
C - Canadian (Winnipeg)
C - Cassel (Germany)
C - Castelsarrasin (France)
C - Catalonia (Spain)
C - Cayenne (French Guiana)
C - Ceuta (Spain)
C - Charlotte (U.S.A.)
C - Chihuahua (Mexico)
C - Civitavecchia (Italy)
C - Clausthal (German States)
C - Cuenca (Spain)
C - Cuiaba (Brazil)
C - Culiacan (Mexico)
C - Dresden (Germany)
C - Frankfurt Am Main (German States)
C - Gunzburg (Austria)
C - Karlsburg (Romania)
C - Ottawa (Canada)
C - Prague (Czechoslovakia)
C - Saint Lo (France)
C - Spoleto (Yugoslavia)
C - Surabaya (Indonesia)
C - Vienna (Austria)
C crowned - Cadiz (Spain)
C and eagle head - Cassel (German States)
C and lion - Geneva (Swiss Cantons)
C-A - Carlsburg (Austria)
CA - Camora
Ca - Chihuahua (Mexico)
CA - Cuenca (Spain)
CA - Vienna (Austria)
CA - Zaragoza (Mexico)
CADIZ - Spain

CALCUTTA - Australia, India-British, India-Republic, Kenya, Malaya, Mombasa
C.A.M. - San Salvador
CANBERRA - Australia, New Zealand
CANNANORE - India-British
CANTON - China
CARACAS - Venezuela
CARLSBURG - Austria, Austrian Netherlands
CASSEL - German States
CASTELSARRASIN - France, French Indo-China
CATALONIA - Spain
CC - (First C is backward) Besancon (France)
CC - Carson City (U.S.A.)
CC - Genoa (Italy)
CE - Ceuta (Morocco)
Ce - Real del Catorce (Mexico)
CENTRAL AMERICAN - El Salvador
CENTRAL GOVERNMENT - Korea
CH - Chalons (France)
CH - Chihuahua (Mexico)
CH - Pressburg (Hungary)
CHALONS - France
CHAMPANER - India-Independent Kingdom
CHANDA - India-Independent Kingdom
CHANDERI - Indian Princely States
CHANDOR - Indian Princely States
CHANGDE - China
CHANGSHA - China
CHANGTE - China
CHE - China
CHEFOO - China
CHEKIANG - China
CHENGTU - China
CHHACHRAULI - India-Mughal
CHHATARPUR - Indian Princely States
CHI - China
CHI - Valcambi (Switzerland)
CHICHOW - China
CHIHUAHUA - Mexico, Spain
CHIHLI - China
CHIKODI - Independent Kingdom
CHINAN - China
CHINAPATTAN - India-British, India-Mughal
CHINCHWAR - India-Independent Kingdom
CHING - China
CHING CHOW - China
CHITARKOT - Indian Princely States
CHITOR - India-Mughal, Indian Princely States
CHUQUISACA - Bolivia
CIVITAVECCHIA - Vatican Papal City States
CL - Chihuahua (Mexico)
CL - Genoa (Italy)
CL and prow - Genoa (Italy)
CLAUSTHAL - German States
CLERMONT - France
C/M - Calcutta (India-British)
CM - St. Petersburg (Russia)
CM - Sestroretsk (Russia)
CM - Souzan (Russia)
Cn - Culiacan (Mexico)
Co - Coimbra (Portugal)
Co - Cuzco (Peru)
COCHIN - India-Dutch, India-French
CONSTANIYAH - Turkey
CONSTANTINE - Algeria, Turkey
CONSTANTINOPLE - Turkey
COPENHAGEN - Danish West Indies, Denmark, Finland, Greenland, Iceland
COQUIMBO - Chile
CORDOBA - Argentina
CORDOVA - Argentina
CORNUCOPIA & torch - Bulgaria
CR - San Jose (Costa Rica)
CRAILSHEIM - German States
CREUSSEN - German States
CUBA - Vietnam (South)
CUENCA - Spain
CUIABA - Brazil
CULIACAN - Mexico
CUTTACK - India-Independent Kingdom, India-Mughal
CUZ or CUZO plain - Cuzco (Peru)
CUZO monogram - Cuzco (Peru)

D

D - Aurich (German States)
D - Dahlonega (U.S.A.)
D - Damao (India-Portuguese)
D - Denver (U.S.A.)
D - Durango (Mexico)
D - Dusseldorf (German States)
D - Graz (Austria)
D - Lyon (France)
D - Munich (Germany)
D - Salzburg (Austria)
D - Surabaya (Indonesia)
D - Stuttgart (Swiss Cantons)
DACCA - India-British
DACHSBACH - German States
DALIPNAGAR - India Princely States
DAMAO - India-Portuguese
DAMASCUS - Syria, Turkey
DAMASK - Turkey
DAR AL-ISLAM - India Princely States
DAR AL-MULK - Afghanistan, India-Mughal
DAR AS SULTANAT - Afghanistan
DAR EL-KHILAFAT - Iran, Yemen
DAR ES-SALAM - Thailand
DAR ES-SULTANAT - Afghanistan, India-Mughal
DAR ES-SURER - Afghanistan, Indian Princely States
DARFUR - Sudan
DARMSTADT - German States, Germany
DAR UL-AMAN - India-Independent Kingdom, Indian Princely States
DAULATABAD - India-Mughal, Indian Princely States
DB - Schwyz (Swiss Cantons)
D-B - Damao (India-Portuguese)
D-D - Diu (India-Portuguese)
DEHLI - Afghanistan, India-Mughal
DEMOCRATIC REPUBLIC - Afghanistan
DENVER - Australia, Ecuador, Liberia, Netherlands, Netherlands East Indies, Philippines, Venezuela
DEOGARH - Indian Princely States
DEOGIR - India-Mughal, Indian Princely States
DERA - Afghanistan, India-Mughal
DERA GHAZI KHAN - Afghanistan
DERA ISHMAEL KHAN - Afghanistan, India-Mughal
DEZFUL - Iran
DHOLPUR - Indian Princely States
DI - Diu (India-Portuguese)
DIEPPE - France
DIG - Indian Princely States
DIJON - France
DILSHADABAD - India-Mughal
DIMISHK - Turkey
DIO - Diu (India-Portuguese)
D-O - Diu (India-Portuguese)
Do - Durango (Mexico)
DODE - Tibet
DODPAL - Tibet
DOGU - Tibet
DOHAD - Indian Princely States
DORDRECHT - Netherlands, Netherlands East Indies
DRESDEN - German States, Germany
DT - Dordrecht (Netherlands)
DURANGO - Mexico, Spain
DUSSELDORF - German States
DVOR ZAMOSKVORETSKY - Russia

E

E - Carlsburg (Austria)
E - Dresden (Germany)
E - Einkhuizen (Netherlands)
E - Ekaterinburg (Russia)
E - Karlsburg (Romania)
E - Konigsberg (German States)
E - Muldenhutten (Germany)
E - Tours (France)
EDINBURGH - Great Britain
EDIRNE - Turkey
EINKHUIZEN - Netherlands East Indies
EKATERINBURG - Russia
ELICHPUR - India-Mughal, Indian Princely States
EM - Ekaterinburg (Russia)
EM - Essaouir Mogador (Morocco)
ENGLAND - Cyprus, Dominican Rep., Egypt
ENKHUIZEN - Netherlands, Netherlands East Indies
EoMo - Estado de Mexico (Mexico)
ERAVAN - Iran
EREVAN - Turkey
EREWAN - Turkey
ERLANGEN - German States
ESSAOUIR MOGADOR - Morocco
ESTADO DE MEXICO - Mexico

F

F - Angers (France)
F - Cassel
F - Dresden (Germany)
F - Feres (Romania)
F - Florence (Italy)
F - Gunzburg (Austria)
F - Hall (Austria)
F - Magdeburg (German States)
F - Stuttgart (Germany)
FAIZ HISAR - India-Independent Kingdom
FANO - Vatican Papal City States
FARKHANDA BUNYAD - India-Mughal, Indian Princely States
FARRUKHABAD - India-British, India-Mughal
FARRUKHI - India-Independent Kingdom
FARRUKHNAGAR - India-Mughal
FARRUKHYAB - India-Independent Kingdom
FAS - Morocco
AL-FASHER - Sudan
FENGTIEN - China
FEODESIA - Russia
FERES - Romania
FERGANA - Russian Turkestan-Khoqand
FERMO - Vatican Papal City States
FERRARA - Vatican Papal City States
FES - Morocco
FES HAZRAT - Morocco
FEZ - Morocco
FF - Altona (Germany)
FF - Stuttgart (Germany)
FH - Fes Hazrat (Morocco)
FIRENZE - Italian States
FIROZA - India-Mughal
FLORENCE - Italian States, Italy
FM monogram - Franklin Mint
FOLIGNO - Vatican Papal City States
FOUMAN - Iran
FRANCE - Uruguay
FRANKFURT - German States, Germany
FRANKLIN MINT - Bahamas, Barbados, Belize, Bermuda, British Virgin Islands, Cayman Islands, Cook Islands, Ethiopia, Guyana, Jamaica, Jordan, Liberia, Malaysia, Malta, Netherlands Antilles, Panama, Papua New Guinea, Philippines, Romania, Solomon Islands, Surinam, Trinidad & Tobago, Tunisia
FRIBOURG - Swiss Cantons
FRIEDBERG - German States
FS - Fez (Morocco)
FS - Santa Fe-Nuevo Reino (Colombia)
FU - China
FUCHOU - China
FUCHOW - China
FUKAGAWA - Japan
FUKIEN - China
FURTH MINT - German States

G

G - Dresden (Germany)
G - Galle (Sri Lanka)
G - J.R. Gaunt & Sons (Birmingham)
G - Geneva (Switzerland)
G - Glatz (Poland)
G - Goa (India-Portuguese)
G - Goias (Brazil)
G - Graz (Austria)
G - Guadalajara (Mexico)
G - Guanajuato (Mexico)
G - Guatemala
G - Gunzburg (Austria)
G Harderwijk (Gelderland-Netherlands)
G - Karlsruhe (Germany)
G - Nagybanya (Austria, Hungary)
G - Poitiers (France)
G - Schwerin (German State)
G - Stettin (German State)
G-A - Goa (India-Portuguese)
Ga - Guadalajara (Mexico)
GADWAL - Indian Princely States
GAEKWARS - Indian Princely States
GANJAH - Iran
GANJIKOT - India-Mughal
GARHAKOTA - Indian Princely States
GAUNT & SONS - British West Africa
GC - Gualalupe y Calvo (Mexico)
GCR - Philadelphia (USA)
GCR - San Jose (Costa Rica)
GEL - Harderwijk (Gelderland-Netherlands)
GENEVA - France, Swiss Cantons
GENEVE - France
GENOA - France, Italian States, Italy
GHAZNI - Afghanistan
GHENT - Ghent
GHULSHANABAD - India-Mughal
GIAMDA - Tibet
GIJON - Spain
GILAN - Iran
GLATZ - East Prussia, German States
G.M. - Mantua (Italian States)
GN - Nagybanya (Romania)
GN-BW - Bamberg (German States)
Go - Guanajuato (Mexico)
GOA - India-Portuguese
GOHAD - India-Mughal, Indian Princely States
GOIAS - Brazil
GOKULGARH - India-Mughal
GOOTY - India-Independent Kingdom
GORHAM MFG. CO. - Serbia
GR - Graz (Austria)
GRAZ - Austria, Italian States
GRENOBLE - France
GUADALAJARA - Mexico, Spain
GOKUL - Indian Princely State
GORHAM MFG. CO. - Yugoslavia
GUADALUPE Y CALVO - Mexico
GUANAJUATO - Mexico, Spain
GUATEMALA - Central American Republic, Guatemala, Spain
GUBBIO - Vatican Papal City States
GUERNICA - Spain
GULJA - China
GULSHANABAD - India-Independent Kingdom, India-Mughal
GUNZBURG - Austria, Austrian Netherlands, Burgau, German States, Italian States, Luxembourg
GUTY - India-Mughal
GWALIAR - India-Mughal, Indian Princely States
GWALIOR FORT - Indian Princely States
GYF - Karlsburg (Romania)

H

H - Amsterdam (Netherlands)
H - Birmingham: Belize, England
H - Darmstadt (Germany)
H - Dresden (Germany)
H - Geneva (Swiss Cantons)
H - Gunzburg (Austria)
H - Hall (Austria)
H - Heaton (England)
H - Hermosillo (Mexico)
H - Heus (Amsterdam)
H - La Rochelle (France)
H - Schwyz (Swiss Cantons)
HA - Hall (Austria)
HABANA - Vietnam (South)
HAIDARABAD - India-Mughal, Indian Princely States
HAIDARABAD SIND - Afghanistan, Independent Kingdom
HAIDARNAGAR - India-Independent Kingdom
HALEB (ALEPPO) - Syria, Turkey
HALL - Austria, Austrian Netherlands, Austrian States, German States, Hungary, Italian States
HAMADAN - Iran
HAMBURG - German East Africa, German States, Germany, Romania, Tanzania
HANCHENG - China
HANGCHOW - China
HANNOVER - German States, Germany
HANOI - French Indo-China
EL-HARAR - Ethiopia-Eritrea
HARDERWIJK - Netherlands, Netherlands East Indies
HASANABAD - India-Mughal
HATHRAS - Indian Princely States
HAVANA - Afghanistan, Cuba, Kampuchea, Laos, Vietnam
HEATON - Australia, Belgian Congo, Bolivia, British North Borneo, British West Africa, Bulgaria, Canada, Ceylon, Costa Rica, Cyprus, Dominican Republic, East Africa, Ecuador, Egypt, El Salvador, Finland, French Indo China, Great Britain, Greece, Guatemala, Guernsey, Haiti, Hong Kong, India-British, India-Republic, Jamaica, Jersey, Kenya, Liberia, Malaya, Malaya & British North Borneo, Mauritius, Nicaragua, Paraguay, Romania, Sarawak, Serbia, Straits Settlements, Thailand, Uruguay, Venezuela, Zaire
HELSINKI - Finland
HERAT - Afghanistan, Iran
HERMANNSTADT - Transylvania
HERMOSILLO - Mexico
HEUS - Netherlands East Indies
HF - LeLocle (Switzerland)
HILLE - Mesopotamia
HINGANGHAT - India-Independent Kingdom
HIROSHIMA - Japan
HISAR FIROZA - India-Mughal
HK - Harderwijk (Netherlands)
HK - Rostock
HN - Hoorn (Netherlands)
Ho - China
Ho - Hermosillo (Mexico)
HOCHENG - China
HOL - Holland (Netherlands)

HOLL - Holland (Netherlands)
HONAN - China
HOORN - Netherlands, Netherlands East Indies
HQ - China
HOTAN - China
HOTIEN - China
HU - China
HUGUENIN - LA LOCOLE - Romania
HUI YUAN - China
HUNAN - China
HUNGARY - Egypt
HUPEH - China
HUSA - Sweden
HUWAYZA - Iran
HWEIYUAN - China
HYDERABAD - India-Mughal, India-Republic, Indian Princely States
HYDERABAD SIND - Afghanistan, India-Independent Kingdom

I

I - Bombay (India-British)
I - Calcutta (India)
I - Graz (Austria)
I - Hamburg (Germany)
I - Limoges (France)
ICHI-NO-SE - Japan
ILI - China
IMPERIAL NAVAL YARD - China
INDORE - Indian Princely States
INDRAPUR - India-Mughal
I/P Potosi (Mexico)
IRAVAN - Iran, Ottoman Empire
ISAGARH - Indian Princely States
ISE - Japan
ISFAHAN - Iran
ISLAMBUL - Turkey
ISTANBUL - Turkey
ITAWA - India-Independent Kingdom, India-Mughal, Indian Princely States
IZHORA - Russia

J

J - Hamburg (Germany)
J - Jubia (Spain)
J - Paris
J - Surabaya (Indonesia)
J and horse head - Cassel (German States)
J and horse head - Paris
JA - Jubia (Spain)
JABBALPORE - India-Mughal
J'AFARABAD URF CHANDOR - Indian Princely States
JAIPUR SUWAI - Indian Princely States
JAISALMIR - Indian Princely States
JALALABAD - Afghanistan
JALAUN - India-Independent Kingdom
JALNAPUR - India-Mughal
JAMMU - Independent Kingdom, Indian Princely States
JAORA - Indian Princely States
JAWAD - Indian Princely States
JAZA-IR - Algeria
JAZA'IR GARP - Algeria, Turkey
JAZA-IRIYAT - Algeria
JEHOL - China
JELOU - Iran
JERUSALEM - Israel
JHABUA - Indian Princely States
JHALAWAR - Indian Princely States
JHANG - India-Independent Kingdom
JHANSI - India-Independent Kingdom, India-Mughal, Indian Princely States
JIUMAN TSUBO - Japan
JODHPUR - India-Mughal, Indian Princely States
JOHN PINCHES - Bahamas
JP - John Pinches (England)
JUBIA - Spain
JUNAGADH - Indian Princely States

K

K - Bordeaux (France)
K - Kampen (Netherlands)
K - King's Norton (Great Britain)
K - Kormoczbanya (Czechoslovakia)
K - Kremnitz (Czechoslovakia)
K - St. Gall (Swiss Cantons)
KABUL - Afghanistan, India-Mughal
KADAPA - Indian Princely States
KAFFA Russia-Krim
KAIFENG - China
KALAT - Indian Princely States
KALAYANI - Indian Princely States
KALCUTTA - India-British, India-Mughal
KALIKUT - India-Independent Kingdom
KALKATAH - India-British
KALPI - India-Independent Kingdom, India-Mughal
KAMBAYAT - India-Mughal
KAMPEN - Netherlands, Netherlands East Indies
KANAUJ - Indian Princely States
KANSU - China
KARA AMID - Turkey
KARAULI Indian Princely States
KARIMABAD - India-Mughal
KARLSBURG - Austria, Hungary, Transylvania
KARLSRUHE - Germany
KARLSBURG - Transylvania
KARLSRUHE - German States, Germany
KARPA - India-Mughal
KASHAN - Iran
KASHGAR - China
KASHI - China
KASHMIR - Afghanistan, India-Independent Kingdom, India-Mughal, Indian Princely States
KASHQAR - China-Sinkiang
KB - Berlin (Germany)
KB - Kormoczbanya (Bulgaria)
K-B or K.B. - Kremnitz (Czechoslovakia)
KENGIS - Sweden
KERMAN - Iran
KERMANSHAHAN - Iran
KEY - Vietnam (South)
KH - Kitaoua Hazrat (Morocco)
KHALIQABAD - India-Independent Kingdom
KHALSA - India-Independent Kingdom
KHANBAYAT - Indian Princely States
KHANABAD - Afghanistan
KHANPUR - Indian Princely States
KHETRI - Indian Princely States
KHARTOUM - Sudan
KHOQAND - Russian Turkestan
KHOTAN - China
KHOY - Iran
KHUI - Iran
KHUJISTA BUNYAD - India-Mughal, Indian Princely States
AL-KHURFAH - Yemen
KHURSHED-SAWAD - India-Independent Kingdom
KHUTAN - China-Sinkiang
KHWAREZM - Russian Turkestan
KIANGSI - China
KIANGSU - China
KING'S NORTON - Angola, Bolivia, British Borneo, British West Africa, East Africa, Egypt, Great Britain, Greece, Hong Kong, Malaya, Romania
KIRCHBERG - German States
KIRIN - China
KIRMAN - Iran
KIRMANSHAHAN - Iran
KISHANGARH - Indian Princely States
KITAOUA HAZRAT - Morocco
KITZINGEN - German States
KLAUSENBURG - Transylvania
KM - Copenhagen (Denmark)
KM - Kaschau (Czechoslovakia)
KM - Kolpina (Russia)
KM - Kolyvan (Russia)
KN - King's Norton (Great Britain)
KOLPINA - Russia
KOLYVAN - Russia, Russia-Siberia
KONGSBERG - Danish West Indies, Norway
KONIGSBERG - East Prussia, German States
KORA - India-Independent Kingdom, India-Mughal, Indian Princely States
KORMOCZBANYA - Bulgaria
KOSOVAH - Turkey
KOTAH - Indian Princely States
KOTSHA - China
KOUME MURA - Japan
KOVNICA - Yugoslavia
KRASHNY DVOR - Russia
KREMNITZ - Austria, Austrian Netherlands, Hungary, Italian States, Transylvania
KUCHA - China
KUCHAR - China
KUCHE - China
KUELIN - China
KUJI - Japan
KULDJA - China
KULDSHA - China
KULMBACH - German States
KUMBER - Indian Princely States
KUNAR - India-Independent Kingdom
KUNCH - India-Independent Kingdom, Indian Princely States
KUNGCHANG - China
KUQA - China (Sinkiang)
KUTCH - Indian Princely States
KUTTENBERG - Austria
KWANGSI - China
KWANGTUNG - China
KWEICHOW - China
KWEIYANG - China
KWLJA - China

L

L Bayonne (France)
L - Lahore (India)
L - Leipzig (German States)
L - Lima (Peru)
L - Lippoldsberg
L - Lisbon (Portugal)
L - London (England)
LADAKH - Afghanistan, Indian Princely States
LAHIJAN - Iran
LAHORE - Afghanistan, India-British, India-Independent Kingdom, India-Mughal, Iran
LANCHOW - China
LANGENBURG - German States
LA PAZ - Bolivia
LA PLATA - Bolivia
LARACHE - Morocco
LA ROCHELLE - France, French Colonies, Windward Islands
LASHKAR - Indian Princely States
LAUSANNE - Swiss Cantons
LEGHORN - Italian States
LEIPZIG - German States
LELOCLE - Ecuador, Paraguay, Romania
LENINGRAD - Laos, Russia
LHASA - Tibet
LILLE - France
LIMA - Chile, Ecuador, Peru, Peru-North, Spain
LIMAE monogram - Lima (Peru), Spain
LIMOGES - France
LIPPOLDSBERG - German States
LISBON - Brazil, Portugal
LIVORNO - Italian States
LJUSNEDAL - Sweden
LLANTRISANT - New Zealand, Philippines
LM monogram - Lima (Peru)
Ln - London (Great Britain)
LONDON - Albania, Australia, Bahamas, Costa Rica, France, Great Britain, Greece, Iceland, India-Republic, Liberia, Morocco, Peru, Russia, Venezuela, Yugoslavia
LOTUS - Madras (India-British)
LPA - La Plata (Bolivia)
Lr - Larache (Morocco)
LUCKNOW - Indian Princely States
LUZERN - Swiss Cantons
LYON - France, French Colonies, Uruguay

M

M - Aargau (Swiss Cantons)
M - Madras (India-British)
M - Madrid (Spain)
M - Manila (Philippines)
M - Maranhao (Brazil)
M - Medallic Art Co.
M - Medellin (Colombia)
M - Melbourne (Australia)
M - Mendoza (Argentina)
M - Mexico
M - Meyer (Danzig)
M - Milan (Italy)
M - Minas Gerais (Brazil)
M - Monaco
M - Moscow (Russia)
M - Munich (Germany)
M - Salzburg (Austria)
M - Toulouse (France)
M crowned - Madrid (Spain)
Ma - Manila (Philippines)
MA - (ligate) Marseilles (France)
MACERATA - Vatican City Papal States
MACHHLIPATAN-BANDAR - India-British
MACHILIPATNAM - India-British
MADHOPUR SAWAI - Indian Princely States
MADRAS - India-British
MADRAS-TIRUVALLUR - Indian Princely States
MADRIS - India-British, Indian Princely States
MADRID - France, Morocco, Philippines, Spain
MADURAL - Indian Princely States
MAGDEBURG - German States
MAHE INDRAPUR - Indian Princely States
MAHESHWAR - Indian Princely States
MAHINDARPUR - India-Mughal
MAHOBA - India-Independent Kingdom
MALHARNAGAR - Indian Princely States
MALKARIAN - India-Independent Kingdom
MALNAPUR - India-Mughal
MALUKA - Indonesia
MANDISOR - Indian Princely States
MANDLA Independent Kingdom
MANILA - Philippines, Culion Leper Colony, Spain
MANISTIR - Turkey
MANTUA - Austria, Italian States
MARAGHEH - Iran
MARAKESH HAZRAT - Morocco
MARRAKESH - Morocco
MARSEILLES - France
MARWAR - Indian Princely States
MASCARA - Algeria, Turkey
MASHHAD - Afghanistan, Iran
MASULIPATAM - India British
MASULIPATNAM - India-British, India-Dutch, India-French
MATELICA - Vatican Papal City States
MATHURA - Indian Princely States
MAZANDARAN - Iran
MAZULIPATAM - India-British, India-Dutch, India-French
MB - (ligate) Birmingham (Great Britain)
MC - Brunswick
MC - Monaco
MD - Madrid (Spain)
MECCA - Saudi Arabia, Turkey
MEDALLIC ART CO. - Marshall Islands
MEDEA - Algeria, Turkey
MEDELLIN - Colombia
MEDEMBLIK - Netherlands
MEKHA - Saudi Arabia
MEKNASAH - Morocco
MEKNES - Morocco
MEKYI - Tibet
MELBOURNE - Australia, Great Britain
MERTA - Indian Princely States
METZ - France, French Colonies
MEXICO CITY - Dominican Republic, Ecuador, El Salvador, Mexico, Nicaragua, Spain, Uruguay
MEYER - Danzig
MH - Marakesh Hazrat (Morocco)
MH - Vienna (Austria)
MIDDELBURG - Netherlands
MIKNAS - Morocco
MIKNASAH - Morocco
MILAN - Austria, Danzig, Eritrea, Italian States, Italy, San Marino
MINAS GERAIS - Brazil
MIRAJ - India-Independent Kingdom
MISR - Egypt, Turkey
MITO - Japan
MK - Meknes (Morocco)
MM - Moscow, Russia
Mo - Mexico City (Mexico)
MOHAMMADABAD - India-Mughal
MONACO - Monaco
MONTALTO - Vatican Papal City States
MONTE CARLO - Monaco
MONTPELLIER - France
MORIOKA - Japan
MOSCOW - Russia
MOULAY - Brahim (Morocco)
MOXOUDABAT - India-French
MR - Marrakesh (Morocco)
MUBARAK - Afghanistan, Iran
MUHAMMABAD - India-Mughal, Indian Princely States
MUHAMMADABAD - India-Independent Kingdom
MUJAHIDBAD - India-Mughal
MUKDEN - China
MULDENHUTTEN - German States, Germany
MULTAN - Afghanistan, India-Mughal, India-Independent Kingdom
MUNBAI (Bombay) - India-British, India-Mughal
MUNICH - Austria
MUNICH - German States, Germany, Leichtenstein, Paraguay
MURADABAD - Afghanistan, India-Independent Kingdom, India-Mughal, Indian Princely States
MURSHIDABAD - British-India, India-French, India-Mughal
MUSTAFABAD - India-Independent Kingdom
MV or MW - Warsaw (Poland)
Mxo - Mexico
MYSORE - India-Independent Kingdom, Indian Princely States

N

N - Bern (Swiss Cantons)
N - Montpellier (France)
N - Nagybanya (Romania)
N - Naples (Italy)
N above VOC - Negapatnam (India)
NABHA - Indian Princely States
NABEREZHNY DVOR - Russia
NAGAR - India-Independent Kingdom, Indian Princely States
NAGASAKI - Japan
NAGOR - India-Mughal, Indian Princely States
NAGPUR - India-Independent Kingdom
NAGYBANYA - Austria, Austrian Netherlands, German States, Hungary, Italian States, Transylvania
NAHAN - India-Independent Kingdom
NAHTARNAGAR - Indian Princely States
NAJAFGARH - India-Independent Kingdom
NAJIBABAD - Afghanistan, India-Independent Kingdom, India Mughal, Indian Princely States
NAKAPATTANAM - India-Dutch
NAKHCHAWAN - Iran
NANCHANG - China
NANTES - France
NAPLES - Italy
NARBONNE - France
NARWAR - India-Mughal, Indian Princely States
NASIRI - Iran
NASRULLANAGAR - India-Independent Kingdom
NAZARBAR - India-Independent Kingdom
N-B or N.B. - Nagybanya (Romania)
NEGAPATNAM - India-Dutch, India-French
NG - Nueva Guatemala
NIENBURG - German States
NIHAWAND - Iran
NIMAK - India-Independent Kingdom
NINGYUANSEN - China
NIPANI - India-Independent Kingdom
NOIDA - India-Republic
NoRo - Santa Fe-Nuevo Reino (Colombia)
NR - Santa Fe-Nuevo Reino (Colombia)
NUEVA GRENADA - Spain
NUEVA GUATEMALA - Guatemala
NUEVA VIZCAYA - Mexico
NUEVO REINO (Bogota) - Colombia, Spain
NUKHA - Russian Caucasia
NUKHWI - Iran
NUREMBURG - German States

O

O - Clermont (France)
O - New Orleans (U.S.A.)
O - Oaxaca (Mexico)
O - Oravicza (Romania)
O crowned between pillars - Oaxaca (Mexico)
O - Riom (France)
Oa - Oaxaca (Mexico)
OAXACA - Mexico
OM - Strasbourg (France)
OMDURMAN - Sudan
ONOLZBACH - German States
OPPELIN - Austria
OR - Oruro (Bolivia)
ORAVICZA - Austria
ORAVITZA - Italian States
ORLEANS - France
ORURO - Bolivia
OSAKA - French Indo-China, Japan
OTTAWA (RCM) - Canada, Great Britain, Iceland, India-Republic, Israel, Jamaica, Newfoundland, New Zealand

P

P - Dijon (France)
P - Pamplona (Spain)
P - Parma (Italy)
P - Pernambuco (Brazil)
P - Perth (Australia)
P - Perugia (Italy)
P - Philadelphia (U.S.A.)
P - Popayan (Colombia)
P - Porto (Portugal)
P - Potosi (Mexico)
P - Prague (Austria)
P - Pretoria (South Africa)
P - Semur (France)
PA - Pamplona (Spain)
Pa - Paris (France)
PALERMO - Italian States
PALI - Indian Princely States
PAMPLONA - Spain
PANAHABAD - Iran, Russian Caucasia-Karabegh
PAOTING - China
PARENDA - India-Mughal
PARIS - Bolivia, Cochin China, Colombia, Comoros, Crete, Dominican Republic, Ethiopia, France, French Cochin China, French Colonies, French Guiana, French IndoChina, German States, Greece, Haiti, Honduras, Italy, Luxembourg, Monaco, Peru, Portugal, Russia, Serbia, Switzerland, Tunis, Tunisia, Uruguay, Venezuela, Vietnam, Yugoslavia
PARIS - Privy Marks Only - Algeria, Bolivia, Brazil, Bulgaria, Cambodia, Cameroon, Central African Republic, Central African States, Chad, Comoros, Congo People's Republic, Crete, Equatorial African States, Equatorial Guinea, Ethiopia, France, French Afars & Issas, French Equatorial Africa, French Indo-China, French Oceania, French Polynesia, French Somaliland, French West Africa, Gabon, Greece, Haiti, Italy, Kampuchia, Laos, Lebanon, Luxembourg, Madagascar, Malagasy Republic, Mali, Malta (Order of), Monaco Montenegro, Morocco, New Caledonia, New Hebrides, Reunion, Romania, Russia, Rwanda, Saarland, St. Pierre & Miquelon, Serbia, South Korea, South Vietnam, Syria, Togo, Tonkin, Tunis, Tunisia, Uruguay, Venezuela, Vietnam-French Cochin China, West African States, Yugoslavia
PARTABGARH - Indian Princely States
PASCO - Peru
PATAN - India-Independent Kingdom
AL-PATANI - Thailand
PATHANKOT - India-Independent Kingdom
PATNA - East India Company, India-British, India-Mughal
PAU - France
PAZ - Bolivia, Peru
PDV - Valladolid Michoacan (Mexico)
PEIYANG ARSENAL - China
PEKING - China
PERGOLA - Vatican Papal City States
PERNAMBUCO - Brazil
PERPIGNAN - France, French Colonies
PERTH - Australia, Great Britain
PERUGIA - Vatican Papal City States
PESHAWAR - Afghanistan, India-Independent Kingdom, India-Mughal, Iran
PETLAD - Indian Princely States
PETROGRAD - Russia
PHALICHERY - India-French
PHILADELPHIA - Canada, Costa Rica, Ecuador, Netherlands, Netherlands East Indies, Nicaragua, Peru, Surinam, United States, Venezuela
Pi - San Luis Potosi (Mexico)
PINCHES - Bahamas
PISIS - Italian States
PL - London (England)
PL - Pamplona (Spain)
PM - Manila (Philippines)
PM - Pobjoy (England)
PN or Pn - Popayan (Colombia)
PO - Pasco (Peru)
POBJOY - Ascension Islands, Isle of Man, Macao, St. Helena & Ascension, Tristan Da Cunha
POISSY - Bulgaria, France, French Equatorial Africa, French Indo-China, Gabon, Greece, Monaco, Morocco, Romania, Uruguay, Yugoslavia
POITTERS - France
PONDICHERY - India-French
POONA - India-Independent Kingdom
POPAYAN - Colombia, Spain
PORTO - Portugal
POTOSI - Argentina, Bolivia, Chile, Spain
PP - Pamplona (Spain)
PR - Dusseldorf
P-R - Gunzburg (Austria)
PRAGUE - Austria, Austrian Netherlands, Bohemia
PRESSBURG - Austria, Hungary
PRETORIA - British West Africa, Cameroon, East Africa, French Equatorial Africa, Great Britain, India-British, Madagascar, Mauritius, South Africa
PROVIDENCE, RI - Yugoslavia
PTA monogram - La Plata
PTS monogram - Potosi
PUEBLA - Mexico
PULICAT - India-Dutch, India-French

Q

Q - Narbonne (France)
Q - Perpignan (France)
QANDAHAR - Afghanistan, India-Mughal
QASBAH PANIPAT - India-Independent Kingdom
QAZWIN - Iran
QILA MUQAM - Indian Princely States
QOMM - Iran
QUITO - Ecuador
QUM - Iran
QUSANTINAN - Algeria
QUSANTINAT - Algeria
QUSTINTINIYAH - Turkey

R

R - London (England)
R - Orleans (France)
R - Rio de Janeiro (Brazil)
R - Rioja (Argentina)
R - Rome (Italy)
R - Saint Andre (France)
R crowned - Rome (Italy)
RA - Rioja (Argentina)
RABAT - Morocco
RABAT AL-FATH - Morocco
RADHANPUR - Indian Princely States
RAJGARH - Indian Princely States
RAJOD - Indian Princely States
RAMNAD - Indian Princely States
RAMPUR - Independent Kingdom, Indian Princely States
RA'NASH - Iran
RASHT - Iran
RATHAMBHOR - India-Mughal, Indian Princely States
RATHGAR - Indian Princely States
RAVENNA - Vatican Papal City States
RAVISHNAGAR - India-Independent Kingdom
Rb - Rabat (Morocco)
REAL DE CATORCE - Mexico
REGENSBURG - German States
REKAB - Iran
RENNES - France
REVAN - Turkey
REZA'IYEH - Iran
RF - Rabat al-Fath (Morocco)
RIKAB - Afghanistan, Iran
RIO - Mozambique
RIO DE JANEIRO - Brazil, Mozambique
RIOJA - Argentina
RIOM - France
RIOXA - Argentina
ROME - Albania, Eritrea, France, Italian Somaliland, Italy, Malta (Order of), Papal States, San Marino, Somalia, Vatican Papal City States, Vatican Papal States
RONCIGLIONE - Vatican Papal City States
ROSTOCK - German States
Roth - German States
ROUEN - France, French Colonies
ROYAL CANADIAN MINT - Dominican Rep.
ROYAL MINT (London & Llantrisant) - Bahamas, Barbados, Belize, British West Africa, Canada, Fiji, Great Britain, Jamaica, Malaya, Malaya & British Borneo, Philippines
Rs - Brussels (Belgium)
RS - Brussels (Belgium)
Rs - Rio de Janeiro (Brazil)

S

S - Dresden (Germany)
S - Durlach (German States)
S - Gunzburg (Austria)
S - Hall in Tyrol (Austria)
S - Hannover (Germany)
S - Helsinki (Finland)
S - Reims (France)
S - San Francisco (U.S.A.)
S - Santiago (Chile)
S - Schmollnitz (Hungary)
S - Schwabach (German States)
S - Seville (Spain)
S - Solothurn (Switzerland)
S - Sourabaya
S - Sydney (Australia)
S - Troyes (France)
S - Utrecht (Indonesia)
S crowned between pillars - Sombrerete de Vargas
SA - Pretoria (South Africa)
Sa - Surabaya
Sa - Utrecht
SACHE - China
SADO - Japan
SAFI - Morocco
SAGAR - East India Company, India-British
SAGUR - Sagur
SAHARANPUR - India-British, India-Mughal
SAHIBABAD - Indian Princely States
SAINT ANDRE - France
SAINT LO - France
SAINT MALO - France
SALAMABAD - India-Independent Kingdom
SALONIKA - Turkey
SALONIKI - Turkey
SALZBURG - Austria
SANA'A - Yemen
SAN FRANCISCO - Australia, El Salvador, Fiji, French Indo-China, Liberia, Netherlands, Netherlands East Indies, Peru, Philippines, Venezuela
SANGLI - India-Independent Kingdom
SAN JOSE - Central American Republic, Costa Rica
SANKT VEIT - Austria
SAN LUIS POTOSI - Mexico
SAN SALVADOR (C.A.M.) - El Salvador
SANTANDER - Spain
SANTIAGO - Bolivia, Chile, Ecuador, Peru, Spain, Uruguay
SAO PAULO - Brazil
SAN SEVERINO - Vatican Papal City States
SARAKHS - Iran
SAHRIND - Afghanistan
SALONIKA - Turkey
SARANGPUR - India Mughal
SARHIND - Afghanistan
SARI - Iran
SARI POL - Afghanistan
SASHTI - India-Independent Kingdom
SAUDI ARABIA - Turkey
SAUGAR - India-Independent Kingdom
SA'UJBULAGH - Iran
SCHMOLLNITZ - Austria, Galicia & Lodomeria, Hungary, Italian States
SCHWABACH - German States
SCHWERIN - German States
SCHWYZ - Swiss Cantons
SD - Santo Domingo (Dominican Republic)
SE - Santiago del Estero (Chile)
SEGOVIA - Spain
SELANIK - Turkey
SEMLAN - Sweden
SEMUR - France
SENDAI - Japan
SEOUL - India-Republic
SERINGAPATAN - India-Independent Kingdom
SER-KHANG - Tibet
SESTRORETSK - Russia
SEVILLE - Spain
SF - Santa Fe-Nuevo Reino (Colombia)
SGV - Madrid (Spain)
Sh - Suwairah (Morocco)
SHACHE - China (Sinkiang)
SHADORAH - Indian Princely States
SHAHABAD - Indian Princely States
SHAHJAHANABAD - Afghanistan, India-Mughal
SHAM - Turkey
SHAMAKHI - Iran, Russian Caucasia
SHAN - China
SHANGHAI - China
SHANSI - China
SHANTUNG - China
SHAW - Heaton (England)
SHEKI - Iran
SHENGYANG - China
SHENSI - China
SHEOPUR - Indian Princely States
SHERRITT - Nicaragua, Philippines
SHIKARPUR - India-Independent Kingdom
SHIRAZ - Iran
SHUFU - China
SHUSHA - Russian Caucasia-Karabagh
SHUSHTAR - Iran
Si - Sijilmasah (Morocco)
SIAN - China
SIBER - Lausanne (Swiss Cantons)
SIEBENBURGEN - Austria
SIJILMASAH - Morocco
SIMNAN - Iran
SIND - Afghanistan, India-Independent Kingdom, India-Mughal, Iran
SINGAPORE - Macao, Singapore
SINKIANG - China
SIPRI - Indian Princely States
SIRHIND - Indian Princely States
SIRONJ - India-Mughal, Indian Princely States
SL - Seville (Spain)
SLAN - China
SLP - San Luis Potosi (Mexico)
SM - Santa Marta (Colombia)
SM - St. Petersburg (Russia)
S-M-O-M - Malta (Order of)

CHART OF COIN SIZES BY MILLIMETERS

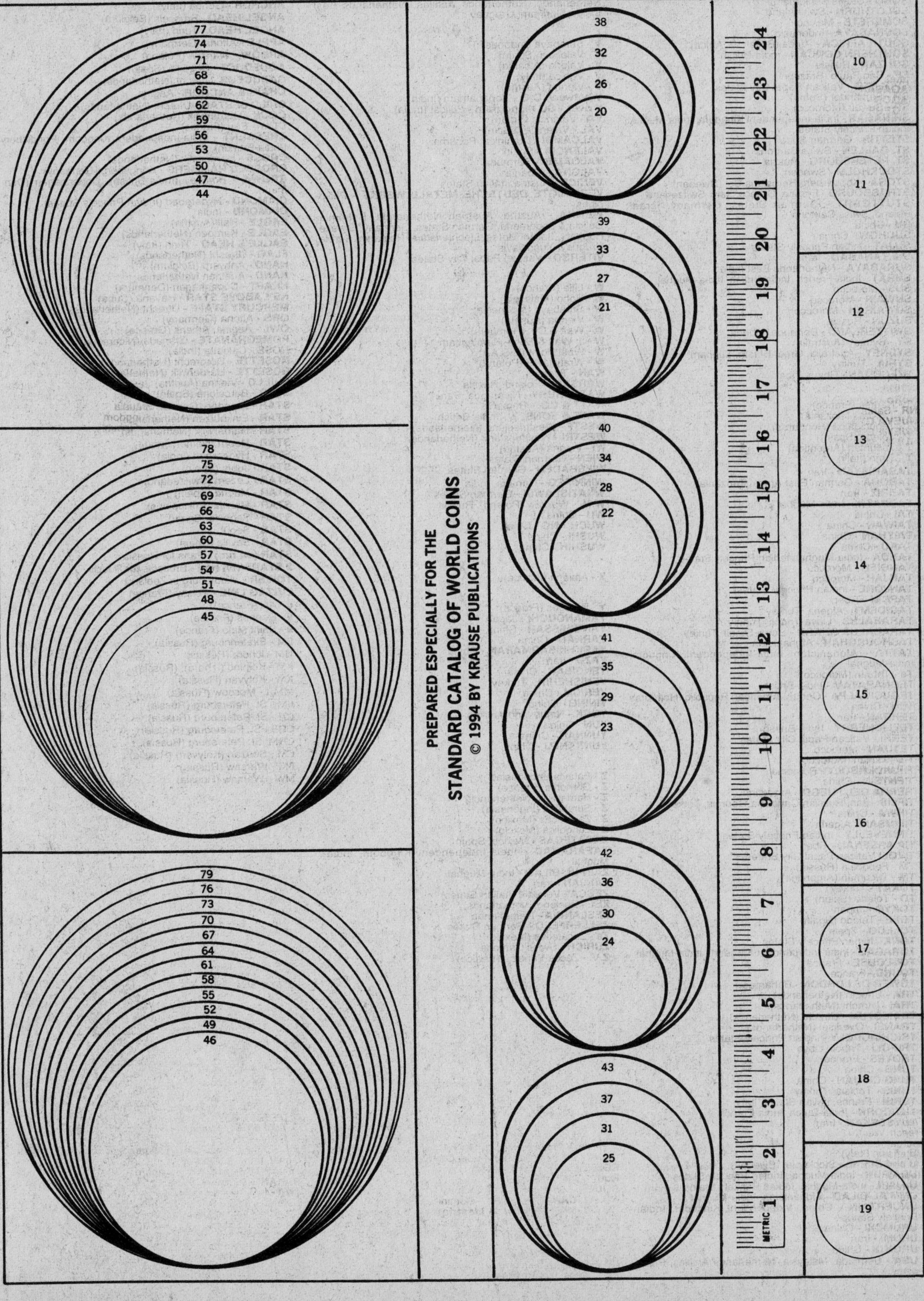

77 74 71 68 65 62 59 56 53 50 47 44

78 75 72 69 66 63 60 57 54 51 48 45

79 76 73 70 67 64 61 58 55 52 49 46

PREPARED ESPECIALLY FOR THE
STANDARD CATALOG OF WORLD COINS

38 32 26 20

39 33 27 21

40 34 28 22

41 35 29 23

42 36 30 24

43 37 31 25

METRIC 1 2 3 4 5 6 7 8 9 10 11 12 13 14 15 16 17 18 19 20 21 22 23 24

10 11 12 13 14 15 16 17 18 19

So - (O above S) Santiago (Chile)
SOCHE - China
SOHO - Straits Settlements
SOLOTHURN - Switzerland
SOMBRETE - Mexico
SOURABAYA - Indonesia
SOUTH AFRICA - Africa (British W. Africa)
SOUTHERN CONCAN - India-British
SOUZAN - Russia
SP - Sao Paulo (Brazil)
SPOLETO - Vatican Papal City States
SR - Santander (Spain)
SR - Suwair (Morocco)
SRINAGAR - India-Independent Kingdom, India-Mughal, Indian Princely States
STETTIN - German States
ST. GALLEN - Swiss Cantons
ST. PETERSBURG - Russia
STOCKHOLM - Sweden
STORA - Kopparberg Bergslags Co. (Sweden)
STRASBOURG - France, Greece, Italy, Switzerland
STUTTGART - German States, Germany, Israel, Poland, Swiss Cantons
SU - China
SUCHOW - China
SUJAT - Indian Princely States
SULTANABAD - Iran
SURABAYA - Netherlands East Indies
SURAT - India-French, India-British, India-Mughal
SUS - Morocco
SUWAIR - Morocco
SUWAIRAH - Morocco
SUZUN - Russia
SWITZERLAND - Bermuda, Liberia
SY - Sydney (Australia)
SYDNEY - Australia, Great Britain, Surinam
SYRIA - Turkey
SZECHUAN - China, Tibet

T

T - Nantes (France)
T - Tabora (Tanzania)
T - Tegucigalpa (Honduras)
T - Toledo (Spain)
T - Tucuman (Argentina)
T - Turin (Italy)
TABARISTAN - Iran
TABORA - German East Africa, Tanzania
TABRIZ - Iran
TADPATRI - India-Mughal
TAI - China
TAIWAN - China
TAIYUAN - China
TAKU - China
TANDA - India-Mughal, Indian Princely States
TANGIER - Morocco
TANJAH - Morocco
TANJORE - Indian Princely States
TAPCHI - Tibet
TAQIDEMT - Algeria, Turkey
TARABALUS - Libya-Tripoli, Turkey
TARABALUS GHARB - Libya-Tripoli, Turkey
TASHQURGHAN - Afghanistan
TATTA - Afghanistan, India-Independent Kingdom, India-Mughal
Te - Tetuan (Morocco)
TEGNAPATAM - India-British
TEGUCIGALPA - Central American Republic, Honduras
TEH - China
TEHRAN - Iran
TELLICHERRY - India-British
TERNI - Vatican Papal City States
TETUAN - Morocco
TG - Tanjah (Morocco)
THUNDERBOLT - Romania
TIENTSIN - China
TIERRA DEL FUEGO - Argentina
TIFLIS - Iran, Russian Caucasia-Georgia, Turkey
TIHWA - China
TILIMSAN - Algeria
TINNEVELLY - Indian Princely States
TIP ARSENAL - Tibet
TIVOLI Vatican Papal City States
TM - Feodosia (Russia)
TM - Tucuman (Argentina)
TOKAT - Turkey
TO - Toledo (Spain)
TOKYO - Japan
TOLE - Toledo (Spain)
TOLEDO - Spain
TONK - Indian Princely States
TORAGAL - India-Independent Kingdom, India-Mughal
TOULOUSE - France
TOURS - France
TOWER OF LONDON - Bahamas
TRA - Utrecth (Netherlands)
TRAI - Utrecht (Netherlands)
TRAIECTUM - Utrecht (Netherlands)
TRANSI - Overijsel (Netherlands)
TRICHINOPOLY - Indian Princely States
TRIPOLI - Tripoli, Libya
TROYES - France
TUNG - China
TUNG CH'UAN - China
TUNIS - Tunisia, Turkey
TURIN - France, Italian States, Italy
TUTICORN - India-Dutch, India-French
TUYSERKAN - Iran

U

U - Turin (Italy)
U and St Eric - Stockholm (Sweden)
UDAIPUR - India-Mughal, Indian Princely States
UJJAIN - India-Mughal, Indian Princely States
UMM AL-BILAD - Afghanistan, India-Mughal
UNCERTAIN - China, Independent Kingdom, Indian Princely States
URUMCHI - China
URUMI - Iran
URUMQI - China
USA - Bermuda, Malaysia, Netherlands Antilles, Philippines
USHI - China
UTRECHT - Aruba, France, Lebanon, Luxembourg, Netherlands, Netherlands Antilles, Netherlands East Indies, Surinam, Uruguay

V

V - Surabaya (Indonesia)
V - Valencia (Spain)
V - Valona (Albania)
V - Venice (Italy)
V - Vienna (Austria)
V between C-O - Negapatnam (India)
V over VOC monogram - Pulicat (India)
VA - Valencia (Spain)
VAL - Valencia (Spain)
VALCAMBI - Dominica, Panama
VALENCIA - Spain
VALOAMBI - Bermuda
VALONA - Albania
VENICE - Austria, Italian States
VEREINIGTE DEUTSCHE METALL WERKS - Philippines
VIENNA - Austria, Austrian Netherlands, Bohemia, Galicia & Lodomeria, German States, Germany, Greece, Hungary, Italian States, Liechtenstein, Romania, Serbia, Uruguay, Yugoslavia
VITERBO - Vatican Papal City States

W

W - Lille (France)
W - Soho (Malaysia)
W - Surabaya (Indonesia)
W - Vienna (Austria)
W - Watt & Co. (Romania)
W - J. Watt & Sons, Birmingham
W - West Point (U.S.A.)
W - Wratislawis (Poland)
WAN - Turkey
WARSAW - Poland, Russia
WATERBURY - Nicaragua, Peru
WATT & CO. - Romania
WATT & SONS, J. - India-British
WESTF - Westfriesland (Netherlands)
WESTRI - Westfriesland (Netherlands)
WI - Vienna (Austria)
WIEN - German States
WIESBADEN - German States
WINNIPEG - Canada, India
WRATISLAWIA - German States
W.M. - Warsaw (Poland), Russia
WU - China
WUCH'ANG - China
WUSHI - China
WUSHIH - China

X

X - Amiens (France)

Y

Y - Bourges (France)
YAMANOUCHI - Japan
YANGIHISSAR - China
YARKAN - China
YARKHISSARMARAN - China
YAZD - Iran
YENGISAR - China
YENISHEHIR - Turkey
YERKIM - China
YINING - China
YORK - Netherland Antilles
YUN - China
YUNNAN - China
YUNNANFU - China

Z

Z - Batavia (Indonesia)
Z - Grenoble (France)
Z - Harderwijk (Netherlands)
Z - Surabaya (Indonesia)
Z - Zacatecas (Mexico)
Z - Zongolica (Mexcio)
ZACATECAS - Mexico, Spain
ZAFARABAD - India-Independent Kingdom, India-Mughal
ZAIN-UL-BILAD - India-Mughal
ZANJAN - Iran
ZECCA - Venezia (Italian States)
ZEL - Zeeland (Netherlands)
ZEELANDIA - Netherlands
ZELLERFELD - German States
Zs - Zacatecas (Mexico)
ZURICH - Swiss Cantons
Z.V. - Zecca Venezia (Venice)

SYMBOLS

ANCHOR - Genoa (Italy)
ANGEL HEAD - Brussels (Belgium)
ANGEL HEAD - Turin (Italy)
APPLE - Altona (Germany)
ARROW - Warsaw (Poland)
AQUEDUCT - Segovia (Spain)
CADUCEUS -Utrecht (Netherlands)
CHAIN & ANCHOR - Aegina
CHILD or STAR - Utrecht (Netherlands)
COCK - Harderwijk (Netherlands)
COW - Pau (France)
CRESCENT - India-Independent Kingdom, Pondichery (India-French)
CROSS - Harderwijk (Netherlands)
CROSSED HAMMERS - Kongsberg (Germany)
CROWN - Bombay (India-British), Copenhagen (Denmark)
DIAMOND - Hyderabad (Indian Princely States)
DIAMOND - India
EAGLE - Hall (Austria)
EAGLE - Kampen (Netherlands)
EAGLE'S HEAD - Turin (Italy)
FLAG - Utrecht (Netherlands)
HAND - Antwerp (Belgium)
HAND - Austrian Netherlands
HEART - Copenhagen (Denmark)
KEY ABOVE STAR - Havana (Cuba)
MERCURY STAFF - Utrecht (Netherlands)
ORB - Altona (Germany)
OWL - Aegina, Athens (Greece)
POMEGRANATE - Granada (Nicaragua)
ROSE - Calcutta (India)
ROSETTE - Dordrecht (Netherlands)
ROSETTE - Harderwijk (Netherlands)
SHIELD - Vienna (Austria)
STAR - Barcelona (Spain)
STAR - Dresden (German State)
STAR - Einkhuizen (Netherlands)
STAR - Harderwijk (Netherlands)
STAR - Hoorn (Netherlands)
STAR - Hyderabad (India)
STAR - Jubia (Spain)
STAR - Luzern (Switzerland)
STAR - Madrid (Spain)
STAR - Manilla (Philippines)
STAR - Segovia (Spain)
STAR - Seoul
STAR - Seville (Spain)
STAR (on rim) - Paris for Russia
2 STARS (on rim) - Brussels for Russia
TOWER - Middleburg in Zeeland
ZIGZAG LINE - Poissy (France)
¢ - Aix (France)
9 - Rennes (France)
9 - Saint Malo (France)
ЕМ - Ekaterinburg (Russia)
ИМ - Ichora (Russia)
КМ - Kolpino (Izhora), (Russia)
КМ - Kolyvan (Russia)
ММД - Moscow (Russia)
БМ - St. Petersburg (Russia)
СП - St. Petersburg (Russia)
СПБ - St. Petersburg (Russia)
СПМ St. Petersburg (Russia)
СМ - Souzan (Kolyvan) (Russia)
ВМ - Warsaw (Russia)
MW - Warsaw (Russia)

AFGHANISTAN

The Islamic Republic of Afghanistan, which occupies a mountainous region of Southwest Asia, has an area of 250,000 sq. mi. (657,000 sq. km.) and a population of 17.6 million. Presently about a fourth of the total population are living (mostly in Pakistan) in exile as refugees. Capital: Kabul. It is bordered by Iran, Pakistan, Russia, and China's Sinkiang Province. Agriculture and herding are the principal industries; textile mills and cement factories are additions to the industrial sector. Cotton, wool, fruits, nuts, oil, sheepskin coats and hand-woven carpets are normally exported but foreign trade has been interrupted since 1979.

Because of its strategic position astride the ancient land route to India, Afghanistan (formerly known as Aryana and Khorasan) was invaded by Darius I, Alexander the Great, various Scythian tribes, the Arabs, the Turks, Genghis Khan, Tamerlane, the Mughals, the Persians, and in more recent times by Great Britain. It was a powerful empire under the Kushans, Hephthalites, Ghaznavids and Ghorids. The name Afghanistan, "Land of the Afghans," came into use in the eighteenth and nineteenth centuries to describe the realm of the Afghan kings. For a short period, this mountainous region was the easternmost frontier of the Iranian world, with strong cultural influences from the Turks and Mongols to the north and India to the south.

Previous to 1747, many Afghan Kings not only ruled in Afghanistan, but also in India, of which Sher Shah Suri was one. Ahmad Shah Abdali, founder of the Durrani dynasty, established his rule at Qandahar in 1747. He conquered large territories in India and eastern Iran, which were lost by his grandson Zaman Shah. A new family, the Barakzays, drove the Durrani king out of Kabul, the capital, in 1819, but the Durranis were not eliminated completely until 1858. Further conflicts among the Barakzays prevented full unity until the reign of 'Abd al-Rahman in 1880. In 1929 the last Barakzay was driven out of the country by a commoner known as Bach-i Saqao, "Son of the Water-Carrier," who ruled as Habib Allah for less than a year before he was defeated by Muhammad Nadir Shah, a relative of the Barakzays. The last king, Muhammad Zahir, became a constitutional, though still autocratic, monarch in 1964. In 1973 a coup d'etat displaced him and created the Republic of Afghanistan. A subsequent military coup established the pro-Soviet Democratic Republic of Afghanistan in 1978. Mounting resistance in the countryside and violence within the government led to the Soviet invasion of late 1979 and the installation of Babrak Karmal as prime minister. A brutal civil war ensued, which continues to the present, even after Soviet forces withdrew in 1989 and Karmal's government was defeated in 1992.

Afghanistan's traditional coinage was much like that of its neighbors Iran and India. There were four major mints: Kabul, Qandahar, Balkh and Herat. The early Durranis also controlled mints in Iran and India, which are included here. On gold and silver coins, the inscriptions in Persian (called Dari in Afghanistan) included the name of the mint city and, normally, of the ruler recognized there, but some issues are anonymous. The arrangement of the inscriptions, and frequently the name of the ruler, was different at each mint. Copper coins were controlled locally and usually did not name any ruler. For these reasons, it is easier to treat the coinage of each mint separately. The relative values of gold, silver, and copper coins were not fixed but were determined in the marketplace.

In 1890 'Abd al-Rahman had a modern mint set up in Kabul with the help of British advisors. The other mints were closed down, except for the issue of local coppers. The new system had sixty paisa to the rupee, but most intermediate denominations also had special names. In 1901 the name Afghanistan appeared on coins for the first time. A decimal system, 100 puls to the afghani, was introduced in 1925. The gold amani, rated at 20 afghanis, was a bullion coin.

The national symbol on most coins of the kingdom is a stylized mosque, within which is seen the mihrab, a niche indicating the direction of Mecca, and the minbar, the pulpit, with a flight of steps leading up to it. Inscriptions in Pashtu, were first used under the rebel Habib Allah, but did not become standard until 1950.

Until 1919, coins were dated by the lunar Islamic Hijri calendar (AH), often with the king's regnal year as a second date. The solar Hijri (SH) calendar was introduced in 1919 (1337 AH, 1298 SH). The rebel Habib Allah reinstated lunar Hijri dating (AH 1347-50), but the solar calendar was used thereafter. The solar Hijri year begins on the first day of spring, about March 21. Adding 621 to the SH year yields the AD year in which it begins.

RULERS

Names of rulers are shown in Perso-Arabic script in the style usually found on their coins, but are not always in a straight line.

DURRANI DYNASTY

Shah Shuja al-Mulk, 1st reign,
AH1216/1801AD (no coins)

شاه شجاع الملک

Mahmud Shah, 1st reign,
AH1216-1218/1801-1803AD

محمود شاه

Qaisar Shah,
AH1218/1803AD

قیصر شاه

Shah Shuja al-Mulk, 2nd reign,
AH1218-1224/1803-1808AD

Mahmud Shah, 2nd reign,
AH1224-1233/1808-1817AD

Ayyub Shah, Puppet of Dost Muhammad,
AH1233-1245/1817-1826AD

ایوب شاه

Sultan Muhammad, at Peshawar
AH1247-1250/1831-1834AD

سلطان محمد

Kohandil Khan, at Qandahar
AH1256-1271/1840-1855AD

کهندل خان

Shah Shuja al-Mulk, as nominee of British East India Co., 3rd reign,
AH1255-1258/1839-1842AD

Fath Jang
AH1258/1842AD

فتح جنگ

Shahpur Shah
AH1258/1842AD

شاپور شاه

Succession at Kashmir, AH1221-1234

Qaisar Shah,
AH1221-1223/1806-1808AD

Ata Muhammad, called Shah Nur al Din on coins,
AH1223-1228/1808-1813AD

شاه نور الدین

Azim Khan, coins in name of Mahmud Shah,
AH1228-1234/1813-1818AD

Succession at Herat, AH1216-1298

Mahmud Shah,
AH1216-1245/1801-1829AD

Kamran Shah,
AH1245-1258/1829-1842AD

کامران شاه

Yar Muhammad Khan Barakzai,
AH1258-1267/1842-1851AD

یار محمد خان بارکزای

Muhammad Yusuf Khan Sadozai,
AH1267-1272/1851-1856AD

محمد یوسف خان سادوزای

Iranian Occupation of Herat (coins in name of Nasir al-Din Shah):
AH1272-1280/1856-1863AD

Sher Ali, AH1280-1296/1863-1879AD
Muhammad Yaqub,
AH1296-1298/1879-1881AD
thereafter, as in the rest of Afghanistan

BARAKZAI DYNASTY

Dost Muhammad, 1st reign, anonymous coinage
AH1239-1255/1824-1839AD

دوست محمد

British Occupation
AH1255-1258/1839-1842AD

Dost Muhammad, 2nd reign, "Akbar Amir" (Great King) in center of obv.
AH1258-1280/1842-1863AD

اکبر امیر

Sher Ali, 1st reign,
AH1280-1283/1863-1866AD

شیر علی

Muhammad Afzal,
AH1283-1284/1866-1867AD

محمد افضل

Muhammad A'zam,
AH1283-1285/1866-1868AD

محمد اعظم

Sher Ali, 2nd reign,
AH1285-1296/1868-1879AD

Muhammad Yaqub,
AH1296-1297/1879-1880AD

محمد یعقوب

Wali Muhammad, at Kabul
AH1297/1880AD

والی محمد

Wali Sher Ali, at Qandahar
AH1297/1880AD

والی شیر علی

Abdur Rahman,
AH1297-1319/1880-1901AD

عبد الرحمن

Muhammad Ishaq, rebel at Balkh,
AH1305-1306/1889AD

محمد اسحاق

Habibullah,
AH1319-1337/1901-1919AD

حبیب الله

Amanullah,
AH1337, SH1298-1307/1919-1929AD

امان الله

Habibullah (rebel, known as Baccha-i-Saqao),
AH1347-1348/1929AD

حبیب الله
١٣٤٧(٥٢٨)

Muhammed Nadir Shah
AH1348-1350, SH1310-1312
1929-1933AD

محمد نادر شاه

Muhammad Zahir Shah,
SH1312-1352/1933-1973AD

محمد ظاهر شاه

Republic, SH1352-1358/1973-1979AD
Democratic Republic, SH1358/1979AD

MINTNAMES

Hammered coins were struck at numerous mints in Afghanistan and adjacent lands. These are listed below, together with their honorific titles, and shown in the style ordinarily found on the coins.

Afghanistan — افغانستان

Ahmadpur Mint
See Bahawalpur Mint — احمد پور

Ahmadshahi Mint
See Qandahar Mint — احمد شاهی

'Ashraf al-Bilad'
Most Noble of Cities — اشرف البلاد

Badakhshan Mint — بوخشان

Bahawalpur Mint — بهاولپور

'Dar as-Surur'
Abode of Happiness — دار السرور

Balkh Mint — بلخ

'Umm al-Bilad'
Mother of Cities — ام البلاد

Bhakhar Mint — بهکر

Dera
Dera Ghazi Khan ديره

Derajat
Dera Isma'il Khan ديره جات

Ghazni غزني

Herat Mint هرات

Dar al-Nusrat
Seat of Victory دارالنصرت

'Dar as-Sultanat'
Abode of the Sultanate دار السلطنة

Jalalabad جلا ل ا باد

Kabul كابل

'Dar al-Mulk'
Abode of the King دار لملك

'Dar as-Sultanat' (see Herat)

Kashmir كشمير

Khanabad لداخ

Ladakh
(Not usually clear on coins) خان اباد

Mashhad مشهد

Multan ملتان

'Dar al-Aman'
Abode of Security دار الامان

Peshawar پشاور

Qandahar Mint
See Ahmadshahi Mint قندهار

Sar-i Pol سرَپل

Tashqurghan تاش قورغان

ANONYMOUS HAMMERED COPPER COINAGE

Afghan copper coins, prior to the beginning of machine-struck coinage in 1891, were not regulated by the central authorities. Mintmasters produced many types of hand-struck coinage including the use of old Afghan coins as blanks. Consequently, weights are quite random, and there are no denominations in the true sense of the term. All were known as 'Falus', and lots of mixed sizes were accounted by weight. Every few years, sometimes every year, coppers were recalled and recoined, at a fee, often substantial, which was paid to the mintmaster and formed his salary. This accounts for the large number of overstruck pieces, which are generally less desirable than clear singly struck specimens.

Hundreds of varieties were issued at the principal mints of Kabul and Ahmadshahi/Qandahar, and the following listing is only a representation of what exists. It is arranged chronologically by mint, to the extent that coins bear dates. A more detailed, but still very fragmentary listing is given by W.H. Valentine, in 'Modern Copper Coins of the Muhammadan States'. No attempt at a complete listing has ever been undertaken.

Prices are for well-struck specimens with clear design and date. Partial or overstruck coins are worth considerably less. Unrepresented types are worth about the same as listed pieces of the same mint.

IMPORTANT: Most types were used at one time or other at all mints. The type cannot therefore be used to determine the mint, which can ordinarily only be ascertained by reading the Persian inscription.

NOTE: Copper coins bearing the name of the issuing ruler are included under "Named Hammered Coinage", below, by mint. For later anonymous issues, see the local coppers listed after the milled coinage.

Ahmadshahi Mint

(See also Qandahar)

Obv: Lion right.

KM#	Date	Good	VG	Fine	VF
11	AH1227	2.50	4.00	7.00	12.00

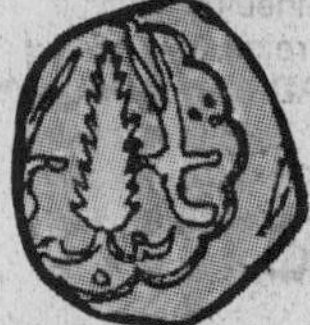

Obv: 8-petalled flower.

KM#	Date	Good	VG	Fine	VF
14	AH1240	3.00	6.00	10.00	17.00

Obv: Leaf between swords.

KM#	Date	Good	VG	Fine	VF
15	AH1240	3.50	7.00	12.00	20.00

Obv: Flower between swords.

KM#	Date	Good	VG	Fine	VF
16	AH1241	3.50	7.00	12.00	20.00

Obv: 3 flowers on 1 stem.

KM#	Date	Good	VG	Fine	VF
18	AH1245	3.50	7.00	12.00	20.00

Obv: 3 swords.

KM#	Date	Good	VG	Fine	VF
20	AH1249	4.50	9.00	15.00	25.00

Obv: Flower.

KM#	Date	Good	VG	Fine	VF
21	AH1252	2.00	4.00	7.00	12.00

Obv: Sunface.

KM#	Date	Good	VG	Fine	VF
22	AH1253	2.00	4.00	7.00	12.00

Obv: Crossed swords.

KM#	Date	Good	VG	Fine	VF
23	ND	2.50	5.00	8.00	13.00
	AH1253	3.00	6.00	10.00	17.00

Obv: Leaf between 2 swords.

KM#	Date	Good	VG	Fine	VF
24	AH1254	3.00	6.00	10.00	17.00

Obv: Ornate borders.

KM#	Date	Good	VG	Fine	VF
25	AH1255	4.50	9.00	15.00	25.00

Obv: 2 bladed sword.

KM#	Date	Good	VG	Fine	VF
26	AH1255	2.50	5.00	8.00	13.00

Obv: Sword between 2 leaves.

KM#	Date	Good	VG	Fine	VF
27	AH1256	2.50	5.00	8.00	13.00
	1257	2.50	5.00	8.00	13.00

Obv: Bird.

KM#	Date	Good	VG	Fine	VF
28	ND	2.00	4.00	7.00	12.00
29	AH1264	3.00	6.00	10.00	17.00

Badakhshan Mint

Rev. leg: ***Badakhshan.***

KM#	Date	Good	VG	Fine	VF
30	ND	7.50	15.00	25.00	40.00

Balkh Mint

Obv: Flower between 2 swords.

KM#	Date	Good	VG	Fine	VF
32	AH1228	2.00	4.00	7.00	12.00
	1233	2.00	4.00	7.00	12.00
	1234	2.00	4.00	7.00	12.00
	1238	2.00	4.00	7.00	12.00

Obv: Lion right.

KM#	Date	Good	VG	Fine	VF
35	AH1267	2.50	5.00	8.00	13.00

Obv: Plant between 2 swords.

KM#	Date	Good	VG	Fine	VF
37	AH1274	3.00	6.00	10.00	16.00
	1277	4.50	9.00	15.00	25.00

Crude, irregular flan.

KM#	Date	Good	VG	Fine	VF
38.1	AH1295	2.50	5.00	8.00	13.00

Obv: Small lion and inscriptions.

KM#	Date	Good	VG	Fine	VF
38.2	AH1295	1.75	3.50	6.00	10.00

NOTE: This type struck by machine over a number of years without change of date. Lion usually faces right, rarely left.

Ghazni Mint

KM#	Date	Good	VG	Fine	VF
39	ND(ca 1860-80)	3.50	7.00	12.00	20.00

Obv: Floral design.

KM#	Date	Good	VG	Fine	VF
40	ND	3.00	6.00	10.00	17.00

Herat Mint

Obv: Leaf and 2 swords.

KM#	Date	Good	VG	Fine	VF
43	AH1224	2.00	4.00	7.00	12.00
	1226	2.00	4.00	7.00	12.00

Obv: Sunface.

KM#	Date	Good	VG	Fine	VF
44	AH1227	2.00	4.00	7.00	12.00

Obv: Crab.

KM#	Date	Good	VG	Fine	VF
45	AH(12)95	2.00	4.00	7.00	12.00

Obv: Fish ?

KM#	Date	Good	VG	Fine	VF
47	AH1297	2.00	4.00	7.00	12.00

Obv: 4 ovals in the shape of a cross within double circle.

KM#	Date	Good	VG	Fine	VF
50	AH1305	5.00	9.00	15.00	25.00

Jalalabad Mint

Obv: Large flower.
Rev. leg: ***Falus*** above mintname.

KM#	Date	Good	VG	Fine	VF
52	AH—	13.00	26.00	45.00	75.00

NOTE: Crudely overstruck on earlier types.

Kabul Mint

Obv: Lily blossom.

KM#	Date	Good	VG	Fine	VF
53	AH(1)222	3.50	7.00	12.00	20.00

Obv: Leaf and swords, *J* in center, large size.

KM#	Date	Good	VG	Fine	VF
54	AH1229	2.50	5.00	8.00	13.00

Obv: Flower.

KM#	Date	Good	VG	Fine	VF
55	AH1232	3.00	6.50	12.00	20.00

Obv: Crossed swords.

KM#	Date	Good	VG	Fine	VF
56	AH1234	2.50	5.00	8.00	13.00

Obv: Crossed swords.

KM#	Date	Good	VG	Fine	VF
58	AH1236	3.00	6.00	10.00	16.00

Obv: Star between 2 swords.

KM#	Date	Good	VG	Fine	VF
59	AH1236	3.50	7.00	12.00	20.00
	ND	3.00	6.00	10.00	16.00

Obv: Flower between 2 leaves.

KM#	Date	Good	VG	Fine	VF
60	AH1236	4.00	7.00	12.00	20.00

Obv: Floral pattern.

KM#	Date	Good	VG	Fine	VF
66	AH12xx	2.00	4.00	7.00	12.00
	ND	2.00	4.00	7.00	12.00

Obv: Sword and stars.

KM#	Date	Good	VG	Fine	VF
68	AH1252	2.00	4.00	7.00	12.00
	126x	2.00	4.00	7.00	12.00
	ND	2.00	4.00	7.00	12.00

Obv: Sword right.

KM#	Date	Good	VG	Fine	VF
69	AH1258	3.00	6.00	10.00	16.00

Obv: Sword and floral ornaments.

KM#	Date	Good	VG	Fine	VF
70	AH1254	2.00	4.00	7.00	12.00
	1258	3.00	6.00	10.00	16.00

Obv: Flower.

KM#	Date	Good	VG	Fine	VF
71	AH1254	2.00	4.00	7.00	12.00

Obv: Flower and swords.

KM#	Date	Good	VG	Fine	VF
72	AH1254-58	2.00	4.00	7.00	12.00
	1256	2.00	4.00	7.00	12.00

Obv: Sword.

KM#	Date	Good	VG	Fine	VF
73	AH1254	2.50	5.00	8.00	13.00

Obv: Flower and swords.

KM#	Date	Good	VG	Fine	VF
75	AH1261	2.50	5.00	8.00	13.00
	1265	2.50	5.00	8.00	13.00

Obv: Star within circle.

KM#	Date	Good	VG	Fine	VF
A76	AH—	2.75	5.50	9.00	15.00

Obv: Flower within chevron border.

KM#	Date	Good	VG	Fine	VF
76	AH1261	4.00	8.00	13.00	22.00

Obv: Flower within star.

KM#	Date	Good	VG	Fine	VF
A77	AH1262	4.00	8.00	13.00	22.00

Obv: Floral spray.

KM#	Date	Good	VG	Fine	VF
77	AH1267	4.50	9.00	15.00	25.00

Obv: Flower.

KM#	Date	Good	VG	Fine	VF
78	AH1268	2.00	4.00	7.00	12.00

Obv: Flower.

KM#	Date	Good	VG	Fine	VF
79	ND	3.50	7.00	12.00	20.00

Khanabad Mint

KM#	Date	Good	VG	Fine	VF
80	AH1301	8.00	16.00	27.00	45.00
	1302	8.00	16.00	27.00	45.00

KM#	Date	Good	VG	Fine	VF
81	AH(1)302	—	—	—	—

Peshawar Mint

KM#	Date	Good	VG	Fine	VF
83	AH1249	4.50	9.00	15.00	25.00

Qandahar Mint

(See also Ahmadshahi)

Obv: Large date and legend.

KM#	Date	Good	VG	Fine	VF
85	AH1228	2.00	4.00	7.00	12.00

Obv: 4 petaled flower within 4 swords.

KM#	Date	Good	VG	Fine	VF
87	ND	2.00	4.00	7.00	12.00

Obv: 3 flowers on 1 stem. Rev: Sword.

KM#	Date	Good	VG	Fine	VF
88	ND	4.00	7.00	12.00	20.00

Obv: Flower w/fancy border.

KM#	Date	Good	VG	Fine	VF
89	AH1289	8.00	16.00	27.00	45.00

NOTE: This type evidently served as the prototype for the British occupation issue dated AH1296, KM#94.

Obv: Flower within wreath.

KM#	Date	Good	VG	Fine	VF
90	AH1294	3.00	6.00	10.00	17.00

Obv: Hand of Ali?

KM#	Date	Good	VG	Fine	VF
91	AH1295	2.50	5.00	8.00	13.00

Obv: Leaf between 2 swords.

KM#	Date	Good	VG	Fine	VF
92	AH1295	2.50	5.00	8.00	13.00

Obv. leg: *Adl* (Justice) in hexagram.

KM#	Date	Good	VG	Fine	VF
95	AH1296	1.00	2.00	3.50	6.00

Obv: Peacock.

KM#	Date	Good	VG	Fine	VF
96	AH1297	1.00	2.00	3.50	6.00

Obv: Flower.

KM#	Date	Good	VG	Fine	VF
97	AH1300	2.50	5.00	8.00	13.00

British Occupation

Obv: Crown.

KM#	Date	Good	VG	Fine	VF
94	AH1296	16.00	32.50	55.00	90.00

NOTE: Issued during the British occupation of Qandahar 1878-79.

KM#	Date	Good	VG	Fine	VF
101	AH1296	17.50	35.00	60.00	100.00

Obv: 4 leaves joined.

KM#	Date	Good	VG	Fine	VF
102	AH1307	2.50	5.00	8.00	13.00

Sar-i Pol Mint

Obv: Lion.

KM#	Date	Good	VG	Fine	VF
98	AH1297	7.50	15.00	25.00	40.00
	ND	7.50	15.00	25.00	40.00

Tashqurghan Mint

Obv: Stem with leaves.

KM#	Date	Good	VG	Fine	VF
99	AH1300	8.00	16.00	28.00	45.00

Obv: Flower.

KM#	Date	Good	VG	Fine	VF
100	AH1300	10.00	20.00	35.00	60.00

NAMED HAMMERED COINAGE

Unlike the anonymous copper coinage, which was purely local, the silver and gold coins, as well as some of the early copper coins, bear the name or characteristic type of the ruler. Because the sequence of rulers often varied at different mints, each ruled by different princes, the coins are best organized according to mint. Each mint employed characteristic types and calligraphy, which continued from one ruler to the next. It is hoped that this system will facilitate identification of these coins.

The following listings include not only the mints situated in contiguous territories under Durrani and Barakzai rule for extended periods of time, but also mints in Kashmir or in other parts of India which the Afghans occupied for relatively brief intervals.

Ahmadpur Mint

(In Bahawalpur)

MAHMUD SHAH

AH1216-1218/1801-1803AD

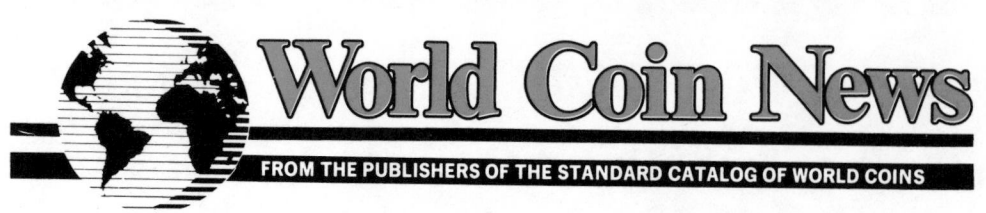

LIGHT RUPEE

SILVER, 8.20-8.40 g

KM#	Date	Year	VG	Fine	VF	XF
108	AH1217	48	22.00	40.00	50.00	60.00
	—	49	22.00	40.00	50.00	60.00

NOTE: Posthumous issue. Reverse only shown.

Ahmadshahi/Qandahar Mint

Ashraf-al-Bilad

Until AH1273, this mint was almost always given on the coins as *Ahmadshahi*, a name given it by Ahmad Shah in honor of himself in AH1171, often with the honorific *Ashraf al-Bilad* (meaning 'Most Noble of Cities'). On later issues, after AH1271, the traditional name *Qandahar* is generally used.

MAHMUD SHAH

AH1216-1218/1801-1803AD, 1st reign

RUPEE

SILVER, 11.40-11.60 g

KM#	Date	Year	VG	Fine	VF	XF
143	AH1216	—	15.00	30.00	45.00	60.00
	1217	2	15.00	30.00	45.00	60.00
	1217	3	15.00	30.00	45.00	60.00
	1218	3	15.00	30.00	45.00	60.00

ASHRAFI

GOLD, 25mm, 3.50 g

KM#	Date	Year	VG	Fine	VF	XF
144	AH1218	3	—	275.00	400.00	500.00

MOHUR

GOLD, 10.90 g

KM#	Date	Year	VG	Fine	VF	XF
145	AH1218	2	—	275.00	350.00	400.00
	1218	3	—	275.00	350.00	400.00

QAISAR SHAH

AH1218/1803AD

RUPEE

SILVER, 11.50-11.60 g

KM#	Date	Year	VG	Fine	VF	XF
148	AH1218	—	20.00	50.00	70.00	85.00

MOHUR

GOLD, 10.90 g

KM#	Date	Year	VG	Fine	VF	XF
149	AH1218	—	—	350.00	475.00	600.00

SHAH SHUJA AL-MULK

AH1218-1224/1803-1808AD, 2nd reign

1/4 RUPEE

SILVER, 2.80-3.00 g

KM#	Date	Year	VG	Fine	VF	XF
151	AH1218	2	20.00	40.00	60.00	90.00

RUPEE

SILVER, 11.40-11.60 g

KM#	Date	Year	VG	Fine	VF	XF
153	AH1218	—	7.50	15.00	20.00	27.50
	1219	1	7.50	15.00	20.00	27.50
	1220	2	7.50	15.00	20.00	27.50
	1221	3	7.50	15.00	20.00	27.50
	1222	—	7.50	15.00	20.00	27.50
	1223	—	7.50	15.00	20.00	27.50
	1224	—	7.50	15.00	20.00	27.50

NOTE: Varieties of the obverse exist.

ASHRAFI

GOLD, 3.00-3.50 g

KM#	Date	Year	VG	Fine	VF	XF
154	AH1220	3	—	175.00	200.00	350.00
	1222	—	—	175.00	200.00	350.00

MOHUR

GOLD, 10.90 g

KM#	Date	Year	VG	Fine	VF	XF
155	AH—	2	—	—	300.00	375.00
	AH1220	3	—	—	325.00	400.00
	1222	—	—	—	325.00	400.00

MAHMUD SHAH

AH1224-1233/1808-1817AD, 2nd reign

1/2 RUPEE

SILVER, 5.40-5.80 g

KM#	Date	Year	VG	Fine	VF	XF
156	AH1224	—	20.00	45.00	65.00	85.00

RUPEE

SILVER, 11.40-11.60 g
Rev: In cartouche or circle.

KM#	Date	Year	VG	Fine	VF	XF
157	AH1222 (error date)					
		—	7.00	14.00	20.00	30.00
	1224	—	7.00	14.00	20.00	28.00
	1225	—	7.00	14.00	20.00	28.00
	1226	—	7.00	14.00	20.00	28.00
	1227	—	7.00	14.00	20.00	28.00
	1228	—	7.00	14.00	20.00	28.00
	1230	—	7.00	14.00	20.00	28.00
	1232	—	7.00	14.00	20.00	28.00

10.20-10.40 g
Rev: In toughra.

KM#	Date	Year	VG	Fine	VF	XF
158.1	AH1229	—	—	10.00	16.00	25.00
	1230	—	—	10.00	16.00	25.00
	1231	—	—	10.00	16.00	25.00
	1232	—	—	10.00	16.00	25.00

Rev: Legend in a circle.

KM#	Date	Year	VG	Fine	VF	XF
158.2	AH1232	—	8.00	15.00	25.00	35.00
	1233	—	8.00	15.00	25.00	35.00
	1234	—	8.00	15.00	25.00	35.00

ASHRAFI

GOLD, 28mm, 2.40 g

KM#	Date	Year	VG	Fine	VF	XF
159	AH1224	—	—	—	Rare	—

AYYUB SHAH

AH1233-1245/1817-1826AD

RUPEE

SILVER
Rev: Mint in center circled by Kalimah.

KM#	Date	Year	VG	Fine	VF	XF
162	AH1234	—	—	—	—	—

SILVER, 11.20-11.60 g

KM#	Date	Year	VG	Fine	VF	XF
163	AH1235	—	15.00	30.00	40.00	50.00
	1236	—	—	Reported, not confirmed		
	1237	—	15.00	30.00	40.00	50.00
	1239	—	15.00	30.00	40.00	50.00

NOTE: Reverses differ each year. Coins dated AH1239 are struck in debased silver.

KM#	Date	Year	VG	Fine	VF	XF
164	AHxxxx	—	25.00	50.00	—	—

ANONYMOUS COINAGE

During the reign of Ayyub Shah

AH1233-1245/1817-1826AD

FALUS

BRONZE
Obv. leg: ***Ya Ghaus ol Azam.***

KM#	Date	Year	VG	Fine	VF	XF
165	AH1240	—	15.00	35.00	55.00	90.00
	1241	—	15.00	35.00	55.00	90.00

During the reign of Dost Muhammad, 1st reign

AH1239-1255/1824-1839AD

RUPEE

SILVER
Obv: Kalimah.

KM#	Date	Year	VG	Fine	VF	XF
168	AH1243	—	10.00	20.00	30.00	40.00
	1244	—	7.00	15.00	20.00	30.00
	1245	—	—	10.00	15.00	25.00
	1246	—	—	10.00	15.00	25.00
	1247	—	—	10.00	15.00	25.00
	1248	—	—	10.00	15.00	25.00
	1249	—	—	9.00	14.00	23.00
	1250	—	—	9.00	14.00	23.00
	1251	—	—	9.00	14.00	23.00
	1252	—	7.00	13.00	20.00	30.00
	1253	—	7.00	13.00	20.00	30.00
	1254	—	7.00	13.00	20.00	30.00

NOTE: Minor variations exist on both sides.

SHAH SHUJA AL-MULK

AH1255-1258/1839-1842AD, 3rd reign

1/4 RUPEE

SILVER, 2.30 g

KM#	Date	Year	VG	Fine	VF	XF
171	AH1255	—	25.00	32.50	45.00	60.00

1/2 RUPEE

SILVER

KM#	Date	Year	VG	Fine	VF	XF
172	AH1255	—	25.00	32.50	45.00	60.00

RUPEE

SILVER, 9.00-9.20 g

KM#	Date	Year	VG	Fine	VF	XF
173	AH1255	—	10.00	20.00	25.00	35.00
	1256	—	12.50	30.00	40.00	50.00

FATH JANG

AH1258/1842AD

RUPEE

SILVER, 9.15-9.35 g

KM#	Date	Year	VG	Fine	VF	XF
178	AH1258	—	20.00	50.00	75.00	100.00

ANONYMOUS COINAGE

During the reign of Kohandil Khan

AH1256-1271/1840-1855AD

1/2 RUPEE

SILVER

KM#	Date	Year	VG	Fine	VF	XF
182	AH1260	—	4.00	10.00	14.00	20.00
	1261	—	4.00	10.00	14.00	20.00
	1262	—	4.00	10.00	14.00	20.00
	1263	—	4.00	10.00	14.00	20.00
	1264	—	4.00	10.00	14.00	20.00
	1265	—	4.00	10.00	14.00	20.00
	1267	—	5.00	12.00	19.00	25.00
	1268	—	6.50	16.00	25.00	35.00
	1269	—	6.50	16.00	25.00	35.00
	1270	—	6.50	16.00	25.00	35.00
	1271	—	6.50	16.00	25.00	35.00
	1272	—	6.50	16.00	25.00	35.00

NOTE: Both obverse and reverse have legends differently arranged in different years.

RUPEE

SILVER

KM#	Date	Year	VG	Fine	VF	XF
183	AH1259	—	12.50	27.50	35.00	50.00

RAHAMDIL KHAN

AH1271-1272/1855-1856AD

1/2 RUPEE

SILVER

Mintname: *Ahmadshahi*

KM#	Date	Year	VG	Fine	VF	XF
184	AH1272	—	15.00	35.00	50.00	70.00

DOST MUHAMMAD

AH1258-1280/1842-1863AD, 2nd reign

In name of Amir Kabir

1/2 RUPEE

SILVER

Mintname: *Ahmadshahi*

Dated on both sides.

KM#	Date	Year	VG	Fine	VF	XF
186	AH1272	—	3.00	6.00	10.00	15.00
	1273	—	3.00	6.00	10.00	15.00

Mintname: *Qandahar*

Dated on both sides.

KM#	Date	Year	VG	Fine	VF	XF
187.1	AH1273	—	3.00	6.00	8.50	13.50
	1274	—	3.00	6.00	8.50	13.50
	1275	—	3.00	6.00	8.50	13.50
	1276	—	3.00	6.00	9.00	15.00
	1277	—	3.00	6.00	9.00	15.00
	1278	—	3.00	6.00	9.00	15.00
	1279	—	— Reported, not confirmed			

Rev: *Qandahar* **above,** *Zuriba* **below.**

KM#	Date	Year	VG	Fine	VF	XF
187.2	AH1281	—	15.00	35.00	50.00	—

RUPEE

SILVER

Mintname: *Ahmadshahi*

Dated on both sides.

KM#	Date	Year	VG	Fine	VF	XF
188	AH1272	—	10.00	25.00	35.00	50.00
	1273	—	10.00	25.00	35.00	50.00

SHER ALI

AH1280-1283/1863-1866AD, 1st reign

1/2 RUPEE

SILVER

Obv: Couplet. Rev: Title of ruler and mint.

KM#	Date	Year	VG	Fine	VF	XF
191	AH1280	—	5.00	10.00	17.00	30.00
	1281	—	6.00	13.00	20.00	30.00
	1282	—	5.00	8.00	15.00	30.00
	1285	—	9.00	15.00	25.00	45.00

Obv: Couplet. Rev: Mint only.

KM#	Date	Year	VG	Fine	VF	XF
192	AH1283	—	10.00	20.00	30.00	40.00

NOTE: Arrangement of rev. legend varies.

TILLA

GOLD

KM#	Date	Year	VG	Fine	VF	XF
194	AH1283	—	—	150.00	200.00	250.00
	1284	—	—	150.00	200.00	250.00
	1285	—	—	150.00	200.00	250.00

MUHAMMAD AFZAL

AH1283-1284/1866-1867AD

1/2 RUPEE

SILVER

KM#	Date	Year	VG	Fine	VF	XF
196	AH1283	—	25.00	50.00	75.00	100.00

Obv: KM#196. Rev: KM#201.

KM#	Date	Year	VG	Fine	VF	XF
197	AH1283	—	30.00	60.00	95.00	110.00

MUHAMMAD A'ZAM

AH1283-1285/1866-1868AD

1/2 RUPEE

SILVER

KM#	Date	Year	VG	Fine	VF	XF
201	AH1283	—	25.00	50.00	75.00	100.00
	1284	—	25.00	50.00	75.00	100.00

SHER ALI

AH1285-1296/1868-1879AD, 2nd reign

1/2 RUPEE

SILVER

KM#	Date	Year	VG	Fine	VF	XF
205.1	AH1284	—	6.00	13.00	20.00	30.00
	1285	—	6.00	13.00	20.00	30.00

NOTE: Resumption of type identical to KM#191 of first reign.

KM#	Date	Year	VG	Fine	VF	XF
205.2	AH1287	—	12.50	20.00	30.00	40.00

KM#	Date	Year	VG	Fine	VF	XF
206	AH1277 (error) for 1288	—	5.50	12.50	20.00	30.00
	1288	—	4.00	7.00	10.00	15.00
	1289	—	5.00	12.50	20.00	30.00

KM#	Date	Year	VG	Fine	VF	XF
207.1	AH1290	—	3.00	6.00	10.00	15.00
	1291	—	3.00	6.00	10.00	15.00
	1292	—	3.00	6.00	10.00	15.00
	1293	—	3.00	6.00	10.00	15.00

Obv: Teardrop design.

KM#	Date	Year	VG	Fine	VF	XF
207.2	AH1294	—	3.00	6.00	10.00	15.00
	1295	—	3.00	6.00	10.00	15.00

KM#	Date	Year	VG	Fine	VF	XF
208	AH1295	—	3.50	13.50	22.50	37.50

MUHAMMAD YAQUB

AH1296-1297/1879-1880AD

1/2 RUPEE

SILVER

KM#	Date	Year	VG	Fine	VF	XF
212	AH1296	—	6.00	16.00	25.00	35.00
	1297	—	12.00	25.00	35.00	45.00

RUPEE

SILVER

KM#	Date	Year	VG	Fine	VF	XF
213	AH1298	—	—	Reported, not confirmed		

WALI SHER ALI

AH1297/1880AD

1/2 RUPEE

SILVER
Dated on both sides.

KM#	Date	Year	VG	Fine	VF	XF
217	AH1297	—	8.50	17.50	25.00	35.00

RUPEE

SILVER
Type of 1/2 Rupee

KM#	Date	Year	VG	Fine	VF	XF
218	AH1297	—	15.00	30.00	40.00	60.00

TILLA

GOLD

KM#	Date	Year	VG	Fine	VF	XF
219	AH1297	—	—	—	Rare	—

ANONYMOUS COINAGE

1/2 RUPEE

SILVER
Dated on both sides.
Obv. leg: *Al-Mulk Lillah*.

KM#	Date	Year	VG	Fine	VF	XF
221	AH1297	—	10.00	20.00	30.00	40.00

NOTE: It is not known under whose authority this type was struck.

ABDUR RAHMAN

AH1297-1319/1880-1901AD

1/2 RUPEE

SILVER
Mintname: *Ahmadshahi*

KM#	Date	Year	VG	Fine	VF	XF
222	AH1298	—	15.00	30.00	40.00	50.00

Mintname: *Qandahar*

KM#	Date	Year	VG	Fine	VF	XF
225	AH1298	—	20.00	35.00	50.00	70.00
	1304	—	20.00	35.00	50.00	70.00

RUPEE

SILVER
Mintname: *Ahmadshahi*

KM#	Date	Year	VG	Fine	VF	XF
227	ND(AH1298)	—	—	—	—	—

Mintname: *Qandahar*

KM#	Date	Year	VG	Fine	VF	XF
223	AH1298	—	35.00	65.00	85.00	120.00

NOTE: Variety with only 1 leaf on obverse exists.

KM#	Date	Year	VG	Fine	VF	XF
224	AH1298	—	7.50	12.50	20.00	30.00
	1299	—	10.00	16.00	25.00	40.00
	1300	—	10.00	16.00	25.00	40.00
	1301	—	10.00	16.00	25.00	40.00
	1302	—	10.00	16.00	25.00	40.00
	1303	—	6.00	10.00	15.00	25.00
	1304	—	—	6.00	10.00	17.50
	1305	—	—	6.00	10.00	17.50
	1306	—	—	6.00	10.00	17.50
	1307	—	—	6.00	10.00	17.50
	1308	—	—	6.00	10.00	17.50

TILLA

GOLD

KM#	Date	Year	VG	Fine	VF	XF
226	AH1298	—	—	—	Rare	—

Bahawalpur Mint

Dar as-Surur

Most Bahawalpur coins have crude oblique milling on the edge.

MAHMUD SHAH

AH1216-1218/1801-1803AD, 1st reign

RUPEE

SILVER, 11.40-11.60 g
Rev: Mint and epithet.

KM#	Date	Year	VG	Fine	VF	XF
242	AH1217	—	30.00	65.00	80.00	100.00

Rev: Mint and *Julus* formula.

KM#	Date	Year	VG	Fine	VF	XF
243	AH1217	1	—	30.00	50.00	65.00
	1217	2	—	30.00	50.00	65.00
	1218	2	—	30.00	50.00	65.00

2 RUPEES

SILVER, 23.00-23.20 g

KM#	Date	Year	VG	Fine	VF	XF
244	AH1217	1	85.00	140.00	200.00	275.00

NOTE: Regnal year written as numeral, not ***Ahad***.

MOHUR

GOLD, 11.00 g

KM#	Date	Year	VG	Fine	VF	XF
245	AH1218	2	—	—	400.00	500.00

2 MOHURS

GOLD, 22.00-22.20 g

KM#	Date	Year	VG	Fine	VF	XF
246	AH1217	1	—	—	750.00	1000.
	1217	2	—	—	750.00	1000.
	1218	2	—	—	750.00	1000.

SHAH SHUJA AL-MULK

AH1218-1224/1803-1808AD, 2nd reign

RUPEE

SILVER, 11.20-11.60 g

KM#	Date	Year	VG	Fine	VF	XF
253	AH1218	1	—	30.00	50.00	65.00
	1218	2	—	30.00	50.00	65.00
	1219	1	—	30.00	50.00	65.00
	1220	—	—	30.00	50.00	65.00
	1222	—	—	30.00	50.00	65.00
	1212 (error for 1221 ?)	—	—	35.00	55.00	75.00

2 RUPEES

SILVER, 23.00 g

KM#	Date	Year	VG	Fine	VF	XF
254	AH1218	1	50.00	100.00	200.00	275.00

MOHUR

GOLD, 11.00-11.10 g

KM#	Date	Year	VG	Fine	VF	XF
255	AH1218	1	—	—	350.00	450.00

2 MOHURS

GOLD, 22.00 g

KM#	Date	Year	VG	Fine	VF	XF
256	AH1218	1	—	—	850.00	1100.

MAHMUD SHAH

AH1224-1233/1808-1817AD, 2nd reign

RUPEE

SILVER, 21.5-26mm, 11.00-11.20 g

KM#	Date	Year	VG	Fine	VF	XF
263	AH1224	1	25.00	55.00	75.00	110.00
	1239	—	15.00	30.00	40.00	60.00
	1240	—	15.00	30.00	40.00	60.00
	1241	—	15.00	30.00	40.00	60.00
	1242	—	15.00	30.00	40.00	60.00
	1244	—	15.00	30.00	40.00	60.00
	1244//1245	—	15.00	30.00	40.00	60.00
	1249	—	15.00	30.00	40.00	60.00
	1249//1250	—	15.00	30.00	40.00	60.00
	1250	—	15.00	30.00	40.00	60.00

NOTE: Coins dated after AH1233 are struck in Mahmud's name by the virtually independent Nawabs of Bahawalpur.

MOHUR

GOLD, 21.5mm, 11.00 g

KM#	Date	Year	VG	Fine	VF	XF
265	AH1225	1	—	—	Rare	—

Bhakhar Mint

The mint is found variously spelled, as *Bhakhar* (most common), *Bakhar*, and *Bakkar*.

MAHMUD SHAH

AH1216-1218/1801-1803AD, 1st reign

RUPEE

SILVER, 11.40-11.60 g
Broad flan, nazarana style.

KM#	Date	Year	VG	Fine	VF	XF
308	ND	—	40.00	90.00	150.00	200.00

SHAH SHUJA AL-MULK

AH1218-1224/1803-1808AD, 2nd reign

FALUS

COPPER

KM#	Date	Year	VG	Fine	VF	XF
308a	AH1218	—	4.50	10.00	15.00	25.00
	1222	—	4.50	10.00	15.00	25.00

RUPEE

SILVER, 11.40-11.60 g

KM#	Date	Year	VG	Fine	VF	XF
309.1	AH1218	—	15.00	25.00	35.00	50.00
	1219	—	15.00	25.00	35.00	50.00
	1220	—	15.00	25.00	35.00	50.00
	1221	12	15.00	25.00	35.00	50.00
	1222	—	15.00	25.00	35.00	50.00
	1223	—	15.00	25.00	35.00	50.00
	1224	—	15.00	25.00	35.00	50.00
	ND	—	6.00	12.00	18.00	25.00

Obv: King's name circled within couplet.

KM#	Date	Year	VG	Fine	VF	XF
309.2	AH1223	—	50.00	100.00	150.00	180.00

MAHMUD SHAH

AH1224-1233/1809-1817AD, 2nd reign

RUPEE

SILVER, 11.40-11.60 g

KM#	Date	Year	VG	Fine	VF	XF
307	AH1228	—	15.00	25.00	35.00	50.00
	1229	—	15.00	25.00	35.00	50.00
	ND	—	6.00	10.00	18.00	25.00

Dera Mint

Dera Ghazi Khan

The mint of Dera was located at Dera Ghazi Khan, taken by the Sikhs in AH1235 (1819AD), and now within Pakistan.

MAHMUD SHAH

AH1216-1218/1801-1803AD, 1st reign

RUPEE

SILVER, 11.40-11.60 g

KM#	Date	Year	VG	Fine	VF	XF
338	AH1216	1	12.50	32.50	45.00	60.00
	1217	2	12.50	32.50	45.00	60.00

SHAH SHUJA AL-MULK

AH1218-1224/1803-1808AD, 2nd reign

RUPEE

SILVER, 11.40-11.60 g

KM#	Date	Year	VG	Fine	VF	XF
343	—	1	12.50	32.50	45.00	60.00
	—	4	12.50	32.50	45.00	60.00
	—	5	12.50	32.50	45.00	60.00

MOHUR

GOLD

KM#	Date	Year	VG	Fine	VF	XF
345	AH1218	1	—	—	400.00	450.00

Derajat Mint

Dera Ismail Khan

The mint of Derajat was located at Dera Ismail Khan, which fell to the Sikhs in (AH1236) 1820-21AD. Issues in the name of Mahmud Shah dated AH1236 and later are actually Sikh issues. The Sikhs formally annexed Derajat in 1835AD (AH1281).

MAHMUD SHAH

AH1216-1218/1801-1803AD, 1st reign

RUPEE

SILVER, 11.00-11.20 g

KM#	Date	Year	VG	Fine	VF	XF
363	AH1216	1	18.00	38.00	50.00	70.00
	1217	2	18.00	38.00	50.00	70.00

SHAH SHUJA AL-MULK

AH1218-1224/1803-1808AD, 2nd reign

RUPEE

SILVER, 20-21.5mm, 10.80-11.20 g

KM#	Date	Year	VG	Fine	VF	XF
368	AH1218	1	12.50	20.00	30.00	40.00
	1218	2	12.50	20.00	30.00	40.00
	1219	2	12.50	20.00	30.00	40.00
	1220	2	12.50	20.00	30.00	40.00
	1220	3	12.50	20.00	30.00	40.00
	1221	3	12.50	20.00	30.00	40.00
	1221	4	12.50	20.00	30.00	40.00
	1221	5	12.50	20.00	30.00	40.00
	—	6	12.50	20.00	30.00	40.00
	1223	—	12.50	20.00	30.00	40.00

MAHMUD SHAH

AH1224-1233/1808-1817AD, 2nd reign

FALUS

COPPER

KM#	Date	Year	Good	VG	Fine	VF
370	AH124(9)	—	5.00	8.00	12.00	18.00

RUPEE

SILVER, 10.60-11.20 g

KM#	Date	Year	VG	Fine	VF	XF
373	AH1224	1	12.50	30.00	40.00	50.00
	1226	3	12.50	30.00	40.00	50.00
	1227	3	12.50	30.00	40.00	50.00
	1228	4	12.50	30.00	40.00	50.00
	1231	4	7.50	15.00	25.00	35.00
	1234	—	7.50	15.00	25.00	35.00
	1236	—	7.50	15.00	25.00	35.00
	1237	—	7.50	15.00	25.00	35.00
	1238	14	7.50	15.00	25.00	35.00
	1239	—	7.50	15.00	25.00	35.00
	1240	—	7.50	15.00	25.00	35.00
	1241	—	7.50	15.00	25.00	35.00
	1242	—	7.50	15.00	25.00	35.00
	1244	—	7.50	15.00	25.00	35.00
	1245	—	7.50	15.00	25.00	35.00
	1246	—	7.50	15.00	25.00	35.00
	1247	—	7.50	15.00	25.00	35.00
	1248	—	7.50	15.00	25.00	35.00
	1250	—	7.50	15.00	25.00	35.00
	1251	—	7.50	15.00	25.00	35.00

NOTE: Coins after AH1235 were issued under Sikh protectorate.

Herat Mint

Dar as-Sultanat

After AH1254, rupees ceased to be coined at Herat. Later emissions, beginning with anonymous issues of Yar Muhammad Khan, were 1/2 rupees. From AH1272-80 (1856-63AD), Herat was occupied by the Persians, who struck coins there in the name of Nasir al-Din Shah. The mint was closed in AH1308 (1891AD), except for a few later coins in copper.

MAHMUD SHAH

AH1216-1245/1801-1829AD

1/12 RUPEE

SILVER, 0.90 g

KM#	Date	Year	VG	Fine	VF	XF
392	AH1230	—	15.00	35.00	50.00	65.00

1/6 RUPEE

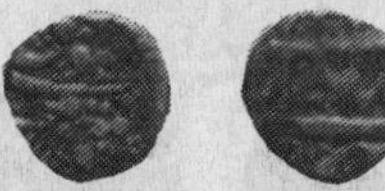

SILVER, 1.80 g

KM#	Date	Year	VG	Fine	VF	XF
393	AH1225	—	15.00	35.00	50.00	70.00
	1238	—	15.00	35.00	50.00	70.00

1/4 RUPEE

SILVER, 11.5mm, 2.80 g

KM#	Date	Year	VG	Fine	VF	XF
395	AH1242	—	25.00	55.00	75.00	100.00

1/2 RUPEE

SILVER, 5.00-5.60 g

KM#	Date	Year	VG	Fine	VF	XF
396	AH1242	—	25.00	45.00	60.00	85.00
	1243	—	25.00	45.00	60.00	85.00

RUPEE

SILVER, 11.00-11.60 g

KM#	Date	Year	VG	Fine	VF	XF
398.1	AH1216	—	—	6.00	9.00	15.00
	1217	—	—	6.00	9.00	15.00
	1218	—	—	6.00	9.00	15.00

KM#	Date	Year	VG	Fine	VF	XF
398.2	AH1219	—	—	6.00	9.00	15.00
	1220	—	—	6.00	9.00	15.00
	1221	—	—	6.00	9.00	15.00
	1222	—	—	6.00	9.00	15.00
	1223	—	—	6.00	9.00	15.00
	1224	—	—	6.00	9.00	15.00
	1225	—	—	6.00	9.00	15.00
	1226	—	—	6.00	9.00	15.00
	1227	—	—	6.00	9.00	15.00
	1228	—	—	6.00	9.00	15.00
	1229	—	—	6.00	9.00	15.00
	1230	—	—	6.50	10.00	16.50
	1231	—	6.00	11.50	18.00	28.00
	1232	—	6.00	11.50	18.00	28.00
	1233	—	6.00	11.50	18.00	28.00
	1234	—	6.00	11.50	18.00	28.00
	1235	—	6.00	11.50	18.00	28.00
	1236	—	6.00	11.50	18.00	28.00
	1237	—	6.00	11.50	18.00	28.00
	1238	—	6.00	11.50	18.00	28.00
	1240	—	6.00	11.50	18.00	28.00
	1242	—	8.00	14.00	20.00	30.00

KM#	Date	Year	VG	Fine	VF	XF
398.3	AH1244	—	8.00	14.00	20.00	30.00
	1254 (error date)	—	8.00	14.00	20.00	30.00

KAMRAN SHAH

AH1245-1258/1829-1842AD

1/6 RUPEE

SILVER, 1.80 g

KM#	Date	Year	VG	Fine	VF	XF
400	AH1257	—	25.00	50.00	80.00	125.00

1/4 RUPEE

SILVER, 2.60-2.80 g

KM#	Date	Year	VG	Fine	VF	XF
401	AH1248	—	35.00	75.00	100.00	135.00

1/2 RUPEE

SILVER, 5.20-5.60 g

KM#	Date	Year	VG	Fine	VF	XF
402	AH125x	—	20.00	30.00	45.00	75.00

RUPEE

SILVER, 10.20-11.00 g

KM#	Date	Year	VG	Fine	VF	XF
403	AH1244	—	30.00	65.00	100.00	125.00
	1245	—	30.00	65.00	100.00	125.00
	1246	—	30.00	65.00	100.00	125.00
	1248	—	30.00	65.00	100.00	125.00
	1249	—	30.00	65.00	100.00	125.00
	1251	—	30.00	65.00	100.00	125.00
	1252	—	30.00	65.00	100.00	125.00
	1254	—	30.00	65.00	100.00	125.00
	1255	—	30.00	65.00	100.00	125.00

YAR MUHAMMAD KHAN SADOZAI

AH1258-1267/1842-1851AD

Anonymous coinage struck with the Kalimah on obv. and mint and date on rev.

1/6 RUPEE

SILVER

KM#	Date	Year	VG	Fine	VF	XF
404	AH1258	—	25.00	35.00	50.00	75.00
	1259	—	25.00	35.00	50.00	75.00
	1260	—	25.00	35.00	50.00	75.00

1/2 RUPEE

SILVER

KM#	Date	Year	VG	Fine	VF	XF
405.1	AH1261	—	10.00	25.00	35.00	50.00
	1263	—	10.00	25.00	35.00	50.00
	1264	—	10.00	25.00	40.00	60.00
	1265	—	10.00	25.00	40.00	60.00

Rev: Legend in circle.

KM#	Date	Year	VG	Fine	VF	XF
405.2	AH1269(sic)	—	12.50	30.00	50.00	70.00

MUHAMMAD YUSUF KHAN SADOZAI

AH1267-1272/1851-1856AD

1/2 RUPEE

SILVER

Rev: Mint in circular area.

KM#	Date	Year	VG	Fine	VF	XF
406	AH1271	—	35.00	60.00	80.00	100.00

Rev: Mint in square.

KM#	Date	Year	VG	Fine	VF	XF
407	AH1271	—	40.00	70.00	90.00	125.00

Obv: Kalimah.

KM#	Date	Year	VG	Fine	VF	XF
408	AH1272	—	20.00	50.00	90.00	120.00

TILLA

GOLD

KM#	Date	Year	VG	Fine	VF	XF
409	AH1272	—	—	—	450.00	500.00

SHER ALI

AH1280-1296/1863-1879AD

1/2 RUPEE

SILVER

Rev: Legend in square.

KM#	Date	Year	VG	Fine	VF	XF
410	AH1280	—	—	—	—	—

Obv: *Amir* at top. Rev: Date.

KM#	Date	Year	VG	Fine	VF	XF
411	AH1280	—	10.00	20.00	35.00	50.00
	1281	—	10.00	20.00	35.00	50.00

Obv: *Amir* at bottom, date both sides.

KM#	Date	Year	VG	Fine	VF	XF
412	AH1281	—	8.00	15.00	25.00	40.00
	1282	—	8.00	15.00	25.00	40.00
	1283	—	8.00	15.00	25.00	40.00
	1284	—	8.00	15.00	25.00	40.00
	1287	—	8.00	15.00	25.00	40.00

Obv: *Amir* at top, legend rearranged.

KM#	Date	Year	VG	Fine	VF	XF
414	AH1287	—	15.00	30.00	45.00	65.00
	1288	—	10.00	23.00	40.00	55.00
	1290	—	10.00	23.00	40.00	55.00

Obv: Shorter inscription (Ruler's name only).

KM#	Date	Year	VG	Fine	VF	XF
413	AH1292	—	12.50	20.00	30.00	40.00
	1295	—	—	5.00	10.00	16.00

NOTE: Several varieties exist.

NOTE: A tilla dated AH1284 of Sher Ali has been reported.

MUHAMMAD YAQUB

AH1296-1298/1879-1881AD

1/6 RUPEE

SILVER, 11mm, 1.80 g

KM#	Date	Year	VG	Fine	VF	XF
415	AH1297	—	—	—	Rare	—

1/2 RUPEE

SILVER

KM#	Date	Year	VG	Fine	VF	XF
417	AH1296	—	3.00	5.00	7.00	13.50
	1297	—	3.00	5.00	7.00	13.50
	1298	—	3.00	5.00	7.00	13.50

Obv: Date below ?
Rev: Date in *Z*.

KM#	Date	Year	VG	Fine	VF	XF
416	AH1298	—	—	—	—	—

ABDUR RAHMAN

AH1297-1319/1880-1901AD

1/8 RUPEE

SILVER, 13mm

KM#	Date	Year	VG	Fine	VF	XF
418	AH1307	—	—	—	Rare	—

1/2 RUPEE

SILVER

KM#	Date	Year	VG	Fine	VF	XF
419	AH1297	—	3.00	5.00	8.00	14.00
	1298	—	5.00	10.00	15.00	25.00
	1299	—	8.00	14.00	20.00	30.00
	1300	—	2.50	5.00	8.00	14.00
	1301	—	2.50	5.00	8.00	14.00
	1302	—	2.50	5.00	8.00	14.00
	1303	—	1.50	3.00	6.00	12.00
	1304	—	1.50	3.00	6.00	12.00
	1305	—	1.50	3.00	6.00	12.00
	1306	—	1.50	3.00	6.00	12.00
	1307	—	1.50	3.00	6.00	12.00
	1308	—	1.50	3.00	6.00	12.00

NOTE: Many coins of this type KM#419 are found with blundered dates. Such coins are worth the same as normal dates. Mulings of dates exist.

Kabul Mint

Dar al-Mulk (until AH1163)
Dar as-Sultanat (after AH1164)

MAHMUD SHAH

AH1216-1218/1801-1803AD, 1st reign

RUPEE

SILVER, 11.40-11.60 g

KM#	Date	Year	VG	Fine	VF	XF
448	AH1216	1	11.00	25.00	35.00	45.00
	1217	1	11.00	25.00	35.00	45.00
	1217	2	11.00	25.00	35.00	45.00
	1218	2	11.00	25.00	35.00	45.00

MOHUR

GOLD, 10.80-11.00 g

KM#	Date	Year	VG	Fine	VF	XF
450	AH(1216)	1	—	—	400.00	450.00
	1218	3	—	—	350.00	400.00

QAISAR SHAH

AH1218/1803AD

Rebel issue

RUPEE

SILVER, 11.65 g

KM#	Date	Year	VG	Fine	VF	XF
453	AH1222	1	45.00	100.00	150.00	200.00

MOHUR

GOLD, 11.00 g

KM#	Date	Year	VG	Fine	VF	XF
455	AH1222	—	—	—	Rare	—

SHAH SHUJA AL-MULK

AH1218-1224/1803-1808AD, 2nd reign

RUPEE

SILVER, 11.50-11.60 g

KM#	Date	Year	VG	Fine	VF	XF
457	AH1218	1	13.50	30.00	40.00	55.00
	1219	2	13.50	30.00	40.00	55.00
	1220	—	13.50	30.00	40.00	55.00
	1222	—	13.50	30.00	40.00	55.00
	1223	—	13.50	30.00	40.00	55.00

MOHUR

GOLD, 10.95 g

KM#	Date	Year	VG	Fine	VF	XF
459	AH1222	4	—	—	350.00	400.00
	1223	—	—	—	350.00	400.00

MAHMUD SHAH

AH1224-1233/1808-1817AD, 2nd reign

RUPEE

SILVER, 10.75-11.60 g
Rev: Mintname as on previous reign, KM#457.

KM#	Date	Year	VG	Fine	VF	XF
461.1	AH1225	2	10.00	20.00	30.00	40.00
	1226	3	10.00	20.00	30.00	40.00
	1227	4	10.00	20.00	30.00	40.00

KM#	Date	Year	VG	Fine	VF	XF
461.2	AH122x	6	10.00	20.00	30.00	40.00

Rev: Mintname in small circle.

KM#	Date	Year	VG	Fine	VF	XF
462	AH1228	5	9.00	18.00	25.00	35.00

Rev: Mintname in toughra form.

KM#	Date	Year	VG	Fine	VF	XF
463	AH(122)6	—	10.00	20.00	30.00	40.00
	1231	8	10.00	20.00	30.00	40.00
	1233	—	10.00	20.00	30.00	40.00

2 RUPEES

SILVER, 23.00-23.20 g

KM#	Date	Year	VG	Fine	VF	XF
464	AH1225	1	65.00	115.00	150.00	200.00

MOHUR

GOLD, 10.90-11.00 g

KM#	Date	Year	VG	Fine	VF	XF
465	AH1224	2	—	—	300.00	375.00
	122x	8	—	—	300.00	375.00

AYYUB SHAH

AH1233-1245/1817-1826AD

RUPEE

SILVER, 10.70-11.40 g

KM#	Date	Year	VG	Fine	VF	XF
468	AH1234	1	12.50	30.00	40.00	50.00
	1234	2	12.50	30.00	40.00	50.00
	1235	2	12.50	30.00	40.00	50.00
	1236	2	12.50	30.00	40.00	50.00
	1236	3	12.50	30.00	40.00	50.00
	1237	3	12.50	30.00	40.00	50.00
	1238	3	12.50	30.00	40.00	50.00

NOTE: Various arrangements of obverse legend.

ANONYMOUS COINAGE

RUPEE

SILVER, 11.00-11.40 g
Obv: Kalimah.

KM#	Date	Year	VG	Fine	VF	XF
473	AH1239	4	15.00	35.00	50.00	70.00

DOST MUHAMMAD

AH1239-1255/1824-1839AD, 1st reign

In the name of Mahmud Shah Durrani

RUPEE

SILVER

KM#	Date	Year	VG	Fine	VF	XF
475	AH1239	—	20.00	50.00	75.00	100.00

Anonymous, with title Sultan al-Zaman

KM#	Date	Year	VG	Fine	VF	XF
476	AH1239	—	20.00	50.00	75.00	100.00

Anonymous, with title Sahib al-Zaman

Rev: Mintname in toughra form.

KM#	Date	Year	VG	Fine	VF	XF
477	AH1240	1	8.50	12.50	20.00	30.00
	1241	2	8.50	12.50	20.00	30.00

Obv: Cartouche in center.

KM#	Date	Year	VG	Fine	VF	XF
478	AH1241	—	6.00	10.00	15.00	22.50
	1242	—	6.00	10.00	15.00	22.50
	1243	—	6.00	10.00	15.00	22.50
	1244	—	6.00	10.00	15.00	22.50

Rev: Mintname in ordinary form.

KM#	Date	Year	VG	Fine	VF	XF
479	AH1244	—	8.00	15.00	22.50	35.00
	1245	—	8.00	15.00	22.50	35.00

In the name of his father, Payinda Khan.

KM#	Date	Year	VG	Fine	VF	XF
480.1	AH1245	—	5.00	8.00	12.00	20.00
	1246	—	5.00	8.00	12.00	20.00
	1247	—	5.00	8.00	12.00	20.00
	1248	—	5.00	8.00	12.00	20.00
	1249	—	5.00	8.00	12.00	20.00
	1250	—	5.00	8.00	12.00	20.00

NOTE: Various arrangements of obverse couplet and various borders on reverse.

KM#	Date	Year	VG	Fine	VF	XF
480.2	AH1247	—	5.00	8.00	12.00	20.00
	1248	—	5.00	8.00	12.00	20.00

In his own name

KM#	Date	Year	VG	Fine	VF	XF
481	AH1250	—	4.50	8.00	12.00	20.00
	1251	—	4.50	8.00	12.00	20.00
	1252	—	4.50	8.00	12.00	20.00
	1253	—	4.50	8.00	12.00	20.00
	1254	—	4.50	8.00	12.00	20.00
	1255	—	4.50	8.00	12.00	20.00

SHAH SHUJA AL-MULK

AH1255-1258/1839-1842AD, 3rd reign

RUPEE

SILVER, 11.50 g
Obv: Short inscription, title *Sultan*. Broad flan.

KM#	Date	Year	VG	Fine	VF	XF
482	AH1255	—	—	—	Rare	—

9.20 g
Obv: Long inscription.

KM#	Date	Year	VG	Fine	VF	XF
483	AH1255	—	10.00	18.00	25.00	35.00

9.20-9.50 g
Obv: Short inscription, title *Sultan*.

KM#	Date	Year	VG	Fine	VF	XF
484.1	AH1255	—	—	6.50	10.00	17.00
	1256	—	—	6.50	10.00	17.00
	1257	—	6.00	12.00	18.00	28.00
	1258	—	6.00	12.00	18.00	28.00

NOTE: Varieties exist, some on broad planchets.

Obv: *Dur-e-Duran* above *Sultan*.

KM#	Date	Year	VG	Fine	VF	XF
484.2	AH1255	—	6.00	12.00	18.00	28.00

Anonymous in name of Sahib al-Zaman

KM#	Date	Year	VG	Fine	VF	XF
485	AH1257	—	12.50	25.00	36.00	50.00

In the name of Shah Zaman

KM#	Date	Year	VG	Fine	VF	XF
486	AH1258	—	16.00	35.00	50.00	70.00

MOHUR

GOLD, 10.70-10.80 g

KM#	Date	Year	VG	Fine	VF	XF
487	AH1255	—	—	—	285.00	350.00
	1258	—	—	—	285.00	350.00

FATH JANG

AH1258/1842AD

RUPEE

SILVER, 9.30-9.40 g
Obv: Couplet, name *Fath Jung* at top.

KM#	Date	Year	VG	Fine	VF	XF
488.1	AH1258	—	18.00	38.00	60.00	80.00

Obv: Couplet, name *Fath Jung* in center.

KM#	Date	Year	VG	Fine	VF	XF
488.2	AH1258	—	25.00	50.00	70.00	100.00

Obv: Name only w/title *Durr-i Durran*.

KM#	Date	Year	VG	Fine	VF	XF
488.3	AH1258	—	18.00	38.00	60.00	80.00

Obv: Name only w/title *Padshah-i Ghazi*.

KM#	Date	Year	VG	Fine	VF	XF
488.4	AH1258	—	18.00	38.00	60.00	80.00

SHAHPUR SHAH

AH1258/1842AD

RUPEE

SILVER, 9.40 g

KM#	Date	Year	VG	Fine	VF	XF
489	AH1258	—	35.00	65.00	100.00	150.00

DOST MUHAMMAD

AH1258-1280/1842-1863AD, 2nd reign

Anonymous

RUPEE

SILVER
Obv: Kalimah

KM#	Date	Year	VG	Fine	VF	XF
493	AH1258	—	9.00	16.00	25.00	35.00

In his own name

Obv: Long couplet.

KM#	Date	Year	VG	Fine	VF	XF
496	AH1259	—	13.50	30.00	40.00	55.00

Obv: Couplet ending *Khaliq-i-Akbar*
Many varieties

KM#	Date	Year	VG	Fine	VF	XF
497	AH1259	—	10.00	15.00	22.50	40.00
	1262	—	7.00	11.00	15.00	25.00
	1263	—	4.50	7.00	10.00	18.00
	1264	—	—	—	—	—
	1265	—	—	5.00	8.00	16.00
	1266	—	—	5.00	8.00	16.00
	1267	—	—	5.00	8.00	16.00

KM#	Date	Year	VG	Fine	VF	XF
497	1268	—	4.50	7.00	12.00	20.00
	1269	—	4.50	7.00	10.00	18.00
	1270	—	—	5.00	8.00	16.00
	1271	—	—	5.00	8.00	16.00
	1272	—	—	5.00	8.00	16.00
	1273	—	—	5.00	8.00	16.00
	1274	—	—	5.00	8.00	16.00
	1275	—	—	5.00	8.00	16.00
	1276	—	4.00	7.00	10.00	18.00
	1277	—	4.00	7.00	10.00	18.00
	1278	—	4.00	7.00	10.00	18.00
	1279	—	4.00	7.00	10.00	18.00
	1280	—	12.50	20.00	30.00	40.00

NOTE: Mulings exist with different dates on obverse and reverse.

TILLA

GOLD

KM#	Date	Year	VG	Fine	VF	XF
499	AH1269	—	—	—	235.00	300.00

SHER ALI

AH1280-1283/1863-1866AD, 1st reign

RUPEE

SILVER

Obv: New couplet, *Bi-Valayi Amir.*

KM#	Date	Year	VG	Fine	VF	XF
502	AH1280	—	—	—	Rare	—

Obv: Couplet starting *Za Aini Marhamat. . .*

KM#	Date	Year	VG	Fine	VF	XF
503	AH1280	—	5.00	9.00	13.00	20.00
	1281	—	5.00	9.00	13.00	20.00
	1282	—	5.00	9.00	13.00	20.00

NOTE: Two varieties of obv. exist.

Anonymous, with title Sahib al-Zaman

KM#	Date	Year	VG	Fine	VF	XF
504	AH1282	—	12.50	25.00	35.00	50.00

MUHAMMAD AFZAL

AH1283-1284/1866-1867AD

RUPEE

SILVER

KM#	Date	Year	VG	Fine	VF	XF
507	AH1283	—	9.00	15.00	20.00	30.00
	1284	—	9.00	15.00	20.00	30.00

NOTE: 2 varieties are known dated AH1283.

MUHAMMAD A'ZAM

AH1283-1285/1866-1868AD

RUPEE

SILVER

KM#	Date	Year	VG	Fine	VF	XF
508.1	AH1284	—	10.00	15.00	20.00	30.00
	1285	—	10.00	15.00	20.00	30.00

KM#	Date	Year	VG	Fine	VF	XF
508.2	AH1284	—	15.00	30.00	45.00	60.00

KM#	Date	Year	VG	Fine	VF	XF
509	AH1285	—	13.00	25.00	35.00	45.00

SHER ALI

AH1285-1296/1868-1879AD, 2nd reign

1/6 RUPEE

SILVER, 1.50 g

KM#	Date	Year	VG	Fine	VF	XF
511	AH1287	—	25.00	50.00	65.00	85.00

1/2 RUPEE

NOTE: KM#512, which was reported for AH1288, 1292, 1293 and 1294, is a misreading of the Qandahar Mint.

SILVER

Large, thin planchet; fine engraving.

KM#	Date	Year	VG	Fine	VF	XF
513	AH1292	—	—	5.00	10.00	18.00

Small, thick planchet; coarse engraving.

KM#	Date	Year	VG	Fine	VF	XF
514	AH1295	—	—	4.00	8.00	15.00

RUPEE

SILVER

Obv: Couplet starting *Za Iltifat-i. . .*

KM#	Date	Year	VG	Fine	VF	XF
516	AH1285	—	7.50	12.50	20.00	30.00

Obv: 3-stem toughra.

KM#	Date	Year	VG	Fine	VF	XF
517	AH1285	—	6.00	10.00	15.00	25.00
	1286	—	3.00	6.00	10.00	20.00
	1286/87	—	6.00	10.00	15.00	25.00
	1287	—	6.00	10.00	15.00	25.00

Obv: 5-stem toughra.

KM#	Date	Year	VG	Fine	VF	XF
518	AH1285	—	40.00	60.00	90.00	140.00
	1286	—	30.00	50.00	80.00	125.00

KM#	Date	Year	VG	Fine	VF	XF
519	AH1287	—	3.50	6.00	10.00	18.00
	1288	—	—	5.00	7.50	15.00
	1289	—	—	5.00	7.50	15.00
	1290	—	—	5.00	7.50	15.00
	1291	—	—	5.00	7.50	15.00
	1292	—	—	5.00	7.50	15.00
	1293	—	—	5.00	7.50	15.00
	1294	—	—	5.00	7.50	15.00
	1295	—	—	5.00	7.50	15.00
	1295//1296	—	—	5.00	7.50	15.00
	1296	—	5.00	7.50	12.50	20.00

NOTE: Other examples bearing different obverse and reverse dates exist.

Fine style

KM#	Date	Year	VG	Fine	VF	XF
520	AH1292	—	4.50	9.00	15.00	25.00
	1293	—	4.50	9.00	15.00	25.00

Coarse style

KM#	Date	Year	VG	Fine	VF	XF
521	AH1293	—	3.50	6.00	10.00	18.00
	1294	—	3.50	6.00	10.00	18.00
	1295	—	3.50	6.00	10.00	18.00

TOMAN

GOLD, 3.45 g

KM#	Date	Year	VG	Fine	VF	XF
524	AH1294	—	—	180.00	225.00	275.00
	1295	—	—	165.00	200.00	250.00
	1296	—	—	165.00	200.00	250.00

MOHUR

GOLD, 10.90 g

KM#	Date	Year	VG	Fine	VF	XF
525	AH1288	—	—	225.00	300.00	400.00

MUHAMMAD YAQUB

AH1296-1297/1879-1880AD

1/3 RUPEE

SILVER

KM#	Date	Year	VG	Fine	VF	XF
531	AH1296	—	25.00	55.00	75.00	100.00

RUPEE

SILVER

KM#	Date	Year	VG	Fine	VF	XF
533	AH1296	—	—	5.00	8.00	16.00
	1297	—	— Reported, not confirmed			

WALI MUHAMMAD

AH1297/1880AD

RUPEE

SILVER

KM#	Date	Year	VG	Fine	VF	XF
538	AH1297	—	10.00	16.00	25.00	40.00

ABDUR RAHMAN

AH1297-1319/1880-1901AD

1/3 RUPEE

SILVER, 15mm

KM#	Date	Year	VG	Fine	VF	XF
541	AH1298	—	30.00	60.00	75.00	100.00

RUPEE

SILVER
Obv: Rudimentary toughra.

KM#	Date	Year	VG	Fine	VF	XF
543	AH1297	—	25.00	45.00	60.00	85.00

Obv: Name of ruler in fancy border.

KM#	Date	Year	VG	Fine	VF	XF
A544	AH1297	—	20.00	40.00	55.00	75.00

Obv: Ornate toughra.

KM#	Date	Year	VG	Fine	VF	XF
B544	AH1298	—	30.00	60.00	90.00	120.00

Obv: Name of ruler within dotted circle.

KM#	Date	Year	VG	Fine	VF	XF
C544	AH1297	—	30.00	60.00	90.00	120.00

Obv: Name of ruler in plain border.

KM#	Date	Year	VG	Fine	VF	XF
544	AH1297	—	4.00	6.00	10.00	18.00
	1298	—	7.50	10.00	13.00	22.50
	1299	—	12.50	20.00	30.00	45.00
	1300	—	12.50	18.00	25.00	35.00
	1301	—	3.00	6.00	10.00	18.00
	1302	—	3.50	6.00	10.00	18.00
	1303	—	—	4.00	7.00	15.00
	1304	—	—	4.00	7.00	15.00
	1305	—	—	2.75	6.00	15.00
	1306	—	—	4.00	7.00	15.00
	1307	—	—	4.00	7.00	15.00
	1308	—	7.00	10.00	15.00	25.00

NOTE: Obverses are often muled with reverses bearing a different date. For machine struck coins dated AH1303//1304 and 1304//1304 see KM#805.

NOTE: The year AH1297 has been observed struck over an 1876 British India 1/4 rupee, probably a mint sport.

NAZARANA RUPEE

SILVER

KM#	Date	Year	VG	Fine	VF	XF
545	AH1303	—	25.00	50.00	75.00	100.00

MUHAMMAD ISHAQ

AH1305-1306/1889AD

RUPEE

SILVER
Struck at Balkh, but inscribed *Kabul*.
W/o title of *Khan*.

KM#	Date	Year	VG	Fine	VF	XF
548	AH1305	—	— Reported, not confirmed			
	1306	—	30.00	55.00	75.00	100.00

Title *Khan* added.

KM#	Date	Year	VG	Fine	VF	XF
549	AH1305	—	35.00	70.00	100.00	125.00
	1306	—	35.00	70.00	100.00	125.00

Kashmir Mint

MAHMUD SHAH

AH1216-1218/1801-1803AD, 1st reign
AH1223-1233/1808-1818AD, 2nd reign

FRACTIONAL FALUS

COPPER, 3.80-4.40 g
First Reign

KM#	Date	Year	Good	VG	Fine	VF
580	AH1217	2	3.00	4.00	5.00	7.00

20mm, 7.20-7.80 g
Second Reign
Obv: King's name in toughra style.

KM#	Date	Year	Good	VG	Fine	VF
581	AH—	1	3.00	4.00	5.00	7.00

FALUS

COPPER, 25.5mm, 10.20 g
First Reign

KM#	Date	Year	Good	VG	Fine	VF
583	AH1216	1	4.00	7.00	10.00	16.00

20mm, 9.40-9.80 g
Second Reign
Obv: Toughra style. Rev: Legend.

KM#	Date	Year	Good	VG	Fine	VF
584	AH—	1	3.00	4.50	7.00	10.00
	1229	—	3.00	4.50	7.00	10.00
	1230	6	3.00	4.50	7.00	10.00

10.00 g
Rev: Swords and plume.

KM#	Date	Year	Good	VG	Fine	VF
585	AH1233	11	4.00	6.00	10.00	15.00

1/4 RUPEE

SILVER, 2.50-2.60 g

KM#	Date	Year	VG	Fine	VF	XF
586	AH1217	2	18.50	40.00	60.00	80.00

RUPEE

SILVER, 10.80-11.00 g
1st Reign

KM#	Date	Year	VG	Fine	VF	XF
588	AH1216	1	8.50	15.00	25.00	35.00
	1217	2	8.50	15.00	25.00	35.00
	1218	3	8.50	15.00	25.00	35.00

KM#	Date	Year	VG	Fine	VF	XF
589	AH1218	3	10.00	20.00	30.00	45.00

KM#	Date	Year	VG	Fine	VF	XF
591	AH1228	6	4.50	9.00	14.00	20.00
	1229	6	4.50	9.00	14.00	20.00
	1229	7	4.50	9.00	14.00	20.00
	1230	7	4.50	9.00	14.00	20.00
	1230	8	4.50	9.00	14.00	20.00
	1230	10	4.50	9.00	14.00	20.00
	1232	10	4.50	9.00	14.00	20.00
	1233	10	6.50	12.50	20.00	30.00
	1233	11	6.50	12.50	20.00	30.00

NOTE: The sequence of regnal years at Kashmir is very confused.

SHAH SHUJA AL-MULK

AH1218-1223/1803-1808AD, 2nd reign

FALUS

COPPER, 7.40-9.00 g
Rev: Sword.

KM#	Date	Year	Good	VG	Fine	VF
594	AH1218	1	2.50	3.50	5.00	7.00
	—	2	3.00	4.50	6.50	9.00

Rev: 2 swords.

KM#	Date	Year	Good	VG	Fine	VF
A595	AH1219	—	5.00	8.50	15.00	22.50

Rev: Crossed swords.

KM#	Date	Year	Good	VG	Fine	VF
595	AH(12)19	—	3.00	4.00	6.00	8.50
596	AH1220	3	3.00	4.00	6.00	8.50

Rev: Sword.

KM#	Date	Year	Good	VG	Fine	VF
597	AH1221	4	3.50	5.00	7.50	10.00

Reign in Kashmir

AH1227-1228/1812-1813AD

RUPEE

SILVER, 10.80-11.20 g

KM#	Date	Year	VG	Fine	VF	XF
598	AH1218	1	—	6.00	10.00	17.50
	1219	2	—	6.00	10.00	17.50
	1220	3	—	6.00	10.00	17.50
	1221	4	—	6.00	10.00	17.50
	1222	5	—	6.00	10.00	17.50
	1223	6	4.50	7.50	12.50	20.00

QAISAR SHAH

AH1222-1223/1807-1808AD

RUPEE

SILVER, 11.00-11.20 g

KM#	Date	Year	VG	Fine	VF	XF
600	AH1222	1	20.00	40.00	60.00	80.00
	1223	1	20.00	40.00	60.00	80.00
	1223	2	20.00	40.00	60.00	80.00

ATA MUHAMMAD BAMIZAI KHAN

Rebel governor of Kashmir

AH1223-1228/1808-1813AD

In the name of Shah Nur al-Din, the patron 'saint' of Kashmir.

FALUS

COPPER, 16.5mm, 7.50 g

KM#	Date	Year	Good	VG	Fine	VF
601	AH1225	3	8.00	15.00	22.50	35.00
	1228	—	8.00	15.00	22.50	35.00

RUPEE

SILVER, 10.70-11.10 g

KM#	Date	Year	VG	Fine	VF	XF
603	AH1223	1	6.50	12.50	20.00	30.00
	1224	1	6.50	12.50	20.00	30.00
	1224	2	6.50	12.50	20.00	30.00
	1225	2	6.50	12.50	20.00	30.00

KM#	Date	Year	VG	Fine	VF	XF
603	1225	3	6.50	12.50	20.00	30.00
	1226	4	6.50	12.50	20.00	30.00
	1227	4	6.50	12.50	20.00	30.00
	1227	5	6.50	12.50	20.00	30.00
	1228	5	6.50	12.50	20.00	30.00

HEAVY RUPEE

(1-1/4 Rupee)

SILVER, 14.50 g

KM#	Date	Year	VG	Fine	VF	XF
604	AH1223	1	—	200.00	250.00	300.00

2 MOHURS

GOLD, 21.60-21.80 g

KM#	Date	Year	VG	Fine	VF	XF
607	AH1225	2	—	—	5000.	6500.

KM#	Date	Year	VG	Fine	VF	XF
608	AH1225	3	—	—	Rare	—

MUHAMMAD A'ZIM

(Governor for Ayub Shah)

AH1228-1234/1813-1819AD

FALUS

COPPER, 7.50 g

KM#	Date	Year	Good	VG	Fine	VF
609	AH1228	1	5.00	9.00	16.00	25.00

AYYUB SHAH

AH1233-1245/1818-1829AD

FALUS

COPPER, 7.00-8.00 g

KM#	Date	Year	Good	VG	Fine	VF
610	AH1233	—	7.00	12.00	18.00	27.50

RUPEE

SILVER, 11.00-11.20 g
Rev: Mint name and regnal year.

KM#	Date	Year	VG	Fine	VF	XF
613	AH1233	1	15.00	30.00	50.00	75.00
	1234	1	12.50	25.00	40.00	60.00

Rev: Mint, regnal year and *Julus* formula.

KM#	Date	Year	VG	Fine	VF	XF
614	AH1234	2	15.00	30.00	50.00	75.00

NOTE: Kashmir fell to the Sikhs in AH1234 (1819AD), ending the Durrani dominion in India.

Mashhad Mint

Mashhad, entitled Muqaddas (holy), was the chief city of Iranian Khorasan. From AH1161/1748AD until AH1218/1803AD, it was the capital of the Afsharid principality, which remained under nominal Durrani suzerainty from AH1163/1750AD onwards. Coins were struck in the name of Durrani rulers in AH1163, 1168-1186, 1198-1218. Issues in the name of Iranian rulers will be listed in a future edition of this catalog under Iran.

MAHMUD SHAH

AH1216-1218/1801-1803AD, First Reign

RUPEE

SILVER, 11.00-11.50 g

KM#	Date	Year	VG	Fine	VF	XF
G640	AH1218	—	60.00	125.00	160.00	200.00

NOTE: In AH1218/1803AD, Mashhad was seized by Fath Ali Shah and permanently annexed to Iran.

Multan Mint

Known as *Dar al-Aman*, ('Abode of Security'), Multan was annexed by Ahmad Shah in AH1165/1752AD, and held under Afghan rule until lost to the Sikhs in AH1233/1818AD, except for an interval of Maratha control in AH1173/1759AD and Sikh control from AH1185-1194/1771-1780AD.

MAHMUD SHAH

AH1216-1218/1801-1803AD, 1st reign

RUPEE

SILVER, 11.50-11.60 g

KM#	Date	Year	VG	Fine	VF	XF
668	AH1216	1	20.00	40.00	60.00	85.00
	1218	1	20.00	40.00	60.00	85.00

SHAH SHUJA AL-MULK

AH1218-1224/1803-1808AD, 2nd reign

RUPEE

SILVER, 20.5mm, 11.40-11.60 g

KM#	Date	Year	VG	Fine	VF	XF
673	AH1218	1	20.00	40.00	60.00	85.00
	1219	—	20.00	40.00	60.00	85.00

MOHUR

GOLD, 10.90-11.00 g

KM#	Date	Year	VG	Fine	VF	XF
675	AH1218	1	—	—	Rare	—
	1224	8	—	—	Rare	—

NOTE: Multan fell to the Sikhs in AH1233/1818AD.

MAHMUD SHAH

AH1224-1233/1808-1817AD, 2nd reign

FALUS

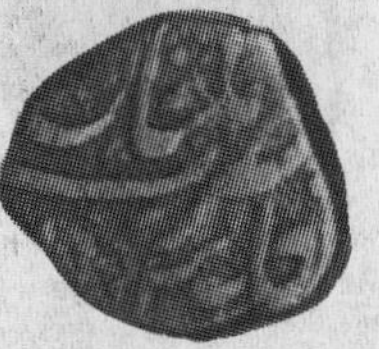

COPPER, 11.60-12.80 g

KM#	Date	Year	Good	VG	Fine	VF
677	AH1226	1	3.75	7.50	10.00	16.50
	1227	1	3.75	7.50	10.00	16.50
	1227	2	3.75	7.50	10.00	16.50
	1228	3	3.75	7.50	10.00	16.50
	1228	5	3.75	7.50	10.00	16.50
	1229	—	3.75	7.50	10.00	16.50
	1230	7	3.75	7.50	10.00	16.50
	1231	7	3.75	7.50	10.00	16.50
	1235	—	3.75	7.50	10.00	16.50
	1253	—	3.75	7.50	10.00	16.50
	1254	—	3.75	7.50	10.00	16.50
	1257	—	3.75	7.50	10.00	16.50
	1260	—	3.75	7.50	10.00	16.50
	1263	—	3.75	7.50	10.00	16.50
	1264	—	3.75	7.50	10.00	16.50
	1267	—	3.75	7.50	10.00	16.50
	1270	—	3.75	7.50	10.00	16.50

NOTE: Issues dated after AH1233 are posthumous issues struck by the Sikhs.

AYYUB SHAH

AH1233-1245/1817-1826AD

RUPEE

SILVER, 11.20-11.40 g
Obv: Kalima, mint and date.

KM#	Date	Year	VG	Fine	VF	XF
680	AH1239	—	—	—	Rare	—

Peshawar Mint

Peshawar passed to Ahmad Shah after the death of Nadir Shah Afshar, who had seized it from the Mughals in AH1151/1738AD. It was lost to the Sikhs in AH1250/1834AD. Although the winter capital of the Durranis, it was never granted an honorific epithet.

MAHMUD SHAH

AH1216-1218/1801-1803AD, 1st reign

RUPEE

SILVER, 11.40-11.60 g
Rev: Mint name w/*Julus* formula.

KM#	Date	Year	VG	Fine	VF	XF
718	AH1216	1	10.00	13.50	20.00	30.00

Rev: Mint name.

KM#	Date	Year	VG	Fine	VF	XF
719	AH1217	2	10.00	13.50	20.00	30.00
	1218	3	10.00	13.50	20.00	30.00

SHAH SHUJA AL-MULK

AH1218-1224/1803-1808AD, 2nd reign

As local ruler at Peshawar

1/10 RUPEE

SILVER, 1.00 g

KM#	Date	Year	VG	Fine	VF	XF
720	AH1227	7	—	—	Rare	—

RUPEE

SILVER, 11.40-11.60 g

KM#	Date	Year	VG	Fine	VF	XF
722	AH1218	1	7.00	12.00	18.00	28.00
	1219	2	7.00	12.00	18.00	28.00
	1220	3	7.00	12.00	18.00	28.00
	1221	4	7.00	12.00	18.00	28.00
	1222	5	7.00	12.00	18.00	28.00
	1223	6	7.00	12.00	18.00	28.00
	1224	7	7.00	12.00	18.00	28.00

As local ruler at Peshawar

KM#	Date	Year	VG	Fine	VF	XF
723	AH1227	1	40.00	70.00	100.00	130.00

Shah Shuja briefly at Peshawar in AH1233/1818AD.

KM#	Date	Year	VG	Fine	VF	XF
724	AH1233	1	40.00	70.00	100.00	130.00
	1234	1	40.00	70.00	100.00	130.00

NOTE: This coin may be distinguished from KM#722 and 723 by the octagon and calligraphy of the rev. and by the date.

MAHMUD SHAH

AH1224-1233/1808-1817AD, 2nd reign

FALUS

COPPER, 11.40 g

KM#	Date	Year	Good	VG	Fine	VF
726	AH123x	—	—	—	Rare	—

RUPEE

SILVER, 10.60-11.50 g
Rev: Legend w/beaded circle.

KM#	Date	Year	VG	Fine	VF	XF
A727	AH1224	1	—	20.00	45.00	80.00

Obv: Linear legends. Rev: Legend in octagon.

KM#	Date	Year	VG	Fine	VF	XF
727.1	AH1225	1	—	11.00	18.00	26.00
	1226	2	—	11.00	18.00	26.00
	1227	2	—	11.00	18.00	26.00
	(122)7	3	—	11.00	18.00	26.00

KM#	Date	Year	VG	Fine	VF	XF
727.2	AH1224	1	—	—	—	—
	1227	3	—	11.00	18.00	26.00
	1227	4	—	11.00	18.00	26.00
	1228	4	—	11.00	18.00	26.00
	1228	5	—	11.00	18.00	26.00
	1229	5	—	11.00	18.00	26.00
	1229	6	—	11.00	18.00	26.00
	1230	6	—	11.00	18.00	26.00
	1230	7	—	11.00	18.00	26.00
	1231	7	—	11.00	18.00	26.00
	1231	8	—	11.00	18.00	26.00

Rev: Legend within square.

KM#	Date	Year	VG	Fine	VF	XF
727.3	AH1227	7	—	40.00	50.00	75.00

Obv: Circular legend around central cartouche.

KM#	Date	Year	VG	Fine	VF	XF
728	AH1231	8	10.00	20.00	30.00	40.00
	1232	8	10.00	20.00	30.00	40.00
	1232	9	10.00	20.00	30.00	40.00
	1233	9	10.00	20.00	30.00	40.00
	1233	10	10.00	20.00	30.00	40.00

AYYUB SHAH

AH1233-1245/1817-1826AD

FALUS

COPPER, 10.40-12.20 g

KM#	Date	Year	Good	VG	Fine	VF
730	AH1234	2	6.00	10.00	17.50	30.00
	1236	4	6.00	10.00	17.50	30.00
	1237	—	5.00	8.50	15.00	25.00
	1238	6	5.00	8.50	15.00	25.00
	1239	—	5.00	8.50	15.00	25.00
	1240	—	6.50	11.00	18.00	32.50

RUPEE

SILVER, 10.40-10.60 g
Obv: Ruler's name in fancy diamond.

KM#	Date	Year	VG	Fine	VF	XF
732	AH1233	1	23.00	45.00	65.00	85.00

Obv: Couplet in 3 lines.

KM#	Date	Year	VG	Fine	VF	XF
733	AH1233	1	8.00	13.00	20.00	30.00
	1233	2	8.00	13.00	20.00	30.00
	1234	2	8.00	13.00	20.00	30.00
	(123)4	6	8.00	13.00	20.00	30.00
	1235	2	8.00	13.00	20.00	30.00
	1235	3	8.00	13.00	20.00	30.00
	1236	3	8.00	13.00	20.00	30.00
	1236	4	8.00	13.00	20.00	30.00
	1237	4	8.00	13.00	20.00	30.00
	1237	5	8.00	13.00	20.00	30.00
	1238	5	8.00	13.00	20.00	30.00
	1238	6	8.00	13.00	20.00	30.00
	1239	6	8.00	13.00	20.00	30.00
	1239	7	8.00	13.00	20.00	30.00
	1240	6	8.00	13.00	20.00	30.00
	1240	7	8.00	13.00	20.00	30.00
	1240	8	8.00	13.00	20.00	30.00
	1241	7	8.00	13.00	20.00	30.00
	1242	9	8.00	13.00	20.00	30.00
	1243	9	8.00	13.00	20.00	30.00
	1243	10	8.00	13.00	20.00	30.00
	1244	11	8.00	13.00	20.00	30.00
	1245	11	5.00	8.50	14.00	20.00

Obv: Name in foliated diamond.

KM#	Date	Year	VG	Fine	VF	XF
734	AH124x	12	25.00	45.00	65.00	85.00

MOHUR

GOLD, 21.5mm, 10.50-10.60 g

KM#	Date	Year	VG	Fine	VF	XF
735	AH—	6	—	—	325.00	375.00
	—	7	—	—	325.00	375.00

DOST MUHAMMAD

AH1239-1255/1824-1839AD, 1st reign

RUPEE

SILVER, 23mm, 10.40 g

KM#	Date	Mintage	VG	Fine	VF	XF
738	AH1246	—	22.50	50.00	75.00	120.00
	1249	—	22.50	50.00	75.00	120.00

SULTAN MUHAMMAD

AH1247-1250/1831-1834AD at Peshawar

Anonymous couplet type.

RUPEE

SILVER

KM#	Date	Mintage	VG	Fine	VF	XF
739	AH1247	—	12.50	25.00	35.00	60.00
	1248	—	12.50	25.00	35.00	60.00
	1249	—	12.50	25.00	35.00	60.00

NOTE: Peshawar fell to the Sikhs in AH1250/1834AD. For later issues, see India, Sikhs.

Qandahar Mint

Issues of this mint are listed together with those of Ahmadshahi, which was a name of Qandahar granted in honor of Ahmad Shah, founder of the Durrani Kingdom.

Rikab Mint

The Camp mint, brought with the royal entourage while traveling, entitled *Mubarak*, 'Auspicious'.

SHAH SHUJA AL-MULK

AH1218-1224/1803-1808AD, 2nd reign

MOHUR

GOLD, 10.80-10.90 g

KM#	Date	Mintage	VG	Fine	VF	XF
749	AH1219	—	—	—	Rare	—

MILLED COINAGE

MONETARY SYSTEM

10 Dinar = 1 Paisa
5 Paise = 1 Shahi
2 Shahi = 1 Sanar
2 Sanar = 1 Abbasi
1-1/2 Abbasi = 1 Qiran
2 Qiran = 1 Kabuli Rupee

PAISA

BRONZE, 25mm

KM#	Date	Mintage	VG	Fine	VF	XF
800	AH1309	—	25.00	40.00	120.00	225.00

Thicker variety of KM#802.

KM#	Date	Mintage	VG	Fine	VF	XF
801	AH1309	—	20.00	30.00	50.00	70.00

BRONZE or BRASS, 20mm

KM#	Date	Mintage	VG	Fine	VF	XF
802	AH1309	—	2.50	5.00	7.50	20.00
	1312	—	2.00	4.00	6.50	15.00
	1313	—	2.50	5.00	7.50	20.00
	1314	—	2.00	4.00	6.50	15.00
	1316	—	3.00	5.00	7.50	20.00
	1317	—	4.00	6.00	10.00	30.00

NOTE: Coins dated AH1313 and 1317 are known in two varieties. 3 varieties are known for AH1314.

KM#	Date	Mintage	VG	Fine	VF	XF
827	AH1317	—	3.50	6.00	12.00	35.00

NOTE: 2 varieties are known.

Mule. Obv: KM#827. Rev: KM#802.

KM#	Date	Mintage	VG	Fine	VF	XF
828	AH1317	—	10.00	15.00	30.00	50.00

KM#	Date	Mintage	VG	Fine	VF	XF
848	AH1329	—	6.00	12.00	20.00	30.00
	1329/17 on KM#828 obverse die	—	8.00	15.00	30.00	50.00

21mm

KM#	Date	Mintage	VG	Fine	VF	XF
849	AH1329	—	2.00	4.00	7.50	15.00
	1331	—	2.00	4.00	7.50	15.00
	1332	—	2.50	4.75	9.00	16.00
	1334	—	3.00	6.00	11.50	20.00

Thick flan, reduced size: 19mm

KM#	Date	Mintage	VG	Fine	VF	XF
854	AH1336	—	2.50	5.00	10.00	25.00

Thin flan

KM#	Date	Mintage	VG	Fine	VF	XF
855	AH1336	—	1.75	3.00	5.00	12.50
	1337	—	1.75	3.00	5.00	12.50

Thick flan, 20mm

KM#	Date	Mintage	VG	Fine	VF	XF
857	AH1337	—	6.50	10.00	20.00	35.00

Thin flan, 19-20mm

KM#	Date	Year	VG	Fine	VF	XF
858	AH1337	—	3.00	6.00	10.00	20.00
	SH1298	(1919)	4.50	8.00	15.00	32.50

NOTE: 3 varieties are known dated AH1337.

KM#	Date	Year	VG	Fine	VF	XF
880	SH1299	(1920)	1.75	4.00	8.00	12.50
	1300	(1921)	2.50	5.00	9.00	15.00
	1301	(1922)	2.50	5.00	9.00	15.00
	1302	(1923)	1.75	4.00	8.00	12.50
	1303	(1924)	1.75	4.00	8.00	12.50

NOTE: 2 varieties are known dated AH1301.

SHAHI

(5 Paisa)

COPPER or BRASS

KM#	Date	Mintage	VG	Fine	VF	XF
803	AH1309	—	15.00	25.00	55.00	140.00

Thick flan

KM#	Date	Mintage	VG	Fine	VF	XF
859	AH1337	—	9.00	16.00	25.00	55.00

Thin flan

KM#	Date	Mintage	VG	Fine	VF	XF
860	AH1337	—	8.00	15.00	22.50	40.00

100 DINARS

(10 Paisa)

COPPER

KM#	Date	Mintage	VG	Fine	VF	XF
809	AH1311	—	125.00	200.00	350.00	600.00

SANAR

(10 Paisa)

1.5500 g, .500 SILVER, .0249 oz ASW
Obv: Date in loop of toughra.

KM#	Date	Mintage	VG	Fine	VF	XF
823	AH1315	—	7.00	10.00	20.00	40.00
	ND	—	8.50	13.00	25.00	45.00

Rev: Date below mosque.

KM#	Date	Mintage	VG	Fine	VF	XF
824	AH1315	—	9.00	14.00	25.00	45.00
	ND	—	8.50	13.50	25.00	45.00

KM#	Date	Mintage	VG	Fine	VF	XF
846	AH1325	—	10.00	20.00	35.00	60.00
	1326	—	5.00	7.50	12.50	20.00
	1328	—	5.00	7.50	12.50	20.00
	1329	—	5.75	8.50	14.00	25.00

KM#	Date	Mintage	VG	Fine	VF	XF
850	AH1329	—	4.00	7.00	11.00	16.00
	1330	—	3.00	6.00	10.00	15.00
	1331	—	3.00	6.00	10.00	15.00
	1333	—	3.00	5.00	9.00	14.00
	1335	—	3.00	5.00	9.00	14.00
	1337	—	3.00	6.00	10.00	15.00

NOTE: Coins dated AH1333 and 1337 are known in 2 varieties.

COPPER or BRASS
Thick flan

KM#	Date	Mintage	VG	Fine	VF	XF
861	AH1337	—	10.00	17.50	30.00	55.00

Thin flan

KM#	Date	Mintage	VG	Fine	VF	XF
862	AH1337	—	9.00	14.00	20.00	35.00

10 PAISE

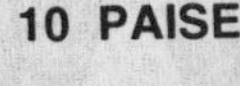

COPPER

KM#	Date	Mintage	VG	Fine	VF	XF
901	AH1348	—	5.00	9.00	17.50	30.00

3 SHAHI
(15 Paisa)

COPPER, 32-33mm
Obv: W/o *Al-Ghazi*.
Rev: Mosque in 8-pointed star.

KM#	Date	Year	VG	Fine	VF	XF
863	AH1337	—	3.00	7.00	14.00	20.00

NOTE: 3 varieties are known.

Obv: *Shamsi* left and below date.

KM#	Date	Year	VG	Fine	VF	XF
869	SH1298	(1919)	2.00	4.00	8.00	13.00

NOTE: ***Shamsi*** (= Solar) is an additional word written on some of the coins dated SH1298, to show the change from a lunar to solar calendar.

Obv: *Al-Ghazi*, w/o *Shamsi* by date.
Rev: Mosque in 8-pointed star.

KM#	Date	Year	VG	Fine	VF	XF
870	SH1298	(1919)	3.00	5.00	8.00	13.00
	1299	(1920)	— Reported, not confirmed			
	1300	(1921)	— Reported, not confirmed			

Thick flan, 11.5 g.
Obv: *Al-Ghazi, Shamsi*.

KM#	Date	Year	VG	Fine	VF	XF
871.1	SH1298	(1919)	10.00	14.00	18.00	24.00

Thin flan, 9 g.

KM#	Date	Year	VG	Fine	VF	XF
871.2	SH1298	(1919)	2.00	4.00	8.00	14.00

Obv: *Shamsi*.
Rev: Mosque in 7-pointed star.

KM#	Date	Year	VG	Fine	VF	XF
872	SH1298	(1919)	2.00	4.00	8.00	14.00

Obv: W/o *Shamsi*.

KM#	Date	Year	VG	Fine	VF	XF
881	SH1298	(1919)	4.00	15.00	22.00	25.00
	1299	(1920)	2.00	4.00	7.00	15.00
	1300	(1921)	2.00	4.00	7.00	15.00
	1302	(1923)	2.00	4.00	7.00	15.00

NOTE: 4 varieties for date 1299 and 3 varieties for date 1300 are known.

Obv. and rev.: 8 stars around perimeter.

KM#	Date	Year	VG	Fine	VF	XF
891	SH1300	(1921)	—	—	—	—

BRASS

KM#	Date	Year	VG	Fine	VF	XF
892	SH1300	(1921)	4.00	8.00	12.00	20.00

COPPER

KM#	Date	Year	VG	Fine	VF	XF
893	SH1300	(1921)	1.25	3.00	5.00	10.00
	1301 (2 vars.)					
893		(1922)	1.25	3.00	5.00	10.00
	130x(error)		—	—	—	—
	1303	(1924)	1.25	3.00	5.00	10.00

ABBASI
(20 Paisa)

3.1100 g, .500 SILVER, .0499 oz ASW
Obv: Date above toughra.

KM#	Date	Mintage	VG	Fine	VF	XF
810	AH1313	—	3.00	5.00	8.00	14.00

Rev: Date below mosque.

KM#	Date	Mintage	VG	Fine	VF	XF
811	AH1313	—	10.00	17.50	27.50	50.00

Rev: New style mosque.

KM#	Date	Mintage	VG	Fine	VF	XF
816	AH1314	—	4.00	8.00	15.00	25.00

KM#	Date	Mintage	VG	Fine	VF	XF
837	AH1320	—	12.50	22.50	35.00	50.00
845	AH1324	—	7.00	12.00	18.00	30.00
	1328	—	7.00	12.00	18.00	30.00

KM#	Date	Mintage	VG	Fine	VF	XF
851	AH1329	—	6.00	11.00	16.00	22.50
	1330	—	4.00	7.00	10.00	15.00
	1333	—	3.00	6.00	9.00	14.00
	1334	—	3.00	6.00	9.00	14.00
	1335	—	3.00	5.00	8.00	13.00
	1337	—	3.00	5.00	8.00	13.00

BILLON

KM#	Date	Year	VG	Fine	VF	XF
874	SH1298	(1919)	50.00	75.00	90.00	150.00

25mm

KM#	Date	Year	VG	Fine	VF	XF
882	SH1299	(1920)	15.00	30.00	50.00	75.00

COPPER or BILLON

KM#	Date	Year	VG	Fine	VF	XF
883	SH1299	(1920)	2.00	5.00	10.00	20.00
	1300	(1921)	2.00	5.00	10.00	20.00
	1301	(1922)	2.00	5.00	10.00	20.00
	1302	(1923)	2.00	5.00	10.00	20.00
	2031(error)		—	—	—	—
	1303	(1924)	2.00	5.00	10.00	20.00

NOTE: Varieties exist.

20 PAISE

BRONZE or BRASS

KM#	Date	Mintage	VG	Fine	VF	XF
895	AH1347	—	3.00	5.00	7.50	17.50

QIRAN
(1/2 Rupee)

4.6500 g, .500 SILVER, .0747 oz ASW
Rev: Star above mosque.

KM#	Date	Mintage	VG	Fine	VF	XF
804	AH1308	—	5.00	7.50	10.00	20.00
	1309	—	5.00	8.00	12.00	25.00
	1310	—	5.00	8.00	12.00	25.00

Rev: *Kabul* above mosque.

KM#	Date	Mintage	VG	Fine	VF	XF
812	AH1313	—	6.00	8.50	12.50	27.50

Rev: *Yak Mesqhal* above mosque.

KM#	Date	Mintage	VG	Fine	VF	XF
817	AH1314	—	7.50	13.50	28.00	60.00

NOTE: The half rupee dated AH1314 bears the denomination of 1 Qiran; all others have Half Rupee.

Rev: Crossed swords and cannons below mosque.

KM#	Date	Mintage	VG	Fine	VF	XF
825	AH1316	—	4.50	8.50	15.00	30.00
	1317	—	— Reported, not confirmed			
	1318	—	— Reported, not confirmed			

Rev: Crossed cannons below mosque.

KM#	Date	Mintage	VG	Fine	VF	XF
831	AH1319	—	14.00	25.00	40.00	65.00

Obv: Date below toughra.

KM#	Date	Mintage	VG	Fine	VF	XF
838	AH1320	—	8.00	14.00	22.50	35.00
	1325	—	7.00	11.00	18.00	27.50

Obv: Date at upper right of toughra.

KM#	Date	Mintage	VG	Fine	VF	XF
841	AH1321	—	7.00	10.00	14.00	22.50

Rev. dated: AH1320

KM#	Date	Mintage	VG	Fine	VF	XF
844	AH1323	—	4.00	6.00	10.00	18.00
	1324	—	4.00	6.00	9.00	16.00
	1326	—	4.00	6.00	9.00	16.00
	1327	—	4.00	6.00	9.00	16.00
	1328	—	4.00	6.00	9.00	16.00
	1329	—	4.00	6.00	10.00	19.00

NOTE: 2 varieties are known.
NOTE: Varieties exist w/1326 on obverse and reverse.

4.6000 g, .500 SILVER, .0739 oz ASW

KM#	Date	Mintage	VG	Fine	VF	XF
852	AH1329	—	3.50	5.50	8.50	14.00
	1333	—	3.50	5.50	8.50	14.00
	1334	—	4.50	7.50	12.50	20.00
	1335	—	4.50	7.50	12.50	20.00
	1337	—	3.50	5.50	8.50	14.00

5.00 g
Obv. leg: Name of *Habibullah*.
Rev: Star of Solomon.

KM#	Date	Mintage	VG	Fine	VF	XF
864	AH1335	—	—	300.00	500.00	—

Obv: Uncircled inscription.

KM#	Date	Year	VG	Fine	VF	XF
865	AH1337	—	4.00	9.00	13.00	20.00

NOTE: 5 varieties are known.

25mm
Obv. leg: Within circle and wreath.

KM#	Date	Year	VG	Fine	VF	XF
866	AH1337	—	150.00	300.00	500.00	725.00

4.7500 g, .500 SILVER, .0763 oz ASW
Obv: Star above inscription, *Shamsi*.

KM#	Date	Year	VG	Fine	VF	XF
875	SH1298	(1919)	3.00	5.00	8.00	14.00

NOTE: 2 varieties are known.

Obv: *Al-Ghazi* above inscription, *Shamsi*.

KM#	Date	Year	VG	Fine	VF	XF
876	SH1298	(1919)	15.00	30.00	50.00	75.00

Obv: W/o *Shamsi*.

KM#	Date	Year	VG	Fine	VF	XF
884	SH1299	(1920)	3.00	4.00	7.00	12.00
	1300	(1921)	3.00	4.00	7.00	12.00

NOTE: 2 varieties are known dated 1299.

KM#	Date	Year	VG	Fine	VF	XF
894	SH1300	(1921)	2.00	4.00	7.00	11.00
	1301	(1922)	2.00	4.00	7.00	10.00
	1302	(1923)	2.00	4.00	7.00	10.00
	1303	(1924)	2.00	4.00	7.00	10.00

4.7000 g, .500 SILVER, .0755 oz ASW

KM#	Date	Mintage	VG	Fine	VF	XF
896	AH1347	—	4.00	7.00	12.00	20.00

KM#	Date	Mintage	VG	Fine	VF	XF
902	AH1348	—	14.00	25.00	35.00	50.00

RUPEE

SILVER

KM#	Date	Mintage	VG	Fine	VF	XF
805	AH1304/1303	—	25.00	35.00	55.00	115.00
	1304	—	25.00	35.00	55.00	115.00

NOTE: Similar to KM#544 these machine struck Rupees were produced by the Birmingham Mint as patterns.

9.2000 g, .900 SILVER, .2662 oz ASW
Obv: Star above toughra.
Rev: Star above, *Kabul* below mosque.

Toughra of Abdur Rahman Khan. Above the toughra between the ends of the wreath, appear stars, a single star, the name *Kabul* or a blank space.

KM#	Date	Mintage	VG	Fine	VF	XF
806	AH1308	—	5.00	8.00	14.00	25.00
	1309	—	4.00	6.00	10.00	20.00
	1310/09	—	4.00	6.00	10.00	25.00
	1310	—	5.00	8.00	14.00	25.00
	1311	—	4.00	6.00	10.00	20.00
	1311/09	—	4.00	6.00	10.00	20.00
	1312/1/9	—	4.00	7.00	14.00	25.00
	1312/1	—	4.00	6.00	10.00	20.00
	1312	—	4.00	6.00	10.00	20.00
	1313	—	4.00	6.00	10.00	20.00
	1391(error)		12.00	15.00	17.50	25.00

NOTE: 2 varieties each are known for dates AH1311-13

Rev: *Kabul* to right of mosque.

KM#	Date	Mintage	VG	Fine	VF	XF
813	AH1313	—	5.00	7.50	10.00	20.00

Rev: *Kabul* above mosque.

KM#	Date	Mintage	VG	Fine	VF	XF
814	AH1312	—	10.00	20.00	50.00	75.00
	1313	—	5.00	7.00	9.00	20.00

Rev: *Du Mesqal* above mosque.

KM#	Date	Mintage	VG	Fine	VF	XF
818	AH1314	—	6.00	10.00	20.00	40.00

Obv: *Kabul* above toughra, undivided dates.

KM#	Date	Mintage	VG	Fine	VF	XF
819.1	AH1314	—	4.00	10.00	17.50	35.00
	1315	—	4.00	5.50	8.50	20.00

Obv: Divided dates, last 2 digits above toughra.

KM#	Date	Mintage	VG	Fine	VF	XF
819.2	AH1315	—	20.00	50.00	100.00	150.00
	1316	—	4.00	6.00	10.00	25.00

Obv: Divided dates, "17" below toughra.

KM#	Date	Mintage	VG	Fine	VF	XF
819.4	AH1317	—	20.00	50.00	100.00	150.00

Obv: Date at right of toughra.

KM#	Date	Mintage	VG	Fine	VF	XF
819.3	AH1317	—	15.00	40.00	60.00	110.00

Obv: 3 stars above toughra, date in toughra.

KM#	Date	Mintage	VG	Fine	VF	XF
829	AH1317	—	6.00	10.00	25.00	50.00

Obv: Date at right of toughra.
Rev: New style mosque.

KM#	Date	Mintage	VG	Fine	VF	XF
830	AH1318	—	5.00	8.00	12.00	20.00

Obv: Toughra of Habibullah in wreath, star above.

KM#	Date	Mintage	VG	Fine	VF	XF
832	AH1319	—	8.00	12.00	25.00	70.00

NOTE: 2 varieties are known.

Obv: *Afghanistan* above small toughra, star at right. Rev: Large inverted pyramid dome.

KM#	Date	Mintage	VG	Fine	VF	XF
833.1	AH1319	—	4.00	5.50	10.00	25.00
	1325	—	4.00	5.50	15.00	40.00

Obv: W/o star.

KM#	Date	Mintage	VG	Fine	VF	XF
833.2	AH1319	—	4.00	5.50	10.00	25.00
	1320	—	4.00	5.50	8.50	20.00
	1325	—	4.00	5.50	15.00	40.00

Obv: *Afghanistan* divided by a star above large toughra. Rev: Inverted pyramid dome.

KM#	Date	Mintage	VG	Fine	VF	XF
839	AH1320	—	4.00	6.00	10.00	20.00

Rev: Small dome mosque.

KM#	Date	Mintage	VG	Fine	VF	XF
840.1	AH1320	—	5.00	8.00	15.00	35.00

Obv: Date in loop of toughra.

KM#	Date	Mintage	VG	Fine	VF	XF
840.2	AH1321	—	10.00	15.00	25.00	50.00

Rev: *Afghanistan* above mosque, crossed swords and cannons.

KM#	Date	Mintage	VG	Fine	VF	XF
842.1	AH1321	—	4.00	7.00	10.50	22.00
	1322	—	4.00	7.00	10.50	22.00

NOTE: 2 varieties exist for AH1321 date.

Rev: Crossed cannons.

KM#	Date	Mintage	VG	Fine	VF	XF
842.2	AH1322	—	4.00	5.00	7.50	18.00
	1324	—	4.00	5.00	7.50	18.00
	1325	—	5.00	8.00	12.00	25.00
	1326	—	4.00	6.00	10.00	19.00
	1327	—	4.00	6.00	10.00	20.00
	1328	—	6.00	8.00	15.00	30.00
	1329	—	5.00	7.50	12.50	25.00

NOTE: 2 varieties exist for AH1328 date.

Rev: Large dome mosque w/o *Afghanistan*.

KM#	Date	Mintage	VG	Fine	VF	XF
847	AH1328	—	7.00	12.00	20.00	40.00

NOTE: Varieties exist.

Obv: Name and titles of Habibullah in wreath.
Rev: Mosque within sunburst.

KM#	Date	Mintage	VG	Fine	VF	XF
853	AH1329	—	4.00	6.00	10.00	17.50
	1330	—	4.00	6.00	9.00	15.00
	1331	—	4.00	6.00	9.00	15.00
	1332	—	4.00	6.00	9.00	15.00
	1333	—	4.00	6.00	9.00	15.00
	1334	—	4.00	6.00	9.00	15.00
	1335	—	4.00	6.00	9.00	15.00
	1337	—	4.00	6.00	10.00	17.50

NOTE: 2 varieties exist for AH1330, 1331 and 1337 and 3 varieties exist for AH1333.

Obv: Name and titles of Amanullah, star above inscription.

KM#	Date	Year	VG	Fine	VF	XF
867	AH1337	—	6.00	10.00	18.00	30.00

NOTE: 7 varieties are known.

9.0000 g, .900 SILVER, .2604 oz ASW
Obv: *Al-Ghazi* above inscription.

KM#	Date	Year	VG	Fine	VF	XF
877	SH1298	(1919)	4.50	6.50	10.00	17.00
	1299	(1920)	4.50	6.50	10.00	17.00

NOTE: 4 varieties are known for date SH1298. 2 varieties are known for date SH1299.

9.2500 g, .900 SILVER, .2676 oz ASW
Obv: Toughra of Amanullah.

KM#	Date	Year	VG	Fine	VF	XF
885	SH1299	(1920)	4.00	5.00	7.50	15.00
	1300	(1921)	4.00	5.00	7.50	15.00
	1301	(1922)	4.00	5.00	7.50	15.00
	1302	(1923)	4.00	5.00	7.50	15.00
	1303	(1924)	4.00	5.00	7.50	15.00

9.1000 g, .900 SILVER, .2633 oz ASW
Obv: Name and titles of Amir Habibullah (The Usurper).

KM#	Date	Mintage	VG	Fine	VF	XF
897	AH1347	—	4.00	8.00	16.00	32.00

Obv: Title in circle.

KM#	Date	Mintage	VG	Fine	VF	XF
898	AH1347	—	25.00	35.00	55.00	90.00

2-1/2 RUPEES

22.9200 g, .900 SILVER, .6632 oz ASW

KM#	Date	Year	VG	Fine	VF	XF
878	SH1298	(1919)	12.50	16.50	20.00	40.00
	1299	(1920)	8.50	12.50	16.50	30.00
	1300	(1921)	8.50	12.50	16.50	30.00
	1301	(1922)	8.50	12.50	15.00	30.00
	1302	(1923)	8.50	12.50	15.00	35.00
	1303	(1924)	8.50	12.50	15.00	40.00

NOTE: 2 varieties each are known for dates SH 1298-1300.

5 RUPEES

46.0500 g, .900 SILVER, 1.3325 oz ASW

KM#	Date	Mintage	VG	Fine	VF	XF
820	AH1314	—	20.00	30.00	60.00	115.00

45.6000 g, .900 SILVER, 1.3194 oz ASW
Obv: Similar to KM#820.

KM#	Date	Mintage	VG	Fine	VF	XF
826	AH1316	—	17.50	27.50	50.00	110.00

Rev: Similar to KM#826.

KM#	Date	Mintage	VG	Fine	VF	XF
834.1	AH1319	—	25.00	45.00	85.00	150.00

Obv: Date at left of toughra.

KM#	Date	Mintage	VG	Fine	VF	XF
834.2	AH1319	—	25.00	45.00	85.00	150.00

KM#	Date	Mintage	VG	Fine	VF	XF
843	AH1322	—	20.00	25.00	38.00	80.00
	1323	—	Reported, not confirmed			
	1324	—	15.00	20.00	32.00	75.00
	1326	—	15.00	20.00	32.00	75.00
	1327/6	—	15.00	20.00	32.00	75.00
	1328	—	22.50	30.00	45.00	90.00
	1329	—	25.00	40.00	60.00	115.00

NOTE: Most dates are recut dies. 2 varieties are known for each date, AH1324 and 1327.

1/2 AMANI

(5 Rupees)

2.3000 g, .900 GOLD, .0665 oz AGW

KM#	Date	Year	VG	Fine	VF	XF
886	SH1299	(1920)	BV	45.00	65.00	100.00

TILLA

(10 Rupees)

4.6000 g, .900 GOLD, 22mm, .1331 oz AGW
Rev. leg: *Allah Akbar* above mosque.

KM#	Date	Mintage	VG	Fine	VF	XF
807	AH1309	—	BV	70.00	110.00	210.00

19mm
Rev. leg: *Allah Akbar* above.

KM#	Date	Mintage	VG	Fine	VF	XF
815	AH1313	—	70.00	90.00	140.00	280.00

Rev: Date below mosque.

KM#	Date	Mintage	VG	Fine	VF	XF
821	AH1314	—	BV	70.00	100.00	150.00
	1316	—	BV	85.00	110.00	175.00

Obv: Date below toughra.

KM#	Date	Mintage	VG	Fine	VF	XF
822	AH1314	—	BV	75.00	100.00	165.00
	1316	—	BV	70.00	100.00	165.00

Obv: Star above toughra.

KM#	Date	Mintage	VG	Fine	VF	XF
835	AH1319	—	70.00	95.00	140.00	240.00

Obv. leg: *Afghanistan* divided by star above toughra.

KM#	Date	Mintage	VG	Fine	VF	XF
836.1	AH1319	—	75.00	100.00	150.00	250.00

Obv. leg: *Afghanistan* above toughra w/star to right.

KM#	Date	Mintage	VG	Fine	VF	XF
836.2	AH1320	—	75.00	100.00	150.00	250.00

Obv: Date divided.

KM#	Date	Mintage	VG	Fine	VF	XF
A856	AH1325	—	—	450.00	650.00	900.00

Obv. leg: Name of *Habibullah*.

KM#	Date	Mintage	VG	Fine	VF	XF
856	AH1335	—	170.00	200.00	260.00	330.00
	1336	—	100.00	120.00	175.00	240.00
	1337	—	110.00	130.00	180.00	220.00

Obv. leg: Name of *Amanullah*.
Rev: Crossed swords below mosque.

KM#	Date	Mintage	VG	Fine	VF	XF
868.1	AH1337	—	100.00	125.00	160.00	225.00

Rev: 6-pointed star below mosque.

KM#	Date	Mintage	VG	Fine	VF	XF
868.2	AH1337	—	100.00	135.00	175.00	250.00

AMANI

(10 Rupees)

4.6000 g, .900 GOLD, 22mm, .1331 oz AGW

KM#	Date	Year	VG	Fine	VF	XF
887	SH1299	(1920)	BV	60.00	80.00	140.00

2 TILLAS

(20 Rupees)

9.2000 g, .900 GOLD, 22mm, .2661 oz AGW

KM#	Date	Mintage	VG	Fine	VF	XF
808	AH1309	—	BV	140.00	210.00	265.00

KM#	Date	Year	Fine	VF	XF	Unc
879	SH1298	(1919)	BV	140.00	240.00	380.00

2 AMANI

(20 Rupees)

9.2000 g, .900 GOLD, .2662 oz AGW

KM#	Date	Year	VG	Fine	VF	XF
888	SH1299	(1920)	BV	140.00	200.00	275.00
	1300	(1921)	BV	140.00	200.00	275.00
	1301	(1922)	BV	140.00	200.00	275.00
	1302	(1923)	BV	140.00	200.00	275.00
	1303	(1924)	BV	140.00	200.00	275.00

HABIBI

(30 Rupees)

4.6000 g, .900 GOLD, .1331 oz AGW

KM#	Date	Mintage	VG	Fine	VF	XF
899	AH1347	—	75.00	125.00	200.00	325.00

Obv: Small star replaces '30 Rupees' in leg.

KM#	Date	Mintage	VG	Fine	VF	XF
900	AH1347	—	75.00	125.00	200.00	325.00

5 AMANI

(50 Rupees)

23.0000 g, .900 GOLD, 34mm, .6656 oz AGW
Obv: Persian *5* above toughra; *Al Ghazi*

at right. Rev. leg: *Amaniya* above mosque.

KM#	Date	Year	VG	Fine	VF	XF
889	SH1299	(1920)	BV	400.00	675.00	1500.

Obv: Star above toughra. Rev: Persian *5* above mosque.

890	SH1299	(1920)	BV	400.00	675.00	1500.

60 RUPEES

6.9000 g, .900 GOLD, .1997 oz AGW

903	AH1337	—	—	550.00	800.00	1600.

DECIMAL COINAGE

100 Pul = 1 Afghani
20 Afghani = 1 Amani

PUL

BRONZE or BRASS

KM#	Date	Year	Fine	VF	XF	Unc
A922 (922)	AH1349	—	.75	1.25	1.75	2.50

Obv: Toughra.

922	AH1349	—	100.00	250.00	300.00	400.00

NOTE: On these and many other Afghan copper coins, various alloys were used quite indiscriminately, depending upon what was immediately at hand. Thus one finds bronze, brass, and various shades in between. For this reason, bronze and brass coins are not given separate types, but are indicated as a single listing.

2 PUL

BRONZE or BRASS, 2.00 g

905	SH1304	(1925)	2.00	3.00	4.50	10.00
	1305	(1926)	2.00	3.00	4.50	10.00

917	AH1348	—	1.25	2.50	3.50	8.00

928	SH1311	(1932)	2.00	3.00	4.00	12.00
	1312	(1933)	1.50	2.25	3.00	10.00
	1313	(1934)	1.75	2.75	3.75	10.00
	1314	(1935)	2.00	3.00	4.00	12.00

BRONZE

936	SH1316	(1937)	.15	.20	.35	1.00

3 PUL

BRONZE

KM#	Date	Year	Fine	VF	XF	Unc
937	SH1316	(1937)	.35	.50	.75	2.00

5 PUL

BRONZE or BRASS, 3.00 g

906	SH1304	(1925)	1.75	3.50	6.00	12.00
	1305	(1926)	1.50	3.00	5.50	12.00

923	AH1349	—	1.75	2.75	4.50	10.00
	1350	—	1.25	2.25	3.50	10.00

NOTE: 2 varieties are known dated AH1350.

929	SH1311	(1932)	2.00	3.50	5.00	15.00
	1312	(1933)	2.00	3.50	5.00	15.00
	1313	(1934)	2.00	3.50	5.00	15.00
	1314	(1935)	2.00	3.50	5.00	15.00

BRONZE

938	SH1316	(1937)	.35	.50	.75	2.50

10 PUL

COPPER, 6.00 g

907	SH1304	(1925)	2.00	3.50	5.50	15.00
	1305	(1926)	2.50	4.00	6.00	20.00
	1306	(1927)	2.50	4.00	6.00	20.00
	ND	—	— Reported, not confirmed			

COPPER or BRASS

918	AH1348	—	2.00	3.50	5.00	15.00
	1349(2 vars.)		2.25	4.00	5.50	15.00

NOTE: Illustration shows an example struck off-center; prices are for properly struck specimens.

BRASS

KM#	Date	Year	Fine	VF	XF	Unc
930	SH1311	(1932)	1.50	2.50	4.00	15.00
	1312	(1933)	1.50	2.50	4.00	15.00
	1313	(1934)	1.50	2.50	4.00	15.00
	1314	(1935)	1.50	2.50	4.00	15.00

COPPER-NICKEL

939	SH1316	(1937)	.40	.65	1.00	3.00

20 PUL

BILLON, 2.00 g

908	SH1304	(1925)	75.00	95.00	125.00	170.00
	ND	—	60.00	85.00	110.00	160.00

COPPER or BRASS

919	AH1348	—	2.00	4.00	10.00	15.00
	1349	—	3.00	5.00	12.00	18.00

25 PUL

COPPER or BRASS

KM#	Date	Mintage	Fine	VF	XF	Unc
924	AH1349	—	2.00	3.50	9.00	14.00

NOTE: 2 varieties are known dated AH1349.

BRONZE or BRASS

KM#	Date	Year	Fine	VF	XF	Unc
931	SH1312	(1933)	1.50	2.50	9.00	15.00
	1313	(1934)	1.50	2.50	9.00	15.00
	1314	(1935)	1.75	2.75	12.00	17.50
	1315	(1936)	— Reported, not confirmed			
	1316	(1937)	1.75	2.75	4.00	17.50

COPPER-NICKEL

940	SH1316	(1937)	.60	.75	1.25	3.50

BRONZE

941	SH1330	(1951)	.15	.25	.50	1.00
	1331	(1952)	.15	.25	.50	1.00
	1332	(1953)	.15	.25	.50	1.00

NICKEL-CLAD STEEL, 20mm, reeded edge

943	SH1331	(1952)	1.00	2.00	3.50	6.00
	1332	(1953)	1.50	3.00	5.00	7.50

Plain edge

KM#	Date	Year	Fine	VF	XF	Unc
944	SH1331	(1952)	.30	.50	.60	1.00
	1332	(1953)	.30	.50	.60	1.00
	1333	(1954)	.30	.50	.60	1.00
	1334	(1955)	.30	.50	.60	1.50

ALUMINUM

KM#	Date	Year	Fine	VF	XF	Unc
945	SH1331	(1952)	.50	1.00	3.00	20.00

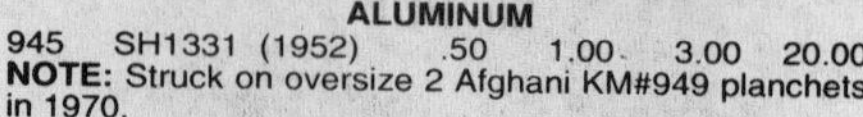

NOTE: Struck on oversize 2 Afghani KM#949 planchets in 1970.

1/2 AFGHANI

(50 Pul)

5.0000 g, .500 SILVER, .0803 oz ASW
Obv: Date below toughra.

KM#	Date	Year	Fine	VF	XF	Unc
909	SH1304	7	2.00	3.50	6.50	20.00
	1305	8	2.00	3.50	6.50	20.00
	1306	9	2.00	3.50	6.50	20.00

NOTE: 2 varieties are known dated SH1304.

Rev: Date below mosque.

KM#	Date	Year	Fine	VF	XF	Unc
915	SH1307	10	3.00	5.50	10.00	30.00

KM#	Date	Year	Fine	VF	XF	Unc
920	AH1348	1	1.50	2.25	4.00	12.50
(919)	1349	2	1.50	2.25	4.00	12.50
	1350	3	1.50	2.25	4.00	12.50

4.7500 g, .500 SILVER, .0763 oz ASW

KM#	Date	Year	Fine	VF	XF	Unc
926	SH1310	(1931)	1.50	2.25	4.00	12.50
	1311	(1932)	1.50	2.25	4.00	12.50
	1312	(1933)	1.50	2.25	4.00	12.50

Obv: Smaller dotted circle.

KM#	Date	Year	Fine	VF	XF	Unc
932.1	SH1312	(1933)	1.75	2.50	4.50	13.00
	1313	(1934)	1.75	2.50	4.50	13.00
	1314	(1935)	1.75	2.50	4.50	13.00

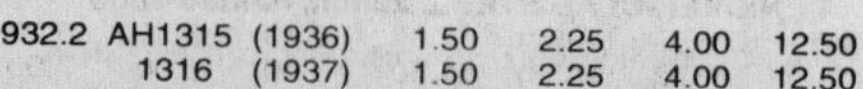

KM#	Date	Year	Fine	VF	XF	Unc
932.2	AH1315	(1936)	1.50	2.25	4.00	12.50
	1316	(1937)	1.50	2.25	4.00	12.50

BRONZE, 21.5mm
Obv: Denomination in numerals.

KM#	Date	Year	Fine	VF	XF	Unc
942.1	SH1330	(1951)	.35	.55	.85	2.00
	133x	(195x)	—	—	—	—

24mm

KM#	Date	Year	Fine	VF	XF	Unc
942.2	SH1330	(1951)	20.00	30.00	40.00	50.00

NICKEL-CLAD STEEL

KM#	Date	Year	Fine	VF	XF	Unc
946	SH1331	(1952)	.20	.35	.65	2.00
	1332	(1953)	.20	.35	.65	2.00
	1333	(1954)	.30	.50	.85	3.00
	1334	(1955)	.20	.35	.65	2.00

Obv: Denomination in words.

KM#	Date	Year	Fine	VF	XF	Unc
947	SH1331	1952	.40	.65	.85	2.50

AFGHANI

(100 Pul)

10.0000 g, .900 SILVER, .2893 oz ASW
Obv: Date below toughra.

KM#	Date	Year	Fine	VF	XF	Unc
910	SH1304	7	3.00	5.00	10.00	22.00
	1305	8	3.00	5.00	10.00	22.00
	1305	9	3.00	5.00	10.00	22.00
	1306	9	3.00	5.00	10.00	22.00

NOTE: 3 varieties are known for date SH1304. 2 varieties each are known for dates SH1305-06.

Rev: Date below mosque.

916 SH1307 (1928) — Reported, not confirmed

9.9500 g, .900 SILVER, .2879 oz ASW

KM#	Date	Year	Fine	VF	XF	Unc
921	AH1348	1	3.00	4.50	9.00	16.50
	1349	2	3.00	4.50	9.00	16.50
	1350	3	3.00	4.50	9.00	16.50

10.0000 g, .900 SILVER, .2893 oz ASW

KM#	Date	Year	Fine	VF	XF	Unc
927.1	SH1310	(1931)	50.00	65.00	80.00	115.00
	1311	(1932)	110.00	160.00	180.00	260.00

Thick flan, 22.5mm

KM#	Date	Year	Fine	VF	XF	Unc
927.2	SH1310	(1931)	250.00	375.00	500.00	700.00

NICKEL-CLAD STEEL

KM#	Date	Year	Fine	VF	XF	Unc
953	SH1340	(1961)	.15	.20	.30	.50

2 AFGHANI

ALUMINUM

KM#	Date	Year	Fine	VF	XF	Unc
949	SH1337	(1958)	.60	1.00	1.50	2.00

NOTE: The above issue was withdrawn and demonetized due to extensive counterfeiting.

NICKEL-CLAD STEEL
Coin type.

KM#	Date	Year	Fine	VF	XF	Unc
954.1	SH1340	(1961)	.20	.30	.50	.85

NOTE: 2 varieties, normal coin type and medallic die orientation.

Medallic die orientation.

KM#	Date	Year	Fine	VF	XF	Unc
954.2	SH1340	(1961)	.20	.30	.50	.85

2-1/2 AFGHANI

25.0000 g, .900 SILVER, .7234 oz ASW

KM#	Date	Year	Fine	VF	XF	Unc
913	SH1305	8	15.00	25.00	50.00	125.00
	1306	9	15.00	20.00	40.00	80.00

NOTE: 2 varieties are known for each date.

5 AFGHANI

ALUMINUM

KM#	Date	Year	Fine	VF	XF	Unc
950	SH1337	(1958)	1.00	1.75	2.25	3.00

NOTE: The above issue was withdrawn and demonetized due to extensive counterfeiting.

NICKEL-CLAD STEEL
Shah Mohammed Sahir

KM#	Date	Year	Fine	VF	XF	Unc
955	SH1340	AH1381	.25	.40	.75	1.50

10 AFGHANI

ALUMINUM

KM#	Date	Year	Fine	VF	XF	Unc
948	SH1336 (1957)	—	—		—	900.00

1/2 AMANI

3.0000 g, .900 GOLD, .0868 oz AGW

KM#	Date	Year	Fine	VF	XF	Unc
911	SH1304	7	BV	40.00	60.00	100.00
	1305	8	BV	40.00	60.00	100.00
	1306	9	BV	40.00	60.00	100.00

4 GRAMS

4.0000 g, .900 GOLD, .1157 oz AGW

KM#	Date	Year	Fine	VF	XF	Unc
935	SH1315 (1936)		BV	75.00	100.00	160.00
	1317 (1938)		BV	75.00	100.00	160.00

AMANI

6.0000 g, .900 GOLD, .1736 oz AGW

KM#	Date	Year	Fine	VF	XF	Unc
912	SH1304	7	BV	90.00	110.00	160.00
	1305	8	BV	90.00	130.00	200.00
	1306	9	BV	90.00	110.00	160.00

20 AFGHANI

6.0000 g, .900 GOLD, .1736 oz AGW

KM#	Date	Year	Fine	VF	XF	Unc
925	AH1348	—	125.00	175.00	200.00	300.00
	1349	2	BV	110.00	165.00	240.00
	1350	3	BV	110.00	165.00	240.00

TILLA

6.0000 g, .900 GOLD, .1736 oz AGW

KM#	Date	Year	Fine	VF	XF	Unc
933	SH1313	(1934)	125.00	150.00	175.00	250.00

8 GRAMS

8.0000 g, .900 GOLD, .2314 oz AGW

KM#	Date	Year	Fine	VF	XF	Unc
934	SH1314	(1935)	BV	130.00	175.00	240.00
	1315	(1936)	BV	130.00	175.00	240.00
	1317	(1938)	BV	130.00	175.00	240.00

KM#	Date	Year	Mintage	VF	XF	Unc
952	SH1339	AH1380	200 pcs.	—	300.00	800.00

NOTE: Struck for royal presentation purposes. Specimens struck with the same dies (including the "8 grams", the "8" having been effaced after striking), but on thin planchets weighing 3.9-4 grams, exist. They are regarded as "mint sports". Market value $300.00 in unc.

2-1/2 AMANI

15.0000 g, .900 GOLD, .4340 oz AGW

KM#	Date	Year	Fine	VF	XF	Unc
914	SH1306	9	—	—	3000.	4500.

LOCAL COINAGE

With the inception of machine struck coinage in AH1308/AD1891, the provincial mints were closed and all minting was centralized at Kabul. However, few base metal coins were struck at Kabul, and old copper coins, as well as foreign copper coins, circulated in Afghanistan. After nine years, the Kabul Mint suspended the production of copper coins (AH1317/AD1900). The consequence was the sanctioning of private striking at Herat and Qandahar, where coins were struck from about AH1322 until AH1333. Royal coinage in copper and brass resumed in AH1329/AD1911, and the private mints were soon afterwards suppressed. Further private strikings took place in AH1337-38/SH1298-99. The minting place, probably Kabul, is not shown on these coins. The local coinage is quite crude, and is usually counterstruck on older Afghan and foreign coins. The listings below may be incomplete.

Ghazni

PAISA

COPPER
Struck over British East India Co., 1/4 Anna.

KM#	Date	Good	VG	Fine	VF
963	AH1322	10.00	20.00	35.00	75.00

Herat

PAISA

COPPER, round or irregular flan

KM#	Date	Good	VG	Fine	VF
956.1	AH1322	2.50	4.00	7.50	12.50
	1328	2.50	4.00	7.50	12.50
	1329	2.50	4.00	7.50	12.50
	1330	2.50	4.00	7.50	12.50
	1331	2.50	4.00	7.50	12.50
	1332	2.50	4.00	7.50	12.50
	Date off flan	1.50	2.50	5.00	8.00

Rev: In a rayed circle.

KM#	Date	Good	VG	Fine	VF
956.2	AH1332	3.00	5.00	8.50	15.00

Obv: Scroll symbol.

KM#	Date	Good	VG	Fine	VF
956.3	AH1325	3.00	5.00	8.50	15.00

Struck over Iran, 50 Dinars, Y#4.

KM#	Date	Good	VG	Fine	VF
957	AH1322	4.00	6.50	12.50	16.00
	1328	3.00	5.00	10.00	12.50

Obv: *Dar al-Nusrat* added, date above.

KM#	Date	Good	VG	Fine	VF
958.1	AH1331	2.50	4.00	7.50	12.50

Rev: Date below mosque.

KM#	Date	Good	VG	Fine	VF
958.2	AH1331	3.50	5.00	8.50	15.00

5 PAISE

In the name of Baccha-i-Saqao

BRASS

KM#	Date	Good	VG	Fine	VF
969	AH1347	5.00	8.50	15.00	22.50

10 PAISE

In the name of Baccha-i-Saqao

BRASS
Rev: Denomination *Dah* written above *Paisa*.

KM#	Date	Good	VG	Fine	VF
970.1	AH1347	6.00	10.00	16.50	25.00

Rev: Denomination *Dah* written at right of *Paisa*.

KM#	Date	Good	VG	Fine	VF
970.2	AH1347	7.50	12.50	20.00	30.00

20 PAISE

In the name of Baccha-i-Saqao

BRASS

KM#	Date	Good	VG	Fine	VF
972	AH1347	7.50	12.50	20.00	30.00

Qandahar

PAISA

COPPER, dump

960.1	AH1322	4.50	7.50	12.50	17.50

c/s: On Iran, 50 Dinars, Y#4.

960.2	AH1322	3.00	5.00	8.00	12.50

c/s: On Muscat & Oman, 1/4 Anna, KM#4.

960.3	AH1322	3.75	6.50	10.00	15.00

964	AH1333	2.00	3.50	6.00	10.00

Without Mint Name

Believed struck at Kabul

PAISA

COPPER, crudely struck.
Obv: Denomination *Yek Paisa*.

KM#	Date	Year	Good	VG	Fine	VF
965	SH1298	(1919)	4.50	7.50	12.50	20.00
	1299	(1920)	4.50	7.50	12.50	20.00

Obv: With name of ruler *Amanullah*.

966	SH1299	(1920)	6.00	10.00	16.50	24.00

2 PAISE

COPPER
Similar to Paisa, KM#965, but inscribed *Do Paisa* below mosque.

KM#	Date	Good	VG	Fine	VF
959	AH1329	3.00	5.00	8.50	13.50

5 PAISE

(1 Shahi)

COPPER, crudely struck.
Rev: Both denominations.

KM#	Date	Year	Good	VG	Fine	VF
967	SH1298					
		AH1338	6.00	10.00	16.50	24.00
	1299	1338	7.50	12.50	20.00	30.00
	1299	1339	6.00	10.00	16.50	24.00

REPUBLIC

SH1352-1357/1973-1978AD

25 PUL

BRASS CLAD STEEL

KM#	Date	Mintage	Fine	VF	XF	Unc
975	SH1352	45.950	.25	.50	1.00	2.50

50 PUL

COPPER CLAD STEEL

976	SH1352	24.750	.75	1.50	2.50	5.00

5 AFGHANI

COPPER-NICKEL CLAD STEEL

977	SH1352	34.750	1.75	3.50	5.00	10.00

250 AFGHANI

28.5700 g, .925 SILVER, .8496 oz ASW
Conservation - Snow Leopard

978	1978	4,370	—	—	—	28.00

28.2800 g, .925 SILVER, .8410 oz ASW

979	1978	4,387	—	—	Proof	38.00

500 AFGHANI

35.3000 g, .925 SILVER, 1.0498 oz ASW
Conservation - Siberian Crane

KM#	Date	Mintage	Fine	VF	XF	Unc
980	1978	4,374	—	—	—	30.00

35.0000 g, .925 SILVER, 1.0408 oz ASW

981	1978	4,218	—	—	Proof	40.00

10,000 AFGHANI

33.4370 g, .900 GOLD, .9676 oz AGW
Conservation - Marco Polo Sheep

982	1978	694 pcs.	—	—	—	550.00
	1978	181 pcs.	—	—	Proof	950.00

DEMOCRATIC REPUBLIC

SH1357/1978AD

MINT MARK

(K) - Key/* = Havana, Cuba

25 PUL

ALUMINUM-BRONZE

KM#	Date	Year	Fine	VF	XF	Unc
990	SH1357	(1978)	.25	.50	1.00	2.00

996	SH1359	(1980)	.20	.40	.80	1.50

50 PUL

ALUMINUM-BRONZE, 3.00 g

992	SH1357	(1978)	.50	.80	1.50	3.00

997	SH1359	(1980)	.25	.50	1.00	2.00

AFGHANI

COPPER-NICKEL

KM#	Date	Year	Fine	VF	XF	Unc
993	SH1357	(1978)	.60	1.00	1.75	3.50

KM#	Date	Year	Fine	VF	XF	Unc
998	SH1359	(1980)	.50	.80	1.50	2.50

2 AFGHANIS

COPPER-NICKEL

KM#	Date	Year	Fine	VF	XF	Unc
994	SH1357	(1978)	1.00	1.50	2.00	4.00

Obv: Similar to 1 Afghani, KM#998.

KM#	Date	Year	Fine	VF	XF	Unc
999	SH1359	(1980)	.60	1.00	1.50	3.00

5 AFGHANIS

COPPER-NICKEL, 7.40 g

KM#	Date	Year	Fine	VF	XF	Unc
995	SH1357	(1978)	1.00	2.00	4.00	6.00

KM#	Date	Year	Fine	VF	XF	Unc
1000	SH1359	(1980)	1.00	1.50	2.00	4.00

BRASS
F.A.O. Issue - World Food Day

KM#	Date	Year	Fine	VF	XF	Unc
1001	SH1360	(1981)	.25	.50	1.00	1.50

10 AFGHANIS

BRASS
70th Anniversary of Independence

KM#	Date	Mintage	Fine	VF	XF	Unc
1015	1989	—	—	—	—	3.50

50 AFGHANIS

COPPER-NICKEL
100 Years of the Automobile

KM#	Date	Mintage	Fine	VF	XF	Unc
1016	1986	—	—	—	—	12.00

World Wildlife Fund Leopard

KM#	Date	Mintage	Fine	VF	XF	Unc
1006	1987	.028	—	—	—	12.00

100 AFGHANIS

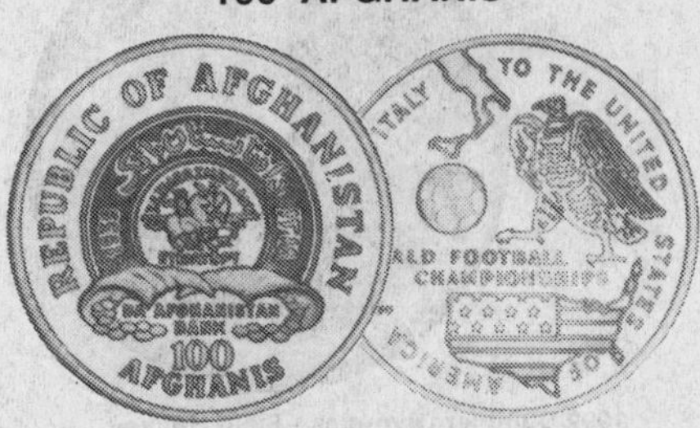

COPPER-NICKEL
World Soccer Championship - Italy to U.S.A.

KM#	Date	Mintage	Fine	VF	XF	Unc
1014	1990	—	—	—	Proof	14.00

250 AFGHANI

20.3100 g, .925 SILVER, .8716 oz ASW
Conservation - Snow Leopard

KM#	Date	Mintage	Fine	VF	XF	Unc
1017	1978	—	—	—	—	28.00

500 AFGHANIS

35.4400 g, .925 SILVER, 1.0539 oz ASW
Conservation - Siberian Crane

KM#	Date	Mintage	Fine	VF	XF	Unc
1018	1978	—	—	—	—	30.00

9.0600 g, .900 SILVER, .2622 oz ASW
F.A.O. Issue - World Food Day

KM#	Date	Year	Fine	VF	XF	Unc
1002	SH1360	1981	—	—	Proof	20.00

12.0000 g, .999 SILVER, .3855 oz ASW
100th Anniversary of the Automobile

KM#	Date	Mintage	Fine	VF	XF	Unc
1003	1986	2,000	—	—	—	40.00

1988 Winter Olympics - Skaters

KM#	Date	Mintage	Fine	VF	XF	Unc
1004	ND(1986)	.010	—	—	—	35.00

Wildlife Preservation - Leopard

KM#	Date	Mintage	Fine	VF	XF	Unc
1005	1986	5,000	—	—	—	45.00

European Soccer Championship - West Germany

KM#	Date	Mintage	Fine	VF	XF	Unc
1007	1988(K)	*5,000	—	—	—	55.00

16.0000 g, .999 SILVER, .5145 oz ASW
1992 Winter Olympics - Bobsledding
Obv: Short thick letters.

KM#	Date	Mintage	Fine	VF	XF	Unc
1008.1	1989	*.010	—	—	Proof	50.00

Obv: Tall thin letters.

KM#	Date	Mintage	Fine	VF	XF	Unc
1008.2	1989	Inc. Ab.	—	—	Proof	75.00

1986 World Soccer Championship - Mexico

KM#	Date	Mintage	Fine	VF	XF	Unc
1009	ND(1988)	5,000	—	—	—	60.00

12.0000 g, .999 SILVER, .3855 oz ASW
1988 Summer Olympics - Volley Ball

KM#	Date	Mintage	Fine	VF	XF	Unc
1010	1987(K)	.010	—	—	—	35.00

16.0000 g, .999 SILVER, .5145 oz ASW
1990 World Soccer Championship - Italy

KM#	Date	Mintage	Fine	VF	XF	Unc
1011	1989	.010	—	—	Proof	50.00

1992 Summer Olympics - Field Hockey

KM#	Date	Mintage	Fine	VF	XF	Unc
1012	1989	.010	—	—	Proof	50.00

12.0000 g, .999 SILVER, .3855 oz ASW
1994 World Cup Soccer Games - USA

KM#	Date	Mintage	Fine	VF	XF	Unc
1013	1991	—	—	—	—	30.00

16.0000 g, .999 SILVER, .5145 oz ASW
Prehistoric Animals - Deinotherium - Elephant

KM#	Date	Mintage	Fine	VF	XF	Unc
1020	1993	—	—	—	Proof	50.00

10,000 AFGHANI

33.6600 g, .900 GOLD, .9739 oz AGW
Conservation - Marco Polo Sheep

KM#	Date	Mintage	Fine	VF	XF	Unc
1019	1978	—	—	—	—	550.00

Listings For

AJMAN: refer to United Arab Emirates

The Peoples Socialist Republic of Albania, a Balkan communist republic bounded by Yugoslavia, Greece, and the Adriatic Sea, has an area of 11,100 sq. mi. (28,748 sq. km.) and a population of 3 million. Capital: Tirane. The country is predominantly agricultural, although recent progress has been made in the manufacturing and mining sectors. Petroleum, chrome, iron, copper, cotton textiles, tobacco and wood products are exported.

Since it had been part of the Greek and Roman empires little is known of the early history of Albania. After the disintegration of the Roman Empire, Albania was overrun by Goths, Byzantines, Venetians, and Turks. Skanderbeg, the national hero, resisted the Turks and established an independent Albania in 1443, but in 1468 the country again fell to the Turks and remained part of the Ottoman Empire for more than 400 years.

Independence was re-established by revolt in 1912, and the present borders established in 1913 by a conference of European powers which, in 1914, placed Prince William of Wied on the throne; popular discontent forced his abdication within months. In 1920, following World War I occupancy by several nations, a republic was set up. Ahmed Zogu seized the presidency in 1925, and in 1928 proclaimed himself king with the title of Zog I. King Zog fled when Italy occupied Albania in 1939 and enthroned King Victor Emanuel of Italy. Upon the surrender of Italy to the Allies in 1943, German troops occupied the country. They withdrew in 1944, and communist partisans seized power, naming Gen. Enver Hoxha provisional president. In 1946, following a victory by the communist front in the 1945 elections, a new constitution modeled on that of the USSR was adopted. In accordance with the constitution of Dec. 28, 1976, the official name of Albania was changed from the Peoples Republic of Albania to the Peoples Socialist Republic of Albania.

RULERS

Ahmed Bey Zogu - King Zog I, 1928-1939
Vittorio Emanuele III, 1939-1943

MINT MARKS

L - London
R - Rome
V - Vienna

MONETARY SYSTEM

100 Qindar Leku = 1 Lek
100 Qindar Ari = 1 Franga Ari
= 5 Lek

KINGDOM

5 QINDAR LEKU

BRONZE

KM#	Date	Mintage	Fine	VF	XF	Unc
1	1926R	.512	15.00	35.00	65.00	140.00

QINDAR AR

BRONZE

KM#	Date	Mintage	Fine	VF	XF	Unc
14	1935R	2.000	2.00	5.00	10.00	20.00

10 QINDAR LEKU

BRONZE

KM#	Date	Mintage	Fine	VF	XF	Unc
2	1926R	.511	10.00	22.00	55.00	120.00

2 QINDAR AR

BRONZE

KM#	Date	Mintage	Fine	VF	XF	Unc
15	1935R	1.500	3.00	8.00	14.00	30.00

1/4 LEKU

NICKEL

KM#	Date	Mintage	Fine	VF	XF	Unc
3	1926R	.506	3.00	6.00	14.00	32.00
	1927R	.756	3.00	6.00	12.00	30.00

1/2 LEK

NICKEL

KM#	Date	Mintage	Fine	VF	XF	Unc
4	1926R	1.002	2.50	5.00	10.00	22.00

KM#	Date	Mintage	Fine	VF	XF	Unc
13	1930V	.500	2.00	4.00	9.00	18.00
	1931L	.500	2.00	4.00	9.00	18.00
	1931L	—	—	—	Proof	—

LEK

NICKEL

KM#	Date	Mintage	Fine	VF	XF	Unc
5	1926R	1.004	2.50	5.00	10.00	25.00
	1927R	.506	3.00	7.00	16.00	32.00
	1930V	1.250	2.00	4.00	8.50	23.50
	1931L	1.000	2.50	5.00	10.00	25.00
	1931L	—	—	—	Proof	—

FRANG AR

5.0000 g, .835 SILVER, .1342 oz ASW

KM#	Date	Mintage	Fine	VF	XF	Unc
6	1927R	.100	50.00	75.00	125.00	275.00
	1927V	.050	— Reported, not confirmed			
	1928R	.060	50.00	85.00	145.00	300.00

KM#	Date	Mintage	Fine	VF	XF	Unc
16	1935R	.700	6.00	12.00	25.00	65.00
	1937R	.600	6.00	14.00	28.00	75.00

25th Anniversary of Independence

KM#	Date	Mintage	Fine	VF	XF	Unc
18	1937R	.050	10.00	20.00	40.00	85.00

2 FRANGA AR

10.0000 g, .835 SILVER, .2684 oz ASW

KM#	Date	Mintage	Fine	VF	XF	Unc
7	1926R	.050	45.00	85.00	140.00	300.00
	1927R	.050	55.00	100.00	150.00	320.00
	1928R	.060	45.00	85.00	130.00	280.00

KM#	Date	Mintage	Fine	VF	XF	Unc
17	1935R	.150	10.00	25.00	50.00	100.00

25th Anniversary of Independence

KM#	Date	Mintage	Fine	VF	XF	Unc
19	1937R	.025	12.50	27.50	52.50	110.00

5 FRANGA AR

25.0000 g, .900 SILVER, .7234 oz ASW

KM#	Date	Mintage	Fine	VF	XF	Unc
8.1	1926R	.060	75.00	150.00	300.00	550.00

Obv: Star below bust.

KM#	Date	Mintage	Fine	VF	XF	Unc
8.2	1926R	Inc. Ab.	115.00	250.00	370.00	650.00

10 FRANGA AR

3.2258 g, .900 GOLD, .0933 oz AGW

KM#	Date	Mintage	Fine	VF	XF	Unc
9	1927R	6,000	100.00	130.00	180.00	250.00

20 FRANGA AR

6.4516 g, .900 GOLD, .1867 oz AGW

KM#	Date	Mintage	Fine	VF	XF	Unc
10	1926R	—	120.00	140.00	225.00	300.00
	1927R	6,000	120.00	150.00	250.00	325.00

George Kastrioti "Skanderbeg"

KM#	Date	Mintage	Fine	VF	XF	Unc
12	1926R	5,900	125.00	160.00	290.00	450.00
	1926 fasces					
		*100 pcs.	—	—	3000.	5000.
	1927V	5,053	—	130.00	200.00	275.00

***NOTE:** 90 pieces were reported melted.

25th Anniversary of Independence

KM#	Date	Mintage	Fine	VF	XF	Unc
20	1937R	2,500	—	150.00	280.00	450.00

King Zog Marriage

KM#	Date	Mintage	Fine	VF	XF	Unc
22	1938R	2,500	—	150.00	250.00	440.00

King Zog 10th Anniversary of Reign

KM#	Date	Mintage	Fine	VF	XF	Unc
24	1938R	1,000	—	200.00	300.00	650.00

NOTE: This piece was struck in 1969 from new dies and is possibly counterfeit.

50 FRANGA AR

16.1290 g, .900 GOLD, .4667 oz AGW
King Zog 10th Anniversary of Reign

KM#	Date	Mintage	Fine	VF	XF	Unc
25	1938R	600 pcs.	—	600.00	1250.	2000.

NOTE: This piece was struck in 1969 from new dies and is possibly counterfeit.

100 FRANGA AR

32.2580 g, .900 GOLD, .9335 oz AGW

KM#	Date	Mintage	Fine	VF	XF	Unc
11.1	1926R	*6,614	—	550.00	750.00	1100.

Obv: Star below bust.

KM#	Date	Mintage	Fine	VF	XF	Unc
11.2	1926R	Inc. Ab.	—	550.00	750.00	1100.

Obv: 2 stars below bust.

KM#	Date	Mintage	Fine	VF	XF	Unc
11.3	1926R	Inc. Ab.	—	550.00	750.00	1100.

KM#	Date	Mintage	Fine	VF	XF	Unc
11a.1	1927R	*5,000	—	550.00	750.00	1100.

Obv: Star below bust.

KM#	Date	Mintage	Fine	VF	XF	Unc
11a.2	1927R	Inc. Ab.	—	650.00	850.00	1200.

Obv: 2 stars below bust.

KM#	Date	Mintage	Fine	VF	XF	Unc
11a.3	1927R	Inc. Ab.	—	650.00	850.00	1200.

25th Anniversary of Independence

KM#	Date	Mintage	Fine	VF	XF	Unc
21	1937R	500 pcs.	—	850.00	1500.	1900.

King Zog Marriage

KM#	Date	Mintage	Fine	VF	XF	Unc
23	1938R	500 pcs.	—	800.00	1400.	1700.

King Zog 10th Anniversary of Reign

KM#	Date	Mintage	Fine	VF	XF	Unc
26	1938R	500 pcs.	—	800.00	1400.	1700.

NOTE: This piece was restruck in 1969 from new dies and is possibly counterfeit.

ITALIAN OCCUPATION WW II

MONETARY SYSTEM

1 Lek = 1 Lira

0.05 LEK

ALUMINUM-BRONZE

KM#	Date	Mintage	Fine	VF	XF	Unc
27	1940R	1.400	1.50	3.50	7.00	15.00
	1941R	.200	3.00	9.00	22.00	55.00

0.10 LEK

ALUMINUM-BRONZE

KM#	Date	Mintage	Fine	VF	XF	Unc
28	1940R	.800	2.00	5.00	9.00	22.00
	1941R	.250	17.50	35.00	65.00	125.00

0.20 LEK

NOTE: KM#29-32 each exist in 2 varieties, magnetic and non-magnetic, the latter being the scarcer.

STAINLESS STEEL

KM#	Date	Mintage	Fine	VF	XF	Unc
29	1939R	.900	1.00	2.00	2.50	7.50
	1940R	.700	1.00	2.00	3.50	9.00
	1941R	1.400	1.00	2.50	4.50	10.00

0.50 LEK

STAINLESS STEEL

KM#	Date	Mintage	Fine	VF	XF	Unc
30	1939R	.100	1.25	3.00	7.00	12.50
	1940R	.500	1.25	2.50	5.50	12.00
	1941R	.900	1.25	2.50	6.00	13.50

LEK

STAINLESS STEEL

KM#	Date	Mintage	Fine	VF	XF	Unc
31	1939R	2.100	.50	1.50	3.50	12.00
	1940R	—	60.00	120.00	230.00	360.00
	1941R	—	—	—	Rare	—

NOTE: Coins dated after 1939 were not struck for circulation.

2 LEK

STAINLESS STEEL

KM#	Date	Mintage	Fine	VF	XF	Unc
32	1939R	1.300	1.50	2.50	6.00	17.00
	1940R	—	60.00	135.00	240.00	450.00
	1941R	—	—	—	Rare	—

NOTE: Coins dated after 1939 were not struck for circulation.

5 LEK

5.0000 g, .835 SILVER, .1342 oz ASW

KM#	Date	Mintage	Fine	VF	XF	Unc
33	1939R	1.350	5.00	10.00	25.00	60.00

10 LEK

10.0000 g, .835 SILVER, .2684 oz ASW

KM#	Date	Mintage	Fine	VF	XF	Unc
34	1939R	.175	35.00	75.00	120.00	230.00

PEOPLES SOCIALIST REPUBLIC

MONETARY SYSTEM

100 Qindarka = 1 Lek

5 QINDARKA

ALUMINUM

KM#	Date	Mintage	Fine	VF	XF	Unc
39	1964	—	.10	.25	.50	1.25

25th Anniversary of Liberation

KM#	Date	Mintage	Fine	VF	XF	Unc
44	1969	—	.10	.20	.30	1.00

Plain edges.

KM#	Date	Mintage	Fine	VF	XF	Unc
71	1988	—	—	—	—	.50

10 QINDARKA

ALUMINUM

KM#	Date	Mintage	Fine	VF	XF	Unc
40	1964	—	.15	.30	.60	1.50

25th Anniversary of Liberation

KM#	Date	Mintage	Fine	VF	XF	Unc
45	1969	—	.10	.20	.35	1.25

KM#	Date	Mintage	Fine	VF	XF	Unc
60	1988	—	—	—	—	.65

20 QINDARKA

ALUMINUM

KM#	Date	Mintage	Fine	VF	XF	Unc
41	1964	—	.20	.40	.60	1.75

25th Anniversary of Liberation

KM#	Date	Mintage	Fine	VF	XF	Unc
46	1969	—	.15	.30	.50	1.50

KM#	Date	Mintage	Fine	VF	XF	Unc
65	1988	—	—	—	—	.85

1/2 LEKU

ZINC

KM#	Date	Mintage	Fine	VF	XF	Unc
35	1947	—	.40	.80	1.50	3.00
	1957	—	.40	.80	1.50	3.00

50 QINDARKA

ALUMINUM

KM#	Date	Mintage	Fine	VF	XF	Unc
42	1964	—	.50	.75	2.00	4.00

25th Anniversary of Liberation

KM#	Date	Mintage	Fine	VF	XF	Unc
47	1969	—	.30	.50	1.00	2.50

Plain edges.

KM#	Date	Mintage	Fine	VF	XF	Unc
72	1988	—	—	—	—	1.25

LEK

ZINC

KM#	Date	Mintage	Fine	VF	XF	Unc
36	1947	—	.60	1.00	2.00	4.50
	1957	—	.50	1.00	1.75	4.00

ALUMINUM

KM#	Date	Mintage	Fine	VF	XF	Unc
43	1964	—	.50	1.00	2.00	4.25

25th Anniversary of Liberation

KM#	Date	Mintage	Fine	VF	XF	Unc
48	1969	—	.35	.75	1.25	3.00

ALUMINUM-BRONZE

KM#	Date	Mintage	Fine	VF	XF	Unc
66	1988	—	—	—	—	1.50

2 LEKE

ZINC

KM#	Date	Mintage	Fine	VF	XF	Unc
37	1947	—	.45	1.00	2.00	4.50
	1957	—	.40	.80	1.75	4.00

COPPER-NICKEL
45th Anniversary of WW II.

KM#	Date	Mintage	Fine	VF	XF	Unc
67	1989	—	—	—	—	2.50

KM#	Date	Mintage	Fine	VF	XF	Unc
73	1989	—	—	—	—	2.50

5 LEKE

ZINC

KM#	Date	Mintage	Fine	VF	XF	Unc
38	1947	—	.85	1.50	3.20	6.00
	1957	—	.75	1.20	2.50	4.50

16.7500 g, .999 SILVER, .5385 oz ASW
500th Anniversary of Death of Prince Skanderberg

KM#	Date	Mintage	Fine	VF	XF	Unc
49	1968	8,540	—	—	Proof	20.00
	1969	1,500	—	—	Proof	30.00
	1970	500 pcs.	—	—	Proof	35.00

COPPER-NICKEL
Seaport of Durazzo

KM#	Date	Mintage	Fine	VF	XF	Unc
57	1987	*.050	—	—	—	6.00

42nd Anniversary of First Railroad

KM#	Date	Mintage	Fine	VF	XF	Unc
61	1988	.020	—	—	—	7.00

10 LEKE

32.8000 g, .999 SILVER, 1.0545 oz ASW
500th Anniversary of Death of Prince Skanderberg
Rev: Similar to 5 Leke, KM#49.

KM#	Date	Mintage	Fine	VF	XF	Unc
50	1968	8,540	—	—	Proof	40.00
	1969	1,500	—	—	Proof	50.00
	1970	500 pcs.	—	—	Proof	120.00

52.5000 g, .925 SILVER, 1.5613 oz ASW
1992 Olympics - Equestrian Right - Incuse Design

KM#	Date	Mintage	Fine	VF	XF	Unc
68	1991	980 pcs.	—	—	—	125.00

1992 Olympics - Equestrian Left - Raised Design

KM#	Date	Mintage	Fine	VF	XF	Unc
69	1991	980 pcs.	—	—	—	125.00

28.4600 g, .925 SILVER, .8464 oz ASW
Olympics - Boxer

KM#	Date	Mintage	Fine	VF	XF	Unc
70	1992	—	—	—	Proof	45.00

20 LEKE

3.9500 g, .900 GOLD, .1143 oz AGW
500th Anniversary of Death of Prince Skanderberg
Obv: Date on ribbon. Rev: Fineness c/m at left of LEKE.

KM#	Date	Mintage	Fine	VF	XF	Unc
51.1	1968	2,920	—	—	Proof	90.00

Rev: Fineness c/m at left, close to LEKE.

KM#	Date	Mintage	Fine	VF	XF	Unc
51.2	1968	Inc.Ab.	—	—	Proof	90.00

Rev: Fineness c/m at right of LEKE.

KM#	Date	Mintage	Fine	VF	XF	Unc
51.3	1968	Inc.Ab.	—	—	Proof	90.00

Rev: W/o fineness c/m.

KM#	Date	Mintage	Fine	VF	XF	Unc
51.4	1968	Inc.Ab.	—	—	Proof	90.00

Rev: Date added below arms.

KM#	Date	Mintage	Fine	VF	XF	Unc
51.5	1969	650 pcs.	—	—	Proof	130.00
	1970	500 pcs.	—	—	Proof	140.00

Rev: Cornucopia c/m at right of LEKE.

KM#	Date	Mintage	Fine	VF	XF	Unc
51.6	1968 Paris	24 pcs.	—	—	—	400.00

25 LEKE

82.8000 g, .999 SILVER, 2.6621 oz ASW
500th Anniversary of Death of Prince Skanderberg
Rev: Similar to KM#52.2 but w/o date.

KM#	Date	Mintage	Fine	VF	XF	Unc
52.1	1968	8,540	—	—	Proof	90.00
	1969	1,500	—	—	Proof	115.00

Rev: Date below arms.

KM#	Date	Mintage	Fine	VF	XF	Unc
52.2	1970	500 pcs.	—	—	Proof	175.00

50 LEKE

9.8700 g, .900 GOLD, .2856 oz AGW
500th Anniversary of Death of Prince Skanderberg

KM#	Date	Mintage	Fine	VF	XF	Unc
53	1968	3,120	—	—	Proof	180.00
	1969	500 pcs.	—	—	Proof	250.00
	1970	100 pcs.	—	—	Proof	285.00

168.1500 g, .925 SILVER, 5.0012 oz ASW
Illustration reduced. Actual size: 65mm.
Obv: Similar to 5 Leke, KM#57.
Seaport of Durazzo

KM#	Date	Mintage	Fine	VF	XF	Unc
58	1987	*.015	—	—	Proof	150.00

Illustration reduced. Actual size: 65mm.
42nd Anniversary of First Railroad

KM#	Date	Mintage	Fine	VF	XF	Unc
62	1988	7,500	—	—	Proof	200.00

100 LEKE

19.7500 g, .900 GOLD, .5715 oz AGW
500th Anniversary of Death of Prince Skanderberg

KM#	Date	Mintage	Fine	VF	XF	Unc
54	1968	3,470	—	—	Proof	350.00
	1969	450 pcs.	—	—	Proof	400.00
	1970	Inc. Ab.	—	—	Proof	500.00

6.4500 g, .900 GOLD, .1866 oz AGW
Seaport of Durazzo
Similar to 5 Leke, KM#57.

KM#	Date	Mintage	Fine	VF	XF	Unc
59	1987	5,000	—	—	Proof	165.00

42nd Anniversary of First Railroad

Similar to 50 Leke, KM#62 but w/o hole in coin.

KM#	Date	Mintage	Fine	VF	XF	Unc
63	1988	2,000	—	—	Proof	275.00

200 LEKE

39.4900 g, .900 GOLD, 1.1427 oz AGW
500th Anniversary of Death of Prince Skanderberg
Rev: Similar to 100 Leke, KM#54.

KM#	Date	Mintage	Fine	VF	XF	Unc
55	1968	2,170	—	—	Proof	600.00
	1969	200 pcs.	—	—	Proof	725.00
	1970	Inc. Ab.	—	—	Proof	800.00

500 LEKE

98.7400 g, .900 GOLD, 2.8574 oz AGW
500th Anniversary of Death of Prince Skanderberg
Rev: Similar to 100 Leke, KM#54.

KM#	Date	Mintage	Fine	VF	XF	Unc
56	1968	1,520	—	—	Proof	1500.
	1969	200 pcs.	—	—	Proof	1700.
	1970	Inc. Ab.	—	—	Proof	1800.

7500 LEKE

483.7500 g, .900 GOLD, 13.9992 oz AGW
42nd Anniversary of First Railroad
Similar to 50 Leke, KM#62.

KM#	Date	Mintage	Fine	VF	XF	Unc
64	1988	50 pcs.	—	—	Proof	8000.

PROOF SETS (PS)

KM#	Date	Mintage	Identification	Issue Price	Mkt. Val.
PS1	1968(5)	1,540	KM51,53-56	470.00	2750.
PS2	1968(3)	8,540	KM49,50,52	44.00	150.00
PS3	1969(5)	—	KM51,53-56	470.00	3200.
PS4	1969(3)	1,500	KM49,50,52	45.00	195.00
PS5	1970(5)	—	KM51.5,53-56	516.00	3525.
PS6	1970(3)	500	KM49,50,52	45.00	330.00
PS7	1991(2)	980	KM68-69	—	250.00

ALDERNEY

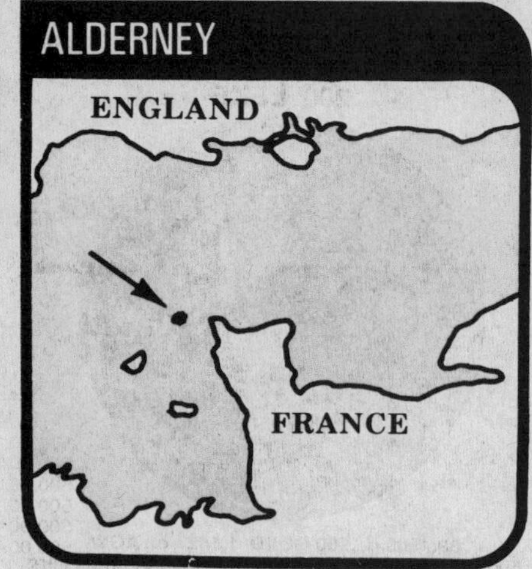

Alderney, the northernmost and third largest of the Channel Islands, separated from the coast of France by the dangerous 8 mile wide tidal channel, has an area of 3 sq. mi. (8 km.) and a population of 1,686. Capital: St. Anne. Principal industries are agriculture and cattle raising.

There is evidence of settlement in prehistoric times and Roman coins are reported to have been found on the island along with evidence of their buildings. Toward the close of the reign of Henry VIII, France began making plans to sieze the Island of Sark. The English, realizing its strategic importance, began to build a defensive fort, which was abandoned some years later when Edward VI died. France constructed a large naval base at its northern tip which incited the English into making Alderney the "Gibraltar of the Channel."

Most of the Islanders were evacuated before the German occupation in 1940 but returned in 1945 when the Germans surrendered.

The Channel Islands have never been subject to the British Parliament and are self-governing units under the direct rule of the Crown acting through the Privy Council. Legislation was only recently introduced for the issue of its own coinage, a right it now shares with Jersey and Guernsey.

RULERS

British

MONETARY SYSTEM

5 New Pence = 1 Shilling
25 New Pence = 1 Crown
100 New Pence = 1 Pound

POUND

9.5000 g, .925 SILVER, .2826 oz ASW
40th Anniversary of Coronation

KM#	Date	Mintage	VF	XF	Unc
4	1993	*.020	—	Proof	30.00

2 POUNDS

COPPER-NICKEL
Royal Visit

KM#	Date	Mintage	VF	XF	Unc
1	1989	—	—	—	7.00
	28.2800 g, .925 SILVER, .8411 oz ASW				
1a	1989	5,000	—	Proof	50.00
	47.5400 g, .917 GOLD, 1.4011 oz AGW				
1b	1989	100 pcs.	—	Proof	900.00

COPPER-NICKEL
90th Birthday of Queen Mother

KM#	Date	Mintage	VF	XF	Unc
2	1990	—	—	—	8.00
	28.2800 g, .925 SILVER, .8411 oz ASW				
2a	1990	5,000	—	Proof	50.00
	47.5400 g, .917 GOLD, 1.4011 oz AGW				
2b	1990	90 pcs.	—	Proof	1150.

COPPER-NICKEL
40th Anniversary of Reign

KM#	Date	Mintage	VF	XF	Unc
3	1992	—	—	—	7.50
	28.2800 g, .925 SILVER, .8411 oz ASW				
3a	1992	5,000	—	Proof	50.00
	47.5400 g, .917 GOLD, 1.4011 oz AGW				
3b	1992	150 pcs.	—	Proof	1000.

COPPER-NICKEL
40th Anniversary of Coronation

KM#	Date	Mintage	VF	XF	Unc
5	1993	—	—	—	7.00
	28.2800 g, .925 SILVER, .8411 oz ASW				
5a	1993	*5,000	—	Proof	50.00

25 POUNDS

8.5130 g, .917 GOLD, .2507 oz AGW
40th Anniversary of Coronation

KM#	Date	Mintage	VF	XF	Unc
6	1993	*1,000	—	Proof	200.00

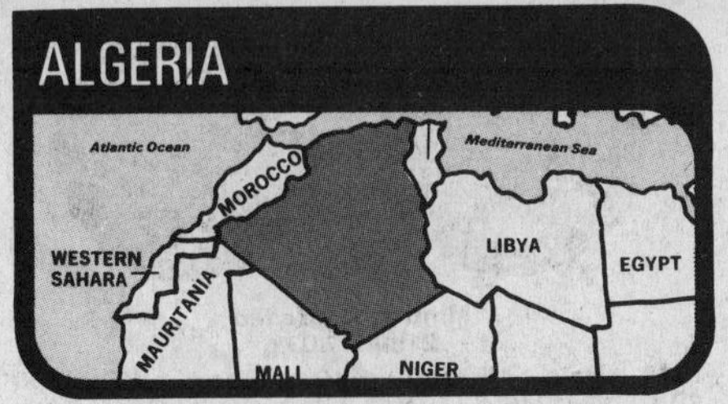

The Democratic and Popular Republic of Algeria, a North African country fronting on the Mediterranean Sea between Tunisia and Morocco, has an area of 919,595 sq. mi. (2,381,740 sq. km.) and a population of 25 million. Capital: Algiers. Most of the country's working population is engaged in agriculture although a recent industrial diversification, financed by oil revenues, is making steady progress. Wines, fruits, iron and zinc ores, phosphates, tobacco products, liquified natural gas, and petroleum are exported.

Algiers, the capital and chief seaport of Algeria, was the site of Phoenician and Roman settlements before the present Moslem city was founded about 950. Nominally part of the sultanate of Tilimsan, Algiers had a large measure of independence under amirs of its own. In 1492 the Jews and Moors who had been expelled from Spain settled in Algiers and enjoyed an increasing influence until the imposition of Turkish control in 1518. For the following three centuries Algiers was the headquarters of the notorious Barbary pirates as Turkish control became more and more nominal. The French took Algiers in 1830, and after a long and wearisome war completed the conquest of Algeria and annexed it to France, 1848, becoming a colony, then a territory, and finally, in the northern provinces, French departments. The inability to obtain equal rights with Frenchmen led to an organized revolt which began on Nov. 1, 1954 and lasted until a ceasefire was signed on July I, 1962. Independence was proclaimed on July 3, 1962, following a self-determination referendum, and the Republic was declared on September 25, 1962.

RULERS

Ottoman, until 1830
Abd-el-Kader (rebel)
AH1250-1264/1834-1847AD

ALGIERS

MINTNAMES

Jaza'Ir جزاير

Jaza'Ir Gharb لجزاير غرب

AH1012-1115/1603-1703AD

al-Mascara المعسكر

During revolt of Abd-el-Kader
AH1250-1264/1834-1847AD

Medea مديه

AH1246/1830AD

Qusantinah
Constantine قسنطينة

AH1245-1254/1830-1837AD

Taqidemt تاقدمت

During revolt of Abd-el-Kader
AH1250-1264/1834-1847AD

NOTE: The dots above and below the letters are integral parts of the letters, but for stylistic reasons, are occasionally omitted.

MONETARY SYSTEM
(Until 1847)

14-1/2 Asper (Akche, Dirham Saghir)
= 1 Kharub
2 Kharuba = 1 Muzuna
24 Muzuna = 1 Budju

NOTE: Coin denominations are not expressed on the coins, and are best determined by size and weight. The silver Budju weighed about 13.5 g until AH1236/1821AD, when it was reduced to about 10.0 g. The fractional pieces varied in proportion to the Budju. They had secondary names, which are given in the text. In 1829 three new silver coins were introduced and Budju became Tugrali-rial, Tugrali-batlaka = 1/3 Rial = 8 Muzuna and Tugrali-nessflik = 1/2 Batlaka = 4 Muzuna. The gold Sultani was officially valued at 108 Muzuna, but varied in accordance with the market price of gold expressed in silver. It weighed 3.20-3.40 g.

OTTOMAN COINAGE

SELIM III

AH1203-1222/1789-1807AD

FELS

COPPER, 1.73 g
Obv. leg: ***Sultan Selim.***
Rev: Mintname: ***Jaza'Ir*** **within octogram.**

KM#	Date	Mintage	Good	VG	Fine	VF
52	AH122x	—	45.00	90.00	150.00	—

1/8 BUDJU

(3 Mazuna)

SILVER, 1.65-1.70 g
Mintname: ***Jaza'Ir***

KM#	Date	Mintage	VG	Fine	VF	XF
40	AH1216	—	20.00	40.00	60.00	100.00
	1218	—	20.00	40.00	60.00	100.00
	1220	—	20.00	40.00	60.00	100.00

NOTE: Earlier dates (AH1200-1215) exist for this type.

Rev: Mintname within octagram.

KM#	Date	Mintage	VG	Fine	VF	XF
47	AH1221	—	40.00	60.00	125.00	175.00
	1222	—	40.00	60.00	125.00	175.00

1/4 BUDJU

SILVER, 2.90-3.40 g, 19-20mm
Mintname: ***Jaza'Ir***

KM#	Date	Mintage	VG	Fine	VF	XF
42	AH1216	—	20.00	35.00	60.00	100.00
	1217	—	20.00	35.00	60.00	100.00
	1218	—	20.00	35.00	60.00	100.00
	1219	—	20.00	35.00	60.00	100.00
	1220	—	20.00	35.00	60.00	100.00

NOTE: Earlier dates (AH1205-1215) exist for this type.

Rev: Mintname within octagram.

KM#	Date	Mintage	VG	Fine	VF	XF
48	AH1221	—	40.00	75.00	125.00	175.00
	1222	—	40.00	75.00	125.00	175.00
	1223	—	40.00	75.00	125.00	175.00

1/2 BUDJU

SILVER, 5.80-6.80 g
Mintname: ***Jaza'Ir***

KM#	Date	Mintage	VG	Fine	VF	XF
45	AH1216	—	60.00	100.00	150.00	225.00
	1217	—	60.00	100.00	150.00	225.00
	1218	—	60.00	100.00	150.00	225.00
	1219	—	60.00	100.00	150.00	225.00
	1220	—	60.00	100.00	150.00	225.00

NOTE: Earlier dates (AH1213-1215) exist for this type.

1/4 SULTANI

GOLD, 15-16mm, 0.85 g
Mintname: ***Jaza'Ir***
Obv. leg: 2 lines. Rev: Mintname above date.

KM#	Date	Mintage	VG	Fine	VF	XF
44	AH1217	—	65.00	100.00	200.00	250.00
	1219	—	65.00	100.00	200.00	250.00

NOTE: Earlier dates (AH1209-1214) exist for this type.

Rev: Mintname within octagram.

KM#	Date	Mintage	VG	Fine	VF	XF
49	AH1221	—	150.00	225.00	300.00	375.00
	1222	—	150.00	225.00	300.00	375.00

1/2 SULTANI

GOLD, 1.54-1.70 g, 18-19mm
Mintname: ***Jaza'Ir***

KM#	Date	Mintage	VG	Fine	VF	XF
46	AH1216	—	100.00	150.00	200.00	275.00
	1217	—	100.00	150.00	200.00	275.00
	1218	—	100.00	150.00	200.00	275.00
	1219	—	100.00	150.00	200.00	275.00

NOTE: Earlier date (AH1215) exists for this type.

Rev: Mintname within octagram.

KM#	Date	Mintage	VG	Fine	VF	XF
50	AH1221	—	200.00	275.00	375.00	500.00
	1222	—	200.00	275.00	375.00	500.00

SULTANI

GOLD, 3.25-3.40 g, 22-25mm
Mintname: ***Jaza'Ir***

KM#	Date	Mintage	VG	Fine	VF	XF
41	AH1216	—	200.00	275.00	375.00	500.00
	1217	—	200.00	275.00	375.00	500.00
	1218	—	200.00	275.00	375.00	500.00
	1219	—	200.00	275.00	375.00	500.00
	1220	—	200.00	275.00	375.00	500.00
	1221	—	200.00	275.00	375.00	500.00

NOTE: Earlier dates (AH1204-1215) exist for this type.

3.10 g
Rev: Mintname within octagram.

KM#	Date	Mintage	VG	Fine	VF	XF
51	AH1221	—	—	—	Rare	—
	1222	—	—	—	Rare	—

MUSTAFA IV

AH1222-1223/1807-1808AD

1/8 BUDJU

SILVER, 16mm, 1.48 g
Mintname: ***Jaza'Ir***

KM#	Date	Mintage	VG	Fine	VF	XF
53	AH1222	—	100.00	150.00	250.00	350.00
	1223	—	100.00	150.00	250.00	350.00

1/4 BUDJU

SILVER, 2.88-3.40 g
Mintname: ***Jaza'Ir***

KM#	Date	Mintage	VG	Fine	VF	XF
54	AH1222	—	100.00	150.00	250.00	350.00
	1223	—	100.00	150.00	250.00	350.00

1/4 SULTANI

GOLD, 0.80 g
Mintname: ***Jaza'Ir***

KM#	Date	Mintage	VG	Fine	VF	XF
55	AH1222	—	—	—	Rare	—
	1223	—	—	—	Rare	—

1/2 SULTANI

GOLD, 1.60-1.73 g
Mintname: ***Jaza'Ir***

KM#	Date	Mintage	VG	Fine	VF	XF
56	AH1222	—	—	—	Rare	—
	1223	—	—	—	Rare	—

SULTANI

GOLD, 3.15-3.40 g
Mintname: ***Jaza'Ir***

KM#	Date	Mintage	VG	Fine	VF	XF
57	AH1222	—	—	—	Rare	—
	1223	—	—	—	Rare	—

MAHMUD II

AH1223-1255/1808-1839AD

NOTE: Asper previously listed here was in error and is correctly listed as a Burben under Tunis.

2 ASPERS

COPPER, 0.80 g
Mintname: *Jaza'Ir*

KM#	Date	Mintage	VG	Fine	VF	XF
70	AH1237	—	15.00	25.00	36.50	70.00
	1238	—	15.00	25.00	36.50	70.00
	1240	—	15.00	25.00	36.50	70.00
	1242	—	15.00	25.00	36.50	70.00
	1243	—	15.00	25.00	36.50	70.00
	1244	—	15.00	25.00	36.50	70.00

Mintname: *Constantine*

KM#	Date	Mintage	Good	VG	Fine	VF
81	AH1247	—	40.00	60.00	90.00	135.00
	1250	—	40.00	60.00	90.00	135.00

NOTE: Varieties exist.

5 ASPERS

(Valued at 1/3 Kharuba)

COPPER, 1.80-2.20 g
Mintname: *Jaza'Ir*

KM#	Date	Mintage	VG	Fine	VF	XF
71	AH1237	—	12.50	22.50	35.00	50.00
	1238	—	12.50	22.50	35.00	50.00
	1239	—	12.50	22.50	35.00	50.00
	1240	—	15.00	25.00	40.00	60.00
	1244	—	10.00	20.00	30.00	45.00

NOTE: The 5 Aspers formerly listed as C#140 is probably an example of the 1/8 Budju, KM#74, of very base metal.

10 ASPERS

COPPER

KM#	Date	Mintage	VG	Fine	VF	XF
72	AH1237	—	—	—	Unc.	1500.

NOTE: Possibly a pattern issue.

KHARUB

BILLON, 14mm, 0.70-0.80 g
Mintname: *Jaza'Ir*

KM#	Date	Mintage	VG	Fine	VF	XF
73	AH1237	—	10.00	15.00	30.00	75.00
	1238	—	10.00	15.00	30.00	75.00
	1240	—	10.00	15.00	30.00	75.00
	1242	—	10.00	15.00	30.00	75.00

0.70-0.90 g
Mintname: *Constantine*

KM#	Date	Mintage	VG	Fine	VF	XF
76	AH1245	—	50.00	100.00	175.00	275.00
	1246	—	50.00	100.00	175.00	275.00
	1247	—	50.00	100.00	175.00	275.00
	1250	—	50.00	100.00	175.00	275.00
	1252	—	50.00	100.00	175.00	275.00

1/8 BUDJU

(Temin Budju = 3 Muzuna)

SILVER, 1.65-1.70 g
Mintname: *Jaza'Ir*

KM#	Date	Mintage	VG	Fine	VF	XF
61	AH1225	—	25.00	45.00	75.00	125.00
	1226	—	25.00	45.00	75.00	125.00
	1227	—	25.00	45.00	75.00	125.00
	1228	—	25.00	45.00	75.00	125.00
	1229	—	25.00	45.00	75.00	125.00
	1230	—	25.00	45.00	75.00	125.00
	1231	—	25.00	45.00	75.00	125.00
	1232	—	25.00	45.00	75.00	125.00
	1233	—	25.00	45.00	75.00	125.00
	1234	—	25.00	45.00	75.00	125.00
	1235	—	25.00	45.00	75.00	125.00

Reduced standard, 1.20-1.30 g

KM#	Date	Mintage	VG	Fine	VF	XF
74	AH1237	—	10.00	15.00	30.00	65.00
	1238	—	10.00	15.00	30.00	65.00
	1239	—	10.00	15.00	30.00	65.00
	1240	—	10.00	15.00	30.00	65.00
	1242	—	10.00	15.00	30.00	65.00
	1243	—	10.00	15.00	30.00	65.00
	1244	—	10.00	15.00	30.00	65.00
	1245	—	10.00	15.00	30.00	65.00

1/6 BUDJU

(Tugrali-ness-flik)
(4 Muzuna = 1/2 Batlaka)

SILVER, 1.50 g

KM#	Date	Mintage	Fine	VF	XF	Unc
77	AH1245	—	35.00	70.00	120.00	200.00

SILVER or BILLON, 18-19mm, 1.40-1.50 g
Mintname: *Constantine*

KM#	Date	Mintage	VG	Fine	VF	XF
82	AH1247	—	50.00	100.00	175.00	250.00
	1248	—	50.00	100.00	175.00	250.00
	1252	—	50.00	100.00	175.00	250.00

1/4 BUDJU

(6 Muzuna = Rebi Budju)

SILVER, 20mm, 3.40 g
Mintname: *Jaza'Ir*
Octagram type

KM#	Date	Mintage	VG	Fine	VF	XF
59	AH1223	—	40.00	75.00	125.00	200.00
	1224	—	40.00	75.00	125.00	200.00

KM#	Date	Mintage	VG	Fine	VF	XF
62	AH1225	—	35.00	60.00	100.00	150.00
	1226	—	35.00	60.00	100.00	150.00
	1227	—	35.00	60.00	100.00	150.00
	1228	—	35.00	60.00	100.00	150.00
	1229	—	35.00	60.00	100.00	150.00
	1230	—	35.00	60.00	100.00	150.00
	1231	—	35.00	60.00	100.00	150.00
	1232	—	35.00	60.00	100.00	150.00
	1233	—	35.00	60.00	100.00	150.00
	1234	—	35.00	60.00	100.00	150.00
	1235	—	35.00	60.00	100.00	150.00

Reduced standard, 2.40 g

KM#	Date	Mintage	Fine	VF	XF	Unc
67	AH1236	—	15.00	30.00	55.00	90.00
	1237	—	12.50	22.00	35.00	60.00
	1238	—	12.50	22.00	35.00	60.00
	1239	—	12.50	22.00	35.00	60.00
	1240	—	12.50	22.00	35.00	60.00
	1241	—	12.50	22.00	35.00	60.00
	1242	—	12.50	22.00	35.00	60.00
	1243	—	12.50	22.00	35.00	60.00
	1244	—	12.50	22.00	35.00	60.00
	1245	—	15.00	27.50	50.00	85.00
	1246	—	20.00	35.00	60.00	100.00

Mintname: *Medea*
21mm, 2.03 g

KM#	Date	Mintage	VG	Fine	VF	XF
80.1	AH1246	—	—	—	Rare	—

Mintname: *Constantine*
21mm, 2.00 g
Obv: Ornament and Sultan's name around.
Rev: Similar to KM#67.

KM#	Date	Mintage	VG	Fine	VF	XF
80.2	AH1246	—	—	—	Rare	—

1/3 BUDJU

(Tugrali-batlaka)

SILVER, 3.10 g
Toughra type

KM#	Date	Mintage	Fine	VF	XF	Unc
78	AH1245	—	45.00	75.00	135.00	245.00

NOTE: Varieties exist.

BUDJU

SILVER, 9.80-10.10 g
Mintname: *Jaza'Ir*

KM#	Date	Mintage	VG	Fine	VF	XF
68	AH1236	—	20.00	45.00	100.00	175.00
	1237	—	16.00	30.00	65.00	110.00
	1238	—	16.00	30.00	65.00	110.00
	1239	—	16.00	30.00	65.00	110.00
	1240	—	16.00	30.00	65.00	110.00
	1241	—	16.00	30.00	65.00	110.00
	1242	—	20.00	30.00	65.00	110.00
	1243	—	25.00	45.00	100.00	175.00
	1244	—	40.00	45.00	100.00	175.00
	1245	—	45.00	100.00	200.00	350.00

(Tugrali-rial)

10.020 g
Mintname: *Jaza'Ir*

KM#	Date	Mintage	VG	Fine	VF	XF
79	AH1245	—	70.00	120.00	200.00	300.00

SILVER or BILLON, 7.90-9.80 g
Mintname: *Constantine*

KM#	Date	Mintage	VG	Fine	VF	XF
83	AH1247	—	100.00	150.00	350.00	750.00
	1248	—	100.00	150.00	350.00	750.00
	1249	—	100.00	170.00	380.00	900.00
	1250	—	100.00	170.00	380.00	900.00
	1253	—	100.00	150.00	350.00	750.00

2 BUDJU

(Zudj Budju)

SILVER, 19.50-20.00 g
Mintname: *Jaza'Ir*

KM#	Date	Mintage	VG	Fine	VF	XF
75	AH1236	—	30.00	50.00	80.00	120.00
	1237	—	30.00	50.00	80.00	120.00
	1238	—	30.00	50.00	80.00	120.00
	1239	—	30.00	50.00	80.00	120.00
	1240	—	35.00	60.00	90.00	130.00
	1241	—	30.00	50.00	80.00	120.00
	1242	—	30.00	50.00	80.00	120.00
	1243	—	40.00	60.00	100.00	175.00
	1244	—	65.00	95.00	170.00	275.00

NOTE: Varieties exist.

1/4 SULTANI

GOLD, 14-15mm, 0.78-0.85 g
Mintname: *Jaza'Ir*
Obv: *Sultan Mahmud.*

KM#	Date	Mintage	VG	Fine	VF	XF
63.1	AH1224	—	—	—	Rare	—
	1228	—	—	—	Rare	—
	1234	—	—	—	Rare	—

Obv: *Sultan Mahmud Han.*

KM#	Date	Mintage	VG	Fine	VF	XF
63.2	AH1231	—	85.00	125.00	175.00	250.00
	1238	—	85.00	125.00	175.00	250.00
	1240	—	85.00	125.00	175.00	250.00
	1243	—	85.00	125.00	175.00	250.00

GOLD, 0.705 g

KM#	Date	Mintage	VG	Fine	VF	XF
64.1	AH1246	1 known	—	—	2500.	—

Mintname: *Medea*

KM#	Date	Mintage	VG	Fine	VF	XF
64.2	AH1246	—	—	—	Rare	—

1/2 SULTANI

GOLD, 1.15-1.60 g
Mintname: *Jaza'Ir*

KM#	Date	Mintage	VG	Fine	VF	XF
65	AH1231	—	100.00	140.00	200.00	275.00
	1232	—	100.00	140.00	200.00	275.00
	1234	—	100.00	140.00	200.00	275.00
	1236	—	100.00	140.00	200.00	275.00
	1237	—	100.00	140.00	200.00	275.00
	1238	—	100.00	140.00	200.00	275.00
	1239	—	100.00	140.00	200.00	275.00
	1240	—	100.00	140.00	200.00	275.00

NOTE: Varieties exist.

SULTANI

GOLD, 22-24mm, 3.20 g
Mintname: *Jaza'Ir*

Rev: Year in fourth line.

KM#	Date	Mintage	VG	Fine	VF	XF
60	AH1223	—	250.00	350.00	450.00	575.00
	1224	—	250.00	350.00	450.00	575.00
	1225	—	250.00	350.00	450.00	575.00
	1226	—	250.00	350.00	450.00	575.00
	1228	—	250.00	350.00	450.00	575.00
	1231	—	250.00	350.00	450.00	575.00
	1232	—	250.00	350.00	450.00	575.00
	1234	—	250.00	350.00	450.00	575.00

Rev: Year in third line.

KM#	Date	Mintage	VG	Fine	VF	XF
66	AH1235	—	165.00	225.00	300.00	400.00
	1236	—	165.00	225.00	300.00	400.00
	1237	—	165.00	225.00	300.00	400.00
	1238	—	165.00	225.00	300.00	400.00
	1239	—	165.00	225.00	300.00	400.00
	1240	—	165.00	225.00	300.00	400.00
	1241	—	165.00	225.00	300.00	400.00
	1243	—	165.00	225.00	300.00	400.00
	3421(error)	—	165.00	225.00	300.00	400.00
	1244	—	165.00	225.00	300.00	400.00
	1245	—	275.00	400.00	550.00	750.00

Mintname: *Constantine*
2.38 g
Obv: Toughra. Rev: 4-line leg. w/20 above *ibn*.

KM#	Date	Mintage	VG	Fine	VF	XF
69	AH1246	—	—	—	Rare	—

REVOLUTIONARY COINAGE

ABDEL KADER

AH1250-1264/1834-1847AD

5 ASPERS/KHARUBA

(Mohammadiya)

COPPER-BILLON, .73-1.30 g
Mintname: *Taqidemt*
12-18mm

KM#	Date	Mintage	VG	Fine	VF	XF
85	AH1250	—	25.00	40.00	60.00	120.00
	1252	—	25.00	40.00	60.00	120.00
	1253	—	25.00	40.00	60.00	120.00
	1254, Arabic '4'	—	22.50	35.00	45.00	90.00
	1254, Persian '4'	—	22.50	35.00	45.00	90.00
	1255	—	22.50	35.00	45.00	90.00
	1256	—	22.50	35.00	45.00	90.00
	1257	—	25.00	40.00	60.00	120.00

Reduced size. 8mm, 0.40-0.70 g
Obv: Different legend.

KM#	Date	Mintage	VG	Fine	VF	XF
86	AH1258	—	17.50	35.00	55.00	110.00

KHARUBA

BILLON
Mintname: *Al Mascara*

KM#	Date	Mintage	VG	Fine	VF	XF
87	AH1254	—	70.00	100.00	150.00	250.00

1/6 BUDJU

(3 Muzuna-Nasfia)

BILLON, 1.00 g
Mintname: *Taqidemt*

KM#	Date	Mintage	VG	Fine	VF	XF
88	AH1254	—	100.00	160.00	285.00	465.00

1/2 BUDJU

Silver, 2.88 g
Mintname: *Taqidemt*
Obv: *Victory of God and Conquest is Near.*

KM#	Date	Mintage	VG	Fine	VF	XF
90	AH1256	—	—	—	Rare	—

BUDJU

SILVER, 27-28mm, 5.57-6.03 g
Mintname: *Taqidemt*
Denomination uncertain
Obv: 3 lines. Rev: 4 lines.

KM#	Date	Mintage	VG	Fine	VF	XF
89	AH1256	—	150.00	300.00	600.00	900.00

NOTE: This coin has also been considered to be a 1/2 Budju, but its weight apparently indicates a reduced Budju in debased metal. Varieties exist.

ALGERIA

FRENCH OCCUPATION

(until July, 1962)

MINT MARKS
(a) Paris - Privy marks only

MONETARY SYSTEM
100 Centimes = 1 Franc

20 FRANCS

COPPER-NICKEL

KM#	Date	Mintage	Fine	VF	XF	Unc
91	1949(a)	25.566	.50	1.00	2.50	8.50
	1956(a)	7.500	.50	1.00	3.00	12.50

50 FRANCS

COPPER-NICKEL

KM#	Date	Mintage	Fine	VF	XF	Unc
92	1949(a)	18.000	2.00	3.00	8.00	15.00

100 FRANCS

COPPER-NICKEL

KM#	Date	Mintage	Fine	VF	XF	Unc
93	1950(a)	22.189	1.50	3.00	6.50	20.00
	1952(a)	12.000	2.00	3.50	7.50	25.00

NOTE: During World War II homeland coins were struck at the Paris Mint and the France 2 Francs, Y#89 were struck at the Philadelphia Mint for use in French African Territories.

REPUBLIC

MONETARY SYSTEM
100 Centimes = 1 Dinar

CENTIME

ALUMINUM

KM#	Date	Year	Mintage	VF	XF	Unc
94	AH1383	1964	35.000	—	—	.10

2 CENTIMES

ALUMINUM

KM#	Date	Year	Mintage	VF	XF	Unc
95	AH1383	1964	50.000	—	.10	.25

5 CENTIMES

ALUMINUM

KM#	Date	Year	Mintage	VF	XF	Unc
96	AH1383	1964	40.000	—	.10	.25

1st Four Year Plan and F.A.O. Issue

KM#	Date	Mintage	VF	XF	Unc
101	1970/73	10.000	—	.15	.50

2nd Four Year Plan and F.A.O. Issue

KM#	Date	Mintage	VF	XF	Unc
106	1974/77	10.000	—	.15	.50

1st Five Year Plan and F.A.O. Issue

KM#	Date	Mintage	VF	XF	Unc
113	ND(1980/84)	—	—	.20	.70

2nd Five Year Plan and F.A.O. Issue

KM#	Date	Mintage	VF	XF	Unc
116	1985/89	—	—	.20	.70

NOTE: Varieties exist.

10 CENTIMES

ALUMINUM-BRONZE

KM#	Date	Year	Mintage	VF	XF	Unc
97	AH1383	1964	—	.10	.20	.40

ALUMINUM

KM#	Date	Mintage	VF	XF	Unc
115	1984	—	.10	.20	.40

NOTE: Varieties exist.

20 CENTIMES

ALUMINUM-BRONZE

KM#	Date	Year	Mintage	VF	XF	Unc
98	AH1383	1964	—	.10	.25	.60

BRASS

Agricultural Revolution and F.A.O. Issue

KM#	Date	Mintage	VF	XF	Unc
103	1972	20.000	.10	.25	.65

ALUMINUM-BRONZE
F.A.O. Issue

KM#	Date	Mintage	VF	XF	Unc
107.1	1975	50.000	.15	.30	1.35

Obv: Small flower above 20.

KM#	Date	Mintage	VF	XF	Unc
107.2	1975	Inc. Ab.	.15	.30	1.35

F.A.O. Issue

KM#	Date	Mintage	VF	XF	Unc
118	1987	60.000	.15	.30	1.25

50 CENTIMES

ALUMINUM-BRONZE

KM#	Date	Year	Mintage	VF	XF	Unc
99	AH1383	1964	—	.20	.30	.75

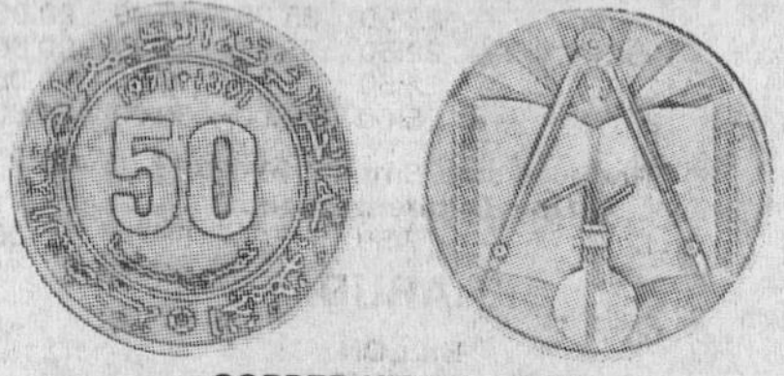

COPPER-NICKEL-ZINC

KM#	Date	Year	Mintage	VF	XF	Unc
102	AH1391	1971	10.000	.15	.25	.60
	1393	1973	—	.15	.25	.60

BRASS
30th Anniversary French-Algerian Clash

KM#	Date	Mintage	VF	XF	Unc
109	ND(1975)	18.000	.20	.50	2.00

ALUMINUM-BRONZE
1400th Anniversary of Mohammad's Flight

KM#	Date	Year	Mintage	VF	XF	Unc
111	AH1400	1980	—	.20	.50	2.50
	1401	1981	—	.20	.50	2.50

25th Anniversary of Constitution

KM#	Date	Mintage	VF	XF	Unc
119	1988	—	.15	.30	1.50

DINAR

COPPER-NICKEL

KM#	Date	Year	Mintage	VF	XF	Unc
100	AH1383	1964	15.000	.40	.80	1.50

F.A.O. Issue

KM#	Date	Mintage	VF	XF	Unc
104.1	1972	20.000	.35	.75	2.25

Legend touches inner circle.

KM#	Date	Mintage	VF	XF	Unc
104.2	1972	Inc. Ab.	.35	.75	2.25

20th Anniversary of Independence

KM#	Date	Mintage	VF	XF	Unc
112	1983	—	.50	1.00	3.50

25th Anniversary of Independence - Monument

KM#	Date	Mintage	VF	XF	Unc
117	1988	—	—	—	4.00

3.2200 g, .920 GOLD, .0953 oz AGW
Historical Coin - 5 Aspers of Abd-el-Kader

KM#	Date	Year	Mintage	VF	XF	Unc
120	AH1411	1991	—	—	—	125.00

2 DINARS

6.4500 g, .920 GOLD, .1908 oz AGW
Historical Coin - Dinar of 762 A.D. Rostomiden Dynasty

KM#	Date	Year	Mintage	VF	XF	Unc
121	AH1411	1991	—	—	—	250.00

5 DINARS

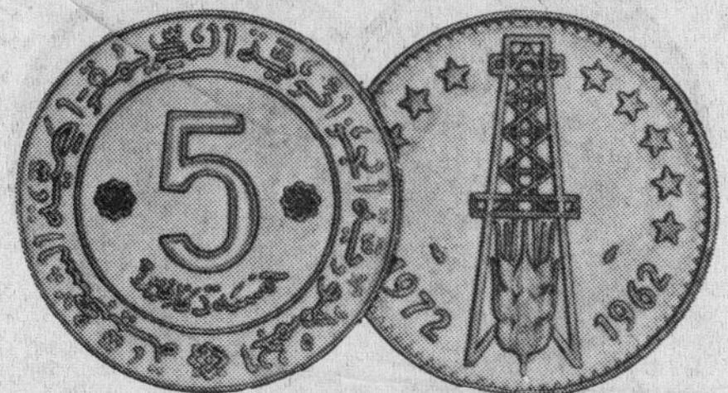

12.0000 g, .750 SILVER, .2893 oz ASW
Privy mark: Owl
10th Anniversary & F.A.O. Issue

KM#	Date	Mintage	VF	XF	Unc
105	1972(a)	—	5.00	10.00	15.00
	NICKEL				
105a.1	1972(a)	—	4.00	8.00	12.50
	Privy mark: Dolphin				
105a.2	1972(a)	—	4.00	8.00	12.50

20th Anniversary of Revolution

KM#	Date	Mintage	VF	XF	Unc
108	1974	—	4.00	8.00	12.50

30th Anniversary of Revolution

KM#	Date	Mintage	VF	XF	Unc
114	1984	—	4.00	8.00	15.00

16.1200 g, .920 GOLD, .4768 oz AGW
Historical Coin - Denar of Numidian King Massinissa, 238-148 B.C.

KM#	Date	Year	Mintage	VF	XF	Unc
122	AH1411	1991	—	—	—	550.00

10 DINARS

BRONZE, 11.37 g

KM#	Date	Mintage	VF	XF	Unc
110	1979	25.001	2.75	4.50	7.00
	1981(a)	40.000	2.75	4.50	7.00
	14.6000 g, .925 SILVER, .4342 oz ASW				
110a	1979	1,000	—	—	35.00
	24.5000 g, .900 GOLD, .7090 oz AGW				
110b	1979	100 pcs.	—	—	1250.

AMERICAN SAMOA

The Territory of American Samoa consists of seven major islands with a total land area of 76 sq. mi. (199 sq. km.) which are located about 2300 miles south-southwest of Hawaii. Population of 41,000. It was first settled by Polynesians around 600 BC. Capital: Pago Pago.

Samoa's long isolation from the western world ended in 1722 when the Dutch explorer, Jacob Roggeveen, came upon the islands. However, it wasn't until 1831 that European influence had any real impact. In that year, John Williams of the London Missionary Society arrived with eight Tahitian missionaries.

By 1900 the Samoan islands were being claimed by both Germany and the United States. Germany annexed several islands which now comprise Western Samoa; the U.S. took Tutuila to use Pago Pago Bay as a coaling station for naval ships.

As Japan began emerging as an international power in the mid-1930's, the U.S. Naval station on Tutuila began to acquire new strategic importance; and in 1940 the Samoan Islands became a training and staging area for the U.S. Marine Corps.

A. P. Lutali, Governor of American Samoa, signed a historic proclamation on May 23, 1988 that authorized the minting of the first numismatic issue for this unincorporated territory administered by the United States Department of the Interior.

MONETARY SYSTEM

100 Cents = 1 Dollar

DOLLAR

BRONZE
America's Cup

KM#	Date	Mintage	VF	XF	Unc
1	1988	2,000	—	Proof	12.50

5 DOLLARS

31.1000 g, .999 SILVER, 1.0000 oz ASW

America's Cup

KM#	Date	Mintage	VF	XF	Unc
2	1988	1,000	—	Proof	35.00

Olympics

KM#	Date	Mintage	VF	XF	Unc
6	1988	1,000	—	Proof	50.00

25 DOLLARS

155.5150 g, .999 SILVER, 5.0000 oz ASW
America's Cup
Illustration reduced. Actual size: 63mm.

KM#	Date	Mintage	VF	XF	Unc
3	1988	100 pcs.	—	Proof	150.00

Olympics - Gov. Lutali
Illustration reduced. Actual size: 63mm.

KM#	Date	Mintage	VF	XF	Unc
7	1988	100 pcs.	—	Proof	200.00

Olympics - Symbols
Illustration reduced. Actual size: 63mm.

KM#	Date	Mintage	VF	XF	Unc
9	1988	100 pcs.	—	Proof	175.00

Olympics
Similar to KM#7 but denomination: TWENTY-FIVE.

KM#	Date	Mintage	VF	XF	Unc
10	1988	—	—	Proof	150.00

GOLD BULLION ISSUES

50 DOLLARS

(1/4 Ounce)

8.6397 g, .900 GOLD, .2500 oz AGW
America's Cup

KM#	Date	Mintage	VF	XF	Unc
4	1988	100 pcs.	—	Proof	275.00

100 DOLLARS

(1 Ounce)

31.1000 g, .999 GOLD, 1.0000 oz AGW
America's Cup
Obv: State seal.
Rev: USA ship passing New Zealand's ship.

KM#	Date	Mintage	VF	XF	Unc
5	1988	50 pcs.	—	Proof	850.00

Olympics
Obv: State seal.
Rev: Olympic rings and stadium above denomination.

KM#	Date	Mintage	VF	XF	Unc
8	1988	50 pcs.	—	Proof	850.00

PROOF SETS (PS)

KM#	Date	Mintage	Identification	Issue Price	Mkt. Val.
PS1	1988(3)	—	KM2-4	315.00	460.00

ANDORRA

Principality of Andorra (Principat d'Andorra), situated on the southern slopes of the Pyrenees Mountains between France and Spain, has an area of 175 sq. mi. (453 sq. km.) and a population of 45,000. Capital: Andorra la Vella. Tourism is the chief source of income. Timber, cattle and derivatives, and furniture are exported.

According to tradition, the independence of Andorra derives from a charter Charlemagne granted the people of Andorra in 806 in recognition of their help in battling the Moors. An agreement between the Count of Foix (France) and the Bishop of Seo de Urgel (Spanish) in 1278 to recognize each other as Co-Princes of Andorra gave the state what has been its political form and territorial extent continuously to the present day. Over the years, the title on the French side passed to the Kings of Navarre, then to the Kings of France, and is now held by the President of France. In 1806 Napoleon declared Andorra a republic, but today it is referred to as a principality.

RULERS

Joan D.M. Bisbe D'urgell I

MONETARY SYSTEM

100 Centims = 1 Diner

MINT MARKS

Crowned M = Madrid

25 CENTIMS

BRONZE

KM#	Date	Mintage	Fine	VF	XF	Unc
33	1986	.010	.—	—	—	3.50

DINER

BRASS

KM#	Date	Mintage	Fine	VF	XF	Unc
14	1983	.028	—	—	—	4.50

CAST COPPER - ZINC

KM#	Date	Mintage	Fine	VF	XF	Unc
15	1984	7,500	—	—	—	2.50

BRASS

KM#	Date	Mintage	Fine	VF	XF	Unc
35	1986	.010	—	—	—	2.00

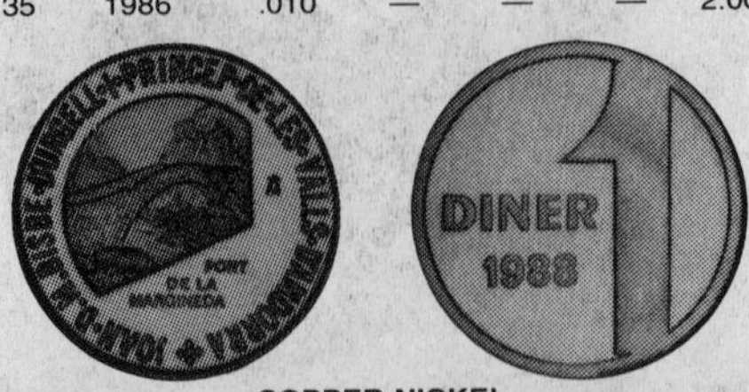

COPPER-NICKEL
Pont De La Margineda

KM#	Date	Mintage	Fine	VF	XF	Unc
49	1988	5,000	—	—	—	2.00

2 DINERS

COPPER-NICKEL RING, BRONZE CENTER
Wildlife - Bear

KM#	Date	Mintage	Fine	VF	XF	Unc
19	1984	5,000	—	—	—	6.00

Wildlife - Squirrel

KM#	Date	Mintage	Fine	VF	XF	Unc
20	1984	5,000	—	—	—	6.00

Wildlife - Ibex

KM#	Date	Mintage	Fine	VF	XF	Unc
21	1984	5,000	—	—	—	6.00

1988 Winter Olympics - Skier

KM#	Date	Mintage	Fine	VF	XF	Unc
27	1985	.011	—	—	—	10.00

1988 Summer Olympics - High Jumper

KM#	Date	Mintage	Fine	VF	XF	Unc
28	1985	.011	—	—	—	10.00

BRASS

KM#	Date	Mintage	Fine	VF	XF	Unc
36	1986	.010	—	—	—	4.00

COPPER-NICKEL
1988 Summer Olympics - Tennis

KM#	Date	Mintage	Fine	VF	XF	Unc
40	1987	.020	—	—	—	14.00

1992 Winter Olympics - Kayak & Skier

KM#	Date	Mintage	Fine	VF	XF	Unc
46	1987	.020	—	—	—	13.50

Santa Coloma

KM#	Date	Mintage	Fine	VF	XF	Unc
50	1988	5,000	—	—	—	4.00

5 DINERS

CAST COPPER

KM#	Date	Mintage	Fine	VF	XF	Unc
16	1984	7,500	—	—	—	5.00

2nd Congress of the Catalan Language

KM#	Date	Mintage	Fine	VF	XF	Unc
29	1986	6,000	—	—	—	5.00

BRONZE

KM#	Date	Mintage	Fine	VF	XF	Unc
37	1986	.010	—	—	—	9.00

COPPER-NICKEL
St. Climent De Pal

KM#	Date	Mintage	Fine	VF	XF	Unc
51	1988	5,000	—	—	—	10.00

10.0000 g, .500 SILVER, .1608 oz ASW
Olympics - Cross Country Skier

KM#	Date	Mintage	Fine	VF	XF	Unc
80	1993	.050	—	—	Proof	12.00

10 DINERS

8.0000 g, .900 CAST SILVER, .2315 oz ASW

KM#	Date	Mintage	Fine	VF	XF	Unc
17	1984	7,500	—	—	—	12.50

World Cup Soccer Games

KM#	Date	Mintage	Fine	VF	XF	Unc
34	1986	.010	—	—	P/L	30.00

7.9300 g, .900 SILVER, .2295 oz ASW

KM#	Date	Mintage	Fine	VF	XF	Unc
38	1986	.010	—	—	—	18.50

8.0000 g, .900 SILVER, .2315 oz ASW
St. Joan De Caselles

KM#	Date	Mintage	Fine	VF	XF	Unc
52	1988	5,000	—	—	—	20.00

12.0000 g, .925 SILVER, .3569 oz ASW
1990 Soccer Games in Italy

KM#	Date	Mintage	Fine	VF	XF	Unc
53	1989	.020	—	—	Proof	27.50

1992 Winter Olympics - Downhill Skier

KM#	Date	Mintage	Fine	VF	XF	Unc
55	1989	.015	—	—	Proof	35.00

1992 Summer Olympics - Soccer

KM#	Date	Mintage	Fine	VF	XF	Unc
56	1989	.015	—	—	Proof	35.00

1990 Soccer Games in Italy

KM#	Date	Mintage	Fine	VF	XF	Unc
60	1989	.020	—	—	Proof	35.00

31.4700 g, .925 SILVER, .9359 oz ASW
Charlemagne - ECU

KM#	Date	Mintage	Fine	VF	XF	Unc
71	1991	.015	—	—	Proof	65.00

31.1035 g, .925 SILVER, .9250 oz ASW
Wildlife - Squirrel

KM#	Date	Mintage	Fine	VF	XF	Unc
74	1992	.015	—	—	Proof	60.00

Wildlife - Chamois

KM#	Date	Mintage	Fine	VF	XF	Unc
75	1992	.015	—	—	Proof	60.00

Wildlife - Bears

KM#	Date	Mintage	Fine	VF	XF	Unc
76	1992	.015	—	—	Proof	60.00

Discovery of America - Stylized Ship on Globe

KM#	Date	Mintage	Fine	VF	XF	Unc
78	1992	.015	—	—	Proof	60.00

31.4700 g, .925 SILVER, .9359 oz ASW
Stylized Tree and Birds
Obv: Crowned arms above denomination & date.

KM#	Date	Mintage	Fine	VF	XF	Unc
84	1993	.015	—	—	Proof	65.00

Space Exploration - Tethered Space Walker

KM#	Date	Mintage	Fine	VF	XF	Unc
85	1993	.015	—	—	Proof	65.00

Soccer - Player Before World Map

KM#	Date	Mintage	Fine	VF	XF	Unc
86	1993	.020	—	—	Proof	65.00

Pioneer Edward White

KM#	Date	Mintage	Fine	VF	XF	Unc
87	1993	*.010	—	—	Proof	65.00

20 DINERS

16.0000 g, .835 SILVER, .4296 oz ASW
Wildlife - Bear

KM#	Date	Mintage	Fine	VF	XF	Unc
22	1984	5,000	—	—	Proof	28.00

Protection of Nature - Squirrel

KM#	Date	Mintage	Fine	VF	XF	Unc
23	1984	5,000	—	—	Proof	28.00

Protection of Nature - Ibex
Obv: Similar to KM#23.

KM#	Date	Mintage	Fine	VF	XF	Unc
24	1984	5,000	—	—	Proof	28.00

16.0000 g, .900 SILVER, .4630 oz ASW
Los Angeles Olympics

KM#	Date	Mintage	Fine	VF	XF	Unc
25	1984	.010	—	—	Proof	30.00

Christmas

KM#	Date	Mintage	Fine	VF	XF	Unc
26	1985	7,000	—	—	Proof	20.00

Olympic Tennis

KM#	Date	Mintage	Fine	VF	XF	Unc
39	1987	.010	—	—	—	40.00

16.0000 g, .999 SILVER, .4501 oz ASW
Seoul Olympics - Stadium

43	1988	.012	—	—	—	75.00

16.0000 g, .925 SILVER, .4759 oz ASW
1992 Winter Olympics - Pairs Figure Skating

47	1988	.015	—	—	Proof	60.00

1992 Summer Olympics - Gymnast on Rings

48	1988	.015	—	—	Proof	60.00

1992 Summer Olympics - Wind Surfer

KM#	Date	Mintage	Fine	VF	XF	Unc
54	1989	.015	—	—	Proof	60.00

1992 Summer Olympics - Kayaker
Obv: Similar to KM#47.

57	1989	.015	—	—	Proof	60.00

1992 Summer Olympics - Hurdler
Obv: Similar to KM#47.

58	1990	.015	—	—	Proof	65.00

1992 Summer Olympics - Equestrian
Obv: Similar to KM#47.

59	1990	.015	—	—	Proof	60.00

21.0000 g, .925 SILVER, .6246 oz ASW
European Small States Games - Cyclist

67	1991	5,000	—	—	Proof	50.00

26.5000 g, .925 SILVER, .7435 oz ASW w/.917 GOLD inlay, .0442 oz AGW
Charlemagne ECU
Obv: Similar to 10 Diners, KM#71.

KM#	Date	Mintage	Fine	VF	XF	Unc
72	1991	5,000	—	—	Proof	155.00

25 DINERS

20.0000 g, .900 SILVER, .5787 oz ASW

18	1984	4,450	—	—	—	40.00
	1984	550 pcs.	—	—	Proof	45.00

Andorra's Governing Charter

44	1988	.010	—	—	Proof	45.00

Millenary of the Bishop of Sala

KM#	Date	Mintage	Fine	VF	XF	Unc
61	1989	*5,000	—	—	Proof	50.00

28.2800 g, .925 SILVER, .8411 oz ASW
Red Cross

KM#	Date	Mintage	Fine	VF	XF	Unc
65	1991	3,000	—	—	Proof	60.00

22.5000 g, .800 SILVER, .5401 oz ASW w/.917 GOLD inlay, .0442 oz AGW
20th Anniversary of Episcopal Coprince

KM#	Date	Mintage	Fine	VF	XF	Unc
69	1991	2,500	—	—	—	50.00

7.7700 g, .583 GOLD, .1456 oz AGW
St. Ermengol - ECU

KM#	Date	Mintage	Fine	VF	XF	Unc
73	1992	3,000	—	—	Proof	90.00

Olympics - Downhill Skier

KM#	Date	Mintage	Fine	VF	XF	Unc
81	1993	6,000	—	—	Proof	80.00

50 DINERS

17.0250 g, .917 GOLD, .5000 oz AGW
Antoni Gaudi

KM#	Date	Mintage	Fine	VF	XF	Unc
62	1990	3,000	—	—	Proof	350.00

15.5500 g, .999 GOLD, .5000 oz AGW
Environmental Protection - Squirrel

KM#	Date	Mintage	Fine	VF	XF	Unc
64	1990	2,500	—	—	Proof	275.00

Endangered Animals - Chamois

KM#	Date	Mintage	Fine	VF	XF	Unc
68	1991	*2,500	—	—	Proof	350.00

13.3400 g, .585 GOLD, .2509 oz AGW
Olympics - Gymnast on Rings

KM#	Date	Mintage	Fine	VF	XF	Unc
70	1991	3,000	—	—	Proof	250.00

19.9650 g, .916 GOLD, .4996 oz AGW
Pau Casals - Musician

KM#	Date	Mintage	Fine	VF	XF	Unc
82	1993	5,000	—	—	Proof	325.00

Joan Miro

KM#	Date	Mintage	Fine	VF	XF	Unc
83	1993	5,000	—	—	Proof	325.00

100 DINERS

5.0000 g, .999 GOLD, .1607 oz AGW

KM#	Date	Mintage	Fine	VF	XF	Unc
41	1987	2,000	—	—	—	100.00

KM#	Date	Mintage	Fine	VF	XF	Unc
42	1988	2,000	—	—	—	100.00

250 DINERS

12.0000 g, .999 GOLD, .3858 oz AGW
Andorra's Governing Charter

KM#	Date	Mintage	Fine	VF	XF	Unc
45	1988	3,000	—	—	Proof	220.00

SOVEREIGN

8.0000 g, .918 GOLD, .2361 oz AGW
Latin Legend

KM#	Date	Mintage	Fine	VF	XF	Unc
30	1982	1,500	—	—	—	150.00

Catalan Legend

KM#	Date	Mintage	Fine	VF	XF	Unc
31	1982	1,500	—	—	—	150.00

Latin Legends

KM#	Date	Mintage	Fine	VF	XF	Unc
32	1983	1,500	—	—	—	150.00

SILVER BULLION ISSUES

DINER

(1/3 Ounce)

10.3000 g, .9999 SILVER, .3312 oz ASW

KM#	Date	Mintage	VF	XF	Unc
66	1990	5,000	—	—	15.00

GOLD BULLION ISSUES

50 DINERS

(1/2 Ounce)

15.5500 g, .999 GOLD, .5000 oz AGW

KM#	Date	Mintage	VF	XF	Unc
63	1989	3,000	—	—	220.00
	1989	—	—	Proof	250.00

Wildlife - Bears

KM#	Date	Mintage	VF	XF	Unc
77	1992	2,500	—	Proof	250.00

100 DINERS

(Ounce)

31.1035 g, .999 GOLD, 1.0000 oz AGW

KM#	Date	Mintage	VF	XF	Unc
79	1989	3,000	—	—	450.00

MINT SETS (MS)

KM#	Date	Mintage	Identification	Issue Price	Mkt. Val.
MS1	1986(5)	—	KM33,35-38	31.00	35.00

PROOF SETS (PS)

KM#	Date	Mintage	Identification	Issue Price	Mkt. Val.
PS1	1963(2)	1,000	M3,M4	51.00	55.00
PS2	1964(2)	—	M5,M6	51.00	50.00
PS3	1964(2)	4	M5a,M6a	—	1400.
PS4	1964(2)	—	M7,M8	80.00	55.00
PS5	1964(2)	—	M7a,M8a	—	1400.

ANGOLA

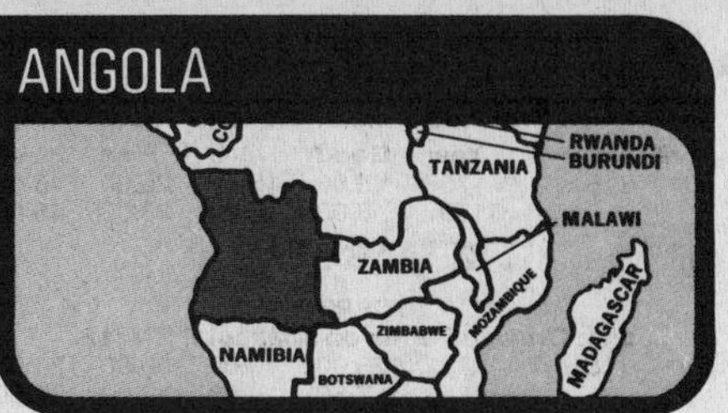

The Peoples Republic of Angola, a country on the west coast of southern Africa bounded by Zaire, Zambia, and Namibia (South-West Africa), has an area of 481,354 sq. mi. (1,246,700 sq. km.) and a population of 7 million, predominantly Bantu in origin. Capital: Luanda. Most of the people are engaged in subsistence agriculture. However, important oil and mineral deposits make Angola potentially one of the richest countries in Africa. Iron and diamonds are exported.

Angola was discovered by Portuguese navigator Diogo Cao in 1482. Portuguese settlers arrived in 1491, and established Angola as a major slaving center which sent about 3 million slaves to the New World.

A revolt, characterized by guerrilla warfare, against Portuguese rule began in 1961 and continued until 1974, when a new regime in Portugal offered independence. The independence movement was actively supported by three groups, the National Front, based in Zaire, the Soviet-backed Popular Movement, and the moderate National Union. Independence was proclaimed on Nov. 11, 1975, and the Portuguese departed, leaving the Angolan people to work out their own political destiny. Within hours, each of the independence groups proclaimed itself Angola's sole ruler. A bloody intertribal civil war erupted in which the Communist Popular Movement, assisted by Soviet arms and Cuban mercenaries, was the eventual victor.

RULERS

Portuguese until 1975

MINT MARKS

KN - King's Norton

MONETARY SYSTEM

(Until 1860)

50 Reis = 1 Macuta

(Commencing 1910)

100 Centavos = 20 Macutas = 1 Escudo

1/4 MACUTA

COPPER

KM#	Date	Mintage	VG	Fine	VF	XF
38	1814	—	10.00	25.00	40.00	70.00
	1815	—	85.00	175.00	350.00	600.00
	1816	—	— Reported, not confirmed			

1/2 MACUTA

COPPER

KM#	Date	Mintage	VG	Fine	VF	XF
39	1814	—	10.00	20.00	35.00	60.00
	1815	.018	75.00	150.00	300.00	500.00
	1819	—	—	—	Rare	—

KM#	Date	Mintage	VG	Fine	VF	XF
42	1848	.417	6.00	12.00	20.00	50.00
	1851	.104	3.00	6.00	12.00	30.00
	1853	.143	3.00	6.00	12.00	30.00

Obv. leg: PETRUS V D.G. . . .

KM#	Date	Mintage	VG	Fine	VF	XF
43	1858	.226	2.50	5.00	10.00	30.00
	1860	.398	2.50	5.00	10.00	30.00

MACUTA

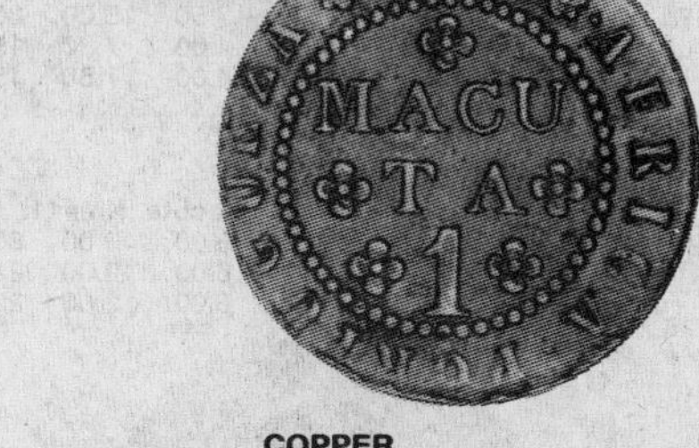

COPPER

KM#	Date	Mintage	VG	Fine	VF	XF
40	1814	*	5.00	10.00	15.00	35.00
	1816	6,110	30.00	65.00	125.00	250.00
	1819	—	—	—	Rare	—

***NOTE:** Lightweight coins exist weighing 10.96 g.

Similar to 1/2 Macuta, KM#42.

KM#	Date	Mintage	VG	Fine	VF	XF
44	1860	.194	7.00	15.00	25.00	45.00

2 MACUTAS

COPPER

Similar to 1 Macuta, KM#40.

KM#	Date	Mintage	VG	Fine	VF	XF
41	1815	—	25.00	50.00	90.00	175.00
	1816	3,175	35.00	65.00	120.00	250.00
	1819	—	—	—	Rare	—

COUNTERMARKED COINAGE

In 1814 various copper coins were countermarked with the crowned arms of Portugal to double their face value.

10 REIS

COPPER

c/m: Crowned arms on V Reis, KM#7.

KM#	Date	Year	Good	VG	Fine	VF
45	(1814)	1752	4.00	7.50	15.00	30.00
		1753	1.50	3.00	5.00	10.00
		1757	2.00	4.00	7.50	15.00

20 REIS

COPPER

c/m: Crowned arms on X Reis, KM#8.

KM#	Date	Year	Good	VG	Fine	VF
46	(1814)	1752	4.50	7.50	12.50	25.00
		1753	4.50	7.50	12.50	25.00
		1757	5.50	10.00	15.00	30.00

1/2 MACUTA

COPPER

c/m: Crowned arms on 1/4 Macuta, KM#10.

KM#	Date	Year	Good	VG	Fine	VF
49	(1814)	1762	3.00	6.50	14.00	27.50
		1763	2.00	4.00	7.50	15.00
		1770	2.00	4.00	7.50	15.00
		1771	6.50	12.50	20.00	40.00

c/m: Crowned arms on 1/4 Macuta, KM#27.

KM#	Date	Year	Good	VG	Fine	VF
53	(1814)	1785	2.50	5.00	12.00	22.50

c/m: Crowned arms on 1/4 Macuta, KM#29.

KM#	Date	Year	Good	VG	Fine	VF
55	(1814)	1789	2.50	5.00	12.00	22.50

40 REIS

COPPER

c/m: Crowned arms on XX Reis, KM#9.

KM#	Date	Year	Good	VG	Fine	VF
47	(1814)	1752	4.00	7.50	15.00	30.00
		1753	2.00	4.00	7.50	15.00
		1757	2.00	4.00	7.50	15.00

MACUTA

COPPER

c/m: Crowned arms on 1/2 Macuta, KM#11.

KM#	Date	Year	Good	VG	Fine	VF
50	(1814)	1762	15.00	25.00	40.00	80.00
		1763	3.00	6.00	12.00	22.50
		1770	3.00	6.00	12.00	22.50

c/m: Crowned arms on 1/2 Macuta, KM#28.

KM#	Date	Year	Good	VG	Fine	VF
54	(1814)	1785	5.00	9.00	14.00	27.50
		1786	5.00	9.00	14.00	27.50

c/m: Crowned arms on 1/2 Macuta, KM#30.

KM#	Date	Year	Good	VG	Fine	VF
56	(1814)	1789	5.00	8.00	14.00	27.50

80 REIS

COPPER

c/m: Crowned arms on XL Reis, KM#9.

KM#	Date	Year	Good	VG	Fine	VF
48	(1814)	1753	8.00	15.00	25.00	45.00
		1757	8.00	15.00	25.00	45.00

2 MACUTAS

COPPER

c/m: Crowned arms on 1 Macuta, KM#12.

KM#	Date	Year	Good	VG	Fine	VF
51	(1814)	1762	25.00	40.00	60.00	120.00
		1763	7.50	10.00	15.00	30.00
		1770	5.00	7.50	10.00	25.00

c/m: Crowned arms on 1 Macuta, KM#20.

KM#	Date	Year	Good	VG	Fine	VF
52	(1814)	1783	40.00	65.00	90.00	175.00
		1785	5.00	10.00	15.00	35.00
		1786	7.50	12.50	20.00	45.00

c/m: Crowned arms on 1 Macuta, KM#31.

KM#	Date	Year	Good	VG	Fine	VF
57	(1814)	1789	5.00	10.00	15.00	35.00

c/m: Crowned arms on 1 Macuta, KM#40.

KM#	Date	Year	Good	VG	Fine	VF
58	(1814)	1814	—	—	Rare	—
		1816	—	—	Rare	—

4 MACUTAS

COPPER

c/m: Crowned arms on 2 Macutas, KM#41.

KM#	Date	Year	Good	VG	Fine	VF
59	(1814)	1815	—	—	Rare	—
		1816	—	—	Rare	—

DECIMAL COINAGE

100 Centavos = 1 Escudo

CENTAVO

BRONZE

KM#	Date	Mintage	Fine	VF	XF	Unc
60	1921	1.360	7.50	12.50	30.00	60.00

2 CENTAVOS

BRONZE

KM#	Date	Mintage	Fine	VF	XF	Unc
61	1921	.530	10.00	15.00	50.00	100.00

5 CENTAVOS

(1 Macuta)

BRONZE

KM#	Date	Mintage	Fine	VF	XF	Unc
62	1921	.720	5.00	10.00	30.00	75.00
	1922	5.680	4.00	8.00	20.00	50.00
	1923	5.840	4.00	8.00	20.00	50.00
	1924	—	12.00	25.00	60.00	125.00

NICKEL-BRONZE

KM#	Date	Mintage	Fine	VF	XF	Unc
66	1927	2.002	1.50	3.50	7.50	15.00

10 CENTAVOS

(2 Macutas)

COPPER-NICKEL

KM#	Date	Mintage	Fine	VF	XF	Unc
63	1921	.160	10.00	17.50	35.00	90.00
	1922	.340	7.50	15.00	30.00	75.00
	1923	2.960	3.50	8.00	17.50	45.00

KM#	Date	Mintage	Fine	VF	XF	Unc
67	1927	2.003	2.00	4.00	12.50	25.00
	1928	1.000	2.00	4.00	12.50	25.00

BRONZE

300th Anniversary of Revolution of 1648

KM#	Date	Mintage	Fine	VF	XF	Unc
70	1948	10.000	.75	2.00	5.00	8.00
	1949	10.000	.20	.50	3.00	6.00

ALUMINUM

KM#	Date	Mintage	Fine	VF	XF	Unc
82	1974	4.000	—	—	—	12.00

NOTE: Not released for circulation, but relatively available.

20 CENTAVOS

(4 Macutas)

COPPER-NICKEL

KM#	Date	Mintage	Fine	VF	XF	Unc
64	1921	2.115	4.00	9.00	18.00	40.00
	1922	1.730	4.00	9.00	18.00	40.00

KM#	Date	Mintage	Fine	VF	XF	Unc
68	1927	2.001	2.25	4.00	7.00	15.00
	1928	.500	3.00	5.00	10.00	20.00

BRONZE
300th Anniversary of Revolution of 1648

KM#	Date	Mintage	Fine	VF	XF	Unc
71	1948	7.850	.40	.75	1.00	2.50
	1949	2.150	4.00	7.50	12.50	20.00

KM#	Date	Mintage	Fine	VF	XF	Unc
78	1962	3.000	—	—	.50	1.00

50 CENTAVOS

NICKEL

KM#	Date	Mintage	Fine	VF	XF	Unc
65	1922	6.000	2.50	7.50	12.50	35.00
	1923 KN	6.000	—	—	225.00	375.00
	1923	Inc. Ab.	2.50	7.50	12.50	35.00

NICKEL-BRONZE

KM#	Date	Mintage	Fine	VF	XF	Unc
69	1927	1.608	3.00	12.00	22.00	65.00
	1928	1.600	3.00	12.00	22.00	65.00

300th Anniversary of Revolution of 1648

KM#	Date	Mintage	Fine	VF	XF	Unc
72	1948	4.000	.35	.75	2.00	4.50
	1950	4.000	.35	.75	2.00	4.50

BRONZE

KM#	Date	Mintage	VF	XF	Unc
75	1953	5.000	.20	.40	2.00
	1954	11.731	.20	.35	1.50
	1955	1.126	3.00	5.00	15.00
	1957	8.873	.20	.40	1.75
	1958	17.520	.15	.30	1.25
	1961	8.750	.20	.40	1.75

COPPER-NICKEL

KM#	Date	Mintage	VF	XF	Unc
75a	1974	150 pcs.	—	125.00	250.00

NOTE: Not released for circulation.

ESCUDO

BRONZE

KM#	Date	Mintage	VF	XF	Unc
76	1953	2.001	.50	1.50	5.00
	1956	2.989	.50	1.25	3.00
	1963	5.000	.50	1.25	3.50
	1965	5.000	.50	1.25	3.50
	1972	10.000	.50	1.25	3.00
	1974	6.214	.50	1.25	3.00

COPPER-NICKEL

KM#	Date	Mintage	VF	XF	Unc
76a	1972	—	—	Rare	—
	1974	—	—	Rare	—

NOTE: Not released for circulation.

2-1/2 ESCUDOS

COPPER-NICKEL

KM#	Date	Mintage	VF	XF	Unc
77	1953	6.008	.40	1.20	5.00
	1956	9.992	.35	.75	4.00
	1967	6.000	.35	.75	4.00
	1968	5.000	.35	.75	4.00
	1969	5.000	.35	.75	4.00
	1974	19.999	.25	.50	3.00

5 ESCUDOS

COPPER-NICKEL

KM#	Date	Mintage	VF	XF	Unc
81	1972	8.000	12.50	25.00	50.00
	1974	*3.343	—	100.00	200.00

***NOTE:** Not released for circulation.

10 ESCUDOS

5.0000 g, .720 SILVER, .1157 oz ASW

KM#	Date	Mintage	VF	XF	Unc
73	1952	2.023	2.50	5.00	8.00
	1955	1.977	2.50	5.00	8.00

COPPER-NICKEL

KM#	Date	Mintage	VF	XF	Unc
79	1969	3.022	1.50	3.00	6.00
	1970	.978	2.00	4.00	7.00

20 ESCUDOS

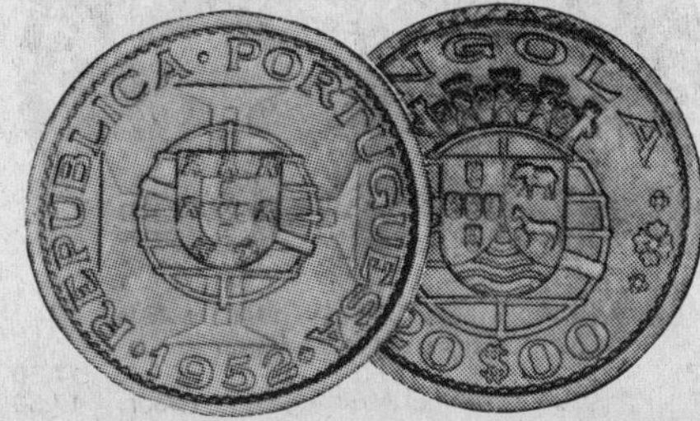

10.0000 g, .720 SILVER, .2315 oz ASW

KM#	Date	Mintage	VF	XF	Unc
74	1952	1.003	2.50	6.00	9.00
	1955	.997	2.50	5.00	8.00

NICKEL

KM#	Date	Mintage	VF	XF	Unc
80	1971	1.572	.75	2.00	4.00
	1972	.428	1.00	2.50	5.00

PEOPLES REPUBLIC

MONETARY SYSTEM

100 Lwei = 1 Kwanza

50 LWEI

COPPER-NICKEL

KM#	Date	Mintage	VF	XF	Unc
90	ND	—	.10	.30	.85
(82)	1979	—	.10	.30	.85

KWANZA

COPPER-NICKEL

KM#	Date	Mintage	VF	XF	Unc
83	ND	—	.30	.50	1.00
	1978	—	.25	.40	1.00
	1979	—	.25	.40	1.00

2 KWANZAS

COPPER-NICKEL

KM#	Date	Mintage	VF	XF	Unc
84	ND	—	.40	.60	1.25

5 KWANZAS

COPPER-NICKEL

KM#	Date	Mintage	VF	XF	Unc
85	ND	—	.65	1.00	2.00

10 KWANZAS

COPPER-NICKEL

Obv: Small date. Rev: Dots near rim.

KM#	Date	Mintage	VF	XF	Unc
86.1	ND	—	1.25	1.75	3.00
	1978	—	1.25	1.75	3.00

Obv: Large date. Rev: Dots away from rim.

KM#	Date	Mintage	VF	XF	Unc
86.2	1978	—	1.25	1.75	3.00

20 KWANZAS

COPPER-NICKEL

KM#	Date	Mintage	VF	XF	Unc
87	1978	—	1.50	2.50	5.00

50 KWANZAS

COPPER
Obv: State emblem. Rev: Denomination.

KM#	Date	Mintage	VF	XF	Unc
91	ND	—	2.00	3.50	7.00

100 KWANZAS

COPPER
Obv: State emblem. Rev: Denomination.

KM#	Date	Mintage	VF	XF	Unc
92	ND	—	2.50	4.50	10.00

500 KWANZAS

21.0000 g, SILVER
Independence - Augostinho Neto

KM#	Date	Mintage	
88	1978	7,500	Reported, not confirmed

1000 KWANZAS

25.0000 g, SILVER
Independence - Augostinho Neto

KM#	Date	Mintage	
89	1978	7,500	Reported, not confirmed

ANGUILLA

The British colony of Anguilla, a self-governing British territory situated in the east Caribbean Sea about 60 miles (100 km.) northwest of St. Kitts, has an area of 35 sq. mi. (91 sq. km.) and a population of 6,000. Capital: The Valley. In recent years, tourism has replaced the traditional fishing, stock raising and salt production as the main industry.

Anguilla was discovered by Columbus in 1493 and became a British colony in 1650. As the other British areas in the West Indies did, Anguilla officially adapted to Sterling beginning in 1825. From 1950 to 1965, Anguilla was a member of the British Caribbean Territories (Eastern Group) Currency Board, whose coinage it used. In March 1967, Anguilla was joined politically with St. Christopher (St. Kitts) -as it had been for much of its colonial history -and Nevis to form a British associated state.

On June 16, 1967, the Provisional Government of Anguilla unilaterally declared its independence and seceded from the Federation. Later, on July 11, 1967, a vote of confidence was taken and the results favored independence. Britain refused to accept the declaration (nor did any other country recognize it) and appointed a British administrator whom Anguilla accepted. However, in Feb. 1969 Anguilla ousted the British emissary, voted to sever all ties with Britain, and established the Republic of Anguilla. The following month Britain landed a force of paratrocpers and policemen. This bloodless counteraction ended the self-proclaimed republic and resulted in the installation of a governing commissioner. The troops were withdrawn in Sept. 1969, and the Anguilla Act of July 1971 placed Anguilla directly under British control. A new constitution in 1976 established Anguilla as a self-governing British colony. Britain retains power over defense, police and civil service, and foreign affairs. Since 1981, Anguilla has empolyed the coinage of the East Caribbean States.

RULERS

British

1/2 DOLLAR

3.6100 g, .999 SILVER, .1160 oz ASW
St. Mary's Church

KM#	Date	Mintage	VF	XF	Unc
15	1969	4,200	—	Proof	10.00
	1970	Inc. Ab.	—	Proof	10.00

DOLLAR

7.1800 g, .999 SILVER, .2308 oz ASW
Map Flora and Fauna

KM#	Date	Mintage	VF	XF	Unc
16	1969	4,450	—	Proof	12.50
	1970	Inc. Ab.	—	Proof	12.50

2 DOLLARS

14.1400 g, .999 SILVER, .4546 oz ASW
National Flag and Map

KM#	Date	Mintage	VF	XF	Unc
17	1969	4,150	—	Proof	17.50
	1970	Inc. Ab.	—	Proof	17.50

4 DOLLARS

28.4800 g, .999 SILVER, .9156 oz ASW
Ship - Atlantic Star

KM#	Date	Mintage	VF	XF	Unc
18	1969	5,100	—	Proof	60.00
	1970	Inc. Ab.	—	Proof	60.00

5 DOLLARS

2.4600 g, .900 GOLD, .0711 oz AGW
Methodist Church of West End

KM#	Date	Mintage	VF	XF	Unc
20	1969	1,925	—	Proof	60.00
	1970	Inc. Ab.	—	Proof	60.00

10 DOLLARS

4.9300 g, .900 GOLD, .1426 oz AGW
Dolphin and Sea Creatures

KM#	Date	Mintage	VF	XF	Unc
21	1969	1,615	—	Proof	110.00
	1970	Inc. Ab.	—	Proof	110.00

20 DOLLARS

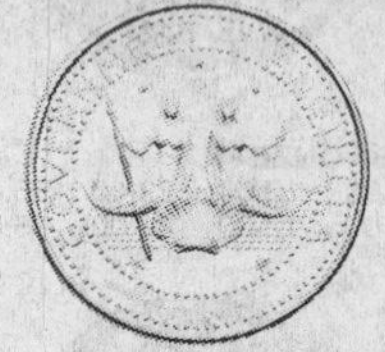

9.8700 g, .900 GOLD, .2856 oz AGW
Mermaids

KM#	Date	Mintage	VF	XF	Unc
22	1969	1,395	—	Proof	275.00
	1970	Inc. Ab.	—	Proof	275.00

100 DOLLARS

49.3700 g, .900 GOLD, 1.4287 oz AGW
Demonstrating Population

KM#	Date	Mintage	VF	XF	Unc
23	1969	710 pcs.	—	Proof	950.00
	1970	Inc. Ab.	—	Proof	950.00

PROOF SETS (PS)

KM#	Date	Mintage	Identification	Issue Price	Mkt. Val.
PS1	1969(8)	—	KM15-18,20-23	225.50	1500.

KM#	Date	Mintage	Identification	Issue Price	Mkt. Val.
PS2	1969(4)	—	KM15-18	25.50	115.00
PS3	1969(4)	—	KM20-23	200.00	1400.
PS4	1970(8)	—	KM15-18,20-23	225.50	1550.
PS5	1970(4)	—	KM15-18	25.50	100.00
PS6	1970(4)	—	KM20-23	200.00	1400.

The Independent State of Antigua and Barbuda, located on the eastern edge of the Leeward Islands in the Caribbean Sea, has an area of 171 sq. mi. (440 sq. km.) and a population of *86,000. Capital: St. John's. Prior to 1967 Antigua and its dependencies, Barbuda and Redonda, comprised a presidency of the Leeward Islands. The mountainous island produces sugar, molasses, rum, cotton and fruit. Tourism is making an increasingly valuable contribution to the economy.

Antigua was discovered by Columbus in 1493, settled by British colonists from St. Kitts in 1632, occupied by the French in 1666, and ceded to Britain in 1667. It became an associated state with internal self-government on February 27, 1967. On November 1, 1981 it became independent as Antigua and Barbuda.

Spanish silver coinage and French colonial "Black Dogs" were used throughout the islands' early history; however, late in the seventeenth century the introduction of British tin farthings was attempted with complete lack of success. In 1822, British colonial Anchor Money was introduced.

From 1825 to 1955, Antigua was on the sterling standard and used British coins. Coins of the British Caribbean Territories (Eastern Group) and East Caribbean States circulated from 1955, and banknotes of East Caribbean Currency Authority are now used on the island. The earlier coinage was augmented in 1981 by that of the East Caribbean States.

RULERS

British

ANTIGUA

MONETARY SYSTEM

100 Cents = 1 Dollar

4 DOLLARS

COPPER-NICKEL
F.A.O. Issue

KM#	Date	Mintage	VF	XF	Unc
1	1970	.014	—	5.00	8.00
	1970	2,000	—	Proof	25.00

NOTE: For similar issues see Barbados, Dominica, Grenada, Montserrat, St. Kitts, St. Lucia and St. Vincent.

ANTIGUA & BARBUDA

10 DOLLARS

COPPER-NICKEL
Royal Visit

KM#	Date	Mintage	VF	XF	Unc
5	1985	.100	—	—	5.00
	28.2800 g, .925 SILVER, .8409 oz ASW				
5a	1985	5,000	—	Proof	35.00
	47.5400 g, .917 GOLD, 1.4013 oz AGW				
5b	1985	250 pcs.	—	Proof	1200.

30 DOLLARS

31.1000 g, .500 SILVER, .5000 oz ASW
George Washington - Yorktown 1781

KM#	Date	Mintage	VF	XF	Unc
2	1982	1,200	—	Proof	40.00

George Washington - Inauguration - 1789
Obv: Similar to KM#2.

KM#	Date	Mintage	VF	XF	Unc
3	1982	1,125	—	Proof	45.00

George Washington - Verplanck's Point - 1790
Obv: Similar to KM#2.

KM#	Date	Mintage	VF	XF	Unc
4	1982	675 pcs.	—	Proof	55.00

Listings For

ANNAM: refer to Vietnam
ANTWERP: refer to France
ANVERS: refer to France

100 DOLLARS

129.5900 g, .925 SILVER, 3.8543 oz ASW
Tropical Birds - Cattle Egret
Obv: Arms in circle, country name above, date below.

KM#	Date	Mintage	VF	XF	Unc
6	1988	*.010	—	Proof	125.00

The Argentine Republic, located in southern South America, has an area of 1,068,301 sq. mi. (2,766,890 sq. km.) and a population of 28.5 million. Capital: Buenos Aires. Its varied topography ranges from the subtropical lowlands of the north to the towering Andean Mountains in the west and the wind-swept Patagonian steppe in the south. The rolling, fertile pampas of central Argentina are ideal for agriculture and grazing, and support most of the republic's population. Meat packing, flour milling, textiles, sugar refining and dairy products are the principal industries. Oil is found in Patagonia, but most mineral requirements must be imported.

Argentina was discovered in 1516 by the Spanish navigator Juan de Solis. A permanent Spanish colony was established at Buenos Aires in 1580, but the colony developed slowly. When Napoleon conquered Spain, the Argentines set up their own government on May 25, 1810. Independence was formally declared on July 9, 1816. A strong tendency toward local autonomy, fostered by difficult transportation, resulted in a federalized union with much authority left to the states or provinces, which resulted in the coinage of 1817-1867.

Internal conflict through the first half century of Argentine independence resulted in a provisional national coinage, chiefly of crown-sized silver. This was supplemented by provincial issues, mainly of minor denominations.

RULERS

Spanish until 1810

MINT MARKS

BA = Buenos Aires
CORDOBA, CORDOVA
Potosi monogram (Bolivia)
R, RA, RIOJA, RIOXA
SE = Santiago del Estero
T, TM = Tucuman
TIERRA DEL FUEGO

In Colonial times, Potosi-struck coinage was used in Argentina and the mint was captured in 1813 by Argentine forces. The coinage of the Independence forces was struck there until 1815 when the mint was retaken by a Spanish army. With independence secured, the Argentine states turned elsewhere for their coinage.

MONETARY SYSTEM

8 Reales = 8 Soles = 1/2 Escudo
16 Reales or Soles = 1 Escudo
10 Decimos = 1 Real
100 Centavos = 1 Peso
10 Pesos = 1 Argentino
(Commencing 1970)
100 Old Pesos = 1 New Peso
(Commencing June 1983)
10,000 New Pesos = 1 Peso Argentino
1,000 Pesos Argentino = 1 Austral

PROVINCIAS DEL RIO DE LA PLATA

1/4 REAL

SILVER
1/4 Real of Rondeau

KM#	Date	Mintage	VG	Fine	VF	XF
A1	ND(1815-16)	4-6 pcs.	—	—	Rare	—

1/2 REAL

SILVER
Mint mark: Potosi monogram
Obv: Flame tips end counter clockwise.

KM#	Date	Mintage	VG	Fine	VF	XF
1.1	1813 J	—	10.00	15.00	30.00	65.00

Obv: Flame tips end clockwise.

KM#	Date	Mintage	VG	Fine	VF	XF
1.2	1815 F	—	12.50	17.50	35.00	70.00

1/2 SOL

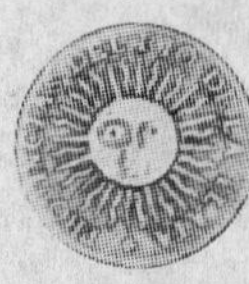

SILVER
Mint mark: Potosi monogram

KM#	Date	Mintage	VG	Fine	VF	XF
10	1815 FL	—	15.00	25.00	60.00	125.00

REAL

SILVER
Mint mark: Potosi monogram

KM#	Date	Mintage	VG	Fine	VF	XF
2	1813 J	—	10.00	15.00	30.00	70.00
	1815 F	—	10.00	15.00	30.00	70.00

Mint mark: RA
Similar to 2 Soles, KM#18.

KM#	Date	Mintage	VG	Fine	VF	XF
17	1824 DS	—	10.00	17.00	35.00	80.00
	1825 CA	—	—	—	Rare	—

SOL

SILVER
Mint mark: Potosi monogram
Similar to 1/2 Sol, KM#10.

KM#	Date	Mintage	VG	Fine	VF	XF
11	1815 FL	—	17.50	37.50	85.00	175.00

2 REALES

SILVER
Mint mark: Potosi monogram

KM#	Date	Mintage	VG	Fine	VF	XF
3	1813 J	—	15.00	25.00	55.00	100.00
	1815 F	—	15.00	25.00	55.00	100.00

2 SOLES

SILVER
Mint mark: Potosi monogram
Similar to 2 Reales, KM#3.

KM#	Date	Mintage	VG	Fine	VF	XF
12	1815 FL	—	30.00	50.00	100.00	200.00

Mint mark: RA

KM#	Date	Mintage	VG	Fine	VF	XF
18	1824 DS	—	12.00	16.50	25.00	45.00
	1825 CA	—	25.00	45.00	75.00	155.00
	1825 CA. DE B. AS.	—	14.00	25.00	45.00	85.00
	1826/5 P	—	15.00	27.50	60.00	120.00
	1826 'P' omitted from rev. leg.	—	9.00	14.00	25.00	45.00
	1826 P medal alignment	—	14.00	25.00	50.00	90.00
	1826 P coin alignment	—	20.00	40.00	75.00	150.00

4 REALES

SILVER
Mint mark: Potosi monogram

KM#	Date	Mintage	VG	Fine	VF	XF
4	1813 J	—	30.00	50.00	85.00	160.00
	1815 F	—	30.00	55.00	90.00	180.00

NOTE: Size of sunface varies for 1815 dated coins.

4 SOLES

SILVER
Mint mark: Potosi monogram

KM#	Date	Mintage	VG	Fine	VF	XF
13	1815 FL	—	40.00	75.00	140.00	275.00

Mint mark: RA

KM#	Date	Mintage	VG	Fine	VF	XF
22	1828 P coin alignment					
		—	20.00	30.00	50.00	90.00
	1828 P medal alignment					
		—	25.00	35.00	55.00	100.00
	1832 P	—	20.00	30.00	50.00	90.00

8 REALES

SILVER
Mint mark: Potosi monogram
Obv: Flame tips end clockwise.

KM#	Date	Mintage	VG	Fine	VF	XF
5	1813 J	—	50.00	75.00	125.00	250.00
	1813 J PRORVINCIAS (error)					
		—	—	—	Rare	—

NOTE: Traces of earlier Spanish colonial edge designs are occasionally encountered and are considered rare.

Obv: Flame tips end counterclockwise.

KM#	Date	Mintage	VG	Fine	VF	XF
14	1815 F	—	50.00	75.00	125.00	250.00
	1815 F PROVICIAS (error)					
		—	75.00	125.00	200.00	350.00

Mint mark: RA

KM#	Date	Mintage	VG	Fine	VF	XF
20	1826 P	—	40.00	80.00	160.00	290.00
	1827 P	—	45.00	90.00	240.00	375.00
	1828 P	—	35.00	75.00	120.00	225.00
	1830 P	—	70.00	160.00	450.00	900.00
	1831/0 P	—	50.00	140.00	390.00	750.00
	1831 P	—	50.00	130.00	360.00	650.00
	1832 P	—	35.00	80.00	160.00	330.00
	1833 P	—	35.00	75.00	120.00	225.00
	1834 P	—	35.00	75.00	120.00	225.00
	1835 P	—	35.00	75.00	120.00	225.00
	1836 P	—	35.00	75.00	120.00	225.00
	1837 P	—	35.00	75.00	120.00	240.00

8 SOLES

SILVER
Mint mark: Potosi monogram

KM#	Date	Mintage	VG	Fine	VF	XF
15	1815 FL	—	50.00	100.00	150.00	275.00
	1815 FL S/R	—	60.00	120.00	180.00	350.00

ESCUDO

3.3750 g, .875 GOLD, .0949 oz AGW
Mint mark: Potosi monogram

KM#	Date	Mintage	VG	Fine	VF	XF
6	1813 J	—	—	—	Rare	—

2 ESCUDOS

6.7500 g, .875 GOLD, .1899 oz AGW
Mint mark: Potosi monogram

KM#	Date	Mintage	VG	Fine	VF	XF
7	1813 J	—	—	—	Unique	—

Mint mark: RA

KM#	Date	Mintage	VG	Fine	VF	XF
19.1	1824 DS	—	175.00	275.00	450.00	750.00
	1825 CA. DE B. AS.					
		—	175.00	275.00	450.00	750.00
	1826 P	—	175.00	275.00	450.00	750.00

Rev: P omitted from legend.

KM#	Date	Mintage	VG	Fine	VF	XF
19.2	1826	—	175.00	275.00	450.00	750.00

NOTE: Struck in medal and coin alignment.

4 ESCUDOS

13.5000 g, .875 GOLD, .3798 oz AGW
Mint mark: Potosi monogram

KM#	Date	Mintage	VG	Fine	VF	XF
8	1813 J	—	—	Reported, not confirmed		

8 ESCUDOS

27.0000 g, .875 GOLD, .7596 oz AGW
Mint mark: Potosi monogram

KM#	Date	Mintage	VG	Fine	VF	XF
9	1813 J	—	4000.	6000.	10,000.	20,000.

NOTE: Superior Casterline sale 5-89 choice VF realized $11,000.

Mint mark: RA

KM#	Date	Mintage	VG	Fine	VF	XF
21	1826 P	—	650.00	1250.	1950.	2750.
	1828 P	—	650.00	1250.	1950.	2750.
	1829 P	2 known	—	—	Rare	—
	1830 P	—	1500.	3000.	4500.	6000.
	1831/0	—	—	—	Rare	—
	1831 P	—	600.00	1200.	1850.	2700.
	1832 P	—	600.00	1200.	1850.	2700.
	1833 P	—	700.00	1350.	2000.	3000.
	1834 P	—	700.00	1350.	2000.	3000.
	1835 P	—	700.00	1350.	2000.	3000.

CONFEDERACION ARGENTINA

CENTAVO

COPPER

KM#	Date	Mintage	VG	Fine	VF	XF
23	1854	—	2.50	5.00	15.00	40.00

2 CENTAVOS

COPPER

KM#	Date	Mintage	VG	Fine	VF	XF
24	1854	—	3.00	7.50	20.00	50.00

NOTE: Struck in medal and coin alignment.

4 CENTAVOS

COPPER

KM#	Date	Mintage	VG	Fine	VF	XF
25	1854	—	5.00	12.50	27.50	75.00

NOTE: Struck in medal and coin alignment.

PROVINCIAL COINAGE

BUENOS AIRES

Buenos Aires, a city and province in eastern Argentina, was the first province to have coins made outside the country. Governor Martin Rodriguez initiated negotiations with Boulton & Watt (Soho Mint) in 1821. The Banco Nacional was dissolved in 1836 and the Casa de Moneda took its place.

NOTE: National Bank 5/10 reales are frequently struck over Soho decimos of 1822-1823.

MONETARY SYSTEM

10 Decimos = 1 Real

DECIMO

COPPER

KM#	Date	Mintage	VG	Fine	VF	XF
1	1822	—	1.25	4.00	15.00	35.00
	1823	—	1.00	3.00	12.00	25.00

NOTE: Officially retired in 1827, in favor of Banco Nacional issues, KM#2-5.

1/4 REAL

COPPER
Obv: Fraction in shaded circle.
Rev: BUENOS AYRES 1827 within branches.

KM#	Date	Mintage	VG	Fine	VF	XF
2	1827	—	15.00	25.00	45.00	100.00

5/10 REAL

COPPER

KM#	Date	Mintage	VG	Fine	VF	XF
3	1827	—	1.00	3.00	6.00	20.00
	1828	—	1.00	3.00	6.00	20.00
3	1830	—	3.00	5.00	10.00	30.00
	1831/27	—	—	—	—	—
	1831	—	1.00	3.00	6.00	20.00

NOTE: Struck in medal and coin alignment.

KM#	Date	Mintage	VG	Fine	VF	XF
6	1840	—	5.00	10.00	25.00	55.00

10 DECIMOS

COPPER

KM#	Date	Mintage	VG	Fine	VF	XF
4	1827	—	4.00	9.00	22.00	50.00
	1828	—	10.00	22.50	45.00	75.00
	1830	—	4.00	9.00	22.00	50.00

REAL

COPPER

KM#	Date	Mintage	VG	Fine	VF	XF
7	1840	—	1.00	3.00	7.00	15.00

KM#	Date	Mintage	VG	Fine	VF	XF
10	1854	—	4.00	10.00	15.00	35.00

20 DECIMOS

COPPER

KM#	Date	Mintage	VG	Fine	VF	XF
5	1827	—	4.00	9.00	22.00	55.00
	1830	—	3.00	5.00	17.50	50.00
	1831	—	12.50	30.00	50.00	100.00

NOTE: Struck in medal and coin alignment.

2 REALES

COPPER

KM#	Date	Mintage	VG	Fine	VF	XF
8	1840	—	2.00	4.00	11.00	25.00
	1844	—	2.00	4.00	11.00	25.00

KM#	Date	Mintage	VG	Fine	VF	XF
9	1853	—	1.00	2.50	6.00	20.00
	1854	—	1.00	2.75	7.50	22.50
	1855	—	1.00	2.50	6.00	20.00
	1856	—	2.00	4.00	10.00	30.00

KM#	Date	Mintage	VG	Fine	VF	XF
11	1860	—	2.00	5.00	10.00	25.00
	1861	—	2.00	5.00	10.00	25.00

CORDOBA

Cordoba, a city and province in central Argentina, was the most prolific of the provincial issuers. The provincial government contracted with concessionaires to make coins. The contractors for 1833 are not known, but all the private makers' coinage is relatively crude and replete with variations, die-sinking inconguities and minor errors. On many pieces it is almost impossible to find the same pairing of dies, i.e., 1/4 Reales, 1/2 Reales and 1 Reales of the 1839-41 type.

On February 2, 1844 a provincial mint was authorized by Governor Manuel Lopez. It operated from 1844 to 1852.

CONCESSIONAIRES

Letter	Date	Name
PP, PNP	1839-41	Pedro Nolasco Pizarro
JPP	1841-44	Jose Policarpo Patino

1/4 REAL

SILVER
Obv: Castle, date below.
Rev: Sun face.

KM#	Date	Mintage	VG	Fine	VF	XF
1	1833	—	15.00	25.00	45.00	75.00
	1838	—	15.00	25.00	45.00	75.00

Obv: Castle flanked by Prize Cup.

KM#	Date	Mintage	VG	Fine	VF	XF
2.1	1839 lg. eight/small sun face	—	1000.	—	—	—
	1839 sm. eight/small sun face	—	—	—	Rare	—

Obv: Castle flanked by P-P, date below.

KM#	Date	Mintage	VG	Fine	VF	XF
2.2	1839 PP	—	6.00	12.50	22.50	45.00
	1840 PP	—	10.00	22.50	45.00	80.00
	1841 PP	—	15.00	27.50	60.00	100.00

NOTE: Many legend and die varieties exist.

Obv: Fraction.

KM#	Date	Mintage	VG	Fine	VF	XF
33	ND(1853-54)	—	10.00	15.00	25.00	50.00

NOTE: Die varieties exist.

1/2 REAL

SILVER
Obv: Arms in wreath, leg: EN UNION Y LIBERTAD.
Rev: Sun face, leg: PROVINCIA DE CORDOVA.

KM#	Date	Mintage	VG	Fine	VF	XF
3	1839 PNP	—	22.50	50.00	65.00	125.00
	1839 PNP LIVERTAD	—	25.00	55.00	75.00	150.00
	1839 PNP CORDOBA on rev.	—	25.00	55.00	75.00	150.00

KM# Date Mintage VG Fine VF XF
3 1840 PNP LIVERTAD
— 15.00 37.50 60.00 115.00
1840 PNP LIVEITAD
— — — Rare —

Obv. leg: EN UNION Y LIVERTAD.
Rev. leg: CONFEDERADA.
4 1839 PNP — 22.50 50.00 70.00 125.00

Obv. leg: CONFEDERADA.
Rev. leg: PROVINCIA DE CORDOVA.
5 1840 PNP — 25.00 50.00 70.00 125.00

Obv. leg: PROVINCIA DE CORDOV.
Rev. leg: PROVINCIA DE CORDOV.
15 1841 PNP — 22.50 50.00 70.00 125.00
1841 — 22.50 50.00 70.00 125.00

Obv: Banner above castle; date below, leg: CORDOVA.
Rev: Sun face, leg: CONFEDERADA.
6 1840 PNP crossed lances below castle
— 25.00 55.00 75.00 —

Obv. leg: CONFEDERADA.
Rev. leg: PROVINCIA DE CORDOVA.
16 1841 PNP — 22.50 50.00 70.00 —
1841 — 22.50 50.00 70.00 —

Obv: Denomination. Rev: Sun face.
29 1850 — 5.00 10.00 20.00 45.00
1850 error: CONFEDRRADA
— 5.00 10.00 20.00 45.00
1851 — 30.00 75.00 120.00 225.00
1853 — 5.00 10.00 20.00 45.00
1854 — 5.00 10.00 20.00 45.00
NOTE: Many legend and die varieties exist.

REAL

SILVER
Obv: Arms (shaded) in wreath; date below, leg: PROVINCIA DE CORDOVA.
Rev: Sun face, leg: CONFEDERADA.
7 1840 PNP — 3.25 6.50 12.50 25.00
1841/0 PNP — — — — —
1841 PNP — 3.25 6.50 12.50 25.00
1841 PNP CORDOBA
— 32.50 55.00 90.00 200.00
1841 PNP CORDOBA & inverted 4
— 42.50 72.50 95.00 200.00
1841 JPP — 3.25 6.50 12.50 25.00
1842 JPP — 3.25 6.50 12.50 25.00
1842 JPP PROVINCI
— 5.00 10.00 22.50 50.00
1842 JPP PROVINCA
— 5.00 10.00 18.00 45.00
1843 JPP — 3.25 6.50 12.50 25.00
1843 JPP inverted 3
— 4.50 8.50 16.00 32.50
3481 JPP (error for 1843)
— 8.50 20.00 32.50 70.00
1843 JPP PROVICIA
— 5.00 10.00 18.00 45.00
1843 JPP CORDOV
— 3.25 6.50 12.50 25.00
4481 JPP (error for 1844)
— 40.00 70.00 100.00 200.00
NOTE: Many legend and die varieties exist.

Obv. leg: PROVINCIA DE CORDOVA.
Rev. leg: PROVINCIA DE CORDOVA.
8 1840 PNP — 15.00 35.00 65.00 110.00
1841 PNP — 15.00 35.00 65.00 110.00

Obv. leg: PROVINCIA DE CORDOVA.
Rev. leg: EN UNION Y LIBERTAD.
9 1840 PNP — 3.25 6.50 12.50 30.00
1841 PNP — 3.25 6.50 12.50 30.00
1841 PNP CORDOBA
— 30.00 50.00 80.00 120.00

Obv. leg: CONFEDERADA.
Rev. leg: CONFEDERADA.
10 1840 PNP — 30.00 50.00 80.00 120.00

Obv. leg: CONFEDERADA.
Rev. leg: PROVINCIA DE CORDOVA.
11 1840 PNP — 30.00 50.00 80.00 120.00

Obv. leg: EN UNION Y LIBERTAD.
Rev. leg: PROVINCIA DE CORDOVA.
12 1840 PNP — 30.00 50.00 80.00 120.00

Obv. leg: EN UNION Y LIVERTAD.
Rev. leg: CONFEDERADA.
13 1840 PNP — 30.00 50.00 80.00 120.00

Obv. leg: PROVINCIA DE CORDOVA, arms w/o shading and 2 rosettes.
Rev. leg: CONFEDERADA, sun face.
KM# Date Mintage VG Fine VF XF
17 1841 PNP — 3.25 6.50 12.50 25.00
1843 JPP — 3.25 6.50 12.50 25.00
1843 JPP PROVINCI
— 3.25 6.50 12.50 25.00
1843 JPP CONFEDERDA
— 3.25 6.50 12.50 25.00
1843 JPP CORDOV
— 3.25 6.50 12.50 25.00

Rev. leg: LIBRE YNDEPENDIENTE.
20 1843 JPP — 6.00 12.00 22.00 45.00

Obv. leg: PROVINCIA DE CORDOVA; banner above castle. Rev. leg: CONFEDERADA, sun face.
14 1840 PNP — 50.00 80.00 120.00 180.00
1841 PNP — 6.00 12.00 22.00 45.00
1841 PNP CORDOBA
— 35.00 60.00 100.00 150.00
1841 PNP CORDOV, inverted 4
— 4.50 8.50 16.00 32.50
1841 PNP inverted 4
— 4.50 8.50 16.00 32.50
1841 PNP CORDOV
— 7.50 15.00 27.50 50.00
NOTE: Many legend and die varieties exist.

Obv. leg: PROVINCIA DE CORDOVA.
Rev. leg: EN UNION Y LIBERTAD.
18 1841 PNP — 12.50 22.50 40.00 75.00

Obv. leg: PROVINCIA DE CORDOVA.
Rev. leg: PROVINCIA DE CORDOVA.
19 1841 PNP rosette below castle
— 22.50 45.00 75.00 135.00

Obv. leg: PROVINCIA DE CORDOVA, arms w/o shading; date below.
Rev. leg: CONFEDERADA, sun face.
21 1843 JPP — 3.25 6.50 12.50 25.00
1843 JPP CONFEDERDA
— 3.25 6.50 12.50 25.00
1843 JPP CORDOV
— 3.25 6.50 12.50 25.00
1843 JPP CORDOV & CONFEDERDA
— 3.25 6.50 12.50 25.00
1843 JPP CORDOV & PROVINCI
— 5.50 10.00 17.50 35.00
1843 JPP CORDO
— 3.25 6.50 12.50 25.00
1843 JPP CORDO & CONFEDERDA
— 3.25 6.50 12.50 25.00
1844 JPP — 3.25 6.50 12.50 25.00
1844 JPP CORDOV
— 22.50 45.00 80.00 130.00
NOTE: Many legend and die varieties exist.

Obv. leg: PROVINCIA DE CORDOVA.
Rev. leg: LIBRE YNDEPENDIENTE.
22 1843 JPP — 6.50 12.50 18.00 37.50
NOTE: Many legend and die varieties exist.

Obv. leg: PROVINCIA DE CORDOBA, denomination.
Rev. leg: CONFEDERADA, sun face, date below.
26 1848 — 6.00 12.00 17.50 35.00
NOTE: Many legend and die varieties exist.

2 REALES

.750 SILVER
Obv: Castle among flags in sprays, leg: PROVINCIA DE CORDOBA.
Rev: Sun face in sprays, date below, leg: CONFEDERADA.
23 1844 — 6.00 11.00 20.00 40.00
1844 CONFEDRADA
— 18.00 37.50 75.00 135.00
1845 — 5.50 11.00 18.00 30.00
NOTE: Many legend and die varieties exist.

KM# Date Mintage VG Fine VF XF
25 1846 — 7.00 13.00 20.00 35.00
1848 — — — Rare —
NOTE: Many legend and die varieties exist.

27 1849 — 6.00 11.00 20.00 35.00

28 1849 — 6.00 11.00 20.00 35.00
1850 — 6.00 11.00 20.00 35.00
NOTE: Many legend and die varieties exist.

Similar to 4 Reales, KM#31.
30 1852 — 15.00 30.00 45.00 85.00
1854 — 15.00 30.00 45.00 85.00

4 REALES

.750 SILVER
Rev. weight: 9 Ds.
24.1 1844 — 100.00 200.00 325.00 575.00

Larger dies.
24.2 1845 obv. w/portcullis
— 30.00 55.00 85.00 160.00
1845 obv. w/o portcullis
— 22.50 40.00 70.00 100.00
1846 die of 1845
— 80.00 120.00 160.00 300.00

24.3 1846 milled edge
— 47.50 85.00 125.00 175.00
1846 laureate edge
— 30.00 55.00 85.00 160.00
1847 — 20.00 30.00 55.00 90.00
1850 — 20.00 30.00 55.00 90.00
1851 sm. 5mm sunface, wgt: 9.D.
— 20.00 30.00 55.00 90.00
1851 lg. 6.5mm sunface, wgt: 9.D.
— 20.00 30.00 55.00 90.00

Rev: Flatter sunface w/even length sunburst.

KM#	Date	Mintage	VG	Fine	VF	XF
24.4	1852		—	—	—	—

NOTE: Die and edge varieties exist.

KM#	Date	Mintage	VG	Fine	VF	XF
31	1852	—	30.00	50.00	80.00	150.00

8 REALES

.750 SILVER
Obv: High spear tips at left.

KM#	Date	Mintage	VG	Fine	VF	XF
32	1852	—	50.00	80.00	150.00	300.00

NOTE: 9 known varieties of obverses w/differences in width of base, size of and distance between leaves and positions of flag poles in relation to letters in inscription. Spelling differences are known w/CORDOBA the common one and Cordova the rare one.

ENTRE RIOS

Entre Rios (Colonia San Jose) was a settlement of Swiss and Italian families in northeast Argentina on the Uruguayan border. General Urquiza (deposer of Rosas) was a political power in the province. As governor, during the war with Paraguay, he authorized an Italian, Pablo Cataldi, to make coins for the settlement during a coin shortage in 1867.

1/2 REAL

SILVER

KM#	Date	Mintage	VG	Fine	VF	XF
1	1867	—	50.00	75.00	125.00	225.00

LA RIOJA

La Rioja (Rioxa), a city and province in northwest Argentina, was the source of rich mineral wealth. Governor Nicolas Davila, authorized a mint at Chilecito to take advantage of the rich mines at Famatina in 1820. The mint made "cob" types, with and without the name RIOXA from 1821 to 1823. The cobs were officially recalled in 1824.

In Chilecito, another city in La Rioja province, gold 1 Escudos and silver 1 Reales were struck in 1823. This mint was transferred to La Rioja in 1824, where coins were struck until 1860.

***NOTE:** Virtually all of the early pieces are false. All pieces dated between 1820 and 1824 should only be bought with certification of two or more authorities.

1/2 REAL

SILVER
Cob type w/RIOXA.

KM#	Date	Mintage	Good	VG	Fine	VF
3	1822	—	—	—	Rare	—

Obv: Arms in branches. Rev: Sun above mountain.

KM#	Date	Mintage	Good	VG	Fine	VF
18	1844 B	—	3.50	6.50	15.00	25.00

Obv. leg: REPUB. ARGENT. CONFEDERADA.
Rev. leg: PROV. DE LA. RIOJA.

KM#	Date	Mintage	Good	VG	Fine	VF
22	1854 B	—	2.00	3.00	7.50	15.00

Rev. leg: CRED. PUB. DE LA RIOJA.

KM#	Date	Mintage	Good	VG	Fine	VF
23	1854 B	—	2.00	4.00	10.00	20.00

Obv. leg: CONFEDERACION ARGENTINA.
Rev. leg: PROV. DE LA. RIOJA.

KM#	Date	Mintage	Good	VG	Fine	VF
24	1854 B	—	2.00	3.00	7.50	15.00

Rev. leg: CRED. PUB. DE LA RIOJA.

KM#	Date	Mintage	Good	VG	Fine	VF
25	1854 B	—	2.00	3.00	7.50	15.00
	1860 B	—	2.50	5.00	12.50	25.00

REAL

SILVER
Mint: Chilecito
Cob type w/RIOXA.

KM#	Date	Mintage	Good	VG	Fine	VF
4	1822	—	—	—	Rare	—

NOTE: 1821 dated coins are counterfeit.

Mint: La Rioja
Obv: Sun above arms.
Rev. leg: SVR AMERICA RIOXA.

KM#	Date	Mintage	Good	VG	Fine	VF
5	ND (1823)	—	—	—	Rare	—

Rev. leg: SUD AMERICA 1823 RIOXA

KM#	Date	Mintage	Good	VG	Fine	VF
6	1823	—	—	—	Rare	—

2 REALES

SILVER
Cob Type

KM#	Date	Mintage	Good	VG	Fine	VF
1	(1)821	—	—	—	Rare	—
	(1)822	—	—	—	Rare	—
	(1)823	—	—	—	Rare	—

General Rosas

KM#	Date	Mintage	Good	VG	Fine	VF
12	1842	—	15.00	25.00	42.50	85.00

Mountain type

KM#	Date	Mintage	Good	VG	Fine	VF
15	1843 RB	—	6.00	12.50	22.50	35.00

Mountain and sun type

KM#	Date	Mintage	Good	VG	Fine	VF
16	1843 RB	—	6.00	13.50	30.00	60.00
	1844 RB	—	5.00	10.00	20.00	45.00

NOTE: Struck in coin and medal rotation.

KM#	Date	Mintage	Good	VG	Fine	VF
26	1859 B	—	17.50	32.50	50.00	80.00
	1860 B	—	5.00	10.00	15.00	40.00

4 REALES

SILVER
Cob Type
Obv: Pillars, RIOXA, date. Rev: Castles & lions.

KM#	Date	Mintage	Good	VG	Fine	VF
2.1	(1)821	—	100.00	200.00	330.00	480.00
	(1)822	—	—	—	Rare	—

Obv: W/o RIOXA

KM#	Date	Mintage	Good	VG	Fine	VF
2.2	(1)823	—	125.00	250.00	375.00	550.00

KM#	Date	Mintage	VG	Fine	VF	XF
20	1846 RV	—	15.00	25.00	40.00	65.00
	1849 RV	—	—	—	—	—
	1849 RB	—	15.00	25.00	40.00	65.00
	1850 RB	—	20.00	30.00	50.00	85.00

KM#	Date	Mintage	VG	Fine	VF	XF
21	1852 B	—	55.00	85.00	130.00	200.00

8 REALES

SILVER

KM#	Date	Mintage	VG	Fine	VF	XF
8	1838 R	—	35.00	70.00	150.00	275.00
	1839 R	—	35.00	70.00	150.00	275.00
	1840 R	—	40.00	80.00	170.00	325.00

NOTE: Struck in coin and medal rotation.

Obv. leg: REPUBLICA ARGENTINA.

KM#	Date	Mintage	VG	Fine	VF	XF
10	1840 R	—	300.00	500.00	900.00	1750.

ESCUDO

3.3750 g, .875 GOLD, .0949 oz AGW
Obv: Sun above arms in branches.
Rev. leg: SUD AMERICA 1823 RIOXA in wreath.

KM#	Date	Mintage	VG	Fine	VF	XF
7	1823	—	—	—	Unique	—

2 ESCUDOS

6.7500 g, .875 GOLD, .1899 oz AGW
General Rosas

KM#	Date	Mintage	VG	Fine	VF	XF
13	1842 R	—	250.00	500.00	800.00	1500.

KM#	Date	Mintage	VG	Fine	VF	XF
17	1843 RB	—	200.00	400.00	600.00	1000.

8 ESCUDOS

27.0000 g, .875 GOLD, .7596 oz AGW
General Rosas

KM#	Date	Mintage	VG	Fine	VF	XF
A9	1836 R	—	—	—	Rare	—

KM#	Date	Mintage	VG	Fine	VF	XF
9	1838 R	—	650.00	1150.	2000.	3500.
	1840 R	—	750.00	1250.	2150.	3750.

Obv. leg: REPUBLICA ARGENTINA.

KM#	Date	Mintage	VG	Fine	VF	XF
11	1840 R	—	850.00	1350.	2250.	4000.

General Rosas

KM#	Date	Mintage	VG	Fine	VF	XF
14	1842 R	—	—	—	*Rare	—

***NOTE:** Superior Heifetz sale 12-89 VF realized $18,700.

KM#	Date	Mintage	VG	Fine	VF	XF
19	1845 B	—	1250.	1850.	2750.	5000.

MENDOZA

Mendoza, a province in western Argentina, was one of the first to make coins designed to resemble the Spanish Colonial cobs of Potosi. The mint was established in 1822, under Governor Pedro Molina. These local cobs were put in circulation in December 1823 and retired from circulation less than a year later.

In 1835 Molina again saw that coins were needed, and decided to award contracts for production rather than have the provincial mint make them. Abel Bucci and Manuel Espeys, who had the contract failed to supply any volume of coinage for circulation and were retired in 1836.

DECIMO

COPPER
Obv: Date and denomination within wreath.
Rev: Arms within branches.

KM#	Date	Mintage	Good	VG	Fine	VF
4	1823	—	—	—	Unique	—

1/8 REAL

COPPER

KM#	Date	Mintage	Good	VG	Fine	VF
5	1835	—	—	—	Rare	—

1/4 REAL

SILVER
Obv: Arms divide value.
Rev: Small animal.

KM#	Date	Mintage	Good	VG	Fine	VF
6	1836	—	—	—	Unique	—

SALTA

Salta, a province in northwest Argentina, was a frequent battleground during the War of Independence. Governor Martin Guemes fought the Spaniards without help from the patriotic forces in Buenos Aires. There was no money with which to pay the troops and what was circulating was counterfeit. Low morale and frequent desertions were one result. In desperation, Guemes decided to countermark the false coins with the word PATRIA and to guarantee them as genuine.

When this action became known to the patriot government in Buenos Aires, it was declared to be a violation of national laws and all the pieces were to be withdrawn.

Meanwhile, Guemes had gained valuable time, culminating with a victory at Castanares which finally rid the north of Spanish influence.

All genuine Salta countermarks are only found on counterfeit Potosi cobs.

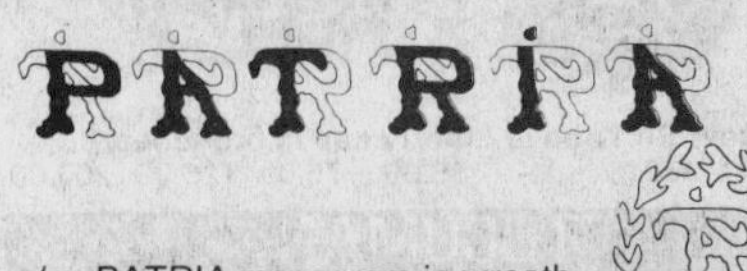

c/m: PATRIA monogram in wreath.

2 REALES

SILVER
c/m: PATRIA monogram in wreath on Potosi Mint cobs.

KM#	Date	Mintage	Good	VG	Fine	VF
2	ND(1817)	—	50.00	100.00	150.00	—

4 REALES

SILVER
c/m: PATRIA monogram in wreath on Potosi Mint cobs.

KM#	Date	Mintage	Good	VG	Fine	VF
3	ND(1817)	—	—	—	Rare	—

8 REALES

All known specimens are considered fantasies.

SANTIAGO DEL ESTERO

Santiago del Estero is a province in north central Argentina. In 1823, during the governorship of Felipe Ibarra, coinage began in an effort to replace the fast-disappearing cob coins of the Potosi mint. The pieces were not well received and coining was soon halted. Another effort, in 1836, faired no better.

1/2 REAL

SILVER
Obv: SoEo in angles of crossed arrows, date below.
Rev: Sun in branches.

KM#	Date	Mintage	Good	VG	Fine	VF
1	(1)823 So Eo	—	—	—	Unique	—

Obv: S E in angles of crossed arrows, date below.

KM#	Date	Mintage	Good	VG	Fine	VF
2	(1)823	—	75.00	150.00	225.00	300.00

REAL

SILVER
Obv: SoEo in angles of crossed arrows, date below.
Rev: Cross.

KM#	Date	Mintage	Good	VG	Fine	VF
3	(1)823	—	—	—	Unique	—

Rev: Sun in branches.

KM#	Date	Mintage	Good	VG	Fine	VF
4	(1)823	—	100.00	200.00	350.00	600.00

Obv: S E in angles of crossed arrows, date below.

KM#	Date	Mintage	Good	VG	Fine	VF
5	(1)823	—	50.00	100.00	150.00	250.00

Rev: Sun above Liberty cap in branches.

KM#	Date	Mintage	Good	VG	Fine	VF
6	(1)836	—	35.00	75.00	125.00	200.00

TUCUMAN

Tucuman is a province in northwestern Argentina. Due to the large quantity of false Potosi cobs circulating in the province, Governor Bernabe Araoz established a mint in 1823 to make cobs that would be distinctive to the area. Their circulation was brief due to the introduction of Confederation coins.

2 REALES

SILVER
Mint mark: TN
Similar to Potosi Cob 2 Reales.

KM#	Date	Mintage	Good	VG	Fine	VF
1	ND(1823)	—	35.00	75.00	100.00	125.00

NOTE: Most coins exist without the TN mint mark. Coins with the T discernable are generally worth two times the above values, with TN visable four times. Those with fictitious dates are attributed to Venezuela. Virtually all have the date 752 but there are 2 known pieces dated 753. These are similar to Potosi coins but can be easily distinguished by the Pillars of Hercules on the obverse.

REPUBLIC

Decimal Coinage

100 Centavos = 1 Peso
5 Pesos = 1 Argentino

CENTAVO

BRONZE

KM#	Date	Mintage	Fine	VF	XF	Unc
7	1882	.108	6.50	13.50	22.50	35.00
	1883	.786	.75	1.75	4.50	18.00
	1884	4.604	.50	1.00	2.50	6.50
	1885	1.314	.50	1.00	3.50	9.00
	1886	.444	.75	1.75	4.50	20.00
	1888	.413	.75	2.25	5.50	22.50
	1889	.568	.75	2.25	5.50	22.50
	1890	2.137	.50	1.00	2.50	6.50
	1891	.605	.75	1.75	4.50	18.00
	1892	.205	1.00	2.25	5.50	22.50
	1893	.754	.50	1.75	4.50	18.00
	1894	.532	1.00	1.75	4.50	18.00
	1895	.423	.75	2.25	5.50	18.00
	1896	.174	4.50	11.00	15.50	27.00

KM#	Date	Mintage	Fine	VF	XF	Unc
12	1939	3.488	.15	.35	.70	1.50
	1940	3.140	.15	.35	.70	1.50
	1941	4.572	.15	.35	.70	1.50
	1942	.496	.30	.75	1.50	7.50
	1943	1.294	.20	.50	1.00	2.00
	1944	3.104	.10	.25	.50	1.25

COPPER
Cruder diework

KM#	Date	Mintage	Fine	VF	XF	Unc
12a	1945	.420	.20	.50	1.00	4.00
	1946	4.450	.15	.35	.50	1.00
	1947	5.630	.15	.35	.50	1.00
	1948	4.420	.15	.35	.50	1.00

2 CENTAVOS

BRONZE

KM#	Date	Mintage	Fine	VF	XF	Unc
8	1882	.088	6.00	13.50	22.50	54.00
	1883	1.389	.75	1.75	3.50	13.50
	1884	5.667	.75	1.75	2.50	6.50
	1885	3.065	.75	1.75	3.00	9.00
	1887	.363	4.50	11.50	18.00	32.50
	1888	.659	1.75	3.50	7.00	21.50
	1889	2.391	.75	1.75	3.00	9.00
	1890	3.609	.75	1.75	3.00	9.00
	1891	8.050	.50	1.75	3.00	6.50
	1892	3.497	.75	1.75	3.00	9.00
	1893	5.473	.75	1.75	3.00	9.00
	1894	2.233	.75	1.75	3.00	9.00
	1895	.593	1.25	3.50	7.00	21.50
	1896	.596	1.75	4.50	8.00	25.00

KM#	Date	Mintage	Fine	VF	XF	Unc
13	1939	5.490	.10	.25	.50	1.25
	1940	4.625	.10	.25	.50	1.75
	1941	4.567	.10	.25	.50	1.75
	1942	2.082	.10	.25	.50	1.75
	1944	.387	.25	.50	1.00	6.50
	1945	4.585	.10	.25	.50	1.75
	1946	3.395	.10	.25	.50	1.75
	1947	4.395	.10	.25	.50	1.50

COPPER
Cruder diework

KM#	Date	Mintage	Fine	VF	XF	Unc
13a	1947	Inc. Ab.	.15	.30	.50	1.50
	1948	3.645	.15	.30	.50	1.50
	1949	7.290	.15	.30	.50	1.50
	1950	.903	.25	.65	1.25	3.00

5 CENTAVOS

COPPER-NICKEL

KM#	Date	Mintage	Fine	VF	XF	Unc
9	1896	1.499	.75	2.00	5.00	15.00
	1897	3.981	.50	1.00	4.00	10.00
	1898	2.661	.50	1.00	4.00	10.00
	1899	2.835	.25	.50	3.00	9.00
	1903	2.502	.25	.50	3.00	9.00
	1904	2.518	.25	.50	3.00	9.00
	1905	4.359	.25	.50	3.00	9.00
	1906	3.939	.25	.50	3.00	9.00
	1907	1.682	.50	1.00	5.00	15.00
	1908	1.693	.50	1.00	5.00	15.00
	1909	4.650	.25	.50	3.00	9.00
	1910	1.469	.75	2.00	5.00	17.50
	1911	1.431	.25	.75	4.00	10.00
	1912	2.377	.25	.75	4.00	10.00
	1913	1.477	.25	.75	4.00	10.00
	1914	1.097	.50	1.00	5.00	15.00
	1915	1.903	.30	.75	3.50	10.00
	1916	1.310	.30	.75	3.50	9.00
	1917	1.009	.75	1.50	4.00	10.00
	1918	2.287	.25	.50	3.00	7.00
9	1919	2.476	.25	.50	3.00	7.00
	1920	5.235	.25	.50	3.00	7.00
	1921	7.040	.20	.35	2.00	6.00
	1922	9.427	.20	.35	2.00	6.00
	1923	6.256	.20	.35	2.00	6.00
	1924	6.355	.20	.35	2.00	6.00
	1925	3.955	.20	.35	2.00	6.00
	1926	3.560	.20	.35	2.00	6.00
	1927	5.650	.20	.35	2.00	6.00
	1928	6.380	.20	.35	2.00	6.00
	1929	11.831	.20	.35	2.00	6.00
	1930	7.110	.20	.35	2.00	6.00
	1931	.506	.75	1.50	4.00	12.50
	1933	5.537	.10	.25	1.00	3.00
	1934	1.288	.25	.50	3.00	7.00
	1935	3.052	.10	.25	1.00	3.00
	1936	7.175	.10	.25	1.00	3.00
	1937	7.063	.10	.25	1.00	3.00
	1938	10.252	.10	.25	1.00	3.00
	1939	7.171	.10	.25	1.00	3.00
	1940	10.191	.10	.25	1.00	3.00
	1941	.951	.25	.75	2.00	8.00
	1942	8.692	.10	.25	1.00	3.00

ALUMINUM-BRONZE

KM#	Date	Mintage	Fine	VF	XF	Unc
15	1942	2.130	.15	.35	1.00	3.00
	1943	15.778	.10	.25	.50	2.00
	1944	21.081	.10	.25	.50	2.00
	1945	21.600	.10	.25	.50	2.00
	1946	20.460	.10	.25	.50	2.00
	1947	22.520	.10	.25	.50	2.00
	1948	42.790	.10	.25	.50	2.00
	1949	35.470	.10	.25	.50	2.00
	1950	13.500	.10	.25	.50	2.00

COPPER-NICKEL
Jose de San Martin
Reeded edge

KM#	Date	Mintage	Fine	VF	XF	Unc
18	1950	3.460	.20	.50	.75	2.50

KM#	Date	Mintage	Fine	VF	XF	Unc
21	1951	34.994	—	.20	.30	.50
	1952	33.110	—	.20	.30	.50
	1953	20.129	—	.20	.30	.50

COPPER-NICKEL-CLAD STEEL
Plain edge

KM#	Date	Mintage	Fine	VF	XF	Unc
21a	1953	56.300	—	.15	.20	.30

Rev: Smaller head.

KM#	Date	Mintage	Fine	VF	XF	Unc
25	1954	50.640	—	.15	.20	.30
	1955	42.200	—	.15	.20	.30
	1956	36.870	—	.15	.20	.30

KM#	Date	Mintage	Fine	VF	XF	Unc
28	1957	26.930	—	.15	.20	.30
	1958	13.108	—	.15	.20	.30
	1959	14.971	—	.15	.20	.30

10 CENTAVOS

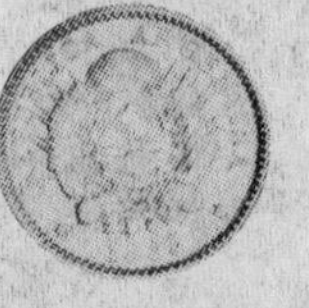

2.5000 g, .900 SILVER, .0723 oz ASW

KM#	Date	Mintage	Fine	VF	XF	Unc
1	1881	1,020	75.00	150.00	225.00	375.00
	1882	.778	5.00	10.00	15.00	40.00
	1883	2.786	2.00	4.00	8.00	16.00

COPPER-NICKEL

KM#	Date	Mintage	Fine	VF	XF	Unc
10	1896	1.877	1.00	2.50	6.00	22.50
	1897	8.582	.50	1.50	4.50	10.00
	1898	8.534	.50	1.50	4.50	10.00
	1899	8.889	.50	1.50	4.50	10.00
	1905	3.785	.50	1.00	3.50	8.00
	1906	3.854	.50	1.00	3.50	8.00
	1907	2.355	.50	1.00	4.50	10.00
	1908	2.280	.50	1.00	4.50	10.00
	1909	3.738	.50	1.00	3.50	8.00
	1910	3.026	.50	1.00	3.50	8.00
	1911	2.142	.75	2.00	5.00	12.00
	1912	2.993	.75	2.00	5.00	12.00
	1913	1.828	1.00	2.50	5.50	15.00
	1914	.751	1.00	2.50	5.50	15.00
	1915	2.607	.50	1.00	3.50	8.00
	1916	.835	1.00	2.50	5.50	15.00
	1918	3.897	.50	1.00	3.50	8.00
	1919	2.517	.50	1.00	3.50	8.00
	1920	7.509	.25	.75	2.50	7.00
	1921	11.564	.25	.60	2.00	3.75
	1922	6.542	.20	.50	1.50	3.50
	1923	5.301	.20	.50	1.50	3.50
	1924	3.489	.20	.50	1.50	3.50
	1925	5.415	.20	.50	1.50	3.50
	1926	5.055	.15	.35	1.00	3.00
	1927	5.205	.15	.35	1.00	3.00
	1928	8.255	.15	.35	1.00	3.00
	1929	2.501	.15	.35	1.00	3.00
	1930	14.586	.15	.35	1.00	2.50
	1931	.893	.50	1.00	2.50	7.50
	1933	5.394	.15	.35	1.00	2.50
	1934	3.319	.15	.35	1.00	2.50
	1935	1.018	.30	.75	2.00	5.00
	1936	3.000	.15	.35	1.00	4.50
	1937	11.766	.15	.35	1.00	2.00
	1938	10.494	.15	.35	1.00	2.00
	1939	5.585	.15	.35	1.00	3.00
	1940	3.955	.15	.35	1.00	3.00
	1941	4.101	.15	.35	1.00	3.00
	1942	2.962	.15	.25	1.00	3.00

ALUMINUM-BRONZE

KM#	Date	Mintage	Fine	VF	XF	Unc
16	1942	15.541	.15	.25	.75	2.00
	1943	13.916	.15	.25	.75	2.00
	1944	16.411	.15	.25	.75	2.00
	1945	12.500	.15	.25	.75	2.00
	1946	15.790	.15	.25	.75	2.00
	1947	36.430	.15	.25	.75	2.00
	1948	54.685	.15	.25	.75	2.00
	1949	57.740	.15	.25	.75	2.00
	1950	42.825	.15	.25	.75	2.00

COPPER-NICKEL
Jose de San Martin
Reeded edge

KM#	Date	Mintage	Fine	VF	XF	Unc
19	1950	17.505	.30	.75	1.00	2.50

KM#	Date	Mintage	Fine	VF	XF	Unc
22	1951	98.521	—	.20	.30	.50
	1952	67.328	—	.20	.30	.50

NICKEL-CLAD STEEL
Plain edge

KM#	Date	Mintage	Fine	VF	XF	Unc
22a	1952	33.240	—	.10	.15	.25
	1953	106.685	—	.10	.15	.25

Obv: Smaller head.

KM#	Date	Mintage	Fine	VF	XF	Unc
26	1954	117.200	—	.10	.15	.25
26	1955	97.045	—	.10	.15	.25
	1956	122.630	—	.10	.15	.25

KM#	Date	Mintage	Fine	VF	XF	Unc
29	1957	52.810	—	.10	.15	.25
	1958	41.916	—	.10	.15	.25
	1959	29.183	—	.10	.15	.25

20 CENTAVOS

5.0000 g, .900 SILVER, .1446 oz ASW

KM#	Date	Mintage	Fine	VF	XF	Unc
2	1881	2,018	40.00	70.00	100.00	150.00
	1882	.762	7.50	12.50	25.00	50.00
	1883/2 inverted 2	1.511	9.00	17.50	35.00	75.00
	1883	Inc. Ab.	4.00	8.00	16.00	35.00

COPPER-NICKEL

KM#	Date	Mintage	Fine	VF	XF	Unc
11	1896	2.030	.75	2.00	5.00	20.00
	1897	5.263	.75	2.00	5.00	20.00
	1898	1.264	1.50	4.00	8.00	30.00
	1899	.840	2.75	6.00	12.00	50.00
	1905	4.455	.75	2.00	5.00	20.00
	1906	4.331	.75	2.00	5.00	20.00
	1907	3.730	1.00	3.00	7.00	25.00
	1908	.719	2.25	5.00	10.00	30.00
	1909	1.329	.50	1.50	4.00	15.00
	1910	1.845	.50	1.50	4.00	15.00
	1911	1.110	.50	1.50	4.00	15.00
	1912	2.402	.50	1.50	4.00	15.00
	1913	1.579	.50	1.00	2.50	10.00
	1914	.527	2.25	5.00	10.00	45.00
	1915	1.921	.50	1.00	2.50	7.50
	1916	.985	.50	1.25	2.50	17.50
	1918	1.638	.40	.75	2.00	7.50
	1919	2.280	.40	.75	2.00	7.50
	1920	7.572	.40	.75	2.00	6.25
	1921	5.286	.25	.60	1.75	5.00
	1922	2.324	.25	.60	1.75	5.00
	1923	4.416	.25	.60	1.75	5.00
	1924	3.676	.25	.60	1.75	5.00
	1925	3.799	.25	.60	1.75	5.00
	1926	3.250	.25	.50	1.25	3.75
	1927	2.880	.25	.50	1.25	3.75
	1928	2.886	.25	.50	1.25	3.75
	1929	8.361	.25	.50	1.25	3.00
	1930	8.281	.25	.50	1.25	3.00
	1931	.315	2.25	5.00	10.00	20.00
	1935	1.127	.25	.60	1.75	5.00
	1936	.855	.50	1.25	2.50	12.50
	1937	3.314	.25	.50	1.50	3.75
	1938	6.449	.25	.50	1.25	3.00
	1939	3.555	.25	.50	1.25	3.00
	1940	4.465	.25	.50	1.25	3.00
	1941	.600	.50	1.00	2.00	10.00
	1942	4.844	.25	.50	1.25	3.00

ALUMINUM-BRONZE

KM#	Date	Mintage	Fine	VF	XF	Unc
17	1942	10.255	.15	.25	.75	2.00
	1943	13.775	.15	.25	.75	2.00
	1944	12.225	.15	.25	.75	2.00
	1945	13.340	.15	.25	.75	2.00
	1946	14.625	.15	.25	.75	2.00
	1947	23.165	.15	.25	.75	2.00
	1948	32.245	.15	.25	.75	2.00
	1949	67.115	.15	.25	.75	2.00
	1950	40.071	.15	.25	.75	2.00

COPPER-NICKEL
Jose de San Martin
Reeded edge

KM#	Date	Mintage	Fine	VF	XF	Unc
20	1950	86.770	.25	.50	.75	2.00

KM#	Date	Mintage	Fine	VF	XF	Unc
23	1951	85.782	.10	.20	.30	.50
	1952	69.796	.10	.20	.30	.50

NICKEL CLAD STEEL
Plain edge

KM#	Date	Mintage	Fine	VF	XF	Unc
23a	1952	12.863	—	.15	.40	1.00
	1953	36.893	—	.15	.25	.50

Head size reduced slightly

KM#	Date	Mintage	Fine	VF	XF	Unc
27	1954	52.563	—	.15	.20	.25
	1955	46.952	—	.15	.20	.25
	1956	35.995	—	.15	.20	.25

KM#	Date	Mintage	Fine	VF	XF	Unc
30	1957	89.365	—	.15	.20	.25
	1958	52.710	—	.15	.20	.25
	1959	56.585	—	.15	.20	.25
	1960	21.254	—	.15	.20	.25
	1961	2.083	—	.25	.50	1.50

50 CENTAVOS

12.5000 g, .900 SILVER, .3617 oz ASW

KM#	Date	Mintage	Fine	VF	XF	Unc
3	1881	1,020	125.00	225.00	375.00	650.00
	1882	.476	20.00	30.00	60.00	150.00
	1883	2.273	8.00	16.00	30.00	65.00

NICKEL
Reeded edge

KM#	Date	Mintage	Fine	VF	XF	Unc
14	1941	10.961	.40	1.00	1.25	2.00

NICKEL-CLAD STEEL
Jose de San Martin
Plain edge

KM#	Date	Mintage	Fine	VF	XF	Unc
24	1952	29.736	.10	.20	.35	.75

KM#	Date	Mintage	Fine	VF	XF	Unc
24	1953	62.814	.10	.20	.35	.75
	1954	132.224	.10	.20	.35	.75
	1955	75.490	.10	.20	.35	.75
	1956	19.120	.10	.20	.45	1.00

KM#	Date	Mintage	Fine	VF	XF	Unc
31	1957	18.139	—	.10	.25	.30
	1958	51.750	.10	.20	.30	.40
	1959	13.997	—	.10	.20	.30
	1960	26.038	.10	.20	.30	.40
	1961	11.106	—	.10	.20	.35

PESO

25.0000 g, .900 SILVER, .7234 oz ASW

KM#	Date	Mintage	Fine	VF	XF	Unc
4	1881	.062	100.00	150.00	220.00	350.00
	1882	.414	50.00	75.00	125.00	250.00
	1883	.098	100.00	150.00	220.00	350.00

NICKEL-CLAD STEEL

KM#	Date	Mintage	Fine	VF	XF	Unc
32	1957	118.118	.10	.20	.40	.75
	1958	118.151	.10	.20	.40	.75
	1959	237.733	.10	.20	.30	.50
	1960	75.048	.10	.30	.50	1.00
	1961	76.897	.10	.30	.50	1.00
	1962	30.006	.10	.30	.50	1.00

150th Anniversary of Removal of Spanish Viceroy

KM#	Date	Mintage	Fine	VF	XF	Unc
33	1960	98.751	.20	.50	.75	1.25

1/2 ARGENTINO

4.0322 g, .900 GOLD, .1167 oz AGW

KM#	Date	Mintage	Fine	VF	XF	Unc
5	1881	9 pcs.	—	—	Rare	—
	1884	421 pcs.	550.00	900.00	1250.	1850.

ARGENTINO

8.0645 g, .900 GOLD, .2334 oz AGW

KM#	Date	Mintage	Fine	VF	XF	Unc
6	1881	.037	125.00	150.00	200.00	275.00
	1882	.252	100.00	125.00	150.00	225.00
	1883	.906	100.00	125.00	150.00	225.00
	1884	.448	100.00	125.00	150.00	225.00
	1885	.204	100.00	125.00	150.00	225.00
	1886	.398	100.00	125.00	150.00	225.00
	1887	1.835	100.00	120.00	140.00	200.00
	1888	1.663	100.00	120.00	140.00	200.00
	1889	.404	175.00	275.00	400.00	550.00
	1896	.197	100.00	125.00	150.00	225.00

5 PESOS

NICKEL-CLAD STEEL
Sailing Ship - Presidente Sarmiento

KM#	Date	Mintage	Fine	VF	XF	Unc
34	1961	37.423	.10	.20	.30	.50
	1962	42.362	.10	.20	.30	.50
	1963	71.769	.10	.20	.30	.50
	1964	12.302	.15	.25	.40	.75
	1965	19.450	.10	.20	.30	.50
	1966	17.259	.10	.20	.30	.50
	1967	17.806	.10	.20	.30	.50
	1968	12.634	.10	.20	.30	.50

10 PESOS

NICKEL-CLAD STEEL
Gaucho

KM#	Date	Mintage	Fine	VF	XF	Unc
35	1962	57.401	.10	.20	.30	.65
	1963	136.792	.10	.20	.30	.65
	1964	46.576	.10	.20	.30	.65
	1965	40.640	—	.15	.30	.65
	1966	50.733	.10	.20	.30	.65
	1967	43.050	.10	.20	.30	.75
	1968	36.588	—	.15	.30	.65

150th Anniversary of Declaration of Independence

KM#	Date	Mintage	Fine	VF	XF	Unc
37	1966	29.336	.10	.15	.35	1.00

25 PESOS

NICKEL-CLAD STEEL
1st Issue of National Coinage in 1813

KM#	Date	Mintage	Fine	VF	XF	Unc
36	1964	20.485	.10	.25	.50	1.25
	1965	14.884	.10	.25	.50	1.25
	1966	16.426	.10	.25	.50	1.25
	1967	15.734	.10	.25	.50	1.25
	1968	4.446	.10	.25	.75	1.65

80th Anniversary of Death of D. Faustino Sarmiento

KM#	Date	Mintage	Fine	VF	XF	Unc
38	1968	15.804	.25	.60	.85	1.50

MONETARY REFORM

1970 - 1983
100 Old Pesos = 1 New Peso

CENTAVO

ALUMINUM

KM#	Date	Mintage	Fine	VF	XF	Unc
39	1970	47.801	—	—	.10	.20
	1971	44.644	—	—	.10	.20
	1972	92.430	—	—	.10	.20
	1973	29.515	—	—	.10	.20
	1974	5.162	—	—	.10	.25
	1975	3.840	—	.10	.20	.50

5 CENTAVOS

ALUMINUM

KM#	Date	Mintage	Fine	VF	XF	Unc
40	1970	56.174	—	.10	.15	.25
	1971	3.798	.10	.20	.35	.50
	1972	84.250	—	.10	.15	.25
	1973	113.912	—	.10	.15	.25
	1974	18.150	—	.10	.15	.25
	1975	6.940	.10	.20	.35	.50

10 CENTAVOS

BRASS

KM#	Date	Mintage	Fine	VF	XF	Unc
41	1970	52.903	—	.10	.15	.25
	1971	135.623	—	.10	.15	.25
	1973	19.930	—	.10	.15	.25
	1974	79.156	—	.10	.15	.25
	1975	31.270	—	.10	.15	.25
	1976	.730	.10	.20	.35	1.00

20 CENTAVOS

BRASS

KM#	Date	Mintage	Fine	VF	XF	Unc
42	1970	27.029	—	.10	.15	.25
	1971	32.211	—	.10	.15	.25
	1972	.220	2.00	6.00	10.00	20.00
	1973	9.676	—	.10	.15	.25
	1974	41.024	—	.10	.15	.25
	1975	26.540	—	.10	.15	.25
	1976	.960	—	.10	.15	.25

50 CENTAVOS

BRASS

KM#	Date	Mintage	Fine	VF	XF	Unc
43	1970	44.748	.10	.15	.30	.50
	1971	34.947	.10	.15	.30	.50
	1972	40.960	.10	.15	.30	.50
	1973	69.472	.10	.15	.30	.50
	1974	63.063	.10	.15	.30	.50
	1975	64.859	.10	.15	.30	.50
	1976	9.768	.10	.15	.30	.50

PESO

ALUMINUM-BRASS

KM#	Date	Mintage	Fine	VF	XF	Unc
44	1974	77.292	—	.10	.25	.75
	1975	423.000	—	.10	.20	.50
	1976	100.075	—	.10	.20	.50

NOTE: Wide and narrow rim varieties exist.

5 PESOS

ALUMINUM-BRONZE

KM#	Date	Mintage	Fine	VF	XF	Unc
46	1976	118.353	—	.10	.20	.65
	1977	64.738	—	.10	.20	.65

Admiral G. Brown Bicentennial

KM#	Date	Mintage	Fine	VF	XF	Unc
48	1977	Inc. Ab.	.10	.15	.25	.50

10 PESOS

ALUMINUM-BRONZE

KM#	Date	Mintage	Fine	VF	XF	Unc
47	1976	128.965	.10	.15	.35	1.00
	1977	113.400	.10	.15	.35	1.00
	1978	253.863	.10	.15	.35	1.00

Admiral G. Brown Bicentennial

KM#	Date	Mintage	Fine	VF	XF	Unc
49	1977	Inc. Ab.	.10	.20	.50	1.20

20 PESOS

ALUMINUM-BRONZE
1978 World Soccer Championship

KM#	Date	Mintage	Fine	VF	XF	Unc
50	1977	1.506	.15	.35	.75	1.25
	1978	2.000	.10	.25	.50	1.00

50 PESOS

ALUMINUM-BRONZE
1978 World Soccer Championship

KM#	Date	Mintage	Fine	VF	XF	Unc
51	1977	1.506	.15	.35	.75	1.25
	1978	2.000	.10	.25	.50	1.00

200th Anniversary of Birth of Jose de San Martin

KM#	Date	Mintage	Fine	VF	XF	Unc
56	1978	40.601	.20	.50	1.00	2.00

Jose de San Martin

KM#	Date	Mintage	Fine	VF	XF	Unc
58	1979	103.491	.10	.25	.75	1.50.

BRASS CLAD STEEL

KM#	Date	Mintage	Fine	VF	XF	Unc
58a	1980	94.730	.10	.25	.75	1.25
	1981	4.372	.10	.25	.75	1.25

ALUMINUM-BRONZE
Conquest of Patagonia Centennial

KM#	Date	Mintage	Fine	VF	XF	Unc
59	1979	Inc. Ab.	.10	.25	.75	1.25

100 PESOS

ALUMINUM-BRONZE
1978 World Soccer Championship

KM#	Date	Mintage	Fine	VF	XF	Unc
52	1977	1.506	.25	.50	1.00	1.50
	1978	2.000	.25	.50	1.00	1.50

200th Anniversary of Birth of Jose de San Martin

KM#	Date	Mintage	Fine	VF	XF	Unc
57	1978	113.826	—	.50	1.00	2.00

Jose de San Martin

KM#	Date	Mintage	Fine	VF	XF	Unc
60	1979	207.572	.15	.30	.75	1.25
	1980	154.260	.15	.30	.75	1.25
	1981	145.680	.15	.30	.75	1.25

BRASS CLAD STEEL

KM#	Date	Mintage	Fine	VF	XF	Unc
60a	1980	Inc. Ab.	.15	.30	.75	1.50
	1981	Inc. Ab.	.15	.30	.75	1.50

ALUMINUM-BRONZE
Conquest of Patagonia Centennial

KM#	Date	Mintage	Fine	VF	XF	Unc
61	1979	Inc. Ab.	.15	.30	.75	1.50

1000 PESOS

10.0000 g, .900 SILVER, .2893 oz ASW
1978 World Soccer Championship

KM#	Date	Mintage	Fine	VF	XF	Unc
53	1977	.106	—	—	5.00	7.50
	1977	1,000	—	—	Proof	17.50
	1978	.141	—	—	5.00	7.50
	1978	1,750	—	—	Proof	17.50

2000 PESOS

15.0000 g, .900 SILVER, .4340 oz ASW
1978 World Soccer Championship

KM#	Date	Mintage	Fine	VF	XF	Unc
54	1977	.106	—	—	7.50	10.00
	1977	1,000	—	—	Proof	22.50
	1978	.141	—	—	7.50	10.00
	1978	1,750	—	—	Proof	22.50

3000 PESOS

25.0000 g, .900 SILVER, .7234 oz ASW
1978 World Soccer Championship

KM#	Date	Mintage	Fine	VF	XF	Unc
55	1977	.106	—	—	10.00	15.00
	1977	1,000	—	—	Proof	35.00
	1978	.141	—	—	10.00	15.00
	1978	1,750	—	—	Proof	35.00

MONETARY REFORM

1983 - 1985
10,000 Pesos = 1 Peso Argentino
100 Centavos = 1 Peso Argentino

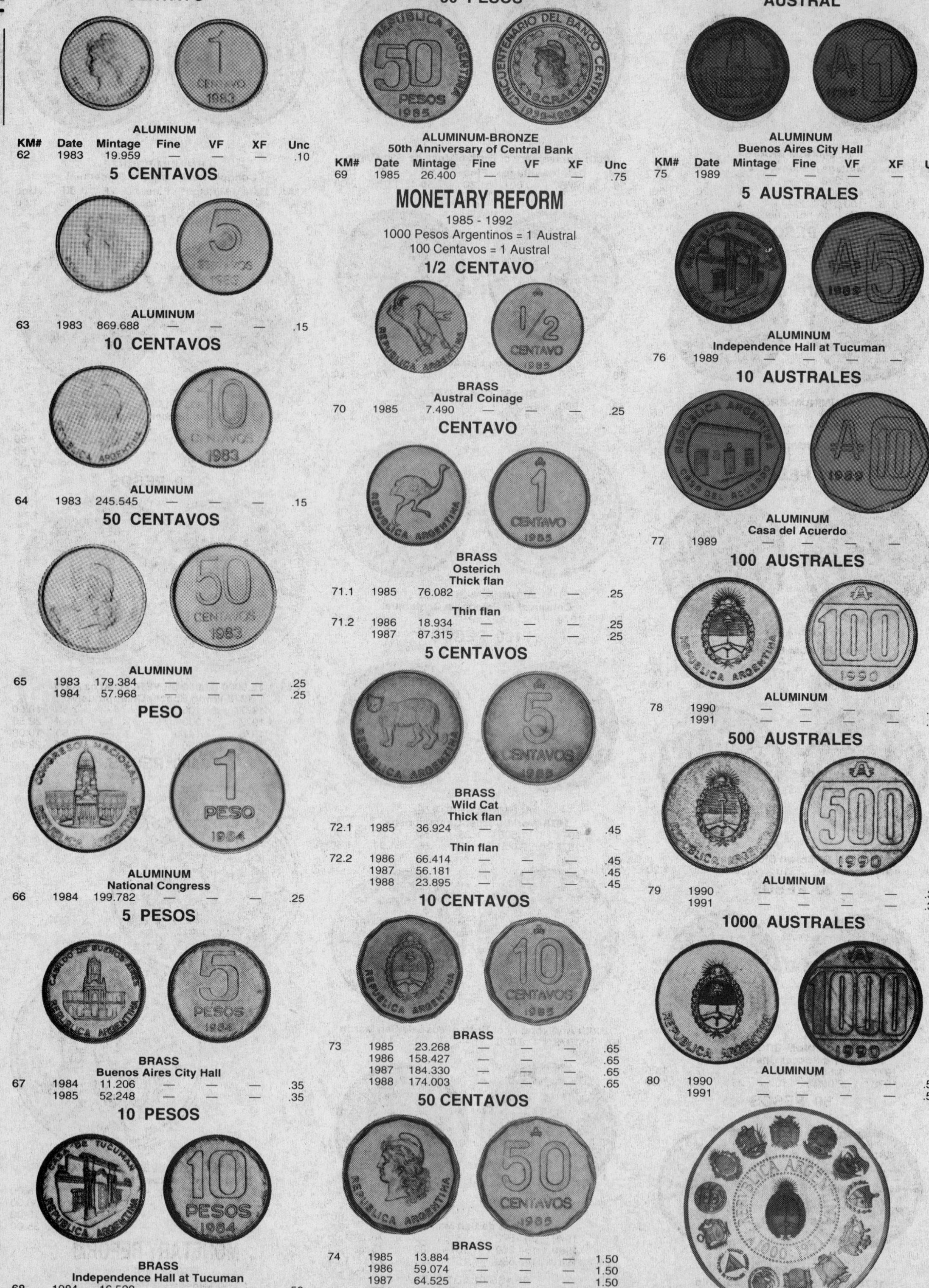

CENTAVO

ALUMINUM

KM#	Date	Mintage	Fine	VF	XF	Unc
62	1983	19.959	—	—	—	.10

5 CENTAVOS

ALUMINUM

KM#	Date	Mintage	Fine	VF	XF	Unc
63	1983	869.688	—	—	—	.15

10 CENTAVOS

ALUMINUM

KM#	Date	Mintage	Fine	VF	XF	Unc
64	1983	245.545	—	—	—	.15

50 CENTAVOS

ALUMINUM

KM#	Date	Mintage	Fine	VF	XF	Unc
65	1983	179.384	—	—	—	.25
	1984	57.968	—	—	—	.25

PESO

ALUMINUM
National Congress

KM#	Date	Mintage	Fine	VF	XF	Unc
66	1984	199.782	—	—	—	.25

5 PESOS

BRASS
Buenos Aires City Hall

KM#	Date	Mintage	Fine	VF	XF	Unc
67	1984	11.206	—	—	—	.35
	1985	52.248	—	—	—	.35

10 PESOS

BRASS
Independence Hall at Tucuman

KM#	Date	Mintage	Fine	VF	XF	Unc
68	1984	16.528	—	—	—	.50
	1985	33.214	—	—	—	.50

50 PESOS

ALUMINUM-BRONZE
50th Anniversary of Central Bank

KM#	Date	Mintage	Fine	VF	XF	Unc
69	1985	26.400	—	—	—	.75

MONETARY REFORM

1985 - 1992
1000 Pesos Argentinos = 1 Austral
100 Centavos = 1 Austral

1/2 CENTAVO

BRASS
Austral Coinage

KM#	Date	Mintage	Fine	VF	XF	Unc
70	1985	7.490	—	—	—	.25

CENTAVO

BRASS
Osterich
Thick flan

KM#	Date	Mintage	Fine	VF	XF	Unc
71.1	1985	76.082	—	—	—	.25
	Thin flan					
71.2	1986	18.934	—	—	—	.25
	1987	87.315	—	—	—	.25

5 CENTAVOS

BRASS
Wild Cat
Thick flan

KM#	Date	Mintage	Fine	VF	XF	Unc
72.1	1985	36.924	—	—	—	.45
	Thin flan					
72.2	1986	66.414	—	—	—	.45
	1987	56.181	—	—	—	.45
	1988	23.895	—	—	—	.45

10 CENTAVOS

BRASS

KM#	Date	Mintage	Fine	VF	XF	Unc
73	1985	23.268	—	—	—	.65
	1986	158.427	—	—	—	.65
	1987	184.330	—	—	—	.65
	1988	174.003	—	—	—	.65

50 CENTAVOS

BRASS

KM#	Date	Mintage	Fine	VF	XF	Unc
74	1985	13.884	—	—	—	1.50
	1986	59.074	—	—	—	1.50
	1987	64.525	—	—	—	1.50
	1988	62.388	—	—	—	1.50

NOTE: Varieties exist.

AUSTRAL

ALUMINUM
Buenos Aires City Hall

KM#	Date	Mintage	Fine	VF	XF	Unc
75	1989	—	—	—	—	.15

5 AUSTRALES

ALUMINUM
Independence Hall at Tucuman

KM#	Date	Mintage	Fine	VF	XF	Unc
76	1989	—	—	—	—	.25

10 AUSTRALES

ALUMINUM
Casa del Acuerdo

KM#	Date	Mintage	Fine	VF	XF	Unc
77	1989	—	—	—	—	.35

100 AUSTRALES

ALUMINUM

KM#	Date	Mintage	Fine	VF	XF	Unc
78	1990	—	—	—	—	.20
	1991	—	—	—	—	.20

500 AUSTRALES

ALUMINUM

KM#	Date	Mintage	Fine	VF	XF	Unc
79	1990	—	—	—	—	.30
	1991	—	—	—	—	.30

1000 AUSTRALES

ALUMINUM

KM#	Date	Mintage	Fine	VF	XF	Unc
80	1990	—	—	—	—	.50
	1991	—	—	—	—	.50

27.0000 g, .925 SILVER, .8029 oz ASW
Ibero - American Series

KM#	Date	Mintage	Fine	VF	XF	Unc
81	1991	.070	—	—	Proof	40.00

MONETARY REFORM

1992 -
10,000 Australes = 1 Peso

CENTAVO

BRASS

KM#	Date	Mintage	Fine	VF	XF	Unc
83	1992	—	—	—	—	.25

5 CENTAVOS

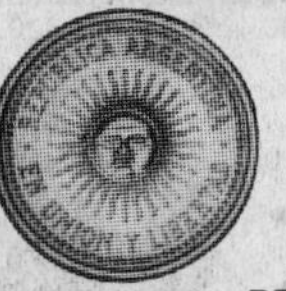

BRASS
Radiant Sunface

KM#	Date	Mintage	Fine	VF	XF	Unc
84	1992	—	—	—	—	.45

10 CENTAVOS

ALUMINUM-BRONZE

KM#	Date	Mintage	Fine	VF	XF	Unc
82	1992	400.000	—	—	—	.65

25 CENTAVOS

BRASS
Towered Building

KM#	Date	Mintage	Fine	VF	XF	Unc
85	1992	—	—	—	—	1.25

50 CENTAVOS

BRASS
Tucuman Province Capital Building

KM#	Date	Mintage	Fine	VF	XF	Unc
86	1992	—	—	—	—	1.50

MINT SETS (MS)

KM#	Date	Mintage	Identification	Issue Price	Mkt. Val.
MS1	1879(4)	—	KM Pn9-12	—	3375.
MS2	1970(5)	—	KM39-43	—	2.00
MS3	1977(6)	—	KM50-55	—	37.50
MS4	1978(6)	—	KM50-55	—	37.50
MS5	1983(4)	—	KM62-65	—	2.00

PROOF SETS (PS)

KM#	Date	Mintage	Identification	Issue Price	Mkt. Val.
PS1	1977(3)	1,000	KM53-55	—	75.00
PS2	1978(3)	1,750	KM53-55	153.00	75.00

ARUBA

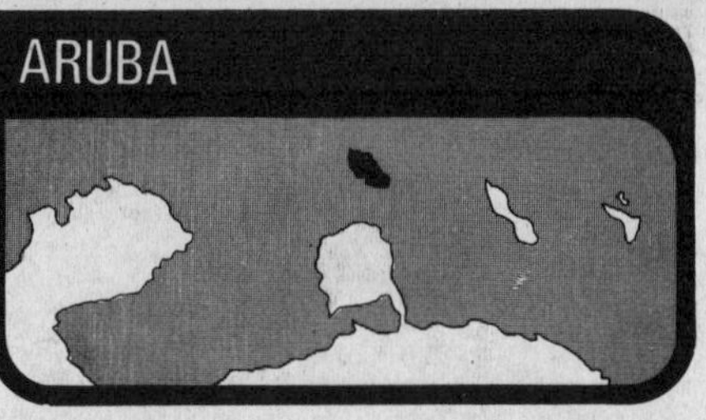

Aruba, formerly a part of the Netherlands Antilles, achieved on Jan. 1, 1986 a special status "status aparte" as the third state under the Dutch crown, together with the Netherlands and the remaining five islands of the Netherlands Antilles. On Dec. 15, 1954 the Netherlands Antilles were given complete domestic autonomy and granted equality within the Kingdom of the Netherlands. The "status aparte" is a step towards total independence of Aruba, scheduled for 1996. Aruba, the second largest island of the Netherlands Antilles, is situated near the Venezuelan coast. The island has an area of 74-1/2 sq. mi. (193 sq. km.) and a population of *63,000. Capital: Oranjestad, named after the Dutch royal family. Aruba was important in the processing and transportation of petroleum products in the first part of the twentieth century, but today the chief industry is tourism.

For earlier issues see Curacao and the Netherlands Antilles.

RULERS

Dutch

MINT MARKS

(u) Utrecht - Privy marks only

MONETARY SYSTEM

100 Cents = 1 Florin

5 CENTS

NICKEL BONDED STEEL

KM#	Date	Mintage	Fine	VF	XF	Unc
1	1986(u)	.276	—	—	.10	.30
	1987(u)	.232	—	—	.10	.30
	1988(u)	.656	—	—	—	.30
	1989(u)	.770	—	—	—	.30
	1990(u)	.612	—	—	—	.30
	1991(u)	.411	—	—	—	.30
	1992(u)	.810	—	—	—	.30
	1993(u)	.708	—	—	—	.30
	1994(u)	—	—	—	—	.30

10 CENTS

NICKEL BONDED STEEL

KM#	Date	Mintage	Fine	VF	XF	Unc
2	1986(u)	.356	—	—	.10	.40
	1987(u)	.222	—	—	.10	.40
	1988(u)	.986	—	—	—	.40
	1989(u)	.610	—	—	—	.40
	1990(u)	.762	—	—	—	.40
	1991(u)	.511	—	—	—	.40
	1992(u)	.610	—	—	—	.40
	1993(u)	1.008	—	—	—	.40
	1994(u)	—	—	—	—	.40

25 CENTS

NICKEL BONDED STEEL

KM#	Date	Mintage	Fine	VF	XF	Unc
3	1986(u)	.356	—	—	.20	.60
	1987(u)	.222	—	—	.20	.60
	1988(u)	.116	—	—	.20	.60
	1989(u)	.360	—	—	—	.60
	1990(u)	.512	—	—	—	.60
	1991(u)	.611	—	—	—	.60
	1992(u)	.460	—	—	—	.60
	1993(u)	.608	—	—	—	.60
	1994(u)	—	—	—	—	.60

50 CENTS

NICKEL BONDED STEEL

KM#	Date	Mintage	Fine	VF	XF	Unc
4	1986(u)	.236	—	—	.40	.80
	1987(u)	.122	—	—	.40	.80
	1988(u)	.216	—	—	.40	.80
	1989(u)	.110	—	—	—	.80
	1990(u)	.262	—	—	—	.80
	1991(u)	.311	—	—	—	.80
	1992(u)	.311	—	—	—	.80
	1993(u)	.458	—	—	—	.80
	1994(u)	—	—	—	—	.80

FLORIN

NICKEL BONDED STEEL

KM#	Date	Mintage	Fine	VF	XF	Unc
5	1986(u)	.336	—	—	.75	1.75
	1987(u)	.222	—	—	.75	1.75
	1988(u)	.566	—	—	—	1.75
	1989(u)	.410	—	—	—	1.75
	1990(u)	.412	—	—	—	1.75
	1991(u)	.161	—	—	—	1.75
	1992(u)	.611	—	—	—	1.75
	1993(u)	.408	—	—	—	1.75
	1994(u)	—	—	—	—	1.75

2-1/2 FLORIN

NICKEL BONDED STEEL

KM#	Date	Mintage	Fine	VF	XF	Unc
6	1986(u)	.086	—	—	1.75	2.50
	1987(u)	.032	—	—	—	2.50
	1988(u)	.026	—	—	—	2.50
	1989(u)	.015	—	—	—	2.50
	1990(u)	.017	—	—	—	2.50
	1991(u)	.016	—	—	—	2.50
	1992(u)	.013	—	—	—	2.50
	1993(u)	.010	—	—	—	2.50
	1994(u)	—	—	—	—	2.50

25 FLORIN

25.0200 g, .925 SILVER, .7441 oz ASW
Commonwealth of Aruba

KM#	Date	Mintage	Fine	VF	XF	Unc
7	1986(u)	5,000	—	—	—	45.00
	1986(u)	.010	—	—	Proof	50.00

Independence

KM#	Date	Mintage	Fine	VF	XF	Unc
8	1991(u)	2,500	—	—	—	35.00
	1991(u)	4,600	—	—	Proof	50.00

Olympics - Windsurfing

KM#	Date	Mintage	Fine	VF	XF	Unc
10	1992(u)	2,000	—	—	—	30.00
	1992(u)	.015	—	—	Proof	47.50

50 FLORIN

6.7200 g, .900 GOLD, .1945 oz AGW
Independence

KM#	Date	Mintage	Fine	VF	XF	Unc
9	1991(u)	2,600	—	—	Proof	180.00

MINT SETS (MS)

KM#	Date	Mintage	Identification	Issue Price	Mkt. Val.
MS1	1986(6)	36,200	KM1-6	8.95	10.00
MS2	1987(6)	21,650	KM1-6	9.95	11.00
MS3	1988(6)	16,000	KM1-6	12.95	13.00
MS4	1989(6)	10,000	KM1-6	12.00	12.00
MS5	1990(6)	12,000	KM1-6	—	12.00
MS6	1991(6)	11,000	KM1-6	14.50	14.50
MS7	1992(6)	10,500	KM1-6	—	14.50
MS8	1993(6)	8,000	KM1-6	—	15.00

Listings For

ASCENSION ISLANDS: refer to St. Helena

AUSTRALIA

Australia, the smallest continent and largest island in the world, is located south of Indonesia between the Indian and Pacific oceans. It has an area of 2,967,909 sq. mi. (7,686,850 sq. km.) and a population of I7 million. Capital: Canberra. Due to its early and sustained isolation, Australia is the habitat of such curious and unique fauna as the kangaroo, koala, platypus, wombat, echidna and frilled-necked lizard. The continent possesses extensive mineral deposits, the most important of which are iron ore, coal, gold, silver, nickel, uranium, lead and zinc. Livestock raising, mining and manufacturing are the principal industries. Chief exports are wool, meat, wheat, iron ore, coal and nonferrous metals.

The first whites to see Australia probably were Portuguese and Spanish navigators of the late 16th century. In 1770, Captain James Cook explored the east coast and annexed it for Great Britain. New South Wales was founded as a penal colony, following the loss of British North America, by Capt. Arthur Phillip on January 26, 1788, a date now celebrated as Australia Day. Dates of creation of the six colonies that now comprise the states of the Australian Commonwealth are: New South Wales, 1823; Tasmania, 1825; Western Australia, 1838; South Australia, 1842; Victoria, 1851; Queensland, 1859. A constitution providing for federation of the colonies was approved by the British Parliament in 1900; the Commonwealth of Australia came into being in 1901. Australia passed the Statute of Westminster Adoption Act on October 9, 1942, which officially established Australia's complete autonomy in external and internal affairs, thereby formalizing a situation that had existed for years. Australia is a member of the Commonwealth of Nations. Elizabeth II is Chief of State.

Australia's currency system was changed from PoundsShillings-Pence to a decimal system of Dollars and Cents on Feb. 14, 1966.

RULERS

British

MINT MARKS

Abbr.	Mint	Mint Marks and Locations
(b)	Bombay	"I" below bust; dots before and after HALF PENNY, 1942-43
(b)	Bombay	"I" below bust dots before and after PENNY, 1942-43
(c)	Calcutta	"I" above date, 1916-18
(c)	Canberra	None, 1966 to date
D	Denver	"D" above date 1/-& 2/-, below date on 3d
D	Denver	"D" below date on 6d
H	Heaton	"H" below date on silver coins, 1914-15
H	Heaton	"H" above date on bronze coins
(L)	London	None, 1910-1915, 1966
M	Melbourne	"M" below date on silver coins, 1916-21
M	Melbourne	"M" above date on the ground on gold coins w/St. George
(m)	Melbourne	Dot below scroll on penny, 1919-20
(m)	Melbourne	Two dots; below lower scroll and above upper, 1919-20
(m)	Melbourne	None, 1922-1964
P	Perth	"P" above date on the ground on gold coins w/St. George
(p)	Perth	Dot between KG (designer's Initials), 1940-41
(p)	Perth	Dot after PENNY, 1941-51 1954-64
(p)	Perth	Dot after AUSTRALIA, 1952-53
(p)	Perth	Dot before SHILLING, 1946
(p)	Perth	None, 1922 penny, 1966
P	Perth	Nuggets, 1986
PL	London	"PL" after PENNY in 1951
PL	London	"PL" on bottom folds of ribbon, 1951 threepence
PL	London	"PL" above date on sixpence, 1951
S	San Francisco	"S" above or below date, 1942-44
S	Sydney	"S" above date on the ground on gold coins w/St. George
(sy)	Sydney	Dot above bottom scroll on penny 1920
(sy)	Sydney	None, 1919-1926

Mint designations are shown in ( ). Ex. 1878(m).
Mint marks are shown after date. Ex. 1878M.

MONETARY SYSTEM

12 Pence = 1 Shilling
2 Shillings = 1 Florin
5 Shillings = 1 Crown
20 Shillings = 1 Pound

NEW SOUTH WALES

CUT AND COUNTERSTAMPED COINAGE

15 PENCE

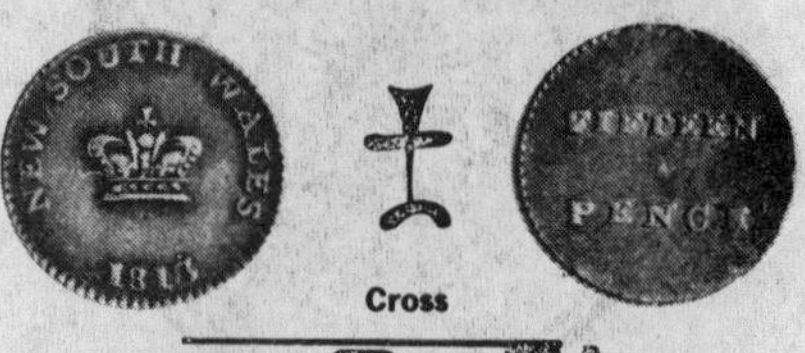

Cross

A

Crown band

Mira type A/1. Rev: FIFTEEN/4.5mm/PENCE.
.903 SILVER
Struck over center plugs of cut Spanish or Spanish Colonial 8 Reales.

KM#	Date	Mintage	Good	VG	Fine	VF
1.1	1813	*.026	500.00	1000.	2250.	4500.

Cross

C

Crown band

Mira type C/4.
Obv: Pearls in band of crown diamond shaped.

KM#	Date	Mintage	Good	VG	Fine	VF
1.2	1813	*1,600	1000.	3500.	4500.	7500.

Cross

D

Crown band

Mira type D/2. Rev: FIFTEEN/5.0mm/PENCE.

KM#	Date	Mintage	Good	VG	Fine	VF
1.3	1813	*8,000	750.00	1500.	3000.	5000.

Cross

E

Crown band

Mira type E/3. Rev: FIFTEEN/3.0mm/PENCE.

KM#	Date	Mintage	Good	VG	Fine	VF
1.4	1813	*4,400	1200.	2500.	4000.	6500.

***NOTE:** Estimated original mintage.
REFERENCE: "A Classification of the New South Wales Dumps", 1977 by Dr. W. J. D. Mira.

'HOLEY DOLLAR'

(5 Shillings)

.903 SILVER
c/s: NEW SOUTH WALES-1813/FIVE SHILLINGS on holed Bolivia, Potosi 8 Reales KM#55.

KM#	Date	Mintage	Good	VG	Fine	VF
2.1	1813(1773-89)	*.040	3000.	6500.	13,500.	26,500.

c/s: On holed Bolivia, Potosi 8 Reales KM#73.

KM#	Date	Mintage	Good	VG	Fine	VF
2.3	1813(1791-1808)	—	2500.	4500.	11,000.	20,000.

c/s: On holed Mexico City 8 Reales, KM#104.

KM#	Date	Mintage	Good	VG	Fine	VF
2.5	1813(1757)	1 known	—	—	Rare	—

M. R. Roberts 1988 sale, unique, realized A $45,000.

c/s: On holed Mexico City 8 Reales, KM#106.

KM#	Date	Mintage	Good	VG	Fine	VF
2.6	1813(1772-89)	Inc. Ab.	2500.	4500.	11,000.	20,000.

c/s: On holed Mexico City 8 Reales, KM#107.

KM#	Date	Mintage	Good	VG	Fine	VF
2.7	1813(1789-90)	Inc. Ab.	2500.	4500.	11,000.	20,000.

c/s: On holed Mexico City 8 Reales, KM#109.

KM#	Date	Mintage	Good	VG	Fine	VF
2.9	1813(1791-1808)	Inc. Ab.	2250.	3750.	7500.	16,000.

c/s: On holed Mexico City 8 Reales, KM#110.

KM#	Date	Mintage	Good	VG	Fine	VF
2.10	1813(1809-10)	Inc. Ab.	2500.	4500.	11,000.	20,000.

c/s: On holed Peru, Lima 8 Reales, KM#117.1.

KM#	Date	Mintage	Good	VG	Fine	VF
2.11	1813(1772-89)	Inc. Ab.	3000.	6000.	12,500.	23,000.

c/s: On holed Peru, Lima 8 Reales, KM#117.1.

KM#	Date	Mintage	Good	VG	Fine	VF
2.13	1813(1791-1808)	Inc. Ab.	3000.	6000.	12,500.	23,000.

c/s: On holed Peru, Lima 8 Reales, KM#117.1.

KM#	Date	Mintage	Good	VG	Fine	VF
2.14	1813(1810)	2 known	—	—	Rare	—

M. R. Roberts 1988 sale, AEF realized A $50,000.

c/s: On holed Spain, Madrid 8 Reales C#71.1.

KM#	Date	Mintage	Good	VG	Fine	VF
2.15	1813(1788-1808)	Inc. Ab.	7500.	12,500.	25,000.	32,000.

c/s: On holed Spain, Seville 8 Reales, C#71.2.

KM#	Date	Mintage	Good	VG	Fine	VF
2.16	1813(1788-1803)	Inc. Ab.	7500.	12,500.	25,000.	32,000.

SOUTH AUSTRALIA

ADELAIDE POUND

8.7500 g, .917 GOLD, .2579 oz AGW

KM#	Date	Mintage	Fine	VF	XF	Unc
1	1852	*20-50 pcs.	—	22,000.	37,000.	55,000.

Rev: Dentilated inner circle.

KM#	Date	Mintage	Fine	VF	XF	Unc
2	1852	.025	2000.	3500.	6500.	10,000.

COMMONWEALTH OF AUSTRALIA

1/2 PENNY

BRONZE

KM#	Date	Mintage	Fine	VF	XF	Unc
22	1911(L)	2.832	.30	2.50	25.00	110.00
	1911(L)	—	—	—	Proof	1600.
	1912H	2.400	.30	2.50	32.00	150.00
	1912H	—	—	—	Proof	1600.
	1913(L)	2.160	.35	4.00	37.50	200.00
	1914(L)	1.440	2.00	6.00	50.00	215.00
	1914H	1.200	2.50	7.00	60.00	230.00
	1915H	.720	20.00	55.00	250.00	1250.
	1916-I(c)	3.600	.30	1.25	16.50	115.00
	1916-I(c)	—	—	—	Proof	1600.
	1917-I(c)	5.760	.30	1.50	16.50	115.00
	1918-I(c)	1.440	3.50	20.00	150.00	1150.
	1919(sy)	3.326	.20	1.50	20.00	110.00
	1919(sy)	—	—	—	Proof	1600.
	1920(sy)	4.114	.65	3.00	22.00	215.00
	1920(m)	—	—	—	Proof	1600.
	1921(sy)	5.280	.30	2.00	15.00	100.00
	1922(sy)	6.924	.30	2.00	15.00	100.00
	1923(sy)	*1.113	800.00	500.00	1000.	15,000.
	1923(sy)	—	—	—	Proof	25,000.
	1924(m)	.682	2.00	6.00	60.00	325.00
	1924(m)	—	—	—	Proof	1600.
	1925(m)	1.147	1.00	3.00	40.00	275.00
	1925(m)	—	—	—	Proof	2750.
	1926(m&sy)	4.139	.20	1.25	25.00	100.00
	1926(m)	—	—	—	Proof	1550.
	1927(m)	3.072	.20	.75	25.00	100.00
	1927(m)	50 pcs.	—	—	Proof	1500.
	1928(m)	2.318	1.25	3.50	35.00	275.00
	1928(m)	—	—	—	Proof	1500.
	1929(m)	2.635	.20	.75	25.00	100.00
	1929(m)	—	—	—	Proof	1600.
	1930(m)	.638	2.50	5.00	45.00	300.00
	1930(m)	—	—	—	Proof	10,000.
	1931(m)	.370	2.50	5.00	45.00	275.00
	1931(m)	—	—	—	Proof	1500.
	1932(m)	2.554	.20	.75	12.00	65.00
	1932(m)	—	—	—	Proof	1500.
	1933(m)	4.608	.20	.75	10.00	65.00
	1933(m)	—	—	—	Proof	1250.
	1934(m)	3.816	.20	.75	12.00	65.00
	1934(m)	100 pcs.	—	—	Proof	750.00
	1935(m)	2.916	.20	.75	8.00	55.00
	1935(m)	100 pcs.	—	—	Proof	750.00
	1936(m)	2.562	.20	.75	8.00	55.00
	1936(m)	—	—	—	Proof	1000.

***NOTE:** Dies dated 1922 were used for the majority of the calendar year 1923, leaving only a small portion of this mintage figure as 1923 dated coins.

Mule. Obv: India 1/4 Anna, KM#511. Rev: KM#465.

KM#	Date	Mintage	Fine	VF	XF	Unc
30	1916-I(c)	*10	2000.	3000.	6000.	—

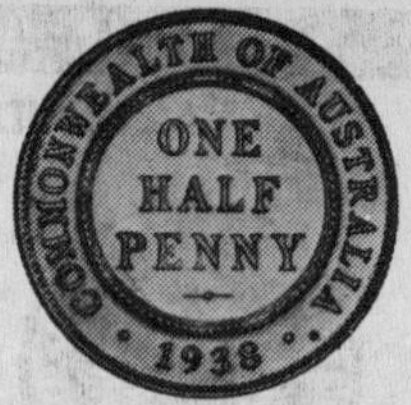

KM#	Date	Mintage	Fine	VF	XF	Unc
35	1938(m)	3.014	.20	.50	2.50	25.00
	1938(m)	250 pcs.	—	—	Proof	650.00
	1939(m)	4.382	.20	.50	5.00	30.00
	1939(m)	—	—	—	Proof	1400.

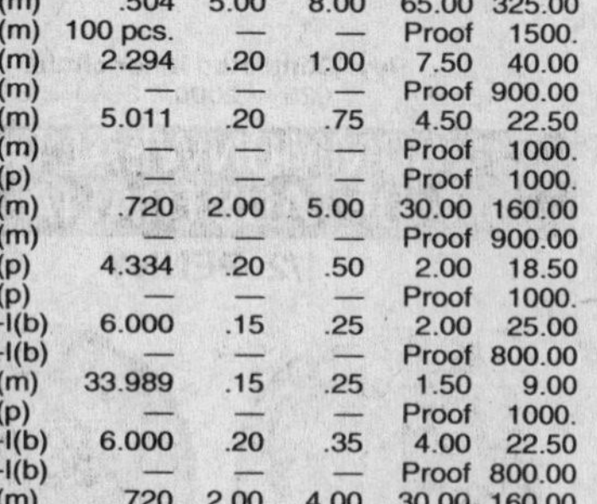

KM#	Date	Mintage	Fine	VF	XF	Unc
41	1939(m)	.504	5.00	8.00	65.00	325.00
	1939(m)	100 pcs.	—	—	Proof	1500.
	1940(m)	2.294	.20	1.00	7.50	40.00
	1940(m)	—	—	—	Proof	900.00
	1941(m)	5.011	.20	.75	4.50	22.50
	1941(m)	—	—	—	Proof	1000.
	1941(p)	—	—	—	Proof	1000.
	1942(m)	.720	2.00	5.00	30.00	160.00
	1942(m)	—	—	—	Proof	900.00
	1942(p)	4.334	.20	.50	2.00	18.50
	1942(p)	—	—	—	Proof	1000.
	1942-I(b)	6.000	.15	.25	2.00	25.00
	1942-I(b)	—	—	—	Proof	800.00
	1943(m)	33.989	.15	.25	1.50	9.00
	1943(p)	—	—	—	Proof	1000.
	1943-I(b)	6.000	.20	.35	4.00	22.50
	1943-I(b)	—	—	—	Proof	800.00
	1944(m)	.720	2.00	4.00	30.00	160.00
	1944(m)	—	—	—	Proof	1200.
	1945(p)	3.033	1.50	3.50	20.00	100.00
	1945(p) w/o dot					
		Inc. Ab.	1.50	3.50	20.00	100.00
	1945(p)	—	—	—	Proof	850.00
	1946(p)	13.747	.15	.25	2.00	10.00
	1946(p)	—	—	—	Proof	850.00
	1947(p)	9.293	.15	.25	2.00	10.00
	1947(p)	—	—	—	Proof	850.00
	1948(m)	4.608	.25	.50	4.00	25.00
	1948(m)	—	—	—	Proof	1000.
	1948(p)	25.553	.15	.25	2.00	10.00
	1948(p)	—	—	—	Proof	850.00

Obv. leg: IND:IMP: dropped.

KM#	Date	Mintage	Fine	VF	XF	Unc
42	1949(m)	—	—	—	Proof	1000.
	1949(p)	22.310	.15	.25	2.75	10.00
	1949(p)	—	—	—	Proof	1000.
	1950(p)	12.014	.15	.50	5.00	15.00
	1950(p)	—	—	—	Proof	850.00
	1951(p)	29.422	.15	.25	2.00	9.00
	1951(p)	—	—	—	Proof	850.00
	1951(p) w/o dot					
		Inc. Ab.	.15	.50	3.00	12.50
	1951PL	*17.040	.15	.35	2.00	6.50
	1951PL	—	—	—	Proof	1000.
	1952(p)	1.832	.50	3.00	10.00	50.00
	1952(p)	—	—	—	Proof	850.00

***NOTE:** 5.040 Struck at the Birmingham Mint.

KM#	Date	Mintage	Fine	VF	XF	Unc
49	1953(p)	23.967	.15	.25	1.25	7.00
	1953(p)	16 pcs.	—	—	Proof	850.00
	1954(p)	21.963	.15	.25	1.00	6.00
	1954(p)	—	—	—	Proof	850.00
	1955(p)	9.343	.15	.25	1.00	6.00
	1955(p)	301 pcs.	—	—	Proof	600.00

Obv. leg: F:D: added.

KM#	Date	Mintage	Fine	VF	XF	Unc
61	1959(m)	10.166	.10	.15	.25	3.00
	1959(m)	1,506	—	—	Proof	65.00
	1960(p)	17.812	.10	.15	.25	1.25
	1960(p)	1,030	—	—	Proof	85.00
	1961(p)	20.183	.10	.15	.25	1.00
	1961(p)	1,040	—	—	Proof	85.00
	1962(p)	10.259	.10	.15	.25	1.00
	1962(p)	1,064	—	—	Proof	75.00
	1963(p)	16.410	.10	.15	.25	1.00
	1963(p)	1,060	—	—	Proof	75.00
	1964(p)	18.230	.10	.15	.25	1.00
	1964(p)	1 known	—	—	Proof	3000.

PENNY

Bronze

KM#	Date	Mintage	Fine	VF	XF	Unc
23	1911(L)	3.768	1.00	5.00	30.00	110.00
	1911(L)	—	—	—	Proof	1800.
	1912H	3.600	1.00	5.00	35.00	135.00
	1912H	—	—	—	Proof	1800.
	1913(L)	2.520	1.50	10.00	40.00	225.00
	1914(L)	.720	5.00	20.00	110.00	400.00
	1915(L)	.960	2.50	25.00	100.00	650.00
	1915H	1.320	2.00	15.00	85.00	550.00
	1916-I(c)	3.324	.50	2.00	25.00	125.00
	1916-I(c)	—	—	—	Proof	1800.
	1917-I(c)	6.240	.40	1.50	22.50	120.00
	1918-I(c)	1.200	5.00	20.00	110.00	700.00
	1919(m) w/o dots					
		5.810	.50	3.00	30.00	250.00
	1919(m) dot below bottom scroll					
		Inc. Ab.	1.50	5.00	50.00	275.00
	1919(m) dots below bottom scroll and above					
	upper	I.A.	12.50	35.00	160.00	—
	1919(m)	—	—	—	Proof	1800.
	1920(m&sy) w/o dots					
		8.250	.75	9.00	150.00	1600.
	1920(m) dot below bottom scroll					
		Inc. Ab.	2.50	10.00	65.00	400.00
	1920(m)	—	—	—	Proof	1800.
	1920(sy) dot above bottom scroll					
		Inc. Ab.	5.00	10.00	65.00	500.00
	1920(m) dots below bottom scroll and above					
	upper	I.A.	7.00	40.00	160.00	—
	1921(m&sy)	7.438	.25	4.00	40.00	220.00
	1922(m&p)	12.697	.25	3.50	32.50	200.00
	1923(m)	5.654	.25	3.50	35.00	210.00
	1923(m)	—	—	—	Proof	1600.
	1924(m&sy)	4.656	.25	2.00	37.50	210.00
	1924(m)	—	—	—	Proof	1500.
	1925(m)	1.639	20.00	40.00	300.00	3750.
	1925(m)	—	—	—	Proof	8000.
	1926(m&sy)	1.859	1.50	5.00	50.00	350.00
	1926(m)	—	—	—	Proof	1800.
	1927(m)	4.922	.30	3.00	17.50	150.00
	1927(m)	50 pcs.	—	—	Proof	1200.
	1928(m)	3.038	.30	4.50	35.00	210.00
	1928(m)	—	—	—	Proof	1800.
	1929(m)	2.599	.30	3.25	35.00	210.00
	1929(m)	—	—	—	Proof	1750.
	1930(m)	*3,000	4500.	6000.	12,000.	30,000.
	1930(m)	—	—	—	Proof	75,000.
	1931(m)	.494	2.00	6.00	65.00	650.00
	1931(m)	—	—	—	Proof	1750.
	1932(m)	2.117	.30	3.50	65.00	125.00
	1933/2(m)	5.818	4.00	15.00	80.00	450.00
	1933(m)	Inc. Ab.	.25	2.00	20.00	90.00
	1933(m)	—	—	—	Proof	1400.
	1934(m)	5.808	.25	1.00	15.00	65.00
	1934(m)	100 pcs.	—	—	Proof	900.00
	1935(m)	3.725	.25	1.25	10.00	60.00
	1935(m)	100 pcs.	—	—	Proof	900.00
	1936(m)	9.890	.25	1.00	8.00	60.00
	1936(m)	—	—	—	Proof	1000.

KM#	Date	Mintage	Fine	VF	XF	Unc
36	1938(m)	5.552	.25	.50	5.50	25.00
	1938(m)	250 pcs.	—	—	Proof	750.00
	1939(m)	6.240	.25	.50	5.50	27.50
	1939(m)	—	—	—	Proof	1250.
	1940(m)	4.075	.30	1.50	9.00	60.00
	1940(p)K.G	1.114	2.00	4.00	50.00	210.00
	1941(m)	1.588	.30	1.25	12.50	60.00
	1941(p)K.G	12.794	1.00	2.50	30.00	150.00
	1941(p)	—	—	—	Proof	1600.
	1941(p)Y.	I.A.	.25	1.00	9.00	50.00
	1941 high dot after 'Y'					
		Inc. Ab.	.50	1.50	12.50	60.00
	1942(p)	12.245	.15	.75	6.00	40.00
	1942(p)	—	—	—	Proof	1200.
	1942-I(b)	9.000	.15	.50	5.00	25.00
	1942(b) w/o 'I'					
		Inc. Ab.	2.00	5.00	15.00	75.00
	1942(b)	—	—	—	Proof	1200.
	1943(m)	11.112	.20	.50	5.00	25.00
	1943(p)	33.086	.15	.50	5.00	20.00
	1943(p)	—	—	—	Proof	1000.
	1943-I(b)	9.000	.20	.50	6.50	27.50
	1943-I(b) w/o (I)					
		Inc. Ab.	2.00	5.00	10.00	75.00
	1943(b)	—	—	—	Proof	800.00
	1944(m)	2.112	.50	2.50	25.00	120.00
	1944(p)	27.830	.15	.50	5.00	20.00
	1944(p)	—	—	—	Proof	1200.
	1945(p)	15.173	.20	.50	5.00	30.00
	1945(p)	—	—	—	Proof	1400.
	1945-I(b)	6 pcs.	—	—	Rare	—
	1945(m)	—	—	—	—	15,000.
	1946(m)	.240	15.00	30.00	100.00	800.00
	1947(m)	6.864	.15	.40	2.75	16.50
	1947(p)	4.49	.50	1.50	9.50	60.00
	1947(p)	—	—	—	Proof	1400.
	1948(m)	26.616	.15	.40	2.75	16.50
	1948(p)	1.534	1.00	4.00	50.00	185.00
	1948(p)	—	—	—	Proof	1500.

Obv. leg: IND:IMP. dropped.

KM#	Date	Mintage	Fine	VF	XF	Unc
43	1949(m)	27.065	.15	.25	2.50	15.00
	1949(m)	—	—	—	Proof	2000.
	1950(m)	36.359	.15	.25	2.50	15.00
	1950(m)	—	—	—	Proof	2000.
	1950(p)	21.488	.20	.30	2.75	30.00
	1950(p)	—	—	—	Proof	1200.
	1951(m)	21.240	.15	.20	1.25	10.00
	1951(p)	12.888	.20	.40	1.75	25.00
	1951(p)	—	—	—	Proof	1200.
	1951PL	18.000	.15	.25	1.00	10.00
	1951PL	—	—	—	Proof	1250.
	1952(m)	12.408	.15	.30	1.25	10.00
	1952(m)	—	—	—	Proof	2500.
	1952(p)	45.514	.15	.30	1.25	12.50
	1952(p)	—	—	—	Proof	1250.

KM#	Date	Mintage	Fine	VF	XF	Unc
50	1953(m)	6.936	.20	1.00	4.00	22.50
	1953(m)	—	—	—	Proof	800.00
	1953(p)	6.203	.20	.75	2.00	15.00
	1953(p)	16 pcs.	—	—	Proof	1400.

Obv. leg: F:D: added.

KM#	Date	Mintage	Fine	VF	XF	Unc
56	1955(m)	6.336	.25	1.25	3.25	20.00
	1955(m)	1,200	—	—	Proof	90.00
	1955(p)	11.110	.10	.20	1.00	10.00
	1955(p)	301 pcs.	—	—	Proof	900.00
	1956(m)	13.872	.10	.20	1.00	8.00
	1956(m)	1,500	—	—	Proof	65.00
	1956(p)	12.121	.10	.20	1.00	8.00
	1956(p)	417 pcs.	—	—	Proof	750.00
	1957(p)	15.978	.10	.20	1.00	5.00
	1957(p)	1,112	—	—	Proof	120.00
	1958(m)	10.012	.10	.20	1.00	5.50
	1958(m)	1,506	—	—	Proof	65.00
	1958(p)	14.428	.10	.20	1.00	5.00
	1958(p)	1,028	—	—	Proof	110.00
	1959(m)	1.617	.50	1.50	10.00	35.00
	1959(m)	1,506	—	—	Proof	65.00
	1959(p)	14.428	.10	.20	1.00	7.00
	1959(p)	1,030	—	—	Proof	100.00
	1960(p)	20.515	.10	.20	1.00	2.00
	1960(p)	1,030	—	—	Proof	90.00
	1961(p)	30.607	.10	.20	.40	1.50
	1961(p)	1,040	—	—	Proof	90.00
	1962(p)	34.851	.10	.20	.40	1.50
	1962(p)	1,064	—	—	Proof	85.00
	1963(p)	10.258	.10	.20	.40	1.50
	1963(p)	1,100	—	—	Proof	85.00
	1964(p)	54.590	.10	.20	.50	1.25
	1964(m)	49.130	.10	.20	.50	1.25
	1964(p)	1 known	—	—	Proof	4000.

THREEPENCE

1.4100 g, .925 SILVER, .0419 oz ASW

KM#	Date	Mintage	Fine	VF	XF	Unc
18	1910(L)	4.000	3.00	10.00	20.00	55.00
	1910(L)	—	—	—	Proof	700.00

KM#	Date	Mintage	Fine	VF	XF	Unc
24	1911(L)	2.000	6.00	16.00	75.00	275.00
	1911(L)	—	—	—	Proof	2000.
	1911(L) reeded edge		—	—	Proof	10,000.
	1912(L)	2.400	10.00	20.00	90.00	375.00
	1914(L)	1.600	15.00	40.00	150.00	725.00
	1915(L)	.800	20.00	60.00	250.00	900.00
	1916M	1.913	10.00	20.00	80.00	375.00
	1916M	25 pcs.	—	—	Proof	1000.
	1917M	3.808	2.00	8.00	27.00	175.00
	1918M	3.119	2.00	10.00	32.00	175.00
	1919M	3.201	3.00	12.50	35.00	190.00
	1919M	—	—	—	Proof	1000.
	1920M	4.196	10.00	22.50	85.00	375.00
	1920M	—	—	—	Proof	1000.
	1921M	7.378	2.00	6.50	20.00	125.00
	1921(m)plain	I.A.	10.00	20.00	75.00	275.00
	1922/1(m)	5.531	1250.	3500.	10,000.	20,000.
	1922(m)	Inc. Ab.	2.00	7.50	25.00	155.00
	1922(m)	—	—	—	Proof	1000.
	1923(m)	.815	15.00	40.00	125.00	650.00
	1924(m&sy)	2.014	10.00	20.00	50.00	160.00
	1924(m)	—	—	—	Proof	900.00
	1925(m&sy)	4.347	1.50	7.50	22.00	140.00
	1925(m)	—	—	—	Proof	900.00
	1926(m&sy)	6.158	1.50	3.00	18.00	125.00
	1926(m)	—	—	—	Proof	900.00
	1927(m)	6.720	1.50	3.00	16.00	95.00
	1927(m)	50 pcs.	—	—	Proof	900.00
	1928(m)	5.000	1.50	3.00	20.00	100.00
	1928(m)	—	—	—	Proof	900.00
	1934/3(m)	1.616	15.00	40.00	150.00	400.00
	1934(m)	Inc. Ab.	1.50	3.00	20.00	105.00
	1934(m)	100 pcs.	—	—	Proof	450.00
	1935(m)	2.800	1.50	3.00	15.00	95.00
	1935(m)	—	—	—	Proof	550.00
	1936(m)	3.600	1.00	2.00	12.00	60.00
	1936(m)	—	—	—	Proof	650.00

KM#	Date	Mintage	Fine	VF	XF	Unc
37	1938(m)	4.560	.75	2.00	9.00	22.50
	1938(m)	250 pcs.	—	—	Proof	300.00
	1939(m)	3.856	.75	2.50	12.00	55.00
	1939(m)	—	—	—	Proof	450.00
	1940(m)	3.840	.75	2.50	10.00	40.00
	1941(m)	7.584	.75	1.75	5.50	22.50
	1942(m)	.528	10.00	20.00	150.00	675.00
	1942D	16.000	BV	.50	1.25	5.00
	1942S	8.000	BV	1.00	1.50	6.50
	1943(m)	24.912	BV	.50	1.00	4.50
	1943D	16.000	BV	.50	1.25	5.00
	1943S	8.000	BV	1.00	1.50	6.00
	1944S	32.000	BV	.50	1.00	5.00

1.4100 g, .500 SILVER, .0226 oz ASW

KM#	Date	Mintage	Fine	VF	XF	Unc
37a	1947(m)	4.176	1.00	2.50	10.00	35.00
	1948(m)	26.208	BV	.50	2.00	7.50

Obv. leg: IND:IMP. dropped.

KM#	Date	Mintage	Fine	VF	XF	Unc
44	1949(m)	26.400	BV	.50	2.00	7.50
	1949(m)	—	—	—	Proof	700.00
	1950(m)	35.456	BV	.50	2.00	10.00
	1951(m)	15.856	BV	1.00	3.00	15.00
	1951PL	40.000	BV	.25	1.25	4.50
	1951PL	—	—	—	Proof	500.00
	1952(m)	21.560	BV	.25	2.00	12.00

KM#	Date	Mintage	Fine	VF	XF	Unc
51	1953(m)	7.664	.25	2.00	6.50	30.00
	1953(m)	—	—	—	Proof	500.00
	1954(m)	2.672	2.00	4.00	10.00	60.00
	1954(m)	—	—	—	Proof	600.00

Obv. leg: F:D: added.

KM#	Date	Mintage	Fine	VF	XF	Unc
57	1955(m)	27.088	BV	.25	1.50	6.00
	1955(m)	1,040	—	—	Proof	40.00
	1956(m)	14.088	BV	.25	1.50	7.00
	1956(m)	1,500	—	—	Proof	35.00
	1957(m)	26.704	BV	.25	1.00	4.50
	1957(m)	1,256	—	—	Proof	35.00
	1958(m)	11.248	BV	.25	2.00	6.00
	1958(m)	1,506	—	—	Proof	35.00
	1959(m)	19.888	BV	.25	1.00	3.50
	1959(m)	1,506	—	—	Proof	35.00
	1960(m)	19.600	BV	.25	.75	1.50
	1960(m)	1,509	—	—	Proof	30.00
	1961(m)	33.840	BV	.25	.75	1.50
	1961(m)	1,506	—	—	Proof	30.00
	1962(m)	15.968	BV	.25	.75	1.50
	1962(m)	2,016	—	—	Proof	30.00
	1963(m)	44.016	BV	.25	.50	1.50
	1963(m)	5,042	—	—	Proof	20.00
	1964(m)	20.320	BV	.25	.50	1.50

SIXPENCE

2.8200 g, .925 SILVER, .0838 oz ASW

KM#	Date	Mintage	Fine	VF	XF	Unc
19	1910(L)	3.046	7.50	20.00	45.00	150.00
	1910(L)	—	—	—	Proof	800.00

KM#	Date	Mintage	Fine	VF	XF	Unc
25	1911(L)	1.000	12.00	30.00	140.00	550.00
	1911(L)	—	—	—	Proof	2000.
	1912(L)	1.600	20.00	50.00	200.00	750.00
	1914(L)	1.800	10.00	20.00	80.00	375.00
	1916M	1.769	10.00	30.00	175.00	700.00

KM#	Date	Mintage	Fine	VF	XF	Unc
25	1916M	25 pcs.	—	—	Proof	1750.
	1917M	1.632	10.00	30.00	170.00	650.00
	1918M	.915	25.00	75.00	250.00	1000.
	1919M	1.521	10.00	25.00	95.00	500.00
	1919M	—	—	—	Proof	1600.
	1920M	1.476	20.00	50.00	200.00	825.00
	1920M	—	—	—	Proof	2500.
	1921(m)	—	—	—	Proof	2000.
	1921(m&sy)	3.795	7.50	15.00	60.00	375.00
	1922(sy)	1.488	25.00	60.00	225.00	850.00
	1922(sy)	—	—	—	Proof	2500.
	1923(m&sy)	1.458	12.50	32.50	175.00	600.00
	1924(m)	—	—	—	Proof	2000.
	1924(m&sy)	1.038	15.00	45.00	175.00	650.00
	1925(m)	—	—	—	Proof	900.00
	1925(m&sy)	3.266	3.00	12.00	35.00	180.00
	1926(m)	—	—	—	Proof	900.00
	1926(m&sy)	3.609	2.50	10.00	35.00	155.00
	1927(m)	3.592	2.50	8.50	30.00	150.00
	1927(m)	50 pcs.	—	—	Proof	900.00
	1928(m)	2.721	2.50	8.50	30.00	165.00
	1928(m)	—	—	—	Proof	900.00
	1934(m)	1.024	3.50	9.00	45.00	200.00
	1934(m)	100 pcs.	—	—	Proof	700.00
	1935(m)	.392	8.00	20.00	100.00	400.00
	1935(m)	—	—	—	Proof	1000.
	1936(m)	1.800	2.00	5.00	20.00	125.00
	1936(m)	—	—	—	Proof	900.00

KM#	Date	Mintage	Fine	VF	XF	Unc
38	1938(m)	2.864	1.75	3.50	12.50	45.00
	1938(m)	250 pcs.	—	—	Proof	400.00
	1939(m)	1.600	1.75	4.00	20.00	125.00
	1939(m)	—	—	—	Proof	900.00
	1940(m)	1.600	1.75	4.00	15.00	85.00
	1941(m)	2.912	1.50	2.50	8.00	45.00
	1942(m)	8.968	BV	1.75	5.00	25.00
	1942D	12.000	BV	.75	3.00	15.00
	1942S	4.000	BV	.75	3.00	20.00
	1943D	8.000	BV	.75	3.00	15.00
	1943S	4.000	BV	.75	3.00	18.00
	1944S	4.000	BV	1.75	3.50	16.50
	1945(m)	10.096	BV	1.75	3.50	15.00

2.8200 g, .500 SILVER, .0453 oz ASW

KM#	Date	Mintage	Fine	VF	XF	Unc
38a	1946(m)	10.024	BV	1.00	5.00	25.00
	1946(m)	—	—	—	Proof	900.00
	1948(m)	1.584	.50	2.00	6.00	26.00

Obv. leg: IND:IMP. dropped.

KM#	Date	Mintage	Fine	VF	XF	Unc
45	1950(m)	10.272	BV	2.50	5.00	27.50
	1950(m)	—	—	—	Proof	1500.
	1951(m)	13.760	BV	2.00	4.00	22.50
	1951PL	20.024	BV	.50	2.50	10.00
	1951PL	—	—	—	Proof	650.00
	1952(m)	2.112	2.00	6.00	30.00	300.00

KM#	Date	Mintage	Fine	VF	XF	Unc
52	1953(m)	1.152	2.00	5.00	25.00	150.00
	1953(m)	—	—	—	Proof	700.00
	1954(m)	7.672	BV	1.50	2.25	6.00
	1954(m)	—	—	—	Proof	750.00

Obv. leg: F:D: added.

KM#	Date	Mintage	Fine	VF	XF	Unc
58	1955(m)	14.248	BV	.75	2.50	12.50
	1955(m)	1,200	—	—	Proof	60.00
	1956(m)	7.904	.50	3.00	6.00	35.00
	1956(m)	1,500	—	—	Proof	50.00
	1957(m)	13.752	BV	.50	1.00	6.00
	1957(m)	1,256	—	—	Proof	50.00
	1958(m)	17.944	BV	.50	1.00	4.00
	1958(m)	1,506	—	—	Proof	45.00
	1959(m)	11.728	BV	.50	1.50	7.00
	1959(m)	1,506	—	—	Proof	45.00
	1960(m)	18.592	BV	.50	1.00	6.50
	1960(m)	1,509	—	—	Proof	40.00
	1961(m)	9.152	BV	.50	1.00	3.00
	1961(m)	1,506	—	—	Proof	40.00
	1962(m)	44.816	BV	.50	.75	2.00

KM#	Date	Mintage	Fine	VF	XF	Unc
58	1962(m)	2,016	—	—	Proof	40.00
	1963(m)	25.056	BV	.50	.75	2.00
	1963(m)	5,042	—	—	Proof	25.00

SHILLING

5.6500 g, .925 SILVER, .1680 oz ASW

KM#	Date	Mintage	Fine	VF	XF	Unc
20	1910(L)	2.536	10.00	25.00	120.00	200.00
	1910(L)	—	—	—	Proof	900.00

KM#	Date	Mintage	Fine	VF	XF	Unc
26	1911(L)	1.700	20.00	45.00	215.00	650.00
	1911(L)	—	—	—	Proof	5000.
	1912(L)	1.000	30.00	110.00	350.00	950.00
	1913(L)	1.200	25.00	80.00	225.00	900.00
	1914(L)	3.300	8.00	30.00	110.00	325.00
	1915(L)	.800	35.00	120.00	400.00	2500.
	1915H	.500	50.00	180.00	600.00	4000.
	1916M	5.141	4.00	12.00	50.00	200.00
	1916M	25 pcs.	—	—	Proof	1750.
	1917M	5.274	4.00	12.00	60.00	200.00
	1918M	3.761	8.00	17.50	65.00	225.00
	1919M	—	—	—	Proof	20,000.
	1920M	.520	10.00	35.00	140.00	600.00
	1920M	—	—	—	Proof	6000.
	1921star(sy)	1.641	50.00	130.00	550.00	2200.
	1921star(m)	—	—	—	Proof	7500.
	1922(m)	2.040	15.00	30.00	115.00	450.00
	1922(m)	—	—	—	Proof	2700.
	1924(m&sy)	.674	20.00	55.00	300.00	700.00
	1924(m)	—	—	—	Proof	4000.
	1925/3(m&sy)	1.448	4.00	15.00	50.00	180.00
	1925(m)	—	—	—	Proof	1500.
	1926(m&sy)	2.352	4.00	12.50	40.00	140.00
	1926(m)	—	—	—	Proof	2000.
	1927(m)	1.146	6.00	15.00	45.00	150.00
	1927(m)	50 pcs.	—	—	Proof	1850.
	1928(m)	.664	15.00	30.00	200.00	600.00
	1928(m)	—	—	—	Proof	3000.
	1931(m)	1.000	6.00	12.50	60.00	170.00
	1931(m)	—	—	—	Proof	—
	1933(m)	.220	50.00	150.00	550.00	2500.
	1933(m)	—	—	—	Proof	10,000.
	1934(m)	.480	10.00	25.00	150.00	375.00
	1934(m)	100 pcs.	—	—	Proof	900.00
	1935(m)	.500	7.50	15.00	45.00	185.00
	1935(m)	—	—	—	Proof	1000.
	1936(m)	2.000	4.00	10.00	40.00	190.00
	1936(m)	—	—	—	Proof	1250.

KM#	Date	Mintage	Fine	VF	XF	Unc
39	1938(m)	1.484	3.00	6.00	12.50	50.00
	1938(m)	250 pcs.	—	—	Proof	500.00
	1939(m)	1.520	3.00	6.00	15.00	100.00
	1939(m)	—	—	—	Proof	2000.
	1940(m)	.760	7.00	15.00	50.00	275.00
	1941(m)	3.040	BV	5.00	10.00	45.00
	1942(m)	1.380	BV	4.00	8.00	28.00
	1942S	4.000	BV	1.50	4.00	12.00
	1943(m)	2.720	3.00	6.00	15.00	80.00
	1943S	16.000	BV	1.50	3.00	8.50
	1944(m)	14.576	BV	3.00	8.00	35.00
	1944S	8.000	BV	1.50	3.00	8.50

5.6500 g, .500 SILVER, .0908 oz ASW

KM#	Date	Mintage	Fine	VF	XF	Unc
39a	1946(m)	10.072	BV	3.50	7.00	20.00
	1946(p)	1.316	6.00	15.00	40.00	130.00
	1948(m)	4.132	BV	4.00	8.00	22.50

Obv. leg: IND:IMP. dropped.

KM#	Date	Mintage	Fine	VF	XF	Unc
46	1950(m)	7.188	BV	3.50	6.00	15.00
	1952(m)	19.644	BV	3.00	5.00	10.00

KM#	Date	Mintage	Fine	VF	XF	Unc
53	1953(m)	12.204	BV	2.50	5.00	10.00
	1953(m)	—	—	—	Proof	700.00
	1954(m)	16.188	BV	2.50	5.00	12.00
	1954(m)	—	—	—	Proof	800.00

Obv. leg: F:D: added.

KM#	Date	Mintage	Fine	VF	XF	Unc
59	1955(m)	7.492	BV	2.00	5.00	18.00
	1955(m)	1,200	—	—	Proof	60.00
	1956(m)	6.064	BV	1.00	4.00	25.00
	1956(m)	1,500	—	—	Proof	50.00
	1957(m)	12.668	BV	.75	2.50	9.00
	1957(m)	1,256	—	—	Proof	50.00
	1958(m)	7.412	BV	.75	2.00	8.00
	1958(m)	1,506	—	—	Proof	45.00
	1959(m)	10.876	BV	.75	1.50	6.00
	1959(m)	1,506	—	—	Proof	45.00
	1960(m)	14.512	—	BV	1.25	4.00
	1960(m)	1,509	—	—	Proof	40.00
	1961(m)	31.864	—	BV	.75	2.50
	1961(m)	1,506	—	—	Proof	40.00
	1962(m)	6.592	—	BV	.75	2.50
	1962(m)	2,016	—	—	Proof	40.00
	1963(m)	10.072	—	BV	.75	3.00
	1963(m)	5,042	—	—	Proof	30.00

FLORIN

11.3100 g, .925 SILVER, .3363 oz ASW

KM#	Date	Mintage	Fine	VF	XF	Unc
21	1910(L)	1.259	50.00	175.00	375.00	1000.
	1910(L)	—	—	—	Proof	1500.

KM#	Date	Mintage	Fine	VF	XF	Unc
27	1911(L)	.950	60.00	260.00	1000.	2500.
	1911(L)	—	—	—	Proof	7000.
	1912(L)	1.000	55.00	240.00	950.00	2750.
	1913(L)	1.200	50.00	225.00	750.00	2250.
	1914(L)	2.300	15.00	40.00	180.00	600.00
	1914H	.500	65.00	280.00	1000.	4500.
	1914H	—	—	—	Proof	9500.
	1915(L)	.500	100.00	300.00	850.00	4000.
	1915H	.750	65.00	200.00	700.00	2250.
	1916M	2.752	12.00	35.00	150.00	700.00
	1916M	25 pcs.	—	—	Proof	2250.
	1917M	4.305	12.00	35.00	150.00	625.00
	1918M	2.095	15.00	50.00	160.00	700.00
	1919M	1.677	45.00	150.00	600.00	1800.
	1920M star	—	—	—	Proof	40,000.
	1921(m)	1.247	30.00	115.00	500.00	1600.
	1921(m) w/o star	—	—	—	Proof	6000.
	1922(m)	2.058	15.00	70.00	300.00	1200.
	1922(m)	—	—	—	Proof	3700.
	1923(m)	1.038	20.00	75.00	320.00	1350.
	1924(m)	—	—	—	Proof	2500.
	1924(m&sy)	1.582	15.00	70.00	250.00	1000.
	1925(m&sy)	2.960	12.50	35.00	150.00	600.00
	1925(m)	—	—	—	Proof	2300.
	1926(m&sy)	2.487	10.00	40.00	160.00	900.00
	1926(m)	—	—	—	Proof	3000.
	1927(m)	3.420	8.00	20.00	120.00	450.00
	1927(m)	50 pcs.	—	—	Proof	1850.
	1928(m)	1.962	12.00	30.00	135.00	460.00
	1928(m)	—	—	—	Proof	2000.
	1931(m)	3.129	6.00	15.00	50.00	215.00
	1931(m)	—	—	—	Proof	1850.
	1932(m)	.188	170.00	450.00	1800.	5500.
	1933(m)	.488	35.00	200.00	900.00	4000.
	1934(m)	1.674	8.00	20.00	125.00	400.00
	1934(m)	100 pcs.	—	—	Proof	1250.
	1935(m)	.915	8.00	17.50	100.00	400.00
	1935(m)	—	—	—	Proof	1250.
	1936(m)	2.382	4.00	8.00	40.00	195.00
	1936(m)	—	—	—	Proof	1350.

Opening of Parliament House, Canberra

KM#	Date	Mintage	Fine	VF	XF	Unc
31	1927(m)	2.000	3.50	7.50	16.00	75.00
	1927(m)	400 pcs.	—	—	Proof	1500.

Centennial of Victoria and Melbourne

KM#	Date	Mintage	Fine	VF	XF	Unc
33	"1934-35"	*.054	100.00	130.00	175.00	325.00
	"1934-35"	—	—	—	Proof	2500.

***NOTE:** 21,000 pcs. were melted.

KM#	Date	Mintage	Fine	VF	XF	Unc
40	1938(m)	2.990	5.00	10.00	22.00	85.00
	1938(m)	—	—	—	Proof	700.00
	1939(m)	.630	15.00	35.00	160.00	700.00
	1939(m)	—	—	—	Proof	2500.
	1940(m)	8.410	BV	4.00	12.00	37.50
	1941(m)	7.614	BV	4.00	10.00	35.00
	1942(m)	17.986	BV	4.00	6.50	22.50
	1942S	6.000	BV	4.50	8.00	27.50
	1943(m)	12.762	BV	4.00	5.50	22.50
	1943S	11.000	BV	4.00	5.50	22.50
	1944(m)	22.440	BV	4.00	5.50	25.00
	1944S	11.000	BV	4.00	5.50	22.50
	1945(m)	11.970	BV	5.00	10.00	50.00

11.3100 g, .500 SILVER, .1818 oz ASW

KM#	Date	Mintage	Fine	VF	XF	Unc
40a	1946(m)	22.154	BV	2.50	5.50	20.00
	1946(m)	—	—	—	Proof	600.00
	1947(m)	39.292	BV	2.50	5.00	18.50
	1947(m)	—	—	—	Proof	600.00

50th Year Jubilee

KM#	Date	Mintage	Fine	VF	XF	Unc
47	1951(m)	2.000	BV	3.00	5.00	12.50

COPPER-NICKEL

KM#	Date	Mintage	Fine	VF	XF	Unc
47a	1951(L)	—	—	—	Proof	5000.

11.3100 g, .500 SILVER, .1818 oz ASW
Obv. leg: IND:IMP. dropped.

KM#	Date	Mintage	Fine	VF	XF	Unc
48	1951(m)	10.068	3.00	7.00	15.00	45.00
	1952(m)	10.044	4.00	8.00	16.00	50.00

KM#	Date	Mintage	Fine	VF	XF	Unc
54	1953(m)	12.658	BV	4.50	7.50	16.50
	1953(m)	—	—	—	Proof	900.00
	1954(m)	15.366	BV	4.50	7.50	22.50
	1954(m)	—	—	—	Proof	1000.

Royal Visit

KM#	Date	Mintage	Fine	VF	XF	Unc
55	1954(m)	4.000	BV	2.50	5.00	12.50

Obv. leg: F:D: added.

KM#	Date	Mintage	Fine	VF	XF	Unc
60	1956(m)	8.090	3.00	5.00	15.00	55.00
	1956(m)	1,500	—	—	Proof	75.00
	1957(m)	9.278	BV	3.00	4.00	8.50
	1957(m)	1,256	—	—	Proof	50.00
	1958(m)	8.972	BV	3.00	4.00	8.50
	1958(m)	1,506	—	—	Proof	45.00
	1959(m)	3.500	BV	3.00	4.00	8.50
	1959(m)	1,506	—	—	Proof	40.00
	1960(m)	15.760	BV	2.50	3.50	6.00
	1960(m)	1,509	—	—	Proof	35.00
	1961(m)	9.452	BV	2.50	3.50	6.00
	1961(m)	1,506	—	—	Proof	35.00
	1962(m)	13.748	BV	2.50	3.50	6.00
	1962(m)	2,016	—	—	Proof	35.00
	1963(m)	12.002	BV	2.50	3.50	6.00
	1963(m)	5,042	—	—	Proof	25.00

CROWN

28.2800 g, .925 SILVER, .8411 oz ASW

KM#	Date	Mintage	Fine	VF	XF	Unc
34	1937(m)	1.008	7.00	11.00	20.00	75.00
	1937(m)	100 pcs.	—	—	Proof	2000.
	1938(m)	.102	40.00	70.00	175.00	500.00
	1938(m)	250 pcs.	—	—	Proof	2500.

TRADE COINAGE

MINT MARKS

M - Melbourne
P - Perth
S - Sydney
(sy) - Sydney

1/2 SOVEREIGN

3.9940 g, .917 GOLD, .1177 oz AGW
Obv: Fillet head.

KM#	Date	Mintage	Fine	VF	XF	Unc
1	1855(sy)	.021	7000.	15,000.	40,000.	90,000.
	1856(sy)	.478	400.00	1500.	4000.	10,000.

Obv: Hair tied with banksia wreath.

KM#	Date	Mintage	Fine	VF	XF	Unc
3	1857(sy)	.537	200.00	600.00	1500.	5000.
	1857(sy)	—	—	—	Proof	27,500.
	1858(sy)	.483	200.00	600.00	1750.	6500.
	1859(sy)	.341	200.00	600.00	2000.	9000.
	1860(sy)	.156	350.00	1500.	4000.	12,500.
	1861(sy)	.186	200.00	600.00	1750.	6000.
	1862(sy)	.210	165.00	675.00	2000.	7000.
	1863(sy)	.348	155.00	600.00	2000.	7000.
	1864(sy)	.141	155.00	675.00	1750.	6500.
	1865(sy)	.062	300.00	700.00	2000.	9000.
	1866(sy)	.154	200.00	600.00	2000.	9000.
	1866(sy)	—	—	—	Proof	20,000.

HALF SOVEREIGN MINT MARKS

KM#5 & #9: S or M on reverse below shield.
All others have S, M or P (from 1900) on reverse on ground below dragon.

Obv: Young head.

KM#	Date	Mintage	Fine	VF	XF	Unc
5	1871S	.180	80.00	160.00	750.00	2250.
	1871S	—	—	—	Proof	13,500.
	1872S	.356	80.00	160.00	750.00	2250.
	1873M	.165	80.00	160.00	850.00	2500.
	1875S	.252	80.00	160.00	750.00	2250.
	1877M	.140	120.00	200.00	850.00	2500.
	1879S	.220	80.00	160.00	600.00	1800.
	1880S	.080	80.00	200.00	900.00	2750.
	1880S	—	—	—	Proof	12,000.
	1881S	.062	80.00	220.00	1000.	3000.
	1881M	.042	90.00	250.00	1200.	3500.
	1881M	—	—	—	Proof	12,000.
	1882S	.052	145.00	275.00	1750.	6000.
	1882M	.106	90.00	220.00	800.00	2250.
	1883S	.220	80.00	160.00	500.00	1400.
	1883S	—	—	—	Proof	12,000.
	1884M	.048	90.00	250.00	1500.	4500.
	1884M	—	—	—	Proof	12,000.
	1885M	.011	250.00	550.00	2500.	8000.
	1886S	.082	80.00	165.00	700.00	2500.
	1886M	.038	90.00	200.00	900.00	2750.
	1886M	—	—	—	Proof	12,000.
	1887S	.134	80.00	165.00	700.00	2500.
	1887S	—	—	—	Proof	12,000.
	1887M	.064	145.00	275.00	1750.	6000.

Obv: Jubilee head.

KM#	Date	Mintage	Fine	VF	XF	Unc
9	1887S	Inc. Ab.	70.00	110.00	250.00	750.00
	1887S	—	—	—	Proof	10,000.
	1887M	Inc. Ab.	80.00	120.00	300.00	850.00
	1887M	—	—	—	Proof	10,000.
	1888M	—	—	—	Proof	11,500.
	1889S	.064	80.00	120.00	500.00	1500.
	1889M	—	—	—	Proof	11,500.
	1890M	—	—	—	Proof	11,500.
	1891S w/J.E.B.	.154	90.00	150.00	650.00	2000.
	1891S w/o J.E.B.	Inc. Ab.	80.00	120.00	500.00	1500.
	1891M	—	—	—	Proof	11,500.
	1892S	—	—	—	Proof	11,500.
	1892M	—	—	—	Proof	11,500.
	1893S	—	—	—	Proof	11,500.
	1893M	.110	70.00	115.00	450.00	1500.
	1893M	—	—	—	Proof	10,000.

Obv: Older veiled head.

KM#	Date	Mintage	Fine	VF	XF	Unc
12	1893S	.250	65.00	100.00	300.00	850.00
	1893S	—	—	—	Proof	10,000.
	1893M	2 known	1000.	—	—	—
	1893M	—	—	—	Proof	11,500.
	1894M	—	—	—	Proof	11,500.
	1895M	—	—	—	Proof	11,500.
	1896M	.218	70.00	125.00	450.00	1500.
	1896M	—	—	—	Proof	10,000.
	1897S	.230	65.00	100.00	300.00	950.00
	1897M	—	—	—	Proof	11,500.
	1898M	—	—	—	Proof	11,500.
	1899M	.090	70.00	125.00	450.00	1500.
	1899M	—	—	—	Proof	10,000.
	1899P	1 known	—	—	Proof	—
	1900S	.260	65.00	100.00	275.00	850.00
	1900M	.113	70.00	125.00	450.00	1500.
	1900M	—	—	—	Proof	10,000.
	1900P	.119	70.00	125.00	450.00	1500.
	1901M	—	—	—	Proof	11,500.
	1901P	—	—	—	Proof	20,000.

KM#	Date	Mintage	Fine	VF	XF	Unc
14	1902S	.084	65.00	100.00	200.00	650.00
	1902S	—	—	—	Proof	7500.
	1903S	.231	60.00	80.00	140.00	450.00
	1904P	.060	120.00	250.00	650.00	2000.
	1906S	.308	60.00	80.00	110.00	400.00
	1906M	.082	60.00	80.00	120.00	425.00
	1907M	.400	60.00	75.00	100.00	400.00
	1908S	.538	60.00	75.00	100.00	400.00
	1908M	Inc. 1907M	60.00	75.00	125.00	500.00
	1908P	.025	140.00	275.00	475.00	2000.
	1909M	.186	60.00	75.00	125.00	500.00
	1909P	.044	125.00	250.00	425.00	1750.
	1910S	.474	60.00	75.00	120.00	400.00

KM#	Date	Mintage	Fine	VF	XF	Unc
28	1911S	.252	60.00	70.00	90.00	125.00
	1911S	—	—		Matte Proof	11,500.
	1911P	.130	BV	60.00	100.00	150.00
	1912S	.278	BV	60.00	90.00	120.00
	1914S	.322	BV	60.00	80.00	110.00
	1915S	.892	BV	60.00	80.00	110.00
	1915M	.125	BV	60.00	80.00	115.00
	1915P	.138	BV	60.00	90.00	135.00
	1916S	.448	BV	60.00	80.00	110.00
	1918P	*200-250 pcs.	300.00	450.00	550.00	800.00

SOVEREIGN

7.9881 g, .917 GOLD, .2354 oz AGW
Obv: Fillet head.

KM#	Date	Mintage	Fine	VF	XF	Unc
2	1855(sy)	.502	1250.	3500.	9000.	25,000.
	1856(sy)	.981	1250.	3500.	9000.	25,000.

Obv: Hair tied with banksia wreath.

KM#	Date	Mintage	Fine	VF	XF	Unc
4	1857(sy)	.499	250.00	500.00	1750.	4500.
	1857(sy)	(plain or milled edge)			Proof	30,000.
	1858(sy)	1.101	250.00	600.00	1850.	7000.
	1859(sy)	1.050	250.00	600.00	1850.	4500.
	1860(sy)	1.573	350.00	850.00	2500.	7500.
	1861(sy)	1.626	200.00	400.00	1200.	3000.
	1862(sy)	2.477	225.00	475.00	1750.	4500.

KM#	Date	Mintage	Fine	VF	XF	Unc
4	1863(sy)	1.255	175.00	425.00	1400.	3500.
	1864(sy)	2.698	150.00	325.00	1000.	2750.
	1865(sy)	2.130	150.00	375.00	1350.	3500.
	1866(sy)	2.911	125.00	275.00	750.00	1750.
	1866(sy)	—	—	—	Proof	25,000.
	1867(sy)	2.370	135.00	325.00	850.00	1800.
	1868(sy)	3.522	125.00	325.00	850.00	1800.
	1870(sy)	1.220	125.00	200.00	550.00	1500.
	1870(sy)	—	—	—	Proof	50,000.

NOTE: 1,202,600 pcs. reported in 1869 are dated 1868.

SOVEREIGN MINT MARKS

KM#6: S or M on obverse below truncation.
All others have S, M or P from 1899 on reverse on ground below dragon.

Obv: Young head.
NOTE: Mintage figures include St. George and shield types. No separate mintage figures are known.

KM#	Date	Mintage	Fine	VF	XF	Unc
6	1871S	2.814	BV	100.00	250.00	700.00
	1871S	—	—	—	Proof	13,500.
	1872S	1.815	BV	100.00	250.00	750.00
	1872/1M	.748	200.00	350.00	600.00	2000.
	1872M	Inc. Ab.	BV	100.00	225.00	650.00
	1873S	1.478	BV	100.00	225.00	650.00
	1873M	3 pcs.		—	Reported, not confirmed	
	1874M	1.373	BV	100.00	250.00	750.00
	1875S	2.122	BV	100.00	200.00	600.00
	1875S	—	—	—	Proof	13,000.
	1877S	1.590	BV	95.00	200.00	600.00
	1878S	1.259	BV	95.00	200.00	600.00
	1879S	1.366	BV	95.00	200.00	600.00
	1879M	1 pc.		—	Reported, not confirmed	
	1880S	1.459	BV	95.00	200.00	600.00
	1880S	—	—	—	Proof	13,000.
	1880M	3.053	500.00	1000.	2500.	7000.
	1880M	—	—	—	Proof	12,500.
	1881S	1.360	BV	95.00	175.00	450.00
	1881M	2.324	BV	135.00	300.00	1200.
	1882S	1.298	BV	95.00	175.00	450.00
	1882M	2.466	BV	95.00	175.00	450.00
	1883S	1.108	BV	95.00	175.00	450.00
	1883S	—	—	—	Proof	12,500.
	1883M	2.050	150.00	350.00	1000.	2500.
	1883M	—	—	—	Proof	12,500.
	1884S	1.595	BV	95.00	175.00	400.00
	1884M	2.942	BV	95.00	175.00	400.00
	1884M	—	—	—	Proof	12,500.
	1885S	1.486	BV	95.00	175.00	400.00
	1885M	2.957	BV	95.00	175.00	400.00
	1885M	—	—	—	Proof	12,500.
	1886S	1.677	BV	95.00	175.00	450.00
	1886S	—	—	—	Proof	12,500.
	1886M	2.902	1500.	3000.	6000.	9000.
	1886M	—	—	—	Proof	14,000.
	1887S	1.000	BV	100.00	325.00	900.00
	1887S	—	—	—	Proof	12,500.
	1887M	1.915	500.00	900.00	3000.	6000.
	1887M	—	—	—	Proof	12,500.

Obv: Young head.
NOTE: Mintage figures include St. George and shield types. No separate mintage figures are known.

KM#	Date	Mintage	Fine	VF	XF	Unc
7	1871S	2.814	—	BV	300.00	900.00
	1871S	—	—	—	Proof	13,500.
	1872S	1.815	—	BV	250.00	800.00
	1872M	.748	—	200.00	500.00	1750.
	1873S	1.478	—	BV	300.00	1000.
	1873M	.752	—	BV	250.00	700.00
	1873M	—	—	—	Proof	12,000.
	1874S	1.899	—	BV	200.00	600.00
	1874M	1.373	—	BV	200.00	600.00
	1874M	—	—	—	Proof	12,000.
	1875S	2.122	—	BV	160.00	550.00
	1875M	1.888	—	BV	160.00	550.00
	1875M	—	—	—	Proof	12,000.
	1876S	1.613	—	BV	150.00	500.00
	1876M	2.124	—	BV	150.00	500.00
	1877S	2 pcs.	—	—	Rare	—
	1877M	1.487	—	BV	150.00	500.00
	1878M	2.171	—	BV	150.00	475.00
	1879S	1.366	—	BV	350.00	1200.
	1879M	2.740	—	BV	150.00	450.00
	1880S	1.459	—	BV	200.00	600.00
	1880S	—	—	—	Proof	12,000.
	1880M	3.053	—	BV	150.00	400.00
	1881S	1.360	—	BV	200.00	600.00
	1881M	2.324	—	BV	150.00	475.00
	1881M	—	—	—	Proof	12,000.
	1882S	1.298	—	BV	150.00	400.00
	1882M	2.466	—	BV	150.00	475.00
	1883S	1.108	—	BV	150.00	475.00
	1883M	2.050	—	BV	150.00	475.00
	1883M	—	—	—	Proof	12,000.
	1884S	1.595	—	BV	150.00	425.00
	1884M	2.942	—	BV	150.00	425.00
	1884M	—	—	—	Proof	12,000.
	1885S	1.486	—	BV	150.00	425.00
	1885M	2.957	—	BV	150.00	425.00
	1885M	—	—	—	Proof	12,000.
	1886S	1.677	—	BV	150.00	425.00
	1886M	2.902	—	BV	150.00	425.00
	1886M	—	—	—	Proof	12,000.
	1887S	1.000	—	BV	190.00	600.00
	1887M	1.915	—	BV	190.00	600.00
	1887M	—	—	—	Proof	12,000.

NOTE: Designers initials on reverse omitted on some pieces 1880S-1882S and 1881M-1882M.

Obv: Jubilee head.

KM#	Date	Mintage	Fine	VF	XF	Unc
10	1887S	1.002	BV	175.00	350.00	800.00
	1887S	—	—	—	Proof	11,000.
	1887M	.940	—	BV	125.00	250.00
	1887M	—	—	—	Proof	10,000.
	1888S	2.187	—	BV	125.00	250.00
	1888M	2.830	—	BV	125.00	225.00
	1888M	—	—	—	Proof	10,000.
	1889S	3.262	—	BV	120.00	200.00
	1889M	2.732	—	BV	120.00	200.00
	1889M	—	—	—	Proof	10,000.
	1890S	2.808	—	BV	120.00	225.00
	1890M	2.473	—	BV	120.00	225.00
	1890M	—	—	—	Proof	10,000.
	1891S	2.596	—	BV	120.00	225.00
	1891M	2.749	—	BV	120.00	225.00
	1892S	2.837	—	BV	120.00	225.00
	1892M	3.488	—	BV	120.00	225.00
	1893S	1.498	—	BV	120.00	225.00
	1893S	—	—	—	Proof	10,000.
	1893M	1.649	—	BV	120.00	225.00
	1893M	—	—	—	Proof	10,000.

Obv: Older veiled head.

KM#	Date	Mintage	Fine	VF	XF	Unc
13	1893S	1.346	—	BV	100.00	175.00
	1893S	—	—	—	Proof	10,000.
	1893M	1.914	—	BV	100.00	175.00
	1893M	—	—	—	Proof	10,000.
	1894S	3.067	—	BV	100.00	180.00
	1894S	—	—	—	Proof	10,000.
	1894M	4.166	—	BV	100.00	175.00
	1894M	—	—	—	Proof	10,000.
	1895S	2.758	—	BV	100.00	180.00
	1895M	4.165	—	BV	100.00	175.00
	1895M	—	—	—	Proof	10,000.
	1896S	2.544	—	BV	100.00	180.00
	1896M	4.456	—	BV	100.00	175.00
	1896M	—	—	—	Proof	10,000.
	1897S	2.532	—	BV	100.00	200.00
	1897M	5.130	—	BV	100.00	175.00
	1897M	—	—	—	Proof	10,000.
	1898S	2.548	—	BV	100.00	200.00
	1898M	5.509	—	BV	100.00	175.00
	1898M	—	—	—	Proof	10,000.
	1899S	3.259	—	BV	100.00	150.00
	1899M	5.579	—	BV	100.00	150.00
	1899M	—	—	—	Proof	10,000.
	1899P	.690	BV	120.00	160.00	375.00
	1899P	—	—	—	Proof	12,500.
	1900S	3.586	—	BV	100.00	150.00
	1900M	4.305	—	BV	100.00	150.00
	1900M	—	—	—	Proof	10,000.
	1900P	1.886	—	BV	100.00	165.00
	1901S	3.012	—	BV	100.00	150.00
	1901M	3.987	—	BV	100.00	150.00
	1901M	—	—	—	Proof	10,000.
	1901P	2.889	—	BV	100.00	165.00
	1901P	—	—	—	Proof	12,500.

KM#	Date	Mintage	Fine	VF	XF	Unc
15	1902S	2.813	—	—	BV	115.00
	1902S	—	—	—	Proof	12,500.
	1902M	4.267	—	—	BV	115.00
	1902P	4.289	—	—	BV	115.00
	1902P	—	—	—	Proof	12,500.
	1903S	2.806	—	—	BV	115.00
	1903M	3.521	—	—	BV	115.00
	1903P	4.674	—	—	BV	115.00
	1904S	2.986	—	—	BV	115.00
	1904M	3.743	—	—	BV	115.00
	1904M	—	—	—	Proof	12,500.
	1904P	4.506	—	—	BV	115.00
	1905S	2.778	—	—	BV	115.00
	1905M	3.633	—	—	BV	115.00
	1905P	4.876	—	—	BV	115.00
	1906S	2.792	—	—	BV	115.00
	1906M	3.657	—	—	BV	115.00
	1906P	4.829	—	—	BV	115.00
	1907S	2.539	—	—	BV	115.00
	1907M	3.332	—	—	BV	115.00
	1907P	4.972	—	—	BV	115.00
	1908S	2.017	—	—	BV	115.00
	1908M	3.080	—	—	BV	115.00
	1908P	4.875	—	—	BV	115.00
	1909S	2.057	—	—	BV	115.00
	1909M	3.029	—	—	BV	115.00
	1909P	4.524	—	—	BV	115.00
	1910S	2.135	—	—	BV	115.00
	1910M	3.054	—	—	BV	115.00
	1910M	—	—	—	Proof	12,500.
	1910P	4.690	—	—	BV	115.00

KM#	Date	Mintage	Fine	VF	XF	Unc
29	1911S	2.519	—	—	BV	110.00
	1911S	—	—	—	Proof	12,500.
	1911M	2.851	—	—	BV	110.00
	1911M	—	—	—	Proof	12,500.
	1911P	4.373	—	—	BV	110.00
	1912S	2.227	—	—	BV	110.00
	1912M	2.467	—	—	BV	110.00
	1912P	4.278	—	—	BV	110.00
	1913S	2.249	—	—	BV	110.00
	1913M	2.323	—	—	BV	110.00
	1913P	4.635	—	—	BV	110.00
	1914S	1.774	—	—	BV	110.00
	1914S	—	—	—	Proof	11,500.
	1914M	2.012	—	—	BV	110.00
	1914P	4.815	—	—	BV	110.00
	1915S	1.346	—	—	BV	110.00
	1915M	1.637	—	—	BV	110.00
	1915P	4.373	—	—	BV	110.00
	1916S	1.242	—	—	BV	110.00
	1916M	1.277	—	—	BV	110.00
	1916P	4.906	—	—	BV	110.00
	1917S	1.666	—	—	BV	110.00
	1917M	.934	—	—	BV	110.00
	1917P	4.110	—	—	BV	110.00
	1918S	3.716	—	—	BV	110.00
	1918M	4.969	—	—	BV	110.00
	1918P	3.812	—	—	BV	110.00
	1919S	1.835	—	—	BV	110.00
	1919M	.514	BV	110.00	140.00	170.00
	1919P	2.995	—	—	BV	110.00
	1920S	.360	3000.	6000.	15,000.	45,000.
	1920M	.530	400.00	1200.	1800.	3000.
	1920P	2.421	—	—	BV	110.00
	1921S	.839	300.00	900.00	1200.	2000.
	1921M	.240	800.00	3000.	6000.	9500.
	1921P	2.314	—	—	BV	110.00
	1922S	.578	800.00	3000.	7000.	12,000.
	1922M	.608	500.00	2000.	5500.	9000.
	1922P	2.298	—	—	BV	110.00
	1923S	.416	400.00	1750.	5500.	9000.
	1923M	.510	BV	105.00	125.00	140.00
	1923P	2.124	—	—	BV	110.00
	1924S	.394	200.00	500.00	1000.	1600.
	1924M	.278	BV	105.00	125.00	140.00
	1924P	1.464	—	BV	150.00	200.00
	1925S	5.632	—	—	BV	110.00
	1925M	3.311	—	—	BV	110.00
	1925P	1.837	—	BV	150.00	200.00
	1926S	1.031	2500.	5000.	10,000.	15,000.
	1926S	—	—	—	Proof	22,500.
	1926M	.211	—	BV	125.00	140.00
	1926P	1.131	—	BV	125.00	190.00
	1927M	.310	—	—	—	—
	1927P	1.383	—	BV	130.00	200.00
	1928M	.413	500.00	900.00	1600.	2750.
	1928P	1.333	—	BV	130.00	200.00

Obv: Smaller head.

KM#	Date	Mintage	Fine	VF	XF	Unc
32	1929M	.436	250.00	750.00	1350.	2000.
	1929M	—	—	—	Proof	10,000.
	1929P	1.606	—	BV	120.00	135.00
	1930M	.077	100.00	150.00	200.00	275.00

KM#	Date	Mintage	Fine	VF	XF	Unc
32	1930M	—	—	—	Proof	10,000.
	1930P	1.915	—	BV	120.00	135.00
	1931M	.057	150.00	225.00	350.00	450.00
	1931M	—	—	—	Proof	10,000.
	1931P	1.173	—	BV	120.00	135.00

2 POUNDS

15.9761 g, .917 GOLD, .4707 oz AGW
50th Anniversary of Reign

KM#	Date	Mintage	Fine	VF	XF	Unc
8	1887S	*11 pcs.	—	—	Proof	27,500.

***NOTE:** Spink Australia Sale #30 11-89 nearly FDC realized $16,940.

KM#	Date	Mintage	Fine	VF	XF	Unc
16	1902S	4 pcs.	—		Matte Proof	35,000.

5 POUNDS

39.9403 g, .917 GOLD, 1.1771 oz AGW
50th Anniversary of Reign

KM#	Date	Mintage	Fine	VF	XF	Unc
11	1887S	*3 pcs.	—	—	Proof	Rare

***NOTE:** Spink Australia Sale #30 11-89 nearly FDC realized $62,370.

KM#	Date	Mintage	Fine	VF	XF	Unc
17	1902S	*3 pcs.	—	—	Proof	Rare
	1902S	Inc. Ab.	—		Matte Proof	*Rare

***NOTE:** Spink Australia Sale #30 11-89 nearly FDC realized $38,500.

DECIMAL COINAGE

100 Cents = 1 Dollar

CENT

BRONZE
Ring-tailed Opossum

KM#	Date	Mintage	Fine	VF	XF	Unc
62	1966(c)	146.457	—	—	.15	.50
	1966(c)	.018	—	—	Proof	4.00
	1966(m) blunted whisker on right					
		238.990	—	.15	.25	1.50
	1966(p) blunted 2nd whisker from right					
		26.620	.15	.30	1.50	8.00
	1967	110.055	—	.15	.25	2.00
	1968	19.930	—	.15	.55	7.00
	1969	87.680	—	—	.15	.60
	1969	.013	—	—	Proof	4.25
	1970	72.560	—	—	.15	.55
	1970	.015	—	—	Proof	4.25
	1971	102.455	—	—	.15	.50
	1971	.010	—	—	Proof	5.00
	1972	82.400	—	—	.10	.50
	1972	.010	—	—	Proof	4.75
	1973	140.710	—	—	.10	.30
	1973	.010	—	—	Proof	5.75
	1974	131.720	—	—	.10	.30
	1974	.011	—	—	Proof	5.00
	1975	134.775	—	—	—	.20
	1975	.023	—	—	Proof	1.00
	1976	172.935	—	—	—	.20
	1976	.021	—	—	Proof	1.75
	1977	153.430	—	—	—	.20
	1977	.055	—	—	Proof	1.50
	1978	97.253	—	—	—	.15
	1978	.039	—	—	Proof	1.00
	1979	130.339	—	—	—	.15
	1979	.036	—	—	Proof	1.00
	1980	137.892	—	—	—	.15
	1980	.068	—	—	Proof	1.00
	1981	223.900	—	—	—	.15
	1981	.086	—	—	Proof	1.00
	1982	134.290	—	—	—	.15
	1982	.100	—	—	Proof	1.00
	1983	205.625	—	—	—	.15
	1983	.080	—	—	Proof	1.25
	1984	74.735	—	—	—	.15
	1984	.061	—	—	Proof	1.50

KM#	Date	Mintage	Fine	VF	XF	Unc
78	1985	38.300	—	—	—	.10
	1985	.075	—	—	Proof	1.00
	1986	.180	—	—	—	2.50
	1986	.067	—	—	Proof	3.00
	1987	127.000	—	—	—	.10
	1987	.070	—	—	Proof	1.00
	1988	56.910	—	—	—	.10
	1988	.106	—	—	Proof	1.00
	1989	—	—	—	—	.10
	1989	—	—	—	Proof	1.00
	1990	—	—	—	—	.10
	1990	—	—	—	Proof	1.00
	1991	—	—	—	—	.10
	1991	—	—	—	Proof	1.00

2 CENTS

BRONZE
Frilled Lizard

KM#	Date	Mintage	Fine	VF	XF	Unc
63	1966(c)	145.226	—	—	.10	.50
	1966(c)	.018	—	—	Proof	7.00
	1966(m) blunted 3rd left claw					
		66.575	—	.15	.35	2.50
	1966(p) blunted 1st right claw					
		217.735	—	.15	.25	1.50
	1967	73.250	—	.15	.30	4.00
	1968	17.000	—	.15	.55	5.00
	1969	12.940	—	.15	.30	2.50
	1969	.013	—	—	Proof	7.75
	1970	39.872	—	—	.15	1.00
	1970	.015	—	—	Proof	7.75
	1971	60.735	—	—	.15	1.00
	1971	.010	—	—	Proof	7.75
	1972	77.570	—	—	.10	.75
	1972	.010	—	—	Proof	7.75
	1973	94.058	—	—	.10	.60
	1973	.010	—	—	Proof	8.75
	1974	177.723	—	—	.10	.60
	1974	.011	—	—	Proof	8.75
	1975	100.045	—	—	.10	.40
	1975	.023	—	—	Proof	1.50
63	1976	121.882	—	—	.10	.25
	1976	.021	—	—	Proof	2.50
	1977	102.000	—	—	—	.25
	1977	.055	—	—	Proof	1.50
	1978	128.253	—	—	—	.25
	1978	.039	—	—	Proof	1.50
	1979	69.705	—	—	.10	.25
	1979	.036	—	—	Proof	1.50
	1980	145.603	—	—	—	.15
	1980	.068	—	—	Proof	1.50
	1981	219.176	—	—	—	.15
	1981	.086	—	—	Proof	1.50
	1982	121.770	—	—	—	.15
	1982	.100	—	—	Proof	1.50
	1983	177.227	—	—	—	.15
	1983	.080	—	—	Proof	1.50
	1984	57.963	—	—	—	.15
	1984	.061	—	—	Proof	2.00

KM#	Date	Mintage	Fine	VF	XF	Unc
79	1985	34.500	—	—	—	.10
	1985	.075	—	—	Proof	1.00
	1986	.180	—	—	—	2.75
	1986	.067	—	—	Proof	4.00
	1987	.200	—	—	—	1.00
	1987	.070	—	—	Proof	1.00
	1988	28.905	—	—	—	.10
	1988	.106	—	—	Proof	1.00
	1989	—	—	—	—	.10
	1989	—	—	—	Proof	1.00
	1990	—	—	—	—	.10
	1990	—	—	—	Proof	1.00
	1991	—	—	—	—	.10
	1991	—	—	—	Proof	1.00

5 CENTS

COPPER-NICKEL
Short-beaked Spiny Ant-eater

KM#	Date	Mintage	Fine	VF	XF	Unc
64	1966(c)	45.427	—	.15	.25	1.50
	1966(c)	.018	—	—	Proof	10.00
	1966(L)	30.000	—	.15	.25	1.50
	1966(L)	—	—	—	Proof	15.00
	1967	62.144	—	.15	.35	2.50
	1968	67.336	—	.15	.40	3.50
	1969	38.170	—	.15	.20	2.00
	1969	.013	—	—	Proof	16.00
	1970	46.058	—	—	.15	2.50
	1970	.015	—	—	Proof	16.00
	1971	39.516	—	.15	.25	3.00
	1971	.010	—	—	Proof	16.00
	1972	8.256	.15	.30	1.30	17.00
	1972	.010	—	—	Proof	15.00
	1973	48.816	—	.15	.20	1.00
	1973	.010	—	—	Proof	17.00
	1974	64.248	—	.15	.20	1.00
	1974	.011	—	—	Proof	14.00
	1975	44.256	—	—	.10	.40
	1975	.023	—	—	Proof	3.00
	1976	113.180	—	—	.10	.30
	1976	.021	—	—	Proof	4.50
	1977	108.800	—	—	.10	.30
	1977	.055	—	—	Proof	3.75
	1978	25.210	—	—	.10	.20
	1978	.039	—	—	Proof	2.00
	1979	44.533	—	—	.10	.20
	1979	.036	—	—	Proof	2.75
	1980	115.042	—	—	.10	.20
	1980	.068	—	—	Proof	2.75
	1981	162.264	—	—	.10	.20
	1981	.086	—	—	Proof	3.25
	1982	139.468	—	—	.10	.20
	1982	.100	—	—	Proof	2.25
	1983	131.568	—	—	.10	.20
	1983	.080	—	—	Proof	3.25
	1984	35.436	—	—	.10	.20
	1984	.061	—	—	Proof	4.00

KM#	Date	Mintage	Fine	VF	XF	Unc
80	1985	.170	(in mint sets only)			
			—	—	—	15.00
	1985	.075	—	—	Proof	25.00
	1986	.180	(in mint sets only)			
			—	—	—	3.00
	1986	.067	—	—	Proof	5.00
	1987	73.500	—	—	—	.20

KM#	Date	Mintage	Fine	VF	XF	Unc
80	1987	.070	—	—	Proof	2.25
	1988	65.424	—	—	—	.20
	1988	.106	—	—	Proof	2.25
	1989	—	—	—	—	.20
	1989	—	—	—	Proof	2.25
	1990	—	—	—	—	.20
	1990	—	—	—	Proof	2.25
	1991	—	—	—	—	.20
	1991	—	—	—	Proof	2.25
	1992	—	—	—	—	.20
	1992	—	—	—	Proof	2.25
	1993	—	—	—	—	.20
	1993	—	—	—	Proof	2.25

10 CENTS

COPPER-NICKEL
Superb Lyre-bird

KM#	Date	Mintage	Fine	VF	XF	Unc
65	1966(c)	10.984	—	.15	.30	2.00
	1966(c)	.018	—	—	Proof	12.00
	1966(L)	30.000	—	.15	.30	2.00
	1966(L)	—	—	—	Proof	16.00
	1967	51.032	—	.15	.55	7.00
	1968	57.194	—	.15	.45	5.00
	1969	22.146	—	.15	.25	2.50
	1969	.013	—	—	Proof	14.00
	1970	22.306	—	.15	.25	2.50
	1970	.015	—	—	Proof	14.00
	1971	20.726	—	.10	.25	3.50
	1971	.010	—	—	Proof	14.00
	1972	12.502	—	.10	.25	4.00
	1972	.010	—	—	Proof	14.00
	1973	27.320	—	.10	.15	1.50
	1973	.010	—	—	Proof	14.00
	1974	46.550	—	.10	.15	1.50
	1974	.011	—	—	Proof	14.00
	1975	50.900	—	.10	.15	.80
	1975	.023	—	—	Proof	2.50
	1976	57.060	—	.10	.15	.80
	1976	.021	—	—	Proof	3.75
	1977	10.940	—	.10	.15	1.00
	1977	.055	—	—	Proof	3.00
	1978	48.400	—	.10	.15	.45
	1978	.039	—	—	Proof	2.50
	1979	36.950	—	.10	.15	.45
	1979	.036	—	—	Proof	2.50
	1980	55.084	—	.10	.15	.45
	1980	.068	—	—	Proof	2.50
	1981	116.060	—	.10	.15	.40
	1981	.086	—	—	Proof	.45
	1982	61.492	—	.10	.15	.35
	1982	.100	—	—	Proof	2.00
	1983	82.318	—	.10	.15	.35
	1983	.080	—	—	Proof	3.00
	1984	25.728	—	.10	.15	.30
	1984	.061	—	—	Proof	3.50

NOTE: One 1981 coin was struck on a Sri Lanka 50 cents planchet, KM#135.1. It carries an approximate value of $600.

KM#	Date	Mintage	Fine	VF	XF	Unc
81	1985	2.100	—	—	.10	.20
	1985	.075	—	—	Proof	1.00
	1986	.180	—	—	—	3.50
	1986	.067	—	—	Proof	8.00
	1987	.200	—	—	—	1.50
	1987	.070	—	—	Proof	2.25
	1988	35.095	—	—	—	.20
	1988	.106	—	—	Proof	2.25
	1989	—	—	—	—	.20
	1989	—	—	—	Proof	2.25
	1990	—	—	—	—	.20
	1990	—	—	—	Proof	2.25
	1991	—	—	—	—	.20
	1991	—	—	—	Proof	2.25
	1992	—	—	—	—	.20
	1992	—	—	—	Proof	2.25
	1993	—	—	—	—	.20
	1993	—	—	—	Proof	2.25

20 CENTS

COPPER-NICKEL
Duckbill Platypus

KM#	Date	Mintage	Fine	VF	XF	Unc
66	1966(c)	28.223	—	.20	1.00	10.00
	1966(c)	.018	—	—	Proof	15.00
	1966(L)	30.000	—	.20	.75	8.00
	1966(L)	—	—	—	Proof	15.00
	1967	83.848	—	.20	1.35	15.00
	1968	40.537	—	.20	1.10	13.00
	1969	16.502	—	.20	1.10	18.00
	1969	.013	—	—	Proof	18.00
	1970	23.271	—	.20	.65	7.00
	1970	.015	—	—	Proof	18.00
	1971	8.947	—	.15	.75	18.00
	1971	.010	—	—	Proof	17.50
	1972	16.643	—	.15	.50	12.00
	1972	.010	—	—	Proof	17.50
	1973	23.356	—	.15	.45	8.00
	1973	.010	—	—	Proof	17.50
	1974	33.548	—	.15	.45	7.50
	1974	.011	—	—	Proof	17.50
	1975	53.300	—	.15	.20	2.00
	1975	.023	—	—	Proof	3.25
	1976	59.774	—	.15	.20	.90
	1976	.021	—	—	Proof	4.50
	1977	41.272	—	.15	.20	.80
	1977	.055	—	—	Proof	3.75
	1978	38.781	—	.15	.20	.80
	1978	.039	—	—	Proof	3.00
	1979	22.300	—	.15	.20	1.00
	1979	.036	—	—	Proof	3.00
	1980	77.673	—	.15	.20	.40
	1980	.068	—	—	Proof	3.25
	1981	164.500	—	.15	.20	.40
	1981	.086	—	—	Proof	3.25
	1982	76.600	—	.15	.20	.40
	1982	.100	—	—	Proof	2.50
	1983	55.113	—	.15	.20	.40
	1983	.080	—	—	Proof	3.50
	1984	27.820	—	.15	.20	.35
	1984	.061	—	—	Proof	5.00

NOTE: Some 1981 dated coins were struck on a Hong Kong 2 Dollar planchet, KM#37. 6 pcs. are reported. Each carries an approximate value of $800.

KM#	Date	Mintage	Fine	VF	XF	Unc
82	1985	27.000	—	.15	.20	.30
	1985	.075	—	—	Proof	2.00
	1986	.180	—	—	—	4.00
	1986	.067	—	—	Proof	10.00
	1987	.200	—	—	—	2.00
	1987	.070	—	—	Proof	2.50
	1988	.240	—	—	—	.30
	1988	.106	—	—	Proof	2.50
	1989	—	—	—	—	.30
	1989	—	—	—	Proof	2.50
	1990	—	—	—	—	.30
	1990	—	—	—	Proof	2.50
	1991	—	—	—	—	.30
	1991	—	—	—	Proof	2.50
	1992	—	—	—	—	.30
	1992	—	—	—	Proof	2.50
	1993	—	—	—	—	.30
	1993	—	—	—	Proof	2.50

50 CENTS

13.2800 g, .800 SILVER, .3416 oz ASW

KM#	Date	Mintage	Fine	VF	XF	Unc
67	1966	36.454	—	—	BV	6.50
	1966	.018	—	—	Proof	150.00

COPPER-NICKEL

KM#	Date	Mintage	Fine	VF	XF	Unc
68	1969	14.015	—	.45	1.25	11.50
	1969	.013	—	—	Proof	75.00
	1971	21.056	—	.45	2.00	12.50
	1971	.010	—	—	Proof	60.00
	1972	5.586	—	.45	2.25	18.00
	1972	.010	—	—	Proof	55.00
	1973	4.009	—	.45	2.25	18.00
	1973	.010	—	—	Proof	60.00
	1974	8.962	—	.45	.85	7.50
	1974	.011	—	—	Proof	50.00
	1975	19.025	—	.40	.50	3.50
	1975	.023	—	—	Proof	18.00
	1976	27.280	—	.40	.50	2.50
	1976	.021	—	—	Proof	21.00
	1978	25.765	—	.40	.50	1.00
	1978	.039	—	—	Proof	16.00
	1979	24.886	—	.40	.50	1.00
	1979	.036	—	—	Proof	17.00
	1980	38.681	—	.40	.50	1.00
	1980	.068	—	—	Proof	7.00
	1981	24.168	—	.40	.50	.80
	1981	.086	—	—	Proof	10.00
	1983	48.923	—	—	.40	.75
	1983	.080	—	—	Proof	10.00
	1984	26.281	—	—	.40	.75
	1984	.061	—	—	Proof	15.00

200th Anniversary of Cook's Australian Voyage
Obv: Similar to KM#68.

KM#	Date	Mintage	Fine	VF	XF	Unc
69	1970	17.100	—	.40	1.50	4.00
	1970	.015	—	—	Proof	50.00

Queen's Silver Jubilee

KM#	Date	Mintage	Fine	VF	XF	Unc
70	1977	25.076	—	.40	.50	1.25
	1977	.055	—	—	Proof	15.00

Wedding of Prince Charles and Lady Diana

KM#	Date	Mintage	Fine	VF	XF	Unc
72	1981	44.100	—	.40	.50	1.25

XII Commonwealth Games Brisbane

KM#	Date	Mintage	Fine	VF	XF	Unc
74	1982	23.287	—	.40	.50	1.25
	1982	.100	—	—	Proof	8.00

KM#	Date	Mintage	Fine	VF	XF	Unc
83	1985	1.000	—	—	.40	.60
	1985	.075	—	—	Proof	4.00
	1986	.180	—	—	—	5.00
	1986	.067	—	—	Proof	15.00
	1987	.200	—	—	—	5.00
	1987	.070	—	—	Proof	15.00
	1989	—	—	—	—	5.00
	1989	—	—	—	Proof	15.00
	1990	—	—	—	—	5.00
	1990	—	—	—	Proof	15.00
	1991	—	—	—	—	5.00
	1991	—	—	—	Proof	15.00
	1992	—	—	—	—	5.00
	1992	—	—	—	Proof	15.00
	1993	—	—	—	—	5.00
	1993	—	—	—	Proof	15.00

Australian Bicentennial

KM#	Date	Mintage	Fine	VF	XF	Unc
99	1988	2.793	—	—	—	2.00
	1988	.106	—	—	Proof	12.00

18.0000 g, .925 SILVER, .5353 oz ASW

KM#	Date	Mintage	Fine	VF	XF	Unc
99a	1988	.025	—	—	Proof	25.00
	1989	.025	—	—	Proof	25.00

Cook Commemorative
Obv: Similar to KM#99.
Rev: Similar to KM#69.

KM#	Date	Mintage	Fine	VF	XF	Unc
127	1989	.025	—	—	Proof	25.00

Queen's Silver Jubilee
Obv: Similar to KM#99.
Rev: Similar to KM#70.

KM#	Date	Mintage	Fine	VF	XF	Unc
128	1989	.025	—	—	Proof	25.00

Wedding of Prince Charles and Lady Diana
Obv: Similar to KM#99.
Rev: Similar to KM#72.

KM#	Date	Mintage	Fine	VF	XF	Unc
129	1989	.025	—	—	Proof	25.00

XII Commonwealth Games Brisbane
Obv: Similar to KM#99.
Rev: Similar to KM#74.

KM#	Date	Mintage	Fine	VF	XF	Unc
130	1989	.025	—	—	Proof	25.00

COPPER-NICKEL
25th Anniversary of Decimal Currency - Merino Ram

KM#	Date	Mintage	Fine	VF	XF	Unc
139	1991	—	—	—	—	2.00
	1991	—	—	—	Proof	12.00

DOLLAR

NICKEL-ALUMINUM-COPPER
Kangaroos

KM#	Date	Mintage	Fine	VF	XF	Unc
77	1984	185.985	—	—	.85	2.50
	1984	.159	—	—	Proof	10.00

KM#	Date	Mintage	Fine	VF	XF	Unc
84	1985	91.400	—	—	.85	3.25
	1985	.075	—	—	Proof	25.00
	1987	.200	—	—	—	3.00
	1987	.070	—	—	Proof	25.00
	1989	—	—	—	—	3.00
	1989	—	—	—	Proof	25.00
	1990	—	—	—	—	3.00
	1990	—	—	—	Proof	25.00
	1991	—	—	—	—	3.00
	1991	—	—	—	Proof	25.00

11.4900 g, .925 SILVER, .3417 oz ASW
Masterpieces in Silver

KM#	Date	Mintage	Fine	VF	XF	Unc
84a	1990	.025	—	—	Proof	35.00

ALUMINUM-BRONZE
International Year of Peace

KM#	Date	Mintage	Fine	VF	XF	Unc
87	1986	25.100	—	—	.85	2.00
	1986	.067	—	—	Proof	22.50

11.4900 g, .925 SILVER, .3417 oz ASW
Masterpieces in Silver

KM#	Date	Mintage	Fine	VF	XF	Unc
87a	1990	.025	—	—	Proof	35.00

ALUMINUM-BRONZE
Aboriginal Art

KM#	Date	Mintage	Fine	VF	XF	Unc
100	1988	1.564	—	—	—	2.50
	1988	.106	—	—	Proof	22.50

11.4900 g, .925 SILVER, .3417 oz ASW
Masterpieces in Silver

KM#	Date	Mintage	Fine	VF	XF	Unc
100a	1988	.025	—	—	Proof	35.00
	1990	.025	—	—	Proof	35.00

ALUMINUM-BRONZE
Olympics - Female Javelin Thrower

KM#	Date	Mintage	Fine	VF	XF	Unc
175	1992	—	—	—	—	3.50
	1992	—	—	—	Proof	12.50

Landcare Australia - Stylized Tree

KM#	Date	Mintage	Fine	VF	XF	Unc
208	1993	—	—	—	—	2.50
	1993	—	—	—	Proof	12.50
	1993 C	—	—	—	—	3.00
	1993 M	—	—	—	—	3.00
	1993 S	—	—	—	—	3.00

NOTE: Visitors at mints and coin shows were allowed to strike a coin for a fee at the following: C - Canberra, M - Hall of Manufacturers Pavilion Coin Show, Melbourne and S - Sydney International Coin Fair.

2 DOLLARS

ALUMINUM-BRONZE
Aborigine Male

KM#	Date	Mintage	Fine	VF	XF	Unc
101	1988	59.679	—	—	—	4.50
	1988	.106	—	—	Proof	10.00
	1989	—	—	—	—	4.50
	1989	—	—	—	Proof	10.00
	1990	—	—	—	—	4.50
	1990	—	—	—	Proof	10.00
	1991	—	—	—	—	4.50
	1991	—	—	—	Proof	10.00
	1992	—	—	—	—	4.50
	1992	—	—	—	Proof	10.00
	1993	—	—	—	—	4.50
	1993	—	—	—	Proof	10.00

8.4300 g, .925 SILVER, .2507 oz ASW

KM#	Date	Mintage	Fine	VF	XF	Unc
101a	1988	.025	—	—	Proof	15.00
	1991	—	—	—	Proof	15.00

5 DOLLARS

ALUMINUM-BRONZE
Parliament House

KM#	Date	Mintage	Fine	VF	XF	Unc
102	1988	—	—	—	—	5.00
	1988	.080	—	—	Proof	17.50

35.7900 g, .925 SILVER, 1.0645 oz ASW

KM#	Date	Mintage	Fine	VF	XF	Unc
102a	1988	.025	—	—	Proof	20.00

ALUMINUM-BRONZE
ANZAC Memorial

KM#	Date	Mintage	Fine	VF	XF	Unc
134	1990	—	—	—	—	6.50
	1990	—	—	—	Proof	28.00

Australian Role In Space Industry

KM#	Date	Mintage	Fine	VF	XF	Unc
190	1992	—	—	—	—	10.00

10 DOLLARS

20.0000 g, .925 SILVER, .5949 oz ASW
XII Commonwealth Games Brisbane

KM#	Date	Mintage	Fine	VF	XF	Unc
75	1982	.126	—	—	—	23.00
	1982	.085	—	—	Proof	43.00

150th Anniversary of the State of Victoria

KM#	Date	Mintage	Fine	VF	XF	Unc
85	1985	.082	—	—	—	17.50
	1985	.056	—	—	Proof	50.00

150th Anniversary of South Australia

KM#	Date	Mintage	Fine	VF	XF	Unc
88	1986	.078	—	—	—	17.50
	1986	.052	—	—	Proof	45.00

New South Wales

KM#	Date	Mintage	Fine	VF	XF	Unc
93	1987	.065	—	—	—	20.00
	1987	.050	—	—	Proof	65.00

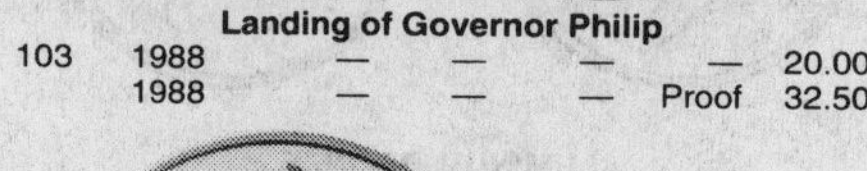

Landing of Governor Philip

KM#	Date	Mintage	Fine	VF	XF	Unc
103	1988	—	—	—	—	20.00
	1988	—	—	—	Proof	32.50

Queensland

KM#	Date	Mintage	Fine	VF	XF	Unc
114	1989	—	—	—	—	20.00
	1989	—	—	—	Proof	32.50

Kookaburra
Obv: Portrait of Queen Elizabeth II.

KM#	Date	Mintage	Fine	VF	XF	Unc
133	1989	—	—	—	Proof	30.00

Sulphur Crested Cockatoo
Obv: Portrait of Queen Elizabeth II.

KM#	Date	Mintage	Fine	VF	XF	Unc
136	1990	—	—	—	Proof	35.00

Western Australia
Obv: Portrait of Queen Elizabeth II.
Rev: Western Australia coat of arms.

KM#	Date	Mintage	Fine	VF	XF	Unc
137	1990	—	—	—	—	18.00
	1990	—	—	—	Proof	32.50

Tasmania

KM#	Date	Mintage	Fine	VF	XF	Unc
153	1991	—	—	—	—	16.50
	1991	—	—	—	Proof	30.00

Birds of Australia - Jabiru Stork

KM#	Date	Mintage	Fine	VF	XF	Unc
156	1991	.050	—	—	Proof	30.00

Northern Territory

KM#	Date	Mintage	Fine	VF	XF	Unc
188	1992	—	—	—	—	16.50
	1992	—	—	—	Proof	30.00

Emperor Penguin

KM#	Date	Mintage	Fine	VF	XF	Unc
199	1992	*.035	—	—	Proof	40.00

Australian Capital Territory

KM#	Date	Mintage	Fine	VF	XF	Unc
210	1993	—	—	—	—	17.50
	1993	—	—	—	Proof	42.50

25 DOLLARS

33.6300 g, .925 SILVER, 1.0001 oz ASW
40th Anniversary of Reign of Queen Elizabeth II - Queen Mother
Obv: Portrait of Queen Elizabeth II.

KM#	Date	Mintage	Fine	VF	XF	Unc
200	1992	—	—	—	Proof	35.00

40th Anniversary of Reign of Queen Elizabeth II - Princess Diana

KM#	Date	Mintage	Fine	VF	XF	Unc
201	1992	—	—	—	Proof	35.00

40th Anniversary of Reign of Queen Elizabeth II - Princess Anne

KM#	Date	Mintage	Fine	VF	XF	Unc
202	1992	—	—	—	Proof	35.00

40th Anniversary of Reign of Queen Elizabeth II - Princess Margaret

KM#	Date	Mintage	Fine	VF	XF	Unc
203	1992	—	—	—	Proof	35.00

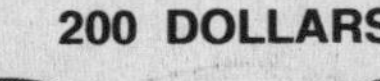

200 DOLLARS

10.0000 g, .917 GOLD, .2948 oz AGW
Koala

KM#	Date	Mintage	Fine	VF	XF	Unc
71	1980	.208	—	—	—	150.00
	1980	.050	—	—	Proof	165.00
	1983	.088	—	—	—	155.00
	1983	.016	—	—	Proof	160.00
	1984	.049	—	—	—	155.00
	1984	.013	—	—	Proof	185.00

Wedding of Prince Charles and Lady Diana

KM#	Date	Mintage	Fine	VF	XF	Unc
73	1981	.078	—	—	—	155.00

XII Commonwealth Games Brisbane

KM#	Date	Mintage	Fine	VF	XF	Unc
76	1982	.077	—	—	—	150.00
	1982	.030	—	—	Proof	155.00

Koala

KM#	Date	Mintage	Fine	VF	XF	Unc
86	1985	.029	—	—	—	160.00
	1985	.017	—	—	Proof	185.00
	1986	.015	—	—	—	160.00
	1986	.017	—	—	Proof	200.00

Arthur Phillip

KM#	Date	Mintage	Fine	VF	XF	Unc
94	1987	.021	—	—	—	170.00
	1987	.020	—	—	Proof	200.00

Bicentennial of Australia

KM#	Date	Mintage	Fine	VF	XF	Unc
115	1988	.011	—	—	—	170.00
	1988	.020	—	—	Proof	200.00

Pride of Australia - Frilled Neck Lizard
Obv: Similar to KM#115.

KM#	Date	Mintage	Fine	VF	XF	Unc
116	1989	*.010	—	—	—	175.00
	1989	*.025	—	—	Proof	210.00

Pride of Australia - Platypus

KM#	Date	Mintage	Fine	VF	XF	Unc
135	1990	—	—	—	—	170.00
	1990	—	—	—	Proof	210.00

Pride of Australia - Emu

KM#	Date	Mintage	Fine	VF	XF	Unc
160	1991	—	—	—	—	170.00
	1991	—	—	—	Proof	210.00

250 DOLLARS

16.9500 g, .917 GOLD, .4995 oz AGW
40th Anniversary of Reign of Queen Elizabeth II - Queen Mother
Rev: Portrait of Queen Mother right in circle of crowns.

KM#	Date	Mintage	Fine	VF	XF	Unc
204	1992	*5,000	—	—	Proof	400.00

40th Anniversary of Reign of Queen Elizabeth II - Princess Diana
Rev: Portrait of Princess Diana right in circle of crowns.

KM#	Date	Mintage	Fine	VF	XF	Unc
205	1992	*5,000	—	—	Proof	400.00

40th Anniversary of Reign of Queen Elizabeth II - Princess Anne
Rev: Portrait of Princess Anne right in circle of crowns.

KM#	Date	Mintage	Fine	VF	XF	Unc
206	1992	*5,000	—	—	Proof	400.00

40th Anniversary of Reign of Queen Elizabeth II - Princess Margaret
Rev: Portrait of Princess Margaret left in circle of crowns.

KM#	Date	Mintage	Fine	VF	XF	Unc
207	1992	*5,000	—	—	Proof	400.00

SILVER BULLION ISSUES

25 CENTS

(The Dump)

7.7750 g, .999 SILVER, .2500 oz ASW
Holey Dollar and Aboriginal Culture

KM#	Date	Mintage	Fine	VF	XF	Unc
113	1988	—	—	—	—	10.00

Wandjina of Aboriginal Mythology

KM#	Date	Mintage	Fine	VF	XF	Unc
132	1989	*.100	—	—	—	10.00

3 Mythological Creatures

KM#	Date	Mintage	Fine	VF	XF	Unc
155	1990	—	—	—	—	10.00

DOLLAR

31.1000 g, .999 SILVER, 1.0000 oz ASW
Holey Dollar and Aboriginal Culture

KM#	Date	Mintage	Fine	VF	XF	Unc
112	1988	—	—	—	—	25.00

Holey Dollar and Crocodiles

KM#	Date	Mintage	Fine	VF	XF	Unc
131	1989	*.100	—	—	—	25.00

Stylized Natives and Jungle

KM#	Date	Mintage	Fine	VF	XF	Unc
154	1990	—	—	—	—	25.00

Australian Kookaburra

KM#	Date	Mintage	Fine	VF	XF	Unc
164	1992	.300	—	—	—	12.50
	1993	.300	—	—	—	12.50

Australian Kookaburra

KM#	Date	Mintage	Fine	VF	XF	Unc
209	1992	—	—	—	Proof	40.00
	1993	*.300	—	—	—	12.50

31.5700 g, .999 SILVER, 1.0140 oz ASW
Kangaroo

KM#	Date	Mintage	Fine	VF	XF	Unc
211	1993	.150	—	—	—	12.00

31.1035 g, .999 SILVER, 1.0000 oz ASW
Pair of Kookaburras

KM#	Date	Mintage	Fine	VF	XF	Unc
212	1994	—	—	—	Proof	15.00

2 DOLLARS

62.2140 g, .999 SILVER, 2.0000 oz ASW
Australian Kookaburra - On Stump

KM#	Date	Mintage	Fine	VF	XF	Unc
179	1992	—	—	—	—	25.00
	1992	5,000	—	—	Proof	95.00

5 DOLLARS

31.1030 g, .999 SILVER, 1.0000 oz ASW
Australian Kookaburra

KM#	Date	Mintage	Fine	VF	XF	Unc
189 (127)	1990	.300	—	—	—	10.00

Australian Kookaburra

KM#	Date	Mintage	Fine	VF	XF	Unc
138	1990	1,000	—	—	Proof	32.50
	1991	.300	—	—	—	10.00
	1991	—	—	—	Proof	32.50

10 DOLLARS

62.2140 g, .999 SILVER, 2.0000 oz ASW
Australian Kookaburra
Rev: Kookaburra bird.

KM#	Date	Mintage	Fine	VF	XF	Unc
161	1991	—	—	—	—	15.00
	1991	5,000	—	—	Proof	65.00

311.0670 g, .999 SILVER, 10.0000 oz ASW
Australian Kookaburra - On Stump
Similar to 30 Dollars, KM#181.

KM#	Date	Mintage	Fine	VF	XF	Unc
180	1992	—	—	—	—	90.00
	1992	2,500	—	—	Proof	350.00

30 DOLLARS

1,100.1000 g, .999 SILVER, 32.1575 oz ASW
Illustration reduced. Actual size: 100mm.
Australian Kookaburra - On Stump

KM#	Date	Mintage	Fine	VF	XF	Unc
181	1992	—	—	—	—	275.00
	1992	1,000	—	—	Proof	900.00
	1993	—	—	—	—	275.00

50 DOLLARS

311.0670 g, .999 SILVER, 10.0000 oz ASW
Australian Kookaburra
Obv: Queen Elizabeth II above denomination.
Rev: Kookaburra bird.

KM#	Date	Mintage	Fine	VF	XF	Unc
162	1991	—	—	—	—	65.00
	1991	2,500	—	—	Proof	350.00

150 DOLLARS

1,000.1000 g, .999 SILVER, 32.1575 oz ASW (Kilo)
Australian Kookaburra
Obv: Queen Elizabeth II above denomination.
Rev: Kookaburra bird.

KM#	Date	Mintage	Fine	VF	XF	Unc
163	1991	—	—	—	—	225.00
	1991	1,000	—	—	Proof	900.00

GOLD BULLION ISSUES

5 DOLLARS

(1/20 Ounce)

1.5710 g, .999 GOLD, .0500 oz AGW
Red Kangaroo
Obv: Elizabeth II.

KM#	Date	Mintage	Fine	VF	XF	Unc
117	1989	2,200	—	—	Proof	35.00
	1990	*.200	—	—		*BV + 25%*

Gray Kangaroo

KM#	Date	Mintage	Fine	VF	XF	Unc
140	1990	7,000	—	—	Proof	32.50
	1991	.200	—	—		*BV + 25%*

Common Wallaroo
Obv: Elizabeth II.
Rev: Similar to 100 Dollars, KM#169.

KM#	Date	Mintage	Fine	VF	XF	Unc
165	1991	3,000	—	—	Proof	32.50
	1992	.200	—	—		*BV + 25%*

15 DOLLARS

(1/10 Ounce)

3.1103 g, .999 GOLD, .1000 oz AGW
Little Hero
Obv: Elizabeth II.

KM#	Date	Mintage	Fine	VF	XF	Unc
89	1986P	.015	—	—	Proof	70.00
	1987	.266	—	—		*BV + 15%*
	1988	.104	—	—		*BV + 15%*
	1989	—	—	—		*BV + 15%*

Golden Aussie

KM#	Date	Mintage	Fine	VF	XF	Unc
95	1987P	.015	—	—	Proof	70.00

Jubilee Nugget

KM#	Date	Mintage	Fine	VF	XF	Unc
104	1988P	*.010	—	—	Proof	70.00

Red Kangaroo

KM#	Date	Mintage	Fine	VF	XF	Unc
118	1989	2,200	—	—	Proof	70.00
	1990	.200	—	—		*BV + 15%*

Gray Kangaroo

KM#	Date	Mintage	Fine	VF	XF	Unc
141	1990	7,000	—	—	Proof	65.00
	1991	.150	—	—		*BV + 15%*

Common Wallaroo
Obv: Elizabeth II.
Rev: Similar to 100 Dollars, KM#169.

KM#	Date	Mintage	Fine	VF	XF	Unc
166	1991	3,000	—	—	Proof	65.00
	1992	.150	—	—		*BV + 15%*

25 DOLLARS

(1/4 Ounce)

7.7508 g, .999 GOLD, .2500 oz AGW
Gold Eagle
Obv: Elizabeth II.

KM#	Date	Mintage	Fine	VF	XF	Unc
90	1986P	.015	—	—	Proof	150.00
	1987	.233	—	—		*BV + 12%*
	1988	.075	—	—		*BV + 12%*
	1989	—	—	—		*BV + 12%*

Father's Day

KM#	Date	Mintage	Fine	VF	XF	Unc
96	1987P	.015	—	—	Proof	150.00

Ruby Well Nugget

KM#	Date	Mintage	Fine	VF	XF	Unc
105	1988P	*.010	—	—	Proof	150.00

Red Kangaroo

KM#	Date	Mintage	Fine	VF	XF	Unc
119	1989	2,200	—	—	Proof	170.00
	1990	*.200	—	—		*BV + 12%*

Gray Kangaroo

KM#	Date	Mintage	Fine	VF	XF	Unc
142	1990	7,000	—	—	Proof	150.00
	1991	.100	—	—		*BV + 12%*

Common Wallaroo
Obv: Elizabeth II.
Rev: Similar to 100 Dollars, KM#169.

KM#	Date	Mintage	Fine	VF	XF	Unc
167	1991	3,000	—	—	Proof	150.00
	1992	.100	—	—		*BV + 12%*

50 DOLLARS

(1/2 Ounce)

15.5017 g, .999 GOLD, .5000 oz AGW
Hand of Faith
Obv: Elizabeth II.

KM#	Date	Mintage	Fine	VF	XF	Unc
91	1986P	.015	—	—	Proof	300.00
	1987	.188	—	—		*BV + 7%*
	1988	.075	—	—		*BV + 7%*
	1989	.100	—	—		*BV + 7%*

Bobby Dazzler

KM#	Date	Mintage	Fine	VF	XF	Unc
97	1987P	.015	—	—	Proof	300.00

Welcome Nugget

KM#	Date	Mintage	Fine	VF	XF	Unc
106	1988P	*.010	—	—	Proof	300.00

Red Kangaroo

KM#	Date	Mintage	Fine	VF	XF	Unc
120	1989	2,200	—	—	Proof	325.00
	1990	*.240	—	—		*BV + 7%*

Gray Kangaroo

KM#	Date	Mintage	Fine	VF	XF	Unc
143	1990	5,000	—	—	Proof	300.00
	1991	.100	—	—		*BV + 7%*

Common Wallaroo
Obv: Elizabeth II.
Rev: Similar to 100 Dollars, KM#169.

KM#	Date	Mintage	Fine	VF	XF	Unc
168	1991	2,000	—	—	Proof	300.00
	1992	.100	—	—		*BV + 7%*

100 DOLLARS

(Ounce)

31.1035 g, .999 GOLD, 1.0000 oz AGW
Welcome Stranger

KM#	Date	Mintage	Fine	VF	XF	Unc
92	1986P	.015	—	—	Proof	500.00
	1987	.259	—	—		*BV + 5%*
	1988	.116	—	—		*BV + 5%*
	1989	—	—	—		*BV + 5%*

Poseidon

KM#	Date	Mintage	Fine	VF	XF	Unc
98	1987P	.015	—	—	Proof	500.00

Pride of Australia Nugget

KM#	Date	Mintage	Fine	VF	XF	Unc
107	1988P	*.010	—	—	Proof	500.00

Red Kangaroo

KM#	Date	Mintage	Fine	VF	XF	Unc
121	1989	2,200	—	—	Proof	650.00
	1990	—	—	—		*BV + 5%*

Gray Kangaroo

KM#	Date	Mintage	Fine	VF	XF	Unc
144	1990	8,000	—	—	Proof	500.00
	1991	.250	—	—		*BV + 5%*

Common Wallaroo

KM#	Date	Mintage	Fine	VF	XF	Unc
169	1991	3,000	—	—	Proof	500.00
	1992	.250	—	—		*BV + 5%*

200 DOLLARS

62.2140 g, .9999 GOLD, 2.0000 oz AGW
Red Kangaroo
Obv: Portrait of Queen Elizabeth II.

KM#	Date	Mintage	Fine	VF	XF	Unc
182	1992	—	—	—		*BV + 5%*
	1992	—	—	—	Proof	1650.

500 DOLLARS

62.2140 g, .999 GOLD, 2.0000 oz AGW
Red Kangaroo
Similar to 100 Dollars, KM#121.

KM#	Date	Mintage	Fine	VF	XF	Unc
150	1991	—	—	—		*BV + 5%*
	1991	250 pcs.	—	—	Proof	1650.

1000 DOLLARS

311.0670 g, .9999 GOLD, 10.0000 oz AGW
Red Kangaroo
Similar to 200 Dollars, KM#182.

KM#	Date	Mintage	Fine	VF	XF	Unc
183	1992	—	—	—		*BV + 4%*
	1992	—	—	—	Proof	7950.

2500 DOLLARS

311.0670 g, .999 GOLD, 10.0000 oz AGW
Red Kangaroo
Similar to 100 Dollars, KM#121.

KM#	Date	Mintage	Fine	VF	XF	Unc
151	1991	—	—	—		*BV + 4%*
	1991	100 pcs.	—	—	Proof	7950.

3000 DOLLARS

1,000.1000 g, .9999 GOLD, 32.1575 oz AGW
Red Kangaroo
Similar to 200 Dollars, KM#182.

KM#	Date	Mintage	Fine	VF	XF	Unc
184	1992	—	—	—		*BV + 3.5%*
	1992	—	—	—	Proof	23,500.

10,000 DOLLARS

1000.1000 g, .999 GOLD, 32.1575 oz AGW
Koala
Similar to 100 Dollars, KM#121.

KM#	Date	Mintage	Fine	VF	XF	Unc
152	1991	—	—	—		*BV + 3.5%*
	1991	50 pcs.	—	—	Proof	23,500.

PLATINUM BULLION ISSUES

5 DOLLARS

1.5710 g, .999 PLATINUM, .0500 oz APW
Similar to 100 Dollars, KM#126.

KM#	Date	Mintage	Fine	VF	XF	Unc
122	1989	2,400	—	—	Proof	35.00
	1990	—	—	—	Proof	35.00

Koala
Obv: Similar to 100 Dollars, KM#149.

KM#	Date	Mintage	Fine	VF	XF	Unc
145	1990	2,500	—	—	Proof	35.00
	1991	.020	—	—		*BV + 20%*
	1991	1,000	—	—	Proof	35.00

Koala
Obv: Elizabeth II.
Rev: Similar to 100 Dollars, KM#174.

KM#	Date	Mintage	Fine	VF	XF	Unc
170	1992	.020	—	—		*BV + 20%*

Obv: Similar to 100 Dollars, KM#195.

KM#	Date	Mintage	Fine	VF	XF	Unc
191	1993	*.020	—	—		*BV + 2%*

15 DOLLARS

(1/10 Ounce)

3.1370 g, .999 PLATINUM, .1000 oz APW
Similar to 100 Dollars, KM#111.

KM#	Date	Mintage	Fine	VF	XF	Unc
108	1988	—	—	—		*BV + 15%*
	1989	—	—	—	Proof	70.00

Similar to 100 Dollars, KM#126.

KM#	Date	Mintage	Fine	VF	XF	Unc
123	1989	2,400	—	—	Proof	70.00
	1990	—	—	—	Proof	70.00

Koala
Obv: Similar to 100 Dollars, KM#149.

KM#	Date	Mintage	Fine	VF	XF	Unc
146	1990	2,500	—	—	Proof	70.00
	1991	.020	—	—		*BV + 15%*
	1991	1,000	—	—	Proof	80.00

Koala
Obv: Elizabeth II.
Rev: Similar to 100 Dollars, KM#174.

KM#	Date	Mintage	Fine	VF	XF	Unc
171	1992	.020	—	—		*BV + 15%*

Obv: Similar to 100 Dollars, KM#195.

KM#	Date	Mintage	Fine	VF	XF	Unc
192	1993	*.020	—	—		*BV + 2%*

25 DOLLARS

(1/4 Ounce)

7.8150 g, .999 PLATINUM, .2500 oz APW
Similar to 100 Dollars, KM#111.

KM#	Date	Mintage	Fine	VF	XF	Unc
109	1988	—	—	—		*BV + 10%*
	1989	—	—	—	Proof	225.00

Similar to 100 Dollars, KM#126.

KM#	Date	Mintage	Fine	VF	XF	Unc
124	1989	2,400	—	—	Proof	225.00
	1990	—	—	—	Proof	225.00

Koala
Obv: Similar to 100 Dollars, KM#149.

KM#	Date	Mintage	Fine	VF	XF	Unc
147	1990	2,500	—	—	Proof	225.00
	1991	.020	—	—		*BV + 10%*
	1991	1,000	—	—	Proof	235.00

Koala
Obv: Elizabeth II.
Rev: Similar to 100 Dollars, KM#174.

KM#	Date	Mintage	Fine	VF	XF	Unc
172	1992	.020	—	—		*BV + 10%*

Obv: Similar to 100 Dollars, KM#195.

KM#	Date	Mintage	Fine	VF	XF	Unc
193	1993	*.020	—	—		*BV + 2%*

50 DOLLARS

(1/2 Ounce)

15.6050 g, .999 PLATINUM, .5000 oz APW

KM#	Date	Mintage	Fine	VF	XF	Unc
110	1988	—	—	—		*BV + 5%*
	1988	.012	—	—	Proof	350.00
	1989	—	—	—	Proof	325.00

Similar to 100 Dollars, KM#126.

KM#	Date	Mintage	Fine	VF	XF	Unc
125	1989	2,400	—	—	Proof	350.00
	1990	8,000	—	—	Proof	325.00

Koala

KM#	Date	Mintage	Fine	VF	XF	Unc
148	1990	5,500	—	—	Proof	325.00
	1991	.020	—	—		*BV + 5%*
	1991	2,000	—	—	Proof	350.00

Koala
Obv: Elizabeth II.
Rev: Similar to 100 Dollars, KM#174.

KM#	Date	Mintage	Fine	VF	XF	Unc
173	1992	.020	—	—		*BV + 5%*

Obv: Similar to 100 Dollars, KM#195.

KM#	Date	Mintage	Fine	VF	XF	Unc
194	1993	*.020	—	—		*BV + 2%*

100 DOLLARS

(1 Ounce)

31.1850 g, .999 PLATINUM, 1.0000 oz APW

KM#	Date	Mintage	Fine	VF	XF	Unc
111	1988	—	—	—		*BV + 4%*
	1989	—	—	—	Proof	650.00

KM#	Date	Mintage	Fine	VF	XF	Unc
126	1989	2,400	—	—	Proof	650.00
	1990	—	—	—	Proof	650.00

Koala

KM#	Date	Mintage	Fine	VF	XF	Unc
149	1990	3,500	—	—	Proof	650.00
	1991	.075	—	—		*BV + 4%*
	1991	1,000	—	—	Proof	650.00

Koala
Obv: Elizabeth II.

KM#	Date	Mintage	Fine	VF	XF	Unc
174	1992	.075	—	—		*BV + 4%*

KM#	Date	Mintage	Fine	VF	XF	Unc
195	1993	*.080	—	—		*BV + 2%*

200 DOLLARS

62.2140 g, .9995 PLATINUM, 2.0000 oz APW
Koala
Obv: Portrait of Queen Elizabeth II.

KM#	Date	Mintage	Fine	VF	XF	Unc
185	1992	—	—	—		BV + 5%
	1992	—	—	—	Proof	1850.

Obv: Similar to 100 Dollars, KM#195.

KM#	Date	Mintage	Fine	VF	XF	Unc
196	1993	—	—	—		BV + 2%

500 DOLLARS

62.2140 g, .999 PLATINUM, 2.0000 oz APW
Koala
Obv: Queen Elizabeth II.
Rev: Koala in tree.

KM#	Date	Mintage	Fine	VF	XF	Unc
157	1991	—	—	—		BV + 5%
	1991	250 pcs.	—	—	Proof	1850.

1000 DOLLARS

311.0670 g, .9995 PLATINUM, 10.0000 oz APW
Koala
Similar to 200 Dollars, KM#185.

KM#	Date	Mintage	Fine	VF	XF	Unc
186	1992	—	—	—		BV + 4%
	1992	—	—	—	Proof	8500.

Illustration reduced. Actual size: 60.3mm
Obv: Similar to 100 Dollars, KM#195.

KM#	Date	Mintage	Fine	VF	XF	Unc
197	1993	—	—	—		BV + 2%

2500 DOLLARS

311.0670 g, .999 PLATINUM, 10.0000 oz APW
Koala
Obv: Queen Elizabeth II.
Rev: Koala in tree.

KM#	Date	Mintage	Fine	VF	XF	Unc
158	1991	—	—	—		BV + 4%
	1991	100 pcs.	—	—	Proof	8500.

3000 DOLLARS

1,000.1000 g, .9995 PLATINUM, 32.1575 oz APW
Koala
Similar to 200 Dollars, KM#185.

KM#	Date	Mintage	Fine	VF	XF	Unc
187	1992	—	—	—		BV + 3.5%
	1992	—	—	—	Proof	25,500.

Illustration reduced. Actual size: 75.3mm
Obv: Similar to 100 Dollars, KM#195.

KM#	Date	Mintage	Fine	VF	XF	Unc
198	1993	—	—	—		BV + 2%

10,000 DOLLARS

1000.1000 g, .999 PLATINUM, 32.1575 oz APW
Koala
Obv: Queen Elizabeth II.
Rev: Koala in tree.

KM#	Date	Mintage	Fine	VF	XF	Unc
159	1991	—	—	—		BV + 3.5%
	1991	50 pcs.	—	—	Proof	25,500.

MINT SETS (MS)

KM#	Date	Mintage	Identification	Issue Price	Mkt. Val.
MS1	1966(6)	16,359	KM62-67 (Card)	2.00	32.00
MS2	1969(6)	31,176	KM62-66,68	2.50	53.00
MS3	1970(6)	40,230	KM62-66,69	2.50	32.00
MS4	1971(6)	28,572	KM62-66,68	2.50	43.00
MS5	1972(6)	39,068	KM62-66,68	2.75	50.00
MS6	1973(6)	30,928	KM62-66,68	3.40	40.00
MS7	1974(6)	25,948	KM62-66,68	3.60	35.00
MS8	1975(6)	30,121	KM62-66,68	3.30	20.00
MS9	1976(6)	40,004	KM62-66,68	3.80	17.50
MS10	1977(6)	128,000	KM62-66,70	4.20	12.00
MS11	1978(6)	70,000	KM62-66,68	4.20	10.00
MS12	1979(6)	70,000	KM62-66,68	4.50	10.00
MS13	1980(6)	100,000	KM62-66,68	5.75	10.00
MS14	1981(6)	120,010	KM62-66,68	6.50	10.00
MS15	1982(6)	195,950	KM62-66,74	6.50	5.50
MS16	1983(6)	155,700	KM62-66,68	5.00	9.00
MS17	1984(6)	150,014	KM62-66,68	7.00	9.00
MS18	1985(7)	170,000	KM78-84	4.00	30.00
MS19	1986(7)	180,000	KM78-83,87	5.50	20.00
MS20	1987(7)	200,000	KM78-84	8.00	11.00
MS21	1988(8)	240,000	KM78-82,99-101	12.00	12.50
MS22	1989(8)	—	KM78-84,101	12.00	11.50
MS23	1990(8)	—	KM78-84,101	12.00	42.00
MS24	1991(8)	—	KM78-82,84,101,139	13.00	16.50
MS25	1992(6)	—	KM80-83,101,175	10.00	10.00
MS26	1993(6)	—	KM80-83,101,208	10.00	10.00

PROOF SETS (PS)

KM#	Date	Mintage	Identification	Issue Price	Mkt. Val.
PSA1	1887S(4)	2 known	KM8-11	—	Rare
PS1	1902S(4)	—	KM14-17	—	Rare
PS2	1911L(4)	—	KM24-27	—	25,000.
PS3	1916M(4)	25	KM24-27	—	6250.
PS4	1925M(5)	—	KM22-26	—	13,650.
PS5	1926M(6)	—	KM22-27	—	9400.
PS6	1927M(6)	50	KM22-27	—	7150.
PS7	1928M(6)	—	KM22-27	—	9550.
PS8	1929M(2)	—	KM22-23	—	3250.
PSA9	1931m(4)	—	KM22-27	—	7000.
PS9	1930M(2)	—	KM22-23	—	85.00
PS10	1933M(2)	—	KM22-23	—	2000.
PS11	1934M(6)	100	KM22-27	—	4500.
PS12	1935M(6)	100	KM22-27	—	4800.
PS13	1936M(6)	—	KM22-27	—	6350.
PS14	1938M(6)	250	KM35-40	—	5150.
PS15	1953P(2)	—	KM49-50	—	3500.
PS16	1955M(4)	1,200	KM56-59	—	200.00
PS17	1955P(2)	301	KM49,56	—	1250.
PS18	1956M(5)	1,500	KM56-60	—	225.00
PS19	1957M(4)	1,256	KM57-60	—	170.00
PS20	1958M(5)	1,506	KM56-60	—	200.00
PS21	1959M(5)	1,506	KM56-61	—	240.00
PS22	1960M(4)	1,509	KM57-60	—	125.00
PS23	1960P(2)	1,030	KM56,61	—	160.00
PS24	1961M(4)	1,506	KM57-60	—	125.00
PS25	1961P(2)	1,040	KM56,61	—	160.00
PS26	1962M(4)	2,016	KM57-60	—	125.00
PS27	1962P(2)	1,064	KM56,61	—	140.00
PS28	1963M(4)	5,042	KM57-60	—	85.00
PS29	1963P(2)	1,064	KM56,61	—	140.00
PS30	1966C(6)	18,110	KM62-67	15.70	250.00
PS31	1969C(6)	12,696	KM62-66,68	11.25	210.00
PS32	1970C(6)	15,112	KM62-66,69	11.30	115.00
PS33	1971C(6)	10,066	KM62-66,68	11.30	125.00
PS34	1972C(6)	10,272	KM62-66,68	14.00	120.00
PS35	1973C(6)	10,090	KM62-66,68	15.50	130.00
PS36	1974(6)	11,103	KM62-66,68	18.00	110.00
PS37	1975(6)	23,021	KM62-66,68	17.00	35.00
PS38	1976(6)	21,200	KM62-66,68	20.20	50.00
PS39	1977(6)	55,000	KM62-66,70	20.20	22.50
PS40	1978(6)	38,513	KM62-66,68	—	22.50
PS41	1979(6)	36,000	KM62-66,68	—	22.50
PS42	1980(6)	68,000	KM62-66,68	—	16.50
PS43	1981(6)	86,008	KM62-66,68	48.00	16.50
PS44	1982(6)	100,000	KM62-66,74	50.00	15.00
PS45	1983(6)	80,000	KM62-66,68	39.00	22.50
PS46	1984(6)	61,398	KM62-66,77	39.00	22.50
PS47	1985(7)	74,809	KM78-84	27.50	50.00
PS48	1986(7)	67,000	KM78-83,87	40.00	40.00
PS49	1986P(4)	12,000	KM89-92	1445.	1200.
PS50	1986P(2)	3,000	KM89,90	305.00	310.00
PS51	1987(7)	69,684	KM78-84	40.00	40.00
PS52	1987(4)	12,000	KM95-98	1440.	1000.
PS53	1987(2)	3,000	KM95,96	305.00	350.00
PS54	1988(8)	101,000	KM78-82,99-101	—	40.00
PS55	1988(8)	5,000	KM78-82,99-101 Coin Fair	—	80.00
PS56	1988(4)	25,000	KM99a-102a	85.00	130.00
PS57	1988(4)	9,000	KM104-107	—	1000.
PS58	1988(2)	1,000	KM104-105	—	200.00
PS59	1988(2)	—	KM112-113	50.00	42.50
PS60	1989(8)	2,500	KM78-84,101	—	40.00
PS61	1989(8)	—	KM78-84,101 Coin Fair	—	70.00
PS62	1989(5)	2,200	KM117-121	1595.	1100.
PS63	1989(5)	2,400	KM122-126	1995.	1300.
PS64	1989(5)	25,000	KM99a,127-130	—	130.00
PS65	1989(2)	—	KM131,132	—	42.50
PS66	1990(8)	—	KM78-84,101	55.00	65.00
PS67	1990(8)	—	KM78-84, 101 Coin Fair	—	80.00
PS68	1990(5)	5,000	KM140-144	—	1050.
PS69	1990(5)	2,500	KM145-149	—	1300.
PS70	1990(3)	2,000	KM140-142	464.00	250.00
PS71	1990(3)	1,000	KM138,144,149	1900.	1200.
PS72	1991(8)	—	KM78-82,84,101,139	55.00	80.00
PS73	1991(8)	—	KM78-82,84,101a,139	—	75.00
PS74	1991(5)	2,000	KM140-144	—	1050.
PS75	1991(5)	1,000	KM145-149	—	1300.
PS76	1991(3)	25,000	KM84a,87a,100a,Sydney Coin Fair	135.00	110.00
PS77	1991(3)	1,000	KM140-142	—	250.00
PS78	1992(6)	—	KM80-83,101,175	40.00	43.00
PS79	1992(4)	—	KM200-203 + medal	120.00	120.00
PS80	1992(4)	5,000	KM204-207 + medal	1520.	1520.
PS81	1993(6)	—	KM80-83,101,208	—	43.00

KEELING-COCOS ISLANDS

The Territory of Cocos (Keeling) Islands, an Australian territory, comprises a group of 27 coral islands located (see arrow on map of Australia) in the Indian Ocean 1,300 miles northwest of Australia. Only Direction and Home Islands are regularly inhabited. The group has an area of 5.4 sq. mi. and a population of about 569. Calcium, phosphate and coconut products are exported.

The islands were discovered by Capt. William Keeling of the British East India Co. in 1609. Alexander Hare, an English adventurer, established a settlement on one of the southern islands in 1823, but it lasted less than a year. A permanent settlement was established on Direction Island in 1827 by Hare and Capt. John Clunies Ross, a Scot, for the purpose of storing East Indian spices for reshipment to Europe during periods of shortage. When the experiment in spice futures did not develop satisfactorily, Hare left the islands (1829 or 1830), leaving Ross as sole owner. The coral group became a British protectorate in 1856; was attached to the colony of Ceylon in 1878; and was placed under the administration of the Straits Settlements in 1882. In 1903 the group was annexed to the Straits Settlements and incorporated into the colony of Singapore until Nov. of 1955, when it was placed under the administration of Australia.

RULERS

British

MONETARY SYSTEM

100 Cents = 1 Rupee

5 CENTS

BRONZE

KM#	Date	Mintage	VF	XF	Unc
1	1977	—	—	10.00	20.00

10 CENTS

BRONZE

KM#	Date	Mintage	VF	XF	Unc
2	1977	—	—	12.50	25.00

25 CENTS

BRONZE

KM#	Date	Mintage	VF	XF	Unc
3	1977	—	—	12.50	25.00

50 CENTS

BRONZE

KM#	Date	Mintage	VF	XF	Unc
4	1977	—	—	15.00	30.00

RUPEE

COPPER-NICKEL

KM#	Date	Mintage	VF	XF	Unc
5	1977	—	—	20.00	40.00

2 RUPEES

COPPER-NICKEL

KM#	Date	Mintage	VF	XF	Unc
6	1977	—	—	20.00	42.50

5 RUPEES

COPPER-NICKEL

KM#	Date	Mintage	VF	XF	Unc
7	1977	—	—	22.50	45.00

10 RUPEES

6.5000 g, .925 SILVER, .1933 oz ASW
150th Anniversary of Keeling-Cocos Islands

KM#	Date	Mintage	VF	XF	Unc
8	1977	6,000	—	—	50.00
	1977	4,000	—	Proof	70.00

25 RUPEES

16.2500 g, .925 SILVER, .4833 oz ASW
150th Anniversary of Keeling-Cocos Islands
Similar to 10 Rupees, KM#9.

KM#	Date	Mintage	VF	XF	Unc
9	1977	6,000	—	—	90.00
	1977	4,000	—	Proof	140.00

150 RUPEES

.750 GOLD
150th Anniversary of Keeling-Cocos Islands

KM#	Date	Mintage	VF	XF	Unc
10	1977	2,000	—	—	—
	1977	2,000	—	Proof	—

NOTE: The entire issue of KM#10 was stolen with only 290 pieces being recovered.

8.4800 g, .916 GOLD, .2497 oz AGW

KM#	Date	Mintage	VF	XF	Unc
10a	1977	2,000	—	—	200.00
	1977	2,000	—	Proof	300.00

MINT SETS (MS)

KM#	Date	Mintage	Identification	Issue Price	Mkt. Val.
MS1	1977(7)	—	KM1-7	—	230.00
MS2	1977(2)	6,000	KM8-9	—	140.00

PROOF SETS (PS)

KM#	Date	Mintage	Identification	Issue Price	Mkt. Val.
PS1	1977(2)	4,000	KM8-9	28.00	210.00

AUSTRIA

The Republic of Austria, a parliamentary democracy located in mountainous central Europe, has an area of 32,374 sq. mi. (83,850 sq. km.) and a population of *7.6 million. Capital: Vienna. Austria is primarily an industrial country. Machinery, iron and steel, textiles, yarns and timber are exported.

The territories later to be known as Austria were overrun in pre-Roman times by various tribes, including the Celts. Upon the fall of the Roman Empire, the country became a margravate of Charlemagne's Empire. Premysl Otaker, King of Bohemia, gained possession in 1252, only to lose the territory to Rudolf of Hapsburg in 1276. Thereafter, until World War I, the story of Austria was that of the ruling Hapsburgs.

During World War I, the Austro-Hungarian Empire was one of the Central Powers with Germany, Bulgaria and Turkey. At the end of the war, the Empire was dismembered and Austria established as an independent republic. In March, 1938, Austria was incorporated into Hitler's short-lived Greater German Reich. Allied forces of both East and West occupied Austria in April, 1945, and subsequently divided it into 4 zones of military occupation. On May 15, 1955, the 4 powers formally recognized Austria as a 'sovereign independent democratic state'.

A number of coin-issuing entities that were or are a part of Austria continue to be of interest to collectors of world coins.

Francis I died on August 18, 1765. His wife Maria Theresa, decreed on July 21, 1766 that coins would be issued with the portrait of Francis and bearing the year of his death (1765). Also to be included were letters of the alphabet to indicate the actual year of issue: i.e. A-1766, G-1772, P-1780.

The posthumous coins were issued rather erratically as to denominations, years and mints. 5 denominations were made and 7 mints were used. Only the Ducat and 20 Kreuzer were made until 1780, the year in which Maria Theresa died. The other denominations were 3, 10 and 17 Kreuzer.

RULERS

Franz II (I), 1792-1835
(as Franz I, Austrian Emperor, 1806-1835)
Ferdinand I, 1835-1848
Franz Joseph I, 1848-1916
Karl I, 1916-1918

MINT MARKS

A, W, WI - Vienna
(a) - Vienna
AI,AL-IV,C-A,E,GA - Karlsburg (Transylvania)
B,K,K-B - Kremnitz (Hungary)
C - Prague (Bohemia)
CB,CI,CI-BI(NI),HS - Hermannstadt (Transylvania)
CV,FT,KV - Klausenburg (Transylvania)
D - Salzburg
D,G,GR - Graz (Styria)
F, HA - Hall
GM - Mantua
H,P-R - Gunzburg
(h) Shield - Vienna
M - Milan (Lombardy)
N-B-Nagybanya (Hungary)
O - Oravicza (Hungary)
P - Prague (Bohemia)
S - Schmollnitz (Hungary)
V - Venice (Venetia)
(v) Eagle - Hall
W - Breslau (Poland)

MINTMASTERS INITIALS

GUNZBURG MINT

Initials	Years	Mintmaster
F,IF	1774-1805	Josef Faby

SALZBURG MINT

Initials	Years	Mintmaster
M	1803-1806	Franz Xaver Matzenkopf

MONETARY SYSTEM

Before 1857

8 Heller = 4 Pfennig = 1 Kreuzer
60 Kreuzer = 1 Florin (Gulden)
2 Florin = 1 Species or Convention Thaler

1857-1892

100 Kreuzer = 1 Florin (Gulden)
1-1/2 Florin = 1 Vereinsthaler

1/4 KREUZER

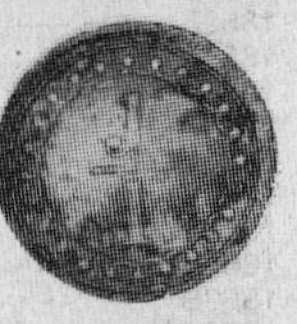

COPPER

KM#	Date	Mintage	Fine	VF	XF	Unc
2106	1812A	—	2.00	4.00	8.00	25.00
	1812B	1.725	3.00	6.00	12.50	35.00
	1812S	—	— Reported, not confirmed			

KM#	Date	Mintage	Fine	VF	XF	Unc
2107	1816A	—	1.50	2.50	5.00	30.00
	1816B	6.652	1.50	2.50	5.00	30.00
	1816E	—	—	—	Rare	—
	1816G	—	—	—	Rare	—
	1816O	—	3.00	6.00	12.00	35.00
	1816S	—	1.00	2.00	4.00	25.00

NOTE: The above 6 issues struck until 1852 w/1816 date.

KM#	Date	Mintage	Fine	VF	XF	Unc
2180	1851A	—	.50	1.00	2.00	7.50
	1851B	9.637	1.00	3.50	6.00	10.00
	1851G	—	10.00	30.00	60.00	120.00

1/2 KREUZER

COPPER

KM#	Date	Mintage	Fine	VF	XF	Unc
2109	1812A	—	2.00	6.00	12.00	40.00
	1812B	—	—	—	Rare	—
	1812	—	3.00	8.00	20.00	50.00

KM#	Date	Mintage	Fine	VF	XF	Unc
2110	1816A	—	1.00	2.00	4.00	25.00
	1816B	6.652	1.50	5.00	10.00	40.00
	1816E	—	—	—	Rare	—
	1816G	—	—	—	Rare	—
	1816O	—	2.00	8.00	20.00	50.00
	1816S	—	2.00	6.00	12.50	40.00

NOTE: The above 6 issues were struck until 1852 w/1816 date.

KM#	Date	Mintage	Fine	VF	XF	Unc
2181	1851A	—	1.00	2.00	4.00	10.00
	1851B	27.733	1.00	2.00	5.00	11.00
	1851C	—	100.00	150.00	300.00	600.00
	1851G	—	10.00	20.00	40.00	100.00

5/10 KREUZER

COPPER, 1.67 g
Obv: Small eagle.

KM#	Date	Mintage	Fine	VF	XF	Unc
2182	1858A	—	1.50	3.00	6.00	9.00
	1858B	11.058	2.00	3.00	6.50	10.00
	1858E	—	15.00	35.00	60.00	130.00
	1858M	—	3.50	8.00	20.00	35.00
	1858V	—	5.00	10.00	20.00	40.00
	1859A	—	.75	1.50	3.00	7.00

KM#	Date	Mintage	Fine	VF	XF	Unc
2182	1859B	13.397	3.50	6.50	10.00	20.00
	1859E	—	15.00	30.00	60.00	120.00
	1859M	—	8.00	16.00	24.00	40.00
	1859V	—	15.00	30.00	60.00	100.00
	1860A	—	1.00	3.00	7.50	15.00
	1860E	—	15.00	30.00	60.00	120.00
	1860V	—	5.00	7.50	18.00	40.00
	1861A	—	5.00	10.00	25.00	50.00
	1861B	3.474	3.50	7.50	15.00	30.00
	1863B	—	6.00	12.00	20.00	40.00
	1864A	—	2.00	5.00	10.00	25.00
	1864B	7.598	2.50	5.00	10.00	20.00
	1864V	—	15.00	30.00	60.00	100.00
	1865A	—	2.00	5.00	10.00	20.00
	1865B	7.182	6.50	13.50	22.50	50.00
	1866A	—	2.00	5.00	10.00	20.00

Reduced weight, 1.60 g

KM#	Date	Mintage	Fine	VF	XF	Unc
2183	1877	—	5.00	10.00	15.00	25.00
	1881	4.200	2.00	4.00	6.00	10.00
	1885	2.000	.75	1.50	3.00	7.00

Obv: Large eagle.

KM#	Date	Mintage	Fine	VF	XF	Unc
2184	1885	Inc. Ab.	.50	1.00	2.00	5.00
	1891	2.000	3.00	6.00	12.50	15.00

KREUZER

COPPER

KM#	Date	Mintage	Fine	VF	XF	Unc
2112	1812A	—	3.00	6.00	15.00	40.00
	1812B	92.163	3.00	6.00	12.00	30.00
	1812C	—	— Reported, not confirmed			
	1812E	—	2.50	5.00	10.00	30.00
	1812G	—	3.00	8.00	20.00	40.00
	1812O	—	6.00	20.00	35.00	60.00
	1812S	—	1.50	4.00	10.00	30.00

KM#	Date	Mintage	Fine	VF	XF	Unc
2113	1816A	—	1.00	2.00	4.00	25.00
	1816B	54.516	1.00	2.00	5.00	25.00
	1816E	—	7.50	15.00	25.00	40.00
	1816G	—	2.00	6.00	12.00	30.00
	1816O	—	2.00	6.00	12.00	30.00
	1816S	—	2.00	6.00	12.00	30.00
	1816S.	—	2.00	6.00	12.00	30.00

NOTE: The above 6 issues were struck until 1852 w/1816 date.

KM#	Date	Mintage	Fine	VF	XF	Unc
2185	1851A	—	.50	.75	1.50	5.00
	1851B	106.458	1.00	1.50	3.00	6.00
	1851C	—	40.00	60.00	120.00	250.00
	1851E	—	8.00	15.00	30.00	80.00
	1851 sm.G	—	2.00	5.00	20.00	60.00
	1851 lg.G	—	2.00	5.00	20.00	60.00

Obv: Small eagle

KM#	Date	Mintage	Fine	VF	XF	Unc
2186	1858A	—	.50	1.00	2.00	4.00
	1858B	23.497	1.00	2.00	3.00	5.00
	1858E	—	5.00	10.00	20.00	45.00
	1858M	—	4.00	7.00	15.00	40.00
	1858V	—	11.00	20.00	40.00	75.00
	1859A	—	.50	1.00	2.00	4.00
	1859B	93.406	1.00	2.00	3.50	6.00

KM#	Date	Mintage	Fine	VF	XF	Unc
2186	1859E	—	2.50	5.00	10.00	17.50
	1859M	—	2.50	5.00	12.00	20.00
	1859V	—	7.00	14.00	25.00	45.00
	1860A	—	.50	1.00	2.00	4.00
	1860B	87.955	.50	1.00	2.00	4.00
	1860E	—	5.00	10.00	20.00	45.00
	1860V	—	4.00	9.00	20.00	35.00
	1861A	—	.75	1.50	2.50	5.00
	1861B	54.201	.50	1.00	3.00	5.00
	1861E	—	2.50	6.00	12.50	27.50
	1862B	11.599	5.00	10.00	25.00	50.00
	1862E	—	10.00	20.00	40.00	90.00
	1863E	—	15.00	35.00	75.00	160.00
	1873A	—	2.00	4.00	7.00	15.00
	1878	—	.50	1.00	2.00	3.00
	1879	—	.50	1.00	2.00	4.00
	1881	37.900	.25	.50	1.50	3.00

Obv: Large eagle.

KM#	Date	Mintage	Fine	VF	XF	Unc
2187	1885	29.000	.25	.50	1.25	3.00
	1891	23.800	.25	.50	1.25	3.00

2 KREUZER

COPPER
Revolution 1848-1849

KM#	Date	Mintage	Fine	VF	XF	Unc
2188	1848A	7.755	5.00	10.00	17.50	45.00

KM#	Date	Mintage	Fine	VF	XF	Unc
2189	1851A	—	3.00	7.50	15.00	30.00
	1851B	22.419	3.50	8.00	16.00	32.50
	1851C	—	300.00	500.00	700.00	1000.
	1851 lg. G	—	8.00	15.00	30.00	85.00
	1851 sm. G	—	8.00	15.00	30.00	85.00

3 KREUZER

.346 SILVER
Obv: Bust of Franz I right.
Rev: Crowned imperial eagle.

KM#	Date	Mintage	Fine	VF	XF	Unc
2114	1801E	—	30.00	60.00	120.00	225.00
	1810A	—	— Reported, not confirmed			

NOTE: Earlier dates (1792-1799) exist for this type.

COPPER, 17.07 g
Obv: Bust of Franz I right.
Rev: Crowned imperial eagle.

KM#	Date	Mintage	Fine	VF	XF	Unc
2115.3	1801E	—	15.00	30.00	75.00	150.00
	1801F	2.762	10.00	15.00	35.00	100.00
	1803F	—	20.00	40.00	60.00	140.00

NOTE: Varieties of tail feathers and heads exist.
NOTE: Earlier date (1800) exists for this type.

COPPER

KM#	Date	Mintage	Fine	VF	XF	Unc
2116	1812A	—	15.00	25.00	40.00	100.00
	1812B	13.594	2.00	4.00	8.00	25.00
	1812B(error)UH	—	5.00	10.00	20.00	40.00
	1812E	—	9.00	15.00	30.00	65.00
	1812G	—	6.00	12.50	20.00	50.00
	1812O	—	6.00	12.50	20.00	50.00
	1812S	—	3.00	5.00	10.00	30.00

1.7000 g, .344 SILVER, .0188 oz ASW

KM#	Date	Mintage	Fine	VF	XF	Unc
2117	1814A	—	—	—	Rare	—
	1815A	—	7.50	15.00	30.00	60.00
	1815B	—	10.00	20.00	40.00	90.00
	1815V	—	7.50	15.00	30.00	60.00

.346 SILVER

KM#	Date	Mintage	Fine	VF	XF	Unc
2118	1817A	—	50.00	80.00	150.00	300.00
	1818B	.538	12.00	25.00	40.00	90.00
	1818V	—	—	—	Rare	—
	1819A	—	12.00	25.00	50.00	100.00
	1820A	—	7.50	15.00	30.00	55.00
	1820B	1.457	7.50	15.00	30.00	55.00
	1820G	—	—	—	Rare	—
	1820V	—	—	—	—	—
	1821A	—	7.50	15.00	30.00	60.00
	1821B	4.894	7.50	15.00	30.00	60.00
	1821E	—	25.00	50.00	75.00	200.00
	1821G	—	25.00	50.00	75.00	175.00
	1822A	.079	12.00	25.00	50.00	100.00
	1823A	.035	25.00	45.00	75.00	150.00
	1823B	I.A.	—	—	Rare	—
	1824A	.037	—	—	Rare	—
	1824G	I.A.	25.00	50.00	75.00	175.00

KM#	Date	Mintage	Fine	VF	XF	Unc
2119	1825A	.051	25.00	50.00	75.00	175.00
	1826A	—	8.00	15.00	30.00	50.00
	1826B	.375	8.00	15.00	30.00	60.00
	1826E	—	25.00	40.00	75.00	175.00
	1827A	.118	40.00	80.00	150.00	250.00
	1827B	—	45.00	75.00	150.00	250.00
	1828A	—	8.00	15.00	30.00	50.00
	1828B	.965	8.00	15.00	30.00	60.00
	1828E	—	35.00	60.00	120.00	200.00
	1828G	—	40.00	70.00	140.00	225.00
	1829A	—	8.00	15.00	30.00	50.00
	1829B	.133	22.50	40.00	75.00	160.00
	1829E	—	17.50	30.00	60.00	140.00
	1829G	—	40.00	70.00	140.00	225.00
	1830A	—	8.00	15.00	30.00	55.00
	1830B	.076	40.00	80.00	150.00	250.00
	1830E	—	40.00	70.00	140.00	225.00
	1831A	—	— Reported, not confirmed			

Struck in a collar, short braids.

KM#	Date	Mintage	Fine	VF	XF	Unc
2120	1831A	—	40.00	75.00	130.00	225.00

Obv: Larger head

KM#	Date	Mintage	Fine	VF	XF	Unc
2121	1831A	—	— Reported, not confirmed			
	1832A	—	5.00	10.00	20.00	50.00
	1833A	—	5.00	10.00	20.00	50.00
	1833C	—	8.00	15.00	30.00	60.00
	1834A	—	20.00	40.00	70.00	130.00
	1834C	—	30.00	50.00	80.00	175.00
	1835A	—	20.00	40.00	70.00	130.00

Obv: Head of Ferdinand I right.
Rev: Eagle, value on chest.

KM#	Date	Mintage	Fine	VF	XF	Unc
2190	1835A	—	20.00	30.00	65.00	140.00
	1835E	—	30.00	50.00	100.00	250.00
	1836A	—	10.00	20.00	40.00	80.00
	1836E	—	25.00	40.00	90.00	240.00

KM#	Date	Mintage	Fine	VF	XF	Unc
2191	1837A	—	3.50	7.50	15.00	40.00
	1837C	—	25.00	40.00	75.00	150.00
	1837E	—	25.00	40.00	75.00	150.00
	1838A	—	3.50	7.50	15.00	45.00

KM#	Date	Mintage	Fine	VF	XF	Unc
2191	1838B	.130	15.00	25.00	40.00	100.00
	1838C	—	10.00	20.00	35.00	75.00
	1838E	—	15.00	25.00	50.00	110.00
	1839A	—	4.00	8.00	15.00	40.00
	1839C	—	12.50	25.00	50.00	100.00
	1839E	—	12.50	25.00	50.00	100.00
	1840A	—	2.50	5.00	10.00	30.00
	1840E	—	12.50	25.00	45.00	90.00
	1841A	—	15.00	25.00	50.00	110.00
	1841E	—	35.00	60.00	100.00	175.00
	1842A	—	6.00	12.00	20.00	50.00
	1842E	—	15.00	25.00	50.00	110.00
	1843A	—	10.00	15.00	30.00	80.00
	1843E	—	15.00	25.00	50.00	110.00
	1844A	—	6.00	10.00	20.00	50.00
	1844E	—	15.00	25.00	50.00	110.00
	1845A	—	3.00	7.50	15.00	35.00
	1845E	—	15.00	30.00	55.00	120.00
	1846A	—	2.50	5.00	12.50	30.00
	1846E	—	15.00	30.00	55.00	120.00
	1847A	—	2.50	5.00	12.50	30.00
	1847C	—	5.00	10.00	20.00	45.00
	1847E	—	15.00	30.00	55.00	120.00
	1848/5A	—	3.50	7.00	15.00	35.00
	1848A	—	2.50	5.00	12.50	30.00
	1848E	—	22.50	40.00	75.00	150.00
2192	1848GM swan above mint mark	—	200.00	350.00	700.00	1200.
	1848GM w/o swan above mint mark	—	200.00	350.00	700.00	1200.

NOTE: The above issue was struck in Mantua by the Austrian garrison under General Josef Radetzky during the siege of March 18-22, 1848 by Italian rebels.

COPPER

KM#	Date	Mintage	Fine	VF	XF	Unc
2193	1851A	—	5.00	10.00	20.00	50.00
	1851B	7.173	5.00	10.00	20.00	50.00
	1851C	36 pcs.	300.00	400.00	700.00	1300.
	1851G	—	10.00	20.00	50.00	150.00

NOTE: Varieties of size of mint mark exist.

4 KREUZER

COPPER

KM#	Date	Mintage	Fine	VF	XF	Unc
2194	1860A	—	2.00	6.00	12.00	30.00
	1860B	—	2.00	6.00	12.00	30.00
	1860E	—	10.00	25.00	50.00	150.00
	1861A	—	2.00	6.00	12.00	30.00
	1861B	18.470	2.00	6.00	12.00	30.00
	1861E	—	5.00	15.00	40.00	115.00
	1862B	.383	2.50	8.00	15.00	35.00
	1864B	6.666	2.50	8.00	15.00	35.00
	1865B	.224	2.50	8.00	15.00	35.00

5 KREUZER

.438 SILVER

KM#	Date	Mintage	Fine	VF	XF	Unc
2122	1815A	—	7.50	15.00	25.00	55.00

KM#	Date	Mintage	Fine	VF	XF	Unc
2123	1817A	—	25.00	40.00	75.00	175.00
	1818A	—	10.00	20.00	30.00	75.00
	1818B	.538	10.00	20.00	30.00	75.00
	1819A	—	—	—	Rare	—
	1820A	—	10.00	20.00	30.00	75.00
	1820B	1.457	10.00	20.00	30.00	75.00
	1820G	—	—	—	Rare	—
	1820V	—	15.00	35.00	60.00	125.00
	1821A	—	10.00	20.00	30.00	75.00
	1821B	4.894	10.00	25.00	40.00	90.00
	1821E	—	25.00	50.00	75.00	175.00
	1821G	—	20.00	40.00	70.00	140.00
	1822E	5,791	—	—	Rare	—
	1822G		1 known	—	Rare	—
	1823A	—	30.00	50.00	75.00	125.00
	1824A	—	—	—	Rare	—
	1824G		1 known	—	Rare	—

Obv: Bust w/short hair, 1 ribbon on neck.

KM#	Date	Mintage	Fine	VF	XF	Unc
2124	1825A	.015	75.00	100.00	200.00	400.00
	1826A	.053	60.00	90.00	175.00	350.00
	1826E	I.A.	—	—	Rare	—
	1827A	.018	—	—	Rare	—
	1828A	.044	60.00	90.00	175.00	350.00
	1830A	—	—	—	—	—

Obv: Bust w/short hair, both ribbons on neck.

KM#	Date	Mintage	Fine	VF	XF	Unc
2125	1831A	—	—	—	—	—

Obv: Larger head

KM#	Date	Mintage	Fine	VF	XF	Unc
2126	1832A	—	20.00	35.00	60.00	125.00
	1833A	.029	20.00	40.00	70.00	150.00
	1834A	.031	20.00	35.00	60.00	125.00
	1835A	—	15.00	25.00	50.00	100.00

KM#	Date	Mintage	Fine	VF	XF	Unc
2195	1835A	—	25.00	50.00	100.00	185.00
	1836A	—	12.50	25.00	50.00	110.00

KM#	Date	Mintage	Fine	VF	XF	Unc
2196	1837A	—	5.00	10.00	20.00	45.00
	1838A	—	5.00	10.00	20.00	45.00
	1838B	.130	— Reported, not confirmed			
	1839A	—	5.00	10.00	20.00	45.00
	1839C	—	7.50	15.00	30.00	60.00
	1840A	—	5.00	12.50	25.00	60.00
	1840C	—	5.00	10.00	20.00	45.00
	1842A	—	15.00	30.00	60.00	125.00
	1844A	—	10.00	20.00	40.00	80.00
	1846A	—	5.00	12.50	30.00	60.00
	1847A	—	7.50	15.00	30.00	70.00
	1848A	90.472	5.00	10.00	20.00	50.00

1.3333 g, .375 SILVER, .0161 oz ASW

KM#	Date	Mintage	Fine	VF	XF	Unc
2197	1858A	—	2.00	3.50	7.50	15.00
	1858B	851 pcs.	250.00	350.00	600.00	1100.
	1858V	—	200.00	300.00	450.00	750.00
	1859A	—	1.00	2.00	4.00	10.00
	1859M	—	10.00	15.00	25.00	40.00
	1859V	—	10.00	15.00	25.00	40.00
	1860A	—	—	—	—	—
	1860B	851 pcs.	250.00	350.00	600.00	1100.
	1860V	—	50.00	75.00	100.00	175.00
	1863A	1.013	5.00	8.00	16.00	40.00
	1864A	1.922	1.50	3.00	6.00	12.50

Obv: Head w/heavier whiskers.

KM#	Date	Mintage	Fine	VF	XF	Unc
2198	1867A	.069	90.00	125.00	200.00	500.00

6 KREUZER

COPPER

Obv: Bust of Franz I right.

KM#	Date	Mintage	Fine	VF	XF	Unc
2128	1803F	—	—	—	Rare	—

NOTE: Earlier date (1800) exists for this issue.

2.2300 g, .428 SILVER, .0306 oz ASW
Revolution 1848-1849

KM#	Date	Mintage	Fine	VF	XF	Unc
2199	1848A	90.400	3.00	5.00	10.00	20.00
	1848B	—	20.00	30.00	50.00	90.00
	1848C	—	4.00	7.50	15.00	40.00

1.9100 g, .438 SILVER, .0268 oz ASW

KM#	Date	Mintage	Fine	VF	XF	Unc
2200	1849A	—	1.00	2.00	3.00	10.00
	1849B	—	15.00	25.00	40.00	90.00
	1849C	—	4.00	7.50	15.00	40.00

NOTE: The above 1849 dated issues were struck from 1849-1852 and 1859-1870.

7 KREUZER

4.6800 g, .250 SILVER, .0376 oz ASW

KM#	Date	Mintage	Fine	VF	XF	Unc
2129	1802A	—	5.00	10.00	20.00	50.00
	1802B	102.034	5.00	10.00	20.00	50.00
	1802C	—	5.00	10.00	25.00	75.00
	1802E	—	12.50	25.00	40.00	110.00
	1802F	—	25.00	50.00	80.00	185.00
	1802G	—	17.50	35.00	60.00	130.00

NOTE: The above 6 issues were overstruck on 1795 dated 12 Kreuzer pieces, KM#2137.

10 KREUZER

.500 SILVER
Obv: Crowned bust in wreath. Rev: Eagle, leg:. . . . . D. LO. SAL. WIRC.

KM#	Date	Mintage	Fine	VF	XF	Unc
2131	1809A	—	40.00	75.00	160.00	275.00
	1810A	—	35.00	70.00	140.00	225.00

Rev. leg:. . . . . LO: WI: ET IN FR: D:

KM#	Date	Mintage	Fine	VF	XF	Unc
2132	1814A	—	—	—	Rare	—
	1815A	—	15.00	30.00	60.00	120.00
	1815B	1.800	15.00	30.00	60.00	120.00
	1815C	—	20.00	40.00	75.00	160.00

Rev. leg:. . . . . GAL. LOD. IL. REX. A. A.

KM#	Date	Mintage	Fine	VF	XF	Unc
2133	1817A	—	45.00	80.00	150.00	275.00
	1818A	—	—	—	Rare	—
	1818B	—	—	—	Rare	—
	1818G	—	—	—	Rare	—
	1818V	—	25.00	50.00	100.00	175.00
	1819A	.012	—	—	Rare	—
	1820A	—	—	—	Rare	—
	1820B	—	—	—	Rare	—
	1820G	—	—	—	Rare	—
	1821B	—	—	—	Rare	—
	1821G	—	50.00	90.00	150.00	275.00
	1821V	—	—	—	Rare	—
	1822G	—	—	—	Rare	—
	1823A	—	30.00	50.00	80.00	175.00
	1823G	—	30.00	60.00	120.00	225.00
	1824A	—	30.00	60.00	100.00	200.00
	1824G	—	—	—	Rare	—

Obv: Older head of Franz I right, 1 ribbon on neck. Rev: Eagle, value below.

KM#	Date	Mintage	Fine	VF	XF	Unc
2134	1825A	—	—	—	Rare	—
	1826A	—	35.00	70.00	140.00	225.00
	1827A	—	35.00	70.00	140.00	225.00
	1828A	—	35.00	70.00	140.00	200.00
	1828E	—	45.00	90.00	175.00	300.00
	1829A	.020	—	—	Rare	—
	1829E	I.A.	35.00	75.00	150.00	250.00
	1830A	—	35.00	75.00	150.00	250.00
	1830B	.045	150.00	275.00	350.00	450.00
	1830E	—	40.00	80.00	160.00	265.00

Obv: Both ribbons on neck.

KM#	Date	Mintage	Fine	VF	XF	Unc
2135	1831A	—	— Reported, not confirmed			

Obv: Larger head

KM#	Date	Mintage	Fine	VF	XF	Unc
2136	1832A	—	20.00	30.00	60.00	135.00
	1833A	—	20.00	30.00	65.00	150.00
	1834A	—	20.00	30.00	70.00	160.00
	1835A	—	35.00	60.00	120.00	250.00

Obv: Head of Ferdinand I right. Rev: Eagle, value below.

KM#	Date	Mintage	Fine	VF	XF	Unc
2201	1835A	—	20.00	35.00	70.00	175.00
	1835E	—	—	—	Rare	—
	1836/5A	—	20.00	30.00	60.00	160.00
	1836A	—	10.00	20.00	40.00	120.00
	1836E	—	—	—	Rare	—

KM#	Date	Mintage	Fine	VF	XF	Unc
2202	1837A	—	7.00	15.00	30.00	60.00
	1837C	—	10.00	20.00	40.00	80.00
	1837E	—	17.50	35.00	65.00	150.00
	1838A	—	17.50	35.00	65.00	150.00
	1838C	—	8.00	20.00	40.00	70.00
	1839A	—	7.50	15.00	30.00	60.00
	1839C	—	5.00	10.00	20.00	50.00
	1839E	—	15.00	30.00	50.00	120.00
	1840A	—	5.00	12.50	25.00	60.00
	1840E	—	17.50	35.00	65.00	150.00
	1841E	—	17.50	35.00	65.00	150.00
	1842A	—	5.00	12.50	25.00	60.00
	1842E	—	15.00	30.00	50.00	120.00
	1843/2A	—	5.00	10.00	20.00	50.00
	1843A	—	5.00	10.00	20.00	50.00
	1843E	—	17.50	35.00	65.00	150.00
	1844A	—	5.00	10.00	20.00	50.00
	1844E	—	17.50	35.00	65.00	150.00
	1845A	—	5.00	10.00	20.00	50.00
	1845E	—	10.00	25.00	50.00	100.00
	1846A	—	5.00	10.00	20.00	50.00
	1846E	—	15.00	30.00	50.00	120.00
	1847A	—	7.00	15.00	30.00	60.00
	1847E	—	12.00	25.00	50.00	100.00
	1848A	—	20.00	40.00	70.00	160.00
	1848E	—	20.00	40.00	70.00	160.00

2.1600 g, .900 SILVER, .0625 oz ASW

KM#	Date	Mintage	Fine	VF	XF	Unc
2203	1852A	—	10.00	20.00	40.00	60.00
	1853A	—	7.50	15.00	30.00	50.00
	1853B	.031	25.00	50.00	100.00	160.00
	1854A	—	15.00	30.00	50.00	120.00
	1855A	—	7.50	15.00	25.00	50.00

2.0000 g, .500 SILVER, .0322 oz ASW

KM#	Date	Mintage	Fine	VF	XF	Unc
2204	1858A	—	6.00	12.00	25.00	37.50
	1858V	—	100.00	150.00	250.00	500.00
	1859A	—	—	—	—	—
	1859M	—	5.00	10.00	20.00	40.00
	1859V	—	8.00	16.00	30.00	60.00
	1860V	—	9.00	18.00	40.00	75.00
	1861V	—	15.00	30.00	50.00	110.00
	1862V	—	30.00	50.00	80.00	180.00
	1863A	—	7.00	15.00	30.00	45.00
	1864A	1.050	10.00	20.00	30.00	65.00
	1864V	.036	150.00	250.00	400.00	650.00
	1865V	1.198	10.00	20.00	30.00	80.00

Obv: Head of Franz Joseph I right w/heavier whiskers.

KM#	Date	Mintage	Fine	VF	XF	Unc
2205	1867A	.059	100.00	200.00	300.00	550.00

1.6667 g, .400 SILVER, .0214 oz ASW

KM#	Date	Mintage	Fine	VF	XF	Unc
2206	1868	12.000	.75	1.00	3.00	8.00
	1869	30.000	.75	1.00	3.00	10.00
	1870	35.000	.75	1.00	2.50	8.00
	1871	2.000	10.00	20.00	40.00	90.00
	1872	70.000	.25	.50	1.00	6.00

15 KREUZER

COPPER

KM#	Date	Mintage	Fine	VF	XF	Unc
2138	1807A	—	3.00	5.00	10.00	50.00
	1807B	22.007	3.00	5.00	10.00	50.00
	1087B (error for 1807)					
		—	45.00	90.00	150.00	300.00
	1807E	—	10.00	20.00	40.00	110.00
	1807G	—	10.00	17.50	30.00	100.00
	1807S	—	3.00	5.00	10.00	55.00

20 KREUZER

6.6800 g, .583 SILVER, .1252 oz ASW

KM#	Date	Mintage	Fine	VF	XF	Unc
2139	1802A	—	9.00	20.00	40.00	90.00
	1802B	1.359	7.00	15.00	27.50	60.00
	1802C	—	7.00	15.00	27.50	60.00
	1802E	—	15.00	35.00	60.00	120.00
	1802G	—	12.00	25.00	50.00	90.00
	1802H	—	9.00	20.00	40.00	85.00
	1803A	—	7.00	15.00	27.50	55.00
	1803B	8.469	7.00	15.00	27.50	60.00
	1803C	5.925	7.00	15.00	30.00	70.00
	1803E	—	7.00	15.00	30.00	75.00
	1803F	—	7.00	15.00	30.00	70.00
	1803G	—	9.00	20.00	40.00	80.00
	1803H	—	12.00	25.00	50.00	100.00
	1804A	—	9.00	20.00	40.00	80.00
	1804B	5.693	7.00	15.00	27.50	60.00
	1804C	.566	7.00	15.00	30.00	70.00
	1804E	—	7.00	15.00	27.50	65.00
	1804F	.651	7.00	15.00	30.00	70.00
	1804G	—	7.00	15.00	30.00	60.00

NOTE: Earlier dates (1792-1797) exist for this type.

Rev. leg:. . . . . D. LOTH. VEN. SAL.

KM#	Date	Mintage	Fine	VF	XF	Unc
2140	1804A	—	25.00	45.00	80.00	175.00
	1804F	Inc.KM2139				
			—	—	—	—
	1804H	—	—	—	Rare	—
	1805A	—	6.00	12.00	25.00	60.00
	1805B	8.402	5.00	10.00	20.00	60.00
	1805C	1.993	7.00	15.00	30.00	80.00
	1805E	—	7.00	15.00	25.00	60.00
	1805G	—	10.00	20.00	40.00	90.00
	1806A	—	5.00	10.00	20.00	55.00
	1806B	19.090	5.00	10.00	20.00	60.00
	1806C	2.977	6.00	12.00	25.00	60.00
	1806D	—	10.00	20.00	40.00	85.00
	1806E	—	—	—	Rare	—
	1806G	—	10.00	20.00	40.00	90.00

Rev. leg:. . . . . D. LO. SAL. WIRC.

KM#	Date	Mintage	Fine	VF	XF	Unc
2141	1806A	—	7.00	15.00	30.00	75.00
	1806B					
		Inc.KM2140	15.00	30.00	60.00	120.00
	1806C	—	25.00	55.00	100.00	175.00
	1807A	—	7.00	15.00	30.00	75.00
	1807B	6.723	12.00	25.00	45.00	95.00
	1807C	2.421	12.00	25.00	45.00	95.00

KM#	Date	Mintage	Fine	VF	XF	Unc
2141	1807D	—	12.00	25.00	45.00	100.00
	1808A	—	5.00	10.00	20.00	50.00
	1808B	3.235	7.00	15.00	30.00	75.00
	1808C	1.188	5.00	10.00	20.00	55.00
	1808D	—	10.00	20.00	40.00	80.00
	1808E	—	7.00	15.00	35.00	80.00
	1808G	—	7.00	15.00	30.00	70.00
	1809A	—	5.00	10.00	20.00	55.00
	1809B	7.239	7.00	15.00	27.50	65.00
	1809C	2.381	7.00	15.00	27.50	60.00
	1809D	—	12.00	25.00	50.00	100.00
	1809E	—	7.00	15.00	35.00	80.00
	1809G	—	5.00	10.00	20.00	50.00
	1810A	—	5.00	10.00	20.00	50.00
	1810C	.714	—	—	—	—
	1810E	—	50.00	100.00	150.00	200.00
	1810G	—	12.00	25.00	50.00	100.00
	1812C	.092	—	—	—	—
	1813C	.055	—	—	—	—
	1814C	—	12.00	25.00	50.00	100.00

Rev. leg:. . . . . LO WI: ET IN FR D.

KM#	Date	Mintage	Fine	VF	XF	Unc
2142	1811A	—	5.00	10.00	20.00	45.00
	1811B	.580	9.00	20.00	40.00	80.00
	1811E	—	12.00	25.00	50.00	100.00
	1812A	—	5.00	10.00	20.00	45.00
	1812B	.774	20.00	40.00	80.00	120.00
	1812E	—	10.00	20.00	40.00	80.00
	1812G	—	10.00	20.00	40.00	80.00
	1813A	—	5.00	10.00	20.00	50.00
	1813B	1.103	6.00	12.00	25.00	50.00
	1813E	—	6.00	12.00	25.00	55.00
	1813G	—	100.00	150.00	200.00	300.00
	1814A	—	5.00	10.00	20.00	45.00
	1814B	1.021	7.00	15.00	35.00	70.00
	1814C	—	7.00	15.00	30.00	60.00
	1814E	—	10.00	20.00	40.00	80.00
	1814G	—	7.00	15.00	35.00	70.00
	1815A	—	5.00	10.00	20.00	45.00
	1815B	1.043	4.00	8.00	15.00	45.00
	1815C	.128	6.00	12.00	25.00	50.00
	1815E	—	7.00	15.00	30.00	65.00
	1815G	—	6.00	12.00	25.00	50.00
	1815	—	15.00	30.00	60.00	120.00
	1816B	5.773	10.00	20.00	40.00	80.00
	1816C	.785	— Reported, not confirmed			

.583 SILVER

Rev. leg:. . . . . GAL. LOD. IL. REX. A. A.

KM#	Date	Mintage	Fine	VF	XF	Unc
2143	1817A	—	5.00	10.00	20.00	45.00
	1818A	—	5.00	10.00	20.00	45.00
	1818B	2.703	5.00	10.00	20.00	55.00
	1818C	.033	10.00	20.00	40.00	80.00
	1818E	—	7.00	15.00	30.00	60.00
	1818G	—	10.00	20.00	40.00	80.00
	1818V	—	6.00	12.00	25.00	55.00
	1818V FNANCISCUS (error)					
		—	60.00	100.00	150.00	375.00
	1819A	—	5.00	10.00	20.00	45.00
	1819C	.081	25.00	45.00	75.00	140.00
	1819E	—	8.00	15.00	30.00	60.00
	1819M	—	7.00	15.00	25.00	50.00
	1820A	—	5.00	10.00	20.00	45.00
	1820B	1.118	12.00	25.00	50.00	100.00
	1820C	.028	10.00	20.00	40.00	80.00
	1820E	—	7.00	15.00	30.00	65.00
	1820G	—	25.00	45.00	75.00	140.00
	1821A	—	6.00	12.00	25.00	55.00
	1821B	1.075	10.00	20.00	40.00	80.00
	1821C	.116	20.00	40.00	70.00	130.00
	1821E	—	7.00	15.00	30.00	70.00
	1821G	—	25.00	45.00	75.00	140.00
	1822A	—	6.00	12.00	25.00	55.00
	1822B	.269	10.00	20.00	40.00	80.00
	1822C	.165	20.00	40.00	70.00	130.00
	1822E	—	7.00	15.00	30.00	75.00
	1822G	—	12.00	25.00	45.00	85.00
	1823A	—	5.00	10.00	20.00	45.00
	1823B	.324	25.00	45.00	75.00	140.00
	1823C	.096	30.00	50.00	90.00	150.00
	1823E	—	6.00	12.00	25.00	55.00
	1823G	—	12.00	25.00	50.00	100.00
	1824A	—	5.00	10.00	20.00	45.00
	1824B	.014	40.00	60.00	90.00	175.00
	1824E	—	6.00	12.00	25.00	60.00
	1824G	—	6.00	12.00	25.00	55.00

Obv: Small bust w/short hair.

KM#	Date	Mintage	Fine	VF	XF	Unc
2144	1825A	—	3.50	7.00	15.00	35.00
	1825B	.373	20.00	40.00	70.00	120.00
	1825E	—	6.00	12.00	25.00	50.00
	1826A	—	3.50	7.00	15.00	35.00
	1826B	—	6.00	12.00	25.00	50.00
	1826C	—	— Reported, not confirmed			
	1826E	—	6.00	12.00	25.00	50.00
	1826G	—	—	—	Rare	—
	1827A	—	3.50	7.00	15.00	35.00
	1827B	1.053	7.00	15.00	30.00	60.00
	1827C	.924	5.00	10.00	20.00	40.00
	1827E	—	6.00	12.00	25.00	50.00
	1827G	—	7.00	15.00	30.00	60.00
	1828A	—	3.50	7.00	15.00	35.00
	1828B	2.402	6.00	12.00	25.00	50.00
	1828E	—	6.00	12.00	25.00	50.00

Obv: Large bust w/short hair.

KM#	Date	Mintage	Fine	VF	XF	Unc
2145	1829A	—	3.00	6.00	12.00	30.00
	1829B	2.319	4.00	8.00	16.00	40.00
	1829E	—	5.00	10.00	20.00	40.00
	1830A	—	3.00	6.00	12.00	30.00
	1830B small	2.348	3.00	6.00	12.00	25.00
	1830B large	Inc. Ab.	3.00	6.00	12.00	25.00
	1830C	1.754	3.00	6.00	12.00	25.00
	1830E	—	3.50	7.00	15.00	35.00

Obv: Ribbons on wreath forward across neck.

KM#	Date	Mintage	Fine	VF	XF	Unc
2146	1831A	—	20.00	40.00	80.00	200.00

Obv: Ribbons on wreath behind neck.

KM#	Date	Mintage	Fine	VF	XF	Unc
2147	1831A	—	3.00	6.00	12.00	30.00
	1831C	—	10.00	20.00	40.00	80.00
	1831M	—	6.00	12.00	25.00	50.00
	1831V	—	7.00	15.00	30.00	55.00
	1832A	—	3.00	6.00	12.00	25.00
	1832B	—	100.00	150.00	250.00	400.00
	1832C	5.122	5.00	10.00	20.00	45.00
	1832M	—	7.00	15.00	30.00	60.00
	1833A	—	6.00	12.00	25.00	50.00
	1833B	—	7.00	15.00	30.00	60.00
	1833C	1.818	6.00	12.00	25.00	50.00
	1833E	—	12.00	25.00	45.00	90.00
	1834A	—	3.50	7.00	15.00	40.00
	1834B	—	6.00	12.00	25.00	50.00
	1834C	1.517	6.00	12.00	25.00	50.00
	1834E	—	6.00	12.00	25.00	50.00
	1835A	—	5.00	10.00	20.00	45.00
	1835B	—	5.00	10.00	20.00	45.00
	1835C	1.489	6.00	12.00	25.00	50.00
	1835E	—	5.00	10.00	20.00	45.00

KM#	Date	Mintage	Fine	VF	XF	Unc
2207	1835A	—	15.00	30.00	60.00	120.00
	1835C	.295	15.00	30.00	60.00	130.00
	1835E	—	35.00	75.00	125.00	250.00
	1836A	—	10.00	20.00	45.00	90.00
	1836E	—	25.00	50.00	100.00	225.00

KM#	Date	Mintage	Fine	VF	XF	Unc
2208	1837A	—	5.00	10.00	20.00	45.00
	1837B	—	7.50	15.00	30.00	60.00
	1837C	.484	10.00	20.00	40.00	80.00
	1837E	—	10.00	22.00	45.00	100.00
	1837M	—	30.00	60.00	100.00	225.00
	1838A	—	5.00	10.00	20.00	45.00
	1838B	—	5.00	10.00	20.00	45.00
	1838C	.625	10.00	20.00	40.00	80.00
	1838/7E	—	8.00	16.50	35.00	80.00
	1838E	—	6.00	12.00	25.00	60.00
	1838M	—	30.00	60.00	100.00	225.00
	1839A	—	5.00	10.00	20.00	45.00
	1839B	—	8.00	18.00	35.00	70.00
	1839C	.220	15.00	30.00	60.00	120.00
	1839E	—	4.00	9.00	20.00	60.00
	1840A	—	2.50	4.00	8.00	30.00
	1840C	1.122	3.00	7.00	15.00	35.00
	1840E	—	10.00	20.00	40.00	80.00
	1840M	—	25.00	50.00	90.00	160.00
	1841A	—	2.50	4.00	8.00	30.00
	1841C	2.543	5.00	10.00	20.00	45.00
	1841E	—	4.00	9.00	20.00	60.00
	1842A	—	2.50	5.00	10.00	35.00
	1842C	.644	5.00	10.00	20.00	45.00
	1842E	—	12.00	25.00	50.00	100.00
	1842M	—	10.00	20.00	40.00	80.00
	1843A	—	20.00	40.00	70.00	130.00
	1843C	1.257	5.00	10.00	20.00	45.00
	1843E	—	5.00	15.00	30.00	80.00
	1843M	—	5.00	10.00	20.00	45.00
	1844A	—	2.50	4.00	8.00	30.00
	1844C	1.492	5.00	10.00	20.00	45.00
	1844E	—	4.00	9.00	20.00	80.00
	1844M	—	7.00	15.00	30.00	60.00
	1845A	—	2.50	5.00	10.00	35.00
	1845C	1.461	3.00	6.00	14.00	35.00
	1845E	—	9.00	18.00	35.00	90.00
	1845M	—	7.00	15.00	30.00	60.00
	1846A	—	2.50	5.00	10.00	35.00
	1846C	1.549	3.00	6.00	14.00	35.00
	1846/5E	—	15.00	35.00	60.00	135.00
	1846E	—	13.50	27.50	50.00	120.00
	1846M	—	7.00	15.00	35.00	70.00
	1847A	—	2.50	4.00	8.00	30.00
	1847C	1.528	3.00	6.00	15.00	35.00
	1847E	—	7.00	15.00	30.00	70.00
	1847M	—	14.00	30.00	60.00	100.00
	1848A	13.632	2.50	4.00	8.00	30.00
	1848C	2.241	3.00	6.00	10.00	30.00
	1848E	—	12.00	25.00	45.00	100.00

Obv: Head of Ferdinand I right.

KM#	Date	Mintage	Fine	VF	XF	Unc
2209	1848GM	7,799	125.00	250.00	350.00	800.00

NOTE: The above issue was struck in Mantua by the Austrian garrison under General Josef Radetzky during the siege of March 18-22, 1848 by Italian rebels.

KM#	Date	Mintage	Fine	VF	XF	Unc
2210	1852A	—	25.00	50.00	100.00	150.00
	1852C	.114	60.00	100.00	200.00	400.00

4.3200 g, .900 SILVER, .1250 oz ASW

KM#	Date	Mintage	Fine	VF	XF	Unc
2211	1852A	—	4.00	8.00	18.00	30.00
	1852B	4.926	5.00	8.00	15.00	32.00
	1852C	1.687	50.00	100.00	150.00	325.00
	1852E	—	40.00	80.00	150.00	275.00
	1853A	—	4.00	8.00	18.00	35.00
	1853C	1.590	5.50	11.00	22.00	45.00
	1853E	—	12.50	25.00	50.00	75.00
	1854A	—	4.00	8.00	18.00	30.00
	1854B	2.287	5.00	8.00	15.00	36.00
	1854C	2.098	6.50	13.00	24.00	45.00
	1854E	—	10.00	20.00	40.00	60.00
	1855A	—	4.00	8.00	18.00	35.00
	1855B	2.198	5.00	8.00	15.00	30.00
	1855C	1.904	10.00	20.00	30.00	47.50
	1855E	—	7.00	15.00	22.50	35.00
	1856A	—	20.00	35.00	50.00	100.00
	1856B	3.654	5.00	8.00	15.00	30.00
	1856C	.048	35.00	75.00	100.00	135.00
	1856E	—	10.00	20.00	37.50	65.00
	1869B	3.224	5.00	8.00	15.00	30.00
	1870B	9.487	5.00	8.00	15.00	30.00
	1871B	4.092	5.00	8.00	15.00	30.00
	1872B	.335	5.00	8.00	15.00	30.00
	1873B	1.286	5.00	8.00	15.00	30.00

2.6667 g, .500 SILVER, .0429 oz ASW

KM#	Date	Mintage	Fine	VF	XF	Unc
2212	1868	30.000	1.00	2.00	4.00	15.00
	1869	30.000	1.00	2.00	4.00	13.00
	1870	30.000	1.00	2.00	4.00	10.00
	1872	.576	15.00	30.00	50.00	85.00

1/4 FLORIN

5.3450 g, .520 SILVER, .0893 oz ASW

KM#	Date	Mintage	Fine	VF	XF	Unc
2213	1857A	—	7.50	15.00	25.00	40.00
	1857B	—	12.00	22.50	37.50	60.00
	1857E	—	35.00	70.00	100.00	140.00
	1857M	—	50.00	75.00	125.00	250.00
	1857V	—	22.00	40.00	60.00	140.00
	1858A	31.197	4.50	9.00	15.00	25.00
	1858B	2.982	6.50	13.00	25.00	50.00
	1858E	Inc. Ab.	6.50	13.00	20.00	35.00
	1858M	Inc. Ab.	25.00	45.00	80.00	160.00
	1859M	27.415	45.00	75.00	115.00	200.00

KM#	Date	Mintage	Fine	VF	XF	Unc
2214	1859A	27.415	3.00	7.00	15.00	25.00
	1859B	13.109	3.00	6.00	10.00	25.00
	1859E	—	4.00	8.00	15.00	25.00
	1859M	—	30.00	60.00	125.00	300.00
	1859V	—	9.00	20.00	40.00	80.00
	1860A	—	11.50	23.00	40.00	55.00
	1860B	21.247	2.00	4.00	6.50	20.00
	1860E	—	35.00	60.00	90.00	180.00
	1860V	—	10.00	20.00	40.00	80.00
	1861A	—	3.00	7.00	15.00	40.00
	1861B	1.656	30.00	50.00	80.00	120.00
	1861E	—	90.00	180.00	250.00	425.00
	1861V	—	15.00	40.00	70.00	150.00
	1862A	—	3.00	7.00	15.00	40.00
	1862B	2.796	7.50	15.00	25.00	75.00
	1862E	—	8.00	16.00	30.00	75.00
	1862V	—	10.00	20.00	40.00	90.00
	1863A	—	15.00	35.00	60.00	120.00
	1863V	.800	17.50	35.00	60.00	140.00
	1864A	4.843	3.00	7.00	15.00	30.00
	1864V	.165	17.50	30.00	50.00	120.00
	1865A	.080	27.50	50.00	80.00	135.00

Obv: Head of Franz Joseph I right w/heavier side whiskers. Rev: Eagle, value below.

KM#	Date	Mintage	Fine	VF	XF	Unc
2215	1866A	—	150.00	250.00	400.00	850.00
	1866V	—	120.00	225.00	400.00	950.00

Rev. leg: HUNGAR, BOHEM. GAL. - LOD. ILL. . . . .

KM#	Date	Mintage	Fine	VF	XF	Unc
2216	1867A	—	75.00	150.00	250.00	500.00
	1868A	—	65.00	110.00	200.00	315.00
	1869A	—	55.00	90.00	150.00	250.00
	1870A	7,956	120.00	200.00	400.00	700.00
	1871A	—	100.00	175.00	300.00	600.00
2217	1872	.100	50.00	100.00	200.00	375.00
	1873	.050	40.00	75.00	150.00	300.00
	1874	.100	80.00	150.00	250.00	425.00
	1875	.020	100.00	250.00	350.00	550.00

30 KREUZER

COPPER

KM#	Date	Mintage	Fine	VF	XF	Unc
2149	1807A	—	4.00	8.00	15.00	40.00
	1807B	15.787	4.00	8.00	15.00	40.00
	1807B (error) inverted C in ERBLAENDISCH					
		—	40.00	70.00	100.00	200.00
	1807E	—	15.00	30.00	50.00	100.00
	1807G	—	10.00	20.00	40.00	80.00
	1807S	—	4.00	8.00	15.00	40.00

NOTE: The above 5 issues struck until 1811.

FLORIN

12.3400 g, .900 SILVER, .3571 oz ASW

KM#	Date	Mintage	Fine	VF	XF	Unc
2219	1857A	—	20.00	35.00	70.00	150.00
	1857B	—	100.00	210.00	350.00	600.00
	1857E	—	100.00	225.00	375.00	675.00
	1857V	—	135.00	240.00	400.00	775.00
	1858A	—	7.50	15.00	22.50	35.00
	1858B	1.920	9.00	18.00	27.50	45.00
	1858E	—	15.00	25.00	40.00	75.00
	1858M	—	20.00	45.00	90.00	200.00
	1858V	—	14.00	30.00	60.00	120.00
	1859A	—	5.00	7.00	14.00	30.00
	1859B	7.537	6.00	11.00	25.00	40.00
	1859E	—	10.00	20.00	35.00	60.00
	1859M	—	12.00	18.00	45.00	125.00
	1859V	—	12.50	25.00	45.00	90.00
	1860A	—	3.00	5.00	10.00	25.00
	1860B	1.883	12.50	25.00	40.00	70.00
	1860E	—	10.00	20.00	35.00	50.00
	1860V	—	17.50	30.00	60.00	120.00
	1861A	—	3.00	5.00	10.00	25.00
	1861B	.815	75.00	150.00	300.00	500.00
	1861E	—	15.00	30.00	60.00	120.00
	1861V	—	20.00	35.00	75.00	150.00
	1862A	—	6.00	10.00	15.00	27.50
	1862B	.314	11.00	25.00	50.00	90.00
	1862E	—	60.00	150.00	225.00	450.00
	1862V	—	25.00	60.00	95.00	190.00
	1863A	—	7.00	12.00	17.50	35.00
	1863B	.287	17.50	35.00	60.00	100.00
	1863E	—	17.50	32.50	65.00	95.00
	1863V	—	17.50	37.50	65.00	130.00
	1864A	—	15.00	30.00	50.00	120.00
	1864B	.340	40.00	75.00	140.00	350.00
	1864E	.150	40.00	100.00	175.00	275.00
	1864V	.130	55.00	110.00	200.00	400.00
	1865A	—	15.00	30.00	50.00	120.00
	1865B	.291	20.00	35.00	65.00	110.00
	1865E	—	15.00	32.50	70.00	100.00
	1865V	.031	120.00	240.00	400.00	675.00

NOTE: Varieties exist.

Obv: Head of Franz Joseph I right w/heavier side whiskers. Rev: Eagle, value below.

KM#	Date	Mintage	Fine	VF	XF	Unc
2220	1866A	—	25.00	50.00	85.00	150.00
	1866B	.359	27.50	60.00	90.00	150.00
	1866E	—	70.00	150.00	250.00	450.00
	1866V	—	80.00	150.00	250.00	450.00

Rev. leg: HUNGAR, BOHEN. GAL. - LOD. ILL. . . . .

KM#	Date	Mintage	Fine	VF	XF	Unc
2221	1867A	—	25.00	40.00	80.00	150.00
	1867B	.714	15.00	30.00	50.00	85.00
2221	1867E	—	150.00	250.00	400.00	650.00
	1868A	—	30.00	50.00	90.00	160.00
	1869A	—	22.50	35.00	70.00	150.00
	1870A	—	15.00	30.00	50.00	90.00
	1871A	—	12.50	25.00	40.00	70.00
	1872A	—	150.00	250.00	400.00	800.00

KM#	Date	Mintage	Fine	VF	XF	Unc
2222	1872	4.725	12.50	25.00	40.00	100.00
	1873	7.880	8.00	16.00	30.00	75.00
	1874	2.479	22.50	40.00	70.00	100.00
	1875/3	5.053	—	—	—	—
	1875	Inc. Ab.	6.00	10.00	15.00	30.00
	1876	7.283	6.00	9.00	14.00	27.50
	1877	13.963	5.00	8.00	13.00	25.00
	1878	18.963	5.00	8.00	13.00	25.00
	1878 plain edge					
		—	—	—	—	—
	1879	37.485	5.00	8.00	13.00	25.00
	1880	6.505	7.50	12.00	20.00	35.00
	1881	6.128	7.50	12.00	20.00	35.00
	1882	5.476	9.00	15.00	25.00	45.00
	1883	6.036	7.00	10.00	14.00	25.00
	1884	4.303	7.00	10.00	14.00	25.00
	1885	3.395	7.00	12.00	16.00	25.00
	1886	6.710	6.00	10.00	14.00	25.00
	1887	5.692	6.00	10.00	14.00	25.00
	1888	6.572	6.00	10.00	14.00	25.00
	1889	5.053	6.00	10.00	14.00	25.00
	1890	4.164	6.00	10.00	14.00	25.00
	1891	4.235	6.00	10.00	14.00	25.00
	1892	2.504	10.00	15.00	25.00	50.00

1/2 THALER

14.0300 g, .833 SILVER, .3757 oz ASW

Obv. leg: FRANCISCVS II. D. G. R. IMP. . . . .

KM#	Date	Mintage	Fine	VF	XF	Unc
2149	1801A	—	60.00	100.00	150.00	225.00
	1802A	—	60.00	100.00	150.00	225.00
	1803A	—	100.00	175.00	275.00	350.00
	1804A	—	60.00	100.00	150.00	225.00

NOTE: Earlier dates (1792-1800) exist for this type.

Obv. leg: FRANCISCVS II. D. G. ROM ET. . . . .

KM#	Date	Mintage	Fine	VF	XF	Unc
2150	1804A	—	—	—	Rare	—
	1805A	—	150.00	250.00	400.00	750.00
	1805V	—	—	—	—	—
	1806A	—	120.00	225.00	375.00	700.00

Obv. leg: FRANCISCVS I. D. G. AVSTRIAE. . . . .
Rev. leg:. . . . . D. LO. SAL. WIRC.

KM#	Date	Mintage	Fine	VF	XF	Unc
2151	1807A	—	—	—	Rare	—
	1808A	—	125.00	200.00	400.00	675.00
	1809A	—	125.00	200.00	400.00	675.00
	1809C	—	150.00	225.00	450.00	750.00
	1810A	—	150.00	225.00	450.00	750.00

Rev. leg:. . . . . LO: WI: ET IN. FR: DVX

KM#	Date	Mintage	Fine	VF	XF	Unc
2152	1811A	2,186	60.00	100.00	150.00	250.00
	1812A	1,930	65.00	110.00	175.00	275.00
	1813A	1,718	65.00	110.00	175.00	275.00
	1814A	1,533	50.00	80.00	125.00	225.00
	1815A	7,849	30.00	50.00	90.00	150.00
	1815B	.057	40.00	70.00	130.00	200.00

Rev. leg:. . . . . GAL. LOD. IL. REX. A. A.

KM#	Date	Mintage	Fine	VF	XF	Unc
2153	1817A	.012	40.00	70.00	115.00	175.00
	1818A	3,695	50.00	80.00	125.00	185.00
	1818B	—	50.00	80.00	125.00	185.00
	1818V	—	35.00	60.00	100.00	150.00
	1819A	—	40.00	65.00	110.00	165.00
	1819B	.015	—	—	Rare	—
	1819C	—	45.00	75.00	125.00	185.00
	1819E	—	—	—	Rare	—
	1819G	—	50.00	80.00	135.00	200.00
	1820A	—	40.00	70.00	115.00	175.00
	1820B	.023	—	—	Rare	—
	1820C	—	40.00	70.00	115.00	175.00
	1820E	—	50.00	80.00	125.00	185.00
	1820G	—	—	—	Rare	—
	1821A	—	40.00	70.00	115.00	175.00
	1821B	9,650	40.00	70.00	115.00	175.00
	1821C	—	35.00	60.00	100.00	150.00
	1821E	—	50.00	80.00	125.00	185.00
	1821G	—	50.00	80.00	125.00	185.00
	1821V	—	—	—	Rare	—
	1822A	—	35.00	60.00	100.00	150.00
	1822B	.013	—	—	Rare	—
	1822C	—	40.00	70.00	115.00	175.00
	1822E	—	50.00	80.00	125.00	185.00
	1822G	—	50.00	80.00	125.00	185.00
	1823A	—	35.00	60.00	100.00	150.00
	1823B	.015	50.00	80.00	125.00	185.00
	1823C	—	50.00	80.00	125.00	185.00
	1823E	—	50.00	80.00	125.00	185.00
	1823G	—	35.00	65.00	110.00	165.00
	1824A	—	35.00	60.00	100.00	150.00
	1824B	.013	40.00	70.00	115.00	175.00
	1824C	—	30.00	55.00	100.00	135.00
	1824G	—	65.00	115.00	150.00	225.00

Obv: Bust w/short hair.

KM#	Date	Mintage	Fine	VF	XF	Unc
2154	1825A	—	50.00	80.00	125.00	185.00
	1825B	.015	50.00	80.00	125.00	185.00
	1825C	—	50.00	80.00	125.00	185.00
	1826A	—	30.00	50.00	80.00	125.00
	1826B	.013	40.00	70.00	115.00	175.00
	1826C	—	35.00	60.00	100.00	150.00
	1826G	—	80.00	150.00	250.00	450.00
	1827A	—	25.00	40.00	60.00	120.00
	1827B	5,230	—	—	Rare	—
	1827C	—	60.00	100.00	175.00	250.00
	1828A	—	30.00	55.00	85.00	130.00
	1829A	—	30.00	50.00	80.00	125.00
	1830A	—	25.00	45.00	75.00	112.00
	1830E	—	—	—	Rare	—

KM#	Date	Mintage	Fine	VF	XF	Unc
2155	1831A	—	60.00	100.00	165.00	225.00

KM#	Date	Mintage	Fine	VF	XF	Unc
2156	1832A	—	40.00	75.00	125.00	200.00
	1832A plain edge					
		—	—	—	—	—
	1833A	—	40.00	75.00	125.00	200.00

KM#	Date	Mintage	Fine	VF	XF	Unc
2156	1833A plain edge					
		—	—	—	—	—
	1833E	—	—	—	Rare	—
	1834A	—	40.00	75.00	125.00	200.00
	1835A	—	35.00	60.00	100.00	175.00

Obv: Head of Ferdinand I right. Rev: Eagle.

KM#	Date	Mintage	Fine	VF	XF	Unc
2224	1835A	—	250.00	400.00	600.00	1200.
	1835C	—	—	—	Rare	—
	1836A	—	250.00	400.00	600.00	1200.
	1836C	—	275.00	550.00	1100.	1700.

KM#	Date	Mintage	Fine	VF	XF	Unc
2225	1837A	—	50.00	100.00	200.00	400.00
	1838A	—	50.00	100.00	200.00	400.00
	1839A	—	45.00	90.00	175.00	350.00
	1840A	—	30.00	65.00	135.00	275.00
	1841A	—	45.00	90.00	175.00	350.00
	1842A	—	40.00	80.00	160.00	300.00
	1843A	—	40.00	80.00	160.00	300.00
	1844A	—	45.00	90.00	175.00	350.00
	1845A	—	40.00	80.00	160.00	300.00
	1846A	—	30.00	65.00	135.00	275.00
	1847A	—	30.00	65.00	135.00	275.00
	1848A	3,964	50.00	100.00	225.00	500.00

KM#	Date	Mintage	Fine	VF	XF	Unc
2226	1848GM	3,947	275.00	450.00	675.00	1350.

NOTE: The above issue was struck in Mantua by the Austrian garrison under General Josef Radetzky during the siege of March 18-22, 1848 by Italian rebels.

Obv: Young head of Franz Joseph I left.

KM#	Date	Mintage	Fine	VF	XF	Unc
2227	1848A	—	700.00	1450.	2000.	3250.
	1849A	—	700.00	1450.	2000.	3250.
	1850A	—	850.00	1750.	2250.	3750.
	1851A	—	650.00	1250.	1800.	3000.

.900 SILVER
Obv: Young head of Franz Joseph I right.
Edge lettering: VIRIBVS VN!TIS.

KM#	Date	Mintage	Fine	VF	XF	Unc
2228.1	1852A	—	125.00	250.00	400.00	800.00
	1853A	—	200.00	375.00	500.00	1000.
	1854A	—	200.00	375.00	500.00	1000.
	1855A	—	150.00	325.00	450.00	950.00
	1856A	—	150.00	325.00	425.00	900.00

Edge lettering: VIRIBUS-VIRIBUS

KM#	Date	Mintage	Fine	VF	XF	Unc
2228.2	1856A	—	150.00	275.00	450.00	750.00

2 FLORINS

24.6900 g, .900 SILVER, .7145 oz ASW

KM#	Date	Mintage	Fine	VF	XF	Unc
2230	1859A	—	75.00	125.00	175.00	275.00
	1859B	.511	40.00	70.00	120.00	200.00
	1860A	—	550.00	950.00	1500.	2250.
	1860V	—	175.00	350.00	700.00	1100.
	1861A	—	—	—	—	—
	1862A	.015	100.00	180.00	300.00	450.00
	1863A	.024	50.00	90.00	150.00	250.00
	1864A	.031	50.00	90.00	150.00	250.00
	1865A	.072	50.00	90.00	150.00	250.00
	1866A	—	— Reported, not confirmed			

KM#	Date	Mintage	Fine	VF	XF	Unc
2231	1866A	.011	175.00	350.00	700.00	1100.

KM#	Date	Mintage	Fine	VF	XF	Unc
2232	1867A	.045	50.00	100.00	150.00	250.00
	1868A	—	50.00	100.00	150.00	250.00
	1869A	—	40.00	75.00	125.00	200.00
	1870A	—	40.00	75.00	125.00	200.00
	1871A	—	50.00	100.00	150.00	250.00
	1872A	—	75.00	150.00	250.00	375.00

KM#	Date	Mintage	Fine	VF	XF	Unc
2233	1872	.045	35.00	65.00	110.00	200.00
	1873	.099	35.00	65.00	120.00	225.00
	1874	.079	25.00	50.00	80.00	150.00
	1875	.106	30.00	60.00	85.00	150.00
	1876	.092	35.00	65.00	90.00	170.00
	1877	.105	25.00	55.00	80.00	150.00
	1878	.147	30.00	60.00	80.00	150.00
	1879	.501	25.00	50.00	70.00	150.00
	1880	.083	30.00	60.00	80.00	140.00
	1881	.104	30.00	60.00	80.00	140.00
	1882	.121	25.00	50.00	70.00	130.00
	1883	.070	35.00	65.00	95.00	160.00
	1884	.087	25.00	50.00	70.00	130.00
	1885	.078	25.00	50.00	70.00	140.00
	1886	.093	25.00	50.00	70.00	140.00
	1887	.117	25.00	50.00	70.00	140.00
	1888	.073	25.00	50.00	70.00	140.00
	1889	.147	35.00	65.00	90.00	170.00
	1890	.104	35.00	65.00	90.00	150.00
	1891	.117	35.00	65.00	90.00	150.00
	1892	.032	30.00	60.00	70.00	140.00

THALER

28.0600 g, .833 SILVER, .7514 oz ASW
Obv. leg: FRANCISCVS II. D.G.R. IMP. S.A. . . .

KM#	Date	Mintage	Fine	VF	XF	Unc
2158	1801A	—	85.00	175.00	325.00	650.00
	1802A	—	110.00	225.00	450.00	850.00
	1803A	—	125.00	250.00	475.00	950.00
	1804A	—	75.00	150.00	275.00	550.00

NOTE: Earlier dates (1792-1800) exist for this type.

Obv. leg: FRANCISCVS II D.G. ROM. ET. . . .

KM#	Date	Mintage	Fine	VF	XF	Unc
2159	1804A	—	60.00	125.00	250.00	475.00
	1805A	—	60.00	125.00	250.00	475.00
	1806A	—	60.00	125.00	250.00	475.00

Obv. leg: FRANCISCVS I.D.G. AVSTRIAE. . . .
Rev. leg:. . . . D. LO. SAL. WIRC.

KM#	Date	Mintage	Fine	VF	XF	Unc
2160	1806A	—	—	—	Rare	—
	1807A	—	40.00	80.00	160.00	325.00
	1808A	—	40.00	80.00	160.00	325.00
	1809A	—	40.00	80.00	160.00	325.00
	1809B (restrike 1841)					
	1809C	—	35.00	70.00	140.00	275.00
	1810A	—	30.00	60.00	120.00	150.00

NOTE: 1810A exists as a klippe.

Rev. leg:. . . . . LO: WI: ET IN. FR: DVX.

KM#	Date	Mintage	Fine	VF	XF	Unc
2161	1811A	—	30.00	65.00	130.00	250.00
	1811C	—	30.00	65.00	130.00	250.00
	1812A	—	175.00	350.00	725.00	1100.
	1812C	—	50.00	100.00	200.00	400.00
	1813A	—	50.00	100.00	200.00	400.00
	1813C	—	50.00	100.00	200.00	400.00
	1813G	—	55.00	100.00	200.00	325.00
	1814A	—	25.00	50.00	100.00	200.00
	1814B	—	—	—	Rare	—
	1814C	—	40.00	80.00	160.00	325.00
	1814G	—	55.00	100.00	200.00	325.00
	1815A	—	25.00	50.00	100.00	200.00
	1815B	—	50.00	110.00	225.00	325.00
	1815C	—	35.00	75.00	150.00	250.00

Rev. leg:. . . . . GAL. LOD. IL. REX. A. A.

KM#	Date	Mintage	Fine	VF	XF	Unc
2162	1817A	—	25.00	50.00	100.00	250.00
	1818A	—	25.00	50.00	100.00	250.00
	1818B	—	30.00	55.00	110.00	200.00
	1818V	—	35.00	70.00	150.00	275.00
	1819A	—	35.00	70.00	135.00	300.00
	1819B	.153	—	—	Rare	—
	1819C	—	35.00	70.00	150.00	275.00
	1819E	—	35.00	70.00	150.00	275.00
	1819G	—	30.00	60.00	125.00	250.00
	1819M	—	45.00	90.00	180.00	300.00
	1820A	—	20.00	40.00	80.00	200.00
	1820B	.250	—	—	Rare	—
	1820C	—	30.00	55.00	100.00	200.00
	1820E	—	50.00	100.00	200.00	325.00
	1820G	—	65.00	130.00	250.00	375.00
	1820M	—	30.00	60.00	125.00	250.00
	1821A	—	25.00	50.00	100.00	250.00
	1821B	.150	20.00	40.00	85.00	150.00
	1821C	—	20.00	40.00	85.00	150.00
	1821E	—	27.50	55.00	125.00	225.00
	1821G	—	25.00	50.00	100.00	200.00
	1821M	—	50.00	100.00	200.00	300.00
	1821V	—	45.00	80.00	175.00	275.00
	1822A	—	20.00	40.00	80.00	200.00
	1822B	.215	25.00	50.00	100.00	200.00
	1822C	—	25.00	50.00	100.00	200.00
	1822E	—	30.00	60.00	125.00	250.00
	1822G	—	25.00	50.00	100.00	200.00
	1822M	—	50.00	100.00	200.00	400.00
	1822V	—	—	—	Rare	—
	1823A	—	20.00	40.00	80.00	200.00
	1823B	.201	25.00	50.00	100.00	200.00
	1823C	—	35.00	70.00	150.00	275.00
	1823E	—	30.00	60.00	125.00	250.00
	1823G	—	30.00	60.00	125.00	250.00
	1824A	—	25.00	50.00	100.00	250.00
	1824B	.282	25.00	50.00	100.00	200.00
	1824C	—	30.00	60.00	125.00	250.00
	1824E	—	35.00	70.00	150.00	275.00
	1824G	—	30.00	60.00	125.00	250.00

KM#	Date	Mintage	Fine	VF	XF	Unc
2163	1824A	—	40.00	80.00	155.00	250.00
	1824C	—	—	—	—	—
	1825A	—	30.00	60.00	125.00	250.00
	1825B	.336	30.00	60.00	125.00	250.00
	1825C	—	35.00	70.00	145.00	270.00
	1825G	—	30.00	60.00	125.00	250.00
	1826A	—	25.00	55.00	100.00	225.00
	1826B	.269	30.00	60.00	125.00	250.00
	1826C	—	30.00	60.00	125.00	250.00
	1826G	—	35.00	70.00	145.00	275.00
	1827A	—	30.00	60.00	125.00	250.00
	1827B	.089	80.00	175.00	325.00	475.00
	1827C	—	25.00	50.00	100.00	200.00
	1828A	—	25.00	50.00	100.00	225.00
	1829A	—	25.00	50.00	100.00	225.00
	1830A	—	20.00	40.00	80.00	175.00
	1830E	—	75.00	150.00	275.00	425.00

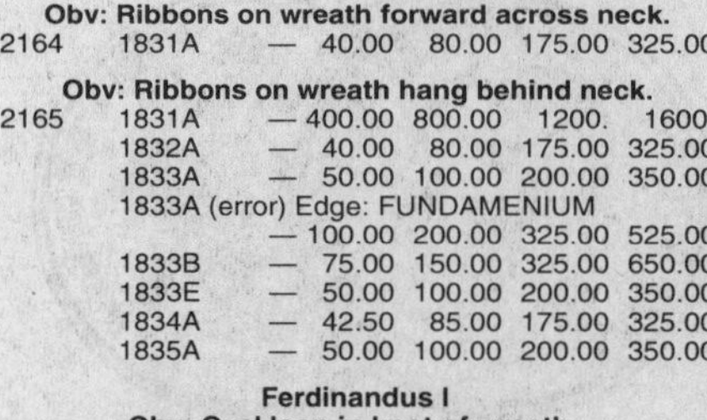

Obv: Ribbons on wreath forward across neck.

KM#	Date	Mintage	Fine	VF	XF	Unc
2164	1831A	—	40.00	80.00	175.00	325.00

Obv: Ribbons on wreath hang behind neck.

KM#	Date	Mintage	Fine	VF	XF	Unc
2165	1831A	—	400.00	800.00	1200.	1600.
	1832A	—	40.00	80.00	175.00	325.00
	1833A	—	50.00	100.00	200.00	350.00
	1833A (error) Edge: FUNDAMENIUM					
		—	100.00	200.00	325.00	525.00
	1833B	—	75.00	150.00	325.00	650.00
	1833E	—	50.00	100.00	200.00	350.00
	1834A	—	42.50	85.00	175.00	325.00
	1835A	—	50.00	100.00	200.00	350.00

Ferdinandus I

Obv: Oval loop in knot of wreath.

KM#	Date	Mintage	Fine	VF	XF	Unc
2238	1835A	—	125.00	250.00	400.00	800.00
	1835C	—	—	—	Rare	—
	1836A	—	75.00	150.00	250.00	500.00
	1836C	—	250.00	400.00	800.00	1500.

Obv: Sharp cornered loop in knot of wreath.

KM#	Date	Mintage	Fine	VF	XF	Unc
2239	1835A	—	375.00	600.00	1100.	1700.

KM#	Date	Mintage	Fine	VF	XF	Unc
2240	1837A	—	50.00	100.00	200.00	350.00
	1837M	—	275.00	500.00	1000.	1700.
	1838A	—	50.00	100.00	200.00	350.00
	1838M	—	550.00	1150.	1750.	2400.
	1839A	—	50.00	100.00	200.00	350.00
	1840A	—	45.00	90.00	175.00	325.00
	1841A	—	40.00	80.00	150.00	275.00
	1842A	—	40.00	80.00	150.00	275.00
	1843A	—	40.00	80.00	150.00	275.00
	1844A	—	40.00	80.00	150.00	275.00
	1845A	—	40.00	80.00	150.00	275.00
	1846A	—	40.00	80.00	150.00	275.00
	1847A	—	40.00	80.00	150.00	275.00
	1848A	.119	30.00	60.00	100.00	225.00

Obv. leg: FRANC.IOS.I.D.G.AVSTR. IMP.HVNG.BOH.REX.
Rev: Similar to KM#2240.

KM#	Date	Mintage	Fine	VF	XF	Unc
2241	1848A	—	500.00	1000.	1500.	2250.
	1849A	—	500.00	1000.	1500.	2250.
	1850A	—	700.00	1350.	1950.	2650.
	1851A	—	500.00	1000.	1500.	2250.

Obv. leg:. . . . . AVSTRIAE.IMPERATOR.
Rev: Similar to KM#2240.

KM#	Date	Mintage	Fine	VF	XF	Unc
2242	1852A	—	600.00	1250.	2250.	3000.

25.9900 g, .900 SILVER, .7520 oz ASW
Edge lettering: VIRIBVS VNITIS.

KM#	Date	Mintage	Fine	VF	XF	Unc
2243.1	1852A	—	60.00	120.00	225.00	350.00
	1853A	—	45.00	100.00	200.00	300.00
	1853B	—	160.00	275.00	450.00	700.00
	1854A	—	45.00	100.00	200.00	375.00
	1855A	—	40.00	90.00	175.00	325.00
	1856A	—	40.00	90.00	175.00	325.00
	Edge lettering: VIRIBUS-VIRIBUS.					
2243.2	1856A	—	—	—	—	—

(Vereins)

18.5186 g, .900 SILVER, .5359 oz ASW

KM#	Date	Mintage	Fine	VF	XF	Unc
2244	1857A	9.154	15.00	30.00	60.00	100.00
	1857B	—	50.00	100.00	200.00	425.00
	1857E	—	40.00	80.00	165.00	325.00
	1857V	—	75.00	150.00	300.00	550.00
	1858A	Inc. Ab.	15.00	30.00	60.00	100.00
	1858B	—	20.00	40.00	80.00	150.00
	1858E	—	50.00	100.00	200.00	425.00
	1858M	—	37.50	75.00	150.00	300.00
	1858V	—	37.50	75.00	150.00	300.00
	1859A	4.949	20.00	40.00	70.00	125.00
	1859B	—	20.00	40.00	80.00	150.00
	1859E	—	40.00	80.00	160.00	350.00
	1859M	—	37.50	75.00	150.00	300.00
	1860A	1.620	20.00	40.00	70.00	150.00
	1860V	.043	37.50	75.00	150.00	300.00
	1861A	3.140	20.00	40.00	70.00	150.00
	1861B	—	20.00	40.00	75.00	150.00
	1861E	—	20.00	40.00	75.00	150.00
	1861V	—	25.00	50.00	100.00	175.00
	1862A	.998	25.00	50.00	90.00	175.00
	1862B	—	25.00	50.00	85.00	175.00
	1862V	—	25.00	50.00	100.00	175.00
	1863A	2.209	20.00	40.00	70.00	125.00
	1863B	—	25.00	50.00	85.00	175.00
	1863E	—	25.00	50.00	90.00	175.00
	1863V	—	25.00	50.00	100.00	175.00
	1864A	2.636	17.50	35.00	65.00	110.00
	1864B	—	27.50	55.00	100.00	200.00
	1864E	.556	17.50	35.00	65.00	125.00
	1864V	.107	62.50	125.00	250.00	450.00
	1865A	2.085	17.50	35.00	65.00	110.00
	1865B	—	20.00	40.00	75.00	125.00
	1865E	—	17.50	35.00	60.00	100.00
	1865V	—	75.00	150.00	275.00	525.00

NOTE: Varieties in asterisk size on edge exist on 1863 and 1864 dated coins.

Obv: Head w/heavier whiskers.

KM#	Date	Mintage	Fine	VF	XF	Unc
2245	1866A	1.236	25.00	50.00	90.00	150.00
	1866B	Inc. Ab.	35.00	60.00	100.00	175.00
	1866E	Inc. Ab.	40.00	80.00	150.00	275.00
	1867A	.850	30.00	60.00	110.00	200.00
	1867B	Inc. Ab.	40.00	85.00	150.00	275.00
	1867E	Inc. Ab.	40.00	80.00	150.00	275.00
	1868E	.168	— Reported, not confirmed			

2 THALER

37.0371 g, .900 SILVER, 1.0718 oz ASW

KM#	Date	Mintage	Fine	VF	XF	Unc
2249	1865A	7,425	350.00	600.00	1000.	1800.

KM#	Date	Mintage	Fine	VF	XF	Unc
2250	1866A	.010	175.00	350.00	500.00	850.00
	1867A	8,300	175.00	350.00	500.00	850.00

1/2 KRONE

5.5555 g, .900 GOLD, .1608 oz AGW

KM#	Date	Mintage	Fine	VF	XF	Unc
2251	1858A	.020	350.00	650.00	950.00	1400.
	1858E	.025	300.00	525.00	800.00	1200.
	1858V	947 pcs.	1300.	1800.	2250.	3000.
	1859A	.402	275.00	600.00	800.00	1300.
2251	1859B	4,376	350.00	700.00	1100.	1600.
	1859E	.017	350.00	700.00	1100.	1600.
	1860A	.201	175.00	325.00	575.00	850.00
	1860B	.043	325.00	600.00	875.00	1400.
	1861A	2,868	525.00	875.00	1250.	1800.
	1861B	.018	350.00	700.00	1100.	1600.
	1861E	.055	275.00	500.00	700.00	1150.
	1863A	40 pcs.	2000.	4000.	8000.	10,000.
	1864A	980 pcs.	1000.	1500.	2000.	2500.
	1865A	2,690	750.00	1250.	1750.	2250.

KM#	Date	Mintage	Fine	VF	XF	Unc
2252	1866A	4,000	425.00	700.00	1100.	1600.

KRONE

11.1111 g, .900 GOLD, .3215 oz AGW

KM#	Date	Mintage	Fine	VF	XF	Unc
2253	1858A	.047	450.00	800.00	1150.	2250.
	1858E	.031	350.00	575.00	850.00	1500.
	1858V	600 pcs.	1750.	2500.	3500.	4500.
	1859A	.010	350.00	650.00	825.00	1750.
	1859M	3,974	650.00	1250.	1750.	3000.
	1859V	1,885	1250.	2000.	2750.	3500.
	1860A	557 pcs.	875.00	1400.	1750.	3000.
	1861A	2,010	650.00	1100.	1500.	2750.
	1863A	1,000	700.00	1250.	1750.	3000.
	1864A	1,530	650.00	1100.	1400.	2750.
	1865A	2,800	650.00	1100.	1400.	2750.

Obv: Large bust.

KM#	Date	Mintage	Fine	VF	XF	Unc
2255	1866A	3,000	875.00	1500.	2000.	3500.

TRADE COINAGE

4 FLORIN-10 FRANCS

3.2258 g, .900 GOLD, .0933 oz AGW

KM#	Date	Mintage	Fine	VF	XF	Unc
2260	1870	7,440	60.00	100.00	160.00	250.00
	1871	6,665	60.00	100.00	160.00	250.00
	1872	4,960	60.00	90.00	140.00	225.00
	1877	3,004	80.00	160.00	250.00	350.00
	1878	6,820	55.00	90.00	140.00	225.00
	1881	8,370	55.00	90.00	140.00	200.00
	1883	3,720	65.00	120.00	180.00	325.00
	1884	7,518	55.00	90.00	115.00	200.00
	1885	.038	55.00	60.00	110.00	165.00
	1888	4,145	55.00	100.00	140.00	250.00
	1889	5,707	55.00	90.00	135.00	225.00
	1890	2,947	65.00	120.00	180.00	300.00
	1891	.011	55.00	65.00	90.00	175.00
	1892	(restrike)	—	—	BV	55.00

DUCAT

3.4909 g, .986 GOLD, .1106 oz AGW
Obv: Bust right, leg: FRANC. II. D. G. R. . . . . . .
Rev: Crowned imperial eagle.

KM#	Date	Mintage	Fine	VF	XF	Unc
2166	1801A	—	120.00	200.00	290.00	450.00
	1802A	—	110.00	180.00	260.00	400.00
	1802B	—	100.00	160.00	250.00	375.00
	1802G	—	110.00	170.00	250.00	375.00
	1803A	—	120.00	200.00	290.00	450.00
	1804A	—	110.00	180.00	260.00	400.00
	1804E	—	100.00	160.00	250.00	375.00

NOTE: Earlier dates (1792-1800) exist for this type.

Obv. leg: FRANCISCVS II D. G. ROM. . . . .
Rev. leg: . . . . .D. LOTH. VEN. SAL.

KM#	Date	Mintage	Fine	VF	XF	Unc
2167	1804A	—	325.00	650.00	1000.	1750.
	1805A	—	325.00	650.00	1000.	1750.
	1806A	—	300.00	600.00	900.	1600.
	1806B	—	325.00	650.00	1000.	1750.
	1806C	—	750.00	1500.	2250.	3000.
	1806D	—	325.00	650.00	1000.	1750.

Rev. leg: . . . . . D. LO. SAL. WIRC.

KM#	Date	Mintage	Fine	VF	XF	Unc
2168	1806A	—	160.00	250.00	375.00	550.00
	1806D	—	750.00	1250.	1500.	2000.
	1807A	—	125.00	200.00	275.00	450.00
	1807C	—	180.00	275.00	425.00	650.00
	1808A	—	125.00	200.00	275.00	450.00
	1808D	—		—	Rare	—
	1809A	—	125.00	200.00	275.00	450.00
	1809B	—	160.00	250.00	375.00	575.00
	1809D	—	500.00	700.00	950.00	1200.
	1810A	—	125.00	200.00	275.00	450.00

Rev. leg: . . . . . .LO: WI: ET IN. FR: DVX.

KM#	Date	Mintage	Fine	VF	XF	Unc
2169	1811A	—	80.00	120.00	200.00	300.00
	1811B	—	80.00	120.00	200.00	300.00
	1812A	—	80.00	120.00	200.00	300.00
	1812B	—	80.00	120.00	200.00	300.00
	1812G	—		—	Rare	—
	1813A	—	100.00	140.00	225.00	325.00
	1813B	—	80.00	120.00	200.00	300.00
	1813E	—	100.00	140.00	225.00	325.00
	1813G	—		—	Rare	—
	1814A	—	80.00	120.00	200.00	300.00
	1814B	—	100.00	140.00	225.00	325.00
	1814E	—	100.00	140.00	225.00	325.00
	1814G	—		—	Rare	—
	1815A	—	80.00	120.00	200.00	300.00
	1815B	—	80.00	120.00	200.00	300.00
	1815E	—	80.00	120.00	200.00	300.00
	1815G	—	100.00	140.00	225.00	325.00

Rev. leg: . . . . . .GAL. LOB. IL. REX. A. A.

KM#	Date	Mintage	Fine	VF	XF	Unc
2170	1816A	—	100.00	140.00	225.00	350.00
	1817A	—	100.00	140.00	225.00	350.00
	1818A	—	100.00	140.00	225.00	350.00
	1818B	—	100.00	140.00	225.00	350.00
	1818E	—	100.00	140.00	225.00	350.00
	1818G	—	110.00	160.00	275.00	375.00
	1819A	—	100.00	140.00	225.00	350.00
	1819B	—	110.00	160.00	250.00	375.00
	1819E	—	100.00	140.00	225.00	350.00
	1819G	—	110.00	160.00	275.00	375.00
	1819V	—	350.00	525.00	700.00	1050.
	1820A	—	100.00	140.00	225.00	350.00
	1820B	—	100.00	140.00	225.00	350.00
	1820E	—	100.00	140.00	225.00	350.00
	1820G	—	100.00	140.00	225.00	350.00
	1821A	—	100.00	140.00	225.00	350.00
	1821B	—	100.00	140.00	225.00	350.00
	1821E	—	100.00	140.00	225.00	350.00
	1821G	—	100.00	140.00	225.00	350.00
	1822A	—	100.00	140.00	225.00	350.00
	1822B	—	100.00	140.00	225.00	350.00
	1822E	—	100.00	140.00	225.00	350.00
	1822G	—	100.00	140.00	225.00	350.00
	1823A	—	100.00	140.00	225.00	350.00
	1823B	—	100.00	140.00	225.00	350.00
	1823E	—	100.00	140.00	225.00	350.00
	1823G	—	100.00	140.00	225.00	350.00
	1824A	—	100.00	140.00	225.00	350.00
	1824B	—	100.00	140.00	225.00	350.00
	1824E	—	100.00	140.00	225.00	350.00
	1824G	—	110.00	160.00	275.00	375.00
	1824V	—	250.00	375.00	550.00	800.00

Obv: Ribbons on wreath forward across neck.

KM#	Date	Mintage	Fine	VF	XF	Unc
2171	1825A	—	80.00	120.00	200.00	300.00
	1825B	—	100.00	130.00	225.00	325.00
	1825E	—	110.00	160.00	250.00	375.00
	1825G	—	—	—	—	—
	1826A	—	80.00	120.00	200.00	300.00
	1826B	—	110.00	160.00	250.00	375.00
	1826E	—	90.00	130.00	200.00	300.00
2171	1826G	—	—	—	Rare	—
	1827A	—	80.00	120.00	200.00	300.00
	1827B	—	110.00	160.00	250.00	375.00
	1827E	—	110.00	160.00	250.00	375.00
	1828A	—	100.00	130.00	225.00	325.00
	1828B	—	100.00	130.00	200.00	300.00
	1828E	—	90.00	130.00	200.00	300.00
	1829A	—	80.00	120.00	180.00	275.00
	1829B	—	100.00	130.00	200.00	300.00
	1829E	—	90.00	130.00	200.00	300.00
	1830A	—	80.00	120.00	180.00	275.00
	1830B	—	100.00	130.00	200.00	300.00
	1830E	—	90.00	130.00	200.00	300.00
	1831A	—	1100.	1600.	2400.	3200.

Obv: Ribbons on wreath behind neck.

KM#	Date	Mintage	Fine	VF	XF	Unc
2172	1831A	—	110.00	160.00	250.00	375.00
	1832A	—	100.00	130.00	200.00	300.00
	1832B	—	100.00	130.00	225.00	325.00
	1833A	—	100.00	130.00	200.00	300.00
	1833B	—	100.00	130.00	200.00	300.00
	1833E	—	110.00	160.00	250.00	375.00
	1834A	—	100.00	130.00	200.00	300.00
	1834B	—	100.00	130.00	200.00	300.00
	1834E	—	110.00	160.00	250.00	375.00
	1835A	—	100.00	130.00	200.00	300.00
	1835B	—	100.00	130.00	200.00	300.00
	1835E	—	110.00	160.00	250.00	375.00

Obv. leg: . . . . . .AVSTRIAE IMPERATOR.

KM#	Date	Mintage	Fine	VF	XF	Unc
2261	1835A	—	275.00	500.00	800.00	1200.
	1835E	—	275.00	500.00	800.00	1200.
	1836A	—	160.00	275.00	450.00	650.00
	1836E	—	200.00	325.00	525.00	800.00

Obv. leg: . . . . .AVSTRI. IMP.

KM#	Date	Mintage	Fine	VF	XF	Unc
2262	1837A	—	60.00	80.00	130.00	200.00
	1837B	—	80.00	115.00	200.00	275.00
	1837E	—	80.00	115.00	200.00	275.00
	1838A	—	60.00	80.00	200.00	275.00
	1838B	—	80.00	115.00	200.00	275.00
	1838E	—	80.00	115.00	200.00	275.00
	1839A	—	60.00	80.00	130.00	200.00
	1839B	—	80.00	115.00	200.00	275.00
	1839E	—	80.00	115.00	200.00	275.00
	1840A	—	60.00	80.00	130.00	200.00
	1840B	—	60.00	80.00	130.00	200.00
	1840E	—	60.00	80.00	140.00	225.00
	1840V	—	475.00	650.00	975.00	1275.
	1841A	—	60.00	80.00	130.00	200.00
	1841B	—	60.00	80.00	110.00	180.00
	1841E	—	60.00	80.00	110.00	180.00
	1841V	—	250.00	350.00	525.00	725.00
	1842A	—	65.00	100.00	160.00	250.00
	1842B	—	100.00	130.00	200.00	350.00
	1842E	—	60.00	80.00	110.00	180.00
	1842V	—	200.00	275.00	700.00	1000.
	1843A	—	60.00	80.00	110.00	180.00
	1843B	—	60.00	80.00	130.00	200.00
	1843E	—	60.00	80.00	130.00	200.00
	1843V	—	200.00	275.00	700.00	1350.
	1844A	—	60.00	80.00	110.00	180.00
	1844B	—	60.00	80.00	110.00	180.00
	1844E	—	60.00	80.00	110.00	180.00
	1844V	—	200.00	275.00	700.00	1350.
	1845A	—	60.00	80.00	110.00	180.00
	1845B	—	60.00	80.00	110.00	180.00
	1845E	—	60.00	80.00	130.00	200.00
	1845V	—	200.00	275.00	700.00	1200.
	1846A	—	60.00	80.00	130.00	200.00
	1846B	—	60.00	80.00	130.00	200.00
	1846E	—	60.00	80.00	130.00	200.00
	1846V	—	200.00	275.00	700.00	1000.
	1847A	—	60.00	80.00	110.00	180.00
	1847B	—	60.00	80.00	110.00	180.00
	1847E	—	80.00	100.00	180.00	250.00
	1847V	—	250.00	350.00	550.00	775.00
	1848A	—	60.00	80.00	110.00	180.00
	1848B	—	60.00	80.00	110.00	180.00
	1848E	—	60.00	80.00	110.00	180.00
	1848V	—	60.00	80.00	110.00	180.00

KM#	Date	Mintage	Fine	VF	XF	Unc
2263	1852A	—	80.00	100.00	160.00	225.00
	1853A	—	90.00	120.00	180.00	250.00
	1853B	.114	90.00	110.00	180.00	250.00
	1853E	—	100.00	130.00	200.00	250.00
	1854A	—	60.00	80.00	120.00	180.00
	1854B	.087	110.00	135.00	225.00	350.00
	1854E	—	100.00	130.00	200.00	250.00
	1854V	—	250.00	450.00	800.00	1200.
	1855A	—	60.00	80.00	120.00	180.00
	1855B	.133	160.00	225.00	350.00	550.00
	1855E	—	90.00	110.00	180.00	250.00
	1855V	—	250.00	450.00	800.00	1200.
	1856A	—	60.00	80.00	140.00	200.00
	1856B	.121	80.00	110.00	180.00	250.00
	1856E	—	60.00	80.00	140.00	200.00
	1856V	—	250.00	450.00	800.00	1200.
	1857A	—	60.00	80.00	130.00	180.00
	1857B	.086	60.00	80.00	130.00	200.00
	1857E	—	100.00	140.00	225.00	350.00
	1857V	—	250.00	450.00	800.00	1200.
	1858A	—	60.00	80.00	110.00	160.00
	1858B	.071	100.00	130.00	180.00	250.00
	1858E	—	90.00	110.00	180.00	250.00
	1858M	—	275.00	800.00	1750.	2500.
	1858V	—	250.00	450.00	800.00	1200.
	1859A	—	60.00	80.00	110.00	160.00
	1859B	.034	60.00	80.00	140.00	200.00
	1859E	—	60.00	80.00	110.00	180.00
	1859V	—	250.00	450.00	800.00	1200.

KM#	Date	Mintage	Fine	VF	XF	Unc
2264	1860A	—	70.00	100.00	140.00	225.00
	1860B	.056	80.00	120.00	180.00	275.00
	1860E	—	100.00	140.00	200.00	325.00
	1860V	—	250.00	400.00	800.00	1200.
	1861A	—	60.00	80.00	120.00	200.00
	1861B	.121	60.00	100.00	160.00	250.00
	1861E	—	90.00	120.00	200.00	325.00
	1861V	—	325.00	800.00	1750.	2500.
	1862A	—	60.00	80.00	120.00	225.00
	1862B	.068	60.00	90.00	140.00	225.00
	1862E	—	60.00	100.00	160.00	225.00
	1862V	—	200.00	400.00	800.00	1200.
	1863A	—	60.00	80.00	120.00	225.00
	1863B	.058	60.00	80.00	120.00	225.00
	1863E	—	60.00	80.00	120.00	225.00
	1863V	—	175.00	375.00	600.00	1000.
	1864A	—	60.00	100.00	160.00	250.00
	1864B	.099	75.00	120.00	180.00	275.00
	1864E	—	60.00	100.00	160.00	250.00
	1864V	—	275.00	800.00	1750.	2500.
	1865A	—	60.00	100.00	160.00	250.00
	1865B	.081	60.00	100.00	160.00	250.00
	1865E	—	60.00	100.00	160.00	250.00
	1865V	—	250.00	475.00	800.00	1200.

Obv: Head of Franz Joseph I right w/heavier side whiskers.

KM#	Date	Mintage	Fine	VF	XF	Unc
2265	1866A	—	75.00	115.00	200.00	350.00
	1866B	.076	75.00	140.00	225.00	400.00
	1866E	—	75.00	115.00	200.00	350.00
	1866V	—	275.00	575.00	1100.	1700.

KM#	Date	Mintage	Fine	VF	XF	Unc
2266	1867A	—	60.00	90.00	130.00	180.00
	1867B	.112	60.00	100.00	140.00	200.00
	1867E	—	70.00	110.00	160.00	225.00
	1868A	—	60.00	90.00	130.00	180.00
	1869A	—	60.00	90.00	130.00	180.00
	1870A	—	60.00	90.00	130.00	180.00
	1871A	—	60.00	90.00	130.00	180.00
	1872A	—	60.00	90.00	130.00	180.00

KM#	Date	Mintage	Fine	VF	XF	Unc
2267	1872	.460	60.00	100.00	125.00	175.00
	1873	.516	60.00	100.00	125.00	175.00
	1874	.353	60.00	100.00	125.00	175.00
	1875	.184	60.00	100.00	125.00	175.00
	1876	.680	60.00	80.00	125.00	150.00
	1877	.823	60.00	80.00	125.00	175.00
	1878	.281	60.00	80.00	125.00	175.00
	1879	.362	60.00	80.00	125.00	175.00
	1880	.341	60.00	100.00	150.00	225.00
	1881	.477	60.00	80.00	125.00	175.00
	1882	.390	60.00	100.00	125.00	175.00
	1883	.409	60.00	100.00	125.00	175.00
	1884	.238	60.00	80.00	125.00	175.00
	1885	.257	60.00	80.00	125.00	150.00
	1886	.291	60.00	80.00	125.00	150.00
	1887	.223	60.00	80.00	100.00	150.00
	1888	.309	60.00	80.00	100.00	150.00
	1889	.335	60.00	80.00	100.00	150.00
	1890	.374	60.00	80.00	100.00	150.00
	1891	.325	60.00	80.00	100.00	150.00
	1892	.361	60.00	80.00	100.00	150.00
	1893	.285	60.00	80.00	100.00	150.00
	1894	.293	60.00	80.00	100.00	150.00
	1895	.330	60.00	80.00	100.00	150.00
	1896	.414	60.00	80.00	100.00	150.00
	1897	.256	60.00	80.00	100.00	150.00
	1898	.350	60.00	80.00	100.00	150.00
	1899	.412	60.00	80.00	100.00	150.00
	1900	.356	60.00	100.00	125.00	175.00
	1901	.349	60.00	100.00	125.00	175.00
	1902	.311	60.00	100.00	125.00	175.00
	1903	.380	60.00	100.00	125.00	175.00
	1904	.517	60.00	100.00	125.00	175.00
	1905	.392	60.00	125.00	150.00	200.00
	1906	.492	60.00	125.00	150.00	200.00
	1907	.554	60.00	125.00	175.00	250.00
	1908	.409	60.00	80.00	125.00	175.00
	1909	.366	60.00	80.00	100.00	150.00
	1910	.440	60.00	80.00	100.00	150.00
	1911	.591	60.00	80.00	100.00	125.00
	1912	.495	60.00	80.00	100.00	125.00
	1913	.320	60.00	80.00	100.00	125.00
	1914	.378	60.00	80.00	100.00	125.00
	1915 (restrike)*		—	—		*BV + 10%*
	1951 (error for 1915)	—	75.00	125.00	150.00	225.00

NOTE: 996,721 pieces were struck from 1920-1936.

50th Jubilee
Rev: Second date below eagle.

KM#	Date	Mintage	Fine	VF	XF	Unc
2268	1848/1898A	.027	150.00	250.00	350.00	500.00
	1849/1898A	2,292	500.00	1000.	1300.	1800.
	1850/1898A	2,292	500.00	1000.	1300.	1800.
	1851/1898A	2,292	500.00	1000.	1300.	1800.

8 FLORIN-20 FRANCS

6.4516 g, .900 GOLD, .1867 oz AGW
Obv: Joseph I, value below.

KM#	Date	Mintage	Fine	VF	XF	Unc
2269	1870	.025	BV	100.00	175.00	250.00
	1871	.034	BV	100.00	150.00	200.00
	1872	5,185	100.00	175.00	275.00	375.00
	1873	.023	BV	100.00	175.00	250.00
	1874	.042	BV	100.00	150.00	200.00
	1875	.086	BV	100.00	150.00	200.00
	1876	.146	BV	100.00	150.00	200.00
	1877	.125	BV	100.00	150.00	200.00
	1878	.125	BV	100.00	150.00	200.00
	1879	.043	BV	100.00	175.00	250.00
	1880	.062	BV	100.00	150.00	200.00
	1881	.062	BV	100.00	150.00	200.00
	1882	.115	BV	100.00	150.00	200.00
	1883	.031	BV	100.00	150.00	200.00
	1884	.091	BV	100.00	150.00	200.00
	1885	.178	BV	100.00	150.00	200.00
	1886	.140	BV	100.00	150.00	200.00
	1887	.174	BV	100.00	150.00	200.00

KM#	Date	Mintage	Fine	VF	XF	Unc
2269	1888	.114	BV	100.00	150.00	200.00
	1889	.208	BV	100.00	150.00	175.00
	1890	.043	BV	100.00	150.00	200.00
	1891	.019	100.00	150.00	225.00	325.00
	1892	(restrike)	—	—	BV	110.00

2 DUCAT

7.0000 g, .986 GOLD, .2219 oz AGW
Obv: Head right.
Rev: Crowned double-headed eagle.

KM#	Date	Mintage	Fine	VF	XF	Unc
2173	1803A	—	—	—	Rare	—

NOTE: Earlier date (1799) exists for this type.

Similar to 1 Ducat, KM#2167.

KM#	Date	Mintage	Fine	VF	XF	Unc
2179	1804A	—	—	—	Rare	—

4 DUCAT

14.0000 g, .986 GOLD, .4438 oz AGW
Obv. leg: FRANCISCVS II. D. G. R. IMP. . . .
Rev. leg: . . . . .LOTH. M. D. HET.

KM#	Date	Mintage	Fine	VF	XF	Unc
2174	1801A	—	300.00	750.00	1800.	2500.
	1802A	—	300.00	800.00	2000.	3000.
	1803A	—	300.00	750.00	1800.	2500.
	1804A	—	300.00	750.00	1800.	2500.

NOTE: Earlier dates (1793-1800) exist for this date.

Obv. leg: FRANCISCVS II. D. G. ROM. ET. . . .
Rev. leg: . . . . .D. LOTH. VEN. SAL.

KM#	Date	Mintage	Fine	VF	XF	Unc
2175	1804A	—	325.00	900.00	2200.	3000.
	1805A	—	325.00	900.00	2200.	3000.
	1806A	—	300.00	750.00	1800.	2500.

Obv. leg: . . . . .AVSTRIAE IMPERATOR.
Rev. leg: . . . . .D. LO. SAL. WIRC.

KM#	Date	Mintage	Fine	VF	XF	Unc
2176	1807A	—	350.00	1000.	2250.	3200.
	1808A	—	325.00	900.00	2200.	3000.
	1809A	—	300.00	750.00	1800.	2500.
	1810A	—	350.00	1000.	2250.	3200.

Rev. leg: . . . . .LO: WI: ET IN. FR: DVX.

KM#	Date	Mintage	Fine	VF	XF	Unc
2177	1811A	—	300.00	750.00	1600.	2200.
	1812A	—	350.00	800.00	1800.	2500.
	1813A	—	300.00	750.00	1600.	2200.
	1814A	—	350.00	800.00	1800.	2500.
	1815A	—	300.00	750.00	1600.	2200.

Rev. leg: . . . . .GAL. LOD. IL. REX. A. A.

KM#	Date	Mintage	Fine	VF	XF	Unc
2178	1816A	—	300.00	550.00	1500.	2500.
	1817A	—	300.00	550.00	1500.	2500.
	1818A	—	325.00	675.00	1800.	2750.
	1819A	—	300.00	550.00	1500.	2500.
	1820A	—	300.00	550.00	1500.	2500.
	1821A	—	300.00	550.00	1500.	2500.
	1822A	—	300.00	550.00	1500.	2500.
	1823A	—	300.00	550.00	1500.	2500.
	1824A	—	300.00	550.00	1500.	2500.
	1825A	—	250.00	500.00	1200.	2000.
	1826A	—	300.00	550.00	1500.	2500.
	1827A	—	300.00	550.00	1500.	2500.
	1828A	—	250.00	500.00	1275.	2000.
	1829A	—	250.00	500.00	1275.	2000.
	1830A	—	250.00	500.00	1275.	2000.

13.9636 g, .986 GOLD, .4430 oz AGW

KM#	Date	Mintage	Fine	VF	XF	Unc
2270	1835A	—	—	—	Rare	—
	1837A	—	250.00	400.00	1000.	2000.
	1838A	—	250.00	400.00	1000.	2000.
	1839A	—	250.00	400.00	1000.	2000.
	1840A	—	250.00	400.00	1000.	2000.
	1841A	—	250.00	400.00	1000.	2000.
	1842A	—	250.00	400.00	1000.	2000.
	1843A	—	250.00	400.00	1000.	2000.
	1844A	—	250.00	400.00	1000.	2000.
	1845A	—	250.00	400.00	1000.	2000.
	1846A	—	250.00	400.00	1000.	2000.
	1847A	—	250.00	400.00	1000.	2000.
	1848A	4,411	250.00	400.00	1000.	2000.
	1848E	—	250.00	500.00	1250.	2500.

KM#	Date	Mintage	Fine	VF	XF	Unc
2271.1	1852A	—	—	No specimens known		

KM#	Date	Mintage	Fine	VF	XF	Unc
2271.1	1853A	—	—	No specimens known		
	1854A	—	250.00	500.00	1250.	2500.
	1855A	—	250.00	500.00	1250.	2500.
	1856A	—	250.00	500.00	1250.	2500.
	1857A	—	250.00	400.00	1000.	2000.
	1858A	—	250.00	400.00	1000.	2000.
	1859A	.013	250.00	400.00	1000.	2000.

Obv: Laurel wreath w/o berries.

KM#	Date	Mintage	Fine	VF	XF	Unc
2271.2	1854A	—	350.00	850.00	1750.	2100.
	1855A	—	—	—	Rare	—
	1857V	—	800.00	1600.	3000.	4000.

KM#	Date	Mintage	Fine	VF	XF	Unc
2272	1860A	6,303	250.00	600.00	1500.	2750.
	1861A	7,664	250.00	600.00	1500.	2750.
	1862A	8,944	250.00	500.00	1250.	2250.
	1863A	.022	250.00	400.00	1000.	2000.
	1864A	.045	250.00	400.00	1000.	2000.
	1864V	4,463	400.00	800.00	1750.	2750.
	1865A	.013	250.00	400.00	1000.	2000.
	1865V	.010	250.00	400.00	1000.	2000.

Obv: Laureate bust w/heavier side whiskers.

KM#	Date	Mintage	Fine	VF	XF	Unc
2273	1866A	8,463	250.00	500.00	1250.	2250.

KM#	Date	Mintage	Fine	VF	XF	Unc
2274	1867A	.016	250.00	400.00	1000.	2000.
	1868A	.017	250.00	400.00	1000.	2000.
	1869A	.019	250.00	400.00	1000.	2000.
	1870A	.012	250.00	400.00	1000.	2000.
	1871A	.019	250.00	400.00	1000.	2000.
	1872A	*.012	250.00	400.00	1000.	2000.

Obv: Similar to KM#2272, but w/o mint mark.

KM#	Date	Mintage	Fine	VF	XF	Unc
2276	1872	*.012	250.00	525.00	725.00	1200.
	1873	.024	225.00	400.00	600.00	1000.
2276	1874	.015	225.00	325.00	600.00	1000.
	1875	.012	225.00	325.00	600.00	1000.
	1876	5,243	250.00	450.00	800.00	1300.
	1877	5,970	250.00	450.00	800.00	1300.
	1878	.023	225.00	325.00	550.00	800.00
	1879	.029	225.00	325.00	550.00	800.00
	1880	.023	225.00	325.00	550.00	800.00
	1881	.035	225.00	325.00	550.00	800.00
	1882	.029	225.00	325.00	550.00	800.00
	1883	.037	225.00	325.00	550.00	800.00
	1884	.035	225.00	325.00	550.00	800.00
	1885	.028	225.00	325.00	550.00	800.00
	1886	.018	225.00	300.00	525.00	800.00
	1887	.027	225.00	300.00	525.00	800.00
	1888	.036	225.00	300.00	525.00	800.00
	1889	.031	225.00	300.00	525.00	800.00
	1890	.047	225.00	300.00	525.00	750.00
	1891	.054	225.00	300.00	525.00	750.00
	1892	.058	225.00	300.00	525.00	750.00
	1893	.054	225.00	275.00	550.00	800.00
	1894	.035	225.00	275.00	550.00	800.00
	1895	.040	225.00	275.00	550.00	800.00
	1896	.049	225.00	250.00	500.00	800.00
	1897	.035	225.00	275.00	550.00	800.00
	1898	.054	225.00	250.00	500.00	800.00
	1899	.054	225.00	250.00	500.00	600.00
	1900	.047	225.00	250.00	500.00	600.00
	1901	.052	225.00	250.00	450.00	600.00
	1902	.069	225.00	250.00	400.00	600.00
	1903	.073	225.00	250.00	400.00	600.00
	1904	.080	225.00	250.00	400.00	600.00
	1905	.091	225.00	250.00	400.00	550.00
	1906	.123	225.00	250.00	300.00	450.00
	1907	.104	225.00	250.00	300.00	500.00
	1908	.080	225.00	250.00	450.00	600.00
	1909	.084	225.00	250.00	375.00	500.00
	1910	.101	225.00	250.00	275.00	400.00
	1911	.142	225.00	250.00	275.00	350.00
	1912	.151	225.00	250.00	275.00	350.00
	1913	.119	225.00	250.00	275.00	350.00
	1914	.102	225.00	250.00	275.00	350.00
	1915 (restrike)*		—	—	*BV + 8%*	

NOTE: 496,501 pieces were struck from 1920-1936.

TRADE COINAGE

THALER

28.0668 g, .833 SILVER, .7517 oz ASW

KM#	Date	Mintage	Fine	VF	XF	Unc
T1	1780 SF (restrike-1853-present)					
		—	—	—		7.00
	1780 SF	(restrike)	—	Proof		9.00

An unofficial trade dollar, the final date of the famous Maria Theresa Thaler has been restruck intermittently since 1781 to modern times at many world mints. It has been used in many areas that lacked a firm local coinage, particularly in north and east Africa and the Near East. Gunzburg Mint was where the original talers were struck. (Listings for these can be found under Burgau-Austrian States, KM#21-23). Since then the talers have been restruck at the following mints, Vienna, Prague, Milan, Venice, Gunzburg, London, Paris, Brussels, Kremnitz, Karlsburg, Rome, Bombay and Florence with an estimated 800 million struck to date. For original Thaler listings refer to BURGAU.

Period	Mintage	Mint
1920-1937	52,069,465	Vienna
1935-1939	19,496,729	Rome
1935-1957	11,809,956	Paris
1936-1961	20,159,070	London
1937-1957	10,995,024	Brussels
1940-1941	18,864,576	Bombay
1949-1955	3,488,500	Birmingham
1956-1975	9,924,151	Vienna

MONETARY REFORM

1892-1918

100 Heller = 1 Corona

HELLER

BRONZE

KM#	Date	Mintage	Fine	VF	XF	Unc
2800	1892	—	30.00	40.00	80.00	180.00
	1893	29.000	.20	.35	.50	4.00
	1894	30.100	.20	.35	.50	4.00
	1895	49.500	.20	.35	.50	2.00
	1896	15.600	.35	1.50	3.00	6.00
	1897	12.400	.35	2.00	4.00	8.00
	1898	6.780	5.00	10.00	20.00	35.00
	1899	1.901	3.00	12.00	25.00	45.00
	1900	26.981	.20	.50	1.50	4.00
	1901	52.096	.20	.35	.50	2.00
	1902	20.553	.20	.50	1.25	3.00
	1903	13.779	.20	.35	.50	2.50
	1909	12.668	.20	.35	.50	2.50
	1910	21.900	.20	.35	.50	2.50
	1911	18.387	.20	.35	.50	2.50
	1912	27.053	.20	.35	.50	2.50
	1913	8.782	.20	.35	.50	2.50
	1914	9.906	.20	.35	.50	2.50
	1915	5.670	.20	.35	.75	2.50
	1916	12.484	.35	.75	1.50	4.00

Obv: Austrian shield on eagle's breast.

KM#	Date	Mintage	Fine	VF	XF	Unc
2823	1916	Inc. Ab.	4.00	6.00	10.00	17.50

2 HELLER

BRONZE

KM#	Date	Mintage	Fine	VF	XF	Unc
2801	1892	.260	50.00	80.00	150.00	300.00
	1893	41.507	.20	.50	1.75	5.00
	1894	78.036	.15	.25	.75	2.50
	1895	25.610	.20	.50	2.25	6.25
	1896	43.080	.15	.25	.75	3.00
	1897	98.000	.15	.25	.75	2.50
	1898	10.720	.75	1.50	4.00	8.00
	1899	42.734	.15	.25	.75	3.00
	1900	7.942	.50	1.00	3.00	8.00
	1901	12.157	2.00	3.00	6.00	12.50
	1902	18.760	.15	.50	1.50	3.00
	1903	26.983	.50	1.50	3.00	8.00
	1904	12.863	.15	.50	1.75	4.00
	1905	6.679	.75	2.75	5.50	12.50
	1906	20.104	.50	1.00	3.00	8.00
	1907	23.804	.15	.25	.75	3.00
	1908	21.984	.15	.25	.75	3.00
	1909	25.975	.15	.25	.75	3.00
	1910	28.406	.50	1.00	3.00	8.00
	1911	50.007	.15	.25	.50	2.00
	1912	74.234	.15	.20	.25	2.00
	1913	27.432	.35	.75	2.25	6.00
	1914	60.674	.15	.20	.25	2.00
	1915	7.870	.15	.20	.25	2.00

IRON

Obv: Austrian shield on eagle's breast.

KM#	Date	Mintage	Fine	VF	XF	Unc
2824	1916	61.909	.50	1.00	2.00	6.00
	1917	81.186	.25	.50	.75	4.00
	1918	66.353	.25	.50	.75	4.00

10 HELLER

NICKEL

KM#	Date	Mintage	Fine	VF	XF	Unc
2802	1892	—	100.00	175.00	250.00	375.00
	1892	—	—	—	Proof	650.00
	1893	43.524	.25	.50	1.50	3.00
	1894	45.558	.25	.50	1.25	3.00
	1895	79.918	.25	.50	1.00	2.50

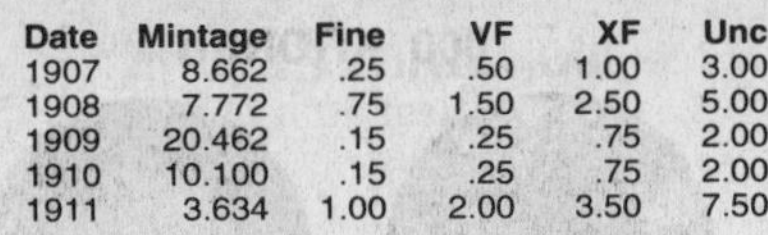

KM#	Date	Mintage	Fine	VF	XF	Unc
2802	1907	8.662	.25	.50	1.00	3.00
	1908	7.772	.75	1.50	2.50	5.00
	1909	20.462	.15	.25	.75	2.00
	1910	10.100	.15	.25	.75	2.00
	1911	3.634	1.00	2.00	3.50	7.50

COPPER-NICKEL-ZINC

KM#	Date	Mintage	Fine	VF	XF	Unc
2822	1915	18.366	.15	.25	.50	1.50
	1916	27.487	.15	.25	.50	1.50

Obv: Austrian shield on eagle's breast.

KM#	Date	Mintage	Fine	VF	XF	Unc
2825	1916	14.804	.50	1.00	2.00	4.00

20 HELLER

NICKEL

KM#	Date	Mintage	Fine	VF	XF	Unc
2803	1892	1.500	7.50	15.00	35.00	75.00
	1892	—	—	—	Proof	250.00
	1893	41.457	.25	.50	1.00	3.00
	1894	50.116	.25	.50	1.00	3.00
	1895	32.927	.25	.35	.50	2.50
	1907	7.650	.75	1.50	3.00	10.00
	1908	7.469	.75	1.25	2.50	8.00
	1909	7.592	1.00	2.00	4.00	10.00
	1911	19.560	.25	.35	.50	2.00
	1914	2.342	5.00	15.00	25.00	50.00

IRON
Obv: Austrian shield on eagle's breast.

KM#	Date	Mintage	Fine	VF	XF	Unc
2826	1916	130.770	.50	1.00	1.50	5.00
	1917	127.420	.50	1.00	1.50	5.00
	1918	48.985	.25	.50	.75	4.00

CORONA

5.0000 g, .835 SILVER, .1342 oz ASW

KM#	Date	Mintage	Fine	VF	XF	Unc
2804	1892	.235	80.00	160.00	250.00	425.00
	1893	50.124	1.75	3.00	5.00	10.00
	1894	28.003	1.75	3.00	5.00	12.00
	1895	15.115	3.75	6.00	12.00	20.00
	1896	3.068	7.50	15.00	25.00	50.00
	1897	2.142	20.00	30.00	60.00	100.00
	1898	5.855	2.50	5.00	8.00	15.00
	1899	11.820	1.75	2.75	5.00	10.00
	1900	3.745	2.50	5.00	8.00	14.00
	1901	10.387	1.75	2.75	5.00	10.00
	1902	2.947	2.00	4.25	7.50	14.00
	1903	2.198	2.00	4.25	7.50	14.00
	1904	.993	4.00	8.50	17.50	25.00
	1905	.505	10.00	25.00	50.00	75.00
	1906	.165	80.00	125.00	200.00	300.00
	1907	.244	30.00	60.00	100.00	200.00

60th Anniversary of Reign

KM#	Date	Mintage	Fine	VF	XF	Unc
2808	1908	4.784	2.00	3.00	5.00	10.00

KM#	Date	Mintage	Fine	VF	XF	Unc
2820	1912	8.457	1.50	2.00	3.00	8.00
	1913	9.345	1.50	2.00	3.00	7.00
	1914	37.897	1.50	2.00	3.00	6.00
	1915	23.000	1.50	2.00	3.00	6.00
	1916	12.415	1.50	2.00	3.00	6.00

2 CORONA

10.0000 g, .835 SILVER, .2684 oz ASW

KM#	Date	Mintage	Fine	VF	XF	Unc
2821	1912	10.245	3.50	5.00	7.00	10.00
	1913	7.256	3.50	5.00	7.00	10.00

5 CORONA

24.0000 g, .900 SILVER, .6945 oz ASW

KM#	Date	Mintage	Fine	VF	XF	Unc
2807	1900	8.525	8.00	12.50	25.00	65.00
	1907	1.539	10.00	15.00	30.00	90.00
	1907	—	—	—	Proof	500.00

60th Anniversary of Reign

KM#	Date	Mintage	Fine	VF	XF	Unc
2809	1908	5.090	8.00	12.50	25.00	55.00
	1908	—	—	—	Proof	500.00

Obv: Large head.

KM#	Date	Mintage	Fine	VF	XF	Unc
2813	1909	1.709	10.00	15.00	35.00	95.00

Obv: Similar to KM#2809.
Rev: Similar to KM#2807.

KM#	Date	Mintage	Fine	VF	XF	Unc
2814	1909	1.776	10.00	15.00	35.00	75.00

10 CORONA

3.3875 g, .900 GOLD, .0980 oz AGW
Obv: Laureate head of Franz Joseph I right.
Rev: Eagle w/value and date below.

KM#	Date	Mintage	Fine	VF	XF	Unc
2805	1892	—	1000.	1500.	2500.	3500.
	1893	—	—	—	Rare	—
	1896	.211	BV	55.00	60.00	80.00
	1897	1.803	BV	55.00	60.00	90.00
	1905	1.933	BV	55.00	60.00	90.00
	1906	1.081	BV	55.00	60.00	90.00

60th Anniversary of Reign
Obv: Small plain head of Franz Joseph I right.
Rev: Eagle, value below, 2 dates above.

KM#	Date	Mintage	Fine	VF	XF	Unc
2810	1908	.654	BV	60.00	70.00	100.00

Rev: Eagle, value and date below.

KM#	Date	Mintage	Fine	VF	XF	Unc
2815	1909	2.320	BV	55.00	60.00	80.00

Obv: Large head.

KM#	Date	Mintage	Fine	VF	XF	Unc
2816	1909	.192	55.00	60.00	80.00	100.00
	1910	1.005	BV	50.00	60.00	80.00
	1911	1.286	BV	50.00	60.00	80.00
	1912	(restrike)	—	—		*BV + 10%*

20 CORONA

6.7751 g, .900 GOLD, .1960 oz AGW

KM#	Date	Mintage	Fine	VF	XF	Unc
2806	1892	.653	—	BV	125.00	150.00
	1893	7.872	—	BV	100.00	115.00
	1894	6.714	—	BV	100.00	115.00
	1895	2.266	—	BV	100.00	115.00
	1896	6.868	—	BV	100.00	115.00
	1897	5.133	—	BV	100.00	115.00

KM#	Date	Mintage	Fine	VF	XF	Unc
2806	1898	1.874	—	BV	100.00	115.00
	1899	.098	100.00	110.00	130.00	150.00
	1900	.027	200.00	400.00	600.00	800.00
	1901	.049	150.00	225.00	325.00	400.00
	1902	.441	BV	110.00	140.00	160.00
	1903	.323	BV	110.00	140.00	160.00
	1904	.494	BV	110.00	140.00	160.00
	1905	.146	100.00	120.00	150.00	170.00

60th Anniversary of Reign
Rev: 2 dates above eagle.

KM#	Date	Mintage	Fine	VF	XF	Unc
2811	1908	.188	100.00	125.00	150.00	200.00

KM#	Date	Mintage	Fine	VF	XF	Unc
2817	1909	.228	450.00	750.00	1250.	1750.

KM#	Date	Mintage	Fine	VF	XF	Unc
2818	1909	.102	575.00	850.00	1250.	1750.
	1910	.386	120.00	150.00	250.00	350.00
	1911	.059	125.00	175.00	275.00	375.00
	1912	4,460	250.00	325.00	400.00	500.00
	1913	.028	350.00	500.00	750.00	1000.
	1914	.082	135.00	225.00	300.00	500.00
	1915	(restrike)	—	—		*BV + 5%*
	1916	.072	2500.	3500.	5500.	7500.

Rev: Austrian shield on eagle.

KM#	Date	Mintage	Fine	VF	XF	Unc
2827	1916	Inc. Ab.	450.00	550.00	900.00	1200.

Obv: Head of Kaiser Karl I. Rev: Similar to KM#2818.

KM#	Date	Mintage	Fine	VF	XF	Unc
2828	1918	*2,000	—	—	Unique	—

***NOTE:** All but one specimen were remelted.

100 CORONA

33.8753 g, .900 GOLD, .9803 oz AGW
60th Anniversary of Reign

KM#	Date	Mintage	Fine	VF	XF	Unc
2812	1908	.016	500.00	600.00	900.00	1300.
	1908	—	—	—	Proof	1750.

KM#	Date	Mintage	Fine	VF	XF	Unc
2819	1909	3,203	500.00	650.00	950.00	1400.
	1910	3,074	500.00	650.00	950.00	1400.
	1911	11,165	500.00	650.00	950.00	1400.
	1912	3,591	550.00	850.00	1150.	1900.
	1913	2,696	500.00	800.00	1200.	1650.
	1914	1,195	500.00	650.00	1000.	1500.
	1915	(restrike)	—	—		*BV + 2%*
	1915	(restrike)	—	—	Proof	—

REPUBLIC

MONETARY SYSTEM

10,000 Kronen = 1 Schilling

20 KRONEN

6.7751 g, .900 GOLD, .1960 oz AGW

KM#	Date	Mintage	Fine	VF	XF	Unc
2830	1923	6,988	700.00	1500.	2000.	2500.
	1924	10,337	700.00	1500.	2000.	2500.

100 KRONEN

33.8753 g, .900 GOLD, .9802 oz AGW

KM#	Date	Mintage	Fine	VF	XF	Unc
2831	1923	617 pcs.	750.00	1250.	2000.	2500.
	1923	—	—	—	Proof	2750.
	1924	2,851	750.00	1250.	2000.	2500.

BRONZE

KM#	Date	Mintage	Fine	VF	XF	Unc
2832	1923	6.404	4.00	8.00	15.00	30.00
	1924	43.014	.25	.50	1.50	4.00

200 KRONEN

BRONZE

KM#	Date	Mintage	Fine	VF	XF	Unc
2833	1924	57.160	.50	1.00	2.00	6.00

1000 KRONEN

COPPER-NICKEL

KM#	Date	Mintage	Fine	VF	XF	Unc
2834	1924	72.353	.75	1.50	3.00	7.50

PRE WWII DECIMAL COINAGE

100 Groschen = 1 Schilling

GROSCHEN

BRONZE

KM#	Date	Mintage	Fine	VF	XF	Unc
2836	1925	30.465	.10	.20	.50	2.00
	1926	15.487	.10	.30	.75	2.00
	1927	9.318	.10	.30	.75	2.50
	1928	17.189	.10	.30	.75	2.50
	1929	11.400	.10	.30	.75	2.50
	1930	8.893	.10	.30	.75	2.50
	1931	.971	10.00	20.00	30.00	60.00
	1932	3.040	1.00	2.50	5.00	7.50
	1933	3.940	.50	1.00	2.00	6.00
	1934	4.232	.15	.50	1.00	4.00
	1935	3.740	.15	.50	1.00	4.00
	1936	6.020	.50	1.00	3.00	9.00
	1937	5.830	.50	1.00	2.00	7.50
	1938	1.650	2.00	3.00	6.00	15.00

2 GROSCHEN

BRONZE

KM#	Date	Mintage	Fine	VF	XF	Unc
2837	1925	29.892	.10	.25	.50	1.50
	1926	17.700	.10	.30	.75	2.00
	1927	7.757	.20	.75	2.00	5.00
	1928	19.478	.10	.30	.75	2.00
	1929	16.184	.10	.30	.75	2.00
	1930	5.709	.20	.60	1.50	4.00
	1934	.812	7.00	12.00	15.00	25.00
	1935	3.148	.20	.60	1.50	4.00
	1936	4.410	.15	.30	1.00	3.00
	1937	3.790	.20	.40	1.25	3.50
	1938	.860	2.50	4.00	6.50	12.50

5 GROSCHEN

COPPER-NICKEL

KM#	Date	Mintage	Fine	VF	XF	Unc
2846	1931	16.631	.15	.40	.80	2.00
	1932	4.700	.25	1.00	2.00	5.00
	1934	3.210	.30	1.00	2.50	6.00
	1936	1.240	2.00	4.00	7.50	15.00
	1937	1.540	20.00	30.00	45.00	80.00
	1938	.870	125.00	175.00	250.00	425.00

10 GROSCHEN

COPPER-NICKEL

KM#	Date	Mintage	Fine	VF	XF	Unc
2838	1925	66.199	.10	.25	.50	3.00
	1928	11.468	.50	1.00	4.00	12.00
	1929	12.000	.40	.75	1.50	4.00

1/2 SCHILLING

3.0000 g, .640 SILVER, .0617 oz ASW

KM#	Date	Mintage	Fine	VF	XF	Unc
2839	1925	18.370	1.00	2.00	3.00	7.50
	1926	12.943	2.50	4.00	6.00	11.00

50 GROSCHEN

COPPER-NICKEL

KM#	Date	Mintage	Fine	VF	XF	Unc
2850	1934	8.225	20.00	35.00	50.00	90.00
	1934	Inc. Ab.	—	—	Proof	125.00

KM#	Date	Mintage	Fine	VF	XF	Unc
2854	1935	11.435	.50	.75	1.50	3.00
	1935	Inc. Ab.	—	—	Proof	80.00
	1936	1.000	30.00	40.00	60.00	115.00
	1936	Inc. Ab.	—	—	Proof	140.00

SCHILLING

7.0000 g, .800 SILVER, .1800 oz ASW

KM#	Date	Mintage	Fine	VF	XF	Unc
2835	1924	11.086	1.25	2.00	3.00	7.00

6.0000 g, .640 SILVER, .1235 oz ASW

KM#	Date	Mintage	Fine	VF	XF	Unc
2840	1925	38.209	1.25	2.00	3.00	6.00
	1926	20.157	1.25	2.00	4.00	8.00
	1932	.700	30.00	40.00	60.00	100.00

COPPER-NICKEL

KM#	Date	Mintage	Fine	VF	XF	Unc
2851	1934	30.641	.75	1.50	3.00	7.00
	1934	—	—	—	Proof	150.00
	1935	11.987	3.00	6.00	12.50	30.00

2 SCHILLING

12.0000 g, .640 SILVER, .2469 oz ASW
Centennial of Death of Franz Schubert

KM#	Date	Mintage	Fine	VF	XF	Unc
2843	1928	6.900	4.00	5.00	6.00	10.00
	1928	Inc. Ab.	—	—	Proof	275.00

100th Anniversary of Birth of Dr. Theodor Billroth

KM#	Date	Mintage	Fine	VF	XF	Unc
2844	1929	2.000	6.00	8.00	14.00	27.50

7th Centennial of Death
of Walther von der Vogelweide

KM#	Date	Mintage	Fine	VF	XF	Unc
2845	1930	.500	5.00	6.00	7.50	12.50
	1930	Inc. Ab.	—	—	Proof	115.00

175th Anniversary of Birth of Wolfgang Mozart

KM#	Date	Mintage	Fine	VF	XF	Unc
2847	1931	.500	8.00	14.00	18.00	27.50
	1931	Inc. Ab.	—	—	Proof	200.00

200th Anniversary of Birth of Joseph Haydn

KM#	Date	Mintage	Fine	VF	XF	Unc
2848	1932	.300	20.00	30.00	50.00	80.00
	1932	Inc. Ab.	—	—	Proof	350.00

Death of Dr. Ignaz Seipel

KM#	Date	Mintage	Fine	VF	XF	Unc
2849	ND(1933)	.400	10.00	15.00	25.00	45.00
	1933	Inc. Ab.	—	—	Proof	300.00

Death of Dr. Engelbert Dollfuss

KM#	Date	Mintage	Fine	VF	XF	Unc
2852	1934	1.500	7.00	11.00	16.00	25.00
	1934	Inc. Ab.	—	—	Proof	190.00

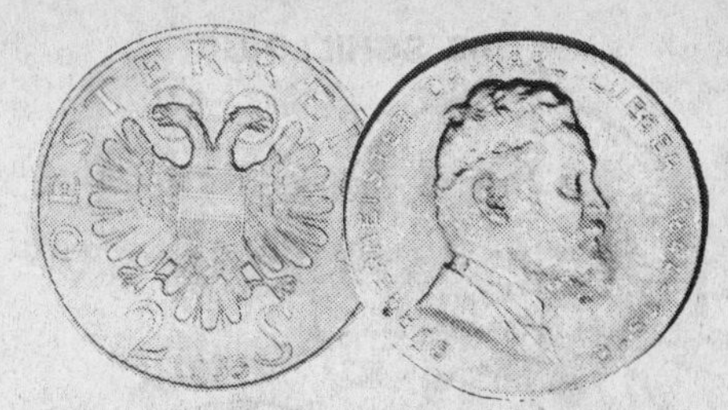

Dr. Karl Lueger

KM#	Date	Mintage	Fine	VF	XF	Unc
2855	1935	.500	8.00	12.50	17.50	27.50
	1935	Inc. Ab.	—	—	Proof	180.00

Bicentennial of Death of Prince Eugen of Savoy

KM#	Date	Mintage	Fine	VF	XF	Unc
2858	1936	.500	6.00	8.00	12.00	20.00
	1936	Inc. Ab.	—	—	Proof	160.00

Bicentennial of Completion of St. Charles Church

KM#	Date	Mintage	Fine	VF	XF	Unc
2859	1937	.500	6.00	8.00	12.00	20.00
	1937	Inc. Ab.	—	—	Proof	135.00

5 SCHILLING

15.0000 g, .835 SILVER, .4027 oz ASW
Madonna of Mariazell

KM#	Date	Mintage	Fine	VF	XF	Unc
2853	1934	3.066	12.50	18.50	22.50	40.00
	1934	—	—	—	Proof	200.00
	1935	5.377	12.50	18.50	22.50	40.00
	1936	1.557	40.00	75.00	100.00	180.00

25 SCHILLING

5.8810 g, .900 GOLD, .1702 oz AGW

KM#	Date	Mintage	Fine	VF	XF	Unc
2841	1926	.276	—	—	P/L	125.00
	1927	.073	—	—	P/L	165.00
	1928	.134	—	—	P/L	125.00
	1929	.243	—	—	P/L	125.00
	1930	.130	—	—	P/L	125.00
	1931	.169	—	—	P/L	125.00
	1933	4,944	—	—	P/L	1750.
	1934	.011	—	—	P/L	575.00

St. Leopold

KM#	Date	Mintage	Fine	VF	XF	Unc
2856	1935	2,880	—	—	P/L	600.00
	1936	7,260	—	—	P/L	550.00
	1937	7,660	—	—	P/L	550.00
	1938	1,360	—	—	P/L	15,000.

100 SCHILLING

23.5245 g, .900 GOLD, .6806 oz AGW

KM#	Date	Mintage	Fine	VF	XF	Unc
2842	1926	.064	—	—	P/L	480.00
	1927	.069	—	—	P/L	480.00
	1928	.040	—	—	P/L	480.00
	1929	.075	—	—	P/L	480.00
	1930	.025	—	—	P/L	480.00
	1931	.102	—	—	P/L	480.00
	1933	4,700	—	—	P/L	1200.
	1934	9,383	—	—	P/L	500.00

Madonna of Mariazell

KM#	Date	Mintage	Fine	VF	XF	Unc
2857	1935	951 pcs.	—	—	P/L	2500.
	1936	.012	—	—	P/L	1400.
	1937	2,900	—	—	P/L	1500.
	1938	1,400	—	—	P/L	12,000.

GERMAN OCCUPATION

1938-1945

MONETARY SYSTEM

150 Schillings = 100 Reichsmark

NOTE: During this time period German Reichsmark coins and banknotes circulated.

POST WWII DECIMAL COINAGE

100 Groschen = 1 Schilling

GROSCHEN

ZINC

KM#	Date	Mintage	Fine	VF	XF	Unc
2873	1947	23.574	—	.10	.25	1.00

2 GROSCHEN

ALUMINUM

KM#	Date	Mintage	VF	XF	Unc
2876	1950	21.600	.10	.25	.50
	1950	—	—	Proof	15.00
	1951	7.370	.20	.50	1.00
	1951	—	—	Proof	30.00
	1952	37.800	.10	.25	.50
	1952	—	—	Proof	15.00
	1954	20.000	.10	.25	.50
	1954	—	—	Proof	30.00
	1957	21.300	.10	.25	.50
	1957	—	—	Proof	30.00
	1962	5.430	.15	.25	.50
	1962	—	—	Proof	17.50
	1964	.173	—	Proof	3.00
	1965	14.475	.10	.15	.25
2876	1965	—	—	Proof	2.00
	1966	7.454	.10	.15	.25
	1966	—	—	Proof	4.00
	1967	.013	—	Proof	50.00
	1968	1.803	.10	.15	.25
	1968	.022	—	Proof	.75
	1969	.057	—	Proof	.75
	1970	.260	—	Proof	.50
	1971	.145	—	Proof	.50
	1972	2.763	—	.10	.20
	1972	.132	—	Proof	.50
	1973	5.883	—	.10	.20
	1973	.149	—	Proof	.50
	1974	1.387	—	.10	.20
	1974	.093	—	Proof	.50
	1975	1.394	—	.10	.20
	1975	.052	—	Proof	.50
	1976	3.309	—	—	.10
	1976	.045	—	Proof	.50
	1977	3.674	—	—	.10
	1977	.047	—	Proof	.50
	1978	1.560	—	—	.10
	1978	.043	—	Proof	.50
	1979	2.473	—	—	.10
	1979	.044	—	Proof	.50
	1980	1.861	—	—	.10
	1980	.048	—	Proof	.50
	1981	.981	—	—	.10
	1981	.049	—	Proof	.50
	1982	3.967	—	—	.10
	1982	.050	—	Proof	.50
	1983	2.665	—	—	.10
	1983	.065	—	Proof	.50
	1984	.564	—	—	.10
	1984	.065	—	Proof	.50
	1985	1.060	—	—	.10
	1985	.045	—	Proof	.50
	1986	1.800	—	—	.10
	1986	.042	—	Proof	.50
	1987	1.000	—	—	.10
	1987	.042	—	Proof	.50
	1988	1.100	—	—	.10
	1988	.039	—	Proof	.50
	1989	.999	—	—	.10
	1989	.038	—	Proof	.50
	1990	.035	—	Proof	.50
	1991	2.600	—	—	.10
	1991	.027	—	Proof	.50
	1992	.025	—	—	.10
	1993	.035	—	—	.10

5 GROSCHEN

ZINC

KM#	Date	Mintage	VF	XF	Unc
2875	1948	17.200	.15	.50	1.25
	1950	19.400	.15	.50	1.25
	1950	—	—	Proof	10.00
	1951	12.400	.15	.50	1.25
	1951	—	—	Proof	10.00
	1953	84.900	.10	.50	1.00
	1955	17.000	.10	.50	1.00
	1957	20.700	.10	.50	1.00
	1957	—	—	Proof	20.00
	1961	3.420	.15	.75	1.50
	1961	—	—	Proof	15.00
	1962	5.990	.15	.50	1.50
	1963	13.295	.10	.25	1.00
	1963	—	—	Proof	10.00
	1964	4.659	.10	.25	1.00
	1964	—	—	Proof	.50
	1965	13.704	.10	.15	.25
	1965	—	—	Proof	.50
	1966	9.348	.10	.15	.25
	1966	—	—	Proof	3.00
	1967	4.404	.10	.15	.25
	1967	—	—	Proof	3.00
	1968	31.422	—	.10	.15
	1968	.016	—	Proof	2.00
	1969	—	—	.10	.15
	1969	.040	—	Proof	2.00
	1970	—	—	.10	.15
	1970	.144	—	Proof	.50
	1971	—	—	.10	.25
	1971	.125	—	Proof	.50
	1972	10.879	—	—	.10
	1972	.116	—	Proof	.50
	1973	10.336	—	—	.10
	1973	.120	—	Proof	.50
	1974	2.911	—	—	.10
	1974	.087	—	Proof	.50
	1975	7.559	—	—	.10
	1975	.051	—	Proof	.50
	1976	12.230	—	—	.10
	1976	.045	—	Proof	.50
	1977	3.200	—	—	.10
	1977	.045	—	Proof	.50
	1978	2.690	—	—	.10
	1978	.043	—	Proof	.50
	1979	4.966	—	—	.10
	1979	.044	—	Proof	.50
	1980	3.068	—	—	.10
	1980	.048	—	Proof	.50
2875	1981	.481	—	—	.10
	1981	.049	—	Proof	.50
	1982	3.967	—	—	.10
	1982	.050	—	Proof	.50
	1983	.501	—	—	.10
	1983	.065	—	Proof	.50
	1984	1.052	—	—	.10
	1984	.065	—	Proof	.50
	1985	1.910	—	—	.10
	1985	.045	—	Proof	.50
	1986	1.010	—	—	.10
	1986	.042	—	Proof	.50
	1987	1.500	—	—	.10
	1987	.042	—	Proof	.50
	1988	1.300	—	—	.10
	1988	.039	—	Proof	.50
	1989	2.640	—	—	.10
	1989	.038	—	Proof	.50
	1990	2.610	—	—	.10
	1990	.035	—	Proof	.50
	1991	2.400	—	—	.10
	1991	.027	—	Proof	.50
	1992	.670	—	—	.10
	1993	.035	—	—	.10

10 GROSCHEN

ZINC

KM#	Date	Mintage	Fine	VF	XF	Unc
2874	1947	6.840	.50	1.50	3.00	10.00
	1947	—	—	—	Proof	20.00
	1948	66.200	—	.10	.50	3.00
	1948	—	—	—	Proof	30.00
	1949	51.200	—	.10	.50	3.00
	1949	—	—	—	Proof	35.00

ALUMINUM

KM#	Date	Mintage	VF	XF	Unc
2878	1951	9.570	.20	.50	2.25
	1951	—	—	Proof	75.00
	1952	45.900	.10	.25	1.00
	1952	—	—	Proof	20.00
	1953	39.000	.10	.25	1.00
	1953	—	—	Proof	75.00
	1955	27.500	.10	.25	1.00
	1955	—	—	Proof	15.00
	1957	33.500	.10	.20	1.00
	1957	—	—	Proof	50.00
	1959	80.700	.10	.20	.75
	1959	—	—	Proof	30.00
	1961	11.100	.10	.25	.75
	1961	—	—	Proof	—
	1962	24.600	.10	.20	.75
	1962	—	—	Proof	25.00
	1963	38.062	.10	.20	.60
	1963	—	—	Proof	10.00
	1964	34.928	.10	.20	.45
	1964	—	—	Proof	.50
	1965	40.615	.10	.20	.40
	1965	—	—	Proof	.50
	1966	24.991	.10	.15	.35
	1966	—	—	Proof	3.00
	1967	32.553	—	.15	.30
	1967	—	—	Proof	2.00
	1968	42.396	—	.10	.25
	1968	.016	—	Proof	2.00
	1969	19.953	—	.10	.25
	1969	.027	—	Proof	.75
	1970	36.998	—	.10	.25
	1970	.102	—	Proof	.50
	1971	57.450	—	.10	.25
	1971	.082	—	Proof	.50
	1972	75.661	—	.10	.25
	1972	.081	—	Proof	.50
	1973	60.244	—	.10	.25
	1973	.097	—	Proof	.50
	1974	55.924	—	.10	.15
	1974	.078	—	Proof	.50
	1975	70.196	—	.10	.15
	1975	.049	—	Proof	.50
	1976	42.379	—	.10	.15
	1976	.044	—	Proof	.50
	1977	107.264	—	.10	.15
	1977	.044	—	Proof	.50
	1978	57.890	—	.10	.15
	1978	.043	—	Proof	.50
	1979	103.724	—	—	.15
	1979	.044	—	Proof	.50
	1980	79.816	—	—	.15
	1980	.048	—	Proof	.50
	1981	92.299	—	—	.15

KM#	Date	Mintage	VF	XF	Unc
2878	1981	.049	—	Proof	.50
	1982	99.967	—	—	.15
	1982	.050	—	Proof	.50
	1983	93.768	—	—	.15
	1983	.065	—	Proof	.50
	1984	86.667	—	—	.15
	1984	.065	—	Proof	.50
	1985	86.300	—	—	.15
	1985	.045	—	Proof	.50
	1986	108.910	—	—	.15
	1986	.042	—	Proof	.50
	1987	114.100	—	—	.15
	1987	.042	—	Proof	.50
	1988	114.500	—	—	.15
	1988	.039	—	Proof	.50
	1989	127.820	—	—	.15
	1989	.038	—	Proof	.50
	1990	182.050	—	—	.15
	1990	.035	—	Proof	.50
	1991	.145	—	—	.15
	1991	.027	—	Proof	.50
	1992	.120	—	—	.15
	1993	—	—	—	.15

20 GROSCHEN

ALUMINUM-BRONZE

KM#	Date	Mintage	Fine	VF	XF	Unc
2877	1950	1.610	.10	.25	.50	6.50
	1950	—	—	—	Proof	25.00
	1951	7.780	.10	.25	.50	2.00
	1951	—	—	—	Proof	25.00
	1954	5.340	.10	.25	.50	2.00
	1954	—	—	—	Proof	100.00

50 GROSCHEN

ALUMINUM

KM#	Date	Mintage	Fine	VF	XF	Unc
2870	1946	13.000	.10	.25	.50	1.75
	1946	—	—	—	Proof	60.00
	1947	26.900	.10	.25	.50	1.25
	1947	—	—	—	Proof	20.00
	1952	7.450	.40	1.00	2.00	5.00
	1952	—	—	—	Proof	35.00
	1955	10.500	.20	.40	.75	3.50
	1955	—	—	—	Proof	30.00

ALUMINUM-BRONZE

KM#	Date	Mintage	VF	XF	Unc
2885	1959	14.100	.10	.20	.50
	1959	—	—	Proof	15.00
	1960	22.400	.10	.20	.50
	1960	—	—	Proof	35.00
	1961	19.800	.10	.20	.50
	1961	—	—	Proof	30.00
	1962	10.000	.10	.25	.75
	1962	—	—	Proof	30.00
	1963	9.483	.10	.15	.50
	1963	—	—	Proof	15.00
	1964	5.331	.10	.25	.75
	1964	—	—	Proof	.75
	1965	15.007	—	.15	.40
	1965	—	—	Proof	1.00
	1966	7.322	.10	.15	.40
	1966	—	—	Proof	5.00
	1967	8.237	.10	.10	.40
	1967	—	—	Proof	7.00
	1968	7.742	—	.10	.25
	1968	.015	—	Proof	3.00
	1969	7.076	—	.10	.25
	1969	.026	—	Proof	1.00
	1970	2.994	—	.10	.20
	1970	.129	—	Proof	.50
	1971	14.217	—	.10	.15
	1971	.084	—	Proof	.50
	1972	17.367	—	.10	.15
	1972	.080	—	Proof	.50
	1973	17.902	—	.10	.15
	1973	.090	—	Proof	.50
	1974	15.852	—	.10	.15
	1974	.076	—	Proof	.50
	1975	9.916	—	.10	.15
	1975	.049	—	Proof	.50

KM#	Date	Mintage	VF	XF	Unc
2885	1976	12.396	—	.10	.15
	1976	.044	—	Proof	.50
	1977	14.516	—	.10	.15
	1977	.044	—	Proof	.50
	1978	12.440	—	.10	.15
	1978	.043	—	Proof	.50
	1979	16.389	—	—	.15
	1979	.044	—	Proof	.50
	1980	29.852	—	—	.15
	1980	.048	—	Proof	.50
	1981	13.024	—	—	.15
	1981	.049	—	Proof	.50
	1982	9.967	—	—	.15
	1982	.050	—	Proof	.50
	1983	15.182	—	—	.15
	1983	.065	—	Proof	.50
	1984	20.740	—	—	.15
	1984	.065	—	Proof	.50
	1985	15.650	—	—	.15
	1985	.045	—	Proof	.50
	1986	17.020	—	—	.15
	1986	.042	—	Proof	.50
	1987	7.300	—	—	.15
	1987	.042	—	Proof	.50
	1988	16.300	—	—	.15
	1988	.039	—	Proof	.50
	1989	17.390	—	—	.15
	1989	.038	—	Proof	.50
	1990	29.650	—	—	.15
	1990	.035	—	Proof	.50
	1991	44.990	—	—	.15
	1991	.027	—	Proof	.50
	1992	20.000	—	—	.15
	1993	20.000	—	—	.15

SCHILLING

ALUMINUM

KM#	Date	Mintage	Fine	VF	XF	Unc
2871	1946	27.300	.20	.35	.50	1.50
	1946	—	—	—	Proof	135.00
	1947	35.800	.20	.35	.50	1.50
	1947	—	—	—	Proof	25.00
	1952	23.300	.25	.50	.75	2.50
	1952	—	—	—	Proof	50.00
	1957	28.600	.25	.50	.75	3.00
	1957	—	—	—	Proof	90.00

ALUMINUM-BRONZE

KM#	Date	Mintage	VF	XF	Unc
2886	1959	46.700	.15	.25	.75
	1959	—	—	Proof	10.00
	1960	46.100	.15	.25	.75
	1960	—	—	Proof	25.00
	1961	51.100	.15	.25	.75
	1961	—	—	Proof	20.00
	1962	9.300	.20	.35	1.00
	1962	—	—	Proof	25.00
	1963	24.845	.15	.25	.75
	1963	—	—	Proof	20.00
	1964	11.709	.20	.35	1.00
	1964	—	—	Proof	1.50
	1965	23.925	.15	.20	.40
	1965	—	—	Proof	1.50
	1966	18.688	.15	.20	.75
	1966	—	—	Proof	7.00
	1967	22.214	.10	.15	.40
	1967	—	—	Proof	9.00
	1968	30.860	.10	.15	.35
	1968	.017	—	Proof	5.00
	1969	10.285	.10	.15	.35
	1969	.028	—	Proof	3.00
	1970	10.679	.10	.15	.25
	1970	.100	—	Proof	1.00
	1971	27.974	.10	.15	.20
	1971	.082	—	Proof	.75
	1972	54.577	.10	.15	.20
	1972	.078	—	Proof	.75
	1973	41.332	.10	.15	.20
	1973	.090	—	Proof	.75
	1974	43.712	.10	.15	.20
	1974	.077	—	Proof	.75
	1975	18.564	.10	.15	.20
	1975	.049	—	Proof	.75
	1976	37.642	.10	.15	.20
	1976	.044	—	Proof	.75
	1977	39.172	.10	.15	.20
	1977	.044	—	Proof	.75
	1978	35.665	—	.10	.20

KM#	Date	Mintage	VF	XF	Unc
2886	1978	.043	—	Proof	.75
	1979	64.840	—	.10	.20
	1979	.044	—	Proof	.75
	1980	49.823	—	.10	.20
	1980	.048	—	Proof	2.50
	1981	37.533	—	.10	.20
	1981	.049	—	Proof	1.50
	1982	29.967	—	—	.20
	1982	.050	—	Proof	.75
	1983	38.186	—	—	.20
	1983	.065	—	Proof	.75
	1984	31.995	—	—	.20
	1984	.065	—	Proof	.75
	1985	49.150	—	—	.20
	1985	.045	—	Proof	.75
	1986	57.580	—	—	.20
	1986	.042	—	Proof	.75
	1987	44.200	—	—	.20
	1987	.042	—	Proof	.75
	1988	51.600	—	—	.20
	1988	.039	—	Proof	1.50
	1989	62.860	—	—	.20
	1989	.038	—	Proof	.75
	1990	103.710	—	—	.20
	1990	.035	—	Proof	.75
	1991	117.700	—	—	.20
	1991	.027	—	Proof	.75
	1992	55.000	—	—	.20
	1993	—	—	—	.20

2 SCHILLING

ALUMINUM

KM#	Date	Mintage	Fine	VF	XF	Unc
2872	1946	10.082	.35	.75	1.00	5.00
	1946	—	—	—	Proof	100.00
	1947	20.140	.35	.75	1.00	4.50
	1947	—	—	—	Proof	35.00
	1952	.149	55.00	80.00	135.00	215.00
	1952	—	—	—	Proof	600.00

5 SCHILLING

ALUMINUM

KM#	Date	Mintage	Fine	VF	XF	Unc
2879	1952	29.873	.75	1.25	2.00	7.50
	1952	—	—	—	Proof	50.00
	1957	.240	65.00	125.00	200.00	300.00
	1957	—	—	—	Proof	400.00

5.2000 g, .640 SILVER, .1070 oz ASW
Reeded edge

KM#	Date	Mintage	Fine	VF	XF	Unc
2889	1960	12.618	—	BV	2.50	5.00
	1960	1,000	—	—	Proof	55.00
	1961	17.902	—	BV	2.50	4.00
	1961	—	—	—	Proof	25.00
	1962	6.771	—	BV	2.50	4.00
	1962	—	—	—	Proof	20.00
	1963	1.811	BV	2.00	4.00	7.50
	1963	—	—	—	Proof	80.00
	1964	4.030	—	BV	2.25	4.00
	1964	—	—	—	Proof	4.00
	1965	4.759	—	BV	2.25	4.00
	1965	—	—	—	Proof	4.00
	1966	4.481	—	BV	2.25	4.00
	1966	—	—	—	Proof	6.00
	1967	1.900	BV	2.00	4.00	5.00
	1967	—	—	—	Proof	7.50
	1968	4.792	—	BV	2.25	4.00
	1968	.020	—	—	Proof	6.50

COPPER-NICKEL
Plain edge

KM#	Date	Mintage	VF	XF	Unc
2889a	1968	2.075	.60	.75	2.00
	1969	41.222		.50	1.00

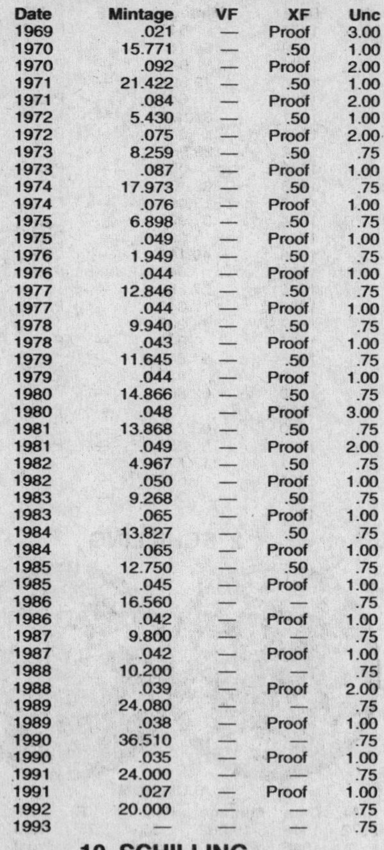

KM#	Date	Mintage	VF	XF	Unc
2889a	1969	.021	—	Proof	3.00
	1970	15.771	—	.50	1.00
	1970	.092	—	Proof	2.00
	1971	21.422	—	.50	1.00
	1971	.084	—	Proof	2.00
	1972	5.430	—	.50	1.00
	1972	.075	—	Proof	2.00
	1973	8.259	—	.50	.75
	1973	.087	—	Proof	1.00
	1974	17.973	—	.50	.75
	1974	.076	—	Proof	1.00
	1975	6.898	—	.50	.75
	1975	.049	—	Proof	1.00
	1976	1.949	—	.50	.75
	1976	.044	—	Proof	1.00
	1977	12.846	—	.50	.75
	1977	.044	—	Proof	1.00
	1978	9.940	—	.50	.75
	1978	.043	—	Proof	1.00
	1979	11.645	—	.50	.75
	1979	.044	—	Proof	1.00
	1980	14.866	—	.50	.75
	1980	.048	—	Proof	3.00
	1981	13.868	—	.50	.75
	1981	.049	—	Proof	2.00
	1982	4.967	—	.50	.75
	1982	.050	—	Proof	1.00
	1983	9.268	—	.50	.75
	1983	.065	—	Proof	1.00
	1984	13.827	—	.50	.75
	1984	.065	—	Proof	1.00
	1985	12.750	—	.50	.75
	1985	.045	—	Proof	1.00
	1986	16.560	—	—	.75
	1986	.042	—	Proof	1.00
	1987	9.800	—	—	.75
	1987	.042	—	Proof	1.00
	1988	10.200	—	—	.75
	1988	.039	—	Proof	2.00
	1989	24.080	—	—	.75
	1989	.038	—	Proof	1.00
	1990	36.510	—	—	.75
	1990	.035	—	Proof	1.00
	1991	24.000	—	—	.75
	1991	.027	—	Proof	1.00
	1992	20.000	—	—	.75
	1993	—	—	—	.75

10 SCHILLING

7.5000 g, .640 SILVER, .1543 oz ASW

KM#	Date	Mintage	Fine	VF	XF	Unc
2882	1957	15.636	—	BV	2.50	6.00
	1957	—	—	—	Proof	60.00
	1958	27.280	—	BV	2.50	8.00
	1958	—	—	—	Proof	315.00
	1959	4.740	—	BV	2.50	9.00
	1959	—	—	—	Proof	30.00
	1964	.187	7.00	10.00	15.00	25.00
	1964	.027	—	—	Proof	8.00
	1965	1.721	—	BV	2.50	5.00
	1965	—	—	—	Proof	4.00
	1966	3.392	—	BV	2.50	4.00
	1966	—	—	—	Proof	7.50
	1967	1.394	—	BV	2.50	4.00
	1967	—	—	—	Proof	8.00
	1968	1.525	—	BV	2.50	4.00
	1968	.015	—	—	Proof	7.00
	1969	1.200	—	BV	2.50	4.00
	1969	.020	—	—	Proof	7.00
	1970	4.600	—	BV	2.50	4.00
	1970	.089	—	—	Proof	5.00
	1971	7.100	—	BV	2.50	4.00
	1971	.080	—	—	Proof	5.00
	1972	14.300	—	BV	2.50	4.00
	1972	.075	—	—	Proof	5.00
	1973	14.600	—	BV	2.50	4.00
	1973	.080	—	—	Proof	5.00

COPPER-NICKEL

KM#	Date	Mintage	VF	XF	Unc
2918	1974	79.000	—	1.00	1.75
	1974	.076	—	Proof	3.50
	1975	16.941	—	1.00	1.75
	1975	.049	—	Proof	2.50
	1976	15.970	—	1.00	1.75
	1976	.044	—	Proof	2.50
	1977	7.652	—	1.00	1.75
	1977	.044	—	Proof	2.50
	1978	6.846	—	1.00	1.75
	1978	.043	—	Proof	2.50
	1979	11.740	—	1.00	1.50
	1979	.044	—	Proof	2.50
	1980	10.852	—	1.00	1.50
	1980	.048	—	Proof	4.50
	1981	8.021	—	1.00	1.50
	1981	.049	—	Proof	4.00
	1982	4.967	—	1.00	1.50
	1982	.050	—	Proof	2.50
	1983	8.993	—	1.00	1.50
	1983	.065	—	Proof	2.50
	1984	8.000	—	1.00	1.50
	1984	.065	—	Proof	2.50
	1985	9.010	—	1.00	1.50
	1985	.045	—	Proof	2.50
	1986	8.770	—	—	1.25
	1986	.042	—	Proof	2.50
	1987	9.300	—	—	1.25
	1987	.042	—	Proof	2.50
	1988	9.050	—	—	1.25
	1988	—	—	Proof	4.50
	1989	—	—	—	1.25
	1989	—	—	Proof	2.50
	1990	—	—	—	1.25
	1990	—	—	Proof	2.50
	1991	18.000	—	—	1.25
	1991	—	—	Proof	2.50
	1992	10.950	—	—	1.25
	1993	—	—	—	1.25

20 SCHILLING

COPPER-ALUMINUM-NICKEL

KM#	Date	Mintage	VF	XF	Unc
2946	1980	9.850	—	2.00	2.50
	1980	.048	—	Proof	3.50
	1981	2.987	—	2.00	2.50
	1981	.049	—	Proof	3.50
	1991	—	—	2.00	2.50
	1992	.100	—	2.00	2.50
	1993	—	—	2.00	2.50

250th Anniversary of Birth of Joseph Haydn

KM#	Date	Mintage	VF	XF	Unc
2955	1982	3.150	—	2.00	2.50
	1982	.050	—	Proof	3.50
	1991	—	—	2.00	2.50
	1992	.100	—	2.00	2.50
	1993	—	—	2.00	2.50

Hochosterwitz Castle

KM#	Date	Mintage	VF	XF	Unc
2960	1983	1.070	—	2.00	2.50
	1983	.065	—	Proof	3.50
	1991	—	—	2.00	2.50
	1992	.100	—	2.00	2.50
	1993	—	—	2.00	2.50

Grafenegg Palace

KM#	Date	Mintage	VF	XF	Unc
2965	1984	1.270	—	2.00	2.50
	1984	.065	—	Proof	3.50
	1991	—	—	2.00	2.50
	1992	.100	—	2.00	2.50
	1993	—	—	2.00	2.50

ALUMINUM-BRONZE
200th Anniversary of Diocese of Linz

KM#	Date	Mintage	VF	XF	Unc
2970	1985	.860	—	2.00	2.50
	1985	.045	—	Proof	3.50
	1991	—	—	2.00	2.50
	1992	.100	—	2.00	2.50
	1993	—	—	2.00	2.50

800th Anniversary of Georgenberger Treaty

KM#	Date	Mintage	VF	XF	Unc
2975	1986	.840	—	2.00	2.50
	1986	.042	—	Proof	3.50
	1991	—	—	2.00	2.50
	1992	—	—	2.00	2.50
	1993	—	—	2.00	2.50

COPPER-ALUMINUM-NICKEL
300th Anniversary of Birth of
Salzburg's Archbishop Thun

KM#	Date	Mintage	VF	XF	Unc
2980	1987	.550	—	—	2.50
	1987	.042	—	Proof	3.50
	1991	—	—	—	2.50
	1992	.100	—	—	2.50
	1993	—	—	—	2.50

Tyrol

KM#	Date	Mintage	VF	XF	Unc
2988	1989	.280	—	—	2.50
	1989	.038	—	Proof	3.50
	1991	—	—	—	2.50
	1992	.100	—	—	2.50
	1993	—	—	—	2.50

Martinsturm in Bregenz Vorarlberg

KM#	Date	Mintage	VF	XF	Unc
2993	1990	.250	—	—	2.50
	1990	.035	—	Proof	3.50
	1991	—	—	—	2.50
	1992	.100	—	—	2.50
	1993	—	—	—	2.50

200th Anniversary of Birth of Franz Grillparzer

KM#	Date	Mintage	VF	XF	Unc
2995	1991	—	—	—	2.50
	1991	.027	—	Proof	3.50
	1992	.100	—	—	2.50
	1993	—	—	—	2.50

25 SCHILLING

13.0000 g, .800 SILVER, .3344 oz ASW
Reopening of the National Theater in Vienna

KM#	Date	Mintage	Fine	VF	XF	Unc
2880	1955	1.499	BV	7.50	9.50	15.00
	1955	*5,000	—	—	Proof	65.00

200th Anniversary of Birth of Wolfgang Mozart

KM#	Date	Mintage	Fine	VF	XF	Unc
2881	1956	4.999	—	BV	3.50	5.00
	1956	*1,500	—	—	Proof	225.00

8th Centennial of Mariazell Basilica

KM#	Date	Mintage	Fine	VF	XF	Unc
2883	1957	4.999	—	BV	3.50	5.00
	1957	*1,500	—	—	Proof	200.00

100th Anniversary of Birth of Auer von Welsbach

KM#	Date	Mintage	Fine	VF	XF	Unc
2884	1958	4.999	—	BV	3.50	5.00
	1958	*500 pcs.	—	—	Proof	1500.

Centennial of Death of Archduke Johann

KM#	Date	Mintage	Fine	VF	XF	Unc
2887	1959	1.899	—	BV	3.50	5.00
	1959	*1,000	—	—	Proof	225.00

40th Anniversary of Carinthian Plebescite

KM#	Date	Mintage	Fine	VF	XF	Unc
2890	1960	1.599	—	BV	3.50	5.00
	1960	pcs.	—	—	Proof	225.00

40th Anniversary of Burgenland

KM#	Date	Mintage	Fine	VF	XF	Unc
2891	1961	1.399	—	BV	3.50	5.00
	1961	*1,200	—	—	Proof	200.00

Anton Bruckner

KM#	Date	Mintage	Fine	VF	XF	Unc
2892	1962	2.399	—	BV	3.50	5.00
	1962	*3,000	—	—	Proof	125.00

300th Anniversary of Birth of Prince Eugen

KM#	Date	Mintage	Fine	VF	XF	Unc
2893	1963	1.994	—	BV	3.50	5.00
	1963	5,931	—	—	Proof	85.00

Franz Grillparzer

KM#	Date	Mintage	Fine	VF	XF	Unc
2895.1	1964	1.664	—	BV	3.50	5.00
	1964	.036	—	—	Proof	7.00

9 shield obverse (error)

KM#	Date	Mintage	Fine	VF	XF	Unc
2895.2	1964	3,660	—	—	Proof	350.00

150th Anniversary of Vienna Technical High School

KM#	Date	Mintage	Fine	VF	XF	Unc
2897	1965	1.563	—	BV	3.50	5.00
	1965	.037	—	—	Proof	7.00

130th Anniversary of Death of Ferdinand Raimund

KM#	Date	Mintage	Fine	VF	XF	Unc
2899	1966	1.388	—	BV	3.50	5.00
	1966	11,800	—	—	Proof	35.00

250th Anniversary of Birth of Maria Theresa

KM#	Date	Mintage	Fine	VF	XF	Unc
2901	1967	2.472	—	BV	3.50	5.00
	1967	.028	—	—	Proof	12.50

300th Anniversary of Birth of Von Hildebrandt

KM#	Date	Mintage	Fine	VF	XF	Unc
2903	1968	1.258	BV	3.50	6.50	8.00
	1968	.042	—	—	Proof	10.00

Peter Rosegger

KM#	Date	Mintage	Fine	VF	XF	Unc
2905	1969	1.356	—	BV	3.50	5.00
	1969	.044	—	—	Proof	10.00

100th Anniversary of Birth of Franz Lehar

KM#	Date	Mintage	Fine	VF	XF	Unc
2907	1970	1.661	—	BV	3.50	5.00
	1970	.139	—	—	Proof	6.00

200th Anniversary of Vienna Bourse

KM#	Date	Mintage	Fine	VF	XF	Unc
2910	1971	1.804	—	BV	3.50	5.00
	1971	.196	—	—	Proof	6.00

50th Anniversary of Death of Carl M. Ziehrer

KM#	Date	Mintage	Fine	VF	XF	Unc
2912	1972	1.955	—	BV	3.50	5.00
	1972	.145	—	—	Proof	6.00

100th Anniversary of Birth of Max Reinhardt

KM#	Date	Mintage	Fine	VF	XF	Unc
2915	1973	2.323	—	BV	3.50	5.00
	1973	.177	—	—	Proof	6.00

50 SCHILLING

20.0000 g, .900 SILVER, .5787 oz ASW
150th Anniversary of Liberation of Tyrol

KM#	Date	Mintage	VF	XF	Unc
2888	1959	2.999	5.00	6.00	9.00
	1959	*800 pcs.	—	Proof	450.00

600th Anniversary Union with Tirol

KM#	Date	Mintage	VF	XF	Unc
2894	1963	2.994	5.00	6.00	7.50
	1963	6,000	—	Proof	150.00

Winter Olympics - Innsbruck

KM#	Date	Mintage	VF	XF	Unc
2896	1964	2.832	5.00	6.00	7.50
	1964	.068	—	Proof	12.00

600th Anniversary Vienna University

KM#	Date	Mintage	VF	XF	Unc
2898	1965	2.163	5.00	6.00	7.50
	1965	.037	—	Proof	12.00

150th Anniversary of National Bank

KM#	Date	Mintage	VF	XF	Unc
2900	1966	1.782	5.00	6.00	7.50
	1966	17,400	—	Proof	60.00

Centennial of the Blue Danube Waltz

KM#	Date	Mintage	VF	XF	Unc
2902	1967	2.974	5.00	6.00	7.50
	1967	.026	—	Proof	45.00

50th Anniversary of the Republic

Rev: Matte surface between pillars.

KM#	Date	Mintage	VF	XF	Unc
2904.1	1968	1.660	5.00	6.00	7.50
	1968	.040	—	Proof	15.00

Rev: Proof surface between pillars.

KM#	Date	Mintage	VF	XF	Unc
2904.2	1968	—	—	Proof	75.00

450th Anniversary of Death of Maximilian I

KM#	Date	Mintage	VF	XF	Unc
2906	1969	2.045	5.00	6.00	7.50
	1969	.055	—	Proof	12.00

300th Anniversary of the Innsbruck University

KM#	Date	Mintage	VF	XF	Unc
2908	1970	2.087	5.00	6.00	7.50
	1970	.113	—	Proof	9.00

100th Anniversary of Birth of Dr. Karl Renner

KM#	Date	Mintage	VF	XF	Unc
2909	1970	2.214	5.00	6.00	7.50
	1970	.286	—	Proof	9.00

80th Anniversary of Birth of Julius Raab

KM#	Date	Mintage	VF	XF	Unc
2911	1971	2.317	5.00	6.00	7.50
	1971	.183	—	Proof	9.00

350th Anniversary of Salzburg University

KM#	Date	Mintage	VF	XF	Unc
2913	1972	2.863	5.00	6.00	7.50
	1972	.136	—	Proof	9.00

100th Anniversary of Institute of Agriculture

KM#	Date	Mintage	VF	XF	Unc
2914	1972	1.891	5.00	6.00	7.50
	1972	.109	—	Proof	9.00

500th Anniversary of Bummerl House

KM#	Date	Mintage	VF	XF	Unc
2916	1973	2.842	5.00	6.00	7.50
	1973	.158	—	Proof	9.00

100th Anniversary of Birth of Dr. Theodor Korner

KM#	Date	Mintage	VF	XF	Unc
2917	1973	2.868	5.00	6.00	7.50
	1973	.132	—	Proof	9.00

20.0000 g, .640 SILVER, .4115 oz ASW
International Garden Exhibition

KM#	Date	Mintage	VF	XF	Unc
2919	1974	2.279	—	5.00	6.00
	1974	.221	—	Proof	7.50

125th Anniversary of Austrian Police Force

KM#	Date	Mintage	VF	XF	Unc
2920	1974	2.259	—	5.00	6.00
	1974	.241	—	Proof	7.50

1200th Anniversary of Salzburg Cathedral

KM#	Date	Mintage	VF	XF	Unc
2921	1974	2.293	—	5.00	6.00
	1974	.207	—	Proof	7.50

50th Year Austrian Broadcasting

KM#	Date	Mintage	VF	XF	Unc
2922	1974	2.290	—	5.00	6.00
	1974	.210	—	Proof	7.50

150th Anniversary of Death of Schubert

KM#	Date	Mintage	VF	XF	Unc
2937	1978	1.868	—	5.00	6.00
	1978	.132	—	Proof	7.50

100 SCHILLING

23.9300 g, .640 SILVER, .4924 oz ASW
150th Anniversary of Birth of Johann Strauss

KM#	Date	Mintage	VF	XF	Unc
2923	1975	2.646	—	—	10.00
	1975	.209	—	Proof	12.00

20th Anniversary of State Treaty

KM#	Date	Mintage	VF	XF	Unc
2924	1975	3.215	—	—	10.00
	1975	.225	—	Proof	12.00

50th Anniversary of Schilling

KM#	Date	Mintage	VF	XF	Unc
2925	1975	3.234	—	—	10.00
	1975	.201	—	Proof	12.00

Winter Olympics - Emblem

KM#	Date	Mintage	VF	XF	Unc
2926	1976	2.826	—	—	10.00
	1976	.374	—	Proof	12.00

Winter Olympics - Buildings and Olympic Rings

KM#	Date	Mintage	VF	XF	Unc
2927	1976(h)	2.718	—	—	10.00
	1976(h)	.232	—	Proof	12.00
	1976(v)	2.692	—	—	10.00
	1976(v)	.223	—	Proof	12.00

Winter Olympics - Skier

KM#	Date	Mintage	VF	XF	Unc
2928	1976(h)	2.641	—	—	10.00
	1976(h)	.184	—	Proof	12.00
	1976(v)	2.636	—	—	10.00
	1976(v)	.179	—	Proof	12.00

Winter Olympics - Ski Jump and Symbols

KM#	Date	Mintage	VF	XF	Unc
2929	1976(h)	2.627	—	—	10.00
	1976(h)	.188	—	Proof	12.00
	1976(v)	2.611	—	—	10.00
	1976(v)	.179	—	Proof	12.00

200th Anniversary of Burgtheater

KM#	Date	Mintage	VF	XF	Unc
2930	1976	1.630	—	—	10.00
	1976	.220	—	Proof	12.00

1000th Anniversary of Carinthia

KM#	Date	Mintage	VF	XF	Unc
2931	1976	1.632	—	—	10.00
	1976	.168	—	Proof	12.00

175th Anniversary of Birth of Johann Nestroy

KM#	Date	Mintage	VF	XF	Unc
2932	1976	1.761	—	—	10.00
	1976	.139	—	Proof	12.00

1200th Anniversary of Kremsmunster Monastery

KM#	Date	Mintage	VF	XF	Unc
2934	1977	1.865	—	—	10.00
	1977	.135	—	Proof	12.00

900th Anniversary of Hohensalzburg Fortress

KM#	Date	Mintage	VF	XF	Unc
2935	1977	1.878	—	—	10.00
	1977	.122	—	Proof	12.00

500th Anniversary of Mint in Hall

KM#	Date	Mintage	VF	XF	Unc
2936	1977	1.868	—	—	10.00
	1977	.132	—	Proof	16.00

700th Anniversary of Gmunden

KM#	Date	Mintage	VF	XF	Unc
2938	1978	1.870	—	—	10.00
	1978	.130	—	Proof	12.00

700th Anniversary Battle of Durnkrut and Jedenspeigen

KM#	Date	Mintage	VF	XF	Unc
2939	1978	1.677	—	—	10.00
	1978	.123	—	Proof	12.00

1100th Anniversary of Founding of Villach

KM#	Date	Mintage	VF	XF	Unc
2940	1978	1.569	—	—	10.00
	1978	.131	—	Proof	12.00

Opening of Arlberg Tunnel

KM#	Date	Mintage	VF	XF	Unc
2941	1978	1.844	—	—	10.00
	1978	.156	—	Proof	12.00

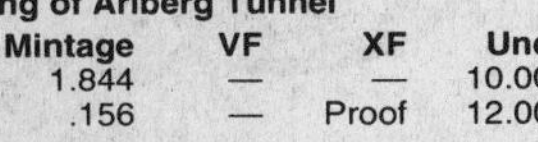

700th Anniversary of Cathedral of Wiener Neustadt

KM#	Date	Mintage	VF	XF	Unc
2942	1979	1.866	—	—	10.00
	1979	.134	—	Proof	12.00

200th Anniversary of Inn District

KM#	Date	Mintage	VF	XF	Unc
2943	1979	1.870	—	—	10.00
	1979	.130	—	Proof	12.00

Vienna International Center

KM#	Date	Mintage	VF	XF	Unc
2944	1979	1.855	—	—	10.00
	1979	.145	—	Proof	12.00

Festival and Congress Hall at Bregenz

KM#	Date	Mintage	VF	XF	Unc
2945	1979	1.573	—	—	10.00
	1979	.161	—	Proof	12.00

18.0000 g, .900 SILVER, .5209 oz ASW
Mozart - Salsburg

KM#	Date	Mintage	VF	XF	Unc
2996	1991	.100	—	Proof	45.00

Mozart's Vienna Years - Burg Theater

KM#	Date	Mintage	VF	XF	Unc
2998	1991	.100	—	Proof	45.00

Rudolph I

KM#	Date	Mintage	VF	XF	Unc
3001	1991	.075	—	Proof	37.50

Maximilian I

KM#	Date	Mintage	VF	XF	Unc
3003	1992	.075	—	Proof	37.50

20.0000 g, .900 SILVER, .5788 oz ASW
Otto Nicolia

KM#	Date	Mintage	VF	XF	Unc
3005	1992	.075	—	Proof	40.00

18.0000 g, .900 SILVER, .5209 oz ASW
Karl V

KM#	Date	Mintage	VF	XF	Unc
3007	1992	.075	—	Proof	40.00

Kaiser Lepold I

KM#	Date	Mintage	VF	XF	Unc
3009	1993	.075	—	Proof	40.00

500 SCHILLING

23.9600 g, .640 SILVER, .4930 oz ASW
Millenium of City of Steyr

KM#	Date	Mintage	VF	XF	Unc
2947	1980	.888	—	—	55.00
	1980	.111	—	Proof	65.00

25th Anniversary of State Treaty

KM#	Date	Mintage	VF	XF	Unc
2948	1980	.866	—	—	50.00
	1980	.134	—	Proof	60.00

Bicentennial of Death of Maria Theresa

KM#	Date	Mintage	VF	XF	Unc
2949	1980	.928	—	—	50.00
	1980	.172	—	Proof	60.00

Centennial of Austrian Red Cross

KM#	Date	Mintage	VF	XF	Unc
2950	1980	.950	—	—	50.00
	1980	.200	—	Proof	60.00

800th Anniversary of Verdun Altar

KM#	Date	Mintage	VF	XF	Unc
2951	1981	.950	—	—	50.00
	1981	.200	—	Proof	60.00

100th Anniversary of Birth of Anton Wildgans

KM#	Date	Mintage	VF	XF	Unc
2952	1981	.983	—	—	50.00
	1981	.167	—	Proof	60.00

100th Anniversary of Birth of Otto Bauer

KM#	Date	Mintage	VF	XF	Unc
2953	1981	.994	—	—	50.00
	1981	.156	—	Proof	60.00

200th Anniversary of Religious Tolerance

KM#	Date	Mintage	VF	XF	Unc
2954	1981	.852	—	—	50.00
	1981	.148	—	Proof	60.00

1500th Anniversary of Death of St. Severin

KM#	Date	Mintage	VF	XF	Unc
2956	1982	.880	—	—	50.00
	1982	.120	—	Proof	60.00

500 Years of Austrian Printing

KM#	Date	Mintage	VF	XF	Unc
2957	1982	.632	—	—	50.00
	1982	.118	—	Proof	60.00

825 Years of the Mariazell Shrine

KM#	Date	Mintage	VF	XF	Unc
2958	1982	.632	—	—	50.00
	1982	.118	—	Proof	60.00

80th Anniversary of Birth of Leopold Figl

KM#	Date	Mintage	VF	XF	Unc
2959	1982	.384	—	—	50.00
	1982	.116	—	Proof	60.00

23.9600 g, .925 SILVER, .7125 oz ASW
World Cup Horse Jumping Championship

KM#	Date	Mintage	VF	XF	Unc
2961	1983	.368	—	—	50.00
	1983	.132	—	Proof	60.00

Centennial of Vienna City Hall

KM#	Date	Mintage	VF	XF	Unc
2962	1983	.466	—	—	50.00
	1983	.134	—	Proof	60.00

Catholic Day - Pope's Visit

KM#	Date	Mintage	VF	XF	Unc
2963	1983	.660	—	—	50.00
	1983	.140	—	Proof	60.00

Centennial of Parliament Building

KM#	Date	Mintage	VF	XF	Unc
2964	1983	.463	—	—	50.00
	1983	.137	—	Proof	60.00

175th Anniversary of Tirolean Revolution

KM#	Date	Mintage	VF	XF	Unc
2966	1984	.454	—	—	50.00
	1984	.146	—	Proof	60.00

100th Anniversary Commercial Shipping on Lake Constance

KM#	Date	Mintage	VF	XF	Unc
2967	1984	.455	—	—	50.00
	1984	.145	—	Proof	60.00

700th Anniversary of Stams Stift in Tirol

KM#	Date	Mintage	VF	XF	Unc
2968	1984	.459	—	—	50.00
	1984	.141	—	Proof	60.00

Centennial of Death of Fanny Elssler

KM#	Date	Mintage	VF	XF	Unc
2969	1984	.462	—	—	50.00
	1984	.138	—	Proof	60.00

400th Anniversary of Graz University.

KM#	Date	Mintage	VF	XF	Unc
2971	1985	.600	—	—	50.00
	1985	.122	—	Proof	60.00

40 Years of Peace In Austria

KM#	Date	Mintage	VF	XF	Unc
2972	1985	.500	—	—	50.00
	1985	.118	—	Proof	60.00

500th Anniversary of Canonization of Leopold III

KM#	Date	Mintage	VF	XF	Unc
2973	1985	.500	—	—	50.00
	1985	.113	—	Proof	60.00

2000th Anniversary of Bregenz

KM#	Date	Mintage	VF	XF	Unc
2974	1985	.500	—	—	50.00
	1985	.116	—	Proof	60.00

300th Anniversary of St. Florian's Cathedral

KM#	Date	Mintage	VF	XF	Unc
2976	1986	.300	—	—	50.00
	1986	.100	—	Proof	60.00

500th Anniversary of First Thaler Coin Struck at Hall Mint

KM#	Date	Mintage	VF	XF	Unc
2977	1986	.400	—	—	50.00
	1986	.101	—	Proof	60.00

250th Anniversary of Birth of
Prince Eugene of Savoy

KM#	Date	Mintage	VF	XF	Unc
2978	1986	.400	—	—	50.00
	1986	.102	—	Proof	60.00

European Conference on Security and Cooperation

KM#	Date	Mintage	VF	XF	Unc
2979	1986	.200	—	—	50.00
	1986	.099	—	Proof	60.00

150th Anniversary of Austrian Railroad

KM#	Date	Mintage	VF	XF	Unc
2981	1987	.210	—	—	50.00
	1987	.095	—	Proof	60.00

400th Anniversary of Birth of
Salzburg's Archbishop von Raitenau

KM#	Date	Mintage	VF	XF	Unc
2982	1987	.210	—	—	50.00
	1987	.094	—	Proof	60.00

800th Anniversary of Holy Cross Church

KM#	Date	Mintage	VF	XF	Unc
2983	1987	.210	—	—	50.00
	1987	.095	—	Proof	60.00

850th Anniversary of St. Georgenberg Abbey

KM#	Date	Mintage	VF	XF	Unc
2984	1988	.300	—	—	50.00
	1988	Inc. Ab.	—	Proof	60.00

Pope's Visit to Austria

KM#	Date	Mintage	VF	XF	Unc
2985	1988	.300	—	—	50.00
	1988	Inc. Ab.	—	Proof	60.00

100th Anniversary of Birth of Victor Adler

KM#	Date	Mintage	VF	XF	Unc
2986	1988	.300	—	—	50.00
	1988	Inc. Ab.	—	Proof	60.00

Gustav Klimt - Artist

KM#	Date	Mintage	VF	XF	Unc
2987	1989	.325	—	—	60.00
	1989	.088	—	Proof	70.00

Koloman Moser - Stained Glass

KM#	Date	Mintage	VF	XF	Unc
2991	1989	.311	—	—	60.00
	1989	.082	—	Proof	70.00

Egon Schiele - Expressionism

KM#	Date	Mintage	VF	XF	Unc
2992	1990	.328	—	—	60.00
	1990	.083	—	Proof	70.00

Oskar Kokoschka - Expressionism

KM#	Date	Mintage	VF	XF	Unc
2994	1990	.326	—	—	60.00
	1990	.081	—	Proof	70.00

8.0000 g, .986 GOLD, .2536 oz AGW

Mozart

KM#	Date	Mintage	VF	XF	Unc
2997	1991	.050	—	Proof	400.00

24.0000 g, .925 SILVER, .7125 oz ASW
Herbert von Karajan - Salzburg Festspielhaus

KM#	Date	Mintage	VF	XF	Unc
3000	1991	.350	—	—	60.00
	1991	.074	—	Proof	70.00

Karl Bohm

KM#	Date	Mintage	VF	XF	Unc
3002	1991	.320	—	—	50.00
	1991	.071	—	Proof	65.00

8.1000 g, .986 GOLD, .2540 oz AGW
150th Anniversary of Vienna Philharmonic

KM#	Date	Mintage	VF	XF	Unc
3006	1992	.050	—	Proof	250.00

1000 SCHILLING

13.5000 g, .900 GOLD, .3906 oz AGW
Austrian Millenium

KM#	Date	Mintage	VF	XF	Unc
2933	1976	1.800	—	—	215.00

NOTE: Exists in shades of red to yellow gold.

16.0000 g, .986 GOLD, .5072 oz AGW
Mozart - The Magic Flute Opera

KM#	Date	Mintage	VF	XF	Unc
2999	1991	.030	—	Proof	750.00

Johann Strauss - Violinist

KM#	Date	Mintage	VF	XF	Unc
3008	1992	.050	—	Proof	475.00

GOLD BULLION ISSUES

200 SCHILLING

3.1100 g, .9999 GOLD, .1000 oz AGW
Vienna Philharmonic Orchestra

KM#	Date	Mintage	VF	XF	Unc
3004	1991	—	—	—	100.00

500 SCHILLING

7.8000 g, .9999 GOLD, .2500 oz AGW
Vienna Philharmonic Orchestra
Obv: Similar to 2000 Schilling, KM#2990.

KM#	Date	Mintage	VF	XF	Unc
2989	1989	—	—	—	150.00

2000 SCHILLING

31.1000 g, .9999 GOLD, 1.0000 oz AGW
Vienna Philharmonic Orchestra

KM#	Date	Mintage	VF	XF	Unc
2990	1989	—	—	—	550.00

SPECIAL SELECTS (S/S)

NOTE: These are proof-like in appearance.

KM#	Date	Mintage	Identification	Issue Price	Mkt. Val.
723	1975	—	100 Schilling, Strauss	—	10.00
724	1975	—	100 Schilling, State Treaty	—	10.00
725	1975	—	100 Schilling, 50th Anniversary of Schilling	—	10.00
727.1	1976	—	100 Schilling, Winter Olympics II, Vienna Mint	—	10.00
727.2	1976	—	100 Schilling, Winter Olympics II, Hall Mint	—	10.00
728.1	1976	—	100 Schilling, Winter Olympics III, Vienna Mint	—	10.00
728.2	1976	—	100 Schilling, Winter Olympics III, Hall Mint	—	10.00
729.1	1976	—	100 Schilling, Winter Olympics IV, Vienna Mint	—	10.00
729.2	1976	—	100 Schilling, Winter Olympics IV, Hall Mint	—	10.00
730	1976	—	100 Schilling, Burgtheater	—	10.00
731	1976	—	100 Schilling, Herzogstuhl	—	10.00
732	1976	—	100 Schilling, Nestroy	—	10.00
734	1977	—	100 Schilling, Kremsmunster	—	10.00
735	1977	—	100 Schilling, Hohensalzb	—	10.00
736	1977	—	100 Schilling, Hall Mint	—	10.00
738	1978	—	100 Schilling, Gmunder	—	10.00
739	1978	—	100 Schilling, Durnkrut	—	10.00
740	1978	—	100 Schilling, Villach	—	10.00
741	1978	80,000	100 Schilling, Arlberg	—	10.00
742	1979	70,000	100 Schilling, Wiener Neustadt	—	10.00
743	1979	75,000	100 Schilling, Inn District	8.50	10.00
744	1979	75,000	100 Schilling, Vienna Center	—	10.00
745	1979	75,000	100 Schilling, Bregenz Hall	—	10.00
747	1980	63,000	500 Schilling, Steyr	—	40.00
748	1980	79,000	500 Schilling, Treaty	—	40.00
749	1980	86,400	500 Schilling, Maria Theresa	—	40.00
750	1980	90,000	500 Schilling, Red Cross	—	40.00
751	1981	85,000	500 Schilling, Verdun	—	40.00
752	1981	72,000	500 Schilling, Anton Wildgans	—	40.00
753	1981	65,000	500 Schilling, Otto Bauer	38.00	40.00
754	1981	60,000	500 Schilling, Religious Tolerance	—	40.00
756	1982	42,600	500 Schilling, St. Severin	—	40.00
757	1982	42,200	500 Schilling, Printing	—	40.00
758	1982	41,600	500 Schilling, Maria Zell Shrine	—	40.00
759	1982	39,600	500 Schilling, Leopold Figl	—	40.00
763	1983	60,000	500 Schilling, Pope's Visit	—	40.00

MINT SETS (MS)

KM#	Date	Mintage	Identification	Issue Price	Mkt. Val.
MS1	1992(8)	25,000	KM2875-2876,2878,2885-2886,2889a, 2918,2946	—	9.00
MS2	1993(8)	35,000	KM2875-2876,2878,2885-2886,2889a, 2918,2946	—	15.00

PROOF SETS (PS)

KM#	Date	Mintage	Identification	Issue Price	Mkt. Val.
PS1	1959(2)	1,000	KM2887-2888	—	575.00
PS2	1964(9)	69,731	KM2875-2876,2878,2882,2885-2886, 2889,2895.1,2896	—	25.00
PS3	1964(9)	2,700	KM2875-2876,2878,2882,2885-2886, 2889,2895.2,2896 (error set)	—	275.00
PS4	1964(7)	—	KM2875-2876,2878,2882,2885-2886, 2889	—	12.00
PS5	1965(7)	83,000	KM2875-2876,2878,2882,2885-2886, 2889	—	7.00
PS6	1965(4)	38,000	KM2882,2889,2897-2898	5.00	25.00
PS7	1966(9)	1,765	KM2875-2876,2878,2882,2885-2886, 2889,2899-2900	—	100.00
PS8	1966(7)	—	KM2875-2876,2878,2882,2885-2886, 2889	—	15.00
PS9	1967(9)	1,163	KM2875-2876,2878,2882,2885-2886, 2889,2901-2902	5.50	100.00
PS10	1967(7)	—	KM2875-2876,2878,2882,2885-2886, 2889	—	40.00
PS11	1968(9)	15,200	KM2875-2876,2878,2882,2885-2886, 2889,2903,2904.1	5.75	40.00
PS12	1968(7)	20,000	KM2875-2876,2878,2882,2885-2886, 2889	—	15.00
PS13	1969(9)	20,000	KM2875-2876,2878,2882,2885-2886, 2889a,2905-2906	7.50	30.00
PS14	1969(7)	21,000	KM2875-2876,2878,2882,2885-2886, 2889a	—	11.00
PS15	1970(9)	—	KM2875-2876,2878,2882,2885-2886, 2889a,2907-2908	8.25	20.00
PS16	1970(9)	—	KM2875-2876,2878,2882,2885-2886, 2889a,2907,2909	8.25	20.00
PS17	1970(7)	92,000	KM2875-2876,2878,2882,2885-2886, 2889a	—	8.50
PS18	1970(3)	—	KM2907-2909	7.00	20.00
PS19	1971(9)	—	KM2875-2876,2878,2882,2885-2886, 2889a,2910-2911	8.25	17.50
PS20	1971(7)	84,000	KM2875-2876,2878,2882,2885-2886, 2889a	—	8.50
PS21	1972(9)	—	KM2875-2876,2878,2882,2885-2886, 2889a,2912-2913	8.50	20.00
PS22	1972(9)	—	KM2875-2876,2878,2882,2885-2886, 2889a,2912,2914	8.50	20.00
PS23	1972(7)	75,000	KM2875-2876,2878,2882,2885-2886, 2889a	—	8.50
PS24	1972(3)	—	KM2912-2914	7.50	20.00
PS25	1973(10)	—	KM2875-2876,2878,2882,2885-2886, 2889a,2915-2917	—	25.00
PS26	1973(7)	87,000	KM2875-2876,2878,2882,2885-2886, 2889a	—	8.50
PS27	1973(3)	—	KM2912-2914	—	20.00
PS28	1974(12)	—	KM2875-2876,2878,2885-2886,2889a, 2918-2923	29.70	35.00
PS29	1974(8)	—	KM2875-2876,2878,2885-2886,2889a, 2918,2921	—	10.00
PS30	1974(7)	76,000	KM2875-2876,2878,2885-2886,2889a, 2918	—	7.50
PS31	1974(5)	—	KM2919-2923	27.00	30.00
PS32	1975(10)	—	KM2875-2876,2878,2885-2886,2889a, 2918,2924-2926	30.00	30.00
PS33	1975(7)	49,000	KM2875-2876,2878,2885-2886,2889a, 2918	—	6.50
PS34	1975(3)	—	KM2924-2926	27.00	25.00
PS35	1976(7)	44,000	KM2875-2876,2878,2885-2886, 2889a,2918	3.00	6.50
PS36	1977(7)	44,000	KM2875-2876,2878,2885-2886,		

KM#	Date	Mintage	Identification	Issue Price	Mkt. Val.
PS36			2889a,2918	3.15	6.50
PS37	1977(6)	—	KM2930-2932,2934-2936	27.00	60.00
PS38	1978(7)	43,000	KM2875-2876,2878,2885-2886,2889a, 2918	—	6.50
PS39	1979(7)	44,000	KM2875-2876,2878,2885-2886,2889a, 2918	—	6.50
PS40	1980(8)	48,000	KM2875-2876,2878,2885-2886,2889a, 2918,2946	—	12.50
PS42	1981(8)	49,000	KM2875-2876,2878,2885-2886,2889a, 2918,2946	—	12.50
PS43	1982(8)	50,000	KM2875-2876,2878,2885-2886,2889a, 2918,2955	—	9.00
PS44	1983(8)	65,000	KM2875-2876,2878,2885-2886,2889a, 2918,2960	—	9.00
PS45	1984(8)	65,000	KM2875-2876,2878,2885-2886,2889a, 2918,2965	—	9.00
PS46	1985(8)	45,000	KM2875-2876,2878,2885-2886,2889a, 2918,2970	—	9.00
PS47	1986(8)	42,000	KM2875-2876,2878,2885-2886,2889a, 2918,2975	—	9.00
PS48	1987(8)	42,000	KM2875-2876,2878,2885-2886,2889a, 2918,2980	—	9.00
PS49	1988(7)	39,000	KM2875-2876,2878,2885-2886,2889a, 2918	—	14.00
PS50	1989(8)	38,000	KM2875-2876,2878,2885-2886,2889a, 2918,2988	—	9.00
PS51	1990(8)	35,000	KM2875-2876,2878,2885-2886,2889a, 2918,2993	—	9.00
PS52	1991(8)	—	KM2875-2876,2878,2885-2886,2889a, 2918,2995	—	9.00

AUERSPERG

Auersberg

The Auersperg princes were princes of estates in Austrian Carniola, a former duchy with estates in Laibach and Silesia, a former province in southwestern Poland and Swabia, one of the stem-duchies of medieval Germany. They were elevated to princely rank in 1653, and the following year were made dukes of Muensterberg, which they ultimately sold to Prussia.

RULERS

Wilhelm, 1800-1822

MONETARY SYSTEM

120 Kreuzer = 1 Convention Thaler

THALER

(Convention)

SILVER

KM#	Date	Mintage	VG	Fine	VF	XF
5	1805	—	80.00	175.00	275.00	500.00

GURK

A bishopric in the Austrian Alpine province of Carinthia, was founded in 1071. In 1806 it was mediatized and assigned to Austria.

RULERS

Franz Xavier V, Count Salm-Reifferscheid, (later Prince), 1783-1822

20 KREUZER

SILVER

KM#	Date	Mintage	VG	Fine	VF	XF
1	1806	—	37.50	75.00	90.00	125.00

THALER

(Convention)

SILVER

KM#	Date	Mintage	VG	Fine	VF	XF
2	1801	—	90.00	150.00	200.00	375.00

TRADE COINAGE

DUCAT

3.5000 g, .986 GOLD, .1109 oz AGW
Obv: Bust of Franz Xavier right.
Rev: Crowned and mantled arms.

KM#	Date	Mintage	VG	Fine	VF	XF
3	1806	—	200.00	375.00	700.00	1750.

OLMUTZ

IN MORAVIA

Olmutz (Olomouc), a bishopric in the eastern part of the Czechoslovakian Republic which was, until 1640, the recognized capital of Moravia, obtained the right to mint a coinage in 1144, but exercised it sparingly until the 17th century.

RULERS

Anton Theodor, Count von Colloredo, 1777-1811
Maria Thaddaus, Count von Trauttmansgorff, 1811-1819
Rudolph Johann, Archduke of Austria, 1819-1831

RUDOLPH JOHANN

1819-1831

20 KREUZER

SILVER

KM#	Date	Mintage	VG	Fine	VF	XF
195	1820	—	15.00	25.00	40.00	60.00

1/2 CONVENTION THALER

SILVER

KM#	Date	Mintage	VG	Fine	VF	XF
196	1820	—	50.00	90.00	150.00	200.00

THALER

SILVER

KM#	Date	Mintage	VG	Fine	VF	XF
197	1820	—	75.00	175.00	325.00	550.00

TRADE COINAGE

DUCAT

3.5000 g, .986 GOLD, .1109 oz AGW

KM#	Date	Mintage	VG	Fine	VF	XF
198	1820	—	175.00	250.00	500.00	800.00

SALZBURG

A town on the Austro-Bavarian frontier which grew up around a monastery and bishopric that was founded circa 700. It was raised to the rank of archbishopric in 798. In 1803 Salzburg was secularized and given to an archduke of Austria. In 1803 it was annexed to Austria but years later passed to Bavaria, returning to Austria in 1813. It became a crownland in 1849, remaining so until becoming part of the Austrian Republic in 1918.

RULERS

Hieronymus, 1772-1803
Ferdinand, Elector, 1803-1805

ENGRAVERS INITIALS

FM, M - Franz Xavier Matzenkopf, Jr. 1755-1805

MONETARY SYSTEM

4 Pfenning = 1 Kreutzer
120 Kreutzer = 1 Convention Thaler

HIERONYMUS

1772-1803

COPPER

KM#	Date	Mintage	VG	Fine	VF	XF
474	1801	—	3.00	5.00	9.00	18.00
	1802	—	3.00	5.00	9.00	18.00

NOTE: Earlier dates (1792-1800) exist for this type.

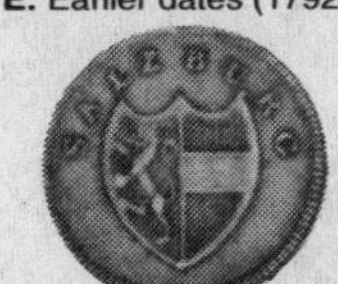

KM#	Date	Mintage	VG	Fine	VF	XF
480	1802	—	5.00	7.00	10.00	20.00

ZWEI (2) PFENNING

COPPER

KM#	Date	Mintage	VG	Fine	VF	XF
472	1801	—	3.00	6.00	12.00	25.00

NOTE: Earlier dates (1791-1800) exist for this type.

KM#	Date	Mintage	VG	Fine	VF	XF
481	1802	—	5.00	8.50	17.00	35.00

EIN (1) KREUZER

COPPER

KM#	Date	Mintage	VG	Fine	VF	XF
470	1801	—	2.00	3.00	5.00	15.00
	1802	—	2.00	3.00	5.00	15.00

NOTE: Earlier dates (1790-1800) exist for this type.

KM#	Date	Mintage	VG	Fine	VF	XF
482	1802	—	5.00	10.00	20.00	40.00

5 KREUZER

BILLON

KM#	Date	Mintage	VG	Fine	VF	XF
477	1801	—	7.50	20.00	50.00	130.00
	1802	—	7.50	20.00	50.00	130.00

NOTE: Earlier dates (1793-1800) exist for this type.

10 KREUZER

3.8900 g, .500 SILVER, .0625 oz ASW

KM#	Date	Mintage	VG	Fine	VF	XF
464	1801 M	—	15.00	30.00	55.00	110.00
	1802 M	—	15.00	30.00	55.00	110.00

NOTE: Earlier dates (1788-1800) exist for this type.

20 KREUZER

6.6800 g, .583 SILVER, .1252 oz ASW

KM#	Date	Mintage	VG	Fine	VF	XF
460	1801 M	—	3.00	6.00	15.00	30.00
	1802 M	—	3.00	6.00	15.00	30.00
	1803 M	—	5.00	15.00	20.00	50.00

NOTE: Varieties exist.
NOTE: Earlier dates (1787-1800) exist for this type.

1/2 THALER

14.0300 g, .833 SILVER, .3757 oz ASW

KM#	Date	Mintage	VG	Fine	VF	XF
461	1802 M	—	50.00	100.00	175.00	325.00

NOTE: Earlier dates (1787-1797) exist for this type.

THALER

28.0600 g, .833 SILVER, .7515 oz ASW

KM#	Date	Mintage	Fine	VF	XF	Unc
465	1801 M	—	65.00	110.00	150.00	325.00
	1802 M	—	75.00	110.00	150.00	325.00
	1803 M	—	75.00	110.00	150.00	325.00

NOTE: Varieties exist.
NOTE: Earlier dates (1789-1800) exist for this type.

TRADE COINAGE

DUCAT

3.5000 g, .986 GOLD, .1109 oz AGW
Obv: Bust right. Rev: Crowned, mantled arms.

KM#	Date	Mintage	VG	Fine	VF	XF
463	1801 M	—	80.00	125.00	250.00	375.00
	1802 M	—	80.00	125.00	250.00	375.00

NOTE: Earlier dates (1787-1800) exist for this type.

Similar to KM#463.

KM#	Date	Mintage	VG	Fine	VF	XF
486	1803 M	—	—	—	Rare	—

NOTE: Varieties exist.

FERDINAND

1803-1805

EIN (1) PFENNING

COPPER
Rev: 1 PFENNING.

KM#	Date	Mintage	VG	Fine	VF	XF
488	1804	—	5.00	7.00	10.00	20.00

Rev: EIN PFENNING.

KM#	Date	Mintage	VG	Fine	VF	XF
489	1804	—	1.50	3.00	5.00	15.00
	1805	—	1.50	3.00	5.00	15.00

NOTE: Varieties exist.

ZWEI (2) PFENNING

COPPER
Rev: II PFENNING.

KM#	Date	Mintage	VG	Fine	VF	XF
490	1804	—	4.50	8.50	17.00	35.00

Rev: ZWEI PFENNING.

KM#	Date	Mintage	VG	Fine	VF	XF
493	1805	—	3.50	7.50	15.00	30.00
(C116a)	1806	—	3.50	7.50	15.00	30.00

EIN (1) KREUZER

COPPER

KM#	Date	Mintage	VG	Fine	VF	XF
491	1804	—	3.00	6.00	12.00	25.00
	1805	—	1.50	4.00	10.00	20.00
	1806	—	1.50	4.00	10.00	20.00

3 KREUZER

BILLON

KM#	Date	Mintage	VG	Fine	VF	XF
483	1803	—	10.00	20.00	40.00	80.00
	1804	—	10.00	20.00	40.00	80.00

Rev: Date in lozenge.

KM#	Date	Mintage	VG	Fine	VF	XF
494	1805	—	10.00	20.00	40.00	85.00

NOTE: Varieties exist with and without mint mark.

6 KREUZER

BILLON

KM#	Date	Mintage	VG	Fine	VF	XF
484	1803	—	10.00	30.00	65.00	130.00
	1804	—	10.00	30.00	60.00	120.00
	1805	—	10.00	25.00	50.00	100.00

Rev: Date in lozenge.

KM#	Date	Mintage	VG	Fine	VF	XF
495	1805	—	10.00	25.00	50.00	100.00
	1806	—	10.00	25.00	50.00	100.00

20 KREUZER

6.6800 g, .583 SILVER, .1252 oz ASW

KM#	Date	Mintage	VG	Fine	VF	XF
492	1804 M	—	10.00	20.00	40.00	90.00

KM#	Date	Mintage	VG	Fine	VF	XF
496	1805 M	—	10.00	25.00	50.00	100.00
	1806 M	—	10.00	25.00	50.00	100.00

THALER

28.0600 g, .833 SILVER, .7515 oz ASW

KM#	Date	Mintage	Fine	VF	XF	Unc
485	1803	—	100.00	175.00	400.00	750.00

KM#	Date	Mintage	Fine	VF	XF	Unc
497	1805 M	—	150.00	250.00	450.00	850.00

Rev. leg: . . . PAS ETBER S R IP ELECTOR.

KM#	Date	Mintage	Fine	VF	XF	Unc
499	1806 M	—	150.00	250.00	450.00	850.00

TRADE COINAGE

DUCAT

3.5000 g, .986 GOLD, .1109 oz AGW

KM#	Date	Mintage	VG	Fine	VF	XF
487	1803 M	—	100.00	250.00	700.00	1100.
	1804 M	—	125.00	275.00	800.00	1250.

KM#	Date	Mintage	VG	Fine	VF	XF
498	1805 M	—	100.00	250.00	600.00	1000.
	1806 M	—	100.00	250.00	600.00	1000.

TYROL

Tirol

A princely county situated in Austria between Germany and Italy. In 1363 Margaret Maultasch, countess of Tyrol, handed over Tyrol to Rudolph, Duke of Austria. Except for a period of Bavarian occupation, 1805-14, Tyrol remained a Hapsburg possession until the breakup of the Austrian Empire at the end of World War I. The world's first dollar-size silver crown was struck at Hall, Tyrol, in 1486.

RULERS

Napoleon, (France) 1805-1809
Maximilian Joseph I, (Bavaria) 1805-1814
Andreas Hofer, Rebellion, 1809
Franz I, (Austria), 1814-1835
Ferdinand, (Austria), 1835-1848
Franz Joseph, (Austria), 1848-1916

The world's first dollar-size silver crown was struck at Hall, Tyrol, in 1486.

MINT MARKS

F, FH, G, H, HA - Hall

MONETARY SYSTEM

120 Kreuzer = 1 Convention Thaler

INSURRECTION COINAGE

1809

EIN (1) KREUZER

COPPER
Issue of Andreas Hofer

KM#	Date	Mintage	VG	Fine	VF	XF
148	1809	—	10.00	15.00	35.00	80.00

NOTE: Varieties exist.

20 KREUZER

SILVER
Issue of Andreas Hofer

KM#	Date	Mintage	VG	Fine	VF	XF
149	1809	—	15.00	20.00	35.00	70.00

NOTE: Three varieties exist.

AZERBAIJAN

The Republic of Azerbaijan (formerly Azerbaijan S.S.R.) includes the Nakhichevan Autonomous Republic and Nagomo-Karabakh Autonomous Region (which was abolished in 1991). Situated in the eastern area of Transcaucasia, it is bordered in the west by Armenia, in the north by Georgia and Dagestan, to the east by the Caspian Sea and to the south by Iran. It has an area of 33,430 sq. mi. (86,600 sq. km.) and a population of 7.1 million. Capital: Baku. The area is rich in mineral deposits of aluminum, copper, iron, lead, salt and zinc, with oil as its leading industry. Agriculture and livestock follow in importance.

In ancient times home of Scythian tribes and known under the Romans as Albania and to the Arabs as Arran, the country of Azerbaijan formed at the time of its invasion by Seliuk Turks a prosperous state under Persian suzerainty. From the 16th century the country was a theatre of fighting and political rivalry between Turkey, Persia and later Russia. Baku was first annexed to Russia by Czar Peter I in 1723 and remained under Russian rule for 12 years. After the Russian retreat the whole of Azerbaijan north of the Aras River became a khanate under Persian control until Czar Alexander I, after an eight-year war with Persia, annexed it in 1813 to the Russian empire.

Until the Russian Revolution of 1905 there was no political life in Azerbaijan. A Mussavat (Equality) party was formed in 1911 by Mohammed Emin, Rasulzade, a former Social Democrat. After the Russian Revolution of March 1917, the party started a campaign for independence, but Baku, the capital, with its mixed population, constituted an alien enclave in the country. While a national Azerbaijani government was established at Gandzha (Elizavetpol), a Communistcontrolled council assumed power at Baku with Stepan Shaumian, an Armenian, at its head. The Gandzha government joined first, on Sept. 20, 1917, a Transcaucasian federal republic, but on May 28, 1918, proclaimed the independence of Azerbaijan. On June 4, 1918, at Batum, a peace treaty was signed with Turkey and a Turko-Azerbaijani force started an offensive against Baku, but it was occupied on Aug. 17, 1918 by 1,400 British troops coming by sea from Anzali, Persia. On Sept. 14 the British evacuated Baku, returning to Anzali, and three days later the Azerbaijan government, headed by Fath Khoysky, established itself at Baku.

After the collapse of the Ottoman empire the British returned to Baku, at first ignoring the Azerbaijan government. A general election with universal suffrage for the Azerbaijan constituent assembly took place on Dec. 7, 1918 and out of 120 members there were 84 Mussavat supporters; Ali Marden Topchibashev was elected speaker, and Nasib Usubekov formed a new government. On Jan. 15, 1920, the Allied powers recognized Azerbaijan de facto, but on April 27 of the same year the Red army invaded the country, and a Soviet republic of Azerbaijan was proclaimed the next day. Later it became a member of the Transcaucasian Federation joining the U.S.S.R. on Dec. 30, 1922; it became a self-constituent republic in 1936.

The Azerbaijan Communist party held its first congress at Baku in Feb. 1920. From 1921 to 1925 its first secretary was a Russian, S.M. Kirov, who directed a mass deportation to Siberia of about 120,000 Azerbaijani "nationalist deviationists," among them the country's first two premiers.

In 1990 it adopted a declaration of republican sovereignty and in Aug. 1991 declared itself formally independent; this action was approved by a vote of referendum in Jan. 1992. It announced its intention of joining the CIS in Dec. 1991, but a parliamentary resolution of Oct. 1992 declined to confirms its involvement.

MONETARY SYSTEM

100 Qapik = 1 Manat

5 QAPIK

ALUMINUM

KM#	Date	Mintage	VF	XF	Unc
1	1993	—	—	—	.50

10 QAPIK

ALUMINUM

KM#	Date	Mintage	VF	XF	Unc
2	1992	—	—	—	.50

20 QAPIK

KM#	Date	Mintage	VF	XF	Unc
BRASS					
3	1992	—	—	—	1.50
ALUMINUM					
3a	1992	—	—	—	.75
	1993	—	—	—	.75

50 QAPIK

KM#	Date	Mintage	VF	XF	Unc
COPPER-NICKEL					
4	1992	—	—	—	2.00
ALUMINUM					
4a	1993	—	—	—	.75

AZORES

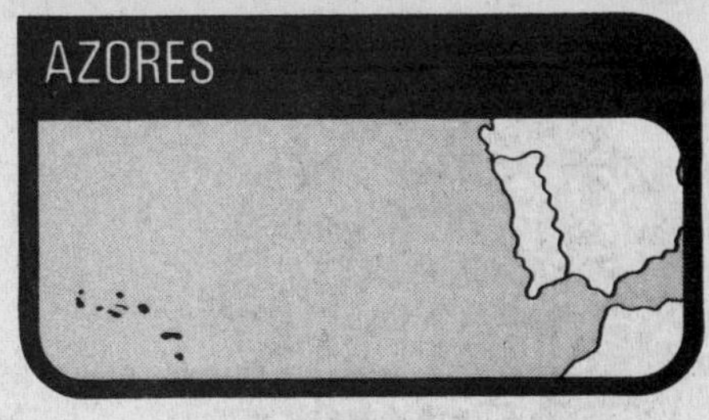

The Azores, an archipelago of nine islands of volcanic origin, are located in the Atlantic Ocean 740 miles (1,190 km.) west of Cape de Roca, Portugal. They are the westernmost region of Europe under the administration of Portugal and have an area of 902 sq. mi. (2,305 sq. km.) and a population of 330,000. Principal city: Ponta Delgada. The natives are mainly of Portuguese descent and earn their livelihood by fishing, wine making, basket weaving and the growing of fruit, grains and sugar cane. Pineapples are the chief item of export. The climate is particularly temperate, making the islands a favorite winter resort.

The Azores were discovered about 1427 by the Portuguese navigator Diogo de Silves. Portugal secured the islands in the 15th century and established the first settlement, on Santa Maria, about 1439. From 1580 to 1640 the Azores were subject to Spain.

The Azores first provincial coinage was ordered by law of August 19, 1750. Copper coins were struck for circulation in both the Azores and Madeira Islands. Keeping the same technical specifications, but with different designs. In 1795 a second provincial coinage was introduced but the weight was reduced by 50 percent.

Angra on Terceira Island became the capital of the captaincy-general of the Azores in 1766 and it was here in 1826 that the constitutionalists set up a pro-Pedro government in opposition to King Miguel in Lisbon. The whole Portuguese fleet attacked Terceira and was repelled at Praia, after which Azoreans, Brazilians and British mercenaries defeated Miguel in Portugal. Maria de Gloria, Pedro's daughter, was proclaimed queen of Portugal on Terceira in 1828.

A U.S. naval base was established at Ponta Delgada in 1917.

After World War II, the islands acquired a renewed importance as a refueling stop for transatlantic air transport. The United States maintains defense bases in the Azores as part of the collective security program of NATO.

In 1976 the archipelago became the Autonomous Region of Azores.

RULERS

Portuguese

MONETARY SYSTEM

1000 Reis (Insulanos) = 1 Milreis

TERCEIRA ISLAND

MARIA II IN EXILE

1828-1833

In 1828 Pedro declined the Portuguese throne in favor of his daughter, Maria da Gloria, who was therefore forced to live in exile 1828-1834 until Miguel was completely defeated.

5 REIS

COPPER

KM#	Date	Mintage	VG	Fine	VF	XF
5	1830	—	1.50	3.00	7.50	25.00

10 REIS

COPPER

KM#	Date	Mintage	VG	Fine	VF	XF
6	1830	—	2.00	4.00	9.00	30.00

80 REIS

BRONZE
Rev: Large leg. and large stars.

KM#	Date	Mintage	VG	Fine	VF	XF
4.1	1829	—	30.00	50.00	80.00	140.00

Rev: Small leg. and small stars.

KM#	Date	Mintage	VG	Fine	VF	XF
4.2	1829	—	15.00	30.00	45.00	75.00

NOTE: Cast from gun or bell metal with varying degrees of planchet thickness and porosity.

AZORES

PROVINCIAL COINAGE

5 REIS

COPPER
Maria II

KM#	Date	Mintage	VG	Fine	VF	XF
10	1843	—	2.50	6.00	12.00	40.00

Luiz I

KM#	Date	Mintage	Fine	VF	XF	Unc
13	1865	.090	6.00	15.00	30.00	75.00
	1866	.100	15.00	25.00	50.00	150.00
	1880	.040	3.00	6.00	15.00	35.00

Carlos I

KM#	Date	Mintage	Fine	VF	XF	Unc
16	1901	.800	1.00	2.00	4.00	12.00

10 REIS

COPPER
Maria II

KM#	Date	Mintage	VG	Fine	VF	XF
11	1843	—	2.50	6.00	15.00	45.00

Luiz I

KM#	Date	Mintage	Fine	VF	XF	Unc
14	1865	.350	2.00	4.50	12.50	30.00
	1866	.175	30.00	50.00	80.00	200.00

Carlos I

KM#	Date	Mintage	Fine	VF	XF	Unc
17	1901	.600	1.00	2.00	4.00	12.00

20 REIS

COPPER
Maria II

KM#	Date	Mintage	VG	Fine	VF	XF
12	1843	—	2.50	6.00	12.00	40.00

Luiz I

KM#	Date	Mintage	Fine	VF	XF	Unc
15	1865	.178	2.50	5.00	12.00	35.00
	1866	.150	3.00	6.00	15.00	45.00

COUNTERMARKED COINAGE

Decree of June 14, 1871

This first decree ordained that the circulating Brazilian Patacas of 2000 Reis, including the fractions of 1000, 500 and 200 Reis, which at the time locally had a value of 1200, 600, 300 and 120 Reis (Portuguese) respectively, were to be countermarked with a royal crown. These were eventually to be replaced or exchanged by current Portuguese coinage upon their entry into the public treasury. This countermark is also known on copper coins and on various silver coins of other nations that were circulating at the time. The following list is a basic guide with samples of known examples. Grades noted are for the basic coin as the countermark is normally found in better condition.

10 REIS

COPPER

c/m: Crown on Azores 5 Reis, KM#9.

KM#	Date	Good	VG	Fine	VF
30	ND(1795)	10.00	15.00	25.00	50.00

20 REIS

COPPER

KM#	Date	Good	VG	Fine	VF
	c/m: Crown on Azores X Reis, KM#6.				
18.1	ND(1830)	10.00	20.00	30.00	60.00
	c/m: Crown on Mozambique X Reis, KM#482 (Portugal)				
18.2	ND(1852)	10.00	20.00	30.00	60.00

KM#	Date	Good	VG	Fine	VF
	c/m: Crown on St. Thomas 20 Reis, KM#D1.				
18.3	ND(1819)	10.00	20.00	30.00	60.00

40 REIS

COPPER
c/m: Crown on St. Thomas 40 Reis, KM#E1.

KM#	Date	Good	VG	Fine	VF
22.1	ND(1819)	10.00	20.00	30.00	60.00
	ND(1825)	10.00	20.00	30.00	60.00

KM#	Date	Good	VG	Fine	VF
	c/m: Crown on Mozambique 40 Reis, KM#22.				
22.2	ND(1840)	10.00	20.00	30.00	60.00

120 REIS

COPPER
c/m: Crown on Angola Macuta, KM#12.

KM#	Date	Good	VG	Fine	VF
19.3	ND(1770)	20.00	30.00	50.00	80.00

KM#	Date	Good	VG	Fine	VF
	c/m: Crown on Azores 80 Reis, KM#4.2.				
19.4	ND(1829)	20.00	30.00	50.00	80.00

SILVER
c/m: Crown on Brazilian 200 Reis, KM#469.

KM#	Date	Good	VG	Fine	VF
19.1	ND(1854-67)	10.00	20.00	30.00	50.00

KM#	Date	Good	VG	Fine	VF
	c/m: Crown on Brazilian 200 Reis, KM#471.				
19.2	ND(1867-69)	10.00	20.00	30.00	50.00

300 REIS

SILVER
c/m: Crown on Brazilian 500 Reis, KM#458.

KM#	Date	Good	VG	Fine	VF
20.1	ND(1848-52)	12.50	25.00	40.00	60.00

KM#	Date	Good	VG	Fine	VF
	c/m: Crown on Brazilian 500 Reis, KM#464.				
20.2	ND(1853-67)	12.50	25.00	40.00	60.00
	c/m: Crown on Brazilian 500 Reis, KM#472.				
20.3	ND(1867-68)	12.50	25.00	40.00	60.00

600 REIS

SILVER

c/m: Crown on Brazilian 1000 Reis, KM#459.

KM#	Date	Good	VG	Fine	VF
28.1	ND(1849-52)	15.00	27.50	45.00	65.00

c/m: Crown on Brazilian 1000 Reis, KM#465.

28.2	ND(1853-66)	15.00	27.50	45.00	65.00

c/m: Crown on Brazilian 1000 Reis, KM#476.

28.3	ND(1869)	17.50	30.00	50.00	75.00

c/m: Crown on East India Co. Bengal Rupee, KM#108.

28.4	ND(1819-32)	12.00	30.00	60.00	100.00

1200 REIS

SILVER

c/m: Crown on Austria-Burgau Thaler, KM#23.

21.1	ND(1780*SF)	30.00	50.00	75.00	125.00

c/m: Crown on Brazilian 1200 Reis, KM#454.

21.4	ND(1834)	100.00	165.00	275.00	450.00

c/m: Crown on Brazilian 2000 Reis, KM#462.

21.2	ND(1851-52)	17.50	30.00	50.00	75.00

c/m: Crown on Brazilian 2000 Reis, KM#466.

21.3	ND(1853-67)	15.00	27.50	45.00	65.00

Decree of March 31, 1887

Countermark crowned G.P., 8mm. Illustration is twice normal size.

This second decree ordained that all foreign silver and copper coinage circulating in the Azores was to be countermarked with a crowned G.P. (Governo Portugues) within a circle. These also were eventually to be replaced or exchanged by current Portuguese coinage upon their entry into the public treasury. This countermark for general use is found on a profusion of Portuguese Brazilian, and foreign issues. The largest crown or dollar size includes the Portuguese 1000 Reis, Brazilian 2000 Reis, obsolete 960 Reis, 1200 Reis, Austrian Thaler, English 5 Shilling or Crown, Spanish American 8 Reales and Spanish 2 Escudos for comparison to the United States dollar. This countermark has been heavily counterfeited and should be approached with caution. The following list is a basic guide with samples of known examples. Grades noted are for the basic coin and the countermark is normally found in better condition than the coin bearing it.

15 REIS

COPPER

c/m: Crowned G.P. on Portuguese India (Goa) 15 Reis, KM#263.

KM#	Date	Good	VG	Fine	VF
23	ND	10.00	20.00	30.00	60.00

120 REIS

SILVER

c/m: Crowned G.P. on Portuguese 80 Reis, KM#238.

24	ND	15.00	25.00	40.00	70.00

300 REIS

SILVER

c/m: Crowned G.P. on Spanish or Spanish Colonial 2 Reales.

25	ND	20.00	30.00	50.00	80.00

600 REIS

SILVER

c/m: Crowned G.P. on Bolivia 4 Reales, KM#54.

26.1	ND(1773-89)	30.00	50.00	75.00	125.00

c/m: Crowned G.P. on Portuguese 400 Reis, KM#331.

26.2	ND(1802-16)	25.00	45.00	70.00	110.00

c/m: Crowned G.P. on Portuguese 400 Reis, KM#386.

26.3	ND(1828-34)	35.00	60.00	100.00	150.00

1200 REIS

SILVER

c/m: Crowned G.P. on Brazilian (Minas Gerais) 960 Reis, KM#242.

KM#	Date	Good	VG	Fine	VF
29.1	ND(1791-1808)	55.00	90.00	135.00	200.00

c/m: Crowned G.P. on Brazilian 960 Reis, KM#307.1.

KM#	Date	VG	Fine	VF	XF
29.2	ND(1809-18)	40.00	60.00	100.00	150.00

c/m: Crowned G.P. on Brazilian 960 Reis, KM326.1.

29.5	ND(1818-22)	40.00	60.00	100.00	150.00

c/m: Crowned G.P. on Peru 8 Reales, KM#142.3.

29.3	ND(1828-40)	40.00	60.00	100.00	150.00

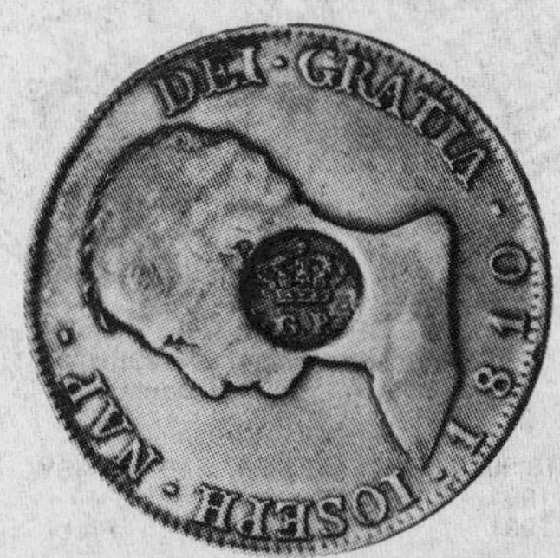

c/m: Crowned G.P. on Spain 20 Reales, C#92.

KM#	Date	Good	VG	Fine	VF
29.4	ND(1808-13)	65.00	95.00	175.00	300.00

NOTE: The above examples as noted are listed only to determine relative size and do not reflect a current price for other foreign types found with genuine countermarks.

REPUBLIC

25 ESCUDOS

COPPER-NICKEL
Regional Autonomy

KM#	Date	Mintage	VF	XF	Unc
43	1980	.770	—	1.50	3.50
	11.0000 g, .925 SILVER, .3272 oz ASW				
43a	1980	.012	—	Proof	20.00

100 ESCUDOS

COPPER-NICKEL
Regional Autonomy

KM#	Date	Mintage	VF	XF	Unc
44	1980	.270	—	3.00	7.50
	16.5000 g, .925 SILVER, .4908 oz ASW				
44a	1980	.012	—	Proof	45.00

COPPER-NICKEL
10th Anniversary of Regional Autonomy - Flower

KM#	Date	Mintage	VF	XF	Unc
45	1986	.750	—	—	4.00
	16.5000 g, .925 SILVER, .4908 oz ASW				
45a	1986	.020	—	—	22.50
	1986	.010	—	Proof	35.00

COPPER-NICKEL
100th Anniversary of Death
of Poet Antero de Quental

KM#	Date	Mintage	VF	XF	Unc
46	1991	1.000	—	—	3.50
	18.5000 g, .925 SILVER, .5502 oz ASW				
46a	1991	.030	—	—	20.00
	1991	.015	—	Proof	32.50

PROOF SETS (PS)

KM#	Date	Mintage	Identification	Issue Price	Mkt. Val.
PS1	1980	12,000	KM43a-44a	40.00	65.00

BAHAMAS

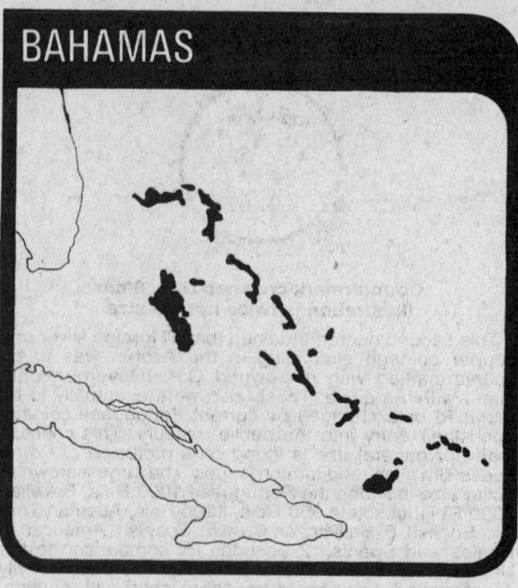

The Commonwealth of the Bahamas is an archipelago of about 3,000 islands, cays and rocks located in the Atlantic Ocean east of Florida and north of Cuba. The total land area of the 800 mile (1,287 km.) long chain of islands is 5,380 sq. mi. (13,935 sq. km.). They have a population of 245,000. Capital: Nassau. The Bahamas import most of their food and manufactured products and export cement, refined oil, pulpwood and lobsters. Tourism is the principal industry.

The Bahamas were discovered by Columbus in October, 1492, upon his sighting of the island of San Salvador, but Spain made no attempt to settle them. British influence began in 1626 when Charles I granted them to the lord proprietors of Carolina, with settlement in 1629 at New Providence by colonists from the northern territory. Although the Bahamas were temporarily under Spanish control in 1641 and 1703, they continued under British proprietors until 1717, when, as the result of political and economic mismanagement, the civil and military governments were surrendered to the King and the islands designated a British Crown Colony. Full international agreement on British possession of the islands resulted from the Treaty of Versailles in 1783. The Bahamas obtained complete internal self-government under the constitution of Jan. 7, 1964. Full independence was achieved on July 10, 1973. The Bahamas is a member of the Commonwealth of Nations. The Queen of England is Chief of State.

The coinage of Great Britain was legal tender in the Bahamas from 1825 to the issuing of a definitive coinage in 1966.

RULERS

British

MINT MARKS

Through 1969 all decimal coinage of the Bahamas was executed at the Royal Mint in England. Since that time issues have been struck at both the Royal Mint and at the Franklin Mint (FM) in the U.S.A. While the mint mark of the latter appears on coins dated 1971 and subsequently, it is missing from the 1970 issues.

JP - John Pinches, London

None - Royal Mint

(t) - Tower of London

FM - Franklin Mint, U.S.A.*

***NOTE:** From 1975 the Franklin Mint has produced coinage in up to 3 different qualities. Qualities of issue are designated in ( ) after each date and are defined as follows:

(M) MATTE - Normal circulation strike or a dull finish produced by sandblasting special uncirculated (polish finish) or proof quality dies.

(U) SPECIAL UNCIRCULATED - Polished or proof-like in appearance without any frosted features.

(P) PROOF - The highest quality obtainable having mirror-like fields and frosted features.

MONETARY SYSTEM

12 Pence = 1 Shilling

PENNY

COPPER

KM#	Date	Mintage	Fine	VF	XF	Unc
1	1806 engrailed edge					
		.120	30.00	70.00	140.00	250.00
	1806 engrailed edge			—	Proof	250.00
	1806 plain edge			(restrike)	Proof	150.00
	1807 engrailed edge			—	Proof	3000.

GILT

KM#	Date	Mintage	Fine	VF	XF	Unc
1a	1806 engrailed edge			(restrike)	Proof	350.00

DECIMAL COINAGE

100 Cents = 1 Dollar

CENT

NICKEL-BRASS
Starfish

KM#	Date	Mintage	VF	XF	Unc
2	1966	7.312	—	.10	.25
	1968	.800	—	.10	.50
	1969	4.036	—	.10	.25
	1969	.010	—	Proof	.50

 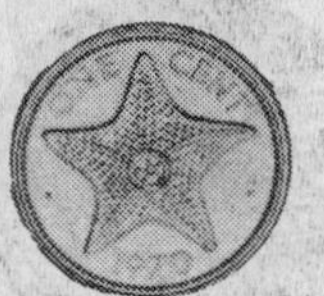

BRONZE

KM#	Date	Mintage	VF	XF	Unc
15	1970	.125	.10	.25	.50
	1970	.023	—	Proof	.50

NOTE: Proof specimens of this date are struck in 'special brass' which looks like a pale bronze.

KM#	Date	Mintage	VF	XF	Unc
16	1971FM	1.007	—	.10	.15
	1971FM(P)	.031	—	Proof	.50
	1972FM	1.037	—	.10	.15
	1972FM(P)	.035	—	Proof	.50
	1973	7.000	—	.10	.15
	1973FM	1.040	—	.10	.15
	1973FM(P)	.035	—	Proof	.50

BRASS

KM#	Date	Mintage	VF	XF	Unc
59	1974	.011	—	.10	.25
	1974FM	.071	—	.10	.20
	1974FM(P)	.094	—	Proof	.50
	1975FM(M)	.060	—	.10	.15
	1975FM(U)	3,845	—	.10	.50
	1975FM(P)	.029	—	Proof	.50
	1976FM(M)	.060	—	.10	.20
	1976FM(U)	1,453	—	.10	.50
	1976FM(P)	.023	—	Proof	.50
	1977	3.000	—	.10	.15
	1977FM(M)	.060	—	.10	.20
	1977FM(U)	713 pcs.	—	.50	1.50
	1977FM(P)	.011	—	Proof	.50
	1978FM(M)	.060	—	.10	.20
	1978FM(U)	767 pcs.	—	.50	1.50
	1978FM(P)	6,931	—	Proof	.75
	1979	—	—	.10	.15
	1979FM(P)	2,053	—	Proof	1.00
	1980	4.000	—	.10	.15
	1980FM(P)	2,084	—	Proof	1.00
	1981	5.000	—	.10	.15
	1981FM(M)	—	—	.10	.15
	1981FM(P)	1,980	—	Proof	1.00
	1982	5.000	—	.10	.15
	1982FM(M)	—	—	.10	.15
	1982FM(P)	1,217	—	Proof	1.00
	1983	8.000	—	.10	.15
	1983FM(P)	1,020	—	Proof	1.00
	1984	—	—	.10	.15
	1984FM(P)	7,500	—	Proof	.75
	1985	12.000	—	.10	.15
	1985FM(P)	7,500	—	Proof	.50
	COPPER PLATED ZINC				
59a	1985	—	—	.10	.25
	1987	12.000	—	.10	.25
	1989	12.000	—	.10	.25
	1989	—	—	Proof	.75
	1990	—	—	.10	.25
	1991	—	—	.10	.25
	1992	—	—	.10	.25

5 CENTS

COPPER-NICKEL
Pineapple

KM#	Date	Mintage	VF	XF	Unc
3	1966	2.571	—	.10	.20
	1968	.600	—	.10	.30
	1969	2.026	—	.10	.20
	1969	.075	—	Proof	.50
	1970	.026	—	.10	.30
	1970	.023	—	Proof	.50

NOTE: The obverse of the above also comes muled with the reverse of a New Zealand 2-cent piece KM#32. The undated 1967 error is listed as New Zealand KM#33.

KM#	Date	Mintage	VF	XF	Unc
17	1971FM	.013	—	.10	.35
	1971FM(P)	.031	—	Proof	.50
	1972FM	.011	—	.10	.35
	1972FM(P)	.035	—	Proof	.50
	1973FM	.021	—	.10	.35
	1973FM(P)	.035	—	Proof	.50

Obv. leg: THE COMMONWEALTH OF THE BAHAMAS

KM#	Date	Mintage	VF	XF	Unc
38	1973	1.000	—	.10	.65

KM#	Date	Mintage	VF	XF	Unc
60	1974FM	.023	—	.10	.25
	1974FM(P)	.094	—	Proof	.50
	1975	—	—	.10	.30
	1975FM(M)	.012	—	.10	.25
	1975FM(U)	3,845	—	.15	.50
	1975FM(P)	.029	—	Proof	.50
	1976FM(M)	.012	—	.10	.25
	1976FM(U)	1,453	—	.15	.75
	1976FM(P)	.023	—	Proof	.50
	1977FM(M)	.012	—	.10	.35
	1977FM(U)	713 pcs.	—	.50	1.50
	1977FM(P)	.011	—	Proof	.50
	1978FM(M)	.012	—	.10	.35
	1978FM(U)	767 pcs.	—	.50	1.50
	1978FM(P)	6,931	—	Proof	.50
	1979FM(P)	2,053	—	Proof	.75
	1980FM(P)	2,084	—	Proof	.75
	1981	—	—	.10	.25
	1981FM(P)	1,980	—	Proof	.75
	1982FM(P)	1,217	—	Proof	.75
	1983	2.000	—	.10	.25
	1983FM(P)	1,020	—	Proof	.75
	1984	—	—	.10	.25
	1984FM(P)	1,036	—	Proof	.75
	1985FM(P)	7,500	—	Proof	.75
	1987	4.000	—	.10	.25
	1989	—	—	.10	.25
	1989	—	—	Proof	.75
	1991	—	—	.10	.25
	1992	—	—	.10	.25

10 CENTS

COPPER-NICKEL
Bone Fish

KM#	Date	Mintage	VF	XF	Unc
4	1966	2.198	—	.10	.25
	1968	.550	—	.50	4.00
	1969	2.026	—	.10	.25
	1969	.010	—	Proof	.50
4	1970	.027	—	.10	.35
	1970	.023	—	Proof	.50

KM#	Date	Mintage	VF	XF	Unc
18	1971FM	.013	—	.15	.50
	1971FM(P)	.031	—	Proof	.50
	1972FM	.011	—	.15	.50
	1972FM(P)	.035	—	Proof	.50
	1973FM	.015	—	.15	.50
	1973FM(P)	.035	—	Proof	.50

Obv. leg: THE COMMONWEALTH OF THE BAHAMAS

KM#	Date	Mintage	VF	XF	Unc
39	1973	1.000	—	.15	.85

KM#	Date	Mintage	VF	XF	Unc
61	1974FM	.017	—	.10	.35
	1974FM(P)	.094	—	Proof	.50
	1975	3.000	—	.10	.25
	1975FM(M)	6,000	—	.15	.50
	1975FM(U)	3,845	—	.15	.50
	1975FM(P)	.029	—	Proof	.50
	1976FM(M)	6,000	—	.15	.50
	1976FM(U)	1,453	—	.25	1.00
	1976FM(P)	.023	—	Proof	.50
	1977FM(M)	6,000	—	.15	.50
	1977FM(U)	713 pcs.	—	.50	1.50
	1977FM(P)	.011	—	Proof	.50
	1978FM(M)	6,000	—	.15	.50
	1978FM(U)	767 pcs.	—	.50	1.50
	1978FM(P)	6,931	—	Proof	.75
	1979FM(P)	2,053	—	Proof	1.00
	1980	2.500	—	.10	.35
	1980FM(P)	2,084	—	Proof	1.00
	1981FM(P)	1,980	—	Proof	1.00
	1982	2.000	—	.10	.35
	1982FM(P)	1,217	—	Proof	1.00
	1983FM(P)	1,020	—	Proof	1.00
	1984FM(P)	1,036	—	Proof	1.00
	1985	2.000	—	.10	.35
	1985FM(M)	—	—	.15	.50
	1985FM(P)	7,500	—	Proof	.75
	1987	3.000	—	.15	.50
	1989	—	—	.15	.50
	1989	—	—	Proof	.75
	1991	—	—	.15	.50
	1992	—	—	.15	.50

15 CENTS

COPPER-NICKEL
Hibiscus

KM#	Date	Mintage	VF	XF	Unc
5	1966	.930	—	.15	.35
	1969	1.026	—	.15	.35
	1969	.010	—	Proof	.50
	1970	.028	—	.15	.35
	1970	.023	—	Proof	.50

KM#	Date	Mintage	VF	XF	Unc
19	1971FM	.013	—	.15	.35
	1971FM(P)	.031	—	Proof	.50
	1972FM	.011	—	.15	.35
	1972FM(P)	.035	—	Proof	.50
	1973FM	.014	—	.15	.35
	1973FM(P)	.035	—	Proof	.50

KM#	Date	Mintage	VF	XF	Unc
62	1974FM	.015	—	.15	.35
	1974FM(P)	.094	—	Proof	.50
	1975FM(M)	3,500	—	.20	1.00
	1975FM(U)	3,845	—	.20	1.00
	1975FM(P)	.029	—	Proof	.50
	1976FM(M)	3,500	—	.20	1.00
	1976FM(U)	1,453	—	.25	1.50
	1976FM(P)	.023	—	Proof	.50
	1977FM(M)	3,500	—	.20	1.00
	1977FM(U)	713 pcs.	—	.50	2.00
	1977FM(P)	.011	—	Proof	.50
	1978FM(M)	3,500	—	.20	1.00
	1978FM(U)	767 pcs.	—	.50	2.00
	1978FM(P)	6,931	—	Proof	.75
	1979FM(P)	2,053	—	Proof	1.00
	1980FM(P)	2,084	—	Proof	1.00
	1981FM(P)	1,980	—	Proof	1.00
	1982FM(P)	1,217	—	Proof	1.25
	1983FM(P)	1,020	—	Proof	1.25
	1984FM(P)	1,036	—	Proof	1.25
	1985FM(P)	7,500	—	Proof	.75
	1989	—	—	.15	.50
	1989	—	—	Proof	1.00
	1991	—	—	.15	.50
	1992	—	—	.15	.50

25 CENTS

NICKEL
Bahaminian Sloop

KM#	Date	Mintage	VF	XF	Unc
6	1966	3.685	—	.25	.50
	1969	1.026	—	.25	.50
	1969	.010	—	Proof	.75
	1970	.026	—	.25	.50
	1970FM	.023	—	Proof	.75
	1970FM(M)	—	—	—	—

KM#	Date	Mintage	VF	XF	Unc
20	1971FM	.013	—	.25	.50
	1971FM(P)	.031	—	Proof	.75
	1972FM	.011	—	.25	.50
	1972FM(M)	—	—	.25	.50
	1972FM(P)	.035	—	Proof	.75
	1973FM	.012	—	.25	.50
	1973FM(P)	.035	—	Proof	.75

KM#	Date	Mintage	VF	XF	Unc
63	1974FM	.013	—	.25	.50
	1974FM(P)	.094	—	Proof	.75
	1975FM(M)	2,400	—	.25	1.00
	1975FM(U)	3,845	—	.25	1.00
	1975FM(P)	.029	—	Proof	.75
	1976FM(M)	2,400	—	.25	1.00
	1976FM(U)	1,453	—	.30	1.25
	1976FM(P)	.023	—	Proof	.75
	1977	—	—	.25	.50
	1977FM(M)	2,400	—	.25	1.00
	1977FM(U)	713 pcs.	—	.50	3.00
	1977FM(P)	.011	—	Proof	.75
	1978FM(M)	2,400	—	.25	1.00
	1978FM(U)	767 pcs.	—	.50	3.00
	1978FM(P)	6,931	—	Proof	1.00
	1979	—	—	.25	.50
	1979FM(P)	2,053	—	Proof	1.25
	1980FM(P)	2,084	—	Proof	1.25
	1981	1.600	—	.25	.50
	1981FM(P)	1,980	—	Proof	1.25
	1982FM(P)	1,217	—	Proof	1.50
	1983FM(P)	1,020	—	Proof	1.50

KM#	Date	Mintage	VF	XF	Unc
63	1984FM(P)	1,036	—	Proof	1.50
	1985	2.000	—	.25	.50
	1985FM(P)	7,500	—	Proof	1.00
	1989	—	—	.25	.50
	1989	—	—	Proof	1.25
	1991	—	—	.25	.50
	1992	—	—	.25	.50

50 CENTS

10.3700 g, .800 SILVER, .2667 oz ASW
Blue Marlin

KM#	Date	Mintage	VF	XF	Unc
7	1966	.701	BV	1.50	2.00
	1969	.026	BV	1.75	2.50
	1969	.010	—	Proof	3.00
	1970	.025	BV	1.75	2.50
	1970	.023	—	Proof	3.00
21	1971FM	.014	BV	1.75	2.50
	1971FM(P)	.031	—	Proof	3.00
	1972FM	.012	BV	1.75	2.50
	1972FM(P)	.035	—	Proof	3.00
	1973FM	.011	BV	1.75	2.50
	1973FM(P)	.035	—	Proof	3.00

COPPER-NICKEL

KM#	Date	Mintage	VF	XF	Unc
64	1974FM	.012	—	.50	1.25
	1975FM(M)	1,200	—	1.00	8.00
	1975FM(U)	3,828	—	.65	4.00
	1976FM(M)	1,200	—	.75	5.00
	1976FM(U)	1,453	—	.65	4.00
	1977FM(M)	1,200	—	.75	5.00
	1977FM(U)	713 pcs.	—	1.25	10.00
	1978FM(M)	1,200	—	1.00	8.00
	1978FM(U)	767 pcs.	—	1.25	10.00
	1981FM(P)	1,980	—	Proof	3.00
	1982FM(P)	1,217	—	Proof	3.50
	1983FM(P)	1,020	—	Proof	3.50
	1984FM(P)	1,036	—	Proof	3.50
	1985FM(P)	7,500	—	Proof	2.50
	1989	—	—	.75	2.00
	1989	—	—	Proof	2.50
	1991	—	—	.75	2.00
	1992	—	—	.75	2.00

10.3700 g, .800 SILVER, .2667 oz ASW

KM#	Date	Mintage	VF	XF	Unc
64a	1974FM(P)	.094	—	Proof	4.00
	1975FM(P)	.029	—	Proof	4.00
	1976FM(P)	.023	—	Proof	4.00
	1977FM(P)	.011	—	Proof	4.00
	1978FM(P)	6,931	—	Proof	4.50
	1979FM(P)	2,053	—	Proof	5.00
	1980FM(P)	2,084	—	Proof	5.00

DOLLAR

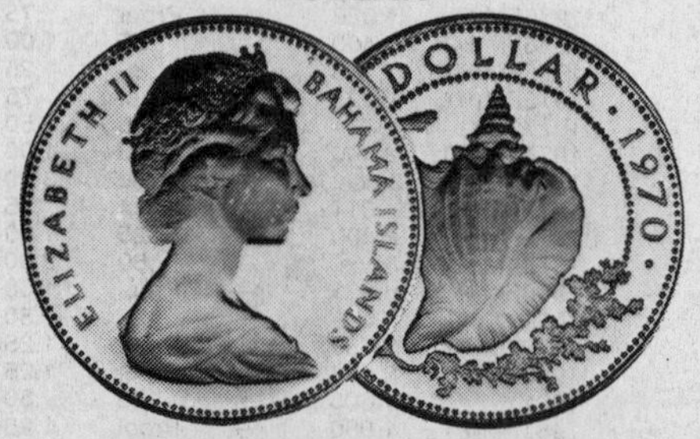

18.1400 g, .800 SILVER, .4666 oz ASW
Conch Shell

KM#	Date	Mintage	VF	XF	Unc
8	1966	.406	BV	3.00	5.00
	1969	.026	BV	3.00	5.00
	1969	.010	—	Proof	6.00
	1970	.027	BV	3.00	5.00
	1970	.023	—	Proof	6.00
22	1971FM	.015	BV	3.00	5.00
	1971FM(P)	.031	—	Proof	6.00
	1972FM	.018	BV	3.00	5.00
	1972FM(P)	.035	—	Proof	6.00
	1973FM	.010	BV	3.00	5.00
	1973FM(P)	.035	—	Proof	6.00

COPPER-NICKEL

KM#	Date	Mintage	VF	XF	Unc
65	1974FM	.012	—	1.00	3.00
	1975FM(M)	600 pcs.	—	7.50	20.00
	1975FM(U)	3,845	—	1.00	3.00
	1976FM(M)	600 pcs.	—	7.50	20.00
	1976FM(U)	1,453	—	1.00	3.50
	1977FM(M)	600 pcs.	—	7.50	20.00
	1977FM(U)	713 pcs.	—	5.00	15.00
	1978FM(U)	1,367	—	2.00	10.00

18.1400 g, .800 SILVER, .4666 oz ASW

KM#	Date	Mintage	VF	XF	Unc
65a	1974FM(P)	.094	—	Proof	6.00
	1975FM(P)	.029	—	Proof	6.00
	1976FM(P)	.023	—	Proof	6.00
	1977FM(P)	.011	—	Proof	6.00
	1978FM(P)	6,931	—	Proof	7.00
	1979FM(P)	2,053	—	Proof	8.00
	1980FM(P)	2,084	—	Proof	8.00

COPPER-NICKEL, 32mm

KM#	Date	Mintage	VF	XF	Unc
65b	1981FM(P)	1,980	—	Proof	8.00
	1989	—	—	1.50	3.50
	1989	*2,000	—	Proof	10.00
	1991	—	—	1.50	3.50
	1992	—	—	1.50	3.50

Poinciana Flower

KM#	Date	Mintage	VF	XF	Unc
89	1982FM(P)	1,217	—	Proof	11.50

10th Anniversary of Independence
Allamanda

KM#	Date	Mintage	VF	XF	Unc
93	1983FM(P)	1,020	—	Proof	12.50

Bougainvillea Flower

KM#	Date	Mintage	VF	XF	Unc
104	1984FM(P)	1,036	—	Proof	12.50
	1985FM(P)	7,500	—	Proof	7.50

2 DOLLARS

29.8000 g, .925 SILVER, .8863 oz ASW
National Bird - Flamingos

KM#	Date	Mintage	VF	XF	Unc
9	1966	.104	BV	5.00	7.00
	1969	.026	BV	5.00	7.00
	1969	.010	—	Proof	9.00
	1970	.032	BV	5.00	7.00
	1970	.023	—	Proof	9.00

KM#	Date	Mintage	VF	XF	Unc
23	1971FM	.088	BV	5.00	7.00
	1971FM(P)	.060	—	Proof	8.00
	1972FM	.065	BV	5.00	7.00
	1972FM(P)	.059	—	Proof	8.00
	1973FM	.043	BV	5.00	7.00
	1973FM(P)	.050	—	Proof	8.00

COPPER-NICKEL

KM#	Date	Mintage	VF	XF	Unc
66	1974FM	.037	—	2.00	4.00
	1975FM(M)	300 pcs.	—	9.00	22.00
	1975FM(U)	8,810	—	2.00	4.50
	1976FM(M)	300 pcs.	—	9.00	22.00
	1976FM(U)	4,381	—	2.00	5.00
	1977FM(M)	300 pcs.	—	9.00	22.00
	1977FM(U)	946 pcs.	—	3.00	15.00
	1978FM(U)	1,067	—	3.00	15.00
	1979FM(U)	300 pcs.	—	7.50	25.00
	29.8000 g, .925 SILVER, .8863 oz ASW				
66a	1974FM(P)	.129	—	Proof	8.00
	1975FM(P)	.045	—	Proof	8.00
	1976FM(P)	.035	—	Proof	8.00
	1977FM(P)	.015	—	Proof	10.00
	1978FM(P)	.011	—	Proof	10.00
	1979FM(P)	2,053	—	Proof	15.00
	1980FM(P)	2,084	—	Proof	15.00
	COPPER-NICKEL, 34mm				
66b	1981FM(P)	1,980	—	Proof	10.00
	1989	—	—	2.00	6.00

16.8500 g, .925 SILVER, .5012 oz ASW

KM#	Date	Mintage	VF	XF	Unc
66c	1989	*4,000	—	Proof	40.00
	1991	600 pcs.	—	—	125.00

COPPER-NICKEL
Bahama Swallows

KM#	Date	Mintage	VF	XF	Unc
90	1982FM(P)	1,217	—	Proof	15.00

10th Anniversary of Independence
Honeycreepers

KM#	Date	Mintage	VF	XF	Unc
94	1983FM(P)	1,020	—	Proof	15.00

Flamingos

KM#	Date	Mintage	VF	XF	Unc
105	1984FM(P)	1,036	—	Proof	17.50
	1985FM(P)	7,500	—	Proof	12.50

5 DOLLARS

42.1200 g, .925 SILVER, 1.2527 oz ASW

KM#	Date	Mintage	VF	XF	Unc
10	1966	.100	BV	7.00	9.00
	1969	.036	BV	7.00	9.00
	1969	.010	—	Proof	10.00
	1970	.043	BV	7.00	9.00
	1970	.023	—	Proof	10.00

KM#	Date	Mintage	VF	XF	Unc
24	1971FM	.029	BV	7.00	9.00
	1971FM(P)	.031	—	Proof	10.00

Obv: Similar to KM#24.

KM#	Date	Mintage	VF	XF	Unc
33	1972FM	.032	BV	7.00	9.00
	1972FM(P)	.035	—	Proof	10.00
	1973FM	.032	BV	7.00	9.00
	1973FM(P)	.035	—	Proof	10.00

COPPER-NICKEL

KM#	Date	Mintage	VF	XF	Unc
67	1974FM	.032	—	—	6.00
	1975FM(M)	200 pcs.	—	—	40.00
	1975FM(U)	7,058	—	—	7.50
	1976FM(M)	200 pcs.	—	—	40.00
	1976FM(U)	2,591	—	—	15.00
	1977FM(M)	200 pcs.	—	—	40.00
	1977FM(U)	801 pcs.	—	—	20.00
	1978FM(U)	1,244	—	—	15.00
	42.1200 g, .925 SILVER, 1.2527 oz ASW				
67a	1974FM(P)	.094	—	Proof	9.00
	1975FM(P)	.029	—	Proof	10.00
	1976FM(P)	.023	—	Proof	10.00
	1977FM(P)	.011	—	Proof	15.00
	1978FM(P)	6,931	—	Proof	20.00
	1979FM(P)	2,053	—	Proof	25.00
	1980FM(P)	2,084	—	Proof	25.00
	42.1200 g, .500 SILVER, .6771 oz ASW **Reduced diameter.**				
67b	1981FM(P)	1,980	—	Proof	27.50

Columbus Memorial

KM#	Date	Mintage	VF	XF	Unc
91	1982FM(P)	1,217	—	Proof	50.00

10th Anniversary of Independence
Flamingos

KM#	Date	Mintage	VF	XF	Unc
95	1983FM(P)	1,020	—	Proof	50.00

Historical Map

KM#	Date	Mintage	VF	XF	Unc
106	1984FM(P)	1,036	—	Proof	50.00

Christopher Columbus

KM#	Date	Mintage	VF	XF	Unc
107	1985FM(P)	7,847	—	Proof	30.00

19.4400 g, .925 SILVER, .5782 oz ASW
Christopher Columbus - Sword and Flag

KM#	Date	Mintage	VF	XF	Unc
132	1989	*4,000	—	Proof	50.00
	1991	750 pcs.	—	Proof	135.00
	1992	*.025	—	Proof	45.00

15.4400 g, .925 SILVER, .5782 oz ASW
Discovery of America - Columbus' Ships
Obv: Coat of arms.

KM#	Date	Mintage	VF	XF	Unc
138	1992	*.025	—	Proof	45.00

500th Anniversary of the Americas - Columbus and King and Queen

KM#	Date	Mintage	VF	XF	Unc
139	1991	*.025	—	Proof	32.50

500th Anniversary of the Americas - Columbus Sighting Land

KM#	Date	Mintage	VF	XF	Unc
140	1991	*.025	—	Proof	32.50

500th Anniversary of the Americas - Columbus Claiming the Land

KM#	Date	Mintage	VF	XF	Unc
141	1991	*.025	—	Proof	32.50

500th Anniversary of the Americas - Jacques Cartier and Map

KM#	Date	Mintage	VF	XF	Unc
142	1991	*.025	—	Proof	32.50

500th Anniversary of the Americas - Thomas Jefferson and Independence Hall

KM#	Date	Mintage	VF	XF	Unc
143	1991	*.025	—	Proof	32.50

500th Anniversary of the Americas - Simon Bolivar and Jose San Martin

KM#	Date	Mintage	VF	XF	Unc
144	1991	*.025	—	Proof	32.50

500th Anniversary of the Americas - Abraham Lincoln and 2 Seated Negroes

KM#	Date	Mintage	VF	XF	Unc
145	1991	*.025	—	Proof	32.50

500th Anniversary of the Americas - Thomas Edison and Electric Light Demonstration

KM#	Date	Mintage	VF	XF	Unc
146	1991	*.025	—	Proof	32.50

500th Anniversary of the Americas - Wright Brothers' First Airplane

KM#	Date	Mintage	VF	XF	Unc
147	1991	*.025	—	Proof	32.50

500th Anniversary of the Americas - Henry Ford and Automobiles

KM#	Date	Mintage	VF	XF	Unc
148	1991	*.025	—	Proof	32.50

500th Anniversary of the Americas - Teddy Roosevelt

KM#	Date	Mintage	VF	XF	Unc
149	1991	*.025	—	Proof	32.50

500th Anniversary of the Americas - First Manned Moonlanding

KM#	Date	Mintage	VF	XF	Unc
150	1991	*.025	—	Proof	32.50

10 DOLLARS

3.9943 g, .917 GOLD, .1177 oz AGW

Adoption of New Constitution - Fortress

KM#	Date	Mintage	VF	XF	Unc
11	1967	6,200	—	—	60.00
	1967	850 pcs.	—	Proof	90.00
25	1971	.023	—	—	50.00
	1971(t)	1,250	—	Proof	80.00

Rev: Hallmark and fineness stamped near bottom.

KM#	Date	Mintage	VF	XF	Unc
26	1971	—	—	—	60.00

NOTE: The above coins were struck by the Gori & Zucchi Mint, Italy.

3.1950 g, .917 GOLD, .0940 oz AGW

KM#	Date	Mintage	VF	XF	Unc
34	1972	.011	—	—	60.00
	1972	1,250	—	Proof	70.00

1.4500 g, .750 GOLD, .0349 oz AGW
Independence Day - July 10
Tobacco Dove
Rev: W/o fineness and date.

KM#	Date	Mintage	VF	XF	Unc
40	1973	—	—	—	25.00
	1973	—	—	Proof	40.00

1.4500 g, .585 GOLD, .0272 oz AGW
Rev: .585 fineness

KM#	Date	Mintage	VF	XF	Unc
41	1973	9,960	—	—	25.00
	1973	1,260	—	Proof	40.00

49.7500 g, .925 SILVER, 1.4795 oz ASW
Independence Day - July 10
Obv: Similar to 2500 Dollars, KM#101.

KM#	Date	Mintage	VF	XF	Unc
42	1973FM	.028	—	—	15.00
	1973FM(P)	.063	—	Proof	20.00

COPPER-NICKEL
First Anniversary of Independence
Obv: Similar to 5 Dollars, KM#67.

KM#	Date	Mintage	VF	XF	Unc
68	1974FM	4,825	—	—	12.00

50.4200 g, .925 SILVER, 1.4994 oz ASW

KM#	Date	Mintage	VF	XF	Unc
68a	1974FM(P)	.043	—	Proof	14.00

COPPER-NICKEL
Anniversary of Independence
Yellow Elder
Obv: Similar to 5 Dollars, KM#67.

KM#	Date	Mintage	VF	XF	Unc
76	1975FM(M)	100 pcs.	—	—	90.00
	1975FM(U)	5,325	—	—	12.50
	1976FM(M)	100 pcs.	—	—	90.00
	1976FM(U)	100 pcs.	—	—	90.00
	1977FM(M)	100 pcs.	—	—	90.00
	1977FM(U)	369 pcs.	—	—	30.00

49.1000 g, .925 SILVER, 1.4602 oz ASW

KM#	Date	Mintage	VF	XF	Unc
76a	1975FM(P)	.063	—	Proof	16.50
	1976FM(P)	.010	—	Proof	18.50
	1977FM(P)	4,424	—	Proof	22.50

45.3600 g, .500 SILVER, .7291 oz ASW
Fifth Anniversary of Independence
Obv: Similar to 5 Dollars, KM#67.

KM#	Date	Mintage	VF	XF	Unc
78.1	1978	.050	—	Proof	18.00

Rev: Tower mint mark after DOLLARS.

KM#	Date	Mintage	VF	XF	Unc
78.2	1978(t)	—	—	Proof	18.00

Fifth Anniversary of Independence
Obv: Arms.

KM#	Date	Mintage	VF	XF	Unc
79	1978	.050	—	Proof	16.00

30.2800 g, .500 SILVER, .4868 oz ASW
Tenth Anniversary Caribbean Development Bank

KM#	Date	Mintage	VF	XF	Unc
84	1980FM(P)	1,001	—	Proof	22.50

28.2800 g, .925 SILVER, .8410 oz ASW
Wedding of Prince Charles and Lady Diana

KM#	Date	Mintage	VF	XF	Unc
85	1981	.039	—	Proof	18.00

30.2800 g, .500 SILVER, .4867 oz ASW
30th Anniversary of Coronation of Queen Elizabeth II

KM#	Date	Mintage	VF	XF	Unc
96	1983FM(P)	3,374	—	Proof	25.00

23.3300 g, .925 SILVER, .6939 oz ASW
10th Anniversary of Independence

KM#	Date	Mintage	VF	XF	Unc
97	1983	800 pcs.	—	Proof	42.50

Los Angeles Olympics - Sprinter

KM#	Date	Mintage	VF	XF	Unc
114	1984	2,100	—	Proof	50.00

29.1700 g, .500 SILVER, .4690 oz ASW
10th Anniversary of Central Bank

KM#	Date	Mintage	VF	XF	Unc
127	1984	1,001	—	Proof	70.00

28.2800 g, .925 SILVER, .8411 oz ASW
Royal Visit

KM#	Date	Mintage	VF	XF	Unc
109	1985	1,060	—	Proof	27.50

47.5400 g, .917 GOLD, 1.4013 oz AGW

KM#	Date	Mintage	VF	XF	Unc
109a	1985	*250 pcs.	—	Proof	800.00

28.2800 g, .500 SILVER, .4546 oz ASW
Commonwealth Games

KM#	Date	Mintage	VF	XF	Unc
113	1986	899 pcs.	—	—	17.50

28.2800 g, .925 SILVER, .8411 oz ASW

KM#	Date	Mintage	VF	XF	Unc
113a	1986	1,343	—	Proof	27.50

Queen Isabella and Columbus
Similar to 250 Dollars, KM#121.

KM#	Date	Mintage	VF	XF	Unc
120	1987	1,800	—	Proof	60.00

Columbus Discovering America
Obv: Queen Elizabeth.
Rev: Columbus sighting America.

KM#	Date	Mintage	VF	XF	Unc
123	1988	1,704	—	Proof	60.00

Christopher Columbus
Obv: Queen Elizabeth.
Rev: Similar to 100 Dollars, KM#130.

KM#	Date	Mintage	VF	XF	Unc
128	1989	*.010	—	Proof	45.00

Discovery of New World - Columbus

KM#	Date	Mintage	VF	XF	Unc
133	1990	550 pcs.	—	—	145.00
	1990	.010	—	Proof	50.00

20 DOLLARS

7.9880 g, .917 GOLD, .2355 oz AGW
Adoption of New Constitution - Lighthouse

KM#	Date	Mintage	VF	XF	Unc
12	1967	6,200	—	—	125.00
	1967	850 pcs.	—	Proof	160.00

KM#	Date	Mintage	VF	XF	Unc
27	1971	.022	—	—	100.00
	1971(t)	1,250	—	Proof	150.00

Rev: Hallmark and fineness stamped at bottom

KM#	Date	Mintage	VF	XF	Unc
28	1971	—	—	—	110.00

NOTE: The above coins were struck by the Gori & Zucchi Mint, Italy.

6.4800 g, .917 GOLD, .1880 oz AGW

KM#	Date	Mintage	VF	XF	Unc
35	1972	.010	—	—	100.00
	1972	1,250	—	Proof	140.00

2.9000 g, .750 GOLD, .0699 oz AGW
Independence Day - July 10
Flamingos
Rev: W/o fineness and date.

KM#	Date	Mintage	VF	XF	Unc
43	1973	—	—	—	35.00
	1973	—	—	Proof	45.00

2.9000 g, .585 GOLD, .0545 oz AGW
Rev: .585 fineness.

KM#	Date	Mintage	VF	XF	Unc
44	1973	8,660	—	—	35.00
	1973	1,260	—	Proof	45.00

25 DOLLARS

37.3800 g, .925 SILVER, 1.1117 oz ASW
250th Anniversary of Parliament
Obv: Similar to 10 Dollars, KM#96.

KM#	Date	Mintage	VF	XF	Unc
82	1979FM	3,002	—	Proof	40.00

120.0000 g, .925 SILVER, 3.5687 oz ASW
Columbus' Discovery of America
Obv: Similar to 10 Dollars, KM#113.

KM#	Date	Mintage	VF	XF	Unc
110	1985	1,950	—	Proof	70.00

129.6000 g, .925 SILVER, 3.8547 oz ASW
Bird Conservation - Flamingos
Obv: Similar to 10 Dollars, KM#113.

KM#	Date	Mintage	VF	XF	Unc
115	1985	1,060	—	Proof	90.00

Queen Isabella and Columbus
Similar to 250 Dollars, KM#121.

KM#	Date	Mintage	VF	XF	Unc
118	1987	1,750	—	Proof	85.00

136.0000 g, .925 SILVER, 4.0446 oz ASW
Columbus Discovering America
Obv: Similar to 250 Dollars, KM#121.

KM#	Date	Mintage	VF	XF	Unc
124	1988	954 pcs.	—	Proof	160.00

136.0800 g, .925 SILVER, 4.0470 oz ASW
Christopher Columbus
Obv: Queen Elizabeth.

KM#	Date	Mintage	VF	XF	Unc
129	1989	*.010	—	Proof	65.00

Illustration reduced. Actual size: 63mm.
Discovery of New World - Indian
Obv: Similar to 10 Dollars, KM#133.

KM#	Date	Mintage	VF	XF	Unc
134	1990	5,000	—	Proof	125.00

Illustration reduced. Actual size: 63mm.
Discovery of New World - Columbus

KM#	Date	Mintage	VF	XF	Unc
153	1991	*500 pcs.	—	Proof	200.00

50 DOLLARS

19.9710 g, .917 GOLD, .5888 oz AGW
Adoption of New Constitution - Santa Maria

KM#	Date	Mintage	VF	XF	Unc
13	1967	1,200	—	—	270.00
	1967	850 pcs.	—	Proof	320.00

KM#	Date	Mintage	VF	XF	Unc
29	1971	6,800	—	—	225.00
	1971(t)	1,250	—	Proof	275.00

Rev: Hallmark and fineness stamped at bottom

KM#	Date	Mintage	VF	XF	Unc
30	1971	—	—	—	250.00

NOTE: The above coins were struck by the Gori & Zucchi Mint, Italy.

15.9700 g, .917 GOLD, .4708 oz AGW

KM#	Date	Mintage	VF	XF	Unc
36	1972	2,250	—	—	220.00
	1972	1,250	—	Proof	250.00

7.2700 g, .750 GOLD, .1753 oz AGW
Independence Day - July 10
Lobster
Rev: W/o fineness, date below lobster.

KM#	Date	Mintage	VF	XF	Unc
45	1973	—	—	—	75.00
	1973	—	—	Proof	100.00

7.2700 g, .585 GOLD, .1367 oz AGW
Rev: .585 fineness to left, date to right.

KM#	Date	Mintage	VF	XF	Unc
46	1973	5,160	—	—	80.00
	1973	1,260	—	Proof	90.00

Rev: W/o date or fineness

KM#	Date	Mintage	VF	XF	Unc
47	1973	—	—	—	90.00

15.6448 g, .500 GOLD, .2515 oz AGW
Independence Day - July 10

KM#	Date	Mintage	VF	XF	Unc
48	1973JP	.023	—	—	125.00
	1973JP	.018	—	Proof	135.00

2.7300 g, .917 GOLD, .0804 oz AGW
1st Anniversary of Independence
Tobacco Dove
Rev: W/o fineness

KM#	Date	Mintage	VF	XF	Unc
69	1974	.034	—	—	45.00
	1974	.020	—	Proof	50.00
	1975	.026	—	—	45.00
	1975	.015	—	Proof	50.00
	1976	2,207	—	—	45.00
	1976	Inc. Ab.	—	Proof	50.00
	1977	1,090	—	—	75.00
	1977	—	—	Proof	75.00

Rev: .917 fineness

KM#	Date	Mintage	VF	XF	Unc
70	1974	—	—	—	60.00

2.6800 g, .500 GOLD, .0430 oz AGW
Flamingos in Flight

KM#	Date	Mintage	VF	XF	Unc
86	1981FM(P)	2,050	—	Proof	80.00

Marlin (Swordfish)

KM#	Date	Mintage	VF	XF	Unc
92	1982FM(P)	841 pcs.	—	Proof	120.00

10th Anniversary of Independence
Flamingo

KM#	Date	Mintage	VF	XF	Unc
98	1983FM(P)	962 pcs.	—	Proof	100.00

Golden Allamanda

KM#	Date	Mintage	VF	XF	Unc
103	1984FM(P)	3,716	—	Proof	60.00

Santa Maria

KM#	Date	Mintage	VF	XF	Unc
108	1985FM(P)	1,575	—	Proof	80.00

100 DOLLARS

39.9400 g, .917 GOLD, 1.1776 oz AGW
Adoption of New Constitution - Columbus

KM#	Date	Mintage	VF	XF	Unc
14	1967	1,200	—	—	600.00
	1967	850 pcs.	—	Proof	625.00

KM#	Date	Mintage	VF	XF	Unc
31	1971	6,800	—	—	500.00
	1971(t)	1,250	—	Proof	600.00

Rev: Hallmark and fineness at bottom right.

KM#	Date	Mintage	VF	XF	Unc
32.1	1971	—	—	—	525.00

Rev: Hallmark at bottom right, w/o fineness.

KM#	Date	Mintage	VF	XF	Unc
32.2	1971	—	—	—	—

NOTE: The above coins were struck by the Gori & Zucchi Mint, Italy.

31.9500 g, .917 GOLD, .9420 oz AGW

KM#	Date	Mintage	VF	XF	Unc
37	1972	2,250	—	—	400.00
	1972	1,250	—	Proof	500.00

NOTE: The 1972 proof $100 is serially numbered on the edge.

14.5400 g, .750 GOLD, .3506 oz AGW
Independence Day - July 10
Rev: W/o fineness, date at bottom.

KM#	Date	Mintage	VF	XF	Unc
49.1	1973	—	—	—	150.00

Rev: W/o date or fineness.

KM#	Date	Mintage	VF	XF	Unc
49.2	1973	—	—	Proof	190.00

14.5400 g, .585 GOLD, .2735 oz AGW
Rev: .585 fineness to left, date to right.

KM#	Date	Mintage	VF	XF	Unc
50.1	1973	4,660	—	—	140.00
	1973 serial no. on reverse				
		1,260	—	Proof	160.00

Rev: Date and fineness at right, serial no. at left.

KM#	Date	Mintage	VF	XF	Unc
50.2	1973	—	—	—	170.00

18.0145 g, .500 GOLD, .2896 oz AGW
First Anniversary of Independence

KM#	Date	Mintage	VF	XF	Unc
71	1974	4,486	—	—	145.00
	1974	4,153	—	Proof	165.00

5.4600 g, .917 GOLD, .1609 oz AGW
Rev: Broken waves behind flamingos legs.

KM#	Date	Mintage	VF	XF	Unc
72	1974	.029	—	—	100.00
	1975	—	—	—	115.00

Rev: Unbroken waves behind flamingos legs.

KM#	Date	Mintage	VF	XF	Unc
73	1974	.017	—	Proof	100.00
	1975	—	—	Proof	100.00
	1976	—	—	—	100.00
	1976	—	—	Proof	115.00
	1977	—	—	—	100.00
	1977	—	—	Proof	120.00

Rev: .917 fineness in oval.

KM#	Date	Mintage	VF	XF	Unc
74	1974	—	—	—	100.00

18.0145 g, .500 GOLD, .2896 oz AGW
Second Anniversary of Independence

KM#	Date	Mintage	VF	XF	Unc
77	1975	3,694	—	—	125.00
	1975	3,145	—	Proof	150.00
	1976	761 pcs.	—	Proof	200.00
	1977	2,023	—	Proof	160.00

13.6000 g, .963 GOLD, .4211 oz AGW
Fifth Anniversary of Independence
Obv: Arms. Rev: Portrait of H.R.H. Prince Charles.

KM#	Date	Mintage	VF	XF	Unc
80	1978	3,275	—	Proof	220.00

Fifth Anniversary of Independence
Obv: Arms. Rev: Portrait of Sir Milo B. Butler.

KM#	Date	Mintage	VF	XF	Unc
81	1978	.025	—	Proof	220.00

6.4800 g, .900 GOLD, .1875 oz AGW
Wedding of Prince Charles and Lady Diana

KM#	Date	Mintage	VF	XF	Unc
87	1981	.010	—	Proof	110.00

10th Anniversary of Independence

KM#	Date	Mintage	VF	XF	Unc
99	1983	400 pcs.	—	Proof	185.00

Columbus' Discovery of America

KM#	Date	Mintage	VF	XF	Unc
111	1985	450 pcs.	—	Proof	225.00

Queen Isabella and Christopher Columbus

KM#	Date	Mintage	VF	XF	Unc
119	1987	849 pcs.	—	Proof	210.00

Columbus Discovering America
Obv: Queen Elizabeth.
Rev: Columbus sighting America.

KM#	Date	Mintage	VF	XF	Unc
125	1988	854 pcs.	—	Proof	225.00

Christopher Columbus
Obv: Queen Elizabeth.

KM#	Date	Mintage	VF	XF	Unc
130	1989	*5,000	—	Proof	210.00

Discovery of New World - Columbus
Obv: Queen Elizabeth II, date below.

KM#	Date	Mintage	VF	XF	Unc
135	1990	500 pcs.	—	—	270.00
	1990	5,000	—	Proof	215.00

Discovery of New World - 5 Man Row Boat

KM#	Date	Mintage	VF	XF	Unc
151	1991	500 pcs.	—	P/L	270.00

Discovery of New World - Columbus' Ships

KM#	Date	Mintage	VF	XF	Unc
152	1992	*5.000	—	Proof	215.00

150 DOLLARS

8.1900 g, .917 GOLD, .2414 oz AGW
Independence Day - July 10
Lobster

KM#	Date	Mintage	VF	XF	Unc
51	1973	—	—	—	125.00
51	1973	—	—	Proof	150.00
	1974	7,128	—	—	160.00
	1974	4,787	—	Proof	165.00
	1975	3,141	—	—	165.00
	1975	2,770	—	Proof	165.00
	1976	168 pcs.	—	Proof	230.00
	1977	327 pcs.	—	Proof	180.00

Rev: Waves under lobster extend to its two front legs.

KM#	Date	Mintage	VF	XF	Unc
52	1974	—	—	Proof	200.00

Rev: .917 fineness in oval.

KM#	Date	Mintage	VF	XF	Unc
53	1974	—	—	—	175.00

200 DOLLARS

10.9200 g, .917 GOLD, .3219 oz AGW
Independence Day - July 10

KM#	Date	Mintage	VF	XF	Unc
54	1973	—	—	—	180.00
	1973	—	—	Proof	200.00
	1974	5,528	—	—	175.00
	1974	3,587	—	Proof	200.00
	1975	1,545	—	—	200.00
	1975	1,570	—	Proof	220.00
	1976	168 pcs.	—	Proof	300.00
	1977	321 pcs.	—	Proof	260.00

KM#	Date	Mintage	VF	XF	Unc
55	1974	—	—	Proof	215.00

Rev: .917 fineness in oval.

KM#	Date	Mintage	VF	XF	Unc
56	1974	—	—	—	175.00

Rev: .916 fineness at left, serial number stamped below arms.

KM#	Date	Mintage	VF	XF	Unc
57	1974	—	—	—	185.00

Rev: W/o fineness, serial number to left.

KM#	Date	Mintage	VF	XF	Unc
58	1974	—	—	—	185.00

250 DOLLARS

10.5800 g, .900 GOLD, .3061 oz AGW
250th Anniversary of Parliament

KM#	Date	Mintage	VF	XF	Unc
83	1979	1,835	—	Proof	280.00

47.5400 g, .917 GOLD, 1.4017 oz AGW
Royal Visit

KM#	Date	Mintage	VF	XF	Unc
137	1985	100 pcs.	—	Proof	900.00

Commonwealth Games
Similar to 10 Dollars, KM#113.

KM#	Date	Mintage	VF	XF	Unc
117	1985	101 pcs.	—	Proof	900.00

Queen Isabella and Columbus

KM#	Date	Mintage	VF	XF	Unc
121	1987	100 pcs.	—	Proof	1500.

Columbus Discovering America
Obv: Queen Elizabeth.
Rev: Columbus sighting America.

KM#	Date	Mintage	VF	XF	Unc
126	1988	53 pcs.	—	Proof	1300.

Christopher Columbus
Obv: Queen Elizabeth.
Rev: Similar to 100 Dollars, KM#130.

KM#	Date	Mintage	VF	XF	Unc
131	1989	*250 pcs.	—	Proof	1200.

Discovery of New World - Indian
Obv: Queen Elizabeth II, date below.

KM#	Date	Mintage	VF	XF	Unc
136	1990	500 pcs.	—	Proof	1300.

500 DOLLARS

25.9200 g, .900 GOLD, .7500 oz AGW
Wedding of Prince Charles and Lady Diana

KM#	Date	Mintage	VF	XF	Unc
88	1981	5,000	—	Proof	525.00

1000 DOLLARS

41.4700 g, .900 GOLD, 1.2001 oz AGW
America's Cup Challenge

KM#	Date	Mintage	VF	XF	Unc
100	1983	300 pcs.	—	Proof	1100.

2500 DOLLARS

407.2600 g, .917 GOLD, 12.0082 oz AGW
Illustration reduced. Actual size: 72mm

KM#	Date	Mintage	VF	XF	Unc
75	1974	204 pcs.	—	Proof	7000.
	1977	168 pcs.	—	Proof	7500.

10th Anniversary of Independence
Illustration reduced. Actual size: 72mm.

KM#	Date	Mintage	VF	XF	Unc
101	1983	55 pcs.	—	Proof	8000.

Columbus' Discovery of America
Illustration reduced. Actual size: 72mm.

KM#	Date	Mintage	VF	XF	Unc
112	1985	37 pcs.	—	Proof	8000.

Columbus and Isabella
Illustration reduced. Actual size: 72mm.

KM#	Date	Mintage	VF	XF	Unc
116	1987	20 pcs.	—	Proof	8500.

Columbus
Obv: Queen Elizabeth.
Rev: Columbus sighting "New World."

KM#	Date	Mintage	VF	XF	Unc
122	1988	32 pcs.	—	Proof	8000.

MINT SETS (MS)

KM#	Date	Mintage	Identification	Issue Price	Mkt. Val.
MS1	1966(9)	75,050	KM2-10	16.00	20.00
MS2	1966(7)	500,000	KM2-8	5.25	9.00
MS3	1967(4)	1,200	KM11-14	180.00	1150.
MS4	1969(9)	26,221	KM2-10	20.25	25.00
MS5	1970(9)	25,135	KM3-10,15	20.25	25.00
MS6	1971(9)	12,895	KM16-24	20.25	20.00
MS7	1971(4)	6,800	KM25,27,29,31	185.00	1050.
MS8	1972(9)	10,128	KM16-23,33	22.75	20.00
MS9	1972(4)	2,250	KM34-37	185.00	750.00
MS10	1973(9)	9,853	KM16-23,33	23.75	20.00
MS11	1973(4)	4,660	KM41,44,46,50	—	310.00
MS12	1973(2)	—	KM40,43	—	85.00
MS13	1974(9)	11,004	KM59-67	22.50	18.00
MS14	1974(4)	5,528	KM51,54,69,72	—	500.00
MS15	1974(2)	—	KM68,71	—	170.00
MS16	1975(9)	3,845	KM59-67	27.00	20.00
MS17	1975(4)	1,545	KM51,54,69,72	—	535.00
MS18	1976(9)	1,453	KM59-67	27.00	30.00
MS19	1977(9)	731	KM59-67	27.00	55.00
MS20	1978(9)	767	KM59-67	27.00	50.00
MS21	1991(7)	5,000	KM59a,60-64,65b	—	25.00
MS22	1992(7)	—	KM59a,60-64,65b	24.00	25.00

PROOF SETS (PS)

KM#	Date	Mintage	Identification	Issue Price	Mkt. Val.
PS1	1967(4)	850	KM11-14	252.00	1245.
PS2	1969(9)	10,381	KM2-10	35.00	30.00
PS3	1970(9)	22,827	KM3-10,15	35.00	30.00
PS4	1971(9)	30,507	KM16-24	35.00	25.00
PS5	1971(4)	1,250	KM25,27,29,31	298.00	1220.
PS6	1972(9)	34,789	KM16-23,33	35.00	25.00
PS7	1972(4)	1,250	KM34-37	565.00	1000.
PS8	1973(9)	34,815	KM16-23,33	35.00	25.00
PS9	1973(4)	1,260	KM41,44,46,50	402.00	355.00
PS10	1974(9)	93,776	KM59-63,64a-67a	45.00	25.00
PS11	1974(4)	3,587	KM51,54,69,73	1000.	550.00
PS12	1975(9)	29,095	KM59-63,64a-67a	59.00	30.00
PS13	1975(4)	1,570	KM51,54,69,73	1000.	555.00
PS14	1976(9)	22,570	KM59-63,64a-67a	59.00	32.00
PS15	1976(4)	—	KM51,54,69,73	1000.	695.00
PS16	1977(9)	10,812	KM59-63,64a-67a	59.00	40.00
PS17	1977(4)	—	KM51,54,69,73	—	625.00
PS18	1978(9)	6,931	KM59-63,64a-67a	59.00	50.00
PS19	1979(9)	2,053	KM59-63,64a-67a	115.00	75.00
PS20	1979(2)	—	KM82-83	445.00	300.00
PS21	1980(9)	2,084	KM59-63,64a-67a	145.00	75.00
PS22	1981(9)	1,980	KM59-66,65b-67b	62.00	65.00
PS23	1982(9)	—	KM59-64,89-91	67.00	80.00
PS24	1983(9)	1,009	KM59-64,93-95	67.00	80.00
PS25	1984(9)	7,500	KM59-64,104-106	72.00	60.00
PS26	1985(9)	1,576	KM59-64,104,105,107	—	55.00
PS27	1989(9)	2,000	KM59a,60-64,66c,104, 132	106.50	100.00
PS28	1991(12)	*25,000	KM139-150	425.00	400.00

BAHRAIN

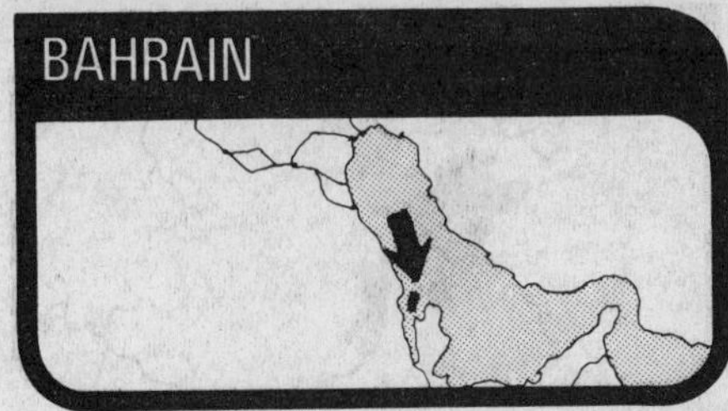

The State of Bahrain, a group of islands in the Persian Gulf off Saudi Arabia, has an area of 240 sq. mi. (622 sq. km.) and a population of 445,000. Capital: Manama. Prior to the depression of the 1930s, the economy was based on pearl fishing. Petroleum and aluminum industries and transit trade are the vital factors in the economy today.

The Portuguese occupied the islands in 1507 but were driven out in 1602 by Arab subjects of Persia. They in turn were ejected by Arabs of the Ataiba tribe from the Arabian mainland who have maintained possession up to the present time. The ruling sheikh of Bahrain entered into relations with Great Britain in 1805 and concluded a binding treaty of protection in 1861. In 1968 Great Britain decided to terminate treaty relations with the Persian Gulf sheikhdoms. Unable to agree on terms of union with the other skeikhdoms, Bahrain decided to seek independence as a separate entity and became fully independent on August 14, 1971.

The coinage of the State of Bahrain was struck at the Royal Mint, London, England.

RULERS

Isa Bin Sulman, 1961

MINT MARKS

بحرين

Bahrain

البحرين

al-Bahrain
of the Two Seas

MONETARY SYSTEM

Falus, Fulus *Fals, Fils* *Falsan*

1000 Fils = 1 Dinar

FILS

BRONZE

KM#	Date	Year	Mintage	VF	XF	Unc
1	AH1385	1965	1.500	.10	.15	.30
	1385	1965	.012	—	Proof	1.00
	1386	1966	1.500	.10	.15	.30
	1386	1966	—	—	Proof	2.00

1.5000 g, .925 SILVER, .0446 oz ASW

KM#	Date	Year	Mintage	VF	XF	Unc
1a	AH1403	1983	*.015	—	Proof	3.00

5 FILS

BRONZE

KM#	Date	Year	Mintage	VF	XF	Unc
2	AH1385	1965	8.000	.10	.15	.30
	1385	1965	.012	—	Proof	1.00

2.0000 g, .925 SILVER, .0595 oz ASW

KM#	Date	Year	Mintage	VF	XF	Unc
2a	AH1403	1983	*.015	—	Proof	3.00

BRASS
Palm Tree

KM#	Date	Year	Mintage	VF	XF	Unc
16	AH1412	1992	—	—	—	.50

10 FILS

BRONZE

KM#	Date	Year	Mintage	VF	XF	Unc
3	AH1385	1965	8.500	.10	.20	.45
	1385	1965	.012	—	Proof	1.50

4.7500 g, .925 SILVER, .1413 oz ASW

KM#	Date	Year	Mintage	VF	XF	Unc
3a	AH1403	1983	*.015	—	Proof	4.00

BRASS
Palm Tree

KM#	Date	Year	Mintage	VF	XF	Unc
17	AH1412	1992	—	—	—	.75

25 FILS

COPPER NICKEL

KM#	Date	Year	Mintage	VF	XF	Unc
4	AH1385	1965	11.250	.15	.30	.65
	1385	1965	.012	—	Proof	2.00

1.7500 g, .925 SILVER, .0521 oz ASW

KM#	Date	Year	Mintage	VF	XF	Unc
4a	AH1403	1983	*.015	—	Proof	4.00

COPPER-NICKEL
Ancient Painting

KM#	Date	Year	Mintage	VF	XF	Unc
18	AH1412	1992	—	—	—	1.25

50 FILS

COPPER-NICKEL

KM#	Date	Year	Mintage	VF	XF	Unc
5	AH1385	1965	6.909	.20	.50	1.00
	1385	1965	.012	—	Proof	2.50

3.1000 g, .925 SILVER, .0922 oz ASW

KM#	Date	Year	Mintage	VF	XF	Unc
5a	AH1403	1983	*.015	—	Proof	5.00

COPPER-NICKEL
Stylized Sail Boats

KM#	Date	Year	Mintage	VF	XF	Unc
19	AH1412	1992	—	—	—	1.50

100 FILS

COPPER-NICKEL

KM#	Date	Year	Mintage	VF	XF	Unc
6	AH1385	1965	8.300	.25	.65	1.25
	1385	1965	.012	—	Proof	3.00

6.5000 g, .925 SILVER, .1933 oz ASW

KM#	Date	Year	Mintage	VF	XF	Unc
6a	AH1403	1983	*.015	—	Proof	6.00

COPPER-NICKEL CENTER IN BRASS RING
Coat of Arms

KM#	Date	Year	Mintage	VF	XF	Unc
15	AH1412	1992	—	—	—	2.50

250 FILS

COPPER-NICKEL
F.A.O. Issue

KM#	Date	Year	Mintage	VF	XF	Unc
7	AH1389	1969	.050	.75	1.50	4.00
	1389	1969	—	—	Proof	5.00
	1403	1983	3,000	1.50	2.50	8.00

15.0000 g, .925 SILVER, .4461 oz ASW

KM#	Date	Year	Mintage	VF	XF	Unc
7a	AH1403	1983	*.015	—	Proof	10.00

500 FILS

18.3000 g, .800 SILVER, .4707 oz ASW
Opening of Isa Town

KM#	Date	Year	Mintage	VF	XF	Unc
8	AH1385	1965	.012	—	Proof	12.50
	1388	1968	.050	2.00	4.00	7.00
	1388	1968	—	—	Proof	12.50

18.0600 g, .925 SILVER, .5372 oz ASW

KM#	Date	Year	Mintage	VF	XF	Unc
8a	AH1403	1983	*.015	—	Proof	35.00

5 DINARS

19.4400 g, .925 SILVER, .5782 oz ASW
World Wildlife Fund - Gazelle

KM#	Date	Year	Mintage	VF	XF	Unc
13	AH1406	1986	*.025	—	Proof	20.00

Save the Children

KM#	Date	Year	Mintage	VF	XF	Unc
14	AH1410	1990	*.020	—	Proof	40.00

10 DINARS

16.0000 g, .917 GOLD, .4717 oz AGW
Opening of Isa Town

KM#	Date	Year	Mintage	VF	XF	Unc
9	AH1388	1968	3,000	—	—	400.00

15.9800 g, .917 GOLD, .4712 oz AGW
Independence Commemorative

KM#	Date	Year	Mintage	VF	XF	Unc
10	AH1391	1971	3,000	—	—	400.00

Opening of Hamad Town

KM#	Date	Year	Mintage	VF	XF	Unc
15	AH1404	1983	—	—	Proof	450.00

50 DINARS

15.9800 g, .917 GOLD, .4712 oz AGW
50th Anniversary of Bahrain Monetary Agency

KM#	Date	Year	Mintage	VF	XF	Unc
11	AH1398	1978	5,000	—	Proof	300.00

100 DINARS

31.9600 g, .917 GOLD, .9424 oz AGW
50th Anniversary of Bahrain Monetary Agency

KM#	Date	Year	Mintage	VF	XF	Unc
12	AH1398	1978	5,000	—	Proof	600.00

PROOF SETS (PS)

KM#	Date	Mintage	Identification	Issue Price	Mkt. Val.
PS1	Mixed (8)	20,000	KM1-6,1965;KM7,1969; KM8,1968	32.00	22.50
PS2	1965(8)	12,000	KM1-8	—	28.50
PS3	1983(7)	15,000	KM1a-8a	99.00	70.00

Listings For

BALTIC REGIONS -
- COURLAND: refer to Latvia
- ESTONIA: refer to Estonia
- LATVIA: refer to Latvia
- LITHUANIA: refer to Lithuania
- LIVONIA: refer to Livonia
- LIVONIA & ESTONIA: refer to Russian Baltics

BANGLADESH

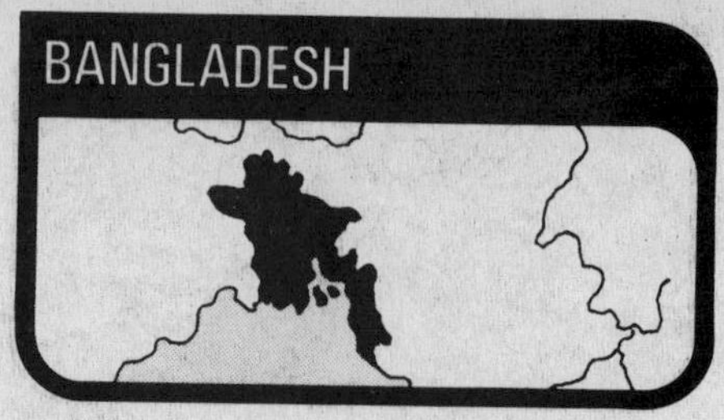

The Peoples Republic of Bangladesh (formerly East Pakistan), a parliamentary democracy located on the Bay of Bengal bordered by India and Burma, has an area of 55,598 sq. mi. (143,998 sq. km.) and a population of 104 million. Capital: Dhaka. The economy is predominantly agricultural. Jute products, jute and tea are exported.

British rule over the vast Indian sub-continent ended in 1947 when British India attained independence and was partitioned into the two successor states of India and Pakistan. Pakistan consisted of East and West Pakistan, two areas united by the Moslem religion but separated by culture and 1,000 miles of Indian territory. Restive under the de facto rule of the militant but fewer West Pakistanis, the East Pakistanis unsuccessfully demanded greater economic benefits and political reforms. The inability of the leaders of East and West Pakistan to resolve a political breakdown occasioned by the East Pakistan success in the general elections of 1970 precipitated massive civil disobedience in East Pakistan which West Pakistan sought to suppress militarily. East Pakistan seceded from Pakistan, March 26, 1971, and with the support of India declared an independent Peoples Republic of Bangladesh.

Bangladesh is a member of the Commonwealth of Nations. The president is the Head of State and of the Government.

MONETARY SYSTEM

100 Poisha = 1 Taka

DATING

Christian era using Bengali numerals.

POISHA

ALUMINUM

KM#	Date	Mintage	VF	XF	Unc
5	1974	300.000	—	.10	.15

5 POISHA

ALUMINUM

KM#	Date	Mintage	VF	XF	Unc
1	1973	*47.088	—	.10	.20
	1974	—	—	.10	.20

F.A.O. Issue

KM#	Date	Mintage	VF	XF	Unc
6	1974	5.000	—	.10	.20
	1975	3.000	—	.10	.20
	1976	3.000	—	.10	.20

F.A.O. Issue

KM#	Date	Mintage	VF	XF	Unc
10	1977	90.000	—	.10	.15
	1978	52.432	—	.10	.25
	1979	120.096	—	.10	.15
	1980	127.008	—	.10	.15
	1981	72.992	—	.10	.15

10 POISHA

ALUMINUM

KM#	Date	Mintage	VF	XF	Unc
2	1973	*21.500	—	.10	.35
	1974	—	—	.10	.35

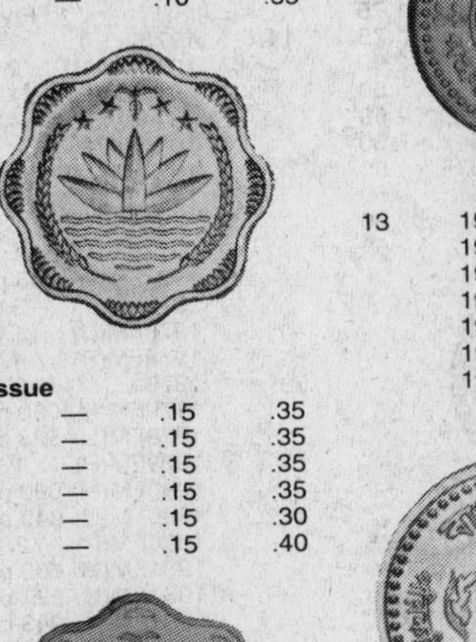

F.A.O. Issue

KM#	Date	Mintage	VF	XF	Unc
7	1974	5.000	—	.15	.35
	1975	4.000	—	.15	.35
	1976	4.000	—	.15	.35
	1977	4.000	—	.15	.35
	1978	141.744	—	.15	.30
	1979	—	—	.15	.40

F.A.O. Issue

KM#	Date	Mintage	VF	XF	Unc
11.1	1977	48.000	—	.15	.30
	1978	77.518	—	.15	.30
	1979	170.112	—	.15	.30
	1980	200.000	—	.15	.30
		21.9 mm			
11.2	1983	142.848	—	.15	.30
	1984	57.152	—	.15	.30

25 POISHA

STEEL

KM#	Date	Mintage	VF	XF	Unc
3	1973	*25.072	—	.25	.50

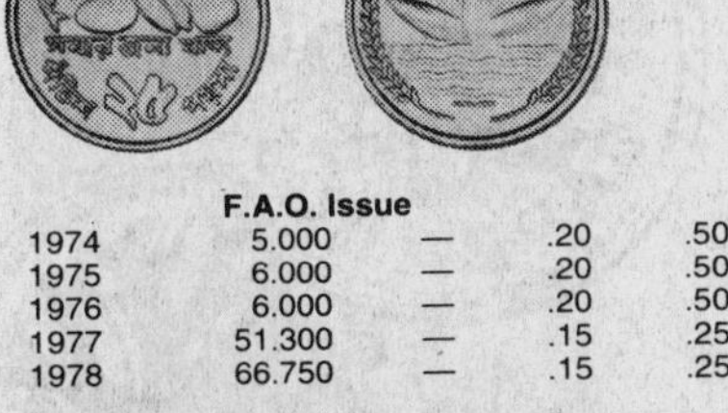

F.A.O. Issue

KM#	Date	Mintage	VF	XF	Unc
8	1974	5.000	—	.20	.50
	1975	6.000	—	.20	.50
	1976	6.000	—	.20	.50
	1977	51.300	—	.15	.25
	1978	66.750	—	.15	.25

F.A.O. Issue

KM#	Date	Mintage	VF	XF	Unc
12	1977	45.300	—	.15	.40
	1978	66.750	—	.15	.40
	1979	56.704	—	.15	.40
	1980	228.992	—	.15	.40
	1981	45.072	—	.15	.40
	1983	96.128	—	.15	.25
	1984	203.872	—	.15	.25

50 POISHA

COPPER-NICKEL

KM#	Date	Mintage	VF	XF	Unc
4	1973	18.000	—	.40	1.00

STEEL
F.A.O. Issue

KM#	Date	Mintage	VF	XF	Unc
13	1977	12.700	—	.20	.75
	1978	37.300	—	.20	.75
	1979	2.208	—	.20	.75
	1980	124.512	—	.20	.50
	1981	36.680	—	.20	.75
	1983	31.392	—	.20	.75
	1984	168.608	—	.20	.50

TAKA

COPPER-NICKEL
F.A.O. Issue

KM#	Date	Mintage	VF	XF	Unc
9	1975	4.000	.15	.45	1.00
	1976	—	.15	.45	1.00
	1977	—	.15	.45	1.00

31.4700 g, .925 SILVER, .9359 oz ASW
Olympics - Runners with Torch

KM#	Date	Mintage	VF	XF	Unc
14	1992	*.040	—	Proof	50.00

Endangered Wildlife - Deer

KM#	Date	Mintage	VF	XF	Unc
15	1993	*.015	—	Proof	50.00
		Soccer - World Cup 1994			
16	1993	*.010	—	Proof	50.00

BARBADOS

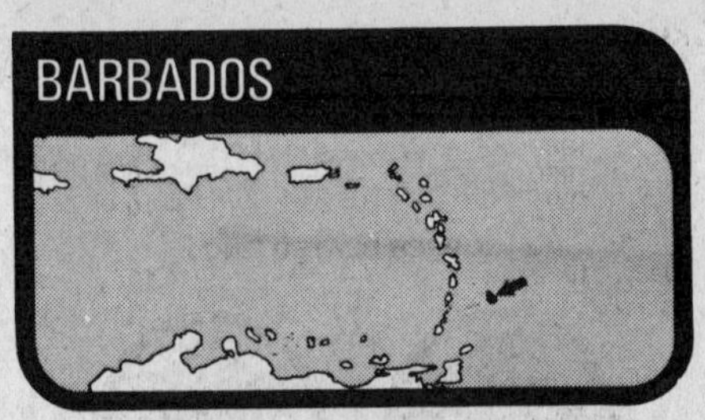

Barbados, an independent state within the British Commonwealth, is located in the Windward Islands of the West Indies east of St. Vincent. The coral island has an area of 166 sq. mi. (430 sq. km.) and a population of 266,000. Capital: Bridgetown. The economy is based on sugar and tourism. Sugar, petroleum products, molasses, and rum are exported.

Barbados was named by the Portuguese who achieved the first landing on the island in 1563. British sailors landed at the site of present-day Holetown in 1624. Barbados was under uninterrupted British control from the time of the first British settlement in 1627 until it obtained independence on Nov. 30, 1966. It is a member of the Commonwealth of Nations. The Queen of England is Chief of State.

Unmarked 'side cut' pieces of Spanish and Spanish Colonial 1, 2 and 8 reales were the principal coinage medium of 18th-century Barbados. The "Neptune" tokens issued by Sir Phillip Gibbs, a local plantation owner, circulated freely but were never established as legal coinage. The coinage and banknotes of the British Caribbean Territories (Eastern Group) were employed prior to 1973 when Barbados issued a decimal coinage.

RULERS

British, until 1966

MINT MARKS

FM - Franklin Mint, U.S.A.*
None - Royal Mint

***NOTE:** From 1975 the Franklin Mint has produced coinage in up to 3 different qualities. Qualities of issue are designated in ( ) after each date and are defined as follows:

(M) MATTE - Normal circulation strike or a dull finish produced by sandblasting special uncirculated (polish finish) or proof quality dies.

(U) SPECIAL UNCIRCULATED - Polished or proof-like in appearance without any frosted features.

(P) PROOF - The highest quality obtainable having mirror-like fields and frosted features.

MONETARY SYSTEM

100 Cents = 1 Dollar

CENT

BRONZE

KM#	Date	Mintage	VF	XF	Unc
10	1973	5.000	—	.10	.25
	1973FM(M)	7,500	—	—	1.00
	1973FM(P)	.097	—	Proof	.50
	1974	7.000	—	.10	.25
	1974FM(M)	8,708	—	—	1.00
	1974FM(P)	.036	—	Proof	.50
	1975	8.000	—	.10	.25
	1975FM(M)	5,000	—	—	.75
	1975FM(U)	1,360	—	—	1.00
	1975FM(P)	.020	—	Proof	.50
	1977FM(M)	2,102	—	—	.75
	1977FM(U)	468 pcs.	—	—	3.00
	1977FM(P)	5,014	—	Proof	.50
	1978	4.807	—	—	—
	1978FM(M)	2,000	—	—	1.00
	1978FM(U)	2,517	—	—	1.50
	1978FM(P)	4,436	—	Proof	1.00
	1979	5.606	—	.10	.25
	1979FM(M)	1,500	—	—	1.00
	1979FM(U)	523 pcs.	—	—	2.50
	1979FM(P)	4,126	—	Proof	1.00
	1980	14.400	—	.10	.25
	1980FM(M)	1,500	—	—	1.00
	1980FM(U)	649 pcs.	—	—	2.00
	1980FM(P)	2,111	—	Proof	1.50
	1981	10.160	—	.10	.25
	1981FM(M)	1,500	—	—	1.00
	1981FM(U)	327 pcs.	—	—	2.00
	1981FM(P)	943 pcs.	—	Proof	1.50
	1982	5.040	—	.10	.25
	1982FM(U)	1,500	—	—	1.25
	1982FM(P)	843 pcs.	—	Proof	1.50
	1983FM(M)	1,500	—	—	1.00
	1983FM(U)	—	—	—	1.25
	1983FM(P)	459 pcs.	—	Proof	1.50
	1984	5.008	—	.10	.25
	1984FM(M)	868 pcs.	—	—	1.25
	1984FM(P)	—	—	Proof	2.00
	1985	—	—	.10	.25

KM#	Date	Mintage	VF	XF	Unc
10	1986	—	—	.10	.25
	1987	10.000	—	.10	.25
	1988	12.136	—	.10	.25
	1989	—	—	.10	.25
	1990	—	—	.10	.25
	1991	—	—	.10	.25

COPPER PLATED ZINC

KM#	Date	Mintage	VF	XF	Unc
10a	1992	—	—	.10	.25

10th Anniversary of Independence

KM#	Date	Mintage	VF	XF	Unc
19	1976	6.406	—	.10	.20
	1976FM(M)	5,000	—	—	.50
	1976FM(U)	996 pcs.	—	—	1.00
	1976FM(P)	.012	—	Proof	.50

5 CENTS

BRASS
South Point Lighthouse

KM#	Date	Mintage	VF	XF	Unc
11	1973	3.000	.10	.15	.35
	1973FM(M)	7,500	—	—	1.25
	1973FM(P)	.097	—	Proof	.75
	1974	4.600	.10	.15	.35
	1974FM(M)	8,708	—	—	1.25
	1974FM(P)	.036	—	Proof	.75
	1975FM(M)	5,000	—	—	1.00
	1975FM(U)	1,360	—	—	1.25
	1975FM(P)	.020	—	Proof	.75
	1977FM(M)	2,100	—	—	2.00
	1977FM(U)	468 pcs.	—	—	3.00
	1977FM(P)	5,014	—	Proof	.75
	1978FM(M)	2,000	—	—	.75
	1978FM(U)	2,517	—	—	2.75
	1978FM(P)	4,436	—	Proof	1.25
	1979	4.800	.10	.15	.35
	1979FM(M)	1,500	—	—	.75
	1979FM(U)	523 pcs.	—	—	2.75
	1979FM(P)	4,126	—	Proof	1.25
	1980FM(M)	1,500	—	—	1.00
	1980FM(U)	649 pcs.	—	—	2.25
	1980FM(P)	2,111	—	Proof	1.75
	1981FM(M)	1,500	—	—	1.00
	1981FM(U)	327 pcs.	—	—	2.25
	1981FM(P)	943 pcs.	—	Proof	1.75
	1982	2.100	.10	.15	.35
	1982FM(U)	1,500	—	—	1.50
	1982FM(P)	843 pcs.	—	Proof	1.75
	1983FM(M)	1,500	—	—	1.50
	1983FM(U)	—	—	—	1.50
	1983FM(P)	459 pcs.	—	Proof	1.75
	1984FM	1,737	—	—	1.50
	1984FM(P)	—	—	Proof	2.25
	1985	—	—	—	.25
	1986	—	—	—	.25
	1988	4.200	—	—	.25
	1989	—	—	—	.25

10th Anniversary of Independence

KM#	Date	Mintage	VF	XF	Unc
20	1976FM(M)	5,000	—	—	1.00
	1976FM(U)	.012	—	—	1.00
	1976FM(P)	—	—	Proof	.75

10 CENTS

COPPER-NICKEL
Bonaparte Tern

KM#	Date	Mintage	VF	XF	Unc
12	1973	4.000	.10	.15	.50
	1973FM(M)	5,000	—	—	1.50
	1973FM(P)	.097	—	Proof	1.00
	1974	4.000	.10	.15	.50
	1974FM(M)	6,208	—	—	1.50
	1974FM(P)	.036	—	Proof	1.00
	1975FM(M)	2,500	—	—	1.00
	1975FM(U)	1,360	—	—	1.50
	1975FM(P)	.020	—	Proof	1.00
	1977FM(M)	2,100	—	—	1.00
12	1977FM(U)	468 pcs.	—	—	4.00
	1977FM(P)	5,014	—	Proof	1.00
	1978FM(M)	2,000	—	—	1.00
	1978FM(U)	2,517	—	—	3.00
	1978FM(P)	4,436	—	Proof	1.50
	1979	2.500	.10	.20	.60
	1979FM(M)	1,500	—	—	2.50
	1979FM(U)	523 pcs.	—	—	3.00
	1979FM(P)	4,126	—	Proof	1.50
	1980	3.500	.10	.15	.50
	1980FM(M)	1,500	—	—	1.00
	1980FM(U)	649 pcs.	—	—	2.50
	1980FM(P)	2,111	—	Proof	2.00
	1981FM(M)	1,500	—	—	1.00
	1981FM(U)	327 pcs.	—	—	2.50
	1981FM(P)	943 pcs.	—	Proof	2.00
	1982FM(U)	1,500	—	—	1.75
	1982FM(P)	843 pcs.	—	Proof	2.00
	1983FM(M)	1,500	—	—	1.75
	1983FM(U)	—	—	—	1.75
	1983FM(P)	459 pcs.	—	Proof	2.00
	1984	3.400	.10	.15	.50
	1984FM(P)	—	—	Proof	2.50
	1985	—	.10	.15	.50
	1986	—	.10	.15	.50
	1987	3.500	.10	.15	.50
	1988	—	.10	.15	.50
	1989	—	.10	.15	.50

10th Anniversary of Independence

KM#	Date	Mintage	VF	XF	Unc
21	1976FM(M)	2,500	—	—	.75
	1976FM(U)	996 pcs.	—	—	1.50
	1976FM(P)	.012	—	Proof	1.00

25 CENTS

COPPER-NICKEL
Morgan Lewis Sugar Mill

KM#	Date	Mintage	VF	XF	Unc
13	1973	6.000	.15	.30	.60
	1973FM(M)	4,300	—	—	1.75
	1973FM(P)	.097	—	Proof	1.25
	1974	1.000	.20	.40	.80
	1974FM(M)	5,508	—	—	1.75
	1974FM(P)	.036	—	Proof	1.25
	1975FM(M)	1,800	—	—	1.25
	1975FM(U)	1,360	—	—	1.75
	1975FM(P)	.020	—	Proof	1.25
	1977FM(M)	2,100	—	—	1.00
	1977FM(U)	468 pcs.	—	—	4.25
	1977FM(P)	5,014	—	Proof	1.25
	1978	2.407	.20	.40	.80
	1978FM(M)	2,000	—	—	1.00
	1978FM(U)	2,517	—	—	3.25
	1978FM(P)	4,436	—	Proof	1.75
	1979	1.200	.20	.40	.80
	1979FM(M)	1,500	—	—	1.00
	1979FM(U)	523 pcs.	—	—	3.00
	1979FM(P)	4.126	—	Proof	1.75
	1980	2.700	.15	.30	.60
	1980FM(M)	1,500	—	—	3.00
	1980FM(U)	649 pcs.	—	—	2.75
	1980FM(P)	2,111	—	Proof	2.25
	1981	4.365	.15	.30	.60
	1981FM(M)	1,500	—	—	3.00
	1981FM(U)	327 pcs.	—	—	2.75
	1981FM(P)	943 pcs.	—	Proof	2.25
	1982FM(U)	1,500	—	—	2.00
	1982FM(P)	843 pcs.	—	Proof	2.25
	1983FM(M)	1,500	—	—	2.00
	1983FM(U)	—	—	—	2.00
	1983FM(P)	459 pcs.	—	Proof	2.25
	1984FM	868 pcs.	—	—	2.00
	1984FM(P)	—	—	Proof	3.00
	1985	—	.15	.30	.60
	1986	—	.15	.30	.60
	1987	3.150	—	—	2.00
	1988	—	.15	.30	.60
	1989	—	.15	.30	.60
	1990	—	.15	.30	.60

10th Anniversary of Independence

KM#	Date	Mintage	VF	XF	Unc
22	1976FM(M)	1,800	—	—	1.25
22	1976FM(U)	996 pcs.	—	—	1.75
	1976FM(P)	.012	—	Proof	1.25

DOLLAR

COPPER-NICKEL
Flying Fish

KM#	Date	Mintage	VF	XF	Unc
14.1	1973	3.955	.60	.75	1.00
	1973FM(M)	3,000	—	—	2.00
	1973FM(P)	.097	—	Proof	1.00
	1974FM(M)	4,208	—	—	2.00
	1974FM(P)	.036	—	Proof	1.00
	1975FM(M)	500 pcs.	—	—	3.50
	1975FM(U)	1,360	—	—	2.00
	1975FM(P)	.020	—	Proof	1.00
	1977FM(M)	600 pcs.	—	—	5.00
	1977FM(U)	468 pcs.	—	—	4.50
	1977FM(P)	5,014	—	Proof	1.50
	1978FM(U)	1,017	—	—	3.50
	1978FM(P)	4,436	—	Proof	2.00
	1979	2.000	.75	1.25	1.75
	1979FM(M)	600 pcs.	—	—	3.00
	1979FM(U)	523 pcs.	—	—	3.50
	1979FM(P)	4,126	—	Proof	2.00
	1980FM(M)	600 pcs.	—	—	3.50
	1980FM(U)	649 pcs.	—	—	3.50
	1980FM(P)	2,111	—	Proof	2.50
	1981FM(M)	600 pcs.	—	—	3.00
	1981FM(U)	327 pcs.	—	—	3.50
	1981FM(P)	943 pcs.	—	Proof	3.00
	1982FM(U)	600 pcs.	—	—	3.00
	1982FM(P)	843 pcs.	—	Proof	3.00
	1983FM(M)	600 pcs.	—	—	3.00
	1983FM(U)	—	—	—	3.00
	1983FM(P)	459 pcs.	—	Proof	4.00
	1984FM	469 pcs.	—	—	3.50
	1984FM(P)	—	—	Proof	4.50
	1985	—	—	—	1.00
	1986	—	—	—	1.00

25.5mm

KM#	Date	Mintage	VF	XF	Unc
14.2	1988	3.145	—	—	1.25
	1989	—	—	—	1.25

10th Anniversary of Independence

KM#	Date	Mintage	VF	XF	Unc
23	1976FM(M)	500 pcs.	—	—	4.00
	1976FM(U)	996 pcs.	—	—	2.00
	1976FM(P)	.012	—	Proof	1.50

2 DOLLARS

COPPER-NICKEL
Staghorn Coral

KM#	Date	Mintage	VF	XF	Unc
15	1973FM(M)	3,000	—	—	2.25
	1973FM(P)	.097	—	Proof	2.50
	1974FM(M)	4,208	—	—	2.25
	1974FM(P)	.036	—	Proof	2.50
	1975FM(M)	500 pcs.	—	—	4.00
	1975FM(U)	1,360	—	—	2.25
	1975FM(P)	.020	—	Proof	2.50

KM#	Date	Mintage	VF	XF	Unc
15	1977FM(M)	600 pcs.	—	—	3.50
	1977FM(U)	468 pcs.	—	—	4.75
	1977FM(P)	5,014	—	Proof	2.50
	1978FM(U)	1,017	—	—	3.75
	1978FM(P)	4,436	—	Proof	2.50
	1979FM(M)	600 pcs.	—	—	3.50
	1979FM(U)	523 pcs.	—	—	3.75
	1979FM(P)	4,126	—	Proof	2.50
	1980FM(M)	600 pcs.	—	—	3.50
	1980FM(U)	649 pcs.	—	—	3.25
	1980FM(P)	2,111	—	Proof	2.75
	1981FM(M)	600 pcs.	—	—	3.00
	1981FM(U)	327 pcs.	—	—	3.25
	1981FM(P)	943 pcs.	—	Proof	2.75
	1982FM(U)	600 pcs.	—	—	3.00
	1982FM(P)	843 pcs.	—	Proof	2.75
	1983FM(U)	—	—	—	3.00
	1983FM(P)	459 pcs.	—	Proof	2.75
	1984FM	473 pcs.	—	—	3.00
	1984FM(P)	—	—	Proof	3.50

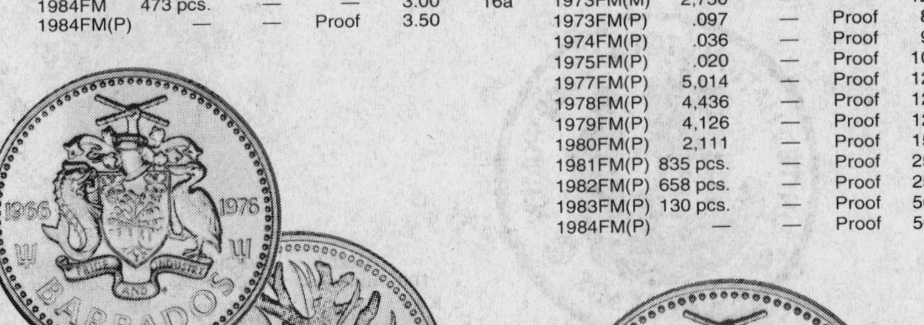

10th Anniversary of Independence

KM#	Date	Mintage	VF	XF	Unc
24	1976FM(M)	500 pcs.	—	—	3.00
	1976FM(U)	996 pcs.	—	—	2.25
	1976FM(P)	.012	—	Proof	2.50

4 DOLLARS

COPPER-NICKEL
F.A.O. Issue

KM#	Date	Mintage	VF	XF	Unc
9	1970	.030	—	2.50	4.00
	1970	2,000	—	Proof	12.00

5 DOLLARS

COPPER-NICKEL
Shell Fountain in Bridgetown's Trafalgar Square
Obv: Similar to 2 Dollars, KM#15.

KM#	Date	Mintage	VF	XF	Unc
16	1974FM(M)	3,958	—	—	5.00
	1975FM(M)	250 pcs.	—	—	8.00
16	1975FM(U)	1,360	—	—	5.00
	1977FM(M)	600 pcs.	—	—	5.00
	1977FM(U)	468 pcs.	—	—	5.00
	1978FM(U)	1,017	—	—	5.00
	1979FM(M)	600 pcs.	—	—	5.00
	1979FM(U)	523 pcs.	—	—	5.00
	1980FM(M)	600 pcs.	—	—	5.00
	1980FM(U)	649 pcs.	—	—	5.00
	1981FM(M)	600 pcs.	—	—	5.00
	1981FM(U)	1,156	—	—	5.00
	1982FM(U)	600 pcs.	—	—	5.00
	1982FM(P)	843 pcs.	—	—	5.00
	1983FM(M)	600 pcs.	—	—	5.00
	1983FM(U)	261 pcs.	—	—	5.00
	1984FM	470 pcs.	—	—	5.00

31.1000 g, .800 SILVER, .7999 oz ASW

KM#	Date	Mintage	VF	XF	Unc
16a	1973FM(M)	2,750	—	—	12.50
	1973FM(P)	.097	—	Proof	8.00
	1974FM(P)	.036	—	Proof	9.00
	1975FM(P)	.020	—	Proof	10.00
	1977FM(P)	5,014	—	Proof	12.50
	1978FM(P)	4,436	—	Proof	12.50
	1979FM(P)	4,126	—	Proof	12.50
	1980FM(P)	2,111	—	Proof	15.00
	1981FM(P)	835 pcs.	—	Proof	25.00
	1982FM(P)	658 pcs.	—	Proof	25.00
	1983FM(P)	130 pcs.	—	Proof	50.00
	1984FM(P)	—	—	Proof	50.00

COPPER-NICKEL
10th Anniversary of Independence
Rev: Similar to KM#16.

KM#	Date	Mintage	VF	XF	Unc
25	1976FM(M)	250 pcs.	—	—	25.00
	1976FM(U)	996 pcs.	—	—	12.50

31.1000 g, .800 SILVER, .7999 oz ASW

KM#	Date	Mintage	VF	XF	Unc
25a	1976FM(P)	.012	—	Proof	15.00

10 DOLLARS

COPPER-NICKEL
Neptune, God of the Sea
Obv: Similar to 2 Dollars, KM#15.

KM#	Date	Mintage	VF	XF	Unc
17	1974FM(M)	3,958	—	—	10.00
	1975FM(M)	250 pcs.	—	—	20.00
	1975FM(U)	1,360	—	—	12.50
	1977FM(M)	600 pcs.	—	—	12.50
	1977FM(U)	468 pcs.	—	—	12.50
	1978FM(U)	1,017	—	—	12.50
	1979FM(M)	600 pcs.	—	—	12.50
	1979FM(U)	523 pcs.	—	—	12.50
	1980FM(M)	600 pcs.	—	—	12.50
	1980FM(U)	649 pcs.	—	—	12.50
	1981FM(M)	600 pcs.	—	—	12.50
	1981FM(U)	1,156	—	—	12.50

37.9000 g, .925 SILVER, 1.1271 oz ASW

KM#	Date	Mintage	VF	XF	Unc
17a	1973FM(M)	2,750	—	—	15.00
	1973FM(P)	.097	—	Proof	12.50
	1974FM(P)	.057	—	Proof	12.50
	1975FM(P)	.029	—	Proof	12.50
	1977FM(P)	7,212	—	Proof	15.00
	1978FM(P)	7,079	—	Proof	15.00
	1979FM(P)	6,534	—	Proof	15.00
	1980FM(P)	3,618	—	Proof	17.50
	1981FM(P)	835 pcs.	—	Proof	45.00

COPPER-NICKEL
10th Anniversary of Independence
Rev: Similar to KM#17.

KM#	Date	Mintage	VF	XF	Unc
26	1976FM(M)	250 pcs.	—	—	30.00
	1976FM(U)	996 pcs.	—	—	15.00

37.9000 g, .925 SILVER, 1.1271 oz ASW

KM#	Date	Mintage	VF	XF	Unc
26a	1976FM(P)	.016	—	Proof	15.00

COPPER-NICKEL
10th Anniversary of the Central Bank of Barbados
Obv: Similar to KM#26.

KM#	Date	Mintage	VF	XF	Unc
34	1982FM(U)	600 pcs.	—	—	20.00

35.5200 g, .925 SILVER, 1.0564 oz ASW

KM#	Date	Mintage	VF	XF	Unc
34a	1982FM(P)	851 pcs.	—	Proof	45.00

COPPER-NICKEL
Pelican

KM#	Date	Mintage	VF	XF	Unc
36	1983FM(M)	600 pcs.	—	—	20.00
	1983FM(U)	141 pcs.	—	—	60.00

35.5200 g, .925 SILVER, 1.0564 oz ASW

KM#	Date	Mintage	VF	XF	Unc
36a	1983FM(P)	679 pcs.	—	Proof	100.00

Dolphins

KM#	Date	Mintage	VF	XF	Unc
40	1984FM(P)	469 pcs.	—	Proof	125.00

28.2800 g, .925 SILVER, .8411 oz ASW
International Cricket Belt Buckle

KM#	Date	Mintage	VF	XF	Unc
50	1991	5,000	—	Proof	55.00

23.3300 g, .925 SILVER, .6938 oz ASW
Discovery of America - Columbus and Indian - Ship and Scroll

KM#	Date	Mintage	VF	XF	Unc
52	1991	750 pcs.	—	—	145.00
	1991	*.025	—	Proof	60.00

Discovery of America -
Columbus and Indian Chief - Scroll

KM#	Date	Mintage	VF	XF	Unc
53	1992	*.025	—	Proof	60.00

20 DOLLARS

23.3300 g, .925 SILVER, .6938 oz ASW
Decade For Women

KM#	Date	Mintage	VF	XF	Unc
46	1985	.020	—	Proof	25.00

Summer Olympics - Hurdler

KM#	Date	Mintage	VF	XF	Unc
49	1988	—	—	—	55.00

25 DOLLARS

28.2800 g, .925 SILVER, .8410 oz ASW
Coronation Jubilee
Obv: Portrait of Queen Elizabeth II.

KM#	Date	Mintage	VF	XF	Unc
27	1978FM(M)	300 pcs.	—	—	90.00
	1978FM(U)	69 pcs.	—	—	250.00
	1978FM(P)	8,728	—	Proof	18.00

30.2800 g, .500 SILVER, .4868 oz AGW
10th Anniversary of Caribbean Development Bank

KM#	Date	Mintage	VF	XF	Unc
30	1980FM(P)	2,345	—	Proof	28.00

Caribbean Festival of Arts
Obv: Similar to KM#30.

KM#	Date	Mintage	VF	XF	Unc
31	1981FM(P)	1,008	—	Proof	35.00

30th Anniversary Coronation of Queen Elizabeth II

KM#	Date	Mintage	VF	XF	Unc
37	1983FM(P)	2,951	—	Proof	32.00

28.2800 g, .925 SILVER, .8410 oz ASW
Royal Visit

KM#	Date	Mintage	VF	XF	Unc
43	1985	*5,000	—	—	35.00

47.5400 g, .917 GOLD, 1.4013 oz AGW

KM#	Date	Mintage	VF	XF	Unc
43a	1985	*250 pcs.	—	Proof	950.00

28.2800 g, .500 SILVER, .4546 oz ASW
Commonwealth Games

KM#	Date	Mintage	VF	XF	Unc
44	1986	*.050	—	—	25.00

28.2800 g, .925 SILVER, .8410 oz ASW

KM#	Date	Mintage	VF	XF	Unc
44a	1986	*.020	—	Proof	30.00

50 DOLLARS

27.3500 g, .500 SILVER, .4397 oz ASW
World Food Day - Black Belly Sheep

KM#	Date	Mintage	VF	XF	Unc
32	1981FM(U)	6,012	—	—	25.00

16.8500 g, .500 SILVER, .2709 oz ASW
F.A.O. Issue - Fourwing Flying Fish

KM#	Date	Mintage	VF	XF	Unc
42	1984FM(P)	3,600	—	Proof	27.50

33.6250 g, .925 SILVER, 1.0000 oz ASW
350th Anniversary of Parliament

KM#	Date	Mintage	VF	XF	Unc
47	1989	*5,000	—	Proof	30.00

15.9800 g, .917 GOLD, .4709 oz AGW
International Cricket Belt Buckle
Similar to 10 Dollars, KM#50.

KM#	Date	Mintage	VF	XF	Unc
51	1991	500 pcs.	—	Proof	530.00

100 DOLLARS

6.2100 g, .500 GOLD, .0998 oz AGW
350th Anniversary - Olive Blossom

KM#	Date	Mintage	VF	XF	Unc
18	1975FM(M)	50 pcs.	—	—	250.00
	1975FM(U)	.016	—	—	60.00
	1975FM(P)	.023	—	Proof	70.00

4.0600 g, .900 GOLD, .1174 oz AGW
Human Rights

KM#	Date	Mintage	VF	XF	Unc
28	1978	1,114	—	—	90.00

5.0500 g, .900 GOLD, .1461 oz AGW

KM#	Date	Mintage	VF	XF	Unc
28a	1978	Inc. Ab.	—	Proof	120.00

6.2100 g, .500 GOLD, .0998 oz AGW
Neptune, God of the Sea

KM#	Date	Mintage	VF	XF	Unc
38	1983FM(U)	3 pcs.	—	—	—
	1983FM(P)	484 pcs.	—	Proof	220.00

Triton, Son of Neptune

KM#	Date	Mintage	VF	XF	Unc
39	1984FM(P)	1,103	—	Proof	165.00

Amphitrite, Wife of Neptune

KM#	Date	Mintage	VF	XF	Unc
41	1985FM(P)	1,276	—	Proof	165.00

15.9760 g, .917 GOLD, .4709 oz AGW
350th Anniversary of Parliament

KM#	Date	Mintage	VF	XF	Unc
48	1989	*500 pcs.	—	Proof	350.00

150 DOLLARS

7.1300 g, .500 GOLD, .1146 oz AGW
National Flower - Poinciana

KM#	Date	Mintage	VF	XF	Unc
33	1981FM(U)	7 pcs.	—	—	—
	1981FM(P)	1,140	—	Proof	125.00

200 DOLLARS

8.1200 g, .900 GOLD, .2349 oz AGW
Year of the Child

KM#	Date	Mintage	VF	XF	Unc
29	1979	1,121	—	—	225.00

10.1000 g, .900 GOLD, .2922 oz AGW

KM#	Date	Mintage	VF	XF	Unc
29a	1979	Inc. Ab.	—	Proof	275.00

250 DOLLARS

6.6000 g, .900 GOLD, .1910 oz AGW
250th Anniversary of Birth of George Washington

KM#	Date	Mintage	VF	XF	Unc
35	1982FM(P)	802 pcs.	—	Proof	150.00

47.5400 g, .917 GOLD, 1.4017 oz AGW
Commonwealth Games
Similar to 25 Dollars, KM#44.

KM#	Date	Mintage	VF	XF	Unc
45	1986	150 pcs.	—	Proof	1000.

MINT SETS (MS)

KM#	Date	Mintage	Identification	Issue Price	Mkt. Val.
MS1	1973(8)	2,500	KM10-15,16a,17a	25.00	25.00
MS2	1974(8)	3,708	KM10-17	25.00	20.00
MS3	1975(8)	1,360	KM10-17	27.50	25.00

KM#	Date	Mintage	Identification	Issue Price	Mkt. Val.
MS4	1976(8)	996	KM19-26	27.50	30.00
MS5	1977(8)	468	KM10-17	27.50	30.00
MS6	1978(8)	517	KM10-17	29.00	30.00
MS7	1979(8)	523	KM10-17	29.00	30.00
MS8	1980(8)	649	KM10-17	30.00	30.00
MS9	1981(8)	327	KM10-17	30.00	35.00
MS10	1982(8)	—	KM10-16,34	35.00	50.00
MS11	1983(8)	141	KM10-16,36	35.50	80.00
MS12	1989(5)	—	KM10-14.1	17.00	17.00

PROOF SETS (PS)

KM#	Date	Mintage	Identification	Issue Price	Mkt. Val.
PS1	1973(8)	97,454	KM10-15,16a,17a	37.50	30.00
PS2	1974(8)	35,600	KM10-15,16a,17a	50.00	30.00
PS3	1975(8)	20,458	KM10-15,16a,17a	55.00	30.00
PS4	1976(8)	11,929	KM19-24,25a,26a	55.00	37.50
PS5	1977(8)	5,014	KM10-15,16a,17a	55.00	35.00
PS6	1978(8)	4,436	KM10-15,16a,17a	58.00	37.50
PS7	1979(8)	4,126	KM10-15,16a,17a	60.00	37.50
PS8	1980(8)	2,011	KM10-15,16a,17a	117.00	45.00
PS9	1980(2)	—	KM16a,17a	115.00	32.50
PS10	1981(8)	—	KM10-15,16a,17a	117.00	85.00
PS11	1982(8)	—	KM10-15,16a,34a	117.00	85.00
PS12	1983(8)	—	KM10-15,16a,36a	—	170.00
PS13	1984(8)	—	KM10-15,16a,40	132.00	200.00

Listings For

BELGIAN CONGO: refer to Zaire

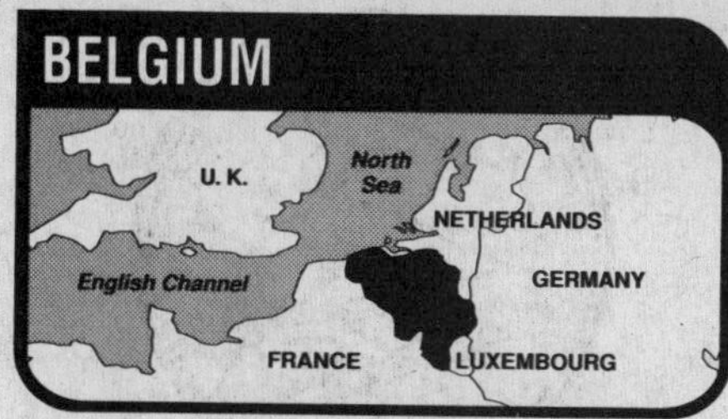

The Kingdom of Belgium, a constitutional monarchy in northwest Europe, has an area of 11,781 sq. mi. (30,519 sq. km.) and a population of 9.9 million, chiefly Dutch-speaking Flemish and French-speaking Walloons. Capital: Brussels. Agriculture, dairy farming, and the processing of raw materials for re-export are the principal industries. Beurs voor Diamant in Antwerp is the world's largest diamond trading center. Iron and steel, machinery motor vehicles, chemicals, textile yarns and fabrics comprise the principal exports.

The Celtic tribe called 'Belgae', from which Belgium derived its name, was described by Caesar as the most courageous of all the tribes of Gaul. The Belgae eventually capitulated to Rome and the area remained for centuries as a part of the Roman Empire known as Belgica.

As Rome began its decline Frankish tribes migrated westward and established the Merovingian, and subsequently, the Carolingian empires. At the death of Charlemagne Europe was divided among his three sons Karl, Lothar and Ludwig. The eastern part of today's Belgium lies in the Duchy of Lower Lorraine while much of the western parts eventually became the County of Flanders. After further divisions the area came under the control of the Duke of Burgundy from whence it passed under Hapsburg control when Marie of Burgundy married Maximilian of Austria. Phillip I (the Fair), son of Maximilian and Marie then added Spain to the Hapsburg empire by marrying Johanna, daughter of Ferdinand and Isabella. Charles and Ferdinand, sons of Phillip and Johanna, began the separate Spanish and Austrian lines of the Hapsburg family. The Burgundian lands, along with the northern provinces which make up present day Netherlands, became the Spanish Netherlands. The northern provinces successfully rebelled and broke away from Hapsburg rule in the late 16th century and early 17th century. The southern provinces along with the Duchy of Luxembourg remained under the influence of Spain until the year 1700 when Charles II, last of the Spanish Hapsburg line, died without leaving an heir and the Spanish crown went to the Bourbon family of France. The Spanish Netherlands then reverted to the control of the Austrian line of Hapsburgs and became the Austrian Netherlands. The Austrian Netherlands along with the Bishopric of Liege fell to the French Republic in 1794.

At the Congress of Vienna in 1815 the area was reunited with the Netherlands, but in 1830 independence was gained and the constitutional monarchy of Belgium was established. A large part of the Duchy of Luxembourg was incorporated into Belgium and the first king was Leopold I of Saxe-Coburg-Gotha.

RULERS

Leopold I, 1831-1865
Leopold II, 1865-1909
Albert I, 1909-1934
Leopold III, 1934-1950
Baudouin I, 1951

MINT MARKS

Angel head - Brussels
St. Michael's head Brussels

MONETARY SYSTEM

100 Centimes = 1 Franc
43 Francs = 1 Ecu

LEGENDS

Belgian coins are inscribed either in Dutch, French or both. The language used is best told by noting the spelling of the name of the country.

(Fr) French: BELGIQUE or BELGES
(Du) Dutch: BELGIE or BELGEN

Many Belgian coins are collected by what is known as Position A and Position B edges. Some dates command a premium depending on the position which are as follows:

Position A: Coins with portrait side down having up right edge lettering.

Position B: Coins with portrait side up having upright edge lettering.

CENTIME

COPPER
Wide rims.

KM#	Date	Mintage	VG	Fine	VF	XF
1.1	1832	—	20.00	50.00	150.00	300.00
	1833/2	5.007	2.50	20.00	100.00	140.00
	1833	Inc. Ab.	2.00	10.00	30.00	60.00
	1835	4.367	2.50	10.00	35.00	90.00

Narrow rims.

KM#	Date	Mintage	VG	Fine	VF	XF
1.2	1835/2	I.A.	3.00	14.00	50.00	95.00
	1835	Inc. Ab.	1.25	4.00	15.00	20.00
	1836/2	4.256	1.25	4.50	20.00	37.50
	1836	Inc. Ab.	1.25	4.50	15.00	32.50
	1837	—	22.50	65.00	200.00	400.00
	1838	—	22.50	65.00	200.00	400.00
	1841	—	22.50	65.00	200.00	400.00
	1844	1.822	2.75	10.00	35.00	70.00
	1845	8.324	.75	3.00	10.00	35.00
	1846/1	8.241	— Reported, not confirmed			
	1846	Inc. Ab.	.75	3.50	12.50	35.00
	1847	5.138	.75	3.50	12.50	35.00
	1848/1	.383	70.00	150.00	230.00	425.00
	1848	Inc. Ab.	70.00	150.00	230.00	425.00
	1849	1.218	1.50	12.50	45.00	100.00
	1850	2.309	1.50	5.00	20.00	60.00
	1855	2.428	50.00	100.00	250.00	400.00
	1856	Inc. Ab.	.75	5.00	20.00	40.00
	1857	.948	3.00	10.00	35.00	80.00
	1858	.916	3.00	10.00	35.00	80.00
	1859	.982	3.00	10.00	35.00	80.00
	1860	1.581	1.00	3.00	9.00	30.00
	1861	1.696	1.00	3.00	9.00	30.00
	1862	11.907	.50	1.50	4.00	15.00
	1863	Inc. Ab.	40.00	75.00	175.00	375.00
	Rev: W/o dash below CENT.					
1.3	1857	Inc. Ab.	20.00	45.00	115.00	245.00
	1858	Inc. Ab.	20.00	45.00	115.00	245.00
	1859	Inc. Ab.	40.00	90.00	225.00	320.00
	1860	Inc. Ab.	15.00	25.00	45.00	135.00
	Rev: W/o stop in signature.					
1.4	1862	Inc. Ab.	4.50	10.00	20.00	40.00

NOTE: Until 1838 these were often struck over Netherlands 1/2 Cent, KM#51. If the date of the Netherlands coin is still visible, add up to 50 percent to the value, except for the date 1838 which is extremely rare.

Obv. French leg: DES BELGES

KM#	Date	Mintage	Fine	VF	XF	Unc
33.1	1869	5.064	1.00	2.00	8.00	20.00
	1870	3.930	1.00	2.00	8.00	20.00
	1873	2.036	1.00	2.00	8.00	20.00
	1874	3.907	1.00	2.00	8.00	20.00
	1875	2.970	1.00	2.00	8.00	20.00
	1876	2.966	1.00	2.00	8.00	20.00
	1882	5.000	1.00	1.50	4.00	12.50
	1833	—	60.00	400.00	850.00	1250.
	1899	2.500	1.00	1.50	3.50	10.00
	1901/801 near 1	3.743	.50	1.50	3.50	10.00
	1901/801 far 1	Inc. Ab.	.50	1.50	3.50	10.00
	1901	Inc. Ab.	.50	1.50	3.50	10.00
	1902/802 near 2	2.847	1.00	2.00	7.50	20.00
	1902/802 far 2	Inc. Ab.	1.00	2.00	7.50	20.00
	1902/801	I.A.	1.00	2.00	7.50	20.00
	1902/1	I.A.	1.00	2.00	7.50	20.00
	1902	Inc. Ab.	.35	.75	1.50	8.00
	1907	3.967	.35	.75	1.50	8.00
	Thick flan.					
33.2	1882	Inc. Ab.	1.50	6.00	20.00	40.00
	1901	Inc. Ab.	.50	2.00	4.00	12.50
	Thin flan.					
33.3	1901	Inc. Ab.	4.00	25.00	60.00	100.00
	Rev: W/o stop in signature.					
33.4	1902	Inc. Ab.	1.00	5.00	15.00	40.00

Obv. Dutch leg: DER BELGEN

KM#	Date	Mintage	Fine	VF	XF	Unc
34.1	1882	Inc. Ab.	50.00	150.00	325.00	550.00
	1887	5.000	1.00	1.50	3.00	12.00
	1892	—	50.00	150.00	300.00	500.00
	1894	5.000	.50	1.25	3.00	10.00
	1899	2.500	.50	1.25	3.00	10.00
	1901/899	I.A.	.75	2.25	4.50	10.00
	1901	Inc. Ab.	.25	.75	1.50	8.00
	1902/1	2.482	1.25	3.50	9.00	15.00
	1902	Inc. Ab.	.25	.75	1.50	8.00
	1907	3.966	.25	.75	1.50	8.00
	Thick flan.					
34.2	1902	Inc. Ab.	.50	2.00	4.00	12.50

Obv. French leg: DES BELGES

KM#	Date	Mintage	Fine	VF	XF	Unc
76	1912	2.540	.20	.50	1.00	2.50
	1914	.870	.25	.75	1.25	4.00

Obv. Dutch leg: DER BELGEN

KM#	Date	Mintage	Fine	VF	XF	Unc
77	1912	2.542	.20	.50	1.00	2.50

2 CENTIMES

COPPER
Wide rims.

KM#	Date	Mintage	VG	Fine	VF	XF
4.1	1833	16.748	2.50	6.00	25.00	50.00
	1834	3.268	3.00	7.00	25.00	50.00
	1835	26.774	2.50	6.00	22.50	45.00

Medal alignment.

KM#	Date	Mintage	VG	Fine	VF	XF
4.3	1833	Inc. Ab.	60.00	225.00	600.00	775.00
	1834	Inc. Ab.	100.00	425.00	1000.	1300.

Narrow rims.

KM#	Date	Mintage	VG	Fine	VF	XF
4.2	1835/3	Inc. Ab.	30.00	70.00	170.00	150.00
	1835	Inc. Ab.	.75	2.00	8.00	14.00
	.1835.	Inc. Ab.	6.50	15.00	40.00	65.00
	1836/3	27.539	15.00	40.00	100.00	160.00
	1836	Inc. Ab.	.75	2.00	8.00	14.00
	1837	—	30.00	65.00	210.00	375.00
	1838/7	—	120.00	500.00	1200.	1500.
	1838	—	30.00	65.00	210.00	375.00
	1841	2.226	1.50	6.00	15.00	25.00
	1842	2.824	1.50	7.00	15.00	30.00
	1844	1.802	1.00	6.00	15.00	25.00
	1845 lg.dt.	8.324	.75	2.50	10.00	17.50
	1845 sm.dt.	I.A.	.75	2.50	10.00	17.50
	1846	8.008	.75	2.50	10.00	17.50
	1847	3.432	1.00	3.50	12.00	20.00
	1848	.420	8.00	20.00	45.00	75.00
	1849	3.690	1.00	3.50	12.00	20.00
	1850	.404	8.00	20.00	50.00	80.00
	1851	2.407	.75	3.00	10.00	20.00
	1852 lg.dt.	.731	5.00	15.00	40.00	65.00
	1852 sm.dt.	I.A.	5.00	15.00	40.00	65.00
	1853	.466	12.00	30.00	75.00	150.00
	1855	.172	22.00	50.00	100.00	200.00
	1856	6.255	.75	2.00	8.00	15.00
	1857	4.612	.75	2.00	8.00	17.00
	1857 w/o signature	Inc. Ab.	20.00	45.00	100.00	160.00
	1858/47	3.177	1.50	3.00	15.00	25.00
	1858/57	I.A.	1.50	3.00	15.00	25.00
	1858	Inc. Ab.	.75	2.00	8.00	27.50
	1859	4.074	.75	2.00	8.00	27.50
	1860	3.070	.75	2.00	8.00	27.50
	1861	2.924	.75	2.00	8.00	15.00
	1862 lg.dt.	6.586	.50	2.00	8.00	15.00
	1862 sm.dt.	I.A.	.50	2.00	8.00	15.00
	1863/2	18.621	.75	2.50	12.00	20.00
	1863	Inc. Ab.	.50	1.00	4.00	6.00
	1864/1	16.840	6.00	12.00	25.00	45.00
	1864	Inc. Ab.	.50	1.00	4.00	6.00
	1865	2.447	.50	2.00	8.00	15.00

NOTE: Until 1836 these were commonly struck over Netherlands 1 Cent, KM#47. If the date of the Netherlands coin is still visible, add up to 50 percent to the value.

Rev: W/o stop in signature.

KM#	Date	Mintage	VG	Fine	VF	XF
4.4	1844	Inc. Ab.	1.00	6.00	15.00	25.00
	1845	Inc. Ab.	.75	2.50	10.00	17.50
	1851	Inc. Ab.	.75	3.00	10.00	20.00
	1861	Inc. Ab.	.75	2.00	8.00	15.00

BRONZE

KM#	Date	Mintage	VG	Fine	VF	XF
4.2a	1845	Inc. Ab.	100.00	250.00	600.00	900.00
	1859	Inc. Ab.	100.00	250.00	600.00	900.00

COPPER
c/s: Script *L* monogram on Netherlands, 1 Cent, KM#47.

KM#	Date	Mintage	VG	Fine	VF	XF
84	ND	—	120.00	450.00	900.00	1400.

Obv. French leg: DES BELGES

KM#	Date	Mintage	Fine	VF	XF	Unc
35.1	1869	2.972	2.50	14.00	30.00	60.00
	1869 plain edge (restrike)		—	—	—	—

KM#	Date	Mintage	Fine	VF	XF	Unc
35.1	1870	5.654	.75	1.50	4.00	10.00
	1870/1	I.A.	1.25	2.00	12.50	30.00
	1871	Inc.1870	1.25	3.00	15.00	40.00
	1873	7.491	.75	1.50	4.00	10.00
	1874 sm. wide date	7.876	.75	1.50	4.00	10.00
	1874 lg. narrow date	Inc. Ab.	.75	1.50	4.00	10.00
	1875	7.932	.75	1.50	4.00	10.00
	1876	10.472	.50	1.50	4.00	10.00
	1902	2.490	.50	1.50	4.00	10.00
	1905	4.981	.50	1.00	2.00	6.00
	1909/5	4.983	.75	1.50	2.50	7.00
	1909	Inc. Ab.	.50	1.00	2.00	6.00

Thin flan.

KM#	Date	Mintage	Fine	VF	XF	Unc
35.2	1902	Inc. Ab.	6.00	40.00	80.00	160.00

Obv. Dutch leg: DER BELGEN

KM#	Date	Mintage	Fine	VF	XF	Unc
36	1902	2.488	.50	1.50	3.00	10.00
	1905/2	4.986	3.00	10.00	25.00	50.00
	1905	Inc. Ab.	.50	1.00	2.00	6.00
	1909	.565	1.00	3.00	9.00	20.00

Obv. French leg: DES BELGES

KM#	Date	Mintage	Fine	VF	XF	Unc
64	1911	.645	2.50	4.00	8.00	17.50
	1912/1	4.928	1.00	5.00	15.00	30.00
	1912	Inc. Ab.	.25	.50	1.00	3.50
	1914	.491	2.50	4.00	8.00	17.50
	1919/4	5.000	3.00	5.00	10.00	35.00
	1919	Inc. Ab.	.25	.50	1.00	3.00

Obv. Dutch leg: DER BELGEN

KM#	Date	Mintage	Fine	VF	XF	Unc
65	1910	1.248	.50	.75	1.75	5.00
	1911 large date	6.441	.25	.50	1.00	3.50
	1911 small date	Inc. Ab.	.25	.50	1.00	3.50
	1912	1.602	.75	1.00	2.00	6.00
	1919	4.998	.25	.50	.75	3.00

5 CENTIMES

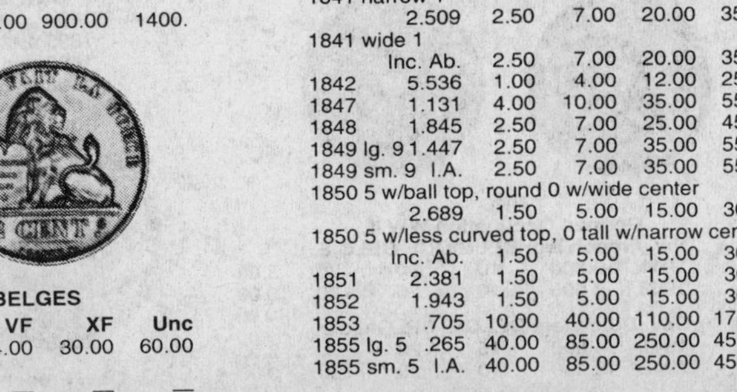

COPPER

KM#	Date	Mintage	VG	Fine	VF	XF
5.1	1811 (error)	—	60.00	120.00	350.00	800.00
	1833	4.437	2.50	6.00	20.00	55.00
	1834	2.515	3.00	7.00	25.00	50.00
	1835	—	60.00	120.00	275.00	550.00
	1837	12.038	1.00	3.00	10.00	25.00
	1838	Inc. Ab.	60.00	175.00	450.00	800.00
	1841 narrow 1	2.509	2.50	7.00	20.00	35.00
	1841 wide 1	Inc. Ab.	2.50	7.00	20.00	35.00
	1842	5.536	1.00	4.00	12.00	25.00
	1847	1.131	4.00	10.00	35.00	55.00
	1848	1.845	2.50	7.00	25.00	45.00
	1849 lg. 9	1.447	2.50	7.00	35.00	55.00
	1849 sm. 9	I.A.	2.50	7.00	35.00	55.00
	1850 5 w/ball top, round 0 w/wide center	2.689	1.50	5.00	15.00	30.00
	1850 5 w/less curved top, 0 tall w/narrow center	Inc. Ab.	1.50	5.00	15.00	30.00
	1851	2.381	1.50	5.00	15.00	30.00
	1852	1.943	1.50	5.00	15.00	30.00
	1853	.705	10.00	40.00	110.00	175.00
	1855 lg. 5	.265	40.00	85.00	250.00	450.00
	1855 sm. 5	I.A.	40.00	85.00	250.00	450.00

KM#	Date	Mintage	VG	Fine	VF	XF
5.1	1856	5.656	1.00	2.00	7.00	20.00
	1857	2.299	1.50	4.00	12.50	25.00
	1858	2.712	1.50	4.00	12.50	25.00
	1858 w/o cross on crown	Inc. Ab.	10.00	35.00	80.00	150.00
	1859	2.591	1.50	4.00	12.50	25.00
	1860	.199	60.00	175.00	300.00	550.00
	1861	Inc. Ab.	70.00	200.00	350.00	650.00

BRONZE

KM#	Date	Mintage	VG	Fine	VF	XF
5.1a	1833	Inc. Ab.	175.00	450.00	1300.	1850.
	1834	—	— Reported, not confirmed			
	1837	—	— Reported, not confirmed			
	1848	Inc. Ab.	120.00	300.00	850.00	1200.
	1850	Inc. Ab.	175.00	450.00	1300.	1850.
	1858	Inc. Ab.	150.00	400.00	1100.	1600.
	1859	Inc. Ab.	120.00	300.00	850.00	1200.

COPPER
Rev: W/o stop in signature.

KM#	Date	Mintage	VG	Fine	VF	XF
5.2	1833	Inc. Ab.	10.00	45.00	110.00	170.00
	1834	Inc. Ab.	15.00	55.00	130.00	190.00
	1837	Inc. Ab.	6.50	30.00	50.00	110.00
	1841	Inc. Ab.	10.00	40.00	85.00	150.00
	1842	Inc. Ab.	7.50	35.00	60.00	120.00
	1847	Inc. Ab.	15.00	55.00	140.00	200.00
	1848	Inc. Ab.	10.00	40.00	60.00	120.00
	1849	Inc. Ab.	15.00	45.00	140.00	200.00
	1850	Inc. Ab.	7.50	30.00	50.00	120.00
	1851	Inc. Ab.	6.00	20.00	40.00	100.00
	1852	Inc. Ab.	7.50	30.00	45.00	110.00

Rev: Large S in CENTS.

KM#	Date	Mintage	VG	Fine	VF	XF
5.3	1858	Inc. Ab.	7.50	30.00	70.00	140.00
	1859	Inc. Ab.	6.00	20.00	60.00	110.00

COPPER-NICKEL

KM#	Date	Mintage	VG	Fine	VF	XF
21	1861	8.259	.25	.60	2.00	4.00
	1862/1	14.149	.25	.60	2.00	4.00
	1862	Inc. Ab.	.25	.50	1.50	3.00
	1863/2	16.055	.25	1.00	2.50	7.50
	1863	Inc. Ab.	.25	.60	2.00	7.00
	1864	2.513	7.50	20.00	40.00	70.00

NOTE: Varieties exist.

Obv. French leg: DES BELGES

KM#	Date	Mintage	Fine	VF	XF	Unc
40	1894	3.111	1.00	2.50	5.00	15.00
	1895	3.693	1.00	2.50	5.00	15.00
	1898	1.004	12.50	22.00	35.00	55.00
	1900/891	1.666	12.50	22.00	35.00	55.00
	1900	Inc. Ab.	10.00	15.00	30.00	45.00

Rev: Lion of different design.

KM#	Date	Mintage	Fine	VF	XF	Unc
44	1901	2.494	5.00	12.00	40.00	60.00

Obv. Dutch leg: DER BELGEN

KM#	Date	Mintage	Fine	VF	XF	Unc
41	1894	1.658	1.00	2.50	5.00	15.00
	1895/4	—	2.00	5.00	15.00	25.00
	1895	4.957	1.00	2.50	5.00	15.00
	1898	.985	12.50	22.00	35.00	55.00
	1900	1.670	10.00	15.00	25.00	45.00

Rev: Lion of different design.

KM#	Date	Mintage	Fine	VF	XF	Unc
45	1901	2.491	5.00	12.00	30.00	60.00

Obv. French leg: BELGIQUE, small date.

KM#	Date	Mintage	Fine	VF	XF	Unc
46	1901	.202	25.00	37.50	47.50	80.00
	1902/1	1.416	.50	1.00	5.00	12.00

KM#	Date	Mintage	Fine	VF	XF	Unc
46	1902	Inc. Ab.	.25	.75	2.50	7.00
	1903	.864	1.00	5.00	10.00	20.00

Obv: Large date.

KM#	Date	Mintage	Fine	VF	XF	Unc
54	1904	5.814	.15	.25	2.00	7.00
	1905/4	9.575	.30	.50	3.00	12.00
	1905	Inc. Ab.	.15	.25	2.00	7.00
	1905 WICHAUX (error)	Inc. Ab.	—	—	—	—
	1905 A. MICHAUX	Inc. Ab.	1.00	3.50	15.00	30.00
	1906/5	8.463	.30	.50	3.00	12.00
	1906	Inc. Ab.	.15	.25	2.00	7.00
	1907	.993	.25	.50	3.00	12.00

Obv. Dutch leg: BELGIE, small date.

KM#	Date	Mintage	Fine	VF	XF	Unc
47	1902/1	1.485	1.75	5.50	22.50	45.00
	1902	Inc. Ab.	.15	.25	2.50	7.00
	1903	1.002	.35	.75	5.00	12.00

Obv: Large date.

KM#	Date	Mintage	Fine	VF	XF	Unc
55	1904	5.812	.15	.25	2.00	7.00
	1905/3	7.002	.35	.65	3.50	12.00
	1905/4	I.A.	.30	.50	3.00	12.00
	1905	Inc. Ab.	.15	.25	2.00	7.00
	1905 w/o cross	Inc. Ab.	—	—	—	—
	1906	11.016	.15	.25	2.00	7.00
	1906 w/o cross	Inc. Ab.	—	—	—	—
	1907	.998	.15	.25	3.00	12.00

Obv. French leg: BELGIQUE

KM#	Date	Mintage	Fine	VF	XF	Unc
66	1910	8.011	.10	.25	1.25	5.00
	1913/0	5.005	.10	.25	2.25	10.00
	1913	Inc. Ab.	.10	.25	1.50	5.00
	1914	1.004	.10	.50	4.00	12.00
	1920/10	10.040	.10	.25	1.00	5.00
	1920	Inc. Ab.	.10	.25	.75	4.00
	1922/0	12.640	.10	.25	1.00	4.00
	1922/1	I.A.	.10	.25	1.25	5.00
	1922	Inc. Ab.	.10	.25	.75	4.00
	1923/13	9.000	.10	.25	2.00	6.00
	1923	Inc. Ab.	.10	.25	.75	4.00
	1925/13	15.860	.10	.25	1.00	4.00
	1925	Inc. Ab.	.10	.25	.75	4.00
	1926/5	7.000	.10	.25	1.00	4.00
	1926	Inc. Ab.	.10	.25	.75	4.00
	1927	2.000	.10	.25	1.00	4.00
	1928	12.507	.10	.25	.75	4.00
	1932	Inc. KM93	5.00	12.50	25.00	80.00

Obv. Dutch leg: BELGIE

KM#	Date	Mintage	Fine	VF	XF	Unc
67	1910	8.033	.10	.25	1.25	7.00
	1914	6.040	.10	.25	1.25	7.00
	1920/10	10.030	.10	.25	1.25	7.00
	1920	Inc. Ab.	.10	.25	.75	5.00
	1921/11	4.200	.10	.25	1.25	7.00
	1921	Inc. Ab.	.10	.25	1.25	7.00
	1922/12	13.180	.10	.25	2.50	8.00

KM#	Date	Mintage	Fine	VF	XF	Unc
67	1922/0	I.A.	.10	.25	1.25	7.00
	1922	Inc. Ab.	.10	.25	1.25	5.00
	1923/13	3.530	.10	.25	1.25	7.00
	1923	Inc. Ab.	.10	.25	1.25	5.00
	1924/11	5.260	.10	.25	1.25	5.00
	1924/14	I.A.	.10	.25	1.25	5.00
	1924	Inc. Ab.	.10	.25	1.25	5.00
	1925/13	13.000	.10	.25	1.25	5.00
	1925/15 high 2	Inc. Ab.	.10	.25	2.00	6.00
	1925/15 level 2	Inc. Ab.	.10	.25	2.00	6.00
	1925/3	I.A.	.10	.25	2.00	6.00
	1925	Inc. Ab.	.10	.25	.75	4.00
	1926/5	I.A.	.10	.25	1.25	5.00
	1927	6.938	.10	.25	.75	4.00
	1928/3	6.252	.10	.25	1.25	5.00
	1928	Inc. Ab.	.10	.25	.75	4.00
	1930	Inc. KM94	5.00	12.50	25.00	80.00
	1931	Inc. KM94	7.50	15.00	30.00	100.00

ZINC
German Occupation WW I
Obv. French leg: BELGIQUE-BELGIE

KM#	Date	Mintage	Fine	VF	XF	Unc
80	1915	10.199	.15	.50	3.00	10.00
	1916 dots	45.464	.10	.30	2.00	5.00

NICKEL-BRASS
Obv. French leg: BELGIQUE
Rev: Star added above 5.

KM#	Date	Mintage	Fine	VF	XF	Unc
93	1932	5.520	.10	.20	.35	3.00

Obv. Dutch leg: BELGIE

KM#	Date	Mintage	Fine	VF	XF	Unc
94	1930	3.000	.10	.20	.35	3.00
	1931	7.430	.10	.20	.35	3.00

Obv. French leg: BELGIQUE-BELGIE

KM#	Date	Mintage	Fine	VF	XF	Unc
110.1	1938	4.970	.10	.20	.75	2.00
	1939 (restrike)	—	—	—	—	—

Medal alignment.

KM#	Date	Mintage	Fine	VF	XF	Unc
110.2	1938	Inc. Ab.	1.25	6.00	12.50	30.00

Obv. Dutch leg: BELGIE-BELGIQUE

KM#	Date	Mintage	Fine	VF	XF	Unc
111	1939	3.000	.10	.20	.75	2.00
	1940	1.970	.20	.40	1.00	3.00

ZINC
German Occupation WW II
Obv. French leg: BELGIQUE-BELGIE

KM#	Date	Mintage	Fine	VF	XF	Unc
123	1941	10.000	.10	.20	.30	3.00
	1943	7.606	.10	.20	.30	3.00

Obv. Dutch leg: BELGIE-BELGIQUE

KM#	Date	Mintage	Fine	VF	XF	Unc
124	1941	4.000	.15	.20	.60	3.00
	1942	18.430	.10	.20	.30	3.00

10 CENTIMES

COPPER

KM#	Date	Mintage	VG	Fine	VF	XF
2.1	1832	.993	9.00	30.00	90.00	200.00
	1833	.994	9.00	30.00	90.00	200.00
	1835	—	125.00	250.00	750.00	1500.
	1838	—	125.00	250.00	750.00	1500.
	1841	—	125.00	250.00	750.00	1500.
	1847/37	.135	16.00	50.00	115.00	250.00
	1847	Inc. Ab.	16.00	50.00	115.00	250.00
	1848/38	.777	20.00	55.00	120.00	200.00
	1848	Inc. Ab.	20.00	55.00	120.00	200.00
	1849/39	I.A.	—	—	—	—
	1849	Inc. Ab.	125.00	150.00	500.00	1200.
	1855	.191	50.00	100.00	200.00	400.00
	1856	Inc. Ab.	100.00	200.00	400.00	1000.

Medal alignment.

KM#	Date	Mintage	VG	Fine	VF	XF
2.2	1838	Inc. Ab.	275.00	750.00	1900.	2600.

COPPER-NICKEL

KM#	Date	Mintage	VG	Fine	VF	XF
22	1861	9.080	.25	.75	1.50	5.00
	1862/61	15.129	.35	1.00	2.00	8.00
	1862	Inc. Ab.	.10	.50	1.25	6.00
	1862 dot after PREMIER	Inc. Ab.	5.00	30.00	75.00	100.00
	1863	14.482	.10	.50	1.25	6.00
	1864	3.202	2.50	5.00	10.00	25.00

Obv. French leg: DES BELGES

KM#	Date	Mintage	Fine	VF	XF	Unc
42	1894	11.886	.75	3.00	5.00	15.00
	1895	.736	30.00	60.00	110.00	160.00
	1898	3.499	3.00	6.00	12.00	30.00
	1901	.551	20.00	30.00	100.00	230.00

Obv. Dutch leg: DER BELGEN

KM#	Date	Mintage	Fine	VF	XF	Unc
43	1894	9.209	.75	3.00	5.00	15.00
	1895/4	3.529	2.00	3.50	10.00	30.00
	1895	Inc. Ab.	1.00	3.50	7.50	25.00
	1898	3.500	3.00	6.00	15.00	30.00
	1901	.556	20.00	40.00	95.00	200.00

Obv. French leg: BELGIQUE, small date.

KM#	Date	Mintage	Fine	VF	XF	Unc
48	1901	.582	6.00	15.00	25.00	45.00
	1902/1	5.866	.50	1.25	7.00	15.00
	1902	Inc. Ab.	.15	.40	2.00	9.00
	1903	.763	1.00	3.00	7.00	15.00

Obv: Large date.

KM#	Date	Mintage	Fine	VF	XF	Unc
52	1903	Inc. Ab.	2.00	6.00	15.00	40.00
	1904	16.354	.15	.25	1.50	7.50
	1905/4	14.392	.25	.50	3.00	10.00
	1905	Inc. Ab.	.15	.25	1.50	7.00
	1906/5	1.483	.50	.75	4.00	10.00
	1906	Inc. Ab.	.25	.50	2.00	8.00

Obv. Dutch leg: BELGIE, small date.

KM#	Date	Mintage	Fine	VF	XF	Unc
49	1902	1.560	.20	.50	2.00	8.00
	1903/2	—	.50	1.25	7.00	15.00
	1903	5.658	.15	.25	1.50	7.00

Obv: Large date.

KM#	Date	Mintage	Fine	VF	XF	Unc
53	1903	Inc. Ab.	1.00	4.00	10.00	20.00
	1904	16.834	.20	.35	1.50	7.00
	1905/3	13.758	.35	.75	2.50	9.00
	1905/4	I.A.	.30	.70	2.00	8.00
	1905	Inc. Ab.	.20	.35	1.50	7.00
	1906/5 point above center of 6	2.017	.50	.75	4.00	12.50
	1906/5 point above right side of 6	Inc. Ab.	.50	.75	4.00	12.50
	1906	Inc. Ab.	.10	.30	1.75	8.00

ZINC
German Occupation
Obv. French leg: BELGIQUE-BELGIE

KM#	Date	Mintage	Fine	VF	XF	Unc
81	1915	9.681	.25	.50	2.50	10.00
	1916.	37.382	.15	.25	1.50	8.00
	1916	Inc. Ab.	10.00	17.50	40.00	80.00
	1917	1.447	17.50	25.00	35.00	85.00

COPPER-NICKEL
Obv. French leg: BELGIQUE

KM#	Date	Mintage	Fine	VF	XF	Unc
85.1	1911 (restrike)	—	—	—	—	—
	1920	6.520	.15	.20	.75	3.00
	1921	7.215	.15	.20	.75	3.00
	1923	20.625	.10	.20	.75	3.00
	1926/3	6.916	.20	.25	1.00	3.50
	1926/5	I.A.	.20	.25	1.00	3.50
	1926	Inc. Ab.	.15	.20	.75	3.00
	1927	8.125	.15	.20	.75	3.00
	1928/3	6.895	.20	.25	1.00	3.50
	1928	Inc. Ab.	.15	.20	.75	3.00
	1929	12.260	.15	.20	.75	3.00

Rev: Single line below ES of CES.

KM#	Date	Mintage	Fine	VF	XF	Unc
85.2	1920	Inc. Ab.	1.50	3.50	7.00	15.00
	1921	Inc. Ab.	2.00	7.50	15.00	30.00

Obv. Dutch leg: BELGIE

KM#	Date	Mintage	Fine	VF	XF	Unc
86	1920	5.050	.15	.20	.75	3.00
	1921	7.580	.15	.20	.75	3.00
	1922	6.250	.15	.20	.75	3.00
	1924	5.825	.15	.20	.75	3.00
	1925/4	8.160	.20	.25	1.00	3.00
	1925	Inc. Ab.	.10	.20	.75	3.00
	1926/5	6.250	.20	.25	1.00	3.00
	1926	Inc. Ab.	.15	.20	.75	3.00
	1927	10.625	.15	.20	.75	3.00
	1928/5	6.750	.20	.25	1.00	3.00
	1928	Inc. Ab.	.15	.20	.75	3.00
	1929	4.668	.15	.20	.75	3.00

NICKEL-BRASS
Obv. French leg: BELGIQUE
Rev: Star added above 10.

KM#	Date	Mintage	Fine	VF	XF	Unc
95.1	1930/20	2.000	110.00	200.00	300.00	375.00
	1930	Inc. Ab.	50.00	100.00	175.00	250.00
	1931	6.270	3.00	5.00	8.00	15.00
	1932	1.270	65.00	100.00	175.00	250.00
	1932 A instead of signature	Inc. Ab.	130.00	225.00	325.00	400.00

Rev: Single line below ES of CES.

KM#	Date	Mintage	Fine	VF	XF	Unc
95.2	1931	Inc. Ab.	2.00	10.00	20.00	40.00
	1932	Inc. Ab.	120.00	210.00	310.00	385.00

Obv. Dutch leg: BELGIE

KM#	Date	Mintage	Fine	VF	XF	Unc
96	1930	1.581	.30	.75	2.00	6.00
	1931	5.000	40.00	80.00	140.00	190.00

Obv. French leg: BELGIQUE-BELGIE

KM#	Date	Mintage	Fine	VF	XF	Unc
112	1938	6.000	.10	.25	.50	1.50
	1939	7.000	.50	1.00	3.00	5.00

Obv. Dutch leg: BELGIE-BELGIQUE

KM#	Date	Mintage	Fine	VF	XF	Unc
113.1	1939	8.425	.10	.25	.50	1.50

Thin flan

KM#	Date	Mintage	Fine	VF	XF	Unc
113.2	1939	Inc. Ab.	1.75	12.50	27.50	50.00

ZINC
German Occupation WW II
Obv. French leg: BELGIQUE-BELGIE

KM#	Date	Mintage	Fine	VF	XF	Unc
125	1941	10.000	.15	.25	1.00	1.50
	1942	17.000	.15	.25	1.00	1.50
	1943	22.500	.15	.25	1.00	1.50
	1945 (restrike)	—	—	—	—	—
	1946	*10.370	—	—	—	—

***NOTE:** Not released for circulation.

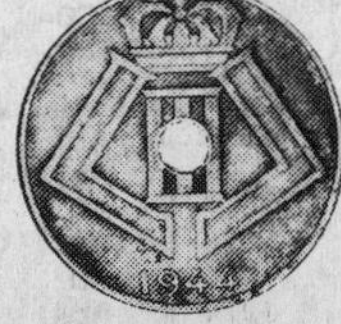

Obv. Dutch leg: BELGIE-BELGIQUE

KM#	Date	Mintage	Fine	VF	XF	Unc
126	1941	7.000	.15	.25	1.00	1.50
	1942	21.000	.15	.25	1.00	1.50
	1943	22.000	.15	.25	1.00	1.50
	1944	28.140	.15	.25	1.00	1.50
	1945	8.000	.15	.25	1.00	1.50
	1946	5.370	.15	.25	1.00	1.50

20 CENTIMES

1.0000 g, .900 SILVER, 0289 oz ASW

KM#	Date	Mintage	VG	Fine	VF	XF
19	1852	.301	8.00	20.00	75.00	125.00
	1853	1.965	3.00	8.00	25.00	80.00
	1858	.865	40.00	125.00	350.00	600.00

NOTE: Varieties w/ and w/o periods after signature exist.

COPPER-NICKEL

KM#	Date	Mintage	VG	Fine	VF	XF
20	1860	1.804	10.00	20.00	70.00	100.00
	1860 I.	I.A.	90.00	250.00	500.00	700.00
	1861	Inc. Ab.	1.00	3.00	10.00	27.50

BRONZE
Obv. French leg: BELGIQUE

KM#	Date	Mintage	Fine	VF	XF	Unc
146	1953	14.150	—	.10	.20	.50
	1953 CENTIMES not touching rim	—	—	.10	.50	1.00
	1954	—	—	400.00	600.00	800.00
	1957	13.300	—	—	.10	.25
	1958	8.700	—	—	.10	.25
	1959	19.670	—	—	.10	.25
	1962	.410	—	6.00	10.00	12.50
	1963	2.550	.10	.20	.50	1.00

Obv. Dutch leg: BELGIE

KM#	Date	Mintage	Fine	VF	XF	Unc
147.1	1954	50.130	—	—	.10	.20
	1960	7.530	—	—	.10	.25

Obv: CENTIEMEN touching rim.

KM#	Date	Mintage	Fine	VF	XF	Unc
147.2	1954	Inc. Ab.	—	.15	.75	2.50
	1960	Inc. Ab.	—	.15	.75	2.50

1/4 FRANC

1.2500 g, .900 SILVER, .0362 oz ASW

KM#	Date	Mintage	VG	Fine	VF	XF
8	1834 signature	.762	15.00	30.00	100.00	150.00
	1834 w/o signature	Inc. Ab.	20.00	40.00	150.00	200.00
	1835 signature	.640	15.00	35.00	125.00	200.00
	1835 w/o signature	Inc. Ab.	22.00	45.00	160.00	225.00
	1841	8,000	175.00	250.00	725.00	1500.
	1843	Inc. Ab.	50.00	100.00	200.00	700.00
	1844	.966	8.00	20.00	90.00	120.00

KM#	Date	Mintage	VG	Fine	VF	XF
14	1849	.101	200.00	750.00	1100.	2000.
	1850	Inc. Ab.	85.00	250.00	600.00	1500.

NOTE: Varieties exist w/ and w/o periods in signature.

25 CENTIMES

COPPER-NICKEL
Obv. French leg: BELGIQUE

KM#	Date	Mintage	Fine	VF	XF	Unc
62	1908	4.007	.50	1.00	12.50	35.00
	1909/8	1.998	4.00	30.00	90.00	200.00
	1909	Inc. Ab.	.50	1.50	15.00	50.00

Obv. Dutch leg: BELGIE

KM#	Date	Mintage	Fine	VF	XF	Unc
63	1908	4.011	.50	1.00	8.00	35.00

Obv. French leg: BELGIQUE

KM#	Date	Mintage	Fine	VF	XF	Unc
68.1	1913	2.011	.15	.30	2.50	7.50
	1920	2.844	.15	.25	2.00	5.00
	1921	7.464	.10	.15	1.00	4.00
	1922	7.600	.10	.20	1.00	4.00
	1923	11.356	.15	.25	1.00	4.00
	1926/3	1.300	1.00	2.50	7.50	17.50
	1926	Inc. Ab.	1.00	2.50	7.50	17.50
	1927/3	8.800	.20	.30	1.00	4.00
	1927	Inc. Ab.	.15	.25	1.00	4.00
	1928	4.351	.10	.15	1.00	4.00
	1929	9.600	.10	.15	1.00	4.00

Rev: Single line below ES of CES.

KM#	Date	Mintage	Fine	VF	XF	Unc
68.2	1920	Inc. Ab.	2.00	6.00	12.50	25.00
	1921	Inc. Ab.	1.75	4.00	8.00	15.00

Obv. Dutch leg: BELGIE

KM#	Date	Mintage	Fine	VF	XF	Unc
69	1910	2.006	.15	.30	2.50	7.50
	1911 (restrike)		—	—	—	—
	1913	2.010	.15	.30	2.00	5.00
	1921	11.173	.15	.25	1.00	4.00
	1922/1	14.200	.20	.30	1.00	4.00
	1922	Inc. Ab.	.15	.25	1.00	4.00
	1926/3	6.400	.75	1.50	5.00	12.50
	1926	Inc. Ab.	.10	.20	1.00	4.00
	1927/3	3.799	.20	.30	1.00	4.00
	1927	Inc. Ab.	.10	.15	1.00	4.00
	1928	9.200	.15	.25	1.00	4.00
	1929	8.980	.15	.25	1.00	4.00

ZINC
German Occupation WW I
Obv. French leg: BELGIQUE-BELGIE

KM#	Date	Mintage	Fine	VF	XF	Unc
82	1915	8.080	.25	1.25	4.00	12.50
	1916	10.671	.25	1.25	4.00	12.50
	1917	3.555	1.50	5.00	10.00	22.50
	1918	5.489	.50	2.50	7.00	15.00

NICKEL-BRASS
Obv. French leg: BELGIQUE-BELGIE

KM#	Date	Mintage	Fine	VF	XF	Unc
114.1	1938	7.200	—	.15	1.00	3.00
	1939	7.732	—	.15	1.00	4.00

Medal alignment.

KM#	Date	Mintage	Fine	VF	XF	Unc
114.2	1939	Inc. Ab.	1.75	9.00	50.00	100.00

Obv. Dutch leg: BELGIE-BELGIQUE

KM#	Date	Mintage	Fine	VF	XF	Unc
115.1	1938	14.932	—	.15	1.00	4.00

Medal alignment.

KM#	Date	Mintage	Fine	VF	XF	Unc
115.2	1939	Inc. Ab.	1.75	9.00	50.00	100.00

ZINC
German Occupation WW II
Obv. French leg: BELGIQUE-BELGIE

KM#	Date	Mintage	Fine	VF	XF	Unc
131	1942	14.400	—	.10	.75	2.00
	1943	21.600	—	.10	.75	2.00
	1945 (restrike)		—	—	—	—
	1946	21.428	—	.10	.75	2.00
	1947	*.300	—	—	—	—

***NOTE:** Not released for circulation.

Obv: Dutch leg: BELGIE-BELGIQUE

KM#	Date	Mintage	Fine	VF	XF	Unc
132	1942	14.400	—	.10	.75	2.00
	1943	21.600	—	.10	.75	2.00
	1944	25.960	—	.10	.75	2.00
	1945	8.200	—	.10	.75	2.00
	1946	11.652	—	.10	.75	2.00
	1947	*.316	—	—	—	—

***NOTE:** Not released for circulation.

COPPER-NICKEL
Obv. French leg: BELGIQUE

KM#	Date	Mintage	Fine	VF	XF	Unc
153.1	1964	21.770	—	—	.10	.15
	1965	11.440	—	—	.10	.15
	1966	19.990	—	—	.10	.15
	1967	6.820	—	—	.10	.15
	1968	25.250	—	—	.10	.15
	1969	7.670	—	—	.10	.15
	1970	27.000	—	—	.10	.15
	1971	16.000	—	—	.10	.15
	1972	20.000	—	—	.10	.15
	1973	12.500	—	—	.10	.15
	1974	20.000	—	—	.10	.15
	1975	12.000	—	—	.10	.15

Medal alignment.

KM#	Date	Mintage	Fine	VF	XF	Unc
153.2	1964	Inc. Ab.	—	—	1.00	1.50
	1965	Inc. Ab.	—	—	1.00	1.50
	1967	Inc. Ab.	—	—	1.00	1.50
	1970	Inc. Ab.	—	—	1.00	1.50
	1971	Inc. Ab.	—	—	1.00	1.50
	1974	Inc. Ab.	—	—	1.00	1.50

Obv. Dutch leg: BELGIE

KM#	Date	Mintage	Fine	VF	XF	Unc
154.1	1964	21.300	—	—	.10	.15
	1965	7.900	—	—	.10	.15
	1966	23.420	—	—	.10	.15
	1967	7.720	—	—	.10	.15
	1968	22.750	—	—	.10	.15
	1969	25.190	—	—	.10	.15
	1970	12.000	—	—	.10	.15
	1971	16.000	—	—	.10	.15
	1972	20.000	—	—	.10	.15
	1973	12.500	—	—	.10	.15
	1974	20.000	—	—	.10	.15
	1975	12.000	—	—	.10	.15

Medal alignment.

KM#	Date	Mintage	Fine	VF	XF	Unc
154.2	1964	Inc. Ab.	—	—	1.00	1.50
	1966	Inc. Ab.	—	—	1.00	1.50
	1969	Inc. Ab.	—	—	1.00	1.50
	1971	Inc. Ab.	—	—	1.00	1.50
	1972	Inc. Ab.	—	—	1.00	1.50

1/2 FRANC

2.5000 g, .900 SILVER, .0723 oz ASW

KM#	Date	Mintage	VG	Fine	VF	XF
6	1833	.058	50.00	120.00	400.00	1000.
	1834	1.578	15.00	40.00	175.00	275.00
	1835	.805	20.00	50.00	200.00	400.00
	1838	.550	30.00	60.00	275.00	700.00
	1840	.347	30.00	60.00	275.00	700.00
	1841	Inc. Ab.	300.00	450.00	1000.	2000.
	1843	.366	30.00	65.00	300.00	800.00
	1844	1.584	15.00	40.00	130.00	250.00

NOTE: Varieties exist.

KM#	Date	Mintage	VG	Fine	VF	XF
15	1847 (restrike)		—	—	—	—
	1849	.210	150.00	450.00	1000.	2000.
	1850	Inc. Ab.	125.00	325.00	700.00	1500.

50 CENTIMES

2.5000 g, .835 SILVER, .0671 oz ASW
Obv. French leg: DES BELGES

KM#	Date	Mintage	Fine	VF	XF	Unc
26	1866	6.806	4.00	20.00	60.00	125.00
	1867	1.014	12.00	40.00	120.00	225.00
	1868	1.076	50.00	85.00	400.00	700.00
	1881/61	.200	90.00	300.00	700.00	1100.
	1881	Inc. Ab.	70.00	225.00	650.00	950.00
	1886/61	1.250	12.00	30.00	80.00	125.00
	1886	Inc. Ab.	2.00	12.00	40.00	110.00
	1898	.499	2.00	15.00	65.00	135.00
	1899	.500	2.00	15.00	65.00	135.00

Obv. Dutch leg: DER BELGEN

KM#	Date	Mintage	Fine	VF	XF	Unc
27	1866 (restrike)		—	—	—	—
	1886	3.750	2.00	7.00	35.00	110.00
	1898	.501	2.50	12.00	65.00	135.00
	1899	.500	2.50	12.00	65.00	135.00

Obv. French leg: DES BELGES

KM#	Date	Mintage	Fine	VF	XF	Unc
50	1901	3.000	1.00	5.00	20.00	45.00

Obv. Dutch leg: DER BELGEN

KM#	Date	Mintage	Fine	VF	XF	Unc
51	1901	3.000	1.00	5.00	20.00	45.00

Obv. French leg: DES BELGES

KM#	Date	Mintage	Fine	VF	XF	Unc
60.1	1907	.545	3.00	10.00	25.00	40.00
	1909	2.503	2.00	4.00	9.00	25.00

Obv: W/o period in signature.

KM#	Date	Mintage	Fine	VF	XF	Unc
60.2	1907	Inc. Ab.	4.00	14.00	35.00	70.00
	1909	Inc. Ab.	2.00	8.00	17.50	35.00

Obv. Dutch leg: DER BELGEN

KM#	Date	Mintage	Fine	VF	XF	Unc
61.1	1907	.545	3.00	10.00	25.00	40.00
	1909	2.510	2.00	4.00	9.00	25.00

Medal alignment.

KM#	Date	Mintage	Fine	VF	XF	Unc
61.2	1909	Inc. Ab.	12.50	45.00	125.00	225.00

Obv. French leg: DES BELGES

KM#	Date	Mintage	Fine	VF	XF	Unc
70	1910	1.900	1.00	3.00	7.00	12.50
	1911	2.063	1.00	3.00	7.00	17.50
	1912	1.000	.75	1.50	3.00	6.00
	1914	.240	5.00	10.00	25.00	45.00

Obv. Dutch leg: DER BELGEN

KM#	Date	Mintage	Fine	VF	XF	Unc
71	1910	1.900	1.00	3.00	7.00	20.00
	1911	2.063	.75	1.50	3.00	6.00
	1912	1.000	.75	1.50	3.00	6.00

ZINC

German Occupation WW I

Obv. Dutch leg: BELGIE-BELGIQUE

KM#	Date	Mintage	Fine	VF	XF	Unc
83	1918	7.394	.50	3.00	5.00	15.00

NICKEL

Obv. French leg: BELGIQUE

KM#	Date	Mintage	Fine	VF	XF	Unc
87	1922	6.180	.15	.25	.50	1.50
	1923	8.820	.15	.25	.50	1.50
	1927	1.750	.15	.30	.50	1.50
	1928	3.000	.15	.25	.75	2.50
	1929	1.000	.25	1.50	3.50	10.00
	1930	1.000	.25	1.50	3.50	10.00
	1932/23	2.530	1.75	4.75	10.00	15.00
	1932	Inc. Ab.	.15	.30	.75	3.00
	1933	2.861	.15	.25	.75	2.50

Obv. Dutch leg: BELGIE

KM#	Date	Mintage	Fine	VF	XF	Unc
88	1922 (restrike)	—	—	—	—	—
	1923	15.000	.20	.25	.50	1.50
	1928/3	10.000	.25	.50	.90	4.00
88	1928	Inc. Ab.	.20	.25	.50	1.50
	1930/23	2.252	.50	2.00	3.50	7.00
	1930	Inc. Ab.	.20	.30	.75	3.00
	1932	2.000	.20	.30	.75	2.50
	1933	1.189	1.00	4.00	6.00	12.00
	1934	.935	50.00	90.00	120.00	180.00

Obv. French leg: BELGIQUE-BELGIE

KM#	Date	Mintage	Fine	VF	XF	Unc
118	1939	15.500	175.00	300.00	400.00	600.00

NOTE: Striking interrupted by the war. Never officially released into circulation.

BRONZE

Obv. French leg: BELGIQUE. Rev: Large head.

KM#	Date	Mintage	Fine	VF	XF	Unc
144	1952	3.520	—	.10	.25	1.00
	1953	22.620	—	—	.10	.35

Rev: Smaller head.

KM#	Date	Mintage	Fine	VF	XF	Unc
148.1	1955	29.160	—	—	.10	.25
	1958	9.750	—	—	.10	.25
	1959	17.350	—	—	.10	.20
	1962	6.160	—	—	.10	.15
	1964	5.860	—	—	.10	.15
	1965	10.320	—	—	.10	.15
	1966	11.040	—	—	.10	.15
	1967	7.200	—	—	.10	.15
	1968	2.000	—	—	.10	.20
	1969	10.000	—	—	.10	.15
	1970	16.000	—	—	.10	.15
	1971	1.250	—	—	.10	.20
	1972	3.000	—	—	.10	.15
	1973	3.000	—	—	.10	.15
	1974	5.000	—	—	.10	.15
	1974 wide rim	Inc. Ab.	—	—	.10	.15
	1975	7.000	—	—	.10	.15
	1976	8.000	—	—	.10	.15
	1977	13.000	—	—	.10	.15
	1978	2.500	—	—	.10	.15
	1979	20.000	—	—	.10	.15
	1980	20.000	—	—	.10	.15
	1981	2.000	—	—	.10	.15
	1982	7.000	—	—	.10	.15
	1983	14.100	—	—	.10	.15
	1985	6.000	—	—	.10	.15
	1987	9.000	—	—	.10	.15
	1988	4.500	—	—	.10	.15
	1989	—	—	—	.10	.15
	1990	—	—	—	.10	.15
	1991	—	—	—	.10	.15

Medal alignment.

KM#	Date	Mintage	Fine	VF	XF	Unc
148.2	1953	Inc. Ab.	—	—	1.00	3.50
	1959	Inc. Ab.	—	—	1.00	2.00
	1965	Inc. Ab.	—	—	1.00	1.50
	1966	Inc. Ab.	—	—	1.00	1.50
	1969	Inc. Ab.	—	—	1.00	1.50
	1974	Inc. Ab.	—	—	1.00	1.50
	1976	Inc. Ab.	—	—	1.00	1.50

Obv. Dutch leg: BELGIE. Rev: Large head.

KM#	Date	Mintage	Fine	VF	XF	Unc
145	1952	5.830	—	.10	.25	1.00
	1953	22.930	—	—	.10	.35
	1954	15.730	—	—	.10	.35

Rev: Smaller head.

KM#	Date	Mintage	Fine	VF	XF	Unc
149.1	1956	5.640	—	—	.10	.25
	1957	13.800	—	—	.10	.25
	1958	19.480	—	—	.10	.20
	1962	4.150	—	—	.10	.15
	1963	1.110	—	—	.10	.15
	1964	10.340	—	—	.10	.15
	1965	9.590	—	—	.10	.15
	1966	6.930	—	—	.10	.15
	1967	6.970	—	—	.10	.15
	1968	2.000	—	—	.10	.20
	1969	10.000	—	—	.10	.15
	1970	12.000	—	—	.10	.15
	1971	1.250	—	—	.10	.20
	1972	7.000	—	—	.10	.15
	1973	3.000	—	—	.10	.15
	1974	5.000	—	—	.10	.15
	1975	7.000	—	—	.10	.15
	1976	8.000	—	—	.10	.15
	1977	13.000	—	—	.10	.15
	1978	2.500	—	—	.10	.15
	1979	40.000	—	—	.10	.15
	1980	20.000	—	—	.10	.15
	1981	2.000	—	—	.10	.15
	1982	7.000	—	—	.10	.15
	1983	14.100	—	—	.10	.15
	1985	6.000	—	—	.10	.15
	1987	18.000	—	—	.10	.15
	1988	9.000	—	—	.10	.15
149.1	1989	—	—	—	.10	.15
	1990	—	—	—	.10	.15
	1991	—	—	—	.10	.15
	1992	—	—	—	.10	.15

Medal alignment.

KM#	Date	Mintage	Fine	VF	XF	Unc
149.2	1953	Inc. Ab.	—	—	1.00	3.50
	1967	Inc. Ab.	—	—	1.00	1.50
	1969	Inc. Ab.	—	—	1.00	1.50
	1979	Inc. Ab.	—	—	1.00	1.50

FRANC

5.0000 g, .900 SILVER, .1447 oz ASW

KM#	Date	Mintage	VG	Fine	VF	XF
7.1	1833	.061	110.00	225.00	500.00	1200.
	1834	.482	30.00	50.00	150.00	400.00
	1835	.861	35.00	70.00	250.00	500.00
	1838	.525	35.00	75.00	280.00	700.00
	1838 lg.star	I.A.	110.00	650.00	1500.	2200.
	1840	.261	40.00	80.00	210.00	800.00
	1841	Inc. Ab.	135.00	375.00	1100.	2000.
	1843	2.196	65.00	165.00	550.00	1200.
	1844	Inc. Ab.	18.00	35.00	110.00	300.00

Medal alignment.

KM#	Date	Mintage	VG	Fine	VF	XF
7.2	1833	Inc. Ab.	200.00	1200.	2800.	4000.

KM#	Date	Mintage	VG	Fine	VF	XF
16.1	1849	.041	150.00	350.00	1000.	2200.
	1850	.162	125.00	300.00	800.00	2000.

NOTE: Edge varieties exist.

Obv: W/o period in signature.

KM#	Date	Mintage	VG	Fine	VF	XF
16.2	1850	Inc. Ab.	225.00	1300.	3300.	4200.

5.0000 g, .835 SILVER, .1342 oz ASW

Obv. French leg: DES BELGES

KM#	Date	Mintage	Fine	VF	XF	Unc
28.1	1866	3.041	5.00	20.00	85.00	175.00
	1867	6.652	3.00	15.00	60.00	140.00
	1868	.675	— Reported, not confirmed			
	1869	1.394	5.00	30.00	130.00	350.00
	1881/67	.119	100.00	250.00	950.00	1500.
	1881	Inc. Ab.	75.00	250.00	800.00	1400.
	1886/66	1.250	4.00	20.00	100.00	175.00
	1886	Inc. Ab.	3.00	15.00	35.00	120.00

Obv: W/o period in signature.

KM#	Date	Mintage	Fine	VF	XF	Unc
28.2	1886	Inc. Ab.	7.00	30.00	75.00	175.00

Obv. Dutch leg: DER BELGEN

KM#	Date	Mintage	Fine	VF	XF	Unc
29.1	1886	1.026	3.00	15.00	45.00	130.00
	1887	2.724	2.00	7.50	25.00	100.00

Obv: W/o period in signature.

KM#	Date	Mintage	Fine	VF	XF	Unc
29.2	1886	Inc. Ab.	12.50	35.00	75.00	150.00
	1887	Inc. Ab.	12.50	35.00	75.00	150.00

50th Anniversary Independence

KM#	Date	Mintage	Fine	VF	XF	Unc
38	1880	.545	8.00	25.00	65.00	110.00

Obv. French leg: DES BELGES

KM#	Date	Mintage	Fine	VF	XF	Unc
56.1	1904	.803	3.00	7.00	20.00	55.00
	1909	2.250	1.25	3.00	9.00	35.00

Obv: W/o period in signature.

KM#	Date	Mintage	Fine	VF	XF	Unc
56.2	1904	Inc. Ab.	6.00	15.00	40.00	80.00
	1909	Inc. Ab.	2.50	6.00	20.00	35.00

Obv. Dutch leg: DER BELGEN

KM#	Date	Mintage	Fine	VF	XF	Unc
57.1	1904	.803	3.00	7.00	20.00	55.00
	1909	2.250	1.25	3.00	9.00	35.00

Obv: W/o period in signature.

KM#	Date	Mintage	Fine	VF	XF	Unc
57.2	1904	Inc. Ab.	6.00	15.00	40.00	80.00
	1909	Inc. Ab.	4.00	10.00	25.00	45.00

Obv. French leg: DES BELGES

KM#	Date	Mintage	Fine	VF	XF	Unc
72	1910	2.190	1.00	3.00	6.00	15.00
	1911	2.810	1.00	2.50	5.00	12.00
	1912	3.250	1.00	2.00	3.00	7.00
	1913	3.000	1.00	2.00	3.00	7.00
	1914	10.563	1.00	2.00	3.00	7.00
	1917	8.540	—	—	—	2000.
	1918	1.469	—	—	—	2000.

Obv. Dutch leg: DER BELGEN

KM#	Date	Mintage	Fine	VF	XF	Unc
73.1	1910	2.750	1.00	3.00	6.00	15.00
	1911	2.250	1.00	2.50	5.00	12.00
	1912	3.250	1.00	2.00	3.00	7.00
	1913	3.000	1.00	2.00	3.00	7.00
	1914	10.222	1.00	2.00	3.00	7.00
	1918	—	—	—	—	2000.

Medal alignment

KM#	Date	Mintage	Fine	VF	XF	Unc
73.2	1914	Inc. Ab.	4.50	12.50	25.00	50.00

NICKEL

Obv. French leg: BELGIQUE

KM#	Date	Mintage	Fine	VF	XF	Unc
89	1922	14.000	.15	.25	.75	3.00
	1923	22.500	.15	.25	.75	3.00
	1928/3	5.000	.20	.75	2.00	5.00
	1928/7	I.A.	.20	.75	2.00	5.00
	1928	Inc. Ab.	.15	.25	.75	3.00
	1929	7.415	.15	.25	.75	3.50
	1930	5.365	.20	.50	1.00	3.50
	1931	—	250.00	450.00	900.00	1500.
	1933	1.998	.50	1.50	3.50	9.00
	1934/24	10.263	.20	.75	2.00	5.00
	1934	Inc. Ab.	.15	.25	.75	3.00

Obv. Dutch leg: BELGIE

KM#	Date	Mintage	Fine	VF	XF	Unc
90	1922	19.000	.15	.25	.75	3.00
	1923/2	17.500	.20	.75	2.00	4.00
	1923	Inc. Ab.	.15	.25	.75	3.00
	1928/3	4.975	.20	.75	2.00	4.00
	1928/7	I.A.	.20	.75	2.00	4.00
	1928	Inc. Ab.	.15	.25	1.50	4.00
	1929	10.365	.15	.25	.75	3.00
	1933	.786	200.00	300.00	450.00	750.00
	1934/24	8.025	.20	.75	2.00	5.00
	1934	Inc. Ab.	.15	.25	.75	3.00
	1935/23	2.238	.35	.75	2.50	7.50
	1935	Inc. Ab.	.30	.50	2.00	6.00

Obv. French leg: BELGIQUE-BELGIE

KM#	Date	Mintage	Fine	VF	XF	Unc
119	1939	46.865	.15	.25	.50	1.50
	1940 (restrike)		—	—	—	—

Obv. Dutch leg: BELGIE-BELGIQUE

KM#	Date	Mintage	Fine	VF	XF	Unc
120	1939	36.000	.15	.25	.50	1.50
	1940	10.865	.20	.40	.75	2.50

ZINC

German Occupation WW II

Obv. French leg: BELGIQUE-BELGIE

KM#	Date	Mintage	Fine	VF	XF	Unc
127	1941	16.000	.15	.25	.50	2.00
	1942	25.000	.15	.25	.50	2.00
	1943	28.000	.15	.25	.50	2.00
	1947	3.175	60.00	100.00	250.00	375.00

Obv. Dutch leg: BELGIE-BELGIQUE

KM#	Date	Mintage	Fine	VF	XF	Unc
128	1942	42.000	.15	.25	.50	2.00
	1943	28.000	.15	.25	.50	2.00
	1944	24.190	.15	.25	.50	2.00
	1945	15.930	.15	.25	.50	2.00
	1946	36.000	.15	.25	.50	2.00
	1947	3.000	30.00	60.00	100.00	175.00

COPPER-NICKEL

Obv. French leg: BELGIQUE

KM#	Date	Mintage	Fine	VF	XF	Unc
142.1	1950	13.630	—	—	.10	3.00
	1951	51.025	—	—	.10	2.00
	1952	53.205	—	—	.10	2.00
	1954	4.980	—	.10	.25	4.00
	1955	3.960	—	.10	.25	4.00
	1956	10.000	—	—	.10	1.00
	1958	31.750	—	—	.10	1.00
	1959	9.000	—	—	.10	1.00
	1960	10.000	—	—	.10	.15
	1961	5.030	—	—	.10	.15
	1962	12.250	—	—	.10	.15
	1963	18.700	—	—	.10	.15
	1964	10.110	—	—	.10	.15
	1965	10.185	—	—	.10	.15
	1966	16.430	—	—	.10	.15
	1967	32.945	—	—	.10	.15
	1968	8.000	—	—	.10	.15
	1969	21.950	—	—	.10	.15
	1970	35.500	—	—	.10	.15
	1971	10.000	—	—	.10	.15
	1972	35.000	—	—	.10	.15
	1973	42.500	—	—	.10	.15
	1974	30.000	—	—	.10	.15
	1975	80.000	—	—	.10	.15
	1976	18.000	—	—	.10	.15
	1977	68.500	—	—	.10	.15
	1978	47.500	—	—	.10	.15
	1979	25.000	—	—	.10	.15
	1980	66.500	—	—	.10	.15
	1981	2.000	—	—	.10	.15
	1988	17.500	—	—	.10	.15

Medal alignment.

KM#	Date	Mintage	Fine	VF	XF	Unc
142.2	1952	Inc. Ab.	—	—	1.00	20.00
	1959	Inc. Ab.	—	—	1.00	10.00
	1963	Inc. Ab.	—	—	1.00	1.50
	1965	Inc. Ab.	—	—	1.00	1.50
	1970	Inc. Ab.	—	—	1.00	1.50
	1974	Inc. Ab.	—	—	1.00	1.50
	1977	Inc. Ab.	—	—	1.00	1.50
	1978	Inc. Ab.	—	—	1.00	1.50
	1979	Inc. Ab.	—	—	1.00	1.50

Obv. Dutch leg: BELGIE

KM#	Date	Mintage	Fine	VF	XF	Unc
143.1	1950	10.000	—	—	.10	3.00
	1951	53.750	—	—	.10	2.00
	1952	49.145	—	—	.10	2.00
	1953	9.915	—	—	.10	2.00
	1954	4.940	—	.10	.25	4.00
	1955	3.960	—	.10	.25	4.00
	1956	10.040	—	—	.10	1.00
	1957	18.315	—	—	.10	1.00
	1958	17.365	—	—	.10	1.00
	1959	5.830	—	—	.10	1.00
	1960	5.555	—	—	.10	.15
	1961	9.350	—	—	.10	.15
	1962	10.720	—	—	.10	.15
	1963	23.460	—	—	.10	.15
	1964	7.430	—	—	.10	.15
	1965	11.190	—	—	.10	.15
	1966	20.990	—	—	.10	.15
	1967	27.470	—	—	.10	.15
	1968	8.170	—	—	.10	.15
	1969	21.730	—	—	.10	.15
	1970	35.730	—	—	.10	.15
	1971	10.000	—	—	.10	.15
	1972	35.000	—	—	.10	.15
	1973	42.500	—	—	.10	.15
	1974	30.000	—	—	.10	.15
	1975	80.000	—	—	.10	.15
	1976	18.000	—	—	.10	.15
	1977	68.500	—	—	.10	.15
	1978	47.500	—	—	.10	.15
	1979	50.000	—	—	.10	.15
	1980	66.500	—	—	.10	.15
	1981	2.000	—	—	.10	.15
	1988	17.500	—	—	.10	.15

Medal alignment.

KM#	Date	Mintage	Fine	VF	XF	Unc
143.2	1951	Inc. Ab.	—	—	1.00	20.00
	1952	Inc. Ab.	—	—	1.00	20.00
	1958	Inc. Ab.	—	—	1.00	10.00
	1970	Inc. Ab.	—	—	1.00	1.50
	1971	Inc. Ab.	—	—	1.00	1.50
	1979	Inc. Ab.	—	—	1.00	1.50

NICKEL-PLATED IRON

Rev: French legend: BELGIQUE.

KM#	Date	Mintage	Fine	VF	XF	Unc
170	1989	—	—	—	—	.35
	1990	—	—	—	—	.35
	1991	—	—	—	—	.35

Rev: Dutch legend: BELGIE.

KM#	Date	Mintage	Fine	VF	XF	Unc
171	1989	—	—	—	—	.35
	1990	—	—	—	—	.35
	1991	—	—	—	—	.35

2 FRANCS

10.0000 g, .900 SILVER, .2894 oz ASW

Edge inscription inclined to left.

KM#	Date	Mintage	VG	Fine	VF	XF
9.1	1834 Pos. A	276	175.00	400.00	900.00	2200.
	1834 Pos. A	—	—	—	Proof	3500.
	1834 Pos. B					

KM#	Date	Mintage	VG	Fine	VF	XF
9.1		Inc. Ab.	175.00	400.00	900.00	2200.
	1835 Pos. A	225	200.00	450.00	950.00	2300.
	1835 Pos. B	Inc. Ab.	225.00	500.00	1000.	2800.
	1840 Pos. A	236	300.00	700.00	1500.	3500.
	1840 Pos. B	Inc. Ab.	300.00	700.00	2000.	4000.
	1841 Pos. A	—	500.00	1200.	4000.	6000.
	1843 Pos. A	735	150.00	300.00	850.00	2000.
	1843 Pos. B	Inc. Ab.	150.00	300.00	850.00	2000.
	1844 Pos. A	483	175.00	450.00	900.00	2200.
	1844 Pos. B	Inc. Ab.	175.00	450.00	900.00	2200.

Edge inscription inclined to right.

KM#	Date	Mintage	VG	Fine	VF	XF
9.2	1834 Pos. A	Inc. Ab.	175.00	450.00	900.00	2200.
	1834 Pos. B	Inc. Ab.	175.00	475.00	1000.	2500.
	1835 Pos. A	Inc. Ab.	175.00	400.00	900.00	2200.
	1835 Pos. B	Inc. Ab.	200.00	500.00	1000.	2500.
	1838 Pos. A	300	220.00	500.00	1000.	2600.
	1838 Pos. B	Inc. Ab.	220.00	500.00	1000.	2600.
	1840 Pos. A	Inc. Ab.	175.00	400.00	900.00	2200.
	1840 Pos. B	Inc. Ab.	175.00	400.00	900.00	2200.
	1841 Pos. A	—	300.00	650.00	2200.	3200.
	1843 Pos. A	Inc Ab.	175.00	400.00	900.00	2100.
	1843 Pos. B	Inc. Ab.	175.00	400.00	900.00	2200.
	1844 Pos. A	Inc. Ab.	175.00	400.00	900.00	2200.
	1844 Pos. B	Inc. Ab.	200.00	450.00	1100.	2600.

KM#	Date	Mintage	VG	Fine	VF	XF
10	1848 (restrike)		—	—	—	—
	1849	—	400.00	900.00	2800.	4700.
	1865	—	450.00	1100.	3200.	5200.

NOTE: The above type was not officially released into circulation.

10.0000 g, .835 SILVER, .2685 oz ASW
Obv. French leg: DES BELGES

KM#	Date	Mintage	Fine	VF	XF	Unc
30.1	1866	1.942	7.00	35.00	175.00	400.00
	1867	3.789	5.00	30.00	125.00	250.00
	1868	2.164	7.00	35.00	150.00	300.00

NOTE: Edge varieties exist.

Rev: W/o cross on crown.

KM#	Date	Mintage	VG	Fine	VF	XF
30.2	1866	Inc. Ab.	15.00	225.00	475.00	850.00
	1867	Inc. Ab.	12.50	190.00	425.00	750.00
	1868	Inc. Ab.	17.50	250.00	500.00	900.00

Obv. Dutch leg: DER BELGEN

KM#	Date	Mintage	Fine	VF	XF	Unc
31	1887	.150	75.00	300.00	1000.	2000.

NOTE: Edge varieties exist.

50th Anniversary Independence
Rev. French leg: DE BELGIQUE

KM#	Date	Mintage	Fine	VF	XF	Unc
39	1880	.118	30.00	100.00	225.00	500.00

Obv. French leg: DES BELGES

KM#	Date	Mintage	Fine	VF	XF	Unc
58.1	1904	.400	6.00	12.00	50.00	90.00
	1909	1.088	2.50	6.00	25.00	45.00

Obv: W/o period in signature.

KM#	Date	Mintage	Fine	VF	XF	Unc
58.2	1904	Inc. Ab.	10.00	30.00	60.00	110.00
	1909	Inc. Ab.	12.50	60.00	160.00	300.00

Obv. Dutch leg: DER BELGEN

KM#	Date	Mintage	Fine	VF	XF	Unc
59.1	1904	.400	5.00	12.00	50.00	90.00
	1909	1.088	2.50	6.00	25.00	45.00

Obv: W/o period in signature.

KM#	Date	Mintage	Fine	VF	XF	Unc
59.2	1904	Inc. Ab.	12.50	60.00	160.00	300.00
	1909	Inc. Ab.	10.00	30.00	60.00	110.00

Obv. French leg: DES BELGES

KM#	Date	Mintage	Fine	VF	XF	Unc
74	1910	.800	4.00	8.00	17.00	40.00
	1911	1.000	2.50	7.00	15.00	35.00
	1912	.375	5.00	12.00	22.00	40.00

Obv. Dutch leg: DER BELGEN

KM#	Date	Mintage	Fine	VF	XF	Unc
75	1911	1.775	2.50	7.00	15.00	35.00
	1912	.375	5.00	12.00	22.00	40.00

NICKEL
Obv. French leg: BELGIQUE

KM#	Date	Mintage	Fine	VF	XF	Unc
91.1	1923	7.500	.25	1.00	2.00	10.00
	1930/20	1.250	22.50	40.00	70.00	135.00
	1930	Inc. Ab.	17.50	35.00	60.00	115.00

Medal alignment.

KM#	Date	Mintage	Fine	VF	XF	Unc
91.2	1923	Inc. Ab.	8.50	25.00	60.00	150.00

Obv. Dutch leg: BELGIE

KM#	Date	Mintage	Fine	VF	XF	Unc
92	1923	6.500	.25	1.00	2.00	10.00
	1924	1.000	12.50	25.00	40.00	75.00
	1930/20	1.252	20.00	35.00	65.00	125.00
	1930	Inc. Ab.	15.00	30.00	55.00	110.00

ZINC COATED STEEL
Allied Occupation Issue
Obv. French leg: BELGIQUE-BELGIE

KM#	Date	Mintage	Fine	VF	XF	Unc
133	1944	25.000	.25	.50	.75	3.00

NOTE: Made in U.S.A. on blanks for 1943 cents.

2-1/2 FRANCS

12.5000 g, .900 SILVER, .3617 oz ASW
Obv. French leg: ROI DES BELGES

KM#	Date	Mintage	VG	Fine	VF	XF
11	1848	.559	45.00	150.00	225.00	350.00
	1849	2.003	30.00	100.00	200.00	300.00

Larger head.

KM#	Date	Mintage	VG	Fine	VF	XF
12	1848	Inc. Ab.	125.00	350.00	1200.	2000.
	1849	Inc. Ab.	30.00	110.00	225.00	500.00
	1849	—	—	—	Proof	1500.
	1850	.065	175.00	400.00	800.00	1500.
	1865	—	350.00	750.00	2000.	3250.

NOTE: Coins dated 1865 were not released into circulation.

5 FRANCS

25.0000 g, .900 SILVER, .7234 oz ASW
Incuse lettered edge.

KM#	Date	Mintage	VG	Fine	VF	XF
3.1	1832 Pos. A	.037	60.00	150.00	800.00	1200.
	1832 Pos. B	Inc. Ab.	55.00	135.00	600.00	1000.
	1833 Pos. A	1.126	16.00	30.00	100.00	600.00
	1833 Pos. B	Inc. Ab.	17.50	35.00	110.00	620.00
	1834 Pos. A	.350	45.00	90.00	250.00	700.00
	1834 Pos. B	Inc. Ab.	45.00	90.00	250.00	700.00
	1835 Pos. A	.370	45.00	90.00	250.00	900.00
	1835 Pos. B	Inc. Ab.	45.00	90.00	250.00	900.00
	1838 Pos. A	5,203	450.00	1200.	3000.	8000.
	1838 Pos. B	Inc. Ab.	500.00	1500.	4000.	9000.
	1840	—	500.00	1700.	3400.	6300.
	1841	—	500.00	1700.	3400.	6300.
	1844 Pos. A	.483	60.00	135.00	400.00	850.00
	1844 Pos. B	Inc. Ab.	150.00	800.00	2000.	4000.

Raised lettered edge.

KM#	Date	Mintage	VG	Fine	VF	XF
3.2	1847	.700	20.00	40.00	85.00	400.00
	1848	2.516	12.00	30.00	65.00	250.00
	1849	3.014	10.00	17.50	45.00	225.00

KM#	Date	Mintage	VG	Fine	VF	XF
17	1849	3.909	12.50	17.50	50.00	75.00
	1850 dot above date					
		5.265	12.50	17.50	50.00	75.00
	1850 w/o dot above date					
		Inc. Ab.	10.00	15.00	40.00	65.00
	1850	—	—	—	Proof	500.00
	1851/0	3.708	15.00	20.00	40.00	60.00
	1851 dot above date					
		Inc. Ab.	10.00	17.50	30.00	45.00
	1851 w/o dot above date					
		Inc. Ab.	10.00	17.50	30.00	45.00
	1852/1	4.605	15.00	25.00	35.00	75.00
	1852	Inc. Ab.	10.00	17.50	30.00	45.00
	1853	2.427	15.00	30.00	40.00	75.00
	1858	.018	60.00	150.00	250.00	550.00
	1865/55 broken M in PREMIER					
		.907	15.00	25.00	60.00	110.00
	1865/55	I.A.	15.00	25.00	60.00	110.00
	1865	Inc. Ab.	10.00	20.00	45.00	90.00
	1865 dot after F on reverse					
		Inc. Ab.	15.00	30.00	65.00	100.00

Obv: Smaller head, engravers name near rim, below truncation.

KM#	Date	Mintage	Fine	VF	XF	Unc
24	1865	Inc. 1867	100.00	225.00	350.00	650.00
	1866	Inc. 1867	175.00	250.00	425.00	725.00
	1866 dot after F on reverse					
		Inc. 1867	175.00	325.00	525.00	800.00
	1867	3.693	7.50	15.00	35.00	100.00
	1867 dot after F on reverse					
		Inc. Ab.	10.00	35.00	50.00	110.00
	1868 Pos. A					
		6.751	7.50	20.00	40.00	100.00
	1868 Pos. B					
		Inc. Ab.	85.00	135.00	330.00	825.00
	1869	12.658	7.50	10.00	40.00	75.00
	1870	10.486	7.50	10.00	40.00	75.00
	1871	4.783	7.50	12.50	45.00	80.00
	1872	2.045	7.50	12.50	45.00	85.00
	1873 Pos. A					
		22.341	6.50	10.00	30.00	60.00
	1873 Pos. B					
		Inc. Ab.	75.00	375.00	900.00	1600.
	1874	2.400	7.50	10.00	40.00	85.00
	1875	2.981	7.50	10.00	35.00	85.00
	1876	2.160	7.50	10.00	40.00	85.00
	1878	3 known	—	—	Rare	—

Obv: Larger head, engravers name below truncation.

KM#	Date	Mintage	Fine	VF	XF	Unc
25	1865	Inc. Ab.	450.00	900.00	1350.	2500.
	1866	Inc. Ab.	550.00	1150.	1800.	3400.
	1867	Inc. Ab.	400.00	800.00	1100.	2300.
	1868	Inc. Ab.	550.00	1100.	1650.	3100.

Un or Een (1) Belga

NICKEL
Obv. French leg: DES BELGES
Rev. value: UN BELGA

KM#	Date	Mintage	Fine	VF	XF	Unc
97.1	1930	1.600	1.50	2.50	5.00	15.00
	1931	9.032	1.00	2.00	3.00	10.00
	1932	3.600	4.00	7.00	10.00	20.00
	1933	1.387	8.00	15.00	25.00	40.00
	1934	1.000	45.00	75.00	110.00	175.00

Medal alignment.

KM#	Date	Mintage	Fine	VF	XF	Unc
97.2	1930	Inc. Ab.	17.50	32.50	75.00	300.00

NOTE: Edge varieties exist.

Obv. Dutch leg: DER BELGEN
Rev. value: EEN BELGA

KM#	Date	Mintage	Fine	VF	XF	Unc
98	1930	5.086	1.00	2.50	5.00	12.50
	1931	5.336	1.00	2.50	5.00	12.50
	1932	3.683	1.50	3.00	7.50	20.00
	1933	2.514	8.00	15.00	20.00	40.00

NOTE: Edge varieties exist.

Rev. French leg: BELGIQUE

KM#	Date	Mintage	Fine	VF	XF	Unc
108.1	1936	.650	6.00	17.50	25.00	50.00
	1937	1.848	6.00	17.50	25.00	50.00

Medal alignment.

KM#	Date	Mintage	Fine	VF	XF	Unc
108.2	1936	Inc. Ab.	17.50	55.00	150.00	350.00

NOTE: Edge varieties exist.

Rev. Dutch leg: BELGIE

KM#	Date	Mintage	Fine	VF	XF	Unc
109.1	1936	2.498	4.00	15.00	20.00	45.00
	1937	—	—	—	—	—

Medal alignment.

KM#	Date	Mintage	Fine	VF	XF	Unc
109.2	1936	Inc. Ab.	15.00	45.00	130.00	300.00

NOTE: Edge varieties exist.

Obv. French leg: BELGIQUE-BELGIE
Milled edge, lettering w/crown.

KM#	Date	Mintage	Fine	VF	XF	Unc
116.1	1938 Pos. A					
		11.419	.15	.60	1.75	6.00
	1938 Pos. B					
		Inc. Ab.	.30	1.00	3.00	6.00
		Inc. Ab.	30.00	50.00	100.00	175.00

Milled edge, lettering w/star.

KM#	Date	Mintage	Fine	VF	XF	Unc
116.2	1939 Pos. A					
		Inc. Ab.	175.00	350.00	600.00	1250.
	1939 Pos. B					
		Inc. Ab.	200.00	425.00	750.00	1550.

Milled edge, w/o lettering (error).

KM#	Date	Mintage	Fine	VF	XF	Unc
116.3	1938					

Obv. Dutch leg: BELGIE-BELGIQUE
Milled edge, lettering w/crown.

KM#	Date	Mintage	Fine	VF	XF	Unc
117.1	1938 Pos. A					
		3.200	5.00	15.00	50.00	125.00
	1938 Pos. B					
		Inc. Ab.	5.00	15.00	50.00	125.00
	1939 Pos. A					
		8.219	7.50	20.00	70.00	150.00
	1939 Pos. B					
		Inc. Ab.	7.50	20.00	70.00	150.00

Milled edge, lettering w/star.

KM#	Date	Mintage	Fine	VF	XF	Unc
117.2	1938 Pos. A					
		Inc. Ab.	6.00	17.50	55.00	135.00
	1938 Pos. B					
		Inc. Ab.	6.00	17.50	55.00	135.00
	1939 Pos. A					
		Inc. Ab.	.10	.50	1.50	5.00
	1939 Pos. B					
		Inc. Ab.	.10	.50	1.50	5.00

Milled edge, w/o lettering (error).

KM#	Date	Mintage	Fine	VF	XF	Unc
117.3	1939	Inc. Ab.	30.00	60.00	135.00	250.00

ZINC
German Occupation WW II
Obv. French leg: DES BELGES

KM#	Date	Mintage	Fine	VF	XF	Unc
129.1	1941	15.200	.35	.75	1.50	5.00
	1943	16.236	.35	.75	1.50	5.00
	1944	1.868	.75	2.00	5.00	12.00
	1945	3.200	.50	1.00	2.50	7.50
	1946	4.452	1.00	2.50	5.00	12.00
	1947	3.100	30.00	65.00	110.00	190.00

Medal alignment.

KM#	Date	Mintage	Fine	VF	XF	Unc
129.2	1943	Inc. Ab.	7.50	35.00	100.00	200.00

Obv. Dutch leg: DER BELGEN

KM#	Date	Mintage	Fine	VF	XF	Unc
130	1941	27.544	.30	.75	1.50	5.00
	1945	3.200	27.50	60.00	100.00	175.00
	1946	4.000	—	—	Rare	—
	1947	.036	125.00	250.00	375.00	650.00

COPPER-NICKEL
Obv. French leg: BELGIQUE

KM#	Date	Mintage	Fine	VF	XF	Unc
134.1	1948	5.304	—	—	.20	4.00
	1949	38.752	—	—	.20	2.00
	1950	23.948	—	—	.20	2.00
	1958	9.088	—	—	.20	1.00
	1961	6.000	—	—	.20	.50
	1962	6.576	—	—	.20	.50
	1963	11.144	—	—	.20	.35
	1964	3.520	—	—	.20	.40
	1965	11.988	—	—	.20	.35
	1966	6.772	—	—	.20	.40
	1967	13.268	—	—	.20	.35
	1968	5.192	—	—	.20	.40
	1969	22.235	—	—	.20	.35
	1969 w/o engravers name					
		Inc. Ab.	—	1.50	2.50	5.00
	1970	2.000	—	—	.20	.45
	1971	15.000	—	—	.20	.35
	1972	17.500	—	—	.20	.35
	1973	10.000	—	—	.20	.35
	1974	25.000	—	—	.20	.35
	1975	34.000	—	—	.20	.35
	1976	7.500	—	—	.20	.40
	1977	22.500	—	—	.20	.35
	1978	27.500	—	—	.20	.35
	1979	5.000	—	—	.20	.40
	1980	11.000	—	—	.20	.35
	1981	2.000	—	—	.20	.40

Medal alignment.

KM#	Date	Mintage	Fine	VF	XF	Unc
134.2	1949	Inc. Ab.	—	—	1.50	20.00
	1950	Inc. Ab.	—	—	1.50	20.00
	1958	Inc. Ab.	—	—	1.50	10.00
	1963	Inc. Ab.	—	—	1.50	3.00
	1965	Inc. Ab.	—	—	1.50	3.00
	1966	Inc. Ab.	—	—	1.50	4.00
	1969	Inc. Ab.	—	—	1.50	3.00
	1975	Inc. Ab.	—	—	1.50	3.00

Obv. Dutch leg: BELGIE

KM#	Date	Mintage	Fine	VF	XF	Unc
135.1	1948	4.800	—	—	.20	4.00
	1949	31.500	—	—	.20	2.00
	1950	34.728	—	—	.20	2.00
	1958	2.672	—	—	.20	4.00
	1960	5.896	—	—	.20	.75
	1961	4.120	—	—	.20	.50
	1962	7.624	—	—	.20	.50
	1963	6.136	—	—	.20	.40
	1964	8.128	—	—	.20	.40
	1965	9.956	—	—	.20	.40
	1966	7.136	—	—	.20	.40
	1967	16.132	—	—	.20	.35
	1968	3.200	—	—	.20	.40
	1969	21.500	—	—	.20	.35
	1970	2.000	—	—	.20	.45
	1971	15.000	—	—	.20	.35
	1972	17.500	—	—	.20	.35
	1972 w/o engravers name					
		Inc. Ab.	—	1.50	2.50	5.00
	1973	10.000	—	—	.20	.35
	1974	25.000	—	—	.20	.35
	1975	34.000	—	—	.20	.35
	1976	7.500	—	—	.20	.40
	1977	22.500	—	—	.20	.35
	1978	27.500	—	—	.20	.35
	1979	10.000	—	—	.20	.35
	1980	11.000	—	—	.20	.35
	1981	2.000	—	—	.20	.40

Medal alignment.

KM#	Date	Mintage	Fine	VF	XF	Unc
135.2	1950	Inc. Ab.	—	—	1.50	20.00
	1962	Inc. Ab.	—	—	1.50	5.00
	1963	Inc. Ab.	—	—	1.50	4.00
	1965	Inc. Ab.	—	—	1.50	4.00
	1966	Inc. Ab.	—	—	1.50	4.00
	1974	Inc. Ab.	—	—	1.50	3.00

BRASS or ALUMINUM-BRONZE
Rev: French leg: BELGIQUE.

KM#	Date	Mintage	Fine	VF	XF	Unc
163	1986	104.250	—	—	.35	.65
	1987	50.720	—	—	.35	.65
	1988	26.500	—	—	.35	.65
	1989	—	—	—	.35	.65
	1990	—	—	—	.35	.65
	1991	—	—	—	.35	.65

Rev: Dutch leg: BELGIE.

KM#	Date	Mintage	Fine	VF	XF	Unc
164	1986	104.250	—	—	.35	.65
	1987	50.720	—	—	.35	.65
	1988	26.500	—	—	.35	.65
	1989	—	—	—	.35	.65
	1990	—	—	—	.35	.65
	1991	—	—	—	.35	.65

10 FRANCS

3.1662 g, .900 GOLD, .0916 oz AGW

KM#	Date	Mintage	Fine	VF	XF	Unc
18	1849	.037	500.00	1200.	2250.	3300.
	1850	.063	400.00	1000.	2000.	3000.

NOTE: 54,890 pcs. dated 1849 and 1850 were withdrawn from circulation.

KM#	Date	Mintage	Fine	VF	XF	Unc
A33	1865 (restrike)		—	—	—	—
	1867	—	1800.	3200.	6500.	11,000.

Deux or Twee (2) Belgas

NICKEL
Independence Centennial
Rev. French leg: BELGIQUE

KM#	Date	Mintage	Fine	VF	XF	Unc
99	1930	2.699	25.00	50.00	80.00	110.00

NOTE: Edge varieties exist.

Rev. Dutch leg: BELGIE

KM#	Date	Mintage	Fine	VF	XF	Unc
100	1930	3.000	30.00	60.00	90.00	125.00

NOTE: Edge varieties exist.

Rev. French leg: BELGIQUE

KM#	Date	Mintage	Fine	VF	XF	Unc
155.1	1969	22.235	—	—	.40	.70
	1970	9.500	—	—	.40	.70
	1971	15.000	—	—	.40	.70
	1972	10.000	—	—	.40	.70
	1973	10.000	—	—	.40	.70
	1974	5.000	—	—	.40	.70
	1975	5.000	—	—	.40	.70
	1976	7.500	—	—	.40	.70
	1977	7.000	—	—	.40	.70
	1978	2.500	—	—	.40	.70
	1979	5.000	—	—	.40	.70

Medal alignment.

KM#	Date	Mintage	Fine	VF	XF	Unc
155.2	1974	Inc. Ab.	—	1.50	3.00	6.00

Rev. Dutch leg: BELGIE

KM#	Date	Mintage	Fine	VF	XF	Unc
156.1	1969	21.500	—	—	.40	.70
	1970	10.000	—	—	.40	.70
	1971	15.000	—	—	.40	.70
	1972	10.000	—	—	.40	.70
	1973	10.000	—	—	.40	.70
	1974	5.000	—	—	.40	.70
	1975	5.000	—	—	.40	.70
	1976	7.500	—	—	.40	.70
	1977	7.000	—	—	.40	.70
	1978	2.500	—	—	.40	.70
	1979	10.000	—	—	.40	.70

Medal alignment.

KM#	Date	Mintage	Fine	VF	XF	Unc
156.2	1971	Inc. Ab.	—	1.50	3.00	6.00
	1976	Inc. Ab.	—	1.50	3.00	6.00

20 FRANCS

6.4516 g, .900 GOLD, .1867 oz AGW
Lettered edge.

KM#	Date	Mintage	Fine	VF	XF	Unc
A23.1	1834	—	950.00	4800.	12,000.	15,000.
	1835	—	1200.	6000.	15,000.	18,500.
	1838	1 known	—	—	—	—
	1841	—	1300.	6500.	16,000.	20,000.

Milled edge.

KM#	Date	Mintage	Fine	VF	XF	Unc
A23.2	1834 (restrike)		—	—	—	—
	1835 (restrike)		—	—	—	—
	1838 (restrike)		—	—	—	—
	1841 (restrike)		—	—	—	—

Plain edge.

KM#	Date	Mintage	Fine	VF	XF	Unc
A23.3	1834 (restrike)		—	—	—	—
	1835 (restrike)		—	—	—	—
	1838 (restrike)		—	—	—	—
	1841 (restrike)		—	—	—	—

KM#	Date	Mintage	Fine	VF	XF	Unc
23	1862	—	1300.	6500.	16,000.	20,000.
	1864	—	1500.	3000.	5000.	8000.
	1865	1.558	BV	100.00	125.00	175.00

NOTE: Varieties exist.

NOTE: 1864 dated coins were not released for circulation and are considered patterns.

KM#	Date	Mintage	Fine	VF	XF	Unc
32	1866 Pos. A	—	1000.	2000.	5000.	8000.
	1866 Pos. B	—	900.00	1800.	4000.	6000.
	1866 Pos. B (error) WINNER	—	900.00	1800.	4000.	6000.
	1867	1.341	—	BV	95.00	110.00
	1868	1.382	—	BV	95.00	110.00
	1869 Pos. A	1.234	—	BV	95.00	110.00
	1869 Pos. B	Inc. Ab.	100.00	175.00	250.00	325.00
	1870	3.191	—	BV	95.00	110.00

NOTE: 1866 dated coins were not released for circulation and are considered patterns.

Obv: Smaller bust.

KM#	Date	Mintage	Fine	VF	XF	Unc
37	1870 Pos. A	Inc. Ab.	—	BV	95.00	110.00
	1870 Pos. B	Inc. Ab.	150.00	250.00	400.00	600.00
	1871 long beard	Inc. Ab.	BV	90.00	115.00	150.00
	1871	2.259	—	BV	95.00	110.00
	1874	3.046	—	BV	95.00	110.00
	1875 Pos. A	4.134	—	BV	95.00	110.00
	1875 Pos. B	Inc. Ab.	275.00	600.00	1000.	1500.
	1876 Pos. A	2.070	—	BV	95.00	110.00
	1876 Pos. B	Inc. Ab.	250.00	400.00	550.00	1000.
	1877 Pos. A	5.906	—	BV	95.00	110.00
	1877 Pos. B	Inc. Ab.	275.00	600.00	1000.	1500.
	1878 Pos. A	2.505	—	BV	95.00	110.00
	1878 Pos. B	Inc. Ab.	550.00	1100.	1650.	2200.
	1882	.522	—	BV	95.00	110.00

Obv. French leg: DES BELGES

KM#	Date	Mintage	Fine	VF	XF	Unc
78	1914 Pos. A	.125	—	BV	100.00	125.00
	1914 Pos B.	Inc. Ab.	125.00	200.00	300.00	450.00

Obv. Dutch leg: DER BELGEN

KM#	Date	Mintage	Fine	VF	XF	Unc
79	1914 Pos. A	.125	—	BV	100.00	125.00
	1914 Pos. B	Inc. Ab.	BV	110.00	150.00	175.00

Vier or Quatre (4) Belgas

NICKEL

Obv. French leg: DES BELGES

KM#	Date	Mintage	Fine	VF	XF	Unc
101.1	1931	3.957	30.00	60.00	75.00	125.00
	1932	5.472	25.00	55.00	70.00	120.00
	1934 (restrike)		—	—	—	—

NOTE: Edge varieties exist.

Medal alignment.

KM#	Date	Mintage	Fine	VF	XF	Unc
101.2	1932	Inc. Ab.	65.00	175.00	300.00	500.00

NOTE: Edge varieties exist.

Obv. Dutch leg: DER BELGEN

KM#	Date	Mintage	Fine	VF	XF	Unc
102	1931	2.600	30.00	60.00	75.00	125.00
	1932	6.950	25.00	55.00	70.00	120.00
	1934 (restrike)		—	—	—	—

NOTE: Edge varieties exist.

11.0000 g, .680 SILVER, .2405 oz ASW

Obv. French leg: DES BELGES

KM#	Date	Mintage	Fine	VF	XF	Unc
103.1	1933 Pos. A	.200	22.50	45.00	80.00	135.00
	1933 Pos. B	Inc. Ab.	25.00	50.00	90.00	150.00
	1934 Pos. A	12.300	BV	3.50	5.00	9.00
	1934 Pos. B	Inc. Ab.	1.50	4.50	7.50	20.00

Medal alignment.

KM#	Date	Mintage	Fine	VF	XF	Unc
103.2	1934	Inc. Ab.	35.00	115.00	190.00	400.00

Obv. Dutch leg: DER BELGEN

KM#	Date	Mintage	Fine	VF	XF	Unc
104.1	1933 Pos. A	.200	17.50	40.00	60.00	85.00
	1933 Pos. B	Inc. Ab.	18.50	42.50	65.00	90.00
	1934 Pos. A	12.300	BV	3.00	4.50	8.00
	1934 Pos. B	Inc. Ab.	1.50	4.50	7.50	20.00

Medal alignment.

KM#	Date	Mintage	Fine	VF	XF	Unc
104.2	1934	Inc. Ab.	35.00	115.00	190.00	400.00

KM#	Date	Mintage	Fine	VF	XF	Unc
105	1934	1.250	4.00	7.00	10.00	20.00
	1935	10.760	BV	3.00	6.00	8.00

NOTE: Edge varieties exist. Coins dated 1934 exist w/and w/o umlauts above E in BELGIE.

8.0000 g, .835 SILVER, .2148 oz ASW

Obv: French leg: BELGIQUE

KM#	Date	Mintage	Fine	VF	XF	Unc
140.1	1949	4.600	BV	2.50	5.00	8.00
	1950	12.957	BV	2.50	5.00	8.00
	1953	3.953	BV	3.50	6.00	10.00
	1954	4.835	12.00	20.00	55.00	90.00
	1955	1.730	150.00	275.00	400.00	650.00

Medal alignment.

KM#	Date	Mintage	Fine	VF	XF	Unc
140.2	1949	Inc. Ab.	15.00	35.00	75.00	125.00
	1950	Inc. Ab.	15.00	35.00	75.00	125.00

Obv. Dutch leg: BELGIE

KM#	Date	Mintage	Fine	VF	XF	Unc
141.1	1949	5.545	BV	2.50	5.00	8.00
	1950	—	150.00	400.00	600.00	1000.
	1951	7.885	BV	2.50	5.00	8.00
	1953	6.625	BV	3.00	6.00	10.00
	1954	5.323	8.00	14.00	25.00	45.00
	1955	3.760	10.00	35.00	100.00	150.00

Medal alignment.

KM#	Date	Mintage	Fine	VF	XF	Unc
141.2	1949	Inc. Ab.	20.00	45.00	75.00	125.00
	1951	Inc. Ab.	15.00	37.50	85.00	150.00

BRONZE

Rev. French leg: BELGIQUE

KM#	Date	Mintage	Fine	VF	XF	Unc
159	1980	30.000	—	—	.70	1.00
	1981	60.000	—	—	.70	1.00
	1982	54.000	—	—	.70	1.00
	1989	—	—	—	.70	1.00
	1990	—	—	—	.70	1.00
	1991	—	—	—	.70	1.00
	1992	—	—	—	.70	1.00

Rev. Dutch leg: BELGIE

KM#	Date	Mintage	Fine	VF	XF	Unc
160	1980	30.000	—	—	.70	1.00
	1981	60.000	—	—	.70	1.00
	1982	54.000	—	—	.70	1.00
	1989	—	—	—	.70	1.00
	1990	—	—	—	.70	1.00
	1991	—	—	—	.70	1.00

25 FRANCS

7.9155 g, .900 GOLD, .2291 oz AGW

KM#	Date	Mintage	Fine	VF	XF	Unc
13.1	1848	*.321	650.00	1500.	2200.	3000.
	1849	**.150	750.00	2000.	4000.	5000.

*NOTE: 268,411 melted.
**NOTE: 125,217 melted.

Obv: Larger head.

KM#	Date	Mintage	Fine	VF	XF	Unc
13.2	1850	.074	850.00	2250.	4500.	6000.

NOTE: 61,910 melted.

40 FRANCS

GOLD

Lettered edge.

KM#	Date	Mintage	Fine	VF	XF	Unc
B23.1	1834	—	1500.	7500.	16,750.	23,500.
	1835	—	1500.	7500.	16,750.	23,500.
	1838	—	2500.	13,500.	30,000.	43,000.
	1841	—	1600.	8000.	18,500.	26,000.

Medal alignment.

KM#	Date	Mintage	Fine	VF	XF	Unc
B23.2	1834	—	1500.	7500.	16,750.	23,500.

50 FRANCS

22.0000 g, .680 SILVER, .4810 oz ASW
Brussels Exposition And Railway Centennial
Obv. leg: DE BELGIQUE.
Rev. French leg: DE FER BELGES.

KM#	Date	Mintage	Fine	VF	XF	Unc
106.1	1935	.140	45.00	90.00	130.00	200.00

Medal alignment.

KM#	Date	Mintage	Fine	VF	XF	Unc
106.2	1935	Inc. Ab.	250.00	600.00	1250.	2000.

NOTE: Edge varieties exist.

Obv. leg: BELGIE.
Rev. Dutch leg: DER BELGISCHE.

KM#	Date	Mintage	Fine	VF	XF	Unc
107.1	1935	.140	50.00	120.00	160.00	240.00

Medal alignment.

KM#	Date	Mintage	Fine	VF	XF	Unc
107.2	1935	Inc. Ab.	400.00	900.00	1500.	2300.

NOTE: Edge varieties exist.

20.0000 g, .835 SILVER, .5369 oz ASW
Rev. French leg: BELGIQUE: BELGIE

KM#	Date	Mintage	Fine	VF	XF	Unc
121.1	1939	1.000	BV	7.00	11.00	18.00
	1940	.631	BV	10.00	20.00	32.50

NOTE: Edge varieties exist.

Rev: W/o cross on crown.

KM#	Date	Mintage	Fine	VF	XF	Unc
121.2	1939	Inc. Ab.	7.50	17.50	25.00	50.00
	1940	Inc. Ab.	10.00	25.00	35.00	70.00

NOTE: Edge varieties exist.

Rev. Dutch leg: BELGIE: BELGIQUE

KM#	Date	Mintage	Fine	VF	XF	Unc
122.1	1939	1.000	BV	8.00	12.00	18.00
	1940	.631	BV	10.00	20.00	32.50

NOTE: Edge varieties exist.

Rev: W/o cross on crown.

KM#	Date	Mintage	Fine	VF	XF	Unc
122.2	1939	Inc. Ab.	6.00	15.00	20.00	40.00
	1940	Inc. Ab.	30.00	70.00	120.00	200.00

NOTE: Edge varieties exist.

Rev: Triangle in 3rd arms from left, cross on crown.

KM#	Date	Mintage	Fine	VF	XF	Unc
122.3	1940	Inc. Ab.	20.00	50.00	70.00	140.00

NOTE: Edge varieties exist.

Rev: W/o cross on crown.

KM#	Date	Mintage	Fine	VF	XF	Unc
122.4	1940	Inc. Ab.	40.00	85.00	130.00	225.00

NOTE: Edge varieties exist.

12.5000 g, .835 SILVER, .3356 oz ASW
Obv. French leg: BELGIQUE

KM#	Date	Mintage	Fine	VF	XF	Unc
136.1	1948	2.000	BV	2.50	5.00	9.00
	1949	4.354	BV	2.50	5.00	9.00
	1950	—	200.00	400.00	800.00	1750.
	1951	2.904	BV	2.50	5.00	10.00
	1954	3.232	BV	6.00	12.00	25.00

Medal alignment.

KM#	Date	Mintage	Fine	VF	XF	Unc
136.2	1949	Inc. Ab.	10.00	30.00	90.00	175.00

Obv. Dutch leg: BELGIE

KM#	Date	Mintage	Fine	VF	XF	Unc
137	1948	3.000	BV	2.50	5.00	9.00
	1950	4.110	BV	2.50	5.00	9.00
	1951	1.698	BV	2.50	5.50	10.00
	1954	2.978	BV	2.50	5.00	9.00

Brussels World Fair
Obv. French leg: DES BELGES

KM#	Date	Mintage	Fine	VF	XF	Unc
150.1	1958	.476	BV	6.00	7.00	12.00

Medal alignment.

KM#	Date	Mintage	Fine	VF	XF	Unc
150.2	1958	Inc. Ab.	10.00	27.50	35.00	65.00

Obv. Dutch leg: DER BELGEN

KM#	Date	Mintage	Fine	VF	XF	Unc
151.1	1958	.382	BV	6.00	7.00	12.00

Medal alignment.

KM#	Date	Mintage	Fine	VF	XF	Unc
151.2	1958	Inc. Ab.	10.00	27.50	35.00	65.00

King Baudouin Marriage

KM#	Date	Mintage	Fine	VF	XF	Unc
152.1	1960	.500	BV	4.00	6.00	10.00

Medal alignment.

KM#	Date	Mintage	Fine	VF	XF	Unc
152.2	1960	Inc. Ab.	12.50	30.00	40.00	75.00

NICKEL
Rev. French leg: BELGIQUE

KM#	Date	Mintage	Fine	VF	XF	Unc
168	1987	30.000	—	—	—	4.50
	1988	.550	—	—	—	4.50
	1989	—	—	—	—	4.50
	1990	—	—	—	—	4.50
	1991	—	—	—	—	4.50

Rev. Dutch leg: BELGIE

KM#	Date	Mintage	Fine	VF	XF	Unc
169	1987	30.000	—	—	—	4.50
	1988	.550	—	—	—	4.50
	1989	—	—	—	—	4.50
	1990	—	—	—	—	4.50
	1991	—	—	—	—	4.50

100 FRANCS

18.0000 g, .835 SILVER, .4832 oz ASW
Obv. French leg: BELGIQUE

KM#	Date	Mintage	Fine	VF	XF	Unc
138.1	1948	1.000	BV	4.00	8.00	12.00
	1949	.106	12.50	20.00	30.00	50.00
	1950	2.807	BV	4.00	7.00	10.00
	1954	2.517	BV	4.00	7.00	10.00

Medal alignment.

KM#	Date	Mintage	Fine	VF	XF	Unc
138.2	1948	Inc. Ab.	10.00	30.00	90.00	175.00
	1950	Inc. Ab.	10.00	30.00	90.00	175.00

Obv. Dutch leg: BELGIE

KM#	Date	Mintage	Fine	VF	XF	Unc
139.1	1948	1.000	BV	4.00	8.00	12.00
	1949	2.271	BV	4.00	7.00	10.00
	1950	—	300.00	500.00	650.00	800.00
	1951	4.691	BV	4.00	7.00	10.00

Medal alignment.

KM#	Date	Mintage	Fine	VF	XF	Unc
139.2	1948	Inc. Ab.	10.00	30.00	90.00	175.00
	1949	Inc. Ab.	7.50	25.00	75.00	140.00
	1951	Inc. Ab.	10.00	30.00	90.00	175.00

250 FRANCS

25.0000 g, .835 SILVER, .6711 oz ASW
Silver Jubilee of King Baudouin.
Obv. French leg: ROI DES BELGES, reeded edge.

KM#	Date	Mintage	Fine	VF	XF	Unc
157.1	1976 large B					
		1.000	—	BV	8.00	10.00
	1976 small B					
		Inc. Ab.	BV	12.50	17.50	25.00

Stars on edge.

KM#	Date	Mintage	Fine	VF	XF	Unc
157.2	1976	.100	—	—	P/L	40.00

Obv. Dutch leg: KONING DER BELGEN, reeded edge.

KM#	Date	Mintage	Fine	VF	XF	Unc
158.1	1976 large B					
		1.000	—	BV	8.00	10.00
	1976 small B					
		Inc. Ab.	BV	12.50	17.50	25.00

Stars on edge.

KM#	Date	Mintage	Fine	VF	XF	Unc
158.2	1976	.100	—	—	P/L	40.00

500 FRANCS

SILVER CLAD COPPER-NICKEL
150th Anniversary of Independence
Rev: French legend.

KM#	Date	Mintage	Fine	VF	XF	Unc
161	1980	1.000	—	—	—	16.50

25.0000 g, .510 SILVER, .4099 oz ASW
Rev: French legend.

KM#	Date	Mintage	Fine	VF	XF	Unc
161a	1980	.053	—	—	Proof	35.00

SILVER CLAD COPPER-NICKEL
Rev: Dutch legend.

KM#	Date	Mintage	Fine	VF	XF	Unc
162	1980	1.000	—	—	—	16.50

25.0000 g, .510 SILVER, .4099 oz ASW
Rev: Dutch legend.

KM#	Date	Mintage	Fine	VF	XF	Unc
162a	1980	.052	—	—	Proof	35.00

Mule. Obv: KM#161. Rev: KM#162.

KM#	Date	Mintage	Fine	VF	XF	Unc
165	1980	—	—	—	Rare	—

22.8500 g, .833 SILVER, .6120 oz ASW
60th Birthday of King Baudouin
Rev: Dutch legends.

KM#	Date	Mintage	Fine	VF	XF	Unc
178	1990	.475	—	—	—	20.00
	1990	.010	—	—	Proof	35.00

60th Birthday of King Baudouin
Rev: French legends.

KM#	Date	Mintage	Fine	VF	XF	Unc
179	1990	.475	—	—	—	20.00
	1990	.010	—	—	Proof	35.00

60th Birthday of King Baudouin
Rev: German legends.

KM#	Date	Mintage	Fine	VF	XF	Unc
180	1990	.050	—	—	—	20.00
	1990	.010	—	—	Proof	35.00

22.8600 g, .835 SILVER, .6120 oz ASW
Europalaia - Mexico Exposition

KM#	Date	Mintage	Fine	VF	XF	Unc
186	1993	—	—	—	—	20.00

EUROPEAN CURRENCY UNITS

5 ECU

22.8500 g, .833 SILVER, .6120 oz ASW
30th Anniversary of Treaties of Rome - Charles V

KM#	Date	Mintage	Fine	VF	XF	Unc
166	1987	.985	—	—	—	20.00
	1987	.015	—	—	Proof	50.00
	1988	—	—	—	—	20.00
	1988	.015	—	—	Proof	50.00

Charlemagne

KM#	Date	Mintage	Fine	VF	XF	Unc
183	1991	.010	—	—	Proof	70.00

22.8500 g, .925 SILVER, .6796 oz ASW
King Baudouin

KM#	Date	Mintage	Fine	VF	XF	Unc
185	1993	.025	—	—	Proof	35.00

10 ECU

3.1100 g., .999 GOLD, .1000 oz AGW
Charles V
Obv: Similar to 5 Ecu, KM#166.

KM#	Date	Mintage	Fine	VF	XF	Unc
172	1989	—	—	—	Proof	250.00

5.3000 g, .900 GOLD, .1000 oz AGW in
.833 SILVER COLLAR
60th Birthday of King Baudouin

KM#	Date	Mintage	Fine	VF	XF	Unc
176	1990	—	—	—	Proof	150.00

40th Year of Reign of King Baudouin

KM#	Date	Mintage	Fine	VF	XF	Unc
181	1991	—	—	—	Proof	150.00

20 ECU

10.5000 g, .900 GOLD, .2000 oz AGW in
.833 SILVER COLLAR
60th Birthday of King Baudouin

KM#	Date	Mintage	Fine	VF	XF	Unc
177	1990	—	—	—	Proof	275.00

40th Year of Reign of King Baudouin
Similar to 10 Ecu, KM#181.

KM#	Date	Mintage	Fine	VF	XF	Unc
182	1991	—	—	—	Proof	275.00

25 ECU

7.7750 g, .999 GOLD, .2500 oz AGW

Diocletian

KM#	Date	Mintage	Fine	VF	XF	Unc
173	1989	—	—	—	—	175.00
	1989	—	—	—	Proof	450.00

50 ECU

17.2800 g, .900 GOLD, .5000 oz AGW
30th Anniversary of Treaties of Rome - Charles V

KM#	Date	Mintage	Fine	VF	XF	Unc
167	1987	1.185	—	—	—	225.00
	1987	.015	—	—	Proof	330.00
	1988	.285	—	—	—	225.00
	1988	.015	—	—	Proof	330.00

15.5550 g, .999 GOLD, .5000 oz AGW
Charlemagne

KM#	Date	Mintage	Fine	VF	XF	Unc
174	1989	—	—	—	Proof	600.00

Charlemagne - Portrait
Rev: Unflattering portrait of Charlemagne.

KM#	Date	Mintage	Fine	VF	XF	Unc
184	1991	4,000	—	—	Proof	450.00

100 ECU

31.1030 g, .999 GOLD, 1.0000 oz AGW
Maria Theresa

KM#	Date	Mintage	Fine	VF	XF	Unc
175	1989	—	—	—	—	550.00
	1989	—	—	—	Proof	950.00

FLEUR DE COIN SETS (SS)

KM#	Date	Mintage	Identification	Issue Price	Mkt. Val.
SS1	1970(5)	5,000	KM135,143,149,154,156 DU	.60	35.00
SS2	1970(5)	5,000	KM134,142,148,153,155 FR	.60	35.00
SS3	1971(5)	20,000	KM135,143,149,154,156 DU	.63	12.50
SS4	1971(5)	20,000	KM134,142,148,153,155 FR	.63	12.50
SS5	1972(5)	10,000	KM135,143,149,154,156 DU	.70	25.00
SS6	1972(5)	10,000	KM134,142,148,153,155 FR	.70	25.00
SS7	1973(5)	31,773	KM135,143,149,154,156 DU	.80	12.50
SS8	1973(5)	31,773	KM134,142,148,153,155 FR	.80	12.50
SS9	1974(5)	39,609	KM135,143,149,154, 156 DU	1.10	6.00
SS10	1974(5)	39,609	KM134,142,148,153, 155 FR	1.10	6.00
SS11	1975(10)	100,000	KM135,143,149,154,156 DU, 134,142,148,153,155 FR	2.50	6.00
SS12	1976(10)	15,000	KM135,143,149,154,156 DU, 134,142,148,153,155FR	20.75	70.00
SS13	1977(8)	50,000	KM135,143,149,156 DU, 134,142,148,155 FR	2.65	6.00
SS14	1978(8)	50,000	KM135,143,149,156 DU, 134,142,148,155 FR	4.00	6.00
SS15	1979(8)	50,000	KM135,143,149,156 DU, 134,142,148,155 FR	4.00	6.00
SS16	1980(8)	60,000	KM135,143,149,160 DU, 134,142,148,159 FR	4.00	6.00
SS17	1981(8)	62,000	KM135,143,149,160 DU, 134,142,148,159 FR	3.25	6.00

MINT SETS (MS)

KM#	Date	Mintage	Identification	Issue Price	Mkt. Val.
MS1	1989(10)	—	KM149,160,164,169,171 DU, 148,159,163,168,170 FR	—	13.00
MS2	1990(10)	60,000	KM149,160,164,169,171 DU, 148,159,163,168,170 FR	—	13.00

PROOF SETS (PS)

KM#	Date	Mintage	Identification	Issue Price	Mkt. Val.
PS1	1987(2)	15,000	KM166-167	395.00	380.00
PS2	1988(2)	15,000	KM166-167	—	380.00
PS3	1989(4)	—	KM172-175	—	2250.

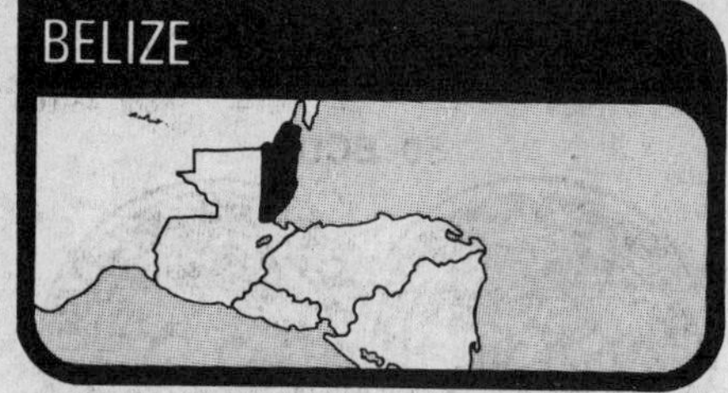

Belize, formerly British Honduras, but now an independent member of the British Commonwealth, is situated in Central America south of Mexico and east and north of Guatemala, with an area of 8,867 sq. mi. (22,960 sq. km.) and a population of *179,400. Capital: Belmopan. Tourism now augments Belize's economy, in addition to sugar, citrus fruits, chicle and hard woods which are exported.

The area, site of the ancient Mayan civilization, was sighted by Columbus in 1502, and settled by shipwrecked English seamen in 1638. British buccaneers settled the former capital of Belize in the 17th century. Britain claimed administrative right over the area after the emancipation of Central America from Spain. In 1825, Imperial coins were introduced into the colony and were rated against the Spanish dollar and Honduran currency. It was declared a colony subordinate to Jamaica in 1862 and was established as the separate Crown Colony of British Honduras in 1884. In May, 1885 an order in Council authorized coins for the colony, with the first shipment arriving in July. While the Guatemalan peso was originally the standard of value, in 1894 the colony changed to the gold standard, based on the U.S. gold dollar. The anti-British Peoples United Party, which attained power in 1954, won a constitution, effective in 1964 which established self-government under a British appointed governor. British Honduras became Belize on June 1, 1973, following the passage of a surprise bill by the Peoples United Party, but the constitutional relationship with Britain remained unchanged.

In Dec. 1975, the U.N. General Assembly adopted a resolution supporting the right of the people of Belize to self-determination, and asking Britain and Guatemala to renew their negotiations on the future of Belize. They obtained independence on Sept. 21, 1981.

RULERS

British

MINT MARKS

H - Birmingham Mint
No mm - Royal Mint

MONETARY SYSTEM

Circa 1765-1855
6 Shillings 8 Pence (Jamaican) = 8 Reales
1855-1864
1 Dollar = 8 Rials = 4 Shillings (Sterling)
Commencing 1864
100 Cents = 1 Dollar

BRITISH HONDURAS

COUNTERMARKED COINAGE

It is generally believed that the crowned "GR" monogram was placed on certain coins to make them acceptable as trade items with local indigenous peoples. This mark did not affect their currency status, although in light of the Revolutionary War of 1810-1820 it may have been an attempt to localize and keep coins in the colony at a time when the supply of Spanish coins dwindled.

1810-1818

6 SHILLINGS 1 PENCE

.916 SILVER

c/m: Crowned script GR in rectangular indent on Mexico City 8 Reales, KM#109.

KM#	Date	Good	VG	Fine	VF
1.1	ND(1791-1808)	75.00	150.00	250.00	400.00

c/m: Crowned script GR in rectangular indent on Mexico City 8 Reales, KM#110.

KM#	Date	Good	VG	Fine	VF
1.2	ND(1808-1811)	75.00	150.00	250.00	400.00

c/m: Crowned script GR in rectangular indent on Peru (Lima) 8 Reales, KM#97.

KM#	Date	Good	VG	Fine	VF
5	ND(1791-1808)	75.00	150.00	250.00	400.00

c/m: Crowned script GR in oval indent on Mexico City 8 Reales, KM#111.

KM#	Date	Good	VG	Fine	VF
2	ND(1811-1818)	60.00	120.00	200.00	325.00

c/m: Crowned script GR in oval indent on France 5 Francs, C#138.

KM#	Date	Good	VG	Fine	VF
3	ND(L'an 4-11)	100.00	175.00	300.00	500.00

c/m: Incuse crowned script GR on Mexico City 8 Reales, KM#111.

KM#	Date	Good	VG	Fine	VF
4	ND(1811-1818)	75.00	150.00	250.00	400.00

NOTE: KM#4 is considered a local issue. The c/m crowned GR in octagonal indent is considered a modern fabrication. Refer to "UNUSUAL WORLD COINS", third edition, Krause Publications.

DECIMAL COINAGE

CENT

BRONZE

KM#	Date	Mintage	Fine	VF	XF	Unc
6	1885	.072	4.00	10.00	22.00	75.00
	1885	—	—	—	Proof	250.00
	1888	.100	3.00	8.50	25.00	85.00
	1888	—	—	—	Proof	275.00
	1889	.050	4.00	10.00	25.00	70.00
	1889	—	—	—	Proof	275.00
	1894	.050	8.00	20.00	50.00	275.00
	1894	*25 pcs.	—	—	Proof	300.00

KM#	Date	Mintage	Fine	VF	XF	Unc
11	1904	.050	6.00	15.00	35.00	70.00
	1904	—	—	—	Proof	200.00
	1904	—	—	Matte Proof		1550.
	1906	.050	8.00	22.50	65.00	225.00
	1906	—	—	Matte Proof		1050.
	1909	.025	35.00	80.00	150.00	350.00

KM#	Date	Mintage	Fine	VF	XF	Unc
15	1911	.050	50.00	90.00	170.00	400.00
	1912H	.050	85.00	160.00	225.00	400.00
	1913	.025	75.00	135.00	200.00	350.00

KM#	Date	Mintage	Fine	VF	XF	Unc
19	1914	.175	2.25	7.50	25.00	120.00
	1916H	.125	2.50	8.50	27.50	125.00
	1918	.040	5.00	15.00	40.00	95.00
	1919	.050	5.00	15.00	40.00	150.00
	1924	.050	4.00	12.00	30.00	90.00
	1924	—	—	—	Proof	250.00
	1926	.050	4.00	12.00	35.00	125.00
	1926	—	—	—	Proof	225.00
	1936	.040	2.00	5.00	20.00	65.00
	1936	50 pcs.	—	—	Proof	170.00

KM#	Date	Mintage	Fine	VF	XF	Unc
21	1937	.080	.50	4.00	12.00	75.00
	1937	—	—	—	Proof	170.00
	1939	.050	.50	2.00	10.00	25.00
	1939	—	—	—	Proof	100.00
	1942	.050	1.00	5.00	15.00	150.00
	1942	—	—	—	Proof	125.00
	1943	.100	.50	2.50	12.00	125.00
	1943	—	—	—	Proof	135.00
	1944	.100	.50	5.00	15.00	150.00
	1944	—	—	—	Proof	200.00
	1945	.130	.50	1.00	7.50	50.00
	1945	—	—	—	Proof	120.00
	1947	.100	.50	1.00	10.00	70.00
	1947	—	—	—	Proof	150.00

Obv. leg: W/o EMPEROR OF INDIA

KM#	Date	Mintage	Fine	VF	XF	Unc
24	1949	.100	.60	1.25	3.50	15.00
	1949	—	—	—	Proof	135.00
	1950	.100	.40	1.00	2.50	5.00
	1950	—	—	—	Proof	135.00
	1951	.100	.60	1.50	4.00	15.00
	1951	—	—	—	Proof	135.00

KM#	Date	Mintage	Fine	VF	XF	Unc
27	1954	.200	.50	.75	1.00	5.00
	1954	—	—	—	Proof	85.00

KM#	Date	Mintage	Fine	VF	XF	Unc
30	1956	.200	.10	.25	.50	3.50
	1956	—	—	—	Proof	80.00
	1958	.400	.50	1.00	5.00	30.00
	1958	—	—	—	Proof	80.00
	1959	.200	.50	1.00	5.00	50.00
	1959	—	—	—	Proof	80.00
	1961	.800	—	.15	.25	.50
	1961	—	—	—	Proof	80.00
	1964	.300	—	.10	.30	.90
	1965	.400	—	—	.10	.50
	1966	.100	—	—	.10	.50
	1967	.400	—	—	.10	.50
	1968	.200	—	—	.10	.50
	1969	.520	—	—	.10	.40
	1970	.120	—	—	.10	.40
	1971	.800	—	—	.10	.40
	1972	.800	—	—	.10	.40
	1973	.400	—	—	.10	.40

5 CENTS

1.1620 g, .925 SILVER, .0346 oz ASW

KM#	Date	Mintage	Fine	VF	XF	Unc
7	1894	.128	5.00	15.00	30.00	75.00
	1894	*25 pcs.	—	—	Proof	350.00

COPPER-NICKEL

KM#	Date	Mintage	Fine	VF	XF	Unc
14	1907	.010	25.00	50.00	100.00	250.00
	1909	.010	25.00	50.00	100.00	250.00

KM#	Date	Mintage	Fine	VF	XF	Unc
16	1911	.010	10.00	30.00	75.00	190.00
	1912H	.020	5.00	22.50	55.00	175.00
	1912H	—	—	—	Proof	550.00
	1916H	.020	5.00	20.00	55.00	175.00
	1918	.020	5.00	18.00	50.00	160.00
	1919	.020	4.00	15.00	50.00	160.00
	1936	.060	2.00	5.00	20.00	75.00
	1936	50 pcs.	—	—	Proof	450.00

KM#	Date	Mintage	Fine	VF	XF	Unc
22	1939	.020	3.00	5.00	20.00	50.00
	1939	—	—	—	Proof	275.00

NICKEL-BRASS

KM#	Date	Mintage	Fine	VF	XF	Unc
22a	1942	.030	5.00	15.00	65.00	200.00
	1942	—	—	—	Proof	300.00
	1943	.040	1.50	7.50	35.00	130.00
	1944	.050	1.50	10.00	50.00	175.00
	1944	—	—	—	Proof	275.00
	1945	.065	1.00	5.00	15.00	75.00
	1945	—	—	—	Proof	150.00
	1947	.040	1.50	5.00	15.00	85.00
	1947	—	—	—	Proof	185.00

Obv. leg: W/o EMPEROR OF INDIA

KM#	Date	Mintage	Fine	VF	XF	Unc
25	1949	.040	1.00	2.00	7.50	35.00
	1949	—	—	—	Proof	150.00
	1950	.225	.40	1.00	4.00	30.00
	1950	—	—	—	Proof	200.00
	1952	.100	.50	1.00	5.00	25.00
	1952	—	—	—	Proof	250.00

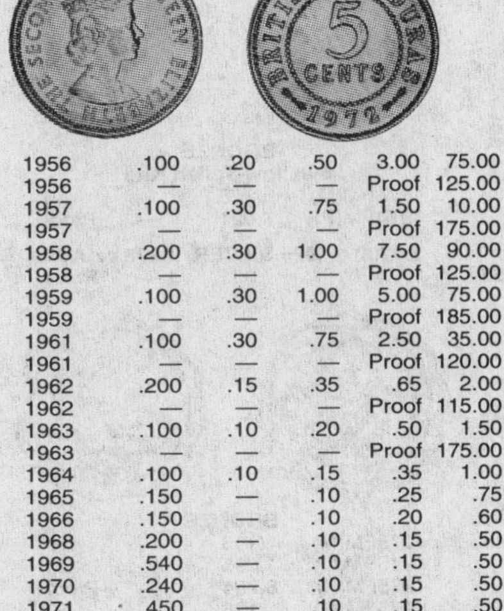

KM#	Date	Mintage	Fine	VF	XF	Unc
31	1956	.100	.20	.50	3.00	75.00
	1956	—	—	—	Proof	125.00
	1957	.100	.30	.75	1.50	10.00
	1957	—	—	—	Proof	175.00
	1958	.200	.30	1.00	7.50	90.00
	1958	—	—	—	Proof	125.00
	1959	.100	.30	1.00	5.00	75.00
	1959	—	—	—	Proof	185.00
	1961	.100	.30	.75	2.50	35.00
	1961	—	—	—	Proof	120.00
	1962	.200	.15	.35	.65	2.00
	1962	—	—	—	Proof	115.00
	1963	.100	.10	.20	.50	1.50
	1963	—	—	—	Proof	175.00
	1964	.100	.10	.15	.35	1.00
	1965	.150	—	.10	.25	.75
	1966	.150	—	.10	.20	.60
	1968	.200	—	.10	.15	.50
	1969	.540	—	.10	.15	.50
	1970	.240	—	.10	.15	.50
	1971	.450	—	.10	.15	.50
	1972	.200	—	.10	.15	.50
	1973	.210	—	.10	.15	.75

10 CENTS

2.3240 g, .925 SILVER, .0691 oz ASW

KM#	Date	Mintage	Fine	VF	XF	Unc
8	1894	.126	5.00	15.00	50.00	125.00
	1894	*25 pcs.	—	—	Proof	450.00

KM#	Date	Mintage	Fine	VF	XF	Unc
20	1918	.010	10.00	25.00	100.00	350.00
	1919	.010	10.00	25.00	100.00	350.00
	1936	.030	4.00	10.00	25.00	100.00
	1936	50 pcs.	—	—	Proof	300.00

KM#	Date	Mintage	Fine	VF	XF	Unc
23	1939	.020	3.00	7.00	20.00	60.00
	1939	—	—	—	Proof	300.00
	1942	.010	3.50	12.00	60.00	150.00
	1943	.020	3.00	6.00	45.00	250.00
	1944	.030	2.50	5.00	40.00	150.00
	1944	—	—	—	Proof	250.00
	1946	.010	3.50	8.00	35.00	175.00
	1946	—	—	—	Proof	450.00

COPPER-NICKEL

KM#	Date	Mintage	Fine	VF	XF	Unc
32	1956	.100	.40	1.00	2.00	7.50
	1956	—	—	—	Proof	200.00
	1959	.100	.60	1.50	2.00	37.50
	1959	—	—	—	Proof	135.00
	1961	.050	.30	.75	1.25	3.00
	1961	—	—	—	Proof	135.00
	1963	.050	.20	.50	.75	2.00
	1963	—	—	—	Proof	135.00
	1964	.060	.15	.25	.50	1.00
	1965/6	.200	5.00	10.00	20.00	40.00
	1965	Inc. Ab.	—	.10	.15	.50
	1970	—	—	.10	.15	.75

25 CENTS

5.8100 g, .925 SILVER, .1728 oz ASW

KM#	Date	Mintage	Fine	VF	XF	Unc
9	1894	.048	8.00	20.00	65.00	285.00
	1894	*25 pcs.	—	—	Proof	600.00
	1895	.047	10.00	25.00	75.00	300.00
	1897	.040	10.00	25.00	85.00	375.00
	1901	.020	15.00	30.00	110.00	375.00
	1901	30 pcs.	—	—	Proof	600.00

KM#	Date	Mintage	Fine	VF	XF	Unc
12	1906	.030	10.00	30.00	110.00	375.00
	1907	.060	7.50	25.00	95.00	325.00

KM#	Date	Mintage	Fine	VF	XF	Unc
17	1911	.014	15.00	40.00	125.00	350.00
	1919	.040	6.00	15.00	75.00	250.00

COPPER-NICKEL

KM#	Date	Mintage	Fine	VF	XF	Unc
26	1952	.075	1.40	3.50	25.00	150.00
	1952	—	—	—	Proof	250.00

KM#	Date	Mintage	Fine	VF	XF	Unc
29	1955	.075	.40	1.00	3.50	15.00
	1955	—	—	—	Proof	150.00
	1960	.075	.40	1.00	5.00	100.00
	1960	—	—	—	Proof	250.00
	1962	.050	.30	.50	1.00	2.50
	1962	—	—	—	Proof	150.00
	1963	.050	.30	.50	2.00	8.00
	1963	—	—	—	Proof	150.00
	1964	.100	.30	.50	.75	1.50
	1965	.075	—	.50	1.00	2.00
	1966	.075	.30	.75	1.50	6.00
	1968	.125	.25	.50	1.00	2.00
	1970	—	.20	.35	.75	1.50
	1971	.150	.20	.30	.50	1.50
	1972	.200	.20	.30	.50	1.50
	1973	.100	.20	.30	.60	1.75

50 CENTS

11.6200 g, .925 SILVER, .3456 oz ASW

KM#	Date	Mintage	Fine	VF	XF	Unc
10	1894	.038	12.00	25.00	85.00	375.00
	1894	*25 pcs.	—	—	Proof	1250.
	1895	.036	12.00	25.00	100.00	400.00
	1897	.020	12.00	30.00	150.00	550.00
	1901	.010	25.00	60.00	300.00	900.00
	1901	30 pcs.	—	—	Proof	1000.

KM#	Date	Mintage	Fine	VF	XF	Unc
13	1906	.015	15.00	50.00	200.00	550.00
	1907	.019	15.00	50.00	170.00	500.00

KM#	Date	Mintage	Fine	VF	XF	Unc
18	1911	.012	20.00	60.00	200.00	800.00
	1919	.040	10.00	30.00	150.00	850.00
	1919	—	—	—	Proof	1250.

COPPER-NICKEL

KM#	Date	Mintage	Fine	VF	XF	Unc
28	1954	.075	.30	.50	1.00	3.00
	1954	—	—	—	Proof	175.00
	1962	.050	.30	.50	1.50	3.50
	1962	—	—	—	Proof	200.00
	1964	.050	.30	.50	1.50	2.50
	1965	.025	1.00	3.00	5.00	25.00
	1966	.025	.50	1.50	3.00	15.00
	1971	.030	.30	.50	1.50	2.50

PROOF SETS (PS)

KM#	Date	Mintage	Identification	Issue Price	Mkt. Val.
PS1	1894(5)	*25	KM6-10	—	3000.
PS2	1901(2)	30	KM9,10	—	1650.
PS3	1936(3)	50	KM16,19,20	—	950.00
PS4	1939(3)	—	KM21-23	—	675.00
PS5	1949(2)	—	KM24,25	—	285.00
PS6	1950(2)	—	KM24,25	—	335.00
PS7	1954(2)	—	KM27,28	—	260.00
PS8	1956(3)	—	KM30-32	—	400.00
PS9	1958(2)	—	KM30,31	—	200.00

BELIZE

MINT MARKS

No mm - Royal Mint
FM - Franklin Mint, U.S.A.*

***NOTE:** From 1975 the Franklin Mint has produced coinage in 3 different qualities. Qualities of issue are designated in ( ) after each date and are defined as follows:

(M) MATTE - Normal circulation strike or a dull finish produced by sandblasting special uncirculated (polish finish) or proof quality dies.

(U) SPECIAL UNCIRCULATED - Polished or proof-like in appearance without any frosted features.

(P) PROOF - The highest quality obtainable having mirror-like fields and frosted features.

CENT

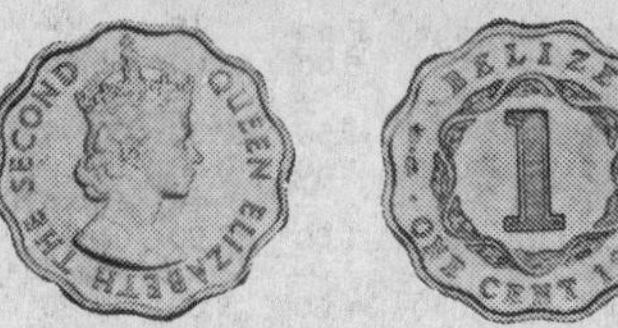

BRONZE

KM#	Date	Mintage	VF	XF	Unc
33	1973	.400	—	.10	.25
	1974	2.000	—	.10	.20
	1975	Inc. Ab.	—	.10	.15
	1976	3.000	—	.10	.15
	ALUMINUM				
33a	1976	2.050	—	.10	.15
	1979	2.505	—	.10	.15
	1980	1.505	—	.10	.15
	1982	—	—	.10	.15
	1983	—	—	.10	.15
	1986	—	—	.10	.15
	1987	—	—	.10	.15
	1989	—	—	.10	.15

BRONZE
Swallow-Tailed Kite

KM#	Date	Mintage	VF	XF	Unc
38	1974FM(M)	.225	—	.40	.75
	1974FM(P)	.021	—	Proof	1.25
	3.0200 g, .925 SILVER, .0898 oz ASW				
38a	1974FM(P)	.031	—	Proof	2.50

BRONZE

KM#	Date	Mintage	VF	XF	Unc
46	1975FM(M)	.118	—	.10	.75
	1975FM(U)	1,095	—	.20	1.00
	1975FM(P)	8,794	—	Proof	1.00
	1976FM(M)	.126	—	.10	.75
	1976FM(U)	759 pcs.	—	.20	1.00
	1976FM(P)	4,893	—	Proof	1.00
	3.0200 g, .925 SILVER, .0898 oz ASW				
46a	1975FM(P)	.013	—	Proof	1.50
	1976FM(P)	5,897	—	Proof	1.50
	1977FM(P)	3,197	—	Proof	1.50
	1978FM(P)	3,342	—	Proof	1.50
	1979FM(P)	2,445	—	Proof	1.50
	1980FM(P)	1,826	—	Proof	1.50
	1981FM(P)	615 pcs.	—	Proof	2.00
	ALUMINUM				
46b	1977FM(U)	.126	—	.10	.15
	1977FM(P)	2,107	—	Proof	1.00
	1978FM(U)	.125	—	.10	.15
	1978FM(P)	1,671	—	Proof	1.00
	1979FM(U)	808 pcs.	—	.15	.75
	1979FM(P)	1,287	—	Proof	1.00
	1980FM(U)	761 pcs.	—	.15	.75
	1980FM(P)	920 pcs.	—	Proof	1.00
	1981FM(U)	297 pcs.	—	.15	.75
	1981FM(P)	643 pcs.	—	Proof	1.00

KM#	Date	Mintage	VF	XF	Unc
83	1982FM(U)	—	—	.15	.75
	1982FM(P)	—	—	Proof	1.00
	1983FM(U)	—	—	.15	.75
	1983FM(P)	—	—	Proof	1.00
	3.0200 g, .925 SILVER, .0898 oz ASW				
83a	1982FM(P)	381 pcs.	—	Proof	6.50
	1983FM(P)	336 pcs.	—	Proof	6.50

ALUMINUM

KM#	Date	Mintage	VF	XF	Unc
90	1984FM(P)	—	—	Proof	1.00
	3.0200 g, .925 SILVER, .0898 oz ASW				
90a	1984FM(P)	—	—	Proof	6.50
	1985	212 pcs.	—	Proof	7.50

ALUMINUM
Obv: Maklouf portrait of Queen Elizabeth II.

KM#	Date	Mintage	VF	XF	Unc
114	1992	—	—	.10	.20

5 CENTS

NICKEL-BRASS

KM#	Date	Mintage	VF	XF	Unc
34	1973	.210	—	.10	.40
	1974	.210	—	.10	.40
	1975	.420	—	.10	.40
	1976	.570	—	.10	.40
	ALUMINUM				
34a	1976	1.000	—	.10	.20
	1979	.960	—	.10	.20
	1980	1.040	—	.10	.20
	1986	—	—	.10	.20
	1987	—	—	.10	.20
	1989	—	—	.10	.20
	1991	—	—	.10	.20

NICKEL-BRASS
Fork-Tailed Flycatcher

KM#	Date	Mintage	VF	XF	Unc
39	1974FM(M)	.050	—	.25	1.25
	1974FM(P)	.021	—	Proof	1.50
	4.3500 g, .925 SILVER, .1293 oz ASW				
39a	1974FM(P)	.031	—	Proof	3.00

NICKEL-BRASS

KM#	Date	Mintage	VF	XF	Unc
47	1975FM(M)	.024	—	.25	1.50
	1975FM(U)	1,095	—	.25	1.50
	1975FM(P)	8,794	—	Proof	1.25
	1976FM(M)	.025	—	.25	1.50
	1976FM(U)	759 pcs.	—	.25	1.50
	1976FM(P)	4,893	—	Proof	1.25
	4.3500 g, .925 SILVER, .1293 oz ASW				
47a	1975FM(P)	.013	—	Proof	2.00
	1976FM(P)	5,897	—	Proof	2.00
	1977FM(P)	3,197	—	Proof	2.00
	1978FM(P)	3,342	—	Proof	2.00
	1979FM(P)	2,445	—	Proof	2.00
	1980FM(P)	1,826	—	Proof	2.00
	1981FM(P)	615 pcs.	—	Proof	2.50
	ALUMINUM				
47b	1977FM(U)	.026	—	.10	.50
	1977FM(P)	2,107	—	Proof	1.50
	1978FM(U)	.025	—	.10	.50
	1978FM(P)	1,671	—	Proof	1.50
	1979FM(U)	808 pcs.	—	.15	.75
	1979FM(P)	1,287	—	.25	1.75
	1980FM(U)	761 pcs.	—	.15	.75
	1980FM(P)	920 pcs.	—	Proof	1.75
	1981FM(U)	297 pcs.	—	.15	.75
	1981FM(P)	643 pcs.	—	Proof	1.75

KM#	Date	Mintage	VF	XF	Unc
84	1982FM(U)	—	—	.15	.75
	1982FM(P)	—	—	Proof	1.75
	1983FM(U)	—	—	.15	.75
	1983FM(P)	—	—	Proof	1.75
	4.3500 g, .925 SILVER, .1293 oz ASW				
84a	1982FM(P)	381 pcs.	—	Proof	12.00
	1983FM(P)	479 pcs.	—	Proof	12.00

ALUMINUM
World Food Day

KM#	Date	Mintage	VF	XF	Unc
64	1981	—	—	.10	.35

KM#	Date	Mintage	VF	XF	Unc
91	1984FM(P)	—	—	Proof	1.75

4.3500 g, .925 SILVER, .1293 oz ASW

KM#	Date	Mintage	VF	XF	Unc
91a	1984FM(P)	—	—	Proof	12.00
	1985	212 pcs.	—	Proof	13.50

ALUMINUM
Obv: Makluf portrait of Queen Elizabeth II.

KM#	Date	Mintage	VF	XF	Unc
115	1992	—	—	.10	.25

10 CENTS

COPPER-NICKEL

KM#	Date	Mintage	VF	XF	Unc
35	1974	.100	.15	.30	.60
	1975	.200	.10	.20	.50
	1976	.700	.10	.15	.45
	1979	.800	.10	.15	.35
	1980	—	.10	.15	.35

Long-Tailed Hermit

KM#	Date	Mintage	VF	XF	Unc
40	1974FM(M)	.027	—	.50	2.00
	1974FM(P)	.021	—	Proof	1.75

2.7900 g, .925 SILVER, .0829 oz ASW

KM#	Date	Mintage	VF	XF	Unc
40a	1974FM(P)	.031	—	Proof	3.50

COPPER-NICKEL

KM#	Date	Mintage	VF	XF	Unc
48	1975FM(M)	.012	—	.25	1.50
	1975FM(U)	1,095	—	.30	2.00
	1975FM(P)	8,794	—	Proof	1.50
	1976FM(M)	.013	—	.25	1.50
	1976FM(U)	759 pcs.	—	.35	2.50
	1976FM(P)	4,893	—	Proof	1.50
	1977FM(U)	.014	—	.25	1.50
	1977FM(P)	2,107	—	Proof	2.00
	1978FM(U)	.013	—	.25	1.50
	1978FM(P)	1,671	—	Proof	2.00
	1979FM(U)	808 pcs.	—	.25	1.50
	1979FM(P)	1,287	—	Proof	2.50
	1980FM(U)	761 pcs.	—	.25	1.50
	1980FM(P)	920 pcs.	—	Proof	2.50
	1981FM(U)	297 pcs.	—	.25	1.50
	1981FM(P)	643 pcs.	—	Proof	2.50

2.7900 g, .925 SILVER, .0829 oz ASW

KM#	Date	Mintage	VF	XF	Unc
48a	1975FM(P)	.013	—	Proof	2.50
	1976FM(P)	5,897	—	Proof	2.50
	1977FM(P)	3,197	—	Proof	2.50
	1978FM(P)	3,342	—	Proof	2.50
	1979FM(P)	2,445	—	Proof	2.50
	1980FM(P)	1,826	—	Proof	2.50
	1981FM(P)	615 pcs.	—	Proof	3.50

COPPER-NICKEL

KM#	Date	Mintage	VF	XF	Unc
85	1982FM(U)	—	—	.25	1.50
	1982FM(P)	—	—	Proof	2.50
	1983FM(U)	—	—	.25	1.50
	1983FM(P)	—	—	Proof	2.50

2.7900 g, .925 SILVER, .0829 oz ASW

KM#	Date	Mintage	VF	XF	Unc
85a	1982FM(P)	381 pcs.	—	Proof	13.50
	1983FM(P)	312 pcs.	—	Proof	13.50

COPPER-NICKEL

KM#	Date	Mintage	VF	XF	Unc
92	1984FM(P)	—	—	Proof	2.50

2.7900 g, .925 SILVER, .0829 oz ASW

KM#	Date	Mintage	VF	XF	Unc
92a	1984FM(P)	—	—	Proof	13.50
	1985	212 pcs.	—	Proof	15.50

COPPER-NICKEL
Obv: Maklouf portrait of Queen Elizabeth II.

KM#	Date	Mintage	VF	XF	Unc
116	1992	—	—	.15	.40

25 CENTS

COPPER-NICKEL

KM#	Date	Mintage	VF	XF	Unc
36	1974	.100	.35	.65	1.25
	1975	.200	.20	.35	.75
	1976	.790	.20	.35	.75
	1979	.500	.20	.35	.75
	1980	—	.20	.35	.75
	1981	—	.20	.35	.75
	1986	—	.20	.35	.75
	1987	—	.20	.35	.75
	1988	—	.20	.35	.75
	1989	—	.20	.35	.75

Blue-Crowned Motmot

KM#	Date	Mintage	VF	XF	Unc
41	1974FM(M)	.013	—	1.00	3.50
	1974FM(P)	.021	—	Proof	2.50

6.6000 g, .925 SILVER, .1962 oz ASW

KM#	Date	Mintage	VF	XF	Unc
41a	1974FM(P)	.031	—	Proof	5.00

COPPER-NICKEL

KM#	Date	Mintage	VF	XF	Unc
49	1975FM(M)	4,716	—	.55	5.00
	1975FM(U)	1,095	—	.40	3.00
	1975FM(P)	8,794	—	Proof	2.50
	1976FM(M)	5,000	—	.50	4.00
	1976FM(U)	759 pcs.	—	.45	3.50
	1976FM(P)	4,893	—	Proof	2.50
	1977FM(U)	5,520	—	.30	2.00
	1977FM(P)	2,107	—	Proof	2.75
	1978FM(U)	5,458	—	.30	2.00
	1978FM(P)	1,671	—	Proof	2.75
	1979FM(U)	808 pcs.	—	.40	3.00
	1979FM(P)	1,287	—	Proof	3.00
	1980FM(U)	761 pcs.	—	.40	3.00
	1980FM(P)	920 pcs.	—	Proof	3.00
	1981FM(U)	297 pcs.	—	.40	3.00
	1981FM(P)	643 pcs.	—	Proof	3.00

6.6000 g, .925 SILVER, .1962 oz ASW

KM#	Date	Mintage	VF	XF	Unc
49a	1975FM(P)	.013	—	Proof	3.50
	1976FM(P)	5,897	—	Proof	3.50
	1977FM(P)	3,197	—	Proof	3.50
	1978FM(P)	3,342	—	Proof	3.50
	1979FM(P)	2,445	—	Proof	3.50
	1980FM(P)	1,826	—	Proof	3.50
	1981FM(P)	615 pcs.	—	Proof	5.00

COPPER-NICKEL

KM#	Date	Mintage	VF	XF	Unc
86	1982FM(U)	—	—	.40	3.00
	1982FM(P)	—	—	Proof	3.00
	1983FM(U)	—	—	.40	3.00
	1983FM(P)	—	—	Proof	3.00

6.6000 g, .925 SILVER, .1962 oz ASW

KM#	Date	Mintage	VF	XF	Unc
86a	1982FM(P)	381 pcs.	—	Proof	18.50
	1983FM(P)	314 pcs.	—	Proof	18.50

COPPER-NICKEL

KM#	Date	Mintage	VF	XF	Unc
93	1984FM(P)	—	—	Proof	3.00

6.6000 g, .925 SILVER, .1962 oz ASW

KM#	Date	Mintage	VF	XF	Unc
93a	1984FM(P)	—	—	Proof	18.50
	1985	212 pcs.	—	Proof	22.50

World Forestry Congress

KM#	Date	Mintage	VF	XF	Unc
77	1985	—	.15	.25	.85

COPPER-NICKEL
Obv: Maklouf portrait of Queen Elizabeth II.

KM#	Date	Mintage	VF	XF	Unc
117	1992	—	—	.25	.75

50 CENTS

COPPER-NICKEL

KM#	Date	Mintage	VF	XF	Unc
37	1974	.123	.40	.75	2.00
	1975	Inc. Ab.	.40	.75	2.00
	1976	.312	.40	.75	2.00
	1979	.125	.40	.75	1.75
	1980	—	.40	.75	1.75
	1989	—	.40	.75	1.75

Frigate Bird

KM#	Date	Mintage	VF	XF	Unc
42	1974FM(M)	8,806	—	.40	4.00
	1974FM(P)	.021	—	Proof	3.50
	9.9400 g, .925 SILVER, .3197 oz ASW				
42a	1974FM(P)	.031	—	Proof	7.50

COPPER-NICKEL

KM#	Date	Mintage	VF	XF	Unc
50	1975FM(M)	2,358	—	.65	6.00
	1975FM(U)	1,095	—	.45	4.50
	1975FM(P)	8,794	—	Proof	4.00
	1976FM(M)	3,259	—	.55	5.00
	1976FM(U)	759 pcs.	—	.55	5.00
	1976FM(P)	4,893	—	Proof	4.00
	1977FM(U)	3,540	—	.45	4.00
	1977FM(P)	2,107	—	Proof	4.00
	1978FM(U)	2,958	—	.45	4.00
	1978FM(P)	1,671	—	Proof	4.00
	1979FM(U)	808 pcs.	—	.55	5.00
	1979FM(P)	1,287	—	Proof	4.00
	1980FM(U)	761 pcs.	—	.55	5.00
	1980FM(P)	920 pcs.	—	Proof	5.00
	1981FM(U)	297 pcs.	—	.55	5.00
	1981FM(P)	643 pcs.	—	Proof	5.00
	9.9400 g, .925 SILVER, .3197 oz ASW				
50a	1975FM(P)	.013	—	Proof	6.50
	1976FM(P)	5,897	—	Proof	6.50
	1977FM(P)	3,197	—	Proof	6.50
	1978FM(P)	3,342	—	Proof	6.50
	1979FM(P)	2,445	—	Proof	6.50
	1980FM(P)	1,826	—	Proof	6.50
	1981FM(P)	615 pcs.	—	Proof	8.50

COPPER-NICKEL

KM#	Date	Mintage	VF	XF	Unc
87	1982FM(U)	—	—	.55	5.00
	1982FM(P)	—	—	Proof	5.00
	1983FM(U)	—	—	.55	5.00
	1983FM(P)	—	—	Proof	5.00
	9.9400 g, .925 SILVER, .3197 oz ASW				
87a	1982FM(P)	381 pcs.	—	Proof	27.50
	1983FM(P)	312 pcs.	—	Proof	27.50

COPPER-NICKEL

KM#	Date	Mintage	VF	XF	Unc
94	1984FM(P)	—	—	Proof	5.00
	9.9400 g, .925 SILVER, .3197 oz ASW				
94a	1984FM(P)	—	—	Proof	27.50
	1985	212 pcs.	—	Proof	32.50

COPPER-NICKEL
Obv: Maklouf portrait of Queen Elizabeth II.

KM#	Date	Mintage	VF	XF	Unc
118	1992	—	—	.75	1.75

DOLLAR

COPPER-NICKEL
Scarlet Macaw

KM#	Date	Mintage	VF	XF	Unc
43	1974FM(M)	6,656	—	.75	6.00
	1974FM(P)	.021	—	Proof	4.00
	1975FM(M)	1,182	—	1.50	8.00
	1975FM(U)	1,095	—	.75	6.00
	1975FM(P)	8,794	—	Proof	5.00
	1976FM(M)	1,250	—	1.50	8.00
	1976FM(U)	759 pcs.	—	1.25	7.50
	1976FM(P)	4,893	—	Proof	5.00
	1977FM(U)	1,770	—	1.00	6.50
	1977FM(P)	2,107	—	Proof	6.50
	1978FM(U)	1,708	—	1.00	6.50
	1978FM(P)	1,671	—	Proof	6.50
	1979FM(U)	808 pcs.	—	1.25	7.50
	1979FM(P)	1,287	—	Proof	6.50
	1980FM(U)	761 pcs.	—	1.25	7.50
	1980FM(P)	920 pcs.	—	Proof	6.50
	1981FM(U)	297 pcs.	—	1.50	8.50
	1981FM(P)	643 pcs.	—	Proof	8.50
	19.8900 g, .925 SILVER, .5915 oz ASW				
43a	1974FM(P)	.031	—	Proof	11.50
	1975FM(P)	.013	—	Proof	11.50
	1976FM(P)	5,897	—	Proof	12.50
	1977FM(P)	3,197	—	Proof	12.50
	1978FM(P)	3,342	—	Proof	12.50
	1979FM(P)	2,445	—	Proof	12.50
	1980FM(P)	1,826	—	Proof	12.50
	1981FM(P)	615 pcs.	—	Proof	13.50

COPPER-NICKEL

KM#	Date	Mintage	VF	XF	Unc
88	1982FM(U)	—	—	1.50	8.50
	1982FM(P)	—	—	Proof	8.50
	1983FM(U)	—	—	1.50	8.50
	1983FM(P)	—	—	Proof	8.50
	19.8900 g, .925 SILVER, .5915 oz ASW				
88a	1982FM(P)	381 pcs.	—	Proof	37.50
	1983FM(P)	1,589	—	Proof	37.50

COPPER-NICKEL

KM#	Date	Mintage	VF	XF	Unc
95	1984FM(P)	—	—	Proof	8.50
	19.8900 g, .925 SILVER, .5915 oz ASW				
95a	1984FM(P)	—	—	Proof	37.50
	1985	212 pcs.	—	Proof	45.00

NICKEL-BRASS
Columbus' Three Ships

KM#	Date	Mintage	VF	XF	Unc
99	1990	—	—	—	2.50
	1992	—	—	—	2.50
	9.0000 g, .925 SILVER, .2676 oz ASW				
99a	1990	*5,000	—	Proof	45.00

2 DOLLARS

COPPER-NICKEL
90th Birthday of Queen Mother

KM#	Date	Mintage	VF	XF	Unc
100	1990	—	—	—	6.00
	28.2800 g, .925 SILVER, .8411 oz ASW				
100a	1990	*.010	—	Proof	50.00

40th Anniversary of Coronation of Queen Elizabeth

KM#	Date	Mintage	VF	XF	Unc
119	1993	*.010	—	Proof	55.00

5 DOLLARS

COPPER-NICKEL
Keel-Billed Toucan

KM#	Date	Mintage	VF	XF	Unc
44	1974FM(M)	4,936	—	2.75	10.00
	1974FM(P)	.021	—	Proof	7.00
	1975FM(M)	237 pcs.	—	5.00	22.50
	1975FM(U)	1,095	—	2.75	9.00
	1975FM(P)	8,794	—	Proof	7.00
	1976FM(M)	250 pcs.	—	5.00	20.00
	1976FM(U)	759 pcs.	—	2.75	10.00
	1976FM(P)	4,893	—	Proof	7.00
	1977FM(U)	720 pcs.	—	2.75	10.00
	1977FM(P)	2,107	—	Proof	8.50
	1978FM(U)	708 pcs.	—	2.75	12.00
	1978FM(P)	1,671	—	Proof	8.50
	1979FM(U)	808 pcs.	—	2.75	10.00
	1979FM(P)	1,287	—	Proof	8.50
	1980FM(U)	761 pcs.	—	2.75	10.00
	1980FM(P)	920 pcs.	—	Proof	8.50
	1981FM(U)	297 pcs.	—	2.75	12.00
	1981FM(P)	643 pcs.	—	Proof	10.00

26.4000 g, .925 SILVER, .7851 oz ASW

KM#	Date	Mintage	VF	XF	Unc
44a	1974FM(P)	.031	—	Proof	9.00
	1975FM(P)	.013	—	Proof	10.00
	1976FM(P)	5,897	—	Proof	12.00
	1977FM(P)	3,197	—	Proof	12.00
	1978FM(P)	3,342	—	Proof	12.00
	1979FM(P)	2,445	—	Proof	12.00
	1980FM(P)	1,826	—	Proof	12.00
	1981FM(P)	615 pcs.	—	Proof	20.00

COPPER-NICKEL

KM#	Date	Mintage	VF	XF	Unc
89	1982FM(U)	—	—	1.50	10.00
	1982FM(P)	—	—	Proof	15.00
	1983FM(U)	—	—	1.50	10.00
	1983FM(P)	—	—	Proof	15.00

26.4000 g, .925 SILVER, .7851 oz ASW

KM#	Date	Mintage	VF	XF	Unc
89a	1982FM(P)	381 pcs.	—	Proof	50.00
	1983FM(P)	311 pcs.	—	Proof	50.00

COPPER-NICKEL

KM#	Date	Mintage	VF	XF	Unc
96	1984FM(P)	—	—	Proof	10.00

26.4000 g, .925 SILVER, .7851 oz ASW

KM#	Date	Mintage	VF	XF	Unc
96a	1984FM(P)	—	—	Proof	50.00
	1985	212 pcs.	—	Proof	60.00

28.2800 g, .925 SILVER, .8411 oz ASW
50th Anniversary of Battle of El Alamein - Field Marshall Rommel
Obv: Portrait of Queen Elizabeth II.
Rev: Similar to 50 Dollars, KM#111.

KM#	Date	Mintage	VF	XF	Unc
107	1992	*5,000	—	Proof	50.00

50th Anniversary of Battle of El Alamein - Lt. Gen. Montgomery
Rev: Similar to 250 Dollars, KM#113.

KM#	Date	Mintage	VF	XF	Unc
108	1992	*5,000	—	Proof	50.00

10 DOLLARS

COPPER-NICKEL
Great Curassow

KM#	Date	Mintage	VF	XF	Unc
45	1974FM(M)	4,726	—	3.50	15.00
	1974FM(P)	.021	—	Proof	8.00
	1975FM(M)	117 pcs.	—	12.50	45.00
	1975FM(U)	1,095	—	3.50	15.00
	1975FM(P)	8,794	—	Proof	9.00
	1976FM(M)	125 pcs.	—	10.00	40.00
	1976FM(U)	759 pcs.	—	4.00	17.50
	1976FM(P)	4,893	—	Proof	10.00
	1977FM(U)	645 pcs.	—	4.00	17.50
	1977FM(P)	2,107	—	Proof	12.50
	1978FM(U)	583 pcs.	—	5.00	20.00
	1978FM(P)	1,671	—	Proof	12.50

29.8000 g, .925 SILVER, .8863 oz ASW

KM#	Date	Mintage	VF	XF	Unc
45a	1974FM(P)	.031	—	Proof	12.00
	1975FM(P)	.013	—	Proof	13.00
	1976FM(P)	5,897	—	Proof	14.00
	1977FM(P)	3,197	—	Proof	15.00
	1978FM(P)	3,342	—	Proof	15.00

COPPER-NICKEL
Flying Jabirus
Obv: Similar to 1 Dollar, KM#43.

KM#	Date	Mintage	VF	XF	Unc
57	1979FM(U)	808 pcs.	—	5.00	25.00
	1979FM(P)	1,287	—	Proof	25.00

29.8000 g, .925 SILVER, .8863 oz ASW

KM#	Date	Mintage	VF	XF	Unc
57a	1979FM(P)	2,445	—	Proof	40.00

COPPER-NICKEL
Scarlet Ibis

KM#	Date	Mintage	VF	XF	Unc
60	1980FM(U)	761 pcs.	—	5.00	25.00
	1980FM(P)	920 pcs.	—	Proof	25.00

25.5000 g, .925 SILVER, .7583 oz ASW

KM#	Date	Mintage	VF	XF	Unc
60a	1980FM(P)	1,826	—	Proof	45.00

COPPER-NICKEL
Roseate Spoonbill
Obv: Similar to 1 Dollar, KM#43.

KM#	Date	Mintage	VF	XF	Unc
65	1981FM(U)	297 pcs.	—	7.50	30.00
	1981FM(P)	643 pcs.	—	Proof	30.00

25.5000 g, .925 SILVER, .7583 oz ASW

KM#	Date	Mintage	VF	XF	Unc
65a	1981FM(P)	615 pcs.	—	Proof	60.00

COPPER-NICKEL
Parrot
Obv: Similar to KM#80.

KM#	Date	Mintage	VF	XF	Unc
69	1982FM(U)	—	—	7.50	30.00
	1982FM(P)	—	—	Proof	40.00

25.5000 g, .925 SILVER, .7583 oz ASW

KM#	Date	Mintage	VF	XF	Unc
69a	1982FM(P)	381 pcs.	—	Proof	110.00

COPPER-NICKEL
Mule. Obv: KM#69. Rev: KM#45.

KM#	Date	Mintage	VF	XF	Unc
80	1982FM(U)	—	—	—	—

Ringed King Fisher

KM#	Date	Mintage	VF	XF	Unc
71	1983FM(U)	—	—	5.00	25.00
	1983FM(P)	—	—	Proof	30.00

25.5000 g, .925 SILVER, .7583 oz ASW

KM#	Date	Mintage	VF	XF	Unc
71a	1983FM(P)	334 pcs.	—	Proof	110.00

COPPER-NICKEL
Laughing Falcon

KM#	Date	Mintage	VF	XF	Unc
75	1984FM(P)	—	—	Proof	30.00

25.5000 g, .925 SILVER, .7583 oz ASW

KM#	Date	Mintage	VF	XF	Unc
75a	1984FM(P)	—	—	Proof	110.00
	1985	212 pcs.	—	Proof	130.00

28.2800 g, .925 SILVER, .8411 oz ASW
10th Anniversary of Independence

KM#	Date	Mintage	VF	XF	Unc
102	1991	*1,000	—	Proof	45.00

10th Anniversary of Central Bank - Jabiru Stork

KM#	Date	Mintage	VF	XF	Unc
104	1992	*1,000	—	Proof	50.00

155.6000 g, .999 SILVER, 5.0032 oz ASW
50th Anniversary of Battle of El Alamein -
Lt. Gen. Montgomery
Obv: Portrait of Queen Elizabeth II.
Rev: Similar to 250 Dollars, KM#113.

KM#	Date	Mintage	VF	XF	Unc
109	1992	*2,500	—	Proof	150.00

20 DOLLARS

23.3300 g, .925 SILVER, .6938 oz ASW
Los Angeles Olympics - Bicyclist

KM#	Date	Mintage	VF	XF	Unc
79	1984	1,050	—	Proof	50.00

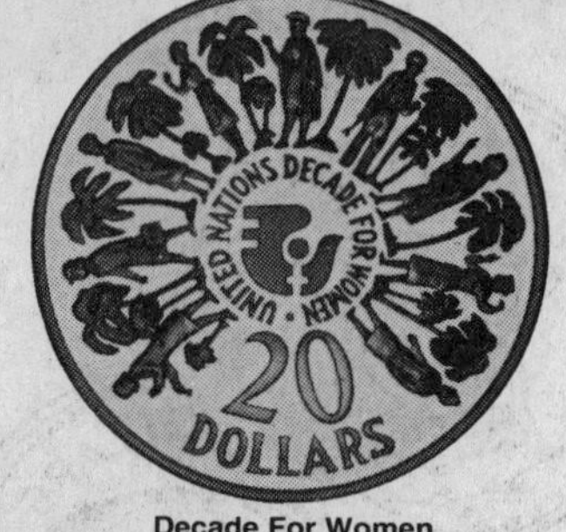

Decade For Women

KM#	Date	Mintage	VF	XF	Unc
82	1985	*.020	—	Proof	25.00

25 DOLLARS

27.8100 g, .925 SILVER, .8270 oz ASW
Coronation Jubilee

KM#	Date	Mintage	VF	XF	Unc
54	1978FM(U)	352 pcs.	—	15.00	40.00
	1978FM(P)	8,438	—	Proof	16.50

30.2800 g, .500 SILVER, .4686 oz ASW
10th Anniversary of Caribbean Development Bank

KM#	Date	Mintage	VF	XF	Unc
61	1980FM(P)	2,647	—	Proof	25.00

30th Anniversary of Coronation of Queen Elizabeth II

KM#	Date	Mintage	VF	XF	Unc
72	1983FM(P)	2,944	—	Proof	25.00

28.2800 g, .925 SILVER, .8411 oz ASW
Royal Visit

KM#	Date	Mintage	VF	XF	Unc
78	1985	*5,000	—	Proof	22.50

500th Anniversary of Columbus Discovery of America

KM#	Date	Mintage	VF	XF	Unc
97	1989	*5,000	—	Proof	50.00

25th Olympic Games - Hurdlers

KM#	Date	Mintage	VF	XF	Unc
106	1992	.030	—	Proof	50.00

3.1300 g, .999 GOLD, .1000 oz AGW
50th Anniversary of Battle of El Alamein - 4 Tanks
Obv: Portrait of Queen Elizabeth II.

KM#	Date	Mintage	VF	XF	Unc
110	1992	*500 pcs.	—	Proof	100.00

50 DOLLARS

1.5000 g, .500 GOLD, .0241 oz AGW
White-necked Jacobin Hummingbird

KM#	Date	Mintage	VF	XF	Unc
66	1981FM(U)	200 pcs.	—	—	65.00
	1981FM(P)	2,873	—	Proof	55.00

129.6000 g, .925 SILVER, 3.8547 oz ASW
Bird Conservation - Redfooted Booby
Obv: Similar to 25 Dollars, KM#72.

KM#	Date	Mintage	VF	XF	Unc
81	1985	*.010	—	Proof	60.00

7.8100 g, .999 GOLD, .2511 oz AGW
50th Anniversary of Battle of El Alamein - Field Marshall Rommel
Obv: Portrait of Queen Elizabeth II.

KM#	Date	Mintage	VF	XF	Unc
111	1992	*500 pcs.	—	Proof	250.00

100 DOLLARS

6.2100 g, .500 GOLD, .0998 oz AGW
30th Anniversary of United Nations

KM#	Date	Mintage	VF	XF	Unc
51	1975FM(M)	100 pcs.	—	—	200.00
	1975FM(U)	2,028	—	—	60.00
	1975FM(P)	8,126	—	Proof	55.00

Ancient Mayan Symbols

KM#	Date	Mintage	VF	XF	Unc
52	1976FM(M)	216 pcs.	—	—	175.00
	1976FM(P)	.011	—	Proof	55.00

Kinich Ahau, Mayan Sun God

KM#	Date	Mintage	VF	XF	Unc
53	1977FM(M)	200 pcs.	—	—	135.00
	1977FM(U)	51 pcs.	—	—	350.00
	1977FM(P)	7,859	—	Proof	55.00

Itzamna Mayan God

KM#	Date	Mintage	VF	XF	Unc
55	1978FM(U)	351 pcs.	—	—	150.00
	1978FM(P)	7,178	—	Proof	55.00

Queen Angelfish

KM#	Date	Mintage	VF	XF	Unc
58	1979FM(U)	400 pcs.	—	—	125.00
	1979FM(P)	4,465	—	Proof	80.00

6.4700 g, .500 GOLD, .1040 oz AGW
Star of Bethlehem

KM#	Date	Mintage	VF	XF	Unc
59	1979FM(U)	—	—	—	120.00
	1979FM(P)	—	—	Proof	70.00

6.2100 g, .500 GOLD, .0998 oz AGW
Moorish Idol Reef Fish

KM#	Date	Mintage	VF	XF	Unc
62	1980FM(U)	400 pcs.	—	—	150.00
	1980FM(P)	3,993	—	Proof	90.00

Orchids

KM#	Date	Mintage	VF	XF	Unc
63	1980FM(U)	250 pcs.	—	—	135.00
	1980FM(P)	2,454	—	Proof	100.00

Yellow Swallowtail Butterfly

KM#	Date	Mintage	VF	XF	Unc
67	1981FM(U)	200 pcs.	—	—	180.00
	1981FM(P)	1,658	—	Proof	240.00

National Independence

KM#	Date	Mintage	VF	XF	Unc
68	1981FM(U)	50 pcs.	—	—	325.00
	1981FM(P)	1,401	—	Proof	150.00

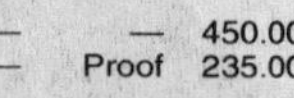

Kinkajou

KM#	Date	Mintage	VF	XF	Unc
70	1982FM(U)	10 pcs.	—	—	450.00
	1982FM(P)	586 pcs.	—	Proof	235.00

Margay Jungle Cat

KM#	Date	Mintage	VF	XF	Unc
73	1983FM(U)	20 pcs.	—	—	400.00
	1983FM(P)	494 pcs.	—	Proof	250.00

White-tail Deer

KM#	Date	Mintage	VF	XF	Unc
74	1984FM(P)	965 pcs.	—	Proof	160.00

Ocelot

KM#	Date	Mintage	VF	XF	Unc
76	1985FM(P)	899 pcs.	—	Proof	250.00

15.9760 g, .917 GOLD, .4708 oz AGW
10th Anniversary of Independence
Similar to 10 Dollars, KM#102.

KM#	Date	Mintage	VF	XF	Unc
103	1991	*500 pcs.	—	Proof	530.00

15.6000 g, .999 GOLD, .5016 oz AGW
50th Anniversary of Battle of El Alamein - Infantry Advancing Left
Obv: Portrait of Queen Elizabeth II.

KM#	Date	Mintage	VF	XF	Unc
112	1992	*500 pcs.	—	Proof	500.00

250 DOLLARS

8.8100 g, .900 GOLD, .2549 oz AGW
Jaguar

KM#	Date	Mintage	VF	XF	Unc
56	1978FM(U)	200 pcs.	—	—	250.00
	1978FM(P)	*3,399	—	Proof	400.00

***NOTE:** 1,712 pieces were used in First Day Covers.

15.9800 g, .917 GOLD, .4708 oz AGW
500th Anniversary of Columbus Discovery of America

KM#	Date	Mintage	VF	XF	Unc
98	1989	*500 pcs.	—	Proof	550.00

10th Anniversary of Central Bank - Jabiru Stork
Similar to 10 Dollars, KM#104.

KM#	Date	Mintage	VF	XF	Unc
105	1992	*500 pcs.	—	Proof	550.00

31.2100 g, .999 GOLD, 1.0035 oz AGW
50th Anniversary of Battle of El Alamein - Lt. Gen. Montgomery
Obv: Portrait of Queen Elizabeth II.

KM#	Date	Mintage	VF	XF	Unc
113	1992	*500 pcs.	—	Proof	750.00

500 DOLLARS

47.5400 g, .917 GOLD, 1.4013 oz AGW
Royal Visit
Similar to 25 Dollars, KM#78.

KM#	Date	Mintage	VF	XF	Unc
101	1985	*250 pcs.	—	Proof	975.00

MINT SETS (MS)

KM#	Date	Mintage	Identification	Issue Price	Mkt. Val.
MS1	1974(8)	4,506	KM38-45	20.00	20.00
MS2	1975(8)	1,095	KM43-50	27.50	27.50
MS3	1976(8)	759	KM43-50	27.50	35.00
MS4	1977(8)	—	KM43-45,46b-47b,48-50	27.50	35.00
MS5	1978(8)	458	KM43-45,46b-47b,48-50	28.50	35.00
MS6	1979(8)	808	KM43-44,46b-47b, 48-50,57	28.50	35.00
MS7	1980(8)	761	KM43-44,46b-47b, 48-50,60	29.50	35.00
MS8	1981(8)	297	KM43-44,46b-47b, 48-50,65	29.50	60.00
MS9	1982(8)	—	KM43-44,46b-47b, 48-50,69	29.50	60.00
MS10	1983(8)	—	KM43-44,46b-47b, 48-50,71	29.50	60.00
MS11	1992(6)	—	KM99,114-118	24.00	24.00

PROOF SETS (PS)

KM#	Date	Mintage	Identification	Issue Price	Mkt. Val.
PS1	1974(8)	21,470	KM38-45	35.00	15.00
PS2	1974(8)	31,368	KM38a-45a	100.00	35.00
PS3	1975(8)	8,794	KM43-50	37.50	17.50
PS4	1975(8)	13,275	KM43a-50a	110.00	35.00
PS5	1976(8)	4,893	KM43-50	37.50	20.00
PS6	1976(8)	5,897	KM43a-50a	110.00	42.00
PS7	1977(8)	2,107	KM43-50	37.50	30.00
PS8	1977(8)	3,197	KM43a-50a	110.00	45.00
PS9	1978(8)	1,671	KM43-50	39.50	35.00
PS10	1978(8)	3,342	KM43a-50a	110.00	45.00
PS11	1979(8)	1,287	KM43-44,46b-47b, 48-50,57	41.50	45.00
PS12	1979(8)	2,445	KM43a-44a,46a-50a,57a	112.00	75.00
PS13	1980(8)	920	KM43-44,46b-47b, 48-50,60	41.50	45.00
PS14	1980(8)	1,826	KM43a-44a,46a-50a,60a	222.00	85.00
PS15	1981(8)	643	KM43-44,46b-47b, 48-50,65	41.50	60.00
PS16	1981(8)	615	KM43a-44a,46a-50a,65a	—	115.00
PS17	1982(8)	—	KM43-44,46b-47b, 48-50,69	49.50	60.00
PS18	1982(8)	381	KM69a,83a-89a	222.00	275.00
PS19	1983(8)	306	KM43-44,46b-47b, 48-50,71	37.00	60.00
PS20	1983(8)	241	KM71a,83a-89a	197.00	300.00
PS21	1984(8)	—	KM43-44,46b-47b, 48-50,75	37.00	50.00
PS22	1984(8)	397	KM75a,90a-96a	197.00	275.00
PS23	1985(8)	212	KM75a,90a-96a	—	325.00
PS24	1992(4)	500	KM110-113	1600.	1600.
PS25	1992(2)	—	KM107-108	100.00	100.00

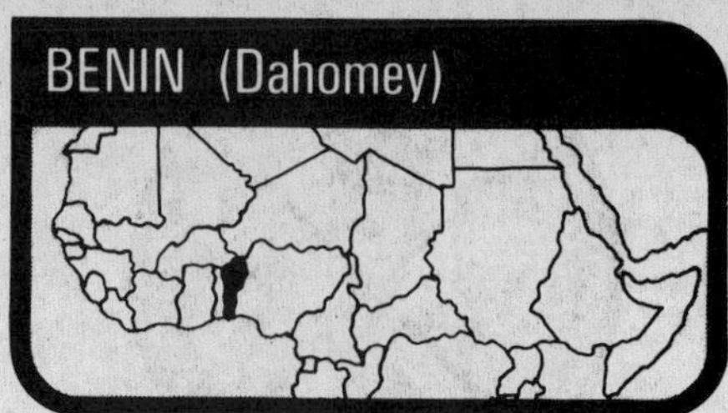

BENIN (Dahomey)

The Peoples Republic of Benin (formerly the Republic of Dahomey), located on the south side of the African bulge between Togo and Nigeria, has an area of 43,484 sq. mi. (112,620 sq. km.) and a population of 4 million. Capital: Porto-Novo. The principal industry of Benin, one of the poorest countries of West Africa, is the processing of palm oil products. Palm kernel oil, peanuts, cotton, and coffee are exported.

Porto-Novo, on the Bight of Benin, was founded as a trading post by the Portuguese in the 17th century. At that time, Benin was composed of an aggregation of mutually suspicious tribes, the majority of which were tributary to the powerful northern Kingdom of Abomey. In 1863, the King of Porto-Novo petitioned France for protection from Abomey. The French subjugated other militant tribes as well, and in 1892 organized the area as a protectorate of France; in 1904 it was incorporated into French West Africa as the Territory of Dahomey. After the establishment of the Fifth French Republic, the Territory at Dahomey became an autonomous state within the French community. On Aug. 1, 1960, it became the fully independent Republic of Dahomey. In 1974, the republic began a transition to a socialist society with MarxismLeninism as its revolutionary philosophy. On Nov. 30, 1975, the name of the Republic of Dahomey was changed to the Peoples Republic of Benin.

DAHOMEY

100 FRANCS

5.1000 g, .999 SILVER, .1638 oz ASW
10th Anniversary of Independence
Obv: Hallmark "999.9" above denomination.

KM#	Date	Mintage	VF	XF	Unc
1.1	1971	4,650	—	Proof	7.50

Obv: Hallmark "999.9" right of denomination.

KM#	Date	Mintage	VF	XF	Unc
1.2	1971	Inc. Ab.	—	Proof	7.50

Obv: Hallmark "1000" lower right S in FRANCS.

KM#	Date	Mintage	VF	XF	Unc
1.3	1971	Inc. Ab.	—	Proof	7.50

200 FRANCS

10.2500 g, .999 SILVER, .3292 oz ASW
10th Anniversary of Independence
Obv: Hallmark "999.9" between 200 and FRANCS.

KM#	Date	Mintage	VF	XF	Unc
2.1	1971	5,150	—	Proof	12.50

Obv: Hallmark "1000" lower right of S in FRANCS.

KM#	Date	Mintage	VF	XF	Unc
2.2	1971	Inc. Ab.	—	Proof	12.50

500 FRANCS

25.2000 g, .999 SILVER, .8094 oz ASW
10th Anniversary of Independence

3	1971	5,550	—	Proof	30.00

1000 FRANCS

51.5000 g, .999 SILVER, 1.6542 oz ASW
10th Anniversary of Independence
Obv: Similar to 500 Francs, KM#3.

4	1971	6,500	—	Proof	75.00

2500 FRANCS

8.8800 g, .900 GOLD, .2569 oz AGW
10th Anniversary of Independence - Dancers

6	1971	960 pcs.	—	Proof	200.00

5000 FRANCS

17.7700 g, .900 GOLD, .5142 oz AGW
10th Anniversary of Independence - Water Buffalos
Obv: Similar to 2500 Francs, KM#6.

KM#	Date	Mintage	VF	XF	Unc
7	1971	610 pcs.	—	Proof	450.00

10,000 FRANCS

35.5500 g, .900 GOLD, 1.0287 oz AGW
10th Anniversary of
Independence - Hippopotamuses
Obv: Similar to 2500 Francs, KM#6.

8	1971	470 pcs.	—	Proof	850.00

25,000 FRANCS

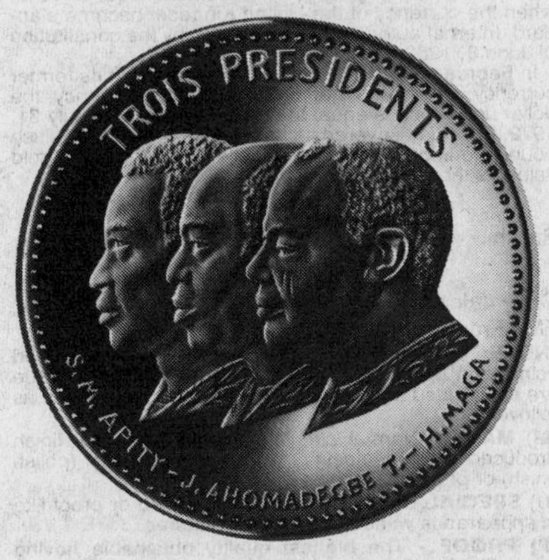

88.8800 g, .900 GOLD, 2.5720 oz AGW
10th Anniversary of Independence - Presidents
Obv: Similar to 2500 Francs, KM#6.

9	1971	380 pcs.	—	Proof	1450.

PROOF SETS (PS)

KM#	Date	Mintage	Identification	Issue Price	Mkt. Val.
PS1	1971(8)	380	KM1-4,6-9	—	3100.
PS2	1971(4)	4,270	KM1-4	36.00	125.00

BENIN

500 FRANCS

12.0000 g, .999 SILVER, .3858 oz ASW
Soccer - Goalie

KM#	Date	Mintage	VF	XF	Unc
3	1992	*.010	—	—	52.00

1000 FRANCS

19.9100 g, .999 SILVER, .6402 oz ASW
5 Hands Holding Jar

KM#	Date	Mintage	VF	XF	Unc
1	ND(1992)	1,000	—	Proof	85.00

Upright National Map in Radiant Sun

2	ND(1992)	1,000	—	Proof	85.00

20.0000 g, .999 SILVER, .6430 oz ASW
Olympics - Gymnast

4	1992	*5,000	—	Proof	55.00

Soccer - Player Kicking Ball

KM#	Date	Mintage	VF	XF	Unc
5	1992	*.010	—	Proof	52.00

Protection of Nature - Elephant

KM#	Date	Mintage	VF	XF	Unc
6	1993	—	—	Proof	42.50

Sailing Ship - Preussen

KM#	Date	Mintage	VF	XF	Unc
7	1993	—	—	Proof	50.00

BERMUDA

The Parliamentary British Colony of Bermuda, situated in the western Atlantic Ocean 660 miles (1,062 km.) east of North Carolina, has an area of 20.5 sq. mi. (53 sq. km.) and a population of 60,000. Capital: Hamilton. Concentrated essences, beauty preparations, and cut flowers are exported. Most Bermudians derive their livelihood from tourism.

Bermuda was discovered by Juan de Bermudez, a Spanish navigator, in about 1503. British influence dates from 1609 when a group of Virginia-bound British colonists under the command of Sir George Somers was shipwrecked on the islands for 10 months. The islands were settled in 1612 by 60 British colonists from the Virginia Colony and became a crown colony in 1684. The earliest coins issued for the island were the "Hogge Money" series of 2, 3, 6 and 12 pence, the name derived from the pig in the obverse design, a recognition of the quantity of such animals then found there. The next issue for Bermuda was the Birmingham coppers of 1793; all locally circulating coinage was demonetized in 1842, when the currency of the United Kingdom became standard. Internal autonomy was obtained by the constitution of June 8, 1968.

In February, 1970, Bermuda converted from its former currency, which was sterling, to a decimal currency, the dollar unit which is equal to one U.S. dollar. On July 31, 1972, Bermuda severed its monetary link with the British pound sterling and pegged its dollar to be the same gold value as the U.S. dollar.

RULERS

British

MINT MARKS

CHI - Valcambi, Switzerland

FM - Franklin Mint, U.S.A.*

***NOTE:** From 1975 the Franklin Mint has produced coinage in up to 3 different qualities. Qualities of issue are designated in ( ) after each date and are defined as follows:

(M) MATTE -Normal circulation strike or a dull finish produced by sandblasting special uncirculated (polish finish) or proof quality dies.

(U) SPECIAL UNCIRCUALTED - Polished or proof-like in appearance without any frosted features.

(P) PROOF - The highest quality obtainable having mirror-like fields and frosted features.

MONETARY SYSTEM

12 Pence = 1 Shilling

20 Shillings = 1 Pound

CROWN

28.2800 g, .925 SILVER, .8411 oz ASW
350th Anniversary of Founding of the Colony

KM#	Date	Mintage	Fine	VF	XF	Unc
13	1959	.100	BV	6.00	8.00	12.00
	1959	6-10 pcs.	—	Matte Proof		1000.

22.6200 g, .500 SILVER, .3636 oz ASW

KM#	Date	Mintage	Fine	VF	XF	Unc
14	1964	.470	—	—	BV	4.50
	1964	.030	—	—	Proof	6.00

DECIMAL COINAGE

100 Cents = 1 Dollar

CENT

BRONZE
Wild Boar

KM#	Date	Mintage	Fine	VF	XF	Unc
15	1970	5.500	—	—	.10	.20
	1970	.011	—	—	Proof	.50
	1971	4.256	—	—	.10	.20
	1972	—	—	Reported, not confirmed		
	1973	2.144	—	—	.10	.20
	1974	.856	—	—	.10	.25
	1975	1.000	—	—	.10	.20
	1976	1.000	—	—	.10	.20
	1977	2.000	—	—	.10	.20
	1978	3.160	—	—	.10	.20
	1980	3.520	—	—	.10	.20
	1981	3.200	—	—	.10	.20
	1982	.320	—	—	.10	.15
	1983	.800	—	—	.10	.15
	1983	.010	—	—	Proof	1.00
	1984	.800	—	—	.10	.15
	1985	—	—	—	.10	.15

KM#	Date	Mintage	Fine	VF	XF	Unc
44	1986	.960	—	—	.10	.15
	1986	Inc. Ab.	—	—	Proof	3.50
	1987	—	—	—	.10	.15
	1988	—	—	—	.10	.15
	1990	—	—	—	.10	.15
	1991	—	—	—	.10	.15

COPPER COATED STEEL

KM#	Date	Mintage	Fine	VF	XF	Unc
44a	1988	—	—	—	—	2.50

COPPER PLATED ZINC

KM#	Date	Mintage	Fine	VF	XF	Unc
44b	1991	—	—	—	.10	.15

5 CENTS

COPPER-NICKEL
Queen Angel Fish

KM#	Date	Mintage	Fine	VF	XF	Unc
16	1970	2.190	—	—	.10	.25
	1970	.011	—	—	Proof	.50
	1974	.310	—	—	.10	.30
	1975	.500	—	—	.10	.30
	1977	.500	—	—	.10	.30
	1979	.500	—	—	.10	.30
	1980	1.100	—	—	.10	.25
	1981	.900	—	—	.10	.25
	1982	.200	—	—	.10	.30
	1983	.800	—	—	.10	.25
	1983	.010	—	—	Proof	1.50
	1984	.500	—	—	.10	.30
	1985	—	—	—	.10	.30

KM#	Date	Mintage	Fine	VF	XF	Unc
45	1986	.700	—	—	.10	.30
	1986	Inc. Ab.	—	—	Proof	4.50
	1987	—	—	—	.10	.25
	1988	—	—	—	.10	.25
	1990	—	—	—	.10	.25

10 CENTS

COPPER-NICKEL
Bermuda Lily

KM#	Date	Mintage	Fine	VF	XF	Unc
17	1970	2.500	—	.10	.15	.30
	1970	.011	—	—	Proof	.50
	1971	2.000	—	.10	.15	.30
	1978	.500	—	.10	.15	.35
	1979	.800	—	.10	.15	.35
	1980	1.100	—	.10	.15	.30
	1981	1.300	—	.10	.15	.30
	1982	.400	—	.10	.15	.35
	1983	1.000	—	.10	.15	.30
	1983	.010	—	—	Proof	2.00
	1984	.500	—	.10	.15	.35
	1985	—	—	.10	.15	.35

KM#	Date	Mintage	Fine	VF	XF	Unc
46	1986	.350	—	.10	.15	.35
	1986	Inc. Ab.	—	—	Proof	6.50
	1987	—	—	.10	.15	.35
	1988	—	—	.10	.15	.35
	1990	—	—	.10	.15	.35

25 CENTS

COPPER-NICKEL
Yellow-Billed Tropical Bird

KM#	Date	Mintage	Fine	VF	XF	Unc
18	1970	1.500	—	.30	.40	.75
	1970	.011	—	—	Proof	1.50
	1973	1.000	—	.30	.40	.75
	1979	.570	—	.30	.40	.85
	1980	1.120	—	.30	.40	.75
	1981	2.200	—	.30	.40	.75
	1982	.160	—	.30	.40	1.00
	1983	.600	—	.30	.40	.85
	1983	.010	—	—	Proof	2.50
	1984	.400	—	.30	.40	.85
	1985	—	—	.30	.40	.85

375th Anniversary of Bermuda
Arms of the Bermudas
Obv: Similar to KM#18.

KM#	Date	Mintage	Fine	VF	XF	Unc
32	1984	—	—	—	.50	2.25

5.9600 g, .925 SILVER, .1772 oz ASW

KM#	Date	Mintage	Fine	VF	XF	Unc
32a	1984	1,750	—	—	Proof	22.50

COPPER-NICKEL
375th Anniversary of Bermuda
City of Hamilton
Obv: Similar to KM#18.

KM#	Date	Mintage	Fine	VF	XF	Unc
33	1984	—	—	—	.50	2.25

5.9600 g, .925 SILVER, .1772 oz ASW

KM#	Date	Mintage	Fine	VF	XF	Unc
33a	1984	1,750	—	—	Proof	22.50

COPPER-NICKEL
375th Anniversary of Bermuda
Town of St. George
Obv: Similar to KM#18.

KM#	Date	Mintage	Fine	VF	XF	Unc
34	1984	—	—	—	.50	2.25

5.9600 g, .925 SILVER, .1772 oz ASW

KM#	Date	Mintage	Fine	VF	XF	Unc
34a	1984	1,750	—	—	Proof	22.50

COPPER-NICKEL
375th Anniversary of Bermuda
Warwick Parish
Obv: Similar to KM#18.

KM#	Date	Mintage	Fine	VF	XF	Unc
35	1984	—	—	—	.50	2.25

5.9600 g, .925 SILVER, .1772 oz ASW

KM#	Date	Mintage	Fine	VF	XF	Unc
35a	1984	1,750	—	—	Proof	22.50

COPPER-NICKEL
375th Anniversary of Bermuda
Smith's Parish
Obv: Similar to KM#18.

KM#	Date	Mintage	Fine	VF	XF	Unc
36	1984	—	—	—	.50	2.25

5.9600 g, .925 SILVER, .1772 oz ASW

KM#	Date	Mintage	Fine	VF	XF	Unc
36a	1984	1,750	—	—	Proof	22.50

COPPER-NICKEL
375th Anniversary of Bermuda
Devonshire Parish
Obv: Similar to KM#18.

KM#	Date	Mintage	Fine	VF	XF	Unc
37	1984	—	—	—	.50	2.25

5.9600 g, .925 SILVER, .1772 oz ASW

KM#	Date	Mintage	Fine	VF	XF	Unc
37a	1984	1,750	—	—	Proof	22.50

COPPER-NICKEL
375th Anniversary of Bermuda
Sandy's Parish
Obv: Similar to KM#18.

KM#	Date	Mintage	Fine	VF	XF	Unc
38	1984	—	—	—	.50	2.25

5.9600 g, .925 SILVER, .1772 oz ASW

KM#	Date	Mintage	Fine	VF	XF	Unc
38a	1984	1,750	—	—	Proof	22.50

COPPER-NICKEL
375th Anniversary of Bermuda
Hamilton Parish
Obv: Similar to KM#18.

KM#	Date	Mintage	Fine	VF	XF	Unc
39	1984	—	—	—	.50	2.25

5.9600 g, .925 SILVER, .1772 oz ASW

KM#	Date	Mintage	Fine	VF	XF	Unc
39a	1984	1,750	—	—	Proof	22.50

COPPER-NICKEL
375th Anniversary of Bermuda
Southampton Parish
Obv: Similar to KM#18.

KM#	Date	Mintage	Fine	VF	XF	Unc
40	1984	—	—	—	.50	2.25

5.9600 g, .925 SILVER, .1772 oz ASW

KM#	Date	Mintage	Fine	VF	XF	Unc
40a	1984	1,750	—	—	Proof	22.50

COPPER-NICKEL
375th Anniversary of Bermuda
Pembroke Parish
Obv: Similar to KM#18.

KM#	Date	Mintage	Fine	VF	XF	Unc
41	1984	—	—	—	.50	2.25

5.9600 g, .925 SILVER, .1772 oz ASW

KM#	Date	Mintage	Fine	VF	XF	Unc
41a	1984	1,750	—	—	Proof	22.50

COPPER-NICKEL
375th Anniversary of Bermuda
Paget Parish
Obv: Similar to KM#18.

KM#	Date	Mintage	Fine	VF	XF	Unc
42	1984	—	—	—	.50	2.25

5.9600 g, .925 SILVER, .1772 oz ASW

KM#	Date	Mintage	Fine	VF	XF	Unc
42a	1984	1,750	—	—	Proof	22.50

COPPER-NICKEL

KM#	Date	Mintage	Fine	VF	XF	Unc
47	1986	.560	—	.30	.40	.75
	1986,	Inc. Ab.	—	—	Proof	10.00
	1987	—	—	.30	.40	.75
	1988	—	—	.30	.40	.75

50 CENTS

COPPER-NICKEL

KM#	Date	Mintage	Fine	VF	XF	Unc
19	1970	1.000	—	.60	.75	1.00
	1970	.011	—	—	Proof	2.00
	1978	.200	—	.60	.85	1.25
	1980	.060	—	.60	.85	1.50
	1981	.100	—	.60	.85	1.25
	1982	.080	—	.60	.85	1.50
	1983	.060	—	.60	.85	1.50
	1983	.010	—	—	Proof	4.50
	1984	.040	—	.60	.85	1.50
	1985	—	—	.60	.85	1.50

KM#	Date	Mintage	Fine	VF	XF	Unc
48	1986	.060	—	.60	.85	1.50
	1986	Inc. Ab.	—	—	Proof	15.00
	1988	—	—	.60	.85	1.50

DOLLAR

28.2800 g, .800 SILVER, .7273 oz ASW

KM#	Date	Mintage	Fine	VF	XF	Unc
20	1970	.011	—	—	Proof	17.50

28.2800 g, .500 SILVER, .4546 oz ASW
Silver Wedding Anniversary

KM#	Date	Mintage	Fine	VF	XF	Unc
22	1972	.075	—	—	—	7.50

28.2800 g, .925 SILVER, .8411 oz ASW

KM#	Date	Mintage	Fine	VF	XF	Unc
22a	1972	.015	—	—	Proof	12.50

COPPER-NICKEL
Wedding of Prince Charles and Lady Diana
Obv: Similar to KM#22.

KM#	Date	Mintage	Fine	VF	XF	Unc
28	1981	.065	—	—	—	3.00

28.2800 g, .925 SILVER, .8411 oz ASW

KM#	Date	Mintage	Fine	VF	XF	Unc
28a	1981	.017	—	—	Proof	15.00

NICKEL-BRASS
Cahow over Bermuda

KM#	Date	Mintage	Fine	VF	XF	Unc
30	1983	.250	—	—	—	2.00
	1983	.010	—	—	Proof	5.00

COPPER-NICKEL
Cruise Ship Tourism

KM#	Date	Mintage	Fine	VF	XF	Unc
43	1985	.011	—	—	—	3.50

28.2800 g, .925 SILVER, .8411 oz ASW

KM#	Date	Mintage	Fine	VF	XF	Unc
43a	1985	2,500	—	—	—	15.00
	1985	4,000	—	—	Proof	22.50

COPPER-NICKEL
World Wildlife Fund - Sea Turtle

KM#	Date	Mintage	Fine	VF	XF	Unc
49	1986	—	—	—	—	4.25

28.2800 g, .925 SILVER, .8411 oz ASW

KM#	Date	Mintage	Fine	VF	XF	Unc
49a	1986	*.010	—	—	—	17.50
	1986	*.025	—	—	Proof	25.00

NICKEL-BRASS
Obv: Similar to KM#43. Rev: Cahow over Bermuda.

KM#	Date	Mintage	Fine	VF	XF	Unc
50	1986	—	—	—	Proof	18.00

COPPER-NICKEL
50th Anniversary of Commercial Aviation

KM#	Date	Mintage	Fine	VF	XF	Unc
52	1987	—	—	—	—	4.25

28.2800 g, .925 SILVER, .8411 oz ASW

KM#	Date	Mintage	Fine	VF	XF	Unc
52a	1987	4,000	—	—	—	20.00
	1987	5,000	—	—	Proof	32.50

COPPER-NICKEL
Railroad

KM#	Date	Mintage	Fine	VF	XF	Unc
55	1988	—	—	—	—	4.25

28.2800 g, .925 SILVER, .8411 oz ASW

KM#	Date	Mintage	Fine	VF	XF	Unc
55a	1988	—	—	—	—	20.00
	1988	—	—	—	Proof	32.50

NICKEL-BRASS
Circulation Type

KM#	Date	Mintage	Fine	VF	XF	Unc
56	1988	—	—	—	—	2.25

8.4000 g, .925 SILVER, .2498 oz ASW

KM#	Date	Mintage	Fine	VF	XF	Unc
56a	1988	*3,000	—	—	Proof	30.00

COPPER-NICKEL
Monarch Conservation Project

KM#	Date	Mintage	Fine	VF	XF	Unc
61	1989	—	—	—	—	5.00

28.2800 g, .925 SILVER, .8411 oz ASW

KM#	Date	Mintage	Fine	VF	XF	Unc
61a	1989	*5,000	—	—	—	22.50
	1989	*5,000	—	—	Proof	35.00

COPPER-NICKEL
90th Birthday of Queen Mother

KM#	Date	Mintage	Fine	VF	XF	Unc
67	1990	—	—	—	—	5.00

28.2800 g, .925 SILVER, .8411 oz ASW

KM#	Date	Mintage	Fine	VF	XF	Unc
67a	1990	*.010	—	—	Proof	60.00

BRONZE
Olympics - Rings
Obv: Portrait of Queen Elizabeth.
Rev: Similar to 5 Dollars, KM#79.

KM#	Date	Mintage	Fine	VF	XF	Unc
78	1992	*250 pcs.	—	—	Proof	25.00

31.4700 g, .925 SILVER, .9359 oz ASW
1992 Olympics - Sailboats

KM#	Date	Mintage	Fine	VF	XF	Unc
85	ND(1993)	*.025	—	—	Proof	50.00

2 DOLLARS

28.2800 g, .925 SILVER, .8411 oz ASW
Cicada Insects

KM#	Date	Mintage	Fine	VF	XF	Unc
64	1990	2,500	—	—	Proof	50.00

Wildlife - Tree Frog

KM#	Date	Mintage	Fine	VF	XF	Unc
65	1990	2,500	—	—	Proof	50.00

Yellow-Crowned Night Heron

KM#	Date	Mintage	Fine	VF	XF	Unc
68	1991	*2,500	—	—	Proof	50.00

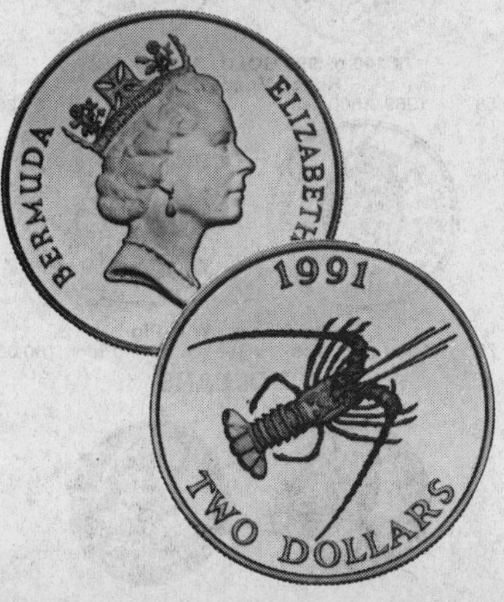

Spiny Lobster

KM#	Date	Mintage	Fine	VF	XF	Unc
69	1991	*2,500	—	—	Proof	50.00

Bluebird Feeding Nestling

KM#	Date	Mintage	Fine	VF	XF	Unc
71	1992	*2,500	—	—	Proof	50.00

Cedar Tree

KM#	Date	Mintage	Fine	VF	XF	Unc
72	1992	*2,500	—	—	Proof	50.00

ELIZABETH II
TWO DOLLARS
1993
BERMUDA
1793

23.0000 g, .925 SILVER, .6840 oz ASW
200 Years of Bermudan Coinage

KM#	Date	Mintage	Fine	VF	XF	Unc
81	1993	5,000	—	—	Proof	50.00

28.2800 g, .925 SILVER, .8411 oz ASW
Humpback Whale

KM#	Date	Mintage	Fine	VF	XF	Unc
83	1993	*2,500	—	—	Proof	60.00

Bermuda Longtail Bird

KM#	Date	Mintage	Fine	VF	XF	Unc
84	1993	*2,500	—	—	Proof	60.00

5 DOLLARS

NICKEL-BRASS

KM#	Date	Mintage	Fine	VF	XF	Unc
31	1983	.100	—	—	—	6.00
	1983	.010	—	—	Proof	8.00

BRASS
Obv: Similar to 1 Dollar, KM#43.
Rev: Onion superimposed over Bermuda map.

KM#	Date	Mintage	Fine	VF	XF	Unc
51	1986	—	—	—	Proof	22.50

10 DOLLARS

3.1340 g, .999 GOLD, .1007 oz AGW
Hogge Money - Wild Pig

KM#	Date	Mintage	Fine	VF	XF	Unc
57	1989	500 pcs.	—	—	Proof	70.00

Hogge Money - Ship

KM#	Date	Mintage	Fine	VF	XF	Unc
74	1990	500 pcs.	—	—	Proof	70.00

Wildlife - Tree Frog
Similar to 2 Dollars, KM#65.

KM#	Date	Mintage	Fine	VF	XF	Unc
66	1990	*2,500	—	—	—	65.00

Yellow-Crowned Night Heron
Obv: Queen Elizabeth II.

KM#	Date	Mintage	Fine	VF	XF	Unc
70	1991	*2,500	—	—	Proof	75.00

Bluebird
Similar to 2 Dollars, KM#71.
Obv: Queen Elizabeth II.
Rev: Bluebird bringing food to nestling in tree trunk.

KM#	Date	Mintage	Fine	VF	XF	Unc
73	1991	*2,500	—	—	—	75.00

20 DOLLARS

7.9881 g, .917 GOLD, .2355 oz AGW
Seagull In Flight

KM#	Date	Mintage	Fine	VF	XF	Unc
21	1970	1,000	—	—	Proof	275.00

25 DOLLARS

COPPER-NICKEL
Royal Visit

KM#	Date	Mintage	Fine	VF	XF	Unc
23	1975FM(M)					
		1,193	—	—	—	20.00
	1975FM(U)		—			
		100 pcs.	—	—	—	60.00

48.7000 g, .925 SILVER, 1.4483 oz ASW

KM#	Date	Mintage	Fine	VF	XF	Unc
23a	1975FM(P)	.015	—	—	Proof	25.00

54.7500 g, .925 SILVER, 1.6283 oz ASW
Queen's Silver Jubilee

KM#	Date	Mintage	Fine	VF	XF	Unc
25	1977CHI	.010	—	—	—	35.00
	1977CHI	.011	—	—	Proof	45.00
	1977	*520 pcs.	—	—	—	250.00
	1977	*550 pcs.	—	—	Proof	300.00

*NOTE: Struck at the Royal Canadian Mint.

7.8140 g, .999 GOLD, .2512 oz AGW
Hogge Money - Ship

KM#	Date	Mintage	Fine	VF	XF	Unc
58	1989	500 pcs.	—	—	Proof	160.00

Hogge Money - Wild Pig

KM#	Date	Mintage	Fine	VF	XF	Unc
75	1990	500 pcs.	—	—	Proof	160.00

50 DOLLARS

4.0500 g, .900 GOLD, .1172 oz AGW
Queen's Silver Jubilee

KM#	Date	Mintage	Fine	VF	XF	Unc
26	1977CHI	3,950	—	—	—	75.00
	1977CHI	4,070	—	—	Proof	100.00
	1977	*520 pcs.	—	—	—	250.00
	1977	*580 pcs.	—	—	Proof	300.00

*NOTE: Struck at the Royal Canadian Mint.

15.6080 g, .999 GOLD, .5018 oz AGW
Hogge Money - Wild Pig

KM#	Date	Mintage	Fine	VF	XF	Unc
59	1989	500 pcs.	—	—	Proof	320.00

Hogge Money - Ship

KM#	Date	Mintage	Fine	VF	XF	Unc
76	1990	500 pcs.	—	—	Proof	320.00

100 DOLLARS

7.0300 g, .900 GOLD, .2034 oz AGW
Royal Visit

KM#	Date	Mintage	Fine	VF	XF	Unc
24	1975FM(M)					
		25 pcs.	—	—	—	300.00
	1975FM(U)	.019	—	—	—	110.00
	1975FM(P)	.027	—	—	Proof	135.00

8.1000 g, .900 GOLD, .2344 oz AGW
Queen's Silver Jubilee

KM#	Date	Mintage	Fine	VF	XF	Unc
27	1977CHI	6,225	—	—	—	125.00
	1977CHI	5,613	—	—	Proof	200.00
	1977	*2,312	—	—	—	250.00
	1977	*1,887	—	—	Proof	300.00

*NOTE: Struck at the Royal Canadian Mint.

31.2100 g, .999 GOLD, 1.0035 oz AGW
Hogge Money - Ship

KM#	Date	Mintage	Fine	VF	XF	Unc
60	1989	500 pcs.	—	—	Proof	700.00

Hogge Money - Wild Pig

KM#	Date	Mintage	Fine	VF	XF	Unc
77	1990	500 pcs.	—	—	Proof	700.00

47.5400 g, .917 GOLD, 1.4017 oz AGW
Olympics - Rings
Obv: Portrait of Queen Elizabeth II.
Rev: Similar to 5 Dollars, KM#79.

KM#	Date	Mintage	Fine	VF	XF	Unc
80	1992	*250 pcs.	—	—	Proof	925.00

200 DOLLARS

28.5000 g, .999 GOLD, .9154 oz AGW
200 Years of Bermudan Coinage

KM#	Date	Mintage	Fine	VF	XF	Unc
82	1993	200 pcs.	—	—	Proof	625.00

250 DOLLARS

15.9760 g, .917 GOLD, .4710 oz AGW
Wedding of Prince Charles and Lady Diana
Obv: Similar to 20 Dollars, KM#21.

KM#	Date	Mintage	Fine	VF	XF	Unc
29	1981	217 pcs.	—	—	—	400.00
	1981	790 pcs.	—	—	Proof	350.00

SILVER BULLION ISSUES

5 DOLLARS

155.5150 g, .999 SILVER, 5.0000 oz ASW
Sailing Ship - Sea Venture Wreck
Illustration reduced. Actual size: 65mm
Obv: Similar to 1 Dollar, KM#43.

KM#	Date	Mintage	Fine	VF	XF	Unc
54	1987	*.020	—	—	Proof	125.00

Sailing Ship - San Antonio
Illustration reduced. Actual size: 65mm
Obv: Portrait of Queen Elizabeth.

KM#	Date	Mintage	Fine	VF	XF	Unc
62	1988	1,500	—	—	Proof	165.00

Illustration reduced. Actual size: 65mm.
Olympics - Rings
Obv: Portrait of Queen Elizabeth II.

KM#	Date	Mintage	Fine	VF	XF	Unc
79	1992	*1,250	—	—	Proof	175.00

PALLADIUM BULLION ISSUES

(Ounce)

25 DOLLARS

31.1000 g, .999 PALLADIUM, 1.0000 oz APW
Ship - Sea Venture

KM#	Date	Mintage	Fine	VF	XF	Unc
53	1987	*.020	—	—	Proof	180.00

Ship Wreck of San Antonio
Obv: Portrait of Queen Elizabeth.

KM#	Date	Mintage	Fine	VF	XF	Unc
63	1988	2,000	—	—	Proof	210.00

MINT SETS (MS)

KM#	Date	Mintage	Identification	Issue Price	Mkt. Val.
MS1	1970(5)	90,000	KM15-19	3.25	2.00
MS2	1977(3)	4,470	KM25-27	175.00	275.00
MS3	1977(2)	—	KM26-27	150.00	240.00
MS4	1984(11)	3,350	KM32-42	24.95	25.00

PROOF SETS (PS)

KM#	Date	Mintage	Identification	Issue Price	Mkt. Val.
PS1	1970(6)	10,000	KM15-20	24.00	25.00
PS2	1970(7)	1,000	KM15-21	216.00	300.00
PS3	1977(3)	—	KM25-27	245.00	420.00
PS4	1977(2)	—	KM26-27	210.00	375.00
PS5	1981(3)	500	KM28a,29(P1) numbered set	1500.	1050.
PS6	1983(7)	6,474	KM15-19,30,31	30.00	25.00
PS7	1984(11)	1,750	KM32a-42a	250.00	250.00
PS8	1986(7)	1,750	KM44-48,50-51	50.00	80.00
PS10	1989(4)	500	KM57-60	1495.	1250.
PS11	1990(4)	500	KM74-77	—	1250.
PS12	1992(3)	250	KM78-80	1075.	1125.
PS13	1992(2)	500	KM71-72	75.00	100.00

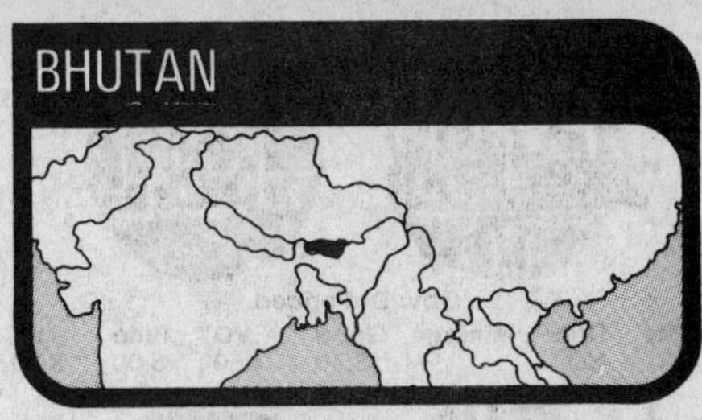

The Kingdom of Bhutan, a landlocked Himalayan country bordered by Tibet and India, has an area of 18,147 sq. mi. (47,000 sq. km.) and a population of 1.4 million. Capital: Thimphu. Virtually the entire population is engaged in agricultural and pastoral activities. Rice, wheat, barley, and yak butter are produced in sufficient quantity to make the country self-sufficient in food. The economy of Bhutan is primitive and many transactions are conducted on a barter basis.

Bhutan's early history is obscure, but is thought to have resembled that of rural medieval Europe. The country was conquered by Tibet, in the 9th century, and a dual temporal and spiritual rule developed which operated until the mid-19th century, when the southern part of the country was occupied by the British and annexed to British India. Bhutan was established as a hereditary monarchy in 1907, and in 1910 agreed to British control of its external affairs. In 1949, India and Bhutan concluded a treaty whereby India assumed Britain's role in subsidizing Bhutan and guiding its foreign affairs. In 1971 Bhutan became a full member of the United Nations.

RULERS

Ugyen Wangchuck, 1907-1926
Jigme Wangchuck, 1926-1952
Jigme Dorji Wangchuck, 1952-1972
Jigme Singye Wangchuck, 1972

DEB (1/2) RUPEE

NOTE: Prior to their own issues the coins (1/2 Rupees) of Cooch Behar circulated freely. After the Cooch Behar Mint closed in 1789, Bhutan began to strike copies of the Cooch Behar coins. As time went on these coins were remelted and increasing amounts of debasing alloys were used until we have a copper or brass issue, some with a slight silver wash.

Period I

C.1790-1820AD

'Ma'

SILVER

KM#	Date	Mintage	Good	VG	Fine	VF
1	ND	—	4.00	6.50	8.50	12.50

'Sa'

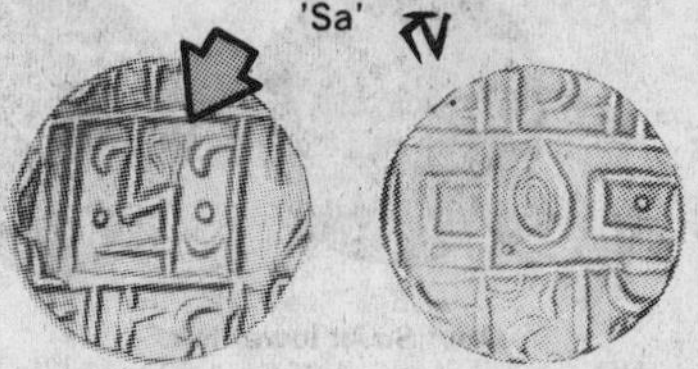

KM#	Date	Mintage	Good	VG	Fine	VF
2	ND	—	4.00	6.50	8.50	12.50

Period II

c.1820-1835AD

"Ma-tam"

'Sa'

SILVER, LEAD alloying

KM#	Date	Mintage	Good	VG	Fine	VF
3	ND	—	3.50	4.50	6.00	8.00

SILVER, COPPER alloying

KM#	Date	Mintage	Good	VG	Fine	VF
4.1	ND	—	3.50	4.50	6.00	8.00

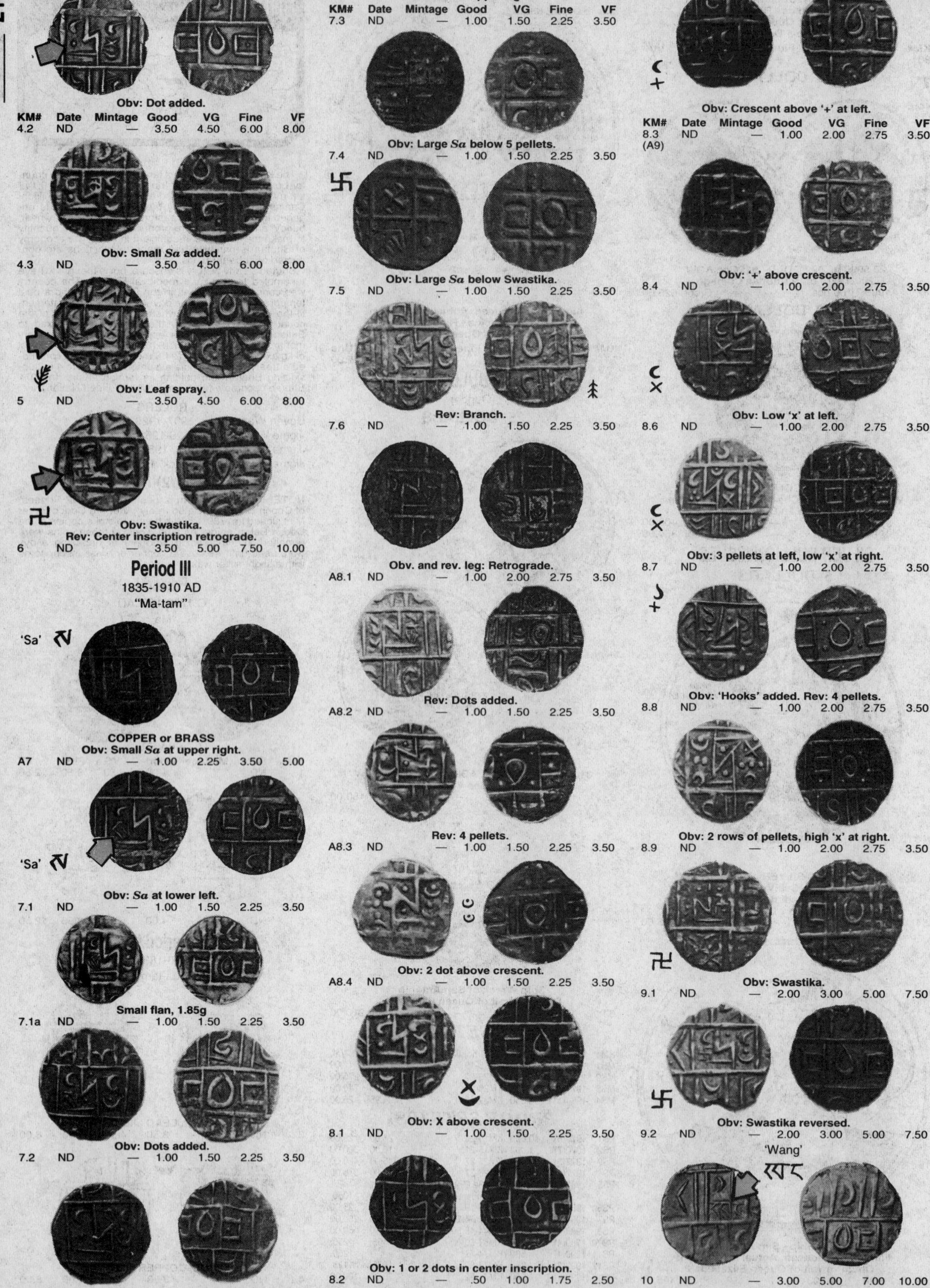

Obv: Dot added.

KM#	Date	Mintage	Good	VG	Fine	VF
4.2	ND	—	3.50	4.50	6.00	8.00

Obv: Small *Sa* added.

4.3	ND	—	3.50	4.50	6.00	8.00

Obv: Leaf spray.

5	ND	—	3.50	4.50	6.00	8.00

Obv: Swastika.
Rev: Center inscription retrograde.

6	ND	—	3.50	5.00	7.50	10.00

Period III

1835-1910 AD
"Ma-tam"

'Sa' ས

COPPER or BRASS
Obv: Small *Sa* at upper right.

A7	ND	—	1.00	2.25	3.50	5.00

'Sa' ས

Obv: *Sa* at lower left.

7.1	ND	—	1.00	1.50	2.25	3.50

Small flan, 1.85g

7.1a	ND	—	1.00	1.50	2.25	3.50

Obv: Dots added.

7.2	ND	—	1.00	1.50	2.25	3.50

Obv: *Sa* at upper right.

KM#	Date	Mintage	Good	VG	Fine	VF
7.3	ND	—	1.00	1.50	2.25	3.50

Obv: Large *Sa* below 5 pellets.

7.4	ND	—	1.00	1.50	2.25	3.50

Obv: Large *Sa* below Swastika.

7.5	ND	—	1.00	1.50	2.25	3.50

Rev: Branch.

7.6	ND	—	1.00	1.50	2.25	3.50

Obv. and rev. leg: Retrograde.

A8.1	ND	—	1.00	2.00	2.75	3.50

Rev: Dots added.

A8.2	ND	—	1.00	1.50	2.25	3.50

Rev: 4 pellets.

A8.3	ND	—	1.00	1.50	2.25	3.50

Obv: 2 dot above crescent.

A8.4	ND	—	1.00	1.50	2.25	3.50

Obv: X above crescent.

8.1	ND	—	1.00	1.50	2.25	3.50

Obv: 1 or 2 dots in center inscription.

8.2	ND	—	.50	1.00	1.75	2.50

Obv: Crescent above '+' at left.

KM#	Date	Mintage	Good	VG	Fine	VF
8.3 (A9)	ND	—	1.00	2.00	2.75	3.50

Obv: '+' above crescent.

8.4	ND	—	1.00	2.00	2.75	3.50

Obv: Low 'x' at left.

8.6	ND	—	1.00	2.00	2.75	3.50

Obv: 3 pellets at left, low 'x' at right.

8.7	ND	—	1.00	2.00	2.75	3.50

Obv: 'Hooks' added. Rev: 4 pellets.

8.8	ND	—	1.00	2.00	2.75	3.50

Obv: 2 rows of pellets, high 'x' at right.

8.9	ND	—	1.00	2.00	2.75	3.50

Obv: Swastika.

9.1	ND	—	2.00	3.00	5.00	7.50

Obv: Swastika reversed.

9.2	ND	—	2.00	3.00	5.00	7.50

'Wang' དབང

10	ND	—	3.00	5.00	7.00	10.00

'Sa dar'

KM#	Date	Mintage	Good	VG	Fine	VF
11	ND	—	3.00	5.00	7.00	10.00
11a	ND	—	3.00	5.00	7.00	10.00
11b	ND	—	3.00	5.00	7.00	10.00

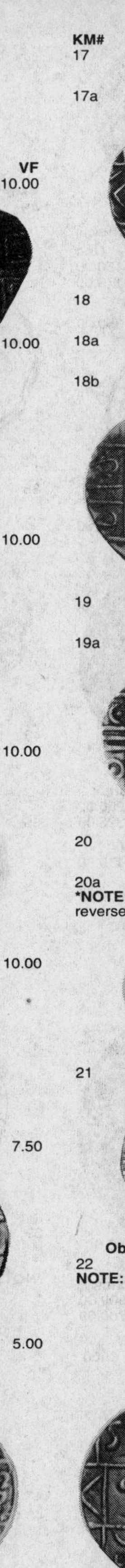

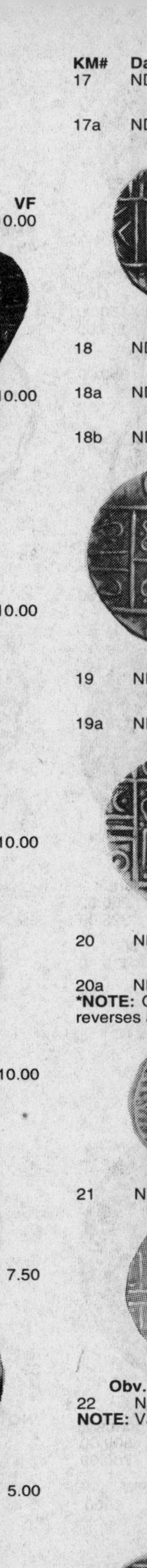

Obv: Rosette. Rev: Swastika.

KM#	Date	Mintage	Good	VG	Fine	VF
12	ND	—	3.00	5.00	7.00	10.00

Obv: Rosette. Rev: 2 fish.

KM#	Date	Mintage	Good	VG	Fine	VF
13	ND	—	3.00	5.00	7.00	10.00

Rev: 2 fish.

KM#	Date	Mintage	Good	VG	Fine	VF
14	ND	—	2.00	3.00	5.00	7.50

NOTE: Varieties exist.

Obv: Knot. Rev: Conch shell.

KM#	Date	Mintage	Good	VG	Fine	VF
15	ND	—	1.50	2.50	3.50	5.00

Period IV

C.1910-1927AD

COPPER

KM#	Date	Mintage	Good	VG	Fine	VF
16	ND	—	2.00	3.50	7.00	10.00

KM#	Date	Mintage	Good	VG	Fine	VF
			SILVER			
17	ND	—	10.00	15.00	25.00	30.00
			COPPER			
17a	ND	*—	2.00	3.50	5.00	7.50
			SILVER			
18	ND	—	10.00	15.00	25.00	30.00
			COPPER			
18a	ND	*—	2.00	3.50	5.00	7.50
			BRASS			
18b	ND	—	2.00	3.50	5.00	7.50
			SILVER			
19	ND	—	10.00	15.00	25.00	30.00
			COPPER			
19a	ND	*—	2.00	3.50	5.00	7.50

KM#	Date	Mintage	Good	VG	Fine	VF
			SILVER			
20	ND	—	10.00	15.00	25.00	30.00
			COPPER			
20a	ND	*—	3.00	4.50	6.00	8.50

***NOTE:** Obverses similar to KM#17-20 but symbols on reverses are encountered arranged differently.

KM#	Date	Mintage	Good	VG	Fine	VF
21	ND	—	1.50	2.50	3.50	5.00

Obv. and rev: Interlacing opposite of KM#21.

KM#	Date	Mintage	Good	VG	Fine	VF
22	ND	—	1.50	2.50	3.50	5.00

NOTE: Varieties exist.

RUPEE

Period I

C.1790-1820AD

'Ma'

SILVER, 11.60 g

KM#	Date	Mintage	Good	VG	Fine	VF
A23	ND	—	—	—	—	250.00

Period II

c.1820-1835AD

'Ma-tam'

SILVER, 9.80 g
Similar to KM#4.

KM#	Date	Mintage	Good	VG	Fine	VF
B23	ND	—	—	—	—	200.00

MODERN COINAGE

64 Pice (Paisa) = 1 Rupee

CYCLICAL DATES

Earth-Dragon Iron-Tiger

(1928) (1950)

OBVERSE LEGENDS

Normal Modified

PICE

BRONZE, 4.90 g

KM#	Date	Mintage	Fine	VF	XF	Unc
23	1928	.010	20.00	35.00	60.00	90.00
	1928	—	—	—	Proof	100.00

3.30 g

KM#	Date	Mintage	Fine	VF	XF	Unc
A27	ND	—	—	—	—	—

2.90 g

KM#	Date	Mintage	Fine	VF	XF	Unc
27	ND	*1.260	.75	1.00	1.50	2.25

***NOTE:** Actually struck in 1951 and 1955.

1/2 RUPEE

SILVER, 5.83-5.85 g

KM#	Date	Mintage	Fine	VF	XF	Unc
24	ND(1928)*	.050	10.00	15.00	22.50	35.00
	ND(1928)	—	—	—	Proof	100.00

NOTE: Actually struck in 1929.

Obv: Leg. modified.

KM#	Date	Mintage	Fine	VF	XF	Unc
25	ND(1928)	I.A.	10.00	15.00	22.50	35.00

NOTE: Actually struck in 1930.

NICKEL, 5.78-5.90 g
Obv: Leg. normal.

KM#	Date	Mintage	Fine	VF	XF	Unc
26	ND(1928)*	.020	2.00	3.00	4.50	7.00
	ND(1950)**	.202	1.50	2.50	3.00	4.50

*NOTE: Actually struck in 1951.
**NOTE: Actually struck in 1955.

NICKEL, reduced wgt., 5.08 g
Obv: Leg. normal.

KM#	Date	Mintage	Fine	VF	XF	Unc
28	ND(1950)***	10.000	.75	1.00	1.50	2.25

***NOTE: Actually struck in 1967/68.

DECIMAL COINAGE

1957-1974
100 Naye Paisa = 1 Rupee
100 Rupees = 1 Sertum

25 NAYA PAISA

COPPER-NICKEL
40th Anniversary Accession of Jigme Wangchuk

KM#	Date	Mintage	VF	XF	Unc
29	1966	.010	.20	.40	.75
	1966	6,000	—	Proof	1.00

50 NAYA PAISA

COPPER-NICKEL
40th Anniversary Accession of Jigme Wangchuk

KM#	Date	Mintage	VF	XF	Unc
30	1966	.010	.25	.50	1.00
	1966	6,000	—	Proof	1.50

RUPEE

COPPER-NICKEL
40th Anniversary Accession of Jigme Wangchuk

KM#	Date	Mintage	VF	XF	Unc
31	1966	.010	.50	.75	1.50
	1966	6,000	—	Proof	1.50

3 RUPEES

COPPER-NICKEL
40th Anniversary Accession of Jigme Wangchuk

KM#	Date	Mintage	VF	XF	Unc
32	1966	5,826	—	—	4.00
	1966	6,000	—	Proof	4.00

28.2800 g, .925 SILVER, .8411 oz ASW

KM#	Date	Mintage	VF	XF	Unc
32a	1966	—	—	—	375.00
	1966	2,000	—	Proof	25.00
	1966	—		Matte Proof	375.00

SERTUM

7.9800 g, .917 GOLD, .2352 oz AGW
40th Anniversary Accession of Jigme Wangchuk

KM#	Date	Mintage	VF	XF	Unc
33	1966	2,300	—	—	150.00
	1966	598 pcs.	—	Proof	175.00

9.8400 g, .950 PLATINUM, .3005 oz APW

KM#	Date	Mintage	VF	XF	Unc
33a	1966	72 pcs.	—	Proof	350.00

7.9800 g, .917 GOLD, .2352 oz AGW

KM#	Date	Mintage	VF	XF	Unc
36	1970	3,111	—	—	150.00

2 SERTUMS

15.9800 g, .917 GOLD, .4711 oz AGW
40th Anniversary Accession of Jigme Wangchuk

KM#	Date	Mintage	VF	XF	Unc
34	1966	800 pcs.	—	—	250.00
	1966	598 pcs.	—	Proof	325.00

19.6700 g, .950 PLATINUM, .6008 oz APW

KM#	Date	Mintage	VF	XF	Unc
34a	1966	72 pcs.	—	Proof	475.00

5 SERTUMS

39.9400 g, .917 GOLD, 1.1776 oz AGW
40th Anniversary Accession of Jigme Wangchuk

KM#	Date	Mintage	VF	XF	Unc
35	1966	800 pcs.	—	—	500.00
	1966	598 pcs.	—	Proof	700.00

49.1800 g, .950 PLATINUM, 1.5022 oz APW

KM#	Date	Mintage	VF	XF	Unc
35a	1966	72 pcs.	—	Proof	1000.

MONETARY REFORM

Commencing 1974
100 Chetrums (Paisa) =
1 Ngultrum (Rupee)
100 Ngultrums = 1 Sertum

5 CHETRUMS

ALUMINUM

KM#	Date	Mintage	VF	XF	Unc
37	1974	—	.10	.20	.50
	1974	1,000	—	Proof	1.25
	1975	—	.10	.15	.20
	1975	—	—	Proof	1.25

5 CHHERTUM

BRONZE

KM#	Date	Mintage	VF	XF	Unc
45	1979	—	.10	.20	.50
	1979	—	—	Proof	1.00

10 CHETRUMS

ALUMINUM

KM#	Date	Mintage	VF	XF	Unc
38	1974	—	.15	.25	.50
	1974	1,000	—	Proof	1.50

F.A.O. Issue and International Women's Year

KM#	Date	Mintage	VF	XF	Unc
43	1975	4.000	.15	.25	.65
	1975	—	—	Proof	2.50

10 CHHERTUM

BRONZE

KM#	Date	Mintage	VF	XF	Unc
46	1979	—	.15	.30	1.00
	1979	—	—	Proof	2.00

20 CHETRUMS

ALUMINUM-BRONZE
F.A.O. Issue

KM#	Date	Mintage	VF	XF	Unc
39	1974	1.194	.15	.25	.50
	1974	*	—	P/L	1.50
	1974	1,000	—	Proof	2.00

*NOTE: In mint set only.

25 CHETRUMS

COPPER-NICKEL
Rev. I

KM#	Date	Mintage	VF	XF	Unc
40.1	1974	—	.10	.20	.75
	1974	1,000	—	Proof	3.00

Rev. II

KM#	Date	Mintage	VF	XF	Unc
40.2	1974	—	.10	.20	.75
	1975	—	.10	.20	.75
	1975	—	—	Proof	3.00

25 CHHERTUM

COPPER-NICKEL

KM#	Date	Mintage	VF	XF	Unc
47	1979	—	.25	.50	1.25
	1979	—	—	Proof	4.00

50 CHHERTUM

COPPER-NICKEL

KM#	Date	Mintage	VF	XF	Unc
48	1979	—	.25	.65	1.50
	1979	—	—	Proof	5.00

NGULTRUM

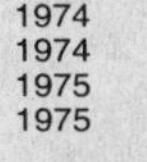

COPPER-NICKEL

KM#	Date	Mintage	VF	XF	Unc
41	1974	—	.20	.50	1.25
	1974	1,000	—	Proof	5.00
	1975	—	.20	.50	1.25
	1975	—	—	Proof	5.00

KM#	Date	Mintage	VF	XF	Unc
49	1979	—	.30	.75	2.00
	1979	—	—	Proof	5.50

3 NGULTRUMS

COPPER-NICKEL

KM#	Date	Mintage	VF	XF	Unc
50	1979	—	1.00	2.00	4.00
	1979	—	—	Proof	7.50

28.2800 g, .925 SILVER, .8411 oz ASW

KM#	Date	Mintage	VF	XF	Unc
50a	1979	*.010	—	Proof	37.50

15 NGULTRUMS

22.3000 g, .500 SILVER, .3584 oz ASW
F.A.O. Issue

KM#	Date	Mintage	VF	XF	Unc
42	1974	.030	—	—	9.00
	1974	*	—	P/L	10.00
	1974	1,000	—	Proof	50.00

***NOTE:** In mint set only.

30 NGULTRUMS

25.0000 g, .500 SILVER, .4018 oz ASW
F.A.O. Issue and International Women's Year

KM#	Date	Mintage	VF	XF	Unc
44	1975	.014	—	—	10.00
	1975	—	—	Proof	20.00

50 NGULTRUMS

28.2800 g, .925 SILVER, .8411 oz ASW
World Food Day

KM#	Date	Mintage	VF	XF	Unc
54	1981	.015	—	—	27.50
	1981	5,000	—	Proof	37.50

100 NGULTRUMS

23.3300 g, .925 SILVER, .6938 oz ASW
Decade For Women

KM#	Date	Mintage	VF	XF	Unc
58	1984	1,050	—	Proof	45.00

200 NGULTRUMS

28.2800 g, .925 SILVER, .8411 oz ASW
75th Anniversary of Monarchy

KM#	Date	Mintage	VF	XF	Unc
55	1982(1983)	.010	—	—	30.00
	1982(1983)	5,000	—	Proof	40.00

International Year of Disabled Persons

KM#	Date	Mintage	VF	XF	Unc
57	1981	.010	—	—	30.00
	1981	.010	—	Proof	35.00

300 NGULTRUMS

28.2800 g, .925 SILVER, .8411 oz ASW
World Championship Soccer

KM#	Date	Mintage	VF	XF	Unc
61	1990	—	—	Proof	50.00

31.4700 g, .925 SILVER, .9359 oz ASW
Endangered Wildlife - Snow Leopard

KM#	Date	Mintage	VF	XF	Unc
65	1991	*.025	—	Proof	55.00

28.2800 g, .925 SILVER, .8411 oz ASW
Solar System

KM#	Date	Mintage	VF	XF	Unc
63	1992	—	—	Proof	45.00

31.4700 g, .925 SILVER, .9359 oz ASW
40th Anniversary of Coronation of Queen Elizabeth

KM#	Date	Mintage	VF	XF	Unc
66	1993	*.010	—	Proof	55.00

Endangered Wildlife - Takin

KM#	Date	Mintage	VF	XF	Unc
67	1993	*.010	—	Proof	50.00

Protect Our World - Elephant, Rhino, Tree and Tiger

KM#	Date	Mintage	VF	XF	Unc
68	1993	*.010	—	Proof	50.00

Protect Our World - Rain Forest

KM#	Date	Mintage	VF	XF	Unc
69	1994	*.010	—	Proof	50.00

SERTUM

7.9800 g, .917 GOLD, .2352 oz AGW
Obv: Similar to 5 Sertums, KM#35.
Rev: 2 dragons around inner circle.

KM#	Date	Mintage	VF	XF	Unc
51	1979	1,000	—	—	135.00
	1979	1,000	—	Proof	160.00

9.8500 g, .950 PLATINUM, .3008 oz APW

KM#	Date	Mintage	VF	XF	Unc
51a	1979	—	—	Proof	250.00

7.9900 g, .917 GOLD, .2356 oz AGW
75th Anniversary of Monarchy

KM#	Date	Mintage	VF	XF	Unc
56	1982(1983)	1,000	—	—	150.00
	1982(1983)	1,000	—	Proof	175.00

2 SERTUMS

15.9800 g, .917 GOLD, .4711 oz AGW
Obv: Similar to 5 Sertums, KM#35.
Rev: 2 dragons around inner circle.

KM#	Date	Mintage	VF	XF	Unc
52	1979	1,000	—	—	235.00
	1979	1,000	—	Proof	300.00

19.7000 g, .950 PLATINUM, .6017 oz APW

KM#	Date	Mintage	VF	XF	Unc
52a	1979	—	—	Proof	500.00

15.9800 g, .917 GOLD, .4711 oz AGW
International Year of Disabled Persons

KM#	Date	Mintage	VF	XF	Unc
60	1981	—	—	—	700.00
	1981	—	—	Proof	900.00

5 SERTUMS

39.9400 g, .917 GOLD, 1.1776 oz AGW
Obv: Similar to 5 Sertums, KM#35.
Rev: 2 dragons around inner circle.

KM#	Date	Mintage	VF	XF	Unc
53	1979	1,000	—	—	620.00
	1979	1,000	—	Proof	700.00

49.2000 g, .950 PLATINUM, 1.5022 oz APW

KM#	Date	Mintage	VF	XF	Unc
53a	1979	—	—	Proof	1000.

7.7760 g, .5833 GOLD, .1458 oz AGW
Endangered Wildlife - Crane

KM#	Date	Mintage	VF	XF	Unc
64	1992	—	—	Proof	125.00

1992 Olympics - Archer

KM#	Date	Mintage	VF	XF	Unc
70	1993	*3,000	—	Proof	150.00

Soccer - World Cup '94

KM#	Date	Mintage	VF	XF	Unc
71	1993	*2,000	—	Proof	150.00

MINT SETS (MS)

KM#	Date	Mintage	Identification	Issue Price	Mkt. Val.
MS1	1966(3)	300	KM33-35	175.00	850.00
MS2	1974(2)	—	KM39,42	4.00	11.50
MS3	1974(4)	—	KM37-38,40-41	6.00	3.00
MS4	1979(3)	1,000	KM51-53	1575.	950.00

PROOF SETS (PS)

KM#	Date	Mintage	Identification	Issue Price	Mkt. Val.
PS1	1966(4)	6,000	KM29-32	11.50	7.50
PS2	1966(3)	598	KM33-35	300.00	1375.
PS3	1966(3)	72	KM33a-35a	685.00	2500.
PS4	1974(6)	1,000	KM37-42	18.00	65.00
PS5	1975(5)	—	KM37,40-41,43-44	—	Rare
PS6	1979(5)	.020	KM45-49	30.00	15.00
PS7	1979(3)	1,000	KM51-53	2100.	1150.
PS8	1979(3)	—	KM51a-53a	2400.	1750.

Listings For

BIAFRA: refer to Nigeria

BOHEMIA & MORAVIA

Bohemia, a province in western Czechoslovakia, was combined with the majority of Moravia in central Czechoslovakia (excluding parts of north and south Moravia which were joined with Silesia in 1938) to form the German protectorate in March, 1939, after the German invasion. Toward the end of war in 1945 the protectorate was dissolved and Bohemia and Moravia once again became part of Czechoslovakia.

MONETARY SYSTEM

100 Haleru = 1 Koruna

10 HALERU

ZINC

KM#	Date	Mintage	Fine	VF	XF	Unc
1	1940	82.114	.25	.50	.75	2.50
	1941	Inc. Ab.	.25	.50	.75	3.50
	1942	Inc. Ab.	.25	.50	.75	3.50
	1943	Inc. Ab.	.50	.75	1.50	4.50
	1944	Inc. Ab.	.75	1.50	2.50	5.50

20 HALERU

ZINC

KM#	Date	Mintage	Fine	VF	XF	Unc
2	1940	106.526	.25	.50	1.00	3.50
	1941	Inc. Ab.	.25	.50	1.00	3.50
	1942	Inc. Ab.	.25	.50	1.00	3.50
	1943	Inc. Ab.	.50	.75	1.50	4.50
	1944	Inc. Ab.	.50	1.00	1.75	4.00

50 HALERU

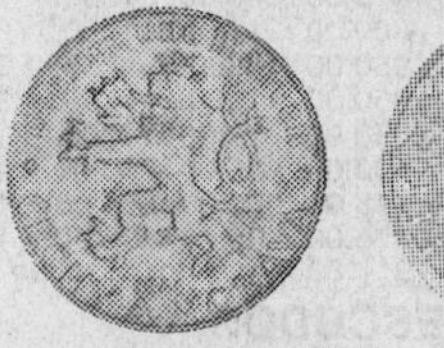 

ZINC

KM#	Date	Mintage	Fine	VF	XF	Unc
3	1940	53.270	.35	.75	1.25	5.00
	1941	Inc. Ab.	.35	.75	1.25	5.00
	1942	Inc. Ab.	.35	.75	1.25	5.00
	1943	Inc. Ab.	.75	1.50	3.00	7.00
	1944	Inc. Ab.	.35	.75	1.25	5.00

KORUNA

ZINC

KM#	Date	Mintage	Fine	VF	XF	Unc
4	1941	102.817	.50	.75	1.50	5.00
	1942	Inc. Ab.	.50	.75	1.50	5.00
	1943	Inc. Ab.	.50	.75	1.50	5.00
	1944	Inc. Ab.	.50	.75	1.50	5.00

BOLIVIA

The Republic of Bolivia, a landlocked country in westcentral South America, has an area of 424,165 sq. mi. (1,098,580 sq. km.) and a population of 6.6 million. Its capitals are: La Paz (administrative) and Sucre (constitutional). Principal exports are tin, zinc, antimony, tungsten, petroleum, natural gas, cotton and coffee.

Much of present day Bolivia was first dominated by the Tiahuanaco Culture ca.400 BC. It had in turn been incorporated into the Inca Empire by 1440AD prior to the arrival of the Spanish, in 1535, who reduced the Indian population to virtual slavery. When Joseph Napoleon was placed upon the throne of occupied Spain in 1809, a fervor of revolutionary activity quickened throughout Alto Peru - culminating in the 1809 Proclamation of Liberty. Sixteen bloody years of struggle ensued before the republic, named for the famed liberator Simon Bolivar, was established on August 6, 1825. Since then Bolivia has suffered through more than 16 constitutions, 69 Presidents and 160 revolutions.

The Imperial City of Potosi, founded by Villaroel in 1546, was established in the midst of what is estimated to have been the world's richest silver mines (having produced in excess of 2 billion dollars worth of silver). While production at the "Casa de Moneda" was enormous, the quality of the coinage was at times so poor that some 50 were condemned to death by their superiors.

Most pre-decimal coinage of independent Bolivia carries the assayers' initials on the reverse near the rim to the right of the date, in 4 to 5 o'clock position. The mint mark or name appears in the 7 to 8 o'clock area.

RULERS

Spanish until 1825

MINT MARKS

A - Paris
(a) - Paris, privy marks only
CHI - Valcambia
H - Heaton
KN - Kings' Norton
PTA monogram - La Plata
OR monogram - Oruro
PAZ - La Paz
P or PTS monogram - Potosi
So - Santiago

ASSAYERS INITIALS

Letter	Date	Name
F	1815	Francisco Jose de Matos
F	1830,1848-1867	Fortunato Equivar
FE	1867-1890	Fortunato Equivar
J	1825-1832	Juan Palomo y Sierra
J	1813-?	Jose Antonio de Sierra
J	1853-1862	Joaquin Zemborain
L	1825-26	Leandro Osio
L	1825,1830-1843	Luis de Aguilar
M	1826-1829,1833-1839	Digo Miguel Lopez
M	1848-1855	Manuel Berrios
P	1776-1802	Pedro de Mazondo
P	1795-1824	Pedro Martin de Albizu
R	1839-1847	Rafael Mariano Bustillo
R	1848	Manuel Telesforo Ramires

NOTE: These names are based on data put forth by Dr. E.A. Sellschopp in *Las Acunaciones de las Cecas de Lima, La Plata Y Potosi*, J. Pelliceri Bru in *Glosario de Maestros de Ceca y Ensayadores* and archival research in the Casa Moneda Nacional de Bolivia.

COLONIAL MILLED COINAGE

1/4 REAL

.8460 g, .896 SILVER, .0243 oz ASW
Mint mark: PTS monogram
Obv: Castle. Rev: Lion.

KM#	Date	Mintage	VG	Fine	VF	XF
82	1801	—	15.00	35.00	75.00	210.00
	1802	—	7.50	12.50	20.00	50.00
	1803	—	10.00	15.00	30.00	65.00
	1804	—	20.00	50.00	150.00	315.00
	1805	—	20.00	50.00	150.00	315.00
	1806	—	7.50	12.50	32.50	60.00
	1807	—	12.50	25.00	50.00	130.00
	1808	—	7.50	12.50	20.00	60.00
	1809	—	10.00	20.00	60.00	160.00

NOTE: There is a variety of 1802 with base of 2 not struck up and frequently miscataloged as 1809.

NOTE: Earlier dates (1796-1800) exist for this type.

1/2 REAL

1.6921 g, .896 SILVER, .0487 oz ASW
Mint mark: PTS monogram
Carolus IIII

KM#	Date	Mintage	VG	Fine	VF	XF
69	1801 PP	—	4.00	7.00	16.00	30.00
	1802 PP	—	4.00	7.00	16.00	30.00
	1803 PJ	—	4.00	7.00	16.00	30.00
	1804 PJ	—	4.00	7.00	16.00	30.00
	1805 PJ	—	4.00	7.00	16.00	30.00
	1806 PJ	—	4.00	7.00	16.00	30.00
	1807 PJ	—	4.00	7.00	16.00	30.00
	1808/7 PJ	—	4.00	7.00	16.00	30.00
	1808 PJ	—	4.00	7.00	16.00	30.00
	1809 PJ	—	20.00	32.50	45.00	85.00

NOTE: Earlier dates (1791-1800) exist for this type.

Ferdinand VII

KM#	Date	Mintage	VG	Fine	VF	XF
90	1814 PJ	—	12.50	20.00	75.00	100.00
	1815 PJ	—	10.00	17.50	70.00	100.00
	1816 PJ	—	4.00	8.00	35.00	55.00
	1817 PJ	—	4.00	7.00	18.50	35.00
	1818 PJ	—	3.50	6.00	17.50	35.00
	1819 PJ	—	3.50	6.00	17.50	35.00
	1820 PJ	—	3.50	6.00	17.50	35.00
	1821 PJ	—	3.50	6.00	17.50	35.00
	1822 PJ	—	3.50	6.00	17.50	35.00
	1823 PJ	—	7.50	15.00	27.50	55.00
	1823 JL	—	3.50	6.00	20.00	50.00
	1824 PJ	—	3.50	6.00	17.50	35.00
	1825 JL	—	3.50	6.00	17.50	35.00

REAL

3.3841 g, .896 SILVER, .0975 oz ASW
Mint mark: PTS monogram
Obv. leg: CAROLUS IIII. . . .
Rev: Pillars.

KM#	Date	Mintage	VG	Fine	VF	XF
70	1801 PP	—	4.50	7.00	14.00	40.00
	1802 PP	—	4.50	8.00	16.50	50.00
	1803 PP	—	5.50	9.00	27.50	65.00
	1803 PJ	—	4.50	7.00	16.00	40.00
	1804 PJ	—	4.50	7.00	14.00	30.00
	1805 PJ	—	4.50	8.00	16.50	45.00
	1806 PJ	—	4.50	8.00	16.50	45.00
	1807 PJ	—	4.50	8.00	16.50	45.00
	1808 PJ	—	4.50	7.00	16.00	40.00
	1808/9 PJ	—	20.00	35.00	65.00	140.00
	1809 PJ	—	25.00	45.00	85.00	115.00

NOTE: Earlier dates (1791-1800) exist for this type.

Obv. leg: FERDIN. VII. . . ., bust.

KM#	Date	Mintage	VG	Fine	VF	XF
87	1813 PJ	—	7.00	12.00	27.50	45.00
	1816 PJ	—	4.50	7.00	14.00	28.00
	1817 PJ	—	4.50	7.00	14.00	28.00
	1818 PJ	—	4.50	7.00	14.00	28.00
	1819 PJ	—	4.50	7.00	14.00	28.00
	1820 PJ	—	4.50	7.00	14.00	28.00
	1821 PJ	—	4.50	7.00	14.00	28.00
	1822 PJ	—	4.50	7.00	14.00	28.00
	1823 PJ	—	4.50	7.00	14.00	28.00
	1824 PJ	—	4.50	7.00	14.00	28.00
	1825 JL	—	4.50	7.00	14.00	28.00

2 REALES

6.7682 g, .896 SILVER, .1950 oz ASW
Mint mark: PTS monogram
Obv. leg: CAROLUS IIII. . . ., bust.
Rev: Pillars.

KM#	Date	Mintage	VG	Fine	VF	XF
71	1801 PP	—	4.50	8.00	22.50	45.00
	1802 PP	—	4.50	8.00	22.50	45.00
	1803/2 PJ	—	4.50	8.00	25.00	65.00
	1803 PJ	—	4.50	8.00	22.50	45.00
	1804 PJ	—	4.50	8.00	22.50	45.00
	1805 PJ	—	4.50	8.00	22.50	45.00
	1806 PJ	—	4.50	8.00	22.50	45.00
	1807 PJ	—	4.50	8.00	22.50	45.00
	1808 PJ	—	4.50	8.00	22.50	45.00

NOTE: Earlier dates (1791-1800) exist for this type.

Obv. leg: FERDIN VII. . . ., bust.

KM#	Date	Mintage	VG	Fine	VF	XF
83	1808 PJ	—	12.00	17.50	45.00	70.00
	1809 PJ	—	4.50	9.00	28.00	45.00
	1813 PJ	—	4.50	9.00	28.00	45.00
	1814 PJ	—	4.50	9.00	28.00	45.00
	1816 PJ	—	4.50	9.00	28.00	50.00
	1817 PJ	—	4.50	9.00	28.00	50.00
	1818 PJ	—	4.50	9.00	28.00	50.00
	1819 PJ	—	4.50	9.00	28.00	45.00
	1820 PJ	—	4.50	9.00	28.00	50.00
	1821 PJ	—	4.50	9.00	28.00	45.00
	1822 PJ	—	4.50	9.00	28.00	45.00
	1823 PJ	—	4.50	9.00	28.00	45.00
	1824 PJ	—	4.50	9.00	28.00	45.00
	1825 PJ	—	9.00	27.50	55.00	115.00
	1825 J	—	27.50	55.00	165.00	275.00
	1825 JL	—	12.50	17.50	45.00	85.00

4 REALES

13.5365 g, .896 SILVER, .3900 oz ASW
Mint mark: PTS monogram
Obv. leg: CAROLUS IIII. . . . ., bust.

KM#	Date	Mintage	VG	Fine	VF	XF
72	1801 PP	—	15.00	25.00	45.00	90.00
	1802 PP	—	17.50	30.00	50.00	90.00
	1803 PJ	—	17.50	30.00	50.00	90.00
	1804 PJ	—	17.50	30.00	50.00	90.00
	1805 PJ	—	30.00	50.00	75.00	100.00
	1806/5 PJ	—	23.50	37.50	65.00	100.00
	1806 PJ	—	15.00	25.00	50.00	90.00
	1807 PJ	—	15.00	25.00	50.00	90.00
	1808 PJ	—	15.00	25.00	50.00	90.00
	1808/9 PJ	—	15.00	25.00	50.00	90.00
	1809 PJ	—	30.00	50.00	75.00	150.00

NOTE: Earlier dates (1791-1800) exist for this type.

Ferdinand VII

KM#	Date	Mintage	VG	Fine	VF	XF
88	1813 PJ	—	—	Reported, not confirmed		
	1814 PJ	—	—	Reported, not confirmed		
	1815 PJ	—	—	Reported, not confirmed		
	1816 PJ	—	17.50	30.00	50.00	90.00
	1817 PJ	—	17.50	30.00	50.00	90.00
	1818 PJ	—	20.00	35.00	60.00	100.00
	1819 PJ	—	20.00	35.00	60.00	100.00
	1820 PJ	—	20.00	35.00	60.00	100.00
	1821 PJ	—	30.00	50.00	75.00	125.00
	1822 PJ	—	20.00	35.00	60.00	100.00
	1823 PJ	—	17.50	30.00	50.00	90.00
	1824 PJ	—	30.00	50.00	75.00	125.00
	1825 PJ	—	225.00	350.00	475.00	650.00
	1825 J	—	175.00	275.00	375.00	500.00
	1825 JL	—	15.00	25.00	50.00	90.00

8 REALES

27.0730 g, .896 SILVER, .7799 oz ASW
Mint mark: PTS monogram

KM#	Date	Mintage	VG	Fine	VF	XF
73.1	1801 PP	—	20.00	35.00	70.00	140.00
	1802 PP	—	20.00	35.00	70.00	140.00
	1803 PJ	—	20.00	35.00	70.00	140.00
	1804 PJ	—	20.00	35.00	70.00	140.00
	1805 PJ	—	20.00	35.00	70.00	140.00
	1806/5 PJ	—	25.00	45.00	95.00	180.00
	1806 PJ	—	20.00	35.00	70.00	140.00
	1807 PJ	—	20.00	35.00	70.00	140.00
	1808 PJ	—	20.00	35.00	70.00	140.00

NOTE: Earlier dates (1791-1800) exist for this type.

KM#	Date	Mintage	VG	Fine	VF	XF
84	1808 PJ	—	25.00	40.00	70.00	175.00
	1809 PJ	—	25.00	40.00	70.00	135.00
	1813 PJ	—	20.00	30.00	50.00	100.00
	1814/13 PJ	—	22.00	45.00	90.00	185.00
	1814 PJ	—	20.00	35.00	70.00	110.00
	1815 PJ	—	20.00	35.00	70.00	110.00
	1816 PJ	—	20.00	35.00	70.00	110.00
	1817 PJ	—	20.00	35.00	70.00	110.00
	1818 PJ	—	20.00	35.00	70.00	110.00
	1819 PJ	—	20.00	35.00	70.00	110.00
	1820 PJ	—	20.00	35.00	70.00	110.00
	1821 PJ	—	20.00	35.00	70.00	110.00
	1822 PJ	—	20.00	35.00	70.00	110.00
	1823/2 PJ	—	50.00	95.00	175.00	350.00
	1823 PJ	—	20.00	35.00	70.00	110.00
	1823 JP	—	25.00	35.00	75.00	175.00
	1824 PJ	—	40.00	65.00	100.00	200.00
	1824 J	—	200.00	350.00	650.00	1250.
	1825 J	—	75.00	150.00	275.00	550.00
	1825 JL	—	20.00	27.50	40.00	75.00

NOTE: 1825 JL are also struck with coin rotation.

Obv. leg: FERDIN IIV (error). . . . .

KM#	Date	Mintage	VG	Fine	VF	XF
89	1813 PJ	—	250.00	450.00	750.00	1200.

ESCUDO

3.3841 g, .875 GOLD, .0952 oz AGW
Mint mark: PTS monogram
Obv. leg: CAROL IIII. . . ., bust.
Rev: Similar to 2 Escudos, KM#79.

KM#	Date	Mintage	VG	Fine	VF	XF
78	1801 PP	—	150.00	200.00	275.00	475.00
	1802 PP	—	150.00	200.00	275.00	475.00
	1803 PJ	—	150.00	200.00	275.00	600.00
	1804 PJ	—	150.00	200.00	275.00	600.00
	1805 PJ	—	150.00	200.00	275.00	600.00
	1806 PJ	—	150.00	200.00	275.00	600.00
	1807 PJ	—	150.00	200.00	275.00	600.00
	1808 PJ	—	150.00	200.00	275.00	600.00

NOTE: Earlier dates (1791-1800) exist for this type.

Obv. leg: FERDIN VII. . . . .

KM#	Date	Mintage	VG	Fine	VF	XF
92	1822 PJ	—	200.00	300.00	450.00	1200.
	1823 PJ	—	250.00	400.00	650.00	1450.
	1824 PJ	—	300.00	500.00	800.00	1750.

2 ESCUDOS

6.7682 g, .875 GOLD, .1904 oz AGW
Mint mark: PTS monogram
Obv. leg: CAROL IIII. . . . .

KM#	Date	Mintage	VG	Fine	VF	XF
79	1801 PP	—	250.00	400.00	525.00	1000.
	1802 PP	—	400.00	550.00	700.00	1300.
	1804 PJ	—	250.00	400.00	525.00	1050.
	1805 PJ	—	325.00	475.00	700.00	1300.
	1806 PJ	—	400.00	550.00	800.00	1300.
	1807 PJ	—	250.00	350.00	525.00	850.00
	1808 PJ	—	325.00	475.00	700.00	1100.

NOTE: Earlier dates (1791-1800) exist for this type.

4 ESCUDOS

13.5365 g, .875 GOLD, .3808 oz AGW
Mint mark: PTS monogram
Obv. leg: CAROL IIII. . . ., bust. Rev: Arms.

KM#	Date	Mintage	VG	Fine	VF	XF
80	1801 PP	—	400.00	525.00	875.00	1900.
	1802 PP	—	475.00	600.00	1000.	1650.
	1803 PP	—	800.00	1100.	1600.	3200.
	1804 PJ	—	950.00	1300.	1750.	3200.
	1804 PP	—	950.00	1300.	1750.	3200.
	1805 PJ	—	550.00	725.00	1000.	1800.
	1806 PJ	—	400.00	525.00	800.00	1800.
	1807 PJ	—	475.00	600.00	875.00	1800.
	1808 PJ	—	475.00	600.00	875.00	1800.

NOTE: Earlier dates (1791-1800) exist for this type.

8 ESCUDOS

27.0730 g, .875 GOLD, .7616 oz AGW
Mint mark: PTS monogram
Obv. leg: CAROL IIII. . . .

KM#	Date	Mintage	VG	Fine	VF	XF
81	1801 PP	—	375.00	450.00	675.00	1100.
	1802 PP	—	375.00	450.00	675.00	1100.
	1803 PJ	—	375.00	450.00	675.00	1100.
	1804 PJ	—	375.00	450.00	675.00	1100.
	1805 PJ	—	375.00	450.00	675.00	1100.
	1806 PJ	—	375.00	450.00	675.00	1100.
	1807 PJ	—	375.00	450.00	675.00	1100.
	1808 PJ	—	375.00	450.00	675.00	1100.

NOTE: Earlier dates (1741-1800) exist for this type.

Obv. leg: FERDIN VII. . . ., uniformed bust.

KM#	Date	Mintage	VG	Fine	VF	XF
86	1809 PJ	—	—	Reported, not confirmed		

Obv. leg: FERDIN. VII. . . .

KM#	Date	Mintage	VG	Fine	VF	XF
91	1817 PJ	—	675.00	900.00	1650.	4800.
	1822 PJ	—	375.00	450.00	675.00	1100.
	1823 PJ	—	500.00	750.00	1250.	3600.
	1824 PJ	—	400.00	550.00	1000.	1800.

REPUBLIC

MONETARY SYSTEM

8 Soles = 1 Peso
16 Soles = 1 Scudo

1/4 SOL

.8500 g, .667 SILVER, .0182 oz ASW
Obv: Llama in plain field, POTOSI below.

KM#	Date	Mintage	VG	Fine	VF	XF
111	1852	—	6.00	12.00	28.00	55.00

Obv: Branches flank Llama.

KM#	Date	Mintage	VG	Fine	VF	XF
117	1853	—	15.00	40.00	65.00	100.00

NOTE: The values above are for holed coins, unholed specimens command a premium of 1-1/2 to 2 times these figures.

1/2 SOL

1.5000 g, .903 SILVER, .0435 oz ASW
Mint mark: PTS monogram
Rev. leg. ends: . . . . CONSTITUCI; 6 pointed stars in field.

KM#	Date	Mintage	VG	Fine	VF	XF
93.1	1827 JM	—	2.50	4.00	7.50	27.00
	1828/7 JM	—	3.00	5.00	8.00	27.50

Rev. leg. ends: . . . . CONSTITUC.

KM#	Date	Mintage	VG	Fine	VF	XF
93.2	1828/7 JM	—	3.50	7.50	12.50	35.00
	1828 JM	—	1.50	3.00	5.00	22.50
	1829 JM	—	2.00	3.50	6.00	22.50

1.5000 g, .667 SILVER, .0322 oz ASW

KM#	Date	Mintage	VG	Fine	VF	XF
93.2a	1830 J close legend					
		—	2.50	4.00	7.50	27.00
	1830 J spaced legend					
		—	2.50	4.00	7.50	27.00
	1830 JF	—	2.50	4.00	7.00	25.00
	1830 JL wide date & large star					
		—	1.00	2.00	3.50	18.00
	1830 JL narrow date & small star					
		—	1.00	2.00	3.50	18.00
	1830 JL (error) CONSTITU(C/.)					
		—	2.50	5.00	9.00	35.00

Rev: 5 pointed stars in field.

KM#	Date	Mintage	VG	Fine	VF	XF
93.3	1830 JL	—	6.00	12.00	28.00	55.00

NOTE: Believed to have been struck after 1853.

Obv: W/o denomination.
Rev: BOLIVAR on truncation.

KM#	Date	Mintage	VG	Fine	VF	XF
118.1	1853 FP	—	2.50	5.00	10.00	28.00
118.1	1853 FP inverted A for V in BOLIVIANA					
		—	3.00	6.00	12.00	35.00
	1854 MJ	—	2.00	3.00	6.00	18.00
	1854 MJ	*	2.50	4.00	7.50	20.00
	1855 MJ	—	2.50	5.00	10.00	28.00
	1856 FJ	—	3.00	5.00	10.00	30.00
	1856 MJ	—	5.00	6.50	11.50	35.00

***NOTE:** Inverted A for V and inverted V for first A in BOLIVIANA for 1854 MJ.

Obv: Denomination added.

KM#	Date	Mintage	VG	Fine	VF	XF
118.2	1856 FJ	—	3.00	5.50	10.00	22.50
	1857/6 FJ	—	3.50	7.00	11.00	25.00
	1857 FJ	—	1.50	3.50	7.50	20.00
	1858/7 FJ	—	2.50	5.50	9.50	22.00
	1858 FJ	—	2.50	5.50	10.00	22.50

NOTE: Varieties exist w/and w/o period after CONSTITUCION.

Rev: BOLIVAR below truncation.

KM#	Date	Mintage	VG	Fine	VF	XF
118.3	1859 FJ	—	8.00	12.00	30.00	70.00
	1859 (error) BOLIVRA					
		—	11.00	17.50	45.00	100.00

Mint mark: PAZ
Rev: Crude "La Paz style" head.

KM#	Date	Mintage	VG	Fine	VF	XF
127	1855 P	—	7.50	12.50	25.00	65.00
	1856/5 P	—	10.00	15.00	30.00	75.00
	1856 P	—	7.50	12.50	25.00	65.00

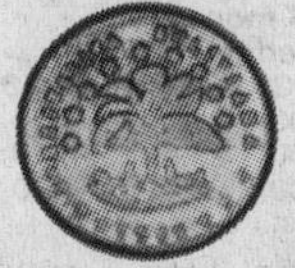

Rev: Crude so-called "ugly head".

KM#	Date	Mintage	VG	Fine	VF	XF
132	1858/7 P	—	10.00	17.50	40.00	80.00
	1858 P	—	8.00	15.00	35.00	70.00
	1859 P	—	12.00	20.00	55.00	100.00

1.3000 g, .667 SILVER, .0279 oz ASW
Mint mark: PTS monogram
Rev. weight: PESO 25 Gs.

KM#	Date	Mintage	VG	Fine	VF	XF
133.1	1859 FJ	—	5.00	10.00	25.00	45.00

1.3000 g, .903 SILVER, .0377 oz ASW
Rev. weight: 25 G.

KM#	Date	Mintage	VG	Fine	VF	XF
133.2	1859 FJ	—	5.00	7.50	15.00	65.00
	1860 FJ	—	5.00	7.50	15.00	45.00
	1861 FJ	—	5.00	7.50	15.00	45.00
	1862 FP	—	5.00	7.50	15.00	60.00
	1863 FP	—	5.00	7.50	15.00	45.00

SOL

3.0000 g, .903 SILVER, .0871 oz ASW
Mint mark: PTS monogram

KM#	Date	Mintage	VG	Fine	VF	XF
94	1827 JM	—	6.00	12.00	28.00	50.00
	1828 JM	—	6.00	12.00	28.00	50.00
	1829 JM	—	5.00	10.00	22.00	45.00

3.0000 g, .667 SILVER, .0643 oz ASW

KM#	Date	Mintage	VG	Fine	VF	XF
94a	1830 J	—	5.00	10.00	20.00	40.00
	1830 JL	—	3.50	5.00	7.50	20.00

2.60-3.60 g, .667 SILVER, .056-.077 oz ASW
Mint mark: Oruro monogram
Obv. leg: . . . . .SOCABON.

KM#	Date	Mintage	VG	Fine	VF	XF
85.1	1849 JM	—	40.00	60.00	90.00	200.00

Obv. leg: . . . . .SOCN.

KM#	Date	Mintage	VG	Fine	VF	XF
85.2	1849 JM	—	40.00	60.00	90.00	200.00

NOTE: The prices above are for holed coins, unholed specimens command a substantial premium.

3.0000 g, .667 SILVER, .0643 oz ASW
Obv: W/o denomination.
Rev: BOLIVAR on truncation.

KM#	Date	Mintage	VG	Fine	VF	XF
119.1	1853 FP	—	4.00	6.00	12.00	28.00
	1853 FP (error) BOLIVLANA					
		—	6.00	12.00	25.00	55.00
	1854 MJ	—	5.00	7.50	15.00	40.00

Obv: Denomination added.

KM#	Date	Mintage	VG	Fine	VF	XF
119.2	1855 MJ	—	4.00	8.00	15.00	35.00
	1856/5 FJ/MJ					
		—	5.00	12.00	27.50	55.00
	1856 FJ	—	4.00	8.00	15.00	35.00
	1857/6 FJ	—	6.00	12.00	27.50	55.00
	1857 FJ	—	4.00	8.00	15.00	35.00
	1858/7 FJ	—	6.00	12.00	27.50	55.00
	1858 FJ	—	4.00	8.00	15.00	35.00

Rev: BOLIVAR below truncation.

KM#	Date	Mintage	VG	Fine	VF	XF
119.3	1859	—	13.50	20.00	45.00	70.00

Mint mark: PAZ
Rev: "Potosi style" laureate head.

KM#	Date	Mintage	VG	Fine	VF	XF
120	1855 P	—	10.00	17.50	35.00	65.00
	1855 F	—	10.00	17.50	35.00	65.00

Rev: Crude "La Paz style" head.

KM#	Date	Mintage	VG	Fine	VF	XF
128	1855 F	—	20.00	50.00	75.00	130.00
	1856 P	—	15.00	25.00	45.00	75.00

Rev: Crude so-called "ugly head".

KM#	Date	Mintage	VG	Fine	VF	XF
131	1857 P	—	15.00	25.00	60.00	90.00
	1858/7 PAZ	—	20.00	30.00	65.00	100.00
	1858 P	—	15.00	25.00	55.00	80.00
	1859/7 P	—	20.00	30.00	70.00	110.00
	1859 P	—	15.00	25.00	50.00	80.00

2.5000 g, .667 SILVER, .0536 oz ASW
Mint mark: PTS monogram
Rev. weight: PESO 50 Gs.

KM#	Date	Mintage	VG	Fine	VF	XF
134.1	1859 FJ	—	10.00	15.00	35.00	70.00
	1859 FJ (error) REP(U/B)BLICA					
		—	15.00	25.00	50.00	100.00

2.5000 g, .903 SILVER, .0726 oz ASW
Rev. weight: 50 G or 50 Gs.

KM#	Date	Mintage	VG	Fine	VF	XF
134.2	1860 FJ	—	3.00	5.00	7.50	15.00
	1860 F/JJ	—	4.00	6.00	10.00	20.00
	1861 FJ	—	3.00	5.00	7.50	15.00
	1862/1 FP	—	4.00	6.00	10.00	20.00
	1862 FJ	—	4.00	6.00	10.00	20.00
	1862 FP	—	3.00	5.00	7.50	15.00
	1863/2 FP	—	4.00	6.00	10.00	20.00
	1863 FP	—	3.00	5.00	7.50	15.00

2 SOLES

6.2000 g, .903 SILVER, .1799 oz ASW
Mint mark: PTS monogram

KM#	Date	Mintage	VG	Fine	VF	XF
95	1827 JM	—	8.00	15.00	35.00	65.00
	1828/7 JM	—	25.00	40.00	65.00	115.00
	1828 JM	—	5.00	7.50	15.00	32.00
	1829 JM	—	12.50	20.00	35.00	60.00

6.2000 g, .667 SILVER, .1324 oz ASW

KM#	Date	Mintage	VG	Fine	VF	XF
95a	1830/27 J	—	20.00	35.00	45.00	90.00
	1830 J	—	6.00	10.00	15.00	32.00
	1830 JF	—	10.00	18.00	27.50	55.00
	1830 JL	—	5.00	7.50	12.50	25.00
	1831 J	—	—	—	Rare	—

Obv: W/o denomination.

KM#	Date	Mintage	VG	Fine	VF	XF
121.1	1853 FP	—	20.00	35.00	70.00	110.00

Obv: Denomination added.

KM#	Date	Mintage	VG	Fine	VF	XF
121.2	1854 MJ	—	5.00	10.00	32.00	60.00
	1855 MJ	—	5.00	10.00	32.00	60.00
	1856 FJ	—	7.50	12.50	40.00	80.00
	1856/5 MJ	—	7.50	12.50	40.00	80.00
	1857 MJ	—	7.50	12.50	40.00	80.00
	1857 FJ	—	5.00	10.00	32.00	60.00
	1858 FJ	—	7.50	12.50	40.00	80.00

Rev: BOLIVAR below truncation.

KM#	Date	Mintage	VG	Fine	VF	XF
121.3	1859/7 FJ	—	15.00	25.00	50.00	100.00
	1859 FJ	—	15.00	25.00	50.00	100.00

Mint mark: PAZ
Rev: Bare head

KM#	Date	Mintage	VG	Fine	VF	XF
122	1853 J	—	500.00	750.00	1000.	1500.

Rev: "Potosi style" laureate head.

KM#	Date	Mintage	VG	Fine	VF	XF
126	1854 F	—	80.00	150.00	260.00	450.00

Rev: Crude "La Paz style" head.

KM#	Date	Mintage	VG	Fine	VF	XF
129	1855 F	4 known	75.00	150.00	250.00	425.00
	1856 P	10 known	75.00	150.00	250.00	400.00

Mint mark: PTS monogram
Rev. weight: PESO 100 Gs.

KM#	Date	Mintage	VG	Fine	VF	XF
135.1	1859 FJ	—	20.00	40.00	80.00	150.00

4.5000 g, .903 SILVER, .1306 oz ASW
Rev. weight: 100 Gs.

KM#	Date	Mintage	VG	Fine	VF	XF
135.2	1859 FJ	—	—	Reported, not confirmed		
	1860 FJ	—	5.00	8.00	12.50	25.00
	1861 FJ	—	7.50	12.50	20.00	35.00
	1862/1 FJ	—	6.00	9.00	15.00	30.00
	1862 FJ	—	5.00	8.00	12.50	25.00
	1862/1 FP	—	5.00	8.00	12.50	25.00
	1862 FP	—	4.00	7.00	10.00	20.00
	1863/2 FP	—	7.50	12.50	20.00	35.00
	1863 FP	—	5.00	8.00	12.50	25.00

4 SOLES

13.5000 g, .903 SILVER, .3918 oz ASW
Mint mark: PTS monogram
Reeded edge,
incuse lettering: AYACUCHO * SUCRE *1824*.

KM#	Date	Mintage	VG	Fine	VF	XF
96	1827 JM	—	12.00	25.00	50.00	85.00
	1828 JM	—	12.00	25.00	50.00	85.00
	1829 JM	—	12.00	25.00	50.00	85.00

NOTE: Many die varieties exist.

13.5000 g, .667 SILVER, .2895 oz ASW

KM#	Date	Mintage	VG	Fine	VF	XF
96a.1	1830 J	—	3.50	8.00	20.00	40.00
	1830/27 JL	—	3.50	8.00	20.00	40.00
	1830 JL	—	2.00	5.00	12.50	25.00

Additional PTS on island.

KM#	Date	Mintage	VG	Fine	VF	XF
96a.2	1830 JL	—	4.00	10.00	25.00	50.00
	1830/3 JL	—	7.00	20.00	50.00	110.00

Obv: W/o denomination

KM#	Date	Mintage	VG	Fine	VF	XF
123.1	1853 FP	—	4.00	10.00	25.00	50.00

Obv: Denomination added

KM#	Date	Mintage	VG	Fine	VF	XF
123.2	1853 MF	—	4.00	10.00	25.00	45.00
	1854 MF	—	4.00	10.00	25.00	45.00
	1854 MJ	—	4.00	10.00	25.00	45.00
	1855 MJ	—	4.00	10.00	25.00	45.00
	1855 MJ (error) CONSTITUCIN	—	6.00	15.00	35.00	55.00
	1855 FJ	—	8.00	20.00	40.00	60.00
	1856 FJ	—	4.00	10.00	25.00	45.00
	1856/5 MJ	—	4.00	10.00	25.00	45.00
	1856 MJ	—	4.00	10.00	25.00	45.00
	1857 FJ	—	4.00	10.00	25.00	45.00
	1857 FJ (error) V in BOLIVIANA inverted A	—	12.00	35.00	65.00	100.00
	1857/F FJ	—	8.00	20.00	35.00	55.00
	1857 FJ (error) CONSTITUCIO	—	8.00	20.00	35.00	55.00
	1858 FJ	—	8.00	20.00	35.00	55.00

Rev: BOLIVAR below truncation.

KM#	Date	Mintage	VG	Fine	VF	XF
123.3	1859 FJ	—	8.00	20.00	35.00	55.00
	1859 FJ (error) A in BOLIVAR inverted V	—	12.00	30.00	55.00	85.00

Mint mark: PAZ

KM#	Date	Mintage	VG	Fine	VF	XF
124.1	1853 J	—	60.00	100.00	175.00	275.00

Mint mark: LA PLATA monogram.

KM#	Date	Mintage	VG	Fine	VF	XF
124.2	1853 J	—	600.00	1200.	2100.	—

Rev: "Potosi style" laureate head.

KM#	Date	Mintage	VG	Fine	VF	XF
125	1853 J	—	15.00	35.00	60.00	120.00
	1854 J	—	—	Reported, not confirmed		
	1854 F	—	15.00	20.00	50.00	110.00
	1855 F	—	10.00	25.00	40.00	95.00

Rev: Crude "La Paz style" head.

KM#	Date	Mintage	VG	Fine	VF	XF
130	1855 F	—	12.50	20.00	35.00	80.00
	1856/5 P/F	—	15.00	25.00	45.00	90.00
	1856 P	—	12.50	20.00	35.00	80.00
	1857/6 P	—	30.00	45.00	65.00	95.00
	1857 P	—	100.00	200.00	300.00	500.00
	1858 P	—	100.00	200.00	300.00	500.00

NOTE: Varieties exist.

KM#	Date	Mintage	VG	Fine	VF	XF
136	1859 P	—	150.00	225.00	300.00	400.00

NOTE: Several distinct bust varieties exist.

13.5000 g, .903 SILVER, .3918 oz ASW
Mint mark: PTS monogram
W/o denomination, only weight indicated as 200 Gs.

KM#	Date	Mintage	VG	Fine	VF	XF
139	1860 FJ	—	30.00	50.00	65.00	100.00

8 SOLES

27.0000 g, .903 SILVER, .7836 oz ASW
Reeded edge,
incuse lettering: AYACUCHO*SUCRE *1824*.

KM#	Date	Mintage	VG	Fine	VF	XF
97	1827 JM	—	15.00	25.00	45.00	75.00
	1828 JM	—	15.00	25.00	45.00	75.00
	1829 JM	—	15.00	25.00	45.00	75.00
	1829 JM V in BOLIVIANA inverted A					
		—	30.00	50.00	225.00	350.00
	1830/20 JF	—	30.00	50.00	80.00	190.00
	1830 JF	—	15.00	25.00	45.00	75.00
	1830 JF/J	—	35.00	55.00	95.00	125.00
	1830 J	—	25.00	35.00	55.00	100.00
	1830 J V in BOLIVIANA inverted A					
		—	30.00	50.00	225.00	350.00
	1830 L	—	— Reported, not confirmed			
	1831 JF	—	15.00	25.00	45.00	75.00
	1831 JL	—	15.00	25.00	45.00	75.00
	1832 JL	—	15.00	25.00	45.00	75.00
	1833 L	—	150.00	225.00	325.00	450.00
	1833 LM	—	15.00	25.00	45.00	75.00
	1834 LM	—	15.00	25.00	45.00	75.00
	1835 LM	—	20.00	30.00	50.00	90.00
	1836/5 LM	—	20.00	30.00	50.00	90.00
	1836 LM	—	15.00	25.00	45.00	75.00
	1837 LM	—	15.00	25.00	45.00	75.00
	1838 LM	—	15.00	25.00	45.00	75.00
	1839 LM	—	15.00	25.00	45.00	75.00
	1839 LR	—	25.00	35.00	55.00	100.00
	1840/4 over inverted 4 LR					
		—	30.00	50.00	90.00	220.00
	1840 LR	—	15.00	25.00	45.00	75.00

NOTE: Varieties exist.

KM#	Date	Mintage	VG	Fine	VF	XF
103	1841 LR	—	15.00	25.00	45.00	75.00
103	1841 LR (error: CONSTITUCIN)					
		—	150.00	250.00	350.00	600.00
	1842 LR	—	15.00	25.00	45.00	75.00
	1843/2 LR	—	20.00	35.00	55.00	100.00
	1843 LR	—	17.50	30.00	50.00	80.00
	1844 R	—	17.50	30.00	50.00	80.00
	1845 R	—	15.00	25.00	45.00	75.00
	1846/5 R	—	25.00	45.00	75.00	155.00
	1846 R	—	17.50	30.00	50.00	80.00
	1847 R	—	17.50	30.00	50.00	80.00
	1848 R	—	50.00	100.00	200.00	300.00
	1848 M	—	—	—	Rare	—
	1848 M/R	—	—	—	Rare	—

NOTE: Varieties exist. Some dates struck in medal rotation.

Obv: w/o denomination. Rev: Bare head.

KM#	Date	Mintage	VG	Fine	VF	XF
109	1848 FM lg. dt.					
		—	15.00	22.50	35.00	70.00
	1848 FM sm. dt.					
		—	15.00	22.50	35.00	70.00
	1849 FM	—	12.50	22.50	35.00	70.00
	1850 FM	—	10.00	20.00	32.50	65.00
	1851/50 FM	—	17.50	25.00	45.00	80.00
	1851 FM	—	10.00	20.00	32.50	65.00
	1851 FR	—	75.00	125.00	175.00	300.00

KM#	Date	Mintage	VG	Fine	VF	XF
112.1	1852 FM	—	17.50	25.00	45.00	90.00
	1853 FP	—	40.00	80.00	125.00	200.00
	1854 M	—	40.00	80.00	125.00	200.00
	1856 FJ	—	25.00	45.00	85.00	140.00

Obv: Denomination added. Rev: Laureate head.

KM#	Date	Mintage	VG	Fine	VF	XF
112.2	1854 MJ	—	17.50	27.50	50.00	90.00
	1855/4 MJ	—	17.50	25.00	50.00	90.00
	1855 MJ	—	12.50	20.00	35.00	75.00

NOTE: Varieties exist.

KM#	Date	Mintage	VG	Fine	VF	XF
137	1859 FJ	—	400.00	600.00	1250.	1750.

20.0000 g, .903 SILVER, .5807 oz ASW
Mint mark: PTS monogram
Rev. weight: Po 400 Gs.

KM#	Date	Mintage	VG	Fine	VF	XF
138.1 (138.3)	1859 FJ	—	1500.	2000.	2800.	—

Rev. weight: PESO/Po 400 Gs.

KM#	Date	Mintage	VG	Fine	VF	XF
138.2	1859 FJ	—	40.00	80.00	160.00	—

Rev. weight: PESO 400 Gs.

KM#	Date	Mintage	VG	Fine	VF	XF
138.3 (138.1)	1859 FJ	—	15.00	30.00	65.00	145.00

Rev. weight: 400 Gs.

KM#	Date	Mintage	VG	Fine	VF	XF
138.4	1859 FJ	—	150.00	250.00	500.00	900.00

Obv: Tree divides 10Ds-20Gs.
Rev. weight: Po 400 Gs.

KM#	Date	Mintage	VG	Fine	VF	XF
138.5	1860 FJ	—	300.00	500.00	1000.	1700.

Rev. weight: 400 Gs.

KM#	Date	Mintage	VG	Fine	VF	XF
138.6	1859 FJ	—	75.00	125.00	200.00	350.00
	1860 FJ small bust and stars					
		—	10.00	15.00	30.00	65.00
	1860 FJ large bust and stars					
		—	10.00	15.00	30.00	65.00
	1861 FJ	—	10.00	15.00	30.00	65.00
	1862/1 FJ	—	10.00	15.00	30.00	65.00
	1862 FJ	—	10.00	15.00	30.00	65.00
	1862 FP	—	10.00	15.00	30.00	65.00
	1863/2 FP	—	10.00	15.00	35.00	70.00
	1863 FP	—	10.00	15.00	35.00	70.00
	1863 FP (error) REPUBLICA BOLIVANA					
		—	50.00	110.00	250.00	500.00

NOTE: Varieties exist.

1/2 SCUDO

1.7000 g, .875 GOLD, .0478 oz AGW

KM#	Date	Mintage	VG	Fine	VF	XF
100	1834 LM	—	—	—	Rare	—
	1838 LM	—	80.00	140.00	210.00	400.00
	1839 LM	—	80.00	130.00	200.00	375.00
	1840 LR	—	80.00	140.00	210.00	400.00

KM#	Date	Mintage	VG	Fine	VF	XF
104	1841 LR/PL	—	65.00	85.00	120.00	200.00
	1841 LR	—	65.00	85.00	120.00	200.00
	1842 LR	—	65.00	85.00	120.00	200.00
	1842 LR (error) "BOLIAR" below bust					
		—	65.00	85.00	120.00	200.00
	1843 LR	—	65.00	85.00	120.00	200.00
	1844 R	—	65.00	85.00	120.00	200.00
	1845 R	—	65.00	85.00	120.00	200.00
	1846 R	—	65.00	85.00	120.00	200.00
	1847 R	—	65.00	85.00	120.00	200.00

KM#	Date	Mintage	Fine	VF	XF	Unc
113	1852/1 FP	—	110.00	185.00	300.00	600.00
	1852 MJ	—	100.00	165.00	250.00	450.00
	1852 FP	—	85.00	140.00	225.00	425.00
	1853 FP	—	85.00	140.00	225.00	425.00
	1854 FP	—	100.00	165.00	250.00	450.00
	1855 MF/FJ	—	85.00	140.00	225.00	425.00
	1855 FP	—	85.00	140.00	225.00	425.00
	1855 M	—	85.00	140.00	225.00	425.00
	1855 MJ	—	85.00	140.00	225.00	425.00
	1855 FS	—	85.00	140.00	225.00	425.00
	1856 FJ	—	85.00	140.00	225.00	425.00
	1856 FS	—	85.00	140.00	225.00	425.00
	1857 FP	—	225.00	385.00	550.00	900.00

1.2500 g, .900 GOLD, .0361 oz AGW

KM#	Date	Mintage	Fine	VF	XF	Unc
140	1868 FE	—	300.00	550.00	650.00	1000.

SCUDO

3.4000 g, .875 GOLD, .0956 oz AGW

KM#	Date	Mintage	VG	Fine	VF	XF
98	1831 JL	—	95.00	130.00	250.00	375.00
	1832 JL	—	95.00	130.00	250.00	350.00
	1833 JL	—	95.00	130.00	250.00	375.00
	1833 LM	—	95.00	130.00	250.00	375.00
	1834 JL	—	75.00	115.00	225.00	350.00
	1834 LM	—	95.00	130.00	250.00	375.00
	1835 LM	—	95.00	130.00	250.00	375.00
	1836 LM	—	95.00	130.00	250.00	375.00
	1837 LM	—	95.00	130.00	250.00	375.00
	1838 LM	—	95.00	130.00	250.00	375.00
	1839 LM	—	95.00	130.00	250.00	375.00
	1840 LR	—	125.00	175.00	325.00	500.00

KM#	Date	Mintage	VG	Fine	VF	XF
105	1841 LR	—	100.00	150.00	200.00	350.00
	1842 LR	—	100.00	150.00	200.00	350.00
	1846 R	—	100.00	150.00	200.00	350.00

KM#	Date	Mintage	Fine	VF	XF	Unc
114	1852 FP	—	100.00	150.00	225.00	400.00
	1853 FP	—	100.00	150.00	225.00	400.00

KM#	Date	Mintage	Fine	VF	XF	Unc
114	1855 LM/J	—	100.00	150.00	225.00	400.00
	1856 FJ	—	100.00	150.00	225.00	400.00

2.5000 g, .900 GOLD, .0723 oz AGW

KM#	Date	Mintage	Fine	VF	XF	Unc
141	1868 FE	—	200.00	300.00	450.00	775.00

2 SCUDOS

6.8000 g, .875 GOLD, .1913 oz AGW

KM#	Date	Mintage	VG	Fine	VF	XF
101	1834 LM	—	250.00	375.00	600.00	900.00
	1835 JM	—	— Reported, not confirmed			
	1835 LM	—	225.00	325.00	550.00	800.00
	1839 JM	—	— Reported, not confirmed			
	1839 LM	—	— Reported, not confirmed			

KM#	Date	Mintage	VG	Fine	VF	XF
106	1841 LR	—	400.00	550.00	825.00	1350.

4 SCUDOS

13.5000 g, .875 GOLD, .3798 oz AGW

KM#	Date	Mintage	VG	Fine	VF	XF
102	1834 JL	—	650.00	1000.	1650.	3150.
	1834 LM	—	—	—	Rare	—

KM#	Date	Mintage	VG	Fine	VF	XF
107	1841 LR	—	900.00	1500.	2500.	3450.

8 SCUDOS

27.0000 g, .875 GOLD, .7596 oz AGW

KM#	Date	Mintage	VG	Fine	VF	XF
99	1831 JL	—	550.00	675.00	1000.	1750.
	1832 JL	—	550.00	675.00	1000.	1750.
	1833 JL	—	550.00	675.00	1000.	1750.
	1833 LM	—	550.00	675.00	1000.	1750.

KM#	Date	Mintage	VG	Fine	VF	XF
99	1834 JL	—	550.00	675.00	1000.	1750.
	1834 JM	—	650.00	780.00	1100.	1850.
	1834 LM	—	550.00	675.00	1000.	1750.
	1835 JM	—	550.00	675.00	1000.	1750.
	1835 LM	—	550.00	675.00	1000.	1750.
	1836 LM	—	650.00	780.00	1100.	1850.
	1837 LM	—	500.00	625.00	950.00	1550.
	1838 LM	—	600.00	675.00	1000.	1750.
	1839 LM	—	500.00	625.00	950.00	1550.
	1840 LR	—	500.00	625.00	950.00	1550.

Large bust.

KM#	Date	Mintage	VG	Fine	VF	XF
108.1	1841 LR	—	600.00	700.00	900.00	1500.

KM#	Date	Mintage	VG	Fine	VF	XF
108.2	1841 LR	—	450.00	550.00	650.00	1000.
	1842 LR	—	450.00	550.00	650.00	1000.
	1843 LR	—	450.00	550.00	650.00	1000.
	1844 LR	—	450.00	550.00	650.00	1000.
	1844 R	—	650.00	750.00	1000.	1750.
	1845 R	—	650.00	750.00	1000.	1750.
	1846 R	—	650.00	750.00	1000.	1750.
	1847 R	—	650.00	750.00	1000.	1750.

KM#	Date	Mintage	VG	Fine	VF	XF
110	1851 MF	—	900.00	1500.	2750.	4500.

KM#	Date	Mintage	Fine	VF	XF	Unc
115	1852 FP	—	3500.	6000.	8500.	12,500.

KM#	Date	Mintage	Fine	VF	XF	Unc
116	1852 FP	—	450.00	650.00	1000.	1850.
	1853 FP	—	450.00	650.00	1000.	1850.
	1854 M	—	450.00	650.00	1000.	1750.
	1854 MJ	—	450.00	650.00	1000.	1750.
	1855 LM	—	450.00	650.00	1000.	1750.
	1855 MJ	—	450.00	650.00	1000.	1750.
	1856 FJ/MJ	—	—	—	—	—
	1856 FJ	—	450.00	650.00	1000.	1750.
	1857/6 FJ	—	450.00	650.00	1000.	1750.
	1857 FJ	—	450.00	650.00	1000.	1750.

ONZA

32.4000 g, .900 GOLD, .9375 oz AGW

KM#	Date	Mintage	Fine	VF	XF	Unc
142	1868 FE	—	—	—	*Rare	—
	1868 FP	—	—	—	Rare	—

***NOTE:** Stack's Hammel sale 9-82 AU realized $13,000., Pacific Coast Auction Galleries, Long Beach sale 6-86 AU realized $15,500., Superior Parker/Casterline sale 12-89 AU realized $15,400.

MELGAREJO COINAGE

1/4 MELGAREJO

5.0000 g, .666 SILVER, .1071 oz ASW

KM#	Date	Mintage	VG	Fine	VF	XF
144	1865	—	8.00	15.00	25.00	90.00

NOTE: Varieties exist.

1/2 MELGAREJO

10.0000 g, .666 SILVER, .2141 oz ASW
Obv: Long beards.

KM#	Date	Mintage	VG	Fine	VF	XF
145.1	1865*	—	10.00	20.00	30.00	80.00

Obv: Short beards.

KM#	Date	Mintage	VG	Fine	VF	XF
145.2	1865	—	10.00	20.00	30.00	80.00
	1865 (error) MELGREJO	—	20.00	40.00	70.00	120.00
	1865 (error) CATERIA	—	20.00	40.00	70.00	120.00
	1868	2 known	275.00	400.00	—	—

***NOTE:** Varieties exist.

MELGAREJO

20.0000 g, .666 SILVER, .4282 oz ASW

KM#	Date	Mintage	VG	Fine	VF	XF
146	1865 FP*	—	40.00	60.00	90.00	210.00

NOTE: Varieties exist.

DECIMAL COINAGE

100 Centecimos (Centavos) = 1 Boliviano

NOTE: In 1870 the weight of the silver coins was modified by adjusting it to the metric system. 9Ds (Decimos) = .900 fineness.

CENTECIMO

COPPER

KM#	Date	Mintage	Fine	VF	XF	Unc
147	1864	.010	50.00	80.00	165.00	275.00

CENTAVO

COPPER

KM#	Date	Mintage	Fine	VF	XF	Unc
162	1878	—	25.00	50.00	100.00	200.00

Obv: Denomination below condor.
Rev: 'LA UNION ES LA FUERZA' in wreath, date below.

KM#	Date	Mintage	Fine	VF	XF	Unc
163	1878	—	100.00	200.00	350.00	650.00

KM#	Date	Mintage	Fine	VF	XF	Unc
167	1883/73 A	.500	4.50	9.00	18.00	45.00
	1883A	Inc. Ab.	3.50	7.50	15.00	35.00

2 CENTECIMOS

COPPER

KM#	Date	Mintage	Fine	VF	XF	Unc
148	1864	.150	50.00	80.00	165.00	275.00

2 CENTAVOS

COPPER

KM#	Date	Mintage	Fine	VF	XF	Unc
164	1878	—	30.00	60.00	90.00	175.00

Obv: Denomination below condor.

KM#	Date	Mintage	Fine	VF	XF	Unc
165	1878	—	150.00	250.00	400.00	800.00

KM#	Date	Mintage	Fine	VF	XF	Unc
168	1883A	.250	3.50	7.50	15.00	50.00

1/20 BOLIVIANO

1.2500 g, .900 SILVER, .0361 oz ASW

KM#	Date	Mintage	Fine	VF	XF	Unc
149	1864 FP	—	6.50	12.50	20.00	70.00
	1865/4 FP	—	10.00	17.50	27.50	100.00
	1865 FP	—	8.00	15.00	22.50	70.00

5 CENTAVOS

1.2500 g, .900 SILVER, .0361 oz ASW
Obv: 11 stars at bottom.
Rev. leg: LA UNION HACE LA FUERZA, w/weight.

KM#	Date	Mintage	Fine	VF	XF	Unc
156.1	1871/0 ER	—	20.00	30.00	70.00	120.00
	1871 ER	—	125.00	—	—	—
	1871 FP	6 known	65.00	125.00	185.00	—

1.1500 g, .900 SILVER, .0333 oz ASW
Obv: 11 stars at bottom. Rev: W/o weight.

KM#	Date	Mintage	Fine	VF	XF	Unc
156.2	1871 ER	—	5.00	8.00	20.00	45.00
	1872 ER	2 known	95.00	185.00	—	—
	1872/1 FE	—	5.00	8.00	12.50	25.00
	1872 FE	3 known	85.00	175.00	—	—

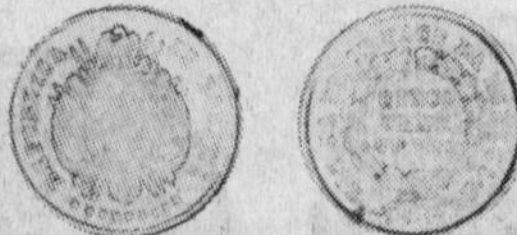

Obv: 9 stars at bottom.

KM#	Date	Mintage	Fine	VF	XF	Unc
156.3	1872 FE	—	4.00	7.00	15.00	40.00

Rev. leg: LA UNION ES LA FUERZA

KM#	Date	Mintage	Fine	VF	XF	Unc
157.1	1872 FE large date	—	2.00	3.50	6.00	12.50
	1872 FE small date	—	2.00	3.50	6.00	12.50
	1873 FE	—	1.50	2.50	5.00	10.00
157.1	1874 FE	—	2.00	4.00	7.50	15.00
	1875 FE	—	1.50	2.50	5.00	10.00
	1876 FE	—	2.00	3.00	6.00	12.00
	1877 FE	—	2.00	3.00	6.00	12.00
	1878 FE	—	2.50	3.50	6.00	12.00
	1878 FE V in BOLIVIANA inverted A	—	4.00	8.00	15.00	30.00
	1879 FE	—	3.50	5.00	10.00	17.50
	1879 FE V in BOLIVIANA inverted A	—	5.00	10.00	17.50	40.00
	1880 FE	—	5.00	10.00	17.50	40.00
	1881 FE	—	2.00	3.50	5.00	12.50
	1882 FE	—	3.75	6.50	10.00	25.00
	1883 FE	—	3.50	4.75	9.00	15.00
	1884 FE	—	4.00	6.00	10.00	20.00
	1884/3 FE	—	4.50	8.50	16.00	35.00

NOTE: Varieties exist in placement of periods in legends.

Reduced size lettering, bar below CENT.

KM#	Date	Mintage	Fine	VF	XF	Unc
157.2	1884 FE	—	—	—	Proof	Rare
	1885 FE	—	3.00	5.00	7.50	17.50
	1886/5 FE	—	3.00	5.00	7.50	17.50
	1886 FE	—	2.75	4.00	6.00	15.00
	1887 FE	—	2.75	4.00	6.00	15.00
	1888 FE	—	3.00	5.00	7.50	17.50
	1889/8 FE	—	7.50	15.00	20.00	27.50
	1889 FE	—	5.00	8.00	11.50	20.00
	1890 CB	—	2.00	5.00	7.50	15.00
	1891/0 CB	—	3.50	7.00	11.00	20.00
	1891 CB	—	3.00	6.50	10.00	17.50
	1893/83 CB	—	2.50	4.00	6.50	15.00
	1893 CB	.070	2.00	3.50	6.00	12.00
	1895 ES/CB	—	10.00	20.00	30.00	50.00
	1895 ES	.020	5.00	15.00	20.00	35.00
	1899 MM	—	2.00	3.50	6.00	12.00
	1900 MM	.050	2.00	5.00	7.50	15.00

NOTE: Varieties exist.

COPPER-NICKEL

KM#	Date	Mintage	Fine	VF	XF	Unc
169.1	1883A	2.200	10.00	20.00	40.00	90.00

NOTE: KM#169.1 was withdrawn from circulation due to confusion with contemporary silver 10 centavos. Eventually most of these Paris Mint pieces were officially hole punched and released back into circulation as KM#169.2.

KM#	Date	Mintage	Fine	VF	XF	Unc
169.2	1883A	Inc. Ab.	2.00	5.00	15.00	30.00

KM#	Date	Mintage	Fine	VF	XF	Unc
171	1892H	2.000	3.00	6.00	18.00	35.00

NOTE: Medal rotation strike.

KM#	Date	Mintage	Fine	VF	XF	Unc
173.1	1893	2.500	3.50	6.00	12.00	27.50
	1893	—	—	—	Proof	100.00
	1899	2.000	1.00	1.75	4.00	12.00
	1909	4.000	.50	1.00	3.00	12.00
	1918	.530	1.25	2.00	4.50	12.00
	1919	4.370	3.00	5.00	10.00	25.00

NOTE: Coins dated 1893, 1918 and 1919 medal rotation strike at Heaton Mint.

Rev: Cornucopia and fasces flank date.

KM#	Date	Mintage	Fine	VF	XF	Unc
173.2	1895	2.000	1.00	1.75	4.00	12.00

Rev: Cornucopia and torch flank date.

KM#	Date	Mintage	Fine	VF	XF	Unc
173.3	1897	1.500	1.00	1.75	4.00	12.00
	1902	2.000	1.00	1.75	4.00	12.00
	1907	2.000	1.75	3.75	6.50	20.00
	1908	3.000	.50	1.00	3.00	12.00

KM#	Date	Mintage	Fine	VF	XF	Unc
178	1935	5.000	.50	1.00	2.50	6.00

1/10 BOLIVIANO

2.5000 g, .900 SILVER, .0723 oz ASW

KM#	Date	Mintage	VG	Fine	VF	XF
150	1864 FP	—	4.00	6.50	10.00	20.00
	1865/4 FP	—	—	—	—	—
	1865 FP	—	4.00	6.00	10.00	20.00
	1866 FP	—	— Reported, not confirmed			
	1867 FP	—	22.50	45.00	75.00	125.00

10 CENTAVOS

2.5000 g, .900 SILVER, .0723 oz ASW
Obv: 11 stars at bottom.
Rev. leg: LA UNION HACE LA FUERZA, weight in grams.

KM#	Date	Mintage	Fine	VF	XF	Unc
153.1	1870 ER	—	1.50	3.00	6.00	12.00
	1870 ER (error) LA UION HACE	—	3.00	5.00	10.00	25.00
	1871 ER	—	2.00	4.00	7.00	15.00
	1871 ER A in REPUBLICA inverted V	—	—	7.00	15.00	30.00
	1871 FP	—	3.00	6.00	12.00	20.00

NOTE: Varieties exist.

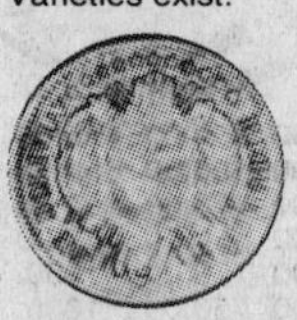

2.3000 g, .900 SILVER, .0666 oz ASW
Obv: 11 stars at bottom. Rev: W/o weight.

KM#	Date	Mintage	Fine	VF	XF	Unc
153.2	1871 ER	—	2.00	5.00	10.00	17.50

Obv: 9 stars at bottom.

KM#	Date	Mintage	Fine	VF	XF	Unc
153.3	1871 ER	—	1.50	3.00	6.00	15.00
	1872 FE	—	1.50	3.00	6.00	15.00
	1872 FE (error) V in BOLIVIA inverted A	—	—	5.00	9.00	25.00

Rev. leg: LA UNION ES LA FUERZA, w/o line below CENTS

KM#	Date	Mintage	Fine	VF	XF	Unc
158.1	1872 FE	—	3.00	6.00	10.00	15.00
	1873 FE	—	1.25	2.25	4.50	9.00
	1874 FE	—	1.25	2.25	4.50	9.00
	1875 FE	—	1.25	2.00	4.00	8.00
	1875 FE (error) LA UNIO ES	—	5.00	10.00	18.00	35.00
	1876 FE	—	1.25	2.00	4.00	8.00
	1877 FE	—	1.25	2.00	4.00	8.00
	1878 FE	—	1.50	2.50	5.00	10.00
	1879 FE	—	1.25	2.00	4.00	8.00
	1880 FE	—	1.25	2.25	4.50	9.00
	1881 FE	—	1.25	2.00	4.00	8.00
	1882 FE	—	1.50	2.50	5.00	10.00
	1883 FE	—	1.50	2.50	5.00	10.00
	1884/3 FE	—	1.50	2.50	5.00	10.00
	1884/3 FE	—	3.00	5.00	10.00	17.50

Rev: W/line below CENTS.

KM#	Date	Mintage	Fine	VF	XF	Unc
158.3	1873 FE	—	3.00	6.00	10.00	15.00
	1874 FE	—	3.00	6.00	10.00	15.00
	1883 FE	—	1.50	2.50	5.00	10.00
	1884/3 FE	—	3.00	5.00	10.00	17.50

Reduced size lettering, bar below CENTS.

KM#	Date	Mintage	Fine	VF	XF	Unc
158.2	1884 FE	—	4.00	7.00	15.00	27.50

KM#	Date	Mintage	VG	Fine	VF	XF
158.2	1884 FE	—	—	—	Proof	Rare
	1885 FE	—	1.50	2.50	5.00	10.00
	1886 FE	—	1.25	2.00	4.00	8.00
	1887 FE	—	5.00	8.00	15.00	27.50
	1888 FE	—	5.00	10.00	18.00	35.00
	1889 FE	—	2.50	5.00	10.00	17.50
	1890 FE	—	2.50	5.00	10.00	17.50
	1890 CB 1 over horizontal 1					
		—	7.50	15.00	25.00	45.00
	1890 CB	—	2.50	5.00	10.00	17.50
	1891 CB	—	1.50	3.00	6.00	12.00
	1893 CB	.050	1.50	3.00	6.00	12.00
	1895 ES	.020	4.00	7.00	13.50	20.00
	1899 MM	—	1.50	3.00	6.00	12.00
	1900 MM	.030	2.00	4.00	7.50	15.00

COPPER-NICKEL

KM#	Date	Mintage	Fine	VF	XF	Unc
170.1	1883A	.800	14.00	30.00	60.00	130.00

NOTE: KM#170.1 was withdrawn from circulation due to confusion with contemporary silver 20 Centavos. Eventually most of these Paris Mint pieces were officially hole punched and released back into circulation as KM#170.2.

KM#	Date	Mintage	Fine	VF	XF	Unc
170.2	1883A	Inc. Ab.	3.00	6.00	15.00	50.00

KM#	Date	Mintage	Fine	VF	XF	Unc
172	1892H	1.000	2.25	5.50	15.00	45.00

NOTE: Medal rotation strike.

Rev: W/o privy marks.

KM#	Date	Mintage	VG	Fine	VF	XF
174.1	1893	1.250	5.00	10.00	15.00	30.00
	1893	—	—	—	Proof	125.00
	1899	3.000	1.00	2.00	4.00	12.00
	1918	1.335	1.00	2.00	4.00	12.00
	1919	6.165	.50	1.00	3.00	12.00

NOTE: Coins dated 1893, 1918 and 1919 medal rotation strike at the Heaton Mint.

Rev: Cornucopia and fasces flank date.

KM#	Date	Mintage	VG	Fine	VF	XF
174.2	1895	1.000	4.00	8.00	17.50	30.00

Rev: Cornucopia and torch flank date.

KM#	Date	Mintage	VG	Fine	VF	XF
174.3	1897	2.250	1.00	2.00	4.00	12.00
	1901	—	17.50	27.50	45.00	75.00
	1902	8.500	.50	1.00	3.00	12.00
	1907/2	4.000	1.25	2.50	5.00	15.00
	1907	Inc. Ab.	.50	1.00	3.00	12.00
	1908	6.000	.50	1.00	3.00	12.00
	1909	8.000	.50	1.00	3.00	12.00

Rev: Wide 0 in value.

KM#	Date	Mintage	Fine	VF	XF	Unc
179.1	1935	10.000	.35	.60	1.50	3.00
	1936	10.000	.35	.60	1.50	3.00

NOTE: Medal rotation strike.

Rev: Narrow 0 in value.

KM#	Date	Mintage	Fine	VF	XF	Unc
179.2	1939	—	.35	.60	1.50	3.00

NOTE: Medal rotation strike.

KM#	Date	Mintage	Fine	VF	XF	Unc
180	1937	20.000	.35	.60	2.00	4.00

NOTE: Medal rotation strike.

ZINC

KM#	Date	Mintage	Fine	VF	XF	Unc
179a	1942	10.000	.45	.75	2.00	4.00

NOTE: Medal rotation strike.

1/5 BOLIVIANO

5.0000 g, .900 SILVER, .1446 oz ASW
Obv: Widely spaced stars.

KM#	Date	Mintage	VG	Fine	VF	XF
151.1	1864 FP	—	5.00	10.00	20.00	45.00
	1864 FP (error) 9.(D/I)S FINO					
		—	7.00	15.00	30.00	60.00

NOTE: Varieties exist in the space between stars.

Obv: Smaller, closely spaced stars.

KM#	Date	Mintage	VG	Fine	VF	XF
151.2	1864 FP	—	3.50	8.00	20.00	45.00
	1865 FP	—	3.50	7.50	15.00	35.00
	1866 FP	—	3.50	7.50	15.00	35.00
	1866/5 FP	—	8.00	17.50	35.00	70.00

20 CENTAVOS

5.0000 g, .900 SILVER, .1446 oz ASW
Obv: 11 stars at bottom.
Rev. leg: LA UNION HACE LA FUERZA, weight.

KM#	Date	Mintage	VG	Fine	VF	XF
154.1	1870 ER	—	25.00	35.00	60.00	90.00
	1871 ER	—	20.00	30.00	50.00	80.00
	1871 ER (error) LA (UN/LA)ION					
		—	25.00	40.00	65.00	100.00
	1871 FP					
		2 known	—	—	Rare	—

4.6000 g, .900 SILVER, .1331 oz ASW
Obv: 11 stars. Rev: W/o weight.

KM#	Date	Mintage	VG	Fine	VF	XF
154.2	1871 ER	—	12.00	25.00	50.00	85.00

Obv: 9 stars at bottom

KM#	Date	Mintage	VG	Fine	VF	XF
154.3	1871 ER	—	8.00	15.00	25.00	45.00
	1872 ER	—	10.00	20.00	35.00	55.00
	1872 FE	—	2.50	5.00	10.00	25.00

Rev. leg: LA UNION ES LA FUERZA

KM#	Date	Mintage	VG	Fine	VF	XF
159.1	1872 FE	—	20.00	40.00	80.00	150.00
	1873 FE	—	1.50	3.00	6.00	10.00
	1874 FE	—	4.00	6.00	12.50	20.00
	1875 FE	—	2.25	3.00	5.00	8.00
	1876 FE	—	2.25	3.00	6.00	9.00
	1876 FE (error) UNI(O/N)N					
		—	6.50	9.00	15.00	25.00
	1877 FE	—	2.25	3.00	5.00	8.00
	1878 FE	—	2.25	3.00	5.00	8.00
	1878 FE (error) BOLI(V/inverted V)IANA					
		—	6.50	9.00	20.00	50.00
	1879/8 FE	—	3.00	6.00	12.00	20.00
	1879 FE	—	2.25	3.00	5.00	8.00
	1880 FE (error) REPUB(L/B)ICA					
		—	6.00	12.00	25.00	45.00
	1880 FE	—	2.25	3.00	5.00	8.00
	1881 FE	—	2.25	3.00	5.00	8.00
	1882 FE	—	2.25	3.00	5.00	8.00
	1883 FE	—	2.25	3.00	5.00	8.00
	1883 EF	—	45.00	75.00	125.00	—
	1884/3 FE	—	4.00	6.00	12.50	20.00
	1884 FE	—	2.25	3.00	5.00	8.00
	1885/75 FE	—	5.00	7.50	10.00	15.00
	1885 FE	—	5.00	7.50	10.00	15.00

Daza Commemorative

KM#	Date	Mintage	VG	Fine	VF	XF
166	1879	—	12.50	27.50	35.00	60.00
	1879 (error) A's in DAZA inverted V's					
		—	15.00	30.00	50.00	80.00

NOTE: Varieties exist.

Reduced size dates and lettering.

KM#	Date	Mintage	VG	Fine	VF	XF
159.2	1884 FE	—	—	—	Proof	Rare
	1885 FE	—	2.25	3.00	5.00	8.00
	1886 FE	—	2.25	3.00	6.00	9.00
	1887 FE	—	2.25	3.00	5.00	8.00
	1888 FE	—	2.25	3.00	5.00	8.00
	1889 FE	—	2.25	3.00	5.00	8.00
	1889/8 FE	—	2.50	4.00	6.50	10.00
	1890 FE	—	2.25	3.00	5.00	8.00
	1890 CB	—	2.25	3.00	5.00	8.00
	1891 CB	—	2.25	3.50	6.00	9.00
	1892/82 CB	—	3.00	5.00	8.00	12.50
	1892 CB	—	2.25	3.50	6.00	9.00
	1893 CB	.500	2.25	3.00	5.00	8.00
	1894 ES	.490	2.25	4.50	7.00	15.00
	1895 ES	—	2.25	3.50	6.00	9.00
	1896 ES	.100	2.25	3.00	5.00	8.00
	1896 CB	I.A.	6.50	10.00	20.00	30.00
	1897 CB	.170	2.25	3.00	5.00	8.00
	1898 CB	—	10.00	15.00	25.00	35.00
	1899 CB	—	—	—	Rare	—
	1899 MM	—	2.25	3.50	6.00	9.00
	1900 MM	.170	2.25	3.50	6.00	9.00
	1901 MM	.040	2.50	4.50	8.00	12.00
	1901 MM/MW					
		—	2.50	5.00	13.50	20.00
	1902 MM	—	6.50	10.00	20.00	30.00
	1903 MM	.010	10.00	15.00	25.00	40.00
	1904 MM	—	7.00	12.00	20.00	30.00
	1907 MM	—	40.00	80.00	125.00	225.00

NOTE: Varieties exist.

4.0000 g, .833 SILVER, .1071 oz ASW

KM#	Date	Mintage	VG	Fine	VF	XF
176	1909H	1.500	1.50	4.00	6.00	11.00

ZINC

KM#	Date	Mintage	VG	Fine	VF	XF
183	1942	10.000	.60	1.20	2.50	5.00

NOTE: Medal rotation strike.

50 CENTAVOS

(1/2 Boliviano)

12.5000 g, .900 SILVER, .3617 oz ASW
Rev. leg: 12 GS. 500 MS. 9 DS. FINO

KM#	Date	Mintage	VG	Fine	VF	XF
161.1	1873 FE	—	5.50	7.00	12.00	20.00

Rev. leg: 12 GMS 500 MMS

KM#	Date	Mintage	VG	Fine	VF	XF
161.2	1873 FE	—	20.00	30.00	50.00	125.00

Rev: W/o 50 Cents and weight.

KM#	Date	Mintage	VG	Fine	VF	XF
161.3	1879/7 FE	—	50.00	100.00	175.00	325.00
	1879 FE	—	50.00	100.00	150.00	275.00
	1882 FE	—	50.00	100.00	150.00	250.00

11.5000 g, .900 SILVER, .3328 oz ASW
Rev: Reduced size lettering w/weight.

KM#	Date	Mintage	VG	Fine	VF	XF
161.4	1884 FE	—	—	—	Proof	Rare
	1887 FE	—	—	—	Rare	—
	1889 MM	—	—	—	Rare	—
	1891 CB	—	45.00	75.00	150.00	300.00

Rev: Reduced size lettering w/o weight.

KM#	Date	Mintage	VG	Fine	VF	XF
161.5	1891 CB	—	BV	3.50	6.50	12.00
	1892 CB	—	BV	3.50	6.50	12.00
	1893 CB	3.150	BV	3.50	6.50	12.00
	1894/1 CB	2.470	BV	5.00	8.50	25.00
	1894 CB	I.A.	BV	3.50	6.50	12.00
	1894/84 ES	—	BV	4.50	7.50	20.00
	1894 ES	I.A.	BV	4.00	7.00	15.00
	1895 ES	3.390	BV	3.50	6.50	12.00
	1896 ES	2.980	BV	3.50	6.50	12.00
	1897 CB	2.300	BV	3.50	6.50	12.00
	1897 ES	—	BV	4.50	7.50	20.00
	1898 CB	—	BV	3.50	6.50	12.00
	1899 CB	—	BV	3.50	6.50	12.00
	1899 MM	—	BV	3.50	6.50	12.00
	1899/69 first 9 over inverted 9	—	BV	4.00	7.00	15.00
	1900 MM	3.820	BV	3.50	6.50	12.00

KM#	Date	Mintage	VG	Fine	VF	XF
175.1	1900 MM	I.A.	BV	3.50	6.50	12.00
	1901/0 MM	2.000	BV	7.00	18.00	35.00
	1901 MM	I.A.	BV	3.50	6.50	12.00
	1902 MM	1.530	BV	3.50	6.50	12.00
	1903/2 MM	.690	BV	4.00	7.00	15.00
	1903 MM	I.A.	BV	3.50	6.50	12.00
	1904 MM	1.290	BV	3.50	6.50	12.00
	1905 MM	1.690	BV	3.50	6.50	12.00
	1905 AB	I.A.	BV	3.50	6.50	12.00
	1906 MM	.630	BV	3.50	6.50	12.00
	1906 AB	5.500	BV	3.50	6.50	12.00
	1907 MM	.050	BV	3.50	6.50	12.00
	1908 MM	—	BV	3.50	6.50	12.00
	1908 MM inverted 8	—	BV	7.00	18.00	35.00

KM#	Date	Mintage	VG	Fine	VF	XF
175.2	1900So	.900	BV	6.50	9.50	20.00

10.0000 g, .833 SILVER, .2678 oz ASW

KM#	Date	Mintage	Fine	VF	XF	Unc
177	1909H	1.400	BV	5.00	7.50	15.00

COPPER-NICKEL

KM#	Date	Mintage	Fine	VF	XF	Unc
181	1937	8.000	10.00	20.00	35.00	65.00

NOTE: Most melted upon receipt in Bolivia.

KM#	Date	Mintage	Fine	VF	XF	Unc
182	1939	—	.25	.50	.75	3.00

NOTE: Medal rotation strike.

BRONZE

KM#	Date	Mintage	Fine	VF	XF	Unc
182a.1	1942	10.000	.35	.60	1.25	5.00

NOTE: Medal rotation strike.

Restrike-poor detail

KM#	Date	Mintage	Fine	VF	XF	Unc
182a.2	1942	5.310	.25	.50	1.00	4.00

NOTE: Medal rotation strike.

BOLIVIANO

25.0000 g, .900 SILVER, .7234 oz ASW
Obv: 9 stars. Rev: I/BOLIVIANO/500 Gs/ 9 Ds FINO inside wide wreath. Raised edge leg: BOLIVIA LIBRE E INDEPENDIENTE 1825.

KM#	Date	Mintage	VG	Fine	VF	XF
152.1	1864 FP	—	12.50	17.50	30.00	70.00
	1864 FP inverted P	—	17.50	30.00	55.00	125.00
	1865/1 FP	—	15.00	25.00	45.00	100.00
	1865/4 FP	—	15.00	25.00	45.00	100.00
	1865 FP	—	10.00	15.00	25.00	60.00
	1866/5 FP	—	12.00	17.00	30.00	65.00
	1866 FP	—	10.00	15.00	25.00	60.00
	1866 PF inverted FP	—	150.00	250.00	450.00	750.00
	1867/6 FP	—	12.50	22.00	40.00	80.00
	1867 FP	—	12.50	20.00	35.00	75.00
	1868 FP	—	—	—	Rare	—

NOTE: Some dates Medal rotation strikes.

Obv: Larger shield.

KM#	Date	Mintage	VG	Fine	VF	XF
152.2	1864 FP	—	30.00	60.00	90.00	140.00

Obv: 11 stars. Rev: Similar to KM#152.1 but inside narrow wreath.

KM#	Date	Mintage	VG	Fine	VF	XF
152.3	1867/6 FP	—	11.50	17.50	25.00	55.00
	1867/6 FE/P	—	10.00	15.00	22.00	50.00
	1867 FE/P	—	11.50	17.50	25.00	55.00
	1867 FE (error) REPUBLICA BOLIVIANO	—	300.00	500.00	850.00	1300.
	1867 FE	—	8.50	12.50	18.00	40.00
	1867 FP	—	10.00	18.00	30.00	65.00
	1868/7 FE	.720	10.00	18.00	30.00	65.00
	1868 FE	I.A.	8.50	12.50	18.00	40.00
	1868 FP	—	8.50	12.50	18.00	40.00
	1869 FE	.260	10.00	18.00	30.00	65.00
	1869 FP	—	12.50	20.00	35.00	70.00

NOTE: Some dates medal rotation strikes.

Rev: Wide wreath, leg: LA UNION HACE LA FUERZA, 25 Gms 9Ds FINO.

KM#	Date	Mintage	VG	Fine	VF	XF
155.1	1870 ER*	—	10.00	12.50	20.00	30.00

Rev: Small wreath. Reeded edge.

KM#	Date	Mintage	VG	Fine	VF	XF
155.2	1870 ER*	—	10.00	12.50	20.00	35.00
	1870 ER	—	—	—	Proof	1000.
	1871/0 ER	—	10.00	16.00	40.00	90.00
	1871 ER*	—	10.00	12.50	20.00	35.00
	1871 FP*	—	12.50	15.00	25.00	40.00

Obv: 9 stars at bottom. Rev: Similar to KM#155.1.

KM#	Date	Mintage	VG	Fine	VF	XF
155.3	1870 ER*	—	15.00	25.00	35.00	65.00
	1871 ER*	—	12.50	17.50	25.00	55.00
	1871 FP*	—	12.50	17.50	25.00	55.00
	1871 EF	—	12.50	17.50	25.00	55.00
	1872 FE	—	20.00	30.00	40.00	70.00
	1872 FE (error) REPUB(L/R)ICA					
		—	20.00	40.00	60.00	100.00

Rev: Wide wreath, leg: 25 G 9D FINO.

KM#	Date	Mintage	VG	Fine	VF	XF
155.4	1870 ER	—	40.00	60.00	120.00	180.00

*NOTE: Several varieties exist.

Rev. leg: LA UNION ES LA FUERZA

KM#	Date	Mintage	VG	Fine	VF	XF
160.1	1872 FE	—	10.00	15.00	25.00	40.00
	1872 FE (error) ES (L/E)A FUERZA					
		—	50.00	80.00	160.00	250.00
	1873 FE	—	10.00	15.00	25.00	40.00
	1874 FE stars widely spaced					
		—	10.00	15.00	25.00	40.00
	1874 FE stars closely spaced					
		—	12.50	17.50	30.00	65.00
	1875 FE	—	10.00	15.00	25.00	40.00
	1877/6 FE	—	100.00	175.00	250.00	500.00
	1877 FE	—	45.00	65.00	120.00	200.00

Rev. leg: 25 Gs 9Ds FINO.

KM#	Date	Mintage	VG	Fine	VF	XF
160.2	1879 F.E.	—	60.00	120.00	225.00	375.00

Rev. leg: 25 GMS, horizontal bar between denomination and weight.

KM#	Date	Mintage	VG	Fine	VF	XF
160.3	1884 FE	—	—	—	Proof	Rare
	1887 FE	—	—	—	Rare	—
	1893 CB					
		4 known	—	1000.	1500.	2500.

BRONZE

KM#	Date	Mintage	Fine	VF	XF	Unc
184	1951	10.000	.10	.20	.40	1.50
	1951	10 pcs.	—	—	Proof	200.00
	1951H	15.000	.10	.20	.40	1.50
	1951KN	15.000	.25	.50	1.00	3.00

NOTE: Medal rotation strike.

5 BOLIVIANOS

BRONZE

KM#	Date	Mintage	Fine	VF	XF	Unc
185	1951	7.000	.25	.50	.75	2.50
	1951	—	—	—	Proof	150.00
	1951H	15.000	.25	.50	.75	2.50
	1951KN	15.000	.60	.90	1.25	3.50

NOTE: Medal rotation strike.

10 BOLIVIANOS

(1 Bolivar)

BRONZE

KM#	Date	Mintage	Fine	VF	XF	Unc
186	1951	40.000	.60	1.00	1.75	3.50
	1951	—	—	—	Proof	—

NOTE: Medal rotation strike.

MONETARY REFORM

100 Centavos = 1 Peso Boliviano

5 CENTAVOS

COPPER-CLAD STEEL

KM#	Date	Mintage	Fine	VF	XF	Unc
187	1965	10.000	.20	.30	.65	1.50
	1970	.100	.20	.30	.65	2.00

10 CENTAVOS

COPPER-CLAD STEEL

KM#	Date	Mintage	Fine	VF	XF	Unc
188	1965	10.000	.10	.25	.50	1.50
	1967	—	.10	.20	.40	1.00
	1969	5.700	.10	.20	.40	1.00
	1971	.200	.15	.25	.50	1.00
	1972	.100	.20	.40	.80	1.50
	1973	6.000	.10	.20	.40	1.00

20 CENTAVOS

NICKEL-CLAD STEEL

KM#	Date	Mintage	Fine	VF	XF	Unc
189	1965	5.000	.20	.40	.70	2.00
	1967	—	.20	.40	.65	1.75
	1970	.400	.20	.40	.80	2.50
	1971	.400	.20	.40	.80	2.50
	1973	5.000	.20	.40	.60	1.50

25 CENTAVOS

NICKEL-CLAD STEEL

KM#	Date	Mintage	Fine	VF	XF	Unc
193	1971	—	.15	.30	.60	1.00
	1972	9.998	.15	.30	.60	1.00

50 CENTAVOS

NICKEL-CLAD STEEL

KM#	Date	Mintage	Fine	VF	XF	Unc
190	1965	10.000	—	.25	.65	1.50
	1967	—	—	.25	.65	1.25
	1972	—	—	.25	.65	1.25
	1973	5.000	—	.25	.65	1.25
	1974	15.000	—	.25	.65	1.25
	1978	5.000	—	.25	.65	1.25
	1980	3.600	—	.25	.65	1.25

PESO BOLIVIANO

NICKEL-CLAD STEEL
F.A.O. Issue

KM#	Date	Mintage	Fine	VF	XF	Unc
191	1968	.040	—	3.00	4.00	7.00

KM#	Date	Mintage	Fine	VF	XF	Unc
192	1968	10.000	.20	.35	.80	1.75
	1969	—	.20	.35	.80	1.75
	1970	10.000	.15	.35	.80	1.75
	1972	—	.20	.35	.80	1.75
	1973	5.000	.15	.25	.80	1.75
	1974	15.000	.15	.25	.80	1.75
	1978	10.000	.15	.25	.80	1.75
	1980	2.993	.15	.25	.80	1.75

5 PESOS BOLIVIANOS

NICKEL-CLAD STEEL

KM#	Date	Mintage	Fine	VF	XF	Unc
197	1976	20.000	.60	1.00	2.00	4.00
	1978	10.000	.60	1.00	2.00	4.00
	1980	5.231	.60	1.00	2.00	4.00

100 PESOS BOLIVIANOS

10.0000 g, .933 SILVER, .3000 oz ASW
150th Anniversary of Independence

KM#	Date	Mintage	Fine	VF	XF	Unc
194	1975	.160	—	—	5.00	8.00

200 PESOS BOLIVIANOS

23.3300 g, .925 SILVER, .6938 oz ASW
International Year of the Child

KM#	Date	Mintage	Fine	VF	XF	Unc
198	1979	.015	—	—	Proof	22.50

250 PESOS BOLIVIANOS

15.0000 g, .933 SILVER, .4500 oz ASW
150th Anniversary of Independence

KM#	Date	Mintage	Fine	VF	XF	Unc
195	1975	.140	—	—	6.00	12.00

500 PESOS BOLIVIANOS

22.0000 g, .933 SILVER, .6600 oz ASW
150th Anniversary of Independence

KM#	Date	Mintage	Fine	VF	XF	Unc
196	1975	.100	—	—	8.50	18.00

4000 PESOS BOLIVIANOS

17.1700 g, .900 GOLD, .4968 oz AGW
International Year of the Child

KM#	Date	Mintage	Fine	VF	XF	Unc
199	1979	6,315	—	—	Proof	225.00

MONETARY REFORM

1,000,000 Peso Bolivianos = 1 Boliviano
100 Centavos = 1 Boliviano

2 CENTAVOS

STAINLESS STEEL

KM#	Date	Mintage	Fine	VF	XF	Unc
200	1987	20.000	—	—	—	.75

5 CENTAVOS

STAINLESS STEEL

KM#	Date	Mintage	Fine	VF	XF	Unc
201	1987	20.000	—	—	—	.75

10 CENTAVOS

STAINLESS STEEL

KM#	Date	Mintage	Fine	VF	XF	Unc
202	1987	20.000	—	—	—	.75
	1991	23.000	—	—	—	.75

20 CENTAVOS

STAINLESS STEEL

KM#	Date	Mintage	Fine	VF	XF	Unc
203	1987	20.000	—	—	—	.75
	1991	20.000	—	—	—	.75

50 CENTAVOS

STAINLESS STEEL

KM#	Date	Mintage	Fine	VF	XF	Unc
204	1987	15.000	—	—	—	1.00
	1991	20.000	—	—	—	1.00

BOLIVIANO

STAINLESS STEEL

KM#	Date	Mintage	Fine	VF	XF	Unc
205	1987	10.000	—	—	—	2.00
	1991	20.000	—	—	—	1.25

2 BOLIVIANOS

STAINLESS STEEL

KM#	Date	Mintage	Fine	VF	XF	Unc
207	1991	18.000	—	—	—	1.50

10 BOLIVIANOS

27.0000 g, .925 SILVER, .8029 oz ASW
Ibero - American Series

KM#	Date	Mintage	Fine	VF	XF	Unc
206	1991	*.050	—	—	Proof	42.50

MINT SETS (MS)

KM#	Date	Mintage	Identification	Issue Price	Mkt. Val.
MS1	1952(4)	—	KM-MB1-MB4	—	800.00

Bophuthatswana

Bophuthatswana is a group of non-contiguous black enclaves located in the north western area of South Africa. Population: 1,382,637. Capital: Mmabatho. The exportation of platinum is their main source of income.

The Botswana people have occupied their general area from the beginnings of their history. In 1871 the British recognized their sovereignty. In 1895, their land known as British Bechuanaland, was claimed by the British and the Boers. The people were scattered across the sub-continent.

In 1977 they achieved their independence from South Africa.

GOLD BULLION ISSUES

NKWE

16.9660 g, .917 GOLD, .5000 oz AGW
10th Anniversary of Independence
Similar to Lowe, KM#2.

KM#	Date	Mintage	VF	XF	Unc
1	1987	—	—	Proof	275.00

PLATINUM BULLION ISSUES

LOWE

31.2100 g, .9995 PLATINUM, 1.0000 oz APW
10th Anniversary of Independence

KM#	Date	Mintage	VF	XF	Unc
2	1987	3,000	—	Proof	600.00

BOSNIA & HERZEGOVINA

The Republic of Bosnia-Herzegovina borders Croatia to the north and west, Serbia to the east and Montenegro in the southeast with only 12.4 mi. of coastline. The total land area is 19,735 sq. mi. (51,129 sq. km.). They have a population of 4,366,000. Capital: Sarajevo. Electricity, mining and agriculture are leading industries.

Under Roman rule Bosnia formed part of Illyria. Bosnia's first ruler of importance was the Bau Kulin, 1180-1204. Stephen Kotromanic was invested with Bosnia, held loyally to Hungary and extended his rule to the principality of Hum or Zahumlje, the future Herzegovina, which until then led a rather independent existance since the 10th century. His daughter Elisabeth married Louis the Great and he died in the same year. His nephew Tvrtko succeeded and during the weakening of Serbian power he assumed the title "Stephen Tvrtko, in Christ God King of the Serbs and Bosnia and the Coastland. Later he assumed the title of "King of Dalmatia and Croatia", but died before he could consolidate power. Successors also asserted their right to the Serbian throne. His brother surrendered Croatia and Dalmatia to Sigismund of Hungary. Interior conflicts led to the invasion of the Turks. In 1459 the Turks invaded Serbia and the King of Bosnia was blamed by Hungary and the pope as being responsible for the disaster. Bosnia was then invaded in 1463 and Herzegovina in 1483. During Turkish rule they had an isolated world from Europe and Constantinople. Islam was accepted to militant Catholicism. During the 16th to 17th centuries Bosnia was an important Turkish outpost in continuing warfare with the Hapsburgs and Venice. When Hungary was freed of the Turkish yoke, the Imperialists penetrated into Bosnia, and in 1697 Prince Eugene captured Sarajevo. Later, by the Treaty of Karlowitz in 1699, the northern boundary of Bosnia became the northernmost limit of the Turkish Empire while the eastern area was ceded to Austria, but later restored to Turkey in 1739 lasting until 1878 following revolts of 1821, 1828, 1831 and 1862. On June 30, 1871 Serbia and Montenegro declared war on Turkey and were quickly defeated. The Turkish war with Russia led to the occupation by Austria-Hungary. Insurgents attempted armed resistance and Austria-Hungary invaded in mass quelling the uprising in 1878. The Austrian Occupation provided a period of prosperity while at the same time prevented relations with Serbia and Croatia. Strengthening political and religious movements from within forced the annexation by Austria on Oct. 7, 1908. Hungary's establishment of a dictatorship in Croatia and following the victories of Serbian forces in the Balkan War roused the whole Yugoslav population of Austria-Hungary to feverish excitement. The Bosnian group, mainly students, devoted their efforts to revolutionary ideas. Jealousy developed between the provincial Government in Sarajevo and the finance ministry if Vienna. In 1913 the Bosnian diet was closed and various Serbian societies were dissolved. During military maneuvers in Bosnia in June 1914 the assasination of the visiting Archduke Francis Ferdinand and his consort, the Duchess of Hohenberg triggered WWI. After Austria's Balkan front collapsed in Oct. 1918, the union with Yugoslavia developed and on Dec. 1, 1918 the former Kingdom of the Serbs, Croats and Slovenes was proclaimed later to become the Kingdom of Yugoslavia on Oct. 3, 1929.

After the defeat of Germany in WWII, during which Bosnia was under the control of Pavelic of Croatia, a new Socialist Republic was formed under Marshall Tito having six constituent republics all subservant, quite similar to the constitution of the U.S.S.R. Military and civil loyalty was with Tito, not with Moscow. In Jan. 1990 the Yugoslav Government announced a rewriting of the Constitution, abolishing the Communist Party's monopoly of power. Opposition parties were legalized in July 1990. On Oct. 15, 1991 the National Assembly adopted a "Memorandum on Sovereignty", the envisaged Bosnian autonomy within a Yugoslav federation. In March 1992 an agreement was reached under EC auspices by Moslems, Serbs and Croats to set up 3 autonomous ethnic communities under a central Bosnian authority. Independence was declared on April 5, 1992. The 2 Serbian members of government resigned and fighting broke out between all 3 ethnic communities. The United Nations is currently providing humanitarian aid while peace talks have resulted in only interrupting the gains being made in territory by Serbian forces.

500 DINARA

COPPER-NICKEL
Preserve Planet Earth - Brontosaurus

KM#	Date	Mintage	VF	XF	Unc
1	1993	—	—	Proof	6.50

Preserve Planet Earth - Tyrannosaurus Rex

KM#	Date	Mintage	VF	XF	Unc
4	1993	—	—	Proof	6.50

750 DINARA

28.2800 g, .925 SILVER, .8411 oz ASW
Preserve Planet Earth - Brontosaurus

KM#	Date	Mintage	VF	XF	Unc
2	1993	*.030	—	Proof	35.00

Preserve Planet Earth - Tyrannosaurus Rex

KM#	Date	Mintage	VF	XF	Unc
5	1993	*.030	—	Proof	35.00

Olympics - Bobsledding

KM#	Date	Mintage	VF	XF	Unc
7	1993	*.030	—	Proof	35.00

Olympics - Downhill Skiing

KM#	Date	Mintage	VF	XF	Unc
9	1993	*.030	—	Proof	35.00

Olympics - Cross Country Skiing

KM#	Date	Mintage	VF	XF	Unc
11	1993	*.030	—	Proof	35.00

Olympics - Pairs Figure Skating

KM#	Date	Mintage	VF	XF	Unc
13	1993	*.030	—	Proof	35.00

10,000 DINARA

6.2200 g, .999 GOLD, .2000 oz AGW
Preserve Planet Earth - Brontosaurus

KM#	Date	Mintage	VF	XF	Unc
3	1993	*5,000	—	Proof	165.00

Preserve Planet Earth - Tyrannosaurus Rex

KM#	Date	Mintage	VF	XF	Unc
6	1993	*5,000	—	Proof	165.00

Olympics - Bobsledding
Similar to 750 Dinara, KM#7.

KM#	Date	Mintage	VF	XF	Unc
8	1993	*5,000	—	Proof	165.00

Olympics - Downhill Skiing
Similar to 750 Dinara, KM#9.

KM#	Date	Mintage	VF	XF	Unc
10	1993	*5,000	—	Proof	165.00

Olympics - Cross Country Skiing
Similar to 750 Dinara, KM#11.

KM#	Date	Mintage	VF	XF	Unc
12	1993	*5,000	—	Proof	165.00

Olympics - Pairs Figure Skating
Similar to 750 Dinara, KM#13.

KM#	Date	Mintage	VF	XF	Unc
14	1993	*5,000	—	Proof	165.00

BULLION ISSUES

1/25 DUKAT

1.2440 g, .9999 GOLD, .0400 oz AGW
Hajj - Kaiaba in Mecca
Similar to 1 Dukat, KM#19.

KM#	Date	Mintage	VF	XF	Unc
15	1993	*.025	—	Proof	40.00

1/10 DUKAT

3.1103 g, .9999 GOLD, .1000 oz AGW
Hajj - Kaiaba in Mecca
Similar to 1 Dukat, KM#19.

KM#	Date	Mintage	VF	XF	Unc
16	1993	*.020	—	Proof	80.00

1/5 DUKAT

6.2200 g, .9999 GOLD, .2000 oz AGW
Hajj - Kaiaba in Mecca
Similar to 1 Dukat, KM#19.

KM#	Date	Mintage	VF	XF	Unc
17	1993	*5,000	—	Proof	160.00

1/2 DUKAT

15.5510 g, .9999 GOLD, .5000 oz AGW
Hajj - Kaiaba in Mecca
Similar to 1 Dukat, KM#19.

KM#	Date	Mintage	VF	XF	Unc
18	1993	*5,000	—	Proof	320.00

DUKAT

31.1030 g, .9999 GOLD, 1.0000 oz AGW
Hajj - Kaiaba in Mecca

KM#	Date	Mintage	VF	XF	Unc
19	1993	*5,000	—	Proof	625.00

MEDALLIC ISSUES

14 ECUS

10.0000 g, .925 SILVER, .8921 oz ASW
International Day of Peace

KM#	Date	Mintage	VF	XF	Unc
M4	1993	*.020	—	Proof	45.00

14 ECUS + 2

9.9700 g, .999 SILVER, .3205 oz ASW
War Relief Funding - Sarajevo Mosque

KM#	Date	Mintage	VF	XF	Unc
M1	1993	.020	—	Proof	35.00

21 ECUS + 3

15.5600 g, .999 SILVER, .5002 oz ASW
War Relief Funding - Sarajevo Mosque
Similar to 14 Ecus + 2, KM#M1.

KM#	Date	Mintage	VF	XF	Unc
M2	1993	*.015	—	Proof	50.00

70 ECUS + 10

6.2200 g, .999 GOLD, .2000 oz AGW
War Relief Funding - Sarajevo Mosque
Similar to 14 Ecus + 2, KM#M1.

KM#	Date	Mintage	VF	XF	Unc
M3	1993	*5,000	—	Proof	165.00

BOTSWANA

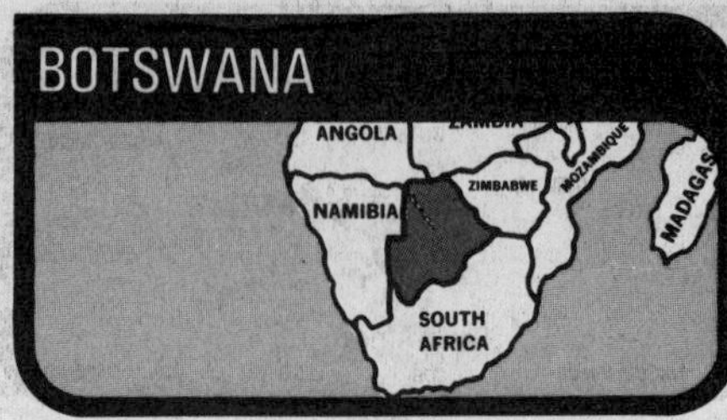

The Republic of Botswana (formerly Bechuanaland), located in south central Africa between Southwest Africa (Namibia) and Zimbabwe, has an area of 231,805 sq. mi. (600,370 sq. km.) and a population of 1.1 million. Capital: Gaborone. Botswana is a member of a Customs Union with South Africa, Lesotho, and Swaziland. The economy is primarily pastoral with a rapidly developing mining industry, of which diamonds, copper and nickel are the chief elements. Meat products and diamonds comprise 85 percent of the exports.

Little is known of the origin of the peoples of Botswana. The early inhabitants, the Bushmen, did not develop a recorded history and are now dying out. The ancestors of the present Botswana residents probably arrived about 1600AD in Bantu migrations from the north and east. Bechuanaland was first united early in the 19th century under Chief Khama III to more effectively resist incursions by the Boer trekkers from Transvaal and by the neighboring Matabeles. As the Boer threat intensified, appeals for protection were made to the British Government, which proclaimed the whole of Bechuanaland a British protectorate in 1885. In 1895, the southern part of the protectorate was annexed to Cape Province. The northern part, known as the Bechuanaland Protectorate, remained under British administration until it became the independent Republic of Botswana on Sept. 30, 1966. Botswana is a member of the Commonwealth of Nations. The president is Chief of State and Head of Government.

MINT MARKS

B - Berne

MONETARY SYSTEM

100 Cents = 1 Thebe

50 CENTS

10.0000 g, .800 SILVER, .2572 oz ASW
Independence Commemorative

KM#	Date	Mintage	VF	XF	Unc
1	1966B	.040	2.50	3.50	5.00
	1966B	.010	—	Proof	7.50

10 THEBE

11.2900 g, .900 GOLD, .3270 oz AGW
Independence Commemorative

KM#	Date	Mintage	VF	XF	Unc
2	1966B	5,100	—	—	160.00

MONETARY REFORM

100 Thebe = 1 Pula

THEBE

ALUMINUM
Turako

KM#	Date	Mintage	VF	XF	Unc
3	1976	15.000	.10	.15	.25
	1976	.026	—	Proof	.75
	1981	.010	—	Proof	1.00
	1983	5.000	.10	.20	.35
	1984	5.000	.10	.20	.35
	1985	—	.10	.20	.35
	1987	—	.10	.20	.30
	1988	—	.10	.20	.30
	1989	—	.10	.20	.30
	1991	—	.10	.20	.30

2 THEBE

BRONZE
World Food Day - Millet

KM#	Date	Mintage	VF	XF	Unc
14	1981	9.990	.15	.25	.50
	1981	.010	—	Proof	1.00
	1985	—	.15	.25	.50

5 THEBE

BRONZE
Toko

KM#	Date	Mintage	VF	XF	Unc
4	1976	3.000	.15	.30	.60
	1976	.026	—	Proof	1.00
	1977	.250	.15	.30	.60
	1979	.200	.15	.30	.60
	1980	1.000	.15	.30	.60
	1981	4.990	.15	.25	.50
	1981	.010	—	Proof	1.25
	1984	2.000	.15	.25	.50
	1985	—	.15	.25	.50
	1988	—	.15	.25	.50
	1989	—	.15	.25	.50

BRONZE CLAD STEEL

KM#	Date	Mintage	VF	XF	Unc
4a	1991	—	.15	.25	.50

10 THEBE

COPPER-NICKEL
South African Oryx

KM#	Date	Mintage	VF	XF	Unc
5	1976	1.500	.25	.40	.75
	1976	.026	—	Proof	1.50
	1977	.500	.25	.40	.75
	1979	.750	.25	.40	.75
	1980	—	.25	.40	.75
	1981	2.590	Reported, not confirmed		
	1981	.010	—	Proof	1.75
	1984	4.000	.20	.30	.60
	1985	—	.20	.30	.60
	1989	—	.20	.30	.60

25 THEBE

COPPER-NICKEL
Zebu

KM#	Date	Mintage	VF	XF	Unc
6	1976	1.500	.25	.55	1.30
	1976	.026	—	Proof	2.00
	1977	.265	.25	.60	1.30
	1980	—	.25	.60	1.30
	1981	.740	.25	.60	1.30
	1981	.010	—	Proof	2.50
	1982	.400	.25	.60	1.30
	1984	2.000	.25	.55	1.30
	1985	—	.30	.60	1.30
	1989	—	.30	.60	1.30

50 THEBE

COPPER-NICKEL
African Fish Eagle

KM#	Date	Mintage	VF	XF	Unc
7	1976	.266	.60	1.25	2.00
7	1976	.026	—	Proof	3.00
	1977	.250	.60	1.25	2.00
	1980	—	.60	1.25	2.00
	1981	—	Reported, not confirmed		
	1981	.010	—	Proof	3.50
	1984	2.000	.60	1.25	2.00
	1985	—	.60	1.25	2.00

NICKEL CLAD STEEL

KM#	Date	Mintage	VF	XF	Unc
7a	1991	—	.60	1.25	2.00

PULA

COPPER-NICKEL
Zebra

KM#	Date	Mintage	VF	XF	Unc
8	1976	.166	1.00	1.75	3.75
	1976	.026	—	Proof	5.00
	1977	.500	1.00	1.75	3.00
	1981	—	1.00	1.75	3.00
	1981	.010	—	Proof	5.50
	1985	—	1.00	1.75	3.00
	1987	—	1.00	1.75	3.00

NICKEL-BRASS
Seven Sided

KM#	Date	Mintage	VF	XF	Unc
24	1991	—	1.00	1.50	3.00

2 PULA

28.2800 g, .500 SILVER, .4546 oz ASW
Commonwealth Games

KM#	Date	Mintage	VF	XF	Unc
17	1986	*.050	—	—	12.50

28.2800 g, .925 SILVER, .8411 oz ASW

KM#	Date	Mintage	VF	XF	Unc
17a	1986	*.020	—	Proof	25.00

Wildlife - Slaty Egret

KM#	Date	Mintage	VF	XF	Unc
18	1986	*.025	—	Proof	22.50

Save The Children Fund

KM#	Date	Mintage	VF	XF	Unc
22	1989	*.020	—	—	50.00

5 PULA

28.2800 g, .500 SILVER, .4546 oz ASW
10th Anniversary of Independence

KM#	Date	Mintage	VF	XF	Unc
9	1976	.031	—	—	15.00

28.2800 g, .925 SILVER, .8411 oz ASW

KM#	Date	Mintage	VF	XF	Unc
9a	1976	.022	—	Proof	25.00

28.5000 g, .500 SILVER, .4582 oz ASW
Conservation Series - Gemsbok
Obv: Similar to KM#15.

KM#	Date	Mintage	VF	XF	Unc
11	1978	4,026	—	—	25.00

28.5000 g, .925 SILVER, .8477 oz ASW

KM#	Date	Mintage	VF	XF	Unc
11a	1978	4,172	—	Proof	32.50

International Year of Disabled Persons

KM#	Date	Mintage	VF	XF	Unc
15	1981	.013	—	—	20.00
	1981	.011	—	Proof	30.00

15.9800 g, .917 GOLD, .4711 oz AGW
Wildlife - Red Lechwes

KM#	Date	Mintage	VF	XF	Unc
19	1986	*5,000	—	Proof	300.00

COPPER-NICKEL
Pope's Visit

KM#	Date	Mintage	VF	XF	Unc
20	1988	*.050	—	—	7.00

28.2800 g, .925 SILVER, .8411 oz ASW

KM#	Date	Mintage	VF	XF	Unc
20a	1988	*5,000	—	Proof	45.00

COPPER-NICKEL
Olympics - Runners

KM#	Date	Mintage	VF	XF	Unc
21	1988	—	—	—	4.00

28.2800 g, .925 SILVER, .8411 oz ASW

KM#	Date	Mintage	VF	XF	Unc
21a	1988	.080	—	Proof	35.00

10.0000 g, .917 GOLD, .2948 oz AGW
Save the Children Fund

KM#	Date	Mintage	VF	XF	Unc
23	1989	*3,000	—	Proof	350.00

10 PULA

35.0000 g, .500 SILVER, .5627 oz ASW
Conservation Series - Klipspringer
Obv: Similar to 5 Pula, KM#21.

KM#	Date	Mintage	VF	XF	Unc
12	1978	4,088	—	—	30.00

35.0000 g, .925 SILVER, 1.0408 oz ASW

KM#	Date	Mintage	VF	XF	Unc
12a	1978	3,989	—	Proof	40.00

150 PULA

15.9800 g, .917 GOLD, .4711 oz AGW
10th Anniversary of Independence

KM#	Date	Mintage	VF	XF	Unc
10	1976	2,520	—	—	200.00
	1976	2,000	—	Proof	250.00

33.4370 g, .900 GOLD, .9676 oz AGW
Conservation Series - Brown Hyaena

KM#	Date	Mintage	VF	XF	Unc
13	1978	664 pcs.	—	—	500.00
	1978	219 pcs.	—	Proof	950.00

15.9800 g, .917 GOLD, .4711 oz AGW
International Year of Disabled Persons

KM#	Date	Mintage	VF	XF	Unc
16	1981	4,158	—	—	240.00
	1981	4,155	—	Proof	300.00

MINT SETS (MS)

KM#	Date	Mintage	Identification	Issue Price	Mkt. Val.
MS1	1978(2)	—	KM11,12	—	55.00

PROOF SETS (PS)

KM#	Date	Mintage	Identification	Issue Price	Mkt. Val.
PS1	1976(6)	20,000	KM3-8	18.00	13.50
PS2	1978(2)	5,850	KM11a,12a	—	72.50
PS3	1981(7)	10,000	KM3-8,14	33.00	16.00

BRAZIL

The Federative Republic of Brazil, which comprises half the continent of South America and is the only Latin American country deriving its culture and language from Portugal, has an area of 3,286,488 sq. mi. (8,511,965 sq. km.) and a population of 138 million. Capital: Brasilia. The economy of Brazil is as varied and complex as any in the developing world. Agriculture is a mainstay of the economy, although but 4 percent of the area is under cultivation. Known mineral resources are almost unlimited in variety and size of reserves. A large, relatively sophisticated industry ranges from basic steel and chemical production to finished consumer goods. Coffee, cotton, iron ore and cocoa are the chief exports.

Brazil was discovered and claimed for Portugal by Admiral Pedro Alvares Cabral in 1500. Portugal established a settlement in 1532 and proclaimed the area a royal colony in 1549. During the Napoleonic Wars, Dom Joao VI established the seat of Portuguese government in Rio de Janeiro. When he returned to Portugal, his son Dom Pedro I declared Brazil's independence on Sept. 7, 1822, and became emperor of Brazil. The Empire of Brazil was maintained until 1889 when the federal republic was established. The Federative Republic was established in 1946 by terms of a constitution drawn up by a constituent assembly. Following a coup in 1964 the armed forces retained overall control under a dictatorship until civilian government was restored on March 15, 1985. The current constitution was adopted in 1988.

RULERS

Portuguese

Maria I, Widow, 1786-1816
Joao, Prince Regent, 1799-1818
Joao VI, 1818-1822

Brazilean

Pedro I, 1822-1831
Pedro II, 1831-1889

MINT MARKS

(a) - Paris, privy marks only
A - Berlin 1913
B - Bahia 1714-1831
C - Cuiaba (Mato Grosso) 1823-1833
G - Goias 1823-1833
M - Minas Gerais 1823-1828
P - Pernambuco (supposedly all counterfeit)
R - Rio de Janeiro 1703-1834
SP - Sao Paulo 1825-1832
W/o mint mark - Lisbon 1715-1805

MONETARY SYSTEM

(Until 1833)

120 Reis = 1 Real
6400 Reis 1 Peca (Dobra = Johannes (Joe) = 4 Escudos

(1833-1942)

1000 Reis = 1 Milreis

(1942-1967)

100 Centavos = 1 Cruzeiro

COLONIAL COINAGE

X or 10 REIS

COPPER
Mint: Lisbon, w/o mint mark.
Obv. leg: JOANNES.D.G.P.E. BRASILIAE. . . .

KM#	Date	Mintage	VG	Fine	VF	XF
232.1	1802	.612	2.50	5.00	9.00	17.50
	1803	1.167	2.50	5.00	9.00	17.50
	1805	1.248	2.50	5.00	9.00	17.50
		Mint mark: R				
232.2	1805	—	3.00	8.00	12.00	20.00
	1806	—	3.00	8.00	12.00	20.00
	1812	—	—	—	Rare	—
	1814	—	3.00	8.00	12.00	20.00
	1815	—	3.00	8.00	12.00	20.00
		Mint mark: B				
232.3	1815	—	3.00	7.50	10.00	30.00
	1816	—	3.00	7.50	10.00	30.00
	1818	—	3.00	7.00	10.00	30.00

Mint mark: R
Obv. leg: JOANNES VI.D.G.PORT. . . .

KM#	Date	Mintage	VG	Fine	VF	XF
314.1	1818	—	2.50	5.00	10.00	20.00
	1819	—	2.50	5.00	10.00	20.00
	1820	—	2.50	5.00	10.00	20.00
	1821	—	2.50	5.00	10.00	20.00
	1822	—	2.50	5.00	10.00	20.00
		Mint mark: B				
314.2	1821	—	2.50	5.00	10.00	20.00
	1822	—	2.50	5.00	10.00	20.00
	1823	—	2.50	5.00	10.00	18.00

XX or 20 REIS

COPPER
Mint: Lisbon, w/o mint mark.
Obv. leg: JOANNES D.G.PORT.ET.BRAS.P. REGENS. . . . . Rev: Globe.

KM#	Date	Mintage	VG	Fine	VF	XF
233.1	1802	.788	2.00	4.00	7.50	15.00
	1803	1.920	2.00	4.00	7.50	15.00

Mint mark: B

KM#	Date	Mintage	VG	Fine	VF	XF
233.2	1812	—	2.00	4.00	10.00	20.00
	1813	—	2.00	4.00	7.50	15.00
	1815	—	2.00	4.00	7.50	15.00
	1816	—	2.00	4.00	7.50	15.00
		Mint mark: R				
233.3	1812	.012	5.00	10.00	20.00	45.00
	1813	.717	3.00	6.00	12.50	17.50
	1813/14	—	5.00	10.00	20.00	35.00
	1814	—	3.00	6.00	12.50	17.50
	1815	.302	3.00	6.00	12.50	17.50
	1817	.116	4.00	8.00	18.00	25.00
	1818	.060	5.00	10.00	20.00	30.00
		Obv. leg: JOANNES D.G.PORT.BRAS.ET ALG.				
309	1816	—	4.00	8.00	18.00	30.00

Minted for Goias and Mato Grosso
Obv. leg: JOANNES D.G.P.E. . . . .crowned value.
Rev. leg: PECUNIA.TOTUM.CIRCUMIT. . . .globe.

KM#	Date	Mintage	VG	Fine	VF	XF
315	1818	—	4.00	7.00	17.00	25.00

Mint mark: R
Obv. leg: JOANNES. VI. D.G.PORT. . . . .

KM#	Date	Mintage	VG	Fine	VF	XF
316.1	1818	—	2.50	5.00	9.00	17.50
	1819	—	2.50	5.00	9.00	17.50
	1820	—	2.50	5.00	9.00	17.50
	1821	—	3.00	6.00	10.00	25.00
	1822	—	2.50	5.00	9.00	17.50
		Mint mark: B				
316.2	1820	—	2.50	5.00	10.00	20.00
	1821	—	2.50	5.00	10.00	20.00

37-1/2 REIS

COPPER
Mint mark: M
Minted for Minas Gerais
Obv. leg: JOANNES.VI.D.G.PORT.BRAS. . . . .
Rev. leg: PECUNIA.TOTUM.CIRCUMIT. . . . .

KM#	Date	Mintage	VG	Fine	VF	XF
317.1	1818	—	10.00	20.00	45.00	75.00
	1819	—	10.00	20.00	45.00	75.00
	1821	—	10.00	20.00	45.00	75.00
		Mint mark: R				
317.2	1818	—	20.00	40.00	110.00	180.00

XL or 40 REIS

COPPER
Mint: Lisbon, w/o mint mark.
Obv. leg: JOANNES D.G.P. ET.BRASILAE. . . . .
Rev: Similar to 10 Reis, KM#232.1.

KM#	Date	Mintage	VG	Fine	VF	XF
234.1	1802	.584	2.50	6.50	12.50	35.00
	1803	1.143	2.50	6.50	12.50	30.00

NOTE: Crown varieties exist for both dates.

Mint mark: B

KM#	Date	Mintage	VG	Fine	VF	XF
234.2	1809	—	4.00	9.00	15.00	35.00
	1810	—	4.00	9.00	15.00	35.00
	1811	—	2.50	6.50	12.50	25.00
	1812	—	2.50	6.50	12.50	22.50
	1814	—	2.50	6.50	12.50	22.50
	1816	—	2.50	6.50	12.50	22.50
		Mint mark: R				
234.3	1812	.252	3.50	7.50	12.50	25.00
	1813	.307	3.50	7.50	12.50	25.00
	1815	.131	3.50	7.50	12.50	25.00
	1816	—	3.50	7.50	12.50	25.00
	1817	.379	6.00	15.00	25.00	45.00

Obv. leg: JOANNES D.G. PORT.BRAS. ET.ALG. . . . .

KM#	Date	Mintage	VG	Fine	VF	XF
311	1816	—	3.00	7.50	15.00	30.00

Minted for Goias and Mato Grosso
Obv. leg: JOANNES.D.G.P.E. . . .
Rev. leg: PECUNIA.TOTUM.CIRCUMIT. . . .

KM#	Date	Mintage	VG	Fine	VF	XF
318	1818	—	15.00	40.00	160.00	200.00

Mint mark: R
Similar to 20 Reis, KM#316.1.

KM#	Date	Mintage	VG	Fine	VF	XF
319.1	1818	—	2.50	6.50	12.00	25.00
	1819	—	5.00	10.00	20.00	40.00
	1820	—	2.50	6.50	12.00	22.50
	1821	—	2.50	6.50	12.00	22.50
	1822	—	2.50	6.50	12.00	22.50

Mint mark: B

KM#	Date	Mintage	VG	Fine	VF	XF
319.2	1820	—	3.50	8.50	22.00	35.00
	1821	—	3.50	8.50	22.00	35.00
	1822	—	3.50	8.50	22.00	35.00
	1823	—	3.50	8.50	25.00	50.00

Minted for Goias and Mato Grosso
Obv. leg: JOANNES.VI.D.G.PORT.BRAS.

KM#	Date	Mintage	VG	Fine	VF	XF
340	1820	—	5.00	35.00	100.00	150.00

75 REIS

COPPER
Mint mark: M
Minted for Minas Gerais
Obv. leg: JOANNES.VI.D.G.PORT.BRAS. . .
Rev. leg: PECUNIA.TOTUM.CIRCUMIT,. . . .
arms on globe.

KM#	Date	Mintage	VG	Fine	VF	XF
320	1818	—	15.00	25.00	45.00	75.00
	1819	—	15.00	25.00	55.00	100.00
	1821	—	15.00	25.00	45.00	75.00

LXXX or 80 REIS

2.2400 g, .917 SILVER, .0660 oz ASW
Mint mark: R
Obv. leg: JOANNES.D.G.PORT.P.REGENS. . . . .

KM#	Date	Mintage	VG	Fine	VF	XF
305	1810	—	—	—	Rare	—
	1814	—	30.00	70.00	150.00	300.00
	1816	—	25.00	50.00	120.00	200.00

COPPER
Similar to 10 Reis, KM#232.2.

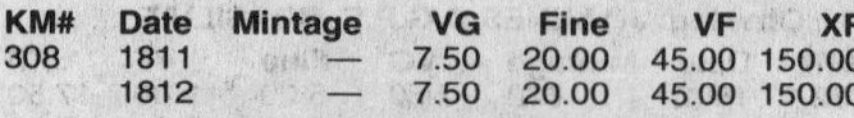

KM#	Date	Mintage	VG	Fine	VF	XF
308	1811	—	7.50	20.00	45.00	150.00
	1812	—	7.50	20.00	45.00	150.00

Mint mark: B
Minted for Goias and Mato Grosso
Obv. leg: JOANNES D.G.PORT. . . crowned value.
Rev. leg: PECUNIA.TOTUM.CIRCUMIT. . . globe.

KM#	Date	Mintage	VG	Fine	VF	XF
321.1	1818	—	2.50	6.00	12.50	30.00

Mint mark: R

KM#	Date	Mintage	VG	Fine	VF	XF
321.2	1818	—	4.00	10.00	20.00	30.00

2.2400 g, .917 SILVER, .0660 oz ASW
Obv: Crowned 80 within wreath, leg: JOANNES.VI. D.G.PORT. BRAS. . . . .

KM#	Date	Mintage	VG	Fine	VF	XF
322.1	1818	—	25.00	50.00	90.00	200.00

Mint mark: B

KM#	Date	Mintage	VG	Fine	VF	XF
322.2	1821	—	20.00	50.00	80.00	220.00

COPPER
Mint mark: R
Minted for Goias and Mato Grosso
Obv. leg: JOANNES.VI.D.G.PORT. . . crowned value.
Rev: Arms on globe.

KM#	Date	Mintage	VG	Fine	VF	XF
341	1820	—	5.00	10.00	20.00	45.00

Mint mark: B

KM#	Date	Mintage	VG	Fine	VF	XF
342.1	1820	—	5.00	10.00	15.00	30.00
	1821	—	5.00	10.00	15.00	30.00
	1822/1	—	7.50	15.00	25.00	45.00
	1822	—	5.00	10.00	17.50	35.00
	1823	—	5.00	10.00	17.50	35.00

Mint mark: R

KM#	Date	Mintage	VG	Fine	VF	XF
342.2	1821	—	4.50	7.50	15.00	27.50
	1822	—	4.50	7.50	15.00	27.50

160 REIS

4.4800 g, .917 SILVER, .1320 oz ASW
Mint mark: R
Obv. leg: JOANNES.D.G.PORT.P. REGENS. . . .,
crowned value. Rev: Globe.

KM#	Date	Mintage	VG	Fine	VF	XF
306.1	1810	—	17.50	35.00	80.00	160.00
	1813	—	6.00	10.00	25.00	50.00
	1813R/B	—	8.50	17.50	30.00	50.00
	1815	—	12.50	25.00	35.00	60.00

Medal strike.

KM#	Date	Mintage	VG	Fine	VF	XF
306.3	1810	—	17.00	40.00	80.00	180.00
	1813	—	17.00	40.00	80.00	180.00

Mint mark: B

KM#	Date	Mintage	VG	Fine	VF	XF
306.2	1811	—	150.00	300.00	900.00	1500.
	1812	—	20.00	70.00	150.00	700.00

4.4509 g, .917 SILVER, .1312 oz ASW
Mint mark: R
Obv. leg: JOANNES.VI.D.G.PORT.BRAS. . . .

KM#	Date	Mintage	VG	Fine	VF	XF
323.1	1818	—	10.00	20.00	40.00	60.00
	1820	—	100.00	200.00	350.00	700.00

Mint mark: B

KM#	Date	Mintage	VG	Fine	VF	XF
323.2	1821	5,639	75.00	125.00	225.00	275.00

320 REIS

8.9018 g, .917 SILVER, .2623 oz ASW
Mint mark: R
Similar to KM#255.1 but obv. leg: MARIA.I.D.G. . . . . .

KM#	Date	Mintage	VG	Fine	VF	XF
221.3	1802	—	11.00	20.00	27.50	45.00

NOTE: Earlier date (1800) exists for this type.

8.9600 g, .917 SILVER, .2641 oz ASW
Obv. leg: JOANNES.D.G.PORT.P.REGENS. . . .

KM#	Date	Mintage	VG	Fine	VF	XF
255.1	1809	—	11.50	22.50	30.00	45.00
	1812	—	9.00	15.00	20.00	40.00
	1813	—	9.00	15.00	20.00	40.00
	1817	—	15.00	30.00	50.00	75.00

Medal strike.

KM#	Date	Mintage	VG	Fine	VF	XF
255.4	1813	—	30.00	50.00	100.00	250.00

Mint mark: B

KM#	Date	Mintage	VG	Fine	VF	XF
255.2	1810	—	17.50	25.00	65.00	160.00
	1816	—	65.00	110.00	200.00	350.00

Mint mark: M

KM#	Date	Mintage	VG	Fine	VF	XF
255.3	1812	—	60.00	130.00	220.00	460.00
	1814	—	75.00	200.00	350.00	750.00
	1816	—	85.00	225.00	450.00	950.00

Obv. leg: JOANNES.VI.D.G.PORT.BRAS. . . .

KM#	Date	Mintage	VG	Fine	VF	XF
324.1	1818	—	750.00	1850.	3500.	8000.

Mint mark: R

KM#	Date	Mintage	VG	Fine	VF	XF
324.2	1818	—	11.00	20.00	50.00	100.00
	1819	—	17.50	35.00	60.00	125.00
	1820	—	9.00	15.00	20.00	35.00

Mint mark: B

KM#	Date	Mintage	VG	Fine	VF	XF
324.3	1821	—	18.50	37.50	55.00	125.00

640 REIS

17.7600 g, .917 SILVER, .5233 oz ASW
Mint mark: R
Similar to KM#231 but obv. leg: MARIA.I.D.G. PORT. REGINA. . . . .

KM#	Date	Mintage	VG	Fine	VF	XF
222.2	1802	56.126	20.00	35.00	45.00	75.00

NOTE: Earlier dates (1791-1800) exist for this type.

Mint mark: B
Rev. leg: SUBQ. . . . .

KM#	Date	Mintage	VG	Fine	VF	XF
231.2	1801	—	18.50	25.00	45.00	70.00

KM#	Date	Mintage	VG	Fine	VF	XF
231.2	1802	—	18.50	25.00	45.00	70.00
	1803	—	18.50	25.00	45.00	70.00
	1804	—	18.50	25.00	45.00	70.00
	1805	—	35.00	65.00	120.00	250.00

NOTE: Earlier dates (1799-1800) exist for this type.

17.9200 g, .917 SILVER, .5280 oz ASW
Obv. leg: JOANNES.D.G.PORT.P.REGENS. . . .

KM#	Date	Mintage	VG	Fine	VF	XF
237	1806	—	30.00	60.00	100.00	250.00
	1807	—	30.00	60.00	100.00	250.00
	1808/7	—	20.00	35.00	60.00	75.00
	1808	—	16.50	25.00	35.00	70.00
256.1	1809	—	16.50	25.00	35.00	70.00
	1810	—	17.50	27.50	40.00	80.00
	1816	—	—	—	Rare	—
	Mint mark: R					
256.2	1809	—	18.50	35.00	45.00	75.00
	1811	—	18.50	35.00	45.00	75.00
	1812	—	25.00	80.00	150.00	300.00
	1813	—	50.00	125.00	250.00	400.00
	1814	—	55.00	150.00	300.00	600.00
	1815	—	55.00	150.00	300.00	600.00
	1816	—	55.00	150.00	300.00	600.00

Mint mark: M

KM#	Date	Mintage	VG	Fine	VF	XF
256.3	1810	—	—	—	Rare	—
	1811	—	50.00	120.00	250.00	400.00
	1812	—	70.00	150.00	275.00	500.00
	1813	—	70.00	150.00	300.00	600.00
	1816	—	70.00	150.00	350.00	800.00

19.3200 g, .917 SILVER, .5693 oz ASW
Obv. leg: JOANNES.VI.

KM#	Date	Mintage	VG	Fine	VF	XF
325.1	1818	—	300.00	650.00	3000.	6000.
	Mint mark: R					
325.2	1818	—	16.50	35.00	75.00	180.00
	1819	—	25.00	60.00	100.00	240.00
	1820	—	16.00	18.50	30.00	60.00
	1821	—	17.50	30.00	35.00	60.00
	1822	—	21.50	50.00	130.00	350.00
	Mint mark: B					
325.3	1821	—	40.00	75.00	150.00	350.00

960 REIS

26.8900 g, .896 SILVER, .7746 oz ASW
Mint mark: B

KM#	Date	Mintage	VG	Fine	VF	XF
307.1	1810	—	17.50	27.50	40.00	55.00
	1810 small crown					
		—	—	—	Rare	—
	1810 . . P.REGENES. . .					
		—	30.00	60.00	100.00	150.00
	1811	—	25.00	40.00	60.00	100.00
	1812	—	17.50	27.50	35.00	60.00
	1813	—	17.50	27.50	35.00	60.00
	1813 . . P.REGENES. . .					
		—	50.00	80.00	150.00	300.00
	1814	—	17.50	27.50	35.00	60.00
	1815	—	17.50	27.50	35.00	60.00
	1816	—	17.50	27.50	35.00	60.00
	Mint mark: M					
307.2	1810	—	—	—	Rare	—
	1816	—	—	—	Rare	—
	Mint mark: R					
307.3	1810	—	17.50	27.50	35.00	60.00
	1811	—	17.50	27.50	35.00	60.00
	1812	—	17.50	27.50	35.00	60.00
	1813/2	—	20.00	30.00	45.00	80.00
	1813	—	17.50	27.50	35.00	60.00
	1814	—	17.50	27.50	35.00	60.00
	1815	—	17.50	27.50	35.00	60.00
	1815 . . STAB.NATA. .					
		—	—	—	Rare	—
	1816	—	17.50	27.50	35.00	60.00
	1817	—	17.50	27.50	35.00	60.00
	1818	—	17.50	27.50	35.00	60.00

27.0700 g, .903 SILVER, .7859 oz ASW
Obv. leg. ends:. . . . . BRAS.ET.ALG. P.REGENS.

KM#	Date	Mintage	VG	Fine	VF	XF
313	1816	—	30.00	50.00	75.00	150.00

KM#	Date	Mintage	VG	Fine	VF	XF
326.1	1818	—	17.50	25.00	35.00	60.00
	1819	—	17.50	25.00	35.00	60.00
	1820	—	17.50	25.00	35.00	60.00
	1820 small castle within zero of denomination					
		—	750.00	1350.	1850.	—
	1821	—	17.50	25.00	35.00	60.00
	1822	—	25.00	35.00	50.00	85.00
	Mint mark: B					
326.2	1819	—	—	—	Rare	—
	1820/19	—	—	—	Rare	—

KM#	Date	Mintage	VG	Fine	VF	XF
326.2	1820	—	17.50	25.00	35.00	60.00
	1820 . . . BARS.ET. . .					
		—	25.00	40.00	60.00	100.00
	1821/0	—	20.00	35.00	45.00	70.00
	1821	—	17.50	25.00	35.00	60.00
	1822	—	375.00	800.00	1800.	2800.

NOTE: KM#307.1-307.3, 313 and 326.1-326.2 are usually found struck over Spanish Colonial 8 Reales. Specimens of Spanish types with original elements visible command the following approximate premiums: 30% for mint mark, 40% for mint mark and assayer initial and 55% for mint mark, assayer initial and date. Specimens of Spanish Colonial types with original elements visible command the following approximate premiums: 10% for mint mark, 20% for mint mark and assayer initial and 35% for mint mark, assayer initial and date. In addition KM#326.1 and 326.2 are sometimes found struck over early South American Republic Peso and 8 Reales types. Specimens of Republic issues with original elements visible command the following approximate premiums: 25% for mint mark, 50% for mint mark and assayer initial and 100% for mint mark, assayer initial and date.

4000 REIS

8.0600 g, .917 GOLD, .2376 oz AGW
Mint: Bahia - w/o mint mark.
Obv. leg: MARIA I.D.G. . . . .

KM#	Date	Mintage	Fine	VF	XF	Unc
225.2	1801	3,705	150.00	275.00	550.00	800.00
	1802	7,738	150.00	275.00	500.00	750.00
	1803	7,807	150.00	275.00	500.00	750.00
	1804/2	Inc. Ab.	150.00	275.00	500.00	750.00
	1805/2	Inc. Be.	150.00	275.00	500.00	750.00

Obv. leg: JOANNES.D.G. . . . ., large crown.
Rev: Dots on either side of date.

KM#	Date	Mintage	Fine	VF	XF	Unc
235.1	1805	.010	125.00	225.00	375.00	500.00
	1806	.012	125.00	225.00	375.00	500.00
	1807	7,725	125.00	225.00	375.00	500.00
	1808	.037	125.00	225.00	375.00	500.00
	1809/8	.019	125.00	225.00	375.00	500.00
	1809	Inc. Ab.	125.00	225.00	375.00	500.00
	1810	.018	125.00	225.00	375.00	500.00
	1811	.019	125.00	225.00	375.00	500.00
	1811 flowers at date					
		Inc. Ab.	125.00	225.00	375.00	500.00
	1813	.011	125.00	225.00	375.00	500.00
	1814	9,494	125.00	225.00	375.00	500.00
	1815	—	125.00	225.00	375.00	500.00
	1816	7,522	125.00	225.00	375.00	500.00

Mint: Rio - w/o mint mark
Obv: Small crown.
Rev: Flower on either side of date.

KM#	Date	Mintage	Fine	VF	XF	Unc
235.2	1808	.128	125.00	225.00	375.00	500.00
	1809/08	.094	125.00	225.00	375.00	500.00
	1809	Inc. Ab.	125.00	225.00	375.00	500.00
	1810/09	.066	125.00	225.00	400.00	500.00
	1810	Inc. Ab.	125.00	225.00	400.00	500.00
	1811/10	.087	125.00	225.00	400.00	500.00
	1811	Inc. Ab.	125.00	225.00	400.00	500.00
	1812	.124	125.00	225.00	400.00	500.00
	181.2	Inc. Ab.	125.00	275.00	400.00	500.00
	1812 PROT (error)					
		Inc. Ab.	150.00	275.00	500.00	700.00
	1813/2	.148	125.00	225.00	400.00	500.00
	1813	Inc. Ab.	125.00	225.00	400.00	500.00
	1814/3	.102	125.00	225.00	400.00	500.00
	1814	Inc. Ab.	125.00	225.00	400.00	500.00
	1815	.083	125.00	225.00	400.00	500.00
	1816	.091	125.00	225.00	400.00	500.00
	1817	.071	125.00	225.00	400.00	500.00
	Obv. leg: PORT.ET.BRAS.(error).					
235.3	1812	Inc. Ab.	150.00	275.00	450.00	600.00

Obv. leg: PORT.BRAS ET ALG.
Rev. leg: PRINCEPS.REGENS. . . .

KM#	Date	Mintage	Fine	VF	XF	Unc
312	1816	Inc. Ab.	175.00	350.00	650.00	900.00

Obv: 6-petal flower on either side of date.

KM#	Date	Mintage	Fine	VF	XF	Unc
327.1	1818	.064	140.00	275.00	500.00	850.00
	1819	.049	200.00	400.00	500.00	850.00
	1820	.087	140.00	275.00	500.00	850.00
	1821/0	.035	140.00	275.00	500.00	850.00
	1821	Inc. Ab.	140.00	275.00	500.00	850.00
	1822/0	.054	150.00	300.00	500.00	800.00
	1822/1	Inc. Ab.	150.00	300.00	500.00	800.00
	1822	Inc. Ab.	150.00	300.00	500.00	800.00

Obv: 4-petal flower on either side of date.

KM#	Date	Mintage	Fine	VF	XF	Unc
327.2	1819	Inc. Ab.	200.00	400.00	650.00	900.00

Mint: Bahia - w/o mint mark.
Obv: Date between crosses.

KM#	Date	Mintage	Fine	VF	XF	Unc
327.3	1819	1,864	600.00	1000.	1500.	2000.
	1820	4,374	850.00	1200.	1800.	2200.

6400 REIS

14.3400 g, .917 GOLD, .4228 oz AGW
Mint mark: R
Obv: Bust right w/bejeweled headdress.
Rev: Crowned arms.

KM#	Date	Mintage	Fine	VF	XF	Unc
226.1	1801	.185	225.00	325.00	420.00	600.00
	1802	.168	225.00	325.00	420.00	650.00
	1803	.176	225.00	325.00	420.00	650.00
	1804	.128	225.00	325.00	420.00	650.00
	1805	.109	225.00	325.00	420.00	650.00

NOTE: Earlier dates (1789-1800) exist for this type.

Mint mark: B

KM#	Date	Mintage	Fine	VF	XF	Unc
226.2	1801	.012	220.00	320.00	700.00	950.00
	1802	3,324	220.00	320.00	700.00	950.00
	1803	3,743	220.00	320.00	700.00	950.00
	1804	3,539	220.00	320.00	700.00	950.00

NOTE: Earlier dates (1790-1800) exist for this type.

Mint mark: R
Obv. leg: JOANNES.D.G.PORT.ET.ALG.P.REGENS.

KM#	Date	Mintage	Fine	VF	XF	Unc
236.1	1805	Inc. Ab.	200.00	300.00	500.00	800.00
	1806	.096	200.00	300.00	500.00	800.00
	1807	.059	200.00	300.00	500.00	800.00
236.1	1808/7	.133	200.00	300.00	500.00	800.00
	1808	Inc. Ab.	200.00	300.00	500.00	800.00
	1809/8	.188	200.00	300.00	500.00	800.00
	1809	Inc. Ab.	200.00	300.00	500.00	800.00
	1810/09	.159	200.00	300.00	500.00	800.00
	1810	Inc. Ab.	200.00	300.00	500.00	800.00
	1811/10	.082	225.00	350.00	550.00	900.00
	1811	Inc. Ab.	225.00	350.00	550.00	900.00
	1812	.064	225.00	350.00	550.00	900.00
	1813	.053	275.00	450.00	650.00	900.00
	1814/3	.042	275.00	450.00	750.00	1000.
	1814	Inc. Ab.	275.00	450.00	750.00	1000.
	1815	.040	275.00	450.00	750.00	1000.
	1816	.039	300.00	500.00	1000.	2000.
	1817	.032	300.00	500.00	1000.	2000.

Obv. leg. ends: . . .PORT.BRAS.ET.ALG.P.REG.

KM#	Date	Mintage	Fine	VF	XF	Unc
236.2	1816	Inc. Ab.	500.00	1000.	1800.	2600.

Obv. leg: JOANNES.VI.D.G.PORT. BRAS.ET.ALG.REX.

KM#	Date	Mintage	Fine	VF	XF	Unc
328	1818	.014	600.00	1200.	2000.	2800.
	1819	9,227	625.00	1250.	2250.	3250.
	1820	3,286	825.00	1650.	2800.	4000.
	1821	2,122	—	—	Unique	—
	1822	599 pcs.	—	—	Rare	—

COUNTERMARKED COINAGE

Shield Countermark

Authorized on April 18, 1809.

The purpose of the shield countermark was to double the value of the earlier Colonial copper coinage and raise the value of the earlier silver coinage. Other Portuguese and Portuguese Colonial coins are known with this countermark.

75 = 80 Reis	300 = 320 Reis
150 = 160 Reis	600 = 640 Reis

10 REIS

COPPER

KM#	Date	Year	Good	VG	Fine	VF
c/m: Shield on V (5) Reis, KM#142.5.						
260	(1809)	1749	2.50	5.00	7.50	15.00
c/m: Shield on V (5) Reis, KM#173.1.						
261	(1809)	1752	10.00	20.00	70.00	140.00
		1753	2.00	3.50	5.50	10.00
		1768	2.00	3.50	7.50	12.50
		1773	2.00	3.50	7.50	12.50
		1774	2.00	3.50	7.50	12.50
c/m: Shield on V (5) Reis, KM#188.						
262	(1809)	1762B	2.50	4.50	7.50	12.50
		1763B	2.50	4.50	7.50	12.50
		1764B	2.00	3.50	6.00	10.00
		1766B	2.00	3.50	6.00	10.00
		1767B	2.00	3.50	6.00	10.00
		1768B	2.00	3.50	6.00	10.00
		1769B	2.00	3.50	6.00	10.00
c/m: Shield on V (5) Reis, KM#200.						
263	(1809)	1778	2.00	3.50	6.00	10.00
		1781	2.00	3.50	6.00	10.00
		1782	2.00	3.50	6.00	10.00
		1784	2.00	3.50	6.00	10.00
		1785	2.00	3.50	6.00	10.00
c/m: Shield on V (5) Reis, w/low flat arch crown, KM#214.1.						
264.1	(1809)	1786	2.00	5.00	12.50	18.00
		1787	2.00	5.00	12.50	18.00
		1790	2.00	5.00	12.50	18.00
		1791	2.00	5.00	12.50	18.00
		1797	5.00	8.50	15.00	32.00
c/m: Shield on V (5) Reis, w/high full arch crown, KM#214.2.						
264.2	(1809)	1786	2.00	5.00	12.50	18.00
		1787	2.00	5.00	12.50	18.00
		1790	2.00	5.00	12.50	15.00
		1791	2.00	5.00	12.50	18.00

20 REIS

COPPER

KM#	Date	Year	Good	VG	Fine	VF
c/m: Shield on X (10) Reis, KM#71.						
265	(1809)	1694P	10.00	25.00	45.00	75.00
265		1696P	8.00	15.00	25.00	45.00
		1697P	6.00	10.00	20.00	35.00
		1699P	6.00	10.00	20.00	35.00
c/m: Shield on X (10) Reis, KM#107.						
266	(1809)	ND	30.00	45.00	85.00	160.00
c/m: Shield on X (10) Reis, KM#108.						
267	(1809)	1715	2.50	5.00	10.00	15.00
		1718	2.50	5.00	10.00	15.00
		1719	2.50	5.00	10.00	15.00
		1720	2.50	5.00	10.00	15.00
c/m: Shield on X (10) Reis, KM#142.1.						
268.1	(1809)	1729B	2.50	4.50	7.50	12.50
		1730B	2.50	4.50	7.50	12.50
		1731B	2.50	4.50	7.50	12.50
c/m: Shield on X (10) Reis, KM#142.2.						
268.2	(1809)	1729	2.50	4.50	7.50	12.50
		1730	2.50	4.50	7.50	12.50
		1731	2.50	4.50	7.50	12.50
		1732	2.50	4.50	7.50	12.50
		1747	8.00	17.00	20.00	30.00
		1748	20.00	40.00	70.00	130.00
c/m: Shield on X (10) Reis, KM#142.3.						
268.3	(1809)	1735	2.00	3.50	6.00	10.00
		1736	2.00	3.50	6.00	10.00
		1746	2.00	3.50	6.00	10.00
c/m: Shield on X (10) Reis, KM#142.4.						
268.4	(1809)	1746	2.00	4.50	7.50	12.50
c/m: Shield on X (10) Reis, KM#142.5.						
268.5	(1809)	1749	2.00	4.50	7.50	12.50
c/m: Shield on X (10) Reis, KM#165.1.						
269	(1809)	1751	18.00	27.00	65.00	110.00
c/m: Shield on X (10) Reis, KM#174.1.						
270	(1809)	1752	4.00	10.00	20.00	30.00
		1753	2.00	5.00	8.00	15.00
		1773	3.00	10.00	20.00	30.00
		1774	2.00	3.50	5.00	7.50
		1775	2.00	3.50	5.00	7.50
		1776	2.00	3.50	5.00	7.50
c/m: Shield on X (10) Reis, KM#174.2.						
271	(1809)	1762B	2.00	3.50	5.00	7.50
c/m: Shield on X (10) Reis, KM#201.						
272	(1809)	1778	2.00	3.50	5.00	7.50
		1781	2.00	3.50	5.00	7.50
		1782	2.00	3.50	5.00	7.50
		1784	2.00	3.50	5.00	7.50
		1785	2.00	3.50	5.00	7.50

KM#	Date	Year	Good	VG	Fine	VF
c/m: Shield on X (10) Reis, w/low flat arch crown, KM#215.1.						
273.1	(1809)	1786	2.00	3.50	5.00	7.50
		1787	2.00	3.50	5.00	7.50
		1790	2.00	3.50	5.00	7.50
		1796	2.00	3.50	5.00	7.50
c/m: Shield on X (10) Reis, w/high full arch crown, KM#215.2.						
273.2	(1809)	1786	2.00	3.50	5.00	7.50
		1787	2.00	3.50	5.00	7.50
		1790	2.00	3.50	5.00	7.50
c/m: Shield on X (10) Reis, KM#228.						
274	(1809)	1799	2.00	3.50	5.00	7.50

40 REIS

COPPER

KM#	Date	Year	Good	VG	Fine	VF
c/m: Shield on XX (20) Reis, KM#70.						
275	(1809)	1693P	15.00	30.00	50.00	90.00
		1694P	7.50	15.00	30.00	45.00
		1695P	6.50	12.50	25.00	35.00
		1697P	6.50	12.50	25.00	30.00
		1698P	6.50	12.50	25.00	30.00
		1699P	6.50	12.50	25.00	30.00
c/m: Shield on XX (20) Reis, KM#109.						
276	(1809)	1715	3.00	5.00	7.50	12.50
		1718	3.00	5.00	7.50	12.50
		1719	3.00	5.00	7.50	12.50
		1729	3.00	5.00	7.50	12.50
c/m: Shield on XX (20) Reis, KM#110.						
277	(1809)	1722	2.50	3.50	7.50	12.50
c/m: Shield on XX (20) Reis, KM#143.1.						
278.1	(1809)	1729B	2.00	3.00	5.00	7.50
		1730B	2.00	3.00	5.00	7.50
		1731B	2.00	3.00	5.00	7.50
		1748B	17.00	35.00	65.00	135.00
c/m: Shield on XX (20) Reis, KM#143.2.						
278.2	(1809)	1729B	2.50	3.50	6.00	10.00
		1730B	2.50	3.50	6.00	10.00
		1731B	2.50	3.50	6.00	10.00

c/m: Shield on XX (20) Reis, KM#143.3.

KM#	Date	Year	Good	VG	Fine	VF
278.3	(1809)	1735	2.50	3.50	6.00	10.00
		1736	2.50	3.50	6.00	10.00

c/m: Shield on XX (20) Reis, KM#143.4.

KM#	Date	Year	Good	VG	Fine	VF
278.4	(1809)	1735	2.00	3.00	5.00	7.50
		1736	2.00	3.00	5.00	7.50
		1746	2.00	3.00	5.00	7.50

c/m: Shield on XX (20) Reis, KM#143.5.

KM#	Date	Year	Good	VG	Fine	VF
278.5	(1809)	1749	2.00	3.00	5.00	7.50

c/m: Shield on XX (20) Reis, KM#166.1.

KM#	Date	Year	Good	VG	Fine	VF
279	(1809)	1751	10.00	25.00	45.00	70.00
		1752	3.00	6.00	12.00	17.50

c/m: 11mm shield on XX (20) Reis, KM#175.1.

KM#	Date	Year	Good	VG	Fine	VF
280.1	(1809)	1752	2.50	4.00	7.50	15.00
		1753	2.50	4.00	7.50	15.00
		1773	2.50	4.00	7.50	15.00
		1774	2.50	4.00	7.50	15.00
		1775	2.50	4.00	7.50	15.00
		1776	2.50	4.00	7.50	15.00

c/m: 8mm shield on XX (20) Reis, KM#175.1.

KM#	Date	Year	Good	VG	Fine	VF
280.2	(1809)	1776	10.00	15.00	20.00	25.00

c/m: Shield on XX (20) Reis, KM#175.2.

KM#	Date	Year	Good	VG	Fine	VF
281	(1809)	1761B	3.00	5.00	7.50	15.00

c/m: Shield on XX (20) Reis, KM#202.

KM#	Date	Year	Good	VG	Fine	VF
282	(1809)	1778	2.50	4.00	7.50	10.00
		1781	2.50	4.00	7.50	10.00
		1782	2.50	4.00	7.50	10.00
		1784	2.50	4.00	7.50	10.00

c/m: Shield on XX (20) Reis w/low flat arch crown, KM#216.1.

KM#	Date	Year	Good	VG	Fine	VF
283.1	(1809)	1786	2.50	5.00	10.00	12.50
		1787	2.50	5.00	10.00	12.50
		1790	2.50	5.00	10.00	12.50
		1796	2.50	5.00	10.00	12.50
		1799	2.50	5.00	10.00	12.50

c/m: Shield on XX (20) Reis w/high full arch crown, KM#216.2.

KM#	Date	Year	Good	VG	Fine	VF
283.2	(1809)	1786	2.00	4.00	7.50	10.00
		1787	2.00	4.00	7.50	10.00
		1790	2.00	4.00	7.50	10.00
		1799	2.00	4.00	7.50	15.00

c/m: Shield on XX (20) Reis, KM#229.

KM#	Date	Year	Good	VG	Fine	VF
284	(1809)	1799	3.00	5.00	7.50	12.50

c/m: Shield on XX (20) Reis, KM#233.1.

KM#	Date	Year	Good	VG	Fine	VF
285	(1809)	1802	2.00	3.50	5.00	7.50
		1803	2.00	3.50	5.00	7.50

80 REIS

COPPER

c/m: Shield on XL (40) Reis, KM#111.

KM#	Date	Year	Good	VG	Fine	VF
286	(1809)	1722	2.00	3.00	5.00	7.50

c/m: Shield on XL (40) Reis, KM#184.1.

KM#	Date	Year	Good	VG	Fine	VF
287	(1809)	1753	2.00	3.00	5.00	7.50
		1760	2.00	3.00	5.00	7.50
		1774	2.00	3.00	5.00	7.50

c/m: Shield on Angola XL Reis, KM#9.

KM#	Date	Year	Good	VG	Fine	VF
301	(1809)	1757	25.00	30.00	40.00	65.00

c/m: Shield on XL (40) Reis, KM#189.

KM#	Date	Year	Good	VG	Fine	VF
288	(1809)	1762B	2.00	3.00	5.00	7.50

c/m: Shield on XL (40) Reis, KM#203.

KM#	Date	Year	Good	VG	Fine	VF
289	(1809)	1778	2.00	3.50	5.00	8.00
		1781	2.00	3.50	5.00	8.00
		1784	2.00	3.50	5.00	8.00

c/m: 11mm shield on XL (40) Reis w/low flat arch crown, KM#217.1.

KM#	Date	Year	Good	VG	Fine	VF
290.1	(1809)	1786	3.00	5.00	7.50	12.50
		1790	4.50	7.50	10.00	20.00
		1791	10.00	15.00	20.00	30.00
		1796	4.50	7.50	10.00	20.00

c/m: 8mm shield on XL (40) Reis w/low flat arch crown, KM#217.1.

KM#	Date	Year	Good	VG	Fine	VF
209.3	(1809)	1796	10.00	15.00	20.00	30.00

c/m: 11mm shield on XL (40) Reis w/high full arch crown, KM#217.2.

KM#	Date	Year	Good	VG	Fine	VF
290.2	(1809)	1786	4.50	7.50	10.00	15.00
		1787	4.50	7.50	10.00	15.00
		1790	4.50	7.50	10.00	15.00
		1791	4.50	7.50	10.00	15.00

c/m: 8mm shield on XL (40) Reis w/high full arch crown, KM#217.2.

KM#	Date	Year	Good	VG	Fine	VF
290.4	(1809)	1787	10.00	15.00	20.00	30.00

c/m: Shield on XL (40) Reis, KM#230.

KM#	Date	Year	Good	VG	Fine	VF
291	(1809)	1799	3.00	5.00	7.00	10.00

c/m: Shield on XL (40) Reis, KM#234.1.

KM#	Date	Year	Good	VG	Fine	VF
292	(1809)	1802	3.00	5.00	7.00	10.00
		1803	3.00	5.00	7.00	10.00

2.2600 g, .917 SILVER, .0666 oz ASW
c/m: Shield on 75 Reis, KM#176.1.

KM#	Date	Year	Good	VG	Fine	VF
293	(1809)	1752B	50.00	150.00	650.00	1000.
		1753B	7.00	20.00	125.00	200.00
		1754B	7.00	20.00	125.00	200.00

c/m: Shield on 75 Reis, KM#176.2.

KM#	Date	Year	Good	VG	Fine	VF
294	(1809)	1754R	20.00	45.00	65.00	200.00
		1755R	20.00	45.00	65.00	200.00
		1760R	27.00	55.00	120.00	400.00

160 REIS

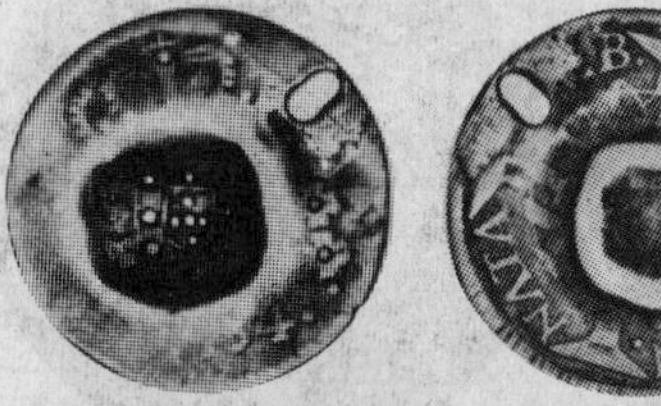

4.5200 g, .917 SILVER, .1332 oz ASW
c/m: Shield on 150 Reis, KM#177.

KM#	Date	Year	Good	VG	Fine	VF
295	(1809)	1752B	9.00	40.00	100.00	1200.
		1753B	9.00	30.00	50.00	160.00
		1754B	9.00	30.00	50.00	160.00
		1756B	70.00	135.00	375.00	1500.
		1768B	—	—	Rare	—

c/m: Shield on 150 Reis, KM#185.

KM#	Date	Year	Good	VG	Fine	VF
296	(1809)	1754R	9.00	20.00	70.00	125.00
		1754 R ATAN NGIS	10.00	22.00	80.00	130.00
		1755R	9.00	15.00	25.00	60.00
		1758R	9.00	15.00	25.00	60.00
		1760R	40.00	85.00	150.00	300.00
		1771R	30.00	50.00	100.00	200.00

320 REIS

9.0500 g, .917 SILVER, .2668 oz ASW
c/m: Shield on 300 Reis, KM#178.

KM#	Date	Year	Good	VG	Fine	VF
297	(1809)	1752B	25.00	45.00	85.00	160.00
		1753B	19.00	35.00	65.00	120.00
		1754B	19.00	35.00	65.00	120.00
		1756B	25.00	45.00	85.00	200.00
		1757B	25.00	50.00	90.00	240.00
		1768B	—	—	Rare	—

c/m: Shield on 300 Reis, KM#186.

KM#	Date	Year	Good	VG	Fine	VF
298	(1809)	1754R	12.50	20.00	30.00	65.00
		1755R	12.50	20.00	30.00	65.00
		1756R	12.50	20.00	30.00	65.00
		1757R	12.50	20.00	30.00	65.00
		1758R	12.50	20.00	30.00	65.00
		1764R	12.50	20.00	30.00	65.00
		1771R	15.00	25.00	45.00	80.00

640 REIS

18.1100 g, .917 SILVER, .5339 oz ASW
c/m: Shield on 600 Reis, KM#179.

KM#	Date	Year	Good	VG	Fine	VF
299	(1809)	1752B	100.00	350.00	500.00	800.00
		1754B	30.00	60.00	105.00	350.00
		1756B	30.00	60.00	105.00	300.00
		1757B	35.00	65.00	110.00	200.00
		1758B	30.00	60.00	100.00	150.00
		1760B	50.00	200.00	350.00	680.00
		1768B	—	—	Rare	—

c/m: Shield on 600 Reis, KM#187.

KM#	Date	Year	Good	VG	Fine	VF
300	(1809)	1754R	25.00	30.00	40.00	65.00
		1755R	30.00	40.00	55.00	90.00
		1756R	30.00	40.00	55.00	90.00
		1758R	30.00	40.00	55.00	90.00
		1760R	80.00	150.00	250.00	550.00
		1764R	25.00	30.00	40.00	65.00
		1765R	65.00	95.00	140.00	320.00
		1770R	40.00	50.00	70.00	220.00
		1771R	30.00	40.00	60.00	200.00
		1774R	30.00	40.00	60.00	200.00

REGIONAL COINAGE

MATO GROSSO

A large state in the center of Brazil. One of the issuers of the counterstamps of the 1808 law. The name of the province appears below the arms on the obverse.

COUNTERSTAMPED COINAGE

TYPE A

Authorized November 4, 1818

c/s: Crowned shield above MATO GROSSO.
Rev. c/s: Banded globe.

NOTE: The c/s having the crown made up of close large pearls is considered a counterfeit.

960 REIS

SILVER

c/s: Type A on Argentina 8 Reales, KM#5.

KM#	Date	Year	VG	Fine	VF	XF
330	ND	(1813-15)	2000.	3500.	—	—

c/s: Type A on Bolivia 8 Reales, KM#73.

KM#	Date	Year	VG	Fine	VF	XF
331.1	ND (1791-1808)		1750.	3000.	—	—

c/s: Type A on Bolivia 8 Reales, KM#84.

KM#	Date	Year	VG	Fine	VF	XF
331.2	ND	(1808-18)	1750.	3000.	—	—

CUIABA

Cuiaba is the present capital of the Mato Grosso state. In 1820 this city name appeared as "CUYABA" or "C" on a counterstamp appearing on Spanish-American 8 Reales coins. This is the rarest Brazilian counterstamp.

COUNTERSTAMPED COINAGE

TYPE B

Authorized 1820

Obv. c/s: Crowned shield above CUYABA. Rev. c/s: Banded globe.

960 REIS

SILVER

c/s: On Spanish Colonial 8 Reales.

KM#	Date	Year	VG	Fine	VF	XF
345	ND(1808)	—	2000.	3500.	—	—

General C/S Issue

TYPE C

Authorized in January, 1821.

Obv. c/s: Crowned 960/C (C. or .C. or C) within branches. Rev. c/s: Shield on globe.

c/s: Type C on Argentina 8 Reales, KM#5.

KM#	Date	Year	VG	Fine	VF	XF
351.1	ND	(1813)	550.00	950.00	1650.	2700.

c/s: Type C on Argentina 8 Reales, KM#14.

KM#	Date	Year	VG	Fine	VF	XF
351.2	ND	(1815)	550.00	950.00	1650.	2700.

c/s: Type C on Bolivia 8 Reales, KM#73.

KM#	Date	Year	VG	Fine	VF	XF
350	ND (1791-1808)		450.00	850.00	1500.	2000.

c/s: Type C on Bolivia 8 Reales, KM#84.

KM#	Date	Year	VG	Fine	VF	XF
352	ND	(1808-18)	350.00	650.00	1000.	1700.

c/s: Type C on Peru 8 Reales, KM#97.

KM#	Date	Year	VG	Fine	VF	XF
353	ND (1791-1808)		550.00	950.00	1650.	2700.

MINAS GERAIS

Minas Gerais is a state in eastern Brazil. In September of 1808 an edict was issued for the authorization of various counterstamps to be used on the many circulating Spanish 8 reales in the country. The Minas Gerais counterstamp was issued both with and w/o the M on the reverse. The silver value was 750 to 800 Reis per coin but they were marked and passed at 960 Reis giving the government a nice profit.

COUNTERSTAMPED COINAGE

Authorized Sept. 1, 1808
until 1810
Obv. c/s: Crowned shield in branches/960.
Rev. c/s: Banded globe with cross.

960 REIS

SILVER

c/s: On Bolivia 8 Reales, KM#55.

KM#	Date	Year Mintage	Fine	VF	XF
240	ND (1773-89)	—	550.00	1000.	1500.

c/s: On Bolivia 8 Reales, KM#64.

KM#	Date	Year Mintage	Fine	VF	XF
241	ND (1789-91)	—	450.00	650.00	1200.

c/s: On Bolivia 8 Reales, KM#73.

KM#	Date	Year Mintage	Fine	VF	XF
242	ND (1791-1808)	—	60.00	170.00	300.00

c/s: On Chile 8 Reales, KM#51.

KM#	Date	Year Mintage	Fine	VF	XF
243	ND (1791-1808)	—	350.00	550.00	800.00

c/s: On Guatemala 8 Reales.

KM#	Date	Year Mintage	Fine	VF	XF
244	ND	—	—	—	Rare	—

c/s: On Mexico City 8 Reales, KM#105.

KM#	Date	Year Mintage	Fine	VF	XF
245	ND (1760-72)	—	—	Rare	—

c/s: On Mexico City 8 Reales, KM#106.

KM#	Date	Year Mintage	Fine	VF	XF
246	ND (1772-89)	—	550.00	1000.	1500.

c/s: On Mexico City 8 Reales, KM#107.

KM#	Date	Year Mintage	Fine	VF	XF
247	ND (1789-90)	—	400.00	600.00	1100.

c/s: On Mexico City 8 Reales, KM#108.

KM#	Date	Year Mintage	Fine	VF	XF
A248	ND (1790)	—	1500.	2000.	—

c/s: On Mexico City 8 Reales, KM#109.

KM#	Date	Year Mintage	Fine	VF	XF
248	ND (1791-1808)	—	400.00	600.00	1000.

c/s: On Peru 8 Reales, KM#78.

KM#	Date	Year Mintage	Fine	VF	XF
249	ND (1772-89)	—	450.00	650.00	1200.

c/s: On Peru 8 Reales, KM#87.

KM#	Date	Year Mintage	Fine	VF	XF
250	ND (1789-91)	—	100.00	200.00	350.00

c/s: On Peru 8 Reales, KM#97.

KM#	Date	Year Mintage	Fine	VF	XF
251	ND (1791-1808)	—	60.00	170.00	300.00

c/s: On Spanish 8 Reales.

KM#	Date	Year Mintage	Fine	VF	XF
252	ND	—	—	—	Rare	—

UNITED KINGDOM

Copper Coinage

The imperial copper coins of Brazil (1823-1833) Were struck to several different standards simultaneously, each intended for a different part of the empire. The following table shows the standards used at each mint:

Weights of Imperial Brazilian copper coins in oitavos:

MINT MARK DENOMINATION (REIS)

	MARK	10	20	40	80	37½	75
Rio De Janeiro	R	1	2	4	8	—	—
Bahia	B	1	2	4	8	—	—
Goias	G	—	1	2	4	—	4
Cuiaba	C	—	1	2	4	—	—
Minas Gerais	M	—	—	—	—	2	—
Sao Paulo	SP	—	—	—	5⅓	—	—

NOTE: 1 Oitavo = 3.586 g,; 8 Oitavos = 1 Onza (28.68

g); thus 5-1/3 Oitavos plus 1 Escropalo) is precisely 2/3 Onza (ounce).

Lightweight Coins: Many coppers are found as much as 15 percent or more below the official weights, and even heavy specimens are occasionally observed. Most of the above coins were counterfeited, as their face value exceeded the cost of the metal and minting. Though usually crude and carelessly engraved, some counterfeits are of decent workmanship, and entirely undistinguishable from government issues. Brazilian collectors generally accept these contemporary counterfeits as collectable, due to their historical value. Before Pedro I began his regular coinage, colonial coppers were revalued with a special countermark, probably in 1822.

Imperial Countermarks

These countermarks consist of a crowned 20, 40 or 80 within a wreath in a circle and opposite a shield in a circle is used.

20 REIS

COPPER
c/m: Crowned 20 in sprays on various Colonial X (10) Reis.

KM#	Date	Year	Good	VG	Fine	VF
355	Various	—	900.00	1500.	2500.	3500.

NOTE: Many authorities consider all known examples of KM#355 to be counterfeit.

40 REIS

COPPER
c/m: Crowned 40 on various X(10) Reis.

KM#	Date	Year	Good	VG	Fine	VF
358	Various	—	750.00	1250.	2000.	3000.

c/m: Crowned 40 in sprays on various Colonial XX (20) Reis.

KM#	Date	Year	Good	VG	Fine	VF
356	Various	—	700.00	1150.	1750.	2500.

NOTE: Three of 8 known dies are believed counterfeit.

80 REIS

COPPER
c/m: 80 on Colonial XX (20) Reis.

KM#	Date	Year	Good	VG	Fine	VF
354	Various	—	1250.	2250.	3500.	5000.

c/m: Crowned 80 in sprays on various Colonial XL (40) Reis.

KM#	Date	Year	Good	VG	Fine	VF
357	Various	—	1500.	2500.	4000.	6000.

NOTE: One of 11 known dies are believed counterfeit.

c/m: Crowned 80 on 75 Reis.

KM#	Date	Year	Good	VG	Fine	VF
359	Various	—	—	—	Rare	—

Regular Coinage

CAUTION: Prices are for specimens without any countermark. Countermarked pieces follow these listings.

10 REIS

COPPER
Mint mark: R

KM#	Date	Mintage	Good	VG	Fine	VF
371.1	1824	.235	1.50	3.50	8.00	15.00
	Mint mark: B					
371.2	1827	.104	3.00	7.50	15.00	30.00
	1828	.728	2.00	5.00	12.00	20.00

20 REIS

COPPER
Mint mark: R
PEDRO I
Weight: 2 oitavos, 7.17 g

KM#	Date	Mintage	Good	VG	Fine	VF
360.1	1822	—	Counterfeit		—	—
	1823	1.700	1.00	2.00	3.50	7.50
	1824	4.956	1.00	2.00	3.50	7.50
	1824 BRSA	I.A.	7.00	10.00	20.00	60.00
	1825	9.054	1.00	2.00	3.50	7.50
	1826	4.419	1.00	2.00	3.50	7.50
	1827	4.648	1.00	2.00	3.50	7.50
	1828	4.474	1.00	2.00	3.50	7.50
	1829	6.806	1.00	2.00	3.50	7.50
	1830	—	1.00	2.00	3.50	7.50
	1831		Counterfeit		—	—
	Mint mark: B					
360.2	1825	.582	2.00	4.00	7.50	12.50
	1827	.044	2.00	4.00	7.50	12.50
	1828	.585	2.00	4.00	7.50	12.50
	1830	.316	2.00	4.00	7.50	12.50

Mint mark: C
PEDRO I
Reduced weight: 1 oitavo = 3.59 g

KM#	Date	Mintage	Good	VG	Fine	VF
375.1	1825	—	15.00	30.00	80.00	150.00
	Mint mark: G					
375.2	1829	—	Counterfeit		—	—

Mint mark: R
PEDRO II
Reduced weight: 2 oitavos = 7.17 g

KM#	Date	Mintage	Good	VG	Fine	VF
380	1832	.014	25.00	60.00	100.00	175.00

37-1/2 REIS

COPPER
Mint mark: M
PEDRO I
Weight: 2 oitavos = 7.17 g

KM#	Date	Mintage	Good	VG	Fine	VF
362	1823	—	10.00	20.00	40.00	60.00
	1824	—	7.50	15.00	30.00	50.00
	1825	—	7.50	15.00	30.00	50.00
	1826	—	7.50	15.00	30.00	50.00
	1827	—	7.50	15.00	30.00	50.00
	1828	—	7.50	15.00	30.00	50.00

40 REIS

COPPER
Mint mark: R
PEDRO I
Weight: 4 oitavos = 14.34 g

KM#	Date	Mintage	VG	Fine	VF	XF
363.1	1823	.920	2.00	4.00	7.50	15.00
	1824	9.170	2.00	3.50	5.00	10.00
	1825	6.774	2.00	3.50	5.00	10.00
	1826	10.507	2.00	3.50	5.00	10.00
	1826 PETRUST	Inc. Ab.	10.00	20.00	30.00	60.00
	1827	17.892	2.00	5.00	8.00	12.00
	1828	15.570	2.00	5.00	8.00	12.00
	1829	8.924	2.00	5.00	8.00	12.00
	1830	—	2.00	5.00	8.00	12.00
	1831/0	—	3.00	6.00	10.00	20.00
	1831	—	2.00	5.00	8.00	12.00
	Mint mark: B					
363.2	1824	.230	2.00	5.00	10.00	15.00
	1825	Inc. Ab	2.00	5.00	10.00	15.00
	1827	.161	2.00	5.00	10.00	15.00
	1828	.051	2.00	5.00	10.00	15.00
	1829	2.052	2.00	5.00	10.00	15.00
	1830	1.032	2.00	5.00	10.00	15.00

NOTE: Most known examples of 1828R, 1829R, and 1830R are counterfeit!

Mint mark: C
PEDRO I
Reduced weight: 2 oitavos = 7.17 g

KM#	Date	Mintage	Good	VG	Fine	VF
364.1	1823	—	6.00	10.00	15.00	30.00
	1824	—	4.50	7.50	12.50	20.00
	1825	—	4.50	7.50	12.50	20.00
	1826	—	4.50	7.50	12.50	20.00
	1827	—	4.50	7.50	12.50	20.00
	1828	—	4.50	7.50	12.50	20.00
	1829	—	4.50	7.50	12.50	20.00
	1830	—	4.50	7.50	12.50	20.00
	1831	—	6.00	10.00	15.00	30.00
	Mint mark: G					
364.2	1823	—	5.00	10.00	20.00	30.00
	1825	—	4.50	7.50	15.00	25.00
	1826	—	5.00	10.00	20.00	30.00
	1827	—	4.50	7.50	15.00	25.00
	1828	—	4.50	7.50	15.00	25.00
	1829	—	4.50	7.50	15.00	25.00
	1830	—	4.50	7.50	15.00	25.00

NOTE: 1823C is considered a counterfeit by many authorities.

Mint mark: R
PEDRO II
Weight: 4 oitavos = 14.34 g

KM#	Date	Mintage	VG	Fine	VF	XF
378	1831	—	Counterfeit issue			—
	1832	.816	2.00	3.50	6.00	12.00

NOTE: 1833R exists as a pattern.

Mint mark: G
PEDRO II
Reduced weight: 2 oitavos = 7.17 g

KM#	Date	Mintage	Good	VG	Fine	VF
381.1	1832 Petrus II	—	3.00	5.00	8.00	20.00
	1832 Petrus 2.o	—	3.00	5.00	8.00	20.00

Mint mark: C

KM#	Date	Mintage	Good	VG	Fine	VF
381.2	1833	—	5.00	8.00	15.00	20.00

75 REIS

COPPER
Mint mark: G
PEDRO I
Weight: 4 oitavos = 14.34 g

KM#	Date	Mintage	Good	VG	Fine	VF
365	1823	—	20.00	40.00	85.00	175.00

80 REIS

COPPER
Mint mark: R
PEDRO I
Weight: 8 oitavos = 28.69 g

KM#	Date	Mintage	VG	Fine	VF	XF
366.1	1823	.100	2.00	3.50	10.00	20.00
	1824	.825	2.00	3.50	10.00	20.00
	1825	1.027	2.00	3.50	10.00	20.00
	1826	10.507	2.00	3.50	10.00	20.00
	1827	17.892	2.00	3.50	10.00	20.00
	1828	26.524	2.00	3.50	10.00	20.00
	1829	20.180	2.00	3.50	10.00	20.00
	1830	—	2.00	3.50	10.00	20.00
	1831	—	2.00	3.50	10.00	20.00

Mint mark: B

KM#	Date	Mintage	VG	Fine	VF	XF
366.2	1824	.879	2.50	4.00	12.50	22.50
	1825	Inc. Ab.	2.50	4.00	12.50	22.50
	1826	.695	2.50	4.00	12.50	22.50
	1827	.352	2.50	4.00	12.50	22.50
	1828	2.539	2.50	4.00	12.50	22.50
	1829	3.993	2.50	4.00	12.50	22.50
	1830	.359	2.50	4.00	12.50	22.50
	1831	—		Counterfeits exist		—

NOTE: Coins with P mint mark are all counterfeit.

Mint mark: SP
PEDRO I
Weight: 5 1/3 oitavos = 19.13 g

KM#	Date	Mintage	Good	VG	Fine	VF
376	1825	—	7.50	12.50	15.00	25.00
	1828	—	4.50	7.50	10.00	15.00
	1829	—	4.50	7.50	10.00	15.00

NOTE: Many varieties of the Sao Paulo coins exist.

Mint mark: C
PEDRO I
Weight: 4 oitavos = 14.34 g

KM#	Date	Mintage	Good	VG	Fine	VF
377.1	1826	—	5.00	7.50	15.00	35.00
	1827	—	15.00	25.00	50.00	100.00
	1828	—	5.00	7.50	15.00	35.00
	1830	—	10.00	30.00	60.00	100.00

Mint mark: G

KM#	Date	Mintage	Good	VG	Fine	VF
377.2	1826	—	5.00	7.50	15.00	25.00
	1828	—	5.00	7.50	15.00	25.00
	1829	—	5.00	7.50	15.00	25.00
	1830	—	5.00	7.50	15.00	25.00
	1831	—	5.00	10.00	20.00	40.00

NOTE: Coins dated 1826G are believed to be counterfeit.

Rev: Arms w/o stars.

KM#	Date	Mintage	Good	VG	Fine	VF
377.3	1828	—	30.00	50.00	70.00	100.00

Mint mark: R
PEDRO II
Weight: 8 oitavos = 28.69 g
Rev: Similar to KM#366.1.

KM#	Date	Mintage	VG	Fine	VF	XF
379	1831	—	2.50	3.50	9.00	17.50
	1832	6.119	2.50	3.50	9.00	17.50
	1833	—	—	Reported, not confirmed		

Mint mark: SP
PEDRO II
Weight: 5 1/3 oitavos = 19.13 g

KM#	Date	Mintage	Good	VG	Fine	VF
382	1832	—	30.00	60.00	100.00	150.00

NOTE: The 1832SP is considered a counterfeit by many authorities.

Mint mark: G
PEDRO II
Weight: 4 oitavos = 14.34 g

KM#	Date	Mintage	Good	VG	Fine	VF
383	1832	—	3.00	5.00	10.00	20.00
	1833	—	3.00	5.00	10.00	20.00
	1833 Petrus I (error)	—	35.00	65.00	120.00	175.00

REGIONAL COUNTERMARKS

NOTE: Due to variations in value from one part of the country to another, copper coins tended to flow to areas where their buying power was greatest. To prevent the outflow, some districts ordered coinage countermarked and reduced in value. There is speculation that silver coins were also ordered to be countermarked, but no documentation is available to substantiate this claim. The following issues are recognized as genuine. Prices are for countermarks on common coins of each variety. Countermarked rare dates bring a premium.

CEARA

Ceara is a state in northeastern Brazil. Due to coin shortages a law was passed October 3, 1833 that copper coins would be countermarked and pass for 1/2 of their face value. In November of 1834 legislation was passed to stop the star countermarks.

Coins of 20, 40, and 80 Reis were countermarked CEARA in a 5-pointed star to indicate a 50 percent reduction in value (to 10, 20, and 40 Reis).

10 REIS

COPPER
c/m: Star on various 20 Reis.

KM#	Date	Year	Good	VG	Fine	VF
396	ND	(1834)	7.50	10.00	12.50	25.00

20 REIS

COPPER
c/m: Star on various 40 Reis.

KM#	Date	Year	Good	VG	Fine	VF
397	ND	(1834)	7.50	10.00	15.00	30.00

40 REIS

COPPER
c/m: Star on various 80 Reis.

KM#	Date	Year	Good	VG	Fine	VF
398	ND	(1834)	10.00	12.50	17.50	45.00

NOTE: A few silver coins bearing this c/m are considered trial pieces and are rare. Many imitations of this c/m exist on various silver coins and are listed in "Unusual World Coins."

MARANHAO

Maranhao is a state in northeastern Brazil. Coin shortages caused 2 issues of countermarked coins. The first was to make the coins pass for 1/4 their face value. These had M and the new value in Roman numerals. Trial impressions of unadopted designs using M and the new value in Arabic numerals are also known. The second issue was to make the coins pass for 1/2 the face value. These were countermarked with an M. These too were soon recalled.

FIRST SERIES (1834)

M and denomination in Roman numerals within a rectangle.

5 REIS

COPPER
c/m: M/V on various 20 Reis.

KM#	Date	Year	Good	VG	Fine	VF
401	ND	(1834)	12.00	15.00	25.00	40.00

10 REIS

COPPER
c/m: M/X on various 40 Reis.

KM#	Date	Year	Good	VG	Fine	VF
402	ND	(1834)	10.00	12.50	22.50	35.00

20 REIS

COPPER
c/m: M/XX on various 80 Reis.

KM#	Date	Year	Good	VG	Fine	VF
403	ND	(1834)	7.50	10.00	20.00	30.00

SECOND SERIES (1835)

Large M on reverse of coin.

10 REIS

COPPER
c/m: M on various 20 Reis.

KM#	Date	Year	Good	VG	Fine	VF
404	ND	(1835)	7.50	10.00	20.00	30.00

20 REIS

COPPER
c/m: M on various 40 Reis.

KM#	Date	Year	Good	VG	Fine	VF
405	ND	(1835)	7.50	10.00	20.00	30.00

40 REIS

COPPER
c/m: M on various 80 Reis.

KM#	Date	Year	Good	VG	Fine	VF
406	ND	(1835)	10.00	15.00	25.00	50.00

NOTE: Second series countermarks are found struck over coins which already have the first series countermark. They are worth about 50 percent more than ordinary second series coins.

PARA

Para is a state in northern Brazil. Two series of countermarks were issued from this state. On January 14, 1835 Governor Malcher authorized a law for the countermarking of the recently withdrawn Mato Grosso coppers to 1/4 of their previous value. On March 6, 1835 Governor Vinagre authorized the countermarking of coppers at 1/2 their face value. Although heavily counterfeited because of their crudeness these coins stayed in circulation until 1868 and even later.

Crude Arabic 10, 20, or 40 countermarked on obverse of coins weighing 2, 4, and 8 oitavos, respectively. The numerals are quite crude and styles vary and are easily distinguished from the general countermarks. Examples of the Para marks are:

10 20 40

10 REIS

COPPER
c/m: 10 on various Colonial XX (20) Reis.

KM#	Date	Year	Good	VG	Fine	VF
407	ND	(1835)	5.00	7.50	10.00	20.00

c/m: 10 on Imperial 20 Reis, R or B mints.

KM#	Date	Year	Good	VG	Fine	VF
408	ND	(1835)	5.00	7.50	10.00	15.00

c/m: 10 on Imperial 40 Reis, C or G mints, KM#364.1 and KM#364.2.

KM#	Date	Year	Good	VG	Fine	VF
409	ND	(1835)	7.50	10.00	15.00	25.00

20 REIS

COPPER
c/m: 20 on Colonial XL (40) Reis.

KM#	Date	Year	Good	VG	Fine	VF
410	ND	(1835)	5.00	7.50	12.50	17.50

c/m: 20 on Imperial 40 Reis, R or B mints.

KM#	Date	Year	Good	VG	Fine	VF
411	ND	(1835)	5.00	7.50	12.50	17.50

c/m: 20 on Imperial 80 Reis, C or G mints, KM#377.1 and KM#377.2.

KM#	Date	Year	Good	VG	Fine	VF
412	ND	(1835)	7.00	10.00	15.00	30.00

40 REIS

COPPER
c/m: 40 on Colonial LXXX (80) Reis.

KM#	Date	Year	Good	VG	Fine	VF
413	ND	(1835)	5.00	7.50	10.00	15.00

c/m: 40 on Imperial 80 Reis, R or B mints.

KM#	Date	Year	Good	VG	Fine	VF
414	ND	(1835)	5.00	7.50	10.00	15.00

REPUBLIC OF PIRATINI

As a result of a revolt in 1835 in the southern Brazilian state of Rio Grande do Sol the "Republic of Piratini" was briefly established and all coins then circulating in the province were countermarked with the arms of the new republic. This series is probably the most counterfeited of all of the elaborate countermarks.

1835-1845

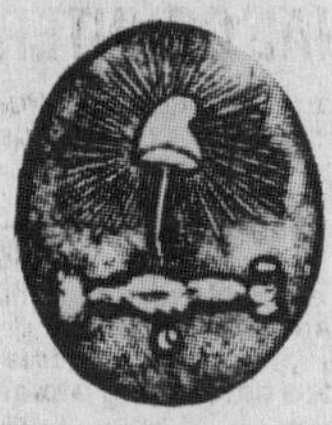

Two hands grasping a sword with Liberty cap on point within oval. Similar countermarks with either the date 1835 or PIRATINI at the bottom or date divided are considered to be fantasies.

20 REIS

COPPER
c/m: On various 20 Reis.

KM#	Date	Year	VG	Fine	VF	XF
A415	ND	—	45.00	90.00	150.00	225.00

40 REIS

COPPER
c/m: On various 40 Reis.

KM#	Date	Year	VG	Fine	VF	XF
B415	ND	—	45.00	90.00	150.00	225.00

80 REIS

COPPER
c/m: On various 80 Reis.

KM#	Date	Year	VG	Fine	VF	XF
C415	ND	—	45.00	90.00	150.00	225.00

320 REIS

SILVER
c/m: On 320 Reis, KM#374.

KM#	Date	Year	VG	Fine	VF	XF
E415	ND(1825R)	—	—	—	Rare	—

640 REIS

SILVER
c/m: On 640 Reis, KM#367.

KM#	Date	Year	VG	Fine	VF	XF
F415	ND(1825R)	—	—	—	Rare	—

960 REIS

SILVER
c/m: On Columbia-Cundinamarca 8 Reales, KM#6.

KM#	Date	Year	VG	Fine	VF	XF
G415	ND(1821)	—	—	—	Rare	—

c/m: On Spain 8 Reales, C#93.

KM#	Date	Year	VG	Fine	VF	XF
H415	ND(1809 IG)	—	—	—	Rare	—

c/m: On Brazil 960 Reis, KM#368.1.

KM#	Date	Year	VG	Fine	VF	XF
I415	ND(1826R)	—	—	—	Rare	—

ICO

Ico is a city in the state of Ceara in northeastern Brazil. It was the center of a revolutionary movement from 1829-1832. Various copper and silver coins countermarked ICO, YCO, JGO and IGO are all considered counterfeit, countermarked after the suppression of the revolt. They have little value, but are collected as curiosities. Average value, about $4.00.

NOTE: In addition to local countermarks, over 280 private countermarks are known. A list of these is given by Kurt Prober, in his "Catalogo das Moedas Brasileiras".

National Countermarks

In order to prevent chaotic conditions resulting from local and private countermarking, the government passed law #54 of 6 October 1835 ordering all coppers countermarked according to the following standards:

2 Oitavos = 7.18 g = 10 Reis

4 Oitavos = 14.34 g = 20 Reis

8 Oitavos = 28.69 g = 40 Reis

The countermarks consist of neat numerals within a circle, having a plain or shaded field. These countermarks were applied to various Brazilian coinage from 1799 to 1833. In addition, wrong countermarks are occasionally found, as well as various Portuguese, Angolan, San Tome, Mozambiquean and pre-1799 Brazilian coins.

10 REIS

COPPER
Mint: Lisbon - w/o mint mark.
c/m: 10 on XX (20) Reis, KM#229.

KM#	Date	Year	Good	VG	Fine	VF
416	ND(1835)	1799	5.00	9.00	18.00	35.00

c/m: 10 on XX (20) Reis, KM#233.1.

KM#	Date	Year	Good	VG	Fine	VF
417.1	ND(1835)	1802	2.50	5.00	10.00	17.50

KM#	Date	Year	Good	VG	Fine	VF
417.1		1803	2.50	5.00	10.00	17.50
		1805	2.50	5.00	10.00	17.50

Mint mark: B

KM#	Date	Year	Good	VG	Fine	VF
417.2	ND(1835)	1812	3.50	6.00	10.00	18.00
		1813	2.50	4.50	7.00	15.00
		1815	2.50	4.50	7.00	15.00
		1816	2.50	4.50	7.00	15.00

Mint mark: R

KM#	Date	Year	Good	VG	Fine	VF
417.3	ND(1835)	1812	3.00	6.00	13.00	25.00
		1813	3.00	6.00	13.00	25.00
		1814	3.00	6.00	13.00	25.00
		1815	3.00	6.00	13.00	25.00

c/m: 10 on XX (20) Reis, KM#309.

KM#	Date	Year	Good	VG	Fine	VF
418	ND(1835)	1816	3.00	6.00	13.00	25.00
		1817	3.00	6.00	13.00	25.00
		1818	4.00	8.00	15.00	30.00

c/m: 10 on XL (40) Reis, KM#318.

KM#	Date	Year	Good	VG	Fine	VF
419	ND(1835)	1818	12.50	18.50	27.50	40.00

c/m: 10 on XX (20) Reis, KM#316.1.

KM#	Date	Year	Good	VG	Fine	VF
420.1	ND(1835)	1818	2.50	5.00	7.50	15.00
		1819	2.50	5.00	7.50	15.00
		1820	2.50	5.00	7.50	15.00
		1821	2.50	5.00	7.50	15.00
		1822	2.50	5.00	7.50	15.00

Mint mark: B

KM#	Date	Year	Good	VG	Fine	VF
420.2	ND(1835)	1820	3.00	6.00	11.00	17.50
		1821	3.00	6.00	11.00	17.50

Mint mark: M
c/m: 10 on 37-1/2 Reis, KM#317.1.

KM#	Date	Year	Good	VG	Fine	VF
421.1	ND(1835)	1818	2.50	8.00	15.00	22.00
		1819	2.50	8.00	15.00	22.00
		1819 medal strike	3.00	10.00	17.50	25.00
		1821	2.50	8.00	15.00	22.00
		1821 medal strike	2.50	8.00	15.00	22.00

Mint mark: R

KM#	Date	Year	Good	VG	Fine	VF
421.2	ND(1835)	1818	12.50	30.00	50.00	110.00

Mint: Lisbon - w/o mint mark.
c/m: 10 on XL (40) Reis, KM#340.

KM#	Date	Year	Good	VG	Fine	VF
422	ND(1835)	1820	25.00	75.00	100.00	150.00

Mint mark: R
c/m: 10 on 20 Reis, Pedro I, KM#360.1.

KM#	Date	Year	Good	VG	Fine	VF
423.1	ND(1835)	1823	2.50	4.50	7.50	15.00
		1824	2.50	4.50	7.50	15.00
		1825	2.50	4.50	7.50	15.00
		1826	2.50	4.50	7.50	15.00
		1827	2.50	4.50	7.50	15.00
		1828	2.50	4.50	7.50	15.00
		1829	2.50	4.50	7.50	15.00
		1830	2.50	4.50	7.50	15.00

Mint mark: B
c/m: 10 on 20 Reis of Pedro I, KM#360.2.

KM#	Date	Year	Good	VG	Fine	VF
423.2	ND(1835)	1825	3.00	5.00	9.00	17.50
		1827	3.00	5.00	9.00	17.50
		1828	3.00	5.00	9.00	17.50
		1830	3.00	5.00	9.00	17.50

Mint mark: C
c/m: 10 on 20 Reis of Pedro I, KM#375.1.

KM#	Date	Year	Good	VG	Fine	VF
424.1	ND(1835)	1825	50.00	100.00	150.00	240.00

Mint mark: G

KM#	Date	Year	Good	VG	Fine	VF
424.2	ND(1835)	1827	20.00	32.50	50.00	100.00

NOTE: The above two pieces were not supposed to have been countermarked, as they only weigh one oitavo-3.59 g.

Mint mark: R
c/m: 10 on 20 Reis of Pedro II, KM#380.

KM#	Date	Year	Good	VG	Fine	VF
425	ND(1835)	1832	30.00	60.00	100.00	150.00

Mint mark: M
c/m: 10 on 37-1/2 Reis of Pedro I.

KM#	Date	Year	Good	VG	Fine	VF
426	ND(1835)	1823	7.50	20.00	40.00	75.00
		1824	7.50	20.00	40.00	75.00
		1825	7.50	20.00	40.00	75.00
		1826	7.50	20.00	40.00	75.00
		1827	7.50	20.00	40.00	75.00
		1828	7.50	20.00	40.00	75.00

Mint mark: C
c/m: 10 on 40 Reis of Pedro I, KM#364.1.

KM#	Date	Year	Good	VG	Fine	VF
427.1	ND(1835)	1823	4.50	7.50	12.50	20.00
		1824	2.00	5.00	7.50	15.00
		1825	2.00	5.00	7.50	15.00
		1826	2.00	5.00	7.50	15.00
		1827	2.00	5.00	7.50	15.00
		1828	2.00	5.00	7.50	15.00
		1829	2.00	5.00	7.50	15.00
		1830	2.00	5.00	7.50	15.00
		1831	2.00	5.00	7.50	15.00

Mint mark: G
c/m: 10 on 40 Reis of Pedro I, KM#364.2.

KM#	Date	Year	Good	VG	Fine	VF
427.2	ND(1835)	1823	3.00	7.50	12.50	25.00
		1825	3.00	7.50	12.50	25.00
		1826	3.00	7.50	12.50	25.00
		1827	2.00	5.00	10.00	17.50
		1828	2.00	5.00	10.00	17.50
		1829	2.00	5.00	10.00	17.50
		1830	2.00	5.00	10.00	17.50

c/m: 10 on 40 Reis of Pedro II, KM#381.1.

KM#	Date	Year	Good	VG	Fine	VF
428.1	ND(1835)	1832 PETRUS II	3.00	7.50	12.50	17.50
		1832 Petrus 2.o	2.00	5.00	7.50	12.50

Mint mark: C

KM#	Date	Year	Good	VG	Fine	VF
428.2	ND(1835)	1833	4.50	7.50	12.50	20.00

c/m: 10 on Mozambique 40 Reis, KM#19.

KM#	Date	Year	Good	VG	Fine	VF
429	ND(1835)	1819	3.00	7.00	12.50	25.00
		1820	3.00	7.00	12.50	25.00
		1821	3.00	7.00	12.50	25.00
		1821	4.00	9.00	17.50	35.00
		1822	4.00	9.00	17.50	35.00
		1825	4.00	9.00	17.50	35.00

20 REIS

COPPER
Mint: Lisbon - w/o mint mark.
c/m: 20 on XL (40) Reis, KM#230.

KM#	Date	Year	Good	VG	Fine	VF
430	ND(1835)	1799	4.50	7.50	12.50	20.00

c/m: 20 on XL (40) Reis, KM#234.1.

KM#	Date	Year	Good	VG	Fine	VF
431.1	ND(1835)	1802	2.00	3.00	5.00	10.00
		1803	2.00	3.00	5.00	10.00

Mint mark: B

KM#	Date	Year	Good	VG	Fine	VF
431.2	ND(1835)	1809	2.50	5.00	8.00	20.00
		1810	2.50	5.00	10.00	20.00
		1811	2.00	4.00	8.00	16.00
		1812	2.00	4.00	8.00	16.00
		1814	2.00	3.00	5.00	10.00
		1816	2.00	3.00	5.00	10.00

Mint mark: R

KM#	Date	Year	Good	VG	Fine	VF
431.3	ND(1835)	1812	2.00	5.00	10.00	20.00
		1813	2.00	5.00	10.00	20.00
		1815	2.00	5.00	10.00	20.00

c/m: 20 on XL (40) Reis, KM#311.

KM#	Date	Year	Good	VG	Fine	VF
432	ND(1835)	1816	2.00	5.00	8.00	20.00
		1817	2.00	5.00	8.00	20.00

c/m: 20 on XL (40) Reis, KM#319.1.

KM#	Date	Year	Good	VG	Fine	VF
433.1	ND(1835)	1818	2.00	3.50	7.00	15.00
		1819	2.00	3.50	7.00	15.00
		1820	2.00	3.50	7.00	15.00
		1821	2.00	3.50	7.00	15.00
		1822	2.00	3.50	7.00	15.00

Mint mark: B

KM#	Date	Year	Good	VG	Fine	VF
433.2	ND(1835)	1820	2.50	5.00	10.00	22.50
		1821	2.50	5.00	10.00	22.50
		1822	2.50	5.00	10.00	22.50
		1823	3.00	6.00	12.50	27.50

Mint mark: M
c/m: 20 on 75 Reis, KM#320.

KM#	Date	Year	Good	VG	Fine	VF
434	ND(1835)	1818	3.00	5.00	12.00	25.00
		1819	3.00	5.00	12.00	25.00
		1819 medal strike	4.00	7.50	15.00	30.00
		1821	3.00	5.00	12.00	25.00

Mint: Lisbon - w/o mint mark.
c/m: 20 on LXXX (80) Reis, KM#341.

KM#	Date	Year	Good	VG	Fine	VF
435	ND(1835)	1820	4.00	8.00	15.00	25.00

Mint mark: R
c/m: 20 on 40 Reis of Pedro I, KM#363.1.

KM#	Date	Year	Good	VG	Fine	VF
436.1	ND(1835)	1823	2.00	5.00	7.50	10.00
		1824	2.00	5.00	7.50	10.00
		1825	2.00	5.00	7.50	10.00
		1826	2.00	5.00	7.50	10.00
		1827	2.00	5.00	7.50	10.00
		1828	2.00	5.00	7.50	10.00
		1829	2.00	5.00	7.50	10.00
		1830	2.00	5.00	7.50	10.00
		1831	2.00	5.00	7.50	10.00

Mint mark: B

KM#	Date	Year	Good	VG	Fine	VF
436.2	ND(1835)	1824	2.00	5.00	7.50	15.00
		1825	2.00	5.00	7.50	15.00
		1827	2.00	5.00	7.50	15.00
		1828	2.00	5.00	7.50	15.00
		1829	2.00	5.00	7.50	15.00
		1830	2.00	5.00	7.50	15.00

Mint mark: R
c/m: 20 on 40 Reis of Pedro II, KM#378.

KM#	Date	Year	Good	VG	Fine	VF
437	ND(1835)	1831	2.00	5.00	7.50	12.50
		1832	2.00	5.00	7.50	12.50

Mint mark: G
c/m: 20 on 75 Reis of Pedro I, KM#365.

KM#	Date	Year	Good	VG	Fine	VF
438	ND(1835)	1823	8.00	12.50	20.00	35.00

Mint mark: C
c/m: 20 on 80 Reis of Pedro I, KM#377.1.

KM#	Date	Year	Good	VG	Fine	VF
439.1	ND(1835)	1826	2.00	3.00	5.00	10.00
		1827	6.00	9.00	16.00	30.00
		1828	3.00	5.00	7.50	12.50
		1830	3.00	5.00	7.50	12.50

Mint mark: G

KM#	Date	Year	Good	VG	Fine	VF
439.2	ND(1835)	1826	2.00	5.00	7.50	12.50
		1828	2.00	3.00	6.50	10.00
		1829	2.00	3.00	6.50	10.00
		1830	2.00	3.00	6.50	10.00
		1831	6.00	10.00	17.50	40.00

c/m: 20 on 80 Reis of Pedro II, KM#383.

KM#	Date	Year	Good	VG	Fine	VF
440	ND(1835)	1832	2.00	3.00	6.00	10.00
		1833	2.00	3.00	6.00	10.00
		1833 Petrus I	10.00	22.00	45.00	95.00

c/m: 20 on Mozambique 80 Reis, KM#20.

KM#	Date	Year	Good	VG	Fine	VF
441	ND(1835)	1819	6.00	12.00	23.00	45.00
		1820	6.00	12.00	23.00	45.00

40 REIS

COPPER
Mint mark: R
c/m: 40 on LXXX (80) Reis, KM#308.

KM#	Date	Year	Good	VG	Fine	VF
442	ND(1835)	1811	4.00	7.00	13.00	25.00
		1812	4.00	7.00	13.00	25.00

Mint mark: B
c/m: 40 on LXXX (80) Reis, KM#342.1.

KM#	Date	Year	Good	VG	Fine	VF
443.1	ND(1835)	1820	2.00	3.50	7.50	12.50
		1821	2.00	3.50	7.50	12.50
		1822	2.00	3.50	7.50	12.50
		1823	2.00	3.50	7.50	15.00

Mint mark: R

KM#	Date	Year	Good	VG	Fine	VF
443.2	ND(1835)	1821	2.00	4.50	7.50	15.00
		1822	2.00	4.50	7.50	15.00

c/m: 40 on 80 Reis of Pedro I, KM#366.1.

KM#	Date	Year	Good	VG	Fine	VF
444.1	ND(1835)	1823	3.50	6.00	9.00	17.50
		1824	2.50	5.00	7.50	10.00
		1825	2.50	5.00	7.50	10.00
		1826	2.50	5.00	7.50	10.00
		1827	2.50	5.00	7.50	10.00
		1828	2.50	5.00	7.50	10.00
		1829	2.50	5.00	7.50	10.00
		1830	2.50	5.00	7.50	10.00
		1831	2.50	5.00	7.50	10.00

Mint mark: B

KM#	Date	Year	Good	VG	Fine	VF
444.2	ND(1835)	1824	2.50	5.00	7.50	12.50
		1825	2.50	5.00	7.50	12.50
		1826	2.50	5.00	7.50	12.50
		1827	2.50	5.00	7.50	12.50
		1828	2.50	5.00	7.50	12.50
		1829	2.50	5.00	7.50	12.50
		1830	2.50	5.00	7.50	12.50
		1831	2.50	5.00	7.50	12.50

Mint mark: SP
c/m: 40 on 80 Reis of Pedro I, KM#376.

KM#	Date	Year	Good	VG	Fine	VF
445	ND(1835)	1825	5.00	7.50	12.50	25.00
		1828	5.00	7.50	12.50	25.00
		1829	5.00	7.50	12.50	25.00

Mint mark: R
c/m: 40 on 80 Reis of Pedro II, KM#379.

KM#	Date	Year	Good	VG	Fine	VF
446	ND(1835)	1831	5.00	7.50	10.00	15.00
		1832	3.50	5.00	7.50	12.50

Mint mark: SP
c/m: 40 on 80 Reis of Pedro II, KM#382.

KM#	Date	Year	Good	VG	Fine	VF
447	ND(1835)	1832	35.00	60.00	100.00	150.00

EMPIRE

80 REIS

2.2400 g, .917 SILVER, .0660 oz ASW
Mint mark: R
Obv. leg: PETRUS I D.G. . . . . around value in floral circle. Rev: Crowned arms in branches.

KM#	Date	Mintage	Fine	VF	XF	Unc
372	1824	—	200.00	375.00	600.00	1400.
	1826	—	200.00	375.00	600.00	1400.

Obv. leg: PETRUS II D.G. . . . .

KM#	Date	Mintage	Fine	VF	XF	Unc
388	1833	418 pcs.	180.00	300.00	600.00	1400.

160 REIS

4.4800 g, .917 SILVER, .1320 oz ASW
Mint mark: R
Obv. leg: PETRUS I D.G. . . . .

KM#	Date	Mintage	Fine	VF	XF	Unc
373	1824	—	180.00	300.00	500.00	1250.
	1826	—	180.00	300.00	500.00	1250.

Obv. leg: PETRUS II D.G. . . . .

KM#	Date	Mintage	Fine	VF	XF	Unc
389	1833	492 pcs.	300.00	600.00	1300.	1800.

320 REIS

8.9600 g, .917 SILVER, .2640 oz ASW
Mint mark: R
Obv. leg: PETRUS I D.G. . . . .

KM#	Date	Mintage	Fine	VF	XF	Unc
374	1824	642 pcs.	500.00	1000.	1800.	2800.
	1825	.018	20.00	30.00	50.00	90.00
	1826	—	100.00	400.00	1300.	2200.
	1827	—	—	—	Unique	—
	1830	4,190	—	—	Rare	—

Obv. leg: PETRUS II D.G. . . . .

KM#	Date	Mintage	Fine	VF	XF	Unc
390	1833	22 pcs.	—	—	Rare	—

640 REIS

17.9200 g, .917 SILVER, .5280 oz ASW
Mint mark: R
Obv. leg: PETRUS I D.G. . . . .

KM#	Date	Mintage	Fine	VF	XF	Unc
367	1823	—	Counterfeit		—	—
	1824/3	.080	10.00	20.00	40.00	80.00
	1824	Inc. Ab.	10.00	20.00	40.00	80.00
	1825	.353	10.00	20.00	40.00	80.00
	1826	9,472	100.00	200.00	400.00	750.00
	1827	Inc. Ab.	100.00	200.00	400.00	750.00

Obv. leg: PETRUS II D.G. . . . .

KM#	Date	Mintage	Fine	VF	XF	Unc
384	1832	118 pcs.	—	—	Rare	—
	1833	5 pcs.	—	—	Rare	—

960 REIS

26.8900 g, .896 SILVER, .7746 oz ASW
Mint mark: R

KM#	Date	Mintage	Fine	VF	XF	Unc
368.1	1823 SIGNO above crown					
		.395	12.50	25.00	45.00	85.00
	1823 IGNO above crown					
		Inc. Ab.	100.00	150.00	250.00	400.00
	1824	.600	12.50	25.00	45.00	85.00
	1825 small 960					
		.600	12.50	25.00	45.00	90.00
	1825 large 960					
		Inc. Ab.	50.00	100.00	300.00	500.00
	1826	.500	12.50	25.00	45.00	90.00
	1827	.018	—	—	Rare	—
	1828	—	Counterfeit		—	—

Mint mark: B

KM#	Date	Mintage	Fine	VF	XF	Unc
368.2	1824	—	40.00	70.00	140.00	200.00
	1825	—	40.00	70.00	140.00	200.00
	1826	—	150.00	400.00	800.00	1200.

NOTE: KM#368 is occasionally found struck over Spanish Colonial 8 Reales. Specimens having the original elements visible command a premium. Discernable mint mark, assayer initial and date all factor into premium values. See note below Colonial 960 Reis, KM#326.2 for additional information.

Mint mark: R

KM#	Date	Mintage	Fine	VF	XF	Unc
385	1832	3,039	200.00	450.00	1150.	1800.
	1833	Inc. Ab.	500.00	1000.	1750.	2750.
	1834	154 pcs.	850.00	1750.	3000.	4500.

4000 REIS

8.2000 g, .917 GOLD, .2417 oz AGW
Mint mark: R

KM#	Date	Mintage	Fine	VF	XF	Unc
369.1	1823	.021	250.00	450.00	650.00	1200.
	1824	.038	250.00	450.00	650.00	1200.
	1825	.020	250.00	450.00	650.00	1400.
	1826	9,142	350.00	550.00	850.00	1800.
	1827/6	7,771	—	—	Rare	—
	1827	Inc. Ab.	—	—	Rare	—

Mint mark: B

KM#	Date	Mintage	Fine	VF	XF	Unc
369.2	1825	—	1100.	2100.	3600.	5200.
	1826	—	1150.	2300.	3900.	5600.
	1828	—	—	—	Rare	—

Mint mark: R

KM#	Date	Mintage	Fine	VF	XF	Unc
386.1	1832	64 pcs.	1200.	2500.	3750.	5400.
	1833/2					
		257 pcs.	1000.	2100.	3500.	5200.

Obv: AZEVEDO below bust.

KM#	Date	Mintage	Fine	VF	XF	Unc
386.2	1832	5 known	—	—	Rare	—

6400 REIS

14.3400 g, .917 GOLD, .4228 oz AGW
Mint mark: R
Pedro I Coronation

KM#	Date	Mintage	Fine	VF	XF	Unc
361	1822	64 pcs.	—	—	*Rare	—

***NOTE:** Spink London sale No. 52, 6-86 near XF realized $87,000.

KM#	Date	Mintage	Fine	VF	XF	Unc
370.1	1823	931 pcs.	950.00	1900.	3500.	5000.
	1824	235 pcs.	1200.	4500.	6000.	9000.
	1825	776 pcs.	950.00	1900.	3500.	5000.
	1827	637 pcs.	950.00	1900.	3500.	5000.
	1828	650 pcs.	1200.	2400.	3500.	5000.
	1830	—	—	—	Unique	—

Mint mark: B

KM#	Date	Mintage	Fine	VF	XF	Unc
370.2	1825	—	1200.	3500.	5500.	7000.
	1826	—	1200.	3500.	5500.	7000.
	1828	423 pcs.	1200.	3500.	5500.	7000.

Mint mark: R

KM#	Date	Mintage	Fine	VF	XF	Unc
387.1	1832	.030	300.00	600.00	1200.	1600.
	1833	.011	300.00	600.00	1300.	1800.

Obv: AZEVEDO below bust.

KM#	Date	Mintage	Fine	VF	XF	Unc
387.2	1832	4,101	500.00	1000.	2000.	3000.

MONETARY REFORM

10 REIS

BRONZE

KM#	Date	Mintage	Fine	VF	XF	Unc
473	1868	89.604	.50	2.00	4.00	7.00
	1869	Inc. Ab.	.50	2.00	4.00	7.00
	1870	—	.50	2.00	5.00	8.00

20 REIS

BRONZE

KM#	Date	Mintage	Fine	VF	XF	Unc
474	1868	90.360	1.50	2.25	4.00	7.00
	1869	Inc. Ab.	1.50	2.25	4.00	7.00
	1870	—	1.75	3.50	7.50	20.00

40 REIS

BRONZE

KM#	Date	Mintage	Fine	VF	XF	Unc
479	1873	3.750	1.00	2.50	5.00	30.00
	1874	.890	1.00	2.50	6.00	35.00
	1875	1.208	1.00	2.50	5.00	30.00
	1876	.549	1.00	4.00	12.00	70.00
	1877	.465	1.00	3.00	10.00	60.00
	1878	1.223	1.00	2.50	6.00	35.00
	1879	2.771	1.00	2.50	5.00	30.00
	1880	1.569	1.00	2.50	5.00	30.00

50 REIS

COPPER-NICKEL

KM#	Date	Mintage	Fine	VF	XF	Unc
482	1886	.590	1.00	2.00	7.00	17.50
	1887	Inc. Ab.	1.00	2.50	7.00	20.00
	1888	.153	1.00	2.50	7.00	35.00

100 REIS

2.2400 g, .917 SILVER, .0660 oz ASW
Obv: Value in floral circle.
Rev: Crowned arms in branches.

KM#	Date	Mintage	Fine	VF	XF	Unc
452	1834	7,709	20.00	35.00	65.00	200.00
	1835	Inc. Ab.	20.00	35.00	65.00	200.00
	1836	5,592	400.00	700.00	1000.	2750.
	1837	9,562	20.00	35.00	65.00	200.00
	1840	910 pcs.	125.00	175.00	250.00	500.00
	1844	—	—	—	Rare	—
	1846	4,699	20.00	35.00	65.00	200.00
	1847/4	682 pcs.	125.00	200.00	350.00	600.00
	1848	486 pcs.	300.00	450.00	700.00	1750.

COPPER-NICKEL

KM#	Date	Mintage	Fine	VF	XF	Unc
477	1871	4.000	.50	1.25	3.00	50.00
	1872	100 pcs.	600.00	900.00	1800.	3000.
	1874	—	.75	2.50	12.00	80.00
	1875	—	5.00	30.00	150.00	600.00
	1876	—	2.50	20.00	150.00	600.00
	1877	—	.75	2.50	12.00	80.00
477	1878	—	1.00	3.00	25.00	200.00
	1879	—	1.00	2.50	12.00	80.00
	1880	—	1.50	5.00	100.00	600.00
	1881	—	.75	2.50	12.00	70.00
	1882	—	.75	2.50	12.00	70.00
	1883	2,700	.75	2.50	12.00	70.00
	1884	—	.75	2.50	12.00	70.00
	1885	—	.75	2.50	12.00	70.00

KM#	Date	Mintage	Fine	VF	XF	Unc
483	1886	.877	.75	2.00	9.50	70.00
	1887	—	.75	2.00	9.50	70.00
	1888	1.696	.75	2.00	9.50	70.00
	1889	.862	.75	2.00	9.50	70.00

200 REIS

4.4800 g, .917 SILVER, .1320 oz ASW

KM#	Date	Mintage	Fine	VF	XF	Unc
455	1835	4,894	20.00	50.00	100.00	300.00
	1837	5,007	20.00	50.00	100.00	300.00
	1840	624 pcs.	125.00	300.00	500.00	800.00
	1844	893 pcs.	100.00	200.00	300.00	500.00
	1846	406 pcs.	150.00	300.00	450.00	500.00
	1847	2,936	25.00	45.00	125.00	300.00
	1848/7	501 pcs.	200.00	400.00	800.00	1000.
	1848	Inc. Ab.	250.00	400.00	800.00	1000.

2.5500 g, .917 SILVER, .0752 oz ASW

KM#	Date	Mintage	Fine	VF	XF	Unc
469	1854	.037	6.00	10.00	30.00	100.00
	1855	.228	3.00	6.00	10.00	25.00
	1856/5	.103	3.00	6.00	10.00	25.00
	1856	Inc. Ab.	3.00	6.00	10.00	25.00
	1857	.128	3.00	6.00	10.00	25.00
	1858	.245	3.00	6.00	10.00	25.00
	1859	.152	3.00	6.00	10.00	25.00
	1860	.028	3.00	6.00	10.00	25.00
	1861	—	4.00	10.00	30.00	100.00
	1862	—	3.00	6.00	10.00	25.00
	1863	—	3.00	6.00	10.00	25.00
	1864	—	3.00	6.00	10.00	25.00
	1865/4	—	—	—	—	—
	1865	—	3.00	6.00	10.00	25.00
	1866	—	3.00	6.00	10.00	25.00
	1867	—	3.00	6.00	10.00	25.00

2.5000 g, .835 SILVER, .0671 oz ASW

KM#	Date	Mintage	Fine	VF	XF	Unc
471	1867	—	2.50	4.00	9.00	25.00
	1868	—	2.50	4.00	9.00	25.00
	1869	—	5.00	10.00	20.00	50.00

COPPER-NICKEL

KM#	Date	Mintage	Fine	VF	XF	Unc
478	1871	3.650	.50	1.25	4.00	50.00
	1874	—	1.00	2.00	5.00	80.00
	1875	—	3.00	10.00	50.00	200.00
	1876	—	1.00	2.00	5.00	80.00
	1877	—	1.00	2.00	5.00	80.00
	1878	—	1.00	2.50	7.00	90.00
	1880	—	1.00	3.00	6.00	80.00
	1882	—	1.00	3.50	6.00	80.00
	1884	—	1.00	1.25	6.00	80.00

KM#	Date	Mintage	Fine	VF	XF	Unc
484	1886	.177	4.50	18.00	65.00	200.00
	1887	—	1.00	2.00	6.00	60.00
	1888	.967	1.00	2.00	6.00	60.00
	1889	.511	1.50	2.50	7.00	65.00

400 REIS

8.9600 g, .917 SILVER, .2640 oz ASW
Obv: Value in floral circle.
Rev: Crowned arms in branches.

KM#	Date	Mintage	Fine	VF	XF	Unc
453	1834	6,197	50.00	100.00	175.00	400.00
	1835	Inc. Ab.	50.00	100.00	175.00	400.00
	1837	7,837	50.00	100.00	175.00	400.00
	1840	—	100.00	300.00	700.00	1200.
	1841	—	200.00	600.00	1000.	1800.
	1843	161 pcs.	400.00	800.00	1600.	2500.
	1844	649 pcs.	100.00	250.00	600.00	1100.
	1845	179 pcs.	100.00	350.00	700.00	1200.
	1847/0	878 pcs.	125.00	250.00	500.00	1000.
	1847	Inc. Ab.	60.00	125.00	200.00	400.00
	1848	510 pcs.	200.00	600.00	1000.	1800.

500 REIS

6.3750 g, .917 SILVER, .1880 oz ASW

KM#	Date	Mintage	Fine	VF	XF	Unc
458	1848	—	—	—	Rare	—
	1849	.026	25.00	50.00	80.00	200.00
	1850	.067	7.50	10.00	18.00	50.00
	1851	.095	7.50	10.00	18.00	50.00
	1852	.167	7.50	10.00	18.00	50.00

KM#	Date	Mintage	Fine	VF	XF	Unc
464	1853	.241	5.00	8.50	10.00	35.00
	1854	.317	5.00	8.50	10.00	35.00
	1855	.212	5.00	8.50	10.00	35.00
	1856	.223	5.00	8.50	10.00	35.00
	1857	.265	5.00	7.50	10.00	35.00
	1858	.791	5.00	7.50	10.00	35.00
	1859	.152	5.00	7.50	10.00	35.00
	1860/50	*.108	5.00	7.50	10.00	50.00
	1860	Inc. Ab.	5.00	7.50	10.00	35.00
	1861	—	5.00	7.50	10.00	35.00
	1862	—	5.00	7.50	10.00	35.00
	1863	—	5.00	7.50	10.00	35.00
	1864	—	5.00	7.50	10.00	35.00
	1865	—	5.00	7.50	10.00	35.00
	1866	—	5.00	7.50	10.00	35.00
	1867	—	5.00	7.50	10.00	35.00

***NOTE:** The 1860 mintage figure includes only first six month's production.

6.2500 g, .835 SILVER, .1678 oz ASW

Obv: C.L. below truncation.

KM#	Date	Mintage	Fine	VF	XF	Unc
472	1867	—	5.00	7.50	10.00	35.00
	1868	—	5.00	7.50	10.00	35.00

6.3750 g, .917 SILVER, .1879 oz ASW
Obv: W/o C.L. Rev. leg: DECRETO DE 1870.

KM#	Date	Mintage	Fine	VF	XF	Unc
480	1876	.076	4.50	10.00	15.00	50.00
	1886	5,283	50.00	100.00	150.00	300.00
	1887	768 pcs.	600.00	900.00	1250.	1750.
	1888	.333	4.50	7.00	10.00	35.00
	1889	.278	4.50	7.00	10.00	35.00

800 REIS

17.9300 g, .917 SILVER, .5283 oz ASW

KM#	Date	Mintage	Fine	VF	XF	Unc
456	1835	1,698	600.00	800.00	1600.	2500.
	1838	497 pcs.	500.00	900.00	1800.	2800.
	1840	145 pcs.	800.00	1200.	2000.	3000.
	1843	127 pcs.	2000.	3000.	4000.	6000.
	1844	628 pcs.	600.00	1000.	1800.	3000.
	1846	672 pcs.	600.00	1000.	1800.	3000.

1000 REIS

12.7500 g, .917 SILVER, .3757 oz ASW

KM#	Date	Mintage	Fine	VF	XF	Unc
459	1849	965 pcs.	600.00	1000.	1500.	2500.
	1850	.169	6.00	8.00	15.00	60.00
	1851	.099	6.00	8.00	15.00	65.00
	1852	.196	6.00	8.00	15.00	60.00

KM#	Date	Mintage	Fine	VF	XF	Unc
465	1853	.266	6.00	8.00	20.00	40.00
	1854	.228	6.00	8.00	20.00	40.00
	1855	.312	6.00	8.00	20.00	40.00
	1856	.426	6.00	8.00	20.00	40.00
	1857	.512	6.00	8.00	20.00	40.00
	1858	.430	6.00	8.00	20.00	40.00
	1859	.996	6.00	8.00	20.00	40.00
	1860/50	.387	8.00	12.00	30.00	60.00
	1860	Inc. Ab.	6.00	8.00	20.00	40.00
	1861	—	6.00	8.00	20.00	40.00
	1862	—	6.00	8.00	20.00	40.00
	1863	—	6.00	8.00	20.00	40.00
	1864	—	6.00	8.00	20.00	40.00
	1865	—	6.00	8.00	20.00	40.00
	1866	—	6.00	8.00	20.00	40.00

12.5000 g, .900 SILVER, .3617 oz ASW

Obv: LUSTER F. below truncation.

KM#	Date	Mintage	Fine	VF	XF	Unc
476	1869	—	15.00	25.00	50.00	85.00

12.7500 g, .917 SILVER, .3759 oz ASW
Obv: W/o LUSTER F. Rev. leg: DECRETO DE 1870.

KM#	Date	Mintage	Fine	VF	XF	Unc
481	1876	.194	7.50	12.50	20.00	60.00
	1877	.012	17.50	30.00	30.00	100.00
	1878	.047	12.50	17.50	30.00	90.00
	1879	.035	12.50	17.50	30.00	85.00
	1880	.020	12.50	17.50	30.00	90.00
	1881	.020	20.00	30.00	45.00	140.00
	1882	.018	25.00	40.00	75.00	175.00
	1883	.031	12.50	17.50	30.00	80.00
	1884	.022	20.00	30.00	65.00	150.00
	1885	.011	30.00	40.00	75.00	175.00
	1886	.048	8.50	15.00	30.00	100.00
	1887	9,875	35.00	60.00	80.00	175.00
	1888	.100	7.50	12.50	20.00	65.00
	1889	.089	50.00	70.00	90.00	200.00

1200 REIS

26.8900 g, .917 SILVER, .7924 oz ASW

KM#	Date	Mintage	Fine	VF	XF	Unc
454	1834	891 pcs.	75.00	250.00	500.00	1250.
	1835	.010	75.00	180.00	450.00	1250.
	1837	6,304	75.00	175.00	450.00	1250.
	1839	186 pcs.	—	—	Rare	—
	1840/37	633 pcs.	250.00	425.00	900.00	2000.
	1840	Inc. Ab.	225.00	450.00	700.00	1500.
	1843	1,803	100.00	450.00	500.00	1250.
	1845	292 pcs.	375.00	750.00	1250.	2500.
	1846	1,898	200.00	450.00	900.00	2000.
	1847	.010	75.00	175.00	500.00	1250.

NOTE: The above type dated 1841 and 1842 are counterfeit.

2000 REIS

25.5000 g, .917 SILVER, .7514 oz ASW

KM#	Date	Mintage	Fine	VF	XF	Unc
462	1851	.256	10.00	15.00	30.00	100.00
	1852	.277	10.00	15.00	30.00	100.00

KM#	Date	Mintage	Fine	VF	XF	Unc
466	1853	.145	10.00	20.00	35.00	80.00
	1854	.086	20.00	30.00	60.00	125.00
	1855	.300	10.00	20.00	35.00	100.00
	1856	.229	10.00	20.00	35.00	80.00
	1857	.105	20.00	30.00	50.00	80.00
	1858	.022	35.00	65.00	100.00	200.00
	1859	.041	400.00	800.00	1250.	1750.
	1863	—	10.00	20.00	35.00	80.00
	1864	—	35.00	65.00	100.00	300.00
	1865	—	20.00	30.00	50.00	80.00
	1866	—	400.00	800.00	1250.	1750.
	1867	—	400.00	800.00	1250.	1750.

25.0000 g, .900 SILVER, .7234 oz ASW
Obv: LUSTER F. below truncation.

KM#	Date	Mintage	Fine	VF	XF	Unc
475	1868	—	20.00	30.00	80.00	200.00
	1869	—	15.00	20.00	50.00	150.00

25.5000 g, .917 SILVER, .7515 oz ASW

KM#	Date	Mintage	Fine	VF	XF	Unc
475a	1875	—	15.00	25.00	50.00	150.00
	1876	—	75.00	125.00	200.00	500.00

Obv: W/o LUSTER F. Rev. leg: DECRETO DE 1870.

KM#	Date	Mintage	Fine	VF	XF	Unc
485	1886	1,190	400.00	600.00	1000.	1400.
	1887	.043	15.00	25.00	45.00	125.00
	1888	.906	10.00	15.00	25.00	60.00
	1889	—	10.00	15.00	25.00	60.00

5000 REIS

4.4824 g, .917 GOLD, .1321 oz AGW

KM#	Date	Mintage	Fine	VF	XF	Unc
470	1854	.021	75.00	100.00	125.00	200.00
	1855	.047	90.00	120.00	150.00	250.00
	1856	.027	75.00	100.00	125.00	200.00
	1857	4,631	150.00	400.00	1150.	1350.
	1858	1,146	250.00	1000.	1750.	2500.
	1859	493	350.00	2000.	2500.	3500.

10,000 REIS

14.3400 g, .917 GOLD, .4228 oz AGW

KM#	Date	Mintage	Fine	VF	XF	Unc
451	1833	7,304	200.00	500.00	700.00	1000.
	1834	5,617	200.00	500.00	700.00	1000.
	1835	.013	200.00	500.00	700.00	1000.
	1836	.011	300.00	550.00	750.00	1800.
	1838	482 pcs.	350.00	1000.	2000.	3000.
	1839	567 pcs.	350.00	1000.	2000.	3000.
	1840	4,462	200.00	900.00	1600.	2200.

Obv: Military bust

KM#	Date	Mintage	Fine	VF	XF	Unc
457	1841	3,454	300.00	800.00	1500.	2000.
	1842	1,146	350.00	1200.	2000.	3000.
	1843	544 pcs.	350.00	1500.	2200.	3200.
	1844	1,989	350.00	1000.	2000.	3000.
	1845	3,834	250.00	600.00	1000.	2000.
	1847	.026	225.00	600.00	1000.	2000.
	1848	4,567	350.00	1000.	2000.	3000.

8.9648 g, .917 GOLD, .2643 oz AGW
Reduced size, 26mm.

KM#	Date	Mintage	Fine	VF	XF	Unc
460	1849	1,678	300.00	750.00	1000.	1500.
	1850	7,359	150.00	250.00	400.00	700.00
	1851	.011	150.00	250.00	400.00	700.00

KM#	Date	Mintage	Fine	VF	XF	Unc
467	1853	.040	BV	140.00	180.00	400.00
	1854	.163	BV	140.00	180.00	400.00
	1855	.041	BV	140.00	180.00	400.00
	1856	.208	BV	140.00	180.00	400.00
	1857	.098	BV	140.00	180.00	400.00
	1858	.055	BV	140.00	180.00	400.00
	1859	.016	150.00	350.00	1850.	3000.
	1861	—	BV	140.00	180.00	450.00
	1863	—	150.00	350.00	1850.	3000.
	1865	—	BV	140.00	180.00	400.00
	1866	—	BV	140.00	180.00	400.00
	1867	—	BV	140.00	180.00	400.00
	1871	—	BV	160.00	200.00	500.00
	1872	—	BV	160.00	200.00	500.00
	1873	—	BV	160.00	200.00	500.00
	1874	—	BV	160.00	200.00	500.00
	1875	—	BV	160.00	200.00	500.00
	1876	.020	BV	160.00	200.00	500.00
	1877	3,441	BV	200.00	300.00	650.00
	1878	.010	BV	150.00	200.00	650.00

KM#	Date	Mintage	Fine	VF	XF	Unc
467	1879	6,431	BV	150.00	200.00	650.00
	1880	9,806	BV	200.00	300.00	650.00
	1882	4,671	BV	220.00	350.00	700.00
	1883	.010	BV	200.00	250.00	600.00
	1884	.011	BV	160.00	200.00	600.00
	1885	7,955	100.00	300.00	650.00	1250.
	1886	3,782	BV	220.00	350.00	700.00
	1887	1,180	100.00	300.00	650.00	1250.
	1888	5,359	BV	250.00	400.00	800.00
	1889	—	BV	220.00	350.00	700.00

20,000 REIS

17.9296 g, .917 GOLD, .5286 oz AGW

KM#	Date	Mintage	Fine	VF	XF	Unc
461	1849	6,464	275.00	600.00	800.00	1000.
	1850	.042	260.00	300.00	500.00	700.00
	1851	.303	260.00	300.00	500.00	700.00

KM#	Date	Mintage	Fine	VF	XF	Unc
463	1851	Inc. Ab.	260.00	300.00	400.00	550.00
	1852	.186	260.00	300.00	400.00	550.00

Obv: Larger bust

KM#	Date	Mintage	Fine	VF	XF	Unc
468	1853	.246	BV	260.00	300.00	650.00
	1854	.026	BV	320.00	450.00	900.00
	1855	.048	BV	260.00	300.00	650.00
	1856	.262	BV	260.00	300.00	650.00
	1857/6	.315	BV	260.00	350.00	700.00
	1857	Inc. Ab.	BV	260.00	350.00	700.00
	1858	.032	BV	260.00	350.00	700.00
	1859	.047	BV	275.00	400.00	850.00
	1860	—	BV	275.00	400.00	800.00
	1861	—	BV	275.00	375.00	750.00
	1862	—	—	—	Rare	—
	1863	—	425.00	550.00	800.00	1300.
	1864	—	300.00	550.00	800.00	1300.
	1865	—	BV	275.00	500.00	800.00
	1867	—	BV	260.00	350.00	700.00
	1889	—	BV	260.00	300.00	600.00

REPUBLIC

20 REIS

BRONZE

KM#	Date	Mintage	Fine	VF	XF	Unc
490	1889	.630	.40	1.00	2.50	15.00
	1893	.250	.40	1.00	2.50	15.00
	1894	Inc. Ab.	.75	1.50	3.00	25.00
	1895	2.118	.50	1.00	2.50	15.00
	1896	.490	5.00	20.00	40.00	100.00
	1897	.273	3.00	8.00	12.50	40.00
	1898	.300	3.00	8.00	12.50	40.00
	1899	1.065	3.00	8.00	12.50	40.00
	1900	1.718	.40	1.00	3.00	20.00
	1901	.713	.50	1.00	3.00	20.00
	1904	.850	.50	1.00	3.00	20.00
	1905	1.075	4.00	8.00	15.00	50.00
	1906	.215	2.00	5.00	10.00	30.00
	1908	4.558	.40	1.00	3.00	20.00
	1909	1.215	5.00	10.00	22.00	50.00

KM#	Date	Mintage	Fine	VF	XF	Unc
490	1910	.828	.75	1.50	3.00	20.00
	1911	1.545	.75	1.50	3.00	20.00
	1912	.480	.85	1.75	4.00	25.00

COPPER-NICKEL

KM#	Date	Mintage	Fine	VF	XF	Unc
516	1918	.373	.25	.50	2.00	5.00
	1919	2.870	.25	.50	1.00	4.00
	1920	.825	.25	.50	1.25	5.00
	1921	1.020	.25	.50	1.25	5.00
	1927	.053	5.00	10.00	30.00	80.00
	1935	100 pcs.	200.00	350.00	700.00	1000.

40 REIS

BRONZE

KM#	Date	Mintage	Fine	VF	XF	Unc
491	1889	1.781	.50	1.00	2.00	15.00
	1893	1.085	1.50	3.00	5.00	22.50
	1894	.770	1.50	3.00	5.00	22.50
	1895	Inc. Ab.	2.00	3.50	6.00	25.00
	1896	.191	10.00	20.00	50.00	100.00
	1897	1.236	.75	2.00	3.50	17.50
	1898	.300	10.00	20.00	50.00	100.00
	1900	2.115	.75	2.50	4.50	20.00
	1901	.525	.75	2.00	3.50	15.00
	1907	.218	.75	2.00	3.50	15.00
	1908	4.639	.75	2.00	3.50	15.00
	1909	4.226	.75	2.00	3.50	17.50
	1910	.848	.75	2.00	4.00	20.00
	1911	1.660	.75	2.00	4.00	20.00
	1912	.819	1.00	2.50	4.50	22.50

50 REIS

COPPER-NICKEL

KM#	Date	Mintage	Fine	VF	XF	Unc
517	1918	.558	.15	.35	.75	6.00
	1919	.558	.15	.35	.75	6.00
	1920	.072	.40	1.00	4.00	18.00
	1921	.682	.15	.35	.75	6.00
	1922	.176	.40	1.00	4.00	18.00
	1925	.128	.40	1.50	5.00	20.00
	1926	.194	.40	1.50	5.00	20.00
	1931	.020	2.00	10.00	30.00	80.00
	1935	100 pcs.	125.00	300.00	450.00	1000.

100 REIS

COPPER-NICKEL

KM#	Date	Mintage	Fine	VF	XF	Unc
492	1889	7.686	.75	3.00	8.50	30.00
	1893	3.589	1.00	3.00	8.50	30.00
	1894	1.881	1.00	3.00	8.50	30.00
	1895	2.308	1.00	3.00	8.50	30.00
	1896	3.390	1.00	3.00	8.50	30.00
	1897	2.875	3.00	6.50	12.00	40.00
	1898	3.685	3.00	6.50	12.00	40.00
	1899	2.990	3.00	6.50	12.00	40.00
	1900	.539	8.00	20.00	60.00	200.00

Date: MCMI = 1901.

KM#	Date	Mintage	Fine	VF	XF	Unc
503	1901	15.775	.40	1.00	2.00	8.00

KM#	Date	Mintage	Fine	VF	XF	Unc
518	1918	.600	.40	1.00	1.50	4.00
	1919	1.219	.40	1.00	1.50	4.00
	1920	1.251	.40	1.00	1.50	4.00
	1921	.853	.40	1.00	1.50	4.00
	1922	.347	.40	1.00	2.00	8.00
	1923	.956	.40	1.00	2.00	8.00
	1924	1.478	1.00	2.00	5.00	10.00
	1925	2.502	.30	.75	1.25	4.00
	1926	1.807	.50	1.00	2.00	8.00
	1927	1.451	.30	.75	1.25	4.00
	1928	1.514	.30	.75	1.25	4.00
	1929	2.503	.30	.75	1.25	4.00
	1930	2.398	.30	.75	1.25	4.00
	1931	2.500	.25	.50	1.00	4.00
	1932	.948	.25	.50	1.00	4.00
	1933	1.314	.25	.50	1.00	4.00
	1934	3.614	.25	.50	1.00	4.00
	1935	3.442	.25	.50	1.00	4.00

Cazique Tibirica
400th Anniversary of Colonization

KM#	Date	Mintage	Fine	VF	XF	Unc
527	1932	1.012	.50	1.00	2.50	7.00

Admiral Marques Tamandare

KM#	Date	Mintage	Fine	VF	XF	Unc
536	1936	3.928	.20	.50	1.50	3.00
	1937	7.905	.10	.25	1.00	2.50
	1938	8.618	.10	.25	1.00	2.50

Dr. Getulio Vargas

KM#	Date	Mintage	Fine	VF	XF	Unc
544	1938	8.106	.10	.20	.50	1.50
	1940	8.797	.10	.20	.50	1.50
	1942	1.285	.10	.20	.50	1.50

NOTE: The 1942 issue has a deeper yellow cast due to higher copper content.

200 REIS

COPPER-NICKEL

KM#	Date	Mintage	Fine	VF	XF	Unc
493	1889	4.829	1.50	3.00	7.50	45.00
	1893	2.586	2.00	4.50	10.00	45.00
	1894	1.562	2.00	4.50	10.00	45.00
	1895	1.633	2.00	4.50	10.00	50.00
	1896	2.850	2.50	5.00	12.50	50.00
	1897	2.405	2.50	5.50	15.00	50.00
	1898	3.925	2.50	5.00	12.50	50.00
	1899	2.724	3.00	6.00	17.50	50.00
	1900	.330	15.00	50.00	100.00	300.00

Date: MCMI = 1901.

KM#	Date	Mintage	Fine	VF	XF	Unc
504	1901	12.625	.60	1.50	2.00	7.50

KM#	Date	Mintage	Fine	VF	XF	Unc
519	1918	.625	.35	.75	1.25	7.50
	1919	.882	.35	.75	1.00	7.50
	1920	1.657	.35	.75	1.00	7.50
	1921	1.135	.35	.75	1.00	7.50
	1922	.678	.35	.75	1.00	7.50
	1923	1.655	.35	.75	1.00	7.50
	1924	1.750	.35	.75	1.00	7.50
	1925	2.082	.35	.75	1.00	7.50
	1926	.324	1.00	3.00	8.00	22.50
	1927	1.806	.35	.75	1.00	6.00
	1928	.782	.35	.75	1.00	6.00
	1929	2.440	.25	.50	.75	5.00
	1930	1.697	.25	.50	.75	5.00
	1931	1.830	.25	.50	.75	5.00
	1932	.761	.25	.50	.75	5.00
	1933	.173	.35	.75	1.00	6.00
	1934	.612	.25	.50	.75	5.00
	1935	1.329	.25	.50	.75	5.00

400th Anniversary of Colonization

KM#	Date	Mintage	Fine	VF	XF	Unc
528	1932	.596	.75	1.50	3.50	8.00

Viscount de Maua

KM#	Date	Mintage	Fine	VF	XF	Unc
537	1936	2.256	.30	.50	1.00	4.00
	1937	6.506	.30	.50	1.00	4.00
	1938	5.787	.30	.50	1.00	4.00

Dr. Getulio Vargas

KM#	Date	Mintage	Fine	VF	XF	Unc
545	1938	7.666	.20	.50	1.00	3.00
	1940	10.161	.15	.40	.60	2.50
	1942	1.966	.15	.40	.60	2.50

NOTE: The 1942 issue has a yellow cast due to higher copper content.

300 REIS

COPPER-NICKEL
Antonio Carlos Gomes

KM#	Date	Mintage	Fine	VF	XF	Unc
538	1936	3.029	.30	.75	1.50	5.00
	1937	4.507	.30	.75	1.50	5.00
	1938	3.753	.30	.75	1.50	5.00

Dr. Getulio Vargas

KM#	Date	Mintage	Fine	VF	XF	Unc
546	1938	12.080	.20	.35	.50	2.50
	1940	8.124	.20	.35	.50	2.50
	1942	2.020	.25	.40	.75	3.50

NOTE: The 1942 issue has a yellow cast due to higher copper content.

400 REIS

5.1000 g, .917 SILVER, .1503 oz ASW
400th Anniversary of Discovery

KM#	Date	Mintage	Fine	VF	XF	Unc
499	1900	.055	10.00	25.00	40.00	80.00

COPPER-NICKEL
Obv: Date: MCMI = 1901.

KM#	Date	Mintage	Fine	VF	XF	Unc
505	1901	5.531	1.25	2.50	6.25	25.00

KM#	Date	Mintage	Fine	VF	XF	Unc
515	1914	.646	15.00	30.00	60.00	100.00

NOTE: This is considered a pattern by many authorities.

KM#	Date	Mintage	Fine	VF	XF	Unc
520	1918	.491	.75	1.50	3.00	6.00
	1919	.891	.75	1.50	3.00	6.00
	1920	1.521	.75	1.50	3.00	6.00
	1921	.871	.50	1.00	3.00	6.00
	1922	1.275	.50	1.00	3.00	6.00
	1923	.764	.50	1.00	3.00	6.00
	1925	2.048	.50	1.00	3.00	6.00
	1926	1.034	.50	1.00	3.00	6.00
	1927	.738	.50	1.00	3.00	6.00
	1929	.869	.50	1.00	3.00	6.00
	1930	1.031	.50	1.00	3.00	6.00
	1931	1.431	.50	1.00	3.00	6.00
	1932	.588	.50	1.00	3.00	6.00
	1935	.225	.50	1.00	3.00	6.00

400th Anniversary of Colonization

KM#	Date	Mintage	Fine	VF	XF	Unc
529	1932	.416	1.00	3.00	5.00	10.00

Oswaldo Cruz

KM#	Date	Mintage	Fine	VF	XF	Unc
539	1936	2.079	.50	.90	1.50	7.50
	1937	3.111	.50	.90	1.50	7.50
	1938	2.681	.50	.90	1.50	7.50

Dr. Getulio Vargas

KM#	Date	Mintage	Fine	VF	XF	Unc
547	1938	10.620	.25	.50	.75	2.50
	1940	7.312	.25	.50	.75	2.50
	1942	1.496	.25	.50	1.00	3.50

NOTE: The 1942 issue has a yellow cast due to higher copper content.

500 REIS

6.3750 g, .917 SILVER, .1879 oz ASW

KM#	Date	Mintage	Fine	VF	XF	Unc
494	1889	4.541	2.50	4.50	8.00	25.00

5.0000 g, .900 SILVER, .1446 oz ASW

KM#	Date	Mintage	Fine	VF	XF	Unc
506	1906	.352	BV	3.00	5.00	15.00
	1907	1.282	BV	3.00	5.00	15.00
	1908	.498	BV	3.00	5.00	15.00
	1911	8,000	20.00	30.00	50.00	80.00
	1912	*.222	20.00	30.00	60.00	90.00

KM#	Date	Mintage	Fine	VF	XF	Unc
509	1912	*Inc. Ab.	3.50	7.50	15.00	40.00

KM#	Date	Mintage	Fine	VF	XF	Unc
512	1913A	—	1.50	3.00	6.00	17.50

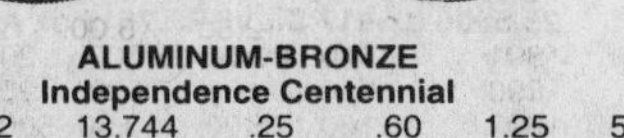

ALUMINUM-BRONZE
Independence Centennial

KM#	Date	Mintage	Fine	VF	XF	Unc
521.1	1922	13.744	.25	.60	1.25	5.00

Error: BBASIL instead of BRASIL

KM#	Date	Mintage	Fine	VF	XF	Unc
521.2	1922	Inc. Ab.	17.50	35.00	55.00	120.00

KM#	Date	Mintage	Fine	VF	XF	Unc
524	1924	7.400	.30	.75	1.25	4.00
	1927	2.725	.30	.75	1.25	4.00
	1928	9.432	.30	.75	1.25	4.00
	1930	.146	1.00	2.00	4.00	10.00

Joao Ramalho
400th Anniversary of Colonization

KM#	Date	Mintage	Fine	VF	XF	Unc
530	1932	.034	1.50	4.00	7.50	13.50

Diogo Feijo
4.00 g

KM#	Date	Mintage	Fine	VF	XF	Unc
533	1935	.014	2.00	7.50	10.00	17.00

5.00 g

KM#	Date	Mintage	Fine	VF	XF	Unc
540	1936	1.326	.60	.90	1.25	4.00
	1937	Inc. Ab.	.60	.90	1.25	4.00
	1938	—	.60	.90	1.25	4.00

Joaquim Machado de Assis

KM#	Date	Mintage	Fine	VF	XF	Unc
549	1939	5.928	.50	.75	1.00	4.00

1000 REIS

12.7500 g, .917 SILVER, .3758 oz ASW

KM#	Date	Mintage	Fine	VF	XF	Unc
495	1889	.296	10.00	15.00	35.00	80.00

400th Anniversary of Discovery

KM#	Date	Mintage	Fine	VF	XF	Unc
500	1900	.033	40.00	65.00	80.00	120.00

10.0000 g, .900 SILVER, .2894 oz ASW

KM#	Date	Mintage	Fine	VF	XF	Unc
507	1906	.420	BV	4.00	7.50	24.00
	1907	1.282	BV	4.00	7.50	24.00
	1908	1.624	BV	4.00	7.50	24.00
	1909	.816	BV	4.00	7.50	24.00
	1910	2.354	BV	4.00	7.50	24.00
	1911	2.810	BV	4.00	7.50	24.00
	1912	*1.570	BV	4.00	7.50	24.00

KM#	Date	Mintage	Fine	VF	XF	Unc
510	1912	*Inc. Ab.	4.00	6.00	10.00	35.00
	1913	2.525	4.00	6.00	10.00	35.00

KM#	Date	Mintage	Fine	VF	XF	Unc
513	1913A	—	BV	3.50	7.00	20.00

ALUMINUM-BRONZE
Independence Centennial

KM#	Date	Mintage	Fine	VF	XF	Unc
522.1	1922	16.698	.40	.60	2.00	5.00

Error: BBASIL instead of BRASIL

KM#	Date	Mintage	Fine	VF	XF	Unc
522.2	1922	Inc. Ab.	2.50	4.00	10.00	20.00

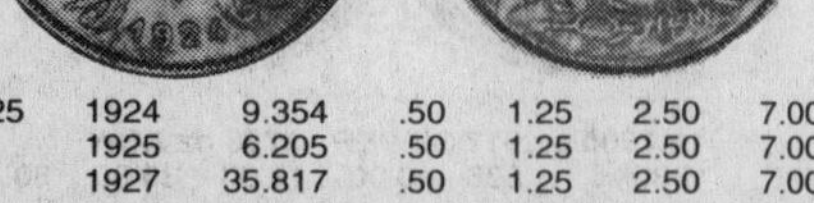

KM#	Date	Mintage	Fine	VF	XF	Unc
525	1924	9.354	.50	1.25	2.50	7.00
	1925	6.205	.50	1.25	2.50	7.00
	1927	35.817	.50	1.25	2.50	7.00

KM#	Date	Mintage	Fine	VF	XF	Unc
525	1928	1.899	.50	1.25	2.50	7.00
	1929	.083	2.50	7.50	15.00	60.00
	1930	.045	2.50	7.50	15.00	60.00
	1931	.200	1.00	5.00	8.50	12.50

Martim Affonso da Sousa
400th Anniversary of Colonization

KM#	Date	Mintage	Fine	VF	XF	Unc
531	1932	.056	2.50	4.50	8.00	14.00

Jose de Anchieta

KM#	Date	Mintage	Fine	VF	XF	Unc
534	1935	.138	1.00	3.00	5.00	12.00

Size reduced

KM#	Date	Mintage	Fine	VF	XF	Unc
541	1936	.926	.50	1.00	2.00	6.00
	1937	Inc. Ab.	.50	1.00	2.00	6.00
	1938	—	.50	1.00	2.00	6.00

Tobias Barreto de Menezes

KM#	Date	Mintage	Fine	VF	XF	Unc
550	1939	9.586	.25	.65	1.25	5.00

2000 REIS

25.5000 g, .917 SILVER, .7515 oz ASW

KM#	Date	Mintage	Fine	VF	XF	Unc
498	1891	.040	500.00	1000.	2000.	3000.
	1896	.010	500.00	1000.	2000.	3000.
	1897	.160	175.00	350.00	500.00	1500.

400th Anniversary of Discovery

KM#	Date	Mintage	Fine	VF	XF	Unc
501	1900	.020	60.00	100.00	200.00	300.00

20.0000 g, .900 SILVER, .5787 oz ASW

KM#	Date	Mintage	Fine	VF	XF	Unc
508	1906	.256	4.50	9.00	17.50	55.00
	1907	2.863	BV	6.00	9.00	45.00
	1908	1.707	BV	6.00	9.00	45.00
	1910	.585	4.50	9.00	17.50	55.00
	1911	1.929	BV	6.00	9.00	45.00
	1912	.741	4.50	9.00	17.50	55.00

KM#	Date	Mintage	Fine	VF	XF	Unc
511	1912	Inc. Ab.	6.50	12.50	25.00	60.00
	1913	.395	6.50	12.50	25.00	60.00

KM#	Date	Mintage	Fine	VF	XF	Unc
514	1913A	—	4.50	9.00	13.00	40.00

7.9000 g, .900 SILVER, .2285 oz ASW
Independence Centennial

KM#	Date	Mintage	Fine	VF	XF	Unc
523	1922	1.560	BV	3.00	4.00	8.00

7.9000 g, .500 SILVER, .1269 oz ASW

KM#	Date	Mintage	Fine	VF	XF	Unc
523a	1922	Inc. Ab.	BV	3.00	4.00	8.00

***NOTE:** Struck in both .900 and .500 fine silver, but can only be distinguished by analysis (and color, on worn specimens).

KM#	Date	Mintage	Fine	VF	XF	Unc
526	1924	9.147	BV	1.50	4.00	13.00
	1925	.723	BV	1.50	4.00	13.00
	1926	1.787	BV	1.50	4.00	13.00
	1927	1.009	BV	2.50	5.00	15.00
	1928	1.250	BV	1.50	4.00	13.00
	1929	1.744	BV	1.50	4.00	13.00
	1930	1.240	BV	1.50	4.00	13.00
	1931	.546	BV	1.50	4.00	13.00
	1934	.938	BV	1.50	4.00	13.00

John III
400th Anniversary of Colonization

KM#	Date	Mintage	Fine	VF	XF	Unc
532	1932	.695	2.00	2.50	5.00	15.00

Duke of Caxias

KM#	Date	Mintage	Fine	VF	XF	Unc
535	1935	2.131	BV	1.50	4.00	13.00

ALUMINUM-BRONZE
Duke of Caxias
Reeded edge.

KM#	Date	Mintage	Fine	VF	XF	Unc
542	1936	.665	.50	.75	2.00	6.00
	1937	Inc. Ab.	.50	.75	2.00	6.00
	1938	—	2.50	4.50	12.50	30.00

Plain edge, polygonal planchet

KM#	Date	Mintage	Fine	VF	XF	Unc
548	1937	—	25.00	50.00	125.00	300.00
	1938	—	.75	1.50	3.50	8.00

Floriano Peixoto

KM#	Date	Mintage	Fine	VF	XF	Unc
551	1939	5.048	.50	.75	2.00	6.00

4000 REIS

51.0000 g, .917 SILVER, 1.5030 oz ASW
400th Anniversary of Discovery
Obv: Star w/16 rays.

KM#	Date	Mintage	Fine	VF	XF	Unc
502.1	1900	6,850	125.00	300.00	500.00	700.00

Obv: Star w/20 rays.

KM#	Date	Mintage	Fine	VF	XF	Unc
502.2	1900	Inc. Ab.	125.00	300.00	500.00	700.00

5000 REIS

10.0000 g, .600 SILVER, .1929 oz ASW
Alberto Santos Dumont

KM#	Date	Mintage	Fine	VF	XF	Unc
543	1936	1.986	BV	2.00	3.00	8.00
	1937	.414	BV	2.00	3.00	8.00
	1938	.994	BV	2.00	3.00	8.00

10,000 REIS

8.9645 g, .917 GOLD, .2643 oz AGW

KM#	Date	Mintage	Fine	VF	XF	Unc
496	1889	7,302	150.00	250.00	600.00	1000.
	1892	2,289	—	—	Rare	—
	1893	—	150.00	250.00	600.00	1000.
	1895	306 pcs.	150.00	250.00	700.00	1100.
	1896	383 pcs.	—	—	Rare	—
	1897	421 pcs.	150.00	250.00	700.00	1100.
	1898	216 pcs.	250.00	500.00	1500.	2000.
	1899	238 pcs.	150.00	250.00	700.00	1100.
	1901	111 pcs.	150.00	250.00	500.00	1000.
	1902	—	—	—	Unique	—
	1903	391 pcs.	150.00	250.00	700.00	1100.
	1904	541 pcs.	150.00	250.00	700.00	1100.
	1906	572 pcs.	150.00	250.00	700.00	1100.
	1907	878 pcs.	150.00	250.00	600.00	1000.
	1908	689 pcs.	150.00	250.00	600.00	1000.
	1909	1,069	150.00	250.00	600.00	1000.
	1911	137 pcs.	175.00	350.00	800.00	1250.

KM#	Date	Mintage	Fine	VF	XF	Unc
496	1914	969 pcs.	250.00	500.00	1500.	2000.
	1915	4,314	250.00	500.00	1500.	2000.
	1916	4,720	150.00	250.00	700.00	1100.
	1919	526 pcs.	150.00	250.00	700.00	1100.
	1921	2,435	150.00	250.00	600.00	1000.
	1922	6 pcs.	—	—	Rare	—

20,000 REIS

17.9290 g, .917 GOLD, .5286 oz AGW

KM#	Date	Mintage	Fine	VF	XF	Unc
497	1889	.091	BV	300.00	550.00	1000.
	1892	7,738	—	—	Rare	—
	1893	4,303	BV	300.00	550.00	1000.
	1894	4,267	BV	300.00	550.00	1000.
	1895	4,811	BV	300.00	550.00	1000.
	1896	7,043	BV	300.00	550.00	1000.
	1897	.011	BV	300.00	550.00	1000.
	1898	.014	BV	300.00	550.00	1000.
	1899	9,558	BV	300.00	550.00	1000.
	1900	7,551	BV	300.00	550.00	1000.
	1901	784 pcs.	BV	350.00	700.00	1200.
	1902	884 pcs.	BV	350.00	700.00	1200.
	1903	675 pcs.	BV	350.00	700.00	1200.
	1904	444 pcs.	BV	350.00	700.00	1200.
	1906	396 pcs.	375.00	750.00	1500.	3000.
	1907	3,310	BV	300.00	550.00	1000.
	1908	6.001	BV	300.00	550.00	1000.
	1909	4,427	BV	300.00	550.00	1000.
	1910	5,119	BV	300.00	550.00	1000.
	1911	8,467	BV	300.00	550.00	1000.
	1912	4,878	BV	300.00	550.00	1000.
	1913	5,182	BV	300.00	600.00	1100.
	1914	1,980	BV	300.00	600.00	1100.
	1917	2,269	BV	300.00	600.00	1100.
	1918	1,216	BV	300.00	600.00	1100.
	1921	5,924	BV	300.00	600.00	1100.
	1922	2,681	BV	300.00	600.00	1100.

MONETARY REFORM

1942-1967
100 Centavos = 1 Cruzeiro

10 CENTAVOS

COPPER-NICKEL
Getulio Vargas

KM#	Date	Mintage	VF	XF	Unc
555	1942	3.826	.35	.50	1.00
	1943	13.565	.25	.35	.75

ALUMINUM-BRONZE

KM#	Date	Mintage	VF	XF	Unc
555a	1943	Inc. Ab.	.25	.35	.75
	1944	12.617	.25	.60	1.00
	1945	24.674	.25	.60	1.00
	1946	35.159	.25	.60	1.00
	1947	20.664	.25	.35	.75

NOTE: KM#555 has a very light yellowish appearance while KM#555a is a deeper yellow.

Jose Bonifacio de Andrada e Silva

KM#	Date	Mintage	VF	XF	Unc
561	1947	Inc. Ab.	.15	.20	.35
	1948	45.041	.15	.20	.35
	1949	21.763	.15	.20	.35
	1950	16.330	.15	.20	.35
	1951	15.561	.10	.15	.35
	1952	10.966	.10	.20	.50
	1953	25.883	.10	.15	.35
	1954	17.031	.10	.15	.35
	1955	25.172	.10	.15	.35

ALUMINUM

KM#	Date	Mintage	VF	XF	Unc
564	1956	.741	.10	.15	.50
	1957	25.311	.10	.15	.25
	1958	5.813	.10	.15	.25

KM#	Date	Mintage	VF	XF	Unc
564	1959	2.611	.10	.15	.25
	1960	.624	.10	.15	.50
	1961	.951	.10	.15	.50

20 CENTAVOS

COPPER-NICKEL
Getulio Vargas

KM#	Date	Mintage	VF	XF	Unc
556	1942	3.007	.25	.50	1.00
	1943	13.392	.15	.40	.75

NOTE: KM#556 has a very light yellowish appearance while KM#556a is a deeper yellow.

ALUMINUM-BRONZE

KM#	Date	Mintage	VF	XF	Unc
556a	1943	Inc. Ab.	.15	.35	.75
	1944	12.673	.15	.35	.75
	1945	61.632	.15	.35	.60
	1946	31.526	.15	.35	.60
	1947	36.422	.15	.35	.75
	1948	39.671	.15	.35	.75

NOTE: Coins dated 1944 exist w/designers initials and straight backed 9 in date or w/o designers initials and curved backed 9 in date.

Ruy Barbosa

KM#	Date	Mintage	VF	XF	Unc
562	1948	Inc. Ab.	.15	.25	.50
	1949	24.805	.15	.25	.50
	1950	15.145	.15	.25	.50
	1951	14.964	.15	.25	.50
	1952	10.942	.15	.25	.50
	1953	25.585	.15	.25	.50
	1954	16.477	.15	.25	.50
	1955	25.122	.15	.25	.50
	1956	6.716	.15	.25	.50

ALUMINUM
National arms

KM#	Date	Mintage	VF	XF	Unc
565	1956	Inc. Ab.	.10	.25	.50
	1957	27.110	.10	.20	.40
	1958	8.552	.10	.20	.40
	1959	4.810	.10	.20	.40
	1960	.510	.10	.25	.50
	1961	2.332	.10	.20	.40

NOTE: Varieties exist in the thickness of the planchet for year 1956.

50 CENTAVOS

COPPER-NICKEL
Getulio Vargas

KM#	Date	Mintage	VF	XF	Unc
557	1942	2.358	.40	.75	1.50
	1943	13.392	.35	.50	1.00

NOTE: KM557 has a very light yellowish appearance while KM#557a is a deeper yellow.

ALUMINUM-BRONZE

KM#	Date	Mintage	VF	XF	Unc
557a	1943	Inc. Ab.	.30	.50	1.00
	1944	12.102	.30	.50	1.00
	1945	73.222	.30	.50	1.00
	1946	13.941	.30	.50	1.00
	1947	23.588	.20	.50	1.00

General Eurico Gaspar Dutra

KM#	Date	Mintage	VF	XF	Unc
563	1948	32.023	.15	.25	.50
	1949	11.392	.15	.25	.50
	1950	7.804	.15	.35	.75
	1951	7.523	.15	.35	.75
	1952	6.863	.15	.35	.75

KM#	Date	Mintage	VF	XF	Unc
563	1953	17.372	.15	.25	.50
	1954	11.353	.15	.25	.50
	1955	27.150	.15	.25	.50
	1956	32.130	.15	.25	.50

National arms

KM#	Date	Mintage	VF	XF	Unc
566	1956	Inc. Ab.	.15	.25	.50

ALUMINUM

KM#	Date	Mintage	VF	XF	Unc
569	1957	49.350	.10	.20	.35
	1958	59.815	.10	.20	.35
	1959	32.891	.10	.20	.35
	1960	15.997	.10	.20	.35
	1961	18.456	.10	.20	.35

CRUZEIRO

ALUMINUM-BRONZE

KM#	Date	Mintage	VF	XF	Unc
558	1942	.381	.50	1.00	3.00
	1943	2.728	.25	.50	1.00
	1944	3.820	.25	.50	1.00
	1945	32.544	.25	.50	.75
	1946	49.794	.25	.50	1.00
	1947	15.391	.25	.50	1.00
	1949	7.889	.25	.50	1.00
	1950	5.163	.25	.50	1.00
	1951	3.757	.25	.50	1.00
	1952	1.769	.50	1.00	2.00
	1953	5.195	.25	.50	1.00
	1954	1.145	.25	.50	1.50
	1955	1.758	.25	.50	1.00
	1956	.668	4.00	6.00	10.00

KM#	Date	Mintage	VF	XF	Unc
567	1956	Inc. Ab.	.15	.25	.50

ALUMINUM

KM#	Date	Mintage	VF	XF	Unc
570	1957	11.849	.10	.20	.45
	1958	15.443	.10	.20	.45
	1959	25.010	.10	.20	.45
	1960	35.267	.10	.20	.45
	1961	22.181	.10	.20	.45

2 CRUZEIROS

ALUMINUM-BRONZE

KM#	Date	Mintage	VF	XF	Unc
559	1942	.276	.75	1.50	4.00
	1943	1.929	.25	.50	1.00
	1944	3.820	.25	.50	1.00
	1945	32.544	.20	.40	1.00
	1946	33.650	.20	.40	1.00
	1947	9.908	.20	.40	1.00
	1949	11.252	.20	.40	1.00
	1950	7.754	.25	.50	1.00
	1951	.390	.40	1.00	3.00
	1952	1.456	1.00	2.00	5.00

KM#	Date	Mintage	VF	XF	Unc
559	1953	3.582	.20	.40	1.00
	1954	1.197	.25	1.00	2.00
	1955	1.838	.20	.50	1.00
	1956	—	.35	1.00	3.50

KM#	Date	Mintage	VF	XF	Unc
568	1956	Inc. Ab.	.20	.40	1.50

ALUMINUM

KM#	Date	Mintage	VF	XF	Unc
571	1957	.194	.20	.30	1.00
	1958	13.687	.15	.25	.60
	1959	20.894	.15	.25	.60
	1960	19.624	.15	.25	.60
	1961	24.924	.15	.25	.60

5 CRUZEIROS

ALUMINUM-BRONZE

KM#	Date	Mintage	VF	XF	Unc
560	1942	.115	.75	1.50	8.00
	1943	.222	.50	1.00	6.50

10 CRUZEIROS

ALUMINUM

KM#	Date	Mintage	VF	XF	Unc
572	1965	19.656	.10	.15	.25

20 CRUZEIROS

ALUMINUM

KM#	Date	Mintage	VF	XF	Unc
573	1965	25.930	.15	.20	.35

50 CRUZEIROS

COPPER-NICKEL

KM#	Date	Mintage	VF	XF	Unc
574	1965	18.001	.15	.25	.50

MONETARY REFORM

1967-1985
1000 Old Cruzeiros = 1 Cruzeiro Novo (New)
100 Centavos = 1 (New) Cruzeiro

CENTAVO

STAINLESS STEEL

KM#	Date	Mintage	VF	XF	Unc
575.1	1967	57.499	—	—	.10

Thinner planchet

KM#	Date	Mintage	VF	XF	Unc
575.2	1969	243.855	—	—	.10
	1975	—	—	.10	.20
	1976	—	—	.10	.20

F.A.O. Issue - Sugar Cane

KM#	Date	Mintage	VF	XF	Unc
585	1975	31.700	—	.10	.20
	1976	18.355	—	—	.10
	1977	.100	—	—	.10
	1978	.050	—	.10	.15
	1979	—	—	.10	.15

F.A.O. Issue - Soja

KM#	Date	Mintage	VF	XF	Unc
589	1979	.100	.10	.25	.75
	1980	.060	.10	.25	.75
	1981	.100	.10	.25	.75
	1982	.100	.10	.25	.75
	1983	—	.10	.25	.75
	1984	—	.10	.25	.75

2 CENTAVOS

STAINLESS STEEL

KM#	Date	Mintage	VF	XF	Unc
576.1	1967	65.226	—	—	.10

Thinner planchet

KM#	Date	Mintage	VF	XF	Unc
576.2	1969	*134.298	—	—	.10
	1975	—	—	.10	.30
	1976	—	—	.10	.30

***NOTE:** Mintage figure includes coins struck through 1974 dated 1969.

F.A.O. Issue - Soja

KM#	Date	Mintage	VF	XF	Unc
586	1975	31.400	—	—	.20
	1976	18.754	—	—	.20
	1977	.100	—	—	.20
	1978	.050	—	.10	.30

5 CENTAVOS

STAINLESS STEEL

KM#	Date	Mintage	VF	XF	Unc
577.1	1967	69.304	—	.10	.15

Thinner planchet

KM#	Date	Mintage	VF	XF	Unc
577.2	1969	*345.071	—	.10	.15
	1975	—	—	.10	.15
	1976	—	—	.10	.15

***NOTE:** Mintage figure includes coins struck through 1974 dated 1969.

F.A.O. Issue - Zebu
Rev: Plain 5

KM#	Date	Mintage	VF	XF	Unc
587.1	1975	44.500	—	.10	.15
	1976	134.267	—	.10	.15
	1977	85.360	—	.10	.15
	1978	34.090	—	.10	.20

Rev: 5 over wavy lines.

KM#	Date	Mintage	VF	XF	Unc
587.2	1975	Inc. Ab.	—	.10	.15
	1976	Inc. Ab.	—	.10	.15

10 CENTAVOS

COPPER-NICKEL

KM#	Date	Mintage	VF	XF	Unc
578.1	1967	22.420	—	.10	.30

Thinner planchet

KM#	Date	Mintage	VF	XF	Unc
578.2	1970	*134.070	—	.10	.20

***NOTE:** Mintage figure includes coins struck through 1974 dated 1970.

STAINLESS STEEL

KM#	Date	Mintage	VF	XF	Unc
578.1a	1974	114.598	—	.10	.20
	1975	—	—	.10	.20
	1976	—	—	.10	.20
	1977	225.213	—	.10	.20
	1978	225.000	—	.10	.20
	1979	.100	—	.10	.20

20 CENTAVOS

COPPER-NICKEL

KM#	Date	Mintage	VF	XF	Unc
579.1	1967	123.610	—	.10	.25
	1970	—	—	.10	.25

Thinner planchet

KM#	Date	Mintage	VF	XF	Unc
579.2	1970	*384.894	—	.10	.30

***NOTE:** Mintage figure includes coins struck through 1974 dated 1970.

STAINLESS STEEL

KM#	Date	Mintage	VF	XF	Unc
579.1a	1975	102.367	—	.10	.25
	1976	—	—	.10	.25
	1977	240.001	—	.10	.25
	1978	255.000	—	.10	.25
	1979	.116	—	.10	.25

50 CENTAVOS

NICKEL

KM#	Date	Mintage	VF	XF	Unc
580	1967	12.987	.25	.50	1.00

COPPER-NICKEL

KM#	Date	Mintage	VF	XF	Unc
580a	1970	503.895	.20	.35	.75
	1975	—	.20	.35	.75

STAINLESS STEEL

KM#	Date	Mintage	VF	XF	Unc
580b	1975	79.062	.20	.35	.75
	1976	—	.20	.35	.75
	1977	160.019	.20	.35	1.00
	1978	200.000	.20	.35	.75
	1979	.104	.20	.35	.75

CRUZEIRO

NICKEL

KM#	Date	Mintage	VF	XF	Unc
581	1970	*48.930	.25	.50	1.00
	1970	.018	—	Proof	3.00
	1974	24.135	.20	.35	.75

***NOTE:** Mintage figure includes coins struck through 1972 dated 1970.

COPPER-NICKEL

KM#	Date	Mintage	VF	XF	Unc
581a	1975	21.613	.20	.35	.75
	1976	—	.20	.35	.75
	1977	.098	.20	.35	.75
	1978	.077	.20	.35	.75

NICKEL
150th Anniversary of Independence

KM#	Date	Mintage	VF	XF	Unc
582	1972 lettered edge	5.600	.35	.75	1.50
	1972 plain edge	Inc. Ab.	.35	.75	1.50
	1972 lettered edge	—	—	Proof	3.00
	1972 plain edge	—	—	Proof	3.00

NOTE: Coins w/plain edge are believed by some to be errors.

STAINLESS STEEL
F.A.O. Issue - Sugar Cane

KM#	Date	Mintage	VF	XF	Unc
590	1979	.596	.10	.20	.50
	1980	690.497	.10	.20	.50
	1981	560.000	.10	.20	.50
	1982	300.000	.10	.20	.50
	1983	.100	.10	.20	.50
	1984	62.100	.10	.20	.50

F.A.O. Issue - Sugar Cane

KM#	Date	Mintage	VF	XF	Unc
598	1985	10.000	—	.15	.45

5 CRUZEIROS

STAINLESS STEEL
Coffee Plant

KM#	Date	Mintage	VF	XF	Unc
591	1980	288.200	.20	.30	.50
	1981	82.000	.20	.30	.50
	1982	108.000	.20	.30	.50
	1983	113.400	.20	.30	.50
	1984	243.000	.20	.30	.50

F.A.O. Issue - Coffee

KM#	Date	Mintage	VF	XF	Unc
599	1985	10.000	.15	.35	.75

10 CRUZEIROS

11.3000 g, .800 SILVER, .2906 oz ASW
10th Anniversary of Central Bank

KM#	Date	Mintage	VF	XF	Unc
588	1975	.020	—	—	55.00

STAINLESS STEEL

KM#	Date	Mintage	VF	XF	Unc
592.1	1980	100.010	—	.40	.50
	1981	200.000	—	.40	.50
	1982	331.000	—	.40	.50
	1983	390.000	—	.40	.50
	1984	390.000	—	.40	.50
		Reduced weight.			
592.2	1985	201.000	—	.40	.50
	1986	—	—	.40	.50

20 CRUZEIROS

18.0000 g, .900 SILVER, .5208 oz ASW, 34mm
150th Anniversary of Independence

KM#	Date	Mintage	VF	XF	Unc
583	1972(a)	.250	BV	6.00	8.00

STAINLESS STEEL
Francis of Assis Church

KM#	Date	Mintage	VF	XF	Unc
593	1981	88.297	—	.20	.75
	1982	158.200	—	.10	.50
	1983	312.000	—	.10	.50
	1984	226.000	—	.10	.50
	1985	205.000	—	.10	.50
	1986	—	—	.10	.50

50 CRUZEIROS

STAINLESS STEEL

KM#	Date	Mintage	VF	XF	Unc
594	1981	57.000	—	.20	.75
	1982	134.000	—	.10	.50
	1983	181.800	—	.10	.50
	1984	292.418	—	.10	.50
	1985	180.000	—	.10	.50
	1986	—	—	.10	.50

100 CRUZEIROS

STAINLESS STEEL

KM#	Date	Mintage	VF	XF	Unc
595	1985	162.000	—	.10	.25
	1986	—	—	—	.20

200 CRUZEIROS

STAINLESS STEEL

KM#	Date	Mintage	VF	XF	Unc
596	1985	55.000	—	.15	.50
	1986	—	—	—	.35

300 CRUZEIROS

16.6500 g, .920 GOLD, .4925 oz AGW
150th Anniversary of Independence

KM#	Date	Mintage	VF	XF	Unc
584	1972(a)	.030	—	—	300.00

500 CRUZEIROS

STAINLESS STEEL

KM#	Date	Mintage	VF	XF	Unc
597	1985	74.000	—	.35	.75
	1986	—	—	—	.50

MONETARY REFORM

1986-1989
1,000 Cruzeiros Novos = 1 Cruzado
100 Centavos = 1 Cruzado

CENTAVO

STAINLESS STEEL

KM#	Date	Mintage	VF	XF	Unc
600	1986	100.000	—	—	.10
	1987	1.000	—	—	.10
	1988	1.000	—	—	.10

5 CENTAVOS

STAINLESS STEEL

KM#	Date	Mintage	VF	XF	Unc
601	1986	99.282	—	—	.10
	1987	1.000	—	—	.10
	1988	1.000	—	—	.10

10 CENTAVOS

STAINLESS STEEL

KM#	Date	Mintage	VF	XF	Unc
602	1986	200.000	—	—	.10
	1987	245.628	—	—	.10
	1988	21.293	—	—	.10

20 CENTAVOS

STAINLESS STEEL

KM#	Date	Mintage	VF	XF	Unc
603	1986	140.000	—	—	.10
	1987	157.500	—	—	.10
	1988	16.000	—	—	.10

50 CENTAVOS

STAINLESS STEEL

KM#	Date	Mintage	VF	XF	Unc
604	1986	200.000	—	—	.15
	1987	201.884	—	—	.15
	1988	131.255	—	—	.15

CRUZADO

STAINLESS STEEL

KM#	Date	Mintage	VF	XF	Unc
605	1986	—	—	—	.25
	1987	383.087	—	—	.25
	1988	321.216	—	—	.25

5 CRUZADOS

STAINLESS STEEL

KM#	Date	Mintage	VF	XF	Unc
606	1986	—	—	—	.35
	1987	141.000	—	—	.35
	1988	291.906	—	—	.35

10 CRUZADOS

STAINLESS STEEL

KM#	Date	Mintage	VF	XF	Unc
607	1987	131.500	—	—	.50
	1988	457.977	—	—	.50

100 CRUZADOS

STAINLESS STEEL
Abolition of Slavery Centennial - Male

KM#	Date	Mintage	VF	XF	Unc
608	1988	.200	—	.75	1.50

Abolition of Slavery Centennial - Female

KM#	Date	Mintage	VF	XF	Unc
609	1988	.200	—	.75	1.50

Abolition of Slavery Centennial - Child

KM#	Date	Mintage	VF	XF	Unc
610	1988	.200	—	.75	1.50

MONETARY REFORM

1989 - 1990

1,000 Old Cruzados = 1 Cruzado Novo

CENTAVO

STAINLESS STEEL

KM#	Date	Mintage	VF	XF	Unc
611	1989	—	—	—	.20
	1990	—	—	—	.20

5 CENTAVOS

STAINLESS STEEL

KM#	Date	Mintage	VF	XF	Unc
612	1989	—	—	—	.25
	1990	—	—	—	.25

10 CENTAVOS

STAINLESS STEEL

KM#	Date	Mintage	VF	XF	Unc
613	1989	—	—	—	.30
	1990	—	—	—	.30

50 CENTAVOS

STAINLESS STEEL

KM#	Date	Mintage	VF	XF	Unc
614	1989	—	—	—	.50
	1990	—	—	—	.50

NOVO (New) CRUZADO

STAINLESS STEEL
Centennial of the Republic

KM#	Date	Mintage	VF	XF	Unc
615	1989	—	—	—	1.00

200 NOVOS CRUZADOS

13.4700 g, .999 SILVER, .4331 oz ASW
Centennial of the Republic

KM#	Date	Mintage	VF	XF	Unc
616	1989	.030	—	Proof	30.00

MONETARY REFORM

1990 - 1993

100 Centavos = 1 Cruzeiro

1 Cruzado Novo = 1 Cruzeiro

CRUZEIRO

STAINLESS STEEL

KM#	Date	Mintage	VF	XF	Unc
617	1990	—	—	—	.10
	1991	—	—	—	.10
	1992	—	—	—	.10

5 CRUZEIROS

STAINLESS STEEL

KM#	Date	Mintage	VF	XF	Unc
618	1990	—	—	—	.20
	1991	—	—	—	.15
	1992	—	—	—	.15

10 CRUZEIROS

STAINLESS STEEL

KM#	Date	Mintage	VF	XF	Unc
619	1990	—	—	—	.30
	1991	—	—	—	.25
	1992	—	—	—	.25

50 CRUZEIROS

STAINLESS STEEL

KM#	Date	Mintage	VF	XF	Unc
620	1990	—	—	—	.40
	1991	—	—	—	.35
	1992	—	—	—	.35

100 CRUZEIROS

STAINLESS STEEL
Manatee

KM#	Date	Mintage	VF	XF	Unc
623	1992	—	—	—	.35
	1993	—	—	—	.35

500 CRUZEIROS

27.0000 g, .925 SILVER, .8029 oz ASW
Ibero - American Series

KM#	Date	Mintage	VF	XF	Unc
621	1991	.070	—	Proof	45.00

STAINLESS STEEL
Leatherback Sea Turtle

KM#	Date	Mintage	VF	XF	Unc
624	1992	—	—	—	.50
	1993	—	—	—	.50

1000 CRUZEIROS

STAINLESS STEEL
Fish - Arcara

KM#	Date	Mintage	VF	XF	Unc
626	1992	—	—	—	.75
	1993	—	—	—	.75

2000 CRUZEIROS

28.2000 g, .925 SILVER, .7977 oz ASW
U.N. Conference on Environment
and Development
Hummingbird and flower.

KM#	Date	Mintage	VF	XF	Unc
622	1992	.050	—	Proof	45.00

5000 CRUZEIROS

STAINLESS STEEL
200th Anniversary of Tiradentes Death

KM#	Date	Mintage	VF	XF	Unc
625	1992	—	—	—	1.25

MONETARY REFORM

1993 -

1,000 Cruzeiros = 1 Cruzeiro Real

5 CRUZEIROS REALS

STAINLESS STEEL
Parrots - Arara

KM#	Date	Mintage	VF	XF	Unc
627	1993	—	—	—	.50

10 CRUZEIROS REALS

STAINLESS STEEL
Anteater - Tamandua

KM#	Date	Mintage	VF	XF	Unc
628	1993	—	—	—	.75

SANTA TEREZA LEPER COLONY

All the following tokens have plain edges. Obverse letters C.S.T. abbreviation for Colonia Santa Tereza.

TOKEN ISSUES (Tn)

100 REIS

BRASS

Tn1	ND	—	—	Rare	—

200 REIS

BRASS

Tn2	ND	—	—	Rare	—

300 REIS

BRASS

Tn3	ND	—	—	Rare	—

500 REIS

BRASS

Tn4	ND	—	—	Rare	—

1000 REIS

BRASS

Tn5	ND	—	—	Rare	—

Listings For

BRITISH EAST CARIBBEAN TERRITORIES: refer to East Caribbean States

BRITISH GUIANA: refer to Guyana

BRITISH HONDURAS: refer to Belize

BRITISH NORTH BORNEO: refer to Malaysia

BRITISH VIRGIN IS.

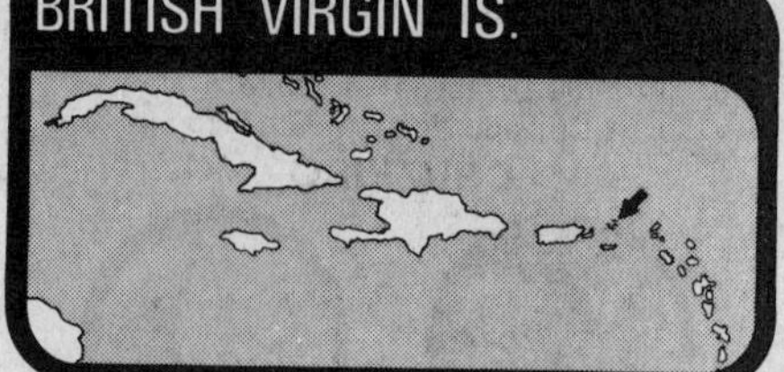

The Colony of the Virgin Islands, a British colony situated in the Caribbean Sea northeast of Puerto Rico and west of the Leeward Islands, has an area of 59 sq. mi. (155 sq. km.) and a population of 14,000. Capital: Road Town. The principal islands of the 36-island group are Tortola, Virgin Gorda, Anegada, and Jost Van Dyke. The chief industries are fishing and stock raising. Fish, livestock and bananas are exported.

The Virgin Islands were discovered by Columbus in 1493, and named by him, Las Virgenes, in honor of St. Ursula and her companions. The British Virgin Islands were formerly part of the administration of the Leeward Islands but received a separate administration as a Crown Colony in 1950. A new constitution promulgated in 1967 provided for a ministerial form of government headed by the Governor.

The Government of the British Virgin Islands issued the first official coinage in its history on June 30, 1973, in honor of 300 years of constitutional government in the islands. U.S. coins and currency continue to be accepted as a medium of exchange, though the coinage of the British Virgin Islands is legal tender and can be exchanged on the islands.

TORTOLA

Tortola, which has an area of about 24 sq. mi. (62 sq. km.), is the largest of thirty-six islands which comprise the British Virgin Islands. It was settled by the Dutch in 1648 and was occupied by the British in 1666. They have held it ever since.

MONETARY SYSTEM

8 Shillings, 3 Pence = 11 Bits = 8 Reales

COUNTERMARKED COINAGE

Tortola

Type I: TORTOLA in odd shaped rectangle.

NOTE: Market valuations listed for "TORTOLA" c/m issues are just for the "TORTOLA" c/m and do not take into consideration any other c/m that may be encountered on the same piece.

1-1/2 PENCE

Black Dog

BILLON
c/m: Incuse 'T' on French Colonial 2 Sous.

KM#	Date	Year	Good	VG	Fine	VF
3	ND	(1801)	22.50	40.00	70.00	125.00

9 PENCE or 1 BIT

SILVER
c/m: Type I on 1/2 cut of Spanish or Spanish Colonial 2 Reales.

4	ND	(1801)	40.00	90.00	180.00	250.00

SHILLING

SILVER
c/m: Type I on 1/8 cut of Spanish or Spanish Colonial 8 Reales.

5	ND	(1801)	70.00	125.00	200.00	275.00

2 SHILLINGS

SILVER
c/m: Type I on 1/4 cut of Spanish or Spanish Colonial 8 Reales.

KM#	Date	Year	Good	VG	Fine	VF
6	ND	(1801)	75.00	150.00	250.00	300.00

4 SHILLINGS, 1-1/2 PENCE

SILVER
c/m: Type I on 1/2 cut of Spanish or Spanish Colonial 8 Reales.

7	ND	(1801)	100.00	200.00	350.00	700.00

Type II: TORTOLA in rectangle

SHILLING

SILVER
c/m: Type II on 1/8 cut of Spanish or Spanish Colonial 8 Reales.

8	ND	(1801-05)	100.00	200.00	320.00	450.00

2 SHILLINGS

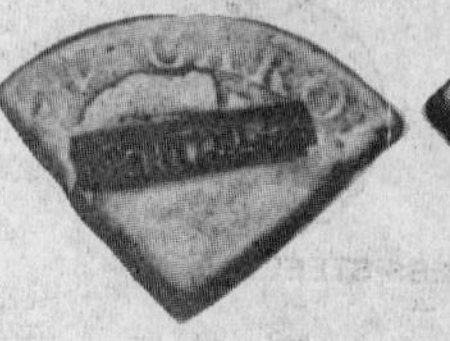

SILVER
c/m: Type II on 1/4 cut of Spanish or Spanish Colonial 8 Reales.

9	ND	(1801-05)	40.00	80.00	150.00	275.00

4 SHILLINGS, 1-1/2 PENCE

SILVER
c/m: Type II on 1/2 cut of Spanish or Spanish Colonial 8 Reales.

10	ND	(1801-05)	50.00	100.00	200.00	370.00

PRIVATE COUNTERMARKED ISSUES

Hodge Plantation

1-1/2 PENCE

Black Dog

BILLON
c/m: Small 3mm incuse 'H' in square indent on French and French Colonial 2 Sous.

KM#	Date	Year	VG	Fine	VF	XF
11	ND	(1801-1811)	10.00	20.00	35.00	65.00

c/m: Large 5mm incuse 'H' in square indent on French and French Colonial 2 Sous.

KM#	Date	Year	Good	VG	Fine	VF
12	ND	(1801-1811)	10.00	20.00	35.00	65.00

Tirtila

Type III: TIRTILA

Type IV: TIRTILA w/inverted V for A.

NOTE: Market valuations listed for TIRTOLA c/m issues are just for the TIRTOLA c/m and do not take into consideration any other c/m that may be encountered on the same piece. Multiple c/m issues tend to have a higher market value.

9 PENCE or 1 BIT

SILVER
c/m: Type III on 1/2 cut of Spanish or Spanish Colonial 2 Reales.

KM#	Date	Year	Good	VG	Fine	VF
13	ND	(1805-24)	125.00	185.00	280.00	450.00

c/m: Type IV on 1/2 cut of Spanish or Spanish Colonial 2 Reales.

KM#	Date	Year	Good	VG	Fine	VF
14	ND	(1805-24)	150.00	225.00	350.00	560.00

SHILLING

SILVER
c/m: Type III on 1/8 cut of Spanish or Spanish Colonial 8 Reales.

KM#	Date	Year	Good	VG	Fine	VF
15	ND	(1805-24)	125.00	185.00	280.00	450.00

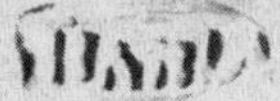

c/m: Type IV on 1/8 cut of Spanish or Spanish Colonial 8 Reales.

KM#	Date	Year	Good	VG	Fine	VF
16	ND	(1805-24)	125.00	185.00	280.00	450.00

2 SHILLINGS

SILVER
c/m: Type III on 1/4 cut of Spanish or Spanish Colonial 8 Reales.

KM#	Date	Year	Good	VG	Fine	VF
17	ND	(1805-24)	85.00	120.00	190.00	300.00

c/m: Type IV on 1/4 cut of Spanish or Spanish Colonial 8 Reales.

KM#	Date	Year	Good	VG	Fine	VF
18	ND	(1805-24)	85.00	120.00	190.00	300.00

4 SHILLINGS, 1-1/2 PENCE

SILVER
c/m: Type III on 1/2 cut of Spanish or Spanish Colonial 8 Reales.

KM#	Date	Year	Good	VG	Fine	VF
19	ND	(1805-24)	125.00	175.00	250.00	400.00

c/m: Type IV on 1/2 cut of Spanish or Spanish Colonial 8 Reales.

KM#	Date	Year	Good	VG	Fine	VF
20	ND	(1805-24)	125.00	175.00	250.00	400.00

BRITISH VIRGIN ISLANDS

RULERS

British

MINT MARKS

FM - Franklin Mint, U.S.A.*

***NOTE:** From 1975 the Franklin Mint has produced coinage in up to 3 different qualities. Qualities of issue are designated in ( ) after each date and are defined as follows:

(M) MATTE -Normal circulation strike or a dull finish produced by sandblasting special uncirculated (polish finish) or proof quality dies.

(U) SPECIAL UNCIRCULATED - Polished or proof-like in appearance without any frosted features.

(P) PROOF - The highest quality obtainable having mirror-like fields and frosted features.

MONETARY SYSTEM

100 Cents = 1 Dollar

CENT

BRONZE
Green-Throated Carib and Antillean Crested Hummingbird

KM#	Date	Mintage	VF	XF	Unc
1	1973FM	.053	—	.10	.50
	1973FM(P)	.181	—	Proof	1.00
	1974FM	.022	—	.10	.50
	1974FM(P)	.094	—	Proof	1.00
	1975FM(M)	6,000	—	.10	.75
	1975FM(U)	2,351	—	.10	.50
	1975FM(P)	.032	—	Proof	1.00
	1976FM(M)	.012	—	.10	.50
	1976FM(U)	996 pcs.	—	.10	.50
	1976FM(P)	.015	—	Proof	1.00
	1977FM(M)	500 pcs.	—	.25	2.00
	1977FM(U)	782 pcs.	—	.10	.50
	1977FM(P)	7,218	—	Proof	1.00
	1978FM(U)	1,443	—	.10	.50
	1978FM(P)	7,059	—	Proof	1.00
	1979FM(U)	680 pcs.	—	.10	.50
	1979FM(P)	5,304	—	Proof	1.00
	1980FM(U)	1,007	—	.10	.50
	1980FM(P)	3,421	—	Proof	1.00
	1981FM(U)	472 pcs.	—	.10	.50
	1981FM(P)	1,124	—	Proof	1.50
	1982FM(U)	—	—	.10	.50
	1982FM(P)	—	—	Proof	1.50
	1983FM(U)	—	—	.10	.50
	1983FM(P)	—	—	Proof	1.50
	1984FM(P)	—	—	Proof	1.50

1.7500 g, .925 SILVER, .0520 oz ASW
Queen's Silver Jubilee

KM#	Date	Mintage	VF	XF	Unc
9	1977FM(P)	.017	—	Proof	2.50

Coronation Jubilee
Similar to KM#1.

KM#	Date	Mintage	VF	XF	Unc
16	1978FM(P)	6,196	—	Proof	3.50

BRONZE
Hawksbill Turtle

KM#	Date	Mintage	VF	XF	Unc
42	1985FM(P)	—	—	Proof	1.00

1.7500 g, .925 SILVER, .0520 oz ASW

KM#	Date	Mintage	VF	XF	Unc
42a	1985FM(P)	1,474	—	Proof	3.00

5 CENTS

COPPER-NICKEL
Zenaida Dove

KM#	Date	Mintage	VF	XF	Unc
2	1973FM	.026	—	.15	.75
	1973FM(P)	.181	—	Proof	1.25
	1974FM	.018	—	.15	.75
	1974FM(P)	.094	—	Proof	1.25
	1975FM(M)	3,800	—	.20	1.00
	1975FM(U)	2,351	—	.15	.75
	1975FM(P)	.032	—	Proof	1.25
	1976FM(M)	4,800	—	.20	1.00
	1976FM(U)	996 pcs.	—	.15	.75
	1976FM(P)	.015	—	Proof	1.25
	1977FM(M)	500 pcs.	—	.35	3.50
	1977FM(U)	782 pcs.	—	.15	.75
	1977FM(P)	7,218	—	Proof	1.25
	1978FM(U)	1,443	—	.15	.75
	1978FM(P)	7,059	—	Proof	1.25
	1979FM(U)	680 pcs.	—	.15	.75
	1979FM(P)	5,304	—	Proof	1.25
	1980FM(U)	1,007	—	.15	.75
	1980FM(P)	3,421	—	Proof	1.25
	1981FM(U)	472 pcs.	—	.15	.75
	1981FM(P)	1,124	—	Proof	1.25
	1982FM(U)	—	—	.15	.75
	1982FM(P)	—	—	Proof	1.25
	1983FM(U)	—	—	.15	.75
	1983FM(P)	—	—	Proof	1.25
	1984FM(P)	—	—	Proof	1.25

3.5500 g, .925 SILVER, .1055 oz ASW
Queen's Silver Jubilee

KM#	Date	Mintage	VF	XF	Unc
10	1977FM(P)	.017	—	Proof	3.00

Coronation Jubilee

KM#	Date	Mintage	VF	XF	Unc
17	1978FM(P)	6,196	—	Proof	4.50

COPPER-NICKEL
Bonito Fish

KM#	Date	Mintage	VF	XF	Unc
43	1985FM(P)	—	—	Proof	1.00

3.5550 g, .925 SILVER, .1055 oz ASW

KM#	Date	Mintage	VF	XF	Unc
43a	1985FM(P)	1,471	—	Proof	4.00

10 CENTS

COPPER-NICKEL
Ringed Kingfisher

KM#	Date	Mintage	VF	XF	Unc
3	1973FM(U)	.023	—	.20	1.00
	1973FM(P)	.181	—	Proof	1.50
	1974FM(U)	.013	—	.20	1.00
	1974FM(P)	.094	—	Proof	1.50
	1975FM(M)	2,000	—	.20	1.25
	1975FM(U)	2,351	—	.20	1.00
	1975FM(P)	.032	—	Proof	1.50
	1976FM(M)	3,000	—	.20	1.00
	1976FM(U)	996 pcs.	—	.20	1.00
	1976FM(P)	.015	—	Proof	1.50
	1977FM(M)	500 pcs.	—	.45	4.00
	1977FM(U)	782 pcs.	—	.20	1.00
	1977FM(P)	7,218	—	Proof	1.50
	1978FM(U)	1,443	—	.20	1.00
	1978FM(P)	7,059	—	Proof	1.50
	1979FM(U)	680 pcs.	—	.20	1.00
	1979FM(P)	5,304	—	Proof	1.50
	1980FM(U)	1,007	—	.20	1.00
	1980FM(P)	3,421	—	Proof	1.50
	1981FM(U)	472 pcs.	—	.20	1.00
	1981FM(P)	1,124	—	Proof	1.50
	1982FM(U)	—	—	.20	1.00
	1982FM(P)	—	—	Proof	1.50
	1983FM(U)	—	—	.20	1.00
	1983FM(P)	—	—	Proof	1.50
	1984FM(P)	—	—	Proof	1.50

6.4000 g, .925 SILVER, .1903 oz ASW
Queen's Silver Jubilee

KM#	Date	Mintage	VF	XF	Unc
11	1977FM(P)	.017	—	Proof	5.00

Coronation Jubilee

KM#	Date	Mintage	VF	XF	Unc
18	1978FM(P)	6,196	—	Proof	6.50

COPPER-NICKEL
Great Barracuda

KM#	Date	Mintage	VF	XF	Unc
44	1985FM(P)	—	—	Proof	1.00

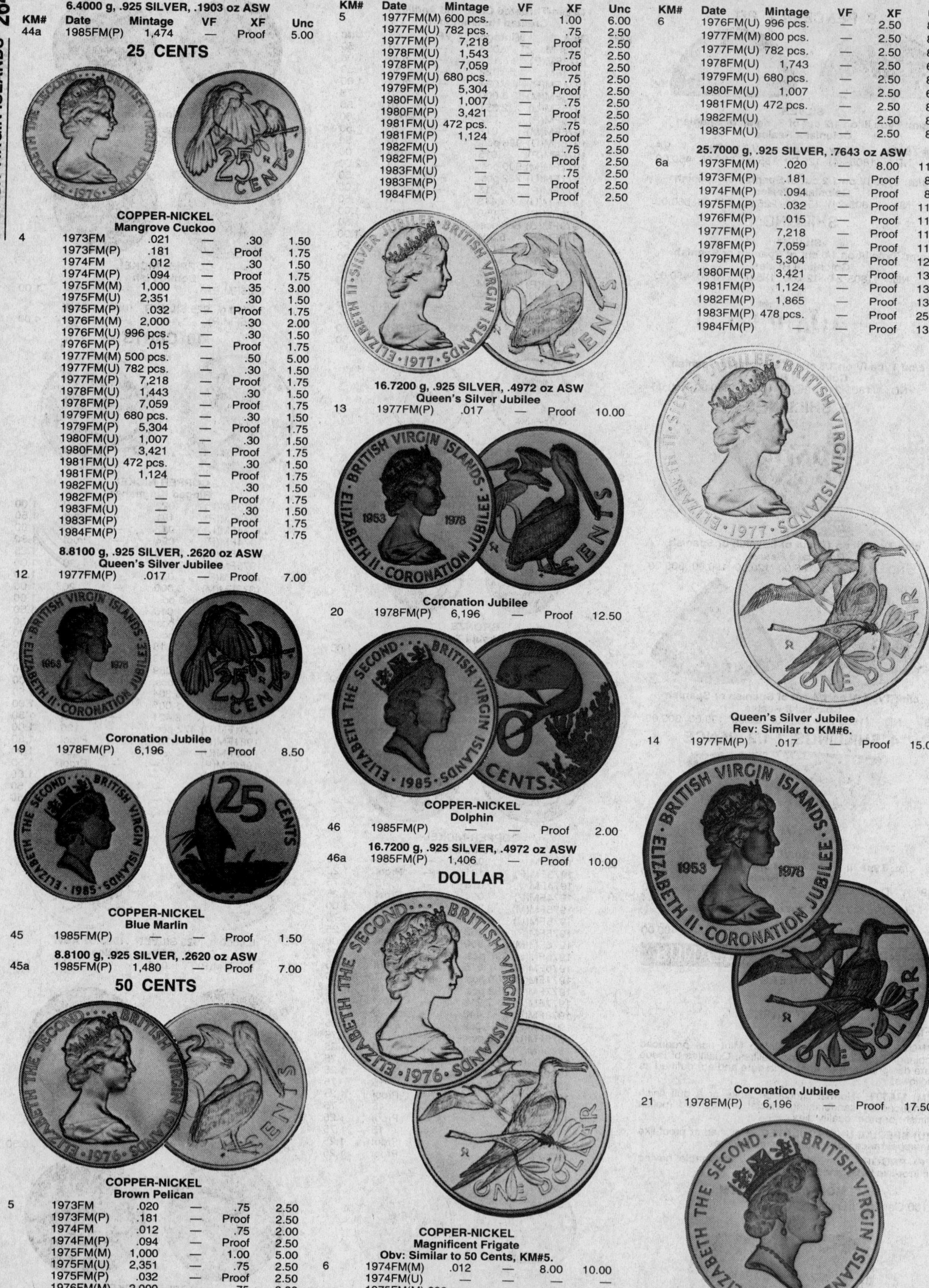

6.4000 g, .925 SILVER, .1903 oz ASW

KM#	Date	Mintage	VF	XF	Unc
44a	1985FM(P)	1,474	—	Proof	5.00

25 CENTS

COPPER-NICKEL
Mangrove Cuckoo

KM#	Date	Mintage	VF	XF	Unc
4	1973FM	.021	—	.30	1.50
	1973FM(P)	.181	—	Proof	1.75
	1974FM	.012	—	.30	1.50
	1974FM(P)	.094	—	Proof	1.75
	1975FM(M)	1,000	—	.35	3.00
	1975FM(U)	2,351	—	.30	1.50
	1975FM(P)	.032	—	Proof	1.75
	1976FM(M)	2,000	—	.30	2.00
	1976FM(U)	996 pcs.	—	.30	1.50
	1976FM(P)	.015	—	Proof	1.75
	1977FM(M)	500 pcs.	—	.50	5.00
	1977FM(U)	782 pcs.	—	.30	1.50
	1977FM(P)	7,218	—	Proof	1.75
	1978FM(U)	1,443	—	.30	1.50
	1978FM(P)	7,059	—	Proof	1.75
	1979FM(U)	680 pcs.	—	.30	1.50
	1979FM(P)	5,304	—	Proof	1.75
	1980FM(U)	1,007	—	.30	1.50
	1980FM(P)	3,421	—	Proof	1.75
	1981FM(U)	472 pcs.	—	.30	1.50
	1981FM(P)	1,124	—	Proof	1.75
	1982FM(U)	—	—	.30	1.50
	1982FM(P)	—	—	Proof	1.75
	1983FM(U)	—	—	.30	1.50
	1983FM(P)	—	—	Proof	1.75
	1984FM(P)	—	—	Proof	1.75

8.8100 g, .925 SILVER, .2620 oz ASW
Queen's Silver Jubilee

KM#	Date	Mintage	VF	XF	Unc
12	1977FM(P)	.017	—	Proof	7.00

Coronation Jubilee

KM#	Date	Mintage	VF	XF	Unc
19	1978FM(P)	6,196	—	Proof	8.50

COPPER-NICKEL
Blue Marlin

KM#	Date	Mintage	VF	XF	Unc
45	1985FM(P)	—	—	Proof	1.50

8.8100 g, .925 SILVER, .2620 oz ASW

KM#	Date	Mintage	VF	XF	Unc
45a	1985FM(P)	1,480	—	Proof	7.00

50 CENTS

COPPER-NICKEL
Brown Pelican

KM#	Date	Mintage	VF	XF	Unc
5	1973FM	.020	—	.75	2.50
	1973FM(P)	.181	—	Proof	2.50
	1974FM	.012	—	.75	2.00
	1974FM(P)	.094	—	Proof	2.50
	1975FM(M)	1,000	—	1.00	5.00
	1975FM(U)	2,351	—	.75	2.50
	1975FM(P)	.032	—	Proof	2.50
	1976FM(M)	2,000	—	.75	3.00
	1976FM(U)	996 pcs.	—	.75	2.50
	1976FM(P)	.015	—	Proof	2.50
5	1977FM(M)	600 pcs.	—	1.00	6.00
	1977FM(U)	782 pcs.	—	.75	2.50
	1977FM(P)	7,218	—	Proof	2.50
	1978FM(U)	1,543	—	.75	2.50
	1978FM(P)	7,059	—	Proof	2.50
	1979FM(U)	680 pcs.	—	.75	2.50
	1979FM(P)	5,304	—	Proof	2.50
	1980FM(U)	1,007	—	.75	2.50
	1980FM(P)	3,421	—	Proof	2.50
	1981FM(U)	472 pcs.	—	.75	2.50
	1981FM(P)	1,124	—	Proof	2.50
	1982FM(U)	—	—	.75	2.50
	1982FM(P)	—	—	Proof	2.50
	1983FM(U)	—	—	.75	2.50
	1983FM(P)	—	—	Proof	2.50
	1984FM(P)	—	—	Proof	2.50

16.7200 g, .925 SILVER, .4972 oz ASW
Queen's Silver Jubilee

KM#	Date	Mintage	VF	XF	Unc
13	1977FM(P)	.017	—	Proof	10.00

Coronation Jubilee

KM#	Date	Mintage	VF	XF	Unc
20	1978FM(P)	6,196	—	Proof	12.50

COPPER-NICKEL
Dolphin

KM#	Date	Mintage	VF	XF	Unc
46	1985FM(P)	—	—	Proof	2.00

16.7200 g, .925 SILVER, .4972 oz ASW

KM#	Date	Mintage	VF	XF	Unc
46a	1985FM(P)	1,406	—	Proof	10.00

DOLLAR

COPPER-NICKEL
Magnificent Frigate
Obv: Similar to 50 Cents, KM#5.

KM#	Date	Mintage	VF	XF	Unc
6	1974FM(M)	.012	—	8.00	10.00
	1974FM(U)	—	—	—	—
	1975FM(M)	800 pcs.	—	2.50	8.00
	1975FM(U)	2,351	—	2.50	6.50
	1976FM(M)	1,800	—	2.50	6.50
6	1976FM(U)	996 pcs.	—	2.50	8.00
	1977FM(M)	800 pcs.	—	2.50	8.00
	1977FM(U)	782 pcs.	—	2.50	8.00
	1978FM(U)	1,743	—	2.50	6.50
	1979FM(U)	680 pcs.	—	2.50	8.00
	1980FM(U)	1,007	—	2.50	6.50
	1981FM(U)	472 pcs.	—	2.50	8.00
	1982FM(U)	—	—	2.50	8.00
	1983FM(U)	—	—	2.50	8.00

25.7000 g, .925 SILVER, .7643 oz ASW

KM#	Date	Mintage	VF	XF	Unc
6a	1973FM(M)	.020	—	8.00	11.00
	1973FM(P)	.181	—	Proof	8.50
	1974FM(P)	.094	—	Proof	8.50
	1975FM(P)	.032	—	Proof	11.00
	1976FM(P)	.015	—	Proof	11.00
	1977FM(P)	7,218	—	Proof	11.00
	1978FM(P)	7,059	—	Proof	11.00
	1979FM(P)	5,304	—	Proof	12.00
	1980FM(P)	3,421	—	Proof	13.00
	1981FM(P)	1,124	—	Proof	13.00
	1982FM(P)	1,865	—	Proof	13.00
	1983FM(P)	478 pcs.	—	Proof	25.00
	1984FM(P)	—	—	Proof	13.00

Queen's Silver Jubilee
Rev: Similar to KM#6.

KM#	Date	Mintage	VF	XF	Unc
14	1977FM(P)	.017	—	Proof	15.00

Coronation Jubilee

KM#	Date	Mintage	VF	XF	Unc
21	1978FM(P)	6,196	—	Proof	17.50

COPPER-NICKEL
Butterfly Fish

KM#	Date	Mintage	VF	XF	Unc
47	1985FM(P)	—	—	Proof	20.00
	24.7400 g, .925 SILVER, .7358 oz ASW				
47a	1985FM(P)	1,372	—	Proof	25.00

5 DOLLARS

COPPER-NICKEL
Snowy Egret
Obv: Similar to 50 Cents, KM#13.

KM#	Date	Mintage	VF	XF	Unc
24	1979FM(U)	680 pcs.	—	—	25.00
	40.5000 g, .925 SILVER, 1.2044 oz ASW				
24a	1979FM(P)	5,304	—	Proof	25.00

COPPER-NICKEL
Great Blue Heron

KM#	Date	Mintage	VF	XF	Unc
26	1980FM(U)	1,007	—	—	25.00
	40.5000 g, .925 SILVER, 1.2044 oz ASW				
26a	1980FM(P)	3,421	—	Proof	25.00

COPPER-NICKEL
Royal Tern
Obv: Similar to 50 Cents, KM#13.

KM#	Date	Mintage	VF	XF	Unc
30	1981FM(U)	472 pcs.	—	—	25.00
	40.5000 g, .925 SILVER, 1.2044 oz ASW				
30a	1981FM(P)	1,124	—	Proof	30.00

COPPER-NICKEL
White-tailed Tropic Birds

KM#	Date	Mintage	VF	XF	Unc
33	1982FM(U)	—	—	—	25.00
	40.5000 g, .925 SILVER, 1.2044 oz ASW				
33a	1982FM(P)	1,865	—	Proof	30.00

COPPER-NICKEL
Yellow Warblers
Obv: Similar to 50 Cents, KM#13.

KM#	Date	Mintage	VF	XF	Unc
35	1983FM(U)	—	—	—	35.00
	40.5000 g, .925 SILVER, 1.2044 oz ASW				
35a	1983FM(P)	478 pcs.	—	Proof	50.00
	1984FM(P)	—	—	Proof	45.00

10 DOLLARS

30.2800 g, .500 SILVER, .4868 oz ASW
30th Anniversary of Coronation of Queen Elizabeth II

KM#	Date	Mintage	VF	XF	Unc
36	1983FM(P)	2,957	—	Proof	22.50

20 DOLLARS

19.0900 g, .925 SILVER, .5678 oz ASW
Crossed Cannons

KM#	Date	Mintage	VF	XF	Unc
48	1985FM(P)	—	—	Proof	20.00

Porcelain Cup
Obv: Similar to KM#48.

KM#	Date	Mintage	VF	XF	Unc
49	1985FM(P)	—	—	Proof	20.00

Sextant
Obv: Similar to KM#48.

KM#	Date	Mintage	VF	XF	Unc
50	1985FM(P)	—	—	Proof	20.00

Emerald and Gold Ring

Obv: Similar to KM#48.

KM#	Date	Mintage	VF	XF	Unc
51	1985FM(P)	—	—	Proof	20.00

Gold Doubloon of 1702
Obv: Similar to KM#48.

KM#	Date	Mintage	VF	XF	Unc
52	1985FM(P)	—	—	Proof	20.00

Anchor
Obv: Similar to KM#48.

KM#	Date	Mintage	VF	XF	Unc
53	1985FM(P)	—	—	Proof	20.00

Brass Nocturnal
Obv: Similar to KM#48.

KM#	Date	Mintage	VF	XF	Unc
54	1985FM(P)	—	—	Proof	20.00

Sword Guillon
Obv: Similar to KM#48.

KM#	Date	Mintage	VF	XF	Unc
55	1985FM(P)	—	—	Proof	20.00

Gold Bar
Obv: Similar to KM#48.

KM#	Date	Mintage	VF	XF	Unc
56	1985FM(P)	—	—	Proof	20.00

Gold Escudo
Obv: Similar to KM#48. Rev: Obv. and rev. of gold escudo of 1733.

KM#	Date	Mintage	VF	XF	Unc
57	1985FM(P)	—	—	Proof	20.00

Ivory Sundial
Obv: Similar to KM#48.

KM#	Date	Mintage	VF	XF	Unc
58	1985FM(P)	—	—	Proof	20.00

Gold Monstrance
Obv: Similar to KM#48.

KM#	Date	Mintage	VF	XF	Unc
59	1985FM(P)	—	—	Proof	20.00

Teapot
Obv: Similar to KM#48.

KM#	Date	Mintage	VF	XF	Unc
60	1985FM(P)	—	—	Proof	20.00

Brass Religious Medallion
Obv: Similar to KM#48.

KM#	Date	Mintage	VF	XF	Unc
61	1985FM(P)	—	—	Proof	20.00

Astrolable
Obv: Similar to KM#48.

KM#	Date	Mintage	VF	XF	Unc
62	1985FM(P)	—	—	Proof	20.00

Bells
Obv: Similar to KM#48.

KM#	Date	Mintage	VF	XF	Unc
63	1985FM(P)	—	—	Proof	20.00

Porcelain Bottle
Obv: Similar to KM#48.

KM#	Date	Mintage	VF	XF	Unc
64	1985FM(P)	—	—	Proof	20.00

Ship and Dutch Cannons
Obv: Similar to KM#48.

KM#	Date	Mintage	VF	XF	Unc
65	1985FM(P)	—	—	Proof	20.00

Spanish Colonial 8 Reales 'Cob' Coin
Obv: Similar to KM#48.

KM#	Date	Mintage	VF	XF	Unc
66	1985FM(P)	—	—	Proof	20.00

Ship's Stern Lantern
Obv: Similar to KM#48.

KM#	Date	Mintage	VF	XF	Unc
67	1985FM(P)	—	—	Proof	20.00

Brass Dividers
Obv: Similar to KM#48.

68	1985FM(P)	—	—	Proof	20.00

Gold Cross
Obv: Similar to KM#48.

69	1985FM(P)	—	—	Proof	20.00

Perfume Bottle
Obv: Similar to KM#48.

70	1985FM(P)	—	—	Proof	20.00

Pocket Watch
Obv: Similar to KM#48.

71	1985FM(P)	—	—	Proof	20.00

Gold Bracelet and Button
Obv: Similar to KM#48.

KM#	Date	Mintage	VF	XF	Unc
72	1985FM(P)	—	—	Proof	20.00

25 DOLLARS

28.1000 g, .925 SILVER, .8356 oz ASW
Coronation Jubilee
Obv: Portrait of Queen.

22	1978FM(P)	8,438	—	Proof	25.00

1.5000 g, .500 GOLD, .0241 oz AGW
Diving Osprey

27	1980FM(P)	.011	—	Proof	50.00

Caribbean Sparrow Hawk

31.1	1981FM(P)	2,513	—	Proof	55.00

Error. Rev: W/o FM mint mark.

31.2	1981(P)	—	—	Proof	60.00

Hawk

41	1982FM(P)	3,819	—	Proof	50.00

Merlin Hawk

37	1983FM(P)	5,949	—	Proof	50.00

Peregrine Falcon

40	1984FM(P)	97 pcs.	—	Proof	110.00

Marsh Hawk

KM#	Date	Mintage	VF	XF	Unc
73	1985FM(P)	1,294	—	Proof	65.00

20.0900 g, .925 SILVER, .5977 oz ASW
Sunken Ship Treasures - Ornamental Lock Plate

90	1988FM(P)	—	—	Proof	26.50

Sunken Ship Treasures - Royal Coat of Arms on Bottle

91	1988FM(P)	—	—	Proof	26.50

Sunken Ship Treasures - Finger Ring

92	1988FM(P)	—	—	Proof	26.50

Sunken Ship Treasures - Hour Glass

93	1988FM(P)	—	—	Proof	26.50

Sunken Ship Treasures - Dagger and Scabbard

KM#	Date	Mintage	VF	XF	Unc
94	1988FM(P)	—	—	Proof	26.50

Sunken Ship Treasures - Jewel Encrusted Cross

KM#	Date	Mintage	VF	XF	Unc
95	1988FM(P)	—	—	Proof	26.50

Sunken Ship Treasures - Crossed Keys

KM#	Date	Mintage	VF	XF	Unc
96	1988FM(P)	—	—	Proof	26.50

Sunken Ship Treasures - Belt Buckle

KM#	Date	Mintage	VF	XF	Unc
97	1988FM(P)	—	—	Proof	26.50

Sunken Ship Treasures - American Bottle

KM#	Date	Mintage	VF	XF	Unc
98	1988FM(P)	—	—	Proof	26.50

Sunken Ship Treasures - Religious Medallion

KM#	Date	Mintage	VF	XF	Unc
99	1988FM(P)	—	—	Proof	26.50

Sunken Ship Treasures - Baby Figurines

KM#	Date	Mintage	VF	XF	Unc
100	1988FM(P)	—	—	Proof	26.50

Sunken Ship Treasures - Insignia of the Royal French Marines

KM#	Date	Mintage	VF	XF	Unc
101	1988FM(P)	—	—	Proof	26.50

Sunken Ship Treasures - Engraved Printing Block

KM#	Date	Mintage	VF	XF	Unc
102	1988FM(P)	—	—	Proof	26.50

Sunken Ship Treasures - Antique Clock

KM#	Date	Mintage	VF	XF	Unc
103	1988FM(P)	—	—	Proof	26.50

Flintlock Pistol

KM#	Date	Mintage	VF	XF	Unc
132	1988FM(P)	—	—	Proof	26.50

Stylized Fish Statue

KM#	Date	Mintage	VF	XF	Unc
133	1988FM(P)	—	—	Proof	26.50

Mortar and Pestle

KM#	Date	Mintage	VF	XF	Unc
134	1988FM(P)	—	—	Proof	26.50

Open Mouthed Dragon Head Sculpture

KM#	Date	Mintage	VF	XF	Unc
135	1988FM(P)	—	—	Proof	26.50

Military Mortar

KM#	Date	Mintage	VF	XF	Unc
136	1988FM(P)	—	—	Proof	26.50

Seated Figure Sculpture

137	1988FM(P)	—	—	Proof	26.50

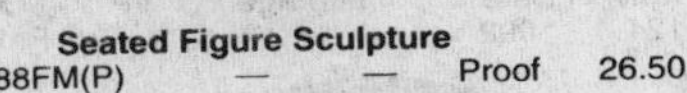

Lion Sculpture

138	1988FM(P)	—	—	Proof	26.50

Violin

139	1988FM(P)	—	—	Proof	26.50

Chalice

140	1988FM(P)	—	—	Proof	26.50

Pitcher

141	1988FM(P)	—	—	Proof	26.50

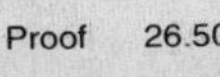

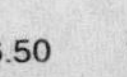

Cannon

KM#	Date	Mintage	VF	XF	Unc
142	1988FM(P)	—	—	Proof	26.50

21.5400 g, .925 SILVER, .6406 oz ASW

Discovery of America - Columbus Planning Voyage

104	1992FM(P)	—	—	Proof	25.00

Discovery of America - Columbus Lecturing

105	1992FM(P)	—	—	Proof	25.00

Discovery of America - Queen Isabella Offering Jewels

106	1992FM(P)	—	—	Proof	25.00

Discovery of America - Columbus Aboard Ship

KM#	Date	Mintage	VF	XF	Unc
107	1992FM(P)	—	—	Proof	25.00

Discovery of America - Columbus on Horseback

108	1992FM(P)	—	—	Proof	25.00

Discovery of America - Ship Under Full Sail

109	1992FM(P)	—	—	Proof	27.50

Discovery of America - Ship At Anchor

110	1992FM(P)	—	—	Proof	27.50

Discovery of America - Natives Offering Gifts

KM#	Date	Mintage	VF	XF	Unc
111	1992FM(P)	—	—	Proof	26.50

Discovery of America - Shipwreck

KM#	Date	Mintage	VF	XF	Unc
112	1992FM(P)	—	—	Proof	27.50

Discovery of America - Royal Banquet

KM#	Date	Mintage	VF	XF	Unc
113	1992FM(P)	—	—	Proof	26.50

Discovery of America - Columbus Explaining Lunar Eclipse to Natives

KM#	Date	Mintage	VF	XF	Unc
114	1992FM(P)	—	—	Proof	26.50

Discovery of America - Columbus on Shore

KM#	Date	Mintage	VF	XF	Unc
115	1992FM(P)	—	—	Proof	27.50

Discovery of America - Spanish Figures

KM#	Date	Mintage	VF	XF	Unc
116	1992FM(P)	—	—	Proof	26.50

Discovery of America - Columbus With Shore Party

KM#	Date	Mintage	VF	XF	Unc
117	1992FM(P)	—	—	Proof	26.50

Discovery of America - Death of Columbus

KM#	Date	Mintage	VF	XF	Unc
118	1992FM(P)	—	—	Proof	25.00

Discovery of America - Columbus Bowing Before King Ferdinand

KM#	Date	Mintage	VF	XF	Unc
122	1992	—	—	Proof	25.00

Discovery of America - Columbus Before Queen Isabella

KM#	Date	Mintage	VF	XF	Unc
123	1992	—	—	Proof	25.00

Discovery of America - Columbus Before King Ferdinand and Queen Isabella

KM#	Date	Mintage	VF	XF	Unc
124	1992	—	—	Proof	25.00

Discovery of America - Columbus Getting Provisions For His Ships

KM#	Date	Mintage	VF	XF	Unc
125	1992	—	—	Proof	26.50

Discovery of America - 4 Sailing Ships

KM#	Date	Mintage	VF	XF	Unc
126	1992	—	—	Proof	27.50

Discovery of America - Columbus Navigating By Stars

KM#	Date	Mintage	VF	XF	Unc
127	1992	—	—	Proof	26.50

Discovery of America - Sighting Land

KM#	Date	Mintage	VF	XF	Unc
128	1992	—	—	Proof	27.50

Discovery of America - Columbus Claiming the Newly Discovered Land

KM#	Date	Mintage	VF	XF	Unc
129	1992	—	—	Proof	26.50

Discovery of America - Columbus Seated on Shore With Ship Wreck Off Shore

KM#	Date	Mintage	VF	XF	Unc
130	1992	—	—	Proof	26.50

Discovery of America - Columbus As Prisoner

KM#	Date	Mintage	VF	XF	Unc
131	1992	—	—	Proof	26.50

50 DOLLARS

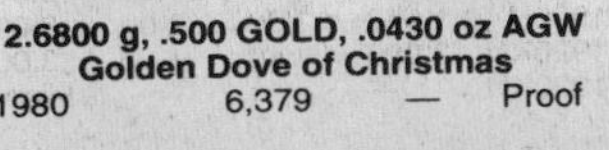

2.6800 g, .500 GOLD, .0430 oz AGW
Golden Dove of Christmas

KM#	Date	Mintage	VF	XF	Unc
28	1980	6,379	—	Proof	60.00

2.0687 g, .500 GOLD, .0332 oz AGW
Flute Player

KM#	Date	Mintage	VF	XF	Unc
75	1988	—	—	Proof	55.00

Bird's Head Staff

KM#	Date	Mintage	VF	XF	Unc
76	1988	—	—	Proof	55.00

Double Spouted Vessel

KM#	Date	Mintage	VF	XF	Unc
77	1988	—	—	Proof	55.00

Deer-top Bell

KM#	Date	Mintage	VF	XF	Unc
78	1988	—	—	Proof	55.00

Two Headed Animal

KM#	Date	Mintage	VF	XF	Unc
79	1988	—	—	Proof	55.00

Turtle

KM#	Date	Mintage	VF	XF	Unc
80	1988	—	—	Proof	55.00

Frog

KM#	Date	Mintage	VF	XF	Unc
81	1988	—	—	Proof	55.00

Mixtec Mask

KM#	Date	Mintage	VF	XF	Unc
82	1988	—	—	Proof	55.00

Chimu Gold Beaker

KM#	Date	Mintage	VF	XF	Unc
83	1988	—	—	Proof	55.00

Bird Vessel

KM#	Date	Mintage	VF	XF	Unc
84	1988	—	—	Proof	55.00

Ceremonial Headdress

KM#	Date	Mintage	VF	XF	Unc
85	1988	—	—	Proof	55.00

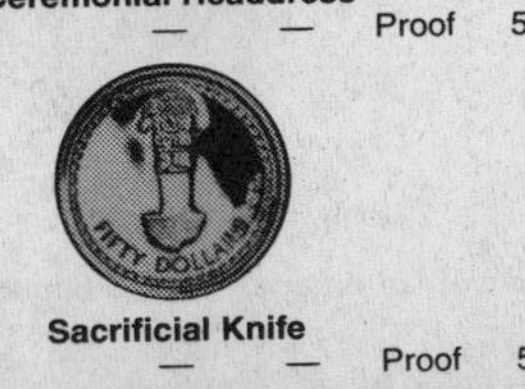

Sacrificial Knife

KM#	Date	Mintage	VF	XF	Unc
86	1988	—	—	Proof	55.00

Ceremonial Dancer

KM#	Date	Mintage	VF	XF	Unc
87	1988	—	—	Proof	55.00

Spanish Colonial Gold Coin

KM#	Date	Mintage	VF	XF	Unc
88	1988	—	—	Proof	55.00

Crossed Hands

KM#	Date	Mintage	VF	XF	Unc
89	1988	—	—	Proof	55.00

100 DOLLARS

7.1000 g, .900 GOLD, .2054 oz AGW
Royal Tern

KM#	Date	Mintage	VF	XF	Unc
7	1975FM(M)	10 pcs.	—	Rare	—
	1975FM(U)	.013	—	—	110.00
	1975FM(P)	*.023	—	Proof	160.00

***NOTE:** Includes 8,754 in First Day Covers.

50th Birthday of Queen Elizabeth II

KM#	Date	Mintage	VF	XF	Unc
8	1976FM(M)	10 pcs.	—	Rare	—
	1976FM(U)	1,752	—	—	125.00
	1976FM(P)	.012	—	Proof	170.00

Queen's Silver Jubilee

KM#	Date	Mintage	VF	XF	Unc
15	1977FM(U)	10 pcs.	—	Rare	—
	1977FM(P)	6,715	—	Proof	185.00

Coronation Jubilee

KM#	Date	Mintage	VF	XF	Unc
23	1978FM(P)	5,772	—	Proof	185.00

Sir Francis Drake

KM#	Date	Mintage	VF	XF	Unc
25	1979FM(P)	3,216	—	Proof	190.00

400th Anniversary of Drake's Voyage

KM#	Date	Mintage	VF	XF	Unc
29	1980FM(P)	5,412	—	Proof	185.00

Knighting of Sir Francis Drake

KM#	Date	Mintage	VF	XF	Unc
32	1981FM(P)	1,321	—	Proof	200.00

30th Anniversary of Queen Elizabeth II Reign

KM#	Date	Mintage	VF	XF	Unc
34	1982FM(P)	620 pcs.	—	Proof	265.00

30th Anniversary of Coronation of Queen Elizabeth II

KM#	Date	Mintage	VF	XF	Unc
38	1983FM(P)	624 pcs.	—	Proof	265.00

Flora - Ginger Thomas

KM#	Date	Mintage	VF	XF	Unc
39	1984FM(P)	25 pcs.	—	Proof	500.00

Sir Francis Drake's West Indian Voyage

KM#	Date	Mintage	VF	XF	Unc
74	1985FM(P)	772 pcs.	—	Proof	325.00

4.1180 g, .500 GOLD, .0662 oz AGW
Discovery of America - King Ferdinand of Spain

KM#	Date	Mintage	VF	XF	Unc
119	ND(1991)	—	—	Proof	150.00

250 DOLLARS

8.0494 g, .500 GOLD, .1294 oz AGW
Discovery of America - Queen Isabella of Spain

KM#	Date	Mintage	VF	XF	Unc
120	ND(1991)	—	—	Proof	275.00

500 DOLLARS

19.8126 g, .500 GOLD, .3185 oz AGW
Discovery of America - Christopher Columbus

KM#	Date	Mintage	VF	XF	Unc
121	ND(1991)	—	—	Proof	525.00

MINT SETS (MS)

KM#	Date	Mintage	Identification	Issue Price	Mkt. Val.
MS1	1973(6)	18,402	KM1-5,6a	11.50	8.00
MS2	1974(6)	9,474	KM1-6	10.00	8.00
MS3	1975(6)	2,351	KM1-6	12.50	10.00
MS4	1976(6)	996	KM1-6	13.50	15.00
MS5	1977(6)	782	KM1-6	12.50	15.00
MS6	1978(6)	943	KM1-6	13.00	20.00
MS7	1979(7)	680	KM1-6,24	20.00	27.50
MS8	1980(7)	1,007	KM1-6,26	21.00	27.50
MS9	1981(7)	472	KM1-6,30	20.00	30.00
MS10	1982(7)	—	KM1-6,33	28.50	35.00
MS11	1983(7)	203	KM1-6,35	22.00	50.00

PROOF SETS (PS)

KM#	Date	Mintage	Identification	Issue Price	Mkt. Val.
PS1	1973(6)	*146,581	KM1-5,6a	15.00	10.00
*NOTE: Includes 34,418 proofs in First Day Covers.					
PS2	1974(6)	93,555	KM1-5,6a	20.00	12.50
PS3	1975(6)	32,244	KM1-5,6a	25.00	15.00
PS4	1976(6)	15,003	KM1-5,6a	25.00	15.00
PS5	1977(6)	7,218	KM1-5,6a	26.00	20.00
PS6	1977(6)	17,366	KM9-14	60.00	50.00
PS7	1978(6)	7,059	KM1-5,6a	25.00	15.00
PS8	1978(6)	6,196	KM16-21	—	50.00
PS9	1979(7)	5,304	KM1-5,6a,24a	39.50	40.00
PS10	1980(7)	3,421	KM1-5,6a,26a	97.00	50.00
PS11	1981(7)	1,124	KM1-5,6a,30a	97.00	55.00
PS12	1982(7)	—	KM1-5,6a,33a	97.00	55.00
PS13	1983(7)	478	KM1-5,6a,35a	77.00	75.00
PS14	1984(7)	5,000	KM1-5,6a,35a	77.00	55.00
PS12	1985(6)	—	KM42-47	20.50	26.50
PS16	1985(6)	—	KM42a-47a	76.00	50.00
PS17	ND(1991)(3)	—	KM119-121	975.00	950.00

BRITISH WEST AFRICA

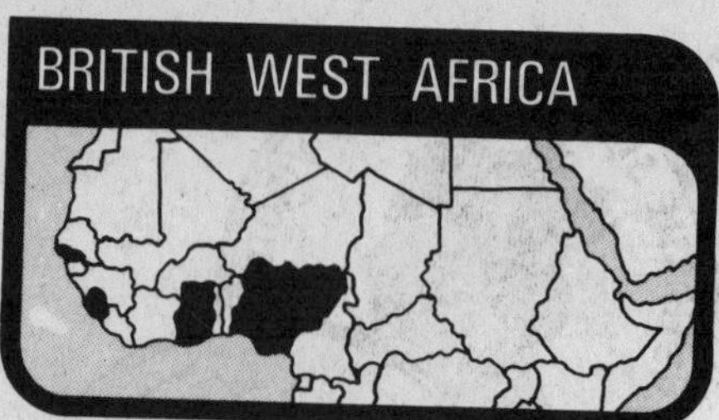

British West Africa was an administrative grouping of the four former British West African colonies of Gambia, Sierra Leone, Nigeria and Gold Coast (now Ghana). All are now independent republics and members of the British Commonwealth of Nations. See separate entries for individual statistics and history.

The four colonies were supplied with a common coinage and banknotes by the West African Currency Board from 1907 through 1958. From 1907 through 1911, the coinage bore the inscription, NIGERIA-BRITISH WEST AFRICA; from 1912 through 1958, BRITISH WEST AFRICA. The coinage, which includes three denominations of 1936 bearing the name of Edward VIII, is obsolete.

For later coinage see Gambia, Ghana, Sierra Leone and Nigeria.

RULERS

British, until 1958

MINT MARKS

G-J.R. Gaunt & Sons, Birmingham
H - Heaton Mint, Birmingham
K, KN - King's Norton, Birmingham
SA - Pretoria, South Africa
No mm - Royal Mint

MONETARY SYSTEM

12 Pence = 1 Shilling
20 Shillings = 1 Pound

1/10 PENNY

ALUMINUM

KM#	Date	Mintage	Fine	VF	XF	Unc
1	1907	1.254	2.00	4.00	7.00	17.50
	1908	8.363	1.00	2.00	4.00	10.00
	1908	—	—	—	Proof	250.00

COPPER-NICKEL

KM#	Date	Mintage	Fine	VF	XF	Unc
3	1908	9.600	.30	.50	1.00	2.00
	1909	4.800	.40	.75	1.50	5.00
	1910	7.200	.50	1.00	2.00	7.50

KM#	Date	Mintage	Fine	VF	XF	Unc
4	1911H	7.200	1.50	3.50	7.50	15.00

Rev. leg: W/o NIGERIA

KM#	Date	Mintage	Fine	VF	XF	Unc
7	1912H	10.800	.30	.75	1.50	4.00
	1913	4.632	1.00	2.00	3.50	6.50
	1913H	1.080	.30	.75	1.50	3.50
	1914	1.200	3.00	5.00	10.00	22.50
	1914H	20.088	.50	1.25	2.00	5.00
	1915H	10.032	.30	.75	1.50	5.00
	1916H	.480	40.00	65.00	100.00	200.00
	1917H	9.384	2.00	3.00	5.00	15.00
	1919H	.912	1.25	2.00	4.00	7.50
	1919KN	.480	10.00	25.00	50.00	80.00
	1920H	1.560	2.00	3.00	5.00	10.00
	1920KN	12.996	.40	1.00	3.00	5.00
	1920KN	—	—	—	Proof	125.00

KM#	Date	Mintage	Fine	VF	XF	Unc
7	1922KN	7.265	1.00	1.75	4.50	12.00
	1923KN	12.000	.30	.75	1.50	5.00
	1925	2.400	5.00	10.00	20.00	40.00
	1925H	12.000	2.00	3.00	5.00	12.00
	1925KN	12.000	.75	1.50	3.00	8.00
	1926	12.000	.75	1.50	2.50	6.00
	1927	3.984	.20	.50	1.50	3.00
	1927	—	—	—	Proof	150.00
	1928	11.760	.20	.50	1.50	3.00
	1928	—	—	—	Proof	150.00
	1928H	2.964	.20	.50	1.50	3.00
	1928KN	3.151	2.00	3.00	5.00	15.00
	1930	9.600	1.75	3.00	6.00	15.00
	1930	—	—	—	Proof	150.00
	1931	9.840	.20	.50	1.00	3.00
	1931	—	—	—	Proof	150.00
	1932	3.600	.20	.50	1.50	5.00
	1932	—	—	—	Proof	150.00
	1933	7.200	.20	.50	5.00	3.50
	1933	—	—	—	Proof	150.00
	1934	4.800	.75	1.50	3.00	6.00
	1934	—	—	—	Proof	150.00
	1935	13.200	.75	1.50	3.00	7.50
	1935	—	—	—	Proof	150.00
	1936	9.720	.30	.50	1.50	3.00
	1936	—	—	—	Proof	150.00

KM#	Date	Mintage	Fine	VF	XF	Unc
14	1936	5.880	.25	.50	1.00	2.50
	1936	—	—	—	Proof	200.00
	1936H	1.404	45.00	85.00	125.00	225.00
	1936H	—	—	—	Proof	350.00
	1936KN	3.000	1.00	2.00	3.50	9.00
	1936KN	—	—	—	Proof	200.00

KM#	Date	Mintage	Fine	VF	XF	Unc
20	1938	12.000	.10	.25	.50	1.50
	1938	—	—	—	Proof	125.00
	1938H	1.596	5.00	8.00	12.00	22.50
	1938H	—	—	—	Proof	100.00
	1939	9.840	.25	.50	1.00	3.50
	1939	—	—	—	Proof	200.00
	1940	13.920	.25	.50	1.00	2.00
	1940	—	—	—	Proof	125.00
	1941	16.560	1.00	2.00	4.00	8.00
	1941	—	—	—	Proof	125.00
	1942	12.360	1.00	2.50	4.50	10.00
	1942	—	—	—	Proof	125.00
	1943	22.560	1.00	2.50	5.00	10.00
	1944	10.440	1.00	2.50	5.00	10.00
	1945	25.706	.50	1.00	1.75	6.00
	1945	—	—	—	Proof	125.00
	1946	2.803	1.00	2.00	4.00	9.00
	1946	—	—	—	Proof	125.00
	1946H	5.004	1.00	2.00	4.00	9.00
	1946KN	1.152	.25	.50	1.00	3.00
	1947	4.202	.25	.50	1.00	3.50
	1947	—	—	—	Proof	125.00
	1947KN	3.900	200.00	300.00	500.00	600.00

Obv. leg: W/o IND: IMP:

KM#	Date	Mintage	Fine	VF	XF	Unc
26	1949H	3.700	1.00	2.00	3.00	6.00
	1949KN	3.036	1.00	2.00	3.00	5.00
	1950KN	13.200	.25	.50	1.00	2.50

BRONZE

KM#	Date	Mintage	Fine	VF	XF	Unc
26a	1952	15.060	.50	1.00	2.00	6.00
	1952	—	—	—	Proof	150.00

KM#	Date	Mintage	Fine	VF	XF	Unc
32	1954	4.800	.50	1.00	2.00	5.00
	1954	—	—	—	Proof	150.00
	1956	2.400	—	—	Rare	—
	1956	—	—	—	Proof	750.00
	1957	7.200	60.00	120.00	220.00	325.00
	1957	—	—	—	Proof	600.00

1/2 PENNY

COPPER-NICKEL

KM#	Date	Mintage	Fine	VF	XF	Unc
5	1911H	3.360	4.00	12.00	25.00	40.00

Rev. leg: W/o NIGERIA

KM#	Date	Mintage	Fine	VF	XF	Unc
8	1912H	3.120	2.00	5.00	7.00	20.00
	1913	—	175.00	250.00	350.00	600.00
	1913H	.216	5.00	10.00	17.50	30.00
	1914	1.622	10.00	20.00	35.00	.60.00
	1914H	.586	10.00	20.00	35.00	60.00
	1914K	3.360	3.00	6.00	17.50	30.00
	1914K*	—	—	—	Proof	225.00
	1915H	3.577	1.00	2.00	4.00	15.00
	1916H	4.046	1.00	3.00	5.00	15.00
	1917H	.214	6.00	12.00	20.00	50.00
	1918H	.490	2.50	5.00	10.00	30.00
	1919H	4.950	1.25	2.50	6.00	20.00
	1919KN	3.861	1.25	2.50	7.50	25.00
	1920H	26.285	1.50	3.00	7.50	15.00
	1920KN	13.844	.50	2.00	3.50	15.00
	1922KN	5.817	300.00	500.00	850.00	1450.
	1927	.528	10.00	20.00	45.00	120.00
	1927	—	—	—	Proof	225.00
	1929	.336	6.00	10.00	17.50	85.00
	1929	—	—	—	Proof	225.00
	1931	.096	600.00	1000.	1200.	1500.
	1931	—	—	—	Proof	225.00
	1932	.960	2.50	5.00	15.00	50.00
	1932	—	—	—	Proof	225.00
	1933	2.122	2.00	3.50	12.00	95.00
	1933	—	—	—	Proof	225.00
	1934	1.694	2.50	5.00	12.50	65.00
	1934	—	—	—	Proof	225.00
	1935	3.271	1.00	3.00	10.00	35.00
	1935	—	—	—	Proof	225.00
	1936	5.400	2.50	5.00	12.00	30.00
	1936	—	—	—	Proof	225.00

***NOTE:** The 1914K was issued with East Africa KM#11 in a double (4 pc.) specimen set.

KM#	Date	Mintage	Fine	VF	XF	Unc
15	1936	14.760	.25	.50	1.00	2.50
	1936	—	—	—	Proof	200.00
	1936H	2.400	1.00	2.00	5.00	12.50
	1936H	—	—	—	Proof	200.00
	1936KN	2.298	.65	1.25	2.25	4.00
	1936KN	—	—	—	Proof	200.00

KM#	Date	Mintage	Fine	VF	XF	Unc
18	1937H	4.800	.40	.85	1.50	4.00
	1937H	—	—	—	Proof	125.00
	1937KN	5.577	.40	.85	3.00	5.00
	1940KN	2.410	1.25	2.50	5.00	15.00
	1940KN	—	—	—	Proof	125.00
	1941H	2.400	.40	2.00	4.00	12.00
	1942	4.800	.40	.85	2.00	8.50
	1943	3.360	.50	1.00	5.00	10.00
	1944	3.600	1.00	3.00	7.00	20.00
	1944	—	—	—	Proof	125.00
	1946	3.600	.25	1.00	3.00	7.00
	1946	—	—	—	Proof	125.00
	1947H	15.218	.35	.75	1.25	5.00
	1947KN	12.000	.40	.85	2.00	6.00

Obv. leg: W/o IND: IMP:

KM#	Date	Mintage	Fine	VF	XF	Unc
27	1949H	5.909	1.50	3.50	8.00	22.00
	1949KN	3.413	1.50	3.50	8.00	25.00
	1951	3.468	1.50	3.50	9.00	25.00
	1951	—	—	—	Proof	250.00

BRONZE

KM#	Date	Mintage	Fine	VF	XF	Unc
27a	1952	11.332	.25	.50	1.50	5.50
	1952	—	—	—	Proof	150.00
	1952H	27.603	.20	.35	.75	2.00
	1952KN	4.800	.50	1.00	3.00	7.50

PENNY

COPPER-NICKEL

KM#	Date	Mintage	Fine	VF	XF	Unc
2	1907	.863	2.00	5.00	9.00	20.00
	1908	3.217	2.00	4.00	8.00	17.50
	1909	.960	3.50	9.00	18.00	45.00
	1910	2.520	2.75	7.00	12.00	25.00

KM#	Date	Mintage	Fine	VF	XF	Unc
6	1911H	1.920	10.00	25.00	60.00	100.00

Rev. leg: W/o NIGERIA

KM#	Date	Mintage	Fine	VF	XF	Unc
9	1912H	1.560	1.50	3.00	7.50	22.50
	1913	1.680	10.00	20.00	30.00	75.00
	1913H	.144	5.00	10.00	17.50	35.00
	1914	3.000	2.50	5.00	10.00	22.50
	1914H	.072	30.00	45.00	80.00	175.00
	1915H	3.295	1.25	2.00	5.00	15.00
	1916H	3.461	1.25	2.00	7.00	14.00
	1917H	.444	3.50	7.00	15.00	45.00
	1918H	.994	5.00	15.00	30.00	65.00
	1919H	21.864	1.25	2.50	5.00	15.00
	1919KN	.264	7.50	14.50	25.00	50.00
	1920H	37.870	1.00	1.75	3.50	12.50
	1920KN	20.685	1.00	2.00	5.00	17.50
	1922KN	3.971	350.00	700.00	1000.	1500.
	1926	8.040	2.00	4.00	10.00	30.00
	1927	.792	25.00	45.00	85.00	200.00
	1927	—	—	—	Proof	225.00
	1928	6.672	2.00	4.00	10.00	25.00
	1928	—	—	—	Proof	225.00
	1929	.636	3.00	5.00	15.00	70.00
	1929	—	—	—	Proof	225.00
	1933	2.806	2.00	4.00	12.50	65.00
	1933	—	—	—	Proof	225.00
	1934	2.640	3.00	4.00	15.00	55.00
	1934	—	—	—	Proof	225.00
	1935	8.551	1.25	3.00	7.50	45.00
	1935	—	—	—	Proof	225.00
	1936	7.368	1.00	2.00	4.50	16.00
	1936	—	—	—	Proof	225.00

KM#	Date	Mintage	Fine	VF	XF	Unc
16	1936	7.992	.50	1.00	3.50	7.00
	1936	—	—	—	Proof	250.00
	1936H	12.600	.35	.75	1.00	3.00
	1936H	—	—	—	Proof	250.00
	1936KN	12.512	.35	.75	1.00	3.00
	1936KN	—	—	—	Proof	250.00

Mule. Obv: East Africa, KM#24. Rev: KM#16.

KM#	Date	Mintage	Fine	VF	XF	Unc
17	1936H	—	125.00	150.00	225.00	350.00

KM#	Date	Mintage	Fine	VF	XF	Unc
19	1937H	11.999	.50	.75	1.25	2.00
	1937H	—	—	—	Proof	200.00
	1937KN	11.999	.50	.75	1.25	2.00
	1937KN	—	—	—	Proof	200.00
	1940	3.840	.50	.75	1.25	2.00
	1940	—	—	—	Proof	—
	1940H	2.400	.50	.75	3.00	8.00
	1940KN	2.400	.75	1.50	4.50	10.00
	1941	6.960	.35	.75	1.25	3.50
	1941	—	—	—	Proof	—
	1942	18.840	.30	.60	1.00	3.00
	1943	28.920	.30	.60	1.00	3.00
	1943H	7.140	2.00	5.00	10.00	20.00
	1944	19.440	.30	.60	1.00	4.00
	1945	6.072	.45	.90	1.75	5.00
	1945	—	—	—	Proof	150.00
	1945H	9.000	1.00	2.00	4.50	10.00
	1945KN	9.557	.75	1.50	3.00	7.00
	1946H	10.446	.85	1.75	3.75	8.00
	1946KN	11.976	.30	.60	1.00	5.00
	1946SA	1.020	250.00	500.00	750.00	1200.
	1947H	12.443	.30	.60	1.00	5.00
	1947KN	9.829	.30	.60	1.00	5.00
	1947SA	58.980	.30	.60	1.00	4.50

Mule. Obv: KM#16. Rev: KM#19.

KM#	Date	Mintage	Fine	VF	XF	Unc
25	1945H	—	750.00	1250.	1850.	2750.

Obv. leg: W/o IND: IMP:

KM#	Date	Mintage	Fine	VF	XF	Unc
30	1951	1.258	7.50	12.50	27.50	45.00
	1951	—	—	—	Proof	250.00
	1951KN	2.692	6.00	10.00	20.00	35.00

BRONZE

KM#	Date	Mintage	Fine	VF	XF	Unc
30a	1952	10.542	.75	1.50	3.00	8.50
	1952	—	—	—	Proof	175.00
	1952H	30.794	.20	.40	.60	3.00
	1952KN	45.398	.20	.40	.60	3.00
	1952 KN	—	—	—	Proof	175.00

KM#	Date	Mintage	Fine	VF	XF	Unc
33	1956	—	.75	1.50	3.00	9.00
	1956H	13.503	.75	1.50	3.00	7.00
	1956KN	13.500	.30	.60	2.00	6.00
	1957	9.000	.75	1.50	5.00	10.00
	1957	—	—	—	Proof	150.00
	1957H	5.340	1.00	2.50	6.50	15.00
	1957KN	5.600	1.00	2.50	5.00	12.50
	1958	12.200	.75	1.50	3.50	10.00
	1958	—	—	—	Proof	125.00
	1958KN	Inc. Ab.	.75	1.50	2.50	8.00

Mule. Obv: KM#30. Rev: KM#33.

KM#	Date	Mintage	Fine	VF	XF	Unc
34	1956H	—	60.00	90.00	140.00	250.00

3 PENCE

1.4138 g, .925 SILVER, .0420 oz ASW

KM#	Date	Mintage	Fine	VF	XF	Unc
10	1913	.240	3.50	7.50	12.50	30.00
	1913	—	—	—	Proof	250.00
	1913H	.496	2.00	4.00	7.50	25.00
	1914H	1.560	1.00	2.00	7.50	25.00
	1915H	.270	15.00	20.00	40.00	85.00
	1916H	.820	10.00	15.00	22.50	65.00
	1917H	3.600	1.50	2.50	7.50	25.00
	1918H	1.722	1.75	3.50	8.00	20.00
	1919H	19.826	1.00	2.00	6.00	15.00
	1919H	—	—	—	Proof	200.00

1.4138 g, .500 SILVER, .0227 oz ASW

KM#	Date	Mintage	Fine	VF	XF	Unc
10a	1920H	3.616	20.00	40.00	60.00	100.00

BRASS

KM#	Date	Mintage	Fine	VF	XF	Unc
10b	1920KN	19.000	1.00	2.50	6.50	25.00
	1920KN	—	—	—	Proof	75.00
	1920KN*	—	—	—	Unique	—
	1925	8.800	1.50	3.00	9.00	40.00
	1926	1.600	10.00	25.00	35.00	85.00
	1927	.800	20.00	40.00	75.00	175.00
	1928	1.760	8.00	20.00	45.00	100.00
	1928	—	—	—	Proof	175.00
	1933	2.800	2.00	4.00	8.00	35.00
	1933	—	—	—	Proof	200.00
	1934	6.400	1.00	2.50	6.00	30.00
	1934	—	—	—	Proof	200.00
	1935	11.560	1.00	2.50	6.00	30.00
	1935	—	—	—	Proof	200.00
	1936	17.160	1.00	2.00	5.00	25.00
	1936	—	—	—	Proof	200.00
	1936H	1.000	20.00	30.00	40.00	100.00
	1936H	—	—	—	Proof	200.00
	1936KN	2.038	10.00	15.00	30.00	65.00

***NOTE:** Mint mark on obverse below bust.

COPPER-NICKEL

KM#	Date	Mintage	Fine	VF	XF	Unc
21	1938H	7.000	.30	.60	2.50	7.50
	1938H	—	—	—	Proof	200.00
	1938KN	9.056	.35	.75	2.50	8.00
	1938KN	—	—	—	Proof	300.00
	1939H	16.500	.30	.60	2.00	5.00
	1939H	—	—	—	Proof	300.00
	1939KN	15.500	.30	.60	2.00	8.00
	1939KN	—	—	—	Proof	200.00

KM#	Date	Mintage	Fine	VF	XF	Unc
21	1940H	3.862	.50	1.00	2.50	7.50
	1940KN	10.000	.30	.60	2.00	5.00
	1941H	5.032	.40	.85	2.00	9.00
	1943H	5.106	.40	.85	2.00	15.00
	1943KN	9.502	.40	.85	2.00	9.00
	1944KN	2.536	.40	.85	2.50	15.00
	1945H	.998	2.00	2.50	5.00	20.00
	1945KN	3.000	.40	.85	2.00	12.50
	1946KN	7.488	.40	.85	2.00	9.00
	1947H	10.000	.35	.75	2.00	8.00
	1947KN	11.248	.40	.85	2.00	8.00

KM#	Date	Mintage	Fine	VF	XF	Unc
35	1957H	.800	50.00	100.00	200.00	350.00

6 PENCE

2.8276 g, .925 SILVER, .0841 oz ASW

KM#	Date	Mintage	Fine	VF	XF	Unc
11	1913	.560	3.00	5.00	8.00	27.50
	1913	—	—	—	Proof	350.00
	1913H	.400	3.00	5.00	9.00	32.50
	1914H	.952	2.75	5.00	12.50	35.00
	1916H	.400	5.00	10.00	15.00	55.00
	1917H	2.400	3.00	5.00	10.00	32.50
	1918H	1.160	2.00	5.00	10.00	35.00
	1919H	8.676	2.00	3.50	7.50	20.00
	1919H	—	—	—	Proof	200.00

2.8276 g, .500 SILVER, .0454 oz ASW

KM#	Date	Mintage	Fine	VF	XF	Unc
11a	1920H	2.948	12.50	30.00	50.00	175.00
	1920H	—	—	—	Proof	275.00

BRASS

KM#	Date	Mintage	Fine	VF	XF	Unc
11b	1920KN	12.000	1.00	5.00	20.00	37.50
	1920KN	—	—	—	Proof	125.00
	1923H	2.000	5.00	12.50	40.00	95.00
	1924	1.000	15.00	30.00	60.00	150.00
	1924H	1.000	12.50	27.50	60.00	125.00
	1924KN	1.000	15.00	30.00	60.00	150.00
	1925	2.800	3.50	7.00	17.50	60.00
	1928	.400	25.00	40.00	95.00	200.00
	1928	—	—	—	Proof	200.00
	1933	1.000	20.00	35.00	90.00	200.00
	1933	—	—	—	Proof	225.00
	1935	4.000	5.00	12.50	25.00	50.00
	1935	—	—	—	Proof	225.00
	1936	10.400	7.50	15.00	25.00	50.00
	1936	—	—	—	Proof	225.00
	1936H	.480	25.00	50.00	75.00	200.00
	1936H	—	—	—	Proof	225.00
	1936KN	2.696	15.00	25.00	35.00	70.00
	1936KN	—	—	—	Proof	225.00

NICKEL-BRASS

KM#	Date	Mintage	Fine	VF	XF	Unc
22	1938	12.114	.50	1.00	2.00	8.00
	1938	—	—	—	Proof	200.00
	1940	17.829	.75	1.50	2.00	10.00
	1940	—	—	—	Proof	200.00
	1942	1.600	1.75	3.50	7.50	18.00
	1943	10.586	.75	1.75	4.00	11.00
	1944	1.814	2.00	3.00	10.00	32.50
	1945	4.000	1.00	2.00	7.50	25.00
	1945	—	—	—	Proof	200.00
	1946	4.000	2.50	5.00	17.50	50.00
	1946	—	—	—	Proof	225.00
	1947	6.120	.50	1.50	5.00	15.00
	1947	—	—	—	Proof	175.00

Obv. leg: W/o IND: IMP:

KM#	Date	Mintage	Fine	VF	XF	Unc
31	1952	2.544	15.00	35.00	75.00	150.00
	1952	—	—	—	Proof	300.00

SHILLING

5.6552 g, .925 SILVER, .1682 oz ASW

KM#	Date	Mintage	Fine	VF	XF	Unc
12	1913	8.800	2.75	4.00	7.50	22.50
	1913	—	—	—	Proof	400.00
	1913H	3.540	2.75	4.00	7.50	30.00
	1914	3.000	2.75	4.00	12.50	35.00
	1914H	11.292	2.75	4.00	10.00	30.00
	1915H	.254	12.50	20.00	37.50	100.00
	1916H	11.838	2.75	4.00	10.00	35.00
	1917H	15.018	2.75	4.00	10.00	35.00
	1918H	9.486	2.75	5.50	12.00	40.00
	1918H	—	—	—	Proof	200.00
	1919	2.000	10.00	15.00	30.00	55.00
	1919H	.992	15.00	22.50	50.00	100.00
	1919H	—	—	—	Proof	200.00
	1920	.828	22.50	40.00	70.00	150.00
			BRASS			
12a	1920G	.016	1400.	2000.	2600.	3500.
	1920KN	38.800	1.50	5.00	12.50	32.50
	1920KN	—	—	—	Proof	200.00
	1920KN*	—	—	—	Unique	—
	1922KN	32.324	2.00	6.50	20.00	70.00
	1923H	24.384	4.00	7.50	17.50	45.00
	1923KN	5.000	8.00	15.00	35.00	90.00
	1924	17.000	2.00	6.50	17.50	60.00
	1924H	9.567	10.00	20.00	50.00	125.00
	1924KN	7.000	7.50	15.00	30.00	80.00
	1925	19.800	4.00	8.00	18.00	45.00
	1926	19.952	2.00	5.00	10.00	40.00
	1927	22.248	1.50	4.00	8.50	35.00
	1927	—	—	—	Proof	225.00
	1928	10.000	15.00	30.00	60.00	200.00
	1928	—	—	—	Proof	300.00
	1936	70.200	3.00	6.50	11.00	32.50
	1936	—	—	—	Proof	225.00
	1936H	10.920	12.50	22.50	35.00	75.00
	1936KN	14.962	2.00	5.00	15.00	42.50
	1936KN	—	—	—	Proof	200.00

***NOTE:** Mint mark on obverse below bust.

NICKEL-BRASS

KM#	Date	Mintage	Fine	VF	XF	Unc
23	1938	57.806	.50	1.25	2.50	10.00
	1938	—	—	—	Proof	200.00
	1939	55.472	.50	1.25	2.50	15.00
	1939	—	—	—	Proof	200.00
	1940	40.311	.50	1.25	2.50	12.50
	1940	—	—	—	Proof	200.00
	1942	42.000	.50	1.25	2.50	15.00
	1943	133.600	.50	1.25	2.50	12.50
	1945	8.010	1.00	1.50	6.00	20.00
	1945	—	—	—	Proof	200.00
	1945H	12.864	2.00	3.50	10.00	30.00
	1945KN	11.120	1.00	2.00	4.00	20.00
	1946	37.350	1.00	2.00	4.50	30.00
	1946	—	—	—	Proof	200.00
	1946H	—	—	—	Rare	—
	1947	99.200	.50	1.00	2.50	10.00
	1947	—	—	—	Proof	200.00
	1947H	10.000	1.50	3.00	9.00	25.00
	1947KN	10.384	.50	1.00	2.50	14.00

TIN-BRASS
Obv. leg: W/o IND: IMP:

KM#	Date	Mintage	Fine	VF	XF	Unc
28	1949	70.000	.50	1.00	4.00	20.00
	1949	—	—	—	Proof	175.00
	1949H	10.000	1.25	2.50	7.50	22.50
	1949KN	10.016	1.25	2.50	7.50	22.50
	1949KN	—	—	—	Proof	200.00
	1951	35.346	1.25	2.50	7.50	25.00
	1951	—	—	—	Proof	175.00
	1951H	10.000	1.25	2.50	7.50	25.00
	1951KN	16.832	1.25	2.50	7.50	25.00
	1952	98.654	.50	1.00	3.00	7.50
	1952	—	—	—	Proof	225.00
	1952H	44.096	.50	1.00	2.00	6.00
	1952KN	41.653	.50	1.00	2.00	5.00
	1952KN	—	—	—	Proof	175.00

2 SHILLINGS

11.3104 g, .925 SILVER, .3364 oz ASW

KM#	Date	Mintage	Fine	VF	XF	Unc
13	1913	2.100	5.00	8.00	15.00	37.50
	1913	—	—	—	Proof	500.00
	1913H	1.176	6.00	12.00	17.50	50.00
	1914	.330	15.00	30.00	75.00	200.00
	1914H	.637	10.00	25.00	35.00	75.00
	1915H	.066	15.00	27.50	40.00	150.00
	1916H	9.824	5.00	8.00	17.50	50.00
	1917H	1.059	15.00	30.00	50.00	150.00
	1917H	—	—	—	Proof	300.00
	1918H	7.294	5.00	12.00	17.50	50.00
	1919	2.000	6.00	12.50	25.00	75.00
	1919H	10.866	4.50	10.00	22.50	55.00
	1919H	—	—	—	Proof	200.00
	1920	.683	30.00	60.00	175.00	250.00
			11.3104 g, .500 SILVER, .1818 oz ASW			
13a	1920H	1.926	30.00	55.00	100.00	275.00
			BRASS			
13b	1920KN	15.856	2.50	5.00	15.00	40.00
	1920KN	—	—	—	Proof	250.00
	1922	10.000	3.00	9.00	17.50	55.00
	1922KN	5.500	6.00	15.00	30.00	75.00
	1922KN	—	—	—	Proof	250.00
	1923H	12.696	4.00	12.00	22.50	65.00
	1924	1.500	7.50	15.00	35.00	90.00
	1925	3.700	4.00	12.00	25.00	70.00
	1926	11.500	4.50	11.00	30.00	80.00
	1927	11.100	4.00	12.00	45.00	100.00
	1927	—	—	—	Proof	250.00
	1928	7.900	—	—	Rare	—
	1928	—	—	—	Proof	350.00
	1936	32.940	5.00	10.00	20.00	60.00
	1936	—	—	—	Proof	250.00
	1936H	8.703	6.00	12.00	35.00	75.00
	1936KN	8.794	6.00	12.00	35.00	75.00

NICKEL-BRASS

KM#	Date	Mintage	Fine	VF	XF	Unc
24	1938H	32.000	1.00	2.00	4.00	15.00
	1938KN	27.852	1.00	2.00	4.00	15.00
	1939H	5.750	1.25	2.50	5.50	25.00
	1939KN	6.250	1.00	2.00	4.00	25.00
	1939KN	—	—	—	Proof	200.00
	1942KN	10.000	1.25	2.50	5.50	25.00
	1946H	10.500	1.25	2.50	5.50	22.50
	1946KN	4.800	1.25	3.00	9.00	35.00
	1947H	5.055	1.00	2.25	5.00	32.50
	1947KN	4.200	1.25	2.75	6.00	35.00

Obv. leg: W/o IND: IMP:

KM#	Date	Mintage	Fine	VF	XF	Unc
29	1949H	7.500	1.25	3.00	8.50	35.00
	1949KN	7.576	1.25	3.00	8.50	30.00
	1951H	6.566	1.25	3.00	8.50	35.00
	1951H	—	—	—	Proof	225.00
	1952H	4.410	2.00	3.50	8.50	35.00
	1952KN	1.236	3.50	6.00	15.00	45.00

SPECIMEN SETS (SS)

KM#	Date	Mintage	Identification	Issue Price	Mkt. Val.
SS1	1913(8)	14	KM10-13, double set	—	1250.
SS2	1913(4)	200	KM10-13	—	550.00
SS3	1919H(8)	2 known	KM10-13, double set	—	1500.
SS4	1920KN(8)	36	KM10b,11b,12a,13b, double set	—	1150.
SS-A5	1920KN(4)	4	KM10b-11b,12a,13b	—	—
SS5	1928(4)	—	KM10b,11b,12a,13b	—	900.00
SS6	1936H(3)	—	KM14-16	—	450.00
SS7	1952(4)	—	KM26a,27a,30a,31	—	750.00

BRITISH WEST INDIES

The 'Anchor Coins' catalogued under this heading do not bear a particular place identification. They were issued for use in various British colonies in both the New World and the Orient. Coins of this type dated 1820 are traditionally assigned to Mauritius and other holdings in the Indian Ocean. Those of 1822 were initially struck for Mauritius but after the introduction of sterling as the denomination of public accounts in Mauritius, they found their widest circulation in Canada and colonies in the Caribbean Sea. In Jamaica they were limited to military transactions only. In the Leeward Islands they were used on all the islands except the Virgin Islands, Windward Islands, Barbados, Tobago and Trinidad.

RULERS

British

ANCHOR COINAGE

1/16 DOLLAR

.892 SILVER

KM#	Date	Mintage	Fine	VF	XF	Unc
1	1820	.162	12.50	30.00	60.00	150.00
	1820	—	—	—	Proof	350.00
	1822/1	.142	15.00	35.00	65.00	175.00
	1822	Inc. Ab.	7.50	15.00	30.00	120.00
	1822	—	—	—	Proof	350.00

1/8 DOLLAR

.892 SILVER

KM#	Date	Mintage	Fine	VF	XF	Unc
2	1820	.120	15.00	35.00	75.00	215.00
	1820	—	—	—	Proof	350.00
	1822/0	.142	12.50	30.00	60.00	190.00
	1822/1	Inc. Ab.	10.00	20.00	45.00	175.00
	1822	Inc. Ab.	7.50	18.00	40.00	160.00
	1822	—	—	—	Proof	350.00

1/4 DOLLAR

.892 SILVER

KM#	Date	Mintage	Fine	VF	XF	Unc
3	1820	.100	30.00	50.00	100.00	275.00
	1820	—	—	—	Proof	400.00
	1822/1	.071	10.00	20.00	45.00	225.00
	1822	Inc. Ab.	7.50	18.00	40.00	200.00
	1822	—	—	—	Proof	400.00

1/2 DOLLAR

.892 SILVER

KM#	Date	Mintage	Fine	VF	XF	Unc
4	1821	—	—	—	Proof	Unique
	1822/1	.089	100.00	200.00	500.00	750.00
	1822	Inc. Ab.	85.00	175.00	300.00	600.00
	1822	—	—	—	Proof	800.00

BRUNEI

Negara Brunei Darussalam (Negeri Brunei), an independent sultanate on the northwest coast of the island of Borneo, has an area of 2,226 sq. mi. (5,765 sq. km.) and a population of 250,000. Capital: Bandar Seri Begawan. Crude oil and rubber are exported.

Magellan was the first European to visit Brunei in 1521. It was a powerful state, ruling over northern Borneo and adjacent islands from the 16th to the 19th century. Brunei became a British protectorate in 1888 and a British dependency in 1905. The Constitution of 1959 restored control over internal affairs to the sultan, while delegating responsibility for defense and foreign affairs to Britain. On January 1, 1984 it became independent.

TITLES

Negri Brunei نكري بروني

RULERS

Sultan Abdul Mumin, 1852-1885
Sultan Hashim Jelal, 1885-1906
British 1906-1950
Sultan Sir Omar Ali Saifuddin III, 1950-1967
Sultan Hassanal Bolkiah I, 1967

MONETARY SYSTEM

100 Cents = 1 Straits Dollar
100 Sen = 1 Dollar

1/2 PITIS

TIN, 24mm

KM#	Date	Mintage	Good	VG	Fine	VF
1	AH1285	—	17.50	27.50	45.00	75.00

PITIS

TIN

Obv: Flag at top to right.

KM#	Date	Mintage	Good	VG	Fine	VF
2.1	AH1285	—	12.50	20.00	32.50	55.00

Obv: Flag at top to left.

KM#	Date	Mintage	Good	VG	Fine	VF
2.2	AH1285	—	12.50	20.00	32.50	55.00

CENT

COPPER

KM#	Date	Mintage	Fine	VF	XF	Unc
3	AH1304	1.000	10.00	20.00	50.00	125.00
	1304	—	—	—	Proof	450.00

DECIMAL COINAGE

100 Sen = 1 Dollar (Ringgit)

SEN

BRONZE

KM#	Date	Mintage	VF	XF	Unc
4	1967	1.000	.10	.20	.50
9	1968	.060	.25	.50	1.50
	1970	.140	.10	.20	.50
	1970	3,234	—	Proof	2.50
	1971	.400	.10	.15	.40
	1973	.120	.10	.30	1.25
	1974	.640	—	.10	.30
	1976	.140	—	.10	.30
	1977	.140	—	.10	.30

Obv. leg: W/o numeral 'I' in title.

KM#	Date	Mintage	VF	XF	Unc
15	1977	.280	—	.10	.20
	1978	.269	—	.10	.15
	1979	.250	.10	.20	.50
	1979	.010	—	Proof	.90
	1980	.260	—	.10	.15
	1981	.540	—	.10	.15
	1982	.100	—	.30	1.50
	1983	.500	—	.10	.15
	1984	.400	—	.10	.15
	1984	3,000	—	Proof	1.00
	1985	.200	—	.10	.15
	1985	—	—	Proof	1.00
	1986	.101	—	—	.15
	1986	7,000	—	Proof	1.00
	COPPER CLAD STEEL				
15a	1986	—	—	—	.30
	1987	.392	—	—	.30
	1988	.502	—	—	.30
	1989	.601	—	—	.30
	1990	.340	—	—	.30
	2.9200 g, .925 SILVER, .0869 oz ASW				
15b	1987	2,000	—	Proof	3.00
	1988	2,000	—	Proof	3.00
	1989	—	—	Proof	3.00

5 SEN

COPPER-NICKEL

KM#	Date	Mintage	VF	XF	Unc
5	1967	1.160	.20	.40	1.25
10	1968	.320	.10	.35	.80
	1970	.760	.10	.30	.60
	1970	3,234	—	Proof	2.50
	1971	.320	.10	.20	.70
	1973	.128	.10	.45	1.85
	1974	.576	.10	.15	.40
	1976	.384	.10	.15	.45
	1977	.384	.10	.15	.45

Obv. leg: W/o numeral 'I' in title.

KM#	Date	Mintage	VF	XF	Unc
16	1977	.920	—	.10	.25
	1978	.640	—	.10	.20
	1979	.650	.10	.20	.50
	1979	.010	—	Proof	1.25
	1980	.640	—	.10	.15
	1981	.960	—	.10	.15
16	1982	.240	—	.45	1.75
	1983	1.280	—	.10	.15
	1984	.800	—	.10	.15
	1984	3,000	—	Proof	1.25
	1985	.800	—	.10	.15
	1985	—	—	Proof	1.25
	1986	.189	—	—	.15
	1986	7,000	—	Proof	1.25
	1987	.960	—	—	.15
	1988	.820	—	—	.15
	1989	1.504	—	—	.15
	1990	.672	—	—	.15
	1.6500 g, .925 SILVER, .0490 oz ASW				
16a	1987	2,000	—	Proof	3.00
	1988	2,000	—	Proof	3.00
	1989	—	—	Proof	3.00

10 SEN

COPPER-NICKEL

KM#	Date	Mintage	VF	XF	Unc
6	1967	3.510	.10	.20	.50
11	1968	.580	.10	.25	.60
	1970	1.360	.10	.20	.50
	1970	3,234	—	Proof	2.50
	1971	.420	.10	.20	.50
	1973	.300	.10	.25	.60
	1974	1.410	.10	.20	.50
	1976	.920	.10	.20	.50
	1977	.920	—	.15	.40

Obv. leg: W/o numeral 'I' in title.

KM#	Date	Mintage	VF	XF	Unc
17	1977	1.800	.10	.15	.40
	1978	1.080	—	.10	.30
	1979	2.050	—	.10	.30
	1979	.010	—	Proof	1.35
	1980	2.840	—	.10	.20
	1981	.976	—	.10	.20
	1983	1.080	—	.10	.20
	1984	1.400	—	.10	.20
	1984	3,000	—	Proof	1.50
	1985	1.540	—	.10	.20
	1985	—	—	Proof	1.50
	1986	2.181	—	—	.20
	1986	7,000	—	Proof	1.50
	1987	2.560	—	—	.20
	1988	.960	—	—	.20
	1989	1.000	—	—	.20
	1990	.900	—	—	.20
	3.3500 g, .925 SILVER, .0996 oz ASW				
17a	1987	2,000	—	Proof	6.00
	1988	2,000	—	Proof	6.00
	1989	—	—	Proof	6.00

20 SEN

COPPER-NICKEL

KM#	Date	Mintage	VF	XF	Unc
7	1967	2.130	.25	1.25	2.00
12	1968	.510	.20	.60	1.25
	1970	.850	.15	.40	1.00
	1970	3,234	—	Proof	2.50
	1971	.450	.20	.60	1.25
	1973	.450	.20	.60	1.25
	1974	.700	.15	.40	1.00

KM#	Date	Mintage	VF	XF	Unc
12	1976	.640	.15	.40	1.00
	1977	.640	.15	.40	1.00

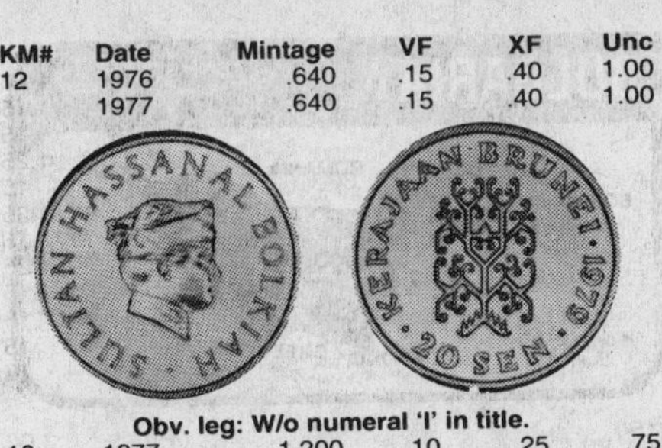

Obv. leg: W/o numeral 'I' in title.

KM#	Date	Mintage	VF	XF	Unc
18	1977	1.200	.10	.25	.75
	1978	.720	.15	.40	1.00
	1979	1.060	.20	.50	1.25
	1979	.010	—	Proof	2.00
	1980	1.540	.10	.20	.50
	1981	2.140	.10	.20	.50
	1982	.120	1.00	4.00	8.00
	1983	1.350	.10	.15	.35
	1984	.750	.10	.15	.35
	1984	3,000	—	Proof	2.25
	1985	1.000	.10	.15	.35
	1985	—	—	Proof	2.25
	1986	2.639	—	—	.35
	1986	7,000	—	Proof	2.25
	1987	2.400	—	—	.35
	1988	.560	—	—	.35
	1989	.500	—	—	.35
	1990	.360	—	—	.35

6.5100 g, .925 SILVER, .1936 oz ASW

KM#	Date	Mintage	VF	XF	Unc
18a	1987	2,000	—	Proof	10.00
	1988	2,000	—	Proof	10.00
	1989	—	—	Proof	10.00

50 SEN

COPPER-NICKEL

KM#	Date	Mintage	VF	XF	Unc
8	1967	.788	.30	1.25	2.00

KM#	Date	Mintage	VF	XF	Unc
13	1968	.212	.30	1.25	2.00
	1970	.300	.30	1.25	2.00
	1970	3,234	—	Proof	5.00
	1971	.320	.30	1.25	2.00
	1973	.140	.50	2.50	4.00
	1974	.244	.30	1.00	1.75
	1976	.240	.30	1.00	1.75
	1977	.240	.30	1.00	1.75

Obv. leg: W/o numeral 'I' in title.

KM#	Date	Mintage	VF	XF	Unc
19	1977	.499	.30	.75	1.45
	1978	.264	.30	.75	1.45
	1979	.730	.30	.75	1.45
	1979	.010	—	Proof	3.50
	1980	.536	.30	.45	.85
	1981	.960	.30	.40	.65
	1982	.136	.50	2.50	6.00
	1983	.408	.30	.40	.65
	1984	.320	.30	.40	.65
	1984	3,000	—	Proof	4.00
	1985	.450	.30	.40	.65
	1985	—	—	Proof	4.00
	1986	1.067	—	—	.65
	1986	7,000	—	Proof	4.00
	1987	1.120	—	—	.65
	1988	.250	—	—	.65
	1989	.500	—	—	.65
	1990	.236	—	—	.65

10.8200 g, .925 SILVER, .3218 oz ASW

KM#	Date	Mintage	VF	XF	Unc
19a	1987	2,000	—	Proof	15.00
	1988	2,000	—	Proof	15.00
	1989	—	—	Proof	15.00

DOLLAR

COPPER-NICKEL

KM#	Date	Mintage	VF	XF	Unc
14	1970	5,000	—	Proof	70.00

Obv. leg: W/o numeral 'I' in title.

KM#	Date	Mintage	VF	XF	Unc
20	1979	.010	—	Proof	15.00
	1984	5,000	—	—	10.00
	1984	3,000	—	Proof	20.00
	1985	.015	—	—	8.00
	1985	.010	—	Proof	15.00
	1986	.010	—	—	8.00
	1986	7,000	—	Proof	20.00
	1987	2,000	—	—	10.00
	1988	2,000	—	—	10.00
	1989	—	—	—	10.00

18.0500 g, .925 SILVER, .5368 oz ASW

KM#	Date	Mintage	VF	XF	Unc
20a	1987	2,000	—	Proof	40.00
	1988	2,000	—	Proof	40.00
	1989	—	—	Proof	40.00

5 DOLLARS

COPPER-NICKEL
Year of Hejira 1400

KM#	Date	Mintage	VF	XF	Unc
23	1980	.010	3.00	12.00	20.00

10 DOLLARS

28.2800 g, .925 SILVER, .8411 oz ASW
10th Anniversary of Brunei Currency Board

KM#	Date	Mintage	VF	XF	Unc
21	1977	.010	—	Proof	80.00

COPPER-NICKEL
Independence Day

KM#	Date	Mintage	VF	XF	Unc
26	1984	.015	—	—	18.00
	1984	5,000	—	Proof	40.00

20 DOLLARS

28.2800 g, .925 SILVER, .8411 oz ASW
20th Anniversary of Coronation

KM#	Date	Mintage	VF	XF	Unc
29	1988	5,000	—	—	20.00
	1988	1,000	—	Proof	80.00

20th Anniversary of Brunei Currency Board

KM#	Date	Mintage	VF	XF	Unc
32	1987	3,000	—	Proof	60.00

50 DOLLARS

28.2800 g, .925 SILVER, .8411 oz ASW
Year of Hejira 1400

KM#	Date	Mintage	VF	XF	Unc
24	1980	3,000	—	Proof	135.00

100 DOLLARS

28.2800 g, .925 SILVER, .8411 oz ASW
Independence Day

KM#	Date	Mintage	VF	XF	Unc
27	1984	5,000	—	—	130.00
	1984	2,000	—	Proof	170.00

31.1000 g, .925 SILVER, .9250 oz ASW
20th Anniversary of Coronation

KM#	Date	Mintage	VF	XF	Unc
30	1988	2,000	—	Proof	140.00

13.5000 g, .917 GOLD, .3976 oz AGW
20th Anniversary of Brunei Currency Board

KM#	Date	Mintage	VF	XF	Unc
33	1987	1,000	—	Proof	600.00

750 DOLLARS

15.9800 g, .917 GOLD, .4711 oz AGW
Year of Hejira 1400

KM#	Date	Mintage	VF	XF	Unc
25	1980	1,000	—	Proof	750.00

1000 DOLLARS

50.0000 g, .917 GOLD, 1.4742 oz AGW
10th Anniversary of Sultan's Coronation

KM#	Date	Mintage	VF	XF	Unc
22	1978	1,000	—	Proof	1800.

Independence Day
Similar to 100 Dollars, KM#27.

KM#	Date	Mintage	VF	XF	Unc
28	1984	4,000	—	—	1150.
	1984	1,000	—	Proof	1350.

20th Anniversary of Coronation

KM#	Date	Mintage	VF	XF	Unc
31	1988	1,000	—	Proof	1250.

SPECIMEN/MINT SETS (MS)

KM#	Date	Mintage	Identification	Issue Price	Mkt. Val.
MS1	1970(5)	4,000	KM9-13	6.60	24.00
MS2	1984(6)	5,000	KM15-20	—	15.00
MS3	1984(3)	500	KM26-28	—	1300.
MS4	1985(6)	15,000	KM15-20	10.00	22.50
MS5	1986(6)	10,000	KM15-20	10.00	22.50
MS6	1987(6)	3,000	KM15a,16-20	15.60	22.50
MS7	1988(6)	2,000	KM15a,16-20	15.60	22.50
MS8	1989(6)	3,000	KM15a,16-20	—	22.50
MS9	1990(6)	3,000	KM15a,16-20	—	22.50

PROOF SETS (PS)

KM#	Date	Mintage	Identification	Issue Price	Mkt. Val.
PS1	1979(6)	10,000	KM15-20	30.00	70.00
PS2	1984(6)	3,000	KM15-20	—	60.00
PS3	1984(3)	500	KM26-28	—	1550.
PS4	1985(6)	10,000	KM15-20	30.00	55.00
PS5	1986(6)	5,000	KM15-20	30.00	65.00
PS6	1987(6)	2,000	KM15b,16a-20a	52.00	75.00
PS7	1988(6)	2,000	KM15b,16a-20a	—	75.00
PS8	1989(6)	2,000	KM15b,16a-20a	—	75.00
PS9	1990(6)	2,000	KM15b,16a-20a	—	75.00

Listings For

BUKHARA: refer to Russian Turkestan

BULGARIA

The Republic of Bulgaria, formerly the Peoples Republic of Bulgaria, a Balkan country on the Black Sea in southeastern Europe, has an area of 42,823 sq. mi. (110,910 sq. km.) and a population of 9 million. Capital: Sofia. Agriculture remains a key component of the economy but industrialization, particularly heavy industry, has been emphasized since the late 1940s. Machinery, tobacco and cigarettes, wines and spirits, clothing and metals are the chief exports.

The area now occupied by Bulgaria was conquered by the Bulgars, an Asiatic tribe, in the 7th century. Bulgarian kingdoms continued to exist on the Bulgarian peninsula until it came under Turkish rule in 1395. In 1878, after nearly 500 years of Turkish rule, Bulgaria was made a principality under Turkish suzerainty. Union seven years later with Eastern Rumelia created a Balkan state with borders approximating those of present-day Bulgaria. A Bulgarian kingdom fully independent of Turkey was proclaimed Sept. 22, 1908. That monarchy was abolished by plebiscite in 1946 and Bulgaria became a Peoples Republic on the Soviet pattern. After democratic reforms in 1989 the name was changed to the Republic of Bulgaria.

Coinage of the Peoples Republic features a number of politically oriented commemoratives.

RULERS

Alexander I, as Prince, 1879-1886
Ferdinand I, as Prince, 1887-1908
As King, 1908-1918
Boris III, 1918-1943

MINT MARKS

A - Berlin
(a) Cornucopia & torch - Paris
BP - Budapest
H - Heaton Mint, Birmingham
KB - Kormoczbanya
(p) Poissy - Thunderbolt

MONETARY SYSTEM

100 Stotinki = 1 Lev

STOTINKA

BRONZE
Rev: Privy marks and designer name below denomination.

KM#	Date	Mintage	Fine	VF	XF	Unc
22.1	1901	20.000	1.00	2.00	6.00	12.50

Rev: W/o privy marks and designer name.

KM#	Date	Mintage	Fine	VF	XF	Unc
22.2	1912	20.000	.50	1.00	3.00	6.00

2 STOTINKI

BRONZE
Rev: HEATON below wreath

KM#	Date	Mintage	Fine	VF	XF	Unc
1	1881	5.000	3.00	6.00	12.00	35.00
	1881	—	—	—	Proof	90.00

Rev: Privy marks and designer name below denomination.

KM#	Date	Mintage	Fine	VF	XF	Unc
23.1	1901(a)	40.000	1.00	2.00	5.00	10.00

Rev: W/o privy marks and designer name.

KM#	Date	Mintage	Fine	VF	XF	Unc
23.2	1912	40.000	.50	1.00	2.00	5.00

2-1/2 STOTINKI

COPPER-NICKEL

KM#	Date	Mintage	Fine	VF	XF	Unc
8	1888	11.647	2.00	5.00	10.00	35.00
	1888	—	—	—	Proof	85.00

5 STOTINKI

BRONZE
Rev: HEATON below ribbon bow.

KM#	Date	Mintage	Fine	VF	XF	Unc
2	1881	10.000	2.00	5.00	10.00	40.00
	1881	—	—	—	Proof	120.00

COPPER-NICKEL

KM#	Date	Mintage	Fine	VF	XF	Unc
9	1888	14.000	.75	2.00	9.00	25.00
	1888	—	—	—	Proof	70.00

KM#	Date	Mintage	Fine	VF	XF	Unc
24	1906	14.000	.20	.60	2.00	5.00
	1912	14.000	.20	.40	1.00	3.00
	1913	20.000	.20	.40	1.00	3.00
	1913	—	—	—	Proof	—

ZINC

KM#	Date	Mintage	Fine	VF	XF	Unc
24a	1917	53.200	.60	1.00	2.50	6.00

10 STOTINKI

BRONZE
Rev: HEATON below ribbon bow.

KM#	Date	Mintage	Fine	VF	XF	Unc
3	1881	15.000	1.50	3.50	7.00	35.00
	1881	—	—	—	Proof	80.00

COPPER-NICKEL

KM#	Date	Mintage	Fine	VF	XF	Unc
10	1888	10.000	.75	2.00	8.50	20.00

KM#	Date	Mintage	Fine	VF	XF	Unc
25	1906	13.000	.50	1.00	2.50	6.00
	1912	13.000	.20	.40	1.00	3.00
	1912	—	—	—	Proof	—
	1913	20.000	.20	.40	1.00	3.00

ZINC

KM#	Date	Mintage	Fine	VF	XF	Unc
25a	1917	59.100	.40	1.00	2.00	5.00
	1917	—	—	—	Proof	125.00

20 STOTINKI

COPPER-NICKEL

KM#	Date	Mintage	Fine	VF	XF	Unc
11	1888	5.000	2.00	5.00	12.00	27.50
	1888	—	—	—	Proof	80.00

KM#	Date	Mintage	Fine	VF	XF	Unc
26	1906	10.000	.50	1.50	3.50	10.00
	1912	10.000	.20	.50	1.25	5.00
	1913	5.000	.20	.50	1.50	5.50
	1913	—	—	—	Proof	—

ZINC

KM#	Date	Mintage	Fine	VF	XF	Unc
26a	1917	40.000	.50	1.75	4.00	8.50
	1917	—	—	—	Proof	125.00

50 STOTINKI

2.5000 g, .835 SILVER, .0671 oz ASW

KM#	Date	Mintage	Fine	VF	XF	Unc
6	1883	3.000	1.50	2.50	6.00	20.00

KM#	Date	Mintage	Fine	VF	XF	Unc
12	1891KB	2.000	1.50	2.50	8.00	25.00

LEV

5.0000 g, .835 SILVER, .1342 oz ASW

KM#	Date	Mintage	Fine	VF	XF	Unc
4	1882	4.500	2.00	5.00	12.00	30.00

KM#	Date	Mintage	Fine	VF	XF	Unc
13	1891KB	4.000	2.00	6.00	15.00	35.00

KM#	Date	Mintage	Fine	VF	XF	Unc
16	1894KB	1.000	2.50	7.00	18.00	40.00

2 LEVA

10.0000 g, .835 SILVER, .2685 oz ASW

KM#	Date	Mintage	Fine	VF	XF	Unc
5	1882	2.000	3.00	8.00	16.00	50.00

KM#	Date	Mintage	Fine	VF	XF	Unc
14	1891KB	1.500	3.00	8.50	18.00	55.00

KM#	Date	Mintage	Fine	VF	XF	Unc
17	1894KB	1.000	3.50	9.00	20.00	60.00
	1894KB	—	—	—	Proof	320.00

5 LEVA

25.0000 g, .900 SILVER, .7234 oz ASW

KM#	Date	Mintage	Fine	VF	XF	Unc
7	1884	.512	10.00	20.00	55.00	165.00
	1885	1.426	8.00	14.00	45.00	135.00

KM#	Date	Mintage	Fine	VF	XF	Unc
15	1892KB	1.001	8.00	12.50	28.00	125.00
	1892KB	—	—	—	Proof	1200.

Obv. leg. rearranged.

KM#	Date	Mintage	Fine	VF	XF	Unc
18	1894KB	1.800	7.00	12.50	25.00	115.00
	1894KB	—	—	—	Proof	1200.

10 LEVA

3.2258 g, .900 GOLD, .0933 oz AGW

KM#	Date	Mintage	Fine	VF	XF	Unc
19	1894KB	.075	45.00	70.00	115.00	240.00
	1894KB	—	—	—	Proof	2000.

20 LEVA

6.4516 g, .900 GOLD, .1867 oz AGW

KM#	Date	Mintage	Fine	VF	XF	Unc
20	1894KB	.100	80.00	110.00	165.00	300.00
	1894KB	—	—	—	Proof	4500.

100 LEVA

32.2580 g, .900 GOLD, .9334 oz AGW

KM#	Date	Mintage	Fine	VF	XF	Unc
21	1894KB	2,500	450.00	650.00	1100.	2200.

KINGDOM

50 STOTINKI

2.5000 g, .835 SILVER, .0671 oz ASW

KM#	Date	Mintage	Fine	VF	XF	Unc
27	1910	.400	1.75	3.50	6.00	14.00

KM#	Date	Mintage	Fine	VF	XF	Unc
30	1912	2.000	1.00	2.00	4.00	10.00
	1913	3.000	1.00	2.00	3.00	7.00
	1916	4.562	50.00	90.00	150.00	220.00

ALUMINUM-BRONZE

KM#	Date	Mintage	Fine	VF	XF	Unc
46	1937	60.200	.10	.35	.75	2.00

LEV

5.0000 g, .835 SILVER, .1342 oz ASW

KM#	Date	Mintage	Fine	VF	XF	Unc
28	1910	3.000	2.00	4.00	7.00	16.00

KM#	Date	Mintage	Fine	VF	XF	Unc
31	1912	2.000	2.00	3.00	5.50	12.50
	1913	3.500	2.00	3.00	5.00	10.00
	1916	4.569	100.00	200.00	350.00	600.00

ALUMINUM

KM#	Date	Mintage	Fine	VF	XF	Unc
35	1923	40.000	2.50	5.00	12.00	35.00

COPPER-NICKEL

KM#	Date	Mintage	Fine	VF	XF	Unc
37	1925	35.000	.20	.50	1.00	2.50
	1925(p)	34.982	.25	.60	1.25	3.00

NOTE: The Poissy issue bears the thunderbolt mint mark.

IRON

KM#	Date	Mintage	Fine	VF	XF	Unc
37a	1941	10.000	3.00	6.00	15.00	40.00

2 LEVA

10.0000 g, .835 SILVER, .2685 oz ASW

KM#	Date	Mintage	Fine	VF	XF	Unc
29	1910	.400	4.50	7.50	16.00	45.00

KM#	Date	Mintage	Fine	VF	XF	Unc
32	1912	1.000	4.00	6.50	12.50	20.00
	1913	.500	4.00	6.50	12.50	20.00
	1916	2.286	125.00	250.00	450.00	750.00

ALUMINUM

KM#	Date	Mintage	Fine	VF	XF	Unc
36	1923	20.000	3.00	6.00	15.00	50.00
	1923H	2 pcs.	—	—	Rare	—

COPPER-NICKEL

KM#	Date	Mintage	Fine	VF	XF	Unc
38	1925	20.000	.30	.60	1.50	3.00
	1925(p)	20.000	.35	.75	1.80	3.50

NOTE: The Poissy issue bears the thunderbolt privy mark.

IRON

KM#	Date	Mintage	Fine	VF	XF	Unc
38a	1941	15.000	.50	1.00	3.00	10.00

KM#	Date	Mintage	Fine	VF	XF	Unc
49	1943	35.000	.50	1.00	4.50	15.00

5 LEVA

KM#	Date	Mintage	Fine	VF	XF	Unc
		COPPER-NICKEL				
39	1930	20.001	.50	1.00	2.25	5.50
		IRON				
39a	1941	15.000	1.00	3.00	6.00	20.00
		NICKEL-CLAD STEEL				
39b	1943	36.000	.40	1.00	2.00	5.00

10 LEVA

KM#	Date	Mintage	Fine	VF	XF	Unc
		COPPER-NICKEL				
40	1930	15.001	.60	1.25	3.00	8.00
		IRON				
40a	1941	2.200	6.00	12.00	25.00	65.00
		NICKEL-CLAD STEEL				
40b	1943	25.000	.60	1.00	3.00	7.00

20 LEVA

6.4516 g, .900 GOLD, .1867 oz AGW
Declaration of Independence

KM#	Date	Mintage	Fine	VF	XF	Unc
33	1912	.075	100.00	125.00	200.00	350.00
	1912	—	—	—	Proof	1500.

4.0000 g, .500 SILVER, .0643 oz ASW

KM#	Date	Mintage	Fine	VF	XF	Unc
41	1930BP	10.016	.75	1.25	2.50	7.50

COPPER-NICKEL

KM#	Date	Mintage	Fine	VF	XF	Unc
47	1940A	6.650	.40	.65	1.25	3.50

50 LEVA

10.0000 g, .500 SILVER, .1607 oz ASW

KM#	Date	Mintage	Fine	VF	XF	Unc
42	1930BP	9.028	1.25	2.50	4.50	12.50

Similar to 100 Leva, KM#45.

KM#	Date	Mintage	Fine	VF	XF	Unc
44	1934	3.001	1.50	3.00	5.00	14.00
	1934	—	—	—	Proof	—

COPPER-NICKEL

KM#	Date	Mintage	Fine	VF	XF	Unc
48	1940A	12.340	.50	1.00	2.00	6.00

NICKEL-CLAD STEEL

KM#	Date	Mintage	Fine	VF	XF	Unc
48a	1943A	15.000	.75	1.50	2.50	7.50

100 LEVA

32.2580 g, .900 GOLD, .9334 oz AGW
Declaration of Independence

KM#	Date	Mintage	Fine	VF	XF	Unc
34	1912	5,000	600.00	900.00	2000.	3000.
	1912	—	—	—	Proof	3500.

20.0000 g, .500 SILVER, .3215 oz ASW

KM#	Date	Mintage	Fine	VF	XF	Unc
43	1930BP	1.556	BV	4.50	8.50	22.00

KM#	Date	Mintage	Fine	VF	XF	Unc
45	1934	2.506	BV	3.00	6.00	12.00
	1934	—	—	—	Proof	—
	1937	2.207	BV	3.00	5.00	10.00

PEOPLES REPUBLIC

STOTINKA

BRASS

KM#	Date	Mintage	Fine	VF	XF	Unc
50	1951	—	—	—	.10	.25

KM#	Date	Mintage	Fine	VF	XF	Unc
59	1962	—	—	—	.10	.25
	1970	—	—	.20	.50	2.00

Obv: 2 dates on arms, '681-1944'

KM#	Date	Mintage	Fine	VF	XF	Unc
84	1974	—	—	—	.10	.15
	1979	2,000	—	—	Proof	1.50
	1980	2,000	—	—	Proof	1.50
	1981	—	—	—	Proof	2.00
	1988	—	—	—	.10	.15
	1989	—	—	—	.10	.15
	1990	—	—	—	.10	.15

NOTE: Edge varieties exist.

1300th Anniversary of Bulgaria

KM#	Date	Mintage	Fine	VF	XF	Unc
111	1981	—	—	.10	.20	.50
	1981	—	—	—	Proof	2.00

2 STOTINKI

BRASS

KM#	Date	Mintage	Fine	VF	XF	Unc
60	1962	—	—	—	.10	.25

Obv: 2 dates on arms, '681-1944'

KM#	Date	Mintage	Fine	VF	XF	Unc
85	1974	—	—	—	.10	.25
	1979	2,000	—	—	Proof	2.00
	1980	2,000	—	—	Proof	2.00
	1988	—	—	—	.10	.25
	1989	—	—	—	.10	.25
	1990	—	—	—	.10	.25

1300th Anniversary of Bulgaria

KM#	Date	Mintage	Fine	VF	XF	Unc
112	1981	—	—	.10	.20	.60
	1981	—	—	—	Proof	2.50

3 STOTINKI

BRASS

KM#	Date	Mintage	Fine	VF	XF	Unc
51	1951	—	—	.10	.25	.75

5 STOTINKI

BRASS

KM#	Date	Mintage	Fine	VF	XF	Unc
52	1951	—	.10	.15	.25	.75

KM#	Date	Mintage	Fine	VF	XF	Unc
61	1962	—	—	.10	.20	.50

Obv: 2 dates on arms '681-1944'

KM#	Date	Mintage	Fine	VF	XF	Unc
86	1974	—	—	.10	.15	.25
	1979	2,000	—	—	Proof	2.00
	1980	2,000	—	—	Proof	2.00
	1981	—	—	—	Proof	3.00
	1988	—	—	—	.15	.25
	1989	—	—	—	.15	.25
	1990	—	—	—	.15	.25

1300th Anniversary of Bulgaria

KM#	Date	Mintage	Fine	VF	XF	Unc
113	1981	—	—	.10	.25	.75
	1981	—	—	—	Proof	2.50

10 STOTINKI

COPPER-NICKEL

KM#	Date	Mintage	Fine	VF	XF	Unc
53	1951	—	—	.10	.20	.40

NICKEL-BRASS

KM#	Date	Mintage	Fine	VF	XF	Unc
62	1962	—	—	.10	.20	.40

Obv: 2 dates on arms, '681-1944'

KM#	Date	Mintage	Fine	VF	XF	Unc
87	1974	—	—	.10	.15	.25
	1979	2,000	—	—	Proof	3.50
	1980	2,000	—	—	Proof	3.50
	1988	—	—	—	.15	.25
	1989	—	—	—	.15	.25
	1990	—	—	—	.15	.25

COPPER-NICKEL
1300th Anniversary of Bulgaria

KM#	Date	Mintage	Fine	VF	XF	Unc
114	1981	—	—	.20	.50	1.50
	1981	—	—	—	Proof	3.50

20 STOTINKI

COPPER-NICKEL

KM#	Date	Mintage	Fine	VF	XF	Unc
55	1952	—	1.00	2.50	7.50	20.00
	1954	—	.10	.25	.75	1.50

NICKEL-BRASS

KM#	Date	Mintage	Fine	VF	XF	Unc
63	1962	—	.10	.20	.30	.75

Obv: 2 dates on arms, '681-1944'

KM#	Date	Mintage	Fine	VF	XF	Unc
88	1974	—	.10	.20	.30	.60
	1979	2,000	—	—	Proof	3.50
	1980	2,000	—	—	Proof	3.50
	1988	—	—	—	.30	.60
	1989	—	—	—	.30	.60
	1990	—	—	—	.30	.60

COPPER-NICKEL
1300th Anniversary of Bulgaria

KM#	Date	Mintage	Fine	VF	XF	Unc
115	1981	—	—	.25	.65	2.00
	1981	—	—	—	Proof	4.00

25 STOTINKI

COPPER-NICKEL

KM#	Date	Mintage	Fine	VF	XF	Unc
54	1951	—	.10	.20	.50	1.00

50 STOTINKI

COPPER-NICKEL

KM#	Date	Mintage	Fine	VF	XF	Unc
56	1959	—	.10	.20	.40	.80

NICKEL-BRASS

KM#	Date	Mintage	Fine	VF	XF	Unc
64	1962	—	.10	.40	.65	1.00

Obv: 2 dates on arms, '681-1944'

KM#	Date	Mintage	Fine	VF	XF	Unc
89	1974	—	.10	.40	.65	1.50
	1979	2,000	—	—	Proof	4.00
	1980	2,000	—	—	Proof	4.00
	1988	—	—	—	.50	1.00
	1989	—	—	—	.50	1.00
	1990	—	—	—	.50	1.00

COPPER-NICKEL
University Games at Sofia

KM#	Date	Mintage	Fine	VF	XF	Unc
98	1977	2.000	.20	.60	1.00	2.00

1300th Anniversary of Bulgaria

KM#	Date	Mintage	Fine	VF	XF	Unc
116	1981	—	—	.30	.60	1.80
	1981	—	—	—	Proof	4.00

LEV

COPPER-NICKEL

KM#	Date	Mintage	Fine	VF	XF	Unc
57	1960	—	.10	.25	.60	1.00

NICKEL-BRASS

KM#	Date	Mintage	Fine	VF	XF	Unc
58	1962	—	—	.50	1.00	1.50

Obv: 2 dates on arms, '681-1944'

KM#	Date	Mintage	Fine	VF	XF	Unc
90	1974	—	—	.50	1.00	2.00
	1979	2,000	—	—	Proof	6.00
	1980	2,000	—	—	Proof	6.00
	1988	—	—	—	.75	2.00
	1989	—	—	—	.75	2.00
	1990	—	—	—	.75	2.00

25th Anniversary of Socialist Revolution

KM#	Date	Mintage	Fine	VF	XF	Unc
74	1969	3.700	.35	.75	1.75	3.50

90th Anniversary Liberation From Turks

KM#	Date	Mintage	Fine	VF	XF	Unc
76	1969	2.150	.40	.80	2.00	4.00

BRONZE
100th Anniversary of the "April Uprising" Against the Turks

KM#	Date	Mintage	Fine	VF	XF	Unc
94	1976	.300	.40	1.00	2.00	5.00
	1976	—	—	—	Proof	9.00

COPPER-NICKEL
World Cup Soccer Games in Spain

KM#	Date	Mintage	Fine	VF	XF	Unc
107	1980	.220	—	1.00	2.00	4.50
	1980	.030	—	—	Proof	6.00

1300th Anniversary of Bulgaria

KM#	Date	Mintage	Fine	VF	XF	Unc
117	1981	—	—	.75	1.50	3.00
	1981	—	—	—	Proof	—

International Hunting Exposition

KM#	Date	Mintage	Fine	VF	XF	Unc
118	1981	—	—	.60	1.50	4.00
	1981	—	—	—	Proof	7.00

Russo-Bulgarian Friendship

KM#	Date	Mintage	Fine	VF	XF	Unc
119	1981	—	—	.60	1.50	4.00
	1981	1,000	—	—	Proof	8.00

1988 Winter Olympics - Hockey

KM#	Date	Mintage	Fine	VF	XF	Unc
175	1987	—	—	—	Proof	6.00

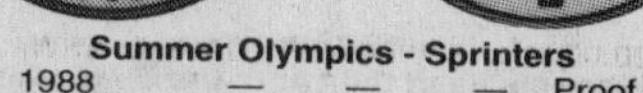

Summer Olympics - Sprinters

KM#	Date	Mintage	Fine	VF	XF	Unc
176	1988	—	—	—	Proof	6.00

2 LEVA

8.8889 g, .900 SILVER, .2572 oz ASW
1100th Anniversary Slavic Alphabet

KM#	Date	Mintage	Fine	VF	XF	Unc
65	1963	.010	—	—	Proof	12.00

20th Anniversary Peoples Republic

KM#	Date	Mintage	Fine	VF	XF	Unc
69	1964	.020	—	—	Proof	12.00

COPPER-NICKEL
1050th Anniversary Death of Ochridsky

KM#	Date	Mintage	Fine	VF	XF	Unc
73	1966	.506	—	1.00	2.00	6.00

25th Anniversary of Socialist Revolution

KM#	Date	Mintage	Fine	VF	XF	Unc
75	1969	1.500	—	.75	1.75	5.00

90th Anniversary Liberation From Turks

KM#	Date	Mintage	Fine	VF	XF	Unc
77	1969	1.900	—	.75	1.75	5.00

NICKEL-BRASS
150th Anniversary of Birth of Dobri Chintulov

KM#	Date	Mintage	Fine	VF	XF	Unc
80	1972	.100	1.00	2.00	4.00	8.00

COPPER-NICKEL
100th Anniversary of the "April Uprising" Against the Turks

KM#	Date	Mintage	Fine	VF	XF	Unc
95.1	1976	*.300	—	.75	2.00	4.50
	1976	—	—	—	Proof	12.00

Lettered edge.

KM#	Date	Mintage	Fine	VF	XF	Unc
95.2	1976	138 pcs.	—	—	—	—

World Cup Soccer Games in Spain

KM#	Date	Mintage	Fine	VF	XF	Unc
108	1980	.220	—	.60	1.20	3.50
	1980	.030	—	—	Proof	7.50

100th Anniversary of Birth of Yordan Yovkov

KM#	Date	Mintage	Fine	VF	XF	Unc
110	1980	.200	—	1.00	3.50	8.00

International Hunting Exposition

KM#	Date	Mintage	Fine	VF	XF	Unc
120	1981	—	—	.75	2.50	6.00
	1981	—	—	—	Proof	10.00

1300th Anniversary of Nationhood
Rev: Equestrian Figure

KM#	Date	Mintage	Fine	VF	XF	Unc
121	1981	—	—	—	—	8.00
	1981	—	—	—	Proof	12.00

1300th Anniversary of Nationhood
Rev: Mother and child.

KM#	Date	Mintage	Fine	VF	XF	Unc
122	1981	—	—	—	Proof	12.00

1300th Anniversary of Nationhood
Rev: Dimitrov.

KM#	Date	Mintage	Fine	VF	XF	Unc
123	1981	—	—	—	—	8.00
	1981	—	—	—	Proof	10.00

1300th Anniversary of Nationhood
Rev: King and saint.

KM#	Date	Mintage	Fine	VF	XF	Unc
124	1981	—	—	—	—	8.00
	1981	—	—	—	Proof	10.00

1300th Anniversary of Nationhood
Rev: Soldier.

KM#	Date	Mintage	Fine	VF	XF	Unc
125	1981	—	—	—	—	8.00
	1981	—	—	—	Proof	10.00

1300th Anniversary of Nationhood
Rev: Clandestine meeting.

KM#	Date	Mintage	Fine	VF	XF	Unc
126	1981	—	—	—	Proof	12.00

1300th Anniversary of Nationhood
Rev: Cyrillic alphabet.

KM#	Date	Mintage	Fine	VF	XF	Unc
127	1981	—	—	—	—	8.00
	1981	—	—	—	Proof	10.00

1300th Anniversary of Nationhood
Rev: Rila Monastary.

KM#	Date	Mintage	Fine	VF	XF	Unc
128	1981	—	—	—	—	8.00
	1981	—	—	—	Proof	10.00

1300th Anniversary of Nationhood
Rev: Russky Monument.

KM#	Date	Mintage	Fine	VF	XF	Unc
129	1981	—	—	—	Proof	12.00

1300th Anniversary of Nationhood
Rev: Bojana Church.

KM#	Date	Mintage	Fine	VF	XF	Unc
130	1981	3,000	—	—	Proof	9.00

1300th Anniversary of Nationhood and the Oboriste Assembly

KM#	Date	Mintage	Fine	VF	XF	Unc
161	1981	—	—	—	Proof	9.00

1300th Anniversary of Nationhood and Uprising of Assen and Peter

KM#	Date	Mintage	Fine	VF	XF	Unc
162	1981	—	—	—	Proof	9.00

1300th Anniversary of Nationhood and 100th Anniversary of Serbo - Bulgarian War

KM#	Date	Mintage	Fine	VF	XF	Unc
163	1985	—	—	—	Proof	9.00

Soccer

KM#	Date	Mintage	Fine	VF	XF	Unc
155	1986	.100	—	—	—	10.00

World Championship of Eurythmics

KM#	Date	Mintage	Fine	VF	XF	Unc
158	1987	.300	—	—	Proof	10.00

Winter Olympics - Skier

KM#	Date	Mintage	Fine	VF	XF	Unc
159	1987	—	—	—	Proof	10.00

100th Anniversary of Sophia University

KM#	Date	Mintage	Fine	VF	XF	Unc
165	1988	—	—	—	Proof	9.00

Soviet - Bulgarian Space Flight

KM#	Date	Mintage	Fine	VF	XF	Unc
166	1988	.300	—	—	Proof	9.00

Summer Olympics - High Jumper

KM#	Date	Mintage	Fine	VF	XF	Unc
177	1988	—	—	—	Proof	9.00

Sophia University
Similar to 20 Leva, KM#173.

KM#	Date	Mintage	Fine	VF	XF	Unc
188	1988	.300	—	—	Proof	9.00

Sports - Rowers

KM#	Date	Mintage	Fine	VF	XF	Unc
178	1989	—	—	—	Proof	9.00

5 LEVA

16.6667 g, .900 SILVER, .4823 oz ASW
1100th Anniversary Slavic Alphabet

KM#	Date	Mintage	Fine	VF	XF	Unc
66	1963	5,000	—	—	Proof	16.50

20th Anniversary Peoples Republic

KM#	Date	Mintage	Fine	VF	XF	Unc
70	1964	.010	—	—	Proof	16.50

20.5000 g, .900 SILVER, .5932 oz ASW
120th Anniversary of Birth of Ivan Vazov

KM#	Date	Mintage	Fine	VF	XF	Unc
78	1970	.370	—	2.50	5.00	12.00
	1970	.110			Proof	20.00

150th Anniversary of Birth of Georgi S. Rakovski

KM#	Date	Mintage	Fine	VF	XF	Unc
79	1971	.300	—	—	Proof	12.00

250th Anniversary of Birth of Paisii Hilendarski

KM#	Date	Mintage	VF	XF	Unc
81	1972	.200	—	Proof	12.00

Centennial of Death of Vasil Levski

KM#	Date	Mintage	VF	XF	Unc
82	1973	.200	—	Proof	12.00

50th Anniversary Anti-Fascist Uprising

KM#	Date	Mintage	VF	XF	Unc
83	1973	.200	—	Proof	15.00

50th Anniversary of Death of Alexander Stamboliiski

KM#	Date	Mintage	VF	XF	Unc
91	1974	.200	—	Proof	16.50

30th Anniversary Socialist Revolution

KM#	Date	Mintage	VF	XF	Unc
92	1974	.200	—	Proof	15.00

Centennial of Death of Khristo Botev

KM#	Date	Mintage	VF	XF	Unc
96	1976	.200	—	Proof	15.00

20.5000 g, .500 SILVER, .3295 oz ASW
100th Anniversary of the "April Uprising" Against the Turks

KM#	Date	Mintage	VF	XF	Unc
97	1976	.200	—	Proof	15.00

150th Anniversary of Birth of Petko Slaveykov

KM#	Date	Mintage	VF	XF	Unc
99	1977	.200	—	Proof	14.00

100th Anniversary of Birth of Peio Javoroff

KM#	Date	Mintage	VF	XF	Unc
100	1978	.200	—	Proof	14.00

100th Anniversary of National Library

KM#	Date	Mintage	VF	XF	Unc
101	1978	.200	—	Proof	14.00

100th Anniversary of Communications Systems

KM#	Date	Mintage	VF	XF	Unc
103	1979	.035	—	—	12.50
	1979	.015	—	Proof	16.00

COPPER-NICKEL
World Cup Soccer Games in Spain

KM#	Date	Mintage	VF	XF	Unc
109	1980	.220	—	—	8.50
	1980	.030	—	Proof	14.00

International Hunting Exposition

KM#	Date	Mintage	VF	XF	Unc
131	1981	—	—	—	9.00
	1981	—	—	Proof	15.00

1300th Anniversary of Bulgarian Statehood

KM#	Date	Mintage	VF	XF	Unc
132	1981	—	—	—	12.00

100th Anniversary of Birth of Vladimir Dimitrov

KM#	Date	Mintage	VF	XF	Unc
140	1982	3,000	—	Proof	14.00

40th Anniversary of Birth of Ljudmila Jivkowa

KM#	Date	Mintage	VF	XF	Unc
141	1982	—	—	Proof	14.00

2nd International Childrens Assembly

KM#	Date	Mintage	VF	XF	Unc
142	1982	—	—	Proof	12.00

3rd International Childrens Assembly

KM#	Date	Mintage	VF	XF	Unc
151	1985	2,500	—	Proof	10.00

90th Anniversary of Tourism Movement

KM#	Date	Mintage	VF	XF	Unc
152	1985	—	—	Proof	10.00

4th Anniversary of UNESCO

KM#	Date	Mintage	VF	XF	Unc
153	1985	—	—	Proof	10.00

Young Inventors Exposition

KM#	Date	Mintage	VF	XF	Unc
154	1985	—	—	Proof	10.00

Chiprovo Uprising

KM#	Date	Mintage	VF	XF	Unc
167	1988	.100	—	Proof	15.00

Dimitar and Karadzha

KM#	Date	Mintage	VF	XF	Unc
168	1988	—	—	Proof	14.00

Kremikovtsi

KM#	Date	Mintage	VF	XF	Unc
169	1988	—	—	Proof	14.00

Childrens Assembly

KM#	Date	Mintage	VF	XF	Unc
170	1988	—	—	Proof	14.00

200th Birthday of Aprilov

KM#	Date	Mintage	VF	XF	Unc
179	1989	—	—	Proof	12.50

250th Anniversary of Birth of Vrachanski

KM#	Date	Mintage	VF	XF	Unc
180	1989	—	—	Proof	12.50

10 LEVA

8.4444 g, .900 GOLD, .2443 oz AGW
1100th Anniversary Slavic Alphabet

KM#	Date	Mintage	VF	XF	Unc
67	1963	7,000	—	Proof	160.00

20th Anniversary Peoples Republic

KM#	Date	Mintage	VF	XF	Unc
71	1964	.010	—	Proof	120.00

29.9500 g, .900 SILVER, .8666 oz ASW
10th Olympic Congress
Edge inscription in Latin

KM#	Date	Mintage	VF	XF	Unc
93.1	1975	.050	—	Proof	32.50

Edge inscription in Cyrillic

KM#	Date	Mintage	VF	XF	Unc
93.2	1975	.050	—	Proof	32.50

29.8500 g, .500 SILVER, .4798 oz ASW
100th Anniversary Liberation from Turks

KM#	Date	Mintage	VF	XF	Unc
102	1978	.200	—	Proof	20.00

23.3280 g, .925 SILVER, .6938 oz ASW
International Year of the Child

KM#	Date	Mintage	VF	XF	Unc
104	1979	.020	—	Proof	27.50

14.0000 g, .500 SILVER, .2251 oz ASW, 32mm
Bulgarian-Soviet Cosmonaut Flight

KM#	Date	Mintage	VF	XF	Unc
105	1979	.035	—	Proof	45.00

23.8500 g, .900 SILVER, .6901 oz ASW, 38mm

KM#	Date	Mintage	VF	XF	Unc
105a	1979	.015	—	Proof	55.00

18.8800 g, .500 SILVER, .3035 oz ASW

Soccer Games - Ball and Net

KM#	Date	Mintage	VF	XF	Unc
143	1982	1,000	—	Proof	45.00

Soccer Games - Players

KM#	Date	Mintage	VF	XF	Unc
144	1982	1,000	—	Proof	45.00

COPPER-NICKEL
Winter Olympics - Skier

KM#	Date	Mintage	VF	XF	Unc
146	1984	1,500	—	Proof	32.00

23.3300 g, .925 SILVER, .6939 oz ASW

KM#	Date	Mintage	VF	XF	Unc
146a	1984	.012	—	Proof	45.00

COPPER-NICKEL
Summer Olympics

KM#	Date	Mintage	VF	XF	Unc
147	1984	2,000	—	Proof	40.00

23.3300 g, .925 SILVER, .6939 oz ASW

KM#	Date	Mintage	VF	XF	Unc
147a	1984	300 pcs.	—	Proof	85.00

International Decade for Women

KM#	Date	Mintage	VF	XF	Unc
149	1984	.018	—	Proof	25.00

18.7500 g, .640 SILVER, .3858 oz ASW
Cosmonauts

KM#	Date	Mintage	VF	XF	Unc
157	1985	2,500	—	Proof	32.00

1988 Winter Olympics - Hockey

KM#	Date	Mintage	VF	XF	Unc
184	1987	—	—	Proof	35.00

Summer Olympics - Sprinters

KM#	Date	Mintage	VF	XF	Unc
185	1988	—	—	Proof	35.00

Summer Olympics - High Jumper

KM#	Date	Mintage	VF	XF	Unc
186	1988	—	—	Proof	40.00

20 LEVA

16.8889 g, .900 GOLD, .4887 oz AGW
1100th Anniversary Slavic Alphabet

KM#	Date	Mintage	Fine	VF	XF	Unc
68	1963	3,000	—	—	Proof	320.00

20th Anniversary Peoples Republic

KM#	Date	Mintage	Fine	VF	XF	Unc
72	1964	5,000	—	—	Proof	250.00

21.8000 g, .500 SILVER, .3505 oz ASW, 37mm
Centennial of Sophia as Capital

KM#	Date	Mintage	Fine	VF	XF	Unc
106	1979	.035	—	—	—	45.00

32.0000 g, .900 SILVER, .9260 oz ASW, 42mm

KM#	Date	Mintage	Fine	VF	XF	Unc
106a	1979	.015	—	—	Proof	55.00

14.0000 g, .500 SILVER, .2250 oz ASW
40th Anniversary of Birth of Ljudmila Jivkowa
Similar to 5 Leva, KM#141.

KM#	Date	Mintage	Fine	VF	XF	Unc
133.1	1982	—	—	—	Proof	35.00

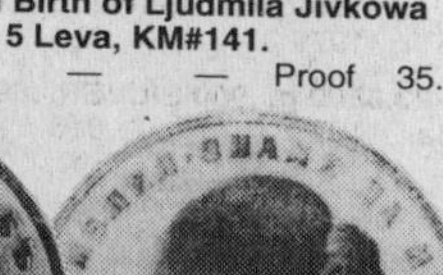

Obv: Denomination between emblems of Chiildren's Assembly and Year of the Child.

KM#	Date	Mintage	Fine	VF	XF	Unc
133.2	1982	—	—	—	Proof	150.00

11.2200 g, .500 SILVER, .1804 oz ASW

Vasil Levsky

KM#	Date	Mintage	Fine	VF	XF	Unc
164	1987	—	—	—	Proof	32.00

11.3900 g, .500 SILVER, .1830 oz ASW
Bulgarian Railways

KM#	Date	Mintage	Fine	VF	XF	Unc
171	1988	—	—	—	Proof	32.00

11.2200 g, .500 SILVER, .1804 oz ASW
110th Anniversary of Liberation

KM#	Date	Mintage	Fine	VF	XF	Unc
172	1988	—	—	—	Proof	28.00

11.5500 g, .500 SILVER, .1855 oz ASW
100th Anniversary of Sophia University

KM#	Date	Mintage	Fine	VF	XF	Unc
173	1988	.100	—	—	Proof	28.00

11.1900 g, .500 SILVER, .1803 oz ASW
Soviet - Bulgarian Space Flight

KM#	Date	Mintage	Fine	VF	XF	Unc
174	1988	.100	—	—	Proof	28.00

COPPER-NICKEL-ZINC

KM#	Date	Mintage	Fine	VF	XF	Unc
181	1989	—	—	—	Proof	20.00

12.1300 g, .500 SILVER, .2138 oz ASW
Academy of Science

KM#	Date	Mintage	Fine	VF	XF	Unc
183	1989	—	—	—	Proof	25.00

14.0000 g, .500 SILVER, .2250 oz ASW
1300th Anniversary of Nationhood

KM#	Date	Mintage	Fine	VF	XF	Unc
134	1981	—	—	—	Proof	25.00

100th Anniversary of Birth of George Dimitrov

KM#	Date	Mintage	Fine	VF	XF	Unc
145	1982	.015	—	—	Proof	22.00

40th Anniversary of Peoples Republic

KM#	Date	Mintage	Fine	VF	XF	Unc
148	1984	—	—	—	Proof	22.00

23.3300 g, .925 SILVER, .6939 oz ASW
Soccer

KM#	Date	Mintage	Fine	VF	XF	Unc
156	1986	.010	—	—	Proof	60.00

Soccer - Player

KM#	Date	Mintage	Fine	VF	XF	Unc
194	1986	.010	—	—	Proof	55.00

Winter Olympics - Skier

KM#	Date	Mintage	Fine	VF	XF	Unc
160	1987	.015	—	—	Proof	55.00

Summer Olympics - High Jump

KM#	Date	Mintage	Fine	VF	XF	Unc
186	1988	—	—	—	—	—

Soccer - Two Players

KM#	Date	Mintage	Fine	VF	XF	Unc
187	1989	*.010	—	—	Proof	55.00

23.3800 g, .925 SILVER, .6954 oz ASW
1992 Summer Olympics - 2 Rowers

KM#	Date	Mintage	Fine	VF	XF	Unc
189	1989	.020	—	—	Proof	50.00

1992 Winter Olympics - Figure Skaters
Obv: Similar to KM#189.

KM#	Date	Mintage	Fine	VF	XF	Unc
190	1989	.020	—	—	Proof	50.00

Wildlife - Mother Bear and Cubs

KM#	Date	Mintage	Fine	VF	XF	Unc
193	1989	—	—	—	Proof	40.00

Soccer - Globe, Net and Shoe

KM#	Date	Mintage	Fine	VF	XF	Unc
191	1990	*.010	—	—	Proof	55.00

Soccer - Ball Design
Obv: Similar to KM#193.

KM#	Date	Mintage	Fine	VF	XF	Unc
192	1990	*.010	—	—	Proof	55.00

Winter Olympics - Cross Country Skiers

KM#	Date	Mintage	Fine	VF	XF	Unc
195	1990	—	—	—	Proof	55.00

Summer Olympics - Runners

KM#	Date	Mintage	Fine	VF	XF	Unc
196	1990	—	—	—	Proof	55.00

Wildlife - Lynx

KM#	Date	Mintage	Fine	VF	XF	Unc
197	1990	—	—	—	Proof	40.00

50 LEVA

20.5000 g, .900 SILVER, .5932 oz ASW
1300th Anniversary of Nationhood
Similar to 2 Leva, KM#121.

KM#	Date	Mintage	Fine	VF	XF	Unc
135	1981	1,000	—	—	Proof	32.00

1300th Anniversary of Nationhood
Rev: Dimitrov.

KM#	Date	Mintage	Fine	VF	XF	Unc
136	1981	1,000	—	—	Proof	35.00

1300th Anniversary of Nationhood

KM#	Date	Mintage	Fine	VF	XF	Unc
137	1981	—	—	—	Proof	40.00

1300th Anniversary of Nationhood
Similar to 2 Leva, KM#124.

KM#	Date	Mintage	Fine	VF	XF	Unc
138	1981	—	—	—	Proof	35.00

COPPER-NICKEL-ZINC

KM#	Date	Mintage	Fine	VF	XF	Unc
182	1989	—	—	—	Proof	25.00

100 LEVA

8.0000 g, .900 GOLD, .2315 oz AGW
International Womens Decade

KM#	Date	Mintage	Fine	VF	XF	Unc
150	1984	500 pcs.	—	—	Proof	260.00

1000 LEVA

16.8800 g, .900 GOLD, .4885 oz AGW
1300th Anniversary of Nationhood
Obv: Similar to 5 Leva, KM#132.

KM#	Date	Mintage	Fine	VF	XF	Unc
139	1981	—	—	—	Proof	380.00

REPUBLIC

10 STOTINKI

NICKEL-BRASS
Ancient Lion Sculpture

KM#	Date	Mintage	VF	XF	Unc
199	1992	—	—	—	.25

20 STOTINKI

NICKEL-BRASS
Ancient Lion Sculpture

KM#	Date	Mintage	VF	XF	Unc
200	1992	—	—	—	.25

50 STOTINKI

NICKEL-BRASS
Ancient Lion Sculpture

KM#	Date	Mintage	VF	XF	Unc
201	1992	—	—	—	.50

LEV

NICKEL-BRASS
Madara Horseman

KM#	Date	Mintage	VF	XF	Unc
202	1992	—	—	—	1.00

2 LEVA

NICKEL-BRASS
Madara Horseman

KM#	Date	Mintage	VF	XF	Unc
203	1992	—	—	—	1.50

5 LEVA

NICKEL-BRASS
Madara Horseman

KM#	Date	Mintage	VF	XF	Unc
204	1992	—	—	—	2.00

10 LEVA

COPPER-NICKEL

Madara Horseman

KM#	Date	Mintage	VF	XF	Unc
205	1992	—	—	—	3.00

50 LEVA

10.0700 g, .925 SILVER, .2995 oz ASW
Olympics - Downhill Skiing

KM#	Date	Mintage	VF	XF	Unc
198	1992	*.040	—	Proof	25.00

100 LEVA

23.3300 g, .925 SILVER, .6939 oz ASW
1994 Olympics - Bobsled

KM#	Date	Mintage	VF	XF	Unc
209	1993	*.030	—	Proof	50.00

Soccer - World Cup 1994

KM#	Date	Mintage	VF	XF	Unc
210	1993	*.015	—	Proof	50.00

500 LEVA

33.6250 g, .925 SILVER, 1.0000 oz ASW
European Community - St. Theodor Stratilat
Obv: Similar to 5000 Leva, KM#207.

KM#	Date	Mintage	VF	XF	Unc
206	1993	5,000	—	Proof	60.00

5000 LEVA

8.6400 g, .900 GOLD, .2500 oz AGW
European Community - Slavonic Alphabet

KM#	Date	Mintage	VF	XF	Unc
207	1993	5,000	—	Proof	200.00

10,000 LEVA

15.5670 g, .999 PLATINUM, .4999 oz APW
European Community - Desislava
Obv: Similar to 5000 Leva, KM#207.

KM#	Date	Mintage	VF	XF	Unc
208	1993	5,000	—	Proof	450.00

PROOF SETS (PS)

KM#	Date	Mintage	Identification	Issue Price	Mkt. Val.
PS1	1912(2)	—	KM33-34	—	5000.
PS2	1962/66(9)	—	KM58-64(1962),73 (1966)	—	—
PS3	1963(2)	5,000	KM65-66	—	27.50
PS4	1964(2)	10,000	KM69-70	—	27.50
PS5	1963/73(8)	—	KM65-66,69-70,78-79, 80-81 mixed date set, REPUBLIQUE DE BULGARIE	—	115.00
PS6	1979(7)	2,000	KM84-90	—	22.50
PS7	1980(7)	2,000	KM84-90	—	22.50

Listings For

BURMA: refer to Myanmar

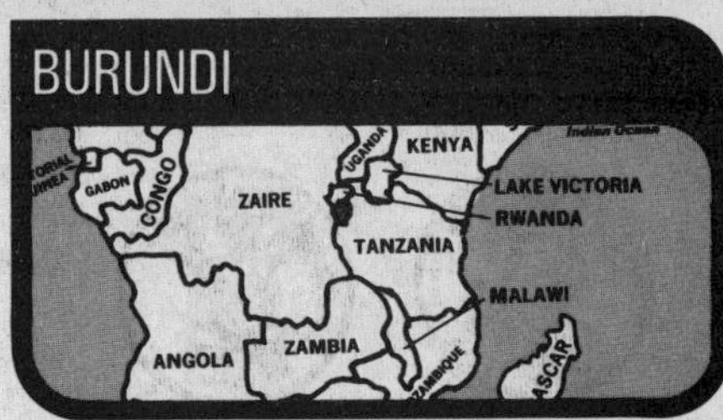

The Republic of Burundi, a landlocked country in central Africa, was a kingdom with a feudalistic society, caste system and Mwami (king) for more than 400 years before independence. It has an area of 10,747 sq. mi. (27,830 sq. km.) and a population of 4.7 million. Capital: Bujumbura. Plagued by poor soil, irregular rainfall and a single-crop economy, coffee, Burundi is barely able to feed itself. Coffee and tea are exported.

Although the area was visited by European explorers and missionaries in the latter half of the 19th century, it wasn't until the 1890s that it, together with Rwanda, fell under European domination as part of German East Africa. Following World War I, the territory was mandated to Belgium by the League of Nations and administered with the Belgian Congo. After World War II it became a U.N. Trust Territory. Limited self-government was established by U.N.-supervised elections in 1961. Burundi gained independence as a kingdom under Mwami Mwambutsa IV on July 1, 1962. The republic was established by military coup in 1966.

NOTE: For earlier coinage see Belgian Congo, and Rwanda and Burundi. For previously listed coinage dated 1966 coins of Mwambutsa IV and Ntare V refer to *UNUSUAL WORLD COINS*, 3rd edition, Krause Publications, 1992.

RULERS

Mwambutsa IV, 1962-1966
Ntare V, 1966

MINT MARKS

(b) - Privy Marks, Brussels

MONETARY SYSTEM

100 Centimes = 1 Franc

KINGDOM

1962-1966

FRANC

BRASS

KM#	Date	Mintage	Fine	VF	XF	Unc
6	1965	10.000	—	.75	1.25	2.50

5 FRANCS

COPPER-NICKEL
Burundi Independence

KM#	Date	Mintage	Fine	VF	XF	Unc
1	1962	—	—	—	—	—
	1962	—	—	—	Proof	—

24.1100 g, .900 SILVER, .6976 oz ASW

KM#	Date	Mintage	Fine	VF	XF	Unc
1a	1962	—	—	—	Proof	—

10 FRANCS

3.2000 g, .900 GOLD, .0926 oz AGW
Burundi Independence

KM#	Date	Mintage	Fine	VF	XF	Unc
2	1962	7,500	—	—	Proof	65.00

3.0000 g, .900 GOLD, .0868 oz AGW
50th Anniversary - Reign of Mwambutsa IV

KM#	Date	Mintage	Fine	VF	XF	Unc
7	1965	—	—	—	—	50.00
	1965	5,000	—	—	Proof	65.00

25 FRANCS

8.0000 g, .900 GOLD, .2315 oz AGW
Burundi Independence

KM#	Date	Mintage	Fine	VF	XF	Unc
3	1962	15,000	—	—	Proof	125.00

7.5000 g, .900 GOLD, .2170 oz AGW
50th Anniversary - Reign of Mwambutsa IV

KM#	Date	Mintage	Fine	VF	XF	Unc
8	1965	—	—	—	—	120.00
	1965	5,000	—	—	Proof	135.00

50 FRANCS

16.0000 g, .900 GOLD, .4630 oz AGW
Burundi Independence

KM#	Date	Mintage	Fine	VF	XF	Unc
4	1962	3,500	—	—	Proof	300.00

15.0000 g, .900 GOLD, .4340 oz AGW
50th Anniversay - Reign of Mwambutsa IV

KM#	Date	Mintage	Fine	VF	XF	Unc
9	1965	—	—	—	—	210.00
	1965	5,000	—	—	Proof	280.00

100 FRANCS

32.0000 g, .900 GOLD, .9260 oz AGW
Burundi Independence

KM#	Date	Mintage	Fine	VF	XF	Unc
5	1962	2,500	—	—	Proof	550.00

30.0000 g, .900 GOLD, .8681 oz AGW
50th Anniversary - Reign of Mwambutsa IV

KM#	Date	Mintage	Fine	VF	XF	Unc
10	1965	—	—	—	—	450.00
	1965	5,000	—	—	Proof	500.00

REPUBLIC

1966

FRANC

ALUMINUM

KM#	Date	Mintage	Fine	VF	XF	Unc
18	1970	10.000	2.00	4.50	7.50	17.50

KM#	Date	Mintage	Fine	VF	XF	Unc
19	1976	5.000	—	.30	.75	1.25
	1980	—	—	.15	.50	1.00
	1990	—	—	.15	.50	1.00
	1993	—	—	.15	.40	.75

5 FRANCS

ALUMINUM

KM#	Date	Mintage	Fine	VF	XF	Unc
16	1968(b)	2.000	—	.25	.80	1.75
	1969(b)	2.000	—	.25	.80	1.75
	1971(b)	2.000	—	.25	.80	1.75

KM#	Date	Mintage	Fine	VF	XF	Unc
20	1976	2.000	—	.25	.75	1.50
	1980	—	—	.25	.75	1.50

10 FRANCS

3.2000 g, .900 GOLD, .0926 oz AGW
1st Anniversary of Republic

KM#	Date	Mintage	Fine	VF	XF	Unc
11	1967	—	—	—	Proof	100.00

COPPER-NICKEL
F.A.O. Issue

KM#	Date	Mintage	Fine	VF	XF	Unc
17	1968	2.000	—	.75	1.25	2.25
	1971	2.000	—	.75	1.25	2.25

20 FRANCS

6.4000 g, .900 GOLD, .1852 oz AGW
1st Anniversary of Republic

KM#	Date	Mintage	Fine	VF	XF	Unc
12	1967	—	—	—	Proof	150.00

25 FRANCS

8.0000 g, .900 GOLD, .2315 oz AGW
1st Anniversary of Republic

KM#	Date	Mintage	Fine	VF	XF	Unc
13	1967	—	—	—	Proof	200.00

50 FRANCS

16.0000 g, .900 GOLD, .4630 oz AGW
1st Anniversary of Republic

KM#	Date	Mintage	Fine	VF	XF	Unc
14	1967	—	—	—	Proof	350.00

100 FRANCS

32.0000 g, .900 GOLD, .9261 oz AGW
1st Anniversary of Republic

KM#	Date	Mintage	Fine	VF	XF	Unc
15	1967	—	—	—	Proof	700.00

PROOF SETS (PS)

KM#	Date	Mintage	Identification	Issue Price	Mkt. Val.
PS1	1962(4)	2,500	KM2-5	—	1040.
PS2	1965(4)	5,000	KM7-10	—	980.
PS3	1967(5)	—	KM11-15	—	1500.

CAMBODIA

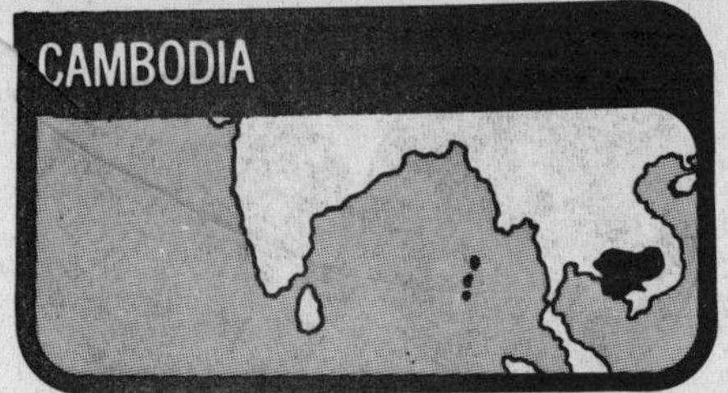

The State of Cambodia, formerly Democratic Kampuchea and the Khmer Republic, a land of paddy fields and forest-clad hills located on the Indo-Chinese peninsula, fronting on the Gulf of Thailand, has an area of 69,898 sq. mi. (181,040 sq. km.) and a population of 7.4 million. Capital: Phnom Penh. Agriculture is the basis of the economy, with rice the chief crop. Native industries include cattle breeding, weaving and rice milling. Rubber, cattle, corn, and timber are exported.

The region was the nucleus of the Khmer empire which flourished from the 5th to the 12th century and attained an excellence in art and architecture still evident in the magnificent ruins at Angkor. The Khmer empire once ruled over much of Southeast Asia, but began to decline in the 13th century as the Thai and Vietnamese invaded the region and attached its territories. At the request of the Cambodian king, a French protectorate attached to Cochin-China was established over the country in 1863, saving it from dissolution, and in 1885, Cambodia was included in the French Union of Indo-China. France established a constitutional monarchy for Cambodia within the French Union in 1949. The 1954 Geneva Convention resulted in full independence for the Kingdom of Cambodia. King Sihanouk abdicated to his father and won the office of Prime Minister.

Prince Sihanouk was toppled by a bloodless coup led by Lon Nol in March of 1970. Sihanouk moved to Peking to head a government-in-exile. On Oct. 9, 1970, Cambodia became the Khmer Republic, and Lon Nol its President. The government of Lon Nol was in turn toppled, April 17, 1975, by the Khmer Rouge insurgents who took control of the government and renamed the country Democratic Kampuchea.

The Khmer Rouge completely eliminated the economy and created a state without money, exchange or barter while exterminating about 2 million Cambodians. These atrocities were finally halted at the beginning of 1979 when the Vietnamese regulars and Cambodian rebels launched an offensive that drove the Khmer Rouge out of Phnom Penh and the country acquired another new title - The Peoples Republic of Kampuchea.

In 1991 Prince Norodom Sihanouk returned to Kampuchea to lead the Supreme National Council.

RULERS

Kings of Cambodia

Norodom I, 1835-1904
Sisowath, 1904-1927
Sisowath Monivong, 1927-1941
Norodom Sihanouk, 1941-1955
Norodom Suramarit, 1955-1960

MINT MARKS

(a) - Paris, privy marks only
(k) - Key, Havana, Cuba

MONETARY SYSTEM

(Until 1860)

2 Att = 1 Pe (Pey)
4 Pe = 1 Fuang (Fuong)
8 Fuang = 1 Tical
4 Salong = 1 Tical

(Commencing 1860)

100 Centimes = 1 Franc

KINGDOM

ATT

COPPER, 1.40-2.50 g, uniface
Similar to 1 Pe, KM#2.

KM#	Date	Year	VG	Fine	VF	XF
1	CS1208	(1847)	4.00	6.50	12.00	25.00

PE

COPPER, 4.00-4.60 g, uniface
W/or w/o silver wash

KM#	Date	Year	VG	Fine	VF	XF
2	CS1208	(1847)	9.00	15.00	27.50	55.00

COPPER or BILLON 0.20-0.90 g, uniface

KM#	Date	Year	VG	Fine	VF	XF
3	ND		6.00	8.50	12.50	27.50

Cocoa bean.

KM#	Date	Year	VG	Fine	VF	XF
4	ND		6.00	9.00	15.00	30.00

Crab

KM#	Date	Year	VG	Fine	VF	XF
5	ND		9.00	15.00	27.50	50.00

2 PE

(1/2 Fuang)

COPPER or BILLON 1.00-2.00 g, uniface
Rooster left.

KM#	Date	Year	VG	Fine	VF	XF
7	ND		3.00	4.50	8.00	20.00

Peacock

KM#	Date	Year	VG	Fine	VF	XF
9	ND		5.50	8.00	15.00	35.00

'Chi' above bird.

KM#	Date	Year	VG	Fine	VF	XF
11	ND		3.00	6.00	10.00	15.00

Cobra

KM#	Date	Year	VG	Fine	VF	XF
13	ND		4.00	7.00	12.00	20.00

Pond Lily

KM#	Date	Year	VG	Fine	VF	XF
14	ND		4.00	7.00	12.00	20.00

Goat

KM#	Date	Year	VG	Fine	VF	XF
15	ND		5.50	8.00	12.50	27.50

Horse

KM#	Date	Year	VG	Fine	VF	XF
17	ND		5.50	8.00	12.50	27.50

Uniface
Similar to 1 Pe, KM#5.

KM#	Date	Year	VG	Fine	VF	XF
19	ND		10.00	15.00	27.50	55.00

Chinze

KM#	Date	Year	VG	Fine	VF	XF
21	ND		10.00	15.00	27.50	55.00

Elephant

KM#	Date	Year	VG	Fine	VF	XF
23	ND		10.00	15.00	27.50	55.00

Garuda bird.
Rev: Leg. in Cambodian script. Hand struck.

KM#	Date	Year	VG	Fine	VF	XF
25	ND		5.00	8.00	15.00	30.00

Obv: Similar to KM#25 but w/o border around Garuda bird. Machine struck.

KM#	Date	Year	VG	Fine	VF	XF
26	ND		2.50	4.00	6.50	12.00

SILVER, 1.85 g, 14.5mm
Uniface
Similar to KM25, but w/o snake in hand.

KM#	Date	Year	VG	Fine	VF	XF
28	ND		—	—	—	300.00

BRASS or COPPER, 23mm
Obv: Similar to KM26, but 3 line legend on rev.

KM#	Date	Year	VG	Fine	VF	XF
30	ND		50.00	100.00	125.00	175.00

FUANG

COPPER or BILLON, 2.70-3.00 g, uniface

KM#	Date	Year	VG	Fine	VF	XF
27	ND		3.00	4.50	7.50	15.00

Uniface
Hippogriff walking to right.
Similar to 2 Pe, KM#21.

KM#	Date	Year	VG	Fine	VF	XF
29	ND		10.00	15.00	27.50	55.00

NOTE: KM#'s 1 through 29 above were struck between 1650 and 1850. All are believed to have been struck at Battambang except KM#25 which is thought to have been made at Siem Reap.

1/8 TICAL

(1 Fuang)

BILLON, 1.50-1.75 g, 11-16mm,
Uniface, w/'Hamza Bird

KM#	Date	Year	VG	Fine	VF	XF
32.1	CS1208	(1847)	4.00	7.00	10.00	20.00

W/o small circle at left.

KM#	Date	Year	VG	Fine	VF	XF
32.2	CS1208	(1847)	—	—	—	—

NOTE: Varieties exist.

SILVER, 14mm
Machine struck

KM#	Date	Year	Fine	VF	XF	Unc
33	ND	(1847)	100.00	150.00	250.00	350.00

NOTE: Modern counterfeits exist in copper, silver and gold.

1/4 TICAL

(1 Salong)

SILVER, 3.20 g, 20mm

KM#	Date	Year	Fine	VF	XF	Unc
34	CS1208	(1847)	150.00	250.00	400.00	550.00

3.60 g, 22mm

KM#	Date	Year	Fine	VF	XF	Unc
35	CS1208	(1847)	150.00	250.00	400.00	550.00

KM#	Date	Year	Fine	VF	XF	Unc
39	CS1209	(1848)	—	—	—	—

TICAL

SILVER, 15.258 g, 30mm, thick flan

KM#	Date	Year	Fine	VF	XF	Unc
36	CS1208	(1847)	50.00	100.00	200.00	500.00

14.209 g, 35mm, thin flan

KM#	Date	Year	Fine	VF	XF	Unc
37	CS1208	(1847)	50.00	100.00	200.00	—

4 TICAL

SILVER, 60.50 g

KM#	Date	Year	Fine	VF	XF	Unc
38	CS1209	(1848)	—	—	—	—

FRENCH PROTECTORATE

MONETARY SYSTEM

100 Centimes = 1 Franc

REGULAR COINAGE

The 1860 dated coins were struck in Belgium in 1875, engraved by C. Wurden whose name appears below the bust.

RESTRIKES

In 1899 after the death of the Queen Mother of Cambodia, all of the 1860 series coins except the 1 Piastre, were restruck with the original dies. These dies were rusty and dirty from long storage and these restrike coins have a grainy appearance to them.

CINQ (5) CENTIMES

BRONZE

KM#	Date	Mintage	Fine	VF	XF	Unc
42.1	1860	11.467	5.00	12.00	35.00	75.00
	1860	—	—	—	Proof	90.00
42.2	1860	(restrike)	—	10.00	30.00	65.00

DIX (10) CENTIMES

BRONZE

KM#	Date	Mintage	Fine	VF	XF	Unc
43.1	1860	10.267	6.00	15.00	40.00	90.00
	1860	—	—	—	Proof	175.00
43.2	1860	(restrike)	—	12.00	35.00	75.00

Local manufacture. Rev: W/error CENTINES

KM#	Date	Mintage	Fine	VF	XF	Unc
43.3	1860	—	15.00	40.00	75.00	150.00

25 CENTIMES

1.2500 g, .900 SILVER, .0361 oz ASW

KM#	Date	Mintage	Fine	VF	XF	Unc
44.1	1860	—	10.00	30.00	100.00	250.00
	1860	—	—	—	Proof	500.00

Reduced weight

KM#	Date	Mintage	Fine	VF	XF	Unc
44.2	1860	(restrike)	—	15.00	30.00	75.00

50 CENTIMES

2.5000 g, .900 SILVER, .0723 oz ASW

KM#	Date	Mintage	Fine	VF	XF	Unc
45.1	1860	—	20.00	60.00	125.00	300.00
	1860	—	—	—	Proof	600.00

Reduced weight, 1.70 g

KM#	Date	Mintage	Fine	VF	XF	Unc
45.2	1860	(restrike)	—	20.00	40.00	100.00

UN (1) FRANC

5.0000 g, .900 SILVER, .1446 oz ASW

KM#	Date	Mintage	Fine	VF	XF	Unc
46.1	1860	—	25.00	70.00	175.00	400.00
	1860	—	—	—	Proof	700.00

Reduced weight, 3.50 g

KM#	Date	Mintage	Fine	VF	XF	Unc
46.2	1860	(restrike)	—	35.00	60.00	125.00

DEUX (2) FRANCS

10.0000 g, .900 SILVER, .2893 oz ASW

KM#	Date	Mintage	Fine	VF	XF	Unc
47.1	1860	—	45.00	125.00	250.00	500.00
	1860	—	—	—	Proof	850.00

Reduced weight, 8.00 g

KM#	Date	Mintage	Fine	VF	XF	Unc
47.2	1860	(restrike)	—	45.00	75.00	225.00

QUATRE (4) FRANCS

20.0000 g, .900 SILVER, .5786 oz ASW

KM#	Date	Mintage	Fine	VF	XF	Unc
48.1	1860	—	75.00	200.00	300.00	600.00
	1860	—	—	—	Proof	1500.

Reduced weight, 15.60 g

KM#	Date	Mintage	Fine	VF	XF	Unc
48.2	1860	(restrike)	—	60.00	120.00	350.00

PIASTRE/PESO/YUAN/5 FRANCS

27.0000 g, .900 SILVER, .7812 oz ASW

KM#	Date	Mintage	Fine	VF	XF	Unc
49	1860	—	300.00	600.00	1200.	2500.
	1860	—	—	—	Proof	3000.

INDEPENDENT KINGDOM

MONETARY SYSTEM

100 Centimes = 1 Riel

100 Sen = 1 Riel (Commencing 1959)

10 CENTIMES

ALUMINUM

KM#	Date	Mintage	Fine	VF	XF	Unc
51	1953(a)	4.000	.25	.50	1.00	3.00

10 SEN

ALUMINUM

KM#	Date	Mintage	Fine	VF	XF	Unc
54	1959(a)	1.000	.10	.20	.40	.75

20 CENTIMES

ALUMINUM

KM#	Date	Mintage	Fine	VF	XF	Unc
52	1953(a)	3.000	.25	.65	1.75	4.00

20 SEN

ALUMINUM

KM#	Date	Mintage	Fine	VF	XF	Unc
55	1959(a)	1.004	.15	.25	.60	1.00

50 CENTIMES

ALUMINUM

KM#	Date	Mintage	Fine	VF	XF	Unc
53	1953(a)	3.170	.45	1.00	2.50	5.00

50 SEN

ALUMINUM

KM#	Date	Mintage	Fine	VF	XF	Unc
56	1959(a)	3.399	.20	.35	.75	1.50

KHMER REPUBLIC

RIEL

COPPER-NICKEL
F.A.O. Issue

KM#	Date	Mintage	Fine	VF	XF	Unc
59	1970	5.000	—	—	10.00	20.00

NOTE: According to the Royal Mint of Great Britain, this coin was minted at the Llantrissant Branch Mint in 1972 but dated 1969. According to the FAO, the coin was to have been dated 1971, but was "not minted" due to the fall of the Cambodian government in 1970. However, this coin was released in limited numbers in 1983. The photograph of the coin, supplied by the FAO, is dated 1970.

5000 RIELS

19.0100 g, .925 SILVER, .5654 oz ASW.
Temple of Angkor-Vath

KM#	Date	Mintage	VF	XF	Unc
60	1974	500 pcs.	—	—	50.00
	1974	800 pcs.	—	Proof	50.00

Cambodian Dancers
Rev: Similar to KM#60.

KM#	Date	Mintage	VF	XF	Unc
61	1974	500 pcs.	—	—	60.00
	1974	800 pcs.	—	Proof	60.00

10,000 RIELS

38.0300 g, .925 SILVER, 1.1310 oz ASW
President Lon Nol
Rev: Similar to 5,000 Riels, KM#60.

KM#	Date	Mintage	VF	XF	Unc
62	1974	500 pcs.	—	—	85.00
	1974	800 pcs.	—	Proof	85.00

Celestial Dancer

Rev: Similar to 5,000 Riels, KM#60.

KM#	Date	Mintage	VF	XF	Unc
63	1974	500 pcs.	—	—	85.00
	1974	800 pcs.	—	Proof	85.00

50,000 RIELS

6.7100 g, .900 GOLD, .1941 oz AGW
Cambodian Dancers

KM#	Date	Mintage	VF	XF	Unc
64	1974	3,250	—	—	150.00
	1974	2,300	—	Proof	225.00

Celestial Dancer

KM#	Date	Mintage	VF	XF	Unc
65	1974	450 pcs.	—	—	250.00
	1974	300 pcs.	—	Proof	350.00

100,000 RIELS

19.1700 g, .900 GOLD, .5547 oz AGW
President Lon Nol
Rev: Similar to 50,000 Riels, KM#65.

KM#	Date	Mintage	VF	XF	Unc
66	1974	250 pcs.	—	—	450.00
	1974	100 pcs.	—	Proof	750.00

NOTE: The above coins were authorized by the Cambodian government shortly before its fall in 1975. The new Communist regime laid claim to the coins and for a time their fate was uncertain. It was not until May 1975, that these coins were offered for sale.

MINT SETS (MS)

KM#	Date	Mintage	Identification	Issue Price	Mkt. Val.
MS1	1974(7)	250	KM60-66	—	1125.
MS2	1974(4)	500	KM60-63	—	280.00

PROOF SETS (PS)

KM#	Date	Mintage	Identification	Issue Price	Mkt. Val.
PS1	1974(7)	100	KM60-66	—	1600.
PS2	1974(4)	800	KM60-63	—	280.00

PEOPLES REPUBLIC OF KAMPUCHEA

5 SEN

ALUMINUM

KM#	Date	Mintage	VF	XF	Unc
69	1979	—	1.50	2.50	4.00

NOTE: Exists w/thick and thin flan.

4 RIELS

COPPER-NICKEL
Cambodian Transportation - Old Sailing Ship

KM#	Date	Mintage	VF	XF	Unc
71	1988(k)	1,500	—	—	12.00

700th Anniversary of Swiss Unity

Similar to 20 Riels, KM#73.

KM#	Date	Mintage	VF	XF	Unc
75	ND(1988)	.015	—	—	10.00

World Championship Soccer - Italy

74	1989	—	—	—	10.00

20 RIELS

12.0600 g, .999 SILVER, .3855 oz ASW
Cambodian Transportation - Old Sailing Ship

70	1988(k)	3,000	—	—	35.00

World Championship Soccer - Mexico

72	1988	5,000	—	—	35.00

16.0000 g, .999 SILVER, .5145 oz ASW
700th Anniversary of Swiss Unity - 1991

73	ND(1988)	2,000	—	Proof	50.00

12.0000 g, .999 SILVER, .3855 oz ASW
European Soccer Championship - Germany

78	1988(k)	5,000	—	—	45.00

16.0000 g, .999 SILVER, .5145 oz ASW
Angkor - Wath Temples

KM#	Date	Mintage	VF	XF	Unc
76	1989	2,000	—	Proof	45.00

World Championship Soccer - Italy

79	1989	.010	—	Proof	50.00

Summer Olympics - Fencers

80	1989	.010	—	Proof	60.00

Winter Olympics - Skier

KM#	Date	Mintage	VF	XF	Unc
81	1989	5,000	—	Proof	60.00

40 RIELS

3.1500 g, .999 GOLD, .1012 oz AGW
Angkor - Wath Temples
Similar to 20 Riels, KM#76.

77	1989	500 pcs.	—	—	160.00

Folklore and Dance

82	1990	—	—	—	140.00

STATE OF CAMBODIA

4 RIELS

NICKEL PLATED STEEL
Olympics - Tennis

83	1991	—	—	—	12.50

COPPER-NICKEL
Prehistoric Animals - Cryptocleidus

86	1993	—	—	—	12.50

20 RIELS

11.9600 g, .999 SILVER, .3845 oz ASW
Soccer - Player Kicking Ball

84	1991	—	—	—	40.00

16.0600 g, .999 SILVER, .5145 oz ASW
Prehistoric Animals - Indricotherium

KM#	Date	Mintage	VF	XF	Unc
87	1993	—	—	Proof	45.00

19.9500 g, .999 SILVER, .6408 oz ASW
Protection of Nature - Asian Elephants

KM#	Date	Mintage	VF	XF	Unc
95	1993	—	—	Proof	45.00

CAMEROON

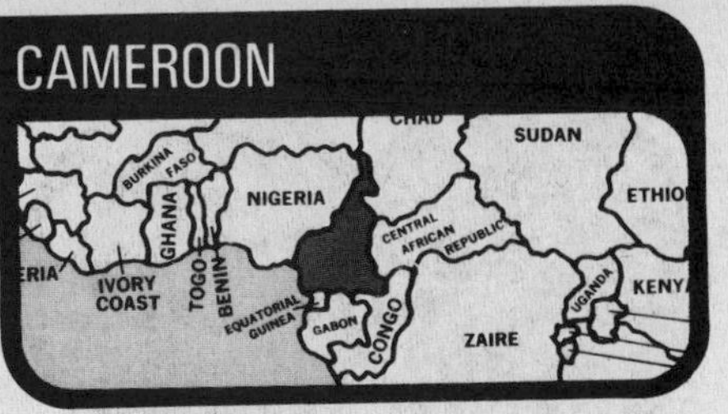

The Republic of Cameroon, located in west-central Africa on the Gulf of Guinea, has an area of 183,569 sq. mi. (475,445 sq. km.) and a population of 10 million. Capital: Yaounde. About 90 percent of the labor force is employed on the land; cash crops account for 80 percent of the country's export revenue. Cocoa, coffee, aluminum, cotton, rubber, and timber are exported.

European contact with what is now the United Republic of Cameroon began in the 16th century with the voyage of Portuguese navigator Fernando Po. The following three centuries saw continuous activity by Spanish, Dutch, and British traders and missionaries. The land was spared colonial rule until 1884, when treaties with tribal chiefs brought German domination. In 1919, the League of Nations divided the Cameroons between Great Britain and France, with the larger eastern area going to France. The French and British mandates were converted into United Nations trusteeships in 1946. French Cameroon became the independent Cameroon Republic on Jan. 1, 1960. The federation of East (French) and West (British) Cameroon was established in 1961 when the southern part of British Cameroon voted for reunification with the Cameroon Republic, and the northern part for union with Nigeria.

Coins of French Equatorial Africa and of the monetary unions identified as the Equatorial African States and Central African States are also current in Cameroon.

MINT MARKS

(a) - Paris, privy marks only
SA - Pretoria, 1943

MONETARY SYSTEM

100 Centimes = 1 Franc

FRENCH MANDATE

50 CENTIMES

ALUMINUM-BRONZE

KM#	Date	Mintage	Fine	VF	XF	Unc
1	1924(a)	4.000	1.50	3.50	20.00	75.00
	1925(a)	2.500	2.00	5.00	25.00	85.00
	1926(a)	7.800	1.00	2.00	12.00	50.00

BRONZE

KM#	Date	Mintage	Fine	VF	XF	Unc
4	1943	4.000	2.00	3.50	7.00	18.00

Obv. leg: LIBRE added

KM#	Date	Mintage	Fine	VF	XF	Unc
6	1943	4.000	2.50	5.50	10.00	20.00

FRANC

ALUMINUM-BRONZE

KM#	Date	Mintage	Fine	VF	XF	Unc
2	1924(a)	3.000	2.00	4.00	20.00	90.00
	1925(a)	1.722	3.00	6.00	30.00	125.00
	1926(a)	11.928	1.00	2.00	12.00	60.00

BRONZE

KM#	Date	Mintage	Fine	VF	XF	Unc
5	1943	3.000	2.50	4.50	17.50	40.00

Obv. leg: LIBRE added

KM#	Date	Mintage	Fine	VF	XF	Unc
7	1943	3.000	3.50	6.50	20.00	45.00

ALUMINUM

KM#	Date	Mintage	Fine	VF	XF	Unc
8	1948(a)	8.000	.10	.25	.75	1.50

2 FRANCS

ALUMINUM-BRONZE

KM#	Date	Mintage	Fine	VF	XF	Unc
3	1924(a)	.500	5.00	15.00	65.00	200.00
	1925(a)	.100	8.00	25.00	100.00	300.00

ALUMINUM

KM#	Date	Mintage	Fine	VF	XF	Unc
9	1948(a)	5.000	.50	1.00	1.50	5.00

5 FRANCS

ALUMINUM-BRONZE

KM#	Date	Mintage	Fine	VF	XF	Unc
24	1958(a)	30.000	.25	.50	1.00	3.00

10 FRANCS

ALUMINUM-BRONZE

KM#	Date	Mintage	Fine	VF	XF	Unc
25	1958(a)	25.000	.25	.50	1.50	4.00

25 FRANCS

ALUMINUM-BRONZE

KM#	Date	Mintage	Fine	VF	XF	Unc
26	1958(a)	12.000	.50	1.00	2.00	6.00

NOTE: KM#24-26 were previously listed in French Equatorial Africa.

REPUBLIC

50 FRANCS

COPPER-NICKEL
Independence Commemorative

KM#	Date	Mintage	Fine	VF	XF	Unc
13	1960(a)	1.154	2.00	3.50	5.50	8.00

100 FRANCS

NICKEL

KM#	Date	Mintage	Fine	VF	XF	Unc
14	1966(a)	9.950	1.00	2.00	4.00	9.00
	1967(a)	10.000	1.00	2.00	4.00	9.00
	1968(a)	11.000	1.00	2.00	4.00	9.00

NOTE: KM#14 was issued double thick and should not be considered a piefort.

KM#	Date	Mintage	Fine	VF	XF	Unc
15	1971(a)	15.000	2.00	3.00	5.00	10.00
	1972(a)	20.000	2.00	3.00	5.00	10.00

NOTE: Refer also to Equatorial African States and Central African States.

Obv: KM#17. Rev: KM#15.

KM#	Date	Mintage	Fine	VF	XF	Unc
16	1972(a)	—	17.50	30.00	40.00	70.00

KM#	Date	Mintage	Fine	VF	XF	Unc
17	1975(a)	—	1.00	2.00	3.00	5.00
	1980(a)	—	1.00	2.00	3.00	5.00
	1982(a)	—	1.00	1.75	2.75	4.50
	1983(a)	—	1.00	1.75	2.75	4.50
	1984(a)	—	1.00	1.75	2.75	3.50
	1986(a)	—	1.00	1.75	2.75	3.50

500 FRANCS

COPPER-NICKEL

KM#	Date	Mintage	Fine	VF	XF	Unc
23	1985(a)	—	2.00	3.50	5.50	10.00
	1986(a)	—	2.00	3.50	5.50	10.00

1000 FRANCS

3.5000 g, .900 GOLD, .1012 oz AGW
10th Anniversary of Independence

KM#	Date	Mintage	Fine	VF	XF	Unc
18	1970	4,000	—	—	Proof	85.00

3000 FRANCS

10.5000 g, .900 GOLD, .3038 oz AGW
10th Anniversary of Independence

KM#	Date	Mintage	Fine	VF	XF	Unc
19	1970	4,000	—	—	Proof	260.00

NOTE: With or without cornucopia mint mark on reverse.

5000 FRANCS

17.5000 g., .900 GOLD, .5064 oz AGW
10th Anniversary of Independence

KM#	Date	Mintage	Fine	VF	XF	Unc
20	1970	4,000	—	—	Proof	425.00

10,000 FRANCS

35.0000 g, .900 GOLD, 1.0128 oz AGW
10th Anniversary of Independence

KM#	Date	Mintage	Fine	VF	XF	Unc
21	1970	4,000	—	—	Proof	950.00

20,000 FRANCS

70.0000 g, .900 GOLD, 2.0257 oz AGW
10th Anniversary of Independence
Obv: Similar to 10,000 Francs, KM#21.

KM#	Date	Mintage	Fine	VF	XF	Unc
22	1970	4,000	—	—	Proof	1600.

PROOF SETS (PS)

KM#	Date	Mintage	Identification	Issue Price	Mkt. Val.
PS1	1970(5)	4,000	KM18-22	—	3325.

1858-59 (5¢ & 10¢ to 1901)

1870-1901

VICTORIA

1902-1910

EDWARD VII

1911

1912-1936

GEORGE V

1935

1937-1947

1948-1952

GEORGE VI

1953-1964

(without straps)

(with straps)

1965 to 1979

1973 and 1988 Olympics

1973, 77 and 79-1989

1978, 1982, 1984

1990—

CANADA

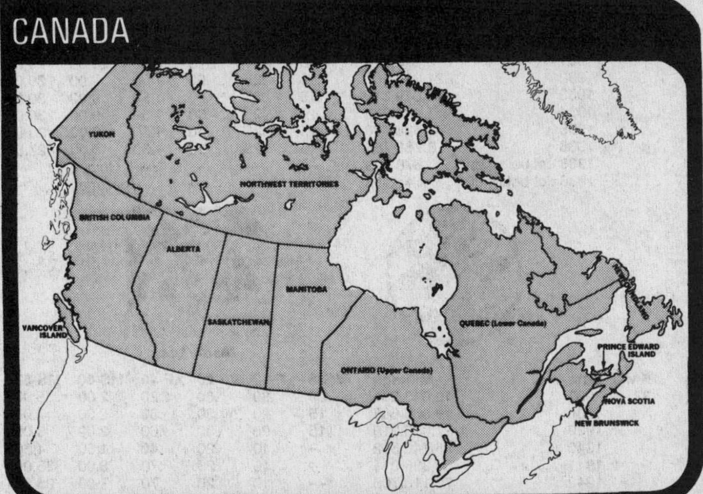

1992

ELIZABETH II

The history of Canadian coinage parallels that of the United States in many respects, although in several aspects it also contrasts quite sharply. Canadian coins are widely collected in the U.S., particularly in the northern tier of states, where at times the issues of our northern neighbors have been encountered in substantial circulating quantities.

This is a most logical situation, as when the dollar was established as the monetary unit of Canada, in 1857, it was given the same intrinsic value as the U.S. dollar. Throughout the years the Canadian dollar had traded on an approximate par with the U.S. dollar, although from time to time one or the other units has traded at a slight premium until in recent years where it is valued at considerably less.

The first Canadian decimal coins were issued in 1858 – 1, 5, 10 and 20 cents – in the name of the Province of Canada (Upper and Lower Canada, or the provinces of Ontario and Quebec as we know them today). The first truly Canadian coinage was offered in 1870 - 5, 10, 25 and 50 cents - following the confederation of these provinces with Nova Scotia and New Brunswick in 1867. Both of the latter had offered their own distinctive coinages in the early 1860s.

Prince Edward Island also offered a single issue of a one cent coin in 1871, prior to its 1873 entry into the confederation. A coinage of Newfoundland was also initiated during this period, in 1865, which continued through 1947, with the British dependency moving into the confederation in 1949.

In contrast to the .900 fine standard of American silver coins, Canada's coinage was originally launched with a .925 fine silver content, and as a result slightly smaller coin sizes. In 1920 the standard was reduced to .800 fine, remaining there until mid-1967 when it was lowered to .500 fine, then abandoned in favor of pure nickel a year later. Another contrast with U.S. coinage was evident in the issue of the large cent from 1858 to 1920, when a small cent of similar size, content and weight to the U.S. cent was introduced.

When Canada's dominion coin issue of 1870 was introduced, the 1858 provincial issue of a decimal 20 cent piece was abandoned in favor of a quasi-decimal 25 cent piece. This move was made, in part, because of the confusion between the 20 cent piece and the U.S. 25 cent piece, which also circulated in Canada, forecasting the similar fate which would befall the U.S. 20 cent piece a few years later. Although tentative steps aimed at the creation of a dollar coin were instituted in 1911, it was not until 1935, the year the issue of silver dollars was halted in the U.S., that Canada launched the issue of a silver dollar.

The first dollar was a commemorative of the silver jubilee of the reign of George V, while the other George V dollar coin (1936) utilized dies which had been prepared at the Royal Mint in London in anticipation of the 1911 dollar which did not materialize. From the beginning, Canada's dollar series has been frequently employed as a vehicle for the commemoration of national events. In addition, a 1951 nickel commemorated the 200th anniversary of the isolation of nickel, of which Canada is the world's leading producer, while the entire 1967 series commemorates the centennial of Canadian confederation.

In the early years, Canada's coins were struck in England at London's Royal Mint or at the Heaton Mint in Birmingham. Issues struck at the Royal Mint do not bear a mint mark, but those produced by Heaton carry an "H". All Canadian coins have been struck since January 2, 1908, at the Royal Canadian Mints at Ottawa and recently at Winnipeg except for some 1968 pure nickel dimes struck at the U.S. Mint in Philadelphia, and do not bear mint marks. Ottawa's mint mark (C) does not appear on some 20th century Newfoundland issues, however, as it does on English type sovereigns struck there from 1908 through 1918.

Canadian coins are graded on MS (Mint State) standards similar to those used for the U.S. series. The points of greatest wear are generally found on the obverses in the bands of the crowns, the sprays of laurel around the head and in the hairlines above or over the ear. The susceptibility of these varying points to wear has decreed that Canadian coins are almost exclusively graded accordingly, with little concentration on the reverses, unless they are abnormally worn or weakly struck.

LARGE CENTS

1858-1910

1911-1920

BRONZE

KM#	Date	Mintage	VG-8	F-12	VF-20	XF-40	MS-60	MS-63
1	1858	421,000	35.00	40.00	55.00	75.00	190.00	475.00
	1859/8 wide 9	I.A.	20.00	25.00	35.00	50.00	125.00	250.00
	1859 narrow 9	9,579,000	1.25	2.00	3.00	5.00	20.00	120.00
	1859 double punched narrow 9 Type I							
		I.A.	170.00	240.00	325.00	500.00	1000.	1800.
	1859 double punched narrow 9 Type II							
		I.A.	25.00	35.00	55.00	75.00	150.00	325.00
7	1876H	4,000,000	1.25	2.00	3.00	5.00	40.00	180.00
	1881H	2,000,000	2.25	3.25	4.75	10.00	50.00	200.00
	1882H	4,000,000	1.25	2.00	3.00	6.00	27.00	120.00
	1884	2,500,000	2.00	3.00	4.00	7.50	40.00	160.00
	1886	1,500,000	3.25	4.50	6.00	11.50	60.00	210.00
	1887	1,500,000	2.25	3.25	5.00	8.00	40.00	170.00
	1888	4,000,000	1.25	2.00	2.75	4.50	27.00	100.00
	1890H	1,000,000	3.75	6.50	11.50	20.00	100.00	300.00
	1891 lg. date	1,452,000	4.50	7.50	11.50	18.50	90.00	275.00
	1891 S.D.L.L.	I.A.	40.00	60.00	70.00	100.00	275.00	750.00
	1891 S.D.S.L.	I.A.	30.00	45.00	60.00	75.00	200.00	550.00
	1892	1,200,000	2.50	4.50	6.00	10.00	35.00	120.00
	1893	2,000,000	1.50	2.50	4.00	7.00	30.00	100.00
	1894	1,000,000	4.50	7.50	12.00	20.00	85.00	215.00
	1895	1,200,000	3.00	5.00	7.00	10.00	50.00	160.00
	1896	2,000,000	1.50	2.00	3.00	5.50	30.00	100.00
	1897	1,500,000	1.50	2.50	3.50	6.00	30.00	110.00
	1898H	1,000,000	3.50	5.50	8.00	11.00	50.00	200.00
	1899	2,400,000	1.50	2.00	3.00	5.00	30.00	100.00
	1900	1,000,000	4.00	8.00	12.00	20.00	65.00	185.00
	1900H	2,600,000	1.25	2.75	3.50	5.00	22.00	70.00
	1901	4,100,000	1.25	2.00	2.75	4.50	22.00	60.00
8	1902	3,000,000	1.00	1.50	2.00	4.00	15.00	40.00
	1903	4,000,000	1.00	1.50	2.00	4.00	20.00	50.00
	1904	2,500,000	1.50	2.00	3.25	5.00	25.00	75.00
	1905	2,000,000	2.50	4.00	6.00	8.50	35.00	95.00
	1906	4,100,000	1.00	1.50	2.00	4.00	20.00	50.00
	1907	2,400,000	1.50	2.50	3.50	5.00	30.00	85.00
	1907H	800,000	7.00	9.00	14.00	20.00	85.00	275.00
	1908	2,401,506	2.00	3.50	4.50	6.00	26.00	80.00
	1909	3,973,339	1.00	1.50	2.00	4.00	20.00	50.00
	1910	5,146,487	1.00	1.25	1.75	3.00	20.00	50.00
15	1911	4,663,486	1.00	1.25	1.75	3.50	20.00	65.00
21	1912	5,107,642	.75	1.00	1.50	2.50	15.00	45.00
	1913	5,735,405	.75	1.00	1.50	2.50	15.00	45.00
	1914	3,405,958	1.15	1.40	2.00	3.50	28.00	90.00
	1915	4,932,134	.75	1.00	1.75	2.75	16.50	60.00
	1916	11,022,367	.45	.65	.90	2.00	12.00	45.00
	1917	11,899,254	.45	.65	.90	1.50	8.00	30.00
	1918	12,970,798	.45	.65	.90	1.50	8.00	30.00
	1919	11,279,634	.45	.65	.90	1.50	8.00	30.00
	1920	6,762,247	.50	.75	1.00	2.00	10.00	40.00

SMALL CENTS

Dot

BRONZE

KM#	Date	Mintage	VG-8	F-12	VF-20	XF-40	MS-60	MS-63
28	1920	15,483,923	.15	.30	.90	2.00	9.00	35.00
	1921	7,601,627	.40	.75	1.75	4.00	14.00	55.00
	1922	1,243,635	8.00	10.00	14.00	22.50	100.00	275.00
	1923	1,019,002	14.00	18.00	24.00	34.00	160.00	500.00
	1924	1,593,195	3.50	5.00	7.50	11.00	75.00	190.00
	1925	1,000,622	11.00	13.00	20.00	28.00	135.00	400.00
	1926	2,143,372	1.75	2.25	4.00	8.00	55.00	175.00
	1927	3,553,928	.75	1.00	2.25	4.00	24.00	90.00
	1928	9,144,860	.15	.25	.65	1.50	10.00	35.00
	1929	12,159,840	.15	.25	.65	1.50	10.00	35.00
	1930	2,538,613	1.60	1.80	3.00	5.00	27.00	90.00
	1931	3,842,776	.60	1.00	1.75	3.50	20.00	70.00
	1932	21,316,190	.15	.25	.60	1.50	9.00	30.00
	1933	12,079,310	.15	.25	.60	1.50	9.00	30.00
	1934	7,042,358	.15	.25	.60	1.50	9.00	30.00
	1935	7,526,400	.15	.25	.60	1.50	9.00	30.00
	1936	8,768,769	.15	.25	.60	1.50	8.00	27.50
	1936 dot below dt	678,823	—	—	—	—	Unique	—
	1936 dot below dt	4 known	—	—	—		Specimen	—

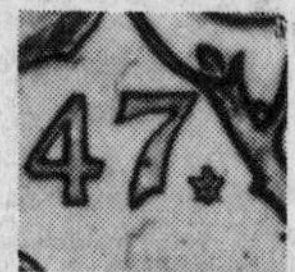

Maple Leaf

KM#	Date	Mintage	VG-8	F-12	VF-20	XF-40	MS-60	MS-63
32	1937	10,040,231	.20	.30	.60	1.20	2.00	5.00
	1938	18,365,608	.15	.20	.30	.60	2.00	7.00
	1939	21,600,319	.15	.20	.30	.60	2.00	6.00
	1940	85,740,532	—	.10	.20	.40	1.50	4.50
	1941	56,336,011	—	.10	.25	.70	8.00	35.00
	1942	76,113,708	—	.10	.20	.70	7.00	25.00
	1943	89,111,969	—	.10	.20	.40	3.00	10.00
	1944	44,131,216	.15	.20	.25	1.00	9.00	30.00
	1945	77,268,591	—	.10	.20	.35	1.25	4.00
	1946	56,662,071	—	.20	.30	.60	1.50	4.50
	1947	31,093,901	—	.10	.20	.35	1.50	5.00
	1947ML	47,855,448	—	.10	.20	.35	1.25	3.50
	Modified Obverse Legend							
41	1948	25,767,779	.10	.20	.35	.60	2.00	7.00
	1949	33,128,933	—	.10	.15	.25	1.25	3.00
	1950	60,444,992	—	.10	.15	.25	1.25	3.00
	1951	80,430,379	—	.10	.15	.25	1.00	2.75
	1952	67,631,736	—	.10	.15	.25	1.00	2.75
	Elizabeth II Effigy							
49	1953 w/o strap	67,806,016	—	.10	.15	.25	.60	2.00
	1953 w/strap	Inc. Ab.	.50	1.00	1.50	3.00	12.00	30.00
	1954 w/strap	22,181,760	.10	.15	.30	.50	2.00	4.50
	1954 w/o strap	Inc. Ab.	Proof-Like Only			—	150.00	250.00
	1955 w/strap	56,403,193	—	.10	.15	.20	.50	1.00
	1955 w/o strap	Inc. Ab.	75.00	125.00	185.00	225.00	475.00	900.00
	1956	78,658,535	—	—	—	.10	.50	.80
	1957	100,601,792	—	—	—	.10	.30	.70
	1958	59,385,679	—	—	—	.10	.30	.70
	1959	83,615,343	—	—	—	.10	.25	.60

KM#	Date	Mintage	VG-8	F-12	VF-20	XF-40	MS-60	MS-63
49	1960	75,772,775	—	—	—	.10	.25	.60
	1961	139,598,404	—	—	—	—	.15	.40
	1962	227,244,069	—	—	—	—	.10	.25
	1963	279,076,334	—	—	—	—	.10	.25
	1964	484,655,322	—	—	—	—	.10	.25
	New Elizabeth II Effigy							
59.1	1965 sm. beads, pointed 5	304,441,082	—	—	—	.10	.45	1.00
	1965 sm. beads, blunt 5	I.A.	—	—	—	—	.10	.25
	1965 lg. beads, pointed 5	I.A.	—	—	1.50	4.00	15.00	30.00
	1965 lg. beads, blunt 5	I.A.	—	—	—	.10	.20	.35
	1966	184,151,087	—	—	—	—	.10	.20
	1968	329,695,772	—	—	—	—	.10	.20
	1969	335,240,929	—	—	—	—	.10	.20
	1970	311,145,010	—	—	—	—	.10	.20
	1971	298,228,936	—	—	—	—	.10	.20
	1972	451,304,591	—	—	—	—	.10	.20
	1973	457,059,852	—	—	—	—	.10	.20
	1974	692,058,489	—	—	—	—	.10	.20
	1975	642,318,000	—	—	—	—	.10	.20
	1976	701,122,890	—	—	—	—	.10	.20
	1977	453,762,670	—	—	—	—	.10	.20
	1978	911,170,647	—	—	—	—	.10	.20
	Smaller Bust							
59.2	1979	754,394,064	—	—	—	—	.10	.20
	Reduced Weight							
127	1980	912,052,318	—	—	—	—	.10	.15
	1981	1,209,468,500	—	—	—	—	.10	.15
	1981	199,000	—	—	—	—	Proof	1.00

New Elizabeth II Effigy

KM#	Date	Mintage	VG-8	F-12	VF-20	XF-40	MS-60	MS-63
132	1982	911,001,000	—	—	—	—	.10	.15
	1982	180,908	—	—	—	—	Proof	1.00
	1983	975,510,000	—	—	—	—	.10	.15
	1983	168,000	—	—	—	—	Proof	1.00
	1984	838,225,000	—	—	—	—	.10	.15
	1984	161,602	—	—	—	—	Proof	1.00
	1985	126,618,000	—	—	—	—	.10	.15
	1985	157,037	—	—	—	—	Proof	1.00
	1986	740,335,000	—	—	—	—	.10	.15
	1986	175,745	—	—	—	—	Proof	1.00
	1987	774,549,000	—	—	—	—	.10	.15
	1987	179,004	—	—	—	—	Proof	1.00
	1988	482,676,752	—	—	—	—	.10	.15
	1988	175,259	—	—	—	—	Proof	1.00
	1989	1,077,347,200	—	—	—	—	.10	.15
	1989	170,928	—	—	—	—	Proof	1.00

New Elizabeth II Effigy

KM#	Date	Mintage	VG-8	F-12	VF-20	XF-40	MS-60	MS-63
181	1990	218,035,000	—	—	—	—	.10	.15
	1990	140,649	—	—	—	—	Proof	1.00
	1991	696,629,000	—	—	—	—	.10	.15
	1991	—	—	—	—	—	Proof	1.00
	1993	—	—	—	—	—	.10	.15
	1993	—	—	—	—	—	Proof	1.00

COMMEMORATIVE CENTS

BRONZE

KM#	Date	Mintage	VG-8	F-12	VF-20	XF-40	MS-60	MS-63
65	1967 Confederation Centennial	345,140,645	—	—	—	—	.10	.20
204	1992 Confederation 125	—	—	—	—	—	.10	.15
		—	—	—	—	—	Proof	1.00

FIVE CENTS

Round 0's

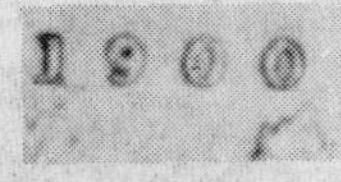

Oval 0's

1.1620 g, .925 SILVER, .0346 oz ASW

KM#	Date	Mintage	VG-8	F-12	VF-20	XF-40	MS-60	MS-63
2	1858 sm. date	1,500,000	8.00	12.00	18.00	35.00	225.00	425.00
	1858 lg. date over sm. date	Inc. Ab.	85.00	135.00	225.00	325.00	700.00	2000.
	1870 flat rim	2,800,000	6.50	10.00	20.00	40.00	175.00	435.00
	1870 wire rim	Inc. Ab.	7.00	11.00	22.50	45.00	200.00	450.00
	1871	1,400,000	7.00	10.00	18.00	35.00	165.00	430.00
	1872H	2,000,000	5.00	9.00	15.00	30.00	185.00	450.00
	1874H plain 4	800,000	12.00	20.00	40.00	75.00	400.00	875.00
	1874H crosslet 4	Inc. Ab.	8.00	12.00	25.00	50.00	300.00	700.00
	1875H lg. date	1,000,000	90.00	150.00	275.00	450.00	1600.	3750.
	1875H sm. date	Inc. Ab.	70.00	110.00	210.00	350.00	1350.	2750.
	1880H	3,000,000	3.00	6.00	12.00	25.00	125.00	400.00
	1881H	1,500,000	3.50	7.00	15.00	30.00	160.00	450.00
	1882H	1,000,000	4.25	8.50	16.50	32.50	180.00	525.00
2	1883H	600,000	10.00	20.00	40.00	65.00	400.00	900.00
	1884	200,000	60.00	100.00	150.00	350.00	1850.	5500.
	1885 sm. 5	1,000,000	4.75	9.50	17.50	40.00	300.00	600.00
	1885 lg. 5	Inc. Ab.	7.00	17.50	35.00	60.00	375.00	800.00
	1885 lg. 5 over sm. 5	Inc. Ab.	30.00	50.00	135.00	400.00	1000.	1900.
	1886 sm. 6	1,700,000	3.75	7.00	14.00	27.50	225.00	500.00
	1886 lg. 6	Inc. Ab.	6.00	9.00	17.50	37.50	275.00	550.00
	1887	500,000	12.00	20.00	35.00	60.00	275.00	675.00
	1888	1,000,000	3.00	5.00	10.00	20.00	125.00	300.00
	1889	1,200,000	14.00	26.00	45.00	90.00	400.00	1000.
	1890H	1,000,000	3.50	6.00	16.00	30.00	165.00	400.00
	1891	1,800,000	2.50	4.00	8.00	16.00	100.00	235.00
	1892	860,000	3.50	6.00	12.00	30.00	175.00	400.00
	1893	1,700,000	2.50	4.00	8.00	16.00	110.00	235.00
	1894	500,000	9.00	18.00	32.00	65.00	325.00	750.00
	1896	1,500,000	3.00	6.00	11.00	20.00	125.00	250.00
	1897	1,319,283	3.00	5.00	10.00	20.00	120.00	225.00
	1898	580,717	6.50	12.00	30.00	45.00	175.00	400.00
	1899	3,000,000	2.00	3.50	7.00	16.00	90.00	210.00
	1900 oval 0's	1,800,000	2.50	4.00	7.00	16.00	100.00	235.00
	1900 round 0's	Inc. Ab.	12.50	25.00	40.00	80.00	285.00	750.00
	1901	2,000,000	2.00	3.50	7.00	16.00	95.00	220.00
9	1902	2,120,000	1.50	2.00	3.00	6.50	35.00	60.00
	1902 lg. broad H	2,200,000	2.00	2.75	4.50	8.00	45.00	70.00
	1902 sm. narrow H	Inc. Ab.	7.50	12.50	22.50	45.00	150.00	225.00
13	1903	1,000,000	4.00	6.00	12.50	25.00	185.00	400.00
	1903H	2,640,000	1.75	3.00	6.00	13.00	80.00	200.00
	1904	2,400,000	1.75	3.00	6.00	14.00	100.00	325.00
	1905	2,600,000	1.75	3.00	6.00	12.00	85.00	200.00
	1906	3,100,000	1.50	2.00	4.00	7.00	70.00	150.00
	1907	5,200,000	1.50	2.00	4.00	7.00	65.00	125.00
	1908	1,220,524	4.00	6.50	12.00	25.00	95.00	200.00
	1909 round leaves	1,983,725	1.75	2.25	6.00	12.00	125.00	325.00
	1909 pointed leaves	Inc. Ab.	8.00	11.00	27.50	55.00	250.00	700.00
	1910 pointed leaves	3,850,325	1.25	1.75	3.00	6.00	45.00	85.00
	1910 round leaves	Inc. Ab.	10.00	15.00	30.00	70.00	290.00	900.00
16	1911	3,692,350	1.75	2.50	5.00	11.00	90.00	175.00
22	1912	5,863,170	1.50	2.00	3.00	6.00	45.00	110.00
	1913	5,488,048	1.25	2.00	3.00	5.00	30.00	60.00
	1914	4,202,179	1.50	2.20	3.50	7.00	55.00	125.00
	1915	1,172,258	7.00	12.00	22.00	40.00	250.00	475.00
	1916	2,481,675	2.75	4.00	6.50	15.00	95.00	225.00
	1917	5,521,373	1.25	1.75	2.50	4.00	40.00	75.00
	1918	6,052,298	1.25	1.75	2.50	4.00	30.00	65.00
	1919	7,835,400	1.25	1.75	2.50	4.00	35.00	65.00

1.1664 g, .800 SILVER, .0300 oz ASW

KM#	Date	Mintage	VG-8	F-12	VF-20	XF-40	MS-60	MS-63
22a	1920	10,649,851	1.25	1.75	2.50	4.00	30.00	60.00
	1921	2,582,495	1250.	1850.	2550.	4750.	11,000.	20,000.

NOTE: Approximately 460 known, balance remelted.
NOTE: Stack's A.G. Carter Jr. Sale 12-89 Choice BU finest known realized $57,200.

Near 6

Far 6

NICKEL

KM#	Date	Mintage	VG-8	F-12	VF-20	XF-40	MS-60	MS-63
29	1922	4,794,119	.25	.75	2.00	7.00	40.00	75.00
	1923	2,502,279	.40	1.25	3.50	10.00	100.00	225.00
	1924	3,105,839	.30	.70	2.50	7.00	75.00	160.00
	1925	201,921	25.00	32.50	55.00	150.00	750.00	1650.
	1926 near 6	938,162	2.50	5.50	12.00	40.00	240.00	600.00
	1926 far 6	Inc. Ab.	50.00	90.00	150.00	300.00	1200.	2200.
	1927	5,285,627	.20	.60	2.00	5.00	45.00	120.00
	1928	4,577,712	.20	.60	2.00	5.00	40.00	80.00
	1929	5,611,911	.20	.60	2.00	5.00	45.00	120.00
	1930	3,704,673	.20	.60	2.00	5.00	70.00	150.00
	1931	5,100,830	.20	.60	2.00	5.00	70.00	150.00
	1932	3,198,566	.20	.60	2.25	6.00	75.00	150.00
	1933	2,597,867	.40	1.00	3.00	8.00	110.00	300.00
	1934	3,827,304	.20	.60	2.00	5.00	80.00	200.00
	1935	3,900,000	.20	.60	2.00	5.00	70.00	160.00
	1936	4,400,450	.20	.60	2.00	5.00	40.00	85.00

KM#	Date	Mintage	VG-8	F-12	VF-20	XF-40	MS-60	MS-63
33	1937 dot	4,593,263	.20	.35	1.75	3.00	10.00	25.00
	1938	3,898,974	.15	.75	1.75	7.00	65.00	150.00
	1939	5,661,123	.20	.50	1.75	4.50	40.00	70.00
	1940	13,920,197	.15	.30	1.00	2.00	14.00	40.00
	1941	8,681,785	.10	.25	1.00	2.50	17.00	42.00
	1942 round	6,847,544	.10	.30	1.00	2.50	14.00	40.00
	Tombac (BRASS)							
39	1942 - 12 sided	3,396,234	.30	.60	1.00	1.50	3.00	9.00

Dot — Maple leaf

NICKEL

KM#	Date	Mintage	VG-8	F-12	VF-20	XF-40	MS-60	MS-63
39a	1946	6,952,684	.15	.25	.50	2.00	10.00	22.50
	1947	7,603,724	.15	.25	.50	1.00	6.00	14.00
	1947 dot	Inc. Ab.	10.00	12.50	20.00	40.00	220.00	600.00
	1947 maple leaf	9,595,124	.15	.25	.50	1.00	6.00	12.00
	Modified Obverse Legend							
42	1948	1,810,789	.50	.80	1.00	2.00	15.00	25.00
	1949	13,037,090	.15	.15	.20	.60	4.00	7.00
	1950	11,970,521	.15	.15	.20	.60	4.00	7.00
	CHROMIUM-PLATED STEEL							
42a	1951 low relief*	4,313,410	.15	.20	.50	1.00	2.50	4.50
	1951 high relief* *	Inc. Ab.	200.00	325.00	500.00	750.00	1150.	2000.
	1952	10,891,148	.15	.20	.50	1.00	3.00	5.00

***NOTE:** A in GRATIA points between denticles.
*** *NOTE:** A in GRATIA points to a denticle.

KM#	Date	Mintage	VG-8	F-12	VF-20	XF-40	MS-60	MS-63
	Elizabeth II Effigy - 12 Sided Coinage							
50	1953 w/o strap	16,635,552	.15	.25	.40	.75	3.00	4.50
	1953 w/strap	Inc.Ab.	.15	.25	.45	1.00	3.50	7.00
	1954	6,998,662	.15	.25	.50	1.00	4.50	7.50
	NICKEL							
50a	1955	5,355,028	.15	.20	.25	.75	3.00	4.50
	1956	9,399,854	—	.20	.30	.45	1.75	3.00
	1957	7,387,703	—	—	.25	.30	1.25	2.75
	1958	7,607,521	—	—	.25	.30	1.25	2.75
	1959	11,552,523	—	—	—	.20	.65	1.25
	1960	37,157,433	—	—	—	.15	.25	.75
	1961	47,889,051	—	—	—	—	.20	.40
	1962	46,307,305	—	—	—	—	.20	.40
	Round Coinage							
57	1963	43,970,320	—	—	—	—	.20	.40
	1964	78,075,068	—	—	—	—	.20	.40
	1964 XWL	—	6.00	8.00	10.00	12.50	22.00	35.00
	New Elizabeth II Effigy							
60.1	1965	84,876,018	—	—	—	—	.20	.30
	1966	27,976,648	—	—	—	—	.20	.30
	1968	101,930,379	—	—	—	—	.20	.30
	1969	27,830,229	—	—	—	—	.20	.30
	1970	5,726,010	—	—	—	.25	.55	.75
	1971	27,312,609	—	—	—	—	.20	.30
	1972	62,417,387	—	—	—	—	.20	.30
	1973	53,507,435	—	—	—	—	.20	.30
	1974	94,704,645	—	—	—	—	.20	.30
	1975	138,882,000	—	—	—	—	.20	.30
	1976	55,140,213	—	—	—	—	.20	.30
	1977	89,120,791	—	—	—	—	.20	.30
	1978	137,079,273	—	—	—	—	.20	.30
	Smaller bust							
60.2	1979	186,295,825	—	—	—	—	.20	.30
	1980	134,878,000	—	—	—	—	.20	.30
	1981	99,107,900	—	—	—	—	.20	.30
	1981	199,000	—	—	—	—	Proof	1.00
	COPPER-NICKEL							
60.2a	1982	64,924,400	—	—	—	—	.20	.30
	1982	180,908	—	—	—	—	Proof	1.00
	1983	72,596,000	—	—	—	—	.20	.30
	1983	168,000	—	—	—	—	Proof	1.00
	1984	84,088,000	—	—	—	—	.20	.30
	1984	161,602	—	—	—	—	Proof	1.00
	1985	126,618,000	—	—	—	—	.20	.30
	1985	157,037	—	—	—	—	Proof	1.00
	1986	156,104,000	—	—	—	—	.20	.30
	1986	175,745	—	—	—	—	Proof	1.00
	1987	106,299,000	—	—	—	—	.10	.15
	1987	179,004	—	—	—	—	Proof	1.00
	1988	75,025,000	—	—	—	—	.10	.15
	1988	175,259	—	—	—	—	Proof	1.00
	1989	141,570,538	—	—	—	—	.10	.15
	1989	170,928	—	—	—	—	Proof	1.00
	New Elizabeth II Effigy							
182	1990	42,537,000	—	—	—	—	.10	.15
	1990	140,649	—	—	—	—	Proof	1.00
	1991	10,931,000	—	—	—	—	.10	.35
	1991	—	—	—	—	—	Proof	1.00
	1993	—	—	—	—	—	.10	.15
	1993	—	—	—	—	—	Proof	1.00

COMMEMORATIVE FIVE CENTS

KM#	Date	Mintage	VG-8	F-12	VF-20	XF-40	MS-60	MS-63
40	1943 Victory, Tombac (Brass)							
		24,760,256	.15	.25	.35	1.00	2.00	6.00

KM#	Date	Mintage	VG-8	F-12	VF-20	XF-40	MS-60	MS-63
	CHROMIUM-PLATED STEEL							
40a	1944	11,532,784	.15	.25	.50	1.00	2.00	4.50
	1945	18,893,216,	.15	.25	.50	1.00	2.00	4.50
48	1951 Nickel Bicentennial, Nickel							
		9,028,507	.15	.20	.25	.50	1.75	3.00

KM#	Date	Mintage	VG-8	F-12	VF-20	XF-40	MS-60	MS-63
66	1967 Confederation Centennial							
		36,876,574	—	—	—	—	.20	.30
205	1992 Confederation 125							
		—	—	—	—	—	.10	.15
		—	—	—	—	—	Proof	1.00

TEN CENTS

1858-1901

1902-1910

2.3240 g, .925 SILVER, .0691 oz ASW

KM#	Date	Mintage	VG-8	F-12	VF-20	XF-40	MS-60	MS-63
3	1858/5	Inc. Below	—	—	—	—	Rare	—
	1858	1,250,000	12.00	22.00	40.00	70.00	275.00	700.00
	1870 narrow 0	1,600,000	10.00	18.00	40.00	75.00	285.00	725.00
	1870 wide 0	Inc. Ab.	15.00	25.00	50.00	100.00	350.00	775.00
	1871	800,000	13.50	25.00	45.00	100.00	325.00	800.00
	1871H	1,870,000	16.00	27.00	60.00	120.00	450.00	900.00
	1872H	1,000,000	50.00	90.00	165.00	350.00	950.00	2400.
	1874H	600,000	6.00	12.00	25.00	60.00	275.00	750.00
	1875H	1,000,000	175.00	300.00	500.00	1050.	3000.	7000.
	1880H	1,500,000	5.00	10.00	20.00	50.00	250.00	600.00
	1881H	950,000	7.00	15.00	32.50	75.00	275.00	700.00
	1882H	1,000,000	6.00	12.00	25.00	60.00	300.00	700.00
	1883H	300,000	20.00	40.00	75.00	165.00	800.00	1800.
	1884	150,000	130.00	250.00	500.00	1250.	3750.	8000.
	1885	400,000	12.00	25.00	65.00	145.00	900.00	2500.
	1886 sm. 6	800,000	9.00	18.00	40.00	80.00	375.00	900.00
	1886 lg. 6	Inc. Ab.	12.00	22.00	55.00	125.00	475.00	1000.
	1887	350,000	17.00	35.00	90.00	200.00	1150.	2750.
	1888	500,000	5.00	9.00	22.00	50.00	235.00	550.00
	1889	600,000	350.00	600.00	1300.	2000.	5000.	10,000.
	1890H	450,000	9.00	17.50	40.00	85.00	325.00	725.00
	1891 21 leaves	800,000	10.00	20.00	45.00	90.00	375.00	825.00
	1891 22 leaves	Inc. Ab.	9.00	17.50	40.00	90.00	350.00	825.00
	1892/1	520,000	85.00	150.00	220.00	—	—	—
	1892	Inc. Ab.	7.00	15.00	30.00	70.00	350.00	800.00
	1893 flat top 3	500,000	12.00	25.00	60.00	120.00	450.00	1250.
	1893 rd. top 3	Inc. Ab.	325.00	750.00	1450.	2850.	6000.	12,500.
	1894	500,000	9.00	20.00	45.00	90.00	350.00	1000.
	1896	650,000	5.00	10.00	20.00	50.00	250.00	550.00
	1898	720,000	5.00	12.00	22.00	55.00	275.00	600.00
	1899 sm. 9's	1,200,000	4.00	8.00	20.00	45.00	210.00	575.00
	1899 lg. 9's	Inc. Ab.	7.00	15.00	30.00	75.00	300.00	850.00
	1900	1,100,000	2.50	5.00	14.00	30.00	150.00	370.00
	1901	1,200,000	2.50	5.00	14.00	30.00	150.00	370.00
10	1902	720,000	3.00	7.00	15.00	40.00	160.00	450.00
	1902H	1,100,000	2.00	4.25	10.00	25.00	100.00	235.00
	1903	500,000	7.00	15.00	40.00	100.00	700.00	1850.
	1903H	1,320,000	2.25	5.00	12.00	40.00	185.00	450.00
	1904	1,000,000	4.00	8.00	18.00	60.00	240.00	500.00
	1905	1,000,000	3.00	6.00	15.00	50.00	275.00	575.00
	1906	1,700,000	1.75	4.00	10.00	32.50	175.00	400.00
	1907	2,620,000	1.75	4.00	9.00	27.50	150.00	350.00
	1908	776,666	4.50	9.00	25.00	60.00	225.00	425.00
	1909 Victorian leaves, similar to 1902-1908 coinage							
		1,697,200	3.00	7.00	15.00	40.00	275.00	650.00
	1909 broad leaves similar to 1910-1912 coinage							
		Inc. Ab.	4.50	9.00	25.00	65.00	375.00	750.00
	1910	4,468,331	1.75	4.00	8.00	20.00	125.00	275.00
17	1911	2,737,584	4.00	9.00	15.00	44.00	140.00	325.00

Small leaves

Broad leaves

KM#	Date	Mintage	VG-8	F-12	VF-20	XF-40	MS-60	MS-63
23	1912	3,235,557	1.75	2.50	6.00	18.00	150.00	375.00
	1913 sm. leaves	3,613,937	1.50	2.25	5.00	15.00	145.00	375.00
	1913 lg. leaves	Inc. Ab.	90.00	160.00	285.00	600.00	3250.	6500.
	1914	2,549,811	1.50	2.50	5.50	16.00	150.00	400.00
	1915	688,057	4.00	9.00	22.00	80.00	400.00	750.00
	1916	4,218,114	1.00	1.50	4.00	9.00	90.00	225.00
	1917	5,011,988	.75	1.25	3.00	7.00	60.00	125.00
	1918	5,133,602	.75	1.25	3.00	7.00	50.00	90.00
	1919	7,877,722	.75	1.25	3.00	7.00	50.00	90.00

KM#	Date	Mintage	VG-8	F-12	VF-20	XF-40	MS-60	MS-63
		2.3328 g, .800 SILVER, .0600 oz ASW						
23a	1920	6,305,345	.75	1.25	3.00	6.50	50.00	100.00
	1921	2,469,562	1.25	2.00	4.00	10.00	60.00	155.00
	1928	2,458,602	1.00	1.75	4.00	9.00	55.00	140.00
	1929	3,253,888	1.00	1.50	3.50	8.50	55.00	130.00
	1930	1,831,043	1.50	2.50	4.50	12.00	60.00	150.00
	1931	2,067,421	1.00	2.00	4.25	9.00	55.00	125.00
	1932	1,154,317	1.50	2.50	5.50	15.00	80.00	175.00
	1933	672,368	2.00	3.50	8.00	25.00	175.00	400.00
	1934	409,067	3.50	6.00	16.00	50.00	375.00	1250.
	1935	384,056	4.00	6.50	18.00	60.00	275.00	600.00
	1936	2,460,871	.60	1.25	3.00	7.00	40.00	80.00
	1936 dot on rev.	4 known	—	—	—		Specimen	—

Maple Leaf

KM#	Date	Mintage	VG-8	F-12	VF-20	XF-40	MS-60	MS-63
34	1937	2,500,095	1.00	1.50	3.00	5.00	14.00	24.00
	1938	4,197,323	1.25	2.50	3.50	8.00	40.00	80.00
	1939	5,501,748	1.00	1.75	2.50	8.00	40.00	80.00
	1940	16,526,470	BV	1.00	1.75	4.00	15.00	30.00
	1941	8,716,386	BV	1.25	3.00	7.00	40.00	85.00
	1942	10,214,011	BV	1.00	2.00	4.00	30.00	45.00
	1943	21,143,229	BV	1.00	2.00	4.00	14.00	30.00
	1944	9,383,582	BV	1.00	2.00	5.00	25.00	45.00
	1945	10,979,570	BV	1.00	2.00	4.00	15.00	25.00
	1946	6,300,066	BV	1.00	2.25	5.00	25.00	45.00
	1947	4,431,926	BV	1.50	3.00	7.00	35.00	50.00
	1947 maple leaf	9,638,793	BV	1.00	2.00	3.50	10.00	18.00
		Modified Obverse Legend						
43	1948	422,741	2.50	4.50	8.00	17.00	45.00	90.00
	1949	11,336,172	—	BV	1.50	2.50	8.00	14.00
	1950	17,823,075	—	BV	1.25	2.00	7.00	12.00
	1951	15,079,265	—	BV	1.00	2.00	6.00	9.00
	1952	10,474,455	—	BV	1.00	2.00	6.00	9.00
		Elizabeth II Effigy						
51	1953 w/o straps	17,706,395	—	BV	1.00	1.50	3.50	6.00
	1953 w/straps	Inc. Ab.	—	BV	1.00	1.75	5.00	6.50
	1954	4,493,150	—	BV	1.00	1.75	7.00	12.00
	1955	12,237,294	—	BV	.75	1.00	3.50	5.00
	1956	16,732,844	—	BV	.75	1.00	2.75	4.00
	1956 dot below date	Inc. Ab.	2.00	3.00	5.00	6.00	12.00	16.00
	1957	16,110,229	—	—	BV	.60	1.50	2.00
	1958	10,621,236	—	—	BV	.60	1.50	2.00
	1959	19,691,433	—	—	BV	.50	1.25	2.00
	1960	45,446,835	—	—	—	BV	.75	1.00
	1961	26,850,859	—	—	—	BV	.75	1.00
	1962	41,864,335	—	—	—	BV	.75	1.00
	1963	41,916,208	—	—	—	BV	.75	1.00
	1964	49,518,549	—	—	—	BV	.75	1.00
		New Elizabeth II Effigy						
61	1965	56,965,392	—	—	—	BV	.75	1.00
	1966	34,567,898	—	—	—	BV	.75	1.00

OTTAWA — Reeding — PHILADELPHIA

KM#	Date	Mintage	VG-8	F-12	VF-20	XF-40	MS-60	MS-63
72	1968 Ottawa, .500 Silver	70,460,000	—	—	—	BV	.60	.75
72a	1968 Ottawa, Nickel	87,412,930	—	—	—	.15	.25	.40
73	1968 Philadelphia, Nickel	85,170,000	—	—	—	.15	.25	.40
	1969 lg.date, lg.ship	4 known	—	—	6500.	—	—	—

Redesigned Smaller Ship

KM#	Date	Mintage	VG-8	F-12	VF-20	XF-40	MS-60	MS-63
77.1	1969	55,833,929	—	—	—	.15	.25	.40
	1970	5,249,296	—	—	—	.25	.65	.95
	1971	41,016,968	—	—	—	.15	.25	.40
	1972	60,169,387	—	—	—	.15	.25	.40
	1973	167,715,435	—	—	—	.15	.25	.40
	1974	201,566,565	—	—	—	.15	.25	.40
	1975	207,680,000	—	—	—	.15	.25	.40
	1976	95,018,533	—	—	—	.15	.25	.40
	1977	128,452,206	—	—	—	.15	.25	.40
	1978	170,366,431	—	—	—	.15	.25	.40
		Smaller bust						
77.2	1979	237,321,321	—	—	—	.15	.25	.40
	1980	170,111,533	—	—	—	.15	.25	.40
	1981	123,912,900	—	—	—	.15	.25	.40
	1981	199,000	—	—	—	—	Proof	1.50
	1982	93,475,000	—	—	—	.15	.25	.40
	1982	180,908	—	—	—	—	Proof	1.50
	1983	111,065,000	—	—	—	.15	.25	.40
	1983	168,000	—	—	—	—	Proof	1.50
	1984	121,690,000	—	—	—	.15	.25	.40
	1984	161,602	—	—	—	—	Proof	1.50
	1985	143,025,000	—	—	—	.15	.25	.40
	1985	157,037	—	—	—	—	Proof	1.50
	1986	168,620,000	—	—	—	.15	.25	.40
	1986	175,745	—	—	—	—	Proof	1.50
	1987	147,309,000	—	—	—	.15	.25	.40
	1987	179,004	—	—	—	—	Proof	1.50
	1988	162,998,558	—	—	—	.15	.25	.40

KM#	Date	Mintage	VG-8	F-12	VF-20	XF-40	MS-60	MS-63
	1988	175,259	—	—	—	—	Proof	1.50
	1989	199,104,414	—	—	—	.15	.25	.40
	1989	170,528	—	—	—	—	Proof	1.50
		New Elizabeth II Effigy						
183	1990	75,023,000	—	—	—	.15	.25	.40
	1990	140,649	—	—	—	—	Proof	1.50
	1991	46,693,000	—	—	—	.15	.25	.40
	1991	—	—	—	—	—	Proof	1.50
	1993	—	—	—	—	.15	.25	.40
	1993	—	—	—	—	—	Proof	1.50

COMMEMORATIVE TEN CENTS

KM#	Date	Mintage	VG-8	F-12	VF-20	XF-40	MS-60	MS-63
67	1967 Confederation Centennial, .800 Silver	62,998,215	—	—	—	BV	.75	1.00
67a	1967 Confederation Centennial, .500 Silver	Inc. Ab.	—	—	—	BV	.75	1.00
206	1992 Confederation 125	—	—	—	—	.15	.25	.40
		—	—	—	—	—	Proof	1.50

TWENTY CENTS

4.6480 g, .925 SILVER, .1382 oz ASW

KM#	Date	Mintage	VG-8	F-12	VF-20	XF-40	MS-60	MS-63
4	1858	750,000	45.00	65.00	100.00	175.00	800.00	1600.

TWENTY-FIVE CENTS

1870-1901

1902-1936

5.8100 g, .925 SILVER, .1728 oz ASW

KM#	Date	Mintage	VG-8	F-12	VF-20	XF-40	MS-60	MS-63
5	1870	900,000	9.00	16.00	40.00	90.00	550.00	1250.
	1871	400,000	12.00	20.00	60.00	150.00	600.00	1750.
	1871H	748,000	14.00	22.00	65.00	170.00	600.00	1450.
	1872H	2,240,000	6.00	8.00	22.50	65.00	325.00	850.00
	1874H	1,600,000	6.00	8.00	22.50	65.00	350.00	900.00
	1875H	1,000,000	200.00	400.00	1000.	2000.	4750.	10,000.
	1880H narrow 0	400,000	27.50	55.00	150.00	300.00	850.00	2000.
5	1880H wide 0	Inc. Ab.	80.00	150.00	325.00	625.00	1800.	4000.
	1880H wide/narrow 0	Inc. Ab.	90.00	160.00	350.00	600.00	—	—
	1881H	820,000	10.00	20.00	45.00	115.00	550.00	1300.
	1882H	600,000	12.50	25.00	55.00	160.00	650.00	1450.
	1883H	960,000	9.00	15.00	37.50	110.00	650.00	1450.
	1885	192,000	70.00	130.00	300.00	600.00	2750.	5500.
	1886/3	540,000	10.00	20.00	60.00	175.00	900.00	2000.
	1886	Inc. Ab.	9.00	18.00	50.00	160.00	775.00	1750.
	1887	100,000	65.00	130.00	300.00	600.00	2750.	5500.
	1888	400,000	9.00	16.00	45.00	110.00	500.00	1100.
	1889	66,324	75.00	165.00	325.00	725.00	3200.	6500.
	1890H	200,000	15.00	25.00	65.00	165.00	900.00	2250.
	1891	120,000	40.00	75.00	175.00	350.00	1100.	2400.
	1892	510,000	8.00	15.00	40.00	120.00	500.00	1400.
	1893	100,000	65.00	110.00	250.00	475.00	1450.	3000.
	1894	220,000	12.50	25.00	60.00	170.00	725.00	1600.
	1899	415,580	5.00	8.00	22.50	70.00	400.00	900.00
	1900	1,320,000	4.00	7.00	20.00	60.00	325.00	750.00
	1901	640,000	4.00	7.00	20.00	60.00	325.00	750.00
11	1902	464,000	5.00	8.00	27.50	80.00	475.00	1350.
	1902H	800,000	3.00	5.00	20.00	50.00	200.00	450.00
	1903	846,150	4.00	7.00	25.00	75.00	400.00	950.00
	1904	400,000	8.00	20.00	65.00	200.00	1000.	2250.
	1905	800,000	5.00	10.00	35.00	115.00	850.00	2000.
	1906 lg. crown	1,237,843	3.50	6.50	20.00	65.00	300.00	950.00
	1906 sm. crown	Inc. Ab.	—	—	—	—	Rare	—
	1907	2,088,000	3.00	6.50	20.00	65.00	300.00	900.00
	1908	495,016	5.00	10.00	35.00	110.00	375.00	850.00
	1909	1,335,929	4.00	8.00	25.00	85.00	475.00	1250.
	1910	3,577,569	3.00	6.00	18.00	50.00	200.00	450.00
18	1911	1,721,341	7.00	16.00	30.00	75.00	375.00	750.00
24	1912	2,544,199	2.50	4.00	9.00	30.00	275.00	850.00
	1913	2,213,595	2.50	4.00	9.00	27.50	250.00	800.00
	1914	1,215,397	3.50	5.00	12.00	35.00	500.00	1250.
	1915	242,382	10.00	22.00	100.00	275.00	1800.	3750.

KM#	Date	Mintage	VG-8	F-12	VF-20	XF-40	MS-60	MS-63
	1916	1,462,566	2.00	4.00	9.00	20.00	200.00	500.00
	1917	3,365,644	1.75	3.50	9.00	18.00	100.00	175.00
	1918	4,175,649	1.75	3.50	9.00	18.00	70.00	175.00
	1919	5,852,262	1.75	3.50	9.00	18.00	70.00	175.00

5.8319 g, .800 SILVER, .1500 oz ASW

KM#	Date	Mintage	VG-8	F-12	VF-20	XF-40	MS-60	MS-63
24a	1920	1,975,278	1.75	2.75	9.00	22.00	120.00	400.00
	1921	597,337	9.00	20.00	65.00	160.00	900.00	2200.
	1927	468,096	20.00	35.00	80.00	200.00	900.00	1800.
	1928	2,114,178	2.00	3.00	8.00	22.00	100.00	300.00
	1929	2,690,562	1.75	2.75	7.50	20.00	100.00	300.00
	1930	968,748	2.00	3.50	10.00	25.00	175.00	475.00
	1931	537,815	2.00	3.50	10.00	25.00	225.00	600.00
	1932	537,994	2.25	4.00	12.00	30.00	190.00	475.00
	1933	421,282	3.50	6.50	16.50	40.00	180.00	400.00
	1934	384,350	4.00	8.00	22.00	60.00	250.00	425.00
	1935	537,772	3.50	7.00	17.50	42.00	200.00	450.00
	1936	972,094	2.00	3.00	9.00	22.00	90.00	200.00

KM#	Date	Mintage	VG-8	F-12	VF-20	XF-40	MS-60	MS-63
24a	1936 dot	153,322	25.00	60.00	135.00	275.00	900.00	2000.

Maple Leaf Variety

KM#	Date	Mintage	VG-8	F-12	VF-20	XF-40	MS-60	MS-63
35	1937	2,690,176	1.50	2.50	4.50	6.00	14.00	32.00
	1938	3,149,245	1.50	3.00	6.00	9.00	70.00	155.00
	1939	3,532,495	1.50	2.50	5.00	7.00	60.00	125.00
	1940	9,583,650	BV	1.75	3.50	5.00	13.00	30.00
	1941	6,654,672	BV	1.75	3.50	5.00	18.00	37.50
	1942	6,935,871	BV	1.75	3.50	5.00	18.00	37.50
	1943	13,559,575	BV	1.25	2.75	3.75	16.00	35.00
	1944	7,216,237	BV	1.25	2.75	4.00	30.00	70.00
	1945	5,296,495	BV	1.25	2.75	4.00	14.00	30.00
	1946	2,210,810	1.50	2.25	3.25	6.50	40.00	70.00
	1947	1,524,554	1.50	2.25	3.50	7.00	55.00	100.00
	1947 dot after 7	Inc. Ab.	30.00	50.00	70.00	125.00	300.00	600.00
	1947 maple leaf	4,393,938	BV	1.50	2.75	5.00	18.00	30.00

Modified Obverse Legend

KM#	Date	Mintage	VG-8	F-12	VF-20	XF-40	MS-60	MS-63
44	1948	2,564,424	1.50	2.25	3.25	6.00	50.00	120.00
	1949	7,988,830	—	BV	1.25	2.25	10.00	22.00
	1950	9,673,335	—	BV	1.25	2.25	9.00	17.50
	1951	8,290,719	—	BV	1.25	2.25	7.00	14.00
	1952	8,859,642	—	BV	1.25	2.25	7.00	14.00

Elizabeth II Effigy

KM#	Date	Mintage	VG-8	F-12	VF-20	XF-40	MS-60	MS-63
52	1953 NSS	10,546,769	—	BV	1.75	2.25	5.00	7.00
	1953 SS	Inc. Ab.	—	BV	1.75	2.25	8.00	14.00
	1954	2,318,891	1.75	2.50	3.50	7.00	25.00	35.00
52	1955	9,552,505	—	—	BV	1.50	4.00	7.00
	1956	11,269,353	—	—	BV	1.25	3.50	5.00
	1957	12,770,190	—	—	BV	1.00	2.25	4.00
	1958	9,336,910	—	—	BV	1.00	2.25	4.00
	1959	13,503,461	—	—	—	BV	2.00	3.00
	1960	22,835,327	—	—	—	BV	2.00	3.00
	1961	18,164,368	—	—	—	BV	2.00	3.00
	1962	29,559,266	—	—	—	BV	2.00	2.25
	1963	21,180,652	—	—	—	BV	1.75	2.25
	1964	36,479,343	—	—	—	BV	1.75	2.25

Machin Portrait

KM#	Date	Mintage	VG-8	F-12	VF-20	XF-40	MS-60	MS-63
62	1965	44,708,869	—	—	—	BV	1.75	2.25
	1966	25,626,315	—	—	—	BV	1.75	2.25

5.8319 g, .500 SILVER, .0937 oz ASW

KM#	Date	Mintage	VG-8	F-12	VF-20	XF-40	MS-60	MS-63
62a	1968	71,464,000	—	—	—	BV	1.50	2.25

NICKEL

KM#	Date	Mintage	VG-8	F-12	VF-20	XF-40	MS-60	MS-63
74.1	1968	88,686,931	—	—	—	.30	.50	.75
	1969	133,037,929	—	—	—	.30	.50	.75
	1970	10,302,010	—	—	—	.30	1.00	1.50
	1971	48,170,428	—	—	—	.30	.50	.75
	1972	43,743,387	—	—	—	.30	.50	.75
	1974	192,360,598	—	—	—	.30	.50	.75
	1975	141,148,000	—	—	—	.30	.50	.75
	1976	86,898,261	—	—	—	.30	.50	.75
	1977	99,634,555	—	—	—	.30	.50	.75
	1978	176,475,408	—	—	—	.30	.50	.75

Smaller bust

KM#	Date	Mintage	VG-8	F-12	VF-20	XF-40	MS-60	MS-63
74.2	1979	131,042,905	—	—	—	.30	.50	.75
	1980	76,178,000	—	—	—	.30	.50	.75
	1981	131,580,272	—	—	—	.30	.50	.75
	1981	199,000	—	—	—	—	Proof	2.00
	1982	171,926,000	—	—	—	.30	.50	.75
	1982	180,908	—	—	—	—	Proof	2.00
	1983	13,162,000	—	—	—	.30	.75	1.50
	1983	168,000	—	—	—	—	Proof	2.00
	1984	121,668,000	—	—	—	.30	.50	.75
	1984	161,602	—	—	—	—	Proof	2.00
	1985	158,734,000	—	—	—	.30	.50	.75
	1985	157,037	—	—	—	—	Proof	2.00
	1986	132,220,000	—	—	—	.30	.50	.75
	1986	175,745	—	—	—	—	Proof	2.00
	1987	53,408,000	—	—	—	.30	.75	1.50
	1987	179,004	—	—	—	—	Proof	2.00
	1988	80,368,473	—	—	—	.30	.75	1.50
	1988	175,259	—	—	—	—	Proof	2.00
	1989	119,796,307	—	—	—	.30	.50	.75
	1989	170,928	—	—	—	—	Proof	2.00

New Elizabeth II Effigy

KM#	Date	Mintage	VG-8	F-12	VF-20	XF-40	MS-60	MS-63
184	1990	31,258,000	—	—	—	.30	.75	1.50
	1990	140,649	—	—	—	—	Proof	2.00
	1991	459,000	—	—	2.00	5.00	9.00	12.00
	1991	—	—	—	—	—	Proof	15.00
	1993	—	—	—	—	.30	.75	1.50
	1993	—	—	—	—	—	Proof	2.00

COMMEMORATIVE TWENTY-FIVE CENTS

KM#	Date	Mintage	VG-8	F-12	VF-20	XF-40	MS-60	MS-63
68	1967 Confederation Centennial, .800 Silver	48,855,500	—	—	—	BV	1.50	2.25
68a	1967 Confederation Centennial, .500 Silver	Inc. Ab.	—	—	—	BV	1.50	2.25
81.1	1973 RCMP Centennial, 120 beads, Nickel	134,958,587	—	—	—	.30	.50	.75
81.2	1973 RCMP Centennial, 132 beads, Nickel	Inc. Ab.	15.00	25.00	35.00	55.00	85.00	120.
207	1992 Confederation 125, Nickel	—	—	—	—	—	—	1.00
		—	—	—	—	—	Proof	2.50

125th Anniversary of Confederation

KM#	Date	Mintage	VG-8	F-12	VF-20	XF-40	MS-60	MS-63
203	1992 New Brunswick, Nickel	10,000,000	—	—	—	—	—	.75
203a	1992 New Brunswick, .925 Silver	—	—	—	—	—	Proof	11.50
212	1992 North West Territories, Nickel	10,000,000	—	—	—	—	—	.75
212a	1992 North West Territories, .925 Silver	—	—	—	—	—	Proof	11.50

KM#	Date	Mintage	VG-8	F-12	VF-20	XF-40	MS-60	MS-63
213	1992 Newfoundland, Nickel	10,000,000	—	—	—	—	—	.75
213a	1992 Newfoundland, .925 Silver	—	—	—	—	—	Proof	11.50
214	1992 Manitoba, Nickel	10,000,000	—	—	—	—	—	.75
214a	1992 Manitoba, .925 Silver	—	—	—	—	—	Proof	10.00
220	1992 Yukon, Nickel	10,000,000	—	—	—	—	—	.75
220a	1992 Yukon, .925 Silver	—	—	—	—	—	Proof	11.50

KM#	Date	Mintage	VG-8	F-12	VF-20	XF-40	MS-60	MS-63
221	1992 Alberta, Nickel	10,000,000	—	—	—	—	—	.75
221a	1992 Alberta, .925 Silver	—	—	—	—	—	Proof	11.50
222	1992 Prince Edward Island, Nickel	10,000,000	—	—	—	—	—	.75
222a	1992 Prince Edward Island, .925 Silver	—	—	—	—	—	Proof	11.50
223	1992 Ontario, Nickel	10,000,000	—	—	—	—	—	.75
223a	1992 Ontario, .925 Silver	—	—	—	—	—	Proof	11.50

KM#	Date	Mintage	VG-8	F-12	VF-20	XF-40	MS-60	MS-63
231	1992 Nova Scotia, Nickel	—	—	—	—	—	—	.75
231a	1992 Nova Scotia, .925 Silver	—	—	—	—	—	Proof	11.50
232	1992 British Columbia, Nickel	—	—	—	—	—	—	.75
232a	1992 British Columbia, .925 Silver	—	—	—	—	—	Proof	11.50

KM#	Date	Mintage	VG-8	F-12	VF-20	XF-40	MS-60	MS-63
233	1992 Saskatchewan, Nickel	—	—	—	—	—	—	.75
233a	1992 Saskatchewan, .925 Silver	—	—	—	—	—	Proof	11.50
234	1992 Quebec, Nickel	—	—	—	—	—	—	.75
234a	1992 Quebec, .925 Silver	—	—	—	—	—	Proof	11.50

FIFTY CENTS

1870-1901 1902-1936

11.6200 g, .925 SILVER, .3456 oz ASW

KM#	Date	Mintage	VG-8	F-12	VF-20	XF-40	MS-60	MS-63
6	1870	450,000	500.00	1000.	2000.	3300.	10,000.	17,000.
	1870 LCW	Inc. Ab.	40.00	65.00	140.00	325.00	3500.	6750.
	1871	200,000	45.00	95.00	220.00	500.00	4500.	7500.
	1871H	45,000	65.00	145.00	300.00	725.00	5750.	9500.
	1872H	80,000	30.00	65.00	170.00	275.00	4000.	7500.
	1872H inverted A for V in VICTORIA	Inc. Ab.	85.00	175.00	375.00	800.00	—	—
	1881H	150,000	40.00	80.00	175.00	300.00	3750.	7250.
	1888	60,000	90.00	200.00	400.00	900.00	5750.	10,000.
	1890H	20,000	600.00	1100.	2000.	3500.	12,000.	22,000.
	1892	151,000	40.00	90.00	200.00	400.00	5000.	9500.
	1894	29,036	200.00	400.00	950.00	1800.	8500.	16,000.
	1898	100 000	40.00	90.00	200.00	400.00	4500.	9000.
	1899	50,000	80.00	165.00	350.00	900.00	6000.	12,500.
	1900	118,000	30.00	55.00	150.00	250.00	4500.	8000.
	1901	80,000	35.00	60.00	150.00	250.00	4500.	7750.

Victorian Leaves

Edwardian Leaves

KM#	Date	Mintage	VG-8	F-12	VF-20	XF-40	MS-60	MS-63
12	1902	120,000	10.00	22.00	70.00	150.00	1000.	3000.
	1903H	140,000	18.00	35.00	110.00	225.00	1400.	3900.
	1904	60,000	70.00	140.00	275.00	600.00	3100.	7000.
	1905	40,000	90.00	200.00	400.00	900.00	5500.	11,000.
	1906	350,000	10.00	22.00	65.00	160.00	1100.	3500.
	1907	300,000	10.00	20.00	55.00	140.00	1100.	3500.
	1908	128,119	20.00	45.00	125.00	300.00	1200.	2750.
	1909	302,118	12.50	35.00	90.00	250.00	1750.	3600.
	1910 Victorian lvs.	649,521	9.00	18.00	50.00	125.00	1000.	3000.
	1910 Edwardian lvs.	Inc. Ab.	9.00	18.00	50.00	125.00	1000.	3000.
	Modified Obverse Legend							
19	1911	209,972	9.00	55.00	225.00	475.00	1300.	2900.
	Modified Obverse Legend							
25	1912	285,867	4.50	16.00	70.00	175.00	1200.	2500.
	1913	265,889	5.00	16.00	70.00	175.00	1400.	3200.
	1914	160,128	15.00	45.00	160.00	400.00	2000.	4250.
	1916	459,070	3.00	14.00	50.00	125.00	750.00	1800.
	1917	752,213	3.00	14.00	35.00	90.00	500.00	1400.
	1918	754,989	3.00	8.00	22.00	70.00	400.00	1000.
	1919	1,113,429	3.00	8.00	22.00	70.00	400.00	1000.

11.6638 g, .800 SILVER, .3000 oz ASW

KM#	Date	Mintage	VG-8	F-12	VF-20	XF-40	MS-60	MS-63
25a	1920	584,691	5.00	10.00	35.00	125.00	600.00	1400.
	1921	75 to 100 pcs.known	10,000.	13,000.	18,000.	24,000.	37,500.	63,800.

NOTE: Bowers and Merena Victoria Sale 9-89 MS-65 realized $110,000.

KM#	Date	Mintage	VG-8	F-12	VF-20	XF-40	MS-60	MS-63
25a	1929	228,328	3.00	10.00	35.00	110.00	550.00	1400.
	1931	57,581	7.00	20.00	60.00	175.00	1200.	2400.
	1932	19,213	30.00	90.00	200.00	475.00	2000.	4000.
	1934	39,539	10.00	25.00	75.00	200.00	900.00	1800.
	1936	38,550	9.00	20.00	65.00	175.00	600.00	1200.

1937-1958 1959-1964 1965-1966

KM#	Date	Mintage	VG-8	F-12	VF-20	XF-40	MS-60	MS-63
36	1937	192,016	2.50	4.00	7.00	10.00	30.00	70.00
	1938	192,018	4.00	8.00	15.00	30.00	140.00	350.00
	1939	287,976	3.00	5.00	8.00	18.00	100.00	275.00
	1940	1,996,566	BV	3.00	3.50	6.00	25.00	70.00
	1941	1,714,874	BV	2.25	3.50	6.00	25.00	70.00
	1942	1,974,164	BV	2.25	3.50	6.00	25.00	70.00
	1943	3,109,583	BV	2.25	3.50	6.00	25.00	70.00
	1944	2,460,205	BV	2.25	3.50	6.00	25.00	70.00
	1945	1,959,528	BV	2.25	3.50	6.00	25.00	70.00
	1946	950,235	BV	5.00	6.50	9.00	75.00	120.00
36	1946 hoof in 6	Inc. Ab.	15.00	22.50	40.00	110.00	900.00	1750.
	1947 straight 7	424,885	3.00	4.00	6.00	14.00	90.00	175.00
	1947 curved 7	Inc. Ab.	2.00	3.50	7.00	14.00	90.00	190.00
	1947ML straight 7	38,433	12.00	16.00	30.00	50.00	150.00	300.00
	1947ML curved 7	Inc. Ab.	750.00	1250.	1700.	2000.	3200.	4750.
	Modified Obverse Legend							
45	1948	37,784	35.00	45.00	60.00	90.00	180.00	275.00
	1949	858,991	2.25	3.00	6.50	10.00	40.00	100.00
	1949 hoof over 9	Inc. Ab.	8.00	12.50	30.00	65.00	350.00	700.00
	1950	2,384,179	3.00	6.00	9.00	20.00	175.00	300.00
	1950 lines in 0	Inc. Ab.	BV	2.50	3.00	4.00	12.00	20.00
	1951	2,421,730	BV	2.00	2.50	3.75	8.00	18.00
	1952	2,596,465	BV	2.50	3.00	3.75	8.00	18.00
	Elizabeth II Effigy							
53	1953 sm. date	1,630,429	BV	2.50	3.00	3.50	8.00	14.00
	1953 lg.dt,straps	Inc. Ab.	BV	2.50	3.50	6.00	24.00	35.00
	1953 lg.dt,w/o straps	I.A.	3.00	5.00	6.00	14.00	90.00	150.00
	1954	506,305	2.25	3.25	4.75	7.00	25.00	35.00
	1955	753,511	BV	3.00	4.00	5.00	14.00	24.00
	1956	1,379,499	—	BV	2.00	3.50	6.00	10.00
	1957	2,171,689	—	—	BV	2.00	4.00	7.00
	1958	2,957,266	—	—	BV	2.00	2.75	6.00
56	1959	3,095,535	—	—	BV	2.00	3.00	5.00
	1960	3,488,897	—	—	—	BV	2.50	3.50
	1961	3,584,417	—	—	—	BV	2.25	3.25
	1962	5,208,030	—	—	—	BV	2.25	3.25
	1963	8,348,871	—	—	—	BV	2.25	3.25
	1964	9,377,676	—	—	—	BV	2.25	3.25
	New Elizabeth II Effigy							
63	1965	12,629,974	—	—	—	BV	2.25	3.25
	1966	7,920,496	—	—	—	BV	2.25	3.25

1968-76 1977 1978-

NICKEL

KM#	Date	Mintage	VG-8	F-12	VF-20	XF-40	MS-60	MS-63
75.1	1968	3,966,932	—	—	—	.50	.65	1.00
	1969	7,113,929	—	—	—	.50	.65	1.00
	1970	2,429,526	—	—	—	.50	.65	1.00
	1971	2,166,444	—	—	—	.50	.65	1.00
	1972	2,515,632	—	—	—	.50	.65	1.00

KM#	Date	Mintage	VG-8	F-12	VF-20	XF-40	MS-60	MS-63
	1973	2,546,096	—	—	—	.50	.65	1.00
	1974	3,436,650	—	—	—	.50	.65	1.00
	1975	3,710,000	—	—	—	.50	.65	1.00
	1976	2,940,719	—	—	—	.50	.65	1.00
	Smaller bust							
75.2	1977	709,839	—	—	.50	.75	1.50	2.00
75.3	1978 square jewels	3,341,892	—	—	—	.50	.75	1.00
	1978 round jewels	Inc. Ab.	—	—	.50	2.50	3.00	4.00
	1979	3,425,000	—	—	—	.50	.65	1.00
	1980	1,574,000	—	—	—	.50	.65	1.00
	1981	2,690,272	—	—	—	.50	.65	1.00
	1981	199,000	—	—	—	—	Proof	3.00
	1982 small beads	2,236,674	—	—	—	.50	.65	1.00
	1982 small beads	180,908	—	—	—	—	Proof	3.00
	1982 large beads	Inc. Ab.	—	—	—	.50	.65	1.00
	1983	1,177,000	—	—	—	.50	.65	1.00
	1983	168,000	—	—	—	—	Proof	3.00
	1984	1,502,989	—	—	—	.50	.65	1.00
	1984	161,602	—	—	—	—	Proof	3.00
	1985	2,188,374	—	—	—	.50	.65	1.00
	1985	157,037	—	—	—	—	Proof	3.00
	1986	781,400	—	—	—	.50	.85	1.25
	1986	175,745	—	—	—	—	Proof	3.00
	1987	373,000	—	—	—	.50	.85	1.25
	1987	179,004	—	—	—	—	Proof	3.00
	1988	220,000	—	—	—	.50	.85	1.25
	1988	175,259	—	—	—	—	Proof	3.00
	1989	266,419	—	—	—	.50	.85	1.25
	1989	170,928	—	—	—	—	Proof	3.00
	New Elizabeth II Effigy							
185	1990	207,000	—	—	—	.50	1.25	2.50
	1990	140,649	—	—	—	—	Proof	3.00
	1991	490,000	—	—	—	.50	1.00	1.75
	1991	—	—	—	—	—	Proof	3.00
	1993	—	—	—	—	.50	1.00	1.75
	1993	—	—	—	—	—	Proof	3.00

COMMEMORATIVE FIFTY CENTS

KM#	Date	Mintage	VG-8	F-12	VF-20	XF-40	MS-60	MS-63
69	1967 Confederation Centennial, .800 Silver	4,211,392	—	—	—	BV	3.00	4.00
208	1992 Confederation 125, Nickel	—	—	—	—	.50	.85	1.75
		—	—	—	—	—	Proof	3.00

VOYAGEUR DOLLARS

23.3276 g, .800 SILVER, .6000 oz ASW

KM#	Date	Mintage	F-12	VF-20	XF-40	AU-50	MS-60	MS-63
31	1936	339,600	10.00	15.00	20.00	27.50	50.00	80.00

Pointed 7 Blunt 7 Maple Leaf (blunt 7 only)

KM#	Date	Mintage	F-12	VF-20	XF-40	AU-50	MS-60	MS-63
37	1937	207,406	10.00	12.00	14.00	17.50	35.00	75.00
	1937	1,295	—	—	—	Proof	—	800.00
	1937	I.A.	—			Matte Proof	—	400.00
	1938	90,304	20.00	30.00	40.00	50.00	85.00	250.00
	1945	38,391	65.00	110.00	135.00	160.00	225.00	550.00
	1945	—	—	—	—		Specimen	2750.
	1946	93,055	12.50	20.00	28.00	35.00	80.00	270.00
	1947 pointed 7	Inc. Bl.	60.00	90.00	120.00	175.00	350.00	1000.
	1947 blunt 7	65,595	30.00	50.00	65.00	80.00	120.00	275.00
	1947 maple leaf	21,135	100.00	130.00	160.00	200.00	275.00	600.00
46	1948	18,780	425.00	525.00	675.00	750.00	900.	1250.
	1950 w/4 water lines	261,002	5.00	6.00	8.00	12.50	16.50	35.00
	1950 w/4 water lines, (1 known)						Matte Proof	—
	1950 Arnprior w/1-1/2 w.l.	I.A.	8.00	10.00	15.00	25.00	45.00	125.00
	1951 w/4 water lines	416,395	5.00	7.00	8.00	9.00	12.50	30.00
	1951 w/4 water lines	—	—	—	—	—	Proof	400.00
	1951 Arnprior w/1-1/2 w.l.	I.A.	22.00	35.00	45.00	70.00	120.00	350.00

KM#	Date	Mintage	F-12	VF-20	XF-40	AU-50	MS-60	MS-63
	1952 w/4 water lines	406,148	5.00	6.00	7.00	8.00	12.00	30.00
	1952 Arnprior	I.A.	35.00	55.00	70.00	120.00	175.00	375.00
	1952 Arnprior	—	—	—	—	—	Proof	Rare
	1952 w/o water lines	I.A.	6.00	7.00	8.00	10.00	13.50	40.00

KM#	Date	Mintage	VF-20	XF-40	AU-50	MS-60	MS-63
54	1953 w/o strap, wire rim	1,074,578	4.00	5.00	6.00	7.00	18.00
	1953 w/strap, flat rim	Inc. Ab.	4.00	5.00	6.00	7.00	20.00
	1954	246,606	5.00	6.00	9.00	16.00	35.00
	1955 w/4 water lines	268,105	5.00	6.00	8.00	14.00	30.00
	1955 Arnprior w/1-1/2 w.l.*	I.A.	70.00	90.00	100.00	125.00	200.00
	1956	209,092	10.00	12.00	14.00	18.00	45.00
	1957 w/4 water lines	496,389	BV	6.00	8.00	10.00	20.00
	1957 w/1 water line	I.A.	7.50	10.00	15.00	20.00	30.00
	1959	1,443,502	—	BV	5.00	6.00	8.00
	1960	1,420,486	—	BV	6.00	7.00	8.00
	1961	1,262,231	—	BV	6.00	7.00	8.00
	1962	1,884,789	—	BV	6.00	7.00	8.00
	1963	4,179,981	—	BV	6.00	7.00	8.00

***NOTE:** All genuine circulation strike 1955 Arnprior dollars have a die break running along the top of TI in the word GRATIA on the obverse.

Small Beads

Medium Beads

Large Beads

New Elizabeth II Effigy

KM#	Date	Mintage	VF-20	XF-40	AU-50	MS-60	MS-63
64.1	1965 sm. beads, pointed 5	10,768,569	—	BV	6.00	7.00	8.00
	1965 sm. beads, blunt 5	Inc. Ab.	—	BV	6.00	7.00	8.00
	1965 lg. beads, blunt 5	Inc. Ab.	—	BV	6.00	7.00	8.00
	1965 lg. beads, pointed 5	Inc. Ab.	BV	4.00	4.25	5.00	8.00
	1965 med. beads, pointed 5	Inc. Ab.	4.00	6.00	7.00	10.00	25.00
	1966 lg. beads	9,912,178	—	BV	6.00	7.00	8.00
	1966 sm. beads	*485 pcs.	—	600.	1000.	1200.	1500.

23.3276 g, .500 SILVER, .3750 oz ASW, 36mm

Smaller bust

KM#	Date	Mintage	MS-63	Mintage	P/L	Spec.
64.2a	1972	—	—	341,598	—	16.00

NICKEL, 32mm

Large bust

KM#	Date	Mintage	MS-63	Mintage	P/L	Spec.
76.1	1968	5,579,714	1.50	1,408,143	2.50	—
	1969	4,809,313	1.50	594,258	2.50	—
	1972	2,676,041	2.00	405,865	2.50	—

Smaller bust

KM#	Date	Mintage	MS-63	Mintage	P/L	Spec.
76.2	1975	3,256,000	2.00	322,325	3.25	—
	1976	2,498,204	2.50	274,106	4.00	—
76.3	1975 mule w/1976 obv.	Inc. Ab.	—	—	*	—

***NOTE:** Only known in proof-like sets w/1976 obv. slightly modified.

KM#	Date	Mintage	MS-63	Mintage	P/L	Spec.
117	1977	1,393,745	2.50	—	4.50	—
120	1978	2,948,488	2.00	—	3.50	—
	1979	2,954,842	2.00	—	5.50	—
	1980	3,291,221	2.00	—	9.00	—

KM#	Date	Mintage	MS-63	Mintage	P/L	Proof
120	1981	2,778,900	2.00	—	5.00	6.50
	1982	1,098,500	2.00	—	5.50	10.00
	1983	2,267,525	2.00	—	6.00	15.00
	1984	1,223,486	2.00	—	6.00	—
	1984	161,602	—	—	—	15.00
	1985	3,104,092	2.00	—	7.00	—
	1985	157,037	—	—	—	35.00
	1986	3,089,225	2.00	—	12.00	—
	1986	175,259	—	—	—	30.00
	1987	287,330	2.00	—	8.00	—
	1987	179,004	—	—	—	30.00

LOON DOLLARS

AUREATE

KM#	Date	Mintage	MS-63	P/L	Proof
157	1987	205,405,000	3.00	—	—
	1987	178,120	—	—	15.00
	1988	138,893,539	2.00	7.50	—
	1988	175,259	—	—	16.50
	1989	184,773,902	2.00	7.50	—
	1989	170,928	—	—	16.50
	New Elizabeth II Effigy				
186	1990	68,402,000	2.00	7.50	—
	1990	140,649	—	—	18.00
	1991	23,156,000	3.00	8.50	—
	1991	—	—	—	20.00
	1993	—	2.00	7.50	—
	1993	—	—	—	20.00

COMMEMORATIVE DOLLARS

23.3276 g, .800 SILVER, .6000 oz ASW

KM#	Date	Mintage	F-12	VF-20	XF-40	AU-50	MS-60	MS-63
30	1935 Jubilee	428,707	15.00	25.00	35.00	45.00	60.00	120.00
38	1939 Royal Visit	1,363,816	6.00	8.00	10.00	15.00	18.00	30.00
	1939 Royal Visit	—	—	—	—	Specimen		600.00
	1939 Royal Visit	—	—	—	—	—	Proof	2500.

KM#	Date	Mintage	F-12	VF-20	XF-40	AU-50	MS-60	MS-63
47	1949 Newfoundland	672,218	9.00	15.00	25.00	30.00	40.00	55.00
	1949 Newfoundland	—	—	—	—	Specimen		425.00
55	1958 Br. Columbia	3,039,630	BV	4.00	5.00	6.00	7.00	14.00

KM#	Date	Mintage	F-12	VF-20	XF-40	AU-50	MS-60	MS-63
58	1964 Charlottetown	7,296,832	—	BV	5.00	6.00	7.00	11.50

KM#	Date	Mintage	MS-63	P/L	Spec.
70	1967 Goose,Confederation Centennial	6,767,496	8.00	11.50	450.00

KM#	Date	Mintage	MS-63	P/L	Spec.
78	1970 Manitoba (Nickel, 32mm)	4,140,058	2.00	—	—
		645,869	—	3.25	—
79	1971 Br. Columbia (Nickel, 32mm)	4,260,781	2.00	3.00	—
		468,729	—	(c) 2.50	—

23.3276 g, .500 SILVER, .3750 oz ASW*

KM#	Date	Mintage	MS-63	P/L	Spec.
80	1971 Br. Columbia (.500 Silver, 36mm)	585,674	—	—	14.50

***NOTE:** All silver dollars dated 1971 to date are minted to this standard.

KM#	Date	Mintage	MS-63	P/L	Spec.
82	1973 Pr. Edward Island (Nickel, 32mm)	3,196,452	2.50	—	—
		466,881	—	(c) 3.25	—

KM#	Date	Mintage	MS-63	P/L	Spec.
83	1973 Mountie (.500 Silver, 36mm)	1,031,271	—	—	15.00
83v	1973 Mountie, with metal crest on case	Inc. Ab.	—	—	17.00
88	1974 Winnipeg (Nickel, 32mm)	2,799,363	3.00	—	—
		363,786	—	(c) 5.00	—
88a	1974 Winnipeg (.500 Silver, 36mm)	728,947	—	—	14.50

KM#	Date	Mintage	MS-63	P/L	Spec.
97	1975 Calgary (.500 Silver, 36mm)	930,956	—	—	9.00
106	1976 Parliament Library (.500 Silver, 36mm)	578,708	—	—	22.50

KM#	Date	Mintage	MS-63	P/L	Spec.
118	1977 Silver Jubilee	744,848	—	—	15.50
121	1978 XI Games (.500 Silver, 36mm)	709,602	—	—	15.50

KM#	Date	Mintage	MS-63	P/L	Spec.
124	1979 Griffon (.500 Silver, 36mm)	826,695	—	—	26.00
128	1980 Arctic Territories (.500 Silver, 36mm)	539,617	—	—	65.00

KM#	Date	Mintage	MS-63	P/L	Proof
130	1981 Railroad (.500 Silver, 36mm)	699,494	50.00	—	35.00
133	1982 Regina (.500 Silver, 36mm)	144,930	37.50	—	—
		758,958	—	—	8.00

KM#	Date	Mintage	MS-63	P/L	Proof
134	1982 Constitution (Nickel, 32mm)	9,709,422	2.00	—	7.00
138	1983 Edmonton University Games (.500 Silver, 36mm)	159,450	32.50	—	—
		506,847	—	—	16.50

KM#	Date	Mintage	MS-63	P/L	Proof
140	1984 Toronto Sesquicentennial (.500 Silver, 36mm)	133,610	37.50	—	—
		732,542	—	—	10.00
141	1984 Cartier (Nickel, 32mm)	7,009,323	2.25	—	—
		87,760	—	—	7.00

KM#	Date	Mintage	MS-63	P/L	Proof
143	1985 National Parks -Moose (.500 Silver, 36mm)	163,314	35.00	—	—
		733,354	—	—	10.00
149	1986 Vancouver (.500 Silver, 36mm)	125,949	40.00	—	—
		680,004	—	—	15.50

KM#	Date	Mintage	MS-63	P/L	Proof
154	1987 John Davis (.500 Silver, 36mm)	118,722	37.50	—	—
		602,374	—	—	22.00
161	1988 Ironworks (.500 Silver, 36mm)	106,872	45.00	—	—
		255,013	—	—	50.00

KM#	Date	Mintage	MS-63	P/L	Proof
168	1989 MacKenzie River (.500 Silver, 36mm)	99,774	27.50	—	—
		244,062	—	—	50.00
170	1990 Henry Kelsey (.500 Silver, 36mm)	99,455	22.50	—	—
		254,959	—	—	23.50

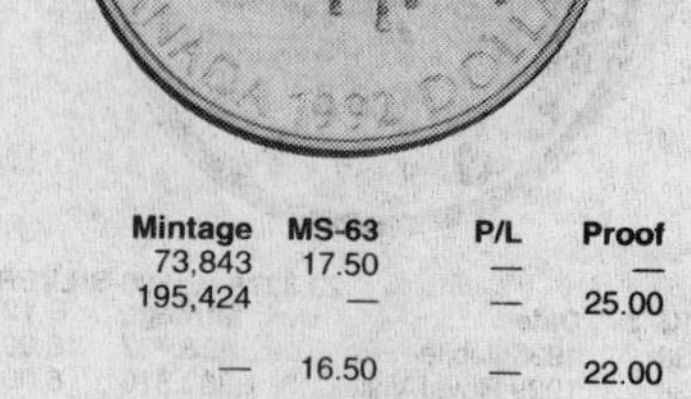

KM#	Date	Mintage	MS-63	P/L	Proof
179	1991 S.S. Frontenac (.500 Silver, 36mm)	73,843	17.50	—	—
		195,424	—	—	25.00
210	1992 Stagecoach Service (.925 Silver, 36mm)	—	16.50	—	22.00

KM#	Date	Mintage	MS-63	P/L	Proof
235	1993 Stanley Cup Hockey (.925 Silver, 36mm)	—	15.00	—	20.00

125th Anniversary of the Confederation

KM#	Date	Mintage	MS-63	P/L	Proof
209	1992 Loon, Aureate	—	2.00	—	20.00
218	1992 Parliament, Aureate	—	2.00	—	18.00

NOTE: (c) Individually cased Proof-likes (P/L), Proofs or Specimens are from broken up Proof-like or specimen sets.

5 DOLLARS

8.3592 g, .900 GOLD, .2419 oz AGW

KM#	Date	Mintage	F-12	VF-20	XF-40	AU-50	MS-60	MS-63
26	1912	165,680	120.00	140.00	165.00	220.00	325.00	600.00
	1913	98,832	120.00	140.00	165.00	220.00	325.00	600.00
	1914	31,122	200.00	300.00	375.00	500.00	750.00	1550.

Olympic Commemoratives

24.3000 g, .925 SILVER, .7227 oz ASW

Series I

KM#	Date	Mintage	MS-63	Proof
84	1973 Sailboats (Kingston)	—	5.50	—
		165,203	—	7.25
85	1973 North America Map	—	5.50	—
		165,203	—	7.25

Series II

KM#	Date	Mintage	MS-63	Proof
89	1974 Olympic Rings	—	5.50	—
		97,431	—	7.25
90	1974 Athlete with torch	—	5.50	—
		97,431	—	7.25

Series III

KM#	Date	Mintage	MS-63	Proof
91	1974 Rowing	—	5.50	—
		104,684	—	7.25
92	1974 Canoeing	—	5.50	—
		104,684	—	7.25

Series IV

KM#	Date	Mintage	MS-63	Proof
98	1975 Marathon	—	5.50	—
		89,155	—	7.25
99	1975 Ladies' javelin	—	5.50	—
		89,155	—	7.25

Series V

KM#	Date	Mintage	MS-63	Proof
100	1975 Swimmer	—	5.50	—
		89,155	—	7.25
101	1975 Diver	—	5.50	—
		89,155	—	7.25

Series VI

KM#	Date	Mintage	MS-63	Proof
107	1976 Fencing	—	5.50	—
		82,302	—	10.00
108	1976 Boxing	—	5.50	—
		82,302	—	10.00

Series VII

KM#	Date	Mintage	MS-63	Proof
109	1976 Olympic Village	—	5.50	—
		76,908	—	11.50
110	1976 Olympic flame	—	5.50	—
		79,102	—	11.50

10 DOLLARS

16.7185 g, .900 GOLD, .4838 oz AGW

KM#	Date	Mintage	F-12	VF-20	XF-40	AU-50	MS-60	MS-63
27	1912	74,759	200.00	300.00	380.00	500.00	750.00	1500.
	1913	149,232	200.00	300.00	380.00	500.00	775.00	1550.
	1914	140,068	210.00	320.00	425.00	625.00	975.00	1950.

Olympic Commemoratives

48.6000 g, .925 SILVER, 1.4454 oz ASW

Series I

KM#	Date	Mintage	MS-63	Proof
86.1	1973 World Map	103,426	11.50	—
		165,203	—	14.00
86.2	1974 World Map (Error-Mule)	320 pcs.	315.00	—
87	1973 Montreal Skyline	—	11.00	—
		165,203	—	14.00

Series II

KM#	Date	Mintage	MS-63	Proof
93	1974 Head of Zeus	—	11.00	—
		104,684	—	14.00
94	1974 Temple of Zeus	—	11.00	—
		104,684	—	14.00

Series III

KM#	Date	Mintage	MS-63	Proof
95	1974 Cycling	—	11.00	—
		97,431	—	14.00
96	1974 Lacrosse	—	11.00	—
		97,431	—	14.00

Series IV

KM#	Date	Mintage	MS-63	Proof
102	1975 Men's hurdles	—	11.00	—
		82,302	—	14.00
103	1975 Ladies' shot put	—	11.00	—
		82,302	—	14.00

Series V

KM#	Date	Mintage	MS-63	Proof
104	1975 Sailing	—	11.00	—
		89,155	—	14.00
105	1975 Paddler	—	11.00	—
		89,155	—	14.00

Series VI

KM#	Date	Mintage	MS-63	Proof
111	1976 Football	—	11.00	—
		76,908	—	17.50
112	1976 Field Hockey	—	11.00	—
		76,908	—	17.50

Series VII

KM#	Date	Mintage	MS-63	Proof
113	1976 Olympic Stadium	—	11.00	—
		79,102	—	18.50
114	1976 Olympic Velodrome	—	11.00	—
		79,102	—	18.50

15 DOLLARS

Olympic Commemoratives

33.6300 g, .925 SILVER, 1.0000 oz ASW

KM#	Date	Mintage	MS-63	Proof
215	1992 Coaching Track	*275,000	—	42.50
216	1992 High Jump, Rings, Speed Skating	*275,000	—	42.50

20 DOLLARS

18.2733 g, .900 GOLD, .5288 oz AGW

KM#	Date	Mintage	MS-63	Proof
71	1967 Centennial	337,688	—	215.00

Olympic Commemoratives

33.6300 g, .925 SILVER, 1.0000 oz ASW

KM#	Date	Mintage	MS-63	Proof
145	1985 Winter Olympics, Downhill Skier, lettered edge	406,360	—	27.50
	1985 Plain edge	Inc. Ab.	—	425.00
146	1985 Winter Olympics, Speed Skater, lettered edge	354,222	—	27.50
	1985 Plain edge	Inc. Ab.	—	340.00

KM#	Date	Mintage	MS-63	Proof
147	1986 Winter Olympics, Biathlon, lettered edge	308,086	—	27.50
	1986 Plain edge	Inc. Ab.	—	340.00
148	1986 Winter Olympics, Hockey, lettered edge	396,602	—	27.50
	1986 Plain edge	Inc. Ab.	—	340.00

KM#	Date	Mintage	MS-63	Proof
150	1986 Winter Olympics, Cross Country Skier	303,199	—	27.50
151	1986 Winter Olympics, Free Style Skier, lettered edge	294,322	—	27.50
	1986 Plain edge	Inc. Ab.	—	340.00

34.1070 g, .925 SILVER, 1.0000 oz ASW

KM#	Date	Mintage	MS-63	Proof
155	1987 Winter Olympics, Figure Skater	334,875	—	27.50
156	1987 Winter Olympics, Curling	286,457	—	27.50

KM#	Date	Mintage	MS-63	Proof
159	1987 Winter Olympics, Ski Jumper	290,954	—	27.50
160	1987 Winter Olympics, Bobsled	274,326	—	27.50

Aviation Commemoratives

31.1030 g, .925 SILVER w/1.0000 GOLD Cameo, 1.0000 oz ASW

KM#	Date	Mintage	MS-63	Proof
172	1990 Lancaster/Fauquier	43,596	—	65.00
173	1990 Anson and Harvard	41,844	—	75.00

31.1030 g, .925 SILVER, .9743 oz ASW

KM#	Date	Mintage	MS-63	Proof
196	1991 Silver Dart	28,791	—	47.50
197	1991 de Haviland "Beaver"	29,399	—	47.50

KM#	Date	Mintage	MS-63	Proof
224	1992 Curtiss JN-4 Canuck ("Jenny")	*50,000	—	47.50
225	1992 de Haviland Gypsy Moth	*50,000	—	47.50

KM#	Date	Mintage	MS-63	Proof
236	1993 Fairchild 71C Float plane	*50,000	—	47.50
237	1993 Lockheed 14	*50,000	—	47.50

100 DOLLARS

13.3375 g, .583 GOLD, .2500 oz AGW

KM#	Date	Mintage	MS-63	Proof
115	1976 Olympics, beaded borders, 27mm	650,000	105.00	—
	16.9655 g, .917 GOLD, .5000 oz AGW			
116	1976 Olympics, reduced size, 25mm, plain borders	337,342	—	200.00
119	1977 Queen's Silver Jubilee	180,396	—	220.00

KM#	Date	Mintage	MS-63	Proof
122	1978 Canadian Unification	200,000	—	210.00
126	1979 Year of the Child	250,000	—	200.00
129	1980 Arctic Territories	300,000	—	215.00

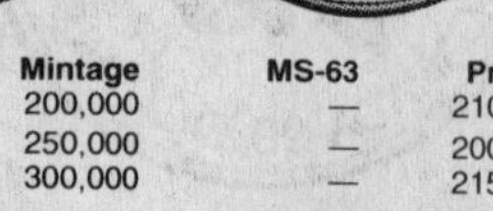

KM#	Date	Mintage	MS-63	Proof
131	1981 National Anthem	102,000	—	225.00
137	1982 New Constitution	121,708	—	215.00
139	1983 St. John's, Newfoundland	83,128	—	220.00

KM#	Date	Mintage	MS-63	Proof
142	1984 Jacques Cartier	67,662	—	220.00
144	1985 National Parks - Big horn sheep	61,332	—	230.00
152	1986 Peace	76,409	—	220.00

13.3375 g, .583 GOLD, .2500 oz AGW

KM#	Date	Mintage	MS-63	Proof
158	1987 1988 Olympics - Torch and logo, lettered edge	142,750	—	120.00
	1987 Plain edge	Inc. Ab.	—	—
162	1988 Whales	52,594	—	240.00
169	1989 Sainte-Marie	59,657	—	135.00

KM#	Date	Mintage	MS-63	Proof
171	1990 Intl. Literacy Year	49,940	—	150.00
180	1991 S.S. Empress of India	*33,966	—	240.00
211	1992 Montreal	—	—	210.00

175 DOLLARS

16.9700 g, .917 GOLD, .5000 oz AGW

KM#	Date	Mintage	MS-63	Proof
217	1992 Olympics - Passing the Torch	*35,000	—	370.00

200 DOLLARS

17.1060 g, .917 GOLD, .5042 oz AGW

KM#	Date	Mintage	MS-63	Proof
178	1990 Canada Flag Silver Jubilee	20,980	—	275.00
202	1991 Hockey	8,741	—	320.00
230	1992 Niagara Falls	*25,000	—	320.00

SOVEREIGN

1908-1910 **7.9881 g, .917 GOLD, .2354 oz AGW** **1911-1919**

C mint mark below horse's rear hooves

KM#	Date	Mintage	F-12	VF-20	XF-40	AU-50	MS-60	MS-63
14	1908C	636 pcs.	1000.	1700.	2300.	2800.	3300.	4100.
	1909C	16,273	175.00	250.00	325.00	550.00	875.00	1400.
	1910C	28,012	125.00	175.00	250.00	400.00	600.00	1200.
20	1911C	256,946	110.00	120.00	130.00	170.00	250.00	300.00
	1911C	—	—	—	—		Specimen	6500.
	1913C	3,715	400.00	550.00	750.00	1000.	1650.	2750.
	1914C	14,871	175.00	250.00	325.00	550.00	875.00	1400.
	1916C	Rare		*About 20 known		20,000.	25,000.	35,000.

NOTE: Stacks's A.G. Carter Jr. Sale 12-89 Gem BU realized $82,500.

KM#	Date	Mintage	F-12	VF-20	XF-40	AU-50	MS-60	MS-63
	1917C	58,845	110.00	120.00	130.00	170.00	250.00	325.00
	1918C	106,516	110.00	120.00	130.00	170.00	250.00	325.00
	1919C	135,889	110.00	120.00	130.00	170.00	250.00	325.00

SILVER BULLION ISSUES
5 DOLLARS

31.1000 g, .9999 SILVER, 1.0000 oz ASW

KM#	Date	Mintage	MS-63	Proof
163	1988 Maple leaf	1,155,931	7.00	—
	1989 Maple leaf	—	7.00	—
	1989 Maple leaf	43,965	—	75.00
	New Elizabeth II Effigy			
187	1990 Maple leaf	1,708,800	7.00	—
	1991 Maple leaf	644,300	15.00	—
	1992 Maple leaf	—	10.00	—
	1993 Maple leaf	—	7.00	—
	1994 Maple leaf	—	7.00	—

GOLD BULLION ISSUES
1 DOLLAR

1.5551 g, .9999 GOLD, .0500 oz AGW

KM#	Date	Mintage	MS-63	Proof
238	1993 Maple Leaf	—	*BV + 20 %*	—

5 DOLLARS

3.1200 g, .9999 GOLD, .1000 oz AGW

KM#	Date	Mintage	MS-63	Proof
135	1982 Maple leaf	246,000	BV + 15%	—
	1983 Maple leaf	304,000	BV + 15%	—
	1984 Maple leaf	262,000	BV + 15%	—
	1985 Maple leaf	398,000	BV + 15%	—
	1986 Maple leaf	529,516	BV + 15%	—
	1987 Maple leaf	459,000	BV + 15%	—
	1988 Maple leaf	506,500	BV + 15%	—
	1989 Maple leaf	—	BV + 15%	—
	1989 Maple leaf	16,992	—	100.00
	New Elizabeth II Effigy			
188	1990 Maple leaf	47,600	BV + 15%	—
	1991 Maple leaf	32,200	BV + 15%	—
	1992 Maple leaf	—	BV + 15%	—
	1993 Maple leaf	—	BV + 15%	—

10 DOLLARS

7.7850 g, .9999 GOLD, .2500 oz AGW

KM#	Date	Mintage	MS-63	Proof
136	1982 Maple leaf	184,000	BV + 11 %	—
	1983 Maple leaf	308,800	BV + 11 %	—
	1984 Maple leaf	242,400	BV + 11 %	—
	1985 Maple leaf	620,000	BV + 11 %	—
	1986 Maple leaf	915,200	BV + 11 %	—
	1987 Maple leaf	376,000	BV + 11 %	—
	1988 Maple leaf	436,000	BV + 11%	—
	1989 Maple leaf	—	BV + 11%	—
	1989 Maple leaf	6,998	—	220.00
	New Elizabeth II Effigy			
189	1990 Maple leaf	63,400	BV + 11%	—
	1991 Maple leaf	41,600	BV + 11%	—
	1992 Maple leaf	—	BV + 11%	—
	1993 Maple leaf	—	BV + 11%	—

20 DOLLARS

15.5515 g, .9999 GOLD, .5000 oz AGW

KM#	Date	Mintage	MS-63	Proof
153	1986 Maple leaf	529,200	BV + 7%	—
	1987 Maple leaf	332,800	BV + 7%	—
	1988 Maple leaf	538,400	BV + 7%	—
	1989 Maple leaf	—	BV + 7%	—
	1989 Maple leaf	6,998	—	365.00
	New Elizabeth II Effigy			
190	1990 Maple leaf	87,200	BV + 7%	—
	1991 Maple leaf	48,100	BV + 7%	—
	1992 Maple leaf	—	BV + 7%	—
	1993 Maple leaf	—	BV + 7%	—

50 DOLLARS

31.1030 g, .999 GOLD, 1.0000 oz AGW
Rev: 999. Maple Leaf. 999.

KM#	Date	Mintage	MS-63	Proof
125.1	1979 Maple leaf	1,000,000	BV + 5%	—
	1980 Maple leaf	1,251,500	BV + 5%	—
	1981 Maple leaf	863,000	BV + 5%	—
	1982 Maple leaf	883,000	BV + 5%	—

31.1030 g, .9999 GOLD, 1.0000 oz AGW
Rev: 9999 Maple Leaf 9999

KM#	Date	Mintage	MS-63	Proof
125.2	1983 Maple leaf	843,000	BV + 5%	—
	1984 Maple leaf	1,067,500	BV + 5%	—
	1985 Maple leaf	1,908,000	BV + 5%	—
	1986 Maple leaf	779,115	BV + 5%	—
	1987 Maple leaf	978,000	BV + 5%	—
	1988 Maple leaf	826,500	BV + 5%	—
	1989 Maple leaf	—	BV + 5%	—
	1989 Maple leaf	17,781	—	700.00
	New Elizabeth II Effigy			
191	1990 Maple leaf	815,000	BV + 5%	—
	1991 Maple leaf	290,000	BV + 5%	—
	1992 Maple leaf	—	BV + 5%	—
	1993 Maple leaf	—	BV + 5%	—

PLATINUM BULLION ISSUES

1 DOLLAR

1.5552 g, .9995 PLATINUM, .0500 oz APW

KM#	Date	Mintage	MS-63	Proof
239	1993 Maple Leaf	—	BV + 22 %	—

5 DOLLARS

3.1203 g, .9995 PLATINUM, .1000 oz APW

KM#	Date	Mintage	MS-63	Proof
164	1988 Maple leaf	74,000	BV + 17%	—
	1989 Maple leaf	—	BV + 17%	—
	1989 Maple leaf	11,999	—	125.00
	New Elizabeth II Effigy			
192	1990 Maple leaf	900 pcs.	BV + 17%	—
	1991 Maple leaf	1,300	BV + 17%	—
	1992 Maple leaf	—	BV + 17%	—

10 DOLLARS

7.7857 g, .9995 PLATINUM, .2500 oz APW

KM#	Date	Mintage	MS-63	Proof
165	1988 Maple leaf	93,600	BV + 12%	—
	1989 Maple leaf	—	BV + 12%	—
	1989 Maple leaf	1,999	—	300.00
	New Elizabeth II Effigy			
193	1990 Maple leaf	400 pcs.	BV + 12%	—
	1991 Maple leaf	1,800	BV + 12%	—
	1992 Maple leaf	—	BV + 12%	—

20 DOLLARS

15.5519 g, .9995 PLATINUM, .5000 oz APW

KM#	Date	Mintage	MS-63	Proof
166	1988 Maple leaf	23,600	BV + 8%	—
	1989 Maple leaf	—	BV + 8%	—
	1989 Maple leaf	1,999	—	550.00
	New Elizabeth II Effigy			
194	1990 Maple leaf	1,300	BV + 8%	—
	1991 Maple leaf	2,800	BV + 8%	—
	1992 Maple leaf	—	BV + 8%	—

30 DOLLARS

3.1100 g, .999 PLATINUM, .1000 oz APW

KM#	Date	Mintage	MS-63	Proof
174	1990 Polar bear swimming	1,928	Proof	80.00
198	1991 Owls	*3,500	Proof	90.00
226	1992 Cougar head and shoulders	*3,500	Proof	100.00
240	1993 Fox	—	Proof	90.00

50 DOLLARS

31.1030 g, .9995 PLATINUM, 1.0000 oz APW

KM#	Date	Mintage	MS-63	Proof
167	1988 Maple leaf	37,500	*BV + 6%*	—
	1989 Maple leaf	1,500	*BV + 6%*	—
	1989 Maple leaf	5,965	—	1000.
	New Elizabeth II Effigy			
195	1990 Maple leaf	15,100	*BV + 6%*	—
	1991 Maple leaf	31,900	*BV + 6%*	—
	1992 Maple leaf	—	*BV + 6%*	—

75 DOLLARS

7.7760 g, .999 PLATINUM, .2500 oz APW

KM#	Date	Mintage	MS-63	Proof
175	1990 Polar bear resting	1,928	Proof	220.00
199	1991 Owls perched on branch	*3,500	Proof	240.00
227	1992 Cougar prowling	*3,500	Proof	250.00
241	1993 Fox	—	Proof	240.00

150 DOLLARS

15.5520 g, .999 PLATINUM, .5000 oz APW

KM#	Date	Mintage	MS-63	Proof
176	1990 Polar bear walking	1,928	Proof	400.00
200	1991 Owl flying	*3,500	Proof	425.00
228	1992 Cougar mother and cub	*3,500	Proof	450.00
242	1993 Fox	—	Proof	425.00

300 DOLLARS

31.1035 g, .999 PLATINUM, 1.0000 oz APW

KM#	Date	Mintage	MS-63	Proof
177	1990 Polar bear mother and cub	1,928	Proof	800.00
201	1991 Owl w/chicks	*3,500	Proof	850.00

KM#	Date	Mintage	MS-63	Proof
229	1992 Cougar resting in tree	*3,500	Proof	875.00
243	1993 Fox	—	Proof	850.00

PROOF-LIKE DOLLARS

23.3276 g, .800 SILVER, .6000 oz ASW

KM#	Date	Mintage	Identification	Issue Price	Mkt Value
D3	1953	1,200	KM54, Canoe w/shoulder fold	—	500.00
D4	1954	5,300	KM54, Canoe	1.25	190.00
D5	1955	7,950	KM54, Canoe	1.25	165.00
D5a	1955	Inc. Ab.	KM54, Arnprior	1.25	320.00
D6	1956	10,212	KM54, Canoe	1.25	120.00
D7	1957	16,241	KM54, Canoe	1.25	50.00
D8	1958	33,237	KM55, British Columbia	1.25	35.00
D9	1959	45,160	KM54, Canoe	1.25	16.50
D10	1960	82,728	KM54, Canoe	1.25	15.00
D11	1961	120,928	KM54, Canoe	1.25	13.50
D12	1962	248,901	KM54, Canoe	1.25	12.00
D13	1963	963,525	KM54, Canoe	1.25	11.00
D14	1964	2,862,441	KM58, Charlottetown	1.25	11.00
D15	1965	2,904,352	KM64, Canoe	—	11.00
D16	1966	672,514	KM64, Canoe	—	12.00
D17	1967	1,036,176	KM70, Confederation	—	17.00

MINT SETS (MS)

Olympic Commemoratives

KM#	Date	Mintage	Identification	Issue Price	Mkt Value
MS1	1973(4)	—	KM84-87, Series I	45.00	32.00
MS2	1974(4)	—	KM89-90,93-94, Series II	48.00	32.00
MS3	1974(4)	—	KM91-92,95-96, Series III	48.00	32.00
MS4	1975(4)	—	KM98-99,102-103, Series IV	48.00	32.00
MS5	1975(4)	—	KM100-101,104-105, Series V	60.00	32.00
MS6	1976(4)	—	KM107-108,111-112, Series VI	60.00	32.00
MS7	1976(4)	—	KM109-110,113-114, Series VII	60.00	35.00

SPECIMEN SETS (SS)

NOTE: Some authorities list these as proof sets. However, the Canadian Mint does not. The coins are double struck with higher than usual pressure, but are considered to have the same quality as proof issue from the Royal Mint, London.

KM#	Date	Mintage	Identification	Issue Price	Mkt Value
SS1	1858(4)	—	KM1-4 Reeded Edge	—	6000.
SS2	1858(4)	—	KM1-4 Plain Edge	—	6000.
SS3	1858(8)	—	KM1-4 Double Set	—	12,500.
SS4	1858(8)	—	KM1(overdate),2-4 Double Set	—	14,000.
SS5	1870(4)	100*	KM2,3,5,6 (reeded edges)	—	12,500.
SS6	1870(8)	—	KM2,3,5,6 Double Set (plain edges)	—	25,000.
SS7	1872H(4)	—	KM2,3,5,6	—	12,500.
SS8	1875H(3)	—	KM2(Large Date),3,5	—	20,000.
SS9	1880H(3)	—	KM2,3,5(Narrow 0)	—	7000.
SS10	1881H(5)	—	KM7,2,3,5,6	—	12,000.
SS11	1892(2)	—	KM3,5	—	10,000.
SS12	1902(5)	100*	KM8-12	—	10,000.
SS13	1902H(3)	—	KM9(Large H),10,11	—	6500.
SS14	1903H(3)	—	KM10,12,13	—	7000.

NOTE: A 1903H double set has been reported on display in Bombay, India.

KM#	Date	Mintage	Identification	Issue Price	Mkt Value
SS15	1908(5)	1,000*	KM8,10-13	—	2800.
SS16	1911(5)	1,000*	KM15-19	—	5500.
SS17	1911/12(8)	5	KM15-20,26-27	—	52,250.
SS18	1921(5)	—	KM22-25,28	—	80,000.
SS19	1922(2)	—	KM28,29	—	800.00
SS20	1923(2)	—	KM28,29	—	800.00
SS21	1924(2)	—	KM28,29	—	800.00
SS22	1925(2)	—	KM28,29	—	1800.
SS23	1926(2)	—	KM28,29 (Near 6)	—	1800.
SS24	1927(3)	—	KM24a,28,29	—	3200.
SS25	1928(4)	—	KM23a,24a,28,29	—	2800.
SS26	1929(5)	—	KM23a-25a,28,29	—	10,000.
SS27	1930(4)	—	KM23a,24a,28,29	—	6500.
SS28	1931(5)	—	KM23a-25a,28,29	—	8500.
SS29	1932(5)	—	KM23a-25a,28,29	—	10,000.
SS30	1934(5)	—	KM23-25,28,29	—	8500.
SS31	1936(5)	—	KM23-25,28,29	—	8500.
SS32	1936(6)	—	KM23a(dot),24a(dot),25a,28(dot), 29,30	—	Rare
SS33	1937(6)	1025*	KM32-37 Matte Finish	—	850.00
SS34	1937(4)	—	KM32-35 Mirror Fields	—	500.00
SS35	1937(6)	75*	KM32-37 Mirror Fields	—	2000.
SS36	1938(6)	—	KM32-37	—	25,000.
SS-A36	1939(6)	—	KM32-35,38 Matte Finish	—	—
SS-B36	1939(6)	—	KM32-35,38 Mirror Fields	—	—
SS-C36	1942(2)	—	KM32,33	—	300.00
SS-D36	1943(2)	—	KM32,40	—	300.00
SS37	1944(5)	3	KM32,34-37,40a	—	20,000.
SS-A37	1944(2)	—	KM32,40a	—	300.00
SS38	1945(6)	6	KM32,34-37,40a	—	6500.
SS-A38	1945(2)	—	KM32,40a	—	300.00

KM#	Date	Mintage	Identification	Issue Price	Mkt Value
SS39	1946(6)	15	KM32,34-37,39a	—	4000.
SS40	1947(6)	—	KM32,34-36(7 curved),37(pointed 7), 39a	—	6000.
SS41	1947(6)	—	KM32,34-36(7 curved),37(blunt 7),39a	—	6000.
SS42	1947ML(6)	—	KM32,34-36(7 curved right),37,39a	—	6000.
SS43	1948(6)	30	KM41-46	—	5000.
SS44	1949(6)	20	KM41-45,47	—	2000.
SS44A	1949(2)	—	KM47	—	1000.
SS45	1950(6)	12	KM41-46	—	2100.
SS46	1950(6)	—	KM41-45,46(Arnprior)	—	2300.
SS47	1951(7)	12	KM41,48,42a,43-46 (w/water lines)	—	3750.
SS48	1952(6)	2,317	KM41,42a,43-46 (water lines)	—	4500
SS48A	1952(6)	—	KM41,42a,43-46 (w/o water lines)	—	4500.
SS49	1953(6)	28	KM49 w/o straps,50-54	—	1800.
SS50	1953(6)	—	KM49 w/straps,50-54	—	1800.
SS51	1964(6)	—	KM49,51,52,56-58	—	450.00
SS52	1965(6)	—	KM59.1-60.1,61-63,64.1	—	450.00

Double Dollar Prestige Sets

KM#	Date	Mintage	Identification	Issue Price	Mkt Value
SS56	1971(7)	66,860	KM59.1-60.1,74.1-75.1,77.1,79(2 pcs.)	12.00	15.00
SS57	1972(7)	36,349	KM59.1-60.1,74.1-75.1,76.1,(2 pcs.), 77.1	12.00	35.00

KM#	Date	Mintage	Identification	Issue Price	Mkt Value
SS58	1973(7)	119,819	KM59.1-60.1,75.1,77.1,81.1,82,83	12.00	20.00
SS59	1973(7)	Inc. Ab.	KM59.1-60.1,75.1,77.1,81.2,82,83	—	150.00
SS60	1974(7)	85,230	KM59.1-60.1,74.1-75.1,77.1,88,88a	15.00	22.00
SS61	1975(7)	97,263	KM59.1-60.1,74.1-75.1,76.2,77.1,97	15.00	15.50
SS62	1976(7)	87,744	KM59.1-60.1,74.1-75.1,76.2,77.1,106	16.00	30.00
SS63	1977(7)	142,577	KM59.1-60.1,74.1,75.2,77.1,117.1,118	16.50	21.50
SS64	1978(7)	147,000	KM59.1-60.1,74.1,75.3,77.1,120,121	16.50	21.50
SS65	1979(7)	155,698	KM59.2-60.2,74.2,75.3,77.2,120,124	18.50	36.50
SS66	1980(7)	162,875	KM60.2,74.2,75.3,77.2,120,127,128	30.50	70.00

Regular Specimen Sets Resumed

KM#	Date	Mintage	Identification	Issue Price	Mkt Value
SS67	1981(6)	71,300	KM60.2,74.2,75.3,77.2,120,123	10.00	10.00
SS68	1982(6)	62,298	KM60.2a,74.2,75.3,77.2,120,123	11.50	10.00
SS69	1983(6)	60,329	KM60.2a,74.2,75.3,77.2,120,132	12.75	10.00
SS70	1984(6)	60,400	KM60.2a,74.2,75.3,77.2,120,132	10.00	10.00
SS71	1985(6)	61,553	KM60.2a,74.2,75.3,77.2,120,132	10.00	10.00
SS73	1986(6)	67,152	KM60.2a,74.2,75.3,77.2,120,132	10.00	12.50
SS72	1987(6)	75,194	KM60.2a,74.2,75.3,77.2,120,132	11.00	14.00
SS73	1988(6)	70,205	KM60.2a,74.2,75.3,77.2,132,157	12.30	15.00
SS74	1989(6)	75,306	KM60.2a,74.2,75.3,77.2,132,157	14.50	20.00
SS75	1990(6)	76,611	KM181-186	15.50	20.00
SS76	1991(6)	54,462	KM181-186	15.50	40.00
SS77	1992(6)	—	KM204-209	16.25	25.00
SS78	1993(6)	—	KM181-186	—	18.00

NOTE: stimated.

Regular Specimen Sets Resumed

V.I.P. SPECIMEN SETS (VS)

NOTE: A very limited number of cased Specimen sets were produced by the Mint beginning in 1969 for presentation to dignitaries visiting the Royal Canadian Mint or other parts of Canada. (A small quantity of 1970 cased Specimen sets were sold to the public for $13.00 each.) The coins, 1¢ to $1.00 were cased in long narrow leather cases (black and other colors).

KM#	Date	Mintage	Identification	Issue Price	Mkt Value
VS1	1969	4 known	—	—	1700.
VS2	1970	100	KM59.1-60.1,74.1-75.1,77.1,78	—	475.00
VS3	1971	69	KM59.1-60.1,74.1-75.1,77.1,79(2 pcs.)	—	375.00
VS4	1972	25	KM59.1-60.1,74.1-75.1,76.1,(2 pcs.),77.1	—	435.00
VS5	1973	26	KM59.1-60.1,75.1,77.1,81.1,82,83	—	435.00
VS6	1974	72	KM59.1-60.1,74.1-75.1,77.1,88,88a	—	375.00
VS7	1975	94	KM59.1-60.1,74.1-75.1,76.2,77.1,97	—	375.00
VS8	1976	—	KM59.1-60.1,74.1-75.1,76.2,77.1,106	—	375.00

PROOF-LIKE SETS (PL)

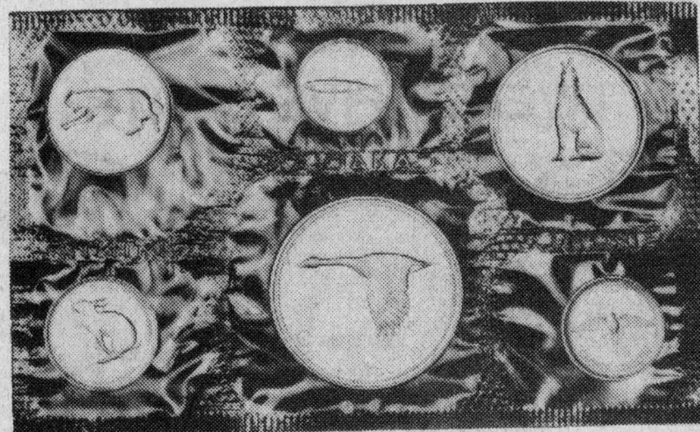

NOTE: These sets do not have the quality of the Proof or Specimen Set, but are specially produced and packaged.

KM#	Date	Mintage	Identification	Issue Price	Mkt Value
PL1	1953(6)	1,200	KM49 w/o straps, 50-54	2.20	1250.
PL2	1953(6)	Inc. Ab.	KM49-54	2.20	750.00
PL3	1954(6)	3,000	KM49-54	2.50	280.00
PL4	1954(6)	Inc. Ab.	KM49 w/o straps, 50-54	2.50	460.00
PL5	1955(6)	6,300	KM49,50a,51-54	2.50	190.00
PL6	1955(6)	Inc. Ab.	KM49,50a,51-54,Arnprior	2.50	280.00
PL7	1956(6)	6,500	KM49,50a,51-54	2.50	110.00
PL8	1957(6)	11,862	KM49,50a,51-54	2.50	65.00
PL9	1958(6)	18,259	KM49,50a,51-53,55	2.50	55.00
PL10	1959(6)	31,577	KM49,50a,51,52,54,56	2.50	25.00
PL11	1960(6)	64,097	KM49,50a,51,52,54,56	3.00	17.50
PL12	1961(6)	98,373	KM49,50a,51,52,54,56	3.00	15.00
PL13	1962(6)	200,950	KM49,50a,51,52,54,56	3.00	10.00
PL14	1963(6)	673,006	KM49,51,52,54,56,57	3.00	8.00
PL15	1964(6)	1,653,162	KM49,51,52,56-58	3.00	8.00
PL16	1965(6)	2,904,352	KM59.1-60.1,61-63,64.1	4.00	8.00
PL17	1966(6)	672,514	KM59.1-60.1,61-63,64.1	4.00	8.00
PL18	1967(6)	961,887	KM65-70 (pliofilm flat pack)	4.00	15.00
PL18A	1967(6)	70,583	KM65-70 and Silver Medal (red box)	12.00	18.00
PL18B	1967(7)	337,688	KM65-71 (black box)	40.00	275.00
PL19	1968(6)	521,641	KM59.1-60.1,72a,74.1-76.1	4.00	2.85
PL20	1969(6)	326,203	KM59.1-60.1,74.1-77.1	4.00	3.10
PL21	1970(6)	349,120	KM59.1-60.1,74.1-75.1,77.1,78	4.00	4.80
PL22	1971(6)	253,311	KM59.1-60.1,74.1-75.1,77.1,79	4.00	3.85
PL23	1972(6)	224,275	KM59.1-60.1,74.1-77.1	4.00	3.50
PL24	1973(6)	243,695	KM59.1-60.1,74.1-75.1 obv. 120 beads, 77.1,81.1,82	4.00	4.25
PL25	1973(6)	Inc. Ab.	KM59.1-60.1,74.1-75.1 obv. 132 beads, 77.1,81.2,82	4.00	145.00
PL26	1974(6)	213,589	KM59.1-60.1,74.1-75.1,77.1,88	5.00	4.25
PL27.1	1975(6)	197,372	KM59.1,60.1,74.1-77.1	5.00	3.85
PL27.2	1975(6)	Inc. Ab.	KM59.1,60.1,74.1-75.1,76.2,77.1	5.00	—
PL28	1976(6)	171,737	KM59.1,60,1,74.1-75.1,76.2,77.1	5.15	5.50
PL29	1977(6)	225,307	KM59.1,60.1,74.1,75.2,77.1,117.1	5.15	4.50
PL30	1978(6)	260,000	KM59.1-60.1,74.1,75.3,77.1,120	5.25	3.50
PL31	1979(6)	187,624	KM59.2-60.2,74.2,75.3,77.2,120	6.25	4.50
PL32	1980(6)	410,842	KM60.2,74.2,75.3,77.2,120,127	6.50	7.00
PL33	1981(6)	186,250	KM60.2,74.2,75.3,77.2,120,123	5.00	5.50
PL34	1982(6)	203,287	KM60.2a,74.2,75.3,77.2,120,123	6.00	4.25
PL36	1983(6)	190,838	KM60.2a,74.2,75.3,77.2,120,132	5.00	10.50
PL37	1984(6)	181,249	KM60.2a,74.2,75.3,77.2,120,132	5.25	9.25
PL38	1985(6)	173,924	KM60.2a,74.2,75.3,77.2,120,132	5.25	9.25
PL40	1986(6)	167,338	KM60.2a,74.2,75.3,77.2,120,132	5.25	12.75
PL39	1987(6)	212,136	KM60.2a,74.2,75.3,77.2,120,132	5.25	7.75
PL41	1988(6)	182,048	KM60.2a,74.2,75.3,77.2,132,157	6.05	9.25
PL42	1989(6)	173,622	KM60.2a,74.2,75.3,77.2,132,157	6.60	14.50
PL43	1990(6)	170,791	KM181-186	7.40	14.50
PL44	1991(6)	130,867	KM181-186	7.40	35.00
PL45	1992(6)	—	KM204-209	8.25	19.50

CUSTOM PROOF-LIKE SETS (CPL)

Each set contains two 1 cent pieces.

KM#	Date	Mintage	Identification	Issue Price	Mkt Value
CPL1	1971(7)	33,517	KM59.1(2 pcs.),60.1,74.1-75.1,77.1,79	6.50	6.00
CPL2	1972(7)	38,198	KM59.1(2 pcs.),60.1,74.1-77.1	6.50	6.00
CPL3	1973(7)	35,676	KM59.1(2 pcs.),60.1,75.1, 77.1,81.1 obv. 120 beads, 82	6.50	5.75
CPL4	1973(7)	Inc. Ab.	KM59.1(2 pcs.),60.1,75.1, 77.1,81.1 obv. 132 beads,82	6.50	160.00
CPL5	1974(7)	44,296	KM59.1(2 pcs.),60.1,74.1-75.1,77.1,88	8.00	5.75
CPL6	1975(7)	36,851	KM59.1(2 pcs.),60.1,74.1-75.1,76.2,77.1	8.00	6.00
CPL7	1976(7)	28,162	KM59.1(2 pcs.),60.1,74.1-75.1,76.2,77.1	8.00	8.75
CPL8	1977(7)	44,198	KM59.1(2 pcs.),60.1,74.1,75.2,77.1,117	8.15	10.00
CPL9	1978(7)	41,000	KM59.1(2 pcs.),60.1,74.1,75.3,77.1,120	—	6.00
CPL10	1979(7)	31,174	KM59.2(2 pcs.),60.2,74.2,75.3,77.2,120	10.75	8.75
CPL11	1980(7)	41,447	KM60.2,74.2,75.3,77.2,120,127(2 pcs.)	10.75	11.50

PROOF SETS (PS)

KM#	Date	Mintage	Identification	Issue Price	Mkt Value
PS1	1981(7)	199,000	KM60.2,74.2,75.3,77.2,120,123,130	36.00	38.00
PS2	1982(7)	180,908	KM60.2a,74.2,75.3,77.2,120,123,133	36.00	15.00
PS3	1983(7)	166,779	KM60.2a,74.2,75.3,77.2,120,132,138	36.00	24.00
PS4	1984(7)	161,602	KM60.2a,74.2,75.3,77.2,120,132,140	30.00	17.50
PS5	1985(7)	157,037	KM60.2a,74.2,75.3,77.2,120,132,143	30.00	18.50
PS6	1986(7)	175,745	KM60.2a,74.2,75.3,77.2,120,132,149	30.00	21.50
PS7	1987(7)	179,004	KM60.2a,74.2,75.3,77.2,120,132,154	34.00	28.00
PS8	1988(7)	175,259	KM60.2a,74.2,75.3,77.2,132,157,161	37.50	63.50
PS9	1989(7)	170,928	KM60.2a,74.2,75.3,77.2,132,157,168	40.00	63.50
PS10	1989(4)	6,823	KM125.2,135-136,153	1190.	1250.
PS11	1989(4)	1,995	KM164-167	1700.	1975.
PS12	1989(3)	2,550	KM125.2,163,167	1530.	1625.
PS13	1989(3)	9,979	KM135,163-164	165.00	225.
PS14	1990(7)	158,068	KM170,181-186	41.00	60.00
PS15	1990(4)	2,629	KM174-177	1720.	1500.
PS16	1991(7)	14,629	KM179,181-186	—	135.00
PS17	1991(4)	873	KM198-201	1760.	1680.
PS18	1992(7)	—	KM204-210	42.75	85.00
PS19	1992 (4)	*3,500	KM226-229	1680.	1680.

Olympic Commemoratives (OCP)

KM#	Date	Mintage	Identification	Issue Price	Mkt Value
OCP1	1973(4)	—	KM84-87,Series I	78.50	42.50
OCP2	1974(4)	—	KM89,90,93,94,Series II	88.50	42.50
OCP3	1974(4)	—	KM91,92,95,96,Series III	88.50	42.50
OCP4	1975(4)	—	KM98,99,102,103,Series IV	88.50	42.50
OCP5	1975(4)	—	KM100,101,104,105,Series V	88.50	42.50
OCP6	1976(4)	—	KM107,108,111,112, Series VI	88.50	55.00
OCP7	1976(4)	—	KM109,110,113,114,Series VII	88.50	60.00

NEWFOUNDLAND

LARGE CENTS

1865-1896 BRONZE 1904-1936

KM#	Date	Mintage	VG-8	F-12	VF-20	XF-40	MS-60	MS-63
1	1865	240,000	1.50	2.75	5.00	11.00	100.00	275.00
	1872H	200,000	1.75	2.75	5.00	11.00	65.00	160.00
	1872H	—	—	—	—	—	Proof	600.00
	1873	200,025	2.00	3.50	7.50	18.00	175.00	550.00
	1873	—	—	—	—	—	Proof	600.00
	1876H	200,000	1.75	2.75	5.00	12.50	150.00	450.00
	1876H	—	—	—	—	—	Proof	600.00
	1880 round O, even date	400,000	1.50	2.50	5.00	11.00	100.00	275.00
	1880 round O, low O	Inc. Ab.	1.75	3.00	6.00	15.00	125.00	375.00
	1880 oval 0	Inc. Ab.	55.00	80.00	120.00	200.00	550.00	1200.
	1885	40,000	15.00	22.00	30.00	70.00	300.00	900.00
	1888	50,000	14.00	18.00	25.00	60.00	275.00	850.00
	1890	200,000	1.75	2.75	4.25	9.00	100.00	250.00
	1894	200,000	1.75	2.75	4.25	9.00	100.00	250.00
	1896	200,000	1.75	2.75	4.25	9.00	100.00	250.00
9	1904H	100,000	4.50	7.50	13.50	18.00	200.00	600.00
	1907	200,000	1.00	2.00	3.00	8.00	110.00	250.00
	1909	200,000	1.00	2.00	3.00	8.00	100.00	200.00
	1909	—	—	—	—	—	Proof	400.00
16	1913	400,000	.75	1.50	2.00	4.00	40.00	100.00
	1917C	702,350	.75	1.50	2.00	4.00	50.00	175.00
	1919C	300,000	.75	1.50	2.25	5.00	75.00	225.00
	1919C	—	—	—	—	—	Proof	150.00
	1920C	302,184	.75	1.50	3.00	7.00	85.00	250.00
	1929	300,000	.75	1.50	2.00	4.00	50.00	160.00
	1929	—	—	—	—	—	Proof	125.00
	1936	300,000	.75	1.25	1.75	3.00	25.00	70.00
	1936	—	—	—	—	—	Proof	250.00

SMALL CENTS

BRONZE

KM#	Date	Mintage	VG-8	F-12	VF-20	XF-40	MS-60	MS-63
18	1938	500,000	.50	1.00	1.50	2.50	16.00	35.00
	1938	—	—	—	—	—	Proof	65.00
	1940	300,000	1.75	2.50	4.00	7.00	35.00	120.00
	1940 re-engraved date	—	15.00	27.50	35.00	45.00	175.00	375.00
	1941C	827,662	.35	.65	1.00	1.50	13.50	40.00
	1941C re-engraved date	—	12.50	20.00	27.50	40.00	150.00	400.00
	1942	1,996,889	.35	.65	1.00	1.50	13.50	40.00
	1943C	1,239,732	.35	.65	1.00	1.50	13.50	40.00
	1944C	1,328,776	1.00	2.00	3.00	4.50	35.00	100.00
	1947C	313,772	1.00	2.00	3.00	4.50	40.00	140.00

FIVE CENTS

1.1782 g, .925 SILVER, .0350 oz ASW

KM#	Date	Mintage	VG-8	F-12	VF-20	XF-40	MS-60	MS-63
2	1865	80,000	20.00	32.50	60.00	125.00	775.00	1500.
	1870	40,000	35.00	50.00	90.00	175.00	1100.	1800.
	1870	—	—	—	—	—	Proof	3900.
	1872H	40,000	22.00	32.00	55.00	135.00	600.00	1200.
	1873	44,260	35.00	45.00	100.00	225.00	1150.	2000.
	1873H	Inc. Ab.	700.00	1150.	1750.	2100.	3750.	—
	1876H	20,000	70.00	100.00	175.00	350.00	1600.	3000.
	1880	40,000	22.00	35.00	75.00	150.00	1000.	1750.
	1881	40,000	15.00	30.00	45.00	110.00	750.00	1500.
	1882H	60,000	12.50	22.50	40.00	100.00	650.00	1300.
	1882H	—	—	—	—	—	Proof	2800.
	1885	16,000	60.00	100.00	180.00	300.00	2000.	4250.
	1888	40,000	20.00	30.00	50.00	125.00	700.00	1200.
	1890	160,000	6.00	12.00	30.00	70.00	500.00	1100.
	1890	—	—	—	—	—	Proof	2100.
	1894	160,000	7.00	12.50	30.00	75.00	500.00	1100.
	1896	400,000	4.00	8.00	20.00	35.00	400.00	1000.
7	1903	100,000	3.00	6.00	18.00	45.00	450.00	1000.
	1904H	100,000	2.00	5.00	14.00	35.00	245.00	500.00
	1908	400,000	1.75	3.50	11.50	25.00	200.00	425.00
13	1912	300,000	1.50	2.50	5.00	16.00	175.00	300.00
	1917C	300,319	1.00	1.75	4.00	14.00	175.00	400.00
	1919C	100,844	2.00	3.00	12.00	30.00	350.00	700.00
	1929	300,000	1.00	1.75	3.25	12.00	150.00	300.00
	1929	—	—	—	—	—	Proof	750.00
19	1938	100,000	1.00	1.50	2.00	4.00	75.00	190.00
	1938	—	—	—	—	—	Proof	350.00
	1940C	200,000	1.00	1.50	2.00	4.00	45.00	140.00
	1941C	621,641	.75	1.50	2.00	3.00	18.00	27.50
	1942C	298,348	1.00	1.50	2.50	3.00	30.00	55.00
	1943C	351,666	.75	1.50	2.00	3.00	18.00	27.50
		1.1664 g, .800 SILVER, .0300 oz ASW						
19a	1944C	286,504	1.00	1.75	2.50	3.00	30.00	90.00
	1945C	203,828	.75	1.50	2.00	3.00	18.00	15.00
	1945C	—	—	—	—	—	Proof	250.00
	1946C	2,041	150.00	200.00	275.00	400.00	1500.	2150.
	1946C	—	—	—	—	—	Proof	4000.
	1947C	38,400	4.00	6.00	9.00	15.00	60.00	125.00
	1947C	—	—	—	—	—	Proof	400.00

TEN CENTS

1865-1896 2.3564 g, .925 SILVER, .0701 oz ASW 1903-1947

KM#	Date	Mintage	VG-8	F-12	VF-20	XF-40	MS-60	MS-63
3	1865	80,000	15.00	22.50	60.00	175.00	1200.	2500.
	1865 plain edge	—	—	—	—	—	Proof	5500.
	1870	30,000	120.00	175.00	325.00	700.00	3000.	6500.
	1872H	40,000	15.00	22.50	55.00	150.00	900.00	1900.
	1873 flat 3	23,614	16.00	30.00	75.00	200.00	1850.	3200.
	1873 round 3	Inc. Ab.	16.00	30.00	75.00	200.00	1850.	3200.
	1876H	10,000	22.50	40.00	80.00	275.00	2000.	3250.
	1880/70	10,000	22.50	40.00	90.00	300.00	2250.	3250.
	1882H	20,000	12.50	25.00	60.00	125.00	1200.	2000.
	1882H	—	—	—	—	—	Proof	3400.
	1885	8,000	55.00	100.00	220.00	500.00	2500.	4500.
	1888	30,000	12.50	22.00	55.00	150.00	1300.	2600.
	1890	100,000	6.00	12.00	22.00	70.00	750.00	1500.
	1890	—	—	—	—	—	Proof	3200.
	1894	100,000	6.00	12.00	22.00	70.00	750.00	1500.
	1894	—	—	—	—	—	Proof	1750.
	1896	230,000	4.00	10.00	20.00	65.00	600.00	1400.
8	1903	100,000	4.00	10.00	27.50	75.00	750.00	1600.
	1904H	100,000	3.00	7.00	20.00	55.00	325.00	550.00
14	1912	150,000	1.50	3.00	9.00	30.00	325.00	550.00
	1917C	250,805	1.25	2.00	6.00	20.00	375.00	900.00
	1919C	54,342	1.50	3.00	9.00	28.00	190.00	350.00
20	1938	100,000	1.00	1.50	2.50	7.00	100.00	250.00
	1938	—	—	—	—	—	Proof	500.00
	1940	100,000	.50	1.00	2.00	5.00	90.00	250.00
	1941C	483,630	.50	1.00	2.00	4.00	35.00	95.00
	1942C	293,736	.50	1.00	2.00	4.00	35.00	100.00
	1943C	104,706	.50	1.00	2.00	4.00	40.00	125.00
		2.3328 g, .800 SILVER, .0600 oz ASW						
20a	1944C	151,471	1.00	1.25	2.00	5.00	55.00	190.00
	1945C	175,833	.60	1.00	2.00	4.00	35.00	100.00
	1946C	38,400	3.00	5.00	10.00	20.00	70.00	300.00
	1947C	61,988	1.75	3.00	7.00	12.00	90.00	220.00

TWENTY CENTS

1865-1900 4.7127 g, .925 SILVER, .1401 oz ASW 1904-1912

KM#	Date	Mintage	VG-8	F-12	VF-20	XF-40	MS-60	MS-63
4	1865	100,000	8.00	14.00	40.00	110.00	950.00	2000.
	1865 plain edge	—	—	—	—	—	Proof	4500.
	1870	50,000	11.00	18.00	60.00	140.00	1250.	2500.
	1872H	90,000	7.00	12.00	30.00	90.00	750.00	1800.
	1873	45,797	9.00	15.00	40.00	120.00	1300.	2600.
	1876H	50,000	10.00	16.00	45.00	125.00	1350.	2700.
	1880/70	30,000	15.00	25.00	60.00	150.00	1350.	3000.
	1881	60,000	4.00	10.00	25.00	75.00	800.00	1800.
	1882H	100,000	5.00	12.00	27.50	80.00	800.00	1800.
	1882H	—	—	—	—	—	Proof	3700.
	1885	40,000	8.00	12.50	30.00	100.00	1300.	2600.
	1888	75,000	4.00	9.00	27.00	90.00	800.00	1750.
	1890	100,000	3.00	6.00	20.00	55.00	550.00	1500.
	1890	—	—	—	—	—	Proof	2750.
	1894	100,000	3.00	6.00	20.00	55.00	550.00	1600.
	1896 small 96	125,000	3.00	6.00	16.00	50.00	550.00	1500.
	1896 large 96	Inc. Ab.	3.50	9.00	20.00	70.00	600.00	1550.
	1899 small 99	125,000	6.00	14.00	30.00	90.00	750.00	1750.
	1899 large 99	Inc. Ab.	2.50	6.00	15.00	50.00	600.00	1750.
	1900	125,000	2.50	5.00	14.00	45.00	600.00	1750.
10	1904H	75,000	9.00	15.00	50.00	125.00	1100.	2500.
	1904H	—	—	—	—	—	Proof	4150.
15	1912	350,000	2.00	3.00	10.00	35.00	350.00	1000.

TWENTY-FIVE CENTS

5.8319 g, .925 SILVER, .1734 oz ASW

KM#	Date	Mintage	VG-8	F-12	VF-20	XF-40	MS-60	MS-63
17	1917C	464,779	1.50	2.00	4.00	8.00	110.00	250.00
	1919C	163,939	1.50	2.25	4.25	12.00	150.00	400.00

FIFTY CENTS

1870-1900 — 11.7818 g, .925 SILVER, .3504 oz ASW — 1904-1919

KM#	Date	Mintage	VG-8	F-12	VF-20	XF-40	MS-60	MS-63
6	1870	50,000	10.00	15.00	40.00	150.00	1250.	2500.
	1870 plain edge	—	—	—	—	—	Proof	5500.
	1872H	48,000	10.00	15.00	40.00	150.00	1250.	2500.
	1873	37,675	22.00	45.00	90.00	350.00	2400.	5000.
	1874	80,000	12.00	20.00	65.00	300.00	2400.	5000.
	1876H	28,000	18.00	30.00	75.00	275.00	2250.	5250.
	1880	24,000	18.00	27.50	75.00	275.00	2250.	5250.
	1881	50,000	10.00	18.00	55.00	200.00	2000.	5250.
	1882H	100,000	8.00	12.50	30.00	130.00	1500.	3500.
	1882H	—	—	—	—	—	Proof	5500.
	1885	40,000	10.00	18.00	55.00	225.00	2000.	5000.
	1888	20,000	15.00	25.00	70.00	300.00	2200.	5200.
	1894	40,000	5.00	8.00	35.00	130.00	1600.	2750.
	1896	60,000	4.00	7.00	25.00	110.00	1400.	2500.
	1898	76,607	4.00	7.00	26.00	120.00	1400.	2400.
	1899 wide 9's	150,000	4.00	7.00	25.00	100.00	1400.	2400.
	1899 narrow 9's	Inc. Ab.	4.00	7.00	25.00	100.00	1400.	2400.
	1900	150,000	4.00	7.00	22.50	100.00	1400.	2400.
11	1904H	140,000	3.00	5.00	16.00	40.00	350.00	900.00
	1907	100,000	5.00	7.00	20.00	45.00	375.00	1000.
	1908	160,000	2.50	4.50	12.50	25.00	175.00	550.00
	1909	200,000	2.50	4.50	12.50	25.00	175.00	550.00
12	1911	200,000	2.00	3.00	8.00	20.00	250.00	600.00
	1917C	375,560	2.00	3.00	6.00	15.00	140.00	350.00
	1918C	294,824	2.00	3.00	6.00	15.00	140.00	350.00
	1919C	306,267	2.00	3.00	6.00	15.00	140.00	350.00

TWO DOLLARS

3.3284 g, .917 GOLD, .0981 oz AGW

KM#	Date	Mintage	F-12	VF-20	XF-40	AU-50	MS-60	MS-63
5	1865	10,000	175.00	225.00	350.00	600.00	1250.	2800.
	1865 plain edge	about 10 known		—	—	—	Proof	10,000.
	1870	10,000	175.00	225.00	350.00	600.00	1250.	3000.
	1870 plain edge	—	—	—	—	—	Proof	10,000.
	1872	6,050	200.00	275.00	400.00	750.00	2500.	5250.
	1880	2,500	1000.	1400.	1800.	2200.	3500.	9000.
	1880	—	—	—	—	—	Proof	18,500.
	1881	10,000	120.00	190.00	235.00	350.00	750.00	1450.
	1882H	25,000	100.00	150.00	185.00	260.00	450.00	1000.
	1882H	—	—	—	—	—	Proof	6000.
	1885	10,000	120.00	190.00	235.00	350.00	750.00	1450.
	1888	25,000	100.00	150.00	185.00	260.00	450.00	1000.

NEW BRUNSWICK

HALF PENNY TOKEN

COPPER

KM#	Date	Mintage	VG-8	F-12	VF-20	XF-40	MS-60	MS-63
1	1843	480,000	3.00	6.00	12.00	25.00	95.00	250.00
	1843	—	—	—	—	—	Proof	750.00

KM#	Date	Mintage	VG-8	F-12	VF-20	XF-40	MS-60	MS-63
3	1854	864,000	3.00	6.00	12.00	25.00	95.00	250.00

ONE PENNY TOKEN

COPPER

KM#	Date	Mintage	VG-8	F-12	VF-20	XF-40	MS-60	MS-63
2	1843	480,000	3.00	6.00	12.00	30.00	150.00	300.00
	1843	—	—	—	—	—	Proof	800.00

KM#	Date	Mintage	VG-8	F-12	VF-20	XF-40	MS-60	MS-63
4	1854	432,000	3.00	6.00	12.00	35.00	160.00	320.00

DECIMAL COINAGE

HALF CENT

BRONZE

KM#	Date	Mintage	VG-8	F-12	VF-20	XF-40	MS-60	MS-63
5	1861	222,800	45.00	70.00	100.00	150.00	350.00	850.00
	1861	—	—	—	—	—	Proof	2200.

ONE CENT

BRONZE

KM#	Date	Mintage	VG-8	F-12	VF-20	XF-40	MS-60	MS-63
6	1861	1,000,000	1.50	2.50	4.00	7.50	60.00	170.00
	1861	—	—	—	—	—	Proof	450.00
	1864 short 6	1,000,000	1.50	2.50	4.00	7.50	60.00	175.00
	1864 long 6	Inc. Ab.	1.50	2.50	4.00	7.50	60.00	165.00

FIVE CENTS

1.1620 g, .925 SILVER, .0346 oz ASW

KM#	Date	Mintage	VG-8	F-12	VF-20	XF-40	MS-60	MS-63
7	1862	100,000	20.00	40.00	90.00	170.00	900.00	1800.
	1862	—	—	—	—	—	Proof	2500.
	1864 small 6	100,000	20.00	40.00	90.00	170.00	900.00	1900.
	1864 large 6	Inc. Ab.	20.00	40.00	90.00	170.00	900.00	1800.

TEN CENTS

2.3240 g, .925 SILVER, .0691 oz ASW

KM#	Date	Mintage	VG-8	F-12	VF-20	XF-40	MS-60	MS-63
8	1862	150,000	22.00	40.00	90.00	170.00	750.00	1600.
	1862 recut 2	Inc. Ab.	22.00	40.00	90.00	170.00	750.00	1600.
	1862	—	—	—	—	—	Proof	2200.
	1864	100,000	22.00	40.00	90.00	170.00	750.00	1600.

TWENTY CENTS

4.6480 g, .925 SILVER, .1382 oz ASW

KM#	Date	Mintage	VG-8	F-12	VF-20	XF-40	MS-60	MS-63
9	1862	150,000	12.00	17.00	30.00	100.00	750.00	1600.
	1862	—	—	—	—	—	Proof	2200.
	1864	150,000	12.00	17.00	30.00	100.00	750.00	1600.

NOVA SCOTIA
STERLING COINAGE
HALF PENNY TOKEN

COPPER

KM#	Date	Mintage	VG-8	F-12	VF-20	XF-40	MS-60	MS-63
1	1823	400,000	2.00	4.00	8.00	15.00	65.00	150.00
	1823 w/o hyphen	Inc. Ab.	5.00	10.00	20.00	35.00	170.00	350.00
	1824	118,636	2.50	5.00	12.50	22.50	100.00	225.00
	1832	800,000	1.50	3.00	7.50	12.50	55.00	150.00
1a	1382(error)	—	150.00	300.00	550.00	—	—	—
	1832/1382	—	500.00	700.00	—	—	—	—
	1832 (imitation)	—	3.25	5.00	8.00	12.50	50.00	100.00

KM#	Date	Mintage	VG-8	F-12	VF-20	XF-40	MS-60	MS-63
3	1840 small 0	300,000	3.50	5.00	8.50	12.50	55.00	165.00
	1840 medium 0	Inc. Ab.	2.50	4.00	6.50	11.00	45.00	125.00
	1840 large 0	Inc. Ab.	4.00	6.00	10.00	16.00	60.00	185.00
	1843	300,000	3.00	5.00	8.00	12.00	50.00	160.00

KM#	Date	Mintage	VG-8	F-12	VF-20	XF-40	MS-60	MS-63
5	1856 w/o LCW	720,000	2.00	4.00	7.50	12.50	55.00	175.00
	1856 w/o LCW	—	—	—	—	—	Proof	600.00
	1856 w/o LCW, inverted A for V in PROVINCE				—	—	Proof	600.00

BRONZE

KM#	Date	Mintage	VG-8	F-12	VF-20	XF-40	MS-60	MS-63
5a	1856 w/LCW	—	—	—	—	—	Proof	600.00

ONE PENNY TOKEN

COPPER

KM#	Date	Mintage	VG-8	F-12	VF-20	XF-40	MS-60	MS-63
2	1824	217,776	3.00	6.00	10.00	22.50	100.00	250.00
	1832	200,000	2.00	4.00	7.50	18.00	80.00	230.00
2a	1832 (imitation)	—	5.50	16.00	24.00	40.00	—	—

KM#	Date	Mintage	VG-8	F-12	VF-20	XF-40	MS-60	MS-63
4	1840	150,000	2.00	4.00	7.00	15.00	60.00	175.00
	1843/0	150,000	9.00	12.50	18.00	30.00	85.00	—
	1843	Inc. Ab.	3.00	6.00	10.00	20.00	75.00	200.00

KM#	Date	Mintage	VG-8	F-12	VF-20	XF-40	MS-60	MS-63
6	1856 w/o LCW	360,000	2.50	4.50	8.50	12.00	55.00	135.00
	1856 w/LCW	Inc. Ab.	2.00	4.00	7.00	10.00	45.00	115.00

BRONZE

KM#	Date	Mintage	VG-8	F-12	VF-20	XF-40	MS-60	MS-63
6a	1856	—	—	—	—	—	Proof	400.00

DECIMAL COINAGE
HALF CENT

BRONZE

KM#	Date	Mintage	VG-8	F-12	VF-20	XF-40	MS-60	MS-63
7	1861	400,000	3.00	5.00	8.00	12.00	55.00	130.00
	1864	400,000	3.00	5.00	8.00	12.00	55.00	130.00
	1864	—	—	—	—	—	Proof	300.00

ONE CENT

BRONZE

KM#	Date	Mintage	VG-8	F-12	VF-20	XF-40	MS-60	MS-63
8	1861	800,000	1.50	2.25	4.50	8.00	60.00	150.00
	1862	(Est.) 100,000	20.00	30.00	50.00	100.00	350.00	750.00
	1864	800,000	1.50	2.25	4.50	8.00	60.00	160.00

NOTE: The Royal Mint Report records mintage of 1,000,000 for 1862 which is considered incorrect.

PRINCE EDWARD ISLAND
ONE CENT

BRONZE

KM#	Date	Mintage	VG-8	F-12	VF-20	XF-40	MS-60	MS-63
4	1871	2,000,000	1.25	2.00	3.50	8.00	70.00	175.00
	1871	—	—	—	—	—	Proof	2000.

CAPE VERDE

The Republic of Cape Verde, Africa's smallest republic, is located in the Atlantic Ocean, about 370 miles (595 km.) west of Dakar, Senegal, off the coast of Africa. The 14-island republic has an area of 1,557 sq. mi. (4,033 sq. km.) and a population of 327,000. Capital: Praia. The refueling of ships and aircraft is the chief economic function of the country. Fishing is important and agriculture is widely practiced, but the Cape Verdes are not self-sufficient in food. Fish products, salt, bananas, and shellfish are exported.

The date of discovery of the islands is uncertain. Possibly they were visited by Venetian captain Alvise Cadamosto in 1456. Portuguese navigator Diogo Gomes claimed them for Portugal in May of 1460. Settlement began two years later. The early importance and wealth of the islands, which caused them to be attacked by Sir Francis Drake and the Dutch, resulted from the monopoly of the Guinea slave trade granted the inhabitants in 1466. Poverty and famine occasioned by frequent periods of severe drought have marked the history of the country since abolition of the slave trade in 1876.

After 500 years of Portuguese rule, the Cape Verdes became independent on July 5, 1975. At the first general election, all seats of the new national assembly were won by the Party for the Independence of Guinea-Bissau and Cape Verde (PAIGC). The PAIGC plans to link the two former colonies into one state.

RULERS

Portuguese, until 1975

MONETARY SYSTEM

100 Centavos = 1 Escudo

COLONIAL COINAGE

5 CENTAVOS

BRONZE

KM#	Date	Mintage	Fine	VF	XF	Unc
1	1930	1.000	.50	1.00	2.00	4.25

10 CENTAVOS

BRONZE

KM#	Date	Mintage	Fine	VF	XF	Unc
2	1930	1.500	.65	1.25	2.25	4.50

20 CENTAVOS

BRONZE

KM#	Date	Mintage	Fine	VF	XF	Unc
3	1930	1.500	.75	1.50	2.50	5.00

50 CENTAVOS

NICKEL-BRONZE

KM#	Date	Mintage	Fine	VF	XF	Unc
4	1930	1.000	6.00	12.00	35.00	175.00

KM#	Date	Mintage	Fine	VF	XF	Unc
6	1949	1.000	.25	.50	1.50	4.00

BRONZE

KM#	Date	Mintage	Fine	VF	XF	Unc
11	1968	1.000	.15	.35	.75	1.50

ESCUDO

NICKEL-BRONZE

KM#	Date	Mintage	Fine	VF	XF	Unc
5	1930	.050	10.00	20.00	50.00	225.00

KM#	Date	Mintage	Fine	VF	XF	Unc
7	1949	.500	.75	1.50	3.00	7.00

BRONZE

KM#	Date	Mintage	Fine	VF	XF	Unc
8	1953	.250	.65	1.25	2.50	5.00
	1968	.500	.35	.75	1.25	3.00

2-1/2 ESCUDOS

NICKEL-BRONZE

KM#	Date	Mintage	Fine	VF	XF	Unc
9	1953	.500	.35	.75	1.50	3.25
	1967	.400	.25	.50	1.25	3.00

5 ESCUDOS

NICKEL-BRONZE

KM#	Date	Mintage	Fine	VF	XF	Unc
12	1968	.200	.50	1.00	2.00	4.00

10 ESCUDOS

5.0000 g, .720 SILVER, .1158 oz ASW

KM#	Date	Mintage	Fine	VF	XF	Unc
10	1953	.400	1.25	2.50	4.50	9.00

REPUBLIC

20 CENTAVOS

ALUMINUM

KM#	Date	Mintage	Fine	VF	XF	Unc
15	1977	—	.10	.25	.40	1.00

50 CENTAVOS

ALUMINUM

KM#	Date	Mintage	Fine	VF	XF	Unc
16	1977	—	.15	.35	.75	1.50

ESCUDO

NICKEL-BRONZE
F.A.O. Issue

KM#	Date	Mintage	Fine	VF	XF	Unc
17	1977	1.000	.25	.50	1.00	2.00
	1980	—	.25	.50	.75	1.50

BRASS PLATED STEEL
10th Anniversary of Independence

KM#	Date	Mintage	Fine	VF	XF	Unc
23	1985	—	—	—	.75	1.50

4.0000 g, .925 SILVER, .1190 oz ASW

KM#	Date	Mintage	Fine	VF	XF	Unc
23a	1985	—	—	—	Proof	—

6.0000 g, .750 GOLD, .1447 oz AGW

KM#	Date	Mintage	Fine	VF	XF	Unc
23b	1985	50 pcs.	—	—	Proof	250.00

2-1/2 ESCUDOS

NICKEL-BRONZE
F.A.O. Issue

KM#	Date	Mintage	Fine	VF	XF	Unc
18	1977	1.200	.25	.50	1.00	2.00
	1982	—	.25	.50	.75	1.50

10 ESCUDOS

COPPER-NICKEL
Eduardo Mondlane

KM#	Date	Mintage	Fine	VF	XF	Unc
19	1977	—	.25	.50	1.00	2.00
	1982	—	.25	.50	.75	1.50

10th Anniversary of Independence

KM#	Date	Mintage	Fine	VF	XF	Unc
24	1985	—	—	—	—	2.00
	9.0000 g, .925 SILVER, .2677 oz ASW					
24a	1985	—	—	—	Proof	—
	9.0000 g, .750 GOLD, .2170 oz AGW					
24b	1985	50 pcs.	—	—	Proof	400.00

20 ESCUDOS

COPPER-NICKEL
Domingos Ramos

KM#	Date	Mintage	Fine	VF	XF	Unc
20	1977	—	.70	1.25	2.25	3.50
	1982	—	.40	.80	1.50	2.00

50 ESCUDOS

COPPER-NICKEL
Amilcar Lopes Cabral

KM#	Date	Mintage	Fine	VF	XF	Unc
21	1977	—	1.25	2.00	3.50	6.00

F.A.O. World Fisheries Conference

KM#	Date	Mintage	Fine	VF	XF	Unc
22	1984	*.115	—	—	—	5.50
	16.0000 g, .925 SILVER, .4759 oz ASW					
22a	1984	*.020	—	—	Proof	35.00
	27.0000 g, .917 GOLD, .7958 AGW					
22b	1984	*100 pcs.	—	—	Proof	1500.

100 ESCUDOS

COPPER-NICKEL
Papal Visit

KM#	Date	Mintage	Fine	VF	XF	Unc
25	1990	—	—	—	—	6.50
	33.4000 g, .900 GOLD, .9666 oz AGW					
25a	1990	—	—	—	Proof	—

250 ESCUDOS

16.4000 g, .900 SILVER, .4745 oz ASW
1st Anniversary of Independence

KM#	Date	Mintage	Fine	VF	XF	Unc
13	1976	.013	—	—	—	17.50
	1976	3,525	—	—	Proof	35.00

2500 ESCUDOS

8.0000 g, .900 GOLD, .2315 oz AGW
1st Anniversary of Independence

KM#	Date	Mintage	Fine	VF	XF	Unc
14	1976	3,409	—	—	Proof	200.00

PROOF SETS (PS)

KM#	Date	Mintage	Identification	Issue Price	Mkt. Val.
PS1	Mixed dates	—	KM13-14 1976, KM17-18 1977	—	300.00
PS2	1985(2)	—	KM23a,24a	—	—

CAYMAN ISLANDS

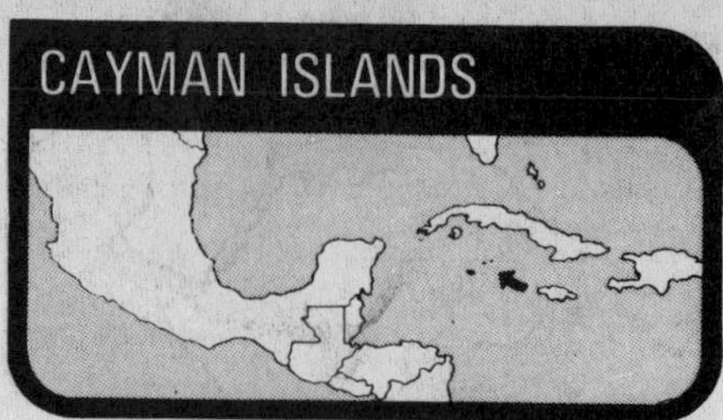

The Cayman Islands, a British dependency situated about 180 miles (290 km.) northwest of Jamaica, consists of three islands: Grand Cayman, Little Cayman, and Cayman Brac. The islands have an area of 100 sq. mi. (259 sq. km.) and a population of 13,000. Capital: Georgtown. Seafaring, commerce, banking, and tourism are the principal industries. Rope, turtle shells, and shark skins are exported.

The islands were discovered by Columbus in 1503, and named by him Tortugas (Spanish for 'turtles') because of the great number of turtles in the nearby waters. Ceded to Britain in 1670, they were colonized from Jamaica by the British and remained dependencies of Jamaica until 1959, when they became a unit territory within the Federation of the West Indies. They became a separate colony when the Federation was dissolved in 1962. Since 1972 a form of self-government has existed, with the Governor responsible for defense and certain other affairs.

While the islands used Jamaican currency for much of their history, the Caymans issued its first national coinage in 1972. The $25 gold and silver commemorative coins issued in 1972 to celebrate the silver wedding anniversary of Queen Elizabeth II and Prince Philip are the first coins in 300 years of Commonwealth coinage to portray a member of the British royal family other than the reigning monarch.

RULERS

British

MINT MARKS

FM - Franklin Mint, U.S.A.*

MONETARY SYSTEM

100 Cents = 1 Dollar

CENT

BRONZE
Great Caiman Thrush

KM#	Date	Mintage	VF	XF	Unc
1	1972	2.155	—	.10	.25
	1972	.011	—	Proof	.50
	1973	9,988	—	Proof	.50
	1974	.030	—	Proof	.50
	1975	7,175	—	Proof	.50
	1976	3,044	—	Proof	.50
	1977	1.800	—	.10	.25
	1977FM	1,970	—	Proof	1.00
	1979FM	4,247	—	Proof	.50
	1980FM	1,215	—	Proof	1.25
	1981FM	865 pcs.	—	Proof	1.50
	1982FM	589 pcs.	—	Proof	1.50
	1982	—	—	.10	.25
	1983FM	—	—	Proof	1.50
	1984FM	—	—	Proof	1.50
	1986	1,000	—	Proof	1.50

25th Anniversary of Coronation

KM#	Date	Mintage	VF	XF	Unc
26	1978	1,303	—	Proof	2.00

KM#	Date	Mintage	VF	XF	Unc
87	1987	—	—	.10	.25
	1987	*500 pcs.	—	Proof	3.00
	1988	*500 pcs.	—	Proof	3.00
	1990	—	—	.10	.25
	BRONZE CLAD STEEL				
87a	1992	—	—	.10	.25

5 CENTS

COPPER-NICKEL
Prawn

KM#	Date	Mintage	VF	XF	Unc
2	1972	.300	—	.10	.25
	1972	.012	—	Proof	.50
	1973	.200	—	.10	.25
	1973	9,988	—	Proof	.50
	1974	.030	—	Proof	.50
	1975	7,175	—	Proof	.50
	1976	3,044	—	Proof	.50
	1977	.600	—	.10	.20
	1977	1,980	—	Proof	.50
	1979FM	4,247	—	Proof	.50
	1980FM	—	—	Proof	2.00
	1981FM	—	—	Proof	2.50
	1982	—	—	.10	.20
	1982FM	—	—	Proof	2.50
	1983FM	—	—	Proof	2.50
	1984FM	—	—	Proof	2.50
	1986	1,000	—	Proof	2.50

NOTE: 1973 Uncs. were not released to circulation.

25th Anniversary of Coronation
Rev: Similar to KM#2.

KM#	Date	Mintage	VF	XF	Unc
27	1978	1,303	—	Proof	3.00

KM#	Date	Mintage	VF	XF	Unc
88	1987	—	—	.10	.25
	1987	*500 pcs.	—	Proof	4.50
	1988	*500 pcs.	—	Proof	4.50
	1990	—	—	.10	.25

10 CENTS

COPPER-NICKEL
Green Turtle

KM#	Date	Mintage	VF	XF	Unc
3	1972	.550	.15	.20	.50
	1972	.011	—	Proof	.75
	1973	.200	.15	.20	.50
	1973	9,988	—	Proof	.75
	1974	.030	—	Proof	.75
	1975	7,175	—	Proof	.75
	1976	3,044	—	Proof	.75
	1977	.960	.15	.20	.50
	1977	1,980	—	Proof	.75
	1979FM	4,247	—	Proof	.75
	1980FM	1,215	—	Proof	3.00
	1981FM	865 pcs.	—	Proof	3.00
	1982	—	.15	.20	.50
	1982FM	589 pcs.	—	Proof	3.00
	1983FM	—	—	Proof	3.00
	1984FM	—	—	Proof	3.00
	1986	1,000	—	Proof	3.00

NOTE: 1973 Uncs. were not released to circulation.

25th Anniversary of Coronation

KM#	Date	Mintage	VF	XF	Unc
28	1978	1,304	—	Proof	3.50

KM#	Date	Mintage	VF	XF	Unc
89	1987	—	.15	.20	.50
	1987	*500 pcs.	—	Proof	5.00
	1988	*500 pcs.	—	Proof	5.00
	1990	—	.15	.20	.50

25 CENTS

COPPER-NICKEL

KM#	Date	Mintage	VF	XF	Unc
4	1972	.350	.30	.50	1.00
	1972	.011	—	Proof	1.00
	1973	.100	.30	.50	1.00
	1973	9,988	—	Proof	1.00
	1974	.030	—	Proof	1.00
	1975	7,175	—	Proof	1.00
	1976	3,044	—	Proof	1.00
	1977	.520	.30	.50	1.00
	1977	1,980	—	Proof	1.00
	1979FM	4,247	—	Proof	1.00
	1980FM	1,215	—	Proof	3.50
	1981FM	865 pcs.	—	Proof	4.00
	1982	—	.30	.50	1.00
	1982FM	589 pcs.	—	Proof	4.00
	1983FM	—	—	Proof	4.00
	1984FM	—	—	Proof	4.00
	1986	1,000	—	Proof	4.00

NOTE: 1973 Uncs. were not released to circulation.

25th Anniversary of Coronation
Rev: Similar to KM#4.

KM#	Date	Mintage	VF	XF	Unc
29	1978	1,303	—	Proof	4.00

KM#	Date	Mintage	VF	XF	Unc
90	1987	—	.30	.50	1.00
	1987	*500 pcs.	—	Proof	6.00
	1988	*500 pcs.	—	Proof	6.00
	1990	—	.30	.50	1.00

50 CENTS

10.3000 g, .925 SILVER, .3063 oz ASW
Caribbean Emperor Fish

KM#	Date	Mintage	VF	XF	Unc
5	1972	500 pcs.	—	—	12.50
	1972	.011	—	Proof	2.50
	1973	9,988	—	Proof	2.50
	1974	.030	—	Proof	2.50
	1975	7,175	—	Proof	3.00
	1976	3,044	—	Proof	4.00
	1977	1,980	—	Proof	4.00
	1979FM	4,247	—	Proof	4.00
	1980FM	1,215	—	Proof	5.00
	1981FM	865 pcs.	—	Proof	6.00
	1982FM	589 pcs.	—	Proof	6.00

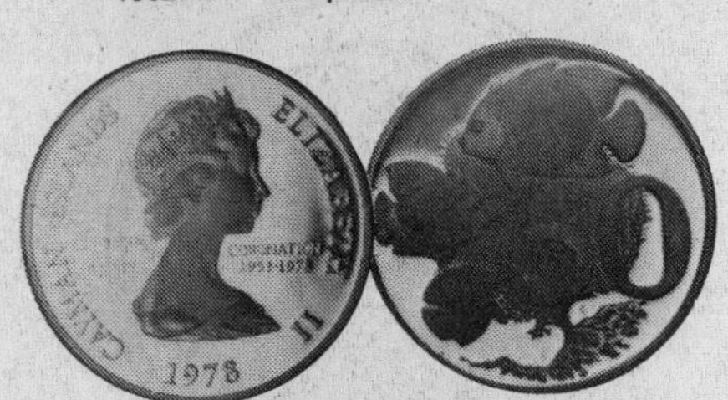

25th Anniversary of Coronation

KM#	Date	Mintage	VF	XF	Unc
30	1978	2,169	—	Proof	8.00

Morning Glory
Obv: Similar to KM#5.

KM#	Date	Mintage	VF	XF	Unc
73	1983FM	—	—	Proof	9.00
	1984FM	411 pcs.	—	Proof	9.00
	1986	1,000	—	Proof	9.00

Obv: Similar to 5 Dollars, KM#81.

KM#	Date	Mintage	VF	XF	Unc
91	1987	*500 pcs.	—	Proof	13.50
	1988	*500 pcs.	—	Proof	13.50

DOLLAR

18.0000 g, .925 SILVER, .5353 oz ASW
Flamboyant

KM#	Date	Mintage	VF	XF	Unc
6	1972	500 pcs.	—	—	15.00
	1972	.011	—	Proof	4.50
	1973	9,988	—	Proof	4.50
	1974	.030	—	Proof	4.50
	1975	7,175	—	Proof	5.00
	1976	3,044	—	Proof	7.00
	1977	1,980	—	Proof	7.00
	1979FM	4,247	—	Proof	7.00
	1980FM	1,215	—	Proof	10.00
	1981FM	865 pcs.	—	Proof	12.00
	1982FM	589 pcs.	—	Proof	12.00

25th Anniversary of Coronation

KM#	Date	Mintage	VF	XF	Unc
31	1978	2,168	—	Proof	12.00

Pineapple
Obv: Similar to 50 Cents, KM#5.

KM#	Date	Mintage	VF	XF	Unc
74	1983FM	1,686	—	Proof	15.00
	1984FM	—	—	Proof	15.00
	1986	1,000	—	Proof	15.00

Obv: Similar to 5 Dollars, KM#81.

KM#	Date	Mintage	VF	XF	Unc
92	1987	*500 pcs.	—	Proof	20.00
	1988	*500 pcs.	—	Proof	20.00

18.1400 g, .925 SILVER, .5395 oz ASW
Green Turtle

KM#	Date	Mintage	VF	XF	Unc
103	1990	*5,000	—	Proof	55.00

Iguanas

KM#	Date	Mintage	VF	XF	Unc
111	1992	*5,000	—	Proof	55.00

2 DOLLARS

29.4500 g, .925 SILVER, .8758 oz ASW
Silver Heron

KM#	Date	Mintage	VF	XF	Unc
7	1972	500 pcs.	—	—	20.00
	1972	.011	—	Proof	7.50
	1973	9,988	—	Proof	7.50
	1974	.030	—	Proof	7.50
	1975	5,390	—	Proof	8.50
	1976	3,044	—	Proof	12.50
	1977	1,980	—	Proof	12.50
	1979FM	4,247	—	Proof	12.50
	1980FM	1,215	—	Proof	20.00
	1981FM	865 pcs.	—	Proof	22.50
	1982FM	589 pcs.	—	Proof	22.50
	1986	1,000	—	Proof	20.00

25th Anniversary of Coronation

KM#	Date	Mintage	VF	XF	Unc
32	1978	2,169	—	Proof	22.50

Parrot
Obv: Similar to 50 Cents, KM#5.

KM#	Date	Mintage	VF	XF	Unc
75	1983FM	409 pcs.	—	Proof	30.00
	1984FM	—	—	Proof	25.00

Obv: Similar to 5 Dollars, KM#81.
Rev: Similar to KM#7.

KM#	Date	Mintage	VF	XF	Unc
93	1987	*500 pcs.	—	Proof	30.00
	1988	*500 pcs.	—	Proof	30.00

5 DOLLARS

35.5000 g, .925 SILVER, 1.0557 oz ASW

KM#	Date	Mintage	VF	XF	Unc
8	1972	500 pcs.	—	—	35.00
	1972	.011	—	Proof	7.50
	1973	.017	—	Proof	7.50
	1974	.026	—	Proof	7.50
	1975	7,753	—	Proof	10.00
	1976	5,177	—	Proof	10.00
	1977	3,525	—	Proof	10.00
	1979FM	—	—	Proof	18.00
	1980FM	—	—	Proof	20.00
	1981FM	—	—	Proof	22.00
	1984FM	—	—	Proof	22.00
	1986	1,000	—	Proof	22.00

25th Anniversary of Coronation

KM#	Date	Mintage	VF	XF	Unc
33	1978	2,168	—	Proof	27.50

150th Anniversary of Parliamentary Government
Obv: Similar to 50 Cents, KM#5.

KM#	Date	Mintage	VF	XF	Unc
70	1982FM	1,105	—	Proof	30.00

Queen's Royal Visit

KM#	Date	Mintage	VF	XF	Unc
76	1983FM	419 pcs.	—	Proof	35.00

28.2800 g, .500 SILVER, .4547 oz ASW
Commonwealth Games

KM#	Date	Mintage	VF	XF	Unc
80	1986	*.050	—	—	12.50

28.2800 g, .925 SILVER, .8411 oz ASW

KM#	Date	Mintage	VF	XF	Unc
80a	1986	*.020	—	Proof	25.00

250th Anniversary of Royal Land Grant

KM#	Date	Mintage	VF	XF	Unc
81	1985	*1,000	—	Proof	30.00

Queen Elizabeth II and Philip's
40th Wedding Anniversary

KM#	Date	Mintage	VF	XF	Unc
85	ND(1987)	*2,000	—	Proof	32.50

35.6400 g, .925 SILVER, 1.0560 oz ASW, 42mm

KM#	Date	Mintage	VF	XF	Unc
85a	ND(1987)	*500 pcs.	—	Proof	120.00

28.2800 g, .925 SILVER, .8411 oz ASW
Seoul Olympics

KM#	Date	Mintage	VF	XF	Unc
94	1988	.020	—	Proof	32.00

35.6400 g, .925 SILVER, 1.0560 oz ASW

KM#	Date	Mintage	VF	XF	Unc
94a	1988	*500 pcs.	—	Proof	120.00

28.2800 g, .925 SILVER, .8411 oz ASW
World Wildlife Fund - Cuban Amazon

KM#	Date	Mintage	VF	XF	Unc
95	1987	—	—	Proof	50.00

500th Anniversary of Columbus'
Discovery of America

KM#	Date	Mintage	VF	XF	Unc
96	1988	*.010	—	Proof	45.00

Visit of Princess Alexandra

KM#	Date	Mintage	VF	XF	Unc
98	1988	*5,000	—	Proof	50.00

100 Years of Postal Service

KM#	Date	Mintage	VF	XF	Unc
100	1989	.010	—	Proof	50.00

Save the Children Fund

KM#	Date	Mintage	VF	XF	Unc
102	1989	*.020	—	Proof	45.00

Queen Mother

KM#	Date	Mintage	VF	XF	Unc
108	1990	*.010	—	Proof	50.00

20th Anniversary of the Currency Board

KM#	Date	Mintage	VF	XF	Unc
109	1991	*2,500	—	Proof	55.00

1992 Olympics - Barcelona

KM#	Date	Mintage	VF	XF	Unc
110	1992	*.050	—	Proof	55.00

40th Anniversary of Coronation of Queen Elizabeth

KM#	Date	Mintage	VF	XF	Unc
112	1993	*.010	—	Proof	55.00

10 DOLLARS

28.2800 g, .925 SILVER, .8411 oz ASW
Wedding of Prince Charles and Lady Diana

KM#	Date	Mintage	VF	XF	Unc
68	1981	.040	—	Proof	20.00

27.8900 g, .925 SILVER, .8295 oz ASW
International Year of the Child

KM#	Date	Mintage	VF	XF	Unc
72	1982	6,616	—	Proof	22.50

23.4500 g, .925 SILVER, .6975 oz ASW
Queen's Royal Visit

KM#	Date	Mintage	VF	XF	Unc
77	1983FM	.010	—	Proof	40.00

25 DOLLARS

51.3500 g, .925 SILVER, 1.5271 oz ASW
Silver Wedding Anniversary

KM#	Date	Mintage	VF	XF	Unc
9	1972	.186	—	—	28.00
	1972	.026	—	Proof	30.00

15.7500 g, .500 GOLD, .2532 oz AGW

KM#	Date	Mintage	VF	XF	Unc
9a	1972	7,706	—	—	80.00
	1972	.021	—	Proof	100.00

51.3500 g, .925 SILVER, 1.5271 oz ASW
Churchill Centenary

KM#	Date	Mintage	VF	XF	Unc
10	1974	1,200	—	—	32.50
	1974	.012	—	Proof	30.00

NOTE: 4300 sets were issued in proof containing KM#10 and Turks & Caicos Islands 20 Crowns KM#2 with an issue price of $80.00.

Queen's Silver Jubilee

KM#	Date	Mintage	VF	XF	Unc
14	1977	3,600	—	—	40.00
	1977	7,854	—	Proof	40.00

Queen Mary I
Obv: Similar to KM#9.

KM#	Date	Mintage	VF	XF	Unc
16	1977	2,720	—	Proof	40.00

Queen Elizabeth I
Obv: Similar to KM#9.

KM#	Date	Mintage	VF	XF	Unc
17	1977	2,677	—	Proof	40.00

Queen Mary II
Obv: Similar to KM#9.

KM#	Date	Mintage	VF	XF	Unc
18	1977	2,653	—	Proof	40.00

Queen Anne
Obv: Similar to KM#9.

KM#	Date	Mintage	VF	XF	Unc
19	1977	2,630	—	Proof	40.00

Queen Victoria
Obv: Similar to KM#9.

KM#	Date	Mintage	VF	XF	Unc
20	1977	2,623	—	Proof	40.00

25th Anniversary of Coronation
Obv: Similar to KM#9. Rev: Ampulla.

KM#	Date	Mintage	VF	XF	Unc
36	1978	5,000	—	Proof	35.00

25th Anniversary of Coronation
Obv: Similar to KM#9. Rev: Orb.

KM#	Date	Mintage	VF	XF	Unc
37	1978	5,000	—	Proof	35.00

25th Anniversary of Coronation
Obv: Similar to KM#9. Rev: St. Edward's crown.

KM#	Date	Mintage	VF	XF	Unc
38	1978	5,000	—	Proof	35.00

25th Anniversary of Coronation
Obv: Similar to KM#9. Rev: Coronation chair.

KM#	Date	Mintage	VF	XF	Unc
39	1978	5,000	—	Proof	35.00

25th Anniversary of Coronation
Obv: Similar to KM#9. Rev: Royal scepter.

KM#	Date	Mintage	VF	XF	Unc
40	1978	5,000	—	Proof	35.00

25th Anniversary of Coronation
Obv: Similar to KM#9. Rev: Spoon.

KM#	Date	Mintage	VF	XF	Unc
41	1978	5,000	—	Proof	35.00

35.6400 g, .500 SILVER, .5729 oz ASW
Saxon Kings
Obv: Similar to KM#9.

KM#	Date	Mintage	VF	XF	Unc
48	1980	.012	—	Proof	32.50

House of Normandy
Obv: Similar to KM#9.

KM#	Date	Mintage	VF	XF	Unc
49	1980	.012	—	Proof	32.50

House of Plantagenet - I
Obv: Similar to KM#9.

KM#	Date	Mintage	VF	XF	Unc
50	1980	.012	—	Proof	32.50

House of Plantagenet - II.
Obv: Similar to KM#9.

KM#	Date	Mintage	VF	XF	Unc
51	1980	.012	—	Proof	32.50

House of Lancaster.
Obv: Similar to KM#9.

KM#	Date	Mintage	VF	XF	Unc
52	1980	.012	—	Proof	32.50

House of York.
Obv: Similar to KM#9.

KM#	Date	Mintage	VF	XF	Unc
53	1980	.012	—	Proof	32.50

House of Tudor
Obv: Similar to KM#9.

KM#	Date	Mintage	VF	XF	Unc
54	1980	.012	—	Proof	32.50

House of Stuart & Orange
Obv: Similar to KM#9.

KM#	Date	Mintage	VF	XF	Unc
55	1980	.012	—	Proof	32.50

House of Hanover
Obv: Similar to KM#9.

KM#	Date	Mintage	VF	XF	Unc
56	1980	.012	—	Proof	32.50

House of Saxe-Coburg and Windsor.
Obv: Similar to KM#9.

KM#	Date	Mintage	VF	XF	Unc
57	1980	.012	—	Proof	32.50

64.8000 g, .925 SILVER, 1.9273 oz ASW
Queen's Royal Visit
Obv: Similar to 50 Cents, KM#5.

KM#	Date	Mintage	VF	XF	Unc
78	1983FM	5,000	—	Proof	45.00

3.1340 g, .999 GOLD, .1006 oz AGW
Winston Churchill - Evacuation of Dunkirk
Obv: Similar to 50 Dollars, KM#105.

KM#	Date	Mintage	VF	XF	Unc
104	1990	*500 pcs.	—	Proof	100.00

50 DOLLARS

64.9400 g, .925 SILVER, 1.9314 oz ASW
Sovereign Queens of England
Obv: Similar to KM#21.

KM#	Date	Mintage	VF	XF	Unc
12	1975	.033	—	—	50.00
	1975	7,800	—	Proof	60.00
	1976	1,292	—	—	60.00
	1976	2,843	—	Proof	60.00
	1977	2,400	—	—	60.00
	1977	Inc, Ab.	—	Proof	60.00

Rev: Coronation Anniversary legend added.

KM#	Date	Mintage	VF	XF	Unc
34	1978	5,775	—	Proof	65.00

11.3400 g, .500 GOLD, .1823 oz AGW
Queen Mary I

KM#	Date	Mintage	VF	XF	Unc
21	1977	1,999	—	Proof	120.00

Queen Elizabeth I

KM#	Date	Mintage	VF	XF	Unc
22	1977	1,969	—	Proof	120.00

Queen Mary II

KM#	Date	Mintage	VF	XF	Unc
23	1977	1,961	—	Proof	120.00

Queen Anne

KM#	Date	Mintage	VF	XF	Unc
24	1977	1,938	—	Proof	120.00

Queen Victoria

KM#	Date	Mintage	VF	XF	Unc
25	1977	1,932	—	Proof	120.00

25th Anniversary of Coronation - Ampulla

KM#	Date	Mintage	VF	XF	Unc
42	1978	771 pcs.	—	Proof	125.00

25th Anniversary of Coronation - Orb

KM#	Date	Mintage	VF	XF	Unc
43	1978	771 pcs.	—	Proof	125.00

25th Anniversary of Coronation - St. Edward's Crown.

KM#	Date	Mintage	VF	XF	Unc
44	1978	771 pcs.	—	Proof	125.00

25th Anniversary of Coronation - Chair

KM#	Date	Mintage	VF	XF	Unc
45	1978	771 pcs.	—	Proof	125.00

25th Anniversary of Coronation - Scepter

KM#	Date	Mintage	VF	XF	Unc
46	1978	771 pcs.	—	Proof	125.00

25th Anniversary of Coronation - Spoon

KM#	Date	Mintage	VF	XF	Unc
47	1978	771 pcs.	—	Proof	125.00

Saxon Kings
Obv: Similar to KM#21.

KM#	Date	Mintage	VF	XF	Unc
58	1980	.010	—	Proof	115.00

House of Normandy
Obv: Similar to KM#21.

KM#	Date	Mintage	VF	XF	Unc
59	1980	.010	—	Proof	115.00

House of Plantagenet - I
Obv: Similar to KM#21.

KM#	Date	Mintage	VF	XF	Unc
60	1980	.011	—	Proof	115.00

House of Plantagenet - II
Obv: Similar to KM#21.

KM#	Date	Mintage	VF	XF	Unc
61	1980	.011	—	Proof	115.00

House of Lancaster
Obv: Similar to KM#21.

KM#	Date	Mintage	VF	XF	Unc
62	1980	.011	—	Proof	115.00

House of York
Obv: Similar to KM#21.

KM#	Date	Mintage	VF	XF	Unc
63	1980	.011	—	Proof	115.00

House of Tudor
Obv: Similar to KM#21.

KM#	Date	Mintage	VF	XF	Unc
64	1980	.011	—	Proof	115.00

House of Stuart and Orange
Obv: Similar to KM#21.

KM#	Date	Mintage	VF	XF	Unc
65	1980	.011	—	Proof	115.00

House of Hanover
Obv: Similar to KM#21.

KM#	Date	Mintage	VF	XF	Unc
66	1980	.011	—	Proof	115.00

House of Saxe-Coburg and Windsor.
Obv: Similar to KM#21.

KM#	Date	Mintage	VF	XF	Unc
67	1980	.011	—	Proof	115.00

5.0000 g, .900 GOLD, .1447 oz AGW
150th Anniversary of Parliamentary Government

KM#	Date	Mintage	VF	XF	Unc
71	1982FM	585 pcs.	—	Proof	130.00

5.1900 g, .917 GOLD, .1530 oz AGW
Queen's Royal Visit

KM#	Date	Mintage	VF	XF	Unc
79	1983	5,000	—	—	120.00

129.6000 g, .925 SILVER, 3.8547 oz ASW
Bird Conservation - Snowy Egret

KM#	Date	Mintage	VF	XF	Unc
83	1985	*.010	—	Proof	75.00

7.8140 g, .999 GOLD, .2509 oz AGW
Winston Churchill - Spitfires Over Dover
Rev: Similar to 250 Dollars, KM#107.

KM#	Date	Mintage	VF	XF	Unc
105	1990	*500 pcs.	—	Proof	200.00

100 DOLLARS

22.6801 g, .500 GOLD, .3646 oz AGW
Churchill Centenary

KM#	Date	Mintage	VF	XF	Unc
11	1974	1,400	—	—	180.00
	1974	6,300	—	Proof	200.00

Sovereign Queens of England
Obv: Similar to 50 Dollars, KM#21.

KM#	Date	Mintage	VF	XF	Unc
13	1975	8,053	—	—	180.00
	1975	4,950	—	Proof	200.00
	1976	2,028	—	—	200.00
	1976	3,560	—	Proof	225.00
	1977	—	—	—	200.00
	1977	2,845	—	Proof	225.00

Queen's Silver Jubilee

KM#	Date	Mintage	VF	XF	Unc
15	1977	562 pcs.	—	—	200.00
	1977	4,386	—	Proof	225.00

Rev: Coronation Anniversary legend.

KM#	Date	Mintage	VF	XF	Unc
35	1978	1,973	—	Proof	240.00

8.0352 g, .917 GOLD, .2369 oz AGW
Wedding of Prince Charles and Lady Diana

KM#	Date	Mintage	VF	XF	Unc
69	1981	.011	—	Proof	150.00

15.9800 g, .917 GOLD, .4708 oz AGW
500th Anniversary of Columbus' Discovery of America

KM#	Date	Mintage	VF	XF	Unc
97	1988	355 pcs.	—	Proof	425.00

100 Years of Postal Service
Rev: Similar to 5 Dollars, KM#100.

KM#	Date	Mintage	VF	XF	Unc
101	1989	500 pcs.	—	Proof	400.00

7.8140 g, .999 GOLD, .2509 oz AGW
Winston Churchill - Evacuation of Dunkirk
Obv: Similar to 50 Dollars, KM#105.

KM#	Date	Mintage	VF	XF	Unc
106	1990	*500 pcs.	—	Proof	400.00

250 DOLLARS

47.5400 g, .917 GOLD, 1.4001 oz AGW
250th Anniversary of Royal Land Grant
Similar to 5 Dollars, KM#81.

KM#	Date	Mintage	VF	XF	Unc
82	1985	*250 pcs.	—	Proof	800.00

Commonwealth Games
Similar to 5 Dollars, KM#80.

KM#	Date	Mintage	VF	XF	Unc
84	1986	*150 pcs.	—	Proof	900.00

Queen Elizabeth II and Philip's 40th Wedding Anniversary
Rev: Similar to 5 Dollars, KM#85.

KM#	Date	Mintage	VF	XF	Unc
86	ND(1987)	75 pcs.	—	Proof	950.00

Visit of Princess Alexandra

KM#	Date	Mintage	VF	XF	Unc
99	1988	86 pcs.	—	Proof	900.00

31.2100 g, .999 GOLD, 1.0014 oz AGW
Winston Churchill - Spitfires Over Dover
Obv: Similar to 50 Dollars, KM#105.

KM#	Date	Mintage	VF	XF	Unc
107	1990	*500 pcs.	—	Proof	950.00

MINT SETS (MS)

KM#	Date	Mintage	Identification	Issue Price	Mkt. Val.
MS1	1987(4)	—	KM87-90	—	5.00

PROOF SETS (PS)

KM#	Date	Mintage	Identification	Issue Price	Mkt. Val.
PS1	1972(8)	10,757	KM1-8	40.00	25.00
PS2	1973(8)	9,988	KM1-8	40.00	25.00
PS3	1974(8)	15,387	KM1-8	40.00	25.00
PS4	1974(2)	2,400	KM10-11	245.00	200.00
PS5	1975(8)	5,390	KM1-8	54.50	28.00
PS6	1975(6)	1,785	KM1-6	31.50	10.00
PS7	1975(2)	3,650	KM12,13	293.00	235.00
PS8	1976(8)	3,044	KM1-8	54.50	30.00
PS9	1976(2)	1,531	KM12,13	293.00	265.00
PS11	1977(8)	1,970	KM1-8	52.50	35.00
PS12	1977(6)	2,445	KM12,16-20	315.00	265.00
PS13	1977(6)	1,932	KM13,21-25	651.00	700.00
PS14	1977(2)	223	KM14,15	290.00	210.00
PS15	1978(8)	1,303	KM26-33	79.50	80.00
PS16	1978(6)	5,000	KM36-41	306.00	210.00
PS17	1978(6)	771	KM42-47	600.00	750.00
PS18	1979(8)	4,247	KM1-8	117.00	50.00
PS19	1980(8)	1,215	KM1-8	147.00	65.00
PS20	1981(8)	865	KM1-8	147.00	75.00
PS21	1982(8)	589	KM1-7,70	147.00	75.00
PS22	1983(8)	348	KM1-4,73-76	157.00	75.00
PS23	1984(8)	—	KM1-4,8,73-75	159.00	80.00
PS24	1986(8)	*1,000	KM1-4,7-8,73-74	150.00	75.00
PS25	1987(8)	*500	KM85a,87-93	160.00	200.00
PS26	1988(8)	*500	KM87-93,94a	170.00	200.00
PS27	1990(4)	*500	KM104-107	1650.	1650.

CENTRAL AFRICAN REPUBLIC

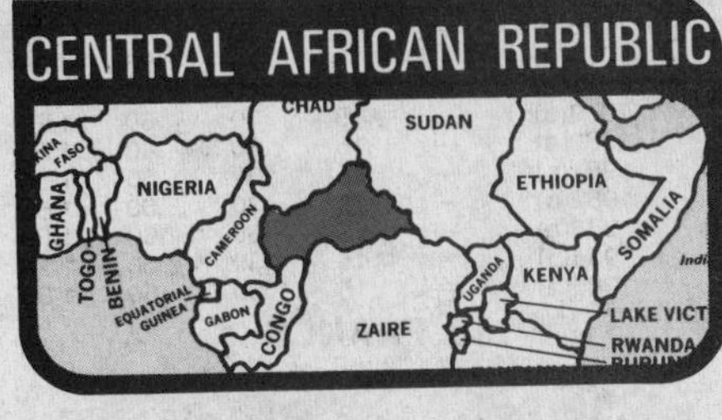

The Central African Republic, a landlocked country in Central Africa, bounded by Chad on the north, Cameroon on the west, Congo (Brazzaville) and Zaire on the south and The Sudan on the east, has an area of 240,535 sq. mi. (622,984 sq. km.) and a population of 2.6 million. Capital: Bangui. Deposits of uranium, iron ore, manganese and copper remain to be developed. Diamonds, cotton, timber and coffee are exported.

The area that is now the Central African Republic was constituted as the French territory of Ubangi-Shari in 1894. It was united with Chad in 1905 and joined with Middle Congo and Gabon in 1910, becoming one of the four territories of French Equatorial Africa. Upon dissolution of the federation on Dec. 1, 1958, the constituent territories became fully autonomous members of the French Community. Ubangi-Shari proclaimed its complete independence as the Central African Republic on Aug. 13, 1960.

On Jan. 1, 1966, Col. Jean-Bedel Bokassa, Chief of Staff of the Armed Forces, overthrew the government of President David Dacko and assumed power as president of the republic. President Bokassa abolished the constitution of 1959 and dissolved the National Assembly. In 1975 the Congress of the sole political party appointed Bokassa president for life. The republic became a constitutional monarchy on Dec. 4, 1976; President Bokassa was named Emperor Bokassa I. Bokassa was ousted as Central African emperor in a bloodless takeover of the government led by former president David Dacko on Sept. 20, 1979, and the African nation proclaimed once again a republic.

NOTE: For earlier coinage see French Equatorial Africa and Equatorial African States. For later coinage see Central African States.

RULERS

French, until 1960
Marshal Jean-Bedel Bokassa, 1976-1979

MINT MARKS

(a) - Paris, privy marks only

MONETARY SYSTEM

100 Centimes = 1 Franc

100 FRANCS

NICKEL

KM#	Date	Mintage	Fine	VF	XF	Unc
6	1971(a)	3.500	4.00	7.50	12.50	27.50
	1972(a)	—	4.00	7.50	12.50	27.50
	1974(a)	—	6.00	12.00	20.00	40.00

KM#	Date	Mintage	Fine	VF	XF	Unc
7	1975(a)	—	3.00	7.00	12.00	20.00
	1976(a)	—	2.00	3.00	5.00	9.00
	1979(a)	—	3.50	7.50	12.50	22.50
	1982(a)	—	2.00	3.50	6.00	10.00
	1983(a)	—	2.00	3.50	6.00	10.00
	1984(a)	—	2.00	3.50	6.00	10.00
	1985(a)	—	2.00	3.50	6.00	10.00
	1988(a)	—	2.00	3.50	6.00	10.00
	1990(a)	—	2.00	3.50	6.00	10.00

1000 FRANCS

3.5000 g, .900 GOLD, .1012 oz AGW
10th Anniversary of Independence
Obv: Bust of Pres. Jean Bedel Bokasso.

KM#	Date	Mintage	Fine	VF	XF	Unc
1	1970	4,000	—	—	Proof	75.00

3000 FRANCS

10.5000 g, .900 GOLD, .3038 oz AGW
10th Anniversary of Independence

KM#	Date	Mintage	Fine	VF	XF	Unc
2	1970	4,000	—	—	Proof	225.00

5000 FRANCS

17.5000 g, .900 GOLD, .5064 oz AGW
10th Anniversary of Independence
Obv: Similar to 3000 Francs, KM#2.

KM#	Date	Mintage	Fine	VF	XF	Unc
3	1970	4,000	—	—	Proof	400.00

10,000 FRANCS

35.0000 g, .900 GOLD, 1.0128 oz AGW
10th Anniversary of Independence
Obv: Similar to 3000 Francs, KM#2.

KM#	Date	Mintage	Fine	VF	XF	Unc
4	1970	4,000	—	—	Proof	800.00

20,000 FRANCS

70.0000 g, .900 GOLD, 2.0257 oz AGW
10th Anniversary of Independence

KM#	Date	Mintage	Fine	VF	XF	Unc
5	1970	4,000	—	—	Proof	1450.

EMPIRE

100 FRANCS

NICKEL
Obv. leg: EMPIRE CENTRAFRICAIN

KM#	Date	Mintage	Fine	VF	XF	Unc
8	1978(a)	—	60.00	100.00	200.00	300.00

REPUBLIC

500 FRANCS

COPPER-NICKEL

KM#	Date	Mintage	Fine	VF	XF	Unc
11	1985(a)	—	2.00	4.00	6.00	10.00
	1986(a)	—	5.00	10.00	20.00	35.00

PROOF SETS (PS)

KM#	Date	Mintage	Identification	Issue Price	Mkt. Val.
PS1	1970(5)	4,000	KM1-5	375.00	2950.

CENTRAL AFRICAN STATES

The Central African States, a monetary union comprising the former French possessions and now independent states of the Republic of Congo (Brazzaville), Gabon, Central African Republic, Chad and Cameroon, issues a common currency for the member states from a common central bank. The monetary unit, the African Financial Community Franc, is tied to and supported by the French franc.

In 1960, an abortive attempt was made to form a union of the newly independent republics of Chad, Congo, Central Africa and Gabon. The proposal was discarded when Chad refused to become a constituent member. The four countries then linked into an Equatorial Customs Unit, to which Cameroon became an associate member in 1961. A more extensive cooperation of the five republics, identified as the Central African Customs and Economic Union, was entered into force at the beginning of 1966.

In 1974 the Central Bank of the Equatorial African States, which had issued coins and paper currency in its own name and with the names of the constituent member nations, changed its name to the Bank of the Central African States. Equatorial Guinea converted to the CFA currency system issuing its first 100 Franc in 1985.

For earlier coinage see French Equatorial Africa.

EQUATORIAL AFRICAN STATES

MINT MARKS

(a) - Paris, privy marks only

MONETARY SYSTEM

100 Centimes = 1 Franc (C.F.A.)

FRANC

ALUMINUM

KM#	Date	Mintage	Fine	VF	XF	Unc
6	1969(a)	2.500	.25	.65	.85	1.50
	1971(a)	3.000	.25	.65	.85	1.50

5 FRANCS

ALUMINUM-BRONZE

KM#	Date	Mintage	Fine	VF	XF	Unc
1	1961(a)	10.000	.35	1.00	1.50	2.50
	1962(a)	5.000	.35	1.00	1.50	2.50
	1965(a)	2.010	.35	1.00	1.50	2.50
	1967(a)	5.795	.35	1.00	1.25	2.00
	1968(a)	5.000	.35	1.00	1.25	2.00
	1969(a)	—	.35	1.00	1.25	2.00
	1970(a)	9.000	.35	1.00	1.25	2.00
	1972(a)	31.010	.35	1.00	1.25	2.00
	1973(a)	5.010	.35	1.00	1.25	2.00

10 FRANCS

ALUMINUM-BRONZE

KM#	Date	Mintage	Fine	VF	XF	Unc
2	1961(a)	10.000	.40	1.00	1.75	3.00
	1962(a)	5.000	.40	1.00	1.75	3.00
	1965(a)	7.000	1.00	1.75	2.75	5.00
	1967(a)	8.000	.40	1.00	1.75	3.00
	1968(a)	2.000	1.50	2.25	3.50	6.00
	1969(a)	10.000	.40	1.00	1.75	3.00
	1972(a)	23.500	.40	1.00	1.75	3.00
	1973(a)	5.000	.75	1.50	2.50	4.50

25 FRANCS

ALUMINUM-BRONZE

KM#	Date	Mintage	Fine	VF	XF	Unc
4	1962(a)	6.000	.50	1.25	2.25	4.00
	1968(a)	—	1.25	2.50	4.00	7.50
	1969(a)	—	1.25	2.50	4.00	7.50
	1970(a)	3.019	.50	1.25	2.25	4.00
	1972(a)	18.516	.50	1.25	2.00	3.00
	1973(a)	—	1.25	2.50	4.00	7.50

50 FRANCS

COPPER-NICKEL

KM#	Date	Mintage	Fine	VF	XF	Unc
3	1961(a)	5.000	2.00	4.00	6.00	10.00
	1963(a)	5.000	2.00	4.00	6.00	10.00

100 FRANCS

NICKEL

KM#	Date	Mintage	Fine	VF	XF	Unc
5	1966(a)	9.948	2.00	4.00	7.00	12.00
	1967(a)	11.000	2.00	4.00	7.00	12.00
	1968(a)	—	2.00	4.00	7.00	12.00

NOTE: For later 100-Francs issues see individual listings under Central African Republic, Congo Peoples Republic, Gabon, Chad, Cameroon and Equatorial Guinea.

CENTRAL AFRICAN STATES

COUNTRY CODE LETTERS

The country in which the coin is intended to circulate in is designated by the following additional code letters.

A = Chad
B = Central African Republic
C = Congo
D = Gabon
E = Cameroon

FRANC

ALUMINUM

KM#	Date	Mintage	Fine	VF	XF	Unc
8	1974(a)	—	.30	.60	1.00	3.00
	1976(a)	—	.30	.60	1.00	3.00
	1978(a)	—	.20	.40	.80	2.50
	1979(a)	—	.20	.40	.80	2.50
	1982(a)	—	.20	.40	.80	2.50
	1985(a)	—	.20	.40	.80	2.50
	1986(a)	—	.20	.40	.80	2.50
	1988(a)	—	.20	.40	.80	2.50
	1990(a)	—	.20	.40	.80	2.50

5 FRANCS

ALUMINUM-BRONZE

KM#	Date	Mintage	Fine	VF	XF	Unc
7	1973(a)	—	.15	.30	.60	1.75
	1975(a)	—	.15	.30	.60	1.75
	1976(a)	—	.15	.30	.60	1.75
	1977(a)	—	.15	.30	.60	1.75
	1978(a)	—	.15	.30	.60	1.75
	1979(a)	—	.15	.30	.60	1.75
	1980(a)	—	.15	.30	.60	1.50
	1981(a)	—	.15	.30	.60	1.50
	1982(a)	—	.15	.30	.60	1.50
	1983(a)	—	.15	.30	.60	1.50
	1984(a)	—	.15	.30	.60	1.50
	1985(a)	—	.15	.30	.60	1.50

10 FRANCS

ALUMINUM-BRONZE

KM#	Date	Mintage	Fine	VF	XF	Unc
9	1974(a)	—	.20	.40	.75	2.00
	1975(a)	—	.20	.40	.75	2.00
	1976(a)	—	.20	.40	.75	2.00
	1977(a)	—	.20	.40	.75	2.00
	1978(a)	—	.20	.40	.75	2.00
	1979(a)	—	.20	.40	.75	2.00
	1980(a)	—	.20	.40	.75	1.50
	1981(a)	—	.20	.40	.75	1.50
	1982(a)	—	.20	.40	.75	1.50
	1983(a)	—	.20	.40	.75	1.50
	1984(a)	—	.20	.40	.75	1.50
	1985(a)	—	.20	.40	.75	1.50

25 FRANCS

ALUMINUM-BRONZE

KM#	Date	Mintage	Fine	VF	XF	Unc
10	1975(a)	—	.50	1.00	1.75	3.00
	1976(a)	—	.50	1.00	1.50	2.75
	1978(a)	—	.50	1.00	1.50	2.75
	1982(a)	—	.35	.75	1.25	2.50
	1983(a)	—	.35	.75	1.25	2.50
	1984(a)	—	.35	.75	1.25	2.50
	1985(a)	—	.35	.75	1.25	2.50

50 FRANCS

NICKEL

KM#	Date	Mintage	Fine	VF	XF	Unc
11	1976A(a)	10.000	1.00	2.00	4.00	7.00
	1976B(a)	I.A.	1.00	2.00	4.00	7.00
	1976C(a)	I.A.	1.00	2.00	4.00	7.00
	1976D(a)	I.A.	1.00	2.00	4.00	7.00
	1976E(a)	I.A.	1.00	2.00	4.00	7.00
	1977A(a)	—	1.25	2.50	5.00	10.00
	1977B(a)	—	1.00	2.00	4.00	7.00
	1977C(a)	—	1.00	2.00	4.00	7.00
	1977D(a)	—	1.00	2.00	4.00	7.00
	1977E(a)	—	1.00	2.00	4.00	7.00
	1978A(a)	—	1.00	2.00	4.00	7.00
	1978B(a)	—	1.00	2.00	4.00	7.00
	1978C(a)	—	1.00	2.00	4.00	7.00
	1978D(a)	—	1.00	2.00	4.00	7.00
	1979E(a)	—	1.00	2.00	4.00	7.00
	1980A(a)	—	.75	1.50	3.50	6.00
	1980C(a)	—	.75	1.50	3.50	6.00
	1981C(a)	—	.75	1.50	3.50	6.00
	1981D(a)	—	.85	1.75	3.75	6.50
	1982A(a)	—	.75	1.50	3.50	6.00
	1983D(a)	—	.75	1.50	3.50	6.00
	1983E(a)	—	.75	1.50	3.50	6.00
	1984A(a)	—	.85	1.75	3.75	6.50
	1984B(a)	—	.85	1.75	3.75	6.50
	1984C(a)	—	.75	1.50	3.50	6.00
	1984D(a)	—	.75	1.50	3.50	6.00
	1985A(a)	—	.75	1.50	3.50	6.00
	1985D(a)	—	.75	1.50	3.50	6.00
	1985B(a)	—	.85	1.75	3.75	6.50
	1986B(a)	—	.85	1.75	3.75	6.50
	1986E(a)	—	.85	1.75	3.75	6.50
	1989A(a)	—	.85	1.75	3.75	6.50
	1990B(a)	—	.85	1.75	3.75	6.50

500 FRANCS

COPPER-NICKEL

KM#	Date	Mintage	Fine	VF	XF	Unc
12	1976A(a)	4.000	4.00	8.00	12.00	18.50
	1976B(a)	I.A.	3.50	7.00	11.00	17.50
	1976C(a)	I.A.	3.50	7.00	11.00	17.50
	1976D(a)	I.A.	3.50	7.00	11.00	17.50
	1976E(a)	I.A.	3.50	7.00	11.00	17.50
	1977A(a)	—	4.00	8.00	12.00	18.50
	1977B(a)	—	3.50	7.00	11.00	17.50
	1977C(a)	—	3.50	7.00	11.00	17.50
	1977D(a)	—	3.50	7.00	11.00	17.50
	1977E(a)	—	3.50	7.00	11.00	17.50
	1979D(a)	—	3.00	6.00	10.00	15.00
	1982D(a)	—	3.00	6.00	10.00	15.00
	1984A(a)	—	3.00	6.00	9.50	13.50
	1984C(a)	—	3.00	6.00	9.50	13.50
	1984E(a)	—	3.00	6.00	9.50	13.50

CENTRAL AMERICAN REP.

The Central American Republic (Provincias Unidas del Centro de America, Republic of the United States of Central America, Central American Confederation) was an 1823-39 confederation of the former provinces of the Captaincy General of Guatemala - Guatemala, Honduras, El Salvador, Nicaragua and Costa Rica - formed after the downfall of the short-lived Mexican empire of Augustin de Iturbide. The confederation, which occupied all of Central America between Mexico and Panama, had a population of fewer than 1.5 million. There was no permanent capital.

On Sept. 15, 1821, the leaders of the Captaincy General that governed the five provinces of Central America for Spain, declared Central America independent from Spain. The following year, Iturbide crowned himself Augustin I of Mexico and invited the Central Americans to join his empire. Guatemala, Honduras, Nicaragua and Costa Rica did so. El Salvador, which desired to become a part of the United States, refused and was invaded and conquered for Mexico by Vicente Filisola, the military governor Iturbide had sent to Guatemala. But almost before El Salvador had been forced into the Mexican empire, Iturbide was ousted and sent into exile by Antonio Lopez de Santa Anna. Filisola then reconvened the National Constituent Assembly that had been called into existence by the Central American declaration of independence of 1821. On July 1, 1823, the Assembly issued a second declaration of independence, from Mexico as well as Spain, and established the Central American Republic.

Historically the confederation, which lasted 15 years, was a triumph of rhetoric over reality. It had neither permanent capital, army nor treasury and was all but powerless to raise funds. Its political leaders managed to write a constitution, but it was as ineffectual as the first constitution of the United States, the Articles of Confederation. The citizens of the Central American Republic had no sense of nationhood and were divided by geography as well as religious and class animosity. By 1827 the entire confederation was embroiled in a civil war. By the end of 1838 every state but El Salvador had seceded from the ill-advised union; however, Costa Rica, Guatemala and Honduras continued to strike coins in the confederation style -until 1850, 1851 and 1861, respectively. Costa Rica then countermarked many coins of this series for continued circulation within its boundaries.

The concept of a unified nation of Central America continues to inspire some interest to this day.

MINT MARKS

CR - San Jose, Costa Rica
G, NG - Guatemala
T - Tegucigalpa, Honduras

MONETARY SYSTEM

16 Reales = 1 Escudo

1/4 REAL

.8500 g, .903 SILVER, .0246 oz ASW
Mint mark: G

KM#	Date	Mintage	VG	Fine	VF	XF
1	1824	—	5.00	12.00	20.00	40.00
	1826	—	3.00	7.50	12.50	25.00
	1828	—	—	—	Rare	—
	1831	—	3.00	7.50	12.50	25.00
	1833	—	—	—	Rare	—
	1837	—	2.25	6.00	12.50	25.00
	1838	—	5.00	12.00	20.00	40.00
	1840/30	—	2.25	5.00	10.00	20.00
	1841	—	—	—	Rare	—

1842/29

KM#	Date	Mintage	VG	Fine	VF	XF
	1842/29	—	2.25	4.00	9.00	18.00
	1842/37	—	2.25	4.00	9.00	17.50
	1843	—	2.25	4.50	10.00	18.50
	1844	—	2.25	4.00	9.00	17.50
	1845	—	40.00	70.00	125.00	250.00
	1846	—	3.50	8.00	15.00	27.50
	1847	—	—	—	Rare	—
	1848	—	—	—	—	—
	1850	—	7.00	17.50	35.00	60.00
	1851	—	—	—	Rare	—

NOTE: 1846 date exists with both coin and medal alignment.

Mint mark: CR

KM#	Date	Mintage	VG	Fine	VF	XF
23	1845	—	35.00	60.00	110.00	225.00

1/2 REAL

1.6900 g., .903 SILVER, .0490 oz ASW
Mint mark: NG

KM#	Date	Mintage	VG	Fine	VF	XF
2	1824 M	—	6.00	13.50	30.00	70.00

Mint mark: T
Similar to KM#20.

KM#	Date	Mintage	VG	Fine	VF	XF
18	1830 F	—	—	—	Rare	—
	1831 F	—	—	Reported, not confirmed		

 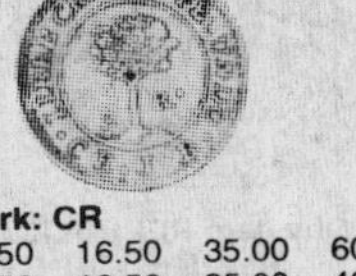

Mint mark: CR

KM#	Date	Mintage	VG	Fine	VF	XF
20	1831 E	—	5.50	16.50	35.00	60.00
	1831 F	—	4.50	12.50	25.00	42.50
	1843 M	—	3.00	7.50	22.50	40.00
	1845 B	—	10.00	22.50	40.00	90.00

1.6900 g, .750 SILVER, .0407 oz ASW

KM#	Date	Mintage	VG	Fine	VF	XF
20a	1846 JB CRESCA	—	5.00	15.00	30.00	60.00
	1846 JB CREZCA	—	20.00	45.00	85.00	180.00
	1847 JB CRESCA	—	20.00	45.00	80.00	170.00
	1847 JB CREZCA	—	5.00	13.50	30.00	60.00
	1848 JB	—	3.00	8.50	22.50	47.50
	1849 JB	—	15.00	30.00	55.00	100.00

REAL

3.3800 g, .903 SILVER, .0981 oz ASW
Mint mark: NG

KM#	Date	Mintage	VG	Fine	VF	XF
3	1824 M	—	6.00	13.50	32.50	55.00
	1828 M	—	15.00	35.00	80.00	155.00

Mint mark: T

KM#	Date	Mintage	VG	Fine	VF	XF
19	1825 M1 known	—	—	—	Rare	—
	1830 F	—	5.00	10.00	25.00	55.00
	1831 F	—	—	Reported, not confirmed		

Mint mark: CR

KM#	Date	Mintage	VG	Fine	VF	XF
21	1831 E	—	11.50	22.50	65.00	130.00
	1831 F	—	9.00	20.00	50.00	100.00
	1848 JB	—	—	—	—	—

3.3800 g, .750 SILVER, .0815 oz ASW

KM#	Date	Mintage	VG	Fine	VF	XF
21a	1848 JB	—	27.50	60.00	125.00	225.00
	1849 JB	—	13.50	30.00	50.00	110.00

2 REALES

6.7700 g, .903 SILVER, .1965 oz ASW
Mint mark: T
Obv. leg: REP.D.CENT.D.AMER.
Rev. leg: LIB.CRESC.FEC.

KM#	Date	Mintage	Good	VG	Fine	VF
10	1825 JD 2 known	—	—	—	Rare	—
	1825 NR	—	75.00	135.00	300.00	525.00

Obv. leg: REPUBLICA DE CENTRO AMERIC.
Rev. leg: LIBRE CRESCA FECUNDO.

KM#	Date	Mintage	VG	Fine	VF	XF
9.1	1825 M	—	—	—	Rare	—

Obv. leg: REPUBLICA DEL CENTRO AMER.
Rev. leg: LIBRE CRESCA FECUND.

KM#	Date	Mintage	VG	Fine	VF	XF
9.2	1825 M	—	—	—	Rare	—

Obv. leg: REPUBLICA DEL CENTRO DE AMER.
Rev. leg: LIBRE CRESCA FECUNDO.

KM#	Date	Mintage	VG	Fine	VF	XF
9.3	1831 F	—	4.50	9.00	20.00	35.00
	1832 F	—	6.50	15.00	32.50	50.00

6.5000 g, .750 SILVER, .1567 oz ASW
Mint mark: CR

KM#	Date	Mintage	VG	Fine	VF	XF
24	1849 JB	—	—	—	Rare	—

8 REALES

27.0700 g, .903 SILVER, .7859 oz ASW
Mint mark: NG

KM#	Date	Mintage	VG	Fine	VF	XF
4	1824 M	—	14.00	30.00	65.00	125.00
	1825 M	—	14.00	30.00	65.00	125.00
	1826 M	—	14.00	30.00	65.00	125.00
	1827 M	—	14.00	32.50	75.00	150.00
	1828 M	—	17.50	37.50	85.00	175.00
	1829 M	—	14.00	30.00	65.00	125.00
	1830 M	—	150.00	250.00	500.00	900.00
	1831 M	—	200.00	400.00	750.00	1200.
	1834 M	—	65.00	120.00	200.00	350.00
	1835 M coin	—	14.00	30.00	65.00	125.00
	1835 M medal	—	14.00	30.00	65.00	125.00
	1836 M	—	14.00	30.00	65.00	125.00
	1836 BA	—	17.50	37.50	75.00	150.00
	1837 BA	—	14.00	30.00	65.00	125.00
	1838 BA	—	— Reported, not confirmed			
	1839/7 MA/BA	—	35.00	75.00	150.00	300.00
4	1840/37 MA/BA	—	15.00	37.50	80.00	150.00
	1840/39 MA	—	14.00	30.00	65.00	125.00
	1840 MA	—	14.00	30.00	65.00	125.00
	1841/37 MA/BA	—	60.00	125.00	250.00	500.00
	1841 MA	—	50.00	100.00	200.00	400.00
	1842/37 MA/BA	—	15.00	32.50	75.00	150.00
	1842/0 MA	—	15.00	32.50	75.00	150.00
	1842 MA	—	14.00	30.00	65.00	125.00
	1846 MA	—	15.00	32.50	75.00	150.00
	1846/2 AE	—	65.00	120.00	200.00	350.00
	1846 AE/MA w/CREZCA over CRESCA	—	65.00	120.00	200.00	350.00
	1846 A	—	15.00	35.00	80.00	150.00
	1847/6 A	—	25.00	50.00	110.00	225.00
	1847 A	—	20.00	40.00	100.00	200.00

Mint mark: CR

KM#	Date	Mintage	VG	Fine	VF	XF
22	1831 E	—	1000.	2000.	4000.	7500.
	1831 F	—	350.00	700.00	1500.	3000.

1/2 ESCUDO

1.6875 g, .875 GOLD, .0474 oz AGW
Mint mark: NG

KM#	Date	Mintage	VG	Fine	VF	XF
5	1824 M	—	45.00	90.00	150.00	300.00
	1825/4 M	—	50.00	100.00	175.00	275.00
	1825 M	—	45.00	75.00	125.00	225.00
	1826 M	—	50.00	100.00	175.00	275.00
	1843 M	—	100.00	200.00	350.00	550.00

Mint mark: CR
Provisional Issue

KM#	Date	Mintage	VG	Fine	VF	XF
11	1825 MU	2 known	—	—	Rare	—

KM#	Date	Mintage	VG	Fine	VF	XF
13.1	1828 F	4,435	75.00	125.00	200.00	350.00
	1843 M	593	90.00	180.00	360.00	600.00
	1846 JB	.013	30.00	50.00	80.00	140.00
	1847 JB	.023	30.00	50.00	80.00	140.00
	1848 JB	.014	30.00	50.00	80.00	140.00
	1849 JB	I.A.	90.00	180.00	350.00	550.00

Mint mark: CR w/inverted C.

KM#	Date	Mintage	VG	Fine	VF	XF
13.2	1847 JB	I.A.	30.00	50.00	80.00	140.00
	1848 JB	I.A.	30.00	50.00	80.00	140.00

ESCUDO

3.3750 g, .875 GOLD, .0949 oz AGW
Mint mark: NG

KM#	Date	Mintage	VG	Fine	VF	XF
6	1824 M	—	100.00	200.00	400.00	600.00
	1825 M	—	75.00	125.00	200.00	400.00

Mint mark: CR

KM#	Date	Mintage	VG	Fine	VF	XF
14	1828 F	—	—	—	Rare	—
	1833 E	.010	50.00	100.00	150.00	250.00
	1833 F	Inc. Ab.	— Reported, not confirmed			
14	1844 M	6,353	50.00	100.00	150.00	250.00
	1845 JB	8,672	90.00	150.00	250.00	375.00
	1846 JB	2,722	50.00	100.00	175.00	260.00
	1847 JB	3,510	50.00	100.00	175.00	260.00
	1848 JB	.010	50.00	80.00	150.00	225.00
	1849 JB	.013	50.00	90.00	150.00	225.00
	1850 JB	—	— Reported, not confirmed			

2 ESCUDOS

6.7500 g, .875 GOLD, .1899 oz AGW
Mint mark: NG

KM#	Date	Mintage	VG	Fine	VF	XF
12	1825 M	—	135.00	180.00	320.00	450.00
	1826 M	—	135.00	180.00	320.00	450.00
	1827 M	—	135.00	180.00	320.00	450.00
	1828 M	—	135.00	180.00	320.00	450.00
	1830 M	—	200.00	250.00	400.00	550.00
	1834 M	—	225.00	375.00	750.00	1000.
	1835 M	—	125.00	190.00	320.00	450.00
	1836 M	—	150.00	200.00	400.00	500.00
	1837 BA	—	150.00	200.00	425.00	750.00
	1840 MA	—	—	—	Rare	—
	1842 MA	—	150.00	200.00	400.00	725.00
	1844 B	—	150.00	200.00	425.00	750.00
	1846 A	—	150.00	200.00	400.00	550.00
	1847 A	—	150.00	200.00	400.00	625.00

Mint mark: CR

KM#	Date	Mintage	VG	Fine	VF	XF
15	1828 F	2,750	100.00	190.00	350.00	700.00
	1835 F	5,452	100.00	170.00	275.00	550.00
	1843 F	4,482	100.00	190.00	350.00	700.00
	1846 JB	—	— Reported, not confirmed			
	1850 JB	7,432	100.00	125.00	225.00	450.00

4 ESCUDOS

13.5000 g, .875 GOLD, .3798 oz AGW
Mint mark: NG

KM#	Date	Mintage	VG	Fine	VF	XF
7	1824 M	—	900.00	1800.	3200.	5500.
	1825 M	—	1200.	2100.	3500.	6000.
	1826 M	—	— Reported, not confirmed			

Mint mark: CR

KM#	Date	Mintage	VG	Fine	VF	XF
16	1828 F	3,048	500.00	750.00	1450.	3500.
	1835 F	697 pcs.	350.00	625.00	1250.	3250.
	1837 E	.011	350.00	650.00	1400.	3750.
	1837 F	Inc. Ab.	—	—	Rare	—
	1849 JB	441 pcs.	1500.	2500.	4500.	7000.

8 ESCUDOS

27.0000 g, .875 GOLD, .7596 oz AGW
Mint mark: NG

KM#	Date	Mintage	VG	Fine	VF	XF
8	1824 M	—	1750.	3500.	7000.	12,000.
	1825 M	—	1750.	3500.	7000.	12,000.

NOTE: Stack's Hammel sale 9-82 Unc 1824 M realized $27,000.

Mint mark: CR

KM#	Date	Mintage	VG	Fine	VF	XF
17	1828 F	5,302	900.00	1500.	2500.	3500.
	1833 F	4,459	900.00	1500.	2500.	3500.
	1837 E	2,028	950.00	1550.	3250.	5500.
	1837 F	Inc. Ab.	1200.	2100.	4000.	6500.

NOTE: Stack's Hammel sale 9-82 AU 1828 F realized $9500.

Listings For

CEYLON: refer to Shri (Sri) Lanka

CHAD

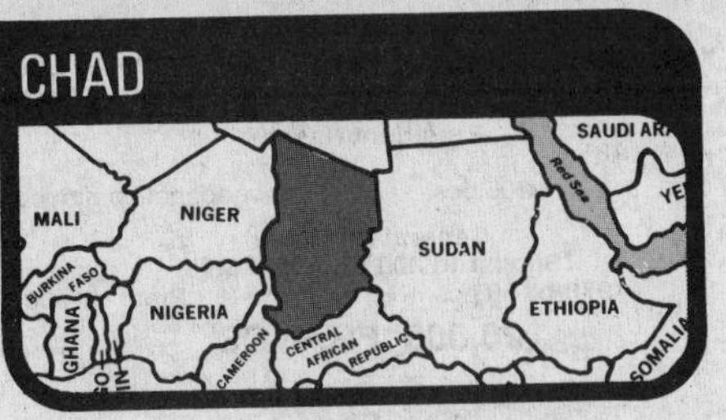

The Republic of Chad, a landlocked country of central Africa, is the largest country of former French Equatorial Africa. It has an area of 495,755 sq. mi. (1,284,000 sq. km.) and a population of 5.1 million. Capital: N'Djamena. An expanding livestock industry produces camels, cattle and sheep. Cotton (the chief product), ivory and palm oil are important exports.

Although supposedly known to Ptolemy, the Chad area was first visited by white men in 1823. Exaggerated estimates of its economic importance led to a race for its possession (1890-93) which resulted in the territory being divided by treaty between Great Britain, France and Germany. As a consequence of World War I, the German area was mandated to France in 1919. Chad was absorbed into the colony of French Equatorial Africa, as part of Ubangi-Shari, in 1910 and became a separate colony in 1920. Upon dissolution of French Equatorial Africa in 1959, the component states became autonomous members of the French Union. Chad became an independent republic on Aug. 11, 1960.

NOTE: For earlier and related coinage see French Equatorial Africa and the Equatorial African States. For later coinage see Central African States.

MINT MARKS

(a) - Paris, privy marks only
(b) = Brussels

COMMEMORATIVE EDGE INSCRIPTIONS

1960 LIBERTE PROGRESS SOLIDARITE
1970/REPUBLIQUE DU TCHAD

100 FRANCS

5.0000 g, .925 SILVER, .0957 oz ASW
10th Anniversary of Independence
Robert Francis Kennedy

KM#	Date	Mintage	Fine	VF	XF	Unc
1	1970(b) 975 pcs.		—	—	Proof	100.00

NICKEL

KM#	Date	Mintage	Fine	VF	XF	Unc
2	1971(a)	5.000	10.00	17.50	27.50	45.00
	1972(a)	5.000	10.00	17.50	27.50	45.00

KM#	Date	Mintage	Fine	VF	XF	Unc
3	1975(a)	—	7.50	12.50	20.00	30.00
	1978(a)	—	8.00	14.00	22.00	35.00
	1980(a)	—	7.00	12.50	17.50	25.00
	1982(a)	—	6.00	10.00	15.00	20.00
	1984(a)	—	6.00	10.00	15.00	20.00
	1985(a)	—	6.00	10.00	15.00	20.00
	1988(a)	—	6.00	10.00	15.00	20.00
	1990(a)	—	6.00	10.00	15.00	20.00

200 FRANCS

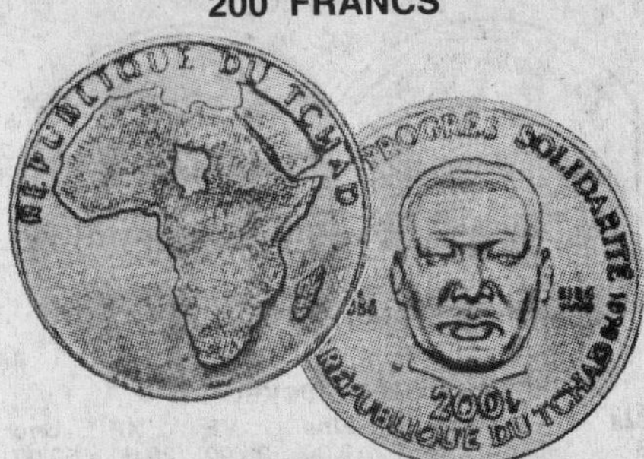

15.0000 g, .925 SILVER, .4461 oz ASW
10th Anniversary of Independence
Martin Luther King, Jr.

KM#	Date	Mintage	Fine	VF	XF	Unc
4	1970(b) 952 pcs.		—	—	Proof	200.00

15.0000 g, .800 SILVER, .3858 oz ASW
10th Anniversary of Independence
General De Gaulle

KM#	Date	Mintage	Fine	VF	XF	Unc
5	1970(b) 442 pcs.		—	—	Proof	225.00

10th Anniversary of Independence
President Nasser

KM#	Date	Mintage	Fine	VF	XF	Unc
6	1970(b) 435 pcs.		—	—	Proof	175.00

300 FRANCS

25.0000 g, .925 SILVER, .8922 oz ASW
10th Anniversary of Independence
John Fitzgerald Kennedy

KM#	Date	Mintage	Fine	VF	XF	Unc
7	1970(b) 504 pcs.		—	—	Proof	450.00

500 FRANCS

COPPER-NICKEL

KM#	Date	Mintage	Fine	VF	XF	Unc
13	1985(a)	—	10.00	20.00	30.00	50.00

1000 FRANCS

3.5000 g, .900 GOLD, .1012 oz AGW
10th Anniversary of Independence
Commandant Lamy

KM#	Date	Mintage	Fine	VF	XF	Unc
8	1970(a)	4,000	—	—	Proof	220.00

3000 FRANCS

10.5000 g, .900 GOLD, .3038 oz AGW
10th Anniversary of Independence
Governor Eboue

KM#	Date	Mintage	Fine	VF	XF	Unc
9	1970(a)	4,000	—	—	Proof	165.00

5000 FRANCS

17.5000 g, .900 GOLD, .5064 oz AGW
10th Anniversary of Independence
General Leclerc

KM#	Date	Mintage	Fine	VF	XF	Unc
10	1970(a)	4,000	—	—	Proof	310.00

10,000 FRANCS

36.0000 g, .900 GOLD, 1.0128 oz AGW
10th Anniversary of Independence

General De Gaulle

KM#	Date	Mintage	Fine	VF	XF	Unc
11	1970(a)	4,000	—	—	Proof	710.00

President Nasser

KM#	Date	Mintage	Fine	VF	XF	Unc
14	1970(b)	205 pcs.	— Reported, not confirmed			

General De Gaulle
Similar to 200 Francs, KM#5.

KM#	Date	Mintage	Fine	VF	XF	Unc
15	1970(b)	90 pcs.	—	—	Proof	1000.

20,000 FRANCS

70.0000 g, .900 GOLD, 2.0257 oz AGW
10th Anniversary of Independence
Francois Tombalbaye

KM#	Date	Mintage	Fine	VF	XF	Unc
12	1970(a)	4,000	—	—	Proof	1350.

PROOF SETS (PS)

KM#	Date	Mintage	Identification	Issue Price	Mkt. Val.
PS1	1970(5)	4,000	KM8-12	412.50	2750.
PS2	1970(3)	—	KM1,4,7	33.00	750.00

CHILE

The Republic of Chile, a ribbon-like country on the Pacific coast of southern South America, has an area of 292,258 sq. mi. (756,950 sq. km.) and a population of 12.2 million. Capital: Santiago. Historically, the economic base of Chile has been the rich mineral deposits of its northern provinces. Copper, of which Chile has 25 percent of the free world's reserves, has accounted for more than 75 percent of Chile's export earnings in recent years. Other important mineral exports are iron ore, iodine and nitrate of soda. Fresh fruits and vegetables, as well as wine are increasingly significant in inter-hemispheric trade.

Diego de Almargo was the first Spaniard to attempt to wrest Chile from the Incas and Araucanian tribes in 1536. He failed, and was followed by Pedro de Valdivia, a favorite of Pizarro, who founded Santiago in 1541. When the Napoleonic Wars involved Spain, leaving the constituent parts of the Spanish Empire to their own devices, Chilean patriots formed a national government and proclaimed the country's independence, Sept. 18, 1810. Independence however, was not secured until Feb. 12, 1818, after a bitter struggle led by Bernardo O'Higgins and San Martin. Though a long steady history of monetary devaluation -reflected in declining weight and fineness in its currency, Chile developed a strong democracy. This was displaced when rampant inflation characterized chaotic and subsequently repressive governments in the late middle 20th century.

RULERS

Spanish until 1818

MINT MARKS

So - Santiago

MINTMASTERS INITIALS

Letter	Date	Name
AJ	1800-1801	Agustin de Infante y Prado and Jose Maria de Bobadilla
D		Domingo Eizaguirre
F		Francisco Rodriguez Brochero
FJ,JF	1803-1817	Francisco Rodriguez Brochero and Jose Maria de Bobadilla

MONETARY SYSTEM

16 Reales = 1 Escudo

COLONIAL MILLED COINAGE

1/4 REAL

.8460 g, .896 SILVER, .0243 oz ASW
Mint mark: So

KM#	Date	Mintage	VG	Fine	VF	XF
63	1801	.057	10.00	15.00	32.00	65.00
	1802	.056	10.00	15.00	32.00	65.00
	1803	.054	10.00	15.00	32.00	65.00
	1804	.056	10.00	15.00	32.00	65.00
	1805	.056	10.00	15.00	32.00	65.00
	1806/5	.054	10.00	15.00	32.00	65.00
	1806	Inc. Ab.	10.00	15.00	32.00	65.00
	1807	.057	10.00	15.00	32.00	65.00
	1808	.057	10.00	15.00	32.00	65.00

NOTE: Earlier dates (1796-1800) exist for this type.

Obv: Lion. Rev: Castle.

KM#	Date	Mintage	VG	Fine	VF	XF
73	1809	.054	15.00	25.00	50.00	100.00
	1810	.054	10.00	15.00	32.00	65.00
	1811	.054	10.00	15.00	32.00	65.00
	1812	.071	10.00	15.00	32.00	65.00
	1813	.063	10.00	15.00	32.00	65.00
	1814	.067	10.00	15.00	32.00	65.00
	1815	.054	10.00	15.00	32.00	65.00
	1816/5	.082	10.00	15.00	32.00	65.00
	1816	Inc.Ab.	10.00	15.00	32.00	65.00
	1817	—	10.00	15.00	32.00	65.00
	1818/6	.403	15.00	20.00	40.00	80.00
	1818	Inc. Ab.	15.00	20.00	40.00	80.00

NOTE: 1817 and 1818 dated coins struck under the Republic.

1/2 REAL

1.6921 g, .896 SILVER, .0487 oz ASW
Obv. leg: CAROLUS IIII. . . ., bust of Charles IIII.
Rev: Similar to KM#64.

KM#	Date	Mintage	VG	Fine	VF	XF
57	1801 AJ	.059	8.00	12.00	22.00	55.00
	1801 AI (broken J)	Inc. Ab.	8.00	12.00	22.00	55.00
	1802 JJ	.078	8.00	12.00	22.00	55.00
	1803 FJ	.036	20.00	40.00	75.00	150.00
	1804/3 FJ	.058	10.00	15.00	30.00	70.00
	1804 FJ	I.A.	8.00	12.00	22.00	70.00
	1805 FJ	.028	12.00	20.00	40.00	80.00
	1806 FJ	.059	8.00	12.00	22.00	55.00
	1807 FJ	.040	8.00	12.00	22.00	55.00
	1808/7 FJ	.058	10.00	15.00	30.00	60.00
	1808 FJ	I.A.	8.00	12.00	22.00	55.00

NOTE: Earlier dates (1792-1800) exist for this type.

Obv. leg: FERDIN VII, bust of Charles IV.

KM#	Date	Mintage	VG	Fine	VF	XF
64	1808 FJ	I.A.	8.00	12.00	25.00	60.00
	1809/8 FJ	.051	12.00	18.00	35.00	65.00
	1809 FJ	I.A.	10.00	17.00	28.00	55.00
	1810 FJ	.050	10.00	17.00	28.00	55.00
	1811 FJ	.018	10.00	17.00	28.00	55.00
	1812 FJ	.125	10.00	17.00	28.00	55.00
	1813 FJ	.218	10.00	17.00	28.00	55.00
	1814 FJ	.077	9.00	14.00	20.00	50.00
	1815 FJ	.099	9.00	14.00	20.00	50.00
	1816 FJ	.119	9.00	14.00	20.00	50.00
	1817 FJ	—	10.00	15.00	30.00	65.00
	1817 FD	—	10.00	15.00	30.00	65.00
	1817 FI	—		—	Rare	—

REAL

3.3841 g, .896 SILVER, .0975 oz ASW
Obv. leg: CAROLUS IIII. . . ., bust of Charles IIII.
Rev: Similar to KM#65.

KM#	Date	Mintage	VG	Fine	VF	XF
58	1801 AJ	.053	8.00	18.00	30.00	60.00
	1801 AI (broken J)	Inc. Ab.	8.00	18.00	30.00	60.00
	1802 JJ	.081	7.50	15.00	27.00	55.00
	1801 AI (broken J)	Inc. Ab.	8.00	18.00	30.00	60.00
	1803 FJ	.018	100.00	200.00	—	—
	1804 FJ	.035	7.50	15.00	27.00	55.00
	1804 FJ/AJ	I.A.	12.00	30.00	45.00	100.00
	1805 FJ	.019	8.00	20.00	35.00	75.00
	1806 FJ	.038	9.00	20.00	45.00	90.00
	1807/6 FJ	.023	12.00	30.00	45.00	100.00
	1807 FJ	I.A.	9.00	20.00	45.00	80.00
	1808/7 FJ	.034	—	—	—	—
	1808 FJ	I.A.	9.00	20.00	35.00	65.00

NOTE: Earlier dates (1792-1800) exist for this type.

Obv. leg: FERDIN. VII. . . ., bust of Charles IV.

KM#	Date	Mintage	VG	Fine	VF	XF
65	1808 FJ	I.A.	25.00	50.00	100.00	200.00
	1809/8 FJ	.029	10.00	20.00	30.00	90.00
	1809 FJ	I.A.	10.00	20.00	30.00	90.00
	1810 FJ	.079	10.00	20.00	30.00	90.00
	1811 FJ	.020	12.00	25.00	50.00	125.00
	1812/1 FJ	.043	15.00	30.00	65.00	135.00
	1812 FJ	I.A.	10.00	20.00	30.00	90.00
	1813 FJ	.213	10.00	20.00	30.00	90.00
	1814 FJ	.054	10.00	20.00	30.00	90.00
	1815 FJ	.041	10.00	20.00	30.00	90.00
	1816 FJ	.123	10.00	20.00	30.00	90.00
	1817 FJ	—	10.00	20.00	30.00	90.00

2 REALES

6.7682 g, .896 SILVER, .1950 oz ASW
Obv. leg: CAROLUS IIII. . . ., bust of Charles IIII.

KM#	Date	Mintage	VG	Fine	VF	XF
59	1801 AJ	.039	15.00	30.00	80.00	160.00
	1802 JJ	.028	15.00	30.00	80.00	160.00
	1803 FJ	.025	15.00	30.00	80.00	160.00
	1803 FJ/JJ	I.A.	18.00	40.00	95.00	200.00
	1804 FJ	.028	15.00	30.00	80.00	160.00
	1804 FJ/inverted mm	Inc. Ab.	20.00	40.00	95.00	200.00
	1805 FJ	.024	15.00	30.00	80.00	160.00
	1806/5 FJ	.066	18.00	40.00	95.00	200.00
	1806 FJ inverted mm	Inc. Ab.	20.00	40.00	95.00	200.00
	1806 FJ	I.A.	15.00	30.00	80.00	160.00
	1807 FJ	.042	15.00	30.00	80.00	160.00
	1808 FJ	.054	15.00	30.00	80.00	160.00

NOTE: Earlier dates (1792-1800) exist for this type.

Obv. leg: FERDIN. VII. . . ., bust of Charles IV.

KM#	Date	Mintage	VG	Fine	VF	XF
66	1808 FJ	I.A.	20.00	40.00	80.00	160.00
	1809 FJ	.041	20.00	40.00	80.00	160.00

Obv. leg: FERDIN. VII. . . ., imaginary laureate military bust.

KM#	Date	Mintage	VG	Fine	VF	XF
74	1810 FJ	.045	25.00	50.00	100.00	200.00
	1810 FJ inverted A for V in VII	Inc. Ab.	50.00	100.00	—	—
	1811 FJ	.027	30.00	60.00	120.00	250.00

Obv. leg: FERDIN. VII. . . ., bust of Ferdinand.

KM#	Date	Mintage	VG	Fine	VF	XF
79	1812 FJ	.069	12.00	20.00	40.00	80.00
	1813 FJ	.136	10.00	18.00	35.00	70.00
	1813 FJ/inverted mm	Inc. Ab.	12.00	20.00	40.00	80.00
	1814 FJ	4,000	40.00	75.00	150.00	325.00
	1815 FJ	.024	15.00	30.00	65.00	130.00
	1816 FJ	.067	10.00	18.00	35.00	70.00
	1817 FJ	—	12.00	20.00	40.00	80.00

4 REALES

13.5365 g, .896 SILVER, .3900 oz ASW
Obv. leg: CAROLUS IIII. . . ., bust of Charles IV.

KM#	Date	Mintage	VG	Fine	VF	XF
60	1801 AJ	2,000	150.00	300.00	480.00	—
	1802 JJ	.018	65.00	150.00	240.00	—
	1803 FJ	9,000	80.00	200.00	320.00	—
	1804/3 FJ	6,000	70.00	150.00	240.00	—
	1804 FJ	I.A.	37.50	75.00	150.00	275.00
	1805 FJ	9,000	75.00	125.00	250.00	400.00
	1806 FJ	.020	32.50	50.00	125.00	250.00
	1807 FJ	.048	32.50	50.00	125.00	250.00
	1808/7 FJ	.025	37.50	75.00	150.00	275.00
	1808 FJ	I.A.	50.00	100.00	175.00	350.00

NOTE: Earlier dates (1792-1800) exist for this type.

Obv. leg: FERDIN. VII. . . ., bust of Charles IV.

KM#	Date	Mintage	VG	Fine	VF	XF
67	1808/7 FJ inverted J	Inc. Ab.	32.50	60.00	125.00	275.00
	1808 FJ	I.A.	32.50	60.00	125.00	275.00
	1808 FJ/inverted J	Inc. Ab.	32.50	60.00	125.00	275.00
	1809 FJ	.015	125.00	200.00	375.00	600.00
	1810 FJ	.010	50.00	80.00	150.00	325.00
	1811 FJ	6,000	50.00	100.00	175.00	350.00
	1811 FJ/inverted J	Inc. Ab.	75.00	100.00	175.00	350.00
	1812 FJ	.027	32.50	50.00	150.00	250.00
	1813 FJ	.034	32.50	50.00	100.00	225.00
	1813 FJ/inverted J	Inc. Ab.	32.50	50.00	100.00	225.00
	1815 FJ	.010	100.00	200.00	350.00	600.00

8 REALES

27.0730 g, .896 SILVER, .7799 oz ASW
Obv. leg: CAROLUS IIII. . . ., bust of Charles IIII.

KM#	Date	Mintage	VG	Fine	VF	XF
51	1801 AJ	.185	100.00	150.00	250.00	400.00
	1802/1 JJ/AJ	—	150.00	250.00	350.00	600.00
	1802 JJ	.160	100.00	150.00	250.00	400.00
	1803/2 FJ/JJ	.111	100.00	175.00	300.00	500.00
	1803 FJ	I.A.	250.00	400.00	600.00	800.00
	1804/3 FJ	.129	150.00	250.00	350.00	600.00
	1804 FJ	I.A.	100.00	150.00	250.00	450.00
	1805 FJ	.159	100.00	150.00	250.00	450.00
	1806/5 FJ	.155	250.00	400.00	500.00	700.00
	1806 FJ	I.A.	250.00	400.00	500.00	700.00
	1807 FJ	.094	250.00	400.00	500.00	750.00
	1808 FJ	.134	200.00	300.00	400.00	700.00

NOTE: Earlier dates (1791-1800) exist for this type.

Obv. leg: FERDIN. VII. . ., imaginary military bust.

KM#	Date	Mintage	VG	Fine	VF	XF
68	1808 FJ	I.A.	600.00	1000.	2000.	5000.
	1809 FJ	.123	100.00	200.00	400.00	700.00

Obv. leg: FERDIN. VII. . . ., imaginary laureate military bust.

KM#	Date	Mintage	VG	Fine	VF	XF
75	1810 FJ	.126	100.00	200.00	400.00	700.00
	1811 FJ	.097	100.00	200.00	400.00	700.00

Obv. leg: FERDIN. VII. ., bust of Ferdinand.

KM#	Date	Mintage	VG	Fine	VF	XF
80	1812 FJ	.307	80.00	125.00	175.00	325.00
	1813 FJ	.415	80.00	125.00	175.00	325.00
	1814 FJ	.368	80.00	125.00	175.00	325.00
	1815 FJ	.388	80.00	125.00	175.00	325.00
	1816 FJ	.386	80.00	125.00	175.00	325.00
	1816/6 FJ	I.A.	100.00	200.00	300.00	500.00
	1817 FJ	.132	750.00	1350.	2250.	3500.

ESCUDO

3.3841 g, .875 GOLD, .0952 oz AGW
Obv. leg. CAROL IIII. . ., bust of Charles IIII.
Rev: Arms, order chain.

KM#	Date	Mintage	VG	Fine	VF	XF
61	1801 AJ	1,088	175.00	250.00	500.00	750.00
	1802 JJ	748 pcs.	275.00	425.00	600.00	850.00
	1803 FJ	1,156	225.00	325.00	500.00	750.00
	1804 FJ	1,428	225.00	325.00	500.00	750.00
	1805 FJ	816 pcs.	225.00	325.00	500.00	750.00
	1806 FJ	544 pcs.	275.00	425.00	600.00	850.00
	1807 FJ	544 pcs.	275.00	425.00	600.00	850.00
	1808 FJ	2,448	175.00	250.00	375.00	600.00

NOTE: Earlier dates (1792-1800) exist for this type.

Obv. leg: FERDIN, VII. . ., imaginary military bust. Rev: Arms.

KM#	Date	Mintage	VG	Fine	VF	XF
69	1808	3,986	—	—	Rare	—
	1809	5,026	—	—	Rare	—

Obv. leg: FERDIN. VII.D.G. . . ., bust of Charles IV.

KM#	Date	Mintage	VG	Fine	VF	XF
76	1810 FJ	816 pcs.	175.00	375.00	500.00	750.00
	1811 FJ	680 pcs.	175.00	375.00	500.00	750.00
	1812 FJ	952 pcs.	175.00	375.00	500.00	750.00
	1813 FJ	4,556	125.00	175.00	250.00	400.00
	1814 FJ	1,152	175.00	375.00	500.00	750.00
	1815 FJ	816 pcs.	175.00	375.00	500.00	750.00
	1816 FJ	408 pcs.	225.00	450.00	600.00	900.00
	1817 FJ	.022	125.00	175.00	250.00	400.00
	1817 JF	I.A.	150.00	250.00	325.00	500.00

NOTE: An additional 17,860 pcs. were struck between 1818-1823; the actual date on the coin is unknown.

2 ESCUDOS

6.7682 g, .875 GOLD, .1904 oz AGW
Obv. leg: CAROL IIII. . ., bust of Charles III.
Rev: Arms.

KM#	Date	Mintage	VG	Fine	VF	XF
53	1801 AJ	680 pcs.	500.00	850.00	1250.	1750.
	1802 JJ	374 pcs.	650.00	1000.	1400.	2000.
	1803 FJ	578 pcs.	500.00	850.00	1250.	1750.
	1804 FJ	544 pcs.	500.00	850.00	1250.	1750.
	1805 FJ	646 pcs.	500.00	850.00	1250.	1750.
	1806 FJ	306 pcs.	650.00	1000.	1400.	2000.
	1807 FJ	340 pcs.	650.00	1000.	1400.	2000.
	1808 FJ	1,020	500.00	850.00	1250.	1750.
	1810 FJ	510 pcs.	500.00	850.00	1250.	1750.
	1811 FJ	340 pcs.	500.00	850.00	1250.	1750.
	1812 FJ	476 pcs.	450.00	650.00	1000.	1500.
	1813 FJ	2,958	450.00	650.00	1000.	1500.

NOTE: Earlier dates (1791-1800) exist for this type.

Obv. leg: FERDIN.VII. . . ., bust of Charles III.

KM#	Date	Mintage	VG	Fine	VF	XF
70	1810 FJ	Inc. Ab.	300.00	475.00	700.00	1250.
	1811 FJ	Inc. Ab.	375.00	600.00	875.00	1550.

Obv. leg: FERDIN. VII. . . ., bust of Charles IV.

KM#	Date	Mintage	VG	Fine	VF	XF
81	1813 FJ	—	150.00	700.00	1000.	1900.
	1814 FJ	682 pcs.	300.00	475.00	700.00	1250.
	1815 FJ	408 pcs.	400.00	600.00	900.00	1500.
	1816 FJ	608 pcs.	400.00	600.00	900.00	1500.
	1817 FJ	168 pcs.	550.00	750.00	1150.	1800.

NOTE: An additional 19,876 pcs. were struck between 1818-1823; the actual dates of these coins are unknown.

4 ESCUDOS

13.5365 g, .875 GOLD, .3808 oz AGW
Obv. leg: CAROL IIII. . ., bust of Charles IIII.
Rev: Arms.

KM#	Date	Mintage	VG	Fine	VF	XF
62	1801 AJ	340 pcs.	500.00	750.00	1000.	1450.
	1802 JJ	374 pcs.	500.00	750.00	1000.	1450.
	1803 FJ	476 pcs.	500.00	750.00	1000.	1450.
	1804 FJ	255 pcs.	575.00	850.00	1250.	1750.
	1805 FJ	323 pcs.	575.00	850.00	1250.	1750.
	1806 FJ	204 pcs.	575.00	850.00	1250.	1750.
	1807 FJ	187 pcs.	600.00	900.00	1500.	2000.
	1808/7 FJ	1,207	550.00	800.00	1200.	1700.
	1808 FJ	I.A.	500.00	750.00	1000.	1450.

NOTE: Earlier dates (1792-1800) exist for this type.

Obv. leg: FERDIN. VII. . ., bust of Ferdinand.
Rev: Arms.

KM#	Date	Mintage	VG	Fine	VF	XF
71	1808 FJ	I.A.	—	—	Rare	—
	1809 FJ	I.A.	—	—	Rare	—

Obv. leg: FERDIN. VII. . . ., bust of Charles IV.

KM#	Date	Mintage	VG	Fine	VF	XF
77	1810 FJ	272 pcs.	425.00	700.00	1250.	1750.
	1811 FJ	170 pcs.	750.00	1250.	1750.	2500.
	1812 FJ	254 pcs.	425.00	700.00	1250.	1750.
	1813 FJ	1,462	375.00	650.00	1100.	1600.
	1814 FJ	340 pcs.	425.00	700.00	1250.	1750.
	1815 FJ	290 pcs.	425.00	700.00	1250.	1750.
	1816 FJ	100 pcs.	650.00	1000.	1500.	2000.
	1817 FJ	68 pcs.	1000.	1500.	2000.	2500.

NOTE: An additional 6,560 pcs. were struck between 1818-1823; the actual date on the coin is unknown.

8 ESCUDOS

27.0730 g, .875 GOLD, .7616 oz AGW
Obv. leg: CAROL IIII. . ., bust of Charles III.

KM#	Date	Mintage	VG	Fine	VF	XF
54	1801 AJ	.046	375.00	550.00	675.00	900.00
	1802 JJ	.049	375.00	550.00	675.00	900.00
	1803/2 FJ/JJ	.044	375.00	600.00	750.00	1100.
	1803 FJ	I.A.	375.00	550.00	675.00	900.00
	1804 FJ	.040	375.00	550.00	675.00	900.00
	1805 FJ	.044	375.00	550.00	675.00	900.00
	1806/5 FJ	.040	375.00	550.00	675.00	900.00
	1806 FJ	I.A.	375.00	550.00	675.00	900.00
	1806 JF	I.A.	400.00	700.00	850.00	1250.
	1807 FJ	.039	375.00	650.00	725.00	1100.
	1807 JF	I.A.	375.00	650.00	725.00	1100.
	1808 FJ	.039	375.00	550.00	675.00	900.00

NOTE: Earlier dates (1791-1800) exist for this type.

Obv. leg: FERDIN. VII. . ., imaginary military bust.

KM#	Date	Mintage	VG	Fine	VF	XF
72	1808 FJ	I.A.	700.00	1200.	1500.	2500.
	1809 FJ	.041	400.00	650.00	1000.	1500.
	1810 FJ	.055	400.00	650.00	1000.	1500.
	1810 FJ inverted mint mark	Inc. Ab.	700.00	1200.	1500.	2500.
	1811 FJ	.044	400.00	650.00	1000.	1500.

Obv. leg: FERDIN. VII. . . ., bust of Charles IIII.

KM#	Date	Mintage	VG	Fine	VF	XF
78	1811 FJ	—	900.00	1500.	2400.	4500.
	1812 FJ	.048	375.00	550.00	675.00	900.00
	1813/2 FT	.037	375.00	550.00	675.00	900.00
	1813 FJ	I.A.	375.00	550.00	675.00	900.00
	1814 FJ	.029	375.00	550.00	675.00	900.00
	1815 FJ	.039	375.00	550.00	675.00	900.00
	1816 FJ	.030	375.00	400.00	500.00	900.00
	1817/6 FJ	.011	375.00	425.00	500.00	900.00
	1817/7/8 FJ	Inc. Ab.	400.00	800.00	1500.	2500.
	1817 FJ	I.A.	375.00	425.00	500.00	900.00

ROYALIST COINAGE

CHILOE

An island off the southwest coast of Chile. The island was the last outpost of the Spanish in their effort to deny Chilean independence. Antonio Quintanilla had coins cast to show that the empire of Ferdinand VII of Spain still exerted some authority in the New World.

COUNTERMARKED COINAGE

(Issued by Antonio Quintanilla)

8 REALES

CAST SILVER
c/m: Chi-loe on sand cast copy of Peru-Lima 8 Reales.

KM#	Date	Mintage	Good	VG	Fine	VF
1	1818	—	600.00	1200.	2200.	3750.

c/m: Chi-loe on sand cast copy of

Bolivia-Potosi 8 Reales.

KM#	Date	Mintage	Good	VG	Fine	VF
2	1822	—	600.00	1200.	2200.	3750.
	1825	—	600.00	1200.	2200.	3750.

PROVISIONAL REPUBLICAN COINAGE

VALDIVIA

Emergency coinage issued by Don Antonio Adriazola by order of the Governor during a shortage of coin with which to pay the local garrison.

REAL

BILLON

KM#	Date	Mintage	Good	VG	Fine	VF
1.1	1822	—	75.00	150.00	280.00	475.00

c/m: APDLVA monogram.

KM#	Date	Mintage	Good	VG	Fine	VF
1.2	1822	—	75.00	150.00	280.00	475.00

2 REALES

BILLON

KM#	Date	Mintage	Good	VG	Fine	VF
2.1	1822	—	75.00	150.00	265.00	450.00

c/m: APDLVA monogram.

KM#	Date	Mintage	Good	VG	Fine	VF
2.2	1822	—	75.00	150.00	265.00	450.00

8 REALES

BILLON

KM#	Date	Mintage	Good	VG	Fine	VF
3.1	1822	—	250.00	400.00	650.00	1000.

c/m: APDLVA monogram.

KM#	Date	Mintage	Good	VG	Fine	VF
3.2	1822	—	250.00	400.00	650.00	1000.

REPUBLIC

MONETARY SYSTEM
8 Reales = 1 Peso
16 Reales = 1 Escudo

UN QUART (1/4) REAL

.900 SILVER

KM#	Date	Mintage	VG	Fine	VF	XF
89	1832/1	.054	13.50	25.00	50.00	100.00
	1832	Inc. Ab.	13.50	25.00	50.00	100.00
	1833	.082	13.50	25.00	50.00	100.00
	1834	.134	60.00	125.00	175.00	350.00

1/2 REAL

.900 SILVER

KM#	Date	Mintage	VG	Fine	VF	XF
90	1833 I	.014	12.00	20.00	40.00	80.00
	1834/3 I	.022	15.00	25.00	45.00	90.00
	1834 I	Inc. Ab.	12.00	20.00	40.00	80.00

NOTE: 1834 dated coins are medal rotation strikes.

Rev. leg: POR LA RAZ. Y LA FUER.

KM#	Date	Mintage	VG	Fine	VF	XF
98.1	1838 IJ	.015	15.00	32.00	50.00	90.00
	1840 IJ	.014	13.50	28.50	47.50	85.00

Rev. leg: POR LA RAZON Y LA FUERZA.

KM#	Date	Mintage	VG	Fine	VF	XF
98.3	1841 IJ	.016	15.00	32.00	50.00	90.00
	1842 IJ	.027	12.00	30.00	45.00	80.00

KM#	Date	Mintage	VG	Fine	VF	XF
98.2	1844 IJ RAZON V (Y) LA	—	3.00	7.50	15.00	25.00
	1845 IJ	—	3.00	7.50	15.00	25.00
	1846/5 IJ	—	5.00	10.00	20.00	30.00
	1846 IJ	—	3.00	7.50	15.00	25.00
	1847 IJ	—	3.00	7.50	15.00	25.00
	1848 JM	—	75.00	150.00	225.00	—
	1849 ML	—	3.00	7.50	15.00	25.00
	1851 LA	—	4.25	9.00	18.50	30.00

UN (1) REAL

3.2000 g, .900 SILVER, .0925 oz ASW

KM#	Date	Mintage	VG	Fine	VF	XF
91	1834 IJ	.016	7.50	15.00	35.00	75.00

Obv: Large plumes, large shield, pointed sprays.

KM#	Date	Mintage	VG	Fine	VF	XF
94.1	1838 IJ	.012	10.00	20.00	40.00	85.00
	1840 IJ	6,800	10.00	20.00	35.00	75.00

Obv: Small shield, blunt sprays w/berries.

KM#	Date	Mintage	VG	Fine	VF	XF
94.3	1841 IJ	7,928	10.00	20.00	35.00	75.00

Obv: Small shield, blunt sprays w/o berries.

KM#	Date	Mintage	VG	Fine	VF	XF
94.4	1842 IJ	4,768	10.00	20.00	35.00	75.00

KM#	Date	Mintage	VG	Fine	VF	XF
94.2	1843 IJ	—	3.50	7.00	12.00	25.00
	1844 IJ	—	3.50	7.00	12.00	25.00
	1845 IJ	—	3.50	7.00	12.00	25.00
	1846 IJ	—	3.50	7.00	12.00	25.00
	1847 IJ	—	15.00	30.00	50.00	80.00
	1848/7/6 JM		6.00	12.00	20.00	40.00
	1848/7 JM	—	5.00	10.00	15.00	30.00
	1848 JM	—	3.50	7.00	12.00	25.00
	1849 ML	—	10.00	20.00	35.00	60.00
	1850/9 LA/ML	—	5.00	10.00	15.00	30.00
	1850 LA	—	3.50	7.00	12.00	25.00

DOS (2) REALES

.900 SILVER

KM#	Date	Mintage	VG	Fine	VF	XF
92	1834 IJ	3,740	20.00	35.00	65.00	100.00

24.5mm

KM#	Date	Mintage	VG	Fine	VF	XF
100.1	1843 IJ	—	5.00	10.00	20.00	40.00

23mm

KM#	Date	Mintage	VG	Fine	VF	XF
100.2	1843 IJ	—	—	—	—	—
	1844 IJ	—	3.00	6.00	10.00	20.00
	1845/3 IJ	—	—	—	—	—
	1845/4 IJ	—	16.00	30.00	40.00	—
	1845 IJ	—	3.00	6.00	10.00	20.00
	1846/5 IJ	—	—	—	—	—
	1846/6 IJ	—	12.00	30.00	40.00	—
	1846 IJ	—	3.00	6.00	10.00	20.00
	1847 IJ	—	3.00	6.00	10.00	20.00
	1848/7 JM	—	2.50	5.00	8.00	15.00
	1848 JM	—	2.50	5.00	8.00	15.00
	1849 ML	—	5.00	10.00	15.00	27.50
	1850/49 LA/ML	—	10.00	20.00	35.00	50.00
	1850 LA	—	8.00	12.50	18.00	30.00
	1850 LA/ML	—	8.00	12.50	18.00	30.00
	1851 LA (error) GHILE	—	10.00	20.00	35.00	50.00
	1852 LA	—	10.00	20.00	35.00	50.00

UN (1) PESO

.900 SILVER
Rev: Y above pillar.

KM#	Date	Mintage	Good	VG	Fine	VF
82.1	1817	—	75.00	125.00	210.00	650.00

Rev: Y to left of pillar.

KM#	Date	Mintage	Good	VG	Fine	VF
82.2	1817 FJ	—	25.00	40.00	85.00	150.00
	1817 FD	—	30.00	55.00	120.00	275.00
	1818/7 FD	.371	35.00	65.00	135.00	300.00
	1818 FD	I.A.	35.00	65.00	135.00	300.00
	1819/8 FD	.236	35.00	65.00	135.00	300.00
	1819 FD	I.A.	30.00	60.00	125.00	275.00
	1820 FD	.116	25.00	45.00	95.00	200.00
	1821 FD	.126	75.00	145.00	325.00	700.00
	1822 FI	.148	25.00	40.00	85.00	175.00
	1823 FI	.045	30.00	60.00	125.00	250.00
	1824 I	.011	100.00	200.00	350.00	800.00
	1825 I	3,400	90.00	150.00	300.00	750.00
	1826 I	6,111	—	—	Rare	—
	1830 I	6,868	80.00	150.00	350.00	750.00
	1831 I	.051	35.00	65.00	135.00	275.00
	1832 I	.040	30.00	55.00	110.00	250.00
	1833 I	.088	25.00	40.00	85.00	175.00
	1834 I	.043	45.00	80.00	180.00	375.00
	1834 IJ	Inc. Ab.	60.00	120.00	250.00	500.00

Coquimbo Mint
Rev: Similar to KM#82.2.

KM#	Date	Mintage	Good	VG	Fine	VF
88	1828TH	—	—	—	—	8000.

8 REALES

27.0700 g, .900 SILVER, .7853 oz ASW, 39mm

KM#	Date	Mintage	VG	Fine	VF	XF
96.1	1837 IJ	5,404	—	—	Rare	—
	1839 IJ	.205	45.00	75.00	125.00	350.00
	1840 IJ	4,556	1200.	1700.	2200.	3850.

Rev: Similar to KM#96.1 but w/larger leg.
Reduced size, 38.5mm, same weight and fineness

KM#	Date	Mintage	VG	Fine	VF	XF
96.2	1848 JM	—	40.00	75.00	125.00	300.00
	1849 ML	—	50.00	90.00	150.00	360.00

ESCUDO

3.4000 g, .875 GOLD, .0956 oz AGW
Obv: Sun above mountains in wreath.
Rev: Crossed flags behind pillar in wreath, date below.

KM#	Date	Mintage	VG	Fine	VF	XF
85	1824 I	3,400	95.00	135.00	170.00	275.00
	1825 I	2,920	95.00	135.00	170.00	275.00
	1826 I	4,280	95.00	135.00	170.00	275.00
	1827 I	408 pcs.	150.00	240.00	300.00	375.00
	1828 I	4,488	95.00	135.00	170.00	275.00
	1830 I	3,328	95.00	135.00	170.00	275.00
	1832 I	2,338	95.00	135.00	170.00	275.00
	1833/0 I	2,620	130.00	200.00	250.00	350.00
	1833 I	Inc. Ab.	115.00	180.00	215.00	300.00
	1834 I	10,614	115.00	180.00	215.00	300.00

Obv: Plumed and supported arms, date below.
Rev: Hand on book below sun rays.

KM#	Date	Mintage	VG	Fine	VF	XF
99	1838 IJ	6,122	125.00	175.00	225.00	375.00

Rev: Liberty standing, column at left, fasces and cornucopia at right.

KM#	Date	Mintage	VG	Fine	VF	XF
101.1	1839 IJ	4,946	100.00	135.00	175.00	250.00
	1840 IJ	4,312	100.00	135.00	175.00	250.00
	1841 IJ	3,992	100.00	135.00	175.00	250.00
	1842 IJ	5,076	100.00	135.00	175.00	250.00

KM#	Date	Mintage	VG	Fine	VF	XF
101.1	1843 IJ	4,632	100.00	135.00	175.00	250.00
	1844 IJ	—	100.00	135.00	175.00	250.00
	1845 IJ	—	100.00	135.00	175.00	250.00

Rev: Liberty standing scene rendered on smaller scale.

KM#	Date	Mintage	VG	Fine	VF	XF
101.2	1847 IJ	—	125.00	175.00	225.00	375.00
	1848 JM	—	100.00	135.00	200.00	350.00
	1849 ML	—	100.00	135.00	200.00	350.00
	1850 LA	—	100.00	135.00	200.00	350.00
	1851 LA	—	125.00	175.00	225.00	375.00

2 ESCUDOS

6.8000 g, .875 GOLD, .1913 oz AGW

KM#	Date	Mintage	VG	Fine	VF	XF
86	1824 I	1,700	150.00	190.00	300.00	450.00
	1825 I	1,460	150.00	190.00	300.00	450.00
	1826 I	1,936	150.00	190.00	300.00	450.00
	1827 I	204 pcs.	200.00	275.00	400.00	550.00
	1832 I	493 pcs.	200.00	275.00	400.00	550.00
	1833 I	224 pcs.	150.00	190.00	325.00	475.00
	1834 IJ	4,648	120.00	150.00	275.00	425.00

KM#	Date	Mintage	VG	Fine	VF	XF
97	1837 IJ	331 pcs.	200.00	255.00	400.00	600.00
	1838 IJ	3,449	150.00	200.00	250.00	450.00

KM#	Date	Mintage	VG	Fine	VF	XF
102.1	1839 IJ	3,064	225.00	275.00	425.00	550.00
	1840 IJ	2,396	225.00	275.00	425.00	550.00
	1841 IJ	2,552	180.00	235.00	375.00	500.00
	1842 IJ	2,986	180.00	235.00	375.00	500.00
	1843 IJ	2,464	180.00	235.00	375.00	500.00
	1844 IJ	—	180.00	235.00	375.00	500.00
	1845 IJ	—	180.00	235.00	375.00	500.00

Rev: Liberty standing scene rendered on smaller scale.

KM#	Date	Mintage	VG	Fine	VF	XF
102.2	1846 IJ	—	150.00	225.00	300.00	375.00
	1847 IJ	—	150.00	225.00	300.00	375.00
	1848 JM	—	150.00	225.00	300.00	375.00
	1849 ML	—	150.00	225.00	300.00	375.00
	1850 LA	—	150.00	225.00	300.00	375.00
	1851 LA	—	150.00	225.00	300.00	375.00

4 ESCUDOS

13.5000 g, .875 GOLD, .3798 oz AGW

KM#	Date	Mintage	VG	Fine	VF	XF
87	1824 FD	1,530	325.00	450.00	700.00	1200.
	1825 I	986 pcs.	350.00	550.00	900.00	1400.
	1826 I	1,326	325.00	450.00	700.00	1200.
	1833 IJ	321 pcs.	350.00	550.00	900.00	1400.
	1834 IJ	2,564	325.00	450.00	700.00	1200.

KM#	Date	Mintage	VG	Fine	VF	XF
95	1836 IJ	1,389	275.00	375.00	575.00	950.00
	1837 IJ	321 pcs.	350.00	550.00	900.00	1400.

KM#	Date	Mintage	VG	Fine	VF	XF
103	1839 IJ	—	1200.	2000.	3500.	—
	1840 IJ	108 pcs.	—	—	Rare	—
	1841 IJ	100 pcs.	—	—	Rare	—

8 ESCUDOS

27.0000 g, .875 GOLD, .7596 oz AGW

KM#	Date	Mintage	VG	Fine	VF	XF
84	1818 FD Constit	.029	375.00	425.00	575.00	800.00
	1818 FD Constitu	Inc. Ab.	400.00	450.00	600.00	900.00
	1819 FD	.037	375.00	425.00	575.00	800.00
	1820 FD	.035	375.00	425.00	575.00	800.00
	1821 FD	.016	375.00	425.00	575.00	800.00
	1822 FI	.031	375.00	425.00	575.00	800.00
	1823 FI	.019	375.00	425.00	575.00	800.00
	1824 I	.010	375.00	425.00	575.00	800.00
	1825 I	8,483	375.00	425.00	575.00	750.00
	1826 I	7,607	375.00	425.00	575.00	750.00
	1827 I	2,176	375.00	425.00	575.00	750.00
	1828/7 I	4,250	475.00	675.00	1125.	2000.
	1828 I	Inc. Ab.	375.00	425.00	575.00	800.00
	1829 I	—	375.00	425.00	575.00	750.00
	1830 I	3,068	375.00	425.00	575.00	750.00
	1831 I	1,745	375.00	450.00	625.00	850.00
	1832/1 I	.011	375.00	425.00	575.00	750.00
	1832 I	Inc. Ab.	375.00	425.00	575.00	750.00
	1833 I	.025	375.00	425.00	575.00	750.00
	1834 IJ	.031	375.00	425.00	575.00	750.00

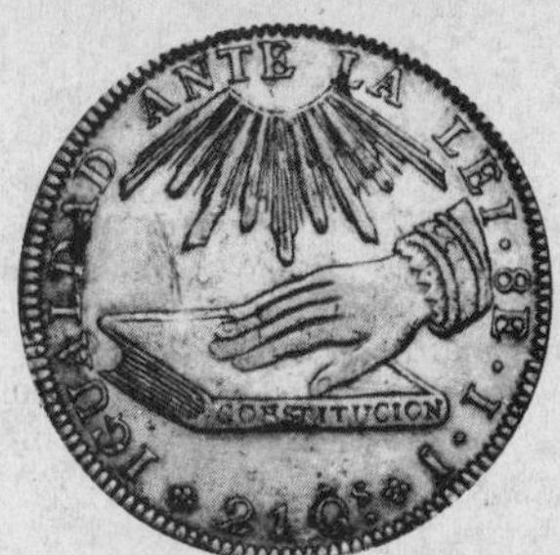

KM#	Date	Mintage	VG	Fine	VF	XF
93	1835 IJ	.028	375.00	425.00	575.00	800.00
	1836 IJ	.027	375.00	425.00	575.00	800.00
	1837 IJ	.017	375.00	425.00	575.00	800.00
	1838 IJ	.033	375.00	425.00	575.00	800.00

NOTE: KM#93 has been rarely encountered struck over KM#84.

Reeded edge

KM#	Date	Mintage	VG	Fine	VF	XF
104.1	1839 IJ	.027	375.00	425.00	575.00	725.00
	1840 IJ	.025	375.00	425.00	575.00	725.00
	1841 IJ	.025	375.00	425.00	575.00	725.00
	1842 IJ	.027	375.00	425.00	575.00	725.00
	1843/2 IJ	.027	375.00	425.00	575.00	725.00
	1843 IJ	Inc. Ab.	375.00	425.00	575.00	725.00

Lettered edge

KM#	Date	Mintage	VG	Fine	VF	XF
104.2	1843 IJ	—	400.00	500.00	600.00	800.00
	1844 IJ	—	400.00	500.00	600.00	800.00
	1845 IJ	—	400.00	500.00	600.00	800.00

KM#	Date	Mintage	VG	Fine	VF	XF
105	1846 IJ	—	375.00	425.00	575.00	750.00
	1847 IJ	—	375.00	425.00	575.00	750.00
	1848/7 JM	—	375.00	425.00	575.00	750.00
	1848 JM	—	375.00	425.00	575.00	750.00
	1849 ML	—	375.00	425.00	575.00	750.00
	1850 LA	—	375.00	425.00	575.00	750.00
	1851 LA	—	375.00	425.00	575.00	750.00

NOTE: For KM#104.2 and 105 edge lettering includes month of issue.

COUNTERMARKED COINAGE

On March 29, 1833, the government ordered the legal circulation of the Argentinian 8 Reales struck at Potosi. The coins struck at Potosi must have the countermark of the coat of arms of Chile and the abbreviation of the place where the countermark was applied.

CHILOE

1 REAL

SILVER

c/m: Mountains/CHIL on Argentina 1 Real, KM#2.

KM#	Date	Year	Good	VG	Fine	VF
A106	ND	(1815)	—	950.00	—	—

NOTE: Sold Bank Leu #51, Bostonian Collection 10-90.

8 REALES

SILVER

c/m: Mountains/CHIL on Argentina 8 Reales, KM#5.

KM#	Date	Year	Good	VG	Fine	VF
106.1	ND	(1813)	1150.	1750.	2250.	2750.

c/m: Mountains/CHIL on Argentina 8 Reales, KM#14.

KM#	Date	Year	Good	VG	Fine	VF
106.2	ND	(1815)	1150.	1750.	2250.	2750.

CONCEPCION

8 REALES

SILVER

c/m: Mountains/CON on Argentina 8 Reales, KM#5.

KM#	Date	Year	Good	VG	Fine	VF
107.1	ND	(1813)	900.00	1500.	2000.	2500.

c/m: Mountains/CON on Argentina 8 Reales, KM#14.

KM#	Date	Year	Good	VG	Fine	VF
107.2	ND	(1815)	900.00	1500.	2000.	2500.

SANTIAGO

2 REALES

SILVER

c/m: Mountains/SAN on Argentina 2 Reales.

KM#	Date	Year	Good	VG	Fine	VF
A108	ND	—	—	—	Rare	—

8 REALES

SILVER

c/m: Mountains/SAN on Argentina 8 Reales, KM#5.

108.1 ND (1813) Reported, not confirmed

c/m: Mountains/SAN on Argentina 8 Reales, KM#14.

108.2 ND (1815) Reported, not confirmed

SERENA

4 REALES

SILVER

c/m: Mountains/SER on Argentina 4 Soles, KM#13.

KM#	Date	Year	Good	VG	Fine	VF
113	ND	(1813)	—	2750.	—	—

NOTE: Sold Bank Leu #51, Bostonian Collection 10-90.

8 REALES

SILVER

c/m: Mountains/SER on Argentina 8 Reales, KM#5.

KM#	Date	Year	Good	VG	Fine	VF
109.1	ND	(1813)	135.00	225.00	375.00	550.00

c/m: Mountains/SER on Argentina 8 Reales, KM#15.

KM#	Date	Year	Good	VG	Fine	VF
109.2	ND	(1815)	135.00	225.00	375.00	550.00

VALDIVIA

4 REALES

SILVER

c/m: Mountains/VALD on Argentina 4 Reales, KM#4.

KM#	Date	Year	Good	VG	Fine	VF
110	ND	(1813)	180.00	300.00	550.00	900.00
	ND	(1815)	180.00	300.00	550.00	900.00

8 REALES

SILVER

c/m: Mountains/VALD on Argentina 8 Reales, KM#5.

KM#	Date	Year	Good	VG	Fine	VF
111.1	ND	(1813)	180.00	300.00	550.00	900.00

c/m: Mountains/VALD on Argentina 8 Reales, KM#14.

KM#	Date	Year	Good	VG	Fine	VF
111.2	ND	(1815)	180.00	300.00	550.00	900.00

VALPARAISO

8 REALES

SILVER

c/m: Mountains/VALP on Argentina 8 Reales, KM#5.

KM#	Date	Year	Good	VG	Fine	VF
112.1	ND	(1813)	180.00	300.00	550.00	900.00

c/m: Mountains/VALP on Argentina 8 REALES, KM#14.

KM#	Date	Year	Good	VG	Fine	VF
112.2	ND	(1815)	180.00	300.00	550.00	900.00

DECIMAL COINAGE

10 Centavos = 1 Decimo
10 Decimos = 1 Peso
10 Pesos = 1 Condor

MEDIO (1/2) CENTAVO

COPPER

KM#	Date	Mintage	VG	Fine	VF	XF
114	1835	2.000	1.00	2.00	3.50	20.00
	1835	Inc. Ab.	—	—	Proof	—

Flat star, stars flank date.

KM#	Date	Mintage	VG	Fine	VF	XF
117	1851	1.620	2.00	4.00	6.00	25.00

Raised star, dots flank date.

KM#	Date	Mintage	VG	Fine	VF	XF
118	1851	2.200	1.00	2.00	4.00	20.00

KM#	Date	Mintage	VG	Fine	VF	XF
126	1853	2.667	1.00	2.00	4.00	20.00

COPPER-NICKEL

KM#	Date	Mintage	VG	Fine	VF	XF
148	1871	.133	2.00	4.50	9.00	17.50
	1872/1	.506	2.00	4.50	9.00	17.50
	1872	Inc. Ab.	3.50	6.00	12.00	22.50
	1873	1.265	2.00	4.50	9.00	17.50

COPPER

KM#	Date	Mintage	VG	Fine	VF	XF
148a	1883/73	.714	1.50	3.00	5.00	12.00
	1883	Inc. Ab.	1.00	2.00	3.50	10.00
	1884	.104	1.50	3.00	6.00	15.00
	1885	.132	1.00	2.00	3.50	10.00
	1886	.469	1.00	2.00	3.50	10.00
	1888/78	.294	1.25	2.50	5.00	12.00
	1888	Inc. Ab.	1.50	3.00	6.00	15.00
	1890/70	.070	2.00	4.00	7.00	16.00
	1890/73	I.A.	2.50	5.00	8.50	18.00
	1890	Inc. Ab.	3.25	6.00	10.00	22.50
	1893/88	.071	2.50	5.00	8.50	18.00
	1893	Inc. Ab.	2.00	4.00	6.00	14.50
	1894	.251	1.00	2.00	3.50	10.00

UN (1) CENTAVO

COPPER, thick flan, 18.01 g

KM#	Date	Mintage	VG	Fine	VF	XF
115	1835	2.000	2.00	4.00	8.00	22.50
	1835	—	—	—	Proof	130.00

Thin flan, 13.35 g

KM#	Date	Mintage	VG	Fine	VF	XF
116	1835	Inc. Ab.	2.00	4.00	8.00	22.50

Obv: Flat star, stars flank date.
Rev: W/o diamond below wreath.

KM#	Date	Mintage	VG	Fine	VF	XF
119	1851	2.430	2.50	5.00	12.50	30.00

Obv: Raised star, dots flank date.
Rev: Diamond below wreath.

KM#	Date	Mintage	VG	Fine	VF	XF
120	1851	3.300	3.00	8.00	17.50	45.00

Rev: Different sprays.

KM#	Date	Mintage	VG	Fine	VF	XF
127	1853	2.667	2.00	5.00	15.00	35.00
	1853	—	—	—	Proof	150.00

NOTE: The 1853 coins were struck with coin and medal rotation.

COPPER-NICKEL

KM#	Date	Mintage	VG	Fine	VF	XF
146	1870/60	—	—	—	—	—
	1871	1.687	1.50	3.00	5.50	12.00
	1872/1	.690	2.50	4.50	7.50	20.00
	1872	Inc. Ab.	2.00	4.00	6.00	17.50
	1873/1	.779	10.00	20.00	35.00	50.00
	1873/2	Inc. Ab.	10.00	20.00	35.00	50.00
	1873	Inc. Ab.	2.00	4.00	6.00	17.50
	1874/1	.263	3.50	6.00	10.00	25.00
	1874	Inc. Ab.	3.00	5.00	7.50	19.00
	1875/1	.113	3.50	6.50	8.50	22.00
	1875	Inc. Ab.	3.00	5.00	8.00	20.00
	1876	.022	12.00	20.00	35.00	60.00
	1877	.016	15.00	30.00	50.00	75.00

COPPER

KM#	Date	Mintage	VG	Fine	VF	XF
146a	1878/1	—	2.25	3.50	7.00	15.00
	1878	.177	2.00	4.00	7.00	25.00
	1879	.793	1.50	3.00	5.50	15.00
	1880/70	.478	2.00	4.00	6.00	20.00
	1880/79	I.A.	2.00	4.00	6.00	20.00
	1880	Inc. Ab.	1.50	3.00	5.50	15.00
	1881	.318	1.75	3.25	6.00	16.00
	1882	.492	1.50	3.00	5.50	15.00
	1883	.274	2.00	4.00	6.00	20.00
	1884/3	.171	2.25	4.50	7.50	25.00
	1884	Inc. Ab.	2.00	4.00	6.00	20.00
	1885	.205	1.50	3.00	5.50	15.00
	1886	.510	1.50	3.00	5.50	15.00
	1887/4	.231	1.75	3.50	7.00	18.00
	1887	Inc. Ab.	1.50	3.00	5.50	15.00
	1888	.141	2.00	4.00	6.00	20.00
	1890	.047	4.25	8.50	15.00	28.00
	1891/81	.099	15.00	30.00	50.00	80.00
	1891	Inc. Ab.	2.50	5.00	10.00	25.00
	1893	.115	1.50	3.00	5.50	15.00
	1894	.244	1.00	2.00	4.00	8.00
	1895	.449	1.00	2.00	3.50	7.00
	1895 1 over inverted 1	Inc. Ab.	4.50	9.00	16.00	30.00
	1896	.139	1.25	2.50	4.00	8.00
	1898	1.605	.50	1.00	2.00	5.00

NOTE: Varieties exist.

KM#	Date	Mintage	VG	Fine	VF	XF
161	1904	.970	.50	1.00	2.00	5.00
	1908	.174	.65	1.25	2.00	7.00
	1919	.173	.25	.50	2.00	7.00

D0S (2) CENTAVOS

COPPER-NICKEL

KM#	Date	Mintage	Fine	VF	XF	Unc
147	1870/60	—	5.00	9.00	18.00	35.00
	1871	.639	3.50	7.50	15.00	30.00
	1872/1	.207	3.50	7.50	15.00	30.00
	1872	Inc. Ab.	12.00	20.00	30.00	60.00
	1873	.461	3.50	7.50	15.00	30.00
	1874	.263	5.00	9.00	18.00	35.00
	1875	.294	5.00	9.00	18.00	35.00
	1876	.108	12.00	20.00	30.00	60.00
	1877	.021	15.00	35.00	50.00	120.00

COPPER

KM#	Date	Mintage	Fine	VF	XF	Unc
147a	1878/6	.112	—	—	—	—
	1878	Inc. Ab.	5.00	9.00	15.00	45.00
	1879	.479	2.50	6.00	10.00	30.00
	1880/70	—	3.00	7.00	12.00	35.00
	1880	.278	2.50	6.00	10.00	30.00
	1881	.172	3.00	7.00	12.00	35.00
	1882	.361	2.50	6.00	10.00	30.00
	1883	.405	2.00	5.00	8.00	25.00
	1884	.182	2.50	6.00	10.00	30.00
	1885	.146	2.50	6.00	10.00	30.00
	1886	.494	2.00	5.00	8.00	25.00
	1887	.106	2.50	6.00	10.00	30.00
	1888	.186	3.00	7.00	12.00	35.00
	1890	.155	5.00	9.00	15.00	40.00
	1891/8	.089	—	—	—	—
	1891	Inc. Ab.	8.00	20.00	30.00	60.00
	1893/1	.141	2.50	6.00	10.00	30.00
	1893	Inc. Ab.	2.50	6.00	10.00	30.00
	1894	.190	3.00	7.00	12.00	35.00

KM#	Date	Mintage	Fine	VF	XF	Unc
164	1919	.147	1.50	3.00	5.00	10.00

DOS I MEDIO (2-1/2) CENTAVOS

COPPER

KM#	Date	Mintage	Fine	VF	XF	Unc
150	1886	.381	2.50	6.00	18.00	45.00
	1887/6	.500	5.00	10.00	25.00	65.00
	1887	Inc. Ab.	2.75	7.00	18.00	45.00
	1895/85	.366	3.00	8.00	20.00	50.00
	1895	Inc. Ab.	2.50	6.00	18.00	45.00
	1896/86	.172	3.00	8.00	20.00	50.00
	1896	Inc. Ab.	2.75	7.00	18.00	50.00
	1898/86	2.177	3.00	8.00	20.00	50.00
	1898/88	I.A.	3.00	8.00	20.00	50.00
	1898/5	Inc. Ab.	3.00	8.00	20.00	50.00
	1898/87	I.A.	3.00	8.00	20.00	50.00
	1898	Inc. Ab.	2.50	6.00	18.00	45.00

KM#	Date	Mintage	Fine	VF	XF	Unc
162	1904	.277	2.75	7.00	18.00	45.00
	1906	.161	3.50	8.50	20.00	50.00
	1907	.262	2.75	7.00	18.00	40.00
	1908	.201	2.50	6.00	18.00	40.00

NOTE: Varieties exist for 1907 dated coins.

MEDIO (1/2) DECIMO

1.2500 g, .900 SILVER, .0361 oz ASW

KM#	Date	Mintage	VG	Fine	VF	XF
121	1851	.233	100.00	200.00	300.00	450.00
	1853	Inc. Ab.	3.00	5.00	9.00	20.00
	1854	.122	20.00	35.00	55.00	80.00
	1855/3	1.257	—	—	—	—
	1855/4	Inc. Ab.	3.50	6.00	12.00	25.00
	1855	Inc. Ab.	3.00	5.00	9.00	20.00
	1856/5	.767	4.00	7.00	15.00	30.00
	1856	Inc. Ab.	3.50	6.00	12.00	25.00
	1857	1.655	3.00	5.00	9.00	20.00
	1858	.318	3.50	6.00	12.00	25.00
	1859/8	.041	3.00	5.00	10.00	22.00
	1859	Inc. Ab.	20.00	35.00	55.00	90.00

1.1500 g, .900 SILVER, .0332 oz ASW

KM#	Date	Mintage	VG	Fine	VF	XF
121a	1860/59	.372	10.00	20.00	27.50	55.00
	1860	Inc. Ab.	7.00	15.00	22.00	50.00
121a	1861	.338	5.00	10.00	18.00	45.00
	1862	4,400	—	—	Rare	—

KM#	Date	Mintage	VG	Fine	VF	XF
137.1	1865	.040	17.50	30.00	45.00	90.00
	1866	.082	10.00	20.00	32.50	50.00

KM#	Date	Mintage	VG	Fine	VF	XF
137.2	1867	.028	4.00	8.00	12.50	25.00
	1868	.181	2.00	4.00	6.00	12.50
	1869	.293	1.50	3.00	4.75	9.50
	1870/69	.540	1.25	2.50	4.00	8.00
	1870	Inc. Ab.	1.25	2.00	3.25	6.50
	1871/0	.171	1.50	3.00	5.00	10.00
	1871	Inc. Ab.	3.00	5.00	7.50	15.00
	1872	.286	2.00	4.00	7.00	12.50
	1873/2	.170	5.00	10.00	25.00	40.00
	1873/9	Inc. Ab.	5.00	10.00	25.00	40.00
	1873	Inc. Ab.	3.00	5.00	7.50	15.00
	1874/3	.588	3.00	7.00	15.00	20.00
	1874	Inc. Ab.	2.00	4.00	7.00	12.50
	1875/2	.097	3.00	7.00	12.00	20.00
	1875/3	I.A.	3.00	7.00	12.00	20.00
	1875/4	I.A.	3.00	7.00	12.00	20.00
	1875	Inc. Ab.	5.00	8.00	12.50	25.00
	1876	.082	3.00	7.00	12.00	16.00
	1877	.327	2.00	6.00	9.00	14.00
	1878	.306	2.00	6.50	10.00	15.00
	1880	.194	3.00	7.00	12.00	16.00
	1881	.264	3.00	7.00	12.00	16.00

1.2500 g, .500 SILVER, .0200 oz ASW
Obv. leg: 0.5 added.

KM#	Date	Mintage	Fine	VF	XF	Unc
137.3	1879	.916	2.00	3.00	6.00	20.00
	1880	1.205	1.50	3.00	5.00	15.00
	1881/0	1.687	1.50	3.00	5.00	15.00
	1881	Inc. Ab.	1.50	3.00	5.00	15.00
	1882	.235	2.50	5.00	8.00	20.00
	1883/2	—	3.00	6.00	12.00	25.00
	1883	.117	3.75	7.50	12.50	25.00
	1884	.664	2.50	3.50	6.50	20.00
	1885/2	.489	2.50	3.50	6.50	20.00
	1885/3	I.A.	2.00	3.00	5.50	18.00
	1885/4	I.A.	2.00	3.00	5.50	18.00
	1885	Inc. Ab.	3.00	6.00	12.00	25.00
	1887	3.081	1.50	3.00	5.00	15.00
	1888/7	2.448	2.50	3.50	6.50	20.00
	1888	Inc. Ab.	1.50	3.00	5.00	15.00
	1892/72	1.684	2.50	3.50	7.50	20.00
	1892/82	I.A.	2.50	3.50	6.50	20.00
	1892/82/72	Inc. Ab.	3.50	6.50	12.50	35.00
	1892/88	I.A.	2.50	4.00	7.00	20.00
	1892	Inc. Ab.	3.50	6.50	12.50	35.00
	1893/73	.850	3.50	6.00	12.00	30.00
	1893/78	I.A.	3.50	6.00	12.00	30.00
	1893/8/7	I.A.	3.50	6.00	12.00	30.00
	1893/83	I.A.	3.50	6.00	12.00	30.00
	1893/2	I.A.	2.00	4.00	6.00	20.00
	1893	Inc. Ab.	1.50	3.00	5.00	15.00
	1894/73	.784	2.00	4.50	7.50	18.00
	1894/84	I.A.	2.00	4.50	7.50	18.00
	1894/3	Inc. Ab.	2.00	4.50	7.50	18.00
	1894	Inc. Ab.	3.50	6.00	12.00	30.00

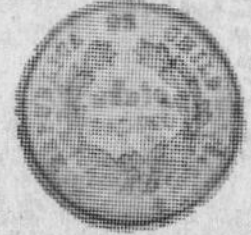

Mule. Obv: KM#137.3. Rev: KM#137.2.

KM#	Date	Mintage	Fine	VF	XF	Unc
149	1884	—	—	—	20.00	50.00

CINCO (5) CENTAVOS

1.0000 g, .835 SILVER, .0268 oz ASW
Obv: O. ROTY on stone below condor.
Rev: Hammer and sickle.

KM#	Date	Mintage	Fine	VF	XF	Unc
155.1	1896 large 6	.888	3.00	6.00	10.00	20.00
	1896 small 6	Inc. Ab.	3.00	6.00	10.00	20.00

1.0000 g, .500 SILVER, .0160 oz ASW
Obv: 0.5 below condor.

KM#	Date	Mintage	Fine	VF	XF	Unc
155.2	1899	1.794	2.00	3.00	5.00	15.00
	1901/801	2.109	3.00	5.00	8.50	20.00
	1901/891	I.A.	3.00	5.00	8.50	20.00
	1901	Inc. Ab.	2.00	3.00	5.00	15.00
	1904/894	2.527	—	—	—	—
	1904/1	I.A.	3.50	7.00	12.50	27.50
	1904	Inc. Ab.	2.00	3.00	5.00	15.00
	1906/4	.713	—	—	—	—
	1906	Inc. Ab.	2.00	3.00	6.00	17.00
	1907	2.791	2.00	3.00	5.00	15.00
	1909/899	—	2.50	4.00	7.00	18.50

NOTE: Varieties exist w/0.5, 0.5. or 05. below condor.

1.0000 g, .400 SILVER, .0128 oz ASW

KM#	Date	Mintage	Fine	VF	XF	Unc
155.2a	1908	3.642	2.00	3.00	5.00	10.00
	1909/8	1.177	—	—	—	—
	1909	Inc. Ab.	2.00	4.00	6.00	12.50
	1910/01	1.587	—	—	—	—
	1910	Inc. Ab.	2.00	3.00	5.00	10.00
	1911	.847	2.00	4.00	6.00	12.50
	1913/2	2.573	2.00	5.00	10.00	20.00
	1913	Inc. Ab.	2.00	3.00	5.00	10.00
	1919	Inc. Be.	1.50	3.00	5.00	10.00

1.0000 g, .450 SILVER, .0144 oz ASW
Obv: 0.45 below condor.

KM#	Date	Mintage	Fine	VF	XF	Unc
155.3	1915	2.250	1.50	3.00	5.00	10.00
	1916/1	4.337	1.50	3.50	6.00	12.00
	1916/5	I.A.	—	—	—	—
	1916	Inc. Ab.	1.50	3.00	5.00	10.00
	1919/1	1.494	3.00	5.00	10.00	20.00
	1919/5	I.A.	3.00	5.00	10.00	20.00
	1919	Inc. Ab.	2.00	4.00	6.00	12.00

NOTE: 1915 exists w/flat and curved top on 5.

COPPER-NICKEL
Obv: O. ROTY deleted.

KM#	Date	Mintage	Fine	VF	XF	Unc
165	1920	.718	1.00	1.50	3.00	6.50
	1921	2.406	.50	1.25	2.00	5.00
	1922	3.872	.50	1.25	2.00	5.00
	1923	2.150	.50	1.25	2.00	5.00
	1925	.994	.50	1.25	2.00	5.00
	1926	.594	1.50	2.50	3.00	6.50
	1927	1.276	.50	1.00	2.00	5.00
	1928	5.197	.50	1.00	2.00	5.00
	1933	3.000	5.00	10.00	17.50	35.00
	1934	Inc. Ab.	.25	.50	1.00	2.00
	1936	2.000	.25	.50	1.00	2.00
	1937	2.000	.25	.50	1.00	2.00
	1938	2.000	.25	.50	1.00	2.00

UN (1) DECIMO

2.5000 g, .900 SILVER, .0723 oz ASW

KM#	Date	Mintage	VG	Fine	VF	XF
124	1852	.211	2.50	5.00	15.00	50.00
	1853	Inc. Ab.	2.50	5.00	15.00	50.00
	1855	.585	2.50	5.00	15.00	50.00
	1856/5	.580	2.50	5.00	15.00	50.00
	1856	Inc. Ab.	2.50	5.00	12.00	35.00
	1857	1.481	2.50	5.00	12.00	35.00
	1858	.540	2.50	5.00	15.00	50.00
	1859	.020	40.00	65.00	100.00	—
	1860/59	—	5.00	10.00	30.00	60.00

2.3000 g, .900 SILVER, .0665 oz ASW

KM#	Date	Mintage	VG	Fine	VF	XF
124a	1860/50	.382	6.00	12.50	22.00	55.00
	1860	Inc. Ab.	2.50	6.00	12.50	30.00
	1861	.236	2.50	6.00	12.50	30.00
	1862	.095	3.00	7.00	15.00	40.00

KM#	Date	Mintage	VG	Fine	VF	XF
136.1	1864 thick flan	.096	5.50	10.00	22.00	40.00
	1864 thin flan	Inc. Ab.	—	—	—	—
	1865/4	.222	6.00	9.00	15.00	30.00
	1865/inverted 5	Inc. Ab.	6.00	9.00	15.00	30.00
	1865	Inc. Ab.	6.00	9.00	15.00	30.00
	1866	.096	5.50	10.00	22.00	40.00

KM#	Date	Mintage	VG	Fine	VF	XF
136.2	1867	.020	7.00	12.00	20.00	40.00
	1868	.207	2.00	3.00	5.00	10.00
	1869/8	.245	—	—	—	—
	1869	Inc. Ab.	2.00	3.00	5.00	10.00
	1870/60	.192	3.00	4.00	7.00	15.00
	1870	Inc. Ab.	2.50	3.50	6.00	12.00
	1871	.091	2.50	3.50	6.00	12.00
	1872/1	.288	—	—	—	—
	1872	Inc. Ab.	2.00	3.00	5.00	10.00
	1873/2	.305	—	—	—	—
	1873/9	I.A.	—	—	—	—
	1873	Inc. Ab.	2.00	3.00	5.00	10.00
	1874/64	.271	—	—	—	—
	1874	Inc.Ab.	2.00	3.00	5.00	10.00
	1875/4	.050	—	—	—	—
	1875	Inc. Ab.	5.00	10.00	20.00	40.00
	1876	.100	2.25	3.25	5.50	11.00
	1877	.096	2.25	3.25	5.50	11.00
	1878	.512	2.00	3.00	5.00	10.00
	1880/70	.243	—	—	—	—
	1880	Inc. Ab.	2.00	3.00	5.00	10.00

2.5000 g, .500 SILVER, .0401 oz ASW
Obv. leg: 0.5 added.

KM#	Date	Mintage	Fine	VF	XF	Unc
136.3	1879/8	1.268	1.25	2.25	3.50	8.00
	1879	Inc. Ab.	1.00	2.00	3.00	7.50
	1880/70	.705	1.50	3.00	5.00	10.00
	1880	Inc. Ab.	1.00	2.00	5.00	10.00
	1881	2.186	1.00	2.00	5.00	10.00
	1882	.233	1.00	2.00	5.00	10.00
	1882/2	I.A.	2.00	5.00	10.00	15.00
	1883	.178	1.00	2.00	5.00	10.00
	1884/2	.319	5.00	10.00	17.00	25.00
	1884	Inc. Ab.	1.00	2.00	5.00	10.00
	1885	.116	6.00	12.00	18.00	25.00
	1887/6	1.514	1.25	2.25	3.50	8.00
	1887 R/B in Republica	Inc. Ab.	1.25	2.25	3.50	8.00
	1887	Inc. Ab.	1.00	2.00	3.00	7.50
	1891	—	—	—	Rare	—
	1892/82	.994	1.00	2.00	5.00	10.00
	1892/0	Inc. Ab.	3.00	6.00	12.00	20.00
	1892	Inc. Ab.	1.00	2.00	3.00	7.50
	1893/83	.516	1.25	2.25	3.50	8.00
	1893/inverted 3	Inc. Ab.	3.50	5.50	10.00	18.00
	1893	Inc. Ab.	1.00	2.00	3.00	7.50
	1894/84	.826	1.00	2.00	3.00	7.50
	1894/3	I.A.	1.00	2.00	3.00	7.50
	1894/3 E/R in REPUBLICA	Inc. Ab.	1.25	2.25	3.50	8.00
	1894	Inc. Ab.	1.00	2.00	3.00	7.50

NOTE: 1 in 10 pieces dated 1887 has R/B in REPUBLICA.

2.0000 g, .500 SILVER, .0321 oz ASW

KM#	Date	Mintage	Fine	VF	XF	Unc
136.3a	1891/81	.264	35.00	80.00	160.00	300.00
	1891	I.A.	35.00	80.00	160.00	300.00

DIEZ (10) CENTAVOS

2.0000 g, .835 SILVER, .0536 oz ASW
Obv: O. ROTY on stone below condor.
Rev: Hammer and sickle.

KM#	Date	Mintage	Fine	VF	XF	Unc
156.1	1896	2.561	2.00	3.50	6.00	10.00

2.0000 g, .500 SILVER, .0321 oz ASW
Obv: 0.5 below condor.

KM#	Date	Mintage	Fine	VF	XF	Unc
156.2	1899	2.013	2.00	3.50	6.00	10.00
	1900	.104	20.00	35.00	50.00	85.00
	1901/891	I.A.	15.00	25.00	35.00	60.00
	1901	Inc. Ab.	10.00	20.00	30.00	50.00
	1904/899	.779	2.00	3.00	5.00	10.00
	1904	Inc. Ab.	2.00	3.50	6.00	10.00
	1906	.139	2.50	4.50	7.50	12.00
	1907	3.151	2.00	3.50	6.00	10.00

NOTE: Varieties exist for 1899 and 1907 dated coins w/0.5, 0,5 or 0.5/9 below condor.

1.5000 g, .400 SILVER, .0192 oz ASW

KM#	Date	Mintage	Fine	VF	XF	Unc
156.2a	1908	4.149	1.00	2.00	3.50	7.00
	1909/8	2.964	1.50	3.00	5.00	10.00
	1909	Inc. Ab.	1.00	2.00	3.50	7.00
	1913	1.269	1.50	3.00	5.00	10.00
	1919	.883	2.50	5.00	7.50	15.00
	1920	2.109	1.00	2.00	3.50	7.00

NOTE: Varieties exist.

1.5000 g, .450 SILVER, .0217 oz ASW
Obv: 0.45 below condor.

KM#	Date	Mintage	Fine	VF	XF	Unc
156.3	1915	1.620	1.00	1.50	2.50	4.00
	1916	2.855	1.00	1.50	2.50	4.00
	1917	.736	1.50	2.50	4.00	8.00
	1918	Inc. Ab.	1.50	2.50	4.00	8.00

COPPER-NICKEL
Obv: O. ROTY deleted.

KM#	Date	Mintage	Fine	VF	XF	Unc
166	1920	.451	1.50	3.50	5.00	10.00
	1921	2.654	.50	.75	1.50	3.00
	1922	4.017	.50	.75	1.50	3.00
	1923	3.356	.50	.75	1.50	3.00
	1924	1.445	.50	.75	1.50	3.00
	1925	2.665	.50	.75	1.50	3.00
	1927	.523	1.00	2.00	3.00	6.00
	1928	3.052	.50	.75	1.50	3.00
	1932	1.500	.75	1.00	2.00	4.00
	1933/2	5.800	—	—	—	—
	1933	Inc. Ab.	.25	.50	1.00	2.00
	1934	.900	.50	.75	1.50	3.00
	1935	1.500	.50	.75	1.50	3.00
	1936	3.300	.25	.50	1.00	2.00
	1937	2.000	.25	.50	1.00	2.00
	1938	5.000	.25	.50	1.00	2.00
	1939	1.200	.25	.50	1.00	2.00
	1940	6.100	.25	.50	1.00	2.00
	1941	.900	1.00	2.00	3.00	6.00

VEINTE (20) CENTAVOS

5.0000 g, .900 SILVER, .1446 oz ASW

KM#	Date	Mintage	VG	Fine	VF	XF
125	1852	.077	10.00	15.00	20.00	35.00
	1853	.906	5.00	6.50	11.00	20.00
	1854	.417	5.00	6.50	11.00	20.00
	1855	.325	5.00	6.50	12.00	22.50
	1856/5	.396	6.00	8.00	12.50	22.50
	1856	Inc. Ab.	5.00	6.50	11.00	20.00
	1857	.748	5.00	6.50	11.00	20.00
	1858	.532	7.50	10.00	15.00	25.00
	1859/8	.120	15.00	25.00	50.00	75.00
	1859	Inc. Ab.	50.00	75.00	—	—

4.6000 g, .900 SILVER, .1331 oz ASW

KM#	Date	Mintage	VG	Fine	VF	XF
125a	1860/50	.388	—	—	—	—
	1860/59	I.A.	3.00	6.00	10.00	20.00

KM#	Date	Mintage	VG	Fine	VF	XF
	1860	Inc. Ab.	3.00	6.00	10.00	20.00
	1861/51	1.471	5.00	7.00	10.00	24.00
	1861/58	I.A.	5.00	7.00	10.00	24.00
	1861/91	I.A.	5.00	7.00	10.00	22.50
	1861	Inc. Ab.	5.00	7.00	10.00	22.50
	1862/52	.324	5.00	7.00	10.00	24.00
	1862	Inc. Ab.	5.00	7.00	10.00	22.50

KM#	Date	Mintage	VG	Fine	VF	XF
135	1863	.160	5.00	7.50	10.00	18.00
	1864	.226	4.50	6.00	10.00	16.00
	1865	1.505	2.00	3.00	5.00	9.00
	1866	4.298	2.00	3.00	5.00	9.00
	1867	Inc. Be.	10.00	15.00	25.00	40.00

Obv: Smaller sprays.

KM#	Date	Mintage	VG	Fine	VF	XF
138.1	1867	.286	4.50	6.00	8.00	12.50
	1868	.197	2.00	3.50	5.00	7.50
	1869/8	.163	3.00	5.00	7.00	10.00
	1869	Inc. Ab.	2.00	3.50	5.00	7.50
	1870/60	.992	3.00	5.00	7.00	10.00
	1870	Inc. Ab.	2.00	3.50	5.00	7.50
	1871	1.144	2.00	3.50	5.00	7.50
	1872/0	1.979	—	—	—	—
	1872	Inc. Ab.	2.00	3.50	5.00	7.50
	1873/2	.846	—	—	—	—
	1873	Inc. Ab.	2.00	3.50	5.00	7.50
	1874 wide date	1.256	2.00	3.50	5.00	7.50
	1874 narrow date	Inc. Ab.	2.00	3.50	5.00	7.50
	1875	.120	5.00	7.50	15.00	25.00
	1876	.749	2.75	4.50	6.00	8.50
	1877	.549	2.75	4.50	6.00	8.50
	1878	2.639	2.75	4.50	6.00	8.50
	1879	9,645	60.00	100.00	175.00	250.00

NOTE: Varieties exist.

5.0000 g, .500 SILVER, .0803 oz ASW
Obv. leg: 0.5 added, w/o dash under S in CENTS.

KM#	Date	Mintage	VG	Fine	VF	XF
138.2	1879	5.073	2.50	4.00	6.00	9.00
	1880/70	6.846	2.75	4.50	7.00	11.00
	1880/79	I.A.	2.75	4.50	7.00	11.00
	1880	Inc. Ab.	2.50	4.00	6.00	9.00
	1881	6.408	2.50	4.00	6.00	9.00
	1893	1.397	2.50	4.00	6.00	9.00

4.0000 g, .500 SILVER, .0643 oz ASW

KM#	Date	Mintage	VG	Fine	VF	XF
138.2a	1890	—	—	—	—	—
	1891/81	2.953	—	—	—	—
	1891	Inc. Ab.	3.00	6.00	15.00	25.00

4.6000 g, .200 SILVER, .0296 oz ASW
Obv. leg: 0.2 added.

KM#	Date	Mintage	VG	Fine	VF	XF
138.3	1891/81	.787	—	—	—	—
	1891	Inc. Ab.	10.00	15.00	20.00	50.00

Obv: Dash under S in CENTS.

KM#	Date	Mintage	VG	Fine	VF	XF
138.4	1892/82	3.719	2.75	4.50	7.00	11.00
	1892	Inc. Ab.	2.50	4.00	6.00	9.00
	1893	Inc. Ab.	2.50	4.00	6.00	9.00

4.0000 g, .835 SILVER, .1073 oz ASW
Obv: O. ROTY below condor.
Rev: Hammer and sickle.

KM#	Date	Mintage	Fine	VF	XF	Unc
151.1	1895	.146	12.50	20.00	30.00	70.00

4.0000 g, .500 SILVER, .0643 oz ASW
Obv: 0.5 below condor.

KM#	Date	Mintage	Fine	VF	XF	Unc
151.2	1899/69	4.343	—	—	—	—
	1899/7	I.A.	—	—	—	—
	1899/8	I.A.	—	—	—	—
	1899	Inc. Ab.	1.00	2.00	3.00	7.00
	1899/sideways 9	Inc. Ab.	—	—	—	—
	1900/899	.334	60.00	80.00	—	—
	1900	Inc. Ab.	30.00	40.00	80.00	150.00
	1906/896	.866	—	—	—	—
	1906	Inc. Ab.	2.00	3.50	4.50	9.00
	1907/895	7.625	2.00	3.00	4.00	8.00
	1907	Inc. Ab.	1.00	2.00	3.00	7.00

NOTE: Varieties with 0.5 or 0.5. exist.

3.0000 g, .400 SILVER, .0385 oz ASW
Obv: W/o 0.5 below condor.

KM#	Date	Mintage	Fine	VF	XF	Unc
151.3	1907	1.201	1.00	1.50	3.00	7.00
	1908	5.869	.75	1.25	2.50	6.00
	1909	1.080	.75	1.25	2.50	6.00
	1913/1	3.507	1.50	2.50	4.00	9.00
	1913/50	I.A.	—	—	—	—
	1913	Inc. Ab.	.75	1.25	2.50	6.00
	1919	3.749	.75	1.25	2.50	6.00
	1920	4.189	.75	1.25	2.50	6.00

3.0000 g, .450 SILVER, .0434 oz ASW
Obv: 0.45 below condor.

KM#	Date	Mintage	Fine	VF	XF	Unc
151.4	1916	3.377	2.00	3.00	4.50	9.50

COPPER-NICKEL
Obv: W/o designer's name. Rev: Large 20.

KM#	Date	Mintage	Fine	VF	XF	Unc
167.1	1920	.499	1.00	2.50	5.00	12.00
	1921	6.547	.25	.50	1.00	3.50
	1922	8.261	.25	.50	1.00	3.50
	1923	5.439	.25	.50	1.00	3.50
	1924	16.096	.25	.50	1.00	3.50
	1925	9.830	.25	.50	1.00	3.50
	1929	9.685	.25	.50	1.00	3.50

Obv: O.ROTY.

KM#	Date	Mintage	Fine	VF	XF	Unc
167.4	1929	Inc. Ab.	1.00	2.50	5.00	10.00

Obv: W/o designer's name. Rev: Small 20.

KM#	Date	Mintage	Fine	VF	XF	Unc
167.2	1925	—	—	—	—	—
	1932	—	.50	1.00	2.00	4.50
	1933/inverted 33	5.900	—	—	—	—
	1933	Inc. Ab.	.25	.50	1.00	3.50
	1937	—	.50	1.00	2.00	4.50

Obv: O. ROTY.

KM#	Date	Mintage	Fine	VF	XF	Unc
167.3	1932	—	.25	.50	1.00	3.50
	1933/inverted 33	1.000	1.00	1.50	2.50	6.00
	1933	Inc. Ab.	.25	.50	1.00	3.50
	1937	—	.25	.50	1.00	3.50
	1938	3.043	.25	.50	1.00	3.50
	1939	5.283	.25	.50	1.00	3.50
	1940	9.300	.25	.50	1.00	3.00
	1941	3.000	.25	.50	1.00	3.00

COPPER

General Bernardo O'Higgens

KM#	Date	Mintage	Fine	VF	XF	Unc
177	1942	30.000	.15	.25	.50	1.50
	1943	39.600	.15	.25	.50	1.50
	1944	29.100	.15	.25	.50	1.50
	1945	11.400	.15	.25	.50	1.50
	1946	13.800	.15	.25	.50	1.50
	1947	15.700	.15	.25	.50	1.50
	1948	15.200	.15	.25	.50	1.50
	1949	14.700	.15	.25	.50	1.50
	1950	15.200	.15	.25	.50	1.50
	1951	14.700	.15	.25	.50	1.00
	1952	15.500	.15	.25	.50	1.00
	1953	7.800	.15	.25	.50	1.00

40 CENTAVOS

6.0000 g, .400 SILVER, .0771 oz ASW

KM#	Date	Mintage	Fine	VF	XF	Unc
163	1907	.056	15.00	25.00	50.00	100.00
	1908	1.452	2.50	6.00	10.00	20.00

50 CENTAVOS

12.5000 g, .900 SILVER, .3617 oz ASW

KM#	Date	Mintage	VG	Fine	VF	XF
128	1853	.769	7.50	10.00	20.00	65.00
	1854	.551	7.50	10.00	20.00	65.00
	1855	1.354	7.50	10.00	20.00	65.00
	1856/5	.606	—	—	—	—
	1856	Inc. Ab.	7.50	10.00	20.00	65.00
	1856 1/inverted 1	Inc. Ab.	—	—	—	—
	1858	.245	13.00	18.00	35.00	90.00
	1859	.489	10.00	15.00	30.00	75.00
	1860/59	.020	—	—	Rare	—
	1860	Inc. Ab.	250.00	350.00	450.00	600.00
	1862	.123	20.00	30.00	60.00	150.00

Obv: Large sprays. Rev: Eagle w/shield.

KM#	Date	Mintage	VG	Fine	VF	XF
134	1862	Inc. Ab.	22.00	30.00	45.00	90.00
	1863/2	.080	13.00	22.00	30.00	52.00
	1863	Inc. Ab.	13.00	22.00	30.00	50.00
	1864/3	.068	13.00	22.00	30.00	50.00
	1864	Inc. Ab.	13.00	22.00	30.00	50.00
	1865/4	.287	7.00	12.00	20.00	32.50
	1865	Inc. Ab.	6.50	11.00	18.00	30.00
	1866/5	.200	6.50	11.00	18.00	30.00
	1866	Inc. Ab.	9.00	13.00	22.00	35.00
	1867	.047	22.00	35.00	55.00	80.00

Obv: Smaller sprays.

KM#	Date	Mintage	VG	Fine	VF	XF
139	1867	Inc. Ab.	15.00	22.00	30.00	50.00
	1868	.147	7.00	9.00	11.00	20.00
	1870/60	.271	—	—	—	—
	1870/68	I.A.	5.50	7.50	10.00	16.50
	1870	Inc. Ab.	5.50	7.00	9.00	15.00
	1872/0	.104	7.00	9.00	11.00	20.00
	1872	Inc. Ab.	7.00	9.00	11.00	20.00

10.0000 g, .700 SILVER, .2250 oz ASW

KM#	Date	Mintage	Fine	VF	XF	Unc
160	1902	2.022	3.50	6.00	10.00	25.00
	1903	1.111	3.50	6.00	10.00	25.00
	1905	1.075	3.50	6.00	10.00	25.00
	1906	.142	— Reported, not confirmed			

NOTE: Varieties with 0.7 or 0.7. exist.

COPPER
General Bernardo O'Higgens

KM#	Date	Mintage	Fine	VF	XF	Unc
178	1942	4.715	.50	1.00	2.00	5.00

UN (1) PESO

25.0000 g, .900 SILVER, .7234 oz ASW

KM#	Date	Mintage	VG	Fine	VF	XF
129	1853	.394	15.00	25.00	45.00	80.00
	1854	.567	15.00	25.00	45.00	80.00
	1855	.683	15.00	25.00	45.00	80.00
	1856/5	.406	24.00	38.00	62.00	150.00
	1856	Inc. Ab.	18.50	28.50	50.00	100.00
	1858	.051	40.00	80.00	140.00	290.00
	1859/8	.330	18.50	28.50	50.00	90.00
	1859	Inc. Ab.	15.00	25.00	45.00	80.00
	1862	.103	45.00	90.00	200.00	340.00

1.5235 g, .900 GOLD, .0441 oz AGW
Crude style.

KM#	Date	Mintage	Fine	VF	XF	Unc
133	1860	.156	30.00	45.00	75.00	110.00
	1861	.176	30.00	45.00	75.00	110.00
	1862	.011	40.00	60.00	80.00	125.00
	1863	.055	30.00	45.00	75.00	110.00
	1864	.029	40.00	60.00	80.00	125.00

Fine style.

KM#	Date	Mintage	Fine	VF	XF	Unc
140	1867	949 pcs.	75.00	100.00	250.00	400.00
	1873	.016	40.00	60.00	80.00	125.00

25.0000 g, .900 SILVER, .7234 oz ASW
Obv. value: 1 PESO. Rev: Eagle w/shield.

KM#	Date	Mintage	Fine	VF	XF	Unc
141	1867	Inc. Be.	1200.	2800.	4000.	6000.

Obv. value: UN PESO

KM#	Date	Mintage	Fine	VF	XF	Unc
142.1	1867	.220	20.00	40.00	60.00	95.00
	1868	1.037	8.00	12.00	20.00	75.00
	1869	.467	10.00	15.00	30.00	75.00
	1870/69	.556	10.00	15.00	30.00	80.00
	1870	Inc. Ab.	10.00	15.00	30.00	75.00
	1871	.795	25.00	45.00	60.00	120.00
	1872	Inc. Ab.	10.00	17.50	30.00	75.00
	1873/2	.323	20.00	35.00	65.00	100.00
	1873	Inc. Ab.	8.00	12.00	20.00	60.00
	1874	1.204	8.00	12.00	20.00	60.00
	1875	2.128	8.00	12.00	20.00	60.00
	1876	1.508	8.00	12.00	20.00	60.00
	1877	1.930	8.00	12.00	20.00	60.00
	1878	.950	8.00	12.00	20.00	60.00
	1879	.780	8.00	12.00	20.00	60.00
	1880	.693	8.00	12.00	20.00	60.00
	1881	1.420	8.00	12.00	20.00	60.00
	1882/1	1.648	10.00	15.00	25.00	75.00
	1882	Inc. Ab.	8.00	12.00	20.00	60.00
	1883/2	1.397	—	—	—	—
	1883 round top 3	Inc. Ab.	8.00	12.00	20.00	70.00
	1884	1.812	8.00	12.00	20.00	60.00
	1885/3	.528	12.50	20.00	40.00	115.00
	1885	Inc. Ab.	10.00	15.00	30.00	95.00
	1886	.966	10.00	15.00	25.00	70.00
	1887	.023	350.00	750.00	1100.	1650.
	1889	.241	20.00	35.00	50.00	145.00
	1890/89	.109	25.00	45.00	65.00	190.00
	1890	Inc. Ab.	20.00	35.00	50.00	145.00
	1891	.109	50.00	100.00	200.00	400.00

Flat top 3, medal alignment.

KM#	Date	Mintage	Fine	VF	XF	Unc
142.2	1883(1925)	.150	—	150.00	300.00	465.00

Flat top 3, coin alignment.

KM#	Date	Mintage	Fine	VF	XF	Unc
142.3	1883(1926)	I.A.	—	150.00	300.00	465.00

NOTE: Above issue minted in 1925-6 and most coins were subsequently melted down.

20.0000 g, .835 SILVER, .5369 oz ASW

KM#	Date	Mintage	Fine	VF	XF	Unc
152.1	1895	6.086	8.00	12.50	16.50	40.00
	1896	1.556	10.00	15.00	28.00	55.00
	1897	.037	25.00	40.00	55.00	90.00

20.0000 g, .700 SILVER, .4501 oz ASW
Obv: 0.7 below condor.

KM#	Date	Mintage	Fine	VF	XF	Unc
152.2	1902	.178	8.00	17.50	35.00	65.00
	1903	.372	6.00	12.50	16.50	40.00
	1905	.429	6.00	12.50	16.50	40.00

12.0000 g, .900 SILVER, .3472 oz ASW
Obv: 0.9 below condor.

KM#	Date	Mintage	Fine	VF	XF	Unc
152.3	1910	2.166	4.00	6.00	12.00	22.50

9.0000 g, .720 SILVER, .2083 oz ASW
Obv: 0.72 below condor.

KM#	Date	Mintage	Fine	VF	XF	Unc
152.4	1915	6.032	3.75	5.00	6.50	15.00
	1917	3.033	4.00	5.50	8.00	17.50

9.0000 g, .500 SILVER, .1446 oz ASW
Obv: 0.5 below condor.

KM#	Date	Mintage	Fine	VF	XF	Unc
152.5	1921	2.287	2.25	3.50	5.00	10.00
	1922	2.718	2.25	3.50	5.00	10.00
152.6	1924	1.748	2.25	3.50	5.00	10.00
	1925	2.037	2.25	3.50	5.00	10.00

NOTE: Struck with medal rotation. Varieties of 1925 dated coins exist w/flat and curved tops.

Mule. Obv: KM#152.5. Rev: KM#171.

KM#	Date	Mintage	Fine	VF	XF	Unc
A171.1	1927	—	15.00	30.00	45.00	90.00

Rev: Thin "1" in denomination.

KM#	Date	Mintage	Fine	VF	XF	Unc
171.1	1927	4.099	4.00	6.00	10.00	18.00

Rev: Thick "1" in denomination.

KM#	Date	Mintage	Fine	VF	XF	Unc
171.2	1927	—	4.00	6.00	10.00	18.00

NOTE: Varieties 0.5 and 0,5 exist.

6.0000 g, .400 SILVER, .0771 oz ASW

KM#	Date	Mintage	Fine	VF	XF	Unc
174	1932	4.000	1.75	2.75	3.50	6.50

COPPER-NICKEL

KM#	Date	Mintage	Fine	VF	XF	Unc
176.1	1933	29.976	.20	.50	1.00	2.00

Obv: O ROTY incuse on rock base.

KM#	Date	Mintage	Fine	VF	XF	Unc
176.2	1940	.150	1.50	2.00	2.50	4.00

COPPER
General Bernardo O'Higgens

KM#	Date	Mintage	Fine	VF	XF	Unc
179	1942	15.150	.10	.35	1.00	4.00
	1943	16.900	.10	.35	1.00	4.00
	1944	12.050	.10	.35	1.00	5.00
	1945	7.600	.10	.35	1.00	5.00
	1946	2.050	.10	.35	1.50	7.50
	1947	2.200	.10	.35	1.50	7.50
	1948	5.900	.10	.25	.75	3.75
	1949	7.100	.10	.20	.45	2.25
	1950	7.250	.10	.20	.45	2.25
	1951	8.150	.10	.20	.45	2.25
	1952	10.400	.10	.20	.45	2.25
	1953	17.200	.10	.20	.40	1.50
	1954	7.566	.10	.20	.40	1.50

ALUMINUM

KM#	Date	Mintage	Fine	VF	XF	Unc
179a	1954	43.550	.10	.15	.25	.40
	1955	69.050	.10	.15	.25	.40
	1956	58.250	.10	.15	.25	.40
	1957	49.250	.10	.15	.25	.40
	1958	29.900	.10	.15	.25	.40

DOS (2) PESOS

3.0506 g, .900 GOLD, .0882 oz AGW
Fine style.

KM#	Date	Mintage	Fine	VF	XF	Unc
132	1857	.207	BV	50.00	75.00	125.00
	1858/7	.056	BV	65.00	100.00	150.00
	1858	Inc. Ab.	BV	50.00	75.00	125.00
	1859	.097	BV	50.00	75.00	125.00
	1860	.078	BV	50.00	75.00	125.00
	1862	.010	BV	50.00	75.00	125.00
	1865	—	—	—	Rare	—

Modified arms.

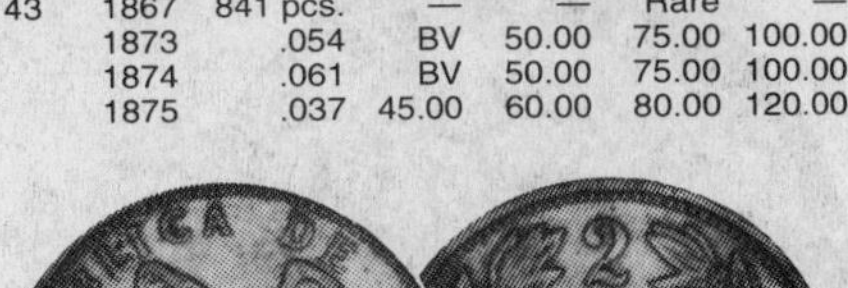

KM#	Date	Mintage	Fine	VF	XF	Unc
143	1867	841 pcs.	—	—	Rare	—
	1873	.054	BV	50.00	75.00	100.00
	1874	.061	BV	50.00	75.00	100.00
	1875	.037	45.00	60.00	80.00	120.00

18.0000 g, .500 SILVER, .2893 oz ASW

KM#	Date	Mintage	Fine	VF	XF	Unc
172	1927	1.112	BV	4.00	8.00	17.50

NOTE: Varieties 0.5 and 0,5 exist.

CINCO (5) PESOS

7.6265 g, .900 GOLD, .2207 oz AGW
Crude style.

KM#	Date	Mintage	Fine	VF	XF	Unc
122	1851	3,735	BV	135.00	160.00	250.00
	1852	.020	BV	125.00	150.00	225.00
	1853	5,987	BV	135.00	160.00	250.00

Fine style.

KM#	Date	Mintage	Fine	VF	XF	Unc
130	1854	953 pcs.	—	—	Rare	—
	1855	7,609	BV	135.00	160.00	250.00
	1856	4,753	BV	135.00	160.00	250.00
	1857	.025	BV	125.00	150.00	225.00
	1858	1.100	BV	125.00	150.00	225.00
	1859/8	.066	BV	125.00	150.00	225.00
	1859	Inc. Ab.	BV	125.00	150.00	225.00
	1862	6,738	BV	135.00	160.00	250.00
	1865	5,110	BV	135.00	160.00	250.00
	1866	6,249	BV	135.00	160.00	250.00
	1867	.010	BV	125.00	150.00	225.00

Modified arms.

KM#	Date	Mintage	Fine	VF	XF	Unc
144	1868	4,065	BV	135.00	160.00	250.00
	1869	5,913	BV	135.00	160.00	250.00
	1870	.013	BV	125.00	150.00	225.00
	1872	.023	BV	125.00	150.00	225.00
	1873	.050	BV	125.00	150.00	225.00

2.9955 g, .917 GOLD, .0883 oz AGW

KM#	Date	Mintage	Fine	VF	XF	Unc
153	1895	3.026	BV	50.00	60.00	90.00
	1896	.024	75.00	150.00	250.00	375.00

KM#	Date	Mintage	Fine	VF	XF	Unc
159	1897	—	—	—	Rare	—
	1898	.426	BV	55.00	85.00	100.00
	1900	1.265	60.00	100.00	120.00	150.00
	1911	1,399	—	—	300.00	450.00

25.0000 g, .900 SILVER, .7234 oz ASW
Rev: Wide 5.

KM#	Date	Mintage	Fine	VF	XF	Unc
173.1	1927	.976	10.00	12.50	17.50	35.00

Rev: Narrow 5.

KM#	Date	Mintage	Fine	VF	XF	Unc
173.2	1927	Inc. Ab.	10.00	12.50	17.50	35.00

NOTE: Varieties 0.9 and 0,9 exist.

ALUMINUM

KM#	Date	Mintage	Fine	VF	XF	Unc
180	1956	1.600	.15	.35	.50	.75

22.5000 g, .999 SILVER, .7228 oz ASW
150th Anniversary of Naval Academy
Obv: Similar to 50 Pesos, KM#184.

KM#	Date	Mintage	VF	XF	Unc
182	1968	1,200	—	Proof	20.00

DIEZ (10) PESOS

15.2530 g, .900 GOLD, .4414 oz AGW
Crude style.

KM#	Date	Mintage	Fine	VF	XF	Unc
123	1851	.050	BV	225.00	275.00	350.00
	1852	.135	BV	225.00	275.00	350.00
	1853	.206	BV	225.00	250.00	300.00

Fine style.

KM#	Date	Mintage	Fine	VF	XF	Unc
131	1854	.195	BV	225.00	275.00	350.00
	1855	.061	BV	225.00	275.00	350.00
	1856	.066	BV	225.00	275.00	350.00
	1857	.020	BV	225.00	275.00	350.00
	1858	.052	BV	225.00	275.00	350.00
	1859	.281	BV	225.00	275.00	350.00
	1860	.031	BV	225.00	275.00	350.00
	1861	.015	BV	225.00	275.00	350.00
	1862	.021	BV	225.00	275.00	350.00
	1863	.025	BV	225.00	275.00	350.00
	1864	.026	BV	225.00	275.00	350.00
	1865	.045	BV	225.00	275.00	350.00
	1866	.066	BV	225.00	275.00	350.00
	1867	.121	BV	225.00	275.00	350.00

Obv: Modified arms.

KM#	Date	Mintage	Fine	VF	XF	Unc
145	1868	.054	BV	225.00	275.00	350.00
	1869	.036	BV	225.00	275.00	350.00
	1870	.076	BV	225.00	275.00	350.00
	1871	.041	BV	225.00	275.00	350.00
	1872	.235	BV	225.00	275.00	350.00
	1873	.112	BV	225.00	275.00	350.00
	1874	1,277	BV	235.00	285.00	375.00
	1876	2,106	BV	235.00	285.00	375.00
	1877	8,208	BV	235.00	285.00	375.00
	1878	7,983	BV	235.00	285.00	375.00
	1879	9,805	BV	235.00	285.00	375.00
	1880	.011	BV	225.00	275.00	350.00
	1881	.013	BV	225.00	275.00	350.00
	1882	.014	BV	225.00	275.00	350.00
	1883	8,381	BV	235.00	285.00	375.00
	1884	9,888	BV	235.00	285.00	375.00
	1885	7,758	BV	235.00	285.00	375.00
	1886	3,721	BV	235.00	285.00	375.00
	1887	5,236	BV	235.00	285.00	375.00
	1888	4,217	BV	235.00	285.00	375.00
	1889	4,650	BV	235.00	285.00	375.00
	1890	2,344	BV	235.00	285.00	375.00
	1892	1,192	BV	235.00	285.00	375.00

5.9910 g, .917 GOLD, .1766 oz AGW

KM#	Date	Mintage	Fine	VF	XF	Unc
154	1895	.808	—	BV	100.00	160.00

KM#	Date	Mintage	Fine	VF	XF	Unc
157	1896	1.163	—	BV	100.00	125.00
	1898	.276	—	BV	100.00	150.00
	1900	—	— Reported, not confirmed			
	1901	1.651	BV	100.00	125.00	200.00

ALUMINUM

KM#	Date	Mintage	Fine	VF	XF	Unc
181	1956	13.100	.15	.35	.50	.75
	1957	28.800	.15	.35	.50	.75
	1958	44.500	.15	.35	.50	.75
	1959	10.220	.25	.50	1.00	1.50

45.0000 g, .999 SILVER, 1.4455 oz ASW
Arrival of Liberation Fleet in 1820

KM#	Date	Mintage	VF	XF	Unc
183	1968	1,215	—	Proof	75.00

VEINTE (20) PESOS

11.9821 g, .917 GOLD, .3532 oz AGW

KM#	Date	Mintage	Fine	VF	XF	Unc
158	1896	.149	—	BV	200.00	250.00
	1906	.041	—	BV	200.00	300.00
	1907	.012	—	BV	200.00	300.00
	1908	.026	—	BV	200.00	300.00
	1910	.028	—	BV	200.00	300.00
	1911	.017	—	BV	200.00	300.00
	1913/11	.018	—	BV	200.00	300.00
	1913	Inc. Ab.	—	BV	200.00	300.00
	1914	.022	—	BV	200.00	300.00
	1915	.065	—	BV	200.00	300.00
	1916	.036	—	BV	200.00	300.00
	1917	.717	—	BV	200.00	300.00

4.0679 g, .900 GOLD, .1177 oz AGW

KM#	Date	Mintage	Fine	VF	XF	Unc
168	1926	.085	—	BV	60.00	90.00
	1958	500 pcs.	BV	60.00	125.00	200.00
	1959	.025	—	—	BV	80.00
	1961	.020	—	—	BV	80.00
	1964	—	—	—	BV	80.00
	1976	.099	—	—	BV	80.00
	1977	.038	—	—	BV	80.00
	1979	.030	—	—	BV	80.00
	1980	.030	—	—	BV	80.00

Rev: Coat of arms on ornamental vines.

KM#	Date	Mintage	Fine	VF	XF	Unc
188	1976	Inc. Ab.	—	BV	70.00	100.00

CINCUENTA (50) PESOS

10.1698 g, .900 GOLD, .2943 oz AGW

KM#	Date	Mintage	Fine	VF	XF	Unc
169	1926	.126	—	BV	150.00	200.00
	1958	.010	—	—	BV	200.00
	1961	.020	—	—	BV	200.00
	1962	.030	—	—	BV	200.00
	1965	—	—	—	BV	200.00
	1966	—	—	—	BV	200.00
	1967	—	—	—	BV	200.00
	1968	—	—	—	BV	200.00
	1969	—	—	—	BV	200.00
	1974	—	—	—	BV	200.00

10.1600 g, .900 GOLD, .2940 oz AGW
150th Anniversary of Military Academy

KM#	Date	Mintage	Fine	VF	XF	Unc
184	1968	2,515	—	—	Proof	200.00

CIEN (100) PESOS

20.3397 g, .900 GOLD, .5886 oz AGW

KM#	Date	Mintage	Fine	VF	XF	Unc
170	1926	.678	—	BV	325.00	375.00

KM#	Date	Mintage	Fine	VF	XF	Unc
175	1932	9,315	—	BV	350.00	450.00
	1946	.380	—	—	BV	350.00
	1947	.500	—	—	BV	350.00
	1948	.405	—	—	BV	350.00
	1949	.245	—	—	BV	350.00
	1950	.020	—	—	BV	350.00
	1951	.190	—	—	BV	350.00
	1952	.240	—	—	BV	350.00
	1953	.150	—	—	BV	350.00
	1954	.250	—	—	BV	350.00
	1955	.085	—	—	BV	350.00
	1956	.070	—	—	BV	350.00
	1957	.020	—	—	BV	350.00
	1958	.178	—	—	BV	350.00
	1959	.100	—	—	BV	350.00
	1960	.345	—	—	BV	350.00
	1961	.195	—	—	BV	350.00
	1962	.250	—	—	BV	350.00
	1963	.145	—	—	BV	350.00
	1964	—	—	—	BV	350.00
	1968	—	—	—	BV	350.00
	1969	—	—	—	BV	350.00
	1970	—	—	—	BV	350.00
	1971	—	—	—	BV	350.00
	1972	—	—	—	BV	350.00
	1973	—	—	—	BV	350.00
	1974	—	—	—	BV	350.00
	1976	.172	—	—	BV	350.00
	1977	.025	—	—	BV	350.00
	1979	.100	—	—	BV	350.00
	1980	.050	—	—	BV	350.00

20.3300 g, .900 GOLD, .5883 oz AGW
150th Anniversary of National Coinage

KM#	Date	Mintage	Fine	VF	XF	Unc
185	1968	1,815	—	—	Proof	400.00

200 PESOS

40.6700 g, .900 GOLD, 1.1769 oz AGW
150th Anniversary of San Martin's Passage
through Andes Mountains

KM#	Date	Mintage	Fine	VF	XF	Unc
186	1968	965 pcs.	—	—	Proof	900.00

500 PESOS

101.6900 g, .900 GOLD, 2.9427 oz AGW
150th Anniversary of National Flag

KM#	Date	Mintage	Fine	VF	XF	Unc
187	1968	—	—	—	Proof	2250.

MONETARY REFORM

10 Pesos = 1 Centesimo
100 Centesimos = 1 Escudo

1/2 CENTESIMO

ALUMINUM

KM#	Date	Mintage	VF	XF	Unc
192	1962	3.750	.10	.30	.50
	1962	—	—	Proof	—
	1963	8.100	.10	.30	.50

CENTESIMO

ALUMINUM

KM#	Date	Mintage	VF	XF	Unc
189	1960	20.160	.35	.75	1.25
	1961	Inc. Ab.	.15	.30	.50
	1962	26.320	.15	.30	.50
	1963	51.360	.15	.30	.50

2 CENTESIMOS

ALUMINUM-BRONZE

KM#	Date	Mintage	VF	XF	Unc
193	1960*	—	—	—	50.00
	1964	4.050	—	.10	1.00
	1965	32.550	—	.10	1.00
	1966	31.800	—	.10	1.00
	1967	34.750	—	.10	1.00
	1968	29.400	—	.10	1.00
	1969	—	—	—	2.50
	1969	—	—	Proof	50.00
	1970	20.250	—	.10	1.00

***NOTE:** Not released for circulation.

5 CENTESIMOS

ALUMINUM-BRONZE

KM#	Date	Mintage	VF	XF	Unc
190	1960	—	—	Proof	100.00
	1961	.012	2.50	5.00	10.00
	1962	Inc. Be.	.10	.15	1.00
	1963	17.280	.10	.15	1.00
	1964	16.628	.10	.15	1.00
	1965	37.680	.10	.15	1.00
	1966	32.360	.10	.15	1.00
	1967	17.640	.10	.15	1.00
	1968	4.338	.10	.15	1.00
	1968	—	—	Proof	50.00
	1969	—	—	—	3.50
	1969	—	—	Proof	50.00
	1970	30.680	.10	.15	1.00

10 CENTESIMOS

ALUMINUM-BRONZE

KM#	Date	Mintage	VF	XF	Unc
191	1960	—	2.00	3.50	6.50
	1961	57.068	.10	.20	1.00
	1962	1.480	.10	.20	1.00

KM#	Date	Mintage	VF	XF	Unc
191	1963	10.920	.10	.20	1.00
	1964	27.020	.10	.20	1.00
	1965	49.480	.10	.20	1.00
	1966	60.360	.10	.20	1.00
	1967	60.680	.10	.25	1.00
	1968	8.040	.10	.20	1.00
	1969	—	—	—	3.50
	1970	42.080	.10	.20	1.00

Bernardo O'Higgins

KM#	Date	Mintage	VF	XF	Unc
194	1971	99.700	—	.10	.15

20 CENTESIMOS

ALUMINUM-BRONZE
Jose Manuel Balmaceda

KM#	Date	Mintage	VF	XF	Unc
195	1971	89.200	—	.10	.20
	1972	—	.10	.20	1.00

50 CENTESIMOS

ALUMINUM-BRONZE
Manuel Rodriguez

KM#	Date	Mintage	VF	XF	Unc
196	1971	58.300	.10	.15	.25

ESCUDO

COPPER-NICKEL
Jose Miguel Carrera

KM#	Date	Mintage	VF	XF	Unc
197	1971	160.900	.10	.20	.40
	1972	Inc. Ab.	.10	.20	.40
	1972	—	—	Proof	50.00

2 ESCUDOS

COPPER-NICKEL
Caupolican, Chief of Araucanian Indians

KM#	Date	Mintage	VF	XF	Unc
198	1971*	106 pcs.	—	—	125.00
	1971	—	—	Proof	50.00

***NOTE:** Not released for circulation.

5 ESCUDOS

COPPER-NICKEL

KM#	Date	Mintage	VF	XF	Unc
199	1971	—	.10	.25	.75
	1972	—	.10	.25	.75
	1972	—	—	Proof	50.00

ALUMINUM

KM#	Date	Mintage	VF	XF	Unc
199a	1972	—	.10	.15	.20

10 ESCUDOS

ALUMINUM

KM#	Date	Mintage	VF	XF	Unc
200	1974	33.750	.10	.15	.20
	1974	—	—	Proof	50.00
	1975	—	.10	.15	.20

50 ESCUDOS

NICKEL-BRASS

KM#	Date	Mintage	VF	XF	Unc
201	1974	6.000	.15	.25	.60
	1975	20.300	.15	.20	.50

100 ESCUDOS

NICKEL-BRASS

KM#	Date	Mintage	VF	XF	Unc
202	1974	32.100	.20	.35	.75
	1975	65.600	.20	.35	.75

MONETARY REFORM

100 Centavos = 1 Peso
1000 Old Escudos = 1 Peso

CENTAVO

ALUMINUM

KM#	Date	Mintage	VF	XF	Unc
203	1975	2.000	.10	.15	.50

5 CENTAVOS

ALUMINUM-BRONZE

KM#	Date	Mintage	VF	XF	Unc
204	1975	12.000	—	.10	.15
	1976	—	—	.10	.15

ALUMINUM

KM#	Date	Mintage	VF	XF	Unc
204a	1976	5.000	—	.10	.15

10 CENTAVOS

ALUMINUM-BRONZE

KM#	Date	Mintage	VF	XF	Unc
205	1975	17.600	—	.10	.15
	1976	—	—	.10	.15

ALUMINUM

KM#	Date	Mintage	VF	XF	Unc
205a	1976	6.600	—	.10	.20
	1977	57.800	—	.10	.15
	1978	58.050	—	.10	.15
	1979	101.950	—	.10	.15

50 CENTAVOS

COPPER-NICKEL

KM#	Date	Mintage	VF	XF	Unc
206	1975	38.000	—	.10	.20
	1976	1.000	.50	1.00	2.00
	1977	10.000	—	.10	.20

ALUMINUM-BRONZE

KM#	Date	Mintage	VF	XF	Unc
206a	1978	19.250	—	.10	.20
	1979	28.000	—	.10	.20

PESO

COPPER-NICKEL
Obv. leg: BERNARDO O'HIGGINS.

KM#	Date	Mintage	VF	XF	Unc
207	1975	51.000	.10	.15	.25

Obv. leg: LIBERTADOR. B.O'HIGGINS.

KM#	Date	Mintage	VF	XF	Unc
208	1976	30.000	—	.10	.25
	1977	20.000	—	.10	.25

ALUMINUM-BRONZE

KM#	Date	Mintage	VF	XF	Unc
208a	1978	39.700	—	.10	.25
	1979	63.000	—	.10	.25

Reduced size, 17mm.

KM#	Date	Mintage	VF	XF	Unc
216	1981	40.000	—	.10	.20
	1984	60.000	—	.10	.20
	1985	20.000	—	.10	.20
	1986	45.000	—	.10	.20
	1987	80.000	—	.10	.20
	1988	105.000	—	.10	.20
	1989	205.000	—	.10	.20
	1990	140.000	—	.10	.20
	1991	140.000	—	.10	.20
	1992	—	—	.10	.20

ALUMINUM

KM#	Date	Mintage	VF	XF	Unc
231	1992	—	—	—	.10
	1993	—	—	—	.10

5 PESOS

COPPER-NICKEL
3rd Anniversary of New Government

KM#	Date	Mintage	VF	XF	Unc
209	1976	2.100	.15	.25	2.00
	1977	28.300	.15	.25	2.00
	1978	11.700	.15	.25	2.00
	1980	8.000	.15	.25	2.00

NICKEL-BRASS, 19mm

KM#	Date	Mintage	VF	XF	Unc
217	1981	17.000	—	.10	.50
	1982	20.000	—	.10	.50
	1984	12.000	—	.10	.50
	1985	16.000	—	.10	.50
	1986	16.000	—	.10	.50
217	1987	8.000	—	.10	.50
	1988	27.000	—	.10	.50
	1989	32.000	—	.10	.50
	1990	23.000	—	.10	.50

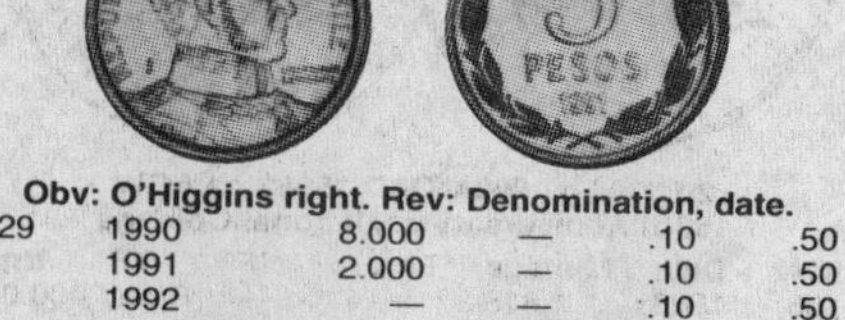

Obv: O'Higgins right. Rev: Denomination, date.

KM#	Date	Mintage	VF	XF	Unc
229	1990	8.000	—	.10	.50
	1991	2.000	—	.10	.50
	1992	—	—	.10	.50

ALUMINUM-BRONZE

KM#	Date	Mintage	VF	XF	Unc
232	1992	—	—	.10	.50
	1993	—	—	.10	.50

10 PESOS

COPPER-NICKEL
3rd Anniversary of New Government

KM#	Date	Mintage	VF	XF	Unc
210	1976	2.100	.10	.20	1.25
	1977	30.000	.10	.20	1.00
	1978	20.000	.10	.20	1.00
	1979	7.000	.10	.20	1.00
	1980	20.000	.10	.20	1.00

44.8000 g, .999 SILVER, 1.4390 oz ASW
3rd Anniversary of New Government

KM#	Date	Mintage	VF	XF	Unc
211	1976	1,000	—	Proof	100.00

NICKEL-BRASS

KM#	Date	Mintage	VF	XF	Unc
218	1981	55.000	.10	.20	.50
	1982	45.000	.10	.20	.50
	1984	30.000	.10	.20	.50
	1985	.400	.50	1.50	3.50
	1986	25.000	.10	.20	.50
	1987	8.000	.10	.20	.50
	1988	45.000	.10	.20	.50
	1989	73.000	.10	.20	.50
	1990	10.000	.10	.20	.50

Obv: Small bust of Higgins right, wide rim.

KM#	Date	Mintage	VF	XF	Unc
228.1	1990	5.000	.10	.20	.50

Obv: Large bust of Higgins right, normal rim.

KM#	Date	Mintage	VF	XF	Unc
228.2	1990	25.000	.10	.20	.50
	1991	—	.10	.20	.50
	1992	—	.10	.20	.50
	1993	—	.10	.20	.50

50 PESOS

10.1500 g, .900 GOLD, .2937 oz AGW
3rd Anniversary of New Government

KM#	Date	Mintage	VF	XF	Unc
212	1976	1,900	—	—	200.00
	1976	Inc. Ab.	—	Proof	225.00

ALUMINUM-BRONZE

KM#	Date	Mintage	VF	XF	Unc
219	1981	12.000	.25	.50	1.25
	1982	14.000	.25	.50	1.25
	1985	.400	.60	1.50	3.50
	1986	1.000	.25	.50	1.25
	1987	4.000	.25	.50	1.25
	1988	4.800	.25	.50	1.25
	1989	4.000	.25	.50	1.25
	1991	10.845	.25	.50	1.25
	1992	—	.25	.50	1.25
	1993	—	.25	.50	1.25

100 PESOS

20.3000 g, .900 GOLD, .5874 oz AGW
3rd Anniversary of New Government

KM#	Date	Mintage	VF	XF	Unc
213	1976	2,900	—	—	350.00
	1976	100 pcs.	—	Proof	825.00

ALUMINUM-BRONZE

KM#	Date	Mintage	VF	XF	Unc
226	1981	10.000	.50	.75	2.50
	1983	—	.50	.75	2.50
	1984	8.000	.50	.75	2.50
	1985	15.000	.50	.75	2.50
	1986	11.000	.50	.75	2.50
	1987	15.000	.50	.75	2.50
	1988	—	.50	.75	2.50
	1989	20.000	.50	.75	2.50
	1991	4.320	.50	.75	2.50

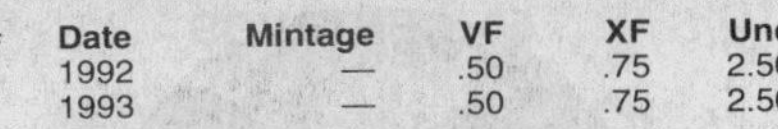

KM#	Date	Mintage	VF	XF	Unc
226	1992	—	.50	.75	2.50
	1993	—	.50	.75	2.50

500 PESOS

102.2700 g, .900 GOLD, 2.9595 oz AGW
3rd Anniversary of New Government
Similar to 100 Pesos, KM#213.

KM#	Date	Mintage	VF	XF	Unc
214	1976	500 pcs.	—	—	1850.
	1976	700 pcs.	—	Proof	1850.

2000 PESOS

8.2000 g, .500 SILVER, .1318 oz ASW
250th Anniversary of the Mint

KM#	Date	Mintage	VF	XF	Unc
233	1993	.050	—	—	16.50

10000 PESOS

27.0000 g, .925 SILVER, .8029 oz ASW
Ibero - American Series

KM#	Date	Mintage	VF	XF	Unc
230	1991	.075	—	Proof	42.50

SILVER BULLION ISSUES

1/4 ONZA

7.7770 g, .999 SILVER, .2500 oz ASW
10th Anniversary of National Liberation

KM#	Date	Mintage	VF	XF	Unc
223	1983	1,000	—	Proof	10.00

1/2 ONZA

15.5530 g, .999 SILVER, .5000 oz ASW
10th Anniversary of National Liberation

KM#	Date	Mintage	VF	XF	Unc
224	1983	1,000	—	Proof	20.00

ONZA

31.1070 g, .999 SILVER, 1.0000 oz ASW
10th Anniversary of National Liberation

KM#	Date	Mintage	VF	XF	Unc
225	1983	1,000	—	Proof	35.00

GOLD BULLION ISSUES

1/4 ONZA

8.6400 g, .900 GOLD, .2500 oz ASW
10th Anniversary of National Liberation
Similar to KM#223.

KM#	Date	Mintage	VF	XF	Unc
220	1983	1,000	—	—	175.00

1/2 ONZA

17.2800 g, .900 GOLD, .5000 oz ASW
10th Anniversary of National Liberation
Similar to KM#224.

KM#	Date	Mintage	VF	XF	Unc
221	1983	1,000	—	—	350.00

ONZA

31.1000 g, .999 GOLD, 1.0000 oz AGW

KM#	Date	Mintage	VF	XF	Unc
227	1948	—	—	—	800.00

KM#	Date	Mintage	VF	XF	Unc
215	1978	8 pcs.	—	Proof	2200.
	1979	1,580	—	—	600.00
	1980	1,730	—	—	600.00
	1981	200 pcs.	—	—	700.00
	1983	999 pcs.	—	—	650.00
	1983	1 pc.	—	Proof	—

34.5590 g, .900 GOLD, 1.0000 oz AGW
10th Anniversary of National Liberation
Similar to KM#225.

KM#	Date	Mintage	VF	XF	Unc
222	1983	1,000	—	—	600.00

PROOF SETS (PS)

KM#	Date	Mintage	Identification	Issue Price	Mkt. Val.
PS1	1968(6)	*	KM182-187	560.00	2200.
PS2	1968(4)	*	KM184-187	528.00	3850.
PS3	1968(2)	*	KM182,183	31.50	95.00
PS4	1971/2(3)	—	KM197(1972),KM198(1971), KM199(1972)	—	150.00

***NOTE:** Total of 12,000 coins struck for each denomination including those available singly.

NECESSITY COINAGE

COPIAPO

Revolution of 1859

Issued by Don Pedro Leon Gallo.

50 CENTAVOS

SILVER, uniface

KM#	Date	Mintage	VG	Fine	VF	XF
1	ND	—	25.00	35.00	50.00	70.00

NOTE: Varieties exist.

PESO

SILVER, uniface

KM#	Date	Mintage	VG	Fine	VF	XF
2.1	ND	—	20.00	30.00	40.00	50.00

Inverted shield.

KM#	Date	Mintage	VG	Fine	VF	XF
2.2	ND	—	20.00	30.00	40.00	50.00

Similar to 50 Centavos, KM#1.

KM#	Date	Mintage	VG	Fine	VF	XF
2.3 (2.2)	ND	—	20.00	30.00	40.00	50.00

NOTE: Denomination appears as either "1.P" or "I.P". Other varieties exist.

Blockade of Puerto de Caldera

Issued during the War of 1865 with Spain.

50 CENTAVOS

SILVER
Obv: COPIAPO-CHILE around shield. Rev: Date.

KM#	Date	Mintage	VG	Fine	VF	XF
3	1865	6 known	—	—	350.00	500.00

NOTE: All known 50 Centavos are restrikes made from original dies circa 1909 by Medina.

PESO

SILVER, 36.5mm

KM#	Date	Mintage	VG	Fine	VF	XF
4	1865(restrike)	—	—	25.00	50.00	75.00

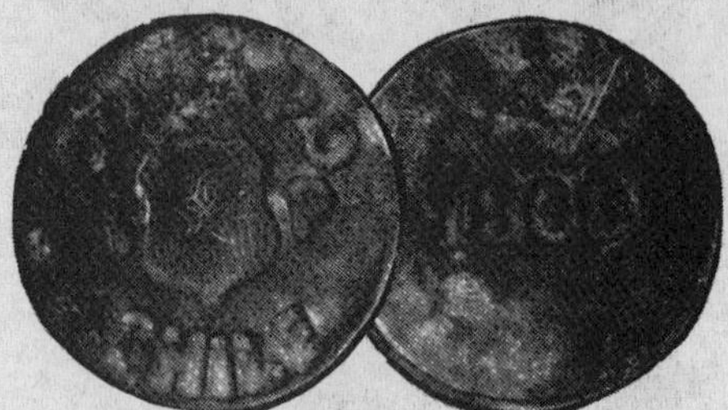

COPPER, 32mm

KM#	Date	Mintage	VG	Fine	VF	XF
4a	1865*	—	850.00	1350.	2000.	—

***NOTE:** Possibly a pattern.

SAN BERNARDO DE MAYPO

1/4 REAL

COPPER
Obv: Mountains (volcano in center) in circle.
Rev: View of Canal de San Bernardo.

KM#	Date	Mintage	VG	Fine	VF	XF
1	1821	—	150.00	300.00	500.00	800.00

NOTE: Struck to pay canal workers.

TARAPACA

Tarapaca is the northernmost province of Chile. It was annexed to Chile from Peru in 1885 after a war between those two countries, in which Chile was the victor. In that same year the Liberal Party came to power in Chile, instituting reforms. In response to these reforms the Conservative Party rebelled and formed a provisional government, and within a few years defeated the Liberals.

REVOLUTIONARY COINAGE

Struck at Iquique by the revolutionary Junta.

PESO

25.0000 g, .620 SILVER, .4983 oz ASW, 37.5mm
Rev. leg: 25 GRs/620 FINO.

KM#	Date	Mintage	Fine	VF	XF	Unc
1	1891	—	250.00	500.00	1000.	1750.

COPPER

KM#	Date	Mintage	Fine	VF	XF	Unc
2	1891*	—	—	880.00	—	—

***NOTE:** Possibly a pattern.

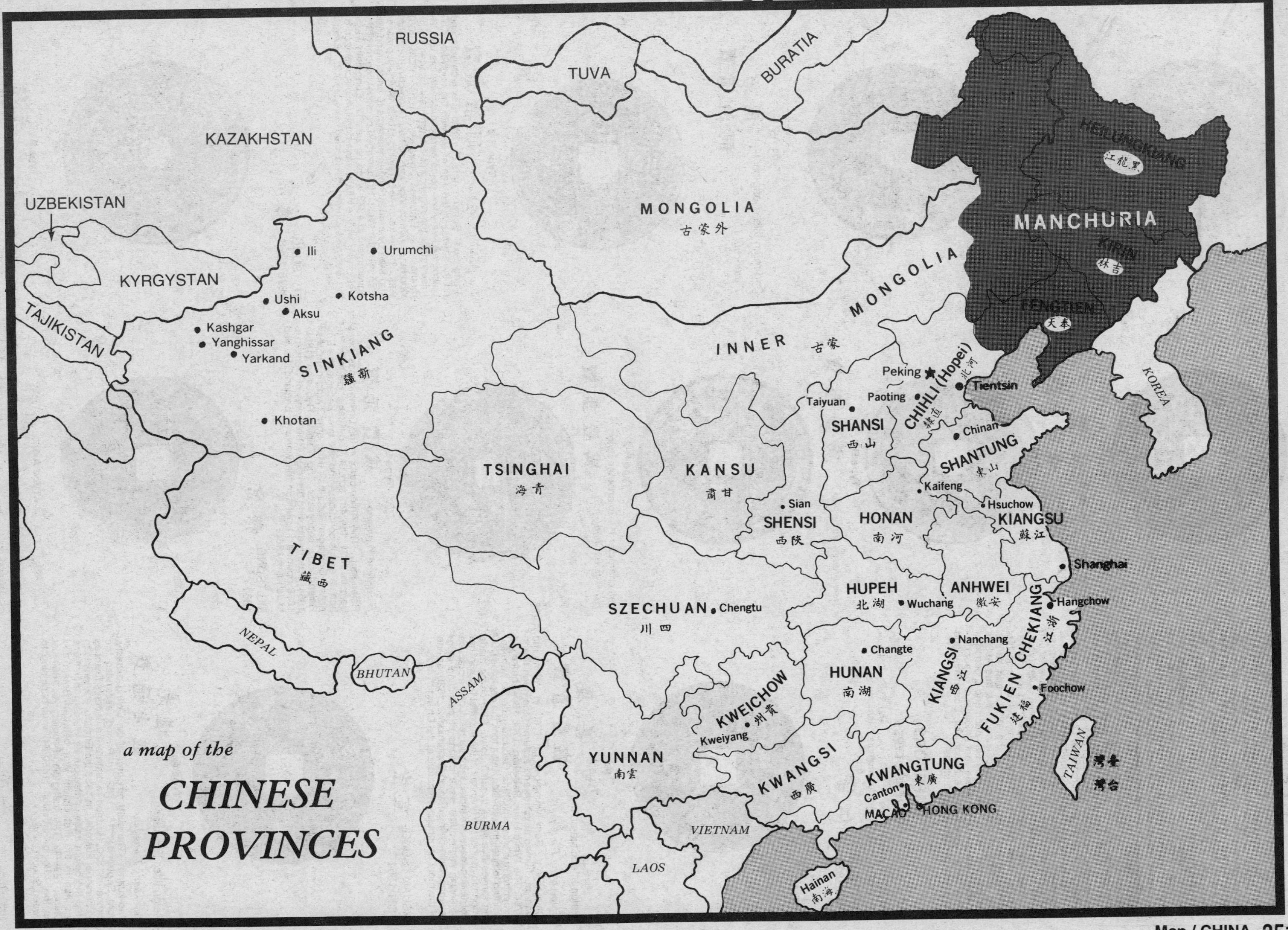

a map of the

CHINESE PROVINCES

RUSSIA
TUVA
BURATIA
KAZAKHSTAN
UZBEKISTAN
KYRGYSTAN
TAJIKISTAN
MONGOLIA 古蒙外
INNER MONGOLIA 古蒙
MANCHURIA
HEILUNGKIANG 江龍黑
KIRIN 林吉
FENGTIEN 天奉
KOREA
SINKIANG 疆新
Ili
Urumchi
Ushi
Aksu
Kotsha
Kashgar
Yanghissar
Yarkand
Khotan
TSINGHAI 海青
KANSU 肅甘
TIBET 藏西
NEPAL
BHUTAN
ASSAM
BURMA
LAOS
VIETNAM
SZECHUAN 川四
Chengtu
SHENSI 西陝
Sian
SHANSI 西山
Taiyuan
CHIHLI (Hopei) 隷直 北河
Peking
Paoting
Tientsin
SHANTUNG 東山
Chinan
Kaifeng
HONAN 南河
KIANGSU 蘇江
Hsuchow
Shanghai
ANHWEI 徽安
HUPEH 北湖
Wuchang
CHEKIANG 江浙
Hangchow
KIANGSI 西江
Nanchang
HUNAN 南湖
Changte
FUKIEN 建福
Foochow
KWEICHOW 州貴
Kweiyang
YUNNAN 南雲
KWANGSI 西廣
KWANGTUNG 東廣
Canton
MACAO
HONG KONG
Hainan 南海
TAIWAN 灣臺 灣台

CHINA

Before 1912, China was ruled by an imperial government. The republican administration which replaced it was itself supplanted on the Chinese mainland by a communist government in 1949, but it has remained in control of Taiwan and other offshore islands in the China Sea with a land area of approximately 14,000 square miles and a population of more than 14 million. The Peoples Republic of China administers some 3.7 million square miles and an estimated 1.16 billion people. This communist government, officially established on October 1, 1949, was admitted to the United Nations, replacing its nationalist predecessor, the Republic of China, in 1971.

Cast coins in base metals were used in China many centuries before the Christian era, but locally struck coinages of the western type in gold, silver, copper and other metals did not appear until 1888. In spite of the relatively short time that modern coins have been in use, the number of varieties is exceptionally large.

Both Nationalist and Communist China, as well as the pre-revolutionary Imperial government and numerous provincial or other agencies, including some foreign-administered agencies and governments, have issued coins in China. Most of these have been in dollar (yuan) or dollar-fraction denominations, based on the internationally used Mexican Pillar Dollar, but coins in tael denominations were issued in the 1920's and earlier. The striking of coins nearly ceased in the late 1930's through the 1940's due to the war effort and a period of uncontrollable inflation while vast amounts of paper currency were issued by the Nationalist, Communist and Japanese occupation institutions.

EMPERORS

OBVERSE TYPES

NOTE: Obverse Type B, *Chung-pao* and Type C *Yuan-pao* were normally used for multiple-cash issues.

JEN TSUNG 仁宗
1796-1820

Type A

Reign title: Chia-ch'ing 嘉慶

Chia-ch'ing T'ung-pao 嘉慶通寶

Chia-ch'ing - Born November 13, 1760, in Peking, he was proclaimed emperor and assumed the reign title in 1796. The White Lotus Rebellion, 1796-1804, broke out in central and western China. Capable generals were appointed to quell the rebellion, but it took the depleted Ch'ing armies five years to put it down. Chia-ch'ing made efforts to restore the finances of the imperial treasury but corruption may have increased as a result of the practice of selling high office as a means of collecting more revenue. Chia-ch'ing died on September 2, 1820, as one of the most unpopular emperors of the Ch'ing dynasty.

HSUAN TSUNG 宣宗
1821-1851

Type A

Reign title: Tao-kuang 道光

Tao-kuang T'ung-pao 道光通寶

Tao-kuang - The sixth emperor of the Ch'ing dynasty, born September 16, 1782, in Peking, ascended the throne in 1820. He tried to restore the nation's finances by personal austerity. In 1838 the Emperor's attempts to stop the opium trade carried out by Western merchants resulted in the first Opium War between Britain and China, 1839-42. Tao-kuang died February 25, 1850 just as the Taiping Rebellion (1850-64) was beginning to sweep South China.

WEN TSUNG 文宗
1851-1861

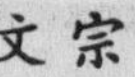

Type A

Reign title: Hsien-feng 咸豐

Hsien-feng T'ung-pao 咸豐通寶

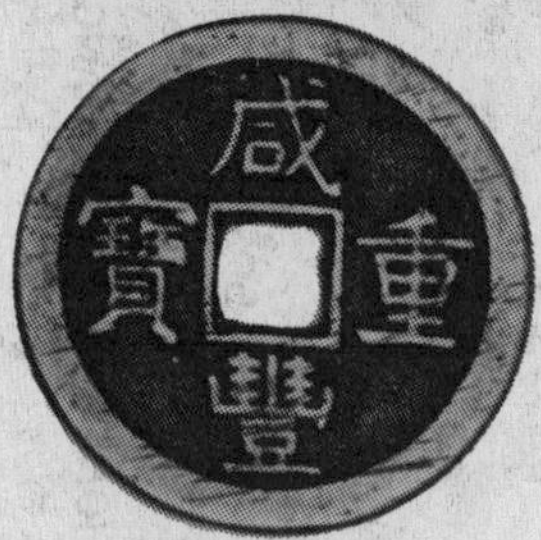

Type B-1

Hsien-feng Chung-pao 咸豐重寶

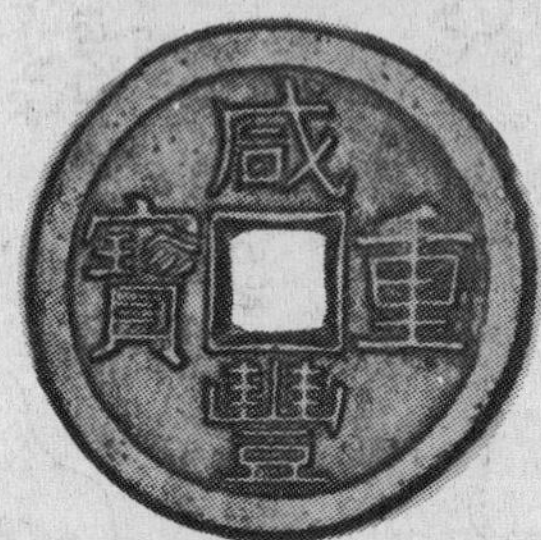

Type B-2

Left character *Pao* in another style.

Hsien-feng Chung-pao 咸豐重寶

Type C

Hsien-feng Yuan-pao 咸豐元寶

Hsien-feng - The 7th emperor in the Ch'ing dynasty was born in 1831, the 4th son of Tao-Kuang. He took Ye-honala as his concubine and she later became the Empress Dowager Tz'u-hsi. Her son T'ung-chih was Hsien-feng's successor. The Taiping Rebellion (1850-1864) occurred during his reign. The Treaty of Tientsin in 1858 opened 11 ports in the war with England. He fled to Jehol in 1860.

MU TSUNG 穆宗
1861

Type A-1

1st reign title: Ch'i-hsiang 祺祥

Ch'i-hsiang T'ung-pao 祺祥通寶

Type B-1

Ch'i-hsiang Chung-pao 祺祥重寶

MU TSUNG 穆宗
1862-1875

Type A-2

2nd reign title: T'ung-chih 同治

T'ung-chih T'ung-pao 同治通寶

Type B-2

T'ung-chih Chung-pao 同治重寶

T'ung-chih - Born on April 27, 1856, T'ung-chih ascended the throne at the age of six with the reign-title Ch'i-hsiang and very few coins were struck with this title. He ruled under the regency of a triumvirate headed by his mother, the Empress Dowager Tz'u-hsi (1835-1908), who made him change to nien-hao T'ung-chih. In the first years of his reign the Taiping rebels were suppressed and the government began attempts to understand and deal with the West. He assumed personal control of the government in 1873 when he was 17. T'ung-chih was a weak ruler whose affairs were constantly scrutinized by the Empress Dowager. He died January 12, 1875, in Peking.

TE TSUNG 德宗
1875-1908

Type A

Reign title: Kuang-hsu 光緒

Kuang-hsu T'ung-pao 光緒通寶

Type B

Kuang-hsu Chung-pao 光緒重寶

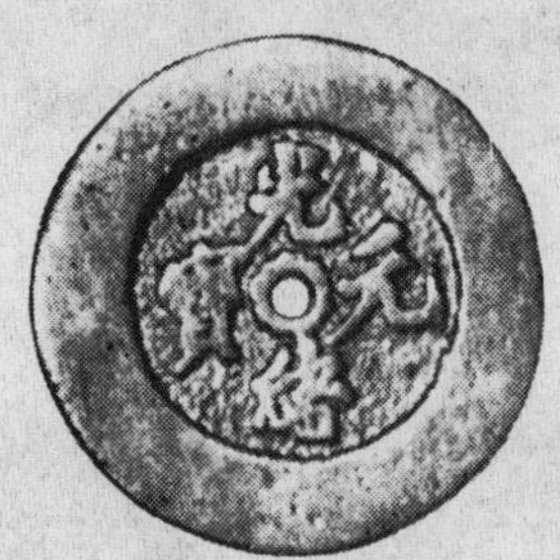

Type C

Kuang-hsu Yuan-pao 光緒元寶

Kuang-hsu - When the previous emperor died, his mother, the Empress Dowager Tz'u-hsi, chose her four-year-old nephew, born August 14, 1871, as emperor. She adopted the boy so that she could act as regent and on February 25, 1875, the young prince ascended the throne, taking the reign title of Kuang-hsu. In 1898 he tried to assert himself and collected a group of progressive officials around him. He issued a series of edicts for revamping of the military, abolition of civil service examinations, improvement of agriculture and restructuring of administrative procedures. During Kuang-hsu's reign (1875-1908) the Empress Dowager totally dominated the government. She confined the emperor to his palace and spread rumors that he was deathly ill. Foreign powers let it be known they would not take kindly to the Emperor's death. This saved his life but thereafter he had no power over the government. On November 15, 1908, Tz'u-hsi died under highly suspicious circumstances and the usually healthy emperor was announced as having died the previous day.

HSUAN T'UNG 宣統
1908-1911

Type A

Reign title: Hsuan-t'ung 宣統

Hsuan-t'ung T'ung-pao 宣統通寶

Hsuan-t'ung - The last emperor of the Ch'ing dynasty in China and Japan's puppet emperor, under the assumed name of K'ang-te, in Manchukuo from 1934 to 1945, was born on February 7, 1906. He succeeded to the throne at the age of three on November 14, 1908. He reigned under a regency for three years but on February 12, 1912, was forced to abdicate the throne. He was permitted to continue living in the palace in Peking until he left secretly in 1924. On March 9, 1932, he was installed as president, and from 1934 to 1945 was emperor of Manchukuo under the reign title of K'ang-te. He was taken prisoner by the Russians in August of 1945 and returned to China as a war criminal in 1950. He was pardoned in 1959 and went to live in Peking where he worked in the repair shop of a botanical garden. He died peacefully in Peking (Beijing) in 1967.

Although Hsuan-t'ung became Emperor in 1908, all the coins of his reign are based on an Accession year of 1909.

YUAN SHIH KAI
Dec. 15, 1915 - March 21, 1916

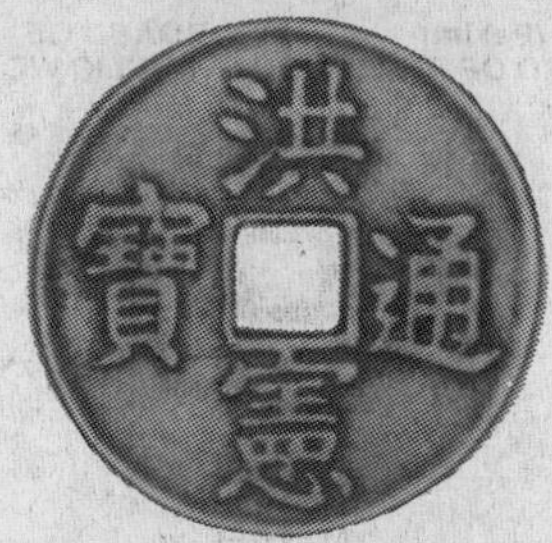

Reign title: Hung-hsien 憲洪

Hung-hsien Tung-pao 憲洪 通寶

Hung-hsien (more popularly known as Yuan Shih Kai) - Born in 1859 in Honan Province, he was the first Han Chinese to hold a viceroyalty and become a grand councillor without any academic qualifications. In 1885 he was made Chinese commissioner at Seoul. During the Boxer Rebellion of 1900, the division under his command was the only remnant of China's army to survive. He enjoyed the trust and support of the dowager empress, Tz'u-hsi, and at her death he was stripped of all his offices. However, when the tide of the revolution threatened to engulf the Manchus Yuan appeared as the only man who could lead the country to peace and unity. Both the Emperor and the provisional president recommended that Yuan be the first president of China. He contrived to make himself president for life and boldly tried to create a new imperial dynasty in 1915-1916. He died of uremia on June 6, 1916.

NOTE: For other legend types refer to Rebel Issues listed after Yunnan-Szechuan.

PROVINCIAL NAMES

(and other source indicators)

Provincial names throughout the catalog are based on the Wade-Giles transliteration of the Chinese word. Current spellings, known as the "Pinyin" form, are widely adopted by the printed media. Example: Sinkiang = Xinjiang.

Name		Single Character (1)	Full Names (Right to left reading)
ANHWEI Also An-hwi, Anhui, now Anhui	(Wan)	皖	徽安
CHEKIANG Also Cheh-kiang, now Zhejiang	(Che)	浙	江浙
CHIHLI Also Hopei (after 1928) now Hebei	(Chih)	直	隸直
CH'ING DYNASTY Also Tsing Dynasty, now Qing Dynasty			清大
CHING-KIANG Also Tsing-kiang now Qingjiang	(Huai)	淮	江清
FENGTIEN Also Fung-tien, Fun-tien, Shengching, Manchurian Provinces, now Liaoning	(Feng)	奉	天奉
FUKIEN Also Foo-kien, F.K., now Fujian	(Min)	閩	建福
HEILUNGKIANG Also Hei Lung Kiang, now Heilongjiang	(Hei)	黑	江龍黑
HONAN Also Ho-nan, now Henan	(Yu)	豫	南河
HOPEH Also Chihli, Hopei, now Hebei	(Chi)	冀	北河
HUNAN Also Hu-nan, now Hunan	(Hsiang)	湘	南湖
HUPEH Also Hupei, Hu-peh, now Hubei	(O)	鄂	北湖
HU PU (Board of Revenue) Also Hu Poo, Hoo Poo	(Hu)	戶	部戶
KANSU Now Gansu	(Kan)		肅甘
KIANGNAN Also Kiang Nan Now Jiangnan	(Ning)	寗	南江
KIANGSI Also Kiang-si, Kiang-see now Jiangxi	(Kan)	贛	西江
KIANGSI (Alternate)	(Kan)		贑贑
KIANGSU Also Kiang-soo, now Jiangsu	(Su)	蘇	蘇江
KIRIN Also Chi-lin Now Jilin	(Chi)	吉	林吉
KWANGSI, KWANGSEA Also Kwang-si, now Guangxi	(Kuei)	桂	西廣
KWANGTUNG Also Kwang-tung, now Guangdong	(Yueh)	粵	東廣
KWEICHOW Also Kweichou, now Guizhou	(Ch'ien)	黔	州貴
PEIYANG MINT (Tientsin) Also Pei-uang, Pei Yang			洋北
SHANSI Now Shanxi	(Shan) or (Chin)	山	西山
SHENSI Also Shen-si, now Shaanxi	(Shan)	陝	西陝
SHANTUNG, SHAN-TUNG Also Shang-tung,	(Tung)	東	東山
now Shandong	(Lu)	魯	
SIKANG			
SINKIANG (Chinese Turkestan) Also Sin-kiang, Hsin kiang Sungarei, now Xinjiang	(Hsin)	新	疆新
SZECHUAN Also Szechwan, Szechuen, Now Sichuan	(Ch'uan) or (Shu)	川 蜀	川四
TAIWAN Also Tai-wan, now Taiwan	(Tai)	臺	弯臺
TAIWAN (Alternate)	(Tai)		灣台
YUNNAN Also Yun-nan, now Yunnan	(Yun)	雲	南雲
YUNNAN (Alternate)	(Tien)	滇	南雲
TUNG SAN SHENG Manchuria			省三東
YUNNAN-SZECHUAN			滇川

GOVERNMENTAL NAMES

(and other source indicators)

Name	Full Names (Right to left reading)
CHITUNG (Japanese puppet)	府政東冀

CHINESE SOVIET REPUBLIC	中華蘇維埃共和國
MANCHUKUO (Japanese puppet)	大滿洲國
MENGCHIANG (Japanese puppet) (2)	蒙疆銀行
PEOPLES REPUBLIC OF CHINA (Communist) (3)	中華人民共和國
REPUBLIC OF CHINA (Nationalist)	中華民國
NORTH CHINA (Japanese puppet)	中國聯合準備銀行

(1) Single-character designators for provincial or regional mints are used primarily on copper coins of the Tai Ching Ti Kuo series.
(2) Vertical readings predominate.
(3) Reads left to right.
(4) For lists of mints in Sinkiang, see that section.

ADDITIONAL CHARACTERS

The additional characters illustrated and defined below are found on the reverse of cast bronze cash coins, usually above the square center hole. In the period covered by this catalog the following mints produced cash coins with these additional marks: Board of Revenue and Board of Works in Peking, Kweichow, Aksu and Ili in Sinkiang, Shantung, Szechuan, and all three mints listed in Yunnan.

一	I,Yi	十	Shih i	心	Hsin
二	Erh	合	Ho	宇	Yu
三	San	工	Kung	宙	Chou
四	Szu	主	Chu	來	Lai
五	Wu	川	Ch'uan	往	Wang
六	Liu	之	Chih	金	Chin
七	Ch'i	正	Cheng	村	Ts'un
八	Pa	又	Yu	日	Jih
九	Chiu	山	Shan	列	Lieh
十	Shih	大	Ta	仁	Jen
主	Chu	中	Chung	丰	Feng
上	Shan	順	Shun	云	Yun
手	Shou	—		—	

MINT MARK IDENTIFIER

There are more than 30 different mints covered in the following text. For ease in identification the more common varieties are illustrated with the Manchu legend.

Boo-Ciowan

Boo Yuwan (Peking)

(Peking) BOARD OF REVENUE

BOARD OF PUBLIC WORKS

Boo Hu
Hu Mint
ANHWEI

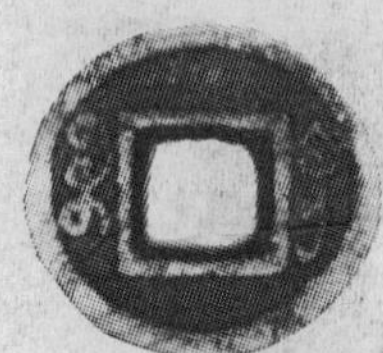

Boo Gung
Kungchang
KANSU

Nanchang
KIANGSI

Boo Je
Che Mint
Hangchow
CHEKIANG

Boo Ji
Chihli Mint
Paoting
CHIHLI

Boo Su
Su Mint
Soohow
KIANGSU

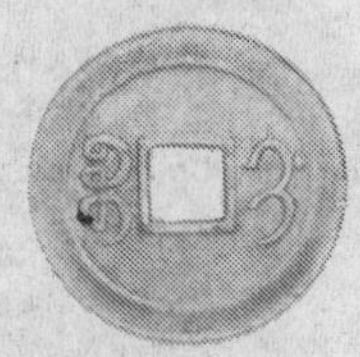

Boo Gi
Chi Mint
KIRIN
(Kuang-hsu era)

Boo Gi
Chi Mint
Chichow
CHIHLI

Boo Jiyen
Ching Mint
Tientsin
CHIHLI
(Until Hsien-Feng era)

Boo Gui
Kuelin
KWANGSI

Boo Guwang
Canton
KWANGTUNG

Boo Fung
FENGTIEN

Boo Fu
Fu Mint
Fuchou
FUKIEN

Boo Giyan
Kweiyang
KWEICHOW

Boo Jin
Taiyuan
SHANSI

Boo Ho
Ho Mint
K'aifeng
HONAN

Boo Ji
Chinan
SHANTUNG

Boo Cuwan
Chengtu
SZECHUAN

Boo Nan
Nan Mint
Ch'ang-sha
HUNAN

Boo San
Shan Mint
Sian
SHENSI

Boo De
Teh Mint
Chengte
CHIHLI

Boo U
Wu Mint
Wuch'ang
HUPEH

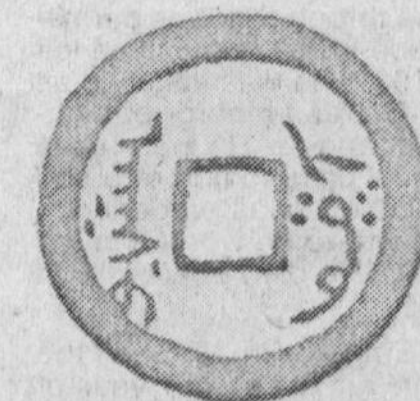

Aksu (Hocheng)
SINKIANG

Ili (Hweiyuan)
SINKIANG

Kotsha (Kuche)
SINKIANG

Kashgar (Shufu)
SINKIANG

Khotan (Hotien)
SINKIANG

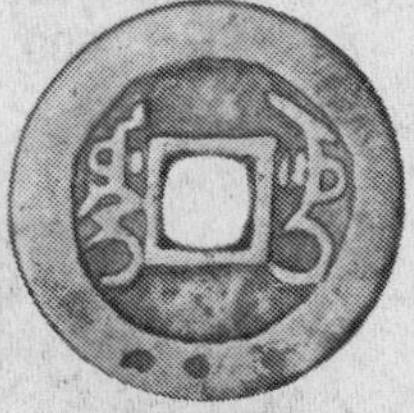

Urumchi (Tihwa)
SINKIANG

Ushi (Wushih)
SINKIANG

Yarkand (Soche)
SINKIANG

Tai Mint
TAIWAN

Boo Yon
Yun Mint
Yunnanfu
YUNNAN

Boo Dong
Tung Mint
Tungch'uan
YUNNAN

Ching Mint
Location unknown

Chou Mint
Location uncertain
(Refer to Yunnan)

NON-CIRCULATING ISSUES

Along with regular circulation coinage produced by the various mints certain cash types were cast in various sizes with the emperor's reign title on the obverse but with various characters and/or symbols not found in our mint identifiers. This listing is not complete but it will benefit the collector as an aid to proper identification.

PALACE ISSUES

Rev. leg: *T'ien-hsia T'ai-p'ing*
"Heaven under Peace".

"An Empire at Peace"
The market value is about $40.00-60.00 in VF condition.

Obv: Chia-ch'ing
Tao-kuang
Hsien-feng
Kuang-hsu
Hsuan-t'ung

Rev: *I-t'ung T'ien-hsia*

"Unify the whole country".
The market value is about $50.00-70.00 in VF condition.

Obv: Hsien-feng

BIRTHDAY CASH

壽 福

These issues have the normal reign title on the obverse but the reverse has two Chinese characters 'Fu' in normal or seal script (happiness), at right and 'Shou' (birthday) at left. The market value is about $40.00-60.00 in VF condition.

Hsien-feng

T'ung-chih

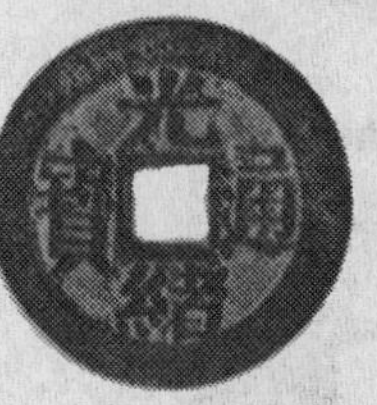

Kuang-hsu

AMULETS

Eight Trigrams

Hsien-feng

The eight trigrams (Pa Kua) of the Book of Changes (I Ching). This book, one of the Five Classics, consists of a set of sixty-four figures known as "trigrams". The trigram is composed of combinations of pairs of eight trigrams each of which represents some power in nature, either active or passive, such as fire, water, thunder, earth, etc. These trigrams are said to have been invented 2000 years and more B.C. by the legendary monarch Fu Hsi, who copied them from the back of a tortoise. Attached to each hexagram are explanatory notes and expository comments. The notes are said to have been written by the Chou King Wen Wang and the comments by Confucius. The notes are made in symbolic language which only mystics could understand, but the comments are written in plain language. These comments have lifted the Book of Changes from a primitive book of divination and oracles to an ethical and philosophical importance. The market value is about $30.00-40.00 in VF condition.

MULTIPLE CASH

The size and weight of multiple cash coins cannot be used to determine the correct denomination as these were issued on various standards. The weights decreased considerably in later years. The values are given in various manners.

Additional character(s) handstamped on the rims are occasionally encountered in this series and are merely private marks.

4 CASH

Ili Mint, Sinkiang

5 CASH

Board of Public Works Mint, Peking

8 CASH

Tihwa Mint, Sinkiang

10 CASH

Normal Ten
Board of Public Works Mint, Peking

Official Ten
Board of Revenue Mint, Peking

Fukien Mint

20 CASH

Fukien Mint

30 CASH

Kiangsu Mint

40 CASH

Chekiang Mint

50 CASH

Fukien Mint
(Weighing) 2 Tael 5 Mace (on rim)

Fukien Mint

100 CASH

Board of Revenue Mint, Peking

500 CASH

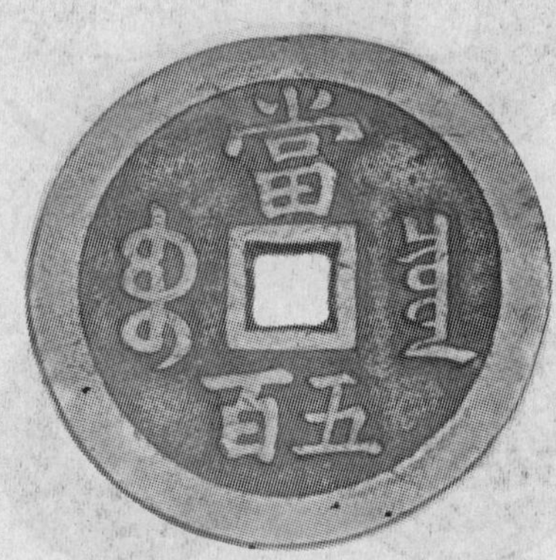

Board of Revenue Mint, Peking

1000 CASH

Board of Revenue Mint, Peking

VARIETIES OF DENOMINATIONS

The denominations for multiple cash may appear in at least three methods. The 50 Cash of Fukien previously illustrated has the 5 above and the 10 below the center hole. The 50 Cash of Kwangsi has the denomination written horizontally below the center hole while the 50 cash of Chekiang has the denomination written vertically below the center hole.

50 CASH

Kwangsi Mint

Chekiang Mint

NUMERALS

NUMBER	CONVENTIONAL	FORMAL	COMMERCIAL
1	一 元	壹 弌	〡
2	二	弍 貳	〢
3	三	叁 弎	〣
4	四	肆	〤
5	五	伍	〥
6	六	陸	〦
7	七	柒	〧
8	八	捌	〨
9	九	玖	〩
10	十	拾 什	十
20	十 二 or 廿	拾貳	〢十
25	五 十 二 or 五 廿	伍拾貳	〢十〥
30	十 三 or 卅	拾叁	〣十
100	百 一	佰壹	〡百
1,000	千 一	仟壹	〡千
10,000	萬 一	萬壹	〡万
100,000	萬 十 億 一	萬拾 億壹	十万
1,000,000	萬百一	萬佰壹	〡百万

NOTE: This table has been adapted from *Chinese Bank Notes* by Ward Smith and Brian Matravers.

MONETARY UNITS

Dollar Amounts		
DOLLAR (*Yuan*)	元 or 員	圓 or 圜
HALF DOLLAR (*Pan Yuan*)	圓 半	元中
50¢ (*Chiao/Hao*)	角伍	毫伍
10¢ (*Chiao/Hao*)	角壹	毫壹
1¢ (*Fen/Hsien*)	分壹	仙壹

Copper and Cash Coin Amounts			
COPPER (*Mei*)	枚	CASH (*Wen*)	文

Tael Amounts	
1 TAEL (*Liang*)	兩
HALF TAEL (*Pan Liang*)	兩半
5 MACE (*Wu Ch'ien*)	錢伍
1 MACE (*I Ch'ien*)	錢壹
1 CANDEREEN (*I Fen*)	分壹

Common Prefixes			
COPPER (*T'ung*)	銅	GOLD (*Chin*)	金
SILVER (*Yin*)	銀	Ku Ping (*Tael*)*	平庫

NOTE: This table has been adapted from *Chinese Bank Notes* by Ward Smith and Brian Matravers.

MONETARY SYSTEM

Cash Coin System

800-1600 Cash = 1 Tael
400 Sinkiang 'red' cash = 1 Tael

In theory, 1000 cash were equal to a tael of silver, but in actuality the rate varied from time to time and place to place.

Dollar System

10 Cash (Wen, Ch'ien) = 1 Cent (Fen, Hsien)
10 Cents = 1 Chiao (Hao)
100 Cents = 1 Dollar (Yuan)
1 Dollar = 0.72 Tael

Imperial silver coins normally bore no denomination, but were inscribed with their weights as follows:

1 Dollar = 7 Mace and 2 Candareens
50 Cents = 3 Mace and 6 Candareens
20 Cents = 1 Mace and 4.4 Candareens
10 Cents = 7.2 Candareens
5 Cents = 3.6 Candareens

NOTE: ***Candareen*** is spelled ***Candarin*** and misspelled as ***Caindarin*** on Kirin Province Imperial coinage.

Tael System

10 Li = 1 Fen (Candareen)
10 Fen (Candareen) = 1 Ch'ien (Mace)
10 Ch'ien (Mace) = 1 Liang (Tael)

DATING

Most struck Chinese coins are dated by year within a given period, such as the regnal eras or the republican periods. A 1907 issue, for example, would be dated in the 33rd year of the Kuang Hsu era (1875 + 33 - 1 = 1907) or a 1926 issue is dated in the 15th year of the Republic (1912 + 15 - 1 = 1926). The mathematical discrepancy in both instances is accounted for by the fact that the first year is included in the elapsed time. Modern Chinese Communist coins are dated in western numerals using the western calendar, but earlier issues use conventional Chinese numerals. Still another method is a 60-year, repeating cycle, outlined in the table below. The date is shown by the combination of two characters, the first from the top row and the second from the column at left. In this catalog, when a cyclical date is used, the abbreviation CD appears before the AD date.

Dates not in parenthesis are those which appear on the coins. For undated coins, dates appearing in parenthesis are the years in which the coin was actually minted. Undated coins for which the year of minting is unknown are listed with ND (No Date) in the date or year column.

CYCLICAL DATES

	庚	辛	壬	癸	甲	乙	丙	丁	戊	己
戌	1850 1910		1862 1922		1874 1934		1886 1946		1838 1898	
亥		1851 1911		1863 1923		1875 1935		1887 1947		1839 1899
子	1840 1900		1852 1912		1864 1924		1876 1936		1888 1948	
丑		1841 1901		1853 1913		1865 1925		1877 1937		1889 1949
寅	1830 1890		1842 1902		1854 1914		1866 1926		1878 1938	
卯		1831 1891		1843 1903		1855 1915		1867 1927		1879 1939
辰	1880 1940		1832 1892		1844 1904		1856 1916		1868 1928	
巳		1881 1941		1833 1893		1845 1905		1857 1917		1869 1929
午	1870 1930		1882 1942		1834 1894		1846 1906		1858 1918	
未		1871 1931		1883 1943		1835 1895		1847 1907		1859 1919
申	1860 1920		1872 1932		1884 1944		1836 1896		1848 1908	
酉		1861 1921		1873 1933		1885 1945		1837 1897		1849 1909

NOTE: This table has been adapted from *Chinese Bank Notes* by Ward Smith and Brian Matravers.

GRADING

Chinese coins should not be graded entirely by western standards. In addition to Fine, Very Fine, Extremely Fine (XF), and Uncirculated, the type of strike should be considered weak, medium or sharp strike. China had no rigid minting rules as we know them. For instance, Kirin (Jilin) and Sinkiang (Xinjiang) Provinces used some dies made of iron - hence, they wore out rapidly. Some communist army issues were apparently struck by crude hand methods on soft dies (it is hard to find two coins of the same die!) In general, especially for some minor coins, dies were used until they were worn well beyond western standards. Subsequently, one could have an uncirculated coin struck from worn dies with little of the design or letters still visible, but still uncirculated! All prices quoted are for well-struck (sharp struck), well-centered specimens. Most silver coins can be found from very fine to uncirculated. Some copper coins are difficult to find except in poorer grades.

NOTE: The following references have been used for this section:

K - Edward Kann - *Illustrated Catalog of Chinese Coins.*
Hsu - T.K. Hsu - *Illustrated Catalog of Chinese Coins*, 1981 edition.
W - A.M. Tracey Woodward - *The Minted Ten-Cash Coins of China.*

NOTE: The die struck 10 and 20 Cash coins are often found silver plated. This was not done at the mint. They were apparently plated to be passed to the unwary as silver coins.

IDENTIFICATION

DRAGON TYPES

(Chinese Imperial Coins)

Side View Dragon-left (Silver Coins)

First used by the Kwangtung Mint in 1889. This was the standard (though not the only) dragon used on silver coins. Normally there is no circle around the dragon. Note the fireball beneath the dragon's chin. Normally there are seven flames on the fireball.

Side View Dragon-left (Copper Coins)

First used on copper coins in 1901 or 1902. The dragon may be circled or uncircled. Many varieties exist, with three to seven flames on the fireball.

Side View Dragon-right (Silver Coins)

First appears on the second series of Fukien. The dragon is redesigned with the dragon's body reversed.

Flying Dragon

Introduced in 1901. Copied from the dragon on Japanese coins. China used this dragon only on copper coins (with one rare exception). Note that the clouds around the dragon's body are curly and snake-like instead of puffy like those around the side view dragon. The fireball now appears as a pearl which the dragon is about to grasp, and normally has no flames. This dragon is normally circled.

Front View Dragon

Introduced about 1904, this type of dragon was not used by many mints. The dragon is usually uncircled and has few clouds around its body. Note the tiny mountain under the cloud beneath the fireball.

Tai Ch'ing Ti Kuo Dragon

In 1905 China carried out a coinage reform which standardized the designs of copper coins. All mints were ordered to use the same obverse and reverse designs, but to place a mint mark in the center of the obverse.

SYCEE (INGOTS)

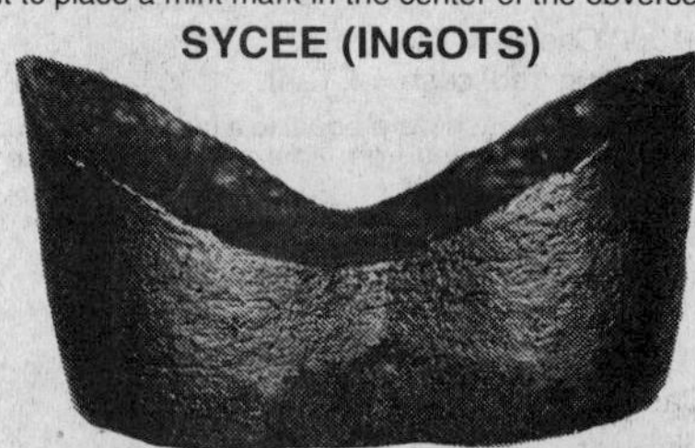

Prior to 1889 the general coinage issued by the Chinese government was the copper-alloy cash coin. Despite occasional shortlived experiments with silver and gold coinage, and disregarding paper money which tended to be unreliable, the government expected the people to get by solely with cash coins. This system worked well for individuals making purchases for themselves, but was unsatisfactory for trade and large business transactions, since a dollar's worth of cash coins weighed about four pounds. As a result, a private currency consisting of silver ingots, usually stamped by the firm which made them, came into use. These were the sycee ingots.

It is not known when these ingots first came into use. Some sources date them to the Yuan (Mongol) dynasty but they are certainly much older. Examples are known from as far back as the Han dynasty (206 BC - 220 AD) but prior to the Sung era (960 - 1280AD) they were used mainly for hoarding wealth. The development of commerce by the Sung dynasty, however, required the use of silver or gold to pay for large purchases. By the Mongol period (1280-1368) silver ingots and paper money had become the dominant currencies, especially for trade. The western explorers who traveled to China during this period (such as Marco Polo) mention both paper money and sycee but not a single one refers to cash coins.

During the Ming dynasty (1368-1644) trade fell off and the use of silver decreased. But toward the end of that dynasty, Dutch and British ships began a new China trade and sycee once again became common. During the 19th and early 20th centuries, the trade in sycee became enormous. Most of the sycee around today are from this period. In 1935 the Chinese government and in 1939 Sinkiang banned the use of sycee and it soon disappeared.

The word sycee (pronounced "sigh - see") is a western corruption of the Chinese word hsi-szu ("fine silk") or hsi yin ("fine silver") and is first known to have appeared in the English language in the late 1600's. By the early 1700's the word appeared regularly in the records of the British East India Company. Westerners also called these ingots "boat money" or "shoe money" owing to the fact that the most common type of ingot resembles a Chinese shoe. The Chinese, however, called the ingots by a variety of names, the most common of which were yuan pao, wen - yin (fine silver) and yin-ting (silver ingot).

The ingots were cast in molds (giving them their characteristic shapes) and while the metal was still semi-liquid, the inscription was impressed. It was due to this procedure that the sides of some sycee are higher than the center. The manufacturers were usually silver firms, often referred to as lu fang's, and after the sycee was finished it was occasionally tested and marked by the kung ku (public assayer).

Sycee were not circulated as we understand it. One didn't usually carry a sycee to market and spend it. Usually the ingots were used as a means of carrying a large amount of money on trips (as we would carry $100 bills instead of $5 bills) or for storing wealth. Large transactions between merchants or banks were paid by means of crates of sycee - each containing 60 fifty tael ingots.

Sycee are known in a variety of shapes the most common of which are the shoe or boat shaped, drum shaped, and loaf shaped (rectangular or hourglass—shaped, with a generally flat surface). Other shapes include one that resembles a double headed axe (this is the oldest type known), one that is square and flat, and others that are "fancy" (in the form of fish, butterflies, leaves, etc.).

Sycee have no denominations as they were simply ingots that passed by weight. Most are in more or less standard weights, however, the most common being 1, 5, 10 and 50 taels. Other weights known include 1/10, 1/5, 1/4, 1/3, 1/2, 2/3, 72/100 (this is the weight of a dollar), 3/4, 2, 3, 4, 6, 7, 8 and 25 taels. Most of the pieces weighing less than 5 taels were used as gifts or souvenirs.

The actual weight of any given value of sycee varied considerably due to the fact that the tael was not a single weight but a general term for a wide range of local weight standards. The weight of the tael varied depending upon location and type of tael in question. For example in one town, the weight of a tael of rice, of silver and of stones may each be different. In addition, the fineness of silver also varied depending upon location and type of tael in question. It was not true, as westerners often wrote, that sycee were made of pure silver. For most purposes, a weight of 37 grams may be used for the tael.

Weights and Current Market Value of Sycee
(Weights are approximate)

1/2 tael	17-19 grams	26.00
72/100 tael	25-27 grams	36.00
1 tael	35-38 grams	46.00
2 taels	70-75 grams	70.00
3 taels	100-140 grams	85.00
5 taels	175-190 grams	110.00
7 taels	240-260 grams	125.00
10 taels	350-380 grams	175.00
25 taels	895-925 grams	550.00
50 taels	1790-1850 grams	850.00
50 taels, square	1790-1850 grams	1600.

SZECHUAN WARLORD ISSUE

200 CASH

Obv: Mirror image of normal coin, Y#459.

NOTE: Certain coins found with degenerate or reversed English legends are usually considered to be local warlord issues while some authorities insist on referring to them as contemporary counterfeits.

GENERAL ISSUE

EMPIRE

Peking Hu Pu Mint

(Board of Revenue)

CASH

CAST BRASS, 21-26mm
Obv. leg: ***Chia-ch'ing T'ung-pao.***

C#	Date	Emperor	Good	VG	Fine	VF
1-2	ND(1796-1820)	Chia-ch'ing	.15	.25	.35	.65

28-30mm

C#	Date	Emperor	Good	VG	Fine	VF
1-2.1	ND(1796-1820)	Chia-ch'ing	10.00	14.00	20.00	30.00

Rev: Dot above.

C#	Date	Emperor	Good	VG	Fine	VF
1-2.2	ND(1796-1820)	Chia-ch'ing	1.25	2.00	3.00	5.00

Rev: Dot below.

C#	Date	Emperor	Good	VG	Fine	VF
1-2.3	ND(1796-1820)	Chia-ch'ing	1.25	2.00	3.00	5.00

CAST BRASS, 20-26 mm
Obv. leg: ***Tao-kuang T'ung-pao.***

C#	Date	Emperor	Good	VG	Fine	VF
1-3	ND(1821-51)	Tao-kuang	.20	.30	.40	.75

28-30mm

C#	Date	Emperor	Good	VG	Fine	VF
1-3.1	ND(1821-51)	Tao-kuang	10.00	14.00	18.00	24.00

Rev: Dot above.

C#	Date	Emperor	Good	VG	Fine	VF
1-3.2	ND(1821-51)	Tao-kuang	1.75	3.00	4.50	8.00

Rev: Dot below.

C#	Date	Emperor	Good	VG	Fine	VF
1-3.3	ND(1821-51)	Tao-kuang	1.75	3.00	4.50	8.00

Obv. leg: ***Hsien-feng T'ung-pao.***

C#	Date	Emperor	Good	VG	Fine	VF
1-4	ND(1851-61)	Hsien-feng	.60	1.00	2.50	4.00

CAST IRON

C#	Date	Emperor	Good	VG	Fine	VF
1-4a	ND(1851-61)	Hsien-feng	7.50	12.50	20.00	35.00

Obv: Type B-2.

C#	Date	Emperor	Good	VG	Fine	VF
1-4.2a	ND(1851-61)	Hsien-feng	—	—	—	—

CAST ZINC

C#	Date	Emperor	Good	VG	Fine	VF
1-4b	ND(1851-61)	Hsien-feng	—	—	Rare	—

CAST BRASS
Obv. leg: ***Ch'i-hsiang T'ung-pao.***

C#	Date	Emperor	Good	VG	Fine	VF
1-12	ND(1861)	Ch'i-hsiang	—	—	Rare	—

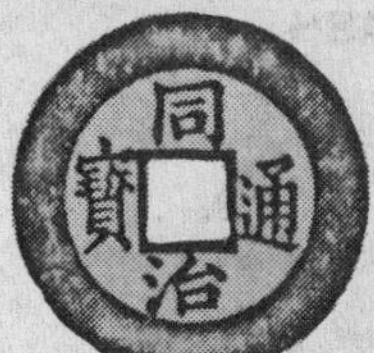

Obv. leg: ***T'ung-chih T'ung-pao.***

C#	Date	Emperor	Good	VG	Fine	VF
1-14	ND(1862-74)	T'ung-chih	3.50	5.50	8.50	15.00

Obv. leg: ***Kuang-hsu T'ung-pao.***

C#	Date	Emperor	Good	VG	Fine	VF
1-16	ND(1875-1908)	Kuang-hsu	1.25	1.75	2.50	4.50

Rev: Dot below.

C#	Date	Emperor	Good	VG	Fine	VF
1-16.8	ND(1899-1901)	Kuang-hsu	1.75	3.00	4.00	6.00

Rev: Dot above.

C#	Date	Emperor	Good	VG	Fine	VF
1-16.9	ND(1899-1901)	Kuang-hsu	1.75	3.00	4.00	6.00

Thousand Character Classic Series

Rev: ***Chih*** **above.**

C#	Date	Emperor	Good	VG	Fine	VF
1-16.1	ND(1875-1908)	Kuang-hsu	6.00	9.00	13.50	18.50

Rev: ***Chou*** **above.**

C#	Date	Emperor	Good	VG	Fine	VF
1-16.2	ND(1875-1908)	Kuang-hsu	6.00	9.00	13.50	18.50

Rev: ***Jih*** **above.**

C#	Date	Emperor	Good	VG	Fine	VF
1-16.3	ND(1875-1908)	Kuang-hsu	6.00	9.00	13.50	18.50

Rev: ***Lai*** **above.**

C#	Date	Emperor	Good	VG	Fine	VF
1-16.4	ND(1875-1908)	Kuang-hsu	9.00	13.50	18.50	25.00

Rev: ***Lieh*** **above.**

C#	Date	Emperor	Good	VG	Fine	VF
1-16.5	ND(1875-1908)	Kuang-hsu	6.00	9.00	13.50	18.50

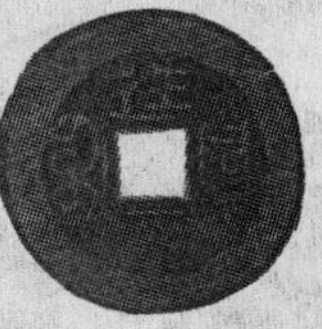

Rev: ***Wang*** **above.**

C#	Date	Emperor	Good	VG	Fine	VF
1-16.6	ND(1875-1908)	Kuang-hsu	9.00	13.50	18.50	25.00

Rev: ***Yu*** **above.**

C#	Date	Emperor	Good	VG	Fine	VF
1-16.7	ND(1875-1908)	Kuang-hsu	9.00	13.50	18.50	30.00

Rev: ***Shou*** **above.**

C#	Date	Emperor	Good	VG	Fine	VF
1-16.10	ND(1875-1908)	Kuang-hsu	6.00	9.00	13.50	18.50

19mm
Obv. leg: ***Hsuan-t'ung T'ung-pao.***

C#	Date	Emperor	Good	VG	Fine	VF
1-19	ND(1909-11)	Hsuan-t'ung	5.00	7.00	9.00	12.00

24mm

C#	Date	Emperor	Good	VG	Fine	VF
1-19.2	ND(1909-11)	Hsuan-t'ung	5.50	9.00	15.00	20.00

IRON, 23mm

C#	Date	Emperor	Good	VG	Fine	VF
1-19a	ND(1909-11)	Hsuan-t'ung	12.00	20.00	30.00	—

5 CASH

CAST BRASS
Obv. leg: ***Hsien-feng Chung-pao.***

C#	Date	Emperor	Good	VG	Fine	VF
1-5	ND(1851-61)	Hsien-feng	—	—	Rare	—

10 CASH

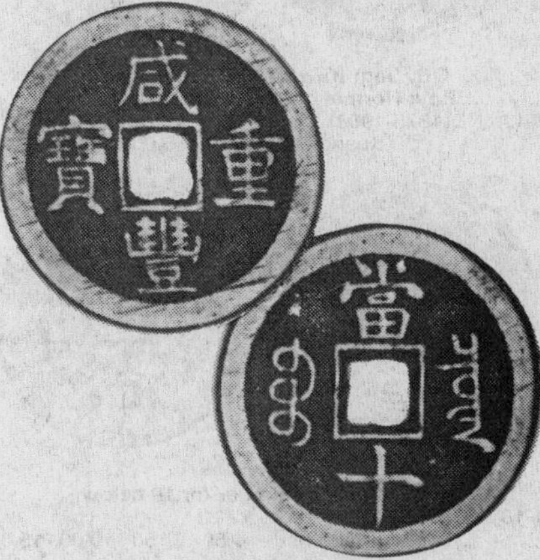

CAST BRASS, 36-39mm
Obv: Type B-1
Obv. leg: ***Hsien-feng Chung-pao.***

C#	Date	Emperor	Good	VG	Fine	VF
1-6	ND(1851-61)	Hsien-feng	4.00	5.00	7.00	9.00

29-35mm

C#	Date	Emperor	Good	VG	Fine	VF
1-6.1	ND(1851-61)	Hsien-feng	3.00	5.00	6.00	8.00

CAST IRON, 37-39mm

C#	Date	Emperor	Good	VG	Fine	VF
1-6a	ND(1851-61)	Hsien-feng	15.00	18.00	28.00	50.00

Obv: Type B-2

C#	Date	Emperor	Good	VG	Fine	VF
1-6.2a	ND(1851-61)	Hsien-feng	100.00	150.00	225.00	275.00

CAST BRASS
Obv: Type B-1

C#	Date	Emperor	Good	VG	Fine	VF
1-13	ND(1861)	Ch'i-hsiang	400.00	500.00	650.00	800.00

28-33mm
Obv. leg: *T'ung-chih Chung-pao.*

C#	Date	Emperor	Good	VG	Fine	VF
1-15	ND(1862-74)	T'ung-chih	1.50	3.00	5.50	10.00

23-27mm

C#	Date	Emperor	Good	VG	Fine	VF
1-15.1	ND(1862-74)	T'ung-chih	1.50	3.00	5.50	8.00

Obv. leg: *Kuang-hsu Chung-pao.*
Rev: Normal character for 10 below.

C#	Date	Emperor	Good	VG	Fine	VF
1-17	ND(1875-1908)	Kuang-hsu	3.00	5.00	8.00	12.00

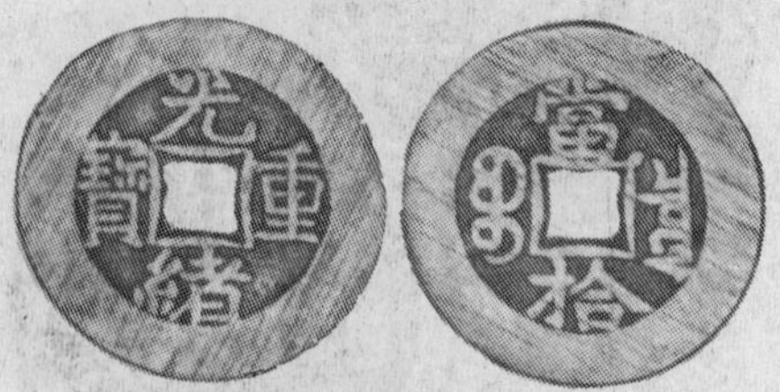

28mm
Rev: Official character for 10 below.

C#	Date	Emperor	Good	VG	Fine	VF
1-18	ND(1875-1908)	Kuang-hsu	4.50	7.50	10.00	15.00

22mm

C#	Date	Emperor	Good	VG	Fine	VF
1-18.1	ND(1875-1908)	Kuang-hsu	—	—	—	—

50 CASH

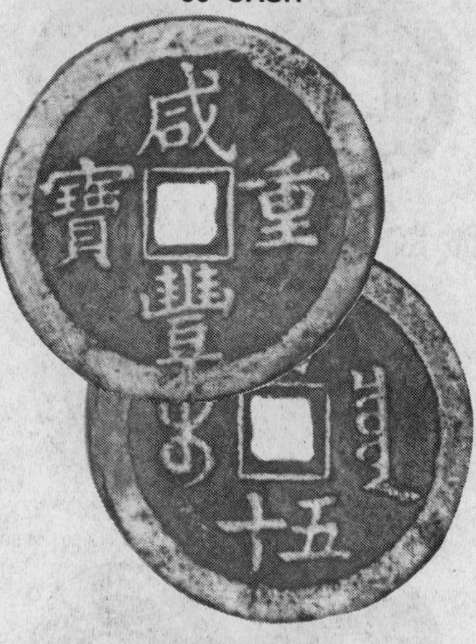

CAST BRASS, 54-58mm
Obv. leg: *Hsien-feng Chung-pao.*

C#	Date	Emperor	Good	VG	Fine	VF
1-7	ND(1851-61)	Hsien-feng	15.00	20.00	30.00	45.00

40-48mm

C#	Date	Emperor	Good	VG	Fine	VF
1-7.1	ND(1851-61)	Hsien-feng	10.00	15.00	25.00	40.00

Rev: Dot to upper right and crescent to upper left.

C#	Date	Emperor	Good	VG	Fine	VF
1-7.2	ND(1851-61)	Hsien-feng	20.00	30.00	60.00	130.00

NOTE: This is one of a series of coins from this mint marked with a dot and crescent to indicate that they were issued by Ching Hui, the Hereditary Prince of K'o Ch'in.

CAST IRON

C#	Date	Emperor	Good	VG	Fine	VF
1.7a	ND(1851-61)	Hsien-feng	—	—	Rare	—

100 CASH

CAST BRASS
Obv. leg: *Hsien-feng Yuan-pao.*

C#	Date	Emperor	Good	VG	Fine	VF
1-8	ND(1851-61)	Hsien-feng	8.00	12.00	20.00	30.00

Rev: Dot and crescent similar to 50 Cash, C#1-7.2.

C#	Date	Emperor	Good	VG	Fine	VF
1-8.1	ND(1851-61)	Hsien-feng	25.00	35.00	45.00	65.00

CAST IRON

C#	Date	Emperor	Good	VG	Fine	VF
1.8a	ND(1851-61)	Hsien-feng	—	—	Rare	—

200 CASH

CAST BRASS
Obv. leg: *Hsien-feng Yuan-pao.*

C#	Date	Emperor	Good	VG	Fine	VF
1-9	ND(1851-61)	Hsien-feng	75.00	125.00	150.00	200.00

Rev: Dot and crescent similar to 50 Cash, C#1-7.2.

C#	Date	Emperor	Good	VG	Fine	VF
1-9.1	ND(1851-61)	Hsien-feng	125.00	175.00	225.00	300.00

500 CASH

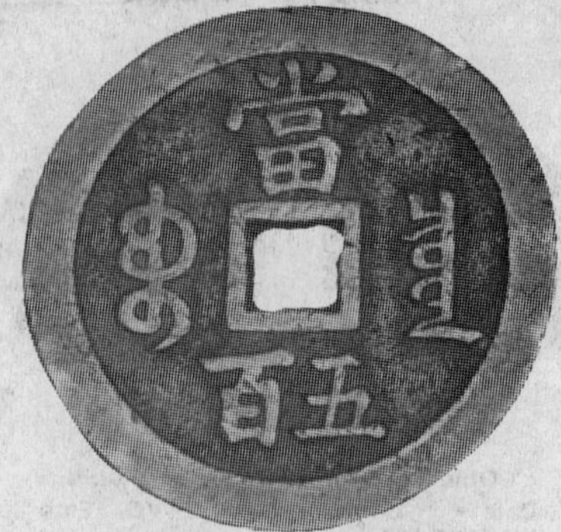

CAST BRASS, 46mm
Obv. leg: *Hsien-feng Yuan-pao.*

C#	Date	Emperor	Good	VG	Fine	VF
1-10	ND(1851-61)	Hsien-feng	20.00	30.00	50.00	75.00

56-58mm

C#	Date	Emperor	Good	VG	Fine	VF
1-10.1	ND(1851-61)	Hsien-feng	25.00	35.00	55.00	85.00

Rev: Dot and crescent similar to 50 Cash, C#1-7.2.

C#	Date	Emperor	Good	VG	Fine	VF
1-10.2	ND(1851-61)	Hsien-feng	45.00	75.00	125.00	185.00

1000 CASH

CAST BRASS
Obv. leg: *Hsien-feng Yuan-pao.*

C#	Date	Emperor	Good	VG	Fine	VF
1-11	ND(1851-61)	Hsien-feng	50.00	75.00	125.00	200.00

Rev: Dot and crescent similar to 50 Cash, C#1-7.2.

C#	Date	Emperor	Good	VG	Fine	VF
1-11.1	ND(1851-61)	Hsien-feng	125.00	175.00	225.00	320.00

FANTASY ISSUES

NOTE: Coins of this mint in denominations of 6, 9, 20, 30, 90, 300, 400, 600, 700, 800, 900, 4000 and 5000 Cash are considered fantasy issues.

Peking Kung Pu Mint

(Board of Public Works)

CASH

CAST BRASS

Obv. leg: *Chia-ch'ing T'ung-pao.*

C#	Date	Emperor	Good	VG	Fine	VF
2-2	ND(1796-1820)	Chia-ch'ing	.20	.30	.50	.75

Rev: Dot above.

C#	Date	Emperor	Good	VG	Fine	VF
2-2.1	ND(1796-1820)	Chia-ch'ing	2.50	4.00	6.00	7.50

Rev: Dot below.

C#	Date	Emperor	Good	VG	Fine	VF
2-2.2	ND(1796-1820)	Chia-ch'ing	2.50	4.00	6.00	7.50

Obv. leg: *Tao-kuang T'ung-pao.*

C#	Date	Emperor	Good	VG	Fine	VF
2-3	ND(1821-51)	Tao-kuang	.20	.30	.50	.75

Rev: Dot above.

C#	Date	Emperor	Good	VG	Fine	VF
2-3.1	ND(1821-51)	Tao-kuang	2.50	4.00	6.00	7.50

Rev: Dot below.

C#	Date	Emperor	Good	VG	Fine	VF
2-3.2	ND(1821-51)	Tao-kuang	2.50	4.00	6.00	7.50

Obv. leg: *Hsien-feng T'ung-pao.*
Wide borders, 27mm.

C#	Date	Emperor	Good	VG	Fine	VF
2-4	ND(1851-61)	Hsien-feng	3.00	5.00	9.00	14.00

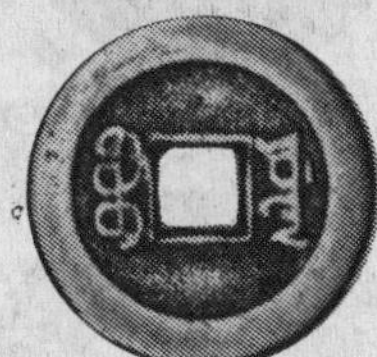

20-24mm

C#	Date	Emperor	Good	VG	Fine	VF
2-4.1	ND(1851-61)	Hsien-feng	.85	1.50	3.00	4.00

CAST IRON

C#	Date	Emperor	Good	VG	Fine	VF
2-4a	ND(1851-61)	Hsien-feng	50.00	60.00	75.00	125.00

CAST ZINC

C#	Date	Emperor	Good	VG	Fine	VF
2-4b	ND(1851-61)	Hsien-feng	—	—	Rare	—

CAST BRASS

Obv. leg: *Ch'i-hsiang T'ung-pao.*

C#	Date	Emperor	Good	VG	Fine	VF
2-11	ND(1861)	Ch'i-hsiang	375.00	650.00	1100.	1800.

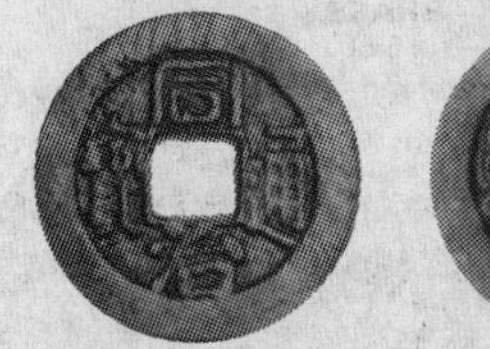
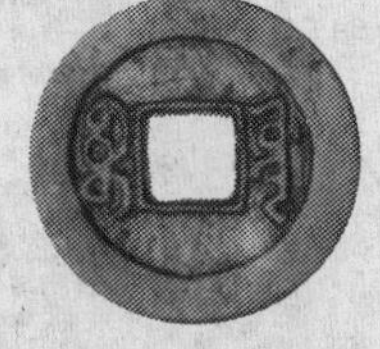

Obv. leg: *T'ung-chih T'ung-pao.*

C#	Date	Emperor	Good	VG	Fine	VF
2-13	ND(1862-74)	T'ung-chih	40.00	60.00	90.00	120.00

Obv. leg: *Kuang-hsu T'ung-pao.*

C#	Date	Emperor	Good	VG	Fine	VF
2-15	ND(1875-1908)	Kuang-hsu	1.50	3.00	6.00	7.00

Thousand Character Classic Series

Rev: *Chou* above.

C#	Date	Emperor	Good	VG	Fine	VF
2-15.1	ND(1899-1901)	Kuang-hsu	6.00	10.00	15.00	20.00

Rev: *Lai* above.

C#	Date	Emperor	Good	VG	Fine	VF
2-15.2	ND(1899-1901)	Kuang-hsu	6.00	10.00	15.00	20.00

Rev: *Lieh* above.

C#	Date	Emperor	Good	VG	Fine	VF
2-15.3	ND(1899-1901)	Kuang-hsu	6.00	10.00	15.00	20.00

Rev: *Yu* above.

C#	Date	Emperor	Good	VG	Fine	VF
2-15.4	ND(1899-1901)	Kuang-hsu	6.00	10.00	15.00	20.00

Rev: *Jih* above.

C#	Date	Emperor	Good	VG	Fine	VF
2-15.5	ND(1899-1901)	Kuang-hsu	6.00	10.00	15.00	20.00

Rev: *Wang* above.

C#	Date	Emperor	Good	VG	Fine	VF
2-15.6	ND(1899-1901)	Kuang-hsu	6.00	10.00	15.00	20.00

Rev: *Jih* above, dot below.

C#	Date	Emperor	Good	VG	Fine	VF
2-15.7	ND(1899-1901)	Kuang-hsu	6.00	10.00	15.00	20.00

5 CASH

CAST BRASS, 28-32mm

Obv. leg: *Hsien-feng Chung-pao.*

C#	Date	Emperor	Good	VG	Fine	VF
2-5	ND(1851-61)	Hsien-feng	10.00	12.50	17.50	35.00

23-25mm

C#	Date	Emperor	Good	VG	Fine	VF
2-5.1	ND(1851-61)	Hsien-feng	12.50	20.00	30.00	50.00

CAST IRON

C#	Date	Emperor	Good	VG	Fine	VF
2-5a	ND(1851-61)	Hsien-feng	Reported, not confirmed			

CAST BRASS

Obv. leg: *Kuang-hsu Chung-pao.*

C#	Date	Emperor	Good	VG	Fine	VF
2-16	ND(1875-1908)	Kuang-hsu	200.00	350.00	500.00	700.00

10 CASH

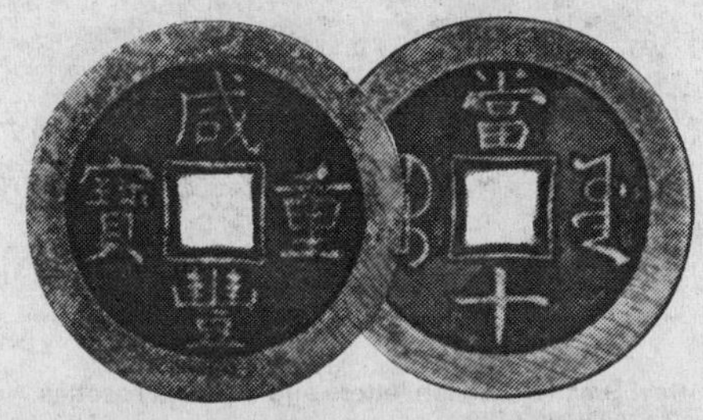

CAST BRASS, 33-38mm

Obv: Type B-1

Obv. leg: *Hsien-feng Chung-pao.*

C#	Date	Emperor	Good	VG	Fine	VF
2-6	ND(1851-61)	Hsien-feng	2.50	5.00	8.00	18.00

29-31mm

C#	Date	Emperor	Good	VG	Fine	VF
2-6.1	ND(1851-61)	Hsien-feng	2.50	5.00	8.00	18.00

CAST IRON

Obv: Type B-2.

C#	Date	Emperor	Good	VG	Fine	VF
2-6a	ND(1851-61)	Hsien-feng	—	—	Rare	—

CAST BRASS

Obv. leg: *Ch'i-hsiang Chung-pao.*

C#	Date	Emperor	Good	VG	Fine	VF
2-12	ND(1861)	Ch'i-hsiang	400.00	550.00	625.00	900.00

Obv. leg: *T'ung-chih Chung-pao.*

C#	Date	Emperor	Good	VG	Fine	VF
2-14	ND(1862-74)	T'ung-chih	4.50	7.50	12.00	25.00

Obv. leg: *Kuang-hsu T'ung-pao.*
Rev: Normal *Shih* (10) below.

C#	Date	Emperor	Good	VG	Fine	VF
2-17	ND(1875-1908)	Kuang-hsu	4.50	7.50	10.00	25.00

Rev: Official *Shih* (10) below.

C#	Date	Emperor	Good	VG	Fine	VF
2-18	ND(1875-1908)	Kuang-hsu	6.00	10.00	15.00	35.00

50 CASH

CAST BRASS, 51-57mm

Obv. leg: *Hsien-feng Chung-pao.*

C#	Date	Emperor	Good	VG	Fine	VF
2-7	ND(1851-61)	Hsien-feng	15.00	20.00	30.00	65.00

42-45mm

C#	Date	Emperor	Good	VG	Fine	VF
2-7.1	ND(1851-61)	Hsien-feng	10.00	15.00	25.00	40.00

100 CASH

CAST BRASS

Obv. leg: *Hsien-feng Yuan-pao.*

C#	Date	Emperor	Good	VG	Fine	VF
2-8	ND(1851-61)	Hsien-feng	13.50	18.00	22.50	50.00

500 CASH

CAST BRASS

Obv. leg: *Hsien-feng Yuan-pao.*

C#	Date	Emperor	Good	VG	Fine	VF
2-9	ND(1851-61)	Hsien-feng	30.00	50.00	75.00	130.00

CAST COPPER

C#	Date	Emperor	Good	VG	Fine	VF
2-9.1	ND(1851-61)	Hsien-feng	60.00	100.00	175.00	250.00

1000 CASH

CAST BRASS

Obv. leg: *Hsien-feng Yuan-pao.*

C#	Date	Emperor	Good	VG	Fine	VF
2-10	ND(1851-61)	Hsien-feng	75.00	130.00	200.00	275.00

FANTASY ISSUES

NOTE: Coins of this mint in denominations of 6, 9, 30, 80 and 90 Cash are considered fantasy issues.

Standard Unified General Issues

A Central mint opened at Tientsin in 1905, was made responsible for producing most of the dies for the Tai Ch'ing "Hupoo" coinage and for the 1910 and 1911 unified coinage. The mint was burned down in 1912 but resumed operations in 1914 with Yuan Shih-kai dollar issues. It continued producing dies for selected branch mints until 1921. It was superseded as the Central mint of China by Nanking in 1927 and by the new Nationalist Government mint at Shanghai in 1933.

CASH

BRASS, struck

Y#	Date	Mintage	VG	Fine	VF	XF
7	CD1908	—	1.00	3.00	6.00	12.00

Y#	Date	Mintage	VG	Fine	VF	XF
18	CD1909	Inc. Y25	20.00	45.00	75.00	110.00

Y#	Date	Mintage	VG	Fine	VF	XF
25	ND	92.126	1.00	1.50	2.00	3.00

2 CASH

COPPER

Y#	Date	Mintage	VG	Fine	VF	XF
8	CD1905	—	2.50	4.50	10.00	17.50
	CD1906	—	3.00	6.00	10.00	25.00

Obv: 4 dots divide leg.

Y#	Date	Mintage	VG	Fine	VF	XF
8.1	CD1907	—	7.00	18.00	25.00	40.00
A18	CD1909	13.353	—	—	Rare	—

24mm

C#	Date	Emperor	Good	VG	Fine	VF
1-19.1	ND(1909-11)	Hsuan-t'ung	15.00	25.00	35.00	60.00

5 CASH

COPPER

Y#	Date	Mintage	VG	Fine	VF	XF
3	ND(1903-05)	3.671	7.00	14.00	21.00	35.00

Rev. leg: Smaller English letters.

3.1 ND(1903-05) — — Reported, not confirmed

Y#	Date	Mintage	VG	Fine	VF	XF
9	CD1905	—	5.00	10.00	20.00	35.00
	CD1906	—	—	—	Rare	—

Obv: 4 dots divide leg.

Y#	Date	Mintage	VG	Fine	VF	XF
9.1	CD1907	—	16.50	40.00	75.00	125.00

Obv. leg: *Hsuan Tung.*

Y#	Date	Mintage	VG	Fine	VF	XF
19	CD1909	2.170	—	—	850.00	1200.

10 CASH

COPPER

Y#	Date	Mintage	Fine	VF	XF	Unc
4	ND(1903-05)					—
		281.171	2.00	3.50	6.00	25.00

Rev: Smaller English letters and different rosettes.

Y#	Date	Mintage	Fine	VF	XF	Unc
4.1	ND(1903-05)					—
		Inc. Ab.	1.00	2.00	3.50	20.00

Y#	Date	Mintage	Fine	VF	XF	Unc
10	CD1905	Inc. Ab.	1.50	3.00	5.00	25.00

Rev: Larger English letters and different dragon.

Y#	Date	Mintage	Fine	VF	XF	Unc
10.1	CD1905	—	25.00	65.00	110.00	—

Y#	Date	Mintage	Fine	VF	XF	Unc
10.2	CD1906	—	.75	1.50	3.00	20.00

Obv: W/o dots. Rev. leg: W/o dot after KUO.

Y#	Date	Mintage	Fine	VF	XF	Unc
10.3	CD1907	—	.50	1.25	2.50	18.00

Rev. leg: Dot after KUO.

Y#	Date	Mintage	Fine	VF	XF	Unc
10.4	CD1907	—	.50	1.25	2.50	18.00

BRASS

Obv: W/o dots.

Y#	Date	Mintage	Fine	VF	XF	Unc
10.4a	CD1907	—	5.50	20.00	35.00	—

COPPER

Obv: 4 dots divide leg.

Y#	Date	Mintage	Fine	VF	XF	Unc
10.5	CD1907	—	.50	1.25	2.50	18.00

BRASS

Y#	Date	Mintage	Fine	VF	XF	Unc
10.5a	CD1907	—	5.50	15.00	30.00	—

COPPER
Rev: Waves below dragon.

Y#	Date	Mintage	Fine	VF	XF	Unc
20	CD1909	—	1.00	2.00	4.00	22.50

Rev: Rosette below dragon, U of KUO inverted A.

20.1	CD1909	—	5.50	12.00	25.00	—

NOTE: Although this coin bears no indication of its origin, it was minted in the Manchurian Provinces ca. 1922.

20x	CD1909	—	20.00	40.00	85.00	—

NOTE: Although this coin bears no indication of its origin, it was minted in Kirin Province.

BRONZE

Y#	Date	Mintage	Fine	VF	XF	Unc
27	Yr.3(1911)	95.585	2.50	4.00	8.00	40.00
	Yr.3(1911)	—	—	—	Proof	Rare

BRASS

27a	Yr.3(1911)	—	30.00	45.00	95.00	150.00

20 CASH

COPPER

Y#	Date	Mintage	VG	Fine	VF	XF
5	(1917)	—	.20	.50	1.50	3.00

NOTE: This coin was struck at the Wuchang Mint in 1917 from unused dies prepared in 1903.

Obv: 4-point rosette in center.

5.1	ND(restrike)	—	2.50	6.00	12.00	25.00

Rev: Head of dragon and clouds redesigned.

Y#	Date	Mintage	VG	Fine	VF	XF
5.2	ND(restrike)	—	2.50	6.00	12.00	25.00

Rev: Dragon in circle of dots.

5a	ND(1903-05)	—	35.00	50.00	85.00	125.00

11	CD1905	—	12.50	30.00	50.00	75.00

11.1	CD1906	—	12.50	30.00	50.00	75.00

Obv: Dots around date, 1.2-1.7mm thick.

11.2	CD1907	—	.60	1.50	2.00	4.00

2.0-2.3mm thick

11.3	CD1907	—	2.50	6.00	12.00	25.00

BRASS

11.3a	CD1907	—	4.00	8.00	15.00	30.00

COPPER
Obv: W/o dots around date.

11.4	CD1907	—	—	Reported, not confirmed

Rev. leg: Dot between KUO and COPPER, 6 waves beneath dragon.

21	CD1909	—	.75	2.00	5.00	8.00

1.2-1.7mm thick
Rev. leg: W/o dot between KUO and COPPER, 6 waves beneath dragon.

Y#	Date	Mintage	VG	Fine	VF	XF
21.1	CD1909	—	1.25	3.00	6.00	10.00

2.0-2.3mm thick

21.2	CD1909	—	1.25	3.00	6.00	10.00

Rev: Rosette beneath dragon.

21.3	CD1909	—	3.00	7.50	20.00	35.00

NOTE: Although this coin bears no indication of its origin, it was minted in the Manchurian Provinces ca. 1922.

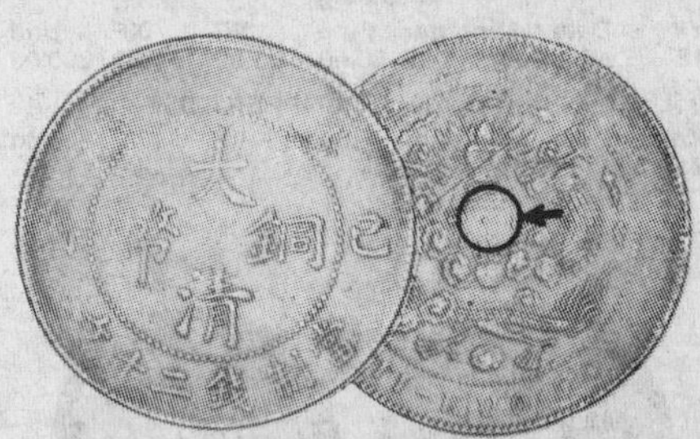

Rev: Dot below dragon's chin.

21.4	CD1909	—	3.50	8.50	16.00	30.00

NOTE: Although this coin bears no indication of its origin, it was minted in the Manchurian Provinces ca. 1922.

Rev: 5 crude waves beneath dragon w/ redesigned forehead.
Inner circle of large dots on obv. and rev.

21.5	CD1909	—	1.20	3.00	6.00	16.00

10 CENTS

2.7000 g, .820 SILVER, .0712 oz ASW
Similar to Y#12.

Kann#	Date	Mintage	Fine	VF	XF	Unc
215	CD1907	—	70.00	125.00	175.00	350.00

12	ND(1908)	—	30.00	40.00	90.00	175.00

3.2000 g, .650 SILVER, .0669 oz ASW
Similar to 50 Cents, Y#23.

222	ND(1910)	—	60.00	125.00	250.00	500.00
	ND(1910)	—	—	—	Proof	650.00

Rev: Larger characters.

222y	ND(1910)	—	—	—	—	—

SILVER, 2.70 g

Y#	Date	Mintage	Fine	VF	XF	Unc
28	Yr.3(1911)	—	10.00	30.00	75.00	150.00

NOTE: Refer to Hunan Republic 10 Cents, K#762.

20 CENTS

5.5000 g, .820 SILVER, .1450 oz ASW

Kann#	Date	Mintage	Fine	VF	XF	Unc
214	CD1907	—	80.00	125.00	200.00	325.00

5.30 g

Y#	Date	Mintage	Fine	VF	XF	Unc
13	ND(1908)	—	50.00	85.00	150.00	200.00

(Error) Rev. leg: "COPPER COIN"

Kann#	Date	Mintage	Fine	VF	XF	Unc
217w	ND(1908)	—	—	—	Rare	—
	Plain edge.					
217y	ND(1908)	—	—	—	—	—

SILVER, 5.40 g

Y#	Date	Mintage	Fine	VF	XF	Unc
29	Yr.3(1911)	—	50.00	100.00	175.00	350.00

25 CENTS

6.7000 g, .800 SILVER, .1724 oz ASW

Kann#	Date	Mintage	Fine	VF	XF	Unc
221	ND(1910)	1.410	200.00	400.00	750.00	1200.
	ND(1910)	—	—	—	Proof	2000.

50 CENTS

13.6000 g, .860 SILVER, .3761 oz ASW

Kann#	Date	Mintage	Fine	VF	XF	Unc
213	CD1907	—	100.00	250.00	400.00	750.00

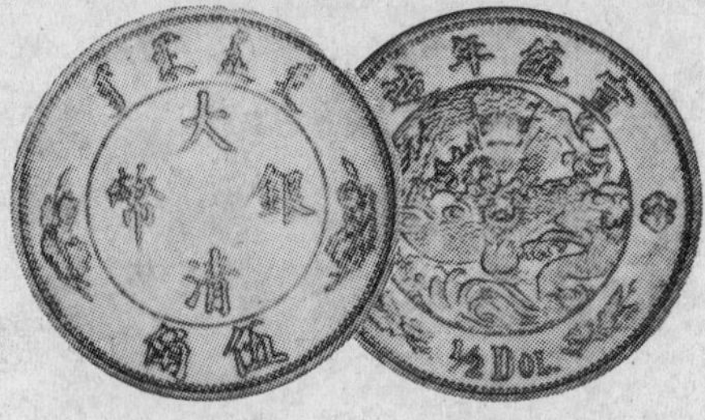

13.4000 g, .800 SILVER, .3447 oz ASW

Y#	Date	Mintage	Fine	VF	XF	Unc
23	ND(1910)	1.571	40.00	70.00	150.00	300.00
	ND(1910)	—	—	—	Proof	750.00

Y#	Date	Mintage	Fine	VF	XF	Unc
30	Yr.3 (1911)	I.A.	200.00	400.00	650.00	1000.
	Yr.3 (1911)	—	—	—	Proof	1200.

DOLLAR

26.9000 g, .900 SILVER, .7785 oz ASW

Kann#	Date	Mintage	Fine	VF	XF	Unc
212	CD1907	—	150.00	350.00	700.00	1000.

Y#	Date	Mintage	Fine	VF	XF	Unc
14	ND(1908)	—	15.00	25.00	50.00	250.00

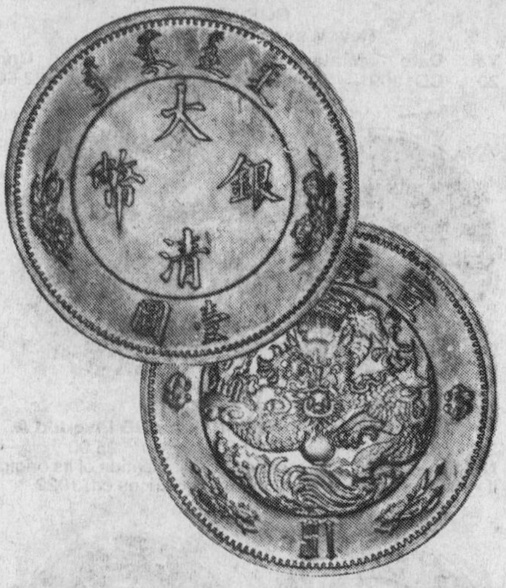

Kann#	Date	Mintage	Fine	VF	XF	Unc
219	ND(1910)	—	125.00	250.00	400.00	800.00
	ND(1910)	—	—	—	Proof	2100.

Y#	Date	Mintage	Fine	VF	XF	Unc
31	Yr.3 (1911)	77.153	15.00	22.00	35.00	200.00

NOTE: Struck at the Tientsin, Nanking and Wuchang Mints without distinctive marks.

Rev: Mint mark "dot" after DOLLAR.

Y#	Date	Mintage	Fine	VF	XF	Unc
31.1	Yr.3 (1911)	I.A.	20.00	25.00	40.00	250.00

PROOF SETS (PS)

KM#	Date	Mintage	Identification	Mkt.Val.
PS1	ND(1910)(4)	—	Y23,K219,K221,K222	—

Rebel Coinage

CASH

CAST COPPER or BRASS, uniface
Obv: *Chin Lung T'ung Pao*

KM#	Date	Emperor	Good	VG	Fine	VF
1	ND(1832)		—	—	Rare	—

NOTE: Issued by Chao Chin Lung.

T'AI P'ING REBELLION

A radical political and religious upheaval that lasted from 1850 to 1864. It ravaged 17 provinces and took an estimated 20,000,000 lives. The rebellion began under the leadership of Hung Hsiu-ch'uan (1814-64), a disappointed civil service examination candidate who believed himself to be the son of God, the younger brother of Jesus Christ, sent to reform China.

Their slogan - to share property in common - attracted many famine-stricken peasants, workers, and miners, as did their propoganda against the foreign Manchu rulers of China. Under the Taipings, the Chinese language was simplified, and equality between men and women was decreed. All property was to be held in common, and equal distribution of the land according to a form of communism was planned. Both the Chinese Communists and the Chinese Nationalists trace their origin to the Taipings.

CASH

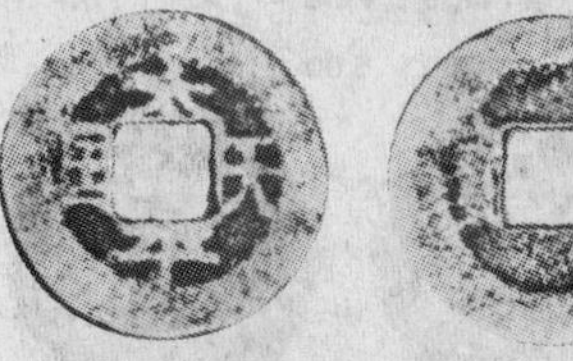

CAST COPPER or BRASS
Obv: *T'ai P'ing T'ien Kuo* (top-bottom-right-left).
Rev: *Sheng Pao* (right-left). 24-25mm.

C#	Date	Good	VG	Fine	VF
38-8	ND(1853-64)	15.00	25.00	35.00	60.00
	31-35mm				
38-7	ND(1853-64)	20.00	35.00	50.00	75.00
	42-45mm				
38-6	ND(1853-64)	25.00	45.00	70.00	100.00

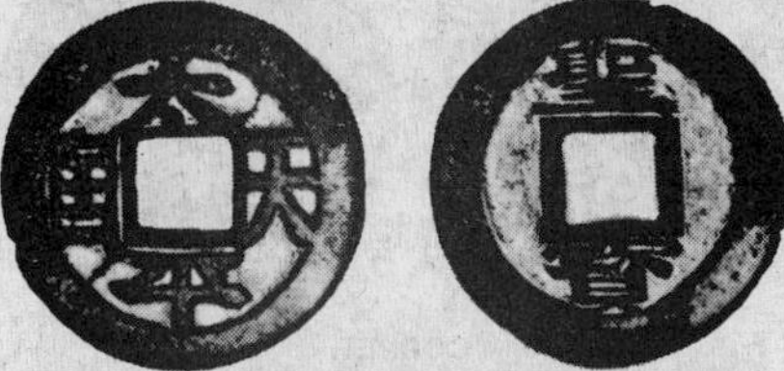

Rev: *Sheng Pao* (top-bottom).
24-26mm. Narrow rims.

C#	Date	Good	VG	Fine	VF
38-5	ND(1853-64)	10.00	25.00	35.00	50.00
	28mm. Wide rims.				
38-5.1	ND(1853-64)	10.00	13.00	20.00	35.00
	31-33mm. Narrow rims.				
38-4	ND(1853-64)	20.00	35.00	50.00	75.00

35mm. Wide rims.

C#	Date	Good	VG	Fine	VF
38-4.1	ND(1853-64)	22.50	40.00	60.00	90.00
	IRON				
38-4.1a	ND(1853-64)	—	—	1000.	—
	BRONZE				
	38-42mm. Narrow rims.				
38-3	ND(1853-64)	60.00	100.00	150.00	220.00
	47-48mm. Wide rims.				
38-3.1	ND(1853-64)	85.00	150.00	225.00	350.00

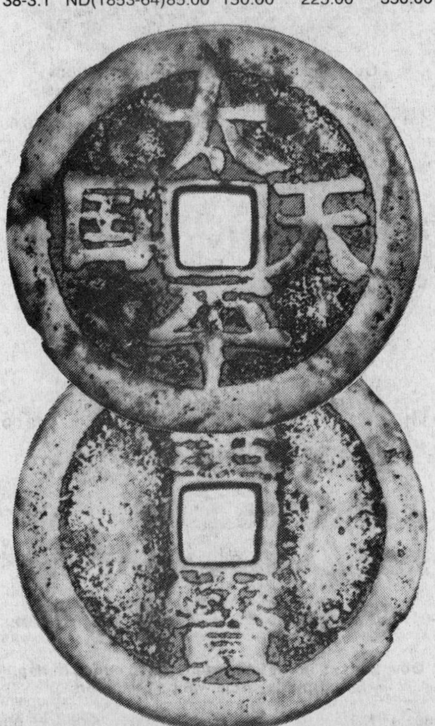

54-56mm. Narrow rims.

C#	Date	Good	VG	Fine	VF
38-2	ND(1853-64)	150.00	250.00	400.00	650.00

Obv: *T'ai P'ing Sheng Pao.*
Rev: *T'ien Kuo.*

C#	Date	Good	VG	Fine	VF
38-12	ND(1853-64)	15.00	20.00	30.00	60.00

Obv: *T'ien Kuo T'ai P'ing.*
Rev: *Sheng Pao.*

C#	Date	Good	VG	Fine	VF
38-14	ND(1853-64)	20.00	30.00	40.00	65.00

Obv: *T'ien Kuo Sheng Pao.*
Rev: *T'ai P'ing.*

C#	Date	Good	VG	Fine	VF
38-13	ND(1853-64)	10.00	15.00	25.00	45.00

Obv: *T'ien Kuo.* Rev: *Sheng Pao.*

C#	Date	Good	VG	Fine	VF
38-11	ND(1853-64)	30.00	40.00	50.00	75.00

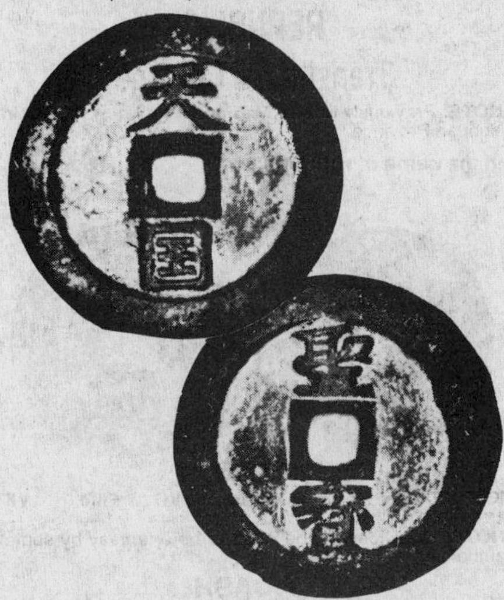

38mm. Large characters.

C#	Date	Good	VG	Fine	VF
38-10	ND(1853-64)	20.00	35.00	50.00	75.00
	36mm. Small characters.				
38-10.1	ND(1853-64)	50.00	70.00	90.00	120.00

Obv: T'ai P'ing. Rev: *Sheng Pao.*

C#	Date	Good	VG	Fine	VF
38-15	ND(1853-64)	20.00	35.00	50.00	75.00

Obv: *P'ing Ching Sheng Pao.*
Rev: *Yu Lin Chun* (Royal Guard).

C#	Date	Good	VG	Fine	VF
39-9	ND(1857)	45.00	75.00	120.00	200.00

Rev: *Ch'ien Ying.*

C#	Date	Good	VG	Fine	VF
39-10	ND(1857)	35.00	60.00	100.00	160.00

Rev: *Ch'ang Sheng Chun.*

C#	Date	Good	VG	Fine	VF
39-11	ND(1857)	35.00	60.00	100.00	160.00

Rev: *Chung Ying.*

C#	Date	Good	VG	Fine	VF
39-12	ND(1857)	35.00	60.00	100.00	160.00

Rev: *Hou Ying.*

C#	Date	Good	VG	Fine	VF
39-13	ND(1857)	35.00	60.00	100.00	160.00

Rev: *Tso Ying.*

C#	Date	Good	VG	Fine	VF
39-14	ND(1857)	35.00	60.00	100.00	160.00

Rev: *Yu Ying.*

C#	Date	Good	VG	Fine	VF
39-15	ND(1857)	35.00	60.00	100.00	160.00

Obv: *P'ing Ching T'ung Pao.*
Rev: *Chung* in seal script.

C#	Date	Good	VG	Fine	VF
39-16	ND(1857)	35.00	60.00	100.00	160.00

NOTE: There are numerous other Cash coins issued by Taiping supporters and military units.

1/4 TAEL

SILVER
Obv: *T'ien Kuo.* **Rev:** *Sheng Pao.*

KM#	Date	Mintage	VG	Fine	VF	XF
2	ND(1853-64)	5 known	—	—	—	2750.

1/2 TAEL

SILVER
Obv: *T'ien Kuo.* **Rev:** *Sheng Pao.*

KM#	Date	Mintage	VG	Fine	VF	XF
3	ND(1853-64)	14 known	—	—	—	2250.

5 TAELS

GOLD

KM#	Date	Mintage	VG	Fine	VF	XF
4	ND(1853-64)	1 known	—	—	—	—

NOTE: For additional listings of Rebel Coins, refer to Sinkiang (Xinjiang) Province.

SMALL SWORD SOCIETY

A Triad group located on the outskirts of Shanghai led by Liu Li-ch'uan. Driven out by the foreign community Shanghai volunteers in 1854.

CASH

COPPER
Obv: *T'ai P'ing T'ung Pao.*
Rev: Crescent above and *Ming* **below.**

C#	Date	Good	VG	Fine	VF
39-1	ND(1853-54)	35.00	50.00	85.00	125.00

Rev: Dot above and crescent below.

C#	Date	Good	VG	Fine	VF
39-2	ND(1853-54)	35.00	50.00	85.00	125.00

Rev: *Wen* **above.**

C#	Date	Good	VG	Fine	VF
39-3	ND(1853-54)	35.00	50.00	85.00	125.00

Rev: *Wen* **at right.**

C#	Date	Good	VG	Fine	VF
39-4	ND(1853-54)	35.00	50.00	85.00	125.00

HEAVEN AND EARTH SOCIETY

A Triad group located in Chekiang Province of which little is known.

CASH

COPPER
Obv: *Huang Ti T'ung Pao.*
Rev: *Sheng* **at right (sideways).**

C#	Date	Good	VG	Fine	VF
39-5	ND(1853-54)	35.00	50.00	85.00	125.00

Obv: *Huang Ti T'ung Pao.*
Rev: *Che Pao.*

C#	Date	Good	VG	Fine	VF
39-6	ND(1853-54)	35.00	75.00	115.00	150.00

Obv: *K'ai Yuan T'ung Pao.* **Rev:** *Wu.*

C#	Date	Good	VG	Fine	VF
39-7	ND(1853-54)	35.00	50.00	85.00	125.00

Obv: *T'ien Ch'ao T'ung Pao.* **Rev:** *Yung.*

C#	Date	Good	VG	Fine	VF
39-8	ND(1853-54)	35.00	50.00	85.00	125.00

REPUBLIC

Transitional Coinage

NOTE: Previously listed KM#5 and KM#4 now appear in Yunnan Province.

In the name of Hung Hsien

5 CASH

COPPER

KM#	Date	Mintage	Good	VG	Fine	VF
1	ND (1916)	—	—	—	—	—

NOTE: Questionable, believed to be a fantasy by some authorities.

10 CASH

COPPER or BRASS, uniface
Obv: Type A.

KM#	Date	Mintage	Good	VG	Fine	VF
2	ND (1916)	—	—	—	—	—

NOTE: Questionable, believed to be a fantasy by some authorities.

Regular Coinage

1/2 CENT

BRONZE

Mint: Tientsin

Y#	Date	Mintage	Fine	VF	XF	Unc
323	Yr.5 (1916)	1.789	5.00	10.00	20.00	45.00

Y#	Date	Mintage	Fine	VF	XF	Unc
346	Yr.25 (1936)	64.720	.60	1.50	3.00	7.50

10 CASH (1 CENT OR 1 FEN)

NOTE: Some sources date these 10 Cash pieces bearing crossed flags ca. 1912, but many were not struck until the 1920's.

COPPER
Mint: Nanking
Rev: Double circle w/small rosettes separating leg.

Y#	Date	Mintage	Fine	VF	XF	Unc
301	ND	—	.20	.50	1.00	15.00

BRASS

Y#	Date	Mintage	Fine	VF	XF	Unc
301a	ND	—	—	—	—	—

COPPER
Mint: Unknown
Obv: 2nd character from right in bottom leg. is rounded. Rev: Double circle w/3 dots separating leg.

Y#	Date	Mintage	Fine	VF	XF	Unc
301.1	ND	—	1.00	2.00	5.00	22.00

Obv: 2nd character from right in bottom leg. rounded. Rev: Double circle w/2 dots separating leg.

Y#	Date	Mintage	Fine	VF	XF	Unc
301.2	ND	—	.30	.75	1.50	16.00

Mint: Nanking
Obv: Small star on flag. Rev: Double circle w/6 pointed stars separating leg.

Y#	Date	Mintage	Fine	VF	XF	Unc
301.3	ND	—	.60	1.50	3.00	18.00

Obv: Large star on flag extending to edges of flag. Rev: Double circle w/6 pointed stars separating leg.

Y#	Date	Mintage	Fine	VF	XF	Unc
301.4	ND	—	10.00	15.00	25.00	65.00

BRASS

Y#	Date	Mintage	Fine	VF	XF	Unc
301.4a	ND	—	—	—	—	—

COPPER

Obv: Flower w/many stems. Rev: Single circle.

Y#	Date	Mintage	Fine	VF	XF	Unc
301.5	ND	—	.50	1.25	3.00	20.00

Obv: Flower w/fewer stems. Rev: Single circle.

Y#	Date	Mintage	Fine	VF	XF	Unc
301.6	ND	—	.50	1.25	3.00	20.00

Mint: Anhwei
Rev: Vine above leaf at 12 o'clock. Wreath tied at bottom. M-shaped leaves at base of wheat ears.

Y#	Date	Mintage	Fine	VF	XF	Unc
302	ND(ca.1920)	—	.40	1.00	2.00	18.00
BRASS						
302a	ND(ca.1920)	—	—	—	—	—

COPPER
Rev: Larger wheat ears.

Y#	Date	Mintage	Fine	VF	XF	Unc
302.1	ND(ca.1920)	—	1.20	3.00	7.50	20.00

Rev: Vine beneath leaf at 12 o'clock. Wreath not tied at bottom. W/o M-shaped leaves at base of wheat ears.

Y#	Date	Mintage	Fine	VF	XF	Unc
302.2	ND(ca.1920)	—	1.60	4.00	8.00	20.00

Rev: Leaves pointing clockwise.

Y#	Date	Mintage	Fine	VF	XF	Unc
302.3	ND(ca.1920)	—	45.00	50.00	75.00	100.00

Obv: Small star shaped rosettes.
Rev: Small 4-petalled rosettes separating leg.

Y#	Date	Mintage	Fine	VF	XF	Unc
303	ND	—	.30	.70	2.00	15.00

Obv: Left flag's star in relief.

Y#	Date	Mintage	Fine	VF	XF	Unc
303.1	ND	—	.30	.70	2.00	15.00

BRASS
Obv: Stars replace rosettes.

Y#	Date	Mintage	Fine	VF	XF	Unc
303a	ND	—	1.60	4.00	10.00	22.50

COPPER
Obv: Large rosettes replace stars.
Rev: Stars separating leg.

Y#	Date	Mintage	Fine	VF	XF	Unc
303.3	ND	—	3.00	6.25	12.50	25.00

Obv: Very small pentagonal rosettes.

Y#	Date	Mintage	Fine	VF	XF	Unc
303.4	ND	—	.75	1.50	3.00	15.00
BRASS						
303.4a	ND	—	3.00	6.25	12.50	25.00

Obv: Large rosettes.
Similar to Y#307a.1.

Y#	Date	Mintage	Fine	VF	XF	Unc
303.5	ND	—	—	—	—	—

COPPER
Mint: Anhwei
Obv: Circled flag flanked by pentagonal rosettes.

Y#	Date	Mintage	Fine	VF	XF	Unc
304	ND(ca.1920)	—	11.50	21.50	42.50	85.00

Mint: Changsha, Hunan
Rev: Chrysanthemum.

Y#	Date	Mintage	Fine	VF	XF	Unc
305	ND	—	15.00	25.00	50.00	115.00

Mint: Changsha, Hunan

Y#	Date	Mintage	Fine	VF	XF	Unc
306.1	ND(ca.1920)	—	.40	1.00	2.00	14.00
BRASS						
306b	ND(ca.1920)	—	1.00	2.50	5.00	18.00
COPPER **Obv: Y#306.1, Rev: Y#306.4**						
306.1b	ND(ca.1920)	—	2.00	3.50	7.00	25.00

Obv: Dot on either side of upper legend.

Y#	Date	Mintage	Fine	VF	XF	Unc
306.2	ND(ca.1920)	—	1.00	2.00	3.50	15.00
BRASS						
306.2b	ND(ca.1920)	—	1.25	3.00	5.00	15.00

COPPER
Obv: Star between flags.

Y#	Date	Mintage	Fine	VF	XF	Unc
306.3	ND(ca.1920)	—	20.00	40.00	75.00	—

Obv: Elongated rosettes, different characters in bottom leg. Rev: Thin leaf blade between lower wheat ears.

Y#	Date	Mintage	Fine	VF	XF	Unc
306.4	ND(ca.1920)	—	17.50	35.00	70.00	175.00

Obv: 5 characters in lower leg.

Y#	Date	Mintage	Fine	VF	XF	Unc
306a	ND(ca.1920)	—	5.00	12.00	25.00	65.00

Mint: Taiyuan, Shensi
Obv: 1 large rosette on either side.
Rev: Slender leaves and short ribbon.

Y#	Date	Mintage	Fine	VF	XF	Unc
307	ND(1919)					
		421.138	.50	1.00	2.00	12.00

Rev: Larger leaves and longer ribbon.

Y#	Date	Mintage	Fine	VF	XF	Unc
307.1	ND(1919)	I.A.	10.00	20.00	40.00	100.00

Obv: 3 rosettes on either side, ornate right flag.
Rev: Long ribbon.

Y#	Date	Mintage	Fine	VF	XF	Unc
307a	ND(1919)	I.A.	1.00	2.00	4.00	12.50

BRASS

Y#	Date	Mintage	Fine	VF	XF	Unc
307b	ND(1919)	—	—	—	—	—

COPPER
Rev: Short ribbon and smaller wheat ears.

Y#	Date	Mintage	Fine	VF	XF	Unc
307a.1	ND(1919)	I.A.	10.00	20.00	40.00	100.00

Mint: Tientsin

Y#	Date	Mintage	Fine	VF	XF	Unc
309	ND(1914-17)	—	10.00	20.00	40.00	120.00

NOTE: Pieces w/L. GIORGI near rim are patterns.

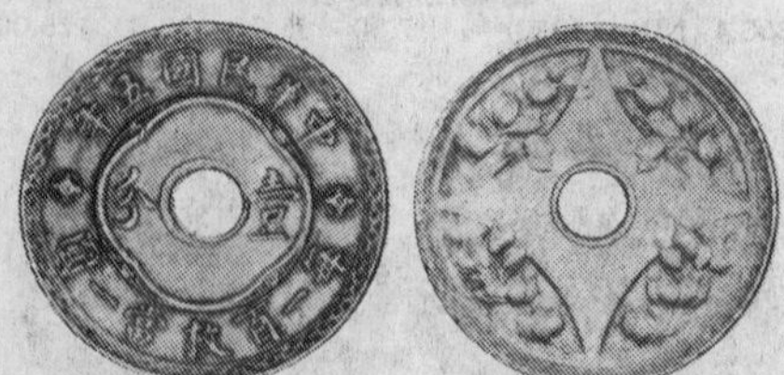

BRONZE
Mint: Tientsin

Y#	Year	Date	Fine	VF	XF	Unc
324	5	(1916)	1.00	2.50	4.50	18.00

NOTE: Pieces w/L. GIORGI near rim are patterns.

COPPER
Mint: Kalgan

Y#	Year	Date	Fine	VF	XF	Unc
311	13	(1924)	175.00	350.00	500.00	850.00

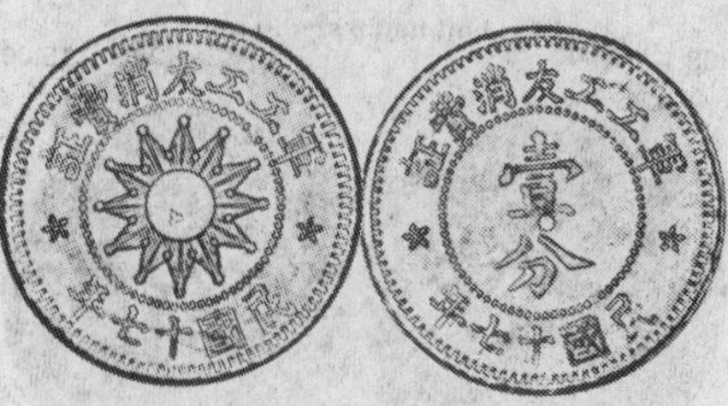

BRASS
Mint: Shansi Arsenal

Y#	Year	Date	Fine	VF	XF	Unc
337	17	(1928)	75.00	125.00	175.00	300.00

NOTE: This coin is usually found with small punch marks near center on obverse and reverse.

BRONZE

Y#	Year	Date	Fine	VF	XF	Unc
324a	22	(1933)	8.00	15.00	30.00	100.00

Y#	Date	Mintage	Fine	VF	XF	Unc
347	Yr.25 (1936)					
		311.780	.20	.50	1.00	2.50
	Yr.26 (1937)					
		307.198	.25	.60	1.25	3.00
	Yr.27 (1938)					
		12.000	1.00	2.00	4.00	8.00
	Yr.28 (1939)					
		75.000	2.00	4.00	8.00	17.50

Y#	Year	Date	Fine	VF	XF	Unc
353	28	(1939)	20.00	45.00	75.00	140.00

ALUMINUM

Y#	Date	Mintage	Fine	VF	XF	Unc
355	Yr.29 (1940)					
		150.000	.10	.25	.50	1.50

BRASS

Y#	Date	Mintage	Fine	VF	XF	Unc
357	Yr.29 (1940)					
		50.000	.30	.75	1.00	2.50

BRONZE

Y#	Year	Date	Fine	VF	XF	Unc
363	37	(1948)	4.00	10.00	15.00	20.00

'PORTRAIT' TEN CASH

NOTE: A number of ten Cash pieces exist w/portraits of Yuan Shih-kai, Sun Yat-sen, Li Yuan-hung or Ni Su-chung and are considered fantasies. Refer to "Unusual World Coins", 3rd edition c. 1992 Krause Publications.

20 CASH (2 CENTS or 2 FEN)

COPPER
Mint: Taiyuan, Shansi

Y#	Date	Mintage	Fine	VF	XF	Unc
308	Yr.8 (1919)					
		200.861	1.00	2.50	6.00	30.00

Y#	Date	Mintage	Fine	VF	XF	Unc
308a	Yr.10 (1921)	I.A.	1.00	2.50	6.00	30.00

Mint: Tientsin

Y#	Date	Mintage	Fine	VF	XF	Unc
310	ND	—	17.50	35.00	60.00	125.00

NOTE: Some sources date these 20 Cash pieces bearing crossed flags ca. 1912, but many were not struck until the 1920's. This coin is usually found weakly struck and lightweight.

Mint: Kalgan

Y#	Year	Date	Fine	VF	XF	Unc
312	13	(1924)	7.00	17.50	35.00	135.00

NOTE: This coin is usually found weakly struck.

Nationalist Commemorative

Hsu#	Date	Mintage	Fine	VF	XF	Unc
9	ND(1927/8)	—	225.00	400.00	650.00	900.00

BRASS
Mint: Shansi Arsenal

Y#	Date	Mintage	Fine	VF	XF	Unc
338	Yr.17(1928)	—	150.00	250.00	400.00	650.00

NOTE: This coin has always been found w/small punch marks near center on obverse and reverse. Similar 5 and 10 Fen pieces have been reported.

BRONZE

Y#	Date	Mintage	Fine	VF	XF	Unc
325a	Yr.22(1933)	—	35.00	55.00	85.00	175.00

BRASS

Y#	Date	Mintage	Fine	VF	XF	Unc
354	Yr.28 (1939)	300.000	3.50	7.50	13.00	22.50

Y#	Date	Mintage	Fine	VF	XF	Unc
358	Yr.29 (1940)	—	.25	.50	.75	1.50

5 CENTS (5 FEN)

BRASS, 27mm
Mint: Shansi Arsenal
Similar to 2 Fen, Y#338.

Y#	Year	Date	Fine	VF	XF	Unc
A339	17	(1928)	450.00	750.00	1250.	—

NOTE: This coin has always been found w/small punch marks near center on obverse and reverse. Similar 5 and 10 Fen pieces have been reported.

NICKEL

Y#	Date	Mintage	Fine	VF	XF	Unc
348	Yr.25 (1936)	72.844	.25	.50	.75	1.75
	Yr.27 (1938)	34.325	.60	1.50	3.00	8.00
	Yr.28 (1939)	6.000	4.00	10.00	15.00	30.00

Rev: A mint mark below spade (Vienna)

Y#	Date	Mintage	Fine	VF	XF	Unc
348.1	Yr.25 (1936)	20.000	.50	1.00	3.25	15.00

Obv: Character *P'ing* on both sides of portrait.

Y#	Year	Date	Fine	VF	XF	Unc
348.2	25	(1936)	50.00	80.00	125.00	175.00

Obv: Character *Ch'ing* on both sides of portrait.

Y#	Year	Date	Fine	VF	XF	Unc
348.3	25	(1936)	50.00	80.00	125.00	175.00

ALUMINUM

Y#	Date	Mintage	Fine	VF	XF	Unc
356	Yr.29 (1940)	350.000	.10	.25	.50	1.00

COPPER-NICKEL

Y#	Date	Mintage	Fine	VF	XF	Unc
359	Yr.29 (1940)	57.000	.25	1.50	2.50	5.00
	Yr.30 (1941)	96.000	.25	1.50	2.50	6.00

10 CENTS
(10 FEN or 1 CHIAO)

SILVER, 2.30 g
Similar to 1 Dollar, Y#318, vertical reeding.

Kann#	Date	Mintage	Fine	VF	XF	Unc
602	ND(1912)	—	150.00	250.00	400.00	1000.

Edge engrailed w/circles.

Kann#	Date	Mintage	Fine	VF	XF	Unc
602b	ND(1912)	—	—	300.00	500.00	1200.

2.7000 g, .700 SILVER, .0607 oz ASW

Y#	Year	Date	Fine	VF	XF	Unc
326	3	(1914)	3.00	7.00	15.00	50.00
	5	(1916)	20.00	40.00	60.00	150.00

SILVER
Pu Yi Wedding

Y#	Year	Date	Fine	VF	XF	Unc
334	15	(1926)	4.00	7.50	15.00	65.00

SILVER, 2.50 g
Death of Sun Yat-sen

Y#	Year	Date	Fine	VF	XF	Unc
339	16	(1927)	20.00	35.00	50.00	150.00

BRASS, 27mm
Mint: Shansi Arsenal
Similar to 2 Fen, Y#338.

Y#	Year	Date	Fine	VF	XF	Unc
B339	17	(1928)	450.00	750.00	1250.	—

NOTE: This coin has always been found w/small punch marks near center on obverse and reverse. Similar 5 and 10 Fen pieces have been reported.

NICKEL

Y#	Date	Mintage	Fine	VF	XF	Unc
349	Yr.25 (1936)	73.866	.60	1.00	3.00	7.50
	Yr.27 (1938)	110.203	2.00	4.25	8.00	12.50
	Yr.28 (1939)	68.000	.80	1.25	3.00	7.50

NON-MAGNETIC NICKEL ALLOY

Y#	Date	Mintage	Fine	VF	XF	Unc
349a	Yr.25 (1936)	1.000	18.00	30.00	35.00	65.00

NOTE: All of the Y#349 coins were supposed to have been minted in pure nickel at the Shanghai Mint. However in 1936 the Tientsin Mint produced about one million 10 Cent pieces of heavily alloyed nickel. The result is that the Shanghai pieces are attracted to a magnet while the Tientsin pieces are not.

 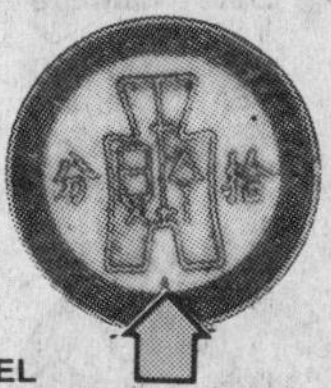

NICKEL
Rev: A mint mark below spade (Vienna Mint)

Y#	Date	Mintage	Fine	VF	XF	Unc
349.1	Yr.25 (1936)A	60.000	.50	1.00	2.50	6.50

COPPER-NICKEL
Reeded edge.

Y#	Date	Mintage	Fine	VF	XF	Unc
360	Yr.29 (1940)	68.000	.50	1.50	2.50	6.00
	Yr.30 (1941)	254.000	.50	1.50	2.50	5.00
	Yr.31 (1942)	10.000	25.00	50.00	80.00	100.00

Plain edge.

Y#	Date	Mintage	Fine	VF	XF	Unc
360.1	Yr.29(1940)	I.A.	—	—	Rare	—
	Yr.30(1941)	I.A.	2.00	5.00	7.50	12.50

20 CENTS
(20 FEN or 2 CHIAO)

SILVER, 5.20 g
Founding of the Republic

Y#	Date	Mintage	Fine	VF	XF	Unc
317	ND(1912)	.155	15.00	20.00	35.00	70.00

5.4000 g, .700 SILVER, .1215 oz ASW

Y#	Year	Date	Fine	VF	XF	Unc
327	3	(1914)	1.00	2.00	5.00	35.00
	5	(1916)	2.00	3.00	10.00	65.00
	9	(1920)	100.00	200.00	250.00	450.00

SILVER, 5.20 g
Pu Yi Wedding

Y#	Year	Date	Fine	VF	XF	Unc
335	15	(1926)	5.00	7.50	15.00	100.00

SILVER, 5.30 g
Death of Sun Yat-sen

Y#	Year	Date	Fine	VF	XF	Unc
340	16	(1927)	15.00	22.50	37.50	100.00

NICKEL

Y#	Date	Mintage	Fine	VF	XF	Unc
350	Yr.25 (1936)	49.620	.50	2.50	3.50	6.00
	Yr.27 (1938)	61.248	1.00	2.00	4.50	8.00
	Yr.28 (1939)	38.000	1.00	2.00	4.50	9.00

Rev: A mint mark below spade (Vienna Mint)

Y#	Date	Mintage	Fine	VF	XF	Unc
350.1	Yr.25 (1936)	40.000	1.00	2.00	3.50	6.00

COPPER-NICKEL

Y#	Date	Mintage	Fine	VF	XF	Unc
361	Yr.31 (1942)	32.300	.40	1.00	2.25	4.00

500 CASH

COPPER
Nationalist Commemorative

Hsu#	Date	Mintage	Fine	VF	XF	Unc
445a	ND(1927/8)	12 pcs. (8 known)	—	—	Rare	—

50 CENTS

13.6000 g, .700 SILVER, .3060 oz ASW

Y#	Year	Date	Fine	VF	XF	Unc
328	3	(1914)	10.00	15.00	30.00	120.00

COPPER-NICKEL

Y#	Date	Mintage	Fine	VF	XF	Unc
362	Yr.30 (1941) milled & smooth edge	—	—	125.00	150.00	—
	Yr.31 (1942)	57.000	.40	.80	1.50	4.00
	Yr.32 (1943)	4.000	2.50	7.50	15.00	27.50

DOLLAR (YUAN)

26.9000 g, .900 SILVER, .7785 oz ASW
Sun Yat-sen Founding of the Republic
Rev: 2 five-pointed stars dividing leg. at top.

Y#	Date	Mintage	Fine	VF	XF	Unc
318	ND(1912)	—	80.00	150.00	225.00	350.00

Obv: Dot below ear.

Y#	Date	Mintage	Fine	VF	XF	Unc
318.1	ND	—	—	—	—	—

NOTE: For similar issue w/rosettes see Y#318a.1 (1927).

27.3000 g, .900 SILVER, .7900 oz ASW
Obv: Similar to Y#318.

Y#	Date	Mintage	Fine	VF	XF	Unc
319	ND(1912)	—	60.00	100.00	150.00	275.00

SILVER, 26.50 g
Li Yuan-hung Founding of Republic
Rev: Similar to Y#319.

Y#	Date	Mintage	Fine	VF	XF	Unc
320	ND(1912)	—	75.00	150.00	250.00	375.00

Rev. leg: OE for OF.

Y#	Date	Mintage	Fine	VF	XF	Unc
320.1	ND(1912)	—	100.00	175.00	275.00	400.00

Rev. leg: CIIINA for CHINA.

Y#	Date	Mintage	Fine	VF	XF	Unc
320.2	ND(1912)	—	100.00	175.00	300.00	400.00

Li Yuan-hung Founding of Republic

Rev: Similar to Y#319.

Y#	Date	Mintage	Fine	VF	XF	Unc
321	ND(1912)	—	25.00	50.00	75.00	100.00

Rev. leg: H of 'THE' engraved as I I, w/o crossbar.

Y#	Date	Mintage	Fine	VF	XF	Unc
321.1	ND(1912)	—	30.00	60.00	85.00	125.00

26.7000 g, .900 SILVER, .7474 oz ASW
39.1mm, thickness 2.8mm
Yuan Shih-kai Founding of Republic

Y#	Date	Mintage	Fine	VF	XF	Unc
322	ND(1914)	.020	—	100.00	150.00	300.00

39.5mm, thickness 3.25mm

Y#	Date	Mintage	Fine	VF	XF	Unc
322.1	ND	—	—	100.00	150.00	300.00

NOTE: A restrike made about 1918 for collectors.

26.4000 g, .890 SILVER, .7555 oz ASW
Yuan Shih-kai
Obv: 6 characters above head.
Vertical reeding.

Y#	Year	Date	Fine	VF	XF	Unc
329	3	(1914)	8.00	12.50	17.50	25.00

Edge engrailed w/circles.

Y#	Year	Date	Fine	VF	XF	Unc
329.1	3	(1914)	30.00	75.00	150.00	300.00

Edge ornamented w/alternating T's.

Y#	Year	Date	Fine	VF	XF	Unc
329.2	3	(1914)	30.00	75.00	150.00	400.00

Plain edge.

Y#	Year	Date	Fine	VF	XF	Unc
329.3	3	(1914)	20.00	40.00	60.00	80.00

Tiny circle in ribbon bow. This is a mint mark, but it is not clear what mint is indicated.

Y#	Year	Date	Fine	VF	XF	Unc
329.4	3	(1914)	15.00	25.00	40.00	75.00

Obv: 7 characters above head.

Y#	Year	Date	Fine	VF	XF	Unc
329.6	8	(1919)	10.00	15.00	35.00	80.00
	9	(1920)	6.00	7.00	10.00	25.00
	10	(1921)	6.00	7.00	10.00	25.00

Oblique edge reeding.

329.5	10	(1921)	17.50	30.00	35.00	50.00

NOTE: Although bearing dates of Yr. 3 (1914) and Yr. 8-10 (1919-21), these Yuan Shi-Kai Dollars were struck for years afterwards. Coins dated Yr. 3 (1914) were struck continuously through 1929 and were also later restruck by the Chinese Communists. Later again in the 1950's this coin was struck for use in Tibet. Coins with dates Yr. 9 and 10 (1920 and 1921) were struck at least until 1929. The total mintage of all four dates of Y#329 is estimated at more than 750 million pieces.

SILVER, 26.80 g
Inauguration of Hung Hsien Regime
Obv: Similar to Y#322.

332	ND	(1916)	—	150.00	200.00	450.00

NOTE: Struck in 1917.

SILVER, 26.50 g
President Hsu Shih-chang
Reeded edge

Kann#	Year	Date	Fine	VF	XF	Unc
676	10	(1921)	—	200.00	300.00	450.00

Plain edge

676.1	10	(1921)	—	500.00	700.00	1000.

SILVER, 26.70 g
President Tsao Kun

Kann#	Date	Mintage	Fine	VF	XF	Unc
677	ND(1923)	.050	—	150.00	200.00	375.00

SILVER, 26.80 g
Pu Yi Wedding
Rev: Value in small characters.

Y#	Year	Date	Fine	VF	XF	Unc
336	12	(1923)	—	250.00	400.00	700.00

Rev: Value in large characters.

336.1	12	(1923)	—	400.00	700.00	1000.

SILVER
President Tuan Chi-jui

Kann#	Date	Mintage	Fine	VF	XF	Unc
683	ND(1924)	—	—	150.00	200.00	375.00

27.0000 g, .890 SILVER, .7727 oz ASW
Incuse edge reeding
Rev: 2 rosettes dividing leg. at top.

Y#	Date	Mintage	Fine	VF	XF	Unc
318a.1	ND(1927)	—	6.00	7.00	8.00	15.00

Edge reeding in relief.

318a.2	ND(1927)	—	6.00	7.00	8.00	15.00

NOTE: Varieties exist with errors in the English legend. For similar coins with 5 pointed stars dividing legends, see Y#318 (1912). In 1949 the Canton Mint restruck Memento dollars.

NOTE: There are modern restrikes in red copper and brass.

SILVER, 26.50 g
General Chu Yu-pu

Kann#	Year	Date	Fine	VF	XF	Unc
690	16	(1927)	—	—	3500.	6000.

27.00 g
Sun Yat-sen Memorial

Kann#	Date	Mintage	Fine	VF	XF	Unc
609	Yr.16 (1927)	480 pcs.	400.00	800.00	1500.	3000.

26.7000 g, .880 SILVER, .7555 oz ASW
Rev: Birds above junk, rising sun.

Y#	Date	Mintage	Fine	VF	XF	Unc
344	Yr.21 (1932)	2.260	60.00	100.00	150.00	300.00

Y#	Date	Mintage	Fine	VF	XF	Unc
345	Yr.22 (1933)	46.400	8.00	10.00	15.00	30.00
	Yr.23 (1934)	128.740	8.00	10.00	12.00	20.00

NOTE: In 1949, three U.S. mints restruck a total of 30 million "Junk Dollars" dated Year 23.

10 DOLLARS

RED GOLD, 7.05 g
Hung Hsien

Y#	Year	Date	Fine	VF	XF	Unc
333	1	(1916)	—	2000.	3000.	4200.

YELLOW GOLD, 7.05 g

Y#	Year	Date	Fine	VF	XF	Unc
333a	1	(1916)	—	2000.	3000.	4200.

8.1500 g, .850 GOLD, .2227 oz AGW

Y#	Year	Date	Fine	VF	XF	Unc
330	8	(1919)	—	—	2500.	4000.

20 DOLLARS

16.3000 g, .850 GOLD, .4456 oz AGW

Y#	Year	Date	Fine	VF	XF	Unc
331	8	(1919)	—	—	4500.	7500.

PROVINCIAL COINAGE

ANHWEI PROVINCE

Anhui

A province located in eastern China. Made a separate province during the Manchu dynasty in the 17th century. Principally agricultural with some mining of coal and iron ore. Spanish-American 8 Reales saw wide circulation in this province until the end of World War I. The provincial mint at Anking began operations in 1897, closed in 1899, and later reopened in 1902. The primary production of the mint was Cash coins but included a series of silver coinage.

EMPIRE

CASH

CAST BRASS
Obv: Type A-1

C#	Date	Emperor	Good	VG	Fine	VF
—	ND (1796-1820)	Chia-ch'ing	—	—	Rare	—

Obv: Type A

C#	Date	Emperor	Good	VG	Fine	VF
—	ND (1820-51)	Tao-kuang	—	—	Rare	—

NOTE: Not to be confused with similar coins from the Changsha Mint in Hunan Province. The Changsha Mint coins have an extra dot or vertical stroke to the left of the mint mark at right of the center hole.

NOTE: For previously listed C#3-1, refer to Honan (Henan) Province for C#3-1.1a and to Taku Mint in Chihli (Hebei) Province for C#3-1.1 and 3-1.2.

MILLED COINAGE

5 CASH

COPPER
Rev: Circled dragon, leg: *AN-HWEI.*

Y#	Date	VG	Fine	VF	XF
35	ND (1902)	125.00	175.00	250.00	350.00

Rev: Uncircled dragon, leg: *AN-HUI.*

Y#	Date	VG	Fine	VF	XF
35.1	ND	—	—	Rare	—

10 CASH

COPPER

Rev: Letter *A* inverted, denomination *ONE SEN.*

Y#	Date	VG	Fine	VF	XF
34a	ND (1902)	50.00	80.00	125.00	350.00

Rev: Letter *A* corrected.

Y#	Date	VG	Fine	VF	XF
34a.1	ND (1902)	40.00	65.00	100.00	250.00

Rev. denomination: *ONE CEN*

Y#	Date	VG	Fine	VF	XF
34	ND (1902)	35.00	50.00	85.00	150.00

NOTE: May show various stages of recutting of 'C' in CEN.

Rev: Rosettes around dragon close together.
Letter *N* backwards in *AN-HWEI* and in *TEN.*

Y#	Date	VG	Fine	VF	XF
36	ND (1902-06)	6.00	12.00	20.00	40.00

Obv: Small Manchu words in center.
Rev: Rosettes close together, letter *N* corrected.
Plain edge

Y#	Date	VG	Fine	VF	XF
36.1	ND (1902-06)	.75	2.00	3.00	10.00

Milled edge

Y#	Date	VG	Fine	VF	XF
36.1a	ND(1902-06)	—	—	Rare	—

Obv: Smaller redesigned rosettes;
larger Manchu words in center.
Rev: Rosettes close together;
larger clouds around redesigned dragon.

Y#	Date	VG	Fine	VF	XF
36.2	ND (1902-06)	.75	2.00	3.00	8.00

Obv: Rosettes crude and heavy.
Rev: Rosettes close together, dragon's head redesigned.

Y#	Date	VG	Fine	VF	XF
36.3	ND (1902-06)	5.00	12.00	17.50	35.00

Rev: Rosettes far apart.

Y#	Date	VG	Fine	VF	XF
36.4	ND (1902-06)	.75	2.00	3.00	8.00

Obv: Small rosette at center; leg. w/5 characters at bottom. Rev: Large English leg. above dragon, w/o TEN CASH.

36a	ND (1902-06)	.75	2.00	3.00	12.00

Obv: Small rosette.
Rev: Small English leg. above dragon.

36a.1	ND (1902-06)	1.00	2.50	5.00	15.00

Rev: Small English leg. w/larger clouds around dragon and only one cloud below dragon's tail.

36a.2	ND (1902-06)	3.00	5.00	8.00	18.00

Obv: Large rosette at center; leg. w/2 characters at bottom.

36a.3	ND (1902-06)	.75	2.00	3.00	6.00

Obv: Large rosette at center; leg. w/5 characters at bottom.

36a.4	ND (1902-06)	1.25	2.50	3.50	7.00

Obv. leg: 2 characters at bottom.
Rev: Small English leg. above dragon.

36a.5	ND (1902-06)	3.50	7.50	15.00	30.00

Obv: Slightly smaller rosette at center w/right Manchu word slightly higher than on Y#36a.5.
Rev: Small English leg. above dragon.

Y#	Date	VG	Fine	VF	XF
36a.6	ND (1902-06)	.75	2.00	3.50	7.00

Obv. leg: 2 characters at bottom.
Rev: Ten spelled *TOEN.*

38a	ND (1902-06)	8.00	15.00	30.00	50.00

Obv. leg: 5 characters at bottom.
Rev: Ten spelled *TOEN.*

38a.1	ND (1902-06)	35.00	70.00	150.00	250.00

Obv. leg: 2 characters at bottom.
Rev: W/o TEN CASH.

38b	ND (1902-06)	5.00	12.00	25.00	65.00

Obv. leg: 5 characters at bottom.

38b.1	ND (1902-06)	15.00	35.00	50.00	140.00

Obv. leg: 7 characters at bottom.
Rev: Rosettes at sides and *AN-HUI* above dragon.

39	ND (1902-06)	—	—	Rare	—

Rev: Stars at sides and *AN-HUI* above dragon.

Y#	Date	VG	Fine	VF	XF
39.1	ND (1902-06)	—	—	Rare	—

Square holed center, *AN-HUI,* upright dragon.

39.2	(1902-06)	—	—	Rare	—

Obv: Large mint mark at center.

Y#	Date	Mintage	VG	Fine	VF	XF
10a	CD1906	—	1.00	2.50	5.00	10.00

Obv: Small mint mark at center.

10a.1	CD1906	—	1.50	3.00	6.00	12.00

Obv. and rev: More finely engraved.
Rev: Cloud near dragon's lower foot shaped like a 3.

10a.2	CD1906	—	.60	1.50	2.50	5.00

20a	CD1909	—	12.00	25.00	50.00	125.00

Rev: Dot after *COIN.*

20a.1	CD1909	—	35.00	65.00	130.00	225.00

20 CASH

COPPER

Y#	Date	Mintage	VG	Fine	VF	XF
37	ND (1902)	—	375.00	750.00	1100.	1500.

Y#	Date	Mintage	VG	Fine	VF	XF
11a	CD1906	—	37.50	75.00	150.00	300.00

5 CENTS

1.3300 g, .820 SILVER, .0351 oz ASW

Y#	Date	Mintage	Fine	VF	XF	Unc
41	ND (1897)	—	40.00	75.00	130.00	250.00

Y#	Year	Date	Fine	VF	XF	Unc
41.1	25	(1899)	35.00	55.00	90.00	175.00

10 CENTS

2.6500 g, .820 SILVER, .0699 oz ASW
Obv: Rosettes divide leg.

Y#	Date	Mintage	Fine	VF	XF	Unc
42	ND (1897)	—	12.00	25.00	50.00	120.00

Obv: W/o rosettes dividing leg.

Y#	Year	Date	Fine	VF	XF	Unc
42.1	24	(1898)	10.00	20.00	40.00	100.00

Obv: Rosettes divide leg.

Y#	Year	Date	Fine	VF	XF	Unc
42.2	24	(1898)	10.00	20.00	40.00	100.00

Obv: A S T C in field.

Y#	Year	Date	Fine	VF	XF	Unc
42.3	24	(1898)	10.00	22.50	45.00	120.00

Obv. leg: 6 characters at top.

Y#	Date	Mintage	Fine	VF	XF	Unc
42.4	CD1898	—	15.00	25.00	50.00	120.00

20 CENTS

5.3000 g, .820 SILVER, .1397 oz ASW
Rev: Large dragon and small English leg.

Y#	Date	Mintage	Fine	VF	XF	Unc
43	ND (1897)	—	15.00	35.00	70.00	140.00

Rev: Smaller dragon and larger English leg.

Y#	Date	Mintage	Fine	VF	XF	Unc
43.1	ND (1897)	—	15.00	35.00	70.00	140.00
43.2	23 (1897)	2 known	—	—	—	—

NOTE: D.K.E. Ching Sale 6-91 AU realized $2,200.

Y#	Year	Date	Fine	VF	XF	Unc
43.3	24	(1898)	15.00	35.00	70.00	160.00

Obv: A S T C in field.

Y#	Year	Date	Fine	VF	XF	Unc
43.4	24	(1898)	15.00	35.00	70.00	160.00

Y#	Year	Date	Fine	VF	XF	Unc
43.5	27	(1901)	1 known	—	—	

NOTE: D.K.E. Ching Sale 6-91 VF+ realized $2,420.

50 CENTS

13.5000 g, .860 SILVER, .3733 oz ASW

Y#	Year	Date	Fine	VF	XF	Unc
44	24	(1898)	70.00	150.00	250.00	550.00

Obv: A S T C in field.

Y#	Year	Date	Fine	VF	XF	Unc
44.1	24	(1898)	65.00	150.00	200.00	500.00

DOLLAR

27.1000 g, .900 SILVER, .7842 oz ASW

Y#	Date	Mintage	Fine	VF	XF	Unc
45	ND (1897)	—	90.00	200.00	300.00	700.00

Y#	Year	Date	Fine	VF	XF	Unc
45.1	23	(1897)	—	—	17,500.	25,000.

Obv: Tall Chinese character '4' in date.
Rev: Similar to Y#45.

Y#	Year	Date	Fine	VF	XF	Unc
45.2	24	(1898)	90.00	200.00	300.00	675.00

Obv: Short Chinese character '4' in date.
Rev: Similar to Y#45.

Y#	Year	Date	Fine	VF	XF	Unc
45.5	24	(1898)	90.00	200.00	300.00	675.00

Obv: Tall Chinese character '4' in date, A S T C in field. Rev: Similar to Y#45.

Y#	Year	Date	Fine	VF	XF	Unc
45.3	24	(1898)	80.00	125.00	200.00	550.00

26.90 g
Obv. leg: 6 characters at top.
Rev: Similar to Y#45.1

Y#	Date	Mintage	Fine	VF	XF	Unc
45.4	CD1898	—	150.00	225.00	350.00	900.00

CHEKIANG PROVINCE

Zhejiang

A province located along the east coast of China. Although the smallest of the Chinese mainland provinces, it is one of the most densely populated. Mostly agricultural with iron and coal mining and some fishing. A small mint opened in 1897. This was replaced by a larger mint which operated briefly 1898-99. Other mints opened in 1903 and 1905. These were merged with the Fukien Mint in 1906-07.

EMPIRE

CASH

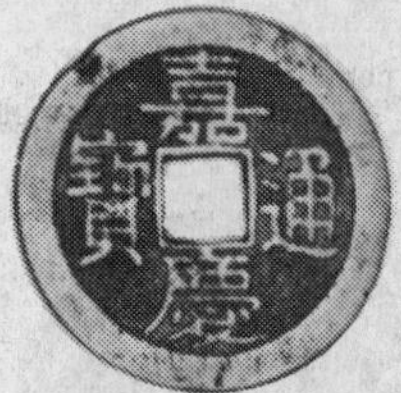

CAST BRASS
Obv: Type A
Rev: Large mint mark and normal rims.

C#	Date	Emperor	Good	VG	Fine	VF
4-2	ND (1796-1820)	Chia-ch'ing	.25	.50	.75	2.00

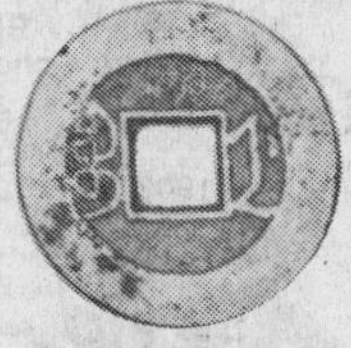

Rev: Small mint mark and wide rims.

C#	Date	Emperor	Good	VG	Fine	VF
4-2.1	ND (1796-1820)	Chia-ch'ing	.25	.50	.75	2.00

CAST IRON

C#	Date	Emperor	Good	VG	Fine	VF
4-2.1a	ND (1796-1820)	Chia-ch'ing	—	—	Rare	—

CAST BRASS
Rev: Dot at bottom.

C#	Date	Emperor	Good	VG	Fine	VF
4-2.2	ND (1796-1820)	Chia-ch'ing	2.00	3.50	5.00	10.00

Obv: Type A
Rev: Large mint mark. 23-25mm.

C#	Date	Emperor	Good	VG	Fine	VF
4-3	ND (1820-51)	Tao-kuang	.25	.50	.75	1.50

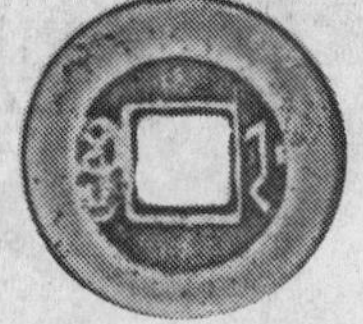

Rev: Small mint mark. 21-23mm.

C#	Date	Emperor	Good	VG	Fine	VF
4-3.1	ND (1820-51)	Tao-kuang	.35	.75	1.00	2.00

21-25mm
Obv: Type A

C#	Date	Emperor	Good	VG	Fine	VF
4-3.5	ND (1851-61)	Hsien-feng	1.00	2.00	3.00	6.00

16-20mm

C#	Date	Emperor	Good	VG	Fine	VF
4-3.6	ND (1851-61)	Hsien-feng	1.00	2.00	3.00	6.00

CAST IRON

C#	Date	Emperor	Good	VG	Fine	VF
4-3.6a	ND (1851-61)	Hsien-feng	6.50	12.50	25.00	55.00

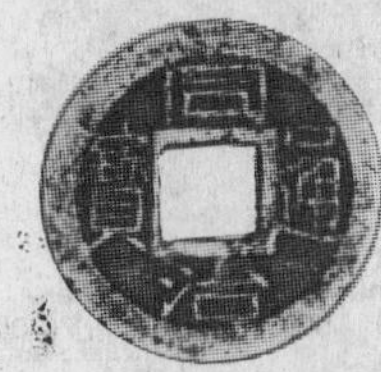

CAST BRASS
Obv: Type A-2

C#	Date	Emperor	Good	VG	Fine	VF
4-17	ND (1862-74)	T'ung-chih	1.25	2.50	4.00	8.00

Obv: Type A
Rev: Mint mark as C#4-2.

C#	Date	Emperor	Good	VG	Fine	VF
4-19	ND (1875-1908)	Kuang-hsu	3.00	4.50	6.50	12.00

Rev: More angular mint mark.

C#	Date	Emperor	Good	VG	Fine	VF
4-19.1	ND (1875-1908)	Kuang-hsu	1.00	2.00	3.00	6.00

CAST ZINC

C#	Date	Emperor	Good	VG	Fine	VF
4-19a	ND (1875-1908)	Kuang-hsu	—	—	Rare	—

10 CASH

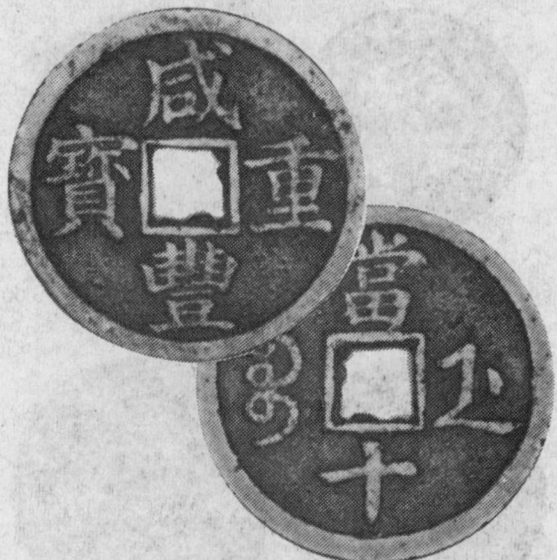

CAST BRASS
Obv: Type B-1
Rev: Manchu mint mark to right as above.
Denomination at bottom in Chinese.

C#	Date	Emperor	Good	VG	Fine	VF
4-4	ND (1851-61)	Hsien-feng	3.00	4.50	6.00	10.00

IRON, 36mm

C#	Date	Emperor	Good	VG	Fine	VF
4-4a	ND(1851-61)	Hsien-feng	—	—	—	—

CAST BRASS
Rev: Chinese character '10' at top.

C#	Date	Emperor	Good	VG	Fine	VF
4-9	ND (1851-61)	Hsien-feng	15.00	25.00	40.00	70.00

Rev: Manchu mint mark left and Chinese mint mark right. Denomination at bottom.

C#	Date	Emperor	Good	VG	Fine	VF
4-11	ND (1851-61)	Hsien-feng	50.00	85.00	140.00	200.00
4-18	ND (1862-74)	T'ung-chih	—	—	Rare	—

Obv: Type A

C#	Date	Emperor	Good	VG	Fine	VF
4-20	ND (1875-1908)	Kuang-hsu	—	—	Rare	—

20 CASH

CAST BRASS
Obv: Type B-1

C#	Date	Emperor	Good	VG	Fine	VF
4-5	ND (1851-61)	Hsien-feng	70.00	120.00	200.00	275.00

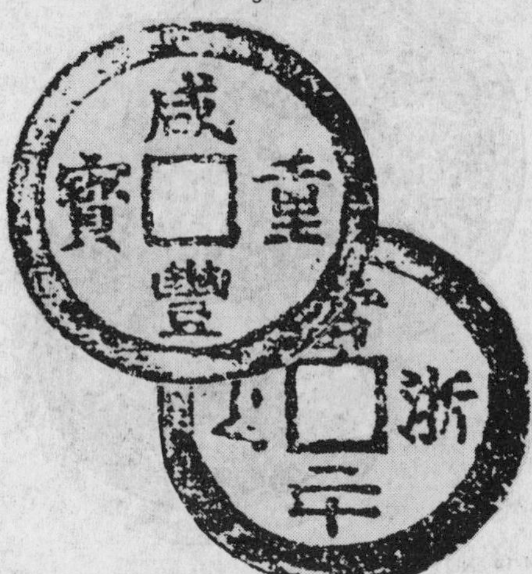

C#	Date	Emperor	Good	VG	Fine	VF
4-12	ND (1851-61)	Hsien-feng	70.00	120.00	200.00	275.00

30 CASH

CAST BRASS
Obv: Type B-1
Rev: Similar to 10 Cash, C#4-4.

C#	Date	Emperor	Good	VG	Fine	VF
4-6	ND (1851-61)	Hsien-feng	90.00	150.00	250.00	350.00

C#	Date	Emperor	Good	VG	Fine	VF
4-13	ND (1851-61)	Hsien-feng	90.00	150.00	250.00	350.00

40 CASH

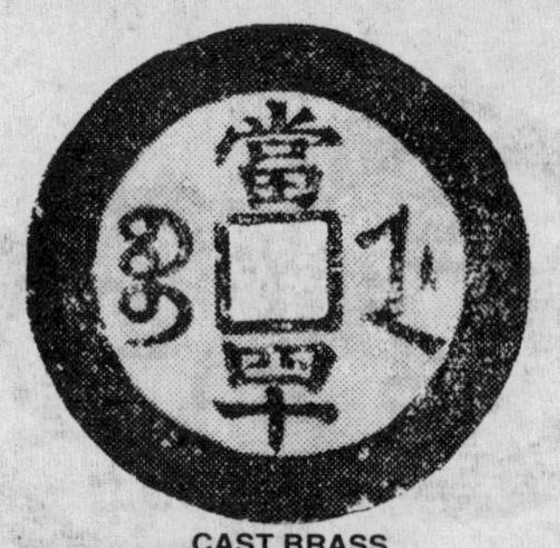

CAST BRASS
Obv: Type B-1

C#	Date	Emperor	Good	VG	Fine	VF
4-7	ND (1851-61)	Hsien-feng	100.00	165.00	275.00	400.00

C#	Date	Emperor	Good	VG	Fine	VF
4-14	ND (1851-61)	Hsien-feng	100.00	165.00	275.00	400.00

50 CASH

CAST BRASS
Obv: Type B-1
Rev: Similar to 10 Cash, C#4-4.

C#	Date	Emperor	Good	VG	Fine	VF
4-8	ND (1851-61)	Hsien-feng	120.00	200.00	350.00	500.00

Rev: Similar to 40 Cash, C#4-14.

C#	Date	Emperor	Good	VG	Fine	VF
4-15	ND (1851-61)	Hsien-feng	90.00	150.00	250.00	350.00

100 CASH

CAST BRASS
Obv: Type B-1

C#	Date	Emperor	Good	VG	Fine	VF
4-10	ND (1851-61)	Hsien-feng	100.00	165.00	275.00	400.00

Rev: Similar to 40 Cash, C#4-14.

C#	Date	Emperor	Good	VG	Fine	VF
4-16	ND (1851-61)	Hsien-feng	100.00	165.00	275.00	400.00

FANTASY ISSUES

NOTE: Coins of this mint in denominations of 400 Cash are considered fantasy issues.

MILLED COINAGE

CASH

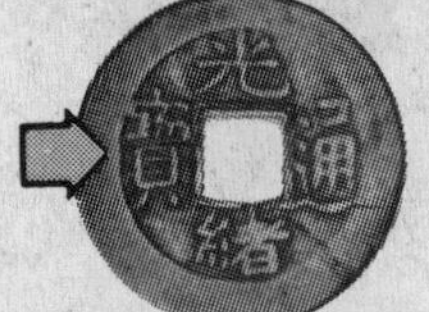

BRASS, struck
Obv: Type A, large *Pao* at left.

Hsu#	Date	Mintage	VG	Fine	VF	XF
151	ND(1887)	—	35.00	50.00	65.00	80.00

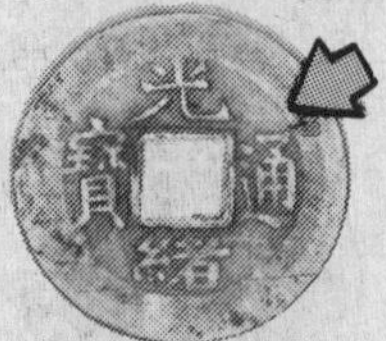

Obv: Top part of *T'ung* shaped like a triangle.

Hsu#	Date	Mintage	VG	Fine	VF	XF
151.1	ND(1897-98)	—	35.00	50.00	60.00	70.00

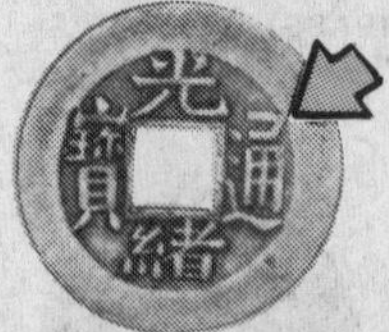
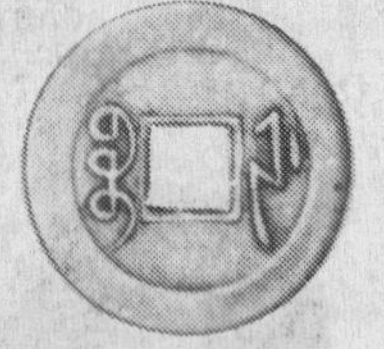

Obv: Top part of *T'ung* shaped like a box.

Hsu#	Date	Mintage	VG	Fine	VF	XF
151.2	ND(1897-98)	—	35.00	50.00	60.00	80.00

2 CASH

COPPER

Y#	Date	Mintage	VG	Fine	VF	XF
8b	CD1906	—	7.50	12.50	20.00	35.00

5 CASH

COPPER

Y#	Date	Mintage	VG	Fine	VF	XF
9b	CD1906	—	5.00	10.00	16.00	35.00

10 CASH

COPPER
Obv: Ball in circle in center.

Y#	Date	Mintage	VG	Fine	VF	XF
49	ND (1903-06)	—	.50	1.00	2.00	4.00

Obv: Rosette at center and large Manchu word at left.

Y#	Date	Mintage	VG	Fine	VF	XF
49.1	ND (1903-06)	—	.25	.50	1.25	2.50

BRASS

Y#	Date	Mintage	VG	Fine	VF	XF
49.1a	ND (1903-06)	—	2.00	4.00	8.00	15.00

COPPER
Similar to Y#49.1a

Y#	Date	Mintage	VG	Fine	VF	XF
49.2	ND (1903-06)	—	.75	1.50	3.00	6.00

Obv: Rosette at center and small Manchu word at left. Rev: Small cramped dragon w/few clouds around body.

Y#	Date	Mintage	VG	Fine	VF	XF
49.3	ND (1903-06)	—	.75	1.50	3.00	6.00

Rev: W/o ball in center circle.

Y#	Date	Mintage	VG	Fine	VF	XF
49.4	ND (1903-06)	—	1.25	2.50	5.00	10.00

BRASS
Obv. leg: 4 characters at bottom.

Y#	Date	Mintage	VG	Fine	VF	XF
49a	ND (1903-06)	—	3.00	6.00	11.00	20.00

COPPER

Y#	Date	Mintage	VG	Fine	VF	XF
49b	ND (1903-06)	—	6.00	12.00	25.00	45.00

Rev. leg: KUO spelled *KIIO*

Y#	Date	Mintage	VG	Fine	VF	XF
10b	CD1906	—	1.00	2.00	4.00	8.00

Rev. leg: KUO spelled *KUO*

Y#	Date	Mintage	VG	Fine	VF	XF
10b.1	CD1906	—	2.50	5.00	10.00	20.00

NOTE: Chekiang and other 10 Cash coin types found struck over Korean 5 Fun coins are counterfeits.

20 CASH

COPPER

Y#	Date	Mintage	VG	Fine	VF	XF
50	ND (1903-04)	—	50.00	100.00	150.00	225.00

NOTE: Exists in two different size planchets.

Y#	Date	Mintage	VG	Fine	VF	XF
11b	CD1906	—	40.00	75.00	125.00	200.00

5 CENTS

1.3500 g, .820 SILVER, .0356 oz ASW
Rev. leg: CHEH-KIANG. . . .,
3.2 CANDAREENS.

Y#	Date	Mintage	Fine	VF	XF	Unc
51	ND (1898-99)	—	15.00	25.00	40.00	100.00

10 CENTS

2.7000 g, .820 SILVER, .0712 oz ASW
Rev. leg: CHEH-KIANG. . . . .

Y#	Year	Date	Fine	VF	XF	Unc
52	22	(1896)	50.00	150.00	200.00	400.00
	Rev. leg: N's retrograde.					
52.1	22	(1896)	55.00	175.00	250.00	500.00
	Rev: Denomination reads 2.7 instead of 7.2.					
52.2	22	(1896)	50.00	100.00	200.00	400.00
52.3	23	(1897)	65.00	125.00	300.00	500.00

Y#	Date	Mintage	Fine	VF	XF	Unc
52.4	ND (1898-99)	—	15.00	25.00	35.00	75.00

20 CENTS

5.4000 g, .820 SILVER, .1424 oz ASW
Rev: 6 rows of scales on dragon.

Y#	Year	Date	Fine	VF	XF	Unc
53	22	(1896)	75.00	150.00	300.00	500.00
	Rev. leg: Letter E retrograde in CHEH-KIANG.					
53.1	22	(1896)	75.00	150.00	300.00	500.00
	Rev. leg: Additional cross-strokes in letter H in CHEH-KIANG. 8 rows of scales on dragon.					
53.2	22	(1896)	75.00	150.00	300.00	500.00
	Rev. leg: W/o hyphen in CHEH KIANG.					
53.3	22	(1896)	75.00	150.00	300.00	500.00
	Rev. leg: Dot in CHEH.KIANG.					
53.4	22	(1896)	75.00	150.00	300.00	500.00

Y#	Year	Date	Fine	VF	XF	Unc
	Rev: Rosettes made of 7 dots dividing leg.					
53.5	23	(1897)	80.00	150.00	300.00	550.00
	Rev: Rosettes replaced by a cross; leg: MACE misspelled NACE.					
53.6	23	(1897)	80.00	150.00	300.00	550.00

Rev. leg: CHEH-KIANG. . . . .

Y#	Date	Mintage	Fine	VF	XF	Unc
53.7	ND (1898-99)	—	15.00	30.00	50.00	150.00

50 CENTS

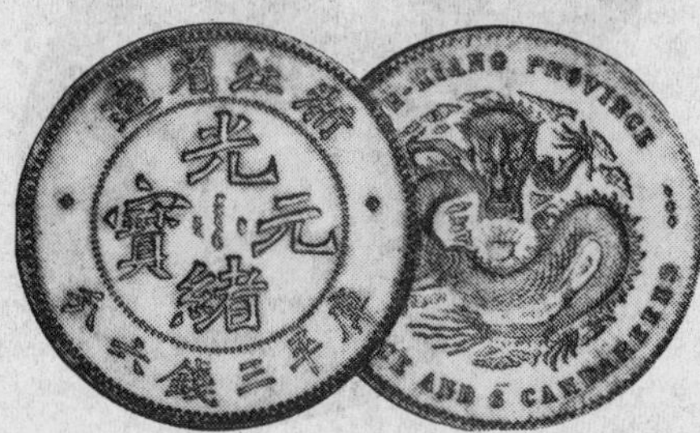

13.5000 g, .860 SILVER, .3733 oz ASW
Rev. leg: CHEH-KIANG. . . . .

Y#	Date	Mintage	Fine	VF	XF	Unc
54	ND (1898-99)	—	150.00	300.00	500.00	1100.

DOLLAR

27.5000 g, .900 SILVER, .7958 oz ASW
Rev. leg: CHEH-KIANG. . . . .

Y#	Date	Mintage	Fine	VF	XF	Unc
56	Yr.23 (1897)	—	—	—	Rare	—

NOTE: Superior Goodman Sale 6-91 AU realized $46,200.

Y#	Date	Mintage	Fine	VF	XF	Unc
55	ND(1898-99)	—	—	—	9900.	13,500.

REPUBLIC

10 CENTS

2.6500 g, .650 SILVER, .0554 oz ASW

Y#	Date	Mintage	Fine	VF	XF	Unc
371	Yr.13 (1924)	4.464	2.00	5.00	7.00	25.00

20 CENTS

SILVER, 5.30 g
Rev: Large 20

Y#	Year	Date	Fine	VF	XF	Unc
373	13	(1924)	300.00	500.00	700.00	1250.

CHIHLI PROVINCE

Hebei, Hopei

A province located in northeastern China which contains the eastern end of the Great Wall. An important producer of coal and some iron ore. In 1928 the provincial name was changed from Chihli to Hopei. The Paoting mint was established in 1745 and only produced cast cash coins.

A mint for struck cash was established in 1888 and the mint for the Peiyang silver coinage was added in 1896. This was destroyed during the Boxer Rebellion. A replacement mint was built in 1902 for the provincial coinage and merged with the Tientsin Central mint in 1910.

EMPIRE

Included here are coins inscribed PEI YANG. These were produced by the mint in the Peiyang Arsenal in Tientsin. For coins inscribed PEKING, see General Issues.

Chengde Mint

(Jehol)

CASH

CAST BRASS
Obv: Type A.

C#	Date	Emperor	Good	VG	Fine	VF
6-1	ND(1851-61)	Hsien-feng	50.00	65.00	75.00	110.00
	CAST IRON					
6-1a	ND(1851-61)	Hsien-feng	20.00	30.00	50.00	—

5 CASH

CAST BRASS

C#	Date	Emperor	Good	VG	Fine	VF
6-2	ND(1851-61)	Hsien-feng	60.00	80.00	125.00	200.00

CAST IRON

C#	Date	Emperor	Good	VG	Fine	VF
6-2a	ND(1851-61)	Hsien-feng	20.00	30.00	50.00	90.00

10 CASH

CAST BRASS
Obv: Type B-1.

C#	Date	Emperor	Good	VG	Fine	VF
6-3	ND(1851-61)	Hsien-feng	30.00	50.00	75.00	100.00

CAST IRON

C#	Date	Emperor	Good	VG	Fine	VF
6-3a	ND(1851-61)	Hsien-feng	32.50	55.00	90.00	150.00

50 CASH

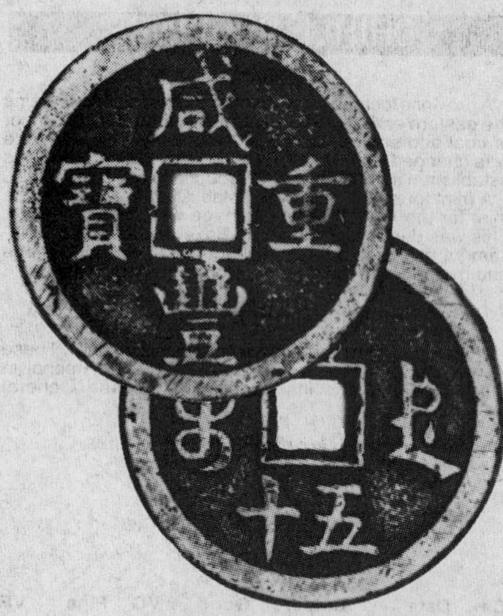

CAST BRASS
Obv: Type B-1.

C#	Date	Emperor	Good	VG	Fine	VF
6-4	ND(1851-61)	Hsien-feng	13.50	22.50	37.50	75.00

100 CASH

CAST BRASS

C#	Date	Emperor	Good	VG	Fine	VF
6-5	ND(1851-61)	Hsien-feng	50.00	70.00	100.00	150.00

FANTASY ISSUES

NOTE: Coins of this mint in denominations of 500 and 1000 Cash are considered fantasy issues.

Chichow Mint

5 CASH

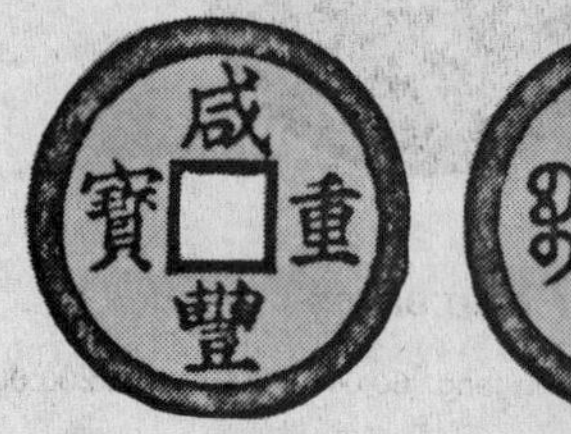

CAST BRASS
Obv: Type B-1

C#	Date	Emperor	Good	VG	Fine	VF
7-1	ND (1851-61)	Hsien-feng	27.50	45.00	75.00	125.00

CAST IRON

C#	Date	Emperor	Good	VG	Fine	VF
7-1a	ND (1851-61)	Hsien-feng	40.00	60.00	85.00	140.00

10 CASH

CAST BRASS
Large size, 35mm.

C#	Date	Emperor	Good	VG	Fine	VF
7-2	ND (1851-61)	Hsien-feng	22.50	37.50	60.00	100.00

Small size, 27mm.

C#	Date	Emperor	Good	VG	Fine	VF
7-2.1	ND (1851-61)	Hsien-feng	20.00	32.50	55.00	90.00

CAST IRON

C#	Date	Emperor	Good	VG	Fine	VF
7-2a	ND (1851-61)	Hsien-feng	27.50	45.00	75.00	125.00

50 CASH

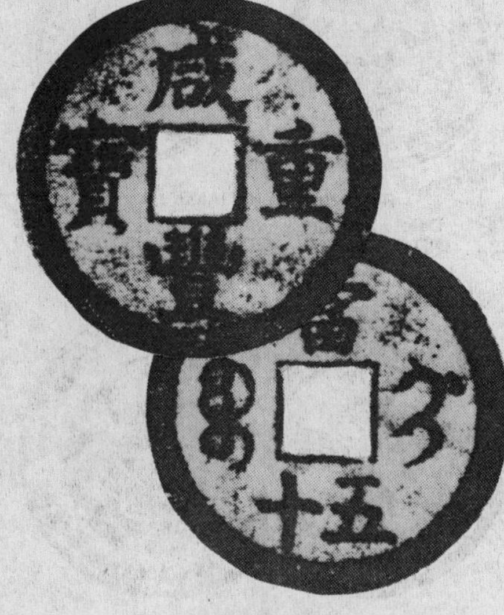

CAST BRASS

C#	Date	Emperor	Good	VG	Fine	VF
7-3	ND (1851-61)	Hsien-feng	20.00	32.50	55.00	100.00

100 CASH

CAST BRASS

C#	Date	Emperor	Good	VG	Fine	VF
7-4	ND (1851-61)	Hsien-feng	25.00	40.00	65.00	135.00

NOTE: This mint mark was later transferred to the Kirin Mint; the Chichow Mint operated through the reign of Hsien Feng.

Paoting Mint

CASH

CAST BRASS
Obv: Type A
26mm

C#	Date	Emperor	Good	VG	Fine	VF
5-2	ND (1796-1820)	Chia-ch'ing	.40	.75	1.25	2.00

31mm

C#	Date	Emperor	Good	VG	Fine	VF
5-2.1	ND(1796-1820)	Chia-ch'ing	60.00	80.00	115.00	175.00

Obv: Type A

C#	Date	Emperor	Good	VG	Fine	VF
5-3	ND (1820-51)	Tao-kuang	.45	.75	1.25	2.00

Rev: Dot below.

C#	Date	Emperor	Good	VG	Fine	VF
5-3.1	ND (1820-51)	Tao-kuang	2.50	3.50	6.00	10.00

Obv: Type A

C#	Date	Emperor	Good	VG	Fine	VF
5-4	ND (1851-61)	Hsien-feng	2.00	3.50	6.00	10.00

CAST IRON

C#	Date	Emperor	Good	VG	Fine	VF
5-4a	ND (1851-61)	Hsien-feng	11.50	18.50	30.00	55.00

CAST BRASS
Obv: Type A-2

C#	Date	Emperor	Good	VG	Fine	VF
5-8	ND (1862-74)	T'ung-chih	3.50	6.00	10.00	16.50

Obv: Type A

C#	Date	Emperor	Good	VG	Fine	VF
5-10	ND (1875-1908)	Kuang-hsu	3.50	6.00	10.00	16.50

Rev: Dot above.

C#	Date	Emperor	Good	VG	Fine	VF
5-10.1	ND (1875-1908)	Kuang-hsu	4.50	7.50	12.50	25.00

Rev: Crescent above.

C#	Date	Emperor	Good	VG	Fine	VF
5-10.2	ND (1875-1908)	Kuang-hsu	4.50	7.50	12.00	20.00

NOTE: The crescent is known in various positions above the center hole.

Rev: Circle above.

C#	Date	Emperor	Good	VG	Fine	VF
5-10.3	ND (1875-1908)	Kuang-hsu	4.50	7.50	12.50	25.00

Rev: Dot below.

C#	Date	Emperor	Good	VG	Fine	VF
5-10.4	ND (1875-1908)	Kuang-hsu	3.50	6.00	10.00	16.00

Rev: Circle below.

C#	Date	Emperor	Good	VG	Fine	VF
5-10.5	ND (1875-1908)	Kuang-hsu	4.50	7.50	12.00	20.00

Rev: Dash above.

C#	Date	Emperor	Good	VG	Fine	VF
5-10.6	ND (1875-1908)	Kuang-hsu	4.50	7.50	12.00	20.00

Rev: Dash below.

C#	Date	Emperor	Good	VG	Fine	VF
5-10.7	ND (1875-1908)	Kuang-hsu	4.50	7.50	12.00	20.00

10 CASH

CAST BRASS
Obv: Type B-1

C#	Date	Emperor	Good	VG	Fine	VF
5-5	ND (1851-61)	Hsien-feng	10.00	17.50	30.00	50.00

CAST IRON

C#	Date	Emperor	Good	VG	Fine	VF
5-5a	ND (1851-61)	Hsien-feng	30.00	45.00	75.00	125.00

CAST BRASS
Rev: Dot above.

C#	Date	Emperor	Good	VG	Fine	VF
5-5.1	ND (1851-61)	Hsien-feng	13.50	21.50	37.50	60.00
5-9	ND (1862-74)	T'ung-chih	—	—	Rare	—
5-11	ND (1875-1908)	Kuang-hsu	—	—	Rare	—

50 CASH

CAST BRASS
Obv: Type B-1

C#	Date	Emperor	Good	VG	Fine	VF
5-6	ND (1851-61)	Hsien-feng	25.00	40.00	65.00	130.00

Rev: Dot at upper right; crescent upper left.

C#	Date	Emperor	Good	VG	Fine	VF
5.6.1	ND (1851-61)	Hsien-feng	27.50	45.00	75.00	140.00

100 CASH

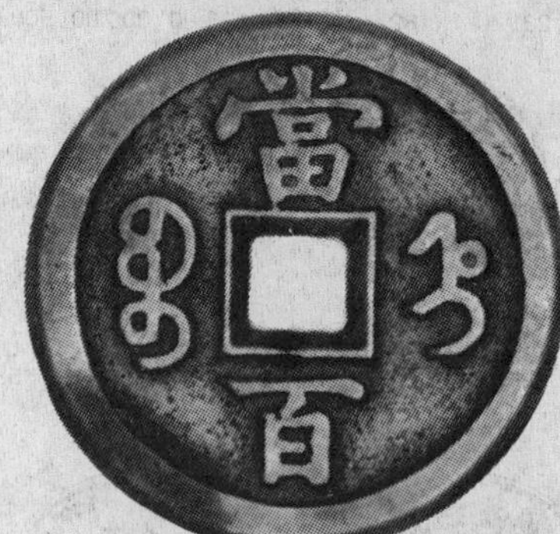

CAST BRASS
Obv: Type C.

C#	Date	Emperor	Good	VG	Fine	VF
5-7	ND (1851-61)	Hsien-feng	25.00	40.00	65.00	130.00

1000 CASH

CAST BRASS

A5-7 ND (1851-61) Hsien-feng — Reported, not confirmed

Peiyang Arsenal Mint

(Tientsin)

CASH

CAST BRASS
Obv: Type A

C#	Date	Emperor	Good	VG	Fine	VF
8-1	ND (1875-1908)	Kuang-hsu	2.50	4.50	7.50	12.00

Rev: Dot above.

C#	Date	Emperor	Good	VG	Fine	VF
8-1.1	ND (1875-1908)	Kuang-hsu	2.75	4.50	7.50	15.00

Rev: Dot below.

C#	Date	Emperor	Good	VG	Fine	VF
8-1.2	ND (1875-1908)	Kuang-hsu	2.00	3.50	6.00	10.00

Rev: 2 dots below.

C#	Date	Emperor	Good	VG	Fine	VF
8-1.3	ND (1875-1908)	Kuang-hsu	3.50	5.50	9.00	15.00

Rev: Circle above.

C#	Date	Emperor	Good	VG	Fine	VF
8-1.4	ND (1875-1908)	Kuang-hsu	3.50	5.50	9.00	18.00

Rev: Circle below.

C#	Date	Emperor	Good	VG	Fine	VF
8-1.5	ND (1875-1908)	Kuang-hsu	3.50	5.50	9.00	18.00

Rev: Crescent above.

C#	Date	Emperor	Good	VG	Fine	VF
8-1.6	ND (1875-1908)	Kuang-hsu	3.50	5.50	9.00	18.00

Rev: Crescent below.

C#	Date	Emperor	Good	VG	Fine	VF
8-1.7	ND (1875-1908)	Kuang-hsu	2.00	3.75	7.50	17.00

Rev: Dash below.

C#	Date	Emperor	Good	VG	Fine	VF
8-1.8	ND (1875-1908)	Kuang-hsu	2.00	3.75	7.50	15.00

NOTE: Varieties exist with dots and crescents in different corners on reverse and also with incuse dots.

MILLED COINAGE

CASH

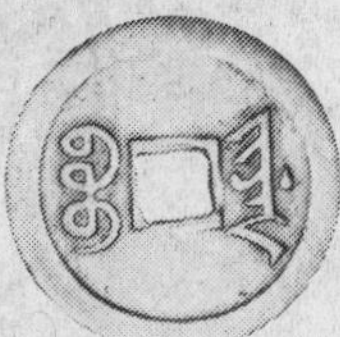

BRASS
Obv: Type A
Obv: Small characters. Rev: Large characters.

Hsu#	Date	Mintage	VG	Fine	VF	XF
410	ND (1888-89)	—	40.00	50.00	75.00	120.00

Obv: Large characters. Rev: Small characters.

Hsu#	Date	Mintage	VG	Fine	VF	XF
410.1	ND (1888-89)	—	40.00	50.00	75.00	120.00

Obv: and rev: Small characters.

Hsu#	Date	Mintage	VG	Fine	VF	XF
410.2	ND (1888-89)	—	10.00	20.00	30.00	45.00

Obv: and rev: Large characters.

Hsu#	Date	Mintage	VG	Fine	VF	XF
410.3	ND (1888-89)	—	40.00	50.00	75.00	110.00

Y#	Date	Mintage	VG	Fine	VF	XF
66	ND(1904-07)	—	1.50	3.00	5.50	10.00

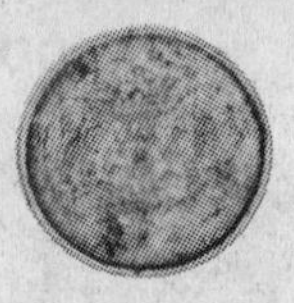

Y#	Date	Mintage	VG	Fine	VF	XF
7c	CD1908	—	2.50	4.50	7.50	13.50

5 CASH

COPPER

Y#	Date	Mintage	VG	Fine	VF	XF
9c	CD1906	—	4.50	8.50	15.00	27.50

10 CASH

COPPER
Rev: Hole in center of rosettes, square mouth dragon.

Y#	Date	Mintage	VG	Fine	VF	XF
67	ND	—	.50	1.00	1.75	3.00

NOTE: Mulings exist with obverse of Kwangtung (-Guangdong) Y#192 and reverse of Chihli Y#67. Refer to Kwangtung listings.

Rev: Round mouth dragon.

Y#	Date	Mintage	VG	Fine	VF	XF
67.1	ND	—	.50	1.00	1.75	3.00

Rev: Dot in center of rosettes, square mouth dragon.

Y#	Date	Mintage	VG	Fine	VF	XF
67.2	ND	—	.50	1.00	1.75	3.00

Rev: Round mouth dragon.

Y#	Date	Mintage	VG	Fine	VF	XF
67.3	ND	—	.50	1.00	1.75	3.00

Rev: Redesigned dragon with smaller body and smaller English legends.

Y#	Date	Mintage	VG	Fine	VF	XF
67.4	ND	—	1.50	3.50	7.00	15.00

Y#	Date	Mintage	VG	Fine	VF	XF
10c	CD1906	—	.50	1.00	2.00	4.00

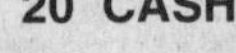

20 CASH

COPPER

Y#	Date	Mintage	VG	Fine	VF	XF
68	ND	—	7.50	15.00	27.50	65.00

BRASS

Y#	Date	Mintage	VG	Fine	VF	XF
68a	ND	—	10.00	20.00	40.00	80.00

COPPER
Rev: Smaller lettering.

Y#	Date	Mintage	VG	Fine	VF	XF
68.1	ND	—	10.00	20.00	40.00	80.00

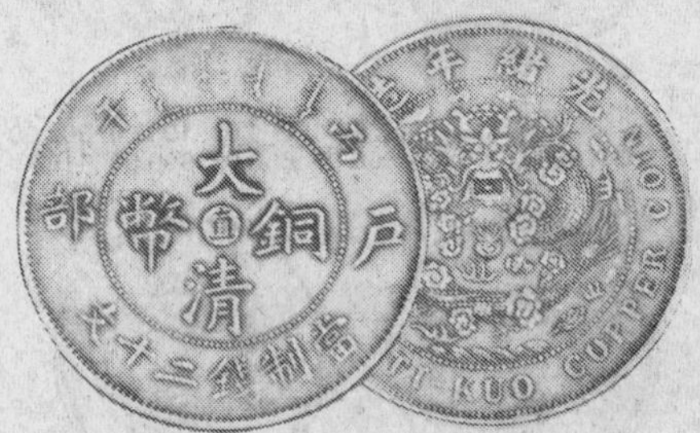

Y#	Date	Mintage	VG	Fine	VF	XF
11c	CD1906	—	15.00	30.00	60.00	120.00

5 CENTS

1.3200 g, .820 SILVER, .0348 oz ASW

Y#	Date	Mintage	Fine	VF	XF	Unc
61	Yr.22 (1896)	7,000	200.00	250.00	300.00	650.00

Obv. leg: ***TAI TSING. . . . .***

Y#	Date	Mintage	Fine	VF	XF	Unc
61.1	Yr.23 (1897)	Inc. Ab.	25.00	50.00	100.00	225.00

Rev: Redesigned dragon.

Y#	Date	Mintage	Fine	VF	XF	Unc
61.2 (61.1)	Yr.23 (1897)	.039	18.00	35.00	55.00	120.00
	Yr.24 (1898)	.231	15.00	25.00	35.00	100.00

Y#	Date	Mintage	Fine	VF	XF	Unc
69	Yr.25 (1899)	.097	20.00	50.00	75.00	125.00
	Yr.26 (1900)	—	125.00	250.00	500.00	1000.

10 CENTS

2.6500 g, .820 SILVER, .0699 oz ASW

Y#	Date	Mintage	Fine	VF	XF	Unc
62	Yr.22 (1896)	5,000	85.00	150.00	200.00	500.00

Obv. leg: ***TAI TSING. . . . .***

Y#	Date	Mintage	Fine	VF	XF	Unc
62.1	Yr.23 (1897)	.148	15.00	25.00	40.00	100.00
	Yr.24 (1898)	.614	12.00	20.00	30.00	100.00
70	Yr.25 (1899)	.153	20.00	50.00	75.00	150.00

20 CENTS

5.3000 g, .820 SILVER, .1397 oz ASW

Y#	Date	Mintage	Fine	VF	XF	Unc
63.1	Yr.22 (1896)	.012	100.00	225.00	400.00	750.00

Obv. leg: *TAI TSING. . . . .*

Y#	Date	Mintage	Fine	VF	XF	Unc
63.2	Yr.23 (1897)	.147	16.50	30.00	45.00	120.00
	Yr.24 (1898)	.350	15.00	25.00	40.00	100.00

Y#	Date	Mintage	Fine	VF	XF	Unc
71	Yr.25 (1899)	.152	25.00	50.00	100.00	300.00
	Yr.26 (1900)	—	500.00	650.00	900.00	1500.

Y#	Date	Mintage	Fine	VF	XF	Unc
71a	Yr.31 (1905)	.161	35.00	75.00	150.00	350.00

50 CENTS

13.3000 g, .860 SILVER, .3678 oz ASW

Y#	Date	Mintage	Fine	VF	XF	Unc
64	Yr.22 (1896)	2,500	400.00	800.00	1250.	2500.

Obv. leg: *TAI TSING. . . . .*
Rev: Dragon w/beady eyes.

Y#	Date	Mintage	Fine	VF	XF	Unc
64.1	Yr.23 (1897)	.021	30.00	65.00	125.00	300.00
	Yr.24 (1898)	I.A.	30.00	65.00	125.00	300.00

Rev: Dragon w/eyelids.

64.2 Yr.24 (1898)

Y#	Date	Mintage	Fine	VF	XF	Unc
72	Yr.25 (1899)	.056	75.00	140.00	225.00	400.00

DOLLAR

26.7000 g, .900 SILVER, .7727 oz ASW

Y#	Date	Mintage	Fine	VF	XF	Unc
65	Yr.22 (1896)	3,000	1000.	2000.	4000.	6500.

Rev: Dragon w/beady eyes.

Y#	Date	Mintage	Fine	VF	XF	Unc
65.1	Yr.23 (1897)	1.120	30.00	90.00	300.00	650.00

Rev: Dragon w/eyelids.

Y#	Date	Mintage	Fine	VF	XF	Unc
65.2	Yr.24 (1898)	2.806	20.00	80.00	200.00	600.00

Obv: Similar to Y#73.2.

Y#	Date	Mintage	Fine	VF	XF	Unc
73	Yr.25 (1899)	1.566	15.00	30.00	50.00	300.00
	Yr.26 (1900)	—	40.00	75.00	125.00	650.00
	Yr.29 (1903)	22.018	8.00	17.00	42.50	200.00

Rev. leg: Period after PEI YANG.

Y#	Date	Mintage	Fine	VF	XF	Unc
73.1	Yr.29 (1903)	I.A.	8.00	17.00	40.00	200.00

Rev: Thinner dragon.

Y#	Date	Mintage	Fine	VF	XF	Unc
73.2	Yr.33 (1907)	2.341	8.00	20.00	45.00	250.00
	Yr.34 (1908)	—	8.00	20.00	35.00	175.00

Rev: Short center spine to tail.

Y#	Date	Mintage	Fine	VF	XF	Unc
73.3	Yr.34 (1908)	—	8.00	12.00	25.00	175.00

Rev: Crosslet 4 in date.

Y#	Date	Mintage	Fine	VF	XF	Unc
73.4	Yr.34 (1908)	—	45.00	100.00	150.00	600.00

NOTE: The 1907 issue has the year as '33th'. The 34th year (1908) issue was restruck during Republican times.

TAEL

SILVER, 51.20 g

Y#	Year	Date	Fine	VF	XF	Unc
74	33	(1907)	—	3250.	4500.	8000.
		Rev: 3 dots on pearl arranged horizontally.				
74.1	33	(1907)	—	3250.	4500.	8000.
		Rev: 3 dots on pearl arranged in arc.				
74.2	33	(1907)	—	3250.	4500.	8000.

Taku Mint

(Imperial Naval Yard)

CASH

CAST BRASS
Obv: Type A. Rev: Type 2 mint mark.

C#	Date	Emperor	Good	VG	Fine	VF
3-1.1	ND (1875-1908)	Kuang-hsu	30.00	55.00	75.00	125.00

Obv: Type A. Rev: Type 2 mint mark.

C#	Date	Emperor	Good	VG	Fine	VF
3-1.2	ND(1875-1908)	Kuang-hsu	15.00	27.50	37.50	70.00

CHINGKIANG

For coins of Chingkiang refer to listings under Kiangsu.

FENGTIEN PROVINCE

(Fungtien)

Liaoning

The southernmost province of the Three Eastern Provinces was known by a variety of names including Fengtien, Shengching, and Liaoning. The modern Mukden (Fengtien Province) Mint operated from 1897 to 1931.

EMPIRE

CASH

CAST BRASS
Obv: Type A.

#	Date	Emperor				
9-1	ND (1875-1908)	Kuang-hsu	—	—	Rare	—

MILLED COINAGE

5 CASH

COPPER

Y#	Date	Mintage	VG	Fine	VF	XF
19e	CD1909	—	37.50	75.00	125.00	200.00

10 CASH

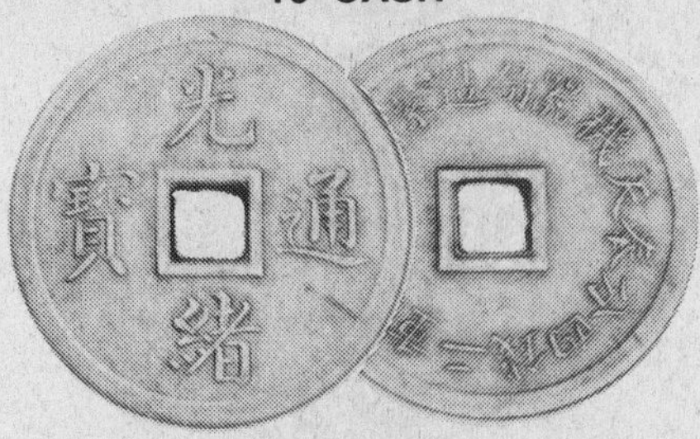

COPPER
Obv: Type A.

Y#	Date	Mintage	VG	Fine	VF	XF
81	ND	—	40.00	60.00	90.00	200.00

NOTE: Seven varieties exist.

BRASS
Province name spelled FEN-TIEN.

Y#	Date	Mintage	VG	Fine	VF	XF
88	CD1903	—	50.00	90.00	135.00	225.00

Province name spelled FUNG-TIEN.

Y#	Date	Mintage	VG	Fine	VF	XF
89	CD1903	—	3.75	7.50	25.00	40.00
	CD1904	—	1.25	3.00	5.00	8.00
	CD1905	—	1.50	4.50	10.00	12.00
	CD1906	35.036	3.00	6.00	25.00	35.00

Obv: Manchu words in center reversed.

Y#	Date	Mintage	Fine	VF	XF	Unc
89.1	CD1903	—	85.00	150.00	250.00	—
	Rev: Large pearl.					
89.2	CD1905	—	2.00	4.00	8.00	24.00

COPPER
Rev: Small pearl.

Y#	Date	Mintage	Fine	VF	XF	Unc
10e	CD1905	—	4.00	8.00	15.00	30.00
	Rev: Large pearl.					
10e.1	CD1905	—	4.00	8.00	15.00	30.00

Obv: Mint mark on spherical disc in center.

Y#	Date	Mintage	Fine	VF	XF	Unc
10e.2	CD1907	130.000	1.50	3.00	6.00	20.00

Obv: Mint mark on flat disc in center.

Y#	Date	Mintage	Fine	VF	XF	Unc
10e.3	CD1907	Inc. Ab.	1.50	3.00	6.00	20.00

Y#	Date	Mintage	Fine	VF	XF	Unc
20e	CD1909	—	8.00	17.50	30.00	—
	Mule. Obv: Y#20e. Rev: Y#10e.					
W286	CD1909	6 known	—	—	Rare	—

20 CASH

BRASS

Y#	Date	Mintage	VG	Fine	VF	XF
90	CD1903	—	75.00	100.00	125.00	175.00
	CD1904	—	5.50	11.00	22.50	55.00
	CD1905	—	9.00	18.00	25.00	60.00

COPPER

Y#	Date	Mintage	VG	Fine	VF	XF
11e	CD1905	—	4.00	7.00	20.00	40.00
	CD1907	—	6.00	12.00	25.00	50.00

Y#	Date	Mintage	VG	Fine	VF	XF
21e	CD1909	—	25.00	60.00	110.00	175.00

5 CENTS

SILVER, 1.20 g

Y#	Year	Date	Fine	VF	XF	Unc
83	25	(1899)	20.00	40.00	70.00	200.00

10 CENTS

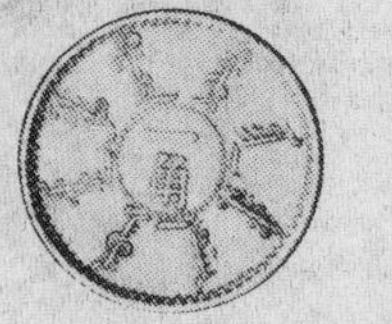

SILVER

Year	Date	Fine	VF	XF	Unc
24	(1898)	20.00	40.00	70.00	200.00

20 CENTS

SILVER, 5.20 g
Rev: 4 rows of scales on dragon.
Clockwise spiral on pearl.

85	24	(1898)	15.00	30.00	55.00	160.00

Rev: 5 rows of scales on dragon.
Counter-clockwise spiral on pearl.

85.1	24	(1898)	15.00	30.00	55.00	160.00

24mm, 8 rows of scales on dragon.

Y#	Date	Mintage	Fine	VF	XF	Unc
91	CD1904	—	8.00	14.00	25.00	70.00

25mm, 5 rows of scales on dragon.

91.1	CD1904	—	9.00	16.00	30.00	80.00

50 CENTS

SILVER, 13.10 g

86	Yr.32(1897)*	—	—	—	Rare	—
	Yr.24(1898)	—	100.00	150.00	250.00	500.00
	Yr.25(1899)	—	200.00	350.00	500.00	800.00

***NOTE:** (error) year 32 should read year 23 (1897).

DOLLAR

26.4000 g, .850 SILVER, .7215 oz ASW

Y#	Year	Date	Fine	VF	XF	Unc
87	24	(1898)	25.00	150.00	300.00	650.00
	25	(1899)	300.00	450.00	550.00	900.00

Obv: 2 center Chinese characters within double circle, 1 of dots around 1 solid.

87.1	25	(1899)	200.00	375.00	500.00	800.00

Y#	Date	Mintage	Fine	VF	XF	Unc
92	CD1903	.262	85.00	150.00	300.00	650.00

Obv: Manchu words in center are reversed.

92.1	CD1903	Inc. Ab.	100.00	175.00	325.00	675.00

MANCHURIAN PROVINCES

Since the 17th century, Manchuria has been divided into three provinces. The two northern provinces were called Heilungkiang and Kirin. Together the three provinces of Manchuria were known as the Manchurian Provinces in English or the Three Eastern Provinces in Chinese. Since the communist takeover in 1949, western Mongol-populated areas of Manchuria have been included in the Inner Mongolia Autonomous Region.

10 CENTS

2.6000 g, .890 SILVER, .0744 oz ASW

Y#	Date	Mintage	Fine	VF	XF	Unc
209	Yr.33 (1907)	1.079	10.00	25.00	40.00	100.00

20 CENTS

5.2000 g, .890 SILVER, .1488 oz ASW
Obv: 1 dot at either side.

210	Yr.33 (1907)		20.00	30.00	60.00	120.00

5.2000 g, .800 SILVER, .1338 oz ASW
Obv: 3 rosettes at either side.

210a.1	Yr.33 (ca.1908)	249.219	9.00	17.50	35.00	70.00

Obv: 1 rosette at either side.

210a.2	Yr.33 (ca.1908)	Inc. Ab.	6.00	12.00	20.00	60.00

Hsuan-t'ung
Obv: 1 large 6 petalled rosette at either side.
Rev: Date as 1ST YEAR.

213.2	Yr.1 (1909)	I.A.	4.00	8.50	15.00	40.00

Obv: 2 small stars flanking 1 large star at either side.
Rev: Date given as FIRST YEAR.

213	Yr.1 (ca.1910)	Inc. Ab.	4.00	7.50	12.50	30.00

Obv: 1 small star at either side.

213.1	Yr.1 (ca.1910)	Inc. Ab.	4.00	8.50	15.00	35.00

Obv: Manchu words at center.
Rev. leg: PROVIENCES (error).

213a	ND (ca.1911)	I.A.	4.00	8.50	15.00	35.00

Obv: W/o Manchu words at center.
Rev: PROVIENCES (error).

213a.6	ND (ca.1912)	I.A.	5.00	10.00	20.00	40.00

5.2000 g, .700 SILVER, .1170 oz ASW
Obv: W/o Manchu at center.
Rev. leg: PROVINCES.

Y#	Date	Mintage	Fine	VF	XF	Unc
213a.4	ND (ca.1913)	I.A.	5.00	10.00	20.00	40.00

Obv: 5 petalled rosette in center w/dot in center of rosette. Dot below side rosettes.

213a.1	ND (ca.1914-15)	Inc. Ab.	4.00	8.50	15.00	30.00

Obv: W/o dot below side rosettes.

213a.2	ND (ca.1914-15)	Inc. Ab.	4.00	8.50	15.00	30.00

Obv: W/o dot in center of 5 petalled rosette.

213a.3	ND (ca.1914-15)	Inc. Ab.	4.00	8.50	15.00	30.00

50 CENTS

13.1000 g, .890 SILVER, .3749 oz ASW

Y#	Year	Date	Fine	VF	XF	Unc
211	33	(1907)	150.00	250.00	350.00	800.00

DOLLAR

26.4000 g, .890 SILVER, .7555 oz ASW

212	33	(1907)	200.00	400.00	700.00	1500.

REPUBLIC
CENT

COPPER

Y#	Year	Date	Fine	VF	XF	Unc
434	18	(1929)	2.00	3.00	5.00	25.00

FUKIEN PROVINCE

Fujian

A province located on the southeastern coast of China, including the island of Taiwan until it became its own separate province in 1885. Although known mainly as an agricultural area, forestry and some mining, particularly iron ore and coal, are also important to the economy. The Foochow Mint operated throughout the Manchu dynasty. The Viceroy's or City mint was opened in 1896 for struck coinage. Two other mints were established in 1905, the Mamoi Arsenal Mint which struck the Custom-House issues until it closed in 1906, and the West Mint which later became the main Fukien (Fujian) Mint. It closed between 1914 and 1920. Various subsidiary mints were in operation from 1924 to 1925.

EMPIRE
Fuchow Mint
CASH

CAST COPPER or BRASS
Obv: Type A

C#	Date	Emperor	Good	VG	Fine	VF
10-2	ND (1796-1820)	Chia-ch'ing	.50	1.00	2.00	3.00

Rev: Thin Manchu at right.

10-2.1	ND (1796-1820)	Chia-ch'ing	.75	2.25	3.25	5.00

Rev: Different Manchu at right.

10-2.2	ND (1796-1820)	Chia-ch'ing	.50	1.00	2.25	4.00

CAST COPPER or BRASS
Obv: Type A

10-3	ND (1821-51)	Tao-kuang	1.00	2.50	3.00	4.50

Obv: Type A
Rev: Line right of mint mark. 26mm.

10-4	ND (1851-61)	Hsien-feng	2.00	3.00	4.00	10.00

Rev: Dot right of mint mark. 22-24mm.

C#	Date	Emperor	Good	VG	Fine	VF
10-4.1	ND (1851-61)	Hsien-feng	2.50	3.50	5.50	12.50

CAST IRON

10-4a.1	ND (1851-61)	Hsien-feng	15.00	27.00	37.50	60.00

Larger size. Wide rims.

10-4a.2	ND (1851-61)	Hsien-feng	20.00	35.00	50.00	75.00

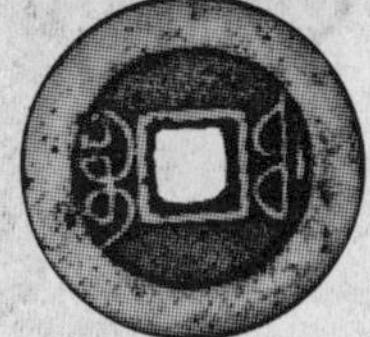

CAST BRASS
Obv: Type A-2

10-22	ND (1862-74)	T'ung-chih	1.25	2.50	4.00	6.00

Obv: Type A

10-25	ND (1875-1908)	Kuang-hsu	1.00	2.00	4.00	6.00

Rev: Dot at top of hole.

10-25.1	ND (1875-1908)	Kuang-hsu	2.50	4.00	6.50	10.00

Rev: Inverted.

10-25.2	ND(1875-1908)	Kuang-hsu	—	—	—	—

5 CASH

BRASS, 31mm
Rev: Weight on the rim similar to 20 Cash, C#10-12.

10-5	ND (1851-61)	Hsien-feng	40.00	70.00	110.00	150.00

Rev: *5 Wen* at top.

10-5.1	ND(1854)	Hsien-feng	—	—	—	—

10 CASH

CAST BRASS, 35-40mm.
Obv: Type A

C#	Date	Emperor	Good	VG	Fine	VF
10-6	ND (1851-61)	Hsien-feng	4.00	8.00	17.00	30.00

Rev: Characters *Ta Ching* appear at upper left and right.

10-6.1	ND (1851-61)	Hsien-feng	—	—	Rare	—

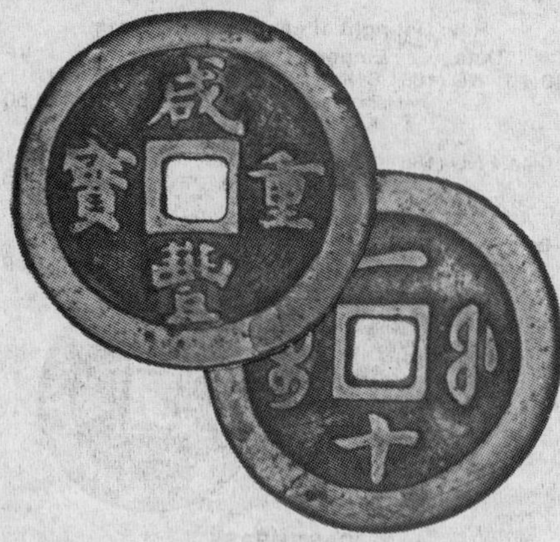

Obv: Type B-1

10-7	ND (1851-61)	Hsien-feng	8.50	15.00	18.50	35.00

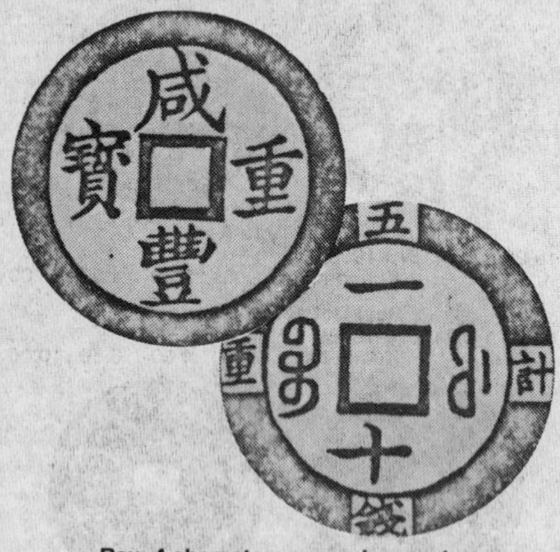

Rev: 4 characters appearing on rim.

10-8	ND (1851-61)	Hsien-feng	12.50	20.00	30.00	100.00

CAST IRON

10-8a	ND (1851-61)	Hsien-feng	—	—	Rare	—

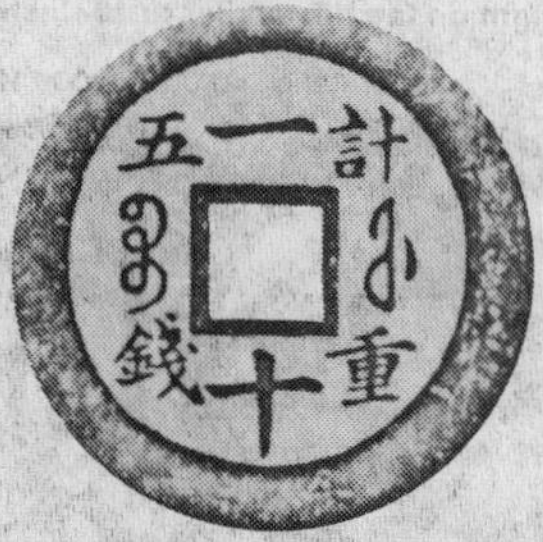

CAST BRASS

10-9	ND (1851-61)	Hsien-feng	70.00	110.00	150.00	275.00

42mm
Rev. leg: 4 characters at top, 4 different characters at bottom. Mint mark (at right) has a crescent at right instead of a dot.

10-9.1	ND (1851-61)	Hsien-feng	—	—	Rare	—

35mm. Rev: Chinese mint mark at right, Manchu mint mark at left.

10-9.2	ND (1851-61)	Hsien-feng	—	—	Rare	—
10-23	ND (1862-74)	T'ung-chih	—	—	Rare	—
10-26	ND (1875-1908)	Kuang-hsu	—	—	Rare	—

NOTE: C#10-9.2, 10-23 and 10-26 are unofficial issues.

20 CASH

CAST BRASS, 45-46mm
Obv: Type A

C#	Date	Emperor	Good	VG	Fine	VF
10-10	ND (1851-61)	Hsien-feng	5.50	10.00	16.50	40.00

CAST IRON

10-10a	ND (1851-61)	Hsien-feng	Reported, not confirmed			

CAST BRASS, 44mm
Obv: Type B-1. Rev: Similar to C10-10.

10-11	ND (1851-61)	Hsien-feng	13,50	22.50	30.00	55.00

Rev: 4 characters appearing on rim.

10-12	ND(1851-61)	Hsien-feng	30.00	50.00	75.00	170.00

CAST IRON

10-12a	ND(1851-61)	Hsien-feng	Reported, not confirmed			

CAST COPPER, 46mm
Rev: 8 characters in the field.

10-13	ND(1851-61)	Hsien-feng	100.00	175.00	250.00	350.00

CAST IRON

10-13a	ND(1851-61)	Hsien-feng	—	—	—	—

50 CASH

CAST COPPER, 55-57mm
Obv: Type A. Rev: 4 characters.

10-14	ND(1851-61)	Hsien-feng	15.00	25.00	30.00	60.00

65mm
Rev: Mint mark w/long vertical stroke at right instead of dot.

10-14.1	ND(1851-61)	Hsien-feng	—	—	Rare	—

55mm
Obv: Type B-1. Rev: 4 characters.

C#	Date	Emperor	Good	VG	Fine	VF
10-15	ND(1851-61)	Hsien-feng	25.00	40.00	55.00	100.00

Rev: 4 characters appearing on rim.

10-16	ND(1851-61)	Hsien-feng	50.00	85.00	150.00	250.00

Rev: 8 characters in field.

10-17	ND(1851-61)	Hsien-feng	175.00	300.00	425.00	550.00

100 CASH

CAST COPPER, 70mm
Obv: Type A. Rev: 4 characters.

10-18	ND(1851-61)	Hsien-feng	35.00	50.00	75.00	135.00

74mm
Rev: Mint mark w/long vertical stroke at right instead of dot.

10-18.1	ND(1851-61)	Hsien-feng	—	—	Rare	—

CAST ZINC
Rev: 4 characters.

10-18a	ND(1851-61)	Hsien-feng	—	—	Rare	—

NOTE: Composition of this coin is reportedly a mixture of zinc, lead and tin. The coin is blue-gray in color and has a large mint mark, written differently from any of the above.

CAST COPPER
Obv: Type B-1. Rev: 4 characters.

C#	Date	Emperor	Good	VG	Fine	VF
10-19	ND(1851-61)	Hsien-feng	25.00	40.00	55.00	90.00

72mm
Rev: 4 characters appearing on rim and small characters in field.

C#	Date	Emperor	Good	VG	Fine	VF
10-20	ND(1851-61)	Hsien-feng	75.00	125.00	175.00	250.00

78mm
Rev: Larger characters in field.

C#	Date	Emperor	Good	VG	Fine	VF
10-20.1	ND(1851-61)	Hsien-feng	35.00	50.00	75.00	125.00

Rev: 8 characters in field.

10-21 ND(1851-61)
Hsien-feng Reported, not confirmed

FANTASY ISSUES

NOTE: 30, 40, 500 and 1000 Cash pieces are reported for this mint, but their existence is doubtful and any encountered would most likely be considered fantasies.

MILLED COINAGE

CASH

BRASS
Obv: Type A

Y#	Date	Emperor	VG	Fine	VF	XF
95	ND(1908)	Kuang-hsu	9.00	12.00	20.00	40.00

Tai Ching Ti Kuo type, Hsu#259.

Y#	Date	Mintage	VG	Fine	VF	XF
7f	CD1908	—	35.00	75.00	110.00	175.00

Obv: Type A

Y#	Date	Emperor	VG	Fine	VF	XF
106	ND(1909/11)	Hsuan-t'ung	20.00	40.00	70.00	100.00

2 CASH

BRASS

Y#	Date	Mintage	VG	Fine	VF	XF
8f	CD1906	—	3.00	8.00	14.00	25.00

5 CASH

COPPER

Y#	Date	Mintage	VG	Fine	VF	XF
99	ND(1901-03)	.590	6.00	12.00	17.50	30.00

BRASS

Y#	Date	Mintage	VG	Fine	VF	XF
99a	ND(1901-03)		12.00	25.00	50.00	75.00

10 CASH

COPPER
Obv: Large characters at left and right.

Y#	Date	Mintage	Fine	VF	XF	Unc
97	ND(1901-05)	417.031	1.50	2.50	8.00	25.00

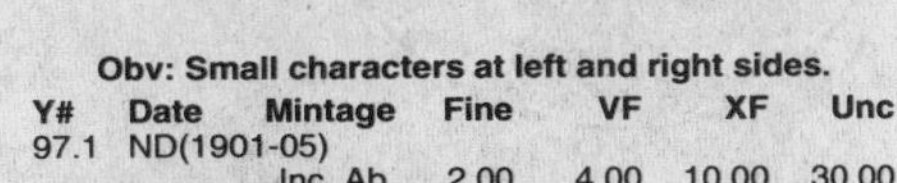

Obv: Small characters at left and right sides.

Y#	Date	Mintage	Fine	VF	XF	Unc
97.1	ND(1901-05)	Inc. Ab.	2.00	4.00	10.00	30.00

Rev: FOO-KIEN CUSTOM.

Y#	Date	Mintage	Fine	VF	XF	Unc
98	ND(1901-05)	Inc. Ab.	100.00	150.00	250.00	—

Rev: 1 cloud left of pearl.

Y#	Date	Mintage	Fine	VF	XF	Unc
100	ND(1901-05)	Inc. Ab.	3.00	6.00	9.00	30.00

Rev: 3 clouds left of pearl and w/o cloud above tip of dragons tail.

Y#	Date	Mintage	Fine	VF	XF	Unc
100.1	ND(1901-05)	Inc. Ab.	2.00	4.00	7.00	25.00

Rev: 3 clouds left of pearl and a cloud above tip of dragon's tail.

Y#	Date	Mintage	Fine	VF	XF	Unc
100.2	ND(1901-05)	Inc. Ab.	1.00	2.00	4.00	25.00

Rev. denomination: 10 CASHES.

Y#	Date	Mintage	Fine	VF	XF	Unc
100.3	ND(1901-05)	Inc. Ab.	12.00	20.00	45.00	—

Y#	Date	Mintage	Fine	VF	XF	Unc
10f	CD1906	—	.75	1.50	3.00	20.00

Y#	Date	Mintage	Fine	VF	XF	Unc
20f	CD1909	—	50.00	85.00	125.00	—

20 CASH

COPPER

Y#	Date	Mintage	VG	Fine	VF	XF
101	ND(1901-02)	.018	12.00	30.00	45.00	75.00

5 CENTS

1.3500 g, .820 SILVER, .0356 oz ASW
Obv. leg: 5 characters at top.
Rev: Side-view dragon-left.

Y#	Date	Mintage	Fine	VF	XF	Unc
102	ND(1896-1903)		8.00	14.00	25.00	50.00

Obv. leg: 4 characters at top.
Rev: Rosette at either side of side-view dragon-right.

Y#	Date	Mintage	Fine	VF	XF	Unc
102.1	ND(1903-08)		3.00	5.00	11.00	30.00

Rev: Rosette above dragon's head.

Y#	Date	Mintage	Fine	VF	XF	Unc
102.2	ND(1903-08)		6.00	12.00	22.50	40.00

10 CENTS

2.7000 g, .820 SILVER, .0712 oz ASW
Obv. leg: 5 characters at top.
Rev: Rosette at either side of side-view dragon-left.

Y#	Date	Mintage	Fine	VF	XF	Unc
103	ND(1896-1903)	13.425	5.00	9.00	17.50	35.00

Rev: Dot at either side of side-view dragon-left.

Y#	Date	Mintage	Fine	VF	XF	Unc
103.1	ND(1896-1903)	Inc. Ab.	8.00	15.00	30.00	60.00

Obv. leg: 4 characters at top.
Rev: Small side-view dragon-right.

Y#	Date	Mintage	Fine	VF	XF	Unc
103.2	ND(1903-08)	Inc. Ab.	3.00	6.00	12.00	30.00

Rev: Large side-view dragon-right.

Y#	Date	Mintage	Fine	VF	XF	Unc
103.3	ND(1903-08)	Inc. Ab.	6.00	12.00	24.00	50.00

20 CENTS

5.4000 g, .820 SILVER, .1424 oz ASW
Obv. leg: 5 characters at top.
Rev: Dot at either side of side-view dragon-left.

Y#	Date	Mintage	Fine	VF	XF	Unc
104	ND(1896-1903)	31.772	3.00	6.00	12.50	30.00

Rev: Rosette at either side of side-view dragon-left.

Y#	Date	Mintage	Fine	VF	XF	Unc
104.1	ND(1898-1903)	Inc. Ab.	3.00	6.00	12.50	30.00

Obv. leg: 4 characters at top.
Rev: Side-view dragon-right.

Y#	Date	Mintage	Fine	VF	XF	Unc
104.2	ND(1903-08)	Inc. Ab.	3.00	6.00	12.50	30.00

DOLLAR

SILVER, 25.70 g
Obv. leg: 4 characters at top "Changchow Soldier's Pay".

Kann#	Date	Mintage	VG	Fine	VF	XF
6	ND(ca.1844)	—	1800.	2500.	3000.	4500.

27.20 g
Obv: Lower character written in different style.

Kann#	Date	Mintage	VG	Fine	VF	XF
5	ND(ca.1844)	—	3000.	4000.	5000.	7500.

26.20 g
Obv. and rev: 2 rosettes.
Obv. leg: 2 characters at top "Soldier's Pay".

Kann#	Date	Mintage	VG	Fine	VF	XF
7	ND(ca.1844)	—	225.00	500.00	800.00	1750.

Obv: 2 rosettes and 2 five petalled flowers.

Kann#	Date	Mintage	VG	Fine	VF	XF
7c	ND(ca.1844)	—	850.00	1250.	1500.	3000.

Kann #5-7 above were issued by military authorities at the city of Changchow. Though Kann dates these pieces in the 1860's they were already circulating in the 1840's.

27.00 g

Y#	Date	Mintage	Fine	VF	XF	Unc
105	ND(ca.1899)	—	—	—	Rare	—

REPUBLIC

CASH

CAST BRASS
Obv. leg: *Fu-chien T'ung-pao.*
Rev: 6 stripes on right flag.

Y#	Date	Mintage	VG	Fine	VF	XF
374	ND(c.1912)	—	65.00	100.00	135.00	200.00

2 CASH

CAST BRASS
Obv. leg: *Fu-chien T'ung-pao.*
Rev: 5 stripes on right flag.

Y#	Date	Mintage	VG	Fine	VF	XF
375	ND(c.1912)	—	12.50	17.50	22.50	30.00

Rev: 6 stripes on right flag.

Y#	Date	Mintage	VG	Fine	VF	XF
375.1	ND(c.1912)	—	40.00	75.00	100.00	150.00

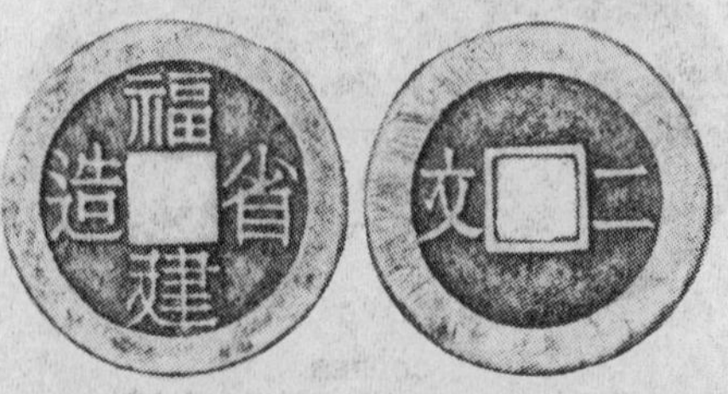

Obv. leg: *Fu-chien Sheng Tsao.*

Y#	Date	Mintage	VG	Fine	VF	XF
376	ND(c.1912)	—	—	—	Rare	—

MILLED COINAGE

10 CASH

COPPER

Y#	Date	Mintage	Fine	VF	XF	Unc
379	ND(ca.1912)	—	3.00	7.00	15.00	35.00

BRASS

Y#	Date	Mintage	Fine	VF	XF	Unc
379a	ND(ca.1912)	—	42.50	60.00	87.50	125.00

10 CENTS

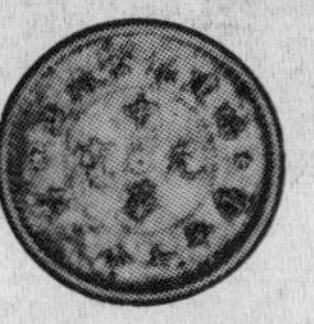

SILVER, 2.60 g

Y#	Date	Mintage	Fine	VF	XF	Unc
380	ND(ca.1912)	—	35.00	60.00	100.00	200.00

Y#	Date	Mintage	Fine	VF	XF	Unc
382	ND(ca.1913)	—	2.50	5.00	9.00	20.00

Similar to Y#380. Obv: Different leg. in center.

Y#	Date	Mintage	Fine	VF	XF	Unc
380a	CD1924	—	30.00	50.00	80.00	150.00

Canton Martyrs

Y#	Year	Date	Fine	VF	XF	Unc
388	17	(1928)	5.00	12.50	25.00	40.00
	20	(1931)	7.00	17.50	30.00	50.00

Canton Martyrs

Y#	Year	Date	Fine	VF	XF	Unc
390	21	(1932)	125.00	175.00	250.00	375.00

20 CENTS

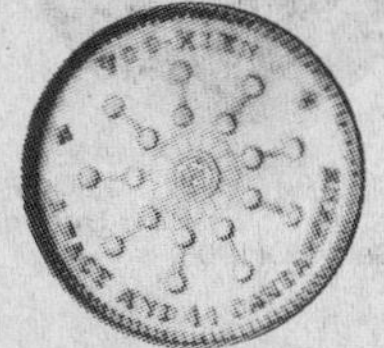

SILVER, 5.00 g

Y#	Date	Mintage	Fine	VF	XF	Unc
377	CD1911	—	10.00	20.00	35.00	125.00

5.40 g

Y#	Date	Mintage	Fine	VF	XF	Unc
A381	ND(1912)	—	3.50	7.00	15.00	25.00

5.20 g

Y#	Date	Mintage	Fine	VF	XF	Unc
383	ND	—	3.00	5.00	10.00	25.00

NOTE: Kann dates this coin 1913, but evidence suggests that it was struck in 1923.

5.70 g

Y#	Year	Date	Fine	VF	XF	Unc
383a	13	(1924)	35.00	50.00	70.00	90.00

5.30 g
Obv. and rev: Rosettes at sides.
Obv: Dot in middle of rosette center.

Y#	Date	Mintage	Fine	VF	XF	Unc
381	CD1923	—	3.50	7.00	10.00	25.00

Rev. leg: MADE spelled MAIE.

Y#	Date	Mintage	Fine	VF	XF	Unc
381.1	CD1923	—	3.50	7.50	12.50	30.00

Rev. leg: MADEIN FOO-KIENMINT.

Y#	Date	Mintage	Fine	VF	XF	Unc
381.2	CD1923	—	3.50	7.50	12.50	30.00

Obv: W/o dot in middle of center rosette, 5 pointed star at sides in place of rosette.

Y#	Date	Mintage	Fine	VF	XF	Unc
381.3	CD1923	—	10.00	12.50	17.50	35.00

Obv: Different leg. in center.

Y#	Date	Mintage	Fine	VF	XF	Unc
381.4	CD1924	—	5.00	8.00	15.00	35.00

Northern Expedition

Y#	Year	Date	Fine	VF	XF	Unc
384	16	(1927)	200.00	300.00	400.00	600.00

5.30 g
Northern Expedition

Y#	Year	Date	Fine	VF	XF	Unc
385	16	(1927)	600.00	950.00	1250.	1750.

Canton Martyrs
Obv: 2 rows of bricks at right of gate.

Y#	Year	Date	Fine	VF	XF	Unc
389.1	17	(1928)	4.00	6.50	10.00	30.00
	20	(1931)	7.00	12.00	20.00	60.00

SILVER, 5.50 g
Obv: Half brick in 3rd row of bricks at right of gate.

Y#	Year	Date	Fine	VF	XF	Unc
389.2	17	(1928)	4.00	6.50	10.00	30.00
	20	(1931)	6.00	10.00	16.50	50.00

Rev: 6 pointed star in legend.

Y#	Year	Date	Fine	VF	XF	Unc
389.3	20	(1931)	—	—	—	—

SILVER, 5.30 g
Canton Martyrs

Y#	Year	Date	Fine	VF	XF	Unc
391	21	(1932)	40.00	65.00	100.00	250.00

HEILUNGKIANG PROVINCE

Heilongjiang

The northwesternmost of the former Three Eastern Provinces, bordering on Siberia. Though very large in extent, it is only sparsely populated, for wide areas are desert land. Economically the district was always backward. Heilungkiang (Heilongjiang) Province had no mint of its own, and seemingly no silver money bearing its name was ever placed in circulation although Imperial patterns in the standard dragon design exist for at least the dollar and 50 cent denominations. During the beginning of the 20th century it was suggested to contract for silver coins from the Berlin Mint.

HONAN PROVINCE

Henan

A province in east-central China. As well as being one of the most densely populated provinces it is also one of the most important agriculturally. It is the area of earliest settlement in China and has housed the capital during various dynasties. The Kaifeng Mint issued coins from its opening in 1647 through most of the rulers of the Manchu dynasty. In 1905 a modern mint opened at Kaifeng but closed in 1914. A mint in Loyang opened in 1924.

EMPIRE

CASH

CAST BRASS
Obv: Type A. Rev: Type 1.

C#	Date	Emperor	Good	VG	Fine	VF
11-1	ND(1851-61)	Hsien-feng	20.00	30.00	40.00	60.00

Rev: Crescent above.

C#	Date	Emperor	Good	VG	Fine	VF
11-1.1	ND(1851-61)	Hsien-feng	20.00	30.00	40.00	60.00

Rev: Circle above.

C#	Date	Emperor	Good	VG	Fine	VF
11-1.2	ND(1851-61)	Hsien-feng	20.00	30.00	40.00	60.00

CAST IRON

C#	Date	Emperor	Good	VG	Fine	VF
11-1a	ND(1851-61)	Hsien-feng	12.50	20.00	30.00	60.00

CAST BRASS
Obv: Type A.

C#	Date	Emperor	Good	VG	Fine	VF
11-9	ND(1875-1908)	Kuang-hsu	4.00	8.00	10.00	12.00

Rev: Circle above.

C#	Date	Emperor	Good	VG	Fine	VF
11-9.1	ND(1875-1908)	Kuang-hsu	5.00	9.00	13.50	35.00

Rev: Circle below.

C#	Date	Emperor	Good	VG	Fine	VF
11-9.2	ND(1875-1908)	Kuang-hsu	5.00	9.00	13.50	25.00

Rev: Crescent above.

C#	Date	Emperor	Good	VG	Fine	VF
11-9.3	ND(1875-1908)	Kuang-hsu	5.00	9.00	13.50	25.00

Rev: Crescent below.

C#	Date	Emperor	Good	VG	Fine	VF
11-9.4	ND(1875-1908)	Kuang-hsu	5.00	9.00	13.50	25.00

Rev: Crescent above, dot below.

C#	Date	Emperor	Good	VG	Fine	VF
11-9.5	ND(1875-1908)	Kuang-hsu	5.00	9.00	13.50	25.00

Rev: Dot above.

C#	Date	Emperor	Good	VG	Fine	VF
11-9.6	ND(1875-1908)	Kuang-hsu	5.00	9.00	13.50	20.00

Rev: Dot below.

C#	Date	Emperor	Good	VG	Fine	VF
11-9.7	ND(1875-1908)	Kuang-hsu	5.00	9.00	13.50	20.00

Rev: Dot at upper left.

C#	Date	Emperor	Good	VG	Fine	VF
11-9.8	ND(1875-1908)	Kuang-hsu	5.00	9.00	13.50	20.00

CAST ZINC

C#	Date	Emperor	Good	VG	Fine	VF
3-1.1a	ND(1875-1908)	Kuang-hsu	—	—	Rare	—

10 CASH

CAST BRASS
Obv: Type B-1

C#	Date	Emperor	Good	VG	Fine	VF
11-2	ND(1851-61)	Hsien-feng	6.00	12.00	20.00	40.00

50 CASH

CAST BRASS
Obv: Type B-1

C#	Date	Emperor	Good	VG	Fine	VF
11-5	ND(1851-61)	Hsien-feng	8.00	15.00	25.00	50.00

100 CASH

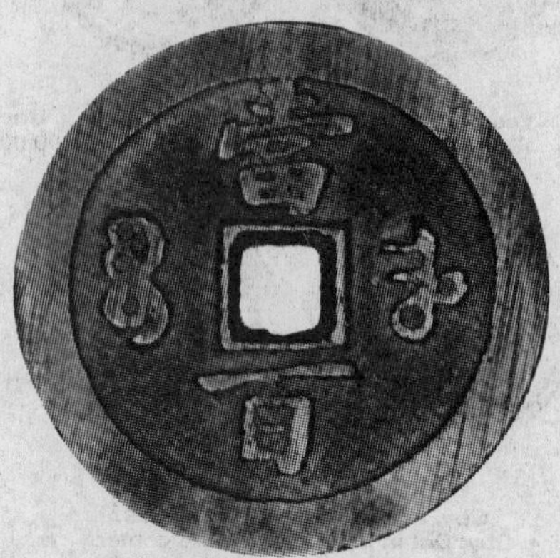

CAST BRASS
Obv: Type C

C#	Date	Emperor	Good	VG	Fine	VF
11-6	ND(1851-61)	Hsien-feng	10.00	20.00	30.00	60.00

500 CASH

CAST BRASS
Obv: Type C

C#	Date	Emperor	Good	VG	Fine	VF
11-7	ND(1851-61)	Hsien-feng	25.00	50.00	75.00	135.00

1000 CASH

CAST BRASS
Obv: Type C

C#	Date	Emperor	Good	VG	Fine	VF
11-8	ND(1851-61)	Hsien-feng	—	—	—	—

FANTASY ISSUES

Coins of this mint in denominations of 20 (C#11-3), 30 (C#11-4), 40 and 70 cash are considered fantasy issues.

MILLED COINAGE

CASH

 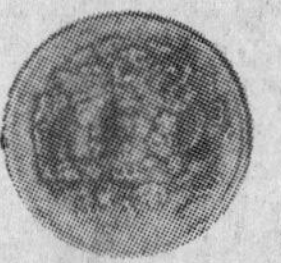

BRASS

Y#	Date	Mintage	VG	Fine	VF	XF
7g	CD1908	—	10.00	25.00	40.00	70.00

5 CASH

BRASS

Y#	Date	Mintage	VG	Fine	VF	XF
19g	CD1909	—	—	—	—	—

10 CASH

COPPER
Rev: Circled dragon w/o mountain below pearl with 3 flames.

Y#	Date	Mintage	VG	Fine	VF	XF
108	ND(1905)	—	4.00	10.00	20.00	40.00

Rev: 5 flames on pearl.

Y#	Date	Mintage	VG	Fine	VF	XF
108.1	ND(1905)	—	.75	1.50	3.00	6.00

Rev: Mountain below pearl, very small English lettering.

Y#	Date	Mintage	VG	Fine	VF	XF
108.2	ND(1905)	—	6.00	15.00	30.00	50.00

Rev: Large English legend.

Y#	Date	Mintage	VG	Fine	VF	XF
108.3	ND(1905)	—	2.50	6.00	10.00	20.00

BRASS
Obv: Raised sphere "Yin-yang" in center.
Rev: Uncircled dragon, Honan spelled HOU-NAN.

Y#	Date	Mintage	VG	Fine	VF	XF
108a	ND(1905)	—	—	—	Rare	—

NOTE: Dies made in Japan.

COPPER
Rev: Uncircled dragon.

Y#	Date	Mintage	VG	Fine	VF	XF
108a.1	ND(1905)	—	.80	2.00	4.00	8.00

Obv: Curved line on raised "Yin-yang" slanted more.

Y#	Date	Mintage	VG	Fine	VF	XF
108a.2	ND(1905)	—	.80	2.00	4.00	8.00

Obv: Flat "Yin-yang". Rev: Plain pearl.

Y#	Date	Mintage	VG	Fine	VF	XF
108a.3	ND(1905)	—	.40	1.00	2.00	4.00
			BRASS			
108a.3a	ND(1905)	—	2.50	5.00	10.00	17.50

COPPER
Rev: Incuse swirl in pearl.

Y#	Date	Mintage	VG	Fine	VF	XF
108a.4	ND(1905)	—	1.00	2.00	4.00	8.00

NOTE: Dies for Y#108a.3 and Y#108a.4 were made in the U.S.

Rev. leg: Period after COIN.

Y#	Date	Mintage	VG	Fine	VF	XF
10g	CD1906	132.000	.60	1.50	3.50	6.00

Rev. leg: Period after COPPER.

Y#	Date	Mintage	VG	Fine	VF	XF
10g.1	CD1906	—	1.20	3.00	6.00	10.00

Y#	Date	Mintage	VG	Fine	VF	XF
20g	CD1909	—	20.00	40.00	60.00	125.00
	1911	—	5.00	15.00	25.00	50.00

NOTE: Normally encountered with weak legends.

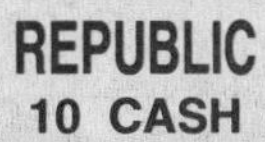

REPUBLIC

10 CASH

COPPER

Y#	Date	Mintage	Fine	VF	XF	Unc
A392	ND(1913-14)	—	1.00	2.00	6.00	20.00

Obv: W/o lines above and below rosettes.

Y#	Date	Mintage	Fine	VF	XF	Unc
A392.1	ND(1913-14)	—	1.00	2.00	6.00	20.00

Rev. leg: TEN CASH in larger letters

Y#	Date	Mintage	Fine	VF	XF	Unc
392	ND	—	.75	1.50	4.00	18.00

Obv: Rosette in center higher in relation to heart shaped leaves below.

Y#	Date	Mintage	Fine	VF	XF	Unc
392.1	ND(ca.1920)	—	2.00	3.50	6.00	20.00

Rev: Letter S in CASH backwards.

Y#	Date	Mintage	Fine	VF	XF	Unc
392.2	ND(ca.1920)	—	10.00	17.50	30.00	—

20 CASH

COPPER
Obv. leg: 6 characters at bottom.

Y#	Date	Mintage	Good	VG	Fine	VF
393	ND(ca.1920)	—	1.25	2.50	5.00	10.00

Obv. leg: 5 characters at bottom.

Y#	Date	Mintage	Good	VG	Fine	VF
393.1	ND(ca.1920)	—	1.00	2.00	4.00	6.00

Rev. leg: CHINA replaces HO-NAN.

Y#	Date	Mintage	Good	VG	Fine	VF
393.2	ND(ca.1921)	—	12.00	25.00	45.00	225.00

Rev: Star above flags.

Y#	Date	Mintage	Good	VG	Fine	VF
A397	Yr.20 (1931)	—	—	—	*Rare	—

***NOTE:** D.K.E. Ching Sale 6-91 VF realized $3,630.

50 CASH

COPPER
Rev: Short flag poles.

Y#	Date	Mintage	Good	VG	Fine	VF
394	ND	—	2.00	3.75	6.50	15.00

Rev: Long flag poles.

Y#	Date	Mintage	Good	VG	Fine	VF
394.1	ND	—	2.00	3.75	6.50	15.00
			BRASS			
394b	ND	—	20.00	40.00	60.00	100.00

Rev. leg: CHINA replaces HONAN.

Y#	Date	Mintage	Good	VG	Fine	VF
394a	ND	—	6.50	12.50	25.00	60.00

Y#	Year	Date	Good	VG	Fine	VF
397	20	(1931)	25.00	50.00	90.00	145.00

100 CASH

COPPER
Rev: Small star in right flag, tassels 4mm long.

Y#	Date	Mintage	Good	VG	Fine	VF
395	ND ca.1928	—	3.00	5.00	10.00	25.00
	Rev: Tassels 5mm long.					
395.1	ND ca.1928	—	3.75	6.50	12.50	30.00
	Rev: Large star in right flag.					
395.2	ND ca.1928	—	—	—	—	—

Y#	Year	Date	Good	VG	Fine	VF
398	20	(1931)	10.00	17.50	35.00	70.00

200 CASH

COPPER
Rev: Large square inside right flag.

Y#	Date	Mintage	Good	VG	Fine	VF
396	ND ca.1928	—	3.00	5.00	10.00	25.00

Rev: Small square and small star inside right flag.

Y#	Date	Mintage	Good	VG	Fine	VF
396.1	ND ca.1928	—	2.50	4.50	9.00	25.00

Rev: Small square and large star inside right flag.

Y#	Date	Mintage	Good	VG	Fine	VF
396.2	ND	—	2.50	4.50	9.00	25.00
	BRASS					
396a	ND ca.1928	—	6.00	15.00	22.50	45.00

NOTE: The Republican coins of Honan (Henan) are usually found weakly struck. Crudely struck specimens with die variations, misspelled leg. are considered war lord issues.

HUNAN PROVINCE

A province in south-central China. Mining of coal, antimony, tungsten and tin is important as well as raising varied agricultural products. The Changsha Mint produced Cash coins from early in the Manchu dynasty. Its facility for struck coinage opened in 1897, and two further copper mints were added in 1905. All three mints were closed down in 1907, but one mint was reopened at a later date and produced vast quantities of republican copper coinage until 1926.

EMPIRE

Changsha Mint

CASH

CAST BRASS
Obv: Type A.

C#	Date	Emperor	Good	VG	Fine	VF
12-2	ND(1796-1820)	Chia-ch'ing	.75	1.50	2.50	5.00
	Obv: Type A.					
12-3	ND(1821-50)	Tao-kuang	2.00	4.00	6.50	10.00
	Obv: Type A.					
12-4	ND(1851-61)	Hsien-feng	2.00	4.00	6.50	10.00
	Obv: Type A-2.					
12-5	ND(1862-74)	T'ung-chih	6.00	12.50	18.50	25.00
	Obv: Type A.					
12-7	ND(1875-1908)	Kuang-hsu	7.50	15.00	21.50	30.00

10 CASH

CAST BRASS

C#	Date	Emperor	Good	VG	Fine	VF
12-6	ND(1862-74)	T'ung-chih	—	—	Rare	—
12-8	ND(1875-1908)	Kuang-hsu	—	—	Rare	—

MILLED COINAGE

NOTE: 2, 5 and 20 Cash Tai Ching Ti Kuo type patterns are reported, not confirmed.

10 CASH

COPPER
Obv: Rosette in center w/center of petals depressed. Manchu words at sides, *Tan Shih* at bottom.
Rev: Narrow spacing in HU-NAN above dragon.

Y#	Date	Mintage	Fine	VF	XF	Unc
112	ND(1902-06)		1.00	2.00	5.00	20.00

Y#	Date	Mintage	Fine	VF	XF	Unc
	Rev: Wide spacing in HU-NAN.					
112.1	ND(1902-06)		2.25	4.00	9.00	30.00
	Obv: Petals of rosette not depressed.					
112.2	ND(1902-06)		1.50	2.50	6.00	20.00

Obv: 2 Manchu words in center, *T'ung Yuan* at bottom.

Y#	Date	Mintage	Fine	VF	XF	Unc
112.3	ND(1902-06)		3.00	6.00	10.00	30.00

Rev: Narrow spacing in HU-NAN.

Y#	Date	Mintage	Fine	VF	XF	Unc
112.4	ND(1902-06)		1.50	2.50	6.00	20.00

Obv: Rosette in center, *Tan Shih* at bottom.
Rev: Ring around pearl.

Y#	Date	Mintage	Fine	VF	XF	Unc
112.5	ND(1902-06)		1.25	2.00	4.00	18.00
	Obv: Centers of petals on rosette depressed.					
112.6	ND(1902-06)		1.50	2.50	6.00	20.00

Obv: 2 Manchu words in center, *T'ung Yuan* at bottom.
Rev: Ring around pearl.

Y#	Date	Mintage	Fine	VF	XF	Unc
112.7	ND(1902-06)		1.50	2.50	6.00	20.00

Obv: Larger characters at left and right, and different characters below. Rev: Dragon redesigned and small star at either side.

Y#	Date	Mintage	Fine	VF	XF	Unc
112.8	ND(1902-06)		5.00	10.00	17.50	40.00

Obv: Rosette in center; leg: 4 characters at bottom. Rev: Redesigned dragon w/o pearl; rosette at either side.

Y#	Date	Mintage	Fine	VF	XF	Unc
112.9	ND(1902-06)		7.50	15.00	30.00	—

Obv: 2 Manchu words in center w/dot between; *T'ung Yuan* at bottom.

Y#	Date	Mintage	Fine	VF	XF	Unc
112.10	ND(1902-06)		1.00	2.00	4.00	18.00

Obv: W/o dot between Manchu words, *T'ung Yuan* at bottom.

Y#	Date	Mintage	Fine	VF	XF	Unc
112.11	ND(1902-06)		1.00	2.00	4.00	18.00

Obv: Smaller 15.5mm inner circle, w/larger beads, *T'ung Yuan* at bottom.

Y#	Date	Mintage	Fine	VF	XF	Unc
112.12	ND(1902-06)		1.00	2.00	4.00	18.00

Obv: 2 Manchu words in center, 18.4mm inner circle. *Huang T;ung Yuan* at bottom.

Y#	Date	Mintage	Fine	VF	XF	Unc
112.13	ND(1902-06)		25.00	45.00	80.00	—

Obv: Smaller 17.5mm inner circle, *Huang T'ung Yuan* at bottom.

Y#	Date	Mintage	Fine	VF	XF	Unc
112.14	ND(1902-06)		25.00	45.00	80.00	—

Obv. leg: 6 characters at bottom. Rev: Flying dragon. Reeded edge.

Y#	Date	Mintage	Fine	VF	XF	Unc
113	ND(1902-06)		4.00	8.00	15.00	40.00

Rev. leg: Inverted U in HU-NAN. Reeded edge.

Y#	Date	Mintage	Fine	VF	XF	Unc
113.1	ND(1902-06)		12.00	25.00	45.00	—

BRASS
Obv. leg: 3 characters at bottom.

Y#	Date	Mintage	Fine	VF	XF	Unc
113a	ND(1904-06)		3.50	6.00	12.50	35.00

COPPER
Obv: Upper and lower parts of character Hu connected. Rev: Dot between Chinese characters above dragon.

Y#	Date	Mintage	Fine	VF	XF	Unc
10h	CD1906	—	17.50	35.00	70.00	—

Obv: Upper and lower part of Hu not connected. Rev: Dot between Chinese characters at top.

Y#	Date	Mintage	Fine	VF	XF	Unc
10h.1	CD1906	—	17.50	35.00	70.00	—

Obv: Similar to Y#10h.1. Rev: 7 flames on pearl.

Y#	Date	Mintage	Fine	VF	XF	Unc
10h.2	CD1906	—	2.00	4.00	8.00	22.00

Rev: 7 flame pearl ornamented w/toothlike projections.

Y#	Date	Mintage	Fine	VF	XF	Unc
10h.3	CD1906	—	1.00	2.00	4.00	18.00

Rev: 4 flames on pearl.

Y#	Date	Mintage	Fine	VF	XF	Unc
10h.4	CD1906	—	2.00	4.00	8.00	22.00

Rev: Redesigned dragon w/high waves beneath.

Y#	Date	Mintage	Fine	VF	XF	Unc
10h.5	CD1906	—	12.00	20.00	40.00	—

Obv: Character Hu connected. Rev: Redesigned dragon; dot between COPPER COIN.

Y#	Date	Mintage	Fine	VF	XF	Unc
10h.6	CD1906	—	12.00	20.00	40.00	—

Rev: Redesigned dragon, w/5 flames on pearl (Woodward #342 and 343).

Y#	Date	Mintage	Fine	VF	XF	Unc
10h.7	CD1906	—	30.00	45.00	75.00	—

5 CENTS

1.3000 g, .820 SILVER, .0343 oz ASW
Similar to 20 Cents, Y#116.

Y#	Date	Mintage	Fine	VF	XF	Unc
—	ND(1897)	—	—	—	Rare	—

10 CENTS

2.5000 g, .820 SILVER, .0659 oz ASW
Obv: 2 rosettes at both sides.

Y#	Date	Mintage	Fine	VF	XF	Unc
115	ND(1897)	—	7.00	15.00	25.00	100.00

Obv: 1 rosette at both sides.

Y#	Date	Mintage	Fine	VF	XF	Unc
115.1	ND(1897)	—	14.00	25.00	45.00	120.00
	CD1898	—	17.50	35.00	60.00	150.00
	CD1899	—	22.50	45.00	75.00	175.00

20 CENTS

5.3000 g, .820 SILVER, .1397 oz ASW

Y#	Date	Mintage	Fine	VF	XF	Unc
116	ND(1897)	—	25.00	65.00	100.00	250.00

TAEL SYSTEM

The following coins, in Tael and Mace (Liang and Ch'ien) denominations, are often called Hunan cakes because of their thickness. Three basic series exist; those issued under provincial authority, those issued by the Ta Ch'ing Bank, and those issued by Changsha merchants.

CH'IEN (MACE)

SILVER, 3.70 g
Provincial Type
Obv: 4 characters. Rev: 2 characters.

Kann#	Date	Mintage	VG	Fine	VF	XF
951	ND(ca.1906)	—	30.00	50.00	70.00	100.00

3.80 g
Merchant Type
Obv: 6 vertical characters. Rev: 6 horizontal characters.

Kann#	Date	Mintage	VG	Fine	VF	XF
971	ND(ca.1908)	—	30.00	50.00	70.00	120.00

Merchant Type
Obv: 4 characters. Rev: 2 vertical characters.

Kann#	Date	Mintage	VG	Fine	VF	XF
973	ND(ca.1908)	—	30.00	50.00	70.00	120.00

Merchant Type
Obv: 6 horizontal characters.
Rev: 2 vertical characters.

Kann#	Date	Mintage	VG	Fine	VF	XF
984/5	ND(ca.1908)	—	30.00	50.00	70.00	120.00

2 CH'IEN (MACE)

SILVER, 7.30 g
Provincial Type
Obv. and rev: 4 characters.

Kann#	Date	Mintage	VG	Fine	VF	XF
950	ND(ca.1906)	—	35.00	55.00	75.00	110.00

Provincial Type
Obv: 6 vertical characters. Rev: 4 characters.

Kann#	Date	Mintage	VG	Fine	VF	XF
960	ND(ca.1906)	—	35.00	55.00	75.00	110.00

Ta Ch'ing Bank Type
Obv: 6 vertical characters.
Rev: 6 horizontal characters.

Kann#	Date	Mintage	VG	Fine	VF	XF
970	ND(ca.1908)	—	35.00	55.00	75.00	130.00

Merchant Type
Obv. and rev: 4 characters.

Kann#	Date	Mintage	VG	Fine	VF	XF
972	ND(ca.1908)	—	35.00	55.00	75.00	130.00

Merchant Type
Obv: 6 horizontal characters. Rev: 4 characters.

Kann#	Date	Mintage	VG	Fine	VF	XF
982/3	ND(ca.1908)	—	35.00	55.00	75.00	110.00

3 CH'IEN (MACE)

SILVER, 10.70 g
Provincial Type
Obv. and rev: 6 horizontal characters.

Kann#	Date	Mintage	VG	Fine	VF	XF
949	ND(ca.1906)	—	37.50	60.00	85.00	120.00

Provincial Type
Obv: 6 vertical characters.
Rev: 6 horizontal characters.

Kann#	Date	Mintage	VG	Fine	VF	XF
959	ND(ca.1906)	—	37.50	60.00	85.00	120.00

Ta Ch'ing Bank Type
Obv: 6 vertical characters.
Rev: 6 horizontal characters.

Kann#	Date	Mintage	VG	Fine	VF	XF
969	ND(ca.1908)	—	37.50	60.00	85.00	140.00

Merchant Type
Obv. and rev: 6 horizontal characters.

Kann#	Date	Mintage	VG	Fine	VF	XF
981	ND(ca.1908)	—	37.50	60.00	85.00	140.00

Merchant Type
"Official" character for "Three".

Kann#	Date	Mintage	VG	Fine	VF	XF
981a	ND(ca.1908)	—	37.50	60.00	85.00	120.00

4 CH'IEN (MACE)

SILVER, 14.3000 g
Provincial Type
Obv. and rev: 6 horizontal characters.

Kann#	Date	Mintage	VG	Fine	VF	XF
948	ND(ca.1906)	—	40.00	65.00	90.00	125.00

Provincial Type
Obv: 6 vertical characters.
Rev: 6 horizontal characters.

Kann#	Date	Mintage	VG	Fine	VF	XF
958	ND(ca.1906)	—	40.00	65.00	90.00	125.00

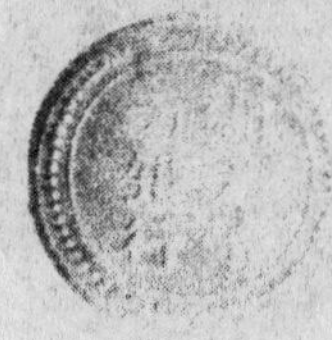

Ta Ch'ing Bank Type
Obv: 6 vertical characters.
Rev: 6 horizontal characters.

Kann#	Date	Mintage	VG	Fine	VF	XF
968	ND(ca.1908)	—	40.00	65.00	90.00	135.00

Merchant Type
Obv. and rev: 6 horizontal characters.

Kann#	Date	Mintage	VG	Fine	VF	XF
980	ND(ca.1908)	—	40.00	65.00	90.00	135.00

5 CH'IEN (MACE)

SILVER, 18.30 g
Provincial Type
Obv. and rev: 6 horizontal characters.

Kann#	Date	Mintage	VG	Fine	VF	XF
947	ND(ca.1906)	—	42.50	70.00	100.00	140.00

Provincial Type
Obv: 6 vertical characters.
Rev: 6 horizontal characters.

Kann#	Date	Mintage	VG	Fine	VF	XF
957	ND(ca.1906)	—	42.50	70.00	100.00	140.00

Ta Ch'ing Bank Type
Obv: 6 vertical characters.
Rev: 6 horizontal characters.

Kann#	Date	Mintage	VG	Fine	VF	XF
967	ND(ca.1908)	—	42.50	70.00	100.00	150.00

Merchant Type
Obv. and rev: 6 horizontal characters.

Kann#	Date	Mintage	VG	Fine	VF	XF
979	ND(ca.1908)	—	42.50	70.00	100.00	150.00

6 CH'IEN (MACE)

SILVER, 21.40 g
Provincial Type
Obv. and rev: 6 horizontal characters.

Kann#	Date	Mintage	VG	Fine	VF	XF
946	ND(ca.1906)	—	45.00	75.00	110.00	150.00

Provincial Type
Obv: 6 vertical characters.
Rev: 6 horizontal characters.

Kann#	Date	Mintage	VG	Fine	VF	XF
956	ND(ca.1906)	—	45.00	75.00	110.00	150.00

Ta Ch'ing Bank Type
Obv: 6 vertical characters.
Rev: 6 horizontal characters.

Kann#	Date	Mintage	VG	Fine	VF	XF
966	ND(ca.1908)	—	45.00	75.00	110.00	185.00

Merchant Type
Obv. and rev: 6 horizontal characters.

Kann#	Date	Mintage	VG	Fine	VF	XF
978	ND(ca.1908)	—	45.00	75.00	110.00	185.00

7 CH'IEN (MACE)

SILVER, 25.90 g
Provincial Type
Obv. and rev: 6 horizontal characters.

Kann#	Date	Mintage	VG	Fine	VF	XF
945	ND(ca.1906)	—	45.00	75.00	110.00	150.00

Provincial Type
Obv: 6 vertical characters.
Rev: 6 horizontal characters.

Kann#	Date	Mintage	VG	Fine	VF	XF
955	ND(ca.1906)	—	45.00	75.00	110.00	150.00

Ta Ch'ing Bank Type
Obv: 6 vertical characters.
Rev: 6 horizontal characters.

Kann#	Date	Mintage	VG	Fine	VF	XF
965	ND(ca.1908)	—	45.00	75.00	110.00	185.00

Merchant Type
Obv. and rev: 6 horizontal characters.

Kann#	Date	Mintage	VG	Fine	VF	XF
977	ND(ca.1908)	—	45.00	75.00	110.00	185.00

8 CH'IEN (MACE)

SILVER, 29.20 g
Provincial Type
Obv. and rev: 6 horizontal characters.

Kann#	Date	Mintage	VG	Fine	VF	XF
944	ND(ca.1906)	—	47.50	72.50	120.00	165.00

Provincial Type
Obv: 6 vertical characters.
Rev: 6 horizontal characters.

Kann#	Date	Mintage	VG	Fine	VF	XF
954	ND(ca.1906)	—	47.50	72.50	120.00	165.00

Ta Ch'ing Bank Type
Obv: 6 vertical characters.
Rev: 6 horizontal characters.

Kann#	Date	Mintage	VG	Fine	VF	XF
964	ND(ca.1908)	—	47.50	72.50	120.00	175.00

Merchant Type
Obv. and rev: 6 horizontal characters.

Kann#	Date	Mintage	VG	Fine	VF	XF
976	ND(ca.1908)	—	47.50	72.50	120.00	175.00

9 CH'IEN (MACE)

SILVER, 32.70 g
Provincial Type
Obv. and rev: 6 horizontal characters.

Kann#	Date	Mintage	VG	Fine	VF	XF
943	ND(ca.1906)	—	50.00	75.00	125.00	175.00

Provincial Type
Obv: 6 vertical characters.
Rev: 6 horizontal characters.

953	ND(ca.1906)	—	50.00	75.00	125.00	175.00

Ta Ch'ing Bank Type
Obv: 6 vertical characters.
Rev: 6 horizontal characters.

963	ND(ca.1908)	—	50.00	75.00	125.00	200.00

Merchant Type
Obv. and rev: 6 horizontal characters.

975	ND(ca.1908)	—	50.00	75.00	125.00	200.00

LIANG (TAEL)

SILVER, 35.90 g
Provincial Type
Obv. and rev: 6 horizontal characters.

942	ND(ca.1906)	—	60.00	100.00	150.00	225.00

Obv: 12 characters. Rev: Blank.

942r	ND(ca.1908)	—	—	—	Rare	—

Provincial Type
Obv: 6 vertical characters.
Rev: 6 horizontal characters.

952	ND(ca.1906)	—	60.00	100.00	140.00	200.00

Ta Ch'ing Bank Type
Obv: 6 vertical characters.
Rev: 6 horizontal characters.

Kann#	Date	Mintage	VG	Fine	VF	XF
962	ND(ca.1908)	—	45.00	75.00	110.00	165.00

Merchant Type
Obv. and rev: 6 horizontal characters.

974	ND(ca.1908)	—	90.00	150.00	225.00	325.00

TRANSITIONAL COINAGE

In the name of Hung Hsien

10 CASH

COPPER

Y#	Year	Date	VG	Fine	VF	XF
401.1	1	(1915)	15.00	30.00	45.00	75.00

NOTE: This coin is dated first year of Hung Hsien which corresponds to 1915.

Rev: Wider spacing in legend.

401.2	1	(1915)	10.00	20.00	30.00	45.00

REPUBLIC

10 CASH

COPPER
Obv: Large rosette. Rev: Center of star convex.

Y#	Date	Mintage	Fine	VF	XF	Unc
399	ND(1912)	—	2.00	4.00	7.50	24.00

BRASS

399a	ND	—	5.00	10.00	17.50	45.00

COPPER
Obv: Small rosette. Rev: Center of star convex.

399.1	ND	—	2.00	4.00	7.00	24.00

Rev: Center of star concave.
Star outlined.

Y#	Date	Mintage	Fine	VF	XF	Unc
399.2	ND	—	2.25	4.50	8.50	26.00

Rev: Star not outlined.

399.3	ND	—	2.25	4.50	8.50	26.00

Obv: Large rosette. Rev: Center of star concave.

399.4	ND	—	2.25	4.50	8.50	26.00

Mule. Obv: General Issue, Y#306.

399.5	ND	—	—	—	—	—

Provincial Constitution
Rev: Rosette above flags.

Y#	Year	Date	VG	Fine	VF	XF
402	11	(1922)	9.00	17.50	27.50	40.00

Rev: Star above flags.

402.1	11	(1922)	7.00	15.00	20.00	35.00

20 CASH

COPPER
Obv: Rosette above flags; leg: 5 characters at bottom.

Y#	Date	Mintage	VG	Fine	VF	XF
400	ND(1919)	—	1.20	3.00	7.50	15.00

BRASS

400b	ND	—	1.60	4.00	10.00	20.00

COPPER
Obv: Dot in rosette above flags; leg: 6 characters at

bottom. Rev: 11 curls in ribbon at base of plant.

Y#	Date	Mintage	VG	Fine	VF	XF
400.2	ND	—	.40	1.00	2.00	4.00

Rev: 25 small curls in ribbon at base of plant.

400.3	ND	—	.40	1.00	2.00	4.00

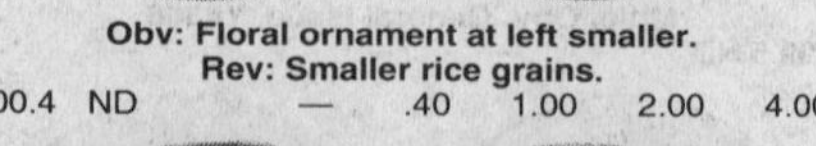

Obv: Floral ornament at left smaller.
Rev: Smaller rice grains.

400.4	ND	—	.40	1.00	2.00	4.00

Rev: Thin ribbon at base of plant.

400.5	ND	—	.40	1.00	2.00	4.00

Obv: Small pentagonal rosette above flags.

400.6	ND	—	.40	1.00	2.00	4.00

Obv: Small star shaped rosette above flags.

400.7	ND	—	.80	2.00	3.00	5.00

BRASS

400.7b	ND	—	1.60	4.00	8.00	15.00

COPPER
Obv: Larger star shaped rosette above flags.

400.8	ND	—	1.00	2.50	4.00	7.00

Obv: Sharp pointed star above flags.

Y#	Date	Mintage	VG	Fine	VF	XF
400.9	ND	—	1.00	2.50	4.00	7.00

Obv: Sharp pointed star above rosette above flags.

400.10	ND	—	20.00	25.00	30.00	35.00

Rev. denomination: 20 CASH.

400a	ND	—	50.00	75.00	100.00	150.00

Provincial Constitution

Y#	Year	Date	VG	Fine	VF	XF
403	11	(1922)	11.00	20.00	30.00	50.00

10 CENTS

SILVER
Hung Hsien

Kann#	Date	Mintage	Fine	VF	XF	Unc
762	ND(1915)	—	250.00	550.00	900.00	1400.

Though Kann calls this coin an Essay, contemporary reports indicate that the coin actually circulated briefly in 1915. Not to be confused with Y#28, the obverse of which has a different legend in Chinese. (See General Issues - Empire).

DOLLAR

SILVER, 27.40 g
Provincial Constitution

Y#	Year	Date	Fine	VF	XF	Unc
404	11	(1922)	125.00	175.00	250.00	400.00

HUPEH PROVINCE

Hubei

A province located in east-central China. Hilly, with some lakes and swamps, it has rich coal and iron deposits plus a varied agricultural program. The Wuchang Mint had been active from early in the Manchu dynasty and its modern equipment began operations in 1895. It probably closed in 1929.

EMPIRE

CASH

CAST BRASS
Obv: Type A

C#	Date	Emperor	Good	VG	Fine	VF
13-2	ND(1796-1820)	Chia-ch'ing	1.00	2.00	3.00	5.00
	Rev: Crescent above.					
13-2.1	ND(1796-1820)	Chia-ch'ing	2.50	5.50	6.50	12.00
	Obv: Type A					
13-3	ND(1821-50)	Tao-kuang	1.00	2.00	3.00	5.00
	Obv: Type A					
13-4	ND(1851-61)	Hsien-feng	3.00	6.00	7.50	10.00
	Obv: Type A-2					
13-9	ND(1862-74)	T'ung-chih	3.50	7.50	11.50	16.50
	Obv: Type A					
13-11	ND(1875-1908)	Kuang-hsu	5.50	12.50	20.00	28.00

5 CASH

CAST BRASS
Obv: Type B-1

13-5	ND(1851-61)	Hsien-Feng	40.00	70.00	100.00	130.00

10 CASH

CAST BRASS
Obv: Type B-1

C#	Date	Emperor	Good	VG	Fine	VF
13-6	ND(1851-61)	Hsien-feng	6.00	12.50	25.00	60.00
	Rev: Crescent in upper right corner.					
13-6.1	ND(1851-61)	Hsien-feng	10.00	20.00	30.00	60.00
	Obv: Type B					
13-10	ND(1862-74)	T'ung-chih	—	—	Rare	—
	Obv: Type B					
13-12	ND(1875-1908)	Kuang-hsu	—	—	Rare	—

50 CASH

CAST BRASS
Obv: Type B
Obv: and rev: Large characters.

C#	Date	Emperor	Good	VG	Fine	VF
13-7	ND(1851-61)	Hsien-feng	10.00	20.00	35.00	60.00
	Rev: Crescent in upper right corner.					
13-7.1	ND(1851-61)	Hsien-feng	52.50	85.00	110.00	175.00

Obv: and rev: Small characters.

C#	Date	Emperor	Good	VG	Fine	VF
13-7.2	ND(1851-61)	Hsien-feng	10.00	20.00	25.00	60.00

100 CASH

CAST BRASS
Obv: Type C

C#	Date	Emperor	Good	VG	Fine	VF
13-8	ND(1851-61)	Hsien-feng	10.00	20.00	30.00	70.00
	Rev: Crescent in upper right corner.					
13-8.1	ND(1851-61)	Hsien-feng	35.00	55.00	75.00	110.00

Chingchow Mint

CASH

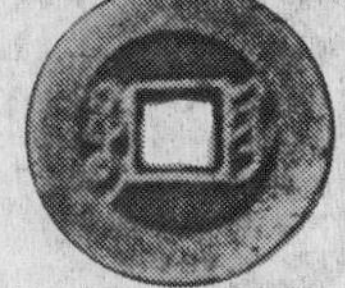

CAST BRASS
Obv: Type A

C#	Date	Emperor	Good	VG	Fine	VF
13-11.1	ND(1875-1908)	Kuang-hsu	12.00	15.00	22.50	30.00

NOTE: Attribution of this mint mark to Chingchow is uncertain.

MILLED COINAGE

CASH

BRASS, struck
Obv: Small characters, 22.5mm.

Hsu#	Date	Mintage	VG	Fine	VF	XF
181	ND(1898)	—	22.50	40.00	50.00	85.00
	Mule. Obv: Hsu#81. Rev: Hsu#82.					
A182	ND(1898)	—	—	—	—	—

Obv: Larger characters, 20.5mm.

Hsu#	Date	Mintage	VG	Fine	VF	XF
182	ND(1898)	—	17.50	25.00	35.00	55.00

Y#	Date	Mintage	VG	Fine	VF	XF
121	ND(1906)	66.474	2.00	3.00	5.00	8.00

Obv: Small mint mark on small disc in center.

Y#	Date	Mintage	VG	Fine	VF	XF
7j	CD1908	I.A.	3.50	8.00	15.00	25.00

Obv: Large mint mark on small disc in center.

Y#	Date	Mintage	VG	Fine	VF	XF
7j.1	CD1908	I.A.	3.50	8.00	15.00	25.00

2 CASH

COPPER

Y#	Date	Mintage	VG	Fine	VF	XF
8j	CD1906	.844	50.00	80.00	125.00	200.00

5 CASH

COPPER, 24mm

Y#	Date	Mintage	VG	Fine	VF	XF
9j	CD1906	9.846	5.00	9.00	15.00	30.00

Dragon redesigned, 23mm.

Y#	Date	Mintage	VG	Fine	VF	XF
9j.1	CD1906	I.A.	6.00	11.00	17.50	35.00

10 CASH

COPPER
Obv: 8 petalled rosette. Rev: Circled dragon.

Y#	Date	Mintage	Fine	VF	XF	Unc
120	ND(1902-05)	4.475	5.00	8.00	15.00	30.00

Rev: Uncircled dragon.

Y#	Date	Mintage	Fine	VF	XF	Unc
120a	ND(1902-05)	Inc. Ab.	3.50	7.00	13.50	30.00

Rev: Slightly larger English letters; wide face on dragon.

Y#	Date	Mintage	Fine	VF	XF	Unc
120a.1	ND(1902-05)	Inc. Ab.	.50	1.00	2.50	20.00

Rev: Large pearl w/many spines, narrower face on dragon.

Y#	Date	Mintage	Fine	VF	XF	Unc
120a.2	ND(1902-05)	Inc. Ab.	.50	1.00	2.50	20.00

Rev: Smaller pearl w/fewer spines on dragon.

Y#	Date	Mintage	Fine	VF	XF	Unc
120a.3	ND(1902-05)	Inc. Ab.	.60	1.25	2.75	20.00

NOTE: Commonly found with medal alignment and also exists with coin alignment.

Obv: 5 petalled rosette, small Manchu word at right. Rev: 4 dots in shape of cross at either side of dragon, PROVINCE spelled PHOVINCE, with V an inverted A.

Y#	Date	Mintage	Fine	VF	XF	Unc
120a.4	ND(1902-05)	Inc. Ab.	.75	1.50	3.00	20.00

Obv: Large Manchu at right.
Rev: R in PROVINCE inverted, V an inverted A.

Y#	Date	Mintage	Fine	VF	XF	Unc
120a.5	ND(1902-05)	Inc. Ab.	.75	1.50	3.00	20.00

Rev: 6 pointed star at either side of dragon; hyphen in HU-PEH.

120a.6	ND(1902-05)	Inc. Ab.	.75	1.50	3.00	20.00

Rev. leg: W/o hyphen in HU PEH.

120a.7	ND(1902-05)	Inc. Ab.	1.50	3.00	6.00	22.00

Obv: 5 petalled rosette and small Manchu.
Rev: Very small pearl.

120a.8	ND(1902-05)	Inc. Ab.	3.50	6.00	12.00	25.00

Obv: Square in circle. Rev. leg: Hyphen in HU-PEH.

120a.9	ND(1902-05)	Inc. Ab.	4.00	7.50	15.00	30.00

Rev. leg: W/o hyphen in HU PEH.

120a.10	ND(1902-05)	Inc. Ab.	1.50	2.50	5.00	20.00

Obv: 2nd character from right at top is larger, 6 petalled rosette. Rev: Front view dragon.

Y#	Date	Mintage	Fine	VF	XF	Unc
122	ND(1902-05)	Inc. Ab.	.60	.85	2.25	20.00

Obv: 2nd character from right *Pei* smaller.

122.1	ND(1902-05)	Inc. Ab.	.50	.75	2.00	20.00

BRASS

Rev: W/o dot at either side of mountain beneath pearl.

122b	ND(1902-05)	Inc. Ab.	—	—	Rare	—

WHITE BRONZE

W#	Date	Mintage	VG	Fine	VF	XF
518	ND(1902-05)		—	—	Rare	—

COPPER

Rev: Clouds above dragons head; 2 clouds below pearl instead of 1.

Y#	Date	Mintage	Fine	VF	XF	Unc
122.3	ND(1902-05)	Inc. Ab.	2.00	5.00	10.00	35.00

Rev: Small circle around lower part of pearl; w/o dots on either side of mountain.

122.4	ND(1902-05)	Inc. Ab.	2.00	5.00	10.00	35.00

Rev: Larger circle around larger pearl; larger English letters.

122.5	ND(1902-05)	Inc. Ab.	2.00	5.00	10.00	35.00

Rev: Circled front view dragon.

122a	ND(1902-05)		125.00	175.00	225.00	—

Rev. leg: TAI CH'ING TI KUO, dragon, w/7 flames on pearl.

Y#	Date	Mintage	Fine	VF	XF	Unc
10j	CD1906	1865.558	.75	1.00	2.00	20.00

Rev: Redesigned dragon w/wide lips; cloud shaped bar below pearl w/5 flames, 28-29mm.

10j.1	CD1906	Inc. Ab.	2.00	5.00	10.00	25.00

30mm

10j.2	CD1906	Inc. Ab.	2.00	5.00	10.00	25.00

Rev: Different dragon w/hook-shaped cloud beneath, pearl w/4 flames; large incuse swirl on pearl.

10j.3	CD1906	Inc. Ab.	.50	.75	1.50	20.00

Rev: Small incuse swirl on pearl w/4 flames.

10j.4	CD1906	Inc. Ab.	.50	.75	1.50	20.00

Rev: Swirl on pearl in relief w/4 flames.

10j.5	CD1906	Inc. Ab.	.75	1.00	2.00	20.00

Rev: Large incuse swirl on pearl.

20j	CD1909	371.577	1.50	3.00	6.00	22.00

Rev: Small swirl in relief on pearl.

Y#	Date	Mintage	Fine	VF	XF	Unc
20j.1	CD1909	Inc. Ab.	1.50	3.00	6.00	22.00

Obv: CD1909 over CD1906.

Y#	Date	Mintage	Fine	VF	XF	Unc
20j.2	CD1909/1906	—	—	—	Rare	—

Rev: Characters *Hsuan T'ung* re-engraved over characters *Kuang Hsu.*

Y#	Date	Mintage	Fine	VF	XF	Unc
20j.3	CD1909	—	—	—	Rare	—

20 CASH

COPPER

Y#	Date	Mintage	VG	Fine	VF	XF
11j	CD1906	3.710	—	250.00	375.00	625.00

5 CENTS

1.3500 g, .820 SILVER, .0356 oz ASW

Y#	Date	Mintage	Fine	VF	XF	Unc
123	ND(1895-1905)	4.278	50.00	100.00	150.00	250.00

10 CENTS

2.7000 g, .820 SILVER, .0712 oz ASW
Rev: Character at either side of dragon *Pen Sheng* indicating coin was for provincial use.

Y#	Date	Mintage	Fine	VF	XF	Unc
124	ND(1894)	—	300.00	700.00	1200.	1750.

Rev: W/o characters beside dragon.

2 varieties of edge milling.

Y#	Date	Mintage	Fine	VF	XF	Unc
124.1	ND(1895-1907)	2.00	4.00	7.50	20.00	

SILVER
Hsuan T'ung

Y#	Date	Mintage	Fine	VF	XF	Unc
129	ND(1909)	—	100.00	200.00	300.00	500.00

20 CENTS

5.3000 g, .820 SILVER, .1397 oz ASW
Rev: Character at either side of dragon *Pen Sheng* indicating coin was for provincial use.

Y#	Date	Mintage	Fine	VF	XF	Unc
125	ND(1894)	—	1500.	3500.	4000.	5000.

Rev: W/o characters beside dragon.

Y#	Date	Mintage	Fine	VF	XF	Unc
125.1	ND(1895-1907)	5.00	10.00	15.00	30.00	

SILVER
Hsuan T'ung

Y#	Date	Mintage	Fine	VF	XF	Unc
130	ND(1909)	—	150.00	350.00	500.00	700.00

50 CENTS

13.5000 g, .860 SILVER, .3733 oz ASW

Y#	Date	Mintage	Fine	VF	XF	Unc
126	ND(1895-1905)	35.00	50.00	85.00	200.00	

DOLLAR

26.7000 g, .900 SILVER, .7727 oz ASW
Obv: Similar to Y#127.1.
Rev: Characters *Pen Sheng* at either side of dragon indicating coin was for provincial use.

Y#	Date	Mintage	Fine	VF	XF	Unc
127	ND(1894)	—	7500.	10,000.	15,000.	25,000.

Rev: W/o *Pen Sheng* at either side of dragon.

Y#	Date	Mintage	Fine	VF	XF	Unc
127.1	ND(1895-1907)	19.935	15.00	22.00	35.00	200.00

27.0000 g, .900 SILVER, .7814 oz ASW
Hsuan T'ung

Y#	Date	Mintage	Fine	VF	XF	Unc
131	ND(1909-11)	2.703	12.00	20.00	30.00	200.00

TAEL SYSTEM

TAEL

37.7000 g, .877 SILVER, 1.0631 oz ASW
Obv: Large central Chinese characters.

Y#	Date	Mintage	Fine	VF	XF	Unc
128.1	Yr.30 (1904)	.648	150.00	250.00	400.00	900.00

Obv: Smaller central Chinese characters.

Y#	Date	Mintage	Fine	VF	XF	Unc
128.2	Yr.30 (1904)	Inc. Ab.	120.00	180.00	280.00	550.00

REPUBLIC

20 CASH

BRASS

Y#	Date	Mintage	VG	Fine	VF	XF
A405	ND	—	40.00	85.00	115.00	165.00

Attribution is uncertain. Probably minted in Szechuan (Sichuan). Former Y#471.

50 CASH

COPPER OR BRASS
Crude Strike

Y#	Year	Date	Good	VG	Fine	VF
405	3	(1914)	375.00	575.00	850.00	1100.
	7	(1918)	175.00	275.00	425.00	650.00

Machine Strike

Y#	Year	Date	Good	VG	Fine	VF
405.1	7	(1918)	375.00	575.00	850.00	1100.

NOTE: Not to be confused with Szechuan (Sichuan) Y#449.

20 CENTS

SILVER, 5.20 g
Obv: Characters *Tsao* at left and *Hu* at right of bust.

Y#	Year	Date	Fine	VF	XF	Unc
406	9	(1920)	75.00	125.00	200.00	500.00

NOTE: Do not confuse with Y#327 (See Republic-General issues.)

KANSU PROVINCE

Gansu

A province located in north-central China with a contrast of mountains and sandy plains. The west end of the Great Wall with its branches lies in Kansu (Gansu). Kansu (Gansu) was the eastern end of the "Silk, Road" that led to central and western Asia. Two mints issued Cash coins. It has been reported, but not confirmed, that the Lanchow Mint operated as late as 1949.

EMPIRE

CASH

CAST BRASS
Obv: Type A

C#	Date	Emperor	Good	VG	Fine	VF
14-1	ND(1851-61)	Hsien-feng	15.00	30.00	45.00	67.50
14-8	ND(1862-74)	T'ung-chih	8.00	16.00	25.00	35.00

5 CASH

CAST BRASS
Obv: Type B-1

C#	Date	Emperor	Good	VG	Fine	VF
14-2	ND(1851-61)	Hsien-feng	20.00	30.00	50.00	80.00

Rev: Large Manchu

C#	Date	Emperor	Good	VG	Fine	VF
14-2.1	ND(1851-61)	Hsien-feng	20.00	30.00	50.00	80.00

Obv: Type B

C#	Date	Emperor	Good	VG	Fine	VF
14-9	ND(1862-74)	T'ung-chih	30.00	40.00	60.00	100.00

10 CASH

CAST BRASS
Obv: Type B

C#	Date	Emperor	Good	VG	Fine	VF
14-3	ND(1851-61)	Hsien-feng	7.00	10.00	20.00	35.00

Obv: Type B

C#	Date	Emperor	Good	VG	Fine	VF
14-10	ND(1862-74)	T'ung-chih	20.00	35.00	45.00	55.00

50 CASH

CAST BRASS, 48mm.
Obv: Type B-1

C#	Date	Emperor	Good	VG	Fine	VF
14-4	ND(1851-61)	Hsien-feng	42.50	70.00	100.00	185.00

43mm

C#	Date	Emperor	Good	VG	Fine	VF
14-4.1	ND(1851-61)	Hsien-feng	40.00	62.50	90.00	165.00

100 CASH

CAST BRASS
Obv: Type C

C#	Date	Emperor	Good	VG	Fine	VF
14-5	ND(1851-61)	Hsien-feng	18.50	30.00	42.50	70.00

500 CASH

CAST BRASS
Obv: Type C

C#	Date	Emperor	Good	VG	Fine	VF
14-6	ND(1851-61)	Hsien-feng	80.00	110.00	150.00	250.00

1000 CASH

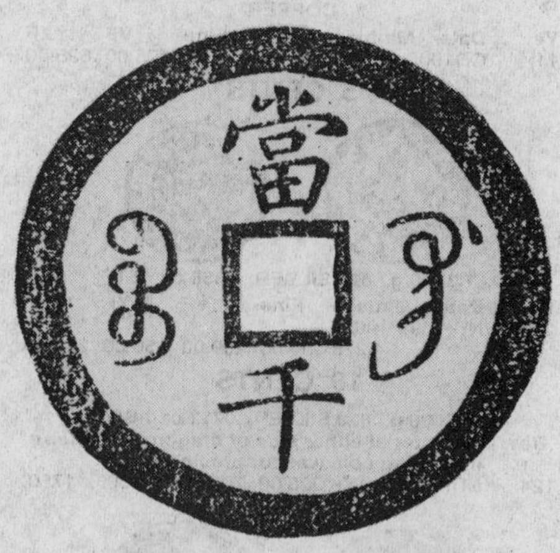

CAST BRASS
Obv: Type C
Illustration reduced, actual size 66mm.

C#	Date	Emperor	Good	VG	Fine	VF
14-7	ND(1851-61)	Hsien-feng	165.00	250.00	350.00	600.00

REPUBLIC

50 CASH

COPPER

Y#	Date	Mintage	VG	Fine	VF	XF
408	Yr.15 (1926)					
		2.564	85.00	175.00	275.00	450.00

100 CASH

COPPER

Y#	Year	Date	VG	Fine	VF	XF
409	15	(1926)	35.00	50.00	100.00	150.00

DOLLAR

SILVER, 26.60 g
Yuan Shih Kai
Obv: Characters *Su* at left, *Kan* at right.

Y#	Year	Date	Fine	VF	XF	Unc
407	3	(1914)	85.00	150.00	300.00	700.00

Sun Yat-sen

Y#	Year	Date	Fine	VF	XF	Unc
410	17	(1928)	100.00	175.00	350.00	700.00

KIANGNAN

A district in eastern China made up of Anhwei (Anhui) and Kiangsu (Jiangsu) provinces. In 1667 the province of Kiangnan was divided into the present provinces of Anhwei (Anhui) and Kiangsu (Jiangsu). In 1723 Nanking, formerly the capital of Kiangnan, was made the capital of Liang-Chiang Chiang (an administrative area consisting of Anhwei (Anhui), Kiangsu (Jiangsu) and Kiangsi (Jiangxi) provinces.

Always highly regarded because of location, agriculture and manufacturing, Kiangnan has frequently been sought after by contending forces.

The Nanking Mint had been active during imperial times. Modern minting facilities began operations in 1897. A second mint was planned for the Kiangnan Arsenal in Shanghai in 1905. Mints for copper coins also operated in Chingkiang (Qingjiang) in central Kiangsu and at Soochow which is further south. A silver mint was planned for Shanghai in 1921. The Nanking Mint, the most important of the group, burned down in 1929. The Nationalist Government Central Mint was completed in Shanghai in 1930 and opened in 1933.

EMPIRE

MILLED COINAGE

CASH

COPPER
Obv: Type A

Hsu#	Date	Mintage	VG	Fine	VF	XF
261	ND(1898)	—	15.00	25.00	35.00	75.00

NOTE: This coin has been erroneously attributed to Ningpo in Chekiang (Zhejang) and to Changchow in Fukien (Fujian). The coin was minted at Nanking from dies produced by the Heaton Mint.

Obv: Smaller characters.
Rev: Mint mark written differently.

Y#	Date	Mintage	VG	Fine	VF	XF
—	ND	—	90.00	135.00	200.00	325.00

BRASS
Obv: Bottom horizontal stroke in mint mark extends beyond outside vertical strokes.

Y#	Date	Mintage	VG	Fine	VF	XF
7k	CD1908	25.450	2.50	4.50	8.50	16.00

Obv: Bottom horizontal stroke in mint mark does not extend beyond outside vertical strokes.

Y#	Date	Mintage	VG	Fine	VF	XF
7k.1	CD1908	Inc. Ab.	3.50	6.50	12.50	21.50

2 CASH

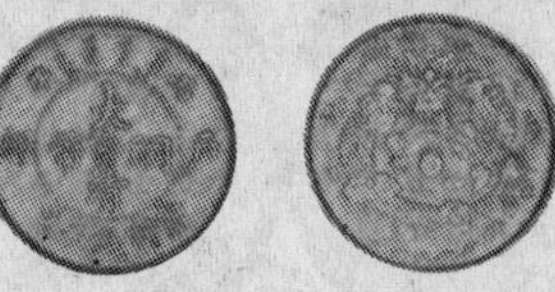

COPPER

Y#	Date	Mintage	VG	Fine	VF	XF
8k	CD1906	—	—	—	—	—

5 CASH

COPPER
Obv: Mint mark incused on raised disk.

Y#	Date	Mintage	VG	Fine	VF	XF
9k.1	CD1906	—	35.00	65.00	100.00	150.00

BRASS

Y#	Date	Mintage	VG	Fine	VF	XF
9k.1a	CD1906	—	45.00	90.00	125.00	200.00

COPPER
Obv: Mint mark in relief at center w/o disc.

Y#	Date	Mintage	VG	Fine	VF	XF
9k.2	CD1906	—	45.00	90.00	125.00	200.00

10 CASH

COPPER
Reeded edge.

Y#	Date	Mintage	Fine	VF	XF	Unc
135	ND	—	30.00	60.00	100.00	—

Plain edge.

Y#	Date	Mintage	Fine	VF	XF	Unc
135.1	ND	—	30.00	60.00	100.00	—

Obv: Small Manchu words in center.

Y#	Date	Mintage	Fine	VF	XF	Unc
135.2	CD1902	—	1.50	3.00	5.00	20.00

Obv: Large Manchu words in center.

Y#	Date	Mintage	Fine	VF	XF	Unc
135.3	CD1902	—	6.00	12.00	25.00	45.00

Y#	Date	Mintage	Fine	VF	XF	Unc
135.4	CD1903	—	4.00	5.00	7.00	24.00

Rev: Cloud above letter T looks like number 3.

Y#	Date	Mintage	Fine	VF	XF	Unc
135.5	CD1904	351.974	1.00	2.00	4.00	20.00

Rev: Cloud above T redesigned.
CASH spelled GASH.

Y#	Date	Mintage	Fine	VF	XF	Unc
135.6	CD1904	I.A.	4.50	9.00	17.50	45.00

Rev: 3rd design of cloud above letter T, thin tailed dragon.

Y#	Date	Mintage	Fine	VF	XF	Unc
135.7	CD1904	I.A.	1.50	3.00	5.00	20.00

Rev: Fewer clouds around dragon, scales on dragons body different, pearl smaller.

Y#	Date	Mintage	Fine	VF	XF	Unc
135.8	CD1904	I.A.	4.50	9.00	17.50	45.00

NOTE: The above coin is believed to be counterfeit.

Rev: Small rosette at either side of dragon.

Y#	Date	Mintage	Fine	VF	XF	Unc
135.9	CD1905	496.020	.75	1.50	3.00	20.00

Rev: Large oblong rosettes at either side of dragon.

Y#	Date	Mintage	Fine	VF	XF	Unc
135.10	CD1905	I.A.	1.50	3.00	5.00	20.00

Obv: Rosette in center.
Rev: denomination: TEN-CASH.

Y#	Date	Mintage	Fine	VF	XF	Unc
138	CD1905	I.A.	3.50	6.00	12.00	30.00

Rev: W/o hyphen in TEN CASH.

Y#	Date	Mintage	Fine	VF	XF	Unc
138.1	CD1905	I.A.	.75	1.50	3.00	20.00

Mule. Obv: Y#10k. Rev: Y#138. raised or incused mint mark.

Y#	Date	Mintage	Fine	VF	XF	Unc
140	CD1906	I.A.	3.00	5.00	12.00	30.00

Mule. Obv: Y#10k.2. Rev: Y#138.

Y#	Date	Mintage	Fine	VF	XF	Unc
A140	CD1906	I.A.	25.00	40.00	60.00	—

Mule. Obv: Y#138. Rev: Y#10k.

Y#	Date	Mintage	Fine	VF	XF	Unc
B140	CD1905	I.A.	30.00	50.00	70.00	—

Mule. Obv: Kiang-nan. Rev: KIANG-SOO. Often confused w/Y#162.

Y#	Date	Mintage	Fine	VF	XF	Unc
C140	ND	—	150.00	200.00	250.00	—
	CD1902	—	—	—	—	—

Mule. Obv: Y#138.1. Rev: Y#135.

Y#	Date	Mintage	Fine	VF	XF	Unc
D140	CD1905	I.A.	100.00	150.00	200.00	—

Other Kiangnan mules exist, dated 1902 and 1903.

Mule. Obv: Y#10.5. Rev: Kiangnan Y#138.1.

Y#	Date	Mintage	Fine	VF	XF	Unc
E140	CD1907	—	100.00	225.00	300.00	—

Obv: Mint mark in relief on raised disc.
Rev: Dragon w/wide face and incuse eyes.

Y#	Date	Mintage	Fine	VF	XF	Unc
10k	CD1906	504.800	1.25	2.50	5.00	20.00

Rev: Dragon w/narrower face and raised dots for eyes.

Y#	Date	Mintage	Fine	VF	XF	Unc
10k.1	CD1906	I.A.	1.25	2.50	5.00	20.00

Obv: Mint mark in relief in field w/o raised disc.
Rev: Dragon w/wide face and incuse eyes.

Y#	Date	Mintage	Fine	VF	XF	Unc
10k.2	CD1906	I.A.	.75	1.50	3.00	20.00

Rev: Dragon w/narrow face and raised dots for eyes.

Y#	Date	Mintage	Fine	VF	XF	Unc
10k.3	CD1906	I.A.	.75	1.50	3.00	20.00

Obv: Mint mark incuse on raised disc.

Y#	Date	Mintage	Fine	VF	XF	Unc
10k.4	CD1906	I.A.	12.00	25.00	45.00	—

BRASS

Y#	Date	Mintage	Fine	VF	XF	Unc
10K.4a	CD1906	—	—	—	—	—

COPPER
Obv: Mint mark incuse on raised disc.
Rev: Dragon w/wide face. 7 flames on pearl.

Y#	Date	Mintage	Fine	VF	XF	Unc
10k.5	CD1907	552.000	1.50	3.00	5.00	20.00

Rev: Different dragon w/narrow face and small mouth, 5 flames on pearl, dot after COIN.

Y#	Date	Mintage	Fine	VF	XF	Unc
10k.6	CD1907	I.A.	.50	1.00	2.50	20.00

BRASS

Y#	Date	Mintage	Fine	VF	XF	Unc
10k.6a	CD1907	I.A.	9.00	17.50	30.00	—

COPPER
Rev: Dragon w/large mouth and redesigned head, flame below pearl has long tail which touches dragon's body, KUO spelled KIIO.

Y#	Date	Mintage	Fine	VF	XF	Unc
10k.7	CD1907	I.A.	.75	1.50	3.00	20.00

Rev: Tail of flame below pearl does not touch body, dash after word COIN. KUO spelled KUO.

Y#	Date	Mintage	Fine	VF	XF	Unc
10k.8	CD1907	I.A.	.75	1.50	3.00	20.00

Rev: Dragon w/square mouth, letter K in KUO larger than other letters, w/o dot or dash after COIN.

Y#	Date	Mintage	Fine	VF	XF	Unc
10k.9	CD1907	I.A.	.50	1.00	2.50	20.00

Rev: Large, flat faced dragon.

Y#	Date	Mintage	Fine	VF	XF	Unc
10k.9a	CD1907	—	—	—	—	—

Obv: Mint mark incuse on raised disc. Rev: Dragon w/small mouth, 5 flame pearl, dot after COIN, KUO spelled KUO.

Y#	Date	Mintage	Fine	VF	XF	Unc
10k.10	CD1908	442.750	.50	1.00	2.50	20.00

Rev: Dragon has large mouth and redesigned head, tail on cloud beneath pearl touches dragon's body, KUO spelled KIIO.

Y#	Date	Mintage	Fine	VF	XF	Unc
10k.11	CD1908	I.A.	1.00	2.00	4.00	20.00

Rev: Dash after COIN, KUO spelled KUO.

Y#	Date	Mintage	Fine	VF	XF	Unc
10k.12	CD1908	I.A.	1.50	3.00	5.00	20.00

Rev: Dragon's head redesigned, w/o dot or dash after COIN, KUO spelled KIIO.

Y#	Date	Mintage	Fine	VF	XF	Unc
10k.13	CD1908	I.A.	1.00	2.00	4.00	20.00

NOTE: Most of the 1907 and 1908 ten cash above have copper spelled GOPPER.

5 CENTS

1.3000 g, .820 SILVER, .0343 oz ASW
Rev: Circled dragon.

Y#	Date	Mintage	Fine	VF	XF	Unc
141	ND(1898)	.100	18.00	30.00	55.00	150.00
	ND(1898)	—	—	—	Proof	700.00

Rev: W/o circle around dragon.

Y#	Date	Mintage	Fine	VF	XF	Unc
141a	ND(1898)	I.A.	7.00	12.00	20.00	40.00
	CD1899	3,812	20.00	35.00	60.00	150.00
	CD1900	.618	7.00	15.00	22.00	50.00
	CD1901	—	25.00	40.00	75.00	150.00

10 CENTS

2.6000 g, .820 SILVER, .0686 oz ASW

Rev: Circled dragon.

Y#	Date	Mintage	Fine	VF	XF	Unc
142	ND(1898)	8.000	12.00	25.00	50.00	150.00
	ND(1898)	—	—	—	Proof	700.00

Y#	Date	Mintage	Fine	VF	XF	Unc
142.1	CD1898	Inc. Ab.	7.00	15.00	25.00	45.00

Rev: W/o circle around dragon w/small rosettes at sides.

Y#	Date	Mintage	Fine	VF	XF	Unc
142a	CD1898	I.A.	3.50	7.00	15.00	30.00

Rev: Large rosettes at sides of dragons.

Y#	Date	Mintage	Fine	VF	XF	Unc
142a.1	CD1898	I.A.	3.50	7.00	15.00	30.00

Obv: Large characters in center, small characters in outer ring.

Y#	Date	Mintage	Fine	VF	XF	Unc
142a.2	CD1899	10.784	2.25	4.50	9.00	30.00

Obv: Small characters in center, large characters in outer ring.

Y#	Date	Mintage	Fine	VF	XF	Unc
142a.3	CD1899	I.A.	2.25	4.50	9.00	30.00

Y#	Date	Mintage	Fine	VF	XF	Unc
142a.4	CD1900	5.460	2.50	5.00	10.00	35.00

Obv: W/o initials. Rev: Large English letters.

Y#	Date	Mintage	Fine	VF	XF	Unc
142a.5	CD1901	7.794	2.25	4.50	9.00	30.00

Rev: Small English letters.

Y#	Date	Mintage	Fine	VF	XF	Unc
142a.6	CD1901	I.A.	2.25	4.50	9.00	30.00

Obv: Initials *HAH*.
Rev: Large rosettes beside dragon.

Y#	Date	Mintage	Fine	VF	XF	Unc
142a.7	CD1901	I.A.	3.50	6.50	12.50	35.00

Rev: Small rosettes beside dragon.

Y#	Date	Mintage	Fine	VF	XF	Unc
142a.8	CD1901	I.A.	3.50	6.50	12.50	35.00

Rev: Large stars beside dragon.

Y#	Date	Mintage	Fine	VF	XF	Unc
142a.9	CD1902	3.778	2.25	4.50	9.00	30.00

Rev: Small stars beside dragon.

Y#	Date	Mintage	Fine	VF	XF	Unc
142a.10	CD1902	I.A.	2.25	4.50	9.00	30.00

Obv: Large rosette.

Y#	Date	Mintage	Fine	VF	XF	Unc
142a.11	CD1903	1.161	3.50	6.50	15.00	50.00

Obv: Small rosette.

Y#	Date	Mintage	Fine	VF	XF	Unc
142a.12	CD1903	I.A.	3.50	6.50	15.00	50.00

Obv: Initials *HAH TH*.

Y#	Date	Mintage	Fine	VF	XF	Unc
142a.13	CD1904	.897	3.75	7.50	15.00	50.00

Obv: Initials *SY* upside down.

Y#	Date	Mintage	Fine	VF	XF	Unc
142a.14	CD1905	.681	3.50	6.50	15.00	50.00

Obv: W/o initials.

Y#	Date	Mintage	Fine	VF	XF	Unc
142a.15	CD1905	I.A.	3.50	6.50	15.00	50.00

Y#	Date	Mintage	Fine	VF	XF	Unc
146	ND(1911)	*.820	7.50	15.00	30.00	75.00

***NOTE:** Includes 590,000 pieces struck in debased silver in 1916.

20 CENTS

5.3000 g, .820 SILVER, .1397 oz ASW
Obv: Rosettes at 2 and 10 o'clock.
Rev: Circle around dragon.

Y#	Date	Mintage	Fine	VF	XF	Unc
143	ND(1898)	7.000	17.50	40.00	70.00	140.00

Y#	Date	Mintage	Fine	VF	XF	Unc
143.1	CD1898	I.A.	15.00	35.00	65.00	100.00

Obv: Large characters in outer ring. Rev: Large English letters, w/o circle around dragon.

Y#	Date	Mintage	Fine	VF	XF	Unc
143a	CD1898	I.A.	3.75	5.50	11.50	25.00

Obv: Small characters in outer ring.
Rev: Small English letters.

Y#	Date	Mintage	Fine	VF	XF	Unc
143a.1	CD1898	I.A.	3.75	5.50	11.50	25.00

Rev: Old type dragon w/long face, flanked by short rosettes.

Y#	Date	Mintage	Fine	VF	XF	Unc
143a.2	CD1899	11.096	3.50	5.00	10.00	20.00

Rev: New type dragon w/shorter face and larger forehead, flanked by long rosettes.

Y#	Date	Mintage	Fine	VF	XF	Unc
143a.3	CD1899	I.A.	5.00	10.00	25.00	50.00

Rev: Old type dragon w/long face, flanked by long rosettes.

Y#	Date	Mintage	Fine	VF	XF	Unc
143a.4	CD1900	5.796	5.00	10.00	25.00	40.00

Rev: New type dragon w/shorter face and larger forehead.

Y#	Date	Mintage	Fine	VF	XF	Unc
143a.5	CD1900	I.A.	5.00	10.00	25.00	50.00

Obv: W/o initials.

Y#	Date	Mintage	Fine	VF	XF	Unc
143a.6	CD1901	47.114	4.50	8.00	15.00	35.00

Rev. leg: . . . . .MACI. . . . .

Y#	Date	Mintage	Fine	VF	XF	Unc
143a.14	CD1901	I.A.	5.00	10.00	25.00	50.00

Obv: Initials *HAH*.

Y#	Date	Mintage	Fine	VF	XF	Unc
143a.7	CD1901	I.A.	3.50	5.00	10.00	30.00
143a.8	CD1902	15.754	4.00	6.50	12.50	30.00

Obv: Rosette in outer leg.

Y#	Date	Mintage	Fine	VF	XF	Unc
143a.9	CD1903	2.432	7.00	17.50	30.00	80.00

Obv: W/o rosette.

Y#	Date	Mintage	Fine	VF	XF	Unc
143a.10	CD1903	I.A.	9.00	22.50	35.00	90.00

Obv: Initials *HAH TH*.

Y#	Date	Mintage	Fine	VF	XF	Unc
143a.11	CD1904	1.172	15.00	35.00	55.00	120.00

Obv: W/o initials.

Y#	Date	Mintage	Fine	VF	XF	Unc
143a.12	CD1905	.828	10.00	25.00	45.00	100.00

Obv: Initials *SY*.

Y#	Date	Mintage	Fine	VF	XF	Unc
143a.13	CD1905	I.A.	9.00	22.00	35.00	85.00

Y#	Date	Mintage	Fine	VF	XF	Unc
147	ND(1911)	2.320	20.00	50.00	80.00	150.00

NOTE: Includes 2,005,000 pieces struck in debased silver in 1916.

50 CENTS

13.2000 g, .860 SILVER, .3650 oz ASW
Rev: Circled dragon

Y#	Date	Mintage	Fine	VF	XF	Unc
144	ND(1898)	.100	175.00	325.00	500.00	1200.
	ND(1898)	—	—	—	Proof	2500.

Rev: W/o circle around dragon.

Y#	Date	Mintage	Fine	VF	XF	Unc
144a	CD1899	155 pcs.	—	800.00	1200.	2000.
	CD1900	—	300.00	800.00	1150.	1700.

DOLLAR

27.0000 g, .900 SILVER, .7814 oz ASW
Rev: Circled dragon. Normal edge reeding.

Y#	Date	Mintage	Fine	VF	XF	Unc
145	ND(1898)	1.603	200.00	350.00	700.00	1400.

Ornamented edge

Y#	Date	Mintage	Fine	VF	XF	Unc
145.1	ND(1898)	I.A.	125.00	175.00	300.00	800.00

Rev: W/o circle around old style dragon.

Y#	Date	Mintage	Fine	VF	XF	Unc
145a.1	CD1898	I.A.	25.00	75.00	150.00	600.00

Similar to Y#145a.1 but w/smaller letters.

Y#	Date	Mintage	Fine	VF	XF	Unc
145a.2	CD1898	I. A.	25.00	75.00	125.00	500.00
	CD1899	2.039	22.50	50.00	120.00	400.00

Obv: Chinese date characters *Wu Shu* reversed.

Y#	Date	Mintage	Fine	VF	XF	Unc
145a.18	CD1898	I.A.	1500.	2750.	—	—

Rev: Redesigned dragon w/shorter face and larger forehead, similar to 1900.

Y#	Date	Mintage	Fine	VF	XF	Unc
145a.3	CD1899	I. A.	100.00	150.00	250.00	750.00

Rev: Large scales on dragon.

Y#	Date	Mintage	Fine	VF	XF	Unc
145a.4	CD1900	2.531	30.00	75.00	150.00	600.00

Rev: Small scales on dragon.

Y#	Date	Mintage	Fine	VF	XF	Unc
145a.20	CD1900	I.A.	22.50	50.00	125.00	600.00

Obv: W/o initials.

Y#	Date	Mintage	Fine	VF	XF	Unc
145a.5	CD1901	2.377	150.00	200.00	300.00	1250.

Obv: Fine initials *HAH* w/o rosette.
Rev: Similar to Y#145a.6.

Y#	Date	Mintage	Fine	VF	XF	Unc
145a.21	CD1901	I.A.	65.00	125.00	200.00	500.00

Obv: Bold initials *HAH* w/o rosette.
Rev: Petals of rosettes separated from each other.

Y#	Date	Mintage	Fine	VF	XF	Unc
145a.6	CD1901	I.A.	65.00	125.00	200.00	500.00

Obv: Cross of 6 dots at upper right.
Rev: Similar to Y#145a.6.

Y#	Date	Mintage	Fine	VF	XF	Unc
145a.22	CD1901	I.A.	100.00	200.00	350.00	1000.

Obv: Initials *HAH* and rosette.
Rev: Petals of rosettes run together.

Y#	Date	Mintage	Fine	VF	XF	Unc
145a.7	CD1901	I.A.	20.00	35.00	75.00	250.00

Obv: Small date, small *HAH*.
Rev: Similar to Y#145a.4

Y#	Date	Mintage	Fine	VF	XF	Unc
145a.8	CD1902	3.562	25.00	50.00	100.00	275.00

Obv: Larger date, larger *HAH*.

Y#	Date	Mintage	Fine	VF	XF	Unc
145a.9	CD1902	I.A.	25.00	50.00	100.00	275.00

Obv: *HAH* and rosette in outer ring.

Y#	Date	Mintage	Fine	VF	XF	Unc
145a.10	CD1903	1.489	40.00	85.00	175.00	400.00

Obv: W/o rosette in outer ring.

Y#	Date	Mintage	Fine	VF	XF	Unc
145a.11	CD1903	I.A.	400.00	600.00	900.00	2000.

Obv: Initials *HAH* and *CH*, w/o dots or rosettes.
Rev: Similar to Y#145a.4.

Y#	Date	Mintage	Fine	VF	XF	Unc
145a.12	CD1904	44.725	10.00	16.00	25.00	100.00

Obv: Dot at either side.

Y#	Date	Mintage	Fine	VF	XF	Unc
145a.13	CD1904	I.A.	10.00	16.00	30.00	125.00

Obv: Dot at either side, w/o 4 central characters.

Y#	Date	Mintage	Fine	VF	XF	Unc
145a.19	CD1904	—	—	—	—	—

Rev: Dot to left of numeral 7.

Y#	Date	Mintage	Fine	VF	XF	Unc
145a.14	CD1904	I.A.	10.00	16.00	30.00	125.00

Obv: 4 petalled rosette at either side *HAH* and *CH*.

Y#	Date	Mintage	Fine	VF	XF	Unc
145a.15	CD1904	I.A.	50.00	125.00	200.00	500.00

Obv: Initials *HAH* and *TH*.

Y#	Date	Mintage	Fine	VF	XF	Unc
145a.16	CD1904	I.A.	50.00	100.00	200.00	500.00

Obv: Initials *SY*.
Rev: Similar to Y#145a.10.

Y#	Date	Mintage	Fine	VF	XF	Unc
145a.17	CD1905	.634	35.00	65.00	125.00	450.00

NOTE: The initials HAH, SY, CH and TH are those of mint officials and were placed on the coins as a guarantee of the coin's fineness. The 5, 10 and 20 Cent coins are often found without a decimal point between the numbers on the reverse. The 1904 dated dollar was restruck during Republican times.

KIANGSI PROVINCE

Jiangxi, Kiangsee

A province located in southeastern China. Mostly hilly with some mountains on the borders that produce coal and tungsten.. Some of China's finest porcelain comes from this province. Kiangsi was visited by Marco Polo. A mint was opened in Nanchang in 1729, closed in 1733, reopened in 1736 and operated with reasonable continuity from that time. Modern machinery was introduced in 1901 although it only produced copper coins. The mint closed amidst internal problems in the 1920's.

EMPIRE

CASH

CAST BRASS
Obv: Type A

C#	Date	Emperor	Good	VG	Fine	VF
15-2	ND(1796-1820)	Chia-ch'ing	.25	.50	1.00	1.50

Rev: Dot in upper left corner.

C#	Date	Emperor	Good	VG	Fine	VF
15-2.1	ND(1796-1820)	Chia-ch'ing	3.50	5.00	7.00	12.00

Obv: Type A

C#	Date	Emperor	Good	VG	Fine	VF
15-3	ND(1821-51)	Tao-kuang	.50	.85	1.50	2.00

CAST ZINC

C#	Date	Emperor	Good	VG	Fine	VF
15-3a	ND(1821-51)	Tao-kuang	—	—	Rare	—

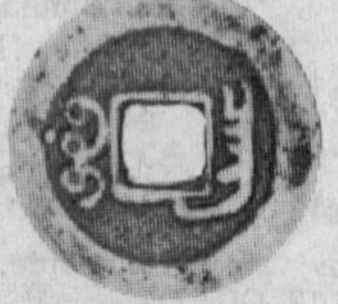

CAST BRASS
Obv: Type A

C#	Date	Emperor	Good	VG	Fine	VF
15-4	ND(1851-61)	Hsien-feng	1.00	2.00	3.00	4.00

Obv: Type A

C#	Date	Emperor	Good	VG	Fine	VF
15-7	ND(1862-74)	T'ung-chih	1.20	3.00	4.00	5.00

Obv: Type A. Rev: Type 1 mint mark.

C#	Date	Emperor	Good	VG	Fine	VF
15-9	ND(1875-1908)	Kuang-hsu	4.50	6.50	12.00	15.00

10 CASH

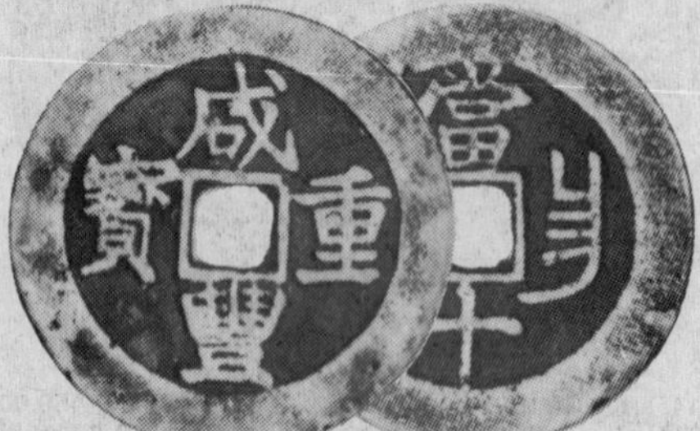

CAST BRASS
Obv: Type B-1

C#	Date	Emperor	Good	VG	Fine	VF
15-5	ND(1851-61)	Hsien-feng	3.00	6.00	10.00	30.00

Obv: Type B

C#	Date	Emperor	Good	VG	Fine	VF
15-8	ND(1862-74)	T'ung-chih	—	—	Rare	—

Obv: Type B

C#	Date	Emperor	Good	VG	Fine	VF
15-10	ND(1875-1908)	Kuang-hsu	—	—	Rare	—

50 CASH

CAST COPPER
Obv: Type B-1

C#	Date	Emperor	Good	VG	Fine	VF
15.6	ND(1851-61)	Hsien-feng	8.00	16.00	30.00	60.00

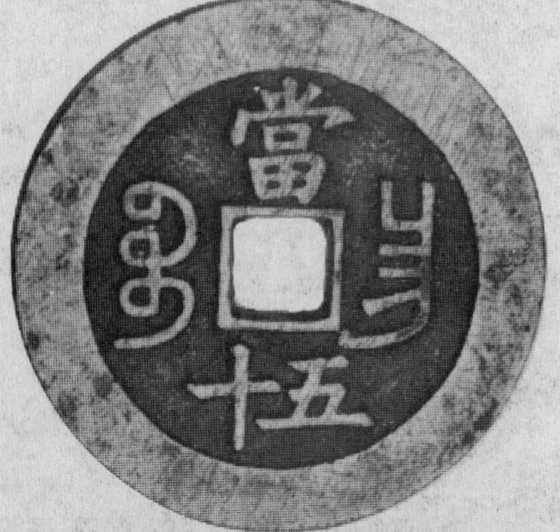

CAST BRASS

C#	Date	Emperor	Good	VG	Fine	VF
15-6.1	ND(1851-61)	Hsien-feng	6.00	12.00	18.00	35.00

MILLED COINAGE

Horizontal rosette   Vertical rosette

10 CASH

COPPER
Obv: Vertical rosette at center.
Rev: Province name spelled KIANG-SEE.

Y#	Date	Mintage	VG	Fine	VF	XF
149	ND	—	3.25	8.00	12.50	22.50

Obv: Horizontal rosette at center.

Y#	Date	Mintage	VG	Fine	VF	XF
149.1	ND	—	3.25	8.00	12.50	22.50

Obv: Different Manchu word at right.
Rev: Circled dragon.

Y#	Date	Mintage	VG	Fine	VF	XF
149.2	ND	—	—	—	Rare	—

NOTE: May be a pattern.

Obv: Manchu reading *Pao Yuan*.
Rev: Province name spelled KIANG-SI; 2 stars at either side of dragon.

Y#	Date	Mintage	Fine	VF	XF	Unc
150	ND	—	6.00	11.00	17.50	35.00

Obv: Manchu reading *Pao Ch'ang* at center and Chinese reading *Ku P'ing* at 3 and 9 o'clock.

Y#	Date	Mintage	Fine	VF	XF	Unc
150.1	ND	—	3.00	6.00	12.00	25.00

Obv: Manchu reading *Pao Ch'ang* at 3 and 9 o'clock, horizontal rosette in center.

Y#	Date	Mintage	Fine	VF	XF	Unc
150.2	ND	—	1.00	2.00	5.00	20.00

BRASS

Y#	Date	Mintage	Fine	VF	XF	Unc
150.2a	ND	—	5.00	10.00	20.00	40.00

COPPER
Obv: Vertical rosette in center.

Y#	Date	Mintage	Fine	VF	XF	Unc
150.3	ND	—	1.00	2.00	4.00	20.00

Obv: Horizontal rosette. Rev: 1 star at either side of dragon, large English lettering.

Y#	Date	Mintage	Fine	VF	XF	Unc
150.4	ND	—	1.00	2.00	4.00	20.00

BRASS

Y#	Date	Mintage	Fine	VF	XF	Unc
150.4a	ND	—	5.00	9.00	17.50	35.00

COPPER
Obv: Vertical rosette.

Y#	Date	Mintage	Fine	VF	XF	Unc
150.5	ND	—	1.00	2.00	4.00	20.00

Rev: Smaller English lettering, 1 star at either side of dragon.

Y#	Date	Mintage	Fine	VF	XF	Unc
150.6	ND	—	1.00	2.00	4.00	20.00

Obv: Small rosette center.
Rev: 1 star at either side of dragon.

Y#	Date	Mintage	Fine	VF	XF	Unc
150.7	ND	—	6.00	11.00	17.50	35.00

Rev: 3 stars at either side of dragon.

Y#	Date	Mintage	Fine	VF	XF	Unc
150.8	ND	—	12.00	20.00	30.00	60.00

Obv: Manchu *Pao Ch'ang* at 3 and 9 o'clock.
Rev: Province name spelled KIANG-SI; front view dragon, mountain below pearl.

Y#	Date	Mintage	VG	Fine	VF	XF
152	ND	—	2.50	4.00	6.00	12.00

Obv: Horizontal rosette in center and Manchu *Pao Ch'ang* at 3 and 9 o'clock.

Y#	Date	Mintage	VG	Fine	VF	XF
152.1	ND	—	2.50	4.00	6.00	12.00

Obv: Horizontal rosette in center and Manchu *Pao Ch'ang* at 3 and 9 o'clock, small character '10'.

Y#	Date	Mintage	VG	Fine	VF	XF
152.2	ND	—	5.00	12.00	17.50	27.50

Obv: Horizontal rosette in center and Manchu *Pao Ch'ang* at 3 and 9 o'clock, large character '10'. Rev: W/o mountain below dragon.

Y#	Date	Mintage	VG	Fine	VF	XF
152.3	ND	—	3.50	8.00	12.00	17.50

Obv: Vertical rosette in center.

152.7	ND	—	—	—	—	—

Obv: Horizontal rosette in center, small character '10'.

152.4	ND	—	3.50	8.00	12.00	17.50

Obv: Manchu *Pao Ch'ang* in center, Chinese *K'u P'ing* at 3 and 9 o'clock. Rev: W/o mountain below pearl, dragon's body repositioned.

152.5	ND	—	3.50	8.00	12.00	17.50

Rev: Mountain below dragon.

152.6	ND	—	3.25	7.50	11.00	16.00

Rev. leg: KIANG-SEE PROVINCE above front view dragon.

153	ND	—	2.00	4.50	7.00	11.00

Obv: Manchu *Pao Ch'ang* at center and Chinese *K'u P'ing* at 3 and 9 o'clock.

153.1	ND	—	.80	2.00	3.50	7.00

Obv: Manchu *Pao Ch'ang* at 3 and 9 o'clock and horizontal rosette in center.

153.2	ND	—	.80	2.00	3.50	7.00

Obv: Small vertical rosette in center.

153.3	ND	—	1.00	2.50	5.25	8.75

NOTE: All 4 varieties of Y#153 are found with and without a swirl on the pearl below dragon's mouth.

Rev. leg: KIANG-SI above flying dragon.

Y#	Date	Mintage	VG	Fine	VF	XF
154	ND	—	40.00	60.00	80.00	100.00

Rev: Eyes of dragon in relief

10m	CD1906	—	1.25	3.00	6.00	12.00

Rev: Dragon's eyes incuse

10m.1	CD1906	—	1.25	3.00	6.00	12.00

Rev: Dragon redesigned, small faint cloud beneath pearl.

10m.2	CD1906	—	5.00	12.00	17.50	30.00

REPUBLIC

10 CASH

COPPER

Obv: Mint mark incused on raised-disc center, w/ Chinese characters on 4 sides *Ta Han T'ung Pi*. 5 character value in outer ring at bottom. Rev: Ring of 9 balls w/o inscription.

411	CD1911	—	—	—	Rare	—

Obv: Date appears at 3 and 9 o'clock. Rev: 9 pointed star inside circle and 5 petalled rosette at 3 and 9 o'clock.

412	CD1912	—	150.00	200.00	325.00	450.00

Obv: Horizontal rosette in center, w/Chinese characters *Chiang Hsi* above and below. Rev: 6 petalled rosette at either side.

412a	CD1912	—	1.25	3.00	5.00	9.00

Obv: Small vertical rosette in center.

Y#	Date	Mintage	VG	Fine	VF	XF
412a.1	CD1912	—	1.25	3.00	5.00	9.00

Obv: Large vertical rosette, thick, large center characters. Rev: Small 5 petalled rosettes at either side.

412a.2	CD1912	—	6.00	12.00	17.50	27.50

Obv: Large vertical rosette in center, thin center characters.

412a.3	CD1912	—	1.25	3.00	5.00	10.00

NOTE: Many Kiangsi (Jiangxi) coins have a 6 petalled rosette in the center of the obverse, arranged so that 2 sides of the rosette are formed by 2 petals in line with each other. The remaining 2 sides have a single petal, standing out from the rest. The direction that these single petals point, determines whether the rosette is horizontal or vertical. A horizontal rosette has the single petals pointing left and right, while the single petals of the vertical rosette point up and down.

KIANGSU/KIANGSOO PROVINCE

Jiangsu

A province located on the east coast of China. One of the smallest and most densely populated of all Chinese provinces. A mint opened in Soochow in 1667, but closed shortly after in 1670. A new mint opened in 1734 for producing cast coins and had continuous operation until about 1870. Modern equipment was introduced in 1898 and a second mint was opened in 1904. Both mints closed down production in 1906. Taels were produced in Shanghai by local silversmiths as early as 1856. These saw limited circulation in the immediate area.

EMPIRE

Kiangsu Mint

CASH

CAST BRASS

Obv: Type A

C#	Date	Emperor	Good	VG	Fine	VF
16-2	ND(1796-1820)	Chia-ch'ing	.50	1.00	1.50	3.00

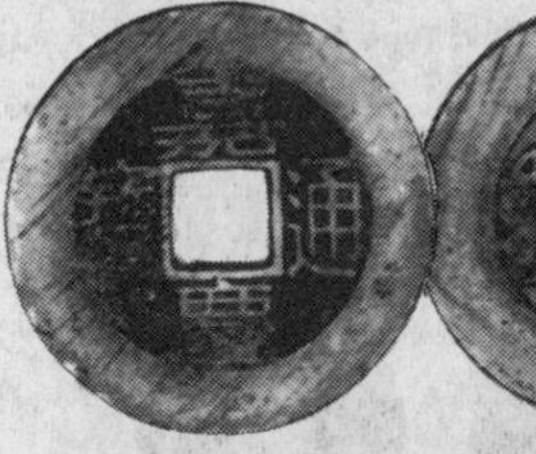

Wide rims.

16-2.1	ND(1796-1820)	Chia-ch'ing	30.00	50.00	70.00	110.00

Obv: Type A Narrow rims.

16-3	ND(1821-51)	Tao-kuang	.50	1.00	2.00	4.00

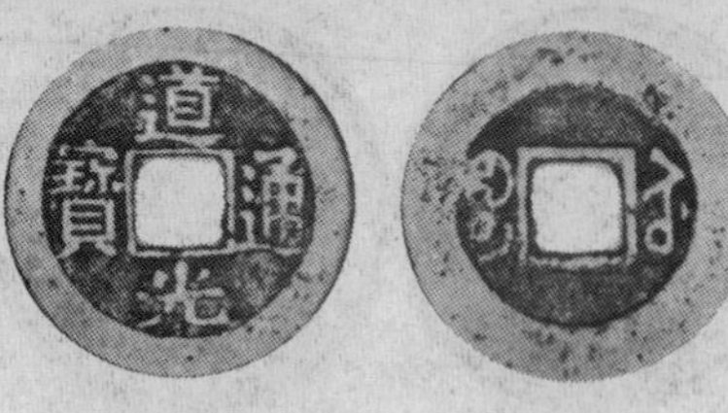

Medium rims.

C#	Date	Emperor	Good	VG	Fine	VF
16-3.1	ND(1821-51)	Tao-kuang	.50	1.00	2.00	4.00

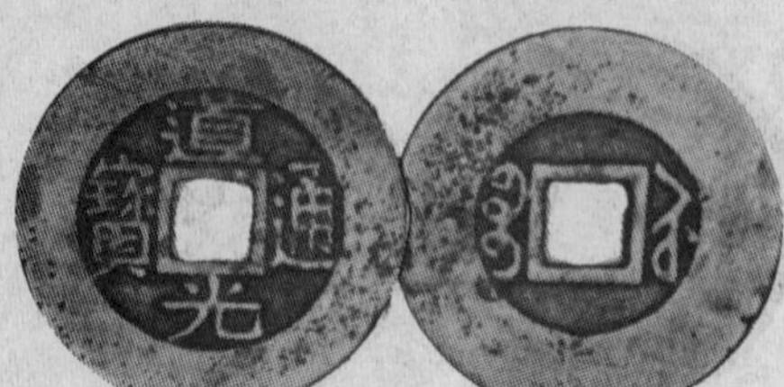

Wide rims.

C#	Date	Emperor	Good	VG	Fine	VF
16-3.2	ND(1821-51)	Tao-kuang	30.00	50.00	70.00	110.00

Narrow rims.

C#	Date	Emperor	Good	VG	Fine	VF
16-4	ND(1851-61)	Hsien-feng	1.00	2.00	3.00	4.50

Medium rims.

C#	Date	Emperor	Good	VG	Fine	VF
16-4.1	ND(1851-61)	Hsien-feng	1.00	2.00	3.00	4.50

Wide rims.

C#	Date	Emperor	Good	VG	Fine	VF
16-4.2	ND(1851-61)	Hsien-feng	—	—	Rare	—

Rev: Crescent above.

C#	Date	Emperor	Good	VG	Fine	VF
16-4.3	ND(1851-61)	Hsien-feng	4.25	8.50	17.50	35.00

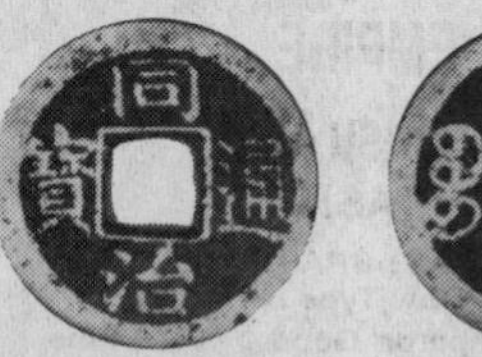

C#	Date	Emperor	Good	VG	Fine	VF
16-11	ND(1862-74)	T'ung-chih	2.75	5.50	9.00	15.00

Obv: Type A

C#	Date	Emperor	Good	VG	Fine	VF
16-12	ND(1875-1908)	Kuang-hsu	2.25	4.50	8.00	13.00

Rev: Circle above.

C#	Date	Emperor	Good	VG	Fine	VF
16-12.1	ND(1875-1908)	Kuang-hsu	3.00	6.00	10.00	16.00

Rev: Crescent above.

C#	Date	Emperor	Good	VG	Fine	VF
16-12.2	ND(1875-1908)	Kuang-hsu	3.00	6.00	10.00	16.00

5 CASH

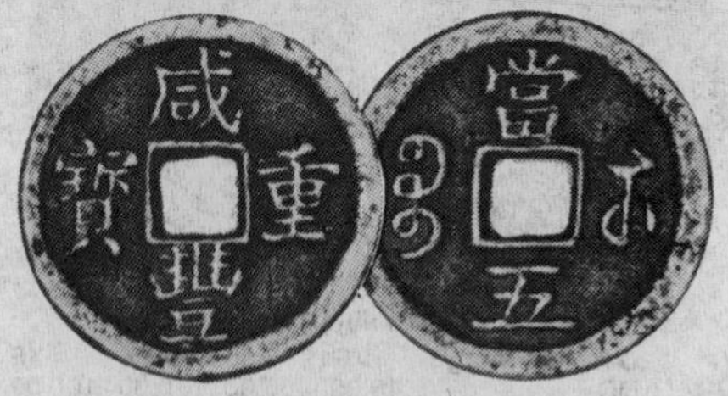

CAST BRASS
Obv: Type B-1

C#	Date	Emperor	Good	VG	Fine	VF
16-5	ND(1851-61)	Hsien-feng	30.00	45.00	65.00	100.00

CAST IRON

C#	Date	Emperor	Good	VG	Fine	VF
16-5a	ND(1851-61)	Hsien-feng	40.00	55.00	80.00	120.00

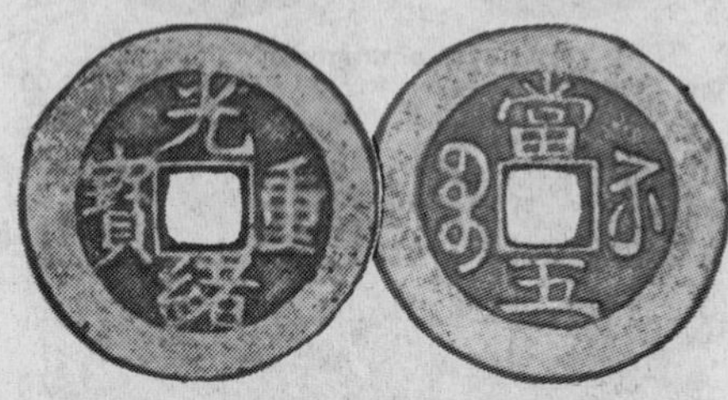

CAST BRASS
Obv: Type B

C#	Date	Emperor	Good	VG	Fine	VF
16-13	ND(1875-1908)	Kuang-hsu	30.00	40.00	50.00	75.00

10 CASH

CAST BRASS, 36-40mm
Obv: Type B-1

C#	Date	Emperor	Good	VG	Fine	VF
16-6	ND(1851-61)	Hsien-feng	5.00	7.50	15.00	25.00

30-34mm

C#	Date	Emperor	Good	VG	Fine	VF
16-6.1	ND(1851-61)	Hsien-feng	5.00	7.50	10.00	20.00

CAST IRON

C#	Date	Emperor	Good	VG	Fine	VF
16-6a	ND(1851-61)	Hsien-feng	27.50	50.00	75.00	100.00

CAST BRASS
Obv: Type B

C#	Date	Emperor	Good	VG	Fine	VF
16-14	ND(1875-1908)	Kuang-hsu	—	—	Rare	—

20 CASH

CAST BRASS, 39mm
Obv: Type B-1

C#	Date	Emperor	Good	VG	Fine	VF
16-7	ND(1851-61)	Hsien-feng	35.00	55.00	75.00	100.00

30 CASH

CAST BRASS, 46mm
Obv: Type B-1

C#	Date	Emperor	Good	VG	Fine	VF
16-8	ND(1851-61)	Hsien-feng	85.00	120.00	150.00	200.00

Rev: Crescent in upper left and right corners; dot in lower left and right corners.

C#	Date	Emperor	Good	VG	Fine	VF
16-8.1	ND(1851-61)	Hsien-feng	250.00	350.00	500.00	750.00

50 CASH

CAST COPPER, 50mm
Obv: Type B-1. Rev: Small characters.

C#	Date	Emperor	Good	VG	Fine	VF
16-9.1	ND(1851-61)	Hsien-feng	8.00	22.00	35.00	60.00

CAST BRASS, 55mm
Rev: Large characters.

C#	Date	Emperor	Good	VG	Fine	VF
16-9.2	ND(1851-61)	Hsien-feng	8.00	22.00	35.00	60.00

100 CASH

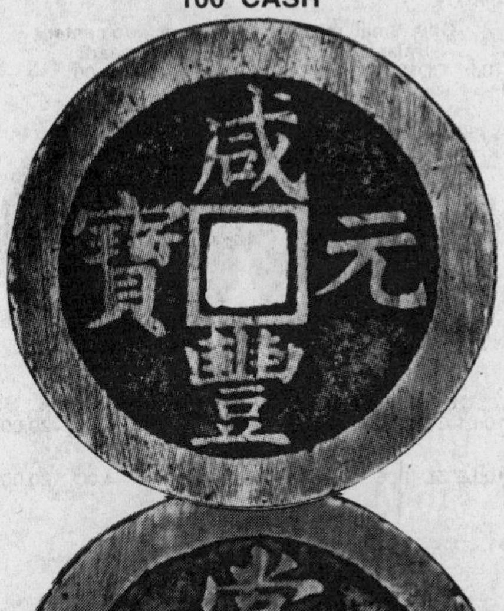

CAST BRASS
Obv: Type C
Obv: and rev: Small characters.

C#	Date	Emperor	Good	VG	Fine	VF
16-10	ND(1851-61)	Hsien-feng	10.00	25.00	35.00	85.00

Obv: and rev: Large characters.

C#	Date	Emperor	Good	VG	Fine	VF
16-10.1	ND(1851-61)	Hsien-feng	10.00	25.00	35.00	85.00

MILLED COINAGE

CASH

BRASS
Obv: Type A

Hsu#	Date	Mintage	Fine	VF	XF	Unc
85	ND ca.1890	—	35.00	55.00	90.00	120.00

5 CASH

COPPER
Rev: Side view dragon, EIVE for FIVE.

Y#	Date	Mintage	Fine	VF	XF	Unc
158	ND(1901)	—	32.50	55.00	100.00	—

BRASS

Y#	Date	Mintage	Fine	VF	XF	Unc
9n	CD1906	—	75.00	125.00	200.00	—

10 CASH

BRASS

Y#	Date	Mintage	Fine	VF	XF	Unc
—	ND(1898)	—	—	—	Rare	—

COPPER
Rev: Cloud below all 3 letters of SOO.

Y#	Date	Mintage	Fine	VF	XF	Unc
160	ND(1904-05)		2.50	4.00	8.00	24.00

Rev: Cloud below first 2 letters of SOO, Manchu word at 9 o'clock higher, dragons body thinner.

Y#	Date	Mintage	Fine	VF	XF	Unc
160.1	ND(1904-05)		2.50	4.00	8.00	24.00

Obv: Manchu words at center, w/o rosettes. Reeded edge.

Y#	Date	Mintage	Fine	VF	XF	Unc
162	ND	—	3.75	6.00	12.00	32.00

Obv: Manchu in center, rosettes at 2 and 10 o'clock.

Y#	Date	Mintage	Fine	VF	XF	Unc
162.1	ND	—	1.00	2.00	4.00	20.00

Unreeded edge.

Y#	Date	Mintage	Fine	VF	XF	Unc
162.2	ND	—	1.00	2.00	4.50	20.00

Obv. and rev: Tiny rosettes. Reeded edge.

Y#	Date	Mintage	Fine	VF	XF	Unc
162.3	ND	—	1.25	2.50	5.00	20.00

Obv: Rosette center, Manchu at 3 and 9 o'clock.

Y#	Date	Mintage	Fine	VF	XF	Unc
162.4	ND	—	.75	1.50	3.50	20.00

Plain edge.

Y#	Date	Mintage	Fine	VF	XF	Unc
162.5	ND	—	.75	1.50	3.50	20.00

Obv: Rosette center, large Manchu at 3 and 9 o'clock, higher than on Y#162.4. Reeded edge.

Y#	Date	Mintage	Fine	VF	XF	Unc
162.6	ND	—	1.50	2.50	5.00	20.00

Plain edge.

Y#	Date	Mintage	Fine	VF	XF	Unc
162.7	ND	—	1.50	2.50	5.00	25.00

BRASS

Y#	Date	Mintage	Fine	VF	XF	Unc
162.7a	ND	—	—	—	Rare	—

COPPER
Obv: Manchu words at center, reeded edge.

Y#	Date	Mintage	Fine	VF	XF	Unc
162.8	CD1902	—	2.00	4.00	7.50	25.00

Plain edge.

Y#	Date	Mintage	Fine	VF	XF	Unc
162.13	CD1902	—	—	—	—	—

Obv: Manchu words at center, reeded edge.

Y#	Date	Mintage	Fine	VF	XF	Unc
162.9	CD1903	—	5.00	7.50	12.00	32.00

Obv: Rosette center, small Manchu at 3 and 9 o'clock. Unreeded edge.

Y#	Date	Mintage	Fine	VF	XF	Unc
162.10	CD1905	—	1.00	2.00	4.50	20.00

Obv: Larger Manchu words.

Y#	Date	Mintage	Fine	VF	XF	Unc
162.11	CD1905	—	2.50	5.00	8.00	25.00

Rev: Kiangsu spelled KIANG-COO.

Y#	Date	Mintage	Fine	VF	XF	Unc
162.12	CD1905	—	250.00	500.00	750.00	—

NOTE: Y#162.12 is considered a contemporary counterfeit by some authorities.

Mule. Obv: Kiangsu Y#162. Rev: Kiangnan Y#135.

Y#	Date	Mintage	Fine	VF	XF	Unc
A162	ND	—	90.00	150.00	250.00	—

Mule. Obv: Kiangsu Y#162.8. Rev: Kiangnan Y#135.

Y#	Date	Mintage	Fine	VF	XF	Unc
B162	CD1902	—	90.00	150.00	250.00	—

Mule. Obv: Kiangsu Y#162.9. Rev: Kiangnan Y#135.

Y#	Date	Mintage	Fine	VF	XF	Unc
C162	CD1903	—	90.00	150.00	250.00	—

Obv: Mint mark incused on raised disc. Plain edge.

Y#	Date	Mintage	Fine	VF	XF	Unc
10n	CD1906	—	2.50	5.00	10.00	30.00
	Reeded edge.					
10n.1	CD1906	—	6.00	11.00	17.50	40.00

Obv: Mint mark in relief in field at center; w/o raised disc. Plain edge.

Y#	Date	Mintage	Fine	VF	XF	Unc
10n.2	CD1906	—	6.00	11.00	17.50	40.00

20 CASH

COPPER

Y#	Date	Mintage	VG	Fine	VF	XF
163	ND	—	17.50	32.50	45.00	65.00

BRASS

Y#	Date	Mintage	VG	Fine	VF	XF
163a	ND	—	30.00	45.00	70.00	110.00

COPPER

Y#	Date	Mintage	VG	Fine	VF	XF
11n.1	CD1906	—	25.00	40.00	60.00	90.00

BRASS

Y#	Date	Mintage	VG	Fine	VF	XF
11n.1a	CD1906	—	35.00	60.00	90.00	150.00

Chingkiang Coinage

Chingkiang is a city in Kiangsu (Jiangsu) province. Some of the coins issued by the mint have the name spelled Tsing-Kiang in English. This is not an error as both spellings were acceptable at the time.

10 CASH

COPPER

Obv: Large character at 3 o'clock. Reeded edge.

Y#	Date	Mintage	Fine	VF	XF	Unc
77	ND(1905)		2.50	4.00	7.50	25.00
	Plain edge.					
77.1	ND(1905)		2.50	4.00	7.50	25.00
	Obv: Ring around center dot in rosette. Reeded edge.					
77.2	ND(1905)		3.00	5.00	10.00	30.00
	Plain edge.					
77.3	ND(1905)		9.00	12.00	15.00	35.00

Obv: Smaller character at 3 o'clock. Reeded edge.

Y#	Date	Mintage	Fine	VF	XF	Unc
77.4	ND(1905)		3.50	6.00	12.00	32.00
	Plain edge.					
77.5	ND(1905)		3.50	6.00	12.00	32.00

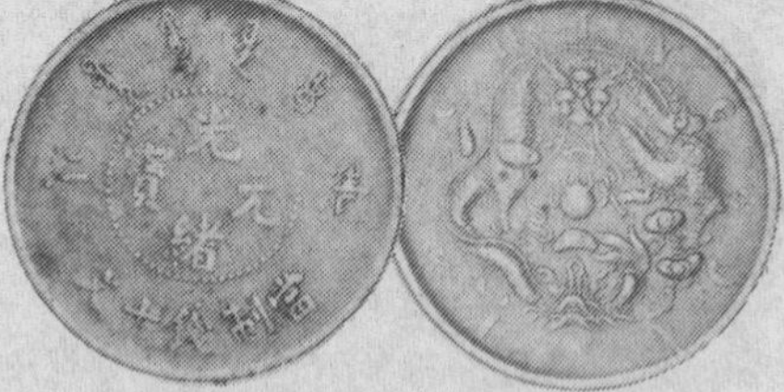

Obv: W/o rosette. Reeded edge.

Y#	Date	Mintage	Fine	VF	XF	Unc
77.6	ND(1905)		3.00	5.00	10.00	30.00
	Plain edge.					
77.7	ND(1905)		8.00	10.00	15.00	35.00

Obv: Large character at 3 o'clock. Reeded edge.

Y#	Date	Mintage	Fine	VF	XF	Unc
78	ND(1905)		1.50	3.00	5.00	20.00

Plain edge.

Y#	Date	Mintage	Fine	VF	XF	Unc
78.1	ND(1905)		3.00	5.00	10.00	30.00

Obv: Small character at 3 o'clock. Reeded edge.

Y#	Date	Mintage	Fine	VF	XF	Unc
78.2	ND(1905)		1.00	1.50	4.50	20.00
	Plain edge.					
78.3	ND(1905)		.75	1.25	4.00	20.00

Obv: W/o rosette. Reeded edge.

Y#	Date	Mintage	Fine	VF	XF	Unc
78.4	ND(1905)		3.50	6.00	15.00	35.00

Obv: Small mint mark in center, w/o center raised disc. Rev: 5 flames on pearl.

Y#	Date	Mintage	Fine	VF	XF	Unc
10d	CD1906	—	25.00	50.00	100.00	—

Obv: Small mint mark. Rev: 7 flames on pearl.

Y#	Date	Mintage	Fine	VF	XF	Unc
10d.1	CD1906	—	1.50	2.50	5.00	20.00
	Rev: 9 flames on pearl.					
10d.2	CD1906	—	1.00	2.00	4.00	20.00

Obv: Large mint mark. Rev: 5 flames on pearl.

Y#	Date	Mintage	Fine	VF	XF	Unc
10d.3	CD1906	—	1.50	2.50	5.00	20.00

Rev: 7 flames on pearl.

Y#	Date	Mintage	Fine	VF	XF	Unc
10d.4	CD1906	—	1.50	2.50	5.00	20.00

Rev: 9 flames on pearl.

Y#	Date	Mintage	Fine	VF	XF	Unc
10d.5	CD1906	—	1.50	2.50	5.00	20.00

Obv: Mint mark incused on raised disc.

10d.6	CD1906	—	—	—	Rare	—

NOTE: A trial piece.

NOTE: The 10 Cash coins of Kiangsu (Jiangsu) and Chingkiang are often found plated with a silvery material. This was not done at the mint. Apparently they were plated to be passed to the unwary as silver coins.

Shanghai Coinage

An important port city in Kiangsu (Jiangsu) province. Although there was no mint in Shanghai prior to the 1930's a number of coins were minted for Shanghai by silversmiths.

5 CH'IEN

SILVER, 18.40 g
Issued by Wang Yung-sheng. Engraved by Wan Ch'uan. Similar to K#902.

Kann#	Year	Date	VG	Fine	VF	XF
908	6	(1856)	—	—	450.00	700.00

Issued by Yu Shen-sheng. Engraved by Wang Shou.

907	6	(1856)	—	—	350.00	550.00

Issued by Ching Cheng-chi. Engraved by Wan Ch'uan.

910	6	(1856)	—	—	350.00	550.00

LIANG (TAEL)

SILVER, 36.70 g
Issued by Wang Yung-sheng. Engraved by Wan Ch'uan.

Kann#	Year	Date	VG	Fine	VF	XF
900	6	(1856)	—	—	800.00	1100.

Issued by Yu Sen-sheng. Engraved by P'ing Cheng.

902	6	(1856)	—	—	700.00	900.00

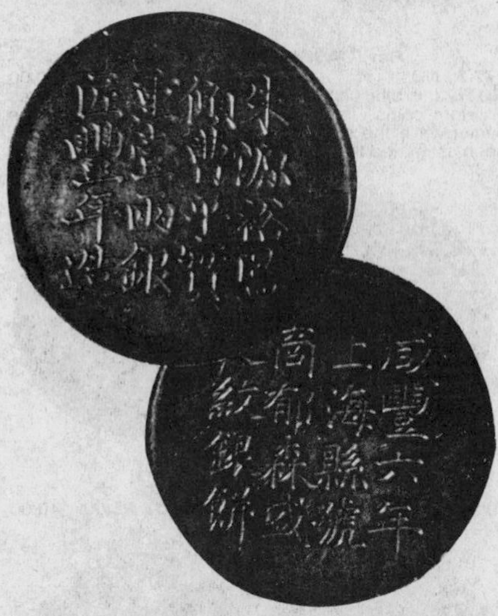

Issued by Yu Sen-sheng. Engraved by Feng Nien.

901	6	(1856)	—	—	700.00	900.00

Issued by Ching Cheng-chi. Engraved by Feng Nien.

903	6	(1856)	—	—	700.00	900.00

K#900-910 above are known as "Silversmith" Taels because each bears the name of a silver smelting firm in Shanghai. The coins were authorized by the taotai (a government official) of Shanghai to facilitate foreign trade and to replace the vanishing Mexican 8 Reales which had become very scarce due to hoarding.

KIRIN PROVINCE

Jilin

A province of northeast China that was formed in 1945. Before that it was one of the three original provinces of Manchuria. Besides growing corn, wheat and tobacco, there is also coal mining. An arsenal in Kirin (Jilin) opened in 1881 and was chosen as a source for coinage attempts. In 1884 Tael trials were struck and regular coinage began in 1895. Modern equipment was installed in a new mint in Kirin (Jilin) in 1901. The issues of this mint were very prolific and many varieties exist due to the use of hand cut dies for the earlier issues. The mint burned down in 1911.

EMPIRE

CASH

CAST BRASS
Obv: Type A

C#	Date	Emperor	Good	VG	Fine	VF
17-1	(1875-1908)	Kuang-hsu	15.00	25.00	35.00	50.00

NOTE: This coin is sometimes erroneously attributed to Chichou (Chichow) in Chihli (Hebei) provinces, which used this mint mark in the Hsein-feng and earlier reigns.

10 CASH

CAST BRASS
Obv: Type C

17-2	(1875-1908)	Kuang-hsu	—	—	Rare	—

MILLED COINAGE

NOTE: Errors in the English legends are very common in the Kirin coinage. It has been estimated there are over 2500 die varieties of Kirin (Jilin) silver coins and more than 1000 varieties of copper 10 Cash. Listed here are basic types and major varieties only.

CASH

BRASS, struck
Obv: Type A

Hsu#	Date	Mintage	Fine	VF	XF	Unc
481	ND	—	200.00	250.00	300.00	425.00

NOTE: This coin is sometimes erroneously attributed to Chichou (Chichow) in Chihli (Hebei) province, which used this mint mark in the Hsein-feng and earlier reigns.

2 CASH

COPPER

Y#	Date	Mintage	VG	Fine	VF	XF
175	ND	—	70.00	110.00	150.00	200.00

10 CASH(ES)

COPPER

Y#	Date	Mintage	VG	Fine	VF	XF
174	ND	—	225.00	275.00	350.00	500.00
176	ND	—	35.00	60.00	90.00	125.00

Rev: Thinner dragon.

Y#	Date	Mintage	VG	Fine	VF	XF
176.1	ND	—	35.00	60.00	90.00	125.00

BRASS
Similar to 50 Cashes, Y#B176.

Y#	Date	Mintage	VG	Fine	VF	XF
C176	CD1901	—	—	—	—	—

COPPER
Obv: Small rosettes. Rev: Large rosettes.

Y#	Date	Mintage	VG	Fine	VF	XF
177	ND	—	5.00	10.00	15.00	25.00

Rev: Small stars.

Y#	Date	Mintage	VG	Fine	VF	XF
177.1	ND	—	5.00	10.00	15.00	25.00

Obv: Small stars. Rev: Large rosettes.

Y#	Date	Mintage	VG	Fine	VF	XF
177.2	ND	—	5.00	10.00	17.50	30.00

Obv. and rev: Small stars.

Y#	Date	Mintage	VG	Fine	VF	XF
177.3	ND	—	5.00	10.00	15.00	25.00

BRASS

Y#	Date	Mintage	VG	Fine	VF	XF
177.3a	ND	—	5.00	10.00	17.50	30.00

COPPER
Obv. and rev: Large stars.

Y#	Date	Mintage	VG	Fine	VF	XF
177.4	ND	—	4.00	7.00	12.00	17.50

Obv: Large stars. Rev: Large rosettes.

Y#	Date	Mintage	VG	Fine	VF	XF
177.5	ND	—	4.00	7.00	12.00	17.50

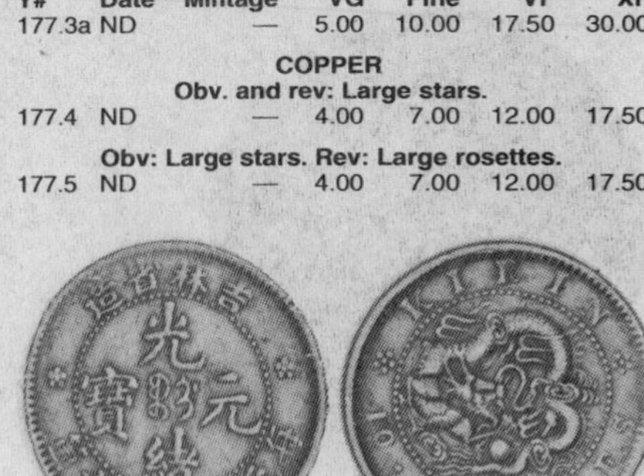

Obv: Medium rosettes.

Y#	Date	Mintage	VG	Fine	VF	XF
177.6	ND	—	4.00	7.00	12.00	17.50

Rev. CASHES spelled CASHIS.

Y#	Date	Mintage	VG	Fine	VF	XF
177.7	ND	—	60.00	100.00	160.00	250.00

NOTE: It is difficult to differentiate the stars and rosettes on worn coins. The rosettes have a raised dot in the center while the stars have a hole in the center. It has been estimated that 1000 varieties of Y#177 exist.

Obv: Very small mint mark.

Y#	Date	Mintage	VG	Fine	VF	XF
20p	CD1909	—	8.00	15.00	25.00	40.00

Obv: Larger mint mark. Rev: Head of dragon redesigned w/more whiskers.

Y#	Date	Mintage	VG	Fine	VF	XF
20p.1	CD1909	—	10.00	17.50	30.00	45.00

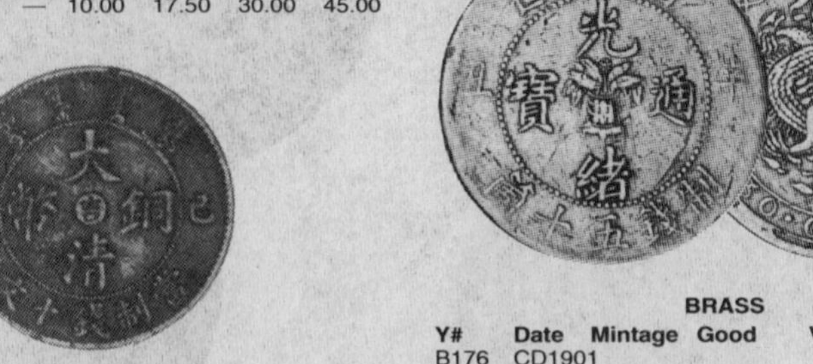

Obv: Larger mint mark.
Rev: Dragon similar to Y#20p.

Y#	Date	Mintage	VG	Fine	VF	XF
20p.2	CD1909	—	10.00	17.50	30.00	45.00

NOTE: For Y#20x refer to General Issues-Empire.

Mule. Obv: Y#20p.
Rev: General Issue - Empire Y#20.1

Y#	Date	Mintage	VG	Fine	VF	XF
20p.3	CD1909	2 known	—	—	Rare	3500.

NOTE: Though dated 1909, minted at Mukden ca.1922.

20 CASH(ES)

COPPER

Y#	Date	Mintage	VG	Fine	VF	XF
178	ND	—	35.00	65.00	100.00	175.00

Obv: Manchu in center, 8 characters below.

Y#	Date	Mintage	VG	Fine	VF	XF
A176	ND	—	80.00	200.00	400.00	700.00

Obv: Rosette in center, 3 characters below.

Y#	Date	Mintage	VG	Fine	VF	XF
A176.1	ND	—	80.00	225.00	425.00	725.00

Y#	Date	Mintage	VG	Fine	VF	XF
21p	CD1909	—	120.00	250.00	450.00	750.00

30 CASHES

BRASS
Similar to 50 Cashes, Y#B176.

Y#	Date	Mintage	VG	Fine	VF	XF
E176	CD1901	—	—	—	—	—

50 CASHES

BRASS

Y#	Date	Mintage	Good	VG	Fine	VF
B176	CD1901	3 known	—	—	Rare	—

NOTE: D.K.E. Ching Sale 6-91 VG-F realized $3,410.
NOTE: A similar 20 Cash and silver 50 Cent have been reported.

100 CASHES

BRASS
Similar to 50 Cashes, Y#B176.

Y#	Date	Mintage	VG	Fine	VF	XF
F176	CD1901	—	—	—	—	—

5 CENTS

SILVER, 1.27 g
Obv: Flower vase center.
Rev: Cross before and after weight:
CANDARINS .36.

Y#	Date	Mintage	Fine	VF	XF	Unc
179	ND	—	10.00	25.00	45.00	85.00

Rev: W/o crosses flanking weight.

Y#	Date	Mintage	Fine	VF	XF	Unc
179.1	ND	—	5.00	10.00	20.00	50.00
	CD1899	—	6.50	12.50	25.00	60.00
	CD1900	—	10.00	20.00	30.00	75.00
	CD1906	—	6.50	12.50	25.00	60.00
	CD1907	—	8.00	15.00	25.00	60.00
	CD1908		—	—	Rare	—

Obv: "Yin-yang" center.

Y#	Date	Mintage	Fine	VF	XF	Unc
179a	CD1900	—	7.50	15.00	30.00	60.00
	CD1901	—	5.50	11.50	25.00	50.00
	CD1902	—	6.50	12.50	25.00	60.00
	CD1903	—	12.50	25.00	50.00	100.00
	CD1904	—	10.00	15.00	30.00	70.00
	CD1905	—	7.50	15.00	30.00	65.00

10 CENTS

SILVER, 2.55 g
Obv: Small flower vase center.
Rev: Cross before and after weight:
CANDARINS .76.

Y#	Date	Mintage	Fine	VF	XF	Unc
180	ND	—	5.50	11.50	22.50	65.00

Obv: Large flower vase center.
Rev: W/o crosses flanking weight.

Y#	Date	Mintage	Fine	VF	XF	Unc
180.1	ND	—	5.50	11.50	22.50	50.00
	CD1899	—	6.50	12.50	25.00	60.00
	CD1900	—	6.50	12.50	25.00	60.00
	CD1906	—	6.50	12.50	25.00	60.00
	CD1907	—	45.00	90.00	150.00	250.00

Obv: "Yin-yang" center.

Y#	Date	Mintage	Fine	VF	XF	Unc
180a	CD1900	—	7.50	15.00	30.00	75.00
	CD1901	—	5.50	11.50	22.50	50.00
	CD1902	—	7.50	15.00	30.00	65.00
	CD1903	—	9.00	18.50	37.50	85.00
	CD1904	—	25.00	40.00	75.00	200.00
	CD1905	—	6.50	11.50	22.50	50.00

Obv: Numeral 1 in center.

Y#	Date	Mintage	Fine	VF	XF	Unc
180c	CD1908	—	60.00	100.00	150.00	250.00

20 CENTS

SILVER, 5.10 g
Obv: Flower vase center.

Y#	Date	Mintage	Fine	VF	XF	Unc
181	ND	—	7.50	15.00	30.00	60.00
	CD1899	—	6.50	12.50	25.00	50.00
	CD1900	—	7.50	15.00	30.00	60.00
	CD1906	Inc. Be.	6.50	12.50	25.00	50.00
	CD1907	Inc. Be.	6.50	12.50	25.00	50.00
	CD1908	Inc. Be.	87.50	175.00	300.00	500.00

Obv: "Yin-yang" center.

Y#	Date	Mintage	Fine	VF	XF	Unc
181a	CD1900	—	7.50	15.00	30.00	60.00
	CD1901	22.508	6.50	12.50	25.00	50.00
	CD1902	Inc.Ab.	6.50	12.50	25.00	50.00
	CD1903	Inc.Ab.	6.50	12.50	25.00	50.00
	CD1904	Inc.Ab.	6.50	12.50	25.00	50.00
	CD1905	Inc.Ab.	6.50	12.50	25.00	50.00

Obv: Manchu words in center.

Y#	Date	Mintage	Fine	VF	XF	Unc
181b	CD1908	Inc.Ab.	35.00	70.00	120.00	225.00

Obv: Numeral 2 center.

Y#	Date	Mintage	Fine	VF	XF	Unc
181c	CD1908	Inc.Ab.	25.00	50.00	85.00	150.00

Obv: Mint mark in relief on raised disc at center.

Y#	Date	Mintage	Fine	VF	XF	Unc
22	(1909)	—	35.00	70.00	125.00	225.00

Obv: Mint mark incuse on raised disc at center.

Y#	Date	Mintage	Fine	VF	XF	Unc
22.1	(1909)	—	35.00	70.00	125.00	225.00

Obv: Mint mark in circle at center.

Y#	Date	Mintage	Fine	VF	XF	Unc
22.2	(1909)	—	35.00	70.00	125.00	225.00

50 CENTS

SILVER, 13.10 g
Obv: Flower vase center w/rosette at either side.
Rev: W/o crosses flanking weight.

Y#	Date	Mintage	Fine	VF	XF	Unc
182	ND	—	15.00	25.00	50.00	150.00

Obv: Rosette at either side. Rev: Crosses before and after weight: *3 CANDARENS 6.*

Y#	Date	Mintage	Fine	VF	XF	Unc
182.1	ND	—	15.00	25.00	50.00	150.00

Obv: W/o rosettes. Rev: W/o crosses flanking weight.

Y#	Date	Mintage	Fine	VF	XF	Unc
182.2	ND	—	—	—	—	—

Y#	Date	Mintage	Fine	VF	XF	Unc
182.3	CD1899	—	25.00	45.00	80.00	200.00
	CD1900	—	20.00	35.00	60.00	150.00
	CD1906	—	20.00	35.00	60.00	150.00
	CD1907	—	20.00	35.00	60.00	150.00
	CD1908	—	50.00	80.00	125.00	300.00

Obv: Figure 8 "Yin-yang" in center.

Y#	Date	Mintage	Fine	VF	XF	Unc
182a	CD1900	—	20.00	35.00	60.00	150.00

Obv: Redesigned "Yin-yang" in center.

Y#	Date	Mintage	Fine	VF	XF	Unc
182a.1	CD1901	—	20.00	35.00	60.00	150.00
	CD1902	—	20.00	35.00	60.00	150.00
	CD1903	—	25.00	40.00	65.00	165.00
	CD1904	—	20.00	35.00	60.00	150.00
	CD1905	—	15.00	30.00	50.00	140.00

Obv: Manchu words in center.

Y#	Date	Mintage	Fine	VF	XF	Unc
182b	CD1908	—	75.00	150.00	275.00	450.00

DOLLAR

SILVER, 26.10 g
Obv: Flower vase center.
Rev: Small rosettes before and after weight 7 CANDARINS 2 or 7 CAINDARINS 2.

Y#	Date	Mintage	Fine	VF	XF	Unc
183	ND	—	60.00	100.00	250.00	500.00
	CD1899	—	60.00	100.00	250.00	500.00
	CD1900	—	60.00	100.00	300.00	600.00
	CD1906	—	60.00	100.00	250.00	500.00
	CD1907	—	125.00	175.00	300.00	650.00
	CD1908	—	350.00	750.00	1500.	3000.

Obv: Large rosettes.
Rev: W/o rosettes flanking weight.

Y#	Date	Mintage	Fine	VF	XF	Unc
183.1	ND	—	750.00	1350.	2500.	4500.

Rev. leg: 3.2 CAINDARINS 2 (error).

Y#	Date	Mintage	Fine	VF	XF	Unc
183.2	CD1906	—	100.00	150.00	250.00	600.00

Obv: Small rosettes. Rev: Small rosettes before and after weight 7 CANDARINS 2.

Y#	Date	Mintage	Fine	VF	XF	Unc
183.3	ND	—	100.00	135.00	175.00	500.00

Obv: Small leaves out of left of basket.
Rev: Similar to Y#183.2.

Y#	Date	Mintage	Fine	VF	XF	Unc
183.4	ND	—	60.00	100.00	150.00	400.00

Obv: Figure '8' Yin-yang in center.

Y#	Date	Mintage	Fine	VF	XF	Unc
183a	CD1900	—	100.00	200.00	350.00	850.00

Obv: Redesigned Yin-yang in center.
Rev: Coarse scaled beady eyed dragon.

Y#	Date	Mintage	Fine	VF	XF	Unc
183a.1	CD1901	—	60.00	100.00	175.00	500.00
	CD1902	—	60.00	100.00	150.00	400.00

Rev: Fine "dot" scaled beady eyed dragon.

Y#	Date	Mintage	Fine	VF	XF	Unc
183a.2	CD1902	—	60.00	100.00	175.00	400.00
	CD1903	—	60.00	100.00	175.00	350.00
	CD1904	—	60.00	100.00	150.00	250.00
	CD1905	—	60.00	100.00	150.00	250.00

Rev: Fine "oval" scaled round eyed dragon.

Y#	Date	Mintage	Fine	VF	XF	Unc
183a.3	CD1905	—	30.00	65.00	135.00	300.00

Obv: Manchu words in center.

Y#	Date	Mintage	Fine	VF	XF	Unc
183b	CD1908	—	300.00	650.00	1150.	2500.

Obv: Numeral 11 in center.

Y#	Date	Mintage	Fine	VF	XF	Unc
183c	CD1908	—	350.00	850.00	1650.	2750.

NOTE: The numeral 11 in center reflects the discount in subsidiary coinage. It took 11 dimes to equal the dollar.

TAEL SERIES

CH'IEN (MACE)

SILVER, 3.60 g
Rev.: Numeral 1 in simple Chinese.

Kann#	Year	Date	Fine	VF	XF	Unc
919	10	(1884)	—	—	500.00	750.00

Rev: Different, more complicated character for 1.

Kann#	Year	Date	Fine	VF	XF	Unc
920	10	(1884)	—	—	400.00	650.00

3 CH'IEN

SILVER, 10.80 g
Vertical edge reeding.

Kann#	Year	Date	Fine	VF	XF	Unc
918	10	(1884)	—	—	500.00	750.00

Diagonal edge reeding.

Kann#	Year	Date	Fine	VF	XF	Unc
918b	10	(1884)	—	—	500.00	750.00

5 CH'IEN

(1/2 Tael)

SILVER, 17.80 g

Kann#	Year	Date	Fine	VF	XF	Unc
917	10	(1884)	—	—	850.00	1500.

7 CH'IEN

SILVER, 25.40 g

Kann#	Year	Date	Fine	VF	XF	Unc
916	10	(1884)	—	—	3500.	5000.

TAEL

SILVER, 35.50 g

Kann#	Year	Date	Fine	VF	XF	Unc
915	10	(1884)	—	—	Rare	—

NOTE: Superior Goodman sale 6-91 AU realized $35,200.

KWANGSI/KWANGSEA

Guangxi

A hilly region in southeast China with many forests. Large amounts of rice are grown adjacent to the many rivers. A mint opened in Kweilin in 1667, closed in 1670, reopened in 1679, closed again in 1681. It reopened in the mid-1700's and was a rather prolific issuer of Cash coins. In 1905 the government allowed modern mints to be established in Kwangsi (Guangxi) at Nanning (1905) and Kweilin (1905). The Nanning Mint began operation in 1919 and closed in 1923. In 1920 a new mint was opened at Wuchow and operated sporadically until 1929. In 1938 part of the Shanghai Central Mint was moved to Kweilin where it operated until at least 1945 and perhaps as late as 1949.

EMPIRE

CASH

CAST BRASS
Obv: Type A

C#	Date	Emperor	Good	VG	Fine	VF
18-2	ND(1796-1820)	Chia-ch'ing	.25	.50	.85	1.25

Obv: Type A

C#	Date	Emperor	Good	VG	Fine	VF
18-3	ND(1821-51)	Tao-kuang	.50	1.00	1.75	3.00

Rev: Dot below left.

C#	Date	Emperor	Good	VG	Fine	VF
18-3.1	ND(1821-51)	Tao-kuang	.60	1.00	2.00	3.00

Obv: Type A

C#	Date	Emperor	Good	VG	Fine	VF
18-4	ND(1851-61)	Hsien-feng	1.00	2.00	3.00	5.00

Obv: Type A-2
Rev: Large Manchu words.

C#	Date	Emperor	Good	VG	Fine	VF
18-7	ND(1862-74)	T'ung-chih	2.50	3.50	6.50	9.00

Rev: Small Manchu words.

C#	Date	Emperor	Good	VG	Fine	VF
18-7.1	ND(1862-74)	T'ung-chih	2.50	3.50	6.50	9.00

Rev: Circle above.

C#	Date	Emperor	Good	VG	Fine	VF
18-7.2	ND(1862-74)	T'ung-chih	5.50	8.50	13.50	25.00

Obv: Type A

C#	Date	Emperor	Good	VG	Fine	VF
18-9	ND(1875-1908)	Kuang-hsu	5.50	8.50	13.50	25.00

10 CASH

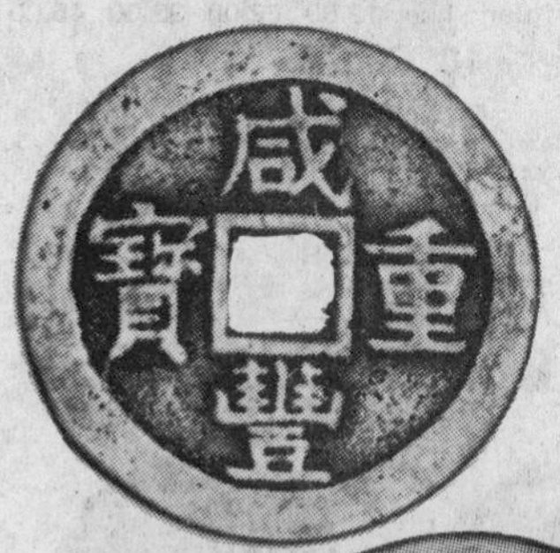

CAST BRASS
Obv: Type B-1

C#	Date	Emperor	Good	VG	Fine	VF
18-5	ND(1851-61)	Hsien-feng	3.00	7.00	9.00	15.00

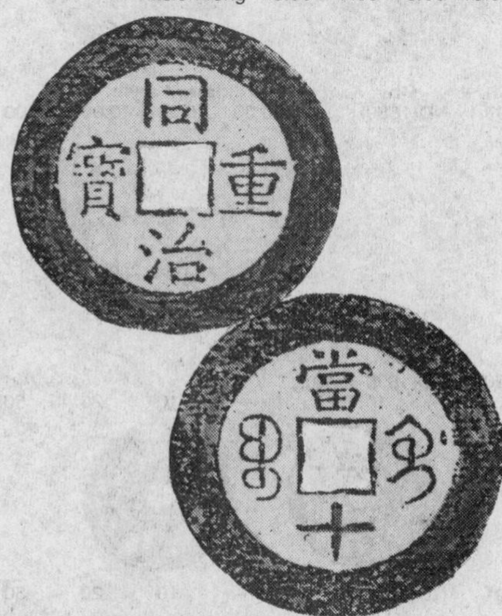

Obv: Type B-2

C#	Date	Emperor	Good	VG	Fine	VF
18-8	ND(1862-74)	T'ung-chih	—	—	Rare	—

Obv: Type B

C#	Date	Emperor	Good	VG	Fine	VF
18-10	ND(1875-1908)	Kuang-hsu	—	—	Rare	—

50 CASH

CAST BRASS
Obv: Type B-1

C#	Date	Emperor	Good	VG	Fine	VF
18-6	ND(1851-61)	Hsien-feng	40.00	60.00	80.00	165.00

REPUBLIC

MILLED COINAGE

CENT

BRASS
Rev. leg: KWANG-SEA.

Y#	Year	Date	Fine	VF	XF	Unc
413	8	(1919)	100.00	150.00	250.00	400.00

Rev. leg: KWANG-SI.

Y#	Year	Date	Fine	VF	XF	Unc
413a	8	(1919)	17.50	37.50	55.00	225.00

Rev: Large *Kuei* mint mark below PU.

Y#	Year	Date	Fine	VF	XF	Unc
347	28	(1939)	—	—	Rare	—

Rev: Small *Kuei* mint mark below PU.

Y#	Year	Date	Fine	VF	XF	Unc
347.1	28	(1939)	—	—	Rare	—

10 CENTS

SILVER, 2.70 g

Y#	Year	Date	Fine	VF	XF	Unc
414	9	(1920)	60.00	100.00	150.00	250.00

20 CENTS

SILVER, 5.30 g
Rev: KWANG-SEA.

Y#	Year	Date	Fine	VF	XF	Unc
415	8	(1919)	50.00	75.00	100.00	175.00
	9	(1920)	70.00	100.00	150.00	250.00
	13	(1924)	100.00	200.00	300.00	500.00

Rev: KWANG-SI.

Y#	Year	Date	Fine	VF	XF	Unc
415a	8	(1919)	10.00	25.00	40.00	125.00
	9	(1920)	10.00	20.00	45.00	100.00
	11	(1922)	10.00	15.00	40.00	100.00
	12	(1923)	4.00	9.00	20.00	40.00
	13	(1924)	4.00	7.50	12.50	25.00
	14	(1925)	4.00	7.50	12.50	25.00

Obv: Tiny character *Hsi* on dot center.
Rev: Wreath added around '20'.

Y#	Year	Date	Fine	VF	XF	Unc
415b	15	(1926)	3.50	6.50	10.00	20.00
	16	(1927)	3.50	6.50	10.00	20.00

Obv: Character *Kuei* in center instead of dot.

Y#	Year	Date	Fine	VF	XF	Unc
415a.113		(1924)	50.00	75.00	100.00	175.00

Rev: Elephant Nose Rock at Kueilin.

Y#	Year	Date	Fine	VF	XF	Unc
416	38	(1949)	75.00	125.00	200.00	350.00

KWANGTUNG PROVINCE

Guangdong

A province located on the southeast coast of China. Kwangtung (Guangdong) lies mostly in the tropics and has both mountains and plains. Its coastline is nearly 800 miles long and provides many good harbors. Because of the location of Guangzhou (Canton) in the province, Kwangtung (Guangdong) was the first to be visited by seaborne foreign traders. Hong Kong was ceded to Great Britain after the First Opium War in 1841. Kowloon was later ceded to Britain in 1860 and the New Territories (100 year lease) in 1898 and Macao to Portugal in 1887, Kwangchowwan was leased to France in 1898 (a property was restored in 1946). A modern mint opened Guangzhou (Canton) in 1889 with Edward Wyon as superintendent. The mint was a large issuer of coins until it closed in 1931. The Nationalists reopened the mint briefly in 1949, striking a few silver dollars, before abandoning the mainland for their retreat to Taiwan.

The large island of Hainan was split off from Kwangtung (Guangdong) Province in 1988 and established as a separate province.

EMPIRE

CASH

CAST BRASS
Obv: Type A

C#	Date	Emperor	Good	VG	Fine	VF
19-2	ND(1796-1820)	Chia-ch'ing	.30	.75	1.50	2.50

CAST IRON

C#	Date	Emperor	Good	VG	Fine	VF
19-2a	ND(1796-1820)	Chia-ch'ing	—	—	Rare	—

CAST BRASS
Obv: Type A

C#	Date	Emperor	Good	VG	Fine	VF
19-3	ND(1821-51)	Tao-kuang	.25	.50	1.00	2.00

Obv: Type A

C#	Date	Emperor	Good	VG	Fine	VF
19-4	ND(1851-61)	Hsien-feng	1.50	2.50	3.50	5.00

Obv: Type A-2

C#	Date	Emperor	Good	VG	Fine	VF
19-5	ND(1862-74)	T'ung-chih	2.00	3.00	4.00	6.00

Obv: Type A

C#	Date	Emperor	Good	VG	Fine	VF
19-7	ND(1875-1908)	Kuang-hsu	12.00	22.00	32.00	45.00

10 CASH

CAST BRASS
Obv: Type B-2

C#	Date	Emperor	Good	VG	Fine	VF
19-6	ND(1862-74)	T'ung-chih	—	—	Rare	—

Obv: Type B

C#	Date	Emperor	Good	VG	Fine	VF
19-8	ND(1875-1908)	Kuang-hsu	—	—	Rare	—

MILLED COINAGE

CASH

BRASS, struck
Obv: Type A

Y#	Date	Mintage	Fine	VF	XF	Unc
189	ND(1889)	—	.25	.45	.85	3.00
	ND(1889)	—	—	—	Proof	275.00

Obv: *Kuang* in a different style.

Y#	Date	Mintage	Fine	VF	XF	Unc
189.1	ND(1889)	—	20.00	25.00	40.00	75.00

Y#	Date	Mintage	Fine	VF	XF	Unc
190	ND(1890-1908)	1059.253	—	.10	.20	.50

Y#	Date	Mintage	Fine	VF	XF	Unc
191	ND(1906-08)	—	—	.10	.20	.50

Obv: Type A

Y#	Date	Mintage	Fine	VF	XF	Unc
204	ND (1909-11)	—	.50	.75	1.00	3.00

CENT (10 CASH)

COPPER
Obv. leg: 6 characters at bottom. Rev: ONE CENT.

Y#	Date	Mintage	Fine	VF	XF	Unc
192	ND(1900-06)		.75	1.50	3.00	20.00

Mule. Obv: Y#192. Rev: Chihli 10 Cash Y#67.

Y#	Date	Mintage	Fine	VF	XF	Unc
A192	ND	—	25.00	35.00	50.00	125.00

Obv. leg: 7 characters at bottom. Rev: TEN CASH.

Y#	Date	Mintage	Fine	VF	XF	Unc
193	ND(1900-06)		1.00	2.00	4.00	20.00

Mule: Obv. Y#192. Rev: Y#193.

Y#	Date	Mintage	Fine	VF	XF	Unc
A193	ND	—	20.00	28.50	40.00	100.00

Mule. Obv: Y#193. Rev: Y#192.

Y#	Date	Mintage	Fine	VF	XF	Unc
B193	ND	—	20.00	28.50	40.00	100.00

W#	Date	Mintage	VG	Fine	VF	XF
896	—	—	65.00	100.00	150.00	225.00

Y#	Date	Mintage	Fine	VF	XF	Unc
10r	CD1906	79.000	1.00	2.00	4.00	20.00
	CD1907	46.000	1.00	2.00	4.00	20.00
	CD1908	62.736	1.00	2.00	4.00	20.00

Y#	Date	Mintage	Fine	VF	XF	Unc
20r	CD1909	—	1.50	3.00	5.00	25.00

5 CENTS

1.3000 g, .820 SILVER, .0343 oz ASW
Obv: 3.65 CANDAREENS.
Rev. leg: Chinese characters around dragon.

Y#	Date	Mintage	Fine	VF	XF	Unc
194	ND(1889)	—	150.00	300.00	450.00	700.00

Obv: 3.6 CANDAREENS.

Y#	Date	Mintage	Fine	VF	XF	Unc
194.1	ND(1889)	—	275.00	550.00	850.00	1200.

Rev: English legend around dragon.

Y#	Date	Mintage	Fine	VF	XF	Unc
199	ND(1890-1905)	—	2.00	3.50	6.00	16.00

10 CENTS

2.7000 g, .820 SILVER, .0712 oz ASW
Obv: 7 3/10 CANDAREENS.

Y#	Date	Mintage	Fine	VF	XF	Unc
195	ND(1889)	—	100.00	175.00	275.00	500.00
	ND(1889)	—	—	—	Proof	—

Obv: 7.2 CANDAREENS.

195.1	ND(1889)	—	2000.	3000.	4500.	—

Rev: English legends around dragon.

200	ND(1890-1900)	—	2.00	3.00	4.00	12.00

20 CENTS

5.3000 g, .820 SILVER, .1397 oz ASW
Obv: 1 MACE AND 4 3/5 CANDAREENS.

196	ND(1889)	—	125.00	225.00	375.00	600.00
	ND(1889)	—	—	—	Proof	—

Obv: 1 MACE AND 4.4 CANDAREENS.

196.1	ND(1889)	—	2500.	3500.	5000.	—

Rev: English legends around dragon.

201	ND(1890-1908)	—	1.50	2.50	3.50	10.00
	ND(1890-1908)	10 known	—	—	Proof	400.00

5.5000 g, .800 SILVER, .1415 oz ASW

205	ND(1909-11)	94.774	4.50	6.00	9.00	20.00

NOTE: Two varieties of edge reeding known.

50 CENTS

13.8000 g, .860 SILVER, .3816 oz ASW

Obv: 3 MACE AND 6-1/2 CANDAREENS.

Y#	Date	Mintage	Fine	VF	XF	Unc
197	ND(1889)	—	325.00	625.00	900.00	1600.

Obv: 3 MACE AND 6 CANDAREENS.

197.1	ND(1889)	—	—	6500.	10,000.	15,000.

13.5000 g, .860 SILVER, .3733 oz ASW
Rev: English legends around dragon.

202	ND(1890-1905)	—	20.00	40.00	75.00	250.00
	ND(1890-1905)	—	—	—	Proof	650.00

DOLLAR

27.4000 g, .900 SILVER, .7929 oz ASW
Obv: 7 MACE AND 3 CANDAREENS.

198	ND(1889)	—	1250.	1750.	2500.	4800.
	ND(1889)	—	—	—	Proof	10,000.

Obv: 7 MACE AND 2 CANDAREENS.

Y#	Date	Mintage	Fine	VF	XF	Unc
198.1	ND(1889)	—	—	—	—	35,000.

NOTE: Considered a pattern.

27.0000 g, .900 SILVER, .7814 oz ASW
Rev: English legends around dragon.

203	ND(1890-1908)	—	15.00	25.00	50.00	350.00
	ND(1890-1908)	—	—	—	Proof	750.00

206	ND(1909-11)	—	15.00	25.00	50.00	300.00

REPUBLIC

CENT

COPPER

417	Yr.1 (1912)	18.836	1.50	2.25	5.00	22.00

Y#	Date	Mintage	Fine	VF	XF	Unc
417	Yr.3 (1914)	14.750	1.50	2.25	5.00	22.00
	Yr.4 (1915)	6.350	4.00	6.00	15.00	35.00
	Yr.5 (1916)	18.388	2.00	3.00	7.50	30.00
	Yr.7 (1918)	—	7.50	12.50	20.00	45.00

BRASS

Y#	Date	Mintage	Fine	VF	XF	Unc
417a	Yr.3 (1914)	I.A.	2.00	5.00	10.00	25.00
	Yr.4 (1915)	I.A.	3.00	7.50	15.00	30.00
	Yr.5 (1916)	I.A.	1.25	3.00	6.00	20.00
	Yr.7 (1918)	—	4.00	10.00	20.00	45.00

2 CENTS

BRASS

Y#	Date	Mintage	Fine	VF	XF	Unc
418	Yr.7 (1918)	—	30.00	50.00	90.00	175.00

COPPER

Y#	Date	Mintage	Fine	VF	XF	Unc
418a	Yr.7 (1918)	—	—	—	Rare	—

5 CENTS

COPPER-NICKEL

Y#	Date	Mintage	Fine	VF	XF	Unc
420	Yr.8 (1919)	.916	.50	1.25	2.25	4.00

Y#	Date	Mintage	Fine	VF	XF	Unc
421	Yr.10 (1921)	.666	1.25	3.00	6.50	12.50

Y#	Date	Mintage	Fine	VF	XF	Unc
420a	Yr.12 (1923)	.480	.50	1.25	2.25	4.00

10 CENTS

SILVER, 2.70 g

Y#	Date	Mintage	Fine	VF	XF	Unc
422	Yr.2 (1913)	8.798	1.50	2.50	4.00	8.00
	Yr.3 (1914)	I.A.	2.00	3.00	4.50	9.00
	Yr.11 (1922)	—	2.50	4.00	6.50	15.00

SILVER, 2.50 g

Y#	Date	Mintage	Fine	VF	XF	Unc
425	Yr.18 (1929)	48.960	1.25	2.00	3.00	6.00

20 CENTS

SILVER, 5.40 g

Y#	Date	Mintage	Fine	VF	XF	Unc
423	Yr.1 (1912)	88.000	BV	2.50	6.00	12.00
	Yr.2 (1913)	109.974	BV	2.50	6.00	12.00
	Yr.3 (1914)	41.691	BV	2.50	6.00	12.00
	Yr.4 (1915)	22.332	4.00	10.00	30.00	65.00
	Yr.7 (1918)	—	BV	2.50	5.00	10.00
	Yr.8 (1919)	195.000	BV	1.25	2.50	5.00
	Yr.9 (1920)	197.000	BV	1.25	2.50	5.00
	Yr.10 (1921)	402.250	BV	1.25	2.50	5.00
	Yr.11 (1922)	350.000	BV	1.25	2.50	5.00
	Yr.12 (1923)	4.400	2.00	3.50	7.00	20.00
	Yr.13 (1924)	55.109	2.00	3.50	8.25	20.00

NOTE: The fineness of many of these 20 cent pieces especially those dated Yr.13 (1924) is as low as .500. In 1924 the Anhwei (Anhui) Mint secretly produced quantities of Kwangtung (Guangdong) 20 cent pieces which were only .400 fine.

SILVER, 5.30 g

Y#	Date	Mintage	Fine	VF	XF	Unc
424	Yr.13 (1924)	I.A.	20.00	40.00	65.00	125.00

Y#	Date	Mintage	Fine	VF	XF	Unc
426	Yr.17 (1928)	28.530	20.00	30.00	50.00	100.00
	Yr.18 (1929)	779.738	BV	1.25	2.25	4.50
	Yr.19 (1930)	1 known	—	—	—	2860.

SPECIMEN SETS (SS)

KM#	Date	Mintage	Identification	Issue Price	Mkt. Val.
SS1	1889(10)	—	Y189,195-198 (2 each)	—	—
SS2	1890(?)	—	Y189-190,199-203	—	2000.

KWEICHOW PROVINCE

Guizhou

A province located in southern China. It is basically a plateau region that is somewhat remote from the general traffic of China. The Kweichow Mint opened in 1730 and produced Cash coins until the end of the reign of Kuang Hsu. The Republic issues for this province are enigmatic as to their origin, as a mint supposedly did not exist in Kweichow (Guizhou) at this time.

EMPIRE

CASH

CAST BRASS
Obv: Type A

C#	Date	Emperor	Good	VG	Fine	VF
20-2	ND(1796-1820)	Chia-ch'ing	.40	1.00	1.25	1.75

Rev: Dot above.

C#	Date	Emperor	Good	VG	Fine	VF
20-2.1	ND(1796-1820)	Chia-ch'ing	.80	2.00	3.00	4.00

Rev: Character *Erh* (two) above.

C#	Date	Emperor	Good	VG	Fine	VF
20-2.2	ND(1796-1820)	Chia-ch'ing	5.50	8.50	13.50	20.00

Obv: Type A

C#	Date	Emperor	Good	VG	Fine	VF
20-3	ND(1821-50)	Tao-kuang	2.00	3.00	4.00	6.00

Rev: Crescent above.

C#	Date	Emperor	Good	VG	Fine	VF
20-3.1	ND(1821-50)	Tao-kuang	3.50	6.00	9.00	13.50

Rev: Circle above.

C#	Date	Emperor	Good	VG	Fine	VF
20-3.2	ND(1821-50)	Tao-kuang	3.50	6.00	9.00	18.00

Rev: Dot inside circle above.

C#	Date	Emperor	Good	VG	Fine	VF
20-3.3	ND(1821-50)	. Tao-kuang	2.50	5.00	6.50	9.00

Rev: Dot above.

C#	Date	Emperor	Good	VG	Fine	VF
20-3.4	ND(1821-50)	Tao-kuang	2.50	5.00	6.50	9.00

Rev: An X above.

C#	Date	Emperor	Good	VG	Fine	VF
20-3.5	ND(1821-50)	Tao-kuang	5.50	8.50	13.50	20.00

Rev: A triangle above.

C#	Date	Emperor	Good	VG	Fine	VF
20-3.6	ND(1821-50)	Tao-kuang	5.50	8.50	13.50	20.00

Rev: Character *Yi* (one) above.

C#	Date	Emperor	Good	VG	Fine	VF
20-3.7	ND(1821-50)	Tao-kuang	5.50	8.50	13.50	20.00

Rev: Character *Ta* (large) above.

C#	Date	Emperor	Good	VG	Fine	VF
20-3.8	ND(1821-50)	Tao-kuang	5.50	8.50	13.50	20.00

NOTE: This coin and C#20-3.14 are difficult to distinguish.

Rev: Crescent below.

C#	Date	Emperor	Good	VG	Fine	VF
20-3.9	ND(1821-50)	Tao-kuang	3.50	6.00	9.00	13.50

Rev: An X below.

C#	Date	Emperor	Good	VG	Fine	VF
20-3.10	ND(1821-50)	Tao-kuang	5.50	50	13.50	25.00

Rev: Dot below.

C#	Date	Emperor	Good	VG	Fine	VF
20-3.11	ND(1821-50)	Tao-kuang	3.00	5.50	8.00	11.50

Rev: Inverted triangle below.

C#	Date	Emperor	Good	VG	Fine	VF
20-3.12	ND(1821-50)	Tao-kuang	5.50	8.50	13.50	20.00

Rev: *Yi* (one) below.

C#	Date	Emperor	Good	VG	Fine	VF
20-3.13	ND(1821-50)	Tao-kuang	5.50	8.50	13.50	20.00

Rev: *Liu* (six) above.

C#	Date	Emperor	Good	VG	Fine	VF
20-3.14	ND(1821-50)	Tao-kuang	5.50	8.50	13.50	20.00

NOTE: This coin and C#20-3.8 are difficult to distinguish.

Rev: *Ch'i* (seven) below.

C#	Date	Emperor	Good	VG	Fine	VF
20-3.15	ND(1821-50)	Tao-kuang	5.50	8.50	13.50	20.00

Obv: Type A

C#	Date	Emperor	Good	VG	Fine	VF
20-4	ND(1851-61)	Hsien-feng	1.50	2.50	4.00	6.00

Rev: Dot above.

C#	Date	Emperor	Good	VG	Fine	VF
20-4.1	ND(1851-61)	Hsien-feng	2.50	4.00	5.00	7.00

Rev: 2 vertical lines above.

C#	Date	Emperor	Good	VG	Fine	VF
20-4.2	ND(1851-61)	Hsien-feng	5.50	8.50	13.50	25.00

Rev: 3 vertical lines above.

C#	Date	Emperor	Good	VG	Fine	VF
20-4.3	ND(1851-61)	Hsien-feng	5.50	8.50	13.50	25.00

Rev: An "X" above.

C#	Date	Emperor	Good	VG	Fine	VF
20-4.4	ND(1851-61)	Hsien-feng	5.50	8.50	13.50	25.00

Rev: Character *Ch'i* (seven) above.

C#	Date	Emperor	Good	VG	Fine	VF
20-4.5	ND(1851-61)	Hsien-feng	5.50	8.50	13.50	25.00

Rev: Character *Shih* (ten) above.

C#	Date	Emperor	Good	VG	Fine	VF
20-4.6	ND(1851-61)	Hsien-feng	5.50	8.50	13.50	25.00

Rev: Character *Wen* (unit) lying on its side above.

C#	Date	Emperor	Good	VG	Fine	VF
20-4.7	ND(1851-61)	Hsien-feng	5.50	8.50	13.50	25.00

Rev: Character *Shih* above and crescent below.

C#	Date	Emperor	Good	VG	Fine	VF
20-4.8	ND(1851-61)	Hsien-feng	5.50	8.50	13.50	25.00

Obv: Type A-2

C#	Date	Emperor	Good	VG	Fine	VF
20-7	ND(1862-74)	T'ung-chih	—	—	Rare	—

Obv: Type A

C#	Date	Emperor	Good	VG	Fine	VF
20-9	ND(1875-1908)	Kuang-hsu	4.00	7.50	10.00	14.00

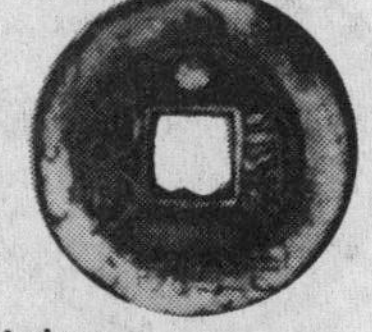

Rev: Dot above.

C#	Date	Emperor	Good	VG	Fine	VF
20-9.1	ND(1875-1908)	Kuang-hsu	5.00	9.00	12.50	17.50

Rev: Character *Kung* above.

C#	Date	Emperor	Good	VG	Fine	VF
20-9.2	ND(1875-1905)	Kuang-hsu	8.50	11.50	16.50	25.00

10 CASH

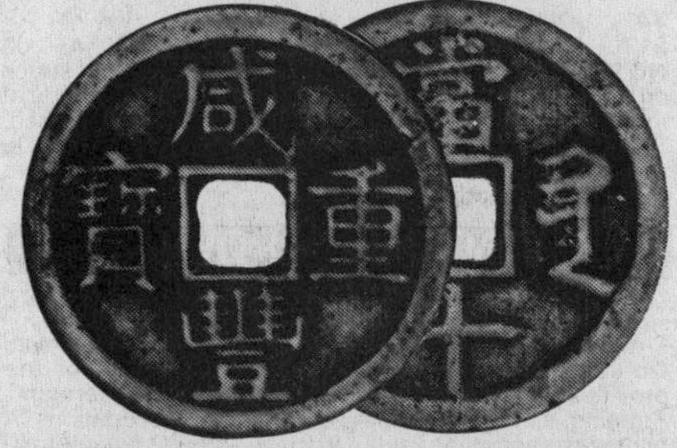

CAST BRASS, 38mm
Obv: Type B-1

C#	Date	Emperor	Good	VG	Fine	VF
20-5	ND(1851-61)	Hsien-feng	18.00	25.00	35.00	60.00

25mm

C#	Date	Emperor	Good	VG	Fine	VF
20-5.1	ND(1851-61)	Hsien-feng	35.00	55.00	75.00	100.00

Obv: Type B-2

C#	Date	Emperor	Good	VG	Fine	VF
20-8	ND(1862-74)	T'ung-chih	—	—	Rare	—

Obv: Type B

C#	Date	Emperor	Good	VG	Fine	VF
20-10	ND(1875-1908)	Kuang-hsu	—	—	Rare	—

50 CASH

CAST BRASS
Obv: Type B-1

C#	Date	Emperor	Good	VG	Fine	VF
20-6	ND(1851-61)	Hsien-feng	60.00	85.00	110.00	165.00

MILLED COINAGE

50 CENTS

SILVER

Kann#	Year	Date	VG	Fine	VF	XF
10	14	(1888)	—	—	Rare	—

DOLLAR

SILVER, 24.80 g

Kann#	Year	Date	VG	Fine	VF	XF
9	14	(1888)	—	—	*Rare	—

***NOTE:** Superior Goodman Sale 6-91 Choice XF realized $46,200.

Kann#	Year	Date	VG	Fine	VF	XF
11	14	(1888)	—	—	Rare	—

22.60 g

Kann#	Year	Date	VG	Fine	VF	XF
12	16	(1890)	—	—	Rare	—

Kann#	Year	Date	VG	Fine	VF	XF
13	16	(1890)	—	—	Rare	—

NOTE: The Kweichow (Guizhou) coins above, obviously copied from contemporary Japanese coins, are still a mystery. Even as late as the 1920's Kweichow (Guizhou) was a very primitive area. It is highly unlikely that the coins were made there in the 1880's and 1890's. It is possible that they were minted elsewhere, possibly in one of the central coastal provinces.

REPUBLIC

1/2 CENT

COPPER

Y#	Year	Date	VG	Fine	VF	XF
A429	38	1949	450.00	750.00	—	—

BRASS

Y#	Year	Date	VG	Fine	VF	XF
A429a	38	1949	300.00	450.00	—	—

10 CENTS

ANTIMONY

Y#	Year	Date	VG	Fine	VF	XF
429	20	(1931)	225.00	425.00	625.00	925.00

20 CENTS

SILVER

Y#	Year	Date	Fine	VF	XF	Unc
430	38	(1949)	100.00	165.00	275.00	400.00

Y#	Year	Date	Fine	VF	XF	Unc
431	38	(1949)	—	—	—	3750.

50 CENTS

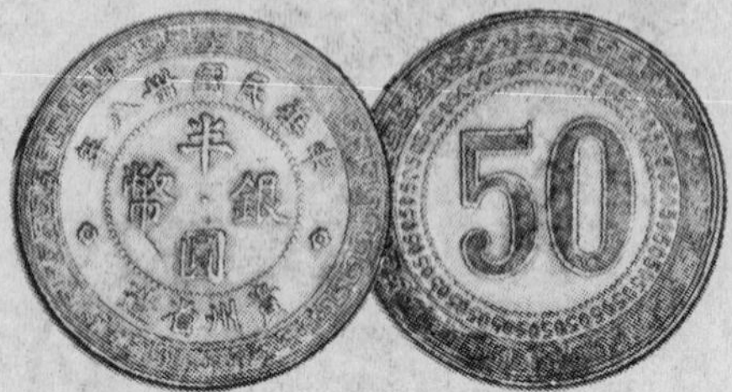

SILVER

Y#	Year	Date	Fine	VF	XF	Unc
432	38	(1949)	—	—	3000.	5300.

DOLLAR

SILVER, 25.80 g
First Road in Kweichow

Y#	Date	Mintage	Fine	VF	XF	Unc
428	Yr.17 (1928)	.648	250.00	500.00	1000.	5000.

NOTE: This coin is known as the 'Auto Dollar' as it purports to portray the governor's automobile. Minor varieties exist in Chinese legends and automobile design.

26.40 g

Y#	Year	Date	Fine	VF	XF	Unc
433	38	(1949)	400.00	700.00	1000.	2500.

NOTE: This coin is known as the 'Bamboo Dollar.'

MANCHURIAN PROVINCES

For coins of Manchuria refer to listings under Fengtien (Liaoning).

PEI YANG

For coins of Pei Yang refer to listings under Chihli (Hebei).

SHANSI PROVINCE

Shanxi

A province located in northeastern China that has some of the richest coal deposits in the world. Parts of the Great Wall cross the province. Extensive agriculture of early China started here. Cited as a "model province" in the new Chinese Republic. Intermittently active mints from 1645. The modern mint was established in 1919. It operated until the mid-1920's and closed because of the public's resistance against the coins that were being produced.

EMPIRE

CASH

CAST BRASS
Obv: Type A

C#	Date	Emperor	Good	VG	Fine	VF
21-2	ND(1796-1820)	Chia-ch'ing	.25	.50	1.00	3.00

Obv: Type A

C#	Date	Emperor	Good	VG	Fine	VF
21-3	ND(1821-50)	Tao-kuang	1.25	2.50	3.00	6.00

Obv: Type A

C#	Date	Emperor	Good	VG	Fine	VF
21-4	ND(1851-61)	Hsien-feng	18.50	27.50	37.50	45.00

Obv: Type A-2

C#	Date	Emperor	Good	VG	Fine	VF
21-6	ND(1862-74)	T'ung-chih	8.50	17.50	25.00	35.00

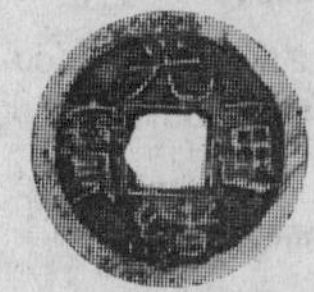

Obv: Type A

C#	Date	Emperor	Good	VG	Fine	VF
21-8	ND(1875-1908)	Kuang-hsu	6.50	11.50	17.50	30.00

10 CASH

CAST BRASS
Obv: Type B-1

C#	Date	Emperor	Good	VG	Fine	VF
21-5	ND(1851-61)	Hsien-feng	12.00	20.00	27.50	50.00

Obv: Type B-2

C#	Date	Emperor	Good	VG	Fine	VF
21-7	ND(1862-74)	T'ung-chih	—	—	Rare	—

REPUBLIC

MILLED COINAGE

10 CASH (1 CENT)

COPPER

Y#	Date	Mintage	Fine	VF	XF	Unc
A435	ND	—	100.00	175.00	225.00	275.00

20 CENTS

SILVER, 4.80 g

Y#	Date	Mintage	VG	Fine	VF	XF
217	ND (ca.1913)	—	100.00	175.00	300.00	450.00

NOTE: Several varieties exist similar to Y#217, but struck cruder, base metal and with different Chinese legends at top of obverse. English legends are usually blundered. Struck about 1913 and thought to be war lord issues. Do not confuse with coins of Fengtien (Liaoning), from which this was copied.

SHANTUNG PROVINCE

Shandong

A province located on the northeastern coast of China. Confucius was born in this province. Parts of the province were leased to Great Britain and to Germany. Farming, fishing and mining are the chief occupations. A mint was opened at Tsinan in 1647 and was an intermittent producer for the empire. A modern mint was opened at Tsinan in 1905, but closed in 1906. Patterns were prepared between 1926-1933 in anticipation of a new coinage, but none were struck for circulation.

EMPIRE

CASH

CAST BRASS
Mint: Chinan
Obv: Type A

C#	Date	Emperor	Good	VG	Fine	VF
22-2	ND(1851-61)	Hsien-feng	16.50	30.00	45.00	60.00

Obv: Type A-2

C#	Date	Emperor	Good	VG	Fine	VF
22-5	ND(1862-74)	T'ung-chih	10.00	18.50	27.50	40.00

Obv: Type A. Rev: Type 1 mint mark.

C#	Date	Emperor	Good	VG	Fine	VF
22-6	ND(1875-1908)	Kuang-hsu	10.00	18.50	27.50	40.00

Mint: Chefoo (now Yantai)
Obv: Type A

C#	Date	Emperor	Good	VG	Fine	VF
27-6	ND(1875-1908)	Kuang-hsu	4.00	6.50	9.00	15.00

Rev: Character *Chin* above.

C#	Date	Emperor	Good	VG	Fine	VF
27-6.1	ND(1875-1908)	Kuang-hsu	5.00	7.50	10.00	15.00

Rev: Character *Ts'un* below.

C#	Date	Emperor	Good	VG	Fine	VF
27-6.2	ND(1875-1908)	Kuang-hsu	5.00	7.50	10.00	15.00

NOTE: C#27 coins were previously listed in Yunnan Province, however some authorities do not attribute these coins to the Chefoo Mint.

MILLED COINAGE

2 CASH

COPPER

Y#	Date	Mintage	VG	Fine	VF	XF
8s	CD1906	—	12.00	25.00	35.00	70.00

10 CASH

COPPER

Y#	Date	Mintage	Fine	VF	XF	Unc
220	ND(1904-05)		8.00	15.00	30.00	55.00

Obv: Thin Manchu words in center.
Rev: SHANTUNG.

Y#	Date	Mintage	Fine	VF	XF	Unc
221	ND(1904-05)		7.00	11.00	17.50	40.00

Obv: Thick Manchu in center.

Y#	Date	Mintage	Fine	VF	XF	Unc
221.1	ND(1904-05)		3.50	7.00	14.00	30.00

Obv: Smaller stars.

Y#	Date	Mintage	Fine	VF	XF	Unc
221.2	ND(1904-05)		3.50	7.00	14.00	30.00

Obv: Similar to Y#220. Rev: Similar to Y#221.

Y#	Date	Mintage	Fine	VF	XF	Unc
221.3	ND(1904-05)		125.00	200.00	300.00	—

Obv: Thick Manchu in center. Rev: SHANG-TUNG.

Y#	Date	Mintage	Fine	VF	XF	Unc
221a	ND(1904-05)		2.50	4.00	7.50	20.00

Obv: Thin Manchu.

Y#	Date	Mintage	Fine	VF	XF	Unc
221a.1	ND(1904-05)		5.00	10.00	17.50	40.00

BRASS
Rev: 6 large waves below dragon.

Y#	Date	Mintage	Fine	VF	XF	Unc
10s	CD1906	—	6.00	10.00	17.50	40.00

COPPER

Y#	Date	Mintage	Fine	VF	XF	Unc
10s.1	CD1906	—	7.00	12.00	25.00	50.00

Rev: 5 small waves below dragon.

Y#	Date	Mintage	Fine	VF	XF	Unc
10s.1a	CD1906	—	5.00	10.00	17.50	40.00

Rev: Dragon w/larger forehead and narrower face, pearl redesigned.

Y#	Date	Mintage	Fine	VF	XF	Unc
10s.2a	CD1906	—	8.00	15.00	30.00	60.00

SHENSI PROVINCE

Shaanxi

A province located in central China that is a rich agricultural area. A very important province in the early development of China. An active imperial mint was located at Sian (Xi'an).

EMPIRE

CASH

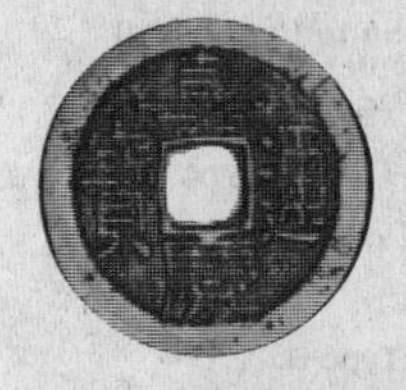
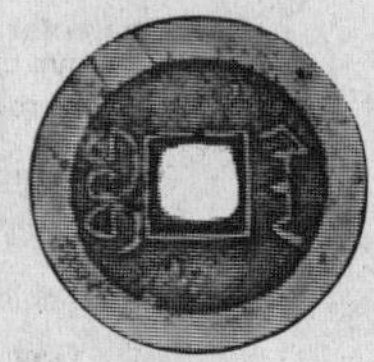

CAST BRASS or COPPER
Obv: Type A

C#	Date	Emperor	Good	VG	Fine	VF
23-2	ND(1796-1820)	Chia-ch'ing	1.50	3.00	4.00	6.00

Obv: Type A

C#	Date	Emperor	Good	VG	Fine	VF
23-3	ND(1821-50)	Tao-kuang	2.50	5.00	7.50	12.50

Obv: Type A

C#	Date	Emperor	Good	VG	Fine	VF
23-4	ND(1851-61)	Hsien-feng	4.00	7.00	12.00	20.00

CAST IRON

C#	Date	Emperor	Good	VG	Fine	VF
23-4a	ND(1851-61)	Hsien-feng	—	—	Rare	—

CAST BRASS
Obv: Type A-2

C#	Date	Emperor	Good	VG	Fine	VF
23-11	ND(1862-74)	T'ung-chih	—	—	Rare	—

Obv: Type A

C#	Date	Emperor	Good	VG	Fine	VF
23-13	ND(1875-1908)	Kuang-hsu	20.00	35.00	50.00	75.00

10 CASH

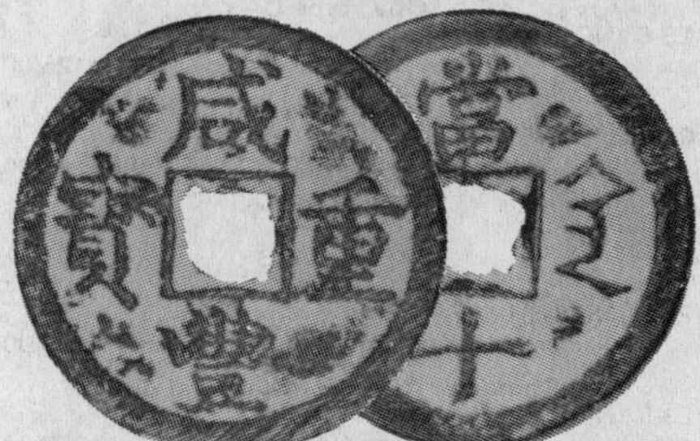

CAST BRASS, 43mm
Obv: Type B-1

C#	Date	Emperor	Good	VG	Fine	VF
23-5	ND(1851-61)	Hsien-feng	10.00	15.00	25.00	45.00

36mm

C#	Date	Emperor	Good	VG	Fine	VF
23-5.1	ND(1851-61)	Hsien-feng	18.50	30.00	50.00	80.00

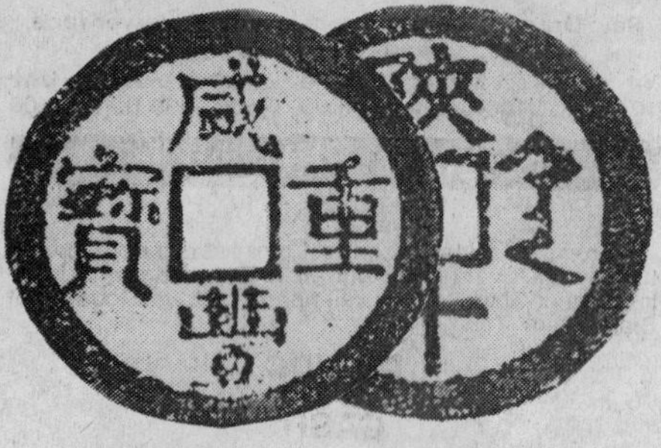

Rev: Character *Shan* (for Shensi) above center hole.

C#	Date	Emperor	Good	VG	Fine	VF
23-6	ND(1851-61)	Hsien-feng	40.00	65.00	90.00	125.00
	Obv: Type B-2					
23-12	ND(1862-74)	Tung-chih	—	—	Rare	—
	Obv: Type B					
23-14	ND(1875-1908)	Kuang-hsu	—	—	Rare	—

50 CASH

CAST BRASS
Obv: Type B-1

C#	Date	Emperor	Good	VG	Fine	VF
23-7	ND(1851-61)	Hsien-feng	10.00	20.00.	35.00	70.00

100 CASH

CAST BRASS, 57-58mm
Obv: Type C

C#	Date	Emperor	Good	VG	Fine	VF
23-8.1	ND(1851-61)	Hsien-feng	35.00	55.00	75.00	125.00
	48-49mm					
23-8.2	ND(1851-61)	Hsien-feng	10.00	17.50	25.00	45.00

500 CASH

CAST BRASS
Obv: Type C

C#	Date	Emperor	Good	VG	Fine	VF
23-9	ND(1851-61)	Hsien-feng	75.00	110.00	150.00	200.00
	Rev: Character *Kuan* (official) cast on rim.					
23-9.1	ND(1851-61)	Hsien-feng	125.00	175.00	250.00	350.00

1000 CASH

CAST BRASS
Obv: Type C

C#	Date	Emperor	Good	VG	Fine	VF
23-10	ND(1851-61)	Hsien-feng	110.00	165.00	225.00	300.00

CAST COPPER

C#	Date	Emperor	Good	VG	Fine	VF
23-10a	ND(1851-61)	Hsien-feng	120.00	175.00	250.00	350.00

CAST BRASS
Rev: Character *Kuan* cast on rim.
Illustration reduced, actual size 74mm.

C#	Date	Emperor	Good	VG	Fine	VF
23-10.1	ND(1851-61)	Hsien-feng	150.00	220.00	300.00	400.00

REPUBLIC

Obv. legends:
IMTYPIF: *I Mei Ta Yuan Pi I* (1) *Fen*
(One Piece Great Dollar Coin = 1 Cent)
IMTYPEF: *I Mei Ta Yuan Pi Ehr* (2) *Fen*
(One Piece Great Dollar Coin = 2 Cent)

CENT

COPPER

Y#	Date	Mintage	VG	Fine	VF	XF
435	ND ca.1928	—	20.00	30.00	50.00	100.00

2 CENTS

COPPER
Dentilated borders.
Obv: Star between flags.

Y#	Date	Mintage	VG	Fine	VF	XF
436	ND ca.1928	—	35.00	60.00	90.00	150.00

Large Chinese legends.
Obv: W/o star between flags.

Y#	Date	Mintage	VG	Fine	VF	XF
436.1	ND ca.1928	—	15.00	25.00	40.00	75.00

Obv. and rev: Star in center.

Y#	Date	Mintage	VG	Fine	VF	XF
436.2	ND ca.1928	—	40.00	75.00	120.00	225.00

Small Chinese legends.
Obv: W/o star between flags.

Y#	Date	Mintage	VG	Fine	VF	XF
436.3	ND ca.1928	—	25.00	50.00	80.00	125.00

Pearled borders.

Y#	Date	Mintage	VG	Fine	VF	XF
436.4	ND ca.1928	—	50.00	80.00	120.00	200.00

SIKANG PROVINCE

Created in 1928 from the western frontier region of Szechuan Province. It was dissolved in 1955, being divided between Szechuan (Sichuan) Province and Tibet.

REPUBLIC

100 CASH

COPPER

KM#	Date	Mintage	VG	Fine	VF	XF
1	Yr.15 (1926)	—	150.00	225.00	300.00	400.00
	Yr.19 (1930)	—	125.00	150.00	200.00	300.00
	BRASS					
2	Yr.19 (1930)	—	125.00	150.00	225.00	375.00

NOTE: Previously listed in Szechuan (Sichuan) Province.

SINKIANG PROVINCE

Hsinkiang, Xinjiang
"New Dominion"

An autonomous region in western China, often referred to as Chinese Turkestan. High mountains surround 2000 ft. tableland on three sides with a large desert in center of this province. Many salt lakes, mining and some farming and oil. Inhabited by early man and was referred to as the "Silk Route" to the West. Sinkiang (Xinjiang) has been historically under the control of many factions, including Genghis Khan. It became a province in 1884. China has made claim to Sinkiang (Xinjiang) for many, many years. This rule has been more nominal than actual. Sinkiang (Xinjiang) had eight imperial mints, only three of which were in operation toward the end of the reign of Kuang Hsu. Only two mints operated during the early years of the republic. In 1949, due to a drastic coin shortage and lack of confidence in the inflated paper money, it was planned to mint some dollars in Sinkiang (Xinjiang). These did not see much circulation, however, due to the defeat of the nationalists, though they have recently appeared in considerable numbers in today's market.

MONETARY SYSTEM

2 Pul = 1 Cash
2 Cash = 5 Li
4 Cash = 10 Li = 1 Fen
25 Cash = 10 Fen = 1 Miscal = 1 Ch'ien, Mace, Tanga
10 Miscals (Mace) = 1 Liang (Tael or Sar)
20 Miscals (Tangas) = 1 Tilla

MINT NAME
LOCAL MINT NAMES AND MARKS

MINT	CHINESE	TURKI	MANCHU
Aksu	城阿	اقصو	

犂伊 الي

Ili
now Yining (Gulja)

什喀 كشقر

Kashgar
now Kashi

闐和 خوتن

Khotan
now Hotan

كوتشر

Kotsha
(Kuche)

車庫 كوچا

Kuche
now Kuqa

化廸

Ti-hua
now Dihua,
refer to Urumchi

化廸 ارومجي

Urumchi
now Urumqi

什烏 اوش

Ushi
now Wushi (Uqturpan)

沙吉英

Yangihissar
now Yengisar

羌爾葉 يارقند

Yarkand
now Shache (Yarkant)

GENERAL COINAGE

EMPIRE

CASH

CAST COPPER
Rev: ***Boo Chiowan*** **(Manchu for Pao Chuan Board of Revenue)**

KM#	Date	Emperor	Good	VG	Fine	VF
10	ND (1875-1908)	Kuang-hsu	1.50	3.50	6.00	9.50

Rev: Similar to KM#10 but ***Boo*** **in mirror image.**

KM#	Date	Emperor	Good	VG	Fine	VF
11	ND (1875-1908)	Kuang-hsu	3.50	6.00	9.00	13.50

Rev: Similar to KM#10 but ***Boo Chiowan*** **in mirror image.**

KM#	Date	Emperor	Good	VG	Fine	VF
12	ND (1875-1908)	Kuang-hsu	1.50	3.50	6.00	9.50

Rev: ***Boo Chaun*** **or** ***Yaun*** **(illiterate Manchu).**

KM#	Date	Emperor	Good	VG	Fine	VF
13	ND (1875-1908)	Kuang-hsu	1.50	3.50	6.00	9.50

Rev: ***Boo Choan*** **(illiterate Manchu).**

KM#	Date	Emperor	Good	VG	Fine	VF
14	ND (1875-1908)	Kuang-hsu	1.50	3.00	5.00	8.50

NOTE: The five one-cash varieties listed above could be confused with Beijing issues C1-16 or C2-15, but they are much more crudely cast, and are made of red copper rather than brass. See Landon Ross, 1986, Numismatics International Bulletin 20(3) for a more detailed review.

10 CASH

CAST COPPER
Rev: ***Pao Yuan?*** **w/*****Hsin*** **(new) above.**

KM#	Date	Emperor	Good	VG	Fine	VF
3	ND(1821-50)	Tao-kuang	5.50	9.00	15.00	25.00

Rev: ***Pao Yuan?*** **w/*****Hsin*** **(new) above.**

KM#	Date	Emperor	Good	VG	Fine	VF
5	ND(1862-74)	T'ung-chih	5.50	9.00	15.00	25.00

NOTE: All of the above were probably cast in the reign of Kuang Hsu (1875-1908).

Obv: Type A
Rev: ***Pao Yuan?*** **w/*****K'a*** **(for Kashgar) above.**

KM#	Date	Emperor	Good	VG	Fine	VF
6	ND(1875-1908)	Kuang-hsu	5.50	8.00	14.00	22.50

Rev: ***Pao Yuan?*** **w/*****K'u*** **(for Kuche) above.**

KM#	Date	Emperor	Good	VG	Fine	VF
7.1	ND(1875-1908)	Kuang-hsu	1.50	3.00	5.00	10.00

Rev: ***Pao*** **at left reversed.**

KM#	Date	Emperor	Good	VG	Fine	VF
7.2	ND(1875-1908)	Kuang-hsu	7.50	13.50	22.50	35.00

Rev: ***Pao Yuan?*** **w/*****Hsin*** **(new) above.**

KM#	Date	Emperor	Good	VG	Fine	VF
8	ND(1875-1908)	Kuang-hsu	3.50	5.00	7.50	15.00

Rev: ***Pao Hsin*** **(for Sinkiang = New Territory) w/** ***Hsin*** **(new) above.**

KM#	Date	Emperor	Good	VG	Fine	VF
9	ND(1875-1908)	Kuang-hsu	3.00	4.50	7.00	15.00

Rev: ***Pao Yuan?*** **w/*****A*** **(for Aksu) above.**

KM#	Date	Emperor	Good	VG	Fine	VF
15	ND (1875-1908)	Kuang-hsu	12.00	15.00	21.50	28.50

Obv. leg: ***Kuang Hsu Ting Wei.***
Rev: ***Pao Yuan?*** **w/*****Hsin*** **(new) above.**

KM#	Date	Emperor	Good	VG	Fine	VF
16	CD1907	Kuang-hsu	17.50	23.50	30.00	45.00

Obv. leg: ***Kuang Hsu Wu Shen.***

KM#	Date	Emperor	Good	VG	Fine	VF
17	CD1908	Kuang-hsu	23.50	32.50	45.00	60.00

HAMMERED COINAGE

1/2 MISCAL

(5 Fen)

SILVER, 1.45 g
Obv. leg: ***On Gumush.***
Rev. leg: ***Besh Fen*** **(5 Fen), w/o mint name.**

Y#	Date	Mintage	VG	Fine	VF	XF
A7.1	ND	—	5.50	9.00	15.00	25.00
	AH1294	—	5.50	9.00	15.00	25.00
	1295	—	5.50	9.00	15.00	25.00

Obv: ***Chu.*** **Rev. Turki leg:** ***Besh Fen.***

Y#	Date	Mintage	VG	Fine	VF	XF
A7.2	AH1295	—	32.50	55.00	90.00	150.00

Obv. leg: Turki. Rev. leg: Manchu.

Y#	Date	Mintage	VG	Fine	VF	XF
A7.3	ND	—	—	—	Rare	—

MILLED COINAGE

Fen and Li Series

FEN, 5 LI

COPPER
Obv: Large dots in circle, dentilated rims.

Y#	Date	Mintage	Good	VG	Fine	VF
1	ND	—	150.00	200.00	350.00	550.00

NOTE: Two varieties are reported.

Obv: Small dots in circle, dotted rims.

Y#	Date	Mintage	Fine	VF	XF	Unc
1a	ND	(modern copy)	—	25.00	35.00	

NOTE: The legend on this coin states that it is valued at 1 Fen 5 Li of silver (about 15 Cash). The coin is the size of a normal 10 Cash piece of Sinkiang (Xinjiang), but these pieces are usually larger than those of the other provinces. For this reason, it is assumed the coin was overvalued to benefit the government.

2 FEN, 5 LI

COPPER

Y#	Date	Mintage	Good	VG	Fine	VF
A1	ND	—	—	—	Rare	—

NOTE: This denomination was recalled shortly after issue and the dies re-engraved 1 Fen and 5 Li to produce Y#1. Do not confuse poorly re-engraved Chinese numeral ***2*** examples of Y#1 for Y#A1. Note the difference in spacing of the Chinese characters below the rosettes between Y#1 and Y#A1.

Y#	Date	Mintage	Good	VG	Fine	VF
B1	ND	—	—	—	Rare	—

NOTE: Status unknown.

Cash Series

10 CASH

COPPER
Rev: W/o Chinese leg. above dragon.

Y#	Date	Mintage	Good	VG	Fine	VF
2.1	ND	—	25.00	42.50	75.00	175.00

Rev: Chinese leg. w/*Nien* (year) added above dragon.

Y#	Date	Mintage	Good	VG	Fine	VF
2.2	CD1910	—	25.00	42.50	75.00	175.00
	1911	—	30.00	50.00	100.00	200.00

Obv: Double ring around star in center.

Y#	Date	Mintage	Good	VG	Fine	VF
2.3	CD1911	—	30.00	50.00	100.00	200.00

Obv: Large characters within center circle.

Y#	Date	Mintage	Fine	VF	XF	Unc
2a	CD1910	(modern copy)	—	25.00	35.00	

MISCAL (MACE)

SILVER
Obv. leg: *Tsu Yin I Ch'ien*
(Fine silver 1 Mace)

Kann#	Date	Mintage	VG	Fine	VF	XF
1000	ND	—	150.00	250.00	425.00	800.00

NOTE: Kann #1000 was minted at the Arsenal of Lanchowfu in Gansu (Kansu) by order of General Tso Tsung-tang when he was campaigning against Yakub Beg's Sinkiang (Xinjiang) armies.

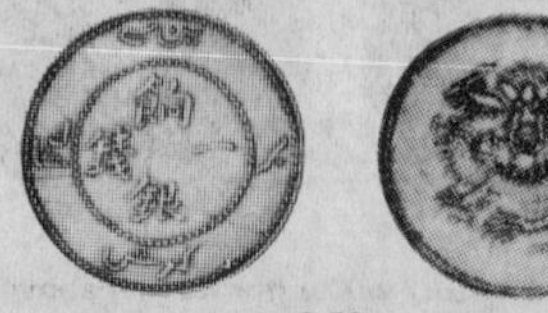

3.50 g
Obv. outer leg: Turki w/o dot in center.
Rev: W/o Turki leg.

Y#	Date	Mintage	VG	Fine	VF	XF
3	ND	—	75.00	125.00	200.00	325.00

Obv. outer leg: Turki w/ dot in center.
Rev: W/o Turki leg.

Y#	Date	Mintage	VG	Fine	VF	XF
3.1	ND	—	75.00	125.00	200.00	325.00

Obv: W/o outer Turki leg. Rev. leg: Turki.

Y#	Date	Mintage	VG	Fine	VF	XF
3.2	ND	—	325.00	550.00	900.00	1500.

Obv. & rev: W/o outer Turki leg.

Y#	Date	Mintage	VG	Fine	VF	XF
3.3	ND	—	90.00	150.00	250.00	400.00

Rev. leg: SUNGAREI above dragon, 1 MACE below.

Y#	Date	Mintage	VG	Fine	VF	XF
10	ND	—	110.00	225.00	400.00	650.00

2 MISCALS (2 MACE)

SILVER, 7.20 g
Obv. outer leg: Turki. Rev: W/o Turki leg.

Y#	Date	Mintage	VG	Fine	VF	XF
4	ND	—	50.00	75.00	150.00	400.00

Obv. outer leg: Continuous Turki. Rev: W/o Turki leg.

Y#	Date	Mintage	VG	Fine	VF	XF
4.1	ND	—	100.00	150.00	250.00	325.00

Obv: W/o outer Turki leg. Rev. leg: Turki.

Y#	Date	Mintage	VG	Fine	VF	XF
4.2	ND	—	150.00	250.00	400.00	650.00

Rev: Redesigned dragon w/o Turki legends.

Y#	Date	Mintage	VG	Fine	VF	XF
4.3	ND	—	150.00	250.00	400.00	650.00

Obv. outer leg: Turki.
Rev: Circled dragon w/o Turki leg.

Y#	Date	Mintage	VG	Fine	VF	XF
4.4	ND	—	—	—	Rare	—

Rev. leg: SUNGAREI above dragon, 2 MACE below.

Y#	Date	Mintage	VG	Fine	VF	XF
11	ND	—	200.00	425.00	850.00	1350.

4 MISCALS (4 MACE)

SILVER, 14.20 g

Y#	Date	Mintage	VG	Fine	VF	XF
5	ND	—	80.00	125.00	200.00	400.00

5 MISCALS (5 MACE)

SILVER, 17.90 g
Obv: W/o dot or rosette in center.
Rev: Uncircled dragon.

Y#	Date	Mintage	VG	Fine	VF	XF
6	ND	—	15.00	25.00	60.00	175.00

Rev: Circled dragon, w/o rosettes.

Y#	Date	Mintage	VG	Fine	VF	XF
6.1	ND	—	15.00	25.00	50.00	90.00

Rev: Large rosettes at sides of dragon.

6.2 ND — 15.00 25.00 50.00 90.00

Obv: Dot in center. Rev: W/o rosettes, circled dragon.

6.3 ND — 15.00 25.00 50.00 90.00

Obv: Cross in center.

6.4 ND — 15.00 25.00 50.00 90.00

Obv: Large rosette in center, middle of which is depressed.

6.5 ND — 15.00 25.00 50.00 90.00

Obv: 8 petalled rosette in center, middle of which is raised. Rev: Small rosettes at sides of dragon.

6.6 ND — 15.00 25.00 50.00 90.00

Rev: Bat above uncircled dragon's head.

6.7 ND — 175.00 300.00 450.00 700.00

Rev: Turki leg. around uncircled dragon.

6.8 ND — 400.00 600.00 — —

Rev. leg: SUNGAREI above uncircled dragon, 5 MACE below.

6.9 ND — — — Rare —

NOTE: Some authorities consider this coin a fantasy.

Rev: W/o SUNGAREI w/4 bats and many clouds around dragon.

6.10 ND — — — Rare —

Obv: Turki leg. rotated. Rev: Bat above dragon's head.

6.11 ND — — — Rare —

SAR (TAEL)

SILVER, 35.50 g
Obv: W/o outer Turki leg. Rev: W/o Turki leg., rosettes at sides of uncircled dragon.

Y#	Date	Mintage	VG	Fine	VF	XF
7	ND	—	25.00	40.00	60.00	140.00

Rev: Turki leg. around circled dragon, w/o rosettes.

7.1 ND — 40.00 65.00 100.00 300.00

Rev: Turki leg. around uncircled dragon.

7.2 ND — 500.00 850.00 1250. 1600.

Obv: Outer Turki leg., rosette in center. Rev: W/o Turki leg., w/rosettes at sides of uncircled dragon.

Y#	Date	Mintage	VG	Fine	VF	XF
7.3	ND	—	35.00	50.00	70.00	150.00

GOLD MISCAL (MACE)

GOLD, 3.90 g
Rev: Turki leg. around uncircled dragon.

Y#	Date	Mintage	Fine	VF	XF	Unc
8	ND	—	600.00	1000.	1400.	2000.

Rev: Turki leg. at left differs.

8.2 ND — 700.00 1200. 1750. 2500.

Rev: W/o Turki leg. around uncircled dragon.

8.1 ND — 1150. 1900. 2800. 4000.

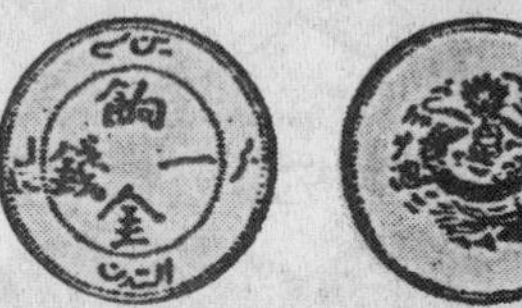

Obv: Turki leg. in outer circle.

8.3 ND — 875.00 1450. 2100. 3000.

GOLD 2 MISCALS

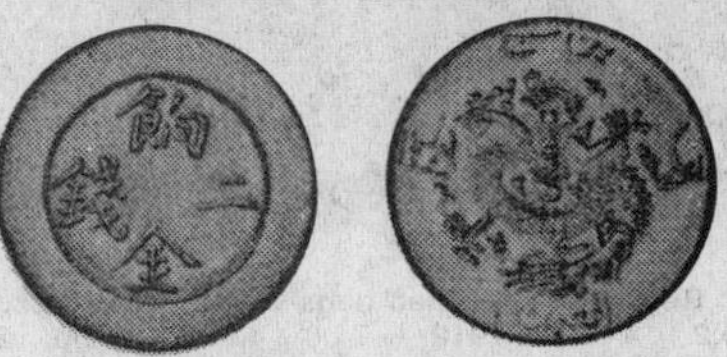

GOLD, 7.80 g
Obv: Narrow spaced Chinese "2".
Rev: Turki leg. around uncircled dragon.

9 ND — 750.00 1350. 2000. 2800.

Obv: Wide spaced Chinese "2".
Rev: Redesigned dragon.

9.1 ND — 750.00 1350. 2000. 2800.

Similar to 2 Miscals (Silver) Y#11.

Kann#	Date	Mintage	Fine	VF	XF	Unc
1505	ND	—	— Reported, not confirmed			

REPUBLIC

10 CASH

COPPER

Obv: Large character *Shih* (ten).

Y#	Date	Mintage	Good	VG	Fine	VF
B39.1	ND	—	8.50	15.00	25.00	37.50

Obv: Small character *Shih* (ten).
Rev: Small crossed flags.

Y#	Date	Mintage	Good	VG	Fine	VF
B39.2	ND	—	12.50	25.00	35.00	50.00

Rev: Large crossed flags w/vertical stripes.

Y#	Year	Date	Good	VG	Fine	VF
A39.1	1	CD1912	7.50	13.50	18.50	28.00

Rev: Small crossed flags w/vertical stripes.

Y#	Year	Date	Good	VG	Fine	VF
A39.2	1	CD1912	7.00	12.00	16.50	25.00

Y#	Date	Mintage	Good	VG	Fine	VF
C39	CD1921	—	—	—	Rare	—

NOTE: Status unknown.

Obv: Chinese leg. *Chung Hua Min Kuo* in inner circle w/*Hsin Kiang* at upper right.
Rev: Flags w/solid sunbursts w/inner circles.

Y#	Date	Mintage	Good	VG	Fine	VF
40.1	CD1929	—	7.00	12.00	16.50	25.00
	1930	—	—	—	Rare	—

NOTE: The cyclical date character at left exists closed and open for CD1929.

Obv: Large starburst in center.
Rev: Long streamers.

Y#	Date	Mintage	Good	VG	Fine	VF
40.2	CD1929	—	7.00	12.00	16.50	25.00

NOTE: Y#40 inscribed "Sheng Ch'eng" in upper legend may refer to Tihwa (Urumchi now Urumqi).

Obv. leg: Cyclical date at upper right.

Y#	Date	Mintage	Good	VG	Fine	VF
40.3	CD1930	—	—	—	Rare	—

20 CASH

COPPER
Obv: 8 petalled rosette in center.
Rev: 2 stripes in flags have arabesques.

Y#	Date	Mintage	VG	Fine	VF	XF
39.1	ND	—	10.00	16.50	20.00	27.50

Obv: 5 petalled rosette in center.

Y#	Date	Mintage	VG	Fine	VF	XF
39.2	ND	—	50.00	100.00	150.00	225.00

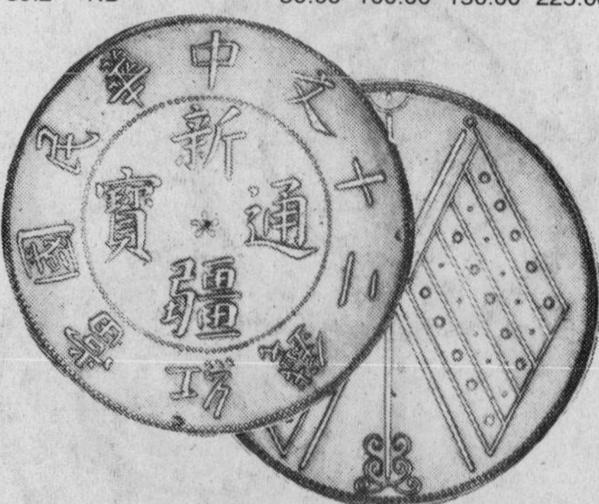

Rev: W/o arabesques in flags.

Y#	Date	Mintage	Fine	VF	XF	Unc
39.3	ND	(restrike)	—	—	50.00	75.00

Obv: Chinese leg. *Chung Hua Min Kuo* in inner circle w/*Hsin Kiang* at upper right.

Y#	Date	Mintage	Good	VG	Fine	VF
A41.1	CD1929	—	75.00	125.00	200.00	300.00
	1930	—	85.00	140.00	225.00	335.00

NOTE: Y#A41.1 inscribed *Sheng Ch'eng* in upper legend may refer to Tihwa (Urumchi now Urumqi).

Obv. leg: Cyclical date at upper right.

Y#	Date	Mintage	Good	VG	Fine	VF
A41.2	CD1930	—	—	—	Rare	—

5 MISCALS (5 MACE)

SILVER, 17.90 g
Rev: 2 stripes in flags have arabesques.

Y#	Year	Date	VG	Fine	VF	XF
41	1	CD1912	40.00	65.00	150.00	200.00

Rev: 4 stripes in flags have arabesques.

Y#	Year	Date	VG	Fine	VF	XF
41a	1	CD1912	40.00	65.00	150.00	200.00

DOLLAR

SILVER
Obv: Similar to Y#46.2 but w/larger Chinese characters. Rev: Thick pointed base "1".

Y#	Year	Date	VG	Fine	VF	XF
46	38	1949	10.00	20.00	30.00	45.00

Obv: Similar to Y#46.2 but w/larger Chinese characters. Rev: Thick pointed base "1" w/large serif.

Y#	Year	Date	VG	Fine	VF	XF
46.1	38	1949	10.00	20.00	30.00	45.00

Obv: Smaller Chinese characters.
Rev: Thin pointed base "1".

Y#	Year	Date	VG	Fine	VF	XF
46.2	38	1949	10.00	20.00	30.00	50.00

Rev: Square based "1".

Y#	Year	Date	VG	Fine	VF	XF
46.3	38	1949	15.00	25.00	45.00	80.00

Obv: Outlined Chinese characters *I Yuan* in center.

Y#	Year	Date	VG	Fine	VF	XF
46.4	38	1949	15.00	25.00	60.00	100.00

Obv: Chinese characters *Min Kuo* *38 Nien* (year) replaced by Chinese numerals 9-4-9-1 (1949) at bottom.

Y#	Year	Date	VG	Fine	VF	XF
46.5	1949	1949	75.00	125.00	175.00	250.00

SAR (TAEL)

SILVER, 35.90 g
Rev: 2 stripes in flags have arabesques.

Y#	Year	Date	VG	Fine	VF	XF
42	1	CD1912	60.00	100.00	200.00	350.00

Obv: Similar to Y#42.
Rev: 4 stripes in flags have arabesques.

Y#	Year	Date	VG	Fine	VF	XF
42a	1	CD1912	60.00	100.00	200.00	350.00

LOCAL COINAGE

Aksu Mint

EMPIRE

CASH

CAST COPPER
Obv: Type A
Rev: Character *Chiu* (nine) above.

C#	Date	Emperor	Good	VG	Fine	VF
30-5	ND(1796-1820)	Chia-ch'ing	1.75	4.25	8.00	10.00

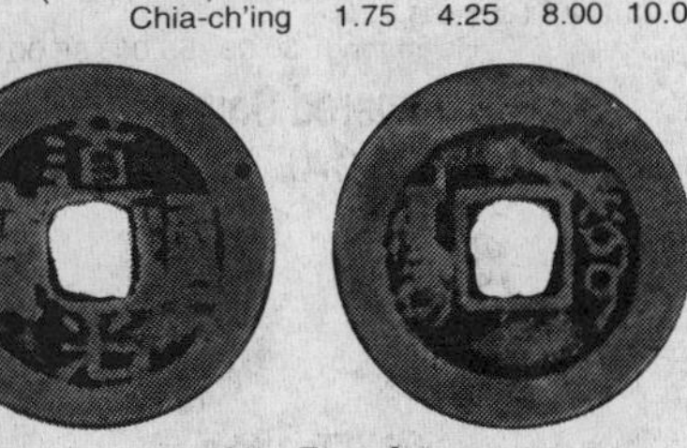

Obv: Type A

C#	Date	Emperor	Good	VG	Fine	VF
30-6	ND(1821-50)	Tao-kuang	1.00	2.00	3.50	6.00

5 CASH

CAST COPPER
Obv: Type A
Rev: Characters *Pa Nien* (= year 8 = 1828) above.

C#	Date	Emperor	Good	VG	Fine	VF
30-7	Yr.8 (1828)	Tao-kuang	1.50	3.00	6.00	10.00

C#	Date	Emperor	Good	VG	Fine	VF
30-10	ND(1851-61)	Hsien-feng	6.00	12.00	22.50	35.00

C#	Date	Emperor	Good	VG	Fine	VF
30-A15	ND(1862-74)	T'ung-chih	75.00	95.00	120.00	150.00

10 CASH

CAST COPPER
Obv: Type A-1
Rev: *Tang* above.

C#	Date	Emperor	Good	VG	Fine	VF
30-2.1	ND(1736-95)	Ch'ien-lung	7.00	10.00	15.00	25.00

Rev: Character *K'a* (Kashgar) above.

C#	Date	Emperor	Good	VG	Fine	VF
30-2.2	ND(1736-95)	Ch'ien-lung	1.75	3.50	4.50	9.00

Rev: Character *A* (for Aksu) above.

C#	Date	Emperor	Good	VG	Fine	VF
30-3	ND(1736-95)	Ch'ien-lung	1.25	3.00	4.50	7.00

NOTE: C#30-2, 30-3 and 30-4 (1 Cash) though bearing the reign title of Ch'ien Lung, were cast during the Kuang Hsu era, (1875-1908).

Obv: Type A
Rev: Characters *Pa Nien* (= year 8 = 1828) above.

C#	Date	Emperor	Good	VG	Fine	VF
30-8	Yr.8 (1828)	Tao-kuang	1.00	1.75	2.75	5.50

NOTE: C#30-7 and 30-8 are commemoratives marking the supression of a revolt in Sinkiang in 1828. Numerous counterfeits, presumably contemporary, have recently come on the market. Many of these modern counterfeits have coin alignment. Refer to page 28 of Ch'en Hung-hsi's 1987 *Hsinchiang Hung Ch'ien Chiako Mulu* for illustrations.

25 mm
Obv: Type A

C#	Date	Emperor	Good	VG	Fine	VF
30-11	ND(1851-61)	Hsien-feng	3.00	5.00	8.00	15.00

CAST COPPER, 25mm
Obv: Type A

C#	Date	Emperor	Good	VG	Fine	VF
30-15	ND(1862-74)	T'ung-chih	3.00	5.00	8.00	15.00

CAST COPPER
Rev: Character *A* (for Aksu) above center hole, *Aksu* in Turki at right, in Manchu at left.

C#	Date	Emperor	Good	VG	Fine	VF
30-18	ND(1875-1908)	Kuang-hsu	1.50	2.50	4.00	8.00

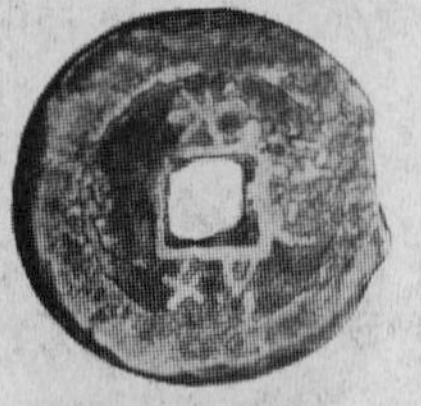

Rev: *Aksu* in Manchu at right, in Turki at left.

C#	Date	Emperor	Good	VG	Fine	VF
30-18.1	ND(1875-1908)	Kuang-hsu	7.50	12.50	19.00	35.00

Rev: Character *K'a* (for Kashgar) above.

C#	Date	Emperor	Good	VG	Fine	VF
30-19	ND(1875-1908)	Kuang-hsu	2.00	4.50	6.50	13.50

50 CASH

CAST BRASS, 36-37mm
Obv: Type B-1

C#	Date	Emperor	Good	VG	Fine	VF
30-12	ND(1851-61)	Hsien-feng	100.00	150.00	200.00	300.00

100 CASH

CAST COPPER, 44-45mm
Obv: Type C

C#	Date	Emperor	Good	VG	Fine	VF
30-13	ND(1851-61)	Hsien-feng	140.00	200.00	275.00	400.00

40-41mm

C#	Date	Emperor	Good	VG	Fine	VF
30-13.1	ND(1851-61)	Hsien-feng	30.00	55.00	85.00	150.00

Hammered Coinage

1/2 MISCAL (5 FEN)

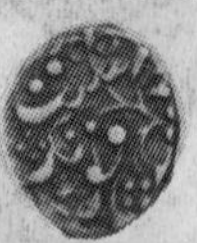

SILVER, 1.45 g
Obv. and rev: Turki script.

Y#	Date	Emperor	VG	Fine	VF	XF
A7.4	ND	—	27.50	45.00	75.00	125.00
	AH1296	—	27.50	45.00	75.00	125.00

Obv: Large Chinese *Kuang* above square w/Turki leg. below. Rev: Turki leg.

Y#	Date	Emperor	VG	Fine	VF	XF
A7.5	AH1296	Kuang-hsu	55.00	90.00	150.00	250.00
	1297	—	11.50	18.50	30.00	50.00
	1298/1297 (mule)	Kuang-hsu	11.50	18.50	30.00	35.00
	1298	Kuang-hsu	11.50	18.50	30.00	50.00

Milled Coinage

MISCAL (MACE)

SILVER, 3.50 g
Similar to 3 Miscals, Y#14.

Y#	Date	Mintage	VG	Fine	VF	XF
A13	AH1310	—	275.00	450.00	750.00	1250.

2 MISCALS (2 MACE)

SILVER, 7.20 g
Similar to 3 Miscals, Y#14.

Y#	Date	Mintage	VG	Fine	VF	XF
13	AH1310	—	40.00	80.00	150.00	225.00
	1311	—	30.00	60.00	100.00	165.00

3 MISCALS (3 MACE)

SILVER, 10.50 g

Y#	Date	Mintage	VG	Fine	VF	XF
14	AH1310	—	40.00	80.00	140.00	225.00
	1311	—	32.50	65.00	110.00	200.00
	1312	—	32.50	65.00	110.00	200.00

5 MISCALS (5 MACE)

SILVER, 17.50 g

Y#	Date	Mintage	VG	Fine	VF	XF
15	AH1310	—	55.00	110.00	190.00	325.00
	1311	—	50.00	100.00	165.00	275.00
	1312	—	40.00	80.00	150.00	250.00

REPUBLIC

10 CASH

CAST COPPER, 32mm.

Y#	Date	Mintage	Good	VG	Fine	VF
37.1	ND	—	35.00	55.00	80.00	—

Reduced size, 29mm.

Y#	Date	Mintage	Good	VG	Fine	VF
37.2	ND	—	35.00	55.00	80.00	—

Milled Coinage

10 CASH

COPPER
Obv: Chinese characters *Shih Wen* (10 Wen) at lower left.
Rev: Upper Turki leg. inverted.

Y#	Date	Mintage	Good	VG	Fine	VF
F38	AH1332	—	35.00	65.00	85.00	125.00

Ili Mint

(Huiyuan, Kuldja, Kuldsha, Kwlja)

EMPIRE

CASH

CAST COPPER

C#	Date	Emperor	Good	VG	Fine	VF
28-2	ND(1796-1820)	Chia-ch'ing	15.00	30.00	55.00	100.00

Rev: Vertical line below.

C#	Date	Emperor	Good	VG	Fine	VF
28-2.1	ND(1796-1820)	Chia-ch'ing	30.00	50.00	85.00	125.00

Rev: Vertical line above.

C#	Date	Emperor	Good	VG	Fine	VF
28-2.2	ND(1796-1820)	Chia-ch'ing	30.00	50.00	85.00	125.00

Obv: Type A

C#	Date	Emperor	Good	VG	Fine	VF
28-3	ND(1821-50)	Tao-kuang	25.00	35.00	50.00	85.00

Rev: Dot above.

C#	Date	Emperor	Good	VG	Fine	VF
28-3.1	ND(1821-50)	Tao-kuang	30.00	50.00	85.00	125.00

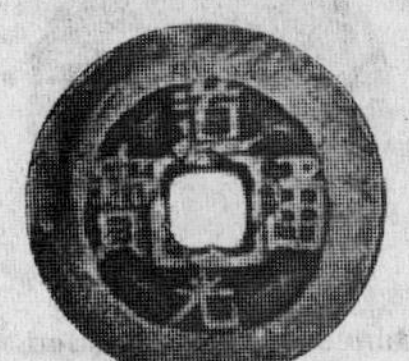

Rev: Vertical line above.

C#	Date	Emperor	Good	VG	Fine	VF
28-3.2	ND(1821-50)	Tao-kuang	30.00	50.00	85.00	125.00

Rev: Character *Shih* (10) above.

C#	Date	Emperor	Good	VG	Fine	VF
28-3.3	ND(1821-50)	Tao-kuang	60.00	75.00	110.00	150.00

Rev: Short vertical lines above and below.

C#	Date	Emperor	Good	VG	Fine	VF
28-3.4	ND(1821-50)	Tao-kuang	35.00	55.00	95.00	140.00

CAST BRASS
Obv: Type A
Narrow rims.

C#	Date	Emperor	Good	VG	Fine	VF
28-4	ND(1851-61)	Hsien-feng	40.00	90.00	150.00	300.00

4 CASH

CAST COPPER, 33mm
Obv: Type B-2

C#	Date	Emperor	Good	VG	Fine	VF
28-5	ND(1851-61)	Hsien-feng	22.50	30.00	42.50	90.00

C#	Date	Emperor	Good	VG	Fine	VF
28-9	ND(1862-74)	T'ung-chih	125.00	200.00	275.00	400.00

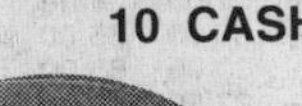

10 CASH

CAST COPPER, 35mm
Obv: Type B-2

C#	Date	Emperor	Good	VG	Fine	VF
28-6	ND(1851-61)	Hsien-feng	125.00	200.00	350.00	500.00

50 CASH

CAST COPPER

C#	Date	Emperor	Good	VG	Fine	VF
28-7	ND(1851-61)	Hsien-feng	100.00	150.00	220.00	300.00

100 CASH

CAST COPPER
Obv: Type C

C#	Date	Emperor	Good	VG	Fine	VF
28-8	ND(1851-61)	Hsien-feng	20.00	30.00	45.00	70.00

NOTE: Numerous counterfeits of C28-8, presumably contemporary, have recently come on the market. Refer to page 39 of Ch'en Hung-hsi's 1987 *Hsinchiang Hung Ch'ien Chiako Mulu* for illustrations. The characters for *Feng* and *Pao* on the obverse are greatly abbreviated, and the bottom horizontal line of the box at the bottom of *Tang* at the top on the reverse is merged with the upper hole frame line.

CAST BRASS

C#	Date	Emperor	Good	VG	Fine	VF
28-8a	ND(1851-61)	Hsien-feng	35.00	55.00	75.00	100.00

500 CASH

CAST COPPER or BRASS

C#	Date	Emperor	Good	VG	Fine	VF
28-11	ND(1851-61)	Hsien-feng	250.00	325.00	400.00	500.00

Kashgar (Shufu) now Kashi Mint

10 CASH

CAST COPPER
Obv: Type A

C#	Date	Emperor	Good	VG	Fine	VF
32-2	ND(1851-61)	Hsien-feng	11.50	18.00	22.50	45.00

Obv: Type A
Rev: *Kashgar* in Turki at left; in Manchu at right, *K'a* (Kashgar) above.

C#	Date	Emperor	Good	VG	Fine	VF
32-6	ND(1875-1908)	Kuang-hsu	5.00	9.50	15.00	25.00

Rev: *Kashgar Pao* (right-left).

C#	Date	Emperor	Good	VG	Fine	VF
32-6.1	ND(1875-1908)	Kuang-hsu	5.00	9.50	15.00	25.00

50 CASH

CAST COPPER

C#	Date	Emperor	Good	VG	Fine	VF
32-3	ND(1851-61)	Hsien-feng	135.00	225.00	350.00	500.00

32mm
Obv: Type B-2
Rev. leg: Stylized Turki mintname.

C#	Date	Emperor	Good	VG	Fine	VF
32-3.1	ND(1851-61)	Hsien-feng	90.00	150.00	250.00	350.00

100 CASH

CAST COPPER, 35mm
Obv: Type B-2
Rev. leg: Stylized Turki mintname.

C#	Date	Emperor	Good	VG	Fine	VF
32-4	ND(1851-61)	Hsien-feng	100.00	160.00	265.00	375.00

Hammered Coinage

1/2 MISCAL (5 FEN)

SILVER, 1.45 g
Obv. leg: Manchu, Chinese and Manchu w/outer border of S's at rim w/o square in center.
Rev: Turki leg.

Y#	Date	Emperor	VG	Fine	VF	XF
A7.6	ND	—	15.00	25.00	40.00	65.00
	AH(12)95	—	15.00	25.00	40.00	65.00

Obv. & rev: Square in center.
Rev. leg: Manchu, Chinese official "5" above Turki.

Y#	Date	Emperor	VG	Fine	VF	XF
A7.7	ND	Kuang-hsu	15.00	25.00	40.00	65.00
	AH(12)95	Kuang-hsu	15.00	25.00	40.00	65.00

Similar to Y#A7.7, but w/normal "5" above.

Y#	Date	Emperor	VG	Fine	VF	XF
A7.23	ND	Kuang-hsu	15.00	25.00	40.00	65.00

Obv: *Kuang* in unusual script, dot in central square.

Y#	Date	Emperor	VG	Fine	VF	XF
A7.24	ND	Kuang-hsu	15.00	25.00	40.00	65.00

Y#	Date	Emperor	VG	Fine	VF	XF
A7.19	ND(1875-1908)	Kuang-hsu	—	—	Rare	—

NOTE: Believed to be degenerate copy of Y#A7.7 by certain authority.

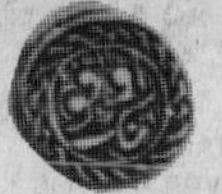 

Obv. & rev: W/o square in center.
Obv. leg: Turki. Rev. leg: Chinese for 5 Fen.

Y#	Date	VG	Fine	VF	XF
A7.8	AH1313	—100.00	175.00	300.00	500.00

Y#	Date	VG	Fine	VF	XF
A7.9	ND	—100.00	175.00	300.00	500.00

Obv: Arabesque, wreath and flower replaces Turki leg. Rev. leg: Chinese for 5 Fen.

Y#	Date	VG	Fine	VF	XF
A7.10	ND	—100.00	175.00	300.00	500.00

Obv. Turki leg: *Besh Fen.*
Rev. Turki leg: *Darb Kashgar.*

Y#	Date	Emperor	VG	Fine	VF	XF
A7.20	ND(1875-1908)	Kuang-hsu	9.00	15.00	25.00	40.00

MISCAL (MACE)

SILVER, 2.90 g
Rev. leg: In Chinese, Turki and Manchu.

Y#	Date	Emperor	VG	Fine	VF	XF
B7	AH1292	Kuang-hsu	250.00	400.00	700.00	1200.
	1295	Kuang-hsu	250.00	400.00	700.00	1200.

Milled Coinage

MISCAL (MACE)

 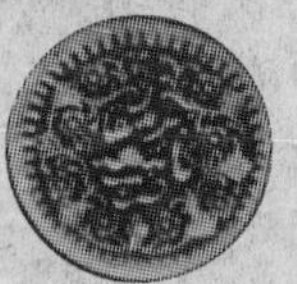

SILVER, 3.50 g
Obv: 6 characters. Rev: Wreath around Turki leg.

Y#	Date	Mintage	VG	Fine	VF	XF
16	ND	—	30.00	55.00	90.00	150.00
	AH1309	—	30.00	55.00	90.00	150.00
	1310	—	27.50	45.00	72.50	120.00
	1311	—	27.50	45.00	72.50	120.00

Obv: Like Y#A16. Rev: Like Y#16.

Y#	Date	Mintage	VG	Fine	VF	XF
D16	AH1310	—	150.00	250.00	400.00	650.00

Obv: 4 characters. Rev: W/o wreath.

Y#	Date	Mintage	VG	Fine	VF	XF
A16	ND	—	90.00	150.00	250.00	400.00
	AH1310	—	90.00	150.00	250.00	400.00

Obv: *Kashgar* at right.

Y#	Date	Mintage	VG	Fine	VF	XF
B16	AH1322	—	32.50	55.00	90.00	150.00
	1331 (error for 1321)	—	32.50	55.00	90.00	150.00

Obv: *Kashgar* in Chinese at right and left.

Y#	Date	Mintage	VG	Fine	VF	XF
C16	AH1322	—	35.00	70.00	125.00	200.00

Obv: Date at lower left. Rev: Dragon.

Y#	Date	Mintage	VG	Fine	VF	XF
A20.1	AH1323	—	200.00	350.00	600.00	1000.

Obv: Date at lower right. Rev: Dragon.

Y#	Date	Mintage	VG	Fine	VF	XF
A20.2	AH1323	—	200.00	350.00	600.00	1000.

Obv: Inverted Turki legends.

Y#	Date	Mintage	VG	Fine	VF	XF
A20.3	AH1323	—	200.00	350.00	600.00	1000.

2 MISCALS (2 MACE)

SILVER, 7.20 g

Y#	Date	Mintage	VG	Fine	VF	XF
17	ND	—	60.00	100.00	175.00	300.00
	AH1310	—	16.50	27.50	45.00	75.00
	1311	—	12.00	20.00	30.00	50.00
	1312	—	10.00	14.00	30.00	65.00
	1313	—	17.50	30.00	45.00	75.00

Obv: Chinese characters *K'a Shih* at right.

Y#	Date	Mintage	VG	Fine	VF	XF
17a	AH1311(error)	—	—	—	—	—
	1313	—	12.50	22.50	32.50	50.00
	1314	—	12.50	22.50	32.50	50.00
	1315	—	12.50	22.50	32.50	50.00
	1317	—	12.50	22.50	32.50	50.00
	1319	—	12.50	22.50	32.50	50.00
	1320	—	17.50	30.00	45.00	75.00

Obv: Chinese characters *K'a Tsao* at right.

Y#	Date	Mintage	VG	Fine	VF	XF
17a.1	AH1320	—	—	—	Rare	—
	1321	—	17.50	30.00	45.00	75.00
	1322	—	20.00	35.00	55.00	100.00

Obv: Chinese and Turki leg.
Rev: Dragon w/tail pointing right.

Y#	Date	Mintage	VG	Fine	VF	XF
B20.1	AH1323	—	175.00	300.00	500.00	850.00

Rev: Dragon w/tail pointing left.

Y#	Date	Mintage	VG	Fine	VF	XF
B20.2	AH1323	—	175.00	300.00	500.00	850.00

Rev: Dragon in circle surrounded by wreath.

Y#	Date	Mintage	VG	Fine	VF	XF
23	AH1324	—	—	—	Rare	—
	1325	—	20.00	40.00	65.00	110.00
	1326	—	20.00	40.00	65.00	110.00
	1327	—	25.00	50.00	80.00	150.00
	1329	—	35.00	65.00	110.00	175.00

Obv: Turki leg. around Chinese within a beaded circle. Rev: Double ring around small dragon, floral pattern outside, w/o leg.

Y#	Date	Mintage	VG	Fine	VF	XF
29	AH1329	—	55.00	90.00	150.00	250.00

Obv: Chinese leg. within circle. Rev: Turki leg. below larger dragon within single circle.

Y#	Date	Mintage	VG	Fine	VF	XF
29.1	AH1329	—	75.00	125.00	200.00	325.00

3 MISCALS

SILVER, 10.50 g

Y#	Date	Mintage	VG	Fine	VF	XF
A18	AH1307	—	1250.	2250.	3750.	5500.

NOTE: Struck at Tihua (Wulumuqi).

Y#	Date	Mintage	VG	Fine	VF	XF
18	ND	—	—	—	Rare	—
	AH1310	—	15.00	25.00	40.00	65.00
	1311	—	17.50	30.00	45.00	75.00
	1312	—	20.00	35.00	55.00	100.00

Obv: Chinese characters *K'a Shih* to right.

Y#	Date	Mintage	VG	Fine	VF	XF
18a	AH1311 (error)	—	—	—	Rare	—
	1313	—	10.00	20.00	32.50	65.00
	1314	—	10.00	20.00	32.50	65.00
	1315	—	10.00	20.00	32.50	65.00
	1316	—	10.00	20.00	32.50	65.00
	1317	—	10.00	20.00	32.50	65.00
	1319	—	10.00	20.00	32.50	65.00
	1320	—	10.00	20.00	32.50	65.00

Obv: Chinese characters *K'a Tsao* to right.

Y#	Date	Mintage	VG	Fine	VF	XF
18a.1	AH1320	—	10.00	20.00	32.50	65.00
	1321	—	10.00	20.00	32.50	65.00
	1322	—	10.00	20.00	32.50	65.00

Obv: Normal 3 in Chinese at bottom.

Y#	Date	Mintage	VG	Fine	VF	XF
20	AH1323	—	85.00	175.00	275.00	450.00

Obv: Official 3 in Chinese at bottom, date at upper left.

Y#	Date	Mintage	VG	Fine	VF	XF
20.1	AH1323	—	100.00	200.00	325.00	550.00

Obv: Official 3 in Chinese at bottom, date at lower right.

Y#	Date	Mintage	VG	Fine	VF	XF
20.2	AH1323	—	100.00	200.00	365.00	600.00

Rev: Turki leg. below small, circled dragon.

Y#	Date	Mintage	VG	Fine	VF	XF
30	AH1329	—	200.00	350.00	600.00	1000.

5 MISCALS

SILVER, 17.20 g
Obv. leg. in Turki, Chinese and Manchu.

Kann#	Date	Mintage	VG	Fine	VF	XF
1040	AH1307	—	1250.	2000.	3500.	5000.

NOTE: Struck at Tihua (Wulumuqi).

Y#	Date	Mintage	VG	Fine	VF	XF
19	AH1310	—	17.50	30.00	55.00	100.00
	1311	—	10.00	20.00	35.00	70.00
	1312	—	15.00	27.50	45.00	90.00
	1313	—	15.00	27.50	45.00	90.00
	1315	—	15.00	27.50	45.00	90.00

Obv: Chinese characters *K'a Shih* at right.

Y#	Date	Mintage	VG	Fine	VF	XF
19a	AH1311(error)	—	—	—	Rare	—
	1313	—	17.50	25.00	40.00	70.00
	1314	—	17.50	25.00	40.00	70.00
	1315	—	17.50	25.00	40.00	70.00
	1316	—	17.50	25.00	40.00	70.00
	1317	—	17.50	25.00	40.00	70.00
	1319	—	17.50	25.00	40.00	70.00
	1320	—	17.50	25.00	40.00	70.00

Obv: Chinese characters *K'a Tsao* at right.

Y#	Date	Mintage	VG	Fine	VF	XF
19a.1	AH1311(error)	—	—	—	Rare	—
	1321	—	10.00	17.50	30.00	60.00
	1322	—	10.00	17.50	30.00	60.00

Obv: Official Chinese and standard Turki leg., date at upper left.
Rev: Dragon's tail points to right.

Y#	Date	Mintage	VG	Fine	VF	XF
21	AH1323	—	20.00	30.00	45.00	75.00

Obv: Date at lower right.

Y#	Date	Mintage	VG	Fine	VF	XF
21.1	AH1323	—	20.00	30.00	45.00	75.00

Obv: Date at upper right.

Y#	Date	Mintage	VG	Fine	VF	XF
21.7	AH1323	—	20.00	30.00	45.00	75.00

Obv: Inverted Turki leg., date at lower right.

Y#	Date	Mintage	VG	Fine	VF	XF
21.2	AH1323	—	22.50	35.00	60.00	100.00

Obv: Simple 5 in Chinese, date at lower right.

Y#	Date	Mintage	VG	Fine	VF	XF
21.3	AH1323	—	—	—	Rare	—

Obv: Official Chinese and standard Turki leg., date at upper left.
Rev: Dragon's tail points to left.

Y#	Date	Mintage	VG	Fine	VF	XF
21.4	AH1323	—	15.00	25.00	50.00	90.00

Obv: Date at lower right.

Y#	Date	Mintage	VG	Fine	VF	XF
21.5	AH1323	—	15.00	25.00	50.00	90.00

Obv: Inverted Turki leg., date at lower right.

Y#	Date	Mintage	VG	Fine	VF	XF
21.6	AH1323	—	20.00	35.00	80.00	135.00

Obv: 3 Chinese characters at top between standard Turki leg.

Y#	Date	Mintage	VG	Fine	VF	XF
25	ND	—	22.50	40.00	85.00	150.00

Obv: Date at left or upper left.

Y#	Date	Mintage	VG	Fine	VF	XF
25.1	AH1325	—	22.50	40.00	85.00	150.00
	1326	—	22.50	40.00	85.00	150.00
(25.6)	1327	—	22.50	40.00	85.00	150.00

Similar to Y#21.1 w/date at upper right, right or lower right.

25.2	AH1325	—	22.50	40.00	85.00	150.00
(25.5)	1326	—	22.50	40.00	85.00	150.00
	1327	—	22.50	40.00	85.00	150.00

Obv: Inverted Turki leg., date at upper right, right or lower right.

25.3	AH1325	—	17.50	25.00	75.00	110.00
(25.7)	1328 (error for 1326)	—	17.50	25.00	75.00	110.00

Obv: Date at upper left or left.

25.8	AH1325	—	17.50	25.00	75.00	110.00

Obv: 2 Chinese characters at top between standard Turki leg. w/date at upper right.

25.4	AH1325	—	20.00	35.00	100.00	150.00

Obv: Similar to Y#25.4.
Rev: Floral sprays reversed.

25.9	AH1325	—	50.00	100.00	165.00	275.00

Obv: Date at upper left.
Rev: Standard florals.

25.10	AH1325	—	50.00	100.00	165.00	275.00

Obv: Date at upper left.
Rev: 3 rosettes at top.

25.11	AH1325	—	600.00	800.00	1000.	1200.

Obv: 3 Chinese characters at top, star in center.

Y#	Date	Mintage	VG	Fine	VF	XF
27	AH1327	—	20.00	30.00	65.00	110.00
	1328	—	25.00	50.00	90.00	150.00

Obv: Official 5 at right, dot in center.

27.1	AH1328	—	35.00	65.00	150.00	225.00

Obv: Rosette in center.

27.2	AH1329	—	50.00	100.00	200.00	275.00

Obv: 2 Chinese characters at top, simple 5 at right, star in center.

27.3	AH1329	—	17.50	25.00	75.00	110.00

Obv: Dot in center.

27.4	AH1329	—	17.50	25.00	75.00	110.00

Obv: Rosette in center.

27.5	AH1329	—	17.50	25.00	75.00	110.00

Obv: Official 5 at right, star in center, leg: *Kashgar*.

27.6	AH1329	—	17.50	25.00	75.00	110.00

Obv: Dot in center, leg: *made in Kashgar*.

31	AH1329	—	25.00	50.00	110.00	175.00

Obv: Star in center.
Rev: Star at center and in outer field.

31.1	AH1321 (error for 1331)	—	20.00	40.00	100.00	150.00
	1329	—	20.00	40.00	100.00	150.00
	1330	—	20.00	40.00	100.00	150.00
	1331	—	20.00	40.00	100.00	150.00

NOTE: Varieties w/2 and 3 tail spines on dragon exist.

Rev: Rosettes in outer field.

Y#	Date	Mintage	VG	Fine	VF	XF
31.2	AH1329	—	50.00	100.00	165.00	275.00

Obv: Rosette in center.

31.3	AH1329	—	22.50	75.00	100.00	150.00

SAR (TAEL)

SILVER, 35.20 g
Obv: 2 Chinese characters at top, w/Turki *Kashgar* to left.

26	AH1325	—	100.00	225.00	475.00	850.00

Obv: 2 Chinese characters at top, w/Turki *Kashgar* to right.

26.2	AH1325	—	300.00	700.00	1100.	1600.

Obv: 3 Chinese characters at top.

26.1	AH1325	—	450.00	1100.	1650.	2200.

REPUBLIC

5 CASH

COPPER
Obv: Large Chinese leg.

Y#	Date	Mintage	Good	VG	Fine	VF
A36.1	ND	—	275.00	375.00	500.00	700.00

Obv: Small Chinese leg.

A36.2	ND	—	275.00	375.00	500.00	700.00

Y#	Date	Mintage	Good	VG	Fine	VF
36	AH1331	—	100.00	135.00	225.00	350.00

10 CASH

COPPER

Obv: Large Chinese leg.

B36.1	ND	—	25.00	37.50	50.00	85.00

Rev: Small Chinese leg.

B36.2	ND	—	25.00	37.50	50.00	85.00

Obv: Chinese leg. *Shih Wen* (10 Wen) at upper left. Rev: Date at upper center.

38.1	ND	—	7.50	15.00	20.00	35.00
	AH1332	—	7.50	15.00	20.00	35.00
	1333	—	7.50	15.00	20.00	35.00
	1334	—	7.50	15.00	20.00	35.00

Rev: Modified Turki leg. w/date at bottom.

38.2	AH1331	—	8.50	12.50	17.50	30.00
	1332	—	8.50	12.50	17.50	30.00
	1334	—	8.50	12.50	17.50	30.00
	1335	—	8.50	12.50	17.50	30.00

Obv: 2 lower right Chinese characters different.

Rev: AH date at top.

Y#	Date	Year	Good	VG	Fine	VF
38.3	AH133-4	1916	50.00	75.00	125.00	200.00

Obv: Outer Chinese leg. w/o *Shih* of *Kashgar* at lower left. Rev: Turki leg. in florals w/*Zarb Kashgar* at top, similar to Y#A38.2.

38.5	AH1334	—	37.50	60.00	100.00	150.00

Rev: Single flower in lower Turki legend.

Y#	Date	Mintage	Good	VG	Fine	VF
38.6	AH1334	—	—	—	—	—

Rev: W/o flowers or florals in Turki legends.

38.7	AH1334	—	—	—	—	—

Obv: Chinese leg. *Hung Hsien T'ung Pi* in inner dotted circle.

A38.1	AH1334	—	20.00	35.00	50.00	100.00

Rev: Smaller Turki leg. in florals.

A38.2	AH1334	—	20.00	35.00	50.00	100.00

NOTE: Y#A38.1 and A38.2 were issued for the brief reign of Yuan Shih-kai as Emperor Hung Hsien (1916).

Obv: Chinese date at upper right w/rosette. Chinese leg. *Chung Hua Min Kuo* in inner circle.

Y#	Date	Year	Good	VG	Fine	VF
38a.1	AH1339	10	5.00	10.00	15.00	25.00
	1340	10	5.00	10.00	15.00	25.00

Obv: Outer Chinese leg. w/o *Shih* of *Kashgar* at upper left.

38a.2	AH134x	11	5.00	10.00	15.00	25.00

Rev: Turki leg. rearranged.

Y#	Date	Year	Good	VG	Fine	VF
38a.3	AH1339	10	5.00	10.00	15.00	25.00
	134x	10	5.00	10.00	15.00	25.00

Obv: Crowded Chinese year '11'.

38a.5	AH1340	11	25.00	40.00	65.00	100.00

Obv: Chinese leg. *Min Kuo T'ung Yuan* in inner circle w/*Kashgar* at right.

Y#	Date	Mintage	Good	VG	Fine	VF
38b.1	AHxxxx	—	15.00	30.00	40.00	65.00

Obv: Outer Chinese leg. rotated.

38b.2	AH13x4	—	15.00	30.00	40.00	65.00

Rev: Chinese character *Jih* in solid sunburst.

B38c.1	CD1928	—	175.00	275.00	425.00	600.00

Obv: Like B38c.1. Rev: Chinese character *Jih* in rayed sunburst.

B38c.2	CD1928	—	175.00	275.00	425.00	600.00

Obv: Like B38b.1. Rev: Like B38c.1.

B38c.3	CD1928	—	175.00	275.00	425.00	600.00

Obv. leg: Cyclic date at left and right like B38.4.

Y#	Date	Mintage	Good	VG	Fine	VF
B38c.4	CD1928	—	175.00	275.00	425.00	600.00

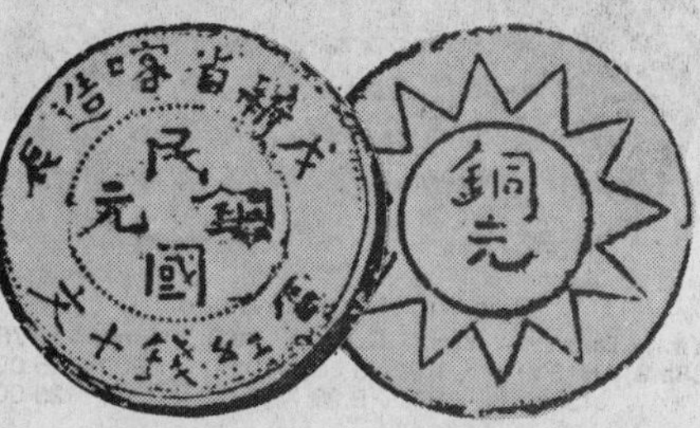

Obv: Chinese leg. *Min Kuo T'ung Yuan* in inner circle. Rev: Chinese characters *T'ung Yuan* in solid sunburst.

B38d	CD1928	—	125.00	175.00	300.00	400.00

Obv: Chinese leg. *Chung Hua Min Kuo* in inner circle. Chinese date at left and right of upper leg. Rev: Chinese characters *T'ung Yuan* in solid sunburst.

B38.1	CD1928	—	17.50	32.50	.45.00	75.00

Obv: Upper leg: *Hsinchiang Kashgar Tsao.* Rev: Small Chinese characters *T'ung Yuan* in outlined sunburst.

B38.2	CD1928	—	15.00	23.00	30.00	50.00

Obv: Upper leg: *Hsinchiang Kash Tsao.* Rev: Large Chinese characters *T'ung Yuan* in outlined sunburst.

B38.3	CD1928	—	15.00	23.00	30.00	50.00

Obv: Chinese date at left and right. Rev: Chinese characters *T'ung Yuan* in outlined sunburst.

B38.4	CD1928	—	3.00	5.50	8.00	16.00
	1929	—	5.00	7.50	15.00	25.00

Rev: Chinese characters *T'ung Yuan* in outlined and finely rayed sunburst.

Y#	Date	Mintage	Good	VG	Fine	VF
B38.5	CD1928	—	35.00	50.00	65.00	100.00

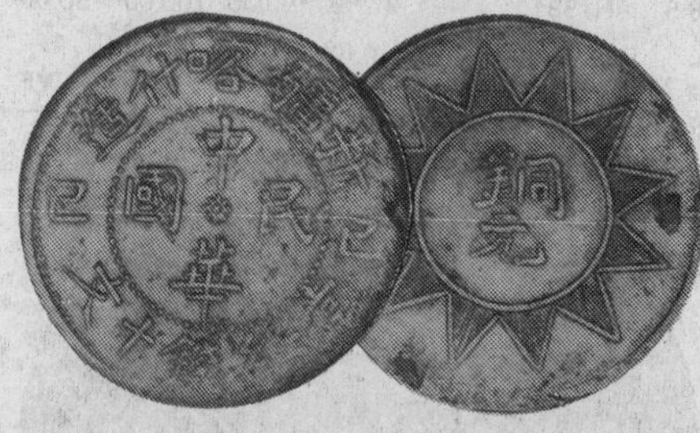

Obv: Upper leg. *Hsinchiang Kashgar Tsao.*

B38.6	CD1929	—	9.50	16.50	32.50	45.00

Obv: Chinese leg. *Min Kuo T'ung Yuan* in inner circle. Rev: Turki leg. in solid sunburst.

B38b.1	CD1928 AH1346	125.00	175.00	300.00	400.00	

Obv: Similar to Y#B38d. Rev: Similar to Y#B38b.1.

B38b.2	CD1928 AH1346	150.00	200.00	350.00	500.00	

Obv: Chinese characters for date to left and right of *Chung Hua Min Kuo* in inner circle. Rev: Turki leg. in outlined sunburst.

B38a.1	CD1929	—	100.00	165.00	250.00	350.00

Obv: Upper leg. *Hsinchiang Kashgar Tsao.*

B38a.2	CD1929	—	75.00	100.00	125.00	150.00

Y#	Date	Year	Good	VG	Fine	VF
A44.1	(1922)	11	50.00	75.00	100.00	125.00

Flags reversed.

A44.2	(1922)	11	50.00	75.00	100.00	125.00

Obv: Upper leg. *Hsinchiang Kashgar Tsao.* Rev: Flags w/wide outlined sunbursts. Flag at right w/inner circle.

44.1	CD1929	—	5.00	8.50	17.50	32.50

Obv: Small 8 petalled rosette in center. Rev: Flag at right w/o inner circle.

44.2	CD1929	—	4.50	7.50	12.00	16.00
	CD1930	—	4.50	7.50	12.00	16.00

Obv: Star w/rays in center.

44.3	CD1930	—	8.50	17.50	22.50	37.50

8 petalled rosette in center. Rev: Flags w/narrow outlined sunbursts.

44.4	CD1930	—	10.00	20.00	35.00	55.00

Reduced size
Rev: Flags w/solid sunbursts.

Y#	Date	Year	Good	VG	Fine	VF
44.5	CD1933	—	4.00	8.00	15.00	20.00

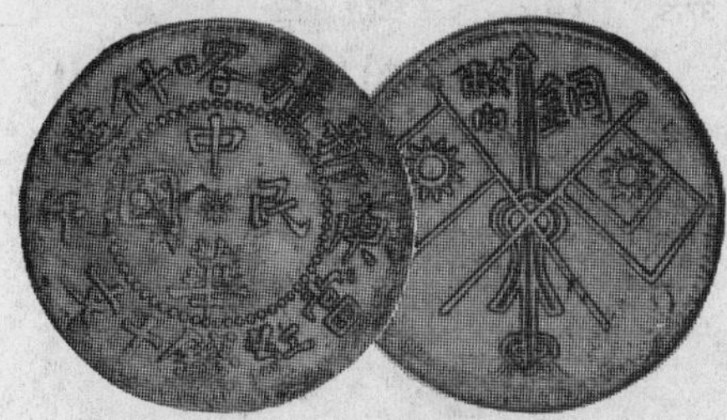

Rev: Reversed flags w/large solid sunbursts.

44.6	CD1929	—	3.00	7.00	13.00	18.00
	1930	—	4.00	8.00	15.00	20.00

Rev: Reversed flags w/small solid sunbursts.

44.7	CD1930	—	25.00	50.00	100.00	165.00

Rev: Reversed flags w/large "flower petal" outlined sunbursts.

44.9	CD1930	—	4.00	8.00	15.00	20.00

Obv. upper leg: *Hsin Chiang Kash Tsao.*

44.8	CD1929	—	75.00	100.00	125.00	150.00

20 CASH

COPPER

Y#	Date	Year	Good	VG	Fine	VF
48	AH1334(?)	10	—	—	Rare	—

5 MISCALS

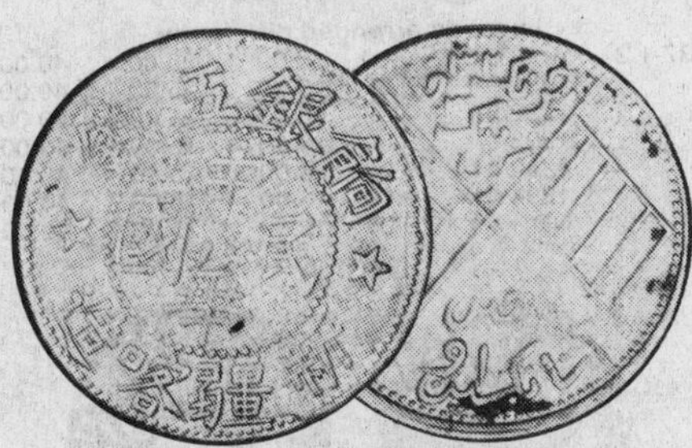

SILVER, 17.30 g
Obv: Stars dividing Chinese legends.
Rev: Crossed flags dividing Turki leg.

Y#	Date	Mintage	VG	Fine	VF	XF
43	AH1331	—	40.00	75.00	160.00	275.00
	1332	—	40.00	75.00	160.00	275.00

Obv: Rosettes dividing Chinese leg.

43.1	AH1330	—	35.00	65.00	135.00	225.00
	1331	—	35.00	65.00	135.00	225.00
	1332	—	35.00	65.00	135.00	225.00
	13-32	—	35.00	65.00	135.00	225.00

NOTE: Varieties exist.

Obv: Rosettes dividing Chinese leg.

43.2	AH1334	—	45.00	85.00	185.00	325.00
	133-4	—	45.00	85.00	185.00	325.00

NOTE: Varieties exist.

Obv: Rosette in center, floral arrangements dividing Chinese leg.

43.3	AH13-32	—	40.00	75.00	160.00	275.00
	133-4	—	45.00	85.00	185.00	325.00

NOTE: Varieties exist.

Obv: Stars divide rotated outer Chinese leg.

Y#	Date	Mintage	VG	Fine	VF	XF
43.4	AHx13x	—	—	—	—	—

Uighuristan Republic

AH1352/1933-1934

10 CASH

COPPER
Rev: Flag at right w/o fringe.

Y#	Date	Mintage	Good	VG	Fine	VF
D38.1	AH1352	—	17.50	35.00	55.00	75.00

Rev: Flag at right w/partial fringe.

D38.2	AH1352	—	17.50	35.00	55.00	75.00

Rev: Flag at right w/full fringe.

D38.3	AH1352	—	17.50	35.00	55.00	75.00

NOTE: Encountered overstruck on various earlier Republican Series 10 Cash.

20 CASH

COPPER, 32-34mm

E38.1	AH1352	—	50.00	100.00	150.00	200.00
	1352 (retrograde)	—	55.00	110.00	165.00	220.00

NOTE: Varieties exist. Also encountered overstruck on 10 Cash, Y#44 varieties.

Flags reversed.

Y#	Date	Mintage	Good	VG	Fine	VF
E38.2	AH1352	—	50.00	100.00	150.00	200.00

ISLAMIC REPUBLIC OF EASTERN TURKESTAN

MISCAL

SILVER
Obv. Turki leg: *Sharket Turkhestan Cumhuriyet Islamiyesi* around central Turki leg. *Muskuk, sanah 1252.*
Rev. Turki leg: *Zarb Kashgar.*

Y#	Date	Mintage	Good	VG	Fine	VF
E39	AH1352	—	—	—	Rare	—

REBEL COINAGE

Yakub Beg

Most of these coins were struck at Kashgar (Kashi) in the name of the Ottoman Sultan Abdul Aziz by the rebel Yakub Beg, who controlled much of Sinkiang (Xinjiang) between 1865 and 1877.

In the name of Abdul Aziz

FALUS

COPPER
Obv. and rev: Date.

C#	Date	Good	VG	Fine	VF
37.4	AH1290	20.00	32.50	40.00	50.00
	1292	20.00	32.50	40.00	50.00

Obv: Date.

C#	Date	Good	VG	Fine	VF
37.5	AH1291	20.00	32.50	40.00	50.00
	1293	20.00	32.50	40.00	50.00
	1294	20.00	32.50	40.00	50.00

Rev: Date.

C#	Date	Good	VG	Fine	VF
37.6	AH1292	20.00	32.50	40.00	50.00

Obv. and rev: W/o date.

C#	Date	Good	VG	Fine	VF
37.7	ND	15.00	21.50	30.00	40.00

1/2 MISCAL (MACE)

SILVER

C#	Date	VG	Fine	VF	XF
37-1.1	AH1290/91	9.00	15.00	25.00	40.00
	1291	9.00	15.00	25.00	40.00
	1291/92	9.00	15.00	25.00	40.00
	1292	9.00	15.00	25.00	40.00
	1293	9.00	15.00	25.00	40.00
	1294	9.00	15.00	25.00	40.00
	ND	9.00	15.00	25.00	40.00

Legends arranged differently.

C#	Date	VG	Fine	VF	XF
37-1.2	AH1291	9.00	15.00	25.00	40.00
	1292	9.00	15.00	25.00	40.00
	1292/93	9.00	15.00	25.00	40.00
	1293	9.00	15.00	25.00	40.00
	1293/94	9.00	15.00	25.00	40.00
	1294	9.00	15.00	25.00	40.00
	ND	9.00	15.00	25.00	40.00

TILLA

GOLD, 4.50 g
Rev. leg: *Zarb Mahrusah Kashgar.*

C#	Date	VG	Fine	VF	XF
37-2.1	AH1290	125.00	250.00	425.00	700.00

3.70 g
Rev. leg: *Zarb Dar us-Sultanat Kashgar.*

C#	Date	VG	Fine	VF	XF
37-2.2	AH1291/1290 (mule)				
		140.00	280.00	475.00	800.00
	1291	110.00	220.00	360.00	600.00

Obv. leg. within dotted border within circles.
Rev. leg. within circle.

C#	Date	VG	Fine	VF	XF
37-2.3	AH1291	110.00	220.00	360.00	600.00

Rev. leg. within segmented circles.

C#	Date	VG	Fine	VF	XF
37-2.4	AH1291	110.00	220.00	360.00	600.00

Obv. leg. within dotted border within circles w/loop.
Rev. leg. within dotted border within circles.

C#	Date	VG	Fine	VF	XF
37-2.5	AH1292	125.00	250.00	425.00	700.00

Obv. leg. within segmented circles w/loop.
Rev. leg. within segmented circles.

C#	Date	VG	Fine	VF	XF
37-2.6	AH1292	90.00	180.00	300.00	500.00
	1293	125.00	250.00	425.00	700.00
	1294	125.00	250.00	425.00	700.00
	1295	125.00	250.00	425.00	700.00

In the name of Abdulhamid II

C#	Date	VG	Fine	VF	XF
37-3	AH12xx	—	—	—	—

Khotan (Hotien) now Hotan Mint

Hammered Coinage

1/2 MISCAL

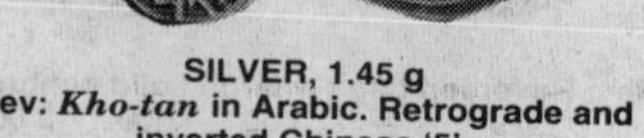

SILVER, 1.45 g
Rev: *Kho-tan* in Arabic. Retrograde and inverted Chinese '5'.

Y#	Date	Mintage	VG	Fine	VF	XF
A7.11	ND (1875-1908)		27.50	45.00	72.50	120.00

Rev: *Zarb Khotan* in Arabic.

Y#	Date	Mintage	VG	Fine	VF	XF
A7.12	ND (1875-1908)		27.50	45.00	72.50	120.00

REBEL COINAGE

Ghazi Rashid

AH1279-84/1862-67AD

A rebel in Sinkiang (Xinjiang) about whom little is known. He was in power from 1862 until his death in 1867.

TENGA

SILVER

C#	Date	VG	Fine	VF	XF
36-5	AH1283	100.00	165.00	250.00	350.00

Kuche (Kucha) Mint

Kuche is west north-west of Aksu and has sometimes been confused with Kulja (Kuldja).

EMPIRE

CASH

CAST COPPER
Rev: Characters *Boo Yuan* left and right, *K'u* above.

C#	Date	Emperor	Good	VG	Fine	VF
33-20	ND(1862-74)					
		T'ung-chih	7.50	14.00	22.00	32.50

C#	Date	Emperor	Good	VG	Fine	VF
33-23	ND(1875-1908)					
		Kuang-Hsu	6.00	8.00	12.00	20.00

5 CASH

CAST COPPER

Obv: Type A

C#	Date	Emperor	Good	VG	Fine	VF
33-8	ND(1851-61)	Hsien-feng	50.00	75.00	100.00	175.00

Obv: Type A-2.

C#	Date	Emperor	Good	VG	Fine	VF
33-22	ND(1862-74)	T'ung-chih	135.00	225.00	350.00	500.00

10 CASH

CAST COPPER

Rev: Character *K'u* (Kuche) above.

C#	Date	Emperor	Good	VG	Fine	VF
33-6	ND(1821-50)	Tao-kuang	2.50	4.00	6.50	13.50

Rev: Character *Hsin* (Sinkiang) above.

C#	Date	Emperor	Good	VG	Fine	VF
33-7	ND(1821-50)	Tao-kuang	2.00	3.00	4.50	8.50

NOTE: C#33-6 and 33-7 were cast during a later reign.

Obv: Type A

C#	Date	Emperor	Good	VG	Fine	VF
33-9	ND(1851-61)	Hsien-feng	2.00	3.00	4.50	8.50

Obv: Type A-2

C#	Date	Emperor	Good	VG	Fine	VF
33-13	ND(1862-74)	T'ung-chih	1.50	3.00	4.00	8.00

Rev: Character *K'u* (Kuche) above.

C#	Date	Emperor	Good	VG	Fine	VF
33-14	ND(1862-74)	T'ung-chih	4.00	6.00	9.00	16.00

Obv: Type A

C#	Date	Emperor	Good	VG	Fine	VF
33-16	ND(1875-1908)	Kuang-hsu	10.00	20.00	30.00	50.00

Rev: Characters *Chiu Nien* (year 9 = 1883) above.

C#	Date	Emperor	Good	VG	Fine	VF
33-17	ND(1883)	Kuang-hsu	10.00	17.50	25.50	45.00

Rev: Character *K'u* above.

C#	Date	Emperor	Good	VG	Fine	VF
33-18	ND(1875-1908)	Kuang-hsu	7.50	12.00	17.50	35.00

Rev: Semi-circle at lower right.

C#	Date	Emperor	Good	VG	Fine	VF
33-18.1	ND(1875-1908)	Kuang-hsu	7.50	13.50	22.50	35.00

C#	Date	Emperor	Good	VG	Fine	VF
33-19	ND(1875-1908)	Kuang-hsu	1.50	2.50	3.50	7.50

NOTE: Other varieties are reported for T'ung Chih and Kuang Hsu reigns.

50 CASH

CAST COPPER

C#	Date	Emperor	Good	VG	Fine	VF
33-10	ND(1851-61)	Hsien-feng	100.00	150.00	250.00	400.00

100 CASH

CAST COPPER, 49mm

C#	Date	Emperor	Good	VG	Fine	VF
33-11	ND(1851-61)	Hsien-feng	100.00	125.00	150.00	225.00

Reduced size, 34mm

C#	Date	Emperor	Good	VG	Fine	VF
33-11a	ND(1851-61)	Hsien-feng	60.00	75.00	90.00	125.00

Hammered Coinage

1/2 MISCAL (5 FEN)

SILVER, 1.45 g

Y#	Date	Emperor	VG	Fine	VF	XF
A7.2	ND(AH1294)	Kuang-hsu	5.50	9.00	15.00	25.00
	(AH1295) yr.4	Kuang-hsu	16.50	27.50	45.00	75.00
	AH1295	Kuang-hsu	5.50	9.00	15.00	25.00

Y#	Date	Emperor	VG	Fine	VF	XF
A7.13	ND (1877)	Kuang-hsu	—	—	Rare	—

Urumchi (Urumqi) Mint

Tihwa, *Ti-hua*, (Dihua)

EMPIRE

8 CASH

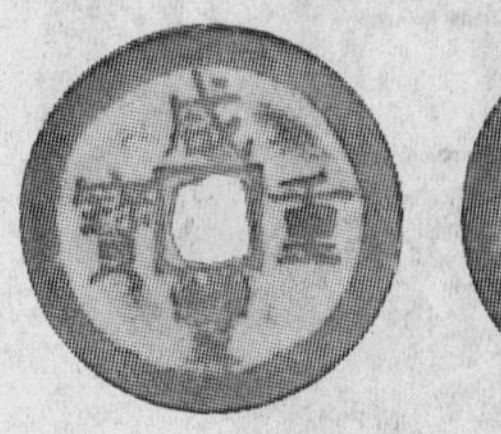

CAST COPPER

Obv: Type B-1

C#	Date	Emperor	Good	VG	Fine	VF
29-1	ND(1851-61)	Hsien-feng	21.50	35.00	50.00	75.00

10 CASH

CAST COPPER, 33mm

Obv: Type B-1

C#	Date	Emperor	Good	VG	Fine	VF
29-2	ND(1851-61)	Hsien-feng	20.00	35.00	50.00	75.00

27mm

C#	Date	Emperor	Good	VG	Fine	VF
29-2.1	ND(1851-61)	Hsien-feng	8.50	15.00	25.00	40.00

50 CASH

CAST COPPER

C#	Date	Emperor	Good	VG	Fine	VF
29-3	ND(1851-61)	Hsien-feng	Reported, not confirmed			

80 CASH

CAST BRASS, 50mm
Obv: Type C

C#	Date	Emperor	Good	VG	Fine	VF
29-5	ND(1851-61)	Hsien-feng	120.00	200.00	275.00	400.00

100 CASH

CAST COPPER

C#	Date	Emperor	Good	VG	Fine	VF
29-4	ND(1851-61)	Hsien-feng	—	—	Rare	—

Milled Coinage

2 MISCALS (2 MACE)

SILVER, 6.60 g
Obv: Simple 2 in Chinese.

Y#	Date	Mintage	VG	Fine	VF	XF
33	AH1321	—	15.00	22.00	55.00	90.00
	1322	—	15.00	22.00	55.00	90.00
	1323	—	17.50	30.00	55.00	90.00

Obv: Official 2 in Chinese.

Y#	Date	Mintage	VG	Fine	VF	XF
33.1	AH1323	—	15.00	22.00	55.00	90.00
	1324	—	15.00	22.00	55.00	90.00
	1325	—	15.00	22.00	55.00	90.00

3 MISCALS

SILVER, 10.30 g
Obv: Simple 3 in Chinese.

Y#	Date	Mintage	VG	Fine	VF	XF
34	AH1321	—	17.50	30.00	75.00	110.00
	1322	—	17.50	30.00	75.00	110.00
	1323	—	17.50	30.00	75.00	110.00

Obv: Official 3 in Chinese.

Y#	Date	Mintage	VG	Fine	VF	XF
34a	AH1323	—	10.00	20.00	32.50	65.00
	1324	—	10.00	20.00	32.50	65.00
	1325	—	10.00	20.00	32.50	65.00

5 MISCALS

SILVER, 17.90 g
Obv: Simple 5 in Chinese.

Y#	Date	Mintage	VG	Fine	VF	XF
35	AH1321	—	20.00	35.00	70.00	125.00
	1322	—	20.00	35.00	70.00	125.00
	1323	—	20.00	35.00	70.00	125.00

Obv: Official 5 in Chinese.

Y#	Date	Mintage	VG	Fine	VF	XF
35a	AH1323	—	20.00	40.00	70.00	125.00
	1324	—	15.00	30.00	60.00	100.00
	1325	—	15.00	30.00	60.00	100.00

REPUBLIC

SAR (TAEL)

SILVER, 35.00 g
Obv: Large characters.
Rev: Rosette at top between wheat ears.

Y#	Date	Year	VG	Fine	VF	XF
45	ND(1917)	6	10.00	12.50	17.50	35.00

Obv: Similar to Y#45 but w/small characters.
Rev: W/o rosette at top.

Y#	Date	Year	VG	Fine	VF	XF
45.1	ND(1917)	6	10.00	12.50	17.50	35.00

Rev: Rosette at top between branches.

Y#	Date	Year	VG	Fine	VF	XF
45.2	ND(1918)	7	12.50	20.00	30.00	60.00

Ushi (Wushih) now Wushi Mint

EMPIRE

10 CASH

CAST COPPER
Rev: *K'u* (Kuche) above, *Ushi* in Manchu and Turki right and left.

C#	Date	Emperor	Good	VG	Fine	VF
34-4	ND(1909-11)	Hsuan-t'ung	50.00	80.00	150.00	—

Yanghissar (Han-cheng) Mint now Yengisar Mint

EMPIRE

1/2 MISCAL

SILVER, 1.45 g

Y#	Date	Mintage	VG	Fine	VF	XF
A7.14	ND(1875-1908)		55.00	90.00	150.00	250.00

Yarkand (Soche) Mint now Shache (Yarkant) Mint

EMPIRE

10 CASH

CAST COPPER, 25mm

C#	Date	Emperor	Good	VG	Fine	VF
35-3	ND(1851-61)	Hsien-feng	4.00	7.00	10.00	16.00

Obv: Type A-2

C#	Date	Emperor	Good	VG	Fine	VF
35-7	ND(1862-74)	T'ung-chih	4.00	7.00	10.00	16.00

50 CASH

CAST BRASS, 37mm
Obv: Type B-1

C#	Date	Emperor	Good	VG	Fine	VF
35-4	ND(1851-61)	Hsien-feng	80.00	135.00	175.00	250.00

32mm

C#	Date	Emperor	Good	VG	Fine	VF
35-4.1	ND(1851-61)	Hsien-feng	65.00	115.00	140.00	200.00

100 CASH

CAST COPPER, 50-56mm
Obv: Type C

C#	Date	Emperor	Good	VG	Fine	VF
35-5.1	ND(1851-61)	Hsien-feng	85.00	125.00	200.00	400.00

45mm

C#	Date	Emperor	Good	VG	Fine	VF
35-5.2	ND(1851-61)	Hsien-feng	85.00	125.00	200.00	400.00

Hammered Coinage

1/2 MISCAL

SILVER, 1.45 g
Rev: Turki and Chinese leg.

Y#	Date	Mintage	VG	Fine	VF	XF
A7.15	ND (1875-1908)		20.00	35.00	60.00	100.00

Rev: Date at left.

Y#	Date	Mintage	VG	Fine	VF	XF
A7.16	AH1295	—	45.00	75.00	120.00	200.00

Rev: Date at right.

Y#	Date	Mintage	VG	Fine	VF	XF
A7.17	AH1295	—	55.00	90.00	150.00	250.00

Rev: Turki, Chinese and Manchu leg.

Y#	Date	Mintage	VG	Fine	VF	XF
A7.18	ND (1875-1908)		15.00	25.00	40.00	65.00

LOCAL COINAGE

In the outset of the Ch'ing Dynasty the Zhungar (Tzungar or Sungar) tribes in the northern sector of Sinkiang were very powerful.

In 1700, the 39th year of Emperor K'ang-hsi Khan Tsewang Arabtan went on a successful expedition to the south conquering Yarkand Khanate. He ordered them to produce the "pul" coppers with his name Tsewang.

After Tsewang's death, his succeeding son Khardan Chirin ordered the minting of new "pul" coppers exchange one new "pul" for two old "pul" of his father.

In 1757, the 22nd year of the Emperor Ch'ien-lung the campaign against the Zhungar Tribes was initiated and Imperial forces finally gained control of the area in the early 1760's.

Ghazi Rashid

A rebel in Sinkiang (Xinjiang) about whom little is known. He was in power from 1862 until his death in 1867.

CASH

COPPER
Small legends

C#	Date	Mint	Good	VG	Fine	VF
36-1	AH1280	Kuche	8.00	14.00	20.00	30.00

NOTE: Exists w/coin or medal rotation.

Large legends

C#	Date	Mint	Good	VG	Fine	VF
36-2	AH1280	Kuche	8.00	14.00	20.00	30.00

NOTE: The date of C#36-1 and 36-2 is found at the top of the reverse. These coins are usually undated or with the date illegible. Even in clearly dated specimens, which are worth a substantial premium, the "0" never seems to be detectable.

C#	Date	Mint	Good	VG	Fine	VF
36-3	—	Aksu	—	—	Rare	—

SZECHUAN PROVINCE

Sichuan

A province located in south-central China. The largest of the traditional Chinese provinces, Szechuan (Sichuan) is a plateau region watered by many rivers. These rivers carry much trading traffic. Agriculture or mining are the occupational choices of most of the populace. In World War II the national capital was moved to Chungking in Szechuan (Sichuan). Chengtu was an active imperial mint that opened in 1732 and was in practically continuous operation until the advent of modern equipment. Modern minting was introduced in the province when Chengtu began milled coinage in 1898. A mint was authorized for Chungking in 1905 but it did not begin operations until 1913. The Chengtu Mint was looted by soldiers in 1925. The last republic issues from Szechuan (Sichuan) were dated 1932.

The machinery for the first Szechuan (Sichuan) Mint was produced in New Jersey and the dies were engraved in Philadelphia. The mint was opened in 1898, but closed within a few months and did not reopen until 1901. There is no doubt now that Y#234-238 (K#145-149) were the first issues of this mint, contrary to the Kann listings.

EMPIRE

CASH

CAST BRASS
Obv: Type A

C#	Date	Emperor	Good	VG	Fine	VF
24-2	ND(1796-1820)	Chia-ch'ing	.50	1.00	1.50	2.00

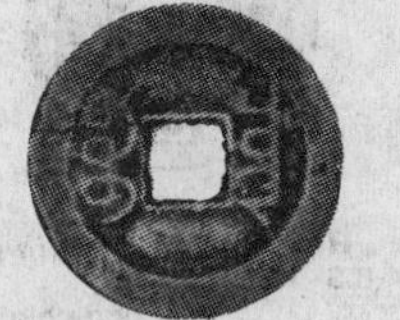

Obv: Type A

C#	Date	Emperor	Good	VG	Fine	VF
24-3	ND(1821-50)	Tao-kuang	.50	1.25	2.00	3.00

C#	Date	Emperor	Good	VG	Fine	VF
24-4	ND(1851-61)	Hsien-feng	4.50	7.50	11.50	18.00

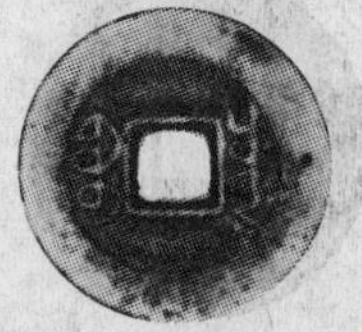

Reduced size.

C#	Date	Emperor	Good	VG	Fine	VF
24-4a	ND(1851-61)	Hsien-feng	1.50	3.00	4.00	5.00

Rev: Character *Shih* (ten) above.

C#	Date	Emperor	Good	VG	Fine	VF
24-4.1	ND(1851-61)	Hsien-feng	5.00	8.00	12.50	20.00

Rev: Character *Wen* above.

C#	Date	Emperor	Good	VG	Fine	VF
24-4.2	ND(1851-61)	Hsien-feng	5.00	8.00	12.50	20.00

Rev: Character *Kung* (work) above.

C#	Date	Emperor	Good	VG	Fine	VF
24-4.3	ND(1851-61)	Hsien-feng	5.00	8.00	12.50	20.00

Rev: Character *Erh* (two) above.

C#	Date	Emperor	Good	VG	Fine	VF
24-4.4	ND(1851-61)	Hsien-feng	5.00	8.00	12.50	20.00

Rev: Circle above.

C#	Date	Emperor	Good	VG	Fine	VF
24-4.5	ND(1851-61)	Hsien-feng	5.00	8.00	12.50	20.00

Rev: Crescent standing on end above.

C#	Date	Emperor	Good	VG	Fine	VF
24-4.6	ND(1851-61)	Hsien-feng	5.00	8.00	12.50	20.00

Rev: 2 horizontal and 1 vertical lines above.

C#	Date	Emperor	Good	VG	Fine	VF
24-4.7	ND(1851-61)	Hsien-feng	5.00	8.00	12.50	20.00

Rev: 2 figures above, possibly 15.

C#	Date	Emperor	Good	VG	Fine	VF
24-4.8	ND(1851-61)	Hsien-feng	5.00	8.00	12.50	20.00

Rev: Crescent below.

C#	Date	Emperor	Good	VG	Fine	VF
24-4.9	ND(1851-61)	Hsien-feng	5.00	8.00	12.50	20.00

Obv: Type A-2

24-8	ND(1862-74)	T'ung-chih	5.00	8.00	12.50	20.00

Rev: Character *Shih* (ten) above and dot below.

24-8.1	ND(1862-74)	T'ung-chih	5.00	8.00	12.50	20.00

Rev: Character *Shih* above and crescent on end below.

24-8.2	ND(1862-74)	T'ung-chih	5.00	8.00	12.50	20.00

Rev: Character *Shih* above and *San* below.

24-8.3	ND(1862-74)	T'ung-chih	5.00	8.00	12.50	20.00

Rev: Character *Shih* above and *Lin* below.

24-8.4	ND(1862-74)	T'ung-chih	5.00	8.00	12.50	20.00

Rev: Character *Wen* above and *Yi.* below.

24-8.5	ND(1862-74)	T'ung-chih	5.00	8.00	12.50	20.00

Rev: Character *Wen* above and *Ch'i* below.

24-8.6	ND(1862-74)	T'ung-chih	5.00	8.00	12.50	20.00

Rev: Character *Wen* above and *Ch'uan* below.

24-8.7	ND(1862-74)	T'ung-chih	5.00	8.00	12.50	20.00

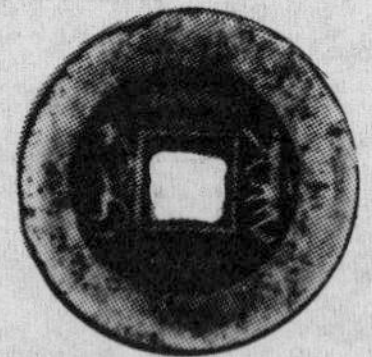

Obv: Type A

24-9	ND(1875-1908)	Kuang-hsu	4.50	7.50	11.50	22.50

NOTE: Refer to "Additional Characters" chart in the introduction to China.

10 CASH

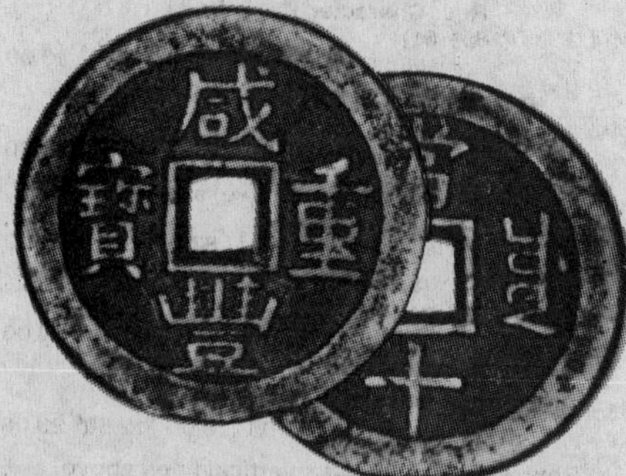

CAST BRASS
Obv: Type B-1
Rev: Type I mint mark.

24-5	ND(1851-61)	Hsien-feng	15.00	25.00	35.00	60.00

Rev: Type II mint mark.

C#	Date	Emperor	Good	VG	Fine	VF
24-5.1	ND(1851-61)	Hsien-feng	35.00	45.00	60.00	85.00

Rev: Type I mint mark.

24-10	ND(1875-1908)	Kuang-hsu	—	—	Rare	—

50 CASH

CAST BRASS
Obv: Type B-1.
Rev: Type II mint mark.

24-6	ND(1851-61)	Hsien-feng	55.00	75.00	100.00	135.00

100 CASH

CAST BRASS
Obv: Type C.
Rev: Type II mint mark.

24-7	ND(1851-61)	Hsien-feng	70.00	90.00	120.00	165.00

MILLED COINAGE

5 CASH

COPPER
Rev: Side view dragon.

Y#	Date	Mintage	VG	Fine	VF	XF
225	ND(1903-04)	.085	60.00	75.00	100.00	135.00

Rev: Flying dragon.

228	ND(1903-04)	Inc. Ab.	100.00	150.00	200.00	275.00

10 CASH

COPPER
Obv: Thick Manchu words in center, large rosettes.

Y#	Date	Mintage	VG	Fine	VF	XF
226	ND(1903-05)	95.960	12.50	25.00	35.00	60.00

Obv: Thin Manchu words, small rosettes.

226.1	ND(1903-05)	Inc. Ab.	22.00	45.00	70.00	125.00

Obv: Large rosettes.

226.2	ND(1903-05)	Inc. Ab.	20.00	40.00	60.00	100.00

Obv. leg: 2 characters at bottom, 6-9mm apart.
Rev: Trident-shaped flame on dragons body below letters CHU.

229	ND(1903-05)	Inc. Ab.	4.00	6.50	10.00	17.50

Obv. leg: Characters at bottom 4-5mm apart.

229.1	ND(1903-05)	Inc. Ab.	4.00	6.50	10.00	17.50

Obv: Manchu at 3 o'clock is lower in relation to center characters.

229.2	ND(1903-05)	Inc. Ab.	4.00	6.50	10.00	17.50

Obv: Characters 6-9mm apart.
Rev: Trident-shaped flame below letters HUE.

229.3	ND(1903-05)	Inc. Ab.	4.00	6.50	10.00	17.50

BRASS

229.3a	ND(1903-05)	Inc. Ab.	4.00	6.50	10.00	17.50

Obv: Characters 4-5mm apart.

229.4	ND(1903-05)	Inc. Ab.	4.00	6.50	10.00	17.50

Obv: Bottom characters 6-9mm apart.
Rev: W/o trident-shaped flame, instead a cloud pointing to the letter U.

229.5	ND(1903-05)	Inc. Ab.	2.50	4.00	7.50	12.00

COPPER

229.5a	ND(1903-05)	Inc. Ab.	3.00	5.00	10.00	15.00

BRASS
Obv: Characters 4-5mm apart.

229.6	ND(1903-05)	Inc. Ab.	4.00	6.00	10.00	17.50

COPPER

229.6a	ND(1903-05)	Inc. Ab.	2.00	3.00	5.50	10.00

BRASS

Obv: Manchu at 3 o'clock is lower.

Y#	Date	Mintage	VG	Fine	VF	XF
229.7	ND(1903-05)	Inc. Ab.	3.75	6.00	10.00	17.50

COPPER

Y#	Date	Mintage	VG	Fine	VF	XF
229.7a	ND(1903-05)	Inc. Ab.	2.00	3.50	6.00	9.00

BRASS

Obv: Characters 4-5mm apart. Rev: W/o cloud below CHU, high point of dragon's body below letter C, tail joins body above letter S in CASH.

Y#	Date	Mintage	VG	Fine	VF	XF
229.8	ND(1903-05)	Inc. Ab.	4.00	6.00	9.00	17.50

COPPER

Y#	Date	Mintage	VG	Fine	VF	XF
229.8a	ND(1903-05)	Inc. Ab.	2.00	3.50	6.00	9.00

Rev: High point of dragons body below letter H, tail joins body above letter C in CASH.

Y#	Date	Mintage	VG	Fine	VF	XF
229.9	ND(1903-05)	Inc. Ab.	2.00	3.50	6.00	9.00

Y#	Date	Mintage	VG	Fine	VF	XF
231	ND(1903-05)	Inc. Ab.	150.00	200.00	225.00	275.00

Y#	Date	Mintage	VG	Fine	VF	XF
10t	CD1906	337.748	1.00	1.50	3.00	6.00

Bottom of Manchu word at 11 o'clock curls to left.

Y#	Date	Mintage	VG	Fine	VF	XF
20t.1	CD1909	231.930	1.00	1.50	3.00	6.00

BRASS

Y#	Date	Mintage	VG	Fine	VF	XF
20t.1a	CD1909	I.A.	3.00	5.00	10.00	15 00

COPPER

Bottom of Manchu word at 11 o'clock curls to right.

Y#	Date	Mintage	VG	Fine	VF	XF
20t.2	CD1909	I.A.	5.00	9.00	12.00	17.50

20 CASH

COPPER

Y#	Date	Mintage	VG	Fine	VF	XF
227	ND(1903-05)	25.319	100.00	125.00	175.00	250.00

Obv: Small Manchu at 3 and 9 o'clock. Rev: Trident flame points to E of SZE.

Y#	Date	Mintage	VG	Fine	VF	XF
230	ND(1903-05)	Inc. Ab.	10.00	15.00	30.00	50.00

Obv: Large Manchu at 3 and 9 o'clock. Rev: Large trident flame points to C of CHUEN.

Y#	Date	Mintage	VG	Fine	VF	XF
230.1	ND(1903-05)	Inc. Ab.	12.00	20.00	35.00	60.00

Obv: Large Manchu. Rev: Trident flame below ZE.

Y#	Date	Mintage	VG	Fine	VF	XF
230.3	ND(1903-05)	Inc. Ab.	15.00	30.00	50.00	80.00

Rev: Trident flame below CHU of CHUEN, large letters.

Y#	Date	Mintage	VG	Fine	VF	XF
230.4	ND	—	30.00	60.00	100.00	160.00

Rev: Trident flame points to E of CHUEN, small letters.

Y#	Date	Mintage	VG	Fine	VF	XF
230.5	ND(1903-05)	Inc. Ab.	—	—	—	—

Obv: Different small Manchu. Rev: Large 5 petalled rosettes, dragon differs.

Y#	Date	Mintage	VG	Fine	VF	XF
230.6	ND(1903-05)	Inc. Ab.	12.00	20.00	35.00	60.00

BRASS

Obv: Small Manchu. Rev: Larger cloud below CHUEN.

Y#	Date	Mintage	VG	Fine	VF	XF
230.7a	ND(1903-05)	Inc. Ab.	15.00	25.00	40.00	70.00

Rev: Front view dragon.

Y#	Date	Mintage	VG	Fine	VF	XF
232	ND	—	— Reported, not confirmed			

COPPER

Y#	Date	Mintage	VG	Fine	VF	XF
11t	CD1906	51.028	10.00	22.50	35.00	60.00

Obv: Bottom of Manchu word at 11 o'clock curls right.

Y#	Date	Mintage	VG	Fine	VF	XF
21t.1	CD1909	33.414	15.00	27.50	40.00	70.00

Obv: Bottom of Manchu word at 11 o'clock curls left.

Y#	Date	Mintage	VG	Fine	VF	XF
21t.2	CD1909	—	15.00	27.50	40.00	70.00

BRASS

Y#	Date	Mintage	VG	Fine	VF	XF
21t.1a	CD1909	I.A.	25.00	35.00	65.00	100.00

5 CENTS

1.3000 g, .820 SILVER, .0343 oz ASW

Y#	Date	Mintage	Fine	VF	XF	Unc
234	ND(1898; 1901-08)	.671	12.00	17.50	30.00	80.00

Errors in the English leg.

Y#	Date	Mintage	Fine	VF	XF	Unc
234.1	ND(1901-08)	Inc. Ab.	15.00	25.00	40.00	90.00

Y#	Date	Mintage	Fine	VF	XF	Unc
239	ND(1910)	.566	20.00	30.00	55.00	120.00

10 CENTS

2.6000 g, .820 SILVER, .0686 oz ASW

Y#	Date	Mintage	Fine	VF	XF	Unc
235	ND(1898; 1901-08)	1.274	10.00	17.50	30.00	90.00

Y#	Date	Mintage	Fine	VF	XF	Unc
240	ND(1909-11)	.278	25.00	30.00	55.00	120.00

20 CENTS

5.3000 g, .820 SILVER, .1397 oz ASW

Rev: 5 flames on pearl.

Y#	Date	Mintage	Fine	VF	XF	Unc
236	ND(1898; 1901-08)	.897	10.00	16.00	27.50	70.00

Rev: 6 flames on pearl.

Y#	Date	Mintage	Fine	VF	XF	Unc
236.1	ND(1898; 1901-08)	Inc. Ab.	10.00	16.00	27.50	70.00

Rev: 7 flames on pearl.

Y#	Date	Mintage	Fine	VF	XF	Unc
236.2	ND(1898; 1901-08)	Inc. Ab.	10.00	16.00	27.50	70.00

Various errors in English leg.

Y#	Date	Mintage	Fine	VF	XF	Unc
236.3	ND(1901-08)	Inc. Ab.	15.00	22.50	35.00	80.00
241	ND(1909-11)	.041	—	—	Rare	—

50 CENTS

13.2000 g, .860 SILVER, .3650 oz ASW
Rev: Dragon w/narrow face, small cross at either side, large fireball.

Y#	Date	Mintage	Fine	VF	XF	Unc
237	ND(1898; 1901-08)	.474	22.00	35.00	65.00	300.00

Various errors in English leg.

Y#	Date	Mintage	Fine	VF	XF	Unc
237.1	ND(1901-08)	Inc. Ab.	25.00	45.00	80.00	225.00

Rev: Dragon w/tapering face and small chin, small fireball, small cross at either side of dragon.

Y#	Date	Mintage	Fine	VF	XF	Unc
237.2	ND(1901-08)	Inc. Ab.	22.00	35.00	65.00	200.00

Rev: Dragon w/wide face and smaller fireball, thicker spines on top of dragon's head, small cross at either side of dragon.

Y#	Date	Mintage	Fine	VF	XF	Unc
237.3	ND(1901-08)	Inc. Ab.	22.00	35.00	65.00	200.00

SILVER, 13.20 g

Y#	Date	Mintage	Fine	VF	XF	Unc
242	ND(1909-11)	.038	75.00	130.00	180.00	325.00

Rev. leg: Inverted A in place of V in PROVINCE.

Y#	Date	Mintage	Fine	VF	XF	Unc
242.1	ND(1909-11)	Inc. Ab.	75.00	130.00	180.00	325.00

DOLLAR

26.8000 g, .900 SILVER, .7756 oz ASW
Rev: Dragon w/narrow face and large fireball, small cross at either side of dragon.

Y#	Date	Mintage	Fine	VF	XF	Unc
238	ND(1898; 1901-08)	6.487	10.00	20.00	30.00	400.00

Rev. leg: Inverted A instead of V in PROVINCE.

Y#	Date	Mintage	Fine	VF	XF	Unc
238.1	ND(1901-08)	Inc. Ab.	10.00	17.00	30.00	350.00

Rev: Dragon w/wider face and flatter pearl, small cross at either side of dragon.

Y#	Date	Mintage	Fine	VF	XF	Unc
238.2	ND(1901-08)	Inc. Ab.	10.00	17.00	30.00	300.00

Rev: 7 MACE and 3 CANDAREENS instead of 2 CANDAREENS.

Y#	Date	Mintage	Fine	VF	XF	Unc
238.3	ND(1901-08)	Inc. Ab.	20.00	40.00	100.00	500.00

Rev: Large spines on dragon's body.

Y#	Date	Mintage	Fine	VF	XF	Unc
243	ND(1909-11)	2.846	12.50	22.50	60.00	300.00

Rev: Inverted A instead of V in PROVINCE.

Y#	Date	Mintage	Fine	VF	XF	Unc
243.1	ND(1909-11)	Inc. Ab.	15.00	25.00	65.00	300.00

Rev: Small spines on dragon's body.

Y#	Date	Mintage	Fine	VF	XF	Unc
243.2	ND(1909-11)	Inc. Ab.	65.00	100.00	200.00	500.00

REPUBLIC

Many coins in silver and minor metals, issued by warlords and Chinese Communists, circulated in such provinces as Kansu (Gansu), Szechuan (Sichuan) and Yunnan. These coins were struck or sometimes cast of silver or copper, but also of debased metals of cruder craftsmanship. Some coins in this category include Y#217, Y#459.3 and many pieces among Y#446 through Y#464. Y#447 through Y#450 come in differing degrees of copper: red copper, debased (yellow) copper and greenish yellow brass. To classify as copper, the color of the coin must be red to brown-red.

5 CASH

COPPER

Y#	Date	Mintage	VG	Fine	VF	XF
441	Yr.1 (1912)	.471	40.00	80.00	130.00	250.00

NOTE: Varieties exist.

BRASS

Y#	Date	Mintage	VG	Fine	VF	XF
441a	Yr.1 (1912)	I.A.	—	—	—	—

SILVER

Y#	Date	Mintage	VG	Fine	VF	XF
441b	Yr.1 (1912)	—	—	—	1000.	1500.

COPPER

Y#	Date	Mintage	VG	Fine	VF	XF
443	Yr.1 (1912)	I.A.	35.00	70.00	110.00	150.00

Y#	Date	Mintage	VG	Fine	VF	XF
446	Yr.1 (1912)	I.A.	—	—	Rare	—

BRASS

Y#	Date	Mintage	VG	Fine	VF	XF
446a	Yr.1 (1912)	I.A.	—	—	Rare	—

10 CASH

COPPER
Obv: 2 rosettes.

Y#	Date	Mintage	VG	Fine	VF	XF
447	Yr.1 (1912)	108.618	1.75	3.00	10.00	20.00
	Yr.2 (1913)	I.A.	6.00	15.00	25.00	50.00
	BRASS					
447a	Yr.1 (1912)	I.A.	.80	1.50	2.50	5.00
	Yr.2 (1913)	I.A.	1.60	4.00	8.00	20.00
	Obv: 3 rosettes.					
447.1a	Yr.2 (1913)	I.A.	—	—	Rare	—

20 CASH

COPPER
Obv: 2 rosettes.

Y#	Date	Mintage	VG	Fine	VF	XF
448	Yr.1 (1912)	115.061	1.00	2.50	5.00	15.00
	Yr.2 (1913)	I.A.	— Reported, not confirmed			
	BRASS					
448a	Yr.1 (1912)	I.A.	.75	1.50	2.50	6.00
	Yr.2 (1913)	I.A.	1.00	2.00	3.50	7.00

COPPER
Obv: 3 rosettes.

Y#	Date	Mintage	VG	Fine	VF	XF
448.1	Yr.2 (1913)	I.A.	250.00	350.00	450.00	800.00
	Yr.3 (1914)	I.A.	250.00	350.00	450.00	800.00
	BRASS					
448.1a	Yr.2 (1913)	I.A.	2.50	6.00	12.00	25.00
	Yr.3 (1914)	I.A.	2.50	6.00	12.00	25.00

NOTE: There are many varieties of this 20 Cash; small and large rosettes; open and closed size characters and exaggerated size character with horns.

2 CENTS

COPPER

Y#	Year	Date	VG	Fine	VF	XF
476	19	(1930)	100.00	225.00	350.00	600.00
		BRASS				
476a	19	(1930)	—	—	—	—

50 CASH

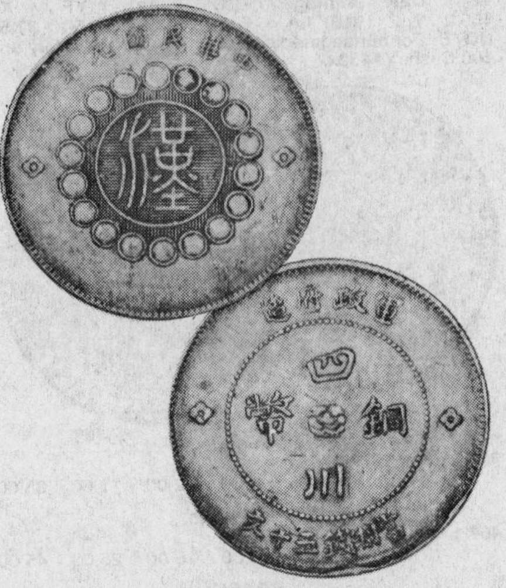

COPPER
Rev: Small flower in center.

Y#	Date	Mintage	VG	Fine	VF	XF
449	Yr.1 (1912)	489.382	2.00	4.00	7.00	15.00
	BRASS					
449a	Yr.1 (1912)	I.A.	1.50	3.50	6.00	10.00

COPPER
Rev: Larger flower in center.

Y#	Date	Mintage	VG	Fine	VF	XF
449.1	Yr.1 (1912)	I.A.	2.00	5.00	10.00	20.00
	BRASS					
449.1a	Yr.1 (1912)	I.A.	2.50	6.00	12.50	25.00

COPPER
Obv: 3 rosettes. Rev: Small flower in center.

Y#	Date	Mintage	VG	Fine	VF	XF
449.2	Yr.2 (1913)	I.A.	2.25	5.50	11.00	22.00
	BRASS					
449.2a	Yr.2 (1913)	I.A.	2.25	5.50	11.00	22.00
	Yr.3 (1914)	I.A.	2.25	5.50	11.00	22.00

200 Cash, Y#459 cut into quarters.

Y#	Date	Mintage	VG	Fine	VF	XF
459y	Yr.2 (1913)	—	30.00	35.00	40.00	50.00

COPPER

Y#	Date	Mintage	VG	Fine	VF	XF
462	Yr.15 (1926)	.090	18.00	35.00	65.00	100.00
	BRASS					
462a	Yr.15 (1926)	I.A.	16.00	32.50	55.00	80.00

100 CASH

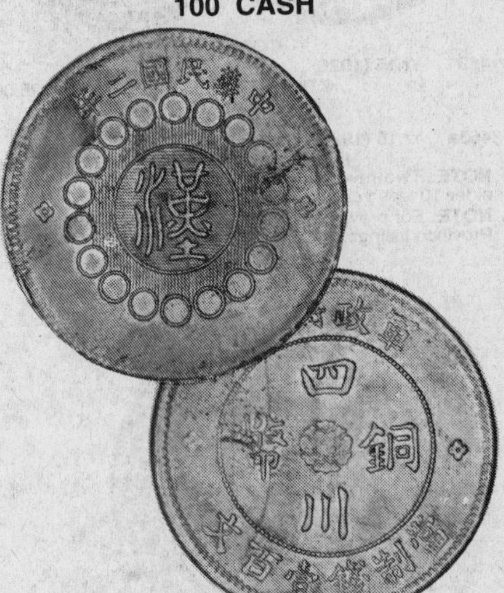

COPPER
Obv: 2 rosettes.
Rev: Large flower in center.

Y#	Date	Mintage	VG	Fine	VF	XF
450	Yr.2 (1913)	399.212	2.50	6.00	8.50	17.50
	Yr.3 (1914)	—	30.00	40.00	50.00	60.00
	BRASS					
450a	Yr.2 (1913)	I.A.	1.50	3.00	6.00	10.00

COPPER
Obv: 3 rosettes.
Rev: Small flower in center.

Y#	Date	Mintage	VG	Fine	VF	XF
450.1	Yr.2 (1913)	I.A.	3.50	9.00	15.00	25.00
	Yr.3 (1914)	—	—	—	—	—

COPPER or BRASS
200 Cash, Y#459 cut in half.

Y#	Date	Mintage	VG	Fine	VF	XF
459x	Yr.2(1913)	—	3.50	9.50	17.00	45.00

COPPER

Y#	Date	Mintage	VG	Fine	VF	XF
463	Yr.15 (1926)	7.055	3.50	9.00	15.00	25.00

BRASS

Y#	Date	Mintage	VG	Fine	VF	XF
463a	Yr.15 (1926)	Inc. Ab.	3.25	8.00	12.50	20.00

NOTE: Two reverse varieties known. Often struck over older 10 Cash coins.

NOTE: For previously listed Y#466-466a refer to Sikang Province listings.

200 CASH

COPPER

Y#	Date	Mintage	VG	Fine	VF	XF
459	Yr.2 (1913)	360.274	— Reported, not confirmed			

BRASS

Y#	Date	Mintage	VG	Fine	VF	XF
459a	Yr.2 (1913)	I.A.	20.00	40.00	80.00	125.00

COPPER
Obv: Tassels draped over flag poles.

Y#	Date	Mintage	VG	Fine	VF	XF
459.1	Yr.2 (1913)	I.A.	6.00	10.00	25.00	40.00

BRASS

Y#	Date	Mintage	VG	Fine	VF	XF
459.1a	Yr.2 (1913)	—	4.50	8.00	20.00	35.00

COPPER
Rev: Smaller stars at sides.

Y#	Date	Mintage	VG	Fine	VF	XF
459.2	Yr.2 (1913)	I.A.	5.00	9.00	22.50	37.50

NOTE: For cut segments refer to 50 Cash, Y#459y and 100 Cash, Y#459x.

Y#	Date	Mintage	VG	Fine	VF	XF
	Plain edge.					
464	Yr.15 (1926)	404.644	4.00	12.00	17.00	35.00
	Reeded edge.					
464.1	Yr.15 (1926)	Inc. Ab.	6.00	15.00	25.00	45.00
	BRASS					
	Plain edge.					
464a	Yr.15 (1926)	Inc. Ab.	4.50	12.00	17.00	35.00
	Reeded edge					
464.1a	Yr.15 (1926)	I.A.	—	—	—	—

Obv: Similar to Y#464. Rev: Dot within first 0 of 200.

Y#	Date	Mintage	VG	Fine	VF	XF
464.2	Yr.15 (1926)	I.A.	—	—	—	—

NOTE: Many varieties: Open and closed buds; overstruck on earlier pieces and on virgin flans; different sizes and thicknesses.

10 CENTS

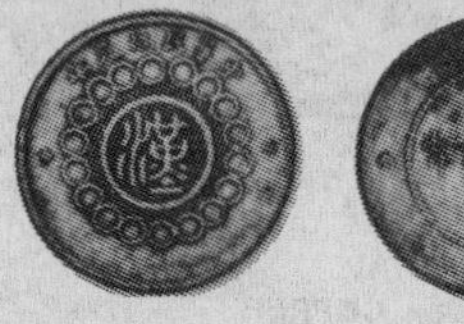

SILVER, 2.60 g

Y#	Date	Mintage	Fine	VF	XF	Unc
453	Yr.1 (1912)	.370	25.00	40.00	75.00	150.00

Y#	Date	Mintage	Fine	VF	XF	Unc
	NICKEL					
468	ND	—	35.00	90.00	110.00	160.00
	SILVER					
468a	ND	—	25.00	60.00	90.00	125.00
	IRON					
468b	ND	—	20.00	50.00	70.00	125.00
	COPPER-NICKEL					
468c	ND	—	12.00	30.00	45.00	70.00

20 CENTS

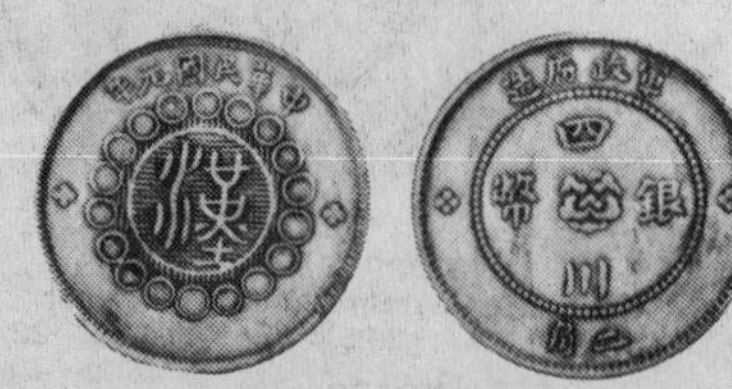

SILVER, 5.20 g

Y#	Date	Mintage	Fine	VF	XF	Unc
454	Yr.1 (1912)	.095	35.00	60.00	100.00	250.00

Tibetan War

Kann#	Date	Mintage	Fine	VF	XF	Unc
795	1932	—	45.00	110.00	165.00	250.00

NOTE: Authenticity not established.

50 CENTS

SILVER, 12.90 g

Y#	Date	Mintage	Fine	VF	XF	Unc
455	Yr.1 (1912)	37.942	10.00	20.00	40.00	125.00
	Yr.2 (1913)	I.A.	—	—	Rare	—

SILVER, 10.50 g
Sun Yat-sen

Y#	Date	Mintage	Fine	VF	XF	Unc
473	Yr.17 (1928)	I.A.	100.00	300.00	475.00	800.00

DOLLAR

SILVER, 25.60 g

Y#	Date	Mintage	Fine	VF	XF	Unc
456	Yr.1 (1912)	55.670	10.00	15.00	25.00	100.00
	Yr.3 (1914)	I.A.	—	—	Rare	—

Rev: Right hand character w/2 dots instead of horizontal stroke.

Y#	Date	Mintage	Fine	VF	XF	Unc
456.1	Yr.1 (1912)	I.A.	25.00	50.00	100.00	250.0

NOTE: Silver content ranged from 0.880 to 0.500 fine.

25.50 g
Sun Yat-sen

Y#	Date	Mintage	Fine	VF	XF	Unc
474	Yr.17 (1928)I.A.		400.00	600.00	850.00	1400.

TAIWAN

For historical information refer to introductory paragraph of the Republic of China following the Peoples Republic of China listings.

Chinese migration to Taiwan began as early as the sixth century. The Dutch established a base on the island in 1624 and held it until 1661, when they were driven out by supporters of the Ming dynasty who used it as a base for their unsuccessful attempt to displace the ruling Manchu dynasty of mainland China. After being occupied by Manchu forces in 1683, Taiwan remained under the suzerainty of China until its cession to Japan in 1895. The island was part of the province of Fukien (Fujian) until established as a separate province in the period 1885-1895. (It took 10 years to complete the conversion to a full-fledged province.)

EMPIRE

CASH

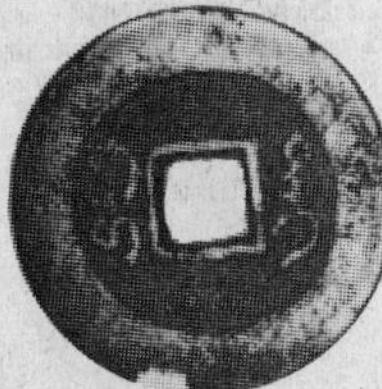

Obv: Type A

C#	Date	Emperor	Good	VG	Fine	VF
25-6	ND(1851-61)	Hsien-feng	60.00	70.00	80.00	100.00

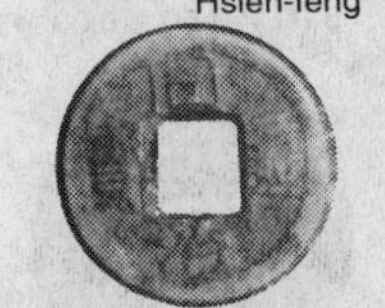

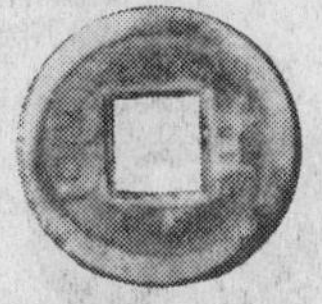

C#	Date	Emperor	Good	VG	Fine	VF
25-9	ND(1862-74)	Tung-chih	—	60.00	90.00	—

MILLED COINAGE

Made in Taiwan 臺灣製局

Made in Tai Province 臺省製造

5 CENTS

1.3000 g, .820 SILVER, .0343 oz ASW
Similar to 10 Cents, Y#247.

Y#	Date	Mintage	Fine	VF	XF	Unc
246	ND(1893-94)		150.00	250.00	400.00	700.00

10 CENTS

2.7000 g, .820 SILVER, .0712 oz ASW
Obv: 4 Chinese characters above meaning: *Made in Taiwan;* large characters in outside circle; small characters inside.

Y#	Date	Mintage	Fine	VF	XF	Unc
247	ND(1893-94)		60.00	100.00	250.00	400.00

Obv: Smaller characters in outside circle, larger characters inside circle.

Y#	Date	Mintage	Fine	VF	XF	Unc
247.1	ND(1893-94)		50.00	100.00	200.00	400.00

Obv: 4 Chinese characters above meaning: *Made in Tai Province.*

Y#	Date	Mintage	Fine	VF	XF	Unc
247.2	ND(1893-94)		80.00	125.00	250.00	500.00

20 CENTS

5.4000 g, .820 SILVER, .1424 oz ASW
Obv: 4 Chinese characters above, meaning *Made in Taiwan.*

Y#	Date	Mintage	Fine	VF	XF	Unc
248	ND(1894)	—	—	—	Rare	—

Obv: 4 Chinese characters above, meaning: *Made in Tai Province.*

Y#	Date	Mintage	Fine	VF	XF	Unc
248.1	ND(1894)	—	—	—	Rare	—

NOTE: These coins were minted at an arsenal in Taiwan.

DOLLAR

"Old Man"

SILVER, 26.80 g

C#	Date	Mintage	VG	Fine	VF	XF
25-3	ND(1837-1845)		200.00	500.00	800.00	2200.

NOTE: C#25-3 normally comes w/2 chops at lower left on the reverse. Many varieties exist.

"Soldier's Pay"

25.00 g
Obv: Chinese *Chia Yi Hsien Tsao.*

Kann#	Year	Date	VG	Fine	VF	XF
3	1	(1862)	1800.	3000.	4500.	6500.

NOTE: Market valuations for the dollar coins above are for specimens with a few light chops. For unchopped specimens, add 10 percent and for heavily chopped specimens deduct 20 percent.

Rev: Crossed lotus flowers.

C#	Date	Mintage	VG	Fine	VF	XF
25-4	ND(1853)	—	300.00	450.00	700.00	2700.

NOTE: C#25-4 normally comes w/2 chops (one being a Chinese numeral *six*) on the reverse.

25.30 g
Rev: Crossed brushes.

C#	Date	Mintage	VG	Fine	VF	XF
25-5	ND(1862)	—	300.00	500.00	800.00	3200.

NOTE: The market values shown for C#25-3/25-5 are for coins which have been lightly chopmarked. Attribution of C#25-4 and C#25-5 to Taiwan is not fully accepted. Other sources attribute these coins to Chihli (Hebei) Province.

YUNNAN PROVINCE

A province located in south China bordering Burma, Laos and Vietnam . It is very mountainous with many lakes. Yunnan was the home of various active imperial mints. A modern mint was established at Kunming in 1905 and the first struck copper coins were issued in 1906 and the first struck silver coins in 1908. General Tang Chi-Yao issued coins in gold, silver and copper with his portrait in 1919. The last Republican coins were struck here in 1949.

EMPIRE

Yunnanfu Mint

CASH

CAST BRASS
Obv: Type A

C#	Date	Emperor	Good	VG	Fine	VF
26-2	ND(1796-1820)	Chia-ch'ing	.25	.50	.75	1.00

Rev: Crescent above.

C#	Date	Emperor	Good	VG	Fine	VF
26-2.1	ND(1796-1820)	Chia-ch'ing	1.00	2.00	3.00	5.00

Obv: Type A

26-3 ND(1821-50) Tao-kuang .25 .50 .75 1.25

Rev: Crescent above.

26-3.1 ND(1821-50) Tao-kuang 2.50 3.50 5.00 7.50

Rev: Horizontal line above.

26-3.2 ND(1821-50) Tao-kuang 1.50 2.00 4.00 6.00

Obv: Type A

26-4 ND(1851-61) Hsien-feng .50 1.00 1.50 2.50

Rev: Crescent above.

26-4.1 ND(1851-61) Hsien-feng 5.00 7.50 10.00 15.00

Rev: Crescent below.

26-4.2 ND(1851-61) Hsien-feng 5.00 7.50 10.00 15.00

Rev: Crescent standing on end above.

26-4.3 ND(1851-61) Hsien-feng 5.00 7.50 10.00 15.00

Rev: Dot within crescent above (Pregnant Moon).

26-4.4 ND(1851-61) Hsien-feng 5.00 7.50 10.00 15.00

Rev: Circle above.

26-4.5 ND(1851-61) Hsien-feng 5.00 7.50 10.00 15.00

Rev: Circle below.

26-4.6 ND(1851-61) Hsien-feng 5.00 7.50 10.00 15.00

Rev: Dot within circle above.

26-4.7 ND(1851-61) Hsien-feng 5.00 7.50 10.00 15.00

Rev: Dot within circle below.

26-4.8 ND(1851-61) Hsien-feng 5.00 7.50 10.00 15.00

Rev: An X above the center.

26-4.9 ND(1851-61) Hsien-feng 5.00 7.50 10.00 15.00

Rev: Character *Ho* above and circle below.

26-4.10 ND(1851-61) Hsien-feng 5.00 7.50 10.00 15.00

Rev: Character *Ho* above and dot within circle below.

26-4.11 ND(1851-61) Hsien-feng 5.00 7.50 10.00 15.00

Rev: Character *Kung* above.

26-4.12 ND(1851-61) Hsien-feng 5.00 7.50 10.00 15.00

Rev: Character *Yi* (one) above.

26-4.13 ND(1851-61) Hsien-feng 5.00 7.50 10.00 15.00

Rev: Character *Erh* (two) above.

26-4.14 ND(1851-61) Hsien-feng Reported, not confirmed

Rev: Character *San* (three) above.

26-4.15 ND(1851-61) Hsien-feng 5.00 7.50 10.00 15.00

Rev: Character *Szu* (four) above.

26-4.16 ND(1851-61) Hsien-feng 5.00 7.50 10.00 15.00

Rev: Character above probably meaning "five".

C#	Date	Emperor	Good	VG	Fine	VF
26-4.17	ND(1851-61)	Hsien-feng	5.00	7.50	10.00	15.00

Rev: Character *Shih* (ten) above and a crescent below.

26-4.18 ND(1851-61) Hsien-feng 5.00 7.50 10.00 15.00

Rev: Character *Chin* above and dot in circle below.

26-4.19 ND(1851-61) Hsien-feng 5.00 7.50 10.00 15.00

Rev: Manchu words above.

26-4.20 ND(1851-61) Hsien-feng 5.00 7.50 10.00 15.00

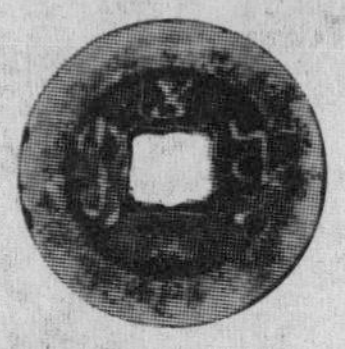

Rev: X above hole in center.

26-4.21 ND(1851-61) Hsien-feng 5.00 7.50 10.00 15.00

Obv: Type A-2

26-7 ND(1862-74) T'ung-chih 1.50 3.00 4.00 6.00

Rev: Circle above.

26-7.1 ND(1862-74) T'ung-chih 5.00 7.50 10.00 15.00

Rev: Dot within circle above.

26-7.2 ND(1862-74) T'ung-chih 5.00 7.50 10.00 15.00

Rev: Dot within crescent above.

26-7.3 ND(1862-74) T'ung-chih 5.00 7.50 10.00 15.00

Rev: Crescent below.

26-7.4 ND(1862-74) T'ung-chih 5.00 7.50 10.00 15.00

Rev: Vertical line above.

26-7.5 ND(1862-74) T'ung-chih 5.00 7.50 10.00 15.00

Rev: Vertical line below.

26-7.6 ND(1862-74) T'ung-chih 5.00 7.50 10.00 15.00

Rev: Character *Kung* above center.

26-7.7 ND(1862-74) T'ung-chih 5.00 7.50 10.00 15.00

Rev: Character *Ho* above.

26-7.8 ND(1862-74) T'ung-chih 5.00 7.50 10.00 15.00

Rev: Character *Ta* above.

26-7.9 ND(1862-74) T'ung-chih 5.00 7.50 10.00 15.00

Rev: Character *Shan* above.

26-7.10 ND(1862-74) T'ung-chih 5.00 7.50 10.00 15.00

Rev: Character *Ch'uan* below.

26-7.11 ND(1862-74) T'ung-chih 5.00 7.50 10.00 15.00

Rev: Character *Yi* (one) above.

26-7.12 ND(1862-74) T'ung-chih 5.00 7.50 10.00 15.00

Rev: Character *Wu* (five) inverted below.

C#	Date	Emperor	Good	VG	Fine	VF
26-7.13	ND(1862-74)	T'ung-chih	5.00	7.50	10.00	15.00

Rev: Character *Liu* (six) above.

26-7.14 ND(1862-74) T'ung-chih 5.00 7.50 10.00 15.00

Rev: Characters *Liu* (six) above, but sideways.

26-7.15 ND(1862-74) T'ung-chih 5.00 7.50 10.00 15.00

Rev: Character *Pa* (eight) above.

26-7.16 ND(1862-74) T'ung-chih 5.00 7.50 10.00 15.00

Rev: Character *Shih* (ten) above.

26-7.17 ND(1862-74) T'ung-chih 5.00 7.50 10.00 15.00

Rev: Character *Shih* (ten) above, crescent below.

26-7.18 ND(1862-74) T'ung-chih 5.00 7.50 10.00 15.00

Rev: Characters *Shih Yi* (eleven) above.

26-7.19 ND(1862-74) T'ung-chih 5.00 7.50 10.00 15.00

Rev: Characters *Shih* (ten) above and *Yi* (one) below.

26-7.20 ND(1862-74) T'ung-chih 5.00 7.50 10.00 15.00

Rev: Characters *Shih* (ten) above *San* (three) below.

26-7.21 ND(1862-74) T'ung-chih 5.00 7.50 10.00 15.00

Rev: Character *Jen* above.

26-7.22 ND(1862-74) T'ung-chih 5.00 7.50 10.00 15.00

Rev: Inverted crescent above.

26-7.23 ND(1862-74) T'ung-chih 5.00 7.50 10.00 15.00

26-9 ND(1875-1908) Kuang-hsu 2.00 4.00 6.50 9.00

Rev: Character *Kung* above.

26-9.1 ND(1875-1908) Kuang-hsu 2.00 5.00 7.50 10.00

Rev: Character *Ssu* (four) above.

26-9.2 ND(1875-1908) Kuang-hsu 2.50 5.00 7.50 10.00

Rev: Character *Chin* above.

C#	Date	Emperor	Good	VG	Fine	VF
26-9.3	ND(1875-1908)	Kuang-hsu	2.50	5.00	7.50	10.00

Rev: Crescent above, dot below.

C#	Date	Emperor	Good	VG	Fine	VF
26-9.4	ND(1875-1908)	Kuang-hsu	2.50	5.00	7.50	12.00

Rev: Dot above hole.

C#	Date	Emperor	Good	VG	Fine	VF
26-9.5	ND(1875-1908)	Kuang-hsu	2.50	5.00	7.50	12.00

Rev: Character *Kung* above hole.

C#	Date	Emperor	Good	VG	Fine	VF
26-11	ND(1909-11)	Hsuan-t'ung	75.00	100.00	150.00	220.00

Rev: Character *Shan* above hole.

C#	Date	Emperor	Good	VG	Fine	VF
26-12	ND(1909-11)	Hsuan-t'ung	30.00	40.00	50.00	100.00

Rev: W/o character above hole.

C#	Date	Emperor	Good	VG	Fine	VF
26-13	ND(1909-11)	Hsuan-t'ung	35.00	45.00	55.00	100.00

Refer to "Additional Characters" chart in the Introduction to China.

10 CASH

CAST BRASS
Obv: Type B-1

C#	Date	Emperor	Good	VG	Fine	VF
26-5	ND(1851-61)	Hsien-feng	2.00	5.00	7.00	15.00

Rev: Dot at upper left.

C#	Date	Emperor	Good	VG	Fine	VF
26-5.1	ND(1851-61)	Hsien-feng	—	—	—	—

37mm

C#	Date	Emperor	Good	VG	Fine	VF
26-8	ND(1862-74)	T'ung-chih	30.00	40.00	45.00	60.00

35mm

C#	Date	Emperor	Good	VG	Fine	VF
26-8.1	ND(1862-74)	T'ung-chih	30.00	40.00	45.00	60.00
26-10	ND(1875-1908)	Kuang-hsu	—	—	Rare	—

50 CASH

CAST BRASS

C#	Date	Emperor	Good	VG	Fine	VF
26-6	ND(1851-61)	Hsien-feng	50.00	60.00	70.00	90.00

Tungch'uan Mint

CASH

CAST BRASS
Obv: Type A-1
Rev: Type 1 mint mark.

C#	Date	Emperor	Good	VG	Fine	VF
27-1	ND(1796-1820)	Chia-ch'ing	1.00	2.00	3.50	6.00

Rev: Type 2 mint mark.

C#	Date	Emperor	Good	VG	Fine	VF
27-1.1	ND(1796-1820)	Chia-ch'ing	15.00	20.00	25.00	30.00

Obv: Type A
Rev: Type 1 mint mark.

C#	Date	Emperor	Good	VG	Fine	VF
27-2	ND(1821-50)	Tao-kuang	.50	1.00	1.50	2.50

Rev: Type 3 mint mark.

C#	Date	Emperor	Good	VG	Fine	VF
27-2.1	ND(1821-50)	Tao-kuang	.50	1.00	1.50	2.50

Obv: Type A

C#	Date	Emperor	Good	VG	Fine	VF
27-3	ND(1851-61)	Hsien-feng	2.00	4.00	5.00	7.00

Rev: Character *Cheng* above.

C#	Date	Emperor	Good	VG	Fine	VF
27-3.1	ND(1851-61)	Hsien-feng	5.00	7.50	10.00	15.00

Obv: Type A-2

C#	Date	Emperor	Good	VG	Fine	VF
27-5	ND(1862-74)	T'ung-chih	5.00	9.00	12.00	18.00

Rev: Character *Cheng* above and crescent below.

C#	Date	Emperor	Good	VG	Fine	VF
27-5.1	ND(1862-74)	T'ung-chih	5.00	7.50	10.00	15.00

Rev: Character *Cheng* above, dot below.

C#	Date	Emperor	Good	VG	Fine	VF
27-5.2	ND(1862-74)	T'ung-chih	5.00	7.50	10.00	15.00

NOTE: Previously listed C#27-6, 27-6.1 and 27-6.2 are now listed under the Chefoo (Yantai) Mint, Shantung (Shandong) Province.

C#	Date	Emperor	Good	VG	Fine	VF
27-7	ND(1909-11)	Hsuan-t'ung	—	—	Rare	—

10 CASH

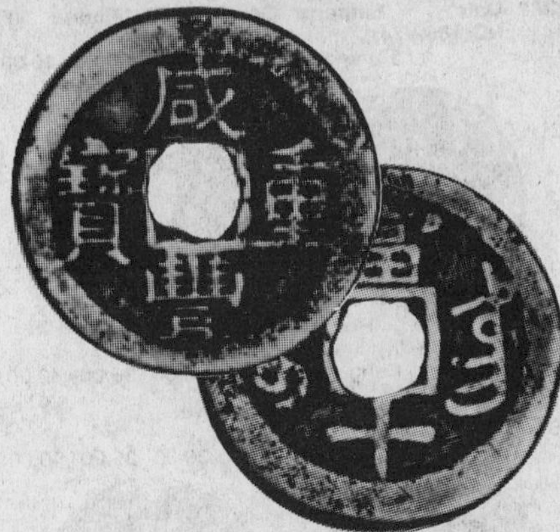

BRASS
Obv: Type B-1

C#	Date	Emperor	Good	VG	Fine	VF
27-4	ND(1851-61)	Hsien-feng	5.00	9.00	16.00	30.00

Uncertain Mint

州

The following coins bear a Manchu mint mark, different from Fukien (Fujian) which reads, 'FU'. though previously attributed to Fukien (Fujian), they are now believed to have been produced at the Chou (district, city or department) Mint while awaiting actual location information. They are not regarded as being produced in Yunnan.

CASH

CAST BRASS
Obv: Type A-2
Rev: Crescent above.

KM#	Date	Emperor	Good	VG	Fine	VF
1	ND(1851-61)	Hsien-feng	10.00	15.00	20.00	25.00

Rev: Circle above.

KM#	Date	Emperor	Good	VG	Fine	VF
2	ND(1851-61)	Hsien-feng	10.00	15.00	20.00	25.00

Obv: Type A-2.
Rev: W/o characters above or below center hole.

KM#	Date	Emperor	Good	VG	Fine	VF
10	ND(1862-74)	T'ung-chih	10.00	15.00	20.00	25.00

Rev: Crescent above.

KM#	Date	Emperor	Good	VG	Fine	VF
11	ND(1862-74)	T'ung-chih	10.00	15.00	20.00	25.00

Rev: Vertical line above.

KM#	Date	Emperor	Good	VG	Fine	VF
12	ND(1862-74)	T'ung-chih	25.00	30.00	35.00	40.00

Rev: Vertical line below.

KM#	Date	Emperor	Good	VG	Fine	VF
13	ND(1862-74)	T'ung-chih	25.00	30.00	35.00	40.00

Rev: Dot above.

KM#	Date	Emperor	Good	VG	Fine	VF
14	ND(1862-74)	T'ung-chih	25.00	30.00	35.00	40.00

Rev: Dot below.

15	ND(1862-74)	T'ung-chih	25.00	30.00	35.00	40.00

Rev: With "X" above.

16	ND(1862-74)	T'ung-chih	25.00	30.00	35.00	40.00

Rev: Character *Cheng* above.

21	ND(1862-74)	T'ung-chih	25.00	30.00	35.00	40.00

Rev: Character *Cheng* above and circle below.

22	ND(1862-74)	T'ung-chih	25.00	30.00	35.00	40.00

Rev: Character *Chih* above.

23	ND(1862-74)	T'ung-chih	25.00	30.00	35.00	40.00

Rev: Character *Chu* above.

25	ND(1862-74)	T'ung-chih	25.00	30.00	35.00	40.00

Rev: Character *Ch'uan* above.

27	ND(1862-74)	T'ung-chih	25.00	30.00	35.00	40.00

Rev: Character *Chung* above.

29	ND(1862-74)	T'ung-chih	25.00	30.00	35.00	40.00

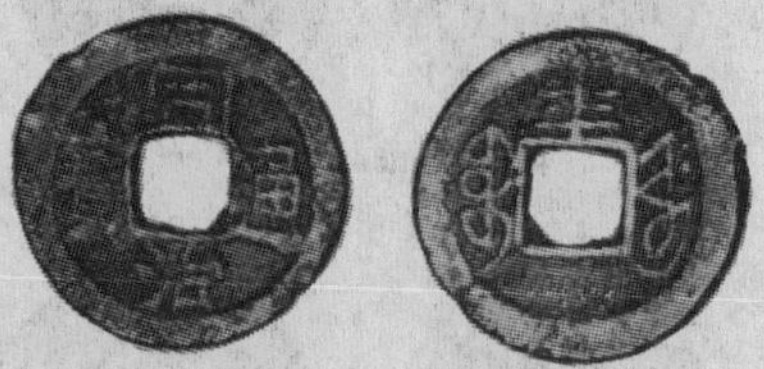

Rev: Character *Feng* above.

31	ND(1862-74)	T'ung-chih	25.00	30.00	35.00	40.00

Rev: Character *Ho* above.

33	ND(1862-74)	T'ung-chih	25.00	30.00	35.00	40.00

Rev: Character *Jen* above.

KM#	Date	Emperor	Good	VG	Fine	VF
35	ND(1862-74)	T'ung-chih	25.00	30.00	35.00	40.00

Rev: Character *Kung* above.

37	ND(1862-74)	T'ung-chih	25.00	30.00	35.00	40.00

Rev: Character *Shang* above.

39	ND(1862-74)	T'ung-chih	25.00	30.00	35.00	40.00

Rev: Character *Shun* above.

41	ND(1862-74)	T'ung-chih	25.00	30.00	35.00	40.00

Rev: Character *Hsin* above.

43	ND(1862-74)	T'ung-chih	25.00	30.00	35.00	40.00

Rev: Character *Ta* above.

45	ND(1862-74)	T'ung-chih	25.00	30.00	35.00	40.00

Rev: Character *Yu* above.

47	ND(1862-74)	T'ung-chih	25.00	30.00	35.00	40.00

Rev: Character *Yun* above.

49	ND(1862-74)	T'ung-chih	25.00	30.00	35.00	40.00

Rev: *Yi* (one) above.

KM#	Date	Emperor	Good	VG	Fine	VF
61	ND(1862-74)	T'ung-chih	25.00	30.00	35.00	40.00

Rev: *Erh* (two) above.

62	ND(1862-74)	T'ung-chih	25.00	30.00	35.00	40.00

Rev: *San* (three) above.

63	ND(1862-74)	T'ung-chih	25.00	30.00	35.00	40.00

Rev: *Wu* (five) above.

65	ND(1862-74)	T'ung-chih	25.00	30.00	35.00	40.00

Rev: Character *Shih* (ten) above.

70	ND(1862-74)	T'ung-chih	25.00	30.00	35.00	40.00

NOTE: Other varieties probably exist. Refer to "Additional Characters" chart in the introduction.

MILLED COINAGE

10 CASH

COPPER

Obv: Large mint mark *Yun* in center.

Y#	Date	Mintage	VG	Fine	VF	XF
10u	CD1906	36.701	10.00	22.00	35.00	60.00

Obv: Small mint mark *Yun* in center.

10u.1	CD1906	I.A.	25.00	55.00	85.00	125.00

Obv: Mint mark *Tien* in center.

Y#	Date	Mintage	VG	Fine	VF	XF
10v	CD1906	I.A.	12.00	30.00	40.00	65.00

20 CASH

COPPER

Obv: Large mint mark *Yun* in center.

11u	CD1906	.645	125.00	175.00	225.00	275.00

Obv: Small mint mark *Yun* in center.

11u.1	CD1906	—	125.00	175.00	225.00	275.00

Obv: Mint mark *Tien* in center.

11v.1	CD1906	I.A.	150.00	275.00	400.00	550.00

BRASS

11v.1a	CD1906	I.A.	175.00	350.00	450.00	600.00

20 CENTS

SILVER, 5.30 g

Y#	Date	Mintage	Fine	VF	XF	Unc
252	ND(1908)	.532	18.00	35.00	60.00	125.00

NOTE: Many minor varieties.

50 CENTS

13.2000 g, .800 SILVER, .3395 oz ASW

253	ND(1908)	—	7.50	15.00	20.00	85.00

Rev: 7 flames on pearl.

Y#	Date	Mintage	Fine	VF	XF	Unc
259	ND(1909-11)	—	7.00	13.50	22.50	90.00

Rev: 9 flames on pearl.

259.1	ND(1909-11)	—	7.00	13.50	22.50	90.00

DOLLAR

26.8000 g, .900 SILVER, .7755 oz ASW

254	ND(1908)	—	15.00	30.00	65.00	300.00

Obv. leg: 4 characters at top.

260	ND(1909-11)	—	15.00	25.00	60.00	300.00

Obv. leg: 7 characters at top.

260.1	CD1910	—	—	—	—	32,500.

REPUBLIC

Transitional Coinage

In the name of the Republic

CASH

CAST COPPER or BRASS

Rev: Mint mark: *Tung Ch'uan* (Yunnan)

at sides of hole.

KM#	Date	Mintage	Good	VG	Fine	VF
5	ND(1912)	—	10.00	20.00	30.00	45.00

10 CASH

BRASS

4	ND (1912)	—	10.00	15.00	20.00	30.00

Restruck Imperial Coinage

The following imperial coins are reign-dated 1875-1908. These coins were apparently restruck from previously unused dies at intervals from 1911 through to 1949, and with a progressively reduced silver content. The dates and silver content shown are approximate.

10 CENTS

2.6500 g, .650 SILVER, .0554 oz ASW

Rev: 2 circles beneath pearl.

Y#	Date	Mintage	Fine	VF	XF	Unc
255	ND(1911-15)	.902	15.00	30.00	45.00	90.00

20 CENTS

5.3000 g, .800 SILVER, .1363 oz ASW

Rev: 2 circles beneath pearl.

256	ND(1911-15)	—	12.50	17.50	32.50	75.00

5.3000 g, .650 SILVER, .1108 oz ASW

Rev: 3 circles beneath pearl.

256a (256.1)	ND(1911-15)	—	12.50	22.50	37.50	75.00

5.3000 g, .400 SILVER, .0682 oz ASW

Rev: 2 or 3 circles beneath pearl.

256b	ND(1920-31)	—	—	—	—	—

50 CENTS

13.2000 g, .800 SILVER, .3395 oz ASW

Rev: 2 circles below pearl.

257	ND(1911-15)	—	5.00	8.00	12.00	30.00

Rev: 3 circles below pearl.

257.1	ND(1911-15)	—	4.50	7.00	10.00	20.00

13.2000 g, .500 SILVER, .2122 oz ASW

Rev: 4 circles below pearl.

257.2	ND(1920-31)	—	4.50	6.00	9.00	20.00

NOTE: There are more than 30 minor varieties of Y#257.

.500* SILVER - BILLON, 13.20 g

Rev: 2 circles beneath pearl,

large circle around center circle of rosettes.

257.3	ND(1949)	—	—	—	—	—

DOLLAR

26.8000 g, .900 SILVER, .7755 oz ASW
Rev: 1 circle below pearl.

Y#	Date	Mintage	Fine	VF	XF	Unc
258	ND(1911-15)	—	15.00	20.00	35.00	250.00

26.8000 g, .600 SILVER, .5170 oz ASW
Rev: 4 circles below pearl.

Y#	Date	Mintage	Fine	VF	XF	Unc
258.1	ND(1920-22)	—	15.00	20.00	35.00	250.00

Regular Coinage

CENT

BRASS
Similar to 2 Cents, Y#489.

Y#	Year	Date	VG	Fine	VF	XF
488	21	(1932)	—	—	Rare	—

2 CENTS

BRASS

Y#	Year	Date	VG	Fine	VF	XF
489	21	(1932)	175.00	325.00	500.00	750.00

50 CASH

BRASS

Y#	Date	Mintage	VG	Fine	VF	XF
478	ND ca.1919	—	10.00	20.00	40.00	70.00

COPPER

Y#	Date	Mintage	VG	Fine	VF	XF
478a	ND ca.1919	—	20.00	40.00	80.00	125.00

5 CENTS

BRASS

Y#	Year	Date	VG	Fine	VF	XF
490	21	(1932)	125.00	175.00	250.00	350.00

COPPER-NICKEL

Y#	Year	Date	VG	Fine	VF	XF
485	12	(1923)	21.50	32.50	47.50	75.00

10 CENTS

COPPER-NICKEL
Reeded edge.

Y#	Year	Date	VG	Fine	VF	XF
486	12	(1923)	1.75	2.50	3.75	7.50

Unreeded edge.

Y#	Year	Date	VG	Fine	VF	XF
486.1	12	(1923)	2.50	4.00	6.50	12.50

20 CENTS

SILVER, 5.60 g

Y#	Year	Date	Fine	VF	XF	Unc
491	21	(1932)	3.00	5.00	8.00	20.00

Rev: Provincial Capitol.

Y#	Year	Date	Fine	VF	XF	Unc
493	38	(1949)	3.50	5.50	8.50	40.00

50 CENTS

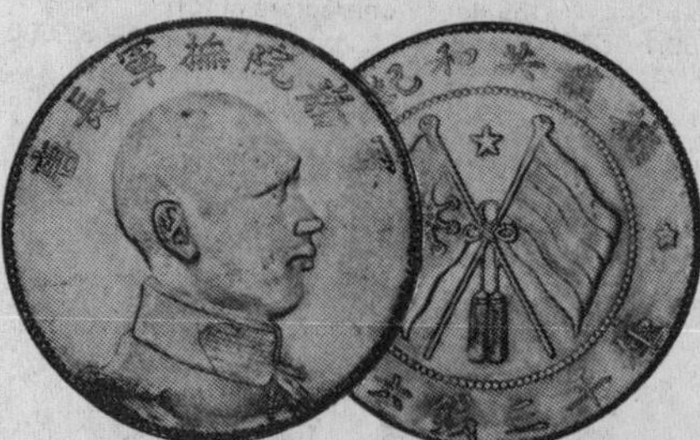

.850* SILVER, 13.10 g
Gen. T'ang Chi-yao

Y#	Date	Mintage	Fine	VF	XF	Unc
480	ND ca.1916	—	10.00	20.00	45.00	120.00

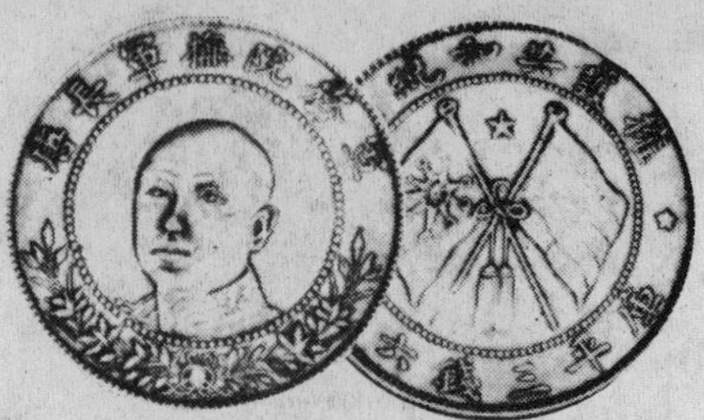

Gen. T'ang Chi-yao

Y#	Date	Mintage	Fine	VF	XF	Unc
479	ND ca.1917	—	7.50	12.00	17.50	35.00

Rev: Circle in center of flag at left.

Y#	Date	Mintage	Fine	VF	XF	Unc
479.1	ND ca.1917	—	7.50	12.00	17.50	35.00

.500* SILVER, 13.10 g

Y#	Year	Date	Fine	VF	XF	Unc
492	21	(1932)	5.00	8.00	10.00	15.00

5 DOLLARS

GOLD, uniface
Similar to 10 Dollars, K#1520.

Kann#	Date	Mintage	Fine	VF	XF	Unc
1521	ND(1917)	—	—	—	Rare	—

.750 GOLD, 4.50 g
Gen. T'ang Chi-yao
Rev: W/numeral 2 below flag tassels.

Y#	Date	Mintage	Fine	VF	XF	Unc
481	ND (1919)	*.060	200.00	400.00	600.00	1250.

Rev: W/o numeral 2 below flag tassels.

Y#	Date	Mintage	Fine	VF	XF	Unc
481.1	ND (1919)	I.A.	—	Reported, not confirmed		

Kann#	Date	Mintage	Fine	VF	XF	Unc
1529	ND(1925)	—	300.00	500.00	800.00	1300.

10 DOLLARS

GOLD, uniface

Kann#	Date	Mintage	Fine	VF	XF	Unc
1520	ND(1917)	—	—	—	Rare	—

.750 GOLD, 8.50 g
Gen. T'ang Chi-yao
Rev: W/numeral 1 below flag tassels.

Y#	Date	Mintage	Fine	VF	XF	Unc
482	ND (1919)	.900	250.00	500.00	800.00	1500.

Rev: W/o numeral 1 below flag tassels.

Y#	Date	Mintage	Fine	VF	XF	Unc
482.1	ND (1919)	I.A.	200.00	400.00	700.00	1250.

Kann#	Date	Mintage	Fine	VF	XF	Unc
1528	ND(1925)	—	300.00	600.00	800.00	1300.

YUNNAN-SZECHUAN

Yunnan-Sichuan

These two coins have a 2-character mint mark in the center of the obverse, indicating the provinces of Yunnan and Szechuan (Sichuan).

EMPIRE

10 CASH

COPPER

Y#	Date	Mintage	VG	Fine	VF	XF
10w	CD1906	—	20.00	40.00	60.00	110.00

20 CASH

COPPER

Y#	Date	Mintage	VG	Fine	VF	XF
11w	CD1906	—	100.00	150.00	200.00	250.00

CHINA-JAP. PUPPET STATES

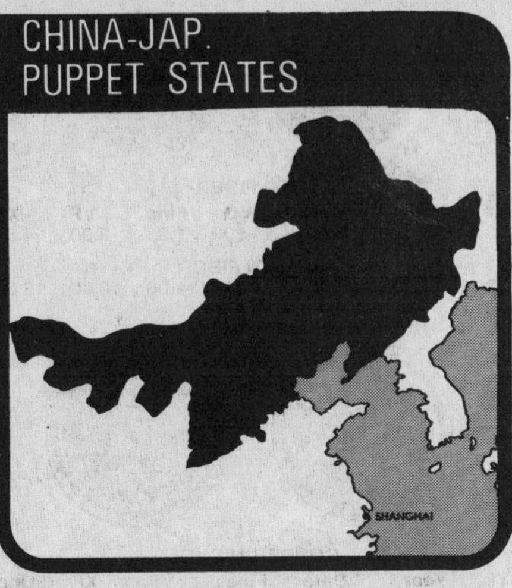

Shortly after World War I the greatest external threat to the territorial integrity of China was posed by Japan, which urgently needed room for an expanding population and raw materials for its industrial and military machines, and which recognized the necessity of controlling all of China if it was to realize its plan of dominating the rest of the Asiatic and South Sea countries. The Japanese had large investments in Manchuria (a name given by non-Chinese to the three northeastern provinces of China) which allowed them privileges that compromised Chinese sovereignty. The educated of China remained unreconciled to Japan's growing power in Manchuria, and the resultant friction occasioned a series of vexing incidents which Japan decided to circumvent by direct action. On the night of Sept. 18-19, 1931, with a contrived incident for an excuse, Japanese forces seized the city of Mukden (Shenyang), and within a few weeks completely demolished Chinese power north of the Great Wall.

In Feb. 1932, after the Japanese occupation of Manchuria, they set up Manchukuo as an independent republic. Jehol (Rehe) was occupied by the Japanese in 1933 and added to Manchukuo. Manchukuo was established as an empire in 1934 with the deposed Manchu emperor Hsuan T'ung (the late Henry Pu Yi) as the puppet emperor K'ang Te. Lacking the means to face the Japanese armies in the field, the Chinese could only trade space for time.

Not content with confining its control of China to the areas north of the Great Wall, the Japanese launched a major campaign in 1937, and by the fall of 1938 had occupied in addition to Manchuria the provinces of Hopei (Hebei) and Chahar, most of the port cities, and the major cities as far west as Hankow (Hankou), now part of Wuhan. In addition, they dominated or threatened the provinces of Suiyuan, Shansi (Shanxi) and Shantung (Shandong).

Still the Chinese did not yield. The struggle was prolonged until the advent of World War II, which brought about the defeat of Japan and the return of the puppet states to Chinese control.

As the victorious Japanese armies swept deeper into China, Japan established central banks under control of the Bank of Japan in the conquered provinces for the purpose of establishing control over banking and finance in the puppet states, and eventually in all of China. These included the Chi Tung Bank which had its main office in Tientsin (Tianjin) with branches in Peking (Beijing), Chinan (Jinan) and Tangshan, the Federal Reserve Bank of China with its main office in Peking (Beijing) and branches in 37 other cities; and the Hua Hsing Bank with its main office in Shanghai and two branches. The puppet states of Manchukuo, previously detailed in this introduction, and Mengchiang, which comprised a greater part of Inner Mongolia, were also major coin-issuing entities.

EAST HOPEI

AUTONOMOUS

Chi Tung Bank

The Chi Tung Bank was the banking institution of the "East Hopei Autonomous Government" established by the Japanese in 1936 to undermine the political position of China in the northwest provinces. It issued both coins and notes between 1937 and 1939 with a restraint uncharacteristic of the puppet banks of the China-Japanese puppet states.

5 LI

COPPER

Y#	Year	Date	Fine	VF	XF	Unc
516	26	(1937)	7.50	12.50	25.00	75.00

FEN

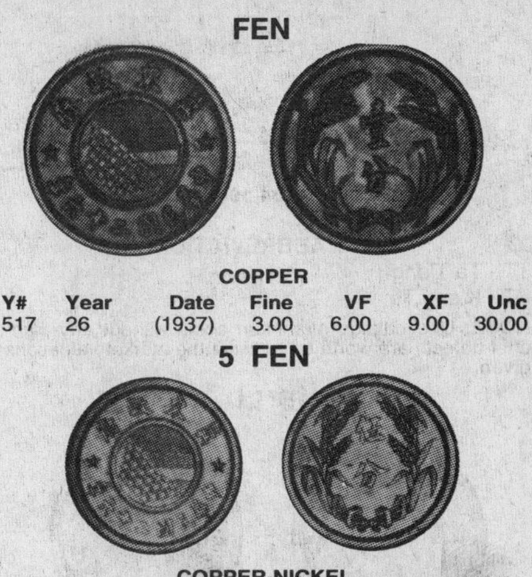

COPPER

Y#	Year	Date	Fine	VF	XF	Unc
517	26	(1937)	3.00	6.00	9.00	30.00

5 FEN

COPPER-NICKEL

Y#	Year	Date	Fine	VF	XF	Unc
518	26	(1937)	2.50	4.50	6.50	25.00

CHIAO

COPPER-NICKEL
Obv: T'ien Ning Pagoda in Peking.

Y#	Year	Date	Fine	VF	XF	Unc
519	26	(1937)	2.50	4.50	6.50	18.00

2 CHIAO

COPPER-NICKEL

Y#	Year	Date	Fine	VF	XF	Unc
520	26	(1937)	3.00	6.00	9.00	30.00

MANCHUKUO

The former Japanese puppet state of Manchukuo (largely Manchuria), comprising the northeastern Chinese provinces of Fengtien (Liaoning), Kirin (Jilin), Heilungkiang (Heilongjiang) and Jehol (Rehe), had an area of 503,143 sq. mi. (1,303,134 sq. km.) and a population of 43.3 million. Capital: Changchun, renamed Hsinking. The area is rich in fertile soil, timber and mineral resources, including coal, iron and gold.

Until the closing years of the 19th century when Chinese influence became predominant, Manchuria was chiefly a domain of the tribal Manchus and their Mongol allies. Coincident with the rise of Chinese influence, foreign imperialistic powers began to appreciate the value of the area to their expansionist philosophy. Japan, overpopulated and poor in resources, desired it as a source of raw materials and for increased living area. Russia wanted it as the eastern terminus of the Trans-Siberian railway that was to unite its Asian empire. The inevitable conflict of Japanese, Chinese and Russian interests required that one or more of the powers be eliminated. After eliminating Russia in 1904, Japan eliminated China on the night of Sept. 18, 1931, when, on the pretext of a contrived incident, it moved militarily to seize control of the Three Eastern Provinces. Early in 1932 Japan declared Manchuria independent by virtue of a voluntary separatist movement and established the state of Manchukuo. To give the puppet state an aura of legitimacy, the deposed emperor of the former Manchu dynasty was recalled from retirement and designated "chief executive ". The area was restored to China at the end of World War II.

RULERS

Ta T'ung, 1932-1934
K'ang Te, 1934-1945

The puppet emperor under the assumed name of K'ang Te was previously the last emperor of China (P'u-yi, or Hsuan T'ung, 1909-11).

MONETARY SYSTEM

10 Li = 1 Fen
10 Fen = 1 Chiao

IDENTIFICATION OF REIGN CHARACTERS

'Nien' Year   1932-1934   Ta T'ung

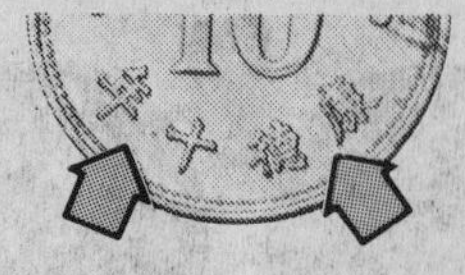

'Nien' Year 1934-1945 K'ang Te

DATE ABBREVIATIONS

TT - Ta T'ung
KT - K'ang Te

NOTE: Uncirculated aluminum coins without any planchet defects are worth up to twice the market valuations given.

5 LI

BRONZE

Y#	Year	Date	Fine	VF	XF	Unc
1	TT 2	(1933)	20.00	35.00	50.00	100.00
	TT 3	(1934)	4.00	9.00	15.00	30.00

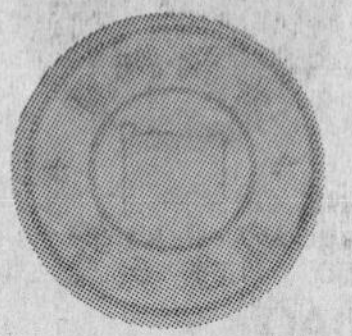
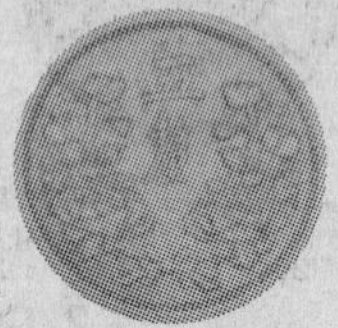

Y#	Year	Date	Fine	VF	XF	Unc
5	KT 1	(1934)	3.00	7.50	10.00	25.00
	KT 2	(1935)	3.00	7.50	10.00	25.00
	KT 3	(1936)	17.50	27.50	40.00	70.00
	KT 4	(1937)	4.00	10.00	12.50	27.50
	KT 6	(1939)	150.00	200.00	275.00	375.00

FEN

BRONZE

Y#	Year	Date	Fine	VF	XF	Unc
2	TT 2	(1933)	2.00	4.00	8.00	25.00
	TT 3	(1934)	1.50	3.00	5.00	20.00

Y#	Year	Date	Fine	VF	XF	Unc
6	KT 1	(1934)	1.00	3.00	6.00	15.00
	KT 2	(1935)	1.00	3.00	5.00	10.00
	KT 3	(1936)	1.00	3.00	5.00	10.00
	KT 4	(1937)	1.00	3.00	5.00	10.00
	KT 5	(1938)	1.00	3.00	5.00	10.00
	KT 6	(1939)	1.00	3.00	6.00	15.00

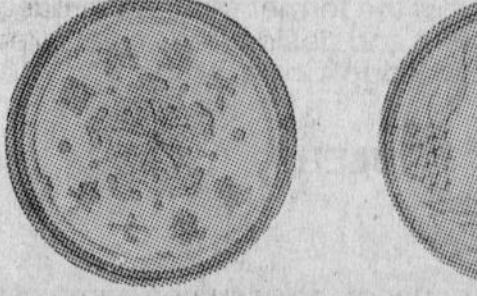

ALUMINUM

Y#	Year	Date	Fine	VF	XF	Unc
9	KT 6	(1939)	.40	.75	2.00	5.00
	KT 7	(1940)	.40	.75	2.00	5.00
	KT 8	(1941)	.40	.75	2.00	5.00
	KT 9	(1942)	.40	.75	2.00	5.00
	KT 10	(1943)	.40	.75	2.00	5.00

Y#	Year	Date	Fine	VF	XF	Unc
13	KT 10	(1943)	.75	2.00	5.00	10.00
	KT 11	(1944)	.75	2.00	5.00	10.00

RED FIBER

Y#	Year	Date	VG	Fine	VF	XF
13a	KT 12	(1945)	.50	1.25	3.00	4.50

BROWN FIBER

Y#	Year	Date	VG	Fine	VF	XF
13a.1	KT 12	(1945)	1.50	4.00	10.00	15.00

5 FEN

COPPER-NICKEL

Y#	Year	Date	Fine	VF	XF	Unc
3	TT 2	(1933)	.75	2.00	5.00	15.00
	TT 3	(1934)	.40	1.00	2.00	10.00

GREEK RIM BORDER VARIETIES

Narrow Design Wide Design

Y#	Year	Date	Fine	VF	XF	Unc
7	KT 1	(1934)	.60	1.50	3.00	6.00
	KT 2	(1935)	.60	1.50	3.00	6.00
	KT 3	(1936)	narrow border design			
			.60	1.50	3.00	6.00
	KT 3	(1936)	wide border design			
			1.25	3.00	6.00	12.00
	KT 4	(1937)	1.00	2.00	4.00	7.50
	KT 6	(1939)	1.00	2.00	4.00	7.50

ALUMINUM

Y#	Year	Date	Fine	VF	XF	Unc
11	KT 7	(1940)	.60	1.50	3.00	6.00
	KT 8	(1941)	.40	.75	2.00	4.00
	KT 9	(1942)	.40	.75	2.00	4.00
	KT 10	(1943)	.40	.75	2.00	4.00

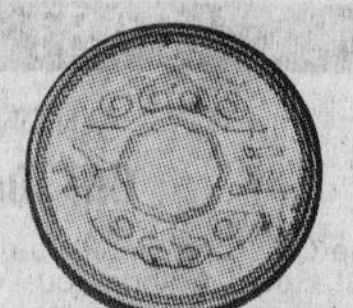

Y#	Year	Date	Fine	VF	XF	Unc
A13	KT 10	(1943)	1.00	2.50	5.00	12.50
	KT 11	(1944)	1.00	2.50	5.00	12.50

RED FIBER

Y#	Year	Date	VG	Fine	VF	XF
A13a						
	KT 11	(1944)	1.00	2.00	3.50	6.00
	KT 12	(1945)	—	—	Rare	—

BROWN FIBER

Y#	Year	Date	VG	Fine	VF	XF
A13a.1						
	KT 11	(1944)	4.00	10.00	15.00	20.00

CHIAO

(10 Fen)

COPPER-NICKEL

Y#	Year	Date	Fine	VF	XF	Unc
4	TT 2	(1933)	1.50	3.00	7.00	15.00
	TT 3	(1934)	.80	2.00	3.75	12.50

Y#	Year	Date	Fine	VF	XF	Unc
8	KT 1	(1934)	.80	2.00	3.00	7.50
	KT 2	(1935)	.80	2.00	3.00	7.50
	KT 5	(1938)	.80	2.00	3.00	7.50
	KT 6	(1939)	.80	2.00	3.00	7.50
	KT 6	(1939)	—	—	Proof	—

Y#	Year	Date	Fine	VF	XF	Unc
10	KT 7	(1940)	1.00	3.00	5.00	12.50

ALUMINUM

Y#	Year	Date	Fine	VF	XF	Unc
12	KT 7	(1940)	.80	2.00	3.00	7.50
	KT 8	(1941)	.80	2.00	3.00	7.50
	KT 9	(1942)	.80	2.00	3.00	7.50
	KT 10	(1943)	275.00	400.00	500.00	600.00

Y#	Year	Date	Fine	VF	XF	Unc
14	KT 10	(1943)	1.50	3.00	5.00	12.50

MENG CHIANG

As Japanese troops moved into North China in 1937, the political situation became fluid in several provinces bordering on Manchukuo, which were sometimes referred to as Inner Mongolia. On September 27, 1937, the Chanan Bank was established. As the situation became more settled the Japanese effected the merger of two local banks with the Bank of Chanan under a new title, Meng Chiang (Mongolian Borderlands or Mongol Territory) Bank. The Meng Chiang Bank was organized on November 27 and opened on December 1, 1937, with headquarters in Kalgan (Zhangjiakou) and branch offices in about a dozen locations throughout the region. Its notes were declared the exclusive currency for the area. The bank closed at the end of the war.

5 CHIAO

COPPER-NICKEL

Y#	Date	Mintage	Fine	VF	XF	Unc
521	Yr.27 (1938)					
		10.800	2.50	5.00	9.00	25.00

PROVISIONAL GOVT OF CHINA

In late 1937 the Japanese North China Expeditionary Army established the "Provisional Government of China" at Peking (Beijing).

FEDERAL RESERVE BANK

The Federal Reserve Bank of China was opened in 1938 by Japanese military authorities in Peking (Beijing). It was the puppet financial agency of the Japanese in northeast China. This puppet bank issued both coins and currency, but in modest amounts.

FEN

ALUMINUM

Y#	Year	Date	Fine	VF	XF	Unc
523	30	(1941)	.50	1.00	2.00	6.00
	31	(1942)	.50	1.00	2.00	6.00
	32	(1943)	3.00	6.00	10.00	30.00

5 FEN

ALUMINUM

Y#	Year	Date	Fine	VF	XF	Unc
524	30	(1941)	.75	2.00	4.00	10.00
	31	(1942)	.75	2.00	4.00	10.00
	32	(1943)	2.00	4.00	8.00	20.00

NOTE: The 5 Fen pieces were struck on both thick and thin planchets.

CHIAO

ALUMINUM

Y#	Year	Date	Fine	VF	XF	Unc
525	30	(1941)	.40	1.00	2.00	6.00
	31	(1942)	.40	1.00	2.00	6.00
	32	(1943)	1.50	3.00	6.00	15.00

NOTE: The 1 Chiao pieces were struck on both thick and thin planchets.

REFORMED GOVERNMENT REPUBLIC OF CHINA

On March 28, 1938 the Japanese Central China Expeditionary Army established the Reformed Government of the Republic of China at Nanking (Nanjing).

HUA HSING COMMERCIAL BANK

The Hua Hsing Commercial Bank was a financial agency created and established by the government of Japan and its puppet authorities in Shanghai in May 1939. Notes and coins were issued until sometime in 1941, with the quantities restricted by Chinese aversion to accepting them.

FEN

BRONZE

Y#	Year	Date	Fine	VF	XF	Unc
A522	29	(1940)	100.00	200.00	300.00	400.00

10 FEN

COPPER-NICKEL

Y#	Year	Date	Fine	VF	XF	Unc
522	29	(1940)	1.00	1.50	2.00	3.50

CHINA/Peoples Republic

The Peoples Republic of China, located in eastern Asia, has an area of 3,691,514 sq. mi. (9,596,960 sq. km.) (including Manchuria and Tibet) and a population of *1.11 billion. Capital: Peking (Beijing). The economy is based on agriculture, mining, and manufacturing. Textiles, clothing, metal ores, tea and rice are exported.

China's ancient civilization began in east-central Henan's Huayang county, 2800-2300 B.C. The warring feudal states comprising early China were first united under Emperor Ch'in Shih (246-210 B.C.) who gave China its name and first central government. Subsequent dynasties alternated brilliant cultural achievements with internal disorder until the Empire was brought down by the revolution of 1911, and the Republic of China installed in its place. Chinese culture attained a pre-eminence in art, literature and philosophy, but a traditional backwardness in industry and administration ill prepared China for the demands of 19th century Western expansionism which exposed it to military and political humiliations, and mandated a drastic revision of political practice in order to secure an accommodation with the modern world.

The Republic of 1911 barely survived the stress of World War I, and was subsequently all but shattered by the rise of nationalism and the emergence of the Chinese Communist movement. Moscow, which practiced a policy of cooperation between Communists and other parties in movements for national liberation, sought to establish an entente between the Chinese Communist Party and the Kuomintang ('National Peoples Party') of Sun Yat-sen. The ensuing cooperation was based on little more than the hope each had of using the other.

An increasingly uneasy association between the Kuomintang and the Chinese Communist Party developed and continued until April 12, 1927, when Chiang Kai-shek, Sun Yat-sen's political heir, instituted a bloody purge to stamp out the Communists within the Kuomintang and the government and virtually paralyzed their ranks throughout China. Some time after the mid-1927 purges, the Chinese Communist Party turned to armed force to resist Chiang Kai-shek and during the period of 1930-34 acquired control over large parts of Kiangsi (-Jiangxi), Fukien (Fujian), Hunan and Hupeh (Hubei). The Nationalist Nanking government responded with a series of campaigns against the soviet power bases and, by October of 1934, succeeded in driving the remnants of the Communist army to a refuge in Shensi (Shaanxi) Province. There the Communists reorganized under the leadership of Mao Tse-tung, defeated the Nationalist forces, and on Sept. 21, 1949, established the Peoples Republic of China. Thereafter relations between Russia and Communist China steadily deteriorated until 1958, when China emerged as an independent center of Communist power.

MONETARY SYSTEM

Before 1949

10 Cash (Wen) = 1 Cent (Fen)

100 Cents (Fen) = 1 Dollar (Yuan)

SOVIET PERIOD

Prior to 1949, the Peoples Republic of China did not exist as such, but the Communists did control areas known as Soviets. Most of the Soviets were established on the borders of two or more provinces and were named according to the provinces involved. Thus there were such soviets as the Kiangsi-Hunan Soviet, the HunanHupeh-Kiangsi Soviet, the Hupeh-Honan-Anhwei Soviet and others. In 1931 some of the soviets in the southern Kiangsi area were consolidated into the Chinese Soviet Republic, which lasted until the Long March of 1934.

CHINESE SOVIET REPUBLIC

In November, 1931, the first congress of the Chinese Soviet proclaimed and established the "Chinese Soviet Republic" under the Chairmanship of Mao Tse-Tung.

CENT

COPPER

Y#	Date	Mintage	VG	Fine	VF	XF
506	ND	—	10.00	20.00	30.00	40.00

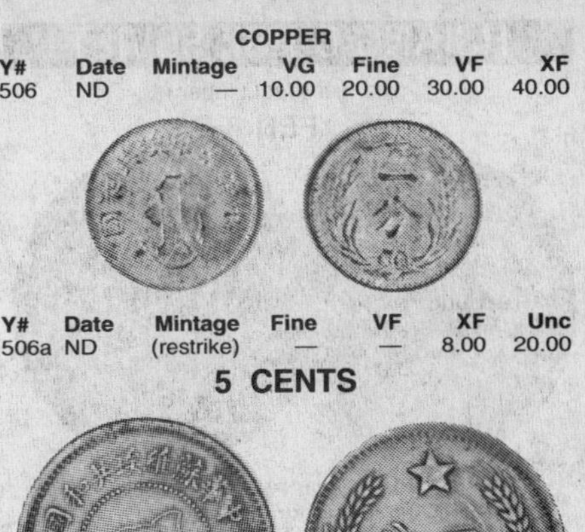

Y#	Date	Mintage	Fine	VF	XF	Unc
506a	ND	(restrike)	—	—	8.00	20.00

5 CENTS

COPPER

Plain edge.

Y#	Date	Mintage	VG	Fine	VF	XF
507	ND	—	20.00	30.00	50.00	70.00
	Reeded edge.					
507.1	ND	—	20.00	30.00	50.00	70.00

NOTE: Varieties exist.

Y#	Date	Mintage	Fine	VF	XF	Unc
507a	ND	(restrike)	—	—	10.00	25.00

20 CENTS

SILVER, 5.50 g

Y#	Date	Mintage	VG	Fine	VF	XF
508	1932	—	15.00	25.00	40.00	60.00
	1933	—	10.00	20.00	30.00	50.00

NOTE: Many minor varieties exist.

DOLLAR

SILVER

Obv: Crude facing portrait of Lenin.

Rev: Hammer, sickle and value within wreath.

KM#	Date	Mintage	VG	Fine	VF	XF
5	1931	—	—	—	Rare	—

NOTE: For previously listed KM#6 refer to Shensi-North Soviet, KM#2.

HSIANG-O-HSI SOVIET

(Kiangsi-West Hupeh)

FEN

COPPER
Obv. leg. around large star.
Rev: Denomination within wreath, leg. around.

KM#	Date	Mintage	VG	Fine	VF	XF
1	ND(1931)	—	—	—	Rare	—

HUNAN SOVIET

DOLLAR

SILVER
Obv. leg: ***Hu Nan Sheng Su Wei Ai Cheng Fu.***

KM#	Date	Mintage	VG	Fine	VF	XF
1	1931	—	1000.	1500.	2000.	—

HUPEH-HONAN-ANHWEI SOVIET

The Hupeh-Honan Anhwei Soviet District was a large revolutionary base. It was formerly made up of three separate special districts: East Hupeh, South Honan and West Anhwei which united until after 1930. Between 1931 and 1932 this Bank has issued a quantity of copper and silver coins as well as banknotes.

DOLLAR

SILVER, 26.80 g
Rev. lower leg: Crude Russian.

Y#	Date	Mintage	VG	Fine	VF	XF
503	1932	—	250.00	575.00	750.00	1000.

27.20 g

Y#	Date	Mintage	VG	Fine	VF	XF
504	1932	—	175.00	275.00	400.00	700.00

NOTE: Attribution of Y#503 to the Hupeh-Honan-Anhwei Soviet is not definite.

MIN-CHE-KAN SOVIET

(Fukien-Chekiang-Kiangsi)

DOLLAR

SILVER
Obv: Profile portrait of Lenin.

KM#	Date	Mintage	VG	Fine	VF	XF
1	1934	—	—	—	—	—

NOTE: Authenticity in doubt.

Obv. leg: 15 characters around globe w/hammer and sickle.

KM#	Date	Mintage	VG	Fine	VF	XF
2	1934	—	—	—	—	—

NOTE: Authenticity in doubt.

NORTH-SHENSI SOVIET

DOLLAR

SILVER
Rev: Value in plain field, yr.5 at bottom.

KM#	Date	Year	VG	Fine	VF	XF
1.1	(1935)	5	1750.	2250.	2850.	—

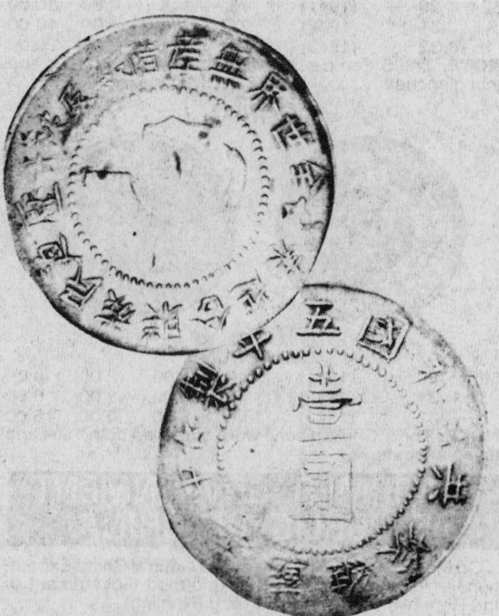

Obv: Star at left, slightly lower.
Rev. leg: Rotated w/yr.5 at top.

KM#	Date	Year	VG	Fine	VF	XF
1.2	(1935)	5	1750.	2250.	2850.	—

Rev: Value within wheat stalks.

KM#	Date	Year	VG	Fine	VF	XF
2	(1935)	5	2500.	3000.	3500.	—

NOTE: Date is given in the 5th year of the Chinese Soviet Republic. They were issued after the "Long March"

P'ING CHIANG COUNTY SOVIET

DOLLAR

SILVER
Obv. leg. 8 characters: *P'ing Chiang. . . . .*

KM#	Date	Mintage	VG	Fine	VF	XF
1	1931	—	—	—	Rare	—

SZECHUAN-SHENSI SOVIET

The Szechuan-Shensi Soviet District was founded in 1933. Within two years and three months from January, 1933 to March, 1935, this Soviet District had issued quite a quantity of banknotes, copper and silver coins. These issues circulated rather popularly throughout the central district.

200 CASH

COPPER, 37mm

Y#	Date	Mintage	Good	VG	Fine	VF
510	1933	—	25.00	50.00	80.00	140.00

34mm
Rev: Small 200 at center.

Y#	Date	Mintage	Good	VG	Fine	VF
510.1	1933	—	25.00	50.00	80.00	140.00

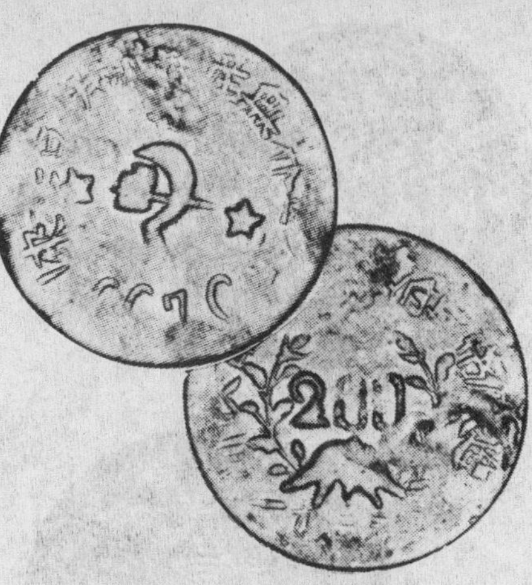

Rev: Large 200 at center.

Y#	Date	Mintage	Good	VG	Fine	VF
510.2	1933	—	25.00	50.00	80.00	140.00

Rev: Square O's in 2OO at center.

Y#	Date	Mintage	Good	VG	Fine	VF
510.3	1933	—	30.00	60.00	100.00	175.00

Obv: Solid hammer and sickle reversed.
Rev: 200 retrograde at center.

Y#	Date	Mintage	Good	VG	Fine	VF
510.4	1933	—	35.00	70.00	115.00	200.00

Obv: Shaded hammer and sickle reversed.

Y#	Date	Mintage	Good	VG	Fine	VF
510.5	1933	—	30.00	60.00	100.00	175.00

Obv: Date w/closed 3 and backwards 4.

Y#	Date	Mintage	VG	Fine	VF	XF
511	1934	—	22.50	45.00	75.00	135.00

Obv: Date w/open 3 and backwards 4.

Y#	Date	Mintage	VG	Fine	VF	XF
511.1	1934	—	22.50	45.00	75.00	135.00

Obv: Date w/4 corrected.

Y#	Date	Mintage	VG	Fine	VF	XF
511.2	1934	—	22.50	45.00	75.00	135.00

Obv: Date w/4 corrected.

Y#	Date	Mintage	Fine	VF	XF	Unc
511a	1934	(restrike)	—	—	12.50	22.50

NOTE: Many varieties of 200 Cash pieces exist. Well struck, usually found in choice condition. Unlisted varieties do not carry a premium.

500 CASH

COPPER, 35mm.
Obv: Small stars flanking date.

Y#	Date	Mintage	VG	Fine	VF	XF
512	1934	—	75.00	100.00	175.00	275.00

32.5mm
Obv: Large stars flanking date, hammer handle across lower leg of star.

Y#	Date	Mintage	VG	Fine	VF	XF
512.1	1934	—	50.00	100.00	160.00	250.00

33-34mm
Obv: Hammer handle extends between right legs of star.

Y#	Date	Mintage	VG	Fine	VF	XF
512.2	1934	—	50.00	100.00	150.00	225.00

NOTE: Many varieties of 500 Cash pieces exist. Unlisted varieties do not carry a premium.

DOLLAR

SILVER, 26.30 g
Obv: Similar to Y#513.1.
Rev: Large decorative solid stars.

Y#	Date	Mintage	VG	Fine	VF	XF
513	1934	—	125.00	225.00	300.00	450.00

Rev: Large solid stars.

Y#	Date	Mintage	VG	Fine	VF	XF
513.5	1934	—	100.00	200.00	275.00	400.00

Rev: Medium solid stars.

Y#	Date	Mintage	VG	Fine	VF	XF
513.1	1934	—	100.00	175.00	250.00	360.00

Rev: Small solid stars.

Y#	Date	Mintage	VG	Fine	VF	XF
513.2	1933	—	—	—	Rare	—
	1934	—	100.00	175.00	250.00	360.00

Rev: Outlined stars.

Y#	Date	Mintage	VG	Fine	VF	XF
513.3	1934	—	100.00	200.00	275.00	375.00

Obv: Similar to Y#513.1.
Rev: Pentagram stars

Y#	Date	Mintage	VG	Fine	VF	XF
513.4	1934	—	75.00	150.00	225.00	325.00

NOTE: Many minor varieties exist.

COINAGE OF UNCERTAIN ORIGIN

DOLLAR

SILVER, 26.40 g
c/m: 3 Chinese characters in rectangular box, meaning *SOVIET* on obv. Y#329.

Kann#	Date	Mintage	VG	Fine	VF	XF
650k	ND	—	125.00	200.00	325.00	600.00

NOTE: For previously listed Y#501 and Y#502 refer to Min-Che-Kan Soviet KM#1 and Hunan Soviet KM#1.

WAN-HSI-PEI SOVIET

(Northwest Anhwei)

50 CASH

COPPER
Obv: Legend around globe w/hammer and sickle.
Rev: Value in star within wreath all within leg.

KM#	Date	Mintage	VG	Fine	VF	XF
1	ND(1931-32)	—	—	—	Rare	—

Rev: Value in circle, Chinese leg. above, Western leg. below.

KM#	Date	Mintage	VG	Fine	VF	XF
2	ND(1931-32)	—	—	—	Rare	—

PEOPLES REPUBLIC

MONETARY SYSTEM

10 Fen (Cents) = 1 Jiao
10 Jiao = 1 Renminbi Yuan

MINT MARKS

(b) - Beijing (Peking)
(s) - Shanghai
(y) - Shenyang (Mukden)

FEN

ALUMINUM

Y#	Date	Mintage	Fine	VF	XF	Unc
1	1955	—	.20	.50	1.50	5.00
	1956	—	.40	1.00	2.50	7.50
	1957	—	.60	1.50	3.50	10.00
	1958	—	.10	.25	.75	2.50
	1959	—	.10	.25	.75	2.50
	1961	—	.10	.25	.75	2.50
	1963	—	.10	.25	.50	1.50
	1964	—	.10	.25	.50	1.00
	1971	—	.10	.25	.50	1.00
	1972	—	.10	.25	.50	1.00
	1973	—	.10	.25	.50	1.50
	1974	—	.10	.25	.50	1.00
	1975	.500	.10	.25	.50	1.00
	1976	—	—	.10	.25	.50
	1977	—	—	.10	.25	.50

Y#	Date	Mintage	Fine	VF	XF	Unc
1	1978	—	—	.10	.25	.50
	1979	—	—	.10	.25	.50
	1980	—	—	.10	.25	.50
	1980	—	—	—	Proof	1.00
	1981	—	—	.10	.25	.50
	1981	—	—	—	Proof	1.00
	1982	—	—	.10	.25	.50
	1982	—	—	—	Proof	1.00
	1983	—	—	—	.10	.25
	1983	2.412	—	—	Proof	1.00
	1984	—	—	—	.10	.25
	1984	3.283	—	—	Proof	1.00
	1985	—	—	—	.10	.25
	1985	—	—	—	Proof	1.00
	1986	—	—	—	.10	.25
	1986	—	—	—	Proof	1.00
	1987	—	—	—	.10	.25
	1991	—	—	—	.10	.25

2 FEN

ALUMINUM

Y#	Date	Mintage	Fine	VF	XF	Unc
2	1956	—	.10	.25	.75	1.50
	1959	—	.20	.50	1.00	4.00
	1960	—	.20	.50	1.00	4.00
	1961	—	.10	.25	.75	1.50
	1962	—	.10	.25	.75	1.50
	1963	—	.10	.25	.75	1.50
	1964	—	.10	.25	.50	1.25
	1974	—	.10	.25	.50	1.50
	1975	—	.10	.25	.50	1.00
	1976	—	.10	.25	.50	1.00
	1977	.360	.10	.25	.50	.75
	1978	—	.10	.20	.40	.60
	1979	—	.10	.20	.40	.60
	1980	—	.10	.20	.40	.60
	1980	—	—	—	Proof	1.00
	1981	—	.10	.20	.40	.60
	1981	—	—	—	Proof	1.00
	1982	—	.10	.20	.40	.60
	1982	—	—	—	Proof	1.00
	1983	—	—	.10	.20	.35
	1983	1.790	—	—	Proof	1.00
	1984	—	—	.10	.20	.35
	1984	1.963	—	—	Proof	1.00
	1985	—	—	.10	.20	.35
	1985	—	—	—	Proof	1.00
	1986	—	—	.15	.35	.75
	1986	—	—	—	Proof	1.00
	1987	—	—	.10	.20	.35
	1988	—	—	.10	.20	.35
	1989	—	—	.10	.20	.35
	1990	—	—	.10	.20	.35

5 FEN

ALUMINUM

Y#	Date	Mintage	Fine	VF	XF	Unc
3	1955	—	.30	.75	2.00	10.00
	1956	—	.15	.35	.75	2.00
	1957	—	.15	.35	.75	2.50
	1974	—	.15	.25	.50	1.50
	1975	—	.15	.25	.50	1.50
	1976	.350	.15	.25	.50	.75
	1979	—	—	—	—	2.00
	1980	—	.15	.25	.50	.75
	1980	—	—	—	Proof	1.00
	1981	—	.15	.25	.50	.75
	1981	—	—	—	Proof	1.00
	1982	—	.15	.25	.50	.75
	1982	—	—	—	Proof	1.00
	1983	—	—	.15	.25	.40
	1983	.484	—	—	Proof	1.00
	1984	—	—	.15	.25	.40
	1984	.600	—	—	Proof	1.00
	1985	—	—	.15	.25	.40
	1985	—	—	—	Proof	1.00
	1986	—	—	.15	.25	.40
	1986	—	—	—	Proof	1.00
	1987	—	—	.15	.25	.40
	1988	—	—	.15	.25	.40
	1989	—	—	.15	.25	.40
	1990	—	—	.15	.25	.40
	1992	—	—	.15	.25	.40

JIAO

COPPER-ZINC

Y#	Date	Mintage	Fine	VF	XF	Unc
24	1980	—	—	—	—	.50
(23)	1980	—	—	—	Proof	1.00
	1981	—	—	—	—	.50
	1981	—	—	—	Proof	1.00
	1982	—	—	—	Proof	1.00
	1983	3.100	—	—	Proof	1.00
	1984	3.500	—	—	Proof	1.00
	1985	—	—	—	Proof	1.00
	1986	—	—	—	Proof	1.00

BRASS

6th National Games - Gymnast

Y#	Date	Mintage	Fine	VF	XF	Unc
148	1987	—	—	—	1.00	2.00

6th National Games - Soccer

Y#	Date	Mintage	Fine	VF	XF	Unc
149	1987	—	—	—	1.00	2.00

6th National Games - Volleyball

Y#	Date	Mintage	Fine	VF	XF	Unc
150	1987	—	—	—	1.00	2.00

ALUMINUM

Y#	Date	Mintage	Fine	VF	XF	Unc
328	1991	—	—	—	—	.50
	1992	—	—	—	—	.50
	1993	—	—	—	—	.50

2 JIAO

COPPER-ZINC

Y#	Date	Mintage	Fine	VF	XF	Unc
25	1980	—	—	—	—	.60
(24)	1980	—	—	—	Proof	1.25
	1981	—	—	—	—	.60
	1981	—	—	—	Proof	1.25
	1982	—	—	—	Proof	1.25
	1983	4.200	—	—	Proof	1.25
	1984	2.500	—	—	Proof	1.25
	1985	—	—	—	Proof	1.25
	1986	—	—	—	Proof	1.25

5 JIAO

COPPER-ZINC

Y#	Date	Mintage	Fine	VF	XF	Unc
26	1980	—	—	—	—	.75
(25)	1980	—	—	—	Proof	1.50
	1981	—	—	—	—	.75

Y#	Date	Mintage	Fine	VF	XF	Unc
(25)	1981	—	—	—	Proof	1.50
	1982	—	—	—	Proof	1.50
	1983	3.000	—	—	Proof	1.50
	1984	3.500	—	—	Proof	1.50
	1985	—	—	—	Proof	1.50
	1986	—	—	—	Proof	1.50

2.2000 g, .900 SILVER, .0637 oz ASW

Marco Polo

Y#	Date	Mintage	VF	XF	Unc
53	1983	7,000	—	Proof	125.00

BRASS

Y#	Date	Mintage	Fine	VF	XF	Unc
329	1991	—	—	—	—	1.00
	1992	—	—	—	—	1.00
	1993	—	—	—	—	1.00

YUAN

COPPER-NICKEL

Y#	Date	Mintage	Fine	VF	XF	Unc
27	1980	—	—	—	—	2.00
(26)	1980	—	—	—	Proof	3.00
	1981	—	—	—	—	2.00
	1981	—	—	—	Proof	3.00
	1982	—	—	—	Proof	3.00
	1983	3.100	—	—	Proof	3.00
	1984	4.100	—	—	Proof	3.00
	1985	—	—	—	—	2.00
	1985	—	—	—	Proof	3.00
	1986	—	—	—	Proof	3.00

COPPER

1980 Olympics - Archery

Y#	Date	Mintage	VF	XF	Unc
10 (9)	1980	.026	—	Proof	5.00

1980 Olympics - Wrestling

Y#	Date	Mintage	VF	XF	Unc
11 (10)	1980	.026	—	Proof	5.00

1980 Olympics - Equestrian

Obv: Similar to Y#14.

Y#	Date	Mintage	VF	XF	Unc
12 (11)	1980	.026	—	Proof	5.00

1980 Olympics - Soccer
Obv: Similar to Y#14.

Y#	Date	Mintage	VF	XF	Unc
13 (12)	1980	.026	—	Proof	5.00

1980 Olympics - Alpine Skiing

Y#	Date	Mintage	VF	XF	Unc
14 (13)	1980	.029	—	Proof	5.00

1980 Olympics - Speed Skating

Y#	Date	Mintage	VF	XF	Unc
15 (14)	1980	.029	—	Proof	5.00

1980 Olympics - Figure Skating

Y#	Date	Mintage	VF	XF	Unc
16 (15)	1980	.029	—	Proof	5.00

1980 Olympics - Biathlon

Y#	Date	Mintage	VF	XF	Unc
17 (16)	1980	.029	—	Proof	5.00

World Cup Soccer

Y#	Date	Mintage	VF	XF	Unc
34	1982	—	—	—	6.00
	1982	.040	—	Proof	7.50

Panda

Y#	Date	Mintage	VF	XF	Unc
58	1983	.030	—	Proof	10.00
	1984	.030	—	Proof	10.00

COPPER-NICKEL
35th Anniversary of Peoples Republic

Y#	Date	Mintage	VF	XF	Unc
85	1984	—	—	—	5.00
	1984	—	—	Proof	6.00

35th Anniversary of Peoples Republic

Y#	Date	Mintage	VF	XF	Unc
86	1984	—	—	—	5.00
	1984	—	—	Proof	6.00

35th Anniversary of Peoples Republic

Y#	Date	Mintage	VF	XF	Unc
87	1984	—	—	—	5.00
	1984	—	—	Proof	6.00

20th Anniversary of Tibet Autonomous Region

Y#	Date	Mintage	VF	XF	Unc
96	1985	*10.000	—	4.00	7.50
	1985	.010	—	Proof	9.00

30th Anniversary Sinkiang Autonomous Region

Y#	Date	Mintage	VF	XF	Unc
109	1985	*10.000	—	2.00	5.50
	1985	.010	—	Proof	7.50

Year of Peace

Y#	Date	Mintage	VF	XF	Unc
151	1986	—	—	—	4.00

40th Anniversary of Mongolian Autonomous Region

Y#	Date	Mintage	VF	XF	Unc
140	1987	—	—	2.00	6.50

30th Anniversary of Kwangsi Autonomous Region

Y#	Date	Mintage	VF	XF	Unc
198	1988	—	—	—	6.50

30th Anniversary of Ninghsia Autonomous Region

Y#	Date	Mintage	VF	XF	Unc
211	1988	—	—	—	6.50

40th Anniversary of Peoples Bank

Y#	Date	Mintage	VF	XF	Unc
212	1988	—	—	4.00	8.50

NICKEL CLAD STEEL
40th Anniversary of the Peoples Republic

Y#	Date	Mintage	VF	XF	Unc
204	1989	—	—	—	3.50

XI Asian Games - Sword Dancer

Y#	Date	Mintage	VF	XF	Unc
264	1990	—	—	—	5.00

XI Asian Games - Female Archer

Y#	Date	Mintage	VF	XF	Unc
265	1990	—	—	—	5.00

Planting Trees Festival - Portrait

Y#	Date	Mintage	VF	XF	Unc
279	1991	—	—	—	2.50

Planting Trees Festival - Globe

Y#	Date	Mintage	VF	XF	Unc
280	1991	—	—	—	2.50

Planting Trees Festival - Seedling

Y#	Date	Mintage	VF	XF	Unc
281	1991	—	—	—	2.50

NICKEL PLATED STEEL
1st Meeting of Chinese Communist Party - House in Shanghai

Y#	Date	Mintage	VF	XF	Unc
284	1991	—	—	—	2.50

Party Meeting During Long March in 1935 - House in Tsunyi, Kweichow Province

Y#	Date	Mintage	VF	XF	Unc
285	1991	—	—	—	2.50

1978 Party Conference - Tian An Men Square

Y#	Date	Mintage	VF	XF	Unc
286	1991	—	—	—	2.50

Women's Soccer Championship - Goalie

Y#	Date	Mintage	VF	XF	Unc
316	1991	—	—	—	2.50

Women's Soccer Championship - Player

Y#	Date	Mintage	VF	XF	Unc
317	1991	—	—	—	2.50

NICKEL CLAD STEEL

Y#	Date	Mintage	VF	XF	Unc
330	1991	—	—	—	2.50

Constitution

Y#	Date	Mintage	VF	XF	Unc
364	1992	—	—	—	2.50

Soong Qingling - Mme. Chiang

Y#	Date	Mintage	VF	XF	Unc
365	1993	—	—	—	2.50

3 YUAN

15.0000 g, .900 SILVER, .4340 oz ASW
Ancient Chinese Coins

Y#	Date	Mintage	VF	XF	Unc
362	1992	*.020	—	Proof	35.00

Ancient Chinese Paper

Y#	Date	Mintage	VF	XF	Unc
363	1992	*.020	—	Proof	35.00

5 YUAN

22.2200 g, .900 SILVER, .6430 oz ASW
Marco Polo

Y#	Date	Mintage	VF	XF	Unc
54	1983	6,100	—	Proof	75.00

8.4500 g, .800 SILVER, .2173 oz ASW
1984 Summer and Winter Olympics - High Jumper

Y#	Date	Mintage	VF	XF	Unc
61	1984	.010	—	Proof	40.00

22.2200 g, .900 SILVER, .6430 oz ASW
Soldier Statues from Archeological Discovery

Y#	Date	Mintage	VF	XF	Unc
68	1984	.014	—	Proof	50.00

Soldier Statues from Archeological Discovery

Y#	Date	Mintage	VF	XF	Unc
69	1984	.014	—	Proof	50.00

Soldier Statues from Archeological Discovery

Y#	Date	Mintage	VF	XF	Unc
70	1984	.014	—	Proof	50.00

Soldier Statues from Archeological Discovery

Y#	Date	Mintage	VF	XF	Unc
71	1984	.014	—	Proof	50.00

Founders of Chinese Culture - Lao-Tse

Y#	Date	Mintage	VF	XF	Unc
90	1985	8,175	—	Proof	55.00

Founders of Chinese Culture - Qu Yuan

Y#	Date	Mintage	VF	XF	Unc
91	1985	8,175	—	Proof	55.00

Founders of Chinese Culture - Sun Wu

Y#	Date	Mintage	VF	XF	Unc
92	1985	8,175	—	Proof	55.00

Founders of Chinese Culture
Chen Sheng and Wu Guang

Y#	Date	Mintage	VF	XF	Unc
93	1985	8,175	—	Proof	55.00

Wildlife - Giant Panda

Y#	Date	Mintage	VF	XF	Unc
106	1986	*.020	—	—	35.00
	1986	.020	—	Proof	50.00

18.6100 g, .925 SILVER, .5535 oz ASW
Soccer

Y#	Date	Mintage	VF	XF	Unc
112	1986	8,500	—	Proof	40.00

22.2200 g, .900 SILVER, .6367 oz ASW
Chinese Culture - Cai Lun - Paper Making

Y#	Date	Mintage	VF	XF	Unc
113	1986	9,675	—	Proof	50.00

Chinese Culture - Zhang Heng - Chemist

Y#	Date	Mintage	VF	XF	Unc
114	1986	9,675	—	Proof	50.00

Chinese Culture - Zu Chon Zhi - Mathematician

Y#	Date	Mintage	VF	XF	Unc
115	1986	9,675	—	Proof	50.00

Chinese Culture - Si Ma Qian - Historian

Y#	Date	Mintage	VF	XF	Unc
116	1986	9,675	—	Proof	50.00

18.6100 g, .925 SILVER, .5535 oz ASW
Year of Peace

Y#	Date	Mintage	VF	XF	Unc
119	1986	1,350	—	Proof	125.00

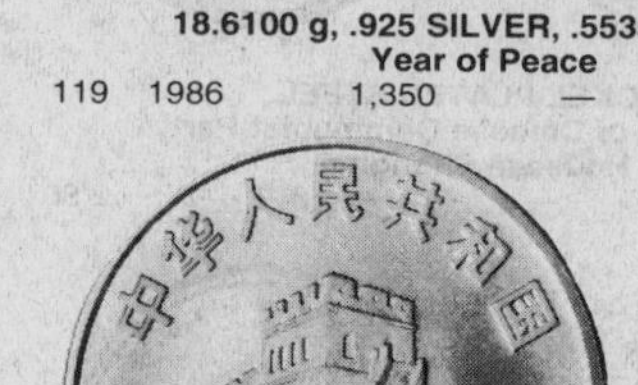

22.2200 g, .900 SILVER, .6367 oz ASW
Great Wall - The Ship Empress of China

Y#	Date	Mintage	VF	XF	Unc
132	1986	.062	—	—	17.50

18.6100 g, .925 SILVER, .5535 oz ASW
Soccer - 2 Players

Y#	Date	Mintage	VF	XF	Unc
197	1986	4,000	—	Proof	35.00

16.8300 g, .800 SILVER, .4328 oz ASW

Y#	Date	Mintage	VF	XF	Unc
197a	1986	1,000	—	—	130.00

31.4700 g, .900 SILVER, .9107 oz ASW
1988 Winter Olympics - Downhill Skier

Y#	Date	Mintage	VF	XF	Unc
129	1988	.011	—	Proof	35.00

1988 Summer Olympics - Woman Hurdler

Y#	Date	Mintage	VF	XF	Unc
130	1988	.015	—	Proof	35.00

Poet Li Bai

Y#	Date	Mintage	VF	XF	Unc
135	1987	4,000	—	Proof	50.00

Poet Du Fu

Y#	Date	Mintage	VF	XF	Unc
136	1987	4,000	—	Proof	50.00

Bridge Builder Li Chun

Y#	Date	Mintage	VF	XF	Unc
137	1987	4,000	—	Proof	50.00

Princess Cheng Wen and Song Zuan Gan Bu

Y#	Date	Mintage	VF	XF	Unc
138	1987	4,000	—	Proof	50.00

22.2200 g, .900 SILVER, .6430 oz ASW
Military Hero of Song Dynasty - Yue Fei

Y#	Date	Mintage	VF	XF	Unc
160	1988	.013	—	Proof	50.00

Bi Sheng - Inventor of Movable-type Printing in China

Y#	Date	Mintage	VF	XF	Unc
161	1988	.014	—	Proof	50.00

Su Shi - Song Dynasty Poet

Y#	Date	Mintage	VF	XF	Unc
162	1988	9,500	—	Proof	50.00

Li Qing-zhao - Poetess of Song Dynasty

Y#	Date	Mintage	VF	XF	Unc
163	1988	.013	—	Proof	50.00

27.0000 g, .900 SILVER, .7812 oz ASW
Olympics - Sailboat Racing

Y#	Date	Mintage	VF	XF	Unc
171	1988	.020	—	Proof	35.00

Olympics - Fencing

Y#	Date	Mintage	VF	XF	Unc
172	1988	.020	—	Proof	35.00

22.2200 g, .900 SILVER, .6431 oz ASW
Kublai Khan - Emperor

Y#	Date	Mintage	VF	XF	Unc
213	1989	.010	—	Proof	50.00

Guan Hanqing - Playwright

Y#	Date	Mintage	VF	XF	Unc
214	1989	8,000	—	Proof	50.00

Guo Shousing - Scientist

Y#	Date	Mintage	VF	XF	Unc
215	1989	8,500	—	Proof	50.00

Huang Daopo - Inventor of Water Wheel

Y#	Date	Mintage	VF	XF	Unc
216	1989	8,000	—	Proof	50.00

Save the Children Fund

Y#	Date	Mintage	VF	XF	Unc
230	1989	*.025	—	Proof	60.00

27.0000 g, .925 SILVER, .8030 oz ASW
Soccer - 2 Players

Y#	Date	Mintage	VF	XF	Unc
243	1989	*.030	—	Proof	40.00

15.0000 g, .900 SILVER, .4341 oz ASW
Bronze Archaeological Finds - Elephant Pitcher

Y#	Date	Mintage	VF	XF	Unc
257	1990	5,000	—	Proof	45.00

Bronze Archaeological Finds - Mythical Creature

Y#	Date	Mintage	VF	XF	Unc
258	1990	5,000	—	Proof	45.00

Bronze Archaeological Finds - Rhinoceros

Y#	Date	Mintage	VF	XF	Unc
259	1990	5,000	—	Proof	45.00

Bronze Archaeological Finds - Leopard

Y#	Date	Mintage	VF	XF	Unc
260	1990	5,000	—	Proof	45.00

27.0000 g, .925 SILVER, .8030 oz ASW
Soccer - 2 Players

Y#	Date	Mintage	VF	XF	Unc
297	1990	—	—	Proof	45.00

Soccer - Goalie

Y#	Date	Mintage	VF	XF	Unc
298	1990	—	—	Proof	45.00

22.2200 g, .900 SILVER, .6431 oz ASW
Luo Guan Zhong - Historian

Y#	Date	Mintage	VF	XF	Unc
302	1990	—	—	—	50.00

Li Zicheng - Revolutionary

Y#	Date	Mintage	VF	XF	Unc
303	1990	—	—	—	50.00

Li Shi Zhen - Naturalist

Y#	Date	Mintage	VF	XF	Unc
304	1990	—	—	—	50.00

Zeng He - Seafarer

Y#	Date	Mintage	VF	XF	Unc
305	1990	—	—	—	50.00

Song Ying Xing - Scientist

Y#	Date	Mintage	VF	XF	Unc
322	1991	*.025	—	Proof	50.00

Cao Xue Qin - Writer

Y#	Date	Mintage	VF	XF	Unc
323	1991	*.025	—	Proof	50.00

Lin Ze Xu - High Ranking Official

Y#	Date	Mintage	VF	XF	Unc
324	1991	*.025	—	Proof	50.00

Hong Xu Quan - Revolutionary

Y#	Date	Mintage	VF	XF	Unc
325	1991	*.025	—	Proof	50.00

Great Wall - Ancient Ships and Shipbuilding

Y#	Date	Mintage	VF	XF	Unc
331	1992	.015	—	Proof	40.00

First Compass

Y#	Date	Mintage	VF	XF	Unc
332	1992	.015	—	Proof	40.00

First Seismograph

Y#	Date	Mintage	VF	XF	Unc
333	1992	.015	—	Proof	40.00

Ancient Kite Flying

Y#	Date	Mintage	VF	XF	Unc
334	1992	.015	—	Proof	40.00

Bronze Age Metal Working Scene

Y#	Date	Mintage	VF	XF	Unc
335	1992	.015	—	Proof	40.00

COPPER
2 Pandas Eating Bamboo

Y#	Date	Mintage	VF	XF	Unc
359	1993	2.000	—	—	6.00

10 YUAN

15.0000 g, .850 SILVER, .4099 oz ASW
Year of the Pig

Y#	Date	Mintage	VF	XF	Unc
44	1983	6,500	—	Proof	375.00

1.2000 g, .900 GOLD, .0347 oz AGW
Marco Polo

Y#	Date	Mintage	VF	XF	Unc
55	1983	.050	—	Proof	65.00

27.0000 g, .900 SILVER, .7813 oz ASW
Pandas

Y#	Date	Mintage	VF	XF	Unc
57	1983	.010	—	Proof	175.00
	1983	Inc. Ab.		Frosted Proof	200.00

15.0000 g, .850 SILVER, .4099 oz ASW
Year of the Rat

Y#	Date	Mintage	VF	XF	Unc
59	1984	9,960	—	Proof	125.00

16.8100 g, .925 SILVER, .5000 oz ASW
Womens Decade

Y#	Date	Mintage	VF	XF	Unc
62	1984	4,000	—	Proof	40.00

Olympics - Volleyball

Y#	Date	Mintage	VF	XF	Unc
63	1984	1,000	—	Proof	35.00

17.0600 g, .800 SILVER, .4388 oz ASW

Y#	Date	Mintage	VF	XF	Unc
63a	1984	1,000	—	—	130.00

Olympics - Speed Skating

Y#	Date	Mintage	VF	XF	Unc
64	1984	6,000	—	Proof	35.00

27.0000 g. .925 SILVER, .8031 oz ASW
Pandas

Y#	Date	Mintage	VF	XF	Unc
67	1984	.010	—	Proof	100.00

15.0000 g, .900 SILVER, .4341 oz ASW
Year of the Ox

Y#	Date	Mintage	VF	XF	Unc
78	1985	9,800	—	Proof	60.00

27.0000 g, .900 SILVER, .7813 oz ASW
110th Anniversary of Birth of Dr. Cheng Jiageng

Y#	Date	Mintage	VF	XF	Unc
88	1984	6,000	—	Proof	55.00

Pandas

Y#	Date	Mintage	VF	XF	Unc
95	1985	.010	—	Proof	100.00

34.5600 g, .900 SILVER, 1.0000 OZ ASW
20th Anniversary of Tibet Autonomous Region

Y#	Date	Mintage	VF	XF	Unc
97	1985	3,000	—	Proof	50.00

15.0000 g, .900 SILVER, .4341 oz ASW
Year of the Tiger

Y#	Date	Mintage	VF	XF	Unc
98	1986	.015	—	Proof	70.00

34.5600 g, .900 SILVER, 1.0000 oz ASW
30th Anniversary Sinkiang Autonomous Region

Y#	Date	Mintage	VF	XF	Unc
110	1985	1,400	—	Proof	40.00

NOTE: For a similar 5 ounce medallic issue refer to *UNUSUAL WORLD COINS*, 3rd edition, Krause Publications, 1992.

29.1900 g, .925 SILVER, .8682 oz ASW
120th Anniversary of Birth of Sun Yat-sen
Rev: Sun Yat-sen's residence.

Y#	Date	Mintage	VF	XF	Unc
111	1986	8,450	—	Proof	50.00

15.0000 g, .900 SILVER, .4341 oz ASW
Year of the Rabbit
Obv: Yellow Crane Pavilion above legend.
Rev: 2 rabbits above denomination.

Y#	Date	Mintage	VF	XF	Unc
121	1987	.010	—	Proof	75.00

Year of the Dragon

Y#	Date	Mintage	VF	XF	Unc
141	1988	.013	—	Proof	75.00

27.0000 g, .925 SILVER, .5056 oz ASW
Rare Animal Protection - Crested Ibis

Y#	Date	Mintage	VF	XF	Unc
165	1988	.050	—	Proof	35.00

Rare Animal Protection - Dolphins

Y#	Date	Mintage	VF	XF	Unc
166	1988	.050	—	Proof	35.00

15.0000 g, .850 SILVER, .4100 oz ASW
Year of the Snake
Obv: Shanhaiguan Pass gate.

Y#	Date	Mintage	VF	XF	Unc
177	1989	.015	—	Proof	125.00

27.0000 g, .925 SILVER, .8031 oz ASW
1990 Asian Games - Weight Lifter
Obv: Monument, stadium, Great Wall segment and sun.

Y#	Date	Mintage	VF	XF	Unc
199	1989	.020	—	Proof	40.00

1990 Asian Games - Diver

Y#	Date	Mintage	VF	XF	Unc
200	1989	.020	—	Proof	40.00

1990 Asian Games - Tennis Player

Y#	Date	Mintage	VF	XF	Unc
201	1989	.020	—	Proof	40.00

1990 Asian Games - Bicyclist

Y#	Date	Mintage	VF	XF	Unc
202	1989	.020	—	Proof	40.00

15.0000 g, .850 SILVER, .4100 oz ASW
Year of the Horse
Obv: Temple of Confucius.

Y#	Date	Mintage	VF	XF	Unc
221	1990	.015	—	Proof	50.00

27.0000 g, .925 SILVER, .8031 oz ASW
40th Anniversary of Peoples Republic - Tian An Men Square

Y#	Date	Mintage	VF	XF	Unc
235	1989	.030	—	Proof	35.00

40th Anniversary of Peoples Republic - Great Wall

Y#	Date	Mintage	VF	XF	Unc
236	1989	.030	—	Proof	35.00

Homer - Poet
Obv: State emblem, legend and date.

Y#	Date	Mintage	VF	XF	Unc
244	1990	*.030	—	Proof	50.00

William Shakespeare

Y#	Date	Mintage	VF	XF	Unc
245	1990	*.030	—	Proof	50.00

Ludwig Van Beethoven

Y#	Date	Mintage	VF	XF	Unc
246	1990	*.030	—	Proof	50.00

Thomas Alva Edison

Y#	Date	Mintage	VF	XF	Unc
247	1990	*.030	—	Proof	50.00

Endangered Animals - Japanese Deer
Obv: State emblem.

Y#	Date	Mintage	VF	XF	Unc
248	1989	.030	—	Proof	40.00

Endangered Animals - Red Crowned Crane
Obv: State emblem.

Y#	Date	Mintage	VF	XF	Unc
249	1989	.030	—	Proof	40.00

XI Asian Games - Javelin Thrower

Y#	Date	Mintage	VF	XF	Unc
251	1990	.020	—	Proof	35.00

XI Asian Games - Baseball Player

Y#	Date	Mintage	VF	XF	Unc
252	1990	.020	—	Proof	35.00

XI Asian Games - Gymnast on Rings

Y#	Date	Mintage	VF	XF	Unc
253	1990	.020	—	Proof	35.00

XI Asian Games - Soccer Player

Y#	Date	Mintage	VF	XF	Unc
254	1990	.020	—	Proof	35.00

15.0000 g, .900 SILVER, .4340 oz ASW
Year of the Goat
Obv: Chinese building and legend.

Y#	Date	Mintage	VF	XF	Unc
270	1990	.015	—	Proof	45.00

27.0000 g, .900 SILVER, .7814 oz ASW
Summer Olympics - Bicycle Racing

Y#	Date	Mintage	VF	XF	Unc
283	1990	—	—	Proof	35.00

Summer Olympics - High Jumping

Y#	Date	Mintage	VF	XF	Unc
300	1990	—	—	Proof	35.00

30.0000 g, .900 SILVER, .8682 oz ASW
Olympics - Diver

Y#	Date	Mintage	VF	XF	Unc
366	1990	—	—	Proof	50.00

27.0800 g, .900 SILVER, .7836 oz ASW
Women's Soccer - 2 Players

Y#	Date	Mintage	VF	XF	Unc
318	1991	—	—	Proof	35.00

27.0200 g, .900 SILVER, .7819 oz ASW
Women's Soccer - 3 Players

Y#	Date	Mintage	VF	XF	Unc
319	1991	—	—	Proof	35.00

27.0000 g, .925 SILVER, .8031 oz ASW
Mozart

Y#	Date	Mintage	VF	XF	Unc
347	1991	—	—	Proof	42.50

Columbus

Y#	Date	Mintage	VF	XF	Unc
348	1991	—	—	Proof	42.50

Einstein

Y#	Date	Mintage	VF	XF	Unc
349	1991	—	—	Proof	42.50

Mark Twain

Y#	Date	Mintage	VF	XF	Unc
350	1991	—	—	Proof	42.50

30.0000 g, .900 SILVER, .8682 oz ASW
Olympics - Downhill Skier

Y#	Date	Mintage	VF	XF	Unc
367	1991	—	—	Proof	50.00

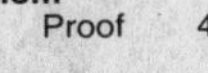

15.0000 g, .900 SILVER, .4340 oz ASW
Winter Olympics - Slalom

Y#	Date	Mintage	VF	XF	Unc
351	1992	—	—	Proof	40.00

Year of the Monkey

Y#	Date	Mintage	VF	XF	Unc
288	1992	—	—	Proof	60.00

26.8300 g, .900 SILVER, .7764 oz ASW
Olympics - Cross Country Skiing

Y#	Date	Mintage	VF	XF	Unc
368	1992	—	—	Proof	45.00

20 YUAN

10.3500 g, .850 SILVER, .2829 oz ASW
1980 Olympics - Wrestling
Obv: Similar to 1 Yuan, Y#10.

Y#	Date	Mintage	VF	XF	Unc
18 (17)	1980	.029	—	Proof	15.00

15.0000 g, .850 SILVER, .4099 oz ASW
Year of the Dog

Y#	Date	Mintage	VF	XF	Unc
38	1982	8,560	—	Proof	150.00

25 YUAN

19.4400 g, .800 SILVER, .5000 oz ASW
World Soccer Cup

Y#	Date	Mintage	VF	XF	Unc
35	1982	.040	—	Proof	40.00

World Soccer Cup

Y#	Date	Mintage	VF	XF	Unc
36	1982	.040	—	Proof	40.00

30 YUAN

15.0000 g, .850 SILVER, .4099 oz ASW
1980 Olympics - Equestrian
Obv: Similar to Y#20.
Rev: Horse racing.

Y#	Date	Mintage	VF	XF	Unc
19 (18)	1980	.029	—	Proof	15.00

1980 Olympics - Soccer

Y#	Date	Mintage	VF	XF	Unc
20 (19)	1980	.029	—	Proof	15.00

1980 Olympics - Speed Skating

Y#	Date	Mintage	VF	XF	Unc
21 (20)	1980	.020	—	Proof	15.00

Year of the Rooster

Y#	Date	Mintage	VF	XF	Unc
32 (34)	1981	.010	—	Proof	375.00

35 YUAN

19.4400 g, .800 SILVER, .5000 oz ASW
UNICEF and IYC

Y#	Date	Mintage	VF	XF	Unc
8	1979	1,000	—	—	170.00
	1979	.014	—	Proof	35.00

33.5800 g, .800 SILVER, .8638 oz ASW
70th Anniversary of 1911 Revolution

Y#	Date	Mintage	VF	XF	Unc
46	1981	3,885	—	Proof	225.00

50 YUAN

155.6800 g, .999 SILVER, 5.0053 oz ASW
Illustration reduced. Actual size: 70.3mm.
1992 Olympics - Speed Skaters

Y#	Date	Mintage	VF	XF	Unc
321	1990	—	—	Proof	225.00

100 YUAN

11.0000 g, .900 GOLD, .3183 oz AGW
Marco Polo

Y#	Date	Mintage	VF	XF	Unc
56	1983	950 pcs.	—	Proof	1000.

11.3180 g, .917 GOLD, .3337 oz AGW
Emperor Qin Shi Huang

Y#	Date	Mintage	VF	XF	Unc
72	1984	9,200	—	Proof	300.00

Founders of Chinese Culture - Confucius

Y#	Date	Mintage	VF	XF	Unc
94	1985	7,000	—	Proof	300.00

Wildlife - Wild Yak

Y#	Date	Mintage	VF	XF	Unc
107	1986	3,000	—	Proof	250.00

Chinese Culture - Liu Bang - Revolutionary Soldier

Y#	Date	Mintage	VF	XF	Unc
117	1986	7,000	—	Proof	300.00

Year of Peace
Similar to 5 Yuan, Y#119.

Y#	Date	Mintage	VF	XF	Unc
120	1986	350 pcs.	—	Proof	1000.

Emperor Li Shih Min
Obv: State emblem and legend.

Y#	Date	Mintage	VF	XF	Unc
139	1987	7,000	—	Proof	300.00

Emperor Zhao Kuangyin

Y#	Date	Mintage	VF	XF	Unc
164	1988	3,750	—	Proof	375.00

8.0000 g, .917 GOLD, .2359 oz AGW
Rare Animal Protection - Monkey

Y#	Date	Mintage	VF	XF	Unc
167	1988	.030	—	Proof	250.00

1990 Asian Games - Ribbon Dancer

Y#	Date	Mintage	VF	XF	Unc
203	1989	*.010	—	Proof	175.00

11.3180 g, .917 GOLD, .3337 oz AGW
Gengus Khan

Y#	Date	Mintage	VF	XF	Unc
217	1989	4,000	—	Proof	375.00

Save the Children Fund

Y#	Date	Mintage	VF	XF	Unc
231	1989	5,000	—	Proof	400.00

8.0000 g, .917 GOLD, .2359 oz AGW
Endangered Animals - Chinese Tiger
Obv: State emblem.

Y#	Date	Mintage	VF	XF	Unc
250	1989	.025	—	Proof	250.00

7.7750 g, .999 GOLD, .2500 oz AGW
40th Anniversary of Peoples Republic

Y#	Date	Mintage	VF	XF	Unc
299	1989	.015	—	Proof	250.00

8.0000 g, .917 GOLD, .2359 oz AGW
XI Asian Games - Swimmer

Y#	Date	Mintage	VF	XF	Unc
256	1990	.010	—	Proof	220.00

10.3700 g, .917 GOLD, .3054 oz AGW
First Emperor - Huang Ti

Y#	Date	Mintage	VF	XF	Unc
287	1990	.020	—	Proof	275.00

11.3180 g, .917 GOLD, .3333 oz AGW
Zhu Yuan Zhang - Emperor

Y#	Date	Mintage	VF	XF	Unc
306	1990	—	—	—	375.00

Olympics - Women's Basketball

Y#	Date	Mintage	VF	XF	Unc
327	1990	—	—	—	275.00

8.6000 g, .917 GOLD, .2533 oz AGW
Women's Soccer

Y#	Date	Mintage	VF	XF	Unc
320	1991	5,000	—	Proof	275.00

Emperor Kang Xi
Obv: State emblem, leg. and date.

Y#	Date	Mintage	VF	XF	Unc
326	1991	*.025	—	Proof	375.00

Ancient Ships and Shipbuilding

Y#	Date	Mintage	VF	XF	Unc
336	1992	1,000	—	Proof	800.00

First Compass

Y#	Date	Mintage	VF	XF	Unc
337	1992	1,000	—	Proof	800.00

First Seismograph

Y#	Date	Mintage	VF	XF	Unc
338	1992	1,000	—	Proof	800.00

First Kite

Y#	Date	Mintage	VF	XF	Unc
339	1992	1,000	—	Proof	800.00

Bronze Age Metal Working

Y#	Date	Mintage	VF	XF	Unc
340	1992	1,000	—	Proof	800.00

150 YUAN

8.0000 g, .917 GOLD, .2359 oz AGW
Year of the Pig

Y#	Date	Mintage	VF	XF	Unc
45	1983	2,185	—	Proof	1950.

Year of the Rat

Y#	Date	Mintage	VF	XF	Unc
60	1984	2,100	—	Proof	2750.

Year of the Ox
Obv: Similar to 10 Yuan, Y#78.

Y#	Date	Mintage	VF	XF	Unc
79	1985	2,200	—	Proof	335.00

Year of the Tiger
Obv: Qing Dynasty Palace

Y#	Date	Mintage	VF	XF	Unc
99	1986	5,049	—	Proof	550.00

Year of the Rabbit

Y#	Date	Mintage	VF	XF	Unc
123	1987	4,750	—	Proof	400.00

Year of the Dragon
Obv: Similar to 10 Yuan, Y#141.

Y#	Date	Mintage	VF	XF	Unc
144	1988	7,500	—	Proof	375.00

Year of the Snake
Obv: Shanhaiguan Pass gate.

Y#	Date	Mintage	VF	XF	Unc
180	1989	7,500	—	Proof	250.00

Year of the Horse
Obv: Temple of Confucius.

Y#	Date	Mintage	VF	XF	Unc
227	1990	7,500	—	Proof	325.00

Year of the Goat
Obv: Chinese building and legend.

Y#	Date	Mintage	VF	XF	Unc
276	1991	7,500	—	Proof	275.00

Year of the Monkey
Obv: Chinese building.

Y#	Date	Mintage	VF	XF	Unc
291	1992	5,000	—	Proof	375.00

200 YUAN

8.4700 g, .917 GOLD, .2497 oz AGW
Chinese Bronze Age Finds - Leopard
Obv: Similar to 800 Yuan, Y#31.

Y#	Date	Mintage	VF	XF	Unc
28 (27)	1981	1,000	—	Proof	600.00

Chinese Bronze Age Finds - Winged Creature

Y#	Date	Mintage	VF	XF	Unc
29 (28)	1981	1,000	—	Proof	1250.

World Cup Soccer

Y#	Date	Mintage	VF	XF	Unc
37	1982	1,261	—	Proof	700.00

Year of the Dog

Y#	Date	Mintage	VF	XF	Unc
39	1982	2,500	—	Proof	800.00

Decade for Women

Y#	Date	Mintage	VF	XF	Unc
89	1985	—	—	—	—

NOTE: Not released.

250 YUAN

8.0000 g, .917 GOLD, .2358 oz AGW
1980 Olympics
Alpine Skiing

Y#	Date	Mintage	VF	XF	Unc
22 (21)	1980	.010	—	Proof	175.00

Year of the Rooster

Y#	Date	Mintage	VF	XF	Unc
33 (35)	1981	4,982	—	Proof	600.00

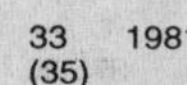

300 YUAN

10.0000 g, .917 GOLD, .2948 oz AGW
1980 Olympics
Archery

Y#	Date	Mintage	VF	XF	Unc
23 (22)	1980	8,800	—	Proof	250.00

400 YUAN

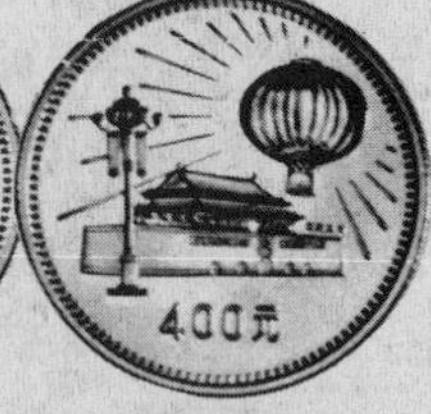

16.9500 g, .917 GOLD, .4997 oz AGW
30th Anniversary of Peoples Republic
Tien An Men

Y#	Date	Mintage	VF	XF	Unc
4	1979	.070	—	Proof	275.00

30th Anniversary of Peoples Republic
Peoples Heroes Monument

Y#	Date	Mintage	VF	XF	Unc
5	1979	.070	—	Proof	275.00

30th Anniversary of Peoples Republic
Chairman Mao Memorial Hall

Y#	Date	Mintage	VF	XF	Unc
6	1979	.070	—	Proof	275.00

30th Anniversary of Peoples Republic
Great Hall of the People

Y#	Date	Mintage	VF	XF	Unc
7	1979	.070	—	Proof	275.00

Chinese Bronze Age Finds - Rhinocerous

Y#	Date	Mintage	VF	XF	Unc
30 (29)	1981	1,000	—	Proof	950.00

13.3600 g, .917 GOLD, .3939 oz AGW
70th Anniversary of 1911 Revolution

Y#	Date	Mintage	VF	XF	Unc
47	1981	1,338	—	Proof	1950.

450 YUAN

17.1700 g, .900 GOLD, .4968 oz AGW
International Year of the Child

Y#	Date	Mintage	VF	XF	Unc
9 (8)	1979	.012	—	Proof	275.00

800 YUAN

33.2000 g, .917 GOLD, .9789 oz AGW
Chinese Bronze Age Finds - Elephant

Y#	Date	Mintage	VF	XF	Unc
31 (30)	1981	1,000	—	Proof	2000.

BI-METALLIC BULLION ISSUES

25 YUAN

11.6700 g, .999 GOLD, .2500 oz AGW
and .999 SILVER, .1250 oz ASW

Y#	Date	Mintage	VF	XF	Unc
301	1991	.010	—	Proof	290.00

50 YUAN

21.7724 g, .999 GOLD, .5000 oz ASW
and .999 SILVER, .2000 oz ASW

Y#	Date	Mintage	VF	XF	Unc
266	1990	2,000	—	Proof	400.00

SILVER BULLION ISSUES

5 JIAO

2.0000 g, .999 SILVER, .0643 oz ASW
Phoenix and Dragon

Y#	Date	Mintage	VF	XF	Unc
205	1990	.050	—	Proof	22.50

10 YUAN
(1 Ounçe)

31.1000 g, .999 SILVER, 1.0000 oz ASW

Y#	Date	Mintage	VF	XF	Unc
133	1987	.030	—	Proof	45.00

Year of the Dragon

Y#	Date	Mintage	VF	XF	Unc
174	1988	.020	—	Proof	75.00

Year of the Snake
Obv: Emblem.

Y#	Date	Mintage	VF	XF	Unc
183	1989	6,000	—	Proof	125.00

Baby Panda

Y#	Date	Mintage	VF	XF	Unc
186	1989	.250	—	—	15.00
	1989	.025	—	Proof	35.00

Year of the Horse

Y#	Date	Mintage	VF	XF	Unc
222	1990	.012	—	Proof	60.00

Y#	Date	Mintage	VF	XF	Unc
237	1990	.200	—	—	15.00
	1990	.020	—	Proof	35.00

Great Wall - Phoenix and Dragon

Y#	Date	Mintage	VF	XF	Unc
261	1990	*.012	—	Proof	50.00

Year of the Goat

Y#	Date	Mintage	VF	XF	Unc
271	1991	8,000	—	Proof	60.00

Panda - Hind Feet in Water
Obv: Date w/bottom serifs.

Y#	Date	Mintage	VF	XF	Unc
308.1	1991	.100	—	—	20.00

Rev: P behind panda.

Y#	Date	Mintage	VF	XF	Unc
308.2	1991	.020	—	Proof	40.00

Obv: Date w/o bottom serifs.

Y#	Date	Mintage	VF	XF	Unc
308.3	1991	Inc. Ab.	—	—	20.00

62.2000 g, .999 SILVER, 2.0000 oz ASW
Panda - Climbing Bamboo Branch

Y#	Date	Mintage	VF	XF	Unc
314	1991	.010	—	Proof	75.00

31.1000 g, .999 SILVER, 1.0000 oz ASW
Year of the Monkey

Y#	Date	Mintage	VF	XF	Unc
294	1992	8,000	—	Proof	60.00

Panda Climbing Right on Bamboo Branch

Y#	Date	Mintage	VF	XF	Unc
346	1992	.100	—	—	20.00
	1992	—	—	Proof	40.00

Temple of Harmony - Peacocks
Obv: Temple of Harmony. Rev: 2 peacocks.

Y#	Date	Mintage	VF	XF	Unc
352	1993	7,000	—	Proof	60.00

31.1000 g, .999 SILVER, 1.0000 oz ASW
Pandas - Mother and Cub
Obv: Similar to KM#361. Rev: Mother Panda nurturing cub.

Y#	Date	Mintage	VF	XF	Unc
360	1993	.020	—	Proof	40.00

Panda On Flat Rock

Y#	Date	Mintage	VF	XF	Unc
361	1993	.120	—	—	15.00

20 YUAN

62.2060 g, .999 SILVER, 2.0000 oz ASW
Phoenix and Dragon

Y#	Date	Mintage	VF	XF	Unc
207	1990	5,000	—	Proof	130.00

50 YUAN

(5 Ounces)

155.5000 g, .999 SILVER, 5.0000 oz ASW
120th Anniversary of Birth of Sun Yat-sen
Illustration reduced. Actual size: 70mm

Y#	Date	Mintage	VF	XF	Unc
108	1986	3,000	—	Proof	160.00

Year of the Rabbit
Similar to 150 Yuan, Y#123.

Y#	Date	Mintage	VF	XF	Unc
122	1987	4,000	—	Proof	325.00

Illustration reduced. Actual size: 70mm.

Y#	Date	Mintage	VF	XF	Unc
134	1987	8,540	—	Proof	100.00

Year of the Dragon
Illustration reduced. Actual size: 70mm
Obv: Similar to 20 Yuan, Y#207.

Y#	Date	Mintage	VF	XF	Unc
142	1988	5,000	—	Proof	275.00

Y#	Date	Mintage	VF	XF	Unc
168	1988	.011	—	Proof	135.00

Summer Olympics - Volleyball
Illustration reduced. Actual size: 70mm.

Y#	Date	Mintage	VF	XF	Unc
170	1988	5,000	—	Proof	275.00

Year of the Snake
Illustration reduced. Actual size: 70mm.
Obv: Similar to 10 Yuan, Y#177.

Y#	Date	Mintage	VF	XF	Unc
178	1989	1,000	—	Proof	350.00

Pandas

Y#	Date	Mintage	VF	XF	Unc
218	1989	9,599	—	Proof	135.00

Year of the Horse
Illustration reduced. Actual size: 70 mm.
Obv: Temple of Confucius.

Y#	Date	Mintage	VF	XF	Unc
223	1990	2,000	—	Proof	300.00

Y#	Date	Mintage	VF	XF	Unc
262	1990	4,000	—	Proof	150.00

Year of the Goat
Obv: Chinese building and legend.

Y#	Date	Mintage	VF	XF	Unc
272	1991	2,000	—	Proof	250.00
Pandas					
373	1991	5,000	—	Proof	160.00
Year of the Monkey					
Similar to 500 Yuan, Y#292.					
289	1992	1,000	—	Proof	375.00
Pandas					
374	1992	4,000	—	Proof	160.00
Temple of Harmony - Peacocks					
Obv: Temple of Harmony. Rev: 2 peacocks.					
353	1993	888 pcs.	—	Proof	350.00
Pandas					
379	1993	—	—	Proof	160.00
Year of the Rooster					
381	1993	1,000	—	Proof	300.00
Year of the Dog					
386	1994	1,000	—	Proof	300.00

100 YUAN
(12 Ounces)

373.2360 g, .999 SILVER, 12.0000 oz ASW
125th Anniversary of Birth of Zhan Tianyou
Illustration reduced. Actual size: 80mm

Y#	Date	Mintage	VF	XF	Unc
131	1987	2,911	—	Proof	300.00

Year of the Dragon
Illustration reduced. Actual size: 80mm
Obv: Similar to 10 Yuan, Y#141.

Y#	Date	Mintage	VF	XF	Unc
143	1988	3,000	—	Proof	600.00

Illustration reduced. Actual size: 70mm.

Y#	Date	Mintage	VF	XF	Unc
169	1988	5,000	—	Proof	275.00

Year of the Snake
Illustration reduced. Actual size: 80mm.
Obv: Similar to 10 Yuan, Y#177.

Y#	Date	Mintage	VF	XF	Unc
179	1989	400 pcs.	—	Proof	1000.

Pandas

Y#	Date	Mintage	VF	XF	Unc
219	1989	3,670	—	Proof	300.00

Year of the Horse
Illustration reduced. Actual size: 80mm.
Obv: Temple of Confucius.

Y#	Date	Mintage	VF	XF	Unc
224	1990	1,000	—	Proof	650.00

Y#	Date	Mintage	VF	XF	Unc
263	1990	2,500	—	Proof	300.00

Year of the Goat
Illustration reduced. Actual size: 80mm.

Y#	Date	Mintage	VF	XF	Unc
273	1991	1,000	—	Proof	550.00
		Pandas			
375	1991	2,500	—	Proof	325.00
		Pandas			
376	1992	2,500	—	Proof	300.00
		Pandas			
380	1993	2,500	—	Proof	300.00

150 YUAN

622.0400 g, .999 SILVER, 20.0000 oz ASW
Phoenix and Dragon

Y#	Date	Mintage	VF	XF	Unc
208	1990	1,500	—	Proof	1150.

373.2360 g, .999 SILVER, 12.0000 oz ASW
Year of the Monkey
Similar to 1000 Yuan, Y#293.

Y#	Date	Mintage	VF	XF	Unc
290	1992	500 pcs.	—	Proof	750.00

Temple of Harmony - Peacocks
Obv: Temple of Harmony. Rev: 2 peacocks.

Y#	Date	Mintage	VF	XF	Unc
355	1993	500 pcs.	—	Proof	750.00
		Year of the Rooster			
383	1993	500 pcs.	—	Proof	600.00
		Year of the Dog			
388	1994	500 pcs.	—	Proof	600.00

GOLD BULLION ISSUES
Temple of Heaven/Panda Series

NOTE: The previously listed non-denominated series of 4 coins 1/10, 1/4, 1/2 and 1 ounce dated 1982 are now listed in *UNUSUAL WORLD COINS*, 3rd edition, Krause Publications, 1992.

3 YUAN

1.0000 g, .999 GOLD, .0321 oz AGW
Obv: Temple of Heaven.

Y#	Date	Mintage	VF	XF	Unc
307	1991	—	—	Proof	30.00

5 YUAN
(1/20 Ounce)

1.5551 g, .999 GOLD, .0500 oz AGW

Y#	Date	Mintage	VF	XF	Unc
48	1983	.058	—	Proof	75.00

Y#	Date	Mintage	VF	XF	Unc
73	1984	.086	—	Proof	45.00
80	1985	.217	—	Proof	70.00

Y#	Date	Mintage	VF	XF	Unc
101	1986	.053	—	—	45.00
	1986P	.098	—	Proof	75.00

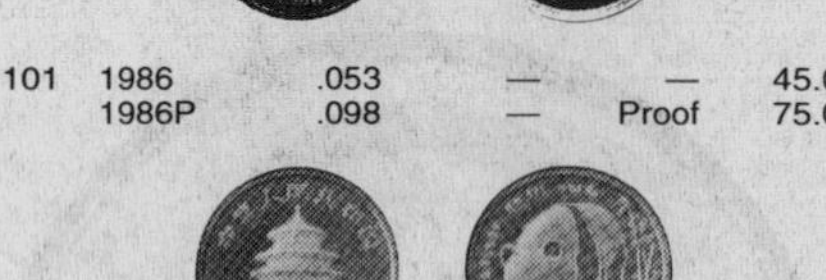

Y#	Date	Mintage	VF	XF	Unc
124	1987(s)	.099	—	—	60.00
	1987(y)	.039	—	—	45.00
	1987P	.010	—	Proof	75.00

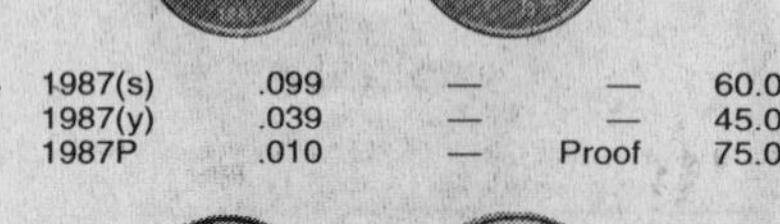

 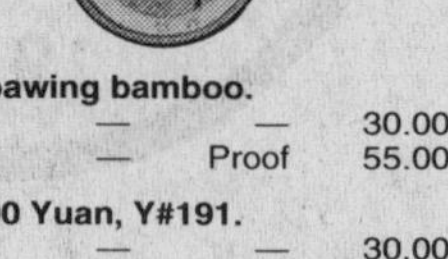

Rev: Panda pawing bamboo.

Y#	Date	Mintage	VF	XF	Unc
152	1988	.482	—	—	30.00
	1988	.475	—	Proof	55.00
		Similar to 100 Yuan, Y#191.			
187	1989	.334	—	—	30.00
	1989	—	—	Proof	55.00
238	1990	—	—	—	30.00
	1990	5,000	—	Proof	55.00
		Similar to 100 Yuan, Y#313.			
309	1991	—	—	—	30.00
	1991	—	—	Proof	55.00
		Similar to 100 Yuan, Y#345.			
341	1992	—	—	—	30.00
	1992	—	—	Proof	55.00

10 YUAN
(1/10 Ounce)

3.1103 g, .999 GOLD, .1000 oz AGW

Y#	Date	Mintage	VF	XF	Unc
49	1983	.074	—	Proof	75.00

Y#	Date	Mintage	VF	XF	Unc
74	1984	.085	—	Proof	55.00

Y#	Date	Mintage	VF	XF	Unc
81	1985	.150	—	Proof	60.00

Y#	Date	Mintage	VF	XF	Unc
102	1986	.045	—	—	55.00
	1986P	.088	—	Proof	125.00

Y#	Date	Mintage	VF	XF	Unc
125	1987(s)	.099	—	—	55.00
	1987(y)	.037	—	—	55.00
	1987P	.010	—	Proof	75.00

Rev: Panda pawing bamboo.

Y#	Date	Mintage	VF	XF	Unc
153	1988	.290	—	—	50.00
	1988	.330	—	Proof	75.00
		Similar to 100 Yuan, Y#191.			
188	1989	.128	—	—	50.00
	1989	—	—	Proof	75.00

1.0000 g, .999 GOLD, .0322 oz AGW
Phoenix and Dragon

Y#	Date	Mintage	VF	XF	Unc
206	1990	.050	—	Proof	50.00
		Panda			
239	1990	—	—	—	50.00
	1990	5,000	—	Proof	75.00

3.1100 g, .999 GOLD, .1000 oz AGW
Similar to 100 Yuan, KM#313.

Y#	Date	Mintage	VF	XF	Unc
310	1991	—	—	—	55.00
	1991	—	—	Proof	80.00
		Similar to 100 Yuan, Y#345.			
342	1992	—	—	—	55.00
	1992	—	—	Proof	80.00

25 YUAN
(1/4 Ounce)

7.7758 g, .999 GOLD, .2500 oz AGW

Y#	Date	Mintage	VF	XF	Unc
50	1983	.039	—	Proof	170.00

Y#	Date	Mintage	VF	XF	Unc
75	1984	.038	—	Proof	170.00

Y#	Date	Mintage	VF	XF	Unc
82	1985	.095	—	Proof	160.00

Y#	Date	Mintage	VF	XF	Unc
103	1986	.033	—	—	100.00
	1986P	.064	—	Proof	185.00

Y#	Date	Mintage	VF	XF	Unc
126	1987(s)	.073	—	—	90.00
	1987(y)	.031	—	—	125.00
	1987P	.010	—	Proof	175.00

Rev: Panda pawing bamboo.

Y#	Date	Mintage	VF	XF	Unc
154	1988	.122	—	—	90.00
	1988	.138	—	Proof	175.00

Similar to 100 Yuan, Y#191.

Y#	Date	Mintage	VF	XF	Unc
189	1989	.071	—	—	90.00
	1989	—	—	Proof	150.00

Panda

Y#	Date	Mintage	VF	XF	Unc
240	1990	—	—	—	120.00
	1990	5,000	—	Proof	150.00

Similar to 100 Yuan, Y#313.

Y#	Date	Mintage	VF	XF	Unc
311	1991	—	—	—	120.00
	1991	—	—	Proof	150.00

Similar to 100 Yuan, Y#345.

Y#	Date	Mintage	VF	XF	Unc
343	1992	—	—	—	120.00
	1992	—	—	Proof	150.00

50 YUAN

(1/2 Ounce)

15.5517 g, .999 GOLD, .5000 oz AGW

Y#	Date	Mintage	VF	XF	Unc
51	1983	.023	—	Proof	350.00

Y#	Date	Mintage	VF	XF	Unc
76	1984	.017	—	Proof	375.00

Y#	Date	Mintage	VF	XF	Unc
83	1985	.076	—	Proof	225.00

Y#	Date	Mintage	VF	XF	Unc
104	1986	.028	—	—	200.00
	1986P	.070	—	Proof	375.00

Y#	Date	Mintage	VF	XF	Unc
127	1987(s)	.078	—	—	200.00
	1987(y)	.017	—	—	400.00
	1987P	.010	—	Proof	375.00

Rev: Panda pawing bamboo.

Y#	Date	Mintage	VF	XF	Unc
155	1988	.104	—	—	200.00
	1988	.118	—	Proof	350.00

Similar to 100 Yuan, Y#191.

Y#	Date	Mintage	VF	XF	Unc
190	1989	.046	—	—	200.00
	1989	—	—	Proof	325.00

Panda

Y#	Date	Mintage	VF	XF	Unc
241	1990	—	—	—	235.00
	1990	5,000	—	Proof	325.00

Similar to 100 Yuan, Y#313.

Y#	Date	Mintage	VF	XF	Unc
312	1991	—	—	—	235.00
	1991	—	—	Proof	325.00

31.1035 g, .999 GOLD, 1.0000 oz AGW
Rev: Panda climbing bamboo branch.

Y#	Date	Mintage	VF	XF	Unc
315	1991	2,500	—	Proof	650.00

15.5517 g, .999 GOLD, .5000 oz AGW
Similar to 100 Yuan, Y#345.

Y#	Date	Mintage	VF	XF	Unc
344	1992	—	—	—	235.00
	1992	—	—	Proof	325.00

100 YUAN

(1 Ounce)

31.1035 g, .999 GOLD, 1.0000 oz AGW

Y#	Date	Mintage	VF	XF	Unc
52	1983	.022	—	Proof	1000.

Y#	Date	Mintage	VF	XF	Unc
77	1984	.023	—	Proof	700.00

Y#	Date	Mintage	VF	XF	Unc
84	1985	.164	—	Proof	425.00

Y#	Date	Mintage	VF	XF	Unc
105	1986	.097	—	—	400.00
	1986P	.137	—	Proof	700.00

Y#	Date	Mintage	VF	XF	Unc
128	1987(s)	.084	—	—	400.00
	1987(y)	.047	—	—	500.00
	1987P	.012	—	Proof	650.00

Rev: Panda pawing bamboo.

Y#	Date	Mintage	VF	XF	Unc
156	1988	.167	—	—	400.00
	1988	.169	—	Proof	600.00

15.5500 g, .999 GOLD, .5000 oz AGW
Olympics - Sword Dancer

Y#	Date	Mintage	VF	XF	Unc
173	1988	.010	—	Proof	375.00

31.1000 g, .999 GOLD, 1.0000 oz AGW
Year of the Dragon
Obv: Temple of Heaven. Rev: 2 floating dragons.

Y#	Date	Mintage	VF	XF	Unc
175	1988	.010	—	Proof	550.00

Year of the Snake
Obv: National emblem.

Y#	Date	Mintage	VF	XF	Unc
184	1989	3,000	—	Proof	625.00

Y#	Date	Mintage	VF	XF	Unc
191	1989	—	—	Proof	550.00

Year of the Horse
Obv: State seal above inscription.

Y#	Date	Mintage	VF	XF	Unc
225	1990	6,000	—	Proof	550.00

Y#	Date	Mintage	VF	XF	Unc
242	1990	5,000	—	Proof	550.00

Year of the Goat
Obv: National emblem above inscription and date.

Y#	Date	Mintage	VF	XF	Unc
274	1991	1,800	—	Proof	900.00

Y#	Date	Mintage	VF	XF	Unc
313	1991	—	—	—	600.00
	1991	—	—	Proof	800.00

Year of the Monkey

Y#	Date	Mintage	VF	XF	Unc
295	1992	1,800	—	Proof	900.00

Y#	Date	Mintage	VF	XF	Unc
345	1992	—	—	—	600.00
	1992	—	—	Proof	800.00

Temple of Harmony - Peacocks
Obv: Temple of Harmony. Rev: 2 peacocks.

Y#	Date	Mintage	VF	XF	Unc
354	1993	1,200	—	Proof	900.00

200 YUAN

(2 Ounces)

62.2060 g, .999 GOLD, 2.0000 oz AGW
Phoenix and Dragon

Y#	Date	Mintage	VF	XF	Unc
209	1990	2,500	—	Proof	1400.

500 YUAN

155.5150 g, .999 GOLD, 5.0000 oz AGW
Illustration reduced. Actual size: 60mm

Y#	Date	Mintage	VF	XF	Unc
147	1987	*3,000	—	Proof	2750.

Year of the Dragon
Illustration reduced. Actual size: 60mm
Obv: Similar to 10 Yuan, Y#141.

Y#	Date	Mintage	VF	XF	Unc
145	1988	3,000	—	Proof	2900.

Y#	Date	Mintage	VF	XF	Unc
233	1988	3,000	—	Proof	2800.

Year of the Snake
Illustration reduced. Actual size: 60mm
Obv: National emblem.

Y#	Date	Mintage	VF	XF	Unc
181	1989	500 pcs.	—	Proof	3500.

Year of the Horse
Illustration reduced. Actual size: 60mm
Obv: Temple of Confucius.

Y#	Date	Mintage	VF	XF	Unc
228	1990	500 pcs.	—	Proof	3200.

Year of the Goat
Illustration reduced. Actual size: 60mm
Obv: Chinese building and legend.

Y#	Date	Mintage	VF	XF	Unc
277	1991	250 pcs.	—	Proof	3500.

Year of the Monkey
Illustration reduced. Actual size: 60mm
Obv: Chinese building.

Y#	Date	Mintage	VF	XF	Unc
292	1992	99 pcs.	—	Proof	6500.
		Pandas			
369	1992	99 pcs.	—	Proof	6000.
		Temple of Harmony - Peacocks			
		Obv: Temple of Harmony. Rev: 2 peacocks.			
356	1993	99 pcs.	—	Proof	5500.
		Year of the Rooster			
384	1993	99 pcs.	—	Proof	6000.
		Year of the Dog			
389	1994	99 pcs.	—	Proof	5500.

1000 YUAN

(12 Ounces)

373.2360 g, .999 GOLD, 12.0000 oz AGW
Illustration reduced. Actual size: 70mm

Y#	Date	Mintage	VF	XF	Unc
66	1984	250 pcs.	—	Proof	18,000.

NOTE: A typical sealed proof exhibits some scuffing and is valued as above, while perfect examples bring a premium.

Illustration reduced. Actual size: 70mm

Y#	Date	Mintage	VF	XF	Unc
118.1	1986	2,550	—	Proof	5750.
		Plain edge			
118.2	1986	2 known	—	Proof	45,000.

Illustration reduced. Actual size: 70mm

Y#	Date	Mintage	VF	XF	Unc
157	1987	2,445	—	Proof	5600.

Year of the Dragon
Illustration reduced. Actual size: 70mm

Y#	Date	Mintage	VF	XF	Unc
146	1988	518 pcs.	—	Proof	9000.
234	1988	3,000	—	Proof	6000.
		Pandas			
370	1988	1,650	—	Proof	6500.

Year of the Snake
Illustration reduced. Actual size: 70mm
Obv: National emblem.

Y#	Date	Mintage	VF	XF	Unc
182	1989	200 pcs.	—	Proof	8500.

Year of the Horse
Illustration reduced. Actual size: 70mm
Obv: Temple of Confucius.

Y#	Date	Mintage	VF	XF	Unc
229	1990	500 pcs.	—	Proof	8000.

Pandas
Obv: Temple of Heaven.

Y#	Date	Mintage	VF	XF	Unc
282	1990	400 pcs.	—	Proof	6000.

Year of the Goat
Illustration reduced. Actual size: 70mm
Obv: Chinese building and legend.

Y#	Date	Mintage	VF	XF	Unc
278	1991	200 pcs.	—	Proof	8000.

Pandas

Y#	Date	Mintage	VF	XF	Unc
371	1991	500 pcs.	—	Proof	7500.

Year of the Monkey
Illustration reduced. Actual size: 70mm
Obv: Chinese building.

Y#	Date	Mintage	VF	XF	Unc
293	1992	99 pcs.	—	Proof	10,000.

Pandas

Y#	Date	Mintage	VF	XF	Unc
372	1992	99 pcs.	—	Proof	9500.

Year of the Rooster

Y#	Date	Mintage	VF	XF	Unc
385	1993	99 pcs.	—	Proof	10,000.

Year of the Dog

Y#	Date	Mintage	VF	XF	Unc
390	1994	99 pcs.	—	Proof	9000.

1500 YUAN

(20 Ounces)

622.6000 g, .999 GOLD, 20.0000 oz AGW
Anniversary of Peoples Republic
Illustration reduced. Actual size: 90mm.
Obv: State emblem above city view w/fireworks in sky.

Y#	Date	Mintage	VF	XF	Unc
232	1989	100 pcs.	—	Proof	13,500.

Phoenix and Dragon

Y#	Date	Mintage	VF	XF	Unc
210	1990	250 pcs.	—	Proof	15,000.

Temple of Harmony - Peacocks
Obv: Temple of Harmony. Rev: 2 peacocks.

Y#	Date	Mintage	VF	XF	Unc
357	1993	66 pcs.	—	Proof	15,000.

10,000 YUAN

4,851.6000 g, .999 GOLD, 156.0000 oz AGW
10th Anniversary of Gold Panda Issue
Obv: Temple of Heaven.
Rev: Panda climbing in bamboo circle, 10 panda design coins in circle around.

Y#	Date	Mintage	VF	XF	Unc
358	1991	10 pcs.	—	—	—

PLATINUM BULLION ISSUES

10 YUAN

(1/10 Ounce)

3.1100 g, .9995 PLATINUM, .1000 oz APW
Panda With Branch

Y#	Date	Mintage	VF	XF	Unc
267	1990	2,500	—	Proof	100.00

25 YUAN

(1/4 Ounce)

7.7758 g, .9995 PLATINUM, .2500 oz APW
Panda Climbing Tree

Y#	Date	Mintage	VF	XF	Unc
268	1990	2,500	—	Proof	250.00

50 YUAN

(1/2 Ounce)

15.5517 g, .9995 PLATINUM, .5000 oz APW
Panda on Rock Eating Bamboo

Y#	Date	Mintage	VF	XF	Unc
269	1990	2,500	—	Proof	400.00

100 YUAN

(1 Ounce)

31.1030 g, .9995 PLATINUM, 1.0000 oz APW
Similar to 100 Yuan, Y#128.

Y#	Date	Mintage	VF	XF	Unc
158	1987	2,000	—	Proof	600.00

Similar to 100 Yuan, Y#156.

Y#	Date	Mintage	VF	XF	Unc
159	1988	2,000	—	Proof	600.00

Year of the Dragon
Obv: Temple of Heaven. Rev: 2 floating dragons.

Y#	Date	Mintage	VF	XF	Unc
176	1988	2,000	—	Proof	750.00

Year of the Snake
Obv: National emblem.

Y#	Date	Mintage	VF	XF	Unc
185	1989	1,000	—	Proof	825.00

Y#	Date	Mintage	VF	XF	Unc
192	1989	5,000	—	Proof	600.00

Year of the Horse
Obv: State seal above inscription.

Y#	Date	Mintage	VF	XF	Unc
226	1990	2,000	—	Proof	650.00

Year of the Goat
Obv: National emblem above inscription and date.

Y#	Date	Mintage	VF	XF	Unc
275	1991	500 pcs.	—	Proof	1000.

Year of the Monkey

Y#	Date	Mintage	VF	XF	Unc
296	1992	300 pcs.	—	Proof	1400.

Year of the Rooster

Y#	Date	Mintage	VF	XF	Unc
382	1993	300 pcs.	—	Proof	1300.

Year of the Dog

Y#	Date	Mintage	VF	XF	Unc
387	1994	300 pcs.	—	Proof	1200.

PALLADIUM BULLION ISSUES

50 YUAN

(1 Ounce)

31.1030 g, .999 PALLADIUM, 1.0000 oz APW

Y#	Date	Mintage	VF	XF	Unc
220	1989	5,000	—	—	250.00

MINT SETS (MS)

KM#	Date	Mintage	Identification	Issue Price	Mkt. Val.
MS1	1979(3)(s)	—	Y1-3, medal	—	7.50
MS2	1980(7)(b)	—	Y24-26(2),27	—	10.00
MS3	1982(4)	—	Y40-43	750.00	3400.
MS4	1991(2)	—	Y316-317	—	—

PROOF SETS (PS)

KM#	Date	Mintage	Identification	Issue Price	Mkt. Val.
PS1	1979(4)	70,000	Y4-7	1695.	1350.
PS2	1980(14)	1,000	Y9-22	1750.	500.00
PS3	1980(7)	—	Y1-3,23-26	Reported, not confirmed	
PS4	1980(4)	—	Y10-13	—	20.00
PS5	1980(4)	—	Y28-31	2950.	6000.
PS6	1980(3)	1,000	Y18-20	—	55.00
PS7	1981(7)(s)	10,000	Y1-3,24-27, medal	—	10.00
PS8	1982(7)(s)	—	Y1-3,24-27, medal	—	10.00
PS9	1983(7)(s)	—	Y1-3,24-27, book	—	12.50
PS9a	1983(7)(s)	—	Y1-3,24-27, medal (paper cover)	—	—
PS10	1984(7)(y)	—	Y1-3,24-27, medal	—	12.50
PS11	1985(7)(y)	—	Y1-3,24-27, medal	—	10.00
PS12	1985(2)	—	Y109-110	45.00	45.00
PS13	1986(7)(y)	—	Y1-3,24-27, medal	10.00	—
PS14	1986(5)	10,000	Y101-105	—	1450.
PS15	1987(5)	10,000	Y124-128	—	1350.
PS16	1987(2)	—	Y133-134	278.00	275.00
PS17	1988(4)	—	Y160-163	200.00	200.00
PS18	1988(5)	10,000	Y152-156	—	1250.
PS19	1989(5)	8,000	Y187-191	—	1150.
PS20	1990(5)	5,000	Y238-242	—	1150.
PS21	1990(3)	2,500	Y267-269	1095.	1150.
PS22	1990(2)	2,000	Y266 and medal	995.00	1000.
PS23	1991(2)	2,000	Y301 and medal	575.00	575.00
PS24	1993(3)	—	Y352-354	—	1300.

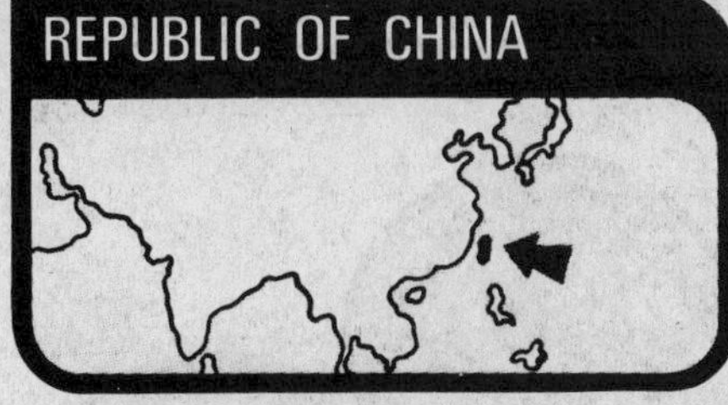

The Republic of China, comprising Taiwan (an island located 90 miles (145 km.) off the southeastern coast of mainland China), the offshore islands of Quemoy and Matsu and nearby islets of the Pescadores chain, has an area of 14,000 sq. mi. (35,980 sq. km.) and a population of 20.2 million. Capital: Taipei. During the past decade, manufacturing has replaced agriculture in importance. Fruits, vegetables, plywood, textile yarns and fabrics and clothing are exported.

Chinese migration to Taiwan began as early as the sixth century. The Dutch established a base on the island in 1624 and held it until 1661, when they were driven out by supporters of the Ming dynasty who used it as a base for their unsuccessful attempt to displace the ruling Manchu dynasty of mainland China. After being occupied by Manchu forces in 1683, Taiwan remained under the suzerainty of China until its cession to Japan in 1895. It was returned to China following World War II. On Dec. 8, 1949, Taiwan became the last remnant of Sun Yat-sen's vast Republic of China. Chiang Kai-Shek had quickly moved his government and nearly exhausted army from the mainland leaving the Communist forces under Mao Tse-tung victorious.

The coins of Nationalist China do not carry A.D. dating, but are dated according to the year of the republic, which was established in 1911. However, republican years are added to 1911 to find the western year. Thus republican year 38 plus 1911 equals Gregorian calendar year 1949AD.

MONETARY SYSTEM

10 Cents = 1 Chiao

10 Chiao = 1 Dollar (Yuan)

10 CENTS

BRONZE
Sun Yat-sen

Y#	Date	Mintage	Fine	VF	XF	Unc
531	Yr.38 (1949)	157.600	.10	.30	1.00	4.00

ALUMINUM

Y#	Date	Mintage	Fine	VF	XF	Unc
533	Yr.44 (1955)	583.980	—	.10	.15	1.50

Y#	Date	Mintage	Fine	VF	XF	Unc
545	Yr.56 (1967)	89.999	—	.10	.15	.75
	Yr.59 (1970)	30.000	—	.10	.25	1.00
	Yr.60 (1971)	19.925	—	.20	.40	1.50
	Yr.61 (1972)	11.141	.10	.40	.60	2.00
	Yr.62 (1973)	111.400	—	—	.10	.75
	Yr.63 (1974)	71.930	—	.10	.25	1.00

20 CENTS

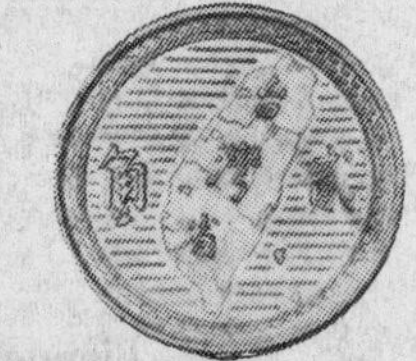

ALUMINUM
Sun Yat-sen

Y#	Date	Mintage	Fine	VF	XF	Unc
534	Yr.39 (1950)	327.495	—	.10	.50	3.00

50 CENTS

5.0000 g, .720 SILVER, .1157 oz ASW
Sun Yat-sen

Y#	Date	Mintage	Fine	VF	XF	Unc
532	Yr.38 (1949)	—	1.50	2.00	3.50	5.00

BRASS

Y#	Date	Mintage	Fine	VF	XF	Unc
535	Yr.43 (1954)	279.624	—	.10	.25	1.00

Y#	Date	Mintage	Fine	VF	XF	Unc
546	Yr.56 (1967)	109.999	—	.10	.15	.50
	Yr.59 (1970)	6.010	.15	.30	.60	1.25
	Yr.60 (1971)	4.434	.20	.40	.80	1.50
	Yr.61 (1972)	21.171	—	.10	.20	1.00
	Yr.62 (1973)	88.840	—	.10	.20	1.00
	Yr.69 (1980)	3.972	—	.10	.20	1.00
	Yr.70 (1981)	100.000	—	.10	.20	1.00

BRONZE

Y#	Date	Mintage	Fine	VF	XF	Unc
550	Yr.70 (1981)	103.800	—	—	.10	.40
	Yr.75 (1986)	22.000	—	—	.10	.40
	Yr.77 (1988)	10.000	—	—	.10	.40

DOLLAR (YUAN)

COPPER-NICKEL-ZINC

Y#	Date	Mintage	Fine	VF	XF	Unc
536	Yr.49 (1960)	321.717	—	.10	.20	.40
	Yr.59 (1970)	48.800	.10	.20	.50	.80
	Yr.60 (1971)	41.532	.10	.20	.50	.80
	Yr.61 (1972)	105.309	—	.10	.20	.40
	Yr.62 (1973)	353.924	—	.10	.20	.40
	Yr.63 (1974)	535.605	—	.10	.20	.40
	Yr.64 (1975)	456.874	—	.10	.20	.40
	Yr.65 (1976)	634.497	—	.10	.20	.40
	Yr.66 (1977)	116.900	—	.10	.20	.40
	Yr.67 (1978)	104.245	—	.10	.20	.40
	Yr.68 (1979)	—	.10	.20	.50	.80
	Yr.69 (1980)	113.900	—	.10	.20	.40

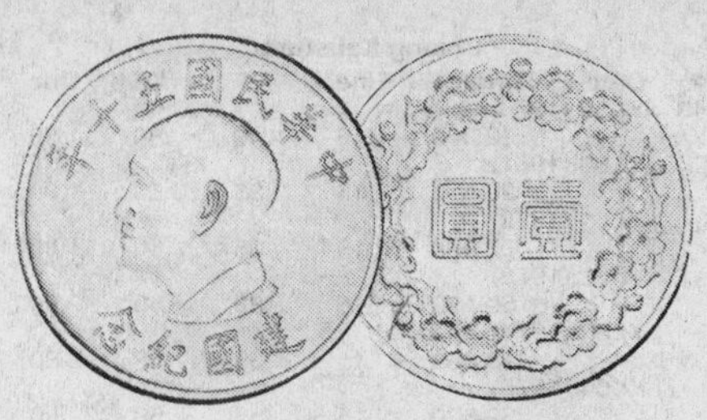

SILVER
50th Anniversary of the Republic
Chiang Kai-shek

Y#	Date	Mintage	Fine	VF	XF	Unc
A537	Yr.50 (1961)	—	—	—	—	280.00

NOTE: This coin was released accidentally or was released and quickly withdrawn and is very scarce today.

COPPER-NICKEL
80th Birthday of Chiang Kai-shek

Y#	Date	Mintage	Fine	VF	XF	Unc
543	Yr.55 (1966)	—	.15	.25	.40	1.00

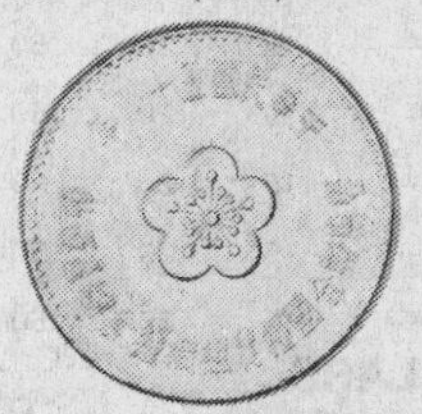

COPPER-NICKEL-ZINC
F.A.O. Issue

Y#	Date	Mintage	Fine	VF	XF	Unc
547	Yr.58 (1969)	10.000	.15	.25	.40	1.00

BRONZE
Chiang Kai-shek

Y#	Date	Mintage	Fine	VF	XF	Unc
551	Yr.70 (1981)	1,080.000	—	—	.10	.15
	Yr.71 (1982)	780.000	—	—	.10	.15
	Yr.72 (1983)	420.000	—	—	.10	.15
	Yr.73 (1984)	110.000	—	—	.10	.15
	Yr.74 (1985)	200.000	—	—	.10	.15
	Yr.75 (1986)	200.000	—	—	.10	.15
	Yr.76 (1987)	110.000	—	—	.10	.15
	Yr.77 (1988)	40.000	—	—	.10	.15

5 DOLLARS

COPPER-NICKEL
Sun Yat-sen

Y#	Date	Mintage	Fine	VF	XF	Unc
537	Yr.54 (1965)	—	.25	.75	1.50	4.00

Chiang Kai-shek

Y#	Date	Mintage	Fine	VF	XF	Unc
548	Yr.59 (1970)	12.360	.15	.40	.80	1.50
	Yr.60 (1971)	20.575	.15	.35	.50	1.00
	Yr.61 (1972)	27.998	.15	.35	.50	.80
	Yr.62 (1973)	50.122	.15	.35	.50	.80
	Yr.63 (1974)	418.068	.15	.35	.50	.80
	Yr.64 (1975)	39.520	.15	.35	.50	.80
	Yr.65 (1976)	140.000	.15	.35	.50	.80
	Yr.66 (1977)	50.260	.15	.35	.50	.80
	Yr.67 (1978)	78.082	.15	.35	.50	.80
	Yr.68 (1979)	—	.15	.35	.50	.80
	Yr.69 (1980)	273.000	.15	.35	.50	.80
	Yr.70 (1981)	162.000	.15	.35	.50	.80

Y#	Date	Mintage	Fine	VF	XF	Unc
552	Yr.70 (1981)	522.432	—	.15	.20	.50
	Yr.71 (1982)	66.000	—	.15	.20	.50
	Yr.72 (1983)	34.000	—	.15	.20	.50
	Yr.73 (1984)	280.000	—	.15	.20	.50
	Yr.77 (1988)	200.000	—	.15	.20	.50

10 DOLLARS

COPPER-NICKEL
Sun Yat-sen

Y#	Date	Mintage	Fine	VF	XF	Unc
538	Yr.54 (1965)	—	.50	1.00	1.75	4.50

Chiang Kai-shek

Y#	Date	Mintage	Fine	VF	XF	Unc
553	Yr.70 (1981)	123.000	—	.30	.40	.65
	Yr.71 (1982)	361.000	—	.30	.40	.65
	Yr.72 (1983)	196.000	—	.30	.40	.65
	Yr.73 (1984)	220.000	—	.30	.40	.65
	Yr.74 (1985)	200.000	—	.30	.40	.65
	Yr.75 (1986)	100.000	—	.30	.40	.65
	Yr.76 (1987)	90.000	—	.30	.40	.65
	Yr.77 (1988)	100.000	—	.30	.40	.65
	Yr.78 (1989)	—	—	.30	.40	.65

50 DOLLARS

17.1000 g, .750 SILVER, .4123 oz ASW
Sun Yat-sen

Y#	Date	Mintage	Fine	VF	XF	Unc
539	Yr.54 (1965)	—	—	—	—	15.00

BRASS

Y#	Date	Year Mintage	VF	XF	Unc
554	1992	81	—	—	3.50

100 DOLLARS

22.2100 g, .750 SILVER, .5335 oz ASW
Sun Yat-sen

Y#	Date	Mintage	Fine	VF	XF	Unc
540	Yr.54 (1965)	—	—	—	—	18.50

1000 DOLLARS

15.0000 g, .900 GOLD, .4340 oz AGW
Sun Yat-sen

Y#	Date	Mintage	Fine	VF	XF	Unc
541	Yr.54 (1965)	—	—	—	—	290.00

2000 DOLLARS

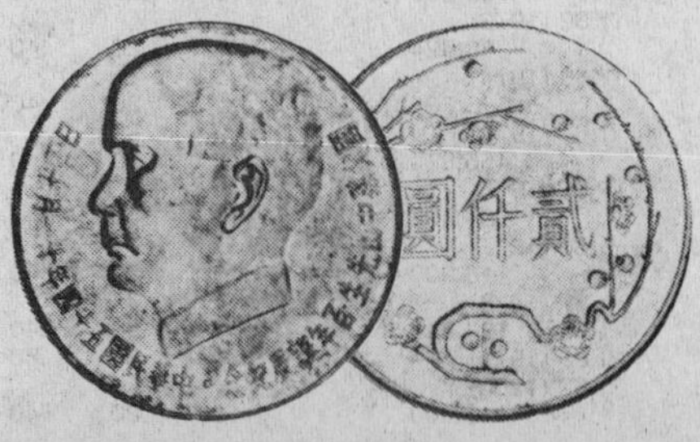

30.0000 g, .900 GOLD, .8681 oz AGW
Sun Yat-sen

Y#	Date	Mintage	Fine	VF	XF	Unc
542	Yr.54 (1965)	—	—	—	—	580.00

31.0600 g, .900 GOLD, .8988 oz AGW
80th Birthday of Chiang Kai-shek

Y#	Date	Mintage	Fine	VF	XF	Unc
544	Yr.55 (1966)	—	—	—	—	600.00

NOTE: For a similar medallic issue struck in silver refer to *UNUSUAL WORLD COINS*, 3rd edition, Krause Publications, 1992.

MINT SETS (MS)

KM#	Date	Mintage	Identification	Issue Price	Mkt. Val.
MS1	1965(4)	—	Y537-540	—	42.00

Listings For

CHINESE TURKESTAN: refer to China/Sinkiang (Xinjiang)

FOREIGN ENCLAVES

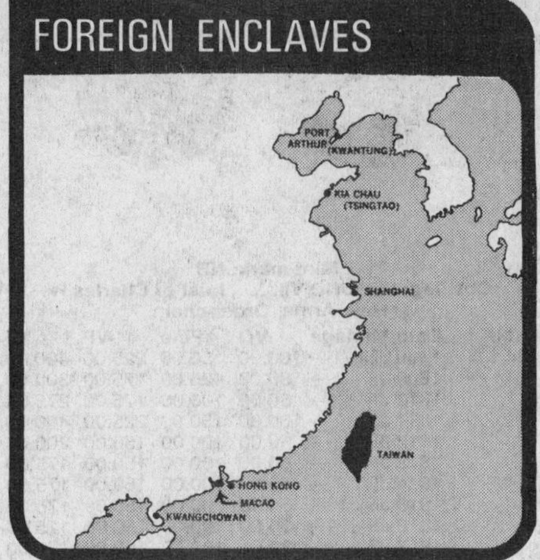

The Age of Exploration brought European traders to China as early as the 16th century. By 1560, the Portuguese were firmly in control of Macao. British, French and Dutch traders soon followed, and in 1784 the first clipper ship of the United States arrived.

Commerce, however, was severely limited by the refusal of the Chinese ruling class to treat the representatives of foreign powers as equals. By the end of the 18th century, only the port of Canton (Guangzhou) had been opened to European merchants, who were forbidden to enter Canton (Guangzhou) proper or travel inland.

The need for raw materials and expanded markets created by the Industrial Revolution brought increased pressure on China to open its doors to foreign traders. Actual military operations between 1839 and 1860, followed in the main by the threat of further attack by the western nations, procured from China extensive trade concessions. Among the more notable were the cession of Hong Kong to Great Britain, and the establishment of foreign enclaves at Kiau Chau (Germany), Kwangchowwan (France), Kuantung (Russia), Shanghai and elsewhere that were virtually sovereign empires within the Chinese Empire.

Military defeats, territorial and trade concessions, and the interference by Christian missionaries in local Chinese governments and customs created mass antagonism toward foreigners, and increased the activities of secret societies who became dedicated to ousting the foreigner from China. Chief among the xenophobic organizations was the I Ho Ch'uan "Righteous Harmony Fists", a society known as the 'Boxers' because its members practiced ritual shadow-boxing to make themselves invulnerable to bullets. In the autumn of 1899, they began to murder Chinese Christians and foreigners. The Empress Dowager T'zu Hsi abetted their work by procrastination and allowing many foreigners in China to be killed. The resulting 'Boxer Uprising' was a fiasco, albeit a bloody one.

Massacring Christians and foreigners as they moved north, the Boxers entered Peking (Beijing) in June 1900. There they beseiged some 1,000 foreigners and 3,000 Chinese Christians in the Legation Quarter until a seven-nation expeditionary force drove them off 55 days later. Although the nations had not declared war on China, they exacted additional concessions and heavy indemnities from the Manchu government. The United States, one of the principal recipients of the Boxer indemnities, later returned a major portion to China for educational development. Another portion was used to establish a fund to assist Chinese students in American schools.

HONG KONG

The free port of Hong Kong, a British-controlled commercial center and entrepot, is located 90 miles (145 km.) southeast of Canton (Guangzhou). For historical background and coin listings, refer to Hong Kong.

KIAU CHAU

Kiau Chau (Kiao Chau, Kiaochow, Kiautscho), a former German trading enclave, was located on the Shantung Peninsula of eastern China. Following the murder of two missionaries in Shantung in 1897, Germany occupied Kiaochow Bay, and during subsequent negotiations with the Chinese government obtained a 99-year lease on 177 sq. mi. of land. The enclave was established as a free port in 1899, and a customs house set up to collect tariffs on goods moving to and from the Chinese interior. The Japanese took the port as their first action in World War I to deprive German sea marauders of their east Asian supply and refitting base and retained possession until 1922, when it was restored to China by the Washington Conference on China and naval armaments. It fell again to Japan in 1938, but not before the Chinese had destroyed its manufacturing facilities. It is presently a part of the Peoples Republic of China. The major city is Tsingtao (Qingdao) is noted for its beer.

RULERS

Wilhelm II, 1897-1918

MONETARY SYSTEM

100 Cents = 1 Dollar

5 CENTS

COPPER-NICKEL

Y#	Date	Mintage	Fine	VF	XF	Unc
1	1909	.610	25.00	35.00	50.00	80.00
	1909	—		—	Proof	325.00

10 CENTS

COPPER-NICKEL

Y#	Date	Mintage	Fine	VF	XF	Unc
2	1909	.670	25.00	35.00	50.00	80.00
	1909	—	—	—	Proof	375.00

KWANGCHOWWAN

Kwangchowwan (Kuang-Chou Wan), a French commercial center including Fort Bayard (Chan-Chiang) and free port, was located on the Luichow (Leizhou) Peninsula which projects southward from China toward the island of Hainan. France acquired a 99-year lease to the 309 sq. mi. (800 sq. km.) enclave, with full territorial jurisdiction, in 1898. It was occupied by Japan during 1943-1945 in accordance with the Vichy-Tokyo agreement of 1941 which gave control of French Indochina to Japan. Upon relinquishment of all French claims in 1946, it became the Chinese municipality of Chankiang (Zhanjiang). In 1949 it was incorporated in the Peoples Republic of China. There are no known coins issued specifically for Kwangchowwan.

KWANTUNG

Kwantung (Kuan-tung), a name applied in the late 19th century to the southern tip of the Liaotung peninsula which projects southward into the Gulf of Chihli from present Liaoning province. The British captured Lushun on the southeast tip of the peninsula in 1860 and renamed it Port Arthur. In 1898, Russia forced a 25-year lease to the 925 sq. mi. enclave from the Ch'ing dynasty, but lost it to Japan as a result of the Russo-Japanese War of 1904-05. Japan controlled the area until defeated in World War II. From 1945 to 1955, Port Arthur was under joint RussianChinese administration, following which it passed to Chinese control. During the Russian occupation, Russian copper and silver coins circulated in the area. Under the Japanese, demonetized silver yen counterstamped *Gin* also circulated. The main city of Kwantung, on which construction was started by the Russians and completed by the Japanese, was Dalny in Russian, Dairen in Japanese, and Ta-lien (Dalian) in Chinese. Dalian and Lushun were merged after World War II into the municipality of Luda.

MACAO

Macao, the oldest European settlement in the Far East, is 35 miles (56 km.) southwest of Hong Kong. For historical background and coin listings, refer to Macao.

SHANGHAI

The port of Shanghai was opened to foreign trade in 1842 as demanded by the foreign victors in the Opium War, and quickly grew to become the most important port in China. Several countries acquired control over certain sections of the city, and beginning in 1854 organized themselves into what was to become the International Settlement. This confederation remained virtually autonomous until occupied by the Japanese in December 1941; the Japanese occupied the surrounding area of Shanghai in 1937. A number of different tokens and encased postage stamps were issued for use in Shanghai.

TAIWAN

The island of Taiwan (Formosa) had been a part of the Chinese empire since the 17th century. In 1895, however, the island was ceded to Japan following the Sino-Japanese War. Japan held the island until 1945 when it was returned to China.

Prior to 1895, Chinese cash coins and dragon silver coins were issued for the island (see Taiwan Province), but under the Japanese no coins were minted specifically for Taiwan. Demonetized Japanese silver yen coins, counterstamped *Gin* were placed in circulation there following the occupation.

COLOMBIA

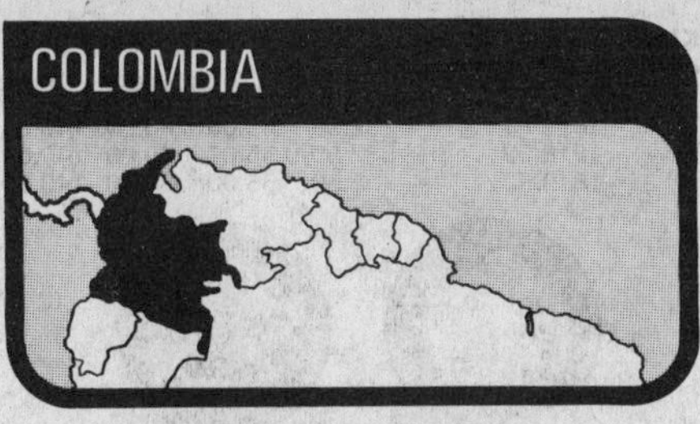

The Republic of Colombia, located in the northwestern corner of South America has an area of 439,737 sq. mi. (1,138,910 sq. km.) and a population of 29 million. Capital: Bogota. The economy is primarily agricultural with a mild, rich coffee being the chief crop. Colombia has the world's largest platinum deposits and important reserves of coal, iron ore, petroleum and limestone, precious metals and emeralds are also mined. Coffee, crude oil, bananas and sugar are exported.

The northern coast of present Colombia was one of the first parts of the American continent to be visited by Spanish navigators, and the site, at Darien in Panama, of the first permanent European settlement on the American mainland in 1510. New Granada, as Colombia was known until 1861, stemmed from the settlement of Santa Marta in 1525. New Granada was established as a Spanish colony in 1549. Independence was declared in 1813, and secured in 1819. In 1819, Simon Bolivar united Colombia, Venezuela, Panama and Ecuador as the Republic of Gran Colombia. Venezuela withdrew from the Republic in 1829; Ecuador in 1830; and Panama in 1903.

RULERS

Spanish, until 1819

MINT MARKS

C, NR, RN - Cartagena
FS, NR, S - Nuevo Reino (Bogota)
M - Medellin
(m) - Medellin, w/o mint mark
P, PN, Pn - Popayan

MONETARY SYSTEM

8 Reales = 1 Peso
2 Pesos = 1 Escudo
8 Escudos = 1 Onza

COLONIAL MILLED COINAGE

1/4 REAL

.8462 g, .896 SILVER, .0243 oz ASW
Mint mark: NR
Obv: Castle. Rev: Lion.

KM#	Date	Mintage	VG	Fine	VF	XF
63	1801	—	5.00	10.00	15.00	50.00
	1802	—	10.00	20.00	35.00	70.00
	1803/2	—	6.00	12.00	20.00	50.00
	1803	—	7.50	15.00	25.00	50.00
	1804	—	5.00	10.00	15.00	50.00
	1805	—	6.00	12.00	20.00	50.00
	1806	—	7.50	15.00	25.00	50.00
	1807	—	12.50	25.00	40.00	65.00
	1808/6	—	20.00	40.00	65.00	110.00
	1808	—	5.00	10.00	15.00	50.00

NOTE: Earlier dates (1796-1800) exist for this type.

KM#	Date	Mintage	VG	Fine	VF	XF
67.1	1809	—	17.50	35.00	55.00	75.00
	1810/09/01	—	10.00	20.00	32.50	60.00
	1810/09	—	10.00	18.50	30.00	55.00
	1810/1	—	10.00	18.50	30.00	55.00
	1810	—	7.50	15.00	25.00	45.00
	1811	—	12.50	25.00	45.00	65.00
	1812	—	7.50	15.00	30.00	50.00
	1813	—	12.50	25.00	45.00	70.00
	1814	—	5.00	10.00	20.00	35.00
	1815	—	10.00	20.00	40.00	65.00
	1816	—	6.00	12.00	25.00	40.00
	1817	—	5.00	10.00	15.00	30.00
	1818/7	—	6.00	13.50	20.00	40.00
	1818	—	5.00	10.00	15.00	35.00
	1819	—	25.00	45.00	65.00	85.00

Mint mark: PN
Similar to KM#63.

KM#	Date	Mintage	VG	Fine	VF	XF
67.2	1816	—	12.00	20.00	40.00	85.00
	1822	—	— Reported, not confirmed			

1/2 REAL

1.6925 g, .896 SILVER, .0487 oz ASW
Mint mark: NR
Obv. leg: FERND. VII. . . ., bust of Charles IV.

KM#	Date	Mintage	VG	Fine	VF	XF
69.1	1810 JJ	—	32.50	55.00	80.00	140.00

KM#	Date	Mintage	VG	Fine	VF	XF
69.1	1812 JF(error)	—	50.00	100.00	150.00	—
	1816 FJ	—	32.50	55.00	80.00	140.00
	1818 FJ	—	32.50	55.00	80.00	140.00
	1819 FJ	—	32.50	55.00	80.00	140.00

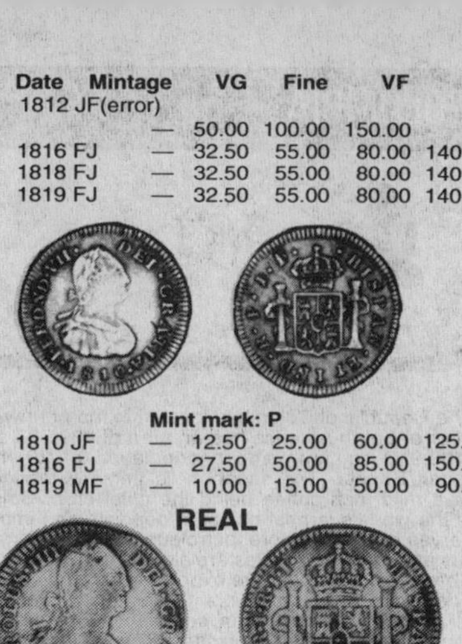

Mint mark: P

KM#	Date	Mintage	VG	Fine	VF	XF
69.2	1810 JF	—	12.50	25.00	60.00	125.00
	1816 FJ	—	27.50	50.00	85.00	150.00
	1819 MF	—	10.00	15.00	50.00	90.00

REAL

3.3834 g, .896 SILVER, .0974 oz ASW
Mint mark: NR
Obv: Bust of Charles IV.

KM#	Date	Mintage	VG	Fine	VF	XF
58	1801/797 JJ	—	10.00	25.00	75.00	—
	1801 JJ	—	6.00	12.50	60.00	125.00
	1802 JJ	—	6.00	12.50	60.00	125.00
	1804 JJ	—	12.50	25.00	65.00	125.00

NOTE: Earlier dates (1792-1800) exist for this type.

Obv. leg: FERDND VII. . . ., bust of Charles IV.

KM#	Date	Mintage	VG	Fine	VF	XF
68.1	1809 FJ	—	— Reported, not confirmed			
	1810 JF	—	6.00	12.50	35.00	80.00
	1810 JJ	—	15.00	30.00	65.00	125.00
	1812 FJ	—	7.50	15.00	40.00	85.00
	1812/4 JF	—	10.00	20.00	55.00	100.00
	1812 JF	—	8.00	20.00	40.00	85.00
	1816 FJ	—	6.00	12.50	35.00	80.00
	1817 FJ	—	7.50	15.00	40.00	85.00
	1818 FJ	—	8.00	17.50	60.00	100.00
	1819 FJ	—	7.50	17.50	40.00	85.00
	1819 FJ (inverted J)	—	6.00	12.50	40.00	85.00
	1819 J	—	6.00	12.50	40.00	85.00
	1820 FJ	—	25.00	50.00	90.00	150.00
	1821 FJ	—	30.00	55.00	100.00	175.00

Mint mark: P

KM#	Date	Mintage	VG	Fine	VF	XF
68.2	1810 JF	—	18.00	35.00	90.00	170.00
	1813 JF	—	30.00	55.00	130.00	225.00
	1820 FM	—	18.00	35.00	90.00	170.00
	1822 FM	—	— Reported, not confirmed			

2 REALES

6.7680 g, .896 SILVER, .1949 oz ASW
Mint mark: NR
Obv. leg: FERDND VII. . . ., bust of Charles IV.

KM#	Date	Mintage	VG	Fine	VF	XF
70.1	1811 JF	—	17.50	35.00	75.00	125.00
	1816 FJ	—	17.50	35.00	75.00	125.00
	1816 JJ/FJ	—	17.50	35.00	75.00	125.00
	1817 FJ	—	17.50	35.00	75.00	125.00
	1818/7 FJ	—	45.00	85.00	150.00	225.00
	1818 FJ	—	25.00	55.00	125.00	200.00
	1819/8 FJ	—	25.00	55.00	125.00	200.00
	1819 FJ	—	25.00	55.00	125.00	200.00

Mint mark: P

KM#	Date	Mintage	VG	Fine	VF	XF
70.2	1810 JF	—	12.00	20.00	40.00	100.00
	1811/0 JF	—	32.50	50.00	70.00	140.00
	1811 JF	—	22.50	40.00	55.00	120.00
	1813 JF	—	22.50	40.00	55.00	120.00
	1814/3 JF	—	75.00	150.00	250.00	500.00

KM#	Date	Mintage	VG	Fine	VF	XF
70.2	1814 JF	—	50.00	100.00	200.00	400.00
	1818 MF	—	22.50	40.00	55.00	120.00
	1819 MF	—	12.00	20.00	40.00	100.00
	1820/10 MF	—	35.00	85.00	150.00	300.00
	1820 MF	—	20.00	35.00	50.00	110.00
	1820 FM	—	20.00	35.00	50.00	110.00

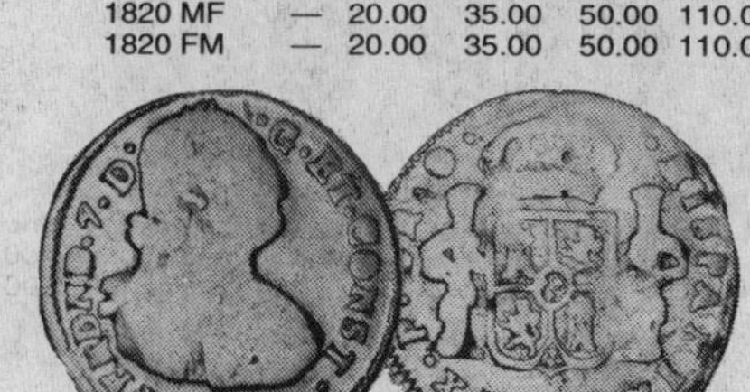

Obv. leg: FERDND. 7.D.G.ET. CONST.

KM#	Date	Mintage	VG	Fine	VF	XF
74	1822 O	—	25.00	50.00	100.00	200.00

8 REALES

27.0730 g, .896 SILVER, .7799 oz ASW
Mint mark: P
Obv. leg: FERDND VII. . . ., bust of Charles IV.

KM#	Date	Mintage	VG	Fine	VF	XF
71	1810 JF	—	1000.	2000.	4250.	9500.
	1811 JF	—	1000.	2000.	4250.	9500.
	1812 JF	—	1000.	2000.	4000.	9000.
	1813/2 JF	—	1000.	2000.	4000.	9000.
	1813 JF	—	1000.	2000.	4000.	9000.
	1813 F	—	—	—	Rare	—
	1814/3 JF	—	450.00	800.00	1600.	3500.
	1814 JF	—	500.00	900.00	1800.	3750.
	1815 JF	—	—	—	Rare	—
	1816 F	—	1200.	2200.	4500.	10,500.
	1820 FM	—	—	—	Rare	—
	1820 MF	—	—	—	Rare	—

ESCUDO

3.3841 g, .875 GOLD, .0952 oz AGW
Mint mark: NR
Obv: Bust of Charles IIII.

KM#	Date	Mintage	VG	Fine	VF	XF
56.1	1801 JJ	—	80.00	125.00	200.00	275.00
	1802/1 JJ	—	80.00	125.00	200.00	275.00
	1802 JJ	—	50.00	100.00	150.00	225.00
	1803 JJ	—	50.00	100.00	150.00	225.00
	1804 JJ	—	50.00	100.00	150.00	225.00
	1805 JJ	—	50.00	100.00	150.00	225.00
	1806 JJ	—	80.00	125.00	175.00	275.00
	1807 JJ	—	100.00	150.00	225.00	325.00
	1808 JJ	—	50.00	100.00	150.00	225.00

NOTE: Earlier dates (1791-1800) exist for this type.

Mint mark: P

KM#	Date	Mintage	VG	Fine	VF	XF
56.2	1801 JF	—	60.00	90.00	130.00	200.00
	1802 JF	—	60.00	90.00	130.00	200.00
	1803 JF	—	80.00	125.00	175.00	275.00
	1804 JF	—	80.00	125.00	175.00	275.00
	1804 JT	—	100.00	150.00	225.00	350.00
	1805 JT	—	80.00	125.00	175.00	275.00
	1805 JF	—	100.00	150.00	225.00	350.00
	1806 JT	—	80.00	125.00	175.00	250.00
	1806 JF	—	80.00	125.00	175.00	250.00
	1807 JF	—	80.00	125.00	175.00	275.00
	1808 JF	—	80.00	125.00	175.00	275.00

NOTE: Earlier dates (1792-1800) exist for this type.

Mint mark: NR
Obv. leg: FERDND VII. . . ., bust of Charles IV.
Rev: Arms, Order chain.

KM#	Date	Mintage	VG	Fine	VF	XF
64.1	1808 JF	—	100.00	150.00	225.00	400.00
	1809 JF	—	80.00	125.00	175.00	300.00
	1810 JF	—	50.00	100.00	175.00	275.00
	1811 JJ	—	100.00	150.00	225.00	400.00
	1812 JF	—	50.00	100.00	150.00	200.00
	1813 JF	—	50.00	100.00	150.00	175.00
	1814 JF	—	50.00	100.00	150.00	175.00
	1815 JF	—	50.00	100.00	150.00	175.00
	1816 JF	—	50.00	100.00	150.00	175.00
	1817 JF	—	50.00	100.00	150.00	175.00
	1818 JF	—	50.00	100.00	150.00	175.00
	1819 JF	—	50.00	100.00	150.00	175.00
	1820 JF	—	80.00	125.00	175.00	275.00

Mint mark: P

KM#	Date	Mintage	VG	Fine	VF	XF
64.2	1808 JF	—	65.00	100.00	150.00	225.00
	1809 JF	—	65.00	100.00	150.00	225.00
	1810 JF	—	65.00	100.00	150.00	225.00
	1812 JF	—	65.00	100.00	150.00	225.00
	1813 JF	—	65.00	100.00	150.00	225.00
	1814 JF	—	65.00	100.00	150.00	225.00
	1816 FM	—	65.00	100.00	150.00	225.00
	1816 FR	—	65.00	100.00	150.00	225.00
	1816 F	—	65.00	100.00	150.00	225.00
	1817 FM	—	65.00	100.00	150.00	225.00
	1818 FM	—	65.00	100.00	150.00	225.00
	1819 FM	—	65.00	100.00	150.00	225.00

2 ESCUDOS

6.7682 g, .875 GOLD, .1904 oz AGW
Mint mark: NR
Obv: Bust right. Rev: Crowned arms, Order chain.

KM#	Date	Mintage	VG	Fine	VF	XF
60.1	1801 JJ	—	125.00	200.00	275.00	350.00
	1803 JJ	—	175.00	225.00	300.00	375.00
	1804 JJ	—	200.00	275.00	325.00	450.00
	1805 JJ	—	100.00	150.00	225.00	300.00
	1806 JJ	—	325.00	400.00	500.00	725.00
	1807 JJ	—	100.00	150.00	225.00	300.00
	1808 JJ	—	125.00	200.00	275.00	350.00

NOTE: Earlier dates (1792-1800) exist for this type.

Mint mark: P

KM#	Date	Mintage	VG	Fine	VF	XF
60.2	1802 JF	—	100.00	150.00	225.00	300.00
	1804 JF	—	125.00	200.00	275.00	350.00
	1804 SF	—	200.00	275.00	350.00	500.00
	1805 JT	—	325.00	425.00	525.00	850.00

NOTE: Earlier dates (1793-1799) exist for this type.

Mint mark: NR
Obv. leg: FERDND VII. . . ., bust of Charles IV.
Rev: Arms, Order chain.

KM#	Date	Mintage	VG	Fine	VF	XF
65.1	1808 JF	—	200.00	275.00	350.00	525.00
	1809 JJ	—	125.00	200.00	275.00	450.00
	1810 JF	—	250.00	325.00	425.00	725.00
	1811 JF	—	225.00	300.00	400.00	675.00

Mint mark: P

KM#	Date	Mintage	VG	Fine	VF	XF
65.2	1817 FM	—	275.00	325.00	400.00	700.00
	1818 FM	—	275.00	325.00	400.00	700.00
	1819 FM	—	275.00	325.00	400.00	700.00

4 ESCUDOS

13.5365 g, .875 GOLD, .3808 oz AGW
Mint mark: NR
Obv. leg: CAROL IIII. . . ., bust of Charles IV.

KM#	Date	Mintage	VG	Fine	VF	XF
61.1	1801 JJ	—	225.00	450.00	550.00	1100.
	1803 JJ	—	225.00	450.00	550.00	1100.
	1804 JJ	—	225.00	450.00	650.00	1300.
	1805 JJ	—	225.00	450.00	600.00	1250.
	1806 JJ	—	225.00	450.00	600.00	1250.
	1807 JJ	—	350.00	650.00	1000.	1650.

NOTE: Earlier dates (1792-1799) exist for this type.

Mint mark: P
Obv. leg: CAROL IIII. . . ., bust of Charles IV.
Rev: Crowned arms in Order chain.

KM#	Date	Mintage	VG	Fine	VF	XF
61.2	1801 JF	—	300.00	600.00	675.00	1375.
	1802 JF	—	250.00	500.00	650.00	1300.
	1807 SF	—	550.00	1100.	1500.	2000.
	1808 JF	—	650.00	1300.	1800.	2600.

NOTE: Earlier dates (1792-1798) exist for this type.

Mint mark: NR
Obv. leg: FERDND VII. . . ., bust of Charles IV.
Rev: Arms, Order chain.

KM#	Date	Mintage	VG	Fine	VF	XF
72	1818 JF	—	300.00	600.00	850.00	1550.
	1819 JF	—	300.00	600.00	850.00	1550.

8 ESCUDOS

27.0730 g, .875 GOLD, .7616 oz AGW
Mint mark: NR
Obv. leg: CAROL IIII. . . ., bust of Charles IV.
Rev: Crowned arms, Order chain.

KM#	Date	Mintage	VG	Fine	VF	XF
62.1	1801 JJ	—	375.00	425.00	650.00	900.00
	1802/1 JJ	—	375.00	425.00	650.00	900.00
	1802 JJ	—	375.00	425.00	650.00	900.00
	1803/2 JJ	—	375.00	425.00	650.00	900.00
	1803 JJ	—	375.00	425.00	650.00	900.00
	1804/3 JJ	—	375.00	425.00	650.00	900.00
	1804 JJ	—	375.00	425.00	650.00	900.00
	1805 JJ	—	375.00	425.00	650.00	900.00
	1806 JJ	—	375.00	425.00	650.00	900.00
	1807 JJ	—	375.00	425.00	650.00	900.00
	1808 JJ	—	375.00	425.00	650.00	900.00
	1808 JF	—	2000.	3500.	6000.	8500.

NOTE: Earlier dates (1792-1800) exist for this type.

Mint mark: P

KM#	Date	Mintage	VG	Fine	VF	XF
62.2	1801 JF	—	375.00	425.00	700.00	1000.
	1802 JF	—	375.00	425.00	700.00	1000.
	1803 JF	—	375.00	425.00	700.00	1000.
	1804 JT	—	1500.	2500.	3500.	4500.
	1804 JF	—	375.00	425.00	700.00	1000.
	1805 JF	—	750.00	1500.	2000.	3000.
	1805 JT	—	500.00	800.00	1200.	2000.
	1806 JF	—	375.00	425.00	700.00	1000.
	1807 JF	—	375.00	425.00	700.00	1000.
	1808 JF	—	550.00	900.00	1300.	2000.

NOTE: Earlier dates (1791-1800) exist for this type.

Mint mark: NR
Obv. leg: FERDND. VII. . . ., bust of Charles IV.

KM#	Date	Mintage	VG	Fine	VF	XF
66.1	1808 JJ	—	600.00	1000.	1400.	2000.
	1808 JF/JJ	—	650.00	1200.	1750.	2250.
	1808 JF	—	650.00	1200.	1750.	2250.
	1809 JF	—	375.00	425.00	650.00	1000.
	1810 JF	—	375.00	425.00	650.00	1000.
	1811/0 JF	—	375.00	425.00	650.00	1000.
	1811 JF	—	375.00	425.00	650.00	1000.
	1812 JF	—	375.00	425.00	650.00	1000.
	1813/2 JF	—	375.00	425.00	800.00	1300.
	1813 JF	—	375.00	425.00	650.00	1000.
	1814/3 JF	—	375.00	425.00	650.00	1000.
	1814 JF	—	375.00	425.00	650.00	1000.
	1815/4 JF	—	375.00	425.00	650.00	1000.
	1815 JF	—	375.00	425.00	650.00	1000.
	1816 JF	—	375.00	425.00	650.00	1000.
	1817 JF	—	375.00	425.00	650.00	1000.
	1818 JF	—	375.00	425.00	650.00	1000.
	1819 JF	—	375.00	425.00	650.00	1000.
	1820 JF	—	375.00	425.00	650.00	1000.

Mint mark: P

KM#	Date	Mintage	VG	Fine	VF	XF
66.2	1808 JF	—	375.00	425.00	650.00	900.00
	1809 JF	—	375.00	425.00	650.00	900.00
	1810/09 JF	—	375.00	425.00	650.00	900.00
	1810 JF	—	375.00	425.00	650.00	900.00
	1811/0 JF	—	375.00	425.00	650.00	900.00
	1811 JF	—	375.00	425.00	650.00	900.00
	1812 JF	—	375.00	425.00	650.00	900.00
	1813 JF	—	375.00	425.00	650.00	900.00
	1814 JF	—	375.00	425.00	650.00	900.00
	1815 JF	—	375.00	425.00	650.00	900.00
	1816 FM	—	450.00	700.00	1000.	1500.
	1816 JF	—	900.00	1500.	2000.	3000.
	1816 F	—	600.00	1000.	1300.	1800.
	1817 FM	—	375.00	425.00	650.00	900.00
	1818 FM	—	375.00	425.00	650.00	900.00
	1819 FM	—	375.00	425.00	650.00	900.00

Mint mark: Pn

KM#	Date	Mintage	VG	Fine	VF	XF
66.3	1814 FR	—	550.00	900.00	1500.	2000.
	1815 FR	—	2750.	4750.	6750.	—
	1816 FR	—	450.00	700.00	1000.	1500.
	1820 FM	—	550.00	900.00	1500.	2000.

POPAYAN

MEDIO (1/2) REAL

COPPER
Obv: P/ANO/1813. Rev: Value.

KM#	Date	Mintage	VG	Fine	VF	XF
1	1813	5 known	200.00	300.00	500.00	750.00

2 REALES

COPPER
Obv: NUEVO REYNO DE GRANADA, ANO/1813
Rev: PROVINCIA DE POPAYAN, value.

KM#	Date	Mintage	VG	Fine	VF	XF
2	1813	—	25.00	35.00	50.00	90.00

8 REALES

COPPER

KM#	Date	Mintage	VG	Fine	VF	XF
3	1813	—	60.00	100.00	175.00	300.00

SANTA MARTA

A city, on the shores of the Caribbean Sea, founded in 1525, is the oldest in Colombia. Santa Marta was one of several areas in Colombia that remained longer under Spanish rule. Royalists, beseiged by Republican forces, made a necessity coinage that copies certain design elements of Spanish Imperial issues.

1/4 REAL

COPPER

KM#	Date	Mintage	Good	VG	Fine	VF
2	1813	—	13.50	27.50	55.00	90.00
	1818	—	— Reported, not confirmed			

KM#	Date	Mintage	Good	VG	Fine	VF
4	1820	—	10.00	17.50	35.00	50.00
	1821	—	— Reported, not confirmed			

NOTE: Varieties exist.

1/2 REAL

COPPER

KM#	Date	Mintage	Good	VG	Fine	VF
1	ND (1812-13)	—	50.00	100.00	200.00	300.00

KM#	Date	Mintage	Good	VG	Fine	VF
3	1813	—	—	—	Rare	—

2 REALES

SILVER

KM#	Date	Mintage	Good	VG	Fine	VF
5	1820	—	200.00	350.00	500.00	700.00

COUNTERMARKED COINAGE

8 REALES

27.0700 g, .903 SILVER, .7859 oz ASW
c/m: S.M. and VPB monogram on Mexico KM#110.

KM#	Date	Mintage	Good	VG	Fine	VF
6	1809 TH	—	350.00	500.00	750.00	1100.

REPUBLICAN COINAGE

CARTAGENA

This port city on Colombia's northern coast was very important for the Spanish colonies and was heavily fortified to ward off British and French privateers. Cartagena was the first major city in Colombia to declare independence from Spain - November 11, 1811. In 1815, after a four month siege, it fell to the Spaniards. In the interim the besieged Republicans struck coins for local use. All these coins are crude in die-work, planchets and striking.

1/2 REAL

COPPER

KM#	Date	Mintage	Good	VG	Fine	VF
2	1812	—	7.50	12.50	22.00	40.00
	1813	—	7.50	15.00	27.50	45.00
	ND	—	6.00	9.00	17.50	35.00

DOS (2) REALES

COPPER

KM#	Date	Mintage	Good	VG	Fine	VF
1	1811	—	12.00	22.50	42.50	80.00
	1812	—	12.00	22.50	42.50	80.00
	1813	—	12.00	22.50	42.50	80.00
	1814	—	8.50	17.50	32.50	65.00
	ND	—	6.00	10.00	22.50	50.00

CUNDINAMARCA STATE

A province in central Colombia, with Bogota as its capital, was the first to declare independence - July 16, 1813. Spain regained control in 1816 and held it until 1819. After the battle of Boyaca the province was again free. Coins made before and after the Spanish re-occupation, and through 1821, when the Gran Colombia plan was put into effect, bear the provincial designation. Imperial Spanish types were struck during the Spanish re-occupation.

1/4 REAL

.7000 g, .583 SILVER, .0131 oz ASW

KM#	Date	Mintage	Good	VG	Fine	VF
2	1814	—	17.50	30.00	50.00	90.00
	1815	—	20.00	35.00	60.00	110.00

1/2 REAL

SILVER
Obv: Indian head. Rev: Pomegranate.

KM#	Date	Mintage	Good	VG	Fine	VF
3	1814 JF	—	40.00	80.00	150.00	275.00

REAL

2.5000 g, .583 SILVER, .0468 oz ASW

KM#	Date	Mintage	Good	VG	Fine	VF
1	1813 JF	—	15.00	40.00	55.00	85.00
	1814 JF	—	15.00	40.00	65.00	100.00
	1815 JF	—	20.00	45.00	75.00	130.00
	1816 JF	—	18.50	42.50	70.00	100.00

2 REALES

4.9000 g, .583 SILVER, .0918 oz ASW

KM#	Date	Mintage	Good	VG	Fine	VF
4	1815 JF	—	12.50	22.50	42.50	80.00
	1816/5 JF	—	15.00	27.50	50.00	95.00
	1816 JF	—	13.50	25.00	45.00	85.00

PROVINCIAL COINAGE

REPUBLIC OF COLOMBIA

1820-1823

Cundinamarca Province

1/2 REAL

1.3000 g, .666 SILVER, .0278 oz ASW

KM#	Date	Mintage	Good	VG	Fine	VF
8	1821 Ba JF	—	10.00	22.50	52.50	115.00

REAL

2.7800 g, .666 SILVER, .0595 oz ASW

KM#	Date	Mintage	Good	VG	Fine	VF
9	1821 Ba JF	—	8.00	17.50	35.00	85.00

2 REALES

4.9800 g, .666 SILVER, .1066 oz ASW

KM#	Date	Mintage	Good	VG	Fine	VF
5	1820 JF	—	32.50	75.00	150.00	325.00
	1820 Ba JF	—	—	—	Rare	—
	1821 Ba JF	—	6.50	15.00	32.50	70.00
	1821 JF	—	27.50	65.00	150.00	300.00
	1823 JF	—	75.00	160.00	275.00	400.00

8 REALES

23.0000 g, .666 SILVER, .4924 oz ASW

KM#	Date	Mintage	Good	VG	Fine	VF
6	1820 JF	—	10.00	30.00	50.00	110.00
	1820 Ba JF	—	50.00	75.00	125.00	250.00
	1821 JF	—	10.00	25.00	45.00	100.00
	1821 Ba JF	—	10.00	30.00	50.00	110.00

Mule. Obv: KM#6. Rev: Similar to Nueva Granada, KM#78.

KM#	Date	Mintage	Good	VG	Fine	VF
7	1820 JF	—	1000.	1500.	2000.	2500.

NATIONAL COINAGE

MINT MARKS

A - Antioquia
AM - Bogota
B, BA, BOGOTA - Santa Fe de Bogota
H - Birmingham
M - Medellin
P, PN, POPAYAN - Popayan

UNITED PROVINCES OF NUEVA GRANADA

PROVISIONAL ISSUE

1819-1822

1/4 REAL

.7000 g, .666 SILVER, .0149 oz ASW
Obv: Liberty cap. Rev: Pomegranate.

KM#	Date	Mintage	Good	VG	Fine	VF
79.1	1820	—	11.50	22.00	40.00	60.00
	1821	—	11.50	22.00	40.00	60.00

Mint mark: BA

KM#	Date	Mintage	Good	VG	Fine	VF
79.2	1821	—	13.50	27.50	60.00	120.00

Mint mark: Pn

KM#	Date	Mintage	Good	VG	Fine	VF
79.3	1822	—	—	—	Rare	—

REAL

3.1500 g, .666 SILVER, .0674 oz ASW
Obv. leg: LIBERTAD AMERICANA around Indian head.
Rev. leg: NUEVA GRANADA around pomegranate.

KM#	Date	Mintage	Good	VG	Fine	VF
75	1819 JF	—	22.50	47.50	100.00	200.00

2 REALES

5.9000 g, .666 SILVER, .1263 oz ASW

KM#	Date	Mintage	Good	VG	Fine	VF
76	1819 JF	—	20.00	40.00	120.00	250.00

Rev: Pomegranate divides value.

KM#	Date	Mintage	Good	VG	Fine	VF
77	1819 JF	—	25.00	50.00	75.00	125.00
	1820 JF	—	30.00	60.00	100.00	175.00

8 REALES

23.0000 g, .666 SILVER, .4924 oz ASW

KM#	Date	Mintage	Good	VG	Fine	VF
78	1819 JF	—	25.00	45.00	90.00	175.00
	1819/20 JF	—	30.00	50.00	100.00	200.00
	1820 JF	—	25.00	45.00	90.00	175.00

COUNTERSTAMPED COINAGE

8 REALES

SILVER
c/s: Pomegranate on Cundinamarca 8 Reales, KM#6.

73	ND (1820 JF)	—	50.00	90.00	150.00	250.00
	ND (1821 Ba JF)	—	50.00	90.00	150.00	250.00

REPUBLIC OF COLOMBIA

1821-1837

1/4 REAL

.7000 g, .666 SILVER, .0149 oz ASW
Mint mark: B
Rev: Mint mark and initials below 1/4.

85.1	1826 TR	—	30.00	50.00	70.00	100.00

NOTE: Counterfeits of the above type with initials RS are reported for 1825-27.

Rev: Mint mark above 1/4, initials.

85.2	1826 RS	—	10.00	17.50	30.00	45.00
	1827 RS	—	4.00	7.50	10.00	22.50
	1828 RS	—	5.00	8.50	11.50	25.00
	1829 RS	—	4.00	7.50	10.00	22.50
	1833 RS	—	5.00	9.00	12.50	27.50
	1834 RS	—	4.00	7.50	10.00	22.50
	1836 RS	—	5.00	8.50	11.50	25.00

Mint mark: P

KM#	Date	Mintage	Good	VG	Fine	VF
85.3	1826 RU	—	5.00	10.00	18.00	30.00
	1832 RU	—	—	—	Rare	—
	1833 RU	—	8.50	15.00	25.00	40.00
	1834 RU	—	5.00	8.50	11.50	25.00
	1836 RU	—	7.00	12.50	20.00	35.00

1/2 REAL

1.5500 g, .666 SILVER, .0331 oz ASW
Mint mark: BA
Obv: Fasces between crossed cornucopias.
Rev: Value in wreath.

88.1	1833 RS	—	8.00	15.00	28.00	55.00
	1834 RS	—	7.50	13.50	22.50	50.00
	1835 RS	—	9.00	17.50	30.00	60.00

Mint mark: PN

88.2	1834 RU	—	9.00	16.50	27.50	50.00
	1835 RU	—	—	—	Rare	—
	1836 RU	—	8.00	15.00	25.00	40.00

REAL

3.1000 g, .666 SILVER, .0663 oz ASW
Mint mark: BA

87.1	1827 B RR	—	22.50	50.00	100.00	200.00
	1827 RR	—	3.50	7.50	12.00	22.00
	1828 RR	—	4.50	10.00	17.50	30.00
	1828 RS	—	3.50	7.50	12.50	22.00
	1829 RS	—	200.00	350.00	—	—
	1833/29 RS	—	5.00	12.00	22.00	45.00
	1833 RS	—	3.00	6.00	10.00	20.00
	1834 RS	—	20.00	40.00	70.00	—
	1835 RS	—	2.50	5.25	9.00	17.50
	1836 RS	—	2.50	5.25	9.00	15.00

Mint mark: PN

87.2	1827 RU	—	—	—	Rare	—
	1828/7 RU	—	6.00	10.00	17.50	30.00
	1828 MF	—	3.00	6.50	12.00	22.00
	1828 RU	—	3.00	6.50	12.00	22.00
	1828 RU/MF	—	—	—	—	—
	1829 MF	—	3.00	6.50	12.00	22.00
	1829 RU	—	3.00	6.50	12.00	22.00
	1830 RU	—	2.00	5.00	9.00	17.50
	1831 RU	—	2.00	5.00	9.00	17.50
	1832 RU	—	3.00	6.50	12.00	22.00
	1833 RU	—	3.00	6.50	12.00	22.00
	1834	—	7.00	13.50	25.00	35.00
	1835	—	—	Reported, not confirmed		

8 REALES

27.0200 g, .835 SILVER, .7253 oz ASW

89	1834 RS	—	30.00	55.00	150.00	300.00
	1835/4 RS	—	20.00	40.00	80.00	175.00
	1835 RS	—	27.50	50.00	135.00	275.00
	1836 RS	—	20.00	40.00	80.00	175.00

PESO

1.6875 g., .875 GOLD, .0474 oz AGW
Mint: Bogota

KM#	Date	Mintage	Good	VG	Fine	VF
80	1821 JF	—	100.00	200.00	350.00	500.00

NOTE: Authenticity currently under study.

KM#	Date	Mintage	VG	Fine	VF	XF
84	1825 JF	—	55.00	60.00	80.00	125.00
	1826 JF	—	55.00	60.00	80.00	125.00
	1826/5 JF	—	55.00	60.00	80.00	125.00
	1826 JR	—	55.00	60.00	80.00	125.00
	1826 PJ	—	55.00	60.00	80.00	125.00
	1827 JF	—	55.00	60.00	80.00	125.00
	1827 RR	—	55.00	60.00	80.00	125.00
	1829/7 PJ	—	55.00	60.00	80.00	125.00
	1829 JF	—	55.00	60.00	80.00	125.00
	1829 RS	—	55.00	60.00	80.00	125.00
	1830 RS	—	55.00	60.00	80.00	125.00
	1833 RS	—	—	Reported, not confirmed		
	1834 RS	—	55.00	60.00	80.00	125.00
	1835 RS	—	55.00	60.00	80.00	125.00
	1836 RS	—	55.00	60.00	80.00	125.00

ESCUDO

3.3841 g, .875 GOLD, .0952 oz AGW
Mint: Bogota

81.1	1822 MF	—	—	Reported, not confirmed		
	1823 JF	—	100.00	125.00	225.00	350.00
	1824 JF	—	—	Reported, not confirmed		
	1825 JF	—	75.00	100.00	200.00	300.00
	1826 JF	—	—	Reported, not confirmed		
	1832 PR	—	—	Reported, not confirmed		
	1832 EM	—	—	Reported, not confirmed		

NOTE: An 1821 dated piece is known and considered to be a contemporary counterfeit.

Mint: Popayan

81.2	1823 FM	—	55.00	65.00	115.00	175.00
	1824 FM	—	55.00	65.00	100.00	150.00
	1825 FM	—	55.00	65.00	100.00	150.00
	1826/5 FM	—	—	Reported, not confirmed		
	1826 FM	—	55.00	65.00	100.00	150.00
	1826 RU	—	—	Reported, not confirmed		
	1827 FM	—	55.00	65.00	100.00	150.00
	1827 RU/FM	—	—	Reported, not confirmed		
	1827 RU	—	55.00	65.00	115.00	175.00
	1828 RU	—	55.00	65.00	115.00	175.00
	1829 RU	—	55.00	65.00	100.00	150.00
	1830 RU	—	55.00	65.00	100.00	150.00
	1831/21 RM	—	65.00	75.00	125.00	200.00
	1831 RU	—	65.00	75.00	125.00	200.00
	1832 RU	—	55.00	65.00	100.00	150.00
	1833/2 RU	—	55.00	65.00	115.00	175.00
	1834 RU	—	55.00	65.00	115.00	175.00
	1835 RU	—	—	Reported, not confirmed		
	1836/4 RU	—	55.00	65.00	115.00	175.00
	1836 RU	—	55.00	65.00	115.00	175.00

2 ESCUDOS

6.7682 g, .875 GOLD, .1904 oz AGW
Mint: Bogota

83	1823 JF	—	150.00	250.00	400.00	600.00
	1824 JF	—	125.00	225.00	350.00	500.00
	1825 JF	—	125.00	225.00	350.00	500.00
	1826 JF	—	135.00	235.00	375.00	550.00
	1829 JF	—	150.00	250.00	400.00	600.00
	1829 PJ	—	150.00	250.00	400.00	600.00
	1829 RS	—	125.00	225.00	350.00	500.00
	1836 RS	—	125.00	225.00	350.00	500.00

4 ESCUDOS

13.5365 g, .875 GOLD, .3808 oz AGW
Mint: Bogota

KM#	Date	Mintage	VG	Fine	VF	XF
86	1826 JF	—	1500.	2000.	3500.	—

8 ESCUDOS

27.0730 g, .875 GOLD, .7616 oz AGW
Mint: Bogota

KM#	Date	Mintage	VG	Fine	VF	XF
82.1	1822 JF	—	400.00	550.00	800.00	1250.
	1823 JF	—	375.00	450.00	650.00	900.00
	1824/3 JF	—	375.00	450.00	650.00	900.00
	1824 JF	—	375.00	450.00	650.00	900.00
	1825 JF	—	375.00	450.00	650.00	900.00
	1826 JF	—	375.00	450.00	650.00	900.00
	1827 JF	—	400.00	550.00	800.00	1250.
	1827 RR	—	400.00	550.00	800.00	1250.
	1828 RR	—	400.00	550.00	800.00	1250.
	1828 RS	—	375.00	450.00	650.00	900.00
	1829 RS	—	375.00	450.00	650.00	900.00
	1830 RS	—	375.00	450.00	650.00	900.00
	1831 RS	—	375.00	450.00	650.00	900.00
	1832 RS	—	375.00	450.00	650.00	900.00
	1833 RS	—	375.00	450.00	650.00	900.00
	1834 RS	—	375.00	450.00	650.00	900.00
	1835 RS	—	375.00	450.00	650.00	900.00
	1836 RS	—	375.00	450.00	650.00	900.00

Mint: Popayan

KM#	Date	Mintage	VG	Fine	VF	XF
82.2	1822 FM	—	400.00	500.00	750.00	1250.
	1823 FM	—	375.00	450.00	650.00	1000.
	1824 FM	—	375.00	450.00	650.00	900.00
	1825 FM	—	375.00	450.00	650.00	900.00
	1826 FM	—	375.00	450.00	650.00	900.00
	1827 FM	—	375.00	450.00	650.00	1000.
	1827 UR	—	400.00	500.00	750.00	1150.
	1828 FM	—	400.00	500.00	750.00	1150.
	1829 FM	—	400.00	550.00	750.00	1150.
	1829 UR	—	375.00	450.00	650.00	900.00
	1830 FW M inverted	—	400.00	600.00	1000.	1500.
	1830 FM	—	400.00	600.00	1000.	1500.
	1830 UR	—	375.00	450.00	650.00	900.00
	1831 UR	—	400.00	600.00	1000.	1500.
	1832/1 UR	—	375.00	450.00	650.00	900.00
	1832 UR	—	375.00	450.00	650.00	900.00
	1833/22 UR	—	425.00	650.00	1250.	2000.
	1833 UR	—	375.00	450.00	650.00	900.00
	1834 UR	—	425.00	650.00	1250.	2000.
	1835 UR	—	375.00	450.00	650.00	900.00
	1836 UR	—	375.00	450.00	650.00	900.00
	1838 UR	—	—	—	Rare	—

REPUBLIC OF NUEVA GRANADA

1837-1859

1/4 REAL

.6800 g, .666 SILVER, .0145 oz ASW
Mint: Bogota

KM#	Date	Mintage	Good	VG	Fine	VF
90.1	1837	—	5.00	10.00	15.00	30.00
	1838	—	5.00	10.00	15.00	30.00
	1839	—	4.00	8.00	12.50	25.00
	1840	—	5.00	10.00	15.00	30.00
	1841	—	4.00	8.00	12.50	25.00
	1842	—	5.00	10.00	15.00	30.00
	1843	—	4.00	8.00	12.50	25.00
	1844	—	4.00	8.00	12.50	25.00
	1845	—	5.00	10.00	15.00	30.00
	1846	—	2.75	6.00	11.00	17.50
	1847	—	3.00	6.50	12.00	20.00
	1848	—	18.00	30.00	55.00	115.00

Mint: Popayan

KM#	Date	Mintage	Good	VG	Fine	VF
90.2	1838	—	10.00	17.50	28.00	45.00
	1841	—	3.50	7.25	12.50	22.00
	1842	—	3.50	7.25	12.50	22.00
	1843	—	3.50	7.25	12.50	22.00
	1844	—	4.50	9.00	15.00	27.50
	1845	—	3.50	7.25	12.50	22.00
	1846	—	3.50	7.00	11.00	20.00

1/2 REAL

1.2600 g, .666 SILVER, .0269 oz ASW
Mint: Bogota

KM#	Date	Mintage	Good	VG	Fine	VF
96.1	1838 RS	—	—	—	Rare	—
	1839 RS	—	2.00	4.00	8.00	17.50
	1840/39 RS	—	4.50	8.50	15.00	27.50
	1840 RS	—	4.00	7.50	12.50	25.00
	1841 RS	—	— Reported, not confirmed			
	1842 RS	—	4.00	7.50	12.50	25.00
	1843 RS	—	4.50	8.50	15.00	27.50
	1844 RS	—	4.00	7.50	12.50	25.00
	1845 RS	—	2.50	5.50	10.00	20.00
	1846 RS	—	3.00	6.50	12.00	22.50
	1847/6 RS	—	2.50	5.50	10.00	20.00
	1847 RS	—	2.25	4.50	8.50	17.50

Mint: Popayan

KM#	Date	Mintage	Good	VG	Fine	VF
96.2	1838 RU	—	3.50	7.50	12.00	22.50
	1839 RU	—	3.00	6.50	11.00	20.00
	1840	—	5.50	12.00	17.50	32.50
	1841 RU	—	4.50	10.00	15.00	30.00
	1841 VU	—	11.50	17.50	40.00	80.00
	1842 UM	—	5.50	12.00	17.50	35.00
	1843 UM	—	7.50	13.00	22.00	45.00
	1844 UE	—	4.00	7.50	13.50	25.00
	1844 UM	—	—	—	Rare	—
	1845 UE	—	5.00	11.00	17.50	35.00
	1846/5 UE	—	4.50	10.00	15.00	30.00
	1846 UE	—	2.00	4.50	9.00	17.50
	1846 UM	—	3.00	6.50	11.00	20.00
	1848 UE	—	18.00	32.50	47.50	85.00
	1848 UE star over last 8 in date	—	—	—	Rare	—

REAL

2.7000 g, .666 SILVER, .0578 oz ASW
Mint: Bogota

KM#	Date	Mintage	Good	VG	Fine	VF
91.1	1837 RS	—	2.00	4.50	9.00	15.00
	1838 RS	—	2.00	4.50	8.00	13.50
	1839 RS	—	2.50	5.00	11.00	17.50
	1840/39 RS	—	4.50	10.00	18.00	27.50
	1841 RS	—	— Reported, not confirmed			
	1842 RS	—	— Reported, not confirmed			
	1843 RS	—	3.50	7.00	13.50	20.00
	1844 RS	—	3.50	7.00	13.50	20.00
	1845 RS	—	2.50	5.00	12.00	18.50
	1846 RS	—	4.00	9.00	16.50	27.50
	1847	—	6.50	13.50	25.00	50.00

Mint: Popayan

KM#	Date	Mintage	Good	VG	Fine	VF
91.2	1839 RU	—	4.00	8.50	15.00	25.00
	1840 RU	—	—	—	—	—
	1841 VU	—	— Reported, not confirmed			
	1844 UM	—	4.00	8.50	14.00	20.00
	1845 UM	—	4.50	9.00	15.00	25.00
	1846/4 UM	—	4.50	9.00	15.00	25.00
	1846 UM	—	6.00	11.50	17.50	32.50

2 REALES

5.5000 g, .666 SILVER, .1177 oz ASW
Mint: Bogota

KM#	Date	Mintage	Good	VG	Fine	VF
97.1	1839 RS	—	9.00	22.00	37.50	70.00
	1840 RS	—	3.00	5.00	11.50	25.00
	1841 RS	—	15.00	35.00	65.00	125.00
	1842 RS	—	—	—	Rare	—
	1843 RS	—	3.00	5.00	11.50	25.00
	1844/3 RS	—	3.75	8.00	17.50	40.00
	1844 RS	—	3.00	7.00	15.00	35.00
	1845 RS	—	4.50	11.00	25.00	50.00
	1846/5 RS	—	15.00	35.00	60.00	100.00

Mint: Popayan

KM#	Date	Mintage	Good	VG	Fine	VF
97.2	1840 RU	—	10.00	22.00	35.00	65.00
	1841 VU	—	8.50	15.00	27.50	50.00
	1842/0/1 UM	—	20.00	37.50	80.00	150.00
	1842 VU	—	22.00	45.00	100.00	175.00
	1842 UM	—	8.50	15.00	27.50	55.00
	1843/2 UM	—	13.50	30.00	45.00	85.00
	1844 UM	—	10.00	22.00	35.00	55.00
	1846 UM	—	—	—	Rare	—

8 REALES

SILVER

KM#	Date	Mintage	VG	Fine	VF	XF
92	1837 RS	—	75.00	200.00	425.00	850.00
	1838 RS	—	—	—	Rare	—

KM#	Date	Mintage	Good	VG	Fine	VF
98	1839 RS	—	7.00	14.00	30.00	60.00
	1840 RS	—	8.00	16.00	35.00	70.00
	1841 RS	—	9.00	19.00	40.00	80.00
	1842 RS	—	9.00	19.00	40.00	80.00
	1843 RS	—	8.00	16.00	35.00	70.00
	1844 RS	—	9.00	19.00	40.00	80.00
	1845 RS	—	9.00	19.00	40.00	80.00

KM#	Date	Mintage	Good	VG	Fine	VF
98	1846/4 RS	—	12.00	22.00	45.00	90.00
	1846/5 RS	—	12.00	22.00	45.00	90.00
	1846 RS	—	9.00	19.00	40.00	80.00

PESO

1.6875 g, .875 GOLD, .0474 oz AGW
Mint: Bogota

KM#	Date	Mintage	VG	Fine	VF	XF
93	1837 RS	—	40.00	60.00	90.00	150.00
	1838 RS	—	60.00	100.00	150.00	250.00
	1839 RS	—	60.00	100.00	150.00	250.00
	1840/39 RS	—	50.00	80.00	120.00	200.00
	1840 RS	—	45.00	70.00	100.00	175.00
	1841 RS	—	— Reported, not confirmed			
	1842 RS	—	40.00	60.00	90.00	150.00
	1844 RS	—	45.00	70.00	100.00	175.00
	1846/3	—	— Reported, not confirmed			
	1846 RS	—	40.00	60.00	90.00	150.00

2 PESOS

3.3750 g, .900 GOLD, .0976 oz AGW
Mint: Popayan

KM#	Date	Mintage	VG	Fine	VF	XF
95	1838 RU	—	55.00	80.00	120.00	200.00
	1842 VU	—	55.00	80.00	160.00	275.00
	1843 UM	—	55.00	80.00	120.00	200.00
	1843 VU	—	55.00	80.00	160.00	275.00
	1844 UM	—	55.00	80.00	130.00	225.00
	1845 UM	—	55.00	80.00	120.00	200.00
	1845 UE	—	55.00	80.00	160.00	275.00
	1846 UE	—	55.00	80.00	120.00	200.00
	1846 UM	—	55.00	80.00	120.00	200.00

3.2258 g, .900 GOLD, .0933 oz AGW
Mint: Bogota

KM#	Date	Mintage	VG	Fine	VF	XF
99	1848	—	— Reported, not confirmed			
	1849	—	500.00	800.00	1200.	1750.
	1851	—	600.00	1200.	1800.	2700.

DIEZ I SEIS (16) PESOS

27.0000 g, .900 GOLD, .7813 oz AGW
Mint: Bogota

KM#	Date	Mintage	VG	Fine	VF	XF
94.1	1837 RS	—	375.00	425.00	500.00	700.00
	1838/7 RS	—	400.00	450.00	550.00	800.00
	1838 RS	—	375.00	425.00	500.00	700.00
	1839/8 RS	—	400.00	450.00	550.00	800.00
	1839 RS	—	375.00	425.00	500.00	700.00
	1840 RS	—	375.00	425.00	500.00	700.00
	1841 RS	—	375.00	425.00	500.00	700.00
	1842 RS	—	375.00	425.00	500.00	700.00
	1843 RS	—	375.00	425.00	500.00	700.00
	1844 RS	—	375.00	425.00	500.00	700.00
	1845 RS	—	375.00	425.00	500.00	700.00
	1846 RS	—	375.00	425.00	550.00	750.00
	1847 RS	—	375.00	425.00	500.00	700.00
	1848 RS	—	450.00	550.00	700.00	1000.
	1849 RS	—	500.00	650.00	850.00	1250.

Mint: Popayan

KM#	Date	Mintage	VG	Fine	VF	XF
94.2	1837 RU	—	375.00	425.00	500.00	700.00
	1838 RU	—	375.00	425.00	500.00	700.00
	1839 RU	—	375.00	425.00	500.00	700.00
	1840 RU	—	375.00	425.00	600.00	1200.
	1841/0 RU	—	450.00	—	—	—
	1841 RU	—	450.00	650.00	—	—
	1841 VU	—	375.00	425.00	500.00	700.00
	1842 VU	—	375.00	425.00	500.00	700.00
	1842 UM	—	375.00	425.00	500.00	700.00
	1843 UM	—	375.00	425.00	500.00	700.00
	1844 UM	—	375.00	425.00	500.00	700.00
	1845 UM	—	375.00	425.00	500.00	700.00
	1846 UM	—	375.00	425.00	550.00	1000.
	1846 UE	—	375.00	425.00	600.00	1200.
	1846 UR	—	450.00	650.00	850.00	—

25.8064 g, .900 GOLD, .7468 oz AGW
Mint: Bogota

KM#	Date	Mintage	VG	Fine	VF	XF
100	1848	—	600.00	1200.	2000.	3500.
	1849	—	600.00	1200.	2000.	3500.
	1850	—	600.00	1200.	2000.	3500.
	1851	—	700.00	1500.	2500.	4000.
	1852	—	600.00	1200.	2000.	3500.
	1853	—	600.00	1200.	2000.	3500.

FIRST DECIMAL COINAGE

MONETARY SYSTEM

10 Decimos de Real = 1 Real (1847-53)
10 Reales = 1 Peso (1847-53)
10 Decimos = 1 Peso (1853-72)

1/2 DECIMO DE REAL

(1/20 Real)

COPPER

KM#	Date	Mintage	Fine	VF	XF	Unc
101	1847	—	4.50	10.00	32.50	50.00
	1847	—	—	—	Proof	90.00
	1848	—	12.50	30.00	75.00	100.00

DECIMO DE REAL

(1/10 Real)

COPPER

KM#	Date	Mintage	Fine	VF	XF	Unc
102	1847	—	5.00	12.50	32.50	55.00
	1847	—	—	—	Proof	150.00
	1848	—	18.50	45.00	80.00	110.00

1/4 REAL

.9000 g, .900 SILVER, .0260 oz ASW
Mint: Bogota

KM#	Date	Mintage	VG	Fine	VF	XF
108.1	1850	—	8.50	15.00	30.00	60.00
	1851	—	3.50	8.50	17.50	45.00

Mint: Popayan

KM#	Date	Mintage	VG	Fine	VF	XF
108.2	1849	—	3.00	7.00	15.00	35.00
	1850	—	2.50	6.50	15.00	35.00
	1851	—	2.50	6.50	15.00	35.00
	1852	—	3.00	7.00	15.00	35.00
	1853	—	3.00	7.00	15.00	35.00
	1855	—	6.00	9.00	20.00	50.00
	1856	—	7.00	15.00	25.00	55.00
	1858	—	13.50	27.50	50.00	110.00

Mint: Bogota
Obv: Similar to KM#108.2. Rev: Caduceus at each side of '1/4' instead of 3 stars below.

KM#	Date	Mintage	VG	Fine	VF	XF
113	1852	—	15.00	35.00	75.00	165.00
	1858	—	—	—	Rare	—

MEDIO (1/2) REAL

1.4000 g, .900 SILVER, .0405 oz ASW
Mint: Bogota

KM#	Date	Mintage	VG	Fine	VF	XF
110	1850	5.000	9.00	18.00	30.00	70.00
	1851	2.500	7.50	15.00	25.00	60.00
	1852/1	—	5.50	11.00	18.00	50.00
	1852	2.500	5.00	10.00	16.50	40.00
	1853	2.500	4.50	8.50	15.00	35.00
	1854	—	— Reported, not confirmed			

MEDIO (1/2) DECIMO

1.5000 g, .900 SILVER, .0434 oz ASW
Mint: Bogota

KM#	Date	Mintage	VG	Fine	VF	XF
114	1853	—	9.00	17.50	25.00	40.00
	1854	—	5.00	10.00	20.00	35.00
	1855	—	5.00	10.00	20.00	35.00
	1856	—	7.00	12.50	22.50	37.50
	1857	—	6.00	11.50	20.00	35.00
	1858	—	6.00	11.50	20.00	35.00

UN (1) REAL

2.7000 g, .900 SILVER, .0781 oz ASW
Mint: Bogota

KM#	Date	Mintage	VG	Fine	VF	XF
103	1847	—	5.00	10.00	17.50	30.00

2.5000 g, .900 SILVER, .0723 oz ASW

KM#	Date	Mintage	VG	Fine	VF	XF
112	1851	—	3.50	7.00	16.50	40.00
	1852	—	2.50	5.50	10.00	17.50
	1853	—	2.75	6.00	15.50	38.00

UN (1) DECIMO

2.5000 g, .900 SILVER, .0723 oz ASW
Mint: Bogota

KM#	Date	Mintage	VG	Fine	VF	XF
115	1853	—	3.75	7.00	10.00	30.00
	1854	—	2.75	4.50	8.00	22.00
	1855/4/3	—	10.00	18.00	30.00	—
	1855/4	—	2.75	5.00	8.50	25.00
	1855	—	2.75	4.50	8.00	22.00
	1856	—	2.25	4.00	7.50	20.00
	1857	—	2.75	5.00	8.50	25.00
	1858/6	—	7.00	12.00	20.00	—
	1858/7	—	3.75	5.50	9.00	30.00
	1858	—	2.75	5.00	8.50	25.00

DOS (2) REALES

5.0000 g, .900 SILVER, .1447 oz ASW
Mint: Bogota

Obv: Date above shield.

KM#	Date	Mintage	VG	Fine	VF	XF
104	1847	—	—	—	Rare	—

NOTE: Probably a pattern.

Obv: Date below shield

KM#	Date	Mintage	VG	Fine	VF	XF
105	1847	—	5.00	10.00	25.00	50.00
	1848	—	3.50	6.50	15.00	35.00
	1849	—	3.50	6.50	15.00	35.00

KM#	Date	Mintage	VG	Fine	VF	XF
109	1849	—	—	—	Rare	—
	1850	—	3.50	7.00	15.00	37.50
	1851	—	3.50	7.00	15.00	37.50
	1852	—	6.00	10.00	25.00	65.00
	1853	—	5.00	9.00	22.00	55.00

DOS (2) DECIMOS

5.0000 g, .900 SILVER, .1447 oz ASW
Mint: Bogota

KM#	Date	Mintage	VG	Fine	VF	XF
117	1854/3	—	7.50	20.00	60.00	150.00
	1854	—	5.00	10.00	25.00	60.00
	1855/3	—	4.50	9.00	35.00	75.00
	1855	—	3.50	7.50	16.50	30.00
	1856/5	—	5.50	12.00	38.00	75.00
	1857	—	3.50	8.00	20.00	45.00
	1858/7	—	20.00	45.00	80.00	165.00

OCHO (8) REALES

20.0000 g, .900 SILVER, .5787 oz ASW
Mint: Bogota

KM#	Date	Mintage	VG	Fine	VF	XF
106	1847	—	30.00	70.00	120.00	250.00

DIEZ (10) REALES

25.0000 g, .900 SILVER, .7234 oz ASW

KM#	Date	Mintage	VG	Fine	VF	XF
107	1847	—	25.00	45.00	70.00	200.00
	1848	—	20.00	35.00	60.00	175.00
	1849/8	—	30.00	60.00	120.00	260.00
	1849	—	25.00	50.00	90.00	225.00

NOTE: Struck at Bogota and Popayan without mint marks.

Mint: Bogota

KM#	Date	Mintage	VG	Fine	VF	XF
111	1850	—	25.00	50.00	100.00	200.00
	1851	—	25.00	50.00	100.00	200.00

PESO

25.0000 g, .900 SILVER, .7234 oz ASW

KM#	Date	Mintage	VG	Fine	VF	XF
118	1855/1	—	18.00	37.50	75.00	125.00
	1855	—	15.00	30.00	45.00	65.00
	1856/5	—	12.50	25.00	40.00	60.00
	1856	—	17.50	32.50	50.00	70.00
	1857/6	—	15.00	30.00	45.00	65.00
	1857	—	12.50	25.00	40.00	60.00
	1858/7	—	15.00	30.00	45.00	65.00
	1858	—	12.50	25.00	40.00	60.00
	1859/6	—	18.00	35.00	65.00	115.00

1.6875 g, .875 GOLD, .0474 oz AGW
Similar to 2 Pesos, KM#121.

KM#	Date	Mintage	VG	Fine	VF	XF
119	1856	—	65.00	150.00	300.00	500.00
	1857	—	— Reported, not confirmed			
	1858	—	65.00	150.00	300.00	500.00

2 PESOS

3.2258 g, .900 GOLD, .0933 oz AGW
Mint mark: P

Rev: Value in wreath.

KM#	Date	Mintage	VG	Fine	VF	XF
121	1857	—	60.00	100.00	175.00	300.00
	1858/48	—	— Reported, not confirmed			
	1858	—	60.00	100.00	175.00	300.00

5 PESOS

8.0648 g, .900 GOLD, .2333 oz AGW
Mint mark: B

KM#	Date	Mintage	VG	Fine	VF	XF
120.1	1849	—	—	—	Unique	—
	1856	—	— Reported, not confirmed			
	1857	—	175.00	400.00	850.00	1350.

Rev: PESOS in small letters.

KM#	Date	Mintage	VG	Fine	VF	XF
120.2	1858	—	200.00	500.00	1000.	1750.

10 PESOS

16.4000 g, .900 GOLD, .4745 oz AGW
Mint: Bogota

KM#	Date	Mintage	VG	Fine	VF	XF
116.1	1853	—	500.00	850.00	1500.	2000.
	1854	—	350.00	700.00	1250.	1500.
	1855	—	350.00	700.00	1250.	1500.
	1856	—	350.00	700.00	1250.	1500.
	1857	—	350.00	700.00	1250.	1500.

Mint: Popayan

KM#	Date	Mintage	VG	Fine	VF	XF
116.2	1853	—	250.00	400.00	600.00	1000.
	1856	—	500.00	850.00	1500.	2000.
	1857	—	—	—	1000.	1500.

16.1290 g, .900 GOLD, .4667 oz AGW
Mint: Bogota
Rev. leg: DIEZ PESOS

KM#	Date	Mintage	VG	Fine	VF	XF
122.1	1857	—	275.00	500.00	900.00	1400.
	1858/7	—	300.00	550.00	1000.	1500.
	1858	—	300.00	550.00	1000.	1500.

Mint: Popayan

KM#	Date	Mintage	VG	Fine	VF	XF
122.2	1853	—	— Reported, not confirmed			
	1856	—	— Reported, not confirmed			
	1857	—	225.00	325.00	500.00	900.00
	1858	—	225.00	325.00	500.00	900.00

GRANADINE CONFEDERATION

1859-1862

MONETARY SYSTEM

10 Reales = 1 Peso
10 Decimos = 1 Peso

1/4 REAL

.9000 g, .666 SILVER, .0192 oz ASW
Mint: Popayan

Rev: 3 stars.

KM#	Date	Mintage	Good	VG	Fine	VF
123	1859	—	3.00	7.00	15.00	32.50
	1860	—	2.50	6.00	13.50	27.50
	1861	—	2.50	6.00	13.50	27.50
	1862/1	—	—	—	—	—
	1862	—	4.00	9.00	17.50	37.50

1/4 DECIMO

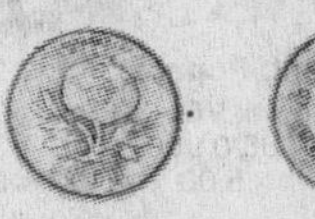

.9000 g, .666 SILVER, .0192 oz ASW
Mint: Bogota
Rev: Caducei flanking fraction.

KM#	Date	Mintage	Good	VG	Fine	VF
131	1860	—	7.50	18.50	40.00	65.00

Rev: 9 stars below fraction.

KM#	Date	Mintage	Good	VG	Fine	VF
132.1	1861	—	3.50	7.50	12.50	27.50
	1862	—	4.50	9.00	15.00	40.00

Mint: Popayan

KM#	Date	Mintage	Good	VG	Fine	VF
132.2	1860	—	12.50	27.50	55.00	125.00

1/2 REAL

1.2500 g, .900 SILVER, .0362 oz ASW
Mint: Popayan

KM#	Date	Mintage	Good	VG	Fine	VF
133	1862	—	5.50	11.50	25.00	55.00
	1862/48	—	5.50	11.50	25.00	55.00

MEDIO (1/2) DECIMO

1.2500 g, .900 SILVER, .0362 oz ASW
Mint: Bogota

KM#	Date	Mintage	VG	Fine	VF	XF
124	1859	—	7.00	17.50	30.00	75.00
	1860/59	—	8.00	20.00	35.00	80.00
	1860	—	6.00	14.00	25.00	55.00
	1861	—	7.00	17.50	30.00	75.00

UN (1) DECIMO

2.5000 g, .900 SILVER, .0723 oz ASW

KM#	Date	Mintage	VG	Fine	VF	XF
125	1859	—	3.75	8.50	20.00	35.00
	1860	—	8.50	22.50	35.00	75.00

DOS (2) REALES

5.0000 g, .900 SILVER, .1447 oz ASW
Mint: Popayan

KM#	Date	Mintage	VG	Fine	VF	XF
134	1862/48/47	—	6.50	15.00	27.50	62.50
	1862/48	—	6.00	13.50	25.00	60.00
	1862/49	—	4.50	10.00	22.50	55.00
	1862/52	—	25.00	45.00	85.00	130.00
	1862	—	6.00	13.50	25.00	55.00

NOTE: These are struck from reworked dies of KM#109.

PESO

25.0000 g, .900 SILVER, .7234 oz ASW
Mint: Bogota

KM#	Date	Mintage	VG	Fine	VF	XF
126	1859	—	15.00	25.00	50.00	100.00
	1860	—	15.00	25.00	50.00	100.00
	1861	—	25.00	50.00	100.00	200.00

1.6129 g, .900 GOLD, .0466 oz AGW
Mint mark: M

KM#	Date	Mintage	VG	Fine	VF	XF
135	1862	2 known	—	—	Rare	—

2 PESOS

3.2258 g, .900 GOLD, .0933 oz AGW
Mint mark: P

KM#	Date	Mintage	VG	Fine	VF	XF
127	1859	—	75.00	150.00	350.00	600.00
	1860	—	125.00	250.00	550.00	1000.

5 PESOS

8.0645 g, .900 GOLD, .2333 oz AGW
Mint mark: P

KM#	Date	Mintage	VG	Fine	VF	XF
128	1859	—	—	—	—	4750.

Mint mark: M

KM#	Date	Mintage	VG	Fine	VF	XF
136	1862	—	—	—	—	5750.

DIEZ (10) PESOS

16.1290 g, .900 GOLD, .4667 oz AGW
Mint: Bogota

KM#	Date	Mintage	VG	Fine	VF	XF
129.1	1859	3,481	250.00	400.00	700.00	1000.
	1860	9,687	225.00	300.00	600.00	900.00
	1861	834 pcs.	275.00	500.00	800.00	1200.

Mint: Popayan

KM#	Date	Mintage	VG	Fine	VF	XF
129.2	1858	—	225.00	300.00	600.00	950.00
	1859/58	—	250.00	400.00	700.00	1100.
	1859	—	225.00	300.00	600.00	950.00
	1860	—	250.00	400.00	700.00	1100.
	1861	—	275.00	450.00	800.00	1250.
	1862	—	250.00	400.00	700.00	1100.

VEINTE (20) PESOS

32.2580 g, .900 GOLD, .9335 oz AGW
Mint: Bogota

KM#	Date	Mintage	VG	Fine	VF	XF
130	1859	2,002	900.00	1750.	3500.	6000.

ESTADOS UNIDOS DE NUEVA GRANADA

1861-1862

UN (1) DECIMO

2.5000 g, .900 SILVER, .0723 oz ASW
Mint: Bogota

KM#	Date	Mintage	VG	Fine	VF	XF
137	1861	—	25.00	55.00	130.00	260.00

PESO

25.0000 g, .900 SILVER, .7234 oz ASW
Mint: Bogota

KM#	Date	Mintage	VG	Fine	VF	XF
138	1861	—	125.00	250.00	400.00	700.00

ESTADOS UNIDOS DE COLOMBIA

1862-1886

1/4 DECIMO

.8500 g, .900 SILVER, .0245 oz ASW
Mint: Bogota

KM#	Date	Mintage	VG	Fine	VF	XF
143.1	1863	.048	3.50	6.50	12.00	27.50
	1864	.435	2.00	4.50	8.00	20.00
	1865	.206	2.00	5.00	10.00	22.00
	1866	.267	2.00	5.00	10.00	22.00
	1867	.208	2.00	5.00	10.00	22.00

.8500 g, .666 SILVER, .0182 oz ASW

KM#	Date	Mintage	VG	Fine	VF	XF
143.1a	1868	.023	—	—	Rare	—
	1869	.183	5.00	10.00	15.00	27.50
	1870	.092	6.00	12.00	17.50	35.00
	1871	.413	5.00	10.00	15.00	27.50
	1873	Inc.KM169	—	—	Rare	—
	1881	Inc.KM169	8.50	17.50	25.00	55.00

.8500 g, .900 SILVER, .0245 oz ASW
Mint: Popayan

KM#	Date	Mintage	VG	Fine	VF	XF
143.2	1863	—	4.50	8.00	12.00	27.50
	1864	.504	4.50	8.00	12.00	27.50
	1865/3	—	10.00	18.00	27.50	50.00
	1865	.291	6.00	12.50	18.00	35.00
	1866	.157	8.00	16.00	25.00	45.00
	1867	.055	8.00	16.00	25.00	45.00

.8500 g, .666 SILVER, .0182 oz ASW

KM#	Date	Mintage	VG	Fine	VF	XF
143.2a	1868	—	6.50	15.00	25.00	47.50
	1869	—	6.00	14.00	20.00	45.00
	1870	—	7.00	16.00	26.50	50.00
	1871	.155	6.00	14.00	20.00	45.00
	1872/1	.041	9.00	18.00	30.00	55.00
	1872	Inc. Ab.	4.50	9.00	15.00	35.00
	1873/2	—	9.00	18.00	30.00	55.00
	1873	—	4.50	9.00	15.00	35.00
	1874	—	7.00	16.00	26.50	50.00
	1875	—	7.00	16.00	26.50	50.00

KM#	Date	Mintage	VG	Fine	VF	XF
143.2a	1876	—	7.00	16.00	26.50	50.00
	1877	.025	7.00	16.00	26.50	50.00
	1878	.025	9.00	18.00	30.00	55.00
	1879	—	6.00	14.00	20.00	45.00
	1880	—	7.00	16.00	27.50	55.00
	1881	—	7.00	16.00	27.50	55.00
	1883	—	— Reported, not confirmed			
	1888	—	—	—	Rare	—

NOTE: Date varieties exist for 1880 and 1881.

Mint: Medellin

KM#	Date	Mintage	VG	Fine	VF	XF
143.3	1874	—	8.00	17.50	30.00	60.00

MEDIO (1/2) DECIMO

1.2500 g, .900 SILVER, .0362 oz ASW
Mint: Bogota

KM#	Date	Mintage	VG	Fine	VF	XF
144	1863	.028	10.00	20.00	40.00	85.00
	1864	Inc. Ab.	12.00	25.00	50.00	100.00
	1865	.029	15.00	30.00	65.00	150.00

1.2500 g, .666 SILVER, .0268 oz ASW

KM#	Date	Mintage	VG	Fine	VF	XF
144a	1867 reverse .666/.900	.363	7.50	18.50	45.00	90.00

KM#	Date	Mintage	VG	Fine	VF	XF
150.1	1868	Inc. KM144a	6.50	17.50	30.00	45.00
	1869	.173	—	—	Rare	—
	1870	.140	12.00	22.50	35.00	60.00
	1871	.100	15.00	25.00	40.00	65.00

Mint: Medellin

KM#	Date	Mintage	VG	Fine	VF	XF
150.2	1868	.062	8.00	16.00	35.00	50.00
	1869	.026	10.00	20.00	45.00	80.00
	1870	—	— Reported, not confirmed			
	1873	.014	8.00	16.00	40.00	60.00
	1874	—	8.00	16.00	40.00	75.00
	1876	—	— Reported, not confirmed			

Mint: Popayan

KM#	Date	Mintage	VG	Fine	VF	XF
150.3	1869	—	5.00	15.00	30.00	50.00
	1870	.382	5.00	15.00	30.00	50.00
	1874	—	5.00	15.00	30.00	50.00
	1875	.573	5.00	15.00	30.00	50.00
	1876	—	6.00	18.00	40.00	75.00
	1878	—	—	—	Rare	—

1.2500 g, .835 SILVER, .0336 oz ASW
Mint: Medellin

KM#	Date	Mintage	VG	Fine	VF	XF
150.2a	1870	Inc. Ab.	7.50	17.50	35.00	55.00
	1871	.061	4.50	10.00	22.50	37.50
	1872/1	Inc. Ab.	6.50	13.50	35.00	55.00
	1872 small head, .835/.666	—	6.50	13.50	35.00	55.00
	1873 AB below large head	—	5.50	12.50	25.00	40.00
	1874/61	—	8.50	13.50	35.00	60.00
	1874	—	4.50	10.00	22.50	37.50

Mint: Popayan

KM#	Date	Mintage	VG	Fine	VF	XF
150.3a	1872 reverse w/0.835/0.666	Inc. Ab.	4.00	10.00	20.00	35.00
	1875/65	—	10.00	25.00	40.00	85.00
	1875	Inc. Ab.	8.50	20.00	37.50	65.00

UN (1) DECIMO

2.5000 g, .900 SILVER, .0723 oz ASW
Mint: Bogota

KM#	Date	Mintage	VG	Fine	VF	XF
145.1	1863	.096	5.00	10.00	20.00	45.00
	1864	.039	6.00	12.00	25.00	50.00
	1866	.112	5.00	10.00	18.00	40.00

Mint: Popayan

KM#	Date	Mintage	VG	Fine	VF	XF
145.2	1863//1848	—	7.50	15.00	30.00	60.00
	1864//1848	.028	6.00	12.50	27.50	58.00
	1864	—	20.00	40.00	60.00	120.00

NOTE: The overdates appear to have been struck from re-cut dies of Un Real, 1848 Popayan, Pn7 w/stars over 1848 on obverse and 1863 or 1864 on reverse.

2.5000 g, .835 SILVER, .0671 oz ASW
Mint: Bogota

KM#	Date	Mintage	VG	Fine	VF	XF
145.1a	1866	.606	5.00	12.00	20.00	45.00

Mint: Popayan

KM#	Date	Mintage	VG	Fine	VF	XF
145.2a	1866	.034	15.00	32.50	55.00	120.00

NOTE: Some, or all, appear to have been struck from re-cut dies of Un Real, 1848 Popayan, Pn7 w/stars over 1848 on obverse and 1866 on reverse.

Mint: Bogota

KM#	Date	Mintage	VG	Fine	VF	XF
151.1	1868	.146	4.00	9.00	22.50	50.00
	1869	.082	3.00	8.00	18.50	45.00
	1871	.144	2.50	6.50	13.50	35.00
	1872	.133	3.00	7.00	16.50	40.00

Mint: Medellin
Obv: AB below bust.

KM#	Date	Mintage	VG	Fine	VF	XF
151.2	1874/3	—	18.50	50.00	85.00	175.00

DOS (2) REALES

5.0000 g, .835 SILVER, .1342 oz ASW
Mint: Popayan

KM#	Date	Mintage	VG	Fine	VF	XF
162	1880	3,000	50.00	100.00	220.00	350.00

NOTE: Apparently, from re-cut dies of 2 Decimos, 1854-1858.

DOS (2) DECIMOS

5.0000 g, .900 SILVER, .1447 oz ASW
Mint: Bogota

KM#	Date	Mintage	VG	Fine	VF	XF
149	1865	—	45.00	115.00	175.00	250.00

5.0000 g, .835 SILVER, .1342 oz ASW

KM#	Date	Mintage	VG	Fine	VF	XF
149a.1	1866	—	4.50	12.00	25.00	55.00
	1867	—	3.00	9.00	17.50	40.00

Mint: Popayan

KM#	Date	Mintage	VG	Fine	VF	XF
149a.2	1867 reverse 0.835/0.900	—	5.00	15.00	30.00	70.00
149b	1867 (error) reverse 0.666	—	10.00	25.00	50.00	90.00
	1867 reverse 0.835/0.666	—	15.00	37.50	75.00	120.00

Mint: Bogota

KM#	Date	Mintage	VG	Fine	VF	XF
155.1	1872	.024	20.00	40.00	60.00	100.00

Mint: Medellin

KM#	Date	Mintage	VG	Fine	VF	XF
155.2	1870	.015	5.50	12.50	25.00	40.00
	1871	.036	16.50	35.00	55.00	85.00
	1872	.045	4.50	10.00	20.00	35.00

NOTE: Each date of KM#155.2 has slightly different head, with 2 varieties for 1872. Varieties in legend spacings also exist.

Obv: Similar to 5 Decimos, KM#153.4.
Rev: Inverted fineness.

KM#	Date	Mintage	VG	Fine	VF	XF
159	1873	800 pcs.	—	—	Rare	—

Obv: Large head. Rev: Large arms.

KM#	Date	Mintage	VG	Fine	VF	XF
160	1874	—	1.25	3.75	12.50	35.00

MEDIO (1/2) PESO

12.5000 g, .835/.900 SILVER, .3356 oz ASW
Mint: Medellin

KM#	Date	Mintage	VG	Fine	VF	XF
152	1868	—	—	—	Rare	—

CINCO (5) DECIMOS

12.5000 g, .835 SILVER, .3356 oz ASW
Edge: DIOS LEI LIBERTAD.
Mint: Bogota

KM#	Date	Mintage	VG	Fine	VF	XF
153.1	1868	9,161	35.00	60.00	130.00	225.00
	1869	.187	7.50	16.50	42.50	90.00
	1870	.206	7.50	16.50	42.50	85.00
	1871	.273	8.50	20.00	50.00	115.00

Mint: Medellin

KM#	Date	Mintage	VG	Fine	VF	XF
153.2	1868	5 known	—	—	Rare	—
	1869	1,054	275.00	500.00	750.00	1000.

KM#	Date	Mintage	VG	Fine	VF	XF
153.3	1872	.030	20.00	45.00	80.00	150.00
	1873	.090	7.50	20.00	40.00	80.00

Obv: Small round head. Rev: Small arms, fineness faces in (counter-clockwise).

KM#	Date	Mintage	VG	Fine	VF	XF
153.4	1873	Inc. Ab.	35.00	75.00	150.00	250.00
	1874	.185	7.00	15.00	35.00	75.00
	1875/4	.197	7.00	15.00	35.00	75.00

Rev: Fineness faces out (clockwise).

KM#	Date	Mintage	VG	Fine	VF	XF
153.5	1875	Inc. Ab.	6.50	12.50	30.00	60.00
	1876/5	—	12.50	25.00	45.00	100.00
	1876	—	6.50	12.50	32.50	70.00
	1877	2 known	—	—	Rare	—

NOTE: Varieties exist.

Mint: Popayan

KM#	Date	Mintage	VG	Fine	VF	XF
153.6	1869	1 known	—	—	Rare	—
	1870/9	7,774	—	Reported, not confirmed		
	1870	Inc. Ab.	115.00	185.00	300.00	475.00
	1871	—	125.00	220.00	400.00	700.00
	1873/69	7,743	—	—	Rare	—
	1873	Inc. Ab.	100.00	175.00	250.00	425.00
	1874	.011	125.00	220.00	375.00	625.00
	1878	3,158	100.00	175.00	250.00	425.00
	1880	2 known	—	—	Rare	—

Mint: Medellin

Obv: Large head. Rev: Large arms.

Edge: DIOS LEI LIBERTAD.

KM#	Date	Mintage	VG	Fine	VF	XF
161.1	1877/4	.168	10.00	18.00	45.00	110.00
	1878/4	.318	7.00	17.50	35.00	65.00
	1878/4 lg.8	I.A.	—	—	Rare	—
	1879/4 pointed tail 9	.379	6.00	15.00	27.50	55.00
	1879/4 ball tailed 9	Inc. Ab.	6.00	15.00	27.50	55.00
	1880/74	.411	25.00	55.00	115.00	225.00
	1880	Inc. Ab.	4.00	7.50	15.00	35.00
	1881	.379	5.00	10.00	20.00	40.00
	1882	—	3.00	6.50	12.50	30.00
	1883	1.096	3.00	6.50	12.50	30.00
	1884/3	1.429	—	—	Rare	—
	1884	Inc. Ab.	3.00	6.50	12.50	30.00
	1885	—	3.75	7.00	12.50	30.00

Edge: DIOS PATRIA LIBERTAD.

KM#	Date	Mintage	VG	Fine	VF	XF
161.1a	1886	—	25.00	55.00	100.00	200.00
	1886 round top 3 in fineness	—	—	—	Rare	—

Obv: 8-pointed stars.

Edge: DIOS LEI LIBERTAD.

KM#	Date	Mintage	VG	Fine	VF	XF
161.2	1880	2 known	—	—	Rare	—
	1882	—	—	—	Rare	—
	1883	—	—	—	Rare	—

12.2000 g, .500/.835 SILVER

KM#	Date	Mintage	VG	Fine	VF	XF
161.2a	1886/4	—	65.00	140.00	250.00	400.00
	1886/6	—	—	—	Rare	—

Edge: DIOS PATRIA LIBERTAD.

KM#	Date	Mintage	VG	Fine	VF	XF
161.2b	1886	—	45.00	125.00	225.00	330.00

Rev: 4 stars.

KM#	Date	Mintage	VG	Fine	VF	XF
161.2c	1886	—	100.00	200.00	350.00	500.00

Obv: Different head. Rev: 3 stars, 1 dot, leg: LEV.

KM#	Date	Mintage	VG	Fine	VF	XF
161.2d	1886	—	—	—	Rare	—

NOTE: The above coins always show traces of 0.835 under 0.500.

Obv: Square Liberty head

Edge: DIOS LEI LIBERTAD.

KM#	Date	Mintage	VG	Fine	VF	XF
161.3	1881	Inc. KM161.1	50.00	85.00	140.00	200.00

12.5000 g, .500 SILVER, .2009 oz ASW

Obv: Modified head w/curl on top, 5-pointed stars.

Rev: 2 stars and 2 dots, leg: LEV.

KM#	Date	Mintage	VG	Fine	VF	XF
164.1	1886	—	—	—	Rare	—

Rev: W/o stars or dots, leg: LEI.

KM#	Date	Mintage	VG	Fine	VF	XF
164.2	1886	—	—	—	Rare	—

.500/.835 SILVER

Rev: W/o stars or dots, leg: LEI.

KM#	Date	Mintage	VG	Fine	VF	XF
164.3	1886	1 known	—	—	Rare	—

PESO

25.0000 g, .900 SILVER, .7234 oz ASW

Mint: Bogota

KM#	Date	Mintage	VG	Fine	VF	XF
139.1	1862	.055	12.50	35.00	60.00	115.00
	1863	.018	10.00	30.00	55.00	100.00
	1864	.104	9.00	25.00	50.00	90.00
	1865	.122	9.00	25.00	50.00	90.00
	1866	.091	9.00	25.00	50.00	90.00
	1867	.044	12.50	35.00	60.00	115.00
	1868	.017	12.50	35.00	60.00	115.00

Mint: Popayan

KM#	Date	Mintage	VG	Fine	VF	XF
139.2	1863	—	200.00	500.00	700.00	1000.

1.6129 g, .900 GOLD, .0466 oz AGW

Mint: Medellin

Obv. leg: ESTADOS UNIDOS DE COLOMBIA.

KM#	Date	Mintage	VG	Fine	VF	XF
146.1	1863	.011	100.00	200.00	350.00	600.00

Obv. leg: COLOMBIA.

KM#	Date	Mintage	VG	Fine	VF	XF
146.2	1864	1,072	600.00	1000.	1500.	2000.

25.0000 g, .900 SILVER, .7234 oz ASW

Mint: Bogota

KM#	Date	Mintage	VG	Fine	VF	XF
154.1	1868	—	300.00	500.00	800.00	1200.
	1869	—	—	—	Rare	—
	1870	.046	55.00	100.00	165.00	300.00
	1871	.040	42.50	85.00	150.00	275.00

Mint: Medellin

KM#	Date	Mintage	VG	Fine	VF	XF
154.2	1869	3,598	65.00	135.00	200.00	400.00
	1870/69	.048	75.00	150.00	225.00	450.00
	1870	Inc. Ab.	50.00	100.00	165.00	300.00
	1871	.055	40.00	75.00	135.00	265.00

1.6129 g, .900 GOLD, .0466 oz AGW

Rev: Arms.

KM#	Date	Mintage	VG	Fine	VF	XF
156	1872/1	.062	45.00	75.00	115.00	175.00
	1872	Inc. Ab.	30.00	60.00	90.00	125.00
	1873	.018	45.00	75.00	115.00	175.00

Rev: Condor

KM#	Date	Mintage	VG	Fine	VF	XF
157.1	1872	Inc. Ab.	30.00	45.00	65.00	100.00
	1873/2	—	80.00	140.00	250.00	500.00
	1873	—	80.00	140.00	250.00	500.00

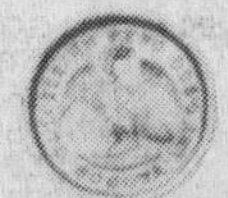

Mint: Bogota

KM#	Date	Mintage	VG	Fine	VF	XF
157.2	1871	—	60.00	120.00	200.00	400.00
	1872	—	30.00	50.00	75.00	115.00
	1873	3,374	30.00	50.00	75.00	115.00
	1874	.014	30.00	50.00	80.00	125.00
	1875	7,002	30.00	50.00	80.00	125.00
	1878	—	75.00	150.00	250.00	350.00

NOTE: The 1871 date is more commonly encountered as a counterfeit than an authentic striking.

2 PESOS

3.2258 g, .900 GOLD, .0933 oz AGW
Mint mark: M

KM#	Date	Mintage	VG	Fine	VF	XF
147	1863	2,996	250.00	450.00	750.00	1250.

Mint: Medellin

KM#	Date	Mintage	VG	Fine	VF	XF
A154	1871	.066	55.00	65.00	80.00	125.00
	1872	.030	65.00	80.00	120.00	175.00
	1876	—	80.00	100.00	140.00	200.00

3.2258 g, .666 GOLD, .0690 oz AGW

KM#	Date	Mintage	VG	Fine	VF	XF
A154a	1885/74	—	—	—	Rare	—

5 PESOS

8.0645 g, .900 GOLD, .2333 oz AGW
Mint: Medellin
Obv. leg: ESTADOS UNIDOS DE COLOMBIA.

KM#	Date	Mintage	VG	Fine	VF	XF
140	1862	—	—	Reported, not confirmed		
	1863	.029	1500.	2500.	4000.	5500.

Obv. leg: COLOMBIA above.

KM#	Date	Mintage	VG	Fine	VF	XF
148	1864	8,035	2000.	3000.	4500.	6000.

8.0645 g, .666 GOLD, .1728 oz AGW

KM#	Date	Mintage	VG	Fine	VF	XF
163	1885/inverted 5					
		—	1000.	1500.	2000.	3000.
	1885/74	—	1000.	1500.	2000.	3000.

10 PESOS

16.1290 g, .900 GOLD, .4667 oz AGW
Mint: Bogota

KM#	Date	Mintage	VG	Fine	VF	XF
141.1	1862	.011	275.00	500.00	850.00	1300.
	1863	.017	275.00	500.00	850.00	1200.
	1864	—	750.00	1250.	2250.	3250.
	1866	—	800.00	1500.	2500.	3500.

Mint: Medellin

KM#	Date	Mintage	VG	Fine	VF	XF
141.2	1863	—	—	Reported, not confirmed		
	1864	—	350.00	500.00	800.00	1250.
	1867	.014	300.00	400.00	700.00	1000.
	1868	.018	225.00	325.00	500.00	800.00
	1869	.018	225.00	350.00	600.00	850.00
	1870	7,786	250.00	375.00	650.00	950.00
	1871	6,018	250.00	375.00	650.00	950.00
	1872	.014	—	Reported, not confirmed		

NOTE: Varieties exist.

Obv: Small date, inverted LEI 0.900.
Rev: Small Phrygian cap.

KM#	Date	Mintage	VG	Fine	VF	XF
141.4	1873	8,623	250.00	375.00	650.00	950.00
	1874	—	250.00	350.00	550.00	850.00
	1875	—	225.00	325.00	500.00	800.00
	1876/5	—	225.00	325.00	500.00	800.00
	1876	—	225.00	325.00	500.00	800.00

NOTE: Varieties exist.

16.1290 g, .666 GOLD, .3453 oz AGW

KM#	Date	Mintage	VG	Fine	VF	XF
141.2a	1886/74	—	—	—	Rare	—

16.1290 g, .900 GOLD, .4667 oz AGW
Mint: Popayan

KM#	Date	Mintage	VG	Fine	VF	XF
141.3	1863	—	250.00	375.00	650.00	900.00
	1864	.010	225.00	325.00	450.00	750.00
	1865	8,727	250.00	375.00	650.00	900.00
	1866	.013	225.00	325.00	450.00	750.00
	1867	—	300.00	400.00	700.00	1000.
	1869	—	300.00	400.00	700.00	1000.
	1870	—	600.00	1000.	2000.	3000.
	1871	2,617	—	Reported, not confirmed		
	1874	—	—	Reported, not confirmed		

20 PESOS

32.2580 g, .900 GOLD, .9335 oz AGW
Mint: Bogota

KM#	Date	Mintage	VG	Fine	VF	XF
142.1	1862	—	475.00	600.00	1250.	2000.
	1863	—	475.00	600.00	1250.	2000.
	1867	—	700.00	1200.	2000.	3250.
	1868	—	500.00	650.00	1400.	2250.
	1869	—	500.00	650.00	1400.	2250.
	1870	.017	500.00	650.00	1400.	2250.
	1871	1,641	550.00	800.00	1600.	2750.
	1872	1,471	500.00	650.00	1400.	2250.
	1873	2,731	500.00	650.00	1400.	2250.
	1874	1,656	500.00	650.00	1400.	2250.
	1875	1,696	500.00	650.00	1400.	2250.
	1876	2,299	700.00	1200.	2000.	3250.
	1877	—	900.00	1500.	2750.	4500.

1868

1869

Mint: Medellin

NOTE: On 1868, arrows in shield on reverse point between zeros in 0.900. On 1869, arrows point at zeros in 0.900.

KM#	Date	Mintage	VG	Fine	VF	XF
142.2	1863	—	—	Reported, not confirmed		
	1867	—	1000.	1700.	3000.	6000.
	1868	7,984	450.00	550.00	1000.	1500.
	1869/8	7,313	475.00	600.00	1200.	1850.
	1869	Inc. Ab.	450.00	550.00	1000.	1500.
	1870	.012	—	Reported, not confirmed		
	1871	5,996	700.00	1200.	2500.	4000.

Mint: Popayan

KM#	Date	Mintage	VG	Fine	VF	XF
142.3	1862	—	—	Reported, not confirmed		
	1863	—	475.00	600.00	1100.	1700.
	1868	—	475.00	600.00	1100.	1700.
	1869	—	475.00	600.00	1100.	1700.
	1870	8,247	475.00	550.00	1000.	1600.
	1871	5,885	475.00	600.00	1150.	1800.
	1872	—	475.00	600.00	1100.	1700.
	1873	—	475.00	600.00	1150.	1800.
	1874/3	5,352	475.00	600.00	1150.	1800.
	1874	Inc. Ab.	475.00	600.00	1150.	1800.
	1875	5,240	475.00	600.00	1150.	1800.
	1877	1,219	900.00	1500.	2750.	5000.
	1878	2,873	500.00	650.00	1400.	2250.

Mint: Medellin
Modified design

KM#	Date	Mintage	VG	Fine	VF	XF
158	1872	.017	900.00	1500.	2750.	5000.
	1873	Inc. Ab.	900.00	1500.	2750.	5000.

MODERN DECIMAL SYSTEM

100 Centavos = 1 Peso

1-1/4 CENTAVOS

COPPER-NICKEL

KM#	Date	Mintage	Fine	VF	XF	Unc
173	1874	2.400	1.00	2.00	4.50	15.00
	1874	—	—	—	Proof	Rare

2-1/2 CENTAVOS

.9000 g, .666 SILVER, .0192 oz ASW

KM#	Date	Mintage	VG	Fine	VF	XF
169	1872	.328	2.00	4.50	8.00	14.00
	1873	.302	2.00	4.50	8.00	14.00
	1874	.075	3.50	8.00	16.00	30.00
	1875	.056	2.50	5.00	9.50	18.00
	1876	.071	3.50	8.00	16.00	30.00
	1877	.078	2.50	5.00	9.50	16.00
	1878	.347	2.00	3.25	4.75	10.00
	1879	.402	2.00	3.25	4.75	10.00
	1880	.123	2.00	3.25	4.75	10.00
	1881	.123	2.00	3.25	4.75	10.00

NOTE: Date varieties exist.

COPPER-NICKEL, 14mm

KM#	Date	Mintage	Fine	VF	XF	Unc
179	1881	24.000	.10	.25	.75	4.50

18mm

KM#	Date	Mintage	Fine	VF	XF	Unc
180	1881	4.000	.65	1.75	3.50	15.00

COPPER
Reeded edge

KM#	Date	Mintage	Fine	VF	XF	Unc
181	1885	—	1.50	4.00	9.00	35.00

NOTE: Date varieties exist.

COPPER-NICKEL

KM#	Date	Mintage	Fine	VF	XF	Unc
182	1886	12.000	.35	1.00	3.00	8.00

CINCO (5) CENTAVOS

1.2500 g, .666 SILVER, .0268 oz ASW

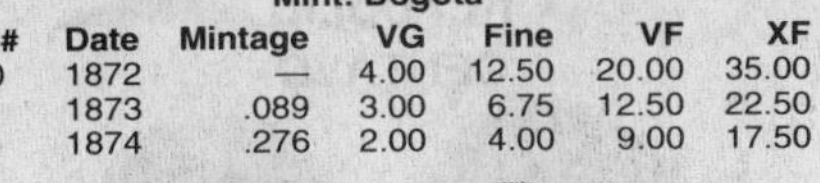

Mint: Bogota

KM#	Date	Mintage	VG	Fine	VF	XF
170	1872	—	4.00	12.50	20.00	35.00
	1873	.089	3.00	6.75	12.50	22.50
	1874	.276	2.00	4.00	9.00	17.50

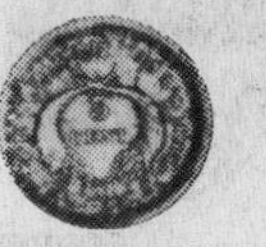

1.2300 g, .835 SILVER, .0330 oz ASW
Mint: Medellin

KM#	Date	Mintage	VG	Fine	VF	XF
174	1874	—	25.00	50.00	100.00	150.00

1.2500 g, .666 SILVER, .0268 oz ASW
Mint: Bogota

KM#	Date	Mintage	VG	Fine	VF	XF
174a.1	1875	.077	1.50	3.00	5.00	15.00
	1876	.019	4.00	10.00	17.50	30.00
	1877	.094	2.50	5.50	8.50	18.00
	1878	.190	1.00	2.75	5.00	15.00
	1879/8	.177	1.00	2.75	5.00	15.00
	1879	Inc. Ab.	1.00	2.75	5.00	15.00
	1880	.044	3.00	8.50	17.50	30.00
	1881	.219	3.00	7.50	15.00	27.50
	1882/1	—	—	—	—	—
	1882	—	1.25	3.00	5.00	15.00
	1883/2	.412	1.50	4.00	7.50	18.00
	1883	Inc. Ab.	1.25	3.00	5.00	15.00
	1884	.220	2.50	5.50	8.50	17.00
	1885	—	1.50	3.50	6.50	15.00

Mint: Medellin

KM#	Date	Mintage	VG	Fine	VF	XF
174a.2	1875	—	20.00	40.00	65.00	120.00

10 CENTAVOS

2.5000 g, .835 SILVER, .0671 oz ASW
Mint: Bogota

KM#	Date	Mintage	VG	Fine	VF	XF
171	1872	Inc. Ab.	3.00	8.00	20.00	42.50
	1873	.043	3.00	8.00	20.00	42.50
	1874	Inc. Be.	2.50	5.00	12.00	17.50

KM#	Date	Mintage	VG	Fine	VF	XF
175.1	1874	.179	1.00	2.50	3.50	8.50
	1875	.265	1.00	2.50	3.50	8.50
	1878	.419	1.50	3.00	6.00	15.00
	1879	Inc. Ab.	1.00	2.50	3.50	8.50
	1880/79	.134	5.00	12.00	16.50	30.00
	1880	Inc. Ab.	4.00	10.00	15.00	27.50
	1881	.020	1.50	3.00	4.00	10.00
	1882	—	2.50	4.00	6.00	15.00
	1883	.202	1.00	2.50	3.50	8.50
	1884/3	—	3.00	9.00	15.00	27.50
	1884	—	1.00	2.50	3.50	8.50
	1885	—	4.00	12.00	17.00	32.50

Mint: Medellin

KM#	Date	Mintage	VG	Fine	VF	XF
175.2	1885(0.835)	—	10.00	15.00	27.50	50.00
	1885(0.835/0.500)	—	12.00	18.00	30.00	65.00

2.5000 g, .500 SILVER, .0402 oz ASW

KM#	Date	Mintage	VG	Fine	VF	XF
175.2a	1885(0.500)	—	15.00	25.00	37.50	80.00
	1885(0.500/0.835)	—	15.00	25.00	37.50	80.00
	1886	—	15.00	25.00	37.50	80.00

20 CENTAVOS

5.0000 g, .835 SILVER, .1342 oz ASW
Mint: Medellin

Obv: Large head. Rev. leg: GRAM 5.

KM#	Date	Mintage	VG	Fine	VF	XF
176.1	1874	—	8.50	20.00	45.00	95.00

Rev. leg: GRAMOS 5.

KM#	Date	Mintage	VG	Fine	VF	XF
176.2	1874	—	20.00	50.00	80.00	150.00
	1882/74	—	13.50	25.00	40.00	60.00

Mint: Bogota
Obv: Small head. Rev. leg: GRAMOS 5.

KM#	Date	Mintage	VG	Fine	VF	XF
176.3	1884/3	—	15.00	32.50	60.00	110.00
	1884	—	13.50	30.00	55.00	100.00

Mint: Medellin
Obv: Small head. Rev. leg: GRAM 5.

KM#	Date	Mintage	VG	Fine	VF	XF
178.1	1875	—	8.50	15.00	22.50	37.50
	1876	—	1.75	3.00	7.50	16.50
	1877	—	5.00	10.00	16.00	27.50
	1882	—	3.50	7.00	12.00	32.50

NOTE: Varieties in sizes of stars exist.

Obv: Small head, tiny B in O of ESTADOS.

KM#	Date	Mintage	VG	Fine	VF	XF
178.2	1875	—	7.50	15.00	24.00	37.50
	1876/5	—	6.50	14.00	22.00	35.00
	1876	—	6.00	12.50	20.00	32.50

Obv: Small head. Rev. leg: GRAMOS 5

KM#	Date	Mintage	VG	Fine	VF	XF
178.3	1882/1	—	2.50	5.50	10.00	15.00
	1882	—	2.00	3.25	6.50	12.50
	1884	—	2.50	5.00	10.00	15.00
	1885/4	—	25.00	50.00	95.00	165.00
	1885	—	15.00	35.00	55.00	90.00
	1885/4 (0.835/0.500)	—	—	—	—	—
	1885(0.835/0.500)	—	20.00	42.50	80.00	150.00

5.0000 g, .500 SILVER, .0804 oz ASW

KM#	Date	Mintage	VG	Fine	VF	XF
178.3a	1886(0.500)	—	30.00	75.00	125.00	200.00
	1886(0.500/0.835)	—	30.00	75.00	125.00	200.00

50 CENTAVOS

12.5000 g, .835 SILVER, .3356 oz ASW
Mint: Bogota
Rev: '50' in numerals
Obv. and rev: Small letters.
Edge: DIOS LEI LIBERTAD.

KM#	Date	Mintage	VG	Fine	VF	XF
172.1	1872	.027	13.50	35.00	65.00	125.00
	1873	.101	8.00	17.50	35.00	75.00

Obv. and rev: Large letters.

KM#	Date	Mintage	VG	Fine	VF	XF
172.2	1874	.280	5.00	12.00	22.00	50.00
	1875	—	—	—	Rare	—

NOTE: Varieties exist.

Rev: CINCUENTA for denomination.

KM#	Date	Mintage	VG	Fine	VF	XF
177.1	1874	Inc. Ab.	3.25	6.00	12.50	22.50
	1875	.621	2.50	7.00	13.00	22.50
	1876	.259	4.50	10.00	20.00	45.00
	1877/6	.133	7.50	15.00	27.50	55.00
	1877	Inc. Ab.	4.50	9.50	20.00	40.00
	1878	.264	4.50	9.50	20.00	40.00
	1879	.307	3.50	8.00	14.00	25.00
	1880	1.249	2.50	6.00	13.00	20.00
	1881	1.086	2.50	6.00	13.00	20.00
	1882/1	—	—	—	Rare	—
	1882	—	3.00	7.00	13.00	22.50
	1883	.221	2.50	7.00	13.00	22.50
	1884	.993	2.50	6.00	12.00	20.00
	1885	—	12.00	20.00	40.00	80.00

Mint: Popayan

KM#	Date	Mintage	VG	Fine	VF	XF
177.2	1880	—	145.00	265.00	450.00	800.00

12.5000 g, .500 SILVER, .2009 oz ASW
Mint: Bogota

KM#	Date	Mintage	VG	Fine	VF	XF
177a.1	1885	—	3.25	7.50	15.00	30.00
	1886/76	—	—	—	Rare	—
	1886/5	—	—	—	Rare	—
	1886	—	5.50	12.50	22.50	45.00

Mint: Medellin

KM#	Date	Mintage	VG	Fine	VF	XF
177a.2	1886	—	80.00	165.00	330.00	700.00

Edge: DIOS PATRIA LIBERTAD.

KM#	Date	Mintage	VG	Fine	VF	XF
177a.3	1886	—	65.00	135.00	275.00	600.00

Obv: KM#161. Rev: KM#177a.2.

KM#	Date	Mintage	VG	Fine	VF	XF
A183	1886	—	—	—	Rare	—

REPUBLIC

CENTAVO

COPPER-NICKEL

KM#	Date	Mintage	Fine	VF	XF	Unc
275	1918	.989	4.00	12.00	20.00	40.00
(197)	1919	.496	12.00	25.00	37.50	65.00
	1920	7.540	2.25	7.50	12.50	25.00
	1921	12.460	1.50	6.00	12.00	20.00
	1933	3.000	.60	3.00	5.00	10.00
	1935	5.000	.60	3.00	5.00	10.00
	1936	1.540	1.75	5.00	7.50	12.00
	1938	7.920	.15	.25	1.00	2.75
	1941B	1.000	.35	.75	1.75	5.50
	1946B	2.096	.30	.55	1.00	3.50
	1947/37B	1.835	—	—	—	—
	1947/6B	I.A.	—	—	—	—
	1947B	Inc. Ab.	.30	.55	1.25	3.75
	1948/38B	1.139	—	—	—	—
	1948B	Inc. Ab.	.35	.75	1.50	4.50

NICKEL-CLAD STEEL

KM#	Date	Mintage	Fine	VF	XF	Unc
275a	1952	8.697	—	Reported, not confirmed		
(197a)	1952B	Inc. Ab.	.10	.15	.25	1.00
	1954B	5.080	.10	.15	.25	1.00
	1956	1.315	.10	.15	.40	1.50
	1957	.900	.15	.25	.50	2.50
	1958/48	—	—	—	—	—
	1958	1.596	.10	.15	.40	2.00

BRONZE

KM#	Date	Mintage	Fine	VF	XF	Unc
205	1942	1.000	.20	.50	1.50	3.50
	1942B	Inc. Ab.	.25	.75	2.00	5.00
	1943B	4.515	.15	.35	1.00	3.00
	1944B	4.515	.15	.35	1.00	3.00
	1945	3.769	.15	.35	1.00	3.00
	1945B	—	.15	.35	1.00	3.00
	1948B	.585	.30	1.00	2.50	6.50
	1949B	4.255	.15	.35	1.00	3.50
	1950B	5.827	.15	.35	1.00	3.50
	1951B	Inc. Ab.	.20	.60	1.75	4.50
	1957	2.500	—	.10	.20	1.00
	1958	.590	.10	.25	.50	2.00
	1959	2.677	—	.10	.20	1.00
	1960	2.500	—	.10	.20	1.00
	1961	3.673	—	.10	.20	1.00
	1962	4.065	—	.10	.20	1.00
	1963	1.845	.10	.15	.30	2.00
	1964/44	3.165	.10	.30	.75	2.50
	1964	Inc. Ab.	—	.10	.20	.75
	1965 large date	5.510	—	.10	.20	.75
	1965 sm. dt.	I.A.	—	.10	.20	.75
	1966	3.910	—	.10	.20	.75

NOTE: Several date varieties exist.

COPPER-CLAD STEEL

KM#	Date	Mintage	Fine	VF	XF	Unc
205a	1967	5.730	—	.10	.15	.25
	1968	7.390	—	.10	.15	.25
	1969	6.870	—	.10	.15	.25
	1970	3.839	—	.10	.15	.25
	1971	3.020	—	.10	.20	.50
	1972	3.100	—	.10	.15	.25
	1973	—	—	—	.10	.20
	1974	2.000	—	—	.10	.20
	1975	1.000	—	—	.10	.20
	1976	1.000	—	—	.10	.20
	1977	.900	—	—	.10	.20
	1978	.224	—	.10	.20	.40

NOTE: Several date varieties exist.

BRONZE
Uprising Sesquicentennial

KM#	Date	Mintage	Fine	VF	XF	Unc
218	1960	.500	.60	1.50	3.00	5.00

NOTE: This and the other issues in the uprising commemorative series offer the usual design of the period with the dates 1810-1960 added at the bottom of the obverse.

DOS, II (2) CENTAVOS

COPPER-NICKEL

KM#	Date	Mintage	Fine	VF	XF	Unc
198	1918	.745	2.50	6.00	15.00	45.00
	1919	.930	7.50	15.00	30.00	80.00
	1920	3.855	1.00	2.25	7.50	15.00
	1921	11.145	.25	.75	2.50	9.00
	1922	10 pcs. known		—	—	400.00
	1933	3.500	.25	.75	3.00	6.00
	1935	2.500	.25	.75	3.00	6.00
	1938	3.872	.20	.50	2.00	5.00
	1941B	.500	.40	1.00	2.50	6.00
	1942B	.500	.50	1.25	2.75	6.50
	1946/36B	2.593	—	—	—	—
	1946B	Inc. Ab.	.30	.85	1.75	4.50
	1947/3B	1.337	—	—	—	—
	1947B	Inc. Ab.	.35	1.00	2.50	5.50

BRONZE

KM#	Date	Mintage	Fine	VF	XF	Unc
210	1948B	2.648	.50	1.00	4.00	7.50
	1949B	1.278	.50	1.00	4.50	8.50
	1950B	2.285	.50	1.00	4.00	8.50

ALUMINUM-BRONZE
Obv: Divided legend

KM#	Date	Mintage	Fine	VF	XF	Unc
211	1952B small date	5.038	—	.10	.25	1.00
	1965/3	1.830	—	.15	.20	.35
	1965 large date	Inc. Ab.	—	.10	.20	.85

Obv: Continuous legend

KM#	Date	Mintage	Fine	VF	XF	Unc
214	1955 large date	2.513	.10	.20	.75	3.00
	1955B large date	Inc. Ab.	—	.10	.20	.85
	1959 small date	4.609	—	.10	.15	.50

Uprising Sesquicentennial

KM#	Date	Mintage	Fine	VF	XF	Unc
219	1960	.250	1.00	1.65	2.25	5.00

2-1/2 CENTAVOS

COPPER-NICKEL

KM#	Date	Mintage	Fine	VF	XF	Unc
190	1902	.400	45.00	120.00	175.00	225.00

CINCO (5) CENTAVOS

COPPER-NICKEL
Rev: Large top 5.

KM#	Date	Mintage	Fine	VF	XF	Unc
183.1	1886	1.000	.25	.75	2.00	6.00

Rev: Small top 5.

KM#	Date	Mintage	Fine	VF	XF	Unc
183.2	1886	—	.25	.75	2.00	6.00
	1886	—	—	—	Proof	185.00
	1888	—	.25	.75	2.00	6.00

KM#	Date	Mintage	Fine	VF	XF	Unc
184	1886	Inc. Ab.	.25	.75	2.25	7.50
	1902	.400	40.00	65.00	125.00	165.00

1.2500 g, .666 SILVER, .0268 oz ASW

KM#	Date	Mintage	Fine	VF	XF	Unc
191	1902	.400	.35	1.00	2.25	7.50

COPPER-NICKEL

KM#	Date	Mintage	Fine	VF	XF	Unc
199	1918	.767	6.50	10.00	15.00	35.00
	1919	1.926	1.75	3.50	8.00	20.00
	1920	2.062	3.50	6.00	10.00	25.00
	1921	1.574	1.50	3.00	6.00	17.50
	1922H	2.623	2.00	3.50	7.00	17.50
	1922H	—	—	—	—	—
	1924	.120	8.00	17.50	27.50	60.00
	1933	2.000	.75	1.50	2.50	5.00
	1933B	—	—	Reported, not confirmed		
	1935	11.616	.50	1.50	2.00	4.00
	1936	—	4.50	7.50	12.50	27.50
	1938B	2.000	.75	2.00	3.50	8.00
	1938	3.867	.50	1.35	2.00	5.00
	1938 large 8 in date	Inc. Ab.	.75	2.00	3.50	8.00
	1939/5	2.000	.75	1.75	3.50	8.00
	1939	Inc. Ab.	.50	1.35	2.50	5.50
	1941	—	2.75	5.00	7.50	18.00
	1941B	.500	1.25	2.50	3.50	7.00
	1946 small date	40.000	.20	.50	.75	2.00
	1946 large date	3.330	2.00	4.00	7.50	15.00
	1949B	2.750	.45	1.00	2.00	4.00
	1949	—	1.75	3.00	4.50	10.00
	1950B large 50 in date	3.611	.45	1.00	2.00	4.00
	1950B small 50 in date	Inc. Ab.	.45	1.00	2.00	4.00

NOTE: Varieties exist.

BRONZE

KM#	Date	Mintage	Fine	VF	XF	Unc
206	1942	—	1.25	2.50	4.00	12.00
	1942B	.800	.50	1.25	2.00	7.00
	1943	—	1.00	1.75	3.50	10.00
	1943B	6.053	.20	.60	1.00	3.00
	1944	—	.25	.75	1.25	4.00
	1944B	9.013	.20	.60	1.00	3.00
	1945/4	—	.50	1.25	2.50	6.50
	1945	—	.50	1.25	2.50	6.50
	1945B	11.101	.25	.75	1.25	3.50
	1946/5	—	1.25	2.50	3.50	9.00
	1946	—	.50	1.25	2.00	5.00
	1952	—	1.25	2.50	3.50	9.00
	1952B	3.985	.15	.40	.75	1.25
	1953B	5.180	.10	.25	.50	1.00
	1954B	1.159	.10	.25	.50	1.00
	1955B	6.819	.10	.25	.50	1.00
	1956	8.772	.10	.25	.50	1.00
	1956B	—	.35	1.25	2.50	6.50
	1957	8.912	.10	.25	.50	1.00
	1958	15.016	.10	.25	.40	.80
	1959	14.271	.10	.25	.40	.80
	1960/660	11.716	.25	.75	1.00	2.00
	1960/70	I.A.	.25	.75	1.00	2.00
	1960	Inc. Ab.	.10	.25	.40	.80
	1961	11.200	.10	.25	.40	.65
	1962	10.928	—	.10	.20	.35
	1963/53	15.113	—	—	—	—
	1963	Inc. Ab.	—	.10	.20	.40
	1964	9.336	—	.10	.20	.35
	1965	6.460	—	.10	.20	.40
	1966	7.170	—	.10	.35	1.00

NOTE: Some coins of 1942-56 have weak "B".

COPPER-CLAD STEEL

KM#	Date	Mintage	Fine	VF	XF	Unc
206a	1967	10.280	—	—	.10	.25
	1968	8.900	—	—	.10	.25
	1969	17.800	—	—	.10	.25
	1970	14.842	—	—	.10	.25
	1971	10.730	—	—	.10	.25
	1972	10.170	—	—	.10	.25
	1973	10.525	—	—	.10	.25
	1974	5.310	—	—	.10	.20
	1975	5.631	—	—	.10	.20
	1976	3.009	—	—	.10	.20
	1977	2.000	—	—	.10	.20
	1978	.468	—	.10	.15	.30
	1979	8.087	—	—	.10	.20

NOTE: Date varieties exist for 1967, 1970 and 1973.

BRONZE
Uprising Sesquicentennial

KM#	Date	Mintage	Fine	VF	XF	Unc
220	1960	.400	1.75	3.50	7.50	25.00

10 CENTAVOS

2.5000 g, .666 SILVER, .0536 oz ASW

KM#	Date	Mintage	Fine	VF	XF	Unc
188	1897 (Brussels)	2.642	.75	1.50	3.00	10.00

2.5000 g, .900 SILVER, .0723 oz ASW
Simon Bolivar

KM#	Date	Mintage	Fine	VF	XF	Unc
196.1	1911	5.065	1.00	1.75	5.00	25.00
	1913	8.305	1.00	1.75	4.00	20.00
	1914	3.840	1.00	1.75	5.00	25.00
	1926	—	—	—	—	—
	1934B on obv.	.140	2.50	4.00	8.00	35.00
	1934/24	I.A.	—	—	—	—
	1934	Inc. Ab.	15.00	25.00	35.00	75.00
	1937	—	8.00	18.50	27.50	50.00
	1938/7	2.055	—	—	—	—
	1938 wide date	I.A.	.50	1.00	2.00	6.50
	1938 narrow date	Inc. Ab.	.50	1.00	2.00	6.50
	1940	.450	1.50	2.50	4.50	15.00
	1941	4.415	.50	1.00	2.00	6.50
	1942	3.140	5.00	10.00	16.50	37.50
	1942B on rev.	I.A.	.50	1.00	2.00	6.50

Obv: Different coat of arms.

KM#	Date	Mintage	Fine	VF	XF	Unc
196.2	1920	2.149	1.50	2.25	6.50	27.50

2.5000 g, .500 SILVER, .0401 oz ASW
Francisco de Paula Santander
Rev: Mint mark at bottom.

KM#	Date	Mintage	Fine	VF	XF	Unc
207.1	1945B	4.830	.50	1.25	2.50	6.00
	1945 B-B	—	—	—	—	—
	1945 backwards B	—	—	—	—	—
	1946/5B	—	.60	1.50	3.00	8.00
	1946B	—	.60	1.50	3.00	8.00
	1947/5B	7.366	1.50	3.00	5.00	10.00
	1947/6B	I.A.	1.50	3.00	5.00	10.00

Rev: Mint mark at top.

KM#	Date	Mintage	Fine	VF	XF	Unc
207.2	1947/5B	I.A.	2.00	4.00	7.50	20.00
	1947B	Inc. Ab.	2.00	4.00	7.50	20.00
	1948/5B	3.629	.60	1.50	3.00	8.00
	1948B	Inc. Ab.	.50	1.00	2.25	6.00
207.2	1949/5B	5.923	2.00	4.00	7.50	20.00
	1949B	Inc. Ab.	.50	1.00	2.00	5.00
	1950B	6.783	.50	1.00	2.25	6.00
	1951/5B	5.185	.50	1.00	2.25	6.00
	1951B	Inc. Ab.	.50	1.00	2.00	5.00
	1952B	1.060	1.00	1.50	3.00	8.00

NOTE: Varieties exist.

COPPER-NICKEL 18mm
Chief Calarca

KM#	Date	Mintage	Fine	VF	XF	Unc
212.1	1952B	6.035	.10	.25	.60	2.25
	1953B	6.985	.10	.25	.60	2.25

18.5mm

KM#	Date	Mintage	Fine	VF	XF	Unc
212.2	1954B	13.006	.10	.20	.30	2.00
	1955B	9.968	.10	.20	.30	1.75
	1956	36.010	.10	.20	.30	1.00
	1958	41.695	.20	.50	1.00	3.00
	1959	36.653	.10	.20	.30	1.00
	1960	32.290	.10	.20	.30	2.00
	1961	17.780	.10	.20	.30	2.00
	1962	8.930	.10	.20	.30	1.50
	1963	37.540	.10	.20	.30	1.00
	1964	61.672	.10	.20	.30	.75
	1965	12.804	.10	.20	.30	1.50
	1966 large date	23.544	.10	.20	.30	.50

NOTE: Varieties exist.

Uprising Sesquicentennial

KM#	Date	Mintage	Fine	VF	XF	Unc
221	1960	1.000	.75	1.25	2.50	8.00

NICKEL-CLAD STEEL
Francisco de Paula Santander

KM#	Date	Mintage	Fine	VF	XF	Unc
226	1967	26.980	—	.10	.15	.50
	1968	23.670	—	.10	.15	.50
	1969	29.450	—	.10	.15	.50

Obv. leg: Divided after REPUBLICA DE

KM#	Date	Mintage	Fine	VF	XF	Unc
236	1969	Inc. Ab.	—	—	.10	.15
	1970	—	—	—	.10	.15
	1971	—	—	.10	.15	.20

Obv. leg: Divided after REPUBLICA

KM#	Date	Mintage	Fine	VF	XF	Unc
243	1970	38.935	—	.10	.15	.20
	1971	53.314	—	.10	.15	.20

Obv. leg: Continuous

KM#	Date	Mintage	Fine	VF	XF	Unc
253	1972	58.000	—	.10	.15	.20
	1973	46.549	—	.10	.15	.20
	1974	49.740	—	.10	.15	.20
	1975	46.037	—	.10	.15	.20
	1976	46.084	—	.10	.15	.20
	1977	8.127	—	.10	.15	.20
	1978	97.081	—	.10	.15	.20

NOTE: Varieties exist.

20 CENTAVOS

5.0000 g, .666 SILVER, .1072 oz ASW

KM#	Date	Mintage	Fine	VF	XF	Unc
189	1897 (Brussels)					
		1.441	1.25	2.50	5.00	15.00

5.0000 g, .900 SILVER, .1446 oz ASW
Simon Bolivar

KM#	Date	Mintage	Fine	VF	XF	Unc
197	1911	1.206	1.50	3.50	7.50	17.50
	1913	1.630	1.50	3.50	7.50	22.50
	1914	2.560	1.50	3.50	9.00	25.00
	1920 wide date					
		1.242	1.75	4.00	10.00	27.50
	1920 narrow date					
		Inc. Ab.	1.75	4.00	10.00	27.50
	1921	.372	4.00	10.00	22.50	55.00
	1922	.045	13.50	32.50	60.00	—
	1933B on obv.					
		.330	2.00	5.00	9.00	25.00
	1933B on rev.					
		Inc. Ab.	12.50	25.00	45.00	125.00
	1933B both sides					
		Inc. Ab.	3.00	6.00	10.00	30.00
	1938/1	1.410	—	—	—	—
	1938	Inc. Ab.	1.25	2.50	5.00	15.00
	1941	—	1.50	3.50	7.50	22.50
	1942	.155	9.00	20.00	32.50	65.00
	1942B	Inc. Ab.	1.50	3.50	7.50	20.00

5.0000 g, .500 SILVER, .0803 oz ASW
Rev: Mint mark in field below CENTAVOS.

KM#	Date	Mintage	Fine	VF	XF	Unc
208.1	1945B	1.675	1.00	2.50	5.00	10.00
	1945BB*	I.A.	4.25	8.00	15.00	32.50
	1946/5B	6.599	1.00	2.50	5.00	10.00
	1946B	Inc. Ab.	1.50	3.00	5.50	12.00
	1946/5(m)	—	3.75	9.50	16.50	37.50
	1946(m)	—	2.75	5.50	10.00	25.00
	1947/5B	9.708	2.50	4.50	8.00	20.00
	1947(m)	—	3.75	6.50	12.00	32.50
	1947B	—	2.50	4.50	8.00	20.00

NOTE: 1945BB has extra B on wreath at bottom.

Rev: Mint mark on wreath at top.

KM#	Date	Mintage	Fine	VF	XF	Unc
208.2	1947/5B	I.A.	5.00	10.00	20.00	50.00
	1947(m)	—	5.00	8.50	15.00	35.00
		1.748	—	—	Rare	—
	1948/5B	I.A.	1.50	3.00	5.00	12.00
	1948B	Inc. Ab.	1.50	3.00	5.00	14.00
	1949/5B	.403	3.75	8.50	17.50	45.00
	1949B	Inc. Ab.	2.50	5.00	10.00	32.50
	1950/45B					
		1.899	2.75	6.75	15.00	50.00
	1950B	Inc. Ab.	2.75	6.00	13.50	37.50
	1951/45B					
		7.498	.75	2.00	4.00	9.00
	1951B	Inc. Ab.	.75	2.00	3.50	7.00

NOTE: Almost all dies for 1946-51 show at least faint traces of overdating from 1945. Coins with absolutely no underdate, and those with very bold underdate, are generally worth more to advanced specialists.

5.0000 g, .300 SILVER, .0482 oz ASW
Simon Bolivar

KM#	Date	Mintage	Fine	VF	XF	Unc
213	1952B	3,887	—	—	Rare	—
	1953B	17.819	.40	.60	1.25	3.50

COPPER-NICKEL
Simon Bolivar
Obv: Small date.

KM#	Date	Mintage	Fine	VF	XF	Unc
215.1	1956	39.778	.10	.15	.20	1.00
215.1	1959	44.779	.10	.15	.20	1.00
	1961	10.740	.15	.25	.50	2.00
	1966	23.060	.10	.15	.20	1.00

Obv: Large date.

KM#	Date	Mintage	Fine	VF	XF	Unc
215.2	1963	12.035	—	.10	.20	.75
	1964	29.075	—	.10	.20	.50
	1965	19.180	.10	.20	.40	1.50

Uprising Sesquicentennial

KM#	Date	Mintage	Fine	VF	XF	Unc
222	1960	.500	.75	1.50	3.00	8.00

Jorge Eliecer Gaitan

KM#	Date	Mintage	Fine	VF	XF	Unc
224	1965	1.000	—	.10	.20	.50

NICKEL-CLAD STEEL
Francisco de Paula Santander

KM#	Date	Mintage	Fine	VF	XF	Unc
227	1967	15.720	—	.10	.20	.75
	1968	26.680	—	.10	.20	.75
	1969	22.470	—	.10	.20	.75

Obv. leg: Divided after REPUBLICA

KM#	Date	Mintage	Fine	VF	XF	Unc
237	1969	Inc.KM227	—	.10	.20	.30
	1970	44.358	—	—	.10	.20

Obv. leg: Divided after REPUBLICA DE

KM#	Date	Mintage	Fine	VF	XF	Unc
245	1971	77.526	—	—	.10	.20

Obv. leg: Continuous

KM#	Date	Mintage	Fine	VF	XF	Unc
246.1	1971	Inc. Ab.	—	—	.10	.20
	1972	41.891	—	—	.10	.20
	1973/1	41.440	—	—	.10	.20
	1973	Inc. Ab.	—	—	.10	.25
	1974/1	45.941	—	—	—	—
	1974	Inc. Ab.	—	—	.10	.20
	1975	28.635	—	—	.10	.20
	1976	29.590	—	—	.10	.20
	1977	2.054	—	—	.10	.25
	1978	10.630	—	—	.10	.20

NOTE: Varieties exist w/ and w/o dots.

Obv: Smaller letters in legend.
Rev: Wreath with larger 20 and smaller CENTAVOS.

KM#	Date	Mintage	Fine	VF	XF	Unc
246.2	1979	16.655	—	—	.10	.20

NOTE: Varieties exist.

25 CENTAVOS

ALUMINUM-BRONZE
Francisco de Paula Santander

KM#	Date	Mintage	Fine	VF	XF	Unc
267	1979	88.874	—	.10	.15	.25

CINCO (5) DECIMOS

12.5000 g, .500 SILVER, .2009 oz ASW
Obv: So-called Greek profile.

KM#	Date	Mintage	VG	Fine	VF	XF
165	1887	.084	27.50	50.00	100.00	185.00
	1888	—	40.00	90.00	200.00	375.00

Obv: Large head.

KM#	Date	Mintage	VG	Fine	VF	XF
166	1888	—	20.00	47.50	75.00	150.00
	1889	—	—	—	Rare	—

Obv: Long-necked Liberty head.

KM#	Date	Mintage	VG	Fine	VF	XF
167	1888	—	—	—	Rare	—

12.5000 g, .835 SILVER, .3356 oz ASW
Obv: Large head. Rev: 2 stars and 2 dots.

KM#	Date	Mintage	VG	Fine	VF	XF
168	1889	—	—	—	Rare	—

50 CENTAVOS

12.5000 g, .500 SILVER, .2009 oz ASW
Mint: Bogota

KM#	Date	Mintage	VG	Fine	VF	XF
185	1887	1.764	6.50	13.50	32.50	85.00
	1888	—	—	—	Rare	—

Similar to KM#186.1a.

KM#	Date	Mintage	VG	Fine	VF	XF
186.1	1888	—	32.50	85.00	175.00	350.00

12.5000 g, .835 SILVER, .3356 oz ASW

KM#	Date	Mintage	VG	Fine	VF	XF
186.1a	1889	.130	12.50	30.00	55.00	100.00
	1898	—	10.00	25.00	47.50	90.00
	1899	—	55.00	125.00	250.00	525.00

Obv: Incuse lettering on head band.

KM#	Date	Mintage	VG	Fine	VF	XF
186.2	1906	.446	6.00	12.00	22.50	50.00
	1907	1.126	5.00	9.00	18.00	40.00
	1908/7	.871	17.50	37.50	70.00	145.00
	1908	Inc. Ab.	7.50	15.00	25.00	55.00

30.4mm
400th Anniversary of Columbus' Discovery of America
Obv: Tip of cap points to left side of A in REPUBLICA.

KM#	Date	Mintage	Fine	VF	XF	Unc
187.1	1892	4.826	5.00	10.00	27.50	75.00

Reduced size, 29.6mm.
Obv: Tip of cap points to right side of A in REPUBLICA.

KM#	Date	Mintage	Fine	VF	XF	Unc
187.2	1892	Inc. Ab.	4.50	9.00	22.50	65.00
	1892	3 known	—	—	Proof	1750.

KM#	Date	Mintage	Fine	VF	XF	Unc
192	1902	.960	6.50	12.00	25.00	65.00

12.5000 g, .900 SILVER, .3617 oz ASW
Mints: Birmingham and Bogota
Simon Bolivar
Obv: Sharper featured bust.
Rev: Left wing and flags far from legend.

KM#	Date	Mintage	Fine	VF	XF	Unc
193.1	1912	1.207	BV	5.00	15.00	50.00
193.1	1913	.417	4.00	7.00	20.00	55.00
	1914 closed 4	.769	BV	6.50	20.00	75.00
	1915 small date	.946	BV	6.00	15.00	40.00
	1916	1.060	BV	6.00	15.00	45.00
	1917 normal 7	.099	10.00	20.00	30.00	65.00
	1917 foot on 7	Inc. Ab.	5.00	9.00	22.50	50.00
	1918	.400	4.00	7.00	20.00	50.00
	1919	Inc. Ab.	15.00	25.00	35.00	80.00
	1922	.150	8.00	14.00	27.50	75.00
	1923	.150	8.00	14.00	27.50	75.00
	1931/21B	—	—	—	—	—
	1931B	.700	BV	4.00	10.00	25.00
	1931	Inc. Ab.	40.00	75.00	120.00	350.00
	1932/12B	.300	8.00	14.00	25.00	50.00
	1932/22B	I.A.	—	—	—	—
	1932B	Inc. Ab.	BV	4.00	9.00	22.50
	1932 flat top 3, w/o B	Inc. Ab.	20.00	30.00	40.00	80.00
	1933/13B	1.000	3.50	5.00	10.00	25.00
	1933/23B	I.A.	5.00	10.00	17.50	35.00
	1933B	Inc. Ab.	BV	4.00	9.00	22.50

Mint: Medellin
Rev: Larger letters, left wing and flags close to legend.

KM#	Date	Mintage	Fine	VF	XF	Unc
193.2	1914 open 4	—	5.00	9.00	22.50	75.00
	1915/4 lg.dt.	—	—	—	—	—
	1915 lg.dt.	—	35.00	65.00	95.00	175.00
	1918/4	—	—	—	—	—
	1918	—	BV	6.00	15.00	40.00
	1919	—	6.00	11.00	25.00	70.00
	1921	.300	6.00	11.00	25.00	70.00
	1922	—	5.00	9.00	22.50	65.00
	1932/22M	1.200	8.00	14.00	25.00	50.00
	1932M	Inc. Ab.	BV	4.00	9.00	22.50
	1932 round top 3, no M	Inc. Ab.	17.50	30.00	45.00	100.00
	1933M	.800	BV	6.00	12.50	35.00
	1933/23 round top 3's, no M	Inc. Ab.	15.00	25.00	35.00	75.00

Obv: Rounded feature bust.

KM#	Date	Mintage	Fine	VF	XF	Unc
274	1916	1.300	BV	6.50	12.00	35.00
	1917	.142	7.00	12.50	25.00	80.00
	1921	1.000	BV	5.50	10.00	25.00
	1922	3.000	BV	5.00	9.00	25.00
	1934	10.000	BV	4.00	7.00	20.00

12.5000 g, .500 SILVER, .2009 oz ASW
Simon Bolivar

KM#	Date	Mintage	Fine	VF	XF	Unc
209	1947/6B	1.240	3.00	6.00	15.00	45.00
	1947B	Inc. Ab.	3.00	6.00	15.00	45.00
	1948/6B	.707	3.00	6.00	15.00	45.00
	1948B	Inc. Ab.	3.00	6.00	15.00	45.00

COPPER-NICKEL
Simon Bolivar

KM#	Date	Mintage	Fine	VF	XF	Unc
217	1958	3.596	.15	.30	.50	2.00
	1959	13.466	.15	.30	.45	1.50
	1960	4.360	.15	.30	.75	8.00
	1961	3.260	.15	.30	.75	7.00
	1962	2.336	.15	.30	.75	6.00
	1963	4.098	.15	.30	.50	1.50
	1964	9.274	.10	.20	.40	1.50
	1965	5.800	.10	.15	.25	1.00
	1966	2.820	.15	.30	.50	1.50

NOTE: Various sizes of date exist.

Uprising Sequicentennial

KM#	Date	Mintage	Fine	VF	XF	Unc
223	1960	.200	1.50	3.00	7.50	15.00

Jorge Eliecer Gaitan

KM#	Date	Mintage	Fine	VF	XF	Unc
225	1965	.600	.10	.20	.30	.60

NICKEL-CLAD STEEL
Francis de Paula Santander

KM#	Date	Mintage	Fine	VF	XF	Unc
228	1967	3.460	.10	.15	.25	.65
	1968	5.460	.10	.15	.25	.65
	1969	1.590	.10	.15	.25	.65

KM#	Date	Mintage	Fine	VF	XF	Unc
244.1	1970	30.906	—	.10	.15	.35
	1971	32.650	—	.10	.15	.30
	1972	25.290	—	.10	.15	.30
	1973	8.060	—	.10	.15	.30
	1974	19.541	—	.10	.15	.25
	1975	4.325	—	.10	.15	.30
	1976	13.181	—	.10	.15	.25
	1977	10.413	—	.10	.15	.25
	1978	10.736	—	.10	.15	.25

KM#	Date	Mintage	Fine	VF	XF	Unc
244.2	1979	22.584	—	.10	.15	.25
	1980	16.433	—	.10	.15	.25
	1982	10.107	—	.10	.15	.25

NOTE: Various sizes of dates exist.

Rev: Larger 50.

KM#	Date	Mintage	Fine	VF	XF	Unc
244.3	1979	—	—	.10	.15	.25

PESO

25.0000 g, .900 SILVER, .7234 oz ASW
200th Anniversary of Popayan Mint

KM#	Date	Mintage	Fine	VF	XF	Unc
216	1956	.012	6.00	9.00	15.00	22.50

COPPER-NICKEL
Simon Bolivar

KM#	Date	Mintage	Fine	VF	XF	Unc
229	1967	4.000	.15	.30	.50	1.00

Simon Bolivar
Obv: Small date.

KM#	Date	Mintage	Fine	VF	XF	Unc
258.1	1974	56.020	—	.10	.15	.40
	1975	117.714	—	.10	.15	.35
	1976	98.728	—	.10	.15	.35

Obv: Large date.

KM#	Date	Mintage	Fine	VF	XF	Unc
258.2	1977	62.083	—	.10	.15	.35
	1978	48.624	—	.10	.15	.35
	1979	83.908	—	.10	.15	.35
	1980	93.406	—	.10	.15	.35
	1981	65.219	—	.10	.15	.35

2 PESOS

BRONZE
Simon Bolivar

KM#	Date	Mintage	Fine	VF	XF	Unc
263	1977	76.661	.10	.15	.25	.50
	1978	69.575	.10	.15	.25	.50
	1979	56.537	.10	.15	.25	.50
	1980	108.521	.10	.15	.25	.50
	1981	40.368	.10	.15	.25	.50
	1983	—	.10	.15	.25	.50
	1987	—	.10	.15	.25	.50
	1988	16.200	.10	.15	.25	.50

NOTE: Varieties exist.

2-1/2 PESOS

3.9940 g, .917 GOLD, .1177 oz AGW

KM#	Date	Mintage	Fine	VF	XF	Unc
194	1913	.018	—	BV	75.00	125.00

Simon Bolivar
Obv: Large head.

KM#	Date	Mintage	Fine	VF	XF	Unc
200	1919A	—	—	BV	60.00	100.00
	1919B	—	—	Reported, not confirmed		
	1919	.034	—	BV	60.00	100.00
	1920/19A	—	—	BV	60.00	100.00
	1920A	—	—	BV	60.00	100.00
	1920	.034	—	BV	85.00	150.00

Simon Bolivar
Obv: Small head, MEDELLIN below bust.

KM#	Date	Mintage	Fine	VF	XF	Unc
203	1924	—	—	BV	60.00	100.00
	1925	—	—	Reported, not confirmed		
	1927	—	—	BV	75.00	125.00
	1928	.014	—	BV	100.00	175.00
	1929	—	—	Reported, not confirmed		

5 PESOS

7.9881 g, .917 GOLD, .2355 oz AGW

KM#	Date	Mintage	Fine	VF	XF	Unc
195	1913	.017	—	BV	110.00	150.00
	1917	.043	—	BV	110.00	150.00
	1918/3	.423	—	BV	110.00	150.00
	1918	Inc. Ab.	—	BV	110.00	150.00
	1919	2.181	—	BV	100.00	135.00

Simon Bolivar
Obv: Large head.

KM#	Date	Mintage	Fine	VF	XF	Unc
201	1919	Inc. Ab.	—	BV	100.00	135.00
	1919A	Inc. Ab.	—	BV	100.00	135.00
	1919B	—	—	BV	110.00	150.00
	1920	.870	—	BV	100.00	135.00
	1920A	Inc.Ab.	—	BV	100.00	135.00
	1920B	.108	—	BV	100.00	135.00
	1921A	—	—	—	—	—

KM#	Date	Mintage	Fine	VF	XF	Unc
201	1922B	.029	—	BV	100.00	135.00
	1923B	.074	—	BV	100.00	135.00
	1924	—	—	Reported, not confirmed		
	1924B	.705	—	BV	100.00	135.00

Simon Bolivar
Obv: Small head, MEDELLIN below bust.

KM#	Date	Mintage	Fine	VF	XF	Unc
204	1924	.120	—	BV	100.00	125.00
	1925/4	.668	—	BV	100.00	125.00
	1925	Inc. Ab.	—	BV	100.00	125.00
	1926	.383	—	BV	100.00	125.00
	1927	.365	—	BV	100.00	125.00
	1928	.314	—	BV	100.00	125.00
	1929	.321	—	BV	100.00	125.00
	1930	.502	—	BV	100.00	125.00

NOTE: 1924 dated coins have several varieties in size of 2 and 4. 1925 dated coins exist with an Arabic and a Spanish style 5. 1930 dated coins have three varieties in size and placement of 3.

COPPER-NICKEL
International Eucharistic Congress

KM#	Date	Mintage	Fine	VF	XF	Unc
230	1968B	.660	.25	.50	.75	1.75

NICKEL-CLAD STEEL
6th Pan-American Games

KM#	Date	Mintage	Fine	VF	XF	Unc
247	1971	2.000	.15	.35	.60	1.50

BRONZE

KM#	Date	Mintage	Fine	VF	XF	Unc
268	1980	146.268	.15	.35	.60	1.25
	1.981 (1981)	9.148	.15	.35	.60	1.25
	1.982 (1982)	84.107	.15	.35	.75	1.50
	1983	—	.15	.35	.60	1.25
	1985	—	.15	.35	.60	1.25
	1987	—	.15	.35	.60	1.25
	1988 small date	45.000	.15	.35	.60	1.25
	1988 large inverted date	Inc. Ab.	.15	.35	.60	1.25
	1989	—	.15	.35	.60	1.25

COPPER-ALUMINUM-NICKEL

KM#	Date	Mintage	Fine	VF	XF	Unc
280	1989	—	—	—	—	1.25
	1990	—	—	—	—	1.25
	1991	—	—	—	—	1.25
	1992	—	—	—	—	1.25

10 PESOS

15.9761 g, .917 GOLD, .4710 oz AGW
Simon Bolivar

KM#	Date	Mintage	Fine	VF	XF	Unc
202	1919	.101	—	BV	250.00	350.00
	1924B	.055	—	BV	250.00	350.00

COPPER-NICKEL-ZINC
Cordoba, San Andreas Island and Providencia

KM#	Date	Mintage	Fine	VF	XF	Unc
270	1.981(1981)					
		20.949	—	.15	.25	1.25
	1982	83.605	—	.15	.25	1.25
	1983	104.051	—	.15	.25	1.25
	1985	80.000	—	.15	.25	1.25
	1988	50.700	—	.15	.25	1.25
	1989	—	—	.15	.25	1.25

NOTE: Date varieties exist.

KM#	Date	Mintage	Fine	VF	XF	Unc
281	1989	—	—	—	—	.50
	1990	—	—	—	—	.50
	1991	—	—	—	—	.50
	1992	—	—	—	—	.50

20 PESOS

ALUMINUM-BRONZE

KM#	Date	Mintage	Fine	VF	XF	Unc
271	1982	—	—	.15	.20	.30
	1984	64.066	—	.15	.20	.30
	1985	100.690	—	.15	.20	.30
	1987	—	—	.15	.20	.30
	1988	72.000	—	.15	.20	.30
	1989	—	—	.15	.20	.30

NOTE: 1985 and 1988 coins exist with large and small dates.

COPPER-ALUMINUM-NICKEL

KM#	Date	Mintage	Fine	VF	XF	Unc
282	1989	—	—	—	—	.50
	1990	—	—	—	—	.50
	1991	—	—	—	—	.50
	1992	—	—	—	—	.50
	1993	—	—	—	—	.50

50 PESOS

COPPER-NICKEL
National Constitution

KM#	Date	Mintage	Fine	VF	XF	Unc
272	1986	14.900	—	—	—	1.25
	1987 lg. dt.	—	—	—	—	1.25
	1988 small date	100.000	—	—	—	1.25
	1989	—	—	—	—	1.25

COPPER-NICKEL-ZINC

KM#	Date	Mintage	Fine	VF	XF	Unc
283	1989	—	—	—	—	1.00
	1990	—	—	—	—	1.00
	1991	—	—	—	—	1.00

100 PESOS

4.3000 g, .900 GOLD, .1244 oz AGW
International Eucharistic Congress

KM#	Date	Mintage	VF	XF	Unc
231	1968	.108	—	—	65.00
	1968	8,000	—	Proof	85.00

Battle of Boyaca - Joachim Paris
Obv: Bust of Bolivar. Rev: Bust of Paris.

KM#	Date	Mintage	VF	XF	Unc
238	1969	6,000	—	Proof	100.00

6th Pan American Games

KM#	Date	Mintage	VF	XF	Unc
248	1971	6,000	—	Proof	100.00

BRASS

KM#	Date	Mintage	Fine	VF	XF	Unc
285	1992		—	—	—	1.50
	1993		—	—	—	1.50

200 PESOS

8.6000 g, .900 GOLD, .2488 oz AGW
International Eucharistic Congress
Rev: Arms and value.

KM#	Date	Mintage	VF	XF	Unc
232	1968	.108	—	—	130.00
	1968	8,000	—	Proof	150.00

Battle of Boyaca - Carlos Soublette
Obv: Bust of Bolivar. Rev: Bust of Soublette.

KM#	Date	Mintage	VF	XF	Unc
239	1969	6,000	—	Proof	175.00

6th Pan American Games

KM#	Date	Mintage	VF	XF	Unc
249	1971	6,000	—	Proof	175.00

300 PESOS

12.9000 g, .900 GOLD, .3733 oz AGW
International Eucharistic Congress

KM#	Date	Mintage	VF	XF	Unc
233	1968	.062	—	—	185.00
	1968	8,000	—	Proof	225.00

Battle of Boyaca - Jose Anzoategui
Obv: Bust of Bolivar. Rev: Bust of Anzoategui.

KM#	Date	Mintage	VF	XF	Unc
240	1969	6,000	—	Proof	225.00

6th Pan American Games

KM#	Date	Mintage	VF	XF	Unc
250	1971	6,000	—	Proof	250.00

500 PESOS

21.5000 g, .900 GOLD, .6221 oz AGW
International Eucharistic Congress
Rev: Arms and value.

KM#	Date	Mintage	VF	XF	Unc
234	1968	.014	—	—	325.00
	1968	8,000	—	Proof	350.00

Battle of Boyaca - Juan Jose Rondon
Obv: Bust of Bolivar. Rev: Bust of Rondon.

KM#	Date	Mintage	VF	XF	Unc
241	1969	6,000	—	Proof	350.00

6th Pan American Games

KM#	Date	Mintage	VF	XF	Unc
251	1971	6,000	—	Proof	400.00

28.2800 g, .925 SILVER, .8411 oz ASW
Conservation - Orinoco Crocodile

KM#	Date	Mintage	VF	XF	Unc
264	1978	2,678	—	—	25.00
	1978	3,233	—	Proof	35.00

750 PESOS

35.0000 g, .925 SILVER, 1.0409 oz ASW
Conservation - Chestnut-Bellied Hummingbird
Obv: Similar to 500 Pesos, KM#264.

KM#	Date	Mintage	VF	XF	Unc
265	1978	2,656	—	—	30.00
	1978	3,100	—	Proof	40.00

1000 PESOS

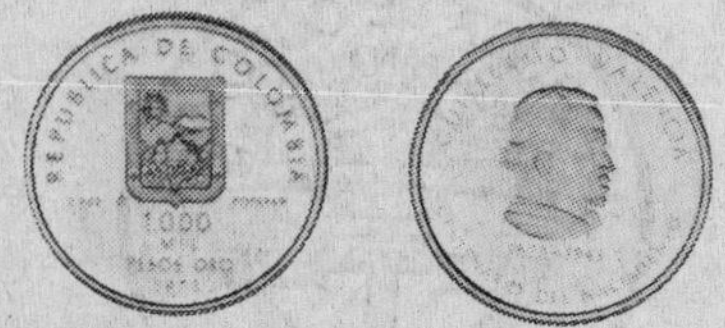

4.3000 g, .900 GOLD, .1244 oz AGW
100th Anniversary of Birth of Guillermo Valencia

KM#	Date	Mintage	VF	XF	Unc
254	1973	10,003	—	Proof	65.00

450th Anniversary of City of Santa Marta

KM#	Date	Mintage	VF	XF	Unc
259	1975	2,500	—	Proof	75.00

Tricentennial of City of Medellin

KM#	Date	Mintage	VF	XF	Unc
260	1975	4,000	—	Proof	75.00

1500 PESOS

64.5000 g, .900 GOLD, 1.8664 oz AGW
International Eucharistic Congress
Obv: Similar to 300 Pesos, KM#233.

KM#	Date	Mintage	VF	XF	Unc
235	1968	5,722	—	—	1000.
	1968	8,000	—	Proof	1200.

Battle of Boyaca - Francisco Santander

KM#	Date	Mintage	VF	XF	Unc
242	1969	6,000	—	Proof	1200.

6th Pan American Games
Obv: Similar to 300 Pesos, KM#250.

KM#	Date	Mintage	VF	XF	Unc
252	1971	6,000	---	Proof	1400.

19.1000 g, .900 GOLD, .5527 oz AGW
50th Anniversary of Gold Museum of Central Bank of Bogata

KM#	Date	Mintage	VF	XF	Unc
255	1973	4,911	—	Proof	275.00

8.6000 g, .900 GOLD, .2488 OZ AGW
100th Anniversary of Birth of Guillermo Valencia

KM#	Date	Mintage	VF	XF	Unc
256	1973	5,000	—	Proof	150.00

2000 PESOS

12.9000 g, .900 GOLD, .3733 oz AGW
100th Anniversary of Birth of Guillermo Valencia

KM#	Date	Mintage	VF	XF	Unc
257	1973	5,003	—	Proof	225.00

8.6000 g, .900 GOLD, .2488 oz AGW
450th Anniversary of City of Santa Marta

KM#	Date	Mintage	VF	XF	Unc
261	1975	2,500	—	Proof	150.00

Tricentennial of City of Medellin

KM#	Date	Mintage	VF	XF	Unc
262	1975	4,000	—	Proof	150.00

10000 PESOS

27.0000 g, .925 SILVER, .8029 oz ASW
Ibero - American Series - Bogota Mint

KM#	Date	Mintage	VF	XF	Unc
284	1991	.070	—	Proof	45.00

15000 PESOS

33.4370 g, .900 GOLD, .9676 oz AGW
Conservation - Ocelot

KM#	Date	Mintage	VF	XF	Unc
266	1978	490 pcs.	—	—	650.00
	1978	148 pcs.	—	Proof	2000.

17.2900 g, .900 GOLD, .5000 oz AGW
150th Anniversary of Death of Jose Maria Cordova

KM#	Date	Mintage	VF	XF	Unc
278 (275)	1980	250 pcs.	—	Proof	350.00

150th Anniversary of Death of
Antonio Jose De Sucre

KM#	Date	Mintage	VF	XF	Unc
276	1980	250 pcs.	—	Proof	350.00

30000 PESOS

34.5800 g, .900 GOLD, 1.0007 oz AGW
Death of Bolivar

KM#	Date	Mintage	VF	XF	Unc
269	1980	500 pcs.	—	Proof	750.00

35000 PESOS

8.6400 g, .900 GOLD, .2500 oz AGW
100th Anniversary of Birth of President Santos

KM#	Date	Mintage	VF	XF	Unc
273	1988	pcs.	—	Proof	200.00

70000 PESOS

17.2800 g, .900 GOLD, .5000 oz AGW
100th Anniversary of Birth of President Santos

KM#	Date	Mintage	VF	XF	Unc
277 (274)	1988	*600 pcs.	—	Proof	400.00

INFLATIONARY COINAGE

P/M - Papel moneda

Beginning about 1886, Colombia fell victim to rampant "printing press" inflation. Deluged by paper money without solid backing the peso gradually declined in value until it was equal to 1 centavo of the old silver-based currency. The 1, 2 and 5 peso p/m coins reflected this inflation, and later circulated at par with the newer 1, 2 and 5 centavo coins.

PESO P/M

COPPER-NICKEL

KM#	Date	Mintage	Fine	VF	XF	Unc
277	1907 AM	2.860	1.25	2.00	5.00	15.00
(271)	1907 AM	—	—	—	Proof	80.00
	1910 AM	1.205	1.75	3.00	7.00	25.00
	1911 AM	2.816	2.00	3.00	8.00	27.50
	1912 AM	6.094	1.50	2.50	6.00	20.00
	1912 H w/o crossbar	2.000	1.50	2.50	6.00	17.50
	1913 AM	.306	3.50	7.00	12.50	30.00
	1914 AM	.552	4.00	8.00	15.00	40.00
	1916 AM	.234	5.00	10.00	18.00	50.00

2 PESOS P/M

COPPER-NICKEL

KM#	Date	Mintage	Fine	VF	XF	Unc
278	1907 AM	4.161	1.75	3.25	8.50	30.00
(272)	1907 AM	—	—	—	Proof	90.00
	1910/07 AM	.649	4.00	6.50	12.50	50.00
	1910 AM	I.A.	4.00	6.50	12.50	50.00
	1911	.458	4.25	7.50	15.00	55.00
	1913	.082	—	Reported, not confirmed		
	1914 AM	1.000	4.00	6.50	12.50	50.00

5 PESOS P/M

COPPER-NICKEL

KM#	Date	Mintage	Fine	VF	XF	Unc
279	1907 AM	6.143	1.25	3.00	6.50	17.50
(273)	1907 AM	—	—	—	Proof	110.00
	1909 AM	4.000	1.50	3.50	7.50	20.00
	1912 H	2.000	1.50	3.50	7.50	20.00
	1912 AM	1.897	2.75	6.50	12.50	35.00
	1913 AM	I.A.	20.00	30.00	50.00	—
	1914 AM	I.A.	10.00	20.00	30.00	50.00

CIVIL WAR COINAGE

Province Of Santander

General Ramon Gonzales Valencia

These coins were struck in Santander in 1902 by General Valencia, to pay his troops after the Battle of Palonegro. Legend has it that they were struck using the brass of expended cartridges. Because the planchets are very thin, the struck uniface surface shows through backwards when examined from the reverse.

10 CENTAVOS

BRASS, uniface

KM#	Date	Mintage	Fine	VF	XF
1	ND(1902)	—	22.50	37.50	60.00

20 CENTAVOS

BRASS, uniface

KM#	Date	Mintage	Fine	VF	XF
2	1902	—	22.50	35.00	52.50

50 CENTAVOS

BRASS, uniface

KM#	Date	Mintage	Fine	VF	XF
3	1902	—	10.00	15.00	35.00

PROOF SETS (PS)

KM#	Date	Mintage	Identification	Issue Price	Mkt. Val.
PS1	1968(5)	8,000	KM231-235	340.00	1950.
PS2	1969(5)	6,000	KM238-242	—	2000.
PS3	1971(5)	6,000	KM248-252	—	2300.
PS4	1973(3)	—	KM254,256,257	—	450.00
PS5	1975(2)	2,500	KM260,262	195.00	235.00
PS6	1975(2)	4,000	KM259,261	195.00	245.00
PS7	1979(2)	—	KM264-265	—	75.00

LEPROSARIUM TOKEN ISSUES (Tn)

BOGOTA MINT

Special coinage for use in the three government

colonies of Agua de Dios, Cano de Lord, and Contratacion. The hospitals were closed in the late 1950's and patients were allowed to exchange these special coins for regular currency at any bank.

CENTAVO

COPPER-NICKEL

KM#	Date	Mintage	Good	VG	Fine	VF
Tn9	1921 RH	.300	.50	1.00	2.75	6.50

2 CENTAVOS

COPPER-NICKEL

KM#	Date	Mintage	Good	VG	Fine	VF
Tn10	1921 RH	.350	.50	1.00	3.50	7.50

2-1/2 CENTAVOS

BRASS

KM#	Date	Mintage	Good	VG	Fine	VF
Tn1	1901	.020	6.00	12.50	20.00	42.50

5 CENTAVOS

BRASS

KM#	Date	Mintage	Good	VG	Fine	VF
Tn2	1901	.015	6.00	12.50	20.00	42.50

COPPER-NICKEL

KM#	Date	Mintage	Good	VG	Fine	VF
Tn11	1921 H	.200	.75	1.50	3.75	8.00

10 CENTAVOS

BRASS

KM#	Date	Mintage	Good	VG	Fine	VF
Tn3	1901	.010	10.00	15.00	25.00	45.00

COPPER-NICKEL

KM#	Date	Mintage	Good	VG	Fine	VF
Tn12	1921 RH	.200	.75	1.50	3.75	8.00

20 CENTAVOS

BRASS

KM#	Date	Mintage	Good	VG	Fine	VF
Tn4	1901	.030	10.00	15.00	25.00	45.00

50 CENTAVOS

BRASS

KM#	Date	Mintage	Good	VG	Fine	VF
Tn5	1901	.026	13.50	20.00	35.00	60.00

COPPER

KM#	Date	Mintage	Good	VG	Fine	VF
Tn5a	1901	2 known	—	—	—	—

COPPER-NICKEL

KM#	Date	Mintage	Good	VG	Fine	VF
Tn13	1921 RH	.120	1.75	3.25	5.50	14.00

BRASS

KM#	Date	Mintage	Good	VG	Fine	VF
Tn14	1928 RH	.050	1.50	4.25	8.00	16.00

COPPER

KM#	Date	Mintage	Good	VG	Fine	VF
Tn14a	1928	Inc. Ab.	—	Rare	—	—

Inflationary Leprosarium T.I. (Tn)

P/M - Papel Moneda

1 Peso was equal in value to 1 Centavo of the old silver currency. It later circulated at par with the newer 1 Centavo coins.

PESO P/M

COPPER-NICKEL

KM#	Date	Mintage	Good	VG	Fine	VF
Tn6	1907	.792	3.00	4.50	10.00	30.00

5 PESOS P/M

COPPER-NICKEL

KM#	Date	Mintage	Good	VG	Fine	VF
Tn7	1907	.159	5.00	10.00	17.50	35.00

10 PESOS P/M

COPPER-NICKEL

KM#	Date	Mintage	Good	VG	Fine	VF
Tn8	1907	.129	6.00	12.00	22.50	45.00

COMOROS

The Federal Islamic Republic of the Comoros, a volcanic archipelago located in the Mozambique Channel of the Indian Ocean 300 miles (483 km.) northwest of Madagascar, has an area of 694 sq. mi. (2,171 sq. km.) and a population of 440,000. Capital: Moroni. The economy of the islands is based on agriculture. There are practically no mineral resources. Vanilla, essence for perfunes, copra, and sisal are exported.

Ancient Phoenician traders were probably the first visitors to the Comoro Islands, but the first detailed knowledge of the area was gathered by Arab sailors. Arab dominion and culture were firmly established when the Portuguese, Dutch, and French arrived in the 16th century. In 1843 a Malagasy ruler ceded the island of Mayotte to France; the other three principal islands of the archipelago--Anjouan, Moheli, and Grand Comore--came under French protection in 1886. The islands were joined administratively with Madagascar in 1912. The Comoros became partially autonomous, with the status of a French overseas territory, in 1946, and achieved complete internal autonomy in 1961. On Dec. 31, 1975, after 133 years of French association, the Comoro Islands became the independent Republic of the Comoros.

Mayotte retained the option of determining its future ties and in 1976 voted to remain French. Its present status is that of a French Territorial Collectivity. French currency now circulates there.

TITLES

Daulat Anjazanchiyah

دولة انجزنجية

RULERS

Said Ali ibn Said Amr, regnant, 1890

French, 1886-1975

MINT MARKS

(a) - Paris, privy marks only

A - Paris

MONETARY SYSTEM

100 Centimes = 1 Franc

ANJOUAN SULTANATE

5 CENTIMES

BRONZE PRIVY MARK

Rev. privy mark: Fasces

KM#	Date	Mintage	Fine	VF	XF	Unc
1.1	AH1308A	.100	6.50	12.00	20.00	65.00

Rev. privy mark: Torch

KM#	Date	Mintage	Fine	VF	XF	Unc
1.2	AH1308A	.200	6.50	12.00	20.00	65.00

10 CENTIMES

BRONZE PRIVY MARK

Rev. privy mark: Fasces

KM#	Date	Mintage	Fine	VF	XF	Unc
2.1	AH1308A	.050	10.00	16.00	30.00	75.00

Rev. privy mark: Torch

KM#	Date	Mintage	Fine	VF	XF	Unc
2.2	AH1308A	.100	10.00	16.00	30.00	75.00

5 FRANCS

.900 SILVER

KM#	Date	Mintage	Fine	VF	XF	Unc
3	AH1308A	2,050	300.00	450.00	675.00	1350.

COLONIAL COINAGE

FRANC

ALUMINUM

KM#	Date	Mintage	Fine	VF	XF	Unc
4	1964(a)	.500	.15	.25	.40	.75

2 FRANCS

ALUMINUM

KM#	Date	Mintage	Fine	VF	XF	Unc
5	1964(a)	.600	.15	.25	.50	1.00

5 FRANCS

ALUMINUM

KM#	Date	Mintage	Fine	VF	XF	Unc
6	1964(a)	1.000	.20	.40	.65	1.25

10 FRANCS

ALUMINUM-BRONZE

KM#	Date	Mintage	Fine	VF	XF	Unc
7	1964(a)	.600	.20	.50	1.00	2.00

20 FRANCS

ALUMINUM-BRONZE

KM#	Date	Mintage	Fine	VF	XF	Unc
8	1964(a)	.500	.30	.65	1.25	2.50

REPUBLIC

Banque Central

5 FRANCS

ALUMINUM
World Fisheries Conference - Coelacanth Fish

KM#	Date	Mintage	Fine	VF	XF	Unc
15	1984(a)	1.000	.25	.50	1.00	2.00

25 FRANCS

NICKEL
F.A.O. Issue - Chickens

KM#	Date	Mintage	Fine	VF	XF	Unc
14	1981(a)	1.000	.75	1.50	3.50	7.00
	1982(a)	—	.20	.40	.75	1.50

50 FRANCS

NICKEL PLATED STEEL

KM#	Date	Mintage	Fine	VF	XF	Unc
16	1990(a)	—	.50	1.00	1.50	2.50

Institut D'Emission

50 FRANCS

NICKEL
Independence of Republic

KM#	Date	Mintage	Fine	VF	XF	Unc
9	1975(a)	—	.40	.75	1.25	2.00

100 FRANCS

NICKEL
F.A.O. Issue

KM#	Date	Mintage	Fine	VF	XF	Unc
13	1977(a)	.500	.60	1.00	2.00	3.50

State of Comoros

5000 FRANCS

44.8300 g, .925 SILVER, 1.3332 oz ASW
Flowers
Rev: Similar to 20,000 Francs, KM#12.

KM#	Date	Mintage	Fine	VF	XF	Unc
10	1976	700 pcs.	—	—	—	60.00
	1976	1,000	—	—	Proof	70.00

10000 FRANCS

3.0700 g, .900 GOLD, .0888 oz AGW
Hummingbird
Obv: Similar to 20,000 Francs, KM#12.

KM#	Date	Mintage	Fine	VF	XF	Unc
11	1976	500 pcs.	—	—	—	110.00
	1976	500 pcs.	—	—	Proof	135.00

20000 FRANCS

6.1400 g, .900 GOLD, .1776 oz AGW
Coelacanth Fish - Said Mohamed Cheikh

KM#	Date	Mintage	Fine	VF	XF	Unc
12	1976	500 pcs.	—	—	—	200.00
	1976	500 pcs.	—	—	Proof	245.00

FLEUR DE COIN SETS (SS)

KM#	Date	Mintage	Identification	Issue Price	Mkt. Val.
SS1	1964(a)	—	KM4-8	—	12.50

NOTE: This set issued with Reunion set.

MINT SETS (MS)

KM#	Date	Mintage	Identification	Issue Price	Mkt. Val.
MS1	1976(3)	500	KM10-12	—	360.00

PROOF SETS (PS)

KM#	Date	Mintage	Identification	Issue Price	Mkt. Val.
PS1	1976(3)	500	KM10-12	229.00	400.00

Listings For

CONGO-BELGE: refer to Zaire

CONGO DEMOCRATIC REPUBLIC: refer to Zaire

The Republic of the Congo (formerly the Peoples Republic of the Congo, located on the equator in west-central Africa, has an area of 132,047 sq. mi. (342,000 sq. km.) and a population of 2.26 million. Capital: Brazzaville. Agriculture forestry, mining, and food processing are the principal industries. Timber, industrial diamonds, potash, peanuts, and cocoa beans are exported.

The Portuguese were the first Europeans to explore the Congo (Brazzaville) area, 14th century. They conducted a slave trade with the tribal kingdoms of Teke, Loango, and Kongo without attempting developmental colonization. French influence was established in 1883 when the king of Teke signed a treaty with Savorgnan de Brazza, thereby placing his kingdom under the protection of France. While a French protectorate, the area was known as Middle Congo. In 1910 Middle Congo became a part of French Equatorial Africa, which also included Gabon, Ubangi-Shari (now the Central African Republic), and Chad. Following World War II, during which it was an important center of Free French activities, the Middle Congo was given a large measure of internal autonomy, and its inhabitants were made French citizens. Upon approval of the constitution of the Fifth French Republic, 1958, it became a member of the new French Community. On Aug. 15, 1960, Middle Congo became the independent Republic of the Congo-Brazzaville. In Jan. 1970 the country's name was changed to Peoples Republic of the Congo. A new constitution which asserts the government's advocacy of socialism was adopted in 1973.

In June and July of 1992, a new 125-member National Assembly was elected. Later that year a new President, Pascal Lissouba was elected. In November, President Lissouba dismissed the previous government and dissolved the National Assembly. A new 23-member government, including members of the opposition, was formed in December 1992 and the name was changed to Republique du Congo.

NOTE: For earlier and related coinage see French Equatorial Africa and the Equatorial African States. For later coinage see Central African States.

RULERS

French

MINT MARKS

(a) - Paris, privy marks only

MONETARY SYSTEM

100 Centimes = 1 Franc

100 FRANCS

NICKEL

KM#	Date	Mintage	Fine	VF	XF	Unc
1	1971(a)	2.500	8.00	15.00	25.00	40.00
	1972(a)	—	8.00	15.00	25.00	40.00

KM#	Date	Mintage	Fine	VF	XF	Unc
2	1975(a)	—	5.00	10.00	17.50	30.00
	1982(a)	—	2.50	5.00	8.00	12.50
	1983(a)	—	2.50	5.00	8.00	12.50
	1985(a)	—	2.00	3.00	6.00	10.00
	1990(a)	—	2.00	3.00	4.00	6.00

COPPER-NICKEL
International Games - Handball

KM#	Date	Mintage	Fine	VF	XF	Unc
3	1984	—	—	—	Proof	22.00

NICKEL PLATED STEEL
Olympics - Boxing

KM#	Date	Mintage	Fine	VF	XF	Unc
7	1991	—	—	—	—	20.00

Olympics - Hurdler

KM#	Date	Mintage	Fine	VF	XF	Unc
8	1991	—	—	—	—	20.00

NICKEL BONDED STEEL
Ancient Sailing Ship

KM#	Date	Mintage	Fine	VF	XF	Unc
10	1991	—	—	—	—	20.00

500 FRANCS

COPPER-NICKEL

KM#	Date	Mintage	Fine	VF	XF	Unc
4	1985(a)	—	3.50	6.00	9.00	15.00
	1986(a)	—	3.50	6.00	9.00	15.00

16.0000 g, .999 SILVER, .5144 oz ASW
Old Style Sailing Ship

KM#	Date	Mintage	Fine	VF	XF	Unc
5	1991	—	—	—	Proof	40.00

12.0000 g, .999 SILVER, .3858 oz ASW
15th Soccer Championship

KM#	Date	Mintage	Fine	VF	XF	Unc
6	1991	—	—	—	—	42.50

16.0700 g, .999 SILVER, .5170 oz ASW
Olympics - Hurdler

KM#	Date	Mintage	Fine	VF	XF	Unc
9	1991	—	—	—	Proof	45.00

20.0000 g, .999 SILVER, .6425 oz ASW

KM#	Date	Mintage	Fine	VF	XF	Unc
9a	1991	—	—	—	—	50.00

20.0000 g, .999 SILVER, .6430 oz ASW
Soccer - Player and Statue of Liberty

KM#	Date	Mintage	Fine	VF	XF	Unc
11	1992	—	—	—	Proof	42.50

19.9500 g, .999 SILVER, .6415 oz ASW
Protection of Nature - Congolese Peacock

KM#	Date	Mintage	Fine	VF	XF	Unc
12	1992	—	—	—	Proof	40.00

1000 FRANCS

20.0000 g, .999 SILVER, .6430 oz ASW
Preservation of Nature - Elephants

KM#	Date	Mintage	Fine	VF	XF	Unc
13	1993	—	—	—	Proof	38.50

15.9000 g, .999 SILVER, .5107 oz ASW
Prehistoric Animals - Brachiosaurus

KM#	Date	Mintage	Fine	VF	XF	Unc
14	1993	—	—	—	Proof	38.50

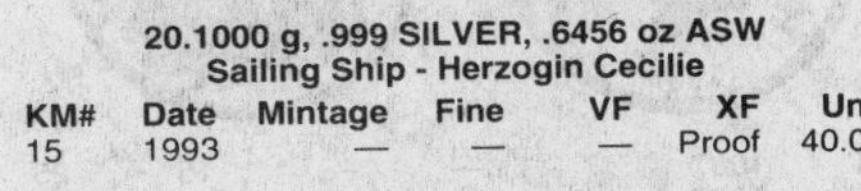

20.1000 g, .999 SILVER, .6456 oz ASW
Sailing Ship - Herzogin Cecilie

KM#	Date	Mintage	Fine	VF	XF	Unc
15	1993	—	—	—	Proof	40.00

COOK ISLANDS

Cook Islands, a political dependency of New Zealand consisting of 15 islands located in the South Pacific Ocean about 2,000 miles (3,218 km.) northeast of New Zealand, has an area of 90 sq. mi. (234 sq. km.) and a population of 21,000. Capital: Avarua. The United States claims the islands of Danger, Manahiki, Penrhyn, and Rakahanga atolls. Citrus and canned fruits and juices, copra, clothing, jewelry, and mother-of-pearl shell are exported.

The islands were first sighted by Spanish navigator Alvaro de Mendada in 1595. Portuguese navigator Pedro Fernandes de Quieros landed on Rakahanga in 1606. English navigator Capt. James Cook sailed to the islands on three occasions: 1773, 1774 and 1777. He named them Hervey Islands, in honor of Augustus John Hervey, a lord of the Admiralty. The islands were declared a British protectorate in 1888, and were annexed to New Zealand in 1901. They were granted internal self-government in 1965. New Zealand provides an annual subsidy and retains responsibility for defense and foreign affairs.

As a territory of New Zealand, Cook Islands are considered to be within the Commonwealth of Nations.

RULERS

British

MINT MARKS

FM - Franklin Mint, U.S.A. *

***NOTE:** From 1975 the Franklin Mint has produced coinage in up to three different qualities. Qualities of issue are designated in () after each date and are defined as follows:

(M) MATTE - Normal circulation strike or a dull finish produced by sandblasting special uncirculated (polish finish) or proof quality dies.

(U) SPECIAL UNCIRCULATED - Polished or proof-like in appearance without any frosted features.

(P) PROOF - The highest quality obtainable having mirror-like fields and frosted features.

MONETARY SYSTEM

(Until 1967)

12 Pence = 1 Shilling
20 Shillings = 1 Pound

(Commencing 1967)

100 Cents = 1 Dollar

CENT

BRONZE
Taro Leaf

KM#	Date	Mintage	VF	XF	Unc
1	1972	.117	—	.10	.20
	1972	.017	—	Proof	.50
	1973	8,500	—	.10	.20
	1973	.013	—	Proof	.50
	1974	.300	—	.10	.20
	1974	7,300	—	Proof	.50
	1975	.429	—	.10	.20
	1975FM(M)	1,000	—	—	.50
	1975FM(U)	2,251	—	—	.20
	1975FM(P)	.021	—	Proof	.50
	1976FM(M)	1,001	—	—	.50
	1976FM(U)	1,066	—	—	.20
	1976FM(P)	.018	—	Proof	.50
	1977FM(M)	1,171	—	—	.50
	1977FM(U)	1,002	—	—	.20
	1977FM(P)	5,986	—	Proof	.50
	1979FM(M)	1,000	—	—	.50
	1979FM(U)	500 pcs.	—	—	1.00
	1979FM(P)	4,058	—	Proof	.50
	1983	—	—	.10	.20
	1983	.010	—	Proof	.50
	Edge: 1728 CAPTAIN COOK 1978.				
1a	1978FM(M)	1,000	—	—	1.00
	1978FM(U)	767 pcs.	—	—	1.00
	1978FM(P)	6,287	—	Proof	.50
	Wedding of Prince Charles and Lady Diana				
	Edge: THE ROYAL WEDDING 29 JULY 1981				
1b	1981FM(M)	1,000	—	—	.50
	1981FM(U)	1,100	—	—	.50
	1981FM(P)	9,205	—	Proof	.40

2 CENTS

BRONZE
Pineapple

KM#	Date	Mintage	VF	XF	Unc
2	1972	.063	.10	.15	.30
	1972	.017	—	Proof	.75
	1973	8,500	.15	.20	.40
	1973	.013	—	Proof	.75
	1974	.120	.10	.15	.30
	1974	7,300	—	Proof	.75
	1975	.129	.10	.15	.25
	1975FM(M)	1,000	—	—	.75
	1975FM(U)	2,251	—	—	.30
	1975FM(P)	.021	—	Proof	.75
	1976FM(M)	1,001	—	—	.75
	1976FM(U)	1,066	—	—	.30
	1976FM(P)	.018	—	Proof	.75
	1977FM(M)	1,171	—	—	.75
	1977FM(U)	1,002	—	—	.30
	1977FM(P)	5,986	—	Proof	.75
	1979FM(M)	1,000	—	—	.75
	1979FM(U)	500 pcs.	—	—	.30
	1979FM(P)	4,058	—	Proof	.75
	1983	—	.10	.15	.25
	1983	.010	—	Proof	.75

Edge: 1728 CAPTAIN COOK 1978.

KM#	Date	Mintage	VF	XF	Unc
2a	1978FM(M)	1,000	—	—	.75
	1978FM(U)	767 pcs.	—	—	.75
	1978FM(P)	6,287	—	Proof	.50

Wedding of Prince Charles and Lady Diana
Edge: THE ROYAL WEDDING 29 JULY 1981

KM#	Date	Mintage	VF	XF	Unc
2b	1981FM(M)	1,000	—	—	.75
	1981FM(U)	1,100	—	—	.75
	1981FM(P)	9,205	—	Proof	.50

5 CENTS

COPPER-NICKEL
Hibiscus

KM#	Date	Mintage	VF	XF	Unc
3	1972	.032	.10	.20	.40
	1972	.017	—	Proof	1.00
	1973	8,500	.15	.25	.50
	1973	.013	—	Proof	1.00
	1974	.080	.10	.20	.40
	1974	7,300	—	Proof	1.00
	1975	.089	.10	.20	.40
	1975FM(M)	1,000	—	—	1.00
	1975FM(U)	2,251	—	—	.40
	1975FM(P)	.021	—	Proof	1.00
	1976FM(M)	1,001	—	—	1.00
	1976FM(U)	1,066	—	—	.40
	1976FM(P)	.018	—	Proof	1.00
	1977FM(M)	1,171	—	—	1.00
	1977FM(U)	1,002	—	—	.40
	1977FM(P)	5,986	—	Proof	1.00
	1979FM(M)	1,000	—	—	1.00
	1979FM(U)	500 pcs.	—	—	.40
	1979FM(P)	4,058	—	Proof	1.00
	1983	—	.10	.20	.40
	1983	.010	—	Proof	1.00

Edge: 1728 CAPTAIN COOK 1978.

KM#	Date	Mintage	VF	XF	Unc
3a	1978FM(M)	1,000	—	—	1.00
	1978FM(U)	767 pcs.	—	—	.75
	1978FM(P)	6,287	—	Proof	.50

Wedding of Prince Charles and Lady Diana
Edge: THE ROYAL WEDDING 29 JULY 1981

KM#	Date	Mintage	VF	XF	Unc
3b	1981FM(M)	1,000	—	—	1.00
	1981FM(U)	1,100	—	—	1.00
	1981FM(P)	9,205	—	Proof	.50

KM#	Date	Mintage	VF	XF	Unc
33	1987	—	—	.10	.25
	1987	—	—	Proof	1.25
	1988	—	—	.10	.25
	1988	—	—	Proof	1.25
	1992	—	—	.10	.25

10 CENTS

COPPER-NICKEL
Orange

KM#	Date	Mintage	VF	XF	Unc
4	1972	.035	.10	.20	.50
	1972	.017	—	Proof	1.25
	1973	.059	.10	.20	.50
	1973	.013	—	Proof	1.25
	1974	.050	.10	.20	.50
	1974	7,300	—	Proof	1.25
	1975	.059	.10	.20	.50
	1975FM(M)	1,000	—	—	1.25
	1975FM(U)	2,251	—	—	.50
	1975FM(P)	.021	—	Proof	1.25
	1976FM(M)	1,001	—	—	1.25
	1976FM(U)	1,066	—	—	.50
	1976FM(P)	.018	—	Proof	1.25
	1977FM(M)	1,171	—	—	1.25
	1977FM(U)	1,002	—	—	.50
	1977FM(P)	5,986	—	Proof	1.25
	1983	—	.10	.20	.50
	1983	.010	—	Proof	1.25

Edge: 1728 CAPTAIN COOK 1978.

KM#	Date	Mintage	VF	XF	Unc
4a	1978FM(M)	1,000	—	—	1.25
	1978FM(U)	767 pcs.	—	—	1.25
	1978FM(P)	6,287	—	Proof	1.00

F.A.O. Issue

KM#	Date	Mintage	VF	XF	Unc
4b	1979FM(M)	9,000	—	—	1.00
	1979FM(U)	500 pcs.	—	—	1.50
	1979FM(P)	4,058	—	Proof	1.25

Wedding of Prince Charles and Lady Diana
Edge: THE ROYAL WEDDING 29 JULY 1981

KM#	Date	Mintage	VF	XF	Unc
4c	1981FM(M)	1,000	—	—	1.25
	1981FM(U)	1,100	—	—	1.25
	1981FM(P)	9,205	—	Proof	.75

KM#	Date	Mintage	VF	XF	Unc
34	1987	—	—	.15	.25
	1987	—	—	Proof	1.25
	1988	—	—	.15	.25
	1988	—	—	Proof	1.25
	1992	—	—	.15	.25

20 CENTS

COPPER-NICKEL
Fairy Tern

KM#	Date	Mintage	VF	XF	Unc
5	1972	.031	.20	.40	.75
	1972	.017	—	Proof	1.50
	1973	.049	.20	.40	.75
	1973	.013	—	Proof	1.50
	1974	5,500	.20	.45	.85
	1974	7,300	—	Proof	1.50
	1975	.060	.20	.40	.75
	1975FM(M)	1,000	—	—	1.50
	1975FM(U)	2,251	—	—	.85
	1975FM(P)	.021	—	Proof	1.50
	1983	—	.20	.40	.85
	1983	.010	—	Proof	1.50

Pacific Triton Shell

KM#	Date	Mintage	VF	XF	Unc
14	1976FM(M)	1,001	—	—	1.50
	1976FM(U)	1,066	—	—	.75
	1976FM(P)	.018	—	Proof	1.50
	1977FM(M)	1,171	—	—	1.50
	1977FM(U)	1,002	—	—	.75
	1977FM(P)	5,986	—	Proof	1.50
	1979FM(M)	1,000	—	—	1.50
	1979FM(U)	500 pcs.	—	—	2.00
	1979FM(P)	4,058	—	Proof	1.50

Edge: 1728 CAPTAIN COOK 1978.

KM#	Date	Mintage	VF	XF	Unc
14a	1978FM(M)	1,000	—	—	1.50
	1978FM(U)	767 pcs.	—	—	2.00
	1978FM(P)	6,287	—	Proof	1.00

Wedding of Prince Charles and Lady Diana
Edge: THE ROYAL WEDDING 29 JULY 1981

KM#	Date	Mintage	VF	XF	Unc
14b	1981FM(M)	1,000	—	—	1.50
	1981FM(U)	1,100	—	—	1.50
	1981FM(P)	9,205	—	Proof	1.00

KM#	Date	Mintage	VF	XF	Unc
35	1987	—	—	.25	.35
	1987	—	—	Proof	1.50
	1988	—	—	.25	.35
	1988	—	—	Proof	1.50
	1992	—	—	.25	.35

50 CENTS

COPPER-NICKEL
Bonito Fish

KM#	Date	Mintage	VF	XF	Unc
6	1972	.031	.40	.75	1.25
	1972	.017	—	Proof	2.00
	1973	.019	.40	.75	1.25
	1973	.013	—	Proof	2.00
	1974	.010	.40	.75	1.25
	1974	7,300	—	Proof	2.00
	1975	.019	.40	.75	1.25
	1975FM(M)	1,000	—	—	2.00
	1975FM(U)	2,251	—	—	1.25
	1975FM(P)	.021	—	Proof	2.00
	1976FM(M)	1,001	—	—	2.00
	1976FM(U)	1,066	—	—	1.25
	1976FM(P)	.018	—	Proof	2.00
	1977FM(M)	1,171	—	—	2.00
	1977FM(U)	1,002	—	—	1.25
	1977FM(P)	5,986	—	Proof	2.00
	1983	—	.40	.75	1.25
	1983	.010	—	Proof	2.00

Edge: 1728 CAPTAIN COOK 1978.

KM#	Date	Mintage	VF	XF	Unc
6a	1978FM(M)	1,000	—	—	2.00
	1978FM(U)	767 pcs.	—	—	2.00
	1978FM(P)	6,287	—	Proof	2.00

F.A.O. Issue

KM#	Date	Mintage	VF	XF	Unc
6b	1979FM(M)	9,000	.50	1.00	1.50
	1979FM(U)	500 pcs.	—	—	2.50
	1979FM(P)	4,058	—	Proof	2.00

Wedding of Prince Charles and Lady Diana
Edge: THE ROYAL WEDDING 29 JULY 1981

KM#	Date	Mintage	VF	XF	Unc
6c	1981FM(M)	1,000	—	—	2.00
	1981FM(U)	1,100	—	—	2.00
	1981FM(P)	9,205	—	Proof	1.50

KM#	Date	Mintage	VF	XF	Unc
36	1987	—	—	.55	.75
	1987	—	—	Proof	2.00
	1992	—	—	.55	.75

50 TENE

COPPER-NICKEL
Turtle

KM#	Date	Mintage	VF	XF	Unc
41	1988	.032	—	—	1.35
	1988	1,000	—	Proof	2.25
	1992	—	—	—	1.35

DOLLAR

COPPER-NICKEL
Tangaroa, Polynesian God of Creation

KM#	Date	Mintage	VF	XF	Unc
7	1972	.031	1.25	2.00	4.00
	1972	.027	—	Proof	4.00
	1973	.049	1.25	2.00	4.00
	1973	.013	—	Proof	6.00
	1974	.020	1.25	2.00	4.00
	1974	7,300	—	Proof	6.00
	1975	.029	1.25	2.00	4.00
	1975FM(M)	1,000	—	—	5.00
	1975FM(U)	2,251	—	—	4.00
	1975FM(P)	.021	—	Proof	6.00
	1976FM(M)	1,001	—	—	5.00
	1976FM(U)	1,066	—	—	5.00
	1976FM(P)	.018	—	Proof	6.00
	1977FM(M)	1,171	—	—	5.00
	1977FM(U)	1,002	—	—	5.00
	1977FM(P)	5,986	—	Proof	8.00
	1979FM(M)	1,000	—	—	5.00
	1979FM(U)	500 pcs.	—	—	6.00
	1979FM(P)	4,058	—	Proof	8.00
	1983	—	1.25	2.00	4.00
	1983	.010	—	Proof	6.00

Edge: 1728 CAPTAIN COOK 1978.

KM#	Date	Mintage	VF	XF	Unc
7a	1978FM(M)	1,000	—	—	6.00
	1978FM(U)	767 pcs.	—	—	6.00
	1978FM(P)	6,287	—	Proof	5.00

Wedding of Prince Charles and Lady Diana

Edge: THE ROYAL WEDDING 29 JULY 1981

KM#	Date	Mintage	VF	XF	Unc
7b	1981FM(M)	1,000	—	—	6.00
	1981FM(U)	1,100	—	—	6.00
	1981FM(P)	9,205	—	Proof	5.00

16th Forum, 2nd P.I.C. and Mini Games

KM#	Date	Mintage	VF	XF	Unc
30	1985	—	—	—	4.00
	27.2200 g, .925 SILVER, .8096 oz ASW				
30a	1985	*2,500	—	Proof	25.00
	39.8000 g, .917 GOLD, 1.1735 oz AGW				
30b	1985	*25 pcs.	—	Proof	3000.

COPPER-NICKEL
60th Birthday of Queen Elizabeth II

KM#	Date	Mintage	VF	XF	Unc
31	1986	.020	—	—	4.50
	27.2200 g, .925 SILVER, .8096 oz ASW				
31a	1986	*2,500	—	Proof	20.00
	44.0000 g, .917 GOLD, 1.2969 oz AGW				
31b	1986	*60 pcs.	—	Proof	1500.

COPPER-NICKEL
Prince Andrew's Marriage

KM#	Date	Mintage	VF	XF	Unc
32	1986	*.020	—	—	4.50
	27.2200 g, .925 SILVER, .8096 oz ASW				
32a	1986	*2,500	—	Proof	17.50
	44.0000 g, .917 GOLD, 1.2969 oz AGW				
32b	1986	*75 pcs.	—	Proof	1250.

COPPER-NICKEL

KM#	Date	Mintage	VF	XF	Unc
37	1987	—	—	1.50	2.50
	1987	—	—	Proof	5.00
	1988	—	—	1.50	2.50
	1988	—	—	Proof	5.00
	1992	—	—	1.50	2.50

Tangaroa, Polynesian God of Fertility
Obv: Portrait of Queen Elizabeth.

KM#	Date	Mintage	VF	XF	Unc
147	1992	—	—	—	4.00

2 DOLLARS

25.7000 g, .925 SILVER, .7643 oz ASW
20th Anniversary of Coronation
Obv: Similar to 50 Cents, KM#6.

KM#	Date	Mintage	VF	XF	Unc
8	1973	.016	—	—	10.00
	1973	.046	—	Proof	10.00

COPPER-NICKEL

KM#	Date	Mintage	VF	XF	Unc
38	1987	—	—	2.25	3.50
	1987	—	—	Proof	7.50
	1988	—	—	2.25	3.50
	1988	—	—	Proof	7.50
	1992	—	—	2.25	3.50

2-1/2 DOLLARS

27.3500 g, .925 SILVER, .8133 oz ASW
Cook 2nd Voyage

KM#	Date	Mintage	VF	XF	Unc
9	1973	6,000	—	—	15.00
	1973	.012	—	Proof	12.00
	1974	2,000	—	—	20.00
	1974	.012	—	Proof	12.00

5 DOLLARS

27.3000 g, .500 SILVER, .4388 oz ASW
Mangara Kingfisher

KM#	Date	Mintage	VF	XF	Unc
15	1976FM(M)	251 pcs.	—	—	35.00
	1976FM(U)	2,192	—	—	15.00
	1976FM(P)	.028	—	Proof	12.00

Atiu Swiftlet

Obv: Similar to 50 Cents, KM#6.

KM#	Date	Mintage	VF	XF	Unc
17	1977FM(M)	252 pcs.	—	—	35.00
	1977FM(U)	4,032	—	—	12.00
	1977FM(P)	.011	—	Proof	12.00

Wildlife Conservation - Polynesian Warbler
Obv: Similar to 50 Cents, KM#6.

KM#	Date	Mintage	VF	XF	Unc
20	1978FM(M)	250 pcs.	—	—	35.00
	1978FM(U)	3,659	—	—	15.00
	1978FM(P)	.011	—	Proof	15.00

Cook Island Conservation Day
Rarotongan Fruit Dove
Obv: Similar to 50 Cents, KM#6.

KM#	Date	Mintage	VF	XF	Unc
24	1979FM(U)	2,500	—	—	22.50
	1979FM(P)	8,612	—	Proof	17.50

ALUMINUM-BRONZE
Conch Shell

KM#	Date	Mintage	VF	XF	Unc
39	1987	—	—	5.00	7.00
	1987	—	—	Proof	15.00
	1988	—	—	5.00	7.00
	1988	—	—	Proof	15.00
	1992	—	—	5.00	7.00

9.9500 g, .500 SILVER, .1600 oz ASW
World Cup Soccer - 3 Players

KM#	Date	Mintage	VF	XF	Unc
149	1991	—	—	Proof	25.00

10.0000 g, .500 SILVER, .1607 oz ASW
Environmental Protection - Child Watching Butterfly

KM#	Date	Mintage	VF	XF	Unc
137	1992	—	—	Proof	25.00

Johann Sebastian Bach

KM#	Date	Mintage	VF	XF	Unc
150	1992	—	—	Proof	25.00

Sailing Ship and Astrolabe

KM#	Date	Mintage	VF	XF	Unc
160	1992	—	—	Proof	25.00

7-1/2 DOLLARS

33.8000 g, .925 SILVER, 1.0052 oz ASW
Cook 2nd Voyage

KM#	Date	Mintage	VF	XF	Unc
10	1973	6,000	—	—	20.00
	1973	.012	—	Proof	18.00
	1974	2,000	—	—	25.00
	1974	.013	—	Proof	18.00

10 DOLLARS

27.9000 g, .925 SILVER, .8297 oz ASW

25th Anniversary of Coronation

KM#	Date	Mintage	VF	XF	Unc
21	1978FM(U)	5,350	—	—	17.50
	1978FM(P)	.011	—	Proof	15.00

10.0000 g, .925 SILVER, .2974 oz ASW
Endangered World Wildlife - Elephant

KM#	Date	Mintage	VF	XF	Unc
72	1990	*.025	—	Proof	35.00

Endangered World Wildlife - Tiger

KM#	Date	Mintage	VF	XF	Unc
73	1990	*.025	—	Proof	35.00

Olympics - Runner

KM#	Date	Mintage	VF	XF	Unc
79	1990	—	—	Proof	30.00

Endangered World Wildlife - Elephants

KM#	Date	Mintage	VF	XF	Unc
80	1990	*.025	—	Proof	35.00

28.0000 g, .925 SILVER, .8327 oz ASW
Save the Children

KM#	Date	Mintage	VF	XF	Unc
81	1990	.020	—	Proof	42.50

10.0000 g, .925 SILVER, .2974 oz ASW
500th Anniversary of Discovery of America

KM#	Date	Mintage	VF	XF	Unc
90	1990	*.010	—	Proof	30.00

1991 Winter Olympics - Cross Country Skier

KM#	Date	Mintage	VF	XF	Unc
91	1990	—	—	Proof	35.00

500th Anniversary of Discovery of America
Columbus and Ship

KM#	Date	Mintage	VF	XF	Unc
121	1990	—	—	Proof	30.00

31.4700 g, .925 SILVER, .9359 oz ASW
Nicolaus Copernicus

KM#	Date	Mintage	VF	XF	Unc
136	1992	—	—	Proof	45.00

20 DOLLARS

28.2800 g, .925 SILVER, .8411 oz ASW
International Year of the Scout

KM#	Date	Mintage	VF	XF	Unc
28	1983	*.010	—	—	35.00
	1983	*.010	—	Proof	45.00

31.4700 g, .925 SILVER, .9359 oz ASW
Friedrich von Schiller

KM#	Date	Mintage	VF	XF	Unc
151	1993	—	—	Proof	40.00

Charles Darwin

KM#	Date	Mintage	VF	XF	Unc
152	1993	*.010	—	Proof	40.00

1996 Olympics - Pole Vault and Sprint

KM#	Date	Mintage	VF	XF	Unc
161	1993	—	—	Proof	40.00

25 DOLLARS

48.8500 g, .925 SILVER, 1.4527 oz ASW
Queen's Silver Jubilee
Obv: Similar to 50 Cents, KM#6.

KM#	Date	Mintage	VF	XF	Unc
18	1977FM(M)	100 pcs.	—	—	75.00
	1977FM(U)	4,068	—	—	30.00
	1977FM(P)	.017	—	Proof	20.00

37.0000 g, .925 SILVER, 1.1005 oz ASW
100th Anniversary of British Rule

42	1988	3,000	—	Proof	50.00

1.2144 g, .999 GOLD, .0400 oz AGW
Endangered Wildlife - Bison

83	1990	—	—	Proof	45.00

Endangered Wildlife - Longhorn Sheep

84	1990	—	—	Proof	45.00

Endangered Wildlife - Tiger

85	1990	—	—	Proof	45.00

Endangered Wildlife - Eagle

86	1990	—	—	Proof	45.00

Endangered Wildlife - Elephant

87	1990	—	—	Proof	45.00

Endangered Wildlife - Lynx

KM#	Date	Mintage	VF	XF	Unc
88	1990	—	—	Proof	45.00

Endangered Wildlife - Przewalski's Horse

138	1992	—	—	P/L	45.00

50 DOLLARS

97.2000 g, .925 SILVER, 2.8907 oz ASW
Winston Churchill Centenary
Obv: Similar to 50 Cents, KM#6.

11	1974	1,202	—	—	45.00
	1974	2,502	—	Proof	50.00

.925 SILVER, GILT

11a	1974	2,002	—	Proof	80.00

3.9400 g, .500 GOLD, .0633 oz AGW
Wedding of Prince Charles and Lady Diana

27	1981	220 pcs.	—	—	75.00
	1981	1,309	—	Proof	100.00

28.2800 g, .925 SILVER, .8411 oz ASW
1988 Olympics - Torch Bearer
Obv: Similar to KM#61.

40	1987P	.020	—	Proof	50.00

20.9400 g, .925 SILVER, .6228 oz ASW
Great Explorers - Stanley & Livingstone

KM#	Date	Mintage	VF	XF	Unc
61	1988 FM(p)	—	—	Proof	47.50

Great Explorers - Capt. James Cook

62	1988 FM(p)	—	—	Proof	47.50

Great Explorers - Balboa

63	1988 FM(p)	—	—	Proof	47.50

Great Explorers - Ferdinand Magellan

64	1988 FM(p)	—	—	Proof	47.50

Great Explorers - Marco Polo

65	1988 FM(p)	—	—	Proof	47.50

Great Explorers - Vasco Da Gama

KM#	Date	Mintage	VF	XF	Unc
66	1988 FM(p)	—	—	Proof	47.50

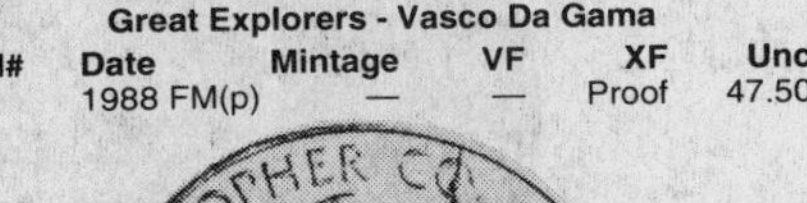

Great Explorers - Christopher Columbus

KM#	Date	Mintage	VF	XF	Unc
67	1988 FM(p)	—	—	Proof	47.50

Great Explorers - Sir Francis Drake

KM#	Date	Mintage	VF	XF	Unc
68	1988 FM(p)	—	—	Proof	47.50

Great Explorers - La Salle

KM#	Date	Mintage	VF	XF	Unc
69	1988 FM(p)	—	—	Proof	47.50

Great Explorers - Alexander The Great

KM#	Date	Mintage	VF	XF	Unc
96	1988 FM(p)	—	—	Proof	47.50

Great Explorers - Leif Ericson

KM#	Date	Mintage	VF	XF	Unc
97	1988 FM(p)	—	—	Proof	47.50

Great Explorers - Amerigo Vespucci

KM#	Date	Mintage	VF	XF	Unc
98	1988 FM(p)	—	—	Proof	47.50

Great Explorers - Bartolomeu Diaz

KM#	Date	Mintage	VF	XF	Unc
99	1988 FM(p)	—	—	Proof	47.50

Great Explorers - Ponce De Leon

KM#	Date	Mintage	VF	XF	Unc
100	1988 FM(p)	—	—	Proof	47.50

Great Explorers - Hernando Cortes

KM#	Date	Mintage	VF	XF	Unc
101	1988 FM(p)	—	—	Proof	47.50

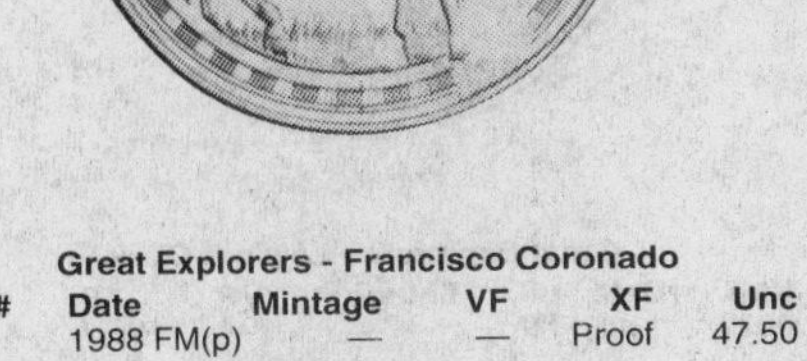

Great Explorers - Francisco Coronado

KM#	Date	Mintage	VF	XF	Unc
102	1988 FM(p)	—	—	Proof	47.50

Great Explorers - Francisco Pizarro

KM#	Date	Mintage	VF	XF	Unc
103	1988 FM(p)	—	—	Proof	47.50

Great Explorers - Samuel De Champlain

KM#	Date	Mintage	VF	XF	Unc
104	1988 FM(p)	—	—	Proof	47.50

Great Explorers - John Cabot

KM#	Date	Mintage	VF	XF	Unc
105	1988 FM(p)	—	—	Proof	47.50

Great Explorers - Abel Janszoon Tasman

KM#	Date	Mintage	VF	XF	Unc
106	1988 FM(p)	—	—	Proof	47.50

Great Explorers - Lewis & Clark

KM#	Date	Mintage	VF	XF	Unc
107	1988 FM(p)	—	—	Proof	47.50

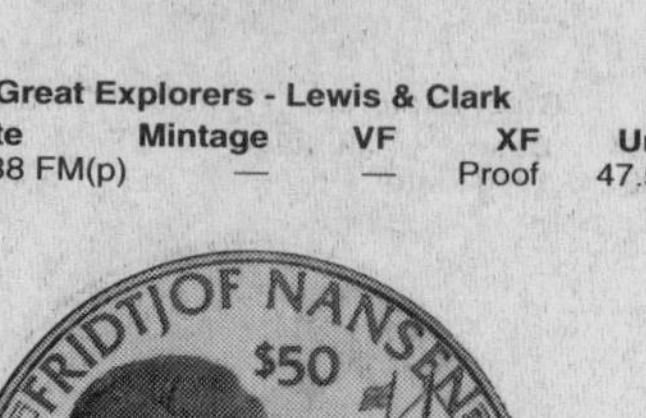

Great Explorers - Fridtjof Nansen

KM#	Date	Mintage	VF	XF	Unc
108	1988 FM(p)	—	—	Proof	47.50

Great Explorers - Robert Peary

KM#	Date	Mintage	VF	XF	Unc
109	1988 FM(p)	—	—	Proof	47.50

Great Explorers - Roald Amundsen

KM#	Date	Mintage	VF	XF	Unc
110	1988 FM(p)	—	—	Proof	47.50

Great Explorers - Richard Byrd

KM#	Date	Mintage	VF	XF	Unc
111	1988 FM(p)	—	—	Proof	47.50

19.4000 g, .925 SILVER, .5770 oz ASW
500th Anniversary of Discovery of America
Sir Francis Drake

KM#	Date	Mintage	VF	XF	Unc
45	1989	*.015	—	Proof	45.00

31.1000 g, .999 SILVER, 1.0000 oz ASW
500th Anniversary of Discovery of America
Capt. James Cook

KM#	Date	Mintage	VF	XF	Unc
46	1989	*.015	—	Proof	45.00

31.1000 g, .925 SILVER, .9250 oz ASW

KM#	Date	Mintage	VF	XF	Unc
46a	1991	—	—	Proof	42.50

500th Anniversary of Discovery of America
Christopher Columbus

KM#	Date	Mintage	VF	XF	Unc
47	1989	*.015	—	Proof	45.00

500th Anniversary of Discovery of America
Ferdinand Magellan

KM#	Date	Mintage	VF	XF	Unc
49	1989	*.015	—	Proof	45.00

19.4000 g, .925 SILVER, .5770 oz ASW
Endangered World Wildlife - Grizzly Bear

KM#	Date	Mintage	VF	XF	Unc
52	1989 PM	—	Reported, not confirmed		
	1990 PM	550 pcs.	—	—	155.00
	1990 PM	*.025	—	Proof	50.00

28.2800 g, .925 SILVER, .8411 oz ASW
1992 Olympics - Runners & Biathlon

KM#	Date	Mintage	VF	XF	Unc
60	1989	*.040	—	—	45.00

Soccer World Championship
Obv: Portrait of Queen Elizabeth.

KM#	Date	Mintage	VF	XF	Unc
70	1989	—	—	Proof	45.00

31.1000 g, .925 SILVER, .9250 oz ASW
500th Anniversary of Discovery of America
Jacques Cartier

KM#	Date	Mintage	VF	XF	Unc
43	1990	*.015	—	Proof	45.00

31.1000 g, .999 SILVER, 1.0000 oz ASW
500th Anniversary of Discovery of America
Vasco Nunez de Balboa

KM#	Date	Mintage	VF	XF	Unc
44	1990	.015	—	Proof	45.00

31.1000 g, .925 SILVER, .9250 oz ASW

KM#	Date	Mintage	VF	XF	Unc
44a	1991	—	—	Proof	42.50

31.1000 g, .999 SILVER, 1.0000 oz ASW
500th Anniversary of Discovery of America
President Abraham Lincoln

KM#	Date	Mintage	VF	XF	Unc
48	1990	*.015	—	Proof	45.00

Endangered World Wildlife - Buffalo

KM#	Date	Mintage	VF	XF	Unc
58	1990 PM	600 pcs.	—	—	155.00
	1990 PM	*.025	—	Proof	50.00

19.8000 g, .925 SILVER, .5888 oz ASW
Endangered World Wildlife - Antelope

KM#	Date	Mintage	VF	XF	Unc
115	1990	—	—	Proof	50.00

19.4000 g, .925 SILVER, .5770 oz ASW
Endangered World Wildlife - African Elephant

KM#	Date	Mintage	VF	XF	Unc
53	1990 PM	1,000	—	—	140.00
	1990 PM	*.025	—	Proof	50.00

Endangered World Wildlife - Chimpanzee

KM#	Date	Mintage	VF	XF	Unc
59	1990 PM	*.025	—	Proof	50.00

Endangered World Wildlife - European Mouflon

KM#	Date	Mintage	VF	XF	Unc
116	1990	—	—	Proof	50.00

Endangered World Wildlife - Lynx

KM#	Date	Mintage	VF	XF	Unc
54	1990 PM	*.025	—	Proof	50.00

31.1000 g, .925 SILVER, .9250 oz ASW
500th Anniversary of Discovery of America
Henry Hudson

KM#	Date	Mintage	VF	XF	Unc
89	1990	—	—	Proof	45.00

Endangered World Wildlife - Dancing Crane

KM#	Date	Mintage	VF	XF	Unc
117	1990	—	—	Proof	50.00

Endangered World Wildlife - Black Rhinocerus

KM#	Date	Mintage	VF	XF	Unc
55	1990 PM	*.025	—	Proof	50.00

Endangered World Wildlife - Big Horn Sheep
Rev: Sheep walking left.

KM#	Date	Mintage	VF	XF	Unc
56	1990 PM	*.025	—	Proof	50.00

19.2000 g, .925 SILVER, .5768 oz ASW
1992 Olympics - Runner

KM#	Date	Mintage	VF	XF	Unc
112	1990	—	—	Proof	45.00

31.1000 g, .925 SILVER, .9250 oz ASW
500th Anniversary of Discovery of America - Cabral

KM#	Date	Mintage	VF	XF	Unc
134	1990	—	—	Proof	45.00

Endangered World Wildlife - Koala

KM#	Date	Mintage	VF	XF	Unc
57	1990 PM	*.025	—	Proof	50.00

500th Anniversary of Discovery of America - Bolivar

KM#	Date	Mintage	VF	XF	Unc
135	1990	—	—	Proof	45.00

31.2600 g, .925 SILVER, .9296 oz ASW
500 Years of America - Samuel Clemens

KM#	Date	Mintage	VF	XF	Unc
139	1990	—	—	Proof	45.00

19.4000 g, .925 SILVER, .5768 oz ASW
Endangered Wildlife - European Hedgehog

KM#	Date	Mintage	VF	XF	Unc
144	1990	*.025	—	Proof	50.00

31.1000 g, .925 SILVER, .9250 oz ASW
500 Years of America - Jacques Cartier

KM#	Date	Mintage	VF	XF	Unc
146	1990	—	—	Proof	45.00

19.8000 g, .925 SILVER, .5888 oz ASW
Endangered World Wildlife - Owl

KM#	Date	Mintage	VF	XF	Unc
93	1991	*.025	—	Proof	50.00

31.1000 g, .925 SILVER, .9250 oz ASW
500th Anniversary of
Discovery of America - Sitting Bull

KM#	Date	Mintage	VF	XF	Unc
94	1991	*.015	—	Proof	45.00

19.2000 g, .925 SILVER, .5768 oz ASW
Endangered Wildlife - Heaviside's Dolphins

KM#	Date	Mintage	VF	XF	Unc
95	1991	—	—	Proof	50.00

Endangered World Wildlife - Weasels

KM#	Date	Mintage	VF	XF	Unc
118	1991	—	—	Proof	50.00

Endangered World Wildlife - Hawk

KM#	Date	Mintage	VF	XF	Unc
119	1991	—	—	Proof	50.00

Endangered World Wildlife - Mountain Goat

KM#	Date	Mintage	VF	XF	Unc
120	1991	—	—	Proof	50.00

19.2000 g, .925 SILVER, .5768 oz ASW
Endangered Wildlife - Lion

KM#	Date	Mintage	VF	XF	Unc
122	1991	—	—	Proof	65.00
	Endangered Wildlife - Deer				
123	1991	*.025	—	Proof	60.00
	Endangered Wildlife Kangaroo				
124	1991	*.025	—	Proof	60.00
	Endangered Wildlife - Cougar and Cub				
125	1991	*.025	—	Proof	60.00
	Endangered Wildlife - 2 Reindeer				
126	1991	*.025	—	Proof	60.00
	Endangered Wildlife - Hummingbird				
127	1991	*.025	—	Proof	60.00
	Endangered Wildlife - 2 Penguins				
128	1991	*.025	—	Proof	60.00

31.2600 g, .925 SILVER, .9296 oz ASW
500 Years of America - Alexander Mackenzie

KM#	Date	Mintage	VF	XF	Unc
141	1991	—	—	Proof	45.00

7.7750 g, .5833 GOLD, .1458 oz AGW
500 Years of America - Columbus Kneeling

KM#	Date	Mintage	VF	XF	Unc
145	1991	—	—	Proof	110.00

31.1000 g, .925 SILVER, .9250 oz ASW
500 Years of America - Indian Priest

KM#	Date	Mintage	VF	XF	Unc
148	1991	*.015	—	Proof	45.00

500th Anniversary of Discovery of America - Coronado Discovering the Grand Canyon

KM#	Date	Mintage	VF	XF	Unc
114	1992	*.015	—	Proof	45.00

7.7760 g, .583 GOLD, .1458 oz AGW
Endangered Wildlife - Eagle Head

KM#	Date	Mintage	VF	XF	Unc
129	1992	—	—	Proof	110.00

Endangered Wildlife - Elephant Head

KM#	Date	Mintage	VF	XF	Unc
131	1992	—	—	Proof	110.00

Endangered Wildlife - Tiger Head

KM#	Date	Mintage	VF	XF	Unc
132	1992	—	—	Proof	110.00

31.2600 g, .925 SILVER, .9296 oz ASW
500 Years of America - Mayflower & Pilgrims

KM#	Date	Mintage	VF	XF	Unc
140	1992	—	—	Proof	45.00

500 Years of America - John Davis

KM#	Date	Mintage	VF	XF	Unc
142	1992	—	—	Proof	45.00

500 Years of America - Vitus Bering

KM#	Date	Mintage	VF	XF	Unc
143	1992	—	—	Proof	45.00

31.1035 g, .925 SILVER, .9250 oz ASW
Pedro de Valdivia

KM#	Date	Mintage	VF	XF	Unc
156	1992	—	—	Proof	45.00

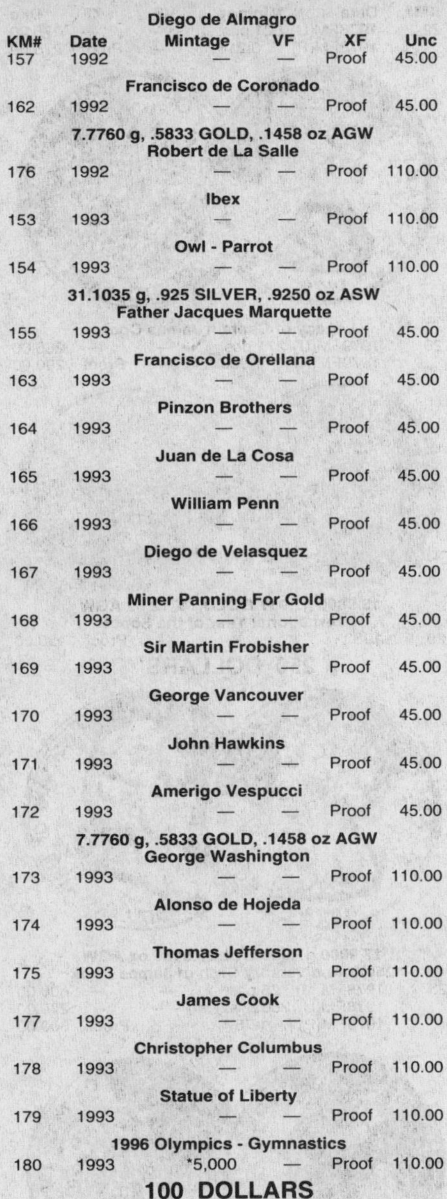

Diego de Almagro

KM#	Date	Mintage	VF	XF	Unc
157	1992	—	—	Proof	45.00

Francisco de Coronado

KM#	Date	Mintage	VF	XF	Unc
162	1992	—	—	Proof	45.00

7.7760 g, .5833 GOLD, .1458 oz AGW
Robert de La Salle

KM#	Date	Mintage	VF	XF	Unc
176	1992	—	—	Proof	110.00

Ibex

KM#	Date	Mintage	VF	XF	Unc
153	1993	—	—	Proof	110.00

Owl - Parrot

KM#	Date	Mintage	VF	XF	Unc
154	1993	—	—	Proof	110.00

31.1035 g, .925 SILVER, .9250 oz ASW
Father Jacques Marquette

KM#	Date	Mintage	VF	XF	Unc
155	1993	—	—	Proof	45.00

Francisco de Orellana

KM#	Date	Mintage	VF	XF	Unc
163	1993	—	—	Proof	45.00

Pinzon Brothers

KM#	Date	Mintage	VF	XF	Unc
164	1993	—	—	Proof	45.00

Juan de La Cosa

KM#	Date	Mintage	VF	XF	Unc
165	1993	—	—	Proof	45.00

William Penn

KM#	Date	Mintage	VF	XF	Unc
166	1993	—	—	Proof	45.00

Diego de Velasquez

KM#	Date	Mintage	VF	XF	Unc
167	1993	—	—	Proof	45.00

Miner Panning For Gold

KM#	Date	Mintage	VF	XF	Unc
168	1993	—	—	Proof	45.00

Sir Martin Frobisher

KM#	Date	Mintage	VF	XF	Unc
169	1993	—	—	Proof	45.00

George Vancouver

KM#	Date	Mintage	VF	XF	Unc
170	1993	—	—	Proof	45.00

John Hawkins

KM#	Date	Mintage	VF	XF	Unc
171	1993	—	—	Proof	45.00

Amerigo Vespucci

KM#	Date	Mintage	VF	XF	Unc
172	1993	—	—	Proof	45.00

7.7760 g, .5833 GOLD, .1458 oz AGW
George Washington

KM#	Date	Mintage	VF	XF	Unc
173	1993	—	—	Proof	110.00

Alonso de Hojeda

KM#	Date	Mintage	VF	XF	Unc
174	1993	—	—	Proof	110.00

Thomas Jefferson

KM#	Date	Mintage	VF	XF	Unc
175	1993	—	—	Proof	110.00

James Cook

KM#	Date	Mintage	VF	XF	Unc
177	1993	—	—	Proof	110.00

Christopher Columbus

KM#	Date	Mintage	VF	XF	Unc
178	1993	—	—	Proof	110.00

Statue of Liberty

KM#	Date	Mintage	VF	XF	Unc
179	1993	—	—	Proof	110.00

1996 Olympics - Gymnastics

KM#	Date	Mintage	VF	XF	Unc
180	1993	*5,000	—	Proof	110.00

100 DOLLARS

16.7185 g, .917 GOLD, .4929 oz AGW
Winston Churchill Centenary

KM#	Date	Mintage	VF	XF	Unc
12	1974	368 pcs.	—	—	325.00
	1974	1,453	—	Proof	250.00

9.6000 g, .900 GOLD, .2778 oz AGW
Bicentennial of Return of Cook from 2nd Voyage

KM#	Date	Mintage	VF	XF	Unc
13	1975FM(M)	100 pcs.	—	—	400.00
	1975FM(U)	7,447	—	—	120.00
	1975FM(P)	.017	—	Proof	175.00

U.S. Bicentennial

KM#	Date	Mintage	VF	XF	Unc
16	1976FM(M)	50 pcs.	—	—	350.00
	1976FM(U)	852 pcs.	—	—	150.00
	1976FM(P)	9,373	—	Proof	200.00

Queen's Silver Jubilee

KM#	Date	Mintage	VF	XF	Unc
19	1977FM(M)	50 pcs.	—	—	350.00
	1977FM(U)	562 pcs.	—	—	150.00
	1977FM(P)	9,364	—	Proof	200.00

Membership in Commonwealth of Nations

KM#	Date	Mintage	VF	XF	Unc
25	1979FM(U)	400 pcs.	—	—	175.00
	1979FM(P)	3,367	—	Proof	275.00

1.2441 g, .999 GOLD, .0400 oz AGW
Endangered World Wildlife - American Bald Eagle

KM#	Date	Mintage	VF	XF	Unc
74	1990	1,320	—	P/L	70.00

Endangered World Wildlife - Bison

KM#	Date	Mintage	VF	XF	Unc
75	1990	320 pcs.	—	P/L	70.00

Endangered World Wildlife - Elephant

KM#	Date	Mintage	VF	XF	Unc
76	1990	720 pcs.	—	P/L	70.00

Endangered World Wildlife - Tiger

KM#	Date	Mintage	VF	XF	Unc
77	1990	420 pcs.	—	P/L	70.00

Endangered World Wildlife - Longhorn Sheep

KM#	Date	Mintage	VF	XF	Unc
78	1990	320 pcs.	—	P/L	70.00

3.4550 g, .900 GOLD, .0999 oz AGW
1992 Summer Olympics - Bicyclists

KM#	Date	Mintage	VF	XF	Unc
92	1990	—	—	Proof	125.00

172.1100 g, SILVER
Illustration reduced. Actual size: 65.2mm.
Discovery of America

KM#	Date	Mintage	VF	XF	Unc
113	1990	—	—	Proof	225.00

155.5175 g, .999 SILVER, 5.0000 oz ASW
Illustration reduced. Actual size: 65mm.
Endangered Wildlife - Cranes

KM#	Date	Mintage	VF	XF	Unc
158	1993	—	—	Proof	200.00

Illustration reduced. Actual size: 65mm.
Mayflower Sailing into New York City

KM#	Date	Mintage	VF	XF	Unc
159	1993	—	—	Proof	200.00

200 DOLLARS

16.6000 g, .900 GOLD, .4803 oz AGW
Bicentennial of Discovery of Hawaii by Capt. Cook

KM#	Date	Mintage	VF	XF	Unc
22	1978FM(M)	26 pcs.	—	—	600.00
	1978FM(U)	621 pcs.	—	—	275.00
	1978FM(P)	3,216	—	Proof	275.00

Legacy of Captain James Cook

KM#	Date	Mintage	VF	XF	Unc
26	1979FM(U)	271 pcs.	—	—	265.00
	1979FM(P)	1,939	—	Proof	290.00

15.9800 g, .917 GOLD, .4712 oz AGW
International Year of the Scout

KM#	Date	Mintage	VF	XF	Unc
29	1983	—	—	Proof	450.00

250 DOLLARS

17.9000 g, .900 GOLD, .5180 oz AGW
250th Anniversary Birth of James Cook

KM#	Date	Mintage	VF	XF	Unc
23	1978FM(M)	25 pcs.	—	—	600.00
	1978FM(U)	200 pcs.	—	—	275.00
	1978FM(P)	1,757	—	Proof	300.00

7.7750 g, .999 GOLD, .2500 oz AGW
500th Anniversary of Discovery of America
Captain James Cook and Benjamin Franklin

KM#	Date	Mintage	VF	XF	Unc
50	1989	*3,000	—	Proof	225.00

500th Anniversary of Discovery of America
Amerigo Vespucci

KM#	Date	Mintage	VF	XF	Unc
51	1989	*3,000	—	Proof	225.00

1991 Olympics - Torch

KM#	Date	Mintage	VF	XF	Unc
71	1990	*3,000	—	Proof	225.00
	1991	—	—	Proof	225.00

9.6000 g, .900 GOLD, .2778 oz AGW
Save the Children

KM#	Date	Mintage	VF	XF	Unc
82	1990	3,000	—	Proof	275.00

MINT SETS (MS)

KM#	Date	Mintage	Identification	Issue Price	Mkt. Val.
MS1	1972(7)	11,045	KM1-7	7.50	5.00
MS2	1973(9)	3,652	KM1-7,9,10	52.50	42.50
MS3	1973(7)	3,023	KM1-7	10.00	8.00
MS4	1973(2)	2,348	KM9,10	45.00	37.50
MS5	1974(9)	913	KM1-7,9,10	52.50	50.00
MS6	1974(7)	2,087	KM1-7	10.00	6.00
MS7	1974(2)	587	KM9,10	45.00	45.00
MS8	1975(7)	2,251	KM1-7	10.00	6.00
MS9	1976(8)	1,066	KM1-4,6,7,14,15	20.00	25.00
MS10	1977(8)	1,171	KM1-4,6,7,14,17	20.00	25.00
MS11	1978(8)	767	KM1a-4a,6a,7a,14a,20	20.00	30.00
MS12	1979(8)	500	KM1-3,4b,6b,7,14,24	—	30.00
MS13	1981(7)	1,100	KM1b-3b,4c,6c,7b,14b	—	15.00
MS14	1983(7)	—	KM1-7	—	6.00
MS15	1987(7)	—	KM33-39	—	15.00
MS16	1988(7)	—	KM33-35,37-39,41	—	16.00

PROOF-LIKE SETS (PLS)

KM#	Date	Mintage	Identification	Issue Price	Mkt. Val.
PLS1	1990	—	KM74-78	325.00	325.00

PROOF SETS (PS)

KM#	Date	Mintage	Identification	Issue Price	Mkt. Val.
PS1	1972(7)	17,101	KM1-7	20.00	10.00
PS2	1973(9)	7,395	KM1-7,9,10	89.50	45.00
PS3	1973(7)	5,136	KM1-7	29.50	10.00
PS4	1973(2)	4,754	KM9,10	60.00	35.00
PS5	1974(9)	4,444	KM1-7,9,10	95.00	50.00
PS6	1974(7)	5,300	KM1-7	32.50	10.00
PS7	1974(2)	2,856	KM9,10	65.00	35.00
PS8	1975(7)	21,290	KM1-7	31.50	10.00
PS9	1976(8)	17,658	KM1-4,6,7,14,15	40.00	22.50
PS10	1977(8)	5,986	KM1-4,6,7,14,17	42.00	25.00
PS11	1978(8)	6,287	KM1a-4a,6a,7a,14a,20	42.00	25.00
PS12	1979(8)	4,058	KM1-3,4b,6b,7,14,24	44.00	25.00
PS13	1981(7)	9,205	KM1b-3b,4c,6c,7b,14b	39.50	12.50
PS14	1983(7)	10,000	KM1-7	29.95	10.00
PS15	1987(7)	—	KM33-39	—	32.50
PS16	1988(7)	—	KM33-35,37-39,41	—	32.50
PS17	1991(12)	1,000	KM93,95,118-120,122-128	—	690.00

COSTA RICA

The Republic of Costa Rica, located in southern Central America between Nicaragua and Panama, has an area of 19,575 sq. mi. (51,100 sq. km.) and a population of 2.8 million. Capital: San Jose. Agriculture predominates and coffee, bananas, beef and sugar contribute heavily to the country's export earnings.

Costa Rica was discovered by Christopher Columbus in 1502, during his last voyage to the new world, and was a colony of Spain from 1522 until independence in 1821. Columbus named the territory Nueva Cartago; the name Costa Rica wasn't generally employed until 1540. Bartholomew Columbus attempted to found the first settlement but was driven off by Indian attacks and the country wasn't pacified until 1530. Costa Rica was absorbed for two years (1821-23) into the Mexican Empire of Augustin de Iturbide. From 1823 to 1848, it was a constituent state of the Central American Republic (q.v.). It was established as a republic in 1848 and adopted democratic reforms in the 1870's and 80's. Today, Costa Rica remains a model of orderly democracy in Latin America, although, like most of the hemisphere its economy is in stress.

MINT MARKS

CR - San Jose 1825-1947
NOTE: Also see Central American Republic.
HEATON - Heaton, Birmingham, England, 1889-93
BIRMm - Heaton, Birmingham, England, 1889-93

ISSUING BANK INITIALS - MINTS

BCCR - Philadelphia 1951-1958,1961
BICR - Philadelphia 1935
BNCR - London 1937,1948
BNCR - San Jose 1942-1947
GCR - Philadelphia 1905-1914,1929
GCR - San Jose 1917-1941

ASSAYERS INITIALS

MM - 1842
JB - 1847-1864
GW - Guillermo Witting, 1850-1890
CY 1902
JCV - 1903

MONETARY SYSTEM

8 Reales = 1 Peso
16 Pesos = 8 Escudos = 1 Onza

REAL SERIES

1/2 REAL

.903 SILVER
Mint: San Jose
Obv: Radiant 6 pointed star in circle above branches.
Rev: Tobacco plant and value in circle, date below.

KM#	Date	Mintage	VG	Fine	VF	XF
32	1842 MM	—	16.00	35.00	65.00	125.00

NOTE: Holed examples are valued at only about 40% of the above figures.

REAL

.903 SILVER
Mint: San Jose

KM#	Date	Mintage	VG	Fine	VF	XF
65	1847 JB	—	5.50	10.00	15.00	32.00
	1847 JB (error) backwards B	—	6.00	12.00	17.50	35.00

.750 SILVER

KM#	Date	Mintage	VG	Fine	VF	XF
66	1849 JB	—	3.50	7.00	10.00	27.50
	1850 JB	—	4.50	9.00	15.00	35.00

1/2 ESCUDO

1.7000 g, .875 GOLD, .0478 oz AGW
Mint: San Jose

KM#	Date	Mintage	VG	Fine	VF	XF
97	1850 JB	3,388	38.50	65.00	100.00	150.00
	1851 JB	6,565	38.50	65.00	100.00	150.00
	1853 JB	8,491	38.50	65.00	100.00	150.00
	1854 JB	4,663	38.50	65.00	100.00	150.00
	1855 JB	8,822	38.50	65.00	100.00	150.00
	1855 GW	I.A.	38.50	65.00	100.00	150.00
	1864 JB	9,018	38.50	65.00	100.00	150.00

ESCUDO

3.3000 g, .875 GOLD, .0928 oz AGW
Mint: San Jose
Rev: Denomination .1-E.

KM#	Date	Mintage	VG	Fine	VF	XF
33.1	1842 MM	.010	300.00	600.00	1200.	2000.

Rev: Denomination 1.-E.

KM#	Date	Mintage	VG	Fine	VF	XF
33.2	1842 MM	I.A.	350.00	800.00	1500.	2250.

KM#	Date	Mintage	VG	Fine	VF	XF
98	1850 JB	6,167	55.00	100.00	150.00	265.00
	1851 JB	4,388	55.00	100.00	150.00	265.00
	1853 JB	2,979	65.00	150.00	250.00	500.00
	1855 JB	4,095	60.00	125.00	200.00	350.00

2 ESCUDOS

6.7500 g, .875 GOLD, .1899 oz AGW
Mint: San Jose

KM#	Date	Mintage	VG	Fine	VF	XF
99	1850 JB	3,641	100.00	150.00	200.00	400.00
	1854 JB	I.A.	100.00	150.00	200.00	400.00
	1854 GW	I.A.	100.00	150.00	200.00	400.00
	1855 JB	.060	100.00	125.00	175.00	400.00
	1855 GW	I.A.	100.00	150.00	200.00	400.00
	1858 GW	.017	100.00	125.00	175.00	400.00
	1862 GW	5,896	110.00	200.00	325.00	550.00
	1863 GW	5,632	110.00	200.00	325.00	550.00

1/2 ONZA

12.6000 g, .875 GOLD, .3545 oz AGW
Mint: San Jose

KM#	Date	Mintage	VG	Fine	VF	XF
100	1850 JB	.018	200.00	300.00	400.00	800.00
	1850 JB	—	—	—	Proof	4200.

COUNTERMARKED COINAGE

1841-1842

Type I
c/m: Radiant 6-pointed star in 7mm circle.
NOTE: An additional plug was cut from each coin to 'pay for the work'. Market valuations are for holed coins.

1/2 REAL

SILVER

c/m: Type I on Mexico 1/2 Real, KM#72.

KM#	Date	Year	Good	VG	Fine	VF
1	ND	(1792-1808)	150.00	200.00	350.00	—

REAL

SILVER
c/m: Type I on Mexico 1 Real, KM#77.

KM#	Date	Year	Good	VG	Fine	VF
4	ND	(1760-1771)	150.00	200.00	350.00	—

2 REALES

SILVER

KM#	Date	Year	Good	VG	Fine	VF
	c/m: Type I on Bolivia (Potosi) 2 Reales, KM#53.					
7	ND	(1773-89)	15.00	30.00	60.00	90.00
	c/m: Type I on Guatemala 2 Reales, KM#34.1.					
8	ND	(1772-76)	15.00	30.00	60.00	90.00
	c/m: Type I on Mexico 2 Reales, KM#91.					
12	ND	(1800)	15.00	30.00	60.00	90.00
	c/m: Type I on Mexico 2 Reales, KM#92.					
9	ND	(1809-12)	15.00	30.00	60.00	90.00
	c/m: Type I on Mexico 2 Reales, KM#372.8.					
10	ND	(1825-41)	15.00	30.00	60.00	90.00

c/m: Type I on Peru 2 Reales, KM#141.1.

KM#	Date	Year	Good	VG	Fine	VF
11	ND	(1825-40)	15.00	30.00	60.00	90.00

c/m: Type I on Peru 2 Reales, KM#95.

KM#	Date	Year	Good	VG	Fine	VF
13	ND	(1791-1808)	15.00	30.00	60.00	90.00

4 REALES

SILVER
c/m: Type I on Bolivia (Potosi) 4 Reales, KM#54.

KM#	Date	Year	Good	VG	Fine	VF
14	ND	(1773-89)	150.00	275.00	425.00	1000.

c/m: Type I on Bolivia (Potosi) 4 Reales, KM#72.

KM#	Date	Year	Good	VG	Fine	VF
15	ND	(1791-1808)	150.00	275.00	425.00	1000.

c/m: Type I on Guatemala, 4 Reales, KM#35.1.

KM#	Date	Year	Good	VG	Fine	VF
16	ND	(1772-76)	750.00	1250.	2500.	—

8 REALES

SILVER

c/m: Type I on Mexico 8 Reales, KM#106.

KM#	Date	Year	Good	VG	Fine	VF
19	ND	(1772-89)	150.00	275.00	425.00	950.00

c/m: Type I on Mexico 8 Reales, KM#376.

KM#	Date	Year	Good	VG	Fine	VF
20	ND	(1824)	200.00	300.00	450.00	1000.

c/m: Type I on Mexico 8 Reales, KM#377.

KM#	Date	Year	Good	VG	Fine	VF
21	ND	(1824-41)	150.00	250.00	400.00	900.00

c/m: Type I on Peru 8 Reales, KM#78.

KM#	Date	Year	Good	VG	Fine	VF
22	ND	(1772-89)	150.00	275.00	425.00	950.00

c/m: Type I on Peru 8 Reales, KM#142.1.

KM#	Date	Year	Good	VG	Fine	VF
23	ND	(1825-28)	150.00	250.00	400.00	900.00

c/m: Type I on Peru 8 Reales, KM#142.3.

KM#	Date	Year	Good	VG	Fine	VF
24	ND	(1828-40)	150.00	250.00	400.00	900.00

c/m: Type I on North Peru 8 Reales, KM#155.

KM#	Date	Year	Good	VG	Fine	VF
25	ND	(1836-39)	150.00	275.00	425.00	950.00

c/m: Type I on Spanish 8 Reales, C#136.

KM#	Date	Year	Good	VG	Fine	VF
26	ND	(1809-30)	150.00	275.00	425.00	950.00

c/m: Type I on Mexico 8 Reales, KM#111.

KM#	Date	Year	Good	VG	Fine	VF
27	ND	(1812-22)	—	—	—	2500.

1841-1842

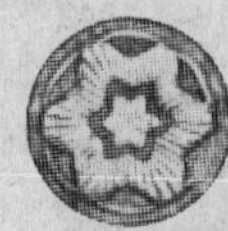

Type II
c/m: Radiant 6-pointed star in 4mm circle.

2 ESCUDOS

GOLD

c/m: Type II on Central American Republic 2 Escudos, KM#15.

KM#	Date	Year	Good	VG	Fine	VF
28	ND	(1825-37)	—	—	Rare	—

4 ESCUDOS

GOLD

c/m: Type II on Central American Republic 4 Escudos, KM#16.

KM#	Date	Year	Good	VG	Fine	VF
29	ND	(1828-37)	—	—	Rare	—

COUNTERSTAMPED COINAGE

1845

Type III
Obv. c/s: COSTA RICA and 2 R. around female head.
Rev. c/s: HABILITADA POR EL GOB. around tree.

2 REALES

SILVER

c/s: Type III on Spanish (Seville) 2 Reales.

KM#	Date	Year	Good	VG	Fine	VF
35	ND	(1732)	20.00	35.00	60.00	100.00

c/s: Type III on Spanish (Madrid) 2 Reales, C#38.

KM#	Date	Year	Good	VG	Fine	VF
36	ND	(1772-88)	8.50	15.00	27.50	50.00

NOTE: The coin illustrated above also has the lattice c/m of the Province of Trinidad (Cuba) and would command a premium.

c/s: Type III on Spanish (Madrid) 2 Reales, C#69.

KM#	Date	Year	Good	VG	Fine	VF
37	ND	(1788-1808)	8.50	15.00	27.50	50.00

c/s: Type III on Spanish (Seville) 2 Reales, C#69.

KM#	Date	Year	Good	VG	Fine	VF
38	ND	(1793-1808)	8.50	15.00	27.50	50.00

c/s: Type III on Spanish 2 Reales, C#89.

KM#	Date	Year	Good	VG	Fine	VF
39	ND	(1811-13)	15.00	25.00	40.00	65.00

c/s: Type III on Spanish 4 Reales, C#90.

KM#	Date	Year	Good	VG	Fine	VF
40	ND	(1808-13)	10.00	15.00	35.00	60.00

c/s: Type III on Spanish (Madrid) 2 Reales, C#134.

KM#	Date	Year	Good	VG	Fine	VF
41	ND	(1814-33)	10.00	17.50	30.00	55.00

c/s: Type III on Spanish (Seville) 2 Reales, C#134.

KM#	Date	Year	Good	VG	Fine	VF
42	ND	(1815-33)	10.00	17.50	30.00	55.00

c/s: Type III on Spanish 4 Reales, C#135.

KM#	Date	Year	Good	VG	Fine	VF
43	ND	(1811-33)	25.00	50.00	95.00	150.00

c/s: Type III on Trinidad, Cuba c/s on Spanish (Seville) 2 Reales, KM#12.

KM#	Date	Year	Good	VG	Fine	VF
44	ND	(1793-1808)	14.00	18.00	32.50	55.00

NOTE: The coin illustrated above also has the lattice c/m of the Province of Trinidad and would command a premium.

1846

Type IV

Obv. c/s: REPUB. DE CENT. DE AMER. 1846 around sun above mountains in a 14mm circle.
Rev. c/s: HABILITADA EN COSTA RICA J.B. . . around tree, 1-R.

REAL

SILVER

c/s: Type IV on Spanish American 'cob' 1 Real.

KM#	Date	Good	VG	Fine	VF
47	1846	8.50	15.00	25.00	45.00

4 REALES

SILVER

c/s: Type IV with additional c/m 4 in square on Guatemala 'cob' 4 Reales, KM#5.

KM#	Date	Year	Good	VG	Fine	VF
50	1846	—	250.00	400.00	600.00	800.00

c/s: Type IV with additional c/m 4 in square on United States Capped Bust 50 Cents, C#32.

KM#	Date	Year	Good	VG	Fine	VF
51.1	1846	(1809)	1250.	2750.	5000.	8000.

c/s: Type IV with additional c/m 4 in square on United State Capped Bust 50 Cents, C#32a.

KM#	Date	Year	Good	VG	Fine	VF
51.2	1846	(1837)	850.00	1750.	3250.	5000.

c/s: Type IV with additional c/m 4 in square on United States Seated Liberty 50 cents.

KM#	Date	Year	Good	VG	Fine	VF
52	1846	(1843)	850.00	1750.	3250.	5000.

1846

Type V

Obv. c/s: REPUB. DE CENT. DE AMER. 1846 around sun above mountains in a 14mm circle.
Rev. c/s: HABILITADA EN COSTA RICA J-B around tree, 2-R.

2 REALES

SILVER

c/s: Type V on Bolivia (Potosi) 'cob' 2 Reales, KM#29.

KM#	Date	Year	Good	VG	Fine	VF
54	1846	(1700-46)	20.00	35.00	60.00	90.00

c/s: Type V on Peru (Lima) 'cob' 2 Reales, KM#30.

KM#	Date	Year	Good	VG	Fine	VF
55	1846	(1700-46)	20.00	35.00	60.00	90.00

c/s: Type V on Guatemula 2 Reales proclamation medal.

KM#	Date	Year	Good	VG	Fine	VF
56	1846	(1808)	150.00	350.00	550.00	900.00

8 REALES

SILVER

c/s: Type V with additional c/m 8 in circle on Bolivia (Potosi) 'cob' 8 Reales, KM#31.

KM#	Date	Year	Good	VG	Fine	VF
58	1846	(1700-46)	400.00	550.00	800.00	1000.

c/s: Type V on Guatemala 'cob' 8 Reales, KM#12.

KM#	Date	Year	Good	VG	Fine	VF
59	1846	(1747-53)	400.00	550.00	800.00	1000.

c/s: Type V on Peru (Lima) 'cob' 8 Reales of Charles II.

KM#	Date	Year	Good	VG	Fine	VF
60	1846	(1665-1700)	400.00	550.00	800.00	1000.

c/s: Type V on Peru (Lima) 'cob' 8 Reales, KM#34.

KM#	Date	Year	Good	VG	Fine	VF
61	1846	(1700-46)	400.00	550.00	800.00	1000.

c/s: Type V on Mexico City 'cob' 8 Reales, KM#48.

KM#	Date	Year	Good	VG	Fine	VF
62	1846	(1733-34)	400.00	550.00	800.00	1000.

COUNTERMARKED COINAGE

1849-1857

Type VI
c/m: HABILITADA POR EL GOBIERNO around lion in 5mm circle.

Local Series

1/2 REAL

SILVER
c/m: Type VI on Central American Republic 1/2 Real, KM#20.

KM#	Date	Year	Good	VG	Fine	VF
67	(1849)	1831 E	5.00	9.00	15.00	22.00
		1831 F	5.00	9.00	15.00	22.00
		1843 M	4.00	6.00	11.00	20.00
		1845 B	4.00	6.00	11.00	20.00

c/m: Type VI on Central American Republic 1/2 Real, KM#20a.

KM#	Date	Year	Good	VG	Fine	VF
68	(1849)	1846 JB 'CRESCA'	3.50	5.00	10.00	17.50
		1846 JB 'CREZCA'	3.50	5.00	10.00	17.50
		1847 JB 'CRESCA'	3.50	5.00	10.00	17.50
		1847 JB 'CREZCA'	3.50	5.00	10.00	17.50
		1848 JB	3.50	5.00	10.00	17.50
		1849 JB	3.50	7.00	12.00	22.00

c/m: Type VI on Costa Rica 1/2 Real, KM#32.

KM#	Date	Year	Good	VG	Fine	VF
69	(1849)	1842 MM	10.00	16.50	30.00	55.00

NOTE: Above values are for unholed pieces, holed examples are worth substantially less.

REAL

SILVER
c/m: Type VI on Central American Republic 1 Real, KM#21.

KM#	Date	Year	Good	VG	Fine	VF
72	(1849)	1831 E	7.50	12.50	27.50	47.50
	(1849)	1831 F	6.00	9.50	25.00	42.50
	(1849)	1848 JB	9.00	18.00	32.50	50.00

c/m: Type VI on Central American Republic 1 Real, KM#21a.

KM#	Date	Year	Good	VG	Fine	VF
72a	(1849)	1848 JB	9.00	18.00	30.00	50.00
		1849 JB	5.50	10.00	25.00	42.50

c/m: Type VI on Costa Rica 1 Real, KM#65.

KM#	Date	Year	Good	VG	Fine	VF
73	(1849)	1847 JB	12.50	22.50	40.00	62.50
		1847 JB (error) backwards B	14.00	27.50	50.00	70.00

c/m: Type VI on Costa Rica 1 Real, KM#66.

KM#	Date	Year	Good	VG	Fine	VF
74	(1849)	1849 JB	12.50	22.50	40.00	67.50
		1850 JB	15.00	27.50	45.00	75.00

2 REALES

SILVER
c/m: Type VI on Central American Republic 2 Reales, KM#24.

KM#	Date	Year	Good	VG	Fine	VF
77	(1849)	1849 JB	4.75	11.00	18.50	32.50

4 REALES

NOTE: Half dollar size coins with Type VI c/m are modern fabrications. Refer to listings in UNUSUAL WORLD COINS, 3rd edition, Krause Publications 1992.

8 REALES

NOTE: Crown size coins with Type VI c/m are modern fabrications. Refer to listings in UNUSUAL WORLD COINS, 3rd edition, Krause Publications, 1992.

1/2 ESCUDO

GOLD
Mint mark: CR
c/m: Type VI on Central American Republic 1/2 Escudo, KM#13.

KM#	Date	Year	VG	Fine	VF	XF
80	(1857)	1828 F	50.00	100.00	150.00	225.00
		1843 M	50.00	100.00	150.00	225.00
		1846 JB	40.00	80.00	125.00	200.00
		1847 JB	40.00	80.00	125.00	200.00
		1848 JB	40.00	80.00	125.00	200.00
		1849 JB	50.00	100.00	150.00	225.00

Mint mark: NG
c/m: Type VI on Central American Republic 1/2 Escudo, KM#5.

KM#	Date	Year	VG	Fine	VF	XF
81	(1857)	1825 M	—	—	—	—

ESCUDO

GOLD
Mint mark: CR
c/m: Type VI on Central American Republic 1 Escudo, KM#14.

KM#	Date	Year	VG	Fine	VF	XF
84	(1857)	1833 E	90.00	175.00	275.00	375.00
		1833 F	90.00	175.00	275.00	375.00
		1844 M	55.00	125.00	225.00	325.00
		1845 JB	90.00	175.00	275.00	375.00
		1846 JB	65.00	125.00	225.00	325.00
		1847 JB	65.00	125.00	225.00	325.00
		1848 JB	65.00	125.00	225.00	325.00
		1849 JB	65.00	125.00	225.00	325.00

English Series

REAL

SILVER
c/m: Type VI on Great Britain 6 Pence, KM#665.

KM#	Date	Year	Good	VG	Fine	VF
87	(1857)	1816-20	6.00	10.00	20.00	35.00

c/m: Type VI on Great Britain 6 Pence, KM#698.

KM#	Date	Year	Good	VG	Fine	VF
88	(1857)	1826-29	8.50	17.50	32.50	55.00

c/m: Type VI on Great Britain 6 Pence, KM#712.

KM#	Date	Year	Good	VG	Fine	VF
89	(1857)	1831,34-37	7.50	15.00	27.50	45.00

c/m: Type VI on Great Britain 6 Pence, KM#733.

KM#	Date	Year	Good	VG	Fine	VF
90	(1857)	1838-46,48-49	5.50	10.00	20.00	35.00

2 REALES

SILVER
c/m: Type VI on Great Britain Shilling, KM#666.

KM#	Date	Year	Good	VG	Fine	VF
93	(1857)	1816-20	7.50	12.50	22.50	40.00

c/m: Type VI on Great Britain Shilling, KM#734.

KM#	Date	Year	Good	VG	Fine	VF
94	(1857)	1838-46,49	6.50	12.00	20.00	37.50

Peso Series

1/16 PESO

1.4600 g, .903 SILVER, .0423 oz ASW

KM#	Date	Mintage	VG	Fine	VF	XF
101	1850 JB	—	7.50	17.50	35.00	65.00
	1855/0 JB	—	10.00	22.50	40.00	75.00
	1855 JB	—	6.00	15.00	30.00	60.00
	1862 JB	—	—	—	Rare	—
	1862 GW	—	27.50	45.00	75.00	150.00

1/8 PESO

2.9500 g, .903 SILVER, .0856 oz ASW

KM#	Date	Mintage	VG	Fine	VF	XF
102	1850 JB	—	5.00	12.50	20.00	45.00
	1853 JB	—	7.50	15.00	32.50	60.00
	1855 JB	—	5.00	12.50	20.00	45.00

1/4 PESO

6.4000 g, .903 SILVER, .1858 oz ASW

KM#	Date	Mintage	VG	Fine	VF	XF
103	1850 JB	—	4.50	10.00	22.50	50.00
	1853 JB	—	8.00	18.00	35.00	65.00
	1855 JB	—	12.00	27.50	50.00	75.00

DECIMAL COINAGE

100 Centavos = 1 Peso (1864-1896)

1/4 CENTAVO

COPPER-NICKEL

KM#	Date	Mintage	VG	Fine	VF	XF
108	ND(1865)	.020	30.00	55.00	90.00	150.00

CENTAVO

COPPER-NICKEL

KM#	Date	Mintage	VG	Fine	VF	XF
109	1865	.033	3.75	10.00	22.50	37.50
	1866	.039	4.50	12.50	25.00	47.50
	1867	.044	7.00	17.50	32.50	62.50
	1868	.020	3.00	8.00	13.50	22.50

KM#	Date	Mintage	Fine	VF	XF	Unc
120	1874	.032	2.75	4.00	8.00	12.50

5 CENTAVOS

1.2680 g, .750 SILVER, .0305 oz ASW

KM#	Date	Mintage	VG	Fine	VF	XF
110	1865 GW	.233	2.50	6.00	15.00	30.00
	1869 GW	—	3.75	10.00	25.00	60.00
	1870 GW	.027	10.00	25.00	55.00	100.00
	1871 GW	.328	5.50	15.00	40.00	75.00
	1872 GW	I.A.	6.50	16.50	45.00	90.00
	1875/1 GW	I.A.	2.00	5.50	13.50	27.50
	1875 GW	I.A.	2.00	5.00	12.00	25.00

KM#	Date	Mintage	Fine	VF	XF	Unc
125	1885 GW	.180	1.50	3.50	8.00	20.00
	1886/5 GW	.251	2.75	6.50	12.50	30.00
	1887 GW	.491	1.25	3.00	7.00	18.00

Mint mark: HEATON BIRMM

KM#	Date	Mintage	Fine	VF	XF	Unc
128	1889	.520	.65	1.75	4.00	15.00
	1889	—	—	—	Proof	150.00
	1890	.431	.65	1.75	4.00	15.00
	1892	.280	.75	2.00	4.50	17.50

10 CENTAVOS

2.5360 g, .750 SILVER, .0611 oz ASW

KM#	Date	Mintage	VG	Fine	VF	XF
111	1865 GW	.185	3.00	8.00	17.50	35.00
	1868 GW	.010	50.00	95.00	175.00	—
	1870 GW	.048	13.50	30.00	55.00	100.00
	1872 GW	.018	45.00	85.00	150.00	—

KM#	Date	Mintage	VG	Fine	VF	XF
121	1875 GW	.286	2.25	5.00	10.00	22.50

2.5000 g, .750 SILVER, .0602 oz ASW

KM#	Date	Mintage	Fine	VF	XF	Unc
126	1886 GW	.120	2.50	6.00	12.00	35.00
	1887 GW	.245	2.25	4.50	10.00	27.50

Mint mark: HEATON BIRMM

KM#	Date	Mintage	Fine	VF	XF	Unc
129	1889	.260	1.00	2.50	4.50	15.00
	1889	—	—	—	Proof	200.00
	1890	.215	1.00	2.75	5.00	17.50
	1892	.140	1.25	3.00	6.50	20.00

25 CENTAVOS

6.2500 g, .750 SILVER, .1507 oz ASW

KM#	Date	Mintage	VG	Fine	VF	XF
105	1864 GW	.223	5.50	17.50	55.00	120.00

KM#	Date	Mintage	VG	Fine	VF	XF
106	1864 GW	I.A.	12.50	27.50	85.00	180.00
	1865 GW	.042	5.00	12.50	25.00	70.00
	1875 GW	.121	3.00	7.50	18.00	45.00

Rev: GW 9Ds

KM#	Date	Mintage	Fine	VF	XF	Unc
127.1	1886 GW	.100	4.50	8.50	17.50	40.00
	1887 GW	.200	5.50	11.50	22.50	52.50

Rev: 9Ds GW

KM#	Date	Mintage	Fine	VF	XF	Unc
127.2	1886 GW	I.A.	6.50	14.00	25.00	60.00
	1887 GW	I.A.	3.00	7.50	18.50	45.00

Mint mark: HEATON BIRMM.

KM#	Date	Mintage	Fine	VF	XF	Unc
130	1889/8	.410	1.50	3.75	9.00	20.00
	1889/99	I.A.	1.50	4.50	11.00	27.50
	1889	Inc. Ab.	1.50	3.00	8.50	20.00
	1889	—	—	—	Proof	250.00
	1890/80	.395	1.50	4.50	11.00	27.50
	1890	Inc. Ab.	1.50	3.75	9.00	22.50
	1892	.440	1.50	3.75	9.00	22.50
	1893	.670	1.25	2.50	6.00	18.00

50 CENTAVOS

12.5000 g, .750 SILVER, .3014 oz ASW

KM#	Date	Mintage	Good	VG	Fine	VF
112	1865 GW	.029	5.00	15.00	42.50	95.00
	1866/5 GW	.117	6.00	16.50	45.00	100.00
	1866 GW	I.A.	7.50	18.50	55.00	115.00
	1867 GW	5,168	50.00	85.00	220.00	375.00
	1870 GW	6,267	75.00	150.00	325.00	—
	1872 GW	I.A.	100.00	225.00	—	—
	1875 GW	.069	4.50	13.50	38.50	80.00

KM#	Date	Mintage	Fine	VF	XF	Unc
124	1880 GW	.389	5.75	13.50	22.50	65.00
	1885 GW	.152	6.00	14.00	25.00	70.00
	1886 GW	.097	6.50	16.50	30.00	75.00
	1887 GW	.208	6.50	16.50	30.00	75.00
	1889 GW*	.205	—	—	Rare	—
	1890/80 GW	.058	5.25	12.00	20.00	60.00
	1890 GW	I.A.	5.25	12.00	20.00	60.00

*NOTE: Not released for circulation.

PESO

1.5253 g, .875 GOLD, .0429 oz AGW

KM#	Date	Mintage	VG	Fine	VF	XF
107	1864 GW	6,383	35.00	70.00	100.00	135.00
	1866 GW	.035	27.50	55.00	85.00	115.00
	1868 GW	—	45.00	85.00	120.00	160.00

NOTE: Several varieties exist dated 1866.

Design modified

KM#	Date	Mintage	VG	Fine	VF	XF
116	1871 GW	.011	28.50	52.50	80.00	115.00
	1872 GW	.037	28.50	52.50	80.00	115.00

2 PESOS

2.9355 g, .875 GOLD, .0825 oz AGW

KM#	Date	Mintage	VG	Fine	VF	XF
113	1866 GW	.013	45.00	70.00	115.00	150.00
	1867 GW	—	60.00	100.00	155.00	200.00
	1868 GW	—	45.00	70.00	115.00	150.00

Design modified (19mm)

KM#	Date	Mintage	VG	Fine	VF	XF
122	1876 GW	2,161	—	—	Rare	—

5 PESOS

7.3387 g, .875 GOLD, 22mm, .2064 oz AGW

KM#	Date	Mintage	VG	Fine	VF	XF
114	1867 GW	.039	100.00	125.00	165.00	250.00
	1868 GW	6,752	100.00	125.00	165.00	250.00
	1869 GW	.011	100.00	125.00	165.00	250.00
	1870 GW	.015	100.00	125.00	165.00	250.00

21mm

KM#	Date	Mintage	VG	Fine	VF	XF
117	1873 GW	5,167	165.00	300.00	650.00	1000.
	1875 GW	I.A.	165.00	300.00	650.00	1000.

8.0645 g, .900 GOLD, .2333 oz AGW

KM#	Date	Mintage	VG	Fine	VF	XF
118	1873 GW	I.A.	1750.	2250.	2750.	3250.

10 PESOS

14.6774 g, .875 GOLD, .4129 oz AGW

KM#	Date	Mintage	VG	Fine	VF	XF
115	1870 GW	.020	225.00	275.00	350.00	500.00

KM#	Date	Mintage	VG	Fine	VF	XF
115	1871 GW	.030	250.00	325.00	400.00	600.00
	1872 GW	4,555	250.00	350.00	425.00	650.00

Design modified

KM#	Date	Mintage	VG	Fine	VF	XF
123	1876 GW	3,389	500.00	1000.	1500.	2000.

20 PESOS

32.2580 g, .900 GOLD, .9334 oz AGW

KM#	Date	Mintage	Fine	VF	XF	Unc
119	1873 GW	—	—	—	*Rare	—

***NOTE:** Stack's Hammel sale 9-82 AU realized $16,000., Pacific Coast Auction Galleries, Long Beach sale 6-86 AU realized $17,000, Superior Galleries Casterline sale 5-89 XF realized $16,500.

COUNTERSTAMPED COINAGE

Necessity issue undertaken in 1889 (and 1890) consequent to supply, by Heaton Mint of underweight 50 centavo coinage of the general type of the Heaton-made 5, 10 & 25 centavos of 1889-93. The host coins were particularly available, due to the adoption by Colombia of a .500 fine debasement of its silver coinage under President Nunez in 1886. This led to runaway inflation, rampant printing press money and hoarding of good (.835-.902 fine) silver.

1889

Type VII
Obv. c/s: COSTA RICA above national arms.
Rev: HABILITADA POR EL GOBIERNO around lion/CR in 7mm circle.

50 CENTAVOS

SILVER
c/s: Type VII on Colombia (Bogota) Cinco Decimos, KM#153.1.

KM#	Date	Year	Good	VG	Fine	VF
136	(1889)	1868	37.50	75.00	150.00	300.00
		1870	25.00	50.00	100.00	200.00

c/s: Type VII on Colombia (Bogota) 50 Centavos, KM#172.1.

KM#	Date	Year	Good	VG	Fine	VF
133.1	(1889)	1872	20.00	35.00	75.00	100.00
		1873	15.00	25.00	50.00	75.00

c/s: Type VII on Colombia (Bogota) 50 Centavos, KM#172.2.

KM#	Date	Year	Good	VG	Fine	VF
133.2	(1889)	1874	12.00	20.00	40.00	60.00

c/s: Type VII on Colombia (Bogota) Cincuenta Centavos, KM#177.1.

KM#	Date	Year	Good	VG	Fine	VF
134	(1889)	1874	17.50	30.00	45.00	65.00
		1875	17.50	30.00	45.00	65.00
		1876	17.50	30.00	45.00	65.00
		1877	17.50	30.00	45.00	65.00
		1878	17.50	30.00	45.00	65.00
		1879	15.00	25.00	40.00	60.00
		1880	15.00	25.00	40.00	60.00
		1881	15.00	25.00	40.00	60.00
		1882	15.00	25.00	40.00	60.00
		1883	15.00	25.00	40.00	60.00
		1884	15.00	25.00	40.00	60.00
		1885	30.00	50.00	80.00	125.00

c/s: Type VII on Colombia (Medellin) Cinco Decimos, KM#161.1.

KM#	Date	Year	Good	VG	Fine	VF
135.1	(1889)	1874	20.00	35.00	50.00	75.00
		1875	20.00	35.00	50.00	75.00
		1876	20.00	35.00	50.00	75.00

c/s: Type VII on Colombia (Medellin) Cinco Decimos, KM#153.6.

KM#	Date	Year	Good	VG	Fine	VF
135.2		1877/4	20.00	35.00	50.00	75.00
		1878/4	20.00	35.00	50.00	75.00
		1879/4	20.00	35.00	50.00	75.00
		1880	20.00	35.00	50.00	75.00
		1881	17.50	30.00	45.00	65.00
		1882	17.50	30.00	45.00	65.00
		1883	17.50	30.00	45.00	65.00
		1884	15.00	25.00	40.00	60.00
		1885	15.00	25.00	40.00	60.00
		1886	45.00	75.00	100.00	150.00

MONETARY REFORM

100 Centimos = 1 Colon

2 CENTIMOS

COPPER-NICKEL

KM#	Date	Mintage	Fine	VF	XF	Unc
144	1903	.360	.50	1.00	2.75	5.00

5 CENTIMOS

1.0000 g, .900 SILVER, .0289 oz ASW

KM#	Date	Mintage	Fine	VF	XF	Unc
145	1905	.500	BV	.75	2.00	8.00
	1910	.400	BV	.75	2.00	9.00
	1912	.540	BV	.75	1.50	5.00
	1914	.510	BV	.75	1.50	5.50

10 CENTIMOS

2.0000 g, .900 SILVER, .0578 oz ASW

KM#	Date	Mintage	Fine	VF	XF	Unc
146	1905	.400	BV	1.00	3.00	10.00
	1910	.400	BV	1.00	3.00	10.00
	1912	.270	BV	1.00	3.00	10.00
	1914	.150	BV	1.25	3.50	12.00

50 CENTIMOS

10.0000 g, .900 SILVER, .2893 oz ASW

KM#	Date	Mintage	Fine	VF	XF	Unc
143	1902CY	.120	15.00	25.00	40.00	85.00
	1903JCV	.380	11.00	18.50	32.50	60.00
	1914GCR	.200	300.00	500.00	850.00	1200.

NOTE: Most specimens were counterstamped UN COLON/ 1923. See KM#164.

DOS (2) COLONES

1.5560 g, .900 GOLD, .0450 oz AGW
Christopher Columbus

KM#	Date	Mintage	Fine	VF	XF	Unc
139	1897	500 pcs.	—	—	Proof	750.00
	1900	.045	30.00	35.00	45.00	55.00
	1915	5,000	40.00	60.00	75.00	90.00
	1916	5,000	40.00	60.00	75.00	90.00
	1921	3,000	50.00	75.00	95.00	125.00
	1922	.013	30.00	40.00	60.00	75.00
	1926	.015	30.00	40.00	60.00	75.00
	1928	.025	30.00	40.00	60.00	75.00

CINCO (5) COLONES

3.8900 g, .900 GOLD, .1125 oz AGW
Christopher Columbus

KM#	Date	Mintage	Fine	VF	XF	Unc
142	1899	.100	BV	60.00	75.00	115.00
	1900	.100	BV	60.00	75.00	115.00

DIEZ (10) COLONES

7.7800 g, .900 GOLD, .2251 oz AGW
Christopher Columbus

KM#	Date	Mintage	Fine	VF	XF	Unc
140	1897	.060	BV	115.00	125.00	175.00
	1899	.050	BV	115.00	125.00	175.00
	1900	.140	BV	115.00	125.00	175.00

VEINTE (20) COLONES

15.5600 g, .900 GOLD, .4502 oz AGW
Christopher Columbus

KM#	Date	Mintage	Fine	VF	XF	Unc
141	1897	.020	BV	225.00	275.00	400.00
	1899	.025	BV	225.00	275.00	400.00
	1900	5,000	BV	250.00	375.00	675.00

MONETARY REFORM

100 Centavos = 1 Colon

5 CENTAVOS

BRASS

KM#	Date	Mintage	Fine	VF	XF	Unc
147	1917	.400	2.25	4.50	11.00	32.50
	1918	1.000	1.25	3.75	9.00	27.50
	1919	.500	2.25	4.50	11.00	32.50

10 CENTAVOS

2.0000 g, .500 SILVER, .0321 oz ASW

KM#	Date	Mintage	Fine	VF	XF	Unc
148	1917	.100	.75	1.50	3.00	7.50

BRASS
Rev: GCR at lower right.

KM#	Date	Mintage	Fine	VF	XF	Unc
149.1	1917	.500	2.00	4.00	9.50	32.50

Rev: GCR at bottom center.

KM#	Date	Mintage	Fine	VF	XF	Unc
149.2	1917	Inc. Ab.	1.75	3.75	8.50	30.00
	1918	.900	1.25	3.00	7.00	27.50
	1919	.250	1.75	4.25	9.50	32.50

50 CENTAVOS

10.0000 g, .500 SILVER, .1607 oz ASW

KM#	Date	Mintage	Fine	VF	XF	Unc
150	1917GCR	9,400	—	—	800.00	1000.
	1918GCR	.030	—	—	—	—

NOTE: All but 10 examples of the 1917 issue and the complete 1918 mintage were counterstamped UN COLON/1923. See KM#165.

MONETARY REFORM

100 Centimos = 1 Colon

5 CENTIMOS

BRASS

KM#	Date	Mintage	Fine	VF	XF	Unc
151	1920	.500	1.50	3.50	8.00	18.50
	1921	.500	1.50	3.50	7.50	17.50
	1922	.500	2.00	4.00	8.50	22.50
	1936	1.500	.40	.75	1.50	7.00
	1938	1.000	.50	1.00	2.00	8.50
	1940	1.300	.40	.75	1.50	7.00
	1941	1.000	.40	.85	2.00	8.50

BRONZE

KM#	Date	Mintage	Fine	VF	XF	Unc
169	1929	1.500	.75	1.50	4.50	12.50

COPPER-NICKEL

KM#	Date	Mintage	Fine	VF	XF	Unc
178	1942	.274	.50	1.00	2.00	4.50

NOTE: Struck over 2 Centimos, KM#144.

BRASS

KM#	Date	Mintage	Fine	VF	XF	Unc
179	1942	1.730	.20	.60	1.50	4.50
	1943	1.000	.20	.60	1.50	4.50
	1946	1.000	.35	.90	2.00	5.50
	1947	3.000	.15	.45	1.00	3.50

COPPER-NICKEL

Rev: Large lettering B.C. - C.R. divided.

KM#	Date	Mintage	Fine	VF	XF	Unc
184.1	1951	3.000	.30	.65	1.25	3.00

Obv: Small ships, 5 stars in shield.
Rev: Small lettering B.C.C.R. not divided.

KM#	Date	Mintage	Fine	VF	XF	Unc
184.2	1951	7.000	.10	.15	.40	1.00

STAINLESS-STEEL

KM#	Date	Mintage	Fine	VF	XF	Unc
184.2a	1953	9.040	—	—	.10	.25
	1958	19.940	—	—	.10	.15
	1967	6.020	—	—	.10	.20

COPPER-NICKEL
Obv: Small ships, 7 stars in shield.

KM#	Date	Mintage	Fine	VF	XF	Unc
184.3	1969	20.000	—	—	.10	.15
	1976	—	—	—	.10	.15
	1976	—	—	—	Proof	.75
	1977	30.000	—	—	.10	.15
	1978	7.520	—	—	.10	.15

NOTE: Varieties exist.

Obv: Large ships, 7 stars in shield.

KM#	Date	Mintage	Fine	VF	XF	Unc
184.4	1972	12.550	—	—	.10	.15
	1973	20.000	—	—	.10	.15
	1976	33.270	—	—	.10	.15

NOTE: Dies vary for each date.

BRASS

KM#	Date	Mintage	Fine	VF	XF	Unc
184.4a	1979	3.060	—	—	.10	.15

10 CENTIMOS

BRASS

KM#	Date	Mintage	Fine	VF	XF	Unc
152	1920	.850	1.00	2.25	4.50	15.00
	1921	.750	1.00	2.25	5.00	16.50
	1922	.750	1.00	2.25	4.50	13.50

BRONZE

KM#	Date	Mintage	Fine	VF	XF	Unc
170	1929	.500	1.00	2.25	4.50	16.00

BRASS

KM#	Date	Mintage	Fine	VF	XF	Unc
174	1936	.750	.35	.75	1.75	10.00
	1941	.500	.50	1.00	2.25	12.00

KM#	Date	Mintage	Fine	VF	XF	Unc
180	1942	1.000	.25	.50	1.50	7.00
	1943	.500	.30	.65	2.00	8.50
180	1946	.500	.45	.85	2.25	8.50
	1947	1.500	.20	.40	1.25	6.00

COPPER-NICKEL
Obv: Small ships, 5 stars in shield.

KM#	Date	Mintage	Fine	VF	XF	Unc
185.1	1951	2.500	.10	.20	.70	1.25

STAINLESS-STEEL

KM#	Date	Mintage	Fine	VF	XF	Unc
185.1a	1953	5.290	—	—	.10	.75
	1958	10.470	—	—	.10	.25
	1967	5.500	—	—	.10	.25

COPPER-NICKEL
Obv: Small ships, 7 stars in field. Rev: Small 10.

KM#	Date	Mintage	Fine	VF	XF	Unc
185.2	1969	10.000	—	—	.10	.15
	1975	5.000	—	—	.10	.15
	1976	40.000	—	—	.10	.15

NOTE: Dies vary for each date.

NICKEL CLAD STEEL

KM#	Date	Mintage	Fine	VF	XF	Unc
185.2b	1979	10.000	—	—	.10	.15

COPPER-NICKEL
Obv: Large ships, 7 stars in field. Rev: Large 10.

KM#	Date	Mintage	Fine	VF	XF	Unc
185.3	1972	20.000	—	—	.10	.15
	1975	Inc. Ab.	—	—	.10	.15
	1976	Inc. Ab.	—	—	.10	.15
	1976	—	—	—	Proof	.75

NICKEL CLAD STEEL

KM#	Date	Mintage	Fine	VF	XF	Unc
185.3a	1979	Inc. Ab.	—	—	.10	.15

ALUMINUM
Obv: Small ships, 7 stars in field.

KM#	Date	Mintage	Fine	VF	XF	Unc
185.2a	1982	40.000	—	—	.10	.15

25 CENTIMOS

3.4500 g, .650 SILVER, .0721 oz ASW

KM#	Date	Mintage	Fine	VF	XF	Unc
168	1924	1.340	1.25	2.25	4.50	16.00

COPPER-NICKEL

KM#	Date	Mintage	Fine	VF	XF	Unc
171	1935	1.200	.25	.75	2.00	12.00

KM#	Date	Mintage	Fine	VF	XF	Unc
175	1937	1.600	.25	.75	1.75	8.00
	1937	—	—	—	Proof	100.00
	1948	9.200	.10	.20	.40	1.25
	1948	—	—	—	Proof	—

BRASS

KM#	Date	Mintage	Fine	VF	XF	Unc
181	1944	.800	.50	1.25	3.50	14.50
	1945	1.200	.50	1.00	2.75	12.50
	1946	1.200	.50	1.00	2.50	10.00

BRONZE

KM#	Date	Mintage	Fine	VF	XF	Unc
181a	1945	Inc. Ab.	1.00	2.00	4.00	20.00

COPPER-NICKEL

Obv: Small ships, 7 stars in shield.

KM#	Date	Mintage	Fine	VF	XF	Unc
188.1	1967	4.000	—	—	.10	.50
	1969	4.000	—	—	.10	.50
	1970	—	—	—	.10	.30
	1974	—	—	—	.10	.30
	1976	—	—	—	.10	.30
	1978	—	—	—	.10	.30

NOTE: Dies vary for each date.

Obv: Large ships, 7 stars in shield.

KM#	Date	Mintage	Fine	VF	XF	Unc
188.2	1972	8.000	—	—	.10	.20
	1974	—	—	—	.10	.20
	1976	12.000	—	—	.10	.20
	1976	—	—	—	Proof	1.00
	1977	12.000	—	—	.10	.20
	1978	—	—	—	.10	.20

NICKEL CLAD STEEL

KM#	Date	Mintage	Fine	VF	XF	Unc
188.2a	1980	30.000	—	—	.10	.20

ALUMINUM

KM#	Date	Mintage	Fine	VF	XF	Unc
188.2b	1982	30.000	—	—	.10	.20

Reeded edge. Reduced size, 17mm.

KM#	Date	Mintage	Fine	VF	XF	Unc
188.3	1983	—	—	—	.10	.20
	1986	—	—	—	.10	.20
	1989	—	—	—	.10	.20

NOTE: Dies vary for each date.

50 CENTIMOS

COPPER-NICKEL

KM#	Date	Mintage	Fine	VF	XF	Unc
172	1935	.700	.50	1.25	4.00	22.50

KM#	Date	Mintage	Fine	VF	XF	Unc
176	1937	.600	.30	1.00	3.00	14.00
	1937	—	—	—	Proof	125.00
182	1948	4.000	.15	.25	.50	2.00
	1948	—	—	—	Proof	—

Obv: Small ships, 7 stars in shield, small 50.

KM#	Date	Mintage	Fine	VF	XF	Unc
189.1	1965	1.000	—	.10	.25	1.00

Obv: Large 50.

KM#	Date	Mintage	Fine	VF	XF	Unc
189.3	1968	2.000	—	.10	.15	.50
	1970	4.000	—	.10	.15	.35
	1976	—	—	.10	.15	.35
	1978	—	—	.10	.15	.35

NOTE: Dies vary for each date.

Obv: Large ships, 7 stars in shield.

KM#	Date	Mintage	Fine	VF	XF	Unc
189.2	1972 lg.dt.	4.000	—	.10	.15	.35
	1972 sm.dt.	I.A.	—	.10	.15	.35
	1975 lg.dt.	.524	—	.10	.15	.35
	1975 sm.dt.	I.A.	—	.10	.15	.35
	1976	6.000	—	.10	.15	.35
	1976	—	—	—	Proof	1.50
	1977	6.000	—	.10	.15	.35

STAINLESS STEEL

Obv: Small ships, letters incuse on ribbon.

KM#	Date	Mintage	Fine	VF	XF	Unc
209.1	1982	12.000	—	—	.10	.20
	1983	—	—	—	.10	.20

Obv: Small ships, letters in relief on ribbon.

KM#	Date	Mintage	Fine	VF	XF	Unc
209.2	1984	—	—	—	.10	.20

Obv: Large ships, letters incuse on ribbon.

KM#	Date	Mintage	Fine	VF	XF	Unc
209.3	1983	—	—	—	.15	.25

UN (1) COLON

COPPER-NICKEL

KM#	Date	Mintage	Fine	VF	XF	Unc
173	1935	.350	.75	2.00	6.50	35.00

KM#	Date	Mintage	Fine	VF	XF	Unc
177	1937	.300	.50	1.25	4.50	20.00
	1937	—	—	—	Proof	150.00
	1948	1.350	.20	.40	.75	2.00
	1948	—	—	—	Proof	—

STAINLESS-STEEL

KM#	Date	Mintage	Fine	VF	XF	Unc
186.1	1954	.990	.20	.35	1.00	7.50

COPPER-NICKEL

Obv: Small ships, 5 stars in shield.

KM#	Date	Mintage	Fine	VF	XF	Unc
186.1a	1961	1.000	.10	.20	.50	2.00

Obv: Small ships, 7 stars in shield.

KM#	Date	Mintage	Fine	VF	XF	Unc
186.2	1965	1.000	.10	.20	.35	1.00
	1968	2.000	.10	.20	.25	.50
	1970	2.000	.10	.20	.25	.50
	1974	—	.10	.20	.25	.50
	1976	12.000	.10	.20	.25	.50
	1976	—	—	—	Proof	2.50
	1977	22.000	.10	.20	.25	.50
	1978	—	.10	.20	.25	.50

NOTE: Dies vary for each date.

Obv: Large ships, 7 stars in shield.

KM#	Date	Mintage	Fine	VF	XF	Unc
186.3	1972	2.000	.10	.20	.25	.50
	1975	1.028	.10	.20	.25	.50

STAINLESS STEEL
Obv: Small ships, letters incuse on ribbon.

KM#	Date	Mintage	Fine	VF	XF	Unc
210.1	1982	12.000	—	—	.10	.25
	1983	—	—	—	.10	.25
	1984	—	—	—	.10	.25
	1991	—	—	—	.10	.25

Obv: Small ships, letters in relief on ribbon.

KM#	Date	Mintage	Fine	VF	XF	Unc
210.2	1984	—	—	—	.10	.25
	1989	—	—	—	.10	.25
	1991	—	—	—	.10	.25

2 COLONES

COPPER-NICKEL

KM#	Date	Mintage	Fine	VF	XF	Unc
183	1948	1.380	.50	.75	1.25	3.00
	1948	—	—	—	Proof	—

STAINLESS-STEEL
Obv: Small ships, 5 stars in shield.

KM#	Date	Mintage	Fine	VF	XF	Unc
187.1	1954	1.030	.25	.50	2.00	10.00

COPPER-NICKEL

KM#	Date	Mintage	Fine	VF	XF	Unc
187.1a	1961	1.000	.15	.30	.50	1.25

Obv: Small ships, 7 stars in shield.

KM#	Date	Mintage	Fine	VF	XF	Unc
187.3	1968	2.000	.15	.30	.40	.90
	1970	1.000	.15	.30	.50	1.00
	1972	2.000	.15	.30	.40	.90
	1976	—	.15	.30	.40	.90
	1978	—	.15	.30	.40	.90

NOTE: Dies vary for each date.

4.3000 g, .999 SILVER, .1381 oz ASW
20th Anniversary of the Central Bank

KM#	Date	Mintage	Fine	VF	XF	Unc
190	1970	5,157	—	—	Proof	7.50

NOTE: Also exists with a small oval w/1000 inside above the S in COLONES.

STAINLESS STEEL

Obv: Large ships.

KM#	Date	Mintage	Fine	VF	XF	Unc
211.1	1982	12.000	—	—	.10	.50
	1983	—	—	—	.10	.50

Obv: Small ships.

KM#	Date	Mintage	Fine	VF	XF	Unc
211.2	1984	—	—	—	.10	.50

5 COLONES

10.7800 g, .999 SILVER, .3463 oz ASW
400th Year of the Founding of New Carthage

KM#	Date	Mintage	Fine	VF	XF	Unc
191	1970	5,157	—	—	Proof	12.50

NICKEL
25th Anniversary of the Central Bank

KM#	Date	Mintage	Fine	VF	XF	Unc
203	1975	2.000	—	.15	.35	1.25
	1975	5,000	—	—	Proof	2.00

STAINLESS STEEL
Obv: Large ships, letters in relief.

KM#	Date	Mintage	Fine	VF	XF	Unc
214.1	1983	—	—	.10	.15	.50

Obv: Small ships, letters incuse.

KM#	Date	Mintage	Fine	VF	XF	Unc
214.2	1985	—	—	.10	.15	.50

Obv: Small ships, letters in relief.

KM#	Date	Mintage	Fine	VF	XF	Unc
214.3	1989	—	—	.10	.15	.50

10 COLONES

21.7000 g, .999 SILVER, .6976 oz ASW
Attempt of Unification of Middle America
Obv: Similar to 5 Colones, KM#191.

KM#	Date	Mintage	Fine	VF	XF	Unc
192	1970	5,157	—	—	Proof	20.00

NICKEL
25th Anniversary of the Central Bank

KM#	Date	Mintage	Fine	VF	XF	Unc
204	1975	.500	.25	.50	1.00	2.00
	1975	5,000	—	—	Proof	4.00

STAINLESS STEEL
Obv: Small ships, letters incuse.

KM#	Date	Mintage	Fine	VF	XF	Unc
215.1	1983	—	—	.20	.30	1.00
	1985	—	—	.20	.30	1.00

Obv: Large ships, letters in relief.

KM#	Date	Mintage	Fine	VF	XF	Unc
215.2	1983	—	—	.20	.30	1.00
	1985	—	—	.20	.30	1.00

20 COLONES

43.7000 g, .999 SILVER, 1.4050 oz ASW
Venus de Milo
Rev: Raised 1000 hallmark in oval below O in MILO.

KM#	Date	Mintage	Fine	VF	XF	Unc
193	1970	7,500	—	—	Proof	40.00

NICKEL
25th Anniversary of the Central Bank

KM#	Date	Mintage	Fine	VF	XF	Unc
205	1975	.250	.50	1.00	2.00	4.00
	1975	5,000	—	—	Proof	9.00

STAINLESS STEEL
Obv: Small ship.

KM#	Date	Mintage	Fine	VF	XF	Unc
216.1	1983	—	—	.35	.60	1.50
	1985	—	—	.35	.60	1.50
	Obv: Large ship.					
216.2	1985	—	—	.35	.60	1.50

25 COLONES

53.9000 g, .999 SILVER, 1.7312 oz ASW
25 Years of Social Legislation
Obv: Similar to 5 Colones, KM#191.

KM#	Date	Mintage	Fine	VF	XF	Unc
194	1970	6,800	—	—	Proof	50.00

50 COLONES

7.4500 g, .900 GOLD, .2155 oz AGW
Inter-American Human Rights Convention

KM#	Date	Mintage	Fine	VF	XF	Unc
195	1970	3,507	—	—	Proof	145.00

25.5500 g, .500 SILVER, .4107 oz ASW
Conservation - Green Turtle

KM#	Date	Mintage	Fine	VF	XF	Unc
200	1974	7,599	—	—	—	17.50
	28.2800 g, .925 SILVER, .8411 oz ASW					
200a	1974	.011	—	—	Proof	20.00

100 COLONES

14.9000 g, .900 GOLD, .4311 oz AGW

KM#	Date	Mintage	Fine	VF	XF	Unc
196	1970	3,507	—	—	Proof	265.00

32.1000 g, .500 SILVER, .5160 oz ASW
Conservation - Manatee
Obv: Similar to 1500 Colones, KM#202.

KM#	Date	Mintage	Fine	VF	XF	Unc
201	1974	7,599	—	—	—	22.50
	35.0000 g, .925 SILVER, 1.0409 oz ASW					
201a	1974	.011	—	—	Proof	25.00

International Year of the Child

KM#	Date	Mintage	Fine	VF	XF	Unc
206	1979	9,500	—	—	—	12.50
	1979	5,000	—	—	Proof	20.00

NICKEL
Dr. Oscar Arias

KM#	Date	Mintage	Fine	VF	XF	Unc
224	1987	.025	—	—	—	7.50

200 COLONES

29.8000 g, .900 GOLD, .8623 oz AGW
Juan Santamaria

KM#	Date	Mintage	Fine	VF	XF	Unc
197	1970	3,507	—	—	Proof	525.00

250 COLONES

30.3300 g, .925 SILVER, .9020 oz ASW
Jaguar

KM#	Date	Mintage	Fine	VF	XF	Unc
212	1982FM(P)	1,109	—	—	Proof	85.00

National Flower

KM#	Date	Mintage	Fine	VF	XF	Unc
217	1983FM(P)	393 pcs.	—	—	Proof	75.00

300 COLONES

10.9700 g, .925 SILVER, .3262 oz ASW
125th Anniversary of Death of Juan Santamaria

KM#	Date	Mintage	Fine	VF	XF	Unc
207	1981	.010	—	—	Proof	10.00

200th Anniversary of Founding of Alajuela

KM#	Date	Mintage	Fine	VF	XF	Unc
223	1981	—	—	—	Proof	10.00

500 COLONES

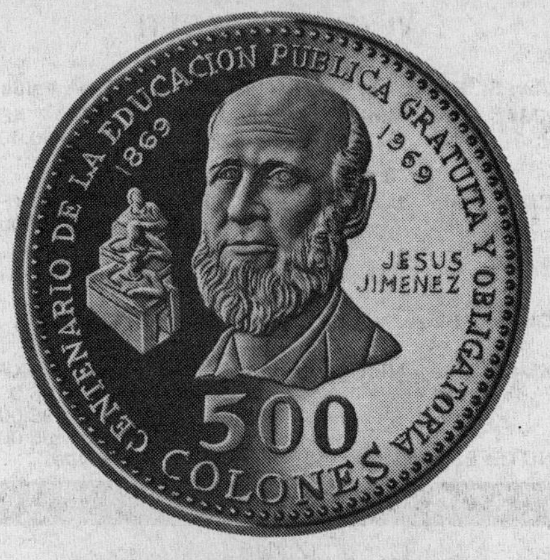

74.5200 g, .900 GOLD, 2.1565 oz AGW
100th Anniversary of Public Education
Obv: Similar to 100 Colones, KM#196.

KM#	Date	Mintage	Fine	VF	XF	Unc
198	1970	3,507	—	—	Proof	1220.

1000 COLONES

149.0400 g, .900 GOLD, 4.3126 oz AGW
150th Anniversary of Central American Independence
Obv: Similar to 100 Colones, KM#196.

KM#	Date	Mintage	Fine	VF	XF	Unc
199	1970	3,507	—	—	Proof	3200.

10.9700 g, .925 SILVER, .3272 oz ASW
Dr. Oscar Arias

KM#	Date	Mintage	Fine	VF	XF	Unc
225	1987	.010	—	—	—	30.00

1500 COLONES

33.4370 g, .900 GOLD, .9676 oz AGW
Conservation - Giant Anteater

KM#	Date	Mintage	Fine	VF	XF	Unc
202	1974	2,418	—	—	—	500.00
	1974	726 pcs.	—	—	Proof	750.00

6.9800 g, .500 GOLD, .1122 oz AGW
Francisco Coronado and Christopher Columbus

KM#	Date	Mintage	Fine	VF	XF	Unc
213	1982FM(P)					
		724 pcs.	—	—	Proof	140.00

KM#	Date	Mintage	Fine	VF	XF	Unc
218	1983FM(P)					
		272 pcs.	—	—	Proof	240.00

5000 COLONES

15.0000 g, .900 GOLD, .4341 oz AGW
125th Anniversary of Death of Juan Santamaria

KM#	Date	Mintage	Fine	VF	XF	Unc
208	1981	—	—	—	—	225.00
	1981	2,000	—	—	Proof	275.00

25,000 COLONES

15.0000 g, .900 GOLD, .4341 oz AGW
Dr. Oscar Arias

KM#	Date	Mintage	Fine	VF	XF	Unc
226	1987	5,000	—	—	Proof	400.00

COUNTERSTAMPED COINAGE

50 CENTIMOS

1923

Type VIII
Obv. c/s: 1923 in 11mm circle.
Rev. c/s: 50 CENTIMOS in 11mm circle.

SILVER
c/s: Type VIII on 25 Centavos, KM#105.

KM#	Date	Year	VG	Fine	VF	XF
155	1923	1864 GW	—	—	Rare	—

c/s: Type VIII on 25 Centavos, KM#106.

KM#	Date	Year	VG	Fine	VF	XF
156	1923	1864 GW	—	—	Rare	—
		1865 GW	22.50	45.00	75.00	125.00
		1875 GW	17.50	35.00	60.00	100.00

c/s: Type VIII on 25 Centavos, KM#127.1.
Rev: GW 9Ds

KM#	Date	Year	VG	Fine	VF	XF
157	1923	1886 GW	3.00	5.00	9.00	15.00
		1887 GW	3.00	5.00	9.00	15.00

c/s: Type VIII on 25 Centavos, KM#127.2.
Rev: 9Ds GW

KM#	Date	Year	VG	Fine	VF	XF
158	1923	1886 GW	4.00	8.00	15.00	25.00
		1887 GW	3.00	5.00	9.00	15.00

c/s: Type VIII on 25 Centavos, KM#130.

KM#	Date	Year	VG	Fine	VF	XF
159	1923	1889	1.50	2.75	5.00	8.50
		1890/80	2.50	3.75	7.00	10.00
		1890	1.50	2.75	5.00	8.50
		1892	1.50	2.75	5.00	8.50
		1893	1.25	2.50	4.50	7.50

NOTE: The entire mintage of 1,866,000 was created by counterstamping the above coins.

UN (1) COLON

1923

Type IX
Obv. c/s: 1923 in 14mm circle.
Rev. c/s: UN COLON in 14mm circle.

SILVER
c/s: Type IX on 50 Centavos, KM#112.

KM#	Date	Year	VG	Fine	VF	XF
162	1923					
		1865 GW	25.00	40.00	65.00	125.00
		1866/5GW	30.00	50.00	80.00	150.00
		1867 GW	—	—	Rare	—
		1870 GW	—	—	Rare	—
		1872 GW	—	—	Rare	—
		1875 GW	25.00	40.00	65.00	125.00

c/s: Type IX on 50 Centavos, KM#124.

KM#	Date	Year	VG	Fine	VF	XF
163	1923	1880 GW	6.50	10.00	25.00	50.00
		1885 GW	6.50	10.00	25.00	50.00
		1886 GW	9.00	17.50	30.00	60.00
		1887 GW	6.50	10.00	27.50	55.00
		1890 GW	6.50	10.00	27.50	55.00

c/s: Type IX on 50 Centimos, KM#143.

KM#	Date	Year	VG	Fine	VF	XF
164	1923	1902 CY	4.00	8.00	13.50	22.50
		1903 JCV	3.00	6.00	10.00	17.50
		1914 GCR	4.00	8.00	13.50	20.00

c/s: Type IX on 50 Centimos, KM#150.

KM#	Date	Year	VG	Fine	VF	XF
165	1923	1917GCR	4.50	8.50	13.50	20.00
		1918GCR	6.00	12.00	17.50	25.00

NOTE: A total of 9,390 of 50 Centimos, KM#150 dated 1917 and 29,800 dated 1918 were counterstamped. The entire mintage of 460,000 was created by counterstamping the above coins.

MINT SETS (MS)

KM#	Date	Mintage	Identification	Issue Price	Mkt. Val.
MS1	1975(3)	—	KM203-205	—	7.50

PROOF SETS (PS)

KM#	Date	Mintage	Identification	Issue Price	Mkt. Val.
PS1	1889(4)	—	KM128-130,KM-Pn3	—	—
PS2	1937(3)	—	KM175-177	—	375.00
PS3	1970(10)	570	KM190-199	—	5480.
PS4	1970(5)	4,650	KM190-194	52.00	130.00
PS5	1970(5)	3,000	KM195-199	832.00	5350.
PS6	1974(2)	30,000	KM200a-201a	50.00	45.00
PS7	1975(3)	—	KM203-205	—	15.00
PS8	1976(5)	5,000	KM184.4,185.3,186.3,188.2, 189.2	10.00	6.00

Listings For

CRETE: refer to Greece

CROATIA

The Republic of Croatia, bordered on the west by the Adriatic Sea and the northeast by Hungary, has an area of 21,829 sq. mi. (56,538 sq. km.) and a population of about 5 million. Capital: Zagreb.

The country was attached to the Kingdom of Hungary until Dec. 1, 1918, when it joined with the Serbs and Slovenes to form the Kingdom of the Serbs, Croats and Slovenes, which changed its name to the Kingdom of Yugoslavia on Oct. 3, 1929. On April 6, 1941, Hitler, angered by the coup d' etat that overthrew the pro-Nazi regime of regent Prince Paul, sent the Nazi armies crashing across the Yugoslav borders from Germany, Hungary, Romania and Bulgaria. Within a week the army of the Balkan Kingdom was prostrate and broken. Yugoslavia was dismembered to reward Hitler's Balkan allies. Croatia, reconstituted as a nominal kingdom, was given to the administration of an Italian princeling, who wisely decided to remain in Italy.

Croatia proclaimed their independence from Yugoslavia on Oct. 8, 1991.

MONETARY SYSTEM

100 Banica = 1 Kuna

The word 'kunas', derived from the Russian 'cunica' which means marten, reflects the use of furs for money in medieval eastern Europe.

KUNA

ZINC
Similar to 2 Kune, KM#2.

KM#	Date	Mintage	Fine	VF	XF	Unc
1	1941	—	—	—	Rare	—

2 KUNE

ZINC

KM#	Date	Mintage	Fine	VF	XF	Unc
2	1941	—	2.50	5.00	9.00	18.00
	1941	—	—	—	Proof	80.00

50 KUNA

NOTE: Dated 1934, this coin is found struck in various metals, 2 sizes - 25 and 26mm - as well as 2 thicknesses. It is considered a modern fantasy issue.

RAGUSA

A port city in Croatia on the Dalmatian coast of the Adriatic Sea. Upon its incorporation in Yugoslavia in 1918, its name was officially changed to Dubrovnik. Ragusa was once a great mercantile power, the merchant fleets of which sailed as far abroad as India and America. The city's present industries include oil-refining, slate mining, and the manufacture of liquers, cheese, silk, leather and soap.

The island rock of Ragusa was colonized during the 7th century by refugees from the destroyed Latin communities of Salona and Epidaurus, and a colony of Slavs. For four centuries Ragusa successfully defended itself against attacks by foreign powers, but from 1205 to 1358 recognized Venetian suzeranity. From 1358 to 1526, Ragusa was a vassal state of Hungary. The fall of Hungary in 1526 freed Ragusa, permitting it to become one of the foremost commercial powers of the Mediterranean and a leader in the development of literature and art. After this period its importance declined, due in part to the discovery of America which reduced the importance of Mediterranean ports. A measure of its former economic importance was regained during the Napoleonic Wars when the republic, by adopting a policy of neutrality (1800-1805), became the leading carrier of the Mediterranean. This favored position was terminated by French seizure in 1805. In 1814 Ragusa was annexed by Austria, remaining a part of the Austrian Empire until its incorporation in the newly formed state of Yugoslavia in 1918. Croatia proclaimed its independence in 1991.

MONETARY SYSTEM

6 Soldi = 1 Grosetto
12 Grosetti = 1 Perpero
36 Grosetti = 1 Scudo
40 Grosetti = 1 Ducato
60 Grosetti = 1 Tallero

VI (6) GROSSETTI

BILLON
Obv: St. Blaze, leg: PROT.RHACUSII. . . . . Rev: Value.

KM#	Date	Mintage	VG	Fine	VF	XF
25.1	1801	—	12.00	20.00	27.50	50.00

Obv. leg: PROT.REIPU.RHACUSI.

C#	Date	Mintage	VG	Fine	VF	XF
25.2	1801	—	12.00	20.00	27.50	50.00

PERPERO

BILLON
Obv: St. Blaze, leg: PROT.RAEIP.RHAGVSINAE. . . . .
Rev: Christ.

KM#	Date	Mintage	VG	Fine	VF	XF
7	1801	—	24.00	40.00	55.00	95.00
	1802	—	24.00	40.00	55.00	95.00
	1803	—	24.00	40.00	55.00	95.00

NOTE: Earlier dates (1683-1750) exist for this type.

ZARA

(Zadar)

Zara, a port and fortress in Dalmatia, Croatia, was occupied by the French during the period of 1807-13. While the French defenders of the city were under siege in 1813, they issued a silver emergency coinage.

FRENCH SIEGE COINAGE

4 FRANCS - 60 CENTIMES

SILVER, 30.59 g

KM#	Date	Mintage	VG	Fine	VF	XF
1	1813	—	400.00	600.00	800.00	1200.

9 FRANCS - 20 CENTIMES

SILVER, 61.12 g

KM#	Date	Mintage	VG	Fine	VF	XF
2	1813	—	500.00	750.00	1000.	1500.

SILVER, 122.38 g
Obv: Large stamp.

KM#	Date	Mintage	VG	Fine	VF	XF
3	1813	—	750.00	1500.	2750.	5000.

Obv: Small stamp.

KM#	Date	Mintage	VG	Fine	VF	XF
4	1813	—	800.00	1600.	2850.	5500.

CUBA

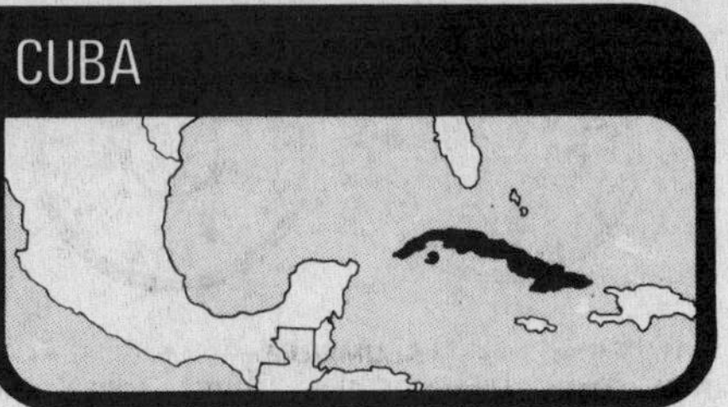

The Republic of Cuba, situated at the northern edge of the Caribbean Sea about 90 miles (145 km.) south of Florida, has an area of 44,218 sq. mi. (110,860 sq. km.) and a population of *10.2 million. Capital: Havana. The Cuban economy is based on the cultivation and refining of sugar, which provides 80 percent of export earnings.

Discovered by Columbus in 1492 and settled by Diego Velasquez in the early 1500s, Cuba remained a Spanish possession until 1898, except for a brief British occupancy of Havana in 1762-63. Cuban attempts to gain freedom were crushed, even while Spain was granting independence to its other American possessions. Ten years of warfare, 1868-78, between Spanish troops and Cuban rebels exacted guarantees of rights which were never implemented. The final revolt, begun in 1895, evoked American sympathy, and with the aid of U.S. troops independence was proclaimed on May 20, 1902. Fulgencio Batista seized the government in 1952 and established a dictatorship. Opposition to Batista, led by Fidel Castro, drove him into exile on Jan. 1, 1959. A communist-type, 25-member collective leadership headed by Castro was inaugurated in March, 1962.

RULERS

Spanish, until 1898

MINT MARKS

Key - Havana, 1977

MONETARY SYSTEM

100 Centavos = 1 Peso

COUNTERMARKED COINAGE

The loss of the Spanish Colonial mints in the new world caused a severe shortage of coinage in Cuba. Clandestine traders introduced the silver inflationary "reales de vellow" of Spain. The ratio was 2 1/2 New Reales to 1 Old Colonial Real. They were accepted easily by the Cuban public, ignorant of the devaluation in Spain where the silver "Peso" was now divided into 20 Reales.

In 1827 the Spanish governor of Cuba banned their importation. Various exchange rates were used until March 22, 1841 when a Royal Order decreed all will be recalled, counted and recorded with receipts issued and devalued with a countermark in the provinces Trinidad, Santiago de Cuba and Puerto Principe. Fifty punches were prepared.

2 REALES

.903 SILVER

KM#	Date	Good	VG	Fine	VF
	c/m: Lattice on Spanish (Madrid) 2 Reales, C#38.1.				
1.1	ND(1772-88)	12.50	22.50	35.00	50.00
	c/m: Lattice on Spanish (Seville) 2 Reales, C#38.2.				
1.2	ND(1773-88)	12.50	22.50	35.00	50.00
	c/m: Lattice on Spanish (Madrid) 2 Reales, C#69.1.				
2	ND(1788-1808)	10.00	20.00	30.00	45.00
	c/m: Lattice on Spanish (Seville) 2 Reales, C#69.2.				
3	ND(1788-1808)	10.00	20.00	30.00	45.00
	c/m: Lattice on Spanish (Catalonia) 2 Reales, C#134.1.				
4.1	ND(1811-14)	13.50	27.00	40.00	60.00
	c/m: Lattice on Spanish (Cadiz) 2 Reales, C#134.2.				
4.2	ND(1810-12)	13.50	27.00	40.00	60.00

c/m: Lattice on Spanish (Madrid)
2 Reales, C#134.3.

KM#	Date	Good	VG	Fine	VF
5	ND(1814-33)	10.00	20.00	30.00	45.00

KM#	Date	Good	VG	Fine	VF
	c/m: Lattice on Spanish (Seville) 2 Reales, C#134.4.				
6	ND(1815-33)	10.00	20.00	30.00	45.00
	c/m: Lattice on Spanish (Madrid) 2 Reales, C#134a.3.				
9	ND(1812-14)	10.00	20.00	30.00	45.00

KM#	Date	Good	VG	Fine	VF
	c/m: Lattice on Spanish (Madrid) 4 Reales, C#90.				
7	ND(1808-13)	10.00	20.00	30.00	45.00
	c/m: Lattice on Spanish (Seville) 4 Reales, C#90.2.				
8	ND(1810-12)	10.00	20.00	30.00	45.00

KM#	Date	Good	VG	Fine	VF
	c/m: Lattice on Spanish (Madrid) 4 Reales, C#137.6.				
10	ND(1822-23)	10.00	20.00	30.00	45.00
	c/m: Lattice on Spanish (Valencia) 4 Reales, C#137.1.				
11	ND(1823)	13.50	27.00	40.00	60.00
	c/m: Lattice on Spanish (Madrid) Proclamation medal of Charles IV.				
12	ND(1789)	—	—	—	—

REPUBLIC

CENTAVO

COPPER-NICKEL

KM#	Date	Mintage	Fine	VF	XF	Unc
9	1915	9.396	.25	1.00	2.00	15.00
	1915	—	—	—	Proof	150.00
	1916	9.318	.25	2.00	3.50	17.50
	1916	—	—	—	Proof	200.00
	1920	19.378	.10	.40	2.50	12.50
	1938	2.000	2.00	4.00	8.00	20.00
	BRASS					
9a	1943	20.000	.10	.40	1.00	2.00
	COPPER-NICKEL					
9b	1946	50.000	—	.10	.50	2.50
	1961	100.000	.15	.25	.60	1.50

BRASS
Birth of Jose Marti Centennial

KM#	Date	Mintage	Fine	VF	XF	Unc
26	1953	50.000	.10	.15	.75	1.75
	1953	—	—	—	Proof	Rare

COPPER-NICKEL

KM#	Date	Mintage	Fine	VF	XF	Unc
30	1958	50.000	—	.10	.40	1.25

ALUMINUM
Obv. leg: PATRIA Y LIBERTAD.

KM#	Date	Mintage	Fine	VF	XF	Unc
33.1	1963	200.020	—	.10	.30	.60
	1966	50.000	—	.10	.40	.80
	1969	50.000	—	.10	.40	.80
	1970	50.000	—	.10	.40	.80
	1971	49.960	.20	.40	.80	1.50
	1972	100.000	—	.10	.40	.80
	1978	50.000	—	.10	.40	.80
	1979	100.000	—	.10	.40	.80
	1981	—	—	.10	.40	.80
	1982	—	—	.10	.40	.80

Obv. leg: PATRIA O MUERTE.

KM#	Date	Mintage	Fine	VF	XF	Unc
33.2	1983	—	—	.10	.40	.80
	1984	—	—	.10	.40	.80
	1985	—	—	.10	.40	.80
	1986	—	—	.10	.40	.80
	1987	—	—	.10	.40	.80

2 CENTAVOS

COPPER-NICKEL

KM#	Date	Mintage	Fine	VF	XF	Unc
10	1915	6.090	.25	1.25	2.50	15.00
	1915	—	—	—	Proof	200.00
	1916	5.322	.25	1.25	3.50	17.50
	1916	—	—	—	Proof	250.00

ALUMINUM
Obv. and rev: Small lettered legends, long edge denticles.

KM#	Date	Mintage	Fine	VF	XF	Unc
104.1	1983	3.996	—	—	—	1.00

Obv. and rev: Large lettered legends, short edge denticles.

KM#	Date	Mintage	Fine	VF	XF	Unc
104.2	1983	Inc. Ab.	—	.10	.20	.50
	1984	—	—	.10	.25	1.00
	1985	—	—	.10	.20	.50
	1986	—	—	.10	.20	.50

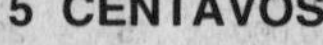

5 CENTAVOS

COPPER-NICKEL

KM#	Date	Mintage	Fine	VF	XF	Unc
11	1915	5.096	.50	1.50	5.00	22.50
	1915	—	—	—	Proof	250.00
	1916	1.714	.75	2.25	7.50	27.50
	1916	—	—	—	Proof	300.00
	1920	10.000	.50	1.25	4.50	17.50

BRASS

KM#	Date	Mintage	Fine	VF	XF	Unc
11a	1943	6.000	1.00	2.50	8.00	30.00

COPPER-NICKEL

KM#	Date	Mintage	Fine	VF	XF	Unc
11b	1946	40.000	.10	.20	.50	3.50
	1960	20.000	.10	.20	.50	5.00
	1961	70.000	.10	.15	.40	1.00

ALUMINUM

KM#	Date	Mintage	Fine	VF	XF	Unc
34	1963	80.000	—	.10	.25	.75
	1966	50.000	—	.15	.35	1.50
	1968	—	—	.15	.35	1.50
	1969	—	—	.25	.50	2.50
	1971	100.020	—	.10	.25	.75
	1972	100.000	—	.10	.25	.75

10 CENTAVOS

2.5000 g, .900 SILVER, .0723 oz ASW

KM#	Date	Mintage	Fine	VF	XF	Unc
12	1915	5.690	1.50	3.00	5.00	20.00
	1915	—	—	—	Proof	350.00
	1916	.560	3.00	6.50	15.00	100.00
	1916	—	—	—	Proof	450.00
	1920	3.090	1.25	2.50	5.50	35.00
	1948	5.120	—	BV	1.50	4.00
	1949	9.880	—	BV	1.50	3.75

50th Year of Republic

KM#	Date	Mintage	Fine	VF	XF	Unc
23	1952	10.000	BV	.50	1.00	2.50

20 CENTAVOS

5.0000 g, .900 SILVER, .1446 oz ASW
Rev: High relief star. Fine edge reeding.

KM#	Date	Mintage	Fine	VF	XF	Unc
13.1	1915	7.915	2.25	4.00	6.00	50.00
	1915	—	—	—	Proof	450.00

Rev: Low relief star.

KM#	Date	Mintage	Fine	VF	XF	Unc
13.2	1915 fine reeding					
		Inc. Ab.	3.50	7.50	20.00	100.00
	1915 coarse reeding					
		Inc. Ab.	2.00	3.50	5.00	35.00
	1916	2.535	3.50	5.00	8.00	70.00
	1916	—	—	—	Proof	600.00
	1920	6.130	1.50	3.00	4.50	25.00
	1932	.184	15.00	40.00	125.00	650.00
	1948	6.830	BV	1.50	2.50	6.00
	1949	13.170	BV	1.25	2.00	4.00

NOTE: Coins with high relief stars normally exhibit a weak key and palm tree on the reverse.

50th Year of Republic

KM#	Date	Mintage	Fine	VF	XF	Unc
24	1952	8.700	BV	.75	1.50	3.00

COPPER-NICKEL
Jose Marti

KM#	Date	Mintage	Fine	VF	XF	Unc
31	1962	83.860	.35	1.00	1.50	4.00
	1968	25.750	.45	1.25	2.00	5.00

ALUMINUM

KM#	Date	Mintage	Fine	VF	XF	Unc
35	1969	25.000	.35	1.00	1.50	3.00
	1970	29.560	.45	1.25	1.75	4.00
	1971	25.000	.35	1.00	1.50	3.00
	1972	—	.35	1.00	1.50	3.00

25 CENTAVOS

6.2500 g, .900 SILVER, .1808 oz ASW
Birth of Jose Marti Centennial

KM#	Date	Mintage	Fine	VF	XF	Unc
27	1953	19.000	—	BV	2.50	6.50
	1953	—	—	—	Proof	Rare

COPPER-NICKEL
Carlos Finlay

KM#	Date	Mintage	Fine	VF	XF	Unc
360	1988	—	—	—	2.00	5.00

Alexander von Humboldt

KM#	Date	Mintage	Fine	VF	XF	Unc
361	1989	—	—	—	2.00	5.00

40 CENTAVOS

10.0000 g, .900 SILVER, .2893 oz ASW
Rev: High relief star.

KM#	Date	Mintage	Fine	VF	XF	Unc
14.1	1915	2.633	5.00	9.00	20.00	125.00
	1915	—	—	—	Proof	600.00
	1920	.540	7.00	12.00	30.00	150.00
	1920	—	—	—	Proof	Rare

Rev: Low relief star.

KM#	Date	Mintage	Fine	VF	XF	Unc
14.2	1915	Inc. Ab.	6.00	10.00	25.00	100.00
	1916	.188	15.00	35.00	150.00	700.00
	1916	—	—	—	Proof	1000.
	1920	Inc. Ab.	8.00	12.50	35.00	145.00

50th Year of Republic

KM#	Date	Mintage	Fine	VF	XF	Unc
25	1952	1.250	BV	2.50	5.00	10.00

COPPER-NICKEL
Camilo Cienfuegos Gornaran

KM#	Date	Mintage	Fine	VF	XF	Unc
32	1962	15.250	2.00	3.00	5.00	8.00

50 CENTAVOS

12.5000 g, .900 SILVER, .3617 oz ASW
Birth of Jose Marti Centennial

KM#	Date	Mintage	Fine	VF	XF	Unc
28	1953	2.000	BV	3.00	6.00	12.50
	1953	—	—	—	Proof	Rare

PESO

26.7295 g, .900 SILVER, .7735 oz ASW

KM#	Date	Mintage	Fine	VF	XF	Unc
8	1898	1,000	300.00	750.00	1750.	3500.
	1898	—	—	—	Proof	4500.

NOTE: Similar "Souvenir Pesos" dated 1897 are listed in *UNUSUAL WORLD COINS*, 3rd edition, Krause Publications, 1992.

Rev: High relief star.

KM#	Date	Mintage	Fine	VF	XF	Unc
15.1	1915	1.976	10.00	17.50	27.50	150.00

Rev: Low relief star.

KM#	Date	Mintage	Fine	VF	XF	Unc
15.2	1915	Inc. Ab.	15.00	25.00	35.00	225.00
	1915	—	—	—	Proof	1350.
	1916	.843	12.50	20.00	40.00	300.00
	1916	—	—	—	Proof	1750.

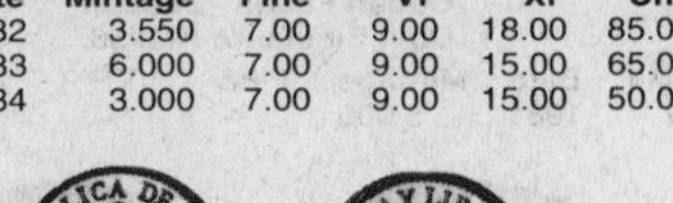

KM#	Date	Mintage	Fine	VF	XF	Unc
15.2	1932	3.550	7.00	9.00	18.00	85.00
	1933	6.000	7.00	9.00	15.00	65.00
	1934	3.000	7.00	9.00	15.00	50.00

1.6718 g, .900 GOLD, .0483 oz AGW
Jose Marti

KM#	Date	Mintage	Fine	VF	XF	Unc
16	1915	6,850	50.00	100.00	200.00	300.00
	1915	—	—	—	Proof	1650.
	1916	.011	50.00	100.00	200.00	275.00
	1916	—	—	—	Proof	1750.

26.7295 g, .900 SILVER, .7735 oz ASW
'ABC'

KM#	Date	Mintage	Fine	VF	XF	Unc
22	1934	7.000	12.00	25.00	45.00	115.00
	1935	12.500	12.00	25.00	50.00	125.00
	1936	16.000	12.00	25.00	50.00	125.00
	1937	11.500	150.00	250.00	400.00	900.00
	1938	10.800	12.00	25.00	50.00	125.00
	1939	9.200	12.00	25.00	45.00	115.00

Birth of Jose Marti Centennial

KM#	Date	Mintage	Fine	VF	XF	Unc
29	1953	1.000	BV	5.00	8.00	15.00
	1953	—	—	—	Proof	Rare

COPPER-NICKEL
Carlos Manuel de Cespedes

KM#	Date	Mintage	Fine	VF	XF	Unc
186	1977	3,000	—	—	—	9.50

Ignacio Agramonte

KM#	Date	Mintage	Fine	VF	XF	Unc
187	1977	3,000	—	—	—	9.50

Maximo Gomez

KM#	Date	Mintage	Fine	VF	XF	Unc
188	1977	3,000	—	—	—	9.50

Antonio Maceo

KM#	Date	Mintage	Fine	VF	XF	Unc
189	1977	3,000	—	—	—	9.50

60th Anniversary of Socialist Revolution - Lenin

KM#	Date	Mintage	Fine	VF	XF	Unc
190	1977	6,000	—	—	—	8.00

Nonaligned Nations Conference

KM#	Date	Mintage	Fine	VF	XF	Unc
191	1979	3,000	—	—	—	9.50

Cuban Flower - Mariposa

KM#	Date	Mintage	Fine	VF	XF	Unc
46	1980	3,000	—	—	—	9.50

Olympics - Athletes in Frames

KM#	Date	Mintage	Fine	VF	XF	Unc
192	1980	3,000	—	—	—	10.00

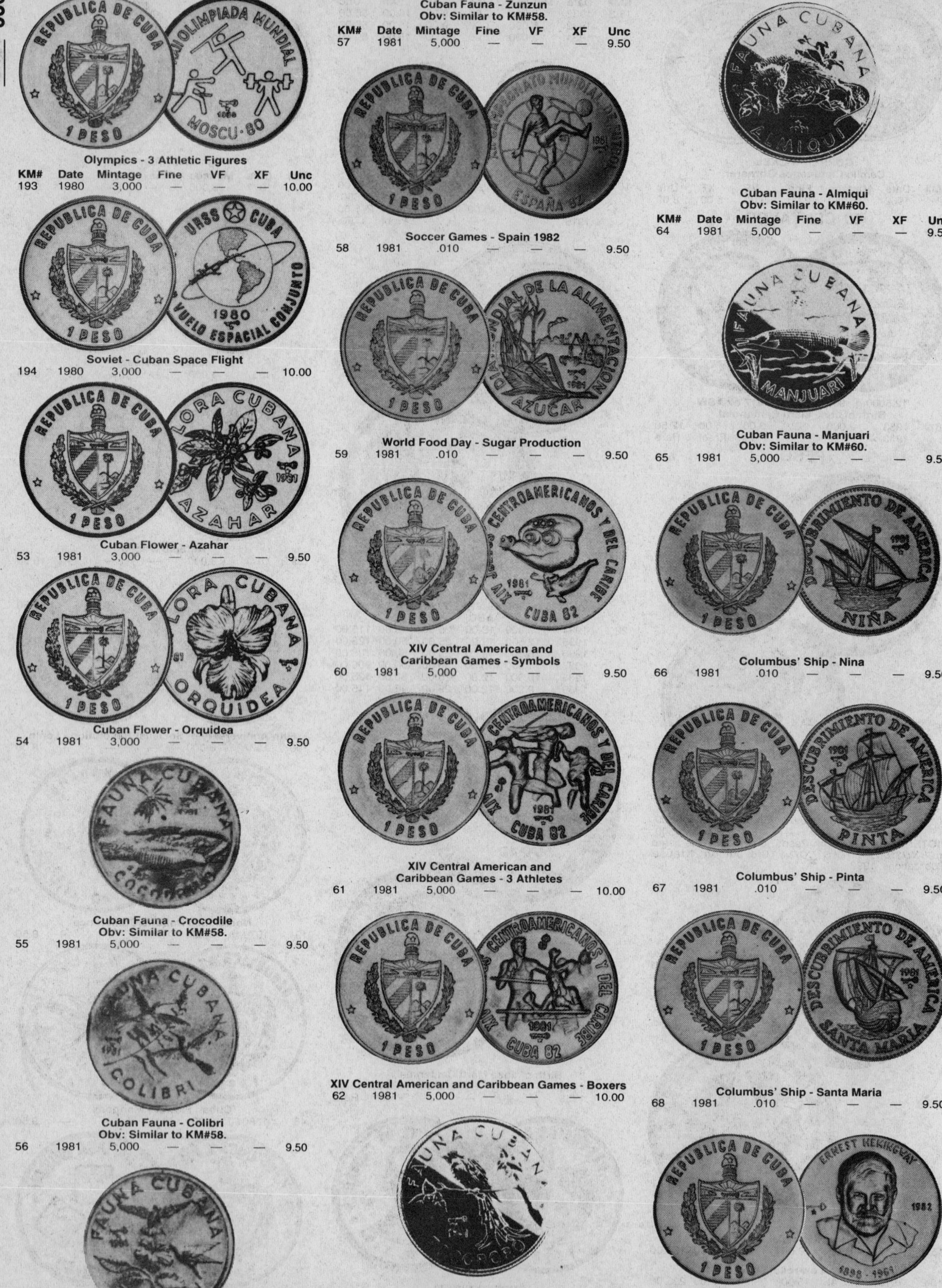

Olympics - 3 Athletic Figures

KM#	Date	Mintage	Fine	VF	XF	Unc
193	1980	3,000	—	—	—	10.00

Soviet - Cuban Space Flight

194	1980	3,000	—	—	—	10.00

Cuban Flower - Azahar

53	1981	3,000	—	—	—	9.50

Cuban Flower - Orquidea

54	1981	3,000	—	—	—	9.50

Cuban Fauna - Crocodile
Obv: Similar to KM#58.

55	1981	5,000	—	—	—	9.50

Cuban Fauna - Colibri
Obv: Similar to KM#58.

56	1981	5,000	—	—	—	9.50

Cuban Fauna - Zunzun
Obv: Similar to KM#58.

KM#	Date	Mintage	Fine	VF	XF	Unc
57	1981	5,000	—	—	—	9.50

Soccer Games - Spain 1982

58	1981	.010	—	—	—	9.50

World Food Day - Sugar Production

59	1981	.010	—	—	—	9.50

XIV Central American and
Caribbean Games - Symbols

60	1981	5,000	—	—	—	9.50

XIV Central American and
Caribbean Games - 3 Athletes

61	1981	5,000	—	—	—	10.00

XIV Central American and Caribbean Games - Boxers

62	1981	5,000	—	—	—	10.00

Cuban Fauna - Tocororo
Obv: Similar to KM#60.

63	1981	5,000	—	—	—	9.50

Cuban Fauna - Almiqui
Obv: Similar to KM#60.

KM#	Date	Mintage	Fine	VF	XF	Unc
64	1981	5,000	—	—	—	9.50

Cuban Fauna - Manjuari
Obv: Similar to KM#60.

65	1981	5,000	—	—	—	9.50

Columbus' Ship - Nina

66	1981	.010	—	—	—	9.50

Columbus' Ship - Pinta

67	1981	.010	—	—	—	9.50

Columbus' Ship - Santa Maria

68	1981	.010	—	—	—	9.50

Ernest Hemingway - Portrait

88	1982	7,000	—	—	—	9.50

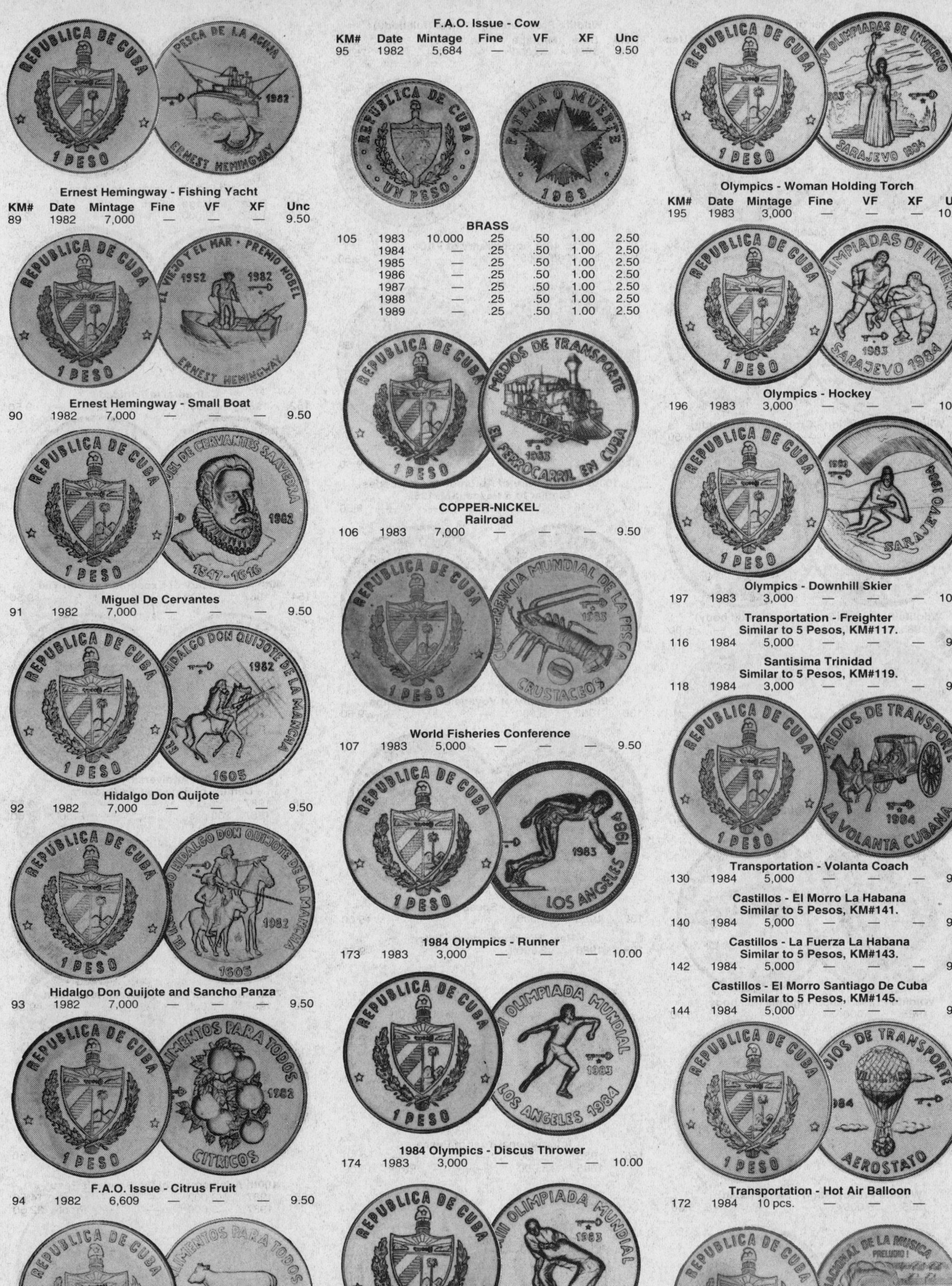

Ernest Hemingway - Fishing Yacht

KM#	Date	Mintage	Fine	VF	XF	Unc
89	1982	7,000	—	—	—	9.50

Ernest Hemingway - Small Boat

KM#	Date	Mintage	Fine	VF	XF	Unc
90	1982	7,000	—	—	—	9.50

Miguel De Cervantes

KM#	Date	Mintage	Fine	VF	XF	Unc
91	1982	7,000	—	—	—	9.50

Hidalgo Don Quijote

KM#	Date	Mintage	Fine	VF	XF	Unc
92	1982	7,000	—	—	—	9.50

Hidalgo Don Quijote and Sancho Panza

KM#	Date	Mintage	Fine	VF	XF	Unc
93	1982	7,000	—	—	—	9.50

F.A.O. Issue - Citrus Fruit

KM#	Date	Mintage	Fine	VF	XF	Unc
94	1982	6,609	—	—	—	9.50

F.A.O. Issue - Cow

KM#	Date	Mintage	Fine	VF	XF	Unc
95	1982	5,684	—	—	—	9.50

BRASS

KM#	Date	Mintage	Fine	VF	XF	Unc
105	1983	10.000	.25	.50	1.00	2.50
	1984	—	.25	.50	1.00	2.50
	1985	—	.25	.50	1.00	2.50
	1986	—	.25	.50	1.00	2.50
	1987	—	.25	.50	1.00	2.50
	1988	—	.25	.50	1.00	2.50
	1989	—	.25	.50	1.00	2.50

COPPER-NICKEL

Railroad

KM#	Date	Mintage	Fine	VF	XF	Unc
106	1983	7,000	—	—	—	9.50

World Fisheries Conference

KM#	Date	Mintage	Fine	VF	XF	Unc
107	1983	5,000	—	—	—	9.50

1984 Olympics - Runner

KM#	Date	Mintage	Fine	VF	XF	Unc
173	1983	3,000	—	—	—	10.00

1984 Olympics - Discus Thrower

KM#	Date	Mintage	Fine	VF	XF	Unc
174	1983	3,000	—	—	—	10.00

1984 Olympics - Judo

KM#	Date	Mintage	Fine	VF	XF	Unc
175	1983	3,000	—	—	—	10.00

Olympics - Woman Holding Torch

KM#	Date	Mintage	Fine	VF	XF	Unc
195	1983	3,000	—	—	—	10.00

Olympics - Hockey

KM#	Date	Mintage	Fine	VF	XF	Unc
196	1983	3,000	—	—	—	10.00

Olympics - Downhill Skier

KM#	Date	Mintage	Fine	VF	XF	Unc
197	1983	3,000	—	—	—	10.00

Transportation - Freighter
Similar to 5 Pesos, KM#117.

KM#	Date	Mintage	Fine	VF	XF	Unc
116	1984	5,000	—	—	—	9.50

Santisima Trinidad
Similar to 5 Pesos, KM#119.

KM#	Date	Mintage	Fine	VF	XF	Unc
118	1984	3,000	—	—	—	9.50

Transportation - Volanta Coach

KM#	Date	Mintage	Fine	VF	XF	Unc
130	1984	5,000	—	—	—	9.50

Castillos - El Morro La Habana
Similar to 5 Pesos, KM#141.

KM#	Date	Mintage	Fine	VF	XF	Unc
140	1984	5,000	—	—	—	9.50

Castillos - La Fuerza La Habana
Similar to 5 Pesos, KM#143.

KM#	Date	Mintage	Fine	VF	XF	Unc
142	1984	5,000	—	—	—	9.50

Castillos - El Morro Santiago De Cuba
Similar to 5 Pesos, KM#145.

KM#	Date	Mintage	Fine	VF	XF	Unc
144	1984	5,000	—	—	—	9.50

Transportation - Hot Air Balloon

KM#	Date	Mintage	Fine	VF	XF	Unc
172	1984	10 pcs.	—	—	—	—

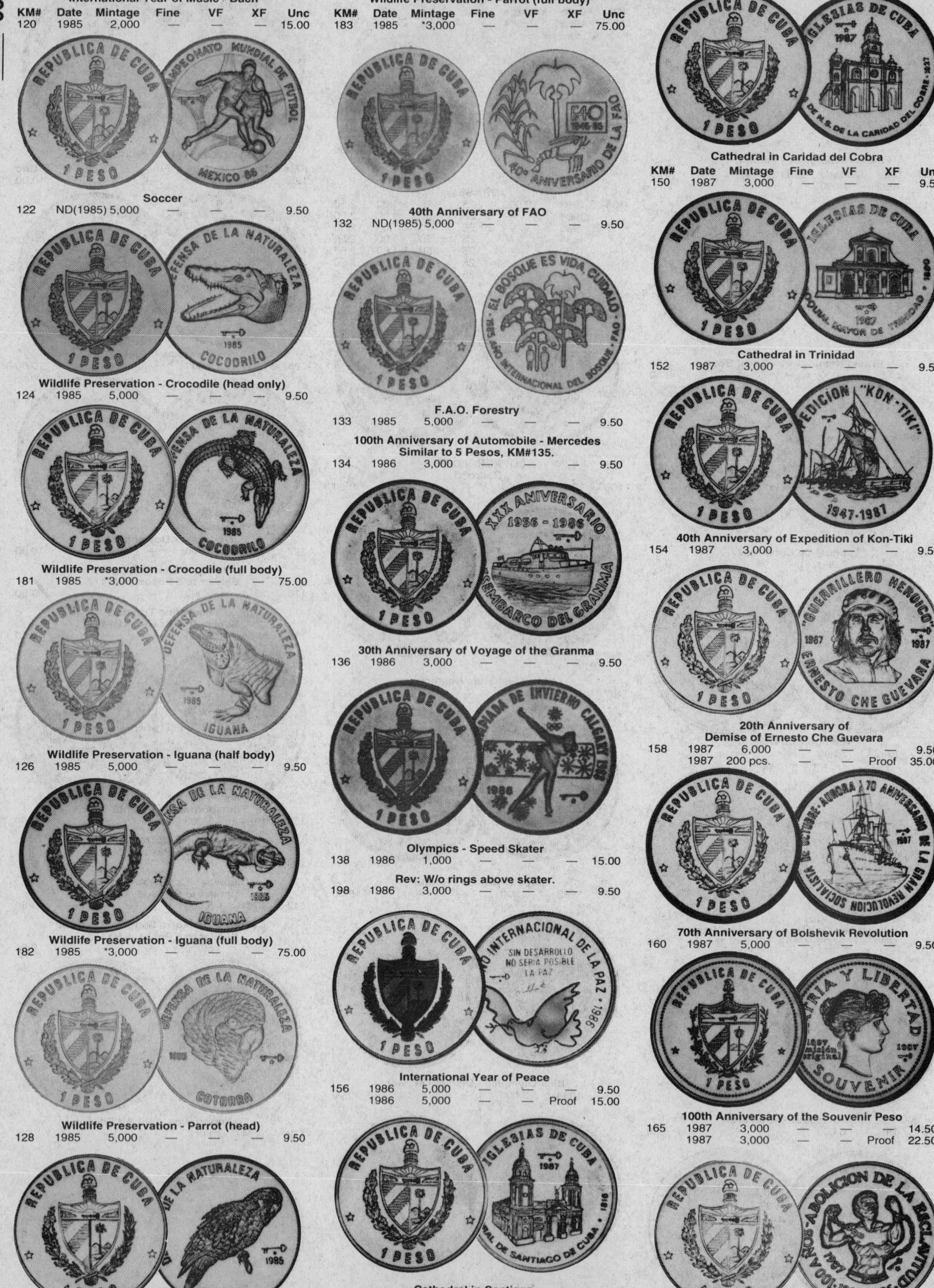

International Year of Music - Bach

KM#	Date	Mintage	Fine	VF	XF	Unc
120	1985	2,000	—	—	—	15.00

Soccer

KM#	Date	Mintage	Fine	VF	XF	Unc
122	ND(1985)	5,000	—	—	—	9.50

Wildlife Preservation - Crocodile (head only)

KM#	Date	Mintage	Fine	VF	XF	Unc
124	1985	5,000	—	—	—	9.50

Wildlife Preservation - Crocodile (full body)

KM#	Date	Mintage	Fine	VF	XF	Unc
181	1985	*3,000	—	—	—	75.00

Wildlife Preservation - Iguana (half body)

KM#	Date	Mintage	Fine	VF	XF	Unc
126	1985	5,000	—	—	—	9.50

Wildlife Preservation - Iguana (full body)

KM#	Date	Mintage	Fine	VF	XF	Unc
182	1985	*3,000	—	—	—	75.00

Wildlife Preservation - Parrot (head)

KM#	Date	Mintage	Fine	VF	XF	Unc
128	1985	5,000	—	—	—	9.50

Wildlife Preservation - Parrot (full body)

KM#	Date	Mintage	Fine	VF	XF	Unc
183	1985	*3,000	—	—	—	75.00

40th Anniversary of FAO

KM#	Date	Mintage	Fine	VF	XF	Unc
132	ND(1985)	5,000	—	—	—	9.50

F.A.O. Forestry

KM#	Date	Mintage	Fine	VF	XF	Unc
133	1985	5,000	—	—	—	9.50

100th Anniversary of Automobile - Mercedes
Similar to 5 Pesos, KM#135.

KM#	Date	Mintage	Fine	VF	XF	Unc
134	1986	3,000	—	—	—	9.50

30th Anniversary of Voyage of the Granma

KM#	Date	Mintage	Fine	VF	XF	Unc
136	1986	3,000	—	—	—	9.50

Olympics - Speed Skater

KM#	Date	Mintage	Fine	VF	XF	Unc
138	1986	1,000	—	—	—	15.00

Rev: W/o rings above skater.

KM#	Date	Mintage	Fine	VF	XF	Unc
198	1986	3,000	—	—	—	9.50

International Year of Peace

KM#	Date	Mintage	Fine	VF	XF	Unc
156	1986	5,000	—	—	—	9.50
	1986	5,000	—	—	Proof	15.00

Cathedral in Santiago

KM#	Date	Mintage	Fine	VF	XF	Unc
148	1987	3,000	—	—	—	9.50

Cathedral in Caridad del Cobra

KM#	Date	Mintage	Fine	VF	XF	Unc
150	1987	3,000	—	—	—	9.50

Cathedral in Trinidad

KM#	Date	Mintage	Fine	VF	XF	Unc
152	1987	3,000	—	—	—	9.50

40th Anniversary of Expedition of Kon-Tiki

KM#	Date	Mintage	Fine	VF	XF	Unc
154	1987	3,000	—	—	—	9.50

20th Anniversary of
Demise of Ernesto Che Guevara

KM#	Date	Mintage	Fine	VF	XF	Unc
158	1987	6,000	—	—	—	9.50
	1987	200 pcs.	—	—	Proof	35.00

70th Anniversary of Bolshevik Revolution

KM#	Date	Mintage	Fine	VF	XF	Unc
160	1987	5,000	—	—	—	9.50

100th Anniversary of the Souvenir Peso

KM#	Date	Mintage	Fine	VF	XF	Unc
165	1987	3,000	—	—	—	14.50
	1987	3,000	—	—	Proof	22.50

KM#	Date	Mintage	Fine	VF	XF	Unc
100th Anniversary of Abolition of Slavery						
167	1987	2,000	—	—	—	16.50
Jose Capablanca Chess Centennial - Player						
179	1988	1,000	—	—	—	17.50
Soccer - 1986 Mexico						
184	1988	—	—	—	—	14.50
Jose Capablanca Chess Centennial - Chess Pieces						
200	1988	6,000	—	—	—	14.50
Soccer - Italy 1990						
244	1988	2,000	—	—	—	14.50
Soccer - West Germany - 3 Players						
245	1988	2,000	—	—	—	14.50
Soccer - West Germany - 4 Players						
246	1988	2,000	—	—	—	14.50

KM#	Date	Mintage	Fine	VF	XF	Unc
40th Anniversary of Cuban National Ballet						
276	1988	2,000	—	—	—	14.50
150th Anniversary of Havana Grand Theater						
277	1988	2,000	—	—	—	14.50
Carlos J. Finlay						
282	1988	2,000	—	—	—	14.50
World Health Organization						
258	1988	2,000	—	—	—	14.50
Transportation - Zeppelin						
269	1988	1,000	—	—	—	16.50
Assault of the Moncada Garrison						
324	1988	2,000	—	—	—	14.50
BRASS						
Jose Marti						
363	1988	—	—	—	—	14.50

COPPER-NICKEL

KM#	Date	Mintage	Fine	VF	XF	Unc
Soccer - Italy - 3 Players						
247	1989	2,000	—	—	—	14.50
Soccer - Italy - Colosseum						
248	1989	2,000	—	—	—	14.50
30th Anniversary of Revolution - Castro						
253	1989	5,000	—	—	—	14.50
30th Anniversary of Revolution - Jose Marti and Castro						
254	1989	5,000	—	—	—	14.50
30th Anniversary of Revolution - Cienfuegos and Castro						
255	1989	5,000	—	—	—	14.50
Triumph of the Revolution						
257	1989	2,000	—	—	—	14.50
Cuban Tobacco						
259	1989	1,000	—	—	—	14.50

160th Anniversary of First Railroad in England

KM#	Date	Mintage	Fine	VF	XF	Unc
260	1989	2,000	—	—	—	14.50

500th Anniversary of Discovery of America

KM#	Date	Mintage	Fine	VF	XF	Unc
261	1989	3,145	—	—	—	14.50

30th Anniversary of the March to Victory

KM#	Date	Mintage	Fine	VF	XF	Unc
270	1989	2,000	—	—	—	14.50

200th Anniversary of French Revolution - Woman

KM#	Date	Mintage	Fine	VF	XF	Unc
271	1989	2,000	—	—	—	14.50

200th Anniversary of French Revolution - Bastille

KM#	Date	Mintage	Fine	VF	XF	Unc
272	1989	2,000	—	—	—	14.50

First Spanish Railroad

KM#	Date	Mintage	Fine	VF	XF	Unc
274	1989	2,000	—	—	—	14.50

First Cuban Railroad

KM#	Date	Mintage	Fine	VF	XF	Unc
275	1989	2,000	—	—	—	14.50

5th Centennial of Discovery of America

KM#	Date	Mintage	Fine	VF	XF	Unc
278	1989	2,000	—	—	—	14.50

Alexander von Humboldt

KM#	Date	Mintage	Fine	VF	XF	Unc
283	1989	2,000	—	—	—	14.50

1992 Olympics - Boxing

KM#	Date	Mintage	Fine	VF	XF	Unc
284	1989	1,000	—	—	—	17.50

Camilo Cienfuegos

KM#	Date	Mintage	Fine	VF	XF	Unc
285	1989	2,000	—	—	—	14.50

Ernesto Che Guevara

KM#	Date	Mintage	Fine	VF	XF	Unc
286	1989	2,000	—	—	—	14.50

Tania La Guerrillera

KM#	Date	Mintage	Fine	VF	XF	Unc
287	1989	2,000	—	—	—	14.50

Columbus Meeting Natives

KM#	Date	Mintage	Fine	VF	XF	Unc
288	1989	2,000	—	—	—	14.50

Esperanto

KM#	Date	Mintage	Fine	VF	XF	Unc
250	1990	6,000	—	—	—	14.50

Discovery of America - Columbus Departing From Spain

KM#	Date	Mintage	Fine	VF	XF	Unc
273	1990	.012	—	—	—	12.50

5th Centennial of Columbus' Arrival in Cuba

KM#	Date	Mintage	Fine	VF	XF	Unc
279	1990	2,000	—	—	—	14.50

Soccer

KM#	Date	Mintage	Fine	VF	XF	Unc
289	1990	—	—	—	—	14.50

500th Anniversary of Discovery of America King Ferdinand of Spain

KM#	Date	Mintage	Fine	VF	XF	Unc
306	1990	3,000	—	—	—	10.00

500th Anniversary of Discovery of America Queen Isabella of Spain

KM#	Date	Mintage	Fine	VF	XF	Unc
307	1990	3,000	—	—	—	10.00

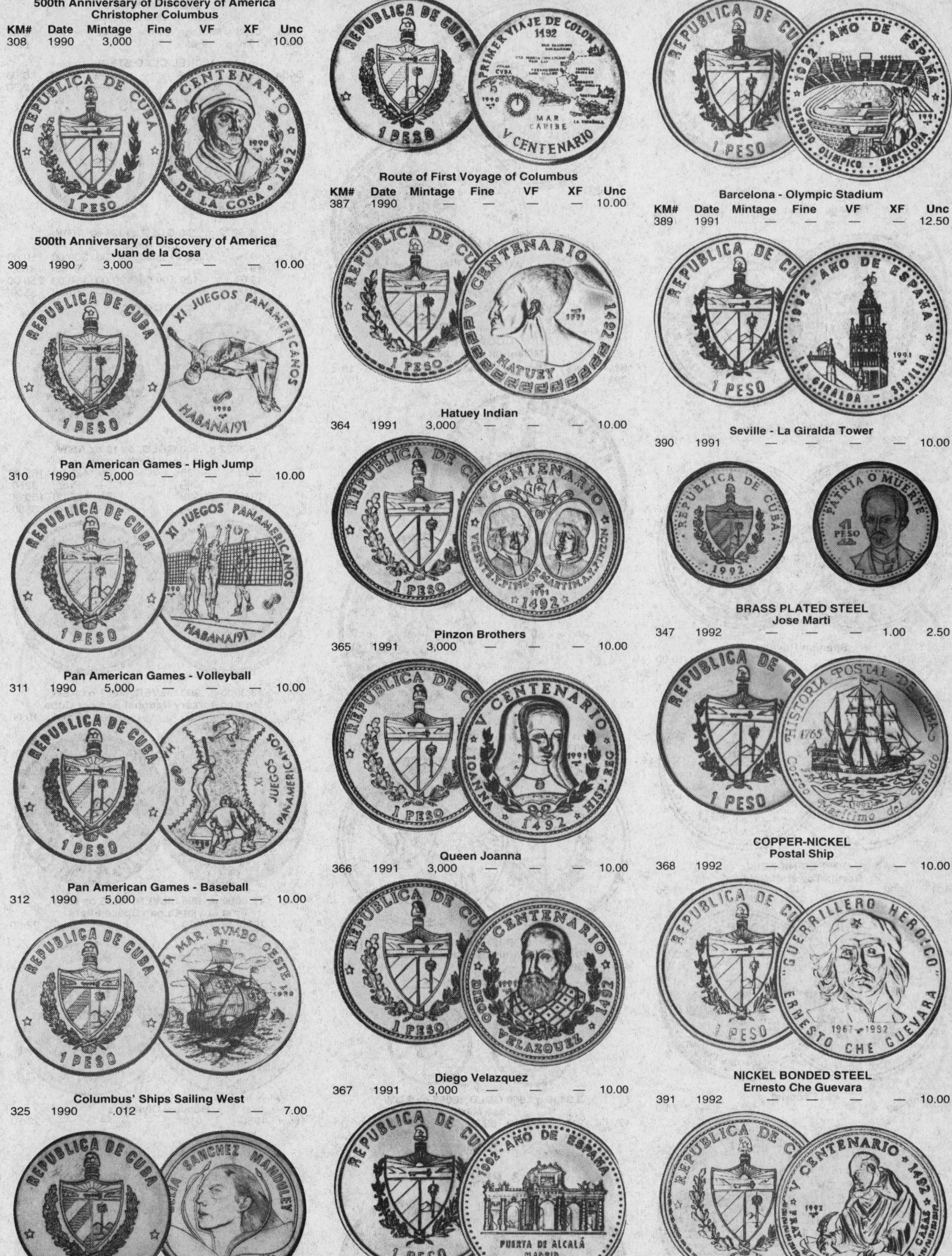

500th Anniversary of Discovery of America
Christopher Columbus

KM#	Date	Mintage	Fine	VF	XF	Unc
308	1990	3,000	—	—	—	10.00

500th Anniversary of Discovery of America
Juan de la Cosa

KM#	Date	Mintage	Fine	VF	XF	Unc
309	1990	3,000	—	—	—	10.00

Pan American Games - High Jump

KM#	Date	Mintage	Fine	VF	XF	Unc
310	1990	5,000	—	—	—	10.00

Pan American Games - Volleyball

KM#	Date	Mintage	Fine	VF	XF	Unc
311	1990	5,000	—	—	—	10.00

Pan American Games - Baseball

KM#	Date	Mintage	Fine	VF	XF	Unc
312	1990	5,000	—	—	—	10.00

Columbus' Ships Sailing West

KM#	Date	Mintage	Fine	VF	XF	Unc
325	1990	.012	—		—	7.00

Celia S. Manduley

KM#	Date	Mintage	Fine	VF	XF	Unc
340	1990	—	—	—		8.00

Route of First Voyage of Columbus

KM#	Date	Mintage	Fine	VF	XF	Unc
387	1990	—	—	—	—	10.00

Hatuey Indian

KM#	Date	Mintage	Fine	VF	XF	Unc
364	1991	3,000	—	—	—	10.00

Pinzon Brothers

KM#	Date	Mintage	Fine	VF	XF	Unc
365	1991	3,000	—	—	—	10.00

Queen Joanna

KM#	Date	Mintage	Fine	VF	XF	Unc
366	1991	3,000	—	—	—	10.00

Diego Velazquez

KM#	Date	Mintage	Fine	VF	XF	Unc
367	1991	3,000	—	—	—	10.00

NICKEL BONDED STEEL
Madrid - Alcala Gate

KM#	Date	Mintage	Fine	VF	XF	Unc
388	1991	—	—	—	—	10.00

Barcelona - Olympic Stadium

KM#	Date	Mintage	Fine	VF	XF	Unc
389	1991	—	—	—	—	12.50

Seville - La Giralda Tower

KM#	Date	Mintage	Fine	VF	XF	Unc
390	1991	—	—	—	—	10.00

BRASS PLATED STEEL
Jose Marti

KM#	Date	Mintage	Fine	VF	XF	Unc
347	1992	—	—	—	1.00	2.50

COPPER-NICKEL
Postal Ship

KM#	Date	Mintage	Fine	VF	XF	Unc
368	1992	—	—	—	—	10.00

NICKEL BONDED STEEL
Ernesto Che Guevara

KM#	Date	Mintage	Fine	VF	XF	Unc
391	1992	—	—	—	—	10.00

Bartolome de Las Casas

KM#	Date	Mintage	Fine	VF	XF	Unc
392	1992	—	—	—	—	10.00

Chief Guama

KM#	Date	Mintage	Fine	VF	XF	Unc
393	1992	—	—	—	—	10.00

King Philipp of Spain

KM#	Date	Mintage	Fine	VF	XF	Unc
394	1992	—	—	—	—	10.00

Spanish Royalty

KM#	Date	Mintage	Fine	VF	XF	Unc
395	ND(1992)	—	—	—	—	10.00

COPPER-NICKEL
Seville Tower of Gold

KM#	Date	Mintage	Fine	VF	XF	Unc
401	1992	—	—	—	—	7.50

El Escorial

KM#	Date	Mintage	Fine	VF	XF	Unc
402	1992	—	—	—	—	7.50

St. Jorge Palace

KM#	Date	Mintage	Fine	VF	XF	Unc
403	1992	—	—	—	—	7.50

COPPER
Millenium of St. Jacobi

KM#	Date	Mintage	Fine	VF	XF	Unc
396	1993	—	—	—	—	10.00

40th Anniversary - Fidel Castro as leader

KM#	Date	Mintage	Fine	VF	XF	Unc
397	1993	—	—	—	—	10.00

COPPER-NICKEL
Prehistoric Animals - Chalicotherium

KM#	Date	Mintage	Fine	VF	XF	Unc
404	1993	—	—	—	—	7.50

2 PESOS

3.3436 g, .900 GOLD, .0967 oz AGW
Jose Marti

KM#	Date	Mintage	Fine	VF	XF	Unc
17	1915	.010	65.00	85.00	115.00	200.00
	1915	—	—	—	Proof	2250.
	1916	.150	60.00	70.00	85.00	120.00
	1916	—	—	—	Proof	2500.

3 PESOS

COPPER-NICKEL
Ernesto Che Guevara

KM#	Date	Mintage	Fine	VF	XF	Unc
346	1990	4.050	—	—	3.00	6.00

NICKEL CLAD STEEL

KM#	Date	Mintage	Fine	VF	XF	Unc
346a	1992	—	—	—	3.00	6.00
	1992	500 pcs.	—	—	Proof	12.50

4 PESOS

6.6872 g, .900 GOLD, .1935 oz AGW
Jose Marti

KM#	Date	Mintage	Fine	VF	XF	Unc
18	1915	6,300	125.00	175.00	300.00	750.00
	1915	—	—	—	Proof	3250.
	1916	.129	100.00	120.00	150.00	250.00
	1916	—	—	—	Proof	3500.

5 PESOS

8.3592 g, .900 GOLD, .2419 oz AGW
Jose Marti

KM#	Date	Mintage	Fine	VF	XF	Unc
19	1915	.696	—	BV	125.00	165.00
	1915	—	—	—	Proof	3250.
	1916	1.132	—	BV	125.00	150.00
	1916	—	—	—	Proof	3500.

13.3300 g, .900 SILVER, .3857 oz ASW
25th Anniversary National Bank of Cuba

KM#	Date	Mintage	Fine	VF	XF	Unc
36	1975	.050	—	—	Proof	10.00

12.0000 g, .999 SILVER, .3855 oz ASW
First Soviet-Cuban Space Flight

KM#	Date	Mintage	Fine	VF	XF	Unc
47	1980	.010	—	—	—	22.50

Moscow Olympics

KM#	Date	Mintage	Fine	VF	XF	Unc
48	1980	.010	—	—	—	22.50

Cuban Flower - Mariposa

KM#	Date	Mintage	Fine	VF	XF	Unc
49	1980	.010	—	—	—	20.00
	1980	3,000	—	—	Proof	30.00

Cuban Flower - Azahar

KM#	Date	Mintage	Fine	VF	XF	Unc
69	1981	.010	—	—	—	20.00
	1981	3,000	—	—	Proof	30.00

Cuban Flower - Orquidea

KM#	Date	Mintage	Fine	VF	XF	Unc
70	1981	.010	—	—	—	20.00
	1981	3,000	—	—	Proof	30.00

Columbus' Ship - Nina

KM#	Date	Mintage	Fine	VF	XF	Unc
71	1981	.010	—	—	—	22.50
	1981	1,000	—	—	Proof	37.50

Columbus' Ship - Pinta

KM#	Date	Mintage	Fine	VF	XF	Unc
72	1981	.010	—	—	—	22.50
	1981	1,000	—	—	Proof	37.50

Columbus' Ship - Santa Maria

KM#	Date	Mintage	Fine	VF	XF	Unc
73	1981	.010	—	—	—	22.50
	1981	1,000	—	—	Proof	37.50

Cuban Fauna - Crocodile

KM#	Date	Mintage	Fine	VF	XF	Unc
74	1981	5,000	—	—	—	22.50
	1981	1,000	—	—	Proof	32.50

Cuban Fauna - Colibri

KM#	Date	Mintage	Fine	VF	XF	Unc
75	1981	5,000	—	—	—	22.50
	1981	1,000	—	—	Proof	32.50

Cuban Fauna - Zunzun

KM#	Date	Mintage	Fine	VF	XF	Unc
76	1981	5,000	—	—	—	22.50
	1981	1,000	—	—	Proof	32.50

Soccer Games - Spain 1982

KM#	Date	Mintage	Fine	VF	XF	Unc
77	1981	4,000	—	—	Proof	22.50

World Food Day - Sugar Production

KM#	Date	Mintage	Fine	VF	XF	Unc
78	1981	7,000	—	—	—	22.50
	1981	1,560	—	—	Proof	30.00

XIV Central American and Caribbean Games - Symbols

KM#	Date	Mintage	Fine	VF	XF	Unc
79	1981	5,000	—	—	—	22.50
	1981	2,000	—	—	Proof	30.00

XIV Central American and Caribbean Games - 3 Athletes

KM#	Date	Mintage	Fine	VF	XF	Unc
80	1981	5,000	—	—	—	25.00
	1981	2,000	—	—	Proof	35.00

XIV Central American and Caribbean Games - Boxers

KM#	Date	Mintage	Fine	VF	XF	Unc
81	1981	5,000	—	—	—	25.00
	1981	2,000	—	—	Proof	35.00

Cuban Fauna - Tocororo
Obv: Similar to KM#81.
Rev: Similar to 1 Peso, KM#63.

KM#	Date	Mintage	Fine	VF	XF	Unc
82	1981	5,000	—	—	—	22.50
	1981	1,000	—	—	Proof	32.50

Cuban Fauna - Almiqui
Obv: Similar to KM#81.
Rev: Similar to 1 Peso, KM#64.

KM#	Date	Mintage	Fine	VF	XF	Unc
83	1981	5,000	—	—	—	22.50
	1981	1,000	—	—	Proof	32.50

Cuban Fauna - Manjuari
Obv: Similar to KM#81.
Rev: Similar to 1 Peso, KM#65.

KM#	Date	Mintage	Fine	VF	XF	Unc
84	1981	5,000	—	—	—	22.50
	1981	1,000	—	—	Proof	32.50

Ernest Hemingway - Portrait

KM#	Date	Mintage	Fine	VF	XF	Unc
96	1982	5,000	—	—	—	22.50
	1982	1,000	—	—	Proof	32.50

Ernest Hemingway - Fishing Yacht

KM#	Date	Mintage	Fine	VF	XF	Unc
97	1982	5,000	—	—	—	22.50
	1982	1,000	—	—	Proof	32.50

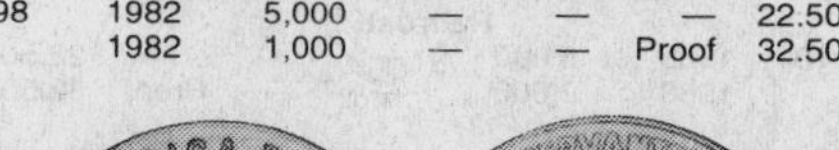

Ernest Hemingway - Small Boat

KM#	Date	Mintage	Fine	VF	XF	Unc
98	1982	5,000	—	—	—	22.50
	1982	1,000	—	—	Proof	32.50

Miguel De Cervantes

KM#	Date	Mintage	Fine	VF	XF	Unc
99	1982	5,000	—	—	—	22.50
	1982	2,000	—	—	Proof	30.00

Hidalgo Don Quijote

KM#	Date	Mintage	Fine	VF	XF	Unc
100	1982	5,000	—	—	—	22.50
	1982	2,000	—	—	Proof	30.00

Hidalgo Don Quijote and Sancho Panza

KM#	Date	Mintage	Fine	VF	XF	Unc
101	1982	5,000	—	—	—	22.50
	1982	2,000	—	—	Proof	30.00

F.A.O. Issue - Citrus Fruit
Similar to 1 Peso, KM#94.

KM#	Date	Mintage	Fine	VF	XF	Unc
102	1982	3,125	—	—	—	22.50
	1982	1,040	—	—	Proof	32.50

F.A.O. Issue - Cow
Similar to 1 Peos, KM#95.

KM#	Date	Mintage	Fine	VF	XF	Unc
103	1982	4,177	—	—	—	22.50
	1982	1,000	—	—	Proof	32.50

1984 Winter Olympics - Hockey
Obv: Similar to KM#99.

KM#	Date	Mintage	Fine	VF	XF	Unc
108	1983	5,000	—	—	Proof	32.50

1984 Summer Olympics - Runner
Obv: Similar to KM#99.

KM#	Date	Mintage	Fine	VF	XF	Unc
109	1983	5,000	—	—	Proof	32.50

Railroad

KM#	Date	Mintage	Fine	VF	XF	Unc
110	1983	5,000	—	—	—	22.50
	1983	2,000	—	—	Proof	32.50

World Fisheries - Saltwater Crayfish

KM#	Date	Mintage	Fine	VF	XF	Unc
111	1983	5,000	—	—	—	22.50
	1983	1,000	—	—	Proof	32.50

Winter Olympics - Woman Holding Torch
Obv: Similar to KM#114.

KM#	Date	Mintage	Fine	VF	XF	Unc
112	1983	5,000	—	—	Proof	32.50

Winter Olympics - Downhill Skier
Obv: Similar to KM#114.

KM#	Date	Mintage	Fine	VF	XF	Unc
113	1983	5,000	—	—	Proof	32.50

Summer Olympics - Discus Thrower

KM#	Date	Mintage	Fine	VF	XF	Unc
114	1983	5,000	—	—	Proof	32.50

Summer Olympics - Judo

KM#	Date	Mintage	Fine	VF	XF	Unc
115	1983	5,000	—	—	Proof	32.50

Transportation - Volanta Coach

KM#	Date	Mintage	Fine	VF	XF	Unc
131	1984	5,000	—	—	—	22.50
	1984	1,000	—	—	Proof	45.00

Transportation - Freighter

KM#	Date	Mintage	Fine	VF	XF	Unc
117	1984	5,000	—	—	—	22.50
	1984	1,000	—	—	Proof	45.00

Santisima Trinidad

KM#	Date	Mintage	Fine	VF	XF	Unc
119	1984	5,000	—	—	—	22.50

Fortress - El Morro La Habana

KM#	Date	Mintage	Fine	VF	XF	Unc
141	1984	5,000	—	—	—	22.50
	1984	1,000	—	—	Proof	45.00

Fortress - La Fuerza La Habana

KM#	Date	Mintage	Fine	VF	XF	Unc
143	1984	5,000	—	—	—	22.50
	1984	1,000	—	—	Proof	45.00

Fortress - El Morro Santiago De Cuba

KM#	Date	Mintage	Fine	VF	XF	Unc
145	1984	5,000	—	—	—	22.50
	1984	1,000	—	—	Proof	45.00

International Year of Music - Bach
Similar to 1 Peso, KM#120.

KM#	Date	Mintage	Fine	VF	XF	Unc
121	1985	2,000	—	—	—	32.50
	1985	—	—	—	Proof	45.00

Soccer
Similar to 1 Peso, KM#122.

KM#	Date	Mintage	Fine	VF	XF	Unc
123	1985	5,000	—	—	—	22.50
	1985	—	—	—	Proof	30.00

Wildlife Preservation - Crocodile

KM#	Date	Mintage	Fine	VF	XF	Unc
125	1985	5,000	—	—	—	22.50

Wildlife Preservation - Iquana

KM#	Date	Mintage	Fine	VF	XF	Unc
127	1985	5,000	—	—	—	22.50

Wildlife Preservation - Parrot

KM#	Date	Mintage	Fine	VF	XF	Unc
129	1985	5,000	—	—	—	22.50

40th Anniversary of FAO
Obv: Similar to KM#129.
Rev: Lobster, palm tree & sugar cane.

KM#	Date	Mintage	Fine	VF	XF	Unc
146	ND(1985)	—	—	—	—	22.50

FAO Issue - Forestry
Obv: Similar to KM#129. Rev: Stylized forest.

KM#	Date	Mintage	Fine	VF	XF	Unc
147	ND(1985)	4,500	—	—	—	22.50
	ND(1985)	500 pcs.	—	—	Proof	50.00

100th Anniversary of the Automobile

KM#	Date	Mintage	Fine	VF	XF	Unc
135	1986	2,500	—	—	—	22.50

30th Anniversary of Voyage of the Granma

KM#	Date	Mintage	Fine	VF	XF	Unc
137	1986	2,500	—	—	—	22.50

Olympics - Skater

KM#	Date	Mintage	Fine	VF	XF	Unc
139	1986	2,500	—	—	—	32.50

Olympics - Skater
Rev: W/o rings above skater.

KM#	Date	Mintage	Fine	VF	XF	Unc
199	1986	.010	—	—	—	22.50

International Year of Peace

KM#	Date	Mintage	Fine	VF	XF	Unc
157	1986	.010	—	—	—	22.50
	1986	2,000	—	—	Proof	32.50

Cathedral in Santiago

KM#	Date	Mintage	Fine	VF	XF	Unc
149	1987	2,500	—	—	—	25.00

Cathedral in Caridad del Cobre

KM#	Date	Mintage	Fine	VF	XF	Unc
151	1987	2,500	—	—	—	25.00

Cathedral in Trinidad

KM#	Date	Mintage	Fine	VF	XF	Unc
153	1987	2,500	—	—	—	25.00

40th Anniversary of Expedition of Kon-Tiki

KM#	Date	Mintage	Fine	VF	XF	Unc
155	1987	5,000	—	—	—	22.50

20th Anniversary of Demise of Ernesto Che Guevara

KM#	Date	Mintage	Fine	VF	XF	Unc
159	1987	5,000	—	—	—	22.50
	1987	200 pcs.	—	—	Proof	30.00

70th Anniversary of Bolshevik Revolution

KM#	Date	Mintage	Fine	VF	XF	Unc
161	1987	3,000	—	—	—	25.00
	1987	1,000	—	—	Proof	45.00

100th Anniversary of Souvenir Peso

KM#	Date	Mintage	Fine	VF	XF	Unc
166	1987	3,000	—	—	—	25.00

12.0000 g, .999 SILVER, .3855 oz ASW
Abolition of Slavery

KM#	Date	Mintage	Fine	VF	XF	Unc
326	1987	2,000	—	—	—	32.50

12.0000 g, .999 SILVER, .3855 oz ASW
Jose Capablanca Chess Championship - Player

KM#	Date	Mintage	Fine	VF	XF	Unc
180	1988	5,000	—	—	—	22.50

Soccer - Mexico 1986

KM#	Date	Mintage	Fine	VF	XF	Unc
185	1988	5,000	—	—	—	20.00
	1988	—	—	—	Proof	30.00

6.0000 g, .999 SILVER, .1927 oz ASW
Soccer - Italy 1990

KM#	Date	Mintage	Fine	VF	XF	Unc
216	1988	—	—	—	—	17.50

12.0000 g, .999 SILVER, .3855 oz ASW

KM#	Date	Mintage	Fine	VF	XF	Unc
216a	1988	5,000	—	—	—	20.00

Soccer - West Germany - 3 Players

KM#	Date	Mintage	Fine	VF	XF	Unc
217	1988	5,000	—	—	—	20.00

Soccer - West Germany - 4 Players

KM#	Date	Mintage	Fine	VF	XF	Unc
218	1988	5,000	—	—	—	20.00

16.0000 g, .999 SILVER, .5145 oz ASW
40th Anniversary of Cuban National Ballet

KM#	Date	Mintage	Fine	VF	XF	Unc
219	1988	2,000	—	—	Proof	45.00

Graf Zeppelin

KM#	Date	Mintage	Fine	VF	XF	Unc
220	1988	3,000	—	—	Proof	45.00

Carlos J. Finlay

KM#	Date	Mintage	Fine	VF	XF	Unc
221	1988	2,000	—	—	Proof	45.00

World Health Organization

KM#	Date	Mintage	Fine	VF	XF	Unc
222	1988	2,000	—	—	Proof	45.00

150th Anniversary of Grand Theater in Havana

KM#	Date	Mintage	Fine	VF	XF	Unc
223	1988	2,000	—	—	Proof	45.00

Olympics - Barcelona - Boxing

KM#	Date	Mintage	Fine	VF	XF	Unc
224	1989	.010	—	—	Proof	65.00

Soccer - Italy - 3 Players

KM#	Date	Mintage	Fine	VF	XF	Unc
225	1989	—	—	—	Proof	55.00

Soccer - Italy - Colosseum

KM#	Date	Mintage	Fine	VF	XF	Unc
226	1989	—	—	—	Proof	55.00

Cuban Tobacco

KM#	Date	Mintage	Fine	VF	XF	Unc
227	1989	—	—	—	Proof	50.00

Alexander von Humboldt

KM#	Date	Mintage	Fine	VF	XF	Unc
231	1989	*3,000	—	—	Proof	50.00

Universal Congress of Esperanto

KM#	Date	Mintage	Fine	VF	XF	Unc
251	1990	6,000	—	—	P/L	45.00

Soccer - Map of Italy and Balls

KM#	Date	Mintage	Fine	VF	XF	Unc
290	1990	—	—	—	Proof	55.00

Soccer Championship

KM#	Date	Mintage	Fine	VF	XF	Unc
338	1991	—	—	—	—	55.00

6.0000 g, .999 SILVER, .1927 oz ASW
Prehistoric Animals - Apatosaurus

KM#	Date	Mintage	Fine	VF	XF	Unc
405	1993	—	—	—	Proof	20.00

10 PESOS

16.7185 g, .900 GOLD, .4838 oz AGW
Jose Marti

KM#	Date	Mintage	Fine	VF	XF	Unc
20	1915	.095	—	BV	275.00	350.00
	1915	—	—	—	Proof	7000.
	1916	1.169	—	BV	250.00	300.00
	1916	—	—	—	Proof	14,500.

26.6600 g, .900 SILVER, .7715 oz ASW
25th Anniversary National Bank of Cuba

KM#	Date	Mintage	Fine	VF	XF	Unc
37	1975	.055	—	—	Proof	20.00

18.0000 g, .999 SILVER, .5782 oz ASW
First Soviet-Cuban Space Flight

KM#	Date	Mintage	Fine	VF	XF	Unc
50	1980	.010	—	—	—	30.00

Moscow Olympics

KM#	Date	Mintage	Fine	VF	XF	Unc
51	1980	.010	—	—	—	30.00

31.1000 g, .999 SILVER, 1.0000 oz ASW
Triumph of the Revolution

KM#	Date	Mintage	Fine	VF	XF	Unc
162	1987	2,000	—	—	Proof	45.00
	1988	4,000	—	—	Proof	40.00
	1989	2,000	—	—	Proof	45.00

60th Anniversary of Birth of Ernesto Che Guevara

KM#	Date	Mintage	Fine	VF	XF	Unc
163	1987	2,000	—	—	Proof	45.00
	1988	4,000	—	—	Proof	40.00
	1989	2,000	—	—	Proof	45.00

30th Anniversary of the March to Victory

KM#	Date	Mintage	Fine	VF	XF	Unc
164	1987	2,000	—	—	Proof	45.00
	1988	4,000	—	—	Proof	40.00
	1989	2,000	—	—	Proof	45.00

150th Anniversary of First Train in Spanish America

KM#	Date	Mintage	Fine	VF	XF	Unc
205	1988	5,000	—	—	Proof	45.00

140th Anniversary of First Train in Spain

KM#	Date	Mintage	Fine	VF	XF	Unc
206	1988	5,000	—	—	Proof	45.00

160th Anniversary of First Train in England

KM#	Date	Mintage	Fine	VF	XF	Unc
207	1988	5,000	—	—	Proof	45.00

3.1100 g, .999 GOLD, .1000 oz AGW
Jose Marti

KM#	Date	Mintage	Fine	VF	XF	Unc
211	1988	50 pcs.	—	—	—	75.00
	1988	15 pcs.	—	—	Proof	125.00
	1989	2,250	—	—	—	55.00
	1989	15 pcs.	—	—	Proof	125.00
	1990	15 pcs.	—	—	—	100.00
	1990	12 pcs.	—	—	Proof	125.00

31.1000 g, .999 SILVER, 1.0000 oz ASW
Tania La Guerrillera

KM#	Date	Mintage	Fine	VF	XF	Unc
228	1988	5,000	—	—	Proof	40.00

Camilo Cienfuegos

KM#	Date	Mintage	Fine	VF	XF	Unc
229	1988	5,000	—	—	Proof	40.00

35th Anniversary of the Assault of the Moncada Garrison

KM#	Date	Mintage	Fine	VF	XF	Unc
230	1988	—	—	—	—	40.00
	1988	5,000	—	—	Proof	40.00

20.0000 g, .999 SILVER, .6431 oz ASW
5th Centennial of Discovery of America

KM#	Date	Mintage	Fine	VF	XF	Unc
238	1989	—	—	—	—	47.50

26.7200 g, .999 SILVER, .8592 oz ASW
200th Anniversary of French Revolution - Female

KM#	Date	Mintage	Fine	VF	XF	Unc
239	1989	—	—	—	—	50.00

200th Anniversary of French Revolution - Bastille

KM#	Date	Mintage	Fine	VF	XF	Unc
240	1989	—	—	—	—	50.00

30th Anniversary of Revolution
Rev: Castro standing.

KM#	Date	Mintage	Fine	VF	XF	Unc
241	1989	—	—	—	—	40.00

30th Anniversary of Revolution
Rev: Jose Marti and Castro.

KM#	Date	Mintage	Fine	VF	XF	Unc
242	1989	—	—	—	—	40.00

30th Anniversary of Revolution
Rev: Camilo Cienfuegos and Fidel Castro.

KM#	Date	Mintage	Fine	VF	XF	Unc
243	1989	—	—	—	—	40.00

20.0000 g, .999 SILVER, .6431 oz ASW
Discovery of America - 3 Sailing Ships

KM#	Date	Mintage	Fine	VF	XF	Unc
249	1989	—	—	—	Proof	55.00

Discovery of America - Ship and Cuba

KM#	Date	Mintage	Fine	VF	XF	Unc
252	1990	—	—	—	Proof	55.00

500th Anniversary of Columbus Meeting Indians

KM#	Date	Mintage	Fine	VF	XF	Unc
256	1990	.010	—	—	Proof	40.00

31.1030 g, .999 SILVER, 1.0000 oz ASW
Celia Sanchez Manduley

KM#	Date	Mintage	Fine	VF	XF	Unc
262	1990	2,000	—	—	Proof	55.00

Discovery of America - King Ferdinand

KM#	Date	Mintage	Fine	VF	XF	Unc
263	1990	5,000	—	—	Proof	45.00

Discovery of America - Queen Isabella

KM#	Date	Mintage	Fine	VF	XF	Unc
264	1990	5,000	—	—	Proof	45.00

Discovery of America Christopher Columbus

KM#	Date	Mintage	Fine	VF	XF	Unc
265	1990	5,000	—	—	Proof	45.00

Discovery of America - Juan De La Cosa

KM#	Date	Mintage	Fine	VF	XF	Unc
266	1990	5,000	—	—	Proof	45.00

Discovery of America - Map of Columbus' Route

KM#	Date	Mintage	Fine	VF	XF	Unc
267	1990	5,000	—	—	Proof	45.00

25.0000 g, .999 SILVER, .8037 oz ASW
Simon Bolivar

KM#	Date	Mintage	Fine	VF	XF	Unc
280	1990	3,300	—	—	Proof	50.00

31.1000 g, .999 SILVER, 1.0000 oz ASW
Pan American Games - High Jumper

KM#	Date	Mintage	Fine	VF	XF	Unc
291	1990	3,000	—	—	Proof	55.00

Pan American Games - Volleyball

KM#	Date	Mintage	Fine	VF	XF	Unc
292	1990	3,000	—	—	Proof	55.00

Pan American Games - Baseball

KM#	Date	Mintage	Fine	VF	XF	Unc
293	1990	3,000	—	—	Proof	55.00

28.0000 g, .925 SILVER, .8327 oz ASW
Summer Olympics - Hurdler

KM#	Date	Mintage	Fine	VF	XF	Unc
336	1990	—	—	—	Proof	80.00

Summer Olympics - Volleyball

KM#	Date	Mintage	Fine	VF	XF	Unc
344	1990	—	—	—	Proof	80.00

Summer Olympics - High Jumper

KM#	Date	Mintage	Fine	VF	XF	Unc
345	1990	—	—	—	Proof	95.00

Olympics - Basketball

KM#	Date	Mintage	Fine	VF	XF	Unc
362	1990	—	—	—	Proof	80.00

28.3000 g, .925 SILVER, .8416 oz ASW
Olympics - Pommel Horse

KM#	Date	Mintage	Fine	VF	XF	Unc
369	1990	*.025	—	—	Proof	80.00

3.1100 g, .999 GOLD, .1000 oz AGW
Olympics - Basketball

KM#	Date	Mintage	Fine	VF	XF	Unc
383	1990	—	—	—	Proof	75.00

28.0000 g, .925 SILVER, .8327 oz ASW
Vicente and Martin Pinzon

KM#	Date	Mintage	Fine	VF	XF	Unc
327	1991	—	—	—	Proof	55.00

Hatuey Indians

KM#	Date	Mintage	Fine	VF	XF	Unc
328	1991	—	—	—	Proof	55.00

American International Monetary Conference

KM#	Date	Mintage	Fine	VF	XF	Unc
329	1991	—	—	—	Proof	55.00

27.0000 g, .925 SILVER, .8029 oz ASW
Ibero - American - Columbus at Gardenas

KM#	Date	Mintage	Fine	VF	XF	Unc
337	1991	.051	—	—	Proof	45.00

31.1000 g, .999 SILVER, 1.0000 oz ASW
Madrid - Alcala Gate

KM#	Date	Mintage	Fine	VF	XF	Unc
348	1991	*3,250	—	—	Proof	50.00

Seville - La Giralda Tower

KM#	Date	Mintage	Fine	VF	XF	Unc
349	1991	*3,250	—	—	Proof	50.00

Barcelona - Olympic Stadium

KM#	Date	Mintage	Fine	VF	XF	Unc
350	1991	—	—	—	Proof	60.00

20.0000 g, .999 SILVER, .6430 oz ASW
Cuban Postal History - Spanish Galleon

KM#	Date	Mintage	Fine	VF	XF	Unc
341	1992	—	—	—	Proof	50.00

3.1100 g, .999 GOLD, .1000 oz AGW
Olympics - Basketball

KM#	Date	Mintage	Fine	VF	XF	Unc
342	1992	*5,000	—	—	—	75.00

31.1000 g, .999 SILVER, 1.0000 oz ASW
Seville - Tower of Gold

KM#	Date	Mintage	Fine	VF	XF	Unc
351	1992	—	—	—	Proof	50.00

El Escorial

KM#	Date	Mintage	Fine	VF	XF	Unc
352	1992	—	—	—	Proof	50.00

Philip I

KM#	Date	Mintage	Fine	VF	XF	Unc
353	1992	—	—	—	Proof	50.00

20.0000 g, .999 SILVER, .6430 oz ASW
Ptolomeo and Toscanelli

KM#	Date	Mintage	Fine	VF	XF	Unc
354	1992	—	—	—	Proof	50.00

31.1000 g, .999 SILVER, 1.0000 oz ASW
Chief Guama

KM#	Date	Mintage	Fine	VF	XF	Unc
355	1992	—	—	—	Proof	55.00

19.9600 g, .999 SILVER, .6411 oz ASW
Postal History - Steam Powered Sailing Ship

KM#	Date	Mintage	Fine	VF	XF	Unc
370	1992	*.010	—	—	Proof	47.50

Introduction of Africans Into America

KM#	Date	Mintage	Fine	VF	XF	Unc
371	1992	—	—	—	Proof	47.50

30.9500 g, .999 SILVER, .9941 oz ASW
Bartolome de Las Casas

KM#	Date	Mintage	Fine	VF	XF	Unc
372	1992	*2,050	—	—	Proof	55.00

31.0000 g, .999 SILVER, 1.0000 oz ASW
Spanish Kings and Queens
Obv: Coat of arms.

KM#	Date	Mintage	Fine	VF	XF	Unc
373	ND(1992)	*2,050	—	—	Proof	55.00

San Jorge Palace

KM#	Date	Mintage	Fine	VF	XF	Unc
374	1992	*2,050	—	—	Proof	55.00

19.8500 g, .999 SILVER, .6375 oz ASW
Abraham Lincoln

KM#	Date	Mintage	Fine	VF	XF	Unc
375	1993	—	—	—	Proof	45.00

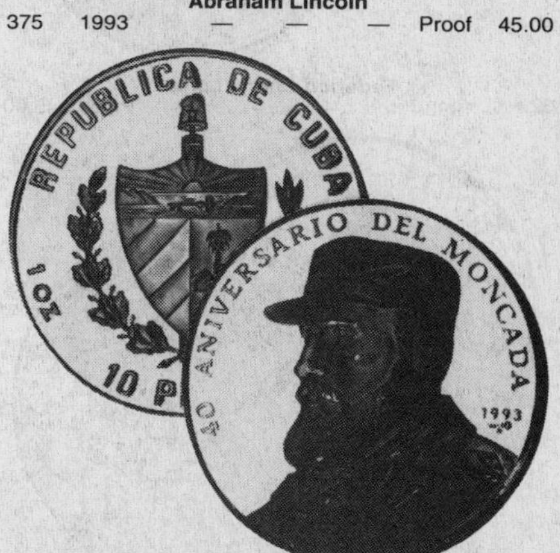

31.1000 g, .999 SILVER, 1.0000 oz ASW
Fidel Castro

KM#	Date	Mintage	Fine	VF	XF	Unc
398	1993	—	—	—	Proof	60.00

St. Jacobi

KM#	Date	Mintage	Fine	VF	XF	Unc
399	1993	—	—	—	Proof	60.00

31.1350 g, .999 SILVER, 1.0000 oz ASW
Bolivar and Marti

KM#	Date	Mintage	Fine	VF	XF	Unc
406	1993	—	—	—	Proof	45.00

Federico Garcia Loreca

KM#	Date	Mintage	Fine	VF	XF	Unc
407	1993	—	—	—	Proof	45.00

Montecristi Manifesto

KM#	Date	Mintage	Fine	VF	XF	Unc
408	1994	—	—	—	Proof	45.00

15 PESOS

3.8800 g, .999 GOLD, .1250 oz AGW
Jose Marti

KM#	Date	Mintage	Fine	VF	XF	Unc
212	1988	50 pcs.	—	—	—	100.00
	1988	15 pcs.	—	—	Proof	150.00
	1989	50 pcs.	—	—	—	100.00
	1989	15 pcs.	—	—	Proof	150.00
	1990	15 pcs.	—	—	—	125.00
	1990	12 pcs.	—	—	Proof	150.00

20 PESOS

33.4370 g, .900 GOLD, .9676 oz AGW
Jose Marti

KM#	Date	Mintage	Fine	VF	XF	Unc
21	1915	.057	BV	475.00	550.00	750.00
	1915	—	—	—	Proof	12,000.
	1916	10 pcs.	—	—	Proof	24,500.

26.0000 g, .925 SILVER, .7732 oz ASW
Ignacio Agramonte

KM#	Date	Mintage	Fine	VF	XF	Unc
38	1977	.025	—	—	Proof	45.00

Maximo Gomez

KM#	Date	Mintage	Fine	VF	XF	Unc
39	1977	.025	—	—	Proof	45.00

Antonio Maceo

KM#	Date	Mintage	Fine	VF	XF	Unc
40	1977	.025	—	—	Proof	45.00

60th Anniversary Socialist Revolution - Lenin

KM#	Date	Mintage	Fine	VF	XF	Unc
41	1977	100 pcs.	—	—	Proof	1000.

Nonaligned Nations Conference

KM#	Date	Mintage	Fine	VF	XF	Unc
44	1979	.020	—	—	—	45.00
	1979	—	—	—	Proof	60.00

62.2000 g, .999 SILVER, 2.0000 oz ASW

Triumph of the Revolution

KM#	Date	Mintage	Fine	VF	XF	Unc
169	1987	333 pcs.	—	—	Proof	85.00
	1988	1,000	—	—	Proof	75.00
	1989	500 pcs.	—	—	Proof	85.00

60th Anniversary of Birth of Ernesto Che Guevara

KM#	Date	Mintage	Fine	VF	XF	Unc
170	1987	333 pcs.	—	—	Proof	85.00
	1988	1,000	—	—	Proof	75.00
	1989	500 pcs.	—	—	Proof	85.00

30th Anniversary of the March to Victory

KM#	Date	Mintage	Fine	VF	XF	Unc
171	1987	333 pcs.	—	—	Proof	85.00
	1988	1,000	—	—	Proof	75.00
	1989	500 pcs.	—	—	Proof	85.00

62.0300 g, .999 SILVER, 1.9945 oz ASW

150th Anniversary of Railroad in Cuba

KM#	Date	Mintage	Fine	VF	XF	Unc
232	1988	*1,000	—	—	P/L	75.00

62.1400 g, .999 SILVER, 1.9980 oz ASW

140th Anniversary of Railroad in Spain

KM#	Date	Mintage	Fine	VF	XF	Unc
233	1988	*1,000	—	—	P/L	75.00

62.1000 g, .999 SILVER, 1.9968 oz ASW

160th Anniversary of Railroad in England

KM#	Date	Mintage	Fine	VF	XF	Unc
234	1988	*1,000	—	—	P/L	75.00

62.0300 g, .999 SILVER, 1.9945 oz ASW

Tania La Guerrillera

KM#	Date	Mintage	Fine	VF	XF	Unc
235	1988	*1,000	—	—	P/L	75.00

62.0600 g, .999 SILVER, 1.9955 oz ASW

Camilo Cienfuegos

KM#	Date	Mintage	Fine	VF	XF	Unc
236	1988	*1,000	—	—	P/L	75.00

35th Anniversary of Assault of the Moncada Garrison

KM#	Date	Mintage	Fine	VF	XF	Unc
237	1988	*1,000	—	—	P/L	75.00

25 PESOS

7.7700 g, .999 GOLD, .2500 oz AGW

Jose Marti

KM#	Date	Mintage	Fine	VF	XF	Unc
213	1988	50 pcs.	—	—	—	200.00
	1988	15 pcs.	—	—	Proof	300.00
	1989	50 pcs.	—	—	—	200.00
	1989	15 pcs.	—	—	Proof	300.00
	1990	12 pcs.	—	—	—	250.00
	1990	12 pcs.	—	—	Proof	300.00

30 PESOS

93.2500 g, .999 SILVER, 2.9951 oz ASW

Vincente and Martin Pinzon

Similar to 10 Pesos KM#327.

KM#	Date	Mintage	Fine	VF	XF	Unc
422	1991	—	—	—	Proof	125.00

Hatuey Indians

Similar to 10 Pesos KM#328.

KM#	Date	Mintage	Fine	VF	XF	Unc
423	1991	—	—	—	Proof	125.00

Chief Guama

KM#	Date	Mintage	Fine	VF	XF	Unc
376	1992	550 pcs.	—	—	Proof	125.00

Bartolome de Las Casas

KM#	Date	Mintage	Fine	VF	XF	Unc
377	1992	550 pcs.	—	—	Proof	125.00

King Philipp

KM#	Date	Mintage	Fine	VF	XF	Unc
378	1992	550 pcs.	—	—	Proof	125.00

Spanish Kings and Queens

KM#	Date	Mintage	Fine	VF	XF	Unc
379	ND(1992) 550 pcs.		—	—	Proof	125.00

50 PESOS

15.5500 g, .999 GOLD, .5000 oz AGW
30th Anniversary of the March to Victory

KM#	Date	Mintage	Fine	VF	XF	Unc
208	1988	150 pcs.	—	—	Proof	285.00

60th Anniversary of Birth of Che Guevara

KM#	Date	Mintage	Fine	VF	XF	Unc
209	1988	150 pcs.	—	—	Proof	285.00

Triumph of the Revolution

KM#	Date	Mintage	Fine	VF	XF	Unc
210	1988	150 pcs.	—	—	Proof	285.00

Jose Marti

KM#	Date	Mintage	Fine	VF	XF	Unc
214	1988	15 pcs.	—	—	Proof	600.00
	1989	150 pcs.	—	—	—	300.00
	1989	15 pcs.	—	—	Proof	600.00
	1990	15 pcs.	—	—	—	450.00
	1990	12 pcs.	—	—	Proof	600.00

Simon Bolivar
Similar to 10 Pesos, KM#280.

KM#	Date	Mintage	Fine	VF	XF	Unc
281	1990	50 pcs.	—	—	P/L	325.00

155.5150 g, .999 SILVER, 5.0000 oz ASW
Illustration reduced. Actual size: 65.3mm.
500th Anniversary of Discovery of America
Christopher Columbus

KM#	Date	Mintage	Fine	VF	XF	Unc
294	1990	*2,000	—	—	Proof	250.00

500th Anniversary of Discovery of America
King Ferdinand of Spain
Similar to 10 Pesos, KM#263.

KM#	Date	Mintage	Fine	VF	XF	Unc
295	1990	*2,000	—	—	Proof	250.00

500th Anniversary of Discovery of America
Queen Isabella of Spain
Similar to 10 Pesos, KM#264.

KM#	Date	Mintage	Fine	VF	XF	Unc
296	1990	*2,000	—	—	Proof	250.00

500th Anniversary of Discovery of America
Juan de la Cosa
Similar to 10 Pesos, KM#266.

KM#	Date	Mintage	Fine	VF	XF	Unc
297	1990	*2,000	—	—	Proof	250.00

15.5500 g, .999 GOLD, .5000 oz AGW
500th Anniversary of Discovery of America
Christopher Columbus
Similar to 10 Pesos, KM#265.

KM#	Date	Mintage	Fine	VF	XF	Unc
298	1990	250 pcs.	—	—	Proof	275.00

500th Anniversary of Discovery of America
King Ferdinand of Spain
Similar to 10 Pesos, KM#263.

KM#	Date	Mintage	Fine	VF	XF	Unc
299	1990	250 pcs.	—	—	Proof	275.00

500th Anniversary of Discovery of America
Queen Isabella of Spain
Similar to 10 Pesos, KM#264.

KM#	Date	Mintage	Fine	VF	XF	Unc
300	1990	250 pcs.	—	—	Proof	275.00

500th Anniversary of Discovery of America
Juan de la Cosa
Similar to 10 Pesos, KM#266.

KM#	Date	Mintage	Fine	VF	XF	Unc
301	1990	250 pcs.	—	—	Proof	275.00

160th Anniversary of First Train in England
Similar to 10 Pesos, KM#207.

KM#	Date	Mintage	Fine	VF	XF	Unc
313	1989	150 pcs.	—	—	P/L	260.00

150th Anniversary of First Train in Spanish America
Similar to 10 Pesos, KM#205.

KM#	Date	Mintage	Fine	VF	XF	Unc
314	1989	150 pcs.	—	—	P/L	260.00

140th Anniversary of First Train in Spain
Similar to 10 Pesos, KM#206.

KM#	Date	Mintage	Fine	VF	XF	Unc
315	1989	150 pcs.	—	—	P/L	260.00

Pan American Games - Baseball
Similar to 10 Pesos, KM#293.

KM#	Date	Mintage	Fine	VF	XF	Unc
321	1990	—	—	—	Proof	285.00

Pan American Games - High Jump
Similar to 10 Pesos, KM#291.

KM#	Date	Mintage	Fine	VF	XF	Unc
322	1990	—	—	—	Proof	285.00

Pan American Games - Volleyball
Similar to 10 Pesos, KM#292.

KM#	Date	Mintage	Fine	VF	XF	Unc
323	1990	—	—	—	Proof	285.00

Tania la Guerrillera
Similar to 10 Pesos, KM#228.

KM#	Date	Mintage	Fine	VF	XF	Unc
330	1989	150 pcs.	—	—	P/L	260.00

Camilo Cienfuegos Gornaran
Similar to 10 Pesos, KM#229.

KM#	Date	Mintage	Fine	VF	XF	Unc
331	1989	150 pcs.	—	—	P/L	260.00

Assault of the Moncada Garrison
Similar to 10 Pesos, KM#230.

KM#	Date	Mintage	Fine	VF	XF	Unc
332	1989	150 pcs.	—	—	P/L	260.00

Hatuey Indians

KM#	Date	Mintage	Fine	VF	XF	Unc
339	1991	—	—	—	—	260.00

Madrid - Alcala Gate
Similar to 10 Pesos, KM#348.

KM#	Date	Mintage	Fine	VF	XF	Unc
356	1991	*1,050	—	—	Proof	265.00

Seville - La Giralda Tower
Similar to 10 Pesos, KM#349.

KM#	Date	Mintage	Fine	VF	XF	Unc
357	1991	*550 pcs.	—	—	Proof	265.00

155.5000 g, .999 SILVER, 5.0000 oz ASW
Illustration reduced. Actual size: 65.2mm.
Olympics - Stadium

KM#	Date	Mintage	Fine	VF	XF	Unc
343	1992	1,050	—	—	Proof	265.00

Philip I
Similar to 10 Pesos, KM#353.

358	1992	—	—	—	Proof	250.00

Chief Guama
Similar to 10 Pesos, KM#355.

359	1992	—	—	—	Proof	250.00

155.7300 g, .999 SILVER, 5.0019 oz ASW
Bartolome de Las Casas
Similar to 10 Pesos, KM#392.

380	1992	550 pcs.	—	—	Proof	265.00

Spanish Kings and Queens
Similar to 10 Pesos, KM#395.

381	ND(1992) 550 pcs.		—	—	Proof	265.00

San Jorge Palace
Similar to 10 Pesos, KM#374.

382	1992	550 pcs.	—	—	Proof	265.00

155.5150 g, .999 SILVER, 5.0000 oz ASW
St. Jacobi
Similar to 10 Pesos, KM#399.

400	1993	—	—	—	Proof	250.00

100 PESOS

12.0000 g, .917 GOLD, .3538 oz AGW
60th Anniversary of Socialist Revolution - Lenin

42	1977	10 pcs.	—	—	Proof	2250.

Carlos Manuel de Cespedes

43	1977	.025	—	—	Proof	200.00

Nonaligned Nations Conference

45	1979	.020	—	—	Proof	200.00

First Soviet-Cuban Space Flight

KM#	Date	Mintage	Fine	VF	XF	Unc
52	1980	1,000	—	—	—	350.00

Columbus' Ship - Nina
Obv: Similar to KM#45.

85	1981	2,000	—	—	—	275.00

Columbus' Ship - Pinta
Obv: Similar to KM#45.

86	1981	2,000	—	—	—	275.00

Columbus' Ship - Santa Maria
Obv: Similar to KM#45.

87	1981	2,000	—	—	—	275.00

31.1030 g, .999 GOLD, 1.0000 oz AGW
30th Anniversary of Revolution

202	1988	100 pcs.	—	—	Proof	650.00

60th Anniversary of Birth of Che Guevara

203	1988	100 pcs.	—	—	Proof	650.00

30th Anniversary of Landing of the Granma

KM#	Date	Mintage	Fine	VF	XF	Unc
204	1988	100 pcs.	—	—	Proof	650.00

Jose Marti

215	1988	50 pcs.	—	—	—	800.00
	1988	15 pcs.	—	—	Proof	1200.
	1989	150 pcs.	—	—	—	650.00
	1989	15 pcs.	—	—	Proof	1200.
	1990	15 pcs.	—	—	—	1000.
	1990	12 pcs.	—	—	Proof	1250.

160th Anniversary of First Train in England
Similar to 10 Pesos, KM#207.

316	1989	150 pcs.	—	—	P/L	650.00

150th Anniversary of First Train in Spanish America
Similar to 10 Pesos, KM#205.

317	1989	150 pcs.	—	—	P/L	650.00

140th Anniversary of First Train in Spain
Similar to 10 Pesos, KM#206.

318	1989	150 pcs.	—	—	P/L	650.00

200th Anniversary of French Revolution - Female
Similar to 10 Pesos, KM#239.

319	1989	—	—	—	Proof	750.00

200th Anniversary of French Revolution - Bastile
Similar to 10 Pesos, KM#240.

320	1989	—	—	—	Proof	750.00

Tania la Guerrillera
Similar to 10 Pesos, KM#228.

333	1989	150 pcs.	—	—	P/L	650.00

Camilo Cienfuegos Gornaran
Similar to 10 Pesos, KM#229.

334	1989	150 pcs.	—	—	P/L	650.00

35th Anniversary of Assault of the Moncada Garrison
Similar to 10 Pesos, KM#230.

335	1989	150 pcs.	—	—	P/L	650.00

500th Anniversary of Discovery of America
Christopher Columbus
Similar to 10 Pesos, KM#265.

302	1990	250 pcs.	—	—	Proof	825.00

500th Anniversary of Discovery of America
King Ferdinand of Spain
Similar to 10 Pesos, KM#263.

303	1990	250 pcs.	—	—	Proof	825.00

500th Anniversary of Discovery of America
Queen Isabella of Spain
Similar to 10 Pesos, KM#264.

304	1990	250 pcs.	—	—	Proof	825.00

500th Anniversary of Discovery of America
Juan de la Cosa
Similar to 10 Pesos, KM#266.

305	1990	250 pcs.	—	—	Proof	825.00

Seville - Tower of Gold
Similar to 10 Pesos, KM#351.

384	1992	*225 pcs.	—	—	Proof	825.00

El Escorial
Similar to 10 Pesos, KM#352.

385	1992	*225 pcs.	—	—	Proof	825.00

500 PESOS

155.5500 g, .999 GOLD, 5.0000 oz AGW
Spanish Kings and Queens
Similar to 10 Pesos, KM#373.

386	ND(1992) *15 pcs.		—	—	Proof	Rare

COUNTERMARKED COINAGE

1872-77 REVOLUTIONARY FUND

It is thought that these c/m were most likely used 1872-1877 by the Cuban revolutionary troops as a fund raising device. Commonly encountered on Mexican coins.

KEY COUNTERMARK VARIETIES

A - Short & thick

B - Long & thin

Values for these pieces vary according to the rarity of the date and type of coin on which the c/m is found.

Prices listed here are for the most common host coins.

REAL SERIES

2 REALES

.903 SILVER
c/m: Key on Mexican 2 Reales, KM#374.

KM#	Date	Good	VG	Fine	VF
1	ND(1825-70)	15.00	25.00	35.00	55.00

4 REALES

.903 SILVER
c/m: Key on Mexican 4 Reales, KM#375.

KM#	Date	Good	VG	Fine	VF
2	ND(1827-70)	20.00	30.00	40.00	60.00

8 REALES

.903 SILVER
c/m: Key on Mexican 8 Reales, KM#377.

KM#	Date	Good	VG	Fine	VF
3	ND(1824-77)	30.00	45.00	60.00	90.00

DECIMAL SERIES

25 CENTAVOS

.903 SILVER
c/m: Key on Mexican 25 Centavos, KM#406.

KM#	Date	Good	VG	Fine	VF
4.1	ND(1869-77)	15.00	20.00	30.00	50.00

c/m: Key on United States Liberty Seated Quarters with arrows at date and rays on reverse.

KM#	Date	Good	VG	Fine	VF
4.2	ND(1853)	65.00	125.00	185.00	275.00

c/m: Key on United States Liberty Seated Quarters plain date without rays on reverse.

KM#	Date	Good	VG	Fine	VF
4.3	ND(1858)	65.00	125.00	185.00	275.00

50 CENTAVOS

.903 SILVER
c/m: Key on Mexican 50 Centavos, KM#407.

KM#	Date	Good	VG	Fine	VF
5.1	ND(1869-77)	20.00	30.00	40.00	60.00

c/m: Key on U.S. Bust Half, C#32.

KM#	Date	Good	VG	Fine	VF
5.2	ND(1833)	550.00	—	—	—

PESO

.903 SILVER
c/m: Key on Mexican Peso, KM#388.

KM#	Date	Good	VG	Fine	VF
6	ND(1866-67)	40.00	75.00	125.00	225.00

c/m: Key on Mexican Peso, KM#408.

KM#	Date	Good	VG	Fine	VF
7	ND(1869-77)	30.00	55.00	80.00	125.00

VISITORS COINAGE

CENTAVO

COPPER-NICKEL

KM#	Date	Mintage	VF	XF	Unc
409	1988	—	.25	.50	1.00

ALUMINUM
Socialist Currency

KM#	Date	Mintage	VF	XF	Unc
410	1988	—	.25	.50	1.00

5 CENTAVOS

COPPER-NICKEL

KM#	Date	Mintage	VF	XF	Unc
411	1981	—	.25	.50	1.00

Hard Currency

KM#	Date	Mintage	VF	XF	Unc
412	1981	—	.25	.50	1.00
	1989	—	.25	.50	1.00

ALUMINUM
Socialist Currency

KM#	Date	Mintage	VF	XF	Unc
413	1988	—	.25	.50	1.00

10 CENTAVOS

COPPER-NICKEL

KM#	Date	Mintage	VF	XF	Unc
414	1981	—	.35	.75	1.50

KM#	Date	Mintage	VF	XF	Unc
415	1981	—	.35	.75	1.50
	1989	—	.35	.75	1.50

ALUMINUM
Socialist Currency

KM#	Date	Mintage	VF	XF	Unc
416	1988	—	.35	.75	1.50

25 CENTAVOS

COPPER-NICKEL

KM#	Date	Mintage	VF	XF	Unc
417	1981	—	.50	1.00	2.00

Hard Currency

KM#	Date	Mintage	VF	XF	Unc
418	1981	—	.50	1.00	2.00
	1989	—	.50	1.00	2.00

ALUMINUM
Socialist Currency

KM#	Date	Mintage	VF	XF	Unc
419	1988	—	.50	1.00	2.00

50 CENTAVOS

COPPER-NICKEL

KM#	Date	Mintage	VF	XF	Unc
420	1981	—	.75	1.50	3.00

PESO

COPPER-NICKEL

KM#	Date	Mintage	VF	XF	Unc
421	1981	—	1.00	2.00	4.50

MINT SETS (MS)

KM#	Date	Mintage	Identification	Issue Price	Mkt. Val.
MS1	1953(4)	—	KM26-29	100.00	—

PROOF SETS (PS)

KM#	Date	Mintage	Identification	Issue Price	Mkt. Val.
PS1	1915(7)	20	KM9-15	—	4500.
PS2	1915(6)	24	KM16-21	—	30,000.
PS3	1916(7)	20	KM9-15	—	5000.
PS4	1916(6)	—	KM16-21	—	50,000.
PS5	1953(4)	—	KM26-29	—	Rare
*NOTE: Spanish or English legends on holders.					
PS6	1975(2)	—	KM36,37	—	30.00
PS7	1977(4)	—	KM38-40,43	290.00	335.00
PS8	1979(2)	—	KM44,45	240.00	260.00
PS9	1988(5)	15	KM211-215	—	1650.

Listings For

CURACAO: refer to Netherlands Antilles
DAHOMEY: refer to Benin

CYPRUS

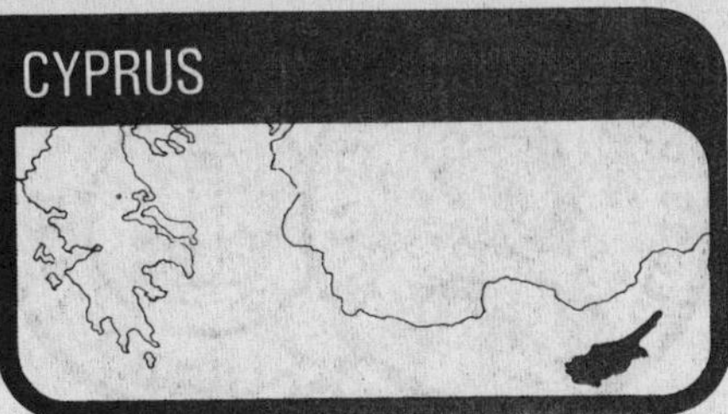

The Republic of Cyprus, a member of the British Commonwealth, lies in the eastern Mediterranean Sea 44 miles (71 km.) south of Turkey and 60 miles (97 km.) west of Syria. It is the third largest island in the Mediterranean Sea, having an area of 3,572 sq. mi. (9,251 sq. km.) and a population of 710,000. Capital: Nicosia. Agriculture, light manufacturing and tourism are the chief industries. Citrus fruit, potatoes, footwear and clothing are exported

The importance of Cyprus dates from the Bronze Age when it was desired as a principal source of copper (from which the island derived its name) and as a strategic trading center. It was during this period that large numbers of Greeks settled on the island and gave it the predominantly Greek character. Its role as an international marketplace made it a prime disseminator of the then prevalent cultures, a role that still influences the civilization of Western man. Because of its fortuitous position and influential role, Cyprus was conquered by a succession of empires: the Assyrian, Egyptian, Persian, Macedonian, Ptolemaic, Roman and Byzantine. It was taken from Isaac Comnenus by Richard the Lion-Heart in 1191, sold to the Templar Knight and for the following 7 centuries was ruled by the Franks, the Venetians and the Ottomans. During the Ottoman period Cyprus acquired its Turkish community (18% of its population). In 1878 the island fell into British hands and was made a crown colony of Britain in 1925. Finally, on Aug. 16, 1960, it became an independent republic.

In 1964, the ethnic Turks withdrew from active participation in the government. Turkish forces invaded Cyprus in 1974, gained control of 40 percent of the island and forcibly separated the Greek and Turkish communities. In 1983, Turkish Cypriots proclaimed their own state in northern Cyprus, which however remains without international recognition.

Cyprus is a member of the Commonwealth of Nations. The president is Chief of State and Head of Government.

RULERS

British, until 1960

MINT MARKS

H - Birmingham, England

MONETARY SYSTEM

9 Piastres = 1 Shilling
20 Shillings = 1 Pound

1/4 PIASTRE

BRONZE, 21.8mm

KM#	Date	Mintage	Fine	VF	XF	Unc
1.1	1879	.150	5.00	15.00	30.00	100.00
	1879	—	—	—	Proof	850.00
	1880	.072	10.00	25.00	50.00	120.00
	1880	—	—	—	Proof	365.00
	1881	.072	10.00	25.00	50.00	120.00
	1881	—	—	—	Proof	350.00
	1881H	.108	5.50	16.00	40.00	110.00
	1881H	—	—	—	Proof	300.00
	1882H	.036	15.00	30.00	90.00	165.00
	1884	.072	10.00	25.00	65.00	160.00
	1885	.036	15.00	40.00	100.00	185.00
	1887	.060	12.50	32.50	80.00	150.00
	1887	—	—	—	Proof	360.00
	1895	.072	12.00	30.00	80.00	150.00
	1898	.072	12.00	30.00	80.00	150.00

Reduced size, 21mm

KM#	Date	Mintage	Fine	VF	XF	Unc
1.2	1900	.036	10.00	25.00	65.00	165.00
	1900	—	—	—	Proof	600.00
	1901	.072	8.00	23.50	60.00	140.00

KM#	Date	Mintage	Fine	VF	XF	Unc
8	1902	.072	5.00	12.50	30.00	125.00
	1905	.422	4.00	12.50	27.50	100.00
	1908	.036	35.00	85.00	150.00	400.00

KM#	Date	Mintage	Fine	VF	XF	Unc
16	1922	.072	5.00	12.50	30.00	80.00
	1926	.360	3.50	7.50	15.00	65.00
	1926	—	—	—	Proof	365.00

1/2 PIASTRE

BRONZE

KM#	Date	Mintage	Fine	VF	XF	Unc
2	1879	.250	7.50	15.00	45.00	165.00
	1879	—	—	—	Proof	850.00
	1881	.054	12.50	25.00	75.00	220.00
	1881	—	—	—	Proof	500.00
	1881H	.072	10.00	20.00	55.00	140.00
	1881H	—	—	—	Proof	325.00
	1882H	.054	10.00	20.00	60.00	180.00
	1882H	—	—	—	Proof	325.00
	1884	.036	20.00	50.00	120.00	275.00
	1884	—	—	—	Proof	325.00
	1885	.054	15.00	30.00	90.00	260.00
	1886	.122	7.50	15.00	45.00	165.00
	1887	.060	10.00	20.00	70.00	200.00
	1887	—	—	—	Proof	325.00
	1889	.054	15.00	35.00	125.00	380.00
	1890	.180	20.00	50.00	100.00	300.00
	1890	—	—	—	Proof	400.00
	1891	.108	27.50	75.00	150.00	300.00
	1896	.036	35.00	110.00	200.00	450.00
	1900	.036	35.00	110.00	200.00	450.00
	1900	—	—	—	Proof	700.00

KM#	Date	Mintage	Fine	VF	XF	Unc
11	1908	.036	40.00	120.00	300.00	600.00

KM#	Date	Mintage	Fine	VF	XF	Unc
17	1922	.036	15.00	40.00	120.00	230.00
	1927	.108	3.50	10.00	35.00	80.00
	1927	—	—	—	Proof	365.00
	1930	.180	3.00	8.00	30.00	75.00
	1930	—	—	—	Proof	365.00
	1931	.090	5.00	15.00	40.00	100.00
	1931	—	—	—	Proof	425.00

COPPER-NICKEL

KM#	Date	Mintage	Fine	VF	XF	Unc
20	1934	1.440	.75	2.50	6.50	16.50
	1934	—	—	—	Proof	325.00

KM#	Date	Mintage	Fine	VF	XF	Unc
22	1938	1.080	.35	1.00	4.00	12.50
	1938	—	—	—	Proof	325.00

BRONZE

KM#	Date	Mintage	Fine	VF	XF	Unc
22a	1942	1.080	.25	1.00	2.50	12.50
	1942	—	—	—	Proof	200.00
	1943	1.620	.25	1.00	2.50	12.50
	1944	2.160	.25	1.00	2.50	12.50
	1945	1.080	.25	1.00	2.50	12.50
	1945	—	—	—	Proof	200.00

KM#	Date	Mintage	Fine	VF	XF	Unc
29	1949	1.080	.15	.35	1.00	3.50
	1949	—	—	—	Proof	150.00

PIASTRE

BRONZE

Rev: Thin '1'

KM#	Date	Mintage	Fine	VF	XF	Unc
3.1	1879	.250	8.00	25.00	50.00	150.00
	1879	—	—	—	Proof	950.00
	1881	.036	15.00	35.00	150.00	325.00
	1881	—	—	—	Proof	600.00
	1881H	.036	15.00	35.00	150.00	500.00
	1881H	—	—	—	Proof	650.00

Rev: Thick '1'

KM#	Date	Mintage	Fine	VF	XF	Unc
3.2	1881	Inc. Ab.	—	—	Proof	1000.
	1881H	Inc. Ab.	10.00	35.00	120.00	500.00
	1881H	—	—	—	Proof	900.00
	1882H	.018	135.00	225.00	450.00	1250.
	1882H	—	—	—	Proof	2000.
	1884	.018	135.00	225.00	450.00	1250.
	1884	—	—	—	Proof	1800.
	1885	.054	25.00	70.00	115.00	275.00
	1885	—	—	—	Proof	1220.
	1886	.227	10.00	30.00	85.00	175.00
	1887	.045	10.00	32.50	100.00	200.00
	1889	.027	30.00	90.00	250.00	500.00
	1890	.090	20.00	70.00	150.00	350.00
	1891	.054	25.00	80.00	200.00	400.00
	1891	—	—	—	Proof	780.00
	1895	.054	25.00	80.00	200.00	400.00
	1896	.054	25.00	80.00	200.00	400.00
	1900	.027	25.00	80.00	200.00	450.00
	1900	—	—	—	Proof	1900.

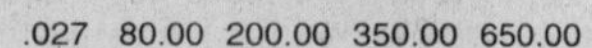

KM#	Date	Mintage	Fine	VF	XF	Unc
12	1908	.027	80.00	200.00	350.00	650.00

KM#	Date	Mintage	Fine	VF	XF	Unc
18	1922	.054	10.00	35.00	125.00	250.00
	1927	.127	5.00	20.00	60.00	150.00
	1927	—	—	—	Proof	400.00
	1930	.096	6.00	22.50	70.00	175.00
	1930	—	—	—	Proof	400.00
	1931	.045	10.00	30.00	80.00	200.00
	1931	—	—	—	Proof	725.00

COPPER-NICKEL

KM#	Date	Mintage	Fine	VF	XF	Unc
21	1934	1.440	1.00	2.50	6.50	16.50
	1934	—	—	—	Proof	325.00

KM#	Date	Mintage	Fine	VF	XF	Unc
23	1938	2.700	.60	1.50	3.00	12.50
	1938	—	—	—	Proof	325.00

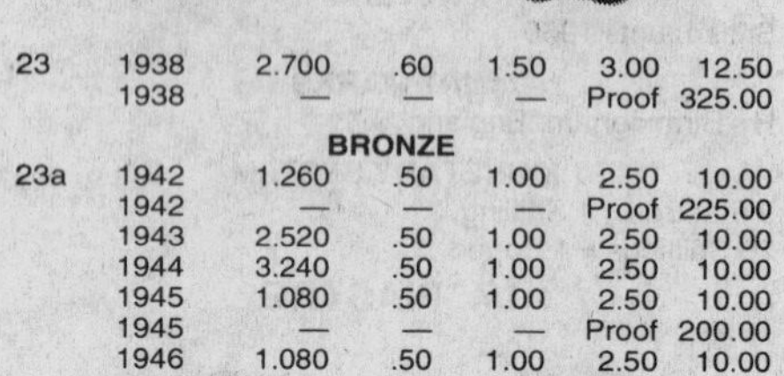

BRONZE

KM#	Date	Mintage	Fine	VF	XF	Unc
23a	1942	1.260	.50	1.00	2.50	10.00
	1942	—	—	—	Proof	225.00
	1943	2.520	.50	1.00	2.50	10.00
	1944	3.240	.50	1.00	2.50	10.00
	1945	1.080	.50	1.00	2.50	10.00
	1945	—	—	—	Proof	200.00
	1946	1.080	.50	1.00	2.50	10.00
	1946	—	—	—	Proof	200.00

Obv. leg: DEI GRATIA REX for REX IMPERATOR.

KM#	Date	Mintage	Fine	VF	XF	Unc
30	1949	1.080	.25	.60	1.50	3.50
	1949	—	—	—	Proof	150.00

3 PIASTRES

1.8851 g, .925 SILVER, .0561 oz ASW

KM#	Date	Mintage	Fine	VF	XF	Unc
4	1901	.300	8.00	20.00	40.00	100.00
	1901	—	—	—	Proof	800.00

4-1/2 PIASTRES

2.8276 g, .925 SILVER, .0841 oz ASW

KM#	Date	Mintage	Fine	VF	XF	Unc
5	1901	.400	5.00	15.00	40.00	100.00
	1901	—	—	—	Proof	950.00

KM#	Date	Mintage	Fine	VF	XF	Unc
15	1921	.600	3.50	10.00	30.00	80.00

KM#	Date	Mintage	Fine	VF	XF	Unc
24	1938	.192	2.00	4.00	12.00	30.00
	1938	—	—	—	Proof	400.00

9 PIASTRES

5.6552 g, .925 SILVER, .1682 oz ASW

KM#	Date	Mintage	Fine	VF	XF	Unc
6	1901	.600	10.00	30.00	80.00	175.00
	1901	—	—	—	Proof	1250.

KM#	Date	Mintage	Fine	VF	XF	Unc
9	1907	.060	35.00	100.00	275.00	500.00

KM#	Date	Mintage	Fine	VF	XF	Unc
13	1913	.050	20.00	70.00	150.00	400.00
	1919	.400	2.50	10.00	30.00	100.00
	1921	.490	2.50	10.00	30.00	100.00

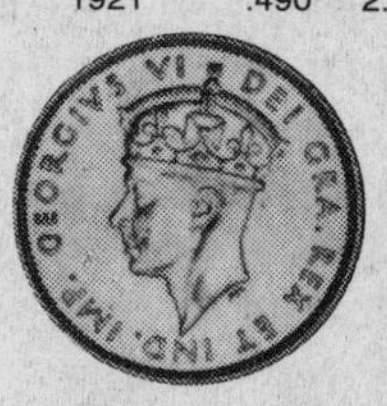

KM#	Date	Mintage	Fine	VF	XF	Unc
25	1938	.504	1.50	3.00	7.00	27.50
	1938	—	—	—	Proof	400.00
	1940	.800	1.50	3.00	7.00	27.50
	1940	—	—	—	Proof	400.00

SHILLING

COPPER-NICKEL

KM#	Date	Mintage	Fine	VF	XF	Unc
27	1947	1.440	.50	1.00	5.00	30.00
	1947	—	—	—	Proof	300.00

Obv. leg: ET IND IMP dropped.

KM#	Date	Mintage	Fine	VF	XF	Unc
31	1949	1.440	.50	1.00	5.00	30.00
	1949	—	—	—	Proof	300.00

18 PIASTRES

11.3104 g, .925 SILVER, .3364 oz ASW

KM#	Date	Mintage	Fine	VF	XF	Unc
7	1901	.200	25.00	100.00	250.00	500.00
	1901	—	—	—	Proof	2450.

KM#	Date	Mintage	Fine	VF	XF	Unc
10	1907	.020	55.00	225.00	485.00	1250.

KM#	Date	Mintage	Fine	VF	XF	Unc
14	1913	.025	35.00	140.00	350.00	650.00
	1921	.155	25.00	60.00	150.00	350.00

KM#	Date	Mintage	Fine	VF	XF	Unc
26	1938	.200	3.50	5.00	10.00	40.00
	1938	—	—	—	Proof	450.00
	1940	.100	3.50	5.00	10.00	40.00
	1940	—	—	—	Proof	450.00

2 SHILLINGS

COPPER-NICKEL

KM#	Date	Mintage	Fine	VF	XF	Unc
28	1947	.720	1.00	2.50	7.50	35.00
	1947	—	—	—	Proof	400.00

Obv. leg: ET IND. IMP. dropped.

KM#	Date	Mintage	Fine	VF	XF	Unc
32	1949	.720	1.00	2.50	7.50	35.00
	1949	—	—	—	Proof	400.00

45 PIASTRES

28.2759 g, .925 SILVER, .8409 oz ASW
50th Anniversary of British Rule

KM#	Date	Mintage	Fine	VF	XF	Unc
19	1928	.080	15.00	25.00	40.00	170.00
	1928	517 pcs.	—	—	Proof	600.00

DECIMAL COINAGE

50 Mils = 1 Shilling
20 Shillings = 1 Pound
1000 Mils = 1 Pound

3 MILS

BRONZE
Flying Fish

KM#	Date	Mintage	VF	XF	Unc
33	1955	6.250	—	.10	.20
	1955	2,000	—	Proof	2.50

5 MILS

BRONZE

KM#	Date	Mintage	VF	XF	Unc
34	1955	10.000	.15	.25	.40
	1955	2,000	—	Proof	3.50
	1956	2.950	.15	.30	.50
	1956	—	—	Proof	285.00

25 MILS

COPPER-NICKEL
Head of Bull

KM#	Date	Mintage	VF	XF	Unc
35	1955	2.500	.25	.35	.50
	1955	2,000	—	Proof	3.50

50 MILS

COPPER-NICKEL
Fern Leaves

KM#	Date	Mintage	VF	XF	Unc
36	1955	4.000	.35	.50	1.00
	1955	2,000	—	Proof	3.50

100 MILS

COPPER-NICKEL

KM#	Date	Mintage	VF	XF	Unc
37	1955	2.500	.50	.75	1.50
	1955	2,000	—	Proof	5.00
	1957	*.500	10.00	15.00	50.00
	1957	—	—	Proof	440.00

***NOTE:** All but 10,000 of 1957 issue were melted down.

REPUBLIC

1960—

MIL

ALUMINUM

KM#	Date	Mintage	VF	XF	Unc
38	1963	5.000	—	—	.10
	1963	.025	—	Proof	.75
	1971	.500	—	.10	.15
	1972	.500	—	.10	.15
	1972	—	—	Proof	1.50

5 MILS

BRONZE

KM#	Date	Mintage	VF	XF	Unc
39	1963	12.000	—	.10	.25
	1963	.025	—	Proof	1.00
	1970	2.500	—	.10	.25
	1971	2.500	—	.10	.25
	1972	2.500	—	.10	.25
	1973	5.000	—	.10	.25
	1974	2.500	—	.10	.25
	1976	2.000	—	.10	.25
	1977	2.000	—	.10	.25
	1978	2.000	—	.10	.25
	1979	2.000	—	.10	.25
	1980	4.000	—	.10	.25
	1980	—	—	Proof	2.00

ALUMINUM
Obv: Small date.

KM#	Date	Mintage	VF	XF	Unc
50.1	1981	12.500	—	—	.15

Obv: Large date.

KM#	Date	Mintage	VF	XF	Unc
50.2	1982	15.000	—	—	.15
	1982	—	—	Proof	1.50

25 MILS

COPPER-NICKEL
Cedar of Lebanon

KM#	Date	Mintage	VF	XF	Unc
40	1963	2.500	.10	.15	.30
	1963	.025	—	Proof	1.25
	1968	1.500	.10	.15	.30
	1971	1.000	.10	.15	.30
	1972	.500	.10	.15	.35
	1973	1.000	.10	.15	.30
	1974	1.000	.10	.15	.30
	1976	2.000	.10	.15	.30
	1977	.500	.10	.15	.30
	1978	.500	.10	.15	.30

KM#	Date	Mintage	VF	XF	Unc
40	1979	1.000	.10	.15	.30
	1980	2.000	.10	.15	.30
	1981	3.000	.10	.15	.30
	1982	1.000	.10	.15	.30
	1982	—	—	Proof	2.50

50 MILS

COPPER-NICKEL
Bunch of Grapes

KM#	Date	Mintage	VF	XF	Unc
41	1963	2.800	.20	.30	.60
	1963	.025	—	Proof	1.50
	1970	.500	.20	.35	.75
	1971	.500	.20	.35	.75
	1972	.750	.20	.30	.60
	1973	.750	.20	.30	.60
	1974	1.500	.20	.30	.60
	1976	1.500	.20	.30	.60
	1977	.500	.20	.30	.60
	1978	.500	.20	.30	.60
	1979	1.000	.20	.30	.60
	1980	3.000	.20	.30	.60
	1981	4.000	.20	.30	.60
	1982	2.000	.20	.30	.60
	1982	—	—	Proof	3.00

100 MILS

COPPER-NICKEL
Cyprus Mouflon

KM#	Date	Mintage	VF	XF	Unc
42	1963	1.750	.40	.65	1.25
	1963	.025	—	Proof	2.00
	1971	.500	.50	.75	1.50
	1973	.750	.40	.65	1.25
	1974	1.000	.50	.75	1.50
	1976	1.500	.40	.65	1.25
	1977	.500	.50	.75	1.50
	1978	1.000	.50	.75	1.50
	1979	1.000	.40	.65	1.25
	1980	1.000	.40	.65	1.25
	1981	2.000	.40	.65	1.25
	1982	2.000	.40	.65	1.25
	1982	—	—	Proof	4.00

500 MILS

COPPER-NICKEL
F.A.O. Issue

KM#	Date	Mintage	VF	XF	Unc
43	1970	.080	1.25	2.00	5.00
	22.6200 g, .800 SILVER, .5818 oz ASW				
43a	1970	5,000	—	Proof	55.00

COPPER-NICKEL
Hercules

KM#	Date	Mintage	VF	XF	Unc
44	1975	.500	1.25	1.75	3.25
	1977	.300	1.25	1.75	3.25
	1977	—	—	Proof	15.00
	14.1400 g, .800 SILVER, .3637 oz ASW				
44a	1975	.010	—	Proof	20.00

COPPER-NICKEL
Refugee Commemorative

KM#	Date	Mintage	VF	XF	Unc
45	1976	.025	1.25	1.75	3.25
	14.1400 g, .925 SILVER, .4205 oz ASW				
45a	1976	.025	—	Proof	15.00

COPPER-NICKEL
Human Rights Commemorative

KM#	Date	Mintage	VF	XF	Unc
48	1978	.050	1.25	1.75	3.25
	14.1400 g, .925 SILVER, .4205 oz ASW				
48a	1978	5,000	—	Proof	65.00

COPPER-NICKEL
Summer Olympic Games

KM#	Date	Mintage	VF	XF	Unc
49	1980	.050	1.25	1.75	4.50
	14.1400 g, .925 SILVER, .4205 oz ASW				
49a	1980	7,500	—	Proof	60.00

COPPER-NICKEL
World Food Day - Swordfish

KM#	Date	Mintage	VF	XF	Unc
51	1981	.050	1.25	1.75	3.25
	14.1400 g, .925 SILVER, .4205 oz ASW				
51a	1981	7,500	—	Proof	35.00

POUND

COPPER-NICKEL
Refugee Commemorative

KM#	Date	Mintage	VF	XF	Unc
46	1976	.025	2.00	2.50	4.00
	28.2800 g, .925 SILVER, .8411 oz ASW				
46a	1976	.025	—	Proof	20.00

50 POUNDS

15.9800 g, .917 GOLD, .4711 oz AGW
Archbishop Makarios

KM#	Date	Mintage	VF	XF	Unc
47	1977	.039	—	—	275.00
	1977	.051	—	Proof	300.00

MONETARY REFORM

100 Cents = 1 Pound

1/2 CENT

ALUMINUM
Cyclamen

KM#	Date	Mintage	VF	XF	Unc
52	1983	10.000	—	.10	.15
	1983	6,250	—	Proof	1.50

CENT

NICKEL-BRASS
Stylized Bird on a Branch

KM#	Date	Mintage	VF	XF	Unc
53.1	1983	15.000	—	.10	.20
	1983	6,250	—	Proof	1.50
	1985	5.000	—	.10	.20
	1987	5.000	—	.10	.20
	1988	5.000	—	.10	.20
	1989	—	—	.10	.20
	1990	—	—	.10	.20

Obv: Altered wreath around arms.

KM#	Date	Mintage	VF	XF	Unc
53.2	1991	—	—	.10	.20
	1992	—	—	.10	.20

2 CENTS

NICKEL-BRASS
Stylized Goats

KM#	Date	Mintage	VF	XF	Unc
54.1	1983	12.000	—	.15	.25
	1983	6,250	—	Proof	1.50
	1985	8.000	—	.15	.25
	1987	—	—	.15	.25
	1988	5.150	—	.15	.25
	1989	—	—	.15	.25
	1990	—	—	.15	.25

Obv: Altered wreath around arms.

KM#	Date	Mintage	VF	XF	Unc
54.2	1991	—	—	.15	.25

5 CENTS

NICKEL-BRASS

KM#	Date	Mintage	VF	XF	Unc
55.1	1983	15.000	—	.20	.50
	1983	6,250	—	Proof	2.00
	1985	5.000	—	.20	.50
	1987	5.000	—	.20	.50
	1988	5.060	—	.20	.50
	1989	—	—	.20	.50
	1990	—	—	.20	.50

Obv: Altered wreath around arms.

KM#	Date	Mintage	VF	XF	Unc
55.2	1991	—	—	.20	.50

10 CENTS

NICKEL-BRASS

KM#	Date	Mintage	VF	XF	Unc
56.1	1983	10.000	—	.35	.75
	1983	6,250	—	Proof	3.00
	1985	5.000	—	.35	.75
	1987	—	—	.35	.75
	1988	5.035	—	.35	.75
	1989	—	—	.35	.75
	1990	—	—	.35	.75

Obv: Altered wreath around arms.

KM#	Date	Mintage	VF	XF	Unc
56.2	1991	—	—	.35	.75

20 CENTS

NICKEL-BRASS
Pied Wheatear

KM#	Date	Mintage	VF	XF	Unc
57	1983	10.000	—	.50	1.00
	1983	6,200	—	Proof	5.00
	1985	5.040	—	.50	1.00
	1987	—	—	.50	1.00
	1988	1.000	—	.50	1.00

BRONZE
Small European States Games

KM#	Date	Mintage	VF	XF	Unc
62.1	1989	—	—	—	1.00
	1989	—	—	Proof	18.00
	1990	—	—	—	1.00

Obv: Altered wreath around arms.

KM#	Date	Mintage	VF	XF	Unc
62.2	1991	—	—	—	1.00
	1992	—	—	—	1.00

50 CENTS

COPPER-NICKEL
Forestry - F.A.O.

KM#	Date	Mintage	VF	XF	Unc
58	1985	.033	1.25	1.75	3.50

14.1400 g, .925 SILVER, .4205 oz ASW

KM#	Date	Mintage	VF	XF	Unc
58a	1985	4,000	—	Proof	20.00

COPPER-NICKEL
Olympics - Symbols

KM#	Date	Mintage	VF	XF	Unc
60	1988	.014	—	—	3.00

14.1400 g, .925 SILVER, .4205 oz ASW

KM#	Date	Mintage	VF	XF	Unc
60a	1988	4,000	—	Proof	20.00

COPPER-NICKEL
Abduction of Europa

KM#	Date	Mintage	VF	XF	Unc
66	1991	3.005	—	—	2.50

7.0000 g, .925 SILVER, .2082 oz ASW

KM#	Date	Mintage	VF	XF	Unc
66a	1991	5,000	—	Proof	20.00

POUND

COPPER-NICKEL
World Wildlife Fund

KM#	Date	Mintage	VF	XF	Unc
59	1986	.039	—	—	5.50

.925 SILVER

KM#	Date	Mintage	VF	XF	Unc
59a	1986	.013	—	Proof	40.00

COPPER-NICKEL
Olympics - Symbols

KM#	Date	Mintage	VF	XF	Unc
61	1988	.014	—	—	5.00

28.2800 g, .925 SILVER, .8411 oz ASW

KM#	Date	Mintage	VF	XF	Unc
61a	1988	4,000	—	Proof	55.00

COPPER-NICKEL
Small European States Games

KM#	Date	Mintage	VF	XF	Unc
63	1989	—	—	—	6.00

28.2800 g, .925 SILVER, .8411 oz ASW

KM#	Date	Mintage	VF	XF	Unc
63a	1989	4,000	—	Proof	50.00

COPPER-NICKEL
Save the Children Fund

KM#	Date	Mintage	VF	XF	Unc
64	1989	—	—	—	6.00
	28.2800 g, .925 SILVER, .8411 oz ASW				
64a	1989	4,000	—	Proof	50.00

COPPER-NICKEL
Olympics - Relay Racing

KM#	Date	Mintage	VF	XF	Unc
67	1992	8,000	—	—	6.50
	28.2800 g, .925 SILVER, .8411 oz ASW				
67a	1992	4,000	—	Proof	55.00

20 POUNDS

7.9881 g, .917 GOLD, .2354 oz AGW
30th Anniversary of the Republic
Obv: State emblem. Rev: Value superimposed on stylized bird.

KM#	Date	Mintage	VF	XF	Unc
65	1990	5,000	—	Proof	250.00

Museum Building Fund

KM#	Date	Mintage	VF	XF	Unc
68	1992	5,000	—	Proof	225.00

MINT SETS (MS)

KM#	Date	Mintage	Identification	Issue Price	Mkt. Val.
MS1	1955(5)	2,550	KM33-37*	2.20	6.50

***NOTE:** MS1 consists of 3 uncirculated and 2 circulated coins.

KM#	Date	Mintage	Identification	Issue Price	Mkt. Val.
MS2	1963(5)	8,050	KM38-42	1.95	5.00
MS3	1971(5)	3,000	KM38-42	1.65	5.00
MS4	1972(4)	3,000	KM39-42	2.35	5.00
MS5	1973(4)	5,000	KM39-42	2.75	5.00
MS6	1974(4)	5,000	KM39-42	3.25	5.00
MS7	1976(3)	5,000	KM40-42	1.25	4.50
MS8	1976(2)	25,000	KM45-46	6.50	6.00
MS9	1977(5)	10,000	KM39-42,44	—	6.50
MS10	1978(5)	—	KM39-42,48	5.50	6.50
MS11	1981(5)	—	KM40-42,50-51	5.00	6.50
MS12	1981(4)	—	KM40-42,50	5.00	6.50
MS13	1982(4)	5,000	KM40-42,50	5.00	6.50
MS14	1983(6)	11,400	KM52-57	15.00	10.00
MS15	1988(5)	—	KM53-57	—	10.00
MS16	1989(5)	—	KM53-56,62	—	10.00
MS17	1990(5)	—	KM53-56,62	10.00	10.00

PROOF SETS (PS)

KM#	Date	Mintage	Identification	Issue Price	Mkt. Val.
PS1	1879(3)	—	KM1.1,2,3.1	—	2750.
PS2	1881(3)	—	KM1.1,2,3.1	—	1550.
PS3	1900(3)	—	KM1.1,2,3.2	—	3250.
PS4	1901(4)	—	KM4-7	—	5500.
PS5	1931(2)	—	KM17-18	—	1175.
PS6	1934(2)	—	KM20-21	—	650.00
PS7	1938(5)	—	KM22-26	—	2000.
PS8	1947(2)	—	KM27-28	—	700.00
PS9	1949(2)	—	KM31-32	—	700.00
PS10	1949(4)	—	KM29-32	—	950.00
PS11	1955(5)	2,000	KM33-37	5.50	18.00
PS12	1963(5)	24,501	KM38-42 with case	9.00	6.50
PS13	1963(5)	500	KM38-42 sealed	8.70	6.50
PS14	1976(2)	25,000	KM45a-46a	50.00	35.00
PS15	Mixed dates(7)	—	KM38(72),39(80), 40-42(82),44(77) 50.2(82)	30.00	30.00
PS16	1983(6)	6,250	KM52-57	40.00	15.00

CZECH REPUBLIC

The Czech Republic, formerly united with Slovakia in the Czechoslavak Federal republic, is bordered in the west by Germany, to the north by Poland, to the east by Slovakia and to the south by Austria. It consists of 3 major regions: Bohemia, Moravia and Silesia. It has an area of 20,431 sq. mi. (78,864 sq. km.) and a population of 10.3 million. Capital: Prague (Praha). Agriculture and livestock are chief occupations while coal deposits are the main mineral resources.

The Czech lands were united with the Slovaks to form the Czechoslovak State, which came into existence on Oct. 28, 1918 upon the dissolution of Austria-Hungary. This territory was broken up for the benefit of Germany, Poland and Hungary by the Munich agreement signed by the United Kingdom, France, Germany and Italy on Sept. 29, 1938. In March 1939 the German influenced Slovak government proclaimed Slovakia independent. Germany incorporated the Czech lands into the Third Reich as the "Protectorate of Bohemia and Moravia." A government-in-exile was set up in London in July 1940. The Soviets and USA forces liberated the area by May 1945. Communist influence increased steadily while pressure for liberalization culminated in the overthrow of the Stalinist leader Antonin Novotny and his associates in 1968. The Communist Party then introduced far reaching reforms which received warnings from Moscow, followed by occupation of Warsaw Pact forces resulting in stationing of Soviet forces. Mass demonstrations for reform began in Nov. 1989 and the Federal Assembly abolished the Communist Party's sole right to govern. New governments followed on Dec. 3 and Dec. 10. The Movement for Democratic Slovakia was apparent in the June 1992 elections with the Slovak National Council adopting a declaration of sovereignty, later a constitution for an independent Slovakia, with the Federal Assembly voting for the dissolution of the Czech and Slovak Federal Republic. This came into effect on Dec. 31, 1992 and both new republics came into being on Jan. 1, 1993.

NOTE: For earlier issues see Czechoslovak Federal Republic and Bohemia and Moravia listings.

MINT MARKS

(c) castle = Hamburg 

(l) - leaf = Royal Canadian 

(m) - monogram - Jablonec nad Nisau 

MONETARY SYSTEM

1 Czechoslovak Koruna (Kcs) = 1 Czech Koruna (Kc)

1 Koruna = 100 Haleru

10 HALERU

ALUMINUM

KM#	Date	Mintage	VF	XF	Unc
6	1993(c)	—	—	—	.25
	1993(m)	—	—	—	.25

20 HALERU

ALUMINUM

KM#	Date	Mintage	VF	XF	Unc
2	1993(c)	—	—	—	.35
	1993(m)	—	—	—	.35

50 HALERU

ALUMINUM

KM#	Date	Mintage	VF	XF	Unc
3	1993(c)	—	—	—	.65
	1993(m)	—	—	—	.65

KORUNA

NICKEL CLAD STEEL

KM#	Date	Mintage	VF	XF	Unc
7	1993(l)	—	—	—	.75

2 KORUN

NICKEL CLAD STEEL

KM#	Date	Mintage	VF	XF	Unc
9	1993(l)	—	—	—	.75

5 KORUN

NICKEL PLATED STEEL

KM#	Date	Mintage	VF	XF	Unc
8	1993(l)	—	—	—	1.00

10 KORUN

COPPER PLATED STEEL
Brno Cathedral

KM#	Date	Mintage	VF	XF	Unc
4	1993(c)	—	—	—	1.50

20 KORUN

BRASS PLATED STEEL
St. Wenceslas on Horse

KM#	Date	Mintage	VF	XF	Unc
5	1993(c)	—	—	—	2.50

50 KORUN

BRASS PLATED STEEL CENTER in
COPPER PLATED STEEL RING
Prague City View

KM#	Date	Mintage	VF	XF	Unc
1	1993(c)	—	—	—	5.50

200 KORUN

13.0000 g, .900 SILVER, .3440 oz ASW
1st Anniversary of Constitution

KM#	Date	Mintage	VF	XF	Unc
10	1993	—	—	—	15.00

MEDALLIC ISSUES

DUCAT

3.5000 g, .986 GOLD, .1109 oz AGW
Architectural Montage of Czech & Moravian Cities

KM#	Date	Mintage	VF	XF	Unc
M1	1993(m)	1,000	—	Proof	85.00

5 DUCAT

17.5000 g, .986 GOLD, .5548 oz AGW
Architectural Montage of Czech & Moravian Cities

KM#	Date	Mintage	VF	XF	Unc
M2	1993(m)	500 pcs.	—	Proof	350.00

14.8400 g, .9999 SILVER, .4771 oz ASW

KM#	Date	Mintage	VF	XF	Unc
M2a	1993(m)	—	—	Proof	25.00

CZECHOSLOVAKIA

The Republic of Czechoslovakia, located in central Europe, has an area of 49,371 sq. mi. (127,870 sq. km.) and a population of 15.6 million. Capital: Prague. Machinery is the chief export of the highly industrialized economy.

Czechoslovakia proclaimed itself a republic on Oct. 28, 1918. When Adolf Hitler became dictator of Nazi Germany he provoked Czechoslovakia's German minority in the Sudetenland to agitate for autonomy. At Munich in Sept. of 1938, France and Britain, vainly seeking to avoid World War II, forced the cession of the Sudetenland to Germany. In March, 1939, Germany invaded Czechoslovakia and established a protectorate over the provinces of Bohemia and Moravia. Bohemia is a historic province in northwest Czechoslovakia that includes the city of Prague, one of the oldest continually occupied sites in Europe; and Moravia is an area of considerable mineral wealth in central Czechoslovakia. Slovakia, a province in southeastern Czechoslovakia that was once a separate country bounded by Poland, Hungary and Austria, was constituted as a puppet republic. World War II defeat of the Axis powers re-established the physical integrity and independence of Czechoslovakia, while bringing it within the Russian sphere of influence. On Feb. 23-25, 1948, the Communists seized control of the government in a coup d'etat, and adopted a constitution making the country a 'people's republic'. A new constitution adopted June 11, 1960, converted the country into a 'socialist republic' which lasted until 1989. On Nov. 11, 1989, demonstrations against the communist government began and in Dec. of that same year, communism was overthrown. In Jan. 1993 Slovakia split away leaving the now smaller Czech Republic.

MONETARY SYSTEM

100 Haleru = 1 Koruna

REPUBLIC

2 HALERE

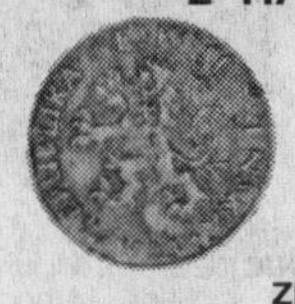

ZINC

KM#	Date	Mintage	Fine	VF	XF	Unc
5	1923	2.700	3.00	5.00	7.50	15.00
	1924	17.300	2.25	3.50	5.00	9.00
	1925	2.000	3.00	5.00	7.50	15.00

5 HALERU

BRONZE

KM#	Date	Mintage	Fine	VF	XF	Unc
6	1923	37.800	.20	.30	.50	2.00
	1924	10 pcs.	—	—	—	1800.
	1925	12.000	.20	.30	.50	2.50
	1926	1.084	1.50	3.25	6.00	12.00
	1927	8.916	.25	.35	.75	2.50
	1928	5.320	.30	.45	.75	2.50
	1929	12.680	.25	.35	.75	2.50
	1930	5.000	.25	.35	.75	2.50
	1931	7.448	.25	.35	.75	2.50
	1932	3.556	.60	1.00	2.00	5.00
	1938	14.244	.25	.35	.75	2.00

10 HALERU

BRONZE

KM#	Date	Mintage	Fine	VF	XF	Unc
3	1922	6.000	.30	.45	1.00	2.75
	1923	24.000	.25	.35	.75	2.00
	1924	5.320	.30	.45	1.00	3.00
	1925	24.680	.25	.35	.60	2.25
	1926	10.000	.25	.35	.75	2.25
	1927	10.000	.25	.35	.75	2.25
	1928	14.290	.25	.35	.75	2.25
	1929	5.710	1.25	2.00	3.50	7.00
	1930	6.980	.30	.45	1.00	2.50
	1931	6.740	.30	.45	1.00	2.50
	1932	11.280	.25	.35	.75	2.00
	1933	4.190	.35	.60	1.25	5.00
	1934	13.200	.25	.35	.75	2.00

KM#	Date	Mintage	Fine	VF	XF	Unc
3	1935	3.420	.50	.75	1.50	5.00
	1936	8.560	.25	.35	.75	2.00
	1937	20.200	.25	.35	.75	2.00
	1938	21.400	.25	.35	.75	2.00

20 HALERU

COPPER-NICKEL

KM#	Date	Mintage	Fine	VF	XF	Unc
1	1921	40.000	.25	.35	.60	2.50
	1922	9,100	.25	.35	.60	2.50
	1924	20.931	.25	.35	.60	2.50
	1925	4.244	.60	1.00	2.00	6.00
	1926	14.825	.25	.35	.60	2.50
	1927	11.757	.25	.35	.60	2.50
	1928	14.018	.25	.35	.60	2.50
	1929	4.225	.30	.50	1.25	3.50
	1930	—	.30	.40	.75	3.00
	1931	5.000	.30	.40	.75	3.00
	1933	Inc. Ab.	2.50	3.50	7.00	14.00
	1937	8.208	.25	.35	.60	2.50
	1938	18.787	.25	.35	.60	2.50

25 HALERU

COPPER-NICKEL

KM#	Date	Mintage	Fine	VF	XF	Unc
16	1933	22.711	.50	1.00	2.00	4.00

50 HALERU

COPPER-NICKEL

KM#	Date	Mintage	Fine	VF	XF	Unc
2	1921	3.000	.25	.50	1.00	3.00
	1922	37.000	.20	.40	.60	2.50
	1924	10.000	.20	.40	.60	2.50
	1925	1.415	.50	1.00	2.00	5.00
	1926	1.585	1.25	2.00	4.00	10.00
	1927	2.000	.50	1.00	2.00	6.00
	1931	6.000	.25	.50	1.00	2.50

KORUNA

COPPER-NICKEL

KM#	Date	Mintage	Fine	VF	XF	Unc
4	1922	50.000	.30	.50	.75	2.00
	1923	15.385	.30	.50	.75	2.00
	1924	21.041	.30	.50	.75	2.00
	1925	8.574	.40	.60	1.00	3.00
	1929	5.000	.50	.75	1.25	3.50
	1930	5.000	1.00	1.50	3.00	8.00
	1937	3.806	.40	.60	1.00	3.00
	1938	8.582	.40	.60	1.00	3.00

5 KORUN

COPPER-NICKEL

KM#	Date	Mintage	Fine	VF	XF	Unc
10	1925	16.475	1.50	2.50	3.00	6.00
	1926	8.912	1.75	2.75	3.50	8.00
	1927	4.614	2.50	4.00	5.75	10.00

7.0000 g, .500 SILVER, .1125 oz ASW

KM#	Date	Mintage	Fine	VF	XF	Unc
11	1928	1.710	2.00	3.00	5.00	10.00
	1929	12.861	1.00	2.00	4.00	8.50
	1930	10.429	1.00	2.00	4.00	8.50
	1931	2.000	2.00	3.00	5.00	10.00
	1932	1.000	5.00	7.50	10.00	35.00

NOTE: Edge varieties exist.

NICKEL

KM#	Date	Mintage	Fine	VF	XF	Unc
11a	1937	—	60.00	100.00	150.00	250.00
	1938	17.200	1.25	2.50	4.00	6.50

10 KORUN

10.0000 g, .700 SILVER, .2250 oz ASW
10th Anniversary of Independence

KM#	Date	Mintage	Fine	VF	XF	Unc
12	1928	1.000	2.00	4.00	5.00	9.00

KM#	Date	Mintage	Fine	VF	XF	Unc
15	1930	4.949	2.00	3.50	6.00	10.00
	1931	6.689	2.00	3.00	5.00	9.00
	1932	11.448	1.75	2.50	4.00	8.00
	1933	.915	7.50	12.50	35.00	125.00

20 KORUN

12.0000 g, .700 SILVER, .2700 oz ASW

KM#	Date	Mintage	Fine	VF	XF	Unc
17	1933	2.280	BV	4.00	7.50	14.00
	1934	3.280	BV	4.00	7.50	14.00

Death of President Masaryk

KM#	Date	Mintage	Fine	VF	XF	Unc
18	1937	1.000	BV	3.00	6.00	9.00

TRADE COINAGE

DUKAT

3.4900 g, .986 GOLD, .1106 oz AGW
Duke Wenceslas

KM#	Date	Mintage	VF	XF	Unc
7	1923	1,000	250.00	600.00	1000.

NOTE: The above coins are serially numbered below the duke.

Similar to KM#7 but w/o serial numbers.

KM#	Date	Mintage	VF	XF	Unc
8	1923	.062	55.00	75.00	100.00
	1924	.033	55.00	75.00	100.00
	1925	.066	55.00	75.00	100.00
	1926	.059	55.00	75.00	100.00
	1927	.026	55.00	75.00	100.00
	1928	.019	55.00	75.00	115.00
	1929	.010	60.00	80.00	150.00
	1930	.011	60.00	80.00	150.00
	1931	.043	55.00	75.00	100.00
	1932	.027	55.00	75.00	100.00
	1933	.058	55.00	75.00	100.00
	1934	9,729	80.00	100.00	160.00
	1935	.013	55.00	75.00	115.00
	1936	.015	55.00	75.00	115.00
	1937	324 pcs.	200.00	400.00	750.00
	1938	56 pcs.	600.00	800.00	1500.
	1939	*276 pcs.	200.00	400.00	750.00
	1951	500 pcs.	150.00	300.00	750.00

***NOTE:** Czech reports show mintage of 20 for Czechoslovakia and 256 for state of Slovakia.

2 DUKATY

6.9800 g, .986 GOLD, .2212 oz AGW
Duke Wenceslas

KM#	Date	Mintage	VF	XF	Unc
9	1923	4,000	150.00	225.00	350.00
	1929	3,262	150.00	225.00	350.00
	1930	Inc. Ab.	150.00	250.00	400.00
	1931	2,994	150.00	225.00	350.00
	1932	5,496	150.00	225.00	350.00
	1933	4,671	150.00	225.00	350.00
	1934	2,403	150.00	225.00	350.00
	1935	2,577	150.00	225.00	350.00
	1936	819 pcs.	300.00	400.00	500.00
	1937	8 pcs.	1500.	2000.	3500.
	1938	*186 pcs.	600.00	800.00	1000.
	1951	200 Pcs.	300.00	500.00	1000.

***NOTE:** Czech reports show mintage of 14 for Czechoslovakia and 172 for state of Slovakia.

5 DUKATU

17.4500 g, .986 GOLD, .5532 oz AGW
Duke Wenceslas

KM#	Date	Mintage	VF	XF	Unc
13	1929	1,827	350.00	450.00	675.00
	1930	543 Pcs.	500.00	700.00	1000.
	1931	1,528	350.00	450.00	675.00
	1932	1,827	350.00	450.00	675.00
	1933	1,752	350.00	450.00	675.00
	1934	1,101	350.00	450.00	675.00
	1935	1,037	350.00	450.00	675.00
	1936	728 pcs.	500.00	700.00	1000.
	1937	4 pcs.	—	—	5000.
	1938	*56 pcs.	1000.	2000.	3000.
	1951	100 pcs.	400.00	800.00	2000.

***NOTE:** Czech reports show mintage of 12 for Czechoslovakia and 44 for state of Slovakia.

10 DUKATU

34.9000 g, .986 GOLD, 1.1064 oz AGW
Duke Wenceslas

KM#	Date	Mintage	VF	XF	Unc
14	1929	1,564	700.00	1000.	1400.
	1930	394 pcs.	1000.	1900.	2800.
	1931	1,239	700.00	1000.	1500.
	1932	1,035	700.00	1000.	1500.
	1933	1,780	700.00	1000.	1500.
	1934	1,298	700.00	1000.	1500.
	1935	600 pcs.	750.00	1200.	1850.
	1936	633 pcs.	750.00	1200.	1850.
	1937	34 pcs.	—	—	8000.
	1938	*192 pcs.	2000.	2800.	4000.
	1951	100 pcs.	2000.	2800.	5000.

***NOTE:** Czech reports show mintage of 20 for Czechoslovakia and 172 for state of Slovakia.

PEOPLES REPUBLIC

20 HALERU

BRONZE

KM#	Date	Mintage	Fine	VF	XF	Unc
20	1947	—	100.00	150.00	185.00	250.00
	1948	24.340	.10	.15	.40	1.00
	1949	25.660	.10	.15	.40	1.00
	1950	11.132	.10	.15	.40	1.00

ALUMINUM

KM#	Date	Mintage	Fine	VF	XF	Unc
31	1951	46.800	.10	.15	.25	.50
	1952	80.340	.10	.15	.25	.50

50 HALERU

BRONZE

KM#	Date	Mintage	Fine	VF	XF	Unc
21	1947	50.000	.15	.25	.40	1.00
	1948	20.000	.15	.25	.40	1.00
	1949	12.715	.15	.25	.40	1.00
	1950	17.415	.15	.25	.40	1.00

ALUMINUM

KM#	Date	Mintage	Fine	VF	XF	Unc
32	1951	60.000	.15	.35	.50	.75
	1952	60.000	.25	.45	.60	1.00
	1953	34.920	.60	1.00	2.00	5.00

KORUNA

COPPER-NICKEL

KM#	Date	Mintage	Fine	VF	XF	Unc
19	1946	88.000	.15	.25	.50	1.00
	1947	12.550	1.50	2.50	3.75	6.50

ALUMINUM

KM#	Date	Mintage	Fine	VF	XF	Unc
22	1947	—	25.00	65.00	100.00	150.00
(32)	1950	62.190	.20	.35	.45	.75
	1951	61.395	.20	.35	.45	.75
	1952	101.105	.20	.30	.40	.65
	1953	73.905	.40	.75	1.75	3.25

2 KORUNY

COPPER-NICKEL

KM#	Date	Mintage	Fine	VF	XF	Unc
23	1947	20.000	.20	.40	.60	1.25
	1948	20.476	.20	.40	.60	1.50

5 KORUN

ALUMINUM

KM#	Date	Mintage	Fine	VF	XF	Unc
34	1952	40.715	17.50	25.00	35.00	45.00

NOTE: Not released for circulation. Almost the entire mintage was melted.

50 KORUN

10.0000 g, .500 SILVER, .1607 oz ASW
1944 Slovak Uprising

KM#	Date	Mintage	Fine	VF	XF	Unc
24	1947	1.000	BV	2.50	3.50	5.00

3rd Anniversary Prague Uprising

KM#	Date	Mintage	Fine	VF	XF	Unc
25	1948	1.000	BV	2.50	3.50	5.00

Stalin 70th Birthday

KM#	Date	Mintage	Fine	VF	XF	Unc
28	1949	1.000	BV	2.50	3.50	5.00

100 KORUN

14.0000 g, .500 SILVER, .2250 oz ASW
600th Anniversary Charles University

KM#	Date	Mintage	Fine	VF	XF	Unc
26	1948	1.000	BV	2.50	3.50	5.50

30th Anniversary of Independence

KM#	Date	Mintage	Fine	VF	XF	Unc
27	1948	1.000	BV	2.50	3.50	5.50

7th Centennial Jihlava Mining Privileges

KM#	Date	Mintage	Fine	VF	XF	Unc
29	1949	1.000	BV	2.50	3.50	5.50

Stalin 70th Birthday

KM#	Date	Mintage	Fine	VF	XF	Unc
30	1949	1.000	BV	2.50	3.50	5.50

30th Anniversary Communist Party

KM#	Date	Mintage	Fine	VF	XF	Unc
33	1951	1.000	BV	2.50	3.50	5.50

MONETARY REFORM

HALER

ALUMINUM

KM#	Date	Mintage	Fine	VF	XF	Unc
35	1953	.030	—	—	.10	.20
	1954	—	—	—	.10	.20
	1955	—	—	—	.10	.20
	1956	—	—	—	.10	.20
	1957	—	—	—	.10	.20
	1958	—	.10	.25	.35	.60
	1959	—	—	—	.10	.20
	1960	—	—	—	.10	.20

3 HALERE

ALUMINUM

KM#	Date	Mintage	Fine	VF	XF	Unc
36	1953	.040	—	.10	.15	.25
	1954	—	—	.10	.15	.25

5 HALERU

ALUMINUM

KM#	Date	Mintage	Fine	VF	XF	Unc
37	1953	.060	.10	.15	.25	.40
	1954	—	.10	.15	.25	.40
	1955	—	.30	.50	.75	2.00

10 HALERU

ALUMINUM

KM#	Date	Mintage	Fine	VF	XF	Unc
38	1953(k)	—	—	.10	.20	.40
	1953(l)	.160	.10	.15	.30	.75
	1953(u)	—	—	—	—	—
	1954	—	—	.10	.20	.40
	1955	—	.50	.75	1.25	2.00
	1956	—	—	.10	.20	.40
	1958	—	—	.10	.20	.40

(k) - Kremnica-130 notches in milled edge.
(l) - Leningrad-133 notches in milled edge.
(u) - Unknown-125 notches in milled edge.

25 HALERU

ALUMINUM

KM#	Date	Mintage	Fine	VF	XF	Unc
39	1953(k)	—	.10	.20	.30	.60
	1953(l)	.160	.30	.50	.60	1.00
	1954	—	.10	.20	.30	.60

(k) - Kremnica-134 notches in milled edge.
(l) - Leningrad-145 notches in milled edge.
(u) - Unknown-135 notches in milled edge.

KORUNA

ALUMINUM-BRONZE

KM#	Date	Mintage	Fine	VF	XF	Unc
46	1957	—	.20	.30	.45	1.00
	1958	—	.20	.30	.45	1.00
	1959	—	.15	.25	.35	.60
	1960	—	.15	.25	.35	.60

10 KORUN

12.0000 g, .500 SILVER, .1929 oz ASW
10th Anniversary Slovak Uprising

KM#	Date	Mintage	Fine	VF	XF	Unc
40	1954	.245	BV	2.00	3.00	4.00
	1954	5,000	—	—	Proof	6.00

10th Anniversary of Liberation From Germany

KM#	Date	Mintage	Fine	VF	XF	Unc
42	1955	.295	BV	2.50	3.50	5.00
	1955	5,000	—	—	Proof	7.00

250th Anniversary Technical College
Raised designer initials.

KM#	Date	Mintage	Fine	VF	XF	Unc
47.1	1957	.075	BV	2.50	3.50	5.50

Incuse designer initials.

KM#	Date	Mintage	Fine	VF	XF	Unc
47.2	1957	5,000	—	—	Proof	8.00

J. A. Komensky

KM#	Date	Mintage	Fine	VF	XF	Unc
48	1957	.150	BV	2.50	3.50	5.50
	1957	5,000	—	—	Proof	8.00

25 KORUN

16.0000 g, .500 SILVER, .2572 oz ASW
10th Anniversary Slovak Uprising

KM#	Date	Mintage	Fine	VF	XF	Unc
41	1954	.245	—	—	5.00	7.00
	1954	5,000	—	—	Proof	10.00

10th Anniversary of Liberation From Germany

KM#	Date	Mintage	Fine	VF	XF	Unc
43	1955	.195	—	—	5.00	7.00
	1955	5,000	—	—	Proof	12.50

50 KORUN

20.0000 g, .900 SILVER, .5787 oz ASW
10th Anniversary of Liberation From Germany

KM#	Date	Mintage	Fine	VF	XF	Unc
44	1955	.120	BV	6.00	10.00	18.00

NOTE: 2 varieties of artists name exist.

100 KORUN

24.0000 g, .900 SILVER, .6945 oz ASW
10th Anniversary of Liberation From Germany

KM#	Date	Mintage	Fine	VF	XF	Unc
45	1955	.075	BV	9.00	16.00	25.00

SOCIALIST REPUBLIC

1960 - 1990

HALER

ALUMINUM

KM#	Date	Mintage	Fine	VF	XF	Unc
51	1962	—	—	—	.10	.15
	1963	—	—	—	.10	.15
	1963	—	—	—	Proof	—
	1986	—	—	—	.10	.15

3 HALERE

ALUMINUM

KM#	Date	Mintage	Fine	VF	XF	Unc
52	1962	—	150.00	200.00	250.00	300.00
	1963	—	—	—	.10	.15
	1963	—	—	—	Proof	—

5 HALERU

ALUMINUM

KM#	Date	Mintage	Fine	VF	XF	Unc
53	1962	—	—	.10	.15	.25
	1963	—	—	.10	.15	.25
	1966	—	—	.10	.15	.25
	1966	—	—	—	Proof	Rare
	1967	—	—	.10	.15	.25
	1970	—	—	.10	.15	.20
	1972	—	—	.10	.15	.20
	1973	—	—	.10	.15	.20
	1974	—	—	.10	.15	.20
	1975	—	—	.10	.15	.20
	1976	—	—	.10	.15	.20

KM#	Date	Mintage	Fine	VF	XF	Unc
86	1977	—	—	—	.10	.25
	1978	—	—	—	.10	.25
	1979	—	—	—	.10	.25
	1980	—	—	—	.10	.25
	1981	—	—	—	.10	.25
	1981	—	—	—	Proof	—
	1982	—	—	In mint set only		.50
	1983	—	—	—	.10	.25
86	1984	—	—	In mint set only		—
	1985	—	—	In mint set only		—
	1986	—	—	—	.10	.25
	1986	—	—	—	Proof	—
	1987	—	—	—	.10	.25
	1988	8.000	—	—	.10	.25
	1989	—	—	—	.10	.25
	1990	—	—	—	.10	.25

10 HALERU

ALUMINUM

KM#	Date	Mintage	Fine	VF	XF	Unc
49.1	1961	—	—	.10	.20	.35
	1962	—	—	.10	.20	.35
	1963	—	—	.10	.20	.35
	1964	—	—	.10	.20	.35
	1965	—	—	.10	.20	.35
	1966	—	—	.10	.20	.35
	1966	—	—	—	Proof	Rare
	1967	—	—	.10	.20	.35
	1968	—	—	.10	.20	.35
	1969	—	—	.10	.15	.35
	1970	—	—	.10	.20	.35
	1971	—	—	.10	.20	.35
	1974	—	—	.10	.20	.35

Obv: Flat top 3 in date.

KM#	Date	Mintage	Fine	VF	XF	Unc
49.2	1963	3,600 est.	12.50	25.00	37.50	65.00

KM#	Date	Mintage	Fine	VF	XF	Unc
80	1974	—	—	—	.10	.25
	1975	—	—	—	.10	.25
	1976	—	—	—	.10	.25
	1977	—	—	—	.10	.25
	1978	—	—	—	.10	.25
	1979	—	—	—	.10	.25
	1980	—	—	—	.10	.25
	1981	—	—	—	.10	.25
	1981	—	—	—	Proof	—
	1982	—	—	—	.10	.25
	1983	—	—	—	.10	.25
	1984	—	—	—	.10	.25
	1985	—	—	—	.10	.25
	1986	—	—	—	.10	.25
	1987	30.000	—	—	.10	.25
	1988	46.320	—	—	.10	.25
	1989	—	—	—	.10	.25
	1990	—	—	—	.10	.25

NOTE: Varieties exist.

20 HALERU

BRASS

KM#	Date	Mintage	Fine	VF	XF	Unc
74	1972	—	—	.10	.20	.40
	1973	—	—	.10	.20	.40
	1974	—	—	.10	.20	.40
	1975	—	—	.10	.20	.40
	1976	—	—	.10	.20	.40
	1977	—	—	.10	.20	.40
	1978	—	—	.10	.20	.40
	1979	—	—	.10	.20	.40
	1980	—	—	.10	.15	.30
	1981	—	—	.10	.15	.30
	1981	—	—	—	Proof	—
	1982	—	—	.10	.15	.30
	1983	—	—	.10	.15	.30
74	1984	—	—	.10	.15	.30
	1985	—	—	.10	.15	.30
	1986	—	—	.10	.15	.30
	1987	26.945	—	.10	.15	.30
	1988	17.000	—	.10	.15	.30
	1989	—	—	.10	.15	.30
	1990	—	—	.10	.15	.30

NOTE: Varieties exist.

25 HALERU

ALUMINUM

KM#	Date	Mintage	Fine	VF	XF	Unc
54	1962	—	.10	.15	.20	.35
	1963	—	.10	.15	.20	.35
	1964	—	.10	.15	.20	.35
	1964	—	—	—	Proof	—

NOTE: 25 Haleru ceased to be legal tender Dec. 31, 1972.

50 HALERU

BRONZE

KM#	Date	Mintage	Fine	VF	XF	Unc
55.1	1963	—	.10	.20	.30	.45
	1964	—	.10	.20	.30	.45
	1965	—	.10	.20	.30	.45
	1965	—	—	—	Proof	—
	1969	—	.10	.20	.30	.45
	1970	—	.10	.20	.30	.40
	1971	—	.10	.20	.30	.40

Obv: Small date, w/o dots.

KM#	Date	Mintage	Fine	VF	XF	Unc
55.2	1969	—	12.50	20.00	35.00	60.00

COPPER-NICKEL

KM#	Date	Mintage	Fine	VF	XF	Unc
89	1978	—	—	—	.10	.50
	1979	—	—	—	.10	.50
	1980	—	—	—	.10	.50
	1981	—	—	—	.10	.50
	1981	—	—	—	Proof	—
	1982	—	—	—	.10	.50
	1983	—	—	—	.10	.50
	1984	—	—	—	.10	.50
	1985	—	—	—	.10	.50
	1986	—	—	—	.10	.50
	1987	5.108	—	—	.10	.50
	1988	5.012	—	—	.10	.50
	1989	—	—	—	.10	.50
	1990	—	—	—	.10	.50

NOTE: Date varieties exist.

KORUNA

ALUMINUM-BRONZE

KM#	Date	Mintage	Fine	VF	XF	Unc
50	1961	—	—	.15	.30	.60
	1962	—	—	.15	.30	.60
	1963	—	—	.15	.30	.60
	1964	—	—	.15	.30	.60
	1965	—	—	.15	.30	.60
	1966	—	.40	.65	.90	1.25
	1966	—	—	—	Proof	Rare
	1967	—	—	.15	.30	.60
	1968	—	—	.15	.30	.60
	1969	—	—	.15	.30	.60
	1970	—	—	.15	.30	.60
	1971	—	—	.15	.30	.60
	1975	—	—	.15	.30	.60
	1976	—	—	.15	.30	.60
	1977	—	—	.15	.30	.75
	1979	—	—	.15	.30	.75
	1980	—	—	.15	.30	.75
	1981	—	—	.15	.30	.75
	1981	—	—	—	Proof	—
	1982	—	—	.15	.30	.75
	1983	—	—	.15	.30	.75

KM#	Date	Mintage	Fine	VF	XF	Unc
50	1984	—	—	.15	.30	.75
	1985	—	—	.15	.30	.75
	1986	—	—	.15	.30	.75
	1987	—	—	.15	.30	.75
	1988	—	—	.15	.30	.75
	1989	—	—	.15	.30	.75
	1990	—	—	.15	.30	.75

NOTE: Date varieties exist.

2 KORUNY

COPPER-NICKEL

KM#	Date	Mintage	Fine	VF	XF	Unc
75	1972	—	—	.25	.35	.75
	1973	—	—	.25	.35	.75
	1974	—	—	.25	.35	.75
	1975	—	—	.25	.35	.75
	1976	—	—	.25	.35	.75
	1977	—	—	.25	.35	.75
	1980	—	—	.25	.35	.75
	1981	—	—	.25	.35	.75
	1981	—	—	—	Proof	—
	1982	—	—	.25	.35	.75
	1983	—	—	.25	.35	.75
	1984	—	—	.25	.35	.75
	1985	—	—	.25	.35	.75
	1986	—	—	.25	.35	.75
	1987	—	—	.25	.35	.75
	1988	—	—	.25	.35	.75
	1989	—	—	.25	.35	.75
	1990	—	—	.25	.35	.75

NOTE: Date and edge varieties exist.

3 KORUNY

COPPER-NICKEL

KM#	Date	Mintage	Fine	VF	XF	Unc
57	1965	—	—	.40	.60	1.00
	1966	—	—	.40	.60	1.00
	1966	—	—	—	Proof	Rare
	1968	—	—	.40	.60	1.00
	1969	—	—	.40	.60	1.00

5 KORUN

COPPER-NICKEL

KM#	Date	Mintage	Fine	VF	XF	Unc
60	1966	—	—	.75	1.00	2.00
	1966	—	—	—	Proof	Rare

1966 Varieties on obverse of coin

Large Date: No space between letter B in REPUBLIC and coat of arms.

Small Date: Space between letter B in REPUBLIC and coat of arms.

Plain Edge: No ornamental inscription on edge.

NOTE: So far there has been no indication of any of the varieties as being scarce.

KM#	Date	Mintage	Fine	VF	XF	Unc
	1967	—	—	—	.75	1.50
	1968	—	—	—	.75	1.50
	1969 straight date	—	—	—	.75	1.50
	1969 date in semi-circle	—	.75	1.25	2.00	3.00
	1970	—	—	—	.75	1.50
	1973 (2 vars.)	—	—	—	.75	1.25
	1974 (3 vars.)	—	—	—	.75	1.25
	1975	—	—	—	.75	1.25
	1978	—	—	—	.75	1.25
	1979	—	—	—	.75	1.25
	1980	—	—	—	.75	1.25
	1981	—	—	—	.75	1.25
	1981	—	—	—	Proof	—
	1982	—	—	—	.75	1.25
	1983	—	—	—	.75	1.25
	1984	—	—	—	.75	1.25
	1985	—	—	—	.75	1.25
	1986	—	—	—	.75	1.25
	1987	—	—	—	.75	1.25
	1988	—	—	—	.75	1.25
	1989	—	—	—	.75	1.25
	1990	—	—	—	.75	1.25

10 KORUN

12.0000 g, .500 SILVER, .1929 oz ASW
20th Anniversary 1944 Slovak Uprising

KM#	Date	Mintage	Fine	VF	XF	Unc
56	1964	.120	—	—	3.00	4.00

550th Anniversary of Death of Jan Hus

KM#	Date	Mintage	Fine	VF	XF	Unc
58	1965	.055	—	—	5.00	7.00
	1965	5,000	—	—	Proof	9.00

1100th Anniversary of Great Moravia

KM#	Date	Mintage	Fine	VF	XF	Unc
61	1966	.115	—	—	4.00	6.00
	1966	5,000	—	—	Proof	9.00

500th Anniversary Bratislava University

KM#	Date	Mintage	Fine	VF	XF	Unc
62	1967	.055	—	—	9.00	12.50
	1967	5,000	—	—	Proof	17.50

Prague National Theater Centennial

KM#	Date	Mintage	Fine	VF	XF	Unc
63	1968	.055	—	—	15.00	20.00
	1968	5,000	—	—	Proof	40.00

20 KORUN

9.0000 g, .500 SILVER, .1446 oz ASW
Centennial Death of Andrej Sladkovic

KM#	Date	Mintage	Fine	VF	XF	Unc
76	1972	.055	—	—	3.00	4.00
	1972	5,000	—	—	Proof	15.00

25 KORUN

16.0000 g, .500 SILVER, .2572 oz ASW
20th Anniversary Czechoslovakian Liberation

KM#	Date	Mintage	Fine	VF	XF	Unc
59	1965	.145	—	—	5.00	8.00
	1965	5,000	—	—	Proof	15.00

Sesquicentennial Prague National Museum

KM#	Date	Mintage	Fine	VF	XF	Unc
64	1968	.055	—	—	5.00	8.00
	1968	5,000	—	—	Proof	50.00

100th Anniversary Death of J. E. Purkinje

KM#	Date	Mintage	Fine	VF	XF	Unc
66	1969	.045	—	—	5.00	8.00
	1969	5,000	—	—	Proof	10.00

NOTE: Edge varieties exist.

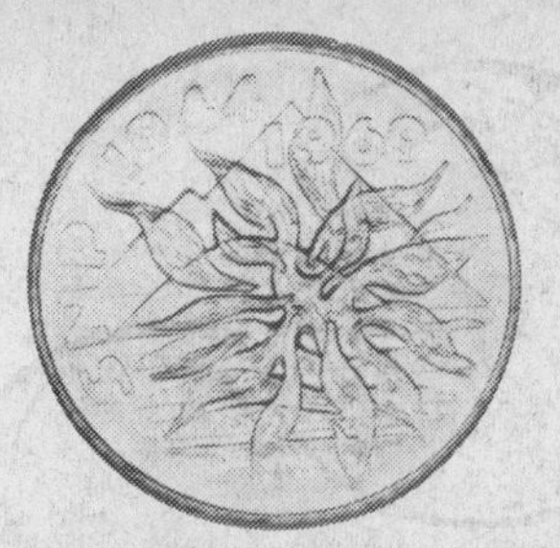

25th Anniversary 1944 Slovak Uprising

KM#	Date	Mintage	Fine	VF	XF	Unc
67	1969	.025	—	—	17.50	30.00
	1969	5,000	—	—	Proof	40.00

NOTE: Edge varieties exist.

10.0000 g, .500 SILVER, .1607 oz ASW
50th Anniversary Slovak National Theater

KM#	Date	Mintage	Fine	VF	XF	Unc
68	1970	.045	—	—	4.00	7.00
	1970	5,000	—	—	Proof	45.00

25th Anniversary of Liberation

KM#	Date	Mintage	Fine	VF	XF	Unc
69	1970	.095	—	—	4.00	6.00
	1970	5,000	—	—	Proof	15.00

50 KORUN

20.0000 g, .900 SILVER, .5787 oz ASW
50th Anniversary of Czechoslovakia
20th Anniversary People's Republic

KM#	Date	Mintage	Fine	VF	XF	Unc
65	1968	.058	—	—	25.00	45.00
	1968	2,000	—	—	Proof	175.00

13.0000 g, .700 SILVER, .2926 oz ASW

Centennial of Birth of Lenin

KM#	Date	Mintage	Fine	VF	XF	Unc
70	1970	.044	—	—	5.00	8.00
	1970	6,200	—	—	Proof	30.00

50th Anniversary Czechoslovak Communist Party

KM#	Date	Mintage	Fine	VF	XF	Unc
71	1971	.045	—	—	5.00	8.00
	1971	5,000	—	—	Proof	40.00

50th Anniv. Death of Pavol Orsagh-Hviezdoslav

KM#	Date	Mintage	Fine	VF	XF	Unc
72	1971	.045	—	—	5.00	8.00
	1971	5,000	—	—	Proof	35.00

50th Anniversary Death of J.V.Myslbek

KM#	Date	Mintage	Fine	VF	XF	Unc
77	1972	.045	—	—	5.00	8.00
	1972	5,000	—	—	Proof	30.00

25th Anniversary Victory of Communist Party

KM#	Date	Mintage	Fine	VF	XF	Unc
78	1973	.055	—	—	5.00	8.00
	1973	5,000	—	—	Proof	30.00

200th Anniversary Birth of Josef Jungmann

KM#	Date	Mintage	Fine	VF	XF	Unc
79	1973	.045	—	—	5.00	8.00
	1973	5,000	—	—	Proof	14.00

Janko Jesensky Birth Centennial

KM#	Date	Mintage	Fine	VF	XF	Unc
81	1974	.055	—	—	5.00	8.00
	1974	5,000	—	—	Proof	14.00

S. K. Neumann Birth Centennial

KM#	Date	Mintage	Fine	VF	XF	Unc
83	1975	.055	—	—	5.00	8.00
	1975	5,000	—	—	Proof	10.00

125th Anniversary of Death of Jan Kollar

KM#	Date	Mintage	Fine	VF	XF	Unc
87	1977	.075	—	—	5.00	8.00
	1977	5,000	—	—	Proof	10.00

Centennial of Birth of Zdenek Nejedly

KM#	Date	Mintage	Fine	VF	XF	Unc
90	1978	.075	—	—	5.00	8.00
	1978	5,000	—	—	Proof	10.00

650th Anniversary of Kremnica Mint

KM#	Date	Mintage	Fine	VF	XF	Unc
91	1978	.093	—	—	5.00	8.00
	1978	7,000	—	—	Proof	10.00

30th Anniversary of 9th Congress

KM#	Date	Mintage	Fine	VF	XF	Unc
98	1979	.094	—	—	5.00	8.00
	1979	6,000	—	—	Proof	10.00

7.0000 g, .500 SILVER, .1125 oz ASW
Prague

KM#	Date	Mintage	Fine	VF	XF	Unc
121	1986	.090	—	—	—	6.00
	1986	.010	—	—	Proof	9.00

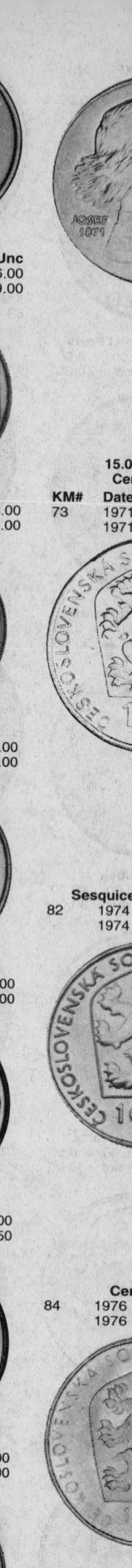

Levoca

KM#	Date	Mintage	Fine	VF	XF	Unc
122	1986	.090	—	—	—	6.00
	1986	.010	—	—	Proof	9.00

Telc

KM#	Date	Mintage	Fine	VF	XF	Unc
124	1986	.090	—	—	—	6.00
	1986	.010	—	—	Proof	9.00

Bratislava

KM#	Date	Mintage	Fine	VF	XF	Unc
125	1986	.090	—	—	—	6.00
	1986	.010	—	—	Proof	9.00

Cesky Krumlov

KM#	Date	Mintage	Fine	VF	XF	Unc
126	1986	.090	—	—	—	6.00
	1986	.010	—	—	Proof	9.00

Environmental Protection - Horses

KM#	Date	Mintage	Fine	VF	XF	Unc
127	1987	.055	—	—	—	6.00
	1987	5,000	—	—	Proof	12.50

300th Anniversary of Birth of Juraj Janosik

KM#	Date	Mintage	Fine	VF	XF	Unc
129	1988	.055	—	—	—	10.00
	1988	5,000	—	—	Proof	16.00

150th Anniversary of Breclav to Brno Railroad

KM#	Date	Mintage	Fine	VF	XF	Unc
133	1989	.057	—	—	—	10.00
	1989	3,000	—	—	Proof	17.50

100 KORUN

15.0000 g, .700 SILVER, .3376 oz ASW
Centennial of Death of Josef Manes

KM#	Date	Mintage	Fine	VF	XF	Unc
73	1971	.045	—	—	12.00	15.00
	1971	5,000	—	—	Proof	27.50

Sesquicentennial of Birth of Bedrich Smetana

KM#	Date	Mintage	Fine	VF	XF	Unc
82	1974	.075	—	—	12.00	15.00
	1974	5,000	—	—	Proof	20.00

Centennial of Death of Janko Kral

KM#	Date	Mintage	Fine	VF	XF	Unc
84	1976	.075	—	—	12.00	15.00
	1976	5,000	—	—	Proof	20.00

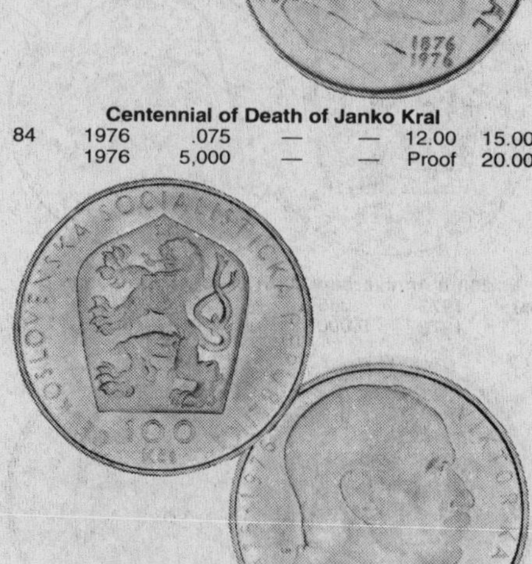

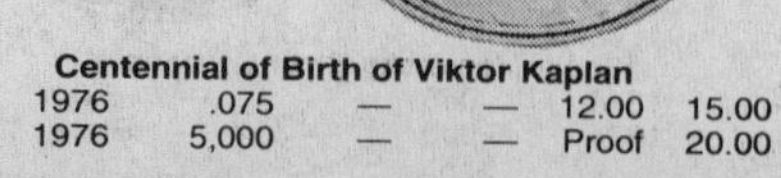

Centennial of Birth of Viktor Kaplan

KM#	Date	Mintage	Fine	VF	XF	Unc
85	1976	.075	—	—	12.00	15.00
	1976	5,000	—	—	Proof	20.00

300th Anniversary of Death of Venceslas Hollar

KM#	Date	Mintage	Fine	VF	XF	Unc
88	1977	.095	—	—	12.00	15.00
	1977	5,000	—	—	Proof	20.00

75th Anniversary of Birth of Julius Fucik

KM#	Date	Mintage	Fine	VF	XF	Unc
92	1978	.075	—	—	12.00	15.00
	1978	5,000	—	—	Proof	20.00

600th Anniversary of Death of King Karel IV

KM#	Date	Mintage	Fine	VF	XF	Unc
93	1978	.090	—	—	12.00	15.00
	1978	.010	—	—	Proof	20.00

150th Anniversary of Birth of Jan Botto

KM#	Date	Mintage	Fine	VF	XF	Unc
99	1979	.075	—	—	12.00	15.00
	1979	5,000	—	—	Proof	20.00

650th Anniversary Birth of Peter Parler

KM#	Date	Mintage	Fine	VF	XF	Unc
100	1980	.091	—	—	12.00	15.00
	1980	9,000	—	—	Proof	20.00

9.0000 g, .500 SILVER, .1446 oz ASW
Fifth Spartakiade Games

KM#	Date	Mintage	Fine	VF	XF	Unc
101	1980	.110	—	—	—	15.00
	1980	.010	—	—	Proof	20.00

Centennial of Birth of Bohumir Smeral

KM#	Date	Mintage	Fine	VF	XF	Unc
102	1980	.074	—	—	—	15.00
	1980	6,000	—	—	Proof	20.00

20th Anniversary of Manned Space Flight

KM#	Date	Mintage	Fine	VF	XF	Unc
103	1981	.095	—	—	—	15.00
	1981	5,000	—	—	Proof	20.00

Centennial of Birth of Prof. Otakar Spaniel

KM#	Date	Mintage	Fine	VF	XF	Unc
104	1981	.115	—	—	—	15.00
	1981	5,000	—	—	Proof	20.00

Centennial of Birth of Ivan Olbracht

KM#	Date	Mintage	Fine	VF	XF	Unc
106	1982	.076	—	—	—	15.00
	1982	4,000	—	—	Proof	20.00

150th Anniversary of Horse Drawn Railway

KM#	Date	Mintage	Fine	VF	XF	Unc
107	1982	.076	—	—	—	15.00
	1982	7,000	—	—	Proof	20.00

100th Anniversary of Death of Karl Marx

KM#	Date	Mintage	Fine	VF	XF	Unc
108	1982	.076	—	—	—	15.00
	1982	4,000	—	—	Proof	20.00

Centennial of Birth of Jaroslav Hasek

KM#	Date	Mintage	Fine	VF	XF	Unc
109	1983	.076	—	—	—	15.00
	1983	4,000	—	—	Proof	20.00

Centennial of Death of Samo Chalupka

KM#	Date	Mintage	Fine	VF	XF	Unc
110	1983	.076	—	—	—	15.00
	1983	4,000	—	—	Proof	20.00

100th Anniversary of Prague Theater

KM#	Date	Mintage	Fine	VF	XF	Unc
111	1983	.140	—	—	—	15.00
	1983	.010	—	—	Proof	20.00

300th Anniversary of Birth of Matej Bel

KM#	Date	Mintage	Fine	VF	XF	Unc
113	1984	.057	—	—	—	15.00
	1984	3,000	—	—	Proof	20.00

150th Anniversary of Birth of Jan Neruda

KM#	Date	Mintage	Fine	VF	XF	Unc
114	1984	.076	—	—	—	15.00
	1984	4,000	—	—	Proof	20.00

Centennial of Birth of Antonin Zapotocky

KM#	Date	Mintage	Fine	VF	XF	Unc
115	1984	.076	—	—	—	15.00
	1984	4,000	—	—	Proof	20.00

200th Anniversary of Birth of Jan Holly

KM#	Date	Mintage	Fine	VF	XF	Unc
116	1985	.062	—	—	—	15.00
	1985	3,000	—	—	Proof	20.00

1985 Ice Hockey Championships

KM#	Date	Mintage	Fine	VF	XF	Unc
117	1985	.066	—	—	—	15.00
	1985	4,000	—	—	Proof	20.00

125th Anniversary of Birth of Martin Kukucin

KM#	Date	Mintage	Fine	VF	XF	Unc
118	1985	.062	—	—	—	15.00
	1985	3,000	—	—	Proof	20.00

10th Anniversary of Helsinki Conference

KM#	Date	Mintage	Fine	VF	XF	Unc
119	1985	.075	—	—	—	15.00
	1985	5,000	—	—	Proof	20.00

250th Anniversary of Death of Petr Brandl

KM#	Date	Mintage	Fine	VF	XF	Unc
120	1985	.071	—	—	—	15.00
	1985	4,000	—	—	Proof	20.00

150th Anniversary of Death of Karel Hynek Macha

KM#	Date	Mintage	Fine	VF	XF	Unc
123	1986	.075	—	—	—	15.00
	1986	5,000	—	—	Proof	20.00

13.0000 g, .500 SILVER, .2090 oz ASW
225th Anniversary of Mining Academy

KM#	Date	Mintage	Fine	VF	XF	Unc
128	1987	.075	—	—	—	15.00
	1987	5,000	—	—	Proof	27.50

Prague Exposition

KM#	Date	Mintage	Fine	VF	XF	Unc
130	1988	.075	—	—	—	15.00
	1988	5,000	—	—	Proof	35.00

Centennial of Birth of Martin Benka

KM#	Date	Mintage	Fine	VF	XF	Unc
132	1988	.065	—	—	—	20.00
	1988	5,000	—	—	Proof	40.00

50th Anniversary of Student Organization Against Occupation and Fascism

KM#	Date	Mintage	Fine	VF	XF	Unc
135	1989	.057	—	—	—	15.00
	1989	3,000	—	—	Proof	30.00

100th Anniversary of Birth of Karel Capek

KM#	Date	Mintage	Fine	VF	XF	Unc
137	1990	.067	—	—	—	15.00
	1990	3,500	—	—	Proof	30.00

250th Anniversary of Death of Jan Kupecky

KM#	Date	Mintage	Fine	VF	XF	Unc
138	1990	.058	—	—	—	15.00
	1990	2,500	—	—	Proof	30.00

500 KORUN

24.0000 g, .900 SILVER, .6944 oz ASW
125th Anniversary of Death of Ludovit Stur

KM#	Date	Mintage	Fine	VF	XF	Unc
105	1981	.051	—	—	—	55.00
	1981	4,000	—	—	Proof	100.00

100th Anniversary of Prague Theater

KM#	Date	Mintage	Fine	VF	XF	Unc
112	1983	.055	—	—	—	80.00
	1983	5,000	—	—	Proof	110.00

100th Anniversary of Birth of Josef Lada

KM#	Date	Mintage	Fine	VF	XF	Unc
136	1987	.045	—	—	—	85.00
	1987	5,000	—	—	Proof	125.00

20th Anniversary of National Federation

KM#	Date	Mintage	Fine	VF	XF	Unc
131	1988	.057	—	—	—	65.00
	1988	3,000	—	—	Proof	120.00

125th Anniversary of Matica Slovenska Institute

KM#	Date	Mintage	Fine	VF	XF	Unc
134	1988	.045	—	—	—	60.00
	1988	5,000	—	—	Proof	110.00

FEDERAL REPUBLIC

1990—

HALER

ALUMINUM

KM#	Date	Mintage	Fine	VF	XF	Unc
149	1991	—	—	—	—	.10
	1992	—	—	—	—	.10

5 HALERU

ALUMINUM

KM#	Date	Mintage	Fine	VF	XF	Unc
150	1991	.010	—	—	—	.20
	1992	Inc. Ab.	—	—	—	.20

10 HALERU

ALUMINUM

KM#	Date	Mintage	Fine	VF	XF	Unc
146	1991	.085	—	—	—	.25
	1992	Inc. Ab.	—	—	—	.25

20 HALERU

ALUMINUM

KM#	Date	Mintage	Fine	VF	XF	Unc
143	1991	.065	—	—	—	.50
	1992	Inc. Ab.	—	—	—	.50

50 HALERU

COPPER-NICKEL

KM#	Date	Mintage	Fine	VF	XF	Unc
144	1991	.030	—	—	—	.75
	1992	Inc. Ab.	—	—	—	.75

KORUNA

COPPER-ALUMINUM

KM#	Date	Mintage	Fine	VF	XF	Unc
151	1991	.040	—	—	—	1.00
	1992	Inc. Ab.	—	—	—	1.00

2 KORUNY

COPPER-NICKEL

KM#	Date	Mintage	Fine	VF	XF	Unc
148	1991	.020	—	—	—	1.25
	1992	—	—	—	—	1.25

5 KORUN

COPPER-NICKEL

KM#	Date	Mintage	Fine	VF	XF	Unc
152	1991	.010	—	—	—	1.50
	1992	—	—	—	—	1.50

10 KORUN

NICKEL-BRONZE
Thomas G. Masaryk
Designer initials below bust

KM#	Date	Mintage	Fine	VF	XF	Unc
139.1	1990	10.000	—	—	—	3.50
	1993	2.500	—	—	—	3.50

Designer name below bust: RONAI

KM#	Date	Mintage	Fine	VF	XF	Unc
139.2	1990	Inc. Ab.	—	—	—	6.50

M.R. Stefanik

KM#	Date	Mintage	Fine	VF	XF	Unc
153	1991	10.000	—	—	—	3.50
	1993	2.526	—	—	—	3.50

A. Rasin

KM#	Date	Mintage	Fine	VF	XF	Unc
159	1992	5.050	—	—	—	3.50

50 KORUN

7.0200 g, .500 SILVER, .1125 oz ASW
St. Agnes

KM#	Date	Mintage	Fine	VF	XF	Unc
140	1990	.157	—	—	—	10.00
	1990	3,000	—	—	Proof	20.00

Steamship Bohemia

KM#	Date	Mintage	Fine	VF	XF	Unc
145	1991	—	—	—	—	10.00

7.0000 g, .700 SILVER, .1575 oz ASW
Piestany Spa

KM#	Date	Mintage	Fine	VF	XF	Unc
155	1991	.077	—	—	—	10.00
	1991	3,000	—	—	Proof	20.00

Marianske Lazne Spa

KM#	Date	Mintage	Fine	VF	XF	Unc
156	1991	.075	—	—	—	10.00
	1991	5,000	—	—	Proof	20.00

Karlovy Vary Spa

KM#	Date	Mintage	Fine	VF	XF	Unc
157	1991	.075	—	—	—	10.00
	1991	5,000	—	—	Proof	20.00

100 KORUN

13.0000 g, .500 SILVER, .2090 oz ASW
Steeple Chase

KM#	Date	Mintage	Fine	VF	XF	Unc
141	1990	.067	—	—	—	15.00
	1990	3,000	—	—	Proof	35.00

Bohuslav Martinu

KM#	Date	Mintage	Fine	VF	XF	Unc
142	1990	.058	—	—	—	15.00
	1990	2,000	—	—	Proof	35.00

13.0000 g, .700 SILVER, .2926 oz ASW
Antonin Dvorak

KM#	Date	Mintage	Fine	VF	XF	Unc
147	1991	.075	—	—	—	12.00
	1991	5,000	—	—	Proof	25.00

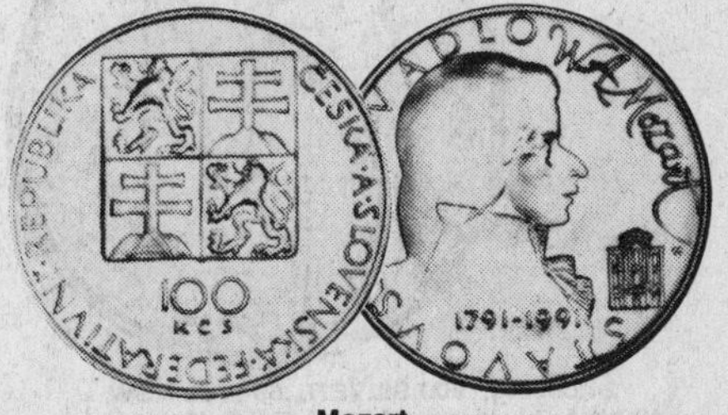

Mozart

KM#	Date	Mintage	Fine	VF	XF	Unc
154	1991	.075	—	—	—	12.00
	1991	5,000	—	—	Proof	25.00

Moravian Museum

KM#	Date	Mintage	Fine	VF	XF	Unc
160	1992	—	—	—	—	10.00
	1992	—	—	—	Proof	25.00

Nazi Massacres at Lidice and Lezaky

KM#	Date	Mintage	Fine	VF	XF	Unc
161	1992	—	—	—	—	10.00
	1992	—	—	—	Proof	25.00

Brevnovsky Monastery

KM#	Date	Mintage	Fine	VF	XF	Unc
162	1993	—	—	—	—	9.00
	1993	—	—	—	Proof	22.50

Spolosnost Slovakian Museum

KM#	Date	Mintage	Fine	VF	XF	Unc
163	1993	—	—	—	—	9.00
	1993	—	—	—	Proof	22.50

500 KORUN

24.0000 g, .900 SILVER, .6944 oz ASW
400th Anniversary of Birth of J.A. Komensky

KM#	Date	Mintage	Fine	VF	XF	Unc
158	1992	—	—	—	—	42.50
	1992	—	—	—	Proof	55.00

Tennis

KM#	Date	Mintage	Fine	VF	XF	Unc
164	1993	—	—	—	—	40.00
	1993	—	—	—	Proof	55.00

MINT SETS (MS)

KM#	Date	Mintage	Identification	Issue Price	Mkt. Val.
MS1	1980(7)	—	KM50,60,74,75,80,86,89	5.00	5.00
MS2	1981(7)	—	KM50,60,74,75,80,86,89	—	5.00
MS3	1982(7)	—	KM50,60,74,75,80,86,89	—	5.00
MS4	1983(7)	—	KM50,60,74,75,80,86,89	—	5.00
MS5	1984(7)	—	KM50,60,74,75,80,86,89	—	5.00
MS6	1985(7)	—	KM50,60,74,75,80,86,89	—	5.00
MS7	1986(7)	—	KM50,60,74,75,80,86,89	—	5.00
MS8	1987(7)	—	KM50,60,74-75,80,86,89	—	5.00
MS9	1988(7)	—	KM50,60,74-75,80,86,89	—	5.00
MS10	1989(7)	—	KM50,60,74-75,80,86,89	—	5.00
MS11	1990(7)	—	KM50,60,74-75,80,86,89	—	5.00
MS12	1991(9)	—	KM143-144,146,148-153	—	10.00
MS13	1991(8)	—	KM143-144,146,148-152	—	6.00
MS14	1992(9)	—	KM143-144,146,148-152,159	—	10.00

PROOF SETS (PS)

KM#	Date	Mintage	Identification	Issue Price	Mkt. Val.
PS1	1981(7)	—	KM50,60,74,75,80,86,89	—	—

BOHEMIA-MORAVIA

For listings previously appearing here refer to Bohemia & Moravia.

DANISH WEST INDIES

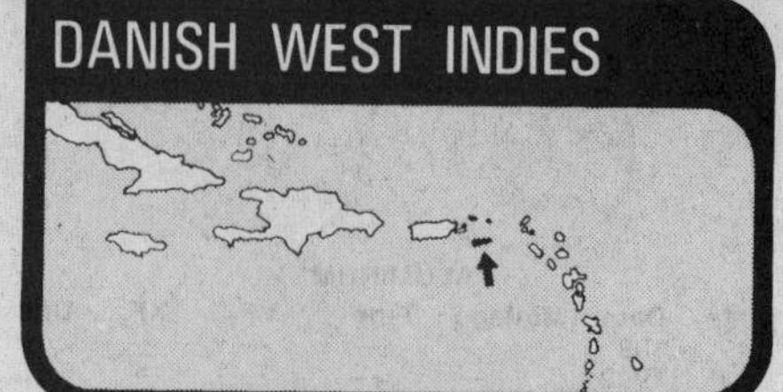

The Danish West Indies (now the U.S. organized unincorporated territory of the Virgin Islands of the United States) consisted of the islands of St. Thomas, St. John, St. Croix, and 62 islets located in the Caribbean Sea 40 miles (64 km.) east of Puerto Rico. The islands have a combined area of 133 sq. mi. (352 sq. km.) and a population of *106,000. Capital: Charlotte Amalie. Tourism is the principal industry. Watch movements, costume jewelry, pharmaceuticals, and rum are exported.

The Virgin Islands were discovered by Columbus in 1493, during his second voyage to America. During the 17th century the islands, actually the peaks of a submerged mountain range, were held at various times by Spain, Holland, England, France and Denmark, and during the same period were favorite resorts of the buccaneers operating in the Caribbean and the coastal waters of eastern North America. Control of the 100-island chain finally passed to Denmark and England. The islands had their own coinage from the early 18th century, based on but not exactly equivalent to, the Danish. In the late 18th and early 19th centuries, Danish minor copper and silver coinage augmented that in use on the islands. The Danish islands were purchased by the United States in 1917 for $25 million, mainly to forestall their acquisition by Germany and because they command the Anegada Passage into the Caribbean Sea, a strategic point on the defense perimeter of the Panama Canal.

RULERS

Danish, until 1917

MONETARY SYSTEM

(Until 1849)

96 Skilling = 1 Daler

NOTE: Skilling denominated issues through 1799 are found on a broad range of planchet sizes and alloys, sometimes even for the same date(s). These "contemporary counterfeits" look to be either silvered copper, copper or low-fineness billon and are not uncommon. It has been reported that some of the 6 and 12 Skillings, dated 1767, were struck in 1782 and 1790 and the 2 Skillings were minted from old dies in 1805. No distinctive features have been identified to segregate these "official restrikes" from those struck in the year on the coins.

II SKILLING

1.2180 g, .250 SILVER, .0098 oz ASW
Obv: Crowned arms. Rev: Value and date.

KM#	Date	Mintage	VG	Fine	VF	XF
13	1816	—	6.50	12.50	25.00	45.00
	1837 flat top 3	*.500	6.50	11.00	22.50	35.00
	1837 round top 3	Inc. Ab.	7.00	13.00	25.00	42.50
18	1847	*.250	6.50	11.00	22.50	35.00

KM#	Date	Mintage	VG	Fine	VF	XF
19	1848	*1.000	4.50	7.50	15.00	27.50

X SKILLING

2.4360 g, .625 SILVER, .0489 oz ASW

KM#	Date	Mintage	VG	Fine	VF	XF
14	1816	*.083	7.50	17.50	30.00	55.00

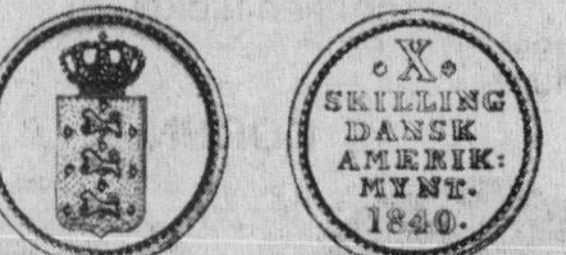

KM#	Date	Mintage	VG	Fine	VF	XF
16	1840	*.110	6.50	15.00	28.00	45.00
	1845	*.100	6.00	13.50	25.00	40.00
	1845	—	—	—	Proof	—
	1847	*.113	6.50	15.00	28.00	45.00
20	1848	*.404	7.50	17.50	30.00	50.00
	1848	—	—	—	Proof	—
	1848 plain edge	Inc. Ab.	8.50	20.00	32.00	55.00

XX SKILLING

4.8720 g, .625 SILVER, .0979 oz ASW
Obv: Crowned arms. Rev: Value and date.

KM#	Date	Mintage	VG	Fine	VF	XF
15	1816	*.020	12.50	30.00	75.00	135.00
17	1840	*.050	10.00	25.00	65.00	120.00
	1845	*.055	10.00	25.00	65.00	120.00
	1847	*.050	10.00	25.00	65.00	120.00
21	1848 incuse edge					
		*.070	10.00	25.00	65.00	120.00
	1848	—	—	—	Proof	315.00
	1848 plain edge					
		Inc. Ab.	17.50	32.50	80.00	150.00

COUNTERMARKED COINAGE

1849-1859

The only countermark authorized for the Danish West Indies was the crowned F R VII monogram, which was used between 1849 through 1859. Although the majority of the coins countermarked in those years were of United States origin, numerous pieces from European and Latin American countries were also employed for this purpose.

COUNTERFEITS: This series has been counterfeited extensively. A common counterfeit countermark lacks the small cross on top of the crown and small shallow striking of c/m especially in beads of crown.

U. S. SERIES

1/2 CENT

COPPER
c/m: Crowned FRVII on U.S. 1/2 Cent.

KM#	Date	Good	VG	Fine	VF
24.1	ND(1808)	—	—	Rare	—
	ND(1809)	—	—	Unique	—
24.2	ND(1834)	—	—	Unique	—

CENT

COPPER
c/m: Crowned FRVII on U.S. Large Cent, C#16.

KM#	Date	Good	VG	Fine	VF
25.1	ND(1795)	250.00	450.00	750.00	1200.

COPPER
c/m: Crowned FRVII on U.S. Large Cent, C#17.

KM#	Date	Good	VG	Fine	VF
25.2	ND(1797)	220.00	425.00	650.00	1000.
	ND(1800)	220.00	425.00	650.00	1000.
	ND(1801)	220.00	425.00	650.00	1000.
	ND(1803)	220.00	425.00	650.00	1000.
	ND(1805)	220.00	425.00	650.00	1000.
	ND(1807)	220.00	425.00	650.00	1000.

c/m: Crowned FRVII on U.S. Large Cent, C#19.

KM#	Date	Good	VG	Fine	VF
25.3	ND(1816)	150.00	300.00	450.00	700.00
	ND(1818)	150.00	300.00	450.00	700.00
	ND(1819)	150.00	300.00	450.00	700.00
	ND(1822)	150.00	300.00	450.00	700.00
	ND(1826)	150.00	300.00	450.00	700.00
	ND(1831)	150.00	300.00	450.00	700.00
	ND(1832)	150.00	300.00	450.00	700.00
	ND(1833)	150.00	300.00	450.00	700.00
	ND(1835)	150.00	300.00	450.00	700.00
	ND(1836)	150.00	300.00	450.00	700.00
	ND(1837)	150.00	300.00	450.00	700.00
	ND(1838)	150.00	300.00	450.00	700.00
	ND(1839)	150.00	300.00	450.00	700.00
	ND(1840)	150.00	300.00	450.00	700.00
	ND(1842)	150.00	300.00	450.00	700.00
	ND(1843)	150.00	300.00	450.00	700.00
	ND(1844)	150.00	300.00	450.00	700.00
	ND(1846)	150.00	300.00	450.00	700.00
	ND(1847)	150.00	300.00	450.00	700.00
	ND(1848)	150.00	300.00	450.00	700.00
	ND(1850)	150.00	300.00	450.00	700.00

25 CENTS

SILVER
c/m: Crowned FRVII on U.S. Liberty Bust 25 Cent, C#29.

KM#	Date	Good	VG	Fine	VF
26.1	ND(1821)	—	—	Unique	—

c/m: Crowned FRVII on U.S. Liberty Bust 25 Cent, C#29a.

KM#	Date	Good	VG	Fine	VF
26.2	ND(1832)	—	—	Unique	—

c/m: Crowned FRVII on U.S. Liberty Seated 25 Cent.

KM#	Date	Good	VG	Fine	VF
26.3	ND(1841)	600.00	1200.	1850.	2800.
	ND(1845)	600.00	1200.	1850.	2800.
	ND(1847)	600.00	1200.	1850.	2800.
	ND(1849)	600.00	1200.	1850.	2800.

50 CENTS

SILVER
c/m: Crowned FRVII on U.S. Liberty bust 50 Cent, C#32.

KM#	Date	Good	VG	Fine	VF
27.1	ND(1810)	600.00	1200.	1850.	2800.
	ND(1812)	600.00	1200.	1850.	2800.
	ND(1823)	600.00	1200.	1850.	2800.
	ND(1824)	600.00	1200.	1850.	2800.
	ND(1826)	600.00	1200.	1850.	2800.
	ND(1831)	600.00	1200.	1850.	2800.
	ND(1833)	600.00	1200.	1850.	2800.
	ND(1834)	600.00	1200.	1850.	2800.
	ND(1836)	600.00	1200.	1850.	2800.

c/m: Crowned FRVII on U.S. Liberty Seated 50 Cent.

KM#	Date	Good	VG	Fine	VF
27.2	ND(1843)	650.00	1300.	2150.	3250.
	ND(1846)	650.00	1300.	2150.	3250.
	ND(1848)	650.00	1300.	2150.	3250.
	ND(1849)	650.00	1300.	2150.	3250.
	ND(1850)	650.00	1300.	2150.	3250.

DOLLAR

SILVER
c/m: Crowned FRVII on U.S. Liberty Seated Dollar.

KM#	Date	Good	VG	Fine	VF
28	ND(1841)	1000.	2000.	3000.	4500.
	ND(1842)	1000.	2000.	3000.	4500.
	ND(1843)	1000.	2000.	3000.	4500.
	ND(1847)	1000.	2000.	3000.	4500.

U.S. COLONIAL VIRGINIA SERIES

1/2 PENNY

COPPER
c/m: Crowned FRVII on Virginia 1/2 Penny.

KM#	Date	Good	VG	Fine	VF
29	ND(1773)	—	—	Unique	—

BARBADOS SERIES

PENNY

COPPER
c/m: Crowned FRVII on Barbados Penny, KM#Tn8.

KM#	Date	Good	VG	Fine	VF
35	ND(1788)	—	—	Unique	—

BRAZIL SERIES

10 REIS

COPPER
c/m: Crowned FRVII on Brazil 10/XX Reis, KM#423.1.

KM#	Date	Good	VG	Fine	VF
36	ND(1830)	—	—	Unique	—

40 REIS

COPPER
c/m: Crowned FRVII on Brazil 40 Reis.

KM#	Date	Good	VG	Fine	VF
31	ND(1826)	—	—	Unique	—

960 REIS

SILVER
c/m: Crowned FRVII on Brazil 960 Reis, KM#307.

KM#	Date	Good	VG	Fine	VF
32.1	ND(1814)	350.00	550.00	850.00	1250.

c/m: Crowned FRVII on Brazil 960 Reis, KM#326.1.

KM#	Date	Good	VG	Fine	VF
32.2	ND(1818)	350.00	550.00	850.00	1250.
	ND(1819)	350.00	550.00	850.00	1250.

ENGLISH SERIES

1/2 PENNY

COPPER

c/m: Crowned FRVII on English 1/2 Penny, KM#662.

KM#	Date	Good	VG	Fine	VF
40	ND(1806)	—	—	Unique	—
	ND(1807)	—	—	Rare	—

PENNY

COPPER

c/m: Crowned FRVII on English Penny, KM#618.

KM#	Date	Good	VG	Fine	VF
37	ND(1797)	60.00	90.00	150.00	250.00

c/m: Crowned FRVII on English Penny, KM#663.

KM#	Date	Good	VG	Fine	VF
38	ND(1807)	—	—	Unique	—

2 PENCE

COPPER

c/m: Crowned FRVII on English 2 Pence, KM#619.

KM#	Date	Good	VG	Fine	VF
41	ND(1797)	—	—	Unique	—

HAITI SERIES

6-1/4 CENTIMES

COPPER

c/m: Crowned FRVII on Haiti 6-1/4 Centimes, KM#38.

KM#	Date	Good	VG	Fine	VF
39	ND(1850)	—	—	Unique	—

IRELAND SERIES

1/2 PENNY

COPPER

c/m: Crowned FRVII on Ireland 1/2 Penny, KM#147.

KM#	Date	Good	VG	Fine	VF
42	ND(1805)	—	—	Unique	—

ISLE OF MAN SERIES

PENNY

COPPER

c/m: Crowned FRVII on Isle of Man Penny, KM#11.

KM#	Date	Good	VG	Fine	VF
43	ND(1813)	—	—	Unique	—

PERU SERIES

4 REALES

SILVER

c/m: Crowned FRVII on South Peru 4 Reales, KM#172.

KM#	Date	Good	VG	Fine	VF
44	ND(1838)	—	—	Unique	—

8 REALES

SILVER

c/m: Crowned FRVII on South Peru 8 Reales, KM#170.4.

KM#	Date	Good	VG	Fine	VF
47	ND(1838)	—	—	Unique	—

DECIMAL COINAGE

20 Cents = 1 Franc

CENT

BRONZE

KM#	Date	Mintage	VG	Fine	VF	XF
63	1859(o)	.216	1.25	3.00	7.00	12.50
	1859(o)	10 pcs.	—	—	Proof	Rare
	1860(o)	.250	2.00	4.50	9.00	18.00

KM#	Date	Mintage	VG	Fine	VF	XF
68	1868(c)	.240	1.25	3.00	7.00	12.50
	1868(c)	—	—	—	Proof	—
	1878(h)	.020	2.50	6.00	12.00	25.00
	1879(h)	.040	125.00	200.00	250.00	450.00
	1883(h)	.210	1.50	4.50	9.00	18.00

3 CENTS

1.0440 g, .625 SILVER, .0210 oz ASW

KM#	Date	Mintage	VG	Fine	VF	XF
64	1859(o)	.291	2.00	5.00	10.00	22.50
	1859(o)	10 pcs.	—	—	Proof	Rare

5 CENTS

1.7400 g, .625 SILVER, .0349 oz ASW

KM#	Date	Mintage	VG	Fine	VF	XF
65	1859(c)	.150	1.75	5.00	10.00	20.00
	1859(c)	10 pcs.	—	—	Proof	Rare

KM#	Date	Mintage	VG	Fine	VF	XF
69	1878(h)	.500	5.00	12.50	25.00	50.00
	1878(h)	—	—	—	Proof	365.00
	1879(h)	Inc. Ab.	5.00	12.50	25.00	50.00

10 CENTS

3.4850 g, .625 SILVER, .0699 oz ASW

KM#	Date	Mintage	VG	Fine	VF	XF
66	1859(c)	.250	1.75	4.50	12.00	25.00
	1859(c)	10 pcs.	—	—	Proof	Rare
	1862/1(c)	.140	—	—	—	—
	1862(c)	Inc. Ab.	5.00	10.00	15.00	30.00
	1862(c)	—	—	—	Proof	225.00

KM#	Date	Mintage	VG	Fine	VF	XF
70	1878(h)	.080	6.00	12.50	25.00	50.00
	1878(h)	—	—	—	Proof	—
	1879(h)	.120	10.00	22.00	47.50	75.00
	1879(h)	—	—	—	Proof	—

20 CENTS

6.9610 g, .625 SILVER, .1399 oz ASW

KM#	Date	Mintage	VG	Fine	VF	XF
67	1859(c)	.430	7.50	15.00	25.00	50.00
	1859(c)	10 pcs.	—	—	Proof	Rare
	1862(c)	.560	7.50	15.00	25.00	50.00
	1862(c)	—	—	—	Proof	375.00

KM#	Date	Mintage	VG	Fine	VF	XF
71	1878(h)	.200	12.50	17.50	35.00	70.00
	1878(h)	—	—	—	Proof	425.00
	1879(h)	.300	40.00	90.00	165.00	250.00

MONETARY REFORM

5 Bit = 1 Cent

5 Francs = 1 Daler

1/2 CENT - 2 1/2 BIT

BRONZE

Mintmasters initials: P-GJ

KM#	Date	Mintage	VG	Fine	VF	XF
74	1905(h)	.190	2.00	5.00	7.50	12.50
	1905(h)	—	—	—	Proof	Rare

CENT - 5 BIT

BRONZE

Mintmasters initials: P-GJ

KM#	Date	Mintage	VG	Fine	VF	XF
75	1905(h)	.500	1.50	3.00	5.00	10.00

Mintmasters Initials: VBP-AH-GJ

KM#	Date	Mintage	VG	Fine	VF	XF
83	1913(h)	.200	3.75	7.50	20.00	40.00

2 CENTS - 10 BIT

BRONZE

Mintmasters Initials: P-GJ

KM#	Date	Mintage	VG	Fine	VF	XF
76	1905(h)	.150	2.25	5.00	10.00	20.00
	1905(h)	20 pcs.	—	—	Proof	Rare

5 CENTS - 25 BIT

NICKEL
Mintmasters Initials: P-GJ

KM#	Date	Mintage	VG	Fine	VF	XF
77	1905(h)	.199	.75	2.25	5.00	10.00
	1905(h)	20 pcs.	—	—	Proof	Rare

10 CENTS - 50 BIT

2.5000 g, .800 SILVER, .0643 oz ASW
Mintmasters Initials: P-GJ

KM#	Date	Mintage	VG	Fine	VF	XF
78	1905(h)	.175	1.25	3.25	7.00	12.50
	1905(h)	20 pcs.	—	—	Proof	Rare

20 CENTS - 1 FRANC

5.0000 g, .800 SILVER, .1286 oz ASW
Mintmasters Initials: P-GJ

KM#	Date	Mintage	VG	Fine	VF	XF
79	1905(h)	.150	4.50	10.00	30.00	60.00
	1905(h)	20 pcs.	—	—	Proof	Rare

Mintmasters Initials: P-GJ

KM#	Date	Mintage	VG	Fine	VF	XF
81	1907(h)	.101	7.50	15.00	30.00	60.00
	1907(h)	10 pcs.	—	—	Proof	Rare

40 CENTS - 2 FRANCS

10.0000 g, .800 SILVER, .2572 oz ASW
Mintmasters Initials: P-GJ

KM#	Date	Mintage	VG	Fine	VF	XF
80	1905(h)	.038	15.00	30.00	60.00	125.00
	1905(h)	20 pcs.	—	—	Proof	Rare

Mintmasters Initials: P-GJ

KM#	Date	Mintage	VG	Fine	VF	XF
82	1907(h)	.025	20.00	45.00	100.00	175.00
	1907(h)	10 pcs.	—	—	Proof	1100.

4 DALER - 20 FRANCS

6.4516 g, .900 GOLD, .1867 oz AGW
Mintmasters Initials: P-GJ

KM#	Date	Mintage	Fine	VF	XF	Unc
72	1904(h)	.121	150.00	250.00	325.00	500.00
	1905(h)	I.A.	150.00	275.00	375.00	600.00

10 DALER - 50 FRANCS

16.1290 g, .900 GOLD, .4667 oz AGW
Mintmasters Initials: P-GJ

KM#	Date	Mintage	Fine	VF	XF	Unc
73	1904(h)	2,005	1250.	2000.	3750.	6000.

PROOF SETS (PS)

KM#	Date	Mintage	Identification	Issue Price	Mkt. Val.
PS1	1859(5)	10	KM63-67	—	Rare
PS2	1862(2)	—	—	—	Rare
PS3	1878	—	—	—	Rare
PS4	1905(5)	20	KM76-80	—	Rare
PS5	1907(2)	10	KM81-82	—	Rare

Listings For

DANZIG: refer to Poland

DENMARK

The Kingdom of Denmark, a constitutional monarchy located at the mouth of the Baltic Sea, has an area of 16,629 sq. mi. (43,070 sq. km.) and a population of 5.1 million. Capital: Copenhagen. Most of the country is arable. Agriculture, which employs the majority of the people, is conducted by small farmers served by cooperatives. The largest industries are food processing, iron and metal, and fishing. Machinery, meats (chiefly bacon), dairy products and chemicals are exported.

Denmark, a great power during the Viking period of the 9th-11th centuries, conducted raids on western Europe and England, and in the 11th century united England, Denmark and Norway under the rule of King Canute. Despite a struggle between the crown and the nobility (13th-14th centuries) which forced the King to grant a written constitution, Queen Margaret (1387-1412) succeeded in uniting Denmark, Norway, Sweden, Finland and Greenland under the Danish crown, placing all of Scandinavia under the rule of Denmark. An unwise alliance with Napoleon contributed to the dismembering of the empire and fostered a liberal movement which succeeded in making Denmark a constitutional monarchy in 1849.

The present decimal system of coinage was introduced in 1874.

RULERS

Christian VII, 1766-1808
Frederik VI, 1808-1839
Christian VIII, 1839-1848
Frederik VII, 1848-1863
Christian IX, 1863-1906
Frederik VIII, 1906-1912
Christian X, 1912-1947
Frederik IX, 1947-1972
Margrethe II, 1972

MINT MARKS

(a) - Altona (1842 issues), apple
(c) - Copenhagen, crown
(h) - Copenhagen, heart
(o) - Altona, orb
KM - Copenhagen
NOTE: (ch) - crossed hammers - Kongsberg.

MINTMASTERS INITIALS

Altona

Letter	Date	Name
MF	1786-1816	Michael Flor
CB	1817-1819	Cajus Branth
FF, IFF	1819-1856	Johan Friedrich Freund
TA	1848-1851	Theodor Andersen
FA	1856-1863	Hans Frederik Alsing

Copenhagen

Letter	Date	Name
HIAB	1797-1810	Hans Jacob Arnold Branth
HIAB	1810-1821	Ole Varberg
CFG	1821-1831	Conrad Frederik Gerlach
VS, WS	1835-1861	Georg Wilhelm Svendsen
RH	1861-1869	Rasmus Hinnerup
CS	1869-1893	Diderik Christian Andreas Svendsen
P, VBP	1893-1918	Vilhelm Buchard Poulsen
HCN	1919-1927	Hans Christian Nielsen
N	1927-1955	Niels Peter Nielsen
C	1956-1971	Alfred Frederik Christiansen
S	1971-1978	Vagn Sorensen
B	1978-1981	Peter M. Bjarno
R, NR	1982-1989	N. Norregaard Rasmussen
LG	1989	Laust Grove

MONEYERS INITIALS

Altona

Letter	Date	Name
FA	1825-1855	Hans Frederik Alsing
FK	1841-1863	Frederik Christopher Krohn
HL	1848-1851	Carl Heinrich Lorenz
PP	1852-1863	Peter Petersen

Copenhagen

Letter	Date	Name
PG	1800-1807	Peter Leonard Gianelli
IC, ICF	1810-1841	Johannes Conradsen
M	1813	Christian Andreas Muller
CC	1836	Christen Christensen
FK	1841-1873	Frederik Christopher Krohn
HC	1873-1901	Harald Conradsen
GI, GJ	1901-1933	Knud Gunnar Jensen
AH	1908-1924	Andreas Frederik Vilhelm Hansen
HS, S	1933-1968	Harald Salomon
B	1968-1983	Frode Bahnsen
A	1986	Johan Alkjaer
HV	1986	Hanne Varming
JP, JPA	1989	Jan Petersen

MONETARY SYSTEM

(Until 1813)

16 Skillings = 1 Mark

64 Skilling Danske = 4 Mark = 1 Krone
96 Skilling Danske = 6 Mark = 1 Daler Specie
12 Marks = 1 Ducat

(Commencing 1813)
96 Rigsbank Skilling = 1 Rigs(bank)daler
30 Schilling Courant = 1 Rigs(bank)daler
2 Rigsbankdaler = 1 Rigsdaler Specie
2 Rigsbankdaler = 1 Specie(daler)
5 Species(daler) = 1 D'Or

1/5 RIGSBANKSKILLING

COPPER
Mint: Altona. Mintmasters Initials: FF.

C#	Date	Mintage	VG	Fine	VF	XF
118	1842	—	4.00	8.00	15.00	30.00

Rev. denomination: 1/5 R.B.S.

C#	Date	Mintage	VG	Fine	VF	XF
118a	1842	—	1.25	2.50	6.00	10.00

1/2 RIGSBANKSKILLING

COPPER

C#	Date	Mintage	VG	Fine	VF	XF
100	1838	—	1.00	2.00	5.00	10.00

Mint: Copenhagen. Mintmasters Intials: VS.

C#	Date	Mintage	VG	Fine	VF	XF
119	1842	—	2.00	4.00	8.00	15.00

Mintmasters Initials: VS.

C#	Date	Mintage	VG	Fine	VF	XF
131	1852	—	1.75	3.00	6.50	11.50

1/2 RIGSMONTSKILLING

BRONZE

C#	Date	Mintage	VG	Fine	VF	XF
134	1857(o)	—	.75	1.25	2.75	5.50
	1857(c)	—	—	—	—	250.00

Y#	Date	Mintage	VG	Fine	VF	XF
1	1868	—	1.00	1.50	3.50	7.00

SKILLING

.9230 g, .138 SILVER, .0041 oz ASW
Mint: Altona. Mintmasters Initials: MF.
Obv: Crowned FR VI monogram.
Rev: Value, DANSK, date.

C#	Date	Mintage	VG	Fine	VF	XF
104	1808	—	2.00	4.25	9.00	15.00
	1809	—	1.50	2.75	6.00	9.00
	1810	—	—	—	Unique	—

COPPER, 15mm
Mintmasters Initials: MF.

C#	Date	Mintage	VG	Fine	VF	XF
87.1	1812	—	1.25	1.50	3.25	5.50

RIGSBANKSKILLING

COPPER

C#	Date	Mintage	VG	Fine	VF	XF
93	1813	—	.75	1.50	5.00	12.00

Obv: Crowned oval arms
Rev: Value and date

C#	Date	Mintage	VG	Fine	VF	XF
101	1818	—	1.25	2.50	6.25	14.00

Mintmasters Initials: FF.

C#	Date	Mintage	VG	Fine	VF	XF
120.1	1842(o)	—	1.75	4.00	8.50	16.00

Mintmasters Initials: VS.

C#	Date	Mintage	VG	Fine	VF	XF
120.2	1842(c)	—	1.75	4.00	8.50	16.00

Mint: Copenhagen. Mintmasters Initials: VS.
Obv: Large bust.

C#	Date	Mintage	VG	Fine	VF	XF
132	1852	—	3.00	6.50	15.00	26.00

Obv: Small bust.

C#	Date	Mintage	VG	Fine	VF	XF
132a	1852	—	—	—	Rare	—

Obv: Medium bust.

C#	Date	Mintage	VG	Fine	VF	XF
132b	1853	—	1.75	3.50	7.00	12.50

RIGSMONTSKILLING

BRONZE

C#	Date	Mintage	VG	Fine	VF	XF
135	1856(o)	—	.75	1.50	3.00	9.00
	1856(c)	—	—	—	—	175.00
	1860(o)	—	1.00	2.00	3.50	10.00
	1863(c)	—	1.25	2.25	5.00	10.00

Y#	Date	Mintage	VG	Fine	VF	XF
2	1867	—	.75	1.50	3.00	6.50
	1869	—	1.00	1.75	3.50	7.00
	1870	—	1.25	2.50	6.00	11.00
	1871	—	1.75	3.25	7.00	12.50
	1872	—	.75	1.50	3.50	7.00

2 SKILLING

1.5000 g, .250 SILVER, .0121 oz ASW
Mint: Copenhagen. Mintmasters Initials: HIAB.

C#	Date	Mintage	VG	Fine	VF	XF
53.1	1801	—	1.25	2.50	4.75	10.00

Mint: Altona. Mintmasters Initials: MF.

C#	Date	Mintage	VG	Fine	VF	XF
53.2	1801	—	2.25	4.00	7.00	12.00
	1805	—	1.50	2.75	5.00	10.00

COPPER
Obv: Truncation in a curved line.

C#	Date	Mintage	VG	Fine	VF	XF
88a	1809	—	1.25	2.50	6.00	11.50
	1810	—	1.25	2.50	5.50	10.50

Obv: Truncation in a broken curved line.

C#	Date	Mintage	VG	Fine	VF	XF
88b	1810	—	1.50	2.75	6.25	12.00
	1811	—	1.50	3.00	7.50	14.00

C#	Date	Mintage	VG	Fine	VF	XF
94	1815	—	1.25	2.50	6.00	12.00

2 RIGSBANKSKILLING

COPPER

C#	Date	Mintage	VG	Fine	VF	XF
102	1818	—	4.00	9.00	15.00	30.00

1.1120 g, .208 SILVER, .0074 oz ASW
Mint: Altona. Mintmasters Initials: IFF.

C#	Date	Mintage	VG	Fine	VF	XF
106	1836	.152	2.00	5.00	7.50	12.50

COPPER
Mint: Copenhagen. Mintmasters Initials: VS.

C#	Date	Mintage	VG	Fine	VF	XF
121	1842	—	15.00	35.00	75.00	140.00

3 SKILLING

COPPER

C#	Date	Mintage	VG	Fine	VF	XF
89	1812	—	1.00	2.00	4.50	8.50
95	1815	—	1.50	3.50	8.00	14.00

3 RIGSBANKSKILLING

1.5190 g, .229 SILVER, .0112 oz ASW
Mint: Altona
Mintmasters Initials: IFF.

C#	Date	Mintage	VG	Fine	VF	XF
107	1836	.130	5.00	12.50	22.50	50.00

Mintmasters Initials: FF.

C#	Date	Mintage	VG	Fine	VF	XF
122	1842	—	1.50	3.00	7.50	15.00

Rev. denomination: 3 R.B.S.

C#	Date	Mintage	VG	Fine	VF	XF
122a	1842	—	1.50	3.00	7.50	14.00

4 SKILLING

2.5980 g, .250 SILVER, .0209 oz ASW
Mint: Altona. Mintmasters Initials: MF.

C#	Date	Mintage	VG	Fine	VF	XF
56	1807	—	3.00	5.50	10.00	20.00

COPPER

C#	Date	Mintage	VG	Fine	VF	XF
96	1815	—	2.50	5.00	14.00	30.00

4 RIGSBANKSKILLING

1.8560 g, .250 SILVER, .0149 oz ASW
Mint: Altona. Mintmasters Initials: IFF.

C#	Date	Mintage	VG	Fine	VF	XF
108	1836	.073	6.00	15.00	27.50	50.00

Mint: Copenhagen.
For use in Schleswig-Holstein
Rev: 1-1/4 SCH.

C#	Date	Mintage	VG	Fine	VF	XF
123.1	1841(h)	—	1.50	3.50	8.50	16.00

Mintmasters Initials: VS.

C#	Date	Mintage	VG	Fine	VF	XF
123.2	1842(c)	—	1.50	2.75	6.50	12.50

Mint: Altona. Mintmasters Initials: FF.

C#	Date	Mintage	VG	Fine	VF	XF
123.3	1842(o)	—	—	—	Rare	—

4 RIGSMONTSKILLING

1.8560 g, .250 SILVER, .0149 oz ASW
Mint: Altona. Mintmasters Initials: FF.

C#	Date	Mintage	VG	Fine	VF	XF
136.1	1854(o)	—	2.00	3.50	11.50	22.00
	1854(o)	—	—	—	Proof	—

Mint: Copenhagen. Mintmasters Initials: VS.

C#	Date	Mintage	VG	Fine	VF	XF
136.2	1856(c)	—	.75	2.00	5.50	13.00

Mint: Copenhagen
Mintmasters Initials: RH.

Y#	Date	Mintage	VG	Fine	VF	XF
4.1	1867	—	1.75	3.50	8.00	15.00
	1867	—	—	—	Proof	—

Mintmasters Initials: CS.

Y#	Date	Mintage	VG	Fine	VF	XF
4.2	1869	—	2.00	4.00	9.00	17.50
	1870	—	1.75	3.50	8.00	15.00
	1871	—	1.75	3.50	8.00	15.00
	1872	—	2.25	5.00	10.00	20.00
	1873	—	2.25	5.00	10.00	20.00
	1874	—	6.25	12.50	30.00	55.00

6 SKILLING

COPPER

C#	Date	Mintage	VG	Fine	VF	XF
97	1813	—	2.50	6.00	15.00	30.00

8 RIGSBANKSKILLING

2.8090 g, .375 SILVER, .0339 oz ASW
Mint: Altona. Mintmasters Initials: FF.
For use in Schleswig-Holstein
Rev: 2-1/2 SCHILL.COUR.

C#	Date	Mintage	VG	Fine	VF	XF
124	1843	—	10.00	20.00	40.00	90.00

NOTE: For 8 Reichsbank Schillinge dated 1816-1819 see Schleswig-Holstein in German States listings.

12 SKILLING

COPPER
Struck over 1 Skilling, C#47.

C#	Date	Mintage	VG	Fine	VF	XF
90	1812	—	5.50	12.50	25.00	50.00

C#	Date	Mintage	VG	Fine	VF	XF
98	1813	—	2.50	6.00	15.00	30.00

1/6 RIGSDALER

5.0490 g, .406 SILVER, .0659 oz ASW
Mint: Altona. Mintmasters Initials: MF.
Offering for Fatherland

C#	Date	Mintage	VG	Fine	VF	XF
105	1808	—	6.00	12.50	20.00	37.50

NOTE: Varieties exist.

16 SKILLING

COPPER

C#	Date	Mintage	VG	Fine	VF	XF
99	1814	—	3.50	7.50	17.50	35.00

16 RIGSBANKSKILLING

4.2140 g, .500 SILVER, .0677 oz ASW
Mint: Copenhagen. Mintmasters Initials: VS.
For use in Schleswig-Holstein
Rev: 5 SCHILL.COURANT.

C#	Date	Mintage	VG	Fine	VF	XF
125	1842	—	12.50	25.00	40.00	80.00
	1844	—	—	—	Rare	—

16 RIGSMONTSKILLING

3.8980 g, .500 SILVER, .0626 oz ASW
Mint: Copenhagen. Mintmasters Initials: VS.

C#	Date	Mintage	VG	Fine	VF	XF
137	1856(c)	—	1.50	3.25	7.75	15.00
	1857(c)	—	2.00	3.50	8.75	16.00
	1858(c)	—	2.25	4.75	10.00	20.00

32 RIGSBANKSKILLING

6.1290 g, .687 SILVER, .1354 oz ASW
Mint: Altona
Mintmasters Initials: CB.

C#	Date	Mintage	VG	Fine	VF	XF
109.1	1818	—	—	—	Rare	—

Mintmasters Initials: IFF

C#	Date	Mintage	VG	Fine	VF	XF
109.2	1820	—	20.00	40.00	70.00	135.00

Mint: Altona. Mintmasters Initials: FF.
For use in Schleswig-Holstein
Rev: 10 SCHILL.COURANT.

C#	Date	Mintage	VG	Fine	VF	XF
126	1842	—	15.00	27.50	45.00	80.00
	1843	—	17.50	30.00	50.00	85.00
	1843 FF/FK	—	60.00	110.00	160.00	250.00

1/2 RIGSDALER

7.2240 g, .875 SILVER, .2032 oz ASW
Mintmasters Initials: VS.

C#	Date	Mintage	VG	Fine	VF	XF
138	1854(c)	—	9.00	20.00	32.50	50.00
	1855(c)	—	8.00	17.50	30.00	45.00

RIGSBANKDALER

14.4470 g, .875 SILVER, .4064 oz ASW
Mint: Copenhagen
Moneyers Initial: M.

C#	Date	Mintage	VG	Fine	VF	XF
110.1	1813	—	45.00	80.00	140.00	225.00
	Moneyers Initials: IC.					
110.2	1813	—	25.00	30.00	55.00	90.00
	Moneyers Initials: IC. Mintmasters Initials: MF.					
110.3	1813	—	30.00	45.00	75.00	140.00
	Moneyers Initials: IC. Mintmasters Initials: CB.					
110.4	1818	—	30.00	37.50	60.00	100.00
	Moneyers Initials: IC. Mintmasters Initials: FF.					
110.5	1819	—	35.00	40.00	70.00	125.00
	Mint: Altona. Mintmasters Initials: FF. Obv: Small head.					
110a.1	1826	—	35.00	80.00	130.00	200.00
	1827	—	40.00	95.00	135.00	210.00
	1828	—	35.00	80.00	130.00	200.00
	1833	—	30.00	70.00	125.00	200.00
	Mint: Copenhagen					
110a.2	1833 KM	—	55.00	100.00	160.00	245.00
	1834 KM	—	55.00	100.00	160.00	245.00

Mint: Altona. Mintmasters Initials: FF.
Obv: Large head.

C#	Date	Mintage	VG	Fine	VF	XF
110b.1	1833	—	40.00	80.00	130.00	210.00
	1834	—	70.00	135.00	200.00	300.00
	1835	—	70.00	135.00	200.00	300.00
	1836	—	40.00	90.00	150.00	220.00
	1839	—	40.00	85.00	135.00	210.00
	Mint: Copenhagen					
110b.2	1834 KM	—	55.00	100.00	155.00	245.00
	Mintmasters Initials: WS.					
110b.3	1835	—	80.00	150.00	220.00	335.00
	1838	—	30.00	60.00	110.00	175.00

Mint: Copenhagen. Mintmasters Initials: VS.
For use in Schleswig-Holstein.
Rev: 30 SCHILL.COURANT.

C#	Date	Mintage	VG	Fine	VF	XF
127.1	1842(c)	—	15.00	32.00	47.50	75.00
	1843(c)	—	20.00	45.00	60.00	90.00
	1843(c)	—	—	—	Proof	—
	1846(c)	—	17.00	35.00	50.00	80.00
	1847(c)	—	12.50	25.00	40.00	65.00
	1847(c)	—	—	—	Proof	—
	1848(c)	—	12.50	27.50	42.50	70.00
	Mint: Altona. Mintmasters Initials: FF.					
127.2	1844(o)	—	18.00	40.00	55.00	85.00
	1845(o)	—	16.00	37.50	55.00	85.00
	1847(o)	—	17.00	35.00	50.00	80.00

Mint: Copenhagen. Mintmasters Initials: VS.

C#	Date	Mintage	VG	Fine	VF	XF
139	1849	—	40.00	90.00	160.00	275.00
	1851	—	35.00	70.00	140.00	235.00

RIGSDALER

14.4470 g, .875 SILVER, .4064 oz ASW
Mint: Copenhagen. Mintmasters Initials: VS.

C#	Date	Mintage	VG	Fine	VF	XF
140.1	1854(c)	—	10.00	17.50	25.00	45.00
	1855(c)	—	15.00	27.50	42.50	65.00
	Mint: Altona. Mintmasters Initials: FF.					
140.2	1855(o)	—	12.50	22.50	35.00	55.00

DALER

(Specie)

28.8930 g, .875 SILVER, .8128 oz ASW
Mintmasters Initials: MF. Moneyers Initial: B.
Obv: Head of Christian VII right.
Rev: Crowned oval arms.

C#	Date	Mintage	VG	Fine	VF	XF
82.1	1801	—	235.00	300.00	430.00	—

NOTE: Earlier dates (1795-1799) exist for this type.

Mint: Altona. Mintmasters Initials: IFF.
Obv: Head of Frederik VI right.

C#	Date	Mintage	VG	Fine	VF	XF
111	1819	—	200.00	500.00	900.00	1550.

Mint: Altona. Mintmasters Initials: FF.

C#	Date	Mintage	VG	Fine	VF	XF
112.1	1820	—	30.00	55.00	85.00	130.00
	1822	—	30.00	55.00	85.00	130.00
	1824	—	30.00	55.00	85.00	130.00
	1825	—	30.00	55.00	80.00	125.00
	1826	—	30.00	55.00	85.00	125.00
	1827	—	40.00	75.00	110.00	160.00
	1828	—	27.00	55.00	85.00	125.00
	1829	—	30.00	55.00	85.00	130.00
	1833	—	27.00	50.00	75.00	115.00
	1834	—	30.00	55.00	80.00	125.00
	1835	—	30.00	55.00	80.00	125.00
	1838	—	27.00	50.00	75.00	115.00
	1839	—	27.00	50.00	75.00	115.00
	Mint: Copenhagen Mintmasters Initials: CFG.					
112.2	1820	—	40.00	70.00	100.00	160.00
	1822	—	40.00	70.00	100.00	160.00
	1824	—	30.00	55.00	85.00	130.00
	1825	—	30.00	55.00	85.00	130.00
112.3	1833KM	—	35.00	65.00	100.00	150.00
	1834KM	—	40.00	70.00	100.00	160.00
	Mintmasters Initials: WS.					
112.4	1835	—	30.00	55.00	80.00	125.00

C#	Date	Mintage	VG	Fine	VF	XF
112.4	1837	—	30.00	55.00	80.00	125.00
	1838	—	27.00	50.00	75.00	115.00
	1838 SW (error)	—	—	—	—	—
	1839	—	27.00	55.00	75.00	115.00

Mint: Altona. Mintmasters Initials: FF.
Obv. leg: CHRISTIANUS. . . . .small letters.

C#	Date	Mintage	VG	Fine	VF	XF
128.1	1840	—	25.00	55.00	85.00	140.00
	1844(o)	—	30.00	70.00	110.00	175.00
	1845(o)	—	25.00	50.00	85.00	140.00
	1847(o)	—	25.00	55.00	100.00	155.00
	Mint: Copenhagen					
128.2	1840(h)	—	25.00	55.00	85.00	140.00
	1841(h)	—	55.00	155.00	195.00	300.00
	Mintmasters Initials: VS.					
128.3	1843(h)	—	75.00	185.00	250.00	350.00
	1843(c)	—	30.00	70.00	110.00	175.00
	1845(h)	—	—	—	Rare	—
	1845(c)	—	25.00	55.00	85.00	140.00
	1846(c)	—	25.00	55.00	85.00	140.00

Mintmasters Initials: VS.
Obv. leg: CHRISTIANVS. . . . .large letters.

C#	Date	Mintage	VG	Fine	VF	XF
128a	1846(c)	—	40.00	60.00	100.00	170.00
	1847(c)	—	40.00	60.00	100.00	170.00
	1848	—	40.00	60.00	100.00	170.00

Mintmasters Initials: VS.
Christian VIII Death
And Accession Of Frederik VII

C#	Date	Mintage	VG	Fine	VF	XF
141	1848	.047	50.00	100.00	170.00	275.00

	Mintmasters Initials: VS.					
142.1	1849(c)	—	35.00	60.00	100.00	200.00
	1853(c)	—	35.00	60.00	100.00	200.00
	1854(c)	—	90.00	140.00	210.00	325.00
	Mint: Altona. Mintmasters Initials: FF.					
142.2	1851(o)	—	—	—	Rare	—
	1853(o)	—	40.00	70.00	115.00	220.00

2 DALER

(Rigs)

28.8930 g, .875 SILVER, .8128 oz ASW
Mint: Altona. Mintmasters Initials: FF.

143.1	1854(o)	—	30.00	45.00	80.00	125.00
	1855(o)	—	30.00	50.00	90.00	140.00
	1856(o)	—	—	—	Rare	—
	Mint: Copenhagen Mintmasters Initials: VS.					
143.2	1854(c)	—	32.50	55.00	100.00	150.00
	1855(c)	—	30.00	47.50	85.00	135.00
	Mintmasters Initials: RH.					
143.3	1863(c)	.360	37.50	70.00	130.00	225.00

Mintmasters Initials: RH.
Frederik VII Death
and Accession of Christian IX

Y#	Date	Mintage	VG	Fine	VF	XF
3	1863	.101	50.00	100.00	160.00	250.00

	Mintmasters Initials: RH.					
5.1	1864	.237	55.00	110.00	180.00	320.00
	1868	.261	60.00	125.00	190.00	350.00
	Mintmasters Initials: CS.					
5.2	1871	.586	65.00	140.00	210.00	380.00
	1872	.149	65.00	140.00	210.00	380.00

TRADE COINAGE

DUCAT SPECIE

3.4900 g, .979 GOLD, .1098 oz AGW
Rev: 5 line leg. in square tablet.

C#	Date	Mintage	Fine	VF	XF	Unc
85.2	1802	—	275.00	625.00	750.00	1000.

NOTE: Earlier dates (1791-1794) exist for this type.

CHR(ISTIANS) D'OR

6.6420 g, .896 GOLD, .1913 oz AGW
Mint: Altona. Mintmasters Initials: FF.

C#	Date	Mintage	VG	Fine	VF	XF
129	1843(o)	.038	250.00	525.00	900.00	1450.
	1844(o)	I.A.	250.00	550.00	975.00	1550.
	1845(o)	I.A.	250.00	550.00	975.00	1550.
	1847(o)	I.A.	250.00	550.00	975.00	1550.

Mint: Copenhagen. Mintmasters Initials: CS.

Y#	Date	Mintage	VG	Fine	VF	XF
6	1869	539 pcs.	500.00	1125.	1800.	2600.

FR(EDERIKS) D'OR

6.6420 g, .896 GOLD, .1913 oz AGW
Mint: Altona
Mintmasters Initials: IFF.

C#	Date	Mintage	VG	Fine	VF	XF
113	1827	—	500.00	1000.	3000.	4000.

	Mintmasters Initials: FF.					
114	1828	.021	400.00	900.00	1500.	2750.

	Mintmasters Initials: FF.					
114a	1829	7,625	300.00	600.00	1500.	2000.
	1830	.012	—	—	Rare	—
	1831	—	300.00	600.00	1500.	2000.
	1833	—	300.00	600.00	1500.	2000.
	1834	—	—	—	Rare	—
	1835	—	300.00	600.00	1500.	2000.
	1837	—	300.00	600.00	1500.	2000.
	1838	—	300.00	600.00	1500.	2000.

	Mintmasters Initials: FF.					
144	1853	678 pcs.	500.00	1100.	1600.	3500.

2 FR(EDERIKS) D'OR

13.2840 g, .896 GOLD, .3827 oz AGW
Mint: Altona
Mintmasters Initials: IFF.

115	1826	—	—	—	Unique	—
	1827	—	500.00	1000.	2000.	3000.

Mintmasters Initials: FF.

C#	Date	Mintage	VG	Fine	VF	XF
116	1828	.168	350.00	800.00	1700.	2450.
	1829	.096	375.00	850.00	1800.	2600.
	1830	.105	375.00	850.00	1800.	2600.
	1833	—	375.00	850.00	1800.	2600.
	1834	—	375.00	850.00	1800.	2600.
	1835	—	400.00	875.00	1850.	2650.
	1836	—	—	—	Rare	—

Mintmasters Initials: FF.

C#	Date	Mintage	VG	Fine	VF	XF
117.1	1836	—	350.00	850.00	1800.	2600.
	1837	—	325.00	800.00	1700.	2350.
	1838	—	325.00	800.00	1700.	2350.
	1839	—	325.00	800.00	1900.	2600.

Mint: Copenhagen. Mintmasters Initials: WS.

C#	Date	Mintage	VG	Fine	VF	XF
117.2	1838	—	650.00	1300.	2300.	3250.

Mint: Copenhagen. Mintmasters Initials: VS.

C#	Date	Mintage	VG	Fine	VF	XF
145.1	1850 KF(c)	—	300.00	700.00	1700.	2550.

Mint: Altona
Mintmasters Initials: FF.

C#	Date	Mintage	VG	Fine	VF	XF
145.2	1851(o)	1.205	325.00	750.00	1800.	2675.
	1852(o)	I.A.	325.00	750.00	1800.	2675.
	1853(o)	I.A.	300.00	700.00	1700.	2550.
	1854(o)	I.A.	325.00	750.00	1800.	2675.
	1855(o)	I.A.	325.00	750.00	1800.	2675.

Mintmasters Initials: FA.

C#	Date	Mintage	VG	Fine	VF	XF
145.3	1856(o)	I.A.	325.00	800.00	1900.	2700.
	1857(o)	I.A.	300.00	700.00	1700.	2550.
	1859(o)	I.A.	300.00	700.00	1700.	2550.

Mint: Copenhagen. Mintmasters Initials: RH.

C#	Date	Mintage	VG	Fine	VF	XF
145.4	1863(c)	*	475.00	950.00	2000.	3000.

*Total mintage 1850VS and 1863RH .031.

2 CHR(ISTIANS) D'OR

13.2840 g, .896 GOLD, .3827 oz AGW
Mint: Copenhagen

C#	Date	Mintage	VG	Fine	VF	XF
130.1	1841(h)	—	350.00	700.00	2100.	3500.

Mint: Altona. Mintmasters Initials: FF.

C#	Date	Mintage	VG	Fine	VF	XF
130.2	1842(o)	—	250.00	575.00	1900.	3100.
	1844(o)	—	375.00	675.00	2100.	3300.

Mint: Copenhagen. Mintmasters Initials: VS.

C#	Date	Mintage	VG	Fine	VF	XF
130.3	1844(c)	—	325.00	650.00	2000.	3200.
	1845(o)	—	250.00	575.00	1900.	3100.
	1847(o)	—	225.00	550.00	1850.	3000.

Total mintage 1841(h) and 1844(c) 9,222 pcs.
Total mintage 1842-47(o) .551.

Mint: Copenhagen. Mintmasters Initials: RH.

Y#	Date	Mintage	VG	Fine	VF	XF
7.1	1866	.042	500.00	1200.	3000.	4000.
	1867	Inc. Ab.	—	—	Rare	—

Mintmasters Initials: CS.

Y#	Date	Mintage	VG	Fine	VF	XF
	1869	Inc. Ab.	500.00	1200.	3000.	4000.
	1870	Inc. Ab.	—	—	Rare	—

DECIMAL COINAGE

100 Ore = 1 Krone

ORE

BRONZE
Mintmasters Initials: CS.

Y#	Date	Mintage	Fine	VF	XF	Unc
8.1	1874(h)	5.540	3.00	5.00	11.00	30.00
	1875(h)	2.361	4.00	6.00	13.00	35.00
	1876(h)	1.483	225.00	300.00	450.00	675.00
	1878(h)	1.016	22.50	37.50	60.00	125.00
	1879(h)	1.491	15.00	22.50	35.00	70.00
	1880(h)	1.989	5.00	10.00	20.00	40.00
	1881(h)	.260	300.00	400.00	625.00	925.00
	1882(h)	1.782	5.00	10.00	20.00	40.00
	1883(h)	2.989	2.00	3.50	9.00	25.00
	1886(h)	.997	30.00	45.00	65.00	110.00
	1887(h)	3.007	5.00	9.00	17.50	35.00
	1888(h)	1.505	5.00	9.00	17.50	35.00
	1889(h)	2.999	2.00	3.50	8.00	22.50
	1891(h)	4.488	1.00	2.00	5.00	15.00
	1892(h)	.492	40.00	70.00	115.00	175.00

Mintmasters Initials: VBP.

Y#	Date	Mintage	Fine	VF	XF	Unc
8.2	1894(h)	4.982	.50	1.00	3.00	14.00
	1897/4(h)	2.988	1.75	3.00	6.50	18.00
	1897(h)	I.A.	1.75	3.00	6.00	17.00
	1899/7(h)	5.012	.55	1.10	4.00	14.00
	1899(h)	I.A.	.50	1.00	3.50	12.00
	1902/802(h)	2.977	.55	1.10	4.00	14.00
	1902(h)	I.A.	.50	1.00	3.50	12.00
	1904/804(h)	4.962	.75	1.50	5.00	16.00
	1904(h)	I.A.	.50	1.00	3.50	12.00

Mintmasters Initials: VBP. Moneyers Initials: GJ.

Y#	Date	Mintage	Fine	VF	XF	Unc
20	1907(h)	5.975	.50	1.00	3.50	12.00
	1909(h)	2.985	.50	1.00	3.50	12.00
	1910(h)	2.994	1.00	2.00	5.00	15.00
	1912(h)	3.006	1.00	2.00	5.00	15.00

Y#	Date	Mintage	Fine	VF	XF	Unc
28.1	1913(h)	5.011	.25	.50	1.00	5.00
	1915(h)	4.940	.50	1.00	1.75	7.50
	1916(h)	2.439	.50	1.00	2.50	8.50
	1917(h)	4.564	8.50	12.50	20.00	35.00

IRON

Y#	Date	Mintage	Fine	VF	XF	Unc
28.1a	1918(h)	6.776	1.00	2.00	6.00	17.50

BRONZE
Mintmasters Initials: HCN. Moneyers Initials: GJ.

Y#	Date	Mintage	Fine	VF	XF	Unc
28.2	1919(h)	4.586	.25	1.00	2.00	6.00
	1920(h)	2.367	4.00	7.50	12.50	20.00
	1921(h)	3.121	.50	1.50	2.50	6.00
	1922(h)	3.267	.50	1.50	2.50	6.00
	1923(h)	2.938	.50	1.50	2.50	6.00

IRON

Y#	Date	Mintage	Fine	VF	XF	Unc
28.2a	1919(h)	.931	3.50	7.50	12.50	25.00

BRONZE

Y#	Date	Mintage	Fine	VF	XF	Unc
46.1	1926(h)	1.572	2.00	4.00	10.00	20.00
	1927(h)	Inc. Ab.	—	.20	1.00	10.00

Mintmasters Initial: N. Moneyers Initials: GJ.

Y#	Date	Mintage	Fine	VF	XF	Unc
46.2	1927(h)	I.A.	4.00	6.00	12.00	25.00
	1928(h)	29.691	.10	.20	1.75	6.00
	1929(h)	5.172	.10	.20	1.75	6.00
	1930(h)	5.306	.10	.20	1.25	6.00
	1932(h)	5.089	.10	.20	1.25	6.00
	1933(h)	2.095	.75	1.50	3.00	10.00
	1934(h)	3.665	—	.10	.50	5.00
	1935(h)	5.668	—	.10	.40	3.50
	1936(h)	5.584	—	.10	.40	2.50
	1937(h)	6.877	—	.10	.40	2.50
	1938(h)	3.850	—	.10	.40	2.50
	1939(h)	5.662	—	.10	.30	1.75
	1940(h)	1.965	—	.10	.30	1.75

NOTE: For coins dated 1941 refer to Faeroe Islands listings at the end of Denmark.

ZINC
Mintmasters Initial: N. Moneyers Initial: S.

Y#	Date	Mintage	Fine	VF	XF	Unc
51	1941(h)	21.570	.15	.30	1.50	10.00
	1942(h)	6.997	.15	.30	1.50	10.00
	1943(h)	15.082	.15	.30	1.50	10.00
	1944(h)	11.981	.15	.30	1.50	10.00
	1945(h)	.916	.75	2.00	4.00	15.00
	1946(h)	.712	2.00	4.00	8.00	20.00

Y#	Date	Mintage	Fine	VF	XF	Unc
56.1	1948(h)	.460	.65	1.00	2.00	7.50
	1949(h)	2.513	.15	.30	.75	5.00
	1950(h)	9.453	.15	.30	.75	5.00
	1951(h)	2.931	.25	.50	.75	5.00
	1952(h)	7.626	.15	.30	.60	3.50
	1953(h)	11.994	.10	.20	.40	3.00
	1954(h)	12.642	.10	.20	.40	3.00
	1955(h)	14.177	.10	.20	.40	3.00

Mintmasters Initial: C. Moneyers Initial: S.

Y#	Date	Mintage	Fine	VF	XF	Unc
56.2	1956(h)	20.211	—	.10	.25	2.50
	1957(h)	20.900	—	.10	.25	2.50
	1958(h)	16.021	—	.10	.25	2.50
	1959(h)	15.929	—	.10	.25	2.00
	1960(h)	23.982	—	—	.15	1.50
	1961(h)	18.986	—	—	.15	1.00
	1962(h)	16.992	—	—	.10	.75
	1963(h)	28.986	—	—	.10	.65
	1964(h)	21.971	—	—	.10	.50
	1965(h)	29.943	—	—	.10	.30
	1966(h)	35.907	—	—	.10	.30
	1967(h)	32.959	—	—	.10	.20
	1968(h)	21.889	—	—	.10	.20
	1969(h)	29.243	—	—	.10	.20
	1970(h)	22.970	—	—	.10	.20
	1971(h)	21.983	—	—	.10	.20

Mintmasters Initial: S. Moneyers Initial: S.

Y#	Date	Mintage	Fine	VF	XF	Unc
56.3	1972(h)	13.000	—	—	.10	.20

BRONZE
Mintmasters Initial: C. Moneyers Initial: S.

Y#	Date	Mintage	Fine	VF	XF	Unc
66	1960(h)	8.990	—	—	.75	1.50
	1962(h)	I.A.	—	—	.75	1.50
	1963(h)	9.980	—	—	.75	1.50
	1964(h)	2.990	—	—	.75	1.50

NOTE: Only an estimated 100,000 of each date of Y#66 were sold, the balance being remelted.

2 ORE

BRONZE
Mintmasters Initial: C. Moneyers Initial: S.

Y#	Date	Mintage	Fine	VF	XF	Unc
9.1	1874(h)	8.828	1.00	2.00	6.00	20.00
	1875(h)	2.817	2.00	4.00	10.00	45.00
	1876(h)	.231	60.00	100.00	150.00	300.00
	1880(h)	1.012	6.00	12.00	25.00	40.00
	1881(h)	1.484	5.00	10.00	22.00	35.00
	1883(h)	1.990	2.00	4.00	7.50	20.00
	1886(h)	1.493	4.00	7.00	12.00	25.00
	1887(h)	I.A.	25.00	40.00	60.00	115.00
	1889/7(h)	1.993	2.50	5.00	7.50	20.00
	1889(h)	I.A.	2.00	3.50	6.00	15.00
	1891(h)	1.903	2.00	3.50	6.00	15.00
	1892(h)	.573	20.00	35.00	50.00	90.00

Mintmasters Initials: VBP.

Y#	Date	Mintage	Fine	VF	XF	Unc
9.2	1894(h)	2.486	1.00	2.00	4.00	10.00
	1897/4(h)	2.479	1.50	3.00	6.00	15.00
	1897(h)	I.A.	1.00	2.00	4.00	10.00
	1899/7(h)	2.504	1.25	2.50	5.00	12.50

Y#	Date	Mintage	Fine	VF	XF	Unc
9.2	1899(h)	I.A.	1.00	2.00	4.00	10.00
	1902/802(h)	3.502	1.50	3.00	6.00	15.00
	1902(h)	I.A.	1.00	2.00	4.00	10.00
	1906(h)	2.498	1.00	2.00	4.00	10.00

Mintmasters Initials: VBP. Moneyers Initials: GJ.

Y#	Date	Mintage	Fine	VF	XF	Unc
21	1907(h)	2.502	.50	1.00	3.00	7.50
	1909(h)	2.485	1.00	2.50	5.00	12.00
	1912(h)	2.480	1.00	2.50	5.00	10.00

Y#	Date	Mintage	Fine	VF	XF	Unc
29.1	1913(h)	.373	12.00	25.00	40.00	70.00
	1914(h)	2.126	1.00	2.50	4.50	9.00
	1915(h)	2.485	1.00	2.50	4.50	9.00
	1916(h)	1.383	1.00	2.50	4.50	9.00
	1917(h)	1.837	6.00	10.00	20.00	35.00

IRON

Y#	Date	Mintage	Fine	VF	XF	Unc
29.1a	1918(h)	4.161	1.00	2.50	5.00	15.00

BRONZE

Mintmasters Initials: HCN. Moneyers Initials: GJ.

Y#	Date	Mintage	Fine	VF	XF	Unc
29.2	1919(h)	5.503	2.00	4.00	6.00	12.00
	1920(h)	2.528	.50	1.00	2.00	5.00
	1921(h)	2.158	1.00	2.50	4.50	8.00
	1923(h)	2.625	1.00	2.50	4.50	8.00

IRON

Y#	Date	Mintage	Fine	VF	XF	Unc
29.2a	1919(h)	1.944	10.00	17.50	25.00	50.00

BRONZE

Y#	Date	Mintage	Fine	VF	XF	Unc
47.1	1926(h)	.301	20.00	30.00	60.00	110.00
	1927(h)	15.359	.10	.20	1.00	6.00

Mintmasters Initial: N. Moneyers Initials: GJ.

Y#	Date	Mintage	Fine	VF	XF	Unc
47.2	1927(h)	I.A.	.50	1.00	2.50	10.00
	1928(h)	5.758	.10	.20	1.50	7.00
	1929(h)	6.817	.10	.20	1.50	7.00
	1930(h)	2.327	.50	1.00	1.50	7.00
	1931(h)	5.135	.10	.20	1.50	6.00
	1932(h)	I.A.	.50	1.00	2.00	10.00
	1934(h)	.756	.25	.75	1.50	6.00
	1935(h)	1.391	.10	.20	.80	4.50
	1936(h)	2.973	.10	.20	.60	4.00
	1937(h)	3.437	.10	.20	.50	3.50
	1938(h)	2.177	—	.10	.25	2.50
	1939(h)	3.165	—	.10	.25	2.50
	1940(h)	1.582	—	.10	.25	2.50

NOTE: For coins dated 1941 refer to Faeroe Islands listings at the end of Denmark.

ALUMINUM

Mintmasters Initial: N. Moneyers Initial: S.

Y#	Date	Mintage	Fine	VF	XF	Unc
52	1941(h)	26.205	.10	.50	1.00	6.00

ZINC

Y#	Date	Mintage	Fine	VF	XF	Unc
52a	1942(h)	12.934	.15	.35	1.00	7.50
	1943(h)	9.603	.15	.35	1.00	7.50
	1944(h)	6.069	.15	.35	1.00	7.50
	1945(h)	.329	2.00	4.00	6.00	20.00
	1947(h)	.589	.50	1.00	2.50	10.00

Y#	Date	Mintage	Fine	VF	XF	Unc
57.1	1948(h)	1.927	.25	.50	1.00	4.00
	1949(h)	1.603	2.00	4.00	6.00	15.00
	1950(h)	4.544	.25	.50	1.00	4.00
	1951(h)	3.766	.25	.50	1.00	5.00

Y#	Date	Mintage	Fine	VF	XF	Unc
57.1	1952(h)	4.874	.10	.20	.75	3.50
	1953(h)	8.112	—	.10	.65	2.50
	1954(h)	6.497	—	.10	.65	2.50
	1955(h)	6.968	—	.10	.30	1.75

Mintmasters Initial: C. Moneyers Initial: S.

Y#	Date	Mintage	Fine	VF	XF	Unc
57.2	1956(h)	10.004	—	.10	.30	1.75
	1957(h)	15.329	—	.10	.30	1.75
	1958(h)	8.120	—	.10	.20	1.50
	1959(h)	10.462	—	.10	.20	1.50
	1960(h)	16.504	—	.10	.20	1.25
	1961(h)	15.504	—	.10	.20	1.00
	1962(h)	10.980	—	.10	.20	1.00
	1963(h)	19.470	—	.10	.20	1.00
	1964(h)	15.411	—	.10	.20	1.00
	1965(h)	20.173	—	—	.10	.75
	1966(h)	21.949	—	—	.10	.40
	1967(h)	22.439	—	—	.10	.40
	1968(h)	17.632	—	—	.10	.40
	1969(h)	29.276	—	—	.10	.20
	1970(h)	23.864	—	—	.10	.20
	1971(h)	35.811	—	—	.10	.20

Mintmasters Initial: S. Moneyers Initial: S.

Y#	Date	Mintage	Fine	VF	XF	Unc
57.3	1972(h)	6.496	—	—	.10	.40

BRONZE

Mintmasters Initial: C. Moneyers Initial: S.

Y#	Date	Mintage	Fine	VF	XF	Unc
67	1960(h)	I.A.	—	—	.75	1.50
	1962(h)	I.A.	—	—	.75	1.50
	1963(h)	.990	—	—	.75	1.50
	1964(h)	3.990	—	—	.75	1.50
	1965(h)	11.980	—	—	.75	1.50
	1966(h)	12.000	—	—	.75	1.50

NOTE: Only an estimated 100,000 of each date of Y#67 were sold, the balance being remelted.

5 ORE

BRONZE

Mintmasters Initials: CS.

Y#	Date	Mintage	Fine	VF	XF	Unc
10.1	1874(h)	2.762	3.00	5.00	14.00	55.00
	1875(h)	.207	15.00	25.00	35.00	90.00
	1882(h)	.076	15.00	25.00	35.00	90.00
	1884(h)	.321	7.50	14.00	22.50	60.00
	1890(h)	.598	25.00	45.00	75.00	140.00
	1891(h)	.787	7.50	14.00	22.50	60.00

Mintmasters Initials: VBP.

Y#	Date	Mintage	Fine	VF	XF	Unc
10.2	1894(h)	.595	5.00	9.00	17.50	40.00
	1898(h)	.397	9.00	17.50	30.00	70.00
	1899(h)	.601	5.00	9.00	15.00	30.00
	1902(h)	.601	5.00	9.00	15.00	30.00
	1904(h)	.397	9.00	14.00	22.50	50.00
	1906(h)	1.000	5.00	9.00	15.00	30.00

Y#	Date	Mintage	Fine	VF	XF	Unc
22	1907(h)	1.000	3.00	5.00	10.00	25.00
	1908(h)	1.198	3.00	5.00	10.00	25.00
	1912(h)	.999	3.00	5.00	10.00	25.00

Mintmasters Initials: VBP. Moneyers Initials: GJ.

Y#	Date	Mintage	Fine	VF	XF	Unc
30.1	1913(h)	.216	30.00	45.00	75.00	125.00
	1914(h)	.785	4.00	6.00	11.00	25.00
	1916(h)	.887	4.00	6.00	11.00	25.00
	1917(h)	.494	4.00	6.00	11.00	25.00

IRON

Y#	Date	Mintage	Fine	VF	XF	Unc
30.1a	1918(h)	1.918	3.00	6.00	12.00	30.00

BRONZE

Mintmasters Initials: HCN. Moneyers Initials: GJ.

Y#	Date	Mintage	Fine	VF	XF	Unc
30.2	1919(h)	.994	2.00	4.00	7.00	12.50
	1920(h)	2.618	2.00	4.00	7.00	12.50
	1921(h)	3.248	2.00	4.00	7.00	12.50
	1923(h)	.369	45.00	90.00	135.00	185.00

IRON

Y#	Date	Mintage	Fine	VF	XF	Unc
30.2a	1919(h)	1.035	6.00	12.00	22.50	50.00

BRONZE

Y#	Date	Mintage	Fine	VF	XF	Unc
48.1	1926(h)	—	—	—	Unique	—
	1927(h)	7.129	.10	.20	1.00	10.00

Mintmasters Initial: N. Moneyers Initials: GJ.

Y#	Date	Mintage	Fine	VF	XF	Unc
48.2	1927(h)	I.A.	2.50	4.50	9.00	25.00
	1928(h)	4.685	.10	.20	1.00	10.00
	1929(h)	1.387	.25	.50	2.00	12.00
	1930(h)	1.339	.25	.50	2.00	12.00
	1932(h)	1.011	.25	.50	2.00	10.00
	1934(h)	.524	.25	.50	1.50	10.00
	1935(h)	1.124	1.00	2.00	4.00	15.00
	1936(h)	1.091	.15	.35	1.00	4.50
	1937(h)	1.209	.15	.35	.75	4.50
	1938(h)	1.093	.30	.50	1.00	4.50
	1939(h)	1.402	.10	.15	.40	2.50
	1940(h)	2.735	.10	.15	.40	2.50

NOTE: For coins dated 1941 refer to Faeroe Islands listings at the end of Denmark.

ALUMINUM

Mintmasters Initial: N. Moneyers Initial: S.

Y#	Date	Mintage	Fine	VF	XF	Unc
53	1941(h)	16.984	.10	.75	2.50	10.00

ZINC

Y#	Date	Mintage	Fine	VF	XF	Unc
53a	1942(h)	2.963	.40	1.00	2.50	10.00
	1943(h)	4.522	.40	1.00	2.50	10.00
	1944(h)	3.744	.40	1.00	2.50	10.00
	1945(h)	.864	2.00	4.00	6.00	15.00

Y#	Date	Mintage	Fine	VF	XF	Unc
58.1	1950(h)	.657	3.00	6.00	10.00	20.00
	1951(h)	1.858	.75	1.25	2.50	10.00
	1952(h)	3.562	.50	1.00	1.75	7.00
	1953(h)	5.944	.50	1.00	1.75	7.00
	1954(h)	3.060	.35	.75	1.50	6.00
	1955(h)	2.314	.35	.75	1.50	6.00

Mintmasters Initial: C. Moneyers Initial: S.

Y#	Date	Mintage	Fine	VF	XF	Unc
58.2	1956(h)	5.888	.25	.75	1.50	5.00
	1957(h)	8.606	.10	.20	.50	3.00
	1958(h)	9.598	.10	.20	.50	3.00
	1959(h)	6.110	.10	.20	.50	3.00
	1960(h)	11.800	—	.10	.35	1.50
	1961(h)	8.995	—	.10	.35	1.50
	1962(h)	9.729	—	.10	.35	1.50
	1963(h)	8.980	—	.10	.35	1.50
	1964(h)	6.738	—	.10	.35	1.50

BRONZE

Y#	Date	Mintage	Fine	VF	XF	Unc
68.1	1960(h)	3.760	.10	.20	.50	1.50
	1962(h)	5.873	.10	.20	.50	1.50
	1963(h)	23.287	—	—	.10	.60
	1964(h)	41.521	—	—	.10	.60
	1965(h)	14.229	—	—	.10	.60
	1966(h)	23.410	—	—	.10	.60
	1967(h)	15.094	—	—	.10	.45
	1968(h)	16.105	—	—	.10	.35
	1969(h)	23.594	—	—	.10	.25
	1970(h)	26.176	—	—	.10	.25
	1971(h)	10.076	—	—	.10	.25

Mintmasters Initial: S. Moneyers Initial: S.

Y#	Date	Mintage	Fine	VF	XF	Unc
68.2	1972(h)	27.938	—	—	.10	.25

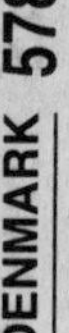

COPPER CLAD IRON
Mintmasters Initial: S. Moneyers Initial: B.

Y#	Date	Mintage	Fine	VF	XF	Unc
78.1	1973(h)	—	—	—	—	.10
	1974(h)	71.796	—	—	—	.10
	1975(h)	45.004	—	—	—	.10
	1976(h)	73.296	—	—	—	.10
	1977(h)	74.066	—	—	—	.10
	1978(h)	52.425	—	—	—	.10

Mintmasters Initial: B. Moneyers Initial: B.

Y#	Date	Mintage	Fine	VF	XF	Unc
78.2	1979(h)	58.953	—	—	—	.10
	1980(h)	54.362	—	—	—	.10
	1981(h)	52.201	—	—	—	.10

Mintmasters Initial: R. Moneyers Initial: B.

Y#	Date	Mintage	Fine	VF	XF	Unc
78.3	1982(h)	74.296	—	—	—	.10
	1983(h)	70.655	—	—	—	.10
	1984(h)	27.599	—	—	—	.10
	1985(h)	56.676	—	—	—	.10
	1986(h)	62.496	—	—	—	.10
	1987(h)	71.798	—	—	—	.10
	1988(h)	48.925	—	—	—	.10

10 ORE

1.4500 g, .400 SILVER, .0186 oz ASW
Mintmasters Initials: CS.

Y#	Date	Mintage	Fine	VF	XF	Unc
11.1	1874(h)	8.975	3.00	5.00	17.50	50.00
	1875(h)	1.387	4.00	6.00	20.00	50.00
	1882(h)	1.057	17.50	25.00	50.00	90.00
	1884(h)	1.019	17.50	25.00	50.00	90.00
	1886(h)	.508	35.00	50.00	75.00	140.00
	1888(h)	.306	50.00	75.00	115.00	170.00
	1889(h)	1.030	5.00	9.00	17.50	35.00
	1891(h)	1.507	4.00	7.50	12.50	25.00

Mintmasters Initials: VBP.

Y#	Date	Mintage	Fine	VF	XF	Unc
11.2	1894(h)	1.521	4.00	7.50	12.50	25.00
	1897(h)	2.044	2.00	4.00	6.00	20.00
	1899(h)	2.050	2.00	4.00	6.00	20.00
	1903/803(h)	3.007	2.00	4.00	6.00	15.00
	1903(h)	I.A.	1.50	3.00	5.00	15.00
	1904(h)	2.449	9.00	17.50	27.50	50.00
	1905(h)	1.571	2.00	4.00	6.00	15.00

Y#	Date	Mintage	Fine	VF	XF	Unc
23	1907(h)	3.068	2.00	3.00	4.50	10.00
	1910(h)	2.530	2.00	3.00	4.50	10.00
	1911(h)	.579	15.00	22.50	35.00	60.00
	1912(h)	1.951	2.00	3.00	5.50	12.50

Mintmasters Initials: VBP. Moneyers Initials: GJ.

Y#	Date	Mintage	Fine	VF	XF	Unc
36.1	1914(h)	2.128	1.25	2.00	4.00	10.00
	1915(h)	.915	3.00	6.00	9.00	15.00
	1916(h)	2.699	1.25	2.00	4.00	10.00
	1917(h)	6.003	1.25	2.00	4.00	10.00
	1918(h)	5.042	.50	1.00	2.50	5.00

Mintmasters Initials: HCN. Moneyers Initials: GJ.

Y#	Date	Mintage	Fine	VF	XF	Unc
36.2	1919(h)	10.184	.50	1.00	2.50	5.00

COPPER-NICKEL

Y#	Date	Mintage	Fine	VF	XF	Unc
31	1920(h)	10.234	2.00	3.00	4.50	11.00
	1921(h)	8.064	2.00	3.00	4.50	11.00
	1922(h)	3.065	8.00	14.00	20.00	37.50
	1923(h)	1.790	125.00	200.00	275.00	350.00

Y#	Date	Mintage	Fine	VF	XF	Unc
49.1	1924(h)	14.661	.10	.30	1.00	7.00
	1925(h)	8.678	.15	.40	1.00	10.00
	1926(h)	4.107	.15	.40	1.00	10.00

Mintmasters Initial: N. Moneyers Initials: GJ.

Y#	Date	Mintage	Fine	VF	XF	Unc
49.2	1929(h)	5.037	.25	.50	1.00	10.00
	1931(h)	3.054	.25	.50	1.00	10.00
	1933(h)	1.274	3.00	4.50	9.00	20.00
	1934(h)	2.013	.25	.50	1.00	10.00
	1935(h)	2.848	.25	.50	1.00	6.00
	1936(h)	3.320	.25	.50	1.00	6.00
	1937(h)	2.234	.25	.50	1.00	6.00
	1938(h)	2.991	.25	.50	1.00	6.00
	1939(h)	2.973	.25	.50	1.00	6.00
	1940(h)	2.998	.25	.50	1.00	5.00
	1941(h)	.748	1.00	2.00	5.00	10.00
	1946(h)	.460	.50	1.00	2.00	5.00
	1947(h)	1.292	60.00	90.00	125.00	175.00

NOTE: For coins dated 1941 without mint mark or initials refer to Faeroe Islands listings at the end of Denmark.

ZINC

Y#	Date	Mintage	Fine	VF	XF	Unc
49.2a	1941(h)	7.706	.25	.75	2.00	10.00
	1942(h)	8.676	.25	.75	2.00	10.00
	1943(h)	2.181	.25	.75	3.00	12.00
	1944(h)	7.994	.25	.75	2.00	10.00
	1945(h)	1.280	15.00	25.00	40.00	75.00

COPPER-NICKEL
Mintmasters Initial: N. Moneyers Initial: S.

Y#	Date	Mintage	Fine	VF	XF	Unc
59.1	1948(h)	5.317	.10	.50	2.00	5.00
	1949(h)	7.595	.10	.20	1.00	3.00
	1950(h)	6.886	.10	.20	1.00	3.00
	1951(h)	8.763	.10	.20	1.00	3.00
	1952(h)	6.810	.10	.20	1.00	3.00
	1953(h)	11.946	—	.10	.50	3.00
	1954(h)	19.739	—	.10	.50	2.50
	1955(h)	17.623	—	.10	.40	2.50

Mintmasters Initial: C. Moneyers Initial: S.

Y#	Date	Mintage	Fine	VF	XF	Unc
59.2	1956(h)	12.323	—	.10	.40	2.50
	1957(h)	13.227	—	.10	.40	1.50
	1958(h)	10.870	—	.10	.40	1.50
	1959(h)	1.255	15.00	20.00	30.00	50.00
	1960(h)	5.107	—	.10	.30	1.00

Y#	Date	Mintage	Fine	VF	XF	Unc
69.1	1960(h)	I.A.	—	.10	.40	1.50
	1961(h)	20.258	—	.10	.15	1.50
	1962(h)	12.785	—	.10	.15	1.50
	1963(h)	17.171	—	.10	.15	1.50
	1964(h)	14.282	—	.10	.15	1.50
	1965(h)	21.857	—	.10	.15	1.50
	1966(h)	24.160	—	.10	.15	1.25
	1967(h)	21.544	—	—	.10	.75
	1968(h)	7.586	—	—	.10	.60
	1969(h)	31.534	—	—	.10	.40
	1970(h)	37.813	—	—	.10	.25
	1971(h)	17.719	—	—	.10	.25

Mintmasters Initial: S. Moneyers Initial: S.

Y#	Date	Mintage	Fine	VF	XF	Unc
69.2	1972(h)	46.959	—	—	.10	.20

Mintmasters Initial: S. Moneyers Initial: B.

Y#	Date	Mintage	Fine	VF	XF	Unc
79.1	1973(h)	37.538	—	—	.10	.20
	1974(h)	38.570	—	—	.10	.20
	1975(h)	62.633	—	—	.10	.20
	1976(h)	64.359	—	—	.10	.20
	1977(h)	61.994	—	—	.10	.20
	1978(h)	30.302	—	—	.10	.20

Mintmasters Initial: B. Moneyers Initial: B.

Y#	Date	Mintage	Fine	VF	XF	Unc
79.2	1979(h)	10.224	—	—	.10	.20
	1980(h)	37.233	—	—	.10	.20
	1981(h)	51.565	—	—	.10	.20

Mintmasters Initial: R. Moneyers Initial: B.

Y#	Date	Mintage	Fine	VF	XF	Unc
79.3	1982(h)	40.195	—	—	.10	.20
	1983(h)	35.634	—	—	.10	.20
	1984(h)	17.828	—	—	.10	.20
	1985(h)	29.317	—	—	.10	.20
	1986(h)	46.254	—	—	.10	.20
	1987(h)	27.898	—	—	.10	.20
	1988(h)	29.400	—	—	.10	.20

25 ORE

2.4200 g, .600 SILVER, .0467 oz ASW
Mintmasters Initials: CS.

Y#	Date	Mintage	Fine	VF	XF	Unc
12.1	1874(h)	8.139	4.00	11.00	25.00	50.00
	1891(h)	1.214	5.00	12.00	25.00	45.00

Mintmasters Initials: VBP.

Y#	Date	Mintage	Fine	VF	XF	Unc
12.2	1894(h)	1.206	4.00	10.00	20.00	35.00
	1900/800(h)	1.206	4.50	11.00	22.50	40.00
	1900(h)	I.A.	4.00	10.00	20.00	35.00
	1904(h)	1.922	6.00	12.00	25.00	40.00
	1905/805(h)	1.722	4.00	7.50	11.50	30.00
	1905(h)	I.A.	3.50	7.00	11.00	27.50

Mintmasters Initials: VBP. Moneyers Initials: GJ.

Y#	Date	Mintage	Fine	VF	XF	Unc
24	1907(h)	2.009	2.25	5.50	11.00	22.50
	1911(h)	2.015	2.25	5.50	11.00	22.50

Y#	Date	Mintage	Fine	VF	XF	Unc
37.1	1913(h)	2.016	2.50	4.00	8.00	17.50
	1914(h)	.347	40.00	70.00	120.00	175.00
	1915(h)	2.862	2.50	3.50	6.00	15.00
	1916(h)	.938	2.50	5.00	10.00	20.00
	1917(h)	1.354	25.00	40.00	75.00	150.00
	1918(h)	2.090	2.50	4.00	6.00	12.50

Mintmasters Initials: HCN. Moneyers Initials: GJ.

Y#	Date	Mintage	Fine	VF	XF	Unc
37.2	1919(h)	9.295	.75	1.25	2.50	5.00

COPPER-NICKEL

Y#	Date	Mintage	Fine	VF	XF	Unc
32	1920(h)	12.288	2.00	4.00	6.00	12.50
	1921(h)	9.444	2.00	4.00	6.00	12.50
	1922(h)	5.701	12.00	17.50	25.00	40.00

Y#	Date	Mintage	Fine	VF	XF	Unc
50.1	1924(h)	8.035	.20	.50	2.00	7.00
	1925(h)	1.906	3.00	5.00	10.00	25.00
	1926(h)	2.659	.20	.50	2.00	17.50

Mintmasters Initial: N. Moneyers Initials: GJ.

Y#	Date	Mintage	Fine	VF	XF	Unc
50.2	1929(h)	.886	.75	2.00	4.00	22.00
	1930(h)	3.423	.75	2.00	4.00	22.00
	1932(h)	.846	3.00	8.00	12.00	30.00
	1933(h)	.479	17.50	25.00	35.00	60.00
	1934(h)	1.660	.50	2.00	4.00	17.50
	1935(h)	1.032	6.00	11.00	17.50	32.50
	1936(h)	1.453	.50	2.00	4.00	14.00
	1937(h)	1.612	2.00	3.50	6.50	16.00
	1938(h)	1.794	.75	2.00	5.00	14.00
	1939(h)	1.972	6.00	11.00	17.50	32.50
	1940(h)	1.356	.50	.75	2.50	7.00
	1946(h)	2.323	.50	.75	2.50	5.00
	1947(h)	1.751	1.50	4.50	6.50	11.00

NOTE: For coins dated 1941 refer to Faeroe Islands listings at the end of Denmark.

ZINC

Y#	Date	Mintage	Fine	VF	XF	Unc
50.2a	1941(h)	15.332	.50	1.25	5.00	16.00
	1942(h)	.997	.50	1.25	3.00	14.00
	1943(h)	5.784	.50	1.25	5.00	17.00
	1944(h)	10.665	.25	.50	1.00	9.00
	1945(h)	4.543	.50	1.25	4.00	15.00

COPPER-NICKEL
Mintmasters Initial: N. Moneyers Initial: S.

Y#	Date	Mintage	Fine	VF	XF	Unc
60.1	1948(h)	1.853	1.00	2.50	4.50	12.00
	1949(h)	15.000	.10	.30	1.00	7.00
	1950(h)	13.771	.10	.30	1.00	7.00
	1951(h)	5.045	.10	.30	1.00	8.00
	1952(h)	2.018	.50	1.00	2.50	12.50
	1953(h)	9.553	.10	.25	.75	2.50

Y#	Date	Mintage	Fine	VF	XF	Unc
60.1	1954(h)	11.337	.10	.25	.75	2.50
	1955(h)	6.385	.15	.25	.75	2.50

Mintmasters Initial: C. Moneyers Initial: S.

Y#	Date	Mintage	Fine	VF	XF	Unc
60.2	1956(h)	10.228	.10	.25	.75	2.50
	1957(h)	7.421	.10	.25	.75	2.50
	1958(h)	3.600	.10	.25	.75	2.50
	1959(h)	2.211	1.50	2.00	2.50	6.00
	1960(h)	3.453	.15	.30	.75	2.50

Y#	Date	Mintage	Fine	VF	XF	Unc
70	1960(h)	I.A.	4.00	6.00	8.00	12.00
	1961(h)	20.860	.10	.20	.40	1.25
	1962(h)	12.563	.10	.20	.40	1.25
	1964(h)	6.175	.10	.20	.40	1.25
	1965(h)	13.492	.10	.20	.40	1.25
	1966(h)	50.220	.10	.20	.40	1.25
	1967(h)	87.468	6.00	10.00	14.00	20.00

Y#	Date	Mintage	Fine	VF	XF	Unc
76.1	1966(h)	I.A.	—	—	.10	.35
	1967(h)	I.A.	—	—	.10	.35
	1968(h)	39.142	—	—	.10	.35
	1969(h)	16.974	—	—	.10	.35
	1970(h)	5.393	—	—	.10	.25
	1971(h)	12.725	—	—	.10	.25

Mintmasters Initial: S. Moneyers Initial: S.

Y#	Date	Mintage	Fine	VF	XF	Unc
76.2	1972(h)	31.422	—	—	.10	.25

Mintmasters Initial: S. Moneyers Initial: B.

Y#	Date	Mintage	Fine	VF	XF	Unc
80.1	1973(h)	30.834	—	—	.10	.25
	1974(h)	22.178	—	—	.10	.25
	1975(h)	28.798	—	—	.10	.25
	1976(h)	48.388	—	—	.10	.25
	1977(h)	32.239	—	—	.10	.25
	1978(h)	17.444	—	—	.10	.25

Mintmasters Initial: B. Moneyers Initial: B.

Y#	Date	Mintage	Fine	VF	XF	Unc
80.2	1979(h)	24.261	—	—	.10	.25
	1980(h)	30.448	—	—	.10	.25
	1981(h)	1.427	—	—	.10	.40

Mintmasters Initial: R. Moneyers Initial: B.

Y#	Date	Mintage	Fine	VF	XF	Unc
80.3	1982(h)	24.671	—	—	.10	.25
	1983(h)	32.706	—	—	.10	.25
	1984(h)	22.882	—	—	.10	.25
	1985(h)	29.048	—	—	.10	.25
	1986(h)	53.496	—	—	.10	.25
	1987(h)	30.575	—	—	.10	.25
	1988(h)	23.370	—	—	.10	.25

BRONZE

Mintmasters Initials: LG. Moneyers Initials: JPA.

Y#	Date	Mintage	Fine	VF	XF	Unc
89	1990	109.084	—	—	.10	.25
	1991	102.162	—	—	.10	.25
	1992	—	—	—	.10	.25

50 ORE

BRONZE

Mintmasters Initials: NR. Moneyers Initials: JP.

Y#	Date	Mintage	Fine	VF	XF	Unc
85.1	1989	92.236	—	—	—	.75

Mintmasters Initials: LG. Moneyers Initials: JPA.

Y#	Date	Mintage	Fine	VF	XF	Unc
85.2	1990	63.358	—	—	—	.75
	1991	11.115	—	—	—	.75
	1992	—	—	—	—	.75

1/2 KRONE

ALUMINUM-BRONZE

Mintmasters Initials: HCN. Moneyers Initials: GJ.

Y#	Date	Mintage	Fine	VF	XF	Unc
33.1	1924(h)	2.150	2.00	5.00	10.00	22.50
	1925(h)	3.432	2.00	5.00	10.00	22.50
	1926(h)	.716	7.50	12.00	20.00	32.50

Mintmasters Initial: N. Moneyers Initials: GJ.

Y#	Date	Mintage	Fine	VF	XF	Unc
33.2	1939(h)	.226	30.00	50.00	70.00	100.00
	1940(h)	1.871	2.00	4.00	6.00	12.50

KRONE

7.5000 g, .800 SILVER, .1929 oz ASW

Mintmasters Initials: CS.

Y#	Date	Mintage	Fine	VF	XF	Unc
13.1	1875(h)	4.040	4.00	15.00	50.00	130.00
	1876(h)	1.284	10.00	22.50	60.00	170.00
	1892(h)	.701	10.00	14.00	25.00	55.00

Mintmasters Initials: VBP.

Y#	Date	Mintage	Fine	VF	XF	Unc
13.2	1898(h)	.201	27.50	40.00	60.00	95.00

Y#	Date	Mintage	Fine	VF	XF	Unc
38	1915(h)	1.410	3.00	4.50	7.50	15.00
	1916(h)	.992	4.00	6.00	10.00	18.00

ALUMINUM-BRONZE

Mintmasters Initials: HCN. Moneyers Initials: GJ.

Y#	Date	Mintage	Fine	VF	XF	Unc
34.1	1924(h)	.999	100.00	150.00	275.00	550.00
	1925(h)	6.314	.75	1.50	10.00	50.00
	1926(h)	2.706	.75	1.50	10.00	50.00

Mintmasters Initial: N. Moneyers Initials: GJ.

Y#	Date	Mintage	Fine	VF	XF	Unc
34.2	1929(h)	.501	4.00	6.00	20.00	60.00
	1930(h)	.540	10.00	20.00	35.00	90.00
	1931(h)	.540	4.00	7.00	20.00	50.00
	1934(h)	.529	2.00	4.00	15.00	40.00
	1935(h)	.505	14.00	22.50	35.00	90.00
	1936(h)	.558	2.25	4.50	12.00	40.00
	1938(h)	.407	9.00	15.00	22.00	60.00
	1939(h)	1.517	.50	1.00	2.50	14.00
	1940(h)	1.496	.50	1.00	2.50	14.00
	1941(h)	.661	2.00	4.00	6.00	25.00

Mintmasters Initial: N. Moneyers Initial: S.

Y#	Date	Mintage	Fine	VF	XF	Unc
54	1942(h)	3.952	.50	1.00	2.25	14.00
	1943(h)	.798	2.50	6.00	15.00	40.00
	1944(h)	1.760	.25	.75	2.00	12.50
	1945(h)	2.581	.25	.75	2.00	12.50
	1946(h)	4.321	.25	.50	1.00	4.50
	1947(h)	5.060	.25	.50	1.00	4.50

Y#	Date	Mintage	Fine	VF	XF	Unc
61.1	1947(h)	I.A.	1.00	2.25	3.75	10.00
	1948(h)	4.248	.25	.50	1.00	5.50
	1949(h)	1.300	.75	2.25	7.00	16.00
	1952(h)	2.124	.50	2.00	5.00	14.00
	1953(h)	.573	.75	2.25	7.00	16.00
	1954(h)	.584	8.00	12.00	18.00	27.50
	1955(h)	1.359	2.00	4.00	7.50	15.00

Mintmasters Initial: C. Moneyers Initial: S.

Y#	Date	Mintage	Fine	VF	XF	Unc
61.2	1956(h)	2.858	.25	.50	1.00	4.00
	1957(h)	10.896	.20	.40	1.00	2.50
	1958(h)	1.507	.20	.40	1.00	2.50
	1959(h)	.243	6.00	8.00	12.50	20.00
	1960(h)	100 pcs.	—	1200.	1400.	2000.

COPPER-NICKEL

Y#	Date	Mintage	Fine	VF	XF	Unc
71.1	1960(h)	1.000	.25	.50	1.00	2.50
	1961(h)	10.348	.20	.25	1.00	3.50
	1962(h)	27.068	.20	.25	1.00	3.50
	1963(h)	32.083	.20	.25	.50	1.50
	1964(h)	5.984	.20	.25	.50	2.00
	1965(h)	13.799	.20	.25	.50	1.50
	1966(h)	10.890	.20	.25	.50	1.50
	1967(h)	18.304	.20	.25	.50	1.00
	1968(h)	8.213	.20	.25	.50	1.00
	1969(h)	9.597	—	.20	.30	.75
	1970(h)	9.460	—	.20	.30	.75
	1971(h)	13.985	—	.20	.30	.60

Mintmasters Initial: S. Moneyers Initial: S.

Y#	Date	Mintage	Fine	VF	XF	Unc
71.2	1972(h)	21.019	—	—	.25	.50

Mintmasters Initial: S. Moneyers Initial: B.

Y#	Date	Mintage	Fine	VF	XF	Unc
81.1	1973(h)	18.268	—	—	.20	.40
	1974(h)	17.742	—	—	.20	.40
	1975(h)	20.136	—	—	.20	.40
	1976(h)	28.049	—	—	.20	.40
	1977(h)	25.685	—	—	.20	.40
	1978(h)	11.286	—	—	.20	.40

Mintmasters Initial: B. Moneyers Initial: B.

Y#	Date	Mintage	Fine	VF	XF	Unc
81.2	1979(h)	25.216	—	—	.20	.40
	1980(h)	25.825	—	—	.20	.40
	1981(h)	8.889	—	—	.20	.40

Mintmasters Initial: R. Moneyers Initial: B.

Y#	Date	Mintage	Fine	VF	XF	Unc
81.3	1982(h)	5.011	—	—	.20	.40
	1983(h)	13.946	—	—	.20	.40
	1984(h)	36.439	—	—	.20	.40
	1985(h)	10.843	—	—	.20	.40
	1986(h)	12.556	—	—	.20	.40
	1987(h)	20.120	—	—	.20	.40
	1988(h)	32.074	—	—	.20	.40
	1989(h)	15.704	—	—	.20	.40

MII Monograms

Y#	Date	Mintage	Fine	VF	XF	Unc
93	1992	125.000	—	—	—	.25
	1993	—	—	—	—	.25

2 KRONER

15.0000 g, .800 SILVER, .3858 oz ASW
Mintmasters Initials: CS.

Y#	Date	Mintage	Fine	VF	XF	Unc
14.1	1875(h)	3.396	7.00	16.00	50.00	125.00
	1876(h)	1.381	7.00	16.00	50.00	125.00

Mintmasters Initials: VBP.

Y#	Date	Mintage	Fine	VF	XF	Unc
14.2	1897(h)	.151	35.00	50.00	80.00	140.00
	1899(h)	.152	25.00	40.00	65.00	110.00

Mintmasters Initials: CS.
25th Anniversary of Reign

Y#	Date	Mintage	Fine	VF	XF	Unc
15	1888(h)	.101	15.00	25.00	35.00	70.00

Mintmasters Initials: CS.
Golden Wedding Anniversary

Y#	Date	Mintage	Fine	VF	XF	Unc
16	1892(h)	.101	15.00	25.00	35.00	70.00

Mintmasters Initial: P.
40th Anniversary of Reign

Y#	Date	Mintage	Fine	VF	XF	Unc
17	1903(h)	.103	10.00	15.00	20.00	37.50

Mintmasters Initials: VBP. Moneyers Initials: GJ.
Christian IX Death
and Accession of Frederik VIII

Y#	Date	Mintage	Fine	VF	XF	Unc
25	1906(h)	.151	6.00	12.00	15.00	27.50

Mintmasters Initials: VBP.
Frederik VIII Death
and Accession of Christian X

Y#	Date	Mintage	Fine	VF	XF	Unc
40	1912(h)	.102	6.00	12.00	18.00	35.00

Y#	Date	Mintage	Fine	VF	XF	Unc
39	1915(h)	.657	12.00	18.00	25.00	45.00
	1916(h)	.402	6.00	10.00	15.00	25.00

Mintmasters Initials: HCN. Moneyers Initials: GJ.
Silver Wedding Anniversary

Y#	Date	Mintage	Fine	VF	XF	Unc
41	1923(h)	.203	5.00	8.00	12.00	16.00

ALUMINUM-BRONZE
Mintmasters Initials: HCN. Moneyers Initials: GJ.

Y#	Date	Mintage	Fine	VF	XF	Unc
35.1	1924(h)	1.128	15.00	30.00	85.00	250.00
	1925(h)	3.248	.75	2.00	15.00	55.00
	1926(h)	1.126	.75	2.00	15.00	55.00

Mintmasters Initial: N. Moneyers Initials: GJ.

Y#	Date	Mintage	Fine	VF	XF	Unc
35.2	1936(h)	.400	4.00	6.00	15.00	40.00
	1938(h)	.191	12.00	18.00	30.00	60.00
	1939(h)	.723	.50	2.00	6.00	25.00
	1940(h)	.743	2.00	4.00	8.00	30.00
	1941(h)	.129	20.00	32.50	55.00	120.00

15.0000 g, .800 SILVER, .3858 oz ASW
Moneyers Initials: HS.
King's 60th Birthday

Y#	Date	Mintage	Fine	VF	XF	Unc
42	1930(h)	.303	4.00	6.00	8.00	14.00

Mintmasters Initial: N. Moneyers Initial: S.
25th Anniversary of Reign

Y#	Date	Mintage	Fine	VF	XF	Unc
43	1937(h)	.209	4.00	6.00	8.00	14.00

King's 75th Birthday

Y#	Date	Mintage	Fine	VF	XF	Unc
55	1945(h)	.157	5.00	7.00	9.00	16.00

ALUMINUM-BRONZE

Y#	Date	Mintage	Fine	VF	XF	Unc
62.1	1947(h)	1.151	.75	1.50	5.00	12.50
	1948(h)	.857	.50	1.00	2.50	8.50
	1949(h)	.272	2.00	3.50	6.50	16.00
	1951(h)	1.576	.50	1.00	2.00	7.50
	1952(h)	1.958	.50	1.00	2.00	6.50
	1953(h)	.432	2.00	3.00	5.00	14.00
	1954(h)	.716	2.00	3.00	5.00	14.00
	1955(h)	.457	2.00	3.00	5.00	14.00

Mintmasters Initial: C. Moneyers Initial: S.

Y#	Date	Mintage	Fine	VF	XF	Unc
62.2	1956(h)	1.444	.35	.55	1.00	7.50
	1957(h)	2.610	.35	.55	.75	3.00
	1958(h)	2.605	.35	.55	.75	3.00
	1959(h)	.192	4.00	9.00	14.00	25.00

15.0000 g, .800 SILVER, .3858 oz ASW
Mintmasters Initial: N. Moneyers Initial: S.
Greenland Commemorative

Y#	Date	Mintage	Fine	VF	XF	Unc
63	1953(h)	.152	7.00	14.00	22.00	30.00

Mintmasters Initial: C. Moneyers Initial: S.
Princess Margrethe's 18th Birthday

Y#	Date	Mintage	Fine	VF	XF	Unc
64	1958(h)	.301	—	4.00	6.00	9.00

COPPER-NICKEL
MII Monogram

Y#	Date	Mintage	Fine	VF	XF	Unc
94	1992	75.000	—	—	—	.50
	1993	—	—	—	—	.50

5 KRONER

17.0000 g, .800 SILVER, .4372 oz ASW
Mintmasters Initial: C. Moneyers Initial: S.
Silver Wedding Anniversary

Y#	Date	Mintage	Fine	VF	XF	Unc
65	1960(h)	.410	—	3.50	4.50	7.00
	1960(h)	—	—	—	P/L	—

COPPER-NICKEL

Y#	Date	Mintage	Fine	VF	XF	Unc
72.1	1960(h)	6.418	—	1.00	1.25	2.00
	1961(h)	9.744	—	1.00	1.75	5.00
	1962(h)	2.074	—	1.00	2.00	6.00
	1963(h)	.709	—	1.00	2.00	7.50
	1964(h)	1.443	—	1.00	2.00	6.50
	1965(h)	2.574	—	1.00	1.50	3.50
	1966(h)	4.370	—	1.00	1.50	3.00
	1967(h)	1.864	—	1.00	1.25	2.50
	1968(h)	4.132	—	1.00	1.25	2.00
	1969(h)	.072	3.00	4.00	5.00	7.50
	1970(h)	2.246	—	1.00	1.20	1.75
	1971(h)	4.767	—	1.00	1.20	1.75

Mintmasters Initial: S. Moneyers Initial: S.

Y#	Date	Mintage	Fine	VF	XF	Unc
72.2	1972(h)	2.599	—	—	1.20	1.75

17.0000 g, .800 SILVER, .4372 oz ASW
Mintmasters Initial: C. Moneyers Initial: S.
Wedding of Princess Anne Marie

Y#	Date	Mintage	Fine	VF	XF	Unc
73	1964(h)	.359	—	—	4.00	6.50

COPPER-NICKEL
Mintmasters Initial: S. Moneyers Initial: B.

Y#	Date	Mintage	Fine	VF	XF	Unc
82.1	1973(h)narrow rim	3.774	—	—	.90	1.50
	1973(h) wide rim					
82.1		Inc. Ab.	—	—	.90	1.25
	1974(h)	5.239	—	—	.90	1.25
	1975(h)	5.810	—	—	.90	1.25
	1976(h)	7.651	—	—	.90	1.25
	1977(h)	6.885	—	—	.90	1.25
	1978(h)	2.984	—	—	.90	1.25

Mintmasters Initial: B. Moneyers Initial: B.

Y#	Date	Mintage	Fine	VF	XF	Unc
82.2	1979(h)	2.861	—	—	.90	1.50
	1980(h)	3.622	—	—	.90	1.50
	1981(h)	1.057	—	—	.90	1.50

Mintmasters Initial: R. Moneyers Initial: B.

Y#	Date	Mintage	Fine	VF	XF	Unc
82.3	1982(h)	1.002	—	—	.90	1.25
	1983(h)	1.044	—	—	.90	1.25
	1984(h)	.713	—	—	.90	1.25
	1985(h)	.621	—	—	.90	1.25
	1986(h)	1.042	—	—	.90	1.25
	1987(h)	.611	—	—	.90	1.25
	1988(h)	.648	—	—	.90	1.25

Mintmasters Initials: LG. Moneyers Initials: JPA.

Y#	Date	Mintage	Fine	VF	XF	Unc
90	1990	46.745	—	—	—	1.00
	1991	—	—	—	—	1.00
	1992	3.752	—	—	—	1.00

10 KRONER

4.4803 g, .900 GOLD, .1296 oz AGW
Mintmasters Initials: CS.

Y#	Date	Mintage	Fine	VF	XF	Unc
18.1	1873(h)	.369	75.00	110.00	145.00	225.00
	1874(h)	I.A.	75.00	125.00	170.00	260.00
	1877(h)	.098	75.00	150.00	185.00	275.00
	1877(h)	—	—	—	Proof	2500.
	1890(h)	.151	75.00	115.00	140.00	210.00

Mintmasters Initials: VBP.

Y#	Date	Mintage	Fine	VF	XF	Unc
18.2	1898(h)	.100	75.00	120.00	150.00	220.00
	1900(h)	.204	75.00	110.00	120.00	180.00

Y#	Date	Mintage	Fine	VF	XF	Unc
26	1908(h)	.308	75.00	85.00	95.00	125.00
	1909(h)	.153	75.00	85.00	95.00	125.00

Y#	Date	Mintage	Fine	VF	XF	Unc
44	1913(h)	.312	75.00	85.00	95.00	125.00
	1917(h)	.132	75.00	85.00	110.00	150.00

20.4000 g, .800 SILVER, .5247 oz ASW
Mintmasters Initial: C. Moneyers Initial: S.
Wedding of Princess Margrethe

Y#	Date	Mintage	Fine	VF	XF	Unc
74	1967(h)	*.498	—	—	5.00	10.00

***NOTE:** 78,383 were melted.

Wedding of Princess Benedikte
Obv: Similar to Y#74.

Y#	Date	Mintage	Fine	VF	XF	Unc
75	1968 C(h)S	*.297	—	—	6.00	12.00

***NOTE:** 42,923 were melted.

Mintmasters Initial: S. Moneyers Initial: S.
Death of Frederik IX
and Accession of Margrethe II

Y#	Date	Mintage	Fine	VF	XF	Unc
77	1972(h)	.400	—	—	5.00	10.00

COPPER-NICKEL
Mintmasters Initial: B. Moneyers Initial: I.

Y#	Date	Mintage	Fine	VF	XF	Unc
83.1	1979(h)	76.801	—	—	1.75	2.50
	1981(h)	10.520	—	—	1.75	2.50

Mintmasters Initial: R. Moneyers Initial: I.

Y#	Date	Mintage	Fine	VF	XF	Unc
83.2	1982(h)	1.065	—	—	1.75	2.50
	1983(h)	1.123	—	—	1.75	2.50
	1984(h)	.748	—	—	1.75	2.50
	1985(h)	.720	—	—	1.75	2.50
	1987(h)	.719	—	—	1.75	2.50
	1988(h)	.718	—	—	1.75	2.50

Mintmasters Initial: R. Moneyers Initial: A.
Crown Prince's Coming of Age

Y#	Date	Mintage	Fine	VF	XF	Unc
84	1986(h)	1.090	—	—	2.00	3.50
	1986(h)	2,000	—	—	Proof	800.00

14.3000 g, .800 SILVER, .3678 oz ASW

Y#	Date	Mintage	Fine	VF	XF	Unc
84a	1986(h)	.024	—	—	Proof	60.00

ALUMINUM-BRONZE

Y#	Date	Mintage	Fine	VF	XF	Unc
86	1989	38.346	—	—	—	3.50
	1990	12.193	—	—	—	3.50
	1991	1.065	—	—	—	3.50
	1992	—	—	—	—	3.50

20 KRONER

8.9606 g, .900 GOLD, .2592 oz AGW
Mintmasters Initials: CS.

Y#	Date	Mintage	Fine	VF	XF	Unc
19.1	1873(h)	1.153	BV	135.00	150.00	200.00
	1874(h)	I.A.	400.00	800.00	1100.	1500.
	1876(h)	.351	BV	135.00	150.00	200.00
	1877(h)	I.A.	BV	135.00	175.00	225.00
	1890(h)	.102	BV	135.00	150.00	200.00
	1890(h)	—	—	—	Proof	3000.

Mintmasters Initials: VBP.

Y#	Date	Mintage	Fine	VF	XF	Unc
19.2	1900(h)	.100	BV	130.00	140.00	200.00
	1900(h)	—	—	—	Proof	3000.

Y#	Date	Mintage	Fine	VF	XF	Unc
27	1908(h)	.243	BV	130.00	140.00	165.00
	1908(h)	—	—	—	Proof	3000.
	1909(h)	.365	BV	130.00	140.00	165.00
	1910(h)	.200	BV	130.00	140.00	165.00
	1911(h)	.183	BV	130.00	140.00	165.00
	1912(h)	.184	BV	130.00	140.00	165.00

Y#	Date	Mintage	Fine	VF	XF	Unc
45.1	1913(h)	.815	BV	125.00	140.00	165.00
	1914(h)	.920	BV	125.00	140.00	165.00
	1914(h)	—	—	—	Proof	3000.
	1915(h)	.532	BV	125.00	140.00	165.00
	1916(h)	1.401	BV	125.00	140.00	165.00
	1917(h)	I.A.	BV	125.00	140.00	165.00

Mintmasters Initials: HCN.

Y#	Date	Mintage	Fine	VF	XF	Unc
45.2	1926(h)	.358	—	—	4000.	12,000.
	1927(h)	I.A.	—	—	4000.	12,000.

Mintmasters Initial: N.

Y#	Date	Mintage	Fine	VF	XF	Unc
45.3	1930(h)	1.285	—	—	—	12,000.
	1931(h)	I.A.	—	—	—	12,000.

NOTE: The 1926-1931 dated 20 Kroners were not released for circulation. Only two each of the 1930 and 1931 dated coins are known.

ALUMINUM-BRONZE
50th Birthday of Queen Margarethe

Y#	Date	Mintage	Fine	VF	XF	Unc
87	1990	1.000	—	—	—	6.50

Mintmasters Initials: LG. Moneyers Initials: JPA.

Y#	Date	Mintage	Fine	VF	XF	Unc
91	1990	34.371	—	—	—	4.50
	1991	11.563	—	—	—	4.50

Silver Wedding Anniversary

Y#	Date	Mintage	Fine	VF	XF	Unc
92	1992	—	—	—	—	6.00

200 KRONER

31.1000 g, .800 SILVER, .8000 oz ASW
50th Birthday of Queen Margarethe

Y#	Date	Mintage	Fine	VF	XF	Unc
88	1990	.130	—	—	—	65.00

31.1000 g, .999 SILVER, 1.0000 oz ASW
Silver Wedding Anniversary

Y#	Date	Mintage	Fine	VF	XF	Unc
95	1992	—	—	—	Proof	50.00

MINT SETS (MS)

KM#	Date	Mintage	Identification	Issue Price	Mkt. Val.
MS1	1956(7)	—	Y56-62	—	185.00
MS2	1957(7)	—	Y56-62	—	145.00
MS3	1958(7)	—	Y56-62	—	145.00
MS4	1959(7)	—	Y56-62	—	375.00
MS5	1960(10)	—	Y56-60,68-72	—	215.00
MS6	1961(7)	—	Y56-58,69-72	—	120.00
MS7	1962(8)	—	Y56-58,68-72	—	100.00
MS8	1963(7)	—	Y56-58,68,69,71,72	—	65.00
MS9	1964(8)	—	Y56-58,68-72	—	65.00
MS10	1965(7)	—	Y56,57,68-72	—	65.00
MS11	1966(8)	—	Y56,57,68-72,76	—	45.00
MS12	1967(8)	—	Y56,57,68-72,76	—	65.00
MS13	1968(7)	—	Y56,57,68,69,71,72,76	—	40.00
MS14	1969(7)	—	Y56,57,68,69,71,72,76	—	40.00
MS15	1970(7)	—	Y56,57,68,69,71,72,76	—	20.00
MS16	1971(7)	—	Y56,57,68,69,71,72,76	—	20.00
MS17	1972(7)	—	Y56,57,68,69,71,72,76	—	9.00
MS18	1973(5)	—	Y78-82	—	10.00
MS19	1974(5)	—	Y78-82	6.00	8.50
MS20	1975(5)	4,300	Y78-82	6.00	125.00
MS21	1976(5)	6,000	Y78-82	3.55	65.00
MS22	1977(5)	6,000	Y78-82	—	60.00
MS23	1978(5)	6,000	Y78-82	—	27.50
MS24	1979(6)	6,000	Y78-83	—	25.00
MS25	1980(5)	4,000	Y78-82	—	225.00
MS26	1981(6)	15,000	Y78-83	—	17.50
MS27	1982(6)	20,000	Y78-83	—	12.00
MS28	1983(6)	20,000	Y78-83	—	12.00
MS29	1984(6)	18,000	Y78-83	—	12.00
MS30	1985(6)	20,000	Y78-83	—	12.00
MS31	1986(6)	20,000	Y78-82,84	—	32.00
MS32	1987(6)	15,000	Y78.3-82.3,83.2	—	32.00
MS33	1988(6)	20,000	Y78.3-82.3,83.2	—	12.00
MS34	1989(3)	27,150	Y81.3, 85-86	12.00	12.00
MS35	1990(6)	45,000	Y85.2,86-87,89-91	27.00	24.00
MS36	1991(5)	50,000	Y85.2,86,89-91	—	16.00
MS37	1992(7)	—	Y85.2,86,89-90,92-94	—	18.00

FAEROE ISLANDS

The Faeroe Islands, a self-governing community within the kingdom of Denmark, are situated in the North Atlantic between Iceland and the Shetland Islands. The 17 inhabited islands and numerous islets and reefs have an area of 540 sq. mi. (1,400 sq. km.) and a population of 47,000. Capital: Thorshavn. The principal industries are fishing and grazing. Fish and fish products are exported.

While it is thought that Irish hermits lived on the islands in the 7th and 8th centuries, the present inhabitants are descended from 6th century Norse settlers. The Faeroe Islands became a Norwegian fief in 1035 and became Danish in 1380 when Norway and Denmark were united. They have ever since remained in Danish possession and were granted self-government (except for an appointed governor-general) with their own legislature, executive and flag in 1948.

The islands were occupied by British troops during World War II, after the German occupation of Denmark. The Faeroe Island coinage was struck in London during World War II.

RULERS

Danish

MONETARY SYSTEM

100 Ore = 1 Krone

ORE

BRONZE

KM#	Date	Mintage	Fine	VF	XF	Unc
1	1941	.100	25.00	40.00	50.00	65.00
	1941	—	—	—	Proof	150.00

2 ORE

BRONZE

KM#	Date	Mintage	Fine	VF	XF	Unc
2	1941	.100	4.00	8.00	14.00	25.00
	1941	—	—	—	Proof	150.00

5 ORE

BRONZE

KM#	Date	Mintage	Fine	VF	XF	Unc
3	1941	.100	4.00	7.00	12.00	22.50
	1941	—	—	—	Proof	150.00

10 ORE

COPPER-NICKEL

KM#	Date	Mintage	Fine	VF	XF	Unc
4	1941	.100	5.00	9.00	15.00	32.50
	1941	—	—	—	Proof	175.00

25 ORE

COPPER-NICKEL

KM#	Date	Mintage	Fine	VF	XF	Unc
5	1941	.100	5.00	9.00	15.00	32.50
	1941	—	—	—	Proof	175.00

SCHLESWIG-HOLSTEIN

Schleswig-Holstein is the border area between Denmark and Germany. The duchy of Schleswig was Danish while Holstein was German. The 1773 Treaty of Zarskoje Selo transferred Holstein to the Danes in exchange for Oldenburg. There was a great deal of trouble in the area during the 19th century. Prussia annexed the territory in 1866. After a plesbicite the area was divided in 1920. North Slesvig went to Denmark and South Schleswig and Holstein went to Germany.

RULERS

Christian VII (of Denmark), 1784-1808
Friedrich VI (of Denmark), 1808-1839
Christian VIII (of Denmark), 1839-1848

ALTONA MINTMASTERS INITIALS

CB - Calus Branth
IFF, FF - Johann Friedrich Freund
MF, M.F, M.F. - Michael Flor
TA - Theodor C.W. Andersen
VS - Georg Vilhelm Svendsen

MONETARY SYSTEM

4 Dreiling = 2 Sechsling = 1 Schilling
60 Schilling = 1 Speciesdaler

JOINT COINAGE

2-1/2 SCHILLING

(1/24 Daler Specie)

2.8090 g, .375 SILVER, .0339 oz ASW
Obv: Crowned CR monogram.
Rev: Value above date.

C#	Date	Mintage	Fine	VF	XF	Unc
4	1801 MF	.211	3.00	7.00	20.00	75.00

NOTE: Earlier dates (1787-1800) exist for this type.

C#	Date	Mintage	Fine	VF	XF	Unc
20	1809 MF	.960	5.00	10.00	30.00	100.00
	1812 MF	.528	5.00	10.00	30.00	100.00

5 SCHILLING

(1/12 Daler Specie)

4.2140 g, .500 SILVER, .0677 oz ASW
Obv: Crowned interlaced CR monogram, VII within.
Rev: Value.

C#	Date	Mintage	Fine	VF	XF	Unc
5	1801 MF	.103	5.00	10.00	30.00	100.00

NOTE: Earlier dates (1787-1800) exist for this type.

8 SCHILLING

2.8090 g, .375 SILVER, .0339 oz ASW

C#	Date	Mintage	Fine	VF	XF	Unc
21	1816 MF	.056	7.00	15.00	40.00	150.00
	1818 CB	.243	7.00	15.00	40.00	150.00
	1819 IFF	.925	7.00	15.00	40.00	150.00

16 SCHILLING

4.2140 g, .500 SILVER, .0677 oz ASW

C#	Date	Mintage	Fine	VF	XF	Unc
22	1816 MF	.031	8.00	20.00	50.00	150.00
	1818 CB	.125	8.00	20.00	50.00	150.00

Rev: 1/12 SP added.

C#	Date	Mintage	Fine	VF	XF	Unc
22a	1831 IFF	.198	8.00	20.00	50.00	150.00
	1839 IFF	.063	8.00	20.00	50.00	150.00

20 SCHILLING

(1/3 Daler Specie)

9.6310 g, .875 SILVER, .2709 oz ASW

C#	Date	Mintage	Fine	VF	XF	Unc
7	1808 MF	.124	8.00	20.00	50.00	200.00

NOTE: Earlier dates (1787-1799) exist for this type.

40 SCHILLING

(2/3 Daler Specie)

19.2630 g, .875 SILVER, .5419 oz ASW
Similar to 20 Schilling, C#7.

C#	Date	Mintage	Fine	VF	XF	Unc
8	1808 MF	—	85.00	150.00	225.00	500.00

NOTE: Earlier dates (1787-1799) exist for this type.

60 SCHILLING

(Daler Specie)

28.8930 g, .875 SILVER, .8128 oz ASW
Similar to 20 Schilling, C#7.

C#	Date	Mintage	Fine	VF	XF	Unc
9	1801 MF	.312	65.00	125.00	300.00	500.00
	1804 MF	.106	65.00	125.00	300.00	500.00
	1805 MF	—	—	—	Rare	—
	1807 MF	.102	65.00	125.00	300.00	500.00
	1808 MF	1.304	100.00	225.00	600.00	1000.

NOTE: Many die varieties exist.
NOTE: Earlier dates (1787-1800) exist for this type.

PROVISIONAL GOVERNMENT

1848-1851

DREILING

COPPER

C#	Date	Mintage	Fine	VF	XF	Unc
23	1850 TA	.200	3.00	6.00	15.00	50.00

SECHSLING

COPPER

C#	Date	Mintage	Fine	VF	XF	Unc
24	1850 TA	.203	5.00	10.00	25.00	85.00
	1851 TA	.163	5.00	10.00	25.00	85.00

SCHILLING

1.4620 g, .250 SILVER, .0117 oz ASW
Obv: Crowned arms in sprays. Rev: Denomination.

C#	Date	Mintage	Fine	VF	XF	Unc
25	1851 TA	—	—	—	Rare	—

DJIBOUTI

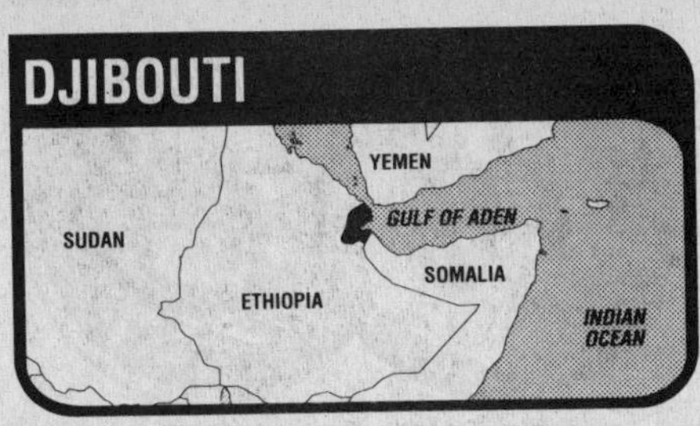

The Republic of Djibouti (formerly French Somaliland and the French Overseas Territory of Afars and Issas), located in northeast Africa at the Bab el Mandeb Strait connecting the Suez Canal and the Red Sea with the Gulf of Aden and the Indian Ocean, has an area of 8,494 sq. mi. (22,000 sq. km.) and a population of 280,000. Capital: Djibouti. The tiny nation has less than one sq. mi. of arable land, and no natural resources except salt, sand, and camels. The commercial activities of the transshipment port of Djibouti and the Addis Abada-Djibouti railroad are the basis of the economy. Salt, fish and hides are exported.

French interest in former French Somaliland began in 1839 with concessions obtained by a French naval lieutenant from the provincial sultans. French Somaliland was made a protectorate in 1884 and its boundaries were delimited by the Franco-British and Ethiopian accords of 1887 and 1897. It became a colony in 1896 and a territory within the French Union in 1946. In 1958 it voted to join the new French Community as an overseas territory, and reaffirmed that choice by a referendum in March, 1967. Its name was changed from French Somaliland to the French Territory of Afars and Issas on July 5, 1967.

The French Tricolor, which had flown over the strategically important territory for 115 years, was lowered for the last time on June 27, 1977, when French Afars and Issas became Africa's 49th independent state, under the name of the Republic of Djibouti.

Djibouti, a seaport and capital city of the Republic of Djibouti (and formerly of French Somaliland and French Afars and Issas) is located on the east coast of Africa at the southernmost entrance to the Red Sea. The capital was moved from Obok to Djibouti in 1892 and established as the transshipment point for Ethiopia's foreign trade via the Franco-Ethiopian railway linking Djibouti and Addis Ababa.

COUNTERMARKED COINAGE

RUPEE-TALER (RYAL) COINAGE SERIES

'Abd Latif Ma'a al-Fazah bi Jibuti

Coins privately countermarked (c/m) around 1900 with 12 scalloped square with Arabic inscription. Sometimes coins have additional c/m's on the coin showing silver fineness.

1/2 RUPEE SIZE

.917 SILVER
c/m: On India 1/2 Rupee, KM#491

KM#	Date	VG	Fine	VF	XF
1	ND(1877-1900)	35.00	60.00	90.00	225.00

RUPEE SIZE

SILVER, dump
c/m: On Murshidabad Rupee, KM#99.

KM#	Date	VG	Fine	VF	XF
2.6	ND(r.y.19)	72.50	120.00	180.00	—

.917 SILVER
c/m: On India Rupee, KM#450.

KM#	Date	VG	Fine	VF	XF
2.1	ND(1835,40)	20.00	35.00	65.00	125.00

c/m: On India Rupee, KM#457.

KM#	Date	VG	Fine	VF	XF
2.2	ND(1840)	20.00	35.00	65.00	125.00

c/m: On India Rupee, KM#458.

KM#	Date	VG	Fine	VF	XF
2.3	ND(1840)	20.00	35.00	65.00	125.00

c/m: On India Rupee, KM#473.

KM#	Date	VG	Fine	VF	XF
2.4	ND(1862-1901)	20.00	35.00	65.00	125.00

RYAL SIZE (TALER)

.833 SILVER

c/m: On Austria M.T. Thaler, KM#T1.

KM#	Date	VG	Fine	VF	XF
3.1	ND(1780)	30.00	50.00	75.00	150.00

c/m: With additional Arabic *"830"*.

KM#	Date	VG	Fine	VF	XF
3.2	ND(1780)	35.00	60.00	90.00	200.00

FRENCH SOMALILAND

MINT MARKS

(a) - Paris (privy marks only)

MONETARY SYSTEM

100 Centimes = 1 Franc

FRANC

ALUMINUM

KM#	Date	Mintage	Fine	VF	XF	Unc
4	1948(a)	.200	6.50	12.50	20.00	40.00
	1949(a)	Inc. Ab.	8.00	15.00	22.50	50.00

KM#	Date	Mintage	Fine	VF	XF	Unc
8	1959(a)	.500	.25	.50	1.50	3.00
	1965(a)	.200	.35	.60	2.00	4.00

2 FRANCS

ALUMINUM

KM#	Date	Mintage	Fine	VF	XF	Unc
5	1948(a)	.200	6.50	12.50	20.00	50.00
	1949(a)	Inc. Ab.	8.00	15.00	22.50	60.00

KM#	Date	Mintage	Fine	VF	XF	Unc
9	1959(a)	.200	.25	.75	2.50	5.00
	1965(a)	.240	.25	.75	2.50	5.00

5 FRANCS

ALUMINUM

KM#	Date	Mintage	Fine	VF	XF	Unc
6	1948(a)	.500	3.00	7.50	15.00	30.00

KM#	Date	Mintage	Fine	VF	XF	Unc
10	1959(a)	.500	.25	.75	2.50	5.00
	1965(a)	.200	.25	.75	3.00	6.50

10 FRANCS

ALUMINUM-BRONZE

KM#	Date	Mintage	Fine	VF	XF	Unc
11	1965(a)	.250	.50	1.00	3.00	6.00

20 FRANCS

ALUMINUM-BRONZE

KM#	Date	Mintage	Fine	VF	XF	Unc
7	1952(a)	.500	1.00	2.00	4.00	10.00

KM#	Date	Mintage	Fine	VF	XF	Unc
12	1965(a)	.200	.50	1.00	3.00	6.00

FLEUR DE COIN SETS (SS)

KM#	Date	Mintage	Identification	Issue Price	Mkt. Val.
SS1	1965(5)	1,898	KM8-12	—	27.50

FRENCH AFARS & ISSAS

MINT MARKS

(a) - Paris (privy marks only)

MONETARY SYSTEM

100 Centimes = 1 Franc

FRANC

ALUMINUM

KM#	Date	Mintage	Fine	VF	XF	Unc
16	1969(a)	.100	1.00	2.00	3.50	6.00
	1971(a)	.100	1.00	2.00	3.50	6.00
	1975(a)	.300	.75	1.25	2.00	3.00

2 FRANCS

ALUMINUM

KM#	Date	Mintage	Fine	VF	XF	Unc
13	1968(a)	.100	1.00	2.00	3.50	6.00
	1975(a)	.180	.75	1.50	2.50	5.00

5 FRANCS

ALUMINUM

KM#	Date	Mintage	Fine	VF	XF	Unc
14	1968(a)	.100	1.00	2.00	3.50	6.00
	1975(a)	.300	.75	1.25	2.00	4.00

10 FRANCS

ALUMINUM-BRONZE

KM#	Date	Mintage	Fine	VF	XF	Unc
17	1969(a)	.100	1.50	3.00	6.00	9.00
	1970(a)	.300	1.00	2.00	4.00	7.00
	1975(a)	.360	.75	1.50	3.00	5.00

20 FRANCS

ALUMINUM-BRONZE

KM#	Date	Mintage	Fine	VF	XF	Unc
15	1968(a)	.300	1.50	2.50	4.50	8.00
	1975(a)	.300	1.00	1.50	3.50	6.00

50 FRANCS

COPPER-NICKEL

KM#	Date	Mintage	Fine	VF	XF	Unc
18	1970(a)	.300	1.25	3.50	6.00	9.50
	1975(a)	.180	1.50	4.00	6.50	10.00

100 FRANCS

COPPER-NICKEL

KM#	Date	Mintage	Fine	VF	XF	Unc
19	1970(a)	.600	2.00	5.00	10.00	15.00
	1975(a)	.400	2.00	5.00	10.00	15.00

DJIBOUTI

FRANC

ALUMINUM

KM#	Date	Mintage	Fine	VF	XF	Unc
20	1977(a)	—	.75	1.25	2.50	4.00

2 FRANCS

ALUMINUM

KM#	Date	Mintage	Fine	VF	XF	Unc
21	1977(a)	—	.75	1.25	2.50	4.00

5 FRANCS

ALUMINUM

KM#	Date	Mintage	Fine	VF	XF	Unc
22	1977(a)	—	.75	1.25	2.00	3.50
	1986(a)	—	.75	1.25	2.00	3.50
	1991(a)	—	.75	1.25	2.00	3.50

10 FRANCS

ALUMINUM-BRONZE

KM#	Date	Mintage	Fine	VF	XF	Unc
23	1977(a)	—	.50	1.00	1.50	3.00
	1983(a)	—	.50	1.00	1.50	4.00
	1991(a)	—	.50	1.00	1.50	2.50

NOTE: Varieties exist.

20 FRANCS

ALUMINUM-BRONZE

KM#	Date	Mintage	Fine	VF	XF	Unc
24	1977(a)	—	.50	1.00	1.50	3.00
	1982(a)	—	.50	1.00	1.50	4.00
	1983(a)	—	.50	1.00	1.50	3.50
	1986(a)	—	.50	1.00	1.50	2.50
	1991(a)	—	.50	1.00	1.50	2.50

NOTE: Varieties exist.

50 FRANCS

COPPER-NICKEL

KM#	Date	Mintage	Fine	VF	XF	Unc
25	1977(a)	—	1.00	2.00	4.00	8.00
	1982(a)	—	.75	1.50	3.00	7.00
	1983(a)	—	.75	1.50	2.50	6.00
	1986(a)	—	.50	1.00	2.25	5.00
	1991(a)	—	.50	1.00	2.00	4.00

100 FRANCS

COPPER-NICKEL

KM#	Date	Mintage	Fine	VF	XF	Unc
26	1977(a)	—	1.00	2.00	3.00	7.00
	1983(a)	—	1.00	2.50	3.50	8.50
	1991(a)	—	1.00	2.00	3.00	6.00

500 FRANCS

ALUMINUM-BRONZE

KM#	Date	Mintage	Fine	VF	XF	Unc
27	1989(a)	—	3.00	4.00	6.00	10.00
	1991(a)	—	3.00	4.00	6.00	10.00

15000 FRANCS

24.3000 g, .999 GOLD, .0103 oz AGW
.999 SILVER, .7710 oz ASW
Republic of Djibouti

KM#	Date	Mintage	VF	XF	Unc
28	1991	*.010	—	—	90.00

DOMINICA

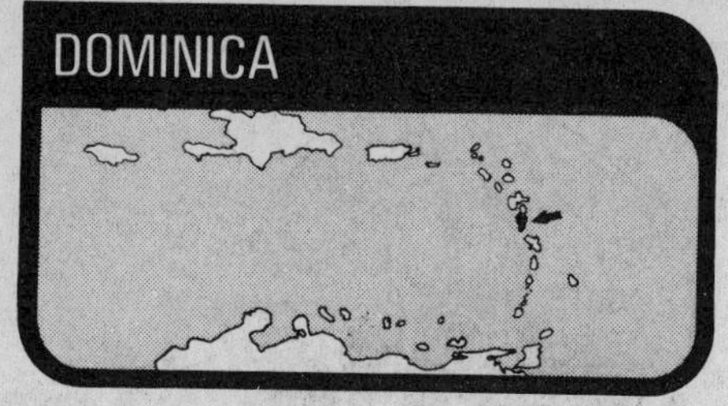

The Commonwealth of Dominica, situated in the Lesser Antilles midway between Guadeloupe to the north and Martinique to the south, has an area of 290 sq. mi. (750 sq. km.) and a population of 87,000. Capital: Roseau. Agriculture is the chief economic activity of the mountainous island. Bananas are the chief export.

Columbus discovered and named the island on Nov. 3, 1493. Spain neglected it and it was finally colonized by the French in 1632. The British drove the French from the island in 1756. Thereafter it changed hands between the French and British a dozen or more times before becoming permanently British in 1805. Beginning in 1761, pierced or mutilated silver was prepared for use on the island. These remained in use until 1862, when they were demonitized and sterling became the standard. Throughout the greater part of its British history, Dominica was a presidency of the Leeward Islands. In 1940 its administration was transferred to the Windward Islands and it was established as a separate colony with considerable local autonomy. From 1955, Dominica was a member of the currency board of the British Caribbean Territories (Eastern Group), which issued its own coins until 1965. Dominica became a West Indies associated state with a built in option for independence in 1967. Full independence was attained on Nov. 3, 1978. Dominica, which has a republican form of government, is a member of the Commonwealth of Nations. The Queen of England is recognized as the head of the Commonwealth, but not as the Chief of State of Dominica.

RULERS

British, until 1978

MINT MARKS

CHI in circle - Valcambi

(ml) - maple leaf - Canadian Royal Mint

MONETARY SYSTEM

(From 1798 until 1813)

11 Bits = 8 Shillings 3 Pence =
= 1 Dollar

(Commemcing 1813)

16 Bits = 12 Shillings = 1 Dollar (Spanish)

100 Cents = 10 Shillings = 1 Dollar (Dominican)

1-1/2 BITS (MOCO)

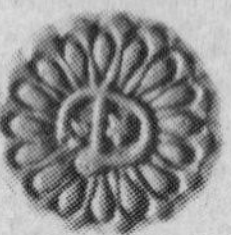

SILVER
c/m: Script 'D' with rays and small star in the loop of the letter overstruck on crenated circular center plug of Spanish or Spanish Colonial 8 Reales.

KM#	Date	Good	VG	Fine	VF
21	ND(1798)	30.00	50.00	75.00	120.00

NOTE: Varieties exist in the shape of the letter and the size and position of the star.

2 BITS

SILVER
Holed Spanish or Spanish Colonial 2 Reales.

KM#	Date	Good	VG	Fine	VF
9	ND(1816)	100.00	180.00	225.00	325.00

3 BITS

SILVER
c/m: Crowned 3 on 1/2 of 23mm center plug cut from Spanish or Spanish Colonial 8 Reales.

KM#	Date	Good	VG	Fine	VF
4	ND(1813)	60.00	100.00	175.00	275.00

2 SHILLINGS 6 PENCE

SILVER
c/m: '2.6' on 1/4 segment of Spanish or Spanish Colonial 8 Reales.

KM#	Date	Good	VG	Fine	VF
10	ND(1816-18)	100.00	200.00	300.00	550.00

4 BITS

SILVER
c/m: Crowned '4' on center ring segment of Spanish or Spanish Colonial 8 Reales.

KM#	Date	Good	VG	Fine	VF
5	ND(1813)	125.00	250.00	600.00	1250.

5-1/2 BITS

(4 Shilling 1-1/2 Pence)

SILVER
Crenated center hole in Bolivia - Potosi 4 Reales, KM#72.

KM#	Date	Good	VG	Fine	VF
2	ND(1791-1809)	500.00	800.00	1250.	1750.

6 BITS

SILVER
c/m: Crowned 'G' on obv. or rev. of center plug cut from Spanish or Spanish Colonial 8 Reales.

KM#	Date	Good	VG	Fine	VF
6	ND(1813)	30.00	50.00	100.00	200.00

11 BITS

SILVER
Crenated center hole in Mexico City 8 Reales, KM#107.

KM#	Date	Good	VG	Fine	VF
3.1	ND(1789-90)	100.00	200.00	300.00	500.00

Crenated center hole in Mexico City 8 Reales, KM#109.

KM#	Date	Good	VG	Fine	VF
3.2	ND(1781-1808)	100.00	200.00	300.00	500.00

NOTE: The center plug was used for the 1-1/2 Bits, KM#21.

12 BITS

SILVER
c/m: Crowned 12 on holed Peru - Lima 8 Reales, KM#97.

KM#	Date	Good	VG	Fine	VF
7	ND(1791-1808)	350.00	950.00	1850.	3800.

16 BITS

SILVER
c/m: Crowned "16" on obv. of holed Mexico City 8 Reales, KM#107.

KM#	Date	Good	VG	Fine	VF
8.1	ND(1789-90)	500.00	1200.	3250.	7500.

c/m: Crowned '16' on obv. and rev. of holed Mexico City 8 Reales, KM#109.

KM#	Date	Good	VG	Fine	VF
8.2	ND(1791-1808)	400.00	1100.	3000.	7000.

MODERN COINAGE

4 DOLLARS

COPPER-NICKEL
F.A.O. Issue

KM#	Date	Mintage	VF	XF	Unc
11	1970	.013	3.00	5.00	7.50
	1970	2,000	—	Proof	15.00

NOTE: These 4 dollar F.A.O. commemorative coins are listed individually under their respective names: Antigua, Barbados, Dominica, Grenada, Montserrat, St. Kitts, St. Lucia and St. Vincent.

10 DOLLARS

20.5000 g, .925 SILVER, .6097 oz ASW
Independence - History of Carnival

KM#	Date	Mintage	VF	XF	Unc
12	1978	1,500	—	7.50	20.00
	1978	2,000	—	Proof	27.50

Visit of Pope John Paul II

KM#	Date	Mintage	VF	XF	Unc
16	1979	1,150	—	7.50	20.00
	1979	3,450	—	Proof	25.00

COPPER-NICKEL
Royal Visit

KM#	Date	Mintage	VF	XF	Unc
20	1985	*.100	—	4.50	7.50
	28.2800 g, .925 SILVER, .8409 oz ASW				
20a	1985	*5,000	—	Proof	25.00
	47.5400 g, .917 GOLD, 1.4013 oz AGW				
20b	1985	*250 pcs.	—	Proof	850.00

20 DOLLARS

40.9100 g, .925 SILVER, 1.2167 oz ASW
Independence & 50th Anniversary of Graf Zeppelin
Obv: Similar to 300 Dollars, KM#15.

KM#	Date	Mintage	VF	XF	Unc
13.1	1978CHI	500 pcs.	—	30.00	65.00
	1978CHI	1,000	—	Proof	75.00
	Maple leaf mint mark and .925 fineness stamp added.				
13.2	1978(ml)	—	—	Proof	—

Israel and Egypt Peace Treaty
Obv: Similar to 300 Dollars, KM#15.

KM#	Date	Mintage	VF	XF	Unc
17	1979	200 pcs.	—	35.00	100.00
	1979	200 pcs.	—	Proof	135.00

100 DOLLARS

129.5900 g, .925 SILVER, 3.8543 oz ASW
Tropical Birds - Sisseran Parrot
Illustration reduced. Actual size: 63mm

KM#	Date	Mintage	VF	XF	Unc
21	1988	*.010	—	Proof	100.00

150 DOLLARS

9.6000 g, .900 GOLD, .2778 oz AGW
Independence - Parrot

KM#	Date	Mintage	VF	XF	Unc
14	1978	300 pcs.	—	—	175.00
	1978	400 pcs.	—	Proof	225.00

Israel and Egypt Peace Treaty

KM#	Date	Mintage	VF	XF	Unc
18	1979	100 pcs.	—	—	950.00
	1979	100 pcs.	—	Proof	1000.

300 DOLLARS

19.2000 g, .900 GOLD, .5556 oz AGW
Independence - Arms

KM#	Date	Mintage	VF	XF	Unc
15	1978	500 pcs.	—	—	375.00
	1978	800 pcs.	—	Proof	400.00

Visit of Pope John Paul II

KM#	Date	Mintage	VF	XF	Unc
19	1979	5,000	—	—	300.00
	1979	300 pcs.	—	—	500.00

DOMINICAN REP.

The Dominican Republic, which occupies the eastern two-thirds of the island of Hispaniola, has an area of 18,816 sq. mi. (48,734 sq. km.) and a population of 6.3 million. Capital: Santo Domingo. The largely agricultural economy produces sugar, coffee, tobacco and cocoa.

Columbus discovered Hispaniola in 1492, and named it La Isla Espanola - 'the Spanish Island'. Santo Domingo, the oldest white settlement in the Western Hemisphere, was the base from which Spain conducted its exploration of the New World. Later, French buccaneers settled the western third of Hispaniola, naming the colony St. Dominique which in 1697 was ceded to France by Spain. In 1804, following a bloody revolt by former slaves, the French colony became the Republic of Haiti - 'mountainous country'. The Spanish called their part of Hispaniola Santo Domingo. In 1822, the Haitians conquered the entire island and held it until 1844, when Juan Pablo Duarte, the national hero of the Dominican Republic, drove them out of Santo Domingo and established an independent Dominican Republic. The republic returned voluntarily to Spanish dominion from 1861 to 1865 after being rejected by France, Britain and the United States. Independence was reclaimed in 1866.

MINT MARKS

A - Paris
(a) - Berlin
(c) - Stylized maple leaf, Royal Canadian Mint
H - Heaton, Birmingham, England
Mo - Mexico
(t) - Tower, Tower Mint, London

RULERS

Spanish, until 1822, 1861-1865
Haiti, 1822-1844

MONETARY SYSTEM

16 Reales = 1 Escudo

SANTO DOMINGO

1/4 REAL

NOTE: Coin previously listed here has been moved to Venezuela, Province of Maracaibo.

COPPER

KM#	Date	Mintage	Good	VG	Fine	VF
2	ND	—	12.50	25.00	40.00	60.00

NOTE: Several varieties exist of fraction and letter arrangement on reverse and the size of the planchet.

2/4 REAL

NOTE: Coin previously listed here has been moved to Venezuela, Province of Maracaibo.

REAL

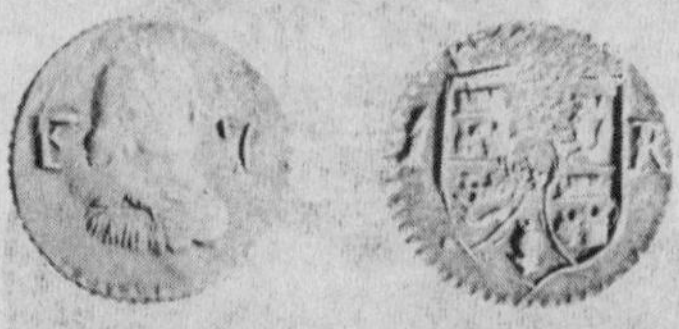

SILVER

KM#	Date	Mintage	Good	VG	Fine	VF
4.1	ND	—	200.00	300.00	450.00	700.00

Rev: Castles and lions reversed in shield.

KM#	Date	Mintage	Good	VG	Fine	VF
4.2	ND	—	200.00	300.00	450.00	700.00

2 REALES

SILVER

KM#	Date	Mintage	Good	VG	Fine	VF
5	ND	—	400.00	600.00	900.00	1350.

COUNTERMARKED COINAGE

REAL

.903 SILVER
c/m: Crowned F.7o on Mexico 1 Real, KM#75.

KM#	Date	Good	VG	Fine	VF
8	ND(1732-47)	40.00	65.00	100.00	175.00

8 REALES

.903 SILVER
c/m: Crowned F.7o on Mexico 8 Reales, KM#109.

KM#	Date	Good	VG	Fine	VF
11	ND(1791-1808)	750.00	1000.	—	—

DOMINICAN REPUBLIC

MONETARY SYSTEM

8 Reales = 1 Peso

1/4 REAL

BRONZE

KM#	Date	Mintage	Fine	VF	XF	Unc
1	1844	1.600	6.00	13.50	37.50	—

BRASS

KM#	Date	Mintage	Fine	VF	XF	Unc
2	1844	—	3.75	8.50	22.50	75.00
	1848 plain 4	—	3.75	8.50	22.50	75.00
	1848 crosslet 4	—	3.75	8.50	22.50	75.00

NOTE: Many varieties exist.

DECIMAL COINAGE

100 Centavos = 1 Peso

CENTAVO

BRASS

KM#	Date	Mintage	Fine	VF	XF	Unc
3	1877	1.000	.50	1.50	3.00	8.50

1-1/4 CENTAVOS

COPPER-NICKEL

KM#	Date	Mintage	Fine	VF	XF	Unc
6	1882	.400	7.00	13.50	30.00	75.00
	1888A	.500	2.50	5.00	12.50	45.00
	1888A	—	—	—	Proof	300.00

2-1/2 CENTAVOS

COPPER-NICKEL

KM#	Date	Mintage	Fine	VF	XF	Unc
4	1877	.021	17.50	25.00	45.00	100.00

KM#	Date	Mintage	Fine	VF	XF	Unc
7	1882	—	4.50	10.00	27.50	60.00
	1888A large date					
		8.000	.75	2.00	6.00	45.00
	1888A lg. date	—	—	—	Proof	275.00
	1888A small date					
		.950	1.25	3.00	7.50	45.00
	1888HH	4.000	.75	2.00	6.00	42.50
	1888HH	—	—	—	Proof	325.00

NOTE: Star on reverse is flanked by H's.

5 CENTAVOS

COPPER-NICKEL

KM#	Date	Mintage	Fine	VF	XF	Unc
5	1877	.130	10.00	20.00	35.00	80.00

MONETARY REFORM

100 Centesimos = 1 Franco

5 CENTESIMOS

BRONZE

KM#	Date	Mintage	Fine	VF	XF	Unc
8	1891A	.400	1.75	5.00	15.00	50.00
	1891A	—	—	—	Proof	—

10 CENTESIMOS

BRONZE

KM#	Date	Mintage	Fine	VF	XF	Unc
9	1891A	.300	2.00	6.00	20.00	60.00
	1891A	—	—	—	Proof	—

50 CENTESIMOS

2.5000 g, .835 SILVER, 0671 oz ASW

KM#	Date	Mintage	Fine	VF	XF	Unc
10	1891A	.150	5.00	13.50	32.50	100.00
	1891A	—	—	—	Proof	—

FRANCO

5.000 g, .835 SILVER, .1342 oz ASW

KM#	Date	Mintage	Fine	VF	XF	Unc
11	1891A	.125	11.50	18.50	40.00	150.00
	1891A	—	—	—	Proof	—

5 FRANCOS

25.0000 g, .900 SILVER, .7234 oz ASW

KM#	Date	Mintage	Fine	VF	XF	Unc
12	1891A	.150	45.00	90.00	145.00	700.00
	1891A	—	—	—	Proof	—

MONETARY REFORM

100 Centavos = 1 Peso

10 CENTAVOS

2.5000 g, .350 SILVER, .0281 oz ASW

KM#	Date	Mintage	Fine	VF	XF	Unc
13	1897A	.764	2.50	10.00	25.00	150.00

20 CENTAVOS

5.0000 g, .350 SILVER, .0563 oz ASW

KM#	Date	Mintage	Fine	VF	XF	Unc
14	1897A	1.395	1.75	7.50	22.50	150.00

1/2 PESO

12.5000 g, .350 SILVER, .1407 oz ASW

KM#	Date	Mintage	Fine	VF	XF	Unc
15	1897A	.917	4.00	15.00	40.00	300.00

PESO

25.0000 g, .350 SILVER, .2813 oz ASW

KM#	Date	Mintage	Fine	VF	XF	Unc
16	1897A	1.455	12.00	30.00	100.00	700.00

MONETARY REFORM

100 Centavos = 1 Peso Oro

CENTAVO

BRONZE

KM#	Date	Mintage	Fine	VF	XF	Unc
17	1937	1.000	.50	1.50	7.50	75.00
	1937	—	—	—	Proof	350.00
	1939	2.000	.50	1.25	5.00	40.00
	1941	2.000	.25	.50	3.00	12.00
	1942	2.000	.25	.50	3.00	15.00
	1944	5.000	.20	.50	1.50	10.00
	1947	3.000	.20	.50	1.00	8.00
	1949	3.000	.20	.40	1.00	8.00
	1951	3.000	.20	.35	.75	8.00
	1952	3.000	.20	.35	.75	8.00
	1955	3.000	.15	.35	.75	6.00
	1956	3.000	.15	.35	.75	6.00
	1957	5.000	.10	.25	.75	5.00
	1959	5.000	.10	.25	.75	5.00
	1961	5.000	.10	.20	.50	2.00
	1961	10 pcs.	—	—	Proof	450.00

100th Anniversary Restoration of the Republic

KM#	Date	Mintage	Fine	VF	XF	Unc
25	1963	13.000	—	—	.10	.40

KM#	Date	Mintage	Fine	VF	XF	Unc
31	1968	5.000	—	—	.10	.20
	1971	6.000	—	—	.10	.20
	1972	3.000	—	—	.10	.20
	1972	500 pcs.	—	—	Proof	20.00
	1975	.500	—	—	.10	.20

F.A.O. Issue

KM#	Date	Mintage	Fine	VF	XF	Unc
32	1969	5.000	—	—	.10	.30

Death of Juan Pablo Duarte Centennial

KM#	Date	Mintage	Fine	VF	XF	Unc
40	1976	3.995	—	—	.10	.20
	1976	5,000	—	—	Proof	1.00

KM#	Date	Mintage	Fine	VF	XF	Unc
48	1978	2.995	—	—	.10	.15
	1978	5,000	—	—	Proof	2.00
	1979	2.985	—	—	.10	.15
	1979	500 pcs.	—	—	Proof	20.00
	1980	.200	—	—	.10	.15
	1980	3,000	—	—	Proof	1.00
	1981	3,000	—	—	Proof	1.00

3.5800 g, .900 SILVER, .1036 oz ASW

KM#	Date	Mintage	Fine	VF	XF	Unc
48a	1978	15 pcs.	—	—	Proof	125.00
	1979	15 pcs.	—	—	Proof	125.00
	1980	15 pcs.	—	—	Proof	125.00
	1981	15 pcs.	—	—	Proof	125.00

COPPER-PLATED-ZINC
Human Rights - Caonabo

KM#	Date	Mintage	Fine	VF	XF	Unc
64	1984Mo	10.000	—	—	—	.25
	1984Mo	1,600	—	—	Proof	1.50
	1986	18.067	—	—	—	.25
	1986	1,600	—	—	Proof	1.50
	1987	15.000	—	—	—	.25
	1987	1,600	—	—	Proof	1.50

2.0000 g, .900 SILVER, .0578 oz ASW

KM#	Date	Mintage	Fine	VF	XF	Unc
64a	1984Mo	100 pcs.	—	—	Proof	20.00
	1986	100 pcs.	—	—	Proof	20.00

COPPER-PLATED-ZINC

KM#	Date	Mintage	Fine	VF	XF	Unc
72	1989	—	—	—	—	.30

3.7000 g, .925 SILVER, .1100 oz ASW

KM#	Date	Mintage	Fine	VF	XF	Unc
72a	1989	2,600	—	—	Proof	—

5 CENTAVOS

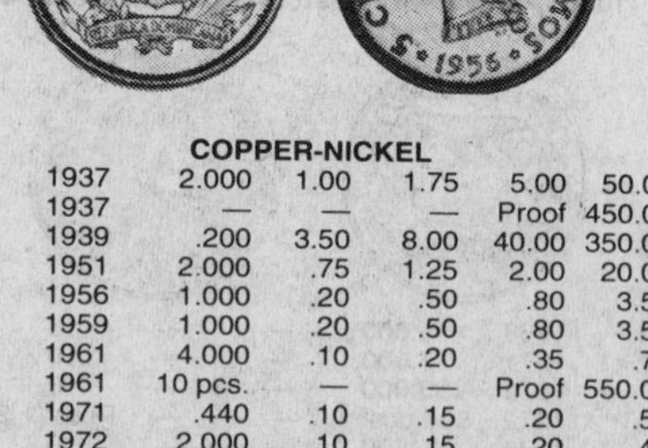

COPPER-NICKEL

KM#	Date	Mintage	Fine	VF	XF	Unc
18	1937	2.000	1.00	1.75	5.00	50.00
	1937	—	—	—	Proof	450.00
	1939	.200	3.50	8.00	40.00	350.00
	1951	2.000	.75	1.25	2.00	20.00
	1956	1.000	.20	.50	.80	3.50
	1959	1.000	.20	.50	.80	3.50
	1961	4.000	.10	.20	.35	.75
	1961	10 pcs.	—	—	Proof	550.00
	1971	.440	.10	.15	.20	.50
	1972	2.000	.10	.15	.20	.40
	1972	500 pcs.	—	—	Proof	20.00
	1974	5.000	—	—	.10	.40
	1974	500 pcs.	—	—	Proof	20.00

5.0000 g, .350 SILVER, .0563 oz ASW

KM#	Date	Mintage	Fine	VF	XF	Unc
18a	1944	2.000	1.50	3.50	7.50	30.00

COPPER-NICKEL
100th Anniversary Restoration of the Republic

KM#	Date	Mintage	Fine	VF	XF	Unc
26	1963	4.000	—	.10	.15	.60

Death of Juan Pablo Duarte Centennial

KM#	Date	Mintage	Fine	VF	XF	Unc
41	1976	5.595	—	—	.10	.50
	1976	5,000	—	—	Proof	2.00

KM#	Date	Mintage	Fine	VF	XF	Unc
49	1978	1.996	—	—	.10	.35
	1978	5,000	—	—	Proof	1.50
	1979	2.988	—	—	.10	.35
	1979	500 pcs.	—	—	Proof	20.00
	1980	5.300	—	—	.10	.35
	1980	3,000	—	—	Proof	2.00
	1981	4.500	—	—	.10	.35
	1981	3,000	—	—	Proof	2.00

5.8600 g, .900 SILVER, .1696 oz ASW

KM#	Date	Mintage	Fine	VF	XF	Unc
49a	1978	15 pcs.	—	—	Proof	125.00
	1979	15 pcs.	—	—	Proof	125.00
	1980	15 pcs.	—	—	Proof	125.00
	1981	15 pcs.	—	—	Proof	125.00

COPPER-NICKEL
Human Rights - Sanchez and Mello

KM#	Date	Mintage	Fine	VF	XF	Unc
59	1983	3.998	—	—	.10	.30
	1983(t)	1,600	—	—	Proof	2.00
	1984Mo	10.000	—	—	.10	.30
	1984Mo	1,600	—	—	Proof	2.00
	1986	12.898	—	—	.10	.30
	1986	1,600	—	—	Proof	2.00
	1987	10.000	—	—	.10	.30
	1987	1,700	—	—	Proof	2.00

5.0000 g, .900 SILVER, .1447 oz ASW

KM#	Date	Mintage	Fine	VF	XF	Unc
59a	1983	100 pcs.	—	—	Proof	30.00
	1984Mo	100 pcs.	—	—	Proof	30.00
	1986	100 pcs.	—	—	Proof	30.00

NICKEL CLAD STEEL
Native Culture - Drummer

KM#	Date	Mintage	Fine	VF	XF	Unc
69	1989	—	—	—	—	.35

5.8300 g, .925 SILVER, .1734 oz ASW

KM#	Date	Mintage	Fine	VF	XF	Unc
69a	1989	2,600	—	—	Proof	—

10 CENTAVOS

2.5000 g, .900 SILVER, .0723 oz ASW

KM#	Date	Mintage	Fine	VF	XF	Unc
19	1937	1.000	BV	2.00	5.00	40.00
	1937	—	—	—	Proof	550.00
	1939	.150	3.00	6.00	20.00	300.00
	1942	2.000	1.00	2.00	3.00	30.00
	1944	1.000	1.00	2.00	4.00	50.00
	1951	.500	1.00	2.00	3.00	10.00
	1952	.500	1.00	2.00	3.00	10.00
	1953	.750	1.00	2.00	3.00	8.00
	1956	1.000	.75	1.50	2.50	8.00
	1959	2.000	BV	1.25	2.25	7.00
	1961	2.000	BV	1.00	2.00	6.00

2.5000 g, .650 SILVER, .0522 oz ASW

100th Anniversary Restoration of the Republic

KM#	Date	Mintage	Fine	VF	XF	Unc
27	1963	4.000	—	BV	1.00	2.00

COPPER-NICKEL
Plain edge

KM#	Date	Mintage	Fine	VF	XF	Unc
19a	1967	10.000	—	—	.15	.50
	1973	8.000	—	—	.15	.50
	1973	500 pcs.	—	—	Proof	25.00
	1975	8.000	—	—	.15	.50

Death of Juan Pablo Duarte Centennial

KM#	Date	Mintage	Fine	VF	XF	Unc
42	1976	5.595	—	—	.10	.75
	1976	5,000	—	—	Proof	2.00

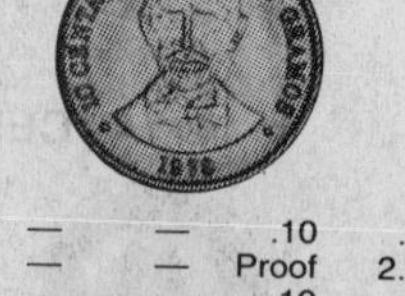

KM#	Date	Mintage	Fine	VF	XF	Unc
50	1978	3.000	—	—	.10	.50
	1978	5,000	—	—	Proof	2.00
	1979	4.020	—	—	.10	.50
	1979	500 pcs.	—	—	Proof	25.00
	1980	4.400	—	—	.10	.35
	1980	3,000	—	—	Proof	3.00
	1981	6.000	—	—	.10	.35
	1981	3,000	—	—	Proof	3.00

2.9500 g, .900 SILVER, .0854 oz ASW

KM#	Date	Mintage	Fine	VF	XF	Unc
50a	1978	15 pcs.	—	—	Proof	125.00
	1979	15 pcs.	—	—	Proof	125.00
	1980	15 pcs.	—	—	Proof	125.00
	1981	15 pcs.	—	—	Proof	125.00

COPPER-NICKEL
Human Rights - Duarte

KM#	Date	Mintage	Fine	VF	XF	Unc
60	1983	4.998	—	—	.10	.35
	1983(t)	4.000	—	—	.10	.35
	1983t)	1,600	—	—	Proof	2.50
	1984 Mo	15.000	—	—	.10	.25
	1984 Mo	1,600	—	—	Proof	2.50
	1986	15.515	—	—	.10	.25
	1986	1,600	—	—	Proof	2.50
	1987	20.000	—	—	.10	.25
	1987	1,700	—	—	Proof	2.50

2.5000 g, .900 SILVER, .0723 oz ASW

KM#	Date	Mintage	Fine	VF	XF	Unc
60a	1983(t)	100 pcs.	—	—	Proof	30.00
	1984 Mo	100 pcs.	—	—	Proof	30.00
	1986	100 pcs.	—	—	Proof	30.00

NICKEL CLAD STEEL

KM#	Date	Mintage	Fine	VF	XF	Unc
70	1989	—	—	—	—	.40
	1991	3.500	—	—	—	.40

2.9000 g, .925 SILVER, .0863 oz ASW

KM#	Date	Mintage	Fine	VF	XF	Unc
70a	1989	2,600	—	—	Proof	—

25 CENTAVOS

6.2500 g, .900 SILVER, .1808 oz ASW

KM#	Date	Mintage	Fine	VF	XF	Unc
20	1937	.560	BV	5.00	15.00	65.00
	1937	—	—	—	Proof	650.00
	1939	.160	4.00	8.00	25.00	500.00
	1942	.560	2.00	4.00	10.00	100.00
	1944	.400	2.00	4.00	8.00	80.00
	1947	.400	2.00	4.00	8.00	80.00
	1951	.400	2.00	4.00	8.00	80.00
	1952	.400	2.00	3.00	5.00	12.50
	1956	.400	2.00	2.50	4.00	10.00
	1960	.600	2.00	2.50	4.00	10.00
	1961	.800	2.00	2.50	4.00	10.00

6.2500 g, .650 SILVER, .1306 oz ASW
100th Anniversary Restoration of the Republic

KM#	Date	Mintage	Fine	VF	XF	Unc
28	1963	2.400	—	BV	1.50	3.00

COPPER-NICKEL
Plain edge

KM#	Date	Mintage	Fine	VF	XF	Unc
20a.1	1967	5.000	—	.10	.20	.75
	1972	.800	—	.10	.40	1.00
	1972	500 pcs.	—	—	Proof	25.00

Reeded edge

KM#	Date	Mintage	Fine	VF	XF	Unc
20a.2	1974	2.000	—	.10	.40	1.00
	1974	500 pcs.	—	—	Proof	25.00

Death of Juan Pablo Duarte Centennial

KM#	Date	Mintage	Fine	VF	XF	Unc
43	1976	3.195	—	.10	.40	1.00
	1976	5,000	—	—	Proof	2.50

KM#	Date	Mintage	Fine	VF	XF	Unc
51	1978	.996	—	—	.35	.75
	1978	5,000	—	—	Proof	3.00
	1979	2.089	—	—	.15	.50
	1979	500 pcs.	—	—	Proof	30.00
	1980	2.600	—	—	.15	.50
	1980	3,000	—	—	Proof	3.00
	1981	3.200	—	—	.15	.50
	1981	3,000	—	—	Proof	3.00

7.3200 g, .900 SILVER, .2118 oz ASW

KM#	Date	Mintage	Fine	VF	XF	Unc
51a	1978	15 pcs.	—	—	Proof	150.00
	1979	15 pcs.	—	—	Proof	150.00
	1980	15 pcs.	—	—	Proof	150.00
	1981	15 pcs.	—	—	Proof	150.00

COPPER-NICKEL
Human Rights - Sisters Mirabel

KM#	Date	Mintage	Fine	VF	XF	Unc
61	1983	.793	—	.10	.20	.50
	1983(t)	5,000	—	—	—	2.50
	1983(t)	1,600	—	—	Proof	8.00
	1984Mo	6.400	—	—	.15	.40
	1984Mo	1,600	—	—	Proof	8.00
	1986	10.132	—	—	.15	.40
	1986	1,600	—	—	Proof	8.00
	1987	6.000	—	—	.15	.40
	1987	1,700	—	—	Proof	8.00

NOTE: Coin and medal rotations and edge reeding varieties exist for the above.

6.2500 g, .900 SILVER, .1808 oz ASW

KM#	Date	Mintage	Fine	VF	XF	Unc
61a	1983(t)	100 pcs.	—	—	Proof	40.00
	1984Mo	100 pcs.	—	—	Proof	40.00
	1986	100 pcs.	—	—	Proof	40.00

NICKEL CLAD STEEL
Native Culture, Ox Cart

KM#	Date	Mintage	Fine	VF	XF	Unc
71.1	1989	—	—	—	—	.60
	1991	38.000	—	—	—	.60

Obv. and rev: Legend and design in beaded circle.

KM#	Date	Mintage	Fine	VF	XF	Unc
71.2	1990	20.000	—	—	—	.60

6.7400 g, .925 SILVER, .2005 oz ASW

KM#	Date	Mintage	Fine	VF	XF	Unc
71.1a	1989	2,600	—	—	Proof	—

1/2 PESO

12.5000 g, .900 SILVER, .3617 oz ASW

KM#	Date	Mintage	Fine	VF	XF	Unc
21	1937	.500	BV	7.50	12.50	70.00
	1937	—	—	—	Proof	750.00
	1944	.100	BV	10.00	25.00	300.00
	1947	.200	BV	7.50	15.00	200.00
	1951	.200	BV	7.50	15.00	150.00
	1952	.140	BV	7.50	12.50	70.00
	1959	.100	BV	6.00	10.00	40.00
	1960	.100	BV	6.00	9.00	30.00
	1961	.400	BV	4.00	6.00	25.00

12.5000 g, .650 SILVER, .2612 oz ASW
100th Anniversary Restoration of the Republic

KM#	Date	Mintage	Fine	VF	XF	Unc
29	1963	.300	—	BV	4.00	7.50

COPPER-NICKEL
Plain edge

KM#	Date	Mintage	Fine	VF	XF	Unc
21a.1	1967	1.500	—	.20	.40	1.50
	1968	.600	—	.30	.50	2.50

Reeded edge

KM#	Date	Mintage	Fine	VF	XF	Unc
21a.2	1973	.600	—	.20	.40	1.50
	1973	500 pcs.	—	—	Proof	35.00
	1975	.600	—	.20	.40	1.50

Death of Juan Pablo Duarte Centennial

KM#	Date	Mintage	Fine	VF	XF	Unc
44	1976	.195	—	.20	.40	1.50
	1976	5,000	—	—	Proof	3.00

KM#	Date	Mintage	Fine	VF	XF	Unc
52	1978	.296	—	.20	.40	1.50
	1978	5,000	—	—	Proof	4.00
	1979	.967	—	.20	.40	1.50
	1979	500 pcs.	—	—	Proof	35.00
	1980	1.000	—	.20	.40	1.50
	1980	3,000	—	—	Proof	5.00
	1981	1.300	—	.20	.40	1.50
	1981	3,000	—	—	Proof	5.00

14.5500 g, .900 SILVER, .4210 oz ASW

KM#	Date	Mintage	Fine	VF	XF	Unc
52a	1978	15 pcs.	—	—	Proof	150.00
	1979	15 pcs.	—	—	Proof	150.00
	1980	15 pcs.	—	—	Proof	150.00
	1981	15 pcs.	—	—	Proof	150.00

COPPER-NICKEL
Human Rights - Bono, Espaillat and Rojas

KM#	Date	Mintage	Fine	VF	XF	Unc
62	1983	.393	—	.20	.40	1.50
	1983(t)	5,000	—	—	—	4.00
	1983(t)	1,600	—	—	Proof	15.00
	1984Mo	3.200	—	.20	.40	1.50
	1984Mo	1,600	—	—	Proof	15.00
	1986	5.225	—	.20	.40	1.50
	1986	1,600	—	—	Proof	15.00
	1987	3.000	—	.20	.40	1.50
	1987	1,700	—	—	Proof	15.00

NOTE: Coin and medal rotations exist for the above.

12.5000 g, .900 SILVER, .3617 oz ASW

KM#	Date	Mintage	Fine	VF	XF	Unc
62a	1983(t)	100 pcs.	—	—	Proof	50.00
	1984Mo	100 pcs.	—	—	Proof	50.00
	1986	100 pcs.	—	—	Proof	50.00

COPPER-NICKEL
Beacon at Colon

KM#	Date	Mintage	Fine	VF	XF	Unc
73.1	1989	—	—	—	—	2.00

Obv. and rev: Legend and design in inner circle.

KM#	Date	Mintage	Fine	VF	XF	Unc
73.2	1990	1.500	—	—	—	2.00

14.6500 g, .925 SILVER, .4357 oz ASW

KM#	Date	Mintage	Fine	VF	XF	Unc
73.1a	1989	2,600	—	—	Proof	—

PESO

26.7000 g, .900 SILVER, .7725 oz ASW
Rev: HP below bust.

KM#	Date	Mintage	Fine	VF	XF	Unc
22	1939	.015	15.00	20.00	45.00	750.00
	1939	—	—	—	Proof	2250.
	1952	.020	BV	7.00	10.00	15.00

25th Anniversary of Trujillo Regime

KM#	Date	Mintage	Fine	VF	XF	Unc
23	1955	.050*	7.50	10.00	15.00	25.00

*30,550 officially melted following Trujillo's assassination in 1961.

26.7000 g, .650 SILVER, .5579 oz ASW
100th Anniversary Restoration of the Republic

KM#	Date	Mintage	Fine	VF	XF	Unc
30	1963	.020	—	—	5.00	7.50
	1963	—	—	—	Proof	—

COPPER-NICKEL
125th Anniversary of the Republic

KM#	Date	Mintage	Fine	VF	XF	Unc
33	1969	.030	—	—	1.50	3.00

26.7000 g, .900 SILVER, .7725 oz ASW
25th Anniversary Central Bank

KM#	Date	Mintage	Fine	VF	XF	Unc
34	1972	.027	—	—	—	8.00
	1972	3,000	—	—	Proof	14.00

12th Central American and Caribbean Games

KM#	Date	Mintage	Fine	VF	XF	Unc
35	1974	.050	—	—	—	8.00
	1974	5,000	—	—	Proof	14.00

COPPER-NICKEL
Death of Juan Pablo Duarte Centennial

KM#	Date	Mintage	Fine	VF	XF	Unc
45	1976	.025	—	—	1.00	2.00
	1976	5,000	—	—	Proof	7.50

KM#	Date	Mintage	Fine	VF	XF	Unc
53	1978	.035	—	—	1.00	2.00
	1978	5,000	—	—	Proof	7.50
	1979	.045	—	—	1.00	2.00
	1979	500 pcs.	—	—	Proof	40.00
	1980	.020	—	—	1.00	2.00
	1980	3,000	—	—	Proof	6.00
	1981	3,000	—	—	Proof	6.00

30.9200 g, .900 SILVER, .8947 oz ASW

KM#	Date	Mintage	Fine	VF	XF	Unc
53a	1978	15 pcs.	—	—	Proof	300.00
	1979	15 pcs.	—	—	Proof	300.00
	1980	15 pcs.	—	—	Proof	300.00
	1981	15 pcs.	—	—	Proof	300.00

COPPER-NICKEL
Human Rights - Montesinos, Enriquillo and Lemba

KM#	Date	Mintage	Fine	VF	XF	Unc
63	1983(t)	.093	—	—	1.00	2.50
	1983	5,000	—	—	—	6.00
	1983(t)	1,600	—	—	Proof	15.00
	1984Mo	.120	—	—	1.00	2.50
	1984Mo	1,600	—	—	Proof	15.00
	1986	—	—	—	1.00	2.50

NOTE: Coin and medal rotations exist for the above.

17.0000 g, .900 SILVER, .4919 oz ASW

KM#	Date	Mintage	Fine	VF	XF	Unc
63a	1983	100 pcs.	—	—	Proof	100.00
	1984	100 pcs.	—	—	Proof	100.00

NICKEL BONDED STEEL
15th Central American and Caribbean Games

KM#	Date	Mintage	Fine	VF	XF	Unc
65	1986	.100	—	—	1.00	3.00
	1986	1,700	—	—	Proof	15.00

COPPER-NICKEL, 6.25 g

KM#	Date	Mintage	Fine	VF	XF	Unc
65a	1986	548 pcs.	—	—	—	40.00
	1986	48 pcs.	—	—	Proof	—

COPPER-NICKEL, 10.00 g

KM#	Date	Mintage	Fine	VF	XF	Unc
65b	1986	550 pcs.	—	—	—	40.00
	1986	50 pcs.	—	—	Proof	—

COPPER-NICKEL, 19.84 g
500th Anniversary of Discovery and Evangelization

KM#	Date	Mintage	Fine	VF	XF	Unc
66	1988(c)	.150	—	—	—	2.50
	1988(c)	1,500	—	—	Proof	12.50

500th Anniversary of Discovery and Evangelization

KM#	Date	Mintage	Fine	VF	XF	Unc
74	1989(c)	—	—	—	—	2.50

31.1000 g, .999 GOLD, 1.0000 oz AGW

KM#	Date	Mintage	Fine	VF	XF	Unc
74a	1989(c)	30 pcs.	—	—	Proof	1250.

COPPER-NICKEL
500th Anniversary of Discovery and Evangelization

KM#	Date	Mintage	Fine	VF	XF	Unc
77	1990	.030	—	—	—	2.50

31.1030 g, .999 GOLD, 1.0000 oz AGW
500th Anniversary of Discovery and Evangelization

KM#	Date	Mintage	Fine	VF	XF	Unc
77a	1990	50 pcs.	—	—	—	1000.

COPPER-ZINC
Juan Pablo Duarte
Obv: DUARTE on bust.

KM#	Date	Mintage	Fine	VF	XF	Unc
80.1	1991	40.000	—	—	—	2.00
	1992	35.000	—	—	—	2.00

Obv: W/o name on bust.

KM#	Date	Mintage	Fine	VF	XF	Unc
80.2	1991	35.000	—	—	—	2.00
	1992	35.000	—	—	—	2.00
	1993	40.000	—	—	—	2.00

COPPER-NICKEL
Pinzon Brothers

KM#	Date	Mintage	Fine	VF	XF	Unc
81	1991	.050	—	—	—	2.50

31.1030 g, .999 GOLD, 1.0000 oz AGW
Pinzon Brothers

KM#	Date	Mintage	Fine	VF	XF	Unc
81a	1991	35 pcs.	—	—	Proof	1150.

COPPER-NICKEL
Christopher Columbus

KM#	Date	Mintage	Fine	VF	XF	Unc
82	1992	.050	—	—	—	2.50

31.1030 g, .999 GOLD, 1.0000 oz AGW
Christopher Columbus

KM#	Date	Mintage	Fine	VF	XF	Unc
82a	1992	35 pcs.	—	—	Proof	1150.

10 PESOS

28.0000 g, .900 SILVER, .8102 oz ASW
International Banker's Conference —
1st Hispaniola Coinage of Carlos and Johanna

KM#	Date	Mintage	Fine	VF	XF	Unc
37	1975	.026	—	—	—	10.00
	1975	4,000	—	—	Proof	14.00

30.0000 g, .900 SILVER, .8681 oz ASW
Pueblo Viejo Mine

KM#	Date	Mintage	Fine	VF	XF	Unc
38	1975	.045	—	—	—	10.00
	1975	5,000	—	—	Proof	14.00

23.3300 g, .925 SILVER, .6938 oz ASW
International Year of the Child

KM#	Date	Mintage	Fine	VF	XF	Unc
57	1982	8,712	—	—	Proof	17.50

25 PESOS

65.0000 g, .925 SILVER, 1.9332 oz ASW
Pope John Paul II's Visit

KM#	Date	Mintage	Fine	VF	XF	Unc
54	1979	3,000	—	—	—	30.00
	1979	6,000	—	—	Proof	35.00

30 PESOS

29.6220 g, .900 GOLD, .8572 oz AGW
25th Anniversary of Trujillo Regime

KM#	Date	Mintage	Fine	VF	XF	Unc
24	1955	.033	—	—	BV	400.00

11.7000 g, .900 GOLD, .3385 oz AGW
12th Central American and Caribbean Games

KM#	Date	Mintage	Fine	VF	XF	Unc
36	1974	.025	—	—	—	150.00
	1974	5,000	—	—	Proof	175.00

78.0000 g, .925 SILVER, 2.3199 oz ASW
30th Anniversary of Central Bank

KM#	Date	Mintage	Fine	VF	XF	Unc
46	1977	5,000	—	—	—	35.00
	1977	2,000	—	—	Proof	45.00

100 PESOS

10.0000 g, .900 GOLD, .2893 oz AGW
Pueblo Viejo Mine

KM#	Date	Mintage	Fine	VF	XF	Unc
39	1975	.018	—	—	—	125.00
	1975	2,000	—	—	Proof	150.00

12.0000 g, .900 GOLD, .3472 oz AGW
Pope John Paul II's Visit

KM#	Date	Mintage	Fine	VF	XF	Unc
55	1979	1,000	—	—	—	160.00
	1979	3,000	—	—	Proof	185.00

155.5000 g, .999 SILVER, 5.0000 oz ASW
Discovery of America - Indians
Illustration reduced. Actual size: 65mm

KM#	Date	Mintage	Fine	VF	XF	Unc
67	1988	5,300	—	—	Proof	90.00

500th Anniversary of Discovery and Evangelization - Columbus and Crew
Obv: Similar to KM#78 of America.

KM#	Date	Mintage	Fine	VF	XF	Unc
75	1989(c)	1,500	—	—	Proof	225.00

155.5000 g, .999 GOLD, 5.0000 oz AGW

KM#	Date	Mintage	Fine	VF	XF	Unc
75a	1989(c)	30 pcs.	—	—	Proof	3500.

155.5000 g, .999 SILVER, 5.0000 oz ASW
500th Anniversary of Discovery and Evangelization of America - Building a Stockade
Illustration reduced. Actual size: 65mm

KM#	Date	Mintage	Fine	VF	XF	Unc
78	1990	1,000	—	—	Proof	150.00

155.5300 g, .999 GOLD, 5.0000 oz AGW

KM#	Date	Mintage	Fine	VF	XF	Unc
78a	1990	50 pcs.	—	—	Proof	3000.

155.5300 g, .999 SILVER, 5.0000 oz ASW
500th Anniversary of Discovery and Evangelization of America - Columbus Presenting Indian to Court
Illustration reduced. Actual size: 65mm.

KM#	Date	Mintage	Fine	VF	XF	Unc
83	1991	1,500	—	—	Proof	150.00

155.5300 g, .999 GOLD, 5.0000 oz AGW

KM#	Date	Mintage	Fine	VF	XF	Unc
83a	1991	35 pcs.	—	—	Proof	3200.

155.5300 g, .999 SILVER, 5.0000 oz ASW
500th Anniversary of Discovery and Evangelization of America - Columbus and Anchored Ship
Illustration reduced. Actual size: 65mm.

KM#	Date	Mintage	Fine	VF	XF	Unc
84	1992	1,500	—	—	Proof	150.00

155.5300 g, .999 GOLD, 5.0000 oz AGW

KM#	Date	Mintage	Fine	VF	XF	Unc
84a	1992	35 pcs.	—	—	Proof	3200.

200 PESOS

31.0000 g, .800 GOLD, .7974 oz AGW
Death of Juan Pablo Duarte Centennial

KM#	Date	Mintage	Fine	VF	XF	Unc
47	1977	*1,000	—	—	—	450.00
	1977	*2,000	—	—	Proof	500.00

NOTE: Large quantity melted for bullion.

17.1700 g, .900 GOLD, .4969 oz AGW
International Year of the Child

KM#	Date	Mintage	Fine	VF	XF	Unc
58	1982	4,303	—	—	Proof	250.00

250 PESOS

31.1000 g, .900 GOLD, .9000 oz AGW
Pope John Paul II's Visit

KM#	Date	Mintage	Fine	VF	XF	Unc
56	1979	1,000	—	—	—	500.00
	1979	3,000	—	—	Proof	575.00

500 PESOS

31.1000 g, .999 GOLD, 1.0000 oz AGW
Discovery of America - Columbus

KM#	Date	Mintage	Fine	VF	XF	Unc
68	1988	2,600	—	—	Proof	700.00

500th Anniversary of Discovery and Evangelization - Ferdinand and Isabella

KM#	Date	Mintage	Fine	VF	XF	Unc
76	1989	600 pcs.	—	—	Proof	850.00

16.9600 g, .917 GOLD, .5000 oz AGW
500th Anniversary of Discovery of America

KM#	Date	Mintage	Fine	VF	XF	Unc
79	1990	1,500	—	—	Proof	375.00

15.5500 g, .999 PLATINUM, .5000 oz APW

KM#	Date	Mintage	Fine	VF	XF	Unc
79a	1990	50 pcs.	—	—	Proof	650.00

16.9600 g, .917 GOLD, .5000 oz AGW
500th Anniversary of Discovery of America
American Fruits

KM#	Date	Mintage	Fine	VF	XF	Unc
85	1991	1,500	—	—	Proof	375.00

15.5500 g, .999 PLATINUM, .5000 oz APW

KM#	Date	Mintage	Fine	VF	XF	Unc
85a	1991	35 pcs.	—	—	Proof	700.00

16.9600 g, .917 GOLD, .5000 oz AGW
500th Anniversary of Discovery of America
Tomb of Christopher Columbus

KM#	Date	Mintage	Fine	VF	XF	Unc
86	1992	2,000	—	—	Proof	350.00

15.5000 g, .999 PLATINUM, .5000 oz APW

KM#	Date	Mintage	Fine	VF	XF	Unc
86a	1992	35 pcs.	—	—	Proof	700.00

MINT SETS (MS)

KM#	Date	Mintage	Identification	Issue Price	Mkt. Val.
MS1	1983(5)	2,000	KM59-63	10.00	15.00
MS2	1984(6)	2,000	KM59-64	—	15.00
MS3	1986(5)	2,000	KM59-62,64	10.00	14.00
MS4	1987(5)	1,000	KM59-62,64	10.00	14.00

PROOF SETS (PS)

KM#	Date	Mintage	Identification	Issue Price	Mkt. Val.
PS1	1937(5)	—	KM17-21	—	2750.
PS2	1972(4)	500	KM18,20a.1,31,34	20.00	85.00
PS3	1973(2)	500	KM19a,21a.2	5.00	60.00
PS4	1974(2)	500	KM18,20a.2	5.00	45.00
PS5	1974(2)	500	KM35-36	120.00	220.00
PS6	1975(2)	500	KM38-39	200.00	200.00
PS7	1976(6)	5,000	KM40-45	10.00	20.00
PS8	1978(6)	5,000	KM48-53	10.00	20.00
PS9	1978(6)	15	KM48a-53a	175.00	900.00
PS10	1979(6)	500	KM48-53	15.00	175.00
PS11	1979(6)	15	KM48a-53a	255.00	900.00
PS12	1980(6)	3,000	KM48-53	15.00	20.00
PS13	1980(6)	15	KM48a-53a	255.00	900.00
PS14	1981(6)	3,000	KM48-53	15.00	20.00
PS15	1981(6)	15	KM48a-53a	300.00	900.00
PS16	1983(t)(2)	1,600	KM59-60	10.00	10.00
PS17	1983(2)	300	Piefonts of KM59 & 60	25.00	50.00
PS18	1983(2)	100	KM59a,60a	45.00	45.00
PS19	1983(t)(3)	1,570	KM61-63	20.00	20.00
PS20	1983(3)	270	Pieforts of KM61-63	45.00	115.00
PS21	1983(3)	70	KM61a-63a	125.00	125.00
PS22	1984Mo(6)	1,570	KM59-64	20.00	45.00
PS23	1984(6)	270	Pieforts of KM59-64	30.00	30.00
PS24	1984(6)	70	KM59a-64a	250.00	250.00
PS25	1986(5)	1,570	KM59-62,64	30.00	20.00
PS26	1986(5)	270	Pieforts of KM59-62,64	40.00	40.00
PS27	1986(5)	70	KM59a-62a,64a	150.00	150.00
PS28	1987(5)	1,600	KM59-62,64	—	30.00
PS29	1987(5)	300	Pieforts of KM59-62,64	—	75.00

SPECIAL SETS (SS)

KM#	Date	Mintage	Identification	Issue Price	Mkt. Val.
SS1	1983(15)	30	KM61-63,61a-63a inc. all mint marks	200.00	200.00
SS2	1984(24)	30	KM59-64	400.00	400.00
SS3	1986(20)	30	KM59-64	300.00	300.00
SS4	1986(2)	1,700	KM65, Nickel-bonded Steel, Proof & Unc	35.00	35.00
SS5	1986(3)	300	KM65, Proof, Unc & Piefort	75.00	75.00
SS6	1986(2)	23	KM65a, Proof & Unc	—	—
SS7	1986(3)	25	KM65a, Proof, Unc & Piefort, 20 g	—	—
SS8	1986(2)	25	KM65b, Proof & Unc	—	—
SS9	1986(3)	25	KM65b, Proof, Unc & Piefort	—	—
SS10	1987(15)	100	KM59-62,64,Proof, Unc & Piefort	—	125.00

EAST AFRICA

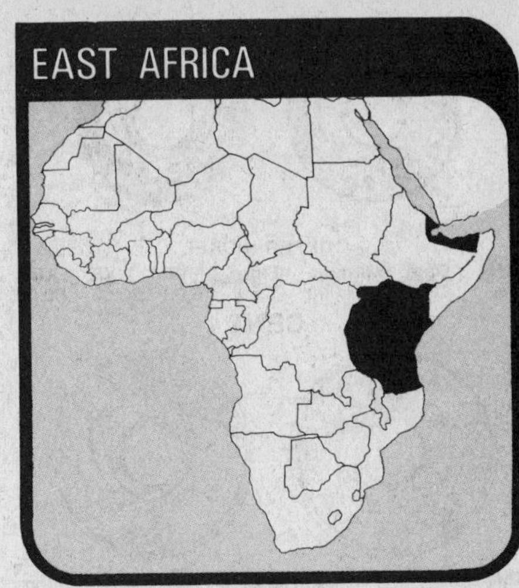

East Africa was an administrative grouping of five separate British territories: Kenya, Tanganyika (now part of Tanzania), the Sultanate of Zanzibar and Pemba (now part of Tanzania), Uganda and British Somaliland (now part of Somalia). See individual entries for specific statistics and history.

The common interest of Kenya, Tanzania and Uganda invited cooperation in economic matters and consideration of political union. The territorial governors, organized as the East Africa High Commission, met periodically to administer such common activities as taxation, industrial development and education. The authority of the Commission did not infringe upon the constitution and internal autonomy of the individual colonies. A common coinage and banknotes, which were also legal tender in Aden, was also legal tender in Aden, was provided for use of the member colonies by the East Africa Currency Board. The coinage through 1919 had the legend "East Africa and Uganda Protectorate".

The East African coinage includes two denominations of 1936 which bear the name of Edward VIII.

NOTE: For later coinage see Kenya, Tanzania and Uganda.

RULERS

British

MINT MARKS

A - Ackroyd & Best, Morley
I - Bombay Mint
H - Heaton Mint, Birmingham, England
K,KN - King's Norton Mint
SA - Pretoria Mint

EAST AFRICA PROTECTORATE

MONETARY SYSTEM

64 Pice = 1 Rupee

PICE

BRONZE

KM#	Date	Mintage	Fine	VF	XF	Unc
1	1897	.640	6.00	12.50	30.00	85.00
	1897	—	—	—	Proof	200.00
	1898	6.400	4.00	10.00	22.50	75.00
	1898	—	—	—	Proof	200.00
	1899	3.200	4.00	10.00	22.50	75.00
	1899	—	—	—	Proof	200.00

EAST AFRICA & UGANDA PROTECTORATE

MONETARY SYSTEM

100 Cents = 1 Rupee

1/2 CENT

ALUMINUM

KM#	Date	Mintage	Fine	VF	XF	Unc
6	1907	—	—	—	Rare	—
	1908	.900	15.00	25.00	50.00	90.00

COPPER-NICKEL

KM#	Date	Mintage	Fine	VF	XF	Unc
6a	1909	.900	7.50	15.00	30.00	60.00

CENT

ALUMINUM

KM#	Date	Mintage	Fine	VF	XF	Unc
5	1906	—	400.00	700.00	1200.	—
	1907	6.948	5.00	10.00	22.50	45.00
	1907	—	—	—	Proof	200.00
	1908	2.871	7.00	12.50	30.00	60.00

COPPER-NICKEL

KM#	Date	Mintage	Fine	VF	XF	Unc
5a	1908	—	—	—	Unique	—
	1909	25.000	.50	1.25	3.00	7.00
	1910	6.000	.50	1.25	4.00	12.00

KM#	Date	Mintage	Fine	VF	XF	Unc
7	1911H	25.000	.25	1.00	2.50	15.00
	1912H	20.000	.25	1.00	2.00	8.00
	1913	4.529	.75	1.50	3.75	20.00
	1914	6.000	.75	1.75	5.00	15.00
	1914H	2.500	1.00	2.50	6.00	17.00
	1916H	1.824	.75	2.00	5.00	20.00
	1917H	3.176	.75	2.50	6.00	17.00
	1918H	10.000	.50	1.00	3.25	12.00

5 CENTS

COPPER-NICKEL

KM#	Date	Mintage	Fine	VF	XF	Unc
11.1	1907	—	—	—	Rare	—

KM#	Date	Mintage	Fine	VF	XF	Unc
11.2	1913H	.300	1.50	4.00	15.00	35.00
	1914K	1.240	.75	3.25	6.00	22.50
	1914K*	—	—	—	Proof	200.00
	1919H	.200	10.00	15.00	40.00	110.00

***NOTE:** The 1914K was issued with British West Africa KM#8 in a double (4 pc.) Specimen Set.

10 CENTS

COPPER-NICKEL

KM#	Date	Mintage	Fine	VF	XF	Unc
2	1906	—	750.00	1500.	2000.	3000.
	1907	1.000	1.50	4.00	10.00	30.00
	1910	.500	3.00	7.00	20.00	55.00

KM#	Date	Mintage	Fine	VF	XF	Unc
8	1911H	1.250	1.50	4.00	7.50	40.00
	1912H	1.050	2.00	5.00	12.50	55.00
	1913	.050	75.00	150.00	250.00	500.00
	1918H	.400	7.50	20.00	40.00	135.00

25 CENTS

2.9160 g, .800 SILVER, .0750 oz ASW

KM#	Date	Mintage	Fine	VF	XF	Unc
3	1906	.400	2.50	6.00	20.00	60.00
	1910H	.200	4.00	8.00	30.00	90.00

KM#	Date	Mintage	Fine	VF	XF	Unc
10	1912	.180	4.00	8.00	25.00	75.00
	1913	.300	2.75	6.50	20.00	50.00
	1914H	.080	20.00	35.00	55.00	100.00
	1914H	—	—	—	Proof	400.00
	1918H	.040	150.00	300.00	500.00	900.00

50 CENTS

5.8319 g, .800 SILVER, .1500 oz ASW

KM#	Date	Mintage	Fine	VF	XF	Unc
4	1906	.200	4.50	12.50	30.00	140.00
	1906	—	—	—	Proof	400.00
	1909	.100	15.00	30.00	85.00	300.00
	1910	.100	10.00	25.00	60.00	225.00

KM#	Date	Mintage	Fine	VF	XF	Unc
9	1911	.150	6.00	12.50	30.00	140.00
	1911	—	—	—	Proof	250.00
	1912	.100	8.00	20.00	60.00	200.00
	1913	.200	5.00	12.50	30.00	130.00
	1914H	.180	5.00	12.50	30.00	130.00
	1918H	.060	60.00	150.00	250.00	500.00
	1919	.100	200.00	300.00	500.00	1200.

PROOF SETS (PS)

KM#	Date	Mintage	Identification	Mkt.Val.
PS1	1906-7(4)	—	KM2-5,Pn2-3	Rare

EAST AFRICA

MONETARY SYSTEM

100 Cents = 1 Florin

CENT

COPPER-NICKEL

KM#	Date	Mintage	Fine	VF	XF	Unc
12	1920H	*2.908	30.00	60.00	100.00	225.00
	1920H	*20-30 pcs.	—	—	Proof	300.00

KM#	Date	Mintage	Fine	VF	XF	Unc
12	1920	—	—	—	—	750.00
	1921	**	—	—	—	425.00

***NOTE:** Only about 30% of total mintage released to circulation.

****NOTE:** Not released for circulation.

5 CENTS

COPPER-NICKEL

KM#	Date	Mintage	Fine	VF	XF	Unc
13	1920H	*.550	65.00	125.00	175.00	350.00
	1920H	*20-30 pcs.	—	—	Proof	400.00

***NOTE:** Only about 30% of total mintage released to circulation.

10 CENTS

COPPER-NICKEL

KM#	Date	Mintage	Fine	VF	XF	Unc
14	1920H	*.700	120.00	170.00	220.00	350.00
	1920H	*20-30 pcs.	—	—	Proof	600.00

***NOTE:** Only about 30% of total mintage released to circulation.

25 CENTS

2.9160 g, .500 SILVER, .0469 oz ASW

KM#	Date	Mintage	Fine	VF	XF	Unc
15	1920H	.748	25.00	35.00	75.00	150.00
	1920H	*20-30 pcs.	—	—	Proof	250.00

50 CENTS

5.8319 g, .500 SILVER, .0937 oz ASW
Fifty Cents-One Shilling

KM#	Date	Mintage	Fine	VF	XF	Unc
16	1920A	*.012	1500.	2000.	3000.	4000.
	1920H	*.062	600.00	1000.	1250.	1600.
	1920H	*20-30 pcs.	—	—	Proof	—

***NOTE:** Not released for circulation.

FLORIN

11.6638 g, .500 SILVER, .1875 oz ASW

KM#	Date	Mintage	Fine	VF	XF	Unc
17	1920	1.479	15.00	35.00	100.00	300.00
	1920A	.542	150.00	250.00	600.00	2000.
	1920H	9.689	12.50	30.00	75.00	250.00
	1920H	*20-30 pcs.	—	—	Proof	—
	1921	2 known	—	—	—	4500.

MONETARY REFORM

(Commencing May, 1921)
100 Cents = 1 Shilling

CENT

BRONZE

KM#	Date	Mintage	Fine	VF	XF	Unc
22	1922	8.250	.25	.85	4.00	10.00
	1922H	43.750	.25	.50	1.50	6.50
	1923	50.000	.25	.50	1.50	6.50
	1924	Inc. Ab.	.25	.75	3.25	10.00
	1924H	17.500	.25	.75	3.25	8.00
	1924KN	10.720	.25	.75	3.25	8.00
	1924KN	—	—	—	Proof	125.00
	1925	6.000	35.00	75.00	150.00	300.00
	1925KN	6.780	2.00	4.00	12.00	35.00
	1927	10.000	.25	.75	3.00	10.00
	1927	—	—	—	Proof	125.00
	1928H	12.000	.25	.75	3.25	8.00
	1928KN	11.764	.35	1.00	3.50	10.00
	1928KN	—	—	—	Proof	125.00
	1930	15.000	.25	.75	2.00	5.00
	1930	—	—	—	Proof	125.00
	1935	10.000	.25	.50	1.25	3.50

KM#	Date	Mintage	Fine	VF	XF	Unc
29	1942	25.000	.10	.25	.85	2.50
	1942I	15.000	.15	.30	1.00	3.00

Obv. leg: ET IND.IMP. dropped.

KM#	Date	Mintage	Fine	VF	XF	Unc
32	1949	4.000	.10	.25	.85	2.50
	1949	—	.10	—	Proof	125.00
	1950	16.000	.10	.25	.85	2.50
	1950	—	—	—	Proof	150.00
	1951H	9.000	.10	.25	.85	2.50
	1951H	—	—	—	Proof	125.00
	1951KN	11.140	.10	.25	.85	2.50
	1951KN	—	—	—	Proof	125.00
	1952	7.000	.10	.25	.85	2.50
	1952H	13.000	.10	.25	.85	2.50
	1952H	—	—	—	Proof	125.00
	1952KN	5.230	.10	.35	1.25	5.00

KM#	Date	Mintage	Fine	VF	XF	Unc
35	1954	8.000	.10	.25	.85	2.50
	1954	—	—	—	Proof	150.00
	1955	5.000	.10	.25	.50	1.75
	1955H	6.384	.10	.20	.65	1.75
	1955KN	4.000	.10	.20	.65	1.75
	1956H	15.616	.10	.15	.30	1.25
	1956KN	9.680	.10	.20	.40	1.25
	1957	15.000	.10	.20	.65	1.75
	1957H	5.000	1.00	2.00	5.00	10.00
	1957KN	Inc. Ab.	.10	.20	.65	1.75
	1959H	10.000	.10	.20	.40	1.25
	1959KN	10.000	.10	.20	.40	1.25
	1961	1.800	.15	.40	2.00	3.50
	1961	—	—	—	Proof	100.00
	1961H	1.800	.15	.40	2.00	3.50
	1962H	10.320	.10	.20	.40	1.25

5 CENTS

BRONZE

KM#	Date	Mintage	Fine	VF	XF	Unc
18	1921	1.000	2.00	4.00	10.00	35.00
	1922	2.500	.50	1.25	4.50	12.50
	1923	2.400	.50	1.25	4.50	12.50
18	1923	—	—	—	Proof	150.00
	1924	4.800	.50	1.00	3.00	15.00
	1925	6.600	.50	1.00	3.00	10.00
	1925	—	—	—	Proof	125.00
	1928	1.200	.50	1.00	3.50	22.50
	1928	—	—	—	Proof	150.00
	1933	5.000	.50	1.00	2.50	10.00
	1934	3.910	.50	1.00	3.50	15.00
	1934	—	—	—	Proof	150.00
	1935	5.800	.50	1.00	3.00	10.00
	1935	—	—	—	Proof	150.00
	1936	1.000	1.50	5.00	7.50	60.00

KM#	Date	Mintage	Fine	VF	XF	Unc
23	1936H	3.500	.25	.50	1.00	4.00
	1936H	—	—	—	Proof	150.00
	1936KN	2.150	.25	.50	1.00	4.00
	1936KN	—	—	—	Proof	150.00

Thick flan

KM#	Date	Mintage	Fine	VF	XF	Unc
25.1	1937H	3.000	.50	1.00	2.00	4.00
	1937KN	3.000	.50	1.00	2.00	6.00
	1939H	2.000	.50	1.00	3.00	13.50
	1939KN	2.000	.50	1.00	3.00	13.50
	1941	—	2.50	6.00	14.00	40.00
	1941I	20.000	.50	1.00	2.00	5.00

Thin flan, reduced weight.

KM#	Date	Mintage	Fine	VF	XF	Unc
25.2	1942	16.000	.50	1.00	2.00	4.00
	1942SA	4.120	1.00	2.00	7.50	30.00
	1943SA	17.880	.50	1.00	5.00	10.00

Obv. leg: ET IND.IMP. dropped.

KM#	Date	Mintage	Fine	VF	XF	Unc
33	1949	4.000	.25	.50	3.00	6.00
	1949	—	—	—	Proof	175.00
	1951H	6.000	.25	.50	2.00	5.00
	1951H	—	—	—	Proof	175.00
	1952	11.200	.20	.40	1.00	3.00
	1952	—	—	—	Proof	150.00

KM#	Date	Mintage	Fine	VF	XF	Unc
37	1955	2.000	.10	.25	.75	2.00
	1955	—	—	—	Proof	150.00
	1955H	4.000	.20	.50	1.25	3.50
	1955H	—	—	—	Proof	150.00
	1955KN	2.000	.35	.80	2.50	5.00
	1956H	3.000	.15	.35	1.00	3.00
	1956KN	3.000	1.50	3.00	5.00	10.00
	1956KN	—	—	—	Proof	125.00
	1957H	5.000	.10	.25	.75	2.00
	1957KN	5.000	.10	.25	.75	2.00
	1961H	4.000	.15	.35	1.00	3.00
	1963	12.600	—	.10	.30	.75
	1963	—	—	—	Proof	150.00

Post-Independence Issue

KM#	Date	Mintage	Fine	VF	XF	Unc
39	1964	7.600	—	.10	.20	.50

10 CENTS

BRONZE

KM#	Date	Mintage	Fine	VF	XF	Unc
19	1921	.130	3.00	7.50	22.50	65.00
	1922	7.120	.75	2.50	5.00	18.50
	1923	1.200	1.25	4.00	15.00	45.00
	1924	4.900	.65	2.25	6.00	25.00
	1925	4.800	.65	2.25	6.00	25.00
	1927	2.000	.75	2.50	6.50	20.00
	1928	3.800	.75	2.50	6.50	30.00
	1928	—	—	—	Proof	175.00
	1933	6.260	.75	2.50	6.50	17.50
	1934	3.649	.75	2.50	6.50	30.00
	1935	7.300	.65	2.00	5.00	15.00
	1936	.500	1.50	5.00	15.00	50.00

KM#	Date	Mintage	Fine	VF	XF	Unc
24	1936	2.000	1.00	3.50	8.00	25.00
	1936	—	—	—	Proof	200.00
	1936H	4.330	.25	.50	1.50	5.00
	1936H	—	—	—	Proof	360.00
	1936KN	4.142	.25	.50	1.50	5.00
	1936KN	—	—	—	Proof	145.00

NOTE: For listing of mule dated 1936H w/obv. of KM#24 and rev. of British West Africa KM#16 refer to British West Africa listings.

COPPER-NICKEL

KM#	Date	Mintage	Fine	VF	XF	Unc
24a	1936KN	—	—	—	—	—

Thick flan

KM#	Date	Mintage	Fine	VF	XF	Unc
26.1	1937	2.000	.25	.75	2.50	6.00
	1937	—	—	—	Proof	175.00
	1937H	2.500	.25	.75	2.50	8.00
	1937H	—	—	—	Proof	175.00
	1937KN	2.500	.25	.75	2.50	8.00
	1937KN	—	—	—	Proof	175.00
	1939H	2.000	.25	.70	3.50	15.00
	1939KN	2.030	.25	.70	3.50	12.50
	1939KN	—	—	—	Proof	175.00
	1941I	15.682	.50	1.50	4.50	17.00
	1941I	—	—	—	Proof	175.00
	1941	—	.50	1.50	4.50	17.00
	1941	—	—	—	Proof	175.00

NOTE: Many dates, including 1941I, exist w/o center hole.

Thin flan, reduced weight.

KM#	Date	Mintage	Fine	VF	XF	Unc
26.2	1942	12.000	.20	.50	1.75	4.00
	1942	—	—	—	Proof	175.00
	1942I	4.317	2.00	4.00	9.00	17.50
	1943SA	14.093	.25	.50	4.50	10.00
	1945SA	5.000	.25	.50	3.00	12.50

Obv. leg: ET IND.IMP. dropped.

KM#	Date	Mintage	Fine	VF	XF	Unc
34	1949	4.000	.20	.40	1.75	4.00

KM#	Date	Mintage	Fine	VF	XF	Unc
34	1949	—	—	—	Proof	175.00
	1950	8.000	.20	.40	1.75	4.00
	1950	—	—	—	Proof	200.00
	1951	14.500	.20	.40	1.25	3.00
	1951	—	—	—	Proof	175.00
	1952	15.800	.20	.40	1.25	3.00
	1952H	2.000	.40	1.25	3.00	10.00

KM#	Date	Mintage	Fine	VF	XF	Unc
38	1956	6.001	.35	1.00	2.50	10.00
	1956	—	—	—	Proof	175.00
	1964H	1 known	—	—	—	1250.

Post-Independence Issue

KM#	Date	Mintage	Fine	VF	XF	Unc
40	1964H	10.002	.10	.15	.30	1.00

50 CENTS

3.8879 g, .250 SILVER, .0312 oz ASW
Fifty Cents-Half Shilling

KM#	Date	Mintage	Fine	VF	XF	Unc
20	1921	6.200	1.00	2.00	7.50	30.00
	1922	Inc. Ab.	1.00	2.00	6.00	27.50
	1923	.396	3.00	6.00	30.00	75.00
	1924	1.000	2.00	4.00	10.00	40.00

KM#	Date	Mintage	Fine	VF	XF	Unc
27	1937H	4.000	.75	1.25	3.50	12.50
	1937H	—	—	—	Proof	275.00
	1942H	5.000	.75	1.25	4.00	20.00
	1943I	2.000	1.50	3.00	7.50	30.00
	1944SA	1.000	2.00	4.00	9.00	32.50

COPPER-NICKEL
Obv. leg: ET INDIA IMPERATOR dropped.

KM#	Date	Mintage	Fine	VF	XF	Unc
30	1948	7.290	.20	.40	1.75	6.00
	1948	—	—	—	Proof	250.00
	1949	12.960	.15	.30	1.25	4.00
	1949	—	—	—	Proof	325.00
	1952KN	2.000	.20	.40	1.75	7.50

KM#	Date	Mintage	Fine	VF	XF	Unc
36	1954	3.700	.15	.35	1.00	3.00
	1954	—	—	—	Proof	225.00
	1955H	1.600	.25	.50	2.50	5.00
	1955H	—	—	—	Proof	225.00
	1955KN	—	.15	.35	1.75	4.50
	1956H	2.000	.15	.25	1.25	3.00
	1956H	—	—	—	Proof	225.00
	1956KN	2.000	.15	.35	1.75	4.00
	1958H	2.600	.15	.40	2.00	5.00

KM#	Date	Mintage	Fine	VF	XF	Unc
36	1960	4.000	.10	.25	1.25	3.25
	1962KN	4.000	.15	.35	1.75	4.50
	1963	6.000	.10	.25	1.25	3.00

SHILLING

7.7759 g, .250 SILVER, .0625 oz ASW

KM#	Date	Mintage	Fine	VF	XF	Unc
21	1921	6.141	1.50	2.75	8.50	20.00
	1921H	4.240	1.75	3.00	10.00	30.00
	1922	18.858	1.25	2.25	6.50	17.50
	1922H	20.052	1.25	2.25	6.50	17.50
	1923	4.000	3.50	7.00	15.00	35.00
	1924	44.604	1.00	2.00	4.50	10.00
	1925	28.405	1.00	2.00	4.50	12.50
	1925	—	—	—	Proof	250.00

KM#	Date	Mintage	Fine	VF	XF	Unc
28	1937H	7.672	1.00	2.00	4.00	12.50
	1937H	—	—	—	Proof	300.00
	1941I	7.000	1.25	2.00	6.00	20.00
	1942H	4.430	1.25	2.00	6.00	20.00
	1942H	—	—	—	Proof	300.00
	1942I	3.900	1.00	2.00	5.00	20.00
	1943I	*25-50 pcs.	250.00	400.00	600.00	1250.
	1944H	10.000	1.25	2.00	7.50	25.00
	1944SA	5.820	1.25	2.00	5.00	22.50
	1945SA	10.080	1.25	2.00	5.00	22.50
	1946SA	18.260	1.25	2.00	3.50	17.50

NOTE: Three varieties of reverse dies exist for above coin.

COPPER-NICKEL
Obv. leg: ET INDIA IMPERATOR dropped.

KM#	Date	Mintage	Fine	VF	XF	Unc
31	1948	19.704	.50	.90	1.50	6.50
	1949	38.318	.50	.90	1.50	6.50
	1949	—	—	—	Proof	250.00
	1949H	12.584	.50	.90	1.50	7.50
	1949KN	15.060	.50	.90	1.50	7.50
	1950	56.362	.35	.60	1.00	3.00
	1950	—	—	—	Proof	250.00
	1950H	12.416	.50	.90	2.25	6.00
	1950KN	10.040	.40	.70	2.00	5.00
	1952	55.605	.35	.60	1.00	3.00
	1952	—	—	—	Proof	175.00
	1952H	8.024	.35	.60	1.25	3.50
	1952KN	9.360	.35	.60	1.25	3.50

SPECIMEN SETS (SS)

KM#	Date	Mintage	Identification	Mkt.Val.
MS1	1921-2(5)	—	KM18-22	2000.

NOTE: The 5 cent coin is dated 1921, all others are 1922.

PROOF SETS (PS)

KM#	Date	Mintage	Identification	Mkt.Val.
PS1	1920H(6)	20-30	KM12-17	—
PS2	1949(5)	—	KM30-34	1000.
PS3	1950(3)	—	KM31,32,34	600.00

EAST CARIBBEAN STATES

The East Caribbean States, formerly the British Caribbean Territories (Eastern group), formed a currency board in 1950 to provide the constituent territories of Trinidad & Tobago, Barbados, British Guiana (now Guyana), British Virgin Islands, Anguilla, St. Kitts, Nevis, Antigua, Dominica, St. Lucia, St. Vincent and Grenada with a common currency, thereby permitting withdrawal of the regular British Pound currency. This was dissolved in 1965 and after the breakup, the East Caribbean Territories, a grouping including Barbados, the Leeward and Windward Islands, came into being. Coinage of the dissolved 'Eastern Group' continues to circulate although paper currency of the East Caribbean Authority was first issued in 1965.

A series of 4-dollar coins tied to the FAO coinage program were released in 1970 under the name of the Caribbean Development Bank by eight loosely federated island groupings in the eastern Caribbean. These issues are listed individually in this volume under Antigua, Barbados, Dominica, Grenada, Montserrat, St. Kitts, St. Lucia and St. Vincent.

RULERS

British

BRITISH EAST CARIBBEAN TERRITORIES

MONETARY SYSTEM

100 Cents = 1 Br. W. Indies Dollar

1/2 CENT

BRONZE

KM#	Date	Mintage	Fine	VF	XF	Unc
1	1955	.500	.30	.50	.75	2.00
	1955	2,000	—	—	Proof	3.00
	1958	.200	.50	.75	1.25	2.50
	1958	20 pcs.	—	—	Proof	145.00

CENT

BRONZE

KM#	Date	Mintage	Fine	VF	XF	Unc
2	1955	8.000	.15	.25	.60	1.00
	1955	2,000	—	—	Proof	3.00
	1957	3.000	.15	.25	1.75	3.00
	1957	—	—	—	Proof	100.00
	1958	1.500	.35	.50	4.50	7.50
	1958	20 pcs.	—	—	Proof	165.00
	1959	.500	.40	.60	6.00	20.00
	1959	—	—	—	Proof	100.00
	1960	2.500	.15	.25	.60	1.25
	1960	—	—	—	Proof	100.00
	1961	2.280	.25	.35	.75	1.25
	1961	—	—	—	Proof	100.00
	1962	2.000	.15	.25	.50	1.25
	1962	—	—	—	Proof	100.00
	1963	.750	.45	.70	1.20	2.50
	1963	—	—	—	Proof	100.00
	1964	2.500	—	—	.20	.35
	1964	—	—	—	Proof	100.00
	1965	4.800	—	—	.20	.35
	1965	—	—	—	P/L	.75
	1965	—	—	—	Proof	5.00

2 CENTS

BRONZE

KM#	Date	Mintage	Fine	VF	XF	Unc
3	1955	5.500	.15	.25	.50	.85
	1955	2,000	—	—	Proof	3.00
	1957	1.250	.15	.25	1.25	2.50
	1957	—	—	—	Proof	110.00
	1958	1.250	.15	.25	2.50	5.00
	1958	20 pcs.	—	—	Proof	185.00
	1960	.750	.15	.25	1.75	3.00
	1960	—	—	—	Proof	110.00
	1961	.788	.15	.25	1.75	3.00
	1961	—	—	—	Proof	110.00
	1962	1.060	.10	.20	.30	.75
	1962	—	—	—	Proof	110.00
	1963	.250	.50	.75	1.50	5.00
	1963	—	—	—	Proof	110.00
	1964	1.188	.10	.20	.30	.65
	1964	—	—	—	Proof	110.00
	1965	2.001	—	.10	.20	.40
	1965	—	—	—	P/L	.75
	1965	—	—	—	Proof	5.00

5 CENTS

NICKEL-BRASS

KM#	Date	Mintage	Fine	VF	XF	Unc
4	1955	8.600	.15	.25	.60	1.25
	1955	2,000	—	—	Proof	4.00
	1956	2.000	.15	.25	.60	1.00
	1956	—	—	—	Proof	300.00
	1960	1.000	.20	.30	.90	1.50
	1960	—	—	—	Proof	150.00
	1962	1.300	.15	.25	.50	1.00
	1962	—	—	—	Proof	150.00
	1963	.200	.25	.35	1.20	2.00
	1963	—	—	—	Proof	150.00
	1964	1.350	—	.10	.30	.75
	1964	—	—	—	Proof	150.00
	1965	2.400	—	.10	.20	.50
	1965	—	—	—	P/L	.75
	1965	—	—	—	Proof	5.00

10 CENTS

COPPER-NICKEL

KM#	Date	Mintage	Fine	VF	XF	Unc
5	1955	5.000	.15	.25	.45	.75
	1955	2,000	—	—	Proof	4.00
	1956	4.000	.15	.25	.45	.75
	1956	—	—	—	Proof	175.00
	1959	2.000	.15	.25	.60	1.00
	1959	—	—	—	Proof	175.00
	1961	1.260	.20	.30	.50	1.00
	1961	—	—	—	Proof	175.00
	1962	1.200	.15	.25	.50	1.00
	1962	—	—	—	Proof	175.00
	1964	1.400	.10	.20	.35	.65
	1965	3.200	.10	.20	.30	.50
	1965	—	—	—	P/L	.75
	1965	—	—	—	Proof	5.00

25 CENTS

COPPER-NICKEL

KM#	Date	Mintage	Fine	VF	XF	Unc
6	1955	7.000	.35	.50	.70	1.00
	1955	2,000	—	—	Proof	6.00
	1957	.800	.75	1.00	2.25	4.50
	1957	—	—	—	Proof	225.00
	1959	1.000	.35	.50	1.25	2.25
	1959	—	—	—	Proof	225.00
	1961	.744	.50	.75	2.50	5.00
	1961	—	—	—	Proof	225.00
	1962	.480	.25	.50	1.25	2.50
	1962	—	—	—	Proof	225.00
6	1963	.480	.25	.50	1.25	2.50
	1963	—	—	—	Proof	225.00
	1964	.480	.25	.50	1.00	1.75
	1964	—	—	—	Proof	225.00
	1965	1.280	.25	.50	.75	1.00
	1965	—	—	—	P/L	1.50
	1965	—	—	—	Proof	7.50

50 CENTS

COPPER-NICKEL

KM#	Date	Mintage	Fine	VF	XF	Unc
7	1955	1.500	.75	1.25	1.75	3.00
	1955	2,000	—	—	Proof	12.00
	1965	.100	2.00	5.00	7.50	15.00
	1965	—	—	—	P/L	7.50
	1965	—	—	—	Proof	10.00

PROOF SETS (PS)

KM#	Date	Mintage	Identification	Issue Price	Mkt. Val.
PS1	1955(7)	2,000	KM1-7	—	30.00
PS2	1958(3)	20	KM1-3	—	500.00
PS3	1965(6)	—	KM2-7	—	35.00

EAST CARIBBEAN TERRITORIES

MONETARY SYSTEM

100 Cents = 1 Dollar

10 DOLLARS

COPPER-NICKEL

10th Anniversary of Caribbean Development Bank

KM#	Date	Mintage	VF	XF	Unc
1	1980	—	—	—	6.00
	28.2800 g, .925 SILVER, .8411 oz ASW				
1a	1980	.010	—	Proof	45.00

COPPER-NICKEL

Wedding of Prince Charles and Lady Diana

KM#	Date	Mintage	VF	XF	Unc
2	1981	.050	—	—	6.00
	28.2800 g, .925 SILVER, .8411 oz ASW				
2a	1981	.030	—	Proof	35.00

PROOF SETS (PS)

KM#	Date	Mintage	Identification	Issue Price	Mkt. Val.
PS1	1970(8)	2,000	4 Dollars	57.60	125.00

EAST CARIBBEAN STATES

CENT

ALUMINUM

KM#	Date	Mintage	VF	XF	Unc
1	1981	—	—	—	.10
	1981	5,000	—	Proof	1.25
	1983	—	—	—	.10
	1984	—	—	—	.10
	1986	—	—	—	.10
	1986	2,500	—	Proof	1.25
	1987	—	—	—	.10
	1989	—	—	—	.10
	1991	—	—	—	.10
	1992	—	—	—	.10

2 CENTS

ALUMINUM

KM#	Date	Mintage	VF	XF	Unc
2	1981	—	—	.10	.15
	1981	5,000	—	Proof	1.50
	1984	—	—	.10	.15
	1986	—	—	.10	.15
	1986	2,500	—	Proof	1.50
	1987	—	—	.10	.15
	1989	—	—	.10	.15
	1991	—	—	.10	.15
	1992	—	—	.10	.15
	1993	—	—	.10	.15

5 CENTS

ALUMINUM

KM#	Date	Mintage	VF	XF	Unc
3	1981	—	—	.10	.20
	1981	5,000	—	Proof	2.25
	1984	—	—	.10	.20
	1986	—	—	.10	.20
	1986	2,500	—	Proof	2.25
	1987	—	—	.10	.20
	1989	—	—	.10	.20
	1991	—	—	.10	.20
	1992	—	—	.10	.20

10 CENTS

COPPER-NICKEL

KM#	Date	Mintage	VF	XF	Unc
4	1981	—	.10	.15	.25
	1981	5,000	—	Proof	3.00
	1986	—	.10	.15	.25
	1986	2,500	—	Proof	3.00
	1987	—	.10	.15	.25
	1989	—	.10	.15	.25
	1991	—	.10	.15	.25

25 CENTS

COPPER-NICKEL

KM#	Date	Mintage	VF	XF	Unc
5	1981	—	.15	.20	.40
	1981	5,000	—	Proof	4.00
	1986	—	.15	.20	.40
	1986	2,500	—	Proof	4.00
	1987	—	.15	.20	.40
	1989	—	.15	.20	.40
	1991	—	.15	.20	.40

DOLLAR

ALUMINUM-BRONZE

KM#	Date	Mintage	VF	XF	Unc
6	1981	—	.50	.75	1.50
	1981	5,000	—	Proof	8.00
	1986	—	.50	.75	1.50
	1986	2,500	—	Proof	8.00

COPPER-NICKEL

KM#	Date	Mintage	VF	XF	Unc
11	1989	—	—	—	3.00
	1991	—	—	—	3.00

2 DOLLARS

COPPER-NICKEL
10th Anniversary of Central Bank

KM#	Date	Mintage	VF	XF	Unc
15	1993	—	—	—	10.00

10 DOLLARS

COPPER-NICKEL
F.A.O. - World Food Day

KM#	Date	Mintage	VF	XF	Unc
7	1981	—	—	—	6.00

28.2800 g, .500 SILVER, .4546 oz ASW

KM#	Date	Mintage	VF	XF	Unc
7a	1981	.010	—	—	10.00
	1981	5,000	—	Proof	32.50

28.2800 g, .925 SILVER, .8411 oz ASW
Queen Mother

KM#	Date	Mintage	VF	XF	Unc
13	1990	—	—	Proof	50.00

40th Anniversary of Coronation of Queen Elizabeth

KM#	Date	Mintage	VF	XF	Unc
14	1993	*.010	—	Proof	50.00

50 DOLLARS

28.2800 g, .925 SILVER, .8411 oz ASW
International Year of the Disabled Persons

KM#	Date	Mintage	VF	XF	Unc
10	1981	.010	—	—	25.00
	1981	.010	—	Proof	30.00

International Year of the Scout

KM#	Date	Mintage	VF	XF	Unc
8	1983	.010	—	—	25.00
	1983	.010	—	Proof	30.00

500 DOLLARS

15.9800 g, .917 GOLD, .4712 oz AGW
International Year of Disabled Persons

KM#	Date	Mintage	VF	XF	Unc
12	1981	—	—	—	650.00
	1981	—	—	Proof	850.00

International Year of the Scout
Obv: Similar to 50 Dollars, KM#8.
Rev: One scout standing, one scout kneeling.

KM#	Date	Mintage	VF	XF	Unc
9	1983	2,000	—	—	400.00
	1983	2,000	—	Proof	500.00

MINT SETS (MS)

KM#	Date	Mintage	Identification	Issue Price	Mkt. Val.
MS1	1986(6)	—	KM1-6	—	7.50
MS2	1991(6)	—	KM1-5,11	19.95	20.00

PROOF SETS (PS)

KM#	Date	Mintage	Identification	Issue Price	Mkt. Val.
PS1	1981(6)	5,000	KM1-6	29.00	20.00
PS2	1986(6)	2,500	KM1-6	30.75	20.00

Listings For

EAST GERMANY: refer to Germany

ECUADOR

The Republic of Ecuador, located astride the equator on the Pacific Coast of South America, has an area of 109,484 sq. mi. (283,560 sq. km.) and a population of 9.5 million. Capital: Quito. Agriculture is the mainstay of the economy but there are appreciable deposits of minerals and petroleum. It is one of the world's largest exporters of bananas and balsa wood. Coffee, cacao and sugar are also valuable exports.

Ecuador was first sighted, 1526, by Francisco Pizarro. Conquest was undertaken by Sebastian de Benalcazar, who founded Quito in 1534. Ecuador was incorporated in the Viceroyalty of New Granada through the 16th and 17th centuries. After previous attempts to attain independence were crushed, Antonio Sucre, the able lieutenant of Bolivar, won Ecuador's freedom on May 24, 1822. It then joined Venezuela and Colombia in a confederacy known as Gran Colombia, and became an independent republic when it left the confederacy in 1830.

MINT MARKS

BIRMm - Birmingham
D - Denver
H - Heaton, Birmingham
HEATON - Heaton, Birmingham
HEATON BIRMINGHAM
HF - LeLocle (Swiss)
LIMA - Lima
Mo - Mexico
PHILA.U.S.A. - Philadelphia
PHILADELPHIA - Philadelphia
QUITO - Quito
SANTIAGO - Chile

ASSAYERS INITIALS

FP - Feliciano Paredes
GJ - Guillermo Jameson
MV - Miguel Vergara
ST - Santiago Taylor

MONETARY SYSTEM

16 Reales = 1 Escudo

COUNTERMARKED COINAGE

1831
M.D.Q. - Moneda de Quito

1/4 REAL

SILVER
c/m: MDQ monogram on Colombia (Nueva Granada) 1/4 Real, KM#79.1.

KM#	Date	Mintage	Good	VG	Fine	VF
1	ND(1820)	—	—	—	Rare	—
	ND(1821)	—	—	—	Rare	—

c/m: MDQ monogram on Colombia (Nueva Granada) 1/4 Real, KM#79.2.

KM#	Date	Mintage	Good	VG	Fine	VF
2	ND(1821 Ba)	—	—	—	Rare	—

1/2 REAL

SILVER
c/m: MDQ monogram on Colombia (Cundinamarca) 1/2 Real, KM#8.

KM#	Date	Mintage	Good	VG	Fine	VF
3	ND(1821)	—	—	—	Rare	—

REAL

SILVER
c/m: MDQ monogram on Colombia (Nueva Granada) Real, KM#75.

KM#	Date	Mintage	Good	VG	Fine	VF
4	ND(1819 JF)	—	—	—	Rare	—

c/m: MDQ monogram on Colombia (Cundinamarca) Real, KM#9.

KM#	Date	Mintage	Good	VG	Fine	VF
5	ND(1821)	—	—	—	Rare	—

2 REALES

SILVER
c/m: MDQ monogram on Colombia (Nueva Granada) 2 Reales, KM#76.

KM#	Date	Mintage	Good	VG	Fine	VF
6	ND(1819 JF)	—	—	—	Rare	—

c/m: MDQ monogram on Colombia (Nueva Granada) 2 Reales, KM#77.

KM#	Date	Mintage	Good	VG	Fine	VF
7	ND(1819 JF)	—	—	—	Rare	—
	ND(1820 JF)	—	—	—	Rare	—

c/m: MDQ monogram on Colombia (Cundinamarca) 2 Reales, KM#5.

KM#	Date	Mintage	Good	VG	Fine	VF
8	ND(1820 JF)	—	—	—	Rare	—
	ND(1820 Ba JF)	—	—	—	Rare	—
	ND(1821 Ba JF)	—	150.00	250.00	350.00	500.00
	ND(1821 JF)	—	100.00	150.00	—	—
	ND(1823 JF)	—	—	—	Rare	—

8 REALES

SILVER
c/m: MDQ monogram on Colombia (Nueva Granada) 8 Reales, KM#78.

KM#	Date	Mintage	Good	VG	Fine	VF
9	ND(1819 JF)	—	—	—	Rare	—
	ND(1820/19 JF)	—	—	—	Rare	—
	ND(1820 JF)	—	—	—	Rare	—

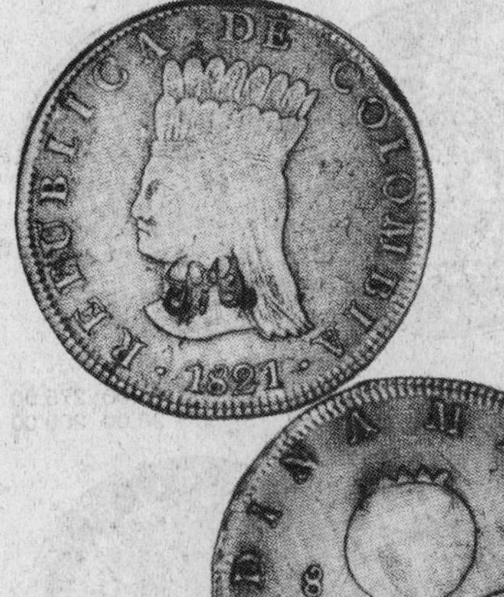

c/m: MDQ monogram on Colombia (Cundinamarca) 8 Reales, KM#6.

KM#	Date	Mintage	Good	VG	Fine	VF
10	ND(1820 JF)	—	—	—	Rare	—
	ND(1820 Ba JF)	—	—	—	Rare	—
	ND(1821 JF)	—	150.00	185.00	225.00	—
	ND(1821 Ba JF)	—	250.00	450.00	650.00	1250.

c/m: MDQ monogram on Colombia (Cundinamarca) 8 Reales, KM#7.

KM#	Date	Mintage	Good	VG	Fine	VF
11	ND(1820 JF)	—	—	—	Rare	—

REGULAR COINAGE

UN QUARTO (1/4) REAL

.333 SILVER, 0.72-.83 g

Obv: Fortress and 2 eliptical lines.

KM#	Date	Mintage	VG	Fine	VF	XF
25	1842 MV	—	300.00	500.00	750.00	1500.

14mm. Obv: Fortress and bird.

KM#	Date	Mintage	VG	Fine	VF	XF
26	1842 MV-S	—	100.00	250.00	400.00	550.00
	1843 MV	—	85.00	175.00	275.00	400.00
	1843 MV-A	—	45.00	115.00	225.00	350.00

NOTE: The A and S above are found on the mountain below the castle.

SILVER

KM#	Date	Mintage	VG	Fine	VF	XF
36	1849 GJ	—	13.50	30.00	60.00	85.00
	1850 GJ	—	25.00	45.00	75.00	145.00
	1851 GJ	—	17.50	40.00	60.00	85.00
	1852 GJ	—	9.00	20.00	45.00	75.00
	1855 GJ	—	15.00	32.50	65.00	90.00
	1856 GJ	—	15.00	32.50	65.00	90.00
	1862 GJ	—	325.00	625.00	850.00	1800.

1/2 REAL

.667 SILVER, 1.30 g
Obv. leg: EL ECUADOR EN COLOMBIA, MoR (Medio Real).

KM#	Date	Mintage	VG	Fine	VF	XF
12.1	1833 GJ	—	15.00	35.00	75.00	200.00
	1835 GJ	—	Reported, not confirmed			

Rev: Denomination 1/2 R

KM#	Date	Mintage	VG	Fine	VF	XF
12.2	1833 GJ	—	20.00	45.00	85.00	250.00
	1835 GJ	—	Reported, not confirmed			

Obv. leg: REPUBLICA DEL ECUADOR.

KM#	Date	Mintage	VG	Fine	VF	XF
22	1838 ST	—	8.50	20.00	45.00	175.00
	1840 MV	—	13.50	35.00	75.00	200.00
	1840 WV W is inverted M	—	37.50	85.00	120.00	200.00
	1843	—	Reported, not confirmed			

1.55-1.85 g, 15-17mm

KM#	Date	Mintage	VG	Fine	VF	XF
35	1848 GJ	—	8.50	18.50	40.00	90.00
	1849 GJ	—	13.50	25.00	55.00	125.00

REAL

.667 SILVER, 3.00-3.40 g
Obv. leg: EL ECUADOR EN COLOMBIA.

KM#	Date	Mintage	VG	Fine	VF	XF
13	1833 GJ	—	15.00	40.00	70.00	150.00
	1834 GJ	—	15.00	40.00	60.00	100.00
	1835 GJ	—	20.00	45.00	75.00	175.00
	1836 GJ	—	—	—	Rare	—

3.40-3.92 g
Obv. leg: REPUBLICA DEL ECUADOR.

KM#	Date	Mintage	VG	Fine	VF	XF
17	1836 GJ	—	15.00	40.00	85.00	175.00
	1836 FP	—	22.50	50.00	95.00	185.00
	1837 FP	—	—	—	Rare	—
	1838 ST	—	15.00	40.00	85.00	175.00
	1838 MV	—	45.00	120.00	225.00	400.00
	1839 MV	—	13.50	35.00	75.00	165.00

KM#	Date	Mintage	VG	Fine	VF	XF
17	1840 MV	—	13.50	35.00	75.00	150.00
	1841 MV	—	—	—	Rare	—

Obv. and rev. legends transposed.

KM#	Date	Mintage	VG	Fine	VF	XF
20	1837 FP	—	250.00	450.00	600.00	800.00
	1838 ST	—	100.00	175.00	275.00	400.00

2 REALES

.667 SILVER, 5.17-5.60 g, 25-27mm
Obv. leg: EL ECUADOR EN COLOMBIA.

KM#	Date	Mintage	VG	Fine	VF	XF
14	1833 GJ	—	60.00	125.00	200.00	400.00
	1834 GJ	—	17.50	35.00	75.00	175.00
	1834 JG	—	—	—	Rare	—
	1835 GJ	—	17.50	35.00	75.00	175.00
	1836 GJ	—	100.00	150.00	275.00	350.00

5.80-6.10 g
Obv. leg: REPUBLICA DEL ECUADOR

KM#	Date	Mintage	VG	Fine	VF	XF
18	1836 GJ	—	13.50	25.00	45.00	125.00
	1836 FP	—	15.00	32.50	60.00	175.00
	1837 FP	—	—	650.00	—	—
	1838 ST	—	17.50	35.00	60.00	175.00
	1838 MV	—	13.50	25.00	45.00	125.00
	1839/8 MV	—	30.00	50.00	—	—
	1839 MV	—	17.50	35.00	60.00	175.00
	1839 MV A is inverted V in LA					
		—	27.50	45.00	95.00	200.00
	1840 MV	—	20.00	40.00	75.00	175.00
	1840 MV V is inverted A					
		—	25.00	50.00	90.00	225.00
	1841 MV	—	30.00	55.00	80.00	200.00

Obv. and rev. legends transposed.

KM#	Date	Mintage	VG	Fine	VF	XF
21	1837 FP	—	22.50	45.00	90.00	225.00
	1838 ST	—	90.00	125.00	200.00	375.00

5.50-6.05 g

KM#	Date	Mintage	VG	Fine	VF	XF
33	1847 GJ	—	12.50	25.00	55.00	200.00
	1848/7 GJ	—	12.50	25.00	65.00	250.00
	1848	—	15.00	30.00	90.00	300.00
	1849 GJ	—	12.50	25.00	55.00	200.00
	1850 GJ	—	12.50	25.00	55.00	200.00
	1851 GJ	—	12.50	25.00	55.00	200.00
	1852 GJ	—	12.50	25.00	55.00	200.00

Obv: 2 R flanking arms.
Rev: Liberty head w/long hair.

KM#	Date	Mintage	VG	Fine	VF	XF
38	1857 GJ	—	500.00	1000.	1800.	3250.
	1862 GJ	—	750.00	1500.	2500.	4500.

6.7600 g, .666 SILVER, .1447 oz ASW
Rev: Liberty head w/short hair.

KM#	Date	Mintage	VG	Fine	VF	XF
40	1862 GJ	—	750.00	1500.	2000.	4000.

4 REALES

.667 SILVER, 12.30-12.75 g

KM#	Date	Mintage	VG	Fine	VF	XF
24	1841 MV	—	15.00	35.00	75.00	250.00
	1841 MV V is inverted A					
		—	25.00	50.00	100.00	300.00
	1842 MV	—	15.00	35.00	75.00	250.00
	1843 MV	—	15.00	35.00	75.00	250.00

12.30 g

KM#	Date	Mintage	VG	Fine	VF	XF
27	1844 MV-A	—	250.00	450.00	750.00	—

NOTE: The A above is found on the breast of the condor.

11.70 g

KM#	Date	Mintage	VG	Fine	VF	XF
29	1845 MV-A	—	250.00	450.00	750.00	—

NOTE: The A above is found on the breast of the condor.

13.35 g

KM#	Date	Mintage	VG	Fine	VF	XF
37	1855 GJ	—	17.50	42.50	125.00	275.00
	1857 GJ	—	12.50	37.50	90.00	200.00

13.4300 g, .666 SILVER, .2876 oz ASW

KM#	Date	Mintage	VG	Fine	VF	XF
37a	1862 GJ	—	900.00	2000.	3000.	4500.

KM#	Date	Mintage	VG	Fine	VF	XF
41	1862	—	60.00	135.00	250.00	500.00

8 REALES

25.0000 g, .900 SILVER, .7234 oz ASW

KM#	Date	Mintage	VG	Fine	VF	XF
32	1846 GJ	—	750.00	1000.	1500.	3000.

5 FRANCOS

25.0000 g, .900 SILVER, .7234 oz ASW

KM#	Date	Mintage	VG	Fine	VF	XF
39	1858 GJ	—	125.00	250.00	375.00	1000.

ESCUDO

3.3000 g, .875 GOLD, .0928 oz AGW

KM#	Date	Mintage	VG	Fine	VF	XF
15	1828	—	—	—	—	—
	1833 GJ	—	90.00	300.00	350.00	525.00
	1834 GJ	—	90.00	300.00	350.00	525.00
	1835 GJ	—	115.00	325.00	400.00	575.00
	1845 GJ	—	—	—	—	—

NOTE: The 1828 dated coins are considered contemporary counterfeits. The 1845 dated coins are suspicious.

DOUBLE ESCUDO

6.7666 g, .875 GOLD, .1903 oz AGW

KM#	Date	Mintage	VG	Fine	VF	XF
16	1833 GJ	—	—	—	Rare	—
	1834 GJ	—	500.00	800.00	1200.	—
	1835 GJ	—	250.00	450.00	750.00	1600.
	1835 FP					
	2 known	—	—	—	Rare	—

4 ESCUDOS

13.5000 g, .875 GOLD, .3798 oz AGW

KM#	Date	Mintage	VG	Fine	VF	XF
19	1836 FP-A	—	250.00	400.00	650.00	1100.
	1837 FP-A	—	225.00	325.00	550.00	950.00
	1838 FP-A	—	700.00	1350.	2100.	3500.
	1838 ST-A	3 to 4 pcs. known		2000.	3500.	—
	1838 MV-A	—	425.00	900.00	1350.	2250.
	1839 MV-A	—	400.00	700.00	1250.	2000.
	1841 MV-A	1 known	—	—	5000.	—

NOTE: Engravers initial A in front drape of bust.

8 ESCUDOS

27.0640 g, .875 GOLD, .7614 oz AGW

KM#	Date	Mintage	VG	Fine	VF	XF
23.1	1838 ST-A	—	750.00	2000.	3000.	4000.
	1838 MV-A	—	750.00	2000.	3500.	5000.
	1839 MV-A	—	550.00	1000.	2000.	3000.
	1840 MV-A	—	500.00	850.00	1700.	2500.
	1841 MV-A	—	400.00	700.00	1500.	2250.

NOTE: Engravers initial A in front drape of bust.

Reduced size.

KM#	Date	Mintage	VG	Fine	VF	XF
23.2	1841 MV-S	—	750.00	2000.	3000.	3500.
	1842 MV-S	—	500.00	850.00	1700.	2500.
	1843 MV-S	—	500.00	850.00	1850.	2800.

NOTE: Engravers initial S sideways in back drape of bust.

KM#	Date	Mintage	VG	Fine	VF	XF
28	1844 MV	—	—	—	*Rare	—
	1845 MV	—	—	—	Rare	—

***NOTE:** Stack's Hammel sale 9-82 VF/G 1844 MV realized $32,000.

Obv: Flagpoles extend below arms.

KM#	Date	Mintage	VG	Fine	VF	XF
30	1845 MV	—	3000.	4500.	5500.	—

Obv: W/o flagpoles below arms.

KM#	Date	Mintage	VG	Fine	VF	XF
31	1845 MV	—	—	3000.	4500.	5750.

KM#	Date	Mintage	VG	Fine	VF	XF
34.1	1847 GJ	—	—	2250.	3250.	5000.
	1848 GJ	—	—	2500.	3500.	5500.
	1849/7 GJ	—	—	Reported, not confirmed		
	1849 GJ	—	—	2500.	3500.	5500.
	1850 GJ	—	—	1500.	2250.	3000.
	1852/0 GJ	—	—	1200.	2000.	2500.
	1854 GJ	—	—	1500.	2250.	3500.
	1855/2 GJ	—	—	1000.	1800.	2200.
	1855 GJ	—	—	1500.	2250.	3500.

Rev: Larger bust w/different hairstyle.

KM#	Date	Mintage	VG	Fine	VF	XF
34.2	1856 GJ	—	—	1500.	2250.	3500.

DECIMAL COINAGE

10 Centavos = 1 Decimo
10 Decimos = 1 Sucre
25 Sucres = 1 Condor

MEDIO (1/2) CENTAVO

COPPER-NICKEL
Mint mark: HEATON BIRMINGHAM

KM#	Date	Mintage	Fine	VF	XF	Unc
47	1884	.600	10.00	15.00	27.50	50.00
	1884	—	—	—	Proof	175.00
	1886	.400	— Reported, not confirmed			

COPPER

KM#	Date	Mintage	Fine	VF	XF	Unc
54	1890H	2.000	5.00	15.00	25.00	60.00

COPPER-NICKEL

KM#	Date	Mintage	Fine	VF	XF	Unc
57	1909H	4.000	2.00	5.00	10.00	30.00

UN (1) CENTAVO

COPPER

KM#	Date	Mintage	Fine	VF	XF	Unc
45	1872HEATON	—	12.50	20.00	50.00	100.00
	1872HEATON	—	—	—	Proof	250.00
	1890H	2.000	4.00	10.00	22.50	75.00

COPPER-NICKEL
Mint mark: HEATON BIRMINGHAM

KM#	Date	Mintage	Fine	VF	XF	Unc
48	1884	.500	7.50	20.00	45.00	100.00
	1884	—	—	—	Proof	175.00
	1886	1.000	5.00	12.50	25.00	65.00

KM#	Date	Mintage	Fine	VF	XF	Unc
58	1909H	3.000	2.00	5.00	11.00	30.00

BRONZE

KM#	Date	Mintage	Fine	VF	XF	Unc
67	1928	2.016	.50	1.00	2.50	5.00

DOS (2) CENTAVOS

COPPER
Mint mark: HEATON

KM#	Date	Mintage	Fine	VF	XF	Unc
46	1872	—	18.00	35.00	70.00	150.00
	1872	—	—	—	Proof	250.00

COPPER-NICKEL

KM#	Date	Mintage	Fine	VF	XF	Unc
59	1909H	2.500	3.00	6.50	15.00	50.00

DOS Y MEDIO (2-1/2) CENTAVOS

COPPER-NICKEL

61	1917	1.600	4.50	12.50	25.00	65.00

NICKEL

68	1928	4.000	1.25	2.75	7.50	22.50

MEDIO (1/2) DECIMO

COPPER-NICKEL
Mint mark: HEATON. BIRMINGHAM.

49	1884	.600	6.50	15.00	32.50	75.00
	1884	—	—	—	Proof	200.00
	1886	.600	5.75	15.00	30.00	70.00

1.2500 g, .900 SILVER, .0361 oz ASW
Mint mark: LIMA

55.1	1893 TF rev: "G.1.250"					
		1.718	1.00	1.75	3.50	8.00
	1893 TF rev: "G.1:250"					
		Inc. Ab.	1.00	1.75	3.50	8.00
	1894/3 TF	.243	2.75	4.50	8.50	20.00
	1897 JF	.800	1.75	2.50	4.50	10.00
	1899/87 JF					
		.560	2.00	4.00	9.00	22.50
	1899 JF	I.A.	1.50	3.00	7.00	15.00
	1899 JF (error) obv: ECUADO.R					
		Inc. Ab.	1.50	3.00	10.00	25.00
	1902/892 JF					
		1.000	1.00	1.75	4.50	10.00
	1902 JF	I.A.	.75	1.25	3.00	7.00
	1905/805 JF					
		.500	2.00	4.00	9.00	22.50
	1905/2 JF	I.A.	2.50	5.00	10.00	25.00
	1905 JF	I.A.	.75	1.25	3.00	8.00
	1912/05 FG					
		.020	2.00	4.00	10.00	25.00
	1912 FG	I.A.	.75	1.25	3.00	7.00
	1912 FG (error) obv: FCUADOR					
		Inc. Ab.	2.00	3.00	5.00	15.00

Mint mark: BIRMm.
Modified reverse.

55.2	1915	2.000	.75	1.25	3.00	8.00

CINCO (5) CENTAVOS

COPPER-NICKEL

Obv: Ribbon tails on flag poles point outward.

KM#	Date	Mintage	Fine	VF	XF	Unc
60.1	1909H	2.000	3.50	10.00	27.50	60.00

Thin planchet
Obv: Ribbon tails on flag poles point downward.

60.2	1917	1.200	4.50	12.50	32.00	70.00
	1918	7.980	1.00	2.50	5.00	10.00

63	1919 rev: 3 berries to left of "C"					
		12.000	.60	1.25	3.50	7.50
	1919 rev: 4 berries loose to left of "C"					
		Inc. Ab.	1.25	2.50	7.00	15.00
	1919 rev: 4 berries tight to left of "C"					
		Inc. Ab.	1.25	2.50	7.00	15.00

65	1924H	10.000	1.00	1.75	4.00	9.00

NICKEL

69	1928	16.000	.75	1.00	2.00	4.50

75	1937HF	15.000	.10	.20	.35	.75

BRASS

75a	1942	2.000	.50	1.25	2.50	5.75
	1944D	3.000	.50	1.00	2.00	3.75

COPPER-NICKEL

75b	1946	40.000	—	—	.10	.25

NICKEL-CLAD STEEL

75c	1970	—	—	—	.10	.25
	1970 obv: ECADOR(error)					
		—	—	—	—	—

UN (1) DECIMO

2.5000 g, .900 SILVER, .0723 oz ASW
Mint mark: HEATON/BIRMINGHAM
Rev: LEI in legend.

KM#	Date	Mintage	VG	Fine	VF	XF
50.1	1884	.050	3.00	6.00	18.00	60.00
	1884	—	—	—	Proof	300.00
	1889	.100	1.00	3.00	15.00	35.00
	1890	.150	2.00	5.00	15.00	40.00

Mint mark: SANTIAGO-CHILE

50.2	1889/789 DT					
		1.000	6.00	10.00	25.00	65.00
	1889 DT	I.A.	2.00	4.00	8.00	20.00

Mint mark: LIMA
Rev. leg: W/o LEI.

50.3	1892 TF	.350	2.00	3.00	10.00	22.50
	1893 TF	.848	.75	1.75	3.00	7.00
	1894 TF	.206	.75	2.00	4.00	12.00
	1899/4 JF/TF					
		.220	2.00	3.00	8.00	20.00

KM#	Date	Mintage	VG	Fine	VF	XF
50.3	1899 JF	I.A.	3.00	6.00	15.00	42.50
	1900 JF/TF rev: w/JR below fasces					
		.480	2.00	3.50	7.00	17.50
	1900 JF	I.A.	1.00	2.50	5.00	10.00
	1900 JF rev: w/o JR below fasces					
		Inc. Ab.	2.00	3.00	6.00	12.50
	1902 JF rev: W/JR below fasces					
		.519	1.00	2.50	5.00	10.00
	1902 JF rev: w/o JR below fasces					
		Inc. Ab.	1.00	2.50	5.00	10.00
	1905 JF	.250	1.00	2.50	5.00	10.00
	1912 FG	.030	2.00	3.00	6.00	15.00

Mint mark: BIRMm
Modified reverse

50.4	1915	1.000	BV	1.25	2.00	7.00

Mint mark: PHILA.

50.5	1916	2.000	BV	1.25	2.00	5.00

DIEZ (10) CENTAVOS

COPPER-NICKEL

KM#	Date	Mintage	Fine	VF	XF	Unc
62	1918	1.000	5.50	11.00	18.50	37.50

64	1919	2.000	1.00	2.00	4.00	10.00

66	1924H	5.000	.75	1.50	3.00	9.00
	1924H	—	—	—	Proof	100.00

NOTE: The H mint mark is very small and is located above the date.

NICKEL

70	1928	16.000	.50	1.00	2.50	8.00

76	1937HF	7.500	.25	.50	1.00	2.50

BRASS

76a	1942	5.000	.60	1.00	1.75	2.50

COPPER-NICKEL

76b	1946	40.000	.10	.15	.25	1.00

NICKEL-CLAD STEEL

76c	1964	20.000	—	—	.10	.25
	1968	15.000	—	—	.10	.25
	1972	20.000	—	—	.10	.15

COPPER-NICKEL CLAD STEEL

76d	1976	10.000	—	—	.10	.15

NOTE: Varieties exist.

DOS (2) DECIMOS

5.0000 g, .900 SILVER, .1446 oz ASW
Mint mark: HEATON/BIRMINGHAM
Rev: LEI in legend.

KM#	Date	Mintage	VG	Fine	VF	XF
51.1	1884	.025	5.00	8.00	15.00	25.00
	1884	—	—	—	Proof	600.00
	1889	.050	6.00	12.00	25.00	40.00
	1890	.075	4.00	7.50	12.50	35.00

Mint mark: SANTIAGO-CHILE

KM#	Date	Mintage	VG	Fine	VF	XF
51.2	1889 DT	1.000	2.00	4.50	8.50	17.50
	1891 DT	.230	4.00	7.50	12.50	25.00

Mint mark: LIMA. or LIMA
Rev. leg: W/o LEI.

KM#	Date	Mintage	VG	Fine	VF	XF
51.3	1889 TF	.075	4.00	7.50	12.50	30.00
	1891/89 TF	.025	5.00	7.50	12.50	30.00
	1892/89 TF	1.138	2.00	4.00	7.50	18.00
	1892 TF	I.A.	6.00	12.00	25.00	40.00
	1893/89 TF	.390	2.00	5.00	8.00	22.00
	1894/89 TF	.409	2.00	5.00	8.00	20.00
	1895/89 TF	.160	3.00	5.00	8.00	20.00
	1896/89 TF	.109	3.00	5.00	8.00	20.00
	1912 FG	.050	5.00	7.50	10.00	25.00
	1914 FG	.110	3.00	5.00	8.00	20.00
	1914 FG	I.A.	2.00	4.00	7.00	15.00
	1915 FG	.157	3.00	5.00	8.00	20.00

NOTE: Small "R" below fasces on rev. 1912-15.

Mint mark: PHILADELPHIA

KM#	Date	Mintage	VG	Fine	VF	XF
51.4	1895 TF	5.000	1.50	3.00	4.00	6.50
	1895 TF	—	—	—	Proof	500.00
	1914 TF	2.500	1.50	3.00	4.50	7.50
	1916 TF	1.000	1.50	3.00	4.50	7.50

20 CENTAVOS

KM#	Date	Mintage	Fine	VF	XF	Unc
		NICKEL				
77	1937HF	7.500	.25	.50	1.00	1.50
		BRASS				
77a	1942	5.000	.60	1.00	2.00	4.50
	1944D	15.000	.40	.75	1.50	3.75
		COPPER-NICKEL				
77b	1946	30.000	.10	.20	.35	.50
		NICKEL-CLAD STEEL				
77c	1959	14.400	—	—	.15	.35
	1962	14.400	—	—	.15	.35
	1966	24.000	—	—	.15	.35
	1969	24.000	—	—	.15	.35
	1971	12.000	—	—	.15	.35
	1972	48.432	—	—	.15	.35

COPPER-NICKEL
Obv: Modified coat of arms.

KM#	Date	Mintage	Fine	VF	XF	Unc
77d	1974	72.000	—	—	.15	.35
		NICKEL-COATED STEEL				
77e	1975	—	—	—	.15	.35
	1980	18.000	—	—	.15	.35
	1981	21.000	—	—	.15	.35
		COPPER-NICKEL COATED STEEL				
77f	1978	37.500	—	—	.15	.35

MEDIO (1/2) SUCRE

12.5000 g, .900 SILVER, .3617 oz ASW
Mint mark: HEATON/BIRMINGHAM

KM#	Date	Mintage	VG	Fine	VF	XF
52	1884	.020	20.00	30.00	60.00	250.00
	1884	—	—	—	Proof	1000.

CINQUENTA (50) CENTAVOS

2.5000 g, .720 SILVER, .0579 oz ASW
Mint mark: PHILA • U • S • A

KM#	Date	Mintage	Fine	VF	XF	Unc
71	1928	1.000	1.00	2.00	3.50	7.50
	1930	.155	2.50	5.00	10.00	25.00

NICKEL-CLAD STEEL

KM#	Date	Mintage	Fine	VF	XF	Unc
81	1963	20.000	—	.15	.25	.60
	1971	5.000	—	.15	.25	.60
	1974	—	—	.15	.25	.60
	1975	—	—	.15	.25	.60
	1977	40.000	—	.10	.20	.50
	1979	25.000	—	.10	.20	.50
	1982	20.000	—	.10	.20	.50

Obv: Modified coat of arms.

KM#	Date	Mintage	Fine	VF	XF	Unc
87	1985	30.000	—	.10	.20	.40

KM#	Date	Mintage	Fine	VF	XF	Unc
90	1988	*	—	—	—	.30
	1988	25 pcs.	—	—	Proof	—

***NOTE:** Withdrawn from circulation and remelted, approximately 100,000 pieces released.

UN (1) SUCRE

25.0000 g, .900 SILVER, .7234 oz ASW
Mint mark: HEATON/BIRMINGHAM

KM#	Date	Mintage	VG	Fine	VF	XF
53.1	1884	.250	6.50	12.50	20.00	40.00
	1884	—	—	—	Proof	2000.
	1888	.100	10.00	20.00	35.00	75.00
	1889	.150	6.50	12.50	20.00	40.00
	1890	.012	40.00	80.00	125.00	300.00
	1892	.060	20.00	40.00	65.00	150.00
	1895	.102	15.00	25.00	35.00	75.00

Mint mark: SANTIAGO-CHILE

KM#	Date	Mintage	VG	Fine	VF	XF
53.2	1888 DT	.373	6.50	12.50	20.00	40.00
	1889 DT	.327	6.50	12.50	20.00	40.00

Mint mark: LIMA

KM#	Date	Mintage	VG	Fine	VF	XF
53.3	1890 TF	.287	6.50	12.50	17.50	35.00
	1891 TF	.143	6.50	12.50	17.50	35.00
	1892 TF	.058	20.00	40.00	60.00	120.00
	1895 TF	.174	6.50	12.50	17.50	35.00
	1896 TF	.148	20.00	30.00	60.00	120.00
	1896 F	Inc. Ab.	20.00	30.00	50.00	100.00
	1897 JF	.462	6.50	12.50	17.50	35.00

5.0000 g, .720 SILVER, .1157 oz ASW
Mint mark: PHILA • U • S • A

KM#	Date	Mintage	Fine	VF	XF	Unc
72	1928	3.000	1.75	2.50	5.00	12.50
	1930	.400	4.00	8.00	16.00	30.00
	1934	2.000	1.75	2.50	5.00	12.50

NICKEL, 26.5mm

KM#	Date	Mintage	Fine	VF	XF	Unc
78.1	1937 HF	9.000	.50	.75	1.50	4.00
		25.9mm				
78.2	1946	18.000	.40	.60	.80	2.00

COPPER-NICKEL
Obv: Different ship in coat of arms.

KM#	Date	Mintage	Fine	VF	XF	Unc
78a	1959	8.400	.25	.50	.65	1.00
	1959	—	—	—	Proof	125.00

NICKEL-CLAD STEEL
Obv: Ship in arms similar to KM#78.

KM#	Date	Mintage	Fine	VF	XF	Unc
78b	1964	20.000	—	.10	.25	.50
	1970	24.000	—	.10	.25	.50
	1971	8.092	—	.10	.25	.50
	1974	40.308	—	.10	.25	.50
	1978	32.000	—	.10	.25	.50
	1979	32.000	—	.10	.25	.50
	1980	110.000	—	.10	.25	.50
	1981	70.000	—	.10	.25	.50

Obv: Modified coat of arms, ship similar to KM#78a.

KM#	Date	Mintage	Fine	VF	XF	Unc
83	1974	23.100	—	.10	.20	.40
	1975	.592	—	.10	.20	.50
	1975	—	—	—	Proof	150.00
	1977	32.000	—	.10	.20	.35

Obv: Modified coat of arms.

KM#	Date	Mintage	Fine	VF	XF	Unc
85	1985	—	—	—	—	.25
	1986	—	—	—	—	.25

KM#	Date	Mintage	Fine	VF	XF	Unc
89	1988	*	—	—	—	.40
	1988	25 pcs.	—	—	Proof	—
	1990	—	—	—	—	.40

*NOTE: Reportedly withdrawn from circulation and remelted, approximately 100,000 pieces released.

DOS (2) SUCRES

10.0000 g, .720 SILVER, .2315 oz ASW
Mint mark: PHILA / U / S / A

KM#	Date	Mintage	Fine	VF	XF	Unc
73	1928	.500	3.50	7.00	15.00	30.00
	1930	.100	10.00	15.00	30.00	60.00

Mint mark: Mo/MEXICO

KM#	Date	Mintage	Fine	VF	XF	Unc
80	1944	1.000	2.50	3.50	4.50	7.00

COPPER-NICKEL

KM#	Date	Mintage	Fine	VF	XF	Unc
82	1973	*2.500	—	—	—	—

*NOTE: Not released to circulation, all but approximately 35 pieces were remelted.

CINCO (5) SUCRES

25.0000 g, .720 SILVER, .5787 oz ASW
Mint mark: Mo/MEXICO

KM#	Date	Mintage	Fine	VF	XF	Unc
79	1943	1.000	—	BV	6.00	10.00
	1944	2.600	—	BV	5.00	8.00

COPPER-NICKEL

KM#	Date	Mintage	Fine	VF	XF	Unc
84	1973	*500 pcs.	—	—	—	—

*NOTE: Only 7 pieces were distributed to Ecuadorian government officials, while 8 pieces (5 of these cancelled) reside in the Central Bank Collection. The remaining 485 pieces have been remelted.

NICKEL-CLAD STEEL

KM#	Date	Mintage	Fine	VF	XF	Unc
91	1988	*	—	—	—	.40
	1988	25 pcs.	—	—	Proof	—
	1991	—	—	—	—	.40

*NOTE: Reportedly withdrawn from circulation and remelted, approximately 100,000 pieces released.

DIEZ (10) SUCRES

8.1360 g, .900 GOLD, .2354 oz AGW
Mint mark: BIRMINGHAM

KM#	Date	Mintage	Fine	VF	XF	Unc
56	1899 JM	.050	100.00	125.00	150.00	275.00
	1900 JM	.050	100.00	125.00	150.00	275.00

NICKEL CLAD STEEL

KM#	Date	Mintage	Fine	VF	XF	Unc
92	1988	*	—	—	—	.75
	1988	25 pcs.	—	—	Proof	—
	1991	—	—	—	—	.75

*NOTE: Withdrawn from circulation and remelted, approximately 100,000 pieces released.

20 SUCRES

NICKEL CLAD STEEL

KM#	Date	Mintage	Fine	VF	XF	Unc
94	1988	—	—	—	—	1.00
	1988	25 pcs.	—	—	Proof	—
	1991	—	—	—	—	1.00

50 SUCRES

NICKEL CLAD STEEL

KM#	Date	Mintage	Fine	VF	XF	Unc
93	1988	*	—	—	—	3.00
	1988	25 pcs.	—	—	Proof	—

*NOTE: Withdrawn from circulation and remelted, approximately 100,000 pieces released.

1000 SUCRES

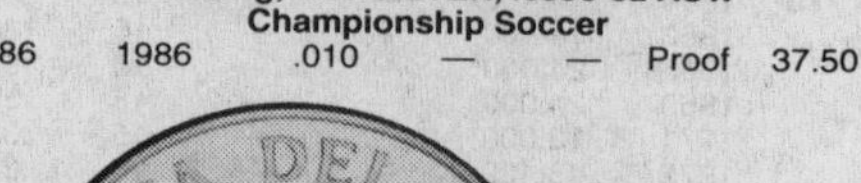

23.3300 g, .925 SILVER, .6938 oz ASW
Championship Soccer

KM#	Date	Mintage	Fine	VF	XF	Unc
86	1986	.010	—	—	Proof	37.50

Championship Soccer

KM#	Date	Mintage	Fine	VF	XF	Unc
88	1986	*.010	—	—	Proof	37.50

5000 SUCRES

27.0000 g, .925 SILVER, .8029 oz ASW
Ibero - American Series

KM#	Date	Mintage	Fine	VF	XF	Unc
95	1991	.050	—	—	Proof	45.00

UN (1) CONDOR

8.3592 g, .900 GOLD, .2419 oz AGW
Mint mark: BIRMINGHAM

KM#	Date	Mintage	Fine	VF	XF	Unc
74	1928	.020	100.00	150.00	200.00	350.00

PROOF SETS (PS)

KM#	Date	Mintage	Identification	Issue Price	Mkt. Val.
PS1	1988(6)	25	KM89-94	—	—

GALAPAGOS ISLANDS

The Galapagos Islands, a territory of Ecuador situated in the Pacific Ocean 650 miles west of Ecuador, have an area of 3,028 sq. mi. (7,842 sq. km.) and a population of 3,100. Capital: San Cristobal, on the island of that name. The archipelago of more than 60 islands scattered over 23,000 sq. mi. of the Pacific was discovered by the Spaniards early in the 16th century, and became part of Ecuador in 1832. The islands are notable for their unique plant and animal life, including 15 species of giant tortoise which are the longest-lived animals on earth, with life spans of more than 200 years.

COUNTERMARKED COINAGE

c/m: Script RA on 1/2 Decimo, KM#55.
c/m: Script RA on 1 Decimo, KM#50.
c/m: Script RA on 2 Decimos, KM#51.
c/m: Script RA on 1/2 Sucre, KM#52.
c/m: Script RA on Un Sucre, KM#53.

Until recently the script RA countermarks, believed to be initials of a well known merchant, Rogelio Alvarado, were attributed to the Galapagos Islands where it was believed the coins were used to pay prisoners in a penal colony. Without documentation these pieces must be considered suspect.

EGYPT

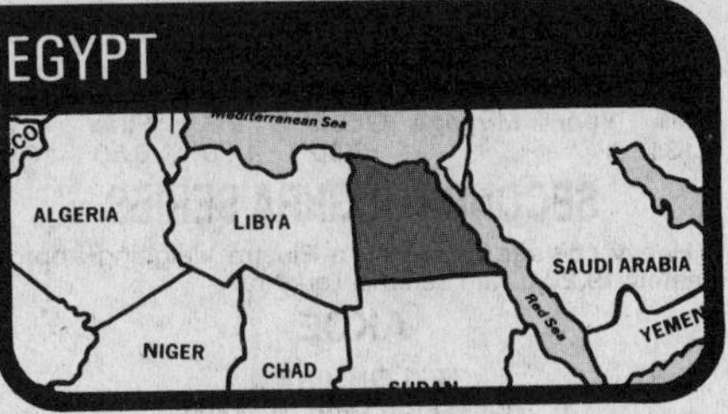

The Arab Republic of Egypt, located on the northeastern corner of Africa, has an area of 386,102 sq. mi. (1,1001,450 sq. km.) and a population of *54.8 million. Capital: Cairo. Although Egypt is an almost rainless expanse of desert, its economy is predominantly agricultural.Cotton, rice and petroleum are exported. Other main sources of income are revenues from the Suez Canal, remittances of Egyptian workers abroad and tourism.

Egyptian history dates back to about 3000 B.C. when the empire was established by uniting the upper and lower kingdoms. Following its 'Golden Age' (16th to 13th centuries B.C.), Egypt was conquered by Persia (525 B.C.) and Alexander the Great (332 B.C.). The Ptolemies, descended from one of Alexander's generals, ruled until the suicide of Cleopatra (30 B.C.) when Egypt became the private domain of the Roman emperor, and subsequently part of the Byzantine world. Various Muslim dynasties ruled Egypt from 641 on, including Ayyubid Sultans to 1250 and Mamluks to 1517, when it was conquered by the Ottoman Turks, interrupted by the occupation of Napoleon (1798-1801). A semi-independent dynasty was founded by Muhammad Ali in 1805 which lasted until 1952. Turkish rule became increasingly casual, permitting Great Britain to inject its influence by purchasing shares in the Suez Canal. British troops occupied Egypt in 1882, becoming the de facto rulers. On Dec. 14, 1914, Egypt was made a protectorate of Britain. British occupation ended on Feb. 28, 1922, when Egypt became a sovereign, independent kingdom. The monarchy was abolished and a republic proclaimed on July 23, 1952.

On Feb. 1, 1958, Egypt and Syria formed the United Arab Republic. Yemen joined on March 8 in an association known as the United Arab States. Syria withdrew from the United Arab Republic on Sept. 29, 1961, and on Dec. 26 Egypt dissolved its ties with Yemen in the United Arab States. On Sept. 2, 1971, Egypt finally shed the name United Arab Republic in favor of the Arab Republic of Egypt.

RULERS

Ottoman, until 1882

Local Viceroys

Muhammad Ali, 1805-1848
Ibrahim Pasha, 1848
Abbas I Pasha, 1848-1854
Sa'id Pasha, 1854-1863

Local Kedives

Isma'il Pasha, 1863-1879
Mohammed Tewfik Pasha, 1879

British, 1882-1922

Local Kedives

Mohammed Tewfik Pasha, 1882
Abbas II Hilmi, 1892-1914

Local Sultans

Hussein Kamil, 1914-1917
Ahmed Fuad I, 1917-1922

Kingdom, 1922-1952
Ahmed Fuad I, 1922-1936
Farouk I, 1936-1952
Fuad II, 1952-1953

Republic, 1952

MONETARY SYSTEM

40 Paras = 1 Qirsh (Piastre) (1885-1916)
10 Ochr-al-Qirsh = 1 Piastre (Commencing 1916)
10 Milliemes = 1 Piastre (Qirsh)
100 Piastres = 1 Pound (Gunayh)

MINT MARKS

Egyptian coins issued prior to the advent of the British Protectorate series of Sultan Hussein Kamil introduced in 1916 were very similar to Turkish coins of the same period. They can best be distinguished by the presence of the Arabic word *Misr* (Egypt) on the reverse, which generally appears immediately above the Muslim accession date of the ruler, which is presented in Arabic numerals. Each coin is individually dated according to the regnal years.

BP - Budapest, Hungary
H - Birmingham, England
KN - King's Norton, England

ENGRAVER

W - Emil Weigand, Berlin

INITIAL LETTERS, NUMERALS

Alif ا i	ba ب ii	ha ح iii	ha ح iv	dal د v
ra ر vi	sin س vii	sad ص viii	(?) sm صم ix	ta ط x
tha ظ xi	'ain ع xii	(hamza) ء xiii	kaf ق xiv	mim م xv
noon ن xvi	noon w/o dot ں xvii	ha هو xviii	(?) ra ر xix	ah اح xx
es اس xxi	ba با xxii	bkr بكر xxiii	ha حا xxiv	raa را xxv
ragib راغب xxvi	sma سما xxvii	msi مصى xxviii	'aa عا xxvix	gha غا xxx
'ab عب xxxi	'abd عبد xxxii	'ad عد xxxiii	'an عن xxxiv	md مد xxxv
mr مر xxxvi	mk مصط xxxvii	mdm مصر xxxviii	mha مها xxxix	ha ه xl
ya يا xli	42a ١٣٤ xlii	md6 مد٦ xliii	6md ٦مد xliv	6mdm ٦مصر xlv

REGNAL YEAR IDENTIFICATION

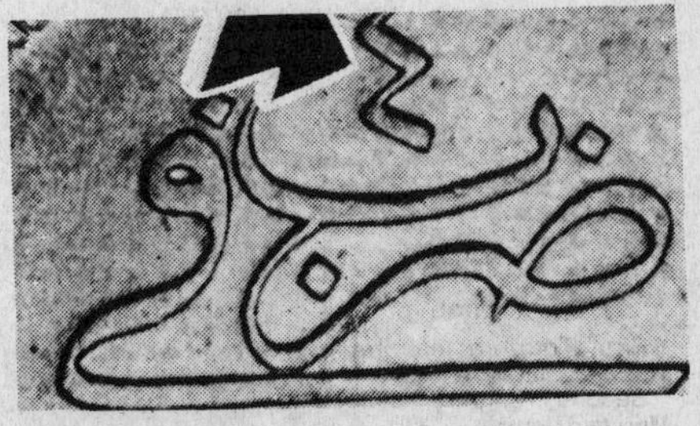

4
Duriba fi

Misr Accession Date

DENOMINATIONS

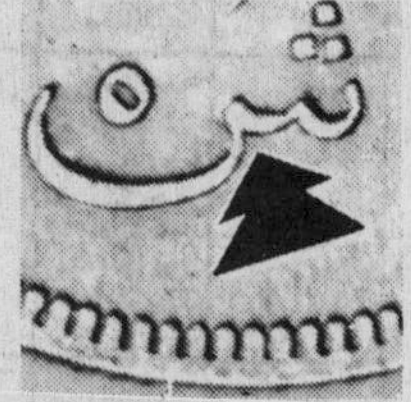

Para *Qirsh*

NOTE: The unit of value on coins of this period is generally presented on the obverse immediately below the toughra, as shown in the illustrations above.

Piastres 1916-1933

Milliemes *Piastres* 1934 -

TITLES

 المصرية

al-Mamlaka *al-Misriya*
(The Kingdom of Egypt)

U.A.R. EGYPT

The legend illustrated is *Jumhuriyat Misr al-'Arabiyya* which translates to 'The Arab Republic of Egypt'. Similar legends are found on the modern issues of Syria.

OTTOMAN COINAGE

SELIM III

AH1203-1212, 1216-1222/
1789-1798, 1801-1807AD

Toughra Types

First Second

First Toughra inscribed *Han Selim bin-Mustafa al-Muzaffer Dai'ma.*
Second Toughra inscribed *Selim Han bin-Mustafa al-Muzaffer Dai'ma.*

FIRST TOUGHRA SERIES

Heavy coinage based on a Piastre weighing approximately 19.20 g with first Toughra.

PARA

BILLON, 0.35 g
Accession Date: AH1203

KM#	Year	Mintage	Good	VG	Fine	VF
A134	1	—	3.00	4.50	6.50	10.00

SECOND TOUGHRA SERIES

Heavy coinage based on a Piastre weighing approximately 19.20 g with second Toughra.

AKCE

BILLON, 0.15 g
Accession Date: AH1203

KM#	Year	Mintage	Good	VG	Fine	VF
133	15	—	— Reported, not confirmed			
	16	—	— Reported, not confirmed			

NOTE: Earlier dates (Yr. 1-11) exist for this type.

PARA

BILLON, 0.35 g
Accession Date: AH1203

KM#	Year	Mintage	Good	VG	Fine	VF
134	14	—	3.00	4.50	6.50	10.00
	15	—	3.00	4.50	6.50	10.00
	16	—	3.00	4.50	6.50	10.00
	17	—	3.00	6.00	10.00	20.00
	18	—	3.00	6.00	10.00	20.00
	19	—	3.00	6.00	10.00	25.00
	20	—	3.00	6.00	10.00	35.00
	21	—	5.00	10.00	20.00	50.00
	22	—	—	—	—	—
	23	—	—	—	—	—

NOTE: Earlier dates (Yr. 1-12) exist for this type.

5 PARA

BILLON, 1.60 g
Accession Date: AH1203

KM#	Year	Mintage	Good	VG	Fine	VF
135	16	—	50.00	100.00	150.00	250.00

NOTE: Earlier date (Yr. 12) exists for this type.

10 PARA

BILLON, 2.45 g
Accession Date: AH1203

KM#	Year	Mintage	Good	VG	Fine	VF
136	16	—	300.00	600.00	1000.	1400.

20 PARA

BILLON, 27.5-29mm, 6.90 g
Accession Date: AH1203
Similar to 5 Para, KM#135.

KM#	Year	Mintage	Good	VG	Fine	VF
137	15	—	150.00	200.00	300.00	500.00
	16	—	120.00	180.00	250.00	400.00

PIASTRE

(40 Para)

BILLON
Accession Date: AH1203

KM#	Year	Mintage	Good	VG	Fine	VF
138	16	—	30.00	50.00	90.00	180.00

1/2 ZERI MAHBUB

GOLD, 1.25-1.30 g
Accession Date: AH1203

KM#	Year	Mintage	VG	Fine	VF	XF
140	20	—	50.00	100.00	200.00	400.00
	21	—	50.00	100.00	200.00	400.00

NOTE: Earlier dates (Yr.2, 4) exist for this type.

ZERI MAHBUB

GOLD, 2.50-2.60 g
Accession Date: AH1203

141	15	—	75.00	125.00	200.00	250.00
	16	—	75.00	125.00	200.00	250.00
	*'aleph-sin'	—	75.00	125.00	200.00	250.00
	*'sad'	—	75.00	125.00	200.00	250.00

***NOTE:** Initial letters.
NOTE: Earlier date (Yr.1) exists for this type.

2 ZERI MAHBUB

GOLD, 4.80-5.00 g
Accession Date: AH1203

142	14	—	200.00	300.00	500.00	900.00
	21	—	200.00	300.00	500.00	900.00
	*'aleph-sin'	—	200.00	300.00	500.00	900.00

***NOTE:** Initial letters.

3 ZERI MAHBUB

GOLD, 7.70 g
Accession Date: AH1203

143	14	—	350.00	500.00	1000.	1500.

MUSTAFA IV

AH1222-1223/1807-1808AD

PARA

BILLON, 14mm, 0.30-0.40 g
Accession Date: AH1222
Obv: Toughra. Rev: Mintname above date.

KM#	Year	Mintage	Good	VG	Fine	VF
155	1	—	10.00	20.00	35.00	60.00

20 PARA

BILLON
Accession Date: AH1222

KM#	Year	Mintage	VG	Fine	VF	XF
156	1	—	500.00	800.00	1300.	2000.

PIASTRE

BILLON, 10.65 g
Accession Date: AH1222

KM#	Year	Mintage	VG	Fine	VF	XF
157	1	—	550.00	1000.	1800.	3100.

1/2 ZERI MAHBUB

GOLD, 20mm, 1.65 g
Accession Date: AH1222

KM#	Year	Mintage	VG	Fine	VF	XF
158	1	—	350.00	500.00	800.00	1200.

ZERI MAHBUB

GOLD, 2.30 g
Accession Date: AH1222

KM#	Year	Mintage	VG	Fine	VF	XF
159	1	—	275.00	400.00	700.00	1000.

2 ZERI MAHBUB

GOLD, 32mm, 4.70 g
Accession Date: AH1222

KM#	Year	Mintage	VG	Fine	VF	XF
160	1	—	400.00	600.00	900.00	1500.

MAHMUD II

AH1223-1255/1808-1839AD

ASPER

BRASS, uniface
Accession Date: AH1223

KM#	Year	Mintage	Good	VG	Fine	VF
—	—	—	50.00	80.00	110.00	150.00

NOTE: The precise status of this piece is undetermined.

AKCHEH

BILLON, 11-12mm, 0.10-0.13 g
Accession Date: AH1223

KM#	Year	Mintage	Good	VG	Fine	VF
A161	16	—	1.00	2.00	3.00	10.00
	17	—	1.00	2.00	3.00	10.00
	18	—	1.00	2.00	3.00	10.00
	19	—	1.00	2.00	3.00	10.00
	20	—	1.00	2.00	3.00	10.00
	21	—	1.00	2.00	3.00	10.00

PARA

BILLON, 12-13mm, 0.15-0.28 g
Accession Date: AH1223

KM#	Year	Mintage	Good	VG	Fine	VF
161	1	—	.75	1.50	4.00	8.50
	2	—	.75	1.50	4.00	8.50
	3	—	.75	1.50	4.00	8.50
	4	—	.75	1.50	4.00	8.50
	5	—	.75	1.50	4.00	8.50
	6	—	.75	1.50	4.00	8.50
	7	—	.75	1.50	4.00	8.50
	8	—	.75	1.50	4.00	8.50
	9	—	.75	1.50	4.00	8.50
	10	—	.75	1.50	4.00	8.50
	11	—	.75	1.50	4.00	8.50
	12	—	.75	1.50	4.00	8.50
	13	—	.75	1.50	4.00	8.50
	14	—	.75	1.50	4.00	8.50
	15	—	.75	1.50	4.00	8.50
	16	—	.75	1.50	4.00	8.50
	17	—	1.00	3.00	10.00	15.00
	18	—	1.00	3.00	10.00	15.00
	19	—	2.00	4.00	15.00	20.00
	20	—	—	—	—	—
	21	—	— Reported, not confirmed			
	25	—	—	—	—	—

COPPER

KM#	Year	Mintage	Good	VG	Fine	VF
162	28	—	8.00	20.00	45.00	100.00
	29	—	8.00	20.00	45.00	100.00

15mm

KM#	Year	Mintage	Good	VG	Fine	VF
163	29	—	8.00	20.00	45.00	100.00

NOTE: KM#163 does not bear any denomination.

15-17mm

KM#	Year	Mintage	Good	VG	Fine	VF
164	29	—	8.00	20.00	45.00	100.00
	30	—	8.00	20.00	45.00	100.00
	31	—	8.00	20.00	45.00	100.00
	32	—	8.00	20.00	45.00	100.00

5 PARA

BILLON, 15-16mm., 0.50-0.70 g
Accession Date: AH1223

KM#	Year	Mintage	Good	VG	Fine	VF
165	5	—	15.00	20.00	30.00	50.00
	6	—	15.00	20.00	30.00	50.00
	7	—	15.00	20.00	30.00	50.00
	8	—	15.00	20.00	30.00	50.00
	9	—	10.00	15.00	25.00	45.00
	10	—	10.00	15.00	25.00	45.00
	11	—	10.00	15.00	25.00	45.00
	12	—	10.00	15.00	25.00	45.00
	13	—	10.00	15.00	25.00	45.00
	14	—	10.00	15.00	25.00	45.00
	15	—	10.00	15.00	25.00	45.00
	16	—	10.00	15.00	25.00	45.00
	17	—	10.00	15.00	25.00	45.00
	18	—	10.00	15.00	25.00	45.00
	19	—	10.00	15.00	25.00	45.00
	20	—	10.00	15.00	25.00	45.00
	21	—	10.00	15.00	25.00	45.00

Obv. and rev: Beaded circle around toughra and legend.

KM#	Year	Mintage	Good	VG	Fine	VF
A166	18	—	35.00	60.00	120.00	200.00

14mm., 0.40 g
Obv: Rose added to right of toughra.

KM#	Year	Mintage	Good	VG	Fine	VF
166	21	—	5.00	15.00	30.00	60.00
	22	—	4.00	10.00	22.50	40.00
	23	—	4.00	10.00	22.50	40.00
	24	—	4.00	10.00	22.50	40.00
	25	—	4.00	10.00	22.50	40.00
	26	—	5.00	15.00	30.00	60.00
	27	—	45.00	70.00	120.00	185.00
	28	—	45.00	70.00	120.00	185.00

COPPER, 22-24mm, 6.14-7.41 g
Floral designs in wreath

KM#	Year	Mintage	Good	VG	Fine	VF
167	28	—	3.00	6.00	12.50	25.00
	29	—	3.00	6.00	12.50	25.00

W/o wreath and denomination.

KM#	Year	Mintage	Good	VG	Fine	VF
168.1	29	—	5.00	7.00	15.00	30.00

Rev: Larger legend.

KM#	Year	Mintage	Good	VG	Fine	VF
168.2	29	—	5.00	7.00	15.00	30.00

Obv: Denomination added below toughra.

KM#	Year	Mintage	Good	VG	Fine	VF
169	29	—	2.00	5.00	10.00	20.00
	30	—	2.00	5.00	10.00	20.00
	31	—	2.00	5.00	10.00	20.00
	32	—	3.00	7.00	15.00	25.00

10 PARA

BILLON, 17-18mm., 0.90-1.40 g
Accession Date: AH1223
Plain dotted borders.

KM#	Year	Mintage	Good	VG	Fine	VF
170.1	8	—	20.00	40.00	80.00	150.00

KM#	Year	Mintage	Good	VG	Fine	VF
170.1	9	—	10.00	20.00	40.00	75.00
	10	—	10.00	20.00	40.00	75.00
	11	—	10.00	20.00	40.00	75.00
	12	—	10.00	20.00	40.00	75.00
	15	—	10.00	20.00	40.00	75.00
	—	—	—	—	Rare	—

NOTE: Border varieties exist.

Ornate borders.

170.2	18	—	3.50	9.00	20.00	32.50
	19	—	3.50	9.00	20.00	32.50
	20	—	3.50	9.00	20.00	32.50
	21	—	5.00	12.50	25.00	40.00

0.75-0.78 g
Wavy borders.

171	21	—	6.00	15.00	25.00	50.00
	22	—	5.00	12.50	20.00	40.00
	23	—	5.00	12.50	20.00	40.00
	24	—	5.00	12.50	20.00	40.00
	25	—	5.00	12.50	20.00	40.00
	26	—	13.50	30.00	75.00	150.00
	27	—	25.00	55.00	120.00	200.00

Obv: *Adli* right of toughra.
Wreath borders, 12mm, 0.30 g

172	28	—	30.00	60.00	125.00	250.00
	29	—	25.00	45.00	85.00	165.00

.833 SILVER, 14mm, 0.35 g
Obv: Denomination below toughra.

KM#	Year	Mintage	VG	Fine	VF	XF
173	29	—	50.00	100.00	180.00	300.00
	30	—	50.00	100.00	180.00	300.00
	31	—	50.00	100.00	180.00	300.00
	32	—	50.00	100.00	180.00	300.00

20 PARA

BILLON, 22-24mm, 2.40-3.80 g
Accession Date: AH1223
Rev: Date

KM#	Year	Mintage	Good	VG	Fine	VF
174	1	—	65.00	115.00	200.00	300.00
	5	—	15.00	25.00	40.00	75.00
	6	—	16.50	27.50	45.00	85.00
	7	—	15.00	25.00	40.00	75.00
	8	—	15.00	25.00	40.00	75.00
	9	—	15.00	25.00	40.00	75.00
	10	—	15.00	25.00	40.00	75.00
	11	—	15.00	25.00	40.00	75.00

Obv: Mintname and date below toughra.

175	5	—	30.00	60.00	150.00	300.00

21mm, 1.38-1.62 g

KM#	Year	Mintage	Good	VG	Fine	VF
176	21	—	10.00	20.00	30.00	50.00
	22	—	7.50	15.00	25.00	40.00
	23	—	7.50	15.00	25.00	40.00
	24	—	7.50	15.00	25.00	40.00
176	25	—	7.50	15.00	25.00	40.00
	26	—	40.00	80.00	150.00	250.00
	27	—	40.00	60.00	100.00	150.00

15mm, 0.58-0.62 g
Obv: *Adli* right of toughra.

177	28	—	12.00	18.00	40.00	75.00
	29	—	12.00	18.00	40.00	75.00

.833 SILVER, 15-16mm, 0.68-0.70 g
Obv: Denomination below toughra.

KM#	Year	Mintage	VG	Fine	VF	XF
178	29	—	20.00	40.00	80.00	160.00
	30	—	20.00	40.00	80.00	160.00
	31	—	20.00	40.00	80.00	160.00
	32	—	20.00	40.00	80.00	160.00

QIRSH

BILLON, 29-31mm, 9.00 g
Accession Date: AH1223

KM#	Year	Mintage	Good	VG	Fine	VF
179.1	1	—	25.00	50.00	100.00	150.00

BILLON, 7.00 g

179.2	3	—	15.00	40.00	50.00	100.00
	5	—	15.00	40.00	50.00	100.00
	6	—	12.50	30.00	45.00	80.00
	7	—	12.50	30.00	45.00	80.00
	8	—	15.00	35.00	50.00	90.00

NOTE: Varieties exist.

Obv: Flower right of toughra.

179.3	7	—	—	—	Rare	—

Obv: Mintname and date below toughra.

180	5	—	40.00	70.00	140.00	250.00

(Yeni Kurus)

2.67-3.08 g
Wavy borders, 26-27mm.

KM#	Year	Mintage	Good	VG	Fine	VF
181	21	—	5.00	10.00	20.00	40.00
	22	—	3.00	7.50	15.00	30.00
	23	—	3.00	7.50	15.00	30.00
181	24	—	3.00	7.50	15.00	30.00
	25	—	3.00	7.50	15.00	30.00
	26	—	5.00	10.00	20.00	40.00
	27	—	15.00	25.00	50.00	100.00

19mm, 1.00-1.31 g
Obv: *Adli* right of toughra.
Wreath borders

182	28	—	9.00	12.00	18.00	30.00
	29	—	12.00	15.00	25.00	35.00

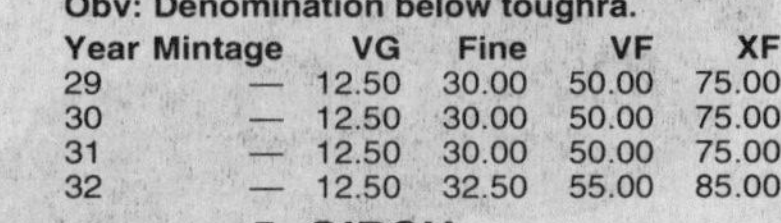

.833 SILVER, 19-20mm, 1.40 g
Obv: Denomination below toughra.

KM#	Year	Mintage	VG	Fine	VF	XF
183	29	—	12.50	30.00	50.00	75.00
	30	—	12.50	30.00	50.00	75.00
	31	—	12.50	30.00	50.00	75.00
	32	—	12.50	32.50	55.00	85.00

5 QIRSH

.833 SILVER, 24-26mm, 7.00 g
Accession Date: AH1223

184	29	—	100.00	200.00	400.00	600.00
	30	—	200.00	300.00	450.00	700.00
	31	—	200.00	300.00	450.00	700.00

10 QIRSH

.833 SILVER, 30mm, 14.00 g
Accession Date: AH1223
Similar to 5 Qirsh, KM#184.

185	29	—	—	—	6500.	7500.

20 QIRSH

.833 SILVER, 37mm, 27.80-28.06 g
Accession Date: AH1223

186	29	—	400.00	700.00	1000.	1450.
	30	—	425.00	750.00	1250.	1650.
	31	—	350.00	650.00	900.00	1350.
	32	—	550.00	900.00	1400.	1900.

GOLD COINAGE

NOTE: The following listings are incomplete, and any information about additional dates, years and types would be appreciated.

PRE-REFORM COINAGE

Prior to AH1251 (1834AD)

The basic unit was the 'Mahbub' or 'Zer Mahbub' (Zer = Gold), which weighed approximately 2.35 g from AH1223 until 1247 (Yr. 15), when it was reduced to about 1.6 g. Fractional denominations were Halves (Nisfiya) and Quarters (Rubiya). The value of the

Mahbub in terms of silver Piastres fluctuated according to the relative value of gold and silver, and the price of debased Egyptian silver coin.

1/4 MAHBUB

(Rubiya)

.875 GOLD, 13-14mm, 0.35-0.60 g
Accession Date: AH1223
Plain borders of dots
Rev. leg: *Azze Nasruhu Duribe Fi. . . . .*

KM#	Year	Mintage	VG	Fine	VF	XF
189	—	—	150.00	225.00	300.00	450.00

KM#	Year	Mintage	VG	Fine	VF	XF
190	7	—	40.00	60.00	85.00	110.00
	8	—	40.00	60.00	85.00	110.00
	9	—	40.00	60.00	85.00	110.00
	10	—	40.00	60.00	85.00	110.00
	11	—	40.00	60.00	85.00	110.00
	12	—	40.00	60.00	85.00	110.00
	13	—	40.00	60.00	85.00	110.00
	14	—	40.00	60.00	85.00	110.00

12-13mm, 0.35-0.40 g
Plain borders of dots.

KM#	Year	Mintage	VG	Fine	VF	XF
191	15	—	25.00	40.00	60.00	85.00
	16	—	17.50	27.50	45.00	65.00
	17	—	25.00	40.00	60.00	85.00
	18	—	17.50	27.50	45.00	65.00
	19	—	20.00	35.00	55.00	80.00
	20	—	20.00	35.00	55.00	80.00
	21	—	20.00	35.00	55.00	80.00

(Saadiya)

Ornamental borders

KM#	Year	Mintage	VG	Fine	VF	XF
192	19	—	30.00	50.00	65.00	75.00
	20	—	40.00	65.00	90.00	115.00
	21	—	60.00	90.00	115.00	140.00

(Coyrek Rumi)

Vine-like borders

KM#	Year	Mintage	VG	Fine	VF	XF
193	21	—	25.00	35.00	50.00	100.00
	22	—	25.00	35.00	50.00	100.00
	23	—	25.00	35.00	50.00	100.00
	24	—	25.00	35.00	50.00	100.00
	25	—	25.00	35.00	50.00	100.00
	26	—	20.00	30.00	40.00	90.00
	27	—	30.00	40.00	70.00	150.00
	28	—	100.00	175.00	275.00	375.00

Different design and w/o year.

KM#	Year	Mintage	VG	Fine	VF	XF
201	—	—	—	—	—	—

1/2 ZERI MAHBUB

(Nisfiya)

.875 GOLD, 19-20mm, 1.15-1.20 g
Accession Date: AH1223

KM#	Year	Mintage	VG	Fine	VF	XF
194	1	—	85.00	140.00	350.00	650.00
	5	—	85.00	140.00	350.00	650.00
	8	—	85.00	140.00	350.00	650.00

(Khayriya)

.875 GOLD, 16mm, 0.70-0.80 g

KM#	Year	Mintage	VG	Fine	VF	XF
195	21	—	20.00	30.00	75.00	150.00
	22	—	20.00	30.00	60.00	125.00
195	23	—	20.00	30.00	60.00	125.00
	24	—	20.00	30.00	60.00	125.00
	25	—	20.00	30.00	60.00	125.00
	26	—	20.00	30.00	75.00	150.00
	27	—	30.00	40.00	100.00	200.00
	28	—	40.00	50.00	125.00	250.00

ZERI MAHBUB

(Altin)

.875 GOLD, 25-26mm, 2.1-2.35 g, crude flan
Accession Date: AH1223

KM#	Year	Mintage	VG	Fine	VF	XF
197	1	—	90.00	175.00	350.00	600.00
	1 dot right of toughra					
		—	—	—	—	—
	2	—	100.00	200.00	400.00	750.00
	3	—	90.00	175.00	350.00	600.00
	5	—	90.00	175.00	350.00	600.00
	7	—	150.00	250.00	425.00	800.00
	8	—	150.00	250.00	425.00	800.00
	10 dot next to toughra					
		—	150.00	250.00	425.00	800.00
	10 rose branch next to toughra					
		—	180.00	300.00	425.00	800.00
	11	—	90.00	175.00	350.00	600.00
	12 rose branch right of toughra					
		—	—	—	—	—
	13	—	150.00	250.00	350.00	600.00
	14	—	90.00	175.00	350.00	600.00

23mm, 2.35 g, thicker & well-shaped flan

KM#	Year	Mintage	VG	Fine	VF	XF
198	15	—	120.00	220.00	425.00	1000.

W/o *Azza Nashruhu.*

KM#	Year	Mintage	VG	Fine	VF	XF
199	5	—	100.00	200.00	375.00	700.00

2 ZERI MAHBUB

.875 GOLD, 28mm, 3.60 g
Accession Date: AH1223

KM#	Year	Mintage	VG	Fine	VF	XF
200	5	—	300.00	500.00	850.00	1750.

NOTE: The above piece may be a medal or token.

TEK RUMI

GOLD, 23mm, 2.35 g
Accession Date: AH1223
Similar to 1/4 Mahbub, KM#193.

KM#	Year	Mintage	VG	Fine	VF	XF
202	11	—	—	—	Rare	—

CHIFTE RUMI

GOLD, 28mm, 3.60 g
Accession Date: AH1223
Similar to 1/4 Mahbub, KM#193.

KM#	Year	Mintage	VG	Fine	VF	XF
203	5	—	—	—	Rare	—

NOUSF or 1/2 MISRIYA

(10 Qirsh)

.875 GOLD, 0.70-0.75 g
Accession Date: AH1223

KM#	Year	Mintage	VG	Fine	VF	XF
213	28	—	30.00	50.00	125.00	200.00
	29	—	30.00	50.00	125.00	200.00

REFORMED COINAGE

AH1251-1326/1834-1908AD

5 QIRSH

(Rubiya, or 1/4 Misriya)

.875 GOLD, 0.30-0.35 g
Accession Date: AH1223

KM#	Year	Mintage	VG	Fine	VF	XF
210	28	—	85.00	140.00	215.00	325.00
	29	—	60.00	100.00	150.00	250.00

0.42 g
Obv: W/o value below toughra.

KM#	Year	Mintage	VG	Fine	VF	XF
211	29	—	60.00	100.00	150.00	250.00

Obv: Denomination added below toughra.

KM#	Year	Mintage	VG	Fine	VF	XF
212	29	—	65.00	100.00	150.00	200.00
	30	—	65.00	100.00	150.00	200.00
	31	—	65.00	100.00	150.00	200.00
	32	—	65.00	100.00	150.00	200.00

10 QIRSH

(Nousf or 1/2 Misriya)

.875 GOLD, 15mm, 0.85 g
Obv: Denomination beneath toughra.

KM#	Year	Mintage	VG	Fine	VF	XF
214	29	—	65.00	100.00	200.00	350.00
	30	—	65.00	100.00	200.00	350.00
	32	—	65.00	100.00	200.00	350.00

20 QIRSH

(Misriya)

.875 GOLD, 18mm, 1.70 g
Accession Date: AH1223

KM#	Year	Mintage	VG	Fine	VF	XF
215	29	—	60.00	100.00	150.00	300.00
	30	—	60.00	100.00	150.00	300.00
	31	—	60.00	100.00	150.00	300.00
	32	—	60.00	100.00	150.00	300.00

Obv. and rev: 4 roses around edge.

KM#	Year	Mintage	VG	Fine	VF	XF
216	32	—	75.00	125.00	200.00	400.00

100 QIRSH

(1 Pound)

.875 GOLD, 22mm, 8.40 g
Accession Date: AH1223

KM#	Year	Mintage	VG	Fine	VF	XF
217	30	—	750.00	1000.	2000.	3000.
	31	—	750.00	1000.	2000.	3000.

ABDUL MEJID

AH1255-1277/1839-1861AD

PARA

COPPER, 16mm, 1.20 g
Accession Date: AH1255

KM#	Year	Mintage	Good	VG	Fine	VF
220	1	—	12.00	30.00	75.00	150.00
	2	—	10.00	20.00	50.00	100.00
	4	—	10.00	20.00	50.00	100.00
	5	—	10.00	20.00	50.00	100.00
	6	—	10.00	20.00	50.00	100.00
	Common date		—	—	Unc	400.00

15mm

KM#	Year	Mintage	Good	VG	Fine	VF
221	8	—	—	—	Rare	—

5 PARA

 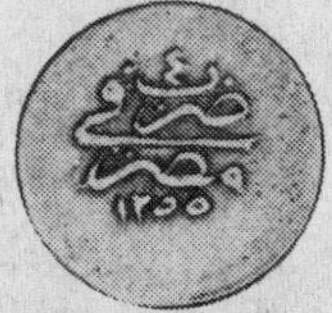

COPPER, 21mm, 6.40 g

Accession Date: AH1255

KM#	Year	Mintage	Good	VG	Fine	VF
222	1	—	1.00	2.00	5.00	12.50
	2	—	1.00	2.00	5.00	12.50
	3	—	1.00	2.00	5.00	12.50
	4	—	1.00	2.00	5.00	12.50
	5	—	1.00	2.00	5.00	12.50
	6	—	1.00	2.00	5.00	12.50

NOTE: Varieties of size of toughra exist.

KM#	Year	Mintage	Good	VG	Fine	VF
223	6	—	2.00	3.00	7.50	17.00
	7	—	1.00	2.00	5.00	16.00
	8	—	4.50	8.50	15.00	27.50

KM#	Year	Mintage	Good	VG	Fine	VF
224	8	—	4.00	7.50	12.50	25.00
	10	—	2.00	5.00	13.50	25.00
	12	—	2.00	5.00	13.50	25.00
	13	—	2.00	5.00	12.50	25.00
	14	—	1.00	2.50	10.00	20.00
	15	—	1.00	2.00	7.50	15.00
	16	—	1.00	2.00	7.50	15.00
	Common date		—	—	Unc	45.00

10 PARA

.833 SILVER, 15mm, 0.37 g
Accession Date: AH1255

KM#	Year	Mintage	VG	Fine	VF	XF
225	1	—	15.00	30.00	60.00	90.00
	2	—	15.00	30.00	60.00	75.00
	3	—	12.50	25.00	50.00	75.00
	4	—	12.50	25.00	50.00	75.00
	5	—	12.50	25.00	50.00	75.00
	6	—	12.50	25.00	50.00	75.00
	7	—	12.50	25.00	50.00	75.00
	8	—	12.50	25.00	50.00	75.00
	9	—	12.50	25.00	50.00	75.00
	10	—	15.00	30.00	60.00	90.00
	11	—	15.00	30.00	60.00	90.00
	12	—	15.00	30.00	60.00	90.00
	13	—	30.00	60.00	120.00	180.00
	14	—	15.00	30.00	60.00	90.00
	15	—	15.00	30.00	60.00	90.00
	18	—	17.50	35.00	65.00	100.00
	19	—	17.50	35.00	65.00	100.00
	20	—	17.50	35.00	65.00	100.00
	21	—	— Reported, not confirmed			
	22	—	17.50	35.00	65.00	100.00
	23	—	15.00	30.00	60.00	90.00

COPPER, 29mm, 12.90 g

KM#	Year	Mintage	Good	VG	Fine	VF
226	15	—	4.50	8.00	15.00	45.00
	16	—	6.00	15.00	22.00	60.00

NOTE: Varieties of size of toughra exist.

20 PARA

.833 SILVER, 16mm, 0.68 g
Accession Date: AH1255

KM#	Year	Mintage	VG	Fine	VF	XF
227	1	—	15.00	30.00	50.00	75.00
	2	—	15.00	30.00	50.00	75.00
	3	—	15.00	30.00	50.00	75.00
	4/3	—	17.50	35.00	60.00	90.00
	4	—	15.00	30.00	50.00	75.00
	5	—	15.00	30.00	50.00	75.00
	6	—	15.00	30.00	50.00	75.00
	7	—	15.00	30.00	50.00	75.00
	8	—	15.00	30.00	50.00	75.00
	9	—	15.00	30.00	50.00	75.00
	10	—	15.00	30.00	50.00	75.00
	11	—	17.50	35.00	60.00	90.00
	12	—	17.50	35.00	60.00	90.00
	13	—	17.50	35.00	60.00	90.00
	14	—	17.50	35.00	60.00	90.00
	15	—	17.50	35.00	60.00	90.00
	18/6	—	20.00	40.00	70.00	110.00
	18	—	20.00	40.00	70.00	110.00
	19	—	30.00	60.00	90.00	150.00
	20	—	20.00	40.00	70.00	110.00
	21	—	20.00	40.00	70.00	110.00
	22	—	20.00	40.00	70.00	110.00
	23	—	17.50	35.00	60.00	90.00
	Common date		—	—	Unc	150.00

QIRSH

.833 SILVER, 19mm, 1.42 g
Accession Date: AH1255

KM#	Year	Mintage	VG	Fine	VF	XF
228	1	—	15.00	30.00	50.00	85.00
	2	—	15.00	30.00	50.00	85.00
	3	—	15.00	30.00	50.00	85.00
	4	—	17.50	35.00	60.00	100.00
	5	—	15.00	30.00	50.00	85.00
	6	—	15.00	30.00	50.00	85.00
	7	—	17.50	35.00	60.00	100.00
	8/7	—	17.50	35.00	60.00	100.00
	8	—	17.50	35.00	60.00	100.00
	9	—	17.50	35.00	60.00	100.00
	10	—	17.50	35.00	60.00	100.00
	11	—	17.50	35.00	60.00	100.00
	12	—	17.50	35.00	60.00	100.00
	13	—	17.50	35.00	60.00	100.00
	14	—	17.50	35.00	60.00	100.00
	15	—	17.50	35.00	60.00	100.00
	16	—	17.50	35.00	60.00	100.00
	17	—	22.50	45.00	75.00	125.00
	18	—	22.50	45.00	75.00	125.00
	19	—	22.50	45.00	75.00	125.00
	20	—	22.50	45.00	75.00	125.00
	21	—	— Reported, not confirmed			
	22	—	22.50	45.00	75.00	125.00
	23	—	17.50	35.00	65.00	110.00
	Common date		—	—	Unc	150.00

5 QIRSH

.833 SILVER, 25-26mm, 6.80-7.00 g
Accession Date: AH1255

KM#	Year	Mintage	VG	Fine	VF	XF
229	1	—	150.00	250.00	500.00	800.00
	2	—	150.00	250.00	500.00	800.00
	3	—	150.00	250.00	500.00	800.00
	4	—	150.00	250.00	500.00	800.00
	5	—	150.00	250.00	500.00	800.00
	6	—	150.00	250.00	500.00	800.00
	16	—	200.00	300.00	750.00	1250.
	23	—	— Reported, not confirmed			

.875 GOLD, 0.427 g

KM#	Year	Mintage	VG	Fine	VF	XF
230	1	—	17.50	30.00	45.00	85.00
	2	—	17.50	30.00	45.00	85.00
	3	—	17.50	30.00	45.00	85.00
	4	—	17.50	30.00	45.00	85.00
	5	—	17.50	30.00	45.00	85.00
	6	—	17.50	30.00	45.00	85.00
	7	—	17.50	30.00	45.00	85.00
	8	—	17.50	30.00	45.00	85.00
	9	—	17.50	30.00	45.00	85.00
	10	—	17.50	30.00	45.00	85.00
	11	—	17.50	30.00	45.00	85.00
	12	—	17.50	30.00	45.00	85.00
	13	—	22.50	37.50	60.00	125.00
	14	—	17.50	30.00	45.00	85.00
	15	—	17.50	30.00	45.00	85.00
	16	—	17.50	30.00	45.00	85.00
	18	—	17.50	30.00	45.00	85.00
	19	—	17.50	30.00	45.00	85.00
	20	—	17.50	30.00	45.00	85.00
	22	—	17.50	30.00	45.00	85.00
	23	—	17.50	30.00	45.00	85.00

10 QIRSH

.833 SILVER, 30mm, 14.00 g
Accession Date: AH1255

KM#	Year	Mintage	VG	Fine	VF	XF
231	1	—	200.00	300.00	650.00	1250.
	2	—	150.00	250.00	600.00	1000.
	3	—	175.00	250.00	600.00	1000.
	4	—	175.00	250.00	550.00	1000.
	5	—	200.00	300.00	600.00	1200.
	6	—	240.00	400.00	900.00	1500.
	10	—	— Reported, not confirmed			
	16	—	— Reported, not confirmed			
	Common date		—	—	Unc	1700.

NOTE: Oblique or vertical milled edges.

.875 GOLD, 15mm, 0.840 g

KM#	Year	Mintage	VG	Fine	VF	XF
231a	1	—	—	—	—	—

20 QIRSH

.833 SILVER, 36-38mm, 27.70-28.00 g
Accession Date: AH1255

KM#	Year	Mintage	VG	Fine	VF	XF
232	1	—	350.00	600.00	1100.	1500.
	2	—	325.00	575.00	1100.	1500.
	3	—	375.00	650.00	1250.	1750.
	4	—	325.00	575.00	1100.	1500.
	Common date		—	—	Unc	3400.

.875 GOLD, 1.71 g

KM#	Year	Mintage	VG	Fine	VF	XF
233	1	—	400.00	650.00	1000.	1750.

50 QIRSH
(1/2 Pound)

.875 GOLD, 4.274 g
Accession Date: AH1255
Beaded border.

KM#	Year	Mintage	VG	Fine	VF	XF
234.1	1	550 pcs.	200.00	300.00	600.00	800.00
	2	—	100.00	150.00	300.00	500.00
	3	—	100.00	125.00	250.00	400.00
	4	—	75.00	100.00	200.00	300.00
	5	—	75.00	100.00	200.00	300.00

Toothed border.

KM#	Year	Mintage	VG	Fine	VF	XF
234.2	6	—	75.00	125.00	250.00	400.00
	7	—	75.00	150.00	300.00	500.00
	8	—	75.00	150.00	300.00	500.00

KM#	Year	Mintage	VG	Fine	VF	XF
234.2	11	—	75.00	150.00	300.00	500.00
	15	—	40.00	75.00	150.00	250.00
	16	—	75.00	100.00	200.00	350.00

100 QIRSH

(1 Pound)

8.5440 g, .875 GOLD, .2404 oz AGW
Accession Date: AH1255
Beaded border.

KM#	Year	Mintage	VG	Fine	VF	XF
235.1	1	—	BV	200.00	300.00	500.00
	2	—	BV	150.00	250.00	475.00
	3	—	BV	125.00	225.00	450.00
	4	—	BV	115.00	200.00	400.00
	5	—	BV	115.00	200.00	400.00

NOTE: For crude copy of regnal year 2 see Sudan Y#3.

Toothed border.

KM#	Year	Mintage	VG	Fine	VF	XF
235.2	6	—	BV	115.00	125.00	275.00
	7	—	BV	125.00	150.00	350.00
	8	—	BV	125.00	150.00	350.00
	9	—	135.00	200.00	240.00	500.00
	10	—	135.00	200.00	240.00	500.00
	11	—	BV	125.00	150.00	350.00
	12	—	BV	125.00	150.00	350.00
	13	—	BV	125.00	150.00	350.00
	14	—	BV	125.00	150.00	350.00
	15	—	BV	115.00	125.00	250.00
	16	—	BV	115.00	135.00	275.00
	17	—	BV	125.00	150.00	350.00
	18	—	— Reported, not confirmed			

ABDUL AZIZ

AH1277-1293/1861-1876AD

4 PARA

BRONZE, 22mm, 2.26 g
Accession Date: AH1277

KM#	Year	Mintage	Fine	VF	XF	Unc
240	4	—	3.50	7.50	15.00	30.00

10 PARA

BRONZE, 30mm, 6.10-6.60 g
Accession Date: AH1277
Obv: W/o flower at right of toughra.

KM#	Year	Mintage	Fine	VF	XF	Unc
241	4	—	1.00	2.50	10.00	25.00
	5	—	1.00	2.50	10.00	25.00
	6	—	2.00	3.50	12.00	35.00
	7	—	2.00	3.50	12.00	40.00
	9	—	1.00	2.50	10.00	25.00
	10	—	2.00	3.50	12.00	35.00

COPPER, 5.80 g
Obv: Flower added at right of toughra.

KM#	Year	Mintage	Fine	VF	XF	Unc
242	8	.204	425.00	650.00	1250.	—
	9	—	350.00	550.00	1200.	—
	11	200 pcs.	—	—	—	5000.

.833 SILVER, 16mm, 0.29-0.33 g

KM#	Year	Mintage	Fine	VF	XF	Unc
243	2	—	20.00	40.00	70.00	160.00
	3	—	15.00	25.00	50.00	125.00
	4	—	15.00	25.00	50.00	125.00
	5	—	20.00	35.00	60.00	150.00
	6	—	10.00	20.00	35.00	75.00
	7	—	7.50	15.00	30.00	60.00
	8	—	6.00	12.50	25.00	40.00
	9	—	6.00	12.50	25.00	50.00

.900 SILVER, 0.30-0.33 g

KM#	Year	Mintage	Fine	VF	XF	Unc
243a	10	—	5.00	10.00	22.00	45.00
	11	—	5.00	10.00	22.00	45.00
	12	—	10.00	15.00	32.00	65.00
	13	—	10.00	15.00	32.00	65.00
	14	—	12.00	20.00	45.00	100.00
	15	—	18.00	32.00	65.00	140.00
	16	—	15.00	30.00	60.00	120.00

20 PARA

BRONZE, 29.5-32mm, 12.10-12.70 g
Accession Date: AH1277
Obv: W/o flower at right of toughra.

KM#	Year	Mintage	Fine	VF	XF	Unc
244	3	—	2.50	6.00	20.00	50.00
	4	—	2.50	6.00	20.00	50.00
	5	—	1.50	4.00	15.00	35.00
	6	—	1.50	4.00	15.00	35.00
	7	—	—	—	Rare	—
	8	—	2.00	5.00	17.50	45.00
	9	—	1.00	3.00	12.00	35.00
	10	—	2.00	5.00	17.50	45.00

12.50 g
Similar, but crude & thick, (struck at Cairo).

KM#	Year	Mintage	Fine	VF	XF	Unc
245	7	1.190	150.00	200.00	400.00	1250.

COPPER, 12.50 g
Obv: Flower at right of toughra.

KM#	Year	Mintage	Fine	VF	XF	Unc
246	7	—	—	—	Rare	—
	8	2.395	15.00	30.00	65.00	180.00
	9	3.089	10.00	25.00	55.00	140.00
	10	.966	12.00	30.00	80.00	150.00
	11	200 pcs.	—	—	Rare	2500.

.833 SILVER, 15-16mm, 0.65-0.70 g

KM#	Year	Mintage	Fine	VF	XF	Unc
247	1	—	50.00	100.00	175.00	350.00
	2	—	25.00	50.00	100.00	175.00
	3	—	12.50	25.00	50.00	125.00
	4	—	10.00	20.00	45.00	100.00
	5	—	12.50	30.00	60.00	125.00
247	6	—	10.00	20.00	45.00	100.00
	7	—	7.50	15.00	35.00	85.00
	8	—	6.00	12.00	20.00	50.00
	9	—	6.00	12.00	20.00	50.00

.900 SILVER, 0.65-0.70 g

KM#	Year	Mintage	Fine	VF	XF	Unc
247a	10	—	6.00	12.00	25.00	50.00
	11	—	6.00	12.00	25.00	50.00
	12	—	6.00	12.00	25.00	50.00
	13	—	10.00	20.00	40.00	80.00
	14	—	10.00	20.00	40.00	80.00
	15	—	20.00	40.00	80.00	150.00
	16	—	— Reported, not confirmed			

40 PARA

(1 Qirsh)

BRONZE, 37mm, 25.63 g
Accession Date: AH1277

KM#	Year	Mintage	Fine	VF	XF	Unc
248	10	—	3.00	10.00	30.00	100.00

NOTE: Exists w/large or small toughra.

COPPER, 36mm, 24.00 g
Obv: Flower added at right of toughra.

KM#	Year	Mintage	Fine	VF	XF	Unc
249	9	125 pcs.	—	—	—	5000.
	10	.150	500.00	750.00	1500.	3000.
	11	200 pcs.	—	—	—	5000.

NOTE: An example of year 10 struck in gold is reported, not confirmed.

QIRSH

.833 SILVER, 18mm, 1.18-1.25 g
Accession Date: AH1277

KM#	Year	Mintage	Fine	VF	XF	Unc
250	1	—	30.00	50.00	100.00	250.00
	2	—	20.00	35.00	75.00	150.00
	3	—	15.00	25.00	50.00	100.00
	4	—	15.00	25.00	50.00	100.00
	5	—	20.00	35.00	75.00	150.00
	6	—	12.50	25.00	45.00	90.00
	7	—	10.00	20.00	40.00	80.00
	8	—	5.00	10.00	20.00	50.00
	9	—	5.00	10.00	20.00	50.00

.900 SILVER, 1.18-1.23 g

KM#	Year	Mintage	Fine	VF	XF	Unc
250a	10	—	5.00	10.00	20.00	60.00
	11/10	—	6.00	12.00	25.00	65.00
	11	—	5.00	10.00	20.00	50.00
	12	—	5.00	10.00	20.00	50.00
	13	—	7.50	15.00	35.00	75.00
	14	—	7.50	15.00	35.00	75.00
	15	—	5.00	10.00	20.00	50.00
	16	—	5.00	10.00	20.00	50.00

Mule. Obv: KM#250a. Rev: KM#270.
Accession Date: AH1293

KM#	Year	Mintage	Fine	VF	XF	Unc
A270	1	—	—	—	Rare	—

2-1/2 QIRSH

3.1500 g, .833 SILVER, .0844 oz ASW
Accession Date: AH1277
Obv: W/o flower at right of toughra.

20mm

KM#	Year	Mintage	Fine	VF	XF	Unc
251	4	3.803	30.00	75.00	150.00	300.00

3.5000 g, .833 SILVER, .0938 oz ASW
Obv: Flower at right of toughra.
22mm

KM#	Year	Mintage	Fine	VF	XF	Unc
252	8	—	175.00	275.00	375.00	650.00
	9	—	150.00	250.00	350.00	600.00

3.6000 g, .900 SILVER, .1013 oz ASW

KM#	Year	Mintage	Fine	VF	XF	Unc
252a	10	—	150.00	250.00	350.00	600.00
	11	—	250.00	450.00	900.00	1500.
	12	—	400.00	750.00	1500.	2750.
	13	—	400.00	750.00	1500.	2750.
	15	—	600.00	1000.	1800.	3000.

5 QIRSH

6.2000 g, .833 SILVER, .1661 oz ASW
Accession Date: AH1277
Obv: W/o flower at right of toughra.
25-26mm

KM#	Year	Mintage	Fine	VF	XF	Unc
253.1	4	4.108	30.00	70.00	125.00	320.00

Rev: Regnal year retrograde.

KM#	Year	Mintage	Fine	VF	XF	Unc
253.2	4	Inc. Ab.	60.00	115.00	175.00	450.00

6.60-7.00 g
Obv: Flower at right of toughra.

KM#	Year	Mintage	Fine	VF	XF	Unc
254	1	—	200.00	350.00	650.00	1150.
	2	—	130.00	280.00	500.00	750.00
	3	—	130.00	280.00	500.00	750.00
	4	—	160.00	300.00	600.00	950.00
	5	—	200.00	450.00	800.00	2000.
	6	—	200.00	450.00	800.00	2000.
	7	—	200.00	450.00	800.00	2000.
	8	—	130.00	230.00	340.00	700.00
	9	—	130.00	230.00	340.00	700.00
	10	—	250.00	450.00	650.00	1200.

.900 SILVER, 6.60-7.00 g

KM#	Year	Mintage	Fine	VF	XF	Unc
254a	10	—	150.00	250.00	350.00	750.00
	11	—	200.00	400.00	750.00	1500.
	12	—	300.00	600.00	1200.	3000.
	13	—	300.00	600.00	1200.	3000.
	15	—	300.00	600.00	1200.	3000.

0.4272 g, .875 GOLD, .0120 oz AGW

KM#	Year	Mintage	VG	Fine	VF	XF
255	3	—	20.00	30.00	40.00	65.00
	4	—	20.00	30.00	40.00	65.00
	5	—	20.00	30.00	40.00	65.00
	6	—	20.00	30.00	40.00	65.00
	7	—	20.00	30.00	40.00	65.00
	8	—	20.00	30.00	40.00	65.00
	9	—	20.00	30.00	40.00	65.00
	10	—	20.00	30.00	40.00	65.00
	11	—	20.00	30.00	40.00	65.00
	12	—	20.00	30.00	40.00	65.00
	13	—	20.00	30.00	40.00	65.00
	14	—	20.00	30.00	40.00	65.00
	15	—	20.00	30.00	40.00	65.00

10 QIRSH

14.0000 g, .900 SILVER, .4051 oz ASW
Accession Date: AH1277
Obv: Flower at right of toughra.

KM#	Year	Mintage	VG	Fine	VF	XF
256	2	—	150.00	250.00	500.00	1000.
	3	—	200.00	350.00	600.00	1250.
	4	—	200.00	350.00	600.00	1250.

12.5000 g, .833 SILVER, .3617 oz ASW
Obv: W/o flower at right of toughra.

KM#	Year	Mintage	Fine	VF	XF	Unc
257	4	3.803	50.00	100.00	180.00	450.00

14.0000 g, .900 SILVER, .4051 oz ASW
Similar to KM#256.

KM#	Year	Mintage	VG	Fine	VF	XF
258	10	—	300.00	600.00	1000.	3000.
	11	—	—	—	Unc	7500.

0.8554 g, .875 GOLD, .0240 oz AGW

KM#	Year	Mintage	VG	Fine	VF	XF
259	10	—	50.00	75.00	90.00	115.00
	11	—	50.00	75.00	90.00	115.00
	12	—	50.00	75.00	90.00	115.00
	14	—	50.00	75.00	90.00	115.00

20 QIRSH

28.0000 g, .833 SILVER, .7500 oz ASW
Accession Date: AH1277
Obv: Flower right of toughra.

KM#	Year	Mintage	VG	Fine	VF	XF
260	1	—	200.00	350.00	850.00	1250.
	2	—	225.00	400.00	1000.	1500.

28.0000 g, .900 SILVER, .8103 oz ASW

KM#	Year	Mintage	VG	Fine	VF	XF
260a	11	—	—	—	Unc	12,500.

25 QIRSH

(1/4 Pound)

2.1360 g, .875 GOLD, .0601 oz AGW
Accession Date: AH1277

KM#	Year	Mintage	VG	Fine	VF	XF
261	8	—	35.00	50.00	75.00	150.00
	9	—	35.00	50.00	75.00	150.00
	10	—	35.00	50.00	75.00	150.00
	11	—	35.00	50.00	75.00	150.00
	12	—	35.00	50.00	75.00	150.00
	13	—	50.00	75.00	125.00	200.00
	14	—	50.00	75.00	125.00	200.00
	15	—	50.00	75.00	125.00	200.00

50 QIRSH

(1/2 Pound)

4.2740 g, .875 GOLD, .1202 oz AGW
Accession Date: AH1277

KM#	Year	Mintage	VG	Fine	VF	XF
262	11	—	100.00	150.00	350.00	500.00
	12	—	80.00	115.00	220.00	325.00
	13	—	100.00	135.00	300.00	450.00
	14	—	80.00	115.00	220.00	325.00
	15	—	80.00	115.00	220.00	325.00
	16	—	80.00	115.00	220.00	325.00

100 QIRSH

(1 Pound)

8.5440 g, .875 GOLD, .2404 oz AGW
Accession Date: AH1277
Obv: Flower at right of toughra.

KM#	Year	Mintage	VG	Fine	VF	XF
263	1	—	—	Reported, not confirmed		
	2	—	150.00	175.00	225.00	300.00
	3	—	—	Reported, not confirmed		
	4	—	BV	120.00	155.00	225.00
	5	—	BV	120.00	155.00	225.00
	6	—	BV	120.00	155.00	225.00
	7	—	BV	120.00	155.00	225.00
	8	—	BV	120.00	155.00	225.00
	9	—	BV	120.00	155.00	225.00
	10	—	BV	120.00	155.00	225.00
	11	—	BV	120.00	155.00	225.00
	12	—	BV	120.00	155.00	225.00
	13	—	BV	120.00	155.00	225.00
	14	—	150.00	200.00	265.00	350.00
	15	—	BV	120.00	155.00	225.00
	16	—	150.00	200.00	265.00	350.00

Obv: W/o flower at right of toughra.

KM#	Year	Mintage	VG	Fine	VF	XF
264	4	.020	150.00	300.00	600.00	1000.

500 QIRSH

(5 Pounds)

42.7200 g, .875 GOLD, 1.2018 oz AGW
Accession Date: AH1277

KM#	Year	Mintage	Fine	VF	XF	Unc
265	8	118 pcs.	3500.	7500.	12,500.	17,500.
	9	Inc. Ab.	3000.	6000.	10,000.	15,000.

KM#	Year	Mintage	Fine	VF	XF	Unc
265	11	200 pcs.	3000.	6000.	10,000.	*15,000.
	15	56 pcs.	3000.	6000.	10,000.	15,000.

*NOTE: Spink Zurich Auction 31 6-89 AU realized $13,400.

MURAD V

AH1293/1876AD

QIRSH

.900 SILVER, 18mm, 1.20 g
Accession Date: AH1293
Obv: Toughra of Murad V.

KM#	Year	Mintage	Fine	VF	XF	Unc
270	1	—	100.00	150.00	300.00	500.00

50 QIRSH

(1/2 Egyptian Pound)

4.2740 g, .875 GOLD, .1202 oz AGW
Accession Date: AH1293
Obv: Toughra of Murad V.

KM#	Year	Mintage	VG	Fine	VF	XF
271	1	—	400.00	650.00	1000.	1500.

100 QIRSH

(1 Egyptian Pound)

8.5440 g, .875 GOLD, .2402 oz AGW
Accession Date: AH1293
Obv: Toughra of Murad V.

KM#	Year	Mintage	VG	Fine	VF	XF
272	1	—	250.00	750.00	1250.	1750.

ABDUL HAMID II

AH1293-1327/1876-1909AD

1/40 QIRSH

BRONZE
Accession Date: AH1293

KM#	Year	Mintage	Fine	VF	XF	Unc
287	10	1.669	.50	1.50	5.00	15.00
	12	2.476	.50	1.50	4.00	15.00
	18	—	40.00	60.00	100.00	160.00
	19	—	.75	1.50	5.00	15.00
	20	—	5.00	10.00	20.00	40.00
	24	1.601	.75	1.50	5.00	15.00
	26	1.999	.50	1.00	4.00	15.00
	27	1.200	1.00	1.50	7.00	18.00
	29	2.000	.50	1.00	4.00	15.00
	31H	2.400	.50	1.00	4.00	15.00
	32H	Inc. Be.	.50	1.00	4.00	15.00
	33H	1.200	.50	1.00	4.00	12.00
	35H	1.200	2.00	3.00	5.00	15.00

1/20 QIRSH

BRONZE
Accession Date: AH1293

KM#	Year	Mintage	Fine	VF	XF	Unc
288	10	4.105	.50	1.50	4.00	12.00
	12	4.457	.50	1.50	4.00	12.00
	18	—	10.00	20.00	30.00	75.00
	19	—	2.50	5.00	10.00	20.00
	20	—	8.00	15.00	30.00	75.00
	21	—	2.00	3.50	10.00	20.00
	24	.801	1.00	3.00	5.00	15.00
	26	1.405	.75	1.50	3.00	12.00
	27	1.402	.75	1.50	3.00	12.00
	29	3.200	.50	1.00	3.00	12.00
288	31H	3.000	.50	1.00	3.00	10.00
	32H	Inc. Be.	.50	1.00	3.00	10.00
	33H	1.400	1.00	2.00	5.00	15.00
	35H	1.400	2.00	5.00	10.00	20.00

1/10 QIRSH

COPPER-NICKEL
Accession Date: AH1293

KM#	Year	Mintage	Fine	VF	XF	Unc
289	10	2.307	.50	1.00	4.00	12.50
	12	3.435	.50	1.00	4.00	12.50
	18	—	6.00	12.00	30.00	75.00
	19	—	.50	1.00	5.00	15.00
	20	—	.50	1.00	5.00	15.00
	21	—	.50	1.00	5.00	15.00
	22	—	4.00	10.00	20.00	60.00
	23	—	.50	1.00	6.00	17.50
	24	1.005	.50	1.00	4.00	12.50
	25	2.000	.50	1.00	5.00	15.00
	27	3.010	.40	.75	3.00	10.00
	28	6.000	.50	1.00	3.00	10.00
	29	1.500	.75	1.50	4.00	15.00
	30	1.000	.50	1.00	3.00	12.50
	31H	3.000	.75	1.50	4.00	15.00
	32H	Inc. Be.	.50	1.00	3.00	12.50
	33H	2.000	.40	.75	2.50	8.50
	35H	2.000	1.00	3.00	6.00	20.00
	Common date		—	—	Proof	100.00

2/10 QIRSH

COPPER-NICKEL
Accession Date: AH1293

KM#	Year	Mintage	Fine	VF	XF	Unc
290	10	3.201	1.00	3.00	6.00	20.00
	12	2.009	1.00	3.00	6.00	20.00
	20	—	8.00	15.00	30.00	75.00
	21	.500	2.00	6.00	12.00	40.00
	24	.500	1.00	3.00	6.00	20.00
	25	.250	3.00	5.00	10.00	35.00
	27	1.002	1.00	3.00	6.00	20.00
	28	2.000	1.00	3.00	6.00	20.00
	29	1.500	1.00	3.00	6.00	20.00
	30	—	3.00	6.00	12.00	40.00
	31H	1.000	1.00	2.50	6.00	20.00
	33H	1.500	1.00	2.50	6.00	20.00
	35H	.750	2.00	6.00	10.00	35.00

10 PARA

.833 SILVER
Accession Date: AH1293

KM#	Year	Mintage	Fine	VF	XF	Unc
275	1	—	75.00	100.00	160.00	325.00
	2	—	80.00	120.00	180.00	430.00
	3	—	75.00	100.00	160.00	325.00
	4	—	—	Reported, not confirmed		
	5	—	—	Reported, not confirmed		

20 PARA

0.5500 g, .833 SILVER, .0147 oz ASW
Accession Date: AH1293

KM#	Year	Mintage	Fine	VF	XF	Unc
276	1	—	75.00	135.00	175.00	425.00
	2	—	70.00	125.00	140.00	400.00
	3	—	75.00	135.00	175.00	425.00
	4	—	—	Reported, not confirmed		
	5	—	—	—	750.00	1000.

5/10 QIRSH

COPPER-NICKEL
Accession Date: AH1293

KM#	Year	Mintage	Fine	VF	XF	Unc
291	10	7.003	2.00	4.00	12.50	40.00
	11	10.005	.50	2.00	6.00	20.00
	13	5.003	.50	2.00	6.00	20.00
	20	1.002	3.00	10.00	20.00	60.00
291	21	3.404	.65	2.50	7.50	25.00
	23	1.000	2.50	5.00	12.50	40.00
	24	3.605	.45	2.00	6.00	20.00
	25	1.998	.45	2.00	6.00	20.00
	27	4.999	.30	1.50	5.00	20.00
	29	12.000	.30	1.50	5.00	20.00
	30	2.000	.50	2.00	6.00	25.00
	33H	1.000	2.00	6.00	12.50	40.00
	Common date		—	—	Proof	145.00

QIRSH

.833 SILVER
Accession Date: AH1293

KM#	Year	Mintage	Fine	VF	XF	Unc
277	1	—	3.00	10.00	20.00	65.00
	2	—	3.00	10.00	18.00	55.00
	3	—	2.50	8.00	15.00	45.00
	4	—	3.00	10.00	18.00	55.00
	5	—	4.00	12.00	20.00	65.00

1.4000 g, .833 SILVER, .0375 oz ASW

KM#	Year	Mintage	Fine	VF	XF	Unc
292	10 W	8.192	1.00	3.00	7.50	20.00
	17 W	.546	1.00	4.00	10.00	30.00
	27 W	.200	1.25	4.00	10.00	27.50
	29 W	.100	1.50	4.00	10.00	30.00
	29H	.100	1.25	3.00	7.50	25.00
	33H	.100	1.25	3.00	7.50	25.00
	33H	—	—	—	Proof	120.00
	Common date		—	—	Proof	135.00

COPPER-NICKEL

KM#	Year	Mintage	Fine	VF	XF	Unc
299	22	.200	10.00	25.00	45.00	100.00
	23	1.500	2.00	6.00	20.00	50.00
	25	.751	3.00	8.00	30.00	60.00
	27	.999	2.00	6.00	20.00	50.00
	29	3.500	2.00	5.00	15.00	40.00
	30	.500	2.50	6.00	20.00	55.00
	33H	1.000	2.00	5.00	15.00	40.00

2 QIRSH

2.8000 g, .833 SILVER, .0750 oz ASW
Accession Date: AH1293
Obv: Flower to right of toughra.

KM#	Year	Mintage	Fine	VF	XF	Unc
293	10 W	4.011	1.00	3.00	7.50	30.00
	11 W	.989	2.00	5.00	12.50	35.00
	17 W	.540	2.00	5.00	12.50	35.00
	19 W	—	—	Reported, not confirmed		
	20 W	1.113	2.00	5.00	12.50	40.00
	24 W	.500	2.00	5.00	12.50	50.00
	27 W	1.000	2.00	4.00	10.00	35.00
	29 W	.450	2.00	4.00	10.00	35.00
	29H	1.250	2.00	4.00	10.00	35.00
	30H	.500	3.00	6.00	15.00	40.00
	31H	Inc. Ab.	3.00	6.00	15.00	40.00
	33H	.450	2.00	4.00	10.00	35.00
	Common date		—	—	Proof	145.00

2-1/2 QIRSH

3.4600 g, .833 SILVER, .0927 oz ASW
Accession Date: AH1293

KM#	Year	Mintage	Fine	VF	XF	Unc
278	6	2 pcs.	—	—	—	4500.

5 QIRSH

6.9200 g, .833 SILVER, .1854 oz ASW
Accession Date: AH1293
Obv: Flower at right of toughra.

KM#	Year	Mintage	Fine	VF	XF	Unc
279	2	—	700.00	1200.	1800.	—
	6	2 pcs.	—	—	—	4000.

7.0000 g, .833 SILVER, .1875 oz ASW

KM#	Year	Mintage	Fine	VF	XF	Unc
294	10 W	4.195	3.00	7.50	15.00	50.00
	11 W	Inc. Ab.	4.00	10.00	25.00	75.00
	15 W	.600	8.00	20.00	40.00	125.00
	16 W	1.205	5.00	12.50	25.00	75.00
	17 W	.872	6.00	15.00	30.00	100.00
	19 W	—	—	Reported, not confirmed		
	20 W	.464	10.00	25.00	50.00	125.00
	21 W	.633	5.00	12.50	20.00	60.00
	22 W	1.118	5.00	12.50	20.00	60.00
	24 W	1.050	5.00	12.50	20.00	60.00
	27 W	.448	5.00	12.50	20.00	50.00
	29 W	.600	5.00	10.00	20.00	50.00
	29H	3.465	5.00	10.00	20.00	50.00
	30H	1.213	5.00	10.00	22.50	60.00
	31H	1.959	5.00	10.00	22.50	60.00
	32H	Inc.Be.	5.00	10.00	20.00	50.00
	33H	2.800	3.00	7.50	20.00	50.00
	Common date		—	—	Proof	285.00

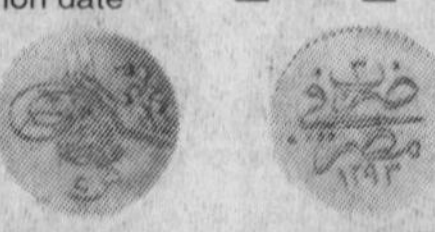

0.4200 g, .875 GOLD, .0118 oz AGW
Obv: Flower at right of toughra.

KM#	Year	Mintage	VG	Fine	VF	XF
280	1	—	—	Reported, not confirmed		
	2	—	100.00	200.00	400.00	800.00
	3	—	40.00	65.00	75.00	100.00
	4	—	—	Reported, not confirmed		
	5	—	100.00	150.00	200.00	250.00
	6	—	150.00	250.00	400.00	650.00
	7	—	40.00	65.00	75.00	100.00
	22	—	100.00	150.00	200.00	300.00

Obv: *Al-Ghazi* at right of toughra.

KM#	Year	Mintage	VG	Fine	VF	XF
298	7	—	—	Reported, not confirmed		
	15	—	100.00	200.00	350.00	600.00
	16	—	20.00	45.00	70.00	90.00
	18	—	15.00	25.00	40.00	65.00
	24	—	25.00	50.00	100.00	150.00
	26	—	25.00	50.00	100.00	150.00
	34	.008	20.00	35.00	65.00	85.00

Rev: Leg. in wreath.

KM#	Year	Mintage	VG	Fine	VF	XF
A299	15	—	100.00	200.00	350.00	600.00

10 QIRSH

14.0000 g, .833 SILVER, .3749 oz ASW
Accession Date: AH1293
Obv: Flower at right of toughra.

KM#	Year	Mintage	Fine	VF	XF	Unc
281	6	2 pcs.	—	—	—	6000.

KM#	Year	Mintage	Fine	VF	XF	Unc
295	10 W	4.030	5.00	10.00	35.00	100.00
	11 W	Inc. Ab.	8.00	15.00	40.00	100.00
	15 W	.300	15.00	30.00	65.00	150.00
	15 W	—	—	—	Proof	450.00
	16 W	.602	8.00	15.00	45.00	125.00
	17 W	.380	10.00	20.00	55.00	150.00
	20 W	.340	15.00	30.00	55.00	150.00
	21 W	.420	10.00	20.00	45.00	125.00
	22 W	.600	10.00	20.00	45.00	125.00
	24 W	.500	10.00	20.00	45.00	125.00
	27 W	.250	15.00	25.00	60.00	150.00
	29 W	*2.450	8.00	15.00	40.00	100.00
	29H	2.950	8.00	15.00	35.00	100.00
	30H	1.000	8.00	15.00	35.00	100.00
	31H	1.250	10.00	20.00	45.00	150.00
	32H	Inc.Be.	8.00	15.00	35.00	100.00
	33H	2.400	8.00	12.50	35.00	100.00
	Common date		—	—	Proof	435.00

stimated.

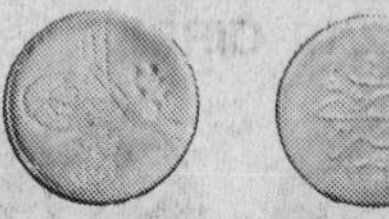

0.8544 g, .875 GOLD, .0240 oz AGW
Obv: Flower at right of touhgra.

KM#	Year	Mintage	VG	Fine	VF	XF
A282	4	—	300.00	500.00	900.00	1500.

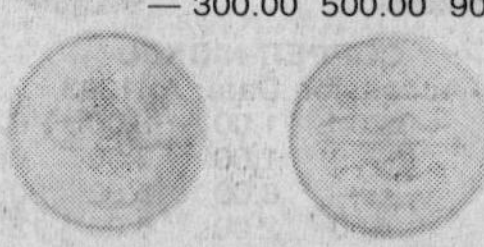

Obv: *Al-Ghazi* at right of toughra.

KM#	Year	Mintage	VG	Fine	VF	XF
282	5	—	—	Reported, not confirmed		
	7	—	—	Reported, not confirmed		
	8	—	—	Reported, not confirmed		
	17	—	20.00	40.00	80.00	120.00
	18	—	25.00	50.00	75.00	125.00
	23	—	40.00	60.00	120.00	200.00
	34	.005	20.00	40.00	80.00	120.00

20 QIRSH

27.5700 g, .833 SILVER, .7385 oz ASW
Accession Date: AH1293

KM#	Year	Mintage	Fine	VF	XF	Unc
283	1	—	550.00	900.00	1500.	2000.
	5	—	650.00	1750.	2500.	3500.
	6	2 pcs.	—	—	—	12,500.

28.0000 g, .833 SILVER, .7499 oz ASW

KM#	Year	Mintage	Fine	VF	XF	Unc
296	10 W	.874	12.00	25.00	70.00	375.00
	11 W	.126	15.00	40.00	100.00	425.00
	15 W	.029	17.50	50.00	150.00	500.00
	16 W	.055	15.00	40.00	100.00	425.00
	17 W	.054	17.50	50.00	150.00	500.00
	17 W	—	—	—	Proof	800.00
	20 W	.172	12.00	40.00	100.00	425.00
	21 W	.158	12.00	30.00	85.00	400.00
	22 W	.287	12.00	30.00	85.00	400.00
	24 W	.500	12.00	30.00	85.00	400.00
	27 W	.250	15.00	40.00	100.00	425.00
	29 W	.500	12.00	30.00	85.00	400.00
	29H	.425	12.00	30.00	80.00	400.00
	30H	.200	12.00	30.00	80.00	400.00
	31H	.250	12.00	30.00	80.00	400.00
	32H	Inc.Be.	12.00	30.00	85.00	400.00
	33H	.300	12.00	30.00	85.00	400.00
	Common date		—	—	Proof	825.00

25 QIRSH

2.1360 g, .875 GOLD, .0601 oz AGW
Accession Date: AH1293
Obv: Flower right of toughra.

KM#	Year	Mintage				
A284	2	—	—	Reported, not confirmed		
	6	2 pcs.	—	—	—	7500.

50 QIRSH

(1/2 Pound)

4.2720 g, .875 GOLD, .1202 oz AGW
Accession Date: AH1293

KM#	Year	Mintage	VG	Fine	VF	XF
284	2	—	—	Reported, not confirmed		
	3	—	—	Reported, not confirmed		
	6	2 pcs.	—	—	—	8000.

NOTE: Previously reported year 1 examples are those of Murad V.

100 QIRSH

(1 Pound)

8.5440 g, .875 GOLD, .2404 oz AGW
Accession Date: AH1293
Obv: Toughra of Abdul Hamid II.

KM#	Year	Mintage	Fine	VF	XF	Unc
285	1	—	400.00	800.00	1350.	2250.
	3	—	—	Reported, not confirmed		
	4	—	400.00	800.00	1350.	2250.
	5	—	—	Reported, not confirmed		
	6	4 pcs.	—	—	—	8200.
	7	—	—	Reported, not confirmed		
	8	—	—	—	Rare	—

8.5000 g, .875 GOLD, .2391 oz AGW
Floral border.

KM#	Year	Mintage	Fine	VF	XF	Unc
297	12	.052	120.00	160.00	190.00	280.00

500 QIRSH

(5 Pounds)

42.7400 g, .875 GOLD, 1.2024 oz AGW
Accession Date: AH1293

KM#	Year	Mintage	Fine	VF	XF	Unc
286	1	—	1250.	3000.	4750.	7500.
	6	**5 pcs.	2500.	5500.	9750.*	14,500.

***NOTE:** Spinks & Son Zurich Auction 18 2-86 superb Unc. realized $14,520.
****NOTE:** Although the mint report documents only 5 pieces, perhaps 10 pieces are thought to exist.

MUHAMMAD V

AH1327-1332/1909-1914AD

1/40 QIRSH

BRONZE
Accession Date: AH1327

KM#	Year	Mintage	Fine	VF	XF	Unc
300	2H	2.000	1.50	3.00	7.50	25.00
	3H	2.000	1.50	3.00	7.50	25.00
	4H	1.200	1.50	3.00	7.50	25.00
	6H	1.200	1.00	2.00	5.00	20.00

1/20 QIRSH

BRONZE
Accession Date: AH1327

KM#	Year	Mintage	Fine	VF	XF	Unc
301	2H	2.000	1.00	3.00	6.00	18.00
	3H	2.000	1.50	4.00	8.00	25.00
	4H	2.400	1.00	3.00	6.00	18.00
	6H	1.400	.75	2.00	6.00	18.00

1/10 QIRSH

COPPER-NICKEL
Accession Date: AH1327

KM#	Year	Mintage	Fine	VF	XF	Unc
302	2H	3.000	3.00	6.00	10.00	25.00
	3	1.000	5.00	12.00	20.00	50.00
	4H	3.000	1.00	2.00	4.00	12.50
	6H	3.000	.75	1.50	3.00	12.50
	Common date		—	—	Proof	110.00

2/10 QIRSH

COPPER-NICKEL
Accession Date: AH1327

KM#	Year	Mintage	Fine	VF	XF	Unc
303	2H	1.000	2.00	4.00	7.00	25.00
	3	.500	3.00	10.00	15.00	35.00
	4H	1.000	2.00	4.00	7.00	25.00
	6H	1.000	1.25	3.00	7.00	25.00
	Common date		—	—	Proof	120.00

5/10 QIRSH

COPPER-NICKEL
Accession Date: AH1327

KM#	Year	Mintage	Fine	VF	XF	Unc
304	2H	2.131	2.50	6.00	15.00	50.00
	3	1.000	5.00	15.00	35.00	75.00
	4H	3.327	1.00	2.50	6.00	25.00
	6H	3.000	1.00	2.50	6.00	25.00

QIRSH

1.4000 g, .833 SILVER, .0375 oz ASW
Accession Date: AH1327

KM#	Year	Mintage	Fine	VF	XF	Unc
305	2H	.251	2.00	4.00	15.00	28.00
	3H	.171	2.25	4.50	16.00	35.00

COPPER-NICKEL

KM#	Year	Mintage	Fine	VF	XF	Unc
306	2H	1.000	2.00	5.00	12.00	35.00
	3	.300	20.00	40.00	75.00	150.00
	4H	.500	4.00	8.00	22.50	65.00
	6H	2.500	2.00	4.00	8.00	28.00

2 QIRSH

2.8000 g, .833 SILVER, .0750 oz ASW
Accession Date: AH1327

KM#	Year	Mintage	Fine	VF	XF	Unc
307	2H	.250	5.00	12.50	28.00	90.00
	3H	.300	5.00	12.50	28.00	90.00

5 QIRSH

7.0000 g, .833 SILVER, .1875 oz ASW
Accession Date: AH1327

KM#	Year	Mintage	Fine	VF	XF	Unc
308	2H	.574	10.00	30.00	60.00	150.00
	3H	2.400	5.00	12.50	30.00	70.00
	4H	1.351	6.00	15.00	35.00	85.00
	6H	7.400	4.00	10.00	20.00	55.00
	Common date		—	—	Proof	350.00

10 QIRSH

14.0000 g, .833 SILVER, .3749 oz ASW
Accession Date: AH1327

KM#	Year	Mintage	Fine	VF	XF	Unc
309	2H	.300	20.00	30.00	60.00	200.00
	3H	1.300	8.00	15.00	30.00	115.00
	4H	.300	10.00	25.00	40.00	200.00
	6H	4.212	6.00	12.50	25.00	100.00
	Common date		—	—	Proof	475.00

20 QIRSH

28.0000 g, .833 SILVER, .7499 oz ASW
Accession Date: AH1327

KM#	Year	Mintage	Fine	VF	XF	Unc
310	2H	.075	30.00	50.00	160.00	500.00
	3H	.600	15.00	30.00	80.00	325.00
	4H	.100	25.00	40.00	90.00	425.00
	6H	.875	12.50	25.00	60.00	300.00
	Common date		—	—	Proof	950.00

BRITISH OCCUPATION

1914-1922

HUSSEIN KAMIL

AH1333-1336/1914-1917AD

1/2 MILLIEME

BRONZE
Accession Date: AH1333

KM#	Date	Year	Mintage	VF	XF	Unc
312	AH1335	1916	—	—	—	—
	1335	1917	4.000	3.50	7.50	25.00

MILLIEME

COPPER-NICKEL
Accession Date: AH1333

KM#	Date	Year	Mintage	VF	XF	Unc
313	AH1335	1917	4.002	3.00	6.00	20.00
	1335	1917H	12.000	1.00	3.00	12.00

2 MILLIEMES

COPPER-NICKEL
Accession Date: AH1333

KM#	Date	Year	Mintage	VF	XF	Unc
314	AH1335	1916H	.300	3.00	7.50	30.00
	1335	1917	3.006	2.50	6.50	22.00
	1335	1917H	9.000	1.00	3.00	14.00

5 MILLIEMES

COPPER-NICKEL
Accession Date: AH1333

KM#	Date	Year	Mintage	VF	XF	Unc
315	AH1335	1916	3.000	5.00	10.00	25.00
	1335	1916H	3.000	3.00	8.00	20.00
	1335	1917	6.776	2.00	6.00	15.00
	1335	1917H	37.000	1.00	2.00	8.00

10 MILLIEMES

COPPER-NICKEL
Accession Date: AH1333

KM#	Date	Year	Mintage	VF	XF	Unc
316	AH1335	1916	1.007	5.00	10.00	35.00
	1335	1916H	1.000	4.00	8.00	25.00
	1335	1917	1.011	5.00	15.00	40.00
	1335	1917H	6.000	2.00	4.00	15.00
	1335	1917KN	4.000	3.00	6.00	20.00

2 PIASTRES

2.8000 g, .833 SILVER, .0749 oz ASW
Accession Date: AH1333

KM#	Date	Year	Mintage	VF	XF	Unc
317.1	AH1335	1916	2.505	4.00	10.00	30.00
	1335	1917	4.461	2.00	5.00	20.00

W/o inner circle.

KM#	Date	Year	Mintage	VF	XF	Unc
317.2	AH1335	1917H	2.180	2.00	5.00	15.00

5 PIASTRES

7.0000 g, .833 SILVER, .1874 oz ASW
Accession Date: AH1333

KM#	Date	Year	Mintage	VF	XF	Unc
318.1	AH1335	1916	6.000	5.00	15.00	40.00
	1335	1917	9.218	4.00	12.50	35.00

W/o inner circle.

KM#	Date	Year	Mintage	VF	XF	Unc
318.2	AH1335	1917H	5.036	4.00	12.50	45.00
	1335	1917H	—	—	Proof	325.00

10 PIASTRES

14.0000 g, .833 SILVER, .3749 oz ASW
Accession Date: AH1333

KM#	Date	Year	Mintage	VF	XF	Unc
319	AH1335	1916	2.900	10.00	25.00	110.00
	1335	1917	4.859	10.00	20.00	95.00

W/o inner circle.

KM#	Date	Year	Mintage	VF	XF	Unc
320	AH1335	1917H	2.000	10.00	30.00	125.00

20 PIASTRES

28.0000 g, .833 SILVER, .7499 oz ASW
Accession Date: AH1333

KM#	Date	Year	Mintage	VF	XF	Unc
321	AH1335	1916	1.500	15.00	25.00	160.00
	1335	1917	.840	15.00	25.00	180.00
	1335	1917	—	—	Proof	750.00

W/o inner circle.

KM#	Date	Year	Mintage	VF	XF	Unc
322	AH1335	1917H	.250	35.00	60.00	300.00

100 PIASTRES

8.5000 g, .875 GOLD, .2391 oz AGW
Accession Date: AH1333

KM#	Date	Year	Mintage	VF	XF	Unc
324	AH1335	1916	.010	100.00	150.00	300.00
	1335	1916	—	—	Proof	1500.

NOTE: Restrikes may exist.

FU'AD I

Sultan, AH1336-1341/1917-1922AD

2 PIASTRES

2.8000 g, .833 SILVER, .0749 oz ASW
Accession Date: AH1335

KM#	Date	Year	Mintage	VF	XF	Unc
325	AH1338	1920H	2.820	75.00	160.00	375.00

5 PIASTRES

7.0000 g, .833 SILVER, .1874 oz ASW
Accession Date: AH1335

KM#	Date	Year	Mintage	VF	XF	Unc
326	AH1338	1920H	1.000	50.00	100.00	350.00

10 PIASTRES

14.0000 g, .833 SILVER, .3749 oz ASW
Accession Date: AH1335

KM#	Date	Year	Mintage	VF	XF	Unc
327	AH1338	1920H	.500	35.00	90.00	360.00

20 PIASTRES

28.0000 g, .833 SILVER, .7499 oz ASW
Accession Date: AH1335

KM#	Date	Year	Mintage	VF	XF	Unc
328	AH1338	1920H	2 known	—	Rare	—

KINGDOM

1922-1952

FU'AD I

King, AH1341-1355/1922-1936AD

1/2 MILLIEME

BRONZE

KM#	Date	Year	Mintage	VF	XF	Unc
330	AH1342	1924H	3.000	5.00	10.00	25.00
	1342	1924H	—	—	Proof	120.00

KM#	Date	Year	Mintage	VF	XF	Unc
343	AH1348	1929BP	1.000	15.00	25.00	50.00
	1351	1932H	1.000	7.50	15.00	30.00
	1351	1932H	—	—	Proof	160.00

MILLIEME

BRONZE

KM#	Date	Year	Mintage	VF	XF	Unc
331	AH1342	1924H	6.500	3.00	7.50	25.00

KM#	Date	Year	Mintage	VF	XF	Unc
344	AH1348	1929BP	4.500	4.00	10.00	25.00
	1351	1932H	2.500	1.25	3.00	15.00
	1351	1932H	—	—	Proof	120.00
	1352	1933H	5.110	3.00	10.00	20.00
	1354	1935H	18.000	.50	2.00	8.00

2 MILLIEMES

COPPER-NICKEL

KM#	Date	Year	Mintage	VF	XF	Unc
332	AH1342	1924H	4.500	3.00	10.00	25.00
	1342	1924H	—	—	Proof	120.00

KM#	Date	Year	Mintage	VF	XF	Unc
345	AH1348	1929BP	*3.500	1.00	3.00	10.00

2-1/2 MILLIEMES

COPPER-NICKEL

KM#	Date	Year	Mintage	VF	XF	Unc
356	AH1352	1933	4.000	3.00	8.00	30.00

5 MILLIEMES

COPPER-NICKEL

KM#	Date	Year	Mintage	VF	XF	Unc
333	AH1342	1924	6.000	3.00	7.50	27.50

KM#	Date	Year	Mintage	VF	XF	Unc
346	AH1348	1929BP	4.000	2.00	8.00	25.00
	1352	1933H	3.000	4.00	12.00	35.00
	1354	1935H	8.000	1.00	5.00	12.50
	1354	1935H	—	—	Proof	120.00

10 MILLIEMES

COPPER-NICKEL

KM#	Date	Year	Mintage	VF	XF	Unc
334	AH1342	1924	2.000	5.00	15.00	50.00

KM#	Date	Year	Mintage	VF	XF	Unc
347	AH1348	1929BP	1.500	4.00	10.00	35.00
	1352	1933H	1.500	4.00	10.00	45.00
	1354	1935H	4.000	2.00	7.50	20.00

2 PIASTRES

2.8000 g, .833 SILVER, .0749 oz ASW

KM#	Date	Year	Mintage	VF	XF	Unc
335	AH1342	1923H	2.500	4.00	10.00	30.00

KM#	Date	Year	Mintage	VF	XF	Unc
348	AH1348	1929BP	.500	2.00	6.00	20.00

NOTE: Edge varieties exist.

5 PIASTRES

7.0000 g, .833 SILVER, .1874 oz ASW

KM#	Date	Year	Mintage	VF	XF	Unc
336	AH1341	1923	.800	10.00	27.00	55.00
	1341	1923H	1.800	6.00	25.00	55.00
	1341	1923H	—	—	Proof	250.00

KM#	Date	Year	Mintage	VF	XF	Unc
349	AH1348	1929BP	.800	10.00	35.00	60.00
	1352	1933	1.300	7.50	25.00	50.00
	1352	1933	—	—	Proof	250.00

10 PIASTRES

14.0000 g, .833 SILVER, .3749 oz ASW

KM#	Date	Year	Mintage	VF	XF	Unc
337	AH1341	1923	.400	10.00	35.00	120.00
	1341	1923H	1.000	10.00	35.00	120.00
	1341	1923H	—	—	Proof	450.00

KM#	Date	Year	Mintage	VF	XF	Unc
350	AH1348	1929BP	.400	12.50	32.50	100.00
	1352	1933	*.350	10.00	30.00	85.00
	1352	1933	—	—	Proof	475.00

20 PIASTRES

28.0000 g, .833 SILVER, .7499 oz ASW

KM#	Date	Year	Mintage	VF	XF	Unc
338	AH1341	1923	.100	30.00	85.00	425.00
	1341	1923H	.050	30.00	85.00	425.00
	1341	1923H	—	—	Proof	875.00

1.7000 g, .875 GOLD, .0478 oz AGW

KM#	Date	Year	Mintage	VF	XF	Unc
339	AH1341	1923	.065	40.00	60.00	125.00

Obv: Bust left.

KM#	Date	Year	Mintage	VF	XF	Unc
351	AH1348	1929	—	40.00	60.00	120.00
	1348	1929	—	—	Proof	—
	1349	1930	—	40.00	60.00	120.00
	1349	1930	—	—	Proof	—

28.0000 g, .833 SILVER, .7499 oz ASW

KM#	Date	Year	Mintage	VF	XF	Unc
352	AH1348	1929BP	.050	35.00	75.00	450.00
	1352	1933	.025	22.50	45.00	300.00
	1352	1933	—	—	Proof	—

50 PIASTRES

4.2500 g, .875 GOLD, .1195 oz AGW

KM#	Date	Year	Mintage	VF	XF	Unc
340	AH1341	1923	.018	70.00	90.00	150.00

KM#	Date	Year	Mintage	VF	XF	Unc
353	AH1348	1929	—	80.00	100.00	160.00
	1348	1929	—	—	Proof	—
	1349	1930	—	70.00	80.00	130.00
	1349	1930	—	—	Proof	—

100 PIASTRES

8.5000 g, .875 GOLD, .2391 oz AGW

KM#	Date	Year	Mintage	VF	XF	Unc
341	AH1340	1922	.025	120.00	150.00	265.00

Obv: Bust left

KM#	Date	Year	Mintage	VF	XF	Unc
354	AH1348	1929	—	120.00	150.00	265.00
	1349	1930	—	120.00	150.00	265.00
	1349	1930	—	—	Proof	—

500 PIASTRES

42.5000 g, .875 GOLD, 1.1957 oz AGW

KM#	Date	Year	Mintage	VF	XF	Unc
342	AH1340	1922	1,800	—	950.00	1600.
	1340	1922	—	—	Proof	1800.

NOTE: Circulation coins were struck in both red and yellow gold.

KM#	Date	Year	Mintage	VF	XF	Unc
355	AH1348	1929	—	—	850.00	1500.
	1349	1930	—	—	850.00	1500.
	1351	1932	—	—	850.00	1500.
	1351	1932	—	—	Proof	1800.

FAROUK I

AH1355-1372/1936-1952AD

1/2 MILLIEME

BRONZE

KM#	Date	Year	Mintage	VF	XF	Unc
357	AH1357	1938	4.000	4.00	7.50	20.00
	1357	1938	—	—	Proof	100.00

MILLIEME

BRONZE

KM#	Date	Year	Mintage	VF	XF	Unc
358	AH1357	1938	26.240	.50	2.00	7.00
	1357	1938	—	—	Proof	120.00
	1364	1945	10.000	3.00	10.00	50.00
	1366	1947	—	3.00	10.00	50.00
	1369	1950	5.000	1.00	3.00	10.00
	1369	1950	—	—	Proof	85.00

COPPER-NICKEL

KM#	Date	Year	Mintage	VF	XF	Unc
362	AH1357	1938	3.500	2.50	5.00	15.00

2 MILLIEMES

COPPER-NICKEL

KM#	Date	Year	Mintage	VF	XF	Unc
359	AH1357	1938	2.500	4.00	10.00	25.00
	1357	1938	—	—	Proof	140.00

5 MILLIEMES

BRONZE

KM#	Date	Year	Mintage	VF	XF	Unc
360	AH1357	1938	—	1.00	3.00	10.00
	1357	1938	—	—	Proof	65.00
	1362	1943	—	1.00	3.00	10.00

COPPER-NICKEL

KM#	Date	Year	Mintage	VF	XF	Unc
363	AH1357	1938	7.000	1.00	3.00	10.00
	1357	1938	—	—	Proof	75.00
	1360	1941	11.500	.50	2.50	8.00

10 MILLIEMES

BRONZE

KM#	Date	Year	Mintage	VF	XF	Unc
361	AH1357	1938	—	1.00	3.00	10.00
	1357	1938	—	—	Proof	140.00
	1362	1943	—	.75	3.00	10.00

COPPER-NICKEL

KM#	Date	Year	Mintage	VF	XF	Unc
364	AH1357	1938	3.500	1.00	3.00	12.50
	1357	1938	—	—	Proof	85.00
	1360	1941	5.322	1.00	3.00	12.50

2 PIASTRES

2.80000 g, .833 SILVER, .0749 oz ASW

KM#	Date	Year	Mintage	VF	XF	Unc
365	AH1356	1937	.500	1.00	2.50	7.50
	1356	1937	—	—	Proof	300.00
	1358	1939	.500	4.00	10.00	75.00
	1358	1939	—	—	Proof	200.00
	1361	1942	10.000	1.50	4.00	10.00
	?	1948	Reported, not confirmed			

NOTE: Rim varieties exist for AH1361 dated coins.

2.8000 g, .500 SILVER, .0450 oz ASW

KM#	Date	Year	Mintage	VF	XF	Unc
369	AH1363	1944	.032	1.00	1.50	4.00

5 PIASTRES

7.0000 g, .833 SILVER, .1874 oz ASW

KM#	Date	Year	Mintage	VF	XF	Unc
366	AH1356	1937	—	3.00	6.00	15.00
	1356	1937	—	—	Proof	275.00
	1358	1939	8.000	3.00	6.00	15.00
	1358	1939	—	—	Proof	275.00

10 PIASTRES

14.0000 g, .833 SILVER, .3749 oz ASW

KM#	Date	Year	Mintage	VF	XF	Unc
367	AH1356	1937	2.800	7.50	10.00	32.00
	1356	1937	—	—	Proof	375.00
	1358	1939	2.850	7.50	10.00	32.00
	1358	1939	—	—	Proof	300.00

20 PIASTRES

28.0000 g, .833 SILVER, .7499 oz ASW

KM#	Date	Year	Mintage	VF	XF	Unc
368	AH1356	1937	—	15.00	35.00	95.00
	1356	1937	—	—	Proof	1000.
	1358	1939	—	15.00	35.00	95.00
	1358	1939	—	—	Proof	1200.

1.7000 g, .875 GOLD, .0478 oz AGW
Royal Wedding

KM#	Date	Year	Mintage	VF	XF	Unc
370	AH1357	1938	.020	30.00	50.00	90.00
	1357	1938	—	—	Proof	R,NC

50 PIASTRES

4.2500 g, .875 GOLD, .1195 oz AGW
Royal Wedding

KM#	Date	Year	Mintage	VF	XF	Unc
371	AH1357	1938	.010	100.00	120.00	225.00
	1357	1938	—	—	Proof	R,NC

100 PIASTRES

8.5000 g, .875 GOLD, .2391 oz AGW
Royal Wedding

KM#	Date	Year	Mintage	VF	XF	Unc
372	AH1357	1938	5,000	150.00	200.00	325.00
	1357	1938	—	—	Proof	R,NC

NOTE: Circulation coins were struck in both red and yellow gold.

500 PIASTRES

42.5000 g, .875 GOLD, 1.1957 oz AGW
Royal Wedding

KM#	Date	Year	Mintage	VF	XF	Unc
373	AH1357	1938	—	—	1500.	2250.
	1357	1938	—	—	Proof	2750.

SPECIMEN SETS (SS)

KM#	Date	Mintage	Identification	Issue Price	Mkt. Val.
SS1	1916/7(10)	—	KM312-316,317.1,318.1, 319,321,324	—	1700.

PROOF SETS (PS)

KM#	Date	Mintage	Identification	Issue Price	Mkt. Val.
PS1	1938(4)	—	KM370-373	4200.	4500.

REPUBLIC

1953-1958

MILLIEME

ALUMINUM-BRONZE
Rev: Small sphinx w/outlined base.

KM#	Date	Year	Mintage	VF	XF	Unc
375	AH1373	1954	—	50.00	100.00	200.00
375	1374	1954	—	3.00	6.00	25.00
	1374	1955	—	2.00	5.00	15.00
	1375	1955	—	2.00	5.00	15.00
	1375	1956	—	2.00	5.00	15.00

Rev: Small sphinx w/o base outlined.

KM#	Date	Year	Mintage	VF	XF	Unc
376	AH1373	1954	—	—	—	—
	1374	1954	—	2.00	5.00	15.00
	1374	1955	—	1.00	2.00	5.00
	1375	1955	—	1.00	2.00	5.00
	1375	1956	—	1.50	2.50	10.00
	1376	1957	—	—	—	—

Rev: Large sphinx.

KM#	Date	Year	Mintage	VF	XF	Unc
377	AH1375	1956	—	.50	1.00	4.00
	1376	1957	—	.75	1.50	5.00
	1377	1958	—	.75	1.50	5.00

5 MILLIEMES

ALUMINUM-BRONZE
Rev: Small sphinx.

KM#	Date	Year	Mintage	VF	XF	Unc
378	AH1373	1954	—	5.00	10.00	35.00
	1374	1954	—	4.00	8.00	25.00
	1374	1955	—	10.00	20.00	50.00
	1375	1956	—	3.00	6.00	15.00

Rev: Large sphinx.

KM#	Date	Year	Mintage	VF	XF	Unc
379	AH1376	1957	—	2.00	4.00	10.00
	1377	1957	—	2.00	4.00	10.00
	1377	1958	—	2.00	4.00	10.00

10 MILLIEMES

Thin *milliemes*

Thick *milliemes*

ALUMINUM-BRONZE
Rev: Small sphinx.

KM#	Date	Year	Mintage	VF	XF	Unc
380	AH1373	1954	thin *milliemes*			
			—	5.00	10.00	25.00
	1374	1954	—	4.00	8.00	20.00
	1374	1955	thick *milliemes*			
			—	3.00	6.00	15.00

Rev: Large sphinx.

KM#	Date	Year	Mintage	VF	XF	Unc
381	AH1374	1955	—	50.00	85.00	150.00
	1375	1956	—	3.00	6.00	15.00
	1376	1957	—	2.00	5.00	12.00
	1377	1958	—	2.00	5.00	12.00

5 PIASTRES

3.5000 g, .720 SILVER, .0810 oz ASW

KM#	Date	Year	Mintage	VF	XF	Unc
382	1375	1956	—	1.50	3.00	6.00
	1376	1956	—	3.00	5.00	10.00
	1376	1957	—	1.50	3.00	6.00

10 PIASTRES

7.0000 g, .625 SILVER, .1406 oz ASW

KM#	Date	Year	Mintage	VF	XF	Unc
383	AH1374	1955	1.408	2.50	6.00	15.00

NOTE: Varieties in date sizes exist.

7.0000 g, .720 SILVER, .1620 oz ASW

KM#	Date	Year	Mintage	VF	XF	Unc
383a	AH1375	1956	—	2.50	6.00	12.00
	1376	1957	—	2.50	5.00	10.00

20 PIASTRES

14.0000 g, .720 SILVER, .3241 oz ASW

KM#	Date	Year	Mintage	VF	XF	Unc
384	AH1375	1956	—	5.00	9.00	18.00

25 PIASTRES

17.5000 g., .720 SILVER, .4051 oz ASW
Suez Canal Nationalization

KM#	Date	Year	Mintage	VF	XF	Unc
385	AH1375	1956	.258	6.00	10.00	20.00

National Assembly Inauguration

KM#	Date	Year	Mintage	VF	XF	Unc
389	AH1376	1957	.246	6.00	9.00	17.00

50 PIASTRES

28.0000 g., .900 SILVER, .8102 oz ASW
Evacuation of the British

KM#	Date	Year	Mintage	VF	XF	Unc
386	AH1375	1956	.250	7.50	15.00	22.00

POUND

8.5000 g, .875 GOLD, .2391 oz AGW
3rd and 5th Anniversaries of Revolution

KM#	Date	Year	Mintage	VF	XF	Unc
387	AH1374	1955	.016	—	135.00	200.00
	1377	1957	.010	—	150.00	225.00

NOTE: Struck in red and yellow gold.

5 POUNDS

42.5000 g, .875 GOLD, 1.1957 oz AGW
3rd and 5th Anniversaries of Revolution

KM#	Date	Year	Mintage	VF	XF	Unc
388	AH1374	1955	—	—	800.00	1400.
	1377	1957	—	—	800.00	1400.

NOTE: Struck in red and yellow gold.

UNITED ARAB REPUBLIC

1958-1971

MILLIEME

ALUMINUM-BRONZE

KM#	Date	Year	Mintage	VF	XF	Unc
393	AH1380	1960	—	.10	.15	.30
	1386	1966	—	—	Proof	3.00

2 MILLIEMES

ALUMINUM-BRONZE

KM#	Date	Year	Mintage	VF	XF	Unc
403	AH1381	1962	—	.15	.35	.60
	1386	1966	—	—	Proof	3.00

5 MILLIEMES

ALUMINUM-BRONZE

KM#	Date	Year	Mintage	VF	XF	Unc
394	AH1380	1960	—	.15	.45	.80
	1386	1966	—	—	Proof	3.00

ALUMINUM

KM#	Date	Year	Mintage	VF	XF	Unc
410	AH1386	1967	—	.15	.40	.65

10 MILLIEMES

ALUMINUM-BRONZE
Obv: *Misr* above denomination.

KM#	Date	Year	Mintage	VF	XF	Unc
395	AH1377	1958	—	15.00	20.00	40.00
	1380	1960	16.080	.80	1.20	2.25
	1386	1966	—	—	Proof	4.00

Obv: W/o *Misr* above denomination.

KM#	Date	Year	Mintage	VF	XF	Unc
396	AH1377	1958	—	15.00	20.00	40.00

ALUMINUM

KM#	Date	Year	Mintage	VF	XF	Unc
411	AH1386	1967	—	.10	.25	.65

20 MILLIEMES

ALUMINUM-BRONZE
Agriculture and Industrial Fair

KM#	Date	Year	Mintage	VF	XF	Unc
390	AH1378	1958	—	.75	1.50	5.00

5 PIASTRES

3.5000 g, .720 SILVER, .0810 oz ASW

KM#	Date	Year	Mintage	VF	XF	Unc
397	AH1380	1960	—	1.75	2.50	4.00
	1386	1966	—	—	Proof	7.50

2.5000 g, .720 SILVER, .0578 oz ASW
Diversion of the Nile

KM#	Date	Year	Mintage	VF	XF	Unc
404	AH1384	1964	.500	1.25	2.00	3.25
	1384	1964	2,000	—	Proof	7.50

COPPER-NICKEL

KM#	Date	Year	Mintage	VF	XF	Unc
412	AH1387	1967	10.800	.50	.75	1.50

NOTE: Edge varieties exist.

International Industrial Fair

KM#	Date	Year	Mintage	VF	XF	Unc
414	AH1388	1968	.500	.75	1.00	2.50

50th Anniversary of International Labor Organization

KM#	Date	Year	Mintage	VF	XF	Unc
417	AH1389	1969	.500	.75	1.00	2.50

10 PIASTRES

7.0000 g, .720 SILVER, .1620 oz ASW
1st Anniversary of U.A.R. Founding

KM#	Date	Year	Mintage	VF	XF	Unc
392	AH1378	1959	—	3.25	6.00	17.50

KM#	Date	Year	Mintage	VF	XF	Unc
398	AH1380	1960	.500	3.00	4.50	7.50
	1386	1966	—	—	Proof	15.00

5.0000 g, .720 SILVER, .1157 oz ASW
Diversion of the Nile

KM#	Date	Year	Mintage	VF	XF	Unc
405	AH1384	1964	.500	2.50	4.00	6.00
	1384	1964	2,000	—	Proof	15.00

COPPER-NICKEL

KM#	Date	Year	Mintage	VF	XF	Unc
413	AH1387	1967	13.200	.60	.90	2.00

Cairo International Agricultural Fair

KM#	Date	Year	Mintage	VF	XF	Unc
419	AH1389	1969	1.000	.75	1.25	3.00

F.A.O. Issue

KM#	Date	Year	Mintage	VF	XF	Unc
418	ND	(1970)	.500	.75	1.25	3.50

Banque Misr 50 Years

KM#	Date	Year	Mintage	VF	XF	Unc
420	AH1390	1970	.500	.60	1.00	2.00

Cairo International Industrial Fair

KM#	Date	Year	Mintage	VF	XF	Unc
421.1	AH1390	1970	.500	.60	1.00	3.25

New shorter Arabic inscriptions

KM#	Date	Year	Mintage	VF	XF	Unc
421.2	AH1391	1971	.500	.60	1.00	2.75

20 PIASTRES

14.0000 g, .720 SILVER, .3241 oz ASW

KM#	Date	Year	Mintage	VF	XF	Unc
399	AH1380	1960	.400	6.00	10.00	25.00
	1386	1966	—	—	Proof	40.00

25 PIASTRES

17.5000 g, .720 SILVER, .4051 oz ASW
3rd Year of National Assembly

KM#	Date	Year	Mintage	VF	XF	Unc
400	AH1380	1960	.250	6.00	8.50	22.00

10.0000 g, .720 SILVER, .2315 oz ASW
Diversion of the Nile

KM#	Date	Year	Mintage	VF	XF	Unc
406	AH1384	1964	.250	3.00	4.50	7.50
	1384	1964	2,000	—	Proof	27.50

6.0000 g, .720 SILVER, .1388 oz ASW
President Nasser

KM#	Date	Year	Mintage	VF	XF	Unc
422	AH1390	1970	.700	2.50	4.00	6.00

12.5000 g, .720 SILVER, .2893 oz ASW
President Nasser

KM#	Date	Year	Mintage	VF	XF	Unc
423	AH1390	1970	.400	3.00	5.00	7.50

50 PIASTRES

20.0000 g, .720 SILVER, .4630 oz ASW
Diversion of the Nile

KM#	Date	Year	Mintage	VF	XF	Unc
407	AH1384	1964	.250	5.00	6.00	8.00
	1384	1964	2,000	—	Proof	45.00

1/2 POUND

4.2500 g, .875 GOLD, .1195 oz AGW
U.A.R. Founding

KM#	Date	Year	Mintage	VF	XF	Unc
391	AH1377	1958	.030	—	—	175.00

POUND

8.5000 g, .875 GOLD, .2391 oz AGW
Aswan Dam

KM#	Date	Year	Mintage	VF	XF	Unc
401	AH1379	1960	.252	—	—	140.00

25.0000 g, .720 SILVER, .5787 oz ASW
Power Station for Aswan Dam

KM#	Date	Year	Mintage	VF	XF	Unc
415	AH1387	1968	.100	5.00	6.00	8.00

Al-Azhar Mosque 1000th Anniversary

KM#	Date	Year	Mintage	VF	XF	Unc
424	AH1359-1361	1970-1972	.100	6.00	7.00	9.00

President Nasser

KM#	Date	Year	Mintage	VF	XF	Unc
425	AH1390	1970	.400	5.00	6.00	8.00

8.0000 g, .875 GOLD, .2251 oz AGW
President Nasser

KM#	Date	Year	Mintage	VF	XF	Unc
426	AH1390	1970	.010	—	—	140.00

5 POUNDS

42.5000 g, .875 GOLD, 1.1957 oz AGW
Aswan Dam

KM#	Date	Year	Mintage	VF	XF	Unc
402	AH1379	1960	5,000	—	—	675.00

26.0000 g, .875 GOLD, .7315 oz AGW
Diversion of the Nile

KM#	Date	Year	Mintage	VF	XF	Unc
408	AH1384	1964	—	—	—	400.00

1400th Anniversary of the Koran

KM#	Date	Year	Mintage	VF	XF	Unc
416	AH1388	1968	.010	—	—	350.00

Al-Azhar Mosque 1000th Anniversary

KM#	Date	Year	Mintage	VF	XF	Unc
427	AH1390	1970	—	—	—	375.00

President Nasser

KM#	Date	Year	Mintage	VF	XF	Unc
428	AH1390	1970	3,000	—	—	350.00

10 POUNDS

52.0000 g, .875 GOLD, 1.4630 oz AGW
Diversion of the Nile

KM#	Date	Year	Mintage	VF	XF	Unc
409	AH1384	1964	2,000	—	—	700.00

PROOF SETS (PS)

KM#	Date	Mintage	Identification	Issue Price	Mkt. Val.
PS2	1964(4)	2,000	KM404-407	18.00	95.00
PS3	1966(7)	2,500	KM393-395,397-399,403	9.00	75.00

ARAB REPUBLIC

1971

MILLIEME

ALUMINUM

KM#	Date	Year	Mintage	VF	XF	Unc
A423	AH1392	1972	—	.10	.30	.50

5 MILLIEMES

ALUMINUM
Mule. Obv: KM#A425. Rev: KM#433.

KM#	Date	Year	Mintage	VF	XF	Unc
A424	AH1392	1972	—	10.00	20.00	45.00

KM#	Date	Year	Mintage	VF	XF	Unc
A425	AH1392	1972	16.000	.20	.50	2.50

BRASS

KM#	Date	Year	Mintage	VF	XF	Unc
432	AH1393	1973	—	.10	.15	.30

ALUMINUM
F.A.O. Issue

KM#	Date	Year	Mintage	VF	XF	Unc
433	AH1393	1973	10.000	.10	.20	.35

BRASS
Mule. Obv: KM#432. Rev: KM#445.

KM#	Date	Year	Mintage	VF	XF	Unc
434	AH1393	1973	—	5.00	10.00	20.00

International Women's Year

KM#	Date	Year	Mintage	VF	XF	Unc
445	AH1395	1975	10.000	.10	.15	.30

F.A.O. Issue

KM#	Date	Year	Mintage	VF	XF	Unc
462	AH1397	1977	5.000	.10	.20	.50

1971 Corrective Revolution

KM#	Date	Year	Mintage	VF	XF	Unc
463	AH1397	1977	2.500	.10	.20	.50
	1399	1979	2.500	.10	.20	.50

ALUMINUM-BRONZE
Sadat's Corrective Revolution

KM#	Date	Year	Mintage	VF	XF	Unc
497	AH1400	1980	2.500	Reported, not confirmed		

10 MILLIEMES

ALUMINUM

KM#	Date	Year	Mintage	VF	XF	Unc
A426	AH1392	1972	20.000	.50	2.00	6.00

NOTE: Edge varieties exist.

BRASS

KM#	Date	Year	Mintage	VF	XF	Unc
435	AH1393	1973	—	.10	.25	.50
	1396	1976	—	.75	1.50	3.00

F.A.O. Issue

446	AH1395	1975	10.000	.10	.20	.35

F.A.O. Issue

449	AH1396	1976	10.000	.10	.20	.30

F.A.O. Issue

464	AH1397	1977	10.000	.10	.20	.85

1971 Corrective Revolution

465	AH1397	1977	2.500	.10	.20	.65
	1399	1979	2.500	.20	.40	1.00

F.A.O. Issue

476	AH1398	1978	2.000	.10	.20	.80

International Year of the Child

483	AH1399	1979	2,000	.10	.20	.65

ALUMINUM-BRONZE
Sadat's Corrective Revolution

498	AH1400	1980	2.500	.10	.25	1.00

F.A.O. Issue

499	AH1400	1980	2.000	.10	.20	.60

PIASTRE

ALUMINUM-BRONZE
Obv: Christian date left of denomination.

KM#	Date	Year	Mintage	VF	XF	Unc
553.1	AH1404	1984	—	—	—	.10

Obv: Islamic date left of denomination.

553.2	AH1404	1984	—	—	—	.10

2 PIASTRES

ALUMINUM-BRONZE

500	AH1400	1980	—	.20	.30	.60

Obv: Christian date left of denomination.

554.1	AH1404	1984	—	—	—	.10

Obv: Islamic date left of denomination.

554.2	AH1404	1984	—	—	—	.10

5 PIASTRES

COPPER-NICKEL
UNICEF 25th Anniversary

A427	AH1392	1972	.500	.75	1.00	3.00

NOTE: Error in spelling "UNICFE"

Rev: Islamic falcon

A428	AH1392	1972	—	.50	.75	2.00

Cairo State Fair

436	AH1393	1973	.500	.60	.75	2.25

National Bank of Egypt 75th Anniversary

KM#	Date	Year	Mintage	VF	XF	Unc
437	AH1393	1973	1.000	.60	.75	2.00

1st Anniversary October War

A441	AH1394	1974	2.000	.60	.75	2.00

International Woman's Year

447	AH1395	1975	2.000	.50	.65	1.00

Mule. Obv: KM#A428. Rev: KM#451.

450	1396	1976	—	5.00	10.00	20.00

1976 Cairo Trade Fair

451	AH1396	1976	.500	.60	.75	2.00

1971 Corrective Revolution

466	AH1397	1977	1.000	.50	.60	1.50
	1399	1979	—	.50	.60	1.25

50th Anniversary of Textile Industry

467	AH1397	1977	1.000	.50	.75	1.65

F.A.O. Issue

468	AH1397	1977	—	.50	.75	1.65

NOTE: Edge varieties exist.

Portland Cement

KM#	Date	Year	Mintage	VF	XF	Unc
477	AH1398	1978	.500	.50	.75	1.65

F.A.O. Issue

KM#	Date	Year	Mintage	VF	XF	Unc
478	AH1398	1978	1.000	.50	.75	1.65

International Year of the Child

KM#	Date	Year	Mintage	VF	XF	Unc
484	AH1399	1979	1.000	.50	.75	1.65

Applied Professions

KM#	Date	Year	Mintage	VF	XF	Unc
501	AH1400	1980	.500	.50	.75	1.35

Sadat's Corrective Revolution of May 15, 1971
Similar to 1 Pound, KM#514.

KM#	Date	Year	Mintage	VF	XF	Unc
502	AH1400	1980	1.000	.50	.75	1.75

ALUMINUM-BRONZE
Obv: Christian date left of denomination.

KM#	Date	Year	Mintage	VF	XF	Unc
555.1	AH1404	1984	—	—	.10	.40

Obv: Islamic date left of denomination.

KM#	Date	Year	Mintage	VF	XF	Unc
555.2	AH1404	1984	—	—	.10	.40

KM#	Date	Year	Mintage	VF	XF	Unc
622	AH1404	1984	—	—	.20	.80

COPPER-NICKEL
Export Trade Show
Similar to 5 Pounds, KM#687.

KM#	Date	Year	Mintage	VF	XF	Unc
694	AH1410	1989	.500	.50	.75	1.35

BRASS
Decorated Vase

KM#	Date	Year	Mintage	VF	XF	Unc
731	AH1413	1992	—	—	—	.75

10 PIASTRES

COPPER-NICKEL
Cairo International Fair

KM#	Date	Year	Mintage	VF	XF	Unc
429	AH1392	1972	.500	.60	1.00	2.00

Rev: Islamic falcon

KM#	Date	Year	Mintage	VF	XF	Unc
430	AH1392	1972	—	.60	1.00	2.00

First Anniversary October War

KM#	Date	Year	Mintage	VF	XF	Unc
442	AH1394	1974	2.000	.60	.90	2.50

F.A.O. Issue

KM#	Date	Year	Mintage	VF	XF	Unc
448	AH1395	1975	2.000	.60	.90	2.25

Reopening of the Suez Canal

KM#	Date	Year	Mintage	VF	XF	Unc
452	AH1396	1976	5.000	.60	.90	3.00

Mule. Obv: KM#452. Rev: KM#430.

KM#	Date	Year	Mintage	VF	XF	Unc
431	AH1392	1972	—	5.50	12.50	27.50

NOTE: Wide and narrow inscriptions exist for obverse.

F.A.O. Issue

KM#	Date	Year	Mintage	VF	XF	Unc
469	AH1397	1977	1.000	.60	.90	2.00

1971 Corrective Revolution

KM#	Date	Year	Mintage	VF	XF	Unc
470	AH1397	1977	1.000	.50	.80	2.25
	1399	1979	1.000	.50	.80	2.25

20th Anniversary Economic Union

KM#	Date	Year	Mintage	VF	XF	Unc
471	AH1397	1977	1.000	.50	.80	2.00

Cairo International Fair

KM#	Date	Year	Mintage	VF	XF	Unc
479	AH1398	1978	—	.50	.80	2.50

25th Anniversary of Abbasia Mint

KM#	Date	Year	Mintage	VF	XF	Unc
485	AH1399	1979	1.000	.50	.80	2.00

National Education Day

KM#	Date	Year	Mintage	VF	XF	Unc
486	AH1399	1979	1.000	.50	.80	2.00

Doctor's Day

KM#	Date	Year	Mintage	VF	XF	Unc
503	AH1400	1980	1.000	.50	.80	2.00

Egyptian-Israeli Peace Treaty

KM#	Date	Year	Mintage	VF	XF	Unc
504	AH1400	1980	1.000	1.50	2.50	4.50

F.A.O. Issue

KM#	Date	Year	Mintage	VF	XF	Unc
505	AH1400	1980	1.000	.50	.80	2.00

Sadat's Corrective Revolution of May 15, 1971

KM#	Date	Year	Mintage	VF	XF	Unc
506	AH1400	1980	1.000	.50	.80	2.00
	1401	1981	—	.50	.80	3.00

Scientist's Day

KM#	Date	Year	Mintage	VF	XF	Unc
520	AH1401	1981	—	.50	.80	2.00

25th Anniversary of Trade Unions

KM#	Date	Year	Mintage	VF	XF	Unc
521	AH1402	1981	—	2.00	3.00	5.50

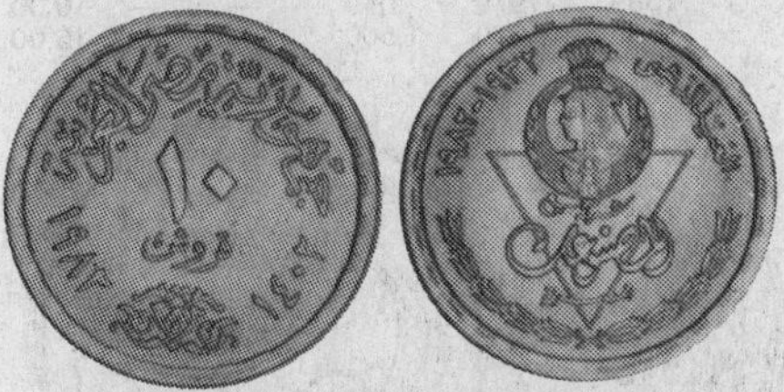

50th Anniversary of Egyptian Products Co.

KM#	Date	Year	Mintage	VF	XF	Unc
599	AH1402	1982	—	.50	.80	2.00

Circulation Coinage

KM#	Date	Year	Mintage	VF	XF	Unc
556	AH1404	1984	—	—	.50	.85

25th Anniversary of National Planning Institute

KM#	Date	Year	Mintage	VF	XF	Unc
570	AH1405	1985	.100	—	—	1.75

60th Anniversary of Egyptian Parliament

KM#	Date	Year	Mintage	VF	XF	Unc
573	AH1405	1985	.250	—	—	1.75

1973 October War

KM#	Date	Year	Mintage	VF	XF	Unc
675	AH1410	1989	.250	—	—	1.75

BRASS
Mosque

KM#	Date	Year	Mintage	VF	XF	Unc
732	AH1413	1992	—	—	—	1.00

20 PIASTRES

COPPER-NICKEL

KM#	Date	Year	Mintage	VF	XF	Unc
507	AH1400	1980	—	.75	1.00	2.35

Circulation Coinage

KM#	Date	Year	Mintage	VF	XF	Unc
557	AH1404	1984	—	—	.70	1.65

25th Anniversary of Cairo International Airport

KM#	Date	Year	Mintage	VF	XF	Unc
596	AH1405	1985	.050	—	—	2.25

Professions

KM#	Date	Year	Mintage	VF	XF	Unc
597	AH1406	1985	.100	—	—	2.25

Soldiers

KM#	Date	Year	Mintage	VF	XF	Unc
606	AH1406	1986	.050	—	—	2.25

Census

KM#	Date	Year	Mintage	VF	XF	Unc
607	AH1407	1986	.500	—	—	2.25

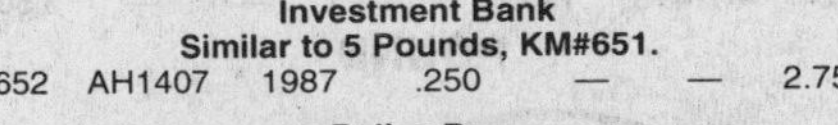

Investment Bank
Similar to 5 Pounds, KM#651.

KM#	Date	Year	Mintage	VF	XF	Unc
652	AH1407	1987	.250	—	—	2.75

Police Day
Similar to 5 Pounds, KM#621.

KM#	Date	Year	Mintage	VF	XF	Unc
646	AH1408	1988	.250	—	—	2.75

Dedication of Cairo Opera House

KM#	Date	Year	Mintage	VF	XF	Unc
650	AH1409	1988	.250	—	—	2.00

1973 October War

KM#	Date	Year	Mintage	VF	XF	Unc
676	AH1410	1989	.250	—	—	2.00

National Health Insurance

KM#	Date	Year	Mintage	VF	XF	Unc
685	AH1409	1989	.250	—	—	2.00

Cairo Subway

KM#	Date	Year	Mintage	VF	XF	Unc
690	AH1409	1989	.250	—	—	3.00

Mohamed Abdel Wahab
Similar to 5 Pounds, KM#727.

KM#	Date	Year	Mintage	VF	XF	Unc
725	AH1412	1991	.100	—	—	3.00

Mosque

KM#	Date	Year	Mintage	VF	XF	Unc
733	AH1413	1992	—	—	—	2.75

25 PIASTRES

6.0000 g, .720 SILVER, .1388 oz ASW
National Bank of Egypt 75th Anniversary

KM#	Date	Year	Mintage	VF	XF	Unc
438	AH1393	1973	.100	4.00	6.00	9.00

COPPER-NICKEL

KM#	Date	Year	Mintage	VF	XF	Unc
734	AH1413	1993	—	—	—	3.50

POUND

25.0000 g, .720 SILVER, .5787 oz ASW
F A O: Aswan Dam

KM#	Date	Year	Mintage	VF	XF	Unc
439	AH1393	1973	.050	5.00	6.00	8.00

8.0000 g, .875 GOLD, .2250 oz AGW
National Bank of Egypt 75th Anniversary

KM#	Date	Year	Mintage	VF	XF	Unc
440	AH1393	1973	7,000	—	—	150.00

15.0000 g, .720 SILVER, .3472 oz ASW
First Anniversary October War

KM#	Date	Year	Mintage	VF	XF	Unc
443	AH1394	1974	.050	—	—	9.00

F.A.O. Issue

KM#	Date	Year	Mintage	VF	XF	Unc
453	AH1396	1976	.050	—	—	9.00

Reopening of Suez Canal

KM#	Date	Year	Mintage	VF	XF	Unc
454	AH1396	1976	.250	—	—	9.00

Om Kalsoum

KM#	Date	Year	Mintage	VF	XF	Unc
455	AH1396	1976	.250	—	—	9.00

8.0000 g, .875 GOLD, .2250 oz AGW

KM#	Date	Year	Mintage	VF	XF	Unc
456	AH1396	1976	5,000	—	—	150.00

15.0000 g, .720 SILVER, .3472 oz ASW
King Faisal

KM#	Date	Year	Mintage	VF	XF	Unc
457	AH1396	1976	.100	—	—	9.00

8.0000 g, .875 GOLD, .2250 oz AGW

KM#	Date	Year	Mintage	VF	XF	Unc
458	AH1396	1976	8,000	—	—	150.00

15.0000 g, .720 SILVER, .3472 oz ASW
F.A.O. Issue

KM#	Date	Year	Mintage	VF	XF	Unc
472	AH1397	1977	.050	—	—	9.00

1971 Corrective Revolution

KM#	Date	Year	Mintage	VF	XF	Unc
473	AH1397	1977	.050	—	—	10.00
	1399	1979	.049	—	—	10.00
	1399	1979	1,500	—	Proof	15.00

20th Anniversary of Economic Union

KM#	Date	Year	Mintage	VF	XF	Unc
474	AH1397	1977	.050	—	—	9.00

8.0000 g, .875 GOLD, .2250 oz AGW

KM#	Date	Year	Mintage	VF	XF	Unc
475	AH1397	1977	5,000	—	—	150.00

15.0000 g, .720 SILVER, .3472 oz ASW
Portland Cement

KM#	Date	Year	Mintage	VF	XF	Unc
480	AH1398	1978	.050	—	—	9.00

25th Anniversary of Ain Shams University

KM#	Date	Year	Mintage	VF	XF	Unc
481	AH1398	1978	.050	—	—	9.00

F.A.O. Issue

482	AH1398	1978	.050	—	—	9.00

25th Anniversary of Abbasia Mint

488	AH1399	1979	.023	—	—	9.00
	1399	1979	2,000	—	Proof	12.00

F.A.O. Issue and I.Y.C.

489	AH1399	1979	.048	—	—	9.00
	1399	1979	2,500	—	Proof	12.00

National Education Day
Rev: Similar to KM#453.

490	AH1399	1979	.098	—	—	9.00
	1399	1979	2,000	—	Proof	12.00

100th Anniversary of Bank of Land Reform

KM#	Date	Year	Mintage	VF	XF	Unc
491	AH1399	1979	.098	—	—	9.00
	1399	1979	2,000	—	Proof	12.00

8.0000 g, .875 GOLD, .2250 oz AGW

492	AH1399	1979	4,200	—	—	125.00
	1399	1979	800 pcs.	—	Proof	225.00

15.0000 g, .720 SILVER, .3472 oz ASW
1400th Anniversary of Mohammed's Flight

493	AH1400	1979	.097	—	—	9.00
	1400	1979	3,000	—	Proof	12.00

8.0000 g, .875 GOLD, .2250 oz AGW

494	AH1400	1979	2,000	—	—	130.00
	1400	1979	2,000	—	Proof	200.00

15.0000 g, .720 SILVER, .3472 oz ASW
Egyptian - Israeli Peace Treaty

508	AH1400	1980	.095	—	—	10.00
	1400	1980	5,000	—	Proof	16.00

8.0000 g, .875 GOLD, .2250 oz AGW

509	AH1400	1980	9,500	—	—	130.00
	1400	1980	500 pcs.	—	Proof	225.00

15.0000 g, .720 SILVER, .3472 oz ASW
Applied Professions in Egypt

510	AH1400	1980	.022	—	—	10.00
	1400	1980	3,000	—	Proof	12.00

Doctor's Day

KM#	Date	Year	Mintage	VF	XF	Unc
511	AH1400	1980	.097	—	—	9.00
	1400	1980	3,000	—	Proof	12.00

8.0000 g, .875 GOLD, .2250 oz AGW

512	AH1400	1980	5,000	—	Proof	185.00

15.0000 g, .720 SILVER, .3472 oz ASW
F.A.O. Issue

513	AH1400	1980	.097	—	—	9.00
	1400	1980	3,000	—	Proof	12.50

Sadat's Corrective Revolution of May 15, 1971

514	AH1400	1980	.047	—	—	9.00
	1400	1980	3,000	—	Proof	12.00

Cairo University Law Facility

515	AH1400	1980	.047	—	—	9.00
	1400	1980	3,000	—	Proof	12.00

8.0000 g, .875 GOLD, .2250 oz AGW

516	AH1400	1980	2,000	—	—	150.00
	1400	1980	—	—	Proof	225.00

15.0000 g, .720 SILVER, .3472 oz ASW
Scientist's Day

KM#	Date	Year	Mintage	VF	XF	Unc
522	AH1401	1981	.025	—	—	10.00

World Food Day

KM#	Date	Year	Mintage	VF	XF	Unc
523	AH1401	1981	.050	—	—	9.00
	1401	1981	1,500	—	Proof	16.50

3rd Anniversary of Suez Canal Reopening

KM#	Date	Year	Mintage	VF	XF	Unc
524	AH1401	1981	.050	—	—	9.00
	1401	1981	2,000	—	Proof	16.50

8.0000 g, .875 GOLD, .2251 oz AGW

KM#	Date	Year	Mintage	VF	XF	Unc
525	AH1401	1981	150 pcs.	—	Proof	225.00

15.0000 g, .720 SILVER, .3472 oz ASW
25th Anniversary of Nationalization of Suez Canal

KM#	Date	Year	Mintage	VF	XF	Unc
528	AH1401	1981	.025	—	—	10.00
	1401	1981	1,500	—	Proof	25.00

8.0000 g, .875 GOLD, .2250 oz AGW

KM#	Date	Year	Mintage	VF	XF	Unc
529	AH1401	1981	3,000	—	—	175.00

15.0000 g, .720 SILVER, .3472 oz ASW
F.A.O. Issue

KM#	Date	Year	Mintage	VF	XF	Unc
532	AH1401	1981	.050	—	—	10.00

25th Anniversary of Egyptian Industry

KM#	Date	Year	Mintage	VF	XF	Unc
526	AH1402	1981	.025	—	—	10.00

25th Anniversary of Trade Unions

KM#	Date	Year	Mintage	VF	XF	Unc
527	AH1402	1981	.025	—	—	12.00

100th Anniversary of Revolt by Arabi Pasha

KM#	Date	Year	Mintage	VF	XF	Unc
530	AH1402	1981	.050	—	—	10.00
	1402	1981	1,500	—	Proof	25.00

8.0000 g, .875 GOLD, .2250 oz AGW

KM#	Date	Year	Mintage	VF	XF	Unc
531	AH1402	1981	3,000	—	—	175.00

15.0000 g, .720 SILVER, .3472 oz ASW
Egypt Air Golden Jubilee

KM#	Date	Year	Mintage	VF	XF	Unc
539	AH1402	1982	.020	—	—	12.00

1000th Anniversary of Al Azhar Mosque

KM#	Date	Year	Mintage	VF	XF	Unc
540	AH1402	1982	.023	—	—	10.00
	1402	1982	4,000	—	Proof	15.00

8.0000 g, .875 GOLD, .2250 oz AGW

KM#	Date	Year	Mintage	VF	XF	Unc
541	AH1402	1982	2,000	—	Proof	175.00

15.0000 g, .720 SILVER, .3472 oz ASW
50th Anniversary of Egyptian Products Co.

KM#	Date	Year	Mintage	VF	XF	Unc
544	AH1402	1982	5,000	—	—	20.00
	1402	1982	2,000	—	Proof	25.00

Return of Sinai to Egypt

KM#	Date	Year	Mintage	VF	XF	Unc
545	AH1402	1982(1983)	.050	—	—	10.00
	1402	1982(1983)	2,000	—	Proof	20.00

50th Anniversary of Air Force

KM#	Date	Year	Mintage	VF	XF	Unc
542	AH1403	1982	.010	—	—	15.00
	1403	1982	2,260	—	Proof	25.00

8.0000 g, .875 GOLD, .2250 oz AGW

KM#	Date	Year	Mintage	VF	XF	Unc
543	AH1403	1982	2,000	—	Proof	175.00

15.0000 g, .720 SILVER, .3472 oz ASW
50th Anniversary of Deaths of Shawky and Hafez

KM#	Date	Year	Mintage	VF	XF	Unc
549	AH1403	1983	.025	—	—	12.00

Misr Insurance Company

KM#	Date	Year	Mintage	VF	XF	Unc
551	AH1404	1984	.020	—	—	12.00

Helwan University Faculty of Fine Arts

KM#	Date	Year	Mintage	VF	XF	Unc
559	AH1404	1984	.025	—	—	12.00
	1404	1984	—	—	Proof	90.00

8.0000 g, .875 GOLD, .2250 oz AGW
50th Anniversary of Egyptian Radio Broadcasting
Similar to 5 Pounds, KM#561.

KM#	Date	Year	Mintage	VF	XF	Unc
583	AH1404	1984	2,000	—	—	175.00
25th Anniversary of National Planning Institute Similar to 5 Pounds, KM#572.						
571	AH1405	1985	200 pcs.	—	—	225.00
60th Anniversary of Egyptian Parliament Similar to 5 Pounds, KM#575.						
574	AH1405	1985	1,000	—	—	200.00
25th Anniversary of Cairo Stadium Similar to 5 Pounds, KM#578.						
577	AH1405	1985	300 pcs.	—	—	200.00
25th Anniversary of Egyptian Television Similar to 5 Pounds, KM#581.						
580	AH1405	1985	150 pcs.	—	—	225.00
Commerce Day Obv: Arabic legends, seals and date. Rev: Stylized depictions of commercial activity.						
604	AH1405	1985	2,000	—	Proof	175.00
Faculty of Economics and Political Science Obv: Arabic legends, seals and date. Rev: Graph within wreath, partial gear wheel.						
605	AH1405	1985	250 pcs.	—	Proof	225.00
25th Anniversary of Cairo International Airport Similar to 5 Pounds, KM#585.						
635	AH1405	1985	200 pcs.	—	—	200.00
Prophet's Mosque Similar to 5 Pounds, KM#584.						
632	AH1406	1985	800 pcs.	—	—	175.00
Cairo University Faculty of Commerce Similar to 5 Pounds, KM#586.						
636	AH1406	1986	200 pcs.	—	—	200.00

25th Anniversary of Egyptian Central Bank
Similar to 5 Pounds, KM#588.

above and below within ornamental border.

KM#	Date	Year	Mintage	VF	XF	Unc
637	AH1406	1986	200 pcs.	—	—	225.00
100th Anniversary of Petroleum Industry Similar to 5 Pounds, KM#602.						
638	AH1406	1986	800 pcs.	—	—	175.00
50th Anniversary of National Theater Similar to 5 Pounds, KM#608.						
640	AH1406	1986	250 pcs.	—	—	200.00
Restoration of Parliament Building Similar to 5 Pounds, KM#614.						
644	AH1406	1986	400 pcs.	—	—	175.00
Census Similar to 5 Pounds, KM#603.						
639	AH1407	1986	200 pcs.	—	—	175.00
40th Anniversary of Engineer's Syndicate Similar to 5 Pounds, KM#610.						
643	AH1407	1986	400 pcs.	—	—	175.00
Parliament Museum Similar to 5 Pounds, KM#617.						
645	AH1407	1987	400 pcs.	—	—	175.00
Investment Bank Similar to 5 Pounds, KM#651.						
653	AH1407	1987	600 pcs.	—	—	175.00
First African Subway Similar to 5 Pounds, KM#620.						
673	AH1408	1987	500 pcs.	—	Proof	225.00
Police Day Similar to 5 Pounds, KM#621.						
647	AH1408	1988	500 pcs.	—	—	175.00
Dedication of Cairo Opera House Similar to 5 Pounds, KM#649.						
654	AH1409	1988	1,500	—	—	225.00
Naquib Mahfouz, Nobel Laureate Similar to 5 Pounds, KM#662.						
661	AH1409	1988	1,000	—	Proof	175.00
United Parliamentary Union Similar to 5 Pounds, KM#665.						
664	AH1409	1989	200 pcs.	—	Proof	225.00
First Arab Olympics Similar to 5 Pounds, KM#667.						
666	AH1409	1989	300 pcs.	—	Proof	200.00
National Research Center Similar to 5 Pounds, KM#669.						
668	AH1409	1989	250 pcs.	—	Proof	225.00
University of Cairo, School of Agriculture Similar to 5 Pounds, KM#678.						
677	AH1410	1989	200 pcs.	—	Proof	250.00
Export Trade Show Similar to 5 Pounds, KM#687.						
695	AH1410	1989	200 pcs.	—	Proof	250.00
Union of African Parliament Similar to 5 Pounds, KM#689.						
696	AH1410	1990	200 pcs.	—	Proof	250.00
5th African Games - Cairo Similar to 5 Pounds, KM#700.						
699	AH1411	1991	200 pcs.	—	Proof	250.00
Mohamed Abdel Wahab Similar to 5 Pounds, KM#728.						
726	AH1412	1991	1,000	—	—	175.00

5 POUNDS

26.0000 g, .875 GOLD, .7315 oz AGW
National Bank of Egypt 75th Anniversary

KM#	Date	Year	Mintage	VF	XF	Unc
441	AH1393	1973	1,000	—	—	400.00
	1393	1973	—	—	Proof	600.00

1973 October War

KM#	Date	Year	Mintage	VF	XF	Unc
444	AH1394	1974	1,000	—	—	450.00

King Faisal Of Saudi Arabia

KM#	Date	Year	Mintage	VF	XF	Unc
459	AH1396	1976	2,500	—	—	600.00
Reopening of Suez Canal						
460	AH1396	1976	2,000	—	—	400.00

Om Kalsoum

KM#	Date	Year	Mintage	VF	XF	Unc
461	AH1396	1976	1,000	—	—	800.00

100th Anniversary of Bank of Land Reform

KM#	Date	Year	Mintage	VF	XF	Unc
495	AH1399	1979	1,750	—	—	450.00
	1399	1979	250 pcs.	—	Proof	600.00

1400th Anniversary of Mohammed's Flight

KM#	Date	Year	Mintage	VF	XF	Unc
496	AH1400	1979	2,000	—	—	400.00

Egyptian-Israeli Peace Treaty

KM#	Date	Year	Mintage	VF	XF	Unc
517	AH1400	1980	2,375	—	—	650.00
	1400	1980	125 pcs.	—	Proof	800.00
Doctor's Day						
518	AH1400	1980	1,000	—	—	550.00

24.0000 g, .925 SILVER, .7138 oz ASW
International Year of the Child

KM#	Date	Year	Mintage	VF	XF	Unc
533	AH1401	1981	.010	—	Proof	27.50

26.0000 g, .875 GOLD, .7315 oz AGW
3rd Anniversary of Suez Canal Reopening

KM#	Date	Year	Mintage	VF	XF	Unc
534	AH1401	1981	925 pcs.	—	—	400.00
	1401	1981	75 pcs.	—	Proof	650.00

25th Anniversary of Nationalization of Suez Canal

KM#	Date	Year	Mintage	VF	XF	Unc
537	AH1401	1981	1,000	—	—	400.00

25th Anniversary of the Ministry of Industry

KM#	Date	Year	Mintage	VF	XF	Unc
535	AH1402	1981	1,500	—	Proof	400.00

100th Anniversary of Revolt by Arabi Pasha

KM#	Date	Year	Mintage	VF	XF	Unc
536	AH1402	1981	1,000	—	—	400.00

1000th Anniversary of Al Azhar Mosque

KM#	Date	Year	Mintage	VF	XF	Unc
546	AH1402	1982	1,500	—	—	400.00

50th Anniversary of Air Force

KM#	Date	Year	Mintage	VF	XF	Unc
547	AH1403	1982	1,000	—	—	400.00

17.5000 g, .720 SILVER, .4051 oz ASW
75th Anniversary of Cairo University

KM#	Date	Year	Mintage	VF	XF	Unc
552	AH1404	1983	.025	—	—	18.00

Los Angeles Olympics

KM#	Date	Year	Mintage	VF	XF	Unc
558	AH1404	1984	.020	—	—	16.50

Academy of Arabic Languages

KM#	Date	Year	Mintage	VF	XF	Unc
560	AH1404	1984	.025	—	—	15.00

50th Anniversary of Egyptian Radio Broadcasting

KM#	Date	Year	Mintage	VF	XF	Unc
561	AH1404	1984	.025	—	—	15.00

26.0000 g, .875 GOLD, .7315 oz AGW
50th Anniversary of Egyptian Radio
Similar to 1 Pound, KM#561.

KM#	Date	Year	Mintage	VF	XF	Unc
671	AH1404	1984	500 pcs.	—	Proof	450.00

17.5000 g, .720 SILVER, .4051 oz ASW
Sculptor Mahmoud Mokhtar

KM#	Date	Year	Mintage	VF	XF	Unc
565	AH1404	1984	.010	—	—	15.00

Golden Jubilee of Petroleum Industry

KM#	Date	Year	Mintage	VF	XF	Unc
566	AH1404	1984	.010	—	—	15.00

Diamond Jubilee of Cooperation

KM#	Date	Year	Mintage	VF	XF	Unc
567	AH1404	1984	.010	—	—	15.00

100th Anniversary of Moharram Printing Press Co.

KM#	Date	Year	Mintage	VF	XF	Unc
563	AH1405	1985	.020	—	—	17.50

40.0000 g, .875 GOLD, 1.1253 oz AGW

KM#	Date	Year	Mintage	VF	XF	Unc
564	AH1405	1985	200 pcs.	—	—	1850.

17.5000 g, .720 SILVER, .4051 oz ASW
25th Anniversary of National Planning Institute

KM#	Date	Year	Mintage	VF	XF	Unc
572	AH1405	1985	.015	—	—	15.00

60th Anniversary of Egyptian Parliament

KM#	Date	Year	Mintage	VF	XF	Unc
575	AH1405	1985	.025	—	—	15.00

26.0000 g, .875 GOLD, .7315 oz AGW

KM#	Date	Year	Mintage	VF	XF	Unc
576	AH1405	1985	500 pcs.	—	—	1850.

17.5000 g, .720 SILVER, .4051 oz ASW
25th Anniversary of Cairo Stadium

KM#	Date	Year	Mintage	VF	XF	Unc
578	AH1405	1985	.025	—	—	15.00

26.0000 g, .875 GOLD, .7315 oz AGW

KM#	Date	Year	Mintage	VF	XF	Unc
579	AH1405	1985	200 pcs.	—	—	1850.

17.5000 g, .720 SILVER, .4051 oz ASW
25th Anniversary of Egyptian Television

KM#	Date	Year	Mintage	VF	XF	Unc
581	AH1405	1985	5,000	—	—	15.00

26.0000 g, .875 GOLD, .7315 oz AGW

KM#	Date	Year	Mintage	VF	XF	Unc
582	AH1405	1985	100 pcs.	—	—	1100.

17.5000 g, .720 SILVER, .4051 oz ASW
25th Anniversary of Cairo International Airport

KM#	Date	Year	Mintage	VF	XF	Unc
585	AH1405	1985	.020	—	—	15.00

Tutankhamun

KM#	Date	Year	Mintage	VF	XF	Unc
592	AH1405	1985	6,000	—	—	15.00
	1405	1985	2,000	—	Proof	30.00

XV UIA Congress

KM#	Date	Year	Mintage	VF	XF	Unc
593	AH1405	1985	.010	—	—	15.00
	1405	1985*	500 pcs.	—	Proof	30.00

Faculty of Economics & Political Science

KM#	Date	Year	Mintage	VF	XF	Unc
598	AH1405	1985	8,000	—	—	15.00

Commerce Day

KM#	Date	Year	Mintage	VF	XF	Unc
600	AH1405	1985	.020	—	—	15.00
	1405	1985	1,000	—	Proof	30.00

The Prophet's Mosque

KM#	Date	Year	Mintage	VF	XF	Unc
584	AH1406	1985	.025	—	—	15.00
	1406	1985	1,000	—	Proof	30.00

26.0000 g, .875 GOLD, .7315 oz AGW
Prophet's Mosque
Similar to KM#584.

633	AH1406	1985	400 pcs.	—	—	450.00

17.5000 g, .720 SILVER, .4051 oz ASW
Professions

587	AH1406	1985	8,000	—	—	15.00

Cairo University Faculty of Commerce

586	AH1406	1986	.020	—	—	15.00

25th Anniversary of Egyptian National Bank

KM#	Date	Year	Mintage	VF	XF	Unc
588	AH1406	1986	6,000	—	—	15.00

17.6800 g, .720 SILVER, .4093 oz ASW
World Soccer Championships

589	AH1406	1986	5,000	—	P/L	15.00
	1406	1986	1,500	—	Proof	30.00

17.5000 g, .720 SILVER, .4051 oz ASW
African Soccer Championship Games

590	AH1406	1986	.015	—	—	15.00
	1406	1986	2,000	—	Proof	30.00

50th Anniversary of Ministry of Health

KM#	Date	Year	Mintage	VF	XF	Unc
594	AH1406	1986	.010	—	—	15.00
	1406	1986*500 pcs.		—	Proof	30.00

Soldiers

601	AH1406	1986	.016	—	—	15.00

100th Anniversary of Petroleum Industry

602	AH1406	1986	6,000	—	—	16.50

50th Anniversary of National Theater

608	AH1406	1986	6,000	—	—	16.50

Census

KM#	Date	Year	Mintage	VF	XF	Unc
603	AH1407	1986	6,000	—	—	16.50

Parliament Museum

KM#	Date	Year	Mintage	VF	XF	Unc
617	AH1407	1987	5,000	—	—	16.50
	26.0000 g, .875 GOLD, .7315 oz AGW					
617a	AH1407	1987	300 pcs.	—	—	350.00

Mecca

KM#	Date	Year	Mintage	VF	XF	Unc
609	AH1406	1986	.030	—	—	15.00
	1406	1986	—	—	Proof	25.00
	26.0000 g, .875 GOLD, .7315 oz AGW					
609a	AH1406	1986	1,400	—	Proof	400.00

40th Anniversary of Engineer's Syndicate

KM#	Date	Year	Mintage	VF	XF	Unc
610	AH1407	1986	6,000	—	—	16.50

17.5000 g, .720 SILVER, .4051 oz ASW
Veterinarian Day

KM#	Date	Year	Mintage	VF	XF	Unc
618	AH1407	1987	5,000	—	—	16.50

17.5000 g, .720 SILVER, .4051 oz ASW
Restoration of Parliament Building

KM#	Date	Year	Mintage	VF	XF	Unc
614	AH1406	1986	5,000	—	—	16.50
	26.0000 g, .875 GOLD, .7315 oz AGW					
614a	AH1406	1986	300 pcs.	—	—	350.00

30th Anniversary of Egyptian Industry

KM#	Date	Year	Mintage	VF	XF	Unc
616	AH1407	1986	5,000	—	—	16.00

75th Anniversary of Misr Petroleum Company

KM#	Date	Year	Mintage	VF	XF	Unc
619	AH1407	1987	.010	—	—	16.50

17.5000 g, .720 SILVER, .4051 oz ASW
30th Anniversary of Atomic Energy Organization

KM#	Date	Year	Mintage	VF	XF	Unc
615	AH1406	1986	5,000	—	—	16.50

Aida Opera

KM#	Date	Year	Mintage	VF	XF	Unc
611	(AH1407)	1987	.025	—	—	35.00

17.5000 g, .900 SILVER, .5084 oz ASW

Faculty of Fine Arts

KM#	Date	Year	Mintage	VF	XF	Unc
630	AH1407	1987	5,000	—	—	16.50

17.7800 g, .720 SILVER, .4052 oz ASW

Investment Bank

KM#	Date	Year	Mintage	VF	XF	Unc
651	AH1407	1987	8,000	—	—	16.50

17.5000 g, .720 SILVER, .4051 oz ASW

First African Subway

KM#	Date	Year	Mintage	VF	XF	Unc
620	AH1408	1987	.015	—	—	16.50

26.0000 g, .875 GOLD, .7315 oz AGW

Similar to KM#620.

KM#	Date	Year	Mintage	VF	XF	Unc
674	AH1408	1987	200 pcs.	—	Proof	550.00

17.5000 g, .720 SILVER, .4051 oz ASW

25th Anniversary of Hellwan Company

KM#	Date	Year	Mintage	VF	XF	Unc
623	AH1408	1987	8,000	—	—	16.50

Police Day

KM#	Date	Year	Mintage	VF	XF	Unc
621	AH1408	1988	.035	—	—	16.50

17.5000 g, .900 SILVER, .5084 oz ASW

Summer Olympics - Pharoah and Athletes

KM#	Date	Year	Mintage	VF	XF	Unc
624	AH1408	1988	.030	—	—	16.50
	1408	1988	2,000	—	Proof	35.00

Summer Olympics - Athletes and Mythological Figures

KM#	Date	Year	Mintage	VF	XF	Unc
626	AH1408	1988	.024	—	—	16.50
	1408	1988	5,000	—	Proof	40.00

Winter Olympics - Ski Jumper and Figure Skater

KM#	Date	Year	Mintage	VF	XF	Unc
628	AH1408	1988	8,000	—	—	16.50
	1408	1988	2,000	—	Proof	40.00

50th Anniversary of Air Travel

KM#	Date	Year	Mintage	VF	XF	Unc
631	AH1408	1988	5,000	—	—	16.50

17.5000 g, .720 SILVER, .4051 oz ASW

Dedication of Cairo Opera House

KM#	Date	Year	Mintage	VF	XF	Unc
649	AH1409	1988	.030	—	—	16.50

26.0000 g, .875 GOLD, .7315 oz AGW

Similar to KM#649.

KM#	Date	Year	Mintage	VF	XF	Unc
655	AH1409	1988	200 pcs.	—	—	550.00

17.5000 g, .720 SILVER, .4051 oz ASW

Ministry of Agriculture

KM#	Date	Year	Mintage	VF	XF	Unc
660	AH1409	1988	5,000	—	—	16.50

Naguib Mahfouz - Nobel Laureate

KM#	Date	Year	Mintage	VF	XF	Unc
662	AH1409	1988	.015	—	—	16.50

Advista Arabia II

KM#	Date	Year	Mintage	VF	XF	Unc
663	AH1409	1989	5,000	—	—	16.50

United Parliamentary Union

KM#	Date	Year	Mintage	VF	XF	Unc
665	AH1409	1989	5,000	—	—	16.50

First Arab Olympics

KM#	Date	Year	Mintage	VF	XF	Unc
667	AH1409	1989	8,000	—	—	16.50

National Research Center
Obv: Similar to KM#667.

KM#	Date	Year	Mintage	VF	XF	Unc
669	AH1409	1989	5,000	—	—	17.50

26.0000 g, .875 GOLD, .7315 oz AGW
Obv: Similar to KM#667. Rev: Similar to KM#669.

KM#	Date	Year	Mintage	VF	XF	Unc
670	AH1408	1988	—	—	Proof	550.00
	1409	1989	200 pcs.	—	Proof	550.00

17.5000 g, .720 SILVER, .4051 oz ASW
National Health Insurance

KM#	Date	Year	Mintage	VF	XF	Unc
686	AH1409	1989	3,000	—	—	18.50

University of Cario School of Agriculture

KM#	Date	Year	Mintage	VF	XF	Unc
678	AH1410	1989	4,000	—	—	25.00

Export Drive

KM#	Date	Year	Mintage	VF	XF	Unc
687	AH1410	1989	4,000	—	—	17.50

17.5000 g, .900 SILVER, .5084 oz ASW
Soccer World Championship - Italy - Ancient Gods

KM#	Date	Year	Mintage	VF	XF	Unc
679	AH1410	1990	600 pcs.	—	—	20.00
	1410	1990	8,000	—	Proof	30.00

Soccer World Championship - Italy - Player Chasing Ball

KM#	Date	Year	Mintage	VF	XF	Unc
682	AH1410	1990	400 pcs.	—	—	20.00
	1410	1990	4,000	—	Proof	35.00

National Population Center

KM#	Date	Year	Mintage	VF	XF	Unc
688	AH1410	1990	5,000	—	—	18.50

Union of African Parliaments

KM#	Date	Year	Mintage	VF	XF	Unc
689	AH1410	1990	5,000	—	—	18.50

17.8200 g, .900 SILVER, .5156 oz ASW
Dar-el-Eloun Faculty

KM#	Date	Year	Mintage	VF	XF	Unc
691	AH1410	1990	5,000	—	—	18.50

17.5000 g, .720 SILVER, .4051 oz ASW
Newly Populated Areas Organization

KM#	Date	Year	Mintage	VF	XF	Unc
697	AH1410	1990	2,000	—	—	45.00

Alexandria Sports Club

KM#	Date	Year	Mintage	VF	XF	Unc
698	AH1411	1990	5,000	—	—	20.00

17.8200 g, .900 SILVER, .5156 oz ASW
Islamic Development Bank

KM#	Date	Year	Mintage	VF	XF	Unc
692	AH1411	1991	5,000	—	—	18.50

5th African Games - Cairo

KM#	Date	Year	Mintage	VF	XF	Unc
700	AH1411	1991	3,000	—	—	30.00

17.5000 g, .900 SILVER, .5084 oz ASW
Summer Olympics - Fencing

KM#	Date	Year	Mintage	VF	XF	Unc
701	AH1412	1992	999 pcs.	—	—	55.00
	1412	1992	2,999	—	Proof	55.00

Summer Olympics - Wrestling

KM#	Date	Year	Mintage	VF	XF	Unc
702	AH1412	1992	999 pcs.	—	—	55.00
	1412	1992	2,999	—	Proof	55.00

Summer Olympics - Archery

KM#	Date	Year	Mintage	VF	XF	Unc
703	AH1412	1992	999 pcs.	—	—	55.00
	1412	1992	2,999	—	Proof	55.00

Summer Olympics - Jumping Over an Ox

KM#	Date	Year	Mintage	VF	XF	Unc
704	AH1412	1992	999 pcs.	—	—	55.00
	1412	1992	2,999	—	Proof	55.00

Summer Olympics - Swimmer Stalking a Duck

KM#	Date	Year	Mintage	VF	XF	Unc
705	AH1412	1992	999 pcs.	—	—	55.00
	1412	1992	2,999	—	Proof	55.00

Summer Olympics - Handball

KM#	Date	Year	Mintage	VF	XF	Unc
706	AH1412	1992	999 pcs.	—	—	55.00
	1412	1992	.025	—	Proof	55.00

Summer Olympics - Field Hockey

KM#	Date	Year	Mintage	VF	XF	Unc
707	AH1412	1992	999 pcs.	—	—	55.00
	1412	1992	.025	—	Proof	55.00

Summer Olympics - Soccer

KM#	Date	Year	Mintage	VF	XF	Unc
708	AH1412	1992	999 pcs.	—	—	55.00
	1412	1992	.025	—	Proof	55.00

17.5000 g, .720 SILVER, .4051 oz ASW
Muhamed Abdel Wahab

KM#	Date	Year	Mintage	VF	XF	Unc
727	AH1412	1991	.030	—	—	17.50

26.0000 g, .875 GOLD, .7315 oz AGW
Obv: Arabic legends and inscriptions.
Rev: Musician's portrait left.

KM#	Date	Year	Mintage	VF	XF	Unc
728	AH1412	1991	400 pcs.	—	—	500.00

10 POUNDS

40.0000 g, .875 GOLD, 1.1254 oz AGW
Egyptian-Israeli Peace Treaty

KM#	Date	Year	Mintage	VF	XF	Unc
519	AH1400	1980	950 pcs.	—	—	900.00
	1400	1980	50 pcs.		Proof	1250.

25th Anniversary of Ministry of Industry

KM#	Date	Year	Mintage	VF	XF	Unc
538	AH1402	1981	18 pcs.	—	—	1500.
	1402	1981	1,000	—	Proof	700.00

1000th Anniversary of al-Azhar Mosque

KM#	Date	Year	Mintage	VF	XF	Unc
548	AH1402	1982	1,322	—	—	700.00

Prophet's Mosque
Similar to 5 Pounds, KM#584.

KM#	Date	Year	Mintage	VF	XF	Unc
634	AH1406	1985	300 pcs.	—	—	600.00

50 POUNDS

8.5000 g, .900 GOLD, .2460 oz AGW
Mecca
Similar to 5 Pounds, KM#609.

KM#	Date	Year	Mintage	VF	XF	Unc
641	AH1406	1986	.014	—	—	185.00

World Soccer Championships
Similar to 5 Pounds, KM#589.

KM#	Date	Year	Mintage	VF	XF	Unc
672	AH1406	1986	250 pcs.	—	—	250.00
	1406	1986	250 pcs.	—	Proof	300.00

Aida Opera
Similar to 5 Pounds, KM#611.

KM#	Date	Year	Mintage	VF	XF	Unc
612	AH1407	1987	.040	—	—	225.00

Summer Olympics - Pharoah and Athletes
Similar to 5 Pounds, KM#624.

KM#	Date	Year	Mintage	VF	XF	Unc
625	AH1408	1988	150 pcs.	—	—	400.00
	1408	1988	50 pcs.	—	Proof	450.00

Summer Olympics - Athletes
Mythological Figures
Similar to 5 Pounds, KM#626.

KM#	Date	Year	Mintage	VF	XF	Unc
627	AH1408	1988	750 pcs.	—	—	300.00
	1408	1988	250 pcs.	—	Proof	350.00

Winter Olympics - Ski Jumper and Figure Skater
Similar to 5 Pounds, KM#628.

KM#	Date	Year	Mintage	VF	XF	Unc
629	AH1408	1988	150 pcs.	—	—	400.00
	1408	1988	50 pcs.	—	Proof	450.00

Soccer World Championship -
Italy - Ancient Gods

KM#	Date	Year	Mintage	VF	XF	Unc
680	AH1410	1990	225 pcs.	—	Proof	450.00

Soccer World Championship - Player Chasing Ball
Similar to 5 Pounds, KM#682.

KM#	Date	Year	Mintage	VF	XF	Unc
683	AH1410	1990	75 pcs.	—	Proof	500.00

Summer Olympics - Fencing

KM#	Date	Year	Mintage	VF	XF	Unc
709	AH1412	1992	49 pcs.	—	—	425.00
	1412	1992	99 pcs.	—	Proof	425.00

Summer Olympics - Wrestling

KM#	Date	Year	Mintage	VF	XF	Unc
710	AH1412	1992	49 pcs.	—	—	425.00
	1412	1992	99 pcs.	—	Proof	425.00

Summer Olympics - Archery

KM#	Date	Year	Mintage	VF	XF	Unc
711	AH1412	1992	49 pcs.	—	—	425.00
	1412	1992	99 pcs.	—	Proof	425.00

Summer Olympics - Jumping Over an Ox

KM#	Date	Year	Mintage	VF	XF	Unc
712	AH1412	1992	49 pcs.	—	—	425.00
	1412	1992	99 pcs.	—	Proof	425.00

Summer Olympics - Swimmer Stalking a Duck

KM#	Date	Year	Mintage	VF	XF	Unc
713	AH1412	1992	49 pcs.	—	—	425.00
	1412	1992	99 pcs.	—	Proof	425.00

Summer Olympics Handball

KM#	Date	Year	Mintage	VF	XF	Unc
714	AH1412	1992	49 pcs.	—	—	425.00
	1412	1992	99 pcs.	—	Proof	425.00

Summer Olympics - Field Hockey

KM#	Date	Year	Mintage	VF	XF	Unc
715	AH1412	1992	49 pcs.	—	—	425.00
	1412	1992	99 pcs.	—	Proof	425.00

Summer Olympics - Soccer

KM#	Date	Year	Mintage	VF	XF	Unc
716	AH1412	1992	49 pcs.	—	—	425.00
	1412	1992	115 pcs.	—	Proof	425.00

100 POUNDS

17.1500 g, .900 GOLD, .4963 oz AGW
Queen Nefertiti

KM#	Date	Year	Mintage	VF	XF	Unc
550	AH—	1983	.016	—	Proof	800.00

Cleopatra VII

KM#	Date	Year	Mintage	VF	XF	Unc
562	AH—	1984	2,121	—	Proof	825.00

The Golden Falcon

KM#	Date	Year	Mintage	VF	XF	Unc
569	AH—	1985	1,800	—	Proof	700.00

Tutankhamun

KM#	Date	Year	Mintage	VF	XF	Unc
591	AH—	1986	7,500	—	Proof	900.00

17.0000 g, .900 GOLD, .4918 oz AGW
Mecca
Similar to 5 Pounds, KM#609.

KM#	Date	Year	Mintage	VF	XF	Unc
642	AH1406	1986	700 pcs.	—	—	350.00

Mythological Golden Ram

KM#	Date	Mintage	VF	XF	Unc
613	1987	7,500	—	Proof	700.00

Golden Warrior

KM#	Date	Mintage	VF	XF	Unc
648	1988	5,500	—	Proof	700.00

17.1500 g, .900 GOLD, .4963 oz AGW
The Golden Cat

KM#	Date	Mintage	VF	XF	Unc
656	1989FM	*7,500	—	Proof	700.00

17.0000 g, .900 GOLD, .4918 oz AGW
Soccer World Championship -
Italy - Ancient Gods

KM#	Date	Year	Mintage	VF	XF	Unc
681	AH1410	1990	125 pcs.	—	Proof	775.00

Soccer World Championship - Player Chasing Ball
Similar to 5 Pounds, KM#682.

KM#	Date	Year	Mintage	VF	XF	Unc
684	AH1410	1990	75 pcs.	—	Proof	800.00

17.1500 g, .900 GOLD, .4963 oz AGW
Ancient Egyptian Culture - Sphinx

KM#	Date	Mintage	VF	XF	Unc
693	1990FM	*5,000	—	Proof	700.00

Pyramids of Giza

KM#	Date	Mintage	VF	XF	Unc
729	1991	*5,000	—	Proof	700.00

17.0000 g, .900 GOLD, .4920 oz AGW
Summer Olympics - Fencing

KM#	Date	Year	Mintage	VF	XF	Unc
717	AH1412	1992	49 pcs.	—	—	800.00
	1412	1992	99 pcs.	—	Proof	800.00

Summer Olympics Wrestling

KM#	Date	Year	Mintage	VF	XF	Unc
718	AH1412	1992	49 pcs.	—	—	800.00
	1412	1992	99 pcs.	—	Proof	800.00

Summer Olympics - Archery

KM#	Date	Year	Mintage	VF	XF	Unc
719	AH1412	1992	49 pcs.	—	—	800.00
	1412	1992	99 pcs.	—	Proof	800.00

Summer Olympics - Jumping Over an Ox

KM#	Date	Year	Mintage	VF	XF	Unc
720	AH1412	1992	49 pcs.	—	—	800.00
	1412	1992	99 pcs.	—	Proof	800.00

Summer Olympics - Swimmer Stalking a Duck

KM#	Date	Year	Mintage	VF	XF	Unc
721	AH1412	1992	49 pcs.	—	—	800.00
	1412	1992	99 pcs.	—	Proof	800.00

Summer Olympics - Handball

KM#	Date	Year	Mintage	VF	XF	Unc
722	AH1412	1992	49 pcs.	—	—	800.00
	1412	1992	99 pcs.	—	Proof	800.00

Summer Olympics - Field Hockey

KM#	Date	Year	Mintage	VF	XF	Unc
723	AH1412	1992	49 pcs.	—	—	800.00
	1412	1992	99 pcs.	—	Proof	800.00

Summer Olympics - Soccer

KM#	Date	Year	Mintage	VF	XF	Unc
724	AH1412	1992	49 pcs.	—	—	800.00
	1412	1992	115 pcs.	—	Proof	800.00

17.1500 g, .900 GOLD, .4963 oz AGW
The Golden Guardians

KM#	Date	Mintage	VF	XF	Unc
730	1992	*5,000	—	Proof	700.00

PROOF SETS (PS)

KM#	Date	Mintage	Identification	Issue Price	Mkt. Val.
PS4	1980(4)	—	KM508-509,517,519	—	2300.
PS5	1980(3)	—	KM509,517,519	—	2275.

EL SALVADOR

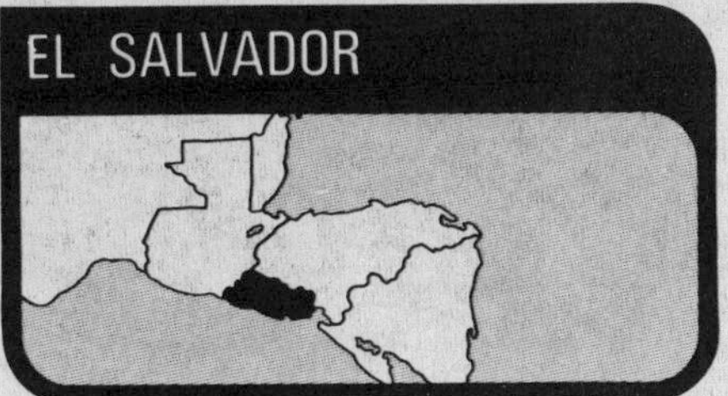

The Republic of El Salvador, a Central American country bordered by Guatemala, Honduras and the Pacific Ocean, has an area of 8,124 sq. mi. (21,040 sq. km.) and a population of 5.6 million. Capital: San Salvador. This most intensely cultivated of Latin America countries produces coffee (the major crop), cotton, sugar and balsam for export. Gold, silver and other metals are largely unexploited.

The first Spanish attempt to subjugate the area was undertaken in 1523 by Pedro de Alvarado, Cortes' lieutenant. He was forced to retreat by superior Indian forces, but returned in 1525 and succeeded in bringing the region under control of the Captaincy General of Guatemala, where it remained until 1821. In 1821, El Salvador and the other Central American provinces jointly declared their independence from Spain. In 1823 the Republic of Central America was formed by the five Central American States. When this federation was dissolved in 1839, El Salvador became an independent republic after its petition to join the United States was not accepted.

Clashes with Honduras occurred over a period of several years. A military coup in 1979 overthrew the Romero government but the ruling military-civilian junta failed to quell the civil war. Leftist insurgents, armed by Cuba and Nicaragua, control about 25% of the country. The U.S. supported the right wing government with military aid.

In the May 1984 presidential election, voters elected Christian Democrat Jose Napoleon Duarte.

MINT MARKS

C.A.M. - Central American Mint, San Salvador
H - Heaton Mint, Birmingham
S - San Francisco
Mo - Mexico

PROVISIONAL COINAGE

MONETARY SYSTEM

16 Reales = 1 Escudo

1/4 REAL

.903 SILVER
Obv: Volcano between S.-S., date below.
Rev: Column w/liberty cap on top between 1/4-1/4.

KM#	Date	Mintage	Good	VG	Fine	VF
1	1828	(3 known)	—	—	Rare	—

1/2 REAL

.903 SILVER
Obv. leg: POR LA LIVERTAD DEL SAL, star,above volcano within branches.
Rev. leg: MONEDA PROVISIONAL, halo above column within branches.

KM#	Date	Mintage	Good	VG	Fine	VF
14	1833	—	100.00	175.00	275.00	400.00

Obv. leg: POR LA LIBERTAD DEL SAL. S - volcano - S above water within circle.
Rev: Liberty cap over 1. - column - 1/2 over water.

KM#	Date	Mintage	Good	VG	Fine	VF
21.1	1835	—	100.00	175.00	275.00	400.00

Obv. leg: POR LA LIBERTAD DEL SAL, S - volcano - S above water within circle.

KM#	Date	Mintage	Good	VG	Fine	VF
21.2	1835	—	110.00	200.00	300.00	425.00
	1835 retrograde 2 in 1/2	—	120.00	225.00	325.00	450.00

Obv. leg: POR LA LIBERTAD DEL SALVA, star above S - volcano - S above water.
Rev. leg: MONEDA PROVISIONAL, Liberty cap over column: 1 - column - M

KM#	Date	Mintage	Good	VG	Fine	VF
21.3	1835	—	90.00	175.00	250.00	375.00

REAL

.903 SILVER
Obv. leg: ESTADO DEL SALVADOR, star above volcano within branches.
Rev. leg: MONEDA PROVISIONAL IND*, star in wreath above 1. - column - R. within branches.

KM#	Date	Mintage	Good	VG	Fine	VF
17	1833	—	75.00	150.00	250.00	350.00

Obv. leg: POR LA LIVERTAD DEL SALVADOR.
Rev: 1. - (thin) column - R. within branches.

KM#	Date	Mintage	Good	VG	Fine	VF
18.1	1833	—	50.00	100.00	175.00	275.00

Obv: Similar to KM#18.1.
Rev: 1. - (thick) column - R. within branches.

KM#	Date	Mintage	Good	VG	Fine	VF
18.2	1833	—	50.00	100.00	175.00	275.00

Obv. leg: POR LA LIVERTAD DEL SALVADOR*
Rev: Similar to KM#18.2.

KM#	Date	Mintage	Good	VG	Fine	VF
18.3	1833	—	50.00	100.00	175.00	275.00

Obv: Star above volcano above water in 1/2 circle of stars.

KM#	Date	Mintage	Good	VG	Fine	VF
18.4	1833	—	75.00	150.00	250.00	350.00

Obv. leg: POR LA LIVERTAD DE SAL, volcano within branches.
Rev. leg: MONEDA PROVISIONAL IND, column within branches.

KM#	Date	Mintage	Good	VG	Fine	VF
18.5	1834	—	75.00	150.00	250.00	350.00

Obv. leg: POR LA LIVERTAD DEL SAL, star above S. - volcano - S. within circle.
Rev. leg: MONEDA PROVISIONAL, Liberty cap above I. - column - R., water below within circle.

KM#	Date	Mintage	Good	VG	Fine	VF
18.6	1835	—	50.00	115.00	175.00	275.00

Obv. leg: POR LA LIVERTAD DEL SAL.

KM#	Date	Mintage	Good	VG	Fine	VF
18.7	1835 NA	—	75.00	150.00	250.00	350.00
	ND	—	—	—	—	—

Obv. leg: POR LA LIBERTAD DEL SAL, star above S - volcano - S above water within circle.

KM#	Date	Mintage	Good	VG	Fine	VF
18.8	1835	—	50.00	115.00	175.00	275.00

NOTE: Varieties also exist with 2 or 3 dots after SAL.

Obv. leg: POR LA LIBERTAD DEL SAL,

star above S - volcano - S above water within circle of dots.

KM#	Date	Mintage	Good	VG	Fine	VF
18.9	1835	—	50.00	115.00	175.00	275.00

Obv. leg: POR LA LIBERTAD DEL SA:

KM#	Date	Mintage	Good	VG	Fine	VF
18.10	1835	—	50.00	115.00	200.00	300.00

Obv. leg: POR LA LIBERTAD DE SALV.

KM#	Date	Mintage	Good	VG	Fine	VF
18.11	1835	—	50.00	115.00	175.00	275.00

2 REALES

.903 SILVER
Obv. leg: POR LA LIVERTAD. SALV, Liberty cap above 2. column - R. above water.
Rev. leg: MONEDA PROVISIONAL, volcano.

KM#	Date	Mintage	Good	VG	Fine	VF
4	1828 FP	—	30.00	55.00	100.00	165.00

Obv: Inner circle added.

KM#	Date	Mintage	Good	VG	Fine	VF
5.1	1828 FP	—	30.00	55.00	100.00	165.00
	1828 F	—	35.00	65.00	125.00	200.00

Obv. leg: POR LA LIBERTAD. SALB.

KM#	Date	Mintage	Good	VG	Fine	VF
5.2	1828 FP	—	30.00	55.00	100.00	165.00

Obv. leg: POR LA LIBERTAD SALVAD.
Rev. leg: MONEDA PROBISIONAL.

KM#	Date	Mintage	Good	VG	Fine	VF
5.3	1829 RL	—	35.00	75.00	150.00	200.00

Obv. leg: POR LA LIBERTAD SALVAD.

KM#	Date	Mintage	Good	VG	Fine	VF
5.4	1829 RL	—	35.00	65.00	125.00	175.00

Obv. leg: POR LA LIBERTAD SALVADOR.

KM#	Date	Mintage	Good	VG	Fine	VF
5.5	1829	—	35.00	65.00	125.00	175.00

Obv. leg: POR LA LIBERTAD DEL SALVADR, star above S - volcano - S. above water.
Rev: Liberty cap above 2 - column - R.

KM#	Date	Mintage	Good	VG	Fine	VF
11.1	1832	—	35.00	65.00	125.00	175.00

Obv. leg: POR LA LIBERTAD DEL SALVADOR
Rev: Liberty cap above 2 - column - R between sprays within dotted circle.

KM#	Date	Mintage	Good	VG	Fine	VF
11.2	1832 RL	—	35.00	65.00	125.00	175.00

Rev: 2 - column - R within solid circle.

KM#	Date	Mintage	Good	VG	Fine	VF
11.3	1832 RL	—	35.00	65.00	125.00	175.00

Obv. leg: POR LA LIBERTAD SALVADOR, w/o waves beneath volcano.

KM#	Date	Mintage	Good	VG	Fine	VF
11.15	1829 RL	—	40.00	80.00	150.00	200.00

Obv. leg: POR LA LIBERTAD SALVADORE

KM#	Date	Mintage	Good	VG	Fine	VF
11.4	1832	—	35.00	65.00	125.00	175.00

Obv. leg: POR LA LIBERTAD DEL SALVADO

KM#	Date	Mintage	Good	VG	Fine	VF
11.5	1832 RL	—	35.00	65.00	125.00	175.00

Obv. leg: POR LA LIVERTAD DEL SALV, star above retrograde S - volcano - S above water.
Rev: Liberty cap above 2. - column - R within branches.

KM#	Date	Mintage	Good	VG	Fine	VF
11.6	1833	—	35.00	65.00	125.00	175.00
	1834/3T	—	40.00	80.00	150.00	200.00

Obv: Regular S' recut above retrograde S'.

KM#	Date	Mintage	Good	VG	Fine	VF
11.7	1834/3	—	40.00	80.00	150.00	200.00

Obv. leg: POR LA LIBERTAD DEL SALVA, star above S - volcano - S above water.

KM#	Date	Mintage	Good	VG	Fine	VF
11.8	1833 RL	—	35.00	65.00	125.00	175.00

NOTE: Varieties exist with 2 or 3 dots after SALVA.

Obv. leg: POR LA LIBERTAD DEL SALVAD

KM#	Date	Mintage	Good	VG	Fine	VF
11.9	1833/2 RL	—	40.00	80.00	150.00	200.00
	1833 RL	—	35.00	65.00	125.00	175.00

Obv. leg: POR LA LIBERTAD DEL SALV

KM#	Date	Mintage	Good	VG	Fine	VF
11.10	1833 L	—	35.00	65.00	125.00	175.00

Obv. leg: LIBERTAD SALVO DORENO

KM#	Date	Mintage	Good	VG	Fine	VF
11.11	1833	—	35.00	65.00	125.00	175.00

Obv. leg: POR LA LIBERTAD DEL SALVADOR.

KM#	Date	Mintage	Good	VG	Fine	VF
11.12	1833 RL	—	35.00	65.00	125.00	175.00

Obv. leg: POR LA LIVERTAD DEL SALV.
Rev. leg: MONEDA PROVISIONAL with retrograde "S".

KM#	Date	Mintage	Good	VG	Fine	VF
11.13	1834	—	40.00	75.00	135.00	200.00

Obv. leg: POR LA LIBERTAD DEL SALV.
Rev. leg: MONEDA PROVISIONAL with retrograde "N".

KM#	Date	Mintage	Good	VG	Fine	VF
11.14	1834	1 known	300.00	485.00	—	—

4 REALES

.903 SILVER
Obv. leg: POR LA LIBERTAD SALV,

Liberty cap above column between retrograde R. - 4.

KM#	Date	Mintage	Good	VG	Fine	VF
8.1	1828 F	—	3250.	4500.	5500.	8000.

Obv. leg: POR LA LIBERTAD DEL SALV, corrected 4. - R.
Rev. leg: MONEDA PROVISIONAL.

8.2	1828 F	—	3250.	4500.	5500.	8000.

COUNTERMARKED COINAGE

2 REALES

SILVER
c/m: SAP monogram on 2 Reales, KM#5.

24.1	ND(1828) FP	—	—	—	—	—
	ND(1829) RL	—	—	—	—	—

c/m: SAP monogram on 2 Reales, KM#11.6.

26	ND(1833-34)	—	50.00	100.00	200.00	300.00

c/m: SAP monogram on Central American Republic 2 Reales, KM#9.

25	ND(1831) F	—	100.00	200.00	400.00	600.00

NOTE: This countermark, appearing to be a SAP monogram has previously been attributed to El Salvador, and also to various Caribbean islands. Inclusion here for reference only.

REPUBLIC

COUNTERMARKED COINAGE

1830

Type I
Volcano, 'S' on either side, '1830' below, in rectangle.

4 REALES

SILVER
c/m: Type I on Mexico 4 Reales, KM#97.

KM#	Date	Year	Mintage	Good	VG	Fine
27	1830	(1772-89)	—	—	Rare	—

1839

Type II
Volcano, '1839' below, in rectangle.
Exists with normal 3 and retrograde 3 in date.

1/2 REAL

SILVER
c/m: Type II on Chile 1/2 Real, KM#90.

30	1839	(1833-4)	—	—	Rare	—

REAL

SILVER
c/m: Type II on Peru 1 Real, KM#145.1.

33	1839	(1826-36)	—	—	Rare	—

2 REALES

SILVER
c/m: Type II on Peru (Lima) 2 Reales, KM#141.1.

36	1839	(1825-36)	—	200.00	350.00	500.00

c/m: Type II on South Peru 2 Reales, KM#169.1.

37	1839	(1837)	—	—	Rare	—

8 REALES

SILVER
c/m: Type II on South Peru 8 Reales, KM#170.2.

40	1839	(1837-39)	—	—	Rare	—

TYPE III-A
Plain Liberty cap above shield on draped flags within 10mm circle.

TYPE III-B
Radiant Liberty cap above shield on draped flags within 12mm circle.

TYPE III-C
Liberty cap above shield within branches in 12mm circle.
NOTE: Other countermark varieties are known to exist.

SPANISH 'REAL' SERIES

1/2 REAL

SILVER
c/m: Type III on Guatemala 1/2 Real, KM#2.

KM#	Date	Year	Good	VG	Fine	VF
43	ND	—	35.00	50.00	70.00	100.00

REAL

SILVER
c/m: Type III on Bolivia (Potosi) 'cob' 1 Real, KM#42.

46	ND	—	17.50	25.00	42.50	65.00

c/m: Type III on Bolivia (Potosi) 1 Real, KM#52.

47	ND	(1773-89)	15.00	20.00	30.00	50.00

c/m: Type III on Chile 1 Real, KM#65.

48	ND	(1808-17)	17.50	25.00	40.00	60.00

c/m: Type III on Colombia 1 Real, KM#91.1.

49	ND	(1837-46)	17.50	25.00	40.00	60.00

c/m: Type III on Mexico Charles and Johanna 1 Real, KM#9.

50	ND	(1536-72)	20.00	30.00	45.00	75.00

c/m: Type III on Mexico City Philip II Real, KM#27.

51	ND	(1556-98)	20.00	30.00	45.00	75.00

c/m: Type III on Peru 1 Real, KM#114.

53	ND	(1839)	15.00	22.50	35.00	50.00

c/m: Type III on Spain 1 Real, C#37.

52	ND	(1772-88)	15.00	22.50	35.00	50.00

2 REALES

SILVER
c/m: Type III on Bolivia (Potosi) 2 Reales, KM#53.

55	ND	(1773-89)	20.00	30.00	45.00	75.00

c/m: Type III on Colombia 2 Reales, KM#97.

56	ND	(1837-46)	22.50	35.00	50.00	85.00

c/m: Type III on Guatemala 2 Reales, KM#34.2.

54	ND	(1787 M)	35.00	60.00	85.00	150.00

c/m: Type III on Mexico 2 Reales, KM#86.

57	ND	(1747-60)	22.50	35.00	50.00	85.00

c/m: Type III on Mexico 2 Reales, KM#89.

KM#	Date	Year	Good	VG	Fine	VF
58	ND	(1789-90)	20.00	30.00	45.00	75.00

c/m: Type III on Mexico 2 Reales, KM#90.

KM#	Date	Year	Good	VG	Fine	VF
59	ND	(1790)	25.00	37.50	55.00	90.00

c/m: Type III on Mexico 2 Reales, KM#91.

KM#	Date	Year	Good	VG	Fine	VF
60	ND	(1792-1808)	20.00	30.00	45.00	75.00

c/m: Type III on Mexico 2 Reales, KM#93.

KM#	Date	Year	Good	VG	Fine	VF
61	ND	(1812-21)	20.00	30.00	45.00	75.00

c/m: Type III on Mexico Iturbide 2 Reales, KM#303.

KM#	Date	Year	Good	VG	Fine	VF
65	ND	(1823 JM)	50.00	100.00	175.00	300.00

c/m: Type III on Peru 2 Reales, KM#53.

KM#	Date	Year	Good	VG	Fine	VF
62	ND	(1752-59)	20.00	30.00	45.00	75.00

c/m: Type III on Peru (Lima) 2 Reales, KM#95.

KM#	Date	Year	Good	VG	Fine	VF
63	ND	(1791-1808)	15.00	22.50	35.00	50.00

c/m: Type III on Spanish 2 Reales, C#134.

KM#	Date	Year	Good	VG	Fine	VF
64	ND	(1810-33)	17.50	25.00	40.00	60.00

4 REALES

SILVER

c/m: Type III on Guatemala 4 Reales, KM#76.1.

KM#	Date	Year	Good	VG	Fine	VF
67	ND	(1747-53)	—	—	Rare	—

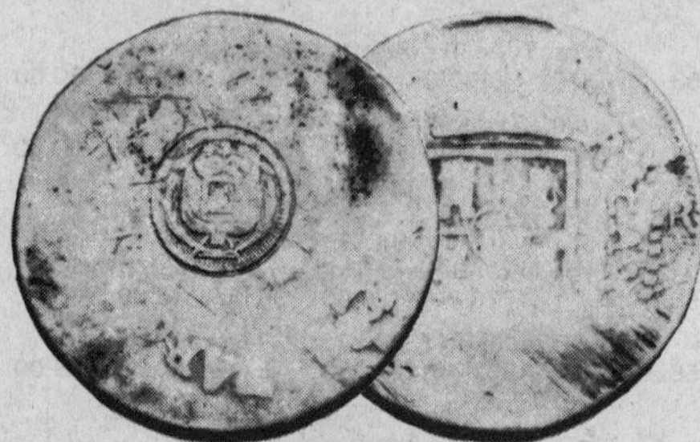

c/m: Type III on Mexico Sombrerte 4 Reales, KM#175.

KM#	Date	Year	Good	VG	Fine	VF
68	ND	(1812)	—	—	Rare	—

8 REALES

SILVER

c/m: Type III on Chile 8 Reales, KM#31.

KM#	Date	Year	Good	VG	Fine	VF
71	ND	(1773-89)	—	—	Rare	—

ENGLISH 'STERLING' SERIES

6 PENCE

.925 SILVER

c/m: Type III on Great Britain 6 Pence, KM#394.

KM#	Date	Year	Good	VG	Fine	VF
74	ND	(1816-20)	22.00	30.00	42.50	55.00

c/m: Type III on Great Britain 6 Pence, KM#425.

KM#	Date	Year	Good	VG	Fine	VF
75	ND	(1831-37)	22.00	30.00	42.50	55.00

SHILLING

.925 SILVER

c/m: Type III on Great Britain Shilling, KM#395.

KM#	Date	Year	Good	VG	Fine	VF
78	ND	(1816-20)	25.00	32.50	45.00	60.00

c/m: Type III on Great Britain Shilling, KM#409.

KM#	Date	Year	Good	VG	Fine	VF
79	ND	(1823-25)	25.00	32.50	45.00	60.00

c/m: Type III on Great Britain Shilling, KM#414.

KM#	Date	Year	Good	VG	Fine	VF
80	ND	(1825-29)	25.00	32.50	45.00	60.00

REVALIDATED GUATEMALA SERIES

Type IV
R in beaded 5mm circle.

1/2 REAL

SILVER

c/m: Type IV on Guatemala 1/2 Real, KM#131.

KM#	Date	Year	Good	VG	Fine	VF
83	ND	(1859-61)	140.00	200.00	275.00	400.00

c/m: Type IV on Guatemala 1/2 Real, KM#138.

KM#	Date	Year	Good	VG	Fine	VF
84	ND	(1862-65)	100.00	150.00	225.00	350.00

REAL

SILVER

c/m: Type IV on Colombia 1 Real, KM#87.

KM#	Date	Year	Good	VG	Fine	VF
87	ND	(1827-36)	15.00	22.00	35.00	50.00

c/m: Type IV on Guatemala 1 Real, KM#132.

KM#	Date	Year	Good	VG	Fine	VF
88	ND	(1859-60)	15.00	22.00	30.00	42.50

c/m: Type IV on Guatemala 1 Real, KM#137.

KM#	Date	Year	Good	VG	Fine	VF
89	ND	(1862-65)	15.00	22.00	30.00	42.50

2 REALES

SILVER

c/m: Type IV on Guatemala 2 Reales, KM#133.

KM#	Date	Year	Good	VG	Fine	VF
91	ND	(1859)	—	—	Rare	—

c/m: Type IV on Guatemala 2 Reales, KM#134.

KM#	Date	Year	Good	VG	Fine	VF
92	ND	(1860-61)	17.50	25.00	32.50	45.00

c/m: Type IV on Guatemala 2 Reales, KM#139.

KM#	Date	Year	Good	VG	Fine	VF
93	ND	(1861-65)	17.50	25.00	32.50	45.00

4 REALES

SILVER

c/m: Type IV on Guatemala 4 Reales, KM#136.

KM#	Date	Year	Good	VG	Fine	VF
96	ND	(1860-61)	100.00	150.00	225.00	350.00

8 REALES

SILVER

c/m: Type IV on Guatemala 1 Peso, KM#178.

KM#	Date	Year	Good	VG	Fine	VF
99	ND	(1859)	—	—	Rare	—

NOTE: Two copper coins of Brazil have also been reported with the Type IV c/m. A 20 Reis dated 1827 and an 80 Reis of the 1820's c/m: '40'.

TYPE V
Zig-Zag Test Mark

2 REALES

SILVER

c/m: Type V on Guatemala 2 Reales, KM#82. (Peru 2 Reales).

KM#	Date	Year	Good	VG	Fine	VF
102	ND	(1825-40)	60.00	85.00	125.00	175.00

c/m: Type V on Peru 2 Reales, KM#141.1.

KM#	Date	Year	Good	VG	Fine	VF
103	ND	(1825-40)	60.00	85.00	125.00	175.00

DECIMAL COINAGE

100 Centavos = 1 Peso

CENTAVO

COPPER-NICKEL

KM#	Date	Mintage	Fine	VF	XF	Unc
106	1889H	1.500	1.00	3.00	5.00	15.00
	1889H	—	—	—	Proof	150.00
	1913H	2.500	1.50	3.50	6.00	20.00

COPPER

KM#	Date	Mintage	Fine	VF	XF	Unc
108	1892/1	.182	45.00	80.00	120.00	225.00
	1892	Inc. Ab.	35.00	70.00	110.00	200.00
	1892	10 pcs.	—	—	Proof	750.00
	1893	—	200.00	300.00	400.00	700.00

COPPER-NICKEL

KM#	Date	Mintage	Fine	VF	XF	Unc
127	1915	5.000	.75	2.50	7.00	20.00
	1919	1.000	1.50	4.00	10.00	35.00
	1920	1.490	1.00	3.00	8.00	25.00
	1925	.200	4.00	8.00	15.00	40.00
	1926	.400	3.00	6.00	12.00	35.00
	1928S	5.000	.75	2.00	6.00	22.50
	1936	2.500	.75	2.00	6.00	22.50

3 CENTAVOS

COPPER-NICKEL

KM#	Date	Mintage	Fine	VF	XF	Unc
107	1889H	.333	1.50	4.50	9.00	25.00
	1889H	—	—	—	Proof	200.00
	1913H	1.000	2.00	6.00	14.00	40.00

KM#	Date	Mintage	Fine	VF	XF	Unc
128	1915	2.700	2.00	5.00	15.00	40.00

1/4 REAL

BRONZE

KM#	Date	Mintage	Fine	VF	XF	Unc
120	1909	—	20.00	30.00	45.00	60.00

NOTE: The decimal value of the above coin was about 3 Centavos. It was apparently struck in response to the continuing use of the Reales monetary system in local market places and rural areas.

5 CENTAVOS

1.2500 g, .835 SILVER, .0336 oz ASW

KM#	Date	Mintage	Fine	VF	XF	Unc
109	1892CAM	.080	6.00	12.50	25.00	50.00
	1892CAM	—	—	—	Proof	500.00
	1893CAM	I.A.	6.00	12.50	25.00	50.00

KM#	Date	Mintage	Fine	VF	XF	Unc
121	1911	1.000	2.00	4.00	8.00	30.00

KM#	Date	Mintage	Fine	VF	XF	Unc
124	1914	2.000	1.50	3.00	6.00	22.50
	1914	20 pcs.	—	—	Proof	150.00

COPPER-NICKEL

KM#	Date	Mintage	Fine	VF	XF	Unc
129	1915	2.500	.75	2.00	6.00	25.00
	1916	1.500	1.25	3.00	8.00	32.50
	1917	1.000	1.50	4.00	10.00	40.00
	1918/7	1.000	1.25	3.00	8.00	30.00
	1918	Inc. Ab.	1.25	3.00	8.00	32.50
	1919	2.000	1.00	3.00	8.00	25.00
	1920	2.000	.75	2.00	6.00	20.00
	1921	1.780	1.00	2.50	7.00	25.00
	1925	4.000	.50	1.50	5.00	17.50

10 CENTAVOS

2.5000 g, .835 SILVER, .0671 oz ASW

KM#	Date	Mintage	Fine	VF	XF	Unc
110	1892CAM	.012	40.00	80.00	150.00	300.00
	1892CAM	—	—	—	Proof	500.00

KM#	Date	Mintage	Fine	VF	XF	Unc
122	1911	1.000	2.25	4.00	8.00	25.00

KM#	Date	Mintage	Fine	VF	XF	Unc
125	1914	1.500	2.00	3.50	6.00	22.50
	1914	20 pcs.	—	—	Proof	250.00

20 CENTAVOS

5.0000 g, .835 SILVER, .1342 oz ASW

KM#	Date	Mintage	Fine	VF	XF	Unc
111	1892CAM	.146	10.00	25.00	65.00	125.00
	1892CAM	—	—	—	Proof	350.00
	1893CAM	—	—	Reported, not confirmed		

25 CENTAVOS

6.2500 g, .835 SILVER, .1678 oz ASW

KM#	Date	Mintage	Fine	VF	XF	Unc
123	1911	.600	4.75	6.00	10.00	30.00

KM#	Date	Mintage	Fine	VF	XF	Unc
126	1914 15 DE SEPT	1.400	5.50	6.50	10.00	25.00
	1914 15 SEP	I.A.	5.50	6.50	10.00	25.00
	1914 15 SET DE 1821	Inc. Ab.	5.50	6.50	10.00	25.00
	1914	20 pcs.	—	—	Proof	600.00

50 CENTAVOS

12.5000 g, .900 SILVER, .3617 oz ASW

KM#	Date	Mintage	Fine	VF	XF	Unc
112	1892CAM	.043	30.00	65.00	150.00	275.00
	1892CAM	—	—	—	Proof	750.00

KM#	Date	Mintage	Fine	VF	XF	Unc
113	1892CAM	.340	10.00	20.00	50.00	120.00
	1893CAM	I.A.	12.00	25.00	55.00	125.00
	1894CAM	I.A.	14.00	27.50	60.00	145.00

UN (1) PESO

25.0000 g, .900 SILVER, .7234 oz ASW

KM#	Date	Mintage	Fine	VF	XF	Unc
114	1892CAM	.041	60.00	150.00	250.00	700.00
	1892CAM	—	—	—	Proof	1000.

KM#	Date	Mintage	Fine	VF	XF	Unc
115.1	1892CAM	.950	25.00	50.00	100.00	200.00
	1893/2 CAM	Inc. Ab.	10.00	22.50	37.50	100.00
	1893CAM	I.A.	6.50	12.00	20.00	80.00
	1894CAM	I.A.	6.50	12.00	20.00	80.00
	1895CAM	I.A.	6.50	12.00	20.00	80.00
	1896CAM	I.A.	100.00	200.00	400.00	—
	1904CAM	.600	6.50	12.00	20.00	80.00
	1908CAM	1.600	6.50	10.00	18.00	65.00
	1911CAM	.500	6.50	12.00	20.00	80.00
	1914CAM	*.700	—	Reported, not confirmed		

***NOTE:** Struck at the Brussels mint, but then remelted for the striking of 1914 minor coinage.

NOTE: Struck in San Salvador and European mints.

Rev: Heavier portrait (wider right shoulder).

KM#	Date	Mintage	Fine	VF	XF	Unc
115.2	1904CAM	.400	8.00	15.00	35.00	100.00
	1909CAM	.690	6.50	12.00	20.00	80.00
	1911CAM	1.020	6.50	12.00	20.00	80.00
	1914CAM	2.100	6.50	12.00	20.00	80.00
	1914CAM	*20 pcs.	—	—	Proof	3000.

NOTE: Struck at United States mints.

2-1/2 PESOS

4.0323 g, .900 GOLD, .1167 oz AGW

KM#	Date	Mintage	Fine	VF	XF	Unc
116	1892CAM	597 pcs.	400.00	600.00	850.00	1500.
	1892CAM	—	—	—	Proof	1750.

5 PESOS

8.0645 g, .900 GOLD, .2334 oz AGW

KM#	Date	Mintage	Fine	VF	XF	Unc
117	1892CAM	558 pcs.	450.00	700.00	1100.	1950.
	1892CAM	—	—	—	Proof	2250.

10 PESOS

16.1290 g, .900 GOLD, .4667 oz AGW

KM#	Date	Mintage	Fine	VF	XF	Unc
118	1892CAM	321 pcs.	800.00	1500.	2000.	3500.
	1892CAM	—	—	—	Proof	3750.

20 PESOS

32.2580 g, .900 GOLD, .9334 oz AGW

KM#	Date	Mintage	Fine	VF	XF	Unc
119	1892CAM	200 pcs.	1500.	2250.	3250.	5500.
	1892CAM	—	—	—	Proof	5750.

MONETARY REFORM

100 Centavos = 1 Colon

CENTAVO

COPPER-NICKEL

KM#	Date	Mintage	Fine	VF	XF	Unc
133	1940	1.000	1.25	3.50	7.00	20.00

BRONZE

KM#	Date	Mintage	Fine	VF	XF	Unc
135	1942	5.000	.20	.50	1.00	4.50
	1943	5.000	.20	.50	1.00	4.50
	1945	5.000	.20	.40	.75	3.00
	1947	5.000	.20	.50	1.00	3.50
	1951	10.000	.10	.30	.75	2.50
	1952	10.000	.10	.20	.40	1.25
	1956	10.000	.10	.20	.40	1.00
	1966	5.000	—	—	.10	.50
	1968	5.000	—	—	.10	.50
	1969	5.000	—	—	.10	.50
	1972	20.000	—	—	.10	.30

BRASS

Obv: Smaller portrait.

KM#	Date	Mintage	Fine	VF	XF	Unc
135a	1976	20.000	—	—	.10	.20
	1977	40.000	—	—	.10	.20

COPPER-ZINC

Obv: Smaller portrait, DH monogram at truncation.
Rev: Denomination in wreath, SM at right base of 1.

KM#	Date	Mintage	Fine	VF	XF	Unc
135c	1981	50.000	—	—	.10	.20

COPPER CLAD STEEL

KM#	Date	Mintage	Fine	VF	XF	Unc
135b	1986	30.000	—	—	.10	.20

BRASS CLAD STEEL

Similar to KM#135.

KM#	Date	Mintage	Fine	VF	XF	Unc
135d	1989	36.000	—	—	.10	.20

2 CENTAVOS

NICKEL-BRASS

KM#	Date	Mintage	Fine	VF	XF	Unc
147	1974	10.002	—	.10	.15	.20

3 CENTAVOS

NICKEL-BRASS

KM#	Date	Mintage	Fine	VF	XF	Unc
148	1974	10.002	.10	.15	.20	.40

5 CENTAVOS

COPPER-NICKEL

KM#	Date	Mintage	Fine	VF	XF	Unc
134	1940	.800	.50	1.00	3.00	8.00
	1951	2.000	.25	.50	1.25	5.00
	1956	8.000	.10	.15	.25	.75
	1959	6.000	.10	.15	.25	.75
	1963	10.000	—	.10	.15	.30
	1966	6.000	.10	.15	.25	.50
	1967	10.000	—	.10	.15	.30
	1972	10.000	—	.10	.15	.30
	1974	10.002	—	.10	.15	.30

COPPER-NICKEL-ZINC

KM#	Date	Mintage	Fine	VF	XF	Unc
134a	1944	5.000	.25	.50	1.50	5.00
	1948	3.000	.25	.50	1.00	2.50
	1950	2.000	.25	.50	1.50	5.00
	1952	4.000	.20	.35	.75	4.00

COPPER-NICKEL CLAD STEEL

KM#	Date	Mintage	Fine	VF	XF	Unc
149.1	1975	15.000	—	.10	.15	.30
	1985	—	—	.10	.15	.30
	1986	30.000	—	.10	.15	.30

NICKEL CLAD STEEL

KM#	Date	Mintage	Fine	VF	XF	Unc
149.2	1976	15.000	—	.10	.15	.30
	1984	15.000	—	.10	.15	.30

COPPER-NICKEL

KM#	Date	Mintage	Fine	VF	XF	Unc
149a	1977	26.000	—	.10	.15	.30

STAINLESS STEEL

Gen. Francisco Morazan

KM#	Date	Mintage	Fine	VF	XF	Unc
154	1987	30.000	—	—	.10	.25
	1991	—	—	—	.10	.25
	1992	—	—	—	.10	.25

10 CENTAVOS

COPPER-NICKEL

KM#	Date	Mintage	Fine	VF	XF	Unc
130	1921	2.000	1.50	5.00	12.00	30.00
	1925	2.000	2.00	6.00	14.00	35.00
	1940	.500	3.50	9.00	20.00	55.00
	1951	1.000	.50	1.50	3.00	8.00
	1967	2.000	—	.10	.50	2.00
	1968	3.000	—	.10	.40	1.00
	1969	3.000	—	.10	.40	1.00
	1972	7.000	—	.10	.25	.75

COPPER-NICKEL-ZINC

KM#	Date	Mintage	Fine	VF	XF	Unc
130a	1952	2.000	.15	.25	.50	1.50
	1985	15.000	—	.10	.15	.30

COPPER-NICKEL CLAD STEEL

KM#	Date	Mintage	Fine	VF	XF	Unc
150	1975	15.000	—	.15	.25	.50

COPPER-NICKEL

KM#	Date	Mintage	Fine	VF	XF	Unc
150a	1977	24.000	—	.10	.20	.40

STAINLESS STEEL

Gen. Francisco Morazan

KM#	Date	Mintage	Fine	VF	XF	Unc
155	1987	30.000	—	—	.15	.35

25 CENTAVOS

7.5000 g, .900 SILVER, .2170 oz ASW

KM#	Date	Mintage	Fine	VF	XF	Unc
136	1943	1.000	1.50	3.00	6.00	10.00
	1944	1.000	1.50	3.00	6.00	10.00

2.5000 g, .900 SILVER, .0723 oz ASW

KM#	Date	Mintage	Fine	VF	XF	Unc
137	1953	14.000	.50	1.00	1.50	3.50

NICKEL

KM#	Date	Mintage	Fine	VF	XF	Unc
139	1970	14.000	—	.10	.20	.60
	1973	28.000	—	.10	.20	.50
	1975	20.000	—	.10	.20	.50
	1977	22.400	—	.10	.20	.50

COPPER-NICKEL

KM#	Date	Mintage	Fine	VF	XF	Unc
139a	1986	21.000	—	.10	.20	.50

STAINLESS STEEL

KM#	Date	Mintage	Fine	VF	XF	Unc
157	1988	20.000	—	.10	.20	.50
	1992	—	—	.10	.20	.50

50 CENTAVOS

5.0000 g, .900 SILVER, .1446 oz ASW

KM#	Date	Mintage	Fine	VF	XF	Unc
138	1953	3.000	1.00	2.00	3.50	6.00

NICKEL, 1.65mm thick

KM#	Date	Mintage	Fine	VF	XF	Unc
140.1	1970	3.000	—	.20	.30	.60

2.00mm thick

KM#	Date	Mintage	Fine	VF	XF	Unc
140.2	1977	1.500	—	.20	.30	.60

UN (1) COLON

25.0000 g, .900 SILVER, .7234 oz ASW
400th Anniversary of Founding of Salvador

KM#	Date	Mintage	Fine	VF	XF	Unc
131	1925Mo	2,000	50.00	100.00	150.00	225.00

2.3000 g, .999 SILVER, .0738 oz ASW
150th Anniversary of Independence

KM#	Date	Mintage	VF	XF	Unc
141	1971	.021	—	Proof	5.50

COPPER-NICKEL
Christopher Columbus

KM#	Date	Mintage	Fine	VF	XF	Unc
153	1984Mo	10.000	—	.50	1.00	2.50
	1985Mo	20.000	—	.50	1.00	2.50

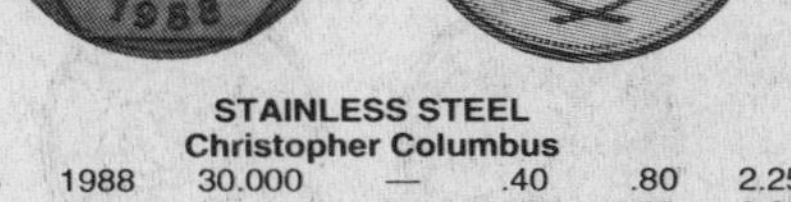

STAINLESS STEEL
Christopher Columbus

KM#	Date	Mintage	Fine	VF	XF	Unc
156	1988	30.000	—	.40	.80	2.25
	1991	—	—	.40	.80	2.25

5 COLONES

11.5000 g, .999 SILVER, .3694 oz ASW
150th Anniversary of Independence

KM#	Date	Mintage	VF	XF	Unc
142	1971	.018	—	Proof	14.50

20 COLONES

15.5600 g, .900 GOLD, .4502 oz AGW
400th Anniversary of Founding of Salvador

KM#	Date	Mintage	Fine	VF	XF	Unc
132	1925Mo					
		100 pcs.	—	1500.	2500.	3500.

25 COLONES

2.9400 g, .900 GOLD, .0850 oz AGW
150th Anniversary of Independence

KM#	Date	Mintage	VF	XF	Unc
143	1971	7,650	—	Proof	90.00

25.0000 g, .900 SILVER, .7234 oz ASW
18th Annual Governors' Assembly

KM#	Date	Mintage	VF	XF	Unc
151	1977	2,000	—	—	20.00
	1977	.020	—	Proof	25.00

50 COLONES

5.9000 g, .900 GOLD, .1707 oz AGW
150th Anniversary of Independence

KM#	Date	Mintage	VF	XF	Unc
144	1971	3,530	—	Proof	125.00

100 COLONES

11.8000 g, .900 GOLD, .3414 oz AGW
150th Anniversary of Independence

KM#	Date	Mintage	VF	XF	Unc
145	1971	2,750	—	Proof	225.00

200 COLONES

23.6000 g, .900 GOLD, .6829 oz AGW
150th Anniversary of Independence

KM#	Date	Mintage	VF	XF	Unc
146	1971	2,245	—	Proof	475.00

250 COLONES

16.0000 g, .917 GOLD, .4717 oz AGW
18th Annual Governors' Assembly

KM#	Date	Mintage	VF	XF	Unc
152	1977	4,000	—	—	250.00
	1977	400 pcs.	—	Proof	350.00

PROOF SETS (PS)

KM#	Date	Mintage	Identification	Issue Price	Mkt. Val.
PS1	1889H(2)	—	KM106-107	—	350.00
PS2	1892(10)	—	KM108-112,114,116-119	—	16,000.
PS3	1914(4)	20	KM115.2,124-126	—	4000.
PS4	1971(6)	—	KM141-146	—	950.00
PS5	1971(4)	—	KM143-146	250.00	915.00
PS6	1971(2)	—	KM141-142	6.00	20.00

Listings For

EQUATORIAL AFRICAN STATES: refer to Central African Republic

EQUATORIAL GUINEA

The Republic of Equatorial Guinea (formerly Spanish Guinea) consists of Rio Muni, located on the coast of westCentral Africa between Cameroon and Gabon, and the off-shore islands of Fernando Po, Annobon, Corisco, Elobey Grande and Elobey Chico. The equatorial country has an area of 10,831 sq. mi. (28,050 sq. km.) and a population of 300,000. Capital: Malabo. The economy is based on agriculture and forestry. Cacao, wood and coffee are exported.

Fernando Po was discovered between 1474 and 1496 by Portuguese navigators charting a route to the spice islands of the Far East. Portugal retained control of it and the adjacent islands until 1778 when they, together with trading rights to the African coast between the Ogooue and Niger Rivers, were ceded to Spain. Fernando Po was administered, with Spanish consent, by the British from 1827 to 1844 when it was reclaimed by Spain. Mainland Rio Muni was granted to Spain by the Berlin Conference of 1885. The name of the colony was changed from Spanish Guinea to Equatorial Guinea in Dec. of 1963. Independence was attained on Oct. 12, 1968.

Equatorial Guinea converted to the CFA currency system as issued for the Central African States issuing its first 100 Franc denomination in 1985.

NOTE: The 1969 coinage carries the actual minting date in the stars at the sides of the large date.

MINT MARKS

(a) - Paris, privy marks only

PESETA

ALUMINUM-BRONZE

KM#	Date	Mintage	Fine	VF	XF	Unc
1	1969(69)	—	.50	1.00	1.50	3.00

5 PESETAS

COPPER-NICKEL

KM#	Date	Mintage	Fine	VF	XF	Unc
2	1969(69)	—	1.50	2.50	3.50	10.00

25 PESETAS

COPPER-NICKEL

KM#	Date	Mintage	Fine	VF	XF	Unc
3	1969(69)	—	2.50	4.00	10.00	15.00

5.0000 g, .999 SILVER, .1606 oz ASW
World Bank

KM#	Date	Mintage	Fine	VF	XF	Unc
5	1970	2,475	—	—	Proof	7.50

United Nations

KM#	Date	Mintage	Fine	VF	XF	Unc
6	1970	2,475	—	—	Proof	7.50

50 PESETAS

COPPER-NICKEL

KM#	Date	Mintage	Fine	VF	XF	Unc
4	1969(69)	—	3.00	5.00	12.00	20.00

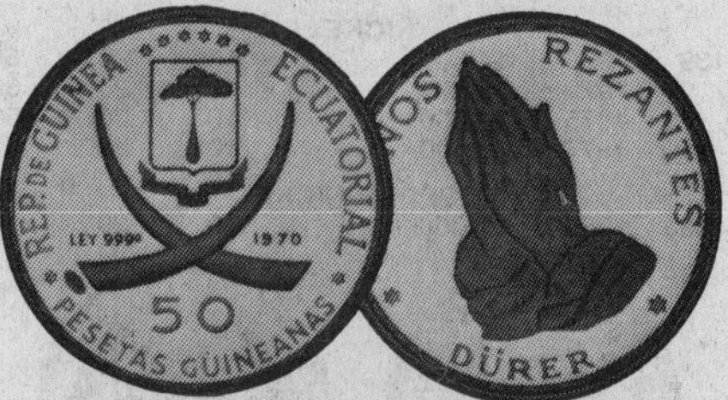

10.0000 g, .999 SILVER, .3212 oz ASW
Praying Hands

KM#	Date	Mintage	Fine	VF	XF	Unc
7	1970	3,840	—	—	Proof	11.50

75 PESETAS

15.0000 g, .999 SILVER, .4818 oz ASW
Pope John XXIII
Obv: Similar to KM#10.

KM#	Date	Mintage	Fine	VF	XF	Unc
8	1970	4,000	—	—	Proof	16.00

Centennial of Birth of Vladimir Ilyich Lenin

KM#	Date	Mintage	Fine	VF	XF	Unc
9	1970	4,000	—	—	Proof	16.00

Abraham Lincoln

KM#	Date	Mintage	Fine	VF	XF	Unc
10	1970	4,390	—	—	Proof	16.00

Centennial of Birth of Mahatma Gandhi
Obv: Similar to KM#10.

KM#	Date	Mintage	Fine	VF	XF	Unc
11	1970	4,000	—	—	Proof	16.00

100 PESETAS

20.0000 g, .999 SILVER, .6430 oz ASW
Praying Hands
Obv: Similar to KM#13.1.

KM#	Date	Mintage	Fine	VF	XF	Unc
12	1970	4,000	—	—	Proof	18.50

Naked Maja

KM#	Date	Mintage	Fine	VF	XF	Unc
13.1	1970	.030	—	—	Proof	40.00

Obv: Fineness stamp at base of right tusk.

KM#	Date	Mintage	Fine	VF	XF	Unc
13.2	1970	Inc. Ab.	—	—	Proof	40.00

Obv: Fineness stamp below base of right tusk.

KM#	Date	Mintage	Fine	VF	XF	Unc
13.3	1970	Inc. Ab.	—	—	Proof	40.00

Obv: Fineness stamp above letters AN.

KM#	Date	Mintage	Fine	VF	XF	Unc
13.4	1970	Inc. Ab.	—	—	Proof	40.00

Obv: 1000 in oval counterstamp at base of right tusk.

KM#	Date	Mintage	Fine	VF	XF	Unc
13.5	1970	Inc. Ab.	—	—	Proof	40.00

150 PESETAS

30.0000 g, .999 SILVER, .9636 oz ASW
Centennial of the Capital Rome, Roma

KM#	Date	Mintage	Fine	VF	XF	Unc
14	1970	3,520	—	—	Proof	27.50

Centennial of the Capital Rome, Coliseum

KM#	Date	Mintage	Fine	VF	XF	Unc
15	1970	3,520	—	—	Proof	27.50

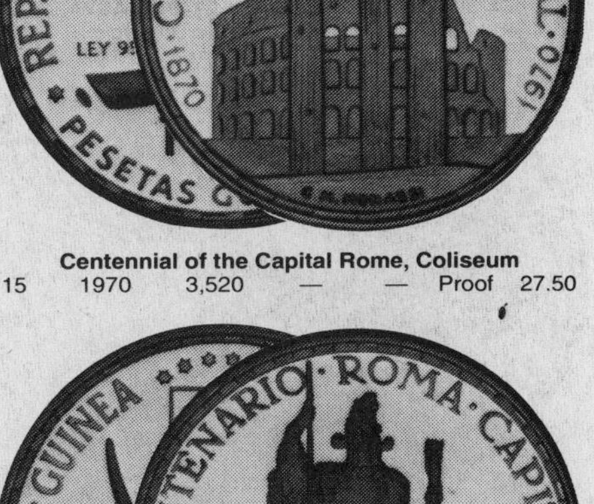

Centennial of the Capital Rome, Athena

KM#	Date	Mintage	Fine	VF	XF	Unc
16	1970	3,520	—	—	Proof	27.50

Centennial of the Capital Rome, Mercury

KM#	Date	Mintage	Fine	VF	XF	Unc
17	1970	3,520	—	—	Proof	27.50

200 PESETAS

40.0000 g, .999 SILVER 1.2848 oz ASW
World Soccer Championship in Mexico
Obv: Similar to 100 Pesetas, KM#13.

KM#	Date	Mintage	Fine	VF	XF	Unc
18	1970	4,280	—	—	Proof	50.00

First President Francisco Macias

KM#	Date	Mintage	Fine	VF	XF	Unc
19	1970	4,000	—	—	Proof	40.00

250 PESETAS

3.5200 g, .900 GOLD, .1018 oz AGW
Naked Maja

KM#	Date	Mintage	Fine	VF	XF	Unc
20	1970	3,500	—	—	Proof	125.00

Praying Hands
Similar to 100 Pesetas, KM#12.

KM#	Date	Mintage	Fine	VF	XF	Unc
21	1970	2,000	—	—	Proof	65.00

500 PESETAS

7.0500 g, .900 GOLD, .2040 oz AGW
Rev: Bust of Pope John XXIII

KM#	Date	Mintage	Fine	VF	XF	Unc
22	1970	1,680	—	—	Proof	140.00

Vladimir Ilyich Lenin
Similar to 75 Pesetas, KM#9.

KM#	Date	Mintage	Fine	VF	XF	Unc
23	1970	1,680	—	—	Proof	140.00

Abraham Lincoln

KM#	Date	Mintage	Fine	VF	XF	Unc
24	1970	1,700	—	—	Proof	140.00

Centennial of Birth of Mahatma Gandhi

KM#	Date	Mintage	Fine	VF	XF	Unc
25	1970	1,680	—	—	Proof	140.00

750 PESETAS

10.5700 g, .900 GOLD, .3058 oz AGW

Centennial of the Capital Rome, Roma
Similar to 150 Pesetas, KM#14.

KM#	Date	Mintage	Fine	VF	XF	Unc
26	1970	1,650	—	—	Proof	225.00

Centennial of the Capital Rome, Coliseum
Similar to 150 Pesetas, KM#15.

KM#	Date	Mintage	Fine	VF	XF	Unc
27	1970	1,550	—	—	Proof	225.00

Centennial of the Capital Rome, Athena
Similar to 150 Pesetas, KM#16.

KM#	Date	Mintage	Fine	VF	XF	Unc
28	1970	1,550	—	—	Proof	225.00

Centennial of the Capital Rome, Mercury
Similar to 150 Pesetas, KM#17.

KM#	Date	Mintage	Fine	VF	XF	Unc
29	1970	1,550	—	—	Proof	225.00

1000 PESETAS

14.1000 g, .900 GOLD, .4080 oz AGW

World Soccer Championship in Mexico
Similar to 200 Pesetas, KM#18.

KM#	Date	Mintage	Fine	VF	XF	Unc
30	1970	1,190	—	—	Proof	250.00

5000 PESETAS

70.5200 g, .900 GOLD, 2.0407 oz AGW

First President Francisco Macias
Similar to 200 Pesetas, KM#19.

KM#	Date	Mintage	Fine	VF	XF	Unc
31	1970	330 pcs.	—	—	Proof	1350.

MONETARY REFORM

EKUELE

BRASS

KM#	Date	Mintage	Fine	VF	XF	Unc
32	1975	3.000	1.00	1.50	2.50	4.00

NOTE: Withdrawn from circulation.

5 EKUELE

COPPER-NICKEL

KM#	Date	Mintage	Fine	VF	XF	Unc
33	1975	2.800	1.25	2.50	3.50	6.00

NOTE: Withdrawn from circulation.

10 EKUELE

COPPER-NICKEL

KM#	Date	Mintage	Fine	VF	XF	Unc
34	1975	1.300	2.25	3.50	5.50	9.00

NOTE: Withdrawn from circulation.

1000 EKUELE

21.4300 g, .925 SILVER, .6373 oz ASW
President Masie Nguema Biyogo

KM#	Date	Mintage	Fine	VF	XF	Unc
35	1978	.031	—	—	Proof	17.50

2000 EKUELE

42.8700 g, .925 SILVER, 1.2749 oz ASW
President Masie Nguema Biyogo

KM#	Date	Mintage	Fine	VF	XF	Unc
36	1978	.031	—	—	Proof	32.50

31.1000 g, .927 SILVER, .9270 oz ASW
XXII Olympics

KM#	Date	Mintage	Fine	VF	XF	Unc
37	ND(1979)	.011	—	—	Proof	25.00

42.8700 g, .925 SILVER, 1.2749 oz ASW
Soccer Games - Argentina 1978

KM#	Date	Mintage	Fine	VF	XF	Unc
38	ND(1979) 195 pcs.		—	—	Proof	120.00

31.0000 g, .927 SILVER, .9270 oz ASW
Zebra

KM#	Date	Mintage	Fine	VF	XF	Unc
55	1980(1983) 1,000		—	—	Proof	30.00

Impalas

KM#	Date	Mintage	Fine	VF	XF	Unc
56	1980(1983) 1,000		—	—	Proof	30.00

Tiger

KM#	Date	Mintage	Fine	VF	XF	Unc
57	1980(1983)	1,000	—	—	Proof	40.00

Cheetah

KM#	Date	Mintage	Fine	VF	XF	Unc
58	1980(1983)	1,000	—	—	Proof	32.50

5000 EKUELE

6.9600 g, .917 GOLD, .2052 oz AGW
President Masie Nguema Biyogo

KM#	Date	Mintage	Fine	VF	XF	Unc
39	1978	.031	—	—	Proof	150.00

10,000 EKUELE

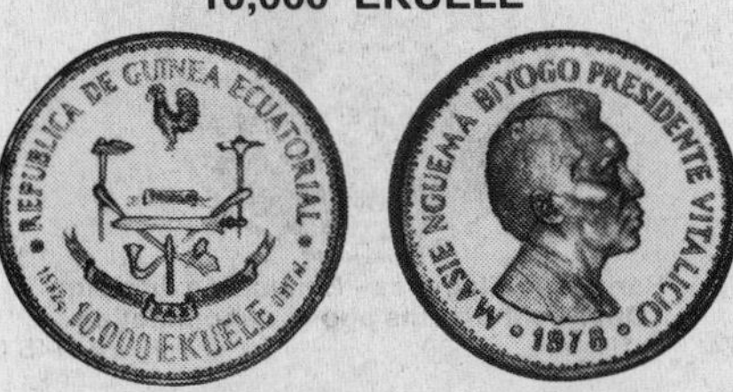

13.9200 g, .917 GOLD, .4104 oz AGW
President Masie Nguema Biyogo

KM#	Date	Mintage	Fine	VF	XF	Unc
40	1978	.031	—	—	Proof	300.00

Soccer Games - Argentina 1978

KM#	Date	Mintage	Fine	VF	XF	Unc
41	ND(1979)	121 pcs.	—	—	Proof	500.00

MONETARY REFORM

EKWELE

ALUMINUM-BRONZE

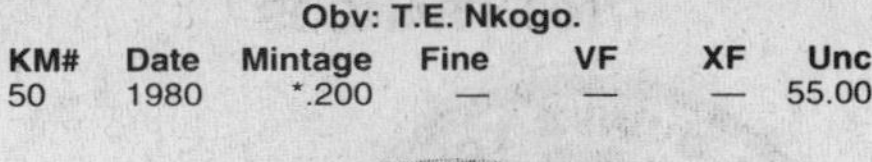

Obv: T.E. Nkogo.

KM#	Date	Mintage	Fine	VF	XF	Unc
50	1980	*.200	—	—	—	55.00

62.2900 g, .999 GOLD, 2.0009 oz AGW
Pope John Paul II
Obv: Coat of arms.

KM#	Date	Mintage	Fine	VF	XF	Unc
54	1982	—	—	—	—	1200.

5 BIPKWELE

COPPER-NICKEL
Obv: T.E. Nkogo right. Rev: Value and arms.

KM#	Date	Mintage	Fine	VF	XF	Unc
51	1980	*.200	—	—	150.00	180.00

25 BIPKWELE

COPPER-NICKEL
T.E. Nkogo

KM#	Date	Mintage	Fine	VF	XF	Unc
52	1980	*.200	—	—	—	30.00
	1981	*.800	—	—	—	—

50 BIPKWELE

COPPER-NICKEL
Obv: T.E. Nkogo right. Rev: Value and arms.

KM#	Date	Mintage	Fine	VF	XF	Unc
53	1980	*.200	—	—	—	32.50
	1981	*.500	—	—	—	—

1000 BIPKWELE

12.5000 g, .925 SILVER, .3717 oz ASW
Royal Couple Visit

KM#	Date	Mintage	Fine	VF	XF	Unc
42	1980	5,125	—	—	—	20.00
	1980	3,000	—	—	Proof	27.50

Juan Carlos I Visit
Rev: Similar to 2000 Bipkwele, KM#45.

KM#	Date	Mintage	Fine	VF	XF	Unc
43	1980	5,125	—	—	—	20.00
	1980	3,000	—	—	Proof	27.50

2000 BIPKWELE

25.0000 g, .925 SILVER, .7435 oz ASW
Royal Couple Visit

KM#	Date	Mintage	Fine	VF	XF	Unc
44	1980	5,125	—	—	—	35.00
	1980	3,000	—	—	Proof	40.00

Juan Carlos I Visit

KM#	Date	Mintage	Fine	VF	XF	Unc
45	1980	5,125	—	—	—	35.00
	1980	3,000	—	—	Proof	40.00

5000 BIPKWELE

4.0000 g, .917 GOLD, .1179 oz AGW
Royal Couple Visit

KM#	Date	Mintage	Fine	VF	XF	Unc
46	1980	4,250	—	—	—	75.00
	1980	2,000	—	—	Proof	100.00

Juan Carlos I Visit

KM#	Date	Mintage	Fine	VF	XF	Unc
47	1980	4,250	—	—	—	75.00
	1980	2,000	—	—	Proof	100.00

10,000 BIPKWELE

8.0000 g, .917 GOLD, .2358 oz AGW
Royal Couple Visit

KM#	Date	Mintage	Fine	VF	XF	Unc
48	1980	4,250	—	—	—	150.00
	1980	2,000	—	—	Proof	175.00

Juan Carlos I Visit

KM#	Date	Mintage	Fine	VF	XF	Unc
49	1980	4,250	—	—	—	150.00
	1980	2,000	—	—	Proof	175.00

MONETARY REFORM

FRANCO

ALUMINUM

KM#	Date	Mintage	Fine	VF	XF	Unc
61	1985	—	— Reported, not confirmed			

5 FRANCOS

ALUMINUM-BRONZE

KM#	Date	Mintage	Fine	VF	XF	Unc
62	1985(a)	—	—	5.00	10.00	15.00

10 FRANCOS

ALUMINUM-BRONZE

KM#	Date	Mintage	Fine	VF	XF	Unc
63	1985	—	— Reported, not confirmed			

25 FRANCOS

ALUMINUM-BRONZE

KM#	Date	Mintage	Fine	VF	XF	Unc
60	1985(a)	—	—	8.00	15.00	25.00

50 FRANCOS

NICKEL

KM#	Date	Mintage	Fine	VF	XF	Unc
64	1985(a)	—	—	20.00	30.00	50.00
	1986(a)	—	—	20.00	30.00	50.00

100 FRANCOS

NICKEL

KM#	Date	Mintage	Fine	VF	XF	Unc
59	1985(a)	—	—	20.00	35.00	55.00
	1986(a)	—	—	20.00	35.00	55.00

500 FRANCOS

COPPER-NICKEL

KM#	Date	Mintage	Fine	VF	XF	Unc
65	1985	—	— Reported, not confirmed			

1000 FRANCOS

COPPER-NICKEL
Brandenburg Gate

KM#	Date	Mintage	Fine	VF	XF	Unc
68	1991	6,000	—	—	Proof	10.00

7000 FRANCOS

26.3000 g, .999 SILVER, .8455 oz ASW
President Mbasogo

KM#	Date	Mintage	Fine	VF	XF	Unc
66	1991	—	—	—	Proof	50.00

25.7000 g, .999 SILVER, .8263 oz ASW
Soccer - Italy 1990

KM#	Date	Mintage	Fine	VF	XF	Unc
67	1991	—	—	—	Proof	45.00

20.0000 g, .999 SILVER, .6430 oz ASW
Discovery of America - Santa Maria

KM#	Date	Mintage	Fine	VF	XF	Unc
69	1991	.015	—	—	Proof	45.00

Seville Expo

KM#	Date	Mintage	Fine	VF	XF	Unc
70	1991	.015	—	—	Proof	45.00

Barcelona Olympics - Athletes on Rings

KM#	Date	Mintage	Fine	VF	XF	Unc
71	1991	.015	—	—	Proof	45.00

15000 FRANCOS

7.0000 g, .917 GOLD, .2063 oz AGW
Discovery of America - Columbus
Obv: Coat of arms above denomination.

KM#	Date	Mintage	Fine	VF	XF	Unc
72	1991	1,500	—	—	Proof	145.00

Expo Seville - Ship and Space Shuttle
Obv: Coat of arms above denomination.

KM#	Date	Mintage	Fine	VF	XF	Unc
73	1991	1,500	—	—	Proof	145.00

Barcelona Olympics - Equestrian Jumping
Obv: Coat of arms above denomination.

KM#	Date	Mintage	Fine	VF	XF	Unc
74	1991	1,500	—	—	Proof	145.00

Endangered Wildlife - Elephant

KM#	Date	Mintage	Fine	VF	XF	Unc
75	1992	—	—	—	Proof	145.00

MINT SETS (MS)

KM#	Date	Mintage	Identification	Issue Price	Mkt. Val.
MS1	1975(3)	—	KM32-34	—	23.00

PROOF SETS (PS)

KM#	Date	Mintage	Identification	Issue Price	Mkt. Val.
PS1	1970(27)	330	KM5-31	—	3600.
PS2	1970(15)	2,475	KM5-19	126.50	360.00
PS3	1970(12)	330	KM20-31	—	3250.

Listings For

ESSEQUIBO & DEMERARY: refer to Guyana

ERITREA

The Republic of Eritrea, a former Ethiopian province fronting on the Red Sea, has an area of 30,466 sq. mi. (117,600 sq. km.) and a population of 2.6 million. It was an Italian colony from 1889 until its incorporation into Italian East Africa in 1936. It was under the British Military Administration from 1941 to Sept. 15, 1952, when the United Nations designated it an autonomous unit within the federation of Ethiopia and Eritrea. On Nov. 14, 1962, it was annexed with Ethiopia. In 1991 the Eritrean Peoples Liberation Front extended its control over the entire territory of Eritrea. Following 2 years of provisional government, Eritrea held a referendum on independence in May 1993. Overwhelming popular approval led to the proclamation of an independent Republic of Eritrea on May 24.

RULERS

Umberto I, 1889-1900
Vittorio Emanuele III, 1900-1945

MINT MARKS

M - Milan
R - Rome

MONETARY SYSTEM

100 Centesimi = 1 Lira
5 Lire = 1 Tallero

COLONIAL COINAGE

50 CENTESIMI

2.5000 g, .835 SILVER, .0671 oz ASW

KM#	Date	Mintage	Fine	VF	XF	Unc
1	1890M	1.800	22.50	45.00	90.00	165.00

LIRA

5.0000 g, .835 SILVER, .1342 oz ASW

KM#	Date	Mintage	Fine	VF	XF	Unc
2	1890R	.598	20.00	40.00	90.00	225.00
	1891R	2.401	20.00	40.00	85.00	210.00
	1896R	1.500	40.00	75.00	150.00	550.00

2 LIRE

10.0000 g, .835 SILVER, .2685 oz ASW

KM#	Date	Mintage	Fine	VF	XF	Unc
3	1890R	1.000	30.00	60.00	125.00	325.00
	1896R	.750	35.00	70.00	140.00	390.00

5 LIRE/TALLERO

28.1250 g, .900 SILVER, .8139 oz ASW

KM#	Date	Mintage	Fine	VF	XF	Unc
4	1891	.196	90.00	185.00	425.00	1200.
	1896	.200	100.00	225.00	450.00	1400.

TALLERO

28.0668 g, .835 SILVER, .7535 oz ASW

KM#	Date	Mintage	Fine	VF	XF	Unc
5	1918R	.510	30.00	60.00	125.00	400.00

REPUBLIC

DOLLAR

COPPER-NICKEL
Independence

KM#	Date	Mintage	VF	XF	Unc
6	1993	—	—	—	6.00

Preserve Planet Earth - Triceratops

KM#	Date	Mintage	VF	XF	Unc
10	1993	—	—	Proof	6.50

Preserve Planet Earth - Ankylosaurus

KM#	Date	Mintage	VF	XF	Unc
13	1993	—	—	—	6.50

10 DOLLARS

31.1030 g, .999 SILVER, 1.0000 oz ASW
Independence

KM#	Date	Mintage	VF	XF	Unc
7	1993	*.030	—	Proof	40.00

28.2800 g, .925 SILVER, .8411 oz ASW
Preserve Planet Earth - Triceratops

KM#	Date	Mintage	VF	XF	Unc
11	1993	*.030	—	Proof	40.00

50 DOLLARS

3.1100 g, .999 GOLD, .1000 oz AGW
Independence

KM#	Date	Mintage	VF	XF	Unc
8	1993	*.020	—	Proof	100.00

100 DOLLARS

6.2200 g, .999 GOLD, .2000 oz AGW
Independence

KM#	Date	Mintage	VF	XF	Unc
9	1993	*5,000	—	Proof	200.00

Preserve Planet Earth - Triceratops

KM#	Date	Mintage	VF	XF	Unc
12	1993	*5,000	—	Proof	175.00

ESTONIA

The Republic of Estonia (formerly the Estonian Soviet Socialist Republic of the U.S.S.R.) is the northernmost of the three Baltic States in Eastern Europe. It has an area of 17,413 sq. mi. (45,100 sq. km.) and a population of *1.5 million. Capital: Tallinn. Agriculture and dairy farming are the principal industries. Butter, eggs, bacon, timber and petroleum are exported.

This small and ancient Baltic state had enjoyed but two decades of independence since the 13th century until the present time. After having been conquered by the Danes, the Livonian Knights, the Teutonic Knights of Germany (who reduced the people to serfdom), the Swedes, the Poles and Russia, Estonia declared itself an independent republic on Feb. 24, 1918 but was not freed until Feb. 1919. The peace treaty was signed Feb. 2, 1920. Shortly after the start of World War II, it was again occupied by Russia and incorporated as the 16th state of the U.S.S.R Germany occupied the tiny state from 1941 to 1944, after which it was retaken by Russia. Most of the nations of the world, including the United States and Great Britain, did not recognize Estonia's incorporation into the Soviet Union.

The coinage, issued during the country's brief independence, is obsolete.

On August 20, 1991, the Parliament of the Estonian Soviet Socialist Republic voted to reassert the republic's independence.

MONETARY SYSTEM

100 Marka = 1 Kroon

MARK

KM#	Date	Mintage	Fine	VF	XF	Unc
		COPPER-NICKEL				
1	1922	5.025	1.50	3.00	5.00	10.00
		NICKEL-BRONZE				
1a	1924	1.985	2.00	4.00	6.00	12.00

KM#	Date	Mintage	Fine	VF	XF	Unc
5	1926	3.979	3.00	5.00	9.00	20.00

3 MARKA

KM#	Date	Mintage	Fine	VF	XF	Unc
		COPPER-NICKEL				
2	1922	2.089	2.00	3.50	5.00	10.00
		NICKEL-BRONZE				
2a	1925	1.134	4.00	7.00	12.00	22.50

KM#	Date	Mintage	Fine	VF	XF	Unc
6	1926	.903	20.00	40.00	65.00	110.00

5 MARKA

KM#	Date	Mintage	Fine	VF	XF	Unc
		COPPER-NICKEL				
3	1922	3.983	2.50	4.00	6.00	16.00
		NICKEL-BRONZE				
3a	1924	1.335	3.00	5.00	7.00	20.00

KM#	Date	Mintage	Fine	VF	XF	Unc
7	1926	1.038	75.00	150.00	200.00	350.00

10 MARKA

KM#	Date	Mintage	Fine	VF	XF	Unc
		NICKEL-BRONZE				
4	1925	2.200	3.00	6.00	10.00	22.50
8	1926	*2.789	650.00	1000.	1500.	2000.

***NOTE:** Most of this issue were melted down. Not released to circulation.

MONETARY REFORM

100 Senti = 1 Kroon

SENT

KM#	Date	Mintage	Fine	VF	XF	Unc
		BRONZE				
10	1929	23.553	.50	1.00	2.00	5.00

KM#	Date	Mintage	Fine	VF	XF	Unc
		1mm thick planchet				
19.1	1939	5.000	5.00	10.00	15.00	30.00
		0.9mm thick planchet				
19.2	1939	Inc. Ab.	5.00	10.00	15.00	30.00

2 SENTI

KM#	Date	Mintage	Fine	VF	XF	Unc
		BRONZE				
15	1934	5.838	1.00	2.25	4.50	8.00

5 SENTI

KM#	Date	Mintage	Fine	VF	XF	Unc
		BRONZE				
11	1931	11.000	1.00	2.25	4.50	8.00

10 SENTI

KM#	Date	Mintage	Fine	VF	XF	Unc
		NICKEL-BRONZE				
12	1931	4.089	1.00	2.25	4.50	8.00

20 SENTI

NICKEL-BRONZE

KM#	Date	Mintage	Fine	VF	XF	Unc
17	1935	4.250	1.00	2.00	4.00	12.00

25 SENTI

NICKEL-BRONZE

KM#	Date	Mintage	Fine	VF	XF	Unc
9	1928	2.025	3.00	6.00	10.00	22.00

50 SENTI

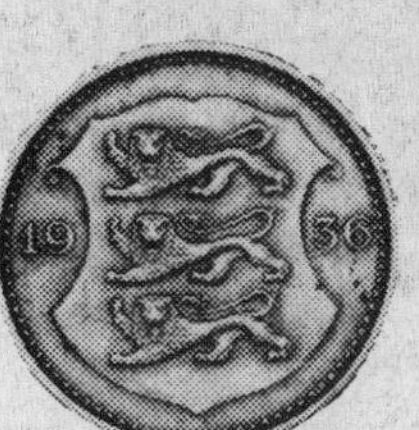

NICKEL-BRONZE

KM#	Date	Mintage	Fine	VF	XF	Unc
18	1936	1.256	3.00	6.00	12.00	25.00

KROON

6.0000 g, .500 SILVER, .0965 oz ASW
Tenth Singing Festival

KM#	Date	Mintage	Fine	VF	XF	Unc
14	1933	.350	8.00	15.00	35.00	65.00

ALUMINUM-BRONZE

KM#	Date	Mintage	Fine	VF	XF	Unc
16	1934	3.304	4.00	7.00	15.00	35.00

NOTE: 1990 restrikes which exist are private issues.

2 KROONI

12.0000 g, .500 SILVER, .1929 oz ASW
Tallinn Castle

KM#	Date	Mintage	Fine	VF	XF	Unc
20	1930	1.276	4.00	7.00	12.50	30.00

University of Tartu Tercentenary

KM#	Date	Mintage	Fine	VF	XF	Unc
13	1932	.100	10.00	20.00	35.00	50.00

NEW REPUBLIC

1991—

5 SENTI

BRASS

KM#	Date	Mintage	Fine	VF	XF	Unc
21	1991	—	—	—	—	.50
	1992	—	—	—	—	.50

10 SENTI

BRASS

KM#	Date	Mintage	Fine	VF	XF	Unc
22	1991	—	—	—	—	.75
	1992	—	—	—	—	.75

20 SENTI

BRASS

KM#	Date	Mintage	Fine	VF	XF	Unc
23	1992	—	—	—	—	1.00

50 SENTI

BRASS

KM#	Date	Mintage	Fine	VF	XF	Unc
24	1992	—	—	—	—	1.25

KROON

COPPER-NICKEL

KM#	Date	Mintage	Fine	VF	XF	Unc
28	1992	.020	—	In sets only		—
	1993	—	—	—	—	1.50

5 KROONI

BRASS
75th Anniversary Declaration of Independence

KM#	Date	Mintage	Fine	VF	XF	Unc
29	1993	—	—	—	—	2.75

10 KROONI

28.2800 g, .925 SILVER, .8411 oz ASW
Olympics - 2 Sail Boats

KM#	Date	Mintage	Fine	VF	XF	Unc
25	1992	*.020	—	—	Proof	50.00

Barn Swallow

KM#	Date	Mintage	Fine	VF	XF	Unc
26	1992	*.010	—	—	Proof	50.00

100 KROONI

Barn Swallows
24.0000 g, .925 SILVER, .7135 oz ASW

KM#	Date	Mintage	Fine	VF	XF	Unc
27	1992	*.050	—	—	Proof	35.00

MINT SETS

KM#	Date	Mintage	Identification	Issue Price	Mkt. Val.
MS1	1992(5)	.020	KM21-24,28	—	38.50

ETHIOPIA

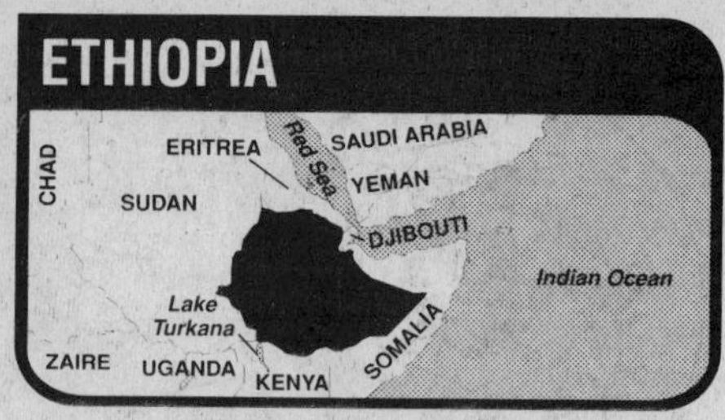

Ethiopia, Africa's oldest independent nation, faces on the Red Sea in East-Central Africa. The country has an area of 441,334 sq. mi. (1,004,390 sq. km.) and a population of *47.7 million people who are divided among 40 tribes and speak 270 languages and dialects. Capital: Addis Ababa. The economy is predominantly agricultural and pastoral. Gold and platinum are mined and petroleum fields are being developed. Coffee, oilseeds, hides and cereals are exported.

Ethiopia was supposedly founded by Menelik I, son of Solomon and the Queen of Sheba in the 10th century B.C. Modern Ethiopian history began with the reign of Emperor Menelik II (1889-1913) under whose guidance the country emerged from medieval isolation. Ethiopia was invaded by Italy in 1935, and together with Italian Somaliland and Eritrea became part of Italian East Africa until liberated by British and Ethiopian troops in 1941. Haile Selassie I, 225th consecutive Solomonic ruler was deposed by a military committee on Sept. 12, 1974. From July 1976 until May 1991, Ethiopia was ruled by a military provisional government. Since that time a transitional government of Ethiopia has been in power. Following 2 years of provisional government, the province of Eritrea held a referendum on independence in May 1993 leading to the proclamation of its independence on May 24.

No coins, patterns or presentation pieces are known bearing Emperor Lij Yasu's likeness or titles. Coins of Menelik II were struck during this period with dates frozen.

RULERS

Menelik II, 1889-1913
Lij Yasu, 1913-1916
Zauditu, Empress, 1916-1930
Haile Selassie I
1930-36, 1941-1974

MINT MARKS

A - Paris
(a) - Paris, privy marks only

Coinage of Menelik II, 1889-1913

NOTE: The first national issue coinage, dated 1887 and 1888 E.E., carried a cornucopia, A, and fasces on the reverse. Subsequent dates have a torch substituted for the fasces, the A being dropped. All issues bearing these marks were struck at the Paris Mint. Coins without mint marks were struck in Addis Ababa.

MONETARY SYSTEM

(Until about 1903)
40 Besa = 20 Gersh = 1 Birr
(After 1903)
32 Besa = 16 Gersh = 1 Birr

DATING

Ethiopian coinage is dated by the Ethiopian Era calendar (E.E.) which commenced 7 years and 8 months after the advent of A.D. dating.

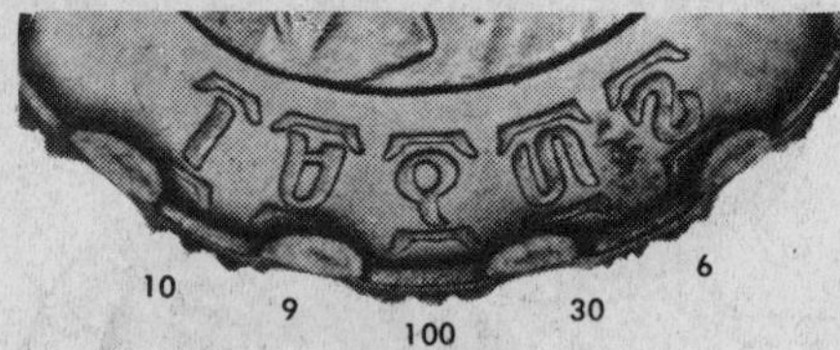

EXAMPLE

1900 (10 and 9 = 19 x 100)
36 (Add 30 and 6)
1936 E.E.
8 (Add)
1943/4 AD

KINGDOM OF ABYSSINIA

MAHALEKI

SILVER, 15mm, 1.04 g
Obv: Crown. Rev: Date, denomination and Ethiopian script.

KM#	Date	Mintage	Fine	VF	XF	Unc
1	EE1885 (1892/93)	—	75.00	150.00	250.00	350.00

NOTE: The above issue has been reported to be the last issue of the Harrar Mint following the capture of that city in 1887 by Menelik's forces.

MONETARY REFORM

1/100 BIRR

(Matonya)

COPPER

KM#	Date	Mintage	Fine	VF	XF	Unc
9	EE1889A (1897)	.500	4.00	8.00	15.00	45.00

1/4 GERSH

(Ya Gersh Rub)

COPPER, 26mm

KM#	Date	Mintage	Fine	VF	XF	Unc
6	EE1888A (1896)	200 pcs.	500.00	900.00	1500.	2500.

1/2 GERSH

(Ya Gersh Alad)

COPPER

KM#	Date	Mintage	Fine	VF	XF	Unc
7	EE1888A (1896)	200 pcs.	350.00	650.00	950.00	1800.

1/32 BIRR

(Ya Birr 32nd)

First Issue

COPPER or BRASS
Enlargement (below lion)

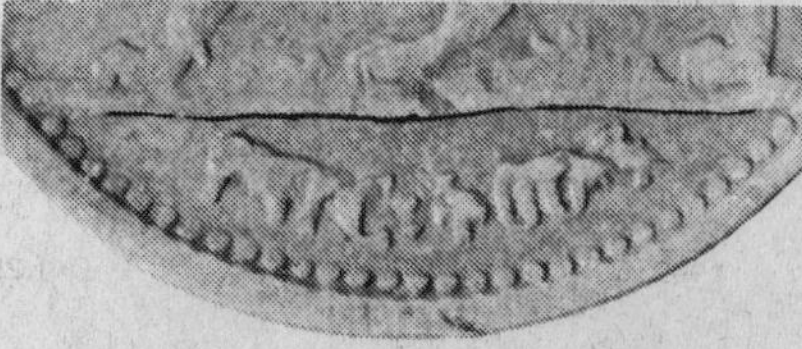

Defaced, with plain and rough edge.

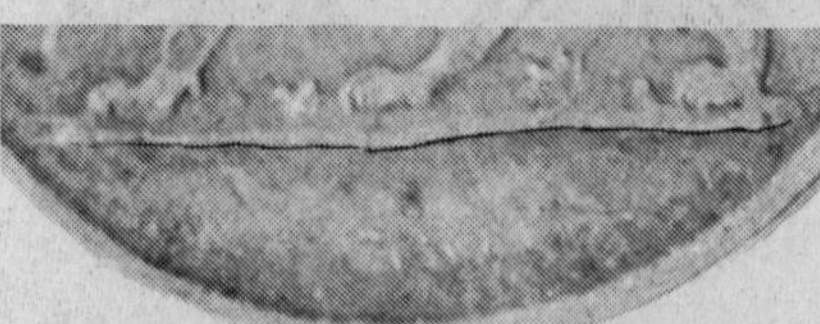

Obliterated, plain and reeded edge.

KM#	Date	Mintage	Fine	VF	XF	Unc
10	EE1889 (1897)	3.50	7.50	15.00	50.00	

NOTE: This issue was struck from dies intended for a silver 1/8 Birr of the die series that included KM#13, 14 and 15. These are found with the denomination partially to almost totally effaced from beneath the lion.

Second Issue

Enlargement (below lion)

KM#	Date	Mintage	Fine	VF	XF	Unc
11	EE1889 (1897)	3.353	4.00	10.00	20.00	60.00

NOTE: Struck at the Addis Ababa Mint in 1922, 1931 and 1933 from newly prepared dies having corrected denominations.

GERSH

(1/20 Birr)

COPPER

KM#	Date	Mintage	Fine	VF	XF	Unc
8	EE1888A (1896)	200 pcs.	400.00	700.00	1150.	2200.

1.4038 g, .835 SILVER, .0377 oz ASW
Rev: Lion's left foreleg raised.

KM#	Date	Mintage	Fine	VF	XF	Unc
12	EE1889A (1897)	1.000	6.00	12.00	20.00	40.00
	1891A (1898)	4.000	4.00	8.00	15.00	25.00
	1895A (1903)	*44.789	2.00	3.50	6.00	20.00

***NOTE:** Struck between 1903-1928.

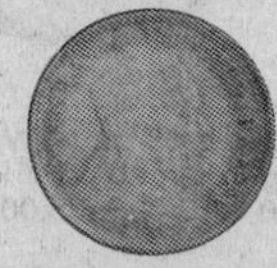

Rev: Lion's right foreleg raised.

KM#	Date	Mintage	Fine	VF	XF	Unc
13	EE1889 (1897)	—	50.00	90.00	150.00	350.00

1/8 BIRR

(Ya Birr Tamun/of Birr Eighth)

3.5094 g, .835 SILVER, .0942 oz ASW
Rev: Lion's left foreleg raised.

KM#	Date	Mintage	Fine	VF	XF	Unc
2	EE1887A (1894)	.025	15.00	25.00	50.00	220.00
	1888A (1896)	200 pcs.	250.00	350.00	550.00	1000.

1/4 BIRR

(Ya Birr Rub/of Birr Fourth)

7.0188 g, .835 SILVER, .1884 oz ASW
Rev: Lion's left foreleg raised.

KM#	Date	Mintage	Fine	VF	XF	Unc
3	EE1887A (1894)	.015	10.00	20.00	40.00	125.00
	1888A (1896)	200 pcs.	150.00	250.00	400.00	900.00
	1889A (1897)	.400	5.00	10.00	25.00	110.00
	1895A (1903)	*.821	4.00	8.00	20.00	100.00

***NOTE:** Struck between 1903 and 1925.

Rev: Lion's right foreleg raised.

KM#	Date	Mintage	Fine	VF	XF	Unc
14	EE1889 (1897)	—	20.00	35.00	60.00	165.00

1/2 BIRR

(Ya Birr Alad/of Birr Half)

14.0375 g, .835 SILVER, .3768 oz ASW
Rev: Lion's left foreleg raised.

KM#	Date	Mintage	Fine	VF	XF	Unc
4	EE1887A (1894)	.010	12.00	25.00	45.00	150.00
	1888A (1896)	200 pcs.	200.00	300.00	500.00	1000.
	1889A (1897)	*.420	10.00	17.50	35.00	125.00

***NOTE:** Struck between 1897 and 1925.

Rev: Lion's right foreleg raised.

KM#	Date	Mintage	Fine	VF	XF	Unc
15	EE1889 (1897)	—	50.00	80.00	150.00	350.00

BIRR

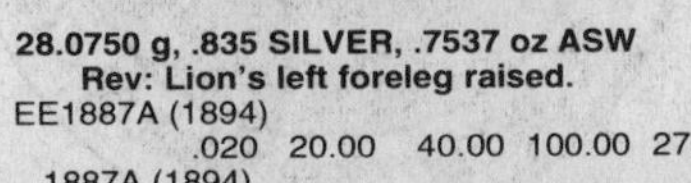

28.0750 g, .835 SILVER, .7537 oz ASW
Rev: Lion's left foreleg raised.

KM#	Date	Mintage	Fine	VF	XF	Unc
5	EE1887A (1894)	.020	20.00	40.00	100.00	275.00
	1887A (1894)	—	—	—	Proof	450.00
	1888A (1896)	200 pcs.	—	—	—	—
	1889A (1897)	.418	15.00	30.00	85.00	250.00

Rev: Lion's right foreleg raised.

KM#	Date	Mintage	Fine	VF	XF	Unc
19	EE1892 (1899)	.401	15.00	30.00	90.00	265.00
	1892 (1899)	—	—	—	Proof	550.00
		—	—	Matte Proof		450.00
	1895 (1903)	*.459	12.50	25.00	85.00	250.00
	1895 (1903)	—	—	—	Proof	500.00

***NOTE:** Struck in 1901, 1903 and 1904.

1/4 WERK

(Ya Werk Rub/of Werk Fourth)

1.7500 g, .900 GOLD, 16mm, .0506 oz AGW

KM#	Date	Mintage	Fine	VF	XF	Unc
16	EE1889 (1897)	—	50.00	125.00	200.00	300.00

1/2 WERK

(Ya Werk Alad/of Werk Half)

3.5000 g, .900 GOLD, .1012 oz AGW

KM#	Date	Mintage	Fine	VF	XF	Unc
17	EE1889 (1897)	—	100.00	165.00	250.00	400.00

KM#	Date	Mintage	Fine	VF	XF	Unc
20	EE1923 (1931)	—	150.00	275.00	425.00	700.00

WERK

7.0000 g, .900 GOLD, .2025 oz AGW

KM#	Date	Mintage	Fine	VF	XF	Unc
18	EE1889 (1897)	—	120.00	185.00	275.00	450.00

NOTE: KM#16-18 vary considerably in weight due to disparities in planchet thicknesses.

KM#	Date	Mintage	Fine	VF	XF	Unc
21	EE1923 (1931)	—	175.00	350.00	600.00	1100.

KINGDOM OF ETHIOPIA

MONETARY SYSTEM

100 Matonas = 100 Santeems
100 Santeems (Cents) = 1 Birr (Dollar)

MATONA

COPPER

KM#	Date	Mintage	Fine	VF	XF	Unc
27	EE1923 (1931)	*1.250	1.50	2.50	5.00	15.00

***NOTE:** Struck by ICI in Birmingham, England. Other denominations in the Matona series were struck in Addis Ababa.

CENT

(An de Santeem)

COPPER

KM#	Date	Mintage	Fine	VF	XF	Unc
32	EE1936 (1944)	20.000	—	.10	.20	.50

NOTE: Coins in the one cent to fifty cent denominations were struck at Philadelphia, Birmingham and the Royal Mint, London between 1944 and 1975 with the date EE1936 frozen.

5 MATONAS

COPPER
Plain edge

KM#	Date	Mintage	Fine	VF	XF	Unc
28.1	EE1923 (1931)	1.363	2.00	3.50	6.00	20.00

Reeded edge

KM#	Date	Mintage	Fine	VF	XF	Unc
28.2	EE1923 (1931)	Inc. Ab.	2.00	3.50	7.00	25.00

5 CENTS

(Amist Santeem)

COPPER

KM#	Date	Mintage	Fine	VF	XF	Unc
33	EE1936 (1944)	*219.000	—	.10	.20	.50

***NOTE:** Struck between 1944-1962 in Philadelphia and 1964-1966 in Birmingham.

10 MATONAS

NICKEL

KM#	Date	Mintage	Fine	VF	XF	Unc
29	EE1923 (1931)	.936	1.50	2.50	4.00	11.00

10 CENTS

(Assir Santeem)

COPPER

KM#	Date	Mintage	Fine	VF	XF	Unc
34	EE1936 (1944)					
		*348.998	—	.10	.25	.75

***NOTE:** Struck between 1945-1963 in Philadelphia, 1964-1966 in Birmingham and 1974-1975 in London.

25 MATONAS

NICKEL

KM#	Date	Mintage	Fine	VF	XF	Unc
30	EE1923 (1931)					
		2.742	1.25	2.00	3.25	8.00

25 CENTS

(Haya Amist Santeem)

COPPER

KM#	Date	Mintage	Fine	VF	XF	Unc
35	EE1936 (1944)					
		*10.000	5.00	10.00	20.00	40.00

***NOTE:** 421,500 issued and 1952 withdrawn and replaced by KM#36.

KM#	Date	Mintage	Fine	VF	XF	Unc
36	EE1936 (1944)					
		*30.000	.25	.50	1.00	3.00

***NOTE:** Issued in 1952 and 1953. Crude and refined edges.

50 MATONAS

NICKEL

KM#	Date	Mintage	Fine	VF	XF	Unc
31	EE1923 (1931)					
		1.621	1.50	2.50	4.50	12.00

50 CENTS

(Hamsa Santeem)

7.0307 g, .800 SILVER, .1808 oz ASW

KM#	Date	Mintage	Fine	VF	XF	Unc
37	EE1936 (1944)					
		*30.000	2.00	3.50	5.50	12.00

***NOTE:** Struck in 1944-1945.

7.0307 g, .700 SILVER, .1582 oz ASW

KM#	Date	Mintage	Fine	VF	XF	Unc
37a	EE1936 (1944)					
		*20.434	2.00	3.50	5.50	12.00

***NOTE:** Struck in 1947.

5 DOLLARS

20.0000 g, .925 SILVER, .5948 oz ASW
Theodros II

KM#	Date	Year	Mintage	VF	XF	Unc
48	EE1964					
		1972F-NI	—	—	—	75.00
	1964	1972NI	.055	—	Proof	40.00

Yohannes IV
Rev: Similar to KM#50.

KM#	Date	Year	Mintage	VF	XF	Unc
49	EE1964					
		1972F-NI	—	—	—	75.00
	1964	1972NI	.055	—	Proof	40.00

Menelik II

KM#	Date	Year	Mintage	VF	XF	Unc
50	EE1964					
		1972F-NI	—	—	—	85.00
	1964	1972NI	.060	—	Proof	45.00

Zauditu

KM#	Date	Year	Mintage	VF	XF	Unc
51	EE1964					
		1972F-NI	—	—	—	90.00
	1964	1972NI	.060	—	Proof	45.00

25.0000 g, .999 SILVER, .8030 oz ASW
Haile Selassie

KM#	Date	Year	Mintage	VF	XF	Unc
52	EE1964	1972HF	3.000	—	Proof	10.00

10 DOLLARS

4.0000 g, .900 GOLD, .1157 oz AGW
75th Anniversary of Birth and 50th Jubilee of Reign of Emperor Haile Selassie I

KM#	Date	Year	Mintage	VF	XF	Unc
38	EE1958	1966NI	.028	—	Proof	80.00

40.0000 g, .925 SILVER, 1.1895 oz ASW

KM#	Date	Year	Mintage	VF	XF	Unc
53	EE1964					
		1972F-NI	—	—	—	175.00
	1964	1972NI	.050	—	Proof	90.00

20 DOLLARS

8.0000 g, .900 GOLD, .2315 oz AGW
75th Anniversary of Birth and 50th Jubilee of Reign of Emperor Haile Selassie I

KM#	Date	Year	Mintage	VF	XF	Unc
39	EE1958	1966NI	.025	—	Proof	125.00

50 DOLLARS

20.0000 g, .900 GOLD, .5787 oz AGW
75th Anniversary of Birth and 50th Jubilee of Reign of Emperor Haile Selassie I

KM#	Date	Year	Mintage	VF	XF	Unc
40	EE1958	1966NI	.015	—	Proof	300.00
	Obv: Bust of Theodros II. Rev: Lion.					
55	EE1964	1972NI	.012	—	Proof	450.00
	Obv: Bust of Yohannes IV.					
56	EE1964	1972NI	.012	—	Proof	450.00
	Obv: Bust of Menelik II.					
57	EE1964	1972NI	.020	—	Proof	450.00
	Obv: Bust of Empress Zauditu.					
58	EE1964	1972NI	.016	—	Proof	450.00

100 DOLLARS

40.0000 g, .900 GOLD, 1.1575 oz AGW
75th Anniversary of Birth and 50th Jubilee of Reign of Emperor Haile Selassie I

KM#	Date	Year	Mintage	VF	XF	Unc
41	EE1958	1966NI	.011	—	Proof	550.00
	Obv: Bust of Selassie. Rev: Lion.					
59	EE1964	1972NI	.010	—	Proof	900.00

200 DOLLARS

80.0000 g, .900 GOLD, 2.3151 oz AGW
75th Anniversary of Birth and 50th Jubilee of Reign of Emperor Haile Selassie I

KM#	Date	Year	Mintage	VF	XF	Unc
42	EE1958	1966NI	8,823	—	Proof	1150.

SOCIALIST ETHIOPIA

CENT

ALUMINUM
F.A.O. Issue
Obv: Small lion head.

KM#	Date	Mintage	Fine	VF	XF	Unc
43.1	EE1969 (1977)					
		35.034	.15	.25	.40	.65

Obv: Large lion head.

KM#	Date	Mintage	Fine	VF	XF	Unc
43.2	EE1969 (1977) FM					
		.012	—	—	Proof	1.00

5 CENTS

COPPER-ZINC
Obv: Small lion head.

KM#	Date	Mintage	Fine	VF	XF	Unc
44.1	EE1969 (1977)					
		201.275	.15	.25	.40	.65

Obv: Large lion head.

KM#	Date	Mintage	Fine	VF	XF	Unc
44.2	EE1969 (1977) FM					
		.012	—	—	Proof	2.00

10 CENTS

COPPER-ZINC
Mountain Nyala
Obv: Small lion head.

KM#	Date	Mintage	Fine	VF	XF	Unc
45.1	EE1969 (1977)					
		202.722	.15	.30	.50	.75

Obv: Large lion head.

KM#	Date	Mintage	Fine	VF	XF	Unc
45.2	EE1969 (1977) FM					
		.012	—	—	Proof	3.00

25 CENTS

COPPER-NICKEL
Obv: Small lion head.

KM#	Date	Mintage	Fine	VF	XF	Unc
46.1	EE1969 (1977)					
		44.983	.20	.30	.60	1.25

Obv: Large lion head.

KM#	Date	Mintage	Fine	VF	XF	Unc
46.2	EE1969 (1977) FM					
		.012	—	—	Proof	4.00

50 CENTS

COPPER-NICKEL
Obv: Small lion head.

KM#	Date	Mintage	Fine	VF	XF	Unc
47.1	EE1969 (1977)					
		27.772	.40	.75	1.25	2.50

Obv: Large lion head.

KM#	Date	Mintage	Fine	VF	XF	Unc
47.2	EE1969 (1977) FM					
		.012	—	—	Proof	7.50

2 BIRR

COPPER-NICKEL
World Soccer Games 1982

KM#	Date	Mintage	Fine	VF	XF	Unc
64	1982	—	—	—	—	4.50

10 BIRR

25.3100 g, .925 SILVER, .7527 oz ASW
Conservation - Bearded Vulture

KM#	Date	Mintage	VF	XF	Unc
61	EE1970(1978)	4,002	—	—	25.00
	28.2800 g, .925 SILVER, .8411 oz ASW				
61a	EE1970(1978)	3,460	—	Proof	35.00

20 BIRR

23.3300 g, .925 SILVER, .6938 oz ASW
International Year of the Child

KM#	Date	Mintage	VF	XF	Unc
54	EE1972(1980)	.016	—	Proof	20.00

Obv: Similar to 2 Birr, KM#64.

KM#	Date	Mintage	VF	XF	Unc
65	1982	.010	—	Proof	27.50

Decade for Women

KM#	Date	Mintage	VF	XF	Unc
73	1984	372 pcs.	—	Proof	65.00

25 BIRR

31.6500 g, .925 SILVER, .9413 oz ASW
Conservation - Mountain Nyala
Obv: Similar to 10 Birr, KM#64.

KM#	Date	Mintage	VF	XF	Unc
62	EE1970(1978)	4,002	—	—	30.00
	35.0000 g, .925 SILVER, 1.0409 oz ASW				
62a	EE1970(1978)	3,295	—	Proof	50.00

50 BIRR

28.2800 g, .925 SILVER, .8411 oz ASW
International Year of Disabled Persons

KM#	Date	Mintage	VF	XF	Unc
66	EE1974(1981)	.011	—	—	20.00
	1974(1981)	.010	—	Proof	25.00

200 BIRR

7.1300 g, .900 GOLD, .2063 oz AGW
World Soccer Games 1982

KM#	Date	Mintage	VF	XF	Unc
67	1982	1,310	—	Proof	220.00

Decade for Women

KM#	Date	Mintage	VF	XF	Unc
72	1984	298 pcs.	—	Proof	350.00

400 BIRR

17.1700 g, .900 GOLD, .4968 oz AGW
International Year of the Child

KM#	Date	Mintage	VF	XF	Unc
60	EE1972(1980)	3,387	—	Proof	225.00

500 BIRR

15.9800 g, .917 GOLD, .5006 oz AGW
International Year of Disabled Persons

KM#	Date	Mintage	VF	XF	Unc
68	EE1974(1981)	2,007	—	—	275.00
	1974(1981)	2,042	—	Proof	350.00

600 BIRR

33.4370 g, .900 GOLD, .9676 oz AGW
Conservation - Walia Ibex

KM#	Date	Mintage	VF	XF	Unc
63	EE1970(1978)	547 pcs.	—	—	600.00
	EE1970(1978)	160 pcs.	—	Proof	1100.

MINT SETS (MS)

KM#	Date	Mintage	Identification	Issue Price	Mkt. Val.
MS1	1972(5)	—	KM48-51-53	—	500.00

PROOF SETS (PS)

KM#	Date	Mintage	Identification	Issue Price	Mkt. Val.
PS1	1894(4)	—	KM2-5	—	2500.
PS2	1966(5)	8,823	KM38-42	—	2200.
PS3	1972(10)	—	KM48-51,53,55-59	—	3000.
PS5	1972(5)	10,000	KM55-59	—	2700.
PS6	1972(5)	50,000	KM48-51,53	46.00	260.00
PS7	1977(5)	11,724	KM43-47	25.00	22.00
PS8	1979(2)	—	KM61a-62a	—	90.00

ERITREA

For coins previously listed here refer to Eritrea.

HARAR

Harar, a province and city located in eastern Ethiopia, was founded by Arab immigrants from Yemen in the 7th century. The sultanate conquered Ethiopia in the mid-16th century, and was in turn conquered by Egypt in 1875 and by Ethiopia in 1887.

TITLES

الهرر

al-Harar

RULERS

Ahmad II,
AH1209-1236/AD1794-1821

'Abd al-Rahman,
AH1236-1240/AD1821-1825

'Abd al-Karim,
AH1240-1250/AD1825-1834

Abu Baker II,
AH1250-1268/AD1834-1852

Muhammad II,
AH1272-1292/AD1856-1875

'Abdallah,
AH1303-1304/AD1885-1887

MONETARY SYSTEM

Not known; 22 Mahallak were said to be equal to one Ashrafi. In the late 18th and the 19th century the Ashrafi in Harar was a fictitious medium used in accounts, which varied in value against the Maria Theresa Dollar from time to time. In the 1st half of the 19th century, 3 Ashrafi were thought to be one Maria Theresa Dollar.

The brass coins are of various sizes, but were probably all called 'Mahallak'. The denominations of the billon and silver are unknown.

MAHALLAK

Anonymous, without name of ruler.

BRASS, 7-10mm, 0.13-0.26 g

KM#	Date	Mintage	Good	VG	Fine	VF
4	AH1222	—	10.00	15.00	25.00	40.00
	1226	—	10.00	15.00	25.00	40.00
	1227	—	10.00	15.00	25.00	40.00

NOTE: Other dates reported to exist.

BRASS, 5-7mm, 0.10-0.20 g

KM#	Date	Mintage	Good	VG	Fine	VF
5	ND	—	4.00	7.50	12.50	20.00

NOTE: Believed to be an issue of 'Abd al-Karim.

Anonymous

About 10-11mm, 0.40-0.65 g

KM#	Date	Mintage	Good	VG	Fine	VF
6	AH1257	—	8.00	15.00	25.00	40.00
	1258	—	8.00	15.00	25.00	40.00

In the name of Muhammad II.

9-11mm, 0.19-0.25 g
Obv: ***Sultan Muhammad bin Ali.***
Rev: ***Al-Sultan abd-al Shakur and date.***

KM#	Date	Mintage	Good	VG	Fine	VF
7	AH1274	—	6.00	12.00	20.00	30.00

10-12mm, 0.35-0.48 g
Obv: ***Sultan Muhammad bin Ali and date.*** **Rev:** ***City of al Harar.***

KM#	Date	Mintage	Good	VG	Fine	VF
8	AH1279	—	7.00	14.00	22.00	35.00

10-14mm, 0.35-0.50 g
Obv: ***Sultan Muhammad bin Ali.***
Rev: ***Struck at Harar and date.***

KM#	Date	Mintage	Good	VG	Fine	VF
9	AH1284	—	3.00	6.00	12.00	20.00

Anonymous, in name of 'THE WEAK SLAVE'

15-19mm, 0.85-1.55 g

KM#	Date	Mintage	Good	VG	Fine	VF
11	AH1303	—	3.00	6.00	11.00	16.00
	1304	—	5.00	10.00	17.50	25.00

SILVER COINS

In the name of Muhammad II

9.5-10mm, 0.05-0.12 g

KM#	Date	Mintage	Good	VG	Fine	VF
10	AH1288	—	35.00	65.00	110.00	185.00

Listings For

FAEROE ISLANDS: refer to Denmark

FALKLAND ISLANDS

The Colony of the Falkland Islands and Dependencies, a British colony located in the South Atlantic about 500 miles northeast of Cape Horn, has an area of 4,700 sq. mi. (12,170 sq. km.) and a population of 2,260. East Falkland, West Falkland, South Georgia, and South Sandwich are the largest of the 200 islands. Capital: Stanley. Sheep grazing is the main industry. Wool, whale oil, and seal oil are exported.

The Falklands were discovered by British navigator John Davis (Davys) in 1592, and named by Capt. John Strong - for Viscount Falkland, treasurer of the British navy - in 1690. French navigator Louis De Bougainville established the first settlement, at Port Louis, in 1764. The following year Capt. John Byron claimed the islands for Britain and left a small party at Saunders Island. Spain later forced the French and British to abandon their settlements but did not implement its claim to the islands. In 1829 the Republic of Buenos Aires, which claimed to have inherited the Spanish rights, sent Louis Vernet to develop a colony on the islands. In 1831 he seized three American sealing vessels, whereupon the men of the corvette, the U.S.S. Lexington, destroyed his settlement and proclaimed the Falklands to be 'free of all governance'. Britain, which had never renounced its claim, then re-established its settlement in 1833.

RULERS

British

MONETARY SYSTEM

100 Pence = 1 Pound

1/2 PENNY

BRONZE
Salmon

KM#	Date	Mintage	VF	XF	Unc
1	1974	.140	—	.10	.25
	1974	.023	—	Proof	1.50
	1980	—	—	.10	.15
	1980	.010	—	Proof	1.50
	1982	—	—	.10	.15
	1982	—	—	Proof	1.50
	1983	—	—	.10	.15

PENNY

BRONZE
Gentoo Penguins

KM#	Date	Mintage	VF	XF	Unc
2	1974	.096	.10	.15	.35
	1974	.023	—	Proof	2.00
	1980	—	.10	.15	.25
	1980	.010	—	Proof	2.00
	1982	—	.10	.15	.25
	1982	—	—	Proof	2.00
	1983	—	.10	.15	.25
	1985	—	.10	.15	.25
	1987	.111	—	.15	.25
	1987	—	—	Proof	2.00
	1992	—	.10	.15	.25
	1992	—	—	Proof	2.00

2 PENCE

BRONZE
Upland Goose

KM#	Date	Mintage	VF	XF	Unc
3	1974	.072	.10	.15	.50
	1974	.023	—	Proof	3.00
	1980	—	.10	.15	.35
	1980	.010	—	Proof	3.00
	1982	—	.10	.15	.35
	1982	—	—	Proof	3.00

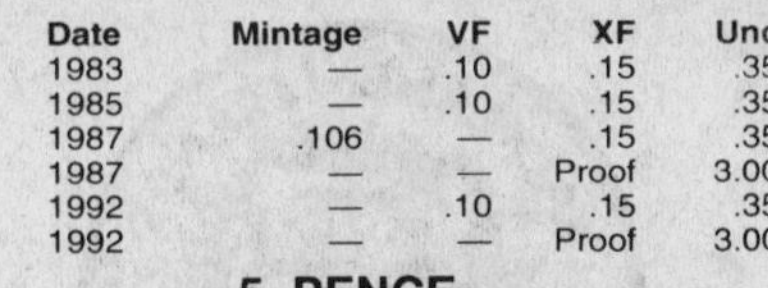

KM#	Date	Mintage	VF	XF	Unc
3	1983	—	.10	.15	.35
	1985	—	.10	.15	.35
	1987	.106	—	.15	.35
	1987	—	—	Proof	3.00
	1992	—	.10	.15	.35
	1992	—	—	Proof	3.00

5 PENCE

COPPER-NICKEL
Blackbrowed Albatross

KM#	Date	Mintage	VF	XF	Unc
4	1974	.067	.10	.25	.65
	1974	.023	—	Proof	3.50
	1980	—	.10	.25	.50
	1980	.010	—	Proof	4.00
	1982	—	.10	.25	.50
	1982	—	—	Proof	4.00
	1983	—	.10	.25	.50
	1985	—	.10	.25	.50
	1987	5,000	—	.25	.50
	1987	—	—	Proof	4.00
	1992	—	.10	.25	.50
	1992	—	—	Proof	4.00

10 PENCE

COPPER-NICKEL
Ursine Seal

KM#	Date	Mintage	VF	XF	Unc
5	1974	.087	.20	.35	1.50
	1974	.023	—	Proof	4.50
	1980	—	.20	.35	1.00
	1980	.010	—	Proof	5.00
	1982	—	.20	.35	1.00
	1982	—	—	Proof	5.00
	1983	—	.20	.35	.75
	1985	—	.20	.35	.75
	1987	4,000	—	.35	.75
	1987	—	—	Proof	5.00
	1992	—	.20	.35	.75
	1992	—	—	Proof	5.00

20 PENCE

COPPER-NICKEL
Romney Marsh Sheep

KM#	Date	Mintage	VF	XF	Unc
17	1982	—	.40	.60	1.00
	1982	—	—	Proof	5.00
	1983	—	.40	.60	1.00
	1985	—	.40	.60	1.00
	1987	4,250	—	.60	1.00
	1987	—	—	Proof	5.00
	1992	—	.40	.60	1.00
	1992	—	—	Proof	5.00

50 PENCE

COPPER-NICKEL
Queen's Silver Jubilee

KM#	Date	Mintage	VF	XF	Unc
10	1977	.100	1.00	1.50	3.00
	28.2800 g, .925 SILVER, .8411 oz ASW				
10a	1977	.022	—	Proof	25.00

COPPER-NICKEL
Fox

KM#	Date	Mintage	VF	XF	Unc
14	1980	—	1.00	1.50	3.50
	1980	—	—	Proof	6.00
	1982	—	1.00	1.50	2.75
	1982	—	—	Proof	6.00
	1983	—	1.00	1.50	2.50
	1985	—	1.00	1.50	2.50
	1987	4,000	1.00	1.50	2.50
	1987	—	—	Proof	6.00
	1992	—	1.00	1.50	2.50
	1992	—	—	Proof	6.00

80th Anniversary of Birth of Queen Mother

KM#	Date	Mintage	VF	XF	Unc
15	1980	—	1.00	1.50	3.00
	28.2800 g, .925 SILVER, .8411 oz ASW				
15a	1980	—	—	Proof	40.00

COPPER-NICKEL
Wedding of Prince Charles and Lady Diana

KM#	Date	Mintage	VF	XF	Unc
16	1981	—	1.00	1.50	3.00
	28.2800 g, .925 SILVER, .8411 oz ASW				
16a	1981	.040	—	Proof	25.00

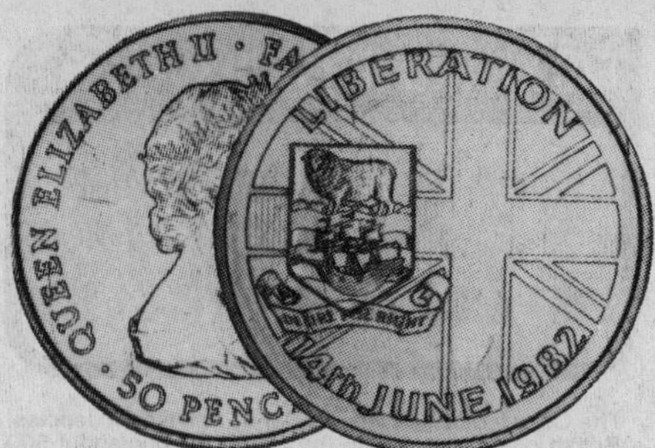

COPPER-NICKEL
Liberation From Argentine Forces

KM#	Date	Mintage	VF	XF	Unc
18	1982	—	1.00	1.50	3.00
	28.2800 g, .925 SILVER, .8411 oz ASW				
18a	1982	*.025	—	Proof	18.00
	47.5000 g, .917 GOLD, 1.4005 oz AGW				
18b	1982	25 pcs.	—	Proof	6000.

COPPER-NICKEL
150th Anniversary of British Rule

KM#	Date	Mintage	VF	XF	Unc
19	1983	*.050	1.00	2.00	5.00
	28.2800 g, .925 SILVER, .8411 oz ASW				
19a	1983	*.010	—	Proof	22.00
	47.5400 g, .917 GOLD, 1.4017 oz AGW				
19b	1983	150 pcs.	—	Proof	2500.

COPPER-NICKEL
Opening of Mount Pleasant Airport

KM#	Date	Mintage	VF	XF	Unc
21	1985	—	—	—	2.50
	28.2750 g, .925 SILVER, .8410 oz ASW				
21a	1985	*5,000	—	Proof	20.00

COPPER-NICKEL
World Wildlife Fund - King Penguins

KM#	Date	Mintage	VF	XF	Unc
25	1987	—	—	—	4.00
	28.2800 g, .925 SILVER, .8411 oz ASW				
25a	1987	*.025	—	Proof	30.00

Children's Fund

KM#	Date	Mintage	VF	XF	Unc
26	1990	*.020	—	Proof	50.00
	COPPER-NICKEL				
26a	1990	—	—	—	5.00

40th Anniversary of Reign

KM#	Date	Mintage	VF	XF	Unc
34	1992	—	—	—	4.50
	28.2800 g, .925 SILVER, .8411 oz ASW				
34a	1992	5,000	—	Proof	50.00

28.2800 g, .925 SILVER, .8411 oz ASW
40th Anniversary of Coronation

KM#	Date	Mintage	VF	XF	Unc
43	ND(1993)	*.010	—	Proof	55.00

1/2 POUND

3.9900 g, .917 GOLD, .1176 oz AGW
Romney Marsh Sheep

KM#	Date	Mintage	VF	XF	Unc
6	1974	2,673	—	Proof	150.00

POUND

7.9900 g, .917 GOLD, .2356 oz AGW
Rommey Marsh Sheep

KM#	Date	Mintage	VF	XF	Unc
7	1974	2,675	—	Proof	250.00

NICKEL-BRASS

KM#	Date	Mintage	VF	XF	Unc
24	1987	—	—	—	3.35
	1987	2,500	—	Proof	10.00
	1992	—	—	—	3.35
	1992	—	—	Proof	10.00

9.5000 g, .925 SILVER, .2825 oz ASW

KM#	Date	Mintage	VF	XF	Unc
24a	1987	*5,000	—	Proof	30.00

19.6500 g, .917 GOLD, .5791 oz AGW

KM#	Date	Mintage	VF	XF	Unc
24b	1987	*200 pcs.	—	Proof	750.00

2 POUNDS

15.9800 g, .917 GOLD, .4712 oz AGW
Romney Marsh Sheep

KM#	Date	Mintage	VF	XF	Unc
8	1974	2,158	—	Proof	550.00

28.2800 g, .500 SILVER, .4546 oz ASW
Commonwealth Games

KM#	Date	Mintage	VF	XF	Unc
22	1986	*.050	—	—	35.00

28.2800 g, .925 SILVER, .8411 oz ASW

KM#	Date	Mintage	VF	XF	Unc
22a	1986	*.020	—	Proof	50.00

10th Wedding Anniversary - Prince Charles

KM#	Date	Mintage	VF	XF	Unc
32	1991	*.010	—	Proof	55.00

COPPER-NICKEL
Heritage Year

KM#	Date	Mintage	VF	XF	Unc
35	1992	—	—	—	9.00

28.2800 g, .925 SILVER, .8411 oz ASW

KM#	Date	Mintage	VF	XF	Unc
35a	1992	*7,500	—	Proof	55.00

5 POUNDS

39.9400 g, .917 GOLD, 1.1773 oz AGW
Romney Marsh Sheep
Obv: Similar to 2 Pounds, KM#8.

KM#	Date	Mintage	VF	XF	Unc
9	1974	2,158	—	Proof	1200.

28.2800 g, .925 SILVER, .8411 oz ASW
Conservation - Humpback Whale

KM#	Date	Mintage	VF	XF	Unc
11	1979	3,998	—	—	35.00
	1979	3,432	—	Proof	65.00

COPPER-NICKEL
90th Birthday of Queen Mother

KM#	Date	Mintage	VF	XF	Unc
27	1990	—	—	—	17.50

28.2800 g, .925 SILVER, .8411 oz ASW

KM#	Date	Mintage	VF	XF	Unc
27a	1990	*.010	—	Proof	50.00

39.9400 g, .917 GOLD, 1.1773 oz AGW
10th Wedding Anniversary - Prince Charles
Similar to 2 Pounds, KM#32.

KM#	Date	Mintage	VF	XF	Unc
33	1991	*200 pcs.	—	Proof	1000.

10th Anniversary of Liberation

KM#	Date	Mintage	VF	XF	Unc
36	1992	100 pcs.	—	Proof	1000.

28.2800 g, .925 SILVER, .8511 oz ASW

KM#	Date	Mintage	VF	XF	Unc
36a	1992	*5,000	—	Proof	50.00

COPPER-NICKEL

KM#	Date	Mintage	VF	XF	Unc
36b	1992	—	—	—	15.00

28.2800 g, .925 SILVER, .8511 oz ASW
400th Anniversary of Discovery - Ship "Desire"

KM#	Date	Mintage	VF	XF	Unc
37	1992	*.020	—	Proof	55.00

10 POUNDS

35.0000 g, .925 SILVER, 1.0409 oz AGW
Conservation - Flightless Steamer Duck

KM#	Date	Mintage	VF	XF	Unc
12	1979	3,996	—	—	45.00
	1979	3,247	—	Proof	85.00

3.1300 g, .999 GOLD, .1000 oz AGW
90th Birthday of Queen Mother
Obv: Portrait of Queen Elizabeth.

KM#	Date	Mintage	VF	XF	Unc
28	1990	*750 pcs.	—	Proof	125.00

400th Anniversary of Discovery
Similar to 5 Pounds, KM#37.

KM#	Date	Mintage	VF	XF	Unc
38	1992	*400 pcs.	—	Proof	125.00

25 POUNDS

150.0000 g, .925 SILVER, 4.4614 oz ASW
100 Years of Self Sufficiency
Illustration reduced. Actual size: 65mm

KM#	Date	Mintage	VF	XF	Unc
20	1985	*.020	—	Proof	75.00

Prince Andrew's Wedding
Illustration reduced. Actual size: 65mm

KM#	Date	Mintage	VF	XF	Unc
23	1986	*.020	—	Proof	60.00

7.8100 g, .999 GOLD, .2500 oz AGW
90th Birthday of Queen Mother
Obv: Portrait of Queen Elizabeth.

KM#	Date	Mintage	VF	XF	Unc
29	1990	*750 pcs.	—	Proof	275.00

400th Anniversary of Discovery - Cathedral and Cross

KM#	Date	Mintage	VF	XF	Unc
40	1992	*400 pcs.	—	Proof	275.00

50 POUNDS

15.6100 g, .999 GOLD, .5000 oz AGW
90th Birthday of Queen Mother
Obv: Portrait of Queen Elizabeth.

KM#	Date	Mintage	VF	XF	Unc
30	1990	750 pcs.	—	Proof	425.00

100th Anniversary of Defense - Soldier

KM#	Date	Mintage	VF	XF	Unc
41	1992	*400 pcs.	—	Proof	450.00

47.5400 g, .917 GOLD, 1.4013 oz AGW
40th Anniversary of Coronation of Queen Elizabeth II

KM#	Date	Mintage	VF	XF	Unc
44	1993	*100 pcs.	—	Proof	1150.

100 POUNDS

31.2100 g, .999 GOLD, 1.0000 oz AGW
90th Birthday of Queen Mother
Obv: Portrait of Queen Elizabeth.

KM#	Date	Mintage	VF	XF	Unc
31	1990	750 pcs.	—	Proof	725.00

400th Anniversary of Discovery - Ship "Desire"
Similar to 5 Pounds, KM#37.

KM#	Date	Mintage	VF	XF	Unc
42	1992	*400 pcs.	—	Proof	725.00

150 POUNDS

33.4370 g, .900 GOLD, .9676 oz AGW
Conservation - Falkland Fur Seal
Obv: Portrait of Queen Elizabeth II.

KM#	Date	Mintage	VF	XF	Unc
13	1979	488 pcs.	—	—	650.00
	1979	164 pcs.	—	Proof	1850.

MINT SETS (MS)

KM#	Date	Mintage	Identification	Issue Price	Mkt. Val.
MS1	1987(7)	—	KM2-5,14,17,24	10.00	10.00
MS2	1992(8)	—	KM2-5,14,17,24,35	24.50	25.00

PROOF SETS (PS)

KM#	Date	Mintage	Identification	Issue Price	Mkt. Val.
PS1	1974(5)	20,000	KM1-5	12.00	15.50
PS2	1974(4)	2,000	KM6-9	1100.	2150.
PS3	1979(2)	10,000	KM11-12	—	125.00
PS4	1980(6)	10,000	KM1-5,14	35.00	20.00
PS5	1982(8)	5,000	KM1-5,14,17,18a	—	50.00
PS6	1982(7)	5,000	KM1-5,14,17	—	26.50
PS7	1987(7)	*2,500	KM2-5,14,17,24	35.00	35.00
PS8	1990(4)	750	KM28-31	1595.	1550.
PS9	1992(8)	*2,500	KM2-5,14,17,24,35a	89.50	90.00
PS10	1992(4)	—	KM38,40-42	1595.	1550.

FIJI ISLANDS

The Republic of Fiji, consists of about 320 islands located in the southwestern Pacific 1,100 miles (1,770 km.) north of New Zealand. The islands have a combined area of 7,056 sq. mi. (18,274 sq. km.) and a population of 715,000. Capital: Suva. Fiji's economy is based on agriculture and mining. Sugar, coconut products, manganese, and gold are exported.

The first European to sight Fiji was the Dutch navigator Abel Tasman in 1643 and the islands were visited by British naval captain James Cook in 1774. The first complete survey of the island was conducted by the United States in 1840. Settlement by mercenaries from Tonga, and traders attracted by the sandalwood trade, began in 1801. Following a lengthy period of intertribal warfare, the islands were unconditionally ceded to Great Britain in 1874 by King Cakobau. Fiji became a sovereign and independent nation on Oct. 10, 1970, the 96th anniversary of the cession of the islands to Queen Victoria.

Fiji was declared a Republic in 1987 following two military coups. It left the British Commonwealth and Queen Elizabeth ceased to be the Head of State. A new constitution was introduced in 1991.

RULERS

British

MINT MARKS

(c) - Royal Australian Mint, Canberra
(o) - Royal Canadian Mint, Ottawa
S - San Francisco, U.S.A.

MONETARY SYSTEM

12 Pence = 1 Shilling
2 Shillings = 1 Florin
20 Shillings = 1 Pound

1/2 PENNY

COPPER-NICKEL

KM#	Date	Mintage	Fine	VF	XF	Unc
1	1934	.096	1.00	3.00	6.00	15.00
	1934	—	—	—	Proof	—

KM#	Date	Mintage	Fine	VF	XF	Unc
14	1940	.024	8.00	15.00	30.00	50.00
	1940	—	—	—	Proof	400.00
	1941	.096	.75	1.50	4.00	13.50
	1941	—	—	—	Proof	250.00

BRASS

KM#	Date	Mintage	Fine	VF	XF	Unc
14a	1942S	.250	.25	.50	5.00	15.00
	1943S	.250	.25	.50	5.00	15.00

COPPER-NICKEL
Obv. leg: EMPEROR dropped.

KM#	Date	Mintage	Fine	VF	XF	Unc
16	1949	.096	.50	1.00	2.00	7.50
	1949	—	—	—	Proof	210.00
	1950	.115	.25	.50	1.50	5.00
	1950	—	—	—	Proof	230.00
	1951	.115	.25	.50	1.50	5.00
	1951	—	—	—	Proof	190.00
	1952	.228	.15	.35	.75	3.00
	1952	—	—	—	Proof	—

KM#	Date	Mintage	Fine	VF	XF	Unc
20	1954	.228	.15	.25	.50	1.00
	1954	—	—	—	Proof	180.00

PENNY

COPPER-NICKEL

KM#	Date	Mintage	Fine	VF	XF	Unc
2	1934	.480	.50	1.00	6.00	18.50
	1934	—	—	—	Proof	—
	1935	.240	.65	1.25	6.50	20.00
	1935	—	—	—	Proof	—
	1936	.240	.65	1.25	6.50	40.00
	1936	—	—	—	Proof	—

KM#	Date	Mintage	Fine	VF	XF	Unc
6	1936	.120	.50	1.00	2.50	7.50
	1936	—	—	—	Proof	225.00

KM#	Date	Mintage	Fine	VF	XF	Unc
7	1937	.360	.50	1.00	3.50	10.00
	1937	—	—	—	Proof	225.00
	1940	.144	2.00	3.00	15.00	40.00
	1940	—	—	—	Proof	225.00
	1941	.228	.50	1.00	2.50	10.00
	1941	—	—	—	Proof	225.00
	1945	.240	2.00	3.00	12.50	30.00
	1945	—	—	—	Proof	225.00

BRASS

KM#	Date	Mintage	Fine	VF	XF	Unc
7a	1942S	1.000	.50	1.00	4.50	20.00
	1943S	1.000	.50	1.00	4.50	20.00

COPPER-NICKEL
Obv. leg: EMPEROR dropped.

KM#	Date	Mintage	Fine	VF	XF	Unc
17	1949	.120	.25	.50	1.00	7.00
	1949	—	—	—	Proof	325.00
	1950	.058	2.00	5.00	15.00	75.00
	1950	—	—	—	Proof	200.00
	1952	.230	.25	.50	1.00	6.50
	1952	—	—	—	Proof	175.00

KM#	Date	Mintage	Fine	VF	XF	Unc
21	1954	.511	.20	.50	1.00	5.00
	1954	—	—	—	Proof	175.00
	1955	.230	.25	.50	1.50	7.50
	1955	—	—	—	Proof	175.00
	1956	.230	.25	.50	1.50	7.50
	1956	—	—	—	Proof	175.00
	1957	.360	.10	.25	.75	3.00

KM#	Date	Mintage	Fine	VF	XF	Unc
21	1957	—	—	—	Proof	175.00
	1959	.864	.10	.20	.35	1.00
	1959	—	—	—	Proof	175.00
	1961	.432	.20	.45	.75	1.50
	1961	—	—	—	Proof	175.00
	1963	.432	.20	.45	.75	1.50
	1963	—	—	—	Proof	175.00
	1964	.864	.10	.20	.35	1.00
	1964	—	—	—	Proof	150.00
	1965	1.440	.10	.15	.25	.50
	1966	.720	.10	.15	.25	.50
	1967	.720	.10	.15	.25	.50
	1968	.720	.10	.15	.25	.50

THREEPENCE

NICKEL-BRASS
Native Hut

KM#	Date	Mintage	Fine	VF	XF	Unc
15	1947	.450	1.25	2.50	7.00	20.00
	1947	—	—	—	Proof	250.00

Obv. leg: EMPEROR dropped.

KM#	Date	Mintage	Fine	VF	XF	Unc
18	1950	.450	.50	1.00	4.00	15.00
	1950	—	—	—	Proof	250.00
	1952	.400	.50	1.00	5.00	22.50
	1952	—	—	—	Proof	250.00

KM#	Date	Mintage	Fine	VF	XF	Unc
22	1955	.400	.50	1.00	4.00	15.00
	1955	—	—	—	Proof	150.00
	1956	.200	.50	1.00	5.00	25.00
	1956	—	—	—	Proof	200.00
	1958	.200	.50	1.00	4.00	15.00
	1958	—	—	—	Proof	185.00
	1960	.240	.25	.50	3.00	12.00
	1960	—	—	—	Proof	185.00
	1961	.240	.25	.50	1.50	7.50
	1961	—	—	—	Proof	185.00
	1963	.240	.15	.30	1.00	5.00
	1963	—	—	—	Proof	150.00
	1964	.240	.15	.30	.50	3.00
	1965	.800	.10	.20	.35	2.00
	1967	.800	.10	.20	.35	2.00

SIXPENCE

2.8276 g, .500 SILVER, .0455 oz ASW
Sea Turtle

KM#	Date	Mintage	Fine	VF	XF	Unc
3	1934	.160	1.50	3.00	20.00	55.00
	1934	—	—	—	Proof	600.00
	1935	.120	2.00	5.00	25.00	80.00
	1935	—	—	—	Proof	—
	1936	.040	3.00	8.00	35.00	90.00
	1936	—	—	—	Proof	—

KM#	Date	Mintage	Fine	VF	XF	Unc
8	1937	.040	3.00	8.00	25.00	90.00
	1937	—	—	—	Proof	400.00

Obv: Smaller head.

KM#	Date	Mintage	Fine	VF	XF	Unc
11	1938	.040	3.00	8.00	25.00	90.00
	1938	—	—	—	Proof	—
	1940	.040	3.00	8.00	25.00	90.00
	1940	—	—	—	Proof	—
	1941	.040	5.00	15.00	40.00	110.00
	1941	—	—	—	Proof	—

2.8276 g, .900 SILVER, .0818 oz ASW

KM#	Date	Mintage	Fine	VF	XF	Unc
11a	1942S	.400	BV	1.00	2.50	7.50
	1943S	.400	BV	1.00	2.50	7.50

COPPER-NICKEL

KM#	Date	Mintage	Fine	VF	XF	Unc
19	1953	.800	.15	.30	1.00	2.50
	1953	—	—	—	Proof	210.00
	1958	.400	.25	.50	1.50	7.50
	1958	—	—	—	Proof	200.00
	1961	.400	.25	.50	1.00	5.00
	1961	—	—	—	Proof	200.00
	1962	.400	.25	.50	1.00	5.00
	1962	—	—	—	Proof	200.00
	1965	.800	.15	.30	.75	4.00
	1967	.800	.15	.30	.75	3.50

SHILLING

5.6552 g, .500 SILVER, .0909 oz ASW
Outrigger

KM#	Date	Mintage	Fine	VF	XF	Unc
4	1934	.360	1.75	6.50	30.00	100.00
	1934	—	—	—	Proof	800.00
	1935	.180	1.75	6.50	30.00	125.00
	1935	—	—	—	Proof	—
	1936	.140	2.00	8.00	35.00	110.00
	1936	—	—	—	Proof	—

KM#	Date	Mintage	Fine	VF	XF	Unc
9	1937	.040	2.75	10.00	40.00	125.00
	1937	—	—	—	Proof	500.00

Obv: Smaller head.

KM#	Date	Mintage	Fine	VF	XF	Unc
12	1938	.040	2.50	10.00	40.00	140.00
	1938	—	—	—	Proof	—
	1941	.040	2.75	12.50	45.00	145.00
	1941	—	—	—	Proof	—

5.6552 g, .900 SILVER, .1636 oz ASW

KM#	Date	Mintage	Fine	VF	XF	Unc
12a	1942S	.500	BV	2.75	4.00	8.50
	1943S	.500	BV	2.75	4.00	8.50

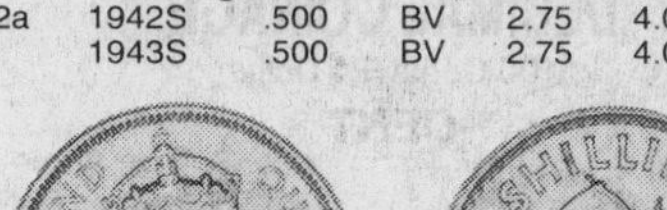

COPPER-NICKEL

KM#	Date	Mintage	Fine	VF	XF	Unc
23	1957	.400	.50	.75	2.00	10.00
	1957	—	—	—	Proof	—
	1958	.400	.50	.75	2.25	12.50
	1958	—	—	—	Proof	—
	1961	.200	.75	1.00	2.25	12.50
	1961	—	—	—	Proof	275.00
	1962	.400	.35	.75	1.25	5.00
	1962	—	—	—	Proof	250.00
	1965	.800	.25	.50	.75	2.50

FLORIN

11.3104 g, .500 SILVER, .1818 oz ASW

KM#	Date	Mintage	Fine	VF	XF	Unc
5	1934	.200	2.00	8.00	40.00	200.00
	1934	—	—	—	Proof	900.00
	1935	.050	3.50	20.00	45.00	300.00
	1935	—	—	—	Proof	—
	1936	.065	3.50	20.00	45.00	300.00
	1936	—	—	—	Proof	—

KM#	Date	Mintage	Fine	VF	XF	Unc
10	1937	.030	4.00	15.00	40.00	210.00
	1937	—	—	—	Proof	750.00

Obv: Smaller head.

KM#	Date	Mintage	Fine	VF	XF	Unc
13	1938	.020	12.50	25.00	55.00	265.00
	1938	—	—	—	Proof	—
	1941	.020	12.50	25.00	55.00	265.00
	1941	—	—	—	Proof	—
	1945	*.100	20.00	35.00	95.00	350.00
	1945	—	—	—	Proof	—

***NOTE:** Quantity believed sunk while in transit during World War II.

11.3104 g, .900 SILVER, .3273 oz ASW

KM#	Date	Mintage	Fine	VF	XF	Unc
13a	1942S	.250	BV	5.50	7.50	17.50
	1943S	.250	BV	6.00	8.00	22.00

COPPER-NICKEL

KM#	Date	Mintage	Fine	VF	XF	Unc
24	1957	.300	.50	1.50	5.00	12.50
	1957	—	—	—	Proof	375.00
	1958	.220	.50	1.50	5.00	15.00
	1958	—	—	—	Proof	375.00
	1962	.200	.25	.50	2.00	11.50
	1962	—	—	—	Proof	375.00
	1964	.200	.25	.50	1.50	7.50
	1964	—	—	—	Proof	400.00
	1965	.400	.25	.50	1.00	3.50

DECIMAL COINAGE

100 Cents = 1 Dollar

CENT

BRONZE
Kava Dish

KM#	Date	Mintage	VF	XF	Unc
27	1969	11.000	—	.10	.20
	1969	.010	—	Proof	.50
	1973	3.000	—	.10	.75
	1975	2.064	—	.10	.35
	1976	2.005	—	.10	.35
	1983	—	—	.10	.35
	1983	3,000	—	Proof	1.00
	1984	2.295	—	.10	.35
	1985	—	—	.10	.35

2.2600 g, .925 SILVER, .0672 oz ASW

KM#	Date	Mintage	VF	XF	Unc
27a	1976	3,012	—	Proof	3.50

BRONZE
F.A.O. Issue - Rice

KM#	Date	Mintage	VF	XF	Unc
39	1977	3.000	—	.10	.50
	1978	3.032	—	.10	.30
	1978	2,000	—	Proof	2.50
	1979	2.500	—	.10	.50
	1980	.314	—	.10	.50
	1980	2,500	—	Proof	1.50
	1981	4.040	—	.10	.50
	1982	5.000	—	.10	.50
	1982	3,000	—	Proof	1.00

KM#	Date	Mintage	VF	XF	Unc
49	1986(c)	3.400	—	—	.25
	1987(c)	3.400	—	—	.25

COPPER PLATED ZINC

KM#	Date	Mintage	VF	XF	Unc
49a	1990(o)	8.500	—	—	.25
	1992	—	—	—	.25

2 CENTS

BRONZE
Fan

KM#	Date	Mintage	VF	XF	Unc
28	1969	8.000	—	.10	.50
	1969	.010	—	Proof	.75
	1973	2.110	.10	.15	.75
	1975	1.500	.10	.15	.50
	1976	1.005	.10	.10	.40
	1977	1.250	—	.10	.40
	1978	1.502	—	.10	.40
	1978	2,000	—	Proof	3.50
	1979	.500	—	.10	.75
	1980	4.020	—	.10	.40
	1980	2,500	—	Proof	2.50
	1981	3.250	—	.10	.40
	1982	4.000	—	.10	.40
	1982	3,000	—	Proof	2.00
	1983	—	—	.10	.40
	1983	3,000	—	Proof	1.50
	1984	1.845	—	.10	.40
	1985	1.700	—	.10	.40

4.5300 g, .925 SILVER, .1347 oz ASW

KM#	Date	Mintage	VF	XF	Unc
28a	1976	3,012	—	Proof	4.50

BRONZE

KM#	Date	Mintage	VF	XF	Unc
50	1986(c)	1.700	—	—	.35
	1987(c)	1.700	—	—	.25

COPPER PLATED ZINC

KM#	Date	Mintage	VF	XF	Unc
50a	1990(o)	5.500	—	—	.25

5 CENTS

COPPER-NICKEL
Native Drum

KM#	Date	Mintage	VF	XF	Unc
29	1969	9.200	.10	.20	.75
	1969	.010	—	Proof	.75
	1973	.600	.10	.30	1.50
	1974	.608	.10	.30	1.25
	1975	1.008	.10	.20	.65
	1976	1.205	.10	.20	.50
	1977	.960	.10	.20	.75
	1978	.880	.10	.20	.60
	1978	2,000	—	Proof	5.00
	1979	1.500	.10	.15	.50
	1980	2.506	.10	.15	.50
	1980	2,500	—	Proof	3.50
	1981	1.980	.10	.15	.35
	1982	2.700	.10	.15	.35
	1982	3,000	—	Proof	3.00
	1983	—	.10	.15	.35
	1983	3,000	—	Proof	2.00
	1984	—	.10	.15	.35

3.2800 g, .925 SILVER, .0975 oz ASW

KM#	Date	Mintage	VF	XF	Unc
29a	1976	3,012	—	Proof	6.00

COPPER-NICKEL

KM#	Date	Mintage	VF	XF	Unc
51	1986(c)	1.200	—	—	.40
	1987(c)	1.200	—	—	.30

NICKEL BONDED STEEL

KM#	Date	Mintage	VF	XF	Unc
51a	1990(o)	2.000	—	—	.30
	1992	—	—	—	.25

10 CENTS

COPPER-NICKEL
Wooden Club

KM#	Date	Mintage	VF	XF	Unc
30	1969	3.500	.20	.40	1.00
	1969	.010	—	Proof	1.00
	1973	.750	.20	.50	2.00
	1975	.752	.20	.50	1.00
	1976	.805	.20	.50	1.00
	1977	.240	.25	.65	1.25
	1978	.664	.20	.50	1.00
	1978	2,000	—	Proof	6.00
	1979	.702	.15	.30	.75
	1980	1.000	.15	.30	.75
	1980	2,500	—	Proof	4.50
	1981	1.200	.20	.45	.85
	1982	1.500	.20	.45	.85
	1982	3,000	—	Proof	4.00
	1983	—	.20	.40	.75
	1983	3,000	—	Proof	3.00
	1984	—	.15	.35	.65
	1985	.660	.15	.35	.65

6.5500 g, .925 SILVER, .1948 oz ASW

KM#	Date	Mintage	VF	XF	Unc
30a	1976	3,012	—	Proof	6.50

COPPER-NICKEL

KM#	Date	Mintage	VF	XF	Unc
52	1986(c)	.740	—	—	.50
	1987(c)	.740	—	—	.35

NICKEL BONDED STEEL

KM#	Date	Mintage	VF	XF	Unc
52a	1990(o)	2.000	—	—	.35

20 CENTS

COPPER-NICKEL
Tabua on Chain

KM#	Date	Mintage	VF	XF	Unc
31	1969	2.000	.30	.80	1.50
	1969	.010	—	Proof	1.75
	1973	.250	.35	1.00	2.25
	1974	.252	.35	.75	1.50
	1975	.352	.35	.75	1.50
	1976	.405	.25	.65	1.00
	1977	.200	.25	.65	1.75
	1978	.406	.25	.50	1.00
	1978	2,000	—	Proof	8.00
	1979	.500	.25	.50	1.00
	1980	1.000	.25	.50	1.00
	1980	2,500	—	Proof	6.50
	1981	1.200	.25	.50	1.00
	1982	1.500	.25	.50	1.00
	1982	3,000	—	Proof	6.00
	1983	—	.25	.50	1.00
	1983	3,000	—	Proof	5.00
	1984	—	.25	.50	1.00
	1985	.240	.20	.35	.70

13.0900 g, .925 SILVER, .3893 oz ASW

KM#	Date	Mintage	VF	XF	Unc
31a	1976	3,012	—	Proof	8.50

COPPER-NICKEL

KM#	Date	Mintage	VF	XF	Unc
53	1986(c)	.260	—	—	.75
	1987(c)	.360	—	—	.50

NICKEL BONDED STEEL

KM#	Date	Mintage	VF	XF	Unc
53a	1990(o)	1.500	—	—	.50

50 CENTS

COPPER-NICKEL
Sailboat - Takia

KM#	Date	Mintage	VF	XF	Unc
36	1975	1.000	.75	1.50	5.00
	1976	.805	.75	1.00	3.00
	1978	4,006	1.25	2.50	7.50
	1978	2,000	—	Proof	13.00
	1980	.316	.75	1.00	2.00
	1980	2,500	—	Proof	11.50
	1981	.511	.75	1.00	2.00
	1982	1.000	.75	1.00	2.00
	1982	3,000	—	Proof	10.00
	1983	—	.60	.85	1.75
	1983	3,000	—	Proof	9.00
	1984	—	.60	.85	1.75

18.0000 g, .925 SILVER, .5353 oz ASW

KM#	Date	Mintage	VF	XF	Unc
36a	1976	3,012	—	Proof	13.50

COPPER-NICKEL
F. A. O. Issue - First Indians in Fiji Centennial

KM#	Date	Mintage	VF	XF	Unc
44	1979	.258	—	—	1.25
	1979	6,004	—	Proof	6.00

10th Anniversary of Independence - Prince Charles

KM#	Date	Mintage	VF	XF	Unc
45	1980	.010	—	—	3.00

KM#	Date	Mintage	VF	XF	Unc
54	1986(c)	.160	—	—	1.50
	1987(c)	.160	—	—	1.50

NICKEL BONDED STEEL

KM#	Date	Mintage	VF	XF	Unc
54a	1990(o)	.800	—	—	1.25

DOLLAR

COPPER-NICKEL

KM#	Date	Mintage	VF	XF	Unc
32	1969	.070	1.00	1.50	3.00
	1969	.010	—	Proof	3.00
	1976	5,007	1.50	3.00	6.50

28.2800 g, .925 SILVER, .8411 oz ASW

KM#	Date	Mintage	VF	XF	Unc
32a	1976	3,012	—	Proof	16.00

COPPER-NICKEL
Independence Commemorative

KM#	Date	Mintage	VF	XF	Unc
33	1970	.015	—	—	5.00
	1970	.015	—	Proof	6.00

28.2800 g, .925 SILVER, .8411 oz ASW

KM#	Date	Mintage	VF	XF	Unc
33a	1970	1,000	—	Proof	80.00

10 DOLLARS

30.3000 g, .925 SILVER, .9012 oz ASW
Queen's Silver Jubilee

KM#	Date	Mintage	VF	XF	Unc
40	1977	3,010	—	Proof	25.00

28.2800 g, .500 SILVER, .4547 oz ASW
Conservation - Pink-billed Parrot Finch

KM#	Date	Mintage	VF	XF	Unc
41	1978	3,582	—	—	25.00

28.2800 g, .925 SILVER, .8411 oz ASW

KM#	Date	Mintage	VF	XF	Unc
41a	1978	4,026	—	Proof	32.00

28.4400 g, .500 SILVER, .4572 oz ASW
10th Anniversary of Independence - Prince Charles

KM#	Date	Mintage	VF	XF	Unc
46	1980	5,001	—	—	15.00

30.4800 g, .925 SILVER, .9066 oz ASW

KM#	Date	Mintage	VF	XF	Unc
46a	1980	3,001	—	Proof	27.50

30.0000 g, .925 SILVER, .8922 oz ASW
Wedding of Prince Charles and Lady Diana
Obv: Similar to KM#41.

KM#	Date	Mintage	VF	XF	Unc
48	1981	5,000	—	Proof	22.50

28.2800 g, .925 SILVER, .8411 oz ASW
25th Anniversary World Wildlife Fund
Fijian Ground Frog
Obv: Similar to KM#41.

KM#	Date	Mintage	VF	XF	Unc
55	1986	*.025	—	Proof	25.00

Save the Children Fund

KM#	Date	Mintage	VF	XF	Unc
60	1991	.020	—	Proof	28.00

40th Anniversary - Coronation of Queen Elizabeth II

KM#	Date	Mintage	VF	XF	Unc
62	1993	*.010	—	Proof	45.00

20 DOLLARS

35.0000 g, .500 SILVER, .5627 oz ASW
Conservation - Golden Cowrie
Obv: Similar to 10 Dollars, KM#41.

KM#	Date	Mintage	VF	XF	Unc
42	1978	3,584	—	—	27.50

35.0000 g, .925 SILVER, 1.0409 oz ASW

KM#	Date	Mintage	VF	XF	Unc
42a	1978	3,869	—	Proof	35.00

25 DOLLARS

48.6000 g, .925 SILVER, 1.4455 oz ASW
100th Anniversary of Cession to Great Britain
Obv: Similar to 10 Dollars, KM#41.

KM#	Date	Mintage	VF	XF	Unc
34	1974	2,400	—	—	25.00
	1974	8,299	—	Proof	22.50

King Cakobau
Obv: Similar to 10 Dollars, KM#41.

KM#	Date	Mintage	VF	XF	Unc
37	1975	836 pcs.	—	—	50.00
	1975	5,157	—	Proof	25.00

100 DOLLARS

31.3600 g, .500 GOLD, .5042 oz AGW
100th Anniversary of Cession to Great Britain
Obv: Similar to 250 Dollars, KM#43.

KM#	Date	Mintage	VF	XF	Unc
35	1974	1,109	—	—	200.00
	1974	2,321	—	Proof	275.00

31.3000 g, .500 GOLD, .5032 oz AGW
King Cakobau
Obv: Similar to 250 Dollars, KM#43.

KM#	Date	Mintage	VF	XF	Unc
38	1975	593 pcs.	—	—	250.00
	1975	3,197	—	Proof	300.00

200 DOLLARS

15.9800 g, .917 GOLD, .4712 oz AGW
10th Anniversary of Independence - Prince Charles

KM#	Date	Mintage	VF	XF	Unc
47	1980	500 pcs.	—	—	285.00
	1980	1,166	—	Proof	265.00

25th Anniversary World Wildlife Fund
Obv: Similar to 10 Cents, KM#31. Rev: Ogmodon.

KM#	Date	Mintage	VF	XF	Unc
56	1986	5,000	—	Proof	325.00

10.0000 g, .917 GOLD, .2948 oz AGW
Save the Children Fund

KM#	Date	Mintage	VF	XF	Unc
61	1991	.032	—	Proof	280.00

250 DOLLARS

33.4370 g, .900 GOLD, .9676 oz AGW
Conservation - Banded Iguana

KM#	Date	Mintage	VF	XF	Unc
43	1978	810 pcs.	—	—	550.00
	1978	252 pcs.	—	Proof	800.00

GOLD BULLION ISSUES

NOTE: Dates are privy marks and are not yet known.

25 DOLLARS

7.7750 g, .750 GOLD, .1875 oz AGW
Fijian Thatched Temple

KM#	Date	Mintage	VF	XF	Unc
57	(1990)	443 pcs.	—	—	150.00
	(1991)	512 pcs.	—	—	150.00
	(1992)	50 pcs.	—	—	200.00

50 DOLLARS

15.5500 g, .750 GOLD, .3750 oz AGW
Fijian Warrior

KM#	Date	Mintage	VF	XF	Unc
58	(1990)	168 pcs.	—	—	275.00
	(1991)	141 pcs.	—	—	275.00
	(1992)	43 pcs.	—	—	350.00

100 DOLLARS

31.1000 g, .750 GOLD, .7500 oz AGW
Tabua on Cord

KM#	Date	Mintage	VF	XF	Unc
59	(1990)	161 pcs.	—	—	550.00
	(1991)	131 pcs.	—	—	550.00
	(1992)	41 pcs.	—	—	650.00

MINT SETS (MS)

KM#	Date	Mintage	Identification	Issue Price	Mkt. Val.
MSA1	1934(3)	—	KM3-5	—	500.00
MSB1	1969(6)	—	KM27-32	—	7.00
MS1	1976(7)	5,001	KM27-32,36	9.00	12.50
MS2	1976(6)	—	KM27-31,36	—	6.50
MS3	1978(6)	4,006	KM28-31,36,39	4.50	8.00
MS4	1978(3)	—	KM41-43	444.00	600.00
MS5	1978(2)	—	KM41-42	44.00	55.00
MS6	1983(6)	3,000	KM27-31,36	5.00	4.50
MS7	1984(6)	5,000	KM27-31,36	3.60	4.50
MS8	1990(6)	—	KM49a-54a	—	5.00
MS9	(1990)(3)	—	KM57-59	905.00	975.00

PROOF SETS (PS)

KM#	Date	Mintage	Identification	Issue Price	Mkt. Val.
PS1	1969(6)	10,000	KM27-32	7.20	7.00
PS2	1976(7)	3,023	KM27a-32a36a	87.50	60.00
PS3	1978(6)	2,000	KM28-31,36,39	31.00	32.00
PS4	1978(2)	—	KM41a,42a	76.00	65.00
PS5	1978(3)	—	KM41a,42a,43	726.00	865.00
PS6	1980(6)	2,500	KM28-31,36,39	45.00	28.00
PS7	1982(6)	3,000	KM28-31,36,39	32.00	22.50
PS8	1983(6)	3,000	KM27-31,36	27.00	20.00

FINLAND

The Republic of Finland, the second most northerly state of the European continent, has an area of 130,543 sq. mi.(338,127 sq. km.) and a population of 5 million. Capital: Helsinki. Lumbering, shipbuilding, metal and woodworking are the leading industries. Paper, timber, woodpulp, plywood and metal products are exported.

The Finns, who probably originated in the Volga region of Russia, took Finland from the Lapps late in the 7th century. They were conquered in the 12th century by Eric IX of Sweden, and brought into contact with Western Christendom. In 1809, Sweden was conquered by Alexander I of Russia, and the peace terms gave Finland to Russia which became a grand duchy within the Russian Empire until Dec. 6, 1917, when, shortly after the Bolshevik revolution it declared its independence. After a brief but bitter civil war between the Russian sympathizers and Finnish nationalists in which the Whites (nationalists) were victorious, a new constitution was adopted, and on Dec. 6, 1917 Finland was established as a republic. In 1939 Soviet troops invaded Finland over disputed territorial concessions which were later granted in the peace treaty of 1940. When the Germans invaded Russia, Finland became involved and in the Armistice of 1944 lost the Petsamo area to the Soviets.

RULERS

Alexander II, 1855-1881
Alexander III, 1881-1894
Nicholas II, 1894-1917

MONETARY SYSTEM

100 Pennia = 1 Markka
Commencing 1963
100 Old Markka = 1 New Markka

MINT MARKS

H - Birmingham 1921
Heart (h) - Copenhagen 1922
No mm - Helsinki

MINTMASTERS INITIALS

Letter	Date	Name
H	1948-1958	Uolevi Helle
H-M	1990	Raimo Heino & Tapio Makkonen
K	1976-1978	Timo Koivuranta
K-H	1977,1979	Timo Koivuranta & Heikki Haivaoja (Designer)
K-M	1983	Timo Koivuranta & Pertti Makinen
K-N	1978	Timo Koivuranta & Antti Neuvonen
K-T	1982	Timo Koivuranta & Erja Tielinen
L	1885-1912	Johan Conrad Lihr
L	1948	V. U. Liuhto
L-M	1991	Arto Lappalainen & Tapio Makkonen
M	1987	Tapio Makkonen
M-L-M	1989	Marjo Lahtinen & Tapio Makkonen
M-S	1992	Tapio Makkonen and Erkki Salmela
N	1983-1987	Tapio Nevalainen
P-M	1989-1990	Reijo Paavilainen & Tapio Makkonen
P-N	1985	Reijo Paavilainen & Tapio Nevalainen
S	1864-1885	Aug. F. Soldan
S	1912-1947	Isac Sundell
S	1958-1975	Allan Soiniemi
S-H	1967-1971	Allan Soiniemi & Heikki Haivaoja (Designer)
S-J	1960	Allan Soiniemi & Toivo Jaatinen

GRAND DUCHY

PENNI

COPPER
Dotted border

KM#	Date	Mintage	Fine	VF	XF	Unc
1.1	1864	.030	1200.	1750.	2500.	4000.
	1865	.515	15.00	25.00	50.00	120.00
	1866/5	3.673	25.00	40.00	85.00	175.00
	1866	Inc. Ab.	8.00	12.00	25.00	50.00
	1867	3.843	7.00	12.00	25.00	50.00
	1869	1.575	15.00	20.00	35.00	70.00
	1870	.500	40.00	60.00	120.00	180.00
	1871	1.500	7.00	12.00	25.00	50.00

Dentilated border

KM#	Date	Mintage	Fine	VF	XF	Unc
1.2	1872	1.000	8.00	15.00	30.00	60.00
	1873	2.000	5.00	8.00	20.00	40.00
	1874	1.450	5.00	8.00	20.00	50.00
	1875	1.550	5.00	8.00	17.00	50.00
	1876	2.005	5.00	8.00	17.00	40.00

KM#	Date	Mintage	Fine	VF	XF	Unc
10	1881	.600	7.00	12.00	20.00	60.00
	1882	.100	30.00	50.00	95.00	145.00
	1883	3.900	1.00	3.00	6.00	20.00
	1884	.404	30.00	60.00	110.00	165.00
	1888	2.290	1.00	3.00	5.00	15.00
	1891	1.008	2.00	5.00	10.00	20.00
	1892	1.510	1.00	2.00	5.00	11.00
	1893	2.290	.75	1.50	4.00	10.00
	1893 dot after date					
		Inc. Ab.	.75	1.50	4.00	10.00
	1894	1.810	.75	1.50	4.00	10.00

KM#	Date	Mintage	Fine	VF	XF	Unc
13	1895	.880	1.50	3.50	7.50	20.00
	1898	1.430	.75	1.25	3.00	10.00
	1899	1.540	.75	1.25	3.00	7.50
	1900	3.550	.50	1.00	2.00	4.00
	1901	1.520	.75	1.25	2.50	5.00
	1902	1.000	.75	1.25	2.50	7.50
	1903 sm.3	1.145	.75	1.25	2.50	7.50
	1903 lg.3	I.A.	1.00	2.00	5.00	12.00
	1904	.500	2.50	5.00	10.00	20.00
	1905	1.390	.50	1.00	2.00	4.00
	1906	1.020	.50	1.00	2.00	4.00
	1907 normal 7					
		2.490	.75	1.25	2.50	7.00
	1907 w/o serif on 7 arm					
		Inc. Ab.	.30	.75	1.75	4.00
	1908	.950	.50	1.00	2.00	5.00
	1909	3.060	.25	.65	1.25	2.50
	1911	2.550	.25	.65	1.25	2.50
	1912	2.450	.25	.65	1.25	2.50
	1913	1.650	.25	.65	1.25	3.00
	1914	1.900	.25	.65	1.25	3.50
	1915	2.250	.25	.65	1.25	2.50
	1916	3.040	.25	.50	1.00	2.00

5 PENNIA

COPPER
Dotted border

KM#	Date	Mintage	Fine	VF	XF	Unc
4.1	1865	.480	6.00	20.00	40.00	120.00
	1866	2.490	1.00	5.00	15.00	70.00
	1867	1.660	2.00	6.00	18.00	80.00
	1870	.300	5.00	15.00	50.00	150.00

NOTE: Varieties exist.

Dentilated border

KM#	Date	Mintage	Fine	VF	XF	Unc
4.2	1872	.500	3.00	10.00	30.00	125.00
	1873	1.000	1.00	5.00	15.00	80.00
	1875	1.000	1.00	5.00	15.00	80.00

NOTE: Varieties exist.

KM#	Date	Mintage	Fine	VF	XF	Unc
11	1888	.600	2.00	7.00	15.00	80.00
	1889	1.070	1.00	5.00	10.00	75.00
	1892	.330	3.00	7.00	20.00	125.00

KM#	Date	Mintage	Fine	VF	XF	Unc
15	1896	.410	2.00	8.00	25.00	80.00

KM#	Date	Mintage	Fine	VF	XF	Unc
15	1897	.590	1.00	5.00	15.00	75.00
	1898	1.150	1.00	4.00	10.00	45.00
	1899	.860	1.00	5.00	15.00	50.00
	1901	.990	1.00	4.00	10.00	40.00
	1905	.620	1.00	4.00	15.00	50.00
	1906	.960	.75	2.50	10.00	40.00
	1907	.770	.75	2.50	10.00	50.00
	1908	1.660	.75	2.50	10.00	30.00
	1910	.060	20.00	35.00	75.00	175.00
	1911	1.050	.75	2.50	6.00	20.00
	1912	.460	1.50	5.00	15.00	40.00
	1913	1.060	.65	1.25	4.00	15.00
	1914	.820	.65	1.25	3.00	15.00
	1915	2.080	.30	.75	3.00	10.00
	1916	4.470	.30	.75	3.00	10.00
	1917	4.070	.30	.75	3.00	10.00

10 PENNIA

COPPER
Dotted border

KM#	Date	Mintage	Fine	VF	XF	Unc
5.1	1865	.250	3.00	12.00	40.00	150.00
	1866/5	.850	5.00	17.00	50.00	175.00
	1866	Inc. Ab.	2.00	8.00	30.00	100.00
	1867	1.440	2.00	7.00	30.00	100.00

Dentilated border

KM#	Date	Mintage	Fine	VF	XF	Unc
5.2	1875	.100	40.00	70.00	150.00	500.00
	1876	.300	3.00	10.00	50.00	150.00

NOTE: Varieties exist.

KM#	Date	Mintage	Fine	VF	XF	Unc
12	1889	.100	10.00	25.00	70.00	300.00
	1890	.106	8.00	20.00	65.00	280.00
	1891	.295	5.00	12.00	35.00	125.00

KM#	Date	Mintage	Fine	VF	XF	Unc
14	1895	.210	3.00	10.00	30.00	125.00
	1896	.294	3.00	10.00	30.00	125.00
	1897	.502	1.50	5.00	20.00	100.00
	1898	.040	25.00	45.00	125.00	350.00
	1899	.440	1.25	5.00	20.00	100.00
	1900	.524	1.25	5.00	15.00	70.00
	1905	.500	1.25	5.00	15.00	70.00
	1907	.503	1.25	5.00	15.00	70.00
	1908	.320	1.50	7.50	17.50	80.00
	1909	.180	2.00	10.00	20.00	100.00
	1910	.241	1.50	7.50	15.00	70.00
	1911	.370	1.00	5.00	10.00	50.00
	1912	.191	1.50	7.50	15.00	70.00
	1913	.150	2.50	7.50	20.00	80.00
	1914	.605	.75	1.50	5.00	25.00
	1915	.420	.50	1.00	3.00	10.00
	1916	1.952	.50	1.00	3.00	10.00
	1917	1.600	.75	1.50	4.00	12.00

25 PENNIA

1.2747 g, .750 SILVER, .0307 oz ASW
Dotted border

KM#	Date	Mintage	Fine	VF	XF	Unc
6.1	1865S	.705	10.00	25.00	50.00	150.00
	1866S	.810	7.00	15.00	40.00	120.00
	1867S	.400	200.00	300.00	600.00	1500.
	1868S	.136	100.00	150.00	350.00	800.00
	1869S	.264	25.00	40.00	80.00	200.00
	1871S	.150	40.00	70.00	150.00	350.00

Dentilated border

KM#	Date	Mintage	Fine	VF	XF	Unc
6.2	1872S	.400	6.00	15.00	40.00	125.00
	1873S	.800	3.00	10.00	30.00	75.00
	1875S	.810	3.00	10.00	30.00	75.00
	1876S	1,200	1000.	1500.	2500.	3500.
	1889L	.404	3.00	8.00	20.00	70.00
	1890L	.800	1.50	3.00	10.00	50.00
	1891L	.280	2.50	6.00	15.00	65.00
	1894L	.820	1.50	3.00	10.00	50.00
	1897L	.450	1.50	3.00	12.00	50.00
	1898L	.444	1.50	3.00	10.00	40.00
	1898L/inverted L	Inc. Ab.	15.00	25.00	40.00	125.00
	1899L	.312	1.50	3.00	15.00	65.00
	1901L	.993	1.00	2.00	5.00	25.00
	1902L	.210	3.00	7.00	15.00	60.00
	1906L	.281	2.00	5.00	10.00	50.00
	1907L	.590	1.00	2.00	5.00	15.00
	1908L	.340	1.00	2.50	5.00	15.00
	1909L	1.099	.75	1.50	3.00	10.00
	1910L	.392	2.50	5.00	10.00	50.00
	1913S	.832	.50	1.00	1.50	3.00
	1915S	2.400	.50	.75	1.00	1.50
	1916S	6.392	.50	.75	1.00	1.50
	1917S	5.820	.50	.75	1.00	1.50

50 PENNIA

2.5494 g, .750 SILVER, .0615 oz ASW
Dotted border

KM#	Date	Mintage	Fine	VF	XF	Unc
2.1	1864S	.104	5.00	15.00	50.00	200.00
	1865S	1.184	3.50	10.00	35.00	125.00
	1866S	.363	10.00	25.00	75.00	250.00
	1868S	.140	40.00	80.00	225.00	650.00
	1869S	.144	15.00	30.00	60.00	250.00
	1869S slanted 9	Inc. Ab.	15.00	30.00	75.00	250.00
	1871S	.320	3.00	8.00	25.00	120.00

Dentilated border

KM#	Date	Mintage	Fine	VF	XF	Unc
2.2	1872S	*.200	3.00	8.00	25.00	120.00
	1874S	.402	2.50	5.00	20.00	100.00
	1876S	600 pcs.	3500.	5000.	6000.	8000.
	1889L	.312	2.50	5.00	25.00	120.00
	1890L	.693	1.00	2.50	15.00	50.00
	1891L	.282	1.00	3.00	15.00	75.00
	1892L	.344	1.00	2.50	12.00	70.00
	1893L	.400	1.00	2.50	12.00	70.00
	1907L	.260	1.00	3.00	15.00	75.00
	1908L	.353	.75	2.00	10.00	30.00
	1911L	.616	.75	1.25	2.50	5.00
	1914S	.600	.75	1.00	1.50	4.00
	1915S	1.000	.75	1.00	1.50	2.50
	1916S	4.752	.75	1.00	1.50	2.50
	1917S	3.972	.75	1.00	1.50	2.50

***NOTE:** Some specimens may appear as proof-like. Proofs were never made officially by the mint.

MARKKA

5.1828 g, .868 SILVER, .1446 oz ASW
Dotted border

KM#	Date	Mintage	Fine	VF	XF	Unc
3.1	1864S	.075	30.00	50.00	100.00	250.00
	1865S	1.673	2.50	5.00	20.00	85.00
	1866S	1.990	2.50	5.00	20.00	75.00
	1867S	.852	10.00	20.00	50.00	250.00
	1870S	5 known	—	—	Rare	—

Dentilated border

KM#	Date	Mintage	Fine	VF	XF	Unc
3.2	1872S	.538	4.00	10.00	35.00	150.00
	1874S	1.002	2.50	6.00	15.00	65.00
	1890L	.841	2.50	6.00	15.00	70.00
	1892L	.484	2.50	6.00	15.00	80.00
	1893L	.254	3.00	7.50	25.00	100.00
	1907L	.350	2.00	3.00	8.00	25.00
	1908L	.153	4.00	10.00	25.00	50.00
	1915S	1.212	2.00	3.00	6.00	10.00

2 MARKKAA

10.3657 g, .868 SILVER, .2893 oz ASW
Dotted border

KM#	Date	Mintage	Fine	VF	XF	Unc
7.1	1865S	.203	5.00	10.00	30.00	150.00
	1866/5S	.820	10.00	25.00	60.00	250.00
	1866S	Inc. Ab.	10.00	25.00	55.00	220.00
	1867S	6 known	—	—	*	—
	1870S	.500	5.00	10.00	30.00	150.00

***NOTE:** Helsingin Numismaattinen Yhdistys Auction 3-1990 VF-EF realized $45,500.

Dentilated border

KM#	Date	Mintage	Fine	VF	XF	Unc
7.2	1872S	.250	5.00	10.00	30.00	150.00
	1874S	.502	5.00	10.00	30.00	120.00
	1905L	.024	60.00	100.00	200.00	600.00
	1906L	.225	5.00	8.00	20.00	50.00
	1907L	.125	8.00	15.00	40.00	80.00
	1908L	.124	5.00	10.00	25.00	50.00

10 MARKKAA

3.2258 g, .900 GOLD, .0933 oz AGW
Regal Issues

KM#	Date	Mintage	Fine	VF	XF	Unc
8	1878S	.254	60.00	85.00	110.00	140.00
	1879/0S	.200	100.00	300.00	1000.	2000.
	1879S	Inc. Ab.	60.00	85.00	110.00	140.00
	1881S	.100	100.00	120.00	140.00	180.00
	1882S	.386	60.00	85.00	110.00	140.00
	1904L	.102	220.00	300.00	450.00	600.00
	1905L	.043	1500.	2000.	2700.	3200.
	1913S	.396	55.00	85.00	110.00	140.00

20 MARKKAA

6.4516 g, .900 GOLD, .1867 oz AGW
Regal Issues

KM#	Date	Mintage	Fine	VF	XF	Unc
9	1878S	*.235	250.00	300.00	350.00	450.00
	1879S	.300	100.00	120.00	140.00	170.00
	1880S	.090	750.00	850.00	1000.	1250.
	1891L	.091	110.00	140.00	200.00	250.00
	1903L	.112	100.00	120.00	170.00	225.00
	1904L	.188	100.00	120.00	140.00	180.00
	1910L	.201	100.00	120.00	140.00	180.00
	1911L	.161	125.00	135.00	190.00	220.00
	1912L	.881	800.00	1000.	1500.	2000.
	1912S	Inc. Ab.	100.00	120.00	140.00	170.00
	1913S	.214	100.00	120.00	140.00	170.00

***NOTE:** Some specimens may appear as proof-like. Proofs were never made officially by the mint.

CIVIL WAR COINAGE

PENNI

COPPER
Kerenski Government Issue

KM#	Date	Mintage	Fine	VF	XF	Unc
16	1917	1.650	.25	.75	1.00	1.50

5 PENNIA

COPPER
Kerenski Government Issue

KM#	Date	Mintage	Fine	VF	XF	Unc
17	1917	Inc. Ab.	.30	.75	2.50	5.00

Finnish Liberated Government Issue
Obv: Wreath knot centered between 9 and 1 of date.

KM#	Date	Mintage	Fine	VF	XF	Unc
21.1	1918	.035	15.00	25.00	35.00	60.00

Obv: Wreath knot above second 1 in 1918.

KM#	Date	Mintage	Fine	VF	XF	Unc
21.2	1918	Inc. Ab.	40.00	60.00	100.00	150.00

NOTE: This type was unofficially struck outside of Finland in the early 1920's.

10 PENNIA

COPPER
Kerenski Government Issue

KM#	Date	Mintage	Fine	VF	XF	Unc
18	1917	Inc. Ab.	.50	1.00	2.50	7.50

25 PENNIA

1.2747 g, .750 SILVER, .0307 oz ASW
Kerenski Government Issue
Obv: Crown above eagle removed.

KM#	Date	Mintage	Fine	VF	XF	Unc
19	1917S	2.310	—	BV	1.00	1.50

50 PENNIA

2.5494 g, .750 SILVER, .0615 oz ASW
Kerenski Government Issue
Obv: Crown above eagle removed.

KM#	Date	Mintage	Fine	VF	XF	Unc
20	1917S	.570	—	BV	1.25	2.00

REPUBLIC

PENNI

COPPER

KM#	Date	Mintage	Fine	VF	XF	Unc
23	1919	1.200	.25	.65	1.75	3.00
	1920	.720	.25	.65	1.75	3.00
	1921	.510	.35	1.00	2.00	4.00
	1922	1.060	.25	.65	1.75	3.00
	1923	.990	.25	.65	1.75	3.00
	1924	2.180	.25	.65	1.75	3.00

KM#	Date	Mintage	Fine	VF	XF	Unc
44	1963 square edge					
		62.460	—	.10	.40	1.00
	1963 round edge					
		118.870	—	.10	.20	.50
	1964	49.300	—	.10	.40	1.00
	1965	43.110	—	.10	.40	1.00
	1966	36.880	—	.10	.40	1.00
	1967	62.790	—	.10	.40	1.00
	1968	73.400	—	—	.20	.50
	1969	51.700	—	—	.20	.50

ALUMINUM

KM#	Date	Mintage	Fine	VF	XF	Unc
44a	1969	28.500	—	—	.20	.50
	1970	85.100	—	—	.10	.25
	1971	70.240	—	—	.10	.25
	1972	95.100	—	—	.10	.25
	1973	115.500	—	—	.10	.25
	1974	100.132	—	—	.10	.25
	1975	111.960	—	—	.10	.25
	1976	34.965	—	—	.10	.25
44a	1977	61.393	—	—	.10	.25
	1978	90.132	—	—	.10	.25
	1979	33.388	—	—	.10	.25

5 PENNIA

COPPER

KM#	Date	Mintage	Fine	VF	XF	Unc
22	1918	4.270	.10	.25	1.00	4.00
	1919	4.640	.10	.25	1.00	4.00
	1920	7.710	.10	.25	1.00	3.00
	1921	5.910	.10	.25	1.00	3.00
	1922	8.540	.10	.25	1.00	3.00
	1927	1.520	.75	1.50	3.50	15.00
	1928	2.110	.25	.50	1.50	8.00
	1929	1.500	.25	.50	1.50	8.00
	1930	2.140	.75	1.25	3.00	12.00
	1932	2.130	.15	.50	1.00	4.00
	1934	2.180	.15	.50	1.00	4.00
	1935	1.610	.15	.35	1.00	3.00
	1936	2.610	.15	.35	1.00	3.00
	1937	3.830	.10	.25	1.00	3.00
	1938	4.300	.10	.25	1.00	3.00
	1939	2.270	.10	.25	1.00	3.00
	1940	1.610	.25	.50	1.50	5.00

Punched center hole

KM#	Date	Mintage	Fine	VF	XF	Unc
64.1	1941	5.950	.10	.20	.50	1.25
(32.1)	1942	4.280	.10	.20	.50	1.25
	1943	1.530	.10	.50	1.25	2.50

W/o punched center hole

KM#	Date	Mintage	Fine	VF	XF	Unc
64.2	1941	Inc. Ab.	25.00	30.00	70.00	100.00
(32.2)	1942	Inc. Ab.	25.00	30.00	70.00	100.00
	1943	Inc. Ab.	50.00	70.00	100.00	125.00

NOTE: The above issues were not authorized by the government and any that exist were illegally removed from the mint.

KM#	Date	Mintage	Fine	VF	XF	Unc
45	1963	60.820	—	.10	.50	1.50
	1964	4.634	.50	1.00	2.00	7.50
	1965	10.264	—	.10	.50	1.50
	1966	8.064	—	.10	.50	1.50
	1967	9.968	—	.10	.50	1.50
	1968	6.144	—	.10	.50	1.50
	1969	3.598	—	.15	.50	2.00
	1970	13.772	—	.10	.15	.50
	1971	20.010	—	—	.15	.50
	1972	24.122	—	—	.15	.50
	1973	25.644	—	—	.15	.50
	1974	21.530	—	—	.15	.50
	1975	25.010	—	—	.15	.50
	1976	25.551	—	—	.15	.50
	1977	1.489	—	.10	.40	1.00

ALUMINUM

KM#	Date	Mintage	Fine	VF	XF	Unc
45a	1977	30.552	—	—	.15	.50
	1978	26.112	—	—	.15	.50
	1979	40.042	—	—	.15	.50
	1980	60.026	—	—	.15	.50
	1981	2.044	—	.20	.40	1.00
	1982	10.012	—	—	.25	.75
	1983	33.885	—	—	—	.10
	1984	25.001	—	—	—	.10
	1985	25.000	—	—	—	.10
	1986	20.000	—	—	—	.10
	1987	2.000	—	—	—	.10
	1988	33.005	—	—	—	.10
	1989	2.200	—	—	—	.10
	1990	2.506	—	—	—	.10

10 PENNIA

COPPER

KM#	Date	Mintage	Fine	VF	XF	Unc
24	1919	3.670	.10	.25	1.00	5.00
	1920	2.380	.10	.25	1.00	5.00
	1921	3.970	.10	.25	1.00	5.00
	1922	2.180	.10	.25	1.00	5.00
	1923	.910	.75	1.50	5.00	15.00
	1924	1.350	.25	.50	2.50	10.00
24	1926	1.690	.25	.50	1.00	6.00
	1927	1.330	.50	1.00	2.50	10.00
	1928	1.006	.50	1.00	2.50	10.00
	1929	1.560	.35	.85	2.00	7.00
	1930	.650	.75	1.50	5.00	12.00
	1931	1.040	1.00	2.00	6.00	15.00
	1934	1.680	.35	.85	1.50	6.00
	1935	1.690	.15	.25	1.00	5.00
	1936	2.010	.15	.25	1.00	5.00
	1937	2.420	.10	.25	.50	3.50
	1938	2.940	.10	.25	.50	3.50
	1939	2.100	.10	.25	.50	3.50
	1940	2.010	.25	.50	1.00	5.00

KM#	Date	Mintage	Fine	VF	XF	Unc
33.1	1941	3.610	.10	.25	.50	1.25
	1942	4.970	.10	.25	.50	1.25
	1943	1.860	.25	.75	1.50	2.50

W/o punched center hole

KM#	Date	Mintage	Fine	VF	XF	Unc
33.2	1941	Inc. Ab.	20.00	30.00	50.00	75.00
	1942	Inc. Ab.	20.00	30.00	50.00	75.00
	1943	Inc. Ab.	30.00	50.00	70.00	100.00

NOTE: The above issues were not authorized by the government and any that exist were illegally removed from the mint.

IRON
Reduced planchet size

KM#	Date	Mintage	Fine	VF	XF	Unc
34.1	1943	1.430	.10	.25	1.00	3.50
	1944	3.040	.10	.25	1.00	3.00
	1945	1.810	.25	.50	2.00	10.00

W/o punched center hole

KM#	Date	Mintage	Fine	VF	XF	Unc
34.2	1943	Inc. Ab.	30.00	50.00	70.00	100.00
	1944	Inc. Ab.	30.00	50.00	70.00	100.00
	1945	Inc. Ab.	50.00	70.00	100.00	150.00

NOTE: The above issues were not authorized by the government and any that exist were illegally removed from the mint.

ALUMINUM-BRONZE

KM#	Date	Mintage	Fine	VF	XF	Unc
46	1963S	38.420	—	.10	.25	1.50
	1964S	6.926	—	.10	.50	2.00
	1965S	4.524	—	.10	.25	1.50
	1966S	3.094	—	.10	.25	1.50
	1967S	1.050	.10	.20	1.00	2.50
	1968S	3.004	—	.10	.20	1.00
	1969S	5.046	—	—	.20	1.00
	1970S	3.996	—	—	.20	1.00
	1971S	15.026	—	—	.10	.50
	1972S	19.900	—	—	.10	.50
	1973S	9.196	—	—	.10	.50
	1974S	8.930	—	—	.10	.50
	1975S	15.064	—	—	.10	.25
	1976K	10.063	—	—	.10	.25
	1977K	10.042	—	—	.10	.25
	1978K	10.062	—	—	.10	.25
	1979K	13.072	—	—	.10	.25
	1980K	23.654	—	—	.10	.25
	1981K	30.036	—	—	.10	.25
	1982K	35.548	—	—	.10	.25

ALUMINUM

KM#	Date	Mintage	Fine	VF	XF	Unc
46a	1983K	6.320	—	—	.25	.50
	1983N	4.191	—	—	.25	.50
	1984N	20.061	—	—	.10	.25
	1985N	20.000	—	—	.10	.25
	1986N	15.000	—	—	.10	.25
	1987N	1.400	—	—	.25	.50
	1987M	2.000	—	—	.25	.50
	1988M	23.197	—	—	.10	.25
	1989M	40.695	—	—	.25	.50
	1990M	2.254	—	—	.25	.50

COPPER-NICKEL
Flower Pods and Stems

KM#	Date	Mintage	Fine	VF	XF	Unc
65	1990M	338.100	—	—	.10	.15
	1991M	158.274	—	—	.10	.15
	1992M	72.267	—	—	.10	.15
	1993M	—	—	—	.10	.15

20 PENNIA

ALUMINUM-BRONZE

KM#	Date	Mintage	Fine	VF	XF	Unc
47	1963S	39.970	—	.10	.20	1.00
	1964S	4.248	.10	.25	.50	2.00
	1965S	5.704	—	.10	.20	1.00
	1966S	4.085	—	.10	.20	1.00
	1967S	1.716	—	.10	.20	1.00
	1968S	1.330	—	.10	.20	1.00
	1969S	.201	.10	.25	1.00	3.00
	1970S	.230	.10	.25	1.00	3.00
	1971S	5.150	—	.10	.15	.50
	1972S	10.001	—	.10	.15	.50
	1973S	9.462	—	.10	.15	.50
	1974S	12.705	—	—	.15	.50
	1975S	12.068	—	—	.10	.50
	1976K	20.058	—	—	.10	.50
	1977K	10.063	—	—	.10	.50
	1978K	10.014	—	—	.10	.50
	1979K	7.513	—	—	.10	.50
	1980K	20.047	—	—	.10	.25
	1981K	30.002	—	—	.10	.25
	1982K	35.050	—	—	.10	.25
	1983K	7.113	—	—	.10	.25
	1983N	12.889	—	—	.10	.25
	1984N	20.029	—	—	.10	.25
	1985N	15.004	—	—	.10	.25
	1986N	20.001	—	—	.10	.25
	1987N	1.200	—	—	.25	.75
	1987M	40.000	—	—	.10	.25
	1988M	13.853	—	—	.10	.25
	1989M	40.695	—	—	.10	.25
	1990M	9.168	—	—	.10	.25

NOTE: Some coins dated 1971 are magnetic and command a higher premium.

25 PENNIA

COPPER-NICKEL

KM#	Date	Mintage	Fine	VF	XF	Unc
25	1921H	20.096	.10	.25	1.00	3.00
	1925S	1.250	.50	1.50	5.00	15.00
	1926S	2.820	.40	1.25	3.00	10.00
	1927S	1.120	.50	1.50	5.00	15.00
	1928S	2.920	.40	1.00	3.00	10.00
	1929S	.200	2.00	4.00	10.00	25.00
	1930S	1.090	.50	1.50	5.00	12.00
	1934S	1.260	.40	.75	2.00	7.00
	1935S	2.190	.30	.50	1.50	6.00
	1936S	2.300	.20	.40	1.00	3.00
	1937S	4.020	.20	.40	1.00	3.00
	1938S	4.500	.20	.40	1.00	3.00
	1939S	2.712	.20	.40	1.00	3.00
	1940S	4.840	.15	.30	.75	2.00

COPPER

KM#	Date	Mintage	Fine	VF	XF	Unc
25a	1940S	.072	.50	1.00	3.00	12.00
	1941S	5.980	.10	.35	1.00	3.00
	1942S	6.464	.10	.35	1.00	3.00
	1943S	4.912	.25	.50	1.50	5.00

IRON

KM#	Date	Mintage	Fine	VF	XF	Unc
25b	1943S	2.700	.15	.50	1.50	7.00
	1944S small closed 4's					
		5.480	.15	.50	1.25	6.00
	1944S large open 4's					
		Inc. Ab.	.15	.50	1.25	6.00
	1945S	6.810	.25	.75	2.00	8.00

50 PENNIA

COPPER-NICKEL

KM#	Date	Mintage	Fine	VF	XF	Unc
26	1921H	10.072	.15	.30	1.00	3.00
	1923S	6.000	.25	1.00	3.00	12.00
	1929S	.984	.75	1.50	5.00	20.00
	1934S	.612	1.00	2.50	7.50	22.00
	1935S	.610	1.00	2.50	7.50	22.00
	1936S	1.520	.30	.50	1.50	6.00
	1937S	2.350	.15	.25	.75	3.50
	1938S	2.330	.15	.25	.75	3.00
	1939S	1.280	.15	.25	.75	3.00
	1940S	3.152	.15	.25	.75	2.50

COPPER

KM#	Date	Mintage	Fine	VF	XF	Unc
26a	1940S	.480	1.25	2.50	5.00	12.00
	1941S	3.860	.15	.40	1.00	3.00
	1942S	5.900	.15	.40	1.00	3.00
	1943S	3.140	.25	.50	1.50	4.00

IRON

KM#	Date	Mintage	Fine	VF	XF	Unc
26b	1943S	1.580	.25	.50	1.50	15.00
	1944S	7.600	.15	.40	1.00	12.00
	1945S	4.700	.15	.40	1.00	12.00
	1946S	2.632	.30	.50	1.50	12.00
	1947S	1.748	.50	1.50	3.50	15.00
	1948L	1.112	3.00	5.00	10.00	20.00

ALUMINUM-BRONZE

KM#	Date	Mintage	Fine	VF	XF	Unc
48	1963S	17.316	—	.20	.50	2.00
	1964S	3.101	—	.25	1.00	3.00
	1965S	1.667	—	.20	.50	2.50
	1966S	1.051	—	.20	.50	2.00
	1967S	.400	.25	.50	1.50	3.00
	1968S	.816	—	.25	1.00	2.50
	1969S	1.341	—	.20	.50	2.00
	1970S	2.250	—	.20	.30	1.50
	1971S	10.003	—	—	.25	.75
	1972S	7.892	—	—	.25	1.00
	1973S	5.430	—	—	.25	.75
	1974S	5.049	—	—	.25	.75
	1975S	4.305	—	—	.25	.75
	1976K	7.022	—	—	.25	.75
	1977K	8.077	—	—	.25	.50
	1978K	8.048	—	—	.25	.50
	1979K	8.004	—	—	.25	.50
	1980K	5.349	—	—	.25	.50
	1981K	20.031	—	—	.25	.50
	1982K	5.042	—	—	.25	.50
	1983K	4.044	—	—	.25	.50
	1983N	1.016	—	—	.25	1.00
	1984N	3.006	—	—	.25	.50
	1985N	10.000	—	—	.20	.35
	1986N	9.002	—	—	.20	.35
	1987N	.700	—	—	.50	1.00
	1987M	10.000	—	—	.20	.35
	1988M	14.735	—	—	.20	.35
	1989M	10.561	—	—	.20	.35
	1990M	5.391	—	—	.20	.35

NOTE: Some 1971 issues are magnetic and command a premium.

COPPER-NICKEL
Polar Bear

KM#	Date	Mintage	Fine	VF	XF	Unc
66	1990M	70.459	—	—	.20	.35
	1991M	78.163	—	—	.20	.35
	1992M	18.930	—	—	.20	.35
	1993M	—	—	—	.20	.35

MARKKA

COPPER-NICKEL

KM#	Date	Mintage	Fine	VF	XF	Unc
27	1921H	10.048	.50	1.00	2.50	5.00
	1922 heart					
		10.000	.75	1.50	3.50	10.00
	1923S	1.780	7.50	15.00	25.00	50.00
	1924S	3.270	3.00	7.00	15.00	30.00

Reduced size

KM#	Date	Mintage	Fine	VF	XF	Unc
30	1928S	3.000	.15	.30	3.00	20.00
	1929S	3.862	.15	.30	3.00	20.00
	1930S	10.284	.15	.30	1.00	12.00
	1931S	2.830	.15	.30	1.00	12.00
	1932S	4.140	.15	.30	1.00	10.00
	1933S	4.032	.15	.30	1.00	10.00
	1936S	.562	.50	1.50	5.00	25.00
	1937S	4.930	.15	.30	1.00	6.00
	1938S	4.410	.15	.25	1.00	6.00
	1939S	3.070	.15	.25	1.00	6.00
	1940S	3.372	.15	.25	1.00	6.00

NOTE: Coins dated 1928S, 1929S and 1930S are known to be restruck on 1921-24, KM#27 coins. (1928S: 2 or 3 known).

COPPER

KM#	Date	Mintage	Fine	VF	XF	Unc
30a	1940S	.084	1.50	3.50	8.00	20.00
	1941S	8.970	.15	.50	1.25	6.00
	1942S	11.200	.15	.50	1.00	4.00
	1943S	7.460	.15	.50	1.25	5.00
	1949H	250 pcs.	1000.	1250.	2000.	3000.
	1950H	.320	.50	1.00	2.00	10.00
	1951H	4.630	.25	.50	1.00	6.00

IRON

KM#	Date	Mintage	Fine	VF	XF	Unc
30b	1943S	7.460	.15	.25	1.00	9.00
	1944S	12.830	.15	.25	1.00	8.00
	1945S	21.950	.15	.25	1.00	8.00
	1946S	2.630	.15	.30	1.25	10.00
	1947S	1.750	.25	.50	1.50	15.00
	1948L	20.500	.15	.25	1.00	8.00
	1949H	17.358	.15	.25	.75	7.00
	1950H	14.654	.15	.25	.75	7.00
	1951H	21.414	.15	.25	.75	7.00
	1952H	5.410	.25	.50	1.50	10.00

KM#	Date	Mintage	Fine	VF	XF	Unc
36	1952	22.050	.15	.35	1.00	7.00
	1953	28.618	.15	.35	1.00	7.00

NICKEL-PLATED IRON

KM#	Date	Mintage	Fine	VF	XF	Unc
36a	1953	6.000	5.00	8.00	12.50	20.00
	1954	36.400	—	.10	.25	.50
	1955	38.100	—	.10	.25	.50
	1956	35.600	—	.10	.25	.50
	1957	29.100	—	.10	.25	.50
	1958	19.940	.10	.20	.35	.70
	1959 thick letters					
		23.920	—	.10	.25	.50
	1959 thin letters					
		Inc. Ab.	—	.10	.25	.50
	1960	22.020	—	.10	.25	.50
	1961	32.220	—	.10	.25	.50
	1962	29.040	—	.10	.25	.50

6.4000 g, .350 SILVER, .0720 oz ASW

KM#	Date	Mintage	Fine	VF	XF	Unc
49	1964S	9.999	—	BV	1.50	4.00
	1965S	15.107	—	BV	1.00	2.00
	1966S	15.183	—	BV	.75	1.50
	1967S	6.249	—	BV	.75	1.50
	1968S	3.063	—	BV	.75	1.50

COPPER-NICKEL

KM#	Date	Mintage	Fine	VF	XF	Unc
49a	1969S	1.308	.35	.45	.60	1.00
	1970S	12.255	—	.35	.45	.75
	1971S	19.676	—	.35	.45	.75
	1972S	19.885	—	.35	.45	.75
	1973S	17.060	—	.35	.45	.75
	1974S	18.065	—	.35	.45	.75
	1975S	11.523	—	—	.35	.60
	1976K	12.048	—	—	.35	.60
	1977K	10.077	—	—	.35	.60
	1978K	10.022	—	—	.35	.60
	1979K	11.311	—	—	.35	.60
	1980K	19.306	—	—	.35	.60
	1981K	32.003	—	—	.35	.60
	1982K	30.001	—	—	.35	.60
	1983K	8.075	—	—	.35	.60
	1983N	11.927	—	—	.35	.60
	1984N	15.000	—	—	.35	.60
	1985N	19.001	—	—	.35	.60
	1986N	10.000	—	—	.35	.60
	1987N	.700	—	—	.50	1.00
	1987M	40.000	—	—	.35	.60
	1988M	27.535	—	—	.35	.60
	1989M	37.520	—	—	.35	.60
	1990M	50.305	—	—	.35	.60
	1991M	125.936	—	—	.35	.60
	1992M	3.628	—	—	.35	.60
	1993M	—	—	—	.35	.60

ALUMINUM-BRONZE

KM#	Date	Mintage	Fine	VF	XF	Unc
76	1993M	—	—	—	.35	.60

5 MARKKAA

ALUMINUM-BRONZE

KM#	Date	Mintage	Fine	VF	XF	Unc
31	1928S	.580	30.00	50.00	100.00	250.00
	1929S	Inc. Ab.	30.00	50.00	90.00	220.00
	1930S	.592	.75	1.75	7.00	35.00
	1931S	3.090	.50	1.00	6.00	30.00
	1932S	.964	5.00	10.00	25.00	70.00
	1933S	1.050	.50	1.00	6.00	30.00
	1935S	.440	1.50	3.00	12.00	50.00
	1936S	.470	1.50	3.00	12.00	45.00
	1937S	1.032	.50	1.00	6.00	15.00
	1938S	.912	.50	1.00	6.00	15.00
	1939S	.752	.50	1.00	6.00	15.00
	1940S	.820	1.25	2.75	8.00	20.00
	1941S	1.452	.50	1.00	4.00	10.00
	1942S	1.390	.50	1.00	5.00	12.00
	1946S	.618	3.50	7.00	20.00	60.00

BRASS

KM#	Date	Mintage	Fine	VF	XF	Unc
31a	1946S	5.538	.20	.50	1.50	3.50
	1947S	6.550	.25	.75	2.00	6.00
	1948L	8.210	.25	.50	1.50	5.00
	1949H thin H	11.014	.50	1.00	3.00	5.00
	1949H wide H	Inc. Ab.	.20	.50	1.50	3.50
	1950H	4.760	.20	.50	1.50	3.50
	1951H	7.8000	.20	.50	1.50	3.50
	1952H	1.210	2.50	6.00	12.00	25.00

IRON

KM#	Date	Mintage	Fine	VF	XF	Unc
37	1952	10.820	.20	.35	2.00	8.00
	1953	9.772	.20	.35	3.00	10.00

NICKEL-PLATED IRON

KM#	Date	Mintage	Fine	VF	XF	Unc
37a	1953	Inc. Ab.	35.00	60.00	80.00	125.00
	1954	6.696	—	.20	.35	1.50
	1955	9.894	—	.20	.35	1.50
	1956	8.220	—	.20	.35	1.00
	1957	4.276	—	.20	.35	1.00
	1958	3.300	—	.20	.35	1.50
	1959	5.874	—	.20	.35	1.00
	1960	3.066	.10	.25	.35	1.50
	1961	7.254	.10	.25	.35	1.50
	1962	4.542	.50	1.00	3.00	6.00

ALUMINUM-BRONZE
Icebreaker - Varma

KM#	Date	Mintage	Fine	VF	XF	Unc
53	1972S	.400	1.50	2.00	2.50	4.00
	1973S	2.188	—	1.25	2.00	3.00
	1974S	.300	—	1.25	2.00	3.00
	1975S	.300	—	1.25	2.00	3.00
	1976K	.400	—	1.25	2.00	3.00
	1977K	.300	—	1.25	2.00	3.00
	1978K	.300	—	1.25	2.00	3.00

Icebreaker - Urho

KM#	Date	Mintage	Fine	VF	XF	Unc
57	1979K	2.005	—	—	1.50	2.25
	1980K	.501	—	1.50	2.00	3.00
	1981K	1.009	—	—	1.50	2.25
	1982K	3.004	—	—	1.50	2.25
	1983K	8.776	—	—	1.50	2.25
	1983N	11.230	—	—	1.50	2.25
	1984N	15.001	—	—	1.50	2.25
	1985N	8.004	—	—	1.50	2.25
	1986N	5.006	—	—	1.50	2.25
	1987N	.660	—	1.50	2.00	3.00
	1987M	10.000	—	—	1.50	2.25
	1988M	3.042	—	—	1.50	2.25
	1989M	10.175	—	—	1.50	2.25
	1990M	9.925	—	—	1.50	2.25
	1991M	5.322	—	—	1.50	2.25
	1992M	.546	—	—	1.50	2.25

COPPER-ALUMINUM-NICKEL
Lake Saimaa Ringed Seal

KM#	Date	Mintage	Fine	VF	XF	Unc
73	1992M	.800	—	—	—	3.50
	1993M	—	—	—	—	3.50

10 MARKKAA

ALUMINUM-BRONZE

KM#	Date	Mintage	Fine	VF	XF	Unc
63 (30)	1928S	.730	2.50	5.00	15.00	75.00
	1929S	Inc. Ab.	2.00	4.00	12.00	70.00
	1930S	.260	1.00	2.50	8.00	65.00
	1931S	1.530	1.00	2.50	8.00	65.00
	1932S	1.010	1.00	2.50	8.00	55.00
	1934S	.154	1.50	3.00	12.00	70.00
	1935S	.081	2.00	4.00	12.00	90.00
	1936S	.304	2.00	4.00	12.00	60.00
	1937S	.181	1.50	2.50	8.00	60.00
	1938S	.631	.75	1.50	5.00	45.00
	1939S	.133	4.00	8.00	15.00	60.00

KM#	Date	Mintage	Fine	VF	XF	Unc
38	1952H	6.390	.20	.50	1.75	5.00
	1953H	22.650	.15	.35	1.00	3.00
	1954H	2.452	.50	1.00	2.00	6.00
	1955H	2.342	.20	.50	1.50	5.00
	1956H	4.240	.20	.40	1.00	4.00
	1958H thin 1	3.292	1.00	2.50	5.00	10.00
	1958H wide 1	Inc. Ab.	.20	.40	1.00	4.00
	1960S	.740	.50	1.00	3.50	8.00
	1961S thin 1	3.580	.20	.50	1.50	5.00
	1961S wide 1	Inc. Ab.	1.00	2.00	3.50	8.00
	1962S	1.852	.30	.60	1.75	5.00

NOTE: The "1" in the denomination on all 1952 to 1956 issues is the thin variety. 1960 issues are the wide variety, and 1962's are thin. Varieties exist in root length of tree.

23.7500 g, .900 SILVER, .6872 oz ASW
50th Anniversary of Independence

KM#	Date	Mintage	Fine	VF	XF	Unc
50	1967SH	1.000	—	—	4.00	6.00

22.7500 g, .500 SILVER, .3657 oz ASW
Paasikivi Birth Centennial

KM#	Date	Mintage	Fine	VF	XF	Unc
51	1970SH	.600	—	—	3.00	5.00

24.2000 g, .500 SILVER, .3890 oz ASW
10th European Athletic Championships

KM#	Date	Mintage	Fine	VF	XF	Unc
52	1971SH	1.000	—	—	3.00	5.00

23.5000 g, .500 SILVER, .3778 oz ASW
75th Birthday of President Kekkonen

KM#	Date	Mintage	Fine	VF	XF	Unc
54	1975SH	1.000	—	—	3.00	5.00

21.7800 g, .500 SILVER, .3501 oz ASW
60th Anniversary of Independence

KM#	Date	Mintage	Fine	VF	XF	Unc
55	1977KH	.400	—	—	3.00	5.00

BI-METALLIC BRASS CENTER, COPPER-NICKEL RING

KM#	Date	Mintage	Fine	VF	XF	Unc
77	1993M	—	—	—	—	4.00

20 MARKKAA

ALUMINUM-BRONZE

KM#	Date	Mintage	Fine	VF	XF	Unc
32	1931S	.016	30.00	40.00	60.00	100.00
	1932S	.014	30.00	40.00	65.00	110.00
	1934S	.390	2.00	5.00	17.50	70.00
	1935S	.250	2.00	5.00	17.50	70.00
	1936S	.110	3.00	5.00	17.50	90.00
	1937S	.510	1.50	2.00	10.00	50.00
	1938S	.360	1.50	2.00	9.00	40.00
	1939S	.960	1.00	2.00	6.00	15.00

KM#	Date	Mintage	Fine	VF	XF	Unc
39	1952H	.083	7.00	10.00	15.00	30.00
	1953H	2.880	.25	.50	1.50	6.00
	1954H	17.034	.15	.50	1.25	5.00
	1955H	2.800	.25	.50	1.50	6.00
	1956H	2.540	.25	.50	1.50	6.00
	1957H	1.050	.50	1.00	3.00	8.00
	1958H	.515	2.50	5.00	10.00	20.00
	1959S	1.580	.25	.50	1.50	6.00
	1960S	3.850	.15	.50	1.00	5.00
	1961S	4.430	.15	.50	1.00	5.00
	1962S	2.280	.15	.50	1.50	6.00

25 MARKKAA

26.3000 g, .500 SILVER, .4228 oz ASW
Winter Games in Lahti

KM#	Date	Mintage	Fine	VF	XF	Unc
56	1978KN	.500	—	—	6.00	8.00

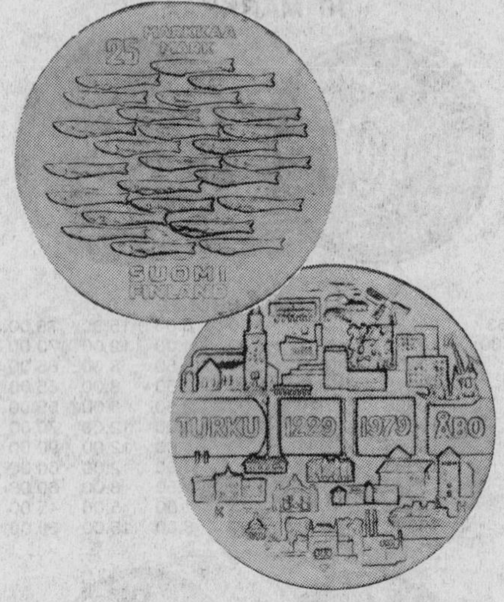

750th Anniversary of Turku

KM#	Date	Mintage	Fine	VF	XF	Unc
58	1979KH	.300	—	—	6.00	8.00

50 MARKKAA

ALUMINUM-BRONZE

KM#	Date	Mintage	Fine	VF	XF	Unc
40	1952H	.991	1.00	3.00	6.00	15.00
	1953H	10.300	.25	.50	2.00	7.00
	1954H	1.170	1.00	3.00	5.00	10.00
	1955H	.583	2.50	5.00	10.00	20.00
	1956H	.792	1.00	3.00	5.00	10.00
	1958H	.242	20.00	25.00	35.00	50.00
	1960S	.110	20.00	30.00	45.00	70.00
	1961S	1.811	1.00	2.00	3.00	7.00
	1962S	.405	2.00	4.00	7.00	15.00

20.0000 g, 500 SILVER, .3216 oz ASW
80th Birthday of President Kekkonen

KM#	Date	Mintage	Fine	VF	XF	Unc
59	1981K	.500	—	—	11.50	13.50

23.0000 g, .500 SILVER, .3698 oz ASW
World Ice Hockey Championship Games

KM#	Date	Mintage	Fine	VF	XF	Unc
60	1982KT	.400	—	—	11.50	13.50

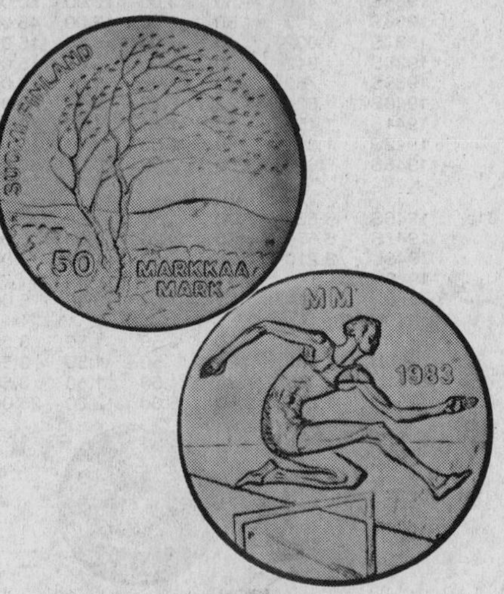

22.0000 g, .500 SILVER, .3537 oz ASW
1st World Athletics Championships

KM#	Date	Mintage	Fine	VF	XF	Unc
61	1983KM	.450	—	—	11.50	13.50

20.0000 g, .500 SILVER, .3216 oz ASW
National Epic - The Kalevala

KM#	Date	Mintage	Fine	VF	XF	Unc
62	1985PN	.300	—	—	12.50	17.00

100 MARKKAA

4.2105 g, .900 GOLD, .1218 oz AGW

KM#	Date	Mintage	Fine	VF	XF	Unc
28	1926S	.050	—	400.00	600.00	850.00

5.2000 g, .500 SILVER, .0836 oz ASW

KM#	Date	Mintage	Fine	VF	XF	Unc
41	1956H	3.012	—	BV	1.50	3.00
	1957H	3.012	—	BV	1.50	3.00
	1958H	1.704	BV	1.50	2.50	4.00
	1959S	1.270	3.00	5.00	7.00	9.00
	1960S	.290	3.50	5.50	7.50	10.00

24.0000 g, .830 SILVER, .6405 oz ASW
World Ski Championships

KM#	Date	Mintage	Fine	VF	XF	Unc
74	1989MLM	.100	—	—	25.00	32.00

Pictorial Arts of Finland

KM#	Date	Mintage	Fine	VF	XF	Unc
75	1989PM	.100	—	—	25.00	32.00

50th Anniversary of Disabled War Veterans Association

KM#	Date	Mintage	Fine	VF	XF	Unc
67	1990PM	.100	—	—	25.00	32.00

350th Anniversary of the University of Helsinki

KM#	Date	Mintage	Fine	VF	XF	Unc
68	1990HM	.150	—	—	25.00	32.00

Ice Hockey World Championship Games

KM#	Date	Mintage	Fine	VF	XF	Unc
69	1991LM	.150	—	—	25.00	32.00
	1991LM					
		*200 pcs.	—	—	Proof	350.00

***NOTE:** Struck w/polished dies to proof or semi-proof quality and encapsulated in hard plastic 60 mm x 83 mm square. These pieces were given out as business gifts to some visitors at the mint.

24.0000 g, .925 SILVER, .7137 oz ASW
Aland

KM#	Date	Mintage	Fine	VF	XF	Unc
70	1991PM	.100	—	—	25.00	32.00
	1991PM					
		*700 pcs.	—	—	Proof	250.00

***NOTE:** Encapsulated as KM#69 above, but struck to higher proof quality.

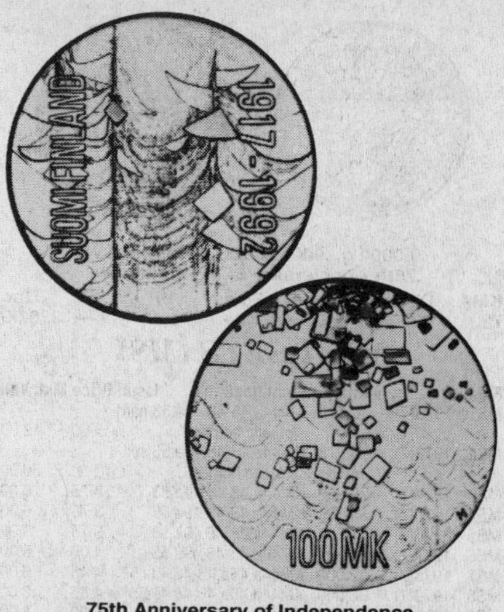

75th Anniversary of Independence

KM#	Date	Mintage	Fine	VF	XF	Unc
71	1992MS	.300	—	—	25.00	35.00

200 MARKKAA

8.4210 g, .900 GOLD, .2436 oz AGW

KM#	Date	Mintage	Fine	VF	XF	Unc
29	1926S	.050	—	550.00	850.00	1000.

8.3000 g, .500 SILVER, .1334 oz ASW

KM#	Date	Mintage	Fine	VF	XF	Unc
42	1956H	1.552	—	BV	2.50	5.00
	1957H	2.157	—	BV	2.50	5.00
	1958H	1.477	BV	2.50	4.00	7.00
	1958S	.034	250.00	300.00	400.00	500.00
	1959S	.070	20.00	25.00	30.00	55.00

500 MARKKAA

12.0000 g, .500 SILVER, .1929 oz ASW
1952 Olympic Games

KM#	Date	Mintage	Fine	VF	XF	Unc
35	1951H	.019	200.00	275.00	350.00	450.00
	1952H	.586	20.00	25.00	35.00	50.00

1000 MARKKAA

14.0000 g, .875 SILVER, .3938 oz ASW
Markka Currency System Centennial - Snellman

KM#	Date	Mintage	Fine	VF	XF	Unc
43	1960SJ	.201	8.00	10.00	15.00	20.00

9.0000 g, .900 GOLD, .2604 oz AGW
75th Anniversary of Independence

KM#	Date	Mintage	Fine	VF	XF	Unc
72	1992MS	.035	—	—	—	330.00

MINT SETS (MS)

KM#	Date	Mintage	Identification	Issue Price	Mkt. Val.
MS1	1973(7)	10,029	KM44a,45-48,49a,53 hard plastic holder	5.00	12.00
MS2	1973(7)	9,978	KM44a,45-48,49a,53 soft plastic holder	10.00	50.00
MS3	1974(7)	79,258	KM44a,45-48,49a,53	3.75	8.00
MS4	1975(7)	58,820	KM44a,45-48,49a,53	3.75	6.00
MS5	1976(7)	45,263	KM44a,45-48,49a,53	3.75	8.00
MS6	1977(7)	40,392	KM44a,45-48,49a,53	4.00	8.00
MS7	1978(7)	42,000	KM44a,45a,46-48,49a,53	4.45	6.00
MS8	1979(7)	36,000	KM44a,45a,46-48,49a,57	4.85	8.00
MS9	1980(6)	37,800	KM45a,46-48,49a,57	5.00	8.00
MS10	1981(6)	35,600	KM45a,46-48,49a,57	5.25	8.00
MS11	1982(6)	34,900	KM45a,46-48,49a,57	5.50	8.00
MS12	1983K(6)	30,100	KM45a,46a,47,48,49a,57	3.25	8.00
MS13	1983N(6)	9,250	KM45a,46a,47,48,49a,57	3.25	15.00
MS14	1984N(6)	29,400	KM45a,46a,47,48,49a,57	3.25	6.00
MS15	1984N(6)	600	KM45a,46a,47,48,49a,57 Russian text	3.75	30.00
MS16	1985N(6)	39,000	KM45a-46a,47-48,49a,57 Finnish text	3.25	6.00
MS17	1985N(6)	1,540	KM45a-46a,47-48,49a,57 Russian text	4.65	15.00
MS18	1985N(6)	1,650	KM45a-46a,47-48,49a,57 English text	3.75	15.00
MS19	1986N(6)	37,100	KM45a-46a,47-48,49a,57 Finnish text	3.25	6.00
MS20	1986N(6)	1,300	KM45a-46a,47-48,49a,57 Russian text	5.00	15.00
MS21	1986N(6)	1,800	KM45a-46a,47-48,49a,57 English text	4.25	15.00
MS22	1987N(6)	34,300	KM45a-46a,47-48,49a,57 Finnish text	—	6.00
MS23	1987N(6)	1,120	KM45a-46a,47-48,49a,57 Russian text	—	15.00
MS24	1987N(6)	1,400	KM45a-46a,47-48,49a,57 English text	—	15.00
MS25	1987M(6)	16,600	KM45a-46a,47-48,49a,57 Finnish text	—	6.00
MS26	1987M(6)	300	KM45a-46a,47-48,49a,57 Russian text	—	25.00
MS27	1987M(6)	180	KM45a-46a,47-48,49a,57 English text	—	25.00
MS28	1988M(6)	34,750	KM45a-46a,47-48,49a,57 Finnish text	—	6.00
MS29	1988M(6)	1,450	KM45a-46a,47-48,49a,57 English text	—	15.00
MS30	1988M(6)	1,220	KM45a-46a,47-48,49a,57 Russian text	—	15.00
MS31	1989M(6)	—	KM45a-46a,47-48,49a,57 Finnish text	—	6.00
MS32	1989M(6)	—	KM45a-46a,47-48,49a,57 English text	—	10.00
MS33	1989M(6)	—	KM45a-46a,47-48,49a,57 Russian text	—	10.00
MS34	1990M(4)	—	KM49a,57,65-66	—	9.00
MS35	1991M(4)	30,000	KM49a,57,65-66 Finnish-Swedish text	—	10.00
MS36	1991M(4)	5,000	KM49a,57,65-66 English text	—	10.00
MS37	1992M(5)	28,000	KM49a,57,65-66,73	—	12.50
MS38	1993M(5)	—	KM65-66,73,76,77	13.30	13.50
MS39	1993M(4)	20,000	KM49a,65-66,73	—	8.00

Listings For

FORMOSA: refer to China, Republic of (Taiwan)

FRANCE

The French Republic, largest of the West European nations, has an area of 211,208 sq. mi. (547,030 sq. km.) and a population of 54.3 million. Capital: Paris. Agriculture, mining and manufacturing are the most important elements of France's diversified economy. Textiles and clothing, iron and steel products, machinery and transportation equipment, agricultural products and wine are exported.

France, the Gaul of ancient times, emerged from the Renaissance as a modern centralized national state which reached its zenith during the reign of Louis XIV (1643-1715) when it became an absolute monarchy and the foremost power in Europe. Although his reign marks the golden age of French culture, the domestic abuses and extravagance of Louis XIV plunged France into a series of costly wars. This, along with a system of special privileges granted the nobility and other favored groups, weakened the monarchy, brought France to bankruptcy - and laid the way for the French Revolution of 1789-94 that shook Europe and affected the whole world.

The monarchy was abolished and the First Republic formed in 1793. The new government fell in 1799 to a coup led by Napoleon Bonaparte who, after declaring himself First Consul for life, had himself proclaimed emperor of France and king of Italy. Napoleon's military victories made him master of much of Europe, but his disastrous Russian campaign of 1812 initiated a series of defeats that led to his abdication in 1814 and exile to the island of Elba. The monarchy was briefly restored under Louis XVIII. Napoleon returned to France in March 1815, but his efforts to regain power were totally crushed at the battle of Waterloo. He was exiled to the island of St. Helena where he died in 1821.

The monarchy under Louis XVIII was again restored in 1815, but the ultrareactionary regime of Charles X (1824-30) was overthrown by a liberal revolution and Louis Philippe of Orleans replaced him as monarch. The monarchy was ousted by the Revolution of 1848 and the Second Republic proclaimed. Louis Napoleon Bonaparte (nephew of Napoleon I) was elected president of the Second Republic. He was proclaimed emperor in 1852. As Napoleon III, he gave France two decades of prosperity under a stable, autocratic regime, but led it to defeat in the Franco-Prussian War of 1870, after which the third Republic was established.

The Third Republic endured until 1940 and the capitulation of France to the swiftly maneuvering German forces. Marshal Henri Petain formed a puppet government that sued for peace and ruled unoccupied France from Vichy. Meanwhile, General Charles de Gaulle escaped to London where he formed a wartime government in exile and the Free French army. De Gaulle's provisional exile government was officially recognized by the Allies after the liberation of Paris in 1944, and De Gaulle, who had been serving as head of the provisional government, was formally elected to that position. In October 1945, the people overwhelmingly rejected a return to the prewar government, thus paving the way for the formation of the Fourth Republic.

De Gaulle was unanimously elected president of the Fourth Republic, but resigned in January 1946 when leftists withdrew their support. In actual operation, the Fourth Republic was remarkably like the Third, with the National Assembly the focus of power. The later years of the Fourth Republic were marked by a burst of industrial expansion unmatched in modern French history. The growth rate, however, was marred by a nagging inflationary trend that weakened the franc and undermined the competitive posture of France's export trade. This and the Algerian conflict led to the recall of De Gaulle to power, the adoption of a new constitution vesting strong powers in the executive, and the establishment in 1958 of the current Fifth Republic.

RULERS

Consulate, 1799-1803, L'an 8-11
Napoleon as Consul, 1799-1804
Napoleon I as Emperor, 1804-1814
(first restoration)
Louis XVIII, 1814-1815
Napoleon I, 1815
(second restoration)
Louis XVIII, 1815-1824
Charles X, 1824-1830
Louis Philippe, 1830-1848
Second Republic, 1848-1852
Napoleon III, 1852-1870
Government of National Defense, 1870-1871
Third Republic, 1871-1940
Vichy State, 1940-1944
De Gaulle's Provisional Govt., 1944-1947
Fourth Republic, 1947-1958
Fifth Republic, 1959-

MINT MARKS AND PRIVY MARKS

In addition to the date and mint mark which are customary on western civilization coinage, most coins manufactured by the French Mints contain two small 'Marques et Differents' as the French call them. These privy marks represent the men responsible for the dies which struck the coins. One privy mark is for the Engraver General (since 1880 the title is Chief Engraver). The other privy mark is the signature of the Mint Director of each mint. Since 1880 this privy mark has represented the office rather than the personage of the Mint Director, and a standard privy mark has been used (cornucopia).

For most dates these privy marks are unimportant minor features. During some issue dates, however, the marks changed. To be even more accurate sometimes the marks changed when the date didn't, even though it should have. These coins can be attributed to the proper mintage report only by considering the privy marks. Previous references have by and large ignored these privy marks. It is entirely possible that unattributed varieties may exist for any privy mark transition. All transition years which may have two varieties of privy marks have the known attribution indicated after the date (if it has been confirmed).

ENGRAVER GENERALS' PRIVY MARKS

Engraver Generals' privy marks may appear on coins of other mints which are dated as follows:

A - PARIS

Date	Privy Mark
AN XI-1816	Tiolier (in script) alternate
AN 13-1815	Tr (in script) signatures
1817-1824	T (in script) on Louis XVIII 1/4 F. only
1816-1824	Horse head on other Louis XVIII (h)
1824-1830	T (in script) (t)
1830-1842	Star (s)
1843-1855	Dog head (d) or D
1855-1879	Anchor (a)
1879	Anchor with bar (ab)
1880-1896	Fasces (f)
1896-1930	Torch (t)
1931-1958	Wing (w)
1958-1974	Owl (o)
1974—	Fish

MINT DIRECTOR PRIVY MARKS

Not all modern coins struck from dies produced at Paris have the 'A' mint mark. In the absence of a mint mark, the cornucopia privy mark serves to attribute a coin to Paris design.

A - PARIS

L'AN 6-1821	Cock
1822-42	Anchor
1843-45	Prow of ship (p)
1845-60	Hand (ha)
1860-79	Bee (b)
1871	(Commune), Trident (t)
1880-98	Cornucopia
1897-1920	None (n)
1901—	Cornucopia (c)

B - ROUEN

L'AN 12-1844	Sheep
1845-46	Hand
1853-57	Pick and shovel

B - BEAUMONT-LE-ROGER

1943-58	Cornucopia

(b) - BRUSSELS

1939	None

BB - STRASBOURG

L'AN 5-1825	Sheaf
1826-34	Beaver (ba)
1834-60	Bee (be)
1860-70	Cross (c)

BD - PAU

C - CASTELSARRASIN

1914, 42-46	Cornucopia

C - SAINT LO

CC, CL - GENOA

1805, 13-14	Prow of ship

CH - CHALONS

D - LYON

L'AN XI-1823	Bee (b)
1823-39	Ark (a)
1839-42	Tower (t)
1848-57	Lion

E - TOURS

F - ANGERS

G - GENEVE

L'AN 12 - 1805	Fish

G - POITIERS

H - LA ROCHELLE

L'AN 11-1817	Monogram
1817-24	Lyre (l)
1824-37	Trident

I - LIMOGES

L'AN XI-1822	Horizontal clasped hands
1823-37	Vertical clasped hands

K - BORDEAUX

L'AN 13-1809	Fish (f)
1809-57	Leaf (l)
1861-68	Pick and hammer
1870	Anchor (a)
1870-1871	M/star (s), die engraver's mark
1870-78	Cross

L - BAYONNE

AN XI-1828	Tulip (t)
1810	Tulip to right of date (tr)
1829-35	Rose
1836-37	Monogram

M - TOULOUSE

AN 14-1811	Hammer (h)
1811-37	Monogram (m)

MA - MARSEILLES

Date	Privy Mark
1787-1809	Star
1809-23	Monogram
1824-38	Palm tree
1853-57	Shell

O - CLERMONT

O - RIOM

P - DIJON

P - SEMUR

Q - NARBONNE

Q - PERPIGNAN

L'AN 4-1837	Grapes

R - LONDON

1815	Lis (no engraver signature)

R - SAINT ANDRE

S - TROYES

T - NANTES

L'AN 4-1818	Anchor
1818-20	Key
1826-35	Olive branch

U - TURIN

U, L'AN 11 - 1814	Heart

W - LILLE

L'AN 4-1840	Caduceus (c)
1840-46	Retort (r)
1853-57	Lamp

X - AMIENS

Y - BOURGES

Z - GRENOBLE

9 - RENNES

9 SAINT MALO

- BESANCON

Flag (u)UTRECHT

1811-14	Fish

Crowned R (R) - ROME

1811-14	Wolf

Thunderbolt (t) - POISSY

1922-24	Cornucopia

Star (s) - MADRID

1916	Cornucopia

MONETARY SYSTEM

(Commencing 1794)

10 Centimes = 1 Decime
10 Decimes = 1 Franc

UN (1) CENTIME

BRONZE
Mint mark: A
Second Republic

Y#	Date	Mintage	Fine	VF	XF	Unc
1	1848	8.615	2.00	5.00	10.00	20.00
	1849	8.664	2.00	5.00	10.00	20.00
	1850	2.721	6.00	12.00	30.00	60.00
	1851	2.712	4.00	7.00	20.00	35.00

Second Empire

Y#	Date	Mintage	Fine	VF	XF	Unc
14.1	1853	4.076	2.00	5.00	9.00	15.00
	1854	2.750	4.00	7.00	15.00	28.00
	1855(d)	6.034	3.00	5.00	12.00	25.00
	1855(a)	I.A.	6.00	15.00	35.00	60.00
	1855(a)	—	—	—	Proof	400.00
	1856	2.878	4.00	10.00	23.00	40.00
	1857	2.000	5.00	12.00	27.00	50.00

Mint mark: B

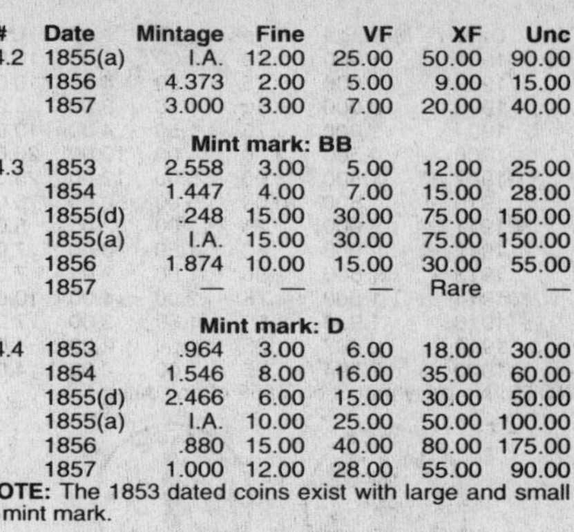

Y#	Date	Mintage	Fine	VF	XF	Unc
14.2	1853	.824	5.00	12.00	22.00	35.00
	1854	1.709	10.00	20.00	40.00	75.00
	1855(d)	1.971	10.00	20.00	40.00	75.00
14.2	1855(a)	I.A.	12.00	25.00	50.00	90.00
	1856	4.373	2.00	5.00	9.00	15.00
	1857	3.000	3.00	7.00	20.00	40.00

Mint mark: BB

Y#	Date	Mintage	Fine	VF	XF	Unc
14.3	1853	2.558	3.00	5.00	12.00	25.00
	1854	1.447	4.00	7.00	15.00	28.00
	1855(d)	.248	15.00	30.00	75.00	150.00
	1855(a)	I.A.	15.00	30.00	75.00	150.00
	1856	1.874	10.00	15.00	30.00	55.00
	1857	—	—	—	Rare	—

Mint mark: D

Y#	Date	Mintage	Fine	VF	XF	Unc
14.4	1853	.964	3.00	6.00	18.00	30.00
	1854	1.546	8.00	16.00	35.00	60.00
	1855(d)	2.466	6.00	15.00	30.00	50.00
	1855(a)	I.A.	10.00	25.00	50.00	100.00
	1856	.880	15.00	40.00	80.00	175.00
	1857	1.000	12.00	28.00	55.00	90.00

NOTE: The 1853 dated coins exist with large and small D mint mark.

Mint mark: K

Y#	Date	Mintage	Fine	VF	XF	Unc
14.5	1853	.405	8.00	18.00	45.00	75.00
	1854	1.150	6.00	14.00	35.00	65.00
	1855(d)	Inc. Ab.	7.00	15.00	45.00	75.00
	1855(a)	1.455	10.00	20.00	50.00	95.00
	1856	2.062	4.00	8.00	20.00	45.00
	1857	1.000	8.00	18.00	40.00	65.00

Mint mark: MA

Y#	Date	Mintage	Fine	VF	XF	Unc
14.6	1853	.225	20.00	35.00	60.00	125.00
	1854	1.976	3.00	6.00	15.00	35.00
	1855(d)	2.839	15.00	25.00	65.00	150.00
	1855(a)	I.A.	3.00	7.00	15.00	35.00
	1856	.305	12.00	30.00	65.00	150.00
	1857	1.500	3.00	10.00	20.00	45.00

Mint mark: W

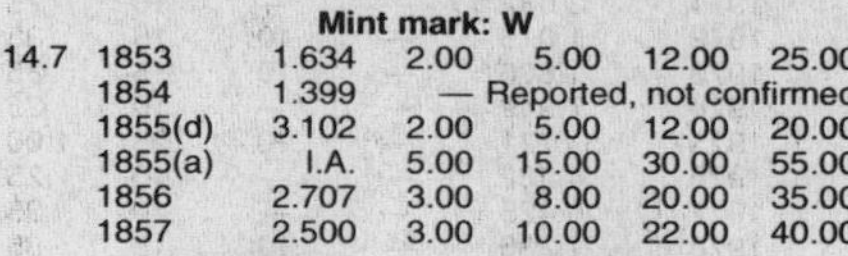

Y#	Date	Mintage	Fine	VF	XF	Unc
14.7	1853	1.634	2.00	5.00	12.00	25.00
	1854	1.399	— Reported, not confirmed			
	1855(d)	3.102	2.00	5.00	12.00	20.00
	1855(a)	I.A.	5.00	15.00	30.00	55.00
	1856	2.707	3.00	8.00	20.00	35.00
	1857	2.500	3.00	10.00	22.00	40.00

Mint mark: A

Y#	Date	Mintage	Fine	VF	XF	Unc
18.1	1861	7.398	.50	2.00	5.00	10.00
	1862	15.561	.50	1.00	2.50	5.00
	1870	1.000	5.00	18.00	30.00	60.00

Mint mark: BB

Y#	Date	Mintage	Fine	VF	XF	Unc
18.2	1861	3.012	1.00	3.00	9.00	15.00
	1862	4.493	1.00	3.00	9.00	15.00

Mint mark: K

Y#	Date	Mintage	Fine	VF	XF	Unc
18.3	1861	1.999	2.00	5.00	10.00	20.00
	1862	7.431	.50	1.00	3.00	5.00

Mint mark: A
Third Republic

Y#	Date	Mintage	Fine	VF	XF	Unc
41.1	1872	1.250	2.00	5.00	9.00	15.00
	1874	1.000	2.00	5.00	9.00	15.00
	1875	1.000	2.00	5.00	9.00	15.00
	1877	1.000	2.00	5.00	9.00	15.00
	1878	1.500	1.50	3.00	7.00	12.00
	1879(ab)	.800	2.00	6.00	11.00	16.00
	1882	.419	3.00	9.00	16.00	30.00
	1884	.400	4.00	10.00	18.00	35.00
	1885	.400	3.00	9.00	16.00	30.00
	1886	.400	3.00	9.00	16.00	30.00
	1887	.400	3.00	9.00	16.00	30.00
	1888	.400	3.00	9.00	16.00	30.00
	1889	.400	3.00	9.00	16.00	30.00
	1890	.400	3.00	9.00	16.00	30.00
	1891	1.400	.75	4.00	8.00	12.00
	1892	.800	1.00	5.00	10.00	18.00
	1893	.300	3.00	9.00	16.00	30.00
	1894	.500	2.00	7.00	14.00	22.00
	1895	3.000	1.50	2.50	5.00	10.00
	1896(f)	3.000	1.50	2.50	5.00	10.00
	1897	2.000	2.00	3.00	6.00	12.00

Mint mark: K

Y#	Date	Mintage	Fine	VF	XF	Unc
41.2	1872	.750	3.00	9.00	16.00	30.00
	1875	2.000	2.00	5.00	9.00	15.00
	1878	.289	10.00	20.00	45.00	80.00

Mint: Paris - w/o mint mark.

Y#	Date	Mintage	Fine	VF	XF	Unc
58	1898	.250	3.00	8.00	15.00	25.00
	1898	—	—	—	Proof	300.00
	1899	1.500	1.00	2.00	4.00	12.00
	1900	.221	15.00	30.00	55.00	100.00
	1900	—	—	—	Proof	300.00

Y#	Date	Mintage	Fine	VF	XF	Unc
58	1901	1.000	1.00	2.00	5.00	12.00
	1902	1.000	.75	1.50	4.00	10.00
	1903	2.000	.50	1.50	3.00	8.00
	1904	1.000	.75	1.50	4.00	10.00
	1908	4.500	2.00	4.00	10.00	20.00
	1909	1.500	3.00	5.00	12.00	25.00
	1910	1.500	10.00	25.00	50.00	75.00
	1911	5.000	.25	1.00	2.00	5.00
	1912	2.000	.50	1.50	3.00	7.00
	1913	1.500	.50	1.50	3.00	7.00
	1914	1.000	.75	2.00	4.00	10.00
	1916	1.996	.50	1.50	3.00	7.00
	1919	2.407	.25	1.00	2.00	4.00
	1920	2.594	.25	1.00	2.00	4.00

NOTE: No privy marks on Y#58 of any date.

CHROME-STEEL
1 New Centime = 1 Old Franc
Fifth Republic

Y#	Date	Mintage	Fine	VF	XF	Unc
102	1962	34.200	—	—	.10	.25
	1963	16.811	—	.10	.15	.35
	1964	22.654	—	—	.10	.25
	1965	47.799	—	—	.10	.25
	1966	19.688	—	—	.10	.25
	1967	52.308	—	—	.10	.25
	1968	40.890	—	—	.10	.25
	1969	35.430	—	—	.10	.25
	1970	29.600	—	—	.10	.25
	1971	3.082	—	—	.10	.25
	1972	1.015	—	.10	.15	.35
	1973	1.806	—	.10	.15	.35
	1974	7.949	—	—	.10	.25
	1975	.771	—	.10	.25	1.00
	1976	4.482	—	—	.10	.25
	1977	6.425	—	—	.10	.25
	1978	1.236	—	.10	.15	.35
	1979	2.213	—	—	.10	.25
	1980	.060	—	—	—	1.00
	1981	.050	—	—	—	1.00
	1982	.069	—	—	—	1.00
	1983	.101	—	—	—	1.00
	1984	.050	—	—	—	1.00
	1985	.020	—	—	—	1.00
	1986	.048	—	—	—	1.00
	1987	.100	—	—	—	1.00
	1988	.100	—	—	—	1.00
	1989	.083	—	—	—	1.00
	1990	.015	—	—	—	1.00
	1991	.015	—	—	—	1.00
	1991	—	—	—	Proof	2.00
	1992	.100	—	—	—	1.00
	1992	—	—	—	Proof	2.00
	1993	—	—	—	—	1.00

DEUX (2) CENTIMES

Small D

Large D

BRONZE
Mint mark: A
Second Empire

Y#	Date	Mintage	Fine	VF	XF	Unc
15.1	1853	.610	4.00	10.00	18.00	30.00
	1854	3.118	.75	2.00	6.00	18.00
	1855(d)	5.417	.25	2.00	6.00	12.00
	1855(a)	I.A.	.25	2.00	6.00	12.00
	1856	1.738	1.00	3.00	7.00	15.00
	1857	1.250	1.50	5.00	10.00	20.00
		Mint mark: B				
15.2	1853	.539	5.00	12.00	20.00	35.00
	1854	1.995	1.00	3.00	7.00	15.00
	1855(d)	1.754	1.50	4.00	8.00	15.00
	1855(a)	I.A.	1.50	4.00	8.00	15.00
	1856	4.324	.25	2.00	6.00	12.00
	1857	2.000	1.50	5.00	15.00	25.00
		Mint mark: BB				
15.3	1853	.168	6.00	15.00	35.00	100.00
	1854	2.003	1.00	3.00	7.00	15.00
	1855(d)	2.135	1.00	3.00	7.00	15.00
	1855(a)	I.A.	2.00	5.00	9.00	18.00
	1856	1.282	1.00	3.00	6.00	12.00
		Mint mark: D				
15.4	1853 sm.D	—	10.00	25.00	40.00	90.00
	1853 lg.D	—	13.00	35.00	55.00	110.00
	1854 small D	2.524	7.00	12.00	25.00	50.00
15.4	1854 lg.D	I.A.	10.00	15.00	30.00	60.00
	1855(d) small D	2.554	4.00	10.00	18.00	30.00
	1855(d) large D	Inc. Ab.	10.00	20.00	35.00	100.00
	1855(a) small D	Inc. Ab.	6.00	12.00	25.00	60.00
	1855(a) large D	Inc. Ab.	1.00	3.00	8.00	15.00
	1856	.774	—	—	—	—
	1857 small D	1.000	10.00	20.00	50.00	125.00
	1857 lg.D	I.A.	6.00	10.00	25.00	50.00
		Mint mark: K				
15.5	1853	.117	10.00	25.00	45.00	100.00
	1854	1.545	1.50	4.00	8.00	20.00
	1855(d)	1.068	2.50	6.00	15.00	30.00
	1855(a)	Inc. Ab.	2.00	5.00	12.00	25.00
	1856	2.281	1.00	3.00	7.00	15.00
	1857	.750	6.00	12.00	25.00	60.00
		Mint mark: MA				
15.6	1853	.163	6.00	16.00	35.00	100.00
	1854	1.312	3.00	8.00	16.00	25.00
	1855(d)	2.438	2.00	6.00	16.00	25.00
	1855(a)	I.A.	4.00	10.00	20.00	35.00
	1856	2.781	1.00	3.00	7.00	15.00
	1857	1.250	7.00	14.00	28.00	65.00
		Mint mark: W				
15.7	1853	.070	20.00	40.00	100.00	135.00
	1854	3.402	1.00	3.00	7.00	15.00
	1855(d)	.939	3.00	7.00	14.00	25.00
	1856	2.581	1.00	3.00	7.00	15.00
	1857	2.250	1.50	3.00	7.00	15.00

Mint mark: A
Obv: Bust points to 1 in date.

Y#	Date	Mintage	Fine	VF	XF	Unc
19.1	1861	4.054	.50	2.00	5.00	10.00
		Mint mark: BB				
19.2	1861	2.440	.75	3.00	6.00	14.00
		Mint mark: K				
19.3	1861	3.291	.75	2.50	5.00	8.00

Mint mark: A
Obv: Recut die (r), bust points to 8 in date.

Y#	Date	Mintage	Fine	VF	XF	Unc
19.4	1861(r)	I.A.	1.00	3.00	5.00	10.00
	1862	7.515	.50	1.50	3.00	5.00
		Mint mark: BB				
19.5	1861(r)	I.A.	1.00	3.00	5.00	10.00
	1862	2.807	1.50	3.50	6.00	12.00
		Mint mark: K				
19.6	1861(r)	I.A.	.25	2.00	4.00	10.00
	1862	13.692	.10	1.50	3.00	5.00

Mint mark: A
Third Republic

Y#	Date	Mintage	Fine	VF	XF	Unc
42.1	1877	.500	3.00	6.00	10.00	18.00
	1878	.750	2.00	4.00	8.00	15.00
	1879(ab)	.600	2.00	4.00	8.00	15.00
	1882	.290	4.00	8.00	18.00	35.00
	1883	.500	3.00	6.00	10.00	18.00
	1884	.300	4.00	8.00	15.00	25.00
	1885	.300	4.00	8.00	15.00	25.00
	1886	.300	4.00	8.00	15.00	25.00
	1887	.300	4.00	8.00	15.00	25.00
	1888	.400	3.00	6.00	12.00	18.00
	1889	.600	2.00	4.00	8.00	15.00
	1890	.300	4.00	8.00	15.00	25.00
	1891	.300	4.00	8.00	15.00	25.00
	1892	.500	3.00	6.00	10.00	18.00
	1893	.250	8.00	15.00	35.00	50.00
	1894	.150	10.00	20.00	40.00	70.00
	1895	1.000	1.00	3.00	5.00	10.00
	1896(f)	1.000	1.00	3.00	5.00	10.00
	1897	1.250	.75	2.00	4.00	8.00
		Mint mark: K				
42.2	1878	.363	3.00	8.00	16.00	25.00

Mint: Paris - w/o mint mark.

Y#	Date	Mintage	Fine	VF	XF	Unc
59	1898	.125	4.00	10.00	15.00	25.00
	1898		—	—	Proof	300.00
	1899	.750	2.00	5.00	10.00	20.00
	1900	.101	40.00	75.00	150.00	200.00
	1900	—	—	—	Proof	300.00
	1901	1.000	1.00	3.00	6.00	12.00
	1902	.750	1.50	4.00	8.00	16.00
	1903	.750	1.50	4.00	8.00	16.00
	1904	.500	2.00	5.00	10.00	18.00
	1907	.250	10.00	20.00	60.00	100.00
	1908	3.500	.50	1.00	3.00	6.00
	1909	1.750	6.00	12.00	40.00	65.00
	1910	1.750	.50	1.00	3.00	6.00
	1911	5.000	.15	1.00	2.00	5.00
	1912	1.500	.25	2.00	4.00	7.00
	1913	1.750	.25	2.00	4.00	7.00
	1914	2.000	.15	1.00	2.00	5.00
	1916	.500	.75	2.00	5.00	8.00
	1919	.902	.50	1.50	4.00	7.00
	1920	.598	.75	2.00	5.00	8.00

NOTE: No privy marks appeared on Y#59 of any date.

CINQ (5) CENTIMES

COPPER
Mint mark: BB

KM#	Date	Mintage	Good	VG	Fine	VF
149	1808	—	20.00	40.00	100.00	225.00

BRONZE
Mint mark: A
Second Empire

Y#	Date	Mintage	Fine	VF	XF	Unc
16.1	1853	13.928	2.00	5.00	16.00	30.00
	1854	28.767	2.00	5.00	14.00	28.00
	1855(d)	26.932	1.00	4.00	12.00	25.00
	1855(a)	I.A.	1.00	4.00	12.00	25.00
	1856	25.799	1.00	4.00	12.00	25.00
	1857	5.729	8.00	18.00	35.00	50.00
		Mint mark: B				
16.2	1853	4.424	4.00	10.00	25.00	45.00
	1854	16.354	2.00	5.00	16.00	30.00
	1855(d)	18.290	2.00	5.00	16.00	30.00
	1855(a)	I.A.	3.00	6.00	18.00	35.00
	1856	14.813	2.00	5.00	16.00	30.00
	1857	1.843	20.00	35.00	100.00	175.00
		Mint mark: BB				
16.3	1853	4.148	4.00	10.00	25.00	45.00
	1854	20.380	2.00	5.00	16.00	30.00
	1855(d)	17.108	2.00	5.00	16.00	30.00
	1855(a)	I.A.	2.00	5.00	16.00	30.00
	1856	10.372	2.00	5.00	14.00	28.00
	1857	1.662	25.00	40.00	125.00	200.00
		Mint mark: D				
16.4	1853	5.013	3.00	6.00	18.00	35.00
	1854	18.597	2.00	5.00	16.00	30.00
	1855(d) small D	14.250	10.00	20.00	45.00	90.00
	1855(d) large D	Inc. Ab.	10.00	20.00	45.00	90.00
	1855(a) small D	Inc. Ab.	3.00	6.00	18.00	35.00
	1855(a) large D	Inc. Ab.	3.00	6.00	18.00	35.00
	1856 small D	7.669	2.00	6.00	15.00	30.00
	1856 large D	Inc Ab.	2.00	6.00	15.00	30.00
	1857 small D	1.531	25.00	40.00	125.00	200.00
	1857 large D	Inc. Ab.	25.00	40.00	125.00	200.00

Mint mark: K

Y#	Date	Mintage	Fine	VF	XF	Unc
16.5	1853	1.652	8.00	18.00	35.00	50.00
	1854	13.608	2.00	5.00	16.00	30.00
	1855(d)	15.761	10.00	20.00	40.00	75.00
	1855(a)	I.A.	3.00	6.00	18.00	35.00
	1856	14.775	2.00	5.00	16.00	30.00
	1857	2.417	12.00	25.00	50.00	90.00

Mint mark: MA

Y#	Date	Mintage	Fine	VF	XF	Unc
16.6	1853	1.654	8.00	18.00	35.00	50.00
	1854	14.835	2.00	5.00	16.00	30.00
	1855(d)	15.417	10.00	20.00	50.00	100.00
	1855(a)	Inc. Ab.	2.00	5.00	14.00	28.00
	1856	16.997	2.00	5.00	16.00	30.00
	1857	4.188	10.00	20.00	45.00	90.00

Mint mark: W

Y#	Date	Mintage	Fine	VF	XF	Unc
16.7	1853	5.398	4.00	10.00	25.00	50.00
	1854	14.957	2.00	5.00	15.00	30.00
	1855(d)	17.473	2.00	5.00	15.00	30.00
	1855(a)	I.A.	2.00	5.00	15.00	30.00
	1856	15.472	2.00	5.00	15.00	30.00
	1857	1.842	25.00	40.00	125.00	200.00

Mint mark: A

Y#	Date	Mintage	Fine	VF	XF	Unc
20.1	1861	6.857	5.00	12.00	25.00	60.00
	1862	5.300	5.00	12.00	25.00	60.00
	1863	12.128	3.00	6.00	20.00	45.00
	1864	3.053	7.00	20.00	40.00	75.00
	1865	2.619	10.00	25.00	50.00	90.00

Mint mark: BB

Y#	Date	Mintage	Fine	VF	XF	Unc
20.2	1861	7.124	4.00	10.00	20.00	50.00
	1862	8.584	4.00	10.00	20.00	50.00
	1863	2.323	20.00	40.00	75.00	100.00
	1864	6.110	5.00	12.00	25.00	60.00
	1865	7.226	4.00	10.00	20.00	50.00

Mint mark: K

Y#	Date	Mintage	Fine	VF	XF	Unc
20.3	1861	6.582	5.00	12.00	25.00	60.00
	1862	7.065	4.00	10.00	20.00	50.00
	1863	9.437	3.00	8.00	18.00	40.00
	1864	5.831	5.00	12.00	25.00	60.00

Mint mark: A
Third Republic

Y#	Date	Mintage	Fine	VF	XF	Unc
43.1	1871	2.238	3.00	8.00	18.00	40.00
	1872	4.263	2.00	5.00	10.00	20.00
	1873	1.492	4.00	10.00	20.00	50.00
	1874	1.730	4.00	10.00	20.00	50.00
	1875	1.193	4.00	10.00	20.00	50.00
	1876	2.481	2.00	5.00	12.00	25.00
	1877	.766	10.00	25.00	40.00	100.00
	1878	.300	25.00	50.00	100.00	175.00
	1879(a)	1.955	2.00	5.00	10.00	20.00
	1879 anchor w/bar					
		Inc. Ab.	30.00	50.00	125.00	200.00
	1880	1.172	4.00	10.00	20.00	50.00
	1881	2.502	2.00	5.00	10.00	20.00
	1882	1.600	3.00	8.00	18.00	40.00
	1883	2.400	2.00	5.00	10.00	20.00
	1884	1.680	3.00	8.00	18.00	40.00
	1885	2.000	2.00	5.00	10.00	20.00
	1886	1.680	3.00	8.00	18.00	40.00
	1887	1.008	4.00	10.00	20.00	50.00
	1888	1.660	2.00	5.00	12.00	25.00
	1889	1.660	2.00	5.00	12.00	25.00
	1890	1.680	2.00	5.00	12.00	25.00
	1891	1.600	2.00	5.00	12.00	25.00
	1892	1.600	2.00	5.00	12.00	25.00
	1893	1.600	2.00	5.00	12.00	25.00
	1894	2.240	1.50	4.00	8.00	18.00
	1896(f)	6.695	1.00	2.00	5.00	12.00
	1896(t)	Inc. Ab.	30.00	60.00	125.00	225.00
	1897	12.600	1.00	2.00	5.00	12.00
	1898	1.200	4.00	10.00	20.00	50.00

Mint mark: K

Y#	Date	Mintage	Fine	VF	XF	Unc
43.2	1871	.016	100.00	200.00	350.00	500.00
	1872	4.064	2.00	5.00	10.00	20.00
	1873	1.997	4.00	10.00	20.00	50.00
	1874	1.326	5.00	12.00	22.00	55.00
	1875	.760	10.00	25.00	40.00	100.00
	1876	1.597	5.00	12.00	22.00	55.00
	1877	1.193	6.00	15.00	25.00	65.00
	1878	.166	40.00	85.00	175.00	325.00

Mint: Paris - w/o mint mark.

Y#	Date	Mintage	Fine	VF	XF	Unc
60	1898	7.900	1.00	3.00	8.00	18.00
	1898	—	—	—	Proof	350.00
	1899	7.400	1.00	3.00	8.00	18.00
	1900	7.400	1.00	3.00	8.00	18.00
	1900	—	—	—	Proof	350.00
	1901(c)	6.000	2.00	4.00	15.00	60.00
	1902	7.900	2.00	4.00	10.00	50.00
	1903	2.879	5.00	10.00	25.00	80.00
	1904	8.000	1.00	3.00	8.00	25.00
	1905	2.100	8.00	18.00	45.00	100.00
	1906	8.394	1.00	3.00	8.00	25.00
	1907	7.900	1.00	3.00	8.00	25.00
	1908	6.090	3.00	7.00	15.00	35.00
	1909	8.000	1.00	3.00	8.00	25.00
	1910	4.000	2.00	4.00	10.00	50.00
	1911	15.386	.50	1.00	3.00	10.00
	1912	20.000	.25	1.00	3.00	10.00
	1913	12.603	.50	1.00	3.00	10.00
	1914	7.000	.25	1.00	3.00	10.00
	1915	6.032	.50	1.00	3.00	10.00
	1916	41.531	.25	1.00	3.00	8.00
	1916(s)	Inc. Ab.	.25	1.00	3.00	8.00
	1917	16.963	.25	1.00	3.00	8.00
	1920	8.152	3.00	7.00	15.00	30.00
	1921	.142	200.00	350.00	550.00	1000.

COPPER-NICKEL

Y#	Date	Mintage	Fine	VF	XF	Unc
71	1914	—	—	—	Rare	—
	1917	10.458	1.00	3.00	10.00	25.00
	1918	35.592	.25	1.00	3.00	10.00
	1919	43.848	.25	1.00	3.00	10.00
	1920	51.321	.25	.50	2.00	7.00

Y#	Date	Mintage	Fine	VF	XF	Unc
72	1920	Inc. Ab.	10.00	20.00	50.00	120.00
	1921	32.908	.25	.50	3.00	7.00
	1922	31.700	.25	.50	3.00	7.00
	1922(t)	17.717	1.50	5.00	10.00	18.00
	1923	23.322	.50	2.00	3.00	10.00
	1923(t)	45.097	.25	.50	1.00	5.00
	1924	47.018	.25	.50	1.00	5.00
	1924(t)	21.210	.50	2.00	3.00	10.00
	1925	66.838	.25	.50	1.00	3.50
	1926	19.820	.25	2.00	3.00	10.00
	1927	6.066	5.00	15.00	40.00	100.00
	1930	31.902	.20	.50	1.00	3.00
	1931	34.711	.20	.50	1.00	3.00
	1932	31.112	.20	.50	1.00	3.00
	1933	12.970	1.00	3.00	8.00	18.00
	1934	27.144	.30	.65	2.00	8.00
	1935	57.221	.25	.50	1.00	3.00
	1936	64.341	.15	.25	.75	3.00
	1937	26.329	.15	.25	.75	3.00
	1938	21.614	.15	.25	.75	3.00

NICKEL-BRONZE

Y#	Date	Mintage	Fine	VF	XF	Unc
72a	.1938.	26.330	.15	.50	1.00	3.00
	.1938. star	I.A.	100.00	200.00	300.00	400.00
	.1939.	52.673	.10	.25	.75	2.00

CHROME-STEEL
5 New Centimes = 5 Old Francs
Fifth Republic

Y#	Date	Mintage	Fine	VF	XF	Unc
103	1961	39.000	.10	.20	.50	2.00
	1962	166.360	.10	.15	.20	.75
	1963	71.900	.10	.20	.40	1.00
	1964	126.480	.10	.15	.30	.75

ALUMINUM-BRONZE

Y#	Date	Mintage	Fine	VF	XF	Unc
A104	1966	502.512	—	—	—	.10
	1967	11.747	—	—	.10	.25
	1968	110.395	—	—	—	.10
	1969	94.955	—	—	—	.10
	1970	58.900	—	—	—	.10
	1971	93.190	—	—	—	.10
	1972	100.515	—	—	—	.10
	1973	100.344	—	—	—	.10
	1974	103.890	—	—	—	.10
	1975	95.835	—	—	—	.10
	1976	148.395	—	—	—	.10
	1977	115.285	—	—	—	.10
	1978	189.804	—	—	—	.10
	1979	180.000	—	—	—	.10
	1980	180.010	—	—	—	.10
	1981	.050	—	—	—	.50
	1982	138.000	—	—	—	.10
	1983	132.000	—	—	—	.10
	1984	150.000	—	—	—	.10
	1985	170.000	—	—	—	.10
	1986	280.000	—	—	—	.10
	1987	310.000	—	—	—	.10
	1988	200.000	—	—	—	.10
	1989	.084	—	—	—	.20
	1990	79.992	—	—	—	.20
	1991	50.000	—	—	—	.20
	1991	—	—	—	Proof	1.00
	1992	180.000	—	—	—	.20
	1992	—	—	—	Proof	1.00
	1993					.20

UN (1) DECIME

STRASBOURG PROVISIONAL ISSUES

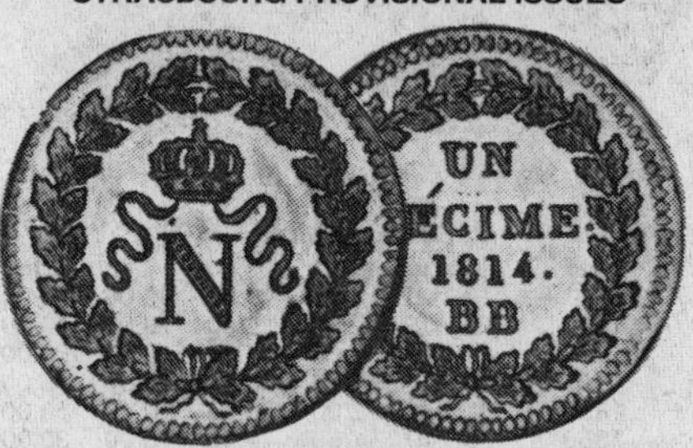

BRONZE
Mint mark: BB

C#	Date	Mintage	VG	Fine	VF	XF
174	1814	.544	7.50	15.00	45.00	125.00
	1814 DECIME.					
		Inc. Ab.	15.00	35.00	90.00	225.00
	1814.	Inc. Ab.	10.00	20.00	50.00	145.00
	1814. DECIME.					
		Inc. Ab.	10.00	20.00	40.00	140.00
	1815	Inc. Ab.	12.50	25.00	55.00	150.00
	1815. DECIME.					
		Inc. Ab.	15.00	30.00	65.00	175.00

C#	Date	Mintage	VG	Fine	VF	XF
175	1814	1.208	15.00	30.00	60.00	150.00
	1814. DECIME.					
		Inc. Ab.	15.00	30.00	60.00	150.00
	1815	I.A.	7.50	15.00	30.00	125.00
	1815. DECIME.					
		Inc. Ab.	10.00	20.00	40.00	140.00

DIX (10) CENTIMES

BILLON
Mint mark: A

C#	Date	Mintage	Fine	VF	XF	Unc
150.1	1807	—	150.00	250.00	500.00	—
	1808	6.269	2.00	10.00	50.00	125.00
	1809	7.529	2.00	10.00	50.00	125.00
	1810	—	—	—	Unique	—

Mint mark: B

C#	Date	Mintage	Fine	VF	XF	Unc
150.2	1808	.163	25.00	60.00	125.00	300.00
	1809	.831	6.00	20.00	60.00	150.00
	1810	1.231	5.00	18.00	55.00	135.00

Mint mark: BB

C#	Date	Mintage	Fine	VF	XF	Unc
150.3	1808	1.425	3.00	15.00	40.00	100.00
	1809	.695	6.00	20.00	60.00	150.00
	1810	—	—	—	Unique	—

Mint mark: H

C#	Date	Mintage	Fine	VF	XF	Unc
150.4	1808	.129	20.00	40.00	150.00	350.00
	1809	.631	7.00	15.00	40.00	125.00
	1810	.673	7.00	15.00	40.00	125.00

Mint mark: I

C#	Date	Mintage	Fine	VF	XF	Unc
150.5	1808	1.062	4.00	10.00	25.00	90.00
	1809	3.473	3.00	7.00	20.00	75.00
	1810	3.066	3.00	7.00	20.00	75.00

Mint mark: M

C#	Date	Mintage	Fine	VF	XF	Unc
150.6	1808	.860	7.00	15.00	40.00	125.00
	1809	1.070	4.00	10.00	25.00	90.00

Mint mark: Q

C#	Date	Mintage	Fine	VF	XF	Unc
150.7	1808	—	—	—	Rare	—
	1809	.555	8.00	25.00	55.00	150.00
	1810	.130	25.00	60.00	125.00	250.00

Mint mark: T

C#	Date	Mintage	Fine	VF	XF	Unc
150.8	1808	.054	40.00	100.00	200.00	500.00
	1809	.134	25.00	50.00	100.00	200.00
	1810	.103	35.00	75.00	150.00	350.00

Mint mark: W

C#	Date	Mintage	Fine	VF	XF	Unc
150.9	1808	1.576	4.00	10.00	25.00	90.00
	1809	1.160	4.00	10.00	25.00	90.00

BRONZE
Mint mark: A
Second Empire

Y#	Date	Mintage	Fine	VF	XF	Unc
17.1	690.00	175.00	18.00	40.00	90.00	175.00
	1853	12.256	2.00	5.00	18.00	50.00
	1854	13.327	2.00	5.00	18.00	50.00
	1855(d)	14.816	2.00	5.00	18.00	45.00
	1855(a)	I.A.	3.00	6.00	20.00	60.00
	1856	19.149	1.50	4.00	15.00	30.00
	1857	3.096	5.00	10.00	25.00	75.00

Mint mark: B

Y#	Date	Mintage	Fine	VF	XF	Unc
17.2	1853	3.546	3.00	7.00	20.00	50.00
	1854	8.065	3.00	9.00	25.00	50.00
	1855(d)	9.960	3.00	10.00	30.00	75.00
	1855(a)	I.A.	2.00	6.00	18.00	45.00
	1856	11.637	2.00	6.00	18.00	45.00
	1857	1.620	15.00	30.00	85.00	200.00

Mint mark: BB

Y#	Date	Mintage	Fine	VF	XF	Unc
17.3	1853	4.582	3.00	7.00	20.00	50.00
	1854	8.433	2.00	6.00	18.00	45.00
	1855(d)	11.953	2.00	6.00	18.00	45.00
	1855(a)	I.A.	1.50	5.00	15.00	40.00
	1856	7.781	2.00	6.00	18.00	45.00
	1857	1.685	15.00	30.00	85.00	200.00

Mint mark: D

Y#	Date	Mintage	Fine	VF	XF	Unc
17.4	1853	3.709	3.00	7.00	20.00	50.00
	1854	8.487	2.00	6.00	18.00	45.00
	1855(d)	12.099	5.00	10.00	30.00	100.00
	1855(a)	I.A.	3.00	8.00	25.00	75.00
	1856	5.118	3.00	8.00	25.00	75.00

Mint mark: K

Y#	Date	Mintage	Fine	VF	XF	Unc
17.5	1853	1.203	5.00	18.00	50.00	135.00
	1854	7.083	10.00	20.00	40.00	90.00
	1855(d)	11.797	5.00	10.00	30.00	100.00
	1855(a)	I.A.	2.00	7.00	20.00	60.00
	1856	8.871	2.00	7.00	18.00	50.00
	1857	1.179	20.00	40.00	100.00	220.00

Mint mark: MA

Y#	Date	Mintage	Fine	VF	XF	Unc
17.6	1853	.889	15.00	30.00	60.00	135.00
	1854	7.995	3.00	7.00	20.00	50.00
	1855(d)					
		11.309	5.00	10.00	30.00	100.00
	1855(a)	I.A.	2.00	7.00	18.00	50.00
	1856	10.937	1.50	5.00	15.00	40.00
	1857	2.052	20.00	40.00	80.00	190.00

Mint mark: W

Y#	Date	Mintage	Fine	VF	XF	Unc
17.7	1853	3.107	2.00	8.00	20.00	60.00
	1854	8.242	2.00	7.00	18.00	50.00
	1855(d)	9.837	4.00	10.00	25.00	65.00
	1855(a)	I.A.	2.00	7.00	18.00	50.00
	1856	11.402	1.50	5.00	15.00	40.00
	1857	1.858	10.00	20.00	60.00	125.00

Mint mark: A

Y#	Date	Mintage	Fine	VF	XF	Unc
21.1	1861	3.638	4.00	12.00	30.00	75.00
	1862	4.736	3.00	10.00	28.00	65.00
	1863	4.873	3.00	10.00	28.00	65.00
	1864	1.556	20.00	50.00	150.00	300.00
	1865	1.608	8.00	20.00	40.00	90.00

Mint mark: BB

Y#	Date	Mintage	Fine	VF	XF	Unc
21.2	1861	4.625	3.00	10.00	28.00	65.00
	1862	4.702	3.00	10.00	28.00	65.00
	1863	1.340	6.00	15.00	35.00	80.00
	1864	3.053	5.00	12.00	30.00	70.00
	1865	4.797	3.00	10.00	28.00	65.00

Mint mark: K

Y#	Date	Mintage	Fine	VF	XF	Unc
21.3	1861	4.363	3.00	10.00	28.00	65.00
	1862	5.244	2.00	10.00	25.00	60.00
	1863	4.521	3.00	10.00	28.00	65.00
	1864	3.075	4.00	12.00	30.00	75.00

Mint mark: A
Third Republic

Y#	Date	Mintage	Fine	VF	XF	Unc
44.1	1870	.889	3.00	10.00	28.00	65.00
	1871	1.840	2.00	8.00	20.00	45.00
	1872	4.399	1.00	4.00	8.00	25.00
	1873	2.096	1.50	5.00	10.00	30.00
	1874	1.194	2.50	7.00	20.00	45.00
	1875	1.434	30.00	65.00	175.00	300.00
	1876	.458	8.00	25.00	50.00	90.00
	1877	.392	12.00	35.00	65.00	135.00
	1878	.150	15.00	40.00	75.00	160.00
	1879	.823	4.00	12.00	28.00	55.00
	1880	1.414	2.00	6.00	18.00	40.00
	1881	.749	4.00	12.00	28.00	55.00
	1882	1.100	2.00	8.00	20.00	45.00
	1883	.700	6.00	20.00	40.00	80.00
	1884	1.060	2.00	8.00	20.00	45.00
	1885	.900	2.50	7.00	20.00	45.00
	1886	1.060	2.00	8.00	20.00	45.00
	1887	.874	2.50	7.00	20.00	45.00
	1888	1.050	2.00	8.00	20.00	45.00
	1889	1.010	2.00	8.00	20.00	45.00
	1890	1.060	2.00	8.00	20.00	45.00
	1891	1.000	2.00	8.00	20.00	45.00
	1892	1.020	2.00	8.00	20.00	45.00
	1893	1.120	2.00	8.00	20.00	45.00
	1894	.800	2.50	10.00	25.00	50.00
	1895	.600	3.00	8.00	28.00	55.00
	1896(f)	4.447	1.00	3.00	8.00	30.00
	1896(t)	Inc. Ab.	30.00	75.00	200.00	300.00
	1897	7.250	.50	3.00	6.00	15.00
	1898	1.400	2.00	6.00	18.00	40.00

Mint mark: K

Y#	Date	Mintage	Fine	VF	XF	Unc
44.2	1871	.027	75.00	175.00	350.00	650.00
	1872	4.359	1.00	4.00	8.00	25.00
	1873	2.001	2.00	6.00	18.00	40.00
	1874	1.337	6.00	20.00	40.00	80.00
	1875	.430	6.00	20.00	40.00	80.00
	1876	.601	5.00	18.00	35.00	75.00
	1877	.403	6.00	20.00	40.00	80.00
	1878	.100	40.00	100.00	175.00	300.00

Mint: Paris - w/o mint mark.

Y#	Date	Mintage	Fine	VF	XF	Unc
61	1898	4.000	1.00	3.00	8.00	20.00
	1898	—	—		Matte Proof	450.00
	1899	4.000	1.00	3.00	8.00	20.00
	1900(n)	5.000	1.00	3.00	8.00	20.00
	1900(n)	—	—	—	Proof	400.00
	1901(c)	2.700	2.00	5.00	15.00	40.00
	1902	3.800	1.50	4.00	10.00	25.00
	1903	3.650	1.50	4.00	10.00	25.00
	1904	3.800	1.50	4.00	10.00	25.00
	1905	.950	35.00	65.00	150.00	275.00
	1906	3.000	2.00	5.00	15.00	40.00
	1907	4.000	1.00	3.00	8.00	20.00
	1908	3.500	1.00	3.00	8.00	20.00
	1909	2.933	1.00	3.00	8.00	25.00
	1910	3.567	1.00	3.00	8.00	20.00
	1911	7.903	.50	1.50	4.00	12.00
	1912	9.500	.50	1.50	4.00	12.00
	1913	9.000	.50	1.50	4.00	12.00
	1914	6.000	.75	2.00	5.00	14.00
	1915	4.362	.50	1.50	4.00	12.00

Y#	Date	Mintage	Fine	VF	XF	Unc
61	1916	22.477	.25	1.00	2.00	7.00
	1916(s)	Inc. Ab.	.25	1.00	2.00	7.00
	1917	11.914	.25	1.00	2.00	7.00
	1920	4.119	2.00	5.00	15.00	40.00
	1921	1.896	10.00	25.00	65.00	125.00

NICKEL

Y#	Date	Mintage	Fine	VF	XF	Unc
73	1914 dash	3,972	400.00	800.00	1200.	2250.

COPPER-NICKEL

Y#	Date	Mintage	Fine	VF	XF	Unc
73a	1917	8.171	1.00	3.00	10.00	25.00
	1918	30.605	.25	.50	2.00	6.00
	1919	33.489	.25	.50	2.00	6.00
	1920	38.845	.25	.50	2.00	6.00
	1921	42.768	.10	.35	.75	5.00
	1922	23.033	.35	.75	2.50	6.00
	1922(t)	12.412	.75	1.50	3.00	10.00
	1923	18.701	.50	1.25	2.50	6.00
	1923(t)	30.016	.25	.50	2.00	5.00
	1924	43.949	.10	.35	.75	4.00
	1924(t)	13.591	2.50	7.50	20.00	50.00
	1925	46.266	.10	.35	.75	4.00
	1926	25.660	.25	.50	2.00	5.00
	1927	16.203	.40	.75	2.50	6.00
	1928	6.967	2.00	6.00	15.00	35.00
	1929	24.531	.10	.35	1.00	4.00
	1930	22.146	.10	.35	1.00	4.00
	1931	49.107	.10	.35	1.00	4.00
	1932	30.317	.10	.35	1.00	4.00
	1933	13.042	.35	.75	2.50	6.00
	1934	24.067	.10	.50	1.00	3.00
	1935	47.487	.10	.50	1.00	3.00
	1936	57.738	.10	.50	1.00	3.00
	1937	25.308	.10	.50	1.00	3.00
	1938	17.063	.25	.75	2.00	5.00

NICKEL-BRONZE

Y#	Date	Mintage	Fine	VF	XF	Unc
73c	.1938.	24.151	.25	.50	1.00	2.00
	1.938.	Inc. Ab.	—	—	—	—
	.1939.	62.269	.15	.30	.65	1.75

Thin flan

Y#	Date	Mintage	Fine	VF	XF	Unc
73c.1	.1939.	Inc. Ab.	.10	.20	.50	1.25

ZINC
Rev: W/o dash below MES in C MES.

Y#	Date	Mintage	Fine	VF	XF	Unc
73b.1	1941	235.875	1.00	2.00	6.00	15.00

Rev: Dash below MES in C MES.

Y#	Date	Mintage	Fine	VF	XF	Unc
73b.2	1941	Inc. Ab.	.75	1.25	4.00	10.00

Rev: Dot before and after date.

Y#	Date	Mintage	Fine	VF	XF	Unc
73b.3	.1941.	Inc. Ab.	.25	.50	1.00	4.00

Vichy French State Issues, thickness 1.5mm.

Y#	Date	Mintage	Fine	VF	XF	Unc
V91.1	1941	70.860	.35	.65	1.50	6.00
	1942	139.598	.30	.60	1.25	4.00
	1943	21.520	1.00	2.00	4.00	10.00

Mint: Paris - w/o mint mark.
Thin flan, 1.3mm.

Y#	Date	Mintage	Fine	VF	XF	Unc
V91.2	1941	Inc. Ab.	.25	.50	1.25	5.00

Y#	Date	Mintage	Fine	VF	XF	Unc
V91.2	1942	Inc. Ab.	.20	.40	1.00	3.00
	1943	Inc. Ab.	.75	1.50	3.00	7.00

Y#	Date	Mintage	Fine	VF	XF	Unc
V93	1943	22.008	.25	.75	2.25	7.00
	1944	58.463	.25	.50	2.00	5.00

Fourth Republic Issues

Y#	Date	Mintage	Fine	VF	XF	Unc
74.1	1945	38.174	1.00	2.00	4.00	12.00
	1946	—	—	—	Rare	—
		Mint mark: B				
74.2	1945	7.246	1.50	3.00	6.00	16.00
	1946	10.566	2.50	5.00	10.00	25.00
		Mint mark: C				
74.3	1945	8.379	2.00	4.00	8.00	25.00

ALUMINUM-BRONZE
Mint: Paris - w/o mint mark.
10 New Centimes = 10 Old Francs
Fifth Republic

Y#	Date	Mintage	Fine	VF	XF	Unc
104	1962	29.100	—	—	.10	.40
	1963	217.601	—	—	—	.10
	1964	93.409	—	—	.10	.20
	1965	41.220	—	—	.10	.30
	1966	16.429	—	.10	.15	.40
	1967	196.728	—	—	—	.10
	1968	111.700	—	—	—	.10
	1969	129.530	—	—	—	.10
	1970	77.020	—	—	—	.10
	1971	26.280	—	—	—	.10
	1972	45.700	—	—	—	.10
	1973	58.000	—	—	—	.10
	1974	91.990	—	—	—	.10
	1975	74.450	—	—	—	.10
	1976	137.320	—	—	—	.10
	1977	140.110	—	—	—	.10
	1978	154.360	—	—	—	.10
	1979	140.000	—	—	—	.10
	1980	140.010	—	—	—	.10
	1981	135.000	—	—	—	.10
	1982	110.000	—	—	—	.10
	1983	150.000	—	—	—	.10
	1984	200.000	—	—	—	.10
	1985	170.000	—	—	—	.10
	1986	150.000	—	—	—	.10
	1987	150.000	—	—	—	.10
	1988	145.000	—	—	—	.10
	1989	179.984	—	—	—	.10
	1990	179.992	—	—	—	.10
	1991	180.000	—	—	—	.10
	1991	—	—	—	Proof	1.00
	1992	130.000	—	—	—	.10
	1992	—	—	—	Proof	1.00
	1993				Proof	.10

VINGT (20) CENTIMES

1.0000 g, .900 SILVER, .0289 oz ASW
Mint mark: A
Second Republic

Y#	Date	Mintage	Fine	VF	XF	Unc
2.1	1849	4,877	125.00	250.00	450.00	700.00
	1850	6.157	3.00	10.00	18.00	45.00
	1851	3.309	5.00	15.00	25.00	55.00
		Mint mark: BB				
2.2	1850	.048	40.00	75.00	200.00	450.00
		Mint mark: K				
2.3	1850	.344	20.00	45.00	100.00	225.00

Mint mark: A
Second Empire - Napoleon III

Y#	Date	Mintage	Fine	VF	XF	Unc
22.1	1853 small head					
22.1		.680	10.00	20.00	50.00	100.00
	1853 large head					
		Inc. Ab.	100.00	200.00	400.00	700.00
	1854	1.683	5.00	12.00	25.00	60.00
	1855(d)	.362	10.00	25.00	45.00	100.00
	1856	.603	8.00	17.50	40.00	80.00
	1857	.840	6.00	15.00	35.00	70.00
	1858	.704	10.00	20.00	40.00	80.00
	1859	3.620	3.00	10.00	20.00	45.00
	1860/50	6.536	6.00	15.00	40.00	100.00
	1860(h)	Inc. Ab.	3.00	6.00	15.00	35.00
	1862	.054	75.00	175.00	300.00	600.00
		Mint mark: BB				
22.2	1856	.013	125.00	275.00	450.00	800.00
	1860(b)					
		2.986	5.00	12.00	25.00	80.00
	1863	.398	20.00	45.00	90.00	200.00
		Mint mark: D				
22.3	1856	.396	12.50	25.00	50.00	125.00

1.0000 g, .835 SILVER, .0268 oz ASW
Mint mark: A

Y#	Date	Mintage	Fine	VF	XF	Unc
27.1	1864	.268	10.00	25.00	75.00	175.00
	1865	—	—	Reported, not confirmed		
	1866	1.460	5.00	10.00	25.00	60.00
		Mint mark: BB				
27.2	1864	.112	15.00	30.00	75.00	175.00
	1866	.843	7.00	15.00	35.00	75.00
		Mint mark: K				
27.3	1864	.058	30.00	60.00	150.00	275.00
	1866	.413	10.00	25.00	55.00	150.00

Mint mark: A

Y#	Date	Mintage	Fine	VF	XF	Unc
28.1	1867	5.611	2.00	4.00	10.00	20.00
	1868	.353	7.00	15.00	35.00	90.00
		Mint mark: BB				
28.2	1867	3.114	2.50	5.00	12.00	25.00
	1868	.200	15.00	30.00	60.00	125.00
	1869	Inc. Ab.	—	—	—	—
		Mint mark: K				
28.3	1867	.091	20.00	50.00	125.00	250.00

1.0000 g, .900 SILVER, 15mm, .0289 oz ASW
Mint mark: A

Y#	Date	Mintage	Fine	VF	XF	Unc
47.1	1878	30 pcs.	—	—	1500.	2000.
		16mm				
47.2	1889	100 pcs.	—	—	1000.	1300.

NOTE: Considered an Essai.

ZINC
Vichy French State Issues

Y#	Date	Mintage	Fine	VF	XF	Unc
V90	1941	54.044	1.00	2.00	5.00	12.00

Thick flan, 3.50 g

Y#	Date	Mintage	Fine	VF	XF	Unc
V92.1	1941	31.397	1.00	2.00	4.00	12.00
	1942	112.868	.50	1.00	3.00	8.00
	1943	64.138	.75	1.50	3.50	10.00

Mint: Paris - w/o mint mark.
Thin flan, 3.00 g

Y#	Date	Mintage	Fine	VF	XF	Unc
V92.2	1941	Inc. Ab.	.50	.75	3.00	10.00
	1943	Inc. Ab.	.50	.75	3.00	7.00
	1944	5.250	15.00	30.00	75.00	150.00

IRON

Y#	Date	Mintage	Fine	VF	XF	Unc
V92a	1944	.695	25.00	60.00	150.00	275.00

ZINC
Fourth Republic Issues

Y#	Date	Mintage	Fine	VF	XF	Unc
75.1	1945	6.003	2.00	5.00	10.00	20.00
	1946	2.662	8.00	18.00	35.00	65.00
		Mint mark: B				
75.2	1945	.100	100.00	200.00	400.00	600.00
	1946	5.525	75.00	150.00	300.00	500.00
		Mint mark: C				
75.3	1945	.299	20.00	50.00	100.00	225.00

ALUMINUM-BRONZE
Mint: Paris - w/o mint mark.
Fifth Republic

Y#	Date	Mintage	Fine	VF	XF	Unc
105	1962	48.200	—	—	.10	.40
	1963	190.330	—	—	.10	.30
	1964	127.521	—	—	.10	.30
	1965	27.024	—	.10	.20	.40
	1966	21.762	—	.10	.20	.40
	1967	138.780	—	—	.10	.15
	1968	77.408	—	—	.10	.20
	1969	50.570	—	—	.10	.20
	1970	70.040	—	—	.10	.15
	1971	31.080	—	—	.10	.15
	1972	39.740	—	—	.10	.15
	1973	45.240	—	—	.10	.15
	1974	54.250	—	—	.10	.15
	1975	40.570	—	—	.10	.15
	1976	117.610	—	—	—	.10
	1977	100.340	—	—	—	.10
	1978	125.015	—	—	—	.10
	1979	70.000	—	—	—	.10
	1980	20.010	—	—	.10	.15
	1981	125.000	—	—	—	.10
	1982	150.000	—	—	—	.10
	1983	110.000	—	—	—	.10
	1984	200.000	—	—	—	.10
	1985	150.000	—	—	—	.10
	1986	40.000	—	—	—	.10
	1987	60.000	—	—	—	.10
	1988	220.000	—	—	—	.10
	1989	139.985	—	—	—	.10
	1990	49.990	—	—	—	.10
	1991	40.000	—	—	—	.10
	1991	—	—	—	Proof	1.00
	1992	90.000	—	—	—	.10
	1992	—	—	—	Proof	1.00
	1993	—	—	—	—	.10

QUART (1/4) FRANC

1.2500 g, .900 SILVER, .0362 oz ASW
Mint mark: A
Obv. leg: BONAPARTE PR. CONSUL.

C#	Date	Mintage	VG	Fine	VF	XF
141.1	AN12	.171	15.00	27.50	65.00	110.00
		Mint mark: BB				
141.2	AN12	1,565	60.00	120.00	300.00	550.00
		Mint mark: D				
141.3	AN12	—	60.00	120.00	300.00	550.00
		Mint mark: I				
141.4	AN12	.041	22.50	45.00	110.00	225.00
		Mint mark: L				
141.5	AN12	.019	30.00	60.00	150.00	275.00
		Mint mark: M				
141.6	AN12	.039	17.50	32.50	80.00	200.00
		Mint mark: MA				
141.7	AN12	9,080	30.00	60.00	150.00	300.00
		Mint mark: Q				
141.8	AN12	.028	25.00	50.00	90.00	250.00
		Mint mark: T				
141.9	AN12	.010	30.00	60.00	150.00	300.00
	Common date				Unc.	275.00

Mint mark: A
Obv. leg: NAPOLEON EMPEREUR.

C#	Date	Mintage	VG	Fine	VF	XF
151.1	AN12	.019	25.00	45.00	85.00	225.00
	AN13	.128	12.50	25.00	45.00	115.00
	AN14	—	—	Reported, not confirmed		

Mint mark: BB

C#	Date	Mintage	VG	Fine	VF	XF
151.8	AN13	2,194	60.00	115.00	225.00	460.00

Mint mark: D

C#	Date	Mintage	VG	Fine	VF	XF
151.2	AN12	5,156	45.00	100.00	175.00	400.00

Mint mark: H

C#	Date	Mintage	VG	Fine	VF	XF
151.3	AN12	.012	30.00	60.00	145.00	350.00
	AN13/12	—	45.00	90.00	225.00	460.00
	AN13	2,744	45.00	90.00	225.00	460.00

Mint mark: I

C#	Date	Mintage	VG	Fine	VF	XF
151.4	AN12	.032	20.00	40.00	85.00	225.00
	AN13	.118	15.00	30.00	75.00	175.00

Mint mark: K

C#	Date	Mintage	VG	Fine	VF	XF
151.5	AN12	8,122	30.00	60.00	145.00	350.00
	AN13	.018	25.00	45.00	100.00	225.00
	AN14	1,757	70.00	140.00	290.00	650.00

Mint mark: L

C#	Date	Mintage	VG	Fine	VF	XF
151.9	AN13	.025	25.00	45.00	85.00	280.00
	AN14	—	70.00	135.00	280.00	575.00

Mint mark: M

C#	Date	Mintage	VG	Fine	VF	XF
151.6	AN12	.016	25.00	45.00	115.00	280.00
	AN13	.039	20.00	40.00	80.00	225.00

Mint mark: MA

C#	Date	Mintage	VG	Fine	VF	XF
151.10	AN13	8,114	30.00	60.00	145.00	350.00

Mint mark: T

C#	Date	Mintage	VG	Fine	VF	XF
151.7	AN12	3,606	60.00	115.00	200.00	425.00
	AN13	6,801	35.00	70.00	140.00	280.00

Mint mark: U

C#	Date	Mintage	VG	Fine	VF	XF
151.11	AN13	.014	60.00	115.00	280.00	575.00
	AN14	100 pcs.	400.00	600.00	1000.	2250.
	Common date				Unc.	325.00

Mint mark: A

C#	Date	Mintage	VG	Fine	VF	XF
151.12	1806	.031	25.00	50.00	90.00	200.00
	1807	—	—	—	—	—

Mint mark: I

C#	Date	Mintage	VG	Fine	VF	XF
151.13	1806	4,583	35.00	70.00	140.00	280.00
	1807	8,356	30.00	60.00	115.00	225.00

Mint mark: K

C#	Date	Mintage	VG	Fine	VF	XF
151.14	1806	4,359	35.00	70.00	140.00	280.00
	1807	5,538	35.00	70.00	140.00	280.00

Mint mark: L

C#	Date	Mintage	VG	Fine	VF	XF
151.15	1806	.018	25.00	50.00	90.00	225.00
	1807	7,618	30.00	75.00	115.00	250.00

Mint mark: M

C#	Date	Mintage	VG	Fine	VF	XF
151.18	1807	1,626	85.00	1750.	300.00	700.00

Mint mark: Q

C#	Date	Mintage	VG	Fine	VF	XF
151.16	1806	8,948	30.00	60.00	115.00	225.00
	1807	9,713	30.00	60.00	115.00	225.00

Mint mark: U

C#	Date	Mintage	VG	Fine	VF	XF
151.17	1806	1,361	85.00	175.00	300.00	700.00
	1807	.013	30.00	50.00	90.00	225.00

Mint mark: A
Negro head.

C#	Date	Mintage	VG	Fine	VF	XF
151a	1807	.041	45.00	100.00	250.00	425.00

Laureate head.

C#	Date	Mintage	VG	Fine	VF	XF
151b.1	1807	.017	45.00	100.00	225.00	400.00
	1808	—	50.00	125.00	250.00	650.00

Mint mark: I

C#	Date	Mintage	VG	Fine	VF	XF
151b.2	1808	1,466	60.00	150.00	300.00	750.00

Mint mark: L

C#	Date	Mintage	VG	Fine	VF	XF
151b.3	1808	4,393	50.00	100.00	225.00	400.00

Mint mark: A

C#	Date	Mintage	VG	Fine	VF	XF
161	1809	.034	30.00	75.00	125.00	250.00

Mint mark: A

C#	Date	Mintage	Fine	VF	XF	Unc
177.1	1817	.100	10.00	25.00	75.00	200.00
	1818	.028	20.00	50.00	100.00	300.00
	1819	.011	25.00	60.00	150.00	400.00
	1820	.012	25.00	60.00	150.00	400.00
	1821	.022	20.00	50.00	100.00	325.00
	1822	.036	20.00	50.00	100.00	250.00
	1823	.044	20.00	50.00	100.00	250.00
	1824	.083	15.00	30.00	75.00	175.00

Mint mark: B

C#	Date	Mintage	Fine	VF	XF	Unc
177.2	1817	.021	22.50	50.00	100.00	300.00
	1818	.016	25.00	60.00	110.00	350.00
	1819	.015	25.00	60.00	110.00	350.00
	1822	.030	22.50	50.00	100.00	325.00
	1823	.013	25.00	60.00	150.00	400.00
	1824	.018	22.50	55.00	110.00	350.00

Mint mark: BB

C#	Date	Mintage	Fine	VF	XF	Unc
177.3	1817	3,772	35.00	90.00	250.00	500.00

Mint mark: D

C#	Date	Mintage	Fine	VF	XF	Unc
177.4	1817	.012	25.00	50.00	100.00	300.00

Mint mark: I

C#	Date	Mintage	Fine	VF	XF	Unc
177.5	1817	.016	30.00	60.00	90.00	275.00
	1823	1,870	75.00	150.00	250.00	600.00

Mint mark: L

C#	Date	Mintage	Fine	VF	XF	Unc
177.6	1817	.014	25.00	50.00	100.00	300.00
	1823	.012	25.00	50.00	100.00	300.00
	1824	.031	20.00	40.00	100.00	300.00

Mint mark: M

C#	Date	Mintage	Fine	VF	XF	Unc
177.7	1817	4,314	35.00	90.00	250.00	500.00
	1823	3,994	40.00	100.00	260.00	525.00
	1824	7,774	35.00	75.00	175.00	425.00

Mint mark: MA

C#	Date	Mintage	Fine	VF	XF	Unc
177.8	1817	2,132	60.00	125.00	225.00	500.00

Mint mark: Q

C#	Date	Mintage	Fine	VF	XF	Unc
177.9	1817	.013	25.00	60.00	150.00	400.00
	1823	.011	25.00	60.00	150.00	400.00

Mint mark: T

C#	Date	Mintage	Fine	VF	XF	Unc
177.10	1817	7,606	35.00	75.00	175.00	500.00

Mint mark: W

C#	Date	Mintage	Fine	VF	XF	Unc
177.11	1817	.014	25.00	60.00	150.00	400.00
	1818	3,294	40.00	100.00	260.00	550.00
	1819	3,170	40.00	100.00	260.00	550.00
	1820	5,894	35.00	75.00	145.00	475.00
	1822	4,486	40.00	100.00	175.00	525.00
	1823	.016	25.00	50.00	120.00	350.00
	1824	.011	25.00	60.00	150.00	400.00

Mint mark: A

C#	Date	Mintage	Fine	VF	XF	Unc
185.1	1825	9,448	35.00	75.00	150.00	350.00
	1826	.083	15.00	30.00	75.00	175.00
	1827	.322	6.00	15.00	60.00	100.00
	1828	.446	6.00	15.00	60.00	100.00
	1829	.154	7.00	17.50	65.00	150.00
	1830	.659	6.00	15.00	40.00	100.00
	1830 reeded edge	Inc.Ab.	60.00	125.00	225.00	425.00

Mint mark: B

C#	Date	Mintage	Fine	VF	XF	Unc
185.2	1826	.023	20.00	35.00	75.00	225.00
	1827	.017	20.00	35.00	75.00	225.00
	1828	.023	20.00	35.00	75.00	225.00
	1829	.032	15.00	25.00	50.00	175.00

Mint mark: BB

C#	Date	Mintage	Fine	VF	XF	Unc
185.9	1827	1,567	60.00	175.00	300.00	550.00
	1828	.013	25.00	60.00	150.00	300.00
	1829	.014	25.00	60.00	150.00	300.00

Mint mark: D

C#	Date	Mintage	Fine	VF	XF	Unc
185.3	1826	.013	25.00	60.00	150.00	300.00
	1827	7,820	35.00	75.00	175.00	350.00
	1828	.013	25.00	60.00	150.00	300.00
	1829	.052	15.00	25.00	50.00	175.00

Mint mark: H

C#	Date	Mintage	Fine	VF	XF	Unc
185.11	1828	.016	20.00	35.00	75.00	225.00

Mint mark: I

C#	Date	Mintage	Fine	VF	XF	Unc
185.10	1827	828	—	—	—	—
	1828	2,226	45.00	125.00	250.00	385.00
	1829	.010	20.00	50.00	100.00	275.00

Mint mark: K

C#	Date	Mintage	Fine	VF	XF	Unc
185.12	1829	.027	20.00	35.00	75.00	200.00
	1830	.021	20.00	35.00	75.00	200.00

Mint mark: L

C#	Date	Mintage	Fine	VF	XF	Unc
185.4	1826	.011	20.00	50.00	100.00	275.00
	1827	7,582	35.00	85.00	175.00	300.00
	1828	.015	20.00	35.00	75.00	225.00
	1829	6,486	35.00	85.00	175.00	300.00
	1830	.015	20.00	35.00	75.00	225.00

Mint mark: M

C#	Date	Mintage	Fine	VF	XF	Unc
185.5	1826	4,861	40.00	100.00	175.00	350.00
	1827	4,292	40.00	100.00	175.00	350.00
	1828	.048	15.00	30.00	65.00	200.00
	1829	.014	20.00	35.00	75.00	225.00

Mint mark: Q

C#	Date	Mintage	Fine	VF	XF	Unc
185.6	1826	7,534	35.00	85.00	175.00	320.00
	1828	.013	20.00	35.00	75.00	225.00

Mint mark: T

C#	Date	Mintage	Fine	VF	XF	Unc
185.7	1826	1,753	—	—	—	—
	1828	6,316	25.00	75.00	175.00	320.00
	1829	6,481	25.00	75.00	175.00	320.00

Mint mark: W

C#	Date	Mintage	Fine	VF	XF	Unc
185.8	1826	.015	20.00	35.00	75.00	225.00
	1827	.022	20.00	35.00	75.00	200.00
	1828	.047	15.00	30.00	65.00	200.00
	1829	.108	10.00	20.00	50.00	125.00
	1830	.074	15.00	25.00	60.00	150.00

Mint mark: A

C#	Date	Mintage	Fine	VF	XF	Unc
196.1	1831	.075	15.00	25.00	60.00	175.00
	1832	.286	7.00	15.00	30.00	80.00
	1833	.155	8.00	18.00	35.00	90.00
	1834	.770	4.00	10.00	20.00	55.00
	1835	.801	4.00	10.00	20.00	55.00
	1836	.898	4.00	7.00	17.50	42.50
	1837	.830	4.00	7.00	17.50	42.50
	1838	.922	4.00	7.00	17.50	42.50
	1839	1.180	4.00	7.00	17.50	42.50
	1840	1.246	4.00	7.00	17.50	42.50
	1841	1.303	4.00	7.00	17.50	42.50
	1842	.647	4.00	7.00	17.50	42.50
	1843	.478	4.00	7.00	17.50	42.50
	1844	.816	4.00	7.00	17.50	42.50
	1845	.396	4.00	7.00	17.50	42.50

Mint mark: B

C#	Date	Mintage	Fine	VF	XF	Unc
196.2	1831	.052	6.00	12.00	27.50	75.00
	1832	.135	5.00	10.00	20.00	55.00
	1833	.080	5.00	10.00	20.00	65.00
	1834	.070	5.00	10.00	20.00	65.00
	1835	3 known	—	500.00	—	—
	1835 (error): PRANCAIS	Inc. Ab.	—	—	400.00	—
	1836	8,413	20.00	40.00	100.00	200.00
	1837	.094	5.00	10.00	20.00	55.00
	1838	.049	10.00	20.00	40.00	90.00
	1839	.053	10.00	20.00	40.00	90.00
	1840/30	1 known	—	750.00	—	—
	1840	.053	10.00	20.00	40.00	90.00
	1841	.289	4.00	8.00	20.00	55.00
	1842	.642	4.00	8.00	17.50	50.00
	1843	.762	4.00	8.00	17.50	50.00
	1844	.018	10.00	20.00	40.00	90.00
	1845	4.603	3.00	6.00	17.50	50.00

Mint mark: BB

C#	Date	Mintage	Fine	VF	XF	Unc
196.3	1831	3,629	30.00	65.00	125.00	250.00
	1832	.011	15.00	30.00	60.00	150.00
	1833	7,890	20.00	40.00	100.00	200.00
	1834	6,063	20.00	40.00	100.00	200.00
	1835	.010	10.00	20.00	40.00	100.00
	1836	.011	10.00	20.00	40.00	100.00
	1837	9,762	20.00	40.00	100.00	200.00
	1838	6,561	20.00	40.00	100.00	225.00
	1839	.013	10.00	20.00	45.00	110.00
	1844	.036	10.00	20.00	40.00	90.00
	1845	.051	10.00	20.00	40.00	90.00

Mint mark: D

C#	Date	Mintage	Fine	VF	XF	Unc
196.4	1831	.034	10.00	20.00	40.00	90.00
	1832	.141	6.00	12.00	28.00	75.00
	1833	.016	15.00	30.00	60.00	150.00
	1834	.030	6.00	12.00	27.50	75.00
	1835	.028	6.00	12.00	27.50	75.00
	1837	8,352	20.00	40.00	100.00	225.00
	1838	6,199	20.00	40.00	100.00	225.00
	1839	5,163	25.00	50.00	125.00	250.00
	1840	.015	15.00	30.00	60.00	150.00

Mint mark: H

C#	Date	Mintage	Fine	VF	XF	Unc
196.5	1831	.026	10.00	20.00	50.00	115.00
	1832	.040	10.00	20.00	40.00	90.00
	1833	.014	15.00	30.00	60.00	150.00
	1834	.046	10.00	20.00	40.00	90.00
	1835	9,989	20.00	40.00	100.00	225.00

Mint mark: I

C#	Date	Mintage	Fine	VF	XF	Unc
196.6	1831	967 pcs.	—	—	—	—
	1832	.034	10.00	20.00	50.00	115.00
	1833	.024	10.00	20.00	50.00	115.00
	1834	.040	6.00	12.00	27.50	75.00
	1835	.044	6.00	12.00	27.50	75.00

C#	Date	Mintage	Fine	VF	XF	Unc
	Mint mark: K					
196.7	1831	.036	6.00	12.00	27.50	75.00
	1832	.020	6.00	12.00	27.50	75.00
	1833	.022	6.00	12.00	27.50	75.00
	1834	.036	6.00	12.00	27.50	75.00
	1835	.041	6.00	12.00	27.50	75.00
	1836	9,500	20.00	40.00	100.00	200.00
	1837	.011	15.00	30.00	60.00	150.00
	1838	.016	15.00	30.00	60.00	150.00
	1839	.016	15.00	30.00	60.00	150.00
	1840	.030	10.00	20.00	40.00	90.00
	1841	.092	8.00	15.00	35.00	80.00
	1842	.023	10.00	20.00	50.00	115.00
	1843	.027	10.00	20.00	50.00	115.00
	1844	.023	10.00	20.00	50.00	115.00
	1845	.016	12.00	25.00	60.00	125.00
	Mint mark: L					
196.8	1831	6,182	20.00	40.00	100.00	225.00
	1832	.022	10.00	20.00	50.00	115.00
	1833	8,927	20.00	40.00	100.00	225.00
	1834	8,789	20.00	40.00	100.00	225.00
	Mint mark: M					
196.9	1831	6,831	20.00	40.00	100.00	225.00
	1832	.035	6.00	12.00	27.50	75.00
	1833	.017	15.00	30.00	60.00	150.00
	1834	8,218	20.00	40.00	100.00	225.00
	1835	.011	15.00	30.00	60.00	150.00
	Mint mark: MA					
196.13	1832	1 known	—	—	Rare	—
	1833	3,452	—	—	—	—
	Mint mark: Q					
196.10	1831	.011	15.00	30.00	60.00	150.00
	1832	.018	12.00	25.00	50.00	125.00
	1834	.014	15.00	30.00	60.00	150.00
	Mint mark: T					
196.12	1832	8,486	20.00	40.00	100.00	225.00
	1833	.018	12.00	25.00	50.00	125.00
	1834	.034	7.00	15.00	30.00	80.00
	Mint mark: W					
196.11	1831	.160	5.00	10.00	20.00	50.00
	1832	.218	5.00	10.00	20.00	60.00
	1833	.141	5.00	10.00	20.00	60.00
	1834	.404	4.00	8.00	18.00	45.00
	1835	.133	5.00	10.00	20.00	55.00
	1836	.089	6.00	12.00	30.00	70.00
	1837	.168	5.00	10.00	20.00	55.00
	1838/3	.100	—	—	—	—
	1838	Inc. Ab.	5.00	10.00	20.00	55.00
	1839	.114	5.00	10.00	20.00	55.00
	1840	.042	10.00	20.00	40.00	90.00
	1841	.168	5.00	10.00	20.00	55.00
	1842	.091	5.00	10.00	20.00	55.00
	1843	.073	5.00	10.00	20.00	55.00
	1844	.367	4.00	8.00	17.50	50.00
	1845	.330	4.00	8.00	17.50	50.00

25 CENTIMES

1.2500 g, .900 SILVER, .0362 oz ASW

C#	Date	Mintage	Fine	VF	XF	Unc
	Mint mark: A					
197.1	1845	Inc. Ab.	5.00	10.00	25.00	85.00
	1846	1.748	4.00	8.00	18.00	55.00
	1847	3.000	3.00	6.00	15.00	45.00
	1848	.142	5.00	10.00	25.00	85.00
	Mint mark: B					
197.2	1845	Inc. Ab.	3.00	6.00	12.50	45.00
	Mint mark: BB					
197.3	1845	Inc. Ab.	5.00	10.00	35.00	125.00
	1846	7,922	20.00	40.00	100.00	250.00
	1847	9,939	20.00	40.00	100.00	250.00
	1848	5,886	25.00	75.00	150.00	300.00
	Mint mark: K					
197.4	1845	Inc. Ab.	15.00	30.00	70.00	200.00
	1846	.012	20.00	40.00	100.00	275.00
	1847	3,905	30.00	75.00	200.00	350.00
	Mint mark: W					
197.5	1845	Inc. Ab.	5.00	10.00	25.00	85.00
	1846	.039	5.00	10.00	35.00	125.00

NICKEL
Mint: Paris - w/o mint mark.
Third Republic

Y#	Date	Mintage	Fine	VF	XF	Unc
69	1903	16.000	.25	1.00	3.00	16.00

Y#	Date	Mintage	Fine	VF	XF	Unc
70	1904	16.000	.25	.75	2.00	15.00
	1905	8.000	.50	1.50	3.50	20.00

Y#	Date	Mintage	Fine	VF	XF	Unc
76	1914(-)	.941	3.00	6.00	10.00	25.00
	1915(-)	.535	4.00	7.00	12.00	35.00
	1916(-)	.100	20.00	35.00	60.00	100.00
	1917(-)	.065	35.00	65.00	100.00	200.00

COPPER-NICKEL

Y#	Date	Mintage	Fine	VF	XF	Unc
76a	1917	3.085	3.00	8.00	18.00	30.00
	1918	18.330	.25	.50	1.50	6.00
	1919	5.106	1.00	2.50	3.50	10.00
	1920	18.108	.15	.50	1.00	5.00
	1921	18.531	.15	.50	1.00	5.00
	1922	17.766	.15	.50	1.00	5.00
	1923	19.718	.15	.50	1.00	5.00
	1924	24.535	.15	.50	1.00	5.00
	1925	17.807	.15	.50	1.00	5.00
	1926	13.226	.15	.50	1.00	5.00
	1927	13.465	.15	.50	1.00	5.00
	1928	9.960	.25	.50	1.50	6.00
	1929	12.887	.15	.50	1.00	4.00
	1930	28.363	.15	.50	1.00	4.00
	1931	22.121	.15	.50	1.00	4.00
	1932	30.364	.15	.50	1.00	4.00
	1933	28.562	.15	.50	1.00	4.00
	1936	4.657	2.00	5.00	12.00	25.00
	1937	7.780	.25	.50	1.50	6.00

NICKEL-BRONZE

Y#	Date	Mintage	Fine	VF	XF	Unc
76b	.1938.	5.170	.25	.50	1.00	3.00
	.1939. thick flan (1.55mm)	42.964	.15	.35	.75	2.00
	.1939. thin flan (1.35mm)	Inc. Ab.	.15	.35	.75	2.00
	.1940.	3.446	6.00	12.00	18.00	35.00

DEMI (1/2) FRANC

2.5000 g, .900 SILVER, .0723 oz ASW
Mint mark: A
Obv. leg: BONAPARTE PREMIER CONSUL.

C#	Date	Mintage	VG	Fine	VF	XF
142.1	ANXI	.031	20.00	50.00	150.00	275.00
	AN12	.280	10.00	20.00	50.00	200.00
	Mint mark: BB					
142.2	AN12	2,125	75.00	150.00	325.00	650.00
	Mint mark: D					
142.3	AN12	.015	25.00	60.00	175.00	300.00
	Mint mark: G					
142.4	AN12	7,407	75.00	175.00	350.00	750.00
	Mint mark: H					
142.5	AN12	1,988	100.00	175.00	350.00	800.00
	Mint mark: I					
142.6	AN12	.416	9.00	18.00	40.00	150.00
	Mint mark: K					
142.7	AN12	.012	30.00	70.00	200.00	375.00
	Mint mark: L					
142.8	AN12	.067	10.00	25.00	65.00	200.00
	Mint mark: M					
142.9	AN12	.136	10.00	20.00	50.00	200.00
	Mint mark: MA					
142.10	AN12	.026	20.00	50.00	125.00	250.00
	Mint mark: Q					
142.11	AN12	.054	15.00	40.00	100.00	225.00
	Mint mark: T					
142.12	AN12	.017	25.00	50.00	175.00	300.00
	Mint mark: U					
142.13	AN12	3,150	80.00	200.00	400.00	850.00
	Common date				Unc.	350.00

Mint mark: A
Obv. leg: NAPOLEON EMPEREUR.

C#	Date	Mintage	VG	Fine	VF	XF
152.1	AN12	.039	12.00	25.00	60.00	250.00
	AN13	.427	9.00	18.00	40.00	150.00
	AN14	.020	25.00	50.00	125.00	350.00
	Mint mark: BB					
152.2	AN12	1,825	50.00	125.00	275.00	500.00
	AN13	895 pcs.	100.00	250.00	400.00	950.00
	Mint mark: D					
152.8	AN13	2,402	35.00	70.00	150.00	350.00
	Mint mark: G					
152.9	AN13	1,181	—	—	Rare	—
	Mint mark: H					
152.3	AN12	7,286	25.00	60.00	125.00	300.00
	AN13	5,036	30.00	75.00	150.00	350.00
	Mint mark: I					
152.4	AN12	.022	20.00	50.00	100.00	225.00
	AN13	.206	12.00	22.00	50.00	200.00
	Mint mark: K					
152.5	AN12	.019	20.00	50.00	100.00	250.00
	AN13	.037	18.00	40.00	80.00	200.00
	AN14	1,757	—	—	Rare	—
	Mint mark: L					
152.10	AN13	.046	15.00	30.00	65.00	180.00
	AN14	3,889	50.00	100.00	225.00	500.00
	Mint mark: M					
152.6	AN12	.099	12.00	25.00	60.00	175.00
	AN13	.212	10.00	20.00	50.00	150.00
	Mint mark: MA					
152.11	AN13	6,103	30.00	75.00	150.00	350.00
	Mint mark: Q					
152.12	AN13	.034	18.00	40.00	80.00	200.00
	Mint mark: T					
152.7	AN12	3,735	35.00	70.00	150.00	350.00
	AN13	6,140	30.00	70.00	140.00	300.00
	Mint mark: U					
152.13	AN13	1,662	50.00	90.00	200.00	400.00
	AN14	—	100.00	200.00	400.00	800.00
	Common date				Unc.	350.00
	Mint mark: A					
152.14	1806	.156	12.00	25.00	60.00	175.00
	Mint mark: I					
152.15	1806	7,027	30.00	75.00	150.00	350.00
	1807	3,848	40.00	90.00	175.00	400.00
	Mint mark: K					
152.16	1806	1,673	50.00	100.00	200.00	450.00
	1807	2,983	40.00	90.00	175.00	400.00
	Mint mark: L					
152.17	1806	.042	15.00	30.00	75.00	200.00
	1807/6	.017	20.00	40.00	100.00	225.00
	1807	Inc. Ab.	20.00	40.00	100.00	250.00
	Mint mark: M					
152.20	1807	1,791	— Reported, not confirmed			
	Mint mark: Q					
152.18	1806	.015	20.00	40.00	100.00	250.00
	1807	.014	20.00	40.00	100.00	250.00
	Mint mark: U					
152.19	1806	9,592	30.00	75.00	150.00	350.00
	1807	4,448	40.00	90.00	175.00	400.00
	Common date				Unc.	325.00

Mint mark: A
Negro head.

C#	Date	Mintage	VG	Fine	VF	XF
152a	1807	.058	75.00	175.00	375.00	800.00

Laureate head.

C#	Date	Mintage	VG	Fine	VF	XF
152b.1	1807	.046	60.00	125.00	250.00	500.00
	1808	6.606	5.00	10.00	20.00	75.00
	Mint mark: B					
152b.2	1808	.559	8.00	15.00	30.00	100.00
	Mint mark: BB					
152b.3	1808	1.596	5.00	10.00	25.00	75.00
	Mint mark: D					
152b.4	1808	.871	6.00	12.00	30.00	90.00
	Mint mark: H					
152b.5	1808	.336	8.00	18.00	45.00	100.00
	Mint mark: I					
152b.6	1808	.298	10.00	20.00	40.00	100.00
	Mint mark: K					
152b.7	1808	.363	8.00	18.00	45.00	100.00
	Mint mark: L					
152b.8	1808	3,394	50.00	100.00	200.00	375.00
	Mint mark: M					
152b.9	1808	.054	20.00	50.00	100.00	200.00
	Mint mark: MA					
152b.10	1808	.028	30.00	60.00	125.00	250.00
	Mint mark: Q					
152b.11	1808	.289	10.00	20.00	40.00	100.00
	Mint mark: T					
152b.12	1808	.128	12.00	25.00	50.00	125.00
	Mint mark: U					
152b.13	1808	3,339	50.00	100.00	200.00	375.00
	Mint mark: W					
152b.14	1808	1.069	5.00	10.00	25.00	75.00
	Common date				Unc.	200.00

C#	Date	Mintage	VG	Fine	VF	XF
	Mint mark: A					
162.1	1809	1.680	5.00	10.00	20.00	75.00
	1810	1.362	5.00	10.00	20.00	75.00
	1811	1.860	5.00	10.00	20.00	75.00
	1812	1.720	5.00	10.00	20.00	75.00
	1813	.627	8.00	15.00	30.00	85.00
	1814	.107	10.00	20.00	50.00	100.00
	Mint mark: B					
162.2	1809	.014	15.00	30.00	90.00	225.00
	1810	.285	8.00	15.00	35.00	100.00
	1811	.252	8.00	15.00	35.00	100.00
	1812	.192	9.00	18.00	40.00	115.00
	Mint mark: BB					
162.10	1810	.011	20.00	40.00	100.00	250.00
	1811	.037	10.00	22.00	55.00	140.00
	Mint mark: CL					
162.16	1813	8,385	50.00	100.00	225.00	550.00
	Mint mark: D					
162.3	1809	.043	10.00	20.00	45.00	125.00
	1810	.071	9.00	18.00	40.00	115.00
	1811	.221	8.00	15.00	35.00	100.00
	1812	.155	8.00	15.00	35.00	100.00
	1813	.110	8.00	18.00	45.00	125.00
	Mint mark: H					
162.11	1810	3,563	40.00	80.00	175.00	350.00
	1811	.120	8.00	15.00	35.00	100.00
	1812	.270	6.00	12.00	30.00	90.00
	1813	.138	8.00	15.00	35.00	100.00
	Mint mark: I					
162.13	1811	.134	8.00	15.00	35.00	100.00
	1812	.137	8.00	15.00	35.00	100.00
	1813	.097	9.00	18.00	40.00	115.00
	Mint mark: K					
162.4	1809	.043	10.00	20.00	45.00	125.00
	1810	.041	10.00	20.00	45.00	125.00
	1811	.016	15.00	30.00	75.00	175.00
	1812	.034	12.00	25.00	60.00	150.00
	1813	.058	10.00	20.00	50.00	125.00
	Mint mark: L					
162.12	1810	.055	10.00	22.00	50.00	125.00
	1810(Tr)	I.A.	— Reported, not confirmed			
	1811	.095	8.00	17.50	40.00	100.00
	1812	.052	10.00	20.00	50.00	125.00
	1813	.044	10.00	22.00	55.00	140.00
	Mint mark: M					
162.5	1809	.021	12.00	25.00	65.00	160.00
	1810	.033	12.00	25.00	60.00	150.00
	1811	.049	10.00	22.00	55.00	140.00
	1812	.105	8.00	17.50	40.00	110.00
	1813	.159	7.00	15.00	35.00	100.00
	1814	.036	40.00	75.00	150.00	350.00
	Mint mark: MA					
162.6	1809	3,176	40.00	75.00	150.00	400.00
	1810	.011	20.00	40.00	100.00	300.00
	1811	.069	10.00	20.00	50.00	125.00
	1812	.052	10.00	20.00	50.00	125.00
	1813	.070	8.00	17.50	45.00	120.00

C#	Date	Mintage	VG	Fine	VF	XF
	Mint mark: Q					
162.7	1809	.070	10.00	22.00	50.00	125.00
	1811	.126	7.50	15.00	35.00	100.00
	1812	.106	8.00	17.50	40.00	110.00
	1813	.044	10.00	22.00	50.00	140.00
	1814	—	— Reported, not confirmed			
	Mint mark: T					
162.14	1811	.114	8.00	17.50	40.00	100.00
	1812	.081	7.00	15.00	45.00	120.00
	1813	.053	10.00	20.00	50.00	125.00
	Mint mark: U					
162.8	1809	5,853	30.00	65.00	125.00	300.00
	1811	.039	12.00	25.00	60.00	150.00
	Mint mark: W					
162.9	1809	.314	6.00	12.00	30.00	100.00
	1810	.240	7.00	14.00	32.00	110.00
	1811	.246	7.00	14.00	32.00	110.00
	1812	.337	6.00	12.00	30.00	100.00
	1813	.058	10.00	20.00	50.00	125.00
	Mint mark: Flag					
162.15	1812	5,084	50.00	100.00	225.00	500.00
	1813	6,894	50.00	100.00	225.00	500.00
	Common date				Unc.	275.00

C#	Date	Mintage	VG	Fine	VF	XF
	Mint mark: A					
178.1	1816	.261	8.00	16.00	40.00	125.00
	1817	.236	8.00	16.00	40.00	125.00
	1818	.050	10.00	20.00	55.00	140.00
	1819	.047	10.00	22.00	55.00	140.00
	1820	.043	10.00	22.00	55.00	140.00
	1821	.082	8.00	17.50	45.00	125.00
	1822	.584	6.00	12.00	35.00	90.00
	1823	.500	6.00	12.00	35.00	90.00
	1824	.613	6.00	12.00	35.00	90.00
	Mint mark: B					
178.2	1816	.019	15.00	30.00	60.00	150.00
	1817	8,759	20.00	40.00	80.00	200.00
	1818	7,803	20.00	40.00	80.00	200.00
	1822	.034	12.00	25.00	55.00	140.00
	1823	.018	15.00	30.00	60.00	150.00
	1824	.042	10.00	22.00	55.00	140.00
	Mint mark: D					
178.11	1824	.018	15.00	30.00	60.00	150.00
	Mint mark: H					
178.9	1817	.086	8.00	17.50	40.00	110.00
	1818	.014	16.00	35.00	70.00	165.00
	1819	2,463	30.00	60.00	125.00	250.00
	1822	1,332	35.00	75.00	125.00	300.00
	1823	3,558	25.00	50.00	110.00	250.00
	1824	.020	15.00	30.00	60.00	150.00
	Mint mark: I					
178.3	1816	2,692	30.00	60.00	125.00	250.00
	1823	3,113	25.00	50.00	110.00	250.00
	1824	.011	16.00	35.00	70.00	165.00
	Mint mark: K					
178.10	1817	.213	8.00	16.00	40.00	125.00
	1820	7,794	20.00	40.00	80.00	200.00
	1823	8,136	20.00	40.00	80.00	200.00
	1824	.053	10.00	20.00	55.00	140.00
	Mint mark: L					
178.4	1816	3,273	25.00	50.00	110.00	250.00
	1817	8,767	20.00	40.00	80.00	200.00
	1818	2,816	30.00	60.00	125.00	250.00
	1823	.036	12.00	25.00	55.00	140.00
	1824	.056	12.00	25.00	60.00	150.00
	Mint mark: M					
178.5	1816	4,682	20.00	40.00	90.00	225.00
	1823	8,632	20.00	40.00	80.00	200.00
	1824	.011	16.00	35.00	70.00	165.00
	Mint mark: Q					
178.6	1816	.012	16.00	35.00	70.00	165.00
	1819	4,488	20.00	40.00	90.00	250.00
	1820	.017	15.00	30.00	60.00	150.00
	1823	.101	9.00	18.00	45.00	135.00
	1824	.170	8.00	16.00	40.00	125.00
	Mint mark: T					
178.7	1816	5,964	20.00	40.00	90.00	225.00
	1819	1,741	35.00	65.00	150.00	300.00
	Mint mark: W					
178.8	1816	8,728	20.00	40.00	80.00	200.00
	1817	.025	12.00	25.00	60.00	150.00
	1818	7,811	20.00	40.00	80.00	200.00
	1819	5,166	20.00	40.00	90.00	250.00
	1821	.037	12.00	25.00	55.00	140.00
	1822	.015	12.00	25.00	60.00	150.00
	1823	.070	8.00	17.50	45.00	125.00
	1824	.102	9.00	18.00	45.00	135.00
	Common date				Unc.	250.00

C#	Date	Mintage	VG	Fine	VF	XF
	Mint mark: A					
186.1	1825	.011	30.00	60.00	125.00	250.00
	1826	.361	6.00	12.00	35.00	90.00
	1827	.786	4.00	10.00	25.00	75.00
	1828	.508	4.00	10.00	25.00	75.00
	1829	.538	4.00	10.00	25.00	75.00
	1830	.377	5.00	12.00	30.00	80.00
	Mint mark: B					
186.2	1826	6,019	20.00	45.00	90.00	225.00
	1827	.019	12.00	25.00	55.00	140.00
	1828	.056	10.00	20.00	40.00	115.00
	1829	.116	6.00	12.00	35.00	100.00
	Mint mark: BB					
186.3	1826	.011	15.00	30.00	60.00	150.00
	1827	2,476	30.00	60.00	120.00	250.00
	1828	.023	10.00	20.00	45.00	125.00
	1829	.022	10.00	20.00	45.00	125.00
	Mint mark: D					
186.4	1826	.020	12.00	25.00	50.00	125.00
	1827	5,629	25.00	50.00	100.00	200.00
	1828	.083	7.50	15.00	35.00	100.00
	1829	.028	10.00	20.00	45.00	120.00
	Mint mark: H					
186.5	1826	.023	10.00	20.00	45.00	120.00
	1827	.014	15.00	30.00	60.00	150.00
	1828	.026	10.00	20.00	45.00	120.00
	1829	.058	7.50	15.00	35.00	100.00
	Mint mark: I					
186.6	1826	1,435	30.00	65.00	150.00	300.00
	1827	1,520	30.00	65.00	150.00	300.00
	1828	2,526	30.00	65.00	150.00	300.00
	1829	.015	12.00	25.00	50.00	125.00
	Mint mark: K					
186.7	1826	.017	12.00	25.00	50.00	125.00
	1827	9,597	22.00	45.00	80.00	200.00
	1828	.027	10.00	20.00	45.00	125.00
	1829	.037	8.00	17.50	40.00	110.00
	1830	.022	10.00	20.00	45.00	125.00
	Mint mark: L					
186.8	1826	.036	8.00	17.50	40.00	100.00
	1827	.031	8.00	17.50	40.00	110.00
	1828	.027	10.00	20.00	45.00	120.00
	1829	.016	12.00	25.00	50.00	125.00
	1830	.018	12.00	25.00	50.00	125.00
	Mint mark: M					
186.9	1826	9,192	20.00	40.00	75.00	200.00
	1827	7,288	22.00	45.00	85.00	225.00
	1828	.072	7.50	15.00	35.00	100.00
	1829	.016	12.00	25.00	50.00	125.00
	1830	7,826	22.00	45.00	85.00	225.00
	Mint mark: MA					
186.13	1829	.032	10.00	22.00	50.00	125.00
	Mint mark: Q					
186.10	1826	.063	7.50	15.00	35.00	100.00
	1827	.011	15.00	30.00	60.00	150.00
	1828	.030	8.00	17.50	40.00	110.00
	1829	.019	10.00	20.00	50.00	125.00
	Mint mark: T					
186.12	1827	8,815	20.00	40.00	75.00	200.00
	1828	.018	12.00	25.00	50.00	125.00
	1829	3,609	25.00	50.00	100.00	250.00
	Mint mark: W					
186.11	1826	.038	8.00	17.50	40.00	100.00
	1827	.030	8.00	17.50	40.00	100.00
	1828	.170	6.00	12.00	30.00	90.00
	1829	.126	6.00	12.00	30.00	90.00
	1830	.131	6.00	12.00	30.00	90.00
	Common date				Unc.	250.00

Mint mark: A

C#	Date	Mintage	Fine	VF	XF	Unc
198.1	1831	.110	7.50	15.00	35.00	100.00
	1832	.345	6.00	12.00	30.00	90.00
	1833	.272	6.00	12.00	30.00	90.00
	1834	.419	6.00	12.00	30.00	90.00
	1835	.831	6.00	12.00	30.00	75.00
	1836	.432	6.00	12.00	30.00	90.00
	1837	.137	7.50	15.00	35.00	100.00
	1838	.385	6.00	12.00	30.00	90.00
	1839	.636	6.00	12.00	30.00	90.00
	1840	1.107	5.00	10.00	25.00	90.00
	1841	1.119	5.00	10.00	25.00	90.00
	1842	.338	7.50	15.00	35.00	100.00
	1843	.152	7.50	15.00	35.00	100.00
	1844	.196	7.50	15.00	35.00	100.00
	1845	.494	7.50	15.00	35.00	90.00

C#	Date	Mintage	Fine	VF	XF	Unc
		Mint mark: B				
198.2	1831	.136	7.50	15.00	35.00	100.00
	1832	.256	6.00	12.00	30.00	100.00
	1833	.093	7.50	15.00	35.00	110.00
	1834	.086	9.00	17.50	35.00	110.00
	1835	.054	10.00	20.00	45.00	125.00
	1836	.043	10.00	20.00	45.00	125.00
	1837	.158	7.50	15.00	35.00	110.00
	1838	.084	9.00	17.50	35.00	110.00
	1839	.116	9.00	17.50	35.00	110.00
	1840	.117	9.00	17.50	35.00	110.00
	1841	.831	6.00	12.00	30.00	90.00
	1842	.250	7.50	15.00	35.00	95.00
	1843	.213	7.50	15.00	35.00	95.00
	1844	.046	10.00	20.00	45.00	125.00
	1845	2.501	5.00	10.00	25.00	75.00
		Mint mark: BB				
198.3	1831	2,767	30.00	60.00	120.00	250.00
	1832	.010	15.00	30.00	60.00	150.00
	1833	.029	10.00	20.00	45.00	125.00
	1834	.020	10.00	20.00	45.00	125.00
	1835	5,346	22.00	45.00	85.00	225.00
	1836	.022	10.00	20.00	45.00	125.00
	1837	5,952	22.00	45.00	85.00	225.00
	1838	5,820	22.00	45.00	85.00	225.00
	1839	6,896	20.00	40.00	75.00	200.00
	1840	770 pcs.	—	—	—	—
	1841	.010	15.00	30.00	60.00	150.00
	1842	.308	7.50	15.00	30.00	90.00
	1844	.025	10.00	20.00	45.00	125.00
	1845	.044	10.00	20.00	45.00	125.00
		Mint mark: D				
198.4	1831	.016	10.00	20.00	45.00	125.00
	1832	.206	7.50	15.00	30.00	90.00
	1833	.032	10.00	20.00	45.00	125.00
	1834	.064	9.00	18.00	35.00	110.00
	1835	.015	15.00	30.00	60.00	150.00
	1836	8,706	20.00	40.00	75.00	200.00
	1837	7,556	20.00	40.00	75.00	200.00
	1838	2,432	25.00	50.00	100.00	250.00
	1840	.019	10.00	20.00	45.00	125.00
		Mint mark: H				
198.5	1831	.018	10.00	20.00	45.00	125.00
	1832	.077	9.00	18.00	35.00	110.00
	1833	.043	10.00	20.00	45.00	125.00
	1834	.086	9.00	18.00	35.00	110.00
		Mint mark: I				
198.6	1831	.013	15.00	30.00	60.00	150.00
	1832	.026	10.00	20.00	45.00	125.00
	1833	.049	8.00	18.00	35.00	100.00
	1834	.025	10.00	20.00	45.00	125.00
	1835	.045	8.00	18.00	35.00	100.00
		Mint mark: K				
198.7	1831	.035	10.00	20.00	45.00	125.00
	1832	.040	8.00	18.00	35.00	100.00
	1833	.029	10.00	20.00	45.00	125.00
	1834	.069	8.00	18.00	35.00	100.00
	1835	.050	8.00	18.00	35.00	100.00
	1836	.015	15.00	30.00	60.00	150.00
	1837	.026	10.00	20.00	45.00	125.00
	1838	.017	12.00	25.00	50.00	135.00
	1839	.018	12.00	25.00	50.00	135.00
	1840	.043	8.00	18.00	35.00	100.00
	1841	.026	10.00	20.00	45.00	125.00
	1842	.035	8.00	18.00	35.00	100.00
	1843	.034	8.00	18.00	35.00	100.00
	1844	.023	10.00	20.00	45.00	125.00
	1845	.022	10.00	20.00	45.00	125.00
		Mint mark: L				
198.8	1831	4,723	22.00	45.00	85.00	225.00
	1832	.034	8.00	18.00	35.00	100.00
	1833	.016	12.00	25.00	50.00	135.00
	1834	.010	15.00	30.00	60.00	150.00
		Mint mark: M				
198.9	1831	8,289	20.00	40.00	75.00	200.00
	1832	.092	9.00	18.00	35.00	110.00
	1833	.026	10.00	20.00	45.00	125.00
	1834	.019	10.00	20.00	45.00	125.00
	1835	.023	10.00	20.00	45.00	125.00
	1836	6,173	22.00	45.00	85.00	225.00
		Mint mark: MA				
198.10	1831	—	400.00	—	—	—
	1832	.052	8.00	18.00	35.00	100.00
	1834	—	—	—	—	—
	1835	.029	10.00	20.00	45.00	125.00
		Mint mark: Q				
198.11	1831	.012	15.00	30.00	60.00	150.00
	1832	.021	10.00	20.00	45.00	125.00
	1833	.055	8.00	18.00	35.00	100.00
	1834	1,824	200.00	400.00	—	—
		Mint mark: T				
198.12	1831	5,573	22.00	45.00	85.00	225.00
	1832	.033	8.00	18.00	35.00	100.00
	1833	.014	15.00	30.00	60.00	150.00
	1834	.055	8.00	18.00	35.00	100.00
		Mint mark: W				
198.13	1831	.125	8.00	15.00	35.00	100.00
	1832	.427	6.00	12.00	25.00	90.00
	1833	.151	8.00	15.00	35.00	100.00
	1834	.683	6.00	12.00	25.00	90.00
	1835	.183	8.00	15.00	35.00	100.00
	1836	.087	8.00	15.00	35.00	100.00
	1837	.267	7.00	14.00	30.00	95.00

C#	Date	Mintage	Fine	VF	XF	Unc
198.13	1838	.132	8.00	15.00	35.00	100.00
	1839	.119	8.00	15.00	35.00	100.00
	1840	.079	9.00	18.00	40.00	110.00
	1841	.234	7.00	14.00	30.00	95.00
	1842	.215	7.00	14.00	30.00	95.00
	1843	.233	7.00	14.00	30.00	95.00
	1844	.408	6.00	12.00	25.00	90.00
	1845	.525	6.00	12.00	25.00	75.00

50 CENTIMES

2.5000 g, .900 SILVER, .0723 oz ASW

C#	Date	Mintage	Fine	VF	XF	Unc
		Mint mark: A				
199.1	1845	.494	10.00	20.00	40.00	90.00
	1846	3.165	7.50	15.00	30.00	80.00
	1847	3.437	7.50	15.00	30.00	80.00
	1848	.218	10.00	20.00	40.00	90.00
		Mint mark: B				
199.2	1845	Inc. C198.2	7.50	15.00	30.00	75.00
	1846	1.000	7.50	15.00	30.00	75.00
		Mint mark: BB				
199.3	1845	Inc. C198.3	12.00	25.00	50.00	135.00
	1846	.017	12.00	25.00	50.00	135.00
	1847	.044	10.00	20.00	40.00	100.00
	1848	.018	12.00	25.00	50.00	135.00
		Mint mark: K				
199.4	1845	Inc. C198.7	35.00	70.00	150.00	300.00
	1846	.022	10.00	20.00	45.00	125.00
	1847	8,915	25.00	50.00	110.00	250.00
		Mint mark: W				
199.5	1845	Inc. C198.13	7.00	15.00	30.00	90.00
	1846	.070	10.00	25.00	40.00	100.00

Mint mark: A
Second Republic

Y#	Date	Mintage	Fine	VF	XF	Unc
3.1	1849	2,655	150.00	300.00	600.00	1000.
	1850	2.165	8.00	18.00	40.00	150.00
	1851	.850	15.00	35.00	100.00	175.00
	1851	—	—	—	Proof	800.00
		Mint mark: BB				
3.2	1850	.040	40.00	110.00	250.00	450.00
		Mint mark: K				
3.3	1850	.031	60.00	125.00	275.00	600.00

Mint mark: A
President Louis-Napoleon

Y#	Date	Mintage	Fine	VF	XF	Unc
11	1852	1.010	35.00	90.00	150.00	325.00

Second Empire

Y#	Date	Mintage	Fine	VF	XF	Unc
23.1	1853	.154	35.00	90.00	200.00	450.00
	1854	1.080	15.00	30.00	75.00	175.00
	1855	.400	25.00	60.00	125.00	250.00
	1856	1.436	15.00	30.00	75.00	175.00
	1857	1.632	15.00	30.00	75.00	175.00
	1858	5.559	8.00	18.00	40.00	125.00
	1859	3.880	9.00	20.00	45.00	135.00
	1860(h)	2.657	10.00	22.00	50.00	150.00
	1862	1.549	15.00	30.00	75.00	175.00
		Mint mark: BB				
23.2	1856	1.196	15.00	30.00	75.00	175.00
	1859	1.112	15.00	30.00	75.00	175.00
	1860	1.555	15.00	30.00	75.00	175.00
	1861	.355	30.00	80.00	175.00	400.00
	1862	1.007	20.00	50.00	125.00	250.00
	1863	.137	45.00	120.00	250.00	500.00
		Mint mark: D				
23.3	1856	1.246	15.00	30.00	75.00	175.00

2.5000 g, .835 SILVER, .0671 oz ASW

Y#	Date	Mintage	Fine	VF	XF	Unc
		Mint mark: A				
29.1	1864	7.598	5.00	10.00	20.00	60.00
	1865	7.398	5.00	10.00	20.00	60.00
	1866	5.921	6.00	12.00	25.00	75.00
	1867	14.528	3.00	6.00	15.00	40.00
	1868	2.789	8.00	18.00	40.00	100.00
		Mint mark: BB				
29.2	1864	4.626	6.00	12.00	25.00	75.00
	1865	5.175	6.00	12.00	25.00	75.00
	1866	5.256	6.00	12.00	25.00	75.00
	1867	9.992	5.00	10.00	20.00	60.00
	1868	Inc. Be.	40.00	100.00	200.00	400.00
	1869	1.800	30.00	75.00	150.00	250.00
		Mint mark: K				
29.3	1864	1.828	15.00	35.00	75.00	150.00
	1865	4.901	6.00	12.00	25.00	75.00
	1866	3.500	8.00	16.00	35.00	100.00
	1867	4.692	6.00	12.00	25.00	75.00

Mint mark: A
Third Republic

Y#	Date	Mintage	Fine	VF	XF	Unc
48.1	1871	.236	15.00	40.00	100.00	225.00
	1872	4.243	4.00	10.00	25.00	60.00
	1873	.926	10.00	25.00	60.00	125.00
	1874	1.228	8.00	15.00	35.00	80.00
	1878	30 pcs.	—	—	Proof	2250.
	1881	5.391	2.00	4.00	15.00	40.00
	1882	2.320	3.00	6.00	20.00	50.00
	1886	.309	15.00	40.00	100.00	225.00
	1887	1.866	6.00	12.00	25.00	65.00
	1888	4.517	1.50	3.00	15.00	40.00
	1889	100 pcs.	—	—	Proof	2000.
	1894	3.600	1.50	3.00	15.00	40.00
	1895	7.200	1.50	3.00	10.00	25.00
		Mint mark: K				
48.2	1871	.723	8.00	15.00	40.00	85.00
	1872	1.643	7.00	14.00	30.00	70.00
	1873	.166	100.00	250.00	450.00	800.00

Mint: Paris - w/o mint mark.

Y#	Date	Mintage	Fine	VF	XF	Unc
62	1897	.088	30.00	75.00	125.00	200.00
	1897	—	—	—	Proof	300.00
	1898	30.000	1.00	2.00	10.00	20.00
	1898	—	—	—	Proof	300.00
	1899	18.000	1.50	3.00	8.00	25.00
	1900	9.195	3.00	6.00	15.00	40.00
	1900	—	—	—	Proof	300.00
	1901	4.960	3.00	6.00	18.00	50.00
	1902	3.778	4.00	8.00	20.00	55.00
	1903	2.222	15.00	30.00	70.00	175.00
	1904	4.000	3.00	6.00	15.00	40.00
	1905	2.381	8.00	15.00	30.00	100.00
	1906	2.679	4.00	8.00	20.00	55.00
	1907	7.332	3.00	6.00	15.00	40.00
	1908	14.304	1.00	2.00	5.00	20.00
	1909	9.900	1.00	2.00	5.00	20.00
	1910	15.923	.75	1.50	4.00	15.00
	1911	1.330	25.00	60.00	150.00	275.00
	1912	16.000	.50	1.00	2.00	8.00
	1913	14.000	.50	1.00	2.00	8.00
	1914	9.657	.50	1.00	2.00	9.00
	1915	20.893	.50	1.00	1.50	5.00
	1916	52.963	.50	1.00	1.50	4.00
	1917	48.629	.50	1.00	1.50	4.00
	1918	36.492	.50	1.00	1.50	4.00
	1919	24.299	.50	1.00	1.50	4.00
	1920	8.509	1.00	2.00	4.00	10.00

ALUMINUM-BRONZE

Y#	Date	Mintage	Fine	VF	XF	Unc
77	1921	8.692	2.00	4.00	10.00	25.00
	1922	86.226	.15	.25	1.50	6.00
	1923	119.584	.15	.25	1.00	4.00
	1924	97.036	.15	.25	1.50	5.00
	1925	48.017	.25	.50	2.00	7.00
	1926	46.447	.25	.50	2.00	7.00

Y#	Date	Mintage	Fine	VF	XF	Unc
77	1927	23.703	.75	2.00	4.00	10.00
	1928	10.329	2.00	4.00	10.00	20.00
	1929	6.669	4.00	10.00	20.00	35.00
80.1	1931	62.775	.15	.25	1.00	4.00
	1932	108.839	.15	.25	.50	3.00
	1932 closed date	Inc. Ab.	.15	.25	.50	3.00
	1933	41.937	.15	.25	.75	4.00
	1933 closed date	Inc. Ab.	.15	.25	.75	4.00
	1936	16.602	.50	1.00	2.00	6.00
	1937	43.950	.15	.25	.75	4.00
	1938	55.707	.15	.25	.75	4.00
	1939	96.594	.15	.25	.50	3.00
	1940	10.854	.50	1.00	2.00	6.00
	1941	82.958	.15	.25	1.00	4.00
	1947	*2.170	65.00	125.00	225.00	350.00

***NOTE:** Struck for Colonial use in Africa.

Mint mark: B

Y#	Date	Mintage	Fine	VF	XF	Unc
80.2	1939	6.200	.50	1.00	2.50	10.00

ALUMINUM
Mint: Paris - w/o mint mark.

Y#	Date	Mintage	Fine	VF	XF	Unc
80a.1	1941	129.758	.15	.25	.50	3.00
	1944	9.898	.50	1.00	3.00	8.00
	1945	26.224	.15	.25	1.00	4.00
	1946	24.605	.15	.25	1.00	4.00
	1947	51.744	.15	.25	.60	3.00

Mint mark: B

Y#	Date	Mintage	Fine	VF	XF	Unc
80a.2	1944	.020	— Reported, not confirmed			
	1945	6.357	.50	1.00	3.00	8.00
	1946	29.344	.15	.25	1.00	4.00
	1947	18.504	2.00	5.00	10.00	20.00

Mint mark: C

Y#	Date	Mintage	Fine	VF	XF	Unc
80a.3	1944	17.220	— Reported, not confirmed			
	1945	2.968	1.00	3.00	6.00	12.00

Mint: Paris - w/o mint mark.
Vichy French State Issues

Y#	Date	Mintage	Fine	VF	XF	Unc
V94.1	1942	50.134	.15	.25	1.00	3.00
	1943	84.462	.15	.25	.75	2.50
	1944	57.410	2.00	4.00	8.00	15.00

Mint mark: B

Y#	Date	Mintage	Fine	VF	XF	Unc
V94.2	1943	21.916	10.00	20.00	40.00	65.00
	1944	27.334	2.00	5.00	10.00	25.00

Mint mark: C

Y#	Date	Mintage	Fine	VF	XF	Unc
V94.3	1944 small C	27.213	3.00	7.00	14.00	35.00
	1944 large C	Inc. Ab.	—	—	—	—

Mint: Paris - w/o mint mark.
Thin flan.

Y#	Date	Mintage	Fine	VF	XF	Unc
V94.4	1942	—	.15	.25	1.00	3.00
	1943	—	.15	.25	.50	1.50

ALUMINUM-BRONZE
50 New Centimes = 50 Old Francs
Obv: 3 folds in collar.

Y#	Date	Mintage	Fine	VF	XF	Unc
106.1	1962	37.560	.30	.60	2.00	4.00
	1963	62.482	.20	.40	1.50	3.00
	1964	41.471	.45	.90	3.00	7.00

Obv: 4 folds in collar.

Y#	Date	Mintage	Fine	VF	XF	Unc
106.2	1962	Inc. Ab.	30.00	75.00	130.00	175.00
	1963	Inc. Ab.	.20	.40	1.00	2.00

1/2 FRANC

NICKEL

Mint: Paris - w/o mint mark.

Y#	Date	Mintage	Fine	VF	XF	Unc
107.1	1965 small legends	184.834	—	—	.15	.30
	1965 large legends	Inc. Ab.	—	—	.15	.30
	1966	88.890	—	—	.15	.30
	1967	28.394	—	—	.15	.40
	1968	57.548	—	—	.15	.30
	1969	47.144	—	—	.15	.30
	1970	42.298	—	—	.15	.30
	1971	36.068	—	—	.15	.30
	1972	42.302	—	—	.15	.30
	1972 w/o O.ROTY	Inc. Ab.	25.00	50.00	100.00	150.00
	1973	48.372	—	—	.15	.30
	1974	37.072	—	—	.15	.30
	1975	22.803	—	—	.15	.40
	1976	115.314	—	—	.15	.30
	1977	131.644	—	—	.15	.30
	1978	63.360	—	—	.15	.30
	1979	.051	—	—	—	.50
	1980	.060	—	—	—	.50
	1981	.050	—	—	—	.50
	1982	.078	—	—	—	.50
	1983	50.000	—	—	.15	.30
	1984	80.000	—	—	.15	.30
	1985	50.000	—	—	—	1.50
	1986	110.000	—	—	—	1.50
	1987	50.000	—	—	—	.30
	1988	.100	—	—	—	.40
	1989	.083	—	—	—	.40
	1990	.015	—	—	—	.40
	1991	50.000	—	—	—	.40
	1992	30.000	—	—	—	.40
	1992	—	—	—	Proof	1.50

Plain edge.

Y#	Date	Mintage	Fine	VF	XF	Unc
107.2	1991	—	—	—	Proof	1.50
	1993	—	—	—	—	.40

FRANC

5.0000 g, .900 SILVER, .1446 oz ASW
Mint mark: A
Obv. leg: BONAPARTE PREMIER CONSUL.

C#	Date	Mintage	VG	Fine	VF	XF
143.1	ANXI	.232	20.00	50.00	125.00	275.00
	AN12	1.311	15.00	30.00	90.00	215.00

Mint mark: BB

C#	Date	Mintage	VG	Fine	VF	XF
143.8	AN12	5,737	100.00	200.00	400.00	800.00

Mint mark: D

C#	Date	Mintage	VG	Fine	VF	XF
143.2	ANXI	.012	75.00	150.00	350.00	650.00
	AN12	.053	35.00	60.00	150.00	350.00

Mint mark: G

C#	Date	Mintage	VG	Fine	VF	XF
143.3	ANXI	.013	100.00	200.00	400.00	900.00
	AN12	7,397	125.00	280.00	500.00	1000.

Mint mark: H

C#	Date	Mintage	VG	Fine	VF	XF
143.9	AN12	.057	35.00	60.00	150.00	350.00

Mint mark: I

C#	Date	Mintage	VG	Fine	VF	XF
143.10	AN12	.279	20.00	45.00	100.00	250.00

Mint mark: K

C#	Date	Mintage	VG	Fine	VF	XF
143.11	AN12	.102	30.00	55.00	125.00	300.00

Mint mark: L

C#	Date	Mintage	VG	Fine	VF	XF
143.4	ANXI	.022	40.00	75.00	200.00	500.00
	AN12	.125	25.00	50.00	115.00	275.00

Mint mark: M

C#	Date	Mintage	VG	Fine	VF	XF
143.12	AN12	.285	20.00	45.00	100.00	250.00

Mint mark: MA

C#	Date	Mintage	VG	Fine	VF	XF
143.5	ANXI	.012	45.00	90.00	250.00	600.00
	AN12	.141	25.00	50.00	115.00	275.00

Mint mark: Q

C#	Date	Mintage	VG	Fine	VF	XF
143.6	ANXI	.034	40.00	75.00	200.00	500.00
	AN12	.140	25.00	50.00	115.00	275.00

Mint mark: T

C#	Date	Mintage	VG	Fine	VF	XF
143.13	AN12	.046	35.00	60.00	150.00	350.00

Mint mark: U

C#	Date	Mintage	VG	Fine	VF	XF
143.14	AN12	5,580	75.00	150.00	350.00	650.00

Mint mark: W

C#	Date	Mintage	VG	Fine	VF	XF
143.7	ANXI	5,756	75.00	150.00	350.00	650.00
	AN12	.028	40.00	75.00	200.00	500.00
	Common date				Unc.	800.00

Mint mark: A

Obv. leg: NAPOLEON EMPEREUR.

C#	Date	Mintage	VG	Fine	VF	XF
153.1	AN12	.326	20.00	40.00	110.00	250.00
	AN13	2.454	15.00	30.00	85.00	200.00
	AN14	.298	25.00	50.00	125.00	300.00

Mint mark: B

C#	Date	Mintage	VG	Fine	VF	XF
153.2	AN12	.030	30.00	60.00	135.00	300.00
	AN13	2,906	65.00	125.00	275.00	600.00

Mint mark: BB

C#	Date	Mintage	VG	Fine	VF	XF
153.13	AN13	3,410	65.00	125.00	275.00	600.00
	AN14	491 pcs.	325.00	750.00	1250.	1850.

Mint mark: D

C#	Date	Mintage	VG	Fine	VF	XF
153.3	AN12	3,968	65.00	125.00	275.00	600.00
	AN13	.010	40.00	75.00	175.00	350.00
	AN14	2,450	65.00	125.00	275.00	650.00

Mint mark: G

C#	Date	Mintage	VG	Fine	VF	XF
153.14	AN13	.011	125.00	250.00	550.00	1250.

Mint mark: H

C#	Date	Mintage	VG	Fine	VF	XF
153.4	AN12	4,398	65.00	125.00	275.00	600.00
	AN13	.043	30.00	60.00	135.00	300.00
	AN14	7,164	65.00	125.00	275.00	600.00

Mint mark: I

C#	Date	Mintage	VG	Fine	VF	XF
153.5	AN12	.043	30.00	60.00	135.00	300.00
	AN13	.390	20.00	40.00	100.00	225.00
	AN14	2,847	100.00	200.00	400.00	800.00

Mint mark: K

C#	Date	Mintage	VG	Fine	VF	XF
153.6	AN12	.024	35.00	65.00	150.00	350.00
	AN13	.061	30.00	60.00	135.00	300.00
	AN14	1,526	100.00	200.00	400.00	900.00

Mint mark: L

C#	Date	Mintage	VG	Fine	VF	XF
153.7	AN12	4,253	65.00	125.00	275.00	600.00
	AN13	.073	30.00	60.00	135.00	300.00
	AN14	4,107	65.00	125.00	275.00	600.00

Mint mark: M

C#	Date	Mintage	VG	Fine	VF	XF
153.8	AN12	.300	20.00	40.00	100.00	225.00
	AN13	.651	15.00	30.00	70.00	200.00
	AN14	1,096	100.00	200.00	400.00	900.00

Mint mark: MA

C#	Date	Mintage	VG	Fine	VF	XF
153.9	AN12	5,582	65.00	125.00	275.00	600.00
	AN13	.028	35.00	65.00	150.00	350.00
	AN14	6,910	65.00	125.00	275.00	600.00

Mint mark: Q

C#	Date	Mintage	VG	Fine	VF	XF
153.10	AN12	.025	35.00	65.00	150.00	350.00
	AN13	.117	25.00	50.00	125.00	275.00

Mint mark: T

C#	Date	Mintage	VG	Fine	VF	XF
153.11	AN12	3,462	65.00	125.00	275.00	700.00
	AN13	.013	40.00	75.00	175.00	350.00

Mint mark: U

C#	Date	Mintage	VG	Fine	VF	XF
153.12	AN12	1,166	100.00	200.00	400.00	900.00
	AN13	.015	60.00	120.00	250.00	650.00
	AN14	4,667	3 known		900.00	—

Mint mark: W

C#	Date	Mintage	VG	Fine	VF	XF
153.15	AN13	.017	40.00	75.00	175.00	350.00
	AN14	4,667	75.00	150.00	300.00	700.00
	Common date				Unc.	1000.

Mint mark: A

C#	Date	Mintage	VG	Fine	VF	XF
153.16	1806	.828	20.00	40.00	100.00	225.00

Mint mark: B

C#	Date	Mintage	VG	Fine	VF	XF
153.26	1807	3,465	65.00	125.00	275.00	600.00

Mint mark: H

C#	Date	Mintage	VG	Fine	VF	XF
153.17	1806	8,472	55.00	100.00	225.00	500.00
	1807	4,728	60.00	110.00	240.00	525.00

Mint mark: I

C#	Date	Mintage	VG	Fine	VF	XF
153.18	1806	.034	35.00	65.00	150.00	350.00
	1807	.011	50.00	100.00	200.00	450.00

Mint mark: K

C#	Date	Mintage	VG	Fine	VF	XF
153.19	1806	3,173	75.00	150.00	400.00	800.00
	1807	2,362	75.00	150.00	400.00	800.00

Mint mark: L

C#	Date	Mintage	VG	Fine	VF	XF
153.20	1806	.253	25.00	50.00	125.00	275.00
	1807	.177	25.00	50.00	125.00	275.00

Mint mark: M

C#	Date	Mintage	VG	Fine	VF	XF
153.21	1806	1,066	100.00	200.00	400.00	900.00
	1807	.023	35.00	65.00	150.00	350.00

Mint mark: MA

C#	Date	Mintage	VG	Fine	VF	XF
153.22	1806	1,010	100.00	200.00	400.00	900.00
	1807	1,493	100.00	200.00	400.00	900.00

Mint mark: Q

C#	Date	Mintage	VG	Fine	VF	XF
153.23	1806	.016	40.00	75.00	175.00	350.00
	1807	9,659	50.00	100.00	225.00	450.00

Mint mark: U

C#	Date	Mintage	VG	Fine	VF	XF
153.24	1806	.015	40.00	75.00	175.00	350.00
	1807	.011	50.00	100.00	225.00	450.00

Mint mark: W

C#	Date	Mintage	VG	Fine	VF	XF
153.25	1806	.028	35.00	65.00	150.00	350.00
	1807	.015	40.00	75.00	175.00	350.00
	Common date				Unc.	800.00

Mint mark: A
Negro head.

C#	Date	Mintage	VG	Fine	VF	XF
153a	1807	.100	150.00	350.00	750.00	1800.

Laureate head.

C#	Date	Mintage	VG	Fine	VF	XF
153b.1	1807	.050	100.00	200.00	350.00	900.00
	1808	4.599	6.00	12.00	55.00	175.00
Mint mark: B						
153b.2	1808	.765	10.00	20.00	65.00	175.00
Mint mark: BB						
153b.3	1808	2.126	8.00	16.00	55.00	150.00
Mint mark: D						
153b.4	1808	.752	10.00	20.00	65.00	175.00
Mint mark: H						
153b.5	1808	.316	12.00	25.00	75.00	200.00
Mint mark: I						
153b.6	1808	.256	12.00	25.00	75.00	200.00
Mint mark: K						
153b.7	1808	.228	12.00	25.00	75.00	200.00
Mint mark: L						
153b.8	1808	.016	40.00	80.00	150.00	325.00
Mint mark: M						
153b.9	1808	.130	20.00	40.00	80.00	200.00
Mint mark: MA						
153b.10	1808	.029	35.00	75.00	135.00	300.00
Mint mark: Q						
153b.11	1808	.064	30.00	65.00	125.00	275.00
Mint mark: T						
153b.12	1808	.106	20.00	40.00	80.00	200.00
Mint mark: U						
153b.13	1808	.013	50.00	125.00	300.00	550.00
Mint mark: W						
153b.14	1808	2.422	8.00	16.00	55.00	150.00
	Common date				Unc.	500.00

Mint mark: A

C#	Date	Mintage	VG	Fine	VF	XF
163.1	1809	.980	8.00	16.00	55.00	150.00
	1810	1.676	8.00	16.00	55.00	150.00
	1811	1.347	8.00	16.00	55.00	150.00
	1812	.563	10.00	20.00	45.00	140.00
	1813	.446	10.00	20.00	45.00	140.00
	1814	.042	35.00	75.00	135.00	300.00
Mint mark: B						
163.2	1809	.202	10.00	20.00	50.00	150.00
	1810	.167	12.00	22.50	60.00	160.00
	1811	.253	10.00	20.00	50.00	150.00
	1812	.118	12.00	25.00	65.00	175.00
	1813	.061	15.00	30.00	75.00	200.00
Mint mark: BB						
163.12	1810	4,336	50.00	100.00	175.00	375.00
	1811	.012	40.00	80.00	150.00	325.00
	1812	5,571	50.00	100.00	175.00	375.00
Mint mark: CL						
163.17	1813	7,229	100.00	200.00	350.00	800.00
Mint mark: D						
163.3	1809	.047	30.00	65.00	125.00	275.00
	1810	.039	30.00	65.00	125.00	275.00
	1811	.242	10.00	20.00	50.00	150.00
	1812	.147	12.00	22.50	60.00	160.00
	1813	.078	15.00	30.00	75.00	200.00
Mint mark: H						
163.4	1809	.034	30.00	65.00	125.00	275.00
	1810	.016	35.00	75.00	150.00	325.00
	1811	.105	12.00	25.00	65.00	175.00
	1812	.165	10.00	22.00	60.00	160.00
	1813	.096	15.00	30.00	75.00	200.00

Mint mark: I

C#	Date	Mintage	VG	Fine	VF	XF
163.13	1810	.018	40.00	80.00	150.00	325.00
	1811	.085	15.00	30.00	75.00	200.00
	1812	.091	15.00	30.00	75.00	200.00
	1813	.076	15.00	30.00	75.00	200.00
Mint mark: K						
163.5	1809	.074	15.00	30.00	75.00	200.00
	1810	.093	15.00	30.00	75.00	200.00
	1811	.048	20.00	40.00	85.00	225.00
	1812	.041	20.00	40.00	85.00	225.00
	1813	.068	15.00	30.00	75.00	200.00
Mint mark: L						
163.6	1809	.028	30.00	65.00	125.00	275.00
	1810	.047	30.00	65.00	125.00	275.00
	1810(Tr)	I.A.	—	—	Unique	—
	1811	.188	10.00	22.00	60.00	160.00
	1812	.047	20.00	40.00	85.00	225.00
	1813	.033	20.00	40.00	85.00	225.00
Mint mark: M						
163.7	1809	8,855	50.00	100.00	175.00	375.00
	1810	.035	30.00	65.00	125.00	275.00
	1811	.081	15.00	30.00	75.00	200.00
	1812	.125	12.00	25.00	65.00	175.00
	1813	.181	12.00	25.00	65.00	175.00
	1814	.029	40.00	80.00	150.00	325.00
Mint mark: MA						
163.8	1809	.020	40.00	80.00	150.00	325.00
	1810	.028	30.00	65.00	125.00	275.00
	1811	.044	25.00	60.00	110.00	250.00
	1812	.036	25.00	60.00	110.00	250.00
	1813	.044	25.00	60.00	110.00	250.00
Mint mark: Q						
163.9	1809	.163	12.00	25.00	65.00	175.00
	1810	.073	15.00	30.00	75.00	200.00
	1811	.161	12.00	25.00	65.00	175.00
	1812	.034	30.00	65.00	125.00	275.00
	1813	.075	15.00	30.00	75.00	200.00
Mint mark: R						
163.15	1812	.012	75.00	150.00	350.00	700.00
	1813	779 pcs.	250.00	500.00	900.00	1350.
Mint mark: T						
163.14	1811	.042	25.00	60.00	110.00	250.00
	1812	.041	25.00	60.00	110.00	250.00
	1813	.020	40.00	80.00	150.00	325.00
Mint mark: U						
163.10	1809	5,549	60.00	125.00	250.00	500.00
	1810	10,200	50.00	100.00	225.00	400.00
	1812	.021	45.00	90.00	200.00	350.00
	1813	6,065	100.00	200.00	350.00	800.00
Mint mark: W						
163.11	1809	.196	12.00	25.00	65.00	175.00
	1810	.187	12.00	25.00	65.00	175.00
	1811	.265	12.00	25.00	65.00	175.00
	1812	.143	12.00	25.00	65.00	175.00
	1813	.093	15.00	30.00	75.00	200.00
Mint mark: Flag						
163.16	1812	.012	100.00	200.00	400.00	800.00
	1813	.069	75.00	150.00	300.00	650.00
	Common date				Unc.	450.00

Mint mark: A

C#	Date	Mintage	VG	Fine	VF	XF
179.1	1816	.253	10.00	20.00	65.00	150.00
	1817	.178	12.00	25.00	75.00	175.00
	1818	.060	15.00	30.00	85.00	200.00
	1819	.027	18.00	35.00	90.00	215.00
	1820	.028	18.00	35.00	90.00	215.00
	1821	.100	12.00	25.00	75.00	175.00
	1822	.635	6.00	12.00	45.00	125.00
	1823	.360	7.50	15.00	50.00	125.00
	1824	.417	6.00	12.00	45.00	125.00
Mint mark: B						
179.2	1816	.016	20.00	40.00	100.00	250.00
	1817	.031	18.00	35.00	90.00	215.00
	1818	3,866	25.00	60.00	150.00	375.00
	1819	.010	20.00	40.00	100.00	250.00
	1820	.016	20.00	40.00	100.00	250.00
	1822	.031	18.00	35.00	90.00	215.00
	1823	7,577	20.00	50.00	125.00	300.00
	1824	.066	12.00	25.00	75.00	175.00
Mint mark: D						
179.9	1817	5,362	22.00	45.00	125.00	275.00
	1823	3,485	25.00	60.00	150.00	375.00
	1824	.030	18.00	35.00	90.00	215.00
Mint mark: H						
179.10	1817	.048	12.00	25.00	75.00	175.00
	1818	8,477	20.00	50.00	125.00	300.00
	1819	8,141	20.00	50.00	125.00	300.00
	1820	6,709	22.00	50.00	125.00	300.00
	1821	5,083	22.00	50.00	125.00	300.00
	1822	.016	20.00	40.00	100.00	250.00
	1823	.014	20.00	40.00	100.00	250.00
	1824	.033	18.00	35.00	90.00	215.00

Mint mark: I

C#	Date	Mintage	VG	Fine	VF	XF
179.3	1816	5,041	22.00	50.00	125.00	300.00
	1823	5,273	22.00	50.00	125.00	300.00
	1824	.033	18.00	35.00	90.00	215.00
Mint mark: K						
179.11	1817	.307	10.00	20.00	65.00	150.00
	1820	.020	20.00	40.00	100.00	250.00
	1823	5,173	22.00	50.00	125.00	300.00
	1824	.123	10.00	20.00	65.00	150.00
Mint mark: L						
179.4	1816	5,770	22.00	50.00	125.00	300.00
	1817	5,059	22.00	50.00	125.00	300.00
	1818	1,450	40.00	85.00	200.00	400.00
	1823	.036	18.00	35.00	90.00	215.00
	1824	.054	12.00	25.00	75.00	175.00
Mint mark: M						
179.5	1816	.070	12.00	25.00	75.00	175.00
	1817	.021	20.00	40.00	100.00	250.00
	1823	.036	18.00	35.00	90.00	215.00
	1824	.059	12.00	25.00	75.00	175.00
Mint mark: MA						
179.12	1824	7,209	20.00	50.00	125.00	300.00
Mint mark: Q						
179.6	1816	.025	20.00	40.00	100.00	250.00
	1817	5,045	22.00	50.00	125.00	300.00
	1819	.013	20.00	40.00	100.00	250.00
	1820	.022	18.00	35.00	90.00	215.00
	1821	4,942	25.00	60.00	150.00	375.00
	1822	3,838	25.00	60.00	150.00	375.00
	1823	.033	18.00	35.00	90.00	215.00
	1824	.052	12.00	25.00	75.00	175.00
Mint mark: T						
179.7	1816	2,240	35.00	75.00	175.00	400.00
	1818	1,728	45.00	100.00	275.00	500.00
	1819	4,094	25.00	60.00	150.00	375.00
Mint mark: W						
179.8	1816	.015	20.00	40.00	100.00	250.00
	1817	.019	20.00	40.00	100.00	250.00
	1818	.016	20.00	40.00	100.00	250.00
	1819	.024	20.00	40.00	100.00	250.00
	1820	.013	25.00	50.00	125.00	275.00
	1821	.200	10.00	20.00	65.00	150.00
	1822	.061	12.00	25.00	75.00	175.00
	1823	.277	10.00	20.00	65.00	150.00
	1824	.388	10.00	20.00	65.00	150.00
	Common date				Unc.	450.00

Mint mark: A

C#	Date	Mintage	VG	Fine	VF	XF
187.1	1825	.335	10.00	20.00	55.00	150.00
	1826	.326	10.00	20.00	55.00	150.00
	1827	.431	10.00	20.00	55.00	150.00
	1828	.517	10.00	20.00	55.00	150.00
	1829	.290	10.00	20.00	55.00	150.00
	1830	.234	10.00	20.00	55.00	150.00
	1830 reeded edge	—	100.00	200.00	400.00	950.00
Mint mark: B						
187.2	1825	.017	20.00	40.00	80.00	200.00
	1826	.020	20.00	40.00	80.00	200.00
	1827	.096	15.00	30.00	70.00	175.00
	1828	.070	15.00	30.00	70.00	175.00
	1829	.124	10.00	20.00	45.00	150.00
	1830	.075	12.00	25.00	70.00	175.00
Mint mark: BB						
187.3	1825	9,256	30.00	60.00	125.00	300.00
	1826	.012	25.00	50.00	100.00	250.00
	1827	.013	25.00	50.00	100.00	250.00
	1828	.024	20.00	40.00	80.00	200.00
	1829	.021	20.00	40.00	80.00	200.00
Mint mark: D						
187.4	1825	.040	15.00	30.00	70.00	170.00
	1826	.028	20.00	40.00	80.00	200.00
	1827	.036	15.00	30.00	70.00	170.00
	1828	.076	12.00	25.00	65.00	150.00
	1829	.031	20.00	40.00	80.00	200.00
Mint mark: H						
187.5	1825	.023	20.00	40.00	80.00	200.00
	1826	.028	20.00	40.00	80.00	200.00
	1827	5,444	35.00	70.00	150.00	350.00
	1828	.027	20.00	40.00	80.00	200.00
	1829	.051	12.00	25.00	65.00	150.00
Mint mark: I						
187.6	1825	6,663	35.00	70.00	150.00	350.00
	1826	4,206	35.00	70.00	150.00	350.00
	1827	6,850	35.00	70.00	150.00	350.00
	1828	5,236	35.00	70.00	150.00	350.00
	1829	.020	20.00	40.00	80.00	200.00
	1830	1,025	60.00	125.00	250.00	500.00
Mint mark: K						
187.7	1825	.024	20.00	40.00	80.00	200.00
	1826	.038	20.00	40.00	80.00	200.00

C#	Date	Mintage	VG	Fine	VF	XF
187.7	1827	.044	18.00	35.00	75.00	185.00
	1828	.132	8.00	17.50	55.00	140.00
	1829	.050	15.00	30.00	70.00	170.00
	1830	.021	20.00	40.00	80.00	200.00

Mint mark: L

C#	Date	Mintage	VG	Fine	VF	XF
187.8	1825	3,830	35.00	70.00	150.00	350.00
	1826	.028	20.00	40.00	80.00	200.00
	1827	.047	18.00	35.00	75.00	185.00
	1828	.044	18.00	35.00	75.00	185.00
	1829	.033	20.00	40.00	80.00	200.00
	1830	.013	22.00	38.00	75.00	185.00

Mint mark: M

C#	Date	Mintage	VG	Fine	VF	XF
187.9	1825	6,069	35.00	70.00	150.00	350.00
	1826	.031	20.00	40.00	80.00	200.00
	1827	.024	20.00	40.00	80.00	200.00
	1828	.072	12.00	25.00	65.00	150.00
	1829	.046	18.00	35.00	75.00	185.00
	1830	.021	20.00	40.00	80.00	200.00

Mint mark: MA

C#	Date	Mintage	VG	Fine	VF	XF
187.13	1829	.066	12.00	25.00	65.00	160.00

Mint mark: Q

C#	Date	Mintage	VG	Fine	VF	XF
187.10	1825	5,653	35.00	70.00	150.00	350.00
	1826	.025	20.00	40.00	80.00	200.00
	1827	.020	20.00	40.00	80.00	200.00
	1828	.018	20.00	40.00	80.00	200.00
	1829	.013	22.00	45.00	90.00	225.00

Mint mark: T

C#	Date	Mintage	VG	Fine	VF	XF
187.12	1826	5,930	35.00	70.00	150.00	350.00
	1827	.014	22.00	45.00	90.00	225.00
	1828	.036	20.00	40.00	80.00	200.00
	1829	.014	22.00	45.00	90.00	225.00
	1830	8,871	30.00	60.00	135.00	300.00

Mint mark: W

C#	Date	Mintage	VG	Fine	VF	XF
187.11	1825	.078	12.00	25.00	65.00	150.00
	1826	.130	8.00	17.50	55.00	140.00
	1827	.519	6.00	12.00	40.00	120.00
	1828	.418	6.00	12.00	45.00	120.00
	1829	.149	8.00	17.50	55.00	140.00
	1830	.078	12.00	25.00	65.00	150.00
	Common date				Unc.	375.00

Mint mark: A

C#	Date	Mintage	VG	Fine	VF	XF
200.1	1831	.202	40.00	100.00	200.00	450.00

Mint mark: B

C#	Date	Mintage	VG	Fine	VF	XF
200.2	1831	.400	30.00	75.00	175.00	400.00

Mint mark: BB

C#	Date	Mintage	VG	Fine	VF	XF
200.3	1831	.018	60.00	150.00	300.00	600.00

Mint mark: D

C#	Date	Mintage	VG	Fine	VF	XF
200.4	1831	.127	40.00	110.00	225.00	450.00

Mint mark: H

C#	Date	Mintage	VG	Fine	VF	XF
200.5	1831	.027	50.00	125.00	275.00	500.00

Mint mark: I

C#	Date	Mintage	VG	Fine	VF	XF
200.6	1831	.021	50.00	125.00	275.00	500.00

Mint mark: K

C#	Date	Mintage	VG	Fine	VF	XF
200.7	1831	.053	40.00	115.00	250.00	475.00

Mint mark: L

C#	Date	Mintage	VG	Fine	VF	XF
200.8	1831	2,406	100.00	250.00	450.00	900.00

Mint mark: M

C#	Date	Mintage	VG	Fine	VF	XF
200.9	1831	.038	45.00	125.00	250.00	475.00

Mint mark: Q

C#	Date	Mintage	VG	Fine	VF	XF
200.10	1831	.018	60.00	150.00	300.00	600.00

Mint mark: T

C#	Date	Mintage	VG	Fine	VF	XF
200.11	1831	.043	40.00	115.00	250.00	475.00

Mint mark: W

C#	Date	Mintage	VG	Fine	VF	XF
200.12	1831	.453	30.00	75.00	175.00	400.00

Mint mark: A
Laureate head

C#	Date	Mintage	Fine	VF	XF	Unc
201.1	1832	.379	10.00	35.00	75.00	250.00
	1833	.114	12.00	40.00	90.00	300.00
	1834	.330	10.00	35.00	75.00	250.00
	1835	.483	10.00	35.00	75.00	250.00
	1836	.138	15.00	40.00	85.00	200.00
	1837	.241	12.00	35.00	75.00	250.00
	1838	.183	15.00	40.00	85.00	200.00
	1839	.243	12.00	35.00	75.00	250.00
	1840	.481	10.00	35.00	75.00	250.00
	1841	.623	10.00	35.00	75.00	250.00

C#	Date	Mintage	Fine	VF	XF	Unc
201.1	1842	.130	15.00	40.00	85.00	200.00
	1843	.074	18.00	40.00	80.00	225.00
	1844	.072	18.00	40.00	80.00	225.00
	1845	.215	15.00	40.00	85.00	200.00
	1846	1.225	8.00	18.00	40.00	150.00
	1847	2.401	8.00	18.00	40.00	150.00
	1848	.228	15.00	40.00	85.00	200.00

Mint mark: B

C#	Date	Mintage	Fine	VF	XF	Unc
201.2	1832	.197	15.00	45.00	90.00	200.00
	1833	.098	12.00	35.00	70.00	200.00
	1834	.146	10.00	25.00	50.00	200.00
	1835	.103	12.00	30.00	60.00	200.00
	1836	.093	12.00	35.00	70.00	200.00
	1837	.212	12.00	30.00	60.00	200.00
	1838	.145	12.00	30.00	60.00	200.00
	1839	.184	12.00	30.00	60.00	200.00
	1840	.148	10.00	25.00	50.00	200.00
	1841	.663	8.00	18.00	40.00	175.00
	1842	.158	12.00	30.00	60.00	200.00
	1843	.130	12.00	30.00	60.00	200.00
	1844	.045	15.00	45.00	90.00	200.00
	1845	.882	8.00	18.00	40.00	175.00
	1846	.818	8.00	18.00	40.00	175.00

Mint mark: BB

C#	Date	Mintage	Fine	VF	XF	Unc
201.3	1832	.042	15.00	45.00	90.00	200.00
	1833	.079	15.00	45.00	90.00	200.00
	1834	.068	15.00	45.00	90.00	200.00
	1835	.046	15.00	45.00	90.00	200.00
	1836	.050	15.00	45.00	90.00	200.00
	1837	.013	20.00	50.00	100.00	200.00
	1838	.024	15.00	40.00	80.00	175.00
	1839	.043	15.00	45.00	90.00	200.00
	1840	.017	20.00	50.00	100.00	200.00
	1841	.053	15.00	45.00	90.00	200.00
	1842	.244	12.00	30.00	60.00	175.00
	1843	.072	15.00	45.00	90.00	200.00
	1844	.076	15.00	45.00	90.00	200.00
	1845	.083	15.00	45.00	90.00	200.00
	1846	.024	15.00	40.00	80.00	175.00
	1847	.068	15.00	45.00	90.00	200.00
	1848	.021	25.00	60.00	125.00	250.00

Mint mark: D

C#	Date	Mintage	Fine	VF	XF	Unc
201.4	1832	.127	10.00	25.00	50.00	160.00
	1833	.024	15.00	40.00	80.00	175.00
	1834	.059	15.00	45.00	90.00	200.00
	1835	.052	15.00	45.00	90.00	200.00
	1836	.019	25.00	60.00	125.00	250.00
	1837	2,531	40.00	100.00	200.00	500.00
	1838	.012	20.00	50.00	100.00	200.00
	1839	.011	20.00	50.00	100.00	200.00
	1840	7,130	40.00	80.00	175.00	350.00

Mint mark: H

C#	Date	Mintage	Fine	VF	XF	Unc
201.5	1832	.080	15.00	45.00	90.00	200.00
	1833	.026	15.00	45.00	90.00	200.00
	1834	.079	15.00	45.00	90.00	200.00
	1835	.017	20.00	50.00	110.00	225.00

Mint mark: I

C#	Date	Mintage	Fine	VF	XF	Unc
201.6	1832	.037	15.00	45.00	90.00	200.00
	1833	.034	15.00	45.00	90.00	200.00
	1834	.045	15.00	45.00	90.00	200.00
	1835	.048	15.00	45.00	90.00	200.00

Mint mark: K

C#	Date	Mintage	Fine	VF	XF	Unc
201.7	1832	.035	15.00	45.00	90.00	200.00
	1833	.030	15.00	45.00	90.00	200.00
	1834	.070	15.00	45.00	90.00	200.00
	1835	.058	15.00	45.00	90.00	200.00
	1836	.040	15.00	40.00	80.00	185.00
	1837	.034	20.00	50.00	100.00	225.00
	1838	.017	20.00	50.00	100.00	225.00
	1839	.048	15.00	45.00	90.00	200.00
	1840	.048	15.00	45.00	90.00	200.00
	1841	.042	15.00	45.00	90.00	200.00
	1842	.032	15.00	45.00	90.00	200.00
	1843	.039	15.00	45.00	90.00	200.00
	1844	.023	15.00	45.00	90.00	200.00
	1845	.023	15.00	45.00	90.00	200.00
	1846	.023	15.00	45.00	90.00	200.00
	1847	*6,787	—	500.00	—	—

***NOTE:** One piece known.

Mint mark: L

C#	Date	Mintage	Fine	VF	XF	Unc
201.8	1832	.031	15.00	45.00	90.00	200.00
	1833	.018	20.00	50.00	100.00	225.00
	1834	.012	20.00	50.00	100.00	225.00
	1835	3,647	80.00	180.00	350.00	—

Mint mark: M

C#	Date	Mintage	Fine	VF	XF	Unc
201.9	1832	.051	15.00	45.00	90.00	200.00
	1833	.049	15.00	45.00	90.00	200.00
	1834	.037	15.00	45.00	90.00	200.00
	1835	.025	18.00	45.00	90.00	200.00

Mint mark: MA

C#	Date	Mintage	Fine	VF	XF	Unc
201.10	1832	.078	15.00	45.00	90.00	200.00
	1833	.057	15.00	45.00	90.00	200.00
	1834	.018	20.00	50.00	100.00	225.00
	1835	.012	20.00	50.00	100.00	225.00
	1837	—	—	—	Rare	—
	1838	.020	20.00	50.00	100.00	225.00

Mint mark: Q

C#	Date	Mintage	Fine	VF	XF	Unc
201.11	1832	—	—	—	Rare	—
	1833	.019	25.00	65.00	125.00	250.00
	1834	.057	15.00	45.00	90.00	200.00

Mint mark: T

C#	Date	Mintage	Fine	VF	XF	Unc
201.12	1832	.034	20.00	50.00	100.00	225.00
	1833	.031	15.00	50.00	100.00	225.00

C#	Date	Mintage	Fine	VF	XF	Unc
201.12	1834	.102	12.00	30.00	60.00	175.00
	1835	.051	15.00	45.00	90.00	200.00

Mint mark: W

C#	Date	Mintage	Fine	VF	XF	Unc
201.13	1832	.155	12.00	30.00	60.00	175.00
	1833	.213	12.00	30.00	60.00	175.00
	1834	.608	8.00	18.00	40.00	150.00
	1835	.206	12.00	30.00	60.00	175.00
	1836	.049	15.00	45.00	90.00	200.00
	1837	.266	12.00	30.00	60.00	175.00
	1838	.162	12.00	30.00	60.00	175.00
	1839	.120	12.00	30.00	60.00	175.00
	1840	.079	15.00	45.00	90.00	200.00
	1841	.321	12.00	30.00	60.00	175.00
	1842	.195	12.00	30.00	60.00	175.00
	1843	.271	12.00	30.00	60.00	175.00
	1844	.381	10.00	25.00	50.00	160.00
	1845	.478	10.00	25.00	50.00	160.00
	1846	.074	15.00	45.00	90.00	200.00

Mint mark: A
Second Republic

Y#	Date	Mintage	Fine	VF	XF	Unc
4.1	1849	1.289	20.00	45.00	90.00	200.00
	1850	1.041	25.00	60.00	115.00	225.00
	1851	.638	40.00	100.00	175.00	300.00

Mint mark: BB

Y#	Date	Mintage	Fine	VF	XF	Unc
4.2	1849	.015	100.00	250.00	600.00	1000.
	1850	.213	60.00	150.00	300.00	600.00

Mint mark: K

Y#	Date	Mintage	Fine	VF	XF	Unc
4.3	1849	.019	100.00	250.00	600.00	1000.
	1850	.035	75.00	200.00	375.00	700.00

Mint mark: A
President Louis-Napoleon

Y#	Date	Mintage	Fine	VF	XF	Unc
12	1852	1.015	45.00	85.00	175.00	375.00
	1852	—	—	—	Proof	1200.

Second Empire - Napoleon III

Y#	Date	Mintage	Fine	VF	XF	Unc
24.1	1853 lg. head					
		.183	150.00	400.00	700.00	1200.
	1853 lg. head	—	—	—	Proof	600.00
	1853 sm. head					
		Inc. Ab.	60.00	125.00	300.00	700.00
	1854	.764	25.00	50.00	150.00	350.00
	1855(d)	.757	35.00	90.00	175.00	300.00
	1855(a)	I.A.	75.00	150.00	225.00	500.00
	1856	1.196	20.00	50.00	125.00	250.00
	1857	1.681	20.00	40.00	100.00	250.00
	1858	5.607	10.00	25.00	75.00	200.00
	1859	3.830	15.00	35.00	90.00	225.00
	1860(h)	2.740	15.00	35.00	90.00	225.00
	1860(b)	I.A.	15.00	35.00	90.00	225.00
	1861	2.012	100.00	200.00	450.00	700.00
	1863	*.019	—	600.00	900.00	—
	1864	.022	— Reported, not confirmed			

***NOTE:** Two pieces known.

Mint mark: BB

Y#	Date	Mintage	Fine	VF	XF	Unc
24.2	1856	1.635	20.00	50.00	125.00	250.00
	1859	1.333	20.00	50.00	125.00	250.00
	1860	I.A.	20.00	50.00	125.00	250.00
	1861	.218	100.00	250.00	500.00	1000.
	1862	1.124	80.00	200.00	400.00	800.00
	1863	.054	125.00	300.00	650.00	900.00

Mint mark: D

Y#	Date	Mintage	Fine	VF	XF	Unc
24.3	1856	1.227	20.00	50.00	725.00	250.00

5.0000 g, .835 SILVER, .1342 oz ASW

Mint mark: A
Laureate head.

Y#	Date	Mintage	Fine	VF	XF	Unc
30.1	1866	14.638	5.00	12.00	25.00	75.00
	1867	12.131	5.00	12.00	25.00	75.00
	1868	14.942	5.00	12.00	25.00	75.00
	1869	2.935	10.00	25.00	75.00	150.00
	1870	.788	—	—	—	—

Mint mark: BB

Y#	Date	Mintage	Fine	VF	XF	Unc
30.2	1866	7.204	6.00	15.00	30.00	90.00
	1867	7.295	6.00	15.00	30.00	90.00
	1868	10.230	5.00	12.00	25.00	75.00
	1869	3.094	10.00	25.00	75.00	150.00
	1870	1.992	15.00	40.00	90.00	200.00

Mint mark: K

Y#	Date	Mintage	Fine	VF	XF	Unc
30.3	1866	1.402	15.00	40.00	90.00	200.00
	1867	6.092	5.00	15.00	35.00	90.00
	1868	.022	150.00	300.00	425.00	1000.

Mint mark: A
Third Republic

Y#	Date	Mintage	Fine	VF	XF	Unc
49.1	1871 small A	2.980	4.00	8.00	25.00	75.00
	1871 large A	Inc. Ab.	3.00	6.00	20.00	60.00
	1872 small A	10.129	2.00	4.00	15.00	50.00
	1872 large A	Inc. Ab.	10.00	25.00	50.00	100.00
	1878	30 pcs.	—	—	Proof	3500.
	1881	2.010	4.00	8.00	25.00	75.00
	1887	3.292	4.00	8.00	25.00	75.00
	1888	3.244	4.00	8.00	25.00	75.00
	1889	100 pcs.	—	—	Proof	2500.
	1894	1.600	4.00	8.00	25.00	75.00
	1895	3.200	4.00	8.00	25.00	75.00

Mint mark: K

Y#	Date	Mintage	Fine	VF	XF	Unc
49.2	1871 small K	1.252	4.00	8.00	25.00	75.00
	1871 large K	Inc. Ab.	3.00	6.00	20.00	60.00
	1872 large K	5.779	15.00	35.00	65.00	150.00
	1872 small K	Inc. Ab.	4.00	8.00	25.00	75.00
	1873	.019	150.00	350.00	700.00	1200.

Mint: Paris - w/o mint mark.

Y#	Date	Mintage	Fine	VF	XF	Unc
63.1	1898	15.000	2.00	3.00	6.00	30.00
	1898	—	—	—	Proof	400.00
	1899	11.000	2.00	4.00	8.00	35.00
	1900	.099	125.00	225.00	450.00	850.00
	1900	—	—	—	Proof	425.00
	1901	6.200	3.00	6.00	15.00	65.00
	1902	6.000	3.00	6.00	15.00	65.00
	1903	.472	50.00	125.00	300.00	600.00
	1904	7.000	3.00	6.00	15.00	65.00
	1905	6.004	3.00	6.00	15.00	65.00
	1906	1.908	10.00	25.00	60.00	150.00
	1907	2.563	8.00	15.00	35.00	100.00
	1908	3.961	4.00	8.00	18.00	65.00
	1909	10.924	2.00	4.00	8.00	35.00
	1910	7.725	2.00	4.00	8.00	35.00
	1911	5.542	2.00	3.00	20.00	50.00
	1912	10.001	2.00	4.00	8.00	35.00
	1913	13.654	2.00	4.00	8.00	35.00
	1914	14.361	2.00	4.00	8.00	35.00
	1915	47.955	1.00	1.50	2.50	8.00
	1916	92.029	1.00	1.25	1.75	5.00
	1917	57.153	1.00	1.25	1.75	5.00
	1918	50.112	1.00	1.25	1.75	5.00
	1919	46.112	1.00	1.25	1.75	5.00
	1920	19.322	1.50	2.50	4.50	8.00

Mint mark: C

Y#	Date	Mintage	Fine	VF	XF	Unc
63.2	1914	.043	150.00	275.00	400.00	600.00

ALUMINUM-BRONZE
Mint: Paris - w/o mint mark.

Chamber of Commerce

Y#	Date	Mintage	Fine	VF	XF	Unc
78	1920	.590	4.00	10.00	25.00	50.00
	1921	54.572	.25	.50	1.50	8.00
	1922	111.343	.15	.25	1.00	6.00
	1923	140.138	.15	.25	1.00	5.00
	1924 open 4	87.715	.15	.25	1.00	6.00
	1924 closed 4	Inc. Ab.	.35	.60	2.00	10.00
	1925	36.523	.25	.50	1.50	8.00
	1926	1.580	5.00	12.00	30.00	60.00
	1927	11.330	1.00	3.00	6.00	12.00
	1928	.405	—	—	—	—

Y#	Date	Mintage	Fine	VF	XF	Unc
81	1931	15.504	.25	.50	2.00	8.00
	1932	29.768	.15	.25	1.00	6.00
	1933	15.356	.25	.50	2.00	8.00
	1934	17.286	.25	.50	2.00	7.00
	1935	1.166	7.50	18.00	30.00	85.00
	1936	23.817	.15	.25	1.00	6.00
	1937	30.940	.15	.25	1.00	5.00
	1938	66.165	.15	.25	1.00	4.00
	1939	48.434	.15	.25	1.00	5.00
	1940	25.525	.15	.25	1.00	6.00
	1941	34.705	.15	.25	1.00	5.00

ALUMINUM

Y#	Date	Mintage	Fine	VF	XF	Unc
81a.1	1941	60.877	.10	.20	1.00	6.00
	1943	4,400	1500.	2000.	—	—
	1944	22.608	.10	.20	1.50	7.00
	1945	61.780	.10	.15	.50	3.00
	1946	52.516	.10	.15	.25	2.50
	1947	110.448	.10	.15	.25	2.50
	1948	96.092	.10	.15	.25	2.50
	1949	41.090	.10	.15	.25	3.00
	1950	27.882	.10	.15	.50	3.50
	1957	16.497	.10	.15	.75	4.00
	1958	21.197	.10	.15	.75	4.00
	1959	41.985	.10	.15	.25	1.50

Mint mark: B

Y#	Date	Mintage	Fine	VF	XF	Unc
81a.2	1944	1.725	— Reported, not confirmed			
	1945	4.251	2.00	6.00	15.00	35.00
	1946	26.493	.10	.20	1.50	7.00
	1947	51.562	.10	.20	1.00	6.00
	1948	45.481	.10	.20	1.00	5.00
	1949	35.840	.10	.20	1.00	6.00
	1950	18.800	1.00	2.00	4.00	20.00
	1957	63.976	.10	.20	1.00	6.00
	1958	13.412	.25	.75	3.00	7.00

Mint mark: C

Y#	Date	Mintage	Fine	VF	XF	Unc
81a.3	1944	33.600	1.00	2.00	5.00	15.00
	1945	5.220	2.00	6.00	15.00	35.00
	1946	9.669	— Reported, not confirmed			

ZINC
Mint mark: A

Y#	Date	Mintage	Fine	VF	XF	Unc
81b	1943	*.017	150.00	300.00	550.00	900.00

***NOTE:** Struck for Colonial use in Africa.

LB (L. Bazor)

ALUMINUM
Mint: Paris - w/o mint mark.
Vichy French State Issues

Y#	Date	Mintage	Fine	VF	XF	Unc
V95.1	1942	152.144	.10	.15	1.00	5.00
	1942 w/o LB	I.A.				
	1943	205.564	.10	.15	.75	3.50
	1943 thin flan	Inc. Ab.	.10	.15	.75	3.50
	1944	50.605	.50	1.25	1.75	8.00

Mint mark: B

Y#	Date	Mintage	Fine	VF	XF	Unc
V95.2	1943	68.082	10.00	15.00	45.00	90.00
	1944	13.622	2.00	5.00	20.00	35.00

Mint mark: C

Y#	Date	Mintage	Fine	VF	XF	Unc
V95.3	1944 lg. C	74.859	.50	1.25	1.75	8.00
	1944 sm. C	Inc. Ab.	20.00	40.00	100.00	300.00

NICKEL
Mint: Paris - w/o mint mark.

1 New Franc = 100 Old Francs
Fifth Republic

Y#	Date	Mintage	Fine	VF	XF	Unc
108	1960	406.375	—	—	.20	.40
	1961	119.611	—	—	.20	.40
	1962	14.014	—	—	.20	.50
	1964	77.425	—	—	.20	.40
	1965	44.252	—	—	.20	.40
	1966	38.038	—	—	.20	.40
	1967	11.322	—	—	.20	.50
	1968	51.550	—	—	.20	.40
	1969	70.595	—	—	.20	.40
	1970	42.560	—	—	.20	.40
	1971	42.475	—	—	.20	.40
	1972	48.250	—	—	.20	.40
	1973	70.000	—	—	.20	.40
	1974	82.235	—	—	.20	.40
	1975	101.685	—	—	.20	.40
	1976	192.520	—	—	.20	.40
	1977	230.085	—	—	.20	.40
	1978	136.580	—	—	.20	.40
	1979	.051	—	—	—	.60
	1980	.060	—	—	—	.60
	1981	.050	—	—	—	.60
	1982	.092	—	—	—	.60
	1983	.101	—	—	—	.60
	1984	.050	—	—	—	.60
	1985	7.002	—	—	—	2.00
	1986	.048	—	—	—	2.00
	1987	.100	—	—	—	.40
	1988	.100	—	—	—	.40
	1989	.083	—	—	—	.40
	1990	.015	—	—	—	.40
	1991	55.000	—	—	—	.40
	1992	30.000	—	—	—	.40
	1992	—	—	—	Proof	2.50
	1993	—	—	—	—	.40

Plain edge.

Y#	Date	Mintage	Fine	VF	XF	Unc
108.2	1991	—	—	—	Proof	2.50

30th Anniversary of Fifth Republic

Y#	Date	Mintage	Fine	VF	XF	Unc
129	1988	49.921	—	—	—	1.00

22.2000 g, .900 SILVER, .6424 oz ASW
30th Anniversary of Fifth Republic
Similar to Y#129.

Y#	Date	Mintage	Fine	VF	XF	Unc
130	1988	.060	—	—	Proof	50.00

9.0000 g, .920 GOLD, .2662 oz AGW
30th Anniversary of Fifth Republic
Similar to Y#129.

Y#	Date	Mintage	Fine	VF	XF	Unc
131	1988	.020	—	—	Proof	275.00

NICKEL
200th Anniversary of Estates General

Y#	Date	Mintage	Fine	VF	XF	Unc
134	1989	5.000	—	—	—	1.75

200th Anniversary of French Republic

Y#	Date	Mintage	Fine	VF	XF	Unc
166.1	1992	30.000	—	—	—	1.25

9.0000 g, .920 GOLD, .2662 oz AGW

Y#	Date	Mintage	Fine	VF	XF	Unc
166.1a	1992	5,000	—	—	Proof	275.00

11.0000 g, .999 PLATINUM, .3537 oz APW

Y#	Date	Mintage	Fine	VF	XF	Unc
166.1b	1992	2,000	—	—	Proof	450.00

15.5500 g, .900 SILVER, .4500 oz ASW, 27.9mm

Y#	Date	Mintage	Fine	VF	XF	Unc
166.2	1992	—	—	—	—	22.50
	1992	.030	—	—	Proof	60.00

2 FRANCS

10.0000 g, .900 SILVER, .2893 oz ASW
Mint mark: A
Obv. leg: BONAPARTE PREMIER CONSUL.

C#	Date	Mintage	VG	Fine	VF	XF
144.1	AN12	.187	40.00	70.00	175.00	500.00
	AN12	—	—	—	Proof	2250.
Mint mark: BB						
144.2	AN12	1,965	200.00	350.00	600.00	1200.
Mint mark: D						
144.3	AN12	2,672	— Reported, not confirmed			
Mint mark: G						
144.4	AN12	2,859	100.00	250.00	400.00	900.00
Mint mark: H						
144.5	AN12	.012	50.00	125.00	250.00	650.00
Mint mark: I						
144.6	AN12	.102	40.00	100.00	200.00	500.00
Mint mark: K						
144.7	AN12	.026	45.00	115.00	225.00	450.00
Mint mark: L						
144.8	AN12	.015	50.00	125.00	250.00	650.00
Mint mark: M						
144.9	AN12	.066	40.00	100.00	200.00	500.00
Mint mark: MA						
144.10	AN12	6,804	60.00	140.00	275.00	700.00
Mint mark: Q						
144.11	AN12	.021	45.00	115.00	225.00	500.00
Mint mark: T						
144.12	AN12	4,484	— Reported, not confirmed			
Mint mark: U						
144.13	AN12	—	—	—	Unique	—
Mint mark: W						
144.14	AN12	5,850	65.00	150.00	300.00	775.00

Mint mark: A
Obv. leg: NAPOLEON EMPEREUR.

C#	Date	Mintage	VG	Fine	VF	XF
154.1	AN12	.060	100.00	250.00	400.00	900.00
	AN13/2	2 known		—	—	—
	AN13	.742	30.00	60.00	125.00	450.00
	AN14	.232	35.00	70.00	150.00	475.00
	1806	.169	35.00	70.00	150.00	475.00
Mint mark: B						
154.2	AN12	.014	45.00	115.00	225.00	500.00
	1807	563	— Reported, not confirmed			
Mint mark: BB						
154.3	AN12	1,798	—	—	—	—
	AN13	4,341	150.00	—	—	—
	1806	1,477	— Reported, not confirmed			
Mint mark: D						
154.11	AN13	2,560	— Reported, not confirmed			
	AN14	204	— Reported, not confirmed			
	1806	530	— Reported, not confirmed			
Mint mark: G						
154.12	AN13	.013	200.00	350.00	600.00	1200.
Mint mark: H						
154.4	AN12	2,800	— Reported, not confirmed			
	AN13	3,727	65.00	150.00	300.00	775.00
	AN14	1,063	200.00	350.00	600.00	1200.
Mint mark: I						
154.5	AN12	3,561	— Reported, not confirmed			
	AN13/2	.124	20.00	40.00	150.00	450.00
	AN13	Inc. Ab.	35.00	70.00	175.00	500.00
	AN14	6,299	150.00	350.00	750.00	—
	1806	.021	45.00	115.00	225.00	450.00
	1807	.082	35.00	70.00	150.00	450.00
Mint mark: K						
154.6	AN12	.010	45.00	115.00	225.00	450.00
	AN13	.036	100.00	250.00	400.00	900.00
	AN14	1,210	—	—	Rare	—
	1806	754	— Reported, not confirmed			
	1807	3,665	200.00	460.00	750.00	1300.
Mint mark: L						
154.7	AN12	1,247	200.00	350.00	600.00	1200.

C#	Date	Mintage	VG	Fine	VF	XF
154.7	AN13	.022	100.00	250.00	400.00	900.00
	AN14	5,183	75.00	200.00	500.00	—
	1806	.072	35.00	70.00	150.00	450.00
	1807	.054	30.00	65.00	160.00	400.00
Mint mark: M						
154.8	AN12	.016	40.00	100.00	200.00	500.00
	AN13	.334	35.00	70.00	150.00	450.00
	1807	8,878	65.00	150.00	300.00	775.00
Mint mark: MA						
154.9	AN12	5,249	— Reported, not confirmed			
	AN13	.011	45.00	115.00	225.00	450.00
	AN14	—	200.00	400.00	800.00	—
	1806	2,289	— Reported, not confirmed			
Mint mark: Q						
154.13	AN13	.052	35.00	70.00	150.00	450.00
	1806	.042	45.00	115.00	225.00	450.00
	1807	.033	45.00	115.00	225.00	450.00
Mint mark: T						
154.10	AN12	1,444	200.00	350.00	600.00	1200.
	AN13	4,600	65.00	150.00	300.00	775.00
Mint mark: U						
154.14	AN13	7,221	200.00	400.00	750.00	1300.
	AN14	—	200.00	400.00	800.00	—
	1806	.010	125.00	300.00	600.00	1200.
	1807	.010	125.00	300.00	600.00	1200.
Mint mark: W						
154.15	AN13	.011	45.00	115.00	225.00	450.00
	AN14	—	200.00	400.00	750.00	1300.
	1806	.010	65.00	150.00	300.00	775.00
	1807	4,114	200.00	400.00	750.00	1300.

Mint mark: A
Negro head.

C#	Date	Mintage	VG	Fine	VF	XF
154a	1807	—	300.00	650.00	1200.	3750.

Laureate head.

C#	Date	Mintage	VG	Fine	VF	XF
154b.1	1807	.019	175.00	325.00	750.00	1850.
	1808	1.100	30.00	60.00	150.00	400.00
Mint mark: B						
154b.2	1808	.161	40.00	80.00	175.00	450.00
Mint mark: I						
154b.3	1808	.106	45.00	90.00	175.00	400.00
Mint mark: K						
154b.4	1808	.038	55.00	90.00	200.00	450.00
Mint mark: L						
154b.5	1808	.019	65.00	110.00	235.00	500.00
Mint mark: M						
154b.6	1808	.028	55.00	90.00	200.00	450.00
Mint mark: MA						
154b.7	1808	7,676	70.00	125.00	250.00	550.00
Mint mark: Q						
154b.8	1808	4,965	75.00	140.00	300.00	600.00
Mint mark: U						
154b.9	1808	2,297	150.00	300.00	550.00	1200.
Mint mark: W						
154b.10	1808	.040	55.00	90.00	200.00	450.00
	Common date				Unc.	650.00

Mint mark: A

C#	Date	Mintage	VG	Fine	VF	XF
164.1	1809	.469	20.00	40.00	100.00	300.00
	1810	.771	17.50	35.00	90.00	275.00
	1811	2.509	15.00	35.00	75.00	250.00
	1812	.308	20.00	40.00	100.00	300.00
	1813	.442	20.00	40.00	100.00	300.00
	1814	.095	35.00	75.00	150.00	350.00

Mint mark: B

C#	Date	Mintage	VG	Fine	VF	XF
164.2	1809	.136	30.00	60.00	125.00	300.00
	1810	.072	35.00	75.00	150.00	350.00
	1811	.290	20.00	40.00	100.00	300.00
	1812	.057	35.00	75.00	150.00	350.00
	1813	.031	35.00	80.00	175.00	450.00
Mint mark: BB						
164.10	1810	1,389	— Reported, not confirmed			
	1811	.012	40.00	100.00	200.00	500.00
	1812	2,835	— Reported, not confirmed			
Mint mark: CL						
164.16	1813	906	400.00	800.00	1500.	3250.
Mint mark: D						
164.11	1810	.018	40.00	100.00	200.00	500.00
	1811	.037	35.00	80.00	175.00	450.00
	1812	.061	35.00	75.00	150.00	350.00
	1813	.033	35.00	80.00	175.00	450.00
Mint mark: H						
164.3	1809	4,534	75.00	150.00	250.00	600.00
	1810	5,710	75.00	150.00	250.00	600.00
	1811	.044	35.00	75.00	150.00	350.00
	1812	.081	35.00	75.00	150.00	350.00
	1813	.080	35.00	75.00	150.00	350.00
Mint mark: I						
164.12	1810	.029	35.00	80.00	175.00	450.00
	1811	.137	30.00	60.00	125.00	300.00
	1812	.209	20.00	40.00	100.00	300.00
	1813	.098	35.00	75.00	150.00	350.00
Mint mark: K						
164.4	1809	3,451	100.00	225.00	350.00	750.00
	1810	3,518	100.00	225.00	350.00	750.00
	1811	.028	35.00	80.00	175.00	450.00
	1812	.021	35.00	80.00	175.00	450.00
	1813	.027	35.00	80.00	175.00	450.00
Mint mark: L						
164.5	1809	.027	35.00	80.00	175.00	450.00
	1810	.032	35.00	80.00	175.00	450.00
	1811	.099	35.00	75.00	150.00	350.00
	1812	.042	35.00	75.00	150.00	350.00
	1813	.033	35.00	80.00	175.00	450.00
Mint mark: M						
164.13	1810	.011	50.00	100.00	225.00	500.00
	1811	.124	20.00	40.00	100.00	300.00
	1812	.145	20.00	40.00	100.00	300.00
	1813	.221	30.00	60.00	125.00	300.00
	1814	.046	35.00	75.00	150.00	350.00
Mint mark: MA						
164.6	1809	.027	35.00	80.00	175.00	450.00
	1810	8,843	50.00	100.00	225.00	500.00
	1811	.039	35.00	75.00	150.00	350.00
	1812	.016	40.00	100.00	200.00	500.00
	1813	.018	40.00	100.00	200.00	500.00
Mint mark: Q						
164.7	1809	.020	50.00	80.00	175.00	450.00
	1810	4,857	75.00	150.00	250.00	600.00
	1811	.075	35.00	75.00	150.00	350.00
	1812	.086	35.00	75.00	150.00	350.00
	1813	.253	20.00	40.00	100.00	300.00
	1814	.016	50.00	100.00	225.00	500.00
Mint mark: T						
164.14	1811	.035	35.00	80.00	175.00	450.00
	1812	.019	40.00	100.00	200.00	500.00
	1813	.011	20.00	40.00	100.00	300.00
Mint mark: U						
164.8	1809	3,149	100.00	200.00	400.00	900.00
	1810	3,077	100.00	200.00	400.00	900.00
	1811	3,893	100.00	200.00	400.00	900.00
Mint mark: W						
164.9	1809	.062	35.00	75.00	150.00	350.00
	1810	.048	35.00	75.00	150.00	350.00
	1811	.118	30.00	60.00	125.00	300.00
	1812	.108	30.00	60.00	125.00	300.00
	1813	.088	35.00	75.00	150.00	350.00
Mint mark: Flag						
164.15	1812	9,493	150.00	300.00	600.00	1350.
	1813/2	.041	—	—	—	—
	1813	Inc. Ab.	100.00	200.00	400.00	900.00
	Common date				Unc.	600.00

Mint mark: A

C#	Date	Mintage	VG	Fine	VF	XF
171	1815	6,783	175.00	350.00	700.00	1500.
	1815	—	—	—	Proof	3500.

Mint mark: A

C#	Date	Mintage	VG	Fine	VF	XF
180.1	1816	.061	25.00	55.00	150.00	375.00
	1817	.214	20.00	40.00	100.00	350.00
	1818	.013	35.00	75.00	200.00	500.00
	1819	2,334	50.00	100.00	250.00	550.00
	1820	.053	25.00	55.00	150.00	375.00
	1821	.139	22.00	45.00	125.00	350.00
	1822	.421	20.00	40.00	100.00	300.00
	1823	.268	20.00	40.00	100.00	250.00
	1824	.284	20.00	40.00	100.00	250.00

Mint mark: B

C#	Date	Mintage	VG	Fine	VF	XF
180.2	1816	4,398	40.00	85.00	250.00	500.00
	1817	.015	35.00	75.00	175.00	450.00
	1818	3,039	45.00	90.00	225.00	500.00
	1819	.012	35.00	75.00	175.00	450.00
	1822	.030	30.00	65.00	150.00	400.00
	1824	.071	25.00	50.00	145.00	375.00

Mint mark: D

C#	Date	Mintage	VG	Fine	VF	XF
180.11	1820	2,282	—	—	—	—
	1822	2,181	50.00	100.00	250.00	500.00
	1823	7,251	40.00	85.00	250.00	500.00
	1824	.108	22.00	45.00	120.00	350.00

Mint mark: H

C#	Date	Mintage	VG	Fine	VF	XF
180.3	1816	7,037	40.00	85.00	250.00	500.00
	1817	.037	30.00	65.00	150.00	400.00
	1818	8,530	40.00	85.00	250.00	500.00
	1819	5,309	40.00	85.00	250.00	500.00
	1820	2,801	—	—	—	—
	1821	2,897	45.00	90.00	225.00	500.00
	1822	9,806	40.00	85.00	250.00	500.00
	1823	.020	30.00	65.00	150.00	400.00
	1824	.027	30.00	65.00	150.00	400.00

Mint mark: I

C#	Date	Mintage	VG	Fine	VF	XF
180.4	1816	3,956	45.00	90.00	225.00	500.00
	1823	.010	40.00	85.00	250.00	500.00
	1824	.053	25.00	55.00	150.00	375.00

Mint mark: K

C#	Date	Mintage	VG	Fine	VF	XF
180.8	1817	.213	20.00	40.00	100.00	250.00
	1820	.011	40.00	85.00	250.00	500.00
	1823	2,545	—	—	—	—
	1824	.038	30.00	65.00	150.00	400.00

Mint mark: L

C#	Date	Mintage	VG	Fine	VF	XF
180.5	1816	1,068	—	—	—	—
	1817	3,026	—	—	—	—
	1818	444 pcs.	—	—	—	—
	1823	.027	30.00	65.00	150.00	400.00
	1824	.048	25.00	55.00	150.00	375.00

Mint mark: M

C#	Date	Mintage	VG	Fine	VF	XF
180.6	1816	1,699	—	—	—	—
	1817	.030	30.00	65.00	150.00	400.00
	1822	1,496	—	—	—	—
	1823	.094	25.00	55.00	150.00	375.00
	1824	.132	22.00	45.00	125.00	350.00

Mint mark: MA

C#	Date	Mintage	VG	Fine	VF	XF
180.12	1824	7,455	40.00	85.00	250.00	500.00

Mint mark: Q

C#	Date	Mintage	VG	Fine	VF	XF
180.7	1816	.013	35.00	75.00	175.00	450.00
	1817	.047	25.00	55.00	150.00	400.00
	1818	.052	25.00	55.00	150.00	400.00
	1819	.064	25.00	55.00	150.00	400.00
	1820	.047	25.00	55.00	150.00	400.00
	1821	.028	30.00	65.00	150.00	400.00
	1822	.011	40.00	85.00	250.00	500.00
	1823	3,399	50.00	100.00	250.00	500.00
	1824	.053	25.00	55.00	150.00	375.00

Mint mark: T

C#	Date	Mintage	VG	Fine	VF	XF
180.9	1817	1,456	—	—	—	—

Mint mark: W

C#	Date	Mintage	VG	Fine	VF	XF
180.10	1817	8,504	40.00	85.00	250.00	500.00
	1818	3,208	—	—	—	—
	1821	.022	30.00	65.00	150.00	400.00
	1822	.102	22.00	45.00	125.00	350.00
	1823	.265	20.00	30.00	75.00	225.00
	1824	.460	20.00	30.00	75.00	225.00
	Common date				Unc.	700.00

Mint mark: A

C#	Date	Mintage	VG	Fine	VF	XF
188.1	1825	.034	30.00	60.00	150.00	400.00
188.1	1826	.122	25.00	50.00	125.00	350.00
	1827	.268	20.00	45.00	100.00	325.00
	1828	.235	20.00	45.00	100.00	325.00
	1829	.145	25.00	50.00	150.00	400.00
	1830	.044	30.00	60.00	150.00	400.00
	1830 reeded edge	Inc. Ab.	150.00	300.00	600.00	1400.

Mint mark: B

C#	Date	Mintage	VG	Fine	VF	XF
188.2	1825	.017	35.00	70.00	175.00	400.00
	1826	.024	35.00	70.00	175.00	400.00
	1827	.138	25.00	50.00	125.00	350.00
	1828	.059	30.00	60.00	150.00	400.00
	1829	.102	25.00	50.00	125.00	250.00
	1830	.064	30.00	60.00	150.00	400.00

Mint mark: BB

C#	Date	Mintage	VG	Fine	VF	XF
188.3	1825	5,856	40.00	80.00	200.00	500.00
	1826	.019	35.00	70.00	175.00	400.00
	1827	.019	35.00	70.00	175.00	400.00
	1828	.025	35.00	70.00	175.00	400.00
	1829	.018	35.00	70.00	175.00	400.00

Mint mark: D

C#	Date	Mintage	VG	Fine	VF	XF
188.4	1825	.027	35.00	70.00	175.00	400.00
	1826	.072	30.00	60.00	150.00	400.00
	1827	.116	25.00	50.00	125.00	250.00
	1828	.108	25.00	50.00	125.00	250.00
	1829	.096	30.00	60.00	150.00	400.00

Mint mark: H

C#	Date	Mintage	VG	Fine	VF	XF
188.5	1825	3,215	—	—	—	—
	1826	.019	35.00	70.00	175.00	400.00
	1827	.019	35.00	70.00	175.00	400.00
	1828	.016	35.00	70.00	175.00	400.00
	1829	.049	30.00	60.00	150.00	400.00

Mint mark: I

C#	Date	Mintage	VG	Fine	VF	XF
188.6	1825	6,239	40.00	80.00	200.00	500.00
	1826	.032	30.00	60.00	150.00	400.00
	1827	.022	35.00	70.00	175.00	400.00
	1828	4,863	45.00	100.00	200.00	500.00
	1829	.016	35.00	70.00	175.00	400.00
	1830	5,635	45.00	100.00	200.00	500.00

Mint mark: K

C#	Date	Mintage	VG	Fine	VF	XF
188.7	1825	.011	35.00	70.00	175.00	400.00
	1826	.011	35.00	70.00	175.00	400.00
	1827	.033	30.00	60.00	150.00	400.00
	1828	.081	30.00	60.00	150.00	400.00
	1829	.033	30.00	60.00	150.00	400.00
	1830	.014	35.00	70.00	175.00	400.00

Mint mark: L

C#	Date	Mintage	VG	Fine	VF	XF
188.8	1825	4,397	45.00	100.00	200.00	500.00
	1826	.025	30.00	60.00	150.00	400.00
	1827	.052	30.00	60.00	150.00	400.00
	1828	.046	30.00	60.00	150.00	400.00
	1829	.021	35.00	70.00	175.00	400.00
	1830	.013	35.00	60.00	150.00	400.00

Mint mark: M

C#	Date	Mintage	VG	Fine	VF	XF
188.9	1825	6,770	40.00	80.00	200.00	500.00
	1826	.040	30.00	60.00	150.00	400.00
	1827	.031	30.00	60.00	150.00	400.00
	1828	.120	25.00	50.00	125.00	250.00
	1829	.049	30.00	60.00	150.00	400.00
	1830	.016	35.00	70.00	175.00	400.00

Mint mark: MA

C#	Date	Mintage	VG	Fine	VF	XF
188.13	1829	.041	30.00	60.00	150.00	400.00

Mint mark: Q

C#	Date	Mintage	VG	Fine	VF	XF
188.10	1825	4,956	50.00	100.00	200.00	500.00
	1826	.021	40.00	60.00	150.00	400.00
	1827	.014	50.00	70.00	175.00	400.00
	1828	.024	50.00	70.00	175.00	400.00
	1829	.011	50.00	70.00	175.00	400.00
	1830	6,688	60.00	125.00	200.00	500.00

Mint mark: T

C#	Date	Mintage	VG	Fine	VF	XF
188.12	1826	9,189	45.00	100.00	200.00	500.00
	1827	.043	30.00	60.00	150.00	400.00
	1828	.031	30.00	60.00	150.00	400.00
	1829	.050	30.00	60.00	150.00	400.00
	1830	.012	35.00	70.00	175.00	400.00

Mint mark: W

C#	Date	Mintage	VG	Fine	VF	XF
188.11	1825	.015	35.00	70.00	175.00	400.00
	1826	.155	25.00	50.00	125.00	250.00
	1827	.481	15.00	35.00	90.00	275.00
	1828	.358	15.00	35.00	90.00	275.00
	1829	.105	25.00	50.00	125.00	400.00
	1830	.109	25.00	50.00	125.00	400.00
	Common date				Unc.	750.00

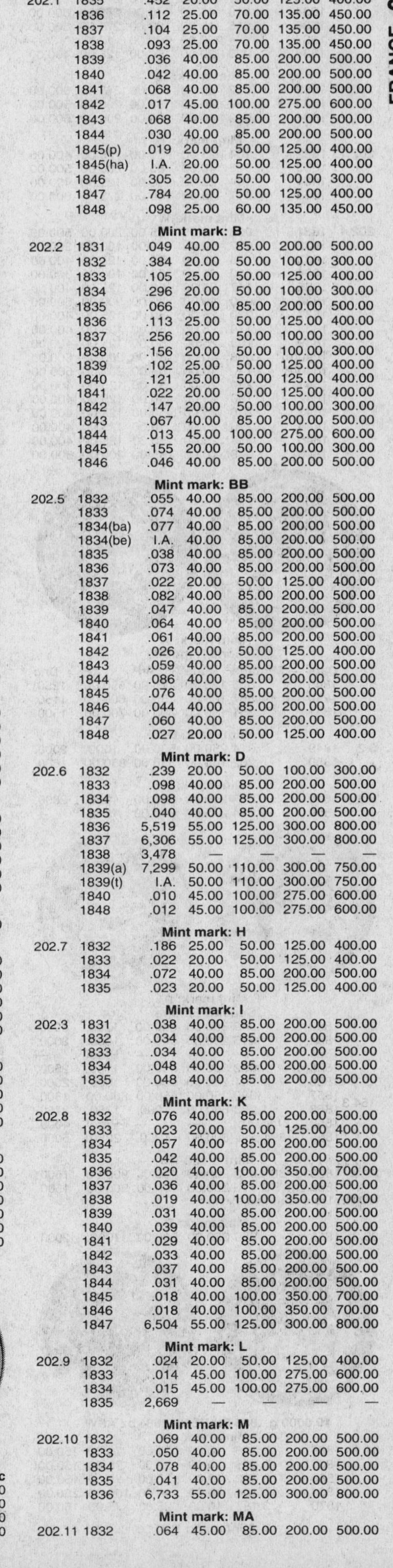

Mint mark: A

C#	Date	Mintage	Fine	VF	XF	Unc
202.1	1831	.010	45.00	100.00	275.00	600.00
	1832	.688	20.00	50.00	125.00	400.00
	1833	.194	25.00	70.00	135.00	450.00
	1834	.493	20.00	50.00	100.00	300.00
202.1	1835	.452	20.00	50.00	125.00	400.00
	1836	.112	25.00	70.00	135.00	450.00
	1837	.104	25.00	70.00	135.00	450.00
	1838	.093	25.00	70.00	135.00	450.00
	1839	.036	40.00	85.00	200.00	500.00
	1840	.042	40.00	85.00	200.00	500.00
	1841	.068	40.00	85.00	200.00	500.00
	1842	.017	45.00	100.00	275.00	600.00
	1843	.068	40.00	85.00	200.00	500.00
	1844	.030	40.00	85.00	200.00	500.00
	1845(p)	.019	20.00	50.00	125.00	400.00
	1845(ha)	I.A.	20.00	50.00	125.00	400.00
	1846	.305	20.00	50.00	100.00	300.00
	1847	.784	20.00	50.00	125.00	400.00
	1848	.098	25.00	60.00	135.00	450.00

Mint mark: B

C#	Date	Mintage	Fine	VF	XF	Unc
202.2	1831	.049	40.00	85.00	200.00	500.00
	1832	.384	20.00	50.00	100.00	300.00
	1833	.105	25.00	50.00	125.00	400.00
	1834	.296	20.00	50.00	100.00	300.00
	1835	.066	40.00	85.00	200.00	500.00
	1836	.113	25.00	50.00	125.00	400.00
	1837	.256	20.00	50.00	100.00	300.00
	1838	.156	20.00	50.00	100.00	300.00
	1839	.102	25.00	50.00	125.00	400.00
	1840	.121	25.00	50.00	125.00	400.00
	1841	.022	20.00	50.00	125.00	400.00
	1842	.147	20.00	50.00	100.00	300.00
	1843	.067	40.00	85.00	200.00	500.00
	1844	.013	45.00	100.00	275.00	600.00
	1845	.155	20.00	50.00	100.00	300.00
	1846	.046	40.00	85.00	200.00	500.00

Mint mark: BB

C#	Date	Mintage	Fine	VF	XF	Unc
202.5	1832	.055	40.00	85.00	200.00	500.00
	1833	.074	40.00	85.00	200.00	500.00
	1834(ba)	.077	40.00	85.00	200.00	500.00
	1834(be)	I.A.	40.00	85.00	200.00	500.00
	1835	.038	40.00	85.00	200.00	500.00
	1836	.073	40.00	85.00	200.00	500.00
	1837	.022	20.00	50.00	125.00	400.00
	1838	.082	40.00	85.00	200.00	500.00
	1839	.047	40.00	85.00	200.00	500.00
	1840	.064	40.00	85.00	200.00	500.00
	1841	.061	40.00	85.00	200.00	500.00
	1842	.026	20.00	50.00	125.00	400.00
	1843	.059	40.00	85.00	200.00	500.00
	1844	.086	40.00	85.00	200.00	500.00
	1845	.076	40.00	85.00	200.00	500.00
	1846	.044	40.00	85.00	200.00	500.00
	1847	.060	40.00	85.00	200.00	500.00
	1848	.027	20.00	50.00	125.00	400.00

Mint mark: D

C#	Date	Mintage	Fine	VF	XF	Unc
202.6	1832	.239	20.00	50.00	100.00	300.00
	1833	.098	40.00	85.00	200.00	500.00
	1834	.098	40.00	85.00	200.00	500.00
	1835	.040	40.00	85.00	200.00	500.00
	1836	5,519	55.00	125.00	300.00	800.00
	1837	6,306	55.00	125.00	300.00	800.00
	1838	3,478	—	—	—	—
	1839(a)	7,299	50.00	110.00	300.00	750.00
	1839(t)	I.A.	50.00	110.00	300.00	750.00
	1840	.010	45.00	100.00	275.00	600.00
	1848	.012	45.00	100.00	275.00	600.00

Mint mark: H

C#	Date	Mintage	Fine	VF	XF	Unc
202.7	1832	.186	25.00	50.00	125.00	400.00
	1833	.022	20.00	50.00	125.00	400.00
	1834	.072	40.00	85.00	200.00	500.00
	1835	.023	20.00	50.00	125.00	400.00

Mint mark: I

C#	Date	Mintage	Fine	VF	XF	Unc
202.3	1831	.038	40.00	85.00	200.00	500.00
	1832	.034	40.00	85.00	200.00	500.00
	1833	.034	40.00	85.00	200.00	500.00
	1834	.048	40.00	85.00	200.00	500.00
	1835	.048	40.00	85.00	200.00	500.00

Mint mark: K

C#	Date	Mintage	Fine	VF	XF	Unc
202.8	1832	.076	40.00	85.00	200.00	500.00
	1833	.023	20.00	50.00	125.00	400.00
	1834	.057	40.00	85.00	200.00	500.00
	1835	.042	40.00	85.00	200.00	500.00
	1836	.020	40.00	100.00	350.00	700.00
	1837	.036	40.00	85.00	200.00	500.00
	1838	.019	40.00	100.00	350.00	700.00
	1839	.031	40.00	85.00	200.00	500.00
	1840	.039	40.00	85.00	200.00	500.00
	1841	.029	40.00	85.00	200.00	500.00
	1842	.033	40.00	85.00	200.00	500.00
	1843	.037	40.00	85.00	200.00	500.00
	1844	.031	40.00	85.00	200.00	500.00
	1845	.018	40.00	100.00	350.00	700.00
	1846	.018	40.00	100.00	350.00	700.00
	1847	6,504	55.00	125.00	300.00	800.00

Mint mark: L

C#	Date	Mintage	Fine	VF	XF	Unc
202.9	1832	.024	20.00	50.00	125.00	400.00
	1833	.014	45.00	100.00	275.00	600.00
	1834	.015	45.00	100.00	275.00	600.00
	1835	2,669	—	—	—	—

Mint mark: M

C#	Date	Mintage	Fine	VF	XF	Unc
202.10	1832	.069	40.00	85.00	200.00	500.00
	1833	.050	40.00	85.00	200.00	500.00
	1834	.078	40.00	85.00	200.00	500.00
	1835	.041	40.00	85.00	200.00	500.00
	1836	6,733	55.00	125.00	300.00	800.00

Mint mark: MA

C#	Date	Mintage	Fine	VF	XF	Unc
202.11	1832	.064	45.00	85.00	200.00	500.00

C#	Date	Mintage	Fine	VF	XF	Unc
202.11	1833	.021	45.00	100.00	275.00	600.00
	1834	.019	45.00	100.00	275.00	600.00
	1835	.015	45.00	100.00	275.00	600.00
	1837	—	250.00	600.00	1200.	—
	1838	.025	20.00	50.00	125.00	400.00

Mint mark: Q

C#	Date	Mintage	Fine	VF	XF	Unc
202.12	1832	.022	45.00	100.00	275.00	600.00
	1833	.037	40.00	85.00	200.00	500.00
	1834	.069	40.00	85.00	200.00	500.00

Mint mark: T

C#	Date	Mintage	Fine	VF	XF	Unc
202.13	1832	.104	25.00	50.00	125.00	400.00
	1833	.028	40.00	85.00	200.00	500.00
	1834	.104	25.00	50.00	125.00	400.00
	1835	.017	45.00	100.00	275.00	600.00

Mint mark: W

C#	Date	Mintage	Fine	VF	XF	Unc
202.4	1831	.033	40.00	85.00	200.00	500.00
	1832	.427	20.00	50.00	100.00	300.00
	1833	.168	25.00	50.00	125.00	400.00
	1834	.583	20.00	50.00	100.00	300.00
	1835	.147	25.00	50.00	125.00	400.00
	1836	.060	40.00	85.00	200.00	500.00
	1837	.230	25.00	50.00	125.00	400.00
	1838	.170	25.00	50.00	125.00	400.00
	1839	.105	25.00	50.00	125.00	400.00
	1840(c)	.063	40.00	85.00	200.00	500.00
	1840(r)	I.A.	40.00	85.00	200.00	500.00
	1841	.290	25.00	50.00	125.00	400.00
	1842	.190	25.00	50.00	125.00	400.00
	1843	.296	25.00	50.00	125.00	400.00
	1844	.290	25.00	50.00	125.00	400.00
	1845	.353	25.00	50.00	125.00	400.00
	1846	.049	40.00	85.00	200.00	500.00

Mint mark: A
Second Republic

Y#	Date	Mintage	Fine	VF	XF	Unc
5.1	1849	.665	125.00	275.00	650.00	1250.
	1850	.857	100.00	250.00	600.00	1150.
	1851	.351	150.00	300.00	700.00	1500.

Mint mark: BB

Y#	Date	Mintage	Fine	VF	XF	Unc
5.2	1849	.014	250.00	500.00	1000.	2000.
	1850	.202	160.00	350.00	850.00	1600.

Mint mark: K

Y#	Date	Mintage	Fine	VF	XF	Unc
5.3	1849	.017	250.00	500.00	1000.	2000.
	1850	9,914	275.00	650.00	1500.	—

Mint mark: A
Second Empire

Y#	Date	Mintage	Fine	VF	XF	Unc
25.1	1853	.049	350.00	600.00	1200.	3000.
	1854	.215	250.00	500.00	1000.	2000.
	1854	—	—	—	Proof	—
	1855(d)	.082	300.00	550.00	1150.	2500.
	1856	.241	250.00	500.00	1000.	2000.
	1857	.389	250.00	450.00	800.00	1800.
	1858	1,288	600.00	1000.	1750.	3750.
	1858	Inc. Ab.	—	—	Proof	4000.
	1859	894 pcs.	800.00	1350.	2250.	5000.

Mint mark: BB

Y#	Date	Mintage	Fine	VF	XF	Unc
25.2	1856 lg. BB	.693	200.00	400.00	900.00	1500.
	1856 sm. BB	I.A.	200.00	400.00	900.00	1500.

NOTE: Date varieties exist.

Mint mark: D

Y#	Date	Mintage	Fine	VF	XF	Unc
25.3	1856	.289	250.00	500.00	1000.	2000.

10.0000 g, .835 SILVER, .2684 oz ASW
Mint mark: A

Y#	Date	Mintage	Fine	VF	XF	Unc
31.1	1866	3.226	10.00	25.00	75.00	150.00
	1867	3.695	10.00	25.00	75.00	150.00
	1868	3.762	10.00	25.00	75.00	150.00
	1869	1.104	20.00	40.00	100.00	250.00
	1870	3.187	10.00	25.00	75.00	150.00

Mint mark: BB

Y#	Date	Mintage	Fine	VF	XF	Unc
31.2	1866	3.090	10.00	25.00	75.00	150.00
	1867	3.471	10.00	25.00	75.00	150.00
	1868	.733	30.00	75.00	175.00	400.00
	1869	.367	35.00	90.00	200.00	500.00
	1870	1.001	—	—	—	—

Mint mark: K

Y#	Date	Mintage	Fine	VF	XF	Unc
31.3	1866	.437	50.00	125.00	250.00	600.00
	1867	1.744	15.00	40.00	100.00	250.00
	1868	.087	—	—	—	—

Mint mark: A
Third Republic

Y#	Date	Mintage	Fine	VF	XF	Unc
45.1	1870	.239	50.00	125.00	350.00	700.00

Mint mark: K

Y#	Date	Mintage	Fine	VF	XF	Unc
45.2	1870(a)	.560	50.00	125.00	300.00	600.00
	1870(s)	I.A.	50.00	125.00	300.00	625.00
	1871	1.256	40.00	100.00	225.00	500.00

Mint mark: A

Y#	Date	Mintage	Fine	VF	XF	Unc
50.1	1870 lg.A	1.324	8.00	18.00	50.00	150.00
	1870 sm.a	I.A.	10.00	20.00	60.00	175.00
	1871 lg.A	4.757	7.00	15.00	40.00	100.00
	1871 sm.a	I.A.	7.00	15.00	40.00	100.00
	1872	2.306	7.00	15.00	40.00	100.00
	1873	.528	30.00	75.00	175.00	400.00
	1878	30 pcs.	—	—	Proof	6000.
	1881	1.014	10.00	30.00	75.00	150.00
	1887	2.343	7.00	15.00	40.00	100.00
	1888	.131	65.00	150.00	300.00	650.00
	1889	100 pcs.	—	—	Proof	5000.
	1894	.300	15.00	40.00	100.00	250.00
	1895	.600	12.00	30.00	75.00	175.00

Mint mark: K

Y#	Date	Mintage	Fine	VF	XF	Unc
50.2	1871 lg. K	1.215	15.00	40.00	100.00	250.00
	1871 sm. k	I.A.	12.00	30.00	75.00	175.00
	1872	1.467	12.00	30.00	75.00	175.00

Mint: Paris - w/o mint mark.

Y#	Date	Mintage	Fine	VF	XF	Unc
64.1	1898	5.000	3.00	5.00	20.00	40.00
	1898	—	—	—	Proof	400.00
	1899	3.500	4.00	7.00	25.00	50.00
	1900	.500	30.00	80.00	200.00	450.00
	1900	—	—	—	Proof	400.00
	1901	1.860	8.00	25.00	60.00	150.00
	1902	2.000	8.00	25.00	60.00	150.00
	1904	1.500	10.00	25.00	50.00	200.00
	1905	2.000	8.00	25.00	60.00	150.00
	1908	2.502	4.00	7.00	25.00	50.00
	1909	1.000	10.00	25.00	50.00	200.00
	1910	2.190	4.00	7.00	25.00	50.00
	1912	1.000	8.00	25.00	60.00	175.00
	1913	.500	20.00	40.00	75.00	200.00
	1914	5.719	2.00	4.00	10.00	25.00
	1915	13.963	1.00	2.00	5.00	15.00
	1916	17.887	1.00	2.00	5.00	15.00
	1917	16.555	1.00	2.00	5.00	15.00
	1918	12.026	1.00	2.00	5.00	15.00
	1919	9.261	2.00	4.00	6.00	12.00
	1920	3.014	3.00	6.00	10.00	25.00

Mint mark: C

Y#	Date	Mintage	Fine	VF	XF	Unc
64.2	1914	.462	10.00	20.00	35.00	50.00
	1914	—	—		Matte Proof	600.00

ALUMINUM-BRONZE
Mint: Paris - w/o mint mark.
French Chamber of Commerce Series

Y#	Date	Mintage	Fine	VF	XF	Unc
79	1920	14.363	8.00	20.00	60.00	100.00
	1921	Inc. Ab.	1.00	2.00	5.00	15.00
	1922	29.463	.50	1.00	2.00	9.00
	1923	43.960	.50	1.00	2.00	9.00
	1924	29.631	.50	1.00	2.00	9.00
	1925	31.607	.50	1.00	2.00	9.00
	1926	2.962	10.00	25.00	75.00	125.00
	1927	1.678	100.00	200.00	450.00	850.00

Y#	Date	Mintage	Fine	VF	XF	Unc
82	1931	1.717	4.00	8.00	16.00	45.00
	1932	8.943	1.00	2.50	4.00	12.00
	1933	8.413	1.00	2.50	4.00	12.00
	1934	6.896	1.50	3.00	8.00	16.00
	1935	.298	15.00	30.00	50.00	100.00
	1936	12.394	.25	1.00	2.00	8.00
	1937	11.055	.25	1.00	2.00	8.00
	1938	28.072	.20	.50	1.00	6.00
	1939	25.403	.20	.50	1.00	6.00
	1940	9.716	1.00	2.50	4.00	12.00
	1941	16.684	.25	1.00	2.00	8.00

ALUMINUM

Y#	Date	Mintage	Fine	VF	XF	Unc
82a.1	1941	Inc. Ab.	.25	.50	1.00	4.00
	1944	7.224	1.00	2.00	6.00	20.00
	1945	16.636	.50	1.00	3.00	10.00
	1946	34.930	.20	.50	1.00	5.00
	1947	78.984	.20	.30	1.00	4.00
	1948	32.354	.20	.50	1.00	5.00
	1949	13.683	.25	.50	1.00	4.00
	1950	12.191	.25	.50	1.00	4.00
	1958	9.906	.20	.50	1.00	5.00
	1959	17.774	.20	.50	1.00	5.00

Mint mark: B

Y#	Date	Mintage	Fine	VF	XF	Unc
82a.2	1944	.170	—	—	—	—
	1945	1.726	4.00	10.00	20.00	50.00
	1946	6.018	2.00	4.00	8.00	30.00
	1947	26.220	.20	.50	1.00	5.00
	1948	39.090	.20	.50	1.00	6.00
	1949	23.955	.20	.50	1.00	5.00
	1950	18.185	.50	1.00	3.00	8.00

Mint mark: C

Y#	Date	Mintage	Fine	VF	XF	Unc
82a.3	1944	9.828	—	—	—	—
	1945	1.165	6.00	12.00	35.00	75.00
	1946	1.533	—	—	—	—

LB (L. Bazor)

Mint: Paris - w/o mint mark.
Vichy French State Issues

Y#	Date	Mintage	Fine	VF	XF	Unc
V96.1	1943	106.997	.20	.50	1.00	6.00
	1944	25.546	1.00	3.00	6.00	9.00

Mint mark: B

Y#	Date	Mintage	Fine	VF	XF	Unc
V96.2	1943	34.131	5.00	10.00	25.00	40.00
	1944	10.298	3.00	6.00	10.00	25.00

Mint mark: C

Y#	Date	Mintage	Fine	VF	XF	Unc
V96.3	1943	7.575	—	Reported, not confirmed		
	1944	19.470	2.50	5.00	10.00	25.00

BRASS
Mint: Philadelphia, U.S.A., w/o mint mark.
Allied Occupation Issue

Y#	Date	Mintage	Fine	VF	XF	Unc
89	1944	50.000	1.00	2.00	7.00	20.00

NICKEL

Y#	Date	Mintage	Fine	VF	XF	Unc
109.1	1979	130.000	—	—	.40	.65
	1980	100.010	—	—	.40	.65
	1981	120.000	—	—	.40	.65
	1982	90.000	—	—	.40	.65
	1983	90.000	—	—	.40	.65
	1984	.050	—	—	—	.75
	1985	.020	—	—	—	2.00
	1986	.048	—	—	—	2.00
	1987	.100	—	—	—	.75
	1988	.100	—	—	—	.75
	1989	.083	—	—	—	.75
	1990	.015	—	—	—	.75
	1991	.015	—	—	—	.75
	1992	.100	—	—	—	.75
	1992	—	—	—	Proof	3.50
	1993	—	—	—	—	.75

Plain edge.

Y#	Date	Mintage	Fine	VF	XF	Unc
109.2	1991	—	—	—	Proof	3.50

5 FRANCS

25.0000 g, .900 SILVER, .7234 oz ASW
Mint mark: A

C#	Date	Mintage	VG	Fine	VF	XF
138.1	L'AN 10	.561	35.00	75.00	175.00	550.00
	L'AN 11	1.558	25.00	60.00	150.00	450.00

NOTE: Earlier dates (L'AN 4 - L'AN 9) exist for this type.

Mint mark: G

C#	Date	Mintage	VG	Fine	VF	XF
138.9	L'AN 10	4,447	125.00	300.00	600.00	2200.

NOTE: Earlier date (L'AN 9) exists for this type.

Mint mark: K

C#	Date	Mintage	VG	Fine	VF	XF
138.3	L'AN 10	.060	40.00	100.00	250.00	700.00
	L'AN 11	.029	60.00	125.00	350.00	1250.

NOTE: Earlier dates (L'AN 5 - L'AN 9) exist for this type.

Mint mark: L

C#	Date	Mintage	VG	Fine	VF	XF
138.4	L'AN 10	.165	35.00	90.00	225.00	550.00
	L'AN 11	.170	35.00	90.00	225.00	550.00

NOTE: Earlier dates (L'AN 5 - L'AN 9) exist for this type.

Mint mark: MA

C#	Date	Mintage	VG	Fine	VF	XF
138.10	L'AN 10	.039	50.00	125.00	300.00	1150.
	L'AN 11	.160	35.00	90.00	225.00	550.00

NOTE: Earlier date (L'AN 9) exists for this type.

Mint mark: Q

C#	Date	Mintage	VG	Fine	VF	XF
138.5	L'AN 10	.134	35.00	90.00	225.00	550.00
	L'AN 11	.360	30.00	80.00	200.00	500.00

NOTE: Earlier dates (L'AN 5 - L'AN 9) exist for this type.

Mint mark: T

C#	Date	Mintage	VG	Fine	VF	XF
138.6	L'AN 10	5,232	— Reported, not confirmed			
	L'AN 11	9,950	70.00	165.00	400.00	1350.

NOTE: Earlier dates (L'AN 5 - L'AN 9) exist for this type.

Mint mark: A
Obv. leg: BONAPARTE PREMIER CONSUL.

C#	Date	Mintage	VG	Fine	VF	XF
145.1	ANXI	3.878	20.00	50.00	150.00	300.00
	ANXI w/o dots flanking privy mark					
		Inc. Ab.	150.00	300.00	700.00	—

Mint mark: D

C#	Date	Mintage	VG	Fine	VF	XF
145.2	ANXI	5,547	100.00	200.00	500.00	900.00

Mint mark: K

C#	Date	Mintage	VG	Fine	VF	XF
145.3	ANXI	.031	50.00	125.00	300.00	800.00

Mint mark: L

C#	Date	Mintage	VG	Fine	VF	XF
145.4	ANXI	.119	35.00	90.00	225.00	550.00

Mint mark: MA

C#	Date	Mintage	VG	Fine	VF	XF
145.5	ANXI	.206	30.00	80.00	200.00	500.00

Mint mark: Q

C#	Date	Mintage	VG	Fine	VF	XF
145.6	ANXI	.309	30.00	80.00	200.00	450.00

Mint mark: T

C#	Date	Mintage	VG	Fine	VF	XF
145.7	ANXI	.018	75.00	200.00	400.00	650.00

Mint mark: A

C#	Date	Mintage	VG	Fine	VF	XF
145.8	AN12	3.454	20.00	40.00	125.00	300.00

Mint mark: B

C#	Date	Mintage	VG	Fine	VF	XF
145.9	AN12	.035	50.00	125.00	300.00	800.00

Mint mark: BB

C#	Date	Mintage	VG	Fine	VF	XF
145.10	AN12	.018	75.00	200.00	400.00	650.00

Mint mark: D

C#	Date	Mintage	VG	Fine	VF	XF
145.11	AN12	.116	35.00	90.00	225.00	550.00

Mint mark: G

C#	Date	Mintage	VG	Fine	VF	XF
145.12	AN12	.014	200.00	500.00	1000.	3000.

Mint mark: H

C#	Date	Mintage	VG	Fine	VF	XF
145.13	AN12	.070	50.00	125.00	300.00	800.00

Mint mark: I

C#	Date	Mintage	VG	Fine	VF	XF
145.14	AN12	.422	30.00	80.00	200.00	350.00

Mint mark: K

C#	Date	Mintage	VG	Fine	VF	XF
145.15	AN12	.462	40.00	80.00	200.00	350.00

Mint mark: L

C#	Date	Mintage	VG	Fine	VF	XF
145.16	AN12	.311	40.00	80.00	200.00	350.00

Mint mark: M

C#	Date	Mintage	VG	Fine	VF	XF
145.17	AN12	1.199	30.00	70.00	175.00	300.00

Mint mark: MA

C#	Date	Mintage	VG	Fine	VF	XF
145.18	AN12	.148	35.00	90.00	225.00	550.00

Mint mark: Q

C#	Date	Mintage	VG	Fine	VF	XF
145.19	AN12	.578	40.00	80.00	200.00	350.00

Mint mark: T

C#	Date	Mintage	VG	Fine	VF	XF
145.20	AN12	.113	35.00	90.00	225.00	550.00

Mint mark: U

C#	Date	Mintage	VG	Fine	VF	XF
145.21	AN12	9,953	150.00	350.00	1000.	2200.

Mint mark: W

C#	Date	Mintage	VG	Fine	VF	XF
145.22	AN12	.028	50.00	125.00	300.00	700.00

Mint mark: A
Obv. leg: NAPOLEON EMPEREUR.

C#	Date	Mintage	VG	Fine	VF	XF
155.1	AN12	.767	50.00	125.00	300.00	500.00

Mint mark: B

C#	Date	Mintage	VG	Fine	VF	XF
155.2	AN12	.010	60.00	150.00	400.00	800.00

Mint mark: D

C#	Date	Mintage	VG	Fine	VF	XF
155.3	AN12	.014	50.00	125.00	300.00	600.00

Mint mark: H

C#	Date	Mintage	VG	Fine	VF	XF
155.4	AN12	.015	50.00	125.00	300.00	600.00

Mint mark: I

C#	Date	Mintage	VG	Fine	VF	XF
155.5	AN12	.090	40.00	100.00	200.00	500.00

Mint mark: K

C#	Date	Mintage	VG	Fine	VF	XF
155.6	AN12	.071	40.00	100.00	200.00	500.00

Mint mark: L

C#	Date	Mintage	VG	Fine	VF	XF
155.7	AN12	.016	50.00	125.00	300.00	600.00

Mint mark: M

C#	Date	Mintage	VG	Fine	VF	XF
155.8	AN12	.427	40.00	100.00	200.00	500.00

Mint mark: MA

C#	Date	Mintage	VG	Fine	VF	XF
155.9	AN12	2,030	— Reported, not confirmed			

Mint mark: Q

C#	Date	Mintage	VG	Fine	VF	XF
155.10	AN12	.055	40.00	100.00	200.00	500.00

Mint mark: T

C#	Date	Mintage	VG	Fine	VF	XF
155.11	AN12	.011	100.00	200.00	400.00	800.00

Mint mark: W

C#	Date	Mintage	VG	Fine	VF	XF
155.12	AN12	4,366	120.00	250.00	500.00	1800.

Mint mark: A
Obv: Monogram below bust.

C#	Date	Mintage	VG	Fine	VF	XF
155a.1	AN13	5.121	20.00	40.00	100.00	300.00
	AN14	1.855	25.00	50.00	125.00	350.00

Mint mark: B

C#	Date	Mintage	VG	Fine	VF	XF
155a.2	AN13	4,901	60.00	150.00	400.00	800.00

Mint mark: BB

C#	Date	Mintage	VG	Fine	VF	XF
155a.3	AN13	7,510	—	—	—	—
	AN14	.831	—	—	—	—

Mint mark: D

C#	Date	Mintage	VG	Fine	VF	XF
155a.4	AN13	.024	40.00	100.00	200.00	500.00
	AN14	3,890	100.00	250.00	500.00	1800.

Mint mark: G

C#	Date	Mintage	VG	Fine	VF	XF
155a.5	AN13	6,487	200.00	400.00	1000.	2500.

Mint mark: H

C#	Date	Mintage	VG	Fine	VF	XF
155a.6	AN13	.035	40.00	100.00	200.00	500.00
	AN14	3,780	100.00	250.00	500.00	1150.

Mint mark: I

C#	Date	Mintage	VG	Fine	VF	XF
155a.7	AN13	.333	40.00	100.00	200.00	500.00
	AN14	.012	—	—	—	—
	Mint mark: K					
155a.8	AN13	.161	50.00	125.00	300.00	600.00
	AN14	2,113	200.00	400.00	700.00	2000.
	Mint mark: L					
155a.9	AN13	.207	40.00	110.00	275.00	475.00
	AN14	.015	50.00	125.00	300.00	600.00
	Mint mark: M					
155a.10	AN13	1.547	30.00	60.00	125.00	300.00
	AN14	.040	40.00	100.00	200.00	500.00
	Mint mark: MA					
155a.11	AN13	.064	40.00	100.00	200.00	450.00
	Mint mark: Q					
155a.12	AN13	.245	35.00	75.00	175.00	375.00
	Mint mark: T					
155a.13	AN13	.025	40.00	100.00	200.00	500.00
	AN14	632	— Reported, not confirmed			
	Mint mark: U					
155a.14	AN13	.021	100.00	200.00	400.00	800.00
	AN14	.014	125.00	250.00	550.00	1150.
	Mint mark: W					
155a.15	AN13	.034	40.00	100.00	200.00	500.00
	AN14	.014	50.00	125.00	300.00	600.00

C#	Date	Mintage	VG	Fine	VF	XF
	Mint mark: A					
155a.16	1806	.826	35.00	75.00	150.00	350.00
	Mint mark: B					
155a.17	1806	.025	40.00	100.00	200.00	500.00
	1807	.044	40.00	100.00	200.00	500.00
	Mint mark: BB					
155a.18	1806	.660	35.00	75.00	150.00	350.00
	1807	1,296	—	—	—	—
	Mint mark: D					
155a.19	1806	2,771	—	—	—	—
	1807	2,423	—	—	—	—
	Mint mark: H					
155a.20	1806	.028	— Reported, not confirmed			
	1807	4,847	100.00	250.00	500.00	1300.
	Mint mark: I					
155a.21	1806	.239	35.00	70.00	150.00	325.00
	1807	.091	35.00	80.00	175.00	400.00
	Mint mark: K					
155a.22	1806	.029	40.00	100.00	200.00	500.00
	1807	.010	60.00	175.00	350.00	800.00
	Mint mark: L					
155a.23	1806	.551	35.00	75.00	150.00	350.00
	1807	.375	35.00	70.00	150.00	325.00
	Mint mark: M					
155a.24	1806	.022	40.00	100.00	200.00	500.00
	1807	.101	35.00	80.00	175.00	400.00
	Mint mark: Q					
155a.25	1806	.078	35.00	70.00	150.00	350.00
	1807	.025	40.00	100.00	200.00	500.00
	Mint mark: T					
155a 26	1806	706 pcs.	— Reported, not confirmed			
	1807	449 pcs.	—	—	Rare	—
	Mint mark: U					
155a.27	1806	.031	100.00	200.00	400.00	800.00
	1807	.030	125.00	250.00	500.00	1400.
	Mint mark: W					
155a.28	1806	.032	40.00	100.00	200.00	500.00
	1807	.029	40.00	100.00	200.00	500.00

Mint mark: A

Obv: Similar to C#155a.1. Rev: Similar to C#155c.

C#	Date	Mintage	VG	Fine	VF	XF
155b	1807	.049	300.00	650.00	1200.	2500.

Rev. leg: REPUBLIQUE FRANCAISE.

C#	Date	Mintage	VG	Fine	VF	XF
155c.1	1807	.041	350.00	700.00	1300.	2000.
	1807	—	—	—	Proof	5000.
	1808	6.462	20.00	35.00	55.00	120.00
	Mint mark: B					
155c.2	1808	1.542	22.00	40.00	65.00	135.00
	Mint mark: BB					
155c.3	1808	.068	35.00	70.00	150.00	325.00
	Mint mark: D					
155c.4	1808	.065	35.00	70.00	150.00	325.00
	Mint mark: H					
155c.5	1808	7,204	— Reported, not confirmed			
	Mint mark: I					
155c.6	1808	.107	35.00	70.00	150.00	300.00
	Mint mark: K					
155c.7	1808	.054	35.00	70.00	150.00	325.00
	Mint mark: L					
155c.8	1808	.144	35.00	70.00	125.00	275.00
	Mint mark: M					
155c.9	1808	.351	25.00	40.00	65.00	150.00
	Mint mark: MA					
155c.10	1808	2,681	100.00	225.00	450.00	900.00
	Mint mark: Q					
155c.11	1808	.012	55.00	95.00	200.00	500.00
	Mint mark: T					
155c.12	1808	2,682	— Reported, not confirmed			
	Mint mark: U					
155c.13	1808	.014	75.00	200.00	400.00	750.00
	Mint mark: W					
155c.14	1808	.550	25.00	40.00	65.00	150.00
	Common date				Unc.	400.00

Mint mark: A

Rev. leg: EMPIRE FRANCAIS.

C#	Date	Mintage	VG	Fine	VF	XF
165.1	1809	3.254	15.00	25.00	50.00	125.00
	1810	8.797	12.50	20.00	45.00	110.00
	1811	31.050	12.50	17.50	40.00	100.00
	1812	9.311	12.50	20.00	45.00	110.00
	1813	9.757	12.50	20.00	45.00	110.00
	1814	1.329	20.00	35.00	85.00	175.00
	Mint mark: B					
165.2	1809	3.036	15.00	25.00	50.00	125.00
	1810	.632	25.00	40.00	65.00	150.00

C#	Date	Mintage	VG	Fine	VF	XF
165.2	1811	3.772	15.00	25.00	50.00	125.00
	1812	3.039	15.00	25.00	50.00	125.00
	1813	.728	25.00	40.00	65.00	150.00
	1814	.020	35.00	75.00	125.00	250.00
	Mint mark: BB					
165.3	1809	2,856	— Reported, not confirmed			
	1810	.028	30.00	60.00	100.00	225.00
	1811	.327	25.00	40.00	65.00	150.00
	1812	.139	30.00	50.00	120.00	200.00
	1813	.025	35.00	75.00	135.00	275.00
	1814	5,382	— Reported, not confirmed			
	Mint mark: CL					
165.18	1813	.014	300.00	500.00	900.00	2500.
	1814	1,191	1500.	2500.	4500.	6500.
	Mint mark: D					
165.4	1809	.011	35.00	75.00	150.00	325.00
	1810	.043	30.00	60.00	100.00	225.00
	1811	1.568	20.00	35.00	85.00	175.00
	1812	2.295	15.00	30.00	50.00	125.00
	1813	.917	20.00	35.00	85.00	175.00
	Mint mark: H					
165.5	1809	9,006	50.00	125.00	250.00	475.00
	1811	1.029	20.00	35.00	85.00	175.00
	1812	1.824	20.00	35.00	85.00	175.00
	1813	1.795	20.00	35.00	85.00	175.00
	1814	.169	30.00	50.00	125.00	200.00
	Mint mark: I					
165.6	1809	.065	30.00	60.00	100.00	225.00
	1810	.026	35.00	75.00	135.00	275.00
	1811	1.830	20.00	35.00	85.00	175.00
	1812	2.672	15.00	30.00	60.00	125.00
	1813	2.555	20.00	35.00	85.00	175.00
	1814	.027	35.00	75.00	135.00	275.00
	Mint mark: K					
165.7	1809	.105	30.00	50.00	125.00	200.00
	1810	.120	30.00	50.00	125.00	200.00
	1811	1.081	20.00	35.00	85.00	175.00
	1812	1.664	20.00	35.00	85.00	175.00
	1813	1.281	20.00	35.00	85.00	175.00
	Mint mark: L					
165.8	1809	.217	30.00	50.00	120.00	200.00
	1810 mint mark at right					
		.185	30.00	50.00	120.00	200.00
	1810 mint mark at left					
		Inc. Ab.	35.00	75.00	135.00	275.00
	1811	1.123	20.00	35.00	85.00	175.00
	1812	.936	20.00	35.00	85.00	175.00
	1813	1.161	20.00	35.00	85.00	175.00
	Mint mark: M					
165.9	1809	.034	30.00	60.00	100.00	225.00
	1810	.072	30.00	60.00	100.00	225.00
	1811	1.101	20.00	35.00	85.00	175.00
	1812	1.617	20.00	35.00	85.00	175.00
	1813	2.213	20.00	35.00	85.00	175.00
	1814	.369	25.00	45.00	90.00	200.00
	Mint mark: MA					
165.10	1809	.012	35.00	75.00	150.00	325.00
	1810	.012	35.00	75.00	150.00	325.00
	1811	.671	25.00	40.00	90.00	200.00
	1812	.612	25.00	40.00	90.00	200.00
	1813	.834	25.00	40.00	90.00	200.00
	1814	.016	40.00	85.00	200.00	300.00
	Mint mark: Q					
165.14	1810	.118	30.00	50.00	125.00	200.00
	1811	1.213	20.00	35.00	85.00	175.00
	1812	1.460	20.00	35.00	85.00	175.00
	1813	1.826	20.00	35.00	85.00	175.00
	1814	.367	25.00	45.00	100.00	190.00
	Mint mark: R					
165.16	1812R/cr	.049	100.00	250.00	550.00	1100.
	1813R/cr	.017	175.00	400.00	850.00	2000.
	Mint mark: T					
165.11	1809	2,218	— Reported, not confirmed			
	1811	.724	20.00	35.00	85.00	175.00
	1812	.926	20.00	35.00	85.00	175.00
	1813	.564	20.00	35.00	85.00	175.00
	1814	8,745	55.00	125.00	275.00	500.00
	Mint mark: U					
165.12	1809	.016	100.00	200.00	450.00	900.00
	1810	.014	100.00	250.00	500.00	1000.
	1811	.169	30.00	60.00	100.00	225.00
	1812/1	—	75.00	150.00	250.00	500.00
	1812	.105	30.00	60.00	100.00	225.00
	1813	.060	35.00	75.00	150.00	325.00
	Mint mark: W					
165.13	1809	1.221	20.00	35.00	85.00	175.00
	1810	.297	30.00	50.00	120.00	200.00
	1811	3.290	15.00	30.00	60.00	125.00
	1812	4.342	15.00	30.00	60.00	125.00
	1813	1.824	20.00	35.00	85.00	175.00
	1814	.033	35.00	75.00	150.00	325.00
	Mint mark: Flag					
165.17	1812	.055	150.00	300.00	650.00	1300.
	1813	.362	125.00	250.00	500.00	1000.
	Common date				Unc.	300.00

C#	Date	Mintage	VG	Fine	VF	XF
		Mint mark: A				
		First Restoration				
168.1	1814	1.466	20.00	45.00	100.00	250.00
	1814	4 known	—	—	Proof	2500.
	1815	.413	25.00	50.00	125.00	275.00
		Mint mark: B				
168.2	1814	.634	25.00	50.00	125.00	275.00
	1815	.254	30.00	65.00	150.00	350.00
		Mint mark: BB				
168.3	1814	4,913	75.00	175.00	400.00	900.00
	1815	1,551	100.00	225.00	500.00	1200.
		Mint mark: D				
168.4	1814	.082	35.00	75.00	175.00	400.00
	1815	7,482	65.00	150.00	325.00	700.00
		Mint mark: H				
168.5	1814	.046	40.00	85.00	200.00	500.00
	1815	.034	40.00	85.00	200.00	500.00
		Mint mark: I				
168.6	1814	1.554	20.00	45.00	100.00	250.00
	1815	1.739	20.00	45.00	100.00	250.00
		Mint mark: K				
168.7	1814	.355	30.00	60.00	120.00	350.00
	1815	.108	30.00	60.00	120.00	350.00
		Mint mark: L				
168.8	1814	1.902	20.00	45.00	100.00	250.00
	1815	1.130	20.00	45.00	100.00	250.00
		Mint mark: M				
168.9	1814	2.377	20.00	45.00	100.00	250.00
	1815	1.406	20.00	45.00	100.00	250.00
		Mint mark: MA				
168.10	1814	.099	35.00	75.00	135.00	300.00
	1815	7,461	75.00	175.00	400.00	900.00
		Mint mark: Q				
168.11	1814	1.182	20.00	45.00	100.00	250.00
	1815/4	.925	30.00	50.00	75.00	200.00
	1815	Inc. Ab.	20.00	45.00	100.00	250.00
		Mint mark: T				
168.12	1814	5,235	75.00	175.00	400.00	900.00
	1815	8,006	— Reported, not confirmed			
		Mint mark: W				
168.13	1814	.104	35.00	75.00	135.00	300.00
	1815	.114	35.00	75.00	135.00	300.00
	Common date				Unc.	600.00

C#	Date	Mintage	VG	Fine	VF	XF
		Mint mark: A				
		"The Hundred Days"				
172.1	1815	.473	75.00	150.00	275.00	650.00
		Mint mark: B				
172.2	1815	.093	100.00	200.00	350.00	1000.
		Mint mark: BB				
172.3	1815	3,723	250.00	600.00	1200.	2500.
		Mint mark: I				
172.4	1815	.596	65.00	125.00	250.00	550.00
		Mint mark: L				
172.5	1815	.097	90.00	200.00	350.00	1000.
		Mint mark: M				
172.6	1815	.080	100.00	225.00	375.00	1250.
		Mint mark: Q				
172.7	1815	.021	120.00	280.00	550.00	1500.
		Mint mark: W				
172.8	1815	.021	120.00	280.00	550.00	1500.

C#	Date	Mintage	VG	Fine	VF	XF
		Mint mark: A				
		Second Restoration				
181.1	1816	3.210	12.00	20.00	45.00	150.00
	1817	3.778	12.00	20.00	45.00	150.00
	1818	.086	20.00	40.00	75.00	225.00
	1819	.658	17.50	30.00	65.00	175.00
	1820	3.226	12.00	20.00	45.00	150.00
	1821	9.526	12.00	20.00	40.00	135.00
	1822	13.453	12.00	20.00	40.00	125.00
	1823	6.536	12.00	20.00	40.00	125.00
	1824	9.066	12.00	20.00	40.00	125.00
		Mint mark: B				
181.2	1816	.922	18.00	30.00	65.00	175.00
	1817	1.580	15.00	25.00	55.00	150.00
	1818	2.190	12.00	20.00	45.00	150.00
	1819	3.437	12.00	20.00	45.00	150.00
	1820	.210	20.00	45.00	100.00	225.00
	1821	.123	30.00	55.00	125.00	250.00
	1822	.897	12.00	20.00	45.00	150.00
	1823	.393	20.00	45.00	100.00	225.00
	1824	1.246	15.00	25.00	55.00	150.00
		Mint mark: BB				
181.3	1816	8,115	40.00	75.00	150.00	475.00
	1817	3,510	55.00	110.00	200.00	600.00
	1818	1,119	55.00	110.00	200.00	600.00
	1819	2,469	55.00	110.00	200.00	600.00
	1820	1,976	55.00	110.00	200.00	600.00
	1821	1,527	60.00	120.00	240.00	720.00
	1823	3,712	55.00	110.00	200.00	600.00
		Mint mark: D				
181.4	1816	6,446	35.00	65.00	125.00	400.00
	1817	3,605	35.00	65.00	125.00	450.00
	1820	.017	—	45.00	75.00	300.00
	1823	.994	12.00	20.00	45.00	150.00
	1824	2.448	12.00	20.00	45.00	150.00
	1824 inverted D	Inc. Ab.	—	—	Rare	—
		Mint mark: H				
181.5	1816	6,575	35.00	80.00	165.00	550.00
	1817	.110	22.00	45.00	85.00	250.00
	1818	.012	55.00	110.00	220.00	500.00
	1819	.033	35.00	65.00	120.00	325.00
	1820	.018	40.00	85.00	165.00	375.00
	1821	.018	55.00	110.00	220.00	450.00
	1822	.077	27.50	60.00	100.00	275.00
	1823	.329	20.00	40.00	75.00	200.00
	1824	.771	12.00	20.00	45.00	150.00
		Mint mark: I				
181.6	1816	.306	20.00	40.00	75.00	200.00
	1817	4,204	45.00	65.00	115.00	400.00
	1818	1,568	55.00	110.00	285.00	575.00
	1819	1,104	55.00	110.00	285.00	575.00
	1820	639	140.00	250.00	400.00	800.00
	1821	6,320	50.00	85.00	145.00	460.00
	1822	8,712	45.00	70.00	145.00	460.00
	1823	.269	20.00	40.00	75.00	200.00
	1824	1.039	12.00	20.00	45.00	150.00
		Mint mark: K				
181.7	1816	.034	25.00	55.00	90.00	250.00

C#	Date	Mintage	VG	Fine	VF	XF
181.7	1817	.386	20.00	40.00	75.00	200.00
	1818	.017	—	65.00	135.00	300.00
	1820	.018	25.00	65.00	135.00	300.00
	1822	.393	20.00	40.00	75.00	200.00
	1823	.800	12.00	20.00	45.00	150.00
	1824	1.010	12.00	20.00	45.00	150.00
		Mint mark: L				
181.8	1816	1.001	12.00	20.00	45.00	150.00
	1817	.377	20.00	40.00	75.00	200.00
	1818	.010	35.00	75.00	150.00	250.00
	1823	.898	12.00	20.00	45.00	150.00
	1824	1.068	12.00	20.00	45.00	150.00
		Mint mark: M				
181.9	1816	.651	12.00	20.00	45.00	150.00
	1817	.188	20.00	40.00	75.00	225.00
	1818	2,920	40.00	80.00	175.00	350.00
	1823	.958	12.00	20.00	45.00	150.00
	1824	1.589	12.00	20.00	40.00	125.00
		Mint mark: MA				
181.10	1816	.018	35.00	75.00	150.00	350.00
	1817	.010	40.00	80.00	165.00	375.00
	1818	7,805	50.00	100.00	200.00	500.00
	1819	1,186	60.00	120.00	250.00	600.00
	1820	440 pcs.	100.00	200.00	350.00	750.00
	1821	198	150.00	250.00	500.00	1000.
	1823	3,847	55.00	110.00	225.00	550.00
	1824	1.422	12.00	20.00	45.00	150.00
		Mint mark: Q				
181.11	1816	.591	18.00	30.00	65.00	175.00
	1817	.105	20.00	40.00	75.00	225.00
	1819	1,618	60.00	120.00	250.00	600.00
	1820	2,770	55.00	110.00	225.00	550.00
	1821	5,626	50.00	100.00	200.00	500.00
	1822	.020	35.00	75.00	150.00	350.00
	1823	.715	12.00	20.00	45.00	150.00
	1824	1.006	12.00	20.00	45.00	150.00
		Mint mark: T				
181.12	1816	.011	40.00	80.00	165.00	325.00
	1817	.025	35.00	70.00	135.00	300.00
	1818	.024	35.00	70.00	135.00	300.00
	1819	.020	35.00	70.00	135.00	300.00
	1820	.011	40.00	80.00	165.00	325.00
		Mint mark: W				
181.13	1816	.072	25.00	55.00	90.00	250.00
	1817	.438	18.00	30.00	65.00	175.00
	1818	.066	25.00	55.00	90.00	250.00
	1819	.034	30.00	65.00	125.00	275.00
	1820	.106	20.00	40.00	75.00	225.00
	1821	3.674	12.00	20.00	45.00	150.00
	1822	4.839	12.00	20.00	45.00	150.00
	1823	4.168	12.00	20.00	45.00	150.00
	1824	9.807	10.00	15.00	35.00	100.00
	Common date				Unc.	400.00

C#	Date	Mintage	VG	Fine	VF	XF
		Mint mark: A				
		Obv: Type I. Rev: Similar to C#181.				
189.1	1824	.408	60.00	125.00	275.00	800.00
	1825	2.492	10.00	15.00	35.00	90.00
	1826	7.171	10.00	15.00	35.00	90.00
		Mint mark: B				
189.2	1825	.113	20.00	50.00	75.00	150.00
	1826	.595	15.00	35.00	60.00	125.00
		Mint mark: BB				
189.3	1825	.157	20.00	50.00	75.00	150.00
	1826	.411	15.00	35.00	60.00	125.00
		Mint mark: D				
189.4	1825	.185	20.00	50.00	75.00	150.00
	1826	1.437	10.00	15.00	35.00	90.00
		Mint mark: H				
189.5	1825	.157	20.00	50.00	75.00	150.00
	1826	.573	15.00	35.00	60.00	125.00
		Mint mark: I				
189.6	1825	.155	20.00	50.00	75.00	150.00
	1826	.536	15.00	35.00	60.00	125.00
		Mint mark: K				

C#	Date	Mintage	VG	Fine	VF	XF
189.7	1825	.326	15.00	35.00	60.00	125.00
	1826	.429	15.00	35.00	60.00	125.00
		Mint mark: L				
189.8	1825	.227	15.00	35.00	60.00	125.00
	1826	.720	10.00	15.00	35.00	90.00
		Mint mark: M				
189.9	1825	.154	20.00	50.00	75.00	150.00
	1826	.670	10.00	15.00	35.00	90.00
		Mint mark: MA				
189.10	1825	.176	20.00	50.00	75.00	150.00
	1826	1.072	10.00	15.00	35.00	90.00
		Mint mark: Q				
189.11	1825	.163	20.00	50.00	75.00	150.00
	1826	.346	15.00	35.00	60.00	125.00
		Mint mark: T				
189.12	1826	.203	15.00	35.00	60.00	125.00
	1826	3.583	10.00	15.00	35.00	90.00
		Mint mark: W				
189.13	1825	1.104	10.00	15.00	35.00	90.00
		Edge inscription in relief.				
189a	1827A	Inc. C189.1	75.00	125.00	250.00	500.00
	1830A	Inc. C189.1	75.00	125.00	250.00	500.00

Mint mark: A
Obv: Type II.

C#	Date	Mintage	VG	Fine	VF	XF
189b.1	1827	6.822	10.00	25.00	50.00	100.00
	1828	8.803	10.00	25.00	50.00	100.00
	1829	4.827	10.00	25.00	50.00	100.00
	1830	6.333	10.00	25.00	50.00	100.00
		Mint mark: B				
189b.2	1827	2.792	10.00	25.00	50.00	100.00
	1828	1.898	10.00	25.00	50.00	100.00
	1829	2.834	10.00	25.00	50.00	100.00
	1830	2.910	10.00	25.00	50.00	100.00
		Mint mark: BB				
189b.3	1827	.393	20.00	45.00	75.00	125.00
	1828	.699	20.00	45.00	75.00	125.00
	1829	.548	20.00	45.00	75.00	125.00
	1830	.112	20.00	45.00	90.00	150.00
		Mint mark: D				
189b.4	1827	1.651	10.00	25.00	50.00	100.00
	1828	2.743	10.00	25.00	50.00	100.00
	1829	1.608	10.00	25.00	50.00	100.00
	1830	.631	15.00	35.00	65.00	125.00
		Mint mark: H				
189b.5	1827	.419	20.00	45.00	75.00	125.00
	1828	.490	20.00	45.00	75.00	125.00
	1829	1.155	10.00	25.00	50.00	100.00
	1830	.574	20.00	45.00	75.00	125.00
		Mint mark: I				
189b.6	1827	.335	20.00	45.00	75.00	125.00
	1828	.124	20.00	45.00	90.00	150.00
	1829	.475	20.00	45.00	75.00	125.00
	1830	.067	35.00	80.00	150.00	300.00
		Mint mark: K				
189b.7	1827	1.147	10.00	25.00	50.00	100.00
	1828	1.632	10.00	25.00	50.00	100.00
	1829	1.011	10.00	25.00	50.00	100.00
	1830	.713	15.00	25.00	45.00	125.00
		Mint mark: L				
189b.8	1827	1.144	10.00	25.00	50.00	100.00
	1828	1.083	10.00	25.00	50.00	100.00
	1829	.857	10.00	25.00	50.00	100.00
	1830	.399	20.00	45.00	75.00	125.00
		Mint mark: M				
189b.9	1827	.806	10.00	25.00	50.00	100.00
	1828	1.818	10.00	25.00	50.00	100.00
	1829	.873	10.00	25.00	50.00	100.00
	1830	.496	20.00	45.00	75.00	125.00
		Mint mark: MA				
189b.10	1827	1.531	10.00	25.00	50.00	100.00

C#	Date	Mintage	VG	Fine	VF	XF
189b.10	1828	1.201	10.00	25.00	50.00	100.00
	1829	1.258	10.00	25.00	50.00	100.00
	1830	1.803	10.00	25.00	50.00	100.00
		Mint mark: Q				
189b.11	1827	.484	20.00	45.00	75.00	125.00
	1828	.394	20.00	45.00	75.00	125.00
	1829	.360	20.00	45.00	75.00	125.00
	1830	.151	20.00	45.00	90.00	150.00
		Mint mark: T				
189b.12	1827	.865	10.00	25.00	50.00	100.00
	1828	.933	10.00	25.00	50.00	100.00
	1829	.888	10.00	25.00	50.00	100.00
	1830	.137	20.00	35.00	55.00	125.00
	Common date				Unc.	350.00
		Mint mark: W				
189b.13	1827	11.525	15.00	25.00	45.00	125.00
	1828	9.610	15.00	25.00	45.00	125.00
	1829	3.235	15.00	25.00	45.00	125.00
	1830	4.134	15.00	25.00	45.00	125.00

Mint mark: A
Incused edge lettering.
Obv. leg: LOUIS PHILIPPE I ROI. . . .

C#	Date	Mintage	VG	Fine	VF	XF
203.1	1830	2.421	12.00	25.00	50.00	175.00
	1831	11.785	10.00	20.00	40.00	100.00
		Mint mark: B				
203.2	1830	1.025	15.00	35.00	75.00	150.00
	1831	7.889	10.00	20.00	40.00	100.00
		Mint mark: BB				
203.3	1830	5,125	75.00	175.00	300.00	600.00
	1831	.983	15.00	35.00	75.00	150.00
		Mint mark: D				
203.4	1830	.368	20.00	40.00	80.00	175.00
	1831	3.460	12.00	25.00	50.00	175.00
		Mint mark: H				
203.5	1830	.030	35.00	75.00	175.00	375.00
	1831	.843	15.00	35.00	75.00	150.00
		Mint mark: I				
203.6	1830	.028	35.00	75.00	175.00	375.00
	1831	.502	20.00	40.00	80.00	175.00
		Mint mark: K				
203.7	1830	.123	25.00	50.00	100.00	200.00
	1831	1.523	15.00	35.00	75.00	175.00
		Mint mark: L				
203.8	1830	8,931	40.00	100.00	200.00	400.00
	1831	.430	20.00	40.00	80.00	175.00
		Mint mark: M				
203.9	1830	.050	35.00	75.00	125.00	275.00
	1831	1.337	15.00	35.00	75.00	175.00
		Mint mark: MA				
203.10	1830	.065	35.00	75.00	125.00	275.00
	1831	2.062	12.00	25.00	50.00	175.00
		Mint mark: Q				
203.11	1830	.012	40.00	80.00	175.00	375.00
	1831	.357	20.00	40.00	80.00	175.00
		Mint mark: T				
203.12	1830	.125	25.00	50.00	100.00	200.00
	1831	1.261	15.00	35.00	75.00	175.00
		Mint mark: W				
203.13	1830	1.020	15.00	35.00	75.00	175.00
	1831	8.226	12.00	20.00	40.00	90.00
	Common date				Unc.	400.00
		Mint mark: A				
		Raised edge lettering.				
203.14	1830	Inc. Ab.	15.00	45.00	90.00	275.00
	1831	Inc. Ab.	15.00	45.00	90.00	275.00
		Mint mark: B				
203.16	1831	Inc. Ab.	75.00	125.00	250.00	—
		Mint mark: W				
203.15	1830	1 known	—	—	—	—
	1831	Inc. Ab.	15.00	45.00	75.00	275.00

Mint mark: A
Incused edge lettering.
Obv. leg: LOUIS PHILIPPE ROI. . . .

C#	Date	Mintage	VG	Fine	VF	XF
203a.1	1830	Inc. Ab.	40.00	90.00	250.00	500.00
		Mint mark: B				
203a.2	1830	Inc. Ab.	50.00	125.00	300.00	600.00
		Mint mark: D				
203a.3	1830	Inc. Ab.	75.00	175.00	450.00	800.00
		Mint mark: W				
203a.4	1830	Inc. Ab.	50.00	125.00	300.00	600.00
		Mint mark: A				
		Raised edge lettering.				
203a.5	1830	Inc. Ab.	100.00	225.00	450.00	900.00

Mint mark: A
Incused edge lettering.

C#	Date	Mintage	VG	Fine	VF	XF
A204.1	1831	Inc. Ab.	40.00	100.00	225.00	450.00
		Mint mark: B				
A204.2	1831	Inc. Ab.	40.00	100.00	225.00	450.00
		Mint mark: BB				
A204.3	1831	Inc. Ab.	20.00	40.00	100.00	300.00
		Mint mark: D				
A204.4	1831	Inc. Ab.	25.00	50.00	125.00	350.00
		Mint mark: I				
A204.5	1831	Inc. Ab.	25.00	50.00	125.00	350.00
		Mint mark: K				
A204.6	1831	Inc. Ab.	25.00	50.00	125.00	350.00
		Mint mark: M				
A204.7	1831	Inc. Ab.	20.00	40.00	100.00	300.00
		Mint mark: MA				
A204.8	1831	Inc. Ab.	25.00	50.00	125.00	350.00
		Mint mark: Q				
A204.9	1831	Inc. Ab.	25.00	50.00	125.00	350.00
		Mint mark: A				
		Raised edge lettering.				
B204.1	1831	Inc. Ab.	12.00	20.00	50.00	125.00
		Mint mark: B				
B204.2	1831	Inc. Ab.	12.00	20.00	50.00	125.00
		Mint mark: BB				
B204.3	1831	Inc. Ab.	20.00	45.00	90.00	175.00
		Mint mark: D				
B204.4	1831	Inc. Ab.	12.00	20.00	50.00	125.00

Mint mark: H

C#	Date	Mintage	VG	Fine	VF	XF
B204.5	1831	Inc. Ab.	20.00	45.00	90.00	175.00

Mint mark: I

C#	Date	Mintage	VG	Fine	VF	XF
B204.12	1831	Inc. Ab.	20.00	45.00	90.00	175.00

Mint mark: K

C#	Date	Mintage	VG	Fine	VF	XF
B204.6	1831	Inc. Ab.	20.00	45.00	90.00	175.00

Mint mark: L

C#	Date	Mintage	VG	Fine	VF	XF
B204.7	1831	Inc. Ab.	25.00	50.00	125.00	275.00

Mint mark: M

C#	Date	Mintage	VG	Fine	VF	XF
B204.8	1831	Inc. Ab.	20.00	45.00	90.00	175.00

Mint mark: MA

C#	Date	Mintage	VG	Fine	VF	XF
B204.9	1831	Inc. Ab.	20.00	45.00	90.00	175.00

Mint mark: Q

C#	Date	Mintage	VG	Fine	VF	XF
B204.13	1831	Inc. Ab.	20.00	45.00	90.00	175.00

Mint mark: T

C#	Date	Mintage	VG	Fine	VF	XF
B204.10	1831	Inc. Ab.	20.00	45.00	90.00	175.00

Mint mark: W

C#	Date	Mintage	VG	Fine	VF	XF
B204.11	1831	Inc. Ab.	12.00	20.00	50.00	125.00

Mint mark: A
Rev: Mint marks at edge outside wreath.

C#	Date	Mintage	Fine	VF	XF	Unc
204.1	1832	7.800	9.00	25.00	50.00	200.00
	1833	8.211	9.00	25.00	50.00	200.00
	1834	11.307	9.00	25.00	50.00	200.00
	1835	5.807	9.00	25.00	50.00	200.00
	1836	1.940	9.00	25.00	50.00	200.00
	1837	6.884	9.00	25.00	50.00	200.00
	1838	4.805	9.00	25.00	50.00	200.00
	1839	5.071	9.00	25.00	50.00	200.00
	1840	4.769	9.00	25.00	50.00	200.00
	1841	1.005	9.00	25.00	50.00	150.00
	1842	.755	15.00	50.00	85.00	250.00
	1843	1.838	9.00	25.00	50.00	200.00
	1844	1.971	9.00	25.00	50.00	200.00
	1845(p)	3.096	9.00	25.00	50.00	200.00
	1845(ha)	I.A.	9.00	25.00	50.00	200.00
	1846	5.434	9.00	25.00	50.00	200.00
	1847	12.578	9.00	25.00	50.00	200.00
	1848	3.196	9.00	25.00	50.00	200.00
	1848	—	—	—	Proof	1500.

Mint mark: B

C#	Date	Mintage	Fine	VF	XF	Unc
204.2	1832	2.852	9.00	25.00	50.00	200.00
	1833	3.791	9.00	25.00	50.00	200.00
	1834	4.453	9.00	25.00	50.00	200.00
	1835	2.793	9.00	25.00	50.00	200.00
	1836	2.631	9.00	25.00	50.00	200.00
	1837	6.075	9.00	25.00	50.00	200.00
	1838	4.002	9.00	25.00	50.00	200.00
	1839	3.467	9.00	25.00	50.00	200.00
	1840	3.337	9.00	25.00	50.00	200.00
	1841	1.652	9.00	25.00	50.00	200.00
	1842	3.489	9.00	25.00	50.00	200.00
	1843	2.472	9.00	25.00	50.00	200.00
	1844	.361	15.00	50.00	85.00	250.00

Mint mark: BB

C#	Date	Mintage	Fine	VF	XF	Unc
204.3	1832	1.725	9.00	25.00	50.00	200.00
	1833	1.799	9.00	25.00	50.00	200.00
	1834(b)	1.621	9.00	25.00	50.00	200.00
	1834 bee	I.A.	15.00	25.00	50.00	200.00
	1835	1.286	9.00	25.00	50.00	200.00
	1836	1.188	9.00	25.00	50.00	200.00
	1837	.600	15.00	50.00	85.00	250.00
	1838	1.535	9.00	25.00	50.00	200.00
	1839	1.064	9.00	25.00	50.00	200.00
	1840	1.186	9.00	25.00	50.00	200.00
	1841	2.082	9.00	25.00	50.00	200.00
	1842	2.471	9.00	25.00	50.00	200.00
	1843	1.422	9.00	25.00	50.00	200.00
	1844	1.890	9.00	25.00	50.00	200.00
	1845	2.041	9.00	25.00	50.00	200.00
	1846	.840	12.00	30.00	65.00	200.00
	1847	1.577	9.00	25.00	50.00	200.00
	1848	.935	12.00	30.00	65.00	200.00

Mint mark: D

C#	Date	Mintage	Fine	VF	XF	Unc
204.4	1832	3.007	9.00	25.00	50.00	200.00
	1833	1.487	9.00	25.00	50.00	200.00
	1834	2.119	9.00	25.00	50.00	200.00
	1835	1.084	9.00	25.00	50.00	200.00
	1836	.200	20.00	50.00	125.00	300.00
	1837	.093	40.00	125.00	250.00	500.00
	1838	.149	20.00	50.00	125.00	300.00
	1839(a)	.519	15.00	30.00	60.00	250.00
	1839(t)	I.A.	15.00	30.00	60.00	250.00
	1840	.070	60.00	150.00	275.00	600.00

Mint mark: H

C#	Date	Mintage	Fine	VF	XF	Unc
204.5	1832	.900	9.00	25.00	50.00	200.00
	1833/2	.844	15.00	30.00	60.00	250.00
	1833	Inc. Ab.	9.00	25.00	50.00	200.00
	1834	2.184	9.00	25.00	50.00	200.00
	1835	.467	15.00	30.00	60.00	250.00

Mint mark: I

C#	Date	Mintage	Fine	VF	XF	Unc
204.6	1832	.703	9.00	25.00	50.00	200.00
	1833	1.014	9.00	25.00	50.00	200.00
	1834	1.933	9.00	25.00	50.00	200.00
	1835	.598	15.00	30.00	60.00	250.00

Mint mark: K

C#	Date	Mintage	Fine	VF	XF	Unc
204.7	1832	.602	15.00	30.00	60.00	250.00
	1833	.749	9.00	25.00	50.00	200.00
	1834	2.157	9.00	25.00	50.00	200.00
	1835	.928	9.00	25.00	50.00	200.00
	1836	.296	20.00	50.00	125.00	300.00
	1837	.813	9.00	25.00	50.00	200.00
	1838	.450	15.00	30.00	60.00	250.00
	1839	.897	9.00	25.00	50.00	200.00
	1840	1.186	9.00	25.00	50.00	200.00
	1841	.995	9.00	25.00	50.00	200.00
	1842	1.026	9.00	25.00	50.00	200.00
	1843	.794	9.00	25.00	50.00	200.00
	1844	.398	15.00	30.00	60.00	250.00
	1845	.537	15.00	30.00	60.00	250.00
	1846	.511	15.00	30.00	60.00	250.00
	1847	.167	20.00	50.00	125.00	300.00
	1848	.166	20.00	50.00	125.00	300.00

Mint mark: L

C#	Date	Mintage	Fine	VF	XF	Unc
204.8	1832	.567	20.00	50.00	125.00	300.00
	1833	.378	20.00	50.00	125.00	300.00
	1834	.359	20.00	50.00	125.00	300.00
	1835	.064	50.00	125.00	250.00	600.00

Mint mark: M

C#	Date	Mintage	Fine	VF	XF	Unc
204.9	1832	.729	20.00	50.00	125.00	300.00
	1833	.669	20.00	50.00	125.00	300.00
	1834	.889	20.00	50.00	125.00	300.00
	1835	.412	20.00	50.00	125.00	300.00
	1836	.072	50.00	125.00	250.00	600.00

Mint mark: MA

C#	Date	Mintage	Fine	VF	XF	Unc
204.10	1832	1.184	9.00	50.00	125.00	300.00
	1833	.872	15.00	50.00	125.00	300.00
	1834	.489	15.00	30.00	60.00	250.00
	1835	.373	15.00	30.00	60.00	250.00
	1836	.362	15.00	30.00	60.00	250.00
	1837	.724	9.00	25.00	50.00	200.00
	1838	2.116	9.00	25.00	50.00	200.00
	1839	.020	100.00	175.00	375.00	800.00

Mint mark: Q

C#	Date	Mintage	Fine	VF	XF	Unc
204.11	1832	.716	9.00	25.00	50.00	200.00
	1833	.663	9.00	25.00	50.00	200.00
	1834	.982	9.00	25.00	50.00	200.00

Mint mark: T

C#	Date	Mintage	Fine	VF	XF	Unc
204.12	1832	1.592	9.00	25.00	50.00	200.00
	1833	1.437	9.00	25.00	50.00	200.00
	1834	2.119	9.00	25.00	50.00	200.00
	1835	.294	20.00	35.00	60.00	250.00

Mint mark: W

C#	Date	Mintage	Fine	VF	XF	Unc
204.13	1832	4.483	9.00	25.00	50.00	180.00
	1833	9.270	9.00	25.00	50.00	180.00
	1834	11.733	9.00	25.00	50.00	180.00
	1835	5.016	9.00	25.00	50.00	180.00
	1836	1.614	9.00	25.00	50.00	180.00
	1837	6.652	9.00	25.00	50.00	180.00
	1838	4.190	9.00	25.00	50.00	180.00
	1839	3.269	9.00	25.00	50.00	180.00
	1840(c)	1.714	9.00	25.00	50.00	180.00
	1840(r)	I.A.	15.00	30.00	60.00	250.00
	1841	8.926	9.00	25.00	50.00	180.00
	1842	5.436	9.00	25.00	50.00	180.00
	1843	7.846	9.00	25.00	50.00	180.00
	1844	8.775	9.00	25.00	50.00	180.00
	1845	11.107	9.00	25.00	50.00	180.00
	1846	1.658	9.00	25.00	50.00	180.00

Mint mark: A
Second Republic

Y#	Date	Mintage	Fine	VF	XF	Unc
7.1	1848	16.648	10.00	20.00	75.00	200.00
	1848 plain edge		—	—	Proof	5000.
	1849	29.338	8.00	15.00	65.00	150.00

Mint mark: BB

Y#	Date	Mintage	Fine	VF	XF	Unc
7.2	1848	2.300	15.00	40.00	125.00	275.00
	1849	2.594	15.00	40.00	125.00	275.00

Mint mark: D

Y#	Date	Mintage	Fine	VF	XF	Unc
7.3	1848	.136	100.00	200.00	400.00	900.00
	1849	9,711	300.00	650.00	1500.	3500.

Mint mark: K

Y#	Date	Mintage	Fine	VF	XF	Unc
7.4	1848	.428	45.00	125.00	275.00	550.00
	1849	.471	45.00	125.00	275.00	550.00

Mint mark: A

Y#	Date	Mintage	Fine	VF	XF	Unc
6.1	1849	7.437	20.00	40.00	125.00	300.00
	1850	14.619	15.00	35.00	100.00	225.00
	1851	13.223	15.00	35.00	100.00	225.00

Mint mark: BB

Y#	Date	Mintage	Fine	VF	XF	Unc
6.2	1849	.916	35.00	80.00	200.00	500.00
	1850	1.169	30.00	70.00	175.00	450.00

Mint mark: K

Y#	Date	Mintage	Fine	VF	XF	Unc
6.3	1850	.332	100.00	200.00	400.00	750.00

Mint mark: A

Y#	Date	Mintage	Fine	VF	XF	Unc
13.1	1852	16.117	12.50	35.00	100.00	350.00
	1852 sign. J.J.Barre	Inc. Ab.	350.00	600.00	1000.	1750.
	1852	—	—	—	Proof	5000.

Mint mark: BB

Y#	Date	Mintage	Fine	VF	XF	Unc
13.2	1852	.041	350.00	650.00	1250.	3000.

Mint mark: A
Second Empire

Y#	Date	Mintage	Fine	VF	XF	Unc
26.1	1854	.011	250.00	500.00	700.00	2000.
	1855	4.075	35.00	85.00	175.00	600.00
	1856	4.683	35.00	85.00	175.00	600.00
	1856	—	—	—	Proof	1250.
	1857	.093	250.00	500.00	800.00	2500.
	1858	.027	275.00	550.00	900.00	2600.
	1859	3,365	400.00	1200.	2000.	3500.

Mint mark: BB

Y#	Date	Mintage	Fine	VF	XF	Unc
26.2	1855	.786	50.00	150.00	275.00	1000.
	1856	2.223	40.00	125.00	275.00	800.00

Mint mark: D

Y#	Date	Mintage	Fine	VF	XF	Unc
26.3	1855	—	60.00	150.00	300.00	1000.
	1856	2.249	40.00	110.00	200.00	800.00

1.6129 g, .900 GOLD, .0467 oz AGW
Mint mark: A
Bare head, 14.4mm.

Y#	Date	Mintage	Fine	VF	XF	Unc
33	1854	3.562	35.00	65.00	100.00	275.00
	1854 plain edge					
		Inc. Ab.	50.00	100.00	150.00	300.00
	1855	.938	65.00	110.00	200.00	400.00

16.7mm.

Y#	Date	Mintage	Fine	VF	XF	Unc
33a.1	1856	2.960	30.00	40.00	65.00	175.00
	1857	3.479	30.00	40.00	65.00	175.00
	1858	2.983	30.00	40.00	65.00	175.00
	1859	5.660	30.00	40.00	65.00	175.00
	1860	4.798	30.00	40.00	65.00	175.00

Mint mark: BB

Y#	Date	Mintage	Fine	VF	XF	Unc
33a.2	1858	—	65.00	125.00	200.00	450.00
	1859	2.279	30.00	40.00	65.00	175.00
	1860	2.022	30.00	40.00	65.00	175.00

25.0000 g, .900 SILVER, .7234 oz ASW
Mint mark: A

Y#	Date	Mintage	Fine	VF	XF	Unc
32.1	1861	.022	225.00	450.00	800.00	2000.
32.1	1861	—	—	—	Proof	7000.
	1862	.021	225.00	450.00	800.00	2000.
	1863	.022	225.00	450.00	800.00	2000.
	1864	.032	225.00	450.00	800.00	2000.
	1865	.025	225.00	450.00	800.00	2000.
	1866	.038	225.00	450.00	800.00	2000.
	1867	6.586	10.00	20.00	90.00	275.00
	1868	6.634	10.00	20.00	90.00	275.00
	1869	2.056	15.00	30.00	125.00	325.00
	1870	6.620	10.00	20.00	90.00	275.00

Mint mark: BB

Y#	Date	Mintage	Fine	VF	XF	Unc
32.2	1865	.073	225.00	450.00	800.00	2000.
	1867	4.224	10.00	20.00	65.00	200.00
	1868	12.090	8.00	15.00	50.00	175.00
	1869	9.597	8.00	15.00	50.00	175.00
	1870	2.055	12.00	30.00	90.00	275.00

1.6129 g, .900 GOLD, .0467 oz AGW
Mint mark: A
Laureate head

Y#	Date	Mintage	Fine	VF	XF	Unc
38.1	1862	1.101	30.00	35.00	65.00	175.00
	1863	1.591	30.00	35.00	65.00	175.00
	1864	2.240	30.00	35.00	65.00	175.00
	1865	.824	30.00	35.00	65.00	175.00
	1866	1.949	30.00	35.00	65.00	175.00
	1867	1.006	30.00	35.00	65.00	175.00
	1868	1.864	30.00	35.00	65.00	175.00

Mint mark: BB

Y#	Date	Mintage	Fine	VF	XF	Unc
38.2	1862	.882	30.00	35.00	65.00	175.00
	1863	1.104	30.00	35.00	65.00	175.00
	1864	1.000	30.00	35.00	65.00	175.00
	1865	.828	30.00	35.00	65.00	175.00
	1866	1.388	30.00	35.00	65.00	175.00
	1867	1.504	30.00	35.00	65.00	175.00
	1868	.439	30.00	35.00	70.00	200.00
	1869	.288	30.00	35.00	75.00	225.00

25.0000 g, .900 SILVER, .7234 oz ASW
Mint mark: A
Obv: E.A.OUDINE F. below truncation.

Y#	Date	Mintage	Fine	VF	XF	Unc
46.1	1870(a)	.064	50.00	125.00	450.00	850.00

Mint mark: K

Y#	Date	Mintage	Fine	VF	XF	Unc
46.2	1870(a)	.544	60.00	150.00	550.00	1000.
	1870 M/star	I.A.	50.00	125.00	450.00	800.00
	1871 M/star	.630	45.00	110.00	400.00	700.00

Obv: A.E.OUDINE F. (error) below truncation.

Y#	Date	Mintage	Fine	VF	XF	Unc
46.3	1870 M/star	I.A.	300.00	650.00	1200.	1800.

Obv: E.A.OUDIИE F. (error) below truncation.

Y#	Date	Mintage	Fine	VF	XF	Unc
46.4	1870 M/star	I.A.	— Reported, not confirmed			

Mint mark: A
Third Republic

Y#	Date	Mintage	Fine	VF	XF	Unc
51	1870	1.185	30.00	125.00	250.00	500.00

Obv: Similar to Y#52a.

Y#	Date	Mintage	Fine	VF	XF	Unc
52.1	1870	.261	45.00	125.00	275.00	600.00
	1871	.238	50.00	150.00	300.00	700.00
	1872	.057	45.00	125.00	275.00	600.00
	1873	27.077	7.00	9.00	12.00	25.00
	1874	7.999	8.00	10.00	25.00	60.00
	1875	13.339	8.00	10.00	18.00	50.00
	1876	8.800	8.00	10.00	25.00	60.00
	1877	2.632	12.00	20.00	40.00	90.00
	1878	1,154	600.00	1200.	2000.	4000.
	1878	30 pcs.	—	—	Proof	6200.
	1889C	20 pcs.	—	—	Proof	6750.

NOTE: Varieties of mint mark size exist for 1875 dated coins.

Mint mark: K

Y#	Date	Mintage	Fine	VF	XF	Unc
52.2	1871	.075	100.00	250.00	500.00	900.00
	1872	.021	300.00	500.00	850.00	2000.
	1873	3.853	8.00	11.00	25.00	60.00
	1874	4.000	8.00	11.00	25.00	60.00
	1875	1.661	15.00	30.00	50.00	150.00
	1876	1.732	15.00	30.00	50.00	150.00
	1877	.661	20.00	35.00	75.00	250.00
	1878	.263	40.00	100.00	200.00	450.00

Trident

Mint mark: A
Edge inscription: DIEU PROTEGE LA FRANCE.
Trident symbol-issued by Commune.

Y#	Date	Mintage	Fine	VF	XF	Unc
52a	1871	.075	200.00	350.00	650.00	170C

Edge inscription: TRAVAIL-GARANTIE-NATIONALE.

Y#	Date	Mintage	Fine	VF	XF	Unc
52b	1871	.010	—	—	—	—

1.6129 g, .900 GOLD, .0467 oz AGW

Y#	Date	Mintage	Fine	VF	XF	Unc
A54	1878	30 pcs.	—	—	Proof	6200.
	1889	40 pcs.	—	—	Proof	6200.

NICKEL
Mint: Paris - w/o mint mark.

Y#	Date	Mintage	Fine	VF	XF	Unc
83	1933(a)	160.078	2.00	3.00	6.00	12.00

Y#	Date	Mintage	Fine	VF	XF	Unc
84	1933(a)	56.686	.50	1.00	4.00	12.00
	1935(a)	54.164	.50	1.00	4.00	12.00
	1936(a)	.117	400.00	700.00	1200.	1850.
	1937(a)	.157	45.00	75.00	150.00	225.00
	1938(a)	4.977	20.00	35.00	65.00	100.00
	1939(a)	—	700.00	1200.	2000.	4000.

ALUMINUM-BRONZE
For Colonial use in Algeria.

Y#	Date	Mintage	Fine	VF	XF	Unc
84a.1	1938(a)	10.144	8.00	15.00	30.00	125.00
	1939(a)	Inc. Ab.	4.00	8.00	20.00	40.00
	1940(a)	38.758	1.00	2.50	5.00	15.00

For Colonial use in Africa.

Y#	Date	Mintage	Fine	VF	XF	Unc
84a.2	1945(a)	13.044	1.50	3.00	6.00	15.00
	1946(a)	21.790	1.50	3.00	6.00	15.00
	1947(a)	2.662	150.00	200.00	350.00	800.00

Mint mark: C

Y#	Date	Mintage	Fine	VF	XF	Unc
84a.3	1945	Inc. Ab.	5.00	12.00	25.00	40.00
	1946	Inc. Ab.	7.00	20.00	40.00	80.00

ALUMINUM
Mint: Paris - w/o mint mark.

Y#	Date	Mintage	Fine	VF	XF	Unc
84b.1	1945(a)	95.399	.20	.35	1.50	8.00
	1946(a)	61.332	.20	.35	1.50	8.00
	1947(a)	46.576	.20	.35	1.50	8.00
	1948(a)	104.473	1.00	3.00	7.00	15.00
	1949(a)	203.252	.20	.35	.75	5.00
	1950(a)	128.372	.20	.35	.75	5.00
	1952(a)	4.000	20.00	50.00	100.00	200.00

NOTE: Exist with open and closed "9's".

Mint mark: B

Y#	Date	Mintage	Fine	VF	XF	Unc
84b.2	1945	6.043	2.00	5.00	10.00	25.00
	1946	13.360	1.00	2.00	4.00	20.00
	1947	30.839	.50	1.50	4.00	10.00
	1948	28.047	30.00	60.00	125.00	200.00
	1949	48.414	.50	1.50	4.00	10.00
	1950	28.952	1.00	3.00	7.00	15.00

NOTE: Exist with open and closed "9's".

Mint mark: C

Y#	Date	Mintage	Fine	VF	XF	Unc
84b.3	1945	2.208	10.00	20.00	40.00	75.00
	1946	1.269	12.00	25.00	50.00	90.00

COPPER-NICKEL
Mint: Paris - w/o mint mark.

Y#	Date	Mintage	Fine	VF	XF	Unc
V97	1941(a)	13.782	65.00	100.00	150.00	250.00

NOTE: Never released for circulation.

12.0000 g, .835 SILVER, .3221 oz ASW
5 New Francs = 500 Old Francs
Fifth Republic

Y#	Date	Mintage	Fine	VF	XF	Unc
110	1960	55.182	—	BV	2.50	5.00
	1961	15.630	—	BV	2.50	5.00
	1962	42.500	—	BV	2.50	5.00
	1963	37.936	—	BV	2.50	5.00
	1964	32.378	—	BV	2.50	5.00
	1965	5.156	—	BV	2.50	9.00
	1966	5.017	—	BV	2.50	9.00
	1967	.502	—	BV	7.00	20.00
	1968	.557	—	BV	6.00	15.00
	1969	.504	—	BV	6.00	15.00

NICKEL-CLAD COPPER-NICKEL

Y#	Date	Mintage	Fine	VF	XF	Unc
110a.1	1970	57.890	—	—	1.00	1.25
	1971	142.204	—	—	1.00	1.25
	1972	45.492	—	—	1.00	1.25
	1973	45.000	—	—	1.00	1.25
	1974	26.888	—	—	1.00	1.25
	1975	16.712	—	—	1.00	1.25
	1976	1.662	—	1.00	1.25	2.00
	1977	.485	—	1.00	1.50	2.25
	1978	30.022	—	—	1.00	1.25
	1979	.051	—	—	—	1.65
	1980	.060	—	—	—	1.65
	1981	.050	—	—	—	1.65
	1982	.060	—	—	—	1.65
	1983	.101	—	—	—	1.65
	1984	.049	—	—	—	1.65
	1985	.020	—	—	—	3.00
	1986	.048	—	—	—	3.00
	1987	20.000	—	—	—	1.65
	1988	.100	—	—	—	1.65
	1989	.083	—	—	—	1.65
	1990	.015	—	—	—	1.65
	1991	7.500	—	—	—	1.65
	1992	10.000	—	—	—	1.65
	1992	—	—	—	Proof	10.00
	1993	—	—	—	—	1.65

Plain edge.

Y#	Date	Mintage	Fine	VF	XF	Unc
110a.2	1991	—	—	—	Proof	10.00

COPPER-NICKEL
Centennial of Erection of Eiffel Tower

Y#	Date	Mintage	Fine	VF	XF	Unc
133	1989	9.910	—	—	—	4.00

12.0000 g, .900 SILVER, .3473 oz ASW

Y#	Date	Mintage	Fine	VF	XF	Unc
133a	1989	.080	—	—	Proof	55.00

14.0000 g, .920 GOLD, .4141 oz AGW

Y#	Date	Mintage	Fine	VF	XF	Unc
133b	1989	.030	—	—	Proof	375.00

16.0000 g, .999 PLATINUM, .5145 oz APW

Y#	Date	Mintage	Fine	VF	XF	Unc
133c	1989	*3,000	—	—	Proof	500.00

***NOTE:** 1,800 pieces were melted by MTB Banking Corporation.

COPPER-NICKEL
Pierre Mendes-France

Y#	Date	Mintage	Fine	VF	XF	Unc
168	1992	10.000	—	—	—	4.00

12.0000 g, .900 SILVER, .3473 oz ASW

Y#	Date	Mintage	Fine	VF	XF	Unc
168a	1992	.010	—	—	Proof	55.00

14.0000 g, .920 GOLD, .4141 oz AGW

Y#	Date	Mintage	Fine	VF	XF	Unc
168b	1992	1,000	—	—	Proof	400.00

12.0000 g, .900 SILVER, .3473 oz ASW
French Antarctic Territories - Albatross Birds

Y#	Date	Mintage	Fine	VF	XF	Unc
178	1992	.015	—	—	Proof	50.00

10 FRANCS

3.2258 g, .900 GOLD, .0933 oz AGW
Mint mark: A

Y#	Date	Mintage	Fine	VF	XF	Unc
9	1850	.592	55.00	100.00	200.00	600.00
	1850	—	—	—	Proof	4000.
	1851	3.115	BV	65.00	150.00	450.00
	1851	—	—	—	Proof	4000.

Bare head, 17.2mm

Y#	Date	Mintage	Fine	VF	XF	Unc
34.1	1854	3.900	BV	75.00	200.00	450.00
	1855	6.117	BV	75.00	200.00	450.00

Plain edge

Y#	Date	Mintage	Fine	VF	XF	Unc
34.2	1854	Inc. Ab.	60.00	125.00	300.00	500.00
	1854	—	—	—	Proof	1250.

19mm

Y#	Date	Mintage	Fine	VF	XF	Unc
34.3	1855	6.117	BV	55.00	75.00	175.00
	1856	10.778	BV	55.00	75.00	175.00
	1857	14.498	BV	55.00	75.00	175.00
	1858	7.534	BV	55.00	75.00	175.00
	1859	10.111	BV	55.00	75.00	175.00
	1860	6.000	BV	55.00	75.00	175.00

Mint mark: BB

Y#	Date	Mintage	Fine	VF	XF	Unc
34.4	1855	32,188	BV	100.00	150.00	500.00
	1858	.677	BV	55.00	75.00	200.00
	1859	2,279	BV	55.00	75.00	175.00
	1860	3.104	BV	55.00	75.00	175.00

Mint mark: A
Laureate head

Y#	Date	Mintage	Fine	VF	XF	Unc
39.1	1861	.363	BV	75.00	125.00	250.00
	1862	2.844	BV	55.00	75.00	175.00
	1863	2.346	BV	55.00	75.00	175.00
	1864	3.339	BV	55.00	75.00	175.00
	1865	1.673	BV	55.00	75.00	175.00
	1866	3.720	BV	55.00	75.00	175.00
	1867	1.205	BV	55.00	75.00	175.00
	1868	3.416	BV	55.00	75.00	175.00

Mint mark: BB

Y#	Date	Mintage	Fine	VF	XF	Unc
39.2	1861	.044	75.00	100.00	150.00	300.00
	1862	1.462	BV	55.00	75.00	175.00
	1863	1.905	BV	55.00	75.00	175.00
	1864	1.449	BV	55.00	75.00	175.00
	1865	1.576	BV	55.00	75.00	175.00
	1866	2.776	BV	55.00	75.00	175.00
	1867	2.346	BV	55.00	75.00	175.00
	1868	1.117	BV	55.00	75.00	175.00
	1869	.109	50.00	75.00	125.00	175.00

Mint mark: A

Y#	Date	Mintage	Fine	VF	XF	Unc
54	1878	30 pcs.	—	—	Proof	8000.
	1889	100 pcs.	—	—	Proof	8000.
	1895	.214	BV	55.00	65.00	200.00
	1896	.585	BV	55.00	65.00	175.00
	1899	1.600	BV	55.00	65.00	175.00

Y#	Date	Mintage	Fine	VF	XF	Unc
65	1899	.699	BV	55.00	70.00	125.00
	1899	—	—	Matte Proof		1200.
	1900	1.570	BV	55.00	60.00	100.00
	1900	—	—	—	Proof	1000.
	1901	2.100	BV	55.00	60.00	100.00
	1905	1.426	BV	55.00	60.00	100.00
	1906	3.665	BV	55.00	60.00	100.00
	1907	3.364	BV	55.00	60.00	100.00
	1908	1.650	BV	55.00	60.00	100.00
	1909	.599	BV	55.00	65.00	125.00

Y#	Date	Mintage	Fine	VF	XF	Unc
65	1910	2.110	BV	55.00	60.00	100.00
	1911	1.881	BV	55.00	60.00	100.00
	1912	1.756	BV	55.00	60.00	100.00
	1914	3.041	BV	55.00	60.00	100.00

10.0000 g, .680 SILVER, .2186 oz ASW
Mint: Paris - w/o mint mark.

Y#	Date	Mintage	Fine	VF	XF	Unc
86	1929	16.292	BV	3.00	10.00	20.00
	1930	36.986	BV	2.50	8.00	15.00
	1931	35.468	BV	2.50	8.00	15.00
	1932	40.288	BV	2.00	6.00	12.00
	1933	31.146	BV	2.00	6.00	12.00
	1934	52.001	BV	2.00	6.00	12.00
	1936	1 known	—	—	—	—
	1937	.052	75.00	125.00	250.00	375.00
	1938	14.090	BV	3.00	10.00	20.00
	1939	8.299	3.00	7.00	15.00	25.00

Long Leaves

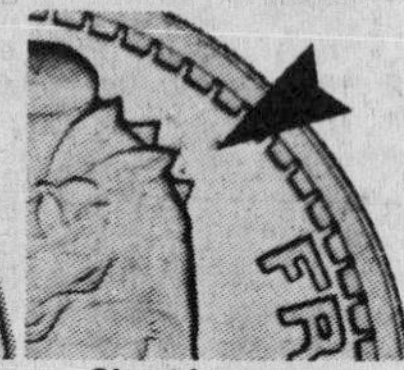
Short Leaves

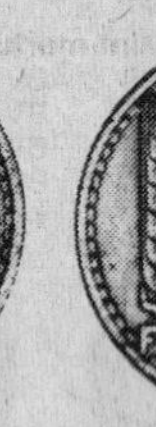

COPPER-NICKEL

Y#	Date	Mintage	Fine	VF	XF	Unc
86a.1	1945(ll)	6.557	.25	.75	2.00	10.00
	1945(sl)	Inc. Ab.	15.00	30.00	50.00	90.00
	1946(ll)	24.409	200.00	350.00	500.00	—
	1946(sl)	Inc. Ab.	.25	.50	2.00	6.00
	1947	41.627	.25	.50	1.00	5.00

Mint mark: B

Y#	Date	Mintage	Fine	VF	XF	Unc
86a.2	1946(ll)	8.452	20.00	35.00	60.00	110.00
	1946(sl)	I.A.	.25	.75	2.00	10.00
	1947	17.188	.25	.50	2.00	6.00

Mint: Paris - w/o mint mark.
Obv: Small head.

Y#	Date	Mintage	Fine	VF	XF	Unc
86b.1	1947	Inc. Ab.	.30	.75	2.00	6.00
	1948	155.945	.20	.35	.75	2.50
	1949	118.149	.20	.35	.75	2.50

Mint mark: B

Y#	Date	Mintage	Fine	VF	XF	Unc
86b.2	1947	Inc. Ab.	1.50	5.00	10.00	25.00
	1948	40.500	.35	1.00	2.50	6.00
	1949	29.518	.35	1.00	2.50	6.00

ALUMINUM-BRONZE
Mint: Paris w/o mint mark.

Y#	Date	Mintage	Fine	VF	XF	Unc
98.1	1950	13.534	.35	.65	3.00	9.00
	1951	153.689	.20	.35	.75	3.00
	1952	76.810	.20	.35	.75	3.00
	1953	46.272	.25	.50	.75	4.00
	1954	2.207	5.00	15.00	30.00	50.00
	1955	47.466	.20	.35	.75	4.00
	1956	2.570	— Reported, not confirmed			
	1957	26.351	.50	1.00	3.00	6.00
	1958(w)	27.213	.50	1.00	3.00	6.00
	1959	.125	— Reported, not confirmed			

Mint mark: B

Y#	Date	Mintage	Fine	VF	XF	Unc
98.2	1950	4.808	2.00	6.00	10.00	25.00
	1951	106.866	.20	.35	.75	4.00
98.2	1952	72.346	.20	.35	.75	4.00
	1953	36.466	.25	.50	1.00	5.00
	1954	21.634	1.00	3.00	6.00	12.00
	1958	1.500	— Reported, not confirmed			

25.0000 g, .900 SILVER, .7234 oz ASW
Mint: Paris - w/o mint mark.
10 New Francs = 1000 Old Francs
Fifth Republic

Y#	Date	Mintage	Fine	VF	XF	Unc
111	1965	8.051	—	BV	6.00	12.00
	1966	9.800	—	BV	6.00	12.00
	1967	10.100	—	BV	6.00	12.00
	1968	3.887	—	BV	8.00	15.00
	1969	.761	—	BV	10.00	18.00
	1970	5.013	—	BV	6.00	12.00
	1971	.513	—	BV	10.00	20.00
	1972	.915	—	BV	8.00	15.00
	1973	.207	—	BV	10.00	25.00

NICKEL-BRASS

Y#	Date	Mintage	Fine	VF	XF	Unc
A112	1974	22.447	—	—	2.00	2.50
	1975	59.013	—	—	2.00	2.50
	1976	104.093	—	—	2.00	2.50
	1977	100.028	—	—	2.00	2.50
	1978	97.590	—	—	2.00	2.50
	1979	110.000	—	—	2.00	2.50
	1980	80.010	—	—	2.00	2.50
	1981	.050	—	—	—	2.75
	1982	.074	—	—	—	2.75
	1983	.101	—	—	—	2.75
	1984	39.988	—	—	2.00	2.50
	1985	30.000	—	—	2.00	2.50
	1986	.013	—	—	—	4.00
	1987	*50.000	—	—	—	2.50

COPPER-NICKEL
100th Anniversary of Death of Leon Gambetta

Y#	Date	Mintage	Fine	VF	XF	Unc
113	1982	3.045	—	—	2.50	4.00

NICKEL-BRONZE
200th Anniversary of Montgolfier Balloon

Y#	Date	Mintage	Fine	VF	XF	Unc
115	1983	3.001	—	—	2.50	4.00

200th Anniversary of Birth of Stendhal

Y#	Date	Mintage	Fine	VF	XF	Unc
116	1983	2.951	—	—	2.50	4.00

200th Anniversary of Birth of Francois Rude

Y#	Date	Mintage	Fine	VF	XF	Unc
118	1984	10.000	—	—	2.50	3.50

Centennial - Death of Victor Hugo

Y#	Date	Mintage	Fine	VF	XF	Unc
119	1985	10.000	—	—	2.50	3.50

12.0000 g, .900 SILVER, .3472 oz ASW

Y#	Date	Mintage	Fine	VF	XF	Unc
119a	1985	.020	—	—	—	35.00

12.0000 g, .999 SILVER, .3854 oz ASW

Y#	Date	Mintage	Fine	VF	XF	Unc
119b	1985	8,000	—	—	Proof	70.00

NICKEL-BRONZE
100th Anniversary - Birth of Robert Schuman

Y#	Date	Mintage	Fine	VF	XF	Unc
122	1986	10.013	—	—	3.00	6.50

7.0000 g, .900 SILVER, .2025 oz ASW

Y#	Date	Mintage	Fine	VF	XF	Unc
122a	1986	.020	—	—	—	25.00

7.0000 g, .950 SILVER, .2138 oz ASW

Y#	Date	Mintage	Fine	VF	XF	Unc
122b	1986	6,000	—	—	Proof	80.00

7.0000 g, .920 GOLD, .2071 oz AGW

Y#	Date	Mintage	Fine	VF	XF	Unc
122c	1986	5,000	—	—	Proof	300.00

NICKEL
Madam Republic

Y#	Date	Mintage	Fine	VF	XF	Unc
123	1986	110.033	—	—	3.00	6.50

NOTE: Recalled and melted, no longer legal tender.

12.0000 g, .900 SILVER, .3473 oz ASW
Millenium of King Capet

Y#	Date	Mintage	Fine	VF	XF	Unc
125	1987	.020	—	—	—	25.00

12.0000 g, .950 SILVER, .3665 oz ASW

Y#	Date	Mintage	Fine	VF	XF	Unc
125a	1987	.010	—	—	Proof	60.00

12.0000 g, .920 GOLD, .3549 oz AGW

Y#	Date	Mintage	Fine	VF	XF	Unc
125b	1987	6,000	—	—	Proof	300.00

14.0000 g, .999 PLATINUM, .4497 oz APW

Y#	Date	Mintage	Fine	VF	XF	Unc
125c	1987	1,000	—	—	Proof	500.00

NICKEL-BRONZE

Y#	Date	Mintage	Fine	VF	XF	Unc
125d	1987	70.000	—	—	3.00	6.50

ALUMINUM-BRONZE RING & STEEL CENTER
Spirit of Bastille

Y#	Date	Mintage	Fine	VF	XF	Unc
127.1	1988	100.000	—	—	3.00	6.00
	1989	249.980	—	—	3.00	6.00
	1990	250.000	—	—	3.00	6.00
	1991	—	—	—	3.00	6.00
	1992	150.000	—	—	3.00	6.00
	1992	—	—	—	Proof	20.00
	1993	—	—	—	3.00	6.00

Plain edge.

Y#	Date	Mintage	Fine	VF	XF	Unc
127.2	1991	—	—	—	Proof	20.00

GOLD RING-GOLD, PALLADIUM & SILVER CENTER

Y#	Date	Mintage	Fine	VF	XF	Unc
127.1a	1988	5,000	—	—	Proof	325.00

ALUMINUM-BRONZE
100th Anniversary of Birth of Roland Garros

Y#	Date	Mintage	Fine	VF	XF	Unc
128	1988	30.000	—	—	2.50	4.00

12.0000 g, .900 SILVER, .3472 oz ASW

Y#	Date	Mintage	Fine	VF	XF	Unc
128a	1988	.010	—	—	—	25.00

12.0000 g, .950 SILVER, .3665 oz ASW

Y#	Date	Mintage	Fine	VF	XF	Unc
128b	1988	.010	—	—	Proof	55.00

12.0000 g, .920 GOLD, .3550 oz AGW

Y#	Date	Mintage	Fine	VF	XF	Unc
128c	1988	3,000	—	—	Proof	350.00

ALUMINUM-BRONZE RING & STEEL CENTER
300th Anniversary of Birth of Montesquieu

Y#	Date	Mintage	Fine	VF	XF	Unc
135	1989	249.964	—	—	2.50	5.00
	1990	249.990	—	—	2.50	5.00
	1991	250.000	—	—	2.50	5.00

GOLD RING-GOLD, PALLADIUM & SILVER CENTER

Y#	Date	Mintage	Fine	VF	XF	Unc
135a	1989	5,000	—	—	Proof	325.00

20 FRANCS

6.4516 g, .900 GOLD, .1867 oz AGW
Mint mark: A
Bare head

C#	Date	Mintage	Fine	VF	XF	Unc
146	ANXI	.058	150.00	225.00	450.00	1400.
	AN12	.988	125.00	150.00	300.00	900.00
	AN12	—	—	—	Proof	5500.

Obv. leg: NAPOLEON EMPEREUR.

C#	Date	Mintage	Fine	VF	XF	Unc
156	AN12	.428	125.00	150.00	350.00	1000.

Redesigned head.

C#	Date	Mintage	Fine	VF	XF	Unc
156a.1	AN13	.519	125.00	150.00	300.00	900.00
	AN14	.148	125.00	175.00	400.00	900.00

Mint mark: I

C#	Date	Mintage	Fine	VF	XF	Unc
156a.2	AN13	—	—	—	—	—
	AN14	1,646	750.00	1250.	2500.	3500.

Mint mark: Q

C#	Date	Mintage	Fine	VF	XF	Unc
156a.3	AN13	522 pcs.	1000.	1500.	3000.	4000.
	AN14	2,710	375.00	625.00	1250.	2250.

Mint mark: T

C#	Date	Mintage	Fine	VF	XF	Unc
156a.4	AN13	918 pcs.	875.00	1400.	2750.	3750.

Mint mark: U

C#	Date	Mintage	Fine	VF	XF	Unc
156a.5	AN14	1,755	500.00	800.00	1500.	2500.

Mint mark: W

C#	Date	Mintage	Fine	VF	XF	Unc
156a.6	AN14	—	—	—	—	—

Mint mark: A

C#	Date	Mintage	Fine	VF	XF	Unc
156a.7	1806	.964	100.00	125.00	225.00	600.00
	1807	.826	100.00	125.00	225.00	600.00

Mint mark: I

C#	Date	Mintage	Fine	VF	XF	Unc
156a.8	1806	8,143	200.00	400.00	800.00	1500.

Mint mark: M

C#	Date	Mintage	Fine	VF	XF	Unc
156a.12	1807	5,296	225.00	450.00	850.00	1500.

Mint mark: Q

C#	Date	Mintage	Fine	VF	XF	Unc
156a.9	1806	3,973	300.00	600.00	1000.	1750.

Mint mark: U

C#	Date	Mintage	Fine	VF	XF	Unc
156a.10	1806	.017	150.00	300.00	600.00	1250.
	1807	2,557	400.00	800.00	1250.	2000.

Mint mark: W

C#	Date	Mintage	Fine	VF	XF	Unc
156a.11	1806	4,242	200.00	400.00	800.00	1500.
	1807	5,181	200.00	400.00	850.00	1500.

Mint mark: A
Laureate head

C#	Date	Mintage	Fine	VF	XF	Unc
156b.1	1807	Inc. Ab.	100.00	125.00	175.00	500.00
	1808	1.450	100.00	125.00	175.00	500.00

Mint mark: K

C#	Date	Mintage	Fine	VF	XF	Unc
156b.2	1808	281 pcs.	—	—	Rare	—

Mint mark: M

C#	Date	Mintage	Fine	VF	XF	Unc
156b.3	1808	.022	150.00	250.00	500.00	900.00

Mint mark: Q

C#	Date	Mintage	Fine	VF	XF	Unc
156b.4	1808	646 pcs.	—	—	Rare	—

Mint mark: U

C#	Date	Mintage	Fine	VF	XF	Unc
156b.5	1808	1,505	375.00	625.00	1250.	1750.

Mint mark: W

C#	Date	Mintage	Fine	VF	XF	Unc
156b.6	1808	8,489	200.00	350.00	750.00	1250.

Mint mark: A

C#	Date	Mintage	Fine	VF	XF	Unc
166.1	1809	.688	100.00	125.00	200.00	550.00
	1810	1.936	100.00	125.00	150.00	400.00
	1811	3.705	100.00	125.00	150.00	400.00
	1812	3.072	100.00	125.00	150.00	400.00
	1813	2.798	100.00	125.00	150.00	400.00
	1814	.328	100.00	150.00	225.00	600.00

Mint mark: CL

C#	Date	Mintage	Fine	VF	XF	Unc
166.10	1813	4,380	500.00	1000.	2000.	4000.
	1814	887 pcs.	750.00	1500.	3000.	6000.

Mint mark: H

C#	Date	Mintage	Fine	VF	XF	Unc
166.2	1809	501 pcs.	750.00	1500.	3000.	4500.
	1810	2,454	500.00	1000.	2000.	3000.
	1811	1,278	625.00	1250.	2500.	5000.

Mint mark: K

C#	Date	Mintage	Fine	VF	XF	Unc
166.3	1809	3,614	250.00	500.00	1000.	1500.
	1810	.015	225.00	450.00	900.00	1750.
	1811	.011	225.00	450.00	900.00	1750.
	1812	2,650	375.00	750.00	1500.	3000.
	1813	869 pcs.	600.00	1200.	2250.	4500.

Mint mark: L

C#	Date	Mintage	Fine	VF	XF	Unc
166.4	1809	2,383	325.00	650.00	1250.	2500.
	1812	.018	125.00	175.00	300.00	800.00
	1813	.019	125.00	175.00	300.00	800.00

Mint mark: M

C#	Date	Mintage	Fine	VF	XF	Unc
166.5	1809	5,007	225.00	450.00	900.00	1750.
	1810	1,983	300.00	600.00	1200.	2500.
	1811	4,971	250.00	400.00	850.00	1750.
	1812	6,498	175.00	300.00	650.00	1400.

Mint mark: Q

C#	Date	Mintage	Fine	VF	XF	Unc
166.8	1810	2,343	450.00	875.00	1750.	3500.
	1812	5,470	250.00	500.00	1000.	2000.
	1813	.013	175.00	350.00	700.00	1400.
	1814	3,289	300.00	600.00	1200.	2400.

Mint mark: R

C#	Date	Mintage	Fine	VF	XF	Unc
166.9	1812(c)	.014	250.00	500.00	750.00	2000.
	1813	5,532	300.00	600.00	1000.	2500.

Mint mark: U

C#	Date	Mintage	Fine	VF	XF	Unc
166.6	1809	3,400	375.00	750.00	1500.	3000.
	1810	5,891	225.00	450.00	900.00	2000.
	1811	.020	150.00	250.00	450.00	1100.
	1812	7,339	175.00	300.00	550.00	1500.
	1813	925 pcs.	750.00	1500.	3000.	4500.

Mint mark: W

C#	Date	Mintage	Fine	VF	XF	Unc
166.7	1809	.017	125.00	200.00	400.00	1000.
	1810	.223	100.00	125.00	175.00	550.00
	1811	.328	100.00	125.00	175.00	550.00

C#	Date	Mintage	Fine	VF	XF	Unc
166.7	1812	.346	100.00	125.00	175.00	550.00
	1813	.104	100.00	125.00	175.00	600.00
	1814	.016	125.00	200.00	350.00	900.00

Mint mark: Flag

C#	Date	Mintage	Fine	VF	XF	Unc
166.11	1813	.090	150.00	250.00	350.00	1100.

Mint mark: A
The Hundred Days

C#	Date	Mintage	Fine	VF	XF	Unc
166.12 (C166.1)	1815	.436	120.00	200.00	300.00	800.00

Mint mark: L

C#	Date	Mintage	Fine	VF	XF	Unc
166.13	1815	.018	150.00	200.00	400.00	1000.

Mint mark: W

C#	Date	Mintage	Fine	VF	XF	Unc
166.14	1815	9,369	200.00	350.00	700.00	1500.

Mint mark: A
Engraver: Tiolier

C#	Date	Mintage	Fine	VF	XF	Unc
170.1	1814	2.684	100.00	125.00	150.00	375.00
	1815	2.113	100.00	125.00	150.00	375.00

Mint mark: B

C#	Date	Mintage	Fine	VF	XF	Unc
170.6	1815	1,539	300.00	600.00	1200.	1500.

Mint mark: K

C#	Date	Mintage	Fine	VF	XF	Unc
170.2	1814	.063	100.00	150.00	200.00	600.00
	1815	.030	100.00	150.00	200.00	600.00

Mint mark: L

C#	Date	Mintage	Fine	VF	XF	Unc
170.3	1814	.045	100.00	150.00	200.00	600.00
	1815	.034	100.00	150.00	200.00	600.00

Mint mark: Q

C#	Date	Mintage	Fine	VF	XF	Unc
170.4	1814	.029	125.00	175.00	250.00	700.00
	1815	.039	100.00	150.00	200.00	600.00

Mint mark: W

C#	Date	Mintage	Fine	VF	XF	Unc
170.5	1814	.060	100.00	150.00	200.00	600.00
	1815	.088	100.00	150.00	200.00	600.00

Mint mark: R
Engraver: T. Wyon, Jr.

C#	Date	Mintage	Fine	VF	XF	Unc
182	1815	.872	100.00	125.00	175.00	450.00

Mint mark: A

C#	Date	Mintage	Fine	VF	XF	Unc
183.1	1816	.522	100.00	125.00	150.00	325.00
	1817	2.135	100.00	125.00	150.00	325.00
	1818	2.681	100.00	125.00	150.00	325.00
	1819	2.350	100.00	125.00	150.00	325.00
	1820	1.317	100.00	125.00	150.00	325.00
	1821	.012	125.00	200.00	300.00	650.00
	1822	.213	100.00	125.00	150.00	325.00
	1823	.012	125.00	200.00	300.00	650.00
	1824	1.510	100.00	125.00	150.00	325.00

Mint mark: B

C#	Date	Mintage	Fine	VF	XF	Unc
183.2	1816	.022	—	—	—	—

Mint mark: H

C#	Date	Mintage	Fine	VF	XF	Unc
183.8	1822	1,253	500.00	850.00	1100.	1850.

Mint mark: K

C#	Date	Mintage	Fine	VF	XF	Unc
183.3	1816	4,947	—	—	—	—
	1817	4,803	175.00	275.00	475.00	900.00

Mint mark: L

C#	Date	Mintage	Fine	VF	XF	Unc
183.4	1816	.022	—	—	—	—
	1817	.036	125.00	200.00	300.00	650.00
	1818	5,394	150.00	225.00	350.00	850.00

Mint mark: MA

C#	Date	Mintage	Fine	VF	XF	Unc
183.9	1824	2,001	625.00	1250.	1500.	1750.

Mint mark: Q

C#	Date	Mintage	Fine	VF	XF	Unc
183.5	1816	.016	100.00	150.00	225.00	550.00
	1817	.097	100.00	125.00	200.00	500.00
	1818	.025	100.00	150.00	200.00	500.00
	1819	.034	100.00	125.00	225.00	550.00
	1820	.060	100.00	125.00	225.00	550.00
	1824	.012	100.00	150.00	275.00	650.00

Mint mark: T

C#	Date	Mintage	Fine	VF	XF	Unc
183.7	1818	.016	100.00	125.00	200.00	550.00
	1819	8,734	100.00	150.00	250.00	625.00
	1820	5,749	100.00	150.00	250.00	625.00

Mint mark: W

C#	Date	Mintage	Fine	VF	XF	Unc
183.6	1816	.054	100.00	125.00	200.00	600.00
	1817	.156	100.00	125.00	150.00	500.00
	1818	1.315	100.00	125.00	150.00	500.00
	1819	.219	100.00	125.00	150.00	500.00
	1820	.044	100.00	125.00	200.00	600.00
	1821	8,446	100.00	150.00	250.00	700.00
	1822	.020	100.00	125.00	200.00	600.00
	1823	7,655	100.00	150.00	250.00	700.00
	1824	.253	100.00	125.00	150.00	500.00

Mint mark: A

C#	Date	Mintage	Fine	VF	XF	Unc
190.1	1825	.664	100.00	125.00	200.00	900.00
	1826	.035	150.00	225.00	375.00	1400.
	1827	.154	100.00	150.00	250.00	1200.
	1828	.279	100.00	150.00	250.00	900.00
	1829	7,783	150.00	250.00	425.00	1700.
	1830	.431	100.00	150.00	250.00	1000.

Mint mark: Q

C#	Date	Mintage	Fine	VF	XF	Unc
190.3	1826	4,574	500.00	1000.	1250.	2250.

Mint mark: T

C#	Date	Mintage	Fine	VF	XF	Unc
190.4	1828	3,175	500.00	1000.	1250.	2250.

Mint mark: W

C#	Date	Mintage	Fine	VF	XF	Unc
190.2	1825	.062	125.00	200.00	350.00	1200.
	1826	6,436	200.00	275.00	450.00	1400.
	1827	3,431	225.00	350.00	550.00	1600.
	1828	.015	150.00	250.00	350.00	1200.
	1829	5,946	200.00	275.00	450.00	1400.
	1830	.015	150.00	250.00	350.00	1200.

Mint mark: A
Incuse edge lettering.

C#	Date	Mintage	Fine	VF	XF	Unc
205.1	1830	.018	125.00	200.00	300.00	1200.
	1831	2.162	100.00	125.00	150.00	1000.

Mint mark: B

C#	Date	Mintage	Fine	VF	XF	Unc
205.2	1831	.088	150.00	300.00	550.00	1500.

Mint mark: W

C#	Date	Mintage	Fine	VF	XF	Unc
205.3	1831	.107	110.00	150.00	200.00	1200.

Mint mark: A
Raised edge lettering.

C#	Date	Mintage	Fine	VF	XF	Unc
205.4	1831	Inc. Ab.	110.00	150.00	200.00	1000.

Mint mark: B

C#	Date	Mintage	Fine	VF	XF	Unc
205.5	1831	—	125.00	175.00	250.00	1000.

Mint mark: T

C#	Date	Mintage	Fine	VF	XF	Unc
205.6	1831	—	500.00	800.00	1250.	2000.

Mint mark: W

C#	Date	Mintage	Fine	VF	XF	Unc
205.7	1831	Inc. Ab.	110.00	150.00	250.00	1500.

Mint mark: A

C#	Date	Mintage	Fine	VF	XF	Unc
206.1	1832	6,360	175.00	350.00	700.00	1500.
	1832	—	—	—	Proof	6000.
	1833	.207	100.00	125.00	175.00	900.00
	1834	.744	100.00	125.00	175.00	700.00
	1835	.097	100.00	125.00	175.00	900.00
	1836	.139	100.00	125.00	175.00	900.00
	1837	.034	100.00	150.00	200.00	900.00
	1838	.173	100.00	125.00	175.00	900.00
	1839	1.012	100.00	125.00	150.00	700.00
	1840	2.045	100.00	125.00	150.00	700.00
	1841	.610	100.00	125.00	175.00	700.00
	1842	.071	125.00	150.00	200.00	900.00
	1843	.106	100.00	125.00	175.00	900.00
	1844	.103	100.00	125.00	175.00	900.00
	1845	939 pcs.	625.00	1250.	1750.	3000.
	1846	.103	100.00	125.00	175.00	900.00
	1847	.385	100.00	125.00	175.00	700.00
	1848	.442	100.00	125.00	150.00	700.00

Mint mark: B

C#	Date	Mintage	Fine	VF	XF	Unc
206.2	1832	.015	100.00	150.00	200.00	900.00
	1833	.155	100.00	125.00	175.00	900.00
	1834	.077	100.00	125.00	175.00	900.00
	1835	.026	100.00	150.00	225.00	900.00

Mint mark: L

C#	Date	Mintage	Fine	VF	XF	Unc
206.5	1834	.021	100.00	150.00	200.00	900.00
	1835	856 pcs.	625.00	1250.	2000.	3000.

Mint mark: T

C#	Date	Mintage	Fine	VF	XF	Unc
206.3	1832	868 pcs.	750.00	1500.	2250.	3250.

Mint mark: W

C#	Date	Mintage	Fine	VF	XF	Unc
206.4	1832	.027	100.00	150.00	200.00	900.00
	1833	.032	100.00	150.00	200.00	900.00
	1834	.041	100.00	150.00	200.00	900.00
	1835	.030	100.00	150.00	200.00	900.00
	1836	.010	100.00	150.00	225.00	900.00
	1837	.011	100.00	150.00	225.00	900.00
	1838	.012	100.00	150.00	225.00	900.00
	1839	.022	100.00	125.00	200.00	900.00
	1840	4,550	150.00	300.00	425.00	1350.
	1841	8,524	125.00	275.00	400.00	1200.
	1842	.022	100.00	125.00	200.00	900.00
	1843	.035	100.00	125.00	200.00	900.00
	1844	.034	100.00	125.00	200.00	900.00
	1845	5,018	125.00	250.00	375.00	1200.
	1846	1,408	375.00	750.00	1250.	1200.

Mint mark: A

Y#	Date	Mintage	Fine	VF	XF	Unc
8	1848	1.543	100.00	125.00	175.00	500.00
	1848	—	—	—	Proof	6000.
	1849	1.303	100.00	125.00	175.00	500.00

Y#	Date	Mintage	Fine	VF	XF	Unc
10	1849	.053	100.00	125.00	200.00	750.00
	1850	3.964	BV	100.00	125.00	450.00
	1850	—	—	—	Proof	5000.
	1851	12.704	BV	100.00	125.00	400.00

Y#	Date	Mintage	Fine	VF	XF	Unc
A13	1852	10.494	BV	100.00	125.00	600.00
	1852	—	—	—	Proof	5000.

Y#	Date	Mintage	Fine	VF	XF	Unc
35.1	1853	5.729	BV	100.00	115.00	175.00
	1853	—	—	—	Proof	5000.
	1854	23.486	BV	100.00	115.00	175.00
	1854	—	—	—	Proof	4000.
	1855(d)	16.595	BV	100.00	115.00	175.00
	1855(a)	Inc. Ab.	BV	100.00	115.00	175.00
	1856	17.303	BV	100.00	115.00	175.00
	1857	19.193	BV	100.00	115.00	175.00
	1858	16.861	BV	100.00	115.00	175.00
	1859	20.295	BV	100.00	115.00	175.00
	1860	10.220	BV	100.00	115.00	175.00

Mint mark: BB

Y#	Date	Mintage	Fine	VF	XF	Unc
35.2	1855	1.760	BV	100.00	125.00	200.00
	1856	1.125	BV	100.00	125.00	200.00
	1858	2.017	BV	100.00	125.00	200.00
	1859	5.871	BV	100.00	115.00	175.00
	1860	5.727	BV	100.00	115.00	175.00

Mint mark: D

Y#	Date	Mintage	Fine	VF	XF	Unc
35.3	1855	.045	100.00	125.00	200.00	450.00

Mint mark: A

Y#	Date	Mintage	Fine	VF	XF	Unc
40.1	1861	2.607	BV	100.00	110.00	175.00
	1861	—	—	—	Proof	5000.
	1862	4.826	BV	100.00	110.00	175.00
	1863	3.920	BV	100.00	110.00	175.00
	1864	7.059	BV	100.00	110.00	175.00
	1865	2.951	BV	100.00	110.00	175.00
	1866	6.992	BV	100.00	110.00	175.00
	1867	2.923	BV	100.00	110.00	175.00
	1868	9.281	BV	100.00	110.00	175.00
	1869	4.046	BV	100.00	110.00	175.00
	1870	.865	BV	100.00	110.00	200.00

Mint mark: BB

Y#	Date	Mintage	Fine	VF	XF	Unc
40.2	1861	1.423	BV	100.00	110.00	175.00
	1862	2.907	BV	100.00	110.00	175.00
	1863	4.753	BV	100.00	110.00	175.00
	1864	3.323	BV	100.00	110.00	175.00
	1865	3.088	BV	100.00	110.00	175.00
	1866	6.979	BV	100.00	110.00	175.00
	1867	4.516	BV	100.00	110.00	175.00
	1868	4.829	BV	100.00	110.00	175.00
	1869	7.317	BV	100.00	110.00	175.00
	1870	1.853	BV	100.00	110.00	200.00

Mint mark: A

Y#	Date	Mintage	Fine	VF	XF	Unc
55	1871	2.508	BV	100.00	110.00	175.00
	1874	1.216	BV	100.00	110.00	125.00
	1875	11.746	BV	100.00	110.00	125.00
	1876	8.825	BV	100.00	110.00	125.00
	1877	12.759	BV	100.00	110.00	125.00
	1878	9.189	BV	100.00	110.00	125.00
	1878	30 pcs.	—	—	Proof	7000.
	1879	1.038	BV	100.00	110.00	125.00
	1886	.985	BV	100.00	110.00	125.00
	1887	1.231	BV	100.00	110.00	125.00
	1887	—	—	—	Proof	5000.
	1888	.028	100.00	125.00	175.00	300.00
	1889	.873	BV	100.00	110.00	125.00
	1889	100 pcs.	—	—	Proof	6000.
	1890	1.030	BV	100.00	110.00	125.00
	1891	.871	BV	100.00	110.00	125.00
	1892	.226	BV	100.00	110.00	125.00
	1893	2.517	BV	100.00	110.00	125.00
	1894	.491	BV	100.00	110.00	125.00
	1895	5.293	BV	100.00	110.00	125.00
	1896	5.330	BV	100.00	110.00	125.00
	1897	11.069	BV	100.00	110.00	125.00
	1898	8.866	BV	100.00	110.00	125.00

Edge inscription: DIEU PROTEGE LA FRANCE.

Y#	Date	Mintage	Fine	VF	XF	Unc
66	1899	1.500	BV	100.00	110.00	125.00
	1900	.615	BV	100.00	110.00	150.00
	1900	Inc. Ab.	—	—	Proof	2000.
	1901	2.643	BV	100.00	110.00	125.00
	1902	2.394	BV	100.00	110.00	125.00
	1903	4.405	BV	100.00	110.00	125.00
	1904	7.706	BV	100.00	110.00	125.00
	1905	9.158	BV	100.00	110.00	125.00
	1906	14.613	BV	100.00	110.00	125.00

Edge inscription: LIBERTE EGALITE FRATERNITE.

Y#	Date	Mintage	Fine	VF	XF	Unc
66a	1906	—	BV	95.00	100.00	115.00
	1907	17.716	BV	95.00	100.00	115.00
	1908	6.721	BV	95.00	100.00	115.00
	1909	9.637	BV	95.00	100.00	115.00
	1910	5.779	BV	95.00	100.00	115.00
	1911	5.346	BV	95.00	100.00	115.00
	1912	10.332	BV	95.00	100.00	115.00
	1913	12.163	BV	95.00	100.00	115.00
	1914	6.518	BV	95.00	100.00	115.00

NOTE: Some dates from 1907-1914 have been officially restruck.

Long Leaves Short Leaves

Mint: Paris - w/o.mint mark.
20.0000 g, .680 SILVER, .4372 oz ASW

Y#	Date	Mintage	Fine	VF	XF	Unc
87	1929(ll)	3.234	BV	7.00	15.00	50.00
	1933(sl)	24.447*	BV	5.00	6.00	25.00
	1933(ll)	Inc. Ab.	BV	5.00	6.00	25.00
	1934(sl)	11.785	BV	5.00	10.00	30.00
	1936(sl)	.048	300.00	450.00	800.00	—
	1937(sl)	1.189	10.00	20.00	40.00	70.00
	1938(sl)	10.910	BV	5.00	10.00	30.00
	1939(sl)	3,918	700.00	1500.	2000.	5000.

*NOTE: Counterfeits exist in bronze-aluminum with thin silver sheath.

3 Feathers 4 Feathers

ALUMINUM-BRONZE
Obv: GEORGES GUIRAUD behind head.

Y#	Date	Mintage	Fine	VF	XF	Unc
99.1	1950 (3 plumes)	5.779	.50	2.00	5.00	12.00
	1950 (4 plumes)	—	200.00	300.00	450.00	—

Mint mark: B

Y#	Date	Mintage	Fine	VF	XF	Unc
99.2	1950 (3 plumes)	—	3.00	6.00	12.00	40.00
	1950 (4 plumes)	—	40.00	85.00	150.00	225.00

Mint: Paris - w/o mint mark.
Obv: G. GUIRAUD behind head.

Y#	Date	Mintage	Fine	VF	XF	Unc
99a.1	1950 (3 plumes)	120.656	3.00	10.00	20.00	50.00
	1950 (4 plumes)	Inc. Ab.	.25	.40	3.00	5.00
	1951 (4 plumes)	97.922	.25	.40	2.00	5.00
	1952 (4 plumes)	130.281	.25	.40	2.00	5.00
	1953 (4 plumes)	60.158	.30	.50	2.00	5.00

Mint mark: B

Y#	Date	Mintage	Fine	VF	XF	Unc
99a.2	1950 (3 plumes)	43.355	25.00	35.00	50.00	115.00
	1950 (4 plumes)	Inc. Ab.	1.00	2.50	5.00	12.00
	1951 (4 plumes)	46.815	.30	.50	2.00	5.00
	1952 (4 plumes)	54.381	.30	.50	2.00	5.00
	1953 (4 plumes)	42.410	.30	.50	2.00	5.00
	1954 (4 plumes)	1.573	175.00	250.00	500.00	900.00

COPPER-ALUMINUM-NICKEL center plug, NICKEL inner ring, COPPER-ALUMINUM-NICKEL outer ring
Mont St. Michel

Y#	Date	Mintage	Fine	VF	XF	Unc
167	1992	60.000	—	—	—	9.00
167	1992	—	—	—	Proof	35.00
	1993	—	—	—	—	9.00

12.6600 g, .750 GOLD center plug, .950 SILVER inner ring, .750 GOLD outer ring

Y#	Date	Mintage	Fine	VF	XF	Unc
167a	1992	.015	—	—	Proof	250.00

.920 GOLD center plug, .750 GOLD inner ring, .920 GOLD outer ring

Y#	Date	Mintage	Fine	VF	XF	Unc
167b	1992	5,000	—	—	Proof	475.00

40 FRANCS

12.9039 g, .900 GOLD, .3734 oz AGW
Mint mark: A

C#	Date	Mintage	Fine	VF	XF	Unc
147	ANXI	.226	200.00	225.00	350.00	1500.
	AN12	.253	200.00	225.00	350.00	1500.

C#	Date	Mintage	Fine	VF	XF	Unc
157.1	AN13	.252	200.00	225.00	350.00	1200.
	AN13	—	—	—	Proof	15,000.
	AN14	121	200.00	225.00	350.00	1200.

Mint mark: U

C#	Date	Mintage	Fine	VF	XF	Unc
157.2	AN14	—	—	—	Rare	—

Mint mark: W

C#	Date	Mintage	Fine	VF	XF	Unc
157.3	AN14	—	—	—	Rare	—

Mint mark: A

C#	Date	Mintage	Fine	VF	XF	Unc
157.4	1806	.196	200.00	225.00	400.00	1000.
	1807	.017	200.00	400.00	800.00	1600.

Mint mark: CL

C#	Date	Mintage	Fine	VF	XF	Unc
157.5	1806	—	—	—	Rare	—

Mint mark: I

C#	Date	Mintage	Fine	VF	XF	Unc
157.6	1806	7,103	250.00	500.00	1250.	2500.
	1807	1,859	350.00	750.00	2000.	3500.

Mint mark: M

C#	Date	Mintage	Fine	VF	XF	Unc
157.7	1806	—	—	—	—	—
	1807	4,994	300.00	600.00	1250.	3000.

Mint mark: U

C#	Date	Mintage	Fine	VF	XF	Unc
157.8	1806	.059	225.00	325.00	650.00	1500.
	1807	619 pcs.	1000.	2000.	3500.	—

Mint mark: W

C#	Date	Mintage	Fine	VF	XF	Unc
157.9	1806	4,336	300.00	650.00	1250.	3000.
	1807	6,043	300.00	650.00	1250.	3000.

Mint mark: A
Laureate head

C#	Date	Mintage	Fine	VF	XF	Unc
157a.1	1807	*.253	200.00	225.00	350.00	1000.
	1808	.044	200.00	225.00	350.00	1000.

Mint mark: H

C#	Date	Mintage	Fine	VF	XF	Unc
157a.2	1808	.012	225.00	450.00	900.00	2250.

Mint mark: M

C#	Date	Mintage	Fine	VF	XF	Unc
157a.3	1808	4,226	300.00	500.00	1000.	2750.

Mint mark: U

C#	Date	Mintage	Fine	VF	XF	Unc
157a.4	1808	346 pcs.	—	—	Rare	—

Mint mark: W

C#	Date	Mintage	Fine	VF	XF	Unc
157a.5	1808	6,356	225.00	450.00	950.00	2750.

Mint mark: A

C#	Date	Mintage	Fine	VF	XF	Unc
167.1	1809	.013	225.00	375.00	700.00	1800.
	1809	—	—	—	Proof	6800.
	1811	1.262	200.00	225.00	300.00	750.00
	1812	.693	200.00	225.00	325.00	1100.
	1813	.045	200.00	300.00	600.00	1500.
	1813	—	—	—	Proof	12,000.

Mint mark: CL

C#	Date	Mintage	Fine	VF	XF	Unc
167.6	1813	3,070	500.00	1000.	2000.	3500.

Mint mark: K

C#	Date	Mintage	Fine	VF	XF	Unc
167.5	1810	886 pcs.	—	—	Rare	—
	1811	6,333	300.00	625.00	1250.	2500.

Mint mark: M

C#	Date	Mintage	Fine	VF	XF	Unc
167.2	1809	1,402	500.00	1000.	1750.	3250.

Mint mark: U

C#	Date	Mintage	Fine	VF	XF	Unc
167.3	1809	—	—	—	Rare	—

Mint mark: W

C#	Date	Mintage	Fine	VF	XF	Unc
167.4	1809	5,925	300.00	600.00	1200.	2400.
	1810	.057	200.00	250.00	450.00	1500.
	1812	.014	200.00	275.00	550.00	1700.

Mint mark: A

C#	Date	Mintage	Fine	VF	XF	Unc
184.1	1816	.041	200.00	300.00	600.00	900.00
	1817	.090	200.00	300.00	500.00	850.00
	1818	.011	200.00	350.00	750.00	1250.
	1820	5,480	250.00	500.00	1000.	2250.
	1822	373 pcs.	—	—	Rare	—
	1823	161 pcs.	—	—	Rare	—
	1824	.015	200.00	275.00	450.00	900.00

Mint mark: B

C#	Date	Mintage	Fine	VF	XF	Unc
184.2	1816	767 pcs.	1000.	2000.	3500.	5000.

Mint mark: H

C#	Date	Mintage	Fine	VF	XF	Unc
184.6	1822	611 pcs.	1000.	2000.	3500.	5000.

Mint mark: L

C#	Date	Mintage	Fine	VF	XF	Unc
184.3	1816	2,923	375.00	675.00	1000.	2750.
	1817	377 pcs.	—	—	Rare	—

Mint mark: Q

C#	Date	Mintage	Fine	VF	XF	Unc
184.4	1816	.011	200.00	300.00	450.00	1250.

Mint mark: W

C#	Date	Mintage	Fine	VF	XF	Unc
184.5	1816	3,210	200.00	300.00	600.00	1200.
	1818	.353	200.00	225.00	300.00	700.00
	1819	4,610	200.00	300.00	600.00	1200.

Mint mark: A

C#	Date	Mintage	Fine	VF	XF	Unc
191.1	1824	.050	225.00	275.00	450.00	2000.
	1826	62 pcs.	—	—	Rare	—
	1827	106 pcs.	—	—	Rare	—
	1828	.052	225.00	275.00	450.00	2000.
	1829	.021	225.00	300.00	500.00	2000.
	1830	.354	225.00	250.00	325.00	1750.

Mint mark: MA

C#	Date	Mintage	Fine	VF	XF	Unc
191.2	1830	1,026	—	—	Rare	—

Mint mark: A

C#	Date	Mintage	Fine	VF	XF	Unc
207.1	1831	.063	200.00	250.00	500.00	1200.

C#	Date	Mintage	Fine	VF	XF	Unc
207.1	1832	.022	200.00	275.00	500.00	1200.
	1832	—	—	—	Proof	9000.
	1833	.221	200.00	250.00	450.00	1200.
	1834	.303	200.00	225.00	400.00	1000.
	1835	.036	200.00	275.00	500.00	1200.
	1836	.053	200.00	275.00	500.00	1200.
	1837	.028	200.00	275.00	500.00	1200.
	1838	.031	200.00	275.00	500.00	1200.
	1839	23 pcs.	—	—	Rare	—

Mint mark: B

C#	Date	Mintage	Fine	VF	XF	Unc
207.2	1832	3,947	300.00	450.00	900.00	2200.
	1833	1,392	450.00	900.00	1750.	3500.

Mint mark: L

C#	Date	Mintage	Fine	VF	XF	Unc
207.3	1834	.012	225.00	325.00	600.00	1800.
	1835	856 pcs.	600.00	1200.	2000.	4500.

50 FRANCS

16.1290 g, .900 GOLD, .4667 oz AGW
Mint mark: A
Bare head

Y#	Date	Mintage	Fine	VF	XF	Unc
36.1	1855	.152	250.00	275.00	300.00	500.00
	1856	.097	250.00	275.00	350.00	500.00
	1857	.320	250.00	275.00	300.00	500.00
	1858	.085	250.00	275.00	350.00	500.00
	1859	.034	250.00	275.00	350.00	500.00

Mint mark: BB

Y#	Date	Mintage	Fine	VF	XF	Unc
36.2	1855	3,051	250.00	350.00	600.00	1000.
	1856	3,803	250.00	375.00	600.00	1000.
	1858	9,135	250.00	350.00	550.00	1000.
	1859	.032	250.00	275.00	400.00	600.00
	1860	.029	—	—	—	—

Mint mark: A
Laureate head

Y#	Date	Mintage	Fine	VF	XF	Unc
A40.1	1862	.024	250.00	275.00	375.00	600.00
	1862	—	—	—	Proof	7500.
	1864	.029	250.00	275.00	375.00	600.00
	1865	3,740	250.00	400.00	600.00	1000.
	1866	.039	250.00	275.00	375.00	600.00
	1867	2,000	250.00	400.00	600.00	1000.
	1868	.016	250.00	275.00	375.00	650.00

Mint mark: BB

Y#	Date	Mintage	Fine	VF	XF	Unc
A40.2	1862	7,310	250.00	300.00	400.00	750.00
	1863	8,251	250.00	300.00	400.00	750.00
	1866	.017	250.00	275.00	375.00	650.00
	1867	.020	250.00	275.00	375.00	650.00
	1868	—	350.00	450.00	650.00	1250.
	1869	1,795	350.00	450.00	650.00	1250.

Mint mark: A

Y#	Date	Mintage	Fine	VF	XF	Unc
56	1878	5,294	350.00	700.00	1200.	2000.
	1887	301 pcs.	550.00	1250.	2250.	4500.
	1889	100 pcs.	—	—	Proof	6500.
	1896	800 pcs.	450.00	900.00	1800.	3500.
	1900	200 pcs.	650.00	1500.	2500.	5000.
	1904	.020	300.00	600.00	900.00	1900.

ALUMINUM-BRONZE

Mint: Paris - w/o mint mark.

Y#	Date	Mintage	Fine	VF	XF	Unc
100.1	1950	.600	75.00	150.00	300.00	575.00
	1951	68.630	1.00	2.00	4.00	8.00
	1952	74.212	.50	2.00	4.00	8.00
	1953	63.172	.50	2.00	4.00	8.00
	1954	.997	15.00	35.00	70.00	120.00
	1958(w)	.501	30.00	65.00	100.00	200.00

Mint mark: B

Y#	Date	Mintage	Fine	VF	XF	Unc
100.2	1951	11.829	1.50	3.00	6.00	12.00
	1952	13.432	2.50	5.50	12.00	30.00
	1953	23.376	1.00	2.50	4.00	10.00
	1954	6.531	5.00	10.00	20.00	40.00

30.0000 g, .900 SILVER, .8682 oz ASW
Mint: Paris - w/o mint mark.
5000 Old Francs = 50 New Francs

Y#	Date	Mintage	Fine	VF	XF	Unc
112	1974	4.299	—	—	—	12.00
	1975	4.551	—	—	—	12.00
	1976	7.739	—	—	—	12.00
	1977	7.884	—	—	—	12.00
	1978	12.028	—	—	—	12.00
	1979	12.041	—	—	—	12.00
	1980	.060	—	—	—	50.00

100 FRANCS

32.2581 g, .900 GOLD, .9335 oz AGW
Mint mark: A

Y#	Date	Mintage	Fine	VF	XF	Unc
37.1	1855	.051	450.00	500.00	550.00	900.00
	1856	.057	450.00	500.00	550.00	900.00
	1857	.103	450.00	500.00	550.00	900.00
	1858	.092	450.00	500.00	550.00	900.00
	1859	.022	450.00	500.00	550.00	900.00

Mint mark: BB

Y#	Date	Mintage	Fine	VF	XF	Unc
37.2	1855	4,173	450.00	500.00	550.00	1100.
	1856	876 pcs.	600.00	1000.	1500.	3000.
	1858	1,928	475.00	525.00	625.00	1300.
	1859	9,305	450.00	500.00	550.00	1100.
	1860	5,405	450.00	500.00	550.00	1100.

Mint mark: A

Y#	Date	Mintage	Fine	VF	XF	Unc
B40.1	1861	—	—	—	Proof	8000.
	1862	6,650	450.00	550.00	800.00	1400.
	1864	5,536	450.00	550.00	800.00	1400.
	1865	1,517	475.00	600.00	1000.	1800.
	1866	9,041	450.00	550.00	750.00	1200.
	1867	4,309	450.00	550.00	800.00	1400.
	1868	2,315	450.00	550.00	1000.	1800.
	1869	.029	450.00	500.00	700.00	1100.
	1870	.010	3000.	6000.	12,000.	20,000.

Mint mark: BB

Y#	Date	Mintage	Fine	VF	XF	Unc
B40.2	1862	3,078	450.00	600.00	800.00	1400.
	1863	3,745	450.00	600.00	800.00	1400.
	1864	1,333	475.00	600.00	850.00	1800.
	1866	3,075	450.00	600.00	850.00	1600.
	1867	2,807	450.00	600.00	850.00	1600.
	1868	789 pcs.	525.00	800.00	1200.	2000.
	1869	.014	450.00	550.00	750.00	1100.

Mint mark: A
Edge inscription: DIEU PROTEGE LA FRANCE.

Y#	Date	Mintage	Fine	VF	XF	Unc
57.1	1878	.013	450.00	475.00	550.00	750.00
	1878	30 pcs.	—	—	Proof	16,000.
	1879	.039	450.00	475.00	550.00	700.00
	1881	.022	450.00	475.00	550.00	700.00
	1882	.037	450.00	475.00	550.00	700.00
	1885	2,894	450.00	650.00	850.00	1250.
	1886	.039	450.00	475.00	550.00	750.00
	1887	234 pcs.	750.00	1750.	3500.	7500.
	1889	100 pcs.	—	—	Proof	13,000.
	1894	143 pcs.	1250.	2750.	5500.	10,000.
	1896	400 pcs.	500.00	1000.	2500.	6000.
	1899	.010	450.00	475.00	550.00	750.00
	1900	.020	450.00	475.00	550.00	750.00
	1901	.010	450.00	475.00	550.00	750.00
	1902	.010	450.00	475.00	550.00	750.00
	1903	.010	450.00	475.00	550.00	750.00
	1904	.020	450.00	475.00	550.00	750.00
	1905	.010	450.00	475.00	550.00	750.00
	1906	.030	450.00	475.00	550.00	750.00

Edge inscription: LIBERTE EGALITE FRATERNITE.

Y#	Date	Mintage	Fine	VF	XF	Unc
57.2	1907	.020	450.00	475.00	500.00	700.00
	1908	.023	450.00	475.00	500.00	700.00
	1909	.020	450.00	475.00	500.00	700.00
	1910	.020	450.00	475.00	500.00	700.00
	1911	.030	450.00	475.00	500.00	700.00
	1912	.020	450.00	475.00	500.00	700.00
	1913	.030	450.00	475.00	500.00	700.00
	1914	1,281	2000.	4500.	7000.	10,000.

6.5500 g, .900 GOLD, .1895 oz AGW
Mint: Paris - w/o mint mark.

Y#	Date	Mintage	Fine	VF	XF	Unc
88	1929	*15 pcs.	—	—	3000.	6500.
	1932	*50 pcs.	—	—	2500.	5000.
	1933	*300 pcs.	—	—	2000.	3000.
	1934	*10 pcs.	—	—	10,000.	16,000.
	1935	6.102	—	—	350.00	850.00
	1936	7.689	—	—	350.00	850.00

COPPER-NICKEL

Y#	Date	Mintage	Fine	VF	XF	Unc
101.1	1954	97.285	.50	1.50	3.50	10.00
	1955	152.517	.25	1.00	2.00	8.00
	1956	7.578	9.00	18.00	27.00	55.00
	1957	11.312	2.50	5.00	10.00	30.00
	1958(w)	3.256	6.00	15.00	25.00	50.00
	1958(o)	Inc. Ab.	25.00	50.00	85.00	150.00

Mint mark: B

Y#	Date	Mintage	Fine	VF	XF	Unc
101.2	1954	86.261	.50	1.50	3.50	8.00
	1955	136.585	.25	1.00	2.00	6.00
	1956	19.154	1.50	3.00	7.00	15.00
	1957	25.702	2.00	4.00	8.00	20.00
	1958	54.072	2.00	4.00	8.00	18.00

15.0000 g, .900 SILVER, .4340 oz ASW
Mint: Paris - w/o mint mark.
Pantheon

Y#	Date	Mintage	Fine	VF	XF	Unc
114.1	1982	3.030	—	—	—	22.50
	1982	.025	—	—	Proof	60.00
	1983	5.001	—	—	—	22.50
	1983	.017	—	—	Proof	65.00
	1984	5.000	—	—	—	22.50
	1985	.999	—	—	—	25.00
	1985	.013	—	—	Proof	60.00
	1986	.519	—	—	—	45.00
	1987	.100	—	—	—	45.00
	1988	.100	—	—	—	45.00
	1989	.083	—	—	—	45.00
	1990	.015	—	—	—	45.00
	1991	.015	—	—	—	45.00
	1991	—	—	—	Proof	65.00
	1992	.015	—	—	—	45.00
	1992	—	—	—	Proof	65.00

Plain edge.

Y#	Date	Mintage	Fine	VF	XF	Unc
114.2	1991	—	—	—	Proof	65.00

50th Anniversary of Death of Marie Curie

Y#	Date	Mintage	Fine	VF	XF	Unc
117	1984	3.964	—	—	—	35.00

15.0000 g, .950 SILVER, .4582 oz ASW

Y#	Date	Mintage	Fine	VF	XF	Unc
117a	1984	1,000	—	—	Proof	225.00

17.0000 g, .920 GOLD, .5029 oz AGW

Y#	Date	Mintage	Fine	VF	XF	Unc
117b	1984	5,000	—	—	Proof	425.00

15.0000 g, .900 SILVER, .4340 oz ASW
Centennial of Emile Zola's Novel, Germinal

Y#	Date	Mintage	Fine	VF	XF	Unc
120	1985	3.980	—	—	—	30.00
	1985	.013	—	—	Proof	60.00

15.0000 g, .950 SILVER, .4582 oz ASW

Y#	Date	Mintage	Fine	VF	XF	Unc
120a	1985	5,000	—	—	Proof	115.00

17.0000 g, .920 GOLD, .5028 oz AGW

Y#	Date	Mintage	Fine	VF	XF	Unc
120b	1985	5,000	—	—	Proof	410.00

15.0000 g, .900 SILVER, .4340 oz ASW
Centennial of Statue of Liberty

Y#	Date	Mintage	Fine	VF	XF	Unc
121	1986	4.427	—	—	—	15.00

15.0000 g, .950 SILVER, .4582 oz ASW

Y#	Date	Mintage	Fine	VF	XF	Unc
121a	1986	.018	—	—	Proof	50.00

17.0000 g, .920 GOLD, .5029 oz AGW

Y#	Date	Mintage	Fine	VF	XF	Unc
121b	1986	.013	—	—	—	210.00
	1986	.017	—	—	Proof	235.00

20.0000 g, .999 PLATINUM, .6430 oz APW

Y#	Date	Mintage	Fine	VF	XF	Unc
121c	1986	9,500	—	—	Proof	375.00

17.0000 g, .900 PALLADIUM, .4920 oz APW

Y#	Date	Mintage	Fine	VF	XF	Unc
121d	1986	1,250	—	—	Proof	225.00

15.0000 g, .900 SILVER, .4340 oz ASW
230th Anniversary of Birth of General Lafayette

Y#	Date	Mintage	Fine	VF	XF	Unc
124	1987	4.801	—	—	—	20.00

15.0000 g, .950 SILVER, .4582 oz ASW

Y#	Date	Mintage	Fine	VF	XF	Unc
124a	1987	.030	—	—	Proof	50.00

17.0000 g, .920 GOLD, .5029 oz AGW

Y#	Date	Mintage	Fine	VF	XF	Unc
124b	1987	.010	—	—	—	250.00
	1987	.020	—	—	Proof	275.00

20.0000 g, .999 PLATINUM, .6430 oz APW

Y#	Date	Mintage	Fine	VF	XF	Unc
124c	1987	8,500	—	—	Proof	600.00

17.0000 g, .900 PALLADIUM, .4920 oz APW

Y#	Date	Mintage	Fine	VF	XF	Unc
124d	1987	7,000	—	—	Proof	150.00

15.0000 g, .900 SILVER, .4340 oz ASW
Fraternity

Y#	Date	Mintage	Fine	VF	XF	Unc
126	1988	4.853	—	—	—	30.00

15.0000 g, .950 SILVER, .4582 oz ASW

Y#	Date	Mintage	Fine	VF	XF	Unc
126a	1988	.020	—	—	Proof	70.00

17.0000 g, .920 GOLD, .5029 oz AGW

Y#	Date	Mintage	Fine	VF	XF	Unc
126b	1988	3,000	—	—	—	450.00
	1988	.012	—	—	Proof	350.00

20.0000 g, .999 PLATINUM, .6430 oz APW

Y#	Date	Mintage	Fine	VF	XF	Unc
126c	1988	5,000	—	—	Proof	650.00

17.0000 g, .900 PALLADIUM, .4920 oz APW

Y#	Date	Mintage	Fine	VF	XF	Unc
126d	1988	7,000	—	—	Proof	225.00

15.0000 g, .900 SILVER, .4340 oz ASW
Human Rights

Y#	Date	Mintage	Fine	VF	XF	Unc
132	1989	4.823	—	—	—	27.50

15.0000 g, .950 SILVER, .4582 oz ASW

Y#	Date	Mintage	Fine	VF	XF	Unc
132a	1989	.040	—	—	Proof	65.00

17.0000 g, .920 GOLD, .5029 oz AGW

Y#	Date	Mintage	Fine	VF	XF	Unc
132b	1989	1,000	—	—	—	600.00
	1989	.020	—	—	Proof	400.00

20.0000 g, .999 PLATINUM, .6430 oz APW

Y#	Date	Mintage	Fine	VF	XF	Unc
132c	1989	1,000	—	—	Proof	950.00

17.0000 g, .900 PALLADIUM, .4920 oz APW

Y#	Date	Mintage	Fine	VF	XF	Unc
132d	1989	1,250	—	—	Proof	250.00

22.2000 g, .900 SILVER, .6424 oz ASW
1992 Olympics - Alpine Skiing
Similar to 500 Francs, Y#137

Y#	Date	Mintage	Fine	VF	XF	Unc
136	1989	*.300	—	—	Proof	47.50

1992 Olympics - Ice Skating Couple
Similar to 500 Francs, Y#139

Y#	Date	Mintage	Fine	VF	XF	Unc
138	1989	*.300	—	—	Proof	47.50

Olympic Speed Skating

Y#	Date	Mintage	Fine	VF	XF	Unc
140	1990	.300	—	—	Proof	47.50

Olympic Bobsledding
Rev: Games logo, value and legend.

Y#	Date	Mintage	Fine	VF	XF	Unc
142	1990	.300	—	—	Proof	47.50

15.0100 g, .900 SILVER, .4340 oz ASW
Charlemagne

Y#	Date	Mintage	Fine	VF	XF	Unc
145	1990	4.950	—	—	—	35.00

22.2000 g, .900 SILVER, .6423 oz ASW
100th Anniversary of Basketball - 2 players

Y#	Date	Mintage	Fine	VF	XF	Unc
146	1991	.013	—	—	Proof	75.00

100th Anniversary of Basketball - 1 player

Y#	Date	Mintage	Fine	VF	XF	Unc
147	1991	.013	—	—	Proof	75.00

1992 Olympics - Free Style Skier

Y#	Date	Mintage	Fine	VF	XF	Unc
149	1990	.300	—	—	Proof	47.50

1992 Olympics - Slalom Skiers

Y#	Date	Mintage	Fine	VF	XF	Unc
151	1990	.300	—	—	Proof	47.50

1992 Olympics - Hockey Players

Y#	Date	Mintage	Fine	VF	XF	Unc
153	1991	.300	—	—	Proof	47.50

1992 Olympics - Cross Country Skier

Y#	Date	Mintage	Fine	VF	XF	Unc
155	1991	.300	—	—	Proof	47.50

1992 Olympics - Ski Jumpers

Y#	Date	Mintage	Fine	VF	XF	Unc
157	1991	.300	—	—	Proof	47.50

15.0100 g, .900 SILVER, .4340 oz ASW
Descartes

Y#	Date	Mintage	Fine	VF	XF	Unc
162	1991	3.985	—	—	—	35.00

22.2000 g, .900 SILVER, .6423 oz ASW

Paralympics - Segmented Flying Birds

Y#	Date	Mintage	Fine	VF	XF	Unc
163	1992	5,000	—	—	Proof	100.00

Bicentennial of the Louvre - Mona Lisa

Y#	Date	Mintage	Fine	VF	XF	Unc
169	1993	—	—	—	—	—
	1993	.200	—	—	Proof	50.00

Bicentennial of the Louvre - Liberty

Y#	Date	Mintage	Fine	VF	XF	Unc
171	1993	—	—	—	—	—
	1993	.020	—	—	Proof	50.00

17.0000 g, .920 GOLD, .5028 oz AGW

Y#	Date	Mintage	Fine	VF	XF	Unc
171a	1993	—	—	—	—	—
	1993	5,000	—	—	Proof	500.00

22.2000 g, .900 SILVER, .6420 oz ASW
Bicentennial of the Louvre - Victory

Y#	Date	Mintage	Fine	VF	XF	Unc
172	1993	—	—	—	—	—
	1993	.020	—	—	Proof	50.00

17.0000 g, .920 GOLD, .5028 oz AGW

Y#	Date	Mintage	Fine	VF	XF	Unc
172a	1993	—	—	—	—	—
	1993	5,000	—	—	Proof	500.00

22.2000 g, .900 SILVER, .6424 oz ASW
French Antarctic Territories - Sea Lions

Y#	Date	Mintage	Fine	VF	XF	Unc
179	1992	.015	—	—	Proof	65.00

French Antarctic Territories - Penguins

Y#	Date	Mintage	Fine	VF	XF	Unc
180	1992	.015	—	—	Proof	60.00

22.2600g, .900 SILVER, .6420 oz ASW
Bicentennial of the Louvre - Venus de Milo

Y#	Date	Mintage	Fine	VF	XF	Unc
174	1993	—	—	—	—	—
	1993	.020	—	—	Proof	50.00

Bicentennial of the Louvre - Marie-Marguerite

Y#	Date	Mintage	Fine	VF	XF	Unc
175	1993	—	—	—	—	—
	1993	.020	—	—	Proof	50.00

17.0000 g, .920 GOLD, .5028 oz AGW

Y#	Date	Mintage	Fine	VF	XF	Unc
175a	1993	—	—	—	—	—
	1993	5,000	—	—	Proof	500.00

22.2600 g, .900 SILVER, .6420 oz ASW
Bicentennial of the Louvre - Napoleon Crowning

Josephine

Y#	Date	Mintage	Fine	VF	XF	Unc
176	1993	—	—	—	—	—
	1993	.020	—	—	Proof	50.00

17.0000 g, .920 GOLD, .5028 oz AGW

Y#	Date	Mintage	Fine	VF	XF	Unc
176a	1993	—	—	—	—	—
	1993	5,000	—	—	Proof	500.00

500 FRANCS

17.0000 g, .920 GOLD, .5029 oz AGW
1992 Olympics - Alpine Skiing
Mint: Paris - w/o mint mark.

Y#	Date	Mintage	Fine	VF	XF	Unc
137	1989	*.030	—	—	Proof	375.00

1992 Olympics - Ice Skating Couple

Y#	Date	Mintage	Fine	VF	XF	Unc
139	1989	*.030	—	—	Proof	375.00

Olympic Speed Skating
Similar to 100 Francs, Y#140.

Y#	Date	Mintage	Fine	VF	XF	Unc
141	1990	.030	—	—	Proof	375.00

Olympic Bobsledding
Similar to 100 Francs, Y#142.

Y#	Date	Mintage	Fine	VF	XF	Unc
143	1990	.030	—	—	Proof	375.00

100th Anniversary of Basketball

Y#	Date	Mintage	Fine	VF	XF	Unc
148	1991	5,000	—	—	Proof	475.00

1992 Olympics - Free Style Skier
Similar to 100 Francs, Y#149.

Y#	Date	Mintage	Fine	VF	XF	Unc
150	1990	.030	—	—	Proof	450.00

1992 Olympics - Slalom Skiers
Similar to 100 Francs, Y#151.

Y#	Date	Mintage	Fine	VF	XF	Unc
152	1990	.030	—	—	Proof	450.00

1992 Olympics - Hockey Players
Similar to 100 Francs, Y#153.

Y#	Date	Mintage	Fine	VF	XF	Unc
154	1991	.030	—	—	Proof	450.00

1992 Olympics - Cross Country Skier
Similar to 100 Francs, Y#155.

Y#	Date	Mintage	Fine	VF	XF	Unc
156	1991	.030	—	—	Proof	450.00

1992 Olympics - Ski Jumpers
Similar to 100 Francs, Y#157.

Y#	Date	Mintage	Fine	VF	XF	Unc
158	1991	.030	—	—	Proof	450.00

1992 Olympics - Pierre de Coubertin

Y#	Date	Mintage	Fine	VF	XF	Unc
159	1991	.030	—	—	Proof	450.00

Mozart in Paris

Y#	Date	Mintage	Fine	VF	XF	Unc
173	1991	*5,000	—	—	Proof	500.00

31.1040 g, .999 GOLD, 1.0000 oz AGW
Bicentennial of the Louvre - Mona Lisa

Y#	Date	Mintage	Fine	VF	XF	Unc
170	1993	—	—	—	—	—
	1993	5,000	—	—	Proof	850.00

Bicentennial of the Louvre - Venus de Milo

Y#	Date	Mintage	Fine	VF	XF	Unc
177	1993	—	—	—	—	—
	1993	5,000	—	—	Proof	850.00

EUROPEAN CURRENCY UNITS

100 FRANCS - 15 ECUS

22.2000 g, .900 SILVER, .6424 oz ASW
Charlemagne

Y#	Date	Mintage	Fine	VF	XF	Unc
144	1990	.030	—	—	Proof	100.00

Descartes

Y#	Date	Mintage	Fine	VF	XF	Unc
160	1991	.020	—	—	Proof	90.00

Jean Monet

Obv: Denomination in center within legend and chain above RF.

Y#	Date	Mintage	Fine	VF	XF	Unc
164	1992	.030	—	—	Proof	75.00

Mediterranean Games - Swimming

Y#	Date	Mintage	Fine	VF	XF	Unc
181	1993	.015	—	—	Proof	55.00

Mediterranean Games - Soccer

Y#	Date	Mintage	Fine	VF	XF	Unc
182	1993	.015	—	—	Proof	55.00

Arc de Triumph

Y#	Date	Mintage	Fine	VF	XF	Unc
183	1993	.020	—	—	Proof	50.00

Brandenburg Gate

Y#	Date	Mintage	Fine	VF	XF	Unc
184	1993	.020	—	—	Proof	50.00

500 FRANCS - 70 ECUS

17.0000 g, .920 GOLD, .5029 oz AGW

Charlemagne

Y#	Date	Mintage	Fine	VF	XF	Unc
A144 (Y143)	1990	5,000	—	—	Proof	500.00

20.0000 g, .999 PLATINUM, .6431 oz APW

Y#	Date	Mintage	Fine	VF	XF	Unc
A144a (Y143)	1990	2,000	—	—	Proof	650.00

17.0000 g, .920 GOLD, .5029 oz AGW

Descartes

Y#	Date	Mintage	Fine	VF	XF	Unc
161	1991	3,000	—	—	Proof	525.00

20.0000 g, .999 PLATINUM, .6431 oz APW

Y#	Date	Mintage	Fine	VF	XF	Unc
161a	1991	1,000	—	—	Proof	675.00

17.0000 g, .920 GOLD, .5029 oz AGW

Jean Monet

Y#	Date	Mintage	Fine	VF	XF	Unc
165	1992	5,000	—	—	Proof	500.00

20.0000 g, .999 PLATINUM, .6431 oz APW

Y#	Date	Mintage	Fine	VF	XF	Unc
165a	1992	2,000	—	—	Proof	650.00

17.0000 g, .920 GOLD, .5029 oz AGW

Mediterranean Games

Y#	Date	Mintage	Fine	VF	XF	Unc
185	1993	3,000	—	—	Proof	475.00

Arc de Triumph

Y#	Date	Mintage	Fine	VF	XF	Unc
186	1993	5,000	—	—	Proof	465.00

19.8000 g, .990 PLATINUM, .6303 oz APW

Y#	Date	Mintage	Fine	VF	XF	Unc
186a	1993	2,000	—	—	Proof	600.00

17.0000 g, .920 GOLD, .5029 oz AGW

Brandenburg Gate

Y#	Date	Mintage	Fine	VF	XF	Unc
187	1993	5,000	—	—	Proof	465.00

19.8000 g, .990 PLATINUM, .6303 oz APW

Y#	Date	Mintage	Fine	VF	XF	Unc
187a	1993	2,000	—	—	Proof	600.00

SPECIMEN 'FDC' SETS(SS)

(Fleur de Coin)

KM#	Date	Mintage	Identification	Issue Price	Mkt. Val.
SS1	1964(7)	25,600	Y102-108,110	4.00	10.00
SS2	1965(7)	35,000	Y102,104,105, 107,108,110,111	7.60	18.00
SS3	1966(8)	7,171	Y102,A104,104,105, 107,108,110,111	9.00	75.00
SS4	1967(8)	2,305	Same as S3	10.00	300.00
SS5	1968(8)	3,000	Same as S3 w/box	10.00	550.00
SS5A	1968(8)	Inc. Ab.	Same as S3 w/o box	—	200.00
SS6	1969(8)	6,050	Same as S3	10.00	150.00
SS7	1970(8)	10,000	Y102,A104,104,105, 107,108,110a,111	9.00	40.00
SS8	1971(8)	12,000	Same as S7	9.00	40.00
SS9	1972(8)	15,000	Same as S7	9.00	40.00
SS10	1973(8)	79,000	Same as S7	12.00	28.00
SS11	1974(9)	98,800	Y102,A104,104,105,107, 108,110a,A112,112	31.00	18.00
SS12	1975(9)	52,000	Same as S11	35.00	28.00
SS13	1976(9)	35,700	Same as S11	35.00	35.00
SS14	1977(9)	25,000	Same as S11	36.00	38.00
SS15	1978(9)	24,000	Same as S11	39.00	45.00
SS16	1979(10)	40,500	Y102,A104,104,105,107-109, 110a,A112,112	55.00	80.00
SS17	1980(10)	60,000	Same as S16	90.00	60.00
SS18	1981(9)	26,000	Y102,A104,104,105,107-109, 110a,A112	—	55.00
SS19	1982(11)	27,500	Y102,A104,104,105,107-109, 110a,A112,113,114	—	90.00
SS20	1983(12)	16,561	Y102,A104,104,105,107-109, 110a,A112,114-116	—	115.00
SS21	1984(12)	13,388	Y102,A104,104-105,107-109, 110a,A112,114,117-118	—	215.00
SS22	1985(12)	12,224	Y102,A104,104-105,107-109, 110a,A112,114,119-120	—	125.00
SS23	1986(12)	13,000	Y102,A104,104-105,107-109, 110a,A112,114,121-122	—	145.00
SS24	1987(10)	15,000	Y102,A104,104-105,107-109, 110a,A112,114	68.00	145.00
SS25	1988(13)	13,000	Y102,A104,104-105,107-109, 110a,114,126-129	—	170.00
SS26	1989(14)	10,000	Y102,A104,104-105,107-109, 110a,114,127,132-135	—	175.00
SS27	1990(13)	10,000	Y102,A104,104-105,107-109, 110a,114,127,140,142,145	—	170.00
SS28	1990(11)	10,000	Y102,A104,104-105,107-109, 110a,114,127,145	—	145.00

MINT SETS (MS)

KM#	Date	Mintage	Identification	Issue Price	Mkt. Val.
MS1	1986(10)	20,000	Y102,A104,104-105,107-109, 110a,A112,122d	—	125.00
MS2	1987(10)	4,000	Y102,A104,104-105,107-109, 110a,A112,125d	—	72.50
MS3	1988(10)	2,000	Y102,A104,104-105,107-109, 110a,127,128	—	75.00
MS4	1989(10)	2,000	Y102,A104,104-105,107-109, 110a,127,135	—	75.00
MS5	1990(11)	10,000	Y102,A104,104-105,107-109, 110a,114,127,144	208.00	210.00
MS6	1991(9)	2,500	Y102,A104,104-105,107.2-109.2, 110a.2,127.2	50.00	50.00
MS7	1992(10)	20,000	Y102,A104,104-105,107.1-109.1, 110a.1,127.1,167	—	55.00
MS8	1993(10)	20,000	Y102,A104,104-105,107.2,108, 109.1,110a.1,127.1,167	—	50.00

NOTE: Coins in MS8 have medal rotation.

PROOF SETS (PS)

KM#	Date	Mintage	Identification	Issue Price	Mkt. Val.
PS1	1830(7)	—	C185-191	—	Rare
PS2	1878(5)	30	Y41-44,48	—	Rare
PS3	1889(4)	20	Y41-44	—	Rare
PS4	1897(5)	—	Y41-44,62	—	Rare
PS5	1900(9)	100	Y58-62,63.1-64.1,65-66	—	Rare
PS6	1991(10)	—	Y102,A104,104-105,107.2-109.2, 110a.2,114.2,127.2	160.00	155.00
PS7	1991(3)	3,000	Y146-148	—	530.00
PS8	1992(11)	15,000	Y102,A104,104-105,107.1-109.1 110a.1,114.1,127.1,167	—	150.00
PS9	1992(3)	2,000	Y178-180	—	225.00

ANTWERP

ANVERS

Antwerp, a town in Belgium, grew from a tiny walled marquisate under Godfrey of Bouillon one of the leaders of the First Crusade in the 11th century to the chief port and commercial center of 15th-century western Europe. Not only was it an acknowledged leader in trade and commerce, but also in the arts. The following centuries carried as much tragedy as triumph. Antwerp was plundered by Spain and its Protestant citizens murdered during the religious troubles of the 16th century. It served as the chief military harbor of Napoleon during the fall of the First Empire. It was the scene of the most famous siege of World War I, and was repeatedly battered by V-bombs during World War II. The French-auspice Antwerp coins of 1814-15 were a necessity money issued while Antwerp, under General Carnot, was besieged by the Allies.

SIEGE COINAGE

The following coins were minted from captured cannons by the French while besieged in Antwerp, Belgium. Some have an *N* for Napoleon while others have a double *L* monogram for King Louis XVIII of France.

ENGRAVERS INITIALS

JLGN - Jean-Louis Gagnepain
R - Ransonnet
V - Van Goor
W - Wolschot Foundry

5 CENTIMES

BRONZE, 29-32mm

Obv: N in wreath.

KM#	Date	Mintage	VG	Fine	VF	XF
1	1814	180 pcs.	100.00	200.00	400.00	800.00

SILVER

KM#	Date	Mintage	VG	Fine	VF	XF
1a	1814	—	—	—	Rare	—

BRONZE, 29-30mm

KM#	Date	Mintage	VG	Fine	VF	XF
2.1	1814	—	15.00	30.00	70.00	150.00

Obv: V above ribbon.

KM#	Date	Mintage	VG	Fine	VF	XF
2.2	1814	.011	12.00	30.00	60.00	120.00
		SILVER				
2.2a	1814	—	—	—	350.00	600.00

BRONZE
Obv: V below ribbon bow.

KM#	Date	Mintage	VG	Fine	VF	XF
2.3	1814	2,800	22.00	45.00	90.00	185.00
		Obv: JLGN on ribbon				
2.4	1814	.017	12.00	30.00	60.00	120.00
		Obv. Type I: Narrow LL monogram.				
3.1	1814	.010	— Reported, not confirmed			

Obv: V below ribbon bow.

KM#	Date	Mintage	VG	Fine	VF	XF
3.2	1814	—	20.00	40.00	100.00	200.00
		Obv: JLGN on ribbon.				
3.3	1814	.031	— Reported, not confirmed			

Obv. Type II: Wide LL monogram, JLGN on ribbon.

KM#	Date	Mintage	VG	Fine	VF	XF
4.1	1814	—	13.00	32.50	65.00	130.00
		SILVER				
4.1a	1814	—	—	—	600.00	1000.
		BRONZE Obv: V below ribbon				
4.2	1814	—	— Reported, not confirmed			

10 CENTIMES

BRONZE
Obv: JEAN LOUIS//GAGNEPAIN on ribbon.

KM#	Date	Mintage	VG	Fine	VF	XF
5.1	1814	.018	20.00	40.00	100.00	210.00
		SILVER				
5.1a	1814	—	—	—	Rare	—

BRONZE
Obv: W/o initials or name on ribbon.

KM#	Date	Mintage	VG	Fine	VF	XF
5.2	1814	7,500	25.00	60.00	150.00	300.00
		Obv: R below ribbon bow.				
5.3	1814	.066	12.00	30.00	60.00	120.00

Obv: W above ribbon bow.

KM#	Date	Mintage	VG	Fine	VF	XF
5.4	1814	.029	15.00	35.00	70.00	150.00
		Obv. Type I: Narrow LL monogram.				
6.1	1814	—	— Reported, not confirmed			

Obv: JEAN LOUIS//GAGNEPAIN on ribbon.

KM#	Date	Mintage	VG	Fine	VF	XF
6.2	1814	.035	18.00	45.00	90.00	190.00
		Obv. Type II: Wide LL monogram, JEAN LOUIS GAGNEPAIN on ribbon.				
7.1	1814	.020	20.00	50.00	100.00	200.00
		Obv: R below ribbon bow.				
7.2	1814	.053	16.00	40.00	80.00	170.00
		SILVER				
7.2a	1814	—	—	—	550.00	900.00

Listings For

FRENCH AFARS & ISSAS: refer to Djibouti

FRENCH COCHIN CHINA: refer to Vietnam

FRENCH COLONIES

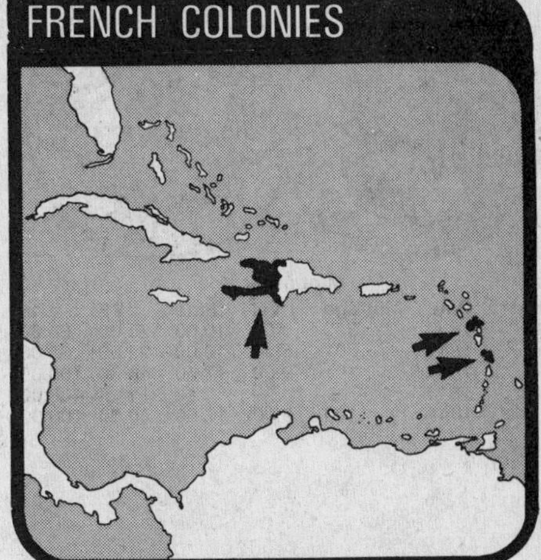

The coins catalogued under this heading were not issued for use in any particular colony but were intended for general use in the West Indies, particularly Martinique, Guadeloupe, and Saint-Dominique (western Hispaniola) until it attained independence as Haiti in 1804.

RULERS

French

MINT MARKS

A Paris
H - LaRochelle

MONETARY SYSTEM

100 Centimes = 1 Franc

5 CENTIMES

BRONZE

KM#	Date	Mintage	VG	Fine	VF	XF
		Mint mark: A				
10.1	1825	.607	2.50	6.00	12.50	35.00
	1828	.501	3.00	7.50	15.00	40.00
	1829	.299	5.00	10.00	30.00	65.00
	1830	.402	4.50	9.00	20.00	50.00
		Mint mark: H				
10.2	1827	.600	2.50	6.00	12.50	35.00

KM#	Date	Mintage	VG	Fine	VF	XF
		Mint mark: A				
12	1839	.600	2.50	6.00	20.00	50.00
	1839	—	—	—	Proof	300.00
	1841	.602	2.50	6.00	20.00	50.00
	1843	.202	7.50	15.00	35.00	70.00
	1844	.201	7.50	15.00	38.00	75.00

10 CENTIMES

BRONZE

KM#	Date	Mintage	VG	Fine	VF	XF
		Mint mark: A				
11.1	1825	.301	5.00	10.00	25.00	55.00
	1828	.253	7.50	15.00	30.00	60.00
	1829	.152	9.00	17.50	35.00	85.00
		Mint mark: H				
11.2	1827	.300	5.00	10.00	25.00	55.00

Mint mark: A

KM#	Date	Mintage	VG	Fine	VF	XF
13	1839	.300	5.00	10.00	25.00	60.00
	1841	.301	5.00	10.00	25.00	60.00
	1843	.101	9.00	17.50	40.00	100.00
	1843	—	—	—	Proof	400.00
	1844	.100	9.00	17.50	40.00	100.00

FRENCH EQ. AFRICA

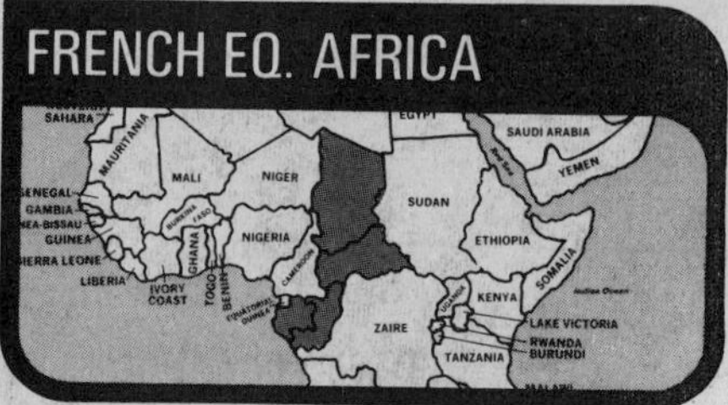

French Equatorial Africa, an area consisting of four self governing dependencies (Middle Congo, Ubangi-Shari, Chad and Gabon) in West-Central Africa, had an area of 969,111 sq. mi. (2,509,987 sq. km.). Capital: Brazzaville. The area, rich in natural resources, exported cotton, timber, coffee, cacao, diamonds and gold.

Little is known of the history of these parts of Africa prior to French occupation - which began with no thought of territorial acquisition. France's initial intent was simply to establish a few supply stations along the west coast of Africa to service the warships assigned to combat the slave trade in the early part of the 19th century. French settlement began in 1839. Gabon (then Gabun) and the Middle Congo were secured between 1885 and 1891; Chad and Ubangi-Shari between 1894 and 1897. The four colonies were joined to form French Equatorial Africa in 1910. The dependencies were changed from colonies to territories within the French Union in 1946, and all the inhabitants were made French citizens. In 1958 they voted to become autonomous republics within the new French Community, and attained full independence in 1960.

For later coinage see Central African States, Congo Peoples Republic, Gabon and Chad.

RULERS

French, until 1960

MINT MARKS

(a) - Paris, privy marks only

(t) - Poissy, privy marks only, thunderbolt

SA - Pretoria (1942-1943)

ENGRAVERS INITIALS

GLS - Steynberg

MONETARY SYSTEM

100 Centimes = 1 Franc

5 CENTIMES

ALUMINUM-BRONZE
Similar to 10 Centimes, KM#4.

KM#	Date	Mintage	Fine	VF	XF	Unc
3	1943	*44.000	90.00	150.00	250.00	500.00

10 CENTIMES

ALUMINUM-BRONZE

KM#	Date	Mintage	Fine	VF	XF	Unc
4	1943	*13.000	75.00	100.00	150.00	350.00

25 CENTIMES

ALUMINUM-BRONZE
Similar to 10 Centimes, KM#4.

KM#	Date	Mintage	Fine	VF	XF	Unc
5	1943	*4.160	200.00	350.00	500.00	850.00

***NOTE:** KM#3-5 were not released for circulation.

50 CENTIMES

BRASS
Mint mark: SA

KM#	Date	Mintage	Fine	VF	XF	Unc
1	1942	8.000	1.50	3.00	7.50	18.00

BRONZE

KM#	Date	Mintage	Fine	VF	XF	Unc
1a	1943	16.000	1.00	2.00	6.00	15.00

FRANC

BRASS
Mint mark: SA

KM#	Date	Mintage	Fine	VF	XF	Unc
2	1942	3.000	2.00	3.50	10.00	30.00

BRONZE

KM#	Date	Mintage	Fine	VF	XF	Unc
2a	1943	6.000	1.50	2.50	8.00	25.00

ALUMINUM

KM#	Date	Mintage	Fine	VF	XF	Unc
6	1948(a)	15.000	.15	.25	.50	2.00

2 FRANCS

ALUMINUM

KM#	Date	Mintage	Fine	VF	XF	Unc
7	1948(a)	5.040	.25	.50	1.50	4.00

NOTE: KM#8-10 previously listed here are now listed in Cameroon, KM#24-26.

FRENCH GUIANA

The French Overseas Department of Guiana, located on the northeast coast of South America, bordered by Surinam and Brazil, has an area of 35,135 sq. mi. (91,000 sq. km.) and a population of *92,038. Capital: Cayenne. Placer gold mining and shrimp processing are the chief industries. Shrimp, lumber, gold, cocoa, and bananas are exported.

The coast of Guiana was sighted by Columbus in 1498 and explored by Amerigo Vespucci in 1499. The French established the first successful trading stations and settlements, and placed the area under direct control of the French Crown in 1674. Portuguese and British forces occupied French Guiana for five years during the Napoleonic Wars. Devil's Island, the notorious penal colony in French Guiana where Capt. Alfred Dreyfus was imprisoned, was established in 1852 - and finally closed in 1947. When France adopted a new constitution in 1946, French Guiana voted to remain within the French Union as an Overseas Department. It now hosts some of the French and Common Market space and satellite stations.

In the late eighteenth century, a series of 2 sous coins was struck for the colony. It is probable that contemporary imitations of these issues, many emanating from Birmingham, England, outnumber the originals. These, both genuine and bogus, host coins for many West Indies counterstamps. As an Overseas Department, Guiana now uses the coins of metropolitan France, however, the franc used in the former colony was always distinct in value from that of the homeland as well as that used in the islands of the French West Indies.

RULERS

French

MINT MARKS

A - Paris

MONETARY SYSTEM

100 Centimes = 10 Decimes = 1 Franc

COLONY OF CAYENNE

2 SOUS

BILLON
Mint mark: A

KM#	Date	Mintage	VG	Fine	VF	XF
3	1816	—	35.00	75.00	150.00	325.00

FRENCH GUIANA

10 CENTIMES

BILLON, 2.50 g
Mint mark: A

KM#	Date	Mintage	VG	Fine	VF	XF
1	1818	2.000	7.00	15.00	35.00	90.00

KM#	Date	Mintage	VG	Fine	VF	XF
2	1846	1.400	7.00	15.00	30.00	75.00

FRENCH INDO-CHINA

French Indo-China, made up of the protectorates of Annam, Tonkin, Cambodia and Laos and the colony of Cochin-China was located on the Indo-Chinese peninsula of Southeast Asia. The colony had an area of 286,194 sq. mi. (741,242 sq. km.). and a population of 30 million. Principal cities: Saigon, Haiphong, Vientiane, Pnom-Penh and Hanoi.

The forebears of the modern Indo-Chinese peoples originated in the Yellow River Valley of northern China, from whence they were driven into the Indo-Chinese peninsula by the Han Chinese. The Chinese followed southward in the second century B.C., conquering the peninsula and ruling it until 938, leaving a lingering heritage of Chinese learning and culture. Indo-Chinese independence was basically maintained until the arrival of the French in the mid-19th century who established control over all of Vietnam, Laos and Cambodia. Activities directed toward obtaining self-determination accelerated during the Japanese occupation of World War II. The dependencies were changed from colonies to territories within the French Union in 1946, and all the inhabitants were made French citizens.

In Aug. of 1945, an uprising erupted involving the French and Vietnamese Nationalists, culminated in the French military disaster at Dien Bien Phu (May, 1954) and the subsequent Geneva Conference that brought an end to French colonial rule in Indo-China.

For later coinage see Kampuchea, Laos and Vietnam.

RULERS

French, until 1954

MINT MARKS

A - Paris
(a) - Paris, privy marks only
B - Beaumont-le-Roger
C - Castlesarrasin
H - Heaton, Birmingham
(p) - Thunderbolt - Poissy
S - San Francisco, U.S.A.
None - Osaka, Japan
None - Hanoi, Tonkin

MONETARY SYSTEM

5 Sapeques = 1 Cent
100 Cents = 1 Piastre

SAPEQUE

BRONZE
Mint mark: A

KM#	Date	Mintage	Fine	VF	XF	Unc
6	1887	5.000	1.50	4.00	15.00	40.00
	1888	5.000	3.00	7.00	20.00	50.00
	1889	100 pcs.	—	—	Proof	500.00
	1892	1.636	60.00	150.00	300.00	500.00
	1893	.864	40.00	100.00	200.00	350.00
	1894	2.500	6.00	15.00	35.00	100.00
	1897	2.829	6.00	15.00	35.00	100.00
	1898	2.171	50.00	125.00	250.00	400.00
	1899	5.000	2.50	7.50	15.00	50.00
	1900	2.657	7.50	25.00	50.00	125.00
	1900	100 pcs.	—	—	Proof	500.00
	1901	4.843	2.50	7.50	15.00	60.00
	1902	2.500	7.50	20.00	40.00	100.00

1/4 CENT

ZINC

KM#	Date	Mintage	Fine	VF	XF	Unc
25	1942	221.800	7.50	17.50	35.00	80.00
	1943	279.450	18.00	40.00	65.00	150.00
	1944	46.122	150.00	250.00	400.00	1000.

NOTE: Lead counterfeits dated 1941 and 1942 are known.

1/2 CENT

BRONZE

KM#	Date	Mintage	Fine	VF	XF	Unc
20	1935(a)	26.365	.25	.50	2.00	10.00
	1936(a)	23.635	.25	.50	2.00	10.00
	1937(a)	10.244	.50	1.50	5.00	15.00
	1938(a)	16.665	.25	.75	2.50	12.00
	1939(a)	17.305	.25	.75	2.50	12.00
	1940(a)	11.218	4.00	8.00	20.00	40.00
	ZINC					
20a	1939(a)	.185	100.00	200.00	300.00	600.00
	1940(a)	—	200.00	300.00	400.00	700.00

CENT

BRONZE
Mint mark: A

KM#	Date	Mintage	Fine	VF	XF	Unc
1	1885	3.673	1.25	4.00	10.00	30.00
	1885	—	—	—	Proof	450.00
	1886	1.883	2.00	6.00	20.00	65.00
	1887	2.362	1.50	5.00	15.00	40.00
	1888	2.564	1.50	5.00	15.00	40.00
	1889	1.573	2.00	6.00	20.00	55.00
	1889	100 pcs.	—	—	Proof	400.00
	1892	2.648	1.50	4.00	20.00	50.00
	1893	1.852	6.00	15.00	45.00	125.00
	1894	.465	10.00	17.50	70.00	175.00
	Rev. leg: UN CENTIEME DE PIASTRE					
7	1895	.290	50.00	100.00	250.00	450.00

KM#	Date	Mintage	Fine	VF	XF	Unc
8	1896	5.690	2.00	3.00	7.50	25.00
	1897	11.055	1.00	2.00	5.00	20.00
	1898	5.000	5.00	7.50	25.00	60.00
	1899	8.000	1.00	2.00	4.00	20.00
	1900	3.000	3.00	5.00	10.00	40.00
	1900	100 pcs.	—	—	Proof	450.00
	1901	9.750	2.00	3.00	7.50	25.00
	1902	5.050	3.00	5.00	10.00	40.00
	1903	8.000	2.50	4.00	8.00	30.00
	1906	2.000	5.00	8.00	25.00	75.00

KM#	Date	Mintage	Fine	VF	XF	Unc
12.1	1908	3.000	10.00	25.00	65.00	225.00
	1909	5.000	25.00	45.00	100.00	275.00
	1910	7.703	1.00	4.00	10.00	25.00
	1911	15.234	.75	3.00	10.00	20.00
	1912	17.027	.75	3.00	10.00	20.00
	1913	3.945	2.00	7.00	20.00	50.00
	1914	11.027	.75	3.00	15.00	30.00
	1916	1.312	8.00	15.00	30.00	60.00
	1917	9.762	1.00	4.00	10.00	20.00
	1918	2.372	6.00	12.50	25.00	50.00
	1919	9.148	1.00	4.00	7.50	20.00
	1920	18.305	.75	3.00	5.00	12.50
	1921	14.722	.75	2.00	3.00	8.00
	1922	8.850	1.00	3.00	5.00	20.00
	1923	1.079	25.00	45.00	75.00	175.00
	1926	11.672	.75	2.00	4.00	10.00
	1927	3.328	5.00	10.00	25.00	50.00
	1930	4.682	1.25	2.75	5.00	10.00
	1931 torch privy mark					
		5.318	25.00	40.00	120.00	350.00
	1931 wing privy mark					

KM#	Date	Mintage	Fine	VF	XF	Unc
12.1		Inc. Ab.	35.00	65.00	160.00	400.00
	1937	8.902	.25	.50	1.50	6.00
	1938	15.499	.25	.50	.75	3.00
	1939	15.599	.25	.50	.75	3.00

Mint: San Francisco - w/o mint mark.

KM#	Date	Mintage	Fine	VF	XF	Unc
12.2	1920	13.290	1.00	2.50	5.00	17.50
	1921	1.610	40.00	80.00	250.00	450.00

Mint mark: Thunderbolt

KM#	Date	Mintage	Fine	VF	XF	Unc
12.3	1922	9.476	1.00	1.75	5.00	12.00
	1923	27.891	.50	.75	1.50	5.00

ZINC
Vichy Government Issues

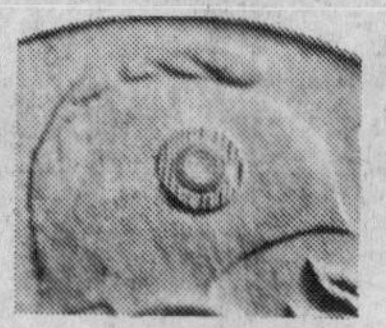
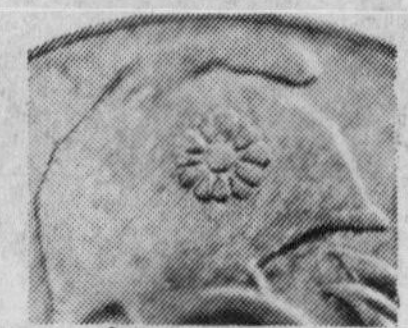

Circles **Rosette**

Type 1, circles on Phrygian cap.

KM#	Date	Mintage	Fine	VF	XF	Unc
24.1	1940 T1	1.990	5.00	10.00	25.00	50.00

Type 2, rosette on Phrygian cap.
Variety 1, 12 petals - Variety 2, 11 petals.

KM#	Date	Mintage	Fine	VF	XF	Unc
24.2	1940 T2 V1	—	5.00	10.00	25.00	50.00

Type 2, rosette on Phrygian cap.

KM#	Date	Mintage	Fine	VF	XF	Unc
24.3	1940 T2 V2	—	5.00	10.00	25.00	60.00
	1941 T2 V2	—	2.00	5.00	15.00	40.00

ALUMINUM

KM#	Date	Mintage	Fine	VF	XF	Unc
26	1943	—	.25	.50	1.00	2.50

NOTE: Edge varieties exist - plain, grooved and partially grooved.

5 CENTS

5.0000 g, COPPER-NICKEL, 1.6mm thick

KM#	Date	Mintage	Fine	VF	XF	Unc
18.1	1923(a)	1.611	3.00	5.00	15.00	40.00
	1924(a)	3.389	1.00	3.00	12.00	35.00
	1925(a)	6.000	1.00	1.75	7.00	20.00
	1930(a)	4.000	1.00	2.00	8.00	25.00
	1937(a)	10.000	.50	1.00	4.00	15.00
	1938(a)	—	10.00	25.00	75.00	175.00
	1938(a)	—	—	—	Proof	250.00

Mint mark: A

KM#	Date	Mintage	Fine	VF	XF	Unc
18.2	1938	1.480	50.00	85.00	150.00	400.00

4.0000 g, NICKEL-BRASS, 1.3mm thick

KM#	Date	Mintage	Fine	VF	XF	Unc
18.1a	1938(a)	50.569	.25	.50	1.00	5.00
	1939(a)	38.501	.25	.50	1.00	5.00

ALUMINUM
Vichy Government Issue

KM#	Date	Mintage	Fine	VF	XF	Unc
27	1943(a)	—	.25	.50	1.00	3.00

NOTE: Edge varieties exist: reeded - rare, plain, grooved and partially grooved.

Postwar Issues

KM#	Date	Mintage	Fine	VF	XF	Unc
30.1	1946(a)	28.000	.25	.60	1.00	3.50

Mint mark: B

KM#	Date	Mintage	Fine	VF	XF	Unc
30.2	1946	22.000	.25	.60	1.00	3.50

10 CENTS

2.7210 g, .900 SILVER, .0787 oz ASW
Mint mark: A
Rev. leg: TITRE 0.900. POIDS 2.721

KM#	Date	Mintage	Fine	VF	XF	Unc
2	1885	2.040	5.00	10.00	30.00	100.00
	1888	1.000	5.00	10.00	40.00	150.00
	1889	100 pcs.	—	—	Proof	600.00
	1892	.200	40.00	75.00	125.00	300.00
	1893	.600	15.00	25.00	65.00	165.00
	1894	.500	20.00	40.00	85.00	200.00
	1895	.600	20.00	40.00	75.00	175.00

2.7000 g, .900 SILVER, .0781 oz ASW
Rev. leg: TITRE 0.900. POIDS 2 GR. 7

KM#	Date	Mintage	Fine	VF	XF	Unc
2a	1895	.300	225.00	350.00	500.00	1000.
	1896 fasces	.650	30.00	75.00	125.00	250.00
	1896 torch	Inc. Ab.	60.00	100.00	175.00	450.00
	1897	.900	20.00	60.00	100.00	175.00

2.7000 g, .835 SILVER, .0725 oz ASW
Rev. leg: TITRE 0,835. POIDS 2 GR. 7

KM#	Date	Mintage	Fine	VF	XF	Unc
9	1898	.500	60.00	120.00	250.00	625.00
	1899	4.100	4.00	10.00	30.00	100.00
	1900	3.600	4.00	10.00	30.00	100.00
	1900	100 pcs.	—	—	Proof	650.00
	1901	2.950	9.00	30.00	75.00	200.00
	1902	7.050	5.00	15.00	35.00	125.00
	1903	1.300	15.00	40.00	100.00	325.00
	1908	1.000	60.00	120.00	250.00	550.00
	1909	1.000	40.00	90.00	175.00	425.00
	1910	2.689	30.00	75.00	125.00	350.00
	1911	2.311	30.00	50.00	100.00	325.00
	1912	2.500	30.00	45.00	90.00	275.00
	1913	4.847	7.50	12.50	35.00	125.00
	1914	2.667	12.00	35.00	75.00	175.00
	1916	2.000	12.00	35.00	75.00	185.00
	1917	1.500	30.00	60.00	115.00	300.00
	1919	1.500	40.00	75.00	150.00	350.00

3.0000 g, .400 SILVER, .0386 oz ASW
Mint: San Francisco - w/o mint mark.
Rev: W/o fineness indicated.

KM#	Date	Mintage	Fine	VF	XF	Unc
14	1920	10.000	10.00	15.00	40.00	100.00

2.7000 g, .680 SILVER, .0590 oz ASW
Mint mark: A
Rev. leg: TITRE 0,680 POIDS 2 GR. 7

KM#	Date	Mintage	Fine	VF	XF	Unc
16.1	1921	12.516	1.50	3.00	8.00	17.50
	1922	22.381	1.50	3.00	8.00	17.50
	1923	21.755	1.50	3.00	8.00	20.00
	1924	2.816	2.00	5.00	15.00	45.00
	1925	4.909	1.75	3.50	12.00	30.00
	1927	6.471	2.50	7.00	17.50	40.00
	1928	1.593	25.00	70.00	150.00	450.00
	1929	5.831	1.50	3.00	10.00	30.00
	1930	6.608	1.50	3.00	10.00	30.00
	1931	100 pcs.	—	—	Proof	300.00
16.2	1937(a)	25.000	1.00	1.50	3.00	8.00

NICKEL

KM#	Date	Mintage	Fine	VF	XF	Unc
21.1	1939(a)	16.841	.25	.50	1.00	5.00
	1940(a)	25.505	.25	.50	1.00	5.00

NOTE: The coins above have no dots left and right of date and are magnetic.

Obv: Date between 2 dots.

KM#	Date	Mintage	Fine	VF	XF	Unc
21.2	.1939.(a)	—	—	—	—	—

COPPER-NICKEL

KM#	Date	Mintage	Fine	VF	XF	Unc
21a.1	1939(a)	2.237	8.00	15.00	30.00	75.00

Obv: Date w/o dots.

KM#	Date	Mintage	Fine	VF	XF	Unc
21a.2	1939(a)	—	35.00	60.00	100.00	175.00
	1941S	50.000	.20	.40	.75	4.00

NOTE: Coins dated 1939 have small dots left and right of date.

ALUMINUM

KM#	Date	Mintage	Fine	VF	XF	Unc
28.1	1945(a)	40.170	.25	.50	1.00	4.50

Mint mark: B

KM#	Date	Mintage	Fine	VF	XF	Unc
28.2	1945	9.830	.50	1.50	3.00	10.00

20 CENTS

5.4430 g, .900 SILVER, .1575 oz ASW
Mint mark: A
Rev. leg: TITRE 0.900. POIDS 5.443

KM#	Date	Mintage	Fine	VF	XF	Unc
3	1885	1.280	10.00	30.00	75.00	250.00
	1887	.250	40.00	100.00	175.00	375.00
	1887	—	—	—	Proof	500.00
	1889	100 pcs.	—	—	Proof	1000.
	1892	.200	50.00	100.00	225.00	500.00
	1893	.200	35.00	100.00	200.00	400.00
	1894	.250	30.00	70.00	150.00	400.00
	1895	.300	25.00	55.00	110.00	300.00

5.4000 g, .900 SILVER, .1562 oz ASW
Rev. leg: TITRE 0.900. POIDS 5 GR. 4

KM#	Date	Mintage	Fine	VF	XF	Unc
3a	1895	.250	50.00	100.00	250.00	700.00
	1896 torch	.300	60.00	125.00	400.00	850.00
	1896 fasces	I.A.	50.00	100.00	350.00	750.00
	1897	.300	50.00	100.00	350.00	700.00

5.4000 g, .835 SILVER, .1450 oz ASW

KM#	Date	Mintage	Fine	VF	XF	Unc
10	1898	.250	50.00	120.00	275.00	550.00
	1899	2.050	7.50	20.00	60.00	200.00
	1900	1.750	10.00	35.00	100.00	275.00

KM#	Date	Mintage	Fine	VF	XF	Unc
10	1900	100 pcs.	—	—	Proof	1000.
	1901	1.375	20.00	50.00	110.00	300.00
	1902	3.525	7.50	20.00	60.00	175.00
	1903	.675	50.00	100.00	200.00	600.00
	1908	.500	100.00	250.00	450.00	850.00
	1909	.200	100.00	200.00	400.00	850.00
	1911	2.340	7.50	20.00	60.00	125.00
	1912	.160	100.00	200.00	450.00	1000.
	1913	1.252	50.00	100.00	200.00	400.00
	1914	2.500	7.50	15.00	25.00	125.00
	1916	1.000	12.50	35.00	100.00	225.00

.835 SILVER
Mule. Obv: KM#10 . Rev: KM#3a.

KM#	Date	Mintage	Fine	VF	XF	Unc
13	1909	Inc. KM10	100.00	250.00	650.00	1200.

6.0000 g, .400 SILVER, .0772 oz ASW
Mint: San Francisco - w/o mint mark.
Rev: W/o fineness indicated.

KM#	Date	Mintage	Fine	VF	XF	Unc
15	1920	4.000	12.50	25.00	50.00	125.00

5.4000 g, .680 SILVER, .1181 oz ASW
Mint mark: A
Rev. leg: TITRE 0.680 POIDS 5 GR. 4

KM#	Date	Mintage	Fine	VF	XF	Unc
17.1	1921	3.663	2.00	4.00	10.00	30.00
	1922	5.812	2.00	4.00	8.00	20.00
	1923	7.109	2.00	4.00	8.00	20.00
	1924	1.400	6.00	12.50	30.00	75.00
	1925	2.556	4.00	10.00	22.50	60.00
	1927	3.245	3.00	7.50	15.00	30.00
	1928	.794	10.00	20.00	60.00	200.00
	1929	.644	15.00	30.00	80.00	225.00
	1930	5.576	1.50	3.00	5.00	10.00
17.2	1937(a)	17.500	1.00	1.50	2.50	7.50

NICKEL
Security edge

KM#	Date	Mintage	Fine	VF	XF	Unc
23	1939(a)	.318	15.00	30.00	70.00	125.00

COPPER-NICKEL
Reeded edge

KM#	Date	Mintage	Fine	VF	XF	Unc
23a.1	1939.(a)	14.676	.25	.50	1.00	6.00

Mint mark: S

KM#	Date	Mintage	Fine	VF	XF	Unc
23a.2	1941.	25.000	.25	.50	1.00	5.00

ALUMINUM

KM#	Date	Mintage	Fine	VF	XF	Unc
29.1	1945(a)	15.412	.50	1.00	2.50	7.50

Mint mark: B

KM#	Date	Mintage	Fine	VF	XF	Unc
29.2	1945	6.665	2.00	4.00	8.00	25.00

Mint mark: C

KM#	Date	Mintage	Fine	VF	XF	Unc
29.3	1945	22.423	.50	1.00	3.00	10.00

50 CENTS

13.6070 g, .900 SILVER, .3937 oz ASW
Mint mark: A
Rev. leg: TITRE 0.900. POIDS 13.607 GR.

KM#	Date	Mintage	Fine	VF	XF	Unc
4	1885	.040	100.00	175.00	400.00	1000.
	1885	—	—	—	Proof	—
	1889	100 pcs.	—	—	Proof	1350.
	1894	.100	35.00	100.00	300.00	675.00
	1895	.100	45.00	125.00	350.00	700.00

13.5000 g, .900 SILVER, .3906 oz ASW
Rev. leg: TITRE 0.900. POIDS 13 GR. 5

KM#	Date	Mintage	Fine	VF	XF	Unc
4a.1	1896	.110	35.00	85.00	250.00	600.00
	1900	—	—	—	—	—
	1900	100 pcs.	—	—	Proof	1500.

KM#	Date	Mintage	Fine	VF	XF	Unc
4a.2	1936(a)	4.000	3.00	4.00	6.00	15.00

COPPER-NICKEL
Rev. leg: BRONZE DE NICKEL

KM#	Date	Mintage	Fine	VF	XF	Unc
31	1946(a)	32.292	2.00	4.00	7.00	20.00

PIASTRE

27.2150 g, .900 SILVER, .7875 oz ASW
Mint mark: A
Rev. leg: TITRE 0.900 POIDS 27.215 GR.

KM#	Date	Mintage	Fine	VF	XF	Unc
5	1885	.800	25.00	50.00	150.00	450.00
	1885	—	—	—	Proof	—
	1886	3.216	10.00	15.00	50.00	175.00
	1886	—	—	—	Proof	4000.
	1887	3.076	10.00	15.00	50.00	175.00
	1888	.948	20.00	40.00	100.00	325.00
	1889	1.240	15.00	25.00	70.00	275.00
	1889	100 pcs.	—	—	Proof	1800.
	1890	6,108	1200.	2200.	3000.	—
	1893	.795	25.00	65.00	125.00	400.00
	1894	1.308	15.00	25.00	75.00	250.00
	1895	1.782	10.00	15.00	50.00	200.00

27.0000 g, .900 SILVER, .7812 oz ASW
Rev. leg: TITRE 0.900. POIDS 27 GR.

KM#	Date	Mintage	Fine	VF	XF	Unc
5a.1	1895	3.798	8.00	12.50	22.50	135.00
	1896	11.858	8.00	10.00	17.50	100.00
	1897	2.511	8.00	12.50	22.50	150.00
	1898	4.304	8.00	12.50	22.50	125.00
	1899	4.681	8.00	12.50	22.50	125.00
	1900	13.319	8.00	10.00	17.50	100.00
	1900	100 pcs.	—	—	Proof	2100.
	1901	3.150	8.00	12.50	22.50	125.00
	1902	3.327	8.00	12.50	22.50	125.00
	1903	10.077	8.00	10.00	17.50	100.00
	1904	5.751	8.00	10.00	17.50	115.00
	1905	3.561	8.00	10.00	17.50	125.00
	1906	10.194	8.00	10.00	17.50	95.00
	1907	14.062	8.00	10.00	17.50	95.00
	1908	13.986	8.00	10.00	17.50	100.00
	1909	9.201	8.00	10.00	17.50	110.00
	1910	.761	30.00	70.00	150.00	300.00
	1913	3.244	8.00	12.50	22.50	125.00
	1924	2.831	8.00	12.50	22.50	150.00
	1925	2.882	8.00	12.50	22.50	150.00
	1926	6.383	8.00	10.00	17.50	100.00
	1927	8.184	8.00	10.00	17.50	95.00
	1928	5.290	8.00	10.00	17.50	95.00

Mint: San Francisco - w/o mint mark.

KM#	Date	Mintage	Fine	VF	XF	Unc
5a.2	1921	4.850	8.00	12.50	25.00	140.00
	1922	1.150	10.00	20.00	40.00	200.00

Mint mark: H

KM#	Date	Mintage	Fine	VF	XF	Unc
5a.3	1921	8.430	8.00	10.00	17.50	125.00
	1922	8.570	8.00	10.00	17.50	100.00

20.0000 g, .900 SILVER, .5787 oz ASW

KM#	Date	Mintage	Fine	VF	XF	Unc
19	1931(a)	16.000	5.00	10.00	15.00	40.00

FEDERATED STATES

(French Union)

PIASTRE

COPPER-NICKEL
Security edge

KM#	Date	Mintage	Fine	VF	XF	Unc
32.1	1946(a)	2.520	7.50	12.50	20.00	85.00
	1947(a)	.261	10.00	17.50	30.00	125.00

Reeded edge.

KM#	Date	Mintage	Fine	VF	XF	Unc
32.2	1947(a)	41.958	.50	1.00	2.00	6.00

NOTE: Similar coins dated 1946 w/rev. leg: INDOCHINE - FRANCAISE are Essais.

PROOF SETS (PS)

KM#	Date	Mintage	Identification	Issue Price	Mkt. Val.
PS1	1889(6)	100	KM1-6	—	6500.
PS2	1900(6)	100	KM4a.1-5a.1,6,8-10	—	6500.

FRENCH OCEANIA

The Colony of French Oceania (now the Territory of French Polynesia), comprising 130 basalt and coral islands scattered among five archipelagoes in the South Pacific, had an area of 1,544 sq. mi. (3,999 sq. km.). Capital: Papeete. The colony produced phosphates, copra and vanilla.

Tahiti of the Society Islands, the hub of French Oceania, was visited by Capt. Cook in 1769 and by Capt. Bligh in the Bounty 1788-89. The Society Islands were claimed by France in 1768, and in 1903 grouped with the Marquesas Islands, the Tuamotu Archipelago, the Gambier Islands and the Austral Islands under a single administrative head located at Papeete, Tahiti, to form the colony of French Oceania.

RULERS

French

MINT MARKS

(a) - Paris, privy marks only

MONETARY SYSTEM

100 Centimes = 1 Franc

50 CENTIMES

ALUMINUM

KM#	Date	Mintage	Fine	VF	XF	Unc
1	1949(a)	.795	.50	.75	1.50	5.50

FRANC

ALUMINUM

KM#	Date	Mintage	Fine	VF	XF	Unc
2	1949(a)	2.000	.20	.35	1.00	4.00

2 FRANCS

ALUMINUM

KM#	Date	Mintage	Fine	VF	XF	Unc
3	1949(a)	1.000	.40	.60	1.50	5.50

5 FRANCS

ALUMINUM

KM#	Date	Mintage	Fine	VF	XF	Unc
4	1952(a)	2.000	.50	.75	1.50	6.00

FRENCH POLYNESIA

The Territory of French Polynesia (formerly French Oceania has an area of 1,544 sq. mi. (3,941 sq. km.) and a population of *185,000. It is comprised of the same five archipelagoes that were grouped administratively to form French Oceania.

The colony of French Oceania became the Territory of French Polynesia by act of the French National Assembly in March, 1957. In Sept. of 1958 it voted in favor of the new constitution of the Fifth Republic, thereby electing to remain within the new French Community.

Picturesque, mountainous Tahiti, the setting of many tales of adventure and romance, is one of the most inspiringly beautiful islands in the world. Robert Louis Stevenson called it 'God's sweetest works'. It was there that Paul Gaugin, one of the pioneers of the Impressionist movement, painted the brilliant, exotic pictures that later made him famous. The arid coral atolls of Tuamotu comprise the most economically valuable area of French Polynesia. Pearl oysters thrive in the warm, limpid lagoons, and extensive portions of the atolls are valuable phosphate rock.

RULERS

French

MINT MARKS

(a) - Paris, privy marks only

MONETARY SYSTEM

100 Centimes = 1 Franc

50 CENTIMES

ALUMINUM

KM#	Date	Mintage	Fine	VF	XF	Unc
1	1965(a)	.895	.10	.25	.50	1.50

FRANC

ALUMINUM

KM#	Date	Mintage	Fine	VF	XF	Unc
2	1965(a)	5.300	—	.10	.20	.75

Obv. leg: I.E.O.M. added

KM#	Date	Mintage	Fine	VF	XF	Unc
11	1975(a)	2.000	—	.10	.15	.50
	1977(a)	1.000	—	.10	.15	.50
	1979(a)	1.500	—	.10	.15	.50
	1981(a)	1.000	—	.10	.15	.50
	1982(a)	2.000	—	.10	.15	.50
	1983(a)	—	—	.10	.15	.50
	1984(a)	—	—	.10	.15	.50
	1985(a)	—	—	.10	.15	.50
	1986(a)	—	—	.10	.15	.50
	1987(a)	—	—	.10	.15	.50
	1989(a)	—	—	.10	.15	.50
	1990(a)	—	—	.10	.15	.50
	1991(a)	—	—	.10	.15	.50
	1992(a)	—	—	.10	.15	.50

2 FRANCS

ALUMINUM

KM#	Date	Mintage	Fine	VF	XF	Unc
3	1965(a)	2.250	—	.10	.25	1.00

Obv. leg: I.E.O.M. added

KM#	Date	Mintage	Fine	VF	XF	Unc
10	1973(a)	.400	—	.10	.25	1.00
	1975(a)	1.000	—	.10	.25	1.00
	1977(a)	1.000	—	.10	.25	1.00
	1979(a)	2.000	—	.10	.25	1.00
	1982(a)	1.000	—	.10	.25	1.00
	1983(a)	—	—	.10	.25	1.00
	1984(a)	—	—	.10	.25	1.00
	1985(a)	—	—	.10	.25	1.00
	1986(a)	—	—	.10	.25	1.00
	1987(a)	—	—	.10	.25	1.00
	1988(a)	—	—	.10	.25	1.00
	1989(a)	—	—	.10	.25	1.00
	1990(a)	—	—	.10	.25	1.00
	1991(a)	—	—	.10	.25	1.00

5 FRANCS

ALUMINUM

KM#	Date	Mintage	Fine	VF	XF	Unc
4	1965(a)	1.520	.10	.25	.50	1.75

Obv. leg: I.E.O.M. added

KM#	Date	Mintage	Fine	VF	XF	Unc
12	1975(a)	.500	.10	.25	.50	1.75
	1977(a)	.500	.10	.25	.50	1.75
	1979(a)	—	.10	.25	.50	1.75
	1982(a)	.500	.10	.25	.50	1.75
	1983(a)	—	.10	.25	.50	1.75
	1984(a)	—	.10	.25	.50	1.75
	1985(a)	—	.10	.25	.50	1.75
	1986(a)	—	.10	.25	.50	1.75
	1988(a)	—	.10	.25	.50	1.75
	1989(a)	—	.10	.25	.50	1.75
	1990(a)	—	.10	.25	.50	1.75
	1991(a)	—	.10	.25	.50	1.75

10 FRANCS

NICKEL

KM#	Date	Mintage	Fine	VF	XF	Unc
5	1967(a)	1.000	.25	.50	.75	2.00

Obv: I.E.O.M. below head

KM#	Date	Mintage	Fine	VF	XF	Unc
8	1972(a)	.300	.25	.50	.75	2.75
	1973(a)	.400	.25	.50	.75	2.75
	1975(a)	1.000	.25	.50	.75	1.75
	1979(a)	.500	.25	.50	.75	1.75
	1982(a)	.500	.25	.50	.75	1.75
	1983(a)	—	.25	.50	.75	1.75
	1984(a)	—	.25	.50	.75	1.75
	1985(a)	—	.25	.50	.75	1.75
	1986(a)	—	.25	.50	.75	1.75
	1991(a)	—	.25	.50	.75	1.75
	1992(a)	—	.25	.50	.75	1.75

20 FRANCS

NICKEL

KM#	Date	Mintage	Fine	VF	XF	Unc
6	1967(a)	.750	.35	.75	1.25	4.00
	1969(a)	.250	.35	1.00	2.00	7.00
	1970(a)	.500	.35	.75	1.25	5.00

Obv: I.E.O.M. below head

KM#	Date	Mintage	Fine	VF	XF	Unc
9	1972(a)	.300	.30	.50	1.00	3.00
	1973(a)	.300	.30	.50	1.00	3.00
	1975(a)	.700	.30	.50	1.00	2.50
	1977(a)	.150	.35	.75	1.50	4.50
	1979(a)	.500	.30	.50	1.00	2.50
	1983(a)	—	.30	.50	1.00	2.50
	1984(a)	—	.30	.50	1.00	2.50
	1986(a)	—	.30	.50	1.00	2.50
	1988(a)	—	.30	.50	1.00	2.50
	1991(a)	—	.30	.50	1.00	2.50

50 FRANCS

NICKEL

KM#	Date	Mintage	Fine	VF	XF	Unc
7	1967(a)	.600	.60	1.00	2.00	5.00

Obv: I.E.O.M. below head.

KM#	Date	Mintage	Fine	VF	XF	Unc
13	1975(a)	.500	.60	.80	1.25	4.00
	1979(a)	—	.60	.80	1.25	4.00
	1982(a)	.500	.60	.80	1.25	4.00
	1984(a)	—	.60	.80	1.25	4.00
	1985(a)	—	.60	.80	1.25	4.00
	1988(a)	—	.60	.80	1.25	4.00
	1991(a)	—	.60	.80	1.25	4.00

100 FRANCS

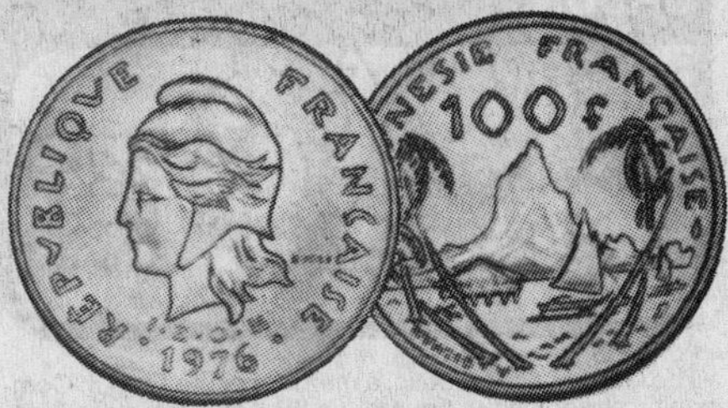

NICKEL-BRONZE

KM#	Date	Mintage	Fine	VF	XF	Unc
14	1976(a)	2.000	1.20	1.50	2.00	4.00
	1979(a)	—	1.20	1.50	2.25	5.00
	1982(a)	1.000	1.20	1.50	2.25	5.00
	1984(a)	—	1.20	1.50	2.25	5.00
	1986(a)	—	1.20	1.50	2.25	5.00
	1987(a)	—	1.20	1.50	2.25	5.00
	1988(a)	—	1.20	1.50	2.25	5.00

FLEUR DE COIN SETS (SS)

KM#	Date	Mintage	Identification	Issue Price	Mkt. Val.
SS1	1965(4)	2,200	KM1-4	—	6.00
SS2	1967(3)	2,200	KM5-7	10.00	10.00

NOTE: KM#SS1 was issued with French Somaliland (Djibouti).

NOTE: KM#SS2 was issued with New Caledonia and New Hebrides.

Listings For

FRENCH SOMALILAND: refer to Djibouti

FRENCH WEST AFRICA

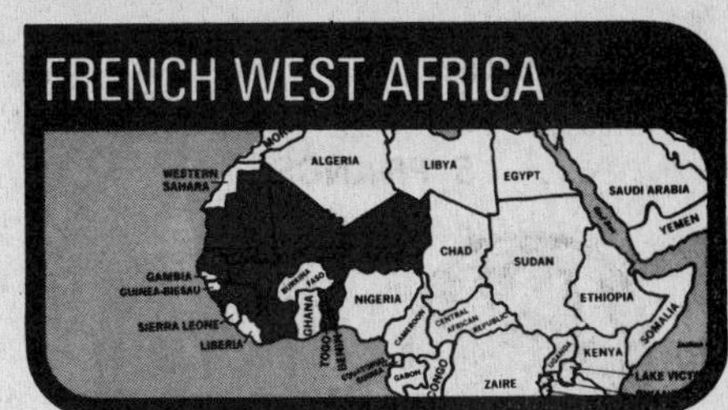

French West Africa (Afrique Occidentale Francaise), a former federation of French colonial territories on the northwest coast of Africa, had an area of 1,831,079 sq. mi. (4,742,495 sq. km.) and a population of about 17.4 million. Capital: Dakar. The constituent territories were Mauritania, Senegal, Dahomey, French Sudan, Ivory Coast, Upper Volta, Niger, French Guinea, and later on the mandated area of Togo. Peanuts, palm kernels, cacao, coffee and bananas were exported.

Prior to the mid-19th century, France, as the other European states, maintained establishments on the west coast of Africa for the purpose of trading in slaves and gum, but made no serious attempt at colonization. From 1854 onward, the coastal settlements were gradually extended into the interior until, by the opening of the 20th century, acquisition ended and organization and development began. French West Africa was formed in 1895 by grouping the several colonies under one administration (at Dakar) while retaining a large measure of autonomy to each of the constituent territories. The inhabitants of French West Africa were made French citizens in 1946. With the exception of French Guinea, all of the colonies voted in 1958 to become autonomous members of the new French Community. French Guinea voted to become the fully independent Republic of Guinea. The present-day independent states are members of the "Union Monetaire Ouest-Africaine".

For later coinage see West African States.

RULERS

French

MINT MARKS

(a) - Paris, privy marks only

MONETARY SYSTEM

100 Centimes = 1 Franc

5 Francs = 1 Unit

50 CENTIMES

ALUMINUM-BRONZE

KM#	Date	Mintage	Fine	VF	XF	Unc
1	1944(a)	10.000	2.00	4.00	10.00	25.00
	1944(a)	—	—	—	Proof	—

FRANC

ALUMINUM-BRONZE

KM#	Date	Mintage	Fine	VF	XF	Unc
2	1944(a)	15.000	1.00	2.00	5.00	20.00
	1944(a)	—	—	—	Proof	—

ALUMINUM

KM#	Date	Mintage	Fine	VF	XF	Unc
3	1948(a)	30.110	.15	.20	.35	1.00
	1955(a)	5.200	.20	.35	.50	1.50

2 FRANCS

ALUMINUM

KM#	Date	Mintage	Fine	VF	XF	Unc
4	1948(a)	12.665	.20	.30	.50	1.75
	1955(a)	1.400	.25	.40	.75	2.00

5 FRANCS

ALUMINUM-BRONZE

KM#	Date	Mintage	Fine	VF	XF	Unc
5	1956(a)	85.000	.25	.40	.75	2.00

10 FRANCS

ALUMINUM-BRONZE

KM#	Date	Mintage	Fine	VF	XF	Unc
6	1956(a)	64.133	.50	1.00	1.50	3.00

KM#	Date	Mintage	Fine	VF	XF	Unc
8	1957(a)	30.000	.50	1.00	1.50	2.75

NOTE: Issued for circulation in French West Africa, including Togo.

25 FRANCS

ALUMINUM-BRONZE

KM#	Date	Mintage	Fine	VF	XF	Unc
7	1956(a)	37.877	.50	1.00	2.00	4.00

KM#	Date	Mintage	Fine	VF	XF	Unc
9	1957(a)	30.000	.50	1.00	2.00	4.50

NOTE: Issued for circulation in French West Africa, including Togo.

Listings For

FUJAIRAH: refer to United Arab Emirates

GABON

The Gabonese Republic, a member of the French Community, straddles the equator on the west coast of Africa. The hot and humid rain forest country has an area of 103,347 sq. mi. (267,670 sq. km.) and a population of 1.2 million, almost all of Bantu origin. Capital: Libreville. Extravagantly rich in resources, Gabon exports crude oil, manganese ore, gold and timbers.

Gabon was first visited by Portuguese navigator Diego Cam in the 15th century. Dutch, French and British traders, lured by the rich stands of hard woods and oil palms, quickly followed. The French founded their first settlement on the left bank of the Gabon River in 1839 and established their presence by signing treaties with the tribal chiefs. After gradually extending their influence into the interior during the last half of the 19th century, France occupied Gabon in 1885 and, in 1910, organized it as one of the four territories of French Equatorial Africa. It became an autonomous republic within the French Union in 1946, and on Aug. 17, 1960, became a completely independent republic within the new French Community.

For earlier coinage see French Equatorial Africa, Central African States and the Equatorial African States.

MINT MARKS

(a) - Paris, privy marks only
(t) - Poissy, privy marks only, thunderbolt

10 FRANCS

4.2000 g, .900 GOLD, .1215 oz AGW
Independence - President Mba

KM#	Date	Mintage	Fine	VF	XF	Unc
1	1960	500 pcs.	—	—	Proof	75.00

25 FRANCS

8.0000 g, .900 GOLD, .2315 oz AGW
Independence - President Mba

KM#	Date	Mintage	Fine	VF	XF	Unc
2	1960	.010	—	—	—	100.00
	1960	500 pcs.	—	—	Proof	125.00

50 FRANCS

16.0000 g, .900 GOLD, .4630 oz AGW
Independence - President Mba

KM#	Date	Mintage	Fine	VF	XF	Unc
3	1960	500 pcs.	—	—	Proof	225.00

100 FRANCS

32.0000 g, .900 GOLD, .9260 oz AGW
Independence - President Mba

KM#	Date	Mintage	Fine	VF	XF	Unc
4	1960	500 pcs.	—	—	Proof	475.00

NICKEL

KM#	Date	Mintage	Fine	VF	XF	Unc
12	1971(a)	1.300	3.50	7.00	15.00	25.00
	1972(a)	2.000	3.50	7.00	15.00	25.00

KM#	Date	Mintage	Fine	VF	XF	Unc
13	1975(a)	—	2.00	4.00	7.50	15.00
	1977(a)	—	3.00	6.50	12.50	22.50
	1978(a)	—	2.50	4.50	9.00	17.50
	1982(a)	—	1.25	2.50	4.50	9.00
	1983(a)	—	1.25	2.50	4.50	9.00
	1984(a)	—	1.00	2.00	4.00	8.00
	1985(a)	—	1.00	2.00	4.00	8.00

500 FRANCS

COPPER-NICKEL
Obv: Denomination above plant, date below.
Rev: Portrait left.

KM#	Date	Mintage	Fine	VF	XF	Unc
14	1985(a)	—	2.00	3.50	5.00	8.00

1000 FRANCS

3.5000 g, .900 GOLD, .1012 oz AGW
1st Manned Moon Landing - Stump of Okume Tree

KM#	Date	Mintage	Fine	VF	XF	Unc
6	1969	4,000	—	—	Proof	75.00

3000 FRANCS

10.5000 g, .900 GOLD, .3038 oz AGW
1st Manned Moon Landing

KM#	Date	Mintage	Fine	VF	XF	Unc
7	1969	4,000	—	—	Proof	200.00

5000 FRANCS

17.5000 g, .900 GOLD, .5064 oz AGW
1st Manned Moon Landing -
Reliquary Figure of Bakota

KM#	Date	Mintage	Fine	VF	XF	Unc
8	1969	4,000	—	—	Proof	325.00

Visit of French President Georges Pompidou

KM#	Date	Mintage	Fine	VF	XF	Unc
11	1971(a)	—	—	—	Proof	550.00

10000 FRANCS

35.0000 g, .900 GOLD, 1.0128 oz AGW
1st Manned Moon Landing - Lunar Module

KM#	Date	Mintage	VF	XF	Unc
9	1969	4,000	—	—	Proof 650.00

20000 FRANCS

70.0000 g, .900 GOLD, 2.0257 oz AGW
1st Manned Moon Landing - Cape Kennedy
Rev: Apollo XI at launching pad.

KM#	Date	Mintage	VF	XF	Unc
10	1969	4,000	—	—	Proof 1350.

PROOF SETS (PS)

KM#	Date	Mintage	Identification	Issue Price	Mkt. Val.
PS1	1960(4)	500	KM1-4	—	900.00
PS2	1969(5)	4,000	KM6-10	—	2600.

GAMBIA

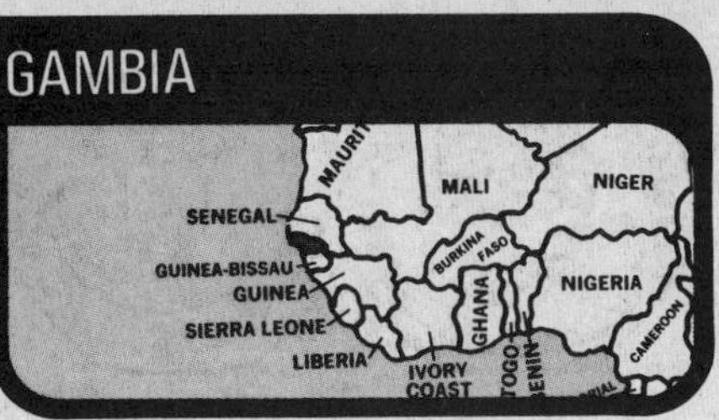

The Republic of The Gambia, an independent member of the British Commonwealth, occupies a strip of land 7 miles (11km.) to 20 miles (32 km.) wide and 200 miles (322 km.) long encompassing both sides of West Africa's Gambia River, and completely surrounded by Senegal. The republic, one of Africa's smallest countries, has an area of 4,361 sq. mi. (11,300 sq. km.) and a population of 720,000. Capital: Banjul. Agriculture and tourism are the principal industries. Peanuts constitute 95 per cent of export earnings.

The Gambia was once part of the great empires of Ghana and Songhay. When Portuguese gold seekers and slave traders visited The Gambia in the 15th century, it was part of the Kingdom of Mali. In 1588 the territory became, through purchase, the first British colony in Africa. English slavers established Fort James, the first settlement, on a small island a dozen miles up the Gambia River in 1664. After alternate periods of union with Sierra Leone and existence as a separate colony The Gambia became a British colony in 1888. On Feb. 18, 1965, The Gambia achieved independence as a constitutional monarchy within the Commonwealth of Nations, with the Queen of England as Chief of State. It became a republic on April 24, 1970, remaining a member of the Commonwealth, but with the president as Chief of State and Head of Government.

Gambia's 8 Shillings coin is a unique denomination in world coinage.

For earlier coinage see British West Africa.

RULERS

Elizabeth II, 1952-1970

MONETARY SYSTEM

12 Pence = 1 Shilling
4 Shillings = 1 Dirham
20 Shillings = 1 Pound

PENNY

BRONZE
Sailing Vessel

KM#	Date	Mintage	VF	XF	Unc
1	1966	3.600	.20	.40	1.00
	1966	6,600	—	Proof	1.00

3 PENCE

NICKEL-BRASS
Double Spurred Francolin

KM#	Date	Mintage	VF	XF	Unc
2	1966	2.000	.30	.50	1.25
	1966	6,600	—	Proof	1.25

6 PENCE

COPPER-NICKEL
Ground Nuts

KM#	Date	Mintage	VF	XF	Unc
3	1966	1.500	.30	.50	1.25
	1966	6,600	—	Proof	1.25

SHILLING

COPPER-NICKEL
Oil Palm

KM#	Date	Mintage	VF	XF	Unc
4	1966	2.500	.50	.80	1.50
	1966	6,600	—	Proof	1.50

2 SHILLINGS

COPPER-NICKEL
African Domestic Ox

KM#	Date	Mintage	VF	XF	Unc
5	1966	1.600	.75	1.50	2.50
	1966	6,600	—	Proof	2.50

4 SHILLINGS

COPPER-NICKEL
Slender-snouted Crocodile

KM#	Date	Mintage	VF	XF	Unc
6	1966	.800	1.50	3.00	6.00
	1966	6,600	—	Proof	4.00

8 SHILLINGS

COPPER-NICKEL
Hippopotamus

KM#	Date	Mintage	VF	XF	Unc
7	1970	.025	2.00	4.00	8.00

32.4000 g, .925 SILVER, .9635 oz ASW

KM#	Date	Mintage	VF	XF	Unc
7a	1970	4,500	—	Proof	28.00

NOTE: VIP issued proofs have a frosted relief, value: $175.00.

DECIMAL COINAGE

100 Bututs = 1 Dalasi

BUTUT

BRONZE

KM#	Date	Mintage	VF	XF	Unc
8	1971	12.449	—	.10	.20
	1971	.032	—	Proof	.50
	1973	3.000	—	.10	.25
	1974	—	—	.35	.50
	1975	—	—	.10	.25

F.A.O. Issue

KM#	Date	Mintage	VF	XF	Unc
14	1974	26.062	—	.10	.20
	1985	4.500	—	.15	.25

5 BUTUTS

BRONZE

KM#	Date	Mintage	VF	XF	Unc
9	1971	5.400	—	.10	.35
	1971	.032	—	Proof	.50
	1977	1.506	—	.10	.35

10 BUTUTS

NICKEL-BRASS

KM#	Date	Mintage	VF	XF	Unc
10	1971	3.000	.10	.15	.50
	1971	.032	—	Proof	1.00
	1977	.750	.10	.15	.50

25 BUTUTS

COPPER-NICKEL

KM#	Date	Mintage	VF	XF	Unc
11	1971	3.040	.15	.30	.75
	1971	.032	—	Proof	1.00

50 BUTUTS

COPPER-NICKEL

KM#	Date	Mintage	VF	XF	Unc
12	1971	1.700	.25	.50	1.25
	1971	.032	—	Proof	1.50

DALASI

COPPER-NICKEL
Obv: Similar to 50 Bututs, KM#12.

KM#	Date	Mintage	VF	XF	Unc
13	1971	1.300	1.25	2.00	3.50
	1971	.032	—	Proof	3.50

KM#	Date	Mintage	VF	XF	Unc
29	1987	—	—	—	3.00

10 DALASIS

28.2800 g, .500 SILVER, .4546 oz ASW
10th Anniversary of Independence

KM#	Date	Mintage	VF	XF	Unc
16	1975	.050	—	—	8.00

28.2800 g, .925 SILVER, .8411 oz ASW

KM#	Date	Mintage	VF	XF	Unc
16a	1975	.020	—	Proof	15.00

28.2800 g, .500 SILVER, .4546 oz ASW
Commonwealth Games - Hurdlers

KM#	Date	Mintage	VF	XF	Unc
23	1986	*.050	—	—	15.00

28.2800 g, .925 SILVER, .8411 oz ASW

KM#	Date	Mintage	VF	XF	Unc
23a	1986	*.020	—	Proof	25.00

Silver Jubilee of Independence

KM#	Date	Mintage	VF	XF	Unc
28	1990	2,000	—	Proof	50.00

COPPER-NICKEL
Papal Visit

KM#	Date	Mintage	VF	XF	Unc
30	1992	—	—	—	7.00

28.2800 g, .925 SILVER, .8411 oz ASW

KM#	Date	Mintage	VF	XF	Unc
30a	1992	5,000	—	Proof	55.00

20 DALASIS

28.6300 g, .925 SILVER, .8514 oz ASW
Conservation Series - Spur-Winged Goose

KM#	Date	Mintage	VF	XF	Unc
17	1977	4,302	—	—	22.50

28.2800 g, .925 SILVER, .8411 oz ASW

KM#	Date	Mintage	VF	XF	Unc
17a	1977	4,404	—	Proof	30.00

World Food Day
Obv: Similar to KM#17.

KM#	Date	Mintage	VF	XF	Unc
20	1981	.010	—	—	20.00
	1981	5,000	—	Proof	27.50

Year of the Scout

KM#	Date	Mintage	VF	XF	Unc
21	1983	*.010	—	—	22.50
	1983	Inc. Ab.	—	Proof	30.00

World Wildlife Fund - Monkey
Obv: Similar to KM#17.

KM#	Date	Mintage	VF	XF	Unc
24	1987	*.025	—	Proof	35.00

Save The Children Fund
Obv: Male portrait left.

KM#	Date	Mintage	VF	XF	Unc
26	1989	*.020	—	Proof	50.00

31.4700 g, .925 SILVER, .9359 oz ASW
40th Anniversary Coronation of Queen Elizabeth II

KM#	Date	Mintage	VF	XF	Unc
32	1993	*.010	—	Proof	50.00

31.2600 g, .925 SILVER, .9296 oz ASW
Olympics - Wrestling

KM#	Date	Mintage	VF	XF	Unc
33	1993	*.040	—	Proof	40.00

31.4700 g, .925 SILVER, .9359 oz ASW
Prince Henry the Navigator

KM#	Date	Mintage	VF	XF	Unc
34	1993	*.015	—	Proof	40.00

Soccer - World Cup 1994

KM#	Date	Mintage	VF	XF	Unc
35	1994	*.015	—	Proof	45.00

Rendezvous In Space

KM#	Date	Mintage	VF	XF	Unc
36	1994	*.010	—	Proof	40.00

40 DALASIS

35.2900 g, .925 SILVER, 1.0495 oz ASW
Conservation Series - Aardvark

KM#	Date	Mintage	VF	XF	Unc
18	1977	4,304	—	—	27.50

35.0000 g, .925 SILVER, 1.0409 oz ASW

KM#	Date	Mintage	VF	XF	Unc
18a	1977	4,183	—	Proof	40.00

250 DALASIS

15.9800 g, .917 GOLD, .4712 oz AGW
Year of the Scout

KM#	Date	Mintage	VF	XF	Unc
22	1983	2,000	—	—	275.00
	1983	2,000	—	Proof	350.00

47.5400 g, .917 GOLD, 1.4011 oz AGW
Papal Visit
Obv: National coat of arms.
Rev: Pope giving a blessing.

KM#	Date	Mintage	VF	XF	Unc
31	1992	100 pcs.	—	Proof	1150.

500 DALASIS

33.4370 g, .900 GOLD, .9676 oz AGW
Conservation Series - Sitatunga

KM#	Date	Mintage	VF	XF	Unc
19	1977	699 pcs.	—	—	550.00
	1977	285 pcs.	—	Proof	750.00

1000 DALASIS

10.0000 g, .917 GOLD, .2948 oz AGW
World Wildlife Fund - Bird

KM#	Date	Mintage	VF	XF	Unc
25	1987	*5,000	—	Proof	250.00

Save the Children Fund

KM#	Date	Mintage	VF	XF	Unc
27	1989	*3,000	—	Proof	325.00

PROOF SETS (PS)

KM#	Date	Mintage	Identification	Issue Price	Mkt. Val.
PS1	1966(6)	5,100	KM1-6	13.00	10.00
PS2	1970/66(7)	1,500	KM1-6,7a	25.00	40.00
PS3	1971(6)	26,249	KM8-13	—	7.50
PS4	1977(2)	—	KM17a,18a	60.00	70.00

Listings For

GERMAN EAST AFRICA: refer to Tanzania

GERMAN NEW GUINEA: refer to Papua-New Guinea

a map of the

GERMAN STATES

1 Aachen
2 Anhalt-Bernburg
3 Anhalt-Dessau
4 Baden
5 Bavaria
6 Berg
7 Birkenfeld
8 Brandenburg-Ansbach Bayreuth
9 Brunswick-Luneburg & Wolfenbuttel
10 Cleve
11 Coesfeld
12 Corvey
13 East Friesland
14 Eichstadt
15 Erfurt
16 Freising
17 Friedberg
18 Fulda
19 Furstenberg
20 Halle
21 Hannover
22 Hesse-Cassel
23 Hesse-Darmstadt
24 Hildesheim
25 Hohenzollern
26 Jever
27 Julich
28 Knyphausen
29 Lauenburg
30 Lippe-Detmold
31 Mainz
32 Mansfeld
33 Mecklenburg-Schwerin
34 Mecklenburg-Strelitz
35 Muhlhausen
36 Munster
37 Nassau
38 Oldenburg
39 Osnabruck
40 Paderborn
41 Passau
42 Prussia
43 Pyrmont
44 Reuss-Greiz
45 Reuss-Schleiz
46 Rhein-Pfalz
47 Saxe-Altenburg
48 Saxe-Coburg-Gotha
49 Saxe-Meiningen
50 Saxe-Weimar-Eisenach
51 Saxony
52 Schaumberg-Hessen & Lippe
53 Schleswig-Holstein
54 Schwarzburg-Rudolstadt
55 Schwarzburg Sonderhausen
56 Stolberg-Wernigerode
57 Trier
58 Wallmoden-Pyrmont
59 Wallmoden-Gimborn
60 Wurttemberg
61 Wurzburg

GERMAN STATES

Although the origin of the German Empire can be traced to the Treaty of Verdun, 843, that ceded Charlemagne's lands east of the Rhine to German Prince Louis, it was for centuries little more than a geographic expression, consisting of hundreds of effectively autonomous big and little states. Nominally the states owed their allegiance to the Holy Roman Emperor, who was also a German king, but as the Emperors exhibited less and less concern for Germany the actual power devolved on the lords of the individual states. The fragmentation of the empire climaxed with the tragic denouement of the Thirty Years War, 1618-48, which devastated much of Germany, destroyed its agriculture and medieval commercial eminence and ended the attempt of the Hapsburgs to unify Germany. Deprived of administrative capacity by a lack of resources, the imperial authority became utterly powerless. At this time Germany contained an estimated 1,800 individual states, some with a population of as little as 300. The German Empire of recent history (the creation of Bismarck) was formed on April 14, 1871, when the king of Prussia became Emperor William I of Germany. The new empire comprised 4 kingdoms, 5 grand duchies, 13 duchies and principalities, 3 free cities and the nonautonomous province of Alsace-Lorraine. The states had the right to issue gold and silver coins of higher value than 1 Mark; coins of 1 Mark and under were general issues of the empire.

MINT MARKS

A - Berlin, 1850-date
A - Clausthal (Hannover) 1832-1849
B - Bayreuth, Franconia (Prussia) 1796-1804
B - Breslau (Prussia, Silesia) 1750-1826
B - Brunswick (Brunswick) 1850-1860
B - Brunswick (Westphalia) 1809-1813
B - Dresden (Saxony) 1861-1872
B - Hannover (Brunswick) 1860-1871
B - Hannover (East Friesland) 1823-1825
B - Hannover (Germany) 1866-1878
B - Hannover (Hannover) 1821-1866
B - Regensburg (Regensburg) 1809
B.H. Frankfurt (Free City of Frankfurt) 1808
B (rosette) H - Regensburg (Rhenish Confederation) 1802-1812
C - Cassel (Westphalia) 1810-1813
C - Clausthal (Brunswick)
C - Clausthal (Hannover) 1813-1834
C - Clausthal (Westphalia) 1810-1811
C - Dresden (Saxony) 1779-1804
C - Frankfurt (Germany) 1866-1879
D - Aurich (East Friesland under Prussia) 1750-1806
D - Dusseldorf, Rhineland (Prussia) 1816-1848
D - Munich (Germany) 1872-date
E - Dresden (Germany) 1872-1887
E - Muldenhutte (Germany) 1887-1953
F - Dresden (Saxony) 1845-1858
FMagdeburg (Prussia) 1750-1806
F - Cassel (Hesse-Cassel) 1803-1807
F - Stuttgart (Germany) 1872-date
G - Dresden (Saxony) 1833-1844, 1850-1854
G - Glatz (Prussian Silesia) 1807-1809
G - Karlsruhe (Germany) 1872-date
G - Stettin In Pomerania (Prussia) 1750-1806
GN-BW - Bamberg (Bamberg)
H - Darmstadt (Germany) 1872-1882
H - Dresden (Saxony) 1804-1812
H.K. - Rostock (Rostock) 1862-1864
I - Hamburg (Germany)
J - Hamburg (Germany) 1873-date
J - Paris (Westphalia) 1808-1809
M.C. - Brunswick (Brunswick) 1813-14, 1820
P.R. - Dusseldorf (Julich-Berg) 1783-1804
S - Dresden (Saxony) 1813-1832
S - Hannover (Hannover) 1839-1844

MONETARY SYSTEM

Until 1871 the Mark (Marck) was a measure of weight.

North German States until 1837

2 Heller = 1 Pfennig
8 Pfennige = 1 Mariengroschen
12 Pfennige = 1 Groschen
24 Groschen = 1 Thaler
2 Gulden = 1-1/3 Reichsthaler
1 Speciesthaler (before 1753)
1 Convention Thaler (after 1753)

North German States after 1837

12 Pfennige = 1 Groschen
30 Groschen = 1 Thaler
1 Vereinsthaler (after 1857)

South German States until 1837

8 Heller = 4 Pfennige = 1 Kreuzer
24 Kreuzer Landmunze = 20 Kreuzer Convention Munze
120 Convention Kreuzer = 2 Convention Gulden = 1 Convention Thaler

South German States after 1837

8 Heller = 4 Pfennige = 1 Kreuzer

German States 1857-1871

As a result of the Monetary Convention of 1857, all the German States adopted a Vereinsthaler of uniform weight being 1/30 fine pound silver. They did continue to use their regional minor coin units to divide the Vereinsthaler for small change purposes.

After the German unification in 1871 when the old Thaler system was abandoned in favor of the Mark system (100 Pfennig = 1 Mark) the Vereinsthaler continued to circulate as a legal tender 3 Mark coin, and the double Thaler as a 6 Mark coin until 1908. In 1908 the Vereinsthalers were officially demonetized and the Thaler coinage was replaced by the new 3 Mark coin which had the same specifications as the old Vereinsthaler. The double Thaler coinage was not replaced as there was no great demand for a 6 Mark coin. Until the 1930's the German public continued to refer to the 3 Mark piece as a "Thaler".

Commencing 1871

100 Pfennig = 1 Mark

ANHALT-BERNBURG

Located in north-central Germany. Appeared as part of the patrimony of Albrecht the Bear of Brandenburg in 1170. Bracteates were first made in the 12th century. It was originally in the inheritance of Heinrich the Fat in 1252 and became extinct in 1468. The division of 1603, among the sons of Joachim Ernst, revitalized Anhalt-Bernburg. Bernburg passed to Dessau after the death of Alexander Carl in 1863.

RULERS

Alexius Friedrich Christian, 1796-1834
Alexander Carl, 1834-1863

MINTMASTERS INITIALS

Letter	Date	Name
HS	1795-1821	Hans Schluter
Z	1821-1848	Johann Carl Ludwig Zincken

PFENNIG

COPPER

KM#	Date	Mintage	Fine	VF	XF	Unc
74	1807	—	7.00	12.50	25.00	70.00

Rev. leg: SCHEIDE MUNTZ

KM#	Date	Mintage	Fine	VF	XF	Unc
76	1808	—	5.00	8.00	15.00	50.00

Rev. leg: SCHEIDEMUNZE

KM#	Date	Mintage	Fine	VF	XF	Unc
77.1	1822	—	5.00	8.00	15.00	40.00
	1823	—	5.00	8.00	15.00	40.00
	1827	—	5.00	8.00	15.00	40.00

Rev. leg: SCHEIDEMUNZE HZL ANHALT

KM#	Date	Mintage	Fine	VF	XF	Unc
77.2	1831 Z	—	5.00	8.00	15.00	40.00

4 PFENNIG

COPPER

KM#	Date	Mintage	Fine	VF	XF	Unc
78.1	1822	—	7.50	15.00	30.00	60.00
	1823	—	7.50	15.00	30.00	60.00

Rev. value: 4 PFENNINGE

KM#	Date	Mintage	Fine	VF	XF	Unc
78.2	1831 Z	—	7.50	15.00	30.00	75.00

1/48 THALER

.9700 g, .250 SILVER, .0077 oz ASW
Obv: Crowned arms in branches. Rev: Value.

KM#	Date	Mintage	Fine	VF	XF	Unc
75	1807	—	8.00	16.00	35.00	80.00

1/24 THALER

1.9800 g, .350 SILVER, .0234 oz ASW
Rev. leg: HANH BERNB . . . . .

KM#	Date	Mintage	Fine	VF	XF	Unc
79	1822	—	7.50	15.00	30.00	65.00
	1823	—	7.50	15.00	30.00	65.00
	1827	—	7.50	15.00	30.00	65.00

Rev. leg: HZL. ANHALT. . . . .

KM#	Date	Mintage	Fine	VF	XF	Unc
81	1831 Z	—	7.50	15.00	30.00	75.00

1/6 THALER

5.3400 g, .520 SILVER, .0892 oz ASW

KM#	Date	Mintage	Fine	VF	XF	Unc
85	1856A	.060	15.00	30.00	50.00	100.00

KM#	Date	Mintage	Fine	VF	XF	Unc
87	1861A	.062	10.00	20.00	40.00	80.00
	1862A	.060	10.00	20.00	40.00	80.00

2/3 THALER

14.0300 g, .833 SILVER, .3757 oz ASW
Rev. leg: HERZOG ZU ANHALT. . . . .

KM#	Date	Mintage	Fine	VF	XF	Unc
72	1806 HS	—	35.00	75.00	125.00	185.00
	1808 HS	—	50.00	100.00	150.00	220.00
	1809 HS	—	35.00	75.00	125.00	185.00

THALER

(Convention)

28.0600 g, .833 SILVER, .7515 oz ASW

KM#	Date	Mintage	Fine	VF	XF	Unc
73	1806 HS	—	250.00	500.00	1200.	3500.
	1809 HS	—	400.00	800.00	2000.	5000.

(Mining)

22.2700 g, .750 SILVER, .5370 oz ASW

KM#	Date	Mintage	Fine	VF	XF	Unc
82	1834	.015	35.00	75.00	175.00	400.00

KM#	Date	Mintage	Fine	VF	XF	Unc
84	1846A	.010	25.00	45.00	85.00	160.00
	1852A	.010	25.00	45.00	85.00	160.00
	1855A	.020	20.00	35.00	65.00	140.00

(Vereins)

18.5200 g, .900 SILVER, .5358 oz ASW

KM#	Date	Mintage	Fine	VF	XF	Unc
86	1859A	.024	40.00	65.00	150.00	325.00

(Mining)

KM#	Date	Mintage	Fine	VF	XF	Unc
88	1861A	.010	25.00	45.00	85.00	160.00
	1862A	.020	20.00	35.00	65.00	140.00

2 THALER

(3-1/2 Gulden)

37.1200 g, .900 SILVER, 1.0741 oz ASW

KM#	Date	Mintage	Fine	VF	XF	Unc
83	1840A	3,600	350.00	500.00	800.00	1750.
	1845A	7,200	300.00	450.00	700.00	1650.
	1855A	5,000	300.00	450.00	700.00	1650.

TRADE COINAGE

DUCAT

3.5000 g, .986 GOLD, .1109 oz AGW
Obv. leg: EX AURO ANHALTINO.
Rev. leg: ALEXIUS FRIED CHRIST. . . .

KM#	Date	Mintage	Fine	VF	XF	Unc
80	1825 Z	116 pcs.	850.00	1400.	2400.	3500.

JOINT COINAGE

UNDER ALEXANDER CARL
FOR ANHALT-COTHEN
AND ANHALT-DESSAU

PFENNIG

COPPER
Rev. leg: 288 EINEN THALER.

KM#	Date	Mintage	Fine	VF	XF	Unc
91	1839	.589	3.00	6.00	15.00	65.00
	1840	.654	3.00	6.00	15.00	65.00

KM#	Date	Mintage	Fine	VF	XF	Unc
96	1856A	.360	2.00	4.00	8.00	35.00
	1862A	.360	2.00	4.00	8.00	35.00
	1864A	.300	2.00	4.00	8.00	35.00
	1867B	.180	2.00	4.00	8.00	35.00

3 PFENNIGE

COPPER

KM#	Date	Mintage	Fine	VF	XF	Unc
92	1839	.386	3.00	6.00	15.00	65.00
	1840	.292	3.00	6.00	15.00	65.00

KM#	Date	Mintage	Fine	VF	XF	Unc
98	1861A	.240	2.50	5.00	12.50	45.00
	1864A	.200	2.50	5.00	12.50	45.00
	1867B	.240	2.50	5.00	12.50	45.00

6 PFENNIGE

.8100 g, .375 SILVER, .0097 oz ASW

KM#	Date	Mintage	Fine	VF	XF	Unc
94	1840	.322	3.00	6.00	18.00	85.00

GROSCHEN

1.6200 g, .375 SILVER, .0195 oz ASW
Obv: Crowned shield. Rev. leg: 24 EINEN THALER.

KM#	Date	Mintage	Fine	VF	XF	Unc
93	1839	.319	2.00	4.50	12.00	45.00
	1840	Inc. Ab.	2.00	4.50	12.00	45.00

SILBERGROSCHEN

2.1900 g, .222 SILVER, .0156 oz ASW

KM#	Date	Mintage	Fine	VF	XF	Unc
95	1851A	.176	2.00	4.50	12.00	45.00
	1852A	.197	2.00	4.50	12.00	45.00
	1855A	.303	2.00	4.50	12.00	45.00
	1859A	.150	2.00	4.50	12.00	45.00
	1862A	.300	2.00	4.50	12.00	45.00

2-1/2 SILBERGROSCHEN

3.2400 g, .375 SILVER, .0390 oz ASW

KM#	Date	Mintage	Fine	VF	XF	Unc
97	1856A	.120	2.50	5.50	15.00	70.00
	1859A	.060	2.50	5.50	15.00	70.00
	1861A	.120	2.50	5.50	15.00	70.00
	1862A	.240	2.50	5.50	15.00	70.00
	1864A	.120	2.50	5.50	15.00	70.00

ANHALT-COTHEN

Cothen has a checkered history after the patrimony of Heinrich the Fat in 1252. It was often ruled with other segments of the House of Anhalt. Founded as a separate line in 1603, became extinct in 1665 and passed to Plotzkau which changed the name to Cothen. It passed to Dessau after the death of Heinrich in 1847.

RULERS

Heinrich, 1830-1847

2 THALER

(3-1/2 Gulden)

37.1200 g, .900 SILVER, 1.0743 oz ASW

KM#	Date	Mintage	Fine	VF	XF	Unc
39	1840A	3,100	400.00	800.00	2500.	6000.

ANHALT-DESSAU

Dessau was part of the 1252 division that included Zerbst and Cothen. In 1396 Zerbst divided into Zerbst and Dessau. In 1508 Zerbst was absorbed into Dessau. Dessau was given to the eldest son of Joachim Ernst in the division of 1603. As other lines became extinct, they fell to Dessau, which united all branches in 1863.

RULERS

Leopold Friedrich Franz, 1751-1817
Leopold Friedrich, 1817-1871
Friedrich I, 1871-1904

Friedrich II, 1904-1918

VI EINEN (1/6) THALER

5.3400 g, .520 SILVER, .0892 oz ASW

KM#	Date	Mintage	Fine	VF	XF	Unc
19	1865A	.120	12.50	25.00	50.00	150.00

EIN (1) THALER

(Vereins)

18.5200 g, .900 SILVER, .5359 oz ASW
Leopold Friedrich

KM#	Date	Mintage	Fine	VF	XF	Unc
14	1858A	.027	30.00	60.00	100.00	350.00

Separation of Anhalt Duchies - 1603
Reunion of Anhalt Duchies - 1863

KM#	Date	Mintage	Fine	VF	XF	Unc
15	1863A	.050	30.00	60.00	100.00	175.00

KM#	Date	Mintage	Fine	VF	XF	Unc
20	1866A	.031	30.00	60.00	100.00	250.00
	1869A	.032	30.00	60.00	100.00	250.00

2 THALER

(3-1/2 Gulden)

37.1200 g, .900 SILVER, 1.0741 oz ASW
Leopold Friedrich

KM#	Date	Mintage	Fine	VF	XF	Unc
13	1839A	4,700	250.00	500.00	800.00	1500.
	1843A	4,700	250.00	500.00	800.00	1500.
	1846A	4,700	250.00	500.00	800.00	1500.

MONETARY REFORM

2 MARK

11.1110 g, .900 SILVER, .3215 oz ASW
Friedrich I

KM#	Date	Mintage	Fine	VF	XF	Unc
22	1876A	.200	100.00	200.00	500.00	1000.

25th Year of Reign of Friedrich I

KM#	Date	Mintage	Fine	VF	XF	Unc
23	1896A	.050	150.00	300.00	500.00	750.00
	1896A	—	—	—	Proof	850.00

Friedrich II

KM#	Date	Mintage	Fine	VF	XF	Unc
27	1904A	.050	125.00	275.00	425.00	700.00
	1904A	150 pcs.	—	—	Proof	800.00

3 MARK

16.6670 g, .900 SILVER, .4823 oz ASW
Friedrich II

KM#	Date	Mintage	Fine	VF	XF	Unc
29	1909A	.100	40.00	75.00	115.00	165.00
	1911A	.100	40.00	75.00	115.00	165.00
	Common date	—	—	—	Proof	250.00

Silver Wedding Anniversary

KM#	Date	Mintage	Fine	VF	XF	Unc
30	1914A	.200	25.00	45.00	65.00	100.00
	1914A	1,000	—	—	Proof	150.00

5 MARK

27.7770 g, .900 SILVER, .8038 oz ASW
25th Year of Reign of Friedrich I

KM#	Date	Mintage	Fine	VF	XF	Unc
24	1896A	.010	500.00	800.00	1500.	2000.
	1896A	—	—	—	Proof	2500.

Silver Wedding Anniversary

KM#	Date	Mintage	Fine	VF	XF	Unc
31	1914A	.030	60.00	175.00	200.00	300.00
	1914A	1,000	—	—	Proof	450.00

10 MARK

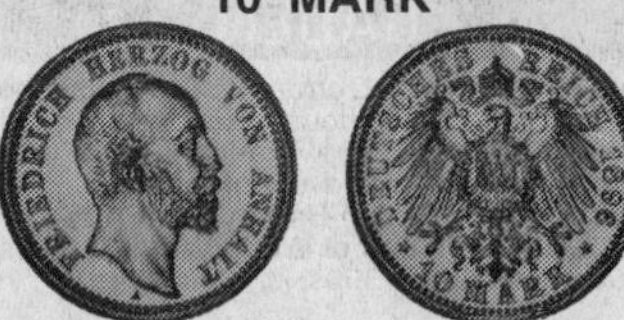

3.9820 g, .900 GOLD, .1152 oz AGW
Friedrich I

KM#	Date	Mintage	Fine	VF	XF	Unc
25	1896A	.020	450.00	750.00	1000.	1500.
	1896A	200 pcs.	—	—	Proof	1600.
	1901A	.020	450.00	750.00	1000.	1500.
	1901A	200 pcs.	—	—	Proof	1600.

20 MARK

7.9650 g, .900 GOLD, .2304 oz AGW
Friedrich I

KM#	Date	Mintage	Fine	VF	XF	Unc
21	1875A	.025	450.00	800.00	1200.	1700.
	1875A	—	—	—	Proof	3500.

KM#	Date	Mintage	Fine	VF	XF	Unc
26	1896A	.015	450.00	750.00	1100.	1500.
	1896A	200 pcs.	—	—	Proof	2000.
	1901A	.015	450.00	750.00	1100.	1400.
	1901A	200 pcs.	—	—	Proof	2000.

Friedrich II

KM#	Date	Mintage	Fine	VF	XF	Unc
28	1904A	.025	450.00	750.00	1000.	1500.
	1904A	200 pcs.	—	—	Proof	2500.

AUGSBURG

FREE CITY

Founded as a Roman colony in the reign of Augustus it

was declared a Free City in 1276. The mint rights were granted in 1521 but the first coins are dated somewhat earlier. Augsburg was given to Bavaria in 1806.

HELLER

COPPER

Obv: Crowned arms. Rev: Value, date.

KM#	Date	Mintage	VG	Fine	VF	XF
188	1801	—	2.00	5.00	10.00	25.00

NOTE: Earlier dates (1780-1798) exist for this type.

Obv: State arms in oval shield.
Rev: Value and date.

KM#	Date	Mintage	Fine	VF	XF	Unc
190	1801	—	1.00	3.00	8.00	50.00
	1803	—	1.00	3.00	8.00	50.00
	1804	—	1.00	3.00	8.00	50.00
	1805	—	1.00	3.00	8.00	50.00

PFENNING

COPPER

Obv: Arms in shield.
Rev. inscription: STADTMYNZ.

KM#	Date	Mintage	VG	Fine	VF	XF
189	1801	—	3.00	6,00	12.00	30.00
	1802	—	3.00	6.00	12.00	30.00
	1803	—	3.00	6.00	12.00	30.00

NOTE: Earlier dates (1780-1800) exist for this type.

Rev. inscription: STADT MUNZ.

KM#	Date	Mintage	Fine	VF	XF	Unc
191	1803	—	2.00	4.00	10.00	50.00
	1804	—	2.00	4.00	10.00	50.00
	1805	—	2.00	4.00	10.00	50.00

BADEN

Located in southwest Germany. The ruling house of Baden began in 1112. Various branches developed and religious wars between the branches were settled in 1648. The branches unified under Baden-Durlach after the extinction of the Baden-Baden line in 1771. The last ruler abdicated at the end of World War I. The first coins were issued in the late 1300s.

RULERS

Carl Friedrich,
Margrave in all Baden, 1771-1803
As Elector, 1803-1806
As Grand Duke, 1806-1811
Carl Ludwig Friedrich, 1811-1818
Ludwig I, 1818-1830
Leopold I, 1830-1852
Ludwig II, 1852-1856, Insane and deposed
Friedrich I as Prince Regent, 1852-1856
As Grand Duke, 1856-1907
Friedrich II, 1907-1918

MINTMASTERS INITIALS

Letter	Date	Name
B	1778-1808	Johann Martin Buckle
B,HB	1790-1812	Johann Heinrich Boltschauser, die-cutter and mint warden
CS,S	1761-1811	Ernst Christoph Steinhauser, mint warden
FE	1802	Franz Eberle, mint warden

1/4 KREUZER

COPPER

KM#	Date	Mintage	Fine	VF	XF	Unc
132	1802	.024	15.00	25.00	150.00	300.00

Obv: Crowned shield. Rev: Value, date within wreath.

KM#	Date	Mintage	Fine	VF	XF	Unc
153	1810	—	—	—	Rare	—

KM#	Date	Mintage	Fine	VF	XF	Unc
181	1821	—	3.00	8.00	20.00	65.00
	1824	.128	3.00	8.00	20.00	65.00

1/2 KREUZER

COPPER

KM#	Date	Mintage	Fine	VF	XF	Unc
133	1803	.027	8.00	15.00	40.00	225.00
	1804	.104	8.00	15.00	25.00	175.00
	1805	.157	8.00	15.00	25.00	175.00

KM#	Date	Mintage	Fine	VF	XF	Unc
139	1806	—	3.00	7.00	15.00	125.00
	1808	—	3.00	7.00	15.00	125.00
	1809	.877	3.00	7.00	15.00	100.00
	1810	.129	3.00	7.00	15.00	125.00
	1812	.105	3.00	7.00	15.00	100.00

Obv: Crowned draped arms.
Rev: Similar to KM#165.

KM#	Date	Mintage	Fine	VF	XF	Unc
164	1814	.078	3.00	7.00	20.00	100.00
	1815	.062	3.00	7.00	20.00	100.00
	1816	.039	3.00	7.00	20.00	100.00
	1817	.102	3.00	7.00	20.00	100.00

Obv: Smaller crowned draped arms.

KM#	Date	Mintage	Fine	VF	XF	Unc
165	1814	Inc. Ab.	3.00	7.00	15.00	80.00

Rev. value: 1/2 KREU/ZER

KM#	Date	Mintage	Fine	VF	XF	Unc
171	1817	—	3.00	7.00	15.00	80.00

KM#	Date	Mintage	Fine	VF	XF	Unc
182	1821	.127	3.00	7.00	15.00	70.00

KM#	Date	Mintage	Fine	VF	XF	Unc
186	1822	.109	3.00	7.00	12.00	65.00
	1823	.035	3.00	7.00	15.00	110.00
	1824	.066	3.00	7.00	15.00	80.00
	1825	.053	3.00	7.00	15.00	90.00
	1826	.191	3.00	7.00	12.00	60.00

Ludwig I

KM#	Date	Mintage	Fine	VF	XF	Unc
188	1827	—	3.00	7.00	15.00	75.00
	1828	.137	3.00	7.00	15.00	75.00
	1829	.204	3.00	7.00	15.00	75.00
	1830	Inc. Ab.	3.00	7.00	15.00	75.00

Leopold I
Obv: D on truncation.

KM#	Date	Mintage	Fine	VF	XF	Unc
194	1830	.024	3.00	7.00	15.00	85.00
	1834	.076	3.00	7.00	12.00	60.00
	1835	.028	3.00	7.00	15.00	90.00

KM#	Date	Mintage	Fine	VF	XF	Unc
213	1842	.101	1.00	4.00	10.00	55.00
	1844	.052	1.00	4.00	10.00	65.00
	1845	.074	1.00	4.00	10.00	60.00
	1846	.090	1.00	4.00	10.00	60.00
	1847	.256	1.00	4.00	10.00	50.00
	1848	.089	1.00	4.00	10.00	60.00
	1849	.102	1.00	4.00	10.00	55.00
	1850	.074	1.00	4.00	10.00	60.00
	1851/0	.087	1.00	4.00	10.00	65.00
	1851	Inc. Ab.	1.00	4.00	10.00	60.00
	1852	.227	1.00	4.00	10.00	50.00

Friedrich I

KM#	Date	Mintage	Fine	VF	XF	Unc
230	1856	.195	1.00	4.00	10.00	45.00

KM#	Date	Mintage	Fine	VF	XF	Unc
241	1859	.219	1.00	2.00	10.00	35.00
	1860	.120	1.00	2.00	10.00	45.00
	1861	.109	1.00	2.00	10.00	45.00
	1862	.117	1.00	2.00	10.00	45.00
	1863	.298	1.00	2.00	10.00	35.00
	1864	.094	2.00	4.00	12.00	50.00
	1865	.349	1.00	2.00	10.00	35.00
	1866	.239	1.00	2.00	10.00	35.00
	1867	—	1.00	2.00	10.00	35.00
	1870	.038	5.00	10.00	25.00	125.00
	1871	—	1.75	6.00	15.00	35.00

EIN (1) KREUZER

COPPER

KM#	Date	Mintage	Fine	VF	XF	Unc
134	1803	.146	10.00	20.00	35.00	200.00
	1805	.096	10.00	20.00	35.00	200.00
	1806	—	—	—	Rare	—

KM#	Date	Mintage	Fine	VF	XF	Unc
141	1807	.096	6.00	14.00	30.00	125.00
	1808	1.704	3.00	7.00	15.00	65.00

KM#	Date	Mintage	Fine	VF	XF	Unc
147	1809	1.263	3.00	7.00	10.00	75.00
	1810	.639	3.00	7.00	10.00	75.00
	1811	.125	3.00	7.00	10.00	75.00

Obv: Crowned arms. Rev: Value, date within wreath.

KM#	Date	Mintage	Fine	VF	XF	Unc
154	1812	.285	3.00	10.00	50.00	125.00

Obv: Leg., crowned arms.
Rev. value: 1 KREUZ/ER, date.

KM#	Date	Mintage	Fine	VF	XF	Unc
157	1813	—	3.00	6.00	15.00	100.00

Rev. value: 1/KREUZER/1813 within circle of dots.

KM#	Date	Mintage	Fine	VF	XF	Unc
158	1813	.320	3.00	6.00	15.00	100.00

KM#	Date	Mintage	Fine	VF	XF	Unc
159	1813	—	3.00	6.00	15.00	100.00

KM#	Date	Mintage	Fine	VF	XF	Unc
160	1813	—	3.00	6.00	15.00	100.00

Obv: Date between dots.

KM#	Date	Mintage	Fine	VF	XF	Unc
166.1	1814	.489	3.00	6.00	15.00	100.00

Obv: Date between stars.

KM#	Date	Mintage	Fine	VF	XF	Unc
166.2	1814	Inc. Ab.	3.00	7.00	10.00	65.00
	1815	.490	3.00	7.00	10.00	65.00
	1816	.464	3.00	7.00	10.00	65.00
	1817	.327	3.00	7.00	10.00	65.00

Obv: Date between crosses.

KM#	Date	Mintage	Fine	VF	XF	Unc
166.3	1815	—	3.00	7.00	10.00	65.00

Rev. value: 1 KREU=/ZER

KM#	Date	Mintage	Fine	VF	XF	Unc
167	1814	—	3.00	7.00	10.00	65.00
	1815	.490	3.00	7.00	10.00	65.00
	1816	.464	3.00	7.00	10.00	65.00
	1817	Inc. Ab.	3.00	7.00	10.00	65.00
	1820	—	3.00	7.00	10.00	65.00

KM#	Date	Mintage	Fine	VF	XF	Unc
183	1821	.055	3.00	7.00	10.00	65.00
	1822	.197	3.00	7.00	10.00	65.00
	1823	.205	3.00	7.00	10.00	65.00
	1824	.253	3.00	7.00	10.00	65.00
	1825	.335	3.00	7.00	10.00	65.00
	1826	—	3.00	7.00	10.00	65.00

Ludwig I

KM#	Date	Mintage	Fine	VF	XF	Unc
189	1827	.515	2.00	7.00	10.00	50.00
	1827 D	Inc. Ab.	2.00	7.00	10.00	50.00
	1828	1.206	2.00	7.00	10.00	50.00
	1828 D	Inc. Ab.	2.00	7.00	10.00	50.00
	1829	.603	2.00	7.00	10.00	50.00

KM#	Date	Mintage	Fine	VF	XF	Unc
189	1829 D	Inc. Ab.	2.00	7.00	10.00	50.00
	1830	.149	2.00	7.00	10.00	50.00
	1830 D	Inc. Ab.	2.00	7.00	10.00	50.00

Leopold I
Obv. leg: Period after BADEN.

KM#	Date	Mintage	Fine	VF	XF	Unc
197.1	1831	.227	1.00	4.00	10.00	50.00

Obv. leg: W/o period after BADEN.

KM#	Date	Mintage	Fine	VF	XF	Unc
197.2	1831	Inc. Ab.	1.00	3.00	6.00	40.00
	1832	.172	1.00	3.00	6.00	40.00
	1833	.181	1.00	3.00	6.00	40.00
	1834	.250	1.00	3.00	6.00	40.00
	1835	.294	1.00	3.00	6.00	40.00
	1836	.163	1.00	3.00	6.00	40.00
	1837	—	1.00	3.00	6.00	40.00

Obv: W/o D on truncation.

KM#	Date	Mintage	Fine	VF	XF	Unc
203	1836	.321	1.00	3.00	6.00	40:00
	1837	Inc. Ab.	1.00	3.00	6.00	40.00
	1838	.642	1.00	3.00	6.00	40.00
	1839	.254	1.00	3.00	6.00	40.00
	1840	.573	1.00	3.00	6.00	40.00
	1841	.423	1.00	3.00	6.00	40.00
	1842	.865	1.00	3.00	6.00	40.00
	1843	.527	1.00	3.00	6.00	40.00
	1844	.663	1.00	3.00	6.00	40.00
	1845	1.442	1.00	3.00	6.00	40.00

Erection of Carl Friedrich's Statue

KM#	Date	Mintage	Fine	VF	XF	Unc
216	1844	.054	15.00	25.00	50.00	125.00

KM#	Date	Mintage	Fine	VF	XF	Unc
218	1845	Inc. Ab.	1.00	3.00	7.00	40.00
	1846	.452	1.00	3.00	7.00	40.00
	1847	.639	1.00	3.00	7.00	40.00
	1848	.232	1.00	3.00	7.00	40.00
	1849	.872	1.00	3.00	7.00	40.00
	1850	.238	1.00	3.00	7.00	40.00
	1851	1.208	1.00	3.00	7.00	40.00
	1852	.821	1.00	3.00	7.00	40.00

Friedrich I
Titles as Prince Regent

KM#	Date	Mintage	Fine	VF	XF	Unc
231	1856	.707	20.00	35.00	65.00	140.00

Titles as Grand Duke

KM#	Date	Mintage	Fine	VF	XF	Unc
232	1856	.660	2.00	4.00	10.00	40.00

Birth of Heir

KM#	Date	Mintage	Fine	VF	XF	Unc
238	1857	—	3.00	6.00	15.00	60.00

KM#	Date	Mintage	Fine	VF	XF	Unc
242	1859	.898	1.00	2.00	6.00	25.00
	1860	.655	1.00	2.00	6.00	25.00
	1861	.726	1.00	2.00	6.00	25.00
	1862	.623	1.00	2.00	6.00	25.00
	1863	.765	1.00	2.00	6.00	25.00
	1864	.724	1.00	2.00	6.00	25.00
	1865	.778	1.00	2.00	6.00	25.00
	1866	.732	1.00	2.00	6.00	25.00
	1867	.698	1.00	2.00	6.00	25.00
	1868	.885	1.00	2.00	6.00	25.00
	1869	.858	1.00	2.00	6.00	25.00
	1870	.918	1.00	2.00	6.00	25.00
	1871	—	1.00	2.00	6.00	25.00

Leopold Memorial

KM#	Date	Mintage	Fine	VF	XF	Unc
244	1861	—	18.00	30.00	50.00	75.00

50th Anniversary Baden's Constitution

KM#	Date	Mintage	Fine	VF	XF	Unc
250	1868	.025	18.00	30.00	50.00	75.00

Church at Seckenheim

KM#	Date	Mintage	Fine	VF	XF	Unc
251	1869	1,000	45.00	75.00	125.00	200.00

Victory in War with France

KM#	Date	Mintage	Fine	VF	XF	Unc
252	1871	—	2.00	4.00	8.00	25.00

Obv: SCHEIDE MUNZE below shield.

KM#	Date	Mintage	Fine	VF	XF	Unc
253	1871	—	32.50	45.00	60.00	80.00

Buehl Commemorating Victory Over France

KM#	Date	Mintage	Fine	VF	XF	Unc
254	1871	—	45.00	75.00	125.00	200.00

Karlsruhe Commemorating Victory Over France
Obv: Arms. Rev: Legend.

KM#	Date	Mintage	Fine	VF	XF	Unc
255	1871	—	18.00	30.00	45.00	75.00

Offenburg Commemorating Victory Over France

KM#	Date	Mintage	Fine	VF	XF	Unc
256	1871	—	35.00	60.00	90.00	150.00

DREI (3) KREUZER

1.4230 g, .313 SILVER, .0143 oz ASW

KM#	Date	Mintage	Fine	VF	XF	Unc
135	1803	.189	10.00	35.00	125.00	350.00
	1805	.445	10.00	25.00	75.00	200.00
	1806	.126	10.00	25.00	100.00	300.00

Obv: Lion in shield faces left.

KM#	Date	Mintage	Fine	VF	XF	Unc
144	1808	.410	10.00	25.00	100.00	300.00

Obv: Lion in shield faces right.

KM#	Date	Mintage	Fine	VF	XF	Unc
148	1809	.208	8.00	20.00	65.00	300.00
	1810	.262	8.00	20.00	65.00	300.00
	1811	.316	8.00	20.00	65.00	300.00

KM#	Date	Mintage	Fine	VF	XF	Unc
155.1	1812	.734	2.00	6.00	15.00	65.00
	1813	.273	2.00	6.00	15.00	65.00

Rev: Z backwards in KREUZER

KM#	Date	Mintage	Fine	VF	XF	Unc
155.2	1812	Inc. Ab.	7.50	18.50	50.00	125.00

1.2470 g, .313 SILVER, .0125 oz ASW
Rev. value: 3 KREUZER within branches

KM#	Date	Mintage	Fine	VF	XF	Unc
161	1813	—	2.00	7.00	15.00	65.00
	1814	.280	2.00	7.00	15.00	65.00
	1815	.214	2.00	7.00	15.00	65.00
	1816	.243	2.00	7.00	15.00	65.00

Rev. value: 3 KREU=/ZER.

KM#	Date	Mintage	Fine	VF	XF	Unc
172	1817	.371	2.00	7.00	15.00	65.00
	1818	.593	2.00	7.00	15.00	65.00
	1819	.815	2.00	7.00	15.00	65.00
	1820	Inc. Ab.	2.00	7.00	15.00	65.00

Obv: Larger shield, w/o drape.

KM#	Date	Mintage	Fine	VF	XF	Unc
178	1820	Inc. Ab.	2.00	7.00	15.00	65.00
	1821	.065	2.00	7.00	15.00	65.00
	1824	.096	2.00	7.00	15.00	65.00
	1825	.073	2.00	7.00	15.00	65.00

1.1400 g, .375 SILVER, .0134 oz ASW
Rev. value: DREI KREUZER

KM#	Date	Mintage	Fine	VF	XF	Unc
191	1829	1.277	2.00	7.00	10.00	40.00
	1830	1.009	2.00	7.00	10.00	40.00

Rev. value: 3 KREUZER

KM#	Date	Mintage	Fine	VF	XF	Unc
199	1832	.729	2.00	7.00	10.00	50.00
	1833	.846	2.00	7.00	10.00	50.00
	1834	.549	2.00	7.00	10.00	50.00
	1835	.476	1.00	4.00	10.00	50.00
	1836	.723	1.00	4.00	10.00	50.00
	1837	—	1.00	4.00	10.00	50.00

1.2990 g, .333 SILVER, .0139 oz ASW

KM#	Date	Mintage	Fine	VF	XF	Unc
211	1841	.328	1.00	4.00	10.00	40.00
	1842	.420	1.00	4.00	10.00	40.00
	1843	.168	1.00	4.00	10.00	40.00
	1844	.361	1.00	4.00	10.00	40.00
	1845	.385	1.00	4.00	10.00	40.00
	1846	.219	1.00	4.00	10.00	40.00
	1847	.392	1.00	4.00	10.00	40.00
	1848	.195	1.00	4.00	10.00	40.00
	1849	.397	1.00	4.00	10.00	40.00

KM#	Date	Mintage	Fine	VF	XF	Unc
211	1850	.212	1.00	4.00	10.00	40.00
	1851	.196	1.00	4.00	10.00	40.00
	1852	.192	1.00	4.00	10.00	40.00

KM#	Date	Mintage	Fine	VF	XF	Unc
226	1853	—	3.00	8.00	15.00	60.00
	1854	—	3.00	8.00	15.00	60.00
	1855	—	3.00	8.00	15.00	60.00
	1856	—	3.00	8.00	15.00	60.00

1.2320 g, .350 SILVER, .0138 oz ASW
Obv: SCHEIDE/MUNZE below arms.

KM#	Date	Mintage	Fine	VF	XF	Unc
246	1866	.240	1.00	3.00	7.00	40.00
	1867	.389	1.00	3.00	7.00	40.00
	1868	.315	1.00	3.00	7.00	40.00
	1869	.285	1.00	3.00	7.00	40.00
	1870	.259	1.00	3.00	7.00	40.00
	1871	—	1.00	3.00	7.00	40.00

6 KREUZER

2.3530 g, .375 SILVER, .0283 oz ASW

KM#	Date	Mintage	Fine	VF	XF	Unc
137	1804	.055	15.00	50.00	150.00	400.00

KM#	Date	Mintage	Fine	VF	XF	Unc
138	1804	Inc. Ab.	15.00	40.00	125.00	300.00
	1805	.461	15.00	40.00	125.00	300.00

Obv: Lion in arms facing left.

KM#	Date	Mintage	Fine	VF	XF	Unc
140	1806	.131	7.00	20.00	60.00	250.00
	1807	.371	7.00	20.00	60.00	250.00
	1808	1.118	6.00	15.00	45.00	200.00

Obv: Lion in arms facing right.

KM#	Date	Mintage	Fine	VF	XF	Unc
149	1809	.539	10.00	25.00	75.00	200.00

Obv. leg: G.H.BADEN. . . .

KM#	Date	Mintage	Fine	VF	XF	Unc
156	1812	.339	5.00	10.00	35.00	125.00
	1813	.559	5.00	10.00	35.00	125.00

Obv. leg: G H BADEN. . . . .
Rev: VI KREUTZER, date within wreath.

KM#	Date	Mintage	Fine	VF	XF	Unc
162	1813	Inc. Ab.	5.00	10.00	45.00	100.00

2.2270 g, .375 SILVER, .0268 oz ASW
Rev. value: 6 KREUT=/ZER within olive branches.

KM#	Date	Mintage	Fine	VF	XF	Unc
168	1814	.115	5.00	10.00	50.00	125.00
	1815	.244	5.00	10.00	50.00	125.00
	1816	1.603	5.00	10.00	50.00	125.00
	1817	.563	5.00	10.00	50.00	125.00

Rev. value: 6 KREU=/ZER within olive branches.

KM#	Date	Mintage	Fine	VF	XF	Unc
170	1816	Inc. Ab.	4.00	10.00	25.00	75.00
	1817	Inc. Ab.	4.00	10.00	25.00	75.00
	1818	.112	4.00	10.00	25.00	75.00

Ludwig I

KM#	Date	Mintage	Fine	VF	XF	Unc
173	1819	.390	5.00	15.00	40.00	150.00

Obv: Larger head right, hair combed forward.
Rev: Crowned shield

KM#	Date	Mintage	Fine	VF	XF	Unc
179	1820	.095	5.00	15.00	40.00	150.00

Rev: Crowned shield within branches.

KM#	Date	Mintage	Fine	VF	XF	Unc
180	1820	Inc. Ab.	5.00	15.00	30.00	125.00
	1821	.186	5.00	15.00	30.00	125.00

Leopold I
Obv: D on truncation.

KM#	Date	Mintage	Fine	VF	XF	Unc
198.1	1831	.862	3.00	7.00	15.00	75.00
	1832	.929	3.00	7.00	15.00	75.00
	1833	1.003	3.00	7.00	15.00	75.00
	1834	.898	3.00	7.00	15.00	75.00
	1835	1.025	3.00	7.00	15.00	75.00
	1836	.917	3.00	7.00	15.00	75.00

Obv: W/o D on truncation.

KM#	Date	Mintage	Fine	VF	XF	Unc
198.2	1835	Inc. Ab.	3.00	8.00	20.00	125.00
	1837	.415	3.00	8.00	20.00	125.00

2.5980 g, .333 SILVER, .0278 oz ASW

KM#	Date	Mintage	Fine	VF	XF	Unc
210	1840	1.317	3.00	5.00	10.00	50.00
	1841	.168	3.00	5.00	10.00	50.00
	1842	.612	3.00	5.00	10.00	50.00
	1843	.615	3.00	5.00	10.00	50.00
	1844	.757	3.00	5.00	10.00	50.00
	1845	.262	3.00	5.00	10.00	50.00
	1846	.368	3.00	5.00	10.00	50.00
	1847	.857	3.00	5.00	10.00	50.00
	1848	.377	3.00	5.00	10.00	50.00
	1849	.371	3.00	5.00	10.00	50.00
	1850	.200	3.00	5.00	10.00	50.00

KM#	Date	Mintage	Fine	VF	XF	Unc
228	1855	—	5.00	10.00	25.00	100.00
	1856	—	5.00	10.00	25.00	100.00

ZEHN (10) KREUZER

3.8980 g, .500 SILVER, .0626 oz ASW
Carl Friedrich

KM#	Date	Mintage	Fine	VF	XF	Unc
145	1808	.068	50.00	175.00	250.00	450.00

Obv: Bust w/short hair.

KM#	Date	Mintage	Fine	VF	XF	Unc
150	1809	Inc. Ab.	15.00	25.00	75.00	250.00

2.7840 g, .500 SILVER, .0447 oz ASW
Ludwig I

KM#	Date	Mintage	Fine	VF	XF	Unc
192	1829	.527	5.00	10.00	30.00	125.00
	1830	.510	5.00	10.00	30.00	125.00

20 KREUZER

6.6820 g, .583 SILVER, .1252 oz ASW
Obv: Carl Fridrich w/long hair. Rev: Lion in shield facing left.

KM#	Date	Mintage	Fine	VF	XF	Unc
142	1807 B	.015	65.00	140.00	275.00	600.00

Rev: Lion in shield facing right.

KM#	Date	Mintage	Fine	VF	XF	Unc
146	1808	—	45.00	100.00	180.00	350.00
	1808 B	—	60.00	150.00	250.00	500.00

Obv: Bust w/short hair.

KM#	Date	Mintage	Fine	VF	XF	Unc
151	1809	—	50.00	100.00	200.00	350.00
	1810	.170	20.00	50.00	100.00	225.00

1/2 GULDEN

5.3030 g, .900 SILVER, .1534 oz ASW
Leopold I

KM#	Date	Mintage	Fine	VF	XF	Unc
209	1838	1.044	12.50	30.00	45.00	125.00
	1839	.500	15.00	35.00	60.00	140.00
	1840	.511	15.00	35.00	60.00	140.00
	1841	.417	15.00	35.00	60.00	140.00
	1842	.362	15.00	35.00	60.00	140.00
	1843	.469	15.00	35.00	60.00	140.00
	1844	.274	15.00	35.00	60.00	140.00
	1845	.322	15.00	35.00	60.00	140.00
	1846	.118	15.00	35.00	60.00	140.00

Obv: W/o D on truncation, larger head.

KM#	Date	Mintage	Fine	VF	XF	Unc
221	1846	Inc. Ab.	15.00	45.00	75.00	180.00
	1847	.537	12.50	40.00	65.00	150.00
	1848	.332	12.50	40.00	65.00	150.00
	1849	.069	15.00	45.00	75.00	180.00

KM#	Date	Mintage	Fine	VF	XF	Unc
221	1850	—	15.00	45.00	75.00	180.00
	1851	.122	15.00	45.00	75.00	180.00
	1852	.026	15.00	45.00	75.00	180.00

Obv: Head of Friedrich I right.

KM#	Date	Mintage	Fine	VF	XF	Unc
233	1856	—	15.00	45.00	75.00	180.00

Obv: VOIGT below head.

KM#	Date	Mintage	Fine	VF	XF	Unc
234	1856	.150	25.00	50.00	100.00	250.00
	1860	.342	25.00	50.00	100.00	250.00

5.2910 g, .900 SILVER, .0850 oz ASW

KM#	Date	Mintage	Fine	VF	XF	Unc
243	1860	Inc. Ab.	25.00	50.00	75.00	200.00
	1861	.264	25.00	50.00	75.00	200.00
	1862	.233	25.00	50.00	75.00	200.00
	1863	.227	25.00	50.00	75.00	200.00
	1864	.117	25.00	50.00	75.00	200.00
	1865	.184	25.00	50.00	75.00	200.00

KM#	Date	Mintage	Fine	VF	XF	Unc
248	1867	.155	25.00	50.00	75.00	200.00
	1868	.070	25.00	50.00	75.00	200.00
	1869	.073	25.00	50.00	75.00	200.00

EIN (1) GULDEN

12.7270 g, .750 SILVER, .3069 oz ASW
Obv: Ludwig I w/short hair.

KM#	Date	Mintage	Fine	VF	XF	Unc
184	1821	.090	150.00	300.00	600.00	1000.
	1822	.045	150.00	300.00	600.00	1000.
	1823	.039	150.00	300.00	600.00	1000.
	1824	.050	150.00	300.00	600.00	1000.
	1825	.022	150.00	300.00	600.00	1000.

Obv: Ludwig I w/curly hair.

KM#	Date	Mintage	Fine	VF	XF	Unc
187	1826	.094	700.00	1200.	1800.	3000.

10.6060 g, .900 SILVER, .3069 oz ASW
Obv: Leopold I w/o period after BADEN.

KM#	Date	Mintage	Fine	VF	XF	Unc
207	1837	.629	25.00	50.00	100.00	250.00
	1838	.210	25.00	50.00	100.00	250.00
	1839	.485	25.00	50.00	100.00	250.00
	1840	.468	25.00	50.00	100.00	250.00
	1841	.387	25.00	50.00	100.00	250.00

Obv: Period after BADEN.

KM#	Date	Mintage	Fine	VF	XF	Unc
214	1842	.390	25.00	50.00	100.00	250.00
	1843	.444	25.00	50.00	100.00	250.00
	1844	.585	25.00	50.00	100.00	250.00
	1845	.439	25.00	50.00	100.00	250.00

KM#	Date	Mintage	Fine	VF	XF	Unc
219	1845	Inc. Ab.	25.00	50.00	100.00	250.00
	1846	—	25.00	50.00	100.00	250.00
	1847	.397	25.00	50.00	100.00	250.00
	1848	.116	25.00	50.00	100.00	250.00
	1849	.021	25.00	50.00	100.00	250.00
	1850	8,652	25.00	50.00	100.00	250.00
	1851	.089	25.00	50.00	100.00	250.00
	1852	.033	75.00	125.00	200.00	300.00

Blessing on the Baden Mines

KM#	Date	Mintage	Fine	VF	XF	Unc
224	1852	Inc. Ab.	75.00	125.00	200.00	300.00

10.5820 g, .900 SILVER, .3062 oz ASW
Obv. leg: FRIEDRICH PRINZ. . . . .

KM#	Date	Mintage	Fine	VF	XF	Unc
235	1856	.149	100.00	225.00	375.00	675.00

Obv. leg: FRIEDRICH GROSHERZOG. . . . .
Rev: Similar to KM#235.

KM#	Date	Mintage	Fine	VF	XF	Unc
236	1856	.342	50.00	75.00	100.00	250.00
	1859	.195	50.00	75.00	100.00	250.00
	1860	.044	50.00	75.00	100.00	250.00

Mint Visit

KM#	Date	Mintage	Fine	VF	XF	Unc
239	1857	776 pcs.	225.00	375.00	500.00	900.00

First Shooting Festival at Mannheim

KM#	Date	Mintage	Fine	VF	XF	Unc
247	1863	.012	60.00	90.00	125.00	200.00

Second Shooting Festival at Karlsruhe

KM#	Date	Mintage	Fine	VF	XF	Unc
249	1867	.014	45.00	90.00	175.00	250.00

ZWEI (2) GULDEN

25.4540 g, .750 SILVER, .6138 oz ASW
Ludwig I

KM#	Date	Mintage	Fine	VF	XF	Unc
185	1821	.030	150.00	250.00	500.00	1500.
	1822	.020	150.00	250.00	500.00	1500.
	1823	7,040	150.00	250.00	500.00	1500.
	1824	.017	150.00	250.00	500.00	1500.
	1825	6,642	150.00	250.00	500.00	1500.

21.2100 g, .900 SILVER, .6138 oz ASW
Leopold I

KM#	Date	Mintage	Fine	VF	XF	Unc
222	1846	.592	50.00	75.00	150.00	400.00
	1847	.232	50.00	75.00	150.00	400.00
	1848	.273	50.00	75.00	150.00	400.00
	1849	.041	50.00	100.00	200.00	500.00
	1850	.140	50.00	75.00	150.00	400.00
	1851	.124	50.00	75.00	150.00	400.00
	1852	.142	50.00	75.00	150.00	400.00

Friedrich I
Rev: Similar to KM#222.

KM#	Date	Mintage	Fine	VF	XF	Unc
237	1856	.084	125.00	250.00	400.00	750.00

5 GULDEN

3.4390 g, .903 GOLD, .0998 oz AGW
Ludwig I

KM#	Date	Mintage	Fine	VF	XF	Unc
176.1	1819 PH	3,000	500.00	1000.	1500.	2000.

Obv: W/o engravers initials below head.

KM#	Date	Mintage	Fine	VF	XF	Unc
176.2	1819	695 pcs.	650.00	1000.	1500.	2000.
	1821	465 pcs.	675.00	1125.	1750.	2400.
	1822	1,718	525.00	875.00	1500.	2000.
	1823	1,854	525.00	875.00	1500.	2000.
	1824	2,763	450.00	750.00	1350.	1750.
	1825	1,508	525.00	875.00	1500.	2000.
	1826	887 pcs.	600.00	1000.	1650.	2250.

Obv: Curly hair.

KM#	Date	Mintage	Fine	VF	XF	Unc
190	1827	2,877	450.00	850.00	2250.	3000.
	1828	2,317	450.00	850.00	2250.	3000.

10 GULDEN

6.8780 g, .903 GOLD, .1997 oz AGW
Ludwig I

KM#	Date	Mintage	Fine	VF	XF	Unc
177.1	1819 PH	4,332	950.00	1500.	2000.	3250.

Obv: W/o engravers initials below head.

KM#	Date	Mintage	Fine	VF	XF	Unc
177.2	1821	812 pcs.	1150.	1800.	2500.	3750.
	1823	373 pcs.	1250.	2000.	2750.	4000.
	1824	328 pcs.	1400.	2200.	3000.	4250.
	1825	Inc. Ab.	1400.	2200.	3000.	4250.

EIN (1) THALER

28.0600 g, .833 SILVER, .7515 oz ASW
Carl Friedrich

KM#	Date	Mintage	Fine	VF	XF	Unc
136	1803 FE HB	675 pcs.	500.00	900.00	1750.	4000.

KM#	Date	Mintage	Fine	VF	XF	Unc
152	1809 B E	6,219	300.00	550.00	1100.	2200.
	1810 B	2,815	250.00	450.00	900.00	2000.
	1811 B E	3,885	225.00	400.00	850.00	1800.

(Krone)

29.5160 g, .871 SILVER, .8266 oz ASW

KM#	Date	Mintage	Fine	VF	XF	Unc
163	1813 D	—	150.00	275.00	600.00	1200.
	1814 D	.036	150.00	275.00	600.00	1200.

Rev: W/o mintmasters initial.

KM#	Date	Mintage	Fine	VF	XF	Unc
169	1814	Inc. Ab.	150.00	225.00	475.00	1000.
	1815	.038	125.00	185.00	375.00	800.00
	1816	.036	100.00	165.00	325.00	700.00
	1817	.052	100.00	165.00	325.00	700.00
	1818	.039	100.00	165.00	365.00	800.00
	1819	—	125.00	200.00	500.00	1200.

Ludwig I
Obv: WD monogram below bust.

KM#	Date	Mintage	Fine	VF	XF	Unc
175.1	1819	—	175.00	325.00	800.00	1750.

Obv: DOELL on truncation.

KM#	Date	Mintage	Fine	VF	XF	Unc
175.2	1819	—	150.00	325.00	700.00	1500.
	1820	.038	150.00	350.00	800.00	1600.
	1821	.019	150.00	375.00	875.00	1800.

18.1480 g, .875 SILVER, .5105 oz ASW

KM#	Date	Mintage	Fine	VF	XF	Unc
193	1829	.168	50.00	100.00	175.00	400.00
	1830	.101	50.00	100.00	175.00	400.00

Leopold
Obv. leg: W/o dot after BADEN.

KM#	Date	Mintage	Fine	VF	XF	Unc
195.1	1830	.238	85.00	175.00	250.00	650.00
	1831	.168	85.00	115.00	200.00	450.00
	1832	.176	85.00	115.00	200.00	450.00
	1832 star	I.A.	85.00	125.00	200.00	475.00

Obv. leg: Dot after BADEN.

KM#	Date	Mintage	Fine	VF	XF	Unc
195.2	1832 star	I.A.	85.00	125.00	200.00	475.00
	1833 star	.115	85.00	125.00	200.00	475.00
	1833	Inc. ab.	75.00	100.00	200.00	450.00
	1834	.036	75.00	100.00	200.00	450.00
	1835	.075	75.00	100.00	200.00	450.00
	1836 lg.6	.085	85.00	135.00	200.00	475.00
	1837	—	75.00	100.00	200.00	450.00

Rev. leg: Hyphen between KRONEN-THALER.

KM#	Date	Mintage	Fine	VF	XF	Unc
195.3	1834	Inc. Ab.	75.00	100.00	200.00	450.00
	1836	Inc. Ab.	100.00	125.00	225.00	700.00

Mint Visit

KM#	Date	Mintage	Fine	VF	XF	Unc
200	1832	—	600.00	850.00	1100.	2000.

Blessings on the Baden Mines

KM#	Date	Mintage	Fine	VF	XF	Unc
202	1834	6,517	200.00	300.00	500.00	1300.

KM#	Date	Mintage	Fine	VF	XF	Unc
204	1836	8,250	175.00	250.00	500.00	1150.

Mule. Obv: KM#195.2 rev. Rev: KM#204.

KM#	Date	Mintage	Fine	VF	XF	Unc
205	1836	—	—	—	Rare	—

Rev: Arms of Ten Customs Union States between 10 caduceus.

KM#	Date	Mintage	Fine	VF	XF	Unc
206	1836	.018	65.00	90.00	150.00	300.00

(Vereins)

18.5190 g, .900 SILVER, .5359 oz ASW
Friedrich I

KM#	Date	Mintage	Fine	VF	XF	Unc
240	1857	.019	50.00	80.00	150.00	350.00
	1858	.232	35.00	65.00	125.00	225.00
	1859	.289	35.00	65.00	125.00	225.00
	1860	.174	35.00	65.00	125.00	225.00
	1861	.358	35.00	65.00	125.00	225.00
	1862	.400	35.00	65.00	125.00	225.00
	1863	.326	35.00	65.00	125.00	225.00
	1864	.322	35.00	65.00	125.00	225.00
	1865	.265	35.00	65.00	125.00	225.00

KM#	Date	Mintage	Fine	VF	XF	Unc
245	1865	Inc. Ab.	35.00	65.00	135.00	275.00
	1866	.149	35.00	65.00	135.00	275.00
	1867	.096	35.00	65.00	135.00	275.00
	1868	.102	35.00	65.00	135.00	275.00
	1869	.062	35.00	65.00	135.00	275.00
	1870	.022	35.00	65.00	135.00	275.00
	1871	—	35.00	65.00	135.00	275.00

2 THALER

(3-1/2 Gulden)

37.1200 g, .900 SILVER, 1.0743 oz ASW
Leopold I

KM#	Date	Mintage	Fine	VF	XF	Unc
212	1841	.231	125.00	175.00	400.00	1000.
	1842	.033	150.00	200.00	550.00	1150.
	1843	.035	150.00	200.00	600.00	1250.

Monument of Carl Friedrich

KM#	Date	Mintage	Fine	VF	XF	Unc
217.1	1844	4,323	125.00	200.00	350.00	750.00

Plain edge.

KM#	Date	Mintage	Fine	VF	XF	Unc
217.2	1844	—	—	—	Rare	—

KM#	Date	Mintage	Fine	VF	XF	Unc
220	1845	.057	150.00	200.00	425.00	800.00
	1846	1,130	300.00	400.00	900.00	1500.
	1847	.031	150.00	200.00	400.00	700.00
	1852	.060	135.00	185.00	350.00	625.00

Friedrich I
Obv: BALBACH below truncation.

KM#	Date	Mintage	Fine	VF	XF	Unc
225	1852	9 pcs.	—	—	Rare	—
	1854	.085	450.00	800.00	2000.	4000.

Obv: Modified head, w/o engravers name below truncation.

KM#	Date	Mintage	Fine	VF	XF	Unc
229	1855	2 pcs.	—	—	Rare	—

FUNF (5) THALER

(500 Kreuzer)

5.7320 g, .903 GOLD, .1664 oz AGW
Ludwig I

KM#	Date	Mintage	Fine	VF	XF	Unc
196	1830	1,788	800.00	1250.	2000.	2500.

MONETARY REFORM

2 MARK

11.1110 g, .900 SILVER, .3215 oz ASW
Friedrich I

KM#	Date	Mintage	Fine	VF	XF	Unc
265	1876G	1.739	35.00	100.00	800.00	1600.
	1877G	.764	35.00	100.00	700.00	1800.
	1880G	.074	60.00	160.00	900.00	2000.
	1883G	.045	65.00	160.00	750.00	2000.
	1888G	.075	70.00	140.00	1000.	2000.

KM#	Date	Mintage	Fine	VF	XF	Unc
269	1892G	.107	35.00	90.00	320.00	600.00
	1894G	.107	35.00	90.00	320.00	600.00
	1896G	.214	25.00	75.00	320.00	700.00
	1898G	.087	30.00	90.00	325.00	1100.
	1899G	.327	30.00	70.00	300.00	650.00
	1900G	.222	25.00	75.00	300.00	600.00
	1901G	.451	25.00	75.00	250.00	500.00
	1902G	5,368	250.00	750.00	1400.	2500.
	1902G	—	—	—	Proof	2250.

50th Year of Reign

KM#	Date	Mintage	Fine	VF	XF	Unc
271	1902G	.375	15.00	25.00	35.00	45.00

KM#	Date	Mintage	Fine	VF	XF	Unc
272	1902G	.198	25.00	60.00	120.00	300.00

KM#	Date	Mintage	Fine	VF	XF	Unc
272	1903G	.494	20.00	45.00	110.00	180.00
	1904G	1.122	20.00	40.00	70.00	140.00
	1905G	.610	20.00	45.00	60.00	160.00
	1906G	.108	45.00	90.00	180.00	350.00
	1907G	.913	20.00	40.00	55.00	120.00

Golden Wedding Anniversary

KM#	Date	Mintage	Fine	VF	XF	Unc
276	1906	.350	15.00	30.00	35.00	50.00
	1906	—	—		Matte Proof	—

Death of Friedrich

KM#	Date	Mintage	Fine	VF	XF	Unc
278	1907	.350	20.00	40.00	50.00	75.00
	1907	—		—	Proof	150.00

Friedrich II

KM#	Date	Mintage	Fine	VF	XF	Unc
283	1911G	.080	125.00	300.00	425.00	750.00
	1913G	.140	100.00	225.00	375.00	650.00
	Common date		—	—	Proof	1000.

3 MARK

16.6670 g, .900 SILVER, .4823 oz ASW
Friedrich II

KM#	Date	Mintage	Fine	VF	XF	Unc
280	1908G	.300	10.00	20.00	30.00	65.00
	1909G	.760	10.00	20.00	30.00	65.00
	1910G	.670	10.00	20.00	30.00	65.00
	1911G	.380	10.00	20.00	35.00	60.00
	1912G	.840	10.00	20.00	30.00	50.00
	1914G	.410	10.00	20.00	25.00	45.00
	1915G	.170	20.00	60.00	80.00	125.00
	Common date		—	—	Proof	175.00

5 MARK

27.7770 g, .900 SILVER, .8038 oz ASW
Friedrich I

KM#	Date	Mintage	Fine	VF	XF	Unc
263.1	1875G	.314	35.00	70.00	800.00	3250.
	1876G	.473	35.00	70.00	950.00	2750.
	1888G	.030	300.00	625.00	1650.	4500.

Obv.leg: Inverted V for 'A' of BADEN.

KM#	Date	Mintage	Fine	VF	XF	Unc
263.2	1875G	Inc. Ab.	35.00	70.00	700.00	2400.

KM#	Date	Mintage	Fine	VF	XF	Unc
263.2	1876G	Inc. Ab.	35.00	70.00	1000.	2500.
	1888G	Inc. Ab.	45.00	100.00	650.00	2000.
	Common date		—	—	Proof	4500.

1.9910 g, .900 GOLD, .0576 oz AGW

KM#	Date	Mintage	Fine	VF	XF	Unc
266	1877G	.345	150.00	250.00	400.00	600.00
	1877G	—	—	—	Proof	1500.

27.7770 g, .900 SILVER, .8038 oz ASW

KM#	Date	Mintage	Fine	VF	XF	Unc
268	1891 inverted V for 'A' in BADEN					
		.043	225.00	450.00	1500.	6000.
	1891 normal 'A' in BADEN					
		Inc. Ab.	30.00	90.00	375.00	1250.
	1893	.043	25.00	65.00	325.00	1000.
	1894	.061	25.00	60.00	225.00	950.00
	1895	.073	25.00	60.00	250.00	950.00
	1898	.131	25.00	60.00	250.00	1000.
	1899	.061	27.50	70.00	375.00	750.00
	1900	.128	27.50	70.00	375.00	900.00
	1901	.128	25.00	70.00	275.00	900.00
	1902	.043	35.00	85.00	250.00	900.00
	Common date		—	—	Proof	900.00

50th Year of Reign

KM#	Date	Mintage	Fine	VF	XF	Unc
273	1902G	.050	40.00	90.00	150.00	200.00
	1902G	—	—	—	Proof	625.00

KM#	Date	Mintage	Fine	VF	XF	Unc
274	1902G	.128	35.00	65.00	225.00	475.00
	1903G	.439	20.00	45.00	175.00	450.00
	1904G	.238	20.00	45.00	175.00	450.00
	1907G	.244	20.00	45.00	175.00	450.00
	Common date		—	—	Proof	400.00

Golden Wedding Anniversary

KM#	Date	Mintage	Fine	VF	XF	Unc
277	1906	.060	50.00	100.00	150.00	200.00
	1906	—	—	—	Proof	275.00

Death of Friedrich

KM#	Date	Mintage	Fine	VF	XF	Unc
279	1907	.060	65.00	125.00	160.00	225.00
	1907	—	—	—	Proof	275.00

Friedrich II

KM#	Date	Mintage	Fine	VF	XF	Unc
281	1908G	.180	35.00	55.00	150.00	600.00
	1913G	.240	30.00	50.00	140.00	425.00
	Common date		—	—	Proof	525.00

10 MARK

3.9820 g, .900 GOLD, .1152 oz AGW
Friedrich I
Rev: Type I.

KM#	Date	Mintage	Fine	VF	XF	Unc
260	1872G	.273	65.00	125.00	200.00	325.00
	1873G	.466	65.00	125.00	200.00	325.00
	1873G	—	—	—	Proof	1750.

Rev: Type II.

KM#	Date	Mintage	Fine	VF	XF	Unc
264	1875G	.339	75.00	150.00	200.00	325.00
	1876G	1.396	65.00	125.00	225.00	350.00
	1877G	.159	65.00	125.00	200.00	325.00
	1878G	.236	65.00	125.00	200.00	325.00
	1879G	.098	100.00	200.00	275.00	400.00
	1880G	1,169	6000.	10,000.	15,000.	30,000.
	1881G	.196	75.00	150.00	250.00	375.00
	1888G	.122	65.00	125.00	200.00	325.00
	Common date		—	—	Proof	1300.

Rev: Type III.

KM#	Date	Mintage	Fine	VF	XF	Unc
267	1890G	.073	125.00	225.00	325.00	500.00
	1891G	.110	125.00	175.00	250.00	350.00
	1893G	.183	125.00	175.00	250.00	325.00
	1896G	.052	125.00	200.00	300.00	450.00
	1897G	.070	125.00	225.00	275.00	400.00
	1898G	.256	115.00	165.00	250.00	325.00
	1900G	.031	150.00	400.00	500.00	800.00
	1901G	.091	125.00	165.00	225.00	325.00
	Common date		—	—	Proof	1300.

KM#	Date	Mintage	Fine	VF	XF	Unc
275	1902G	.030	175.00	300.00	450.00	650.00
	1903G	.110	125.00	200.00	250.00	350.00
	1904G	.150	110.00	150.00	225.00	325.00
	1905G	.096	125.00	200.00	250.00	350.00
	1906G	.120	125.00	150.00	225.00	325.00
	1907G	.120	110.00	150.00	225.00	325.00
	Common date		—	—	Proof	1000.

Friedrich II

KM#	Date	Mintage	Fine	VF	XF	Unc
282	1909G	.086	225.00	500.00	650.00	850.00
	1910G	.061	225.00	500.00	650.00	850.00
	1911G	.029	2000.	4500.	6500.	8000.
	1912G	.026	700.00	1200.	2200.	3000.
	1913G	.042	500.00	800.00	1100.	1900.
	Common date		—	—	Proof	2000.

20 MARK

7.9650 g, .900 GOLD, .2304 oz AGW
Friedrich I
Rev: Type I.

KM#	Date	Mintage	Fine	VF	XF	Unc
261	1872G	.398	125.00	150.00	225.00	325.00
	1873G	.517	125.00	160.00	300.00	350.00
	Common date		—	—	Proof	2250.

Rev: Type II.

KM#	Date	Mintage	Fine	VF	XF	Unc
262	1874G	.155	225.00	400.00	600.00	900.00
	1874G	—	—	—	Proof	3000.

Rev: Type III.

KM#	Date	Mintage	Fine	VF	XF	Unc
270	1894G sm. 4					
		.400	135.00	160.00	250.00	400.00
	1894G lg.4	.400	135.00	160.00	250.00	400.00
	1895G	.100	135.00	225.00	300.00	450.00
	Common date		—	—	Proof	1300.

Friedrich II

KM#	Date	Mintage	Fine	VF	XF	Unc
284	1911G	.190	125.00	150.00	200.00	300.00
	1912G	.310	125.00	140.00	200.00	300.00
	1913G	.085	125.00	150.00	225.00	325.00
	1914G	.280	125.00	150.00	200.00	300.00
	Common date		—	—	Proof	800.00

TRADE COINAGE

DUCAT

3.6600 g, .938 GOLD, .1103 oz AGW
Carl Friedrich

KM#	Date	Mintage	Fine	VF	XF	Unc
143	1807	1,022	—	1500.	2500.	4000.

Leopold

KM#	Date	Mintage	Fine	VF	XF	Unc
201	1832	6,631	—	1000.	1500.	2000.
	1833	2,496	—	1100.	1600.	2100.
	1834	1,992	—	1150.	1650.	2200.
	1835	2,470	—	1100.	1600.	2100.
	1836	1,777	—	1150.	1650.	2200.

Obv: W/o designers initial or star below head.

KM#	Date	Mintage	Fine	VF	XF	Unc
208	1837	1,467	—	1125.	1650.	2200.
	1838	2,095	—	1125.	1650.	2200.
	1839	2,448	—	1100.	1600.	2100.
	1840	2,044	—	1125.	1650.	2200.
	1841	2,145	—	1125.	1650.	2200.
	1842	2,130	—	1125.	1650.	2200.

KM#	Date	Mintage	Fine	VF	XF	Unc
215	1843	1,350	—	1300.	1700.	2200.
	1844	850 pcs.	—	1500.	2000.	2500.
	1845	2,097	—	1200.	1600.	2000.
	1846	1,950	—	1200.	1600.	2000.

Obv: Larger head.

KM#	Date	Mintage	Fine	VF	XF	Unc
223.1	1847	1,870	—	1200.	1600.	2100.
	1848	1,590	—	1200.	1600.	2100.
	1849	1,420	—	1200.	1600.	2100.
	1850	1,390	—	1200.	1600.	2100.
	1851	1,280	—	1200.	1600.	2100.
	1852	1,450	—	1350.	1750.	2250.

Obv: Star below head.

KM#	Date	Mintage	Fine	VF	XF	Unc
223.2	1852	Inc. Ab.	—	1350.	1750.	2250.

NOTE: Posthumous issue.

Friedrich I

KM#	Date	Mintage	Fine	VF	XF	Unc
227	1854	1,820	—	1500.	3000.	4000.

BAMBERG

Bishopric in northern Bavaria. The see was founded in 1007 and the first coinage appeared soon after. The bishops were made princes of the empire in the mid-1200s. It was annexed to Bavaria in 1802.

RULERS

Christoph Franz, Freiherr von Buseck, Bishop, 1795-1802
Georg Karl, von Fechenbach, 1802-1803

TRADE COINAGE

DUCAT

3.5000 g, .986 GOLD, .1109 oz AGW
Union of Bamberg with Bavaria

KM#	Date	Mintage	Fine	VF	XF	Unc
154	1802	—	400.00	800.00	1350.	1900.

BAVARIA

Located in south Germany. In 1180 the Duchy of Bavaria was given to the Count of Wittelsbach by the emperor. He is the ancestor of all who ruled in Bavaria until 1918. Primogeniture was proclaimed in 1506 and in 1623 the dukes of Bavaria were given the electoral right. Bavaria, which had been divided for the various heirs, was reunited in 1799. The title of king was granted to Bavaria in 1805.

RULERS

Maximilian IV, Joseph as Elector, 1799-1805
Maximilian IV,
As King Maximilian I, Joseph, 1806-1825
Ludwig I, 1825-1848
Maximilian II, 1848-1864
Ludwig II, 1864-1886
Otto, 1886-1913
Prince Regent Luitpold, 1886-1912
Ludwig III, 1913-1918

HELLER

COPPER
Obv: Shield and date in diamond.
Rev. value: 1/HEL/LER in diamond.

KM#	Date	Mintage	Fine	VF	XF	Unc
305	1801	—	5.00	10.00	15.00	50.00
	1802	—	5.00	10.00	15.00	50.00
	1803	—	5.00	10.00	15.00	50.00
	1804	—	5.00	10.00	15.00	50.00
	1805	—	5.00	10.00	15.00	50.00

NOTE: Earlier dates (1799-1800) exist for this type.

KM#	Date	Mintage	Fine	VF	XF	Unc
340	1806	—	3.00	5.00	10.00	35.00
	1807	—	3.00	5.00	10.00	35.00
	1808	—	3.00	5.00	10.00	35.00
	1809	—	3.00	5.00	10.00	35.00
	1810	—	3.00	5.00	10.00	35.00
	1811	—	3.00	5.00	10.00	35.00
	1812	—	3.00	5.00	10.00	35.00
	1813	—	3.00	5.00	10.00	35.00
	1814	—	3.00	5.00	10.00	35.00
	1815	—	3.00	5.00	10.00	35.00
	1816	—	3.00	5.00	10.00	35.00
	1817	—	3.00	5.00	10.00	35.00
	1818	—	3.00	5.00	10.00	35.00
	1819	—	3.00	5.00	10.00	35.00
	1820	—	3.00	5.00	10.00	35.00
	1821	—	3.00	5.00	10.00	35.00
	1822	—	3.00	5.00	10.00	35.00
	1823	—	3.00	5.00	10.00	35.00
	1824	—	3.00	5.00	10.00	35.00
	1825	—	3.00	5.00	10.00	35.00

KM#	Date	Mintage	Fine	VF	XF	Unc
383	1828	—	3.00	5.00	10.00	35.00
	1829	—	3.00	5.00	10.00	35.00
	1830	—	3.00	5.00	10.00	35.00
	1831	—	3.00	5.00	10.00	35.00
	1832	—	3.00	5.00	10.00	35.00
	1833	—	3.00	5.00	10.00	35.00
	1834	—	3.00	5.00	10.00	35.00
	1835	—	3.00	5.00	10.00	35.00

KM#	Date	Mintage	Fine	VF	XF	Unc
419	1839	.256	1.00	2.00	5.00	25.00
	1840	.169	1.00	2.00	5.00	25.00
	1841	—	1.00	2.00	5.00	25.00
	1842	—	1.00	2.00	5.00	25.00
	1843	—	1.00	2.00	5.00	25.00
	1844	.190	1.00	2.00	5.00	25.00
	1845	.434	1.00	2.00	5.00	25.00
	1846	—	1.00	2.00	5.00	25.00
	1847	.074	1.00	2.00	5.00	25.00
	1848	.514	1.00	2.00	5.00	25.00

KM#	Date	Mintage	Fine	VF	XF	Unc
449	1849	.346	1.00	2.00	5.00	20.00
	1850	.306	1.00	2.00	5.00	20.00
	1851	.437	1.00	2.00	5.00	20.00
	1852	.206	1.00	2.00	5.00	20.00
	1853	.279	1.00	2.00	5.00	20.00
	1854	.193	1.00	2.00	5.00	20.00
	1855	.132	1.00	2.00	5.00	20.00
	1856	.034	1.00	2.00	5.00	20.00

PFENNIG

COPPER
Obv: Bavaria shield in ornamental cartouche.
Rev: Value above date.

KM#	Date	Mintage	Fine	VF	XF	Unc
306	1801	—	2.00	7.00	15.00	40.00
	1802	—	2.00	7.00	15.00	40.00
	1803	—	2.00	7.00	15.00	40.00
	1804	—	2.00	7.00	15.00	40.00
	1805	—	2.00	7.00	15.00	40.00

NOTE: Earlier dates (1799-1800) exist for this type.

KM#	Date	Mintage	Fine	VF	XF	Unc
341	1806	—	1.00	3.00	7.00	25.00
	1807	—	1.00	3.00	7.00	25.00
	1808	—	1.00	3.00	7.00	25.00
	1809	—	1.00	3.00	7.00	25.00
	1810	—	1.00	3.00	7.00	25.00
	1811	—	1.00	3.00	7.00	25.00
	1812	—	1.00	3.00	7.00	25.00
	1813	—	1.00	3.00	7.00	25.00
	1814	—	1.00	3.00	7.00	25.00
	1815	—	1.00	3.00	7.00	25.00
	1816	—	1.00	3.00	7.00	25.00
	1817	—	1.00	3.00	7.00	25.00
	1818	—	1.00	3.00	7.00	25.00
	1819	—	1.00	3.00	7.00	25.00
	1820	—	1.00	3.00	7.00	25.00
	1821	—	1.00	3.00	7.00	25.00
	1822	—	1.00	3.00	7.00	25.00
	1823	—	1.00	3.00	7.00	25.00
	1824	—	1.00	3.00	7.00	25.00
	1825	—	1.00	3.00	7.00	25.00

KM#	Date	Mintage	Fine	VF	XF	Unc
384	1828	—	1.00	3.00	7.00	20.00
	1829	—	1.00	3.00	7.00	20.00
	1830	—	1.00	3.00	7.00	20.00
	1831	—	1.00	3.00	7.00	20.00
	1832	—	1.00	3.00	7.00	20.00
	1833	—	1.00	3.00	7.00	20.00
	1834	—	1.00	3.00	7.00	20.00
	1835	—	1.00	3.00	7.00	20.00

KM#	Date	Mintage	Fine	VF	XF	Unc
420	1839	.801	1.00	2.00	5.00	15.00
	1840	.732	1.00	2.00	5.00	15.00
	1841	.970	1.00	2.00	5.00	15.00
	1842	.817	1.00	2.00	5.00	15.00
	1843	.892	1.00	2.00	5.00	15.00
	1844	.645	1.00	2.00	5.00	15.00
	1845	1.037	1.00	2.00	5.00	15.00
	1846	1.487	1.00	2.00	5.00	15.00
	1847	1.808	1.00	2.00	5.00	15.00
	1848	1.815	1.00	2.00	5.00	15.00

KM#	Date	Mintage	Fine	VF	XF	Unc
450	1849	2.120	1.00	2.00	5.00	15.00
	1850	2.494	1.00	2.00	5.00	15.00
	1851	2.162	1.00	2.00	5.00	15.00
	1852	2.634	1.00	2.00	5.00	15.00
	1853	1.950	1.00	2.00	5.00	15.00
	1854	1.842	1.00	2.00	5.00	15.00
	1855	1.576	1.00	2.00	5.00	15.00
	1856	1.530	1.00	2.00	5.00	15.00

KM#	Date	Mintage	Fine	VF	XF	Unc
471	1858	—	1.00	2.00	5.00	15.00
	1859	—	1.00	2.00	5.00	15.00
	1860	—	1.00	2.00	5.00	15.00
	1861	—	1.00	2.00	5.00	15.00
	1862	—	1.00	2.00	5.00	15.00
	1863	2.284	1.00	2.00	5.00	15.00
	1864	2.304	1.00	2.00	5.00	15.00

KM#	Date	Mintage	Fine	VF	XF	Unc
486	1865	1.401	1.00	2.00	5.00	15.00
	1866	1.485	1.00	2.00	5.00	15.00
	1867	1.633	1.00	2.00	5.00	15.00
	1868	1.394	1.00	2.00	5.00	15.00
	1869	1.474	1.00	2.00	5.00	15.00
	1870	1.608	1.00	2.00	5.00	15.00
	1871	1.534	1.00	2.00	5.00	15.00

2 PFENNIG

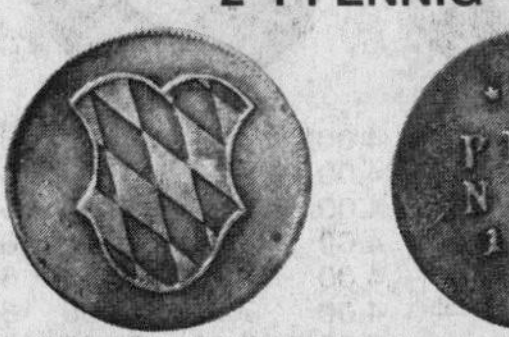

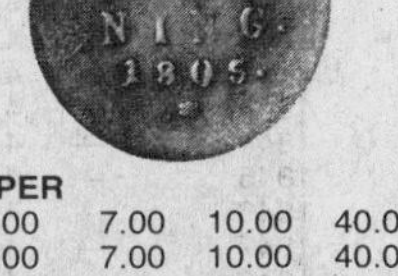

COPPER

KM#	Date	Mintage	Fine	VF	XF	Unc
307	1801	—	3.00	7.00	10.00	40.00
	1802	—	3.00	7.00	10.00	40.00
	1803	—	3.00	7.00	10.00	40.00
	1804	—	3.00	7.00	10.00	40.00
	1805	—	3.00	7.00	10.00	40.00

NOTE: Earlier dates (1799-1800) exist for this type.

KM#	Date	Mintage	Fine	VF	XF	Unc
342	1806	—	1.00	3.00	7.00	30.00
	1807	—	1.00	3.00	7.00	30.00
	1808	—	1.00	3.00	7.00	30.00
	1809	—	1.00	3.00	7.00	30.00
	1810	—	1.00	3.00	7.00	30.00
	1811	—	1.00	3.00	7.00	30.00
	1812	—	1.00	3.00	7.00	30.00
	1813	—	1.00	3.00	7.00	30.00
	1814	—	1.00	3.00	7.00	30.00
	1815	—	1.00	3.00	7.00	30.00
	1816	—	1.00	3.00	7.00	30.00
	1817	—	1.00	3.00	7.00	30.00
	1818	—	1.00	3.00	7.00	30.00
	1819	—	1.00	3.00	7.00	30.00
	1820	—	1.00	3.00	7.00	30.00
	1821	—	1.00	3.00	7.00	30.00
	1822	—	1.00	3.00	7.00	30.00
	1823	—	1.00	3.00	7.00	30.00
	1824	—	1.00	3.00	7.00	30.00
	1825	—	1.00	3.00	7.00	30.00

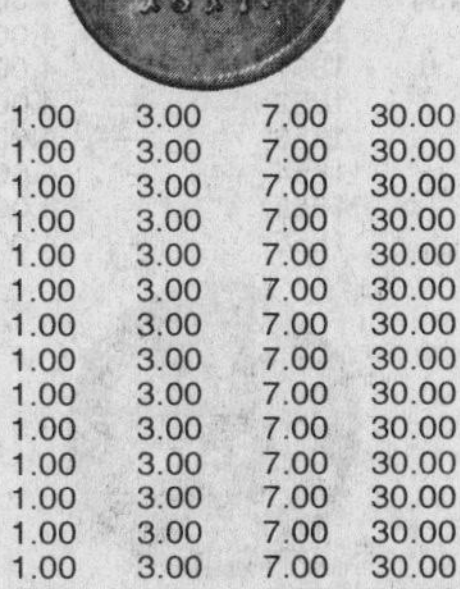

KM#	Date	Mintage	Fine	VF	XF	Unc
385	1828	—	1.00	3.00	7.00	30.00
	1829	—	1.00	3.00	7.00	30.00
	1830	—	1.00	3.00	7.00	30.00
	1831	—	1.00	3.00	7.00	30.00
	1832	—	1.00	3.00	7.00	30.00
	1833	—	1.00	3.00	7.00	30.00
	1834	—	1.00	3.00	7.00	30.00
	1835	—	1.00	3.00	7.00	30.00

KM#	Date	Mintage	Fine	VF	XF	Unc
421	1839	.320	1.00	3.00	7.00	25.00
	1840	.320	1.00	3.00	7.00	25.00
	1841	.442	1.00	3.00	7.00	25.00
	1842	.353	1.00	3.00	7.00	25.00
	1843	.203	1.00	3.00	7.00	25.00
	1844	.226	1.00	3.00	7.00	25.00
	1845	.242	1.00	3.00	7.00	25.00
	1846	.232	1.00	3.00	7.00	25.00
	1847	.663	1.00	3.00	7.00	25.00
	1848	.776	1.00	3.00	7.00	25.00

KM#	Date	Mintage	Fine	VF	XF	Unc
451	1849	.454	1.00	3.00	7.00	25.00
	1850	1.477	1.00	3.00	7.00	25.00

KM#	Date	Mintage	Fine	VF	XF	Unc
472	1858	—	1.00	2.00	4.00	20.00
	1859	—	1.00	2.00	4.00	20.00
	1860	—	1.00	2.00	4.00	20.00
	1861	—	1.00	2.00	4.00	20.00
	1862	—	1.00	2.00	4.00	20.00
	1863	.228	1.00	2.00	4.00	20.00

KM#	Date	Mintage	Fine	VF	XF	Unc
478	1864	.589	1.00	2.00	4.00	20.00
	1865	.358	1.00	2.00	4.00	20.00
	1866	.234	1.00	2.00	4.00	20.00
	1867	.481	1.00	2.00	4.00	20.00
	1868	.208	1.00	2.00	4.00	20.00
	1869	.466	1.00	2.00	4.00	20.00
	1870	.476	1.00	2.00	4.00	20.00
	1871	.466	1.00	2.00	4.00	20.00

1/2 KREUZER

COPPER

KM#	Date	Mintage	Fine	VF	XF	Unc
463	1851	.796	1.00	3.00	5.00	25.00
	1852	.981	1.00	3.00	5.00	25.00
	1853	.797	1.00	3.00	5.00	25.00
	1854	.528	1.00	3.00	5.00	25.00
	1855	.641	1.00	3.00	5.00	25.00
	1856	.462	1.00	3.00	5.00	25.00

KREUZER

.7700 g, .187 SILVER, .0046 oz ASW
Obv: Head right, MAX. IOS.
Rev: Crowned shield within palm branches.

KM#	Date	Mintage	Fine	VF	XF	Unc
308	1802	—	5.00	15.00	40.00	100.00
	1803	—	5.00	15.00	40.00	100.00

NOTE: Earlier dates (1799-1800) exist for this type.

KM#	Date	Mintage	Fine	VF	XF	Unc
317	1801	—	5.00	10.00	30.00	80.00
	1802	—	5.00	10.00	30.00	80.00

Obv. leg: MAX. IOS. H.I.B.C. Rev: W/o numeric value.

KM#	Date	Mintage	Fine	VF	XF	Unc
315	1801	—	5.00	10.00	30.00	80.00
	1802	—	5.00	10.00	30.00	80.00
	1803	—	5.00	10.00	30.00	80.00
	1806/0	—	5.50	11.00	32.50	90.00

NOTE: Earlier date (1800) exists for this type.

Rev: Numeral value separating date.

KM#	Date	Mintage	Fine	VF	XF	Unc
329	1804	—	5.00	10.00	30.00	80.00

Obv. leg: MAX. IOS. C.Z.P.B.
Rev: LAND MUNZ, oval arms separating value.

KM#	Date	Mintage	Fine	VF	XF	Unc
330	1804	—	5.00	10.00	30.00	80.00
	1805	—	5.00	10.00	30.00	80.00

COPPER

KM#	Date	Mintage	Fine	VF	XF	Unc
343	1806	.145	25.00	50.00	125.00	250.00

NOTE: Minted for use in Tyrol, then occupied by Bavaria.

.7700 g, .187 SILVER, .0046 oz ASW

KM#	Date	Mintage	Fine	VF	XF	Unc
344	1806	—	3.00	5.00	10.00	65.00
	1807	—	3.00	5.00	10.00	65.00
	1808	—	3.00	5.00	10.00	65.00
	1809	—	3.00	5.00	10.00	65.00
	1810	—	3.00	5.00	10.00	65.00
	1811	—	3.00	5.00	10.00	65.00
	1812	—	3.00	5.00	10.00	65.00
	1813	—	3.00	5.00	10.00	65.00
	1814	—	3.00	5.00	10.00	65.00
	1815	—	3.00	5.00	10.00	65.00
	1816	—	3.00	5.00	10.00	65.00
	1817	—	3.00	5.00	10.00	65.00
	1818	—	3.00	5.00	10.00	65.00
	1819	—	3.00	5.00	10.00	65.00
	1820	—	3.00	5.00	10.00	65.00
	1821	—	3.00	5.00	10.00	65.00
	1822	—	3.00	5.00	10.00	65.00
	1823	—	3.00	5.00	10.00	65.00
	1824	—	3.00	5.00	10.00	65.00
	1825	—	3.00	5.00	10.00	65.00

Obv. leg: LUDWIG KOENIG. . . . .

KM#	Date	Mintage	Fine	VF	XF	Unc
376	1827	—	3.00	5.00	10.00	75.00
	1828	—	3.00	5.00	10.00	75.00
	1829	—	3.00	5.00	10.00	75.00
	1830	—	3.00	5.00	10.00	75.00

Obv. leg: LUDWIG I KOENIG. . . . .

KM#	Date	Mintage	Fine	VF	XF	Unc
390	1830	—	3.00	5.00	10.00	60.00
	1831	—	3.00	5.00	10.00	60.00
	1832	—	3.00	5.00	10.00	60.00
	1833	—	3.00	5.00	10.00	60.00
	1834	—	3.00	5.00	10.00	60.00
	1835	—	3.00	5.00	10.00	60.00

.8400 g, .166 SILVER, .0044 oz ASW

KM#	Date	Mintage	Fine	VF	XF	Unc
422	1839	1.474	1.00	2.00	5.00	20.00
	1840	1.769	1.00	2.00	5.00	20.00
	1841	1.591	1.00	2.00	5.00	20.00
	1842	1.855	1.00	2.00	5.00	20.00
	1843	1.373	1.00	2.00	5.00	20.00
	1844	1.324	1.00	2.00	5.00	20.00
	1845	1.660	1.00	2.00	5.00	20.00
	1846	1.849	1.00	2.00	5.00	20.00
	1847	1.519	1.00	2.00	5.00	20.00
	1848	1.746	1.00	2.00	5.00	20.00

KM#	Date	Mintage	Fine	VF	XF	Unc
452	1849	1.971	1.00	2.00	5.00	20.00
	1850	3.135	1.00	2.00	5.00	20.00

KM#	Date	Mintage	Fine	VF	XF	Unc
452	1851	2.084	1.00	2.00	5.00	20.00
	1852	1.915	1.00	2.00	5.00	20.00
	1853	1.528	1.00	2.00	5.00	20.00
	1854	1.650	1.00	2.00	5.00	20.00
	1855	1.510	1.00	2.00	5.00	20.00
	1856	1.335	1.00	2.00	5.00	20.00

KM#	Date	Mintage	Fine	VF	XF	Unc
473	1858	2.400	1.00	2.50	4.50	10.00
	1859	—	1.00	2.50	4.50	10.00
	1860	.231	1.00	2.50	4.50	10.00
	1861	3.276	1.00	2.50	4.50	10.00
	1862	3.358	1.00	2.50	4.50	10.00
	1863	3.356	1.00	2.50	4.50	10.00
	1864	3.293	1.00	2.50	4.50	10.00

KM#	Date	Mintage	Fine	VF	XF	Unc
487	1865	1.837	1.00	2.50	4.50	10.00
	1866	2.542	1.00	2.50	4.50	10.00
	1867	2.305	1.00	2.50	4.50	10.00
	1868	2.526	1.00	2.50	4.50	10.00
	1869	2.774	1.00	2.50	4.50	10.00
	1870	2.199	1.00	2.50	4.50	10.00
	1871	2.634	1.00	2.50	4.50	10.00

3 KREUZER

(1 Groschen)

1.3500 g, .333 SILVER, .0144 oz ASW
Obv: Head right, leg: MAX. IOS. P. B.
Rev: Crowned oval arms separating value.

KM#	Date	Mintage	Fine	VF	XF	Unc
309	1801	—	5.00	15.00	50.00	125.00
	1802	—	5.00	15.00	50.00	125.00

NOTE: Earlier dates (1799-1800) exist for this type.

Obv. leg: MAX. IOS. H.I.B.C. &

KM#	Date	Mintage	Fine	VF	XF	Unc
322	1803	—	5.00	15.00	50.00	125.00
	1804	—	5.00	15.00	50.00	125.00

Obv. leg: MAX. IOS. C.Z.P.B.

KM#	Date	Mintage	Fine	VF	XF	Unc
331	1804	—	5.00	15.00	50.00	125.00
	1805	—	5.00	15.00	50.00	125.00

Obv: Head right. Rev: Shield w/crown above crossed scepter and sword.

KM#	Date	Mintage	Fine	VF	XF	Unc
352	1807	—	5.00	15.00	50.00	125.00
	1808	—	5.00	15.00	50.00	125.00
	1809	—	5.00	15.00	50.00	125.00
	1810	—	5.00	15.00	50.00	125.00
	1811	—	5.00	15.00	50.00	125.00
	1812	—	5.00	15.00	50.00	125.00
	1813	—	5.00	15.00	50.00	125.00
	1814	—	5.00	15.00	50.00	125.00
	1815	—	5.00	15.00	50.00	125.00
	1816	—	5.00	15.00	50.00	125.00
	1817	—	5.00	15.00	50.00	125.00
	1818	—	5.00	15.00	50.00	125.00
	1819	—	5.00	15.00	50.00	125.00
	1820	—	5.00	15.00	50.00	125.00
	1821	—	5.00	15.00	50.00	125.00
	1822	—	5.00	15.00	50.00	125.00
	1823	—	5.00	15.00	50.00	125.00
	1824	—	5.00	15.00	50.00	125.00
	1825	—	5.00	15.00	50.00	125.00

1.3000 g, .333 SILVER, .0139 oz ASW
Obv. leg: LUDWIG KOENIG. . . . .

KM#	Date	Mintage	Fine	VF	XF	Unc
377	1827	—	5.00	15.00	50.00	125.00
	1828	—	5.00	15.00	50.00	125.00
	1829	—	5.00	15.00	50.00	125.00
	1830	—	5.00	15.00	50.00	125.00

Obv. leg: LUDWIG I KOENIG. . . . .

KM#	Date	Mintage	Fine	VF	XF	Unc
391	1830	—	5.00	10.00	25.00	75.00
	1831	—	5.00	10.00	25.00	75.00
	1832	—	5.00	10.00	25.00	75.00
	1833	—	5.00	10.00	25.00	75.00
	1834	—	5.00	10.00	25.00	75.00
	1835	—	5.00	10.00	25.00	75.00
	1836	—	5.00	10.00	25.00	75.00

KM#	Date	Mintage	Fine	VF	XF	Unc
423	1839	.456	2.00	5.00	7.00	25.00
	1840	.235	2.00	5.00	7.00	30.00
	1841	.337	2.00	5.00	7.00	30.00
	1842	.370	2.00	5.00	7.00	30.00
	1843	.337	2.00	5.00	7.00	30.00
	1844	.269	2.00	5.00	7.00	30.00
	1845	.361	2.00	5.00	7.00	30.00
	1846	.463	2.00	5.00	7.00	30.00
	1847	.563	2.00	5.00	7.00	30.00
	1848	.447	2.00	5.00	7.00	30.00

KM#	Date	Mintage	Fine	VF	XF	Unc
453	1849	.373	2.00	5.00	7.00	30.00
	1850	.615	2.00	5.00	7.00	30.00
	1851	.582	2.00	5.00	7.00	30.00
	1852	.282	2.00	5.00	7.00	30.00
	1853	.280	2.00	5.00	7.00	30.00
	1854	.388	2.00	5.00	7.00	30.00
	1855	.285	2.00	5.00	7.00	30.00
	1856	.091	2.00	5.00	7.00	30.00

1.2300 g, .350 SILVER, .0138 oz ASW

KM#	Date	Mintage	Fine	VF	XF	Unc
488	1865	.832	2.00	5.00	7.00	30.00
	1866	.566	2.00	5.00	7.00	30.00
	1867	.099	2.00	5.00	7.00	30.00
	1868	.065	2.00	5.00	7.00	30.00

6 KREUZER

2.7000 g, .333 SILVER, .0289 oz ASW
Obv: Head right, leg: MAX. IOS. P.B.
Rev: Crowned arms, date below.

KM#	Date	Mintage	Fine	VF	XF	Unc
310	1802	—	10.00	25.00	50.00	200.00
	1803	—	10.00	25.00	50.00	200.00

NOTE: Earlier dates (1799-1800) exist for this type.

Obv. leg: MAX. IOS. H.I.B.C. &

KM#	Date	Mintage	Fine	VF	XF	Unc
318	1801	—	10.00	20.00	40.00	125.00
	1803	—	10.00	20.00	40.00	125.00
	1804	—	10.00	20.00	40.00	125.00

Obv. leg: MAX. IOS. C.Z.P.B.

KM#	Date	Mintage	Fine	VF	XF	Unc
332	1804	—	20.00	40.00	80.00	200.00
	1805	—	20.00	40.00	80.00	200.00

Obv: Head right.
Rev: Crowned arms w/shield divided.

KM#	Date	Mintage	Fine	VF	XF	Unc
345	1806	—	25.00	50.00	100.00	250.00

KM#	Date	Mintage	Fine	VF	XF	Unc
346	1806	—	5.00	20.00	50.00	125.00
	1807	—	5.00	20.00	50.00	125.00
	1808	—	5.00	20.00	50.00	125.00
	1809	—	5.00	20.00	50.00	125.00
	1810	—	5.00	20.00	50.00	125.00
	1811	—	5.00	20.00	50.00	125.00
	1812	—	5.00	20.00	50.00	125.00
	1813	—	5.00	20.00	50.00	125.00
	1814	—	5.00	20.00	50.00	125.00
	1815	—	5.00	20.00	50.00	125.00
	1816	—	5.00	20.00	50.00	125.00
	1817	—	5.00	20.00	50.00	125.00
	1818	—	5.00	20.00	50.00	125.00
	1819	—	5.00	20.00	50.00	125.00
	1820	—	5.00	20.00	50.00	125.00
	1821/0	—	5.00	20.00	50.00	125.00
	1821	—	5.00	20.00	50.00	125.00
	1822	—	5.00	20.00	50.00	125.00
	1823	—	5.00	20.00	50.00	125.00
	1824	—	5.00	20.00	50.00	125.00
	1825	—	5.00	20.00	50.00	125.00

2.6000 g, .333 SILVER, .0278 oz ASW
Obv. leg: LUDWIG KOENIG. . . . .

KM#	Date	Mintage	Fine	VF	XF	Unc
378	1827	—	5.00	25.00	65.00	125.00
	1828	—	5.00	25.00	65.00	125.00
	1829	—	5.00	25.00	65.00	125.00

Obv. leg: LUDWIG I KOENIG. . . . .

KM#	Date	Mintage	Fine	VF	XF	Unc
392	1830	—	5.00	15.00	50.00	100.00
	1831	—	5.00	15.00	50.00	100.00
	1832	—	5.00	15.00	50.00	100.00
	1833	—	5.00	15.00	50.00	100.00
	1834	—	5.00	15.00	50.00	100.00
	1835	—	5.00	15.00	50.00	100.00

KM#	Date	Mintage	Fine	VF	XF	Unc
424	1839	.800	4.00	7.00	20.00	60.00
	1840	—	4.00	7.00	20.00	60.00
	1841	—	4.00	7.00	20.00	60.00
	1842	—	4.00	7.00	20.00	60.00
	1843	—	4.00	7.00	20.00	60.00
	1844	—	4.00	7.00	20.00	60.00
	1845	—	4.00	7.00	20.00	60.00
	1846	—	4.00	7.00	20.00	60.00
	1847	—	4.00	7.00	20.00	60.00
	1848	—	4.00	7.00	20.00	60.00

KM#	Date	Mintage	Fine	VF	XF	Unc
454	1849	—	4.00	7.00	20.00	60.00
	1850	—	4.00	7.00	20.00	60.00
	1851	—	4.00	7.00	20.00	60.00
	1852	—	4.00	7.00	20.00	60.00
	1853	—	4.00	7.00	20.00	60.00
	1854	—	4.00	7.00	20.00	60.00
	1855	—	4.00	7.00	20.00	60.00
	1856	—	4.00	7.00	20.00	60.00

2.4600 g, .350 SILVER, .0276 oz ASW
Obv. leg: SCHEIDE MUNZE added.

KM#	Date	Mintage	Fine	VF	XF	Unc
491	1866	.087	7.50	15.00	50.00	175.00
	1867	.024	10.00	25.00	75.00	200.00

10 KREUZER

3.9000 g, .500 SILVER, .0626 oz ASW
Obv: Maximillian IV Joseph right in wreath.
Rev: Crowned 3 fold oval arms.

KM#	Date	Mintage	Fine	VF	XF	Unc
316	1801	—	30.00	50.00	125.00	275.00

NOTE: Earlier date (1800) exists for this type.

Rev. leg: POPOLO

KM#	Date	Mintage	Fine	VF	XF	Unc
319	1801	—	40.00	60.00	150.00	375.00

20 KREUZER

6.6800 g, .583 SILVER, .1252 oz ASW
Obv: Maximillian IV Joseph right within wreath.
Rev: Crowned arms within crossed branches, date and value below.

KM#	Date	Mintage	Fine	VF	XF	Unc
311	1801	—	55.00	90.00	150.00	275.00
	1802	—	75.00	130.00	225.00	400.00
	1803	—	55.00	90.00	150.00	275.00

NOTE: Earlier dates (1799-1800) exist for this type.

KM#	Date	Mintage	Fine	VF	XF	Unc
333	1804	—	55.00	100.00	200.00	475.00
	1805	—	55.00	100.00	200.00	475.00

KM#	Date	Mintage	Fine	VF	XF	Unc
347	1806	—	25.00	60.00	125.00	225.00
	1807	—	25.00	60.00	125.00	225.00
	1808	—	25.00	60.00	125.00	225.00
	1809	—	25.00	60.00	125.00	225.00
	1810	—	25.00	60.00	125.00	225.00
	1811	—	25.00	60.00	125.00	225.00
	1812	—	25.00	60.00	125.00	225.00
	1813	—	25.00	60.00	125.00	225.00
	1814	—	25.00	60.00	125.00	225.00
	1815	—	25.00	60.00	125.00	225.00
	1816	—	25.00	60.00	125.00	225.00
	1817	—	25.00	60.00	125.00	225.00
	1818	—	25.00	60.00	125.00	225.00
	1819	—	25.00	60.00	125.00	225.00
	1820	—	25.00	60.00	125.00	225.00
	1821	—	25.00	60.00	125.00	225.00
	1822	—	25.00	60.00	125.00	225.00
	1823	—	25.00	60.00	125.00	225.00
	1824	—	25.00	60.00	125.00	225.00
	1825	—	25.00	60.00	125.00	225.00

1/2 GULDEN

5.3000 g, .900 SILVER, .1533 oz ASW
Ludwig I

KM#	Date	Mintage	Fine	VF	XF	Unc
417	1838	1.750	15.00	25.00	50.00	100.00
	1839	.474	15.00	25.00	50.00	100.00
	1840	.233	15.00	25.00	50.00	125.00
	1841	.243	15.00	25.00	50.00	125.00
	1842	.508	15.00	25.00	50.00	100.00
	1843	.337	15.00	25.00	50.00	125.00
	1844	1.452	15.00	25.00	50.00	100.00
	1845	1.869	15.00	25.00	50.00	100.00
	1846	1.181	15.00	25.00	50.00	100.00
	1847	.241	15.00	25.00	50.00	125.00
	1848	.407	15.00	25.00	50.00	125.00

Maximillian II

KM#	Date	Mintage	Fine	VF	XF	Unc
444	1848	Inc. Ab.	20.00	30.00	50.00	125.00
	1849	.218	20.00	30.00	50.00	125.00
	1850	.189	20.00	30.00	50.00	125.00
	1851	.171	20.00	30.00	50.00	125.00
	1852	.120	20.00	30.00	50.00	125.00
	1853	.206	20.00	30.00	50.00	125.00
	1854	.146	20.00	30.00	50.00	125.00
	1855	.060	20.00	30.00	50.00	100.00
	1856	.074	20.00	30.00	50.00	100.00
	1857	.020	25.00	40.00	65.00	150.00
	1858	.183	20.00	30.00	50.00	100.00
	1859	.405	20.00	30.00	50.00	100.00
	1860	.292	20.00	30.00	50.00	100.00
	1861	.254	20.00	30.00	50.00	100.00
	1862	.141	20.00	30.00	50.00	100.00
	1863	.190	20.00	30.00	50.00	100.00
	1864	.160	20.00	30.00	50.00	100.00

Obv: Ludwig II w/part in hair.

KM#	Date	Mintage	Fine	VF	XF	Unc
479	1864	Inc. Ab.	40.00	75.00	125.00	250.00
	1865	.227	35.00	60.00	100.00	200.00
	1866	.101	40.00	75.00	125.00	250.00

Obv: W/o part in hair.

KM#	Date	Mintage	Fine	VF	XF	Unc
492	1866	Inc. Ab.	40.00	75.00	125.00	250.00
	1867	.100	35.00	60.00	100.00	200.00
	1868	.121	35.00	75.00	100.00	200.00
	1869	.133	35.00	75.00	100.00	200.00
	1870	.111	35.00	75.00	100.00	200.00
	1871	.051	40.00	75.00	125.00	225.00

GULDEN

10.6000 g, .900 SILVER, .3067 oz ASW
Ludwig I

KM#	Date	Mintage	Fine	VF	XF	Unc
414	1837	2.057	15.00	25.00	75.00	125.00
	1838	2.045	15.00	25.00	75.00	125.00
	1839	2.320	15.00	25.00	75.00	125.00
	1840	3.591	15.00	25.00	75.00	125.00
	1841	4.362	15.00	25.00	75.00	125.00
	1842	1.449	15.00	25.00	75.00	125.00
	1843	4.832	15.00	25.00	75.00	125.00
	1844	3.491	15.00	25.00	75.00	125.00
	1845	1.115	15.00	25.00	75.00	125.00
	1846	.686	15.00	25.00	85.00	150.00
	1847	.387	15.00	25.00	85.00	150.00
	1848	.437	15.00	25.00	85.00	150.00

Maximillian I

KM#	Date	Mintage	Fine	VF	XF	Unc
445	1848	Inc. Ab.	20.00	40.00	75.00	125.00
	1849	.366	20.00	40.00	75.00	125.00
	1850	.343	20.00	40.00	75.00	125.00
	1851	.224	20.00	40.00	75.00	125.00
	1852	.453	20.00	40.00	75.00	125.00
	1853	.257	20.00	40.00	75.00	125.00
	1854	.513	20.00	40.00	75.00	125.00
	1855	1.076	20.00	40.00	75.00	125.00
	1856	.455	20.00	40.00	75.00	125.00
	1857	.032	25.00	60.00	100.00	150.00
	1858	.144	25.00	60.00	100.00	150.00
	1859	.529	25.00	60.00	100.00	150.00
	1860	.452	25.00	60.00	100.00	150.00
	1861	.358	25.00	60.00	100.00	150.00
	1862	.266	25.00	60.00	100.00	150.00
	1863	.234	25.00	60.00	100.00	150.00
	1864	.414	25.00	60.00	100.00	150.00

Obv: Ludwig II w/part in hair.

KM#	Date	Mintage	Fine	VF	XF	Unc
480	1864	Inc. Ab.	50.00	100.00	150.00	250.00
	1865	.167	50.00	100.00	150.00	250.00
	1866	.122	50.00	100.00	150.00	250.00

Obv: W/o part in hair.

KM#	Date	Mintage	Fine	VF	XF	Unc
493	1866	Inc. Ab.	50.00	100.00	150.00	250.00
	1867	.086	50.00	100.00	150.00	250.00
	1868	.122	50.00	100.00	150.00	250.00
	1869	.122	50.00	100.00	150.00	250.00
	1870	.072	50.00	100.00	150.00	250.00
	1871	.035	60.00	120.00	175.00	275.00

ZWEY (2) GULDEN

21.2100 g, .900 SILVER, .6138 oz ASW
Obv. leg: LUDWIG I KOENIG V. BAYERN.

KM#	Date	Mintage	Fine	VF	XF	Unc
438	1845	.883	30.00	50.00	125.00	275.00
	1846	1.523	30.00	50.00	125.00	275.00
	1847	1.491	30.00	50.00	125.00	275.00
	1848	.950	30.00	50.00	125.00	275.00

Obv. leg: MAXIMILIAN II KOENIG V. BAYERN.
Rev: Similar to KM#438.

KM#	Date	Mintage	Fine	VF	XF	Unc
446	1848	Inc. Ab.	27.50	50.00	120.00	250.00
	1849	.741	27.50	50.00	120.00	250.00
	1850	.915	27.50	50.00	120.00	250.00
	1851	1.157	27.50	50.00	120.00	250.00
	1852	1.356	27.50	50.00	120.00	250.00
	1853	.634	27.50	50.00	120.00	250.00
	1854	.430	27.50	50.00	120.00	250.00
	1855	.585	30.00	60.00	150.00	300.00
	1856	.510	30.00	60.00	150.00	300.00

Restoration of Madonna Column in Munich

KM#	Date	Mintage	Fine	VF	XF	Unc
465	1855	1.000	20.00	30.00	50.00	125.00

1/2 THALER

14.0300 g, .833 SILVER, .3757 oz ASW
Similar to 1 Thaler, KM#313.

KM#	Date	Mintage	Fine	VF	XF	Unc
312	1801	—	150.00	300.00	600.00	1250.
	1802	—	150.00	300.00	600.00	1250.
	1803	—	150.00	300.00	600.00	1250.

NOTE: Earlier dates (1799-1800) exist for this type.

KM#	Date	Mintage	Fine	VF	XF	Unc
323	1803	—	100.00	200.00	450.00	850.00
	1804	—	100.00	200.00	450.00	850.00
	1805	—	100.00	200.00	450.00	850.00

(Without denomination)

KM#	Date	Mintage	Fine	VF	XF	Unc
324	ND (1799-1805)	—	65.00	165.00	250.00	450.00

KM#	Date	Mintage	Fine	VF	XF	Unc
348	ND (1806-08)	*1,500	100.00	250.00	400.00	750.00

Obv: Script letters.

KM#	Date	Mintage	Fine	VF	XF	Unc
353	ND (1807-08)	—	100.00	200.00	400.00	800.00

Obv: Block or normal letters.

KM#	Date	Mintage	Fine	VF	XF	Unc
357	ND (1808-37)	.025	95.00	200.00	300.00	625.00

THALER

28.0000 g, .833 SILVER, .7500 oz ASW
Maximillian IV Joseph

KM#	Date	Mintage	Fine	VF	XF	Unc
313	1801	—	100.00	175.00	400.00	900.00
	1802	—	120.00	200.00	475.00	1000.

NOTE: Earlier dates (1799-1800) exist for this type.

Obv. leg: D.G. MAXIM. IOSEPH

KM#	Date	Mintage	Fine	VF	XF	Unc
320.1	1802	—	1000.	1500.	3500.	5000.

Obv. leg: D.G. MAX. IOSEPH

KM#	Date	Mintage	Fine	VF	XF	Unc
320.2	1802	—	650.00	1250.	1750.	3000.
	1803	—	650.00	1250.	1750.	3000.

Obv: Uniformed bust right, leg: MAXIMILIAN. . . .

KM#	Date	Mintage	Fine	VF	XF	Unc
321	1802	—	350.00	700.00	1500.	3000.

KM#	Date	Mintage	Fine	VF	XF	Unc
325	1803	—	125.00	200.00	450.00	1000.

Obv. leg. ends: . . . .ZU PFALZBAIERN.

KM#	Date	Mintage	Fine	VF	XF	Unc
326	1803	—	175.00	400.00	1000.	2200.
	1804	—	175.00	400.00	1000.	2200.
	1805	—	175.00	400.00	1000.	2200.

Rev. leg: FUR GOTT UND. . . . .

KM#	Date	Mintage	Fine	VF	XF	Unc
334	1804	—	1500.	3000.	4000.	6000.
	1805	—	125.00	200.00	450.00	1000.

KM#	Date	Mintage	Fine	VF	XF	Unc
349	1806	—	100.00	250.00	600.00	1750.

Rev: Crowned lions facing outward.

KM#	Date	Mintage	Fine	VF	XF	Unc
350	1806	—	200.00	400.00	1000.	2000.

Obv: Bust w/pigtail.

KM#	Date	Mintage	Fine	VF	XF	Unc
354	1807	.100	1500.	3000.	5000.	7500.

KM#	Date	Mintage	Fine	VF	XF	Unc
355	1807	Inc. Ab.	75.00	150.00	250.00	700.00
	1808	.055	75.00	150.00	250.00	700.00
	1809	8,932	85.00	150.00	275.00	750.00
	1810	6,721	90.00	160.00	300.00	900.00
	1811	.011	90.00	160.00	300.00	900.00
	1812	8,432	90.00	160.00	300.00	900.00
	1813	5,888	90.00	160.00	300.00	900.00
	1814	4,579	90.00	160.00	300.00	900.00
	1815	6,913	90.00	160.00	300.00	900.00
	1816	.011	90.00	160.00	300.00	900.00
	1817	4,638	90.00	160.00	300.00	900.00
	1818	—	90.00	160.00	300.00	900.00
	1819	—	90.00	160.00	300.00	900.00
	1820	3,974	90.00	160.00	300.00	900.00
	1821	3,826	90.00	160.00	300.00	900.00
	1822	—	90.00	160.00	300.00	900.00

(Krone)

29.3400 g, .868 SILVER, .8188 oz ASW

KM#	Date	Mintage	Fine	VF	XF	Unc
358.1	1809	.063	40.00	75.00	175.00	325.00
	1810	.924	40.00	75.00	175.00	325.00
	1811	.196	40.00	75.00	200.00	425.00
	1812	.618	40.00	75.00	125.00	325.00
	1813	.656	40.00	75.00	125.00	325.00
	1814	.975	40.00	75.00	125.00	325.00
	1815	.769	40.00	75.00	125.00	325.00
	1816	2.453	40.00	75.00	125.00	325.00
	1817	.399	40.00	75.00	125.00	325.00
	1818	.119	40.00	100.00	200.00	425.00
	1819	.292	40.00	100.00	200.00	425.00
	1820	.132	40.00	100.00	200.00	425.00
	1821	.260	40.00	75.00	185.00	350.00
	1822	.052	40.00	100.00	200.00	425.00
	1823	.016	40.00	100.00	200.00	425.00
	1824	.031	40.00	100.00	200.00	425.00
	1825	.081	40.00	75.00	185.00	350.00

Obv. leg: JOEPHUS (Error).

KM#	Date	Mintage	Fine	VF	XF	Unc
358.2	1813	Inc. Ab.	100.00	225.00	625.00	1250.

(Convention)

28.0600 g, .833 SILVER, .7515 oz ASW
Granting of Bavarian Constitution

KM#	Date	Mintage	Fine	VF	XF	Unc
361	1818	.040	30.00	60.00	100.00	175.00

Rev: Similar to KM#355.

KM#	Date	Mintage	Fine	VF	XF	Unc
367	1822	.051	100.00	200.00	450.00	1000.
	1823	.047	150.00	350.00	750.00	1800.
	1824	3,907	100.00	225.00	500.00	1200.
	1825	1,932	100.00	200.00	450.00	1000.

Coronation of Ludwig I

KM#	Date	Mintage	Fine	VF	XF	Unc
370	1825	—	150.00	200.00	300.00	500.00

Death of Reichenbach and Fraunhofer
Obv: Similar to KM#370.

KM#	Date	Mintage	Fine	VF	XF	Unc
371	1826	—	150.00	200.00	275.00	450.00

Removal of University From Landshut to Munich
Obv: Similar to KM#370.

KM#	Date	Mintage	Fine	VF	XF	Unc
372	1826	—	150.00	200.00	275.00	450.00

(Krone)

29.5400 g, .871 SILVER, .8272 oz ASW

KM#	Date	Mintage	Fine	VF	XF	Unc
373	1826	.051	100.00	150.00	250.00	500.00
	1827	.066	130.00	200.00	300.00	750.00
	1828	.079	100.00	150.00	300.00	500.00
	1829	.094	130.00	200.00	300.00	750.00

(Convention)

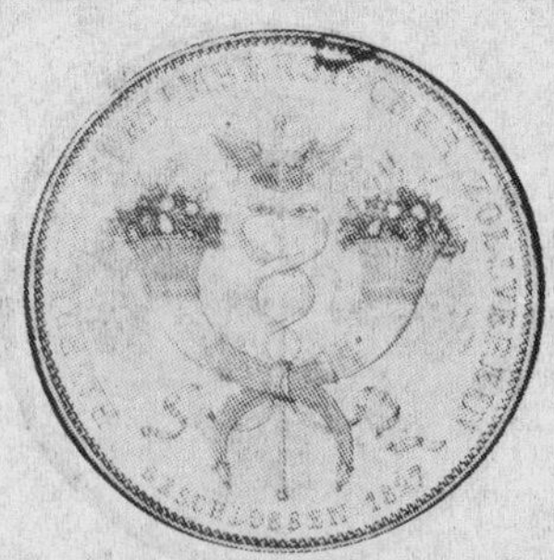

28.0600 g, .833 SILVER, .7515 oz ASW
Bavaria-Wurttemberg Customs Treaty Signing
Obv: Similar to KM#370.

KM#	Date	Mintage	Fine	VF	XF	Unc
379	1827	—	150.00	200.00	275.00	500.00

Founding of Order of Ludwig
Obv: Similar to KM#370.

KM#	Date	Mintage	Fine	VF	XF	Unc
380	1827	—	150.00	200.00	275.00	500.00

Founding of Theresien Order
Obv: Similar to KM#370.

KM#	Date	Mintage	Fine	VF	XF	Unc
381	1827	—	150.00	200.00	275.00	500.00

Blessings of Heaven On Royal Family
Obv: Similar to KM#370.

KM#	Date	Mintage	Fine	VF	XF	Unc
386	1828	—	100.00	125.00	175.00	375.00

Constitution Monument Dedication
Obv: Similar to KM#370.

KM#	Date	Mintage	Fine	VF	XF	Unc
387	1828	—	150.00	200.00	275.00	450.00

Commercial Treaty Between Bavaria, Prussia, Hesse and Wurttemberg
Obv: Similar to KM#370.

KM#	Date	Mintage	Fine	VF	XF	Unc
389	1829	—	150.00	200.00	275.00	500.00

Loyalty of Bavarians to Royal Family
Obv: Similar to KM#370.

KM#	Date	Mintage	Fine	VF	XF	Unc
393	1830	—	150.00	200.00	250.00	450.00

(Krone)

29.5400 g, .871 SILVER, .8272 oz ASW

KM#	Date	Mintage	Fine	VF	XF	Unc
394	1830	.061	75.00	150.00	300.00	650.00
	1831	.064	75.00	150.00	300.00	650.00
	1832	.070	75.00	150.00	300.00	650.00

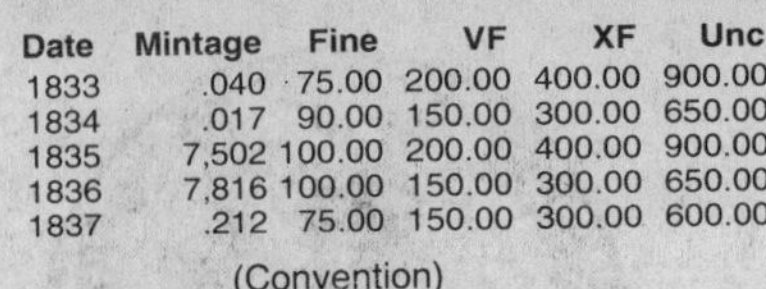

KM#	Date	Mintage	Fine	VF	XF	Unc
	1833	.040	75.00	200.00	400.00	900.00
	1834	.017	90.00	150.00	300.00	650.00
	1835	7,502	100.00	200.00	400.00	900.00
	1836	7,816	100.00	150.00	300.00	650.00
	1837	.212	75.00	150.00	300.00	600.00

(Convention)

28.0600 g, .833 SILVER, .7515 oz ASW
Opening of the Legislature
Similar to KM#370.

KM#	Date	Mintage	Fine	VF	XF	Unc
401	1831	—	150.00	225.00	450.00	650.00

Prince Otto of Bavaria First King of Greece
Obv: Similar to KM#370.

KM#	Date	Mintage	Fine	VF	XF	Unc
402	1832	—	150.00	200.00	250.00	500.00

Formation of Customs Union With Prussia, Saxony, Hesse and Thuringia
Obv: Similar to KM#370.

KM#	Date	Mintage	Fine	VF	XF	Unc
403	1833	—	150.00	200.00	250.00	500.00

Monument For Bavarians Who Fell In Russia
Obv: Similar to KM#370.

KM#	Date	Mintage	Fine	VF	XF	Unc
404	1833	—	150.00	200.00	250.00	500.00

Provincial Legislature
Obv: Similar to KM#370.

KM#	Date	Mintage	Fine	VF	XF	Unc
405	1834	—	150.00	200.00	275.00	500.00

Erection of Monument at Oberwittelsbach
Obv: Similar to KM#370.

KM#	Date	Mintage	Fine	VF	XF	Unc
406	1834	—	150.00	200.00	300.00	550.00

Entry of Baden to German Customs Union
Obv: Similar to KM#370.

KM#	Date	Mintage	Fine	VF	XF	Unc
407	1835	—	150.00	200.00	250.00	550.00

Establishment of Bavarian Mortgage Bank
Obv: Similar to KM#370.

KM#	Date	Mintage	Fine	VF	XF	Unc
408	1835	—	150.00	225.00	300.00	575.00

Monument for King Otto Leaving His Mother
Obv: Similar to KM#370.

KM#	Date	Mintage	Fine	VF	XF	Unc
409	1835	—	150.00	200.00	250.00	450.00

Construction of First Steam Railway
Obv: Similar to KM#370.

KM#	Date	Mintage	Fine	VF	XF	Unc
410	1835	—	150.00	200.00	275.00	500.00

Monument in Munich to King Maximilian Joseph
Obv: Similar to KM#370.

KM#	Date	Mintage	Fine	VF	XF	Unc
411.1	1835	—	150.00	200.00	300.00	500.00

Rev: Sceptre not beyond shoulder.

KM#	Date	Mintage	Fine	VF	XF	Unc
411.2	1835	—	175.00	300.00	450.00	750.00

School Given To Benedictine Order
Obv: Similar to KM#370.

KM#	Date	Mintage	Fine	VF	XF	Unc
412	1835	—	150.00	225.00	350.00	550.00

Erection of Otto Chapel at Kiefersfelden
Obv: Similar to KM#370.

KM#	Date	Mintage	Fine	VF	XF	Unc
413	1836	—	150.00	200.00	275.00	500.00

Order of St. Michael as Order of Merit
Obv: Similar to KM#370.

KM#	Date	Mintage	Fine	VF	XF	Unc
415	1837	—	150.00	200.00	300.00	575.00

(Vereins)

18.5200 g, .900 SILVER, .5360 oz ASW
Maximillian II

KM#	Date	Mintage	Fine	VF	XF	Unc
468	1857	1.560	20.00	40.00	80.00	150.00
	1858	2.283	20.00	40.00	80.00	150.00
	1859	2.661	20.00	40.00	80.00	150.00
	1860	2.471	20.00	40.00	80.00	150.00
	1861	2.682	20.00	40.00	80.00	150.00
	1862	2.587	20.00	40.00	80.00	150.00
	1863	2.587	20.00	40.00	80.00	150.00
	1864	1.458	20.00	40.00	80.00	150.00

Obv: Ludwig II w/part in hair.

KM#	Date	Mintage	Fine	VF	XF	Unc
481	1864	Inc. Ab.	60.00	135.00	250.00	500.00
	1865	1.144	35.00	75.00	150.00	400.00
	1866	1.075	40.00	80.00	175.00	450.00

Obv: W/o part in hair. Rev: Arms.

KM#	Date	Mintage	Fine	VF	XF	Unc
494.1	1866	Inc. Ab.	35.00	50.00	150.00	175.00
	1867	.595	35.00	55.00	160.00	190.00
	1868	.312	35.00	60.00	160.00	325.00
	1869	.277	35.00	75.00	180.00	375.00
	1870	.264	35.00	60.00	160.00	325.00
	1871	.718	35.00	55.00	150.00	300.00

Rev:New arabesques below arms.

KM#	Date	Mintage	Fine	VF	XF	Unc
494.2	1871	—	300.00	600.00	1100.	1800.

Obv: J. REIS below truncation.

KM#	Date	Mintage	Fine	VF	XF	Unc
495	1871	Inc. Ab.	125.00	250.00	400.00	600.00

KM#	Date	Mintage	Fine	VF	XF	Unc
489	ND(1865)	.110	20.00	35.00	75.00	115.00
	1866	Inc. Ab.	20.00	35.00	60.00	100.00
	1867	Inc. Ab.	20.00	35.00	60.00	100.00

KM#	Date	Mintage	Fine	VF	XF	Unc
489	1868	Inc. Ab.	20.00	35.00	60.00	100.00
	1869	Inc. Ab.	20.00	35.00	60.00	100.00
	1870	Inc. Ab.	20.00	35.00	60.00	100.00
	1871	Inc. Ab.	20.00	35.00	60.00	100.00

German Victory In Franco-Prussian War

KM#	Date	Mintage	Fine	VF	XF	Unc
496	1871	.150	30.00	45.00	70.00	130.00
	1871	—	—	—	Proof	375.00

ZWEI (2) THALER

(3-1/2 Gulden)

37.1200 g, .900 SILVER, 1.0743 oz ASW
Monetary Union of Six South German States
Ludwig I

KM#	Date	Mintage	Fine	VF	XF	Unc
416	1837	—	150.00	200.00	275.00	450.00

Reapportionment of Bavaria
Obv: Similar to KM#416.

KM#	Date	Mintage	Fine	VF	XF	Unc
418	1838	—	150.00	300.00	450.00	750.00

Maximilian I, Elector of Bavaria
Obv: Similar to KM#416.

KM#	Date	Mintage	Fine	VF	XF	Unc
425	1839	—	150.00	200.00	375.00	575.00

Obv: Similar to KM#416.

KM#	Date	Mintage	Fine	VF	XF	Unc
426	1839	.113	150.00	250.00	500.00	1400.
	1840	.193	125.00	200.00	400.00	1200.
	1841	.450	150.00	250.00	500.00	1400.

Albrecht Durer
Obv: Similar to KM#416.

KM#	Date	Mintage	Fine	VF	XF	Unc
427	1840	—	150.00	200.00	300.00	550.00

Jean Paul Friedrich Richter
Obv: Similar to KM#416.

KM#	Date	Mintage	Fine	VF	XF	Unc
429	1841	—	150.00	200.00	300.00	550.00

Walhalla Commemorative
Obv: Similar to KM#416.

KM#	Date	Mintage	Fine	VF	XF	Unc
430	1842	—	150.00	200.00	250.00	450.00

Marriage of Crown Prince of Bavaria and Marie, Royal Princess of Prussia
Obv: Similar to KM#416.

KM#	Date	Mintage	Fine	VF	XF	Unc
431.1	1842	—	150.00	200.00	250.00	450.00

Obv: 1 OCTB. 1842 (Error date).

KM#	Date	Mintage	Fine	VF	XF	Unc
431.2	1842	—	150.00	200.00	250.00	450.00

Obv: Similar to KM#416.

KM#	Date	Mintage	Fine	VF	XF	Unc
432	1842	.085	100.00	250.00	450.00	1200.
	1843	.277	100.00	150.00	250.00	700.00
	1844	.122	100.00	175.00	300.00	800.00
	1845	.167	100.00	175.00	300.00	800.00
	1846	.132	100.00	225.00	400.00	1000.
	1847	.012	100.00	225.00	400.00	1000.
	1848	.192	100.00	150.00	250.00	700.00

100th Anniversary Academy of Erlangen
Obv: Similar to KM#416.

KM#	Date	Mintage	Fine	VF	XF	Unc
434	1843	—	150.00	200.00	300.00	550.00

Completion of the General's Hall in Munich
Obv: Similar to KM#416.

KM#	Date	Mintage	Fine	VF	XF	Unc
437	1844	—	150.00	200.00	325.00	600.00

Chancellor Baron von Kreittmayr
Obv: Similar to KM#416.

KM#	Date	Mintage	Fine	VF	XF	Unc
439	1845	—	200.00	325.00	550.00	1000.

Birth of 2 Grandsons
Obv: Similar to KM#416.

KM#	Date	Mintage	Fine	VF	XF	Unc
440	1845	—	150.00	275.00	400.00	650.00

Completion of Canal Between Danube and Main Rivers
Obv: Similar to KM#416.

KM#	Date	Mintage	Fine	VF	XF	Unc
441	1846	—	200.00	325.00	450.00	725.00

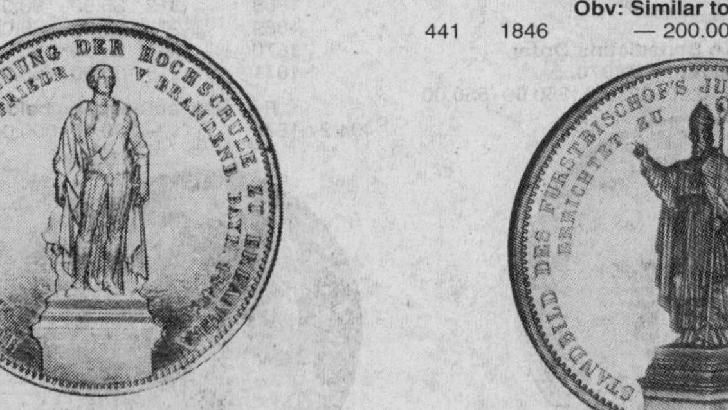

Bishop Julius Echter von Mespelbrunn
Obv: Similar to KM#416.

KM#	Date	Mintage	Fine	VF	XF	Unc
442	1847	—	200.00	400.00	600.00	1300.

Abdication of Ludwig I for Maximilian
Obv: Similar to KM#416.

KM#	Date	Mintage	Fine	VF	XF	Unc
443	1848	—	400.00	900.00	1600.	3200.

New Constitution
Maximillian II
Edge: VEREINSMUNZE

KM#	Date	Mintage	Fine	VF	XF	Unc
447.1	1848	—	175.00	225.00	400.00	700.00

Edge: CONVENTION-VOM

KM#	Date	Mintage	Fine	VF	XF	Unc
447.2	1848	—	175.00	325.00	500.00	775.00

NOTE: Restrike post 1857.

Edge: DREY EIN HALB GULDEN

KM#	Date	Mintage	Fine	VF	XF	Unc
447.3	1848	—	225.00	425.00	700.00	1100.

NOTE: Restrike post 1857.

Johann Christoph von Gluck
Obv: Similar to KM#447.1. Edge: VEREINSMUNZE.

KM#	Date	Mintage	Fine	VF	XF	Unc
448.1	1848	—	500.00	750.00	1500.	3000.

Edge: DREY EIN HALB GULDEN

KM#	Date	Mintage	Fine	VF	XF	Unc
448.2	1848	—	500.00	750.00	1500.	3000.

Orlando Di Lasso
Obv: Similar to KM#447.1. Edge: VEREINSMUNZE.

KM#	Date	Mintage	Fine	VF	XF	Unc
455.1	1849	—	700.00	1250.	1750.	3500.

Edge: DREY EIN HALB GULDEN

KM#	Date	Mintage	Fine	VF	XF	Unc
455.2	1849	—	700.00	1250.	1750.	3500.

KM#	Date	Mintage	Fine	VF	XF	Unc
456	1849	—	125.00	250.00	500.00	1200.
	1850	—	100.00	200.00	400.00	900.00
	1851	—	100.00	175.00	350.00	700.00
	1852	—	100.00	200.00	400.00	900.00
	1853	—	100.00	175.00	350.00	700.00
	1854	—	100.00	150.00	250.00	550.00
	1855	.417	100.00	150.00	250.00	550.00
	1856	.142	100.00	150.00	250.00	550.00

Exhibition of German Products in Crystal Palace
Obv: Similar to KM#447.1. Edge: VEREINS MUNZE.

KM#	Date	Mintage	Fine	VF	XF	Unc
464.1	1854	—	175.00	250.00	350.00	550.00

Edge: CONVENTION-VOM

KM#	Date	Mintage	Fine	VF	XF	Unc
464.2	1854	—	175.00	250.00	350.00	550.00

Erection of Monument to King Maximilian II
Obv: Similar to KM#447.1.

KM#	Date	Mintage	Fine	VF	XF	Unc
467	1856	1,152	300.00	425.00	750.00	1400.

(Vereins)

37.0400 g, .900 SILVER, 1.0717 oz ASW
Obv: Similar to KM#447.1.

KM#	Date	Mintage	Fine	VF	XF	Unc
474	1859	.028	350.00	700.00	1350.	2700.
	1860	.069	200.00	375.00	600.00	1250.

Obv: Different hair style.

KM#	Date	Mintage	Fine	VF	XF	Unc
475	1861	.029	300.00	450.00	800.00	1600.
	1862	8,727	400.00	550.00	1000.	2000.
	1863	.011	350.00	500.00	800.00	1800.
	1864	8,201	350.00	550.00	1000.	2000.

Ludwig II

KM#	Date	Mintage	Fine	VF	XF	Unc
490	1865	2,490	2750.	4500.	6000.	8500.
	1867	1,760	3750.	6500.	8500.	14,000.
	1869	—	3750.	6500.	8500.	14,000.

1/2 KRONE

5.0000 g, .900 GOLD, .1446 oz AGW
Maximillian II

KM#	Date	Mintage	Fine	VF	XF	Unc
469	1857	1,749	—	2500.	4000.	7000.
	1858	1,020	—	3000.	4500.	7500.
	1859	1,200	—	3000.	4500.	7500.
	1860	—	—	—	8000.	12,000.
	1861	32 pcs.	—	—	8000.	12,000.
	1863	—	—	—	8000.	12,000.
	1863	—	—	—	Proof	*
	1864	—	—	—	8000.	12,000.

*NOTE: Stack's Hammel sale 9/82 Proof realized $13,000.

Ludwig II

KM#	Date	Mintage	Fine	VF	XF	Unc
482	1864	—	—	—	Rare	—
	1865	—	—	—	Rare	—
	1866	—	—	—	Rare	—
	1867	12 pcs.	—	—	Rare	—
	1868	—	—	—	Rare	—
	1869	—	—	—	Rare	—
	1869	—	—	—	Proof	*

*NOTE: Stack's Hammel sale 9/82 Proof realized $17,000.

KRONE

10.0000 g, .900 GOLD, .2892 oz AGW
Maximillian II

KM#	Date	Mintage	Fine	VF	XF	Unc
470	1857	771 pcs.	—	5000.	8000.	12,000.
(C249)	1858	753 pcs.	—	5000.	8000.	12,000.
	1859	200 pcs.	—	6000.	10,000.	15,000.
	1860	45 pcs.	—	—	12,000.	18,000.
	1861	65 pcs.	—	—	12,000.	18,000.
	1863	—	—	—	12,000.	18,000.
	1864	—	—	—	12,000.	18,000.

Ludwig II

KM#	Date	Mintage	Fine	VF	XF	Unc
483	1864	—	—	—	Rare	—
	1865	—	—	—	Rare	—
	1865	12 pcs.	—	—	Proof	*
	1866	—	—	—	Rare	—
	1867	12 pcs.	—	—	Rare	—
	1868	—	—	—	Rare	—
	1869	—	—	—	Rare	—

*NOTE: Stack's Hammel sale 9/82 Proof realized $29,000.

MONETARY REFORM

2 MARK

11.1110 g, .900 SILVER, .3215 oz ASW
Ludwig II

KM#	Date	Mintage	Fine	VF	XF	Unc
505	1876D	5.370	30.00	60.00	225.00	550.00
	1877D	1.512	30.00	60.00	250.00	700.00
	1880D	.169	75.00	150.00	600.00	1200.
	1883D	.104	60.00	150.00	325.00	800.00

Otto

KM#	Date	Mintage	Fine	VF	XF	Unc
507	1888D	.172	150.00	300.00	700.00	1200.

KM#	Date	Mintage	Fine	VF	XF	Unc
511	1891D	.246	12.00	32.50	90.00	240.00
	1893D	.246	20.00	37.50	90.00	200.00
	1896D	.492	12.00	25.00	55.00	150.00
	1898D	.201	50.00	100.00	225.00	500.00
	1899D	.753	12.00	25.00	50.00	140.00
	1900D	.722	14.00	25.00	45.00	110.00
	1901D	.809	14.00	25.00	45.00	125.00
	1902D	1.321	10.00	22.00	35.00	110.00
	1903D	1.406	10.00	22.00	35.00	100.00
	1904D	2.320	10.00	22.00	35.00	100.00
	1905D	1.406	10.00	22.00	35.00	85.00
	1906D	1.055	10.00	22.00	45.00	95.00
	1907D	2.106	10.00	22.00	35.00	75.00
	1908D	.633	10.00	22.00	35.00	85.00
	1912D	.214	10.00	22.00	35.00	100.00
	1913D	.098	35.00	70.00	140.00	210.00

90th Birthday of Prince Regent Luitpold

KM#	Date	Mintage	Fine	VF	XF	Unc
516	1911D	.640	10.00	17.50	25.00	40.00
	1911D	—	—	—	Proof	100.00

Ludwig III

KM#	Date	Mintage	Fine	VF	XF	Unc
519	1914D	.574	30.00	60.00	90.00	120.00

3 MARK

16.6670 g, .900 SILVER, .4823 oz ASW
Otto

KM#	Date	Mintage	Fine	VF	XF	Unc
515	1908D	.681	10.00	15.00	25.00	60.00
	1909D	1.827	10.00	15.00	25.00	60.00
	1910D	1.496	10.00	15.00	25.00	60.00
	1911D	.843	10.00	15.00	25.00	60.00
	1912D	1.014	10.00	15.00	25.00	60.00
	1913D	.731	10.00	15.00	25.00	60.00
	1913D	—	—	—	Proof	90.00

90th Birthday of Prince Regent Luitpold

KM#	Date	Mintage	Fine	VF	XF	Unc
517	1911D	.640	12.50	20.00	30.00	60.00
	1911D	—	—	—	Proof	90.00

Ludwig III

KM#	Date	Mintage	Fine	VF	XF	Unc
520	1914D	.717	15.00	30.00	45.00	60.00
	1914D	—	—	—	Proof	125.00

Golden Wedding Anniversary

KM#	Date	Mintage	Fine	VF	XF	Unc
523	1918D	130 pcs.	—	12,500.	20,000.	25,000.

5 MARK

27.7770 g, .900 SILVER, .8038 oz ASW
Ludwig II

KM#	Date	Mintage	Fine	VF	XF	Unc
502	1874D	.085	40.00	70.00	350.00	800.00
	1875D	.657	40.00	70.00	325.00	700.00
	1876D	1.130	35.00	60.00	250.00	600.00

1.9910 g, .900 GOLD, .0576 oz AGW

KM#	Date	Mintage	Fine	VF	XF	Unc
506	1877D	.635	125.00	200.00	275.00	400.00
	1877D	—	—	—	Proof	1500.
	1878D	.128	350.00	800.00	1000.	1400.

27.7770 g, .900 SILVER, .8038 oz ASW
Otto

KM#	Date	Mintage	Fine	VF	XF	Unc
508	1888D	.069	175.00	275.00	900.00	1500.
	1888D	—	—	—	Proof	3500.

Obv: Similar to KM#508.

KM#	Date	Mintage	Fine	VF	XF	Unc
512	1891D	.098	17.50	35.00	100.00	300.00
	1893D	.098	25.00	50.00	120.00	300.00
	1894D	.141	17.50	35.00	120.00	300.00
	1895D	.141	22.50	45.00	110.00	300.00
	1896D	.028	55.00	125.00	600.00	1000.
	1898D	.303	15.00	30.00	60.00	175.00
	1899D	.141	25.00	50.00	90.00	225.00
	1900D	.295	15.00	30.00	90.00	200.00
	1901D	.275	15.00	30.00	90.00	200.00
	1902D	.486	15.00	30.00	65.00	175.00
	1903D	1.012	15.00	30.00	65.00	175.00
	1904D	.548	20.00	40.00	60.00	175.00
	1906D	.070	35.00	75.00	200.00	400.00

KM#	Date	Mintage	Fine	VF	XF	Unc
512	1907D	.753	15.00	25.00	55.00	125.00
	1908D	.537	15.00	25.00	50.00	125.00
	1913D	.420	17.50	25.00	45.00	100.00
	Common date	—	—	—	Proof	900.00

90th Birthday of Prince Regent Luitpold
Rev: Similar to KM#512.

KM#	Date	Mintage	Fine	VF	XF	Unc
518	1911D	.160	25.00	70.00	100.00	135.00
	1911D	—	—	—	Proof	175.00

Ludwig III
Rev: Similar to KM#512.

KM#	Date	Mintage	Fine	VF	XF	Unc
521	1914D	.142	35.00	80.00	130.00	175.00

10 MARK

3.9820 g, .900 GOLD, .1152 oz AGW
Ludwig II
Obv: J. REIS below truncation. Rev: Type I.

KM#	Date	Mintage	Fine	VF	XF	Unc
500	1872D	.626	65.00	125.00	175.00	350.00
	1872D	—	—	—	Proof	1600.
	1873D	1.198	65.00	125.00	175.00	300.00
	1873D	—	—	—	Proof	1600.

Rev: Type II.

KM#	Date	Mintage	Fine	VF	XF	Unc
503	1874D	.407	65.00	120.00	160.00	250.00
	1874D	—	—	—	Proof	1300.
	1875D	.816	65.00	120.00	160.00	250.00
	1876D	.684	65.00	120.00	160.00	250.00
	1877D	.283	65.00	120.00	160.00	250.00
	1878D	.638	65.00	120.00	160.00	250.00
	1879D	.224	65.00	120.00	160.00	250.00
	1880D	.299	65.00	120.00	160.00	250.00
	1881D	.157	65.00	120.00	160.00	250.00
	1881D	—	—	—	Proof	1300.

Otto
Obv. leg: . . . .VON BAYERN. Rev: Type II.

KM#	Date	Mintage	Fine	VF	XF	Unc
509	1888D	.281	100.00	200.00	275.00	450.00
	1888D	—	—	—	Proof	1300.

Rev: Type III.

KM#	Date	Mintage	Fine	VF	XF	Unc
510	1890D	.420	65.00	130.00	150.00	200.00
	1893D	.422	65.00	130.00	150.00	200.00

KM#	Date	Mintage	Fine	VF	XF	Unc
510	1896D	.281	65.00	120.00	170.00	225.00
	1898D	.589	65.00	130.00	150.00	200.00
	1900D	.141	125.00	150.00	225.00	300.00
	1900D	—	—	—	Proof	700.00

Obv. leg:. . . .v. BAYERN

KM#	Date	Mintage	Fine	VF	XF	Unc
514	1900D	Inc. Ab.	65.00	140.00	225.00	325.00
	1901D	.141	65.00	125.00	200.00	300.00
	1902D	.068	65.00	125.00	200.00	300.00
	1903D	.534	65.00	120.00	180.00	250.00
	1904D	.211	65.00	120.00	180.00	250.00
	1905D	.281	65.00	120.00	180.00	250.00
	1906D	.141	65.00	125.00	190.00	250.00
	1907D	.211	65.00	120.00	190.00	250.00
	1909D	.209	65.00	120.00	190.00	250.00
	1910D	.141	65.00	120.00	190.00	250.00
	1911D	.072	65.00	125.00	200.00	300.00
	1912D	.141	65.00	125.00	190.00	250.00
	Common date		—	—	Proof	800.00

20 MARK

7.9650 g, .900 GOLD, .2304 oz AGW
Ludwig II
Rev: Type I.

KM#	Date	Mintage	Fine	VF	XF	Unc
501	1872D	1.556	125.00	150.00	250.00	500.00
	1872D	—	—	—	Proof	1600.
	1873D	2.770	125.00	150.00	250.00	400.00
	1873D	—	—	—	Proof	1600.

Rev: Type II.

KM#	Date	Mintage	Fine	VF	XF	Unc
504	1874D	.615	125.00	150.00	200.00	300.00
	1875D	—	725.00	1400.	2000.	2500.
	1875D	—	—	—	Proof	1500.
	1876D	.454	125.00	150.00	200.00	350.00
	1878D	.050	300.00	625.00	850.00	1400.
	1878D	—	—	—	Proof	1500.

Otto
Rev: Type III.

KM#	Date	Mintage	Fine	VF	XF	Unc
513	1895D	.501	125.00	140.00	160.00	250.00
	1895D	—	—	—	Proof	800.00
	1900D	.501	125.00	140.00	160.00	250.00
	1905D	.501	125.00	140.00	160.00	250.00
	1905D	—	—	—	Proof	800.00
	1913D	*.311	—	17,500.	22,500.	25,000.
	1913D	—	—	—	Proof	35,000.

Ludwig III

KM#	Date	Mintage	Fine	VF	XF	Unc
522	1914D	*.533	—	2000.	2500.	3000.
	1914D	—	—	—	Proof	3600.

***NOTE:** Never officially released.

TRADE COINAGE

DUCAT

3.4900 g, .937 GOLD, .1051 oz AGW
Obv. leg: D.G. MAX. IOS. . . .

KM#	Date	Mintage	Fine	VF	XF	Unc
314.1	1801	—	750.00	1250.	2250.	2850.
	1802	—	1000.	1500.	2500.	3100.

NOTE: Earlier dates (1799-1800) exist for this type.

Obv. leg: D.G. MAXIM. IOSEPH

KM#	Date	Mintage	Fine	VF	XF	Unc
314.2	1801	—	1000.	1500.	2500.	3000.
	1802	—	1000.	1500.	2500.	3000.
	1803	—	1250.	1750.	2750.	3250.

NOTE: Earlier dates (1799-1800) exist for this type.

Obv. leg: MAXIMILIAN IOSEPH. . . .

KM#	Date	Mintage	Fine	VF	XF	Unc
335	1804	—	1750.	2250.	3000.	3750.
	1805	—	1250.	1750.	2500.	3250.

KM#	Date	Mintage	Fine	VF	XF	Unc
351	1806	3,937	1750.	2250.	3250.	4250.

KM#	Date	Mintage	Fine	VF	XF	Unc
356	1807	2,260	650.00	1125.	1750.	2500.
	1808	1,465	500.00	1050.	1600.	2250.
	1809	3,263	750.00	1250.	2000.	2750.
	1810	3,124	850.00	1350.	2250.	3000.
	1811	—	600.00	1100.	1750.	2500.
	1812	—	850.00	1350.	2250.	3000.
	1813	—	600.00	1100.	1750.	2500.
	1814	—	600.00	1100.	1750.	2500.
	1815	—	750.00	1250.	2000.	2750.
	1816	—	600.00	1000.	1600.	2250.
	1817	—	600.00	1100.	1750.	2500.
	1818	—	600.00	1100.	1750.	2500.
	1819	—	750.00	1250.	2000.	2750.
	1820	—	600.00	1100.	1750.	2500.
	1821	—	500.00	1050.	1600.	2250.
	1822	—	600.00	1100.	1750.	2500.

Obv. leg: BAEIRN. . . . .

KM#	Date	Mintage	Fine	VF	XF	Unc
362	1821	—	1250.	1950.	3000.	4200.
	1822	—	750.00	1250.	1850.	2650.

Rev. leg: EX AURO DANUBII above river god.

KM#	Date	Mintage	Fine	VF	XF	Unc
363	1821	—	2250.	3250.	4250.	5500.

Rev. leg: EX AURO OENI above river god.

KM#	Date	Mintage	Fine	VF	XF	Unc
364	1821	—	2500.	3500.	5500.	8500.

Isar - Gold Ducat

KM#	Date	Mintage	Fine	VF	XF	Unc
365	1821	—	1750.	2750.	5000.	7750.

Rhine - Gold Ducat

KM#	Date	Mintage	Fine	VF	XF	Unc
366	1821	—	1000.	1750.	3500.	4750.

Obv: Older head.

KM#	Date	Mintage	Fine	VF	XF	Unc
368	1823	4,400	600.00	1000.	1600.	2250.
	1824	.019	750.00	1250.	2000.	2750.
	1825	3,000	600.00	1100.	1650.	2300.

Ludwig I

KM#	Date	Mintage	Fine	VF	XF	Unc
375	1826	696 pcs.	1250.	1850.	2375.	2850.
	1827	4,200	1750.	2500.	3250.	3850.
	1828	3,090	1750.	2000.	2500.	3000.

Obv. leg: LUDWIG I

KM#	Date	Mintage	Fine	VF	XF	Unc
388.1	1828	1,351	800.00	1300.	1800.	2350.
	1829	1,143	600.00	1000.	1500.	2100.
	1830	1,731	600.00	1000.	1500.	2100.
	1831	3,907	1000.	1500.	2100.	2600.
	1832	1,884	600.00	1000.	1500.	2100.
	1833	1,230	1000.	1500.	2100.	2600.
	1834	1,711	1200.	1800.	2600.	3250.

Struck in collared dies.

KM#	Date	Mintage	Fine	VF	XF	Unc
388.2	1835	2,048	600.00	1000.	1500.	2100.

KM#	Date	Mintage	Fine	VF	XF	Unc
428	1840	5,000	600.00	1000.	1500.	2100.
	1841	2,309	650.00	1150.	1800.	2350.
	1842	810 pcs.	650.00	1150.	1800.	2350.
	1843	2,358	650.00	1150.	1800.	2350.
	1844	4,259	850.00	1500.	2350.	3150.
	1845	2,470	600.00	1000.	1500.	2100.
	1846	3,642	650.00	1150.	1800.	2350.
	1847	5,122	600.00	1000.	1500.	2100.
	1848	1,470	600.00	1000.	1500.	2100.

Rev. leg: EX AURO DANUBII above River God.

KM#	Date	Mintage	Fine	VF	XF	Unc
395.1	1830	—	1500.	3000.	4500.	6250.

Rev: Inverted "C" in date.

KM#	Date	Mintage	Fine	VF	XF	Unc
395.2	1830	—	1500.	3250.	4750.	6500.

Obv. leg: LUDWIG I. . . .

KM#	Date	Mintage	Fine	VF	XF	Unc
396	1830	—	1500.	3000.	4500.	6250.

Inn - Gold Ducat

KM#	Date	Mintage	Fine	VF	XF	Unc
397	1830	—	1500.	3000.	4500.	6250.

Isar - Gold Ducat

KM#	Date	Mintage	Fine	VF	XF	Unc
398	1830	—	1750.	3600.	5350.	7500.

Rhine - Gold Ducat

KM#	Date	Mintage	Fine	VF	XF	Unc
399	1830	—	1000.	2500.	4000.	5750.

Obv. leg: LUDWIG I. . . .

KM#	Date	Mintage	Fine	VF	XF	Unc
400	1830	—	1000.	2500.	4000.	5750.

Rhine - Gold Ducat

KM#	Date	Mintage	Fine	VF	XF	Unc
433	1842	—	500.00	1250.	2250.	3250.
	1846	—	400.00	1000.	2000.	3000.

Maximillian II

Obv. leg: . . . . .KOENIG V BAYERN

KM#	Date	Mintage	Fine	VF	XF	Unc
457	1849	1,470	750.00	1250.	1750.	2250.
	1850	1,519	500.00	1000.	1250.	1750.
	1851	3,815	400.00	600.00	900.00	1200.
	1852	4,396	400.00	600.00	900.00	1200.
	1853	5,603	400.00	600.00	900.00	1200.
	1854	5,707	400.00	600.00	900.00	1200.
	1855	1,540	500.00	1000.	1250.	1750.
	1856	3,782	400.00	600.00	900.00	1200.

Obv. leg: . . . . .BAVARIAE REX

KM#	Date	Mintage	Fine	VF	XF	Unc
461	1850	100 pcs.	1750.	2250.	3500.	5250.

Rev. leg: . . . . .BERGBAU BEI GOLDKRONACH.

KM#	Date	Mintage	Fine	VF	XF	Unc
466	1855	—	12,500.	17,500.	25,000.	35,000.

Rhine - Gold Ducat

KM#	Date	Mintage	Fine	VF	XF	Unc
462	1850	—	500.00	1000.	1700.	2000.
	1851	—	550.00	1200.	2000.	2250.
	1852	—	500.00	1000.	1700.	2000.
	1853	—	500.00	1000.	1700.	2000.
	1854	—	425.00	900.00	1500.	1800.
	1855	—	600.00	1400.	2500.	3000.
	1856	—	425.00	900.00	1500.	1800.

Reduced size

KM#	Date	Mintage	Fine	VF	XF	Unc
477	1863	—	1500.	2500.	4000.	4950.

BERG

Located in western Germany. The first Count of Berg took his title in 1101 and the first coins appeared c. 1135. Not until 1380, did a duke rule in Berg. In 1801 Berg was absorbed by France but in 1806, along with Cleves and Julich, became the Grand Duchy of Berg. It was transferred to Westphalia in 1808 and given to Prussia in 1814.

RULERS

Johann Wilhelm, 1592-1609, 1609-1624
Wolfgang Wilhelm, 1624-1653
Philip Wilhelm, 1653-1690
Johann Wilhelm, 1690-1716
Philip Wilhelm, allowed to return by French, 1690-1693
Carl Philip, 1716-1742
Carl Theodor, 1742-1799
Maximilian IV, Joseph (of Bavaria) 1799-1806
Joachim Murat, 1806-1808

MINTMASTERS INITIALS

Letter	Date	Name
PR,R..,R.	1783-1804	Peter Rudesheim
TS,S,S.,T:s,Sr	1805-1818	Theodor Stockmar

1/2 STUBER

COPPER

KM#	Date	Mintage	Fine	VF	XF	Unc
2	1802.R.	—	5.00	10.00	20.00	80.00
	1803.R.	—	5.00	10.00	20.00	80.00
	1804.R.	—	5.00	10.00	20.00	80.00
5	1805 S	—	5.00	10.00	20.00	80.00

Obv: Monogram w/o rosettes.

KM#	Date	Mintage	Fine	VF	XF	Unc
6	1805 s	—	5.00	10.00	20.00	80.00

3 STUBER

1.8500 g, .220 SILVER, .0130 oz ASW

KM#	Date	Mintage	Fine	VF	XF	Unc
1	1801.R.	—	5.00	10.00	20.00	80.00
	1802.R.	—	5.00	10.00	20.00	80.00
	1803.R.	—	5.00	10.00	20.00	80.00
	1804.R.	—	5.00	10.00	20.00	80.00
	1805.R.	—	5.00	10.00	20.00	80.00
	1806.R.	—	5.00	10.00	20.00	80.00

KM#	Date	Mintage	Fine	VF	XF	Unc
7	1805 S	—	7.50	15.00	30.00	90.00
	1805 T.S.	—	7.50	15.00	30.00	90.00
	1806 S	—	7.50	15.00	30.00	90.00

Obv: Royal crown.

KM#	Date	Mintage	Fine	VF	XF	Unc
9	1806 S	—	10.00	20.00	40.00	125.00

KM#	Date	Mintage	Fine	VF	XF	Unc
10	1806 S	—	6.00	12.50	25.00	90.00
	1806 Sr	—	6.00	12.50	25.00	90.00
	1807 S	—	6.00	12.50	25.00	90.00
	1807 Sr	—	6.00	12.50	25.00	90.00

NOTE: KM#1, 9 and 10 were restruck officially in 1808-09 for circulation and were equal to 10 Centimes.

1/2 THALER

(Reichs)

9.7440 g, .750 SILVER, .2349 oz ASW
Maximillian IV Joseph

KM#	Date	Mintage	Fine	VF	XF	Unc
4	1803 R	—	125.00	250.00	500.00	1000.
	1804 R	—	125.00	250.00	500.00	1000.

THALER

(Reichs)

19.4880 g, .750 SILVER, .4690 oz ASW
Maximillian IV Joseph

KM#	Date	Mintage	Fine	VF	XF	Unc
3	1802 PR	—	225.00	450.00	850.00	2000.
	1803 PR	—	250.00	500.00	900.00	2250.
	1804 PR	—	275.00	550.00	950.00	2500.
	1805 PR	—	300.00	600.00	1000.	2750.

Obv: T. S. below larger head.

KM#	Date	Mintage	Fine	VF	XF	Unc
8	1805 TS	9,396	350.00	550.00	1000.	2500.
	1806 TS	7,044	400.00	600.00	1200.	2750.

Joachim

KM#	Date	Mintage	Fine	VF	XF	Unc
11	1806 TS	8,356	450.00	650.00	1300.	2750.

(Cassa)

17.3230 g, .751 SILVER, .4177 oz ASW

KM#	Date	Mintage	Fine	VF	XF	Unc
12	1807 TS	—	1000.	2000.	3000.	5000.

Obv: Similar to KM#12.

KM#	Date	Mintage	Fine	VF	XF	Unc
13	1807 TS	—	1500.	2500.	5000.	10,000.

BIBERACH

Located in Wurttemberg 22 miles to the southwest of Ulm, Biberach became a free imperial city in 1312. The city came under the control of Baden in 1803 and then of Wurttemberg in 1806.

DUCAT

3.5000 g, .986 GOLD, .1109 oz AGW
Peace of Luneville
Obv: City god kneeling at altar, eye of God w/rays above.
Rev: 9-line inscription w/Roman numeral date.

KM#	Date	Mintage	VG	Fine	VF	XF
20	1801	—	—	850.00	1500.	2250.

BIRKENFELD

Located in southwest Germany. For most of the time prior to 1801, Birkenfeld was in the possession of the Counts Palatine. It was a part of France from 1801-1814, Prussia from 1814-1817 and was made a principality in 1817.

RULERS

Paul Friedrich August (of Oldenburg), 1829-1853
Nikolaus Friedrich Peter (of Oldenburg), 1853-1900

MINT MARKS

B - Hannover

PFENNIG

COPPER

KM#	Date	Mintage	Fine	VF	XF	Unc
6	1848	.158	45.00	80.00	125.00	175.00

KM#	Date	Mintage	Fine	VF	XF	Unc
20	1859B	.072	25.00	60.00	90.00	140.00

2 PFENNIGE

COPPER

KM#	Date	Mintage	Fine	VF	XF	Unc
7	1848	.117	15.00	35.00	65.00	150.00

KM#	Date	Mintage	Fine	VF	XF	Unc
15	1858B	.072	15.00	35.00	60.00	120.00

3 PFENNIGE

COPPER

KM#	Date	Mintage	Fine	VF	XF	Unc
8	1848	.121	17.00	37.50	75.00	150.00

Obv: Crowned NFP monogram.

KM#	Date	Mintage	Fine	VF	XF	Unc
16	1858B	.072	17.00	37.50	75.00	150.00

1/2 SILBER GROSCHEN

1.0900 g, .220 SILVER, .0077 oz ASW

KM#	Date	Mintage	Fine	VF	XF	Unc
17	1858B	.060	40.00	80.00	120.00	275.00

SILBER GROSCHEN

2.1900 g, .220 SILVER, .0154 oz ASW
Obv: Crowned arms. Rev: Value.

KM#	Date	Mintage	Fine	VF	XF	Unc
9	1848	.063	35.00	70.00	110.00	225.00

Obv: Different arms.

KM#	Date	Mintage	Fine	VF	XF	Unc
18	1858B	.060	35.00	70.00	110.00	225.00

2-1/2 SILBER GROSCHEN

(1/12 Thaler)

3.2200 g, .375 SILVER, .0388 oz ASW
Obv: Crowned arms. Rev: Value.

KM#	Date	Mintage	Fine	VF	XF	Unc
10	1848	.023	35.00	70.00	110.00	225.00

Obv: Different arms.

KM#	Date	Mintage	Fine	VF	XF	Unc
19	1858B	.036	35.00	70.00	110.00	225.00

BRANDENBURG-ANSBACH-BAYREUTH

Held by Prussia from 1791 to 1805 and then given to Bavaria.

RULERS

Friedrich Wilhelm III of Prussia, 1797-1805

PFENNIG

.2600 g, .111 SILVER, .0009 oz ASW
Obv: Crowned FWR monogram. Rev: Value.

KM#	Date	Mintage	Fine	VF	XF	Unc
17	1801B	.616	3.00	7.00	15.00	40.00
	1803B	.984	3.00	7.00	15.00	40.00

NOTE: Earlier date (1799) exists for this type.

KREUZER

.7200 g, .163 SILVER, .0037 oz ASW

KM#	Date	Mintage	Fine	VF	XF	Unc
18	1802B	.324	3.00	7.00	20.00	50.00

KM#	Date	Mintage	Fine	VF	XF	Unc
18	1803B	.533	3.00	7.00	20.00	50.00
	1804B	1.243	3.00	7.00	20.00	50.00

3 KREUZER

1.0500 g, .336 SILVER, .0113 oz ASW

KM#	Date	Mintage	Fine	VF	XF	Unc
15	1801B	1.335	7.00	15.00	30.00	100.00
	1802B	1.330	7.00	15.00	30.00	100.00

NOTE: Earlier dates (1798-1800) exist for this type.

6 KREUZER

2.4400 g, .375 SILVER, .0294 oz ASW

KM#	Date	Mintage	Fine	VF	XF	Unc
16	1801B	.340	10.00	20.00	60.00	125.00
	1802B	.249	10.00	20.00	60.00	125.00

NOTE: Earlier dates (1798-1800) exist for this type.

TRADE COINAGE

DUCAT

3.5000 g, .986 GOLD, .1109 oz AGW

KM#	Date	Mintage	Fine	VF	XF	Unc
19	1803B	—	—	—	Rare	—

BREMEN

Located in northwest Germany. The city was founded c. 787 but was nominally under control of the archbishops until 1646 when it became a Free Imperial City. Bremen was granted the mint right in 1369 and there was practically continuous coinage until 1907.

FREE CITY

MINTMASTERS INITIALS

Letter	Date	Name
B	1844-1868	Th. W. Bruel, in Hannover
OHK	1761-1805	Otto Heinrich Knorre

SCHWAREN

COPPER

KM#	Date	Mintage	Fine	VF	XF	Unc
241	1859	.069	2.00	4.00	8.00	27.50

2-1/2 SCHWAREN

COPPER
Rev: D.B. in exergue.

KM#	Date	Mintage	Fine	VF	XF	Unc
220	1802	.196	3.00	6.00	15.00	50.00

NOTE: Earlier date (1797) exists for this type.

KM#	Date	Mintage	Fine	VF	XF	Unc
225	1820	.183	3.00	6.00	15.00	50.00

KM#	Date	Mintage	Fine	VF	XF	Unc
234	1841	.131	7.50	15.00	30.00	70.00
	1853	.177	2.00	4.00	8.00	30.00
	1861	.072	2.00	4.00	8.00	30.00
	1866	.162	2.00	4.00	8.00	30.00
235	1841	Inc. Ab.	—	—	—	—

1/2 GROTE

COPPER

KM#	Date	Mintage	Fine	VF	XF	Unc
236	1841	Inc.KM234	5.00	10.00	25.00	60.00

GROTEN

.7700 g, .281 SILVER, .0069 oz ASW

KM#	Date	Mintage	Fine	VF	XF	Unc
230	1840	.262	2.00	5.00	10.00	35.00

6 GROTE/1/12 THALER

1.9440 g, .740 SILVER, .0462 oz ASW

KM#	Date	Mintage	Fine	VF	XF	Unc
231	1840	.079	5.00	15.00	30.00	75.00

2.9200 g, .494 SILVER, .0463 oz ASW

KM#	Date	Mintage	Fine	VF	XF	Unc
240	1857	.311	4.00	8.00	17.50	45.00

KM#	Date	Mintage	Fine	VF	XF	Unc
245	1861	.127	4.50	9.00	20.00	60.00

12 GROTE

(= 1/6 Thaler)

3.8890 g, .740 SILVER, .0925 oz ASW

KM#	Date	Mintage	Fine	VF	XF	Unc
232	1840	.193	7.00	12.00	30.00	100.00
	1841	.112	7.00	12.00	30.00	110.00
	1845	.063	7.00	12.00	30.00	125.00
	1846	.056	7.00	12.00	30.00	125.00

Obv: Crowned cornered arms.

KM#	Date	Mintage	Fine	VF	XF	Unc
242	1859	.450	4.00	8.00	17.50	65.00
	1860	.150	5.00	10.00	22.50	75.00

36 GROTE

(=1/2 Thaler)

8.7700 g, .986 SILVER, .2780 oz ASW

KM#	Date	Mintage	Fine	VF	XF	Unc
233	1840	.170	20.00	40.00	70.00	160.00
	1841	.044	25.00	50.00	85.00	175.00
	1845	.084	20.00	40.00	70.00	160.00
	1846	.085	20.00	40.00	70.00	160.00
	1859	.121	20.00	40.00	70.00	160.00

KM#	Date	Mintage	Fine	VF	XF	Unc
243	1859	.050	30.00	60.00	100.00	200.00
	1864	.100	25.00	45.00	75.00	160.00

EIN (1) THALER

(Vereins)

17.5390 g, .986 SILVER, .5560 oz ASW
50th Anniversary of Liberation of Germany

KM#	Date	Mintage	Fine	VF	XF	Unc
246	1863	.020	35.00	55.00	90.00	160.00

2nd German Shooting Festival

KM#	Date	Mintage	Fine	VF	XF	Unc
248	1865 B	.050	35.00	55.00	90.00	150.00

Victory Over France

KM#	Date	Mintage	Fine	VF	XF	Unc
249	1871 B	.061	30.00	50.00	85.00	145.00

MONETARY REFORM

2 MARK

11.1110 g, .900 SILVER, .3215 oz ASW

KM#	Date	Mintage	Fine	VF	XF	Unc
250	1904J	.100	17.50	35.00	80.00	120.00
	1904J	200 pcs.	—	—	Proof	300.00

5 MARK

27.7770 g, .900 SILVER, .8038 oz ASW

KM#	Date	Mintage	Fine	VF	XF	Unc
251	1906J	.041	55.00	135.00	210.00	285.00
	1906J	600 pcs.	—	—	Proof	600.00

10 MARK

3.9820 g, .900 GOLD, .1152 oz AGW

KM#	Date	Mintage	Fine	VF	XF	Unc
253	1907J	.020	400.00	500.00	700.00	1000.
	1907J	—	—	—	Proof	1700.

20 MARK

7.9650 g, .900 GOLD, .2304 oz AGW

KM#	Date	Mintage	Fine	VF	XF	Unc
252	1906J	.020	350.00	500.00	750.00	1200.
	1906J	—	—	—	Proof	2500.

BRUNSWICK-LUNEBURG-CALENBERG-HANNOVER

Located in north-central Germany. The first duke began his rule in 1235. The first coinage appeared c. 1175. There was considerable shuffling of territory until 1692 when Ernst August became the elector of Hannover. Georg Ludwig became George I of England in 1714. There was separate coinage for Luneburg until during the reign of George III. The name was changed to Hannover in 1814.

RULERS

Georg III, (King of Great Britain), 1760-1814

After 1814 see Kingdom of Hannover

BRUNSWICK MINTS AND MINTMASTERS

Clausthal Mint

Letter	Date	Name
A	1833-1849	Vacant Mintmastership
C	1751-1753,1790-1792,1800-1802	Commission
GM,GFM	1802-1807	Georg Friedrich Michaelis
IWL	1807-1819	Johann Wilhelm Lunde
WAJA	1821-1838	Wilhelm August Julius Albert

Hannover Mint

Letter	Date	Name
C	1800-1806	Commission

PFENNING

COPPER

Obv: Wildman holding staff. Rev: Value and date.

KM#	Date	Mintage	Fine	VF	XF	Unc
330	1803 GFM	—	6.00	12.00	18.00	50.00
	1804 GFM	—	6.00	12.00	18.00	50.00

NOTE: Earlier dates (1760-1796) exist for this type.

Obv: Crowned GR monogram.
Rev: Denomination: PFENN

KM#	Date	Mintage	Fine	VF	XF	Unc
360	1801 .C.	—	4.00	7.00	10.00	40.00
	1802 .C.	—	4.00	7.00	10.00	40.00
	1802 GFM	—	4.00	7.00	10.00	40.00
	1803 GFM	—	4.00	7.00	10.00	40.00
	1804 GFM	—	4.00	7.00	10.00	40.00
	1806 GFM	—	4.00	7.00	10.00	40.00

NOTE: Earlier dates (1768-1800) exist for this type.

2 PFENNING

COPPER

KM#	Date	Mintage	Fine	VF	XF	Unc
402	1801 .C.	—	3.00	7.00	10.00	70.00
	1802 GFM	—	3.00	7.00	10.00	70.00
	1803 GFM	—	3.00	7.00	10.00	70.00
	1804 GFM	—	3.00	7.00	10.00	70.00
	1807 GFM	—	3.00	7.00	10.00	70.00

NOTE: Earlier dates (1794-1800) exist for this type.

4 PFENNING

BILLON

Obv: Crowned GR monogram. Rev: Value, date.

KM#	Date	Mintage	Fine	VF	XF	Unc
344	1802 .C.	—	3.00	7.00	15.00	40.00
	1804 GFM	—	3.00	7.00	15.00	40.00

NOTE: Earlier dates (1762-1799) exist for this type.

MARIENGROSCHEN

BILLON

Obv: Crowned GR monogram.
Rev: Value, date.

KM#	Date	Mintage	Fine	VF	XF	Unc
345	1802 .C.	—	3.00	7.00	15.00	40.00
	1803 GFM	—	3.00	7.00	15.00	40.00
	1804 GFM	—	3.00	7.00	15.00	40.00

NOTE: Earlier dates (1762-1799) exist for this type.

24 MARIENGROSCHEN

SILVER

Obv: Crowned arms above 2/3 in. oval.
Rev: Value above date.

KM#	Date	Mintage	Fine	VF	XF	Unc
341	1801 PLM	—	30.00	50.00	85.00	185.00

NOTE: Earlier dates (1761-1800) exist for this type.

12 EINEN (1/12) THALER

(2 Groschen)

SILVER

KM#	Date	Mintage	Fine	VF	XF	Unc
336	1801 PLM	—	3.00	7.00	15.00	60.00
	1801 EC	—	3.00	7.00	15.00	60.00
	1801 .C.	8,780	3.00	7.00	15.00	60.00
	1801 GFM	—	3.00	7.00	15.00	60.00
	1802 .C.	—	3.00	7.00	15.00	60.00
	1802 GFM	—	3.00	7.00	15.00	60.00
	1803 GFM	—	3.00	7.00	15.00	60.00
	1804 GFM	—	3.00	7.00	15.00	60.00
	1805 GFM	—	3.00	7.00	15.00	60.00
	1806 GFM	—	3.00	7.00	15.00	60.00
	1807 GFM	—	3.00	7.00	15.00	60.00

NOTE: Earlier dates (1760-1800) exist for this type.

1/6 THALER

SILVER
George III
W/o French arms or titles.

KM#	Date	Mintage	Fine	VF	XF	Unc
415	1802 C.	—	20.00	30.00	60.00	175.00
	1802 GFM	—	20.00	30.00	60.00	175.00
	1803 GFM	—	20.00	30.00	60.00	175.00
	1804/3 GFM	—	37.50	65.00	120.00	250.00
	1804 GFM	—	—	—	—	—

KM#	Date	Mintage	Fine	VF	XF	Unc
419	1804 GFM	—	15.00	25.00	75.00	200.00

KM#	Date	Mintage	Fine	VF	XF	Unc
420	1804 GFM	—	15.00	25.00	75.00	200.00

KM#	Date	Mintage	Fine	VF	XF	Unc
423	1807 GM	—	15.00	20.00	40.00	125.00

1/3 THALER

SILVER
George III

KM#	Date	Mintage	Fine	VF	XF	Unc
417	1803 GFM	—	30.00	50.00	100.00	225.00
	1804 GFM	—	30.00	50.00	100.00	225.00

KM#	Date	Mintage	Fine	VF	XF	Unc
421	1804 GFM	—	40.00	85.00	125.00	300.00

1/2 THALER

(Cassen)

SILVER
George III
Rev. value: CASSEN GELD

KM#	Date	Mintage	Fine	VF	XF	Unc
410	1801 C	372 pcs.	—	—	Rare	—

Rev. value: CASSEN=GELD

KM#	Date	Mintage	Fine	VF	XF	Unc
411	1801 C	—	—	—	Rare	—

2/3 THALER

SILVER
George III

KM#	Date	Mintage	Fine	VF	XF	Unc
412	1801 .C.	—	30.00	50.00	100.00	200.00
	1802 .C.	—	30.00	50.00	100.00	200.00

KM#	Date	Mintage	Fine	VF	XF	Unc
413	1801 .C.	—	30.00	50.00	100.00	200.00
	1802	—	30.00	50.00	100.00	200.00
	1802 .C.	—	30.00	50.00	100.00	200.00
	1802 GFM	—	30.00	50.00	100.00	200.00
	1803 GFM	—	30.00	50.00	100.00	200.00
	1804 GFM	—	30.00	50.00	100.00	200.00
	1805 GFM	—	30.00	50.00	100.00	200.00

KM#	Date	Mintage	Fine	VF	XF	Unc
422	1805 GFM	—	30.00	50.00	100.00	200.00
	1806 GFM	—	30.00	50.00	100.00	200.00
	1807 GFM	—	30.00	50.00	100.00	200.00

THALER

(Cassengeld)

SILVER
George III

KM#	Date	Mintage	Fine	VF	XF	Unc
414	1801 C	126 pcs.	400.00	750.00	1250.	2000.

TRADE COINAGE

DUCAT

3.5000 g, .986 GOLD, .1109 oz AGW

Obv: Large modified arms.
Rev. leg: EX AURO . . . . . above horse.

KM#	Date	Mintage	Fine	VF	XF	Unc
416	1802 .C.	—	350.00	525.00	900.00	1400.
	1802 GFM	—	400.00	600.00	1000.	1600.
	1804 GFM	—	300.00	525.00	800.00	1200.

PISTOLE

6.6500 g, .900 GOLD, .1924 oz AGW

KM#	Date	Mintage	Fine	VF	XF	Unc
418	1803 C	—	350.00	650.00	1100.	2000.

BRUNSWICK-WOLFENBUTTEL

Located in north-central Germany. Wolfenbuttel was annexed to Brunswick in 1257. The Wolfenbuttel line of the Brunswick house was founded in 1318 and was a fairly constant line until 1884 when Prussia installed a government that lasted until 1913. Brunswick was given to the Kaiser's son-in-law, who was the previous duke's grandson, in 1913 and he was forced to abdicate in 1918.

RULERS

Karl Wilhelm Ferdinand, 1780-1806
Friedrich Wilhelm, 1806-1815
Karl II (under regency of George III of Great Britain), 1815-1820
Karl II (under regency of George IV of Great Britain), 1820-1823
Karl II, 1823-1830
Wilhelm, 1831-1884
Prussian rule, 1884-1913
Ernst August, 1913-1918

MINTMASTERS INITIALS

Letter	Date	Name
B,LB	1844-1866	Theodor Wilhelm Bruel, in Hannover
B	1850-1859	Johann W. Chr. Brumleu, in Brunswick
CvC	1820-1850	Cramer von Clausbruch, in Brunswick
FR	1814-1820	Friedrich Ritter, in Brunswick
	1622-1640	Henning Schreiber, in Clausthal
K	1776-1802	Christian Friedrich Krull, die-cutter in Brunswick
MC	1779-1806,1820	Munz - Commission at Brunswick

PFENNIG

COPPER
Obv: Horse left.

KM#	Date	Mintage	Fine	VF	XF	Unc
995	1801 MC	—	2.00	4.00	7.00	50.00
	1802 MC	—	2.00	4.00	7.00	40.00
	1803 MC	—	2.00	4.00	7.00	50.00
	1804 MC	—	2.00	4.00	7.00	50.00
	1805 MC	—	2.00	4.00	7.00	50.00
	1806 MC	—	2.00	4.00	7.00	50.00

NOTE: Earlier dates (1780-1800) exist for this type.

Obv: M.C. below horse.

KM#	Date	Mintage	Fine	VF	XF	Unc
1050.1	1813 MC	—	2.00	3.00	6.00	50.00
	1814 MC	—	2.00	3.00	6.00	50.00

Obv: F.R. below horse.

KM#	Date	Mintage	Fine	VF	XF	Unc
1050.2	1814 FR	—	1.00	2.00	5.00	40.00
	1815 FR	—	1.00	2.00	5.00	40.00

Obv: F.R. below horse, leg: GEORG P.R.T.N.

KM#	Date	Mintage	Fine	VF	XF	Unc
1068	1816 FR	—	3.00	5.00	10.00	60.00
	1818 FR	—	3.00	5.00	10.00	60.00

KM#	Date	Mintage	Fine	VF	XF	Unc
1069	1816 FR	—	2.00	3.00	6.00	50.00
	1817 FR	—	2.00	3.00	6.00	50.00
	1818 FR	—	2.00	3.00	6.00	50.00
	1819 FR	—	2.00	3.00	6.00	50.00
	1820 FR	—	2.00	3.00	6.00	50.00

Obv. leg: FRIEDRICH WILHELM. . . . .

KM#	Date	Mintage	Fine	VF	XF	Unc
1075	1818	—	15.00	30.00	60.00	140.00

Obv. leg: GEORG D.G.

KM#	Date	Mintage	Fine	VF	XF	Unc
1076	1818 FR	—	2.00	4.00	7.00	50.00

Obv. leg: GEORG T.N. . . . . . begins at upper left.

KM#	Date	Mintage	Fine	VF	XF	Unc
1077	1818 FR	—	2.00	4.00	7.00	50.00
	1819 FR	—	2.00	4.00	7.00	50.00
	1820 FR	—	2.00	4.00	7.00	50.00

Obv. leg: GEORG T.N. begins at lower left.

KM#	Date	Mintage	Fine	VF	XF	Unc
1078	1819 FR	—	2.00	4.00	7.00	50.00

Obv: W/o F.R., leg: GEORG IV. R.TVT. . . .
Rev: MC below date.

KM#	Date	Mintage	Fine	VF	XF	Unc
1079	1819 MC	—	2.00	4.00	7.00	50.00
	1820 MC	—	2.00	4.00	7.00	50.00

Obv. leg: GEORGE IV D.G.R.TVT. . . . .

KM#	Date	Mintage	Fine	VF	XF	Unc
1085	1820 MC	—	2.00	4.00	7.00	50.00
	1822 MC	—	2.00	4.00	7.00	50.00
	1823 MC	—	2.00	4.00	7.00	50.00

Obv. leg: GEORGE IV D.G.R.T.N. . . .et.l.

KM#	Date	Mintage	Fine	VF	XF	Unc
1094	1822 CvC	—	2.00	4.00	7.00	50.00
	1823 CvC	—	2.00	4.00	7.00	50.00

Obv. leg. ends: . . . . .BR. U.LUEN.

KM#	Date	Mintage	Fine	VF	XF	Unc
1098	1823 CvC	—	1.00	2.00	3.00	40.00
	1824 CvC	—	1.00	2.00	3.00	40.00
	1825 CvC	—	1.00	2.00	3.00	40.00
	1826 CvC	—	1.00	2.00	3.00	40.00
	1828 CvC	—	1.00	2.00	3.00	40.00
	1829/8 CvC	—	3.00	6.00	12.50	50.00
	1829 CvC	—	1.00	2.00	3.00	40.00
	1830 CvC	—	1.00	2.00	3.00	40.00

Obv. leg. ends: . . . . .BR.U.L.

KM#	Date	Mintage	Fine	VF	XF	Unc
1107	1824 Cvc	—	1.00	2.00	3.00	40.00

Obv. leg. ends: . . . . .BR. U. LUEN.
Rev. value: PFENNIG.

KM#	Date	Mintage	Fine	VF	XF	Unc
1120	1831 CvC	—	1.00	3.00	4.00	40.00
	1832 CvC	—	1.00	3.00	4.00	40.00
	1833 CvC	—	1.00	3.00	4.00	40.00
	1834 CvC	—	1.00	3.00	4.00	40.00

Rev. value: PFENNIG.

KM#	Date	Mintage	Fine	VF	XF	Unc
1127	1834 CvC	—	1.00	3.00	5.00	40.00

KM#	Date	Mintage	Fine	VF	XF	Unc
1142	1851 B	—	1.00	2.00	4.00	35.00
	1852 B	.270	1.00	2.00	4.00	35.00
	1853 B	.139	1.00	2.00	4.00	35.00
	1855 B	.079	1.00	2.00	4.00	35.00
	1856 B	.514	1.00	2.00	4.00	35.00

Rev: W/o B below date.

KM#	Date	Mintage	Fine	VF	XF	Unc
1148	1854	.126	3.00	5.00	10.00	90.00
	1856	Inc.Ab.	3.00	5.00	10.00	90.00

Obv. leg: HERZOGTH.BRAUNSCHWEIG.

KM#	Date	Mintage	Fine	VF	XF	Unc
1154	1859	.103	1.00	2.00	3.50	25.00
	1860	.307	1.00	2.00	3.50	25.00

2 PFENNIGE

COPPER

KM#	Date	Mintage	Fine	VF	XF	Unc
1056	1814 FR	—	2.00	3.00	5.00	45.00
	1815 FR	—	2.00	3.00	5.00	45.00

Obv: W/o F.R. below monogram.

KM#	Date	Mintage	Fine	VF	XF	Unc
1064	1815	—	2.00	3.00	5.00	45.00

Rev: M.C. below date.

KM#	Date	Mintage	Fine	VF	XF	Unc
1086	1820 MC	—	2.00	3.00	5.00	45.00

Rev: C.v.C. below date.

KM#	Date	Mintage	Fine	VF	XF	Unc
1099	1823 CvC	—	2.00	3.00	5.00	45.00

KM#	Date	Mintage	Fine	VF	XF	Unc
1108	1824 CvC	—	2.00	3.00	5.00	45.00
	1826 CvC	—	2.00	3.00	5.00	45.00
	1827 CvC	—	2.00	3.00	5.00	45.00
	1828 CvC	—	2.00	3.00	5.00	45.00
	1829 CvC	—	2.00	3.00	5.00	45.00
	1830 CvC	—	2.00	3.00	5.00	45.00

Obv. leg: WILHELM. . . . .

KM#	Date	Mintage	Fine	VF	XF	Unc
1123	1832 CvC	—	2.00	3.00	5.00	60.00
	1833 CvC	—	2.00	3.00	5.00	60.00
	1834 CvC	—	2.00	3.00	5.00	60.00

Rev. value: PFENNIG.

KM#	Date	Mintage	Fine	VF	XF	Unc
1128	1834 CvC	—	2.00	5.00	10.00	70.00

KM#	Date	Mintage	Fine	VF	XF	Unc
1143	1851 B	—	.75	1.25	2.50	30.00
	1852 B	.135	.75	1.25	2.50	30.00
	1853 B	.124	.75	1.25	2.50	30.00
	1854 B	.063	.75	1.25	2.50	30.00
	1855 B	.189	.75	1.25	2.50	30.00
	1855	—	—	—	—	—
	1856 B	.253	.75	1.25	2.50	30.00

KM#	Date	Mintage	Fine	VF	XF	Unc
1155	1859	.062	.75	1.25	2.50	30.00
	1860	.147	.75	1.25	2.50	30.00

4 PFENNIGE

BILLON
Obv: Horse. Rev: Value

KM#	Date	Mintage	Fine	VF	XF	Unc
997	1801 MC	—	3.00	6.00	12.00	40.00
	1802 MC	—	3.00	6.00	12.00	35.00
	1803 MC	—	3.00	6.00	12.00	40.00
	1804 MC	—	3.00	6.00	12.00	40.00

NOTE: Earlier dates (1780-1800) exist for this type.

1.2300 g, .187 SILVER, .0073 oz ASW
Obv: Prancing horse left, 'F.R.' below, leg. ends: BRIETL. Rev: Value.

KM#	Date	Mintage	Fine	VF	XF	Unc
1087	1820 FR	.035	5.00	15.00	35.00	150.00

Obv: W/o F.R. Rev: C.V.C. below date.

KM#	Date	Mintage	Fine	VF	XF	Unc
1100	1823 CvC	.063	3.00	10.00	15.00	85.00

6 PFENNIGE

BILLON
Obv: Horse. Rev: Value.

KM#	Date	Mintage	Fine	VF	XF	Unc
1019	1802 MC	—	4.00	8.00	15.00	50.00
	1804 MC	—	4.00	8.00	15.00	40.00

NOTE: Earlier dates (1784-1800) exist for this type.

1.3900 g, .250 SILVER, .0111 oz ASW
Obv: M.C. below horse.

KM#	Date	Mintage	Fine	VF	XF	Unc
1057	1814 MC	—	3.00	6.00	15.00	50.00

Obv: B. instead of BR in legend.

KM#	Date	Mintage	Fine	VF	XF	Unc
1058	1814 MC	—	3.00	6.00	15.00	50.00

Obv: F.R. below mound.

KM#	Date	Mintage	Fine	VF	XF	Unc
1059	1814 FR	—	3.00	7.00	20.00	60.00
	1815 FR	.133	3.00	7.00	20.00	60.00

BILLON
Obv. leg: GEORG T.N. CAROLI D. BR.

KM#	Date	Mintage	Fine	VF	XF	Unc
1070	1816 FR	.036	5.00	10.00	25.00	100.00
	1819 FR	.030	5.00	10.00	25.00	100.00

Obv. leg: GEORG IV. . . . . . Rev: C.V.C. below date.

KM#	Date	Mintage	Fine	VF	XF	Unc
1101	1823 CvC	.060	3.00	7.00	20.00	80.00

Obv. leg. ends: . . . . .BR U L.

KM#	Date	Mintage	Fine	VF	XF	Unc
1116	1828 CvC	—	3.00	7.00	15.00	50.00

1/2 GROSCHEN

(1/60 Thaler)
(Vereins)

1.0900 g, .220 SILVER, .0077 oz ASW

KM#	Date	Mintage	Fine	VF	XF	Unc
1151	1858	.576	1.50	3.00	6.00	30.00
	1859	.131	2.00	4.00	8.00	35.00
	1860	.313	1.50	3.00	6.00	30.00

MARIENGROSCHEN

BILLON
Obv: Horse left. Rev: Value, date.

KM#	Date	Mintage	Fine	VF	XF	Unc
1031	1802 MC	—	4.00	8.00	15.00	50.00
	1803 MC	—	4.00	8.00	15.00	40.00
	1804 MC	—	4.00	8.00	15.00	50.00
	1805 MC	—	4.00	8.00	15.00	50.00
	1806 MC	—	4.00	8.00	15.00	50.00

NOTE: Earlier dates (1788-1800) exist for this type.

GROSCHEN

SILVER

KM#	Date	Mintage	VG	Fine	VF	XF
1137	1847 CVC	—	—	—	Rare	—

(1/30 Thaler)
(Vereins)

2.1900 g, .220 SILVER, .0154 oz ASW

KM#	Date	Mintage	Fine	VF	XF	Unc
1150	1857	.039	4.00	8.00	12.00	45.00
	1858	.713	2.00	4.00	8.00	35.00
	1859	.594	2.00	4.00	8.00	35.00
	1860	.095	3.00	6.00	10.00	40.00

2 MARIENGROSCHEN

BILLON

KM#	Date	Mintage	Fine	VF	XF	Unc
1045	1804 M.C.	—	5.00	10.00	20.00	50.00

4 GUTE GROSCHEN

5.3500 g, .521 SILVER, .0896 oz ASW

KM#	Date	Mintage	Fine	VF	XF	Unc
1135	1840 CvC	.060	15.00	30.00	60.00	200.00

8 GUTE GROSCHEN

SILVER

KM#	Date	Mintage	Fine	VF	XF	Unc
1026	1801 MC	—	15.00	30.00	60.00	150.00
	1803 MC	—	15.00	30.00	60.00	150.00
	1804 MC	—	15.00	30.00	60.00	150.00
	1805 MC	—	15.00	30.00	60.00	150.00

NOTE: Earlier dates (1786-1799) exist for this type.

16 GUTE GROSCHEN

SILVER
Obv: Arms. Rev: Value.

KM#	Date	Mintage	Fine	VF	XF	Unc
1020	1801 MC	—	18.00	40.00	90.00	200.00
	1802 MC	—	18.00	40.00	90.00	200.00
	1803 MC	—	18.00	40.00	90.00	200.00
	1804 MC	—	18.00	40.00	90.00	200.00
	1805 MC	—	18.00	40.00	90.00	200.00

NOTE: Earlier dates (1784-1799) exist for this type.

24 MARIENGROSCHEN

(= 2/3 Thaler)

SILVER

KM#	Date	Mintage	Fine	VF	XF	Unc
1034	1801 MC	—	25.00	60.00	140.00	325.00
	1802 MC	—	25.00	60.00	140.00	325.00

KM#	Date	Mintage	Fine	VF	XF	Unc
1034	1803 MC	—	25.00	60.00	140.00	325.00
	1804 MC	—	25.00	60.00	140.00	325.00
	1805 MC	—	25.00	60.00	140.00	325.00
	1806 MC	—	25.00	60.00	140.00	325.00

NOTE: Earlier dates (1789-1800) exist for this type.

13.0800 g, .993 SILVER, .4176 oz ASW
Obv. leg: FRIDERICVS. . . . .

KM#	Date	Mintage	Fine	VF	XF	Unc
1060	1814 FR	—	100.00	175.00	300.00	525.00
	1815 FR	.036	100.00	175.00	300.00	525.00

KM#	Date	Mintage	Fine	VF	XF	Unc
1065	1815 FR	—	90.00	150.00	250.00	450.00
	1816 FR	.027	90.00	150.00	250.00	450.00
	1817 FR	.019	90.00	150.00	250.00	450.00
	1818 FR	.017	90.00	150.00	250.00	450.00

Obv. leg: REX BRITANNIAR.

KM#	Date	Mintage	Fine	VF	XF	Unc
1088	1820 MC	.024	100.00	180.00	300.00	550.00

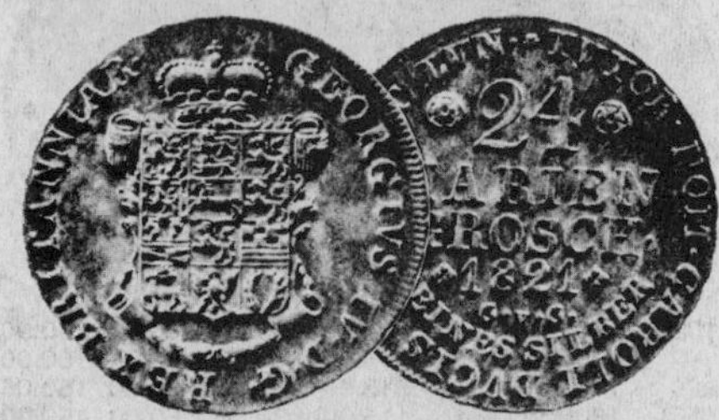

Rev: CvC below date.

KM#	Date	Mintage	Fine	VF	XF	Unc
1091	1821 CvC	.029	85.00	145.00	250.00	450.00
	1823 CvC	.030	85.00	145.00	250.00	450.00

Obv. leg: ZU BRAUNS.

KM#	Date	Mintage	Fine	VF	XF	Unc
1102	1823 CvC	—	75.00	125.00	200.00	375.00
	1824 CvC	—	75.00	125.00	200.00	375.00
	1825 CvC	—	75.00	125.00	200.00	375.00
	1826 CvC	.040	75.00	125.00	200.00	375.00
	1828 CvC	—	75.00	125.00	200.00	375.00
	1829 CvC	.034	75.00	125.00	200.00	375.00

Obv. leg: ZU BRAUNSCHW.

KM#	Date	Mintage	Fine	VF	XF	Unc
1109	1824 CvC	.032	50.00	100.00	150.00	250.00
	1825 CvC	.032	50.00	100.00	150.00	250.00
	1826 CvC	—	50.00	100.00	150.00	250.00
	1828 CvC	—	50.00	100.00	150.00	250.00
	1829 CvC	—	50.00	100.00	150.00	250.00

KM#	Date	Mintage	Fine	VF	XF	Unc
1124	1832 CvC	.032	40.00	80.00	125.00	225.00
	1833 CvC	.027	40.00	80.00	125.00	225.00
	1834 CvC	.030	40.00	80.00	125.00	225.00

24 EINEN (1/24) THALER

BILLON
Obv: Horse. Rev: Value.

KM#	Date	Mintage	Fine	VF	XF	Unc
999	1802 MC	—	3.00	7.00	15.00	50.00

NOTE: Earlier dates (1780-1798) exist for this type.

1.9400 g, .375 SILVER, .0233 oz ASW
Rev: F.R. below date.

KM#	Date	Mintage	Fine	VF	XF	Unc
1061	1814 FR	—	3.00	6.00	10.00	50.00
	1815 FR	.066	3.00	6.00	10.00	50.00

Obv. leg: GEORG T.N.CAROLI D.BR:. Rev: Value.

KM#	Date	Mintage	Fine	VF	XF	Unc
1080	1819 FR	.058	4.00	10.00	40.00	150.00

Obv. leg: GEORG IV. Rev: Value, M.C. below date.

KM#	Date	Mintage	Fine	VF	XF	Unc
1089	1820 MC	—	3.00	7.00	15.00	60.00

Rev: C.v.C. below date.

KM#	Date	Mintage	Fine	VF	XF	Unc
1103	1823 CvC	—	3.00	7.00	20.00	80.00

Obv. leg: BRAUNSCHW. U. LUEN.

KM#	Date	Mintage	Fine	VF	XF	Unc
1112	1825 CvC	—	5.00	15.00	25.00	100.00

1/12 THALER

BILLON
Similar to KM#1051.3.

KM#	Date	Mintage	Fine	VF	XF	Unc
1000	1801 MC	—	4.00	8.00	15.00	60.00
	1802 MC	—	4.00	8.00	15.00	50.00
	1803 MC	—	4.00	8.00	15.00	60.00
	1804 MC	—	4.00	8.00	15.00	60.00
	1805 MC	—	4.00	8.00	15.00	60.00
	1806 MC	—	4.00	8.00	15.00	60.00

NOTE: Earlier dates (1780-1800) exist for this type.

3.3400 g, .437 SILVER, .0469 oz ASW
Obv: Prancing horse left, MC below. Rev: Value.

KM#	Date	Mintage	Fine	VF	XF	Unc
1051.1	1813 MC	—	4.00	8.00	15.00	60.00
	1814 MC	—	4.00	8.00	15.00	60.00

Obv: FR below horse.

KM#	Date	Mintage	Fine	VF	XF	Unc
1051.2	1815 FR	—	3.00	5.00	10.00	50.00

Obv: W/o initials below horse. Rev: FR below date.

KM#	Date	Mintage	Fine	VF	XF	Unc
1051.3	1815 FR	—	3.00	5.00	10.00	50.00

BILLON
Obv. leg: GEORG D.

KM#	Date	Mintage	Fine	VF	XF	Unc
1071	1816 FR	—	3.00	8.00	20.00	80.00
	1817 FR	—	3.00	8.00	20.00	80.00
	1818 FR	—	3.00	8.00	20.00	80.00
	1819 FR	—	3.00	8.00	20.00	80.00

Obv. leg: GEORG IV.

KM#	Date	Mintage	Fine	VF	XF	Unc
1090	1820 MC	—	3.00	7.00	15.00	60.00

Rev: CvC below date.

KM#	Date	Mintage	Fine	VF	XF	Unc
1092	1821 CvC	—	3.00	5.00	10.00	60.00
	1822 CvC	—	3.00	5.00	10.00	60.00
	1823 CvC	—	3.00	5.00	10.00	60.00

Obv. leg: BRAUNSCHW. U. LUEN.

KM#	Date	Mintage	Fine	VF	XF	Unc
1104	1823 CvC	—	3.00	5.00	10.00	60.00
	1824 CvC	—	3.00	5.00	10.00	60.00
	1825 CvC	—	3.00	5.00	10.00	60.00
	1826 CvC	—	3.00	5.00	10.00	60.00
	1827 CvC	—	3.00	5.00	10.00	60.00
	1828 CvC	—	3.00	5.00	10.00	60.00
	1829 CvC	—	3.00	5.00	10.00	60.00
	1830 CvC	—	3.00	5.00	10.00	60.00

Obv. leg: BRAUNSCHW. U.L.

KM#	Date	Mintage	Fine	VF	XF	Unc
1105	1823 CvC	—	7.50	15.00	30.00	125.00
	1824 CvC	—	7.50	15.00	30.00	125.00
	1825 CvC	—	7.50	15.00	30.00	125.00
	1826 CvC	—	7.50	15.00	30.00	125.00

Obv. leg: BRAUNS. U. LUEN.

KM#	Date	Mintage	Fine	VF	XF	Unc
1106	1823 CvC	—	3.00	5.00	10.00	60.00
	1824 CvC	—	3.00	5.00	10.00	60.00
	1828 CvC	—	3.00	5.00	10.00	60.00
	1829 CvC	—	3.00	5.00	10.00	60.00

1/6 THALER

SILVER

KM#	Date	Mintage	Fine	VF	XF	Unc
1001	1801 MC	—	6.00	12.00	30.00	90.00
	1802 MC	—	6.00	12.00	30.00	90.00
	1803 MC	—	6.00	12.00	30.00	90.00
	1804 MC	—	6.00	12.00	30.00	90.00

NOTE: Earlier dates (1780-1799) exist for this type.

5.2000 g, .563 SILVER, .0941 oz ASW
Obv: Prancing horse left, M.C. below.

KM#	Date	Mintage	Fine	VF	XF	Unc
1052	1813 MC	—	7.50	15.00	40.00	125.00
	1814 MC	—	7.50	15.00	40.00	125.00

THALER

SILVER
Obv: Small arms. Rev: Value, date.

KM#	Date	Mintage	Fine	VF	XF	Unc
1030	1801 MC	—	—	—	Rare	—

NOTE: Earlier dates (1787-1796) exist for this coin.

28.0600 g, .833 SILVER, .7516 oz ASW

KM#	Date	Mintage	Fine	VF	XF	Unc
1093	1821 CvC	1,480	400.00	800.00	1200.	2500.

(Convention)

22.2700 g, .750 SILVER, .5371 oz ASW
Wilhelm
Obv: FRITZ.F. at truncation.

KM#	Date	Mintage	Fine	VF	XF	Unc
1129	1837 CvC	2,788	75.00	150.00	400.00	900.00
	1838 CvC	.033	50.00	100.00	300.00	600.00

Obv: Smaller head.

KM#	Date	Mintage	Fine	VF	XF	Unc
1130	1839 CvC	.041	35.00	70.00	200.00	500.00

Obv: Smaller head, w/o name at truncation.

KM#	Date	Mintage	Fine	VF	XF	Unc
1131	1839 CvC	I.A.	25.00	50.00	150.00	400.00
	1840 CvC	.086	25.00	50.00	150.00	400.00
	1841 CvC	.304	20.00	40.00	125.00	350.00
	1842 CvC	.117	20.00	40.00	125.00	350.00
	1848 CvC	.011	30.00	60.00	200.00	550.00
	1850 CvC	5,671	35.00	80.00	250.00	700.00

Obv. leg. ends: U.L.
Rev: Similar to KM#1129.

KM#	Date	Mintage	Fine	VF	XF	Unc
1144	1851 B	5,742	50.00	135.00	325.00	850.00

Obv. leg. ends: LUN.

KM#	Date	Mintage	Fine	VF	XF	Unc
1146	1853 B	.024	35.00	125.00	285.00	750.00
	1854 B	.097	25.00	45.00	160.00	425.00
	1855 B	.010	40.00	135.00	315.00	825.00

(Vereins)

18.5200 g, .900 SILVER, .5360 oz ASW

KM#	Date	Mintage	Fine	VF	XF	Unc
1152	1858 B	.049	30.00	55.00	125.00	250.00
	1859 B	.030	35.00	65.00	150.00	330.00
	1865 B	.020	30.00	55.00	125.00	250.00
	1866 B	.010	25.00	45.00	110.00	215.00
	1867 B	.010	30.00	55.00	125.00	250.00
	1870 B	.107	30.00	55.00	125.00	250.00
	1871 B	.048	25.00	45.00	110.00	215.00

2 THALER

(3-1/2 Gulden)

37.1200 g, .900 SILVER, 1.0743 oz ASW
Wilhelm

KM#	Date	Mintage	Fine	VF	XF	Unc
1136	1842 CvC	.052	100.00	200.00	500.00	1200.
	1843 CvC	.068	100.00	200.00	500.00	1200.
	1844 CvC	.015	125.00	275.00	650.00	1600.
	1845 CvC	.011	125.00	275.00	650.00	1600.
	1846 CvC	.015	125.00	275.00	650.00	1600.
	1847 CvC	.015	125.00	240.00	550.00	1400.
	1848 CvC	.011	125.00	240.00	550.00	1400.

KM#	Date	Mintage	Fine	VF	XF	Unc
1136	1849 CvC	.013	125.00	275.00	650.00	1600.
	1850 CvC	.077	125.00	275.00	650.00	1600.

KM#	Date	Mintage	Fine	VF	XF	Unc
1140	1850	—	—	—	—	—
	1850 B	Inc.Ab.	100.00	150.00	400.00	850.00
	1851 B	.010	125.00	200.00	625.00	1250.
	1852 B	.011	125.00	200.00	625.00	1250.
	1854 B	.253	90.00	125.00	150.00	400.00
	1855 B	.620	90.00	125.00	150.00	400.00

25th Anniversary of Reign

KM#	Date	Mintage	Fine	VF	XF	Unc
1149	1856 B	.017	90.00	125.00	175.00	300.00

2 1/2 THALER

3.3200 g, .900 GOLD, .0961 oz AGW
Similar to KM#1072.

KM#	Date	Mintage	Fine	VF	XF	Unc
1032	1801 MC	—	375.00	750.00	1350.	2000.
	1802 MC	—	300.00	625.00	1150.	1750.
	1806 MC	—	300.00	625.00	1150.	2000.

NOTE: Earlier dates (1788-1800) exist for this type.

Obv: Crowned many quartered arms w/garlands.
Rev: Value, F.R. below.

KM#	Date	Mintage	Fine	VF	XF	Unc
1066	1815 FR	—	600.00	1000.	1650.	2500.

KM#	Date	Mintage	Fine	VF	XF	Unc
1072	1816 FR	—	575.00	800.00	1125.	1750.
	1818 FR	—	825.00	1150.	1350.	2000.
	1819 FR	—	700.00	950.00	1250.	1750.

KM#	Date	Mintage	Fine	VF	XF	Unc
1095	1822 CvC	—	550.00	900.00	1500.	2000.

Rev: W/o legend around border.

KM#	Date	Mintage	Fine	VF	XF	Unc
1113	1825 CvC	—	350.00	500.00	875.00	1500.
	1828 CvC	—	425.00	625.00	1000.	1650.

Karl II

KM#	Date	Mintage	Fine	VF	XF	Unc
1117	1829 CvC	—	400.00	600.00	900.00	1500.
1125	1832 CvC	—	450.00	650.00	1000.	1500.

Wilhelm

KM#	Date	Mintage	Fine	VF	XF	Unc
1145	1851 B	4,138	350.00	500.00	750.00	1100.

5 THALER

6.6500 g, .900 GOLD, .1924 oz AGW
Obv: Similar to KM#1110. Rev: Similar to KM#1062.

KM#	Date	Mintage	Fine	VF	XF	Unc
1025	1801 MC	—	575.00	875.00	1250.	2000.
	1802 MC	—	425.00	625.00	1000.	1800.
	1803 MC	—	—	—	Rare	—
	1804 MC	—	575.00	875.00	1250.	2000.
	1805 MC	—	500.00	750.00	1150.	1850.
	1806 MC	—	500.00	750.00	1150.	1850.

NOTE: Earlier dates (1785-1800) exist for this type.

Obv. leg: FRIDERICVS. . . . .

KM#	Date	Mintage	Fine	VF	XF	Unc
1081	1814 FR	—	—	—	—	—
1062	1814 FR	—	600.00	925.00	1350.	2000.
	1815 FR	—	525.00	800.00	1200.	1850.

Rev. leg. ends: . . . . .BR. ET LVN.

KM#	Date	Mintage	Fine	VF	XF	Unc
1073	1816 FR	—	675.00	1000.	1650.	2250.
	1817 FR	—	575.00	875.00	1500.	2150.
	1818 FR	—	675.00	1000.	1650.	2250.
	1819 FR	—	675.00	1000.	1650.	2250.
1096	1822 CvC	—	675.00	1000.	1650.	2250.
	1823 CvC	—	850.00	1250.	1850.	2750.
1110	1824 CvC	—	425.00	625.00	950.00	1500.
	1825 CvC	—	445.00	675.00	1000.	1650.
	1828 CvC	—	445.00	675.00	1000.	1650.
	1830 CvC	—	500.00	775.00	1150.	1750.
1126	1832 CvC	—	525.00	800.00	1250.	1850.
	1834 CvC	—	575.00	900.00	1500.	2150.

10 THALER

13.3000 g, .900 GOLD, .3848 oz AGW
Similar to KM#1054.

KM#	Date	Mintage	Fine	VF	XF	Unc
1041	1801 MC	—	675.00	1150.	2000.	3000.
	1804 MC	—	750.00	1250.	2000.	3000.
	1805 MC	—	550.00	875.00	1500.	2500.
	1806 MC	—	750.00	1250.	1850.	2750.

NOTE: Earlier dates (1794-1800) exist for this type.

KM#	Date	Mintage	Fine	VF	XF	Unc
1054	1813 MC	—	750.00	1250.	1850.	2750.
	1814 MC	—	675.00	1150.	1750.	2350.
1055	1814 FR	—	750.00	1250.	1850.	3000.

KM#	Date	Mintage	Fine	VF	XF	Unc
1074	1817 FR	—	675.00	1150.	1750.	2500.
	1818 FR	—	550.00	875.00	1500.	2500.
	1819 FR	—	675.00	1150.	1750.	2500.
1097	1822 CvC	—	750.00	1250.	1850.	3000.

KM#	Date	Mintage	Fine	VF	XF	Unc
1111	1824 CvC	—	750.00	1250.	1850.	2750.
	1825 CvC	—	600.00	1000.	1650.	2500.
	1829 CvC	—	825.00	1350.	2000.	2750.
	1830 CvC	—	750.00	1250.	1850.	2500.

Karl II

KM#	Date	Mintage	Fine	VF	XF	Unc
1115	1827 CvC	—	900.00	1500.	2250.	3150.
	1828 CvC	—	900.00	1500.	2250.	3150.
	1829 CvC	—	825.00	1350.	2000.	2750.
	1829 CvC	—	—	—	Proof	5250.

KM#	Date	Mintage	Fine	VF	XF	Unc
1121	1831 CvC	—	750.00	1250.	1850.	2500.

KM#	Date	Mintage	Fine	VF	XF	Unc
1122	1831 CvC	—	525.00	875.00	1350.	2250.
	1832 CvC	—	525.00	875.00	1350.	2250.
	1833 CvC	—	600.00	1000.	1500.	2250.
	1834 CvC	—	450.00	750.00	1250.	2250.

Wilhelm
Obv. leg. ends: . . . . .U.L.

KM#	Date	Mintage	Fine	VF	XF	Unc
1141	1850 B	9,763	975.00	1650.	2150.	2750.

Obv. leg. ends: . . . . .LUN.

KM#	Date	Mintage	Fine	VF	XF	Unc
1147	1853 B	.150	400.00	650.00	1000.	2000.
	1854 B	.163	400.00	650.00	1000.	2000.
	1855 B	.020	750.00	1250.	1750.	2500.
	1856 B	.057	400.00	650.00	1000.	2000.
	1857 B	.054	400.00	650.00	1100.	2250.

KRONE

11.1110 g, .900 GOLD, .3215 oz AGW
Wilhelm

KM#	Date	Mintage	Fine	VF	XF	Unc
1153	1858 B	.032	500.00	900.00	1350.	2350.
	1859 B	.013	600.00	1100.	1750.	2750.

MONETARY REFORM

3 MARK

16.6670 g, .900 SILVER, .4823 oz ASW
Ernst August Wedding and Accession

KM#	Date	Mintage	Fine	VF	XF	Unc
1161	1915A	1,700	500.00	1000.	1500.	2500.
	1915A	—	—	—	Proof	2500.

Obv. leg: U.LUNEB added.

KM#	Date	Mintage	Fine	VF	XF	Unc
1162	1915A	.032	45.00	100.00	150.00	250.00
	1915A	—	—	—	Proof	300.00

5 MARK

27.7770 g, .900 SILVER, .8038 oz ASW
Ernst August Wedding and Accession

KM#	Date	Mintage	Fine	VF	XF	Unc
1163	1915A	1,400	500.00	1000.	1500.	2500.
	1915A	—	—	—	Proof	2500.

Obv. leg: U.LUNEB added.
Rev: Similar to KM#1163.

KM#	Date	Mintage	Fine	VF	XF	Unc
1164	1915A	8,600	150.00	325.00	500.00	750.00
	1915A	—	—	—	Proof	750.00

20 MARK

7.9650 g, .900 GOLD, .2304 oz AGW
Wilhelm
Rev: Type II.

KM#	Date	Mintage	Fine	VF	XF	Unc
1160	1875A	.100	250.00	500.00	1000.	1500.
	1876A	—	—	—	—	3600.

TRADE COINAGE

DUCAT

3.5000 g, .986 GOLD, .1109 oz AGW
Similar to KM#1067.

KM#	Date	Mintage	Fine	VF	XF	Unc
1023	1801 MC	—	450.00	750.00	1250.	1600.

NOTE: Earlier dates (1784-1800) exist for this type.

Obv: Crowned many quartered arms w/garlands.
Rev: Value, EX AVRO HERCINIA.

KM#	Date	Mintage	Fine	VF	XF	Unc
1063	1814 HC	376 pcs.	575.00	1000.	1750.	2350.

KM#	Date	Mintage	Fine	VF	XF	Unc
1067	1815 FR	220 pcs.	725.00	1250.	2000.	2750.
1114	1825 CvC	530 pcs.	750.00	1250.	2100.	2850.

EAST FRIESLAND

A county located on the North Sea coast between the Ems and Weser Rivers in North Germany. The count was raised to rank of prince in 1654. At the death of the last prince in 1744, East Friesland passed to Prussia. From 1815 to 1866 East Friesland was part of Hannover until Hannover was absorbed by Prussia in 1866.

RULERS

Friedrich Wilhelm III (of Prussia), 1797-1807
George IV (of Great Britain), 1815-1820

MINT MARKS

A - Berlin
B - Breslau
D - Aurich
F - Magdeburg
Star - Dresden

MONETARY SYSTEM

Witte = 4 Hohlpfennig = 1/3 Schilling = 1/20 Schaf = 1/10 Stuber
Ciffert = 6 Witten
Stuber = 10 Witten = 1/30 Reichstaler
Schaf = 20 Witten = 2 Stuber
Flindrich = 3 Stuber
Schilling = 6 Stuber
288 Pfennige = 54 Stuber = 36 Mariengroschen = 1 Reichsthaler

1/4 STUBER

COPPER
Obv: Crowned FW monogram. Rev: Value, date.

KM#	Date	Mintage	Fine	VF	XF	Unc
272	1802A	1.296	2.00	5.00	10.00	30.00
	1803A	Inc. Ab.	2.00	5.00	10.00	30.00
	1804A	.216	2.00	5.00	10.00	30.00

NOTE: Earlier date (1799) exists for this type.

KM#	Date	Mintage	Fine	VF	XF	Unc
290	1823	.710	5.00	10.00	25.00	70.00
	1824	Inc. Ab.	5.00	10.00	25.00	70.00
	1825	Inc. Ab.	5.00	10.00	25.00	70.00

STUBER

BILLON

KM#	Date	Mintage	Fine	VF	XF	Unc
280	1804A	.378	20.00	32.50	55.00	100.00

KM#	Date	Mintage	Fine	VF	XF	Unc
291	1823B	.161	12.00	20.00	45.00	85.00

2 STUBER

BILLON
Obv: Bust. Rev: Value.

KM#	Date	Mintage	Fine	VF	XF	Unc
281	1804A	.216	25.00	50.00	100.00	220.00

Obv: Crowned monogram GR. Rev: Value.

KM#	Date	Mintage	Fine	VF	XF	Unc
292	1823B	.081	15.00	30.00	70.00	125.00

ERFURT

A city in central Germany. It was a mint for the archbishops of Mainz in the 11th, 12th and 13th centuries. It also served as an Imperial Mint in the 12th century. Independence was granted in 1255 and the mint right was obtained in 1341 and 1354. Erfurt was occupied by Swedish force from 1631 until 1648, during the Thirty Years War. A local coinage was produced until 1802 when Erfurt fell to Prussia.

RULERS

Friedrich Carl Joseph, Freiherr von und zu Erthal, Archbishop, 1774-1802

MINTMASTERS INITIALS

Letter	Date	Name
C	1779-1804	Julianus Eberhard Volkmar Claus, Mint director
S	1801-1802	Johann Blasius Siegling, Mint director

6 PFENNIG

BILLON
Obv: Wheel in crowned shield. Rev: Value.

KM#	Date	Mintage	Fine	VF	XF	Unc
122	1801 S	—	6.00	12.00	30.00	65.00

GROSCHEN

(1/24 Taler)

BILLON

KM#	Date	Mintage	Fine	VF	XF	Unc
123	1801 S	—	6.00	15.00	35.00	85.00

Obv: Shield within branches.

KM#	Date	Mintage	Fine	VF	XF	Unc
124	1802 S	—	6.00	15.00	35.00	85.00

FRANKFURT

A free city in west-central Germany, founded as a Roman settlement in the 1st century and for several centuries the site of the election of the Holy Roman Emperors. It housed the Imperial Mint from early times and obtained the mint right in 1428 with almost continuous coinage until 1866. Frankfurt am Main was merged into the Confederation of the Rhine in 1806 and was made the Grand Duchy of Frankfurt in 1810. The Congress of Vienna restored its freedom in 1815 but when the city sided with the Austrians in the Austro-Prussian War, victorious Prussia absorbed it in 1866.

RULERS

Carl Theodor v. Dalberg, 1810-15

MINT MARKS

F = Frankfurt

MINTMASTERS INITIALS

Frankfurt Mint

Letter	Date	Name
G.B., I.G.B.	1790-1825	Johann Georg Bunsen
S.T.	1836-1837	Samuel Tomschutz
Z	1843-1856	Johann Philipp Zollman

WARDENS INITIALS

Frankfurt Mint

Letter	Date	Name
GH	1798-1816	Georg Hille

ENGRAVERS

Frankfurt Mint

A.V. NORDHEIM
1857-1866

Wiesbaden Mint

ZOLLMANN
1818-1843 Johann Philipp Zollman

In some instances old dies were used later with initials beyond the date range of the man that held the position.

HELLER

COPPER

KM#	Date	Mintage	Fine	VF	XF	Unc
300	1814 G.B.	.332	8.00	15.00	30.00	65.00

Transitional Issue

KM#	Date	Mintage	Fine	VF	XF	Unc
304	1814	Inc. Ab.	—	—	—	—

Mint mark: F

KM#	Date	Mintage	Fine	VF	XF	Unc
301	1814 GB	I.A.	2.00	4.00	8.00	45.00
	1815 GB	.166	2.00	4.00	8.00	45.00
	1816 GB	—	2.00	4.00	8.00	45.00
	1817 GB	—	2.00	4.00	8.00	45.00
	1818 GB	—	2.00	4.00	8.00	45.00
	1819 GB	—	2.00	4.00	8.00	45.00
	1820/02 GB		2.00	4.00	8.00	50.00
	1820 GB	—	2.00	4.00	8.00	45.00
	1821 GB	—	2.00	4.00	8.00	45.00
	1822 GB	—	2.00	4.00	8.00	45.00
	1824 GB	—	2.00	4.00	8.00	45.00
	1825 GB	—	2.00	4.00	8.00	45.00

NOTE: Varieties exist.

KM#	Date	Mintage	Fine	VF	XF	Unc
310	1836 ST	.120	2.00	4.00	8.00	50.00
	1837 ST	.144	2.00	4.00	8.00	50.00

KM#	Date	Mintage	Fine	VF	XF	Unc
311	1838	—	2.00	4.00	8.00	50.00

KM#	Date	Mintage	Fine	VF	XF	Unc
327	1841	.173	2.00	4.00	8.00	45.00
	1842	.328	2.00	4.00	8.00	45.00
	1843	—	2.00	4.00	8.00	45.00
	1844	.162	2.00	4.00	8.00	45.00
	1845	.169	2.00	4.00	8.00	45.00
	1846	.205	2.00	4.00	8.00	45.00
	1847	.453	2.00	4.00	8.00	45.00
	1849	.396	2.00	4.00	8.00	45.00
	1850	.669	2.00	4.00	8.00	45.00
	1851	.275	2.00	4.00	8.00	45.00
	1852	.325	2.00	4.00	8.00	45.00

Obv. leg: FREIE STADT.

KM#	Date	Mintage	Fine	VF	XF	Unc
332	1843	.038	12.50	25.00	50.00	100.00

KM#	Date	Mintage	Fine	VF	XF	Unc
351	1853	.411	2.00	4.00	6.00	25.00
	1854	.271	2.00	4.00	6.00	25.00
	1855	.430	2.00	4.00	6.00	25.00
	1856	.484	2.00	4.00	6.00	25.00
	1857	.723	2.00	4.00	6.00	25.00
	1858	.377	2.00	4.00	6.00	25.00

KM#	Date	Mintage	Fine	VF	XF	Unc
356	1859	.377	2.00	4.00	6.00	25.00
	1860	.353	2.00	4.00	6.00	25.00
	1861	.378	2.00	4.00	6.00	25.00
	1862	.391	2.00	4.00	6.00	25.00
	1863	.370	2.00	4.00	6.00	25.00
	1864	.390	2.00	4.00	6.00	25.00
	1865	.384	2.00	4.00	6.00	25.00

PFENNIG

COPPER
Mint mark: F
Obv: Displayed eagle. Rev: Value, date.

KM#	Date	Mintage	Fine	VF	XF	Unc
268	1801 GB	—	2.00	4.00	10.00	35.00
	1802 GB	—	2.00	4.00	10.00	35.00
	1803 PB	—	2.00	4.00	10.00	35.00
	1803 GB	—	2.00	4.00	10.00	35.00
	1804 GB	—	2.00	4.00	10.00	35.00
	1805 GB	—	2.00	4.00	10.00	35.00
	1806 GB	—	2.00	4.00	10.00	35.00

NOTE: Varieties exist.
NOTE: Earlier dates (1786-1800) exist for this type.

KREUZER

(Convention)

BILLON

KM#	Date	Mintage	VG	Fine	VF	XF
295	1803 GB GH	—	5.00	15.00	30.00	60.00
	1804 GB GH	—	5.00	15.00	30.00	60.00
	1805 GB GH	—	5.00	15.00	30.00	60.00

Rev: Rosettes at sides of "1".

KM#	Date	Mintage	VG	Fine	VF	XF
296	1804 GB GH	—	5.00	15.00	30.00	60.00
	1805 GN GH	—	5.00	15.00	30.00	60.00

Rev: Dot at sides of "1"

KM#	Date	Mintage	VG	Fine	VF	XF
297	1804 GB GH	—	5.00	15.00	30.00	60.00
	1805 GB GH	—	5.00	15.00	30.00	60.00

Obv: Rosette below date.

KM#	Date	Mintage	VG	Fine	VF	XF
298	1808 GB GH	—	5.00	15.00	30.00	60.00

.8350 g, .167 SILVER, .0044 oz ASW

KM#	Date	Mintage	Fine	VF	XF	Unc
312	1838	.078	2.00	4.00	10.00	30.00
	1841	.123	2.00	4.00	10.00	25.00
	1842	.402	2.00	4.00	10.00	25.00
	1843	.169	2.00	4.00	10.00	25.00
	1844	.215	2.00	4.00	10.00	25.00
	1845	.205	2.00	4.00	10.00	25.00
	1846	.101	2.00	4.00	10.00	25.00
	1847	.553	2.00	4.00	10.00	25.00
	1848	.482	2.00	4.00	10.00	25.00
	1849	.627	2.00	4.00	10.00	25.00
	1850	.612	2.00	4.00	10.00	25.00
	1851	.543	2.00	4.00	10.00	25.00
	1852	.889	2.00	4.00	10.00	25.00
	1853	.526	2.00	4.00	10.00	25.00
	1854	.589	2.00	4.00	10.00	25.00
	1855	.677	2.00	4.00	10.00	25.00
	1856	1.227	2.00	4.00	10.00	25.00
	1857	.774	2.00	4.00	10.00	25.00

BILLON

KM#	Date	Mintage	Fine	VF	XF	Unc
317	ND (1839)	—	1.00	3.00	10.00	30.00

NOTE: Varieties exist.

.8330 g, .167 SILVER, .0044 oz ASW
Obv: Eagle w/long body.

KM#	Date	Mintage	Fine	VF	XF	Unc
357	1859	.358	2.00	4.00	10.00	27.50
	1860	.640	2.00	4.00	10.00	27.50
	1861	.313	2.00	4.00	10.00	27.50
	1862	—	25.00	52.50	80.00	125.00

Obv: Eagle w/heart-shaped body.

KM#	Date	Mintage	Fine	VF	XF	Unc
367	1862	.645	2.00	4.00	8.00	20.00
	1863	.611	2.00	4.00	8.00	20.00
	1864	.344	2.00	4.00	8.00	20.00
	1865	.366	2.00	4.00	8.00	20.00
	1866	.151	2.00	5.00	10.00	25.00

3 KREUZER

1.2990 g, .333 SILVER, .0139 oz ASW

KM#	Date	Mintage	Fine	VF	XF	Unc
313	1838	.080	3.00	7.00	18.00	40.00
	1841	.085	3.00	7.00	18.00	40.00
	1842	.109	3.00	7.00	18.00	40.00
	1843	.089	3.00	7.00	18.00	40.00
	1846	.154	3.00	7.00	18.00	40.00

BILLON
Obv: Crowned eagle. Rev: View of city.

KM#	Date	Mintage	Fine	VF	XF	Unc
318	ND (1839)	—	1.00	3.00	10.00	30.00

1.2990 g, .333 SILVER, .0139 oz ASW

KM#	Date	Mintage	Fine	VF	XF	Unc
334	1846	Inc. Ab.	2.00	5.00	12.50	35.00
	1848	.038	2.00	5.00	12.50	35.00
	1849/6	.950	2.00	5.00	12.50	40.00
	1849	Inc. Ab.	2.00	5.00	12.50	35.00
	1850	.182	2.00	5.00	12.50	35.00
	1851	.158	2.00	5.00	12.50	35.00
	1852	.129	2.00	5.00	12.50	35.00
	1853	.069	2.00	5.00	12.50	35.00
	1854	.154	2.00	5.00	12.50	35.00
	1855	.148	2.00	5.00	12.50	35.00
	1856	.084	2.00	5.00	12.50	35.00

1.2900 g, .350 SILVER, .0145 oz ASW

KM#	Date	Mintage	Fine	VF	XF	Unc
373	1866	.096	5.00	10.00	20.00	60.00

6 KREUZER

2.5900 g, .333 SILVER, .0277 oz ASW

KM#	Date	Mintage	Fine	VF	XF	Unc
314	1838	.110	2.00	6.00	15.00	60.00
	1841	.123	2.00	6.00	15.00	60.00
	1842	.161	2.00	6.00	15.00	60.00
	1843	.260	2.00	6.00	15.00	60.00
	1844	.370	2.00	6.00	15.00	60.00
	1845	.105	2.00	6.00	15.00	60.00
	1846	.211	2.00	6.00	15.00	60.00

.333 SILVER
Obv: Crowned eagle. Rev: View of city.

KM#	Date	Mintage	Fine	VF	XF	Unc
319	ND (1839)	—	6.50	12.50	22.50	60.00

KM#	Date	Mintage	Fine	VF	XF	Unc
335	1846	Inc. Ab.	2.00	6.00	15.00	50.00
	1848	.291	2.00	6.00	15.00	50.00
	1849	.171	2.00	6.00	15.00	50.00
	1850	.152	2.00	6.00	15.00	50.00
	1851	.159	2.00	6.00	15.00	50.00
	1852	.221	2.00	6.00	15.00	50.00
	1853	.106	2.00	6.00	15.00	50.00
	1855	.181	2.00	6.00	15.00	50.00
	1856	.166	2.00	6.00	15.00	50.00

KM#	Date	Mintage	Fine	VF	XF	Unc
350	1852	Inc. Ab.	3.50	10.00	25.00	65.00
	1853	Inc. Ab.	3.50	10.00	25.00	65.00
	1854	.212	3.50	10.00	25.00	65.00
	1856	Inc. Ab.	3.50	10.00	25.00	65.00

2.4600 g, .350 SILVER, .0276 oz ASW

KM#	Date	Mintage	Fine	VF	XF	Unc
374	1866	.038	5.00	10.00	20.00	70.00

1/2 GULDEN

5.3000 g, .900 SILVER, .1533 oz ASW

KM#	Date	Mintage	Fine	VF	XF	Unc
315	1838	.120	25.00	40.00	90.00	200.00
	1838	—	—	—	Proof	225.00
	1840	.391	15.00	30.00	70.00	150.00
	1841	.161	25.00	40.00	90.00	200.00

KM#	Date	Mintage	Fine	VF	XF	Unc
330	1842	.075	25.00	40.00	90.00	200.00
	1843	.056	25.00	40.00	90.00	200.00
	1844	.049	25.00	40.00	90.00	200.00
	1845	.072	25.00	40.00	90.00	200.00
	1846	.047	25.00	40.00	90.00	200.00
	1847	.051	25.00	40.00	90.00	200.00
	1849	.055	25.00	40.00	90.00	200.00

KM#	Date	Mintage	Fine	VF	XF	Unc
368	1862	.014	100.00	200.00	350.00	700.00

GULDEN

10.6000 g, .900 SILVER, .3067 oz ASW

KM#	Date	Mintage	Fine	VF	XF	Unc
316	1838	.120	35.00	75.00	145.00	250.00
	1838	—	—	—	Proof	200.00
	1839	—	—	—	—	2500.
	1840	.391	35.00	75.00	145.00	250.00
	1841	.161	35.00	75.00	145.00	250.00

Obv: Eagle w/large arabesques.

KM#	Date	Mintage	Fine	VF	XF	Unc
331	1842	.123	22.00	45.00	90.00	200.00
	1843	.172	22.00	45.00	90.00	200.00
	1844	.122	22.00	45.00	90.00	200.00
	1845	.101	22.00	45.00	90.00	200.00
	1846	.120	22.00	45.00	90.00	200.00
	1847	.121	22.00	45.00	90.00	200.00
	1848	.078	22.00	45.00	90.00	225.00
	1849	.090	22.00	45.00	90.00	225.00
	1850	.030	30.00	60.00	120.00	250.00
	1851	.064	30.00	60.00	120.00	250.00
	1852	.064	30.00	60.00	120.00	250.00
	1853	.029	30.00	60.00	120.00	250.00
	1854	.034	30.00	60.00	120.00	250.00
	1855	.038	30.00	60.00	120.00	250.00

Obv: Eagle w/small arabesques.

KM#	Date	Mintage	Fine	VF	XF	Unc
358	1859	.059	30.00	60.00	125.00	250.00
	1861	.211	20.00	40.00	80.00	160.00

Obv: Eagle w/o arabesques.

KM#	Date	Mintage	Fine	VF	XF	Unc
369	1862	.011	100.00	200.00	400.00	800.00
	1863	.056	45.00	90.00	165.00	300.00

ZWEY (2) GULDEN

21.2200 g, .900 SILVER, .6138 oz ASW

KM#	Date	Mintage	Fine	VF	XF	Unc
333	1845	.114	50.00	80.00	140.00	290.00
	1846	.281	50.00	80.00	140.00	290.00
	1847	.215	50.00	80.00	140.00	290.00
	1848	.147	50.00	80.00	140.00	290.00
	1849	.023	70.00	90.00	190.00	400.00
	1850	.031	100.00	175.00	325.00	600.00
	1851	.032	70.00	90.00	190.00	400.00
	1852	.026	90.00	125.00	225.00	450.00
	1853	.056	70.00	90.00	190.00	400.00
	1854	6,028	100.00	150.00	250.00	500.00
	1856	.036	70.00	90.00	190.00	400.00

Constitutional Convention, May 1, 1848

KM#	Date	Mintage	Fine	VF	XF	Unc
336	1848	—	—	—	Rare	—

Constitutional Convention, May 18, 1848

KM#	Date	Mintage	Fine	VF	XF	Unc
337	1848	8,600	50.00	100.00	160.00	240.00

NOTE: Coins were struck in anticipation of the Constitutional Convention scheduled to take place May 1, 1848. When the convention was delayed till May 18, 1848 the coins were recalled and the dies were altered to reflect this new date.

Archduke Johann of Austria elected as Vicar

KM#	Date	Mintage	Fine	VF	XF	Unc
338	1848	.036	30.00	50.00	70.00	150.00
	1848	—	—	—	Proof	200.00

Archduke Johann of Austria elected as Vicar

KM#	Date	Mintage	Fine	VF	XF	Unc
339	1848	—	2000.	3500.	5000.	7500.

Opening of German Parliament
Obv: KM#337. Rev: KM#333.

KM#	Date	Mintage	Fine	VF	XF	Unc
340	1848	—	2000.	3500.	5000.	7500.

Friedrich Wilhelm IV of Prussia elected as Emperor of Germany

KM#	Date	Mintage	Fine	VF	XF	Unc
341.1	1849	200 pcs.	2000.	3500.	5000.	7500.

Plain edge.

KM#	Date	Mintage	Fine	VF	XF	Unc
341.2	1849 (1890)	(restrike)		—	—	—

Obv: Similar to KM#333.

KM#	Date	Mintage	Fine	VF	XF	Unc
342	1849	—	—	—	—	8300.

Centenary of Goethe's Birth

KM#	Date	Mintage	Fine	VF	XF	Unc
343	1849	8,500	60.00	90.00	125.00	180.00
	1849	—	—	—	Proof	250.00

300th Anniversary of Religious Peace

KM#	Date	Mintage	Fine	VF	XF	Unc
353	1855	.032	40.00	60.00	100.00	150.00

EIN (1) THALER

(Vereins)

18.5200 g, .900 SILVER, .5360 oz ASW

KM#	Date	Mintage	Fine	VF	XF	Unc
354	1857	1,350	125.00	250.00	550.00	1200.

Obv: House roofs visible around tower at left.

KM#	Date	Mintage	Fine	VF	XF	Unc
355	1857	—	150.00	300.00	600.00	1200.
	1858	.012	50.00	100.00	200.00	400.00

KM#	Date	Mintage	Fine	VF	XF	Unc
360	1859	.283	25.00	45.00	70.00	140.00
	1860	1.700	20.00	40.00	60.00	120.00
	1861	—	50.00	100.00	200.00	400.00

Obv: Different hair-knot.

KM#	Date	Mintage	Fine	VF	XF	Unc
366	1861	.016	150.00	300.00	600.00	1200.

Obv: Different dress.

KM#	Date	Mintage	Fine	VF	XF	Unc
370	1862	.312	20.00	40.00	60.00	125.00
	1863	.021	25.00	50.00	100.00	200.00
	1864	.105	20.00	40.00	60.00	125.00
	1865	.207	20.00	40.00	60.00	125.00

ZWEI (2) THALER

(3-1/2 Gulden)

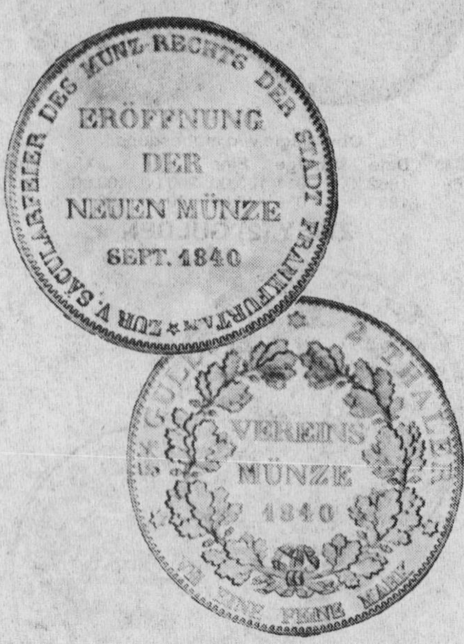

37.1000 g, .900 SILVER, 1.0743 oz ASW
New Mint Opening in 1840

KM#	Date	Mintage	Fine	VF	XF	Unc
325	1840	649 pcs.	425.00	750.00	1250.	2800.

KM#	Date	Mintage	Fine	VF	XF	Unc
326	1840	Inc. KM329	75.00	150.00	265.00	550.00
	1841	Inc. KM329	60.00	130.00	200.00	400.00
	1842	Inc. KM329	—	—	Rare	—
	1843	Inc. KM329	75.00	150.00	275.00	575.00
	1844	Inc. KM329	75.00	150.00	275.00	575.00

Mule. Obv: KM#326. Rev: Obv. of KM#329.

KM#	Date	Mintage	Fine	VF	XF	Unc
328	ND(1838)	—	—	—	—	7500.

Rev: Value.

KM#	Date	Mintage	Fine	VF	XF	Unc
329	1841	.121	60.00	100.00	200.00	400.00
	1841	—	—	—	Proof	450.00
	1842	.287	60.00	100.00	200.00	400.00
	1843	.123	60.00	100.00	200.00	400.00
	1844	.196	60.00	100.00	200.00	400.00
	1845	.036	75.00	125.00	250.00	550.00
	1846	.072	65.00	115.00	225.00	450.00
	1847	.071	65.00	115.00	225.00	450.00
	1851	8,354	100.00	175.00	300.00	600.00
	1854	.107	60.00	100.00	200.00	400.00
	1855	.072	65.00	115.00	225.00	450.00

37.0400 g, .900 SILVER, 1.0717 oz ASW

KM#	Date	Mintage	Fine	VF	XF	Unc
365	1860	.341	40.00	65.00	100.00	180.00
	1861	1.787	40.00	65.00	100.00	180.00
	1862	.344	40.00	65.00	100.00	180.00
	1866	.637	40.00	65.00	100.00	180.00

TRADE COINAGE

DUCAT

3.5000 g, .986 GOLD, .1109 oz AGW
300th Anniversary of the Reformation

KM#	Date	Mintage	Fine	VF	XF	Unc
302	1817	—	75.00	125.00	200.00	400.00

KM#	Date	Mintage	Fine	VF	XF	Unc
352	1853	1,121	300.00	500.00	950.00	1500.
	1856	665 pcs.	325.00	550.00	1000.	1600.

2 DUCAT

7.0000 g, .986 GOLD, .2219 oz AGW
300th Anniversary of Reformation

KM#	Date	Mintage	Fine	VF	XF	Unc
303 (M18)	1817	—	100.00	200.00	400.00	600.00

FRIEDBERG

IMPERIAL CITY

The fortified town of Friedberg, located in Hesse about 14 miles north of Frankfurt am Main, dates from Roman times. It attained free status in 1211 and was the site of an imperial mint until the mid-13th century. In 1349 Friedberg passed to the countship of Schwarzburg, losing its free status shortly thereafter. Local nobles began electing one among themselves to the office of burgrave-for-life. The burgraves obtained the mint right in 1541 and recognized only the emperor as overlord. In 1802 Friedberg passed in fief to Hesse-Darmstadt and was mediatized in 1818.

RULERS

Johann Maria Rudolph von Waldbott Bassenheim, 1777-1805

Clemens August von Westphalen, 1805-1818

MINTMASTERS INITIALS

Letter	Date	Name
GB(F)GH	1790-1833	Johann Georg Bunsen, in Frankfurt
	1798-1816	Georg Hille, warden in Frankfurt

EIN (1) THALER

(Convention)

SILVER
Obv: Titles of Francis II.

KM#	Date	Mintage	Fine	VF	XF	Unc
75	1804 GB(F)GH	—	175.00	300.00	600.00	1300.

NOTE: Legend varieties exist.

FURSTENBERG

A noble family with holdings in Baden and Wurttemberg. The lord of Furstenberg assumed the title of Count in the 13th century which was raised to the rank of Prince in 1664. The Furstenberg possessions were mediatized in 1806.

FURSTENBERG-STUHLINGEN

RULERS

Karl Joachim, 1796-1804

Carl Egon, 1804-1854

MINT MARKS

G - Gunzburg

MINTMASTERS INITIALS

Letter	Date	Name
CH	1784-1808	Christian Heugelin, warden in Stuttgart
ILW,W	1798-1845	Johann Ludwig Wagner, die-cutter in Stuttgart

EIN (1) KREUZER

COPPER

KM#	Date	Mintage	Fine	VF	XF	Unc
35	1804 W.	.040	30.00	70.00	150.00	275.00

3 KREUZER

1.4200 g, .312 SILVER, .0142 oz ASW

KM#	Date	Mintage	Fine	VF	XF	Unc
36	1804 W.	.012	65.00	135.00	250.00	425.00

6 KREUZER

2.3500 g, .375 SILVER, .0283 oz ASW

KM#	Date	Mintage	Fine	VF	XF	Unc
37	1804 W.	6,720	75.00	155.00	275.00	500.00

10 KREUZER

3.8900 g, .500 SILVER, .0625 oz ASW

KM#	Date	Mintage	Fine	VF	XF	Unc
38	1804 W.	6,075	100.00	175.00	300.00	550.00

20 KREUZER

6.6800 g, .583 SILVER, .1252 oz ASW
Obv: Bust right, leg. ends: PRINC. IN FURSTENBERG.
Rev: Crowned arms.

KM#	Date	Mintage	Fine	VF	XF	Unc
39	1804 W.	3,011	135.00	225.00	325.00	600.00

Obv. leg. ends: PRINC FURSTENBERG.

KM#	Date	Mintage	Fine	VF	XF	Unc
40	1804	Inc. Ab.	135.00	225.00	325.00	600.00

EIN (1) THALER

(Convention)

28.0600 g, .833 SILVER, .7515 oz ASW
Karl Joachim

KM#	Date	Mintage	Fine	VF	XF	Unc
41	1804 ILW//CH	388 pcs.	500.00	1000.	1600.	3000.

FURTHER AUSTRIA

Vorderoesterreich

Name given to imperial lands in South Swabia in the 18th century. In 1805 it was divided by Baden and Bavaria.

RULERS

Franz II (Austria), 1792-1805

MINT MARKS

A - Wien

F - Hall

G - Baia Mare (Nagybanya)

H - Gunzburg

HELLER

COPPER

KM#	Date	Mintage	Fine	VF	XF	Unc
21	1801H	—	4.00	7.00	20.00	125.00
	1801.H	—	4.00	7.00	20.00	125.00
	1803H	—	4.00	7.00	20.00	125.00

NOTE: Earlier dates (1793-1799) exist for this type.

1/4 KREUTZER

COPPER, 1.40 g

KM#	Date	Mintage	Fine	VF	XF	Unc
25	1801H	—	—	—	Rare	—
	1802H	—	10.00	25.00	50.00	100.00
	1803H	—	6.50	20.00	40.00	80.00

1/2 KREUTZER

COPPER, 2.80 g

KM#	Date	Mintage	Fine	VF	XF	Unc
26	1801H	—	—	—	Rare	—
	1802H	—	15.00	85.00	125.00	185.00
	1803H	—	8.50	20.00	40.00	75.00
	1804H	—	—	—	Rare	—
31	1805H	—	—	—	Rare	—

EIN (1) KREUTZER

COPPER, 5.70 g
Rev: Small lettering.

KM#	Date	Mintage	Fine	VF	XF	Unc
27	1801H	—	3.00	10.00	25.00	50.00
	1802H	—	3.00	10.00	25.00	50.00
	1803H	—	3.00	10.00	25.00	50.00
	1804H	—	3.00	10.00	25.00	50.00

KM#	Date	Mintage	Fine	VF	XF	Unc
30	1804H	—	—	—	Rare	—
	1805H	—	3.00	10.00	25.00	50.00

3 KREUTZER

1.4100 g, .312 SILVER, .0141 oz ASW

KM#	Date	Mintage	Fine	VF	XF	Unc
28	1802A	—	—	—	Rare	—
	1802G	—	—	—	Rare	—
	1802H	—	—	—	Rare	—
	1803H	—	—	—	Rare	—
	1804H	—	—	—	Rare	—
	1805H	—	—	—	Rare	—

6 KREUTZER

2.3500 g, .375 SILVER, .0283 oz ASW

KM#	Date	Mintage	Fine	VF	XF	Unc
29	1802A	—	—	—	Rare	—
	1802G	—	—	—	Rare	—
	1802H	—	3.00	10.00	30.00	65.00
	1803H	—	3.00	10.00	30.00	65.00
	1804H	—	3.00	10.00	30.00	65.00
	1805A	—	3.00	10.00	30.00	65.00
	1805H	—	3.00	10.00	30.00	65.00

HAMBURG

The city of Hamburg is located on the Elbe River about 75 miles from the North Sea. It was founded by Charlemagne in the 9th century. In 1241 it joined Lubeck to form the Hanseatic League. The mint right was leased to the citizens in 1292, however the first local hohlpfennings had been struck almost 50 years earlier. In 1510 Hamburg was formally made a Free City, though in fact it had been free for about 250 years. It was occupied by the French during the Napoleonic period. In 1866 it joined the North German Confederation and became a part of the German Empire in 1871. The Hamburg coinage is almost continuous up to the time of World War I.

MINTMASTERS INITIALS

Letter	Date	Name
CAIG, CAJG	1813	C.A.J. Ginquembre, French director of mint

Letter	Date	Name
HSK	1805-1842	Hans Schierven Knoph
OHK	1761-1805	Otto Heinrich Knorre

City arms - a triple-turreted gate

DREILING

(3 Pfennig - 1/4 Schilling - 1/128 Thaler)

.5100 g, .187 SILVER, .0030 oz ASW
Obv: Castle w/O.H.K. below.
Rev: 'I' between rosettes.

KM#	Date	Mintage	Fine	VF	XF	Unc
220	1803 OHK	.355	2.00	4.00	10.00	30.00

NOTE: Earlier dates (1783-1800) exist for this type.

Obv: Castle w/H.S.K. below.

KM#	Date	Mintage	Fine	VF	XF	Unc
235	1807 HSK	.384	1.00	3.00	6.00	25.00
	1809 HSK	.768	1.00	3.00	6.00	25.00

Rev: 'I' between dots.

KM#	Date	Mintage	Fine	VF	XF	Unc
250	1823 HSK	.021	1.00	3.00	6.00	25.00
	1832 HSK	.036	1.00	3.00	6.00	25.00
	1833 HSK	.303	1.00	3.00	6.00	25.00
	1836 HSK	.293	1.00	3.00	6.00	25.00
	1839 HSK	.299	1.00	3.00	6.00	25.00

Obv: Redesigned castle. Rev: 'I' between rosettes.

KM#	Date	Mintage	Fine	VF	XF	Unc
260	1841 HSK	.554	1.00	3.00	6.00	25.00

Obv: W/o initials below castle.
Rev: 'I' between 5-pointed stars.

KM#	Date	Mintage	Fine	VF	XF	Unc
264	1846	.574	1.00	3.00	6.00	25.00

Rev: 'I' between 6-pointed stars.

KM#	Date	Mintage	Fine	VF	XF	Unc
270	1851	.578	1.00	3.00	6.00	25.00

Beaded borders.

KM#	Date	Mintage	Fine	VF	XF	Unc
275	1855A	.320	1.00	2.50	5.00	25.00
	1855	2.613	1.00	2.00	4.00	25.00

SECHSLING

(6 Pfennig - 1/2 Schilling - 1/64 Thaler)

.7600 g, .250 SILVER, .0061 oz ASW
Obv: Castle w/O.H.K. below.
Rev: 'I' between rosettes.

KM#	Date	Mintage	Fine	VF	XF	Unc
213	1803 OHK	.182	1.00	3.00	6.00	40.00

NOTE: Earlier dates (1778-1800) exist for this type.

Obv: Small castle w/H.S.K. below.

KM#	Date	Mintage	Fine	VF	XF	Unc
236.1	1807 HSK	.096	2.00	4.00	8.00	50.00
	1809 HSK	.192	1.00	3.00	6.00	40.00
	1817 HSK	.048	2.00	4.00	8.00	50.00

Obv: Large castle.

KM#	Date	Mintage	Fine	VF	XF	Unc
236.2	1823 HSK	.030	2.00	4.00	8.00	50.00
	1833 HSK	.135	1.00	3.00	6.00	40.00
	1836 HSK	.155	1.00	3.00	6.00	40.00
	1839 HSK	.354	1.00	3.00	6.00	40.00

Rev: 'I' between dots.

KM#	Date	Mintage	Fine	VF	XF	Unc
255	1832 HSK	.066	2.00	4.00	8.00	45.00

Obv: Redesigned castle. Rev: 'I' between rosettes.

KM#	Date	Mintage	Fine	VF	XF	Unc
261	1841 HSK	.293	1.00	3.00	6.00	40.00

Obv: W/o initials below castle.
Rev: 'I' between 5-pointed stars.

KM#	Date	Mintage	Fine	VF	XF	Unc
265	1846	.480	1.00	3.00	6.00	30.00

Rev: 'I' between 6-pointed stars.

KM#	Date	Mintage	Fine	VF	XF	Unc
271	1851	.480	1.00	3.00	6.00	30.00

Beaded borders.

KM#	Date	Mintage	Fine	VF	XF	Unc
276	1855A	.098	2.00	4.00	8.00	35.00
	1855	1.841	1.00	3.00	6.00	30.00

SCHILLING

(12 Pfennig - 1/32 Thaler)

1.0800 g, .375 SILVER, .0130 oz ASW
Obv: Castle w/H.S.K. below.

KM#	Date	Mintage	Fine	VF	XF	Unc
246	1817 HSK	.019	2.00	6.00	10.00	60.00
	1818 HSK	.029	2.00	6.00	10.00	60.00
	1819 HSK	.149	2.00	6.00	10.00	60.00

Rev. leg: HAMB. COVR., 'I' between dots.

KM#	Date	Mintage	Fine	VF	XF	Unc
251.1	1823 HSK	.138	1.00	3.00	6.00	35.00
	1828 HSK	.142	1.00	3.00	6.00	35.00
	1832 HSK	.142	1.00	3.00	6.00	35.00

Rev: 'I' between rosettes.

KM#	Date	Mintage	Fine	VF	XF	Unc
251.2	1837 HSK	.153	1.00	3.00	6.00	35.00
	1840 HSK	.144	1.00	3.00	6.00	35.00

Obv: Redesigned castle.

KM#	Date	Mintage	Fine	VF	XF	Unc
262	1841 HSK	.149	1.00	3.00	6.00	35.00

Rev: 'I' between 5-pointed stars.

KM#	Date	Mintage	Fine	VF	XF	Unc
266	1846	.240	1.00	3.00	6.00	35.00

Rev: 'I' between 6-pointed stars.

KM#	Date	Mintage	Fine	VF	XF	Unc
272	1851	.240	1.00	3.00	6.00	35.00

Beaded borders.

KM#	Date	Mintage	Fine	VF	XF	Unc
277	1855A	.112	1.00	2.00	5.00	25.00
	1855	1.841	1.00	2.00	5.00	25.00

32 SCHILLING

18.3200 g, .750 SILVER, .4417 oz ASW

KM#	Date	Mintage	Fine	VF	XF	Unc
238	1808 HSK	.210	30.00	60.00	100.00	300.00

14.1700 g, .968 SILVER, .4410 oz ASW

KM#	Date	Mintage	Fine	VF	XF	Unc
241	1809 HSK	.880	25.00	50.00	90.00	175.00

KM#	Date	Mintage	Fine	VF	XF	Unc
242	1809 CAIG	3.058	20.00	40.00	80.00	150.00

MONETARY REFORM

2 MARK

11.1110 g, .900 SILVER, .3215 oz ASW

KM#	Date	Mintage	Fine	VF	XF	Unc
290	1876J	3.962	20.00	45.00	250.00	450.00
	1877J	.500	25.00	50.00	275.00	550.00
	1878J	.350	25.00	50.00	325.00	625.00
	1880J	.099	40.00	100.00	350.00	750.00
	1883J	.060	40.00	100.00	350.00	675.00
	1888J	.100	30.00	60.00	300.00	575.00

KM#	Date	Mintage	Fine	VF	XF	Unc
294	1892J	.141	15.00	25.00	75.00	325.00
	1893J	.146	15.00	25.00	75.00	275.00
	1896J	.286	15.00	20.00	50.00	175.00
	1898J	.118	25.00	60.00	160.00	400.00
	1899J	.286	15.00	20.00	60.00	175.00
	1900J	.577	12.50	25.00	60.00	175.00
	1901J	.482	12.50	20.00	50.00	150.00
	1902J	.779	12.50	20.00	50.00	125.00
	1903J	.817	12.50	20.00	40.00	125.00
	1904J	1.248	12.50	20.00	40.00	125.00
	1905J	.204	25.00	40.00	75.00	225.00
	1906J	1.225	12.50	20.00	40.00	125.00
	1907J	1.226	12.50	20.00	40.00	100.00
	1908J	.368	12.50	25.00	40.00	125.00
	1911J	.204	12.50	25.00	60.00	125.00
	1912J	.079	15.00	40.00	95.00	250.00
	1913J	.105	12.50	25.00	60.00	125.00
	1914J	.328	10.00	20.00	40.00	100.00
	Common date	—	—	Proof	275.00	

3 MARK

16.6670 g, .900 SILVER, .4823 oz ASW

KM#	Date	Mintage	Fine	VF	XF	Unc
296	1908J	.408	12.50	20.00	25.00	50.00
	1909J	1.389	12.50	20.00	25.00	50.00
	1910J	.526	12.50	20.00	25.00	50.00
	1911J	.922	12.50	20.00	25.00	50.00
	1912J	.491	12.50	20.00	25.00	50.00
	1913J	.344	12.50	20.00	25.00	50.00
	1914J	.575	12.50	20.00	25.00	50.00
	Common date		—	—	Proof	200.00

5 MARK

27.7770 g, .900 SILVER, .8038 oz ASW
Rev: Type I.

KM#	Date	Mintage	Fine	VF	XF	Unc
287	1875J	.286	30.00	75.00	400.00	1250.
	1876J	.930	30.00	50.00	350.00	1000.
	1888J	.040	50.00	150.00	400.00	1250.

1.9910 g, .900 GOLD, .0576 oz AGW

KM#	Date	Mintage	Fine	VF	XF	Unc
291	1877J	.441	125.00	200.00	275.00	450.00
	1877J	—	—	—	Proof	Rare

27.7770 g, .900 SILVER, .8038 oz ASW
Rev: Type II.

KM#	Date	Mintage	Fine	VF	XF	Unc
293	1891J	.059	20.00	65.00	125.00	450.00
	1893J	.055	20.00	50.00	125.00	400.00
	1894J	.082	20.00	50.00	125.00	350.00
	1895J	.082	25.00	50.00	125.00	350.00
	1896J	.016	100.00	250.00	600.00	1200.
	1898J	.176	20.00	50.00	125.00	350.00
	1899J	.082	20.00	50.00	125.00	350.00
	1900J	.172	17.50	40.00	95.00	300.00
	1901J	.172	17.50	40.00	95.00	300.00
	1902J	.294	17.50	35.00	75.00	250.00
	1903J	.588	17.50	35.00	70.00	150.00
	1904J	.319	15.00	30.00	70.00	175.00
	1907J	.326	15.00	30.00	70.00	175.00
	1908J	.458	15.00	30.00	70.00	150.00
	1913J	.327	15.00	30.00	50.00	125.00
	Common date		—	—	Proof	1500.

10 MARK

3.9820 g, .900 GOLD, .1152 oz AGW
Rev: Type I.

KM#	Date	Mintage	Fine	VF	XF	Unc
285	1873B	.025	600.00	900.00	1400.	2500.
	1873B	—	—	—	Proof	Rare

Rev: Type II.

KM#	Date	Mintage	Fine	VF	XF	Unc
286	1874B	.050	400.00	650.00	1000.	1400.

KM#	Date	Mintage	Fine	VF	XF	Unc
288	1875J	.608	65.00	110.00	160.00	250.00
	1875J	—	—	—	Proof	1000.
	1876J	6,321	700.00	1000.	1500.	1900.
	1877J	.221	65.00	110.00	160.00	250.00
	1878J	.316	65.00	110.00	160.00	250.00
	1879J	.255	65.00	110.00	160.00	250.00
	1880J	.139	65.00	110.00	160.00	250.00
	1888J	.163	65.00	110.00	160.00	250.00

KM#	Date	Mintage	Fine	VF	XF	Unc
292	1890J	.245	65.00	110.00	160.00	250.00
	1893J	.246	65.00	110.00	160.00	250.00
	1896J	.164	65.00	110.00	160.00	250.00
	1898J	.344	65.00	110.00	160.00	225.00
	1900J	.082	65.00	110.00	160.00	250.00
	1901J	.082	70.00	110.00	160.00	300.00
	1902J	.041	150.00	250.00	350.00	450.00
	1903J	.310	65.00	110.00	160.00	250.00
	1905J	.164	65.00	110.00	160.00	250.00
	1906J	.164	65.00	110.00	160.00	250.00
	1907J	.111	65.00	110.00	160.00	250.00
	1908J	.032	150.00	250.00	350.00	450.00
	1909J	.122	65.00	110.00	160.00	250.00
	1909J	—	—	—	Proof	600.00
	1910J	.041	150.00	250.00	350.00	450.00
	1911J	.075	70.00	150.00	200.00	350.00
	1911J	—	—	—	Proof	600.00
	1912J	.048	150.00	250.00	350.00	450.00
	1912J	—	—	—	Proof	600.00
	1913J	.041	150.00	200.00	300.00	400.00
	1913J	—	—	—	Proof	600.00

20 MARK

7.9650 g, .900 GOLD, .2304 oz AGW
Rev: Type II.

KM#	Date	Mintage	Fine	VF	XF	Unc
289	1875J	.313	115.00	165.00	200.00	300.00
	1876J	1.723	115.00	135.00	150.00	225.00
	1877J	1.324	115.00	135.00	150.00	225.00
	1878J	2.008	115.00	135.00	150.00	225.00
	1879J	.104	250.00	425.00	750.00	1250.
	1880J	.120	115.00	150.00	275.00	400.00
	1881J	500 pcs.	15,000.	20,000.	25,000.	30,000.
	1883J	.125	115.00	140.00	180.00	350.00
	1884J	.639	115.00	140.00	180.00	350.00
	1887J	.251	115.00	140.00	180.00	350.00
	1889J	.014	500.00	1000.	1250.	1750.

Rev: Type III.

KM#	Date	Mintage	Fine	VF	XF	Unc
295	1893J	.815	115.00	135.00	160.00	225.00
	1894J	.501	115.00	135.00	160.00	225.00
	1895J	.501	115.00	135.00	160.00	225.00
	1897J	.500	115.00	135.00	160.00	225.00
	1899J	1.002	115.00	135.00	160.00	225.00
	1900J	.501	115.00	135.00	160.00	225.00
	1908J	14 pcs.	—	—	Rare	—
	1913J	.491	115.00	130.00	150.00	200.00
	1913J	—	—	—	Proof	900.00

TRADE COINAGE

DUCAT

3.4900 g, .979 GOLD, .1099 oz AGW
Obv: Titles of Francis II.

KM#	Date	Mintage	Fine	VF	XF	Unc
227.1	1801	7,236	375.00	625.00	1150.	1500.
	1802	9,199	375.00	625.00	1150.	1500.
	1803	6,365	375.00	625.00	1150.	1500.
	1804	7,284	375.00	625.00	1150.	1500.
	1805	9,466	375.00	625.00	1150.	1500.

NOTE: Earlier dates (1793-1800) exist for this type.

KM#	Date	Mintage	Fine	VF	XF	Unc
227.2	1806	7,521	375.00	625.00	1150.	1500.

KM#	Date	Mintage	Fine	VF	XF	Unc
237	1807	6,000	375.00	625.00	1150.	1600.

KM#	Date	Mintage	Fine	VF	XF	Unc
239	1808	7,500	350.00	575.00	1000.	1750.
	1809	7,500	300.00	500.00	875.00	1500.
	1810	7,407	300.00	500.00	875.00	1500.

KM#	Date	Mintage	Fine	VF	XF	Unc
245	1811	.011	300.00	500.00	875.00	1250.
	1815	9,965	300.00	500.00	875.00	1250.
	1817	5,000	325.00	550.00	975.00	1350.
	1818	7,000	325.00	550.00	975.00	1350.
	1819	8,901	300.00	500.00	875.00	1250.
	1820	7,000	300.00	500.00	875.00	1250.
	1821	9,900	300.00	500.00	875.00	1250.
	1822	.013	300.00	500.00	875.00	1250.
	1823	8,700	300.00	500.00	875.00	1250.
	1824	6,970	300.00	500.00	875.00	1250.
	1825	.010	300.00	500.00	875.00	1250.
	1826	.012	300.00	500.00	875.00	1250.
	1827	.011	300.00	500.00	875.00	1250.
	1828	8,601	300.00	500.00	875.00	1250.
	1829	9,606	300.00	500.00	875.00	1250.
	1830	.012	300.00	500.00	875.00	1250.
	1831	9,200	300.00	500.00	875.00	1250.
	1832	9,500	300.00	500.00	875.00	1250.
	1833	9,440	300.00	500.00	875.00	1250.
	1834	.010	250.00	400.00	750.00	1000.

KM#	Date	Mintage	Fine	VF	XF	Unc
256	1835	.010	250.00	425.00	750.00	1150.
	1836	8,067	250.00	425.00	750.00	1150.
	1837	8,156	250.00	425.00	750.00	1150.
	1838	9,000	250.00	425.00	750.00	1150.
	1839	9,045	250.00	425.00	750.00	1150.
	1840	9,882	250.00	425.00	750.00	1150.
	1841	.010	250.00	425.00	750.00	1150.
	1842	.012	225.00	375.00	625.00	1000.

Struck in a collar.

KM#	Date	Mintage	Fine	VF	XF	Unc
263	1843	.012	225.00	375.00	625.00	1000.
	1844	9,768	250.00	425.00	750.00	1150.
	1845	.012	200.00	325.00	550.00	875.00
	1846	.011	200.00	325.00	550.00	875.00
	1847	.010	200.00	325.00	550.00	875.00
	1848	.013	200.00	325.00	550.00	875.00
	1849	.010	200.00	325.00	550.00	875.00
	1850	.011	200.00	325.00	550.00	875.00

Obv: Knights shield redesigned.

KM#	Date	Mintage	Fine	VF	XF	Unc
273	1851	8,497	225.00	375.00	750.00	1000.
	1852	9,476	225.00	375.00	750.00	1000.
	1853	.010	225.00	375.00	750.00	1000.

Rev. leg. ends: 979 MILLES

KM#	Date	Mintage	Fine	VF	XF	Unc
274	1854	.012	175.00	250.00	400.00	750.00
	1855	.011	175.00	250.00	400.00	750.00
	1856	.011	175.00	250.00	400.00	750.00
	1857	.012	175.00	250.00	400.00	750.00
	1858	.010	175.00	250.00	400.00	750.00
	1859	.014	175.00	250.00	400.00	750.00
	1860	.015	175.00	250.00	400.00	750.00
	1861	.015	175.00	250.00	400.00	750.00
	1862	.017	150.00	200.00	350.00	700.00
	1863	.020	150.00	200.00	350.00	700.00
	1864	.024	150.00	200.00	350.00	700.00
	1865	.017	150.00	200.00	350.00	700.00
	1866	.024	150.00	200.00	350.00	700.00
	1867	.026	150.00	200.00	350.00	700.00

Rev: Mint mark B below shell.

KM#	Date	Mintage	Fine	VF	XF	Unc
280	1868B	.025	135.00	175.00	300.00	600.00
	1869B	.026	135.00	175.00	300.00	600.00
	1870B	.030	135.00	175.00	300.00	600.00
	1871B	.030	135.00	175.00	300.00	600.00
	1872B	.030	135.00	175.00	300.00	600.00

2 DUCAT

6.9800 g, .979 GOLD, .2197 oz AGW
Obv. leg: FRANCISVS II D.G.ROM.IMP. . .

KM#	Date	Mintage	Fine	VF	XF	Unc
228.1	1801	1,273	650.00	1250.	1750.	2350.
	1802	1,256	650.00	1250.	1750.	2350.
	1803	837 pcs.	650.00	1350.	2350.	3000.
	1804	—	650.00	1300.	2000.	2500.
	1805	Inc. KM227.1	650.00	1250.	1750.	2350.

NOTE: Earlier dates (1793-1800) exist for this type.

Obv. leg: . . . .D.G.R.IMP. . .

KM#	Date	Mintage	Fine	VF	XF	Unc
228.2	1804	1,072	650.00	1250.	1750.	2350.
	1806	1,201	650.00	1250.	1750.	2350.

KM#	Date	Mintage	Fine	VF	XF	Unc
240	1808	1,250	500.00	1000.	1500.	2000.
	1809	1,250	500.00	1000.	1500.	2000.
	1810	1,050	500.00	1000.	1500.	2000.

5 DUCAT

(1/2 Portugaloser)

17.5000 g, .986 GOLD, .5548 oz AGW

KM#	Date	Mintage	Fine	VF	XF	Unc
234	1801	—	—	700.00	1000.	1500.

HANNOVER

KINGDOM

A state located in northwest Germany which became Hannover when Ernst August of Brunswick-Luneberg chose the title of Elector of Hannover after his capital city. During the Napoleonic wars it was first occupied by Prussia and then incorporated into the Kingdom of Westphalia. In 1814 it was raised to the status of a Kingdom. Hannover was absorbed by Prussia in 1866.

RULERS

George III, 1760-1820
Georg IV, 1820-1830
Wilhelm IV, 1830-1837
Ernst August, 1837-1851
Georg V, 1851-1866

MINT MARKS

A - Clausthal, 1832-1849
B - Hannover, 1866-1878
C - Clausthal, 1814-1833

MINTMASTERS INITIALS

Letter	Date	Name
B	1817-1838	Ludwig August Bruel
B	1844-1868	Theodor Wilhelm Bruel
CHH,H	1802-1817	Christian Heinrich Haase
LAB,LB	1817-1838	Ludwig August Bruel
S	1839-1844	Carl Schulter

PFENNIG

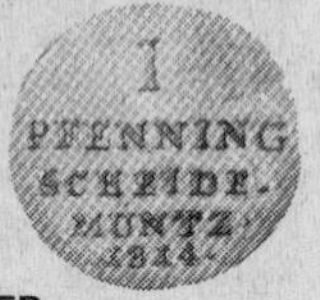

COPPER
Obv: H below crowned GR monogram.

KM#	Date	Mintage	Fine	VF	XF	Unc
103.1	1814 H	—	3.00	5.00	15.00	50.00

Obv: C below crowned monogram.

KM#	Date	Mintage	Fine	VF	XF	Unc
103.2	1814C	—	3.00	5.00	15.00	50.00

KM#	Date	Mintage	Fine	VF	XF	Unc
104	1814C	—	2.50	4.50	10.00	40.00
	1817C	—	2.50	4.50	10.00	40.00
	1818C	—	2.50	4.50	10.00	40.00
	1819C	—	2.50	4.50	10.00	40.00
	1820C	—	2.50	4.50	10.00	40.00

KM#	Date	Mintage	Fine	VF	XF	Unc
125.1	1821C	—	2.00	4.00	8.00	25.00
	1822C	—	2.00	4.00	8.00	25.00
	1823C	—	2.00	4.00	8.00	25.00
	1824C	—	2.00	4.00	8.00	25.00
	1825C	—	2.00	4.00	8.00	25.00
	1826C	—	2.00	4.00	8.00	25.00
	1827 w/o mint mark	—	2.00	4.00	8.00	25.00
	1827C	—	2.00	4.00	8.00	25.00
	1828C	—	2.00	4.00	8.00	25.00
	1829C	—	2.00	4.00	8.00	25.00
	1830C	—	2.00	4.00	8.00	25.00

Rev: B below value.

KM#	Date	Mintage	Fine	VF	XF	Unc
125.2	1826 B	—	2.00	4.00	8.00	25.00
	1828 B	—	2.00	4.00	8.00	25.00
	1829 B	—	2.00	4.00	8.00	25.00
	1830 B	—	2.00	4.00	8.00	25.00

Obv: Date below crowned WR monogram.
Rev: A below value.

KM#	Date	Mintage	Fine	VF	XF	Unc
150.1	1832A	—	2.00	4.00	8.00	30.00
	1833A	—	2.00	4.00	8.00	30.00
	1834A	—	2.00	4.00	8.00	30.00

Rev: B below value.

KM#	Date	Mintage	Fine	VF	XF	Unc
150.2	1832 B	—	2.00	4.00	8.00	30.00
	1833 B	—	2.00	4.00	8.00	30.00
	1834 B	—	2.00	4.00	8.00	30.00
	1835 B	—	2.00	4.00	8.00	30.00

Rev: C below value.

KM#	Date	Mintage	Fine	VF	XF	Unc
150.3	1831/30C	—	2.00	4.00	9.00	35.00
	1831C	—	2.00	4.00	8.00	30.00
	1832C	—	2.00	4.00	8.00	30.00
	1833C	—	2.00	4.00	8.00	30.00

Obv: IV below WR monogram.

KM#	Date	Mintage	Fine	VF	XF	Unc
156	1834A	—	4.00	7.00	20.00	75.00

Obv: Crowned shield w/prancing horse.
Rev: A below value.

KM#	Date	Mintage	Fine	VF	XF	Unc
166.1	1835A	—	2.00	4.00	8.00	30.00
	1836A	—	2.00	4.00	8.00	30.00
	1837A	—	2.00	4.00	8.00	30.00

Rev: B below value.

KM#	Date	Mintage	Fine	VF	XF	Unc
166.2	1835 B	—	2.00	4.00	8.00	30.00
	1836 B	—	2.00	4.00	8.00	30.00
	1837 B	—	2.00	4.00	8.00	30.00

Obv: Crowned EAR monogram. Rev: A below value.

KM#	Date	Mintage	Fine	VF	XF	Unc
173.1	1837A	—	2.00	4.00	8.00	30.00
	1838A	—	2.00	4.00	8.00	30.00
	1839A	—	2.00	4.00	8.00	30.00
	1840A	—	2.00	4.00	8.00	30.00
	1841A	—	2.00	4.00	8.00	30.00
	1842A	—	2.00	4.00	8.00	30.00
	1843A	—	2.00	4.00	8.00	30.00
	1844A	—	2.00	4.00	8.00	30.00
	1845A	—	2.00	4.00	8.00	30.00
	1846A	—	2.00	4.00	8.00	30.00

Rev: B below value.

KM#	Date	Mintage	Fine	VF	XF	Unc
173.2	1838 B	—	3.00	7.00	20.00	75.00

Rev: S below value.

KM#	Date	Mintage	Fine	VF	XF	Unc
173.3	1839 S	—	3.00	7.00	20.00	75.00
	1841 S	—	3.00	7.00	20.00	75.00
	1842 S	—	3.00	7.00	20.00	75.00

Obv: Date below monogram. Rev: SCHEIDEMUNZE below value, B mint mark.

KM#	Date	Mintage	Fine	VF	XF	Unc
176	1838 B	—	20.00	40.00	75.00	150.00

Rev: B below value.

KM#	Date	Mintage	Fine	VF	XF	Unc
201.1	1845 B	—	1.50	3.00	6.00	20.00
	1846 B	—	1.50	3.00	6.00	20.00

KM#	Date	Mintage	Fine	VF	XF	Unc
201.1	1847 B	—	1.50	3.00	6.00	20.00
	1848 B	—	1.50	3.00	6.00	20.00
	1849 B	—	1.50	3.00	6.00	20.00
	1850 B	—	1.50	3.00	6.00	20.00
	1851 B	—	1.50	3.00	6.00	20.00

Rev: A below value.

KM#	Date	Mintage	Fine	VF	XF	Unc
201.2	1846A	—	1.50	3.00	6.00	20.00
	1847A	—	1.50	3.00	6.00	20.00
	1848A	—	1.50	3.00	6.00	20.00
	1849A	—	1.50	3.00	6.00	20.00

Obv: V below monogram.

KM#	Date	Mintage	Fine	VF	XF	Unc
216	1852 B	—	15.00	30.00	60.00	125.00

KM#	Date	Mintage	Fine	VF	XF	Unc
221	1853 B	—	2.00	4.00	8.00	30.00
	1854 B	—	2.00	4.00	8.00	30.00
	1855 B	—	2.00	4.00	8.00	30.00
	1856 B	—	2.00	4.00	8.00	30.00

KM#	Date	Mintage	Fine	VF	XF	Unc
233	1858 B	—	1.50	3.00	6.00	20.00
	1859 B	—	1.50	3.00	6.00	20.00
	1860 B	—	1.50	3.00	6.00	20.00
	1861 B	—	1.50	3.00	6.00	20.00
	1862 B	—	1.50	3.00	6.00	20.00
	1863 B	2.324	1.50	3.00	6.00	20.00
	1864 B	—	1.50	3.00	6.00	20.00

2 PFENNIG

COPPER
Obv: Crowned GR monogram, date below.
Rev: Value.

KM#	Date	Mintage	Fine	VF	XF	Unc
115	1817C	—	5.00	10.00	25.00	100.00
	1818C	—	5.00	10.00	25.00	100.00
126.1	1821C	—	3.00	5.00	15.00	50.00
	1822C	—	3.00	5.00	15.00	50.00
	1823C	—	3.00	5.00	15.00	50.00
	1824C	—	3.00	5.00	15.00	50.00
	1825C	—	3.00	5.00	15.00	50.00
	1826C	—	3.00	5.00	15.00	50.00
	1827C	—	3.00	5.00	15.00	50.00
	1828C	—	3.00	5.00	15.00	50.00
	1829C	—	3.00	5.00	15.00	50.00
	1830C	—	3.00	5.00	15.00	50.00

Rev: B below value.

KM#	Date	Mintage	Fine	VF	XF	Unc
126.2	1826 B	.154	3.00	6.00	18.00	70.00

Obv: Crowned WR monogram above date.
Rev: C below value.

KM#	Date	Mintage	Fine	VF	XF	Unc
147.1	1831C	—	3.00	5.00	15.00	70.00
	1833C	—	3.00	5.00	15.00	70.00
	1834C	—	3.00	5.00	15.00	70.00

Rev: A below value.

KM#	Date	Mintage	Fine	VF	XF	Unc
147.2	1834A	—	4.00	8.00	22.00	70.00

Obv: IV below monogram. Rev: Date.

KM#	Date	Mintage	Fine	VF	XF	Unc
157	1834A	—	4.00	8.00	22.00	70.00

Obv: Crowned shield w/prancing horse.

KM#	Date	Mintage	Fine	VF	XF	Unc
167.1	1835A	—	3.00	6.00	18.00	70.00
	1836A	—	3.00	6.00	18.00	70.00
	1837A	—	3.00	6.00	18.00	70.00

Pearl border

KM#	Date	Mintage	Fine	VF	XF	Unc
167.2	1837A	—	5.00	10.00	25.00	100.00

Obv: Crowned EAR monogram.
Rev: Value, A below date.

KM#	Date	Mintage	Fine	VF	XF	Unc
174.1	1837A	—	2.00	4.00	10.00	40.00
	1838A	—	2.00	4.00	10.00	40.00
	1839A	—	2.00	4.00	10.00	40.00
	1840A	—	2.00	4.00	10.00	40.00
	1841A	—	2.00	4.00	10.00	40.00
	1842A	—	2.00	4.00	10.00	40.00
	1843A	—	2.00	4.00	10.00	40.00
	1844A	—	2.00	4.00	10.00	40.00
	1845A	—	2.00	4.00	10.00	40.00
	1846A	—	2.00	4.00	10.00	40.00

Rev: S below date.

KM#	Date	Mintage	Fine	VF	XF	Unc
174.2	1842 S	—	3.00	6.00	15.00	65.00
	1844 S	—	3.00	6.00	15.00	65.00

Rev: B below date, struck in a ring.

KM#	Date	Mintage	Fine	VF	XF	Unc
202.1	1845 B	—	1.50	3.00	8.00	30.00
	1846 B	—	1.50	3.00	8.00	30.00
	1847 B	—	1.50	3.00	8.00	30.00
	1848 B	—	1.50	3.00	8.00	30.00
	1849 B	—	1.50	3.00	8.00	30.00
	1850 B	—	1.50	3.00	8.00	30.00
	1851 B	—	1.50	3.00	8.00	30.00

Rev: A below date.

KM#	Date	Mintage	Fine	VF	XF	Unc
202.2	1846A	—	1.50	3.00	8.00	30.00
	1847A	—	1.50	3.00	8.00	30.00
	1848A	—	1.50	3.00	8.00	30.00
	1849A	—	1.50	3.00	8.00	30.00

Rev: B below date.

KM#	Date	Mintage	Fine	VF	XF	Unc
217	1852 B	—	1.25	2.50	7.00	30.00
	1853 B	—	1.25	2.50	7.00	30.00
	1854 B	—	1.25	2.50	7.00	30.00
	1855 B	—	1.25	2.50	7.00	30.00
	1856 B	—	1.25	2.50	7.00	30.00

KM#	Date	Mintage	Fine	VF	XF	Unc
234	1858 B	—	1.25	2.50	7.00	30.00
	1859 B	—	1.25	2.50	7.00	30.00
	1860 B	—	1.25	2.50	7.00	30.00
	1861 B	—	1.25	2.50	7.00	30.00
	1862 B	—	1.25	2.50	7.00	30.00
	1863 B	.607	1.25	2.50	7.00	30.00
	1864 B	—	1.25	2.50	7.00	30.00

4 PFENNIG

(1/2 Mariengroschen)

1.2300 g, .187 SILVER, .0073 oz ASW
Obv. C below crowned GR monogram.
Rev. leg: NACH DEM REICHS FUSS

KM#	Date	Mintage	Fine	VF	XF	Unc
105.1	1814C	—	7.50	15.00	30.00	75.00
	1815C	—	7.50	15.00	30.00	75.00

Obv: H below monogram.

KM#	Date	Mintage	Fine	VF	XF	Unc
105.2	1815 H	—	7.50	15.00	30.00	75.00
	1816 H	—	7.50	15.00	30.00	75.00

Obv. leg: CONVENT MUNZE

KM#	Date	Mintage	Fine	VF	XF	Unc
112	1816 H	.071	8.50	17.50	40.00	100.00
	1817 H	Inc. Ab.	8.50	17.50	40.00	100.00

Obv: IV below monogram,
leg: CONVENTIONS MUNZE.

KM#	Date	Mintage	Fine	VF	XF	Unc
135	1822 B	—	6.00	12.00	20.00	50.00
	1826 B	—	6.00	12.00	20.00	50.00
	1828 B	—	6.00	12.00	20.00	50.00
	1830 B	—	6.00	12.00	20.00	50.00

COPPER
Obv: Date below monogram.
Rev: C below SCHEIDEMUNZE.

KM#	Date	Mintage	Fine	VF	XF	Unc
143	1827C	—	50.00	90.00	150.00	350.00

KM#	Date	Mintage	Fine	VF	XF	Unc
148	1831C	—	50.00	85.00	140.00	325.00

.9200 g, .218 SILVER, .0064 oz ASW
Rev: B below date.

KM#	Date	Mintage	Fine	VF	XF	Unc
168	1835 B	—	2.00	4.00	8.00	30.00
	1836 B	—	2.00	4.00	8.00	30.00
	1837 B	—	2.00	4.00	8.00	30.00
177.1	1838 B	—	2.00	4.00	8.00	30.00

Rev: S below date.

KM#	Date	Mintage	Fine	VF	XF	Unc
177.2	1840 S	—	2.00	4.00	8.00	30.00
	1841 S	—	2.00	4.00	8.00	30.00
	1842 S	—	2.00	4.00	8.00	30.00

6 PFENNIG

1.3900 g, .218 SILVER, .0097 oz ASW
Obv: Crowned shield w/prancing horse.
Rev: S below value.

KM#	Date	Mintage	Fine	VF	XF	Unc
198.1	1843 S	—	3.00	7.00	15.00	50.00
	1844 S	—	3.00	7.00	15.00	50.00

Obv: B below shield.

KM#	Date	Mintage	Fine	VF	XF	Unc
198.2	1844 B	—	3.00	7.00	15.00	40.00
	1845 B	—	3.00	7.00	15.00	40.00
	1846 B	—	3.00	7.00	15.00	40.00

KM#	Date	Mintage	Fine	VF	XF	Unc
205	1846 B	—	1.50	3.50	6.00	25.00
	1847 B	—	1.50	3.50	6.00	25.00
	1848 B	—	1.50	3.50	6.00	25.00
	1849 B	—	1.50	3.50	6.00	25.00
	1850 B	—	1.50	3.50	6.00	25.00
	1851 B	—	1.50	3.50	6.00	25.00

KM#	Date	Mintage	Fine	VF	XF	Unc
218	1852 B	—	1.50	3.50	7.00	30.00
	1853 B	—	1.50	3.50	7.00	30.00
	1854 B	—	1.50	3.50	7.00	30.00
	1855 B	—	1.50	3.50	7.00	30.00

1/2 GROSCHEN

1.0900 g, .220 SILVER, .0077 oz ASW

KM#	Date	Mintage	Fine	VF	XF	Unc
235	1858 B	—	1.50	3.00	5.00	25.00
	1859 B	—	1.50	3.00	5.00	25.00
	1861 B	—	1.50	3.00	5.00	25.00
	1862 B	—	1.50	3.00	5.00	25.00
	1863 B	.047	1.50	3.00	5.00	25.00
	1864 B	—	1.50	3.00	5.00	25.00
	1865 B	—	1.50	3.00	5.00	25.00

MARIENGROSCHEN

(1/36 Thaler)

1.4800 g, .312 SILVER, .0148 oz ASW
Obv: C below crowned GR monogram.
Rev: Value, leg: NACH DEM REICHFUSS.

KM#	Date	Mintage	Fine	VF	XF	Unc
106	1814C	—	12.50	30.00	70.00	175.00

Rev: H below date.

KM#	Date	Mintage	Fine	VF	XF	Unc
113	1816 H	.443	5.00	10.00	25.00	75.00
	1817 H	Inc. Ab.	5.00	10.00	25.00	75.00
	1818 H	Inc. Ab.	5.00	10.00	25.00	75.00

GROSCHEN

2.1900 g, .220 SILVER, .0154 oz ASW

KM#	Date	Mintage	Fine	VF	XF	Unc
236	1858 B	—	1.50	2.50	5.00	25.00
	1859 B	—	1.50	2.50	5.00	25.00
	1860 B	—	1.50	2.50	5.00	25.00
	1861 B	—	1.50	2.50	5.00	25.00
	1862 B	—	1.50	2.50	5.00	25.00
	1863 B	.069	1.50	2.50	5.00	25.00
	1864 B	—	1.50	2.50	5.00	25.00
	1865 B	—	1.50	2.50	5.00	25.00
	1866 B	.076	1.50	2.50	5.00	25.00

3 MARIENGROSCHEN

3.3400 g, .437 SILVER, .0469 oz ASW
Obv: C.H.H. below ledge.
Rev. leg: CONVENTIONSMUNZE.

KM#	Date	Mintage	Fine	VF	XF	Unc
114.1	1816 CHH	—	5.00	15.00	40.00	100.00
	1817 CHH	—	5.00	15.00	40.00	100.00
	1818 CHH	12.000	5.00	15.00	40.00	100.00

Obv: .L.A.B. below ledge.

KM#	Date	Mintage	Fine	VF	XF	Unc
114.2	1819 LAB	—	5.00	15.00	40.00	100.00
	1820 LAB	I.A.	5.00	15.00	40.00	100.00

Obv: L.B. below ledge.

KM#	Date	Mintage	Fine	VF	XF	Unc
114.3	1819 LB	I.A.	5.00	15.00	40.00	100.00
	1820 LB	—	5.00	15.00	40.00	100.00

KM#	Date	Mintage	Fine	VF	XF	Unc
120	1820 LB	—	5.00	15.00	40.00	100.00
	1821 LB	I.A.	5.00	15.00	40.00	100.00

16 GUTE GROSCHEN

11.7700 g, .993 SILVER, .3758 oz ASW
Obv: Prancing horse w/M on ledge,
leg: GEORGIUS.III.D.G.BRITAN.&.HANNOV.REX.

KM#	Date	Mintage	Fine	VF	XF	Unc
121.1	1820	—	90.00	150.00	250.00	425.00

Obv. leg: GEORGIUS.III.D.G.BRITANNIARUM.

KM#	Date	Mintage	Fine	VF	XF	Unc
121.2	1820	—	90.00	150.00	250.00	425.00

Obv: Prancing horse, M on ledge
XX.EINE.F.MARK. below,
leg: GEORGIUS.IV.D.G.BRITAN.& HANNOV.REX.
Rev: Value, CONVENTIONS-MUNZE. below.

KM#	Date	Mintage	Fine	VF	XF	Unc
122	1820	—	30.00	60.00	100.00	165.00

Obv: XX.E.F. MARK below ledge.
Rev. leg: CONV-MUNZE FEIN SILBER.

KM#	Date	Mintage	Fine	VF	XF	Unc
123	1820	—	30.00	55.00	90.00	150.00

Obv: XX.EINE.F.MARK. below ledge.

KM#	Date	Mintage	Fine	VF	XF	Unc
124	1820	—	25.00	45.00	75.00	125.00

Obv: XX.E.F.MARK. below ledge.
Rev: FEIN SILB.

KM#	Date	Mintage	Fine	VF	XF	Unc
127	1821	—	25.00	45.00	75.00	125.00

Rev: CONV MUNZE FEIN SILB around bottom.

KM#	Date	Mintage	Fine	VF	XF	Unc
128	1821	—	25.00	50.00	100.00	175.00

NOTE: 7 obverse legend varieties exist.

Rev: FEINES SILB below GROSCHEN.

KM#	Date	Mintage	Fine	VF	XF	Unc
136	1822	—	25.00	50.00	100.00	175.00

NOTE: 2 obverse legend varieties exist.

KM#	Date	Mintage	Fine	VF	XF	Unc
137	1822	—	25.00	50.00	100.00	175.00

NOTE: 2 obverse legend varieties exist.

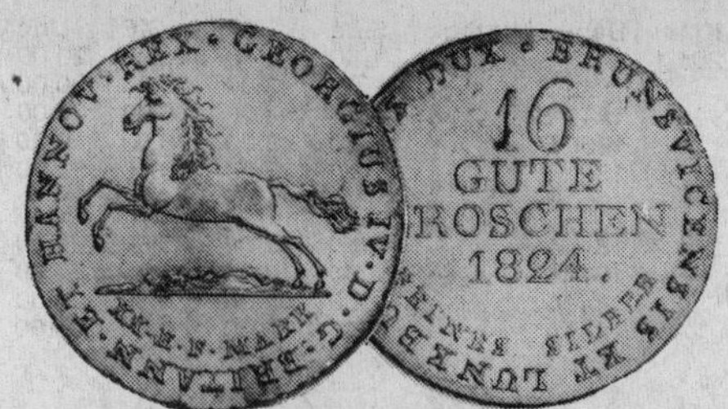

KM#	Date	Mintage	Fine	VF	XF	Unc
138	1822	—	20.00	30.00	60.00	125.00
	1823	—	20.00	30.00	60.00	125.00
	1824	—	20.00	30.00	60.00	125.00
	1825	—	20.00	30.00	60.00	125.00
	1826	—	20.00	30.00	60.00	125.00
	1827	—	20.00	30.00	60.00	125.00
	1828	—	20.00	30.00	60.00	125.00
	1829	—	20.00	30.00	60.00	125.00
	1830	—	20.00	30.00	60.00	125.00

NOTE: 2 obverse legend varieties exist for 1822, 1823 and 1825.

KM#	Date	Mintage	Fine	VF	XF	Unc
145.1	1830	—	20.00	30.00	60.00	125.00

KM#	Date	Mintage	Fine	VF	XF	Unc
145.2	1831	—	20.00	30.00	60.00	125.00
	1832	—	20.00	30.00	60.00	125.00
	1832A	—	20.00	30.00	60.00	125.00

Obv: W/'L' on ledge.

KM#	Date	Mintage	Fine	VF	XF	Unc
145.3	1832A	—	20.00	30.00	60.00	125.00
	1833A	—	20.00	30.00	60.00	125.00
	1834A	—	20.00	30.00	60.00	125.00

Obv: W/'M' on ledge.

KM#	Date	Mintage	Fine	VF	XF	Unc
145.4	1832A	—	20.00	30.00	60.00	125.00

Obv: W/'W' on ledge.

KM#	Date	Mintage	Fine	VF	XF	Unc
145.5	1834A	—	20.00	30.00	60.00	125.00

1/24 THALER

1.9400 g, .312 SILVER, .0194 oz ASW
Obv: Date below prancing horse.
Rev. value, leg: NACH DEM REICHFUSS.

KM#	Date	Mintage	Fine	VF	XF	Unc
107	1814C	—	4.00	8.00	20.00	100.00

KM#	Date	Mintage	Fine	VF	XF	Unc
116	1817 H	.946	4.00	8.00	20.00	100.00
	1818	—	4.00	8.00	20.00	100.00

Obv: IV below monogram.

KM#	Date	Mintage	Fine	VF	XF	Unc
141	1826 B	.139	4.00	7.00	15.00	60.00
	1827 B	.328	4.00	7.00	15.00	60.00
	1828 B	.904	4.00	7.00	15.00	60.00

Rev: B below date.

KM#	Date	Mintage	Fine	VF	XF	Unc
158.1	1834 B	—	2.50	6.00	12.00	40.00
	1834 .B.	—	—	—	—	—
	1835 B	—	2.50	6.00	12.00	40.00
	1836 B	—	2.50	6.00	12.00	40.00
	1837 B	—	2.50	6.00	12.00	40.00

Rev: A below date.

KM#	Date	Mintage	Fine	VF	XF	Unc
158.2	1835A	—	2.50	6.00	12.00	40.00
	1836A	—	2.50	6.00	12.00	40.00

Rev: B below date.

KM#	Date	Mintage	Fine	VF	XF	Unc
178.1	1838 B	—	2.50	6.00	12.00	40.00

Rev: S below date.

KM#	Date	Mintage	Fine	VF	XF	Unc
178.2	1839 S	—	2.50	6.00	12.00	40.00
	1841 S	—	2.50	6.00	12.00	40.00
	1842 S	—	2.50	6.00	12.00	40.00

Rev: A below date.

KM#	Date	Mintage	Fine	VF	XF	Unc
178.3	1839A	—	2.50	6.00	12.00	40.00
	1840A	—	2.50	6.00	12.00	40.00
	1841A	—	2.50	6.00	12.00	40.00
	1842A	—	2.50	6.00	12.00	40.00
	1843A	—	2.50	6.00	12.00	40.00
	1844A	—	2.50	6.00	12.00	40.00
	1845A	—	2.50	6.00	12.00	40.00
	1846A	—	2.50	6.00	12.00	40.00

Obv: B below prancing horse. Rev: Value, SCHEIDEMUNZE.

KM#	Date	Mintage	Fine	VF	XF	Unc
203	1845 B	—	2.50	6.00	12.00	40.00
	1846 B	—	2.50	6.00	12.00	40.00

Obv. leg: NEC ASPERA TERRENT.

KM#	Date	Mintage	Fine	VF	XF	Unc
227	1854 B	—	2.50	6.00	12.00	40.00
	1855 B	—	2.50	6.00	12.00	40.00
	1856 B	—	2.50	6.00	12.00	40.00

1/12 THALER

(3 Mariengroschen)

3.2400 g, .437 SILVER, .0455 oz ASW
Obv: Prancing horse, S on ledge.
Rev: Value, leg: NACH DEM REICHS FUSS.

KM#	Date	Mintage	Fine	VF	XF	Unc
108	1814C	—	5.00	15.00	40.00	100.00
	1815C	—	5.00	15.00	40.00	100.00
	1816C	—	5.00	15.00	40.00	100.00

KM#	Date	Mintage	Fine	VF	XF	Unc
139	1822 LB	1.908	5.00	15.00	40.00	100.00
	1823 L.B.	1.900	5.00	15.00	40.00	100.00
	1823 LB	I.A.	5.00	15.00	40.00	100.00
	1824 LB	.502	5.00	15.00	40.00	100.00

2.6700 g, .520 SILVER, .0446 oz ASW
Obv: B below head.

KM#	Date	Mintage	Fine	VF	XF	Unc
159	1834 B	—	5.00	15.00	40.00	100.00
	1835 B	—	5.00	15.00	40.00	100.00
	1836 B	—	5.00	15.00	40.00	100.00
	1837 B	—	5.00	15.00	40.00	100.00
179.1	1838 B	—	5.00	15.00	40.00	100.00

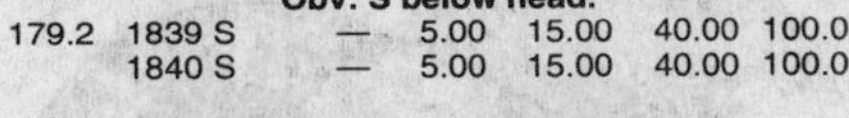

Obv: S below head.

KM#	Date	Mintage	Fine	VF	XF	Unc
179.2	1839 S	—	5.00	15.00	40.00	100.00
	1840 S	—	5.00	15.00	40.00	100.00

KM#	Date	Mintage	Fine	VF	XF	Unc
194.1	1841 S	—	3.00	7.00	15.00	60.00
	1842 S	—	3.00	7.00	15.00	60.00
	1843 S	—	3.00	7.00	15.00	60.00
	1844 S	—	3.00	7.00	15.00	60.00

Obv: B below head.

KM#	Date	Mintage	Fine	VF	XF	Unc
194.2	1844 B	—	3.00	7.00	15.00	40.00
	1845 B	—	3.00	7.00	15.00	40.00
	1846 B	—	3.00	7.00	15.00	40.00
	1847 B	—	3.00	7.00	15.00	40.00

Obv: Larger head.

KM#	Date	Mintage	Fine	VF	XF	Unc
206	1848 B	—	3.00	7.00	15.00	40.00
	1849 B	—	3.00	7.00	15.00	40.00
	1850 B	—	3.00	7.00	15.00	40.00
	1851 B	—	3.00	7.00	15.00	40.00

Obv: BREHMER F at truncation.

KM#	Date	Mintage	Fine	VF	XF	Unc
219	1852 B	—	3.00	7.00	15.00	40.00
	1853 B	—	3.00	7.00	15.00	40.00

3.2200 g, .375 SILVER, .0388 oz ASW
Obv: W/o name at truncation.
Rev. value: SCHEIDEMUNZE.

KM#	Date	Mintage	Fine	VF	XF	Unc
237	1859 B	—	3.00	7.00	15.00	40.00
	1860 B	—	3.00	7.00	15.00	40.00
	1862 B	—	3.00	7.00	15.00	40.00

1/6 THALER

5.8500 g, .500 SILVER, .0940 oz ASW
Obv: B below ledge.

KM#	Date	Mintage	Fine	VF	XF	Unc
129	1821 B	.150	15.00	30.00	75.00	225.00

5.3500 g, .520 SILVER, .0895 oz ASW

KM#	Date	Mintage	Fine	VF	XF	Unc
160	1834	.360	20.00	40.00	75.00	200.00

Obv: S below larger head.
Rev: Crowned arms on cartouche.

KM#	Date	Mintage	Fine	VF	XF	Unc
190	1840 S	.457	20.00	40.00	75.00	225.00

Rev: Shield w/square corners.

KM#	Date	Mintage	Fine	VF	XF	Unc
195	1841 S	Inc. Ab.	20.00	40.00	75.00	200.00

KM#	Date	Mintage	Fine	VF	XF	Unc
199	1844 B	Inc. Ab.	20.00	40.00	75.00	250.00
	1845 B	Inc. Ab.	20.00	40.00	75.00	250.00
	1847 B	Inc. Ab.	20.00	40.00	75.00	250.00

5.3400 g, .520 SILVER, .0893 oz ASW

KM#	Date	Mintage	Fine	VF	XF	Unc
238	1859 B	—	12.00	20.00	35.00	75.00
	1860 B	—	12.00	20.00	35.00	75.00
	1862 B	—	12.00	20.00	35.00	75.00
	1863 B	.087	12.00	20.00	35.00	75.00
	1866 B	5,904	30.00	50.00	90.00	165.00

2/3 THALER

13.0800 g, .993 SILVER, .4176 oz ASW

KM#	Date	Mintage	Fine	VF	XF	Unc
100.1	1813C	—	45.00	100.00	150.00	250.00
	1814C	—	45.00	100.00	150.00	250.00

Obv: M below truncation.

KM#	Date	Mintage	Fine	VF	XF	Unc
100.2	1814	—	50.00	110.00	175.00	275.00

KM#	Date	Mintage	Fine	VF	XF	Unc
140	1822C	—	40.00	80.00	120.00	250.00
	1823C	—	40.00	80.00	120.00	250.00
	1824C	—	40.00	80.00	120.00	250.00
	1825C	—	40.00	80.00	120.00	250.00
	1826C	—	40.00	80.00	120.00	250.00
	1827C	—	40.00	80.00	120.00	250.00
	1828C	—	40.00	80.00	120.00	250.00
	1829C	—	40.00	80.00	120.00	250.00

NOTE: Several varieties exist.

17.3200 g, .750 SILVER, .4177 oz ASW
Rev. value: 18 STUCK EINE MARK FEIN.

KM#	Date	Mintage	Fine	VF	XF	Unc
142	1826 B	—	55.00	125.00	250.00	450.00
	1827 B	—	55.00	125.00	250.00	450.00
	1828 B	—	55.00	125.00	250.00	450.00

13.0800 g, .993 SILVER, .4176 oz ASW
Obv: Ribbon inscribed
HONI SOIT QUI MAL Y PENSE.

KM#	Date	Mintage	Fine	VF	XF	Unc
151	1832	—	37.50	80.00	135.00	225.00
	1833	—	37.50	80.00	135.00	225.00

Rev: Similar to KM#151.

KM#	Date	Mintage	Fine	VF	XF	Unc
154	1833A	.050	140.00	250.00	400.00	650.00

KM#	Date	Mintage	Fine	VF	XF	Unc
161.1	1834A	Inc. Ab.	135.00	250.00	375.00	575.00

Obv. and rev: Raised edge and circle of dots around legend. Struck in collar.

KM#	Date	Mintage	Fine	VF	XF	Unc
161.2	1834A	Inc. Ab.	—	—	—	—

KM#	Date	Mintage	Fine	VF	XF	Unc
162	1834A	Inc. Ab.	550.00	750.00	1250.	1750.

Rev: AUSBEUTE DER GRUBE

KM#	Date	Mintage	Fine	VF	XF	Unc
163	1834A	Inc. Ab.	1350.	2000.	3000.	4500.

Obv: Different head right, A below.

KM#	Date	Mintage	Fine	VF	XF	Unc
180	1838A	—	50.00	110.00	250.00	375.00
	1839A	—	50.00	110.00	250.00	375.00

THALER

23.5400 g, .993 SILVER, .7516 oz ASW
Silver Mines of Clausthal
Rev: Large date.

KM#	Date	Mintage	Fine	VF	XF	Unc
146.1	1830	—	400.00	600.00	900.00	1800.

Rev: Flat 3 in small date.

KM#	Date	Mintage	Fine	VF	XF	Unc
146.2	1830	—	400.00	600.00	900.00	1800.

22.2700 g, .750 SILVER, .5370 oz ASW

KM#	Date	Mintage	Fine	VF	XF	Unc
164	1834 B	.044	40.00	115.00	350.00	1000.

16.8200 g, .993 SILVER, .5370 oz ASW
Obv: Similar to KM#164, A below head.

KM#	Date	Mintage	Fine	VF	XF	Unc
165	1834A	—	45.00	100.00	325.00	850.00
	1835A	—	45.00	90.00	250.00	700.00

Wilhelm IV

KM#	Date	Mintage	Fine	VF	XF	Unc
169	1835A	—	70.00	100.00	375.00	900.00
	1836A	—	30.00	50.00	150.00	450.00
	1837A	—	30.00	50.00	150.00	450.00

22.2700 g, .750 SILVER, .5370 oz ASW

KM#	Date	Mintage	Fine	VF	XF	Unc
172	1836 B	—	70.00	100.00	300.00	800.00

16.8200 g, .993 SILVER, .5370 oz ASW

Ernst August V

KM#	Date	Mintage	Fine	VF	XF	Unc
181	1838A	—	35.00	75.00	185.00	500.00
	1839A	—	35.00	75.00	185.00	500.00

KM#	Date	Mintage	Fine	VF	XF	Unc
182	1838A	—	35.00	75.00	185.00	500.00
	1839A	—	35.00	75.00	185.00	500.00
	1840A	—	45.00	90.00	225.00	600.00

King's Visit to Clausthal Mint

KM#	Date	Mintage	Fine	VF	XF	Unc
184	1839A	—	125.00	225.00	375.00	600.00

Obv: Similar to KM#182.
Rev. leg: FEINES---SILBER

KM#	Date	Mintage	Fine	VF	XF	Unc
191	1840A	—	—	—	Rare	—

KM#	Date	Mintage	Fine	VF	XF	Unc
192	1840A	—	40.00	70.00	175.00	450.00
	1841A	—	40.00	70.00	175.00	450.00

Obv: S below truncation.
Rev: Similar to KM#192.

KM#	Date	Mintage	Fine	VF	XF	Unc
193	1840 S	—	75.00	150.00	500.00	1300.

Obv: BRANDT F. at truncation.

KM#	Date	Mintage	Fine	VF	XF	Unc
196	1841 S	—	40.00	80.00	200.00	625.00

Obv: A below head.

KM#	Date	Mintage	Fine	VF	XF	Unc
197.1	1842A	.620	20.00	40.00	135.00	325.00
	1843A	.638	22.00	50.00	175.00	400.00
	1844A	.622	22.00	50.00	175.00	400.00
	1845A	.656	22.00	50.00	175.00	400.00
	1846A	.650	22.00	50.00	175.00	400.00
	1847A	.625	20.00	40.00	135.00	325.00
	1848A	.661	20.00	40.00	135.00	325.00
	1849A	.357	22.00	50.00	175.00	400.00

Obv: B below head.

KM#	Date	Mintage	Fine	VF	XF	Unc
197.2	1844 B	—	45.00	85.00	200.00	550.00
	1845 B	—	25.00	50.00	135.00	350.00
	1846 B	—	45.00	85.00	200.00	550.00
	1847 B	—	45.00	85.00	200.00	550.00

Wedding of Crown Prince Georg of Hannover and Duchess Marie of Sachsen-Altenburg

KM#	Date	Mintage	Fine	VF	XF	Unc
207	1843 S	1,010	150.00	300.00	500.00	900.00

Obv: BREHMER F. at truncation.

KM#	Date	Mintage	Fine	VF	XF	Unc
208	1848 B	—	22.00	50.00	150.00	400.00
	1849 B	—	22.00	50.00	150.00	400.00

Rev: HARZ SEGEN above crown.

KM#	Date	Mintage	Fine	VF	XF	Unc
209.1	1849 B	—	50.00	125.00	300.00	850.00

Rev: BERGSEGEN DES HARZES above crown.

KM#	Date	Mintage	Fine	VF	XF	Unc
209.2	1850 B	.712	22.00	50.00	100.00	250.00
	1851 B	.453	22.00	50.00	100.00	250.00

KM#	Date	Mintage	Fine	VF	XF	Unc
220	1852 B	.170	22.00	50.00	100.00	250.00
	1853 B	.180	22.00	50.00	100.00	250.00
	1854/3 B	—	—	—	—	—
	1854 B	.951	22.00	50.00	100.00	250.00
	1855 B	.974	22.00	50.00	100.00	250.00
	1856 B	.077	22.00	50.00	100.00	250.00

18.5200 g, .900 SILVER, .5360 oz ASW

KM#	Date	Mintage	Fine	VF	XF	Unc
230	1857 B	.274	20.00	40.00	70.00	140.00
	1858 B	.432	20.00	40.00	70.00	140.00
	1859 B	.554	20.00	40.00	65.00	120.00
	1860 B	.790	20.00	40.00	65.00	120.00
	1861 B	.736	20.00	40.00	65.00	120.00
	1862 B	.133	20.00	40.00	65.00	120.00
	1863 B	.233	20.00	40.00	65.00	120.00
	1864 B	.158	20.00	40.00	65.00	120.00
	1865 B	—	20.00	35.00	55.00	120.00
	1866 B	.159	20.00	35.00	50.00	100.00

50th Anniversary of Battle of Waterloo

KM#	Date	Mintage	Fine	VF	XF	Unc
241	1865 B	.015	30.00	50.00	80.00	135.00

NOTE: This coin was given to veterans of the battle in pension payments.

50th Anniversary Union East Friesia and Hannover

KM#	Date	Mintage	Fine	VF	XF	Unc
242	1865 B	1,000	125.00	200.00	300.00	600.00
	1865 B	—	—	—	Proof	550.00

Frisian Oath Commemorative
Obv: Similar to KM#241.

KM#	Date	Mintage	Fine	VF	XF	Unc
243	1865 B	2,000	125.00	200.00	300.00	500.00

2 THALER

(3-1/2 Gulden)

Obv: Similar to KM#240.

KM#	Date	Mintage	Fine	VF	XF	Unc
229	1854 B	.102	100.00	150.00	200.00	350.00
	1855 B	.842	90.00	125.00	175.00	325.00

37.0400 g, .900 SILVER, 1.0719 oz ASW

KM#	Date	Mintage	Fine	VF	XF	Unc
240	1862 B	.133	100.00	150.00	200.00	350.00
	1866 B	.038	90.00	125.00	175.00	325.00

2-1/2 THALER

3.3400 g, .903 GOLD, .0970 oz AGW

KM#	Date	Mintage	Fine	VF	XF	Unc
109	1814 CHH	—	325.00	500.00	750.00	1150.

KM#	Date	Mintage	Fine	VF	XF	Unc
130	1821 B	—	225.00	450.00	675.00	1100.
	1827 B	—	225.00	450.00	675.00	1100.
	1830 B	—	225.00	450.00	675.00	1100.

KM#	Date	Mintage	Fine	VF	XF	Unc
152	1832 B	—	200.00	400.00	600.00	1000.
	1833 B	—	200.00	400.00	600.00	1000.
	1835 B	—	200.00	400.00	600.00	1000.

3.3200 g, .896 GOLD, .0956 oz AGW

KM#	Date	Mintage	Fine	VF	XF	Unc
152a	1836 B	—	150.00	300.00	550.00	900.00
	1837 B	—	150.00	300.00	550.00	900.00

KM#	Date	Mintage	Fine	VF	XF	Unc
185.1	1839 S	—	225.00	400.00	600.00	1000.
	1840 S	—	225.00	400.00	600.00	1000.
	1843 S	—	225.00	400.00	600.00	1000.

KM#	Date	Mintage	Fine	VF	XF	Unc
185.2	1845 B	—	225.00	400.00	600.00	1000.
	1846 B	—	225.00	400.00	600.00	1000.
	1847 B	—	225.00	400.00	600.00	1000.
	1848 B	—	225.00	400.00	600.00	1000.

KM#	Date	Mintage	Fine	VF	XF	Unc
215	1850 B	—	200.00	300.00	500.00	900.00

Obv: BREHMER F. at truncation, B below.

KM#	Date	Mintage	Fine	VF	XF	Unc
223	1853 B	—	250.00	500.00	1000.	1500.
	1855 B	—	175.00	350.00	700.00	1000.

5 THALER

6.6500 g, .896 GOLD, .1916 oz AGW

KM#	Date	Mintage	Fine	VF	XF	Unc
101	1813 TW	—	200.00	300.00	750.00	1500.
	1814 TW	—	200.00	300.00	750.00	1500.
	1815 TW	—	250.00	400.00	875.00	1750.

6.6800 g, .903 GOLD, .1940 oz AGW

KM#	Date	Mintage	Fine	VF	XF	Unc
110	1814C	—	825.00	1200.	2000.	3250.
	1815C	—	—	—	Rare	—

KM#	Date	Mintage	Fine	VF	XF	Unc
131	1821C	185 pcs.	1500.	2000.	3000.	7500.

KM#	Date	Mintage	Fine	VF	XF	Unc
132	1821 B	—	250.00	450.00	700.00	1000.
	1825 B	—	250.00	450.00	700.00	1000.
	1828 B	—	250.00	450.00	700.00	1000.
	1829 B	—	250.00	450.00	700.00	1000.
	1830 B	—	250.00	450.00	700.00	1000.

6.6500 g, .896 GOLD, .1916 oz AGW

KM#	Date	Mintage	Fine	VF	XF	Unc
170	1835 B	—	350.00	500.00	750.00	1500.

KM#	Date	Mintage	Fine	VF	XF	Unc
186	1839 S	—	400.00	700.00	1000.	1800.

Obv: B below head.

KM#	Date	Mintage	Fine	VF	XF	Unc
204	1845 B	—	300.00	500.00	800.00	1350.
	1846 B	—	375.00	650.00	1000.	1600.
	1848 B	—	375.00	650.00	1000.	1600.

KM#	Date	Mintage	Fine	VF	XF	Unc
210	1849 B	—	300.00	500.00	750.00	1350.
	1851 B	—	300.00	500.00	750.00	1350.

Rev. leg: HARZ GOLD added.

KM#	Date	Mintage	Fine	VF	XF	Unc
211	1849 B	—	350.00	550.00	800.00	1400.
	1850 B	—	300.00	500.00	750.00	1300.

Obv: BREHMER F. at truncation, B below.

KM#	Date	Mintage	Fine	VF	XF	Unc
224	1853 B	—	300.00	500.00	750.00	1200.
	1855 B	—	300.00	500.00	750.00	1200.
	1856 B	—	400.00	800.00	1000.	2000.

Rev. leg: HARZ GOLD added.

KM#	Date	Mintage	Fine	VF	XF	Unc
225	1853 B	—	500.00	875.00	1200.	2250.
	1856 B	—	550.00	1150.	1500.	2650.

10 THALER

13.3600 g, .903 GOLD, .3879 oz AGW

KM#	Date	Mintage	Fine	VF	XF	Unc
102	1813 CHH	—	1000.	1500.	2000.	3250.
	1814 CHH	—	750.00	1100.	1500.	2500.

KM#	Date	Mintage	Fine	VF	XF	Unc
133	1821 B	—	600.00	1000.	1500.	2200.
	1822 B	—	475.00	800.00	1300.	1800.
	1823 B	—	475.00	800.00	1300.	1800.
	1824 B	—	475.00	800.00	1300.	1800.
	1825 B	—	325.00	550.00	1100.	1600.
	1827 B	—	325.00	550.00	1100.	1600.
	1828 B	—	325.00	550.00	1100.	1600.
	1829 B	—	325.00	550.00	1100.	1600.
	1830 B	—	325.00	550.00	1100.	1600.

KM#	Date	Mintage	Fine	VF	XF	Unc
153	1832	—	550.00	900.00	1250.	2500.

KM#	Date	Mintage	Fine	VF	XF	Unc
155	1833	—	550.00	900.00	1250.	2500.

13.3000 g, .896 GOLD, .3832 oz AGW

Obv: B below head.

KM#	Date	Mintage	Fine	VF	XF	Unc
171	1835 B	—	675.00	1150.	1900.	2650.
	1836 B	—	650.00	1125.	1875.	2600.
	1837 B	—	550.00	900.00	1500.	2250.

KM#	Date	Mintage	Fine	VF	XF	Unc
175	1837 B	—	—	—	10,000.	15,000.
	1838 B	—	500.00	900.00	1500.	2250.

Obv: S below head.

KM#	Date	Mintage	Fine	VF	XF	Unc
187	1839 S	—	400.00	600.00	1200.	2000.

Obv: BRANDT F. on truncation.

KM#	Date	Mintage	Fine	VF	XF	Unc
200.1	1844 S	—	600.00	1000.	1500.	2250.

Obv: B below head.

KM#	Date	Mintage	Fine	VF	XF	Unc
200.2	1844 B	—	600.00	1000.	1500.	2500.

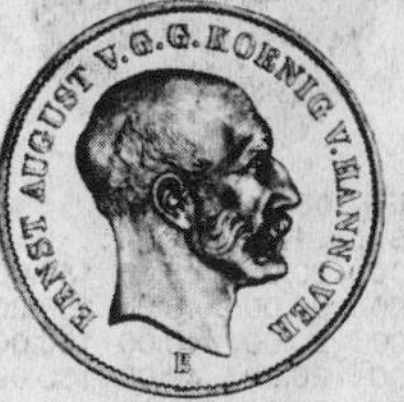 

Obv: W/o markings on truncation, leg. ends: . . . . .V. HANNOVER.

KM#	Date	Mintage	Fine	VF	XF	Unc
200.3	1846 B	—	400.00	800.00	1200.	2000.
	1847 B	—	400.00	800.00	1200.	2000.
	1848 B	—	300.00	600.00	900.00	1500.

Obv. leg. ends: . . . . .VON HANNOVER

KM#	Date	Mintage	Fine	VF	XF	Unc
212	1849 B	—	500.00	1000.	1500.	2250.
	1850 B	—	350.00	600.00	1000.	1500.
	1851 B	—	500.00	1000.	1500.	2250.

KM#	Date	Mintage	Fine	VF	XF	Unc
226	1853 B	—	450.00	750.00	1250.	1750.
	1854 B	—	300.00	500.00	900.00	1250.
	1855 B	—	450.00	750.00	1250.	1750.
	1856 B	—	500.00	900.00	1500.	2150.

TRADE COINAGE

DUCAT

3.5000 g, .986 GOLD, .1109 oz AGW

KM#	Date	Mintage	Fine	VF	XF	Unc
111	1815C	—	525.00	875.00	1400.	2000.
	1818C	—	600.00	1000.	1650.	2250.
134	1821C	252 pcs.	975.00	1650.	2400.	3250.
	1824C	749 pcs.	900.00	1500.	2250.	3000.
	1827C	1,300	825.00	1400.	2000.	2750.

KM#	Date	Mintage	Fine	VF	XF	Unc
149	1831C	1,550	750.00	1250.	1900.	2500.

1/2 KRONE

5.5500 g, .900 GOLD, .1606 oz AGW

KM#	Date	Mintage	Fine	VF	XF	Unc
231	1857 B	4,105	300.00	600.00	1000.	1500.
	1858 B	116 pcs.	900.00	1500.	2000.	3000.
	1859 B	790 pcs.	400.00	800.00	1200.	1750.
	1862 B	96 pcs.	1500.	2000.	2500.	5000.
	1864 B	.013	300.00	600.00	1000.	1500.
	1866 B	2,909	300.00	600.00	850.00	1500.

KRONE

11.1100 g, .900 GOLD, .3215 oz AGW

KM#	Date	Mintage	Fine	VF	XF	Unc
232	1857 B	.145	350.00	500.00	900.00	1500.
	1858 B	.047	450.00	800.00	1200.	1800.
	1859 B	.020	500.00	850.00	1300.	1900.
	1860 B	.015	550.00	1000.	1500.	2250.
	1861 B	780 pcs.	1000.	1500.	2000.	3000.
	1862 B	.020	525.00	875.00	1400.	1900.
	1863 B	.126	350.00	500.00	900.00	1500.
	1864 B	.014	450.00	800.00	1100.	1700.
	1866 B	.383	350.00	500.00	900.00	1500.

HESSE-CASSEL

(Hessen-Kassel)

The Hesse principalities were located for the most part north of the Main River, bounded by Westphalia on the west, the Brunswick duchies on the north, the Saxon duchies on the east and Rhine Palatinate and the bishoprics of Mainz and Fulda on the south. The rule of the landgraves of Hesse began in the second half of the 13th century, the dignity of Prince of the Empire being acquired in 1292. In 1567 the patrimony was divided by four surviving sons, only those of Cassel and Darmstadt surviving for more than a generation. In Hesse-Cassel the landgrave was raised to the rank of elector in 1803. The electorate formed part of the Kingdom of Westphalia from 1806 to 1813. In 1866 Hesse-Cassel fell to Prussia.

RULERS

Wilhelm IX, 1785-1803
Wilhelm I, As Elector, 1803-1821
Wilhelm II, 1821-1847
Friedrich Wilhelm, 1847-1866

MINT MARKS

C - Cassel
(L.) - Lippoldsberg

MINTMASTERS INITIALS

Letter	Date	Name
CP	1820-1861	Christoph Pfeuffer, die-cutter
D.F., F.	1774-1831	Dietrich Flalda
FH	1786-1821	Friedrich Heenwagen
H	1775-1820	Carl Ludwig Holzemer, die-cutter
K	1804-1833	Wilhelm Korner

ARMS

Hessian lion rampant left.

HELLER

COPPER
Similar to KM#553 but 19mm.

KM#	Date	Mintage	Fine	VF	XF	Unc
543	1801	—	2.00	4.00	10.00	55.00
	1802	—	2.00	4.00	10.00	55.00
	1803	—	2.00	4.00	10.00	55.00

NOTE: Earlier dates (1791-1800) exist for this type.

KM#	Date	Mintage	Fine	VF	XF	Unc
553	1803	—	2.00	4.00	10.00	60.00
	1805	—	2.00	4.00	10.00	60.00
	1806	—	2.00	4.00	10.00	60.00
	1814	—	2.00	4.00	10.00	60.00

Obv: Crowned WK monogram w/1 ring at base of W.

KM#	Date	Mintage	Fine	VF	XF	Unc
565	1817	—	2.00	4.00	10.00	60.00
	1818	—	2.00	4.00	10.00	60.00
	1819	—	2.00	4.00	10.00	60.00
	1820	—	2.00	4.00	10.00	60.00
575	1822	—	2.00	4.00	7.00	40.00
575	1823	—	2.00	4.00	7.00	40.00
	1824	—	2.00	4.00	7.00	40.00
	1825	—	2.00	4.00	7.00	40.00
	1827	—	2.00	4.00	7.00	40.00

Obv: Crowned WK monogram w/2 rings at base of W.

KM#	Date	Mintage	Fine	VF	XF	Unc
576	1822	—	2.00	4.00	7.00	40.00
	1825	—	2.00	4.00	7.00	40.00
	1827	—	2.00	4.00	7.00	40.00
	1828	—	2.00	4.00	7.00	40.00
	1829	—	2.00	4.00	7.00	40.00
	1831	—	2.00	4.00	7.00	40.00

Obv: Crowned arms, leg: KURHESSEN.
Rev. value: SCHEIDE MUNZE.

KM#	Date	Mintage	Fine	VF	XF	Unc
602	1842	.037	5.00	10.00	25.00	100.00

Obv. leg: 360 EINEN THALER.

KM#	Date	Mintage	Fine	VF	XF	Unc
605	1843	—	1.00	2.00	5.00	30.00
	1845	—	1.00	2.00	5.00	30.00
	1847	—	1.00	2.00	5.00	30.00

KM#	Date	Mintage	Fine	VF	XF	Unc
613	1849	—	1.00	2.00	3.00	30.00
	1852	—	1.00	2.00	3.00	30.00
	1854	—	1.00	2.00	3.00	30.00
	1856	—	1.00	2.00	3.00	30.00
	1858	—	1.00	2.00	3.00	30.00
	1859	—	1.00	2.00	3.00	30.00
	1860	—	1.00	2.00	3.00	30.00
	1861	—	1.00	2.00	3.00	30.00
	1862	—	1.00	2.00	3.00	30.00
	1863	—	1.00	2.00	3.00	30.00
	1864	—	1.00	2.00	3.00	30.00
	1865	—	1.00	2.00	3.00	30.00
	1866	—	1.00	2.00	3.00	30.00

2 HELLER

COPPER

KM#	Date	Mintage	Fine	VF	XF	Unc
561	1814	—	5.00	10.00	20.00	100.00

Obv: Crowned WK monogram w/1 ring at base of W.

KM#	Date	Mintage	Fine	VF	XF	Unc
564	1816	—	3.00	7.00	15.00	75.00
	1818	—	3.00	7.00	15.00	75.00
	1820	—	3.00	7.00	15.00	75.00
585	1831	—	2.00	4.00	7.00	25.00

Obv: Crowned WK monogram w/2 rings at base of W.

KM#	Date	Mintage	Fine	VF	XF	Unc
589	1833	—	2.00	4.00	7.00	25.00

KM#	Date	Mintage	Fine	VF	XF	Unc
606	1843	—	2.00	4.00	7.00	25.00

3 HELLER

COPPER

KM#	Date	Mintage	Fine	VF	XF	Unc
607	1843	—	2.00	4.00	8.00	35.00

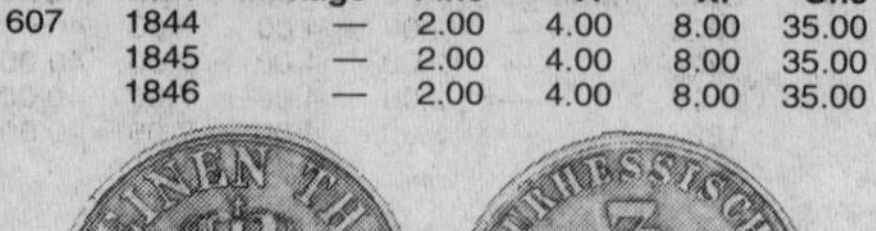

KM#	Date	Mintage	Fine	VF	XF	Unc
607	1844	—	2.00	4.00	8.00	35.00
	1845	—	2.00	4.00	8.00	35.00
	1846	—	2.00	4.00	8.00	35.00

KM#	Date	Mintage	Fine	VF	XF	Unc
612	1848	—	1.50	3.00	6.00	30.00
	1849	—	1.50	3.00	6.00	30.00
	1850	—	1.50	3.00	6.00	30.00
	1851	—	1.50	3.00	6.00	30.00
	1852	—	1.50	3.00	6.00	30.00
	1853	—	1.50	3.00	6.00	30.00
	1854	—	1.50	3.00	6.00	30.00
	1856	—	1.50	3.00	6.00	30.00
	1858	—	1.50	3.00	6.00	30.00
	1859	—	1.50	3.00	6.00	30.00
	1860	—	1.50	3.00	6.00	30.00
	1861	—	1.50	3.00	6.00	30.00
	1862	—	1.50	3.00	6.00	30.00
	1863	—	1.50	3.00	6.00	30.00
	1864	—	1.50	3.00	6.00	30.00
	1865	—	1.50	3.00	6.00	30.00
	1866	—	1.50	3.00	6.00	30.00

4 HELLER

COPPER
Obv: Crowned WK monogram w/1 loop at base of W.

KM#	Date	Mintage	Fine	VF	XF	Unc
562	1815	—	3.00	7.00	20.00	125.00
	1816	—	3.00	7.00	20.00	125.00
	1817	—	3.00	7.00	20.00	125.00
	1818	—	3.00	7.00	20.00	125.00
	1819	—	3.00	7.00	20.00	125.00
	1820	—	3.00	7.00	20.00	125.00
	1821	—	3.00	7.00	20.00	125.00

Obv: Crowned WK monogram w/2 loops at base of W.

KM#	Date	Mintage	Fine	VF	XF	Unc
571	1821	—	2.00	4.00	10.00	65.00
	1822	—	2.00	4.00	10.00	65.00
	1824	—	2.00	4.00	10.00	65.00
	1826	—	2.00	4.00	10.00	65.00
	1827	—	2.00	4.00	10.00	65.00
	1828	—	2.00	4.00	10.00	65.00
	1829	—	2.00	4.00	10.00	65.00
	1830	—	2.00	4.00	10.00	65.00
	1831	—	2.00	4.00	10.00	65.00

1/2 SILBER GROSCHEN

.9700 g, .250 SILVER, .0077 oz ASW
Obv: Crowned arms.
Rev. value: SILBER GROSCHEN.

KM#	Date	Mintage	Fine	VF	XF	Unc
603	1842	1.491	2.00	4.00	10.00	65.00

SILBER GROSCHEN

1.5600 g, .312 SILVER, .0156 oz ASW

KM#	Date	Mintage	Fine	VF	XF	Unc
601	1841	5.925	1.00	3.00	7.00	40.00
	1845	.062	2.00	4.00	8.00	45.00
	1847	.456	2.00	4.00	8.00	45.00

KM#	Date	Mintage	Fine	VF	XF	Unc
615	1851	.262	1.00	3.00	7.00	30.00
	1852	.147	1.00	3.00	7.00	30.00
	1853	.125	1.00	3.00	7.00	30.00
	1854	.098	1.00	3.00	7.00	30.00
	1855	.054	1.00	3.00	7.00	30.00
	1856	.234	1.00	3.00	7.00	30.00
	1857	.119	1.00	3.00	7.00	30.00
	1858	.058	1.00	3.00	7.00	30.00
	1859	.235	1.00	3.00	7.00	30.00
	1860	.156	1.00	3.00	7.00	30.00
	1861	.165	1.00	3.00	7.00	30.00
	1862	—	1.00	3.00	7.00	30.00
	1863	—	1.00	3.00	7.00	30.00
	1864	.122	1.00	3.00	7.00	30.00
	1865	.192	1.00	3.00	7.00	30.00
	1866	.182	1.00	3.00	7.00	30.00

2 SILBER GROSCHEN

2.6000 g, .375 SILVER, .0313 oz ASW

KM#	Date	Mintage	Fine	VF	XF	Unc
604	1842	2.414	10.00	20.00	45.00	90.00

2-1/2 SILBER GROSCHEN

3.2500 g, .375 SILVER, .0391 oz ASW

KM#	Date	Mintage	Fine	VF	XF	Unc
620	1852 CP	.034	3.00	7.00	20.00	75.00
	1853 CP	.049	3.00	7.00	20.00	75.00
	1856 CP	.039	3.00	7.00	20.00	75.00
	1859 CP	.069	3.00	7.00	20.00	75.00
	1860 CP	.042	3.00	7.00	20.00	75.00
	1861 CP	.034	3.00	7.00	20.00	75.00
	1862 CP	.031	3.00	7.00	20.00	75.00
	1865 CP	.023	3.00	7.00	20.00	75.00

24 EINEN (1/24) THALER

BILLON
Obv: Rampant lion left. Rev: Value, date below.

KM#	Date	Mintage	Fine	VF	XF	Unc
529	1801	—	7.00	15.00	35.00	100.00
	1802	—	7.00	15.00	35.00	100.00

NOTE: Earlier dates (1786-1800) exist for this type.

KM#	Date	Mintage	Fine	VF	XF	Unc
554.1	1803 F	.526	7.00	15.00	35.00	100.00
	1804 F	—	7.00	15.00	35.00	100.00
	1805 F	—	7.00	15.00	35.00	100.00
	1806 F	—	7.00	15.00	35.00	100.00
	1807 F	.997	7.00	15.00	35.00	100.00

Obv: Rampant lion left.
Rev: Value, w/o mint mark below date.

KM#	Date	Mintage	Fine	VF	XF	Unc
554.2	1814	—	6.00	12.00	30.00	100.00
	1815	—	6.00	12.00	30.00	100.00
	1816	—	6.00	12.00	30.00	100.00
	1817	—	6.00	12.00	30.00	100.00
	1818	—	6.00	12.00	30.00	100.00
	1819	—	6.00	12.00	30.00	100.00
	1820	—	6.00	12.00	30.00	100.00
	1821	—	6.00	12.00	30.00	100.00
577	1822	—	17.50	35.00	70.00	165.00

VI EINEN (1/6) THALER

SILVER

KM#	Date	Mintage	Fine	VF	XF	Unc
546	1801 F	—	10.00	20.00	40.00	150.00
	1802 F	—	10.00	20.00	40.00	150.00

NOTE: Earlier dates (1798-1800) exist for this type.

.625 SILVER
Obv: Crowned arms within laurel branches.
Rev: Value.

KM#	Date	Mintage	Fine	VF	XF	Unc
555	1803 F	—	10.00	20.00	45.00	165.00

KM#	Date	Mintage	Fine	VF	XF	Unc
556	1803 F	—	10.00	20.00	45.00	165.00
	1804 F	—	10.00	20.00	45.00	165.00
	1805 F	—	10.00	20.00	45.00	165.00
	1806 F	—	10.00	20.00	45.00	165.00
	1807 F	.040	10.00	20.00	45.00	165.00

Obv: Lion in oval shield. Rev: Value, date.

KM#	Date	Mintage	Fine	VF	XF	Unc
572	1821	.038	15.00	30.00	100.00	275.00
	1822	.056	15.00	30.00	100.00	250.00

5.3200 g, .500 SILVER, .0855 oz ASW
Obv. leg: . . . . .KURF S.L.V. HESSEN. . . . .

KM#	Date	Mintage	Fine	VF	XF	Unc
579.1	1823	.182	10.00	20.00	40.00	150.00
	1824	.276	10.00	20.00	40.00	150.00
	1825	.306	10.00	20.00	40.00	150.00
	1826	.147	10.00	20.00	40.00	150.00
	1827	.280	10.00	20.00	40.00	150.00
	1828	.395	10.00	20.00	40.00	150.00
	1829	.590	10.00	20.00	40.00	150.00
	1830	.524	10.00	20.00	40.00	150.00
	1831	.201	10.00	20.00	40.00	150.00

Obv. leg: . . . . .KURF. V. HESSEN. . . . .

KM#	Date	Mintage	Fine	VF	XF	Unc
579.2	1831	.022	75.00	140.00	250.00	475.00

Rev: THAELR (error)

KM#	Date	Mintage	Fine	VF	XF	Unc
579.3	1828	—	50.00	115.00	200.00	325.00

Obv. leg. ends: . . . . . KURPR.U.MITREG.

KM#	Date	Mintage	Fine	VF	XF	Unc
590	1833	.046	5.00	15.00	35.00	145.00
	1834	.599	5.00	10.00	25.00	85.00
	1835	.810	5.00	10.00	25.00	85.00
	1836	.528	5.00	10.00	25.00	85.00
	1837	.624	5.00	10.00	25.00	85.00
	1838	.558	5.00	10.00	25.00	85.00
	1839	.228	5.00	10.00	25.00	100.00
	1840	6,000	5.00	20.00	50.00	225.00
	1841	.192	5.00	10.00	20.00	100.00
	1842	1.404	5.00	10.00	20.00	85.00
	1843	—	5.00	10.00	25.00	100.00
	1844	6,132	5.00	20.00	50.00	225.00
	1845	.095	5.00	10.00	25.00	115.00
	1846	.045	5.00	15.00	35.00	145.00

Obv. leg. ends: . . . . . .KURPR.=MITREG

KM#	Date	Mintage	Fine	VF	XF	Unc
609	1846	Inc.Ab.	75.00	145.00	250.00	475.00
	1847	.103	65.00	125.00	225.00	400.00

5.3500 g, .520 SILVER, .0894 oz ASW
Obv: C.P. at truncation.

KM#	Date	Mintage	Fine	VF	XF	Unc
616	1851 CP	.030	10.00	20.00	30.00	125.00
	1852 CP	.033	10.00	20.00	30.00	125.00
	1854 CP	.013	10.00	20.00	30.00	125.00
	1855 CP	.022	10.00	20.00	30.00	125.00
	1856 CP	—	10.00	20.00	30.00	125.00

1/3 THALER

8.5000 g, .625 SILVER, .1708 oz ASW

KM#	Date	Mintage	Fine	VF	XF	Unc
578	1822	.105	10.00	40.00	75.00	175.00
	1823	.125	10.00	40.00	75.00	175.00
	1824	.099	10.00	40.00	75.00	175.00
	1825	.162	10.00	40.00	75.00	175.00
	1826	.280	10.00	40.00	75.00	175.00
	1827	.278	10.00	40.00	75.00	175.00
	1828	—	10.00	40.00	75.00	175.00
	1829	.219	10.00	40.00	75.00	175.00

1/2 THALER

11.1200 g, .750 SILVER, .2681 oz ASW

KM#	Date	Mintage	Fine	VF	XF	Unc
567	1819	—	25.00	50.00	100.00	300.00
	1820	—	25.00	50.00	100.00	300.00

THALER

SILVER
Obv: Small bust right.
Rev: Crowned oval arms w/griffon supporters.

KM#	Date	Mintage	Fine	VF	XF	Unc
552	1802 FH	—	—	—	Rare	—

KM#	Date	Mintage	Fine	VF	XF	Unc
560	1813 K	—	600.00	1500.	3000.	4500.

NOTE: Possibly a pattern.

22.2700 g, .750 SILVER, .5371 oz ASW
Obv. leg: KURF. SOUV.

KM#	Date	Mintage	Fine	VF	XF	Unc
568	1819	—	60.00	100.00	425.00	1000.
	1820	—	75.00	140.00	575.00	1200.

Obv. leg: SOUV.LANDGR.Z.HESSEN.

KM#	Date	Mintage	Fine	VF	XF	Unc
573.1	1821	2,385	85.00	200.00	700.00	1500.
	1822	3,456	100.00	260.00	900.00	1900.

Obv: W/o period after HESSEN.

KM#	Date	Mintage	Fine	VF	XF	Unc
573.2	1821	Inc. Ab.	85.00	200.00	700.00	1500.

KM#	Date	Mintage	Fine	VF	XF	Unc
587	1832	.020	22.00	50.00	150.00	450.00
	1833	.017	22.00	50.00	150.00	450.00
	1834	.037	22.00	50.00	150.00	450.00
	1835	.014	22.00	50.00	150.00	450.00
	1836	.040	25.00	55.00	175.00	575.00
	1837	.026	25.00	50.00	175.00	450.00
	1838	4,041	40.00	70.00	200.00	800.00
	1839	2,574	25.00	50.00	150.00	450.00
	1841	.025	22.00	50.00	150.00	450.00
	1842	.031	25.00	55.00	175.00	575.00

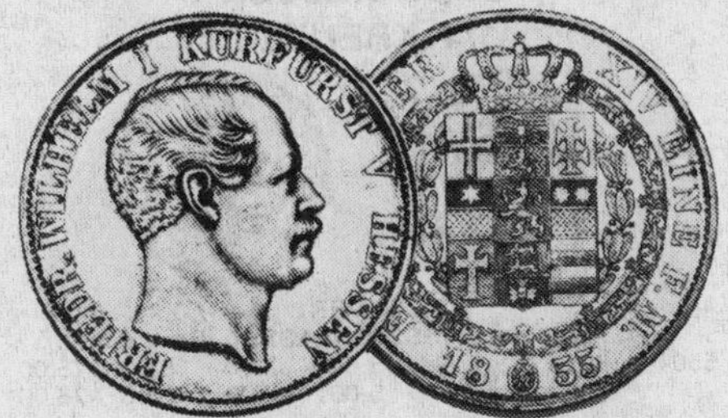

Obv: C.PFEUFFER F. at truncation.

KM#	Date	Mintage	Fine	VF	XF	Unc
617	1851	3,963	75.00	150.00	500.00	1500.
	1854	7,338	60.00	100.00	325.00	1250.
	1855	.028	35.00	65.00	275.00	800.00

18.5200 g, .900 SILVER, .5360 oz ASW
Obv: W/C.P. at truncation.

KM#	Date	Mintage	Fine	VF	XF	Unc
621.1	1858 CP	.062	25.00	55.00	150.00	500.00
	1859 CP	.037	25.00	55.00	150.00	500.00
	1860 CP	.031	25.00	55.00	150.00	500.00
	1862 CP	.032	25.00	55.00	150.00	500.00
	1864 CP	.032	25.00	55.00	150.00	500.00
	1865 CP	.031	25.00	55.00	150.00	500.00

Obv: W/o C.P. at truncation.

KM#	Date	Mintage	Fine	VF	XF	Unc
621.2	1858	Inc. Ab.	25.00	55.00	150.00	500.00
	1859	Inc. Ab.	25.00	55.00	150.00	500.00
	1860	Inc. Ab.	25.00	60.00	150.00	500.00
	1861	.032	25.00	60.00	150.00	500.00
	1862	—	25.00	60.00	150.00	500.00
	1863	.032	25.00	60.00	150.00	500.00
	1864	Inc. Ab.	25.00	55.00	150.00	500.00
	1865	Inc. Ab.	25.00	55.00	150.00	500.00

2 THALER

(Reichs)
(3-1/2 Gulden)

37.1200 g, .900 SILVER, 1.0742 oz ASW

KM#	Date	Mintage	Fine	VF	XF	Unc
600	1840	.019	90.00	150.00	375.00	1200.
	1841	.019	100.00	175.00	425.00	1350.
	1842	.019	100.00	175.00	425.00	1350.
	1843	.018	115.00	185.00	460.00	1425.
	1844	.059	130.00	200.00	500.00	1600.
	1845	—	130.00	200.00	500.00	1600.

Obv: Larger letters.

KM#	Date	Mintage	Fine	VF	XF	Unc
608	1844	Inc. Ab.	90.00	150.00	375.00	1200.
	1845	—	130.00	210.00	500.00	1600.

Obv. leg: KURPRINZ-MITREGENT.

KM#	Date	Mintage	Fine	VF	XF	Unc
610	1847	.010	400.00	750.00	1700.	3800.

Obv: CP on truncation.

KM#	Date	Mintage	Fine	VF	XF	Unc
618	1851 CP	3,996	150.00	300.00	500.00	1100.
	1854 CP	.141	100.00	150.00	325.00	800.00
	1855 CP	.357	85.00	125.00	275.00	600.00

5 THALER

6.6500 g, .900 GOLD, .1924 oz AGW
Obv: Bust right. Rev: Similar to KM#557.

KM#	Date	Mintage	Fine	VF	XF	Unc
545	1801 F	—	300.00	650.00	1000.	1750.

NOTE: Earlier dates (1791-1800) exist for this type.

KM#	Date	Mintage	Fine	VF	XF	Unc
557	1803 F	1,659	650.00	1250.	2250.	3250.
	1805 F	1,941	775.00	1500.	2500.	3750.
	1806 F	875 pcs.	900.00	1750.	3000.	4250.

KM#	Date	Mintage	Fine	VF	XF	Unc
563	1815	2,226	900.00	1500.	2500.	3750.

Obv. leg: WILHELMUS I.ELECT.HASS.

KM#	Date	Mintage	Fine	VF	XF	Unc
566	1817	2,352	900.00	1500.	2500.	3750.
	1819	1,548	1050.	1750.	3000.	4250.

Obv. leg: WILHELM I KURF. . . . .

KM#	Date	Mintage	Fine	VF	XF	Unc
570	1820	534 pcs.	1000.	1850.	3500.	5250.

Obv. leg: . . . . .KURF.S.L. Z. HESSEN. . . . .

KM#	Date	Mintage	Fine	VF	XF	Unc
574.1	1821	1,142	500.00	1200.	2250.	4500.
	1823	1,140	500.00	1200.	2250.	4500.

Obv. leg: . . . . .KURF.S.L.V.HESSEN. . . . .

KM#	Date	Mintage	Fine	VF	XF	Unc
574.2	1823	518 pcs.	750.00	1500.	2500.	4500.
	1825	409 pcs.	750.00	1500.	2500.	4500.
	1828	952 pcs.	675.00	1250.	2250.	4000.
	1829	502 pcs.	750.00	1500.	2500.	4500.

KM#	Date	Mintage	Fine	VF	XF	Unc
591	1834	1,025	500.00	875.00	1500.	2000.
	1836	2,002	500.00	875.00	1500.	2000.
	1837	256 pcs.	575.00	1000.	1750.	2250.
	1839	1,996	500.00	875.00	1500.	2000.
	1840	.017	425.00	750.00	1250.	1750.
	1841	.016	425.00	750.00	1250.	1750.
	1842	6,909	425.00	750.00	1250.	1750.
	1843	1,657	500.00	875.00	1500.	2000.
	1844	1,495	500.00	875.00	1500.	2000.
	1845	1,364	500.00	875.00	1500.	2000.

Obv. leg. ends: . . . . .KURPR.-MITREG.

KM#	Date	Mintage	Fine	VF	XF	Unc
611	1847	1,438	750.00	1250.	2000.	3000.

Obv: CP on truncation.

KM#	Date	Mintage	Fine	VF	XF	Unc
619	1851 CP	596 pcs.	800.00	1300.	2000.	3500.

10 THALER

13.3000 g, .900 GOLD, .3848 oz AGW

KM#	Date	Mintage	Fine	VF	XF	Unc
594	1838	126 pcs.	1400.	2000.	3000.	4000.
	1840	Inc. KM591	1000.	1500.	2500.	3500.
	1841	Inc. KM591	1000.	1500.	2500.	3500.

OBER-HESSEN

1/4 KREUZER

COPPER

Obv: Arms, leg: HESSEN CASSEL. Rev: Value.

KM#	Date	Mintage	Fine	VF	XF	Unc
550	1801	—	5.00	7.00	15.00	75.00
	1802	—	5.00	7.00	15.00	75.00

Obv: Crowned arms. Rev: Value within rosettes.

KM#	Date	Mintage	Fine	VF	XF	Unc
580	1824	—	2.00	4.00	8.00	40.00
	1825	—	2.00	4.00	8.00	40.00
	1827	—	2.00	4.00	8.00	40.00
	1829	—	2.00	4.00	8.00	40.00
	1830	—	2.00	4.00	8.00	40.00

Similar to KM#580.

KM#	Date	Mintage	Fine	VF	XF	Unc
592	1834	—	2.00	4.00	8.00	40.00
	1835	—	2.00	4.00	8.00	40.00

1/2 KREUZER

COPPER

Obv: Arms, HESSEN CASSEL. Rev: Value.

KM#	Date	Mintage	Fine	VF	XF	Unc
551	1801	—	3.00	6.00	15.00	75.00
	1802	—	3.00	6.00	15.00	75.00
	1803	—	3.00	6.00	15.00	75.00

Obv: Elector's cap above arms. Rev: Value.

KM#	Date	Mintage	Fine	VF	XF	Unc
558	1803 F	—	3.00	6.00	15.00	75.00
	1804 F	—	3.00	6.00	15.00	75.00

KM#	Date	Mintage	Fine	VF	XF	Unc
581	1824	—	2.00	4.00	8.00	40.00
	1825	—	2.00	4.00	8.00	40.00
	1826	—	2.00	4.00	8.00	40.00
	1827	—	2.00	4.00	8.00	40.00
	1828	—	2.00	4.00	8.00	40.00
	1829	—	2.00	4.00	8.00	40.00
	1830	—	2.00	4.00	8.00	40.00

Similar to KM#581.

KM#	Date	Mintage	Fine	VF	XF	Unc
593	1834	—	2.00	4.00	8.00	40.00

KREUZER

COPPER

Obv: Crowned arms. Rev: Value within rosettes.

KM#	Date	Mintage	Fine	VF	XF	Unc
582	1825	—	2.00	4.00	8.00	40.00
	1828	—	2.00	4.00	8.00	40.00
	1829	—	2.00	4.00	8.00	40.00

Similar to KM#582.

KM#	Date	Mintage	Fine	VF	XF	Unc
588	1832	—	2.00	4.00	8.00	40.00
	1833	—	2.00	4.00	8.00	40.00
	1835	—	2.00	4.00	8.00	40.00

6 KREUZER

BILLON

Obv: Crowned arms. Rev: Value within rosettes.

KM#	Date	Mintage	Fine	VF	XF	Unc
583	1826	—	5.00	10.00	40.00	90.00
	1827	—	5.00	10.00	40.00	90.00
	1828	—	5.00	10.00	40.00	90.00

Rev: W/o rosettes.

KM#	Date	Mintage	Fine	VF	XF	Unc
586	1831	—	3.00	7.00	30.00	75.00
	1832	—	3.00	7.00	30.00	75.00
	1833	—	3.00	7.00	30.00	75.00
	1834	—	3.00	7.00	30.00	75.00

HESSE-DARMSTADT

A state located in southwest Germany was founded in 1567. The Landgrave was elevated to the status of Grand Duke in 1806. In 1815 the Congress of Vienna awarded Hesse-Darmstadt the cities of Mainz and Worms which were relinquished along with the newly acquired HesseHomburg, to the Prussians in 1866. It became part of the German Empire in 1871 and endured until the abdication of the Grand Duke in 1918.

RULERS

Ludwig X, 1790-1806
As Grand Duke Ludwig I, 1806-1830
Ludwig II, 1830-1848
Ludwig III, 1848-1877
Ludwig IV, 1877-1892
Ernst Ludwig, 1892-1918

MINTMASTERS INITIALS

Letter	Date	Name
HR	1817—	Hector Roessler
RF	1772-1809	Remigius Fehr

HELLER

COPPER

Obv: Crowned pointed arms, G.H.-K.M. Rev: Value.

KM#	Date	Mintage	Fine	VF	XF	Unc
291	1824	—	1.00	2.00	7.00	40.00

KM#	Date	Mintage	Fine	VF	XF	Unc
302	1837	—	1.00	2.00	7.00	35.00
	1840	—	1.00	2.00	7.00	35.00
	1841	—	1.00	2.00	7.00	35.00
	1842	.103	1.00	2.00	7.00	35.00
	1843	.175	1.00	2.00	7.00	35.00
	1844	.241	1.00	2.00	7.00	35.00
	1845	—	1.00	2.00	7.00	35.00
	1846	—	1.00	2.00	7.00	35.00
	1847	—	1.00	2.00	7.00	35.00

Obv: Crowned square arms.

KM#	Date	Mintage	Fine	VF	XF	Unc
322	1847	—	1.00	2.00	5.00	35.00

KM#	Date	Mintage	Fine	VF	XF	Unc
323	1848	—	1.00	2.00	5.00	35.00
	1849	—	1.00	2.00	5.00	35.00
	1850	—	1.00	2.00	5.00	35.00
	1851	—	1.00	2.00	5.00	35.00
	1852	—	1.00	2.00	5.00	35.00
	1853	—	1.00	2.00	5.00	35.00
	1854	—	1.00	2.00	5.00	35.00
	1855	—	1.00	2.00	5.00	35.00

PFENNIG

COPPER

KM#	Date	Mintage	Fine	VF	XF	Unc
251	1801	—	2.00	4.00	8.00	40.00
	1802	—	2.00	4.00	8.00	40.00
	1803	—	2.00	4.00	8.00	40.00
	1804	—	2.00	4.00	8.00	40.00
	1805	—	2.00	4.00	8.00	40.00
	1806 RF	—	2.00	4.00	8.00	40.00

NOTE: Earlier dates (1797-1800) exist for this type.

.333 SILVER

KM#	Date	Mintage	Fine	VF	XF	Unc
280	1811	—	2.00	4.00	8.00	40.00
	1819	—	2.00	4.00	8.00	40.00

Obv: GH-KM.

KM#	Date	Mintage	Fine	VF	XF	Unc
283	1819	—	2.00	5.00	9.00	40.00

KM#	Date	Mintage	Fine	VF	XF	Unc
337	1857	.140	1.00	2.00	3.00	30.00
	1858	.202	1.00	2.00	3.00	30.00
	1859	.257	1.00	2.00	3.00	30.00
	1860	.268	1.00	2.00	3.00	30.00
	1861	.311	1.00	2.00	3.00	30.00
	1862	.324	1.00	2.00	3.00	30.00
	1863	.190	1.00	2.00	3.00	30.00
	1864	—	1.00	2.00	3.00	30.00
	1865	.279	1.00	2.00	3.00	30.00
	1866	.317	1.00	2.00	3.00	30.00
	1867	.296	1.00	2.00	3.00	30.00
	1868	.332	1.00	2.00	3.00	30.00
	1869	.322	1.00	2.00	3.00	30.00
	1870	.526	1.00	2.00	3.00	30.00
	1871	.322	1.00	2.00	3.00	30.00
	1872	.338	1.00	2.00	3.00	30.00

1/4 STUBER

COPPER

KM#	Date	Mintage	Fine	VF	XF	Unc
258	1805 RF	—	3.00	6.00	15.00	50.00

1/2 STUBER

COPPER

Obv: Crowned LLX monogram. Rev: Value.

KM#	Date	Mintage	Fine	VF	XF	Unc
259	1805	—	2.00	4.00	10.00	40.00

1/4 KREUZER

COPPER

KM#	Date	Mintage	Fine	VF	XF	Unc
272	1809	—	1.00	3.00	7.00	40.00
	1816	—	1.00	3.00	7.00	40.00

Obv. leg: G.H.-S.M.

KM#	Date	Mintage	Fine	VF	XF	Unc
273	1809	—	1.00	3.00	7.00	40.00
	1816	—	1.00	3.00	7.00	40.00
	1817	—	1.00	3.00	7.00	40.00

1/2 KREUZER

COPPER

KM#	Date	Mintage	Fine	VF	XF	Unc
274	1809	—	1.00	4.00	8.00	40.00
	1817	—	1.00	4.00	8.00	40.00

Obv. leg: G.H.-S.M.

KM#	Date	Mintage	Fine	VF	XF	Unc
281	1817	—	1.00	4.00	8.00	40.00

KREUZER

.7700 g, .187 SILVER, .0046 oz ASW
Obv: Lion divides H.D. Rev: LAND MUNZE, value.

KM#	Date	Mintage	Fine	VF	XF	Unc
257	1801	—	1.00	3.00	7.00	50.00
	1802	—	1.00	3.00	7.00	50.00
	1803	—	1.00	3.00	7.00	50.00
	1804	—	1.00	3.00	7.00	50.00
	1805	—	1.00	3.00	7.00	50.00

Obv: Crowned lion between H.D.
Rev: Value, LAND MUNZ.

KM#	Date	Mintage	Fine	VF	XF	Unc
260	1806	—	1.00	3.00	7.00	50.00

Obv: Crowned lion w/sword between H.D.

KM#	Date	Mintage	Fine	VF	XF	Unc
261	1806	—	1.00	3.00	8.00	65.00

Obv: Crowned lion between H.D.-L.M. Rev: Value.

KM#	Date	Mintage	Fine	VF	XF	Unc
262	1806	—	1.00	4.00	20.00	110.00
	1807	—	1.00	4.00	20.00	110.00

Obv: Crowned lion w/sword between H.D.-L.M.

KM#	Date	Mintage	Fine	VF	XF	Unc
263	1807	—	1.00	3.00	8.00	65.00

Obv: Crowned lion w/sword between G.H.-L.M.
Rev: Value, LAND MUNZ.

KM#	Date	Mintage	Fine	VF	XF	Unc
264	1807	—	1.00	3.00	8.00	65.00
	1808	—	1.00	3.00	8.00	65.00
	1809	—	1.00	3.00	8.00	65.00

Obv: Crowned arms between G.H.-L.M.

KM#	Date	Mintage	Fine	VF	XF	Unc
275	1809	—	1.00	4.00	8.00	60.00
	1810	—	1.00	4.00	8.00	60.00
	1817	—	1.00	4.00	8.00	60.00

Obv: Crowned arms between G.H.-S.M.

KM#	Date	Mintage	Fine	VF	XF	Unc
284	1819	—	1.00	4.00	8.00	60.00

KM#	Date	Mintage	Fine	VF	XF	Unc
299	1834	—	1.00	3.00	6.00	40.00
	1835	—	1.00	3.00	6.00	40.00
	1836	—	1.00	3.00	6.00	40.00
	1837	—	1.00	3.00	6.00	40.00
	1838	—	1.00	3.00	6.00	40.00

.8300 g, .166 SILVER, .0044 oz ASW

KM#	Date	Mintage	Fine	VF	XF	Unc
303	1837	—	1.00	3.00	6.00	40.00
	1838	—	1.00	3.00	6.00	40.00
	1839	—	1.00	3.00	6.00	40.00
	1840	—	1.00	3.00	6.00	40.00
	1841	—	1.00	3.00	6.00	40.00
	1842	.438	1.00	3.00	6.00	40.00

KM#	Date	Mintage	Fine	VF	XF	Unc
316	1843	.129	1.00	3.00	6.00	40.00
	1844	—	1.00	3.00	6.00	40.00
	1845	.516	1.00	3.00	6.00	40.00
	1847	—	1.00	3.00	6.00	40.00

KM#	Date	Mintage	Fine	VF	XF	Unc
324	1848	.546	1.00	3.00	6.00	40.00
	1849	—	1.00	3.00	6.00	40.00
	1850	—	1.00	3.00	6.00	40.00
	1852	—	1.00	3.00	6.00	40.00
	1854	.236	1.00	3.00	6.00	40.00
	1855	.162	1.00	3.00	6.00	40.00
	1856	.334	1.00	3.00	6.00	40.00

KM#	Date	Mintage	Fine	VF	XF	Unc
339	1858	.271	1.00	3.00	6.00	25.00
	1859	.147	1.00	3.00	6.00	25.00
	1860	.268	1.00	3.00	6.00	25.00
	1861	.207	1.00	3.00	6.00	25.00
	1862	.211	1.00	3.00	6.00	25.00
	1863	.190	1.00	3.00	6.00	25.00
	1864	.376	1.00	3.00	6.00	25.00
	1865	.181	1.00	3.00	6.00	25.00
	1866	.247	1.00	3.00	6.00	25.00
	1867	.273	1.00	3.00	6.00	25.00
	1868	.199	1.00	3.00	6.00	25.00
	1869	.249	1.00	3.00	6.00	25.00
	1870	.349	1.00	3.00	6.00	25.00
	1871	.366	1.00	3.00	6.00	25.00
	1872	.128	1.00	3.00	6.00	25.00

3 KREUZER

1.3900 g, .281 SILVER, .0125 oz ASW
Obv: Lion on pedestal divides H.D.
Rev: LAND MUNZE, value.

KM#	Date	Mintage	Fine	VF	XF	Unc
256	1801	—	3.00	7.00	25.00	100.00
	1802	—	3.00	7.00	25.00	100.00
	1803	—	3.00	7.00	25.00	100.00
	1804	—	3.00	7.00	25.00	100.00
	1805	—	3.00	7.00	25.00	100.00

NOTE: Earlier date (1800) exists for this type.

Obv: Crowned arms G.H.-L.M.
Rev. value: III KREUZER.

KM#	Date	Mintage	Fine	VF	XF	Unc
269	1808	—	3.00	7.00	25.00	100.00
	1809	—	3.00	7.00	25.00	100.00
	1810	—	3.00	7.00	25.00	100.00

Rev. value: 3 KREUZER

KM#	Date	Mintage	Fine	VF	XF	Unc
282	1817	—	3.00	7.00	25.00	100.00
285	1819	—	3.00	7.00	15.00	75.00
	1822	—	3.00	7.00	15.00	75.00

Obv: Crowned arms, GR HERZOGTH.
Rev: Value, SCHEIDEMUNZE.

KM#	Date	Mintage	Fine	VF	XF	Unc
295	1833	—	5.00	10.00	20.00	80.00

KM#	Date	Mintage	Fine	VF	XF	Unc
296	1833	—	2.00	6.00	12.00	70.00
	1834	—	2.00	6.00	12.00	70.00
	1835	—	2.00	6.00	12.00	70.00
	1836	—	2.00	6.00	12.00	70.00

KM#	Date	Mintage	Fine	VF	XF	Unc
305	1838	—	2.00	4.00	8.00	55.00
	1839	—	2.00	4.00	8.00	55.00
	1840	—	2.00	4.00	8.00	55.00
	1841	—	2.00	4.00	8.00	55.00
	1842	.280	2.00	4.00	8.00	55.00

Obv. leg: GROSHERZOGTHUM HESSEN.

KM#	Date	Mintage	Fine	VF	XF	Unc
317	1843	.288	1.00	3.00	6.00	45.00
	1844	—	1.00	3.00	6.00	45.00
	1845	.245	1.00	3.00	6.00	45.00
	1846	—	1.00	3.00	6.00	45.00
	1847	—	1.00	3.00	6.00	45.00

KM#	Date	Mintage	Fine	VF	XF	Unc
325	1848	.082	1.00	3.00	6.00	40.00
	1850	—	1.00	3.00	6.00	40.00
	1851	—	1.00	3.00	6.00	40.00
	1852	—	1.00	3.00	6.00	40.00
	1853	—	1.00	3.00	6.00	40.00
	1854	.076	1.00	3.00	6.00	40.00
	1855	.148	1.00	3.00	6.00	40.00
	1856	.062	1.00	3.00	6.00	40.00

1.2300 g, .250 SILVER, .0138 oz ASW

KM#	Date	Mintage	Fine	VF	XF	Unc
345	1864	.095	1.00	3.00	6.00	40.00
	1865	.087	1.00	3.00	6.00	40.00
	1866	.090	1.00	3.00	6.00	40.00
	1867	.077	1.00	3.00	6.00	40.00

5 KREUZER

(Convention)

2.2300 g, .437 SILVER, .0313 oz ASW
Obv: Crowned L. Rev: Value.

KM#	Date	Mintage	Fine	VF	XF	Unc
265	1807	—	10.00	25.00	50.00	250.00

Obv: Curled edges on L

KM#	Date	Mintage	Fine	VF	XF	Unc
266	1807	—	10.00	30.00	60.00	300.00

Obv: L at truncation. Rev: R.IUSTIRT F. below arms.

KM#	Date	Mintage	Fine	VF	XF	Unc
270	1808	—	10.00	25.00	50.00	250.00

6 KREUZER

2.4300 g, .343 SILVER, .0267 oz ASW

KM#	Date	Mintage	Fine	VF	XF	Unc
286	1819	—	5.00	10.00	25.00	100.00
	1820	—	5.00	10.00	25.00	100.00

KM#	Date	Mintage	Fine	VF	XF	Unc
290	1821	—	3.00	6.00	15.00	60.00
	1824	—	3.00	6.00	15.00	60.00
	1826	—	3.00	6.00	15.00	60.00
	1827	—	3.00	6.00	15.00	60.00
	1828	—	3.00	6.00	15.00	60.00
	1833	—	3.00	6.00	15.00	60.00

KM#	Date	Mintage	Fine	VF	XF	Unc
297	1833	—	3.00	6.00	15.00	60.00
	1834	—	3.00	6.00	15.00	60.00
	1835	—	3.00	6.00	15.00	60.00
	1836	—	3.00	6.00	15.00	60.00
	1837	—	3.00	6.00	15.00	60.00

2.4600 g, .350 SILVER, .0276 oz ASW

KM#	Date	Mintage	Fine	VF	XF	Unc
306	1838	—	2.50	5.00	12.50	50.00
	1839	—	2.50	5.00	12.50	50.00
	1840	—	2.50	5.00	12.50	50.00
	1841	—	2.50	5.00	12.50	50.00
	1842	.816	2.50	5.00	12.50	50.00

KM#	Date	Mintage	Fine	VF	XF	Unc
318	1843	.775	2.50	5.00	15.00	60.00
	1844	.331	2.50	5.00	15.00	60.00
	1845	.235	2.50	5.00	15.00	60.00
	1846	.897	2.50	5.00	15.00	60.00
	1847	—	2.50	5.00	15.00	60.00
326	1848	.243	2.00	5.00	15.00	60.00
	1850	—	2.00	5.00	15.00	60.00
	1851	—	2.00	5.00	15.00	60.00
	1852	—	2.00	5.00	15.00	60.00
	1853	—	2.00	5.00	15.00	60.00
	1854	.033	2.00	5.00	15.00	60.00
	1855	.072	2.00	5.00	15.00	60.00
	1856	.044	2.00	5.00	15.00	60.00

KM#	Date	Mintage	Fine	VF	XF	Unc
346	1864	.052	2.00	5.00	15.00	65.00
	1865	.039	2.00	5.00	15.00	65.00
	1866	.043	2.00	5.00	15.00	65.00
	1867	.060	2.00	5.00	15.00	65.00

10 KREUZER

(Convention)

3.9000 g, .500 SILVER, .0626 oz ASW

KM#	Date	Mintage	Fine	VF	XF	Unc
271	1808 RF	—	15.00	35.00	200.00	350.00

20 KREUZER

(Convention)

6.6800 g, .583 SILVER, .1252 oz ASW
Obv: Head right, FRISCH F. at truncation.
Rev: Crowned arms dividing date, R.F. below.

KM#	Date	Mintage	Fine	VF	XF	Unc
267	1807 RF	—	20.00	50.00	225.00	575.00

Obv. leg: LUDEWIG. . . . .

KM#	Date	Mintage	Fine	VF	XF	Unc
268	1807 RF	—	20.00	50.00	200.00	500.00
	1808 RF	—	20.00	50.00	200.00	500.00
	1809 RF	—	20.00	50.00	200.00	500.00

Obv. leg: LUDWIG. . . . .

KM#	Date	Mintage	Fine	VF	XF	Unc
276	1809 RF	—	20.00	50.00	200.00	500.00

1/2 GULDEN

5.3000 g, .900 SILVER, .1533 oz ASW
Obv: VOIGHT below head.

KM#	Date	Mintage	Fine	VF	XF	Unc
307	1838	1.080	15.00	30.00	65.00	200.00
	1839	Inc. Ab.	15.00	30.00	65.00	200.00
	1840	Inc. Ab.	15.00	30.00	65.00	200.00
	1841	Inc. Ab.	15.00	30.00	65.00	200.00
	1843	.151	15.00	30.00	65.00	200.00
	1844	.081	20.00	40.00	75.00	250.00
	1845	.167	15.00	30.00	65.00	200.00
	1846	.033	20.00	40.00	85.00	300.00

Obv: VOIGHT below head.

KM#	Date	Mintage	Fine	VF	XF	Unc
336	1855	.047	30.00	60.00	150.00	400.00

GULDEN

(2/3 Thaler)

10.6000 g, .900 SILVER, .3067 oz ASW
Obv: Small head left. Rev: Value within wreath.

KM#	Date	Mintage	Fine	VF	XF	Unc
304	1837	1.122	25.00	40.00	85.00	225.00

KM#	Date	Mintage	Fine	VF	XF	Unc
308	1838	Inc. Ab.	30.00	50.00	100.00	275.00

Obv: VOIGT below head.

KM#	Date	Mintage	Fine	VF	XF	Unc
309	1839	Inc. Ab.	20.00	40.00	75.00	200.00
	1840	Inc. Ab.	20.00	40.00	75.00	200.00
	1841	Inc. Ab.	20.00	40.00	75.00	200.00
	1842	.605	20.00	40.00	75.00	200.00
	1843	.314	20.00	40.00	75.00	200.00
	1844	.191	20.00	40.00	75.00	200.00
	1845	.176	20.00	40.00	75.00	200.00
	1846	.144	20.00	40.00	75.00	200.00
	1847	.251	20.00	40.00	75.00	200.00

Visit of Crown Prince of Russia
Obv: VOIGHT below head.

KM#	Date	Mintage	Fine	VF	XF	Unc
319	1843	—	125.00	250.00	400.00	850.00

Public Freedom Through German Parliament

KM#	Date	Mintage	Fine	VF	XF	Unc
327	1848	—	125.00	175.00	275.00	600.00

10.5800 g, .900 SILVER, .3061 oz ASW
Obv: VOIGHT below head.

KM#	Date	Mintage	Fine	VF	XF	Unc
328	1848	.090	40.00	75.00	200.00	400.00
	1854	.044	40.00	75.00	200.00	400.00
	1855	.090	40.00	75.00	200.00	400.00
	1856	.153	20.00	40.00	125.00	300.00

ZWEY (2) GULDEN

21.2100 g, .900 SILVER, .6138 oz ASW
Obv: VOIGHT below head.

KM#	Date	Mintage	Fine	VF	XF	Unc
321	1845	.044	50.00	100.00	225.00	550.00
	1846	.270	45.00	100.00	210.00	500.00
	1847	.030	55.00	115.00	275.00	700.00

Obv: VOIGHT below head.

KM#	Date	Mintage	Fine	VF	XF	Unc
329	1848	.252	70.00	150.00	350.00	900.00
	1849	Inc. Ab.	70.00	150.00	350.00	900.00
	1853	Inc. Ab.	50.00	100.00	270.00	650.00
	1854	.127	40.00	80.00	215.00	500.00
	1855	.149	40.00	80.00	215.00	500.00
	1856	.064	40.00	80.00	215.00	500.00

EIN (1) THALER

28.0600 g, .833 SILVER, .7516 oz ASW

KM#	Date	Mintage	Fine	VF	XF	Unc
277	1809 L	—	200.00	350.00	700.00	1600.

(Krone)

29.5100 g, .871 SILVER, .8264 oz ASW

KM#	Date	Mintage	Fine	VF	XF	Unc
287	1819 HR	.019	275.00	400.00	850.00	1800.

KM#	Date	Mintage	Fine	VF	XF	Unc
292	1825 HR	.171	100.00	165.00	350.00	950.00

Obv: VOIGHT below head.

KM#	Date	Mintage	Fine	VF	XF	Unc
298	1833 HR	.124	75.00	150.00	300.00	800.00
	1835 HR	.558	100.00	175.00	375.00	1100.
	1836 HR	I.A.	75.00	150.00	300.00	800.00
	1837 HR	I.A.	100.00	175.00	375.00	1100.

(Vereins)

18.5200 g, .900 SILVER, .5360 oz ASW

KM#	Date	Mintage	Fine	VF	XF	Unc
338	1857	.091	25.00	60.00	150.00	350.00
	1858	.537	25.00	60.00	150.00	300.00
	1859	.594	25.00	60.00	150.00	300.00
	1860	.608	25.00	60.00	150.00	300.00
	1861	.414	25.00	60.00	150.00	300.00
	1862	.242	25.00	60.00	150.00	300.00
	1863	.215	25.00	60.00	150.00	300.00
	1864	.073	25.00	65.00	175.00	350.00
	1865	.078	25.00	65.00	175.00	350.00
	1866	.059	25.00	65.00	175.00	350.00
	1867	.024	25.00	65.00	175.00	350.00
	1868	.048	25.00	65.00	185.00	425.00
	1869	.034	25.00	65.00	185.00	425.00
	1870	.039	25.00	65.00	175.00	350.00
	1871	.033	35.00	70.00	175.00	350.00

2 THALER

(3-1/2 Gulden)

37.1200 g, .900 SILVER, 1.0742 oz ASW

KM#	Date	Mintage	Fine	VF	XF	Unc
310	1839	.024	100.00	175.00	350.00	800.00
	1840	.368	85.00	140.00	275.00	600.00
	1841	.688	75.00	125.00	200.00	525.00
	1842	.286	90.00	150.00	315.00	700.00

Obv: Similar to KM#310.

KM#	Date	Mintage	Fine	VF	XF	Unc
320	1844	.377	90.00	150.00	300.00	700.00

Rev: Similar to KM#320.

KM#	Date	Mintage	Fine	VF	XF	Unc
335	1854	.043	300.00	500.00	1000.	2200.

5 GULDEN

3.4250 g, .904 GOLD, .0995 oz AGW
Obv: Head left, C.V. below.
Rev: Crowned draped arms, value 5G, leg: AUS HESS. RHEINGOLD.

KM#	Date	Mintage	Fine	VF	XF	Unc
300	1835 CV-HR	60 pcs.	2000.	4000.	7500.	12,500.

KM#	Date	Mintage	Fine	VF	XF	Unc
301	1835 CV-HR	.022	700.00	1500.	2000.	3250.
	1840 CV-HR	I.A.	300.00	500.00	800.00	1550.
	1841 CV-HR	I.A.	300.00	500.00	850.00	1650.
	1842 CV-HR	I.A.	300.00	500.00	800.00	1650.

10 GULDEN

6.8500 g, .904 GOLD, .1991 oz AGW

KM#	Date	Mintage	Fine	VF	XF	Unc
293	1826 HR	1,700	600.00	1500.	2500.	4000.
	1827 HR	1,705	600.00	1500.	2500.	3500.

KM#	Date	Mintage	Fine	VF	XF	Unc
315	1840 CV-HR	.017	300.00	750.00	1250.	2000.
	1841 CV-HR	I.A.	300.00	750.00	1250.	2000.
	1842 CV-HR	I.A.	300.00	750.00	1250.	2000.

MONETARY REFORM

2 MARK

11.1110 g, .900 SILVER, .3215 oz ASW

KM#	Date	Mintage	Fine	VF	XF	Unc
355	1876H	.202	125.00	300.00	2100.	4200.
	1877H	.338	125.00	325.00	2250.	4500.

KM#	Date	Mintage	Fine	VF	XF	Unc
359	1888A	.022	450.00	1250.	2000.	3500.
	1888A	500 pcs.	—	—	Proof	5200.

Rev: Type III.

KM#	Date	Mintage	Fine	VF	XF	Unc
363	1891A	.063	275.00	625.00	1000.	2250.
	1891A	—	—	—	Proof	2750.

KM#	Date	Mintage	Fine	VF	XF	Unc
368	1895A	.054	150.00	300.00	600.00	1000.
	1896A	8,950	300.00	600.00	900.00	1400.
	1896A	200 pcs.	—	—	Proof	2000.
	1898A	.034	175.00	325.00	650.00	1100.
	1898A	360 pcs.	—	—	Proof	1500.
	1899A	.054	175.00	325.00	650.00	1100.
	1899A	128 pcs.	—	—	Proof	1600.
	1900A	8,950	350.00	625.00	950.00	1500.
	1900A	200 pcs.	—	—	Proof	2100.

400th Birthday of Philipp The Magnanimous

KM#	Date	Mintage	Fine	VF	XF	Unc
372	1904	.100	20.00	40.00	65.00	85.00
	1904	2,250	—	—	*Proof	135.00

***NOTE:** Obverse Matte, reverse polished.

3 MARK

16.6670 g, .900 SILVER, .4823 oz ASW

KM#	Date	Mintage	Fine	VF	XF	Unc
375	1910A	.200	30.00	60.00	95.00	140.00
	1910A	—	—	—	Proof	250.00

25 Year Jubilee

KM#	Date	Mintage	Fine	VF	XF	Unc
376	1917A	1,333	—	1750.	2500.	3000.
	1917A	Inc. Ab.	—	—	Proof	3500.

5 MARK

27.7770 g, .900 SILVER, .8038 oz ASW
Rev: Type II.

KM#	Date	Mintage	Fine	VF	XF	Unc
353	1875H	.148	45.00	125.00	1700.	4200.
	1876H	.290	45.00	125.00	1500.	3500.

1.9910 g, .900 GOLD, .0576 oz AGW

KM#	Date	Mintage	Fine	VF	XF	Unc
356	1877H	.103	175.00	400.00	700.00	1200.
	1877H	—	—	—	Proof	Rare

Rev: Type II.

KM#	Date	Mintage	Fine	VF	XF	Unc
357	1877H	.079	300.00	600.00	800.00	1200.
	1877H	—	—	—	Proof	2000.

27.7770 g, .900 SILVER, .8038 oz ASW
Rev: Type II.

KM#	Date	Mintage	Fine	VF	XF	Unc
360	1888A	8,940	425.00	1200.	2250.	4000.
	1888A	400 pcs.	—	—	Proof	4000.

Rev: Type III.

KM#	Date	Mintage	Fine	VF	XF	Unc
364	1891A	.025	225.00	400.00	1500.	3000.
	1891A	—	—	—	Proof	4000.

KM#	Date	Mintage	Fine	VF	XF	Unc
369	1895A	.039	90.00	200.00	750.00	1750.
	1895A	200 pcs.	—	—	Proof	2000.
	1898A	.037	90.00	200.00	750.00	1750.
	1898A	240 pcs.	—	—	Proof	2000.
	1899A	.018	110.00	225.00	800.00	2000.
	1899A	176 pcs.	—	—	Proof	2200.
	1900A	.018	200.00	350.00	1000.	2500.
	1900A	150 pcs.	—	—	Proof	2500.

400th Birthday of Philipp The Magnanimous

KM#	Date	Mintage	Fine	VF	XF	Unc
373	1904	.040	40.00	90.00	135.00	240.00
	1904	700 pcs.	—	—	*Proof	350.00

***NOTE:** Obverse Matte, reverse polished.

10 MARK

3.9820 g, .900 GOLD, .1152 oz AGW

KM#	Date	Mintage	Fine	VF	XF	Unc
350	1872H	.030	120.00	175.00	425.00	700.00
	1872H	—	—	—	Proof	Rare
	1873H	.432	110.00	150.00	325.00	600.00
	1873H	—	—	—	Proof	Rare

Rev: Type II.

KM#	Date	Mintage	Fine	VF	XF	Unc
354	1875H	.191	100.00	170.00	250.00	400.00
	1876H	.513	120.00	150.00	225.00	350.00
	1877H	.094	140.00	180.00	300.00	500.00

KM#	Date	Mintage	Fine	VF	XF	Unc
358	1878H	.132	140.00	275.00	425.00	750.00
	1878H	—	—	—	Proof	2000.
	1879H	.056	200.00	300.00	600.00	1000.
	1879H	—	—	—	Proof	2000.
	1880H	.109	220.00	325.00	625.00	1100.
	1880H	—	—	—	Proof	2000.
361	1888A	.036	220.00	325.00	625.00	1000.
	1888A	500 pcs.	—	—	Proof	2750.

Edge: Vines and stars.

KM#	Date	Mintage	Fine	VF	XF	Unc
362	1890A	.054	275.00	400.00	750.00	1100.

Rev: Type III.

KM#	Date	Mintage	Fine	VF	XF	Unc
366	1893A	.054	275.00	400.00	750.00	1100.
	1893A	450 pcs.	—	—	Proof	2700.

KM#	Date	Mintage	Fine	VF	XF	Unc
370	1896A	.036	200.00	450.00	800.00	1200.
	1896A	230 pcs.	—	—	Proof	2250.
	1898A	.075	175.00	325.00	600.00	1000.
	1898A	500 pcs.	—	—	Proof	2250.

20 MARK

7.9650 g, .900 GOLD, .2304 oz AGW
Rev: Type I.

KM#	Date	Mintage	Fine	VF	XF	Unc
351	1872H	.183	125.00	225.00	400.00	650.00
	1872H	—	—	—	Proof	Rare
	1873H	.521	120.00	175.00	350.00	600.00

Rev: Type II.

KM#	Date	Mintage	Fine	VF	XF	Unc
352	1874H	.134	175.00	300.00	700.00	1000.

KM#	Date	Mintage	Fine	VF	XF	Unc
365	1892A	.025	500.00	750.00	1100.	1800.
	1892A	—	—	—	Proof	4500.

Rev: Type III.

KM#	Date	Mintage	Fine	VF	XF	Unc
367	1893A	.025	500.00	750.00	1000.	1400.
	1893A	—	—	—	Proof	2500.

KM#	Date	Mintage	Fine	VF	XF	Unc
371	1896A	.015	300.00	500.00	900.00	1500.
	1896A	230 pcs.	—	—	Proof	1500.
	1897A	.045	125.00	175.00	350.00	650.00
	1897A	400 pcs.	—	—	Proof	1300.
	1898A	.070	125.00	175.00	350.00	550.00
	1898A	500 pcs.	—	—	Proof	1300.
	1899A	.040	125.00	175.00	400.00	750.00
	1899A	600 pcs.	—	—	Proof	1300.
	1900A	.040	125.00	175.00	350.00	600.00
	1900A	500 pcs.	—	—	Proof	1300.
	1901A	.080	125.00	175.00	325.00	500.00
	1901A	600 pcs.	—	—	Proof	1300.
	1903A	.040	125.00	175.00	350.00	750.00
	1903A	100 pcs.	—	—	Proof	1500.

KM#	Date	Mintage	Fine	VF	XF	Unc
374	1905A	.045	125.00	200.00	300.00	500.00
	1905A	200 pcs.	—	—	Proof	1500.
	1906A	.085	125.00	175.00	275.00	425.00
	1906A	199 pcs.	—	—	Proof	1500.
	1908A	.040	125.00	175.00	275.00	450.00
	1911A	.150	125.00	175.00	300.00	450.00

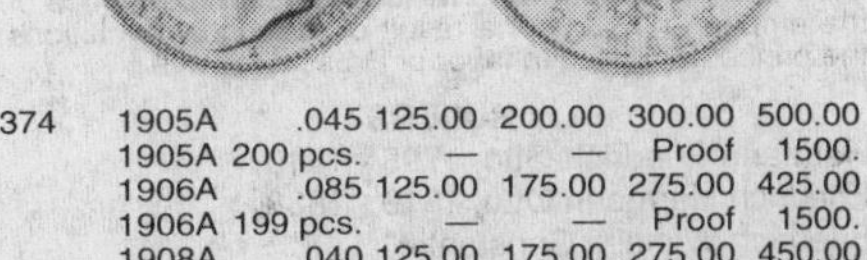

HESSE-HOMBURG

Hesse-Homburg, located in southwest Germany was created from part of Hesse-Darmstadt in 1596 and was mediatized to Darmstadt 1801-1815. In 1815 it was restored to independence and added the Lordships of Meisenheim and Kreuznach. The Homburg line became extinct in 1866, passed to Darmstadt and was almost immediately annexed to Prussia.

RULERS

Friedrich V Ludwig, 1751-1820
Friedrich VI Josef, 1820-1829
Ludwig Wilhelm, 1829-1839
Philipp August, 1839-1846
Gustav Adolph, 1846-1848
Ferdinand Heinrich, 1848-1866

MINTMASTERS INITIALS

Letter	Date	Name
RS	1817-1845	Rudolph Stadelmann, die-cutter in Darmstadt and Homburg
C.SCHNITZSPAHN	d.1877	Christian Schnitzspahn, chief die-cutter and medalleur in Darmstadt
C.VOIGT, VOIGT	1829-?	Carl F. Voigt, chief die-cutter and medalleur in Munich

KREUZER

.8300 g, .166 SILVER, .0044 oz ASW

KM#	Date	Mintage	Fine	VF	XF	Unc
13	1840	.048	30.00	60.00	100.00	250.00

3 KREUZER

1.3800 g, .281 SILVER, .0124 oz ASW

KM#	Date	Mintage	Fine	VF	XF	Unc
14	1840	.015	35.00	75.00	150.00	300.00

SILVER
Obv: Hessian lion in shield, leg: LANDGRAFTHUM HESSEN. Rev: 3/KREUZER/date in oak wreath.

KM#	Date	Mintage	Fine	VF	XF	Unc
19	1856	—	—	—	—	—

6 KREUZER

2.4300 g, .343 SILVER, .0267 oz ASW

KM#	Date	Mintage	Fine	VF	XF	Unc
15	1840	.057	30.00	75.00	150.00	350.00

1/2 GULDEN

5.3000 g, .900 SILVER, .1533 oz ASW

KM#	Date	Mintage	Fine	VF	XF	Unc
11	1838 VOIGT	.011	75.00	150.00	225.00	375.00
	1839	—	—	—	Proof	475.00

Obv: RS at truncation.

KM#	Date	Mintage	Fine	VF	XF	Unc
16	1840 RS	.010	60.00	120.00	200.00	400.00
	1841 RS	6,560	60.00	120.00	200.00	400.00
	1843 RS	6,900	60.00	120.00	200.00	400.00
	1844 RS	.018	60.00	120.00	200.00	400.00
	1845	Inc. Ab.	60.00	120.00	200.00	400.00
	1846 RS	4,300	60.00	120.00	200.00	400.00

GULDEN

10.6000 g, .900 SILVER, .3067 oz ASW

KM#	Date	Mintage	Fine	VF	XF	Unc
12	1838 VOIGT	.011	60.00	140.00	300.00	725.00
	1839	—	—	—	Proof	875.00

KM#	Date	Mintage	Fine	VF	XF	Unc
17	1841 RS	.014	60.00	140.00	300.00	700.00
	1843 RS	6,800	60.00	140.00	300.00	700.00
	1844 RS	.014	60.00	140.00	300.00	700.00
	1845 RS	8,100	60.00	140.00	300.00	700.00
	1846 RS	8,100	60.00	140.00	300.00	700.00

ZWEY (2) GULDEN

21.2100 g, .900 SILVER, .6317 oz ASW

KM#	Date	Mintage	Fine	VF	XF	Unc
18	1846 C.VOIGT					
		.011	300.00	600.00	1200.	3000.

EIN (1) THALER

(Vereins)

18.5200 g, .900 SILVER, .5358 oz ASW

KM#	Date	Mintage	Fine	VF	XF	Unc
20	1858	5,000	50.00	100.00	200.00	500.00
	1859	6,579	50.00	100.00	200.00	500.00
	1860	6,593	50.00	100.00	200.00	500.00
	1861	6,588	50.00	100.00	200.00	500.00
	1862	6,592	50.00	100.00	200.00	500.00
	1863	6,575	50.00	100.00	200.00	500.00

HOHENLOHE

This south German family traces its ancestry to the 900's. In 1209 the house divided but one of the lines became extinct in 1390. Thereafter there were numerous divisions with the last major one being in 1600.

MINTMASTERS INITIALS

Letter	Date	Name
D	1800-1806	Anton Paul Dallinger, die-cutter
ICE	1803	Johann Christoph Eberhardt, in Wertheim

HOHENLOHE-KIRCHBERG

This principality was located in southern Germany. The Kirchberg line was founded in 1701. The count was raised to the rank of prince of the empire in 1764 and the last prince died in 1819.

RULERS

Christian Friedrich Karl, 1767-1806

1/2 THALER

(Convention)

SILVER

KM#	Date	Mintage	Fine	VF	XF	Unc
15	1804 D	—	250.00	450.00	750.00	1250.

HOHENLOHE-NEUENSTEIN-OEHRINGEN

This principality was located in southern Germany. The Neuenstein-Oehringen line was founded in 1610 and the first prince of the empire from this line was proclaimed in 1764. The line became extinct in 1805 and the lands passed to Ingelfingen.

RULERS

Ludwig Friedrich Karl, 1765-1805

10 KREUZER

(Convention)

SILVER

KM#	Date	Mintage	VG	Fine	VF	XF
70	1803 IC-E	—	20.00	40.00	90.00	200.00

TRADE COINAGE

DUCAT

3.5000 g, .986 GOLD, .1109 oz AGW
81st Birthday - L.F. Karl

KM#	Date	Mintage	Fine	VF	XF	Unc
71	1804 D	—	750.00	1750.	3000.	5000.

2 DUCAT

7.0000 g, .986 GOLD, .2219 oz AGW
81st Birthday - L.F. Karl
Obv: Bust right. Rev: Crowned arms.

KM#	Date	Mintage	Fine	VF	XF	Unc
72	1804 D	—	1000.	2000.	3500.	6000.

HOHENZOLLERN-HECHINGEN

Located in southern Germany, the Hechingen line was founded in 1576. The family received the mint right in 1471 and the counts were raised to the rank of prince of the empire in 1623. As a result of the 1848 revolutions the prince abdicated in favor of Prussia in 1849.

RULERS

Hermann Friedrich Otto, 1798 - 1810
Friedrich Hermann Otto, 1810 - 1838
Friedrich Wilhelm Constantin, 1838-1849

MINTMASTERS INITIALS

Letter	Date	Name
CH, ICH	1783-1808	Johann Christian Heuglin
C.VOIGT	1829-1873	Carl Friedrich Voigt, medalist in Munich
ILW, W	1798-1845	Johann Ludwig Wagner, die-cutter

ARMS

Hohenzollern - quartered silver and black
Office of hereditary chamberlain to the emperor - crossed scepters.

3 KREUZER

1.2900 g, .333 SILVER, .0138 oz ASW
Obv: Crowned arms. Rev: Value within wreath.

KM#	Date	Mintage	Fine	VF	XF	Unc
47	1845	.030	10.00	25.00	50.00	160.00
	1846	.030	10.00	25.00	50.00	160.00
	1847	8,000	15.00	30.00	60.00	200.00

6 KREUZER

2.5900 g, .333 SILVER, .0277 oz ASW
Obv: Crowned arms. Rev: Value within wreath.

KM#	Date	Mintage	Fine	VF	XF	Unc
45	1841	.024	15.00	35.00	60.00	175.00
	1842	.026	15.00	35.00	60.00	175.00
	1845	.025	15.00	35.00	60.00	175.00
	1846	.025	15.00	35.00	60.00	175.00
	1847	.026	15.00	35.00	60.00	175.00

1/2 GULDEN

5.3000 g, .900 SILVER, .1533 oz ASW

KM#	Date	Mintage	Fine	VF	XF	Unc
40	1839	.015	35.00	75.00	150.00	300.00
	1841	6,000	35.00	75.00	150.00	325.00
	1842	5,540	35.00	75.00	150.00	325.00
	1843	6,000	35.00	75.00	150.00	325.00
	1844	6,000	35.00	75.00	150.00	325.00
	1845	6,000	35.00	75.00	150.00	325.00
	1846	6,000	35.00	75.00	150.00	325.00
	1847	6,000	35.00	75.00	150.00	325.00

GULDEN

10.6000 g, .900 SILVER, .3067 oz ASW

KM#	Date	Mintage	Fine	VF	XF	Unc
41	1839	.015	50.00	125.00	200.00	450.00
	1841	6,000	50.00	125.00	200.00	500.00
	1842	6,000	50.00	125.00	200.00	500.00
	1843	8,280	50.00	125.00	200.00	500.00
	1844	6,000	50.00	125.00	200.00	500.00
	1845	5,465	50.00	125.00	200.00	500.00
	1846	5,718	50.00	125.00	200.00	500.00
	1847	6,324	50.00	125.00	200.00	500.00

ZWEY (2) GULDEN

21.2100 g, .900 SILVER, .6138 oz ASW

KM#	Date	Mintage	Fine	VF	XF	Unc
48	1846	4,300	175.00	450.00	1000.	1500.
	1847	4,300	175.00	450.00	800.00	1400.

EIN (1) THALER

28.0600 g, .833 SILVER, .7516 oz ASW

KM#	Date	Mintage	Fine	VF	XF	Unc
35	1804 W-CH					
		2,000	400.00	800.00	1400.	3000.

Obv: ILH below shoulder.

KM#	Date	Mintage	Fine	VF	XF	Unc
36	1804 ILH-CH	—	400.00	800.00	1400.	3000.

2 THALER

(3-1/2 Gulden)

37.1200 g, .900 SILVER, 1.0742 oz ASW

KM#	Date	Mintage	Fine	VF	XF	Unc
46	1844	2,346	400.00	800.00	1600.	2800.
	1845	1,000	425.00	925.00	1800.	3200.
	1846	570 pcs.	500.00	1000.	2000.	3600.

HOHENZOLLERN-SIGMARINGEN

Located in southern Germany, the Sigmaringen line was founded in 1576. The counts obtained the mint right in 1471 amd were raised to the rank of Prince of the Empire in 1623. As a result of the 1848 revolutions the princes abdicated in favor of Prussia in 1849.

RULERS

Anton Aloys, 1785-1831
Carl, 1831-1848
Carl Anton, 1848-1849

MINTMASTERS INITIALS

Letter	Date	Name
D	1828-1848	Carl Wilhelm Doell, in Karlsruhe
BALBACH	1848-1856	Othemar Balbach, medalist in Karlsruhe

ARMS

Hohenzollern - quartered black and silver
Sigmaringen - stag left

EIN (1) KREUZER

COPPER
Obv: Crowned arms. Rev. value: EIN KREUZER.

KM#	Date	Mintage	Fine	VF	XF	Unc
21	1842	.180	3.00	7.00	20.00	80.00
	1846	.055	3.00	7.00	20.00	100.00

.6200 g, .250 SILVER, .0049 oz ASW
Rev. value: 1 KREUZER.

KM#	Date	Mintage	Fine	VF	XF	Unc
22	1842	.120	3.00	7.00	20.00	100.00
	1846	.060	3.00	7.00	20.00	100.00

3 KREUZER

1.2900 g, .333 SILVER, .0138 oz ASW

KM#	Date	Mintage	Fine	VF	XF	Unc
17	1839	.052	5.00	10.00	25.00	125.00
	1841	.068	5.00	10.00	25.00	125.00
	1842	.072	5.00	10.00	25.00	125.00
	1844	.170	5.00	10.00	25.00	125.00
	1845	.126	5.00	10.00	25.00	125.00
	1846	.126	5.00	10.00	25.00	125.00
	1847	.060	5.00	10.00	25.00	125.00

6 KREUZER

2.5900 g, .333 SILVER, .0277 oz ASW
Obv: Crowned arms. Rev: Value within wreath.

KM#	Date	Mintage	Fine	VF	XF	Unc
18	1839	.075	7.00	15.00	40.00	135.00
	1840	.075	7.00	15.00	40.00	135.00
	1841	.075	7.00	15.00	40.00	135.00
	1842	.074	7.00	15.00	40.00	135.00
	1844	.140	7.00	15.00	40.00	135.00
	1845	.208	7.00	15.00	40.00	135.00
	1846	.208	7.00	15.00	40.00	135.00
	1847	—	7.00	15.00	40.00	135.00

1/2 GULDEN

5.3000 g, .900 SILVER, .1533 oz ASW

KM#	Date	Mintage	Fine	VF	XF	Unc
15	1838	.012	50.00	75.00	135.00	225.00
	1839	.012	50.00	75.00	135.00	225.00
	1840	.012	50.00	75.00	135.00	225.00
	1841	.012	50.00	75.00	135.00	225.00
	1842	.012	50.00	75.00	135.00	225.00
	1843	.012	50.00	75.00	135.00	225.00
	1844	.012	50.00	75.00	135.00	225.00
	1845	.012	50.00	75.00	135.00	225.00
	1846	.012	50.00	75.00	135.00	225.00
	1847	3,068	70.00	110.00	150.00	300.00
	1848	—	50.00	75.00	135.00	225.00

GULDEN

10.6000 g, .900 SILVER, .3067 oz ASW
Obv: Head left, D below. Rev: Value within wreath.

KM#	Date	Mintage	Fine	VF	XF	Unc
16.1	1838 D	—	65.00	125.00	200.00	350.00

Obv: DOELL below head.

KM#	Date	Mintage	Fine	VF	XF	Unc
16.2	1838	.018	65.00	120.00	200.00	350.00
	1839	.012	65.00	120.00	200.00	350.00
	1840	.012	65.00	120.00	200.00	350.00
	1841	.012	65.00	120.00	200.00	350.00
	1842	.012	65.00	120.00	200.00	350.00
	1843	.012	65.00	120.00	200.00	350.00
	1844	.012	65.00	120.00	200.00	350.00
	1845	.012	65.00	120.00	200.00	350.00
	1846	.012	65.00	120.00	200.00	350.00
	1847	.012	65.00	120.00	200.00	350.00
	1848	3,068	90.00	150.00	250.00	425.00

Obv: BALBACH below head

KM#	Date	Mintage	Fine	VF	XF	Unc
25	1849	5,000	150.00	250.00	450.00	675.00

ZWEI (2) GULDEN

21.2100 g, .900 SILVER, .6138 oz ASW

KM#	Date	Mintage	Fine	VF	XF	Unc
24	1845 D	9,206	125.00	250.00	650.00	1200.
	1846 D	9,206	125.00	250.00	650.00	1200.
	1847 D	9,206	125.00	250.00	650.00	1200.
	1848 D	6,905	125.00	250.00	700.00	1300.

Obv: BALBACH below bust.

KM#	Date	Mintage	Fine	VF	XF	Unc
26	1849	1,213	325.00	600.00	900.00	1800.

2 THALER

(3-1/2 Gulden)

37.1200 g, .900 SILVER, 1.0742 oz ASW

KM#	Date	Mintage	Fine	VF	XF	Unc
20	1841	2,857	325.00	600.00	1200.	2400.
	1842	2,857	325.00	600.00	1200.	2400.
	1843	2,877	325.00	600.00	1200.	2400.

Obv: Similar to KM#20.

KM#	Date	Mintage	Fine	VF	XF	Unc
23	1844	3,300	325.00	600.00	1100.	2000.
	1846	6,600	300.00	550.00	1100.	2200.
	1847	2,000	350.00	650.00	1200.	2200.

HOHENZOLLERN (under Prussia)

In 1849, Prussia obtained the Hohenzollern lands due to the 1848 revolutions and political unrest. One series of coins was issued by Prussia for their Hohenzollern holdings.

RULERS

Friedrich Wilhelm IV (of Prussia), 1849-1861

KREUZER

COPPER

KM#	Date	Mintage	Fine	VF	XF	Unc
1	1852A	.030	15.00	30.00	60.00	100.00

3 KREUZER

1.2900 g, .333 SILVER, .0138 oz ASW

KM#	Date	Mintage	Fine	VF	XF	Unc
2	1852A	.022	15.00	30.00	75.00	150.00
	1852A	—	—	—	Proof	150.00

6 KREUZER

2.5900 g, .333 SILVER, .0277 oz ASW

KM#	Date	Mintage	Fine	VF	XF	Unc
3	1852A	.027	20.00	40.00	100.00	200.00
	1852A	—	—	—	Proof	200.00

1/2 GULDEN

5.3000 g, .900 SILVER, .1537 oz ASW

KM#	Date	Mintage	Fine	VF	XF	Unc
4	1852A	.053	65.00	100.00	150.00	225.00

GULDEN

10.6000 g, .900 SILVER, .3067 oz ASW

KM#	Date	Mintage	Fine	VF	XF	Unc
5	1852A	.050	65.00	100.00	150.00	275.00
	1852A	—	—	—	Proof	350.00

Listings For

HOLSTEIN: refer to Denmark
HOLSTEIN-GOTTORP: refer to Denmark

ISENBURG

The lands of the counts of Isenburg lay on both sides of the Main River to the east of Frankfurt. The dynasty traces its lineage back to the 10th century and began issuing coins in the mid-13th century. The county underwent many divisions in the Middle Ages, but by the early 17th century only one dominant branch was producing coins. This was Isenburg-Birstein, divided once again into Isenburg-Offenbach-Birstein and Isenburg-Budingen in 1635. The latter was further divided into four branches in 1673/1687 and two of the substrata became extinct in 1725 and 1780 respectively. Isenburg-Offenbach-Birstein was raised to the rank of prince in 1744 and all other branches had to relinquish their sovereignty to his descendant in 1806. The latter lost his sole leadership in 1813 because he sided with Napoleon and the lands of Isenburg-Offenbach-Birstein were mediatized to Hesse-Darmstadt in 1815. The subdivisions of Isenburg-Budigen did not issue a regular coinage, but struck the series of the quasi-official snipe hellers during the 19th century.

RULERS

Wolfgang Ernst II, 1754-1803
Karl I, 1803-1820
Wolfgang Ernst III, 1820-1866
Karl II, 1866

Isenburg-Budingen

Ernst Kasimir II, 1775-1801
Ernst Kasimir III, 1801-1848
Adolf II (in Wachtersbach), 1805-1847
Ernst Kasimir IV, 1848-1861
Bruno, 1861-1906

6 KREUZER

BILLON

KM#	Date	Mintage	Fine	VF	XF	Unc
46	1811	1,000	30.00	60.00	125.00	275.00

12 KREUZER

(Kipper)

SILVER
Obv: J. LAROQUE F. at truncation.

KM#	Date	Mintage	Fine	VF	XF	Unc
47	1811	500 pcs.	60.00	125.00	250.00	450.00

EIN (1) THALER

(Reichs)

SILVER

KM#	Date	Mintage	Fine	VF	XF	Unc
48	1811	100 pcs.	500.00	1000.	1750.	3000.

TRADE COINAGE

DUCAT

3.5000 g, .986 GOLD, .1109 oz AGW

KM#	Date	Mintage	Fine	VF	XF	Unc
49	1811	—	—	—	—	—

2 DUCAT

7.0000 g, .986 GOLD, .2218 oz AGW

KM#	Date	Mintage	Fine	VF	XF	Unc
50	1811	—	1500.	3000.	6000.	10,000.

NOTE: Struck w/1 Ducat dies, KM#49.

KNYPHAUSEN

The district of Knyphausen was located in northwestern Germany in East Friesland. Local nobility ruled from the 14th century and until 1623 when it was sold to Oldenburg. It became autonomous in 1653 and was acquired through marriage to the Bentinck family in 1733. Coins were struck c. 1800. It was claimed by both Anhalt and Oldenburg and the arms of Knyphausen appear on coins of both places.

RULERS

Wilhelm Gustav Friedrich, 1774-1835

1/8 THALER

(9 Grote)

SILVER
Obv: Arms.
Rev: Crowned double-headed eagle dividing value.

KM#	Date	Mintage	Fine	VF	XF	Unc
5 (C2)	1807	—	300.00	600.00	1200.	1750.

KM#	Date	Mintage	Fine	VF	XF	Unc
6 (C1)	1807	.016	125.00	250.00	500.00	725.00

LAUENBURG

The line of rulers of this Saxon duchy became extinct in 1689 and passed to Brunswick-Luneburg-Celle, then to Brunswick-Luneburg-Calenberg-Hannover in 1705. After the Napoleonic Wars, Lauenburg went to Prussia in 1813, to Denmark in 1814 and was regained by Prussia as part of the latter's annexation of Holstein in 1864. The Brunswick duches struck special coins for Lauenburg. See Saxe-Lauenburg for coinage prior to 1689.

RULERS

Georg III von Brunswick-Luneburg-Calenberg Hannover, 1760-1818
Frederick VI (of Denmark), 1816-1839

MINTMASTERS INITIALS

Letter	Date	Name
FF	1830	Johann Friedrich Freund

2/3 THALER

17.3200 g, .750 SILVER, .4177 oz ASW

KM#	Date	Mintage	Fine	VF	XF	Unc
25 (C1)	1830 FF	—	150.00	250.00	400.00	800.00

LEININGEN-DAGSBURG-HARTENBURG

Established from an early division of Leiningen in 1317 and further divided in 1541, Leiningen-Dagsburg-Hartenburg was located some 30 miles west-southwest of Mannheim. The count was raised to the rank of prince in 1779 and was the only member of his line to issue any coins. His possessions were taken by France in 1801.

RULERS

Karl Friedrich Wilhelm, 1756-1807

PFENNIG

BILLON
Obv: Eagles below crown within branches.
Rev: Value.

KM#	Date	Mintage	Fine	VF	XF	Unc
7 (C1)	1805	—	35.00	75.00	150.00	300.00

2 PFENNIG

BILLON
Obv: Crowned arms. Rev: Value, branch below.

KM#	Date	Mintage	Fine	VF	XF	Unc
8 (C2)	1805	—	50.00	100.00	200.00	400.00

3 KREUZER

BILLON
Obv: Crowned arms within branches.
Rev: Value, branch below.

KM#	Date	Mintage	Fine	VF	XF	Unc
5 (C3)	1804	—	40.00	90.00	200.00	400.00

KM#	Date	Mintage	Fine	VF	XF	Unc
9 (C3a)	1805	—	35.00	75.00	175.00	350.00

6 KREUZER

BILLON
Obv: Crowned arms within branches.
Rev: Value, branch below.

KM#	Date	Mintage	Fine	VF	XF	Unc
6 (C5)	1804	—	50.00	125.00	300.00	600.00

KM#	Date	Mintage	Fine	VF	XF	Unc
10 (C5a)	1805	—	40.00	90.00	200.00	400.00

LIPPE-DETMOLD

The Counts of Lippe ruled over a small state in northwestern Germany. In 1528/9 they became Counts; in 1720 they were raised to the rank of Princes, but did not use the title until 1789. Another branch of the family ruled the even smaller Schaumburg-Lippe. Lippe joined North German Confederation in 1866, and became part of the German Empire in 1871. When the insane Prince Alexander succeeded to the throne in 1895, the main branch reached an end, and a ten-year testamentary dispute between the Biesterfeld and the SchaumburgLippe lines followed - a Wilhelmine cause celebre. The Biesterfeld line gained the principality in 1905, but abdicated in 1918. In 1947 Lippe was absorbed by the German Land of North Rhine-Westphalia.

RULERS

Friedrich Wilhelm Leopold
Alone, 1789-1802
Paul Alexander Leopold II
under Regency of Pauline of Anhalt-Bernburg, 1802-1820
As Independent Prince, 1820-1851
Paul Friedrich Emil Leopold III, 1851-1875
Woldemar, 1875 - 1895
Alexander, 1895 - 1905
Leopold IV, 1905-1918

MINT MARKS

A - Berlin, 1843-1918

MINTMASTERS INITIALS

Letter	Date	Name
ST	1820-40	Strickling of Blomberg
T	1812-20	Trebbe of Lemgo
	1789-1803	Balthasar Reinhard
	1803	Siegmann

HELLER

COPPER

KM#	Date	Mintage	Fine	VF	XF	Unc
225	1802 T	.166	9.00	15.00	30.00	55.00
(C70)	1802	Inc. Ab.	2.00	4.00	10.00	40.00
	1809 T	.108	2.00	4.00	10.00	40.00
(C70)	1812 T	—	2.00	4.00	10.00	40.00
	1814 T	—	2.00	4.00	10.00	40.00
	1816 T	—	2.00	4.00	10.00	40.00
	1816	—	2.00	4.00	10.00	40.00

Obv: Blooming rose. Rev. value: I HELLER, date.

KM#	Date	Mintage	Fine	VF	XF	Unc
241	1821ST	—	2.00	4.00	10.00	40.00
(C74)	1822ST	—	2.00	4.00	10.00	40.00
	1825ST	—	2.00	4.00	10.00	40.00
	1826ST	—	2.00	4.00	10.00	40.00
	1828ST	—	2.00	4.00	10.00	40.00
	1835ST	—	2.00	4.00	10.00	40.00
	1836ST	—	2.00	4.00	10.00	40.00
	1840ST	—	2.00	4.00	10.00	40.00

Rev. value: 1 HELLER, date.

KM#	Date	Mintage	Fine	VF	XF	Unc
244 (C74a)	1826 ST	—	2.00	4.00	10.00	40.00

PFENNING

COPPER

KM#	Date	Mintage	Fine	VF	XF	Unc
226 (C71.1)	1802	.120	3.00	7.00	20.00	100.00

Rev: T below date.

KM#	Date	Mintage	Fine	VF	XF	Unc
235 (C71.2)	1818 T	—	3.00	7.00	15.00	90.00

Rev: W/o T.

KM#	Date	Mintage	Fine	VF	XF	Unc
236 (C71.3)	1818	—	3.00	7.00	15.00	90.00

Rev: ST below date.

KM#	Date	Mintage	Fine	VF	XF	Unc
240	1820 ST	—	3.00	7.00	15.00	60.00
(C75)	1821 ST	—	3.00	7.00	15.00	60.00
	1824 ST	—	3.00	7.00	15.00	60.00
	1825 ST	—	3.00	7.00	15.00	60.00

Rev. value: PFENNING

KM#	Date	Mintage	Fine	VF	XF	Unc
242	1821 ST	—	—	—	—	—
(C75a)	1824 ST	—	3.00	7.00	20.00	75.00

KM#	Date	Mintage	Fine	VF	XF	Unc
245	1828 ST	—	1.50	3.50	8.00	50.00
(C75b)	1829 ST	—	1.50	3.50	8.00	50.00
	1830 ST	—	1.50	3.50	8.00	50.00
	1836 ST	—	1.50	3.50	8.00	50.00
	1840 ST	—	1.50	3.50	8.00	50.00

KM#	Date	Mintage	Fine	VF	XF	Unc
251 (C77)	1847 A	.972	1.00	3.00	7.00	40.00

KM#	Date	Mintage	Fine	VF	XF	Unc
260	1851 A	1.080	1.00	3.00	7.00	35.00
(C83)	1858 A	.900	1.00	3.00	7.00	35.00

1-1/2 PFENNING

(1/192 Thaler)

COPPER

KM#	Date	Mintage	Fine	VF	XF	Unc
243	1821 T	—	3.00	5.00	10.00	65.00
(C76)	1823 T	—	3.00	5.00	10.00	65.00
	1824 T	—	3.00	5.00	10.00	65.00
	1825 T	—	3.00	5.00	10.00	65.00

2 PFENNING

COPPER
Obv: Blooming rose.
Rev: Value, rosette below date.

KM#	Date	Mintage	Fine	VF	XF	Unc
227 (C72)	1802	.127	4.00	7.00	20.00	100.00

3 PFENNINGE

COPPER
Obv: Crowned shield w/blooming rose. Rev: Value.

KM#	Date	Mintage	Fine	VF	XF	Unc
252 (C78)	1847A	1.020	2.00	5.00	10.00	60.00

KM#	Date	Mintage	Fine	VF	XF	Unc
261 (C84)	1858A	.060	3.00	7.00	15.00	75.00

1/2 SILBER GROSCHEN

.9700 g, .250 SILVER, .0077 oz ASW
Obv: Head right. Rev: Value.

KM#	Date	Mintage	Fine	VF	XF	Unc
253 (C79)	1847A	.321	6.00	12.00	30.00	85.00

MARIENGROSCHEN

BILLON
Obv: Arms. Rev: Value and date.

KM#	Date	Mintage	VG	Fine	VF	XF
228	1802	—	1.00	3.00	6.50	15.00
(C73)	1803	—	1.00	3.00	6.50	15.00

KM#	Date	Mintage	VG	Fine	VF	XF
229 (C73a)	1804	—	1.00	3.00	6.50	15.00

SILBER GROSCHEN

1.5500 g, .312 SILVER, .0155 oz ASW

KM#	Date	Mintage	Fine	VF	XF	Unc
254 (C80)	1847A	.750	5.00	10.00	25.00	60.00

2.1900 g, .220 SILVER, .0154 oz ASW

KM#	Date	Mintage	Fine	VF	XF	Unc
265 (C85)	1860A	.432	2.00	5.00	15.00	50.00

2-1/2 SILBER GROSCHEN

3.2400 g, .375 SILVER, .0390 oz ASW
Obv: Head right. Rev: Value.

KM#	Date	Mintage	Fine	VF	XF	Unc
255 (C81)	1847A	.363	5.00	10.00	25.00	75.00

3.2200 g, .375 SILVER, .0388 oz ASW

KM#	Date	Mintage	Fine	VF	XF	Unc
266 (C86)	1860A	.120	5.00	10.00	25.00	75.00

EIN (1) THALER

18.5200 g, .900 SILVER, .5360 oz ASW

KM#	Date	Mintage	Fine	VF	XF	Unc
267	1860A	.026	40.00	75.00	135.00	285.00
(C87)	1866A	.018	45.00	80.00	150.00	315.00

2 THALER

(3-1/2 Gulden)

37.1200 g, .900 SILVER, 1.0742 oz ASW

KM#	Date	Mintage	Fine	VF	XF	Unc
250 (C82)	1843A	.017	200.00	400.00	700.00	1400.

MONETARY REFORM

2 MARK

11.1110 g, .900 SILVER, .3215 oz ASW

KM#	Date	Mintage	Fine	VF	XF	Unc
270	1906A	.020	100.00	200.00	300.00	450.00
(Y83)	1906A	1,100	—	—	Proof	450.00

3 MARK

16.6670 g, .900 SILVER, .4823 oz ASW

KM#	Date	Mintage	Fine	VF	XF	Unc
275	1913A	.015	125.00	250.00	325.00	475.00
(Y84)	1913A	100 pcs.	—	—	Proof	550.00

LOWENSTEIN-WERTHEIM-ROCHEFORT

Rochefort was the Catholic branch of Lowenstein-Wertheim, established in 1635. From 1622 until about 1650, coinage for Lowenstein-Wertheim-Rochefort was struck at the mint of Cugnon in Luxembourg. The ruler was made Prince of the Empire in 1711. All lands in his possession were mediatized in 1806.

RULERS

Dominik Constantin, 1789-1806

MINT

Cugnon Mint in Luxembourg

PFENNING

COPPER

KM#	Date	Mintage	Fine	VF	XF	Unc
100	1801	—	6.00	12.00	40.00	185.00
(C115a)	1802	—	6.00	12.00	40.00	185.00

NOTE: Earlier date (1800) exists for this type.

LOWENSTEIN-WERTHEIM-VIRNEBURG & ROCHEFORT

JOINT COINAGE

PFENNING

COPPER

KM#	Date	Mintage	Fine	VF	XF	Unc
28	1802	—	2.00	4.00	10.00	50.00
(C133)	1804	—	2.00	4.00	10.00	50.00

Obv: Spade shield

KM#	Date	Mintage	Fine	VF	XF	Unc
30 (C133a)	1804	—	2.00	3.00	8.00	40.00

Obv: (error) L.M. above shield.

KM#	Date	Mintage	Fine	VF	XF	Unc
31 (C133b)	1804	—	4.00	7.00	15.00	100.00

BILLON, uniface

Eagle above 3 roses, 1 PF above.

KM#	Date	Mintage	Fine	VF	XF	Unc
25	1801	—	3.00	7.00	15.00	65.00
(C138)	1802	—	3.00	7.00	15.00	65.00
	1803	—	3.00	7.00	15.00	65.00
	1804	—	3.00	7.00	15.00	65.00

NOTE: Earlier dates (1798-1800) exist for this type.

Tear shaped arms.

KM#	Date	Mintage	Fine	VF	XF	Unc
29	1802	—	4.00	8.00	16.00	70.00

KREUZER

BILLON

KM#	Date	Mintage	Fine	VF	XF	Unc
26	1801	—	3.00	6.00	12.00	60.00
(C140)	1802	—	3.00	6.00	12.00	60.00
	1803	—	3.00	6.00	12.00	60.00
	1804	—	3.00	6.00	12.00	60.00
	1805	—	3.00	6.00	12.00	60.00
	1806	—	3.00	6.00	10.00	50.00

NOTE: Varieties exist.
NOTE: Earlier date (1800) exists for this type.

3 KREUZER

BILLON

Obv: Arms. Rev: Value

KM#	Date	Mintage	Fine	VF	XF	Unc
27.1	1801	—	6.00	15.00	40.00	150.00

KM#	Date	Mintage	Fine	VF	XF	Unc
27.2	1802	—	6.00	15.00	40.00	150.00
	1803	—	6.00	15.00	40.00	150.00

KM#	Date	Mintage	Fine	VF	XF	Unc
27.3	1804	—	6.00	12.00	35.00	120.00
	1805	—	6.00	12.00	35.00	120.00

NOTE: Earlier date (1800) exists for this type.

SILVER

KM#	Date	Mintage	Fine	VF	XF	Unc
32 (C143)	1805	—	—	—	225.00	—

LUBECK

FREE CITY

Lubeck became a free city of the empire in 1188 and from c. 1190 into the 13th century an imperial mint existed in the town. It was granted the mint right in 1188, 1226 and 1340, but actually began its first civic coinage c. 1350. Occupied by the French during the Napoleonic Wars, it was restored as a free city in 1813 and became part of the German Empire in 1871.

2 MARK

11.1110 g, .900 SILVER, .3215 oz ASW

KM#	Date	Mintage	Fine	VF	XF	Unc
210	1901A	.025	100.00	175.00	225.00	350.00
(Y85)	1901A	—	—	—	Proof	450.00

KM#	Date	Mintage	Fine	VF	XF	Unc
212	1904A	.025	45.00	75.00	130.00	185.00
(Y85a)	1904A	200 pcs.	—	—	Proof	275.00
	1905A	.025	45.00	75.00	130.00	225.00
	1905A	178 pcs.	—	—	Proof	275.00
	1906A	.025	45.00	75.00	130.00	225.00
	1906A	200 pcs.	—	—	Proof	275.00
	1907A	.025	45.00	75.00	130.00	225.00
	1911A	.025	45.00	75.00	130.00	225.00
	1911A	—	—	—	Proof	—
	1912A	.025	45.00	75.00	130.00	225.00
	1912A	—	—	—	Proof	—

3 MARK

16.6670 g, .900 SILVER, .4823 oz ASW

KM#	Date	Mintage	Fine	VF	XF	Unc
215	1908A	.033	25.00	70.00	125.00	190.00
(Y86)	1909A	.033	25.00	70.00	125.00	190.00
	1910A	.033	25.00	70.00	125.00	190.00
	1911A	.033	25.00	70.00	125.00	190.00
	1912A	.034	25.00	70.00	125.00	190.00
	1913A	.030	25.00	70.00	125.00	190.00
	1914A	.010	35.00	85.00	150.00	225.00
	Common date	—	—	—	Proof	250.00

5 MARK

27.7770 g, .900 SILVER, .8038 oz ASW

KM#	Date	Mintage	Fine	VF	XF	Unc
213	1904A	.010	100.00	250.00	375.00	500.00
(Y87)	1904A	200 pcs.	—	—	Proof	800.00

KM#	Date	Mintage	Fine	VF	XF	Unc
(Y87)	1907A	.010	100.00	250.00	375.00	500.00
	1908A	.010	100.00	275.00	400.00	550.00
	1913A	6,000	100.00	275.00	400.00	600.00

10 MARK

3.9820 g, .900 GOLD, .1152 oz AGW

KM#	Date	Mintage	Fine	VF	XF	Unc
211 (Y88)	1901A	.010	300.00	500.00	800.00	1100.
	1901A	200 pcs.	—	—	Proof	1800.
	1904A	.010	300.00	500.00	800.00	1100.
	1904A	130 pcs.	—	—	Proof	1800.

KM#	Date	Mintage	Fine	VF	XF	Unc
214 (Y88a)	1905A	.010	300.00	500.00	800.00	1100.
	1905A	247 pcs.	—	—	Proof	2250.
	1906A	.010	300.00	500.00	800.00	1100.
	1906A	216 pcs.	—	—	Proof	2250.
	1909A	.010	300.00	500.00	800.00	1100.
	1910A	.010	300.00	500.00	800.00	1100.

TRADE COINAGE

DUCAT

3.5000 g, .986 GOLD, .1109 oz AGW

KM#	Date	Mintage	Fine	VF	XF	Unc
205 (C24)	1801 HDF	—	400.00	750.00	1250.	1650.

MECKLENBURG-SCHWERIN

The duchy of Mecklenburg was located along the Baltic coast between Holstein and Pomerania. Schwerin was annexed to Mecklenburg in 1357. In 1658 the Mecklenburg dynasty was divided into two lines. The 1815 Congress of Vienna elevated the duchy to the status of grand duchy and it became a part of the German Empire in 1871 until 1918 when the last grand duke abdicated.

RULERS

Friedrich Franz I, 1785-1837
Paul Friedrich, 1837-1842
Friedrich Franz II, 1842-1883
Friedrich Franz III, 1883-1897
Friedrich Franz IV, 1897-1918

MINT MARKS

A - Berlin
B - Hannover

PFENNIG

COPPER

C#	Date	Mintage	Fine	VF	XF	Unc
73	1831	.514	2.50	5.00	10.00	40.00

C#	Date	Mintage	Fine	VF	XF	Unc
102	1872B	2.335	1.00	2.00	4.00	15.00

2 PFENNIG

COPPER

C#	Date	Mintage	Fine	VF	XF	Unc
74	1831	.257	2.50	5.00	10.00	60.00

C#	Date	Mintage	Fine	VF	XF	Unc
103	1872B	1.155	1.50	3.00	6.00	30.00

3 PFENNIG

(1 Dreiling)

.5000 g, .187 SILVER, .0030 oz ASW
Rev. leg: MECK. SCHWERIN: SCHEID

C#	Date	Mintage	Fine	VF	XF	Unc
57	1801	.204	2.00	4.00	10.00	65.00
	1803	.117	2.00	4.00	10.00	65.00
	1804	.113	2.00	4.00	10.00	65.00
	1805	.414	2.00	4.00	10.00	65.00
	1810	.117	2.00	4.00	10.00	65.00
	1811	.273	2.00	4.00	10.00	65.00
	1813	—	2.00	4.00	10.00	80.00
	1814	.060	2.00	4.00	10.00	80.00
	1815	.081	2.00	4.00	10.00	80.00

BILLON
Obv: Crowned FF monogram.
Rev: Value.

C#	Date	Mintage	Fine	VF	XF	Unc
75	1816	.199	2.00	4.00	10.00	70.00
	1817	.083	2.00	4.00	10.00	80.00
	1818	.077	2.00	4.00	10.00	80.00
	1819	.251	2.00	4.00	10.00	70.00

Rev. value: I DREILING, date.

C#	Date	Mintage	Fine	VF	XF	Unc
76	1819	.596	2.00	4.00	8.00	40.00
	1820	.845	2.00	4.00	8.00	40.00
	1821	.516	2.00	4.00	8.00	40.00
	1822	1.021	2.00	4.00	8.00	40.00
	1824	.235	2.00	4.00	8.00	40.00

.4500 g, .125 SILVER, .0018 oz ASW

C#	Date	Mintage	Fine	VF	XF	Unc
76.4	1828	.684	2.00	4.00	8.00	40.00
	1829	.207	2.00	4.00	8.00	40.00
	1830	.793	2.00	4.00	8.00	40.00

C#	Date	Mintage	Fine	VF	XF	Unc
76.7	1831	.064	3.00	5.00	10.00	50.00
	1832	.308	3.00	5.00	8.00	40.00
	1833	.048	3.00	5.00	10.00	50.00
	1836	.452	3.00	5.00	8.00	40.00

C#	Date	Mintage	Fine	VF	XF	Unc
94	1838	—	3.00	5.00	10.00	60.00
	1839	.172	3.00	5.00	10.00	60.00
	1840	.112	3.00	5.00	10.00	60.00
	1841	.100	3.00	5.00	10.00	60.00
	1842	.157	3.00	5.00	10.00	60.00

C#	Date	Mintage	Fine	VF	XF	Unc
105	1842	.203	3.00	5.00	10.00	55.00
	1843	.230	3.00	5.00	10.00	55.00
	1844	.125	3.00	5.00	10.00	55.00
	1845	.170	3.00	5.00	10.00	55.00
	1846	.077	3.00	5.00	10.00	55.00

COPPER

C#	Date	Mintage	Fine	VF	XF	Unc
101	1843	.089	2.00	4.00	8.00	45.00
	1845	.151	2.00	4.00	8.00	45.00
	1846	.073	2.00	4.00	8.00	45.00
	1848	—	2.00	4.00	8.00	45.00

C#	Date	Mintage	Fine	VF	XF	Unc
101a	1852A	—	1.50	2.50	5.00	30.00
101a	1853A	—	1.50	2.50	5.00	30.00
	1854A	—	1.50	2.50	5.00	30.00
	1855A	1.135	1.50	2.50	5.00	30.00
	1858A	—	1.50	2.50	5.00	30.00
	1859A	—	1.50	2.50	5.00	30.00
	1860A	—	1.50	2.50	5.00	30.00
	1861A	—	1.50	2.50	5.00	30.00
	1863A	—	1.50	2.50	5.00	30.00
	1864A	1.076	1.50	2.50	5.00	30.00

5 PFENNIG

COPPER

C#	Date	Mintage	Fine	VF	XF	Unc
104	1872B	.459	7.00	15.00	35.00	75.00

6 PFENNIG

.7600 g, .250 SILVER, .0061 oz ASW

C#	Date	Mintage	Fine	VF	XF	Unc
59	1801	.080	3.00	5.00	10.00	40.00
	1802	.141	3.00	5.00	10.00	40.00
	1803	.060	3.00	5.00	10.00	40.00
	1804	.062	3.00	5.00	10.00	40.00
	1805	.321	3.00	5.00	10.00	40.00
	1809	.084	3.00	5.00	10.00	40.00
	1810	.081	3.00	5.00	10.00	40.00
	1811	.222	3.00	5.00	10.00	40.00
	1813	.254	3.00	5.00	10.00	40.00
	1815	.199	3.00	5.00	10.00	40.00

Obv: Crowned FF monogram. Rev: Value 6 PFEN.

C#	Date	Mintage	Fine	VF	XF	Unc
77	1816	.255	3.00	5.00	10.00	40.00
	1817	.300	3.00	5.00	10.00	40.00

.9000 g, .125 SILVER, .0036 oz ASW
W/o legends

C#	Date	Mintage	Fine	VF	XF	Unc
79	1831	.128	2.00	7.00	15.00	75.00

SECHSLING

.7600 g, .250 SILVER, .0061 oz ASW

C#	Date	Mintage	Fine	VF	XF	Unc
78	1820	.150	2.00	4.00	10.00	55.00
	1821	.249	2.00	4.00	10.00	55.00
	1822	.272	2.00	4.00	10.00	55.00
	1823	.320	2.00	4.00	10.00	55.00
	1824	.419	2.00	4.00	10.00	55.00

.9000 g, .125 SILVER, .0036 oz ASW

C#	Date	Mintage	Fine	VF	XF	Unc
78.4	1828	—	2.00	4.00	10.00	75.00
	1829	.190	2.00	4.00	10.00	75.00

SCHILLING

1.0800 g, .375 SILVER, .0130 oz ASW
Obv: Crowned FF monogram. Rev: 1/SCHILLING/COURANT/MECKLENB/SCHWERIN/MUNZE/date.

C#	Date	Mintage	Fine	VF	XF	Unc
61	1801	1.301	3.00	7.00	15.00	60.00
	1802	2.431	3.00	7.00	15.00	60.00
	1803	2.348	3.00	7.00	15.00	60.00
	1804	2.603	3.00	7.00	15.00	60.00
	1805	2.501	3.00	7.00	15.00	60.00
	1806	1.766	3.00	7.00	15.00	60.00
	1807	.585	3.00	7.00	15.00	60.00
	1808	.243	3.00	7.00	15.00	60.00
	1809	.342	3.00	7.00	15.00	60.00
	1810	.250	3.00	7.00	15.00	60.00

NOTE: Earlier dates (1785-1800) exist for this type.

Rev: Value.

C#	Date	Mintage	Fine	VF	XF	Unc
80	1817	.031	10.00	20.00	50.00	250.00

1.1100 g, .312 SILVER, .0111 oz ASW
Obv. leg: GR. HZ. U.M.S.

C#	Date	Mintage	Fine	VF	XF	Unc
81	1826	.159	3.00	7.00	20.00	80.00
	1827	.342	3.00	7.00	20.00	80.00

Obv. leg: GR. HERZOG V. Rev: Value, legend.

C#	Date	Mintage	Fine	VF	XF	Unc
81.4	1829	.054	4.00	8.00	15.00	90.00
	1830	.501	3.00	6.00	10.00	55.00
	1831	.528	3.00	6.00	10.00	55.00

C#	Date	Mintage	Fine	VF	XF	Unc
81.4	1832	.119	3.00	6.00	10.00	75.00
	1833	.091	3.00	6.00	10.00	75.00
	1834	.118	3.00	6.00	10.00	75.00
	1835	.109	3.00	6.00	10.00	75.00
	1836	.163	3.00	6.00	10.00	70.00
	1837	.082	3.00	6.00	10.00	75.00

Obv: Crowned PF monogram

C#	Date	Mintage	Fine	VF	XF	Unc
95	1838	.021	4.00	7.00	15.00	115.00
	1839	.125	4.00	7.00	15.00	65.00
	1840	.052	4.00	7.00	15.00	75.00
	1841	.046	4.00	7.00	15.00	75.00
	1842	.030	4.00	7.00	15.00	100.00

BILLON

C#	Date	Mintage	Fine	VF	XF	Unc
106	1842	.108	2.00	4.00	8.00	45.00
	1843	.139	2.00	4.00	8.00	45.00
	1844	.116	2.00	4.00	8.00	45.00
	1845	.246	2.00	4.00	8.00	45.00
	1846	.154	2.00	4.00	8.00	45.00

4 SCHILLINGE

3.0600 g, .562 SILVER, .0553 oz ASW

C#	Date	Mintage	Fine	VF	XF	Unc
63	1809	1,408	40.00	60.00	100.00	450.00

NOTE: Earlier date (1785) exists for this type.

3.3000 g, .437 SILVER, .0464 oz ASW

C#	Date	Mintage	Fine	VF	XF	Unc
82	1826	.621	10.00	15.00	35.00	130.00

3.0600 g, .500 SILVER, .0492 oz ASW
Obv: Head left, leg: GR. HERZOG. . . .

C#	Date	Mintage	Fine	VF	XF	Unc
83	1828	.070	15.00	25.00	50.00	185.00

Obv. leg: GROSSHERZOG. . . .

C#	Date	Mintage	Fine	VF	XF	Unc
83a	1829	.200	10.00	15.00	35.00	115.00
	1830	1.793	10.00	15.00	35.00	115.00
	1831	.476	10.00	15.00	35.00	115.00
	1832	.121	10.00	15.00	35.00	115.00
	1833	.049	10.00	20.00	40.00	135.00

Obv: Crowned arms within 2 crossed branches.

C#	Date	Mintage	Fine	VF	XF	Unc
96	1838	.015	10.00	20.00	40.00	120.00
	1839	.039	10.00	20.00	40.00	120.00

8 SCHILLINGE

6.6000 g, .437 SILVER, .0927 oz ASW

C#	Date	Mintage	Fine	VF	XF	Unc
84	1827	.025	20.00	40.00	120.00	250.00

1/48 THALER

1.3000 g, .208 SILVER, .0086 oz ASW

C#	Date	Mintage	Fine	VF	XF	Unc
107	1848	—	3.00	5.00	10.00	45.00

C#	Date	Mintage	Fine	VF	XF	Unc
107a	1852A	—	2.00	4.00	8.00	35.00
	1853A	—	2.00	4.00	8.00	35.00
	1855A	2.819	2.00	4.00	8.00	35.00
	1858A	—	2.00	4.00	8.00	35.00
	1860A	—	2.00	4.00	8.00	35.00
	1861A	—	2.00	4.00	8.00	35.00
	1862A	—	2.00	4.00	8.00	35.00
	1863A	—	2.00	4.00	8.00	35.00
	1864A	—	2.00	4.00	8.00	35.00
	1866A	2.034	2.00	4.00	8.00	35.00

1/12 THALER

2.4400 g, .500 SILVER, .0392 oz ASW

C#	Date	Mintage	Fine	VF	XF	Unc
108	1848	2.047	6.00	12.00	30.00	75.00

NOTE: Varieties exist.

1/6 THALER

5.3500 g, .520 SILVER, .0894 oz ASW

C#	Date	Mintage	Fine	VF	XF	Unc
109	1848A	.137	10.00	25.00	75.00	125.00

2/3 THALER

17.3200 g, .750 SILVER, .4177 oz ASW

C#	Date	Mintage	Fine	VF	XF	Unc
70	1801	.169	30.00	70.00	110.00	250.00
	1808	.655	30.00	70.00	110.00	250.00
	1810	.338	30.00	70.00	110.00	250.00

NOTE: Earlier dates (1789-1800) exist for this type.

C#	Date	Mintage	Fine	VF	XF	Unc
71	1813	9,918	75.00	125.00	250.00	450.00

Obv. leg: . . . . .G.G. HERZOG. . . . .
Rev: Date below value.

C#	Date	Mintage	Fine	VF	XF	Unc
85	1817	6,783	275.00	450.00	750.00	1250.

Obv: leg: . . . . .G.G. GR. HERZ. . . . .

C#	Date	Mintage	Fine	VF	XF	Unc
85a	1825	.035	85.00	175.00	325.00	600.00

Obv. leg. ends: . . . . .SCHW.

C#	Date	Mintage	Fine	VF	XF	Unc
86	1825	.043	100.00	180.00	300.00	600.00
	1826	—	100.00	180.00	300.00	600.00

Obv. leg. ends: . . . . .SCHWERIN.

C#	Date	Mintage	Fine	VF	XF	Unc
86a	1826	.103	100.00	180.00	300.00	600.00

C#	Date	Mintage	Fine	VF	XF	Unc
87	1828	.057	100.00	165.00	330.00	600.00
87a	1829	—	—	—	Rare	—

13.1700 g, .986 SILVER, .4175 oz ASW

C#	Date	Mintage	Fine	VF	XF	Unc
97	1839	.291	30.00	70.00	125.00	250.00
	1840	.856	25.00	50.00	100.00	200.00
	1841	.118	35.00	75.00	150.00	300.00

C#	Date	Mintage	Fine	VF	XF	Unc
110	1845	1,563	375.00	550.00	825.00	1250.

EIN (1) THALER

22.2700 g, .750 SILVER, .5370 oz ASW

C#	Date	Mintage	Fine	VF	XF	Unc
111	1848A	.528	30.00	60.00	120.00	225.00

18.5200 g, .900 SILVER, .5360 oz ASW

C#	Date	Mintage	Fine	VF	XF	Unc
112	1864A	.100	30.00	60.00	140.00	275.00

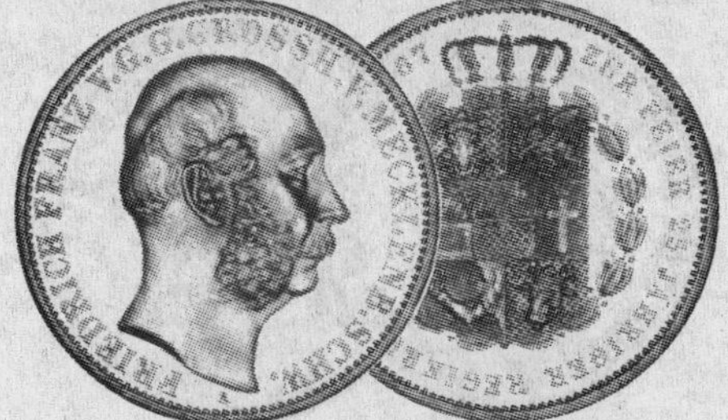

25th Anniversary of Reign

C#	Date	Mintage	Fine	VF	XF	Unc
113	1867A	.010	30.00	60.00	140.00	225.00

ZWEI EIN HALB (2-1/2) THALER

3.3300 g, .896 GOLD, .0959 oz AGW

C#	Date	Mintage	Fine	VF	XF	Unc
90	1831	7,755	375.00	750.00	1250.	2500.
	1833	124 pcs.	600.00	1000.	1750.	2500.
	1835	195 pcs.	600.00	1000.	1750.	2500.

C#	Date	Mintage	Fine	VF	XF	Unc
98	1840	2,910	300.00	500.00	750.00	1100.

FUNF (5) THALER

6.6600 g, .896 GOLD, .1919 oz AGW

C#	Date	Mintage	Fine	VF	XF	Unc
92	1828	1,753	600.00	1200.	1800.	3000.
	1831	3,878	600.00	1200.	1800.	3000.
	1832	3,334	600.00	1200.	1800.	3000.
	1833	125 pcs.	1000.	1200.	3000.	4000.
	1835	100 pcs.	1000.	1200.	3000.	4000.

C#	Date	Mintage	Fine	VF	XF	Unc
99	1840	1,454	650.00	1250.	1750.	3000.

ZEHN (10) THALER

13.3200 g, .896 GOLD, .3837 oz AGW

C#	Date	Mintage	Fine	VF	XF	Unc
93	1828	876 pcs.	1250.	2500.	3750.	5000.
	1831	1,938	1000.	2000.	3250.	4250.
	1832	1,667	1000.	2000.	3250.	4250.
	1833	128 pcs.	1500.	3000.	4500.	6000.

C#	Date	Mintage	Fine	VF	XF	Unc
100	1839	.092	500.00	1100.	1500.	2000.

MONETARY REFORM

2 MARK

11.1110 g, .900 SILVER, .3215 OZ ASW

Y#	Date	Mintage	Fine	VF	XF	Unc
89	1876A	.300	100.00	250.00	750.00	1750.
	1876A	—	—	—	Proof	2000.

Coming of Age of Grand Duke

Y#	Date	Mintage	Fine	VF	XF	Unc
93	1901A	.050	125.00	300.00	450.00	1200.
	1901A	1,000	—	—	Proof	1200.

Friedrich Franz IV Wedding

Y#	Date	Mintage	Fine	VF	XF	Unc
96	1904A	.100	15.00	35.00	65.00	90.00
	1904A	6,000	—	—	Proof	150.00

3 MARK

16.6670 g, .900 SILVER, .4823 oz ASW
100 Years as Grand Duchy

Y#	Date	Mintage	Fine	VF	XF	Unc
98	1915A	.033	40.00	90.00	150.00	200.00
	1915A	—	—	—	Proof	350.00

5 MARK

27.7770 g, .900 SILVER, .8038 oz ASW
Friedrich Franz IV Wedding

Y#	Date	Mintage	Fine	VF	XF	Unc
97	1904A	.040	35.00	100.00	175.00	225.00
	1904A	2,500	—	—	Proof	450.00

100 Years as Grand Duchy

Y#	Date	Mintage	Fine	VF	XF	Unc
99	1915A	.010	125.00	250.00	425.00	700.00
	1915A	—	—	—	Proof	800.00

10 MARK

3.9820 g, .900 GOLD, .1152 oz AGW
Rev: Type I.

Y#	Date	Mintage	Fine	VF	XF	Unc
90	1872A	.016	700.00	1000.	1500.	2750.
	1872A	100 pcs.	—	—	Proof	Rare

Rev: Type II.

Y#	Date	Mintage	Fine	VF	XF	Unc
90a	1878A	.050	300.00	500.00	700.00	1000.
	1878A	—	—	—	Proof	2500.

Y#	Date	Mintage	Fine	VF	XF	Unc
92	1890A	.100	150.00	300.00	500.00	900.00
	1890A	—	—	—	Proof	1800.

Coming of Age of Grand Duke
Rev: Type III.

Y#	Date	Mintage	Fine	VF	XF	Unc
94	1901A	.010	450.00	750.00	1200.	1750.
	1901A	200 pcs.	—	—	Proof	1950.

20 MARK

7.9650 g, .900 GOLD, .2304 oz AGW

Rev: Type I.

Y#	Date	Mintage	Fine	VF	XF	Unc
91	1872A	.069	375.00	650.00	1000.	1750.
	1872A	—	—	—	Proof	Rare

Coming of Age of Grand Duke
Rev: Type III.

95	1901A	5,000	900.00	1750.	2750.	4000.
	1901A	200 pcs.	—	—	Proof	3250.

MECKLENBURG-STRELITZ

The duchy of Mecklenburg was located along the Baltic Coast between Holstein and Pomerania. The Strelitz line was founded in 1658 when the Mecklenburg line was divided into two lines. The 1815 Congress of Vienna elevated the duchy to the status of grand duchy. It became a part of the German Empire in 1871 until 1918 when the last grand duke died.

RULERS

Karl II, 1794-1816
Georg, 1816-1860
Friedrich Wilhelm, 1860-1904
Adolph Friedrich V, 1904-1914
Adolph Friedrich VI, 1914-1918

PFENNIG

COPPER
Obv: Crowned G. Rev: Value.

C#	Date	Mintage	Fine	VF	XF	Unc
40	1838	.058	5.00	10.00	25.00	125.00

46	1872	.118	1.50	3.00	6.00	30.00

1-1/2 PFENNIG

COPPER

41	1838	.040	5.00	10.00	25.00	125.00

2 PFENNIG

COPPER

47	1872 B	.203	1.50	3.00	6.00	35.00

3 PFENNIG

COPPER

42	1832	.290	1.50	3.00	6.00	35.00
	1843	.283	1.50	3.00	6.00	35.00
	1845/3	—	1.50	3.00	6.00	35.00
	1845	.193	1.50	3.00	6.00	35.00
	1847	—	1.50	3.00	6.00	35.00

42a	1855A	1.501	1.50	3.00	6.00	35.00
	1859A	.580	1.50	3.00	6.00	35.00

C#	Date	Mintage	Fine	VF	XF	Unc
45	1862A	Inc. Ab.	1.50	3.00	6.00	35.00
	1864A	Inc. Ab.	1.50	3.00	6.00	35.00

5 PFENNIG

COPPER

48	1872 B	.118	1.50	3.00	6.00	35.00

4 SCHILLINGE

3.2500 g, .375 SILVER, .0392 oz ASW

44	1846	.165	5.00	15.00	30.00	100.00
	1847	.170	5.00	15.00	30.00	100.00
	1849	.135	5.00	15.00	30.00	100.00

1/48 THALER

1.3000 g, .208 SILVER, .0086 oz ASW

43	1838	.145	2.00	4.00	10.00	40.00
	1841	.055	3.00	6.00	12.50	50.00
	1845	.097	2.00	4.00	10.00	40.00
	1847	.231	2.00	4.00	10.00	40.00

43a	1855A	.634	1.50	3.00	6.00	30.00
	1859A	.720	1.50	3.00	6.00	30.00

49	1862A	Inc. Ab.	1.50	3.00	6.00	30.00
	1864A	Inc. Ab.	1.50	3.00	6.00	30.00

EIN (1) THALER

18.5200 g, .900 SILVER, .5360 oz ASW

50	1870A	.050	25.00	40.00	85.00	175.00

MONETARY REFORM

2 MARK

11.1110 g, .900 SILVER, .3215 oz ASW

Y#	Date	Mintage	Fine	VF	XF	Unc
100	1877A	.100	125.00	250.00	1400.	2750.
	1877A	—	—	—	Proof	3000.

103	1905A	.010	135.00	300.00	575.00	750.00
	1905A	2,500	—	—	Proof	750.00

3 MARK

16.6670 g, .900 SILVER, .4823 oz ASW

106	1913A	7,000	200.00	400.00	800.00	1200.
	1913A	—	—	—	Proof	1200.

10 MARK

3.9820 g, .900 GOLD, .1152 oz AGW
Rev: Type I.

101	1873A	1,500	3500.	5000.	6500.	7500.
	1873A	—	—	—	Proof	13,000.

101a	1874A	3,000	2000.	4000.	5000.	7000.
	1880A	4,000	1500.	3250.	4000.	5000.

104	1905A	1,000	1500.	2250.	3000.	4500.
	1905A	150 pcs.	—	—	Proof	3750.

20 MARK

7.9650 g, .900 GOLD, .2304 oz AGW

102	1873A	6,750	1500.	2750.	4000.	6500.

Rev: Type II.

Y#	Date	Mintage	Fine	VF	XF	Unc
102a	1874A	6,000	1500.	2750.	4000.	6500.

Rev: Type III.

Y#	Date	Mintage	Fine	VF	XF	Unc
105	1905A	1,000	2000.	3000.	5000.	6000.
	1905A	160 pcs.	—	—	Proof	5500.

MUNSTER

BISHOPRIC

A Bishopric, located in Westphalia, was established c. 802. The first Munster coinage was struck c. 1228. In 1802 the bishopric was secularized and divided. From 1806-1810 most of Munster belonged to Berg, from 1810-1814 to France and from 1814 onward, to Prussia.

During the 16th and 17th centuries treasury tokens, mostly counterstamped with the arms or initials of the current treasurer were issued. These were replaced in the middle of the 17th century by Cathedral coins, showing St. Paul with a sword. They last appeared at the end of the 18th century.

RULERS

Maximilian Franz of Austria, 1784-1801
Sede Vacante, 1801
Anton Victor of Prussia, 1801-1802

1/24 THALER
(Reichs)

BILLON
Obv: Value. Rev: Date.

C#	Date	Mintage	Fine	VF	XF	Unc
40	1801	—	20.00	40.00	80.00	125.00

1/3 THALER
(Reichs)

SILVER

C#	Date	Mintage	Fine	VF	XF	Unc
41	1801	—	90.00	140.00	200.00	350.00

2/3 THALER
(Reichs)

SILVER

C#	Date	Mintage	Fine	VF	XF	Unc
42	1801	—	150.00	250.00	400.00	650.00

EIN (1) THALER
(Species)

SILVER

C#	Date	Mintage	Fine	VF	XF	Unc
43	1801	200 pcs.	750.00	1200.	2200.	4500.

NASSAU

The duchy of Nassau, located on both sides of the River Lahn in the Middle Rhineland was established in 1158. The lands were frequently divided and combined. The first coins were struck c. 1260. The Weilburg line was founded in 1355 and the Usingen line in 1642. In 1806 they united under a common administration. The Usingen line became extinct in 1816 leaving a fully united duchy under the Weilburg rulers. The house ended with the ouster of the duke in 1866 by Prussia.

JOINT COINAGE

Nassau-Weilburg & Nassau-Usingen

RULERS

Friedrich August, 1803-1816
Friedrich Wilhelm, 1788-1816

MINTMASTERS INITIALS

Letter	Date	Name
CT	—	Christian Teichmann

1/4 KREUZER

COPPER
Obv: Crowned arms, leg: HERZOGL NASS.
Rev: L below date.

C#	Date	Mintage	Fine	VF	XF	Unc
1	1808	.449	1.00	3.00	6.00	40.00

C#	Date	Mintage	Fine	VF	XF	Unc
1a	1808	Inc. Ab.	1.00	3.00	6.00	40.00
	1809	—	1.00	3.00	6.00	40.00
	1810	—	1.00	3.00	6.00	40.00
	1811	—	1.00	3.00	6.00	40.00
	1812	1.470	1.00	3.00	6.00	40.00
	1813	.280	1.00	3.00	6.00	40.00
	1814	.278	1.00	3.00	6.00	40.00

NOTE: Several varieties exist.

1/2 KREUZER

COPPER

C#	Date	Mintage	Fine	VF	XF	Unc
2	1813	.445	2.00	4.00	10.00	65.00

KREUZER

COPPER

C#	Date	Mintage	Fine	VF	XF	Unc
3	1808	.799	15.00	40.00	85.00	275.00
	1809	—	1.00	3.00	7.00	50.00

Rev: L below wreath.

C#	Date	Mintage	Fine	VF	XF	Unc
3a	1808	Inc. Ab.	15.00	40.00	85.00	275.00

Obv. leg: HERZ:

C#	Date	Mintage	Fine	VF	XF	Unc
3b	1809	—	5.00	10.00	25.00	100.00
	1810	—	3.00	5.00	15.00	50.00
	1813	.131	3.00	5.00	15.00	50.00

3 KREUZER
(1 Groschen)

1.3800 g, .281 SILVER, .0124 oz ASW
Obv. leg: HERZ. NASS. SCHEIDE.M.
Rev: Value.

C#	Date	Mintage	Fine	VF	XF	Unc
4a	1809	.010	10.00	25.00	80.00	200.00

Obv. leg: HERZ. NASSAU. SCHEIDEMUNZ.

C#	Date	Mintage	Fine	VF	XF	Unc
4	1810.	.750	7.00	20.00	40.00	125.00
	1811	—	10.00	30.00	60.00	150.00

Obv. leg: HERZ. NASSAU. SCHEIDE. M.

C#	Date	Mintage	Fine	VF	XF	Unc
4b	1811	.270	7.00	15.00	25.00	125.00
	1812	.480	5.00	10.00	20.00	100.00
	1813	.506	5.00	10.00	20.00	90.00
	1814	.844	2.50	5.00	10.00	40.00
	1815	.675	2.50	5.00	10.00	40.00
	1816	.091	2.50	5.00	10.00	40.00
	1817	.259	2.50	5.00	10.00	40.00
	1818	.675	2.50	5.00	10.00	40.00
	1819	.928	2.50	5.00	10.00	40.00

5 KREUZER

2.2200 g, .437 SILVER, .0311 oz ASW
Obv. leg: HERZ. NASSAU. . . . .

C#	Date	Mintage	Fine	VF	XF	Unc
5	1808	4,000	150.00	300.00	600.00	1000.
	1809	—	10.00	20.00	50.00	125.00

Obv. leg: HERZOGL. NASS. . . .

C#	Date	Mintage	Fine	VF	XF	Unc
5a	1808	Inc. Ab.	10.00	20.00	50.00	140.00

Obv. leg: HERZ. NASSAUISCHE.
Rev: Value, L below.

C#	Date	Mintage	Fine	VF	XF	Unc
5b	1808	—	10.00	20.00	50.00	140.00
	1809	—	10.00	20.00	50.00	140.00

10 KREUZER

3.8900 g, .500 SILVER, .0625 oz ASW
Obv. leg: HERZ. NASSAUISCHE CONVENTIONS MUNZ. Rev: L below value.

C#	Date	Mintage	Fine	VF	XF	Unc
6	1809	—	200.00	400.00	750.00	1250.

Obv. leg: HERZ. NASSAU. CONVENT. MUNZ.

C#	Date	Mintage	Fine	VF	XF	Unc
6a	1809	—	20.00	45.00	90.00	150.00

Obv. leg: HERZ. NASSAUISCHE. . . . .

C#	Date	Mintage	Fine	VF	XF	Unc
6b	1809	—	20.00	45.00	90.00	150.00

Obv. leg: HERZ. NASSAU. Rev: W/o L.

C#	Date	Mintage	Fine	VF	XF	Unc
6c	1809	—	20.00	45.00	90.00	150.00

20 KREUZER

6.6800 g, .583 SILVER, .1252 oz ASW
Obv. leg: HERZ. NASSAUISCHE CONVENTIONS MUNZ.

C#	Date	Mintage	Fine	VF	XF	Unc
7	1809	—	100.00	200.00	400.00	750.00

Obv. leg: HERZ. NASSAUISCHE CONVENT. MUNZ.

C#	Date	Mintage	Fine	VF	XF	Unc
7a	1809	—	20.00	40.00	60.00	125.00

Rev: Wreath w/o bow, running horse below.

C#	Date	Mintage	Fine	VF	XF	Unc
7b	1809	—	20.00	40.00	60.00	125.00

Rev: 60 between rosettes

C#	Date	Mintage	Fine	VF	XF	Unc
7c	1809	—	20.00	40.00	60.00	125.00

Obv. leg: . . . . .CONVENTIONS. Rev: Value within branches.

C#	Date	Mintage	Fine	VF	XF	Unc
7d	1809	—	20.00	40.00	60.00	125.00

Obv. leg: . . . . . .CONVENT. Rev: L below wreath.

C#	Date	Mintage	Fine	VF	XF	Unc
7e	1809	—	20.00	40.00	60.00	125.00

Rev: W/o bow on wreath, prancing horse below.

C#	Date	Mintage	Fine	VF	XF	Unc
7f	1809	—	20.00	40.00	60.00	125.00

Obv. leg: HERZ: NASS: CONV: MUNZ:

C#	Date	Mintage	Fine	VF	XF	Unc
7g	1809	—	20.00	40.00	60.00	125.00

TRADE COINAGE

DUCAT

3.5000 g, .986 GOLD, .1109 oz AGW

C#	Date	Mintage	Fine	VF	XF	Unc
8	1809	3,543	500.00	1000.	1600.	3000.

SEPARATE COINAGE

Nassau-Usingen

RULERS
Friedrich August, 1803-1816

10 KREUZER

3.8900 g, .500 SILVER, .0625 oz ASW

C#	Date	Mintage	Fine	VF	XF	Unc
9.1	1809	—	200.00	375.00	700.00	1200.

Obv: L at truncation.

C#	Date	Mintage	Fine	VF	XF	Unc
9.2	1809 L	—	200.00	375.00	700.00	1200.

20 KREUZER

6.6800 g, .583 SILVER, .1252 oz ASW
Obv: Head right, L at truncation. Rev: Crowned arms.

C#	Date	Mintage	Fine	VF	XF	Unc
10	1809 L	—	20.00	45.00	90.00	250.00

C#	Date	Mintage	Fine	VF	XF	Unc
10a	1809 L	—	20.00	45.00	90.00	250.00

1/2 THALER

(Convention)

14.0300 g, .833 SILVER, .3757 oz ASW

C#	Date	Mintage	Fine	VF	XF	Unc
11	1809 L	—	50.00	110.00	200.00	500.00

EIN (1) THALER

(Convention)

28.0600 g, .833 SILVER, .7515 oz ASW
Obv: Head right, L at truncation.
Rev: Similar to C#12c.

C#	Date	Mintage	Fine	VF	XF	Unc
12	1809 L	—	350.00	550.00	1200.	2500.

Rev: Date dividing C.T.

C#	Date	Mintage	Fine	VF	XF	Unc
12c	1810 CT	—	200.00	350.00	800.00	1600.
	1811 CT	—	200.00	275.00	600.00	1200.
	1812 CT	—	200.00	300.00	725.00	1500.
	1813 CT	.042	200.00	300.00	725.00	1500.
	1815 CT	—	200.00	300.00	725.00	1500.

Nassau-Weilburg

RULERS
Friedrich Wilhelm II, 1788-1816

10 KREUZER

3.8900 g, .500 SILVER, .0625 oz ASW

C#	Date	Mintage	Fine	VF	XF	Unc
30	1809	—	25.00	50.00	150.00	250.00

Obv: L at truncation.

C#	Date	Mintage	Fine	VF	XF	Unc
30a	1809	—	25.00	50.00	150.00	250.00

20 KREUZER

6.6800 g, .583 SILVER, .1252 oz ASW

C#	Date	Mintage	Fine	VF	XF	Unc
31	1809	—	25.00	50.00	150.00	250.00
	1810	—	25.00	50.00	150.00	250.00

1/2 THALER

(Convention)

14.0300 g, .833 SILVER, .3757 oz ASW
Obv: L on truncation.

C#	Date	Mintage	Fine	VF	XF	Unc
32	1809 L	—	80.00	160.00	250.00	350.00

EIN (1) THALER

(Convention)

28.0600 g, .833 SILVER, .7515 oz ASW
Obv: L on truncation.

C#	Date	Mintage	Fine	VF	XF	Unc
33	1809 L	—	450.00	850.00	1700.	3400.

Rev: Arms between laurel and palm branches.

C#	Date	Mintage	Fine	VF	XF	Unc
33a	1809 L	—	450.00	850.00	1700.	3400.

Obv: L on truncation.
Rev: Date dividing C.T.

C#	Date	Mintage	Fine	VF	XF	Unc
33b	1810 CT	—	175.00	375.00	900.00	1900.
	1811 CT	—	175.00	275.00	700.00	1500.
	1812 CT	—	175.00	375.00	900.00	1900.

Obv: Long bust.

C#	Date	Mintage	Fine	VF	XF	Unc
33d	1811 CT	—	175.00	275.00	700.00	1500.

C#	Date	Mintage	Fine	VF	XF	Unc
33c	1813 CT	.042	275.00	450.00	1000.	2000.
	1815 CT	—	300.00	560.00	1150.	2400.

United Nassau

RULERS

Duke Wilhelm, 1816-1839
Duke Adolph, 1839-1866

MINTMASTERS INITIALS

Letter	Date	Name
CT	1816-1825	Christian Teichmann

HELLER

COPPER
Obv: Crowned arms. Rev: Value.

C#	Date	Mintage	Fine	VF	XF	Unc
51	1842	.182	2.00	4.00	8.00	35.00

PFENNIG

COPPER

C#	Date	Mintage	Fine	VF	XF	Unc
52	1859	.220	2.00	4.00	8.00	35.00
	1860	.580	2.00	4.00	8.00	35.00
	1862	.490	2.00	4.00	8.00	35.00

1/4 KREUZER

COPPER

C#	Date	Mintage	Fine	VF	XF	Unc
35	1817.	.433	1.00	2.00	4.00	20.00
	1818.	.894	1.00	2.00	4.00	20.00
	1819.	4.932	1.00	2.00	4.00	20.00

Rev: W/o period after date.

C#	Date	Mintage	Fine	VF	XF	Unc
35a	1817	Inc. Ab.	1.00	2.00	4.00	20.00
	1818	—	1.00	2.00	4.00	20.00
	1819	Inc. Ab.	1.00	2.00	4.00	20.00
	1822	4.210	1.00	2.00	4.00	20.00

NOTE: Several varieties exist.

EIN (1) KREUZER

COPPER, 22-24mm
Obv: Crowned spade-shaped arms.
Rev: Value in wreath.

C#	Date	Mintage	Fine	VF	XF	Unc
36	1817	.203	1.00	3.00	6.00	30.00
	1818	.084	1.00	3.00	6.00	30.00

.5300 g, .229 SILVER, .0039 oz ASW
Rev: W/o wreath.

C#	Date	Mintage	Fine	VF	XF	Unc
38	1817	.079	1.00	3.00	6.00	30.00
	1823	.545	1.00	3.00	6.00	30.00
	1824	.564	1.00	3.00	6.00	30.00
	1828	—	1.00	3.00	6.00	30.00

COPPER, 22-24mm

C#	Date	Mintage	Fine	VF	XF	Unc
37	1830	.265	1.00	3.00	6.00	30.00
	1832	.517	1.00	3.00	6.00	30.00
	1834	.326	1.00	3.00	6.00	30.00
	1836	.200	1.00	3.00	6.00	30.00
	1838	.269	1.00	3.00	6.00	30.00

.5300 g, .229 SILVER, .0039 oz ASW

C#	Date	Mintage	Fine	VF	XF	Unc
39	1832	.144	1.00	3.00	6.00	30.00
	1833	1.037	1.00	3.00	6.00	30.00
	1835	.408	1.00	3.00	6.00	30.00

COPPER

C#	Date	Mintage	Fine	VF	XF	Unc
53	1842	.480	1.00	3.00	6.00	30.00
	1844	.188	1.00	3.00	6.00	30.00
	1848	.249	1.00	3.00	6.00	30.00
	1854	.274	1.00	3.00	6.00	30.00
	1855	—	1.00	3.00	6.00	30.00
	1856	.357	1.00	3.00	6.00	30.00

C#	Date	Mintage	Fine	VF	XF	Unc
54	1859	.836	1.00	3.00	6.00	30.00
	1860	.610	1.00	3.00	6.00	30.00
	1861	.556	1.00	3.00	6.00	30.00
	1862	.610	1.00	3.00	6.00	30.00
	1863	.576	1.00	3.00	6.00	30.00

.5300 g, .229 SILVER, .0039 oz ASW

C#	Date	Mintage	Fine	VF	XF	Unc
55	1861	.664	1.00	3.00	6.00	30.00

3 KREUZER

1.3800 g, .281 SILVER, .0124 oz ASW
Obv: Crowned spade-shaped arms, NASSAU.
Rev: Value.

C#	Date	Mintage	Fine	VF	XF	Unc
40	1817	.259	2.50	5.00	10.00	40.00
	1818	.675	2.50	5.00	10.00	40.00
	1819	.928	2.50	5.00	10.00	40.00

C#	Date	Mintage	Fine	VF	XF	Unc
40a	1822	.671	2.50	5.00	10.00	40.00
	1823	.671	2.50	5.00	10.00	40.00
	1824	—	2.50	5.00	10.00	40.00
	1825	.192	2.50	5.00	10.00	40.00
	1826	.352	2.50	5.00	10.00	40.00
	1827	.308	2.50	5.00	10.00	40.00
	1828	.308	2.50	5.00	10.00	40.00

1.2900 g, .281 SILVER, .0116 oz ASW

C#	Date	Mintage	Fine	VF	XF	Unc
41	1831	.509	2.50	5.00	10.00	40.00
	1832	.388	2.50	5.00	10.00	40.00
	1833	.042	2.50	5.00	10.00	40.00
	1834	.292	2.50	5.00	10.00	40.00
	1836	.340	2.50	5.00	10.00	40.00

1.2900 g, .333 SILVER, .0138 oz ASW

C#	Date	Mintage	Fine	VF	XF	Unc
56	1841	—	60.00	100.00	150.00	225.00
	1842	.112	2.00	4.00	8.00	35.00
	1844	.056	2.00	4.00	8.00	35.00
	1845	—	2.00	4.00	8.00	35.00
	1847	.210	2.00	4.00	8.00	35.00
	1848	.541	2.00	4.00	8.00	35.00
	1853	.091	2.00	4.00	8.00	35.00
	1855	.179	2.00	4.00	8.00	35.00

6 KREUZER

2.2200 g, .375 SILVER, .0267 oz ASW
Obv: Crowned square arms, leg: NASSAUISCHE.
Rev: Value in wreath.

C#	Date	Mintage	Fine	VF	XF	Unc
42	1817	.109	3.00	6.00	12.00	40.00
	1818	.263	3.00	6.00	12.00	40.00
	1819	.378	3.00	6.00	12.00	40.00

Obv. leg: NASSAU.

C#	Date	Mintage	Fine	VF	XF	Unc
42a	1822	.306	3.00	6.00	12.00	40.00
	1823	.306	3.00	6.00	12.00	40.00
	1824	.083	4.00	8.00	15.00	50.00
	1825	.176	3.00	6.00	12.00	40.00
	1826	.314	3.00	6.00	12.00	40.00
	1827	.302	3.00	6.00	12.00	40.00
	1828	.303	3.00	6.00	12.00	40.00

C#	Date	Mintage	Fine	VF	XF	Unc
43	1831	1.100	3.00	6.00	12.00	40.00
	1832	.377	3.00	6.00	12.00	40.00
	1833	.641	3.00	6.00	12.00	40.00
	1834	.565	3.00	6.00	12.00	40.00
	1835	.832	3.00	6.00	12.00	40.00
	1836	.452	3.00	6.00	12.00	40.00
	1837	.314	3.00	6.00	12.00	40.00

2.5900 g, .333 SILVER, .0277 oz ASW

C#	Date	Mintage	Fine	VF	XF	Unc
43a	1838	.201	3.00	6.00	12.00	40.00
	1839	.109	3.00	6.00	12.00	40.00

C#	Date	Mintage	Fine	VF	XF	Unc
57	1840	.094	4.00	8.00	15.00	50.00
	1841	.321	3.00	6.00	12.00	40.00
	1844	.073	4.00	8.00	15.00	50.00
	1846	—	3.00	6.00	12.00	40.00
	1847	—	3.00	6.00	12.00	40.00
	1848	.198	3.00	6.00	12.00	40.00
	1855	.190	3.00	6.00	12.00	40.00

1/2 GULDEN

5.3000 g, .900 SILVER, .1533 oz ASW

C#	Date	Mintage	Fine	VF	XF	Unc
44	1838	.108	20.00	40.00	75.00	150.00
	1839	.108	20.00	40.00	75.00	150.00

C#	Date	Mintage	Fine	VF	XF	Unc
58	1840	.095	20.00	40.00	75.00	150.00
	1841	.125	20.00	40.00	75.00	150.00
	1842	.031	20.00	40.00	75.00	150.00
	1843	.104	20.00	40.00	75.00	150.00
	1844	.117	20.00	40.00	75.00	150.00
	1845	.072	20.00	40.00	75.00	150.00

Obv: Head left.

C#	Date	Mintage	Fine	VF	XF	Unc
59	1856	.313	20.00	40.00	75.00	150.00
	1860	.104	20.00	40.00	75.00	150.00

GULDEN

10.6000 g, .900 SILVER, .3067 oz ASW

C#	Date	Mintage	Fine	VF	XF	Unc
45	1838	.190	25.00	50.00	100.00	250.00
	1839	.108	25.00	50.00	100.00	250.00

Obv: ZOLLMANN on truncation.

C#	Date	Mintage	Fine	VF	XF	Unc
60	1840	.117	25.00	50.00	100.00	175.00
	1841	.124	25.00	50.00	100.00	175.00
	1842	.020	25.00	50.00	100.00	175.00
	1843	.236	25.00	50.00	100.00	175.00
	1844	.093	25.00	50.00	100.00	175.00
	1845	.138	25.00	50.00	100.00	175.00
	1846	.048	25.00	50.00	100.00	175.00
	1847	.231	25.00	50.00	100.00	175.00
	1855	.188	25.00	50.00	100.00	175.00

C#	Date	Mintage	Fine	VF	XF	Unc
61	1855	Inc. Ab.	25.00	50.00	100.00	200.00
	1856	.040	25.00	50.00	100.00	200.00

ZWEY (2) GULDEN

21.2100 g, .900 SILVER, .6138 oz ASW
Obv: ZOLLMANN on truncation.

C#	Date	Mintage	Fine	VF	XF	Unc
65	1846	.177	50.00	125.00	300.00	800.00
	1847	.088	60.00	150.00	350.00	875.00

EIN (1) THALER

(Krone)

29.5300 g, .871 SILVER, .8270 oz ASW
Obv: Head right, L below. Rev: Crowned draped arms, date below dividing C.T.

C#	Date	Mintage	Fine	VF	XF	Unc
46	1816 CT	—	—	—	Rare	—

C#	Date	Mintage	Fine	VF	XF	Unc
47	1817 CT-L	.013	250.00	500.00	1200.	2500.

Obv: Similar to C#49 w/P.Z. on truncation.

C#	Date	Mintage	Fine	VF	XF	Unc
48	1818 CT	4,500	250.00	500.00	1200.	2400.
	1825 CT	2,000	300.00	600.00	1400.	2800.

Obv: ZOLLMANN. F on truncation.

C#	Date	Mintage	Fine	VF	XF	Unc
49	1831	9,385	200.00	350.00	500.00	1400.
	1832	567 pcs.	125.00	225.00	350.00	800.00
	1833	—	125.00	225.00	350.00	800.00
	1836	—	125.00	225.00	350.00	800.00
	1837	2,683	125.00	225.00	350.00	800.00

Visit of Duke to the Mint
Obv: Similar to C#49

C#	Date	Mintage	Fine	VF	XF	Unc
49a	1831	Inc. Ab.	500.00	900.00	1600.	2400.

(Vereins)

18.5200 g, .900 SILVER, .5360 oz ASW
Obv: Z on truncation.

C#	Date	Mintage	Fine	VF	XF	Unc
62	1859 Z	.050	45.00	80.00	175.00	400.00
	1860 Z	.030	45.00	80.00	175.00	400.00

Obv: F. KORN on truncation.

C#	Date	Mintage	Fine	VF	XF	Unc
62a	1863	.145	45.00	80.00	200.00	500.00

Visit of Duke to Mint

63	1861	3 pcs.	—	—	Proof 12,000.	

25th Anniversary of Reign

64	1864	6,162	35.00	55.00	115.00	190.00

ZWEI (2) THALER

(3-1/2 Gulden)

37.1200 g, .900 SILVER, 1.0742 oz ASW
Obv: Similar to C#67a, ZOLLMANN on truncation.

66	1840	.056	250.00	450.00	1000.	2000.

C#	Date	Mintage	Fine	VF	XF	Unc
67a	1844	.021	175.00	300.00	650.00	1400.
	1847	—	—	—	Rare	—

Obv: Truncation bare.

67	1844	Inc. Ab.	175.00	300.00	650.00	1400.
	1854	.072	175.00	300.00	600.00	1250.

37.0400 g, .900 SILVER, 1.0719 oz ASW
Obv: C ZOLLMANN on truncation.

68	1860	.130	125.00	225.00	400.00	1000.

TRADE COINAGE

DUCAT

3.5000 g, .986 GOLD, .1109 oz AGW
Obv: Head right. Rev: Crowned draped arms.

50	1818 CT	501 pcs.	650.00	1150.	2150.	4000.

NURNBERG

Nurnberg, in Franconia, was made a Free City in 1219. In that same year an Imperial mint was established there and continued throughout the rest of the century. The mint right was obtained in 1376 and again in 1422. City coins were struck from c. 1390 to 1806 when the city was made part of Bavaria.

MINTMASTERS INITIALS

K.R. - Georg Knoll and Riedner

PFENNIG

BILLON, uniface
State shield between branches above value and date.

10	1806	—	3.00	7.00	15.00	40.00

NOTE: Earlier date (1799) exists for this type.

Oval state shield w/garland draped above urn, value below date.

10a	1806	—	3.00	7.00	15.00	40.00

Oval state shield, garland w/loop above value and date.

10b	1806	—	3.00	7.00	15.00	40.00

Garland hanging from urn on pedestal above state shield, value and date below.

11	1806	—	3.00	7.00	15.00	40.00
	1807	—	3.00	7.00	15.00	40.00

State shield in front of altar, value and date below.

C#	Date	Mintage	Fine	VF	XF	Unc
11a	1806	—	3.00	7.00	15.00	40.00
	1807	—	3.00	7.00	15.00	40.00

KREUZER

BILLON
Obv: Pyramid w/city arms; date below.
Rev: City view.

C#	Date	Mintage	VG	Fine	VF	XF
36	1806	—	2.50	4.00	9.00	20.00

Rev: Rose bush.

36a	1806	—	2.25	3.00	7.50	20.00

Obv: Spade arms w/mural crown and garlands.

37	1806	—	2.25	3.00	7.50	20.00
	1807	—	2.25	3.00	7.50	20.00

Obv: Pyramid w/city arms; date below.
Rev: City view.

38	1807	—	4.00	6.50	10.00	20.00

3 KREUZER

BILLON
Obv: Crowned shield w/garland.
Rev: Value within wreath, date below.

C#	Date	Mintage	Fine	VF	XF	Unc
44	1806	—	2.00	6.00	15.00	50.00

Rev. leg: NURNB: SCHEIDE MUNZ.

44a	1806	—	2.00	6.00	15.00	50.00
	1807	—	2.00	6.00	15.00	50.00

6 KREUZER

BILLON

51	1806	—	4.00	8.00	15.00	50.00
	1807	—	4.00	8.00	15.00	50.00

TRADE COINAGE

DUCAT

3.5000 g, .986 GOLD, .1109 oz AGW

89	1806 KR	—	200.00	400.00	650.00	1000.

2 DUCAT

7.0000 g, .986 GOLD, .2219 oz AGW
Obv: City view. Rev: Lamb w/flag.

90	1806 KR	—	450.00	1000.	1900.	3200.

3 DUCAT

10.5000 g, .986 GOLD, .3329 oz AGW
Obv: City view. Rev: Lamb w/flag.

—	1806 KR	—	1000.	2100.	3600.	6000.

OLDENBURG

The county of Oldenburg, located on the North Sea, near Friesland was established in 1180. The first coins were struck c. 1290. It was ruled by Denmark from 1667 to 1773 and was raised to the status of duchy in 1777. The Bishopric of Lubeck was joined to it in 1803 and the territory was annexed to France in 1810. The 1815 Congress of Vienna elevated Oldenburg to grand duchy. They entered the German Empire in 1871 and remained there until the grand duke abdicated in 1918.

RULERS

Peter Friedrich Wilhelm, 1785-1823
Peter Friedrich Ludwig, 1823-1829
Paul Friedrich August, 1829-1853
Nicolaus Friedrich Peter, 1853-1900
Friedrich August, 1900-1918

MINTMASTERS INITIALS

I.H.M. - Johann Heinrich Madelung

N - Samuel Mathias Neudorf
B - Johann Ephraim Bauert

SCHWAREN

COPPER

C#	Date	Mintage	Fine	VF	XF	Unc
43	1846	.126	2.50	5.00	10.00	45.00

Rev: B below date.

C#	Date	Mintage	Fine	VF	XF	Unc
43a	1852 B	.144	1.50	3.00	6.00	40.00

C#	Date	Mintage	Fine	VF	XF	Unc
54	1854 B	.072	2.00	4.00	8.00	45.00
	1856 B	.072	2.00	4.00	8.00	45.00

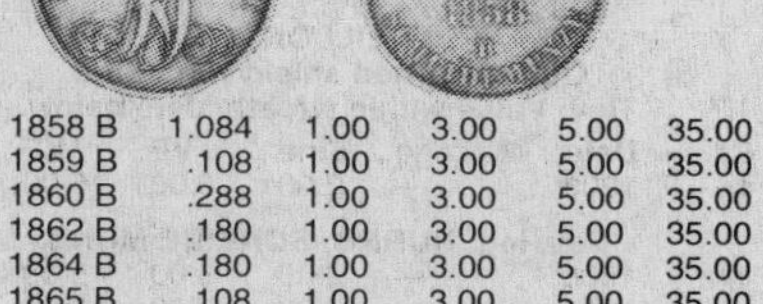

C#	Date	Mintage	Fine	VF	XF	Unc
55	1858 B	1.084	1.00	3.00	5.00	35.00
	1859 B	.108	1.00	3.00	5.00	35.00
	1860 B	.288	1.00	3.00	5.00	35.00
	1862 B	.180	1.00	3.00	5.00	35.00
	1864 B	.180	1.00	3.00	5.00	35.00
	1865 B	.108	1.00	3.00	5.00	35.00
	1866 B	.144	1.00	3.00	5.00	35.00
	1869 B	.180	1.00	3.00	5.00	35.00

3 SCHWAREN

(3 Pfennig)

COPPER

C#	Date	Mintage	Fine	VF	XF	Unc
57	1858 B	.372	1.00	3.00	6.00	35.00
	1859 B	.432	1.00	3.00	6.00	35.00
	1860 B	.060	2.00	4.00	8.00	45.00
	1862 B	.012	2.00	4.00	8.00	45.00
	1864 B	.060	2.00	4.00	8.00	45.00
	1865 B	.060	2.00	4.00	8.00	45.00
	1866 B	.036	2.00	4.00	8.00	45.00
	1869 B	.096	2.00	4.00	8.00	45.00

1/4 GROTE

(1 Pfennig)

COPPER

C#	Date	Mintage	Fine	VF	XF	Unc
44	1846	.090	2.50	5.00	10.00	50.00

1/2 GROTE

COPPER

C#	Date	Mintage	Fine	VF	XF	Unc
25	1802	.078	3.00	7.00	15.00	70.00
	1816	.149	3.00	7.00	15.00	60.00

C#	Date	Mintage	Fine	VF	XF	Unc
45	1831	.072	2.00	5.00	10.00	50.00
	1835	.075	2.00	5.00	10.00	50.00

C#	Date	Mintage	Fine	VF	XF	Unc
45a	1840	.122	2.00	5.00	10.00	50.00

C#	Date	Mintage	Fine	VF	XF	Unc
46	1846	.088	2.00	5.00	10.00	55.00

C#	Date	Mintage	Fine	VF	XF	Unc
56	1853 B	.072	2.00	4.00	7.00	45.00
	1856 B	.072	2.00	4.00	7.00	45.00

GROTE

.9700 g, .208 SILVER, .0064 oz ASW
Obv: Crowned arms w/garland, N.D.C.F.

C#	Date	Mintage	Fine	VF	XF	Unc
28	1817	.391	4.00	7.00	25.00	85.00

.9200 g, .218 SILVER, .0064 oz ASW
Obv. leg: SCHEIDE-M.

C#	Date	Mintage	Fine	VF	XF	Unc
47	1836 B	.361	3.00	6.00	20.00	75.00

C#	Date	Mintage	Fine	VF	XF	Unc
48	1849 B	.043	2.00	5.00	15.00	60.00
	1850 B	.081	2.00	4.00	10.00	50.00

C#	Date	Mintage	Fine	VF	XF	Unc
58	1853 B	.057	2.00	4.00	10.00	45.00
	1856 B	.072	2.00	4.00	10.00	45.00
	1857 B	.027	2.00	4.00	10.00	45.00

2 GROTE

(1/36 Thaler)

1.3900 g, .291 SILVER, .0130 oz ASW
Obv. leg: N.D.C.F.

C#	Date	Mintage	Fine	VF	XF	Unc
33	1815	1.080	5.00	15.00	30.00	150.00

3 GROTE

(1/24 Thaler)

1.9400 g, .312 SILVER, .0194 oz ASW

C#	Date	Mintage	Fine	VF	XF	Unc
49	1840 S	.486	3.00	6.00	20.00	80.00

C#	Date	Mintage	Fine	VF	XF	Unc
61	1856 B	.156	3.00	6.00	15.00	75.00

4 GROTE

(1/18 Thaler)

2.3900 g, .340 SILVER, .0261 oz ASW
Obv: Crowned arms w/garlands, N.D.C.F. Rev: Value.

C#	Date	Mintage	Fine	VF	XF	Unc
35	1816	.393	3.00	5.00	10.00	50.00
	1818	.126	3.00	5.00	10.00	50.00

C#	Date	Mintage	Fine	VF	XF	Unc
50	1840 S	.380	3.00	5.00	10.00	50.00

6 GROTE

(1/12 Thaler)

3.5700 g, .340 SILVER, .0390 oz ASW

C#	Date	Mintage	Fine	VF	XF	Unc
37	1816	.309	3.00	7.00	20.00	75.00
	1818	.060	3.00	7.00	20.00	75.00

12 GROTE

(1/6 Thaler)

4.8700 g, .520 SILVER, .0783 oz ASW

C#	Date	Mintage	Fine	VF	XF	Unc
39	1816	.036	6.00	15.00	25.00	100.00
	1818	.066	6.00	15.00	25.00	100.00

1/2 GROSCHEN

1.0900 g, .220 SILVER, .0077 oz ASW

C#	Date	Mintage	Fine	VF	XF	Unc
59	1858 B	1.020	1.50	3.50	10.00	30.00
	1864 B	.060	2.00	5.00	12.00	40.00
	1865 B	.048	2.00	5.00	12.00	40.00
	1866 B	.168	2.00	5.00	12.00	35.00
	1869 B	.120	2.00	5.00	12.00	35.00

GROSCHEN

2.1900 g, .220 SILVER, .0154 oz ASW

C#	Date	Mintage	Fine	VF	XF	Unc
60	1858 B	.720	3.00	5.00	10.00	60.00

C#	Date	Mintage	Fine	VF	XF	Unc
60a	1858 B	1.080	3.00	5.00	10.00	50.00
	1864 B	.030	3.00	5.00	10.00	60.00
	1865 B	.030	3.00	5.00	10.00	60.00
	1866 B	.120	3.00	5.00	10.00	60.00
	1869 B	.090	3.00	5.00	10.00	60.00

2-1/2 GROSCHEN

(1/12 Thaler)

3.2200 g, .375 SILVER, .0388 oz ASW

C#	Date	Mintage	Fine	VF	XF	Unc
62	1858 B	.600	3.00	7.00	20.00	80.00

1/6 THALER

5.3500 g, .520 SILVER, .0894 oz ASW

C#	Date	Mintage	Fine	VF	XF	Unc
51	1846 B	.164	25.00	50.00	100.00	225.00

1/3 THALER

7.7900 g, .625 SILVER, .1565 oz ASW

C#	Date	Mintage	Fine	VF	XF	Unc
41	1816	.018	60.00	100.00	300.00	450.00
	1818	.033	50.00	80.00	250.00	400.00

EIN (1) THALER

22.2700 g, .750 SILVER, .5370 oz ASW

C#	Date	Mintage	Fine	VF	XF	Unc
52	1846 B	.042	75.00	125.00	500.00	1250.

18.5200 g, .900 SILVER, .5360 oz ASW

C#	Date	Mintage	Fine	VF	XF	Unc
63	1858 B	.017	70.00	130.00	225.00	450.00
	1860 B	.047	60.00	120.00	180.00	375.00
	1866 B	.072	50.00	100.00	150.00	300.00

2 THALER

(3-1/2 Gulden)

37.1200 g, .900 SILVER, 1.0742 oz ASW

C#	Date	Mintage	Fine	VF	XF	Unc
53	1840	.019	700.00	1250.	2500.	4750.
	1840	—	—	—	Proof	4500.

MONETARY REFORM

2 MARK

11.1110 g, .900 SILVER, .3215 oz ASW

Y#	Date	Mintage	Fine	VF	XF	Unc
108	1891A	.100	125.00	250.00	400.00	650.00
	1891A	—	—	—	Proof	650.00

Y#	Date	Mintage	Fine	VF	XF	Unc
109	1900A	.050	100.00	200.00	450.00	850.00
	1900A	—	—	—	Proof	900.00
	1901A	.075	85.00	200.00	450.00	850.00
	1901A	260 pcs.	—	—	Proof	900.00

5 MARK

27.7770 g, .900 SILVER, .8038 oz ASW

Y#	Date	Mintage	Fine	VF	XF	Unc
110	1900A	.020	225.00	500.00	1500.	2500.
	1900A	—	—	—	Proof	3000.
	1901A	.010	250.00	700.00	1600.	3250.
	1901A	170 pcs.	—	—	Proof	3500.

10 MARK

3.9820 g, .900 GOLD, .1152 oz AGW

Y#	Date	Mintage	Fine	VF	XF	Unc
107	1874B	.015	750.00	1250.	2000.	3750.
	1874B	—	—	—	Proof	Rare

OSNABRUCK

The city of Osnabruck is located northeast of Munster. Although the city owed its original growth to the bishopric it achieved considerable independence from the bishops and joined the Hanseatic League. It had its own local coinage from the early 16th century until 1805. It was absorbed by Hannover in 1803.

CITY

HELLER

COPPER

Obv: Wheel. Rev: Value, date below.

C#	Date	Mintage	Fine	VF	XF	Unc
1a	1801	—	3.00	7.00	15.00	75.00

NOTE: Earlier dates (1791-1795) exist for this type.

1-1/2 PFENNING

COPPER

C#	Date	Mintage	Fine	VF	XF	Unc
5	1805	—	3.00	7.00	15.00	75.00

NOTE: Earlier dates (1791-1795) exist for this type.

2 PFENNING

COPPER

Similar to 3 Pfennig, C#11.

C#	Date	Mintage	Fine	VF	XF	Unc
7	1801	—	4.00	8.00	20.00	100.00
	1802	—	4.00	8.00	20.00	100.00
	1803	—	4.00	8.00	20.00	100.00
	1804	—	4.00	8.00	20.00	100.00
	1805	—	4.00	8.00	20.00	100.00

NOTE: Earlier dates (1791-1800) exist for this type.

3 PFENNING

COPPER

C#	Date	Mintage	Fine	VF	XF	Unc
11	1805	—	7.50	15.00	35.00	120.00

PFALZ

(Rhenish Palatinate, Rheinpfalz)

The office of count palatine of the Rhine is first mentioned in the 10th century and the first coins were struck in the 11th century. There were many divisions. The lines of Neuburg, Sulzbach, Zweibrucken and Birkenfeld were founded in 1569 and were culminated in Maximilian Josef of Zweibrucken who became king and elector of Bavaria by 1805.

Rhein Pfalz

RULERS

Maximilian Joseph,
Elector of Pfalz-Bayern,
1799-1805

1/2 KREUZER

COPPER

Obv: Crowned shield w/lion, dividing RP.
Rev: Value and date within wreath.

C#	Date	Mintage	Fine	VF	XF	Unc
1	1802	—	6.00	12.00	30.00	135.00

KREUZER

COPPER

Obv: Crowned shield w/lion, dividing RP.
Rev: Value and date within wreath.

C#	Date	Mintage	Fine	VF	XF	Unc
2	1802	—	7.00	15.00	30.00	160.00

EIN (1) THALER

(Convention)

SILVER

Obv: Head right.
Rev: Crowned shield within branches.

C#	Date	Mintage	Fine	VF	XF	Unc
3	1802	—	2500.	4000.	6500.	10,000.

POMERANIA

A duchy on the Baltic Sea, near modern day Poland, was founded in the late 11th century. After many divisions, Pomerania was annexed to Sweden in 1637. BrandenburgPrussia had an interest in the area and slowly acquired bits until in 1815 all of Pomerania belonged to Prussia. The arms of Pomerania appear on coins of BrandenburgPrussia from the 17th century onward.

RULERS

Gustav IV Adolf of Sweden, 1792-1809

3 PFENNINGE

COPPER

Obv: Griffon left w/sceptor, K.S.P.L.M. above.
Rev: Value above date.

C#	Date	Mintage	VG	Fine	VF	XF
29	1806	.384	3.00	6.00	10.00	25.00
	1808	.258	3.00	6.00	10.00	25.00

NOTE: Earlier date (1792) exists for this type.

Obv. leg: "K. SCHWED. POM. LANDES M".

C#	Date	Mintage	VG	Fine	VF	XF
30	1806	—	—	—	Rare	—

Obv. leg: "K.S.P. LANDESM".

C#	Date	Mintage	VG	Fine	VF	XF
31	1808	—	—	—	Rare	—

PRUSSIA

The Kingdom of Prussia, located in north central Germany, came into being in 1701. The ruler received the title of King in Prussia in exchange for his support during the War of the Spanish Succession. During the Napoleonic Wars, Prussia allied itself with Saxony. When they were defeated in 1806 they were forced to cede a large portion of their territory. In 1813 the French were expelled and their territories were returned to them plus additional territories. After defeating Denmark and Austria, in 1864 and 1866 they acquired more territory. Prussia was the pivotal state of unification of Germany in 1871 and their King was proclaimed emperor of all Germany. World War I brought an end to the Empire and the Kingdom of Prussia in 1918.

RULERS

Friedrich Wilhelm III, 1797-1840
Friedrich Wilhelm IV, 1840-1861
Wilhelm I, 1861-1888
Friedrich III, March 1888-June 1888
Wilhelm II, 1888-1918

MINT MARKS

A - Berlin = Prussia, East Friesland, East Prussia, Posen
B - Bayreuth = Brandenburg-Ansbach Bayreuth
B - Breslau = Silesia, Posen, South Prussia
C - = Cleve
D - Aurich = East Friesland, Prussia
E - Konigsberg = East Prussia
F - Magdeburg
G - Stettin
G - Schwerin, Plon-Rethwisch Mint, 1763 only
S - Schwabach = Brandenburg Ansbach-Bayreuth
Star - Dresden

PFENNIG

COPPER
Mint mark: A

C#	Date	Mintage	VG	Fine	VF	XF
95	1801	—	1.50	3.00	5.00	10.00
	1804	—	1.50	3.00	5.00	10.00
	1806	—	1.50	3.00	5.00	10.00

NOTE: Earlier date (1799) exists for this type.

BILLON
Obv: Crowned FRW monogram.

C#	Date	Mintage	VG	Fine	VF	XF
100	1801	—	1.50	3.00	5.00	10.00
	1802	—	1.50	3.00	5.00	10.00
	1803	—	1.50	3.00	5.00	10.00
	1804	—	1.50	3.00	5.00	10.00

NOTE: Earlier date (1799) exists for this type.

Obv: Smaller W in crowned FRW monogram.

C#	Date	Mintage	VG	Fine	VF	XF
100a	1804	—	1.50	3.00	5.00	10.00
	1806	—	1.50	3.00	5.00	10.00

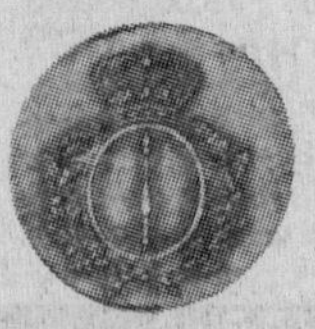

COPPER
Brandenburg Provincial Issue

C#	Date	Mintage	Fine	VF	XF	Unc
97	1810	—	2.50	5.00	10.00	40.00
	1811	—	2.50	5.00	10.00	40.00
	1814	—	2.50	5.00	10.00	40.00
	1816	—	2.50	5.00	10.00	40.00

C#	Date	Mintage	Fine	VF	XF	Unc
123	1821	—	1.50	3.00	6.00	35.00
	1822	—	1.50	3.00	6.00	35.00
	1825	—	1.50	3.00	6.00	35.00
	1826	—	1.50	3.00	6.00	35.00
	1827	—	1.50	3.00	6.00	35.00
	1828	—	1.50	3.00	6.00	35.00
	1832	—	1.50	3.00	6.00	35.00
	1833	—	1.50	3.00	6.00	35.00
	1835	—	1.50	3.00	6.00	35.00
	1836	—	1.50	3.00	6.00	35.00
123	1837	—	1.50	3.00	6.00	35.00
	1838	—	1.50	3.00	6.00	35.00
	1839	—	1.50	3.00	6.00	35.00
	1840	—	1.50	3.00	6.00	35.00

Mint mark: B

C#	Date	Mintage	Fine	VF	XF	Unc
123a	1821	—	2.00	4.00	8.00	40.00
	1822	—	2.00	4.00	8.00	40.00
123b	1826	—	2.00	4.00	8.00	40.00

Mint mark: D

C#	Date	Mintage	Fine	VF	XF	Unc
123c	1821	—	1.50	3.00	6.00	40.00
	1822	—	1.50	3.00	6.00	40.00
	1823	—	1.50	3.00	6.00	40.00
	1824	—	1.50	3.00	6.00	40.00
	1825	—	1.50	3.00	6.00	40.00
	1826	—	1.50	3.00	6.00	40.00
	1827	—	1.50	3.00	6.00	40.00
	1828	—	1.50	3.00	6.00	40.00
	1829	—	1.50	3.00	6.00	40.00
	1830	—	1.50	3.00	6.00	40.00
	1831	—	1.50	3.00	6.00	40.00
	1832	—	1.50	3.00	6.00	40.00
	1833	—	1.50	3.00	6.00	40.00
	1834	—	1.50	3.00	6.00	40.00
	1835	—	1.50	3.00	6.00	40.00
	1836	—	1.50	3.00	6.00	40.00
	1837	—	1.50	3.00	6.00	40.00
	1838	—	1.50	3.00	6.00	40.00
	1839	—	1.50	3.00	6.00	40.00
	1840	—	1.50	3.00	6.00	40.00

Mint mark: A

C#	Date	Mintage	Fine	VF	XF	Unc
136	1841	—	.75	1.50	4.00	35.00
	1842	—	.75	1.50	4.00	35.00

Mint mark: D

C#	Date	Mintage	Fine	VF	XF	Unc
136a	1841	—	.75	1.50	4.00	35.00
	1842	—	.75	1.50	4.00	35.00

Mint mark: A

C#	Date	Mintage	Fine	VF	XF	Unc
140	1843	—	.75	1.50	4.00	35.00
	1844	—	.75	1.50	4.00	35.00
	1845	—	.75	1.50	4.00	35.00

Mint mark: D

C#	Date	Mintage	Fine	VF	XF	Unc
140a	1844	—	.75	1.50	4.00	35.00
	1845	—	.75	1.50	4.00	35.00

Mint mark: A

C#	Date	Mintage	Fine	VF	XF	Unc
140b	1846	—	.75	1.50	4.00	30.00
	1847	—	.75	1.50	4.00	30.00
	1848	—	.75	1.50	4.00	30.00
	1849	—	.75	1.50	4.00	30.00
	1850	—	.75	1.50	4.00	30.00
	1851	—	.75	1.50	4.00	30.00
	1852	—	.75	1.50	4.00	30.00
	1853	—	.75	1.50	4.00	30.00
	1854	—	.75	1.50	4.00	30.00
	1855	—	.75	1.50	4.00	30.00
	1856	—	.75	1.50	4.00	30.00
	1857	—	.75	1.50	4.00	30.00
	1858	—	.75	1.50	4.00	30.00
	1859	—	.75	1.50	4.00	30.00
	1860	—	.75	1.50	4.00	30.00

Mint mark: D

C#	Date	Mintage	Fine	VF	XF	Unc
140c	1846	—	1.00	2.00	5.00	35.00
	1847	—	1.00	2.00	5.00	35.00
	1848	—	1.00	2.00	5.00	35.00

Mint mark: A

C#	Date	Mintage	Fine	VF	XF	Unc
161	1861	—	.50	1.00	2.50	20.00
	1862	—	.50	1.00	2.50	20.00
	1863	—	.50	1.00	2.50	20.00
	1864	—	.50	1.00	2.50	20.00
	1865	—	.50	1.00	2.50	20.00
	1866	—	.50	1.00	2.50	20.00
	1867	—	.50	1.00	2.50	20.00
	1868	—	.50	1.00	2.50	20.00
	1869	—	.50	1.00	2.50	20.00
	1870	—	.50	1.00	2.50	20.00
	1871	—	.50	1.00	2.50	20.00
	1872	—	.50	1.00	2.50	20.00
	1873	—	.50	1.00	2.50	20.00

Mint mark: B

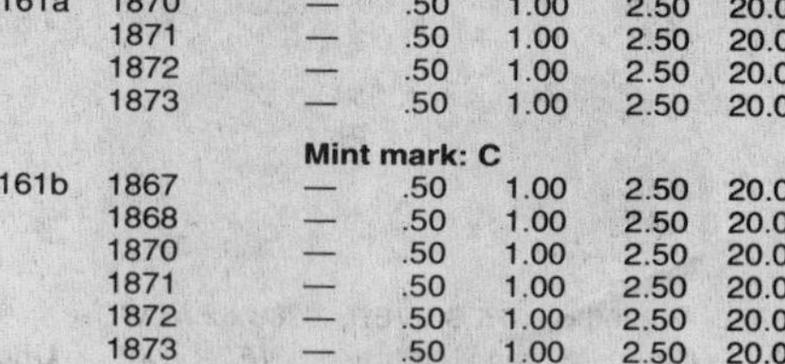

C#	Date	Mintage	Fine	VF	XF	Unc
161a	1867	—	.50	1.00	2.50	20.00
	1868	—	.50	1.00	2.50	20.00
	1869	—	.50	1.00	2.50	20.00
161a	1870	—	.50	1.00	2.50	20.00
	1871	—	.50	1.00	2.50	20.00
	1872	—	.50	1.00	2.50	20.00
	1873	—	.50	1.00	2.50	20.00

Mint mark: C

C#	Date	Mintage	Fine	VF	XF	Unc
161b	1867	—	.50	1.00	2.50	20.00
	1868	—	.50	1.00	2.50	20.00
	1870	—	.50	1.00	2.50	20.00
	1871	—	.50	1.00	2.50	20.00
	1872	—	.50	1.00	2.50	20.00
	1873	—	.50	1.00	2.50	20.00

2 PFENNIG

COPPER
Mint mark: A
Brandenburg Provincial Issue

C#	Date	Mintage	Fine	VF	XF	Unc
98	1810	—	2.50	5.00	10.00	50.00
	1814	—	2.50	5.00	10.00	50.00
	1816	—	2.50	5.00	10.00	50.00

C#	Date	Mintage	Fine	VF	XF	Unc
124	1821	—	2.00	4.00	8.00	45.00
	1822	—	2.00	4.00	8.00	45.00
	1825	—	2.00	4.00	8.00	45.00
	1826	—	2.00	4.00	8.00	45.00
	1827	—	2.00	4.00	8.00	45.00
	1828	—	2.00	4.00	8.00	45.00
	1830	—	2.00	4.00	8.00	45.00
	1832	—	2.00	4.00	8.00	45.00
	1833	—	2.00	4.00	8.00	45.00
	1835	—	2.00	4.00	8.00	45.00
	1836	—	2.00	4.00	8.00	45.00
	1837	—	2.00	4.00	8.00	45.00
	1838	—	2.00	4.00	8.00	45.00
	1839	—	2.00	4.00	8.00	45.00
	1840	—	2.00	4.00	8.00	45.00

Mint mark: B

C#	Date	Mintage	Fine	VF	XF	Unc
124a	1821	—	3.00	5.00	10.00	50.00
	1822	—	3.00	5.00	10.00	50.00

Mint mark: D

C#	Date	Mintage	Fine	VF	XF	Unc
124b	1823	—	2.00	4.00	8.00	40.00
	1824	—	2.00	4.00	8.00	40.00
	1825	—	2.00	4.00	8.00	40.00
	1826	—	2.00	4.00	8.00	40.00
	1827	—	2.00	4.00	8.00	40.00
	1828	—	2.00	4.00	8.00	40.00
	1829	—	2.00	4.00	8.00	40.00
	1830	—	2.00	4.00	8.00	40.00
	1831	—	2.00	4.00	8.00	40.00
	1832	—	2.00	4.00	8.00	40.00
	1833	—	2.00	4.00	8.00	40.00
	1834	—	2.00	4.00	8.00	40.00
	1835	—	2.00	4.00	8.00	40.00
	1836	—	2.00	4.00	8.00	40.00
	1837	—	2.00	4.00	8.00	40.00
	1838	—	2.00	4.00	8.00	40.00
	1839	—	2.00	4.00	8.00	40.00

Mint mark: A

C#	Date	Mintage	Fine	VF	XF	Unc
137	1841	—	1.00	2.00	5.00	40.00
	1842	—	1.00	2.00	5.00	40.00

Mint mark: D

C#	Date	Mintage	Fine	VF	XF	Unc
137a	1841	—	1.00	2.00	5.00	40.00
	1842	—	1.00	2.00	5.00	40.00

Mint mark: A

C#	Date	Mintage	Fine	VF	XF	Unc
141	1843	—	1.00	2.00	5.00	40.00
	1844	—	1.00	2.00	5.00	40.00
	1845	—	1.00	2.00	5.00	40.00

Mint mark: D

C#	Date	Mintage	Fine	VF	XF	Unc
141a	1844	—	1.00	2.00	5.00	40.00
	1845	—	1.00	2.00	5.00	40.00

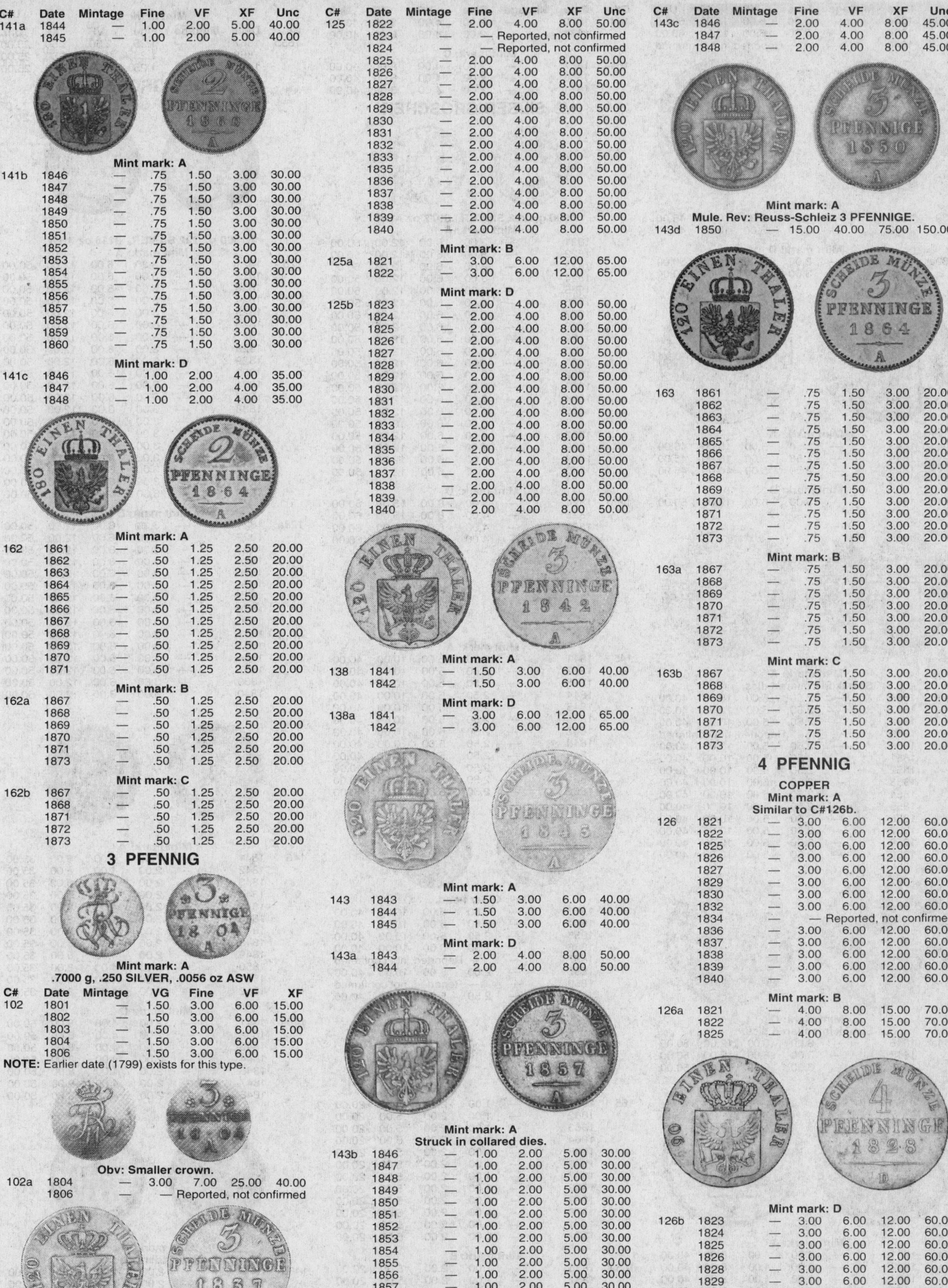

Mint mark: A

C#	Date	Mintage	Fine	VF	XF	Unc
141b	1846	—	.75	1.50	3.00	30.00
	1847	—	.75	1.50	3.00	30.00
	1848	—	.75	1.50	3.00	30.00
	1849	—	.75	1.50	3.00	30.00
	1850	—	.75	1.50	3.00	30.00
	1851	—	.75	1.50	3.00	30.00
	1852	—	.75	1.50	3.00	30.00
	1853	—	.75	1.50	3.00	30.00
	1854	—	.75	1.50	3.00	30.00
	1855	—	.75	1.50	3.00	30.00
	1856	—	.75	1.50	3.00	30.00
	1857	—	.75	1.50	3.00	30.00
	1858	—	.75	1.50	3.00	30.00
	1859	—	.75	1.50	3.00	30.00
	1860	—	.75	1.50	3.00	30.00

Mint mark: D

C#	Date	Mintage	Fine	VF	XF	Unc
141c	1846	—	1.00	2.00	4.00	35.00
	1847	—	1.00	2.00	4.00	35.00
	1848	—	1.00	2.00	4.00	35.00

Mint mark: A

C#	Date	Mintage	Fine	VF	XF	Unc
162	1861	—	.50	1.25	2.50	20.00
	1862	—	.50	1.25	2.50	20.00
	1863	—	.50	1.25	2.50	20.00
	1864	—	.50	1.25	2.50	20.00
	1865	—	.50	1.25	2.50	20.00
	1866	—	.50	1.25	2.50	20.00
	1867	—	.50	1.25	2.50	20.00
	1868	—	.50	1.25	2.50	20.00
	1869	—	.50	1.25	2.50	20.00
	1870	—	.50	1.25	2.50	20.00
	1871	—	.50	1.25	2.50	20.00

Mint mark: B

C#	Date	Mintage	Fine	VF	XF	Unc
162a	1867	—	.50	1.25	2.50	20.00
	1868	—	.50	1.25	2.50	20.00
	1869	—	.50	1.25	2.50	20.00
	1870	—	.50	1.25	2.50	20.00
	1871	—	.50	1.25	2.50	20.00
	1873	—	.50	1.25	2.50	20.00

Mint mark: C

C#	Date	Mintage	Fine	VF	XF	Unc
162b	1867	—	.50	1.25	2.50	20.00
	1868	—	.50	1.25	2.50	20.00
	1871	—	.50	1.25	2.50	20.00
	1872	—	.50	1.25	2.50	20.00
	1873	—	.50	1.25	2.50	20.00

3 PFENNIG

Mint mark: A

.7000 g, .250 SILVER, .0056 oz ASW

C#	Date	Mintage	VG	Fine	VF	XF
102	1801	—	1.50	3.00	6.00	15.00
	1802	—	1.50	3.00	6.00	15.00
	1803	—	1.50	3.00	6.00	15.00
	1804	—	1.50	3.00	6.00	15.00
	1806	—	1.50	3.00	6.00	15.00

NOTE: Earlier date (1799) exists for this type.

Obv: Smaller crown.

C#	Date	Mintage	VG	Fine	VF	XF
102a	1804	—	3.00	7.00	25.00	40.00
	1806	—	Reported, not confirmed			

COPPER

C#	Date	Mintage	Fine	VF	XF	Unc
125	1821	—	2.00	4.00	8.00	50.00
	1822	—	2.00	4.00	8.00	50.00
	1823	—	Reported, not confirmed			
	1824	—	Reported, not confirmed			
	1825	—	2.00	4.00	8.00	50.00
	1826	—	2.00	4.00	8.00	50.00
	1827	—	2.00	4.00	8.00	50.00
	1828	—	2.00	4.00	8.00	50.00
	1829	—	2.00	4.00	8.00	50.00
	1830	—	2.00	4.00	8.00	50.00
	1831	—	2.00	4.00	8.00	50.00
	1832	—	2.00	4.00	8.00	50.00
	1833	—	2.00	4.00	8.00	50.00
	1835	—	2.00	4.00	8.00	50.00
	1836	—	2.00	4.00	8.00	50.00
	1837	—	2.00	4.00	8.00	50.00
	1838	—	2.00	4.00	8.00	50.00
	1839	—	2.00	4.00	8.00	50.00
	1840	—	2.00	4.00	8.00	50.00

Mint mark: B

C#	Date	Mintage	Fine	VF	XF	Unc
125a	1821	—	3.00	6.00	12.00	65.00
	1822	—	3.00	6.00	12.00	65.00

Mint mark: D

C#	Date	Mintage	Fine	VF	XF	Unc
125b	1823	—	2.00	4.00	8.00	50.00
	1824	—	2.00	4.00	8.00	50.00
	1825	—	2.00	4.00	8.00	50.00
	1826	—	2.00	4.00	8.00	50.00
	1827	—	2.00	4.00	8.00	50.00
	1828	—	2.00	4.00	8.00	50.00
	1829	—	2.00	4.00	8.00	50.00
	1830	—	2.00	4.00	8.00	50.00
	1831	—	2.00	4.00	8.00	50.00
	1832	—	2.00	4.00	8.00	50.00
	1833	—	2.00	4.00	8.00	50.00
	1834	—	2.00	4.00	8.00	50.00
	1835	—	2.00	4.00	8.00	50.00
	1836	—	2.00	4.00	8.00	50.00
	1837	—	2.00	4.00	8.00	50.00
	1838	—	2.00	4.00	8.00	50.00
	1839	—	2.00	4.00	8.00	50.00
	1840	—	2.00	4.00	8.00	50.00

Mint mark: A

C#	Date	Mintage	Fine	VF	XF	Unc
138	1841	—	1.50	3.00	6.00	40.00
	1842	—	1.50	3.00	6.00	40.00

Mint mark: D

C#	Date	Mintage	Fine	VF	XF	Unc
138a	1841	—	3.00	6.00	12.00	65.00
	1842	—	3.00	6.00	12.00	65.00

Mint mark: A

C#	Date	Mintage	Fine	VF	XF	Unc
143	1843	—	1.50	3.00	6.00	40.00
	1844	—	1.50	3.00	6.00	40.00
	1845	—	1.50	3.00	6.00	40.00

Mint mark: D

C#	Date	Mintage	Fine	VF	XF	Unc
143a	1843	—	2.00	4.00	8.00	50.00
	1844	—	2.00	4.00	8.00	50.00

Mint mark: A

Struck in collared dies.

C#	Date	Mintage	Fine	VF	XF	Unc
143b	1846	—	1.00	2.00	5.00	30.00
	1847	—	1.00	2.00	5.00	30.00
	1848	—	1.00	2.00	5.00	30.00
	1849	—	1.00	2.00	5.00	30.00
	1850	—	1.00	2.00	5.00	30.00
	1851	—	1.00	2.00	5.00	30.00
	1852	—	1.00	2.00	5.00	30.00
	1853	—	1.00	2.00	5.00	30.00
	1854	—	1.00	2.00	5.00	30.00
	1855	—	1.00	2.00	5.00	30.00
	1856	—	1.00	2.00	5.00	30.00
	1857	—	1.00	2.00	5.00	30.00
	1858	—	1.00	2.00	5.00	30.00
	1859	—	1.00	2.00	5.00	30.00
	1860	—	1.00	2.00	5.00	30.00

Mint mark: D

Struck in collared dies.

C#	Date	Mintage	Fine	VF	XF	Unc
143c	1846	—	2.00	4.00	8.00	45.00
	1847	—	2.00	4.00	8.00	45.00
	1848	—	2.00	4.00	8.00	45.00

Mint mark: A

Mule. Rev: Reuss-Schleiz 3 PFENNIGE.

C#	Date	Mintage	Fine	VF	XF	Unc
143d	1850	—	15.00	40.00	75.00	150.00

C#	Date	Mintage	Fine	VF	XF	Unc
163	1861	—	.75	1.50	3.00	20.00
	1862	—	.75	1.50	3.00	20.00
	1863	—	.75	1.50	3.00	20.00
	1864	—	.75	1.50	3.00	20.00
	1865	—	.75	1.50	3.00	20.00
	1866	—	.75	1.50	3.00	20.00
	1867	—	.75	1.50	3.00	20.00
	1868	—	.75	1.50	3.00	20.00
	1869	—	.75	1.50	3.00	20.00
	1870	—	.75	1.50	3.00	20.00
	1871	—	.75	1.50	3.00	20.00
	1872	—	.75	1.50	3.00	20.00
	1873	—	.75	1.50	3.00	20.00

Mint mark: B

C#	Date	Mintage	Fine	VF	XF	Unc
163a	1867	—	.75	1.50	3.00	20.00
	1868	—	.75	1.50	3.00	20.00
	1869	—	.75	1.50	3.00	20.00
	1870	—	.75	1.50	3.00	20.00
	1871	—	.75	1.50	3.00	20.00
	1872	—	.75	1.50	3.00	20.00
	1873	—	.75	1.50	3.00	20.00

Mint mark: C

C#	Date	Mintage	Fine	VF	XF	Unc
163b	1867	—	.75	1.50	3.00	20.00
	1868	—	.75	1.50	3.00	20.00
	1869	—	.75	1.50	3.00	20.00
	1870	—	.75	1.50	3.00	20.00
	1871	—	.75	1.50	3.00	20.00
	1872	—	.75	1.50	3.00	20.00
	1873	—	.75	1.50	3.00	20.00

4 PFENNIG

COPPER

Mint mark: A

Similar to C#126b.

C#	Date	Mintage	Fine	VF	XF	Unc
126	1821	—	3.00	6.00	12.00	60.00
	1822	—	3.00	6.00	12.00	60.00
	1825	—	3.00	6.00	12.00	60.00
	1826	—	3.00	6.00	12.00	60.00
	1827	—	3.00	6.00	12.00	60.00
	1829	—	3.00	6.00	12.00	60.00
	1830	—	3.00	6.00	12.00	60.00
	1832	—	3.00	6.00	12.00	60.00
	1834	—	Reported, not confirmed			
	1836	—	3.00	6.00	12.00	60.00
	1837	—	3.00	6.00	12.00	60.00
	1838	—	3.00	6.00	12.00	60.00
	1839	—	3.00	6.00	12.00	60.00
	1840	—	3.00	6.00	12.00	60.00

Mint mark: B

C#	Date	Mintage	Fine	VF	XF	Unc
126a	1821	—	4.00	8.00	15.00	70.00
	1822	—	4.00	8.00	15.00	70.00
	1825	—	4.00	8.00	15.00	70.00

Mint mark: D

C#	Date	Mintage	Fine	VF	XF	Unc
126b	1823	—	3.00	6.00	12.00	60.00
	1824	—	3.00	6.00	12.00	60.00
	1825	—	3.00	6.00	12.00	60.00
	1826	—	3.00	6.00	12.00	60.00
	1828	—	3.00	6.00	12.00	60.00
	1829	—	3.00	6.00	12.00	60.00
	1831	—	3.00	6.00	12.00	60.00
	1832	—	3.00	6.00	12.00	60.00
	1833	—	3.00	6.00	12.00	60.00
	1834	—	3.00	6.00	12.00	60.00
	1836	—	3.00	6.00	12.00	60.00
	1837	—	3.00	6.00	12.00	60.00

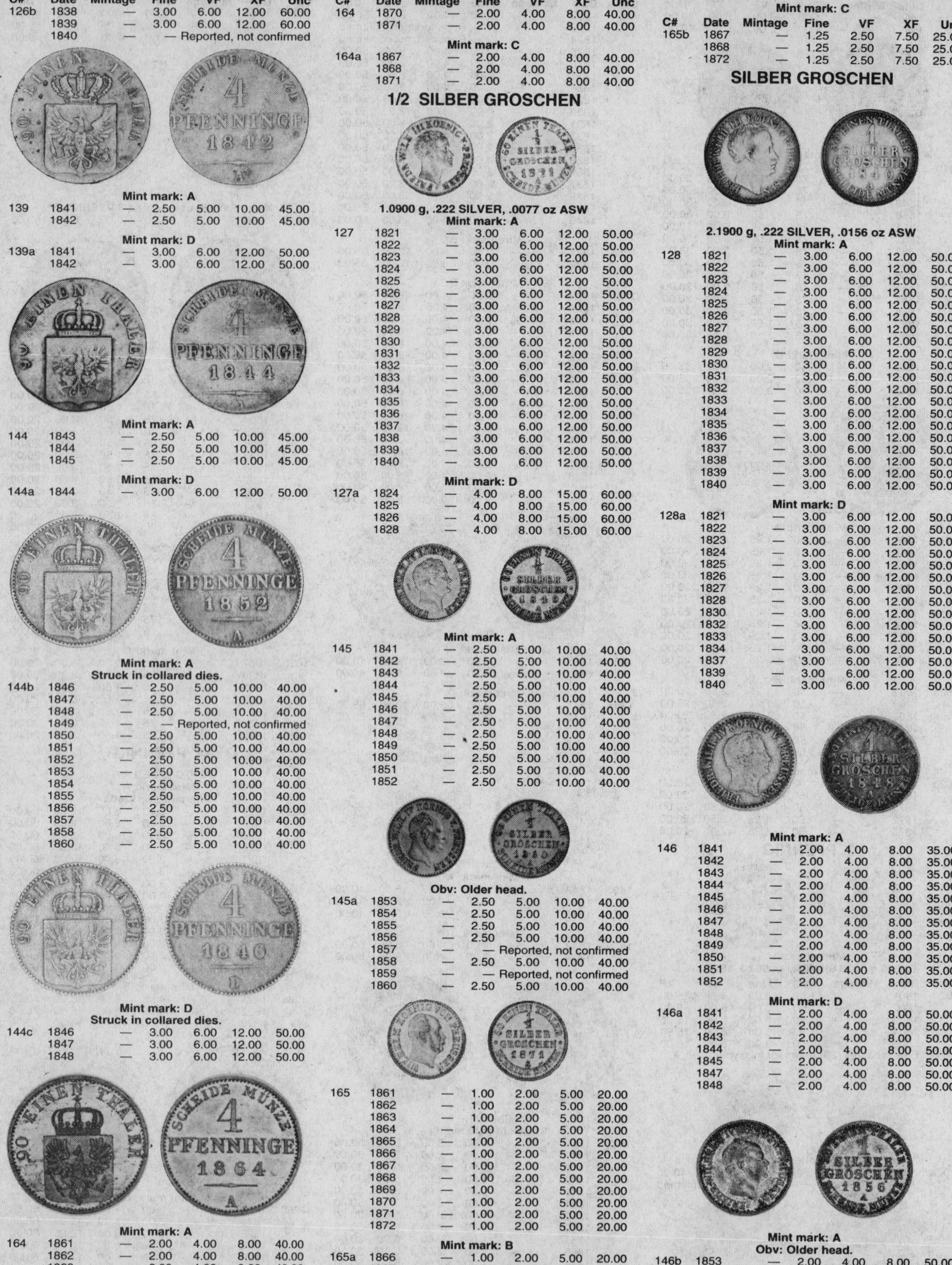

C#	Date	Mintage	Fine	VF	XF	Unc
126b	1838	—	3.00	6.00	12.00	60.00
	1839	—	3.00	6.00	12.00	60.00
	1840	—	— Reported, not confirmed			
	Mint mark: A					
139	1841	—	2.50	5.00	10.00	45.00
	1842	—	2.50	5.00	10.00	45.00
	Mint mark: D					
139a	1841	—	3.00	6.00	12.00	50.00
	1842	—	3.00	6.00	12.00	50.00
	Mint mark: A					
144	1843	—	2.50	5.00	10.00	45.00
	1844	—	2.50	5.00	10.00	45.00
	1845	—	2.50	5.00	10.00	45.00
	Mint mark: D					
144a	1844	—	3.00	6.00	12.00	50.00
	Mint mark: A **Struck in collared dies.**					
144b	1846	—	2.50	5.00	10.00	40.00
	1847	—	2.50	5.00	10.00	40.00
	1848	—	2.50	5.00	10.00	40.00
	1849	—	— Reported, not confirmed			
	1850	—	2.50	5.00	10.00	40.00
	1851	—	2.50	5.00	10.00	40.00
	1852	—	2.50	5.00	10.00	40.00
	1853	—	2.50	5.00	10.00	40.00
	1854	—	2.50	5.00	10.00	40.00
	1855	—	2.50	5.00	10.00	40.00
	1856	—	2.50	5.00	10.00	40.00
	1857	—	2.50	5.00	10.00	40.00
	1858	—	2.50	5.00	10.00	40.00
	1860	—	2.50	5.00	10.00	40.00
	Mint mark: D **Struck in collared dies.**					
144c	1846	—	3.00	6.00	12.00	50.00
	1847	—	3.00	6.00	12.00	50.00
	1848	—	3.00	6.00	12.00	50.00
	Mint mark: A					
164	1861	—	2.00	4.00	8.00	40.00
	1862	—	2.00	4.00	8.00	40.00
	1863	—	2.00	4.00	8.00	40.00
	1864	—	2.00	4.00	8.00	40.00
	1865	—	2.00	4.00	8.00	40.00
	1866	—	2.00	4.00	8.00	40.00
	1867	—	2.00	4.00	8.00	40.00
	1868	—	2.00	4.00	8.00	40.00
	1869	—	2.00	4.00	8.00	40.00
164	1870	—	2.00	4.00	8.00	40.00
	1871	—	2.00	4.00	8.00	40.00
	Mint mark: C					
164a	1867	—	2.00	4.00	8.00	40.00
	1868	—	2.00	4.00	8.00	40.00
	1871	—	2.00	4.00	8.00	40.00

1/2 SILBER GROSCHEN

1.0900 g, .222 SILVER, .0077 oz ASW

C#	Date	Mintage	Fine	VF	XF	Unc
	Mint mark: A					
127	1821	—	3.00	6.00	12.00	50.00
	1822	—	3.00	6.00	12.00	50.00
	1823	—	3.00	6.00	12.00	50.00
	1824	—	3.00	6.00	12.00	50.00
	1825	—	3.00	6.00	12.00	50.00
	1826	—	3.00	6.00	12.00	50.00
	1827	—	3.00	6.00	12.00	50.00
	1828	—	3.00	6.00	12.00	50.00
	1829	—	3.00	6.00	12.00	50.00
	1830	—	3.00	6.00	12.00	50.00
	1831	—	3.00	6.00	12.00	50.00
	1832	—	3.00	6.00	12.00	50.00
	1833	—	3.00	6.00	12.00	50.00
	1834	—	3.00	6.00	12.00	50.00
	1835	—	3.00	6.00	12.00	50.00
	1836	—	3.00	6.00	12.00	50.00
	1837	—	3.00	6.00	12.00	50.00
	1838	—	3.00	6.00	12.00	50.00
	1839	—	3.00	6.00	12.00	50.00
	1840	—	3.00	6.00	12.00	50.00
	Mint mark: D					
127a	1824	—	4.00	8.00	15.00	60.00
	1825	—	4.00	8.00	15.00	60.00
	1826	—	4.00	8.00	15.00	60.00
	1828	—	4.00	8.00	15.00	60.00
	Mint mark: A					
145	1841	—	2.50	5.00	10.00	40.00
	1842	—	2.50	5.00	10.00	40.00
	1843	—	2.50	5.00	10.00	40.00
	1844	—	2.50	5.00	10.00	40.00
	1845	—	2.50	5.00	10.00	40.00
	1846	—	2.50	5.00	10.00	40.00
	1847	—	2.50	5.00	10.00	40.00
	1848	—	2.50	5.00	10.00	40.00
	1849	—	2.50	5.00	10.00	40.00
	1850	—	2.50	5.00	10.00	40.00
	1851	—	2.50	5.00	10.00	40.00
	1852	—	2.50	5.00	10.00	40.00
	Obv: Older head.					
145a	1853	—	2.50	5.00	10.00	40.00
	1854	—	2.50	5.00	10.00	40.00
	1855	—	2.50	5.00	10.00	40.00
	1856	—	2.50	5.00	10.00	40.00
	1857	—	— Reported, not confirmed			
	1858	—	2.50	5.00	10.00	40.00
	1859	—	— Reported, not confirmed			
	1860	—	2.50	5.00	10.00	40.00
165	1861	—	1.00	2.00	5.00	20.00
	1862	—	1.00	2.00	5.00	20.00
	1863	—	1.00	2.00	5.00	20.00
	1864	—	1.00	2.00	5.00	20.00
	1865	—	1.00	2.00	5.00	20.00
	1866	—	1.00	2.00	5.00	20.00
	1867	—	1.00	2.00	5.00	20.00
	1868	—	1.00	2.00	5.00	20.00
	1869	—	1.00	2.00	5.00	20.00
	1870	—	1.00	2.00	5.00	20.00
	1871	—	1.00	2.00	5.00	20.00
	1872	—	1.00	2.00	5.00	20.00
	Mint mark: B					
165a	1866	—	1.00	2.00	5.00	20.00
	1867	—	1.00	2.00	5.00	20.00
	1868	—	1.00	2.00	5.00	20.00
	1869	—	1.00	2.00	5.00	20.00
	1870	—	1.00	2.00	5.00	20.00
	1871	—	1.00	2.00	5.00	20.00
	1872	—	1.00	2.00	5.00	20.00
	1873	—	1.00	2.00	5.00	20.00
	Mint mark: C					
165b	1867	—	1.25	2.50	7.50	25.00
	1868	—	1.25	2.50	7.50	25.00
	1872	—	1.25	2.50	7.50	25.00

SILBER GROSCHEN

2.1900 g, .222 SILVER, .0156 oz ASW

C#	Date	Mintage	Fine	VF	XF	Unc
	Mint mark: A					
128	1821	—	3.00	6.00	12.00	50.00
	1822	—	3.00	6.00	12.00	50.00
	1823	—	3.00	6.00	12.00	50.00
	1824	—	3.00	6.00	12.00	50.00
	1825	—	3.00	6.00	12.00	50.00
	1826	—	3.00	6.00	12.00	50.00
	1827	—	3.00	6.00	12.00	50.00
	1828	—	3.00	6.00	12.00	50.00
	1829	—	3.00	6.00	12.00	50.00
	1830	—	3.00	6.00	12.00	50.00
	1831	—	3.00	6.00	12.00	50.00
	1832	—	3.00	6.00	12.00	50.00
	1833	—	3.00	6.00	12.00	50.00
	1834	—	3.00	6.00	12.00	50.00
	1835	—	3.00	6.00	12.00	50.00
	1836	—	3.00	6.00	12.00	50.00
	1837	—	3.00	6.00	12.00	50.00
	1838	—	3.00	6.00	12.00	50.00
	1839	—	3.00	6.00	12.00	50.00
	1840	—	3.00	6.00	12.00	50.00
	Mint mark: D					
128a	1821	—	3.00	6.00	12.00	50.00
	1822	—	3.00	6.00	12.00	50.00
	1823	—	3.00	6.00	12.00	50.00
	1824	—	3.00	6.00	12.00	50.00
	1825	—	3.00	6.00	12.00	50.00
	1826	—	3.00	6.00	12.00	50.00
	1827	—	3.00	6.00	12.00	50.00
	1828	—	3.00	6.00	12.00	50.00
	1830	—	3.00	6.00	12.00	50.00
	1832	—	3.00	6.00	12.00	50.00
	1833	—	3.00	6.00	12.00	50.00
	1834	—	3.00	6.00	12.00	50.00
	1837	—	3.00	6.00	12.00	50.00
	1839	—	3.00	6.00	12.00	50.00
	1840	—	3.00	6.00	12.00	50.00
	Mint mark: A					
146	1841	—	2.00	4.00	8.00	35.00
	1842	—	2.00	4.00	8.00	35.00
	1843	—	2.00	4.00	8.00	35.00
	1844	—	2.00	4.00	8.00	35.00
	1845	—	2.00	4.00	8.00	35.00
	1846	—	2.00	4.00	8.00	35.00
	1847	—	2.00	4.00	8.00	35.00
	1848	—	2.00	4.00	8.00	35.00
	1849	—	2.00	4.00	8.00	35.00
	1850	—	2.00	4.00	8.00	35.00
	1851	—	2.00	4.00	8.00	35.00
	1852	—	2.00	4.00	8.00	35.00
	Mint mark: D					
146a	1841	—	2.00	4.00	8.00	50.00
	1842	—	2.00	4.00	8.00	50.00
	1843	—	2.00	4.00	8.00	50.00
	1844	—	2.00	4.00	8.00	50.00
	1845	—	2.00	4.00	8.00	50.00
	1847	—	2.00	4.00	8.00	50.00
	1848	—	2.00	4.00	8.00	50.00
	Mint mark: A **Obv: Older head.**					
146b	1853	—	2.00	4.00	8.00	50.00
	1854	—	2.00	4.00	8.00	50.00
	1855	—	2.00	4.00	8.00	50.00
	1856	—	2.00	4.00	8.00	50.00
	1857	—	2.00	4.00	8.00	50.00
	1858	—	2.00	4.00	8.00	50.00
	1859	—	2.00	4.00	8.00	50.00
	1860	—	2.00	4.00	8.00	50.00

C#	Date	Mintage	Fine	VF	XF	Unc
166	1861	—	1.00	2.00	5.00	40.00
	1862	—	1.00	2.00	5.00	40.00
	1863	—	1.00	2.00	5.00	40.00
	1864	—	1.00	2.00	5.00	40.00
	1865	—	1.00	2.00	5.00	40.00
	1866	—	1.00	2.00	5.00	40.00
	1867	—	1.00	2.00	5.00	40.00
	1868	—	1.00	2.00	5.00	40.00
	1869	—	1.00	2.00	5.00	40.00
	1870	—	1.00	2.00	5.00	40.00
	1871	—	1.00	2.00	5.00	40.00
	1872	—	1.00	2.00	5.00	40.00
	1873	—	1.00	2.00	5.00	40.00

Mint mark: B

C#	Date	Mintage	Fine	VF	XF	Unc
166a	1866	—	1.00	2.00	5.00	40.00
	1867	—	1.00	2.00	5.00	40.00
	1868	—	1.00	2.00	5.00	40.00
	1869	—	1.00	2.00	5.00	40.00
	1870	—	1.00	2.00	5.00	40.00
	1871	—	1.00	2.00	5.00	40.00
	1872	—	1.00	2.00	5.00	40.00
	1873	—	1.00	2.00	5.00	40.00

Mint mark: C

C#	Date	Mintage	Fine	VF	XF	Unc
166b	1867	—	1.00	2.00	5.00	40.00
	1868	—	1.00	2.00	5.00	40.00
	1869	—	1.00	2.00	5.00	40.00
	1870	—	1.00	2.00	5.00	40.00
	1871	—	1.00	2.00	5.00	40.00
	1872	—	1.00	2.00	5.00	40.00
	1873	—	1.00	2.00	5.00	40.00

2-1/2 SILBER GROSCHEN

3.2400 g, .375 SILVER, .0390 oz ASW

Mint mark: A

C#	Date	Mintage	Fine	VF	XF	Unc
147	1842	—	3.00	6.00	12.00	55.00
	1843	—	3.00	6.00	12.00	55.00
	1844	—	3.00	6.00	12.00	55.00
	1848	—	3.00	6.00	12.00	55.00
	1849	—	3.00	6.00	12.00	55.00
	1850	—	3.00	6.00	12.00	55.00
	1851	—	3.00	6.00	12.00	55.00
	1852	—	3.00	6.00	12.00	55.00

C#	Date	Mintage	Fine	VF	XF	Unc
147a	1853	—	3.00	6.00	12.00	55.00
	1854	—	3.00	6.00	12.00	55.00
	1855	—	3.00	6.00	12.00	55.00
	1856	—	3.00	6.00	12.00	55.00
	1857	—	3.00	6.00	12.00	55.00
	1858	—	3.00	6.00	12.00	55.00
	1859	—	3.00	6.00	12.00	55.00
	1860	—	3.00	6.00	12.00	55.00

C#	Date	Mintage	Fine	VF	XF	Unc
167	1861	—	2.00	4.00	8.00	50.00
	1862	—	2.00	4.00	8.00	50.00
	1863	—	2.00	4.00	8.00	50.00
	1864	—	2.00	4.00	8.00	50.00
	1865	—	2.00	4.00	8.00	50.00
	1866	—	2.00	4.00	8.00	50.00
	1867	—	2.00	4.00	8.00	50.00
	1868	—	1.50	3.00	6.00	35.00
	1869	—	1.50	3.00	6.00	35.00
	1870	—	1.50	3.00	6.00	35.00
	1871	—	1.50	3.00	6.00	35.00
	1872	—	1.50	3.00	6.00	35.00
	1873	—	1.50	3.00	6.00	35.00

Mint mark: B

C#	Date	Mintage	Fine	VF	XF	Unc
167a	1869	—	1.50	3.00	6.00	40.00
	1870	—	1.50	3.00	6.00	40.00
	1871	—	1.50	3.00	6.00	40.00
	1872	—	1.50	3.00	6.00	40.00
	1873	—	1.50	3.00	6.00	40.00

Mint mark: C

C#	Date	Mintage	Fine	VF	XF	Unc
167b	1867	—	1.50	3.00	6.00	35.00
	1868	—	1.50	3.00	6.00	35.00
	1869	—	1.50	3.00	6.00	35.00
	1870	—	1.50	3.00	6.00	35.00
	1871	—	1.50	3.00	6.00	35.00
	1872	—	1.50	3.00	6.00	35.00
	1873	—	1.50	3.00	6.00	35.00

4 GROSCHEN

5.3450 g, .521 SILVER, .0895 oz ASW

Mint mark: A

C#	Date	Mintage	Fine	VF	XF	Unc
104	1801	—	8.00	15.00	50.00	175.00
	1802	—	8.00	15.00	50.00	175.00
	1803	—	8.00	15.00	50.00	175.00
	1804	—	8.00	15.00	50.00	175.00
	1805	—	8.00	15.00	50.00	175.00
	1806	—	12.00	20.00	100.00	225.00
	1807	—	12.00	20.00	100.00	225.00
	1808	—	12.00	20.00	100.00	225.00
	1809	—	12.00	20.00	100.00	225.00

NOTE: Earlier dates (1798-1800) exist for this type.

Mint mark: B

C#	Date	Mintage	Fine	VF	XF	Unc
104b	1802	—	10.00	20.00	50.00	150.00
	1803	—	10.00	20.00	50.00	150.00
	1804	—	10.00	20.00	50.00	150.00
	1805	—	10.00	20.00	50.00	150.00

Mint mark: G

C#	Date	Mintage	Fine	VF	XF	Unc
104a	1808	—	15.00	20.00	100.00	225.00
	1809	—	15.00	20.00	100.00	225.00

Mint mark: A

C#	Date	Mintage	Fine	VF	XF	Unc
106	1816	11.652	10.00	25.00	65.00	250.00
	1817	14.484	10.00	25.00	65.00	250.00
	1818	—	10.00	25.00	65.00	250.00

Mint mark: D

C#	Date	Mintage	Fine	VF	XF	Unc
106a	1818	—	25.00	50.00	200.00	275.00

1/6 THALER

5.3450 g, .521 SILVER, .0895 oz ASW

Mint mark: A

C#	Date	Mintage	Fine	VF	XF	Unc
105	1809	—	10.00	20.00	50.00	200.00
	1810	—	10.00	20.00	50.00	200.00
	1811	—	10.00	20.00	50.00	200.00
	1812	—	10.00	20.00	50.00	200.00
	1813	—	10.00	20.00	50.00	200.00
	1814	—	10.00	20.00	50.00	200.00
	1815	—	10.00	20.00	50.00	200.00
	1816	—	10.00	20.00	50.00	200.00

Mint mark: B

C#	Date	Mintage	Fine	VF	XF	Unc
105a	1812	—	10.00	20.00	50.00	200.00
	1813	—	10.00	20.00	50.00	200.00
	1814	—	10.00	20.00	50.00	200.00
	1815	—	10.00	20.00	50.00	200.00
	1816	—	10.00	20.00	50.00	200.00
	1817	—	10.00	20.00	50.00	200.00

Mint mark: D

C#	Date	Mintage	Fine	VF	XF	Unc
105b	1817	—	15.00	30.00	70.00	225.00
	1818	—	15.00	30.00	70.00	225.00

Mint mark: A

C#	Date	Mintage	Fine	VF	XF	Unc
129	1822	3.264	4.00	10.00	40.00	100.00
	1823	8.550	4.00	10.00	40.00	100.00
	1824	3.504	4.00	10.00	40.00	100.00
	1825	4.662	4.00	10.00	40.00	100.00
	1826	3.300	4.00	10.00	40.00	100.00
	1827	.972	4.00	10.00	40.00	100.00
	1835	.060	10.00	20.00	70.00	150.00
	1837	.042	10.00	20.00	70.00	150.00
	1838	.048	10.00	20.00	70.00	150.00
	1839	.576	4.00	10.00	40.00	100.00
	1840	.954	4.00	10.00	40.00	100.00

Mint mark: D

C#	Date	Mintage	Fine	VF	XF	Unc
129a	1823	.066	10.00	20.00	70.00	150.00
	1826	.636	4.00	10.00	45.00	125.00
	1827	.924	4.00	10.00	45.00	125.00
	1828	—	4.00	10.00	45.00	125.00
	1835	—	4.00	10.00	45.00	125.00
	1840	.762	4.00	10.00	45.00	125.00

Mint mark: A

C#	Date	Mintage	Fine	VF	XF	Unc
148	1841	.786	4.00	10.00	35.00	125.00
	1842	3.046	4.00	10.00	35.00	125.00
	1843	1.566	4.00	10.00	35.00	125.00
	1844	.948	4.00	10.00	35.00	125.00
	1845	.312	4.00	10.00	35.00	125.00
	1846	.270	4.00	10.00	35.00	125.00
	1847	.240	4.00	10.00	35.00	125.00
	1848	.912	4.00	10.00	35.00	125.00
	1849	2.556	4.00	10.00	35.00	125.00
	1850	.078	5.00	15.00	45.00	150.00
	1851	—	4.00	10.00	35.00	125.00
	1852	.372	4.00	10.00	35.00	125.00

Mint mark: D

C#	Date	Mintage	Fine	VF	XF	Unc
148a	1841	.678	4.00	10.00	35.00	125.00
	1842	.576	4.00	10.00	35.00	125.00
	1843	.426	4.00	10.00	35.00	125.00
	1844	.270	4.00	10.00	35.00	125.00
	1845	.096	5.00	15.00	40.00	150.00

Mint mark: A

Obv: Older head.

C#	Date	Mintage	Fine	VF	XF	Unc
148b	1853	.216	4.00	10.00	35.00	125.00
	1854	.116	4.00	10.00	35.00	125.00
	1855	.030	5.00	15.00	40.00	150.00
	1856	.051	5.00	15.00	40.00	150.00

Rev: Crowned eagle w/sceptre and orb.

C#	Date	Mintage	Fine	VF	XF	Unc
149	1858	.096	10.00	25.00	50.00	150.00
	1859	.032	10.00	25.00	50.00	150.00
	1860	.128	10.00	25.00	50.00	150.00

C#	Date	Mintage	Fine	VF	XF	Unc
168	1861	.249	20.00	40.00	75.00	150.00
	1862	1.180	20.00	40.00	75.00	150.00
	1863	.413	20.00	40.00	75.00	150.00
	1864	.441	20.00	40.00	75.00	150.00

Rev: Eagle w/larger head.

C#	Date	Mintage	Fine	VF	XF	Unc
168a	1865	.194	40.00	75.00	100.00	250.00

C#	Date	Mintage	Fine	VF	XF	Unc
168a	1867	.148	40.00	75.00	100.00	250.00
	1868	.128	40.00	75.00	100.00	250.00

1/3 THALER

8.3520 g, .666 SILVER, .1788 oz ASW

Mint mark: A

C#	Date	Mintage	Fine	VF	XF	Unc
108	1801	—	15.00	30.00	75.00	225.00
	1802	—	15.00	30.00	75.00	225.00
	1804	—	15.00	30.00	75.00	225.00
	1807	—	15.00	30.00	75.00	225.00

NOTE: Earlier date (1800) exists for this type.

Mint mark: G

C#	Date	Mintage	Fine	VF	XF	Unc
108a	1809	—	25.00	50.00	175.00	400.00

Mint mark: A

C#	Date	Mintage	Fine	VF	XF	Unc
109	1809	—	65.00	125.00	300.00	500.00

Mint mark: G

C#	Date	Mintage	Fine	VF	XF	Unc
109a	1809	—	50.00	100.00	250.00	400.00

2/3 THALER

(1 Gulden)

17.3230 g, .750 SILVER, .4177 oz ASW

C#	Date	Mintage	VG	Fine	VF	XF
87	1801	—	25.00	50.00	85.00	185.00

NOTE: Earlier dates (1796-97) exist for this type.

Mint mark: A

Similar to C#87, leg. ends: VON PREUSSEN

C#	Date	Mintage	Fine	VF	XF	Unc
111	1810	—	50.00	100.00	200.00	350.00

THALER

(Reichs)

22.2720 g, .750 SILVER, .5371 oz ASW

Mint mark: A

C#	Date	Mintage	Fine	VF	XF	Unc
113	1801	—	30.00	80.00	200.00	700.00
	1802	—	30.00	80.00	200.00	700.00
	1803	—	30.00	80.00	200.00	700.00
	1803 PRUSSEN(error)	—	—	—	—	—
113	1804	—	50.00	80.00	275.00	800.00
	1805	—	50.00	80.00	275.00	800.00
	1806	—	50.00	80.00	275.00	800.00
	1807	—	50.00	80.00	275.00	800.00
	1809	—	50.00	80.00	275.00	800.00

NOTE: Earlier dates (1797-1800) exist for this type.

Mint mark: B

C#	Date	Mintage	Fine	VF	XF	Unc
113b	1801	—	35.00	125.00	300.00	900.00
	1802	—	35.00	125.00	300.00	900.00
	1803	—	40.00	180.00	400.00	1000.

NOTE: Earlier dates (1799-1800) exist for this type.

Mint mark: G

C#	Date	Mintage	Fine	VF	XF	Unc
113a	1808	.033	200.00	350.00	1400.	3200.
	1809	—	200.00	350.00	7500.	13,000.

C#	Date	Mintage	Fine	VF	XF	Unc
114	1809	—	25.00	50.00	175.00	500.00
	1810	—	25.00	50.00	175.00	500.00
	1810 (error) THAELR	—	—	—	—	—
	1811	—	25.00	50.00	175.00	600.00
	1812	—	25.00	50.00	175.00	600.00
	1813	—	25.00	50.00	150.00	325.00
	1814	—	25.00	50.00	125.00	275.00
	1814 (error) WILHLEM	—	—	—	—	—
	1815	—	25.00	50.00	150.00	325.00
	1816	—	25.00	50.00	150.00	325.00

Mint mark: B

C#	Date	Mintage	Fine	VF	XF	Unc
114a	1812	—	35.00	75.00	300.00	800.00
	1813	—	35.00	75.00	300.00	800.00
	1815	—	50.00	100.00	400.00	1000.
	1816	—	35.00	75.00	300.00	800.00

Visit of Friedrich Wilhelm IV to Berlin Mint

Mint mark: A

C#	Date	Mintage	Fine	VF	XF	Unc
115	1812	—	1500.	3000.	6000.	10,000.

Obv. leg: FR. WILH. . . .

C#	Date	Mintage	Fine	VF	XF	Unc
116	1816	—	200.00	375.00	1400.	4000.
	1817	—	250.00	550.00	1900.	4800.

Obv. leg: FRIEDR. WILHELM . . . .

C#	Date	Mintage	Fine	VF	XF	Unc
116a	1816	—	30.00	100.00	300.00	800.00
	1817	—	30.00	50.00	160.00	400.00
	1818	—	30.00	50.00	160.00	400.00
	1819	—	30.00	50.00	160.00	750.00
	1820	—	30.00	50.00	160.00	750.00
	1821	—	30.00	50.00	160.00	750.00
	1822	—	30.00	100.00	300.00	800.00

Mint mark: D

C#	Date	Mintage	Fine	VF	XF	Unc
116b	1818	—	30.00	60.00	275.00	800.00
	1819	—	30.00	60.00	275.00	800.00
	1820	—	30.00	60.00	275.00	800.00
	1821	—	—	—	Rare	—
	1822	—	30.00	65.00	300.00	850.00

Mint mark: A

C#	Date	Mintage	Fine	VF	XF	Unc
130	1823	.761	25.00	50.00	110.00	400.00
	1824	1.144	25.00	50.00	110.00	400.00
	1825	.405	25.00	50.00	110.00	400.00
	1826	.687	25.00	50.00	110.00	400.00

Mint mark: D

C#	Date	Mintage	Fine	VF	XF	Unc
130a	1823	.013	75.00	125.00	500.00	1200.
	1824	.016	40.00	100.00	300.00	800.00
	1825	.036	50.00	120.00	350.00	950.00

Mint mark: A

Rev: Arms of different design.

C#	Date	Mintage	Fine	VF	XF	Unc
130b	1827	.078	65.00	150.00	500.00	1200.
	1828	1.578	30.00	60.00	185.00	600.00

Mint mark: D

C#	Date	Mintage	Fine	VF	XF	Unc
130c	1828	.012	75.00	200.00	650.00	1600.

Mint mark: A

Obv: Older head.

C#	Date	Mintage	Fine	VF	XF	Unc
130d	1828	1.578	—	—	Rare	—
	1829	4.002	20.00	50.00	90.00	200.00
	1830	6.888	20.00	50.00	90.00	200.00
	1831	4.595	20.00	50.00	90.00	200.00
	1832	.267	25.00	50.00	100.00	300.00
	1833	.448	25.00	50.00	100.00	300.00
	1834	1.299	20.00	50.00	90.00	200.00
	1835	.449	25.00	50.00	100.00	300.00
	1835	—	—	—	Proof	600.00
	1836	.526	25.00	50.00	100.00	300.00
	1837	.466	25.00	50.00	100.00	300.00
	1838	.314	25.00	50.00	100.00	300.00
	1839	.247	25.00	50.00	100.00	300.00
	1840	1.630	20.00	50.00	90.00	200.00
	Common date		—	—	Proof	—

Mint mark: D

C#	Date	Mintage	Fine	VF	XF	Unc
130e	1829	.277	30.00	50.00	225.00	650.00
	1830	.651	30.00	50.00	175.00	550.00
	1831	.045	30.00	50.00	175.00	550.00
	1832	.029	30.00	60.00	225.00	800.00
	1833	.019	30.00	60.00	225.00	800.00
	1834	.021	30.00	60.00	225.00	800.00
	1835	.016	30.00	60.00	225.00	800.00
	1836	.021	30.00	60.00	225.00	800.00
	1837	.015	30.00	60.00	225.00	800.00
	1838	.025	30.00	60.00	225.00	800.00
	1839	.012	30.00	60.00	225.00	800.00
	1840	.011	30.00	60.00	225.00	800.00

(Mining)

Mint mark: A

C#	Date	Mintage	Fine	VF	XF	Unc
131	1826	.050	35.00	80.00	200.00	600.00
	1827	.050	35.00	80.00	200.00	600.00
	1828	.050	35.00	80.00	200.00	600.00

Obv: Older head.

C#	Date	Mintage	Fine	VF	XF	Unc
131a	1829	—	25.00	60.00	110.00	250.00
	1830	—	25.00	60.00	110.00	250.00
	1831	—	25.00	60.00	110.00	250.00
	1832	—	25.00	60.00	110.00	325.00
	1833	—	25.00	60.00	110.00	325.00
	1834	—	25.00	60.00	110.00	300.00
	1835	—	25.00	60.00	110.00	325.00
	1836	—	25.00	60.00	110.00	325.00
	1837	—	25.00	60.00	110.00	325.00
	1838	—	25.00	60.00	110.00	325.00
	1839	—	25.00	60.00	110.00	325.00
	1840	—	25.00	60.00	100.00	225.00

C#	Date	Mintage	Fine	VF	XF	Unc
150	1841	2.280	35.00	85.00	275.00	800.00

(Reichs)

C#	Date	Mintage	Fine	VF	XF	Unc
150b	1842	.518	30.00	60.00	160.00	400.00
	1843	.600	25.00	50.00	100.00	250.00
	1844	.918	25.00	50.00	100.00	250.00
	1845	.720	25.00	50.00	100.00	250.00
	1846	1.115	25.00	50.00	100.00	250.00
	1847	1.283	25.00	50.00	100.00	250.00
	1848	3.743	25.00	50.00	100.00	250.00
	1849	.892	25.00	50.00	100.00	250.00
	1850	.350	25.00	50.00	100.00	250.00
	1851	.731	30.00	60.00	160.00	400.00
	1852	.329	30.00	60.00	160.00	400.00
	Common date		—	—	Proof	—

Obv: Older head.

C#	Date	Mintage	Fine	VF	XF	Unc
150a	1853	.300	30.00	60.00	125.00	250.00
	1854	3.500	25.00	50.00	100.00	225.00
	1855	7.300	25.00	50.00	100.00	225.00
	1856	.940	25.00	50.00	100.00	225.00

(Mining)

C#	Date	Mintage	Fine	VF	XF	Unc
151	1841	.050	50.00	110.00	300.00	950.00

Obv: Larger head. Rev: Dot after THALER.

C#	Date	Mintage	Fine	VF	XF	Unc
151b	1842	.050	30.00	65.00	150.00	350.00
	1843	.050	30.00	65.00	150.00	350.00
	1844	.050	30.00	65.00	150.00	350.00
	1845	.050	30.00	65.00	150.00	350.00
	1846	.050	30.00	65.00	150.00	350.00

Rev: W/o dot after THALER.

C#	Date	Mintage	Fine	VF	XF	Unc
151c	1847	.050	30.00	65.00	150.00	350.00
	1848	.050	30.00	65.00	150.00	350.00
	1849	.050	30.00	65.00	150.00	350.00
	1850	.050	30.00	65.00	150.00	350.00
	1851	.050	30.00	65.00	150.00	350.00
	1852	.050	30.00	65.00	150.00	350.00

Obv: Older head.

C#	Date	Mintage	Fine	VF	XF	Unc
151a	1853	.050	30.00	65.00	150.00	350.00
	1854	.050	30.00	65.00	150.00	350.00
	1855	.050	30.00	65.00	150.00	350.00
	1856	.050	30.00	65.00	150.00	350.00
	Common date		—	—	Proof	—

(Vereins)

18.5200 g, .900 SILVER, .5360 oz ASW

C#	Date	Mintage	Fine	VF	XF	Unc
152	1857	.836	20.00	30.00	60.00	200.00
	1858	1.120	20.00	30.00	60.00	200.00
	1859	17.600	17.50	25.00	50.00	150.00
	1860	17.429	17.50	25.00	50.00	150.00
	1861	.010	40.00	80.00	125.00	250.00
	1861	—	—	—	Proof	250.00

(Mining)

Obv: Similar to C#152.

C#	Date	Mintage	Fine	VF	XF	Unc
153	1857	.047	30.00	65.00	150.00	350.00
	1858	.095	30.00	65.00	150.00	350.00
	1859	.094	30.00	65.00	150.00	350.00
	1860	.298	30.00	65.00	150.00	350.00
	Common date		—	—	Proof	—

(Vereins)

Coronation of Wilhelm and Augusta

C#	Date	Mintage	Fine	VF	XF	Unc
169	1861	1.000	17.50	25.00	40.00	75.00
	1861	—	—	—	Proof	—

Obv: Similar to C#170a. Rev: Similar to C#152.

C#	Date	Mintage	Fine	VF	XF	Unc
170	1861	13.716	20.00	35.00	65.00	150.00
	1862	6.057	20.00	35.00	75.00	160.00
	1863	1.668	20.00	45.00	90.00	200.00

C#	Date	Mintage	Fine	VF	XF	Unc
170a	1864	1.379	25.00	35.00	75.00	160.00
	1865	2.584	20.00	35.00	65.00	150.00
	1866	24.409	20.00	35.00	65.00	150.00
	1867	31.390	20.00	35.00	65.00	150.00
	1868	6.286	20.00	35.00	65.00	150.00
	1869	3.630	20.00	35.00	65.00	150.00
	1870	3.140	20.00	35.00	65.00	150.00
	1871	7.600	20.00	35.00	65.00	150.00
	Common date		—	—	Proof	—

Mint mark: B

C#	Date	Mintage	Fine	VF	XF	Unc
170b	1866	.034	25.00	55.00	150.00	350.00
	1867	.593	25.00	55.00	150.00	350.00
	1868	.048	30.00	75.00	175.00	450.00
	1869	.370	30.00	75.00	175.00	450.00
	1870	.611	25.00	55.00	150.00	350.00
	1871	.245	25.00	55.00	150.00	350.00

Mint mark: C

C#	Date	Mintage	Fine	VF	XF	Unc
170c	1867	.179	50.00	125.00	300.00	700.00
	1868	5,139	75.00	165.00	600.00	1250.
	1869	.044	50.00	125.00	300.00	700.00
	1870	.190	50.00	125.00	300.00	700.00
	1871	.028	50.00	125.00	300.00	700.00
	Common date		—	—	Proof	—

(Mining)

Mint mark: A

C#	Date	Mintage	Fine	VF	XF	Unc
171	1861	.070	35.00	55.00	100.00	300.00
	1862	.145	30.00	50.00	90.00	250.00

(Vereins)

Victory over Austria

C#	Date	Mintage	Fine	VF	XF	Unc
172	1866	.500	30.00	55.00	80.00	125.00

Victory over France

C#	Date	Mintage	Fine	VF	XF	Unc
173	1871	.880	17.50	25.00	40.00	75.00
	1871	—	—	—	Proof	150.00

2 THALER

(3-1/2 Gulden)

37.1190 g, .900 SILVER, 1.0742 oz ASW
Mint mark: A

C#	Date	Mintage	Fine	VF	XF	Unc
132	1839	.172	100.00	150.00	300.00	800.00
	1840	.789	75.00	125.00	225.00	600.00
132a	1841	—	—	—	Rare	—

C#	Date	Mintage	Fine	VF	XF	Unc
154	1841	4.307	55.00	85.00	185.00	400.00
	1842	1.249	55.00	85.00	200.00	475.00
	1843	.193	55.00	85.00	200.00	475.00
	1844	1.069	55.00	85.00	200.00	475.00
	1845	.961	55.00	85.00	200.00	475.00
	1846	1.472	55.00	85.00	200.00	475.00
	1847	.232	—	—	Rare	—
	1848	4,147	—	—	Rare	—
	1850	.221	55.00	85.00	200.00	475.00
	1851	.379	55.00	85.00	200.00	475.00

C#	Date	Mintage	Fine	VF	XF	Unc
154a	1853	2,500	200.00	450.00	1200.	2000.
	1854	.147	90.00	125.00	275.00	500.00
	1855	.100	75.00	110.00	225.00	425.00
	1856	.627	60.00	90.00	160.00	375.00

37.0370 g, .900 SILVER, 1.0718 oz ASW
Obv: Similar to C#154a.

C#	Date	Mintage	Fine	VF	XF	Unc
155	1858	.017	200.00	375.00	1000.	1600.
	1859	.174	150.00	300.00	750.00	1325.

Rev: Similar to C#155.

C#	Date	Mintage	Fine	VF	XF	Unc
174	1861	9,490	500.00	1000.	1800.	3200.
	1862	.058	250.00	460.00	1200.	2000.
	1863	337 pcs.	—	—	Rare	—
	1863	—	—	—	Proof	3000.

Similar to C#174b.

C#	Date	Mintage	Fine	VF	XF	Unc
174a	1865	.023	175.00	350.00	1000.	1500.
	1866	5,110	225.00	425.00	1100.	2000.
	1867	1,195	250.00	550.00	1500.	3200.
	1868	1,584	250.00	550.00	1500.	3200.
	1869	1,901	250.00	550.00	1500.	3200.
	1870	3,155	250.00	550.00	1500.	3200.
	1871	1,134	235.00	350.00	1100.	1750.
	Common date		—	—	Proof	1800

Mint mark: C

C#	Date	Mintage	Fine	VF	XF	Unc
174b	1866	.226	150.00	260.00	425.00	800.00
	1867	1.049	100.00	200.00	350.00	700.00

1/2 KRONE

5.5550 g, .900 GOLD, .1607 oz AGW
Mint mark: A

C#	Date	Mintage	Fine	VF	XF	Unc
159	1858	2,036	800.00	1500.	2000.	3250.

C#	Date	Mintage	Fine	VF	XF	Unc
175	1862	6,365	500.00	900.00	1250.	2000.
	1863	3,642	500.00	900.00	1250.	2000.
	1864	4,840	500.00	900.00	1250.	2000.
	1866	.014	500.00	900.00	1250.	2000.
	1867	5,711	500.00	900.00	1250.	2000.
	1868	.092	400.00	800.00	1200.	1600.
	1869	—	800.00	1500.	2000.	3200.

Mint mark: B

C#	Date	Mintage	Fine	VF	XF	Unc
175a	1868	3,718	800.00	1500.	2000.	3750.

KRONE

11.1110 g, .916 GOLD, .3272 oz AGW
Mint mark: A

C#	Date	Mintage	Fine	VF	XF	Unc
160	1858	6,320	600.00	1400.	1800.	3000.
	1859	.034	550.00	1200.	1600.	2600.
	1860	.016	650.00	1500.	2000.	3250.

C#	Date	Mintage	Fine	VF	XF	Unc
176	1861	2,488	650.00	1200.	1600.	3000.
	1862	5,558	650.00	1200.	1600.	3000.
	1863	2,653	650.00	1200.	1600.	3000.
	1864	792 pcs.	800.00	1400.	2000.	3250.
	1866	720 pcs.	800.00	1400.	2000.	3250.
	1867	4,087	400.00	800.00	1200.	2000.
	1867	—	—	—	Proof	2500.
	1868	.097	400.00	800.00	1200.	2000.
	1869	—	1000.	1400.	2000.	3600.
	1870	1,764	800.00	1400.	2000.	3250.

Mint mark: B

C#	Date	Mintage	Fine	VF	XF	Unc
176a	1867	.015	500.00	1250.	2000.	3000.
	1868	.040	500.00	1250.	2000.	3000.

MONETARY REFORM

2 MARK

11.1110 g, .900 SILVER, .3215 oz ASW

Mint mark: A

Y#	Date	Mintage	Fine	VF	XF	Unc
111	1876	13.368	10.00	40.00	200.00	425.00
	1877	3.634	10.00	35.00	175.00	475.00
	1879	.029	100.00	200.00	800.00	1900.
	1880	.665	25.00	75.00	550.00	1200.
	1883	.164	35.00	115.00	400.00	800.00
	1884	.140	40.00	140.00	450.00	1000.

Mint mark: B

Y#	Date	Mintage	Fine	VF	XF	Unc
111.1	1876	3.985	10.00	40.00	225.00	475.00
	1877	1.301	15.00	50.00	320.00	625.00

Mint mark: C

Y#	Date	Mintage	Fine	VF	XF	Unc
111.2	1876	5.233	10.00	40.00	275.00	500.00
	1877	1.307	15.00	50.00	320.00	625.00

Mint mark: A

Y#	Date	Mintage	Fine	VF	XF	Unc
116	1888	.500	12.50	20.00	40.00	75.00
	1888	—	—	—	Proof	500.00

Y#	Date	Mintage	Fine	VF	XF	Unc
120	1888	.141	100.00	250.00	400.00	600.00
	1888	—	—	—	Proof	750.00

Y#	Date	Mintage	Fine	VF	XF	Unc
120a	1891	.544	10.00	20.00	40.00	150.00
	1891	—	—	—	Proof	500.00
	1892	.182	100.00	200.00	400.00	800.00
	1892	—	—	—	Proof	2500.
	1893	.948	10.00	20.00	40.00	140.00
	1896	1.772	10.00	20.00	40.00	140.00
	1898	1.045	12.50	30.00	60.00	175.00
	1899	2.351	10.00	20.00	40.00	140.00
	1900	2.582	10.00	17.50	40.00	125.00
	1901	.398	40.00	85.00	175.00	350.00
	1901	—	—	—	Proof	2500.
	1902	3.948	8.00	14.00	40.00	115.00
	1903	4.079	8.00	14.00	40.00	115.00
	1904	9.981	8.00	14.00	40.00	115.00
	1905	6.493	8.00	14.00	35.00	80.00
	1905	620 pcs.	—	—	Proof	175.00
	1906	4.019	8.00	14.00	30.00	70.00
	1906	85 pcs.	—	—	Proof	175.00
	1907	8.110	8.00	14.00	25.00	60.00
	1908	2.389	8.00	14.00	30.00	95.00
	1911	1.181	9.00	17.50	30.00	100.00
	1912	.733	9.00	17.50	30.00	100.00

200 Years Kingdom of Prussia

Y#	Date	Mintage	Fine	VF	XF	Unc
128	1901	2.600	5.00	10.00	15.00	30.00
	1901	—	—	—	Proof	70.00

100 Years Defeat of Napoleon

Y#	Date	Mintage	Fine	VF	XF	Unc
132	1913	1.500	10.00	12.50	17.50	30.00
	1913	—	—	—	Proof	60.00

25th Year of Reign

Y#	Date	Mintage	Fine	VF	XF	Unc
134	1913	1.500	10.00	12.50	17.50	30.00
	1913	5,000	—	—	Proof	75.00

3 MARK

16.6670 g, .900 SILVER, .4823 oz ASW

Mint mark: A

Y#	Date	Mintage	Fine	VF	XF	Unc
121	1908	2.859	10.00	15.00	22.50	50.00
	1909	6.344	10.00	15.00	22.50	50.00
	1910	5.591	10.00	15.00	22.50	50.00
	1911	3.242	10.00	15.00	22.50	50.00
	1912	4.626	10.00	15.00	22.50	50.00
	Common date	—	—	—	Proof	150.00

Berlin University

Y#	Date	Mintage	Fine	VF	XF	Unc
130	1910	.200	17.50	35.00	70.00	95.00
	1910	2,000	—	—	Proof	300.00

Breslau University

Y#	Date	Mintage	Fine	VF	XF	Unc
131	1911	.400	12.50	27.50	55.00	80.00
	1911	—	—	—	Proof	250.00

100 Years Defeat of Napoleon

Y#	Date	Mintage	Fine	VF	XF	Unc
133	1913	2.000	12.50	15.00	20.00	40.00
	1913	—	—	—	Proof	100.00

25th Year of Reign

Y#	Date	Mintage	Fine	VF	XF	Unc
135	1913	2.000	12.50	15.00	20.00	40.00
	1913	6,000	—	—	Proof	90.00

Y#	Date	Mintage	Fine	VF	XF	Unc
125	1914	2.564	12.50	15.00	20.00	35.00
	1914	—	—	—	Proof	100.00

Centenary Absorption of Mansfeld

Y#	Date	Mintage	Fine	VF	XF	Unc
136	1915	.030	75.00	250.00	400.00	550.00
	1915	—	—	—	Proof	700.00

5 MARK

27.7770 g, .900 SILVER, .8038 oz ASW

Mint mark: A

Y#	Date	Mintage	Fine	VF	XF	Unc
112	1874	.838	17.50	45.00	275.00	575.00
	1875	.853	17.50	50.00	350.00	1000.
	1876	2.041	15.00	40.00	225.00	525.00
	Common date	—	—	—	Proof	1750.

Mint mark: B

Y#	Date	Mintage	Fine	VF	XF	Unc
112.1	1875	.919	17.50	45.00	350.00	1000.
	1876	2.098	15.00	45.00	225.00	475.00

Mint mark: C

Y#	Date	Mintage	Fine	VF	XF	Unc
112.2	1876	.812	17.50	45.00	225.00	1000.

1.9910 g, .900 GOLD, .0576 oz AGW

Mint mark: A

Y#	Date	Mintage	Fine	VF	XF	Unc
113	1877	1.217	100.00	150.00	200.00	300.00
	1877	—	—	—	Proof	1300.
	1878	.502	100.00	150.00	200.00	300.00
	1878	—	—	—	Proof	1300.

Mint mark: B

Y#	Date	Mintage	Fine	VF	XF	Unc
113.1	1877	.517	100.00	150.00	200.00	350.00
	1877	—	—	—	Proof	1100.

Mint mark: C

Y#	Date	Mintage	Fine	VF	XF	Unc
113.2	1877	.688	100.00	150.00	200.00	325.00

27.7770 g, .900 SILVER, .8038 oz ASW
Mint mark: A

Y#	Date	Mintage	Fine	VF	XF	Unc
117	1888	.200	40.00	75.00	125.00	175.00
	1888	—	—	—	Proof	500.00

Rev: Type II.

Y#	Date	Mintage	Fine	VF	XF	Unc
122	1888	.056	175.00	425.00	800.00	1100.
	1888	—	—	—	Proof	1750.

Y#	Date	Mintage	Fine	VF	XF	Unc
122a	1891	.130	15.00	35.00	130.00	625.00
	1892	.224	15.00	35.00	130.00	625.00
	1893	.215	15.00	35.00	150.00	525.00
	1894	.440	15.00	40.00	110.00	525.00
	1895	.831	15.00	40.00	130.00	525.00
	1896	.046	95.00	175.00	750.00	1800.
	1898	1.134	15.00	30.00	100.00	450.00
	1899	.525	15.00	35.00	140.00	450.00
	1900	1.080	15.00	30.00	140.00	325.00
	1901	.668	15.00	30.00	100.00	325.00
	1902	1.951	15.00	25.00	70.00	225.00
	1903	3.856	15.00	22.50	65.00	225.00
	1904	2.060	15.00	22.50	65.00	200.00
	1906	.231	20.00	35.00	100.00	300.00
	1907	2.902	15.00	22.50	50.00	175.00
	1908	2.231	15.00	22.50	50.00	200.00
	Common date	—	—	—	Proof	550.00

200 Years Kingdom of Prussia

Y#	Date	Mintage	Fine	VF	XF	Unc
129	1901	.460	25.00	45.00	65.00	100.00
	1901	—	—	—	Proof	175.00

Y#	Date	Mintage	Fine	VF	XF	Unc
126	1913	1.962	20.00	25.00	35.00	85.00
	1914	1.587	20.00	25.00	35.00	85.00
	Common date	—	—	—	Proof	350.00

10 MARK

3.9820 g, .900 GOLD, .1152 oz AGW
Mint mark: A

Y#	Date	Mintage	Fine	VF	XF	Unc
114	1872	3.123	60.00	90.00	120.00	200.00
	1872	—	—	—	Proof	1600.
	1873	3.016	60.00	90.00	120.00	200.00
	1873	—	—	—	Proof	1600.

Mint mark: B

Y#	Date	Mintage	Fine	VF	XF	Unc
114b	1872	1.418	60.00	90.00	120.00	275.00
	1873	2.273	60.00	90.00	120.00	275.00

Mint mark: C

Y#	Date	Mintage	Fine	VF	XF	Unc
114c	1872	1.747	60.00	90.00	120.00	275.00
	1873	2.295	60.00	90.00	120.00	275.00

Mint mark: A
Rev: Type II.

Y#	Date	Mintage	Fine	VF	XF	Unc
114a	1874	.833	60.00	90.00	120.00	250.00
	1874	—	—	—	Proof	1100.
	1875	2.430	60.00	90.00	120.00	250.00
	1877	.851	60.00	90.00	120.00	250.00
	1878	1.126	60.00	90.00	120.00	250.00
	1879	1.012	60.00	90.00	120.00	200.00
	1879	—	—	—	Proof	550.00
	1880	1.762	60.00	90.00	120.00	200.00
	1882	8,382	1500.	3300.	4500.	7000.
	1883	.013	1200.	1800.	2200.	3000.
	1883	—	—	—	Proof	10,000.
	1886	.014	1500.	2200.	3200.	5000.
	1888	.189	—	90.00	120.00	250.00
	1888	—	—	—	Proof	1300.

Mint mark: B

Y#	Date	Mintage	Fine	VF	XF	Unc
114d	1874	1.028	60.00	90.00	120.00	300.00
	1875	.456	60.00	90.00	120.00	300.00
	1876	2,800	1000.	1600.	2200.	3000.
	1876	—	—	—	Proof	10,000.
	1877	.247	60.00	90.00	120.00	350.00
	1878	.015	—	—	Rare	—

Mint mark: C

Y#	Date	Mintage	Fine	VF	XF	Unc
114e	1874	.321	60.00	90.00	120.00	250.00
	1874	—	—	—	Proof	1300.
	1875	1.532	60.00	90.00	120.00	250.00
	1876	.027	500.00	1200.	1500.	2500.
	1877	.328	60.00	90.00	120.00	300.00
	1878	.516	60.00	90.00	120.00	300.00
	1879	.282	60.00	90.00	120.00	250.00

Mint mark: A

Y#	Date	Mintage	Fine	VF	XF	Unc
118	1888	.876	60.00	90.00	120.00	175.00
	1888	—	—	—	Proof	600.00

Rev: Type II.

Y#	Date	Mintage	Fine	VF	XF	Unc
123	1889	.024	1400.	2000.	2500.	3500.
	1889	—	—	—	Proof	6000.

Rev: Type III.

Y#	Date	Mintage	Fine	VF	XF	Unc
123a	1890	1.512	BV	90.00	120.00	200.00
	1890	—	—	—	Proof	500.00
	1892	.035	400.00	700.00	1000.	1500.
	1893	1.591	BV	90.00	120.00	200.00
	1894	.018	600.00	1200.	1500.	2000.
	1895	.029	400.00	750.00	1350.	1900.
	1896	1.081	BV	90.00	120.00	200.00
	1897	.114	BV	125.00	250.00	400.00
	1898	2.280	BV	90.00	120.00	200.00
	1899	.300	BV	90.00	165.00	225.00
	1900	.742	BV	90.00	120.00	200.00
	1900	—	—	—	Proof	500.00
	1901	.702	BV	90.00	120.00	200.00
	1901	—	—	—	Proof	500.00
	1902	.271	BV	90.00	120.00	200.00
	1902	—	—	—	Proof	500.00
	1903	1.685	BV	90.00	120.00	200.00
	1903	—	—	—	Proof	500.00
	1904	1.178	BV	90.00	120.00	200.00
	1905	1.063	BV	90.00	120.00	200.00
	1905	117 pcs.	—	—	Proof	500.00
	1906	.542	BV	90.00	120.00	175.00
	1906	150 pcs.	—	—	Proof	500.00
	1907	.813	BV	90.00	120.00	175.00
	1907	—	—	—	Proof	500.00
	1909	.532	BV	90.00	120.00	175.00
	1909	—	—	—	Proof	500.00
	1910	.803	BV	90.00	120.00	175.00
	1911	.271	BV	90.00	120.00	200.00
	1911	—	—	—	Proof	500.00
	1912	.542	BV	90.00	120.00	175.00
	1912	—	—	—	Proof	500.00

20 MARK

7.9650 g, .900 GOLD, .2304 oz AGW
Mint mark: A

Y#	Date	Mintage	Fine	VF	XF	Unc
115	1871	.502	BV	135.00	150.00	300.00
	1871	—	—	—	Proof	1800.
	1872	7.717	BV	135.00	150.00	225.00
	1872	2,491	—	—	Proof	1800.
	1873	9.063	BV	135.00	150.00	225.00
	1873	—	—	—	Proof	1800.

Mint mark: B

Y#	Date	Mintage	Fine	VF	XF	Unc
115b	1872	1.918	BV	135.00	150.00	225.00
	1873	3.441	BV	135.00	150.00	225.00

Mint mark: C

Y#	Date	Mintage	Fine	VF	XF	Unc
115c	1872	3.056	BV	135.00	150.00	225.00
	1873	5.228	BV	135.00	150.00	225.00
	1873	—	—	—	Proof	1800.

Mint mark: A
Rev: Type II.

Y#	Date	Mintage	Fine	VF	XF	Unc
115a	1874	.762	BV	115.00	140.00	200.00
	1874	—	—	—	Proof	1300.
	1875	4.203	BV	115.00	140.00	200.00
	1876	2.673	BV	115.00	140.00	200.00
	1877	1.250	BV	115.00	140.00	200.00
	1878	2.175	BV	115.00	140.00	200.00
	1879	1.023	BV	115.00	140.00	200.00
	1881	.428	BV	115.00	140.00	200.00
	1882	.655	BV	115.00	140.00	200.00
	1882	—	—	—	Proof	1300.
	1883	4.283	BV	115.00	140.00	200.00
	1884	.224	BV	115.00	140.00	200.00
	1885	.407	BV	115.00	140.00	200.00

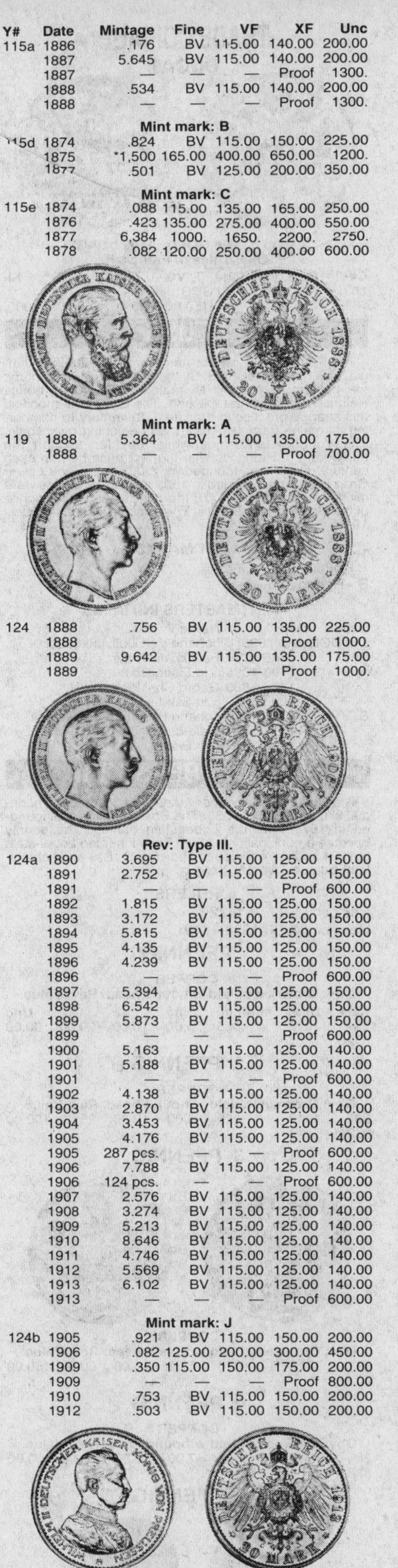

Y#	Date	Mintage	Fine	VF	XF	Unc
115a	1886	.176	BV	115.00	140.00	200.00
	1887	5.645	BV	115.00	140.00	200.00
	1887	—	—	—	Proof	1300.
	1888	.534	BV	115.00	140.00	200.00
	1888	—	—	—	Proof	1300.

Mint mark: B

Y#	Date	Mintage	Fine	VF	XF	Unc
115d	1874	.824	BV	115.00	150.00	225.00
	1875	*1,500	165.00	400.00	650.00	1200.
	1877	.501	BV	125.00	200.00	350.00

Mint mark: C

Y#	Date	Mintage	Fine	VF	XF	Unc
115e	1874	.088	115.00	135.00	165.00	250.00
	1876	.423	135.00	275.00	400.00	550.00
	1877	6,384	1000.	1650.	2200.	2750.
	1878	.082	120.00	250.00	400.00	600.00

Mint mark: A

Y#	Date	Mintage	Fine	VF	XF	Unc
119	1888	5.364	BV	115.00	135.00	175.00
	1888	—	—	—	Proof	700.00

Y#	Date	Mintage	Fine	VF	XF	Unc
124	1888	.756	BV	115.00	135.00	225.00
	1888	—	—	—	Proof	1000.
	1889	9.642	BV	115.00	135.00	175.00
	1889	—	—	—	Proof	1000.

Rev: Type III.

Y#	Date	Mintage	Fine	VF	XF	Unc
124a	1890	3.695	BV	115.00	125.00	150.00
	1891	2.752	BV	115.00	125.00	150.00
	1891	—	—	—	Proof	600.00
	1892	1.815	BV	115.00	125.00	150.00
	1893	3.172	BV	115.00	125.00	150.00
	1894	5.815	BV	115.00	125.00	150.00
	1895	4.135	BV	115.00	125.00	150.00
	1896	4.239	BV	115.00	125.00	150.00
	1896	—	—	—	Proof	600.00
	1897	5.394	BV	115.00	125.00	150.00
	1898	6.542	BV	115.00	125.00	150.00
	1899	5.873	BV	115.00	125.00	150.00
	1899	—	—	—	Proof	600.00
	1900	5.163	BV	115.00	125.00	140.00
	1901	5.188	BV	115.00	125.00	140.00
	1901	—	—	—	Proof	600.00
	1902	4.138	BV	115.00	125.00	140.00
	1903	2.870	BV	115.00	125.00	140.00
	1904	3.453	BV	115.00	125.00	140.00
	1905	4.176	BV	115.00	125.00	140.00
	1905	287 pcs.	—	—	Proof	600.00
	1906	7.788	BV	115.00	125.00	140.00
	1906	124 pcs.	—	—	Proof	600.00
	1907	2.576	BV	115.00	125.00	140.00
	1908	3.274	BV	115.00	125.00	140.00
	1909	5.213	BV	115.00	125.00	140.00
	1910	8.646	BV	115.00	125.00	140.00
	1911	4.746	BV	115.00	125.00	140.00
	1912	5.569	BV	115.00	125.00	140.00
	1913	6.102	BV	115.00	125.00	140.00
	1913	—	—	—	Proof	600.00

Mint mark: J

Y#	Date	Mintage	Fine	VF	XF	Unc
124b	1905	.921	BV	115.00	150.00	200.00
	1906	.082	125.00	200.00	300.00	450.00
	1909	.350	115.00	150.00	175.00	200.00
	1909	—	—	—	Proof	800.00
	1910	.753	BV	115.00	150.00	200.00
	1912	.503	BV	115.00	150.00	200.00

Mint mark: A

Y#	Date	Mintage	Fine	VF	XF	Unc
127	1913	6.102	BV	115.00	135.00	175.00
	1913	—	—	—	Proof	1200.
	1914	2.137	BV	115.00	135.00	175.00
	1914	—	—	—	Proof	1200.
	1915	1.271	750.00	1250.	2500.	3000.

TRADE COINAGE

1/2 FREDERICK D'OR

3.3410 g, .903 GOLD, .0970 oz AGW
Obv: L at truncation.

C#	Date	Mintage	Fine	VF	XF	Unc
118	1802	—	275.00	350.00	800.00	1500.
	1803	—	550.00	800.00	1200.	2000.
	1804	—	300.00	500.00	900.00	1625.
	1806	—	275.00	400.00	800.00	1500.
	1814	—	300.00	500.00	900.00	1625.
	1816	—	350.00	600.00	1000.	1750.

C#	Date	Mintage	Fine	VF	XF	Unc
121	1817	—	300.00	500.00	700.00	1250.

C#	Date	Mintage	Fine	VF	XF	Unc
133	1825	—	300.00	500.00	750.00	1000.
	1827	—	375.00	650.00	875.00	1125.
	1828	—	600.00	1000.	1250.	1500.
	1829	—	500.00	875.00	1125.	1375.
	1830	—	350.00	625.00	875.00	1125.
	1831	—	350.00	625.00	875.00	1125.
	1832	—	350.00	625.00	875.00	1125.
	1833	—	350.00	625.00	875.00	1125.
	1834	—	350.00	625.00	875.00	1125.
	1838	—	350.00	625.00	875.00	1125.
	1839	—	400.00	750.00	1000.	1250.
	1840	—	500.00	875.00	1125.	1375.

C#	Date	Mintage	Fine	VF	XF	Unc
156	1841	—	300.00	500.00	750.00	1000.
	1842	—	300.00	500.00	750.00	1000.
	1843	—	400.00	750.00	1000.	1250.
	1844	—	400.00	750.00	1000.	1250.
	1845	—	400.00	750.00	1000.	1250.
	1846	—	400.00	750.00	1000.	1250.
	1849	—	400.00	750.00	1000.	1250.

C#	Date	Mintage	Fine	VF	XF	Unc
156a	1853	—	400.00	750.00	1000.	1250.

FREDERICK D'OR

6.6820 g, .903 GOLD, .1940 oz AGW
Mint mark: A

C#	Date	Mintage	Fine	VF	XF	Unc
119	1801	—	400.00	600.00	950.00	1400.
	1802	—	450.00	600.00	950.00	1400.
	1803	—	400.00	475.00	800.00	1200.
	1804	—	450.00	600.00	950.00	1400.
	1805	—	350.00	525.00	950.00	1200.
	1806	—	350.00	525.00	950.00	1200.
	1807	—	350.00	525.00	950.00	1200.
	1808	—	550.00	800.00	1200.	1600.
	1809	—	350.00	475.00	800.00	1200.
	1810	—	450.00	600.00	950.00	1400.
	1811	—	450.00	600.00	950.00	1400.
	1812	—	350.00	475.00	800.00	1200.
	1813	—	400.00	525.00	875.00	1300.
	1816	—	450.00	600.00	950.00	1400.

NOTE: Earlier dates (1798-1800) exist for this type.

Mint mark: B

C#	Date	Mintage	Fine	VF	XF	Unc
119a	1801	—	450.00	600.00	1000.	1400.
	1802	—	450.00	600.00	1000.	1400.
	1803	—	550.00	800.00	1200.	1800.
	1804	—	550.00	800.00	1200.	1800.
	1805	—	550.00	800.00	1200.	1800.

NOTE: Earlier date (1800) exists for this type.

Mint mark: A

C#	Date	Mintage	Fine	VF	XF	Unc
122	1817	—	500.00	800.00	1200.	1800.
	1818	—	400.00	550.00	1000.	1500.
	1819	—	650.00	1000.	1500.	2000.
	1822	—	400.00	550.00	1000.	1500.

C#	Date	Mintage	Fine	VF	XF	Unc
134	1825	—	300.00	400.00	800.00	1250.
	1827	—	400.00	600.00	1000.	1500.
	1828	—	300.00	550.00	800.00	1400.
	1829	—	400.00	550.00	1000.	1500.
	1830	—	400.00	550.00	1000.	1500.
	1831	—	300.00	550.00	900.00	1400.
	1832	—	300.00	550.00	900.00	1400.
	1833	—	300.00	550.00	900.00	1400.
	1834	—	300.00	550.00	1000.	1500.
	1836	—	300.00	550.00	1000.	1500.
	1837	—	300.00	550.00	800.00	1400.
	1838	—	300.00	550.00	800.00	1500.
	1839	—	300.00	550.00	800.00	1400.
	1840	—	300.00	550.00	800.00	1250.

C#	Date	Mintage	Fine	VF	XF	Unc
157	1841	—	300.00	550.00	800.00	1250.
	1842	—	300.00	550.00	800.00	1250.
	1843	—	300.00	550.00	800.00	1400.
	1844	—	300.00	550.00	800.00	1250.
	1845	—	300.00	550.00	800.00	1250.
	1846	—	300.00	550.00	800.00	1250.
	1847	—	300.00	550.00	800.00	1400.
	1848	—	300.00	550.00	800.00	1250.
	1849	—	300.00	550.00	800.00	1250.
	1850	—	300.00	550.00	800.00	1400.
	1851	—	300.00	550.00	800.00	1500.
	1852	—	300.00	550.00	800.00	1400.

C#	Date	Mintage	Fine	VF	XF	Unc
157a	1853	—	300.00	550.00	800.00	1250.
	1854	—	300.00	550.00	800.00	1250.
	1855	—	300.00	550.00	800.00	1250.

2 FREDERICK D'OR

13.3630 g, .903 GOLD, .3880 oz AGW
Mint mark: A
Obv: L at truncation.

C#	Date	Mintage	Fine	VF	XF	Unc
120	1801	—	700.00	975.00	1800.	2600.
	1802	—	800.00	1250.	2200.	3000.
	1806	—	800.00	1250.	2200.	3000.
	1811	—	700.00	975.00	1800.	2600.
	1813	—	725.00	1000.	2000.	2800.
	1814	—	800.00	1250.	2200.	3000.

NOTE: Earlier date (1800) exists for this type.

C#	Date	Mintage	Fine	VF	XF	Unc
135	1825	—	800.00	1200.	1600.	2000.
	1826	—	700.00	1100.	1500.	1800.
	1827	—	600.00	1000.	1400.	1600.
	1828	—	600.00	1000.	1400.	1600.
	1829	—	700.00	1100.	1500.	1800.
	1830	—	550.00	900.00	1300.	1500.
	1831	—	550.00	900.00	1300.	1500.
	1832	—	700.00	1100.	1500.	1800.
	1836	—	800.00	1200.	1600.	2000.
	1837	—	550.00	900.00	1300.	1500.
	1838	—	600.00	1000.	1400.	1600.
	1839	—	500.00	800.00	1200.	1400.
	1840	—	500.00	800.00	1200.	1400.

C#	Date	Mintage	Fine	VF	XF	Unc
158	1841	—	500.00	800.00	1200.	1500.
	1842	—	500.00	800.00	1200.	1500.
	1843	—	600.00	1250.	1750.	2000.
	1844	—	800.00	1500.	2000.	2250.
	1845	—	800.00	1500.	2000.	2250.
	1846	—	500.00	800.00	1200.	1500.
	1848	—	500.00	800.00	1200.	1500.
	1849	—	500.00	800.00	1200.	1500.
	1852	—	500.00	800.00	1200.	1500.

C#	Date	Mintage	Fine	VF	XF	Unc
158a	1853	—	500.00	800.00	1200.	2000.
	1854	—	500.00	800.00	1200.	2000.
	1855	—	750.00	1500.	2000.	2500.

PYRMONT

A county, southwest of Hannover, was established c. 1160. Their first coins were struck in the 13th century. In 1625 Pyrmont was incorporated with Waldeck. Occasional issues of special coins for Pyrmont were struck in the 18th and 19th centuries.

RULERS

Georg, Prince, 1805-1812

MINTMASTERS INITIALS

Letter	Date	Name
FW	1807-1829	Friedrich Welle

24 EINEN (1/24) THALER

1.9900 g, .368 SILVER, .0235 oz ASW
Obv: Crowned and mantled 2 shields of arms.
Rev: Value above date.

C#	Date	Mintage	VG	Fine	VF	XF
6	1806 FW	—	25.00	50.00	100.00	175.00
	1807 FW	—	25.00	50.00	100.00	175.00

EIN (1) THALER

(Convention)

28.0600 g, .833 SILVER, .7515 oz ASW

C#	Date	Mintage	Fine	VF	XF	Unc
7	1811 FW	—	850.00	1500.	3250.	6000.

REGENSBURG

Ratisbon

The Bishopric, located in central Bavaria, was established in 470. Regular episcopal coins appeared in the 11th century. Regensburg became a Free City in 1180 and in 1230 received the right to mint its own coins. The dated city coinage extends from c. 1511 to 1802. In 1803 the city was given to the bishop and the city and Bishopric were united with Bavaria.

FREE CITY

RULERS

Holy Roman, until 1802

MINTMASTERS INITIALS

Letter	Date	Name
B,BF,G.C.B.	1773-1803	Georg Christoph Busch
GZ,Z	1791-1802	Johann Leonhard Zollner
K, Kornlein	1773-1802	Johann Nikolaus Kornlein

HELLER

COPPER, uniface
Crossed keys.

C#	Date	Mintage	VG	Fine	VF	XF
2	1801	—	2.50	4.50	7.50	15.00
	1802	—	2.50	4.50	7.50	15.00
	1803	—	2.50	4.50	7.50	15.00

NOTE: Earlier dates (1794-1799) exist for this type.

EIN (1) THALER

SILVER

C#	Date	Mintage	Fine	VF	XF	Unc
57	1801 Z	—	1000.	2000.	2800.	4800.
	1802 Z	—	1000.	2000.	2800.	4800.

TRADE COINAGE

DUCAT

3.5000 g, .986 GOLD, .1109 oz AGW
Obv: Titles of Francis II.

C#	Date	Mintage	VG	Fine	VF	XF
103	ND(1792-1803) GCB	—	150.00	350.00	650.00	1000.

REUSS

The Reuss family, whose lands were located in Thuringia, was founded c. 1035. By the end of the 12th century, the custom of naming all males in the ruling house Heinrich had been established. The Elder Line modified this strange practice in the late 17th century to numbering all males from 1 to 100, then beginning over again. The Younger Line, meanwhile, decided to start the numbering of Heinrichs with the first male born in each century. Greiz was founded in 1303. Upper and Lower Greiz lines were founded in 1535 and the territories were divided until 1768. In 1778 the ruler was made a prince of the Holy Roman Empire. The principality endured until 1918.

MINT MARKS

A - Berlin
B - Hannover

MINTMASTERS INITIALS

Letter	Date	Name
DF, DOELL	(d. 1835)	Johann Veit Doll, die-cutter
FA	1785-1790	Facius, die-cutter
	1790-1835	in Eisenach
L	1803-1833	Georg Christoph Lowel, in Saalfeld
S, ST	1785-1790	Johann Leonhard Stockmar, die-cutter
	1790-1835	in Eisenach

REUSS-EBERSDORF

The Reuss family, whose lands were located in Thuringia, was founded c. 1035. The Ebersdorf line was founded in 1671 from the Lobenstein branch. The county became a principality in 1806. They inherited Lobenstein in 1824 and were forced to abdicate in 1849 and LobensteinEbersdorf went to Schleiz.

RULERS

Heinrich LI, 1779-1822
Heinrich LXXII, 1822-1849

PFENNIG

COPPER
Obv: Crowned shield w/hound head. Rev: Value.

KM#	Date	Mintage	Fine	VF	XF	Unc
25 (C20)	1812	.035	5.00	10.00	20.00	90.00

2 PFENNIG

COPPER
Obv: Crowned shield w/hound head. Rev: Value.

KM#	Date	Mintage	Fine	VF	XF	Unc
26 (C21)	1812	.029	5.00	10.00	25.00	100.00

3 PFENNIG

COPPER
Obv: Crowned shield w/hound head. Rev: Value.

KM#	Date	Mintage	Fine	VF	XF	Unc
27 (C22)	1812	.018	5.00	15.00	60.00	150.00

4 PFENNIG

COPPER
Obv: Crowned shield w/hound head. Rev: Value.

KM#	Date	Mintage	Fine	VF	XF	Unc
28 (C23)	1812	.023	7.00	15.00	30.00	100.00

6 PFENNIG

.9500 g, .250 SILVER, .0076 oz ASW

KM#	Date	Mintage	Fine	VF	XF	Unc
29 (C27)	1812	7,376	7.00	15.00	30.00	100.00

8 PFENNIG

1.3000 g, .250 SILVER, .0104 oz ASW

KM#	Date	Mintage	Fine	VF	XF	Unc
30 (C29)	1812	.011	10.00	20.00	40.00	150.00

GROSCHEN

1.7600 g, .368 SILVER, .0208 oz ASW

KM#	Date	Mintage	Fine	VF	XF	Unc
31	1812	8,962	7.00	20.00	35.00	125.00
(C31)	1814	.087	7.00	20.00	35.00	125.00

EIN (1) THALER

(Species)

28.0600 g, .833 SILVER, .7515 oz ASW

KM#	Date	Mintage	Fine	VF	XF	Unc
32 (C33)	1812 L	1,575	350.00	700.00	1400.	3000.

REUSS-LOBENSTEIN

The Reuss family, whose lands were located in Thuringia, was founded c. 1035. The Lobenstein line was founded in 1635. The county became a principality in 1790. In 1824 Lobenstein was given to Ebersdorf.

RULERS

Heinrich XXXV, 1782-1805
Heinrich LIV, 1805-1824

3 PFENNIG

BILLON
Obv: Crowned lion.

KM#	Date	Mintage	Fine	VF	XF	Unc
15 (C10)	1804	.110	3.00	6.00	10.00	60.00
Different ruler.						
17	1807	.054	3.00	6.00	10.00	60.00
Obv: Uncrowned lion.						
18 (C15)	1807	Inc. Ab.	3.00	6.00	10.00	60.00

1/48 THALER

.9700 g, .250 SILVER, .0077 oz ASW
Obv: Crowned lion. Rev: Value.

KM#	Date	Mintage	Fine	VF	XF	Unc
16 (C12)	1805	.033	6.00	12.00	25.00	75.00

REUSS-LOBENSTEIN-EBERSDORF

This line was formed by the merger between Ebersdorf and Lobenstein in 1824. The prince abdicated during political troubles in 1848 and the lands went to Schleiz in 1849.

RULERS

Heinrich LXXII (as Prince of Reuss Ebersdorf) 1822-1824
(as Prince of Reuss-Lobenstein Ebersdorf), 1824-1849

PFENNIG

COPPER

KM#	Date	Mintage	Fine	VF	XF	Unc
1	1841A	.316	4.00	8.00	15.00	45.00
(C1)	1844A	.381	4.00	8.00	15.00	45.00

3 PFENNIG

COPPER

KM#	Date	Mintage	Fine	VF	XF	Unc
2	1841A	.107	5.00	10.00	20.00	50.00
(C2)	1844A	.180	5.00	10.00	20.00	50.00

1/2 SILBER GROSCHEN

1.0900 g, .222 SILVER, .0077 oz ASW
Obv: Crowned shield w/crowned lion. Rev: Value.

KM#	Date	Mintage	Fine	VF	XF	Unc
3 (C3)	1841A	.070	5.00	10.00	20.00	60.00

SILBER GROSCHEN

2.1900 g, .222 SILVER, .0156 oz ASW
Obv: Crowned shield w/crowned lion. Rev: Value.

KM#	Date	Mintage	Fine	VF	XF	Unc
4	1841A	.059	5.00	10.00	20.00	60.00
(C4)	1844A	.087	5.00	10.00	20.00	60.00

2 THALER

(3-1/2 Gulden)

37.1200 g, .900 SILVER, 1.0742 oz ASW

KM#	Date	Mintage	Fine	VF	XF	Unc
5	1840A	2,750	200.00	400.00	750.00	1700.
(C5)	1847A	2,750	200.00	400.00	750.00	1700.

25th Anniversary of Reign
Obv: Similar to C#5.

KM#	Date	Mintage	Fine	VF	XF	Unc
6 (C6)	1847A	500 pcs.	400.00	700.00	1500.	2750.

REUSS-OBERGREIZ

The other branch of the division of 1535, Obergreiz went through a number of consolidations and further divisions. Upon the extinction of the Ruess-Untergreiz line in 1768, the latter passed to Reuss-Obergreiz and this line continued on into the 20th century, obtaining the rank of count back in 1673 and that of prince in 1778.

RULERS

Heinrich XIII, 1800-1817
Heinrich XIX, 1817-1836
Heinrich XX, 1836-1859
Heinrich XXII, 1859-1902
Heinrich XXIV, 1902-1918

HELLER

COPPER
Obv: Crowned lion on crowned oval shield.
Rev: Value.

KM#	Date	Mintage	Fine	VF	XF	Unc
100	1812	.045	4.00	8.00	15.00	65.00
(C37)	1815	.045	4.00	8.00	15.00	65.00
(C52)	1817	.040	4.00	8.00	15.00	65.00
	1819	.048	4.00	8.00	15.00	65.00

PFENNIG

COPPER

KM#	Date	Mintage	Fine	VF	XF	Unc
92	1806	.187	3.00	6.00	12.00	60.00
(C38)	1808	.273	3.00	6.00	12.00	60.00
Obv: Crowned lion on crowned oval shield.						
95	1808	—	3.00	6.00	12.00	60.00
(C39)	1810	.443	3.00	6.00	12.00	60.00
	1812	—	3.00	6.00	12.00	60.00
	1813	—	3.00	6.00	12.00	60.00
	1814	—	3.00	6.00	12.00	60.00
	1815	—	3.00	6.00	12.00	60.00
	1816	—	3.00	6.00	12.00	60.00

KM#	Date	Mintage	Fine	VF	XF	Unc
102	1817	—	2.50	5.00	10.00	55.00
(C53)	1819	—	2.50	5.00	10.00	55.00
	1820	—	2.50	5.00	10.00	55.00
	1821	—	2.50	5.00	10.00	55.00
	1822	—	2.50	5.00	10.00	55.00
	1823	—	2.50	5.00	10.00	55.00
	1824	—	2.50	5.00	10.00	55.00
	1825	—	2.50	5.00	10.00	55.00
	1826	—	2.50	5.00	10.00	55.00
	1827	—	2.50	5.00	10.00	55.00
	1828	—	2.50	5.00	10.00	55.00
	1829	—	2.50	5.00	10.00	55.00
	1830	—	2.50	5.00	10.00	55.00
	1831	—	2.50	5.00	10.00	55.00
	1832	—	2.50	5.00	10.00	50.00

Obv: King's crown.

KM#	Date	Mintage	Fine	VF	XF	Unc
115 (C57)	1864 A	.360	1.50	3.00	6.00	40.00

Obv: Prince's crown.

KM#	Date	Mintage	Fine	VF	XF	Unc
117 (C57a)	1868 A	.360	1.50	3.00	6.00	35.00

3 PFENNIG

COPPER

KM#	Date	Mintage	Fine	VF	XF	Unc
90	1805	.092	3.00	6.00	12.00	60.00
(C40)	1806	—	3.00	6.00	12.00	60.00
	1808	.256	3.00	6.00	12.00	60.00
	1810	.415	3.00	6.00	12.00	60.00
	1812	.296	3.00	6.00	12.00	60.00
	1813	—	3.00	6.00	12.00	60.00
	1814	—	3.00	6.00	12.00	60.00
	1815	—	3.00	6.00	12.00	60.00
	1816	—	3.00	6.00	12.00	60.00

KM#	Date	Mintage	Fine	VF	XF	Unc
103	1817	.144	2.50	5.00	10.00	55.00
(C54)	1819	—	2.50	5.00	10.00	55.00
	1820	—	2.50	5.00	10.00	55.00
	1821	—	2.50	5.00	10.00	55.00
	1822	—	2.50	5.00	10.00	55.00
	1823	—	2.50	5.00	10.00	55.00
	1824	—	2.50	5.00	10.00	55.00
	1825	—	2.50	5.00	10.00	55.00
	1826	—	2.50	5.00	10.00	55.00
	1827	—	2.50	5.00	10.00	55.00
	1828	—	2.50	5.00	10.00	55.00
	1829	—	2.50	5.00	10.00	55.00
	1830	—	2.50	5.00	10.00	55.00
	1831	—	2.50	5.00	10.00	55.00
	1832	—	2.50	5.00	10.00	55.00
	1833 L	—	2.50	5.00	10.00	55.00

Obv: King's crown.

KM#	Date	Mintage	Fine	VF	XF	Unc
116 (C58)	1864 A	.360	2.00	4.00	8.00	50.00

Obv: Prince's crown.

KM#	Date	Mintage	Fine	VF	XF	Unc
118 (C58a)	1868 A	.240	2.00	4.00	8.00	50.00

GROSCHEN

1.7600 g, .368 SILVER, .0208 oz ASW

KM#	Date	Mintage	Fine	VF	XF	Unc
91	1805	.251	2.50	5.00	10.00	50.00
(C42)	1812	.110	2.50	5.00	10.00	50.00

2.1900 g, .220 SILVER, .0154 oz ASW

KM#	Date	Mintage	Fine	VF	XF	Unc
119 (C59)	1868 A	.090	2.50	5.00	10.00	50.00

1/6 THALER

5.3600 g, .541 SILVER, .0932 oz ASW

KM#	Date	Mintage	Fine	VF	XF	Unc
96 (C45)	1808 L	9,006	75.00	150.00	300.00	500.00

1/3 THALER

7.0100 g, .833 SILVER, .1877 oz ASW

KM#	Date	Mintage	Fine	VF	XF	Unc
97 (C47)	1809 L	1,500	200.00	400.00	800.00	1200.

THALER

28.0600 g, .833 SILVER, .7515 oz ASW
Obv. leg: D.G. HENR. XIII .....

KM#	Date	Mintage	Fine	VF	XF	Unc
93 (C49)	1806 DOELL-L	345 pcs.	750.00	1400.	3200.	7500.
	1807 DOELL-L	200 pcs.	750.00	1400.	3200.	7500.

Obv. leg: V.G.G. HEINRICH .....
Rev: Similar to KM#93.

KM#	Date	Mintage	Fine	VF	XF	Unc
94 (C50)	1807 DF-L	300 pcs.	1000.	1600.	3500.	7500.
	1812 DF-L	2,275	900.00	1500.	2750.	6500.

KM#	Date	Mintage	Fine	VF	XF	Unc
101 (C51)	1812 DF-L	I.A.	350.00	700.00	1250.	3000.

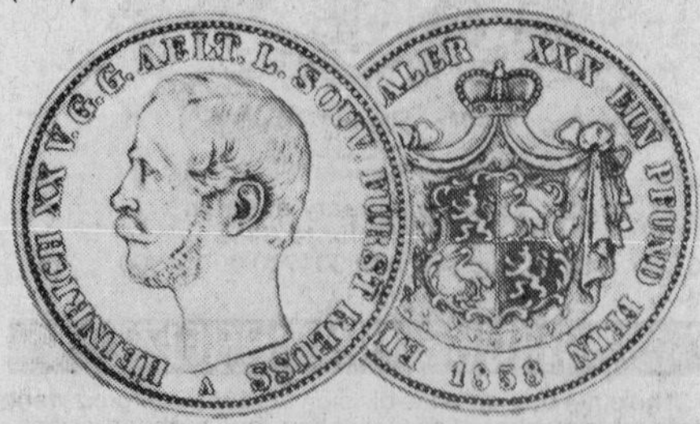

18.5200 g, .900 SILVER, .5360 oz ASW

KM#	Date	Mintage	Fine	VF	XF	Unc
110 (C55)	1858A	9,500	60.00	100.00	200.00	450.00

KM#	Date	Mintage	Fine	VF	XF	Unc
120 (C60)	1868A	7,100	60.00	100.00	200.00	450.00

2 THALER

(3-1/2 Gulden)

37.1200 g, .900 SILVER, 1.0742 oz ASW

KM#	Date	Mintage	Fine	VF	XF	Unc
105	1841A	2,400	200.00	375.00	750.00	1500.
(C56)	1844A	2,400	200.00	375.00	750.00	1500.
	1848A	2,400	200.00	375.00	750.00	1500.
	1851A	2,400	200.00	375.00	750.00	1500.

MONETARY REFORM

2 MARK

11.1110 g, .900 SILVER, .3215 oz ASW
Rev: Type II.

Y#	Date	Mintage	Fine	VF	XF	Unc
126	1877B	.020	150.00	300.00	1500.	2750.
(Y137)	1877B	—	—	—	Proof	3000.

Rev: Type III.

Y#	Date	Mintage	Fine	VF	XF	Unc
127	1892A	.010	125.00	325.00	650.00	950.00
(Y137a)	1892A	—	—	—	Proof	1200.

Y#	Date	Mintage	Fine	VF	XF	Unc
128	1899A	.010	100.00	200.00	400.00	550.00
(Y139)	1899A	120 pcs.	—	—	Proof	600.00

Y#	Date	Mintage	Fine	VF	XF	Unc
(Y139)	1901A	.010	100.00	200.00	400.00	550.00
	1901A	—	—	—	Proof	600.00

3 MARK

16.6670 g, .900 SILVER, .4823 oz ASW

	Date	Mintage	Fine	VF	XF	Unc
130	1909A	.010	100.00	250.00	400.00	550.00
(Y140)	1909A	400 pcs.	—	—	Proof	1000.

20 MARK

7.9650 g, .900 GOLD, .2304 oz AGW
Rev: Type II.

	Date	Mintage	Fine	VF	XF	Unc
125	1875B	1,510	6000.	9000.	12,500.	17,500.
(Y138)	1875B	—	—	—	Proof	25,000.

REUSS-SCHLEIZ

Originally part of the holdings of Reuss-Gera, Schleiz was ruled separately on and off during the first half of the 16th century. When the Gera line died out in 1550, Schleiz passed to Obergreiz. Schleiz was reintegrated into a new line of Gera and a separate countship at Schleiz was founded in 1635, only to last one generation. At its extinction in 1666, Schleiz passed to Reuss-Saalburg which thereafter took the name of Reuss-Schleiz.

RULERS

Heinrich XLII, 1784-1818
Heinrich LXII, 1818-1854
Heinrich LXVII, 1854-1867
Heinrich XIV, 1867-1913
Heinrich XXVII, 1913-1918

1/2 PFENNIG

(1 Heller)

COPPER

KM#	Date	Mintage	Fine	VF	XF	Unc
56 (C25)	1841A	—	15.00	30.00	60.00	175.00

PFENNIG

COPPER

	Date	Mintage	Fine	VF	XF	Unc
57	1841A	.751	4.00	7.00	20.00	75.00
(C26)	1847A	1.138	4.00	7.00	20.00	75.00

	Date	Mintage	Fine	VF	XF	Unc
65 (C27)	1850A	.540	2.00	4.00	8.00	40.00

	Date	Mintage	Fine	VF	XF	Unc
69	1855A	.362	2.00	4.00	8.00	40.00
(C35)	1858A	.360	2.00	4.00	8.00	40.00
	1862A	.202	2.00	4.00	8.00	40.00
	1864A	.540	2.00	4.00	8.00	40.00

KM#	Date	Mintage	Fine	VF	XF	Unc
75 (C40)	1868A	.360	2.00	4.00	8.00	40.00

3 PFENNIG

COPPER
Obv: Oval crowned shield w/crowned lion.
Rev: Value.

	Date	Mintage	Fine	VF	XF	Unc
50	1815	.076	5.00	10.00	20.00	75.00
(C20)	1816	Inc. Ab.	5.00	10.00	20.00	75.00

	Date	Mintage	Fine	VF	XF	Unc
58	1841A	.250	4.00	8.00	15.00	55.00
(C28)	1844A	.379	3.00	6.00	12.50	50.00

	Date	Mintage	Fine	VF	XF	Unc
66 (C29)	1850A	.311	3.00	6.00	12.50	50.00

	Date	Mintage	Fine	VF	XF	Unc
70	1855A	.242	3.00	6.00	12.50	50.00
(C36)	1858A	.360	3.00	6.00	12.50	50.00
	1862A	.125	3.00	6.00	12.50	50.00
	1864A	.240	3.00	6.00	12.50	50.00

	Date	Mintage	Fine	VF	XF	Unc
76 (C41)	1868A	.120	3.00	6.00	12.50	50.00

SILBER GROSCHEN

1.7600 g, .368 SILVER, .0208 oz ASW
Obv: Oval crowned arms, crowned lion w/1 tail.
Rev: Value.

	Date	Mintage	Fine	VF	XF	Unc
51 (C22)	1815	—	5.00	10.00	20.00	125.00

Obv: Uncrowned lion w/1 tail.

	Date	Mintage	Fine	VF	XF	Unc
52 (C22)a	1816S	.033	5.00	10.00	20.00	125.00

Obv: Crowned lion w/2 tails.

	Date	Mintage	Fine	VF	XF	Unc
53 (C22)b	1816S	Inc. Ab.	5.00	10.00	20.00	125.00

2.1900 g, .222 SILVER, .0156 oz ASW

	Date	Mintage	Fine	VF	XF	Unc
59	1841A	.064	4.00	8.00	15.00	90.00
(C30)	1844A	.092	4.00	8.00	15.00	90.00
	1846A	.062	4.00	8.00	15.00	90.00

Obv. leg: JUNGERER LINIE

KM#	Date	Mintage	Fine	VF	XF	Unc
67 (C31)	1850A	.062	4.00	8.00	15.00	100.00

	Date	Mintage	Fine	VF	XF	Unc
71 (C37)	1855A	.031	5.00	10.00	20.00	125.00

2 SILBER GROSCHEN

3.1100 g, .312 SILVER, .0311 oz ASW
Obv: Crowned shield w/crowned lion. Rev: Value.

	Date	Mintage	Fine	VF	XF	Unc
68 (C32)	1850A	.064	5.00	10.00	20.00	125.00

	Date	Mintage	Fine	VF	XF	Unc
72 (C38)	1855A	.031	10.00	20.00	40.00	150.00

THALER

(Vereins)

18.5200 g, .900 SILVER, .5360 oz ASW

	Date	Mintage	Fine	VF	XF	Unc
73	1858A	10,000	45.00	75.00	140.00	350.00
(C39)	1862A	10,000	45.00	75.00	140.00	350.00

	Date	Mintage	Fine	VF	XF	Unc
77 (C42)	1868A	.014	40.00	65.00	125.00	325.00

2 THALER

(3-1/2 Gulden)

37.1200 g, .900 SILVER, 1.0742 oz ASW

	Date	Mintage	Fine	VF	XF	Unc
55	1840A	2,650	250.00	400.00	800.00	1500.
(C33)	1844A	3,000	250.00	400.00	800.00	1500.
	1846A	2,650	250.00	400.00	800.00	1500.
	1853A	2,700	250.00	400.00	800.00	1500.
	1854A	2,700	225.00	450.00	1000.	1600.

25th Anniversary of Reign
Obv: Similar to KM#55.

KM#	Date	Mintage	Fine	VF	XF	Unc
60 (C34)	1843A	500 pcs.	350.00	700.00	1500.	3000.

MONETARY REFORM

2 MARK

11.1110 g, .900 SILVER, .3215 oz ASW

KM#	Date	Mintage	Fine	VF	XF	Unc
82	1884A	.100	150.00	300.00	850.00	1500.
(Y141)	1884A	—	—	—	Proof	2500.

10 MARK

3.9820 g, .900 GOLD, .1152 oz AGW

KM#	Date	Mintage	Fine	VF	XF	Unc
81	1882A	4,800	1250.	2500.	4000.	5000.
(Y142)	1882A	200 pcs.	—	—	Proof	10,000.

20 MARK

7.9650 g, .900 GOLD, .2304 oz AGW

KM#	Date	Mintage	Fine	VF	XF	Unc
80	1881A	.012	1000.	1500.	2500.	3250.
(Y143)	1881A	500 pcs.	—	—	Proof	6000.

Death of Heinrich I's Wife, Maximilane von Hardegg
Similar to 2/3 Thaler, KM#19, but 10-line inscription on obverse.

KM#	Date	Mintage	Fine	VF	XF	Unc
22	1678	—	—	—	—	—

RHENISH CONFEDERATION

Issues for Carl von Dahlberg, 1804-1817

MINTMASTERS INITIALS

Letter	Date	Name
B,CB	1773-1811	Christoph Busch, Regensburg
BH	1790-1825	Johann Georg Bunsen, mint master in Frankfurt
	1798-1816	Johann Georg Hille, mintwarden in Frankfurt

HELLER

COPPER
Obv. leg: FURST PRIM SCHEIDE MUNZ.

C#	Date	Mintage	Fine	VF	XF	Unc
1	1808 BH	.033	10.00	30.00	70.00	150.00
	1810 BH	—	10.00	30.00	70.00	150.00
	1812 BH	—	10.00	30.00	70.00	150.00

Obv. leg: GROSH FRANKF SCHEIDE MUNZ.

C#	Date	Mintage	Fine	VF	XF	Unc
2	1810 BH	—	10.00	30.00	70.00	150.00
	1812 BH	—	10.00	30.00	70.00	150.00

KREUZER

BILLON
Obv. leg: SCHEID.MUNZ.

C#	Date	Mintage	Fine	VF	XF	Unc
3.1	1808 BH	—	8.00	25.00	50.00	150.00
	1809 BH	—	8.00	25.00	50.00	150.00
	1810 BH	—	8.00	25.00	50.00	150.00

Obv. leg: SCHEIDMUNZ.

C#	Date	Mintage	Fine	VF	XF	Unc
3.2	1809 BH	—	8.00	25.00	60.00	150.00

1/2 THALER

(Convention)

.833 SILVER

C#	Date	Mintage	Fine	VF	XF	Unc
5	1809 B	—	65.00	100.00	175.00	300.00

EIN (1) THALER

(Convention)

28.0600 g, .833 SILVER, .7516 oz ASW

C#	Date	Mintage	Fine	VF	XF	Unc
4	1808 BH	—	175.00	375.00	650.00	1200.

C#	Date	Mintage	Fine	VF	XF	Unc
6	1809 B	—	150.00	325.00	1100.	2500.

C#	Date	Mintage	Fine	VF	XF	Unc
7	1809 CB	—	150.00	325.00	800.00	2200.

TRADE COINAGE

DUCAT

3.5000 g, .986 GOLD, .1109 oz AGW

C#	Date	Mintage	Fine	VF	XF	Unc
8	1809 BH	—	500.00	1000.	1750.	2750.

ROSTOCK

A city, near the Baltic Sea in Mecklenburg, has a history from the 12th century. The first municipal charter dates from 1218. In 1325 Rostock obtained the mint right and not long after, joined the Hanseatic League. The city coinage extends to 1864.

MINTMASTERS INITIALS

Letter	Date	Name
AIB	1805	Andreas Joachim Brand
AS	1815-1824	Adam Schiller
BS	1843-1859	Benjamin Steinhorst
FL	1796-1802	Friedrich Lautersack
HK	1862-1864	Heinrich Kehr

PFENNIG

COPPER
Obv: Griffin shield within ring. Rev: Value.

C#	Date	Mintage	Fine	VF	XF	Unc
2a	1801 FL	—	3.50	7.00	20.00	70.00
	1802 FL	—	3.50	7.00	20.00	70.00

NOTE: Earlier dates (1796-1800) exist for this type.

Obv. leg: ROSTOCKER begins at 8 o'clock.

C#	Date	Mintage	Fine	VF	XF	Unc
4	1802 FL	—	3.50	7.00	20.00	70.00
	1805 AIB	—	3.50	7.00	20.00	70.00

Obv: W/o circle between griffin and legend.

C#	Date	Mintage	Fine	VF	XF	Unc
4a	1815 AS	—	3.00	6.00	15.00	70.00
	1824 AS	—	3.00	6.00	15.00	60.00

C#	Date	Mintage	Fine	VF	XF	Unc
5	1848 BS	—	3.50	7.00	20.00	70.00

3 PFENNIG

COPPER

C#	Date	Mintage	Fine	VF	XF	Unc
10	1815 AS	—	3.50	7.00	20.00	75.00
	1824 AS	—	3.50	7.00	20.00	75.00
10a	1843 BS	.192	3.50	7.00	20.00	75.00

C#	Date	Mintage	Fine	VF	XF	Unc
11	1855 BS	—	3.50	7.00	20.00	75.00

C#	Date	Mintage	Fine	VF	XF	Unc
12	1859 BS	—	3.50	7.00	20.00	75.00

C#	Date	Mintage	Fine	VF	XF	Unc
12a	1862 HK	—	3.50	7.00	20.00	75.00
	1864 HK	—	3.50	7.00	20.00	75.00

SAXE-ALTENBURG

A duchy, located in Thuringia in northwest Germany. It came into being in 1826 when Saxe-Gotha-Altenburg became extinct. The duke of Saxe-Hildburghausen ceded Hildburghausen to Meiningen in exchange for SaxeAltenburg. The last duke abdicated in 1918.

RULERS

Joseph, 1834-1848
Georg, 1848-1853
Ernst I, 1853-1908
Ernst II, 1908-1918

MINTMASTERS INITIALS

B - Gustav Julius Buschick
F - Gustav Theodor Fischer
G - Johann Georg Grohmann

PFENNIG

COPPER

Obv: Crowned arms. Rev: Value.

C#	Date	Mintage	Fine	VF	XF	Unc
1	1841 G	.220	1.50	3.00	6.00	40.00

Obv: Crowned heart shaped arms.

C#	Date	Mintage	Fine	VF	XF	Unc
2	1843 G	.089	2.00	4.00	8.00	45.00

Rev: F below date.

C#	Date	Mintage	Fine	VF	XF	Unc
11	1852 F	.120	1.50	3.00	6.00	40.00

Rev: F below date.

C#	Date	Mintage	Fine	VF	XF	Unc
14	1856 F	.041	2.00	4.00	8.00	45.00
	1858 F	.129	1.50	3.00	6.00	40.00

Rev: W/o mintmasters initial.

C#	Date	Mintage	Fine	VF	XF	Unc
14a	1857	—	1.50	3.00	6.00	40.00

Rev: B below date.

C#	Date	Mintage	Fine	VF	XF	Unc
14b	1861 B	.163	1.50	3.00	6.00	40.00
	1863 B	.302	1.50	3.00	6.00	40.00
	1865 B	.150	1.50	3.00	6.00	40.00

2 PFENNIG

COPPER

Obv: Crowned arms. Rev: Value.

C#	Date	Mintage	Fine	VF	XF	Unc
3	1841 G	.150	2.00	4.00	8.00	45.00

Obv: Crowned heart shaped arms.

C#	Date	Mintage	Fine	VF	XF	Unc
4	1843 G	.046	2.50	5.00	10.00	50.00

C#	Date	Mintage	Fine	VF	XF	Unc
12	1852 F	.060	2.50	5.00	10.00	50.00
15	1856 F	.029	2.50	5.00	10.00	50.00

5 PFENNIG

(1/2 Neugroschen)

1.0600 g, .229 SILVER, .0078 oz ASW
Obv: Crowned arms. Rev: Value.

C#	Date	Mintage	Fine	VF	XF	Unc
5	1841 G	.097	4.00	8.00	20.00	75.00
	1842 G	.130	4.00	8.00	20.00	75.00

10 PFENNIG

(1 Neugroschen)

2.1200 g, .229 SILVER, .0156 oz ASW
Obv: Crowned arms. Rev: Value.

C#	Date	Mintage	Fine	VF	XF	Unc
6	1841 G	.146	4.00	8.00	20.00	75.00
	1842 G	.065	4.00	8.00	20.00	75.00

20 PFENNIG

(2 Neugroschen)

3.1100 g, .312 SILVER, .0311 oz ASW

C#	Date	Mintage	Fine	VF	XF	Unc
7	ND	—	5.00	10.00	20.00	60.00
7a	1841 G	.231	6.00	12.00	25.00	80.00

1/6 THALER

5.3450 g, .520 SILVER, .0894 oz ASW

C#	Date	Mintage	Fine	VF	XF	Unc
8	1841 G	.060	10.00	25.00	100.00	250.00
	1842 G	.060	10.00	25.00	100.00	250.00

THALER

22.2720 g, .750 SILVER, .5371 oz ASW

C#	Date	Mintage	Fine	VF	XF	Unc
9	1841 G	.020	75.00	150.00	325.00	1000.

(Vereins)

18.5200 g, .900 SILVER, .5360 oz ASW

C#	Date	Mintage	Fine	VF	XF	Unc
16	1858 F	.032	40.00	75.00	150.00	325.00
	1858 F	—	—	—	Proof	450.00
16	1864 B	.022	30.00	60.00	125.00	300.00
	1869 B	.023	30.00	60.00	125.00	300.00

2 THALER

(3-1/2 Gulden)

37.1190 g, .900 SILVER, 1.0742 oz ASW

C#	Date	Mintage	Fine	VF	XF	Unc
10	1841 G	9,400	200.00	375.00	800.00	1600.
	1842 G	4,700	250.00	500.00	1000.	2000.
	1843 G	4,700	225.00	450.00	900.00	1900.
	1847 F	9,400	200.00	375.00	850.00	1800.

Rev: Similar to 1 Thaler, C#16.

C#	Date	Mintage	Fine	VF	XF	Unc
13	1852 F	9,400	250.00	450.00	900.00	1900.

MONETARY REFORM

2 MARK

11.1110 g, .900 SILVER, .3215 oz ASW
Ernst 75th Birthday

Y#	Date	Mintage	Fine	VF	XF	Unc
144	1901A	.050	100.00	200.00	400.00	600.00
	1901A	500 pcs.	—	—	Proof	700.00

5 MARK

27.7770 g, .900 SILVER, .8038 oz ASW
Ernst 75th Birthday

Y#	Date	Mintage	Fine	VF	XF	Unc
145	1901A	.020	200.00	425.00	800.00	1200.
	1901A	500 pcs.	—	—	Proof	1250.

Ernst 50th Year of Reign

Y#	Date	Mintage	Fine	VF	XF	Unc
147	1903A	.020	100.00	200.00	300.00	425.00
	1903A	300 pcs.	—	—	Proof	500.00

20 MARK

7.9650 g, .900 GOLD, .2304 oz AGW

Y#	Date	Mintage	Fine	VF	XF	Unc
146	1887A	.015	800.00	1000.	1500.	2000.
	1887A	—	—	—	Proof	3750.

SAXE-COBURG-GOTHA

Located in northwest Germany, Saxe-Coburg-Gotha was created for the duke of Saxe-Coburg-Saalfeld after the dispersal of Saalfeld and the acquisition of Gotha in 1826. The last duke abdicated in 1918.

RULERS

Ernst I, 1826-1844
Ernst II, 1844-1893
Alfred, 1893-1900
Carl Eduard, 1900-1918

MINTMASTERS INITIALS

Letter	Date	Name
B	1860-1887	Gustav Julius Buschick
EK	1828-38	Ernst Kleinsteuber
F	1845-60	Gustav Theodor Fischer
G	1826-28	Graupner
G	1838-44	Johann Georg Grohmann
ST	1826-1828	Strebel

PFENNIG

COPPER

C#	Date	Mintage	Fine	VF	XF	Unc
83	1833	—	2.00	4.00	8.00	50.00
	1834	—	2.00	4.00	8.00	50.00
	1835	—	2.00	4.00	8.00	50.00
	1836	—	2.00	4.00	8.00	50.00
	1837	—	2.00	4.00	8.00	50.00

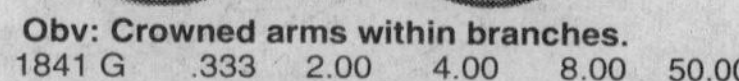

Obv: Crowned arms within branches.

C#	Date	Mintage	Fine	VF	XF	Unc
100	1841 G	.333	2.00	4.00	8.00	50.00

Obv: F above crowned arms.

C#	Date	Mintage	Fine	VF	XF	Unc
109	1847 F	.207	1.50	3.00	6.00	50.00
	1851 F	.059	1.50	3.00	6.00	50.00
	1852 F	.201	1.50	3.00	6.00	50.00
	1856 F	.600	1.50	3.00	6.00	50.00

Obv: B above arms.

C#	Date	Mintage	Fine	VF	XF	Unc
109a	1865 B	.150	1.50	3.00	6.00	50.00

C#	Date	Mintage	Fine	VF	XF	Unc
109b	1868 B	.200	1.50	3.00	6.00	50.00
	1870 B	.096	1.50	3.00	6.00	50.00

1-1/2 PFENNIG

COPPER

C#	Date	Mintage	Fine	VF	XF	Unc
84	1834	—	2.00	4.00	8.00	50.00
	1835	—	2.00	4.00	8.00	50.00

2 PFENNIG

COPPER

C#	Date	Mintage	Fine	VF	XF	Unc
85	1834	—	2.00	4.00	8.00	50.00
	1835	—	2.00	4.00	8.00	50.00

C#	Date	Mintage	Fine	VF	XF	Unc
101	1841 G	.333	2.00	4.00	8.00	50.00

Obv: F and date below bow.

C#	Date	Mintage	Fine	VF	XF	Unc
110	1847 F	.130	1.50	3.00	6.00	50.00
	1851 F	.125	1.50	3.00	6.00	50.00
	1852 F	.146	1.50	3.00	6.00	50.00
	1856 F	.600	1.50	3.00	6.00	50.00

Obv: B and date below bow.

C#	Date	Mintage	Fine	VF	XF	Unc
110a	1868 B	.136	1.50	3.00	6.00	50.00
	1870 B	.118	1.50	3.00	6.00	50.00

3 PFENNIG

COPPER

C#	Date	Mintage	Fine	VF	XF	Unc
86	1834	—	4.00	8.00	17.50	65.00

KREUZER

.7900 g, .125 SILVER, .0031 oz ASW
Obv: ST below crowned E. Rev: Value in script.

C#	Date	Mintage	Fine	VF	XF	Unc
86.5	1827 ST	—	5.00	12.00	30.00	120.00

C#	Date	Mintage	Fine	VF	XF	Unc
87	1827 ST	—	5.00	12.00	30.00	120.00
	1828 ST	—	5.00	12.00	30.00	120.00

Obv: EK below crowned E.

C#	Date	Mintage	Fine	VF	XF	Unc
87a	1829 EK	—	5.00	12.00	30.00	120.00
	1830 EK	—	5.00	12.00	30.00	120.00

Rev: KREUZER along bottom rim.

C#	Date	Mintage	Fine	VF	XF	Unc
88	1831	—	2.00	6.00	10.00	60.00
	1832	—	2.00	6.00	10.00	60.00
	1833	—	2.00	6.00	10.00	60.00
	1834	—	2.00	6.00	10.00	60.00
	1836	—	2.00	6.00	10.00	60.00
	1837	—	2.00	6.00	10.00	60.00

3 KREUZER

1.5000 g, .243 SILVER, .0117 oz ASW
Obv: Crowned E within branches, ST below.
Rev: Value in script.

C#	Date	Mintage	Fine	VF	XF	Unc
89.5	1827 ST	—	10.00	30.00	50.00	200.00

C#	Date	Mintage	Fine	VF	XF	Unc
90	1827 ST	—	8.00	20.00	40.00	175.00
	1828 ST	—	8.00	20.00	40.00	175.00
	1829 S	—	8.00	20.00	40.00	175.00
	1829 ST	—	8.00	20.00	40.00	175.00

Obv: EK below crowned E.

C#	Date	Mintage	Fine	VF	XF	Unc
90a	1828 EK	—	8.00	20.00	40.00	175.00
	1830 EK	—	8.00	20.00	40.00	175.00
	1831 EK	—	8.00	20.00	40.00	175.00

C#	Date	Mintage	Fine	VF	XF	Unc
91	1831	—	2.00	5.00	15.00	80.00
	1832	—	2.00	5.00	15.00	80.00
	1833	—	2.00	5.00	15.00	80.00
	1834	—	2.00	5.00	15.00	80.00
	1835	—	2.00	5.00	15.00	80.00
	1836	—	2.00	5.00	15.00	80.00
	1837	—	2.00	5.00	15.00	80.00

Obv: Crowned arms. Rev: Value within branches.

C#	Date	Mintage	Fine	VF	XF	Unc
101.3	1838	.358	2.00	5.00	15.00	80.00

6 KREUZER

2.7300 g, .305 SILVER, .0267 oz ASW

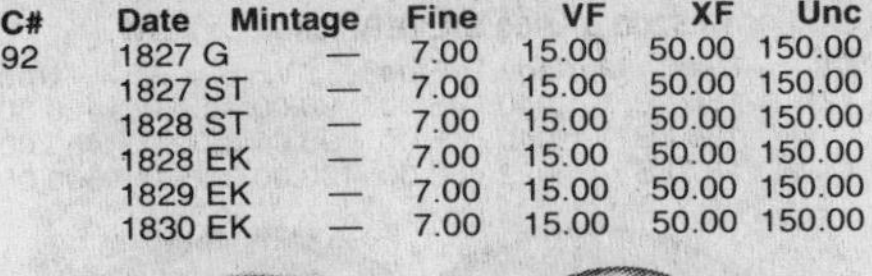

C#	Date	Mintage	Fine	VF	XF	Unc
92	1827 G	—	7.00	15.00	50.00	150.00
	1827 ST	—	7.00	15.00	50.00	150.00
	1828 ST	—	7.00	15.00	50.00	150.00
	1828 EK	—	7.00	15.00	50.00	150.00
	1829 EK	—	7.00	15.00	50.00	150.00
	1830 EK	—	7.00	15.00	50.00	150.00

C#	Date	Mintage	Fine	VF	XF	Unc
93	1831	—	3.00	5.00	20.00	100.00
	1832	—	3.00	5.00	20.00	100.00
	1833	—	3.00	5.00	20.00	100.00
	1834	—	3.00	5.00	20.00	100.00
	1835	—	3.00	5.00	20.00	100.00
	1836	—	3.00	5.00	20.00	100.00
	1837	—	3.00	5.00	20.00	100.00

C#	Date	Mintage	Fine	VF	XF	Unc
101.6	1838	.209	3.00	5.00	20.00	100.00

10 KREUZER

3.8900 g, .500 SILVER, .0625 oz ASW
Similar to C#94b.

C#	Date	Mintage	Fine	VF	XF	Unc
94	1831	—	20.00	35.00	70.00	250.00
	1832	—	20.00	35.00	70.00	250.00
	1833	—	20.00	35.00	70.00	250.00
	1834	—	20.00	35.00	70.00	250.00

C#	Date	Mintage	Fine	VF	XF	Unc
94b	1835	—	15.00	30.00	60.00	200.00
	1836	—	15.00	30.00	60.00	200.00
	1837	—	15.00	30.00	60.00	200.00

20 KREUZER

6.6800 g, .583 SILVER, .1252 oz ASW
Obv. leg: . . . . .COBURG & GOTHA. . . . .
crowned arms. Rev: ST below value.

C#	Date	Mintage	Fine	VF	XF	Unc
95	1827 ST	—	20.00	50.00	125.00	300.00

Obv. leg: . . . . .COBURG UND GOTHA. . . . .

C#	Date	Mintage	Fine	VF	XF	Unc
95a	1827 ST	—	20.00	50.00	125.00	300.00
	1828 ST	—	20.00	50.00	125.00	300.00

Rev: E.K. below branches.

C#	Date	Mintage	Fine	VF	XF	Unc
95b	1828 EK	—	20.00	50.00	125.00	300.00
	1830 EK	—	20.00	50.00	125.00	300.00

Similar to C#96a.

C#	Date	Mintage	Fine	VF	XF	Unc
96	1831	—	20.00	50.00	125.00	300.00
	1834	—	20.00	50.00	125.00	300.00

Obv. leg. ends: . . . . .SACHSEN COBURG-GOTHA

C#	Date	Mintage	Fine	VF	XF	Unc
96a	1835	—	15.00	35.00	60.00	200.00
	1836	—	15.00	35.00	60.00	200.00

1/2 GROSCHEN

1.0600 g, .229 SILVER, .0078 oz ASW

C#	Date	Mintage	Fine	VF	XF	Unc
102	1841 G	.247	5.00	10.00	35.00	125.00
	1844 G	.065	5.00	10.00	35.00	125.00

C#	Date	Mintage	Fine	VF	XF	Unc
111	1851 F	.032	2.00	4.00	8.00	50.00
	1855 F	.130	2.00	4.00	8.00	50.00
	1858 F	.060	2.00	4.00	8.00	50.00

Obv: B below arms.

C#	Date	Mintage	Fine	VF	XF	Unc
114	1868 B	.032	2.00	4.00	8.00	50.00
	1870 B	.052	2.00	4.00	8.00	50.00

GROSCHEN

1.9800 g, .368 SILVER, .0234 oz ASW

C#	Date	Mintage	Fine	VF	XF	Unc
89	1837	—	5.00	10.00	30.00	125.00

2.1200 g, .229 SILVER, .0156 oz ASW

C#	Date	Mintage	Fine	VF	XF	Unc
103	1841 G	.355	8.00	15.00	40.00	175.00

C#	Date	Mintage	Fine	VF	XF	Unc
112	1847 F	.130	2.00	4.00	8.00	50.00
	1851 F	.049	2.00	4.00	8.00	50.00
	1855 F	.130	2.00	4.00	8.00	50.00
	1858 F	.033	2.00	4.00	8.00	50.00

C#	Date	Mintage	Fine	VF	XF	Unc
115	1865 B	.070	2.00	4.00	8.00	50.00
	1868 B	.031	2.00	4.00	8.00	50.00
	1870 B	.030	2.00	4.00	8.00	50.00

2 GROSCHEN

3.1100 g, .312 SILVER, .0311 oz ASW
Obv: Crowned arms within branches. Rev: Value.

C#	Date	Mintage	Fine	VF	XF	Unc
104	1841 G	.214	8.00	20.00	40.00	150.00
	1844 G	.032	8.00	20.00	40.00	150.00

C#	Date	Mintage	Fine	VF	XF	Unc
113	1847 F	.097	6.00	12.00	25.00	75.00
	1851 F	.032	6.00	12.00	25.00	75.00
	1855 F	.081	6.00	12.00	25.00	75.00
	1858 F	.055	6.00	12.00	25.00	75.00

3.2200 g, .300 SILVER, .0310 oz ASW

C#	Date	Mintage	Fine	VF	XF	Unc
116	1865 B	.070	5.00	10.00	20.00	65.00
	1868 B	.030	5.00	10.00	20.00	65.00
	1870 B	.031	5.00	10.00	20.00	65.00

1/6 THALER

5.3450 g, .521 SILVER, .0895 oz ASW

C#	Date	Mintage	Fine	VF	XF	Unc
105	1841 G	.048	15.00	40.00	75.00	225.00
	1842 G	.048	15.00	40.00	75.00	225.00
	1843 G	.048	15.00	40.00	75.00	225.00

Obv: Different head.

C#	Date	Mintage	Fine	VF	XF	Unc
117	1845 F	.123	15.00	35.00	75.00	225.00

C#	Date	Mintage	Fine	VF	XF	Unc
117a	1848 F	.130	10.00	30.00	60.00	200.00

Obv: Head w/beard.

C#	Date	Mintage	Fine	VF	XF	Unc
117b	1852 F	.048	15.00	35.00	75.00	225.00
	1855 F	.060	15.00	35.00	75.00	225.00

5.3400 g, .520 SILVER, .0892 oz ASW

C#	Date	Mintage	Fine	VF	XF	Unc
118	1864 B	.060	10.00	30.00	60.00	200.00

25th Anniversary of Reign

C#	Date	Mintage	Fine	VF	XF	Unc
119	1869 B	.012	10.00	30.00	50.00	150.00

1/2 THALER

(Convention)

(1 Gulden)

14.0300 g, .833 SILVER, .3757 oz ASW

C#	Date	Mintage	Fine	VF	XF	Unc
97	1830 EK	—	65.00	135.00	300.00	650.00
	1831	—	65.00	135.00	300.00	650.00

C#	Date	Mintage	Fine	VF	XF	Unc
97	1832	—	65.00	135.00	300.00	650.00
	1834	—	65.00	135.00	300.00	650.00
	1835 HF	—	65.00	135.00	300.00	650.00
97a	1834 HF	—	65.00	135.00	300.00	650.00

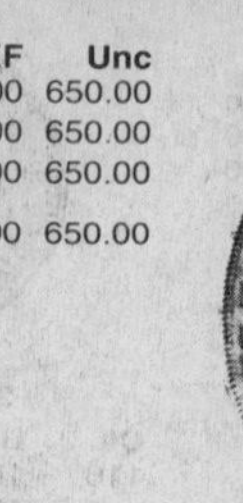

EIN (1) THALER

(Krone)

29.3800 g, .871 SILVER, .8228 oz ASW

98	1827	—	350.00	700.00	1000.	2000.

(Convention)

28.0600 g, .833 SILVER, .7514 oz ASW

99	1828	31 pcs.	—	—	Rare	—
	1828	—	—	—	Proof	10,000.

99a	1829 E-K	1,095	400.00	800.00	1500.	2750.

Rev: W/o mintmasters initials.

C#	Date	Mintage	Fine	VF	XF	Unc
99b	1832	304 pcs.	—	—	Rare	—
	1833	Inc. Ab.	—	—	Rare	—
99c	1835	—	800.00	1700.	3000.	5000.

22.2700 g, .750 SILVER, .5371 oz ASW
Rev: Crowned draped arms within wreath.

106	1841 G	.016	75.00	150.00	400.00	1000.
	1842 G	.016	75.00	150.00	400.00	1000.

120	1846 F	.032	75.00	150.00	400.00	1000.

120a	1848 F	.016	75.00	150.00	400.00	1000.

120b	1851 F	8,000	75.00	150.00	400.00	1000.
	1852 F	8,000	75.00	150.00	400.00	1000.

(Vereins)

18.5200 g, .900 SILVER, .5360 oz ASW

C#	Date	Mintage	Fine	VF	XF	Unc
121	1862 B	.040	45.00	90.00	200.00	450.00
	1864 B	.040	45.00	90.00	200.00	450.00
	1870 B	.022	60.00	100.00	225.00	500.00

25th Anniversary of Reign

122	1869 B	6,000	45.00	85.00	150.00	300.00

2 THALER

(3-1/2 Gulden)

37.1200 g, .900 SILVER, 1.0743 oz ASW

107	1841 G	.011	250.00	500.00	1000.	2200.
	1842 G	5,350	300.00	600.00	1100.	2400.
	1843 G	5,350	300.00	600.00	1100.	2400.

Rev: Similar to C#123a.

123	1847 F	.011	350.00	625.00	1400.	2800.

123a	1854 F	.016	225.00	425.00	1000.	2000.

MONETARY REFORM

2 MARK

11.1110 g, .900 SILVER, .3215 oz ASW

Y#	Date	Mintage	Fine	VF	XF	Unc
149	1895A	.015	250.00	650.00	900.00	1250.

Y#	Date	Mintage	Fine	VF	XF	Unc
152	1905A	.010	125.00	275.00	600.00	950.00
	1905A	2,000	—	—	Proof	850.00
	1911A	100 pcs.	—	—	Proof	9000.

5 MARK

27.7770 g, .900 SILVER, .8038 oz ASW

Y#	Date	Mintage	Fine	VF	XF	Unc
150	1895A	4,000	750.00	1500.	2000.	3000.
	1895A	—	—	—	Proof	3250.

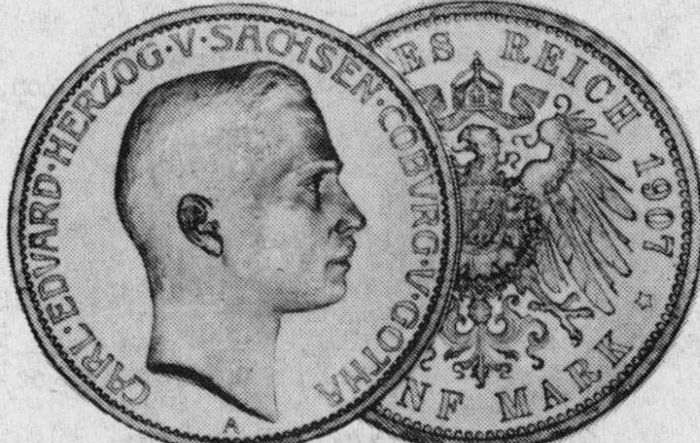

Y#	Date	Mintage	Fine	VF	XF	Unc
153	1907A	.010	300.00	600.00	1000.	1500.
	1907A	—	—	—	Proof	1800.

10 MARK

3.9820 g, .900 GOLD, .1152 oz AGW

Y#	Date	Mintage	Fine	VF	XF	Unc
154	1905A	9,511	400.00	600.00	1000.	1400.
	1905A	489 pcs.	—	—	Proof	3500.

20 MARK

7.9650 g, .900 GOLD, .2304 oz AGW

Rev: Type I.

Y#	Date	Mintage	Fine	VF	XF	Unc
148	1872E	1,000	7000.	11,000.	15,000.	19,000.
	1872E	—	—	—	Proof	Rare

Y#	Date	Mintage	Fine	VF	XF	Unc
148a	1886A	.020	500.00	900.00	1400.	1800.
	1886A	—	—	—	Proof	3750.

Y#	Date	Mintage	Fine	VF	XF	Unc
151	1895A	.010	500.00	1200.	2000.	2750.
	1895A	225 pcs.	—	—	Proof	4500.

Y#	Date	Mintage	Fine	VF	XF	Unc
155	1905A	.010	400.00	750.00	1200.	1800.
	1905A	484 pcs.	—	—	Proof	3750.

TRADE COINAGE

DUCAT

3.5000 g, .986 GOLD, .1109 oz AGW

C#	Date	Mintage	Fine	VF	XF	Unc
108	1831 E-K	600 pcs.	900.00	2000.	3250.	4250.
108a	1836	1,600	600.00	1250.	2500.	3250.
	1842	508 pcs.	600.00	1500.	3000.	3750.

SAXE-COBURG-SAALFELD

A duchy, located in northwest Germany, was founded in 1680 as Saxe-Saalfeld. They obtained Coburg in 1735. In 1826, Saalfeld was given to Meiningen and the ruler became the first duke of Saxe-Coburg-Gotha.

RULERS

Franz, 1800-1806
Ernst I, 1806-1826

MINTMASTERS INITIALS

Letter	Date	Name
L	1803-1816	Georg Christoph Loewel
S	1816-1826	Laurentius Theodor Sommer, warden

HELLER

COPPER

C#	Date	Mintage	Fine	VF	XF	Unc
63	1808	—	2.00	4.00	10.00	50.00
	1809	.112	2.00	4.00	10.00	50.00
	1810	.071	2.00	4.00	10.00	50.00
	1814	.050	2.00	4.00	10.00	50.00
	1815	Inc. Ab.	2.00	4.00	10.00	50.00
	1817	—	2.00	4.00	10.00	50.00
	1818	—	2.00	4.00	10.00	50.00
	1819	—	2.00	4.00	10.00	50.00
	1824	—	2.00	4.00	10.00	50.00
	1826	—	2.00	4.00	10.00	50.00

C#	Date	Mintage	Fine	VF	XF	Unc
68	1809	—	3.00	5.00	10.00	50.00

PFENNIG

COPPER

C#	Date	Mintage	Fine	VF	XF	Unc
47	1804	—	1.50	3.00	6.00	50.00
	1805	—	1.50	3.00	6.00	50.00
	1808	.083	1.50	3.00	6.00	50.00
	1809	.055	1.50	3.00	6.00	50.00
	1814	.043	1.50	3.00	6.00	50.00
	1815	Inc. Ab.	1.50	3.00	6.00	50.00
	1817	—	1.50	3.00	6.00	50.00
	1819	—	1.50	3.00	6.00	50.00
	1820	—	1.50	3.00	6.00	50.00
	1821	—	1.50	3.00	6.00	50.00
	1822	—	1.50	3.00	6.00	50.00
	1823	—	1.50	3.00	6.00	50.00
	1824	—	1.50	3.00	6.00	50.00
	1826	—	1.50	3.00	6.00	50.00

Rev: W/o rosettes on sides of 'I'.

C#	Date	Mintage	Fine	VF	XF	Unc
47a	1805	—	1.50	3.00	6.00	50.00

BILLON

C#	Date	Mintage	Fine	VF	XF	Unc
56	1805	—	1.50	3.00	6.00	50.00
73	1808	.962	4.00	7.00	15.00	70.00

COPPER

C#	Date	Mintage	Fine	VF	XF	Unc
69	1809	—	3.00	5.00	10.00	60.00

2 PFENNIG

COPPER

C#	Date	Mintage	Fine	VF	XF	Unc
70	1810	.124	3.00	10.00	20.00	60.00
	1817	—	3.00	10.00	20.00	60.00
	1818	—	3.00	10.00	20.00	60.00

Rev: W/o rosettes on sides of 2.

C#	Date	Mintage	Fine	VF	XF	Unc
70a	1810	Inc. Ab.	3.00	10.00	20.00	60.00

3 PFENNIG

.7900 g, .125 SILVER, .0031 oz ASW

C#	Date	Mintage	Fine	VF	XF	Unc
49	1804	—	3.00	7.00	15.00	50.00
	1805	—	3.00	7.00	15.00	50.00
	1806	—	3.00	7.00	15.00	50.00

COPPER

Obv: Arms on crowned cartouche w/festoons.

C#	Date	Mintage	Fine	VF	XF	Unc
48	1806	—	3.00	5.00	10.00	45.00

Rev. value: III PFENNIG

C#	Date	Mintage	Fine	VF	XF	Unc
65	1807	—	4.00	8.00	20.00	60.00
	1808	.063	4.00	8.00	20.00	60.00

C#	Date	Mintage	Fine	VF	XF	Unc
65a	1821	—	2.00	6.00	15.00	50.00
	1822	—	2.00	6.00	15.00	50.00
	1823	—	2.00	6.00	15.00	50.00
	1824	—	2.00	6.00	15.00	50.00
	1825	—	2.00	6.00	15.00	50.00
	1826	—	2.00	6.00	15.00	50.00

4 PFENNIG

COPPER

C#	Date	Mintage	Fine	VF	XF	Unc
71	1809	.027	4.00	8.00	20.00	75.00
	1810	8,106	4.00	8.00	20.00	75.00
	1818	—	4.00	8.00	20.00	75.00
	1820	—	4.00	8.00	20.00	75.00

6 PFENNIG

1.2900 g, .229 SILVER, .0094 oz ASW

C#	Date	Mintage	Fine	VF	XF	Unc
66	1808	.047	4.00	8.00	20.00	75.00
	1810	—	4.00	8.00	20.00	75.00
	1818 S	—	4.00	8.00	20.00	75.00
	1820 S	—	4.00	8.00	20.00	75.00

KREUZER

.7900 g, .125 SILVER, .0031 oz ASW

C#	Date	Mintage	Fine	VF	XF	Unc
57	1805	—	3.00	8.00	15.00	70.00

Obv: Crowned E within 2 crossed branches.
Rev: Value, leg: H.S.C.

C#	Date	Mintage	Fine	VF	XF	Unc
74	1808	.068	3.00	7.00	15.00	60.00
	1812	.018	3.00	7.00	15.00	60.00
	1813	.018	3.00	7.00	15.00	60.00
	1815	.021	3.00	7.00	15.00	60.00
	1817	—	3.00	7.00	15.00	60.00
	1818	—	3.00	7.00	15.00	60.00
	1820	—	3.00	7.00	15.00	60.00

Rev. leg: H.S.C.S.

C#	Date	Mintage	Fine	VF	XF	Unc
74a	1824 S	—	3.00	5.00	10.00	60.00
	1825 S	—	3.00	5.00	10.00	60.00
	1826 S	—	3.00	5.00	10.00	60.00

3 KREUZER

1.5000 g, .243 SILVER, .0117 oz ASW
Obv: Crowned oval arms. Rev: Value.

C#	Date	Mintage	Fine	VF	XF	Unc
58	1804	—	2.00	6.00	15.00	60.00

Obv: Pointed arms.

C#	Date	Mintage	Fine	VF	XF	Unc
58a	1805	—	2.00	6.00	15.00	60.00

Rev. leg: H.S. COBURG. L.M.

C#	Date	Mintage	Fine	VF	XF	Unc
59	1805	—	2.00	6.00	15.00	65.00

Rev. leg: H.S. COBURG LAND. M.

C#	Date	Mintage	Fine	VF	XF	Unc
59a	1805	—	2.00	6.00	15.00	65.00

Obv: Crowned E within, L below crossed branches.
Rev: Value, leg: H.S.C.

C#	Date	Mintage	Fine	VF	XF	Unc
75b	1808	—	3.00	7.00	15.00	65.00
75	1808 L	.137	3.00	7.00	15.00	65.00
	1810 L	.151	3.00	7.00	15.00	65.00
	1812 L	.196	3.00	7.00	15.00	65.00
	1813 L	.143	3.00	7.00	15.00	65.00
	1814 L	.116	3.00	7.00	15.00	65.00
	1815 L	.026	3.00	7.00	15.00	65.00

Obv: S below crossed branches.

C#	Date	Mintage	Fine	VF	XF	Unc
75c	1816 S	—	3.00	7.00	15.00	65.00
	1817 S	—	3.00	7.00	15.00	65.00
	1818 S	—	3.00	7.00	15.00	65.00
	1819 S	—	3.00	7.00	15.00	65.00
	1820 S	—	3.00	7.00	15.00	65.00

Rev. leg: H.S.C.S.

C#	Date	Mintage	Fine	VF	XF	Unc
75a	1821 S	—	4.00	8.00	20.00	70.00
	1822 S	—	4.00	8.00	20.00	70.00
	1823 S	—	4.00	8.00	20.00	70.00
	1824 S	—	4.00	8.00	20.00	70.00
	1825 S	—	4.00	8.00	20.00	70.00
	1826 S	—	4.00	8.00	20.00	70.00

Obv: G below crossed branches.

C#	Date	Mintage	Fine	VF	XF	Unc
75d	1826 G	—	4.00	8.00	20.00	70.00

6 KREUZER

2.7200 g, .305 SILVER, .0266 oz ASW
Obv: Crowned shield. Rev: Value.

C#	Date	Mintage	Fine	VF	XF	Unc
60	1804	—	3.00	7.00	20.00	100.00
	1805	—	3.00	7.00	20.00	100.00

Rev. leg: H.S. COBURG. LAND. M.

C#	Date	Mintage	Fine	VF	XF	Unc
61	1805	—	3.00	7.00	20.00	100.00

Obv: Crowned E within, L below crossed branches.
Rev. leg: H.S.C.

C#	Date	Mintage	Fine	VF	XF	Unc
76	1808 L	.075	3.00	7.00	15.00	65.00
	1810 L	.056	3.00	7.00	15.00	65.00
	1812 L	.089	3.00	7.00	15.00	65.00
	1813 L	.042	3.00	7.00	15.00	65.00
	1814 L	.050	3.00	7.00	15.00	65.00
	1815 L	.011	3.00	7.00	15.00	65.00

Obv: S below crossed branches.

C#	Date	Mintage	Fine	VF	XF	Unc
76b	1816 S	—	3.00	7.00	15.00	65.00
	1817 S	—	3.00	7.00	15.00	65.00
	1818 S	—	3.00	7.00	15.00	65.00
	1819 S	—	3.00	7.00	15.00	65.00
	1820 S	—	3.00	7.00	15.00	65.00

Rev. leg: H.S.C.S.

C#	Date	Mintage	Fine	VF	XF	Unc
76a	1821 S	—	4.00	8.00	25.00	100.00
	1822 S	—	4.00	8.00	25.00	100.00
	1823 S	—	4.00	8.00	25.00	100.00
	1824 S	—	4.00	8.00	25.00	100.00
	1825 S	—	4.00	8.00	25.00	100.00
	1826 S	—	4.00	8.00	25.00	100.00

10 KREUZER

3.8900 g, .500 SILVER, .0625 oz ASW
Obv. leg: . . . . .SACHS. SOUV. . . . ., crowned arms.
Rev: Value within bound branches.

C#	Date	Mintage	Fine	VF	XF	Unc
77	1820 S	—	25.00	50.00	150.00	350.00

Obv. leg: . . . . .SACHS. COBURG.

C#	Date	Mintage	Fine	VF	XF	Unc
77a	1824 S	—	50.00	75.00	175.00	400.00

20 KREUZER

6.6800 g, .583 SILVER, .1252 oz ASW

C#	Date	Mintage	Fine	VF	XF	Unc
79	1807 L	—	25.00	65.00	150.00	400.00

Rev: Date below wreath.

C#	Date	Mintage	Fine	VF	XF	Unc
79a	1807	—	30.00	75.00	175.00	450.00

C#	Date	Mintage	Fine	VF	XF	Unc
80	1812 L	.030	15.00	50.00	125.00	375.00
	1813 L	.046	15.00	50.00	125.00	375.00
	1819 S	—	15.00	50.00	125.00	375.00
	1820 S	—	15.00	50.00	125.00	375.00

C#	Date	Mintage	Fine	VF	XF	Unc
80a	1823 S	—	15.00	50.00	125.00	375.00
	1824 S	—	15.00	50.00	125.00	375.00
	1825 S	—	15.00	50.00	125.00	375.00
	1826 S	—	15.00	50.00	125.00	375.00

GROSCHEN

1.9800 g, .368 SILVER, .0234 oz ASW

C#	Date	Mintage	Fine	VF	XF	Unc
67	1808	.026	2.00	4.00	10.00	60.00
	1810	—	2.00	4.00	10.00	60.00
	1818 S	—	2.00	4.00	10.00	60.00

48 EINEN (1/48) THALER

.9700 g, .250 SILVER, .0077 oz ASW

C#	Date	Mintage	Fine	VF	XF	Unc
52	1804	—	4.00	8.00	20.00	125.00

C#	Date	Mintage	Fine	VF	XF	Unc
52a	1804	—	—	—	Rare	—
	1805	—	3.00	7.00	15.00	125.00
	1806	—	—	—	Rare	—

24 EINEN (1/24) THALER

1.9800 g, .368 SILVER, .0234 oz ASW

C#	Date	Mintage	Fine	VF	XF	Unc
54	1805	—	3.00	8.00	20.00	100.00

EIN (1) THALER

(Convention)

28.0600 g, .833 SILVER, .7521 oz ASW

C#	Date	Mintage	Fine	VF	XF	Unc
62	1805 L	600 pcs.	300.00	600.00	1000.	2000.

C#	Date	Mintage	Fine	VF	XF	Unc
81	1817	—	150.00	300.00	600.00	1200.

Edge: EIN SPECIESTHALER

C#	Date	Mintage	Fine	VF	XF	Unc
81a	1817	—	150.00	300.00	700.00	1500.

(Krone)

29.3800 g, .871 SILVER, .8228 oz ASW

C#	Date	Mintage	Fine	VF	XF	Unc
82	1825	—	1000.	2000.	3500.	6000.
	1825	—	—	—		Proof 12,000.

SAXE-HILDBURGHAUSEN

Saxe-Hildburghausen was founded in 1680. During the 1826 reshuffle, it was exchanged for Altenburg.

RULERS

Joseph Friedrich, Prince Regent, 1780-1784
Alone, 1786-1826

HELLER

COPPER

C#	Date	Mintage	Fine	VF	XF	Unc
65a	1804	—	3.00	5.00	15.00	50.00
	1805	—	3.00	5.00	15.00	50.00
	1806	—	3.00	5.00	15.00	50.00

C#	Date	Mintage	Fine	VF	XF	Unc
66	1808	—	1.50	4.00	8.00	40.00
	1809	—	1.50	4.00	8.00	40.00
66	1811	—	1.50	4.00	8.00	40.00
	1812	—	1.50	4.00	8.00	40.00
	1816	—	1.50	4.00	8.00	40.00
	1817	—	1.50	4.00	8.00	40.00
	1818	—	1.50	4.00	8.00	40.00

C#	Date	Mintage	Fine	VF	XF	Unc
67	1820	—	1.50	4.00	8.00	40.00
	1821	—	1.50	4.00	8.00	40.00
	1822	—	1.50	4.00	8.00	40.00
	1823	—	1.50	4.00	8.00	40.00
	1824	—	1.50	4.00	8.00	40.00
	1825	—	1.50	4.00	8.00	40.00

PFENNIG

COPPER

C#	Date	Mintage	Fine	VF	XF	Unc
69	1823	—	3.00	5.00	15.00	50.00
	1825	—	3.00	5.00	15.00	50.00
	1826	—	3.00	5.00	15.00	50.00

Obv: Crowned rectangular arms.

C#	Date	Mintage	Fine	VF	XF	Unc
69.5	1826	—	5.00	10.00	25.00	80.00

1/8 KREUZER

COPPER
Obv: Crowned F within crossed branches.
Rev: Value, leg: KREUZER LANDMUNZE.

C#	Date	Mintage	Fine	VF	XF	Unc
67a	1825	—	3.00	5.00	15.00	60.00

1/4 KREUZER

COPPER

C#	Date	Mintage	Fine	VF	XF	Unc
70	1825	—	4.00	8.00	16.00	60.00

Obv: Crowned heart shaped arms, H.S.H.H.

C#	Date	Mintage	Fine	VF	XF	Unc
71	1825	—	4.00	8.00	16.00	60.00

1/2 KREUZER

COPPER
Obv: Crowned arms. Rev: Value in script.

C#	Date	Mintage	Fine	VF	XF	Unc
72	1808	—	5.00	10.00	20.00	70.00
	1809	—	5.00	10.00	20.00	70.00

Obv: Crowned heart-shaped arms, leg: HERZ.Z.S.
Rev: Value

C#	Date	Mintage	Fine	VF	XF	Unc
73	1823	—	5.00	10.00	25.00	80.00

Obv. leg: HERZOGTHUM

C#	Date	Mintage	Fine	VF	XF	Unc
73b	1823	—	5.00	10.00	25.00	80.00

Rev: Value, leg: KREUZER LANDMUNZE.

C#	Date	Mintage	Fine	VF	XF	Unc
73a	1823	—	6.00	12.00	30.00	90.00

KREUZER

BILLON

C#	Date	Mintage	Fine	VF	XF	Unc
74a	1804	—	7.00	15.00	35.00	125.00
	1805	—	7.00	15.00	35.00	125.00

Obv: Crowned oval arms within branches.
Rev: Value.

C#	Date	Mintage	Fine	VF	XF	Unc
76	1806	—	6.00	15.00	30.00	100.00
	1811	—	6.00	15.00	30.00	100.00

3 KREUZER

BILLON
Obv: Crowned F within wreath.
Rev: Value within ring.

C#	Date	Mintage	Fine	VF	XF	Unc
83	1808	—	4.50	9.00	25.00	100.00
	1810	—	4.50	9.00	25.00	100.00
	1811	—	4.50	9.00	25.00	100.00
	1812	—	4.50	9.00	25.00	100.00
	1815	—	4.50	9.00	25.00	100.00
	1816	—	4.50	9.00	25.00	100.00
	1817	—	4.50	9.00	25.00	100.00
	1818	—	4.50	9.00	25.00	100.00
	1820	—	4.50	9.00	25.00	100.00

6 KREUZER

BILLON

C#	Date	Mintage	Fine	VF	XF	Unc
86	1808	—	6.50	15.00	35.00	125.00
	1811	—	6.50	15.00	35.00	125.00
	1812	—	6.50	15.00	35.00	125.00
	1815	—	6.50	15.00	35.00	125.00
	1816	—	6.50	15.00	35.00	125.00
	1817	—	6.50	15.00	35.00	125.00
	1818	—	6.50	15.00	35.00	125.00

Obv: Crowned F within crossed branches.
Rev: Value.

C#	Date	Mintage	Fine	VF	XF	Unc
88	1820	—	6.50	12.50	30.00	110.00
	1821	—	6.50	12.50	30.00	110.00
	1823	—	6.50	12.50	30.00	110.00
	1824	—	6.50	12.50	30.00	110.00
	1825	—	6.50	12.50	30.00	110.00

SAXE-MEININGEN

Saxe-Meiningen was founded in 1680. It was called Saxe-Coburg-Meiningen until 1826 when it exchanged Coburg for Hildburghausen.

RULERS

Bernhard II Under Regency of Luise
Eleonore, 1803-1821
Bernhard II, 1821-1866
Georg II, 1866-1914
Bernhard III, 1914-1918

MINTMASTERS INITIALS

Letter	Date	Name
F.HELFRICHT	d.1892	Ferdinand Helfricht, die-cutter and chief medaileur
K	1835-1837	Georg Krell, warden then mintmaster
L	1803-1833	Georg Christoph Loewel
VOIGT		J.C. Voigt, die-cutter and medaileur

HELLER

COPPER
Obv: Crowned heart-shaped arms, leg: H.
Rev: Value.

C#	Date	Mintage	Fine	VF	XF	Unc
21	1814	—	2.00	4.00	8.00	60.00

Obv. leg: HERZ.

C#	Date	Mintage	Fine	VF	XF	Unc
21a	1814	—	2.00	4.00	8.00	60.00

PFENNIG

COPPER
Obv. leg: HERZ.

C#	Date	Mintage	Fine	VF	XF	Unc
23	1818	.090	3.00	7.00	15.00	75.00

C#	Date	Mintage	Fine	VF	XF	Unc
34	1832	.275	2.00	4.00	8.00	50.00
	1833	.093	2.00	4.00	8.00	50.00
	1835	.034	2.00	4.00	8.00	50.00

Obv: Crowned arms within branches.

C#	Date	Mintage	Fine	VF	XF	Unc
35	1839	.079	2.00	4.00	8.00	50.00
	1842	.132	2.00	4.00	8.00	50.00

C#	Date	Mintage	Fine	VF	XF	Unc
37	1860	.240	1.50	3.00	6.00	50.00
	1862	.243	1.50	3.00	6.00	50.00
	1863	.240	1.50	3.00	6.00	50.00
	1865	.240	1.50	3.00	6.00	50.00
	1866	.480	1.50	3.00	6.00	50.00

C#	Date	Mintage	Fine	VF	XF	Unc
65	1867	.240	1.50	3.00	6.00	50.00
	1868	.480	1.50	3.00	6.00	50.00

2 PFENNIG

COPPER

C#	Date	Mintage	Fine	VF	XF	Unc
39	1832	.202	1.50	3.00	6.00	50.00
	1833	.101	1.50	3.00	6.00	50.00
	1835	.036	1.50	3.00	6.00	50.00

C#	Date	Mintage	Fine	VF	XF	Unc
40	1839	.075	1.50	3.00	6.00	50.00
	1842	.184	1.50	3.00	6.00	50.00

C#	Date	Mintage	Fine	VF	XF	Unc
42	1860	.361	1.50	3.00	6.00	50.00
	1862	.357	1.50	3.00	6.00	50.00
	1863	.120	1.50	3.00	6.00	50.00
	1864	.480	1.50	3.00	6.00	50.00
	1865	.240	1.50	3.00	6.00	50.00
	1866	.480	1.50	3.00	6.00	50.00

C#	Date	Mintage	Fine	VF	XF	Unc
66	1867	.480	1.50	3.00	6.00	50.00
	1868	.240	1.50	3.00	6.00	50.00
	1869	.240	1.50	3.00	6.00	50.00
	1870	.720	1.50	3.00	6.00	50.00

1/8 KREUZER

COPPER

C#	Date	Mintage	Fine	VF	XF	Unc
30	1828	—	2.50	5.00	10.00	50.00

1/4 KREUZER

COPPER

Obv: Crowned heart shaped arms, leg: HERZ. Rev: Value.

C#	Date	Mintage	Fine	VF	XF	Unc
22	1812	—	2.50	5.00	10.00	50.00
	1814	—	2.50	5.00	10.00	50.00
	1818	.066	2.50	5.00	10.00	50.00

Obv: Crowned heart shaped arms, leg. HERZ. Rev: Value, leg: LANDMUNZE.

C#	Date	Mintage	Fine	VF	XF	Unc
31	1823	—	4.00	8.00	15.00	60.00

C#	Date	Mintage	Fine	VF	XF	Unc
33	1828	—	1.50	3.00	6.00	50.00
	1829	.168	1.50	3.00	6.00	40.00
	1830	.161	1.50	3.00	6.00	40.00
	1831	.321	1.50	3.00	6.00	40.00
	1832	.063	1.50	3.00	6.00	40.00

NOTE: Many varieties in legend size exist.

Obv: Legend below crowned arms.

C#	Date	Mintage	Fine	VF	XF	Unc
33.1	1828	—	1.50	3.00	6.00	40.00

Obv. leg: MEININGEN

C#	Date	Mintage	Fine	VF	XF	Unc
33a	1829	Inc. Ab.	1.50	3.00	6.00	40.00

Rev. value: KREUZER.

C#	Date	Mintage	Fine	VF	XF	Unc
36	1854	.240	1.50	3.00	6.00	40.00

1/2 KREUZER

COPPER

C#	Date	Mintage	Fine	VF	XF	Unc
24	1812	—	2.50	5.00	10.00	50.00
	1814	—	2.50	5.00	10.00	50.00
	1818	.102	2.50	5.00	10.00	50.00

C#	Date	Mintage	Fine	VF	XF	Unc
38	1828	—	2.00	4.00	8.00	45.00
	1831	—	2.00	4.00	8.00	45.00

C#	Date	Mintage	Fine	VF	XF	Unc
38.1	1829	.121	1.50	3.00	6.00	40.00
	1830 L	.144	1.50	3.00	6.00	40.00
	1831 L	.341	1.50	3.00	6.00	40.00
	1832 L	.045	1.50	3.00	6.00	40.00

C#	Date	Mintage	Fine	VF	XF	Unc
41	1854	.240	1.50	3.00	6.00	40.00

KREUZER

(Convention)

.7300 g, .166 SILVER, .0038 oz ASW

Obv: Crowned draped arms, H.S.C.M. Rev: Value.

C#	Date	Mintage	Fine	VF	XF	Unc
26	1808	—	2.50	5.00	10.00	60.00

Obv: Drape extends beneath crown.

C#	Date	Mintage	Fine	VF	XF	Unc
26a	1812	.307	4.00	8.00	15.00	80.00

COPPER

C#	Date	Mintage	Fine	VF	XF	Unc
25	1814	—	4.00	8.00	15.00	60.00
	1818	.090	4.00	8.00	15.00	60.00

Obv: Crowned rectangular arms, leg: HERZ.

C#	Date	Mintage	Fine	VF	XF	Unc
43	1828	—	2.50	5.00	10.00	50.00
43	1829	.144	2.50	5.00	10.00	50.00
	1830	.118	2.50	5.00	10.00	50.00

.7300 g, .166 SILVER, .0038 oz ASW

Obv: Crowned arms dividing S.M.

C#	Date	Mintage	Fine	VF	XF	Unc
47	1828	.211	2.50	5.00	10.00	50.00
	1829	—	2.50	5.00	10.00	50.00
	1829 L	.255	2.50	5.00	10.00	50.00
	1830 L	.092	2.50	5.00	10.00	50.00

COPPER

C#	Date	Mintage	Fine	VF	XF	Unc
43a	1831	.166	2.00	4.00	8.00	40.00
	1832	.032	2.00	4.00	8.00	40.00
	1833	.104	2.00	4.00	8.00	40.00
	1834	.177	2.00	4.00	8.00	40.00
	1835	.035	2.00	4.00	8.00	40.00

.7300 g, .166 SILVER, .0038 oz ASW

Obv: Crowned arms within bound branches, L initial.

C#	Date	Mintage	Fine	VF	XF	Unc
48	1831 L	.212	2.00	4.00	8.00	50.00
	1832 L	.348	2.00	4.00	8.00	50.00
	1833 L	.272	2.00	4.00	8.00	50.00
	1834 L	.162	2.00	4.00	8.00	50.00

Obv: K mintmasters initial.

C#	Date	Mintage	Fine	VF	XF	Unc
48a	1835 K	.059	2.00	4.00	8.00	50.00
	1836 K	.055	2.00	4.00	8.00	50.00
	1837 K	.049	2.00	4.00	8.00	50.00

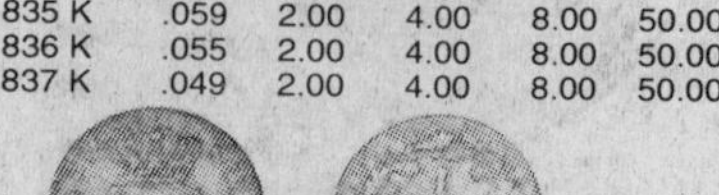

.8300 g, .166 SILVER, .0044 oz ASW

C#	Date	Mintage	Fine	VF	XF	Unc
49	1839	.348	2.00	4.00	8.00	45.00

COPPER

Obv: Crowned arms within branches. Rev: Value.

C#	Date	Mintage	Fine	VF	XF	Unc
44	1842	.180	2.00	4.00	8.00	40.00

Obv: Six point star below crowned arms.

C#	Date	Mintage	Fine	VF	XF	Unc
45	1854	.202	2.00	4.00	8.00	40.00

.8400 g, .165 SILVER, .0044 oz ASW

C#	Date	Mintage	Fine	VF	XF	Unc
50	1864	.240	2.00	4.00	8.00	45.00
	1866	.240	2.00	4.00	8.00	45.00

3 KREUZER

1.3600 g, .305 SILVER, .0133 oz ASW

Obv: Crowned draped arms.

C#	Date	Mintage	Fine	VF	XF	Unc
27	1808	—	6.00	10.00	30.00	125.00

Obv: Drape extends beneath crown.

C#	Date	Mintage	Fine	VF	XF	Unc
27a	1812	.263	3.00	6.00	20.00	100.00
	1813	Inc. Ab.	3.00	6.00	20.00	100.00

Obv: Crowned arms dividing S.M. Rev: Value.

C#	Date	Mintage	Fine	VF	XF	Unc
51	1827	.171	2.00	4.00	8.00	50.00
	1828	.077	2.00	4.00	8.00	50.00
	1829	—	2.00	4.00	8.00	50.00

Obv: L mintmasters initial.

C#	Date	Mintage	Fine	VF	XF	Unc
51a	1829 L	1.263	2.00	4.00	8.00	50.00
	1830 L	.533	2.00	4.00	8.00	50.00

C#	Date	Mintage	Fine	VF	XF	Unc
52	1831 L	.540	2.00	4.00	8.00	50.00
	1832 L	.918	2.00	4.00	8.00	50.00
	1833 L	1.284	2.00	4.00	8.00	50.00
	1834 L	.187	2.00	4.00	8.00	50.00
	1835 L	—	2.00	4.00	8.00	50.00
52a	1835 K	.800	2.00	4.00	8.00	50.00
	1836 K	.399	2.00	4.00	8.00	50.00
	1837 K	.246	2.00	4.00	8.00	50.00

1.2900 g, .333 SILVER, .0138 oz ASW
Obv: Crowned arms, leg: HERZOGTHUM.
Rev: Value within branches.

C#	Date	Mintage	Fine	VF	XF	Unc
53	1840	.207	2.00	4.00	8.00	50.00

6 KREUZER

2.4300 g, .333 SILVER, .0260 oz ASW
Obv: Crowned, draped arms, leg: S.COB.
Rev: Value within wreath.

C#	Date	Mintage	Fine	VF	XF	Unc
28	1808	—	15.00	25.00	50.00	150.00
	1812	—	15.00	25.00	50.00	150.00
	1813	—	15.00	25.00	50.00	150.00

Obv: Drape extends beneath crown.

C#	Date	Mintage	Fine	VF	XF	Unc
28a	1812	.087	10.00	20.00	40.00	150.00
	1813	Inc. Ab.	10.00	20.00	40.00	150.00

2.4400 g, .347 SILVER, .0272 oz ASW

C#	Date	Mintage	Fine	VF	XF	Unc
54	1826	—	5.00	15.00	25.00	80.00
	1827	.486	5.00	15.00	25.00	80.00
	1828	.179	5.00	15.00	25.00	80.00
	1829	—	5.00	15.00	25.00	80.00

Obv: W/L mintmasters initial.

C#	Date	Mintage	Fine	VF	XF	Unc
54a	1828 L	—	5.00	15.00	25.00	80.00
	1829 L	1.513	5.00	15.00	25.00	80.00
	1830 L	.747	5.00	15.00	25.00	80.00

C#	Date	Mintage	Fine	VF	XF	Unc
55	1831 L	.684	3.00	5.00	10.00	60.00
	1832 L	.658	3.00	5.00	10.00	60.00
	1833 L	.723	3.00	5.00	10.00	60.00
	1834 L	.409	3.00	5.00	10.00	60.00
	1835 L	—	3.00	5.00	10.00	60.00

Obv: W/K mintmaster initial.

C#	Date	Mintage	Fine	VF	XF	Unc
55a	1835 K	.512	3.00	5.00	10.00	60.00
	1836 K	.432	3.00	5.00	10.00	60.00
	1837 K	.253	3.00	5.00	10.00	60.00

2.5900 g, .333 SILVER, .0277 oz ASW
Obv: Crowned arms, leg: HERZOGTHUM.
Rev: Value within branches.

C#	Date	Mintage	Fine	VF	XF	Unc
56	1840	.097	4.00	7.00	15.00	75.00

20 KREUZER

.583 SILVER

C#	Date	Mintage	Fine	VF	XF	Unc
29	1812	5 pcs. known	—	Rare	—	

1/2 GULDEN

5.3000 g, .900 SILVER, .1533 oz ASW

C#	Date	Mintage	Fine	VF	XF	Unc
57	1838	.071	20.00	50.00	100.00	250.00
	1839	.045	20.00	50.00	100.00	250.00
	1840	.032	20.00	50.00	100.00	250.00
	1841	.057	20.00	50.00	100.00	250.00

Obv: Different head w/HELFRICHT below.

C#	Date	Mintage	Fine	VF	XF	Unc
57a	1843	.133	20.00	50.00	100.00	225.00
	1846	.106	20.00	50.00	100.00	225.00

C#	Date	Mintage	Fine	VF	XF	Unc
57b	1854	.108	20.00	50.00	100.00	250.00

GULDEN

11.8000 g, .989 SILVER, .3752 oz ASW

C#	Date	Mintage	Fine	VF	XF	Unc
58	1829	2,000	125.00	200.00	325.00	700.00

12.8300 g, .750 SILVER, .3093 oz ASW

C#	Date	Mintage	Fine	VF	XF	Unc
59	1830 L	9,118	65.00	125.00	200.00	350.00
	1831 L	5,511	50.00	100.00	150.00	300.00
	1832 L	4,688	50.00	100.00	150.00	300.00
	1833 L	.010	35.00	75.00	120.00	250.00

C#	Date	Mintage	Fine	VF	XF	Unc
59a	1835 K	2,015	75.00	150.00	200.00	400.00
	1836 K	2,028	75.00	150.00	200.00	400.00
	1837 K	2,148	75.00	150.00	200.00	400.00

10.6000 g, .900 SILVER, .3067 oz ASW

C#	Date	Mintage	Fine	VF	XF	Unc
60	1838	.071	40.00	80.00	160.00	250.00
	1839	.071	40.00	80.00	160.00	250.00
	1840	.032	40.00	80.00	160.00	250.00
	1841	.031	40.00	80.00	160.00	250.00

Obv: HELFRICHT below bust.

C#	Date	Mintage	Fine	VF	XF	Unc
60a	1843	.133	40.00	80.00	160.00	250.00
	1846	.149	40.00	80.00	160.00	250.00

C#	Date	Mintage	Fine	VF	XF	Unc
60b	1854	.108	45.00	90.00	175.00	275.00

2 GULDEN

21.2100 g, .900 SILVER, .6138 oz ASW

C#	Date	Mintage	Fine	VF	XF	Unc
62	1854	.167	50.00	90.00	185.00	375.00

EIN (1) THALER

(Convention)

28.0600 g, .833 SILVER, .7514 oz ASW
Death of Georg I

C#	Date	Mintage	Fine	VF	XF	Unc
19	ND(1803)L	—	300.00	600.00	1200.	2000.

18.5200 g, .900 SILVER, .5360 oz ASW
Obv: HELFRICHT on truncation.

C#	Date	Mintage	Fine	VF	XF	Unc
61	1859	.040	35.00	75.00	135.00	325.00
	1860	.040	35.00	75.00	135.00	325.00
	1861	.040	35.00	75.00	135.00	325.00
	1862	.040	35.00	75.00	135.00	325.00
	1863	.040	35.00	75.00	135.00	325.00
	1866	.040	35.00	75.00	135.00	325.00

Obv: HELFRICHT on truncation.

C#	Date	Mintage	Fine	VF	XF	Unc
67	1867	6,644	90.00	175.00	450.00	900.00

2 THALER

(3-1/2 Gulden)

37.1200 g, .900 SILVER, 1.0743 oz ASW
Obv: VOIGT below bust.

C#	Date	Mintage	Fine	VF	XF	Unc
63	1841	.012	300.00	525.00	1400.	2600.

Obv: Similar to C#63.

C#	Date	Mintage	Fine	VF	XF	Unc
64	1843	.011	200.00	400.00	800.00	1600.
	1846	.015	200.00	350.00	700.00	1500.

Obv: HELFRICHT below bust. Rev: Similar to C#64.

C#	Date	Mintage	Fine	VF	XF	Unc
64a	1853	.014	200.00	350.00	700.00	1500.
	1854	.014	200.00	350.00	700.00	1500.

MONETARY REFORM

2 MARK

11.1110 g, .900 SILVER, .3215 oz ASW
75th Birthday of the Duke

Y#	Date	Mintage	Fine	VF	XF	Unc
159	1901D	.020	100.00	250.00	400.00	650.00

Obv: Long beard.

Y#	Date	Mintage	Fine	VF	XF	Unc
161.1	1902D	.020	225.00	750.00	1200.	2000.

Obv: Short beard.

Y#	Date	Mintage	Fine	VF	XF	Unc
161.2	1902D	Inc. Ab.	100.00	200.00	350.00	700.00
	1913D	5,000	150.00	250.00	450.00	650.00

Death of Georg II

Y#	Date	Mintage	Fine	VF	XF	Unc
166	1915	.030	35.00	60.00	140.00	200.00

3 MARK

16.6670 g, .900 SILVER, .4823 oz ASW

Y#	Date	Mintage	Fine	VF	XF	Unc
162	1908D	.035	35.00	100.00	140.00	200.00
	1908D	—	—	—	Proof	200.00
	1913D	.020	35.00	100.00	140.00	200.00

Death of Georg II

Y#	Date	Mintage	Fine	VF	XF	Unc
167	1915	.030	30.00	75.00	150.00	200.00
	1915	—	—	—	Proof	225.00

5 MARK

27.7770 g, .900 SILVER, .8038 oz ASW
75th Birthday of the Duke

Y#	Date	Mintage	Fine	VF	XF	Unc
160	1901D	.020	85.00	225.00	425.00	725.00
	1901D	—	—	—	Proof	1200.

Obv: Long beard.

Y#	Date	Mintage	Fine	VF	XF	Unc
163.1	1902D	.020	60.00	175.00	325.00	500.00

Obv: Short beard.

Y#	Date	Mintage	Fine	VF	XF	Unc
163.2	1902D	Inc. Ab.	60.00	150.00	325.00	650.00
	1908D	.060	50.00	150.00	275.00	450.00

10 MARK

3.9820 g, .900 GOLD, .1152 oz AGW

Y#	Date	Mintage	Fine	VF	XF	Unc
157	1890D	2,000	1000.	2000.	2500.	3700.
	1890D	—	—	—	Proof	7000.
	1898D	2,000	800.00	1500.	1850.	2750.
	1898D	—	—	—	Proof	7000.

Y#	Date	Mintage	Fine	VF	XF	Unc
164	1902D	2,000	600.00	1400.	2000.	3000.
	1902D	—	—	—	Proof	4250.
	1909D	2,000	600.00	1400.	2000.	3000.
	1909D	—	—	—	Proof	4250.
	1914D	1,002	800.00	1600.	2000.	3000.
	1914D	—	—	—	Proof	4250.

20 MARK

7.9650 g, .900 GOLD, .2304 oz AGW

Rev: Type I.

Y#	Date	Mintage	Fine	VF	XF	Unc
156	1872D	3,000	3000.	6000.	8000.	12,000.
	1872D	—	—	—	Proof	17,500.

Rev: Type II.

Y#	Date	Mintage	Fine	VF	XF	Unc
156a	1882D	3,061	2000.	3500.	4000.	6500.
	1882D	—	—	—	Proof	11,000.

Y#	Date	Mintage	Fine	VF	XF	Unc
158	1889D	4,032	1750.	3000.	4500.	6000.
	1889D	—	—	—	Proof	9000.

Rev: Type III.

Y#	Date	Mintage	Fine	VF	XF	Unc
158a	1900D	1,005	1500.	3000.	3500.	5500.
	1900D	—	—	—	Proof	11,000.
	1905D	1,000	1500.	3000.	3500.	5500.
	1905D	—	—	—	Proof	11,000.

Y#	Date	Mintage	Fine	VF	XF	Unc
165	1910D	1,004	1500.	3000.	3500.	5000.
	1910D	—	—	—	Proof	7000.
	1914D	1,000	1500.	3000.	3500.	5000.
	1914D	—	—	—	Proof	7000.

SAXE-WEIMAR-EISENACH

Saxe-Weimar-Eisenach was founded in 1644. It was raised to the status of a grand duchy in 1814. The last grand duke abdicated in 1918.

RULERS

Carl August, 1775-1828
Carl Friedrich, 1828-1853
Carl Alexander, 1853-1901
Wilhelm Ernst, 1901-1918

MINTMASTERS INITIALS

Letter	Date	Name
JLST, LS, ST	1785-1790 1793-1835	Johann Leonhard Stockmar, mintmaster

HELLER

COPPER

C#	Date	Mintage	Fine	VF	XF	Unc
55c	1801	—	2.00	4.00	8.00	65.00
	1813	—	2.00	4.00	8.00	65.00

PFENNIG

COPPER

Rev: Value and date; line below date.

C#	Date	Mintage	Fine	VF	XF	Unc
56c	1801	—	3.00	7.00	15.00	60.00
	1803	—	3.00	7.00	15.00	60.00
	1807	.030	3.00	7.00	15.00	60.00

NOTE: Earlier date (1799) exists for this type.

Rev: Value and date; 1's in date reversed, line below date.

C#	Date	Mintage	Fine	VF	XF	Unc
56d	1810	.080	3.00	7.00	15.00	60.00
	1813	—	3.00	7.00	15.00	60.00

Rev: Value and date; line below date.

C#	Date	Mintage	Fine	VF	XF	Unc
61	1821	.100	2.00	4.00	8.00	40.00
	1824	—	2.00	4.00	8.00	40.00
	1826	—	2.00	4.00	8.00	40.00
77	1830	—	2.50	5.00	10.00	50.00

C#	Date	Mintage	Fine	VF	XF	Unc
81	1840A	.760	2.00	4.00	8.00	45.00
	1841A	.760	2.00	4.00	8.00	45.00
	1844A	.361	2.00	4.00	8.00	45.00
	1851A	.360	2.00	4.00	8.00	45.00

Denticled border

C#	Date	Mintage	Fine	VF	XF	Unc
89	1858A	.720	1.50	3.00	6.00	40.00
	1865A	.720	1.50	3.00	6.00	40.00

1-1/2 PFENNIG

COPPER

C#	Date	Mintage	Fine	VF	XF	Unc
57	1807	.034	10.00	20.00	35.00	125.00

NOTE: Earlier date (1799) exists for this type.

C#	Date	Mintage	Fine	VF	XF	Unc
62	1824	—	3.00	5.00	10.00	50.00
78	1830	—	3.00	5.00	10.00	50.00

2 PFENNIG

COPPER

C#	Date	Mintage	Fine	VF	XF	Unc
58c	1803	—	4.00	7.00	20.00	125.00
	1807	.036	3.00	6.00	15.00	80.00

Milled edge

C#	Date	Mintage	Fine	VF	XF	Unc
58d	1803	—	4.00	7.00	20.00	125.00
	1807	.036	3.00	6.00	15.00	80.00

Rev: Similar to C#58c but w/rosette below date.

C#	Date	Mintage	Fine	VF	XF	Unc
58e	1813	—	3.00	6.00	15.00	80.00

Obv: Saxon arms; S.W.E. above.
Rev: Value above date; rosette below date.

C#	Date	Mintage	Fine	VF	XF	Unc
63	1821	.068	2.00	5.00	8.00	60.00
	1826	—	2.00	5.00	8.00	60.00

Rev: Line below date.

C#	Date	Mintage	Fine	VF	XF	Unc
79	1830	—	2.00	5.00	8.00	60.00

Denticled border

C#	Date	Mintage	Fine	VF	XF	Unc
90	1858A	—	1.50	3.00	6.00	25.00
	1865A	—	1.50	3.00	6.00	25.00

3 PFENNIG

COPPER
Leaf edge

C#	Date	Mintage	Fine	VF	XF	Unc
59c	1807	.049	5.00	10.00	25.00	100.00

NOTE: Earlier date (1799) exists for this type.

Reeded edge

C#	Date	Mintage	Fine	VF	XF	Unc
59d	1807	Inc. Ab.	4.00	7.00	17.00	60.00

Rev: Rosette below date.

C#	Date	Mintage	Fine	VF	XF	Unc
59e	1804	—	2.00	4.00	8.00	40.00

Leaf edge

C#	Date	Mintage	Fine	VF	XF	Unc
64	1824	—	2.00	4.00	8.00	40.00

Reeded edge

C#	Date	Mintage	Fine	VF	XF	Unc
64a	1824	—	2.00	4.00	8.00	40.00

C#	Date	Mintage	Fine	VF	XF	Unc
80	1830	—	2.00	4.00	8.00	40.00

Straight date

C#	Date	Mintage	Fine	VF	XF	Unc
80.1	1830	—	2.00	4.00	8.00	40.00

Obv: Crowned Saxon arms in circular legend.
Rev: Value above date; SCHEIDE MUNZE above.

C#	Date	Mintage	Fine	VF	XF	Unc
82	1840A	—	2.00	4.00	8.00	40.00

4 PFENNIG

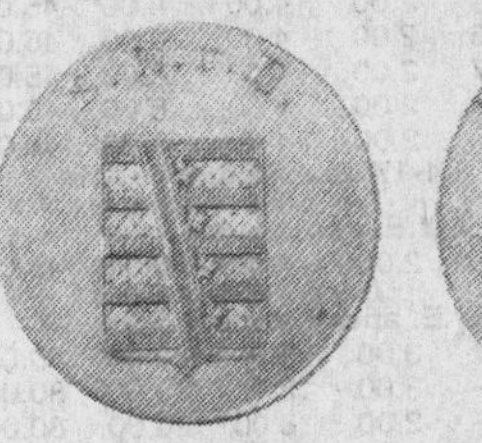

COPPER
Obv: Saxon arms; S.W.u.E. above.
Rev: Value above date; w/o line below date.

C#	Date	Mintage	Fine	VF	XF	Unc
60	1810	.146	5.00	10.00	25.00	125.00

Rev: Line below date.

C#	Date	Mintage	Fine	VF	XF	Unc
60a	1810	Inc. Ab.	5.00	10.00	25.00	125.00
	1812	—	5.00	10.00	25.00	125.00

Rev: Rosette below date.

C#	Date	Mintage	Fine	VF	XF	Unc
60b	1813	—	5.00	10.00	25.00	125.00

Reeded edge

C#	Date	Mintage	Fine	VF	XF	Unc
65	1821	.092	4.00	7.00	15.00	100.00
	1826	—	4.00	7.00	15.00	100.00

Leaf edge

C#	Date	Mintage	Fine	VF	XF	Unc
65a	1821	Inc. Ab.	4.00	7.00	15.00	100.00

1/2 GROSCHEN

1.0900 g, .222 SILVER, .0077 oz ASW
Obv: Crowned arms. Rev: Value.

C#	Date	Mintage	Fine	VF	XF	Unc
85	1840A	2.400	2.00	4.00	8.00	40.00
91	1858A	.300	2.00	4.00	8.00	40.00

GROSCHEN

2.1900 g, .222 SILVER, .0156 oz ASW

C#	Date	Mintage	Fine	VF	XF	Unc
86	1840A	2.408	2.00	4.00	8.00	40.00

C#	Date	Mintage	Fine	VF	XF	Unc
92	1858A	.300	2.00	4.00	8.00	40.00

1/48 THALER

1.0600 g, .229 SILVER, .0078 oz ASW

C#	Date	Mintage	Fine	VF	XF	Unc
67	1801	—	2.00	4.00	8.00	45.00
	1804	—	2.00	4.00	8.00	45.00
	1808	.286	2.00	4.00	8.00	45.00
	1810	.327	2.00	4.00	8.00	45.00
	1813	—	2.00	4.00	8.00	45.00
	1814	—	2.00	4.00	8.00	45.00

NOTE: Earlier dates (1794-1799) exist for this type.

Obv: G.H.S.W.E. above arms.

C#	Date	Mintage	Fine	VF	XF	Unc
68	1815	—	2.00	4.00	8.00	45.00

Obv: S.W.E. above arms.

C#	Date	Mintage	Fine	VF	XF	Unc
69	1821	.243	3.00	6.00	20.00	80.00
	1824	—	3.00	6.00	20.00	80.00
	1826	—	3.00	6.00	20.00	80.00

Obv: Saxon arms w/S.W.E. above.

C#	Date	Mintage	Fine	VF	XF	Unc
83	1831	—	3.00	6.00	15.00	70.00

Rev: Reversed 1's in date.

C#	Date	Mintage	Fine	VF	XF	Unc
83a	1831	—	3.00	6.00	15.00	70.00

1/24 THALER

2.1200 g, .229 SILVER, .0156 oz ASW
Obv: S.W.U.E. above arms. Rev: Value.

C#	Date	Mintage	Fine	VF	XF	Unc
70	1801	—	3.00	7.00	20.00	90.00
	1804	—	3.00	7.00	20.00	90.00
	1808	.199	3.00	7.00	20.00	90.00
	1810	.452	3.00	7.00	20.00	90.00
	1813	—	3.00	7.00	20.00	90.00
	1814 small letters	—	3.00	7.00	20.00	90.00

NOTE: Earlier dates (1794-1799) exist for this type.

Obv: G.H.S.W.E. above arms.

C#	Date	Mintage	Fine	VF	XF	Unc
71	1815	—	8.00	15.00	50.00	175.00

Obv: S.W.E. above arms.

C#	Date	Mintage	Fine	VF	XF	Unc
72	1821	.493	5.00	10.00	25.00	90.00
	1824	—	5.00	10.00	25.00	90.00
	1826	—	5.00	10.00	25.00	90.00

Rev. value: ENIEN

C#	Date	Mintage	Fine	VF	XF	Unc
72a	1821	Inc. Ab.	—	—	—	—

Rev. value: EINEN

C#	Date	Mintage	Fine	VF	XF	Unc
84	1830	—	3.00	6.00	20.00	80.00

1/2 THALER

(Species)

14.0300 g, .833 SILVER, .3757 oz ASW

C#	Date	Mintage	Fine	VF	XF	Unc
74	1813 LS	—	35.00	75.00	125.00	300.00

EIN (1) THALER

(Convention)

28.0600 g, .833 SILVER, .7514 oz ASW

C#	Date	Mintage	Fine	VF	XF	Unc
75	1813 LS	—	125.00	275.00	600.00	1000.

C#	Date	Mintage	Fine	VF	XF	Unc
76	1815	5,273	250.00	450.00	900.00	2000.

22.2700 g, .750 SILVER, .5370 oz ASW

C#	Date	Mintage	Fine	VF	XF	Unc
87	1841A	.203	40.00	75.00	180.00	475.00

(Vereins)

18.5200 g, .900 SILVER, .5360 oz ASW

C#	Date	Mintage	Fine	VF	XF	Unc
93	1858A	.063	40.00	75.00	140.00	300.00
	1866A	.044	40.00	75.00	140.00	300.00
	1870A	.045	40.00	75.00	140.00	300.00

2 THALER

(3-1/2 Gulden)

37.1200 g, .900 SILVER, 1.0742 oz ASW

C#	Date	Mintage	Fine	VF	XF	Unc
88	1840A	.019	150.00	300.00	600.00	1300.
	1842A	.038	150.00	300.00	600.00	1300.
	1843A	Inc. Ab.	200.00	350.00	700.00	1600.
	1848A	.019	150.00	300.00	600.00	1300.

Rev: Similar to C#88.

C#	Date	Mintage	Fine	VF	XF	Unc
94	1855A	.019	225.00	400.00	900.00	1750.

MONETARY REFORM

2 MARK

11.1110 g, .900 SILVER, .3215 oz ASW
Golden Wedding of Carl Alexander

Y#	Date	Mintage	Fine	VF	XF	Unc
168.1	1892A	.050	75.00	150.00	350.00	550.00

80th Birthday of the Grand Duke

Y#	Date	Mintage	Fine	VF	XF	Unc
168.2	1898A	.100	50.00	125.00	325.00	525.00
	1898A	—	—	—	Proof	650.00

Y#	Date	Mintage	Fine	VF	XF	Unc
170	1901A	.100	100.00	300.00	400.00	750.00
	1901A	—	—	—	Proof	800.00

Grand Duke's 1st Marriage

Y#	Date	Mintage	Fine	VF	XF	Unc
172	1903A	.040	35.00	60.00	100.00	140.00
	1903A	*1,000	—	—	Proof	200.00

Jena University 350th Anniversary

Y#	Date	Mintage	Fine	VF	XF	Unc
174	1908A	.050	25.00	50.00	100.00	125.00

3 MARK

16.6670 g, .900 SILVER, .4823 oz ASW
Grand Duke's 2nd Marriage

Y#	Date	Mintage	Fine	VF	XF	Unc
176	1910A	.133	15.00	35.00	70.00	85.00
	1910A	—	—	—	Proof	125.00

Centenary of Grand Duchy

Y#	Date	Mintage	Fine	VF	XF	Unc
177	1915A	.050	25.00	75.00	125.00	175.00
	1915A	200 pcs.	—	—	Proof	400.00

5 MARK

27.7770 g, .900 SILVER, .8038 oz ASW
Grand Duke's 1st Marriage

Y#	Date	Mintage	Fine	VF	XF	Unc
173	1903A	.024	50.00	100.00	225.00	300.00
	1903A	*1,000	—	—	Proof	425.00

Jena University 350th Anniversary

Y#	Date	Mintage	Fine	VF	XF	Unc
175	1908A	.040	75.00	125.00	200.00	250.00
	1908A	—	—	—	Proof	625.00

20 MARK

7.9650 g, .900 GOLD, .2304 oz AGW
Golden Wedding of Carl Alexander

Y#	Date	Mintage	Fine	VF	XF	Unc
169	1892A	5,000	600.00	900.00	1250.	2000.
	1892A	—	—	—	Proof	5000.
	1896A	.015	650.00	1250.	1750.	2250.
	1896A	380 pcs.	—	—	Proof	5000.

Y#	Date	Mintage	Fine	VF	XF	Unc
171	1901A	5,000	750.00	1500.	2000.	3000.
	1901A	—	—	—	Proof	4500.

SAXONY

Saxony, located in southeast Germany was founded in 850. The first coinage was struck c. 990. It was divided into two lines in 1464. The electoral right was obtained by the elder line in 1547. During the time of the Reformation, Saxony was one of the more powerful states in central Europe. It became a kingdom in 1806. At the Congress of Vienna in 1815, they were forced to cede half its territories to Prussia.

RULERS

Friedrich August III, 1763-1806
Later Friedrich August I, 1806-1827
Anton, 1827-1836
Friedrich August II, 1836-1854
Johann, 1854-1873
Albert, 1873-1902
Georg, 1902-1904
Friedrich August III, 1904-1918

MINT MARKS

L - Leipzig

MINTMASTERS INITIALS

Dresden Mint

Letter	Date	Name
B	1860-1887	Gustav Julius Buschick
C,IC,IEC	1779-1804	Johann Ernst Croll
F	1845-1860	Gustav Theodor Fischer
G	1833-1844	Johann Georg Grohmann
GS,IGS,S	1812-1832	Johann Gotthelf Studer
H,SGH	1804-1813	Samuel Gottlieb Helbig

HELLER

COPPER
Obv: Crowned arms. Rev: Value above date.

C#	Date	Mintage	Fine	VF	XF	Unc
90	1801 C	—	1.50	4.00	8.00	40.00
	1805/705 H	—	1.50	4.00	8.00	40.00
	1805 H	—	1.50	4.00	8.00	40.00

NOTE: Earlier dates (1778-1799) exist for this type.

Obv: Crowned arms within branches.
Rev: Value, w/o legends.

C#	Date	Mintage	Fine	VF	XF	Unc
157	1813 H	.562	3.00	5.00	10.00	60.00
	1813 S	Inc. Ab.	3.00	5.00	10.00	60.00

PFENNIG

COPPER
Obv: Crowned arms. Rev: Value above date.

C#	Date	Mintage	Fine	VF	XF	Unc
91	1801 C	—	2.00	4.00	10.00	50.00
	1804/799 C	—	2.00	4.00	10.00	50.00
	1804 C	—	2.00	4.00	10.00	50.00
	1805 H/C	—	2.00	4.00	10.00	50.00
	1805 H	—	2.00	4.00	10.00	50.00
	1806 H/795 C	—	2.00	4.00	10.00	50.00
	1806 H	—	2.00	4.00	10.00	50.00

NOTE: Earlier dates (1772-1800) exist for this type.

Obv: Crowned arms within branches.
Rev: Value, w/o legends, pearl borders both sides.

C#	Date	Mintage	Fine	VF	XF	Unc
158	1807 H	.691	3.00	7.00	20.00	75.00
	1807 H/799 C	—	4.00	8.00	25.00	85.00
	1807/86 H	—	4.00	8.00	25.00	85.00

Obv: Trefoil border.

C#	Date	Mintage	Fine	VF	XF	Unc
158a	1808 H	.014	4.00	8.00	15.00	75.00

C#	Date	Mintage	Fine	VF	XF	Unc
158b	1811 H	1.267	2.00	4.00	10.00	75.00
	1815 S	—	2.00	4.00	10.00	75.00
	1816 S	—	2.00	4.00	10.00	75.00
	1822 S	—	2.00	4.00	10.00	75.00
	1825 S	.230	2.00	4.00	10.00	75.00

C#	Date	Mintage	Fine	VF	XF	Unc
201	1831 S	1.154	2.00	4.00	8.00	45.00
	1832 S	.527	2.00	4.00	8.00	45.00
	1833 G	1.152	2.00	4.00	8.00	45.00

C#	Date	Mintage	Fine	VF	XF	Unc
220	1836 G	.226	1.50	3.00	6.00	40.00
	1837 G	.940	1.50	3.00	6.00	40.00
	1838 G	1.473	1.50	3.00	6.00	40.00

C#	Date	Mintage	Fine	VF	XF	Unc
221	1841 G	.492	1.50	3.00	6.00	30.00
	1842 G	.323	1.50	3.00	6.00	30.00
	1843 G	1.115	1.50	3.00	6.00	30.00
	1846 F	.450	1.50	3.00	6.00	30.00
	1847 F	.546	1.50	3.00	6.00	30.00
	1848 F	1.447	1.50	3.00	6.00	30.00
	1849 F	.783	1.50	3.00	6.00	30.00
	1850 F	.815	1.50	3.00	6.00	30.00
	1851 F	1.556	1.50	3.00	6.00	30.00
	1852 F	.918	1.50	3.00	6.00	30.00
	1853 F	1.164	1.50	3.00	6.00	30.00
	1854 F	.548	1.50	3.00	6.00	30.00

C#	Date	Mintage	Fine	VF	XF	Unc
248	1855 F	.657	1.50	3.00	6.00	30.00
	1856 F	3.457	1.50	3.00	6.00	30.00
	1859 F	2.341	1.50	3.00	6.00	30.00

C#	Date	Mintage	Fine	VF	XF	Unc
248a	1861 B	.338	1.50	3.00	6.00	30.00

C#	Date	Mintage	Fine	VF	XF	Unc
250	1862 B	1.094	1.50	3.00	6.00	30.00
	1863 B	4.484	1.50	3.00	6.00	30.00
	1865 B	3.877	1.50	3.00	6.00	30.00
	1866 B	1.129	1.50	3.00	6.00	30.00
	1868 B	2.084	1.50	3.00	6.00	30.00
	1871 B	.331	1.50	3.00	6.00	30.00
	1872 B	.591	1.50	3.00	6.00	30.00
	1873 B	.549	1.50	3.00	6.00	30.00

2 PFENNIGE

COPPER

C#	Date	Mintage	Fine	VF	XF	Unc
222	1841 G	1.263	2.00	4.00	8.00	40.00

C#	Date	Mintage	Fine	VF	XF	Unc
222a	1841 G	Inc. Ab.	1.50	3.00	6.00	40.00
	1843 G	.112	1.50	3.00	6.00	40.00
	1846 F	.090	1.50	3.00	6.00	40.00
	1847 F	.401	1.50	3.00	6.00	40.00
	1848 F	.518	1.50	3.00	6.00	40.00
	1849 F	.365	1.50	3.00	6.00	40.00
	1850 F	.647	1.50	3.00	6.00	40.00
	1851 F	.271	1.50	3.00	6.00	40.00
	1852 F	.361	1.50	3.00	6.00	40.00
	1853 F	.576	1.50	3.00	6.00	40.00
	1854 F	.056	2.00	4.00	8.00	45.00

C#	Date	Mintage	Fine	VF	XF	Unc
249	1855 F	.536	1.50	3.00	6.00	40.00
	1856 F	2.182	1.50	3.00	6.00	40.00
	1859 F	1.103	1.50	3.00	6.00	40.00

C#	Date	Mintage	Fine	VF	XF	Unc
249a	1861 B	.163	2.00	4.00	8.00	45.00

C#	Date	Mintage	Fine	VF	XF	Unc
251	1862 B	.739	1.25	2.50	5.00	30.00
	1863 B	.456	1.25	2.50	5.00	30.00
	1864 B	3.139	1.25	2.50	5.00	30.00
	1866 B	.551	1.25	2.50	5.00	30.00
	1869 B	2.220	1.25	2.50	5.00	30.00
	1873 B	.262	1.50	3.00	6.00	35.00

3 PFENNIGE

COPPER

C#	Date	Mintage	Fine	VF	XF	Unc
92	1801 C	—	3.00	6.00	15.00	50.00
	1802 C	—	3.00	6.00	15.00	50.00
	1803 C	—	3.00	6.00	15.00	50.00
	1804 H	—	3.00	6.00	15.00	50.00
	1806 H	—	3.00	6.00	15.00	50.00

NOTE: Earlier dates (1797-1800) exist for this type.

C#	Date	Mintage	Fine	VF	XF	Unc
160	1807 H	.317	4.00	8.00	20.00	70.00
	1808 H	.295	4.00	8.00	20.00	70.00
	1809 H	4,800	15.00	30.00	60.00	125.00
	1811 H	.128	4.00	8.00	20.00	70.00
	1812 H	.096	4.00	8.00	20.00	70.00
	1814 S	.211	4.00	8.00	20.00	70.00
	1815 S	.432	4.00	8.00	20.00	70.00
	1822 S	—	4.00	8.00	20.00	70.00
	1823 S	.019	4.00	8.00	20.00	70.00
	1824 S	.123	4.00	8.00	20.00	70.00

Obv: Crowned arched arms.
Rev. value: 3 PFENNIGE.

C#	Date	Mintage	Fine	VF	XF	Unc
161	1825 S	.168	4.00	8.00	20.00	70.00
	1826 S	.031	5.00	10.00	25.00	80.00
202	1831 S	.077	5.00	10.00	15.00	60.00
	1832 S	.226	3.00	6.00	12.00	50.00

Rev: G below date.

C#	Date	Mintage	Fine	VF	XF	Unc
202b	1833 G	.069	4.00	8.00	15.00	60.00
202a	1834 G	.500	3.00	6.00	12.00	40.00

C#	Date	Mintage	Fine	VF	XF	Unc
223	1836 G	.039	4.00	8.00	15.00	60.00
	1837 G	.542	3.00	6.00	12.00	50.00

4 PFENNIGE

COPPER

C#	Date	Mintage	Fine	VF	XF	Unc
162	1808 H	1.548	6.00	12.50	30.00	100.00
	1809/6 H	1.059	6.00	12.50	30.00	100.00
	1809/8 H	I.A.	6.00	12.50	30.00	100.00
	1809 H	Inc. Ab.	6.00	12.50	30.00	100.00
	1810 H	.886	6.00	12.50	30.00	100.00

5 PFENNIGE

COPPER

C#	Date	Mintage	Fine	VF	XF	Unc
252	1862 B	2.468	1.50	3.00	6.00	40.00
	1863 B	.693	1.50	3.00	6.00	40.00
	1864 B	1.090	1.50	3.00	6.00	40.00
	1866 B	.141	1.50	3.00	6.00	40.00
	1867 B	.444	1.50	3.00	6.00	40.00
	1869 B	.860	1.50	3.00	6.00	40.00

8 PFENNIGE

1.2900 g, .250 SILVER, .0103 oz ASW

C#	Date	Mintage	Fine	VF	XF	Unc
165	1808 H	2.594	4.00	8.00	20.00	60.00
	1809 H	4.722	4.00	8.00	20.00	60.00

1/2 NEU-GROSCHEN

(5 Pfennig)

1.0600 g, .229 SILVER, .0078 oz ASW

C#	Date	Mintage	Fine	VF	XF	Unc
224	1841 G	2.248	1.50	3.00	5.00	25.00
	1842 G	2.845	1.50	3.00	5.00	25.00
	1843 G	3.552	1.50	3.00	5.00	25.00
	1844 G	1.354	1.50	3.00	5.00	25.00
	1848 F	.500	1.50	3.00	5.00	25.00
	1849 F	.579	1.50	3.00	5.00	25.00
	1851 F	.506	1.50	3.00	5.00	25.00
	1852 F	.497	1.50	3.00	5.00	25.00
	1853 F	.256	2.00	4.00	6.00	35.00
	1854 F	.107	2.00	4.00	6.00	35.00

C#	Date	Mintage	Fine	VF	XF	Unc
253	1855 F	.444	2.00	3.00	5.00	45.00
	1856 F	.713	2.00	3.00	5.00	45.00

NEU-GROSCHEN

(10 Pfennig)

2.1200 g, .229 SILVER, .0156 oz ASW

C#	Date	Mintage	Fine	VF	XF	Unc
225	1841 G	4.500	1.50	3.00	6.00	40.00
	1842 G	2.463	1.50	3.00	6.00	40.00
	1845 F	.457	1.50	3.00	6.00	40.00
	1846 F	1.656	1.50	3.00	6.00	40.00
	1847 F	1.532	1.50	3.00	6.00	40.00
	1848 F	.105	1.50	3.00	6.00	40.00
	1849 F	1.049	1.50	3.00	6.00	40.00
	1850 F	.505	1.50	3.00	6.00	40.00
	1851 F	.676	1.50	3.00	6.00	40.00
	1852 F	.949	1.50	3.00	6.00	40.00
	1853 F	.798	1.50	3.00	6.00	40.00
	1854 F	.443	1.50	3.00	6.00	40.00

Rev: F below value.

C#	Date	Mintage	Fine	VF	XF	Unc
254	1855 F	1.106	2.00	3.50	6.00	35.00
	1856 F	1.188	2.00	3.50	6.00	35.00

2.1000 g, .230 SILVER, .0155 oz ASW
Rev: B below value.

C#	Date	Mintage	Fine	VF	XF	Unc
254a	1861 B	.395	2.50	5.00	7.50	45.00

C#	Date	Mintage	Fine	VF	XF	Unc
255	1863 B	1.514	1.50	3.00	5.00	30.00
	1865 B	.557	2.00	4.00	6.00	35.00
	1867 B	.296	2.00	4.00	6.00	35.00

C#	Date	Mintage	Fine	VF	XF	Unc
256	1867 B	.897	2.00	4.00	8.00	40.00
	1868 B	.608	2.00	4.00	8.00	40.00
	1870 B	.908	2.00	4.00	8.00	40.00
	1871 B	.293	2.00	4.00	8.00	40.00
	1873 B	.420	2.00	4.00	8.00	40.00

2 NEU-GROSCHEN

(20 Pfennig)

3.1100 g, .312 SILVER, .0311 oz ASW

C#	Date	Mintage	Fine	VF	XF	Unc
226	1841 G	3.125	1.50	3.00	6.00	40.00
	1842 G	1.413	1.50	3.00	6.00	40.00
	1844 G	1.477	1.50	3.00	6.00	40.00
	1846 F	.516	1.50	3.00	6.00	40.00
	1847 F	.425	1.50	3.00	6.00	40.00
	1848 F	1.062	1.50	3.00	6.00	40.00
	1849 F	.656	1.50	3.00	6.00	40.00
	1850 F	.380	1.50	3.00	6.00	40.00
	1851 F	.588	1.50	3.00	6.00	40.00
	1852 F	.974	1.50	3.00	6.00	40.00
	1853 F	.604	1.50	3.00	6.00	40.00
	1854 F	.790	1.50	3.00	6.00	40.00

C#	Date	Mintage	Fine	VF	XF	Unc
257	1855 F	.921	2.50	5.00	10.00	60.00
	1856 F	2.207	2.50	5.00	10.00	60.00

3.2200 g, .300 SILVER, .0310 oz ASW

C#	Date	Mintage	Fine	VF	XF	Unc
258	1863 B	.557	2.50	5.00	10.00	50.00
	1864 B	.447	2.50	5.00	10.00	50.00
	1865 B	.371	2.50	5.00	10.00	50.00
	1866 B	.448	2.50	5.00	10.00	50.00

C#	Date	Mintage	Fine	VF	XF	Unc
259	1868 B	.419	4.00	8.00	15.00	55.00
	1869 B	.599	4.00	8.00	15.00	55.00
	1871 B	.245	4.00	8.00	15.00	55.00
	1873 B	.468	4.00	8.00	15.00	55.00

1/48 THALER

.9700 g, .250 SILVER, .0077 oz ASW
Obv: Crowned shield within crossed laurel branches. Rev: Value, date below.

C#	Date	Mintage	Fine	VF	XF	Unc
97	1802 C	—	3.00	5.00	10.00	75.00
	1803 C	—	3.00	5.00	10.00	75.00
	1805 H	—	3.00	5.00	10.00	75.00
	1806 H	—	3.00	5.00	10.00	75.00

NOTE: Earlier dates (1764-1799) exist for this type.

C#	Date	Mintage	Fine	VF	XF	Unc
163	1806 H	—	3.00	5.00	10.00	75.00
	1806/797 H	—	4.00	7.00	13.50	100.00
	1807 H	2.990	3.00	5.00	10.00	75.00
	1808 H	1.816	3.00	5.00	10.00	75.00
	1811/01 H	4.242	4.00	7.00	13.50	100.00
	1811 H	Inc. Ab.	3.00	5.00	10.00	75.00
	1812 H	5.382	3.00	5.00	10.00	75.00
	1812 S	Inc. Ab.	3.00	5.00	10.00	75.00
	1813 H	.730	3.00	5.00	10.00	75.00
	1813 S	Inc. Ab.	3.00	5.00	10.00	75.00
	1814 S	2.871	3.00	5.00	10.00	75.00
	1815 S	1.059	3.00	5.00	10.00	75.00

1/24 THALER

1.9800 g, .368 SILVER, .0234 oz ASW
Obv: leg: FRID.AVG. . . .

C#	Date	Mintage	Fine	VF	XF	Unc
98	1801 EDC	—	2.50	5.00	10.00	50.00
	1802 EDC	—	2.50	5.00	10.00	50.00
	1806 SGH	—	—	—	—	—

NOTE: Earlier dates (1764-1800) exist for this type.

C#	Date	Mintage	Fine	VF	XF	Unc
166	1816 IGS	.146	2.50	5.00	10.00	50.00
	1817 IGS	.252	2.50	5.00	10.00	50.00
	1818 IGS	.166	2.50	5.00	10.00	50.00

Obv. leg: FRIED. . . . . .

C#	Date	Mintage	Fine	VF	XF	Unc
167	1819 IGS	.337	3.00	7.00	15.00	60.00
	1820 IGS	.268	3.00	7.00	15.00	60.00
	1821 IGS	.321	3.00	7.00	15.00	60.00
	1822 IGS	.439	3.00	7.00	15.00	60.00

Obv. leg: FRIEDR. . . . .

C#	Date	Mintage	Fine	VF	XF	Unc
167a	1823 IGS	.368	3.00	7.00	15.00	60.00

Obv: Crowned arched arms.

C#	Date	Mintage	Fine	VF	XF	Unc
168	1824 S	.332	2.50	5.00	10.00	50.00
	1825 S	.262	2.50	5.00	10.00	50.00
	1826 S	.311	2.50	5.00	10.00	50.00
	1827 S	.067	3.00	6.00	12.00	60.00

Obv: Crowned arched arms within crossed branches.

C#	Date	Mintage	Fine	VF	XF	Unc
203	1827 S	.066	5.00	10.00	20.00	85.00
	1828 S	.100	5.00	10.00	20.00	85.00

1/12 THALER

3.3400 g, .437 SILVER, .0469 oz ASW
Obv: Crowned large oval arms.
Rev: Value above date.

C#	Date	Mintage	Fine	VF	XF	Unc
100	1801 EDC	—	2.50	5.00	10.00	65.00
	1802 EDC	—	2.50	5.00	10.00	65.00

NOTE: Earlier dates (1763-1800) exist for this type.

C#	Date	Mintage	Fine	VF	XF	Unc
169	1806 SGH	.037	5.00	10.00	20.00	90.00
	1807 SGH	.038	5.00	10.00	20.00	90.00
	1808 SGH	.140	4.00	7.00	15.00	75.00
	1809 SGH	1.071	4.00	7.00	15.00	75.00
	1810 SGH	.515	4.00	7.00	15.00	75.00
	1811 SGH	—	4.00	7.00	15.00	75.00
	1812 IGS	5.172	4.00	7.00	15.00	75.00
	1812 SGH	I.A.	4.00	7.00	15.00	75.00
	1813 IGS	2.055	4.00	7.00	15.00	75.00
	1813 SGH	I.A.	4.00	7.00	15.00	75.00
	1814 IGS	.063	5.00	10.00	20.00	90.00
	1816 IGS	—	4.00	7.00	15.00	75.00
	1817 IGS	—	4.00	7.00	15.00	75.00
	1818 IGS	—	4.00	7.00	15.00	75.00

Obv. leg. (error): FRID VGVST. . . .

C#	Date	Mintage	Fine	VF	XF	Unc
169a	1809 SGH	I.A.	4.00	7.00	15.00	75.00

Obv. leg: FRIED. . . .

C#	Date	Mintage	Fine	VF	XF	Unc
170	1819 IGS	—	3.00	6.00	12.00	65.00
	1820 IGS	—	3.00	6.00	12.00	65.00
	1821 IGS	—	3.00	6.00	12.00	65.00
	1822 IGS	—	3.00	6.00	12.00	65.00
	1823 IGS	1.624	3.00	6.00	12.00	65.00

Obv. leg: FRIEDR. . . . .

C#	Date	Mintage	Fine	VF	XF	Unc
170a	1823 IGS	I.A.	3.00	6.00	12.00	65.00

Obv: Crowned arched arms.

C#	Date	Mintage	Fine	VF	XF	Unc
171	1824 S	2.470	2.50	5.00	10.00	50.00
	1825 S	1.721	2.50	5.00	10.00	50.00
	1826 S	.763	2.50	5.00	10.00	50.00
	1827 S	.564	2.50	5.00	10.00	50.00

Obv: Crowned arched arms within crossed branches.

C#	Date	Mintage	Fine	VF	XF	Unc
204	1827 S	.060	4.00	8.00	15.00	65.00
	1828 S	.256	2.50	5.00	10.00	50.00

C#	Date	Mintage	Fine	VF	XF	Unc
204a	1829 S	1.431	2.50	5.00	10.00	50.00
	1830 S	1.684	2.50	5.00	10.00	50.00
	1831 S	.206	2.50	5.00	10.00	50.00
	1832 S	.882	2.50	5.00	10.00	50.00

C#	Date	Mintage	Fine	VF	XF	Unc
227	1836 G	.690	3.00	6.00	12.00	60.00

1/6 THALER

(Reichs)

5.3900 g, .541 SILVER, .0937 oz ASW

C#	Date	Mintage	Fine	VF	XF	Unc
108	1803 IEC	—	7.50	15.00	35.00	110.00
	1804 IEC	—	7.50	15.00	35.00	110.00
	1804 SGH	—	7.50	15.00	35.00	110.00
	1805 SGH	—	7.50	15.00	35.00	110.00
	1806 SGH	—	7.50	15.00	35.00	110.00

C#	Date	Mintage	Fine	VF	XF	Unc
172	1806 SGH	.018	15.00	25.00	50.00	150.00
	1807 SGH	.317	7.50	15.00	35.00	110.00
	1808 SGH	2.421	7.50	15.00	35.00	110.00
	1809 SGH	3.608	7.50	15.00	35.00	110.00
	1810 SGH	2.405	7.50	15.00	35.00	110.00
	1813 SGH	.229	7.50	15.00	35.00	110.00
172a	1813 IGS	—	7.50	15.00	35.00	110.00
	1817 IGS	.119	7.50	15.00	35.00	110.00

5.3400 g, .521 SILVER, .0894 oz ASW

C#	Date	Mintage	Fine	VF	XF	Unc
173	1825 GS	.068	15.00	30.00	60.00	150.00

Death of King Friedrich August

C#	Date	Mintage	Fine	VF	XF	Unc
174	1827 S	.048	7.50	15.00	30.00	60.00

Rev: Crowned arched arms within crossed branches.

C#	Date	Mintage	Fine	VF	XF	Unc
205	1827 S	.019	25.00	50.00	100.00	200.00
	1828 S	.018	25.00	50.00	100.00	200.00

Obv: Older head.

C#	Date	Mintage	Fine	VF	XF	Unc
205a	1829 S	.124	20.00	40.00	80.00	200.00

Death of King Anton

C#	Date	Mintage	Fine	VF	XF	Unc
206	1836 G	.046	15.00	30.00	60.00	125.00

C#	Date	Mintage	Fine	VF	XF	Unc
228	1841 G	.450	6.00	12.00	30.00	90.00
	1842 G	1.322	6.00	12.00	30.00	90.00
	1843 G	.655	6.00	12.00	30.00	90.00
	1846 F	.601	6.00	12.00	30.00	90.00
	1847 F	.366	6.00	12.00	30.00	90.00
	1848 F	.270	6.00	12.00	30.00	90.00
	1849 F	.449	6.00	12.00	30.00	90.00
	1850 F	.134	6.00	12.00	30.00	90.00

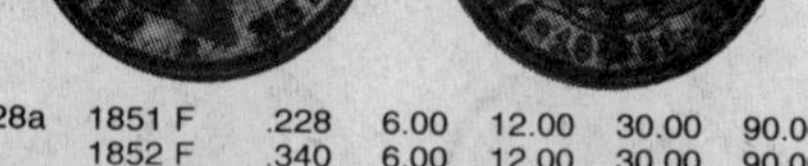

C#	Date	Mintage	Fine	VF	XF	Unc
228a	1851 F	.228	6.00	12.00	30.00	90.00
	1852 F	.340	6.00	12.00	30.00	90.00

Death of King Friedrich August II
Obv. leg: D.9.AUG. 1854 below head.
Rev: ER SAEETE. . . . .in sprays.

C#	Date	Mintage	Fine	VF	XF	Unc
229	1854 F	.521	5.00	10.00	25.00	85.00

C#	Date	Mintage	Fine	VF	XF	Unc
260	1855 F	.476	5.00	10.00	25.00	100.00
	1856 F	1.529	5.00	10.00	25.00	100.00

5.3420 g, .520 SILVER, .0893 oz ASW

C#	Date	Mintage	Fine	VF	XF	Unc
261	1860 B	.871	4.00	8.00	17.50	60.00
	1860 F	.052	6.00	12.50	25.00	100.00
	1861 B	1.099	4.00	8.00	17.50	60.00
	1863 B	.589	4.00	8.00	17.50	60.00
	1864 B	.161	4.00	8.00	17.50	60.00
	1865 B	.683	4.00	8.00	17.50	60.00
	1866/5 B	.475	4.00	8.00	17.50	65.00
	1866 B	Inc. Ab.	4.00	8.00	15.00	60.00
	1869 B	.626	4.00	8.00	15.00	60.00
	1870 B	.280	4.00	8.00	15.00	60.00
	1871 B	.293	4.00	8.00	15.00	60.00

1/3 THALER

(Reichs)

7.0160 g, .833 SILVER, .1880 oz ASW
Obv: Head right.
Rev: Crowned oval arms within crossed branches.

C#	Date	Mintage	Fine	VF	XF	Unc
113	1801 IEC	—	17.50	30.00	60.00	125.00
	1802 IEC	—	17.50	30.00	60.00	125.00

NOTE: Earlier dates (1791-1800) exist for this type.

Obv. leg: FEID, head right.

C#	Date	Mintage	Fine	VF	XF	Unc
175	1806 SGH	.027	40.00	80.00	125.00	225.00
	1808 SGH	.277	20.00	45.00	75.00	135.00
	1809 SGH	.303	20.00	45.00	75.00	135.00
	1810 SGH	.295	20.00	45.00	75.00	135.00
	1811 SGH	.278	20.00	45.00	75.00	135.00
	1812 SGH	.080	30.00	60.00	100.00	175.00
	1815 IGS	5.740	60.00	120.00	200.00	325.00
	1816 IGS	9,049	50.00	100.00	160.00	275.00
	1817 IGS	8,929	50.00	100.00	160.00	275.00

Obv. leg: FEIN.

C#	Date	Mintage	Fine	VF	XF	Unc
175a	1808	Inc. Ab.	30.00	60.00	90.00	175.00

Obv. leg: ACHTZIG

C#	Date	Mintage	Fine	VF	XF	Unc
175b	1808	Inc. Ab.	40.00	85.00	135.00	225.00

C#	Date	Mintage	Fine	VF	XF	Unc
176	1818 IGS	.019	40.00	80.00	150.00	250.00
	1821 IGS	—	40.00	80.00	150.00	250.00

8.2540 g, .708 SILVER, .1880 oz ASW
Obv: Head right. Rev: Crowned arched arms within crossed branches.

C#	Date	Mintage	Fine	VF	XF	Unc
207	1827 S	8,700	50.00	100.00	200.00	350.00
	1828 S	.010	50.00	100.00	200.00	350.00
	1829 S	.021	35.00	70.00	150.00	300.00
	1830 S	.097	35.00	70.00	150.00	300.00

8.3520 g, .667 SILVER, .1790 oz ASW

C#	Date	Mintage	Fine	VF	XF	Unc
230	1852 F	.194	15.00	30.00	60.00	125.00
	1853 F	.403	15.00	30.00	60.00	125.00
	1854 F	1.156	15.00	30.00	60.00	125.00

Death of King Friedrich August II

C#	Date	Mintage	Fine	VF	XF	Unc
231	1854 F	.029	20.00	40.00	80.00	125.00

Obv: Head left.
Rev: Crowned draped rectangular arms.

C#	Date	Mintage	Fine	VF	XF	Unc
262	1856 F	.308	25.00	50.00	100.00	175.00

8.3200 g, .667 SILVER, .1784 oz ASW

C#	Date	Mintage	Fine	VF	XF	Unc
263	1858 F	.326	20.00	40.00	80.00	150.00
	1859 F	.617	20.00	40.00	80.00	150.00

C#	Date	Mintage	Fine	VF	XF	Unc
264	1860 B	.345	17.50	35.00	70.00	125.00

2/3 THALER

(Reichs)

14.0310 g, .833 SILVER, .3760 oz ASW

C#	Date	Mintage	Fine	VF	XF	Unc
121	1801 IEC	—	25.00	40.00	75.00	150.00
	1802 IEC	—	25.00	40.00	75.00	150.00
	1805 SGH	—	25.00	40.00	75.00	150.00
	1806 SGH	—	25.00	40.00	75.00	150.00

NOTE: Earlier dates (1791-1800) exist for this type.

C#	Date	Mintage	Fine	VF	XF	Unc
177	1806 SGH	.084	25.00	35.00	60.00	200.00
	1807 SGH	.075	25.00	35.00	60.00	200.00
	1808 SGH	.171	25.00	35.00	60.00	200.00
	1809 SGH	.165	25.00	35.00	60.00	200.00
	1810 SGH	.165	25.00	35.00	60.00	200.00
	1811 SGH	.161	25.00	35.00	60.00	200.00
	1812 SGH	.086	25.00	35.00	60.00	200.00
	1813 IGS	—	25.00	35.00	60.00	200.00
	1814 IGS	.025	25.00	35.00	60.00	200.00
	1815 IGS	.048	25.00	35.00	60.00	200.00
	1816 IGS	.055	25.00	35.00	60.00	200.00
	1817 IGS	.060	25.00	35.00	60.00	200.00

C#	Date	Mintage	Fine	VF	XF	Unc
178a	1822 IGS	.023	60.00	125.00	250.00	450.00

C#	Date	Mintage	Fine	VF	XF	Unc
208	1827 S	.011	50.00	100.00	200.00	400.00
	1828 S	.012	50.00	100.00	200.00	400.00

Obv: Different head right.

C#	Date	Mintage	Fine	VF	XF	Unc
208a	1829 S	.013	60.00	125.00	250.00	450.00

EIN (1) THALER

(Mining)

28.0630 g, .833 SILVER, .7520 oz ASW
Obv: Head right. Rev: Crowned oval arms, leg: DER SEEGEN DES BERGBAVES.

C#	Date	Mintage	Fine	VF	XF	Unc
136a	1801 IEC	—	75.00	150.00	300.00	600.00
	1802 IEC	—	75.00	150.00	300.00	600.00
	1803 IEC	—	75.00	150.00	300.00	600.00
	1804 IEC	—	75.00	150.00	300.00	600.00
	1804 SGH	—	75.00	150.00	300.00	600.00
	1805 SGH	—	75.00	150.00	300.00	600.00
	1806 SGH	—	75.00	150.00	300.00	600.00

NOTE: Earlier dates (1794-1800) exist for this type.

(Convention)

Rev. leg: X.EINE.FEINE.MARK, date.

C#	Date	Mintage	Fine	VF	XF	Unc
135	1801 IEC	—	35.00	65.00	100.00	300.00
	1802 IEC	—	35.00	65.00	100.00	300.00
	1803 IEC	—	35.00	65.00	100.00	300.00
	1804 IEC	—	35.00	65.00	100.00	300.00
	1804 SGH	—	35.00	65.00	100.00	300.00
	1805 SGH	—	35.00	65.00	100.00	300.00
	1806 SGH	—	35.00	65.00	100.00	300.00

NOTE: Earlier dates (1791-1800) exist for this type.

C#	Date	Mintage	Fine	VF	XF	Unc
180	1806 SGH	.663	750.00	1250.	2500.	5000.

Obv: Small bust.

C#	Date	Mintage	Fine	VF	XF	Unc
180b	1807 SGH	.461	35.00	60.00	100.00	225.00
	1808 SGH	1.534	35.00	60.00	100.00	225.00
	1809 SGH	.563	35.00	60.00	100.00	225.00
	1810 SGH	.368	35.00	60.00	100.00	225.00
	1811 SGH	.395	35.00	60.00	100.00	225.00
	1812 SGH	.134	35.00	60.00	100.00	225.00
	1813 IGS	.773	35.00	60.00	100.00	225.00
	1813 IGS (error) ENIE		100.00	130.00	200.00	300.00
	1813 SGH	I.A.	35.00	60.00	100.00	225.00
	1815 IGS	.510	35.00	60.00	150.00	225.00
	1816 IGS	—	35.00	60.00	100.00	225.00
	1817 IGS	—	35.00	60.00	100.00	225.00

Edge inscription: GOTT SEGNE SACHSEN

C#	Date	Mintage	Fine	VF	XF	Unc
180a	1816 IGS	—	50.00	75.00	125.00	250.00

(Mining)

C#	Date	Mintage	Fine	VF	XF	Unc
179	1807 SGH	—	75.00	175.00	400.00	800.00

C#	Date	Mintage	Fine	VF	XF	Unc
181	1807 SGH	—	75.00	150.00	400.00	800.00
	1808 SGH	—	75.00	150.00	400.00	800.00
	1809 SGH	—	75.00	150.00	400.00	800.00
	1810 SGH	—	75.00	150.00	400.00	800.00
	1811 SGH	—	75.00	150.00	400.00	800.00
	1812 SGH	—	75.00	150.00	400.00	800.00
	1813 SGH	—	75.00	150.00	400.00	800.00
	1813 IGS	—	40.00	80.00	150.00	300.00
	1815 IGS	—	40.00	80.00	150.00	300.00
	1816 IGS	—	40.00	80.00	150.00	300.00
	1817 IGS	—	200.00	300.00	600.00	1250.

Rev: Legend right to left.

C#	Date	Mintage	Fine	VF	XF	Unc
181a	1811 SGH	—	75.00	150.00	400.00	800.00
	1813 SGH	—	75.00	150.00	400.00	800.00
	1811 IGS	—	75.00	150.00	400.00	800.00
	1813 IGS	—	75.00	150.00	400.00	800.00
	1815 IGS	—	75.00	150.00	400.00	800.00
	1816 IGS	—	75.00	150.00	400.00	800.00

(Convention)

Mining Academy at Freiberg

C#	Date	Mintage	Fine	VF	XF	Unc
182	1815	—	1000.	1500.	3000.	4500.

C#	Date	Mintage	Fine	VF	XF	Unc
183	1816 IGS	—	600.00	800.00	1500.	2500.

C#	Date	Mintage	Fine	VF	XF	Unc
184	1817 IGS	—	35.00	60.00	125.00	250.00
	1818 IGS	—	35.00	60.00	125.00	250.00
	1819 IGS	—	35.00	60.00	125.00	250.00
	1820 IGS	—	35.00	60.00	125.00	250.00
	1821 IGS	—	35.00	60.00	125.00	250.00

(Mining)

Rev. leg: DER SEGEN.

C#	Date	Mintage	Fine	VF	XF	Unc
185	1817 IGS	—	75.00	150.00	300.00	600.00
	1818 IGS	—	75.00	150.00	300.00	600.00
	1819 IGS	—	75.00	150.00	300.00	600.00
	1820 IGS	—	75.00	150.00	300.00	600.00
	1821 IGS	—	75.00	150.00	300.00	600.00

(Convention)

Obv: Different bust. Rev. leg: W/o DER SEGEN.

C#	Date	Mintage	Fine	VF	XF	Unc
186	1822 IGS	—	40.00	60.00	150.00	300.00
	1823 IGS	.512	40.00	60.00	150.00	300.00

(Mining)

Obv. leg: W/DER SEGEN added.

C#	Date	Mintage	Fine	VF	XF	Unc
187	1822 IGS	—	50.00	125.00	350.00	625.00
	1823 IGS	—	50.00	125.00	350.00	625.00

(Convention)

C#	Date	Mintage	Fine	VF	XF	Unc
188	1824 S	.546	35.00	60.00	125.00	275.00
	1825 S	.546	35.00	60.00	125.00	250.00
	1826 S	.546	35.00	60.00	125.00	250.00
	1827 S	.423	35.00	60.00	125.00	275.00

(Mining)

C#	Date	Mintage	Fine	VF	XF	Unc
189	1824 S	—	60.00	125.00	225.00	475.00
	1825 S	—	60.00	125.00	225.00	475.00
	1826 S	—	60.00	125.00	225.00	475.00
	1827 S	.018	60.00	125.00	225.00	475.00

C#	Date	Mintage	Fine	VF	XF	Unc
189a	1824 GS	—	150.00	450.00	1200.	2000.

(Convention)

Death of King Friedrich August

C#	Date	Mintage	Fine	VF	XF	Unc
190	1827 S	.014	60.00	100.00	150.00	250.00

(Mining)

Edge inscription: SEGEN DES BERGBAUS

C#	Date	Mintage	Fine	VF	XF	Unc
190a	1827 S	4,357	75.00	150.00	200.00	400.00

(Convention)

C#	Date	Mintage	Fine	VF	XF	Unc
209	1827 S	.107	45.00	80.00	150.00	375.00
	1828 S	.609	40.00	60.00	125.00	300.00

C#	Date	Mintage	Fine	VF	XF	Unc
209a	1829 S	.534	30.00	60.00	100.00	200.00
	1830 S	.620	30.00	60.00	100.00	200.00
	1831 S	.697	30.00	60.00	100.00	200.00
	1832 S	.979	30.00	60.00	100.00	200.00
	1833 G	.190	30.00	60.00	100.00	200.00
	1834 G	.486	30.00	60.00	100.00	200.00
	1835 G	.458	30.00	60.00	100.00	200.00
	1836 G	.585	30.00	60.00	100.00	200.00

(Mining)

Rev. leg: SEGEN DES BERGBAUS.

C#	Date	Mintage	Fine	VF	XF	Unc
210	1828 S	.018	150.00	300.00	750.00	1900.

Obv: Older head.

C#	Date	Mintage	Fine	VF	XF	Unc
210a	1829 S	.019	65.00	175.00	450.00	1000.
	1830 S	.019	65.00	200.00	500.00	1200.
	1831 S	.019	65.00	175.00	450.00	1000.
	1832 S	.013	65.00	175.00	450.00	1000.
	1833 G	3,000	65.00	200.00	500.00	1200.
	1834 G	5,500	65.00	175.00	450.00	1000.
	1835 G	4,986	65.00	175.00	450.00	1000.
	1836 G	4,836	65.00	200.00	500.00	1200.

(Convention)

Prize Thaler - Mining Academy at Freiberg
Obv: Similar to C#209.

C#	Date	Mintage	Fine	VF	XF	Unc
211	1829	200 pcs.	1000.	2000.	4000.	6000.

Prize Thaler - Forestry Institute at Tharant

C#	Date	Mintage	Fine	VF	XF	Unc
212	1830	25 pcs.	—	—	Rare	—

Prize Thaler - Agriculture Educational Establishment at Tharant
Rev: LANDWIRTSCHAFTL

C#	Date	Mintage	Fine	VF	XF	Unc
213	1830	25 pcs.	—	—	Rare	—

New Constitution

C#	Date	Mintage	Fine	VF	XF	Unc
214	1831 S	.014	40.00	80.00	125.00	250.00

Death of King Anton

C#	Date	Mintage	Fine	VF	XF	Unc
215	1836 G	.012	40.00	80.00	125.00	250.00

(Mining)

Edge inscription: SEGEN DES BERGBAUS

C#	Date	Mintage	Fine	VF	XF	Unc
215a	1836 G	2,500	100.00	250.00	500.00	1000.

(Convention)

C#	Date	Mintage	Fine	VF	XF	Unc
232	1836 G	.034	100.00	200.00	600.00	1200.
	1837 G	.031	125.00	275.00	700.00	1400.

Obv. legend continuous.

C#	Date	Mintage	Fine	VF	XF	Unc
232a	1836 G	3,260	450.00	1000.	2200.	4000.
	1837 G	.094	50.00	90.00	225.00	475.00
	1838 G	.139	40.00	75.00	200.00	400.00

(Mining)

Obv. leg: KOENIG. Rev. leg: SEGEN DES, etc.

C#	Date	Mintage	Fine	VF	XF	Unc
233	1836 G	3,262	450.00	1000.	2200.	4000.
	1837 G	5,770	135.00	275.00	700.00	1400.
	1838 G	.036	90.00	175.00	475.00	875.00

(Convention)

22.2720 g, .750 SILVER, .5371 oz ASW
Visit to Dresden Mint
Lettered edge

C#	Date	Mintage	Fine	VF	XF	Unc
234	1839 G	—	900.00	1800.	3000.	4500.

Plain edge

C#	Date	Mintage	Fine	VF	XF	Unc
234a	1839	—	—	—	Rare	—

C#	Date	Mintage	Fine	VF	XF	Unc
235	1839 G	.643	25.00	50.00	100.00	250.00
	1840 G	1.406	25.00	50.00	100.00	250.00
	1841 G	2.505	25.00	50.00	100.00	250.00
	1842 G	.974	25.00	50.00	100.00	250.00
	1843 G	1.251	25.00	50.00	100.00	250.00
	1844 G	1.026	25.00	50.00	100.00	250.00

Obv: F below head.

C#	Date	Mintage	Fine	VF	XF	Unc
235a	1845 F	.973	25.00	50.00	100.00	250.00
	1846 F	.860	25.00	50.00	100.00	250.00
	1847 F	.677	25.00	50.00	100.00	250.00
	1848 F	1.592	25.00	50.00	100.00	250.00
	1849 F	1.368	25.00	50.00	100.00	250.00

C#	Date	Mintage	Fine	VF	XF	Unc
235b	1850 F	1.074	25.00	50.00	125.00	325.00
	1851 F	1.351	25.00	50.00	125.00	325.00
	1852 F	1.105	25.00	50.00	125.00	325.00
	1853 F	1.171	25.00	50.00	125.00	325.00
	1854 F	1.075	25.00	50.00	125.00	325.00

(Mining)

Obv: G below head.

C#	Date	Mintage	Fine	VF	XF	Unc
236	1841 G	.011	75.00	150.00	450.00	1000.
	1842 G	.017	75.00	150.00	450.00	1000.
	1843 G	.017	75.00	150.00	450.00	1000.
	1844 G	.011	75.00	150.00	450.00	1000.

Obv: F below head.

C#	Date	Mintage	Fine	VF	XF	Unc
236b	1845 F	.019	60.00	150.00	300.00	600.00
	1846 F	.022	60.00	150.00	300.00	600.00
	1847 F	.040	60.00	125.00	250.00	500.00
	1848 F	.021	60.00	150.00	300.00	600.00
	1849 F	.038	60.00	150.00	300.00	600.00
236a	1850 F	.034	50.00	125.00	250.00	500.00
	1851 F	.033	50.00	100.00	200.00	400.00
	1852 F	.047	50.00	125.00	250.00	500.00
	1853 F	.055	50.00	100.00	200.00	400.00
	1854 F	.037	50.00	100.00	200.00	400.00

Death of King Friedrich August II

C#	Date	Mintage	Fine	VF	XF	Unc
237	1854 F	.016	30.00	60.00	100.00	200.00

Edge: SEGEN DES BERGBAUS and crossed hammers.

C#	Date	Mintage	Fine	VF	XF	Unc
237a	1854 F	8,829	40.00	75.00	125.00	250.00

(Convention)

C#	Date	Mintage	Fine	VF	XF	Unc
265	1854 F	.525	30.00	60.00	150.00	450.00

(Mining)

Rev: Similar to C#269.

C#	Date	Mintage	Fine	VF	XF	Unc
266	1854 F	.027	90.00	175.00	425.00	1000.

(Convention)

Visit to Mint by King Johann

C#	Date	Mintage	Fine	VF	XF	Unc
267	1855 F	5,250	35.00	65.00	125.00	300.00
	1855 F	—	—	—	Proof	400.00

Rev: Similar to C#265.

C#	Date	Mintage	Fine	VF	XF	Unc
268	1855 F	.863	25.00	40.00	125.00	300.00
	1856 F	1.089	25.00	40.00	100.00	250.00

(Mining)

C#	Date	Mintage	Fine	VF	XF	Unc
269	1855 F	.056	65.00	125.00	350.00	800.00
	1856 F	.056	65.00	125.00	350.00	800.00

(Vereins)

18.5200 g, .900 SILVER, .5360 oz ASW
Obv: Similar to C#269.

C#	Date	Mintage	Fine	VF	XF	Unc
270	1857 F	.969	25.00	45.00	100.00	250.00
	1858 F	.200	25.00	45.00	100.00	250.00
	1859 F	2.490	20.00	35.00	90.00	225.00

(Mining)

Obv: Similar to C#269.

C#	Date	Mintage	Fine	VF	XF	Unc
271	1857 F	.035	75.00	150.00	400.00	800.00
	1858 F	.034	75.00	150.00	400.00	800.00

Obv. leg: Large letters.
Rev. leg: SEGEN DES BERGBAUS.

C#	Date	Mintage	Fine	VF	XF	Unc
272.1	1858 F	.061	35.00	65.00	135.00	325.00
	1859 F	.094	35.00	65.00	135.00	325.00
	1860 B	.298	25.00	50.00	100.00	250.00
	1861 B	.016	40.00	75.00	150.00	350.00

Obv. leg: Small letters.

C#	Date	Mintage	Fine	VF	XF	Unc
272.2	1861 B	.130	75.00	150.00	450.00	1000.

Rev. leg: SEGEN DES BERGBAUES.

C#	Date	Mintage	Fine	VF	XF	Unc
272a	1861 B	.130	25.00	50.00	70.00	150.00
	1862 B	.145	25.00	50.00	70.00	150.00
	1863 B	.135	25.00	50.00	70.00	150.00
	1864 B	.120	25.00	50.00	70.00	150.00
	1865 B	.221	25.00	50.00	70.00	150.00
	1866 B	.185	25.00	50.00	70.00	150.00
	1867 B	.175	25.00	50.00	70.00	150.00

C#	Date	Mintage	Fine	VF	XF	Unc
272b	1868 B	.181	25.00	50.00	70.00	150.00
	1869 B	.190	25.00	50.00	70.00	150.00
	1870 B	.236	25.00	50.00	70.00	150.00
	1871 B	.203	25.00	50.00	70.00	150.00

(Vereins)

C#	Date	Mintage	Fine	VF	XF	Unc
273	1860 B	2.669	25.00	50.00	90.00	200.00
	1861 B	1.409	25.00	50.00	90.00	200.00

Obv: Similar to C#273.

C#	Date	Mintage	Fine	VF	XF	Unc
273a	1861 B	1.070	25.00	50.00	70.00	150.00
	1862 B	2.134	25.00	50.00	70.00	150.00
	1863 B	1.471	25.00	50.00	70.00	150.00
	1864 B	1.904	25.00	50.00	70.00	150.00
	1865 B	1.335	25.00	50.00	70.00	150.00
	1866 B	1.181	25.00	50.00	70.00	150.00
	1867 B	2.020	25.00	50.00	70.00	150.00
	1868 B	1.683	25.00	50.00	70.00	150.00

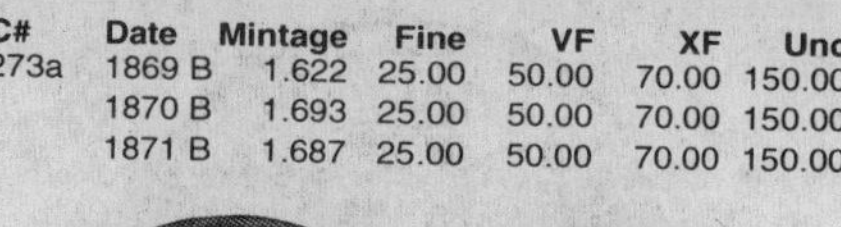

C#	Date	Mintage	Fine	VF	XF	Unc
273a	1869 B	1.622	25.00	50.00	70.00	150.00
	1870 B	1.693	25.00	50.00	70.00	150.00
	1871 B	1.687	25.00	50.00	70.00	150.00

Victory Over France

C#	Date	Mintage	Fine	VF	XF	Unc
274	1871 B	.045	35.00	50.00	100.00	200.00

2 THALER

(3-1/2 Gulden)

37.1200 g, .900 SILVER, 1.0742 oz ASW

C#	Date	Mintage	Fine	VF	XF	Unc
238	1839 G	.020	90.00	125.00	300.00	600.00
	1840 G	.068	90.00	125.00	300.00	600.00
	1841 G	.039	90.00	125.00	300.00	600.00
	1842 G	.071	70.00	100.00	250.00	450.00
	1843 G	.059	70.00	100.00	250.00	450.00

C#	Date	Mintage	Fine	VF	XF	Unc
238a	1847 F	.147	50.00	85.00	185.00	400.00
	1848 F	.078	65.00	125.00	225.00	550.00
	1849 F	.015	65.00	125.00	225.00	550.00
	1850 F	.113	50.00	85.00	185.00	400.00
	1851 F	.246	50.00	85.00	185.00	400.00
	1852 F	.209	50.00	85.00	185.00	400.00
	1853 F	.303	50.00	85.00	185.00	400.00
	1854 F	.886	50.00	85.00	185.00	400.00

Prize Thaler - Mining Academy at Freiberg
Obv: Similar to C#238.

C#	Date	Mintage	Fine	VF	XF	Unc
239	1841 G	200 pcs.	750.00	1500.	3000.	4500.

Prize Thaler - Forest and Agriculture Academy
Obv: Similar to C#238.

C#	Date	Mintage	Fine	VF	XF	Unc
240	1847 F	50 pcs.	3000.	6000.	8500.	12,000.

Death of King Friedrich August II

C#	Date	Mintage	Fine	VF	XF	Unc
241	1854 F	6,148	100.00	200.00	300.00	500.00
	1854 F	—	—	—	Proof	800.00

Rev: Similar to C#238.

C#	Date	Mintage	Fine	VF	XF	Unc
275	1855 F	.462	50.00	90.00	190.00	350.00
	1856 F	.091	75.00	110.00	210.00	400.00

Prize Thaler - Mining Academy at Freiberg
Obv: Similar to C#275 w/F below head.

C#	Date	Mintage	Fine	VF	XF	Unc
276	1857 F	100 pcs.	750.00	1500.	3000.	4500.

Obv: B below head.

C#	Date	Mintage	Fine	VF	XF	Unc
276a	1857 B	206 pcs.	700.00	1400.	2500.	4000.

37.0370 g, .900 SILVER, 1.0718 oz ASW
Obv: Similar to C#275.

C#	Date	Mintage	Fine	VF	XF	Unc
277	1857 F	.351	50.00	80.00	180.00	365.00
	1858 F	.454	50.00	80.00	180.00	365.00
	1859 F	.323	50.00	80.00	180.00	365.00

Rev. value: VEREINSTHAELR

C#	Date	Mintage	Fine	VF	XF	Unc
277a	1858	Inc. Ab.	35.00	90.00	175.00	375.00

Obv: Similar to C#275.

C#	Date	Mintage	Fine	VF	XF	Unc
278	1861 B	.730	65.00	100.00	200.00	400.00

Golden Wedding Anniversary

C#	Date	Mintage	Fine	VF	XF	Unc
279	1872 B	.049	50.00	75.00	125.00	200.00

Plain edge.

C#	Date	Mintage	Fine	VF	XF	Unc
279a	1872 B	Inc. Ab.	100.00	250.00	350.00	500.00

2-1/2 THALER

3.3410 g, .902 GOLD, .0970 oz AGW

C#	Date	Mintage	VF	XF	Unc	
245	1842 G	560 pcs.	300.00	600.00	1000.	2250.
	1845 F	420 pcs.	300.00	600.00	1000.	2250.
	1848 F	2,445	250.00	500.00	1000.	2000.
	1854 F	308 pcs.	400.00	700.00	1200.	2500.

5 THALER

6.6820 g, .902 GOLD, .1940 oz AGW
Obv: Bust right. Rev: Crowned arms.

C#	Date	Mintage	Fine	VF	XF	Unc
150	1801 IEC	—	400.00	900.00	1500.	3750.
	1802 IEC	—	400.00	900.00	1500.	3750.

NOTE: Earlier dates (1791-1800) exist for this type.

C#	Date	Mintage	Fine	VF	XF	Unc
150a	1805 SGH	—	500.00	1000.	1500.	4000.
	1806 SGH	—	500.00	1000.	1500.	4000.

C#	Date	Mintage	Fine	VF	XF	Unc
195	1806 SGH	.044	500.00	1000.	2000.	5000.
	1807 SGH	.152	400.00	900.00	1500.	3500.
	1808 SGH	.135	300.00	600.00	1250.	2750.
	1809 SGH	.054	300.00	600.00	1250.	2750.
	1810 SGH	.235	300.00	600.00	1250.	2750.
	1812 SGH	.098	300.00	600.00	1250.	2750.
	1813 SGH	.118	300.00	600.00	1250.	2750.
	1815 IGS	.020	250.00	500.00	1250.	2500.
	1816 IGS	—	400.00	900.00	1500.	3250.
	1817 IGS	—	250.00	500.00	1250.	2500.

Obv: Uniformed bust left.

C#	Date	Mintage	Fine	VF	XF	Unc
196	1818 IGS	—	800.00	2000.	4000.	7500.

C#	Date	Mintage	Fine	VF	XF	Unc
197	1825 S	.060	250.00	600.00	1500.	3000.
	1826 S	2,590	400.00	1000.	2000.	4000.
	1827 S	700 pcs.	500.00	1000.	2000.	4000.

C#	Date	Mintage	Fine	VF	XF	Unc
218	1827 S	405 pcs.	500.00	1000.	2000.	4000.
	1828 S	855 pcs.	500.00	1000.	2000.	4000.

Obv: Older head.

C#	Date	Mintage	Fine	VF	XF	Unc
218a	1829 S	385 pcs.	500.00	1000.	2000.	4000.
	1830 S	2,800	550.00	1100.	2000.	4250.
	1831 S	245 pcs.	700.00	1500.	3000.	5000.
	1832 S	175 pcs.	700.00	1250.	2500.	4500.
	1834 G	490 pcs.	700.00	1250.	2500.	4500.
	1835 G	380 pcs.	700.00	1250.	2500.	4500.
	1836 G	455 pcs.	700.00	1500.	2500.	5000.

C#	Date	Mintage	Fine	VF	XF	Unc
243	1837 G	490 pcs.	400.00	750.00	2000.	3250.
	1838 G	175 pcs.	500.00	750.00	2000.	3250.
	1839 G	210 pcs.	500.00	850.00	2000.	3500.

C#	Date	Mintage	Fine	VF	XF	Unc
246	1842 G	4,455	250.00	400.00	1000.	2000.
	1845 F	1,483	300.00	500.00	1200.	2250.
	1848 F	1,964	300.00	500.00	1200.	2250.
	1849 F	1,110	300.00	500.00	1200.	2250.
	1853 F	511 pcs.	450.00	800.00	1500.	2500.
	1854 F	4,570	300.00	500.00	1200.	2250.

10 THALER

13.3640 g, .902 GOLD, .3880 oz AGW

C#	Date	Mintage	Fine	VF	XF	Unc
156	1801 IEC	—	800.00	2000.	3000.	5000.
	1802 IEC	—	800.00	2000.	3000.	5000.
	1803 IEC	—	800.00	2000.	3000.	5000.
	1804 IEC	—	600.00	1500.	2750.	4000.
	1804 SGH	—	500.00	1100.	2250.	4000.
	1805 SGH	—	600.00	1500.	2750.	4000.
	1806 SGH	—	500.00	1100.	2250.	4000.

NOTE: Earlier dates (1791-1800) exist for this type.

C#	Date	Mintage	Fine	VF	XF	Unc
198	1806 SGH	—	600.00	1250.	2500.	4000.
	1807 SGH	—	600.00	1250.	2500.	4000.
	1808 SGH	—	500.00	1000.	2000.	4000.
	1809 SGH	—	600.00	1250.	2500.	4000.
	1810 SGH	—	500.00	1000.	2000.	4000.
	1811 SGH	—	500.00	1000.	2000.	3500.
	1812 SGH	—	500.00	1000.	2000.	3500.
	1813 SGH	—	450.00	850.00	1750.	3000.
	1813 IGS	—	500.00	1000.	2000.	3500.
	1815 IGS	—	450.00	850.00	1750.	3000.
	1816 IGS	—	600.00	1250.	2500.	3500.
	1817 IGS	—	450.00	850.00	1750.	3000.

C#	Date	Mintage	Fine	VF	XF	Unc
199	1818 IGS	—	2000.	4000.	7500.	9000.

C#	Date	Mintage	Fine	VF	XF	Unc
200	1825 S	—	800.00	2000.	4000.	5000.
	1826 S	—	700.00	1500.	3000.	4000.
	1827 S	9,250	700.00	1500.	3000.	4000.

Obv: Head right.
Rev: Crowned arched arms within crossed branches.

C#	Date	Mintage	Fine	VF	XF	Unc
219	1827 S	875 pcs.	1200.	3000.	6000.	7500.
	1828 S	5,530	800.00	2250.	5000.	6000.

Obv: Older head.

C#	Date	Mintage	Fine	VF	XF	Unc
219a	1829 S	3,010	800.00	2000.	4000.	5000.
	1830 S	.018	650.00	1600.	3250.	4500.
	1831 S	3,255	1250.	2500.	5000.	7000.
	1832 S	2,625	800.00	2000.	4000.	5000.
	1833 G	—	1250.	2500.	5000.	7000.
	1834 G	3,080	1250.	2500.	5000.	7000.
	1835 G	2,715	1250.	2500.	5000.	7000.
	1836 G	4,655	1250.	2500.	5000.	7000.

Obv: Different head. Rev: Crowned rectangular arms within crossed branches.

C#	Date	Mintage	Fine	VF	XF	Unc
244	1836 G	1,110	600.00	1250.	2500.	3250.
	1837 G	2,400	600.00	1250.	2500.	3250.
	1838 G	1,750	700.00	1500.	3000.	3750.
	1839 G	1,855	700.00	1500.	3000.	3750.

C#	Date	Mintage	Fine	VF	XF	Unc
247	1839 G	1,855	800.00	2000.	4000.	5000.
	1845 F	2,100	600.00	1250.	2500.	3250.
	1848 F	4,761	700.00	1500.	3000.	4000.
	1849 F	1,928	700.00	1500.	3000.	4000.
	1853 F	1,038	700.00	1500.	3000.	4000.
	1854 F	1,620	800.00	2000.	4000.	5000.

1/2 KRONE

5.5560 g, .900 GOLD, .1608 oz AGW

C#	Date	Mintage	Fine	VF	XF	Unc
280	1857 F	4,831	475.00	1000.	2000.	3000.
	1858 F	2,455	475.00	1000.	2000.	3000.
	1862 B	2,177	550.00	1200.	2250.	3000.
	1866 B	1,559	550.00	1200.	2250.	3000.
	1868 B	1,516	550.00	1200.	2500.	3250.
	1870 B	1,740	550.00	1200.	2500.	3250.

KRONE

11.1110 g, .900 GOLD, .3215 oz AGW

C#	Date	Mintage	Fine	VF	XF	Unc
281	1857 F	3,580	525.00	1350.	2500.	3000.
	1858 F	4,610	525.00	1350.	2500.	3000.
	1859 F	9,040	525.00	1350.	2500.	3000.
	1860 B	5,067	525.00	1350.	2750.	3500.
	1861 B	3,908	525.00	1350.	2500.	3000.
	1862 B	3,229	525.00	1350.	2750.	3500.
	1863 B	3,538	525.00	1350.	2750.	3500.
	1865 B	4,371	525.00	1350.	2500.	3000.
	1867 B	2,155	525.00	1350.	2750.	3500.
	1868 B	5,262	525.00	1350.	2500.	3000.
	1870 B	2,700	525.00	1350.	2500.	3000.
	1871 B	2,140	525.00	1350.	2750.	3500.

MONETARY REFORM

2 MARK

11.1110 g, .900 SILVER, .3215 oz ASW

Y#	Date	Mintage	Fine	VF	XF	Unc
180	1876E	1.613	30.00	80.00	500.00	1200.
	1877E	.796	30.00	80.00	450.00	1100.
	1877E	—	—	—	Proof	1000.
	1879E	.036	70.00	175.00	700.00	1900.
	1880E	.058	70.00	125.00	550.00	1900.
	1883E	.056	70.00	125.00	550.00	2000.
	1888E	.091	40.00	100.00	450.00	1700.

Y#	Date	Mintage	Fine	VF	XF	Unc
180a	1891E	.130	25.00	65.00	125.00	300.00
	1893E	.130	25.00	85.00	175.00	325.00
	1895E	.117	30.00	115.00	200.00	375.00
	1896E	.144	25.00	85.00	175.00	350.00
	1898E	.107	25.00	85.00	175.00	400.00
	1899E	.401	15.00	60.00	110.00	225.00
	1900E	.384	15.00	60.00	110.00	200.00
	1901E	.440	12.50	55.00	100.00	200.00
	1902E	.543	10.00	55.00	100.00	175.00

Death of Albert

Y#	Date	Mintage	Fine	VF	XF	Unc
185	1902E	.168	15.00	40.00	65.00	90.00
	1902E	250 pcs.		—	Proof	200.00

Y#	Date	Mintage	Fine	VF	XF	Unc
187	1903E	.746	30.00	60.00	140.00	275.00
	1903E	50 pcs.	—	—	Proof	450.00
	1904E	1.266	17.50	50.00	100.00	200.00

Death of Georg

Y#	Date	Mintage	Fine	VF	XF	Unc
191	1904E	.150	15.00	35.00	60.00	90.00
	1904E	55 pcs.	—	—	Proof	225.00

Y#	Date	Mintage	Fine	VF	XF	Unc
193	1905E	.559	20.00	40.00	80.00	150.00
	1905E	100 pcs.	—	—	Proof	200.00
	1906E	.559	20.00	40.00	80.00	150.00
	1907E	1.118	20.00	40.00	80.00	150.00
	1908E	.336	20.00	45.00	75.00	150.00
	1911E	.186	20.00	45.00	75.00	150.00
	1912E	.168	20.00	45.00	75.00	150.00
	1914E	.298	20.00	40.00	70.00	150.00
	Common date		—	—	Proof	225.00

500th Anniversary Leipzig University

Y#	Date	Mintage	Fine	VF	XF	Unc
198	1909	.125	15.00	30.00	65.00	90.00
	1909	300 pcs.	—	—	Proof	200.00

3 MARK

16.6670 g, .900 SILVER, .4823 oz ASW

Y#	Date	Mintage	Fine	VF	XF	Unc
194	1908E	.276	10.00	25.00	40.00	60.00
	1909E	1.197	10.00	25.00	30.00	50.00
	1910E	.745	10.00	25.00	30.00	50.00
	1911E	.581	10.00	25.00	30.00	50.00
	1912E	.379	10.00	25.00	30.00	50.00
	1913E	.307	10.00	25.00	30.00	50.00
	Common date		—	—	Proof	150.00

Battle of Leipzig Centennial

Y#	Date	Mintage	Fine	VF	XF	Unc
200	1913E	1.000	15.00	20.00	30.00	35.00
	1913E	.017	—	—	Proof	125.00

Jubilee of Reformation

Y#	Date	Mintage	Fine	VF	XF	Unc
201	1917E	100 pcs.	—	Proof	27,500.	40,000.

5 MARK

27.7770 g, .900 SILVER, .8038 oz ASW

Y#	Date	Mintage	Fine	VF	XF	Unc
181	1875E	.494	30.00	60.00	750.00	2200.
	1876E	.635	25.00	50.00	650.00	1900.
	1889E	.036	40.00	100.00	750.00	2700.

1.9910 g, .900 GOLD, .0576 oz AGW

Y#	Date	Mintage	Fine	VF	XF	Unc
182	1877E	.402	100.00	175.00	250.00	400.00
	1877E	—	—	—	Proof	1000.

27.7770 g, .900 SILVER, .8038 oz ASW

Y#	Date	Mintage	Fine	VF	XF	Unc
181a	1891E	.052	30.00	60.00	600.00	1100.
	1893E	.052	30.00	60.00	600.00	1100.
	1894E	.075	30.00	60.00	600.00	1100.
	1895E	.089	30.00	60.00	600.00	1100.
	1898E	.160	25.00	50.00	450.00	800.00
	1899E	.074	25.00	50.00	450.00	900.00
	1900E	.157	25.00	50.00	400.00	800.00
	1901E	.156	25.00	50.00	300.00	700.00
	1902E	.168	20.00	35.00	250.00	500.00

Death of Albert

Y#	Date	Mintage	Fine	VF	XF	Unc
186	1902E	.100	30.00	60.00	125.00	165.00
	1902E	250 pcs.	—	—	Proof	425.00

Y#	Date	Mintage	Fine	VF	XF	Unc
188	1903E	.536	20.00	40.00	125.00	450.00
	1903E	50 pcs.	—	—	Proof	750.00
	1904E	.291	25.00	50.00	160.00	600.00
	1904E	—	—	—	Proof	850.00

Death of Georg

Y#	Date	Mintage	Fine	VF	XF	Unc
192	1904E	.037	40.00	125.00	225.00	275.00
	1904E	70 pcs.	—	—	Proof	400.00

Y#	Date	Mintage	Fine	VF	XF	Unc
195	1907E	.398	20.00	40.00	90.00	150.00
	1908E	.317	20.00	40.00	90.00	175.00
	1914E	.298	17.50	35.00	80.00	150.00

500th Anniversary Leipzig University

Y#	Date	Mintage	Fine	VF	XF	Unc
199	1909	.050	40.00	90.00	175.00	225.00
	1909	300 pcs.	—	—	Proof	525.00

10 MARK

3.9820 g, .900 GOLD, .1152 oz AGW

Rev: Type I.

Y#	Date	Mintage	Fine	VF	XF	Unc
178	1872E	.339	65.00	100.00	150.00	325.00
	1873E	.822	65.00	100.00	150.00	300.00

Rev: Type II.

Y#	Date	Mintage	Fine	VF	XF	Unc
183	1874E	.048	450.00	750.00	1200.	2500.
	1875E	.528	70.00	100.00	150.00	250.00
	1877E	.201	70.00	100.00	150.00	300.00
	1878E	.225	70.00	100.00	150.00	300.00
	1879E	.182	70.00	100.00	150.00	300.00
	1881E	.240	70.00	100.00	150.00	300.00
	1888E	.149	70.00	100.00	150.00	300.00

Rev: Type III.

Y#	Date	Mintage	Fine	VF	XF	Unc
183a	1891E	.224	80.00	125.00	150.00	275.00
	1893E	.224	80.00	125.00	150.00	275.00
	1896E	.150	80.00	125.00	150.00	275.00
	1898E	.313	80.00	125.00	150.00	275.00
	1900E	.074	80.00	125.00	150.00	275.00
	1900E	—	—	—	Proof	1500.
	1901E	.075	80.00	125.00	150.00	275.00
	1902E	.037	80.00	125.00	150.00	325.00

Y#	Date	Mintage	Fine	VF	XF	Unc
189	1903E	.284	80.00	125.00	200.00	300.00
	1903E	100 pcs.	—	—	Proof	1100.
	1904E	.149	80.00	125.00	200.00	300.00

Y#	Date	Mintage	Fine	VF	XF	Unc
196	1905E	.112	70.00	125.00	150.00	275.00
	1905E	100 pcs.	—	—	Proof	800.00
	1906E	.075	70.00	125.00	150.00	275.00
	1907E	.112	70.00	125.00	150.00	275.00
	1909E	.112	70.00	125.00	150.00	275.00
	1910E	.075	70.00	125.00	150.00	275.00
	1910E	—	—	—	Proof	850.00
	1911E	.038	70.00	125.00	150.00	325.00
	1912E	.075	70.00	125.00	150.00	300.00

20 MARK

7.9650 g, .900 GOLD, .2304 oz AGW

Rev: Type I.

Y#	Date	Mintage	Fine	VF	XF	Unc
179.1	1872E	.890	115.00	130.00	150.00	250.00
	1872E	—	—	—	Proof	Rare

Obv: Large letters in legend.

Y#	Date	Mintage	Fine	VF	XF	Unc
179.2	1873E	.203	115.00	135.00	160.00	275.00

Rev: Type II.

Y#	Date	Mintage	Fine	VF	XF	Unc
184	1874E	.153	115.00	135.00	160.00	350.00
	1876E	.482	115.00	135.00	160.00	350.00
	1876E	—	—	—	Proof	1800.
	1877E	1,181	9000.	17,000.	25,000.	35,000.
	1878E	1,564	11,000.	22,000.	38,000.	45,000.

Rev: Type III.

Y#	Date	Mintage	Fine	VF	XF	Unc
184a	1894E	.639	115.00	125.00	150.00	325.00
	1895E	.113	115.00	125.00	225.00	375.00

Y#	Date	Mintage	Fine	VF	XF	Unc
190	1903E	.250	115.00	150.00	225.00	350.00
	1903E	—	—	—	Proof	1800.

Y#	Date	Mintage	Fine	VF	XF	Unc
197	1905E	.500	115.00	125.00	150.00	250.00
	1905E	86 pcs.	—	—	Proof	1100.
	1913E	.121	115.00	140.00	200.00	325.00
	1914E	.325	115.00	165.00	225.00	425.00

TRADE COINAGE

DUCAT

3.5000 g, .986 GOLD, .1109 oz AGW

C#	Date	Mintage	Fine	VF	XF	Unc
145	1801 IEC	—	300.00	600.00	1250.	3000.
	1802 IEC	—	200.00	400.00	750.00	2000.
	1803 IEC	—	300.00	600.00	1250.	3000.
	1804 IEC	—	250.00	500.00	1000.	2500.

NOTE: Earlier dates (1791-1800) exist for this type.

C#	Date	Mintage	Fine	VF	XF	Unc
145a	1804 SGH	—	300.00	700.00	1250.	2500.
	1805 SGH	—	350.00	800.00	1500.	3000.
	1806 SGH	—	300.00	700.00	1250.	2500.

C#	Date	Mintage	Fine	VF	XF	Unc
192	1806 SGH	3,207	200.00	400.00	1000.	2000.
	1807 SGH	2,660	300.00	800.00	1500.	2500.
	1808 SGH	2,010	300.00	800.00	1500.	2500.
	1809 SGH	1,608	300.00	800.00	1500.	2500.
	1810 SGH	1,072	300.00	800.00	1500.	2500.
	1811 SGH	268 pcs.	350.00	800.00	1750.	3000.
	1812 SGH	67 pcs.	400.00	800.00	1750.	3000.
	1813 SGH	—	300.00	600.00	1500.	2500.

C#	Date	Mintage	Fine	VF	XF	Unc
192a	1813 IGS	—	300.00	600.00	1500.	2500.
	1814 IGS	134 pcs.	500.00	1000.	2000.	3500.
	1815 IGS	804 pcs.	350.00	800.00	1750.	3000.
	1816 IGS	2,243	300.00	600.00	1300.	2500.
	1817 IGS	1,812	300.00	600.00	1300.	2500.
	1818 IGS	1,466	300.00	600.00	1300.	2500.
	1819 IGS	1,466	300.00	600.00	1300.	2500.
	1820 IGS	2,502	300.00	600.00	1300.	2500.
	1821 IGS	1,948	300.00	600.00	1300.	2500.
	1822 IGS	1,898	300.00	600.00	1300.	2500.

400th Jubilee of Leipzig University
Obv: Bust in coronet and cape right.
Rev. leg: SALVA SIT.

Fr#	Date	Mintage	Fine	VF	XF	Unc
2586	1809	—	300.00	600.00	1200.	2000.

Obv: Uniformed bust left, leg: FRIEDR.AUGUST. . . .
Rev: Crowned oval arms within crossed branches.

C#	Date	Mintage	Fine	VF	XF	Unc
193	1823 IGS	1,380	300.00	600.00	1200.	2000.

Obv. leg: FRIEDR.AUG.KOEN. . . .

C#	Date	Mintage	Fine	VF	XF	Unc
194	1824 IGS	2,847	300.00	600.00	1000.	1800.
194a	1825 IGS	1,725	300.00	600.00	1200.	2000.
	1826 IGS	2,415	300.00	600.00	1200.	2000.
	1827 IGS	1,639	300.00	600.00	1200.	2000.

C#	Date	Mintage	Fine	VF	XF	Unc
217	1827 S	587 pcs.	400.00	900.00	1500.	2500.
	1828 S	771 pcs.	400.00	900.00	1500.	2500.

C#	Date	Mintage	Fine	VF	XF	Unc
217a	1829 S	2,070	300.00	600.00	1200.	2000.
	1830 S	1,898	300.00	600.00	1200.	2000.
	1831 S	862 pcs.	400.00	900.00	1500.	2500.
	1832 S	776 pcs.	400.00	900.00	1500.	2500.
	1833 G	2,156	400.00	900.00	1500.	2500.
	1834 G	1,582	400.00	900.00	1500.	2500.
	1835 G	119 pcs.	600.00	1250.	2000.	3000.
	1836 G	804 pcs.	600.00	1250.	2000.	3000.

Obv: Different head.

C#	Date	Mintage	Fine	VF	XF	Unc
242	1836 G	100 pcs.	600.00	1250.	2250.	3250.
	1837 G	168 pcs.	600.00	1250.	2250.	3250.
	1838 G	637 pcs.	400.00	1100.	2250.	3250.

SCHAUMBURG-HESSEN

Located in northwest Germany, Schaumburg-Hessen was founded in 1640 when Schaumburg-Gehmen was divided between Hesse-Cassel and Lippe-Alverdissen. The two became known as Schaumburg-Hessen and Schaumburg-Lippe. Cassel struck coins for its half as late as 1832.

RULERS

Wilhelm (of Hesse-Cassel), 1785-1821
Wilhelm II, (of Hesse-Cassel), 1821-1847

MONETARY SYSTEM

12 Gute Pfennig = 1 Groschen

PFENNIG

(Guter)

COPPER
Obv: Crowned shield separating WL. Rev: Value.

C#	Date	Mintage	Fine	VF	XF	Unc
3	1801	—	2.50	5.00	10.00	50.00
	1802	—	2.50	5.00	10.00	50.00
	1803	—	2.50	5.00	10.00	50.00

NOTE: Earlier dates (1787-1800) exist for this type.

Obv: Elector's cap above arms dividing W.K.
Rev: Value, F below.

C#	Date	Mintage	Fine	VF	XF	Unc
4	1804 F	—	3.00	6.00	12.00	60.00
	1805 F	—	3.00	6.00	12.00	60.00
	1806 F	—	3.00	6.00	12.00	60.00
	1807 F	—	3.00	6.00	12.00	60.00
	1814 F	—	3.00	6.00	12.00	60.00

Rev: Rosette below value and date.

C#	Date	Mintage	Fine	VF	XF	Unc
4b	1815	—	3.00	6.00	12.00	60.00

C#	Date	Mintage	Fine	VF	XF	Unc
4a	1816	—	2.00	4.00	8.00	45.00
	1818	—	2.00	4.00	8.00	45.00
	1819	—	2.00	4.00	8.00	45.00
	1820	—	2.00	4.00	8.00	45.00
	1821	—	2.00	4.00	8.00	45.00
5	1824	—	2.00	4.00	8.00	45.00
	1826	—	2.00	4.00	8.00	45.00
	1827	—	2.00	4.00	8.00	45.00
	1828	—	2.00	4.00	8.00	45.00
	1829	—	2.00	4.00	8.00	45.00
	1830	—	2.00	4.00	8.00	45.00
6	1832	—	2.00	4.00	8.00	45.00

SCHAUMBURG-LIPPE

Located in northwest Germany, Schaumburg-Lippe was founded in 1640 when Schaumburg-Gehmen was divided between Hesse-Cassel and Lippe-Alverdissen. The two became known as Schaumburg-Hessen and Schaumburg-Lippe. They were elevated into a county independent of Lippe. Schaumburg-Lippe minted currency into the 20th century. The last prince died in 1911.

RULERS

Georg Wilhelm, 1787-1860
Adolph Georg, 1860-1893
Albrecht Georg, 1893-1911

PFENNIG

(Guter)

COPPER
Obv: Crowned arms. Rev: Value.

C#	Date	Mintage	Fine	VF	XF	Unc
36	1824	—	1.50	3.00	6.00	30.00
	1826	—	1.50	3.00	6.00	30.00

C#	Date	Mintage	Fine	VF	XF	Unc
37	1858A	1.440	2.00	4.00	8.00	35.00

2 PFENNIG

COPPER

C#	Date	Mintage	Fine	VF	XF	Unc
38	1858A	.360	3.00	6.00	10.00	40.00

3 PFENNIG

COPPER

C#	Date	Mintage	Fine	VF	XF	Unc
39	1858A	.360	3.00	6.00	10.00	40.00

4 PFENNIG

COPPER
Obv: Crowned arms, garlands and roses. Rev: Value.

C#	Date	Mintage	Fine	VF	XF	Unc
30	1802	.288	12.00	25.00	45.00	90.00

.7500 g, .186 SILVER, .0044 oz ASW
Obv: Crowned arms.

C#	Date	Mintage	Fine	VF	XF	Unc
41	1821	.491	7.50	17.50	35.00	60.00

C#	Date	Mintage	Fine	VF	XF	Unc
41a	1828	—	7.50	17.50	35.00	60.00

COPPER

C#	Date	Mintage	Fine	VF	XF	Unc
40	1858A	.180	6.00	12.50	25.00	50.00

1/2 SILBER GROSCHEN

(1/60 Thaler)

1.0900 g, .220 SILVER, .0077 oz ASW

C#	Date	Mintage	Fine	VF	XF	Unc
45	1858A	.120	6.00	12.50	25.00	50.00

MARIENGROSCHEN

1.5500 g, .388 SILVER, .0193 oz ASW
Obv: Crowned arms, garlands and roses. Rev: Value.

C#	Date	Mintage	Fine	VF	XF	Unc
32	1802	.144	20.00	45.00	75.00	125.00

C#	Date	Mintage	Fine	VF	XF	Unc
42	1821	.143	7.50	17.50	35.00	60.00
	1828	—	7.50	17.50	35.00	60.00

SILBER GROSCHEN

(1/50 Thaler)

2.1900 g, .220 SILVER, .0154 oz ASW

C#	Date	Mintage	Fine	VF	XF	Unc
46	1858A	.210	6.00	12.50	22.50	45.00

2-1/2 SILBER GROSCHEN

(1/12 Thaler)

3.2200 g, .375 SILVER, .0388 oz ASW

C#	Date	Mintage	Fine	VF	XF	Unc
47	1858A	.061	12.50	25.00	60.00	125.00

1/24 THALER

1.9900 g, .368 SILVER, .0235 oz ASW

C#	Date	Mintage	Fine	VF	XF	Unc
43	1821	.195	12.00	25.00	45.00	90.00
	1826	—	12.00	25.00	45.00	90.00

1/2 THALER

14.0310 g, .833 SILVER, .3760 oz ASW

C#	Date	Mintage	Fine	VF	XF	Unc
44	1821	5,400	75.00	150.00	300.00	450.00

THALER

28.0630 g, .833 SILVER, .7520 oz ASW

C#	Date	Mintage	Fine	VF	XF	Unc
34	1802	4,000	175.00	325.00	750.00	1500.

18.5200 g, .900 SILVER, .5360 oz ASW

C#	Date	Mintage	Fine	VF	XF	Unc
48	1860B	8,356	60.00	100.00	250.00	550.00

C#	Date	Mintage	Fine	VF	XF	Unc
51	1865B	7,000	40.00	75.00	175.00	325.00

2 THALER

37.0370 g, .900 SILVER, 1.0718 oz ASW
50th Anniversary of Reign as Prince
Obv: Similar to 1 Thaler, C#48.

C#	Date	Mintage	Fine	VF	XF	Unc
49	1857B	2,000	150.00	250.00	400.00	800.00

10 THALER

13.2840 g, .900 GOLD, .3826 oz AGW

C#	Date	Mintage	Fine	VF	XF	Unc
50	1829 FF	874 pcs.	4000.	9500.	18,500.*	25,000.
	1829 w/o FF	179 pcs.	4250.	10,000.	20,000.	27,500.

*NOTE: Stack's Hammel sale 9/82 AU realized $20,000.

MONETARY REFORM

2 MARK

11.1110 g, .900 SILVER, .3215 oz ASW

Y#	Date	Mintage	Fine	VF	XF	Unc
203	1898A	5,000	200.00	400.00	600.00	1000.
	1898A	162 pcs.	—	—	Proof	1000.
	1904A	5,000	175.00	350.00	600.00	900.00
	1904A	200 pcs.	—	—	—	900.00

3 MARK

16.6670 g, .900 SILVER, .4823 oz ASW
Death of Prince George

Y#	Date	Mintage	Fine	VF	XF	Unc
206	1911A	.050	30.00	75.00	100.00	150.00
	1911A	—	—	—	Proof	200.00

5 MARK

27.7770 g, .900 SILVER, .8038 oz ASW

Y#	Date	Mintage	Fine	VF	XF	Unc
204	1898A	3,000	350.00	800.00	1100.	1750.
	1898A	90 pcs.	—	—	Proof	2500.
	1904A	3,000	350.00	800.00	1100.	1750.
	1904A	200 pcs.	—	—	Proof	1800.

20 MARK

7.9650 g, .900 GOLD, .2304 oz AGW

Y#	Date	Mintage	Fine	VF	XF	Unc
202	1874B	3,000	2000.	3000.	5000.	8000.
	1874B	—	—	—	Proof	Rare

Y#	Date	Mintage	Fine	VF	XF	Unc
205	1898A	5,000	600.00	1000.	1400.	2000.
	1898A	250 pcs.	—	—	Proof	4000.
	1904A	5,500	600.00	1000.	1400.	2000.
	1904A	132 pcs.	—	—	Proof	4000.

SCHLESWIG-HOLSTEIN

For issues previously listed here refer to Denmark.

SCHWARZBURG-RUDOLSTADT

The Schwarzburg family held territory in central and northern Thuringia. After many divisions, two lines, Sondershausen and Rudolstadt were founded in 1552. The count of Rudolstadt was raised to the rank of prince in 1710. The last prince abdicated in 1918.

RULERS

Ludwig Friedrich II, 1793-1807
Friedrich Gunther, 1807-1867
Albert, 1867-1869
George, 1869-1890
Gunther Viktor, 1890-1918

PFENNIG

COPPER
Obv: SCHWARZB/RUD-LM.
Rev: Value, 1 PF in script.

C#	Date	Mintage	Fine	VF	XF	Unc
50	1801	—	3.00	7.00	15.00	60.00
	1802	—	3.00	7.00	15.00	60.00

C#	Date	Mintage	Fine	VF	XF	Unc
63	1825	—	2.50	6.00	10.00	40.00
	Obv: Crowned arms. Rev. value: SCHEIDE MUNZE.					
65	1842A	—	2.00	5.00	8.00	35.00

2 PFENNIG

COPPER
Obv: Crowned FG monogram within crossed branches. Rev: Value.

C#	Date	Mintage	Fine	VF	XF	Unc
57	1812	—	3.00	7.00	15.00	70.00
	Obv: Crowned arms					
66	1842A	—	3.00	6.00	10.00	45.00

3 PFENNIG

COPPER
Obv. leg: SCHWARZB/RUD-LM.
Rev: Value, 3 PF in script.

C#	Date	Mintage	Fine	VF	XF	Unc
51	1804	—	3.00	5.00	8.00	45.00
	Obv: Monogram FG within crossed branches. Rev: Value.					
58	1813	—	3.00	5.00	8.00	45.00
	Obv: Crown above monogram.					
64	1825	—	3.00	5.00	10.00	50.00
	Obv: Crowned arms. Rev. leg: SCHEIDEMUNZE.					
67	1842A	—	3.00	5.00	8.00	45.00

4 PFENNIG

COPPER
Obv: Monogram FG within crossed branches.
Rev: Value.

C#	Date	Mintage	Fine	VF	XF	Unc
59	1812	—	5.00	8.00	20.00	90.00
	1813	—	5.00	8.00	20.00	90.00

6 PFENNIG

1.3300 g, .250 SILVER, .0106 oz ASW

C#	Date	Mintage	Fine	VF	XF	Unc
53	1801	—	5.00	8.00	20.00	85.00

NOTE: Earlier date (1800) exists for this type.

C#	Date	Mintage	Fine	VF	XF	Unc
60	1808	—	5.00	8.00	20.00	85.00

Obv: Rosette above & ledge below leg: SCHWARZB/RUD-LM.

C#	Date	Mintage	Fine	VF	XF	Unc
60a	1812	—	5.00	8.00	20.00	85.00
	1813	—	5.00	8.00	20.00	85.00

1/8 KREUZER

COPPER
Obv: Crowned arms within branches. Rev: Value.

C#	Date	Mintage	Fine	VF	XF	Unc
73	1840	.024	3.00	7.00	15.00	40.00
	1855	—	3.00	7.00	15.00	40.00

1/4 KREUZER

COPPER

C#	Date	Mintage	Fine	VF	XF	Unc
74	1840	.972	2.00	4.00	8.00	30.00
	1852	—	2.00	4.00	8.00	30.00
	1853	—	2.00	4.00	8.00	30.00
	1855	—	2.00	4.00	8.00	30.00
	1856	—	2.00	4.00	8.00	30.00

C#	Date	Mintage	Fine	VF	XF	Unc
74a	1857	—	2.00	4.00	8.00	25.00
	1859	—	2.00	4.00	8.00	25.00
	1860	—	2.00	4.00	8.00	25.00
	1861	—	2.00	4.00	8.00	25.00
	1863	—	2.00	4.00	8.00	25.00
	1865	—	2.00	4.00	8.00	25.00
	1866	—	2.00	4.00	8.00	25.00
82	1868	.096	3.00	6.00	12.00	45.00

KREUZER

COPPER

C#	Date	Mintage	Fine	VF	XF	Unc
76	1840	.480	3.00	6.00	12.00	40.00

C#	Date	Mintage	Fine	VF	XF	Unc
76a	1864	—	2.00	4.00	8.00	30.00
	1865	—	2.00	4.00	8.00	30.00
	1866	—	2.00	4.00	8.00	30.00

C#	Date	Mintage	Fine	VF	XF	Unc
83	1868	.037	4.00	8.00	15.00	40.00

3 KREUZER

1.2900 g, .333 SILVER, .0138 oz ASW

C#	Date	Mintage	Fine	VF	XF	Unc
77	1839	.155	5.00	10.00	20.00	100.00
	1840	Inc. Ab.	5.00	10.00	20.00	100.00
	1841	Inc. Ab.	5.00	10.00	20.00	100.00
	1842	Inc. Ab.	5.00	10.00	20.00	100.00
	1846	Inc. Ab.	5.00	10.00	20.00	100.00
	1.2300 g, .350 SILVER, .0138 oz ASW Obv. leg: SCHEIDE MUNZE added.					
77a	1866	.010	10.00	15.00	30.00	125.00

6 KREUZER

2.5900 g, .333 SILVER, .0277 oz ASW

C#	Date	Mintage	Fine	VF	XF	Unc
78	1840	.165	5.00	10.00	20.00	125.00
	1842	Inc. Ab.	5.00	10.00	20.00	125.00
	1846	Inc. Ab.	5.00	10.00	20.00	125.00
	2.4600 g, .350 SILVER, .0276 oz ASW Obv. leg: SCHEIDE MUNZE added.					
78a	1866	.010	12.00	20.00	40.00	150.00

1/2 GROSCHEN

1.0900 g, .222 SILVER, .0077 oz ASW
Obv: Crowned arms. Rev: Value.

C#	Date	Mintage	Fine	VF	XF	Unc
68	1841A	—	3.00	7.00	20.00	100.00

GROSCHEN

BILLON
Obv. leg: SCHWARZB. RUD-LM. Rev: Value.

C#	Date	Mintage	Fine	VF	XF	Unc
61	1803	—	3.00	7.00	15.00	70.00
	1808	—	3.00	7.00	15.00	70.00
	Obv: Rosette above, legend below. Rev: Value w/rosettes.					
61a	1812	—	4.00	8.00	17.00	90.00
	2.1900 g, .222 SILVER, .0156 oz ASW Obv: Crowned arms. Rev: Value.					
69	1841A	—	3.00	7.00	15.00	70.00

1/2 GULDEN

5.3030 g, .900 SILVER, .1535 oz ASW

C#	Date	Mintage	Fine	VF	XF	Unc
79	1841	.157	15.00	30.00	75.00	200.00
	1842	Inc. Ab.	15.00	30.00	75.00	200.00
	1843	Inc. Ab.	15.00	30.00	75.00	200.00
	1846	Inc. Ab.	15.00	30.00	75.00	200.00

GULDEN

10.6060 g, .900 SILVER, .3069 oz ASW
Obv: Similar to 1/2 Gulden, C#79.

C#	Date	Mintage	Fine	VF	XF	Unc
80	1841	.163	25.00	50.00	100.00	250.00
	1842	Inc. Ab.	25.00	50.00	100.00	250.00
	1843	Inc. Ab.	25.00	50.00	100.00	250.00
	1846	Inc. Ab.	25.00	50.00	100.00	250.00

ZWEY (2) GULDEN

21.2110 g, .900 SILVER, .6138 oz ASW
Obv: Similar to 1/2 Gulden, C#79.

C#	Date	Mintage	Fine	VF	XF	Unc
81	1846	500 pcs.	250.00	450.00	800.00	1800.

THALER

(Species)

28.0630 g, .833 SILVER, .7520 oz ASW

C#	Date	Mintage	Fine	VF	XF	Unc
62	1812 L	—	90.00	150.00	275.00	600.00
	1813 L	—	100.00	175.00	300.00	650.00

(Vereins)

18.5200 g, .900 SILVER, .5360 oz ASW

C#	Date	Mintage	Fine	VF	XF	Unc
70	1858	.016	40.00	65.00	130.00	275.00
	1859	6,000	50.00	75.00	150.00	300.00

C#	Date	Mintage	Fine	VF	XF	Unc
70a	1862	.048	40.00	65.00	130.00	275.00
	1863	.017	40.00	65.00	130.00	275.00

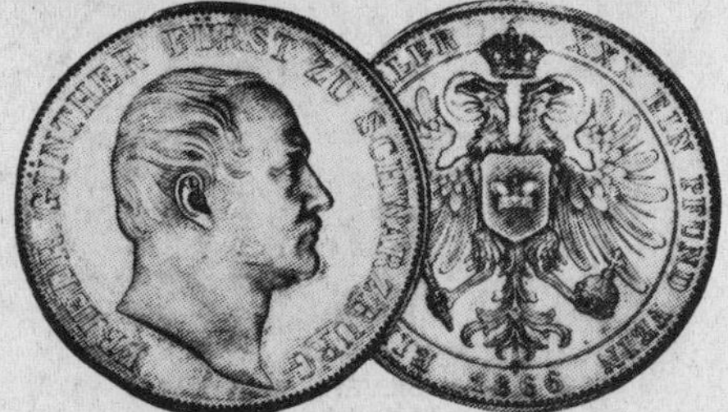

C#	Date	Mintage	Fine	VF	XF	Unc
70b	1866	.027	40.00	65.00	130.00	275.00

50th Anniversary of Reign

C#	Date	Mintage	Fine	VF	XF	Unc
71	1864	4,500	50.00	75.00	150.00	300.00
	1864	—	—	—	Proof	500.00

C#	Date	Mintage	Fine	VF	XF	Unc
84	1867	.013	50.00	80.00	175.00	450.00

2 THALER

(3-1/2 Gulden)

37.1200 g, .900 SILVER, 1.0742 oz ASW

C#	Date	Mintage	Fine	VF	XF	Unc
72	1841 A	.010	100.00	200.00	450.00	1000.
	1845 A	5,100	100.00	200.00	450.00	1000.

MONETARY REFORM

2 MARK

11.1110 g, .900 SILVER, .3215 oz ASW

Y#	Date	Mintage	Fine	VF	XF	Unc
207	1898A	.100	125.00	250.00	500.00	600.00
	1898A	375 pcs.	—	—	Proof	900.00

10 MARK

3.9820 g, .900 GOLD, .1152 oz AGW

Y#	Date	Mintage	Fine	VF	XF	Unc
208	1898A	.010	600.00	1100.	1500.	2000.
	1898A	700 pcs.	—	—	Proof	3500.

TRADE COINAGE

DUCAT

3.5000 g, .986 GOLD, .1109 oz AGW

C#	Date	Mintage	Fine	VF	XF	Unc
55	1803	311 pcs.	600.00	1300.	2500.	4000.

SCHWARZBURG-SONDERHAUSEN

The Schwarzburg family held territory in central and northern Thuringia. After many divisions, two lines, Sondershausen and Rudolstadt were founded in 1552. The count of Sondershausen was raised to the rank of prince in 1709. The last prince died in 1909 and the lands passed to Rudolstadt.

RULERS

Gunther Friedrich Carl I, 1794-1835
Gunther Friedrich Carl II, 1835-1880
Karl Gunther, 1880-1909

PFENNIG

COPPER

C#	Date	Mintage	Fine	VF	XF	Unc
18	1846A	1.613	1.50	3.00	6.00	35.00
	1858A	.360	2.00	4.00	8.00	40.00

3 PFENNIG

COPPER

C#	Date	Mintage	Fine	VF	XF	Unc
19	1846A	.682	3.00	6.00	12.00	50.00
	1858A	.360	3.00	6.00	12.00	50.00
	1870A	.120	3.00	6.00	12.00	50.00

1/2 SILBER GROSCHEN

1.0900 g, .222 SILVER, .0077 oz ASW

C#	Date	Mintage	Fine	VF	XF	Unc
20	1846A	.657	3.00	6.00	12.00	50.00
	1851A	Inc. Ab.	3.00	6.00	12.00	50.00
	1858A	.180	3.00	6.00	12.00	50.00

SILBER GROSCHEN

2.1900 g, .222 SILVER, .0156 oz ASW

C#	Date	Mintage	Fine	VF	XF	Unc
21	1846A	.584	3.00	6.00	12.00	60.00
	1851A	Inc. Ab.	3.00	6.00	12.00	60.00
	1858A	.150	3.00	6.00	12.00	60.00
	1870A	.120	3.00	6.00	12.00	60.00

THALER

(Vereins)

18.5200 g, .900 SILVER, .5360 oz ASW

C#	Date	Mintage	Fine	VF	XF	Unc
22	1859A	.015	50.00	75.00	150.00	400.00
	1865A	.010	50.00	75.00	150.00	400.00
	1870A	.011	50.00	75.00	150.00	400.00

2 THALER

(3-1/2 Gulden)

37.1200 g, .900 SILVER, 1.0741 oz ASW

C#	Date	Mintage	Fine	VF	XF	Unc
23	1841A	4,300	125.00	225.00	500.00	1100.
	1845A	8,600	100.00	200.00	425.00	950.00
	1854A	8,600	100.00	200.00	425.00	950.00

MONETARY REFORM

2 MARK

11.1110 g, .900 SILVER, .3215 oz ASW

Y#	Date	Mintage	Fine	VF	XF	Unc
209	1896A	.050	100.00	250.00	450.00	600.00
	1896A	190 pcs.	—	—	Proof	800.00

25th Anniversary of Reign
Struck w/thick rim.

Y#	Date	Mintage	Fine	VF	XF	Unc
211	1905A	.013	45.00	80.00	175.00	200.00
	1905A	5,000	—	—	Proof	250.00

Struck w/thin rim.

Y#	Date	Mintage	Fine	VF	XF	Unc
211a	1905A	.062	25.00	40.00	95.00	125.00
	1905A	5,000	—	—	Proof	150.00

3 MARK

16.6670 g, .900 SILVER, .4823 oz ASW
Death of Karl Gunther

Y#	Date	Mintage	Fine	VF	XF	Unc
212	1909A	.070	25.00	70.00	90.00	130.00
	1909A	—	—	—	Proof	175.00

20 MARK

7.9650 g, .900 GOLD, .2304 oz AGW

Y#	Date	Mintage	Fine	VF	XF	Unc
210	1896A	5,000	750.00	1250.	2000.	3000.
	1896A	—	—	—	Proof	5500.

SILESIA

A duchy, located in northeastern Germany, was separated into many segments. They were greatly influenced by Bohemia and Austria. The first coins were struck c. 1169. Special coins for Silesian possessions were struck by Bohemia from 1327. From 1526, when Bohemia and its Silesian possessions fell to Austria, a special series of coins were struck by Austria for the area. After the Prussian invasion, in 1740, they also minted coins from 1743 through 1797.

RULERS

Friedrich Wilhelm III, 1797-1840

MINT MARKS

A - Berlin
B - Breslau
G - Glatz, 1807-1809
W - Wratislawia (i.e. Breslau)

NOTE: For similar gold coins dated 1787-1805 refer to Prussian listings.

1/2 KREUZER

COPPER
Obv: Crowned FW monogram. Rev: Value.

C#	Date	Mintage	Fine	VF	XF	Unc
53	1806A	—	12.00	25.00	40.00	70.00

KREUZER

BILLON
Obv: Uniformed bust left.
Rev: Crowned arms w/eagle.

C#	Date	Mintage	Fine	VF	XF	Unc
57	1806A	—	17.50	40.00	90.00	200.00
	1808G	—	17.50	40.00	90.00	200.00

Obv: Crowned arms w/eagle within crossed branches. Rev: Value.

C#	Date	Mintage	Fine	VF	XF	Unc
54	1810A	.055	15.00	30.00	60.00	125.00

9 KREUZER

BILLON

C#	Date	Mintage	Fine	VF	XF	Unc
60	1808G	—	55.00	100.00	175.00	300.00

18 KREUZER

.563 SILVER
Obv: Uniformed bust left.
Rev: Crowned eagle w/scepter and orb.

C#	Date	Mintage	Fine	VF	XF	Unc
61	1808G	—	100.00	200.00	375.00	750.00

GROSCHEL

BILLON
Obv: Crowned FWR monogram. Rev: Value.

C#	Date	Mintage	Fine	VF	XF	Unc
56	1805A	—	20.00	40.00	75.00	150.00
	1806A	—	20.00	40.00	75.00	150.00
	1808G	—	20.00	40.00	75.00	150.00
	1809G	—	20.00	40.00	75.00	150.00

NOTE: Earlier date (1797) exists for this type.

STOLBERG

Stolberg, a county located in the Harz mountains of central Germany, had its own coinage from the 11th century.

MINTMASTERS INITIALS

Letter	Date	Name
EHAZ,Z	1792-1807	Ernst Hermann Agathus Ziegler

STOLBERG-ROSSLA

The Rossla line was founded in 1704.

PFENNIG

COPPER
Obv: Stag left before column.
Rev: Value above date.

C#	Date	Mintage	VG	Fine	VF	XF
47	1801 Z	—	5.00	10.00	15.00	30.00

NOTE: Earlier date (1799) exists for this type.

STOLBERG-WERNIGERODE

Stolberg, a county located in the Harz mountains of central Germany, had its own coinage from the 11th century. The lines of Wernigerode and Stolberg were established in 1641. A division of the lands occurred in 1645 but only the Wernigerode branch issued coins after 1800. Although administered by Prussia from 1714, the country retained a certain amount of sovereignty until 1876.

RULERS

Christian Friedrich, 1778-1824
Henrich XII, 1824-1854

TRADE COINAGE

DUCAT

3.5000 g, .986 GOLD, .1109 oz AGW
Golden Wedding Anniversary.

C#	Date	Mintage	Fine	VF	XF	Unc
25	1818	308 pcs.	500.00	1000.	2000.	4000.

Henrich XII

C#	Date	Mintage	Fine	VF	XF	Unc
26	1824	—	500.00	1000.	2000.	4000.

TEUTONIC ORDER

The Order of Knights was founded during the Third Crusade in 1198. They acquired considerable territory by conquest from the heathen Prussians in the late 13th and early 14th centuries. The seat of the Grand Master moved from Acre to Venice and in 1309 to Marienburg, Prussia. The Teutonic Order began striking coins in the late 13th century. In 1355 permission was granted to strike hellers at Mergentheim. However, the bulk of the Order's coinage until 1525 was schillings and half schoters minted in and for Prussia. In 1809 the Order was suppressed and Mergentheim was annexed to Wurttemberg.

RULERS

Max Franz, 1780-1801
Carl Ludwig, 1801-1804
Anton Victor, 1804-1809

6 KREUZER

SILVER
Death of Grand Master Max Franz

C#	Date	Mintage	VG	Fine	VF	XF
—	1801	—	15.00	30.00	60.00	125.00

1/4 THALER

SILVER
Death of Grand Master Max Franz

26	1801	—	30.00	60.00	125.00	275.00

WALDECK

The county of Waldeck was located on the border of Hesse. Their first coinage appeared c. 1250. Pyrmont was united with Waldeck in 1625 but was ruled separately for a while in the 19th century. They were reunited in 1812. The rulers gained the status of prince in 1712. The administration was turned over to Prussia in 1867 but the princes retained some sovereignty until 1918.

WALDECK-PYRMONT

RULERS
Friedrich Karl August in Waldeck, 1763-1812
Georg (In Pyrmont), 1805-1812
(Refer to Pyrmont for listings)
(In Waldeck-Pyrmont), 1812-1813
Georg Heinrich, 1813-1845
Emma, As Regent For Georg Victor, 1845-1852
Georg Victor, 1852-1893
Friedrich, 1893-1918

MINTMASTERS INITIALS
AW - Albert Welle
FW, F*w, W, .W. - Friedrich Welle

PFENNIG

COPPER
Obv: Crowned F monogram. Rev: Value.

C#	Date	Mintage	Fine	VF	XF	Unc
42b	1809 FW	—	5.00	10.00	20.00	120.00
	1810 FW	—	5.00	10.00	20.00	120.00

Obv: Crowned arms.

43a	1809 FW	—	5.00	10.00	20.00	120.00

Rev. value: 1 PFENNIG.

43b	1810 FW	—	5.00	10.00	20.00	120.00

Obv: Crowned GH monogram.

65	1816 FW	—	4.00	8.00	16.00	80.00
	1817 FW	—	4.00	8.00	16.00	80.00

66	1816 FW	—	4.00	8.00	16.00	80.00
	1817 W	—	4.00	8.00	16.00	80.00

Obv: Crowned Waldeck-Pyrmont arms.

67	1821 FW	—	3.00	6.00	12.00	60.00

Obv: Arms in beaded border.

67a	1821 FW	—	3.00	6.00	12.00	60.00

Obv: Crowned draped arms.

68	1825 FW	—	4.00	8.00	18.00	100.00

C#	Date	Mintage	Fine	VF	XF	Unc
69	1842A	.352	2.50	5.00	10.00	50.00
	1843A	.220	2.50	5.00	10.00	50.00
	1845A	.384	2.50	5.00	10.00	50.00

85	1855A	.366	1.50	3.00	6.00	35.00
	1855A	—	—	—	Proof	100.00

85a	1867B	.540	1.50	3.00	6.00	35.00

3 PFENNIG

COPPER
Obv: Crowned F monogram,
leg: FURSTL. WALDECK SCH. MUNZ.
Rev. value: III PFENNIGE.

44a	1809 FW	—	5.00	10.00	25.00	150.00
	1810 FW	—	5.00	10.00	25.00	150.00

NOTE: Earlier date (1781) exists for this type.

Obv: Crowned star arms.

45	1809 FW	—	5.00	10.00	25.00	150.00

NOTE: Earlier date (1781) exists for this type.

Obv: Arms within pearl circle.

45a	1810 FW	—	7.00	15.00	35.00	165.00

70	1819 FW	—	5.00	10.00	20.00	120.00

Rev. value: PFENNIG

70b	1819 FW	—	5.00	10.00	20.00	120.00

70a	1819 FW	—	5.00	10.00	20.00	120.00

71	1824 FW	—	4.00	8.00	16.00	80.00
	1825 FW	—	4.00	8.00	16.00	80.00

72	1842A	.247	3.00	6.00	12.00	60.00
	1843A	.114	3.00	6.00	12.00	60.00
	1845A	.249	3.00	6.00	12.00	60.00

C#	Date	Mintage	Fine	VF	XF	Unc
86	1855A	.243	2.50	5.00	10.00	50.00

86.1	1867B	.420	2.50	5.00	10.00	50.00

1/2 GROSCHEN

COPPER

46	1809 FW	—	20.00	45.00	90.00	200.00

Obv: Crowned draped arms.

73	1825 FW	—	20.00	40.00	80.00	175.00

GROSCHEN

(Marien)

1.3900 g, .312 SILVER, .0139 oz ASW

74	1814 FW	—	10.00	20.00	40.00	150.00
	1820 FW	—	10.00	20.00	40.00	150.00

74a	1820 FW	—	—	—	Rare	—

Obv: Crowned draped arms.

74b	1820 FW	—	10.00	20.00	40.00	150.00
	1823 FW	—	10.00	20.00	40.00	150.00

(Silber)

2.1900 g, .222 SILVER, .0156 oz ASW
Obv. leg. ends: . . . . .WALDECK U.P.

76	1836 AW	.164	10.00	20.00	40.00	150.00
	1839 AW	.046	10.00	20.00	40.00	150.00

Obv. leg. ends: . . . . .WALDECK U. PYRMONT

C#	Date	Mintage	Fine	VF	XF	Unc
77	1842A	.310	6.00	12.00	25.00	100.00
	1843A	.191	6.00	12.00	25.00	100.00
	1845A	.182	6.00	12.00	25.00	100.00

Rev: A below value and date.

C#	Date	Mintage	Fine	VF	XF	Unc
87	1855A	.156	7.00	15.00	30.00	125.00

C#	Date	Mintage	Fine	VF	XF	Unc
87a	1867B	.180	6.00	12.00	20.00	90.00

2 MARIENGROSCHEN

2.3900 g, .375 SILVER, .0288 oz ASW

C#	Date	Mintage	Fine	VF	XF	Unc
78	1820 FW	—	8.00	16.00	40.00	160.00
	1822 FW	—	8.00	16.00	40.00	160.00
	1823 FW	—	8.00	16.00	40.00	160.00
	1824 FW	—	8.00	16.00	40.00	160.00
	1825 FW	—	8.00	16.00	40.00	160.00

Rev: A.W. below value.

C#	Date	Mintage	Fine	VF	XF	Unc
78a	1827 AW	—	8.00	16.00	40.00	160.00
	1828 AW	—	8.00	16.00	40.00	160.00

24 EINEN (1/24) THALER

1.9800 g, .368 SILVER, .0234 oz ASW

C#	Date	Mintage	Fine	VF	XF	Unc
75	1818 FW	—	10.00	20.00	45.00	165.00
	1819 FW	—	10.00	20.00	45.00	165.00

1/6 THALER

5.3400 g, .520 SILVER, .0892 oz ASW

C#	Date	Mintage	Fine	VF	XF	Unc
79	1837 AW	.034	20.00	40.00	80.00	200.00

C#	Date	Mintage	Fine	VF	XF	Unc
79a	1843A	.038	20.00	40.00	80.00	200.00
	1845A	.038	20.00	40.00	80.00	200.00

IV EINEN (1/4) THALER

7.0000 g, .620 SILVER, .1395 oz ASW

C#	Date	Mintage	Fine	VF	XF	Unc
53	1810 FW	—	100.00	200.00	375.00	700.00

Rev: Date and value in larger letters.

C#	Date	Mintage	Fine	VF	XF	Unc
53a	1810 FW	—	75.00	150.00	300.00	600.00

Obv. leg. ends: . . . . .PYRMONT & .

C#	Date	Mintage	Fine	VF	XF	Unc
62	1812 FW	—	600.00	1250.	1750.	2250.

Obv. leg. ends: . . . . .PYRMONT EC

C#	Date	Mintage	Fine	VF	XF	Unc
62a	1813 FW	—	600.00	1250.	1750.	2250.

3 EINEN (1/3) THALER

8.8000 g, .620 SILVER, .1754 oz ASW

C#	Date	Mintage	Fine	VF	XF	Unc
80	1824 FW	—	50.00	100.00	200.00	350.00

C#	Date	Mintage	Fine	VF	XF	Unc
80a	1824 FW	—	50.00	100.00	200.00	350.00

C#	Date	Mintage	Fine	VF	XF	Unc
81	1824 FW	—	50.00	100.00	200.00	350.00

THALER

28.0600 g, .833 SILVER, .7515 oz ASW

Obv. leg: FRIDERICUS PR. . . . .

C#	Date	Mintage	Fine	VF	XF	Unc
59	1810 FW	—	400.00	700.00	1500.	3500.

Obv. leg: FRIDERICUS D.G. PR. . . . .

C#	Date	Mintage	Fine	VF	XF	Unc
59a	1810 FW	—	600.00	1100.	2500.	5200.

C#	Date	Mintage	Fine	VF	XF	Unc
63	1813 FW	—	600.00	1100.	2500.	5000.

29.5170 g, .868 SILVER, .8237 oz ASW

Similar to C#63.

Edge inscription: KRONEN THALER

C#	Date	Mintage	Fine	VF	XF	Unc
64	1813 FW	—	600.00	1100.	2500.	5000.

Similar to C#63.

Edge inscription: WALDECKISCHER

C#	Date	Mintage	Fine	VF	XF	Unc
64a	1813 FW	—	600.00	1100.	2500.	5000.

Edge: Stars

C#	Date	Mintage	Fine	VF	XF	Unc
64b	1813 FW	—	600.00	1100.	2500.	5000.

29.4500 g, .868 SILVER, .8218 oz ASW

C#	Date	Mintage	Fine	VF	XF	Unc
82	1824 FW	—	200.00	350.00	700.00	1400.

18.5200 g, .900 SILVER, .5358 oz ASW

C#	Date	Mintage	Fine	VF	XF	Unc
88	1859A	.014	40.00	85.00	165.00	325.00
	1867A	.019	40.00	85.00	165.00	325.00

2 THALER
(3-1/2 Gulden)

37.1200 g, .900 SILVER, 1.0742 oz ASW

C#	Date	Mintage	Fine	VF	XF	Unc
83	1842A	4,500	350.00	700.00	1200.	2000.
	1845A	4,500	350.00	700.00	1200.	2000.

Rev: Similar to C#83.

84	1847A	1,000	650.00	1100.	1900.	3250.

89	1856A	.011	200.00	400.00	800.00	1600.

MONETARY REFORM
5 MARK

27.7770 g, .900 SILVER, .8038 oz ASW

213	1903A	2,000	600.00	1300.	2500.	3250.
	1903A	300 pcs.	—	—	Proof	3750.

20 MARK

7.9650 g, .900 GOLD, .2304 oz AGW

C#	Date	Mintage	Fine	VF	XF	Unc
214	1903A	2,000	1000.	2000.	2500.	3250.
	1903A	150 pcs.	—	—	Proof	6500.

WALLMODEN-GIMBORN

The town of Gimborn, located in Westphalia, was purchased from Schwarzenberg in 1782. The following year it was raised to the rank of county. In 1806, Wallmoden-Gimborn was annexed to Berg. In 1815, the land went to Prussia.

RULERS

Johann Ludwig, 1782-1806

1/24 THALER

1.9900 g, .368 SILVER, .0235 oz ASW

1	1802	—	80.00	225.00	375.00	600.00

1/2 THALER

14.0300 g, .833 SILVER, .3757 oz ASW

2	1802	—	375.00	475.00	775.00	—

TRADE COINAGE
DUCAT

3.5000 g, .986 GOLD, .1109 oz AGW

3	1802	400 pcs.	1250.	2500.	4500.	8000.

WESTPHALIA

A kingdom, located in western Germany, created by Napoleon for his brother. It was comprised of parts of Hesse-Cassel, Brunswick, Hildesheim, Paderborn, Halberstadt, Osnabruck, Minden, etc. In 1813 and 1814, Westphalia was divided and returned to its former owners.

RULERS

Jerome (Hieronymus) Napoleon, 1807-1813

MINT MARKS

B - Brunswick
C,C. - Cassel, mm on rev.
C,C. - Clausthal, mm on obv.
F - Cassel

MINTMASTERS MARKS

C & eagle head - Cassel
J & horse head Cassel
J & horse head - Paris

MINTMASTERS INITIALS

Letter	Date	Name
F	1783-1831	Dietrich Heinrich Fulda in Cassel

GERMAN STANDARD
PFENNIG

COPPER

C#	Date	Mintage	Fine	VF	XF	Unc
1	1808C	—	7.00	15.00	30.00	100.00

2 PFENNIG

COPPER
Obv: Crowned HN monogram. Rev: Value.

2	1808C	—	7.00	15.00	30.00	100.00
	1810C	—	7.00	15.00	40.00	120.00

4 PFENNIG

BILLON SILVER

3	1808C	—	15.00	25.00	60.00	175.00
3a	1809C	—	10.00	20.00	45.00	150.00

MARIENGROSCHEN

BILLON SILVER

4	1808C	—	10.00	20.00	40.00	135.00
	1810C	—	10.00	20.00	50.00	165.00

24 MARIENGROSCHEN

17.3200 g, .750 SILVER, .4177 oz ASW

12	1810B	—	60.00	120.00	225.00	375.00

24 EINEN (1/24) THALER

1.9900 g, .368 SILVER, .0235 oz ASW
Obv: Crowned HN monogram w/ribbons. Rev: Value.

17	1807 F	—	12.00	25.00	50.00	125.00
	1808/7 F	—	10.00	25.00	45.00	125.00
	1808 F	—	10.00	20.00	40.00	100.00
	1809 F	—	15.00	25.00	55.00	140.00

Obv: Crown w/o ribbons.

17a	1809C	—	10.00	20.00	40.00	150.00

12 EINEN (1/12) THALER

3.3400 g, .437 SILVER, .0469 oz ASW

5	1808C	—	12.50	25.00	65.00	175.00
	1809C	—	12.50	25.00	65.00	175.00
	1810C	—	12.50	25.00	65.00	175.00

1/6 THALER
(Reichs)

3.1800 g, .994 SILVER, .1016 oz ASW

C#	Date	Mintage	Fine	VF	XF	Unc
6	1808C	—	15.00	30.00	65.00	125.00
	1812C	—	15.00	30.00	65.00	125.00
6a	1810C	—	25.00	65.00	150.00	300.00

5.8500 g, .500 SILVER, .0939 oz ASW

C#	Date	Mintage	Fine	VF	XF	Unc
11	1808B	—	12.50	25.00	55.00	100.00
	1809B	—	12.50	25.00	55.00	100.00
	1810B	—	12.50	25.00	55.00	100.00
	1812B	—	12.50	25.00	55.00	100.00
	1813B	—	12.50	25.00	55.00	100.00

C#	Date	Mintage	Fine	VF	XF	Unc
18	1808 F	—	10.00	20.00	45.00	90.00
	1809 C	—	10.00	20.00	45.00	90.00
	1809 F	—	10.00	20.00	45.00	90.00
	1810 C	—	10.00	20.00	45.00	90.00
	1810 F	—	10.00	20.00	45.00	90.00
	1813 C	—	10.00	20.00	45.00	90.00

2/3 THALER

(Reichs)

13.0800 g, .994 SILVER, .4180 oz ASW

C#	Date	Mintage	Fine	VF	XF	Unc
7	1808C	—	40.00	80.00	150.00	300.00
	1810C	—	40.00	80.00	150.00	300.00

Rev: Similar to C#7.

C#	Date	Mintage	Fine	VF	XF	Unc
7a	1809C	—	75.00	150.00	250.00	400.00
	1810C	—	75.00	125.00	225.00	325.00

C#	Date	Mintage	Fine	VF	XF	Unc
8	1811C	—	50.00	100.00	200.00	400.00

C#	Date	Mintage	Fine	VF	XF	Unc
9	1811C	—	50.00	100.00	150.00	300.00
	1812C	—	60.00	125.00	175.00	350.00
	1813C	—	50.00	100.00	150.00	300.00

THALER

28.0600 g, .833 SILVER, .7515 oz ASW

C#	Date	Mintage	Fine	VF	XF	Unc
19	1810C	5 pcs.	—	—	20,000.	30,000.

C#	Date	Mintage	Fine	VF	XF	Unc
20	1810C	—	100.00	200.00	350.00	850.00
	1811C	—	100.00	200.00	350.00	850.00
	1812C	—	100.00	200.00	350.00	850.00

C#	Date	Mintage	Fine	VF	XF	Unc
20a	1811C	—	100.00	200.00	350.00	850.00
	1812C	—	100.00	200.00	350.00	850.00
	1813C	—	100.00	200.00	350.00	850.00

(Mining)

C#	Date	Mintage	Fine	VF	XF	Unc
10	1811C	—	225.00	450.00	900.00	2250.

Obv: Similar to C#10 but small bust.

C#	Date	Mintage	Fine	VF	XF	Unc
10a	1811C	—	225.00	450.00	900.00	2250.

V (5) THALER

6.6500 g, .900 GOLD, .1924 oz AGW

C#	Date	Mintage	Fine	VF	XF	Unc
13	1810B	—	1000.	2400.	3750.	8500.

Obv: Bust left w/o laurel wreath.

C#	Date	Mintage	Fine	VF	XF	Unc
14	1811B	—	—	—	—	—

C#	Date	Mintage	Fine	VF	XF	Unc
14a	1811B	—	900.00	2000.	4000.	6000.
	1812B	—	800.00	1750.	3500.	5000.
	1813B	—	900.00	2000.	4000.	6000.

X (10) THALER

13.3000 g, .900 GOLD, .3848 oz AGW

C#	Date	Mintage	Fine	VF	XF	Unc
15	1810B	—	1000.	2000.	4000.	6000.

Obv: Bust left, w/o laurel wreath.

C#	Date	Mintage	Fine	VF	XF	Unc
16	1811B	—	—	—	—	—

C#	Date	Mintage	Fine	VF	XF	Unc
16a	1811B	—	725.00	1650.	3000.	5000.
	1812B	—	725.00	1650.	3000.	5000.
	1813B	—	725.00	1650.	2500.	5000.

FRENCH STANDARD

CENTIME

COPPER

C#	Date	Mintage	Fine	VF	XF	Unc
21	1809C	—	2.50	7.50	20.00	50.00
	1812C	—	2.50	7.50	20.00	50.00

2 CENTIMES

COPPER

C#	Date	Mintage	Fine	VF	XF	Unc
22	1808C	—	2.50	5.00	17.50	55.00
	1809C	—	2.50	5.00	17.50	55.00
	1810C	—	2.50	5.00	17.50	55.00
	1812C	—	2.50	5.00	17.50	55.00
22a	1808J	—	25.00	50.00	100.00	225.00

3 CENTIMES

COPPER

C#	Date	Mintage	Fine	VF	XF	Unc
23	1808C	—	2.50	5.00	20.00	55.00
	1809C	—	2.50	5.00	20.00	55.00
	1810C	—	2.50	5.00	17.50	55.00
	1812C	—	2.50	5.00	17.50	55.00
23a	1808J	—	25.00	50.00	100.00	225.00

5 CENTIMES

COPPER

C#	Date	Mintage	Fine	VF	XF	Unc
24	1808C	—	2.50	5.00	25.00	65.00
	1809C	—	2.50	5.00	25.00	65.00
	1812C	—	2.50	5.00	25.00	65.00
24a	1808J	—	30.00	60.00	125.00	325.00
	1809J	—	—	—	Rare	—

10 CENTIMES

1.9700 g, .200 SILVER, .0126 oz ASW

C#	Date	Mintage	Fine	VF	XF	Unc
25	1808C	—	3.00	12.50	35.00	80.00
	1809C	—	3.00	12.50	35.00	80.00
	1810C	—	3.00	12.50	35.00	80.00
	1812C	—	3.00	12.50	35.00	80.00

20 CENTIMES

3.8700 g, .200 SILVER, .0248 oz ASW

C#	Date	Mintage	Fine	VF	XF	Unc
26	1808C	—	4.00	17.50	40.00	110.00
	1810C	—	4.00	17.50	40.00	110.00
	1812C	—	4.00	17.50	40.00	110.00

1/2 FRANK

2.5000 g, .900 SILVER, .0723 oz ASW

C#	Date	Mintage	Fine	VF	XF	Unc
27a	1808J	—	100.00	225.00	450.00	650.00

FRANK

5.0000 g, .900 SILVER, .1447 oz ASW

C#	Date	Mintage	Fine	VF	XF	Unc
28	1808J	—	150.00	325.00	650.00	1150.

2 FRANKEN

10.0000 g, .900 SILVER, .2894 oz ASW

C#	Date	Mintage	Fine	VF	XF	Unc
29	1808J	—	200.00	400.00	750.00	1250.

5 FRANKEN

25.0000 g, .900 SILVER, .7235 oz ASW

C#	Date	Mintage	Fine	VF	XF	Unc
30	1808J	—	500.00	1000.	2000.	3500.
30a	1809J	—	500.00	1000.	2000.	3500.

1.6200 g, .900 GOLD, .0469 oz AGW

C#	Date	Mintage	Fine	VF	XF	Unc
31	1813C	—	225.00	350.00	500.00	1200.

10 FRANKEN

3.2300 g, .900 GOLD, .0936 oz AGW

C#	Date	Mintage	Fine	VF	XF	Unc
32.1	1813C	—	350.00	600.00	900.00	1500.
	Medal alignment.					
32.2	1813C	—	—	—	Proof	Rare

20 FRANKEN

6.4500 g, .900 GOLD, .1868 oz AGW

C#	Date	Mintage	Fine	VF	XF	Unc
	Mintmasters mark: Horses head					
33	1808J	—	225.00	400.00	800.00	1750.
	1809J	—	225.00	400.00	800.00	1750.
	Mintmasters mark: Eagles head					
33a	1808C	.013	225.00	350.00	800.00	1750.
	1809C	9,104	225.00	350.00	800.00	1750.
	1811C	.019	225.00	350.00	800.00	1750.
	1813C	—	500.00	1000.	1500.	4000.
	Mintmasters mark: Horses head					
33b	1809C	—	200.00	300.00	700.00	1800.
	W/o edge inscription (restrikes ca. 1867).					
33c	1813C	—	—	Reported, not confirmed		

40 FRANKEN

12.9000 g, .900 GOLD, .3733 oz AGW

C#	Date	Mintage	Fine	VF	XF	Unc
34	1813C	80 pcs.	3000.	4500.	8000.	12,000.
	W/o edge inscription (restrikes ca. 1867).					
34a	1813C	5,465	—	—	2200.	4000.

WISMAR

A seaport on the Baltic, the city of Wismar is said to have obtained municipal rights from Mecklenburg in 1229. It was an important member of the Hanseatic League in the 13th and 14th centuries. Their coinage began at the end of the 13th century and terminated in 1854. They belonged to Sweden from 1648 to 1803. A special plate money was struck by the Swedes in 1715 when the town was under siege. In 1803, Sweden sold Wismar to Mecklenburg-Schwerin. The transaction was confirmed in 1815.

RULERS

Swedish, 1648-1803
Friedrich Franz I, 1785-1837
Paul Friedrich, 1837-1842
Friedrich Franz II, 1842-1883

MINTMASTERS INITIALS

FL - F. Lautersack
FS - Friedrich Schmidt
HM - Joachim Heinrich Meese
ICM - Carl Johann Joachim Mau
IZ - Johann Joachim Zeller
S - Heinrich Schroeder

UNDER MECKLENBURG-SCHWERIN

3 PFENING

COPPER

C#	Date	Mintage	Fine	VF	XF	Unc
3	1824 FL	—	—	—	—	—
	1824 IZ	—	3.00	6.00	15.00	60.00
	1825 IZ	—	3.00	6.00	15.00	60.00

C#	Date	Mintage	Fine	VF	XF	Unc
3b	1829 HM	—	3.00	6.00	15.00	60.00
	1830 HM	—	3.00	6.00	15.00	60.00
3d	1840 FS	—	3.00	6.00	15.00	60.00
3e	1845 S	—	3.00	6.00	15.00	60.00

C#	Date	Mintage	Fine	VF	XF	Unc
3a	1835 ICM	—	3.00	6.00	15.00	60.00

Obv. leg. ends: . . . . .MOHETA NOVA.

C#	Date	Mintage	Fine	VF	XF	Unc
3c	1840 FS	—	3.00	6.00	15.00	60.00

C#	Date	Mintage	Fine	VF	XF	Unc
4	1854 S	—	3.00	6.00	15.00	60.00

WURTTEMBERG

Located in South Germany, between Baden and Bavaria, Wurttemberg obtained the mint right in 1374. In 1495 the rulers became dukes. In 1802 the duke exchanged some of his land on the Rhine with France for territories nearer his capital city. Napoleon elevated the duke to the status of elector in 1803 and made him a king in 1806. The kingdom joined the German Empire in 1871 and endured until the king abdicated in 1918.

RULERS

Friedrich, as Duke Friedrich II, 1797-1803
As Elector Friedrich I, 1803-1806
As King Friedrich I, 1806-1816
Wilhelm I, 1816-1864
Charles I, 1864-1891
Wilhelm II, 1891-1918

MINTMASTERS INITIALS

AD - Gottlob August Doell
CH,ICH - Johann Christian Heuglin
CS,C,Sch F - Christian Schnitzspahn
C VOIGT - Carl Friedrich Voigt
DFH,DH,FH - Daniel Friedrich Heuglin
IPR,PR,R - Johann Peter Rasp
PB - Peter Bruckman
S,VS - Veit Schrempf
SS - Simon Schnell
W,LW,ILW - Johann Ludwig Wagner

1/4 KREUZER

COPPER

C#	Date	Mintage	Fine	VF	XF	Unc
158	1842	.198	2.00	4.00	8.00	45.00
	1843	.118	2.00	4.00	8.00	45.00
	1852	—	2.00	4.00	8.00	45.00
	1853	—	2.00	4.00	8.00	45.00
	1854	—	2.00	4.00	8.00	45.00
	1855	—	2.00	4.00	8.00	45.00
	1856	—	2.00	4.00	8.00	45.00

C#	Date	Mintage	Fine	VF	XF	Unc
159	1858	—	2.00	4.00	8.00	45.00
	1860	—	2.00	4.00	8.00	45.00
	1861	—	2.00	4.00	8.00	45.00
	1862	—	2.00	4.00	8.00	45.00
	1863	—	2.00	4.00	8.00	45.00
	1864	—	2.00	4.00	8.00	45.00

C#	Date	Mintage	Fine	VF	XF	Unc
203	1865	—	2.00	4.00	8.00	40.00
	1866	—	2.00	4.00	8.00	40.00
	1867	—	2.00	4.00	8.00	40.00
	1868	—	2.00	4.00	8.00	40.00
	1869	—	2.00	4.00	8.00	40.00
	1871	—	2.00	4.00	8.00	40.00
	1872	—	2.00	4.00	8.00	40.00

1/2 KREUZER

BILLON

C#	Date	Mintage	Fine	VF	XF	Unc
138	1812	—	3.00	6.00	15.00	75.00
	1813	.470	3.00	6.00	15.00	75.00
	1816	.126	3.00	6.00	15.00	75.00
	ND	—	3.00	6.00	15.00	75.00

Obv: Crowned W.

C#	Date	Mintage	Fine	VF	XF	Unc
162	ND	—	10.00	15.00	30.00	175.00

Obv: Crowned W dividing date.

C#	Date	Mintage	Fine	VF	XF	Unc
A163	1818	—	7.00	10.00	20.00	120.00

C#	Date	Mintage	Fine	VF	XF	Unc
163	1824	.840	2.50	5.00	10.00	50.00
	1828	—	2.50	5.00	10.00	50.00
	1829	.780	2.50	5.00	10.00	50.00
	1831	.620	2.50	5.00	10.00	50.00
	1833	Inc. 1831	2.50	5.00	10.00	50.00
	1834	Inc. 1831	2.50	5.00	10.00	50.00
	1835	Inc. 1831	2.50	5.00	10.00	50.00
	1836	Inc. 1831	2.50	5.00	10.00	50.00
	1837	Inc. 1831	2.50	5.00	10.00	50.00

COPPER

C#	Date	Mintage	Fine	VF	XF	Unc
160	1840	—	1.50	3.00	6.00	30.00
	1841	—	1.50	3.00	6.00	30.00
	1842	.452	1.50	3.00	6.00	30.00
	1844	—	1.50	3.00	6.00	30.00
	1845	—	1.50	3.00	6.00	30.00
	1846	—	1.50	3.00	6.00	30.00
	1847	—	1.50	3.00	6.00	30.00
	1848	—	1.50	3.00	6.00	30.00
	1849	—	1.50	3.00	6.00	30.00
	1850	—	1.50	3.00	6.00	30.00
	1851	—	1.50	3.00	6.00	30.00
	1852	—	1.50	3.00	6.00	30.00
	1853	—	1.50	3.00	6.00	30.00
	1854	—	1.50	3.00	6.00	30.00
	1855	—	1.50	3.00	6.00	30.00
	1856	—	1.50	3.00	6.00	30.00

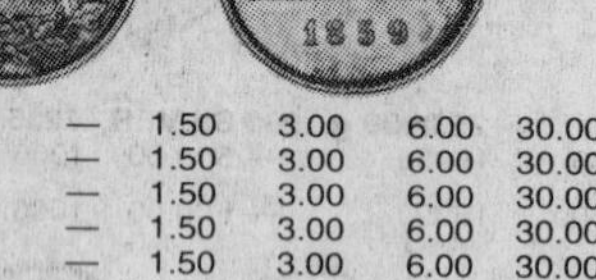

C#	Date	Mintage	Fine	VF	XF	Unc
161	1858	—	1.50	3.00	6.00	30.00
	1859	—	1.50	3.00	6.00	30.00
	1860	—	1.50	3.00	6.00	30.00
	1861	—	1.50	3.00	6.00	30.00
	1862	—	1.50	3.00	6.00	30.00
	1863	—	1.50	3.00	6.00	30.00
	1864	—	1.50	3.00	6.00	30.00

C#	Date	Mintage	Fine	VF	XF	Unc
204	1865	—	1.50	3.00	6.00	30.00
	1866	—	1.50	3.00	6.00	30.00
	1867	—	1.50	3.00	6.00	30.00
	1868	—	1.50	3.00	6.00	30.00
	1869	—	1.50	3.00	6.00	30.00
	1870	.147	1.50	3.00	6.00	30.00
	1871	.290	1.50	3.00	6.00	30.00
	1872	.177	1.50	3.00	6.00	30.00

EIN (1) KREUZER

BILLON
Obv: Crowned FII. Rev: Value, branches reach middle of coin.

C#	Date	Mintage	Fine	VF	XF	Unc
108a	1801	—	7.00	15.00	30.00	125.00
	1802	—	7.00	15.00	30.00	125.00

NOTE: Earlier dates (1799-1800) exist for this type.

Obv: Legends. Rev: Crowned arms.

C#	Date	Mintage	Fine	VF	XF	Unc
122	1803	—	6.00	12.50	25.00	80.00
	1804	—	6.00	12.50	25.00	80.00

Obv: Crowned F II monogram, w/o leg. Rev: Value above branches.

C#	Date	Mintage	Fine	VF	XF	Unc
122a	1805	—	6.00	12.50	25.00	80.00

Obv: Crowned FR monogram.

C#	Date	Mintage	Fine	VF	XF	Unc
139	1807	—	5.00	10.00	20.00	60.00
	1808	—	5.00	10.00	20.00	60.00
	1809	—	5.00	10.00	20.00	60.00
	1810	—	5.00	10.00	20.00	60.00
	1811	—	5.00	10.00	20.00	60.00
	1812	—	5.00	10.00	20.00	60.00
	1813	.530	5.00	10.00	20.00	60.00
	1814	—	5.00	10.00	20.00	60.00
	1816	.630	5.00	10.00	20.00	60.00

Obv: Crowned W within wreath.

C#	Date	Mintage	Fine	VF	XF	Unc
164	1818	—	7.50	15.00	30.00	100.00

C#	Date	Mintage	Fine	VF	XF	Unc
165	1824 W	.780	4.00	8.00	20.00	60.00
	1825 W	.300	4.00	8.00	20.00	60.00
	1826 W	—	4.00	8.00	20.00	60.00
	1827 W	—	4.00	8.00	20.00	60.00
	1828 W	—	4.00	8.00	20.00	60.00
	1829 W	—	4.00	8.00	20.00	60.00
	1830 W	—	4.00	8.00	20.00	60.00
	1831 W	—	4.00	8.00	20.00	60.00
	1832 W	—	4.00	8.00	20.00	60.00
	1833 W	—	4.00	8.00	20.00	60.00
	1834 W	—	4.00	8.00	20.00	60.00
	1835 W	—	4.00	8.00	20.00	60.00
	1836 W	—	4.00	8.00	20.00	60.00
	1837 W	—	4.00	8.00	20.00	60.00
	1838 W	—	4.00	8.00	20.00	60.00

.6200 g, .250 SILVER, .0049 oz ASW
Obv: Crowned arms, leg: WURTTEMBERG.
Rev: Value within wreath.

C#	Date	Mintage	Fine	VF	XF	Unc
166	1839	—	3.00	6.00	15.00	50.00
	1840	—	3.00	6.00	15.00	50.00
	1841	—	3.00	6.00	15.00	50.00
	1842	—	3.00	6.00	15.00	50.00

C#	Date	Mintage	Fine	VF	XF	Unc
166a	1842	—	1.50	3.00	6.00	40.00
	1843	—	1.50	3.00	6.00	40.00
	1844	—	1.50	3.00	6.00	40.00
	1845	—	1.50	3.00	6.00	40.00
	1846	—	1.50	3.00	6.00	40.00
	1847	—	1.50	3.00	6.00	40.00
	1848	—	1.50	3.00	6.00	40.00
	1849	—	1.50	3.00	6.00	40.00
	1850	—	1.50	3.00	6.00	40.00
	1851	—	1.50	3.00	6.00	40.00
	1852	—	1.50	3.00	6.00	40.00
	1853	—	1.50	3.00	6.00	40.00
	1854	—	1.50	3.00	6.00	40.00
	1855	—	1.50	3.00	6.00	40.00
	1856	—	1.50	3.00	6.00	40.00
	1857	—	1.50	3.00	6.00	40.00

.8300 g, .166 SILVER, .0044 oz ASW

C#	Date	Mintage	Fine	VF	XF	Unc
166b	1857	.095	1.50	3.00	6.00	30.00
	1858	.072	1.50	3.00	6.00	30.00
	1859	.050	1.50	3.00	6.00	30.00
	1860	.049	1.50	3.00	6.00	30.00
	1861	.097	1.50	3.00	6.00	30.00
	1862	.056	1.50	3.00	6.00	30.00
	1863	.098	1.50	3.00	6.00	30.00
	1864	.151	1.50	3.00	6.00	30.00

C#	Date	Mintage	Fine	VF	XF	Unc
205	1865/3	.086	1.50	3.00	6.00	30.00
	1865	.086	1.50	3.00	6.00	30.00
	1866	.078	1.50	3.00	6.00	30.00
	1867	.119	1.50	3.00	6.00	30.00
	1868	.119	1.50	3.00	6.00	30.00
	1869	.120	1.50	3.00	6.00	30.00
	1870	.126	1.50	3.00	6.00	30.00
	1871	—	1.50	3.00	6.00	30.00
	1872	.100	1.50	3.00	6.00	30.00
	1873	.080	1.50	3.00	6.00	30.00

3 KREUZER

1.3500 g, .333 SILVER, .0144 oz ASW
Obv: 3 in oval border. Rev: Date divided by W.

C#	Date	Mintage	Fine	VF	XF	Unc
110d	1801	—	10.00	20.00	50.00	100.00
	1802	—	10.00	20.00	50.00	100.00

Obv: F. II. monogram, W below inscription.
Rev: Crowned oval arms.

C#	Date	Mintage	Fine	VF	XF	Unc
124	1803	—	10.00	20.00	50.00	100.00

Rev: Crowned rectangular arms.

C#	Date	Mintage	Fine	VF	XF	Unc
124a	1804	—	5.00	10.00	20.00	100.00
	1805	—	5.00	10.00	20.00	100.00
	1806	—	5.00	10.00	20.00	100.00
	1086(error)	—	6.00	12.50	25.00	125.00

Obv: FR monogram. Rev: Crowned electoral arms.

C#	Date	Mintage	Fine	VF	XF	Unc
140	1806	—	10.00	35.00	75.00	275.00

C#	Date	Mintage	Fine	VF	XF	Unc
141	1807	—	5.00	10.00	20.00	100.00
	1808	—	5.00	10.00	20.00	100.00
	1809	—	5.00	10.00	20.00	100.00
	1810	—	5.00	10.00	20.00	100.00
	1811	—	5.00	10.00	20.00	100.00
	1812	—	5.00	10.00	20.00	100.00
	1813	—	5.00	10.00	20.00	100.00
	1814	.160	5.00	10.00	20.00	100.00

Obv: Crowned W within wreath. Rev: Value.

C#	Date	Mintage	Fine	VF	XF	Unc
167	1818	—	6.00	12.00	25.00	125.00

C#	Date	Mintage	Fine	VF	XF	Unc
168	1823	—	6.00	12.00	25.00	125.00
	1824	—	6.00	12.00	25.00	125.00

Obv: Date and W below head.

C#	Date	Mintage	Fine	VF	XF	Unc
168.1	1823 W	—	6.00	12.00	25.00	125.00
	1824 W	—	6.00	12.00	25.00	125.00
	1825 W	.380	6.00	12.00	25.00	125.00

C#	Date	Mintage	Fine	VF	XF	Unc
168a	1826	—	5.00	10.00	25.00	100.00
	1827	—	5.00	10.00	25.00	100.00
	1828	—	5.00	10.00	25.00	100.00
	1829	—	5.00	10.00	25.00	100.00
	1830	—	5.00	10.00	25.00	100.00
	1831	—	5.00	10.00	25.00	100.00
	1832	—	5.00	10.00	25.00	100.00
	1834	—	5.00	10.00	25.00	100.00
	1835	—	5.00	10.00	25.00	100.00
	1836	—	5.00	10.00	25.00	100.00
	1837	—	5.00	10.00	25.00	100.00

1.2900 g, .333 SILVER, .0138 oz ASW
Obv: Crowned rectangular arms, leg: WURTTEMBERG.
Rev: Value within wreath.

C#	Date	Mintage	Fine	VF	XF	Unc
169	1839	—	5.00	10.00	25.00	100.00
	1840	—	5.00	10.00	25.00	100.00
	1841	—	5.00	10.00	25.00	100.00
	1842	—	5.00	10.00	25.00	100.00

C#	Date	Mintage	Fine	VF	XF	Unc
169a	1842	—	1.50	3.00	6.00	40.00
	1843	—	1.50	3.00	6.00	40.00
	1844	—	1.50	3.00	6.00	40.00
	1845	—	1.50	3.00	6.00	40.00
	1846	—	1.50	3.00	6.00	40.00
	1847	—	1.50	3.00	6.00	40.00
	1848	—	1.50	3.00	6.00	40.00
	1849	—	1.50	3.00	6.00	40.00
	1850	—	1.50	3.00	6.00	40.00
	1851	—	1.50	3.00	6.00	40.00
	1852	—	1.50	3.00	6.00	40.00
	1853	—	1.50	3.00	6.00	40.00
	1854	—	1.50	3.00	6.00	40.00
	1855	—	1.50	3.00	6.00	40.00
	1856	—	1.50	3.00	6.00	40.00

6 KREUZER

2.7000 g, .333 SILVER, .0289 oz ASW

C#	Date	Mintage	Fine	VF	XF	Unc
126	1803W	—	15.00	40.00	100.00	225.00
	1804W	—	15.00	40.00	100.00	225.00

Obv: W/o W below monogram.

C#	Date	Mintage	Fine	VF	XF	Unc
126a	1804	—	15.00	40.00	100.00	225.00
	1805	—	15.00	40.00	100.00	225.00

Rev: Electoral arms.

C#	Date	Mintage	Fine	VF	XF	Unc
142	1806	—	15.00	40.00	100.00	200.00

Rev: Crowned arms w/flags in left half of shield.

C#	Date	Mintage	Fine	VF	XF	Unc
142a	1806	—	15.00	40.00	100.00	200.00

Rev: Arms dividing date.

C#	Date	Mintage	Fine	VF	XF	Unc
142b	1806	—	15.00	40.00	100.00	200.00

C#	Date	Mintage	Fine	VF	XF	Unc
143	1806	—	4.00	8.00	15.00	60.00
	1807	—	4.00	8.00	15.00	60.00
	1808	—	4.00	8.00	15.00	60.00
	1809	—	4.00	8.00	15.00	60.00
	1810	—	4.00	8.00	15.00	60.00
	1811	—	4.00	8.00	15.00	60.00
	1812	—	4.00	8.00	15.00	60.00
	1814	—	4.00	8.00	15.00	60.00

Obv: Crowned W within wreath. Rev: Value.

C#	Date	Mintage	Fine	VF	XF	Unc
170	1817	—	7.50	15.00	30.00	75.00
	1818	—	7.50	15.00	30.00	75.00
170a	1819	—	7.50	15.00	30.00	75.00
	1821	—	7.50	15.00	30.00	75.00

Obv: Head right, date below.
Rev: Crowned circular arms within wreath.

C#	Date	Mintage	Fine	VF	XF	Unc
171.1	1823	—	10.00	20.00	60.00	200.00

Obv: Narrower head.

C#	Date	Mintage	Fine	VF	XF	Unc
171.2	1823	—	10.00	20.00	60.00	200.00

Obv. leg: WILHELM KON. . . .

C#	Date	Mintage	Fine	VF	XF	Unc
171.3	1823	—	10.00	20.00	60.00	200.00
	1825	—	10.00	20.00	60.00	200.00

Rev: Crowned tapered arms within branches.

C#	Date	Mintage	Fine	VF	XF	Unc
171a	1825	—	10.00	20.00	50.00	175.00
	1826	—	10.00	20.00	50.00	175.00
	1827	—	10.00	20.00	50.00	175.00
	1828	—	10.00	20.00	50.00	175.00
	1829	—	10.00	20.00	50.00	175.00
	1830	—	10.00	20.00	50.00	175.00
	1831	—	10.00	20.00	50.00	175.00
	1832	—	10.00	20.00	50.00	175.00
	1833	—	10.00	20.00	50.00	175.00
	1834	—	10.00	20.00	50.00	175.00
	1835	—	10.00	20.00	50.00	175.00
	1836	—	10.00	20.00	50.00	175.00
	1837	—	10.00	20.00	50.00	175.00

2.5900 g, .333 SILVER, .0277 oz ASW

C#	Date	Mintage	Fine	VF	XF	Unc
172	1838	—	5.00	10.00	20.00	85.00
	1839	—	5.00	10.00	20.00	85.00
	1840	—	5.00	10.00	20.00	85.00
	1841	—	5.00	10.00	20.00	85.00
	1842	—	5.00	10.00	20.00	85.00

C#	Date	Mintage	Fine	VF	XF	Unc
172a	1842	—	2.50	5.00	10.00	50.00
	1843	—	2.50	5.00	10.00	50.00
	1844	—	2.50	5.00	10.00	50.00
	1845	—	2.50	5.00	10.00	50.00
	1846	—	2.50	5.00	10.00	50.00
	1847	—	2.50	5.00	10.00	50.00
	1848	—	2.50	5.00	10.00	50.00
	1849	—	2.50	5.00	10.00	50.00
	1850	—	2.50	5.00	10.00	50.00
	1851	—	2.50	5.00	10.00	50.00
	1852	—	2.50	5.00	10.00	50.00
	1853	—	2.50	5.00	10.00	50.00
	1854	—	2.50	5.00	10.00	50.00
	1855	—	2.50	5.00	10.00	50.00
	1856	—	2.50	5.00	10.00	50.00

10 KREUZER

(Convention)

BILLON

C#	Date	Mintage	Fine	VF	XF	Unc
128	1805 ILW	—	80.00	150.00	300.00	550.00

Rev. leg: AD NORMAN.

C#	Date	Mintage	Fine	VF	XF	Unc
144	1808 ILW	.025	80.00	150.00	300.00	550.00
	1809 ILW	.010	90.00	175.00	325.00	575.00

Obv. leg: FRIEDRICH KOENIG. . . . . .
Rev. leg: NACH DEM.

C#	Date	Mintage	Fine	VF	XF	Unc
145	1812 ILW	.026	90.00	175.00	325.00	575.00

Obv. leg: FRID. KOENIG. . . . . .

C#	Date	Mintage	Fine	VF	XF	Unc
145.1	1812 ILW	—	90.00	175.00	325.00	575.00

C#	Date	Mintage	Fine	VF	XF	Unc
173	1818 W	.152	80.00	150.00	300.00	550.00

C#	Date	Mintage	Fine	VF	XF	Unc
174	1823	.011	80.00	150.00	300.00	550.00

12 KREUZER

3.9000 g, .500 SILVER, .0627 oz ASW

C#	Date	Mintage	Fine	VF	XF	Unc
175	1824 W	.045	15.00	30.00	60.00	125.00

C#	Date	Mintage	Fine	VF	XF	Unc
175a	1825 W	.025	15.00	30.00	60.00	125.00

20 KREUZER

(Convention)

6.6800 g, .583 SILVER, .1251 oz ASW
Obv: Bust left, leg: . . . .ELECTOR.
Rev: Crowned oval arms.

C#	Date	Mintage	Fine	VF	XF	Unc
130	1805 ILW	—	17.50	35.00	60.00	125.00

Obv. leg. ends: . . . . .WURTTEMB.

C#	Date	Mintage	Fine	VF	XF	Unc
146	1807 ILW	—	12.50	25.00	40.00	100.00
	1808 ILW	—	12.50	25.00	40.00	100.00
	1809 ILW	—	12.50	25.00	40.00	100.00
	1810 ILW	—	12.50	25.00	40.00	100.00

C#	Date	Mintage	Fine	VF	XF	Unc
147	1810 ILW	—	17.50	35.00	70.00	125.00
	1812 ILW	—	17.50	35.00	70.00	125.00

Obv: Larger head.

C#	Date	Mintage	Fine	VF	XF	Unc
147a	1810 ILW	—	17.50	35.00	60.00	125.00

C#	Date	Mintage	Fine	VF	XF	Unc
148	1812 ILW	.105	12.50	25.00	50.00	100.00

C#	Date	Mintage	Fine	VF	XF	Unc
176	1818 W	.180	50.00	100.00	225.00	375.00

C#	Date	Mintage	Fine	VF	XF	Unc
177	1823 W	.033	50.00	100.00	225.00	375.00

24 KREUZER

6.6800 g, .583 SILVER, .1251 oz ASW

C#	Date	Mintage	Fine	VF	XF	Unc
178	1824 W	—	50.00	100.00	225.00	375.00
	1825 W	—	50.00	100.00	225.00	375.00
	1825	—	50.00	100.00	225.00	375.00

1/2 GULDEN

5.2900 g, .900 SILVER, .1530 oz ASW
Obv: VOIGT below head.

C#	Date	Mintage	Fine	VF	XF	Unc
179	1838	.824	15.00	50.00	100.00	200.00
	1839	.464	80.00	175.00	500.00	900.00
	1840	.516	15.00	35.00	75.00	150.00
	1841	.412	15.00	35.00	75.00	150.00
	1844	.154	100.00	200.00	400.00	800.00
	1845	.280	15.00	35.00	75.00	150.00
	1846	.338	15.00	35.00	75.00	150.00
	1847	.682	15.00	35.00	70.00	140.00
	1848	.498	15.00	35.00	70.00	140.00
	1849	.312	15.00	35.00	75.00	150.00
	1850	.286	15.00	35.00	75.00	150.00
	1852	.228	15.00	35.00	75.00	150.00
	1853	.192	15.00	35.00	75.00	150.00
	1854	.140	15.00	35.00	75.00	150.00
	1855	.112	15.00	35.00	75.00	150.00
	1856	.108	15.00	35.00	75.00	150.00
	1858	—	15.00	35.00	75.00	150.00

Obv: W/o VOIGT below head.

C#	Date	Mintage	Fine	VF	XF	Unc
179a	1858	.219	15.00	90.00	150.00	250.00
	1859	.072	15.00	90.00	150.00	250.00
	1860	.299	15.00	40.00	80.00	160.00
	1861	.693	15.00	40.00	80.00	160.00
	1862	.149	15.00	50.00	100.00	200.00
	1863	—	15.00	50.00	100.00	200.00
	1864	.161	15.00	37.50	75.00	140.00

Obv: Head right w/C.S. on truncation.

C#	Date	Mintage	Fine	VF	XF	Unc
206	1865 CS	.166	15.00	50.00	100.00	250.00
	1866 CS	.276	15.00	50.00	100.00	250.00
	1867 CS	.071	15.00	50.00	100.00	250.00
	1868 CS	.105	15.00	50.00	100.00	250.00

Obv: W/o C.S. on truncation.

C#	Date	Mintage	Fine	VF	XF	Unc
206a	1868	Inc. Ab.	15.00	50.00	100.00	200.00
	1869	.072	15.00	50.00	100.00	200.00
	1870	.044	15.00	60.00	100.00	200.00
	1871	.041	15.00	60.00	100.00	200.00

GULDEN

12.7200 g, .750 SILVER, .3067 oz ASW

C#	Date	Mintage	Fine	VF	XF	Unc
180	1824 W	.021	80.00	175.00	500.00	900.00

C#	Date	Mintage	Fine	VF	XF	Unc
180a	1824	—	—	—	Rare	—

C#	Date	Mintage	Fine	VF	XF	Unc
181	1825 W	—	150.00	300.00	600.00	1000.

10.6000 g, .900 SILVER, .3067 oz ASW
Obv: VOIGT below head.

C#	Date	Mintage	Fine	VF	XF	Unc
182	1838	.712	15.00	50.00	100.00	200.00
	1839	.365	15.00	50.00	100.00	200.00
	1840	2.561	15.00	50.00	100.00	200.00
	1841	—	25.00	100.00	200.00	400.00
	1842	2.493	15.00	50.00	100.00	200.00
	1843	1.983	15.00	50.00	100.00	200.00
	1844	.379	15.00	50.00	100.00	200.00
	1845	.044	15.00	50.00	100.00	200.00
	1846	.042	15.00	50.00	100.00	200.00
	1847	.056	15.00	50.00	100.00	200.00
	1848/6	.058	17.50	60.00	125.00	250.00
	1848	Inc. Ab.	15.00	50.00	100.00	200.00
	1849	.129	15.00	50.00	100.00	200.00
	1850	.114	15.00	50.00	100.00	200.00
	1851	.096	15.00	50.00	100.00	200.00
	1852	.032	15.00	50.00	100.00	200.00
	1853	.235	15.00	50.00	100.00	200.00
	1854	.090	15.00	50.00	100.00	200.00
	1855	.223	15.00	50.00	100.00	200.00
	1856	—	15.00	50.00	100.00	200.00

Obv: A.D. below head.

C#	Date	Mintage	Fine	VF	XF	Unc
182a	1837 AD	.443	25.00	100.00	150.00	300.00
	1838 AD	Inc.Ab.	25.00	100.00	150.00	300.00

Obv: W/o VOIGT below head.

C#	Date	Mintage	Fine	VF	XF	Unc
182b	1839	—	15.00	35.00	75.00	150.00
	1840	—	15.00	35.00	75.00	150.00
	1841	—	25.00	75.00	125.00	250.00
182c	1848	Inc. Ab.	25.00	75.00	125.00	250.00

25th Anniversary of Reign

C#	Date	Mintage	Fine	VF	XF	Unc
183	1841	—	20.00	35.00	60.00	100.00

Visit of King to New Mint

C#	Date	Mintage	Fine	VF	XF	Unc
184	1844	—	650.00	1250.	2000.	3000.

NOTE: Restrikes exist.

Visit of Queen to Mint

C#	Date	Mintage	Fine	VF	XF	Unc
185	1845	17 pcs.	—	—	Rare	—

2 GULDEN

25.4500 gm., .750 SILVER, .6138 oz ASW

C#	Date	Mintage	Fine	VF	XF	Unc
187	1824 W	.015	200.00	350.00	900.00	1800.

Obv: Larger head right.
Rev. leg. ends: SC.

C#	Date	Mintage	Fine	VF	XF	Unc
187a	1824 ILW	Inc. Ab.	—	—	Rare	—

Obv: WAGNER F at truncation, leg: . . . . .WURTTEMB.
Rev: Crowned pointed arms within branches.

C#	Date	Mintage	Fine	VF	XF	Unc
188	1825 W	9,934	300.00	500.00	1200.	2600.

Obv: W/o name at bottom.

C#	Date	Mintage	Fine	VF	XF	Unc
188a	1825 W	Inc. Ab	—	—	Rare	—

21.2100 g, .900 SILVER, .6138 oz ASW

C#	Date	Mintage	Fine	VF	XF	Unc
189	1845	.562	45.00	75.00	150.00	350.00
	1846	.621	45.00	75.00	150.00	350.00
	1847	1.160	45.00	75.00	150.00	350.00
	1848	.336	45.00	75.00	150.00	350.00
	1849	.486	45.00	75.00	150.00	350.00
	1850	.280	45.00	75.00	150.00	350.00
	1851	.140	45.00	75.00	150.00	350.00
	1852	.225	45.00	75.00	150.00	350.00
	1853	.175	45.00	75.00	150.00	350.00
	1854	.074	45.00	75.00	150.00	350.00
	1855	.133	45.00	75.00	150.00	350.00
	1856	.267	45.00	75.00	150.00	350.00

5 GULDEN

3.4250 g, .904 GOLD, .0997 oz AGW

C#	Date	Mintage	Fine	VF	XF	Unc
198	1825 W	5,956	350.00	650.00	1000.	1800.

C#	Date	Mintage	Fine	VF	XF	Unc
198a	1824 W	2,282	500.00	1100.	1800.	2500.
	1835 W	1,443	600.00	1400.	2200.	3000.

C#	Date	Mintage	Fine	VF	XF	Unc
198b	1839 W	822 pcs.	800.00	1600.	2500.	3250.

10 GULDEN

6.8500 g, .904 GOLD, .1990 oz AGW

C#	Date	Mintage	Fine	VF	XF	Unc
199	1824 W	1,896	900.00	1800.	2500.	4000.
	1825 W	1,240	900.00	1800.	2500.	4000.

Visit of King to Mint

C#	Date	Mintage	Fine	VF	XF	Unc
200	1825 W	8 pcs.	—	—	—	15,000.

1/2 THALER

14.0300 g, .833 SILVER, .3759 oz ASW

C#	Date	Mintage	Fine	VF	XF	Unc
132	1805 ILW	—	350.00	750.00	1500.	2000.

THALER

(Convention)

28.0600 g, .833 SILVER, .7515 oz ASW

C#	Date	Mintage	Fine	VF	XF	Unc
134	1803	—	750.00	1200.	2500.	4500.

Obv. leg: . . . . .WURT. S.R.I.AR.VEXILL.ET ELECT.

C#	Date	Mintage	Fine	VF	XF	Unc
149	1806	—	—	—	Rare	—

Obv. leg. ends: . . . . .WURTEMBERGIAE.

C#	Date	Mintage	Fine	VF	XF	Unc
149a	1806	—	—	—	Rare	—

Obv: I.L. WAGNER F. below bust.
Rev: Leg. w/larger letters.

C#	Date	Mintage	Fine	VF	XF	Unc
149b	1806	—	—	—	Rare	—

C#	Date	Mintage	Fine	VF	XF	Unc
150	1809	—	—	—	Rare	—

Obv: I.L.W. below bust,
leg. ends: . . . . .WURTTEMBERGIAE.

C#	Date	Mintage	Fine	VF	XF	Unc
150a	1809 ILW	—	—	—	Rare	—

(Kronen)

29.4900 g, .868 SILVER, .8230 oz ASW
Obv: Military bust; leg:. . . . .D.G.REX . . . .
Rev: Crowned arms between lion and stag.

C#	Date	Mintage	Fine	VF	XF	Unc
151	1810 ILW	—	.—	—	Rare	—

Obv: Bust; leg: FRIDERICH I KOENIG . . . . .

C#	Date	Mintage	Fine	VF	XF	Unc
152	1810 ILW	—	—	—	Rare	—

Obv: Large head.

C#	Date	Mintage	Fine	VF	XF	Unc
A153	1810 ILW	—	300.00	800.00	2000.	4500.

Obv: Small head, w/o period before legend.

C#	Date	Mintage	Fine	VF	XF	Unc
153	1810 ILW	—	300.00	800.00	1750.	4000.

C#	Date	Mintage	Fine	VF	XF	Unc
153a	1811 ILW	2,000	400.00	800.00	2000.	4500.

C#	Date	Mintage	Fine	VF	XF	Unc
154	1812 ILW	.015	300.00	600.00	1200.	2500.

(Convention)

28.0600 g, .833 SILVER, .7515 oz ASW
Obv: Head left, WAGNER F below.
Rev: Value within wreath.

C#	Date	Mintage	Fine	VF	XF	Unc
190	1817	—	—	—	Rare	—

C#	Date	Mintage	Fine	VF	XF	Unc
190a	1818	—	500.00	1000.	2000.	4500.

(Kronen)

29.4900 g, .868 SILVER, .8230 oz ASW

C#	Date	Mintage	Fine	VF	XF	Unc
191	1817	.044	400.00	600.00	1500.	3000.

Rev: Similar to C#191.

C#	Date	Mintage	Fine	VF	XF	Unc
191a	1818	Inc. Ab.	300.00	550.00	1200.	2500.
	1818/7	Inc. Ab.	—	—	—	—

C#	Date	Mintage	Fine	VF	XF	Unc
192	1825	.226	85.00	135.00	300.00	600.00
	1826	—	100.00	150.00	375.00	800.00
	1827	—	100.00	150.00	375.00	800.00
	1828	—	100.00	150.00	375.00	800.00
	1829	—	100.00	150.00	375.00	800.00
	1830 W below bust	6,695	100.00	150.00	375.00	800.00
	1831	9,074	100.00	150.00	375.00	800.00
	1832 W below bust	—	100.00	150.00	375.00	800.00
	1833	—	100.00	150.00	375.00	800.00

NOTE: Varieties exist.

Obv: W below truncation.

C#	Date	Mintage	Fine	VF	XF	Unc
192a	1834 W	—	100.00	150.00	375.00	800.00
	1835 W	—	100.00	150.00	375.00	800.00
	1837 W	.170	85.00	135.00	300.00	600.00

Free Trade
Obv: Similar to C#192a.

C#	Date	Mintage	Fine	VF	XF	Unc
193	1833 W	—	75.00	125.00	225.00	450.00
	1833 LW	—	—	—	—	—

(Vereins)

18.5200 g, .900 SILVER, .5360 oz ASW

C#	Date	Mintage	Fine	VF	XF	Unc
186	1857	.452	25.00	55.00	135.00	275.00
	1858	.644	25.00	55.00	135.00	275.00
	1859	1.333	25.00	55.00	135.00	275.00
	1860	.645	25.00	55.00	135.00	275.00
	1861	.754	25.00	55.00	135.00	275.00
	1862	.648	25.00	55.00	135.00	275.00
	1863	.621	25.00	55.00	135.00	275.00
	1864	.533	25.00	55.00	135.00	275.00

Obv: C. SCHNITZSPAHN F on truncation.

C#	Date	Mintage	Fine	VF	XF	Unc
207	1865	.276	125.00	225.00	650.00	1500.

Rev: Antlers extend into leg.

C#	Date	Mintage	Fine	VF	XF	Unc
207a	1865	Inc. Ab.	40.00	75.00	200.00	475.00
	1866	.346	40.00	75.00	200.00	475.00
	1867	.165	40.00	75.00	200.00	475.00
207b	1868	.078	45.00	90.00	220.00	525.00
	1869	.031	50.00	100.00	240.00	550.00
	1870	.044	50.00	100.00	240.00	550.00

Victorious Conclusion of Franco-Prussian War
Rev: C.SCH.F at 7 o'clock.

C#	Date	Mintage	Fine	VF	XF	Unc
208	1871	.114	25.00	45.00	85.00	150.00
	1871	—	—	—	Proof	—

(3-1/2 Gulden)

37.1200 g, .900 SILVER, 1.0742 oz ASW

C#	Date	Mintage	Fine	VF	XF	Unc
194	1840	.162	125.00	225.00	450.00	1000.
	1842	.051	175.00	300.00	600.00	1200.
	1843	.245	125.00	225.00	450.00	1000.
	1854	.168	125.00	225.00	450.00	1000.
	1855	Inc.Ab.	125.00	225.00	450.00	1000.

Marriage of Crown Prince Carl to Olga,
Grand Duchess of Russia
Rev: Similar to C#194.

C#	Date	Mintage	Fine	VF	XF	Unc
195	1846	5,808	100.00	200.00	375.00	750.00

37.0400 g, .900 SILVER, 1.0717 oz ASW
Restoration of Ulm Cathedral

C#	Date	Mintage	Fine	VF	XF	Unc
209	1869	—	125.00	200.00	425.00	800.00
	1871	4,031	100.00	200.00	400.00	600.00

MONETARY REFORM

2 MARK

11.1110 g, .900 SILVER, .3215 oz ASW

Y#	Date	Mintage	Fine	VF	XF	Unc
215	1876F	1.550	30.00	75.00	525.00	1400.
	1877F	1.107	30.00	125.00	600.00	1700.
	1880F	.129	60.00	175.00	700.00	2300.
	1883F	.074	60.00	150.00	675.00	2000.
	1888F	.123	30.00	120.00	575.00	1600.
	1888F	—	—	—	Proof	1600.

Y#	Date	Mintage	Fine	VF	XF	Unc
220	1892F	.177	16.00	45.00	95.00	200.00

Y#	Date	Mintage	Fine	VF	XF	Unc
220	1893F	.174	16.00	45.00	75.00	175.00
	1896F	.351	12.00	28.00	50.00	125.00
	1898F	.144	20.00	45.00	90.00	195.00
	1899F	.538	12.00	19.00	35.00	125.00
	1900F	.516	10.00	16.00	40.00	100.00
	1901F	.592	12.00	19.00	40.00	100.00
	1902F	.816	10.00	17.00	45.00	100.00
	1903F	.811	12.00	19.00	40.00	100.00
	1904F	1.988	10.00	17.00	35.00	90.00
	1905F	.250	12.00	21.00	35.00	90.00
	1906F	1.505	12.00	21.00	50.00	90.00
	1907F	1.504	10.00	15.00	30.00	90.00
	1908F	.451	10.00	22.00	40.00	100.00
	1912F	.251	10.00	16.00	35.00	90.00
	1913F	.226	10.00	17.00	40.00	100.00
	1914F	.318	10.00	17.00	45.00	100.00
	Common date	—	—	—	Proof	175.00

3 MARK

16.6670 g, .900 SILVER, .4823 oz ASW

Y#	Date	Mintage	Fine	VF	XF	Unc
221	1908F	.300	10.00	17.50	25.00	55.00
	1909F	1.907	10.00	17.50	25.00	50.00
	1910F	.837	10.00	17.50	25.00	50.00
	1911F	.425	10.00	17.50	25.00	50.00
	1912F	.849	10.00	17.50	25.00	45.00
	1913F	.267	10.00	17.50	25.00	65.00
	1914F	.733	10.00	17.50	25.00	45.00
	Common date	—	—	—	Proof	175.00

Silver Wedding Anniversary
Obv: Normal bar in H of CHARLOTTE.

Y#	Date	Mintage	Fine	VF	XF	Unc
225	1911F	.493	12.50	20.00	50.00	60.00
	1911F	—	—	—	Proof	125.00

Obv: High bar in H of CHARLOTTE.

Y#	Date	Mintage	Fine	VF	XF	Unc
225a	1911F	7,000	100.00	250.00	450.00	600.00

25th Year of Reign

Y#	Date	Mintage	Fine	VF	XF	Unc
226	1916F	1,000	—	—	Proof	4000.

NOTE: 650 pieces have been melted.

5 MARK

27.7770 g, .900 SILVER, .8038 oz ASW

Y#	Date	Mintage	Fine	VF	XF	Unc
216	1874F	.113	30.00	60.00	900.00	2400.
	1875F	.318	30.00	60.00	900.00	2000.
	1876F	.897	30.00	60.00	600.00	1700.
	1888F	.049	40.00	100.00	900.00	2100.

1.9910 g, .900 GOLD, .0576 oz AGW

Y#	Date	Mintage	Fine	VF	XF	Unc
217	1877F	.488	100.00	200.00	250.00	425.00
	1877F	—	—	—	Proof	1300.
	1878F	.050	325.00	650.00	1250.	2000.

27.7770 g, .900 SILVER, .8038 oz ASW

Y#	Date	Mintage	Fine	VF	XF	Unc
222	1892F	.069	20.00	70.00	200.00	400.00
	1893F	.071	20.00	70.00	200.00	400.00
	1894F	.020	150.00	400.00	1250.	2000.
	1895F	.201	20.00	40.00	175.00	350.00
	1898F	.216	15.00	30.00	175.00	350.00
	1899F	.112	15.00	30.00	175.00	350.00
	1900F	.211	15.00	30.00	85.00	275.00
	1901F	.211	15.00	30.00	85.00	275.00
	1902F	.361	15.00	30.00	85.00	275.00
	1903F	.722	15.00	30.00	70.00	250.00
	1904F	.391	15.00	30.00	70.00	250.00
	1906F	.064	25.00	60.00	200.00	400.00
	1906F	50 pcs.	—	—	Proof	600.00
	1907F	.417	15.00	30.00	70.00	150.00
	1908F	.532	15.00	30.00	60.00	150.00
	1913F	.401	15.00	30.00	55.00	150.00
	Common date	—	—	—	Proof	300.00

10 MARK

3.9820 g, .900 GOLD, .1152 oz AGW
Rev: Type I.

Y#	Date	Mintage	Fine	VF	XF	Unc
218	1872F	.271	65.00	100.00	200.00	300.00
	1872F	—	—	—	Proof	1300.
	1873F	.675	65.00	100.00	200.00	300.00
	1873F	—	—	—	Proof	1300.

Rev: Type II.

Y#	Date	Mintage	Fine	VF	XF	Unc
218a	1874F	.205	65.00	120.00	170.00	300.00
	1875F	.532	65.00	120.00	150.00	250.00
	1876F	.933	65.00	120.00	160.00	300.00
218a	1876F	—	—	—	Proof	1300.
	1877F	.271	65.00	120.00	170.00	300.00
	1878F	.337	65.00	120.00	160.00	300.00
	1879F	.211	65.00	120.00	160.00	275.00
	1880F	.245	65.00	120.00	170.00	300.00
	1881F	.079	75.00	150.00	200.00	325.00
	1888F	.200	65.00	120.00	160.00	275.00
	1888F	—	—	—	Proof	1300.

Rev: Type III.

Y#	Date	Mintage	Fine	VF	XF	Unc
218b	1890F	.220	90.00	130.00	190.00	275.00
	1891F	.080	100.00	150.00	225.00	400.00

Y#	Date	Mintage	Fine	VF	XF	Unc
223	1893F	.300	65.00	100.00	165.00	225.00
	1896F	.200	65.00	100.00	165.00	225.00
	1898F	.420	65.00	100.00	165.00	225.00
	1900F	.090	80.00	125.00	175.00	225.00
	1901F	.110	65.00	125.00	175.00	225.00
	1902F	.050	125.00	150.00	200.00	250.00
	1903F	.180	65.00	100.00	165.00	225.00
	1904F	.350	65.00	100.00	150.00	225.00
	1904F	—	—	—	Proof	800.00
	1905F	.200	65.00	100.00	150.00	225.00
	1905F	—	—	—	Proof	800.00
	1906F	.100	65.00	100.00	165.00	225.00
	1906F	50 pcs.	—	—	Proof	800.00
	1907F	.150	65.00	100.00	150.00	225.00
	1907F	—	—	—	Proof	800.00
	1909F	.100	65.00	125.00	150.00	225.00
	1909F	—	—	—	Proof	800.00
	1910F	.150	65.00	125.00	175.00	225.00
	1910F	—	—	—	Proof	800.00
	1911F	.050	140.00	275.00	425.00	550.00
	1911F	—	—	—	Proof	800.00
	1912F	.049	140.00	275.00	425.00	650.00
	1912F	—	—	—	Proof	800.00
	1913F	.050	140.00	275.00	425.00	550.00
	1913F	—	—	—	Proof	800.00

20 MARK

7.9650 g, .900 GOLD, .2304 oz AGW
Rev: Type I.

Y#	Date	Mintage	Fine	VF	XF	Unc
219	1872F	.662	115.00	125.00	175.00	425.00
	1872F	—	—	—	Proof	1900.
	1873F	1.357	115.00	125.00	175.00	425.00
	1873F	—	—	—	Proof	1900.

Rev: Type II.

Y#	Date	Mintage	Fine	VF	XF	Unc
219a	1874F	.322	115.00	125.00	200.00	450.00
	1876F	.359	115.00	125.00	200.00	450.00

Rev: Type III.

Y#	Date	Mintage	Fine	VF	XF	Unc
224	1894F	.501	BV	115.00	140.00	250.00
	1897F	.400	BV	115.00	140.00	250.00
	1897F	—	—	—	Proof	700.00
	1898F	.106	BV	115.00	165.00	275.00
	1900F	.500	BV	115.00	140.00	250.00
	1900F	—	—	—	Proof	700.00
	1905F	.506	BV	115.00	140.00	250.00
	1905F	—	—	—	Proof	500.00
	1913F	.043	4000.	8000.	12,500.	20,000.
	1913F	—	—	—	Proof	60,000.
224	1914F	.558	3800.	7500.	12,000.	18,000.
	1914F	—	—	—	Proof	60,000.

TRADE COINAGE

DUCAT

3.5000 g, .986 GOLD, .1109 oz AGW
Visit of Duke to Mint
Obv: Bust right. Rev: IN HOCHST. . . . . within wreath.

C#	Date	Mintage	Fine	VF	XF	Unc
136	1803 ILW	—	—	—	Rare	—

Rev. leg: DEN 9. IAN 1804 added.

C#	Date	Mintage	Fine	VF	XF	Unc
136a	1804 ILW	—	—	—	Rare	—

Rev: Crowned circular arms within branches.

C#	Date	Mintage	Fine	VF	XF	Unc
137	1804 ILW	—	500.00	1000.	2000.	3500.

C#	Date	Mintage	Fine	VF	XF	Unc
155	1808 CH	—	500.00	1000.	2000.	3500.

C#	Date	Mintage	Fine	VF	XF	Unc
156	1813 ILW	—	600.00	1250.	2500.	4000.

C#	Date	Mintage	Fine	VF	XF	Unc
196	1818 W	—	600.00	1250.	2500.	3500.

C#	Date	Mintage	Fine	VF	XF	Unc
197	1840 AD	.081	175.00	350.00	525.00	850.00
	1841	.232	—	—	—	—
	1841/0 AD	I.A.	150.00	300.00	425.00	750.00
	1841 AD	I.A.	150.00	300.00	425.00	750.00
	1842 AD	.025	175.00	350.00	525.00	850.00
	1848 AD	.062	175.00	350.00	525.00	850.00

FREDERICK D'OR = 1 KAROLIN

6.6500 g, .900 GOLD, .1924 oz AGW

C#	Date	Mintage	Fine	VF	XF	Unc
157	1810 ILW	—	1500.	3000.	6000.	9000.

WURZBURG

BISHOPRIC

A Bishopric, located in Franconia, was established in 741. The mint right was obtained in the 11th century. The first coins were struck c. 1040. In 1441 the bishops were confirmed as dukes. In 1803 the area was secularized and granted to Bavaria. It was made a grand duchy in 1806 but the 1815 Congress of Vienna returned it to Bavaria.

RULERS

Georg Carl, Freiherr von Fechenbach, Bishop, 1795-1803
Ferdinand, Grand Duke, 1806-1814

MONETARY SYSTEM

3 Drier (Kortling) = 1 Shillinger
7 Shillinger = 15 Kreuzer
28 Shillinger = 1 Guter Gulden
44-4/5 Shillinger = 1 Convention Thaler

VIERTEL (1/4) KREUZER

COPPER

C#	Date	Mintage	Fine	VF	XF	Unc
151	1811	—	4.00	8.00	35.00	150.00

1/2 KREUZER

COPPER

C#	Date	Mintage	Fine	VF	XF	Unc
152	1810	—	5.00	10.00	40.00	150.00
	1811	—	5.00	10.00	40.00	150.00

KREUZER

SILVER
Obv: Crowned arms, dividing G.W.L.M. above.
Rev: Value.

C#	Date	Mintage	Fine	VF	XF	Unc
153	1808	—	4.00	7.00	25.00	120.00

Obv: W/o legend.

C#	Date	Mintage	Fine	VF	XF	Unc
153a	1808	—	4.00	7.00	25.00	120.00

Rev: G.W.L.M., value.

C#	Date	Mintage	Fine	VF	XF	Unc
153b	1808	—	4.00	7.00	25.00	120.00

3 KREUZER

BILLON, 21mm

C#	Date	Mintage	Fine	VF	XF	Unc
154	1807	—	4.00	8.00	30.00	120.00
	1808	—	4.00	8.00	30.00	120.00
	1809	—	4.00	8.00	30.00	120.00

6 KREUZER

SILVER
Obv: Large crown.

C#	Date	Mintage	Fine	VF	XF	Unc
155	1807	—	7.00	15.00	50.00	150.00
	1808	—	7.00	15.00	50.00	150.00

Obv: Small crown.

C#	Date	Mintage	Fine	VF	XF	Unc
155a	1809	—	7.00	15.00	50.00	150.00

TRADE COINAGE

GOLDGULDEN

3.2500 g, .770 GOLD, .0805 oz AGW
Obv: Head of Ferdinand right.
Rev: Palm tree, arms, value and date.

C#	Date	Mintage	Fine	VF	XF	Unc
159	1807	—	1000.	1800.	2800.	3500.
	1809	—	1000.	1800.	2800.	3500.

C#	Date	Mintage	Fine	VF	XF	Unc
160	1812R	—	1000.	1800.	2800.	3500.

Rev: Crowned battle flag; value and date.

C#	Date	Mintage	Fine	VF	XF	Unc
161	1813R	—	4000.	7000.	10,000.	12,500.

C#	Date	Mintage	Fine	VF	XF	Unc
162	1814R	—	3000.	5000.	8000.	10,000.

GERMANY

The Federal Republic of Germany, located in northcentral Europe, has an area of 137,744 sq. mi. (356,910 sq. km.) and a population of *77.6 million. Capital: Berlin. The economy centers about one of the world's foremost industrial establishments. Machinery, motor vehicles, iron, steel, yarns and fabrics are exported.

Germany, a nation of north-central Europe which from 1871 to 1945 was, successively, an empire, a republic and a totalitarian state, attained its territorial peak as an empire when it comprised a 208,780 sq. mi. (540,740 sq. km.) homeland and an overseas colonial empire.

As the power of the Roman Empire waned, several war like tribes residing in northern Germany moved south and west, invading France, Belgium, England, Italy and Spain. In 800 A.D. the Frankish king Charlemagne, who ruled most of France and Germany, was crowned Emperor of the Holy Roman Empire, a loose federation of an estimated 1,800 German States that lasted until 1806. Modern Germany was formed from the eastern part of Charlemagne's empire.

After 1812, the German States were reduced to a federation of 32, of which Prussia was the strongest. In 1871, Prussian chancellor Otto von Bismarck united the German states into an empire ruled by William I, the Prussian king. The empire initiated a colonial endeavor and became one of the world's greatest powers. Germany disintegrated as a result of World War I, and was reestablished as the Weimar Republic. The humiliation of defeat, economic depression, poverty and discontent gave rise to Adolf Hitler, 1933, who reconstituted Germany as the Third Reich and after initial diplomatic and military triumphs, expanded his goals beyond Europe into Africa and USSR which let it into final disaster in World War II, ending on VE Day, May 7, 1945.

During the post-Normandy phase of World War II, Allied troops occupied the western German provinces of Schleswig-Holstein, Hamburg, Lower Saxony, Bremen, North Rhine-Westphalia, Hesse, Rhineland-Palatinate, Baden-Wurttemberg, Bavaria and Saarland. The conquered provinces were divided into American, British and French occupation zones. Five eastern German provinces were occupied and administered by the forces of the Soviet Union.

The western occupation forces restored the civil status of their zones on Sept. 21, 1949, and resumed diplomatic relations with the provinces on July 2, 1951. On May 5, 1955, nine of the ten western provinces, organized as the Federal Republic of Germany, became fully independent. The tenth, Saarland, was restored to the republic on Jan. 1, 1957.

From the late 14th century until the fall of Napoleon, the city of Saarbrucken was ruled by the counts of Nassau-Saarbrucken, but the surrounding territory was subject to the political and cultural domination of France. At the close of the Napoleonic era, the Saarland came under the control of Prussia. France was awarded the Saar coal mines following World War I, and the Saarland was made an autonomous territory of the League of Nations, its future political affiliation to be determined by referendum. The plebiscite, 1935, chose reincorporation into Germany. France reoccupied the Saarland, 1945, establishing strong economic ties and assuming the obligation of defense and foreign affairs. After sustained agitation by West Germany, France agreed, 1955, to the return of the Saar to Germany by Jan. 1957.

The post-World War II division of Germany was ended Oct. 3, 1990, when the German Democratic Republic (East Germany) ceased to exist and its five constituent provinces were formally admitted to the Federal Republic of Germany. An election Dec. 2, 1990, chose representatives to the united federal parliament (Bundestag), which then conducted its opening session in Berlin in the old Reichstag building. Though Berlin technically is the capital of a united Germany, the actual seat of government remains for the time being in Bonn.

RULERS

Wilhelm I, 1871-1888
Friedrich III, 1888
Wilhelm II, 1888-1918

MINT MARKS

A - Berlin
B - Hannover (1866-1878)
B - Vienna (1938-1944)
C - Frankfurt (1866-1879)

D - Munich
E - Dresden (1872-1887)
E - Muldenhutten (1887-1953)
F - Stuttgart
G - Karlsruhe
H - Darmstadt (1872-1882)
J - Hamburg

MONETARY SYSTEM

(Until 1923)
100 Pfennig = 1 Mark
(During 1923-1924)
100 Rentenpfennig = 1 Rentenmark
(Commencing 1924)
100 Reichspfennig = 1 Reichsmark
(Commencing 1945)
100 Pfennig = 1 Mark

EMPIRE

1871-1918

PFENNIG

COPPER

KM#	Date	Mintage	Fine	VF	XF	Unc
1	1873A	.184	100.00	200.00	400.00	950.00
	1873B	.095	225.00	525.00	800.00	1450.
	1873D	.052	175.00	475.00	700.00	1150.
	1874A	26.760	.75	4.00	15.00	40.00
	1874B	8.743	2.50	10.00	20.00	65.00
	1874C	15.744	2.50	10.00	20.00	65.00
	1874D	7.074	5.00	15.00	25.00	65.00
	1874E	4.522	10.00	15.00	35.00	90.00
	1874F	3.985	2.50	7.50	17.50	65.00
	1874G	4.768	7.50	30.00	50.00	90.00
	1874H	2.013	30.00	55.00	100.00	300.00
	1875A	64.669	.75	1.50	7.50	20.00
	1875B	27.618	1.00	2.50	15.00	40.00
	1875C	22.654	1.00	2.50	15.00	40.00
	1875D	13.342	1.00	2.50	10.00	30.00
	1875E	7.779	5.00	15.00	30.00	60.00
	1875F	15.271	1.00	3.00	12.50	35.00
	1875G	12.021	5.00	10.00	20.00	60.00
	1875H	3.516	30.00	60.00	90.00	200.00
	1875J	7.242	2.50	10.00	20.00	50.00
	1876A	34.542	.75	1.50	7.50	20.00
	1876B	5.995	3.00	5.00	10.00	32.00
	1876C	11.044	3.00	5.00	10.00	32.00
	1876D	12.651	3.00	5.00	10.00	32.00
	1876E	6.532	2.50	7.50	20.00	50.00
	1876F	11.404	3.00	6.00	10.00	32.00
	1876G	3.331	7.50	20.00	35.00	70.00
	1876H	2.998	30.00	50.00	85.00	160.00
	1876J	1.165	50.00	100.00	275.00	475.00
	1877A	.472	60.00	150.00	475.00	750.00
	1877B	.088	325.00	550.00	1250.	1950.
	1885A	5.448	1.50	6.00	15.00	30.00
	1885E	.430	35.00	60.00	100.00	200.00
	1885G	1.100	20.00	50.00	80.00	125.00
	1885J	1.696	10.00	20.00	40.00	65.00
	1886A	14.114	1.00	2.50	10.00	25.00
	1886D	2.873	1.00	2.50	12.50	40.00
	1886E	2.060	3.00	6.00	20.00	65.00
	1886F	1.726	2.50	5.00	17.50	45.00
	1886G	.814	25.00	90.00	130.00	225.00
	1886J	1.593	7.50	15.00	30.00	50.00
	1887A	15.923	1.00	1.50	10.00	25.00
	1887D	5.177	2.50	4.00	10.00	25.00
	1887E	2.315	3.00	6.00	20.00	50.00
	1887E dot after PFENNIG.	25 pcs.	—	—	7000.	10,000.
	1887F	6.345	2.50	5.00	15.00	35.00
	1887G	1.888	3.00	7.50	20.00	40.00
	1887J	2.082	1.50	3.00	10.00	25.00
	1888A	19.936	1.00	2.50	10.00	20.00
	1888D	3.277	6.00	9.00	12.50	40.00
	1888E	1.310	5.00	10.00	20.00	40.00
	1888F	.584	20.00	30.00	95.00	150.00
	1888G	1.385	5.00	10.00	20.00	45.00
	1888J	2.803	4.00	7.50	12.50	45.00
	1889A	20.750	1.00	2.50	12.50	30.00
	1889D	8.454	2.00	3.00	15.00	30.00
	1889E	4.330	1.00	2.50	12.50	25.00
	1889F	5.010	1.00	2.50	12.50	30.00
	1889G	3.411	1.50	3.00	15.00	25.00
	1889J	3.308	2.50	5.00	10.00	30.00
	Common date		—	—	Proof	200.00

KM#	Date	Mintage	Fine	VF	XF	Unc
10	1890A	17.295	.50	1.50	3.50	10.00
	1890D	7.030	1.00	2.50	5.00	12.50
	1890E	3.730	.50	2.00	6.50	12.50
	1890F	4.189	.50	2.00	6.50	15.00
	1890G	3.050	2.00	4.00	6.50	15.00
	1890J	2.247	2.00	4.00	6.50	15.00
	1891A	12.040	2.00	4.00	5.00	10.00
	1891D	.876	10.00	25.00	75.00	115.00
	1891E	.528	20.00	40.00	75.00	115.00
	1891F	1.263	5.00	10.00	20.00	45.00
	1891G	.360	40.00	75.00	145.00	240.00
	1891J	1.837	7.50	25.00	75.00	135.00
	1892A	22.341	.25	.50	1.50	20.00
	1892D	6.139	2.00	4.00	9.00	40.00
	1892E	3.195	2.00	4.00	9.00	35.00
	1892F	5.013	1.00	2.00	5.00	30.00
	1892G	2.689	1.50	2.50	6.00	30.00
	1892J	3.980	.50	1.50	4.00	20.00
	1893A	18.966	.25	.50	2.00	12.00
	1893D	7.027	.25	1.00	4.00	20.00
	1893E	1.218	10.00	20.00	30.00	60.00
	1893F	1.460	1.00	2.00	6.00	30.00
	1893G	.700	12.50	25.00	35.00	70.00
	1893J	1.825	.50	5.00	15.00	30.00
	1894A	17.592	.25	.50	2.00	8.00
	1894D	5.530	.25	1.00	4.00	12.50
	1894E	5.040	.50	1.50	5.00	15.00
	1894F	4.206	.20	1.00	4.00	15.00
	1894G	2.351	.50	1.50	5.00	10.00
	1894J	2.619	.50	2.00	6.00	12.50
	1895A	20.152	.25	1.00	2.50	7.50
	1895D	1.496	10.00	25.00	35.00	70.00
	1895E	1.191	5.00	10.00	25.00	35.00
	1895F	4.366	.25	2.50	6.50	12.50
	1895G	3.051	1.00	3.00	7.50	15.00
	1895J	3.839	2.00	4.00	10.00	20.00
	1896A	27.094	.10	.25	1.50	6.00
	1896D	7.025	.10	.25	1.50	6.00
	1896E	3.725	.25	2.50	5.00	10.00
	1896F	3.450	.10	.20	1.50	6.00
	1896G	3.028	.25	4.00	7.50	10.00
	1897A	8.534	.25	1.00	3.50	7.50
	1897D	2.600	1.00	2.50	6.00	10.00
	1897E	1.294	3.50	7.50	15.00	35.00
	1897F	2.390	2.50	6.50	20.00	50.00
	1897G	1.122	10.00	20.00	35.00	75.00
	1897J	4.941	1.00	2.00	5.00	10.00
	1898A	18.564	.10	.25	1.00	6.00
	1898D	4.430	.25	2.00	5.00	15.00
	1898E	2.432	.50	5.00	10.00	20.00
	1898F	4.193	.20	1.00	2.50	7.00
	1898G	1.951	.25	5.00	15.00	30.00
	1898J	3.231	.25	2.50	5.00	10.00
	1899A	22.009	.10	.25	2.00	4.00
	1899D	4.590	.10	.25	2.00	4.00
	1899E	3.725	.25	2.50	5.00	12.50
	1899F	4.300	.10	.20	1.00	3.50
	1899G	2.550	.20	1.50	5.00	15.00
	1899J	2.416	.20	1.00	4.00	10.00
	1900A	51.804	.10	.25	1.00	3.50
	1900D	14.635	.10	.25	1.00	3.50
	1900E	7.887	.20	1.00	3.50	7.50
	1900F	10.312	.10	.50	1.50	5.00
	1900G	6.138	.20	1.00	3.50	7.50
	1900J	9.917	.20	1.00	3.50	7.50
	1901A	21.045	.10	.25	1.00	3.50
	1901D	5.337	.25	1.00	3.50	7.50
	1901E	1.397	1.00	6.00	9.00	20.00
	1901F	2.925	.25	2.50	5.00	10.00
	1901G	1.977	2.50	5.00	10.00	30.00
	1901J	2.011	3.00	10.00	15.00	35.00
	1902A	7.474	.50	5.00	10.00	15.00
	1902D	2.811	5.00	10.00	15.00	20.00
	1902E	1.183	5.00	10.00	9.00	20.00
	1902F	1.250	2.50	7.50	12.50	22.00
	1902G	.881	7.50	12.50	17.50	35.00
	1902J	150 pcs.	300.00	1100.	1450.	—
	1903A	12.690	.10	.50	1.50	6.00
	1903D	3.140	2.00	4.00	7.50	12.50
	1903E	1.956	2.00	4.00	7.50	12.50
	1903F	2.945	1.50	3.00	6.00	10.00
	1903G	1.377	2.50	10.00	15.00	25.00
	1903J	2.832	.10	.50	2.00	7.00
	1904A	28.625	.10	.25	1.00	4.00
	1904D	4.118	.10	.50	1.50	5.00
	1904E	2.778	.25	2.50	5.00	18.00
	1904F	4.520	.25	2.00	4.00	10.00
	1904G	3.232	.20	3.00	6.00	12.50
	1904J	4.467	.10	.50	1.50	5.00
	1905A	19.631	.10	.25	1.00	4.00
	1905D	6.084	.10	.25	1.00	4.00
	1905E	3.564	.10	.50	1.50	5.00
	1905F	4.153	.10	.20	1.00	4.00
	1905G	3.051	.20	1.00	3.00	6.00
	1905J	4.085	.10	.20	1.00	4.00
	1906A	46.921	.10	.50	1.50	5.00
	1906D	5.633	.10	.50	1.50	5.00
	1906E	7.278	.10	.50	1.50	5.00
	1906F	7.173	.10	.50	1.50	5.00
	1906G	5.194	.10	.50	1.50	5.00
	1906J	3.622	.10	.50	1.50	5.00
	1907A	33.711	.10	.50	1.50	5.00
	1907D	14.691	.10	.50	1.50	5.00
	1907E	3.719	.10	.50	1.50	5.00
	1907F	7.026	.10	.20	1.50	5.00
	1907G	3.052	.10	.50	1.50	5.00
	1907J	6.722	.10	.50	1.50	5.00
	1908A	21.922	.10	.50	1.50	5.00
	1908D	10.629	.10	.50	1.50	5.00
	1908E	3.400	.10	.50	1.50	5.00
	1908F	6.112	.10	.20	1.50	5.00
	1908G	3.663	.10	.50	1.50	5.00
	1908J	5.581	.10	.50	1.50	5.00
	1909A	21.430	.10	.25	1.00	3.00
	1909D	2.814	.20	1.00	2.50	7.50
	1909E	2.562	1.50	4.00	6.00	10.00
	1909F	2.425	1.50	4.00	6.00	10.00
	1909G	1.220	1.50	4.00	7.50	15.00
	1909J	1.634	1.50	4.00	6.50	12.50
	1910A	10.761	.10	.50	1.50	5.00
	1910D	4.221	.10	.25	1.00	3.00
	1910E	1.600	.25	1.50	5.00	10.00
	1910F	3.009	.20	1.50	5.00	7.50
	1910G	1.834	.25	4.00	6.00	10.00
	1910J	2.450	.25	5.00	7.50	15.00
	1911A	38.172	.10	.50	1.50	4.50
	1911D	8.657	.10	.50	1.50	5.00
	1911E	5.236	.10	.50	1.50	5.00
	1911F	5.780	.10	.50	1.50	5.00
	1911G	2.075	.10	.50	1.50	5.00
	1911J	5.594	.10	.50	1.50	5.00
	1912A	42.693	.10	.50	1.50	4.50
	1912D	10.173	.10	.50	1.50	5.00
	1912E	5.689	.10	.50	1.50	5.00
	1912F	7.441	.10	.50	1.50	5.00
	1912G	5.526	.10	.50	1.50	5.00
	1912J	5.615	.10	.50	1.50	5.00
	1913A	32.671	.10	.50	1.50	4.50
	1913D	8.161	.10	.50	1.50	5.00
	1913E	2.258	1.50	4.00	7.50	15.00
	1913F	6.620	.10	.20	1.00	3.00
	1913G	3.209	.10	.50	1.50	5.00
	1913J	1.456	.50	5.00	10.00	20.00
	1914A	9.976	.10	.50	1.50	5.00
	1914D	1.842	.10	.50	1.50	5.00
	1914E	2.926	.20	1.00	2.00	6.00
	1914F	3.316	.10	.50	1.50	5.00
	1914G	2.100	.20	1.00	2.00	6.00
	1914J	4.368	.10	.50	1.50	5.00
	1915A	14.738	.10	.50	1.50	5.00
	1915D	1.771	.10	.25	2.50	6.00
	1915E	2.779	.20	1.50	3.50	7.50
	1915F	1.411	.20	1.50	3.50	10.00
	1915G	2.041	.20	1.50	4.00	9.00
	1915J	2.981	.20	1.50	3.50	7.50
	1916A	5.960	.10	.50	1.50	5.00
	1916D	5.401	.20	1.00	3.00	7.00
	1916E	.818	1.00	5.00	7.50	10.00
	1916F	1.104	.50	2.00	5.00	9.00
	1916G	.671	1.50	7.50	10.00	17.50
	1916J	.898	1.50	6.00	9.00	12.50
	Common date		—	—	Proof	70.00

ALUMINUM

KM#	Date	Mintage	Fine	VF	XF	Unc
24	1916G	—	125.00	225.00	350.00	550.00
	1917A	27.159	.15	.50	2.00	5.00
	1917A	—	—	—	Proof	40.00
	1917D	6.940	.15	.50	2.00	6.00
	1917E	3.862	.50	2.00	4.50	8.00
	1917E	—	—	—	Proof	40.00
	1917F	5.125	.25	2.00	4.00	7.00
	1917G	3.139	.25	2.00	4.50	8.00
	1917G	—	—	—	Proof	40.00
	1917J	4.182	.25	2.00	4.00	8.00
	1917J	—	—	—	Proof	40.00
	1918A	—	150.00	300.00	500.00	900.00
	1918D	.318	10.00	20.00	27.50	40.00
	Common date		—	—	Proof	90.00

2 PFENNIG

COPPER

KM#	Date	Mintage	Fine	VF	XF	Unc
2	1873A	.877	2.50	7.50	35.00	185.00
	1873B	.290	25.00	60.00	120.00	275.00
	1873C	.161	25.00	65.00	135.00	325.00
	1873D	2.358	5.00	25.00	65.00	225.00
	1873F	.022	100.00	250.00	700.00	1450.
	1873G	.118	50.00	140.00	300.00	475.00
	1874A	37.360	.50	2.50	12.50	40.00
	1874B	10.310	1.50	7.50	17.50	45.00
	1874C	17.474	1.00	5.00	15.00	45.00
	1874D	2.943	3.50	15.00	30.00	125.00
	1874E	5.090	2.50	12.50	30.00	125.00
	1874F	6.405	1.00	7.50	25.00	125.00
	1874G	6.128	1.00	7.50	25.00	185.00
	1874H	2.706	10.00	20.00	60.00	165.00
	1875A	28.963	.50	2.50	12.50	40.00
	1875B	15.844	1.00	3.50	20.00	45.00
	1875C	35.541	.50	1.00	25.00	60.00
	1875D	11.160	.50	1.00	45.00	150.00
	1875E	7.872	1.00	1.50	30.00	125.00
	1875F	9.827	.50	1.00	30.00	125.00
	1875G	11.903	.50	1.00	30.00	125.00
	1875H	3.309	3.50	7.50	30.00	125.00
	1875J	14.210	.50	1.00	20.00	70.00
	1876A	18.906	.50	1.00	12.50	40.00
	1876B	7.097	.50	1.00	15.00	40.00
	1876C	12.280	.50	1.00	15.00	40.00

KM#	Date	Mintage	Fine	VF	XF	Unc
2	1876D	10.296	.50	1.00	15.00	40.00
	1876E	4.988	1.00	1.50	15.00	40.00
	1876F	7.207	.50	1.50	15.00	40.00
	1876G	3.502	1.00	2.50	15.00	40.00
	1876H	3.630	1.00	3.00	20.00	50.00
	1876J	1.995	4.00	7.50	17.50	50.00
	1877A	9.827	.50	1.00	15.00	40.00
	1877B	.060	150.00	300.00	600.00	—
	Common date		—	—	Proof	240.00

KM#	Date	Mintage	Fine	VF	XF	Unc
16	1904A	5.414	.10	.25	1.00	12.00
	1904D	1.404	.10	.50	2.00	14.00
	1904E	.744	2.00	6.00	12.50	30.00
	1904F	1.002	.10	1.00	4.00	12.00
	1904G	.495	2.00	6.00	12.50	30.00
	1904J	.044	4.00	10.00	35.00	60.00
	1905A	5.172	.10	.25	1.00	6.00
	1905D	1.570	.10	.50	2.00	7.50
	1905E	.924	.10	1.00	3.50	10.00
	1905F	1.115	.10	1.00	2.50	7.50
	1905G	1.030	.10	1.00	3.00	10.00
	1905J	1.609	.10	1.00	3.00	10.00
	1906A	8.459	.10	.25	1.00	6.00
	1906D	3.539	.10	.25	1.00	6.00
	1906E	2.055	.10	.25	1.00	6.00
	1906F	2.840	.10	.25	1.00	6.00
	1906G	1.527	.10	.25	1.00	6.00
	1906J	1.908	.10	.25	1.00	6.00
	1907A	13.468	.10	.25	1.00	6.00
	1907D	1.921	.10	.25	1.00	6.00
	1907E	.744	.25	2.00	6.00	10.00
	1907F	1.059	.10	.50	1.50	6.00
	1907G	.610	.25	1.00	3.00	6.00
	1907J	.952	.10	.50	1.50	6.00
	1908A	5.421	.10	.25	1.00	6.00
	1908D	1.407	.10	.50	1.50	6.00
	1908E	.745	1.00	5.00	7.50	10.00
	1908F	1.003	.10	.50	2.00	7.50
	1908G	.610	.25	1.00	4.00	7.50
	1908J	.817	.10	.50	2.50	12.50
	1910A	5.421	.10	.25	1.00	6.00
	1910D	1.407	.10	.50	1.50	6.00
	1910E	.745	.25	4.00	6.50	12.00
	1910F	1.003	.25	1.50	4.00	7.50
	1910G	.517	.25	1.50	5.00	12.00
	1910J	.568	.25	1.00	3.50	10.00
	1911A	8.187	.10	1.00	2.50	6.00
	1911D	2.100	.10	.50	2.50	6.00
	1911E	1.133	.10	.50	3.00	6.00
	1911F	1.490	.10	.50	3.00	6.00
	1911G	1.313	.10	.50	3.00	6.00
	1911J	1.883	.10	.50	2.50	6.00
	1912A	13.580	.10	.25	1.00	6.00
	1912D	3.109	.10	.50	2.00	6.00
	1912E	1.808	.10	1.00	3.00	6.00
	1912F	2.366	.10	.50	2.00	6.00
	1912G	1.395	.10	.50	2.50	6.00
	1912J	1.605	.10	.50	2.50	6.00
	1913A	4.212	.10	.25	1.00	6.00
	1913D	2.525	.10	.50	1.50	6.00
	1913E	.413	3.00	15.00	20.00	30.00
	1913F	1.602	.10	.50	2.00	6.00
	1913G	.741	.25	1.00	3.00	6.00
	1913J	1.254	.10	.50	1.50	6.00
	1914A	5.350	.10	.25	1.00	6.00
	1914E	1.201	1.00	3.50	8.50	15.00
	1914F	.158	12.00	45.00	75.00	150.00
	1914G	.610	2.00	6.00	15.00	25.00
	1914J	.817	.10	1.00	3.00	7.50
	1915A	3.897	.10	1.00	3.00	6.00
	1915D	1.407	.10	1.00	2.00	6.00
	1915E	.288	5.00	15.00	25.00	45.00
	1915F	.904	.10	.25	1.00	6.00
	1916A	3.524	.10	1.00	3.00	6.00
	1916D	.915	.25	1.00	2.00	6.00
	1916E	.484	1.00	2.50	6.00	12.50
	1916F	.651	.25	1.00	4.00	7.50
	1916G	.397	.50	2.50	6.00	15.00
	1916J	.531	.50	2.50	6.00	15.00
	Common date		—	—	Proof	80.00

5 PFENNIG

COPPER-NICKEL

KM#	Date	Mintage	Fine	VF	XF	Unc
3	1874A	10.003	.25	1.00	12.50	90.00
	1874B	5.054	.50	2.50	15.00	120.00
	1874C	3.707	.50	2.50	15.00	120.00
	1874D	2.447	.50	2.50	15.00	120.00
	1874E	5.465	.50	2.50	15.00	135.00
	1874F	3.562	1.50	4.00	17.50	135.00
	1874G	2.721	1.50	4.00	17.50	140.00
	1875A	30.844	.25	1.00	12.50	60.00
	1875B	11.658	.50	2.50	15.00	90.00

KM#	Date	Mintage	Fine	VF	XF	Unc
3	1875C	18.082	.50	2.50	15.00	90.00
	1875D	12.380	.50	2.50	15.00	90.00
	1875E	6.745	.50	2.50	15.00	90.00
	1875F	9.758	.50	2.50	15.00	90.00
	1875G	10.220	.50	2.50	15.00	90.00
	1875H	.703	20.00	45.00	75.00	175.00
	1875J	9.781	.50	2.50	15.00	90.00
	1876A	22.342	.25	1.00	12.50	60.00
	1876B	8.925	.50	2.50	15.00	70.00
	1876C	8.680	.50	2.50	15.00	70.00
	1876D	14.467	.50	2.50	15.00	70.00
	1876E	6.899	.50	2.50	15.00	70.00
	1876F	6.826	.50	2.50	15.00	70.00
	1876G	6.942	.50	2.50	15.00	135.00
	1876H	3.027	3.00	6.00	25.00	175.00
	1876J	11.920	.50	2.50	12.50	60.00
	1888A	7.366	.25	1.00	15.00	40.00
	1888/78D	1.967	3.00	6.00	25.00	60.00
	1888D	Inc. Ab.	2.50	5.00	20.00	50.00
	1888E	1.016	3.00	4.00	17.50	45.00
	1888F	1.412	1.00	2.00	12.50	30.00
	1888G	.853	6.00	8.00	22.50	55.00
	1888J	1.130	6.00	8.00	22.50	55.00
	1889A	10.804	.25	1.00	9.00	22.50
	1889D	2.816	1.00	2.50	10.00	35.00
	1889E	1.492	2.00	3.50	12.50	45.00
	1889F	2.010	1.00	2.50	10.00	35.00
	1889G	1.221	2.00	4.00	15.00	45.00
	1889J	1.636	2.50	4.00	17.50	50.00
	Common date		—	—	Proof	225.00

KM#	Date	Mintage	Fine	VF	XF	Unc
11	1890A	4.548	.10	.50	4.00	12.50
	1890D	2.813	.25	1.00	5.00	15.00
	1890E	1.318	.25	1.00	6.00	17.50
	1890F	1.068	.25	1.00	5.00	15.00
	1890G	.948	.25	1.00	6.00	17.50
	1890J	1.629	.20	1.00	5.00	15.00
	1891A	6.313	.10	.50	4.00	12.50
	1891E	.173	12.50	35.00	50.00	80.00
	1891F	.942	.25	1.00	5.00	15.00
	1891G	.271	5.00	17.50	30.00	55.00
	1892A	2.279	.10	1.00	4.00	12.50
	1892D	.920	.25	1.00	5.00	15.00
	1892E	.346	2.50	12.50	20.00	35.00
	1892F	.464	4.00	15.00	25.00	45.00
	1892G	.800	3.00	15.00	22.50	35.00
	1892J	.093	50.00	90.00	150.00	225.00
	1893A	8.572	.10	.50	4.00	15.00
	1893D	1.892	.25	1.00	5.00	16.50
	1893E	1.149	.25	1.00	6.00	17.50
	1893F	1.546	.15	1.00	5.00	15.00
	1893G	.422	4.00	15.00	20.00	40.00
	1893J	1.544	.20	1.00	5.00	15.00
	1894A	10.830	.10	.50	4.00	12.50
	1894D	2.812	.25	1.00	5.00	15.00
	1894E	.802	.25	1.50	6.00	17.50
	1894F	.300	1.00	4.00	10.00	30.00
	1894G	.280	1.00	5.00	12.50	35.00
	1894J	1.634	.20	1.00	5.00	15.00
	1895E	.686	.25	2.50	7.50	22.50
	1895F	1.705	.15	1.50	5.00	15.00
	1895G	.940	.25	2.00	6.00	17.50
	1896A	1.459	.25	1.00	5.00	15.00
	1896E	.658	.25	2.50	7.50	17.50
	1896F	2.009	.10	1.00	5.00	15.00
	1896G	1.221	1500.	2500.	—	—
	1896J	1.634	.20	1.00	5.00	15.00
	1897A	9.390	.10	.50	3.00	10.00
	1897D	2.812	.25	1.00	3.00	10.00
	1897E	.833	.25	2.00	5.00	15.00
	1897G	Inc. Ab.	.10	1.00	4.50	15.00
	1898A	10.836	.10	.30	2.00	8.00
	1898D	2.812	.10	.50	2.00	10.00
	1898E	1.492	.10	.50	2.00	14.00
	1898F	2.007	.10	.50	2.50	14.00
	1898G	1.220	.10	.50	1.50	17.50
	1898J	1.635	.20	1.00	2.00	12.00
	1899A	10.884	.10	.30	1.00	10.00
	1899D	2.812	.10	.50	2.00	14.00
	1899E	1.488	.10	.50	3.00	17.50
	1899F	2.006	.10	.50	2.00	14.00
	1899G	1.222	.10	.50	2.00	12.00
	1899J	1.634	.10	.50	2.00	12.00
	1900A	18.941	.10	.30	1.00	8.00
	1900D	4.254	.10	.50	1.50	12.00
	1900E	2.236	.10	.50	2.00	14.00
	1900F	3.209	.10	.25	1.50	12.00
	1900G	2.136	.10	.50	2.00	12.00
	1900J	2.859	.10	.50	2.00	12.00
	1901A	8.155	.10	.30	1.00	7.00
	1901D	2.779	.10	.20	.75	10.00
	1901E	1.492	.10	.50	2.00	12.00
	1901F	1.810	.10	.25	1.00	10.00
	1901G	.915	.10	.50	2.00	10.00
	1901J	1.226	.10	.25	1.00	10.00
	1902A	8.949	.10	.30	1.00	7.50
	1902D	2.812	.10	.20	.75	12.00
	1902E	1.120	.10	.50	2.00	14.50
	1902F	1.800	.10	.50	2.00	14.50
	1902G	1.220	.10	.50	3.50	17.50
	1902J	1.636	.10	.25	1.50	12.00
	1903A	5.932	.10	.30	1.00	7.50

KM#	Date	Mintage	Fine	VF	XF	Unc
11	1903D	1.406	.10	.50	2.50	8.00
	1903E	1.114	.10	1.00	4.00	12.00
	1903F	1.209	.10	.50	4.00	12.00
	1903G	.610	.10	1.50	5.00	15.00
	1903J	.817	.10	1.00	4.00	12.00
	1904A	6.791	.10	.30	1.50	7.50
	1904D	1.408	.10	.50	2.00	12.00
	1904E	.746	.10	1.50	4.00	12.00
	1904F	1.006	.10	.50	2.50	12.00
	1904G	.610	.10	1.00	3.00	14.00
	1904J	.818	.10	.50	2.50	14.00
	1905A	8.129	.10	.20	.50	8.00
	1905D	2.109	.10	.20	.50	8.00
	1905E	1.117	.10	.20	.50	8.00
	1905F	1.505	.10	.20	.50	8.00
	1905G	.915	.10	.50	2.50	10.00
	1905J	1.226	.10	.20	.50	8.00
	1906A	18.970	.10	.20	.50	7.00
	1906D	4.922	.10	.20	.50	7.50
	1906E	2.605	.10	.20	.50	7.50
	1906F	3.512	.10	.20	.50	7.50
	1906G	2.136	.10	.25	1.00	9.00
	1906J	2.859	.10	.20	.50	7.50
	1907A	11.930	.10	.20	.50	7.00
	1907D	2.113	.10	.20	.50	7.50
	1907E	1.517	.10	.25	1.00	9.00
	1907F	1.845	.10	.20	.50	7.50
	1907G	.915	.10	.50	1.00	9.00
	1907J	1.636	.10	.20	.50	7.50
	1908A	22.114	.10	.20	.50	6.50
	1908D	4.991	.10	.20	.50	7.00
	1908E	2.919	.10	.20	.50	8.00
	1908/7F	5.124	30.00	60.00	80.00	150.00
	1908F	Inc. Ab.	.10	.20	.50	7.50
	1908/108G	3.357	—	—	—	—
	1908G	Inc. Ab.	.10	.15	.50	7.00
	1908J	3.264	.10	.20	.50	6.00
	1909A	5.797	.10	.30	2.00	8.00
	1909D	2.753	.10	.50	2.50	9.00
	1909E	.984	.25	2.50	5.00	15.00
	1909F	.252	2.00	5.00	7.50	17.50
	1909/8J	1.632	1.00	5.00	15.00	45.00
	1909J	Inc. Ab.	.10	2.50	5.00	10.00
	1910A	7.344	.10	.20	1.00	6.50
	1910D	2.814	.10	.20	.50	8.50
	1910E	1.290	.10	.50	1.50	10.00
	1910F	1.721	.10	.20	.50	8.50
	1910G	1.222	.10	.20	.50	8.50
	1910J	.152	10.00	40.00	65.00	130.00
	1911A	15.660	.10	.15	.50	6.50
	1911D	2.221	.10	.20	.50	7.00
	1911E	1.770	.10	.20	.50	7.00
	1911F	2.714	.10	.20	.50	7.00
	1911G	1.833	.10	.20	1.00	7.00
	1911J	3.116	.10	.15	.50	7.00
	1912A	19.320	.10	.15	.50	6.50
	1912D	4.015	.10	.20	.50	7.00
	1912E	2.568	.10	.20	.50	7.00
	1912F	3.679	.10	.15	.50	7.00
	1912G	2.440	.10	.20	.50	7.00
	1912J	3.020	.10	.15	.50	7.00
	1913A	15.506	.10	.15	.50	6.50
	1913D	5.519	.10	.20	.50	7.00
	1913E	2.373	.10	.20	.50	9.00
	1913F	2.054	.10	.20	.50	6.00
	1913G	1.221	.10	.20	.50	6.00
	1913J	.253	5.00	12.50	17.50	30.00
	1914A	23.605	.10	.15	.50	6.00
	1914D	3.014	.10	.20	.50	6.00
	1914E	1.710	.10	.20	.50	6.00
	1914F	2.206	.10	.20	.50	6.00
	1914G	1.218	.10	.20	.50	6.00
	1914J	3.235	.10	.15	.50	6.00
	1915D	3.516	.10	.50	2.00	7.00
	1915E	.834	1.00	6.00	8.00	15.00
	1915F	1.894	.10	.50	2.00	6.00
	1915G	.894	.50	5.00	6.50	10.00
	1915J	1.669	.10	.50	3.50	10.00
	1915	—	1.00	5.00	12.50	25.00
	Common date		—	—	Proof	80.00

IRON

KM#	Date	Mintage	Fine	VF	XF	Unc
19	1915A	34.631	.10	.25	2.00	7.50
	1915D	2.021	.50	7.50	12.50	20.00
	1915E	4.670	.50	5.00	10.00	20.00
	1915F	3.500	.25	2.50	7.50	15.00
	1915G	3.676	.25	2.00	5.00	12.50
	1915J	2.100	.25	2.00	5.00	12.50
	1916A	51.003	.10	.25	1.50	8.50
	1916D	19.590	.10	.50	1.50	8.50
	1916E	2.271	1.00	10.00	15.00	22.50
	1916F	10.479	.15	1.00	2.00	8.50
	1916G	5.599	.25	1.50	3.50	12.00
	1916J	10.253	.25	3.00	7.50	15.00
	1917A	87.315	.10	.50	1.00	7.50
	1917D	19.581	.10	.50	1.00	7.50
	1917E	11.092	.50	5.00	7.50	10.00
	1917F	10.930	.10	.50	2.00	8.50
	1917F mule w/Polish rev. of Y#5, see Poland					
	1917G	6.720	.25	3.00	6.00	10.00
	1917J	11.686	.25	2.00	5.00	10.00

KM#	Date	Mintage	Fine	VF	XF	Unc
19	1918A	223.516	.10	.50	1.00	6.50
	1918D	29.130	.10	.50	1.00	6.50
	1918E	23.600	.25	1.00	6.00	12.50
	1918F	24.598	.10	.25	1.00	6.50
	1918G	12.697	.10	.50	1.00	6.50
	1918J	20.240	.10	.50	1.00	6.50
	1919A	112.102	.10	.20	.50	6.00
	1919D	41.163	.10	.25	1.00	6.50
	1919E	20.608	.25	3.00	6.00	12.50
	1919F	32.700	.10	.25	1.00	6.50
	1919G	13.925	.10	.50	2.50	10.00
	1919J	16.249	.15	1.00	2.00	7.50
	1920A	80.300	.10	.20	.50	6.00
	1920D	25.502	.10	.50	1.00	6.50
	1920E	11.646	.25	2.50	10.00	22.50
	1920F	24.300	.10	.25	1.00	6.50
	1920G	10.244	.20	2.00	3.50	12.50
	1920J	16.857	.10	.20	1.00	6.50
	1921A	143.418	.10	.20	.50	6.00
	1921D	38.133	.10	.25	1.00	6.50
	1921E	21.104	2.50	5.00	10.00	17.00
	1921F	24.800	.10	.25	1.00	6.50
	1921G	21.289	.10	.25	1.00	6.50
	1921J	28.928	.15	1.00	3.00	10.00
	1922A	89.062	—	—	Rare	—
	1922D	31.240	.10	.25	1.00	6.50
	1922E	19.156	2.50	5.00	10.00	18.00
	1922F	16.436	.10	.25	1.00	6.50
	1922G	19.708	.10	.25	1.00	6.50
	1922J	16.820	.25	2.50	6.00	12.50
	Common date		—	—	Proof	70.00

10 PFENNIG

COPPER-NICKEL

KM#	Date	Mintage	Fine	VF	XF	Unc
4	1873A	.931	6.00	10.00	22.50	110.00
	1873B	.333	17.50	25.00	90.00	225.00
	1873C	.522	15.00	20.00	70.00	200.00
	1873D	.472	5.00	10.00	40.00	185.00
	1873F	.476	20.00	30.00	60.00	200.00
	1873G	.519	15.00	20.00	70.00	200.00
	1873H	.044	100.00	200.00	475.00	900.00
	1874A	7.664	.25	2.00	12.50	75.00
	1874B	2.669	2.50	5.00	17.50	90.00
	1874C	12.029	.25	2.00	12.50	70.00
	1874D	3.586	10.00	17.50	65.00	150.00
	1874E	3.157	10.00	17.50	40.00	125.00
	1874F	7.309	1.00	2.50	12.50	75.00
	1874G	5.552	1.00	2.50	12.50	80.00
	1874H	3.323	12.50	20.00	40.00	150.00
	1875A	15.523	.25	2.00	10.00	70.00
	1875B	4.120	1.00	2.50	12.50	75.00
	1875C	8.304	1.00	2.50	12.00	70.00
	1875D	13.365	1.00	2.50	12.00	70.00
	1875E	9.833	1.00	2.50	12.50	70.00
	1875F	7.975	1.00	2.50	12.50	70.00
	1875G	5.390	2.50	5.00	15.00	75.00
	1875H	4.268	12.50	20.00	40.00	100.00
	1875J	9.407	1.00	2.50	12.00	70.00
	1876A	34.175	.25	2.00	10.00	40.00
	1876B	10.120	1.00	2.50	12.00	40.00
	1876C	13.214	.25	2.00	10.00	40.00
	1876D	16.787	.25	2.00	10.00	40.00
	1876E	6.161	1.00	2.50	12.50	45.00
	1876F	7.034	1.00	2.50	12.50	45.00
	1876G	6.222	1.00	2.50	12.50	45.00
	1876H	3.227	17.50	30.00	40.00	75.00
	1876J	11.315	1.00	2.50	12.00	40.00
	1888A	8.519	1.00	2.50	15.00	45.00
	1888D	2.493	.50	2.50	12.00	35.00
	1888E	1.268	1.00	7.50	20.00	50.00
	1888F	1.340	1.00	7.50	20.00	50.00
	1888G	1.081	1.00	7.50	20.00	45.00
	1888J	1.436	.50	2.50	12.00	40.00
	1889A	11.542	.25	2.00	10.00	30.00
	1889D	2.813	.50	2.00	10.00	35.00
	1889E	1.493	.50	2.50	12.00	35.00
	1889F	2.432	.50	2.50	12.00	35.00
	1889G	1.223	.50	5.00	20.00	45.00
	1889J	1.638	.50	2.50	12.00	35.00
	Common date		—	—	Proof	350.00

KM#	Date	Mintage	Fine	VF	XF	Unc
12	1890A	6.878	.10	.25	6.00	18.00
	1890F	.784	.25	1.50	8.00	25.00
	1890G	.976	.25	2.00	8.00	25.00
	1890J	1.637	.25	1.00	8.00	25.00
	1891A	4.239	.10	.25	3.00	15.00
	1891D	2.812	.10	.30	4.00	16.00
	1891E	1.489	.20	1.00	4.00	16.00
	1891F	1.226	.25	2.50	5.00	20.00
	1891G	.247	7.00	20.00	40.00	70.00
	1892A	2.413	.15	.50	4.00	18.00
	1892D	2.812	.15	.50	4.00	18.00
	1892E	.870	.25	2.50	5.00	20.00
	1892F	.663	.25	2.50	5.00	20.00
	1892G	.300	6.00	15.00	30.00	65.00
	1892J	—	2150.	3600.	—	—
	1893A	8.435	.10	.25	2.00	10.00
	1893E	.362	.50	6.00	12.50	35.00
	1893F	1.345	.15	.50	3.00	16.00
	1893G	.921	.25	1.50	5.00	16.00
	1893J	1.636	.20	1.00	5.00	16.00
	1894E	.260	7.50	25.00	40.00	65.00
	1896A	4.996	.10	1.00	2.00	10.00
	1896D	2.812	.20	1.00	4.00	12.00
	1896E	1.495	.20	1.00	4.00	15.00
	1896F	2.009	.15	1.00	4.00	15.00
	1896G	.200	6.00	15.00	25.00	40.00
	1896J	1.632	.10	.30	4.00	15.00
	1897A	5.842	.10	.25	1.50	9.00
	1897G	1.020	.25	1.50	4.00	15.00
	1898A	10.833	.10	.25	1.00	8.00
	1898D	2.814	.10	.25	3.00	12.00
	1898E	.805	.20	.50	3.00	14.00
	1898F	2.007	.15	.50	2.00	14.00
	1898G	.480	.50	3.00	6.00	22.50
	1898J	1.635	.10	.30	1.50	14.00
	1899A	10.838	.10	.25	1.00	8.00
	1899D	3.813	.10	.25	3.00	12.00
	1899E	2.175	.10	.30	3.00	14.00
	1899F	2.008	.10	.25	3.00	12.00
	1899G	1.382	.10	.25	3.00	12.00
	1899J	1.635	.10	.25	3.00	12.00
	1900A	34.559	.10	.25	1.00	7.00
	1900D	8.694	.10	.25	1.00	12.00
	1900E	4.490	.10	.30	1.50	12.00
	1900F	5.933	.10	.25	1.00	12.00
	1900G	4.239	.10	.25	1.50	14.00
	1900J	5.720	.10	.25	1.00	14.00
	1901A	10.200	.10	.25	1.00	7.00
	1901D	3.259	.10	.25	1.00	12.00
	1901E	1.863	.10	.30	1.00	12.00
	1901F	2.594	.10	.25	1.00	12.00
	1901G	1.527	.10	.25	1.00	12.00
	1901J	1.225	.10	.25	1.00	12.00
	1902A	5.878	.10	.25	1.00	6.00
	1902D	1.406	.10	.25	1.00	12.00
	1902E	.502	.25	3.00	6.00	15.00
	1902F	1.003	.10	.25	1.00	14.00
	1902G	.610	.25	1.50	3.50	14.00
	1902J	.815	.25	1.50	3.00	14.00
	1903A	5.131	.10	.25	1.00	7.00
	1903D	1.406	.10	.30	1.50	12.00
	1903E	.988	.15	.30	1.00	12.00
	1903F	1.003	.10	.25	1.00	12.00
	1903G	.610	.25	.50	1.50	14.00
	1903J	.816	.20	.40	1.50	14.00
	1904A	5.189	.10	.25	1.00	6.00
	1904D	1.056	.10	.30	1.00	12.00
	1904E	.559	.25	1.00	2.50	12.00
	1904F	.753	.10	.25	1.00	12.00
	1904G	.457	1.00	5.00	7.50	16.00
	1904J	.612	.25	1.50	3.50	16.00
	1905A	8.650	.10	.25	1.00	6.00
	1905A	250 pcs.	—	—	Proof	100.00
	1905D	1.846	.10	.25	1.00	7.50
	1905E	.980	.15	.30	1.00	7.50
	1905F	1.310	.10	.25	1.00	7.50
	1905G	.642	.25	1.00	2.00	10.00
	1905J	1.430	.10	.25	1.00	7.50
	1906A	14.470	.10	.25	1.00	7.50
	1906D	4.132	.10	.25	1.00	7.50
	1906E	2.189	.10	.25	1.00	7.50
	1906F	2.953	.10	.25	1.00	7.50
	1906G	1.952	.10	.25	1.00	7.50
	1906J	2.042	.10	.25	1.00	7.50
	1907A	17.971	.10	.25	1.00	6.50
	1907D	2.813	.10	.25	1.00	7.50
	1907E	2.291	.10	.25	1.00	7.50
	1907F	3.206	.10	.25	1.00	7.50
	1907G	1.889	.10	.25	1.00	7.50
	1907J	2.750	.10	.25	1.00	7.50
	1908A	20.410	.10	.25	1.00	6.50
	1908D	6.773	.10	.25	1.00	7.50
	1908E	2.490	.10	.25	1.00	7.50
	1908F	3.535	.10	.25	1.00	7.50
	1908G	1.708	.10	.25	1.00	7.50
	1908J	2.649	.10	.25	1.00	7.50
	1909A	2.270	.25	1.00	2.50	12.00
	1909D	.966	.25	1.50	6.00	18.00
	1909E	.806	.50	3.00	6.00	20.00
	1909F	.780	.50	3.00	8.00	20.00
	1909G	.980	.25	2.50	8.00	20.00
	1909J	.725	.25	2.50	8.00	20.00
	1910A	3.734	.10	.20	.50	6.00
	1910D	1.406	.25	.50	1.00	7.50
	1910E	.300	3.50	7.50	15.00	25.00
	1910F	1.003	.25	.50	1.00	7.50
	1910G	.610	.25	.50	1.00	7.50
	1911A	13.554	.10	.15	.50	6.00
	1911D	2.508	.10	.15	.50	7.00
	1911E	2.246	.10	.15	.50	7.00
	1911F	2.235	.10	.15	.50	7.00
	1911G	1.678	.10	.15	.50	7.00
	1911J	3.062	.10	.15	.50	7.00
	1912A	21.312	.10	.15	.50	6.00
	1912D	6.988	.10	.15	.50	7.00
	1912E	2.649	.10	.15	.50	7.00
	1912F	3.787	.10	.15	.50	7.00
	1912G	2.441	.10	.15	.50	7.00
	1912J	2.730	.10	.15	.50	7.00
	1913A	13.466	.10	.15	.50	6.00
	1913D	3.164	.10	.15	.50	7.00
	1913E	1.478	.10	.15	.50	7.00
	1913F	1.991	.10	.15	.50	7.00
	1913G	1.373	.10	.15	.50	7.00
	1913J	1.550	.10	.15	.50	7.00
	1914A	18.570	.10	.15	.50	6.00
	1914D	2.301	.10	.15	.50	7.00
	1914E	3.478	.10	.15	.50	7.00
	1914F	4.515	.10	.15	.50	7.00
	1914G	2.689	.10	.15	.50	7.00
	1914J	1.589	.10	.15	.50	7.00
	1915A	10.639	.10	.15	.50	7.00
	1915D	2.277	.10	.15	.50	7.00
	1915E	1.027	.25	2.50	5.00	15.00
	1915F	1.508	.10	.15	.50	7.00
	1915G	.363	15.00	50.00	75.00	150.00
	1915J	2.677	.20	1.00	2.50	7.50
	1916D	1.128	.15	1.00	2.50	10.00
	Common date		—	—	Proof	95.00

IRON

KM#	Date	Mintage	Fine	VF	XF	Unc
20	1915A	—	125.00	275.00	350.00	475.00
	1916A	69.143	.10	.35	1.50	6.00
	1916D	11.609	.10	.30	1.50	6.50
	1916E	8.280	.15	.50	4.00	8.00
	1916F	7.473	.15	.50	4.00	8.00
	1916G	5.878	.15	.50	4.00	8.00
	1916J	11.683	.15	.50	3.50	6.50
	1916	—	—	—	Rare	—
	1917A	53.198	.10	.20	1.00	2.00
	1917D	16.370	.10	.30	1.50	2.50
	1917E	9.182	.15	.50	2.50	5.00
	1917F	11.341	.15	.50	2.50	5.00
	1917F mule w/Polish rev. of Y#6, see Poland					
	1917G	7.088	.15	.50	3.00	7.50
	1917J	9.205	.15	.50	3.50	7.50
	1918D	.042	300.00	550.00	850.00	1150.
	1921A	16.265	1.00	4.00	6.00	12.50
	1922D	—	2.00	7.50	12.50	20.00
	1922E	2.235	17.50	35.00	50.00	100.00
	1922F	1.928	.50	3.00	5.00	10.00
	1922G	1.358	15.00	30.00	50.00	110.00
	1922J	2.420	1.00	4.00	6.00	12.50
	1922	—	100.00	175.00	250.00	450.00
	Common date		—	—	Proof	95.00

NOTE: The 1915A and 1922 are suspected patterns.

ZINC

Eagle and beaded border similar to KM#12.

KM#	Date	Mintage	Fine	VF	XF	Unc
25	1916F	—	150.00	400.00	600.00	900.00
	1917A	—	75.00	150.00	225.00	325.00
	1917	—	60.00	130.00	170.00	275.00
	1922J	—	—	—	Rare	—

W/o mint mark.
3.10-3.60 g

KM#	Date	Mintage	Fine	VF	XF	Unc
26	1917	75.073	.10	.20	1.00	5.50
	1918	202.008	.10	.20	1.00	5.50
	1918	28 pcs.	—	—	Proof	—
	1919	147.800	.10	.20	1.00	5.50
	1919	50 pcs.	—	—	Proof	—
	1920	223.019	.10	.20	1.00	5.50
	1920	40 pcs.	—	—	Proof	—
	1921	319.334	.10	.20	1.00	5.50
	1921	24 pcs.	—	—	Proof	—
	1922	274.499	.10	.20	1.00	5.50
	1922	12 pcs.	—	—	Proof	—
	Common date		—	—	Proof	80.00

20 PFENNIG

1.1110 g, .900 SILVER, .0321 oz ASW

KM#	Date	Mintage	Fine	VF	XF	Unc
5	1873A	2.159	5.00	12.50	25.00	120.00
	1873B	.664	17.50	40.00	100.00	220.00
	1873C	.904	17.50	25.00	50.00	135.00
	1873D	1.201	8.00	12.50	30.00	125.00
	1873E	100 pcs.	1000.	1400.	1800.	3000.
	1873F	.450	17.50	30.00	90.00	200.00
	1873G	.763	12.50	25.00	70.00	165.00
	1873H	.054	150.00	350.00	750.00	1500.
	1874A	8.830	6.00	10.00	15.00	65.00
	1874B	9.222	6.00	10.00	15.00	75.00
	1874C	1.303	10.00	15.00	25.00	100.00
	1874D	10.087	7.50	10.00	16.00	75.00
	1874E	2.281	7.50	15.00	25.00	90.00
	1874F	7.222	6.50	10.00	16.00	75.00
	1874G	3.281	8.00	12.50	20.00	75.00

KM#	Date	Mintage	Fine	VF	XF	Unc
5	1874H	1.842	12.50	17.50	25.00	100.00
	1875A	9.034	5.00	7.50	10.00	50.00
	1875B	2.768	8.00	12.50	25.00	60.00
	1875C	5.938	6.00	9.00	25.00	60.00
	1875D	15.032	6.00	9.00	12.50	50.00
	1875E	1.486	17.50	27.50	60.00	125.00
	1875F	7.668	6.00	9.00	12.50	60.00
	1875G	3.940	8.00	12.50	25.00	75.00
	1875H	1.340	17.50	27.50	37.50	125.00
	1875J	3.502	10.00	15.00	22.50	60.00
	1876A	6.959	6.00	10.00	15.00	40.00
	1876B	5.089	6.00	10.00	15.00	55.00
	1876C	5.911	6.00	10.00	15.00	70.00
	1876D	14.152	5.00	9.00	12.50	45.00
	1876E	11.648	7.50	12.50	20.00	90.00
	1876F	13.635	5.00	9.00	10.00	65.00
	1876G	7.820	5.00	9.00	10.00	65.00
	1876H	1.433	17.50	35.00	60.00	145.00
	1876J	10.272	6.00	10.00	17.50	40.00
	1877F	.700	125.00	225.00	325.00	550.00
	Common date		—	—	Proof	350.00

COPPER-NICKEL

KM#	Date	Mintage	Fine	VF	XF	Unc
9.1	1887A	2.712	7.50	20.00	27.50	55.00
	1887D	.704	7.50	25.00	35.00	80.00
	1887E	.373	15.00	35.00	50.00	125.00
	1887F	.503	15.00	30.00	45.00	90.00
	1887G	.306	15.00	30.00	50.00	200.00
	1887J	.408	15.00	30.00	50.00	125.00
	1888A	5.426	7.50	25.00	30.00	55.00
	1888D	1.406	10.00	25.00	35.00	75.00
	1888E	.744	10.00	25.00	35.00	100.00
	1888F	1.005	10.00	25.00	35.00	90.00
	1888G	.611	10.00	25.00	40.00	135.00
	1888/7J	.818	25.00	45.00	60.00	125.00
	1888J	Inc. Ab.	10.00	25.00	35.00	75.00
	Common date		—	—	Proof	250.00

Obv: Star below value.

KM#	Date	Mintage	Fine	VF	XF	Unc
9.2	1887E	50 pcs.	—	—	P/L	6000.

NOTE: Struck at the new mint facility at Muldenhutten.

KM#	Date	Mintage	Fine	VF	XF	Unc
13	1890A	2.716	15.00	27.50	45.00	135.00
	1890/80D	.703	15.00	35.00	65.00	150.00
	1890D	Inc. Ab.	15.00	35.00	65.00	150.00
	1890E	.373	17.50	45.00	120.00	250.00
	1890F	.503	15.00	30.00	70.00	200.00
	1890G	.306	17.50	40.00	110.00	250.00
	1890J	.410	15.00	35.00	65.00	250.00
	1892A	2.712	10.00	25.00	45.00	125.00
	1892D	.703	15.00	35.00	45.00	185.00
	1892E	.372	15.00	40.00	70.00	300.00
	1892F	.502	15.00	35.00	65.00	200.00
	1892G	.304	20.00	50.00	130.00	325.00
	1892J	.409	15.00	40.00	120.00	325.00
	Common date		—	—	Proof	270.00

25 PFENNIG

NICKEL

KM#	Date	Mintage	Fine	VF	XF	Unc
18	1909A	.962	2.50	6.00	10.00	20.00
	1909D	1.406	2.50	6.00	10.00	20.00
	1909E	.250	15.00	27.50	40.00	85.00
	1909F	.400	4.00	10.00	20.00	35.00
	1909G	.610	4.00	10.00	20.00	35.00
	1909J	.010	400.00	600.00	900.00	1500.
	1910A	9.522	3.00	8.00	11.50	18.00
	1910D	1.408	3.00	8.00	11.50	18.00
	1910E	1.242	3.00	8.00	11.50	18.00
	1910F	1.605	3.00	8.00	15.00	22.50
	1910G	.330	3.00	8.00	18.50	32.50
	1910J	1.561	3.00	8.00	15.00	20.00
	1911A	3.179	2.50	6.00	10.00	16.00

KM#	Date	Mintage	Fine	VF	XF	Unc
18	1911D	.506	3.00	8.00	18.50	35.00
	1911E	.747	3.00	8.00	18.50	35.00
	1911G	.892	3.00	8.00	18.50	35.00
	1911J	.516	3.00	8.00	18.50	35.00
	1912A	2.590	3.00	8.00	11.50	17.50
	1912D	.900	3.00	8.00	17.50	30.00
	1912F	1.003	3.00	8.00	18.50	32.50
	1912J	.362	12.50	25.00	35.00	70.00
	Common date		—	—	Proof	130.00

50 PFENNIG

2.7770 g, .900 SILVER, .0803 oz ASW

KM#	Date	Mintage	Fine	VF	XF	Unc
6	1875A	7.095	7.50	15.00	30.00	90.00
	1875B	2.799	8.00	16.00	50.00	120.00
	1875C	2.047	7.50	15.00	30.00	90.00
	1875D	4.668	8.00	16.00	32.50	120.00
	1875E	.353	150.00	325.00	650.00	1800.
	1875F	.874	22.50	50.00	80.00	185.00
	1875G	2.034	15.00	17.50	37.50	150.00
	1875H	.175	150.00	300.00	600.00	1800.
	1875J	2.411	12.50	20.00	50.00	160.00
	1876A	34.475	7.50	15.00	30.00	75.00
	1876B	11.016	7.50	15.00	30.00	90.00
	1876C	10.945	7.50	15.00	30.00	90.00
	1876D	3.641	12.50	25.00	45.00	95.00
	1876E	4.127	7.50	15.00	30.00	90.00
	1876F	4.448	12.50	20.00	40.00	90.00
	1876G	1.797	12.50	20.00	40.00	120.00
	1876H	1.877	12.50	25.00	45.00	150.00
	1876J	3.589	8.00	17.50	35.00	90.00
	1877A	3.249	8.00	17.50	35.00	80.00
	1877B	3.691	12.50	20.00	40.00	90.00
	1877C	2.388	15.00	32.50	45.00	95.00
	1877D	3.004	12.50	20.00	40.00	90.00
	1877E	1.121	22.50	45.00	85.00	185.00
	1877F	1.311	25.00	37.50	70.00	125.00
	1877H	.622	75.00	100.00	170.00	300.00
	1877J	1.526	40.00	65.00	150.00	275.00
	Common date		—	—	Proof	250.00

KM#	Date	Mintage	Fine	VF	XF	Unc
8	1877A	6.746	20.00	35.00	80.00	175.00
	1877B	3.097	22.50	40.00	90.00	220.00
	1877C	2.820	20.00	40.00	90.00	220.00
	1877D	5.315	18.00	30.00	80.00	190.00
	1877E	2.296	20.00	35.00	90.00	220.00
	1877F	2.145	20.00	35.00	90.00	220.00
	1877G	2.061	22.50	45.00	100.00	250.00
	1877H	1.510	30.00	70.00	150.00	300.00
	1877J	1.337	22.50	45.00	100.00	250.00
	1878E	.364	200.00	300.00	500.00	950.00
	Common date		—	—	Proof	425.00

KM#	Date	Mintage	Fine	VF	XF	Unc
15	1896A	.389	90.00	190.00	275.00	350.00
	1898A	.387	90.00	190.00	275.00	350.00
	1900J	.192	100.00	200.00	300.00	400.00
	1900J	—	—	—	Proof	500.00
	1901A	.194	100.00	225.00	325.00	425.00
	1902F	.095	150.00	250.00	350.00	750.00
	1902F	—	—	—	Proof	500.00
	1903A	.384	125.00	200.00	250.00	325.00
	Common date		—	—	Proof	475.00

1/2 MARK

2.7770 g, .900 SILVER, .0803 oz ASW

KM#	Date	Mintage	Fine	VF	XF	Unc
17	1905A	37.766	.75	1.00	5.00	12.00
	1905D	7.636	.75	1.50	5.00	12.00
	1905E	4.908	.75	1.50	5.00	12.00
	1905F	6.310	.75	1.50	5.00	12.00
	1905G	3.886	.75	1.50	5.00	15.00
	1905J	6.316	.75	1.50	5.00	12.00
	1906A	29.754	.75	1.50	5.00	12.00
	1906D	11.977	.75	1.50	5.00	12.00
	1906E	5.821	.75	1.50	5.00	15.00
	1906F	8.036	.75	1.50	5.00	12.00

KM#	Date	Mintage	Fine	VF	XF	Unc
17	1906G	4.273	.75	1.50	5.00	18.00
	1906J	2.179	.75	2.50	7.50	22.50
	1907A	14.168	.75	1.50	5.00	12.00
	1907D	2.884	.75	1.50	5.00	12.00
	1907E	.600	2.50	7.50	17.50	45.00
	1907F	1.202	.75	1.50	5.00	12.00
	1907G	.927	2.50	7.50	17.50	30.00
	1907J	3.268	.75	1.50	5.00	18.00
	1908A	5.018	.75	1.50	5.00	12.00
	1908D	.400	7.50	17.50	22.50	50.00
	1908E	.591	1.75	7.50	17.50	30.00
	1908F	1,000	650.00	1250.	2650.	4000.
	1908G	.675	1.25	5.00	10.00	22.50
	1908/7J	1.309	1.25	5.00	10.00	22.50
	1908J	Inc. Ab.	1.25	5.00	10.00	22.50
	1909A	5.404	.75	1.50	5.00	12.00
	1909/5D	1.001	.75	1.50	5.00	12.00
	1909D	Inc. Ab.	.75	1.50	5.00	12.00
	1909E	.745	1.25	5.00	10.00	20.00
	1909F	.999	.75	2.50	7.50	12.00
	1909G	.607	1.25	5.00	10.00	18.00
	1909J	.816	1.25	5.00	10.00	18.00
	1911A	2.710	1.25	5.00	7.50	20.00
	1911/05D	.703	1.25	5.00	7.50	20.00
	1911D	Inc. Ab.	1.25	5.00	7.50	20.00
	1911E	.376	5.00	17.50	25.00	45.00
	1911F	.502	2.50	7.50	17.50	35.00
	1911G	.610	2.50	7.50	17.50	35.00
	1911J	.418	5.00	17.50	27.50	50.00
	1912A	2.709	1.25	5.00	7.50	20.00
	1912/5D	.703	1.50	10.00	15.00	25.00
	1912D	Inc. Ab.	1.50	10.00	15.00	25.00
	1912E	.369	5.00	17.50	25.00	45.00
	1912F	.501	2.50	7.50	12.50	25.00
	1912J	.399	5.00	17.50	27.50	50.00
	1913A	5.419	.75	1.50	5.00	12.00
	1913/05D	1.406	.75	1.50	5.00	12.00
	1913D	Inc. Ab.	.75	1.50	5.00	12.00
	1913E	.745	2.50	5.00	10.00	18.00
	1913F	1.003	.75	1.50	5.00	12.00
	1913G	.610	1.25	5.00	10.00	18.00
	1913J	.817	1.25	5.00	10.00	25.00
	1914A	13.525	.75	1.50	4.00	10.00
	1914/05D	.328	2.50	10.00	15.00	30.00
	1914D	Inc. Ab.	2.50	10.00	15.00	30.00
	1914J	2.292	.75	3.00	5.00	12.00
	1915A	13.015	.75	1.50	3.50	10.00
	1915/05D	5.117	.75	1.50	3.50	10.00
	1915D	Inc. Ab.	.75	1.50	3.50	10.00
	1915E	3.308	.75	1.50	3.50	10.00
	1915F	5.309	.75	1.50	3.50	10.00
	1915G	2.730	.75	1.50	3.50	10.00
	1915J	2.285	.75	1.50	3.50	10.00
	1916A	9.750	.75	1.50	3.50	10.00
	1916/616D					
		4.397	.75	1.50	3.50	10.00
	1916/05D	I.A.	.75	1.50	3.50	10.00
	1916/5D	I.A.	.75	1.50	3.50	10.00
	1916D	Inc. Ab.	.75	1.50	3.50	10.00
	1916E	1.640	.75	1.50	3.50	10.00
	1916F	2.410	.75	1.50	3.50	10.00
	1916G	1.779	.75	1.50	3.50	10.00
	1916J	1.464	.75	1.50	3.50	10.00
	1917A	14.692	.75	1.50	3.50	10.00
	1917/05D	.979	.75	1.50	3.50	10.00
	1917D	Inc. Ab.	.75	1.50	3.50	10.00
	1917E	1.561	.75	1.50	3.50	10.00
	1917F	.450	2.50	10.00	15.00	50.00
	1917G	.619	2.50	10.00	15.00	50.00
	1917J	1.039	1.50	4.00	6.00	15.00
	1918A*	14.622	.75	1.50	3.50	10.00
	1918/05D	3.670	.75	1.50	3.50	10.00
	1918D*	Inc. Ab.	.75	1.50	3.50	10.00
	1918E*	2.807	2.50	7.50	10.00	20.00
	1918E	19 pcs.	—	—	Proof	—
	1918F*	4.010	.75	1.50	4.00	10.00
	1918G*	1.032	1.50	6.00	10.00	15.00
	1918J*	3.452	.75	1.50	5.00	12.00
	1919A*	9.124	.75	1.50	5.00	12.00
	1919/1619D					
		2.195	.75	1.50	5.00	15.00
	1919/05D	I.A.	.75	1.50	5.00	15.00
	1919D*	Inc. Ab.	.75	1.50	5.00	15.00
	1919E*	1.767	2.50	7.50	12.50	20.00
	1919F*	1.559	2.00	6.00	12.00	25.00
	1919J*	1.875	1.00	3.00	5.00	15.00
	Common date		—	—	Proof	120.00

***NOTE:** Some were issued with a black finish to prevent hoarding.

MARK

5.5500 g, .900 SILVER, .1606 oz ASW

KM#	Date	Mintage	Fine	VF	XF	Unc
7	1873A	.930	2.50	5.00	45.00	175.00
	1873B	.089	12.50	25.00	100.00	250.00
	1873C	.018	65.00	125.00	275.00	600.00
	1873D	.244	5.00	12.50	80.00	185.00
	1873F	.109	10.00	20.00	80.00	200.00
	1874A	6.310	2.50	6.00	40.00	90.00
	1874B	2.672	6.00	15.00	65.00	185.00

KM#	Date	Mintage	Fine	VF	XF	Unc
7	1874C	.840	6.00	15.00	80.00	200.00
	1874D	7.079	2.50	6.00	30.00	100.00
	1874E	3.240	6.00	25.00	65.00	125.00
	1874F	6.155	2.50	8.00	40.00	125.00
	1874G	4.210	2.50	10.00	45.00	125.00
	1874H	1.893	4.00	7.50	75.00	200.00
	1875A	30.340	2.50	7.50	35.00	90.00
	1875B	7.690	2.50	7.50	50.00	125.00
	1875C	6.209	2.50	7.50	50.00	140.00
	1875D	7.538	2.50	5.00	30.00	100.00
	1875E	4.646	2.50	7.50	50.00	125.00
	1875F	7.074	2.50	5.00	20.00	90.00
	1875G	6.072	2.50	7.50	40.00	125.00
	1875H	2.300	3.50	10.00	65.00	175.00
	1875J	7.728	2.50	7.50	40.00	110.00
	1876A	17.297	2.50	5.00	30.00	90.00
	1876C	4.790	2.50	7.50	45.00	110.00
	1876D	2.956	2.50	7.50	50.00	150.00
	1876F	4.161	2.50	7.50	45.00	100.00
	1876G	2.333	2.50	7.50	40.00	125.00
	1876H	2.481	2.50	7.50	50.00	150.00
	1876J	1.109	2.50	7.50	70.00	180.00
	1877A	.697	4.00	7.50	45.00	150.00
	1877B	.048	35.00	100.00	275.00	1600.
	1878A	1.527	2.50	7.50	50.00	125.00
	1878B	.582	5.00	12.50	80.00	325.00
	1878C	.600	10.00	25.00	120.00	475.00
	1878E	.318	7.50	20.00	150.00	850.00
	1878F	1.039	5.00	12.50	60.00	125.00
	1878G	.525	5.00	15.00	110.00	275.00
	1878J	.895	5.00	12.50	50.00	120.00
	1879A	.156	45.00	80.00	160.00	650.00
	1880A	1.071	5.00	12.50	60.00	150.00
	1880D	.338	5.00	12.50	85.00	275.00
	1880E	.173	12.00	25.00	125.00	400.00
	1880F	.223	12.00	25.00	125.00	450.00
	1880G	.146	50.00	75.00	150.00	550.00
	1880H	.164	25.00	50.00	150.00	550.00
	1880J	.197	10.00	22.50	110.00	600.00
	1881A	6.386	2.50	5.00	30.00	85.00
	1881D	2.040	2.50	5.00	30.00	75.00
	1881E	1.081	5.00	10.00	70.00	115.00
	1881F	1.455	4.00	10.00	60.00	100.00
	1881G	.426	7.50	12.50	75.00	225.00
	1881H	.387	7.50	12.50	75.00	225.00
	1881J	.790	5.00	10.00	60.00	100.00
	1882A	1.474	2.50	12.50	55.00	150.00
	1882G	.459	10.00	25.00	100.00	400.00
	1882H	.109	35.00	70.00	200.00	600.00
	1882J	.098	10.00	25.00	100.00	400.00
	1883A	.809	5.00	10.00	50.00	100.00
	1883D	.208	30.00	50.00	100.00	300.00
	1883E	.112	30.00	60.00	250.00	800.00
	1883F	.148	20.00	35.00	140.00	700.00
	1883G	.091	65.00	125.00	325.00	1050.
	1883J	.121	25.00	40.00	225.00	900.00
	1885A	1.467	2.50	5.00	35.00	85.00
	1885G	.468	5.00	15.00	75.00	250.00
	1885J	.413	7.50	15.00	90.00	200.00
	1886A	1.101	3.00	7.50	35.00	75.00
	1886D	1.445	3.00	7.50	40.00	90.00
	1886E	.764	7.50	15.00	60.00	120.00
	1886F	1.031	2.50	6.00	40.00	80.00
	1886G	.161	15.00	45.00	135.00	225.00
	1886J	.427	7.50	15.00	75.00	150.00
	1887A	3.006	2.50	7.50	40.00	80.00
	Common date		—	—	Proof	350.00

KM#	Date	Mintage	Fine	VF	XF	Unc
14	1891A	.711	7.50	12.50	20.00	80.00
	1891D	Inc.Be.	350.00	600.00	950.00	1750.
	1892A	.909	5.00	12.50	20.00	80.00
	1892D	.418	5.00	15.00	30.00	110.00
	1892E	.223	10.00	16.00	40.00	175.00
	1892F	.302	5.00	15.00	30.00	135.00
	1892G	.183	12.00	18.00	65.00	175.00
	1892J	.237	15.00	35.00	65.00	140.00
	1893A	1.633	2.50	5.00	10.00	70.00
	1893D	.425	2.50	5.00	30.00	85.00
	1893E	.224	7.50	17.50	40.00	130.00
	1893F	.300	7.50	15.00	30.00	110.00
	1893J	.254	5.00	12.50	40.00	110.00
	1894G	.184	20.00	40.00	90.00	250.00
	1896A	2.160	2.50	5.00	12.50	50.00
	1896D	.562	2.50	6.00	15.00	80.00
	1896E	.297	5.00	15.00	40.00	110.00
	1896F	.401	2.50	6.00	30.00	85.00
	1896G	.243	7.50	20.00	65.00	175.00
	1896J	.326	5.00	15.00	40.00	135.00
	1898A	1.000	5.00	12.50	20.00	85.00
	1899A	1.439	2.50	5.00	12.50	60.00
	1899D	.633	2.50	5.00	15.00	65.00
	1899E	.335	5.00	15.00	25.00	90.00
	1899F	.393	4.00	10.00	20.00	75.00
	1899G	.274	4.00	10.00	25.00	145.00
	1899J	.368	4.00	10.00	25.00	125.00
	1900A	1.625	2.50	5.00	10.00	35.00
	1900/800D	.421	2.50	5.00	10.00	60.00
	1900/801D	.915	2.50	5.00	10.00	60.00
	1900D	Inc. Ab.	2.50	5.00	10.00	60.00
14	1900E	.223	5.00	15.00	20.00	65.00
	1900F	.301	4.00	10.00	20.00	70.00
	1900G	.183	7.50	17.50	60.00	175.00
	1900J	.246	10.00	20.00	40.00	125.00
	1901A	3.821	2.50	5.00	10.00	25.00
	1901D	Inc. Ab.	2.50	5.00	12.00	30.00
	1901E	.484	2.50	6.00	17.50	35.00
	1901F	.802	2.50	5.00	10.00	25.00
	1901G	.579	2.50	5.00	20.00	65.00
	1901J	.531	2.50	5.00	20.00	65.00
	1902A	5.222	1.50	4.00	8.00	22.00
	1902D	1.546	1.50	4.00	8.00	22.00
	1902E	.819	1.50	4.00	10.00	45.00
	1902F	.953	1.50	4.00	8.00	45.00
	1902G	.270	6.00	25.00	35.00	110.00
	1902J	.898	2.50	5.00	10.00	60.00
	1903A	3.965	1.25	2.00	5.00	20.00
	1903/803D	.914	1.25	2.50	6.00	22.00
	1903D	Inc. Ab.	1.25	2.50	6.00	22.00
	1903E	.485	5.00	12.00	20.00	60.00
	1903F	.652	5.00	7.50	12.00	50.00
	1903G	.614	2.50	5.00	12.00	50.00
	1903J	.531	5.00	12.00	20.00	60.00
	1904A	3.243	1.25	2.00	5.00	20.00
	1904D	1.761	1.25	2.00	6.00	25.00
	1904E	.931	2.50	5.00	10.00	27.50
	1904F	1.255	2.50	4.00	7.50	25.00
	1904G	.664	2.50	5.00	10.00	30.00
	1904J	1.021	2.50	5.00	10.00	45.00
	1905A	10.303	1.25	2.00	5.00	15.00
	1905D	1.759	2.50	4.00	7.50	20.00
	1905E	.931	2.50	4.00	10.00	27.50
	1905F	Inc.Ab.	2000.	2800.	4500.	6000.
	1905G	.860	2.50	5.00	10.00	27.50
	1905J	1.021	1.50	5.00	6.00	40.00
	1906A	5.414	1.25	2.50	5.00	20.00
	1906D	1.412	1.25	2.50	7.50	20.00
	1906E	.745	1.50	5.00	10.00	30.00
	1906F	2.257	1.25	2.50	5.00	25.00
	1906G	.609	2.50	5.00	10.00	30.00
	1906G 10-30 pcs.		—	—	Proof	—
	1906J	.372	2.50	6.00	12.50	40.00
	1907A	9.201	1.25	2.50	5.00	20.00
	1907D	2.387	1.25	2.50	5.00	20.00
	1907E	1.265	1.25	2.50	6.00	25.00
	1907F	1.704	1.25	2.50	6.00	25.00
	1907G	1.035	1.25	2.50	6.00	25.00
	1907J	1.833	1.25	2.50	6.00	25.00
	1908A	4.338	1.25	2.50	5.00	15.00
	1908D	1.126	1.25	2.50	5.00	20.00
	1908E	.596	2.50	5.00	10.00	40.00
	1908F	.802	1.25	2.50	5.00	35.00
	1908G	.488	2.50	5.00	10.00	25.00
	1908J	.653	2.50	5.00	10.00	25.00
	1909A	4.151	1.25	2.50	5.00	15.00
	1909D	1.968	1.25	3.00	5.00	20.00
	1909E	Inc.Be.	25.00	75.00	125.00	200.00
	1909G	.854	5.00	20.00	30.00	45.00
	1909J	.053	75.00	150.00	200.00	300.00
	1910A	5.870	1.25	1.50	4.00	15.00
	1910D	1.406	1.25	2.50	5.00	20.00
	1910E	1.050	2.50	5.00	7.50	27.50
	1910F	1.631	2.50	5.00	7.50	27.50
	1910G	.610	2.50	5.00	12.00	25.00
	1910J	1.094	2.50	5.00	12.00	27.50
	1911A	5.693	1.25	2.50	5.00	15.00
	1911D	.126	10.00	20.00	35.00	70.00
	1911E	.738	4.00	6.00	12.50	32.50
	1911F	.773	2.50	6.00	12.50	32.50
	1911G	.305	4.00	6.00	12.50	35.00
	1911J	.812	4.00	6.00	12.50	32.00
	1912A	2.439	1.25	2.50	5.00	15.00
	1912D	.632	1.25	2.50	5.00	20.00
	1912E	.708	2.50	5.00	12.00	25.00
	1912F	.502	2.50	5.00	12.00	27.50
	1912J	.409	2.50	6.00	12.50	40.00
	1913F	.450	10.00	27.50	45.00	70.00
	1913G	.275	20.00	40.00	60.00	90.00
	1913J	.368	15.00	30.00	45.00	70.00
	1914A	11.304	1.25	1.50	3.00	10.00
	1914/9D	3.515	1.25	1.50	3.00	10.00
	1914D	Inc. Ab.	1.25	1.50	3.00	10.00
	1914E	2.235	1.25	1.50	3.00	10.00
	1914F	2.300	1.25	1.50	3.00	10.00
	1914G	1.911	1.25	1.50	3.00	10.00
	1914J	2.978	1.25	1.50	3.00	10.00
	1915A	13.817	1.25	1.50	3.00	10.00
	1915D	4.218	1.25	1.50	3.00	10.00
	1915E	2.235	1.25	1.50	3.00	10.00
	1915F	2.911	1.25	1.50	3.00	10.00
	1915G	1.749	1.25	1.50	3.00	10.00
	1915J	1.634	1.25	1.50	3.00	10.00
	1916F	.306	12.00	22.00	32.00	65.00
	Common date		—	—	Proof	140.00

WW I OCCUPATION COINAGE

Issued under the authority of the German Military Commander of the East for use in Estonia, Latvia, Lithuania, Poland, and Northwest Russia.

KOPEK

IRON

KM#	Date	Mintage	Fine	VF	XF	Unc
21	1916A	11.942	2.50	5.00	10.00	25.00
	1916A	—	—	—	Proof	75.00
	1916J	8.000	2.50	5.00	10.00	25.00
	1916J	—	—	—	Proof	75.00

2 KOPEKS

IRON

KM#	Date	Mintage	Fine	VF	XF	Unc
22	1916A	6.973	2.50	5.00	12.50	30.00
	1916A	—	—	—	Proof	75.00
	1916J	8.000	2.50	5.00	12.50	30.00
	1916J	—	—	—	Proof	75.00

3 KOPEKS

IRON

KM#	Date	Mintage	Fine	VF	XF	Unc
23	1916A	8.670	2.50	5.00	12.50	35.00
	1916A	—	—	—	Proof	75.00
	1916J	8.000	2.50	5.00	12.50	35.00
	1916J	—	—	—	Proof	75.00

WEIMAR REPUBLIC

1919-1933

RENTENPFENNIG

BRONZE

KM#	Date	Mintage	Fine	VF	XF	Unc
30	1923A	12.629	.15	.50	1.50	5.00
	1923D	*2.314	.25	2.00	5.00	22.00
	1923E	2.200	1.50	4.00	12.00	35.00
	1923F	.160	1.50	4.00	12.00	35.00
	1923G	1.004	.25	1.50	8.00	30.00
	1923J	1.470	.25	1.50	6.00	20.00
	1924A	55.273	.15	.50	2.50	7.50
	1924D	17.540	.20	1.50	5.00	10.00
	1924E	6.838	.20	1.50	6.00	12.50
	1924F	10.347	.20	1.50	5.00	10.00
	1924G	7.366	.25	1.50	6.00	12.50
	1924J	11.024	.20	1.50	5.00	10.00
	1925A	—	300.00	500.00	650.00	800.00
	1929F	—	125.00	225.00	350.00	500.00
	Common date		—	—	Proof	120.00

REICHSPFENNIG

BRONZE

KM#	Date	Mintage	Fine	VF	XF	Unc
37	1924A	13.496	.10	.25	1.00	6.00
	1924D	6.206	.10	.25	1.00	6.00
	1924E	1.100	40.00	175.00	250.00	475.00
	1924F	2.650	.15	.30	1.00	6.00
	1924G	5.100	.15	.50	2.00	8.50
	1924J	24.400	.10	.25	1.00	6.00
	1925A	40.925	.10	.25	1.00	5.00
	1925D	1.558	5.00	12.50	22.50	40.00
	1925E	10.460	.10	.25	1.00	6.00
	1925F	5.673	.10	.25	1.00	6.00
	1925G	13.502	.10	.25	1.00	6.00
	1925J	30.300	.10	.25	1.00	6.00

KM#	Date	Mintage	Fine	VF	XF	Unc
37	1927A	4.671	.10	.25	1.00	6.00
	1927D	4.203	.15	.50	2.00	8.50
	1927E	8.000	.15	.50	3.50	12.00
	1927F	2.350	.25	1.00	2.00	8.50
	1927G	3.236	.15	.50	3.50	12.00
	1928A	19.300	.10	.25	1.00	3.50
	1928D	10.200	.10	.25	1.00	3.50
	1928F	8.672	.10	.25	1.00	3.50
	1928G	3.764	.15	.50	2.00	6.00
	1929A	37.170	.10	.25	1.00	3.50
	1929D	9.337	.10	.25	1.00	3.50
	1929E	6.600	.15	.30	1.00	5.00
	1929F	3.150	.10	.25	1.50	6.00
	1929G	1.986	.15	.50	2.00	6.00
	1930A	40.997	.10	.25	1.00	3.50
	1930D	6.441	.10	.25	1.00	3.50
	1930E	1.412	6.00	12.00	25.00	60.00
	1930F	6.415	.10	.50	1.50	6.00
	1930G	5.017	.10	.25	1.00	3.50
	1931A	38.481	.10	.25	1.00	3.50
	1931D	5.998	.10	.25	1.00	3.50
	1931E	12.800	.15	.50	2.00	6.00
	1931F	12.591	.10	.25	1.00	3.50
	1931G	2.622	.15	.50	2.50	7.50
	1932A	17.096	.10	.25	1.00	3.50
	1933A	37.846	.10	.25	1.00	3.50
	1933E	2.945	.35	2.00	4.50	9.00
	1933F	5.023	.10	.50	1.00	5.00
	1934A	51.214	.10	.25	1.00	5.00
	1934D	7.408	.10	.25	1.00	5.00
	1934E	4.628	.50	3.50	7.50	15.00
	1934F	5.667	.10	.25	1.00	5.00
	1934G	2.450	.15	.30	1.00	5.00
	1934J	4.271	.15	.50	3.00	8.50
	1935A	35.894	.10	.25	1.00	5.00
	1935D	15.489	.10	.25	1.00	5.00
	1935E	8.351	.15	.50	2.50	7.50
	1935F	12.094	.10	.25	1.00	5.00
	1935G	7.454	.10	.25	1.00	5.00
	1935J	8.505	.10	.25	1.00	5.00
	1936A	*50.949	.10	.25	1.00	5.00
	1936D	12.262	.10	.25	1.00	5.00
	1936E	2.576	.50	3.00	10.00	15.00
	1936F	6.915	.10	.25	1.00	5.00
	1936G	*2.940	.15	.30	1.00	5.00
	1936J	*5.421	.15	.50	2.00	7.50
	Common date		—	—	Proof	85.00

2 RENTENPFENNIG

BRONZE

KM#	Date	Mintage	Fine	VF	XF	Unc
31	1923A	8.587	.15	.50	2.50	12.50
	1923D	1.490	.15	.50	3.00	10.00
	1923F	Inc.Ab.	.50	5.00	15.00	35.00
	1923G	Inc.Ab.	.25	1.00	6.50	15.00
	1923J	Inc.Ab.	.50	5.00	12.50	25.00
	1924A	80.864	.10	.25	2.50	10.00
	1924D	19.899	.10	.25	2.50	10.00
	1924E	6.595	.15	.50	3.00	12.00
	1924F	14.969	.15	.50	3.00	10.00
	1924G	10.349	.15	.50	3.00	10.00
	1924J	21.196	.25	1.00	5.00	10.00
	Common date		—	—	Proof	140.00

2 REICHSPFENNIG

BRONZE

KM#	Date	Mintage	Fine	VF	XF	Unc
38	1923F	—	400.00	600.00	750.00	1000.
	1924A	19.620	.10	.25	1.00	6.00
	1924D	3.482	.10	.30	1.50	12.00
	1924E	4.253	.15	1.50	7.50	20.00
	1924F	4.567	.10	.20	1.00	10.00
	1924G	7.560	.10	.20	1.00	10.00
	1924J	7.489	.10	.25	1.00	10.00
	1925A	22.433	.10	.25	1.00	6.00
	1925D	2.412	.15	.60	2.50	15.00
	1925E	5.414	.10	.30	1.50	10.00
	1925F	4.851	.10	.30	1.50	10.00
	1925G	2.456	.25	1.50	7.50	20.00
	1936A	3.220	.25	2.00	7.50	17.50
	1936D	6.525	.10	.30	1.50	10.00
	1936E	.573	5.00	15.00	22.50	50.00
	1936F	3.100	.15	.50	1.00	6.00
	Common date		—	—	Proof	90.00

4 REICHSPFENNIG

BRONZE

KM#	Date	Mintage	Fine	VF	XF	Unc
75	1932A	27.101	2.50	6.50	10.00	20.00
	1932A	—	—	—	Proof	150.00
	1932D	7.055	2.50	5.00	12.50	22.50
	1932D	—	—	—	Proof	150.00
	1932E	3.729	2.50	8.50	15.00	40.00
	1932E	—	—	—	Proof	150.00
	1932F	5.022	2.50	8.50	15.00	40.00
	1932F	—	—	—	Proof	150.00
	1932G	3.050	3.00	10.00	17.50	50.00
	1932G	—	—	—	Proof	150.00
	1932J	4.094	2.50	8.50	15.00	40.00
	1932J	—	—	—	Proof	150.00

5 RENTENPFENNIG

ALUMINUM-BRONZE

KM#	Date	Mintage	Fine	VF	XF	Unc
32	1923A	3.083	.20	1.00	2.50	10.00
	1923D	Inc.Be.	.30	1.50	3.00	17.50
	1923F	Inc.Be.	35.00	75.00	125.00	200.00
	1923G	Inc.Be.	25.00	50.00	100.00	160.00
	1924A	171.966	.10	.50	2.00	7.50
	1924D	31.163	.20	.50	1.00	6.00
	1924E	12.206	.20	.50	1.00	7.50
	1924F	29.032	.20	.50	1.00	7.50
	1924G	19.217	.20	.50	1.00	7.50
	1924J	32.332	.20	.50	1.00	7.50
	1925F	1 known	—	4800.	—	—
	Common date		—	—	Proof	90.00

5 REICHSPFENNIG

ALUMINUM-BRONZE

KM#	Date	Mintage	Fine	VF	XF	Unc
39	1924A	14.469	.20	.50	2.50	15.00
	1924D	8.139	.20	.50	2.50	8.00
	1924E	5.976	.20	1.00	5.00	15.00
	1924F	3.134	.20	1.00	5.00	15.00
	1924G	4.790	.20	1.00	7.50	17.50
	1924J	2.200	.25	1.00	3.50	12.00
	1925A	85.239	.15	.40	2.00	7.00
	1925D	39.750	.15	.35	2.00	7.00
	1925E	17.554	.20	1.00	5.00	12.00
	1925F large 5	20.990	.15	.35	2.50	6.00
	1925F small 5	Inc. Ab.	.15	.35	2.50	6.00
	1925G	10.232	.20	1.00	5.00	17.50
	1925J	10.950	.20	1.00	5.00	17.50
	1926A	22.377	.15	.40	2.00	12.00
	1926E	5.990	10.00	20.00	35.00	50.00
	1926F	2.871	5.00	12.50	25.00	35.00
	1930A	7.418	.20	.50	3.00	15.00
	1935A	19.178	.15	.25	.50	6.00
	1935D	5.480	.15	.35	1.00	8.00
	1935E	2.384	.20	.50	3.00	12.00
	1935F	4.585	.15	.40	1.50	8.00
	1935G	2.652	.20	.50	3.00	12.00
	1935J	2.614	.20	.50	3.00	12.00
	1936A	36.992	.15	.25	.50	6.00
	1936D	8.108	.15	.35	1.00	8.00
	1936E	2.981	.20	.50	3.00	12.00
	1936F	6.643	.15	.30	1.00	7.00
	1936G	2.274	.20	.35	1.00	8.00
	1936J	4.470	.20	.50	3.00	12.00
	Common date		—	—	Proof	75.00

10 RENTENPFENNIG

ALUMINUM-BRONZE

KM#	Date	Mintage	Fine	VF	XF	Unc
33	1923A	Inc.Be.	.25	2.50	6.00	17.50
	1923D	Inc.Be.	.50	5.00	10.00	25.00
	1923F	Inc. Be.	45.00	95.00	160.00	275.00
33	1923G	Inc. Be.	2.50	12.50	25.00	50.00
	1924A	169.956	.20	.40	2.50	7.50
	1924D	33.894	.15	.50	1.00	10.00
	1924E	18.679	.20	1.00	1.50	15.00
	1924F	42.237	.15	.50	1.00	10.00
	1924F	—	—	—	Proof	95.00
	1924G	18.758	.20	.50	1.00	15.00
	1924J	33.928	.15	.50	1.00	15.00
	1925F	.013	250.00	500.00	750.00	1000.

10 REICHSPFENNIG

ALUMINUM-BRONZE

KM#	Date	Mintage	Fine	VF	XF	Unc
40	1924A	20.883	.15	.25	1.00	12.50
	1924D	9.639	.15	.50	1.50	15.00
	1924E	5.185	.20	1.00	1.50	17.50
	1924F	2.758	1.00	7.50	15.00	37.50
	1924G	4.363	.20	1.00	1.50	17.50
	1924J	3.993	.15	.50	1.00	15.00
	1925A	102.319	.10	.15	.50	10.00
	1925D	36.853	.10	.15	.50	10.00
	1925E	18.700	.15	.50	1.00	15.00
	1925F	12.516	.10	.15	.50	12.50
	1925G	10.360	.10	.50	1.00	12.50
	1925J	8.755	4.00	12.50	25.00	37.50
	1926A	14.390	.20	2.00	4.00	15.00
	1926G	1.481	2.50	10.00	20.00	37.50
	1928A	2.308	2.00	6.00	9.00	17.50
	1928G	Inc. Be.	40.00	60.00	125.00	180.00
	1929A	25.712	.15	.50	1.50	12.50
	1929D	7.049	.15	.50	1.50	12.50
	1929E	3.138	.20	1.00	2.50	17.50
	1929F	3.740	.20	1.00	2.50	17.50
	1929G	2.729	.30	3.50	6.00	22.00
	1929J	4.086	.20	2.50	5.00	18.50
	1930A	7.540	.20	2.00	2.50	12.50
	1930D	2.148	.25	3.50	5.00	15.00
	1930E	2.090	1.00	5.00	15.00	32.50
	1930F	2.006	1.00	5.00	15.00	32.50
	1930G	1.542	5.00	15.00	30.00	60.00
	1930J	1.637	2.50	5.00	12.50	30.00
	1931A	9.661	.20	2.50	5.00	15.00
	1931D	.664	15.00	35.00	65.00	100.00
	1931F	1.482	2.50	10.00	12.50	32.50
	1931G	.038	150.00	275.00	450.00	600.00
	1932A	4.528	.25	3.50	6.00	17.50
	1932D	2.812	.50	5.00	7.50	17.50
	1932E	1.491	6.00	12.50	17.50	40.00
	1932F	1.806	6.00	12.50	17.50	40.00
	1932G	.137	300.00	600.00	900.00	1100.
	1933A	1.349	15.00	25.00	50.00	100.00
	1933G	1.046	5.00	10.00	16.50	40.00
	1933J	1.634	1.00	8.50	15.00	35.00
	1934A	3.200	.20	1.00	6.00	17.50
	1934D	1.252	1.00	7.50	10.00	25.00
	1934E	Inc. Be.	20.00	35.00	50.00	100.00
	1934F	.100	15.00	30.00	50.00	100.00
	1934G	.150	15.00	30.00	50.00	125.00
	1935A	35.890	.10	.15	1.00	8.50
	1935D	8.960	.10	.25	1.50	12.50
	1935E	5.966	.15	.35	2.00	15.00
	1935F	7.944	.10	.30	1.50	12.50
	1935G	4.847	.10	.50	3.00	15.00
	1935J	8.995	.10	.30	1.50	12.50
	1936A	24.527	.10	.15	.50	7.50
	1936D	8.092	.10	.20	1.00	12.50
	1936E	2.441	.20	.50	2.50	15.00
	1936F	4.889	.10	.30	1.50	12.50
	1936G	1.715	.15	.60	2.50	15.00
	1936J	1.632	.25	3.00	8.00	17.50
	Common date		—	—	Proof	85.00

50 PFENNIG

ALUMINUM

KM#	Date	Mintage	Fine	VF	XF	Unc
27	1919A	7.173	.25	1.50	4.00	6.00
	1919D	.791	.50	1.50	3.50	10.00
	1919E	.930	2.00	7.00	15.00	30.00
	1919E	35 pcs.	—	—	Proof	—
	1919F	.160	5.00	10.00	20.00	50.00
	1919G	.660	.75	5.00	7.50	12.50
	1919J	.800	3.00	8.00	17.00	40.00
	1920A	119.793	.10	.15	.25	1.50
	1920D	28.306	.10	.15	.25	1.50
	1920E	14.400	.25	1.50	4.00	10.00
	1920E	226 pcs.	—	—	Proof	65.00
	1920F	10.932	.10	.15	.25	1.50
	1920G	5.040	.20	1.50	2.50	5.00
	1920J	15.423	.10	.25	1.00	4.00
	1921A	184.468	.10	.15	.25	1.50
	1921D	48.729	.10	.15	.25	1.50

KM#	Date	Mintage	Fine	VF	XF	Unc
27	1921E	31.210	.15	1.50	2.50	5.00
	1921E	332 pcs.	—	—	Proof	65.00
	1921F	46.950	.10	.15	.25	1.50
	1921G	19.107	.10	.20	.50	1.50
	1921J	28.013	.10	.25	1.00	4.00
	1922A	145.215	.10	.15	.25	1.50
	1922D	58.019	.10	.15	.25	1.50
	1922E	33.930	.15	1.50	2.50	5.00
	1922E	333 pcs.	—	—	Proof	65.00
	1922F	33.000	.10	.15	.25	1.50
	1922G	36.745	.10	.20	.50	1.50
	1922J	36.202	.25	2.50	4.50	9.00

50 RENTENPFENNIG

ALUMINUM-BRONZE

KM#	Date	Mintage	Fine	VF	XF	Unc
34	1923A	.451	5.00	15.00	25.00	50.00
	1923D	.192	12.50	17.50	30.00	55.00
	1923F	.120	45.00	90.00	120.00	220.00
	1923G	.120	15.00	25.00	55.00	90.00
	1923J	4,000	600.00	1200.	1600.	2200.
	1924A	117.365	5.00	10.00	15.00	30.00
	1924D	30.971	5.00	10.00	15.00	40.00
	1924E	14.668	5.00	10.00	20.00	45.00
	1924F	21.968	5.00	10.00	15.00	40.00
	1924G	13.349	7.50	15.00	25.00	50.00
	1924J	17.252	5.00	10.00	15.00	40.00
	Common date		—	—	Proof	200.00

50 REICHSPFENNIG

ALUMINUM-BRONZE

KM#	Date	Mintage	Fine	VF	XF	Unc
41	1924A	.801	500.00	850.00	1150.	1750.
	1924A	—	—	—	Proof	1850.
	1924E	Inc.Be.	1000.	2000.	3000.	5000.
	1924F	.055	1250.	2500.	4250.	6750.
	1924F	—	—	—	Proof	10,500.
	1924G	.011	1500.	3250.	5750.	8500.
	1924G	—	—	—	Proof	—
	1925E	1.805	500.00	800.00	1000.	1500.
	1925E	196 pcs.	—	—	Proof	1850.
	1925F	—	—	—	Proof	24,000.

NOTE: Peus Auction #324 4-89 1924F and 1925F proofs realized $10,360 and $23,830 respectively.

NICKEL

KM#	Date	Mintage	Fine	VF	XF	Unc
49	1927A	16.309	2.00	3.50	5.00	10.00
	1927D	2.228	2.50	5.00	7.50	12.50
	1927E	1.070	5.00	10.00	15.00	20.00
	1927F	1.940	2.50	5.00	7.50	12.50
	1927G	1.756	4.00	7.50	10.00	17.50
	1927J	4.056	2.50	5.00	7.50	12.50
	1928A	43.864	.25	1.50	3.50	7.50
	1928D	14.088	.50	2.50	5.00	10.00
	1928E	8.618	.50	3.50	6.00	12.50
	1928F	9.954	.50	2.50	5.00	10.00
	1928G	6.177	.50	4.50	7.50	15.00
	1928J	6.565	.50	2.50	5.00	10.00
	1929A	10.298	.50	2.00	4.00	7.50
	1929D	1.965	.50	3.50	6.00	12.50
	1929E	—		—	Reported, not confirmed	
	1929F	1.162	5.00	12.50	20.00	32.50
	1930A	4.128	.50	4.50	7.50	12.50
	1930D	1.406	2.00	12.00	17.50	30.00
	1930E	.745	5.00	17.50	25.00	45.00
	1930F	.320	20.00	40.00	65.00	100.00
	1930G	.610	5.00	20.00	40.00	50.00
	1930J	.526	3.00	20.00	35.00	45.00
	1930	—	—	—	—	—
	1931A	5.624	.50	4.00	7.50	10.00
	1931D	1.125	1.50	12.50	17.50	30.00
	1931F	1.484	1.50	12.00	16.00	25.00
	1931G	.060	45.00	90.00	135.00	200.00
	1931J	.291	25.00	50.00	65.00	100.00
	1932E	.598	20.00	50.00	70.00	16.00
	1932G	.096	875.00	1500.	1750.	2250.
	1933G	.333	40.00	70.00	100.00	185.00
	1933J	.654	35.00	65.00	90.00	140.00
	1935A	6.390	.50	4.00	6.00	8.50

KM#	Date	Mintage	Fine	VF	XF	Unc
49	1935D	2.812	2.50	7.50	15.00	20.00
	1935E	.745	7.50	30.00	40.00	50.00
	1935F	2.006	2.50	7.50	10.00	15.00
	1935G	.650	12.50	37.50	50.00	70.00
	1935J	1.635	2.00	15.00	20.00	27.50
	1935	—	1.00	6.00	12.50	25.00
	1936A	7.696	2.50	5.00	7.50	12.50
	1936D	.844	4.00	20.00	35.00	70.00
	1936E	1.190	5.00	15.00	30.00	60.00
	1936F	.602	7.50	17.50	35.00	75.00
	1936G	.936	5.00	15.00	30.00	40.00
	1936J	.490	25.00	75.00	100.00	160.00
	1937A	10.842	.25	2.50	5.00	7.50
	1937D	2.814	.50	4.00	7.50	10.00
	1937F	1.700	.50	2.50	10.00	12.50
	1937J	.300	45.00	95.00	120.00	175.00
	1938E	1.200	7.50	12.50	22.50	30.00
	1938G	1.299	7.50	12.50	25.00	35.00
	1938J	1.333	7.50	15.00	25.00	35.00
	Common date		—	—	Proof	150.00

MARK

5.0000 g, .500 SILVER, .0803 oz ASW

KM#	Date	Mintage	Fine	VF	XF	Unc
42	1924A	75.536	4.00	9.00	15.00	35.00
	1924D	17.099	5.00	10.00	22.50	45.00
	1924E	12.293	5.00	10.00	22.50	45.00
	1924E	115 pcs.	—	—	Proof	275.00
	1924F	16.550	5.00	10.00	18.00	40.00
	1924G	10.065	6.00	12.00	25.00	65.00
	1924J	13.481	5.00	10.00	20.00	45.00
	1925A	13.878	6.00	12.00	35.00	100.00
	1925D	6.100	8.00	15.00	35.00	80.00
	Common date		—	—	Proof	200.00

REICHSMARK

5.0000 g, .500 SILVER, .0803 oz ASW

KM#	Date	Mintage	Fine	VF	XF	Unc
44	1925A	34.527	3.00	10.00	20.00	40.00
	1925A	600 pcs.	—	—	Proof	200.00
	1925D	13.854	3.00	12.50	22.50	50.00
	1925E	6.460	7.50	20.00	32.00	60.00
	1925F	8.035	7.50	15.00	27.50	55.00
	1925G	4.520	7.50	15.00	30.00	55.00
	1925J	6.800	7.50	15.00	25.00	55.00
	1926A	35.555	6.50	10.00	22.50	45.00
	1926D	4.424	7.50	15.00	27.50	60.00
	1926E	3.225	7.50	15.00	45.00	90.00
	1926E	31 pcs.	—	—	Proof	200.00
	1926F	3.045	7.50	27.50	40.00	75.00
	1926G	3.410	7.50	27.50	40.00	75.00
	1926J	1.290	25.00	75.00	120.00	225.00
	1927A	.364	100.00	275.00	375.00	700.00
	1927F	1.959	20.00	60.00	100.00	200.00
	1927J	2.451	15.00	45.00	75.00	150.00

2 REICHSMARK

10.0000 g, .500 SILVER, .1608 oz ASW

KM#	Date	Mintage	Fine	VF	XF	Unc
45	1925A	16.145	7.50	12.50	22.00	50.00
	1925D	2.272	10.00	15.00	35.00	60.00
	1925E	1.971	10.00	17.50	40.00	85.00
	1925E	101 pcs.	—	—	Proof	200.00
	1925F	2.414	10.00	17.50	35.00	60.00
	1925G	.929	10.00	20.00	45.00	100.00
	1925J	2.326	10.00	17.50	35.00	60.00
	1926A	31.645	5.00	10.00	20.00	45.00
	1926D	11.322	5.00	10.00	22.00	50.00
	1926E	5.107	7.50	12.50	30.00	60.00
	1926E	30 pcs.	—	—	Proof	—
	1926F	7.115	7.50	12.50	30.00	60.00
	1926G	5.171	7.50	12.50	30.00	60.00
	1926J	5.305	7.50	12.50	30.00	60.00
	1927A	6.399	7.50	12.50	30.00	60.00
	1927D	.466	400.00	850.00	1500.	2250.
	1927E	.373	125.00	325.00	650.00	1200.
	1927E	53 pcs.	—	—	Proof	2150.
	1927F	.502	65.00	125.00	200.00	300.00
	1927J	.540	50.00	100.00	150.00	250.00

KM#	Date	Mintage	Fine	VF	XF	Unc
45	1931D	2.109	20.00	35.00	60.00	115.00
	1931E	1.118	22.50	45.00	75.00	145.00
	1931F	1.505	22.50	45.00	75.00	145.00
	1931G	.915	35.00	75.00	125.00	200.00
	1931J	1.226	22.50	40.00	60.00	125.00
	Common date		—	—	Proof	160.00

3 MARK

ALUMINUM
Reeded edge

KM#	Date	Mintage	Fine	VF	XF	Unc
28	1922A	15.497	.25	2.50	5.00	10.00
	1922A	—	—	—	Proof	75.00
	1922E	2,000	90.00	175.00	300.00	500.00
	1922E	1,000	—	—	Proof	400.00

3rd Anniversary Weimar Constitution

KM#	Date	Mintage	Fine	VF	XF	Unc
29	1922A	32.514	.25	1.00	1.50	2.50
	1922D	8.441	175.00	250.00	350.00	550.00
	1922D	—	—	—	Proof	500.00
	1922E	2.440	.50	5.00	7.50	15.00
	1922E	.022	—	—	Proof	30.00
	1922F	6.023	2.50	12.50	17.50	30.00
	1922G	3.655	.25	2.50	5.00	12.50
	1922J	4.896	.25	1.50	4.00	7.50
	1923E	2.030	17.50	40.00	60.00	85.00
	1923E	2,291	—	—	Proof	75.00

15.0000 g, .500 SILVER, .2411 oz ASW

KM#	Date	Mintage	Fine	VF	XF	Unc
43	1924A	24.386	17.50	30.00	45.00	85.00
	1924D	3.769	12.50	35.00	55.00	110.00
	1924E	3.353	20.00	35.00	55.00	110.00
	1924E	115 pcs.	—	—	Proof	350.00
	1924F	4.518	20.00	35.00	55.00	110.00
	1924G	2.745	20.00	35.00	55.00	110.00
	1924J	3.677	20.00	35.00	55.00	110.00
	1925D	2.558	35.00	75.00	110.00	175.00
	Common date		—	—	Proof	280.00

3 REICHSMARK

15.0000 g, .500 SILVER, .2411 oz ASW
1000th Year of the Rhineland

KM#	Date	Mintage	Fine	VF	XF	Unc
46	1925A	3.052	15.00	30.00	45.00	80.00
	1925A	—	—	—	Proof	150.00
	1925D	1.123	17.50	35.00	50.00	90.00
	1925D	—	—	—	Proof	165.00
	1925E	.441	20.00	40.00	55.00	95.00
	1925E	229 pcs.	—	—	Proof	175.00
	1925F	.173	20.00	40.00	55.00	115.00
	1925F	—	—	—	Proof	250.00
	1925G	.300	20.00	40.00	50.00	90.00
	1925G	—	—	—	Proof	150.00
	1925J	.492	20.00	40.00	50.00	85.00
	1925J	—	—	—	Proof	185.00

700 Years of Freedom for Lubeck

KM#	Date	Mintage	Fine	VF	XF	Unc
48	1926A	.200	60.00	90.00	140.00	215.00
	1926A	—	—	—	Proof	265.00

100th Anniversary of Bremerhaven

KM#	Date	Mintage	Fine	VF	XF	Unc
50	1927A	.150	60.00	90.00	135.00	200.00
	1927A	—	—	—	Proof	330.00

1000th Anniversary - Founding of Nordhausen

KM#	Date	Mintage	Fine	VF	XF	Unc
52	1927A	.100	60.00	90.00	145.00	220.00
	1927A	—	—	—	Proof	400.00

400th Anniversary - Philip University in Marburg

KM#	Date	Mintage	Fine	VF	XF	Unc
53	1927A	.130	60.00	90.00	135.00	200.00
	1927A	—	—	—	Proof	250.00

450th Anniversary - Tubingen University

KM#	Date	Mintage	Fine	VF	XF	Unc
54	1927F	.050	150.00	250.00	400.00	550.00
	1927F	—	—	—	Proof	650.00

900th Anniversary - Founding of Naumburg

KM#	Date	Mintage	Fine	VF	XF	Unc
57	1928A	.100	60.00	90.00	140.00	250.00
	1928A	—	—		Matte Proof	500.00

400th Anniversary - Death of Albrecht Durer

KM#	Date	Mintage	Fine	VF	XF	Unc
58	1928D	.050	150.00	250.00	400.00	550.00
	1928D	—	—		Matte Proof	1500.

1000th Anniversary - Founding of Dinkelsbuhl

KM#	Date	Mintage	Fine	VF	XF	Unc
59	1928D	.040	250.00	450.00	650.00	850.00
	1928D	—	—	—	Proof	2000.

200th Anniversary - Birth of Gotthold Lessing

KM#	Date	Mintage	Fine	VF	XF	Unc
60	1929A	.217	17.50	30.00	60.00	90.00
	1929A	—	—	—	Proof	160.00
	1929D	.056	20.00	35.00	65.00	100.00
	1929D	—	—	—	Proof	250.00
	1929E	.030	20.00	35.00	70.00	110.00
	1929E	—	—	—	Proof	275.00
	1929F	.040	20.00	35.00	65.00	100.00
	1929F	—	—	—	Proof	250.00
	1929G	.024	20.00	35.00	80.00	130.00
	1929G	—	—	—	Proof	300.00
	1929J	.033	20.00	35.00	80.00	120.00
	1929J	—	—	—	Proof	300.00

Waldeck-Prussia Union

KM#	Date	Mintage	Fine	VF	XF	Unc
62	1929A	.170	60.00	90.00	135.00	200.00
	1929A	—	—	—	Proof	275.00

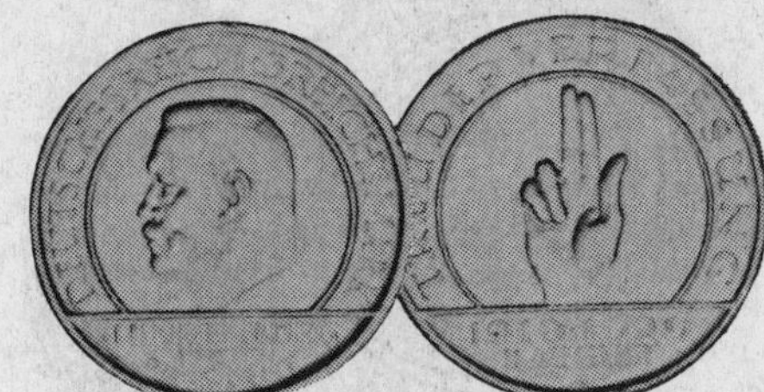

10th Anniversary - Weimar Constitution

KM#	Date	Mintage	Fine	VF	XF	Unc
63	1929A	1.421	17.50	35.00	50.00	75.00
	1929A	—	—	—	Proof	225.00
	1929A	—	—		Matte Proof	—
	1929D	.499	17.50	35.00	55.00	85.00
	1929D	—	—	—	Proof	225.00
	1929E	.122	22.50	45.00	55.00	90.00
	1929E	—	—	—	Proof	300.00
	1929F	.370	17.50	35.00	55.00	90.00
	1929F	—	—	—	Proof	275.00
	1929G	.256	22.50	45.00	60.00	90.00
	1929G	—	—	—	Proof	275.00
	1929J	.342	17.50	35.00	55.00	90.00
	1929J	—	—	—	Proof	275.00

1000th Anniversary - Meissen

KM#	Date	Mintage	Fine	VF	XF	Unc
65	1929E	.200	25.00	45.00	65.00	100.00
	1929E	—	—	—	Proof	300.00

Graf Zeppelin Flight

KM#	Date	Mintage	Fine	VF	XF	Unc
67	1930A	.542	35.00	60.00	85.00	125.00
	1930A	—	—	—	Proof	375.00
	1930D	.141	35.00	60.00	90.00	125.00
	1930D	—	—	—	Proof	250.00
	1930E	.075	35.00	60.00	90.00	150.00
	1930E	—	—	—	Proof	350.00
	1930F	.100	35.00	60.00	90.00	125.00
	1930F	—	—	—	Proof	275.00
	1930G	.061	40.00	65.00	95.00	200.00
	1930G	—	—	—	Proof	350.00
	1930J	.082	40.00	65.00	95.00	190.00
	1930J	—	—	—	Proof	325.00

700th Anniversary - Death of Von Der Vogelweide

KM#	Date	Mintage	Fine	VF	XF	Unc
69	1930A	.163	35.00	55.00	85.00	125.00
	1930A	—	—	—	Proof	225.00
	1930A	—	—		Matte Proof	—
	1930D	.042	35.00	55.00	85.00	135.00
	1930D	—	—	—	Proof	225.00
	1930E	.022	37.50	75.00	100.00	160.00
	1930E	—	—	—	Proof	275.00
	1930F	.030	37.50	75.00	100.00	160.00
	1930F	—	—	—	Proof	325.00
	1930G	.018	45.00	85.00	125.00	170.00
	1930G	—	—	—	Proof	275.00
	1930J	.025	35.00	55.00	85.00	155.00
	1930J	—	—	—	Proof	275.00

Liberation of Rhineland

KM#	Date	Mintage	Fine	VF	XF	Unc
70	1930A	1.734	22.50	35.00	60.00	85.00
	1930A	—	—	—	Proof	150.00
	1930A	—	—		Matte Proof	—
	1930D	.450	22.50	35.00	60.00	85.00
	1930D	—	—	—	Proof	200.00
	1930E	.038	65.00	125.00	175.00	325.00
	1930E	—	—	—	Proof	200.00
	1930F	.321	22.50	35.00	60.00	85.00
	1930F	—	—	—	Proof	160.00
	1930G	.195	22.50	35.00	65.00	120.00
	1930G	—	—	—	Proof	200.00
	1930J	.261	22.50	35.00	65.00	110.00
	1930J	—	—	—	Proof	200.00

300th Anniversary - Magdeburg Rebuilding

KM#	Date	Mintage	Fine	VF	XF	Unc
72	1931A	.100	100.00	150.00	220.00	325.00
	1931A	—	—	—	Proof	450.00

Centenary - Death of vom Stein

KM#	Date	Mintage	Fine	VF	XF	Unc
73	1931A	.150	60.00	90.00	150.00	225.00
	1931A	—	—	—	Proof	300.00

KM#	Date	Mintage	Fine	VF	XF	Unc
74	1931A	13.324	100.00	150.00	275.00	450.00
	1931D	2.232	125.00	200.00	275.00	450.00
	1931E	2.235	125.00	200.00	275.00	450.00
	1931F	2.357	125.00	200.00	275.00	450.00
	1931G	1.468	125.00	200.00	300.00	550.00
	1931J	1.115	125.00	200.00	300.00	550.00
	1932A	2.933	100.00	150.00	275.00	450.00
	1932D	1.986	125.00	200.00	300.00	550.00
	1932F	.653	250.00	450.00	650.00	1000.
	1932G	.210	325.00	900.00	1500.	2250.
	1932J	1.336	125.00	200.00	300.00	550.00
	1933G	*.152	800.00	1450.	2200.	3250.
	Common date		—	—	Proof	1250.

*NOTE: Less than 10 percent of issue was released.

Centenary - Death of Goethe

KM#	Date	Mintage	Fine	VF	XF	Unc
76	1932A	.217	25.00	50.00	85.00	135.00
	1932A	—	—	—	Proof	250.00
	1932D	.056	25.00	50.00	85.00	135.00
	1932D	—	—	—	Proof	250.00
	1932E	.030	40.00	70.00	100.00	165.00
	1932E	—	—	—	Proof	300.00
	1932F	.040	25.00	50.00	85.00	135.00
	1932F	—	—	—	Proof	225.00
	1932F	—	—	Matte Proof		—
	1932G	.024	40.00	70.00	100.00	165.00
	1932G	—	—	—	Proof	300.00
	1932J	.033	30.00	55.00	90.00	165.00
	1932J	—	—	—	Proof	265.00

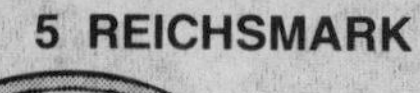

5 REICHSMARK

25.0000 g, .500 SILVER, .4019 oz ASW
1000th Year of the Rhineland

KM#	Date	Mintage	Fine	VF	XF	Unc
47	1925A	.684	35.00	60.00	100.00	170.00
	1925A	—	—	—	Proof	375.00
	1925D	.452	35.00	60.00	100.00	180.00
	1925D	—	—	—	Proof	450.00
	1925E	.204	50.00	75.00	120.00	220.00
	1925E	226 pcs.	—	—	Proof	450.00
	1925F	.212	40.00	65.00	110.00	200.00
	1925F	—	—	—	Proof	475.00
	1925G	.089	45.00	70.00	115.00	210.00
	1925G	—	—	—	Proof	500.00
	1925J	.043	70.00	140.00	175.00	375.00
	1925J	—	—	—	Proof	550.00

100th Anniversary - Bremerhaven

KM#	Date	Mintage	Fine	VF	XF	Unc
51	1927A	.050	175.00	275.00	450.00	700.00
	1927A	—	—	—	Proof	950.00

450th Anniversary - University of Tubingen

KM#	Date	Mintage	Fine	VF	XF	Unc
55	1927F	.040	175.00	275.00	450.00	650.00
	1927F	—	—	—	Proof	750.00

KM#	Date	Mintage	Fine	VF	XF	Unc
56	1927A	7.926	30.00	70.00	100.00	160.00
	1927D	1.471	35.00	80.00	125.00	220.00
	1927E	1.100	40.00	90.00	150.00	300.00
	1927F	.700	30.00	70.00	120.00	200.00
	1927G	.759	60.00	110.00	180.00	325.00
	1927J	1.006	35.00	90.00	150.00	250.00
	1928A	15.466	30.00	70.00	100.00	170.00
	1928D	4.613	30.00	70.00	100.00	170.00
	1928E	2.310	30.00	80.00	125.00	250.00
	1928F	3.771	30.00	70.00	100.00	170.00
	1928G	1.923	35.00	80.00	125.00	220.00
	1928J	2.450	35.00	80.00	125.00	250.00

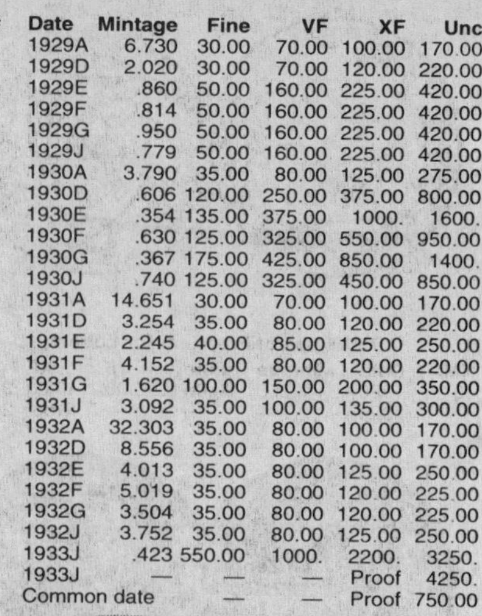

KM#	Date	Mintage	Fine	VF	XF	Unc
56	1929A	6.730	30.00	70.00	100.00	170.00
	1929D	2.020	30.00	70.00	120.00	220.00
	1929E	.860	50.00	160.00	225.00	420.00
	1929F	.814	50.00	160.00	225.00	420.00
	1929G	.950	50.00	160.00	225.00	420.00
	1929J	.779	50.00	160.00	225.00	420.00
	1930A	3.790	35.00	80.00	125.00	275.00
	1930D	.606	120.00	250.00	375.00	800.00
	1930E	.354	135.00	375.00	1000.	1600.
	1930F	.630	125.00	325.00	550.00	950.00
	1930G	.367	175.00	425.00	850.00	1400.
	1930J	.740	125.00	325.00	450.00	850.00
	1931A	14.651	30.00	70.00	100.00	170.00
	1931D	3.254	35.00	80.00	120.00	220.00
	1931E	2.245	40.00	85.00	125.00	250.00
	1931F	4.152	35.00	80.00	120.00	220.00
	1931G	1.620	100.00	150.00	200.00	350.00
	1931J	3.092	35.00	100.00	135.00	300.00
	1932A	32.303	35.00	80.00	100.00	170.00
	1932D	8.556	35.00	80.00	100.00	170.00
	1932E	4.013	35.00	80.00	125.00	250.00
	1932F	5.019	35.00	80.00	120.00	225.00
	1932G	3.504	35.00	80.00	120.00	225.00
	1932J	3.752	35.00	80.00	125.00	250.00
	1933J	.423	550.00	1000.	2200.	3250.
	1933J	—	—	—	Proof	4250.
	Common date		—	—	Proof	750.00

200th Anniversary - Birth of Gotthold Lessing

KM#	Date	Mintage	Fine	VF	XF	Unc
61	1929A	.087	50.00	100.00	125.00	200.00
	1929A	—	—	—	Proof	350.00
	1929D	.022	50.00	100.00	140.00	225.00
	1929D	—	—	—	Proof	350.00
	1929E	.012	60.00	120.00	165.00	285.00
	1929E	—	—	—	Proof	425.00
	1929F	.016	50.00	100.00	140.00	225.00
	1929F	—	—	—	Proof	375.00
	1929G	9,760	60.00	120.00	165.00	285.00
	1929G	—	—	—	Proof	425.00
	1929J	.013	55.00	110.00	140.00	250.00
	1929J	—	—	—	Proof	400.00

10th Anniversary - Weimar Constitution

KM#	Date	Mintage	Fine	VF	XF	Unc
64	1929A	.325	45.00	65.00	125.00	200.00
	1929A	—	—	—	Proof	325.00
	1929D	.084	50.00	90.00	135.00	220.00
	1929D	—	—	—	Proof	400.00
	1929E	.045	50.00	90.00	135.00	220.00
	1929E	—	—	—	Proof	650.00
	1929F	.060	60.00	100.00	140.00	225.00
	1929F	—	—	—	Proof	400.00
	1929G	.037	60.00	100.00	150.00	235.00
	1929G	—	—	—	Proof	500.00
	1929J	.049	50.00	90.00	150.00	235.00
	1929J	—	—	—	Proof	450.00

1000th Anniversary - Meissen

KM#	Date	Mintage	Fine	VF	XF	Unc
66	1929E	.120	150.00	300.00	450.00	650.00
	1929E	—	—	—	Proof	1000.

Graf Zeppelin Flight

KM#	Date	Mintage	Fine	VF	XF	Unc
68	1930A	.217	60.00	100.00	165.00	230.00
	1930A	—	—	—	Proof	450.00
	1930A	—	—	Matte Proof		—
	1930D	.056	70.00	110.00	170.00	265.00
	1930D	—	—	—	Proof	550.00
	1930E	.030	70.00	110.00	180.00	350.00
	1930E	—	—	—	Proof	500.00
	1930F	.040	70.00	110.00	170.00	265.00
	1930F	—	—	—	Proof	475.00
	1930G	.024	75.00	115.00	180.00	350.00
	1930G	—	—	—	Proof	600.00
	1930J	.033	70.00	110.00	175.00	300.00
	1930J	—	—	—	Proof	550.00

Liberation of Rhineland

KM#	Date	Mintage	Fine	VF	XF	Unc
71	1930A	.325	60.00	100.00	160.00	225.00
	1930A	—	—	—	Proof	400.00
	1930D	.084	60.00	100.00	170.00	255.00
	1930D	—	—	—	Proof	550.00
	1930E	.045	70.00	125.00	180.00	285.00
	1930E	—	—	—	Proof	475.00
	1930F	.060	60.00	100.00	165.00	270.00
	1930F	—	—	—	Proof	450.00
	1930G	.037	85.00	165.00	265.00	400.00
	1930G	—	—	—	Proof	550.00
	1930J	.049	70.00	125.00	175.00	285.00
	1930J	—	—	—	Proof	575.00

Centenary -Death of Goethe

KM#	Date	Mintage	Fine	VF	XF	Unc
77	1932A	.011	550.00	1250.	2250.	3200.
	1932A	—	—	—	Proof	3500.
	1932D	2,812	650.00	1350.	2400.	3250.
	1932D	—	—	—	Proof	3700.
	1932E	1,490	700.00	1400.	2500.	3500.
	1932E	—	—	—	Proof	3700.
	1932F	2,006	700.00	1400.	2500.	3500.
	1932F	—	—	—	Proof	3700.
	1932G	1,220	750.00	1500.	2500.	3500.
	1932G	—	—	—	Proof	3700.
	1932J	1,634	750.00	1500.	2500.	3500.
	1932J	—	—	—	Proof	3700.

200 MARK

ALUMINUM

KM#	Date	Mintage	Fine	VF	XF	Unc
35	1923A	174.900	.15	.50	1.50	2.00
	1923A	—	—	—	Proof	40.00
	1923D	35.189	.20	1.00	1.50	2.00
	1923D	—	—	—	Proof	40.00
	1923E	11.250	.25	2.00	3.50	6.50
	1923E	4,095	—	—	Proof	40.00
	1923F	20.090	.20	1.00	2.00	5.00
	1923F	—	—	—	Proof	40.00
	1923G	24.923	.20	.50	1.00	2.00
	1923G	—	—	—	Proof	40.00
	1923J	16.258	.25	1.50	2.50	6.00
	1923J	—	—	—	Proof	40.00

500 MARK

ALUMINUM

KM#	Date	Mintage	Fine	VF	XF	Unc
36	1923A	59.278	.20	1.00	1.50	2.00
	1923A	—	—	—	Proof	70.00
	1923D	13.683	.25	1.00	1.50	3.00
	1923D	—	—	—	Proof	70.00
	1923E	2.128	1.00	7.50	12.50	15.00
	1923E	2,053	—	—	Proof	70.00
	1923F	7.963	.25	1.50	2.00	5.00
	1923F	—	—	—	Proof	70.00
	1923G	4.404	.25	2.50	5.00	7.50
	1923G	—	—	—	Proof	70.00
	1923J	1.008	10.00	18.00	35.00	65.00
	1923J	—	—	—	Proof	250.00

THIRD REICH

1933-1945

REICHSPFENNIG

BRONZE

KM#	Date	Mintage	Fine	VF	XF	Unc
89	1936A	Inc.KM37	1.50	4.00	7.50	15.00
	1936E	.150	25.00	50.00	100.00	150.00
	1936F	4.600	22.50	50.00	95.00	145.00
	1936G	Inc.KM37	15.00	30.00	60.00	90.00
	1936J	Inc.KM37	10.00	30.00	50.00	70.00
	1937A	67.180	.10	.25	.50	2.50
	1937D	14.060	.10	.25	.50	2.50
	1937E	10.700	.15	.35	1.00	5.00
	1937F	11.058	.15	.35	1.00	5.00
	1937G	4.250	.15	.35	1.00	5.00
	1937J	6.714	.15	.35	1.00	5.00
	1938A	75.707	.10	.25	.50	5.00
	1938B	2.378	.50	6.00	9.00	12.50
	1938D	13.930	.10	.25	.50	5.00
	1938E	14.503	.10	.25	.50	5.00
	1938F	11.714	.10	.25	.50	5.00
	1938G	8.390	.10	.25	.50	5.00
	1938J	15.458	.10	.25	.50	6.00
	1939A	97.541	.10	.25	.50	5.00
	1939B	22.732	.15	.35	1.00	7.50
	1939D	20.760	.10	.25	.50	5.00
	1939E	12.478	.10	.25	.50	7.50
	1939F	12.482	.10	.25	.50	5.00
	1939G	12.250	.10	.25	.50	5.00
	1939J	8.368	.10	.25	.50	7.50
	1940A	27.094	.10	.25	.50	6.00
	1940F	7.850	.15	.35	1.00	6.00
	1940G	3.875	1.00	5.00	7.50	15.00
	1940J	7.450	.50	4.00	5.00	8.00
	Common date		—	—	Proof	75.00

ZINC

KM#	Date	Mintage	Fine	VF	XF	Unc
97	1940A	223.948	.10	.20	1.00	5.00
	1940B	62.198	.10	.20	1.00	2.50
	1940D	43.951	.10	.20	1.00	5.00
	1940E	20.749	.20	1.00	5.00	7.50
	1940F	33.854	.10	.20	1.00	5.00
	1940G	20.165	.10	.20	1.00	5.00
	1940J	24.459	.10	.20	1.00	5.00
	1941A	281.618	.10	.15	.50	4.00
	1941B	62.285	.20	1.00	1.50	7.50
	1941D	73.745	.10	.15	.50	5.00
	1941E	49.041	.10	.50	1.50	7.50
	1941F	51.017	.10	.15	.50	5.00
	1941G	44.810	.10	.50	1.00	7.50
	1941J	57.625	.10	.15	.50	5.00
	1942A	558.877	.10	.15	.50	5.00
	1942B	124.740	.10	.20	1.00	6.00
	1942D	134.145	.10	.15	.50	6.00
	1942E	84.674	.15	1.50	2.50	8.50
	1942F	90.788	.10	.15	.50	6.00
	1942G	59.858	.10	.15	.50	6.00
	1942J	122.934	.10	.50	1.00	6.00
	1943A	372.401	.10	.15	.50	6.00
	1943B	79.315	.10	.50	1.00	6.00
	1943D	91.629	.10	.15	.50	6.00
	1943E	34.191	.50	2.50	7.50	10.00
	1943F	70.269	.10	.50	1.00	6.00
	1943G	24.688	.15	1.50	2.50	7.50
	1943J	37.695	.15	1.50	2.50	7.50
	1944A	124.421	.10	.50	2.00	5.00
	1944B	87.850	.20	1.00	2.00	5.00
	1944D	56.755	.20	1.00	2.50	7.00
	1944E	41.729	.20	2.00	5.00	10.00
	1944F	15.580	.50	4.00	6.00	12.00
	1944G	34.967	.10	.50	1.00	4.00
	1945A	17.145	.25	2.50	7.50	15.00
	1945E	6.800	25.00	45.00	70.00	130.00
	Common date		—	—	Proof	80.00

2 REICHSPFENNIG

BRONZE

KM#	Date	Mintage	Fine	VF	XF	Unc
90	1936A	Inc.Be.	.50	3.00	8.00	25.00
	1936D	Inc.Be.	.50	3.00	8.00	25.00
	1936F	3.100	5.00	15.00	30.00	50.00
	1937A	34.404	.10	.50	1.50	7.00
	1937D	9.016	.10	.50	1.50	7.00
	1937E	Inc.Be.	6.00	20.00	45.00	80.00
	1937F	7.487	.10	.50	1.50	7.00
	1937G	.490	2.00	8.50	15.00	35.00
	1937J	.450	2.00	8.50	15.00	30.00
	1938A	27.264	.10	.15	.50	6.00
	1938B	2.714	1.50	4.00	8.00	22.00
	1938D	8.770	.10	.25	1.00	6.00
	1938E	5.450	.25	1.00	2.00	6.00
	1938F	10.090	.10	.25	1.00	6.00
	1938G	3.685	.10	.25	1.00	6.00
	1938J	7.243	.10	.25	1.00	6.00
	1939A	37.348	.10	.25	1.00	6.00
	1939B	9.361	.10	.25	1.00	6.00
	1939D	7.555	.10	.25	1.00	6.00
	1939E	6.650	.25	1.00	4.50	10.00
	1939F	7.019	.10	.25	1.00	6.00
	1939G	4.885	.10	.25	1.00	6.00
	1939J	6.996	.10	.25	1.00	6.00
	1940A	22.681	.10	.25	1.00	6.00
	1940D	3.855	.50	3.00	6.50	12.50
	1940E	3.412	2.50	10.00	15.00	30.00
	1940G	1.161	40.00	70.00	110.00	160.00
	1940J	2.357	1.50	7.50	12.50	25.00
	Common date		—	—	Proof	80.00

5 REICHSPFENNIG

ALUMINUM-BRONZE

KM#	Date	Mintage	Fine	VF	XF	Unc
91	1936A	Inc.Be.	15.00	25.00	55.00	100.00
	1936D	Inc.Be.	10.00	20.00	35.00	60.00
	1936G	Inc.Be.	40.00	80.00	120.00	175.00
	1937A	29.700	.10	.20	1.00	6.00
	1937D	4.992	.10	.20	1.00	7.50
	1937E	4.474	.20	1.00	3.00	10.00
	1937F	2.092	.10	.20	1.00	8.00
	1937G	2.749	2.50	7.50	15.00	20.00
	1937J	6.991	.25	2.50	5.00	12.50
	1938A	54.012	.25	2.50	5.00	7.50
	1938B	3.447	.25	1.50	5.00	10.00
	1938D	17.708	.10	.25	1.50	6.00
	1938E	8.602	.10	.40	4.00	8.00
	1938F	8.147	.10	.25	1.50	7.00
	1938G	7.323	.10	.25	1.50	7.00
	1938J	7.646	.10	.25	1.50	7.00
	1939A	35.337	.10	.25	1.50	7.00
	1939B	8.313	.10	.20	1.00	7.50

KM#	Date	Mintage	Fine	VF	XF	Unc
91	1939D	8.304	.20	1.00	2.00	7.50
	1939E	5.138	.20	1.00	2.00	7.50
	1939F	10.339	.10	.20	1.00	6.00
	1939G	4.266	.25	2.50	7.50	12.50
	1939J	4.177	.20	2.00	7.50	10.00
	Common date		—	—	Proof	95.00

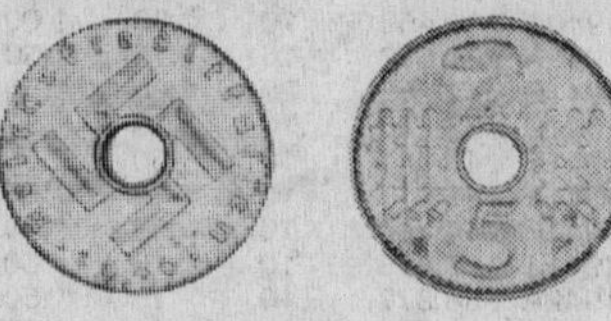

ZINC
Military Issue

KM#	Date	Mintage	Fine	VF	XF	Unc
98	1940A	—	5.00	10.00	20.00	30.00
	1940B	3.020	50.00	100.00	135.00	200.00
	1940D	—	15.00	30.00	60.00	90.00
	1940E	2.445	50.00	100.00	135.00	275.00
	1940F	—	40.00	80.00	165.00	275.00
	1940G	—	40.00	80.00	250.00	325.00
	1940J	—	40.00	80.00	250.00	325.00
	1941A	—	25.00	50.00	100.00	150.00
	1941F	—	40.00	80.00	250.00	325.00
	Common date		—	—	Proof	200.00

NOTE: Circulated only in occupied territories.

KM#	Date	Mintage	Fine	VF	XF	Unc
100	1940A	174.684	.10	.20	1.00	5.00
	1940B	63.469	.20	1.00	1.50	6.00
	1940D	44.364	.20	1.00	1.50	6.00
	1940E	25.800	.30	2.00	4.00	6.00
	1940F	31.381	.20	1.00	2.00	6.00
	1940G	24.148	.20	1.00	2.50	6.00
	1940J	30.518	.20	1.00	2.00	6.00
	1941A	246.216	.10	.20	1.00	5.00
	1941B	60.297	.10	.30	2.00	7.50
	1941D	51.100	.10	.30	2.00	7.50
	1941E	26.354	.10	.30	2.00	7.50
	1941F	36.725	.10	.30	2.00	7.50
	1941G	21.276	.10	.30	2.00	7.50
	1941J	52.872	.10	.30	2.00	7.50
	1942A	161.042	.10	.20	1.00	5.00
	1942B	12.405	.25	1.50	5.00	7.50
	1942D	15.486	.10	.35	2.50	5.00
	1942E	8.800	7.50	17.50	22.50	35.00
	1942F	24.662	.10	.25	1.50	5.00
	1942G	12.749	.10	.35	2.50	7.50
	1943A	46.830	.15	.50	2.00	7.50
	1943B	.833	10.00	20.00	30.00	80.00
	1943D	13.650	.15	.50	4.00	10.00
	1943E	16.581	2.50	7.50	12.50	17.50
	1943F	9.891	.20	1.00	2.50	6.00
	1943G	7.237	.15	.50	2.00	6.00
	1944A	23.699	3.50	15.00	27.50	37.50
	1944D	26.340	.25	1.50	3.00	5.00
	1944E	19.720	.50	4.00	9.00	15.00
	1944F	6.853	.25	1.50	3.00	7.50
	1944G	3.540	65.00	150.00	275.00	350.00
	Common date		—	—	Proof	75.00

10 REICHSPFENNIG

ALUMINUM-BRONZE

KM#	Date	Mintage	Fine	VF	XF	Unc
92	1936A	Inc. Be.	2.50	12.50	20.00	60.00
	1936E	.245	65.00	135.00	175.00	275.00
	1936G	.129	100.00	225.00	300.00	500.00
	1937A	36.830	.10	.50	2.00	7.50
	1937D	6.882	.25	1.50	3.00	10.00
	1937E	3.786	2.00	10.00	18.00	40.00
	1937F	5.934	.50	2.50	5.00	12.50
	1937G	2.131	1.00	5.00	7.50	17.50
	1937J	4.439	.50	2.50	5.00	15.00
	1938A	70.068	.10	.20	1.00	6.00
	1938B	7.852	.50	2.50	5.00	12.50
	1938D	16.990	.10	.50	2.00	8.00
	1938E	10.739	.20	1.00	2.50	9.00
	1938F	12.307	.20	1.00	2.50	9.00
	1938G	8.584	.20	1.00	2.50	9.00
	1938J	10.389	.20	1.00	2.50	9.00
	1939A	40.171	.20	1.00	2.00	8.00
	1939B	7.814	.20	1.00	2.00	9.00
	1939D	11.307	.20	1.00	2.00	9.00
	1939E	5.079	.50	2.50	7.50	15.00
	1939F	6.993	.25	1.50	3.00	10.00
	1939G	5.532	.50	5.00	10.00	20.00
	1939J	5.557	.20	1.00	2.00	6.00
	Common date		—	—	Proof	95.00

ZINC
Military Issue

KM#	Date	Mintage	Fine	VF	XF	Unc
99	1940A	—	6.00	12.50	22.50	35.00
	1940B	.840	50.00	100.00	200.00	300.00
	1940D	—	40.00	75.00	225.00	300.00
	1940E	5.100	50.00	100.00	200.00	300.00
	1940F	—	50.00	100.00	200.00	300.00
	1940G	.150	40.00	75.00	225.00	300.00
	1940J	—	50.00	100.00	200.00	300.00
	1941A	—	50.00	100.00	175.00	250.00
	1941F	—	50.00	100.00	175.00	250.00

NOTE: Circulated only in occupied territories.

KM#	Date	Mintage	Fine	VF	XF	Unc
101	1940A	212.948	.10	.35	1.50	6.00
	1940B	76.274	.15	.50	2.50	7.50
	1940D	45.434	.15	.50	2.00	6.50
	1940E	34.350	.15	.50	2.00	6.50
	1940F	27.603	.15	.50	2.00	6.50
	1940G	27.308	.15	.50	2.00	6.50
	1940J	41.678	.15	.50	2.00	6.50
	1941A	240.284	.10	.35	1.50	6.00
	1941B	70.747	.15	.50	2.50	7.50
	1941D	77.560	.15	.50	2.00	6.50
	1941E	36.548	.15	.50	2.00	6.50
	1941F	42.834	.15	.50	2.00	6.50
	1941G	28.765	.15	.50	2.00	6.50
	1941J	30.525	.15	.50	2.00	6.50
	1942A	184.545	.10	.20	.50	2.00
	1942B	16.329	.25	2.50	3.50	10.00
	1942D	40.852	.20	1.00	2.50	7.50
	1942E	18.334	.25	1.50	3.00	7.50
	1942F	32.690	.10	.35	1.50	6.00
	1942G	20.295	.25	1.50	2.50	6.00
	1942J	29.957	.25	1.50	2.50	7.50
	1943A	157.357	.15	1.50	2.50	7.50
	1943B	11.940	2.50	7.50	15.00	30.00
	1943D	17.304	.25	2.00	3.00	7.50
	1943E	10.445	2.50	7.50	15.00	30.00
	1943F	24.804	.25	2.50	5.00	7.50
	1943G	3.618	.25	2.50	6.00	12.50
	1943J	1.821	15.00	30.00	50.00	85.00
	1944A	84.164	.15	1.00	2.50	7.50
	1944B	40.781	.50	1.50	3.00	8.00
	1944D	30.369	.35	1.50	3.00	8.00
	1944E	29.963	.50	2.00	4.00	8.00
	1944F	19.639	.50	2.00	4.00	8.00
	1944G	13.023	.50	2.00	4.00	8.00
	1945A	7.112	5.00	12.50	17.50	27.50
	1945E	4.897	10.00	15.00	25.00	60.00
	Common date		—	—	Proof	80.00

50 REICHSPFENNIG

ALUMINUM

KM#	Date	Mintage	Fine	VF	XF	Unc
87	1935A	75.912	.25	2.50	6.00	17.50
	1935A	—	—	—	Proof	75.00
	1935D	19.688	.25	1.00	2.50	15.00
	1935D	—	—	—	Proof	75.00
	1935E	10.418	.50	5.00	7.50	20.00
	1935E	—	—	—	Proof	75.00
	1935F	14.061	.25	1.00	3.00	20.00
	1935F	—	—	—	Proof	75.00
	1935G	8.540	.50	4.00	9.00	30.00
	1935G	—	—	—	Proof	75.00
	1935J	11.438	.35	3.50	7.50	25.00
	1935J	—	—	—	Proof	100.00

NICKEL

KM#	Date	Mintage	Fine	VF	XF	Unc
95	1938A	5.051	10.00	20.00	35.00	65.00
	1938B	1.124	15.00	30.00	45.00	75.00
	1938D	1.260	15.00	30.00	45.00	75.00
	1938E	.949	15.00	30.00	45.00	80.00
	1938F	1.210	7.50	20.00	45.00	80.00

KM#	Date	Mintage	Fine	VF	XF	Unc
95	1938G	.460	20.00	40.00	75.00	140.00
	1938J	.730	12.50	27.50	65.00	125.00
	1939A	15.037	12.50	22.00	35.00	50.00
	1939B	2.826	12.50	22.00	40.00	55.00
	1939D	3.648	10.00	22.00	40.00	55.00
	1939E	1.924	10.00	25.00	45.00	65.00
	1939F	2.602	10.00	25.00	45.00	65.00
	1939G	1.565	10.00	25.00	50.00	80.00
	1939J	2.114	10.00	25.00	45.00	75.00
	Common date		—	—	Proof	220.00

ALUMINUM

KM#	Date	Mintage	Fine	VF	XF	Unc
96	1939A	5.000	.35	2.50	5.00	20.00
	1939B	5.482	.35	2.50	5.00	20.00
	1939D	.600	2.50	12.50	25.00	50.00
	1939E	2.000	.50	5.00	7.50	30.00
	1939F	3.600	.35	3.00	6.00	22.50
	1939G	.560	10.00	20.00	50.00	75.00
	1939J	1.000	2.50	10.00	15.00	40.00
	1940A	56.128	.15	.50	2.50	15.00
	1940B	10.016	.35	3.00	5.00	15.00
	1940D	13.800	.25	1.50	3.00	15.00
	1940E	5.618	1.50	10.00	15.00	40.00
	1940F	6.663	.25	1.50	3.00	15.00
	1940G	5.616	1.50	9.00	12.50	35.00
	1940J	7.335	2.00	12.50	17.50	50.00
	1941A	31.263	.25	1.50	3.00	15.00
	1941B	4.291	2.00	5.00	7.00	15.00
	1941D	7.200	.35	3.00	5.00	15.00
	1941E	3.806	.50	4.00	7.50	20.00
	1941F	5.128	.30	2.00	5.00	15.00
	1941G	3.091	2.50	4.00	7.50	20.00
	1941J	4.165	1.00	6.00	8.00	20.00
	1942A	11.580	.15	.50	2.50	7.50
	1942B	2.876	3.50	15.00	25.00	55.00
	1942D	2.247	.35	3.00	6.00	15.00
	1942E	3.810	2.50	5.00	7.50	22.50
	1942F	5.133	1.00	3.50	5.00	15.00
	1942G	1.400	2.50	5.00	10.00	30.00
	1943A	29.325	.15	.50	2.50	8.50
	1943B	8.229	.50	4.50	7.50	15.00
	1943D	5.315	.20	1.00	3.50	15.00
	1943G	2.892	1.25	7.50	12.50	30.00
	1943J	4.166	5.00	10.00	15.00	35.00
	1944B	5.622	1.00	7.50	10.00	22.50
	1944D	4.886	7.50	15.00	25.00	60.00
	1944F	3.739	1.25	7.50	10.00	30.00
	1944G	1.190	65.00	100.00	150.00	200.00
	Common date		—	—	Proof	125.00

REICHSMARK

NICKEL

KM#	Date	Mintage	Fine	VF	XF	Unc
78	1933A	6.030	.75	2.50	7.50	15.00
	1933D	4.562	1.00	3.00	9.00	18.00
	1933E	3.500	2.50	7.50	12.50	25.00
	1933F	1.400	4.00	8.50	15.00	27.50
	1933G	2.000	2.50	7.50	15.00	27.50
	1934A	52.345	.50	1.50	2.50	8.00
	1934D	30.597	.50	1.50	2.50	8.00
	1934E	15.135	1.00	3.00	7.00	15.00
	1934F	23.672	.75	2.50	5.00	12.50
	1934G	13.252	1.50	5.00	10.00	18.00
	1934J	16.820	1.00	3.50	7.50	15.00
	1935A	57.896	.75	2.50	5.00	12.50
	1935J	3.621	2.50	7.50	20.00	40.00
	1936A	20.287	1.25	4.00	7.00	12.50
	1936D	4.940	2.50	7.50	15.00	27.50
	1936E	3.200	2.50	10.00	25.00	35.00
	1936F	2.075	2.50	10.00	25.00	45.00
	1936G	.620	35.00	65.00	125.00	200.00
	1936J	2.975	2.50	7.50	12.50	27.50
	1937A	49.976	.50	1.50	2.50	8.00
	1937D	10.529	1.00	3.00	6.00	12.00
	1937E	2.926	3.00	15.00	30.00	50.00
	1937F	6.221	2.50	6.00	12.00	18.00
	1937G	2.143	2.50	10.00	17.50	40.00
	1937J	4.721	2.50	10.00	17.50	40.00
	1938A	9.829	1.25	4.00	6.50	10.00
	1938E	2.073	4.00	17.50	25.00	45.00
	1938F	2.739	5.00	17.50	22.50	40.00
	1938G	4.381	10.00	20.00	35.00	60.00
	1938J	1.269	27.50	70.00	90.00	135.00
	1939A	52.150	5.00	12.50	15.00	35.00
	1939B	9.836	50.00	125.00	140.00	200.00
	1939D	12.522	9.00	22.50	37.50	65.00
	1939E	6.570	20.00	35.00	80.00	120.00
	1939F	10.033	10.00	20.00	40.00	65.00
	1939G	5.475	60.00	130.00	170.00	350.00
	1939J	8.478	15.00	35.00	60.00	100.00
	Common date		—	—	Proof	185.00

2 REICHSMARK

8.0000 g, .625 SILVER, .1607 oz ASW
450th Anniversary - Birth of Martin Luther

KM#	Date	Mintage	Fine	VF	XF	Unc
79	1933A	.542	8.75	17.50	25.00	45.00
	1933A	—	—	—	Proof	125.00
	1933D	.141	10.00	20.00	25.00	45.00
	1933D	—	—	—	Proof	125.00
	1933E	.075	10.00	20.00	35.00	60.00
	1933E	—	—	—	Proof	225.00
	1933F	.100	10.00	20.00	25.00	45.00
	1933F	—	—	—	Proof	225.00
	1933G	.061	12.00	22.50	40.00	65.00
	1933G	—	—	—	Proof	225.00
	1933J	.082	10.00	20.00	35.00	60.00
	1933J	—	—	—	Proof	200.00

1st Anniversary Nazi Rule
Potsdam Garrison Church

KM#	Date	Mintage	Fine	VF	XF	Unc
81	1934A	2.710	3.50	7.00	20.00	70.00
	1934A	—	—	—	Proof	200.00
	1934D	.703	4.00	8.00	30.00	75.00
	1934D	—	—	—	Proof	200.00
	1934E	.373	6.25	12.50	35.00	100.00
	1934E	—	—	—	Proof	200.00
	1934F	.502	4.50	9.00	25.00	70.00
	1934F	—	—	—	Proof	200.00
	1934G	.305	6.00	12.50	35.00	115.00
	1934G	—	—	—	Proof	200.00
	1934J	.409	6.00	12.50	35.00	110.00
	1934J	—	—	—	Proof	200.00

175th Anniversary - Birth of Schiller

KM#	Date	Mintage	Fine	VF	XF	Unc
84	1934F	.300	25.00	50.00	80.00	120.00
	1934F	—	—	—	Proof	200.00

Swastika-Hindenburg Issue

KM#	Date	Mintage	Fine	VF	XF	Unc
93	1936D	.840	3.00	6.00	15.00	20.00
	1936E	Inc.Be.	8.00	30.00	60.00	100.00
	1936G	Inc.Be.	6.00	20.00	35.00	50.00
	1936J	Inc.Be.	20.00	60.00	120.00	200.00
	1937A	23.425	2.50	3.50	5.00	12.00
	1937D	6.190	2.50	3.50	5.00	12.00
	1937E	3.725	2.50	3.50	5.00	12.00
	1937F	5.015	2.50	3.50	5.00	12.00
	1937G	1.913	2.50	3.50	5.00	12.00
	1937J	2.756	2.50	3.50	5.00	12.00
	1938A	13.201	2.50	3.50	5.00	10.00
	1938B	13.163	2.50	3.50	5.00	10.00
	1938D	3.711	2.50	3.50	5.00	10.00
	1938E	4.731	2.50	3.50	5.00	10.00
	1938F	1.882	3.00	4.00	6.00	12.50
	1938G	2.313	2.50	3.50	5.00	10.00
	1938J	2.306	3.00	4.00	5.00	10.00
	1939A	26.855	2.50	3.50	5.00	10.00
	1939B	3.522	2.50	3.50	5.00	10.00
	1939D	5.357	2.50	3.50	5.00	10.00
	1939E	.251	12.50	30.00	40.00	60.00
	1939F	3.180	2.50	3.50	5.00	8.00
	1939G	2.305	2.50	3.50	7.50	12.50
	1939J	3.414	2.50	3.50	7.50	10.00
	Common date		—	—	Proof	165.00

5 REICHSMARK

13.8800 g, .900 SILVER, .4016 oz ASW
450th Anniversary - Birth of Martin Luther

KM#	Date	Mintage	Fine	VF	XF	Unc
80	1933A	.108	50.00	100.00	150.00	250.00
	1933A	—	—	—	Proof	330.00
	1933D	.028	60.00	125.00	185.00	300.00
	1933D	—	—	—	Proof	400.00
	1933E	.012	70.00	140.00	200.00	350.00
	1933E	—	—	—	Proof	500.00
	1933F	.020	60.00	125.00	175.00	280.00
	1933F	—	—	—	Proof	400.00
	1933G	.012	100.00	175.00	275.00	375.00
	1933G	—	—	—	Proof	500.00
	1933J	.016	75.00	140.00	200.00	350.00
	1933J	—	—	—	Proof	400.00

175th Anniversary - Birth of Schiller

KM#	Date	Mintage	Fine	VF	XF	Unc
85	1934F	.100	85.00	175.00	275.00	425.00
	1934F	—	—	—	Proof	500.00

1st Anniversary Nazi Rule
Potsdam Garrison Church

KM#	Date	Mintage	Fine	VF	XF	Unc
82	1934A	2.168	7.50	10.00	30.00	80.00
	1934D	.562	7.50	10.00	45.00	100.00
	1934E	.298	10.00	18.00	50.00	150.00
	1934F	.401	8.00	12.50	45.00	135.00
	1934G	.244	10.00	18.00	50.00	150.00
	1934J	.327	9.00	18.00	45.00	125.00
	Common date		—	—	Proof	280.00

NOTE: Impaired proofs are common and valued around $200.

Rev: Date 21 MARZ 1933 dropped

KM#	Date	Mintage	Fine	VF	XF	Unc
83	1934A	14.526	4.00	6.00	15.00	40.00
	1934D	6.303	4.00	6.00	15.00	50.00
	1934E	2.739	5.00	7.50	17.50	65.00
	1934F	4.844	4.00	6.00	15.00	50.00
	1934G	2.304	5.00	7.50	17.50	65.00
	1934J	4.294	4.00	6.00	15.00	50.00
	1935A	23.407	4.00	6.00	12.00	35.00
	1935D	3.539	4.00	6.00	15.00	50.00
	1935E	2.476	5.00	7.50	17.50	65.00
	1935F	2.177	5.00	7.50	17.50	75.00
	1935G	1.966	5.00	7.50	17.50	75.00
	1935J	1.425	6.00	10.00	25.00	110.00
	Common date		—	—	Proof	250.00

Hindenburg Issue

KM#	Date	Mintage	Fine	VF	XF	Unc
86	1935A	19.325	3.00	6.00	10.00	25.00
	1935D	6.596	3.00	6.00	10.00	25.00
	1935E	3.260	4.00	6.50	12.50	30.00
	1935F	4.372	3.00	6.00	10.00	27.50
	1935G	2.371	3.00	6.00	12.50	32.50
	1935J	2.830	3.00	6.00	12.50	32.50
	1936A	30.611	3.00	6.00	10.00	16.00
	1936D	7.032	3.00	6.00	10.00	18.00
	1936E	3.320	3.00	6.00	12.50	27.50

KM#	Date	Mintage	Fine	VF	XF	Unc
86	1936F	4.926	3.00	6.00	12.50	27.50
	1936G	2.734	3.00	6.00	12.50	30.00
	1936J	3.706	3.00	6.00	12.50	30.00
	Common date		—	—	Proof	225.00

Swastika-Hindenburg Issue

KM#	Date	Mintage	Fine	VF	XF	Unc
94	1936A	8.430	3.00	6.00	10.00	17.50
	1936D	1.872	3.00	7.00	15.00	27.50
	1936E	.870	5.00	8.00	17.50	30.00
	1936F	1.732	3.00	7.00	15.00	27.50
	1936G	.743	5.00	8.50	20.00	35.00
	1936J	.640	8.00	20.00	30.00	75.00
	1937A	6.662	3.00	6.00	10.00	20.00
	1937D	2.173	3.00	6.00	10.00	15.00
	1937E	1.490	5.00	8.00	15.00	27.50
	1937F	1.578	4.00	7.50	15.00	27.50
	1937G	1.472	5.00	8.00	15.00	27.50
	1937J	2.191	3.00	6.00	12.50	25.00
	1938A	6.789	3.00	6.00	10.00	15.00
	1938D	1.304	3.00	6.00	12.50	17.50
	1938E	.425	5.00	8.00	15.00	27.50
	1938F	.740	3.50	6.50	12.50	22.50
	1938G	.861	4.00	7.50	15.00	25.00
	1938J	1.302	3.50	6.50	12.50	20.00
	1939A	3.428	4.00	7.50	12.50	20.00
	1939B	1.942	5.00	8.00	15.00	25.00
	1939D	1.216	7.50	12.50	20.00	30.00
	1939E	1.320	15.00	20.00	40.00	80.00
	1939F	1.060	7.50	12.50	25.00	45.00
	1939G	.567	12.50	18.00	35.00	75.00
	1939J	1.710	5.00	8.00	15.00	25.00
	Common date		—	—	Proof	200.00

ALLIED OCCUPATION COINAGE

REICHSPFENNIG

ZINC
Modified design, swastika and wreath removed.
Eagle missing tail feathers.

KM#	Date	Mintage	Fine	VF	XF	Unc
A102	1944D	—	—	2000.	3500.	4500.

KM#	Date	Mintage	Fine	VF	XF	Unc
A103	1945F	2.984	5.00	10.00	18.00	35.00
	1946F	1.633	15.00	35.00	80.00	130.00
	1946G	1.500	35.00	75.00	110.00	150.00
	Common date		—	—	Proof	175.00

5 REICHSPFENNIG

ZINC

KM#	Date	Mintage	Fine	VF	XF	Unc
A105	1947A	—	2.50	7.50	15.00	25.00
	1947D	16.528	2.50	4.50	6.50	20.00
	1948A	—	5.00	15.00	25.00	35.00
	1948E	7.666	150.00	300.00	400.00	700.00

10 REICHSPFENNIG

ZINC

KM#	Date	Mintage	Fine	VF	XF	Unc
A104	1945F	5.942	4.50	7.50	15.00	25.00
	1946F	3.738	10.00	20.00	30.00	100.00
	1946G	1.600	35.00	65.00	100.00	150.00
	1947A	—	4.50	10.00	20.00	30.00
	1947E	2.612	175.00	225.00	325.00	450.00
	1947F	1.269	1.50	3.50	8.00	17.50

KM#	Date	Mintage	Fine	VF	XF	Unc
A104	1948A	—	5.00	20.00	25.00	35.00
	1948F	19.579	2.50	4.50	10.00	20.00
	Common date		—	—	Proof	180.00

MONETARY REFORM

100 Pfennig = 1 Deutsche Mark (DM)

PFENNIG

BRONZE-CLAD STEEL
Currency Reform

KM#	Date	Mintage	VF	XF	Unc
A101	1948D	46.325	.50	15.00	35.00
	1948F	68.203	.50	8.00	27.50
	1948F	250 pcs.	—	Proof	150.00
	1948G	45.604	.50	15.00	40.00
	1948J	79.304	.50	15.00	45.00
	1949D	99.863	.50	6.00	22.50
	1949D	—	—	Proof	100.00
	1949F	129.935	.50	6.00	17.50
	1949F	250 pcs.	—	Proof	50.00
	1949G	70.954	.50	10.00	25.00
	1949J	101.932	.50	6.00	22.50
	1949J	—	—	Proof	80.00

COPPER PLATED STEEL
Federal Republic

KM#	Date	Mintage	VF	XF	Unc
105	1950D	772.592	—	.10	1.00
	1950F	898.277	—	.10	1.00
	1950F	620 pcs.	—	Proof	27.50
	1950G	515.673	—	.10	1.00
	1950G	1,800	—	Proof	5.00
	1950J	784.424	—	.10	1.00
	1950J	—	—	Proof	12.00
	1966D	65.063	—	.10	2.00
	1966F	75.031	—	.10	2.00
	1966F	100 pcs.	—	Proof	35.00
	1966G	48.261	—	.10	2.00
	1966G	3,070	—	Proof	4.00
	1966J	66.842	—	.10	3.00
	1966J	1,000	—	Proof	8.00
	1967D	39.082	—	.10	3.00
	1967F	45.003	—	.10	3.00
	1967F	1,500	—	Proof	6.00
	1967G	20.787	—	.10	3.00
	1967G	4,500	—	Proof	3.50
	1967J	42.583	—	.10	4.00
	1967J	1,500	—	Proof	8.00
	1968D	32.797	—	.10	1.00
	1968F	26.338	—	.10	1.00
	1968F	3,000	—	Proof	5.00
	1968G	20.382	—	.10	1.00
	1968G	6,023	—	Proof	4.00
	1968J	23.414	—	.25	1.00
	1968J	2,000	—	Proof	6.50
	1969D	78.177	—	.10	.50
	1969F	90.172	—	.10	.50
	1969F	5,100	—	Proof	1.50
	1969G	61.836	—	.10	.50
	1969G	8,700	—	Proof	1.25
	1969J	80.221	—	.10	.50
	1969J	5,000	—	Proof	1.50
	1970D	91.151	—	.10	.25
	1970F	105.236	—	.10	.25
	1970F	5,240	—	Proof	1.50
	1970G	82.421	—	.10	.25
	1970G	10,200	—	Proof	1.00
	1970 sm.J	93.455	—	.10	.25
	1970 lg.J	Inc. Ab.	—	.10	.25
	1970J	5,000	—	Proof	1.50
	1971D	116.612	—	.10	.25
	1971D	8,000	—	Proof	1.00
	1971F	157.393	—	.10	.25
	1971F	8,000	—	Proof	1.00
	1971G	77.674	—	.10	.25
	1971G	10,200	—	Proof	1.00
	1971J	120.218	—	.10	.25
	1971J	8,000	—	Proof	1.00
	1972D	90.696	—	.10	.25
	1972D	8,000	—	Proof	1.00
	1972F	105.006	—	.10	.25
	1972F	8,000	—	Proof	1.00
	1972G	60.660	—	.10	.25
	1972G	10,000	—	Proof	1.00
	1972J	93.492	—	.10	.25
	1972J	8,000	—	Proof	1.00
	1973D	38.976	—	.10	.25
	1973D	9,000	—	Proof	1.00
	1973F	45.006	—	.10	.25
	1973F	9,000	—	Proof	1.00
	1973G	25.811	—	.10	.25
	1973G	9,000	—	Proof	1.00
	1973J	40.057	—	.10	.25
	1973J	9,000	—	Proof	1.00
	1974D	90.951	—	.10	.25
	1974D	.035	—	Proof	.40
105	1974F	105.091	—	.10	.25
	1974F	.035	—	Proof	.40
	1974G	60.548	—	.10	.25
	1974G	.035	—	Proof	.40
	1974J	93.527	—	.10	.25
	1974J	.035	—	Proof	.40
	1975D	91.053	—	.10	.25
	1975D	.043	—	Proof	.40
	1975F	105.007	—	.10	.25
	1975F	.043	—	Proof	.40
	1975G	60.704	—	.10	.25
	1975G	.043	—	Proof	.40
	1975J	93.495	—	.10	.25
	1975J	.043	—	Proof	.40
	1976D	130.227	—	.10	.25
	1976D	.043	—	Proof	.40
	1976F	150.037	—	.10	.25
	1976F	.043	—	Proof	.40
	1976G	86.586	—	.10	.25
	1976G	.043	—	Proof	.40
	1976J	133.500	—	.10	.25
	1976J	.043	—	Proof	.40
	1977D	143.000	—	.10	.25
	1977D	.052	—	Proof	.40
	1977F	165.000	—	.10	.25
	1977F	.051	—	Proof	.40
	1977G	95.201	—	.10	.25
	1977G	.051	—	Proof	.40
	1977J	146.788	—	.10	.25
	1977J	.051	—	Proof	.40
	1978D	156.000	—	.10	.25
	1978D	.054	—	Proof	.40
	1978F	180.000	—	.10	.25
	1978F	.054	—	Proof	.40
	1978G	103.800	—	.10	.25
	1978G	.054	—	Proof	.40
	1978J	160.200	—	.10	.25
	1978J	.054	—	Proof	.40
	1979D	156.000	—	.10	.25
	1979D	.089	—	Proof	.40
	1979F	180.000	—	.10	.25
	1979F	.089	—	Proof	.40
	1979G	103.800	—	.10	.25
	1979G	.089	—	Proof	.40
	1979J	160.200	—	.10	.25
	1979J	.089	—	Proof	.40
	1980D	200.080	—	.10	.25
	1980D	.110	—	Proof	.40
	1980F	200.620	—	.10	.25
	1980F	.110	—	Proof	.40
	1980G	71.940	—	.10	.25
	1980G	.110	—	Proof	.40
	1980J	143.110	—	.10	.25
	1980J	.110	—	Proof	.40
	1981D	169.550	—	.10	.25
	1981D	.091	—	Proof	.40
	1981F	274.010	—	.10	.25
	1981F	.091	—	Proof	.40
	1981G	178.010	—	.10	.25
	1981G	.091	—	Proof	.40
	1981J	189.090	—	.10	.25
	1981J	.091	—	Proof	.40
	1982D	130.090	—	.10	.20
	1982D	.078	—	Proof	.40
	1982F	108.390	—	.10	.20
	1982F	.078	—	Proof	.40
	1982G	77.740	—	.10	.20
	1982G	.078	—	Proof	.40
	1982J	124.720	—	.10	.20
	1982J	.078	—	Proof	.40
	1983D	46.800	—	.10	.20
	1983D	.075	—	Proof	.40
	1983F	54.000	—	.10	.20
	1983F	.075	—	Proof	.40
	1983G	31.140	—	.10	.20
	1983G	.075	—	Proof	.40
	1983J	48.060	—	.10	.20
	1983J	.075	—	Proof	.40
	1984D	58.500	—	.10	.20
	1984D	.064	—	Proof	.40
	1984F	67.500	—	.10	.20
	1984F	.064	—	Proof	.40
	1984G	38.900	—	.10	.20
	1984G	.064	—	Proof	.40
	1984J	60.100	—	.10	.20
	1984J	.064	—	Proof	.40
	1985D	19.500	—	.10	.20
	1985D	.056	—	Proof	.40
	1985F	22.500	—	.10	.20
	1985F	.054	—	Proof	.40
	1985G	13.000	—	—	.10
	1985G	.055	—	Proof	.40
	1985J	20.000	—	—	.10
	1985J	.054	—	Proof	.40
	1986D	39.000	—	—	.10
	1986D	.044	—	Proof	.40
	1986F	45.000	—	—	.10
	1986F	.044	—	Proof	.40
	1986G	25.900	—	—	.10
	1986G	.044	—	Proof	.40
	1986J	40.100	—	—	.10
	1986J	.044	—	Proof	.40
	1987D	6.500	—	—	.10
	1987D	.045	—	Proof	.40
	1987F	7.500	—	—	.10
	1987F	.045	—	Proof	.40
	1987G	4.330	—	—	.10
	1987G	.045	—	Proof	.40
	1987J	6.680	—	—	.10
	1987J	.045	—	Proof	.40
105	1988D	52.000	—	—	.10
	1988D	.045	—	Proof	.40
	1988F	60.000	—	—	.10
	1988F	.045	—	Proof	.40
	1988G	34.600	—	—	.10
	1988G	.045	—	Proof	.40
	1988J	53.400	—	—	.10
	1988J	.045	—	Proof	.40
	1989D	—	—	—	.10
	1989D	—	—	Proof	.40
	1989F	120.000	—	—	.10
	1989F	.045	—	Proof	.40
	1989G	—	—	—	.10
	1989G	—	—	Proof	.40
	1989J	—	—	—	.10
	1989J	—	—	Proof	.40
	1990D	—	—	—	.10
	1990D	—	—	Proof	.40
	1990F	195.000	—	—	.10
	1990F	.045	—	Proof	.40
	1990G	—	—	—	.10
	1990G	—	—	Proof	.40
	1990J	—	—	—	.10
	1990J	—	—	Proof	.40
	1991A	—	—	—	.10
	1991A	—	—	Proof	.40
	1991D	—	—	—	.10
	1991D	—	—	Proof	.40
	1991F	—	—	—	.10
	1991F	—	—	Proof	.40
	1991G	—	—	—	.10
	1991G	—	—	Proof	.40
	1991J	—	—	—	.10
	1991J	—	—	Proof	.40

2 PFENNIG

BRONZE
Federal Republic

KM#	Date	Mintage	VF	XF	Unc
106	1950D	26.263	.10	1.00	7.50
	1950D	—	—	Proof	50.00
	1950F	30.278	.10	1.00	7.50
	1950F	200 pcs.	—	Proof	—
	1950G	17.151	.10	3.00	45.00
	1950G	—	—	Proof	65.00
	1950J	27.216	.10	1.00	7.50
	1950J	—	—	Proof	40.00
	1958D	19.440	.10	1.00	7.50
	1958F	24.122	.10	1.00	7.50
	1958F	100 pcs.	—	Proof	—
	1958G	15.255	.10	1.00	7.50
	1958J	21.250	.10	1.00	7.50
	1959D	19.690	—	.25	7.50
	1959F	25.017	—	.25	7.50
	1959F	75 pcs.	—	Proof	—
	1959G	12.899	—	.25	7.50
	1959J	25.482	—	.25	7.50
	1960D	21.979	—	.25	5.00
	1960F	13.060	—	.25	5.00
	1960F	75 pcs.	—	Proof	—
	1960G	5.657	.10	.25	5.00
	1960J	17.799	—	.25	5.00
	1961D	26.662	—	.25	5.00
	1961F	24.990	—	.25	5.00
	1961G	18.060	—	.25	5.00
	1961J	22.147	—	.25	5.00
	1962D	21.297	—	.25	5.00
	1962F	42.189	—	.25	3.00
	1962G	17.297	—	.25	3.00
	1962J	30.706	—	.25	3.00
	1963D	7.648	—	.25	5.00
	1963F	18.299	—	.25	2.00
	1963G	35.838	—	.25	2.00
	1963G	—	—	Proof	—
	1963J	42.884	—	.25	2.00
	1964D	20.336	—	.25	3.00
	1964F	31.400	—	.10	1.00
	1964G	18.431	—	.10	1.00
	1964G	*600 pcs.	—	Proof	12.00
	1964J	13.370	—	.10	1.00
	1965D	48.541	—	.10	1.00
	1965F	27.000	—	.10	1.00
	1965F	*80 pcs.	—	Proof	70.00
	1965G	13.584	—	.10	1.00
	1965G	1,200	—	Proof	5.00
	1965J	33.397	—	.10	1.00
	1966D	65.077	—	.10	.25
	1966F	52.543	—	.10	.25
	1966F	100 pcs.	—	Proof	80.00
	1966G	40.804	—	.10	.25
	1966G	3,070	—	Proof	5.50
	1966J	46.754	—	.10	.25
	1966J	1,000	—	Proof	40.00
	1967D	25.997	—	.10	2.00
	1967F	30.004	—	.10	1.00
	1967F	1,500	—	Proof	7.00
	1967G	6.280	—	1.00	3.00
	1967G	4,500	—	Proof	4.50
	1967J	26.725	—	.10	1.00
	1967J	1,500	—	Proof	10.00
	1968D	19.523	—	1.00	3.00
	1968G	15.357	—	.10	1.00

KM#	Date	Mintage	VF	XF	Unc
106	1968G	3,651	—	Proof	4.00
	1968J	—	150.00	225.00	350.00
	1969J	—	150.00	225.00	350.00

BRONZE CLAD STEEL

KM#	Date	Mintage	VF	XF	Unc
106a	1967G	520 pcs.	—	Proof	720.00
	1968D	19.523	—	.10	.25
	1968F	30.000	—	.10	.25
	1968F	3,000	—	Proof	6.00
	1968G	13.004	—	.10	.25
	1968G	2,372	—	Proof	4.00
	1968J	20.026	—	.10	.25
	1968J	2,000	—	Proof	7.50
	1969D	39.012	—	.10	.25
	1969D	—	—	Proof	1.25
	1969F	45.029	—	.10	.25
	1969F	5,100	—	Proof	1.25
	1969G	32.157	—	.10	.25
	1969G	8,700	—	Proof	1.25
	1969J	40.102	—	.10	.25
	1969J	5,000	—	Proof	2.50
	1970D	45.525	—	.10	.25
	1970F	73.851	—	.10	.25
	1970F	5,140	—	Proof	1.25
	1970G	30.330	—	.10	.25
	1970G	10,200	—	Proof	1.25
	1970 sm.J	46.730	—	.10	.25
	1970 lg.J	Inc. Ab.	—	.10	.25
	1970J	5,000	—	Proof	1.75
	1971D	71.755	—	.10	.25
	1971D	8,000	—	Proof	1.25
	1971F	82.765	—	.10	.25
	1971F	8,000	—	Proof	1.25
	1971G	47.850	—	.10	.25
	1971G	.010	—	Proof	1.25
	1971J	73.641	—	.10	.25
	1971J	8,000	—	Proof	1.25
	1972D	52.403	—	.10	.25
	1972D	8,000	—	Proof	1.00
	1972F	60.272	—	.10	.25
	1972F	8,000	—	Proof	1.00
	1972G	34.864	—	.10	.25
	1972G	.010	—	Proof	1.00
	1972J	53.673	—	.10	.25
	1972J	8,000	—	Proof	1.00
	1973D	26.190	—	.10	.25
	1973D	9,000	—	Proof	1.00
	1973F	30.160	—	.10	.25
	1973F	9,000	—	Proof	1.00
	1973G	17.379	—	.10	.25
	1973G	9,000	—	Proof	1.00
	1973J	26.830	—	.10	.25
	1973J	9,000	—	Proof	1.00
	1974D	58.667	—	.10	.25
	1974D	.035	—	Proof	.50
	1974F	67.596	—	.10	.25
	1974F	.035	—	Proof	.50
	1974G	39.007	—	.10	.25
	1974G	.035	—	Proof	.50
	1974J	60.195	—	.10	.25
	1974J	.035	—	Proof	.50
	1975D	58.634	—	.10	.25
	1975D	.043	—	Proof	.50
	1975F	67.685	—	.10	.25
	1975F	.043	—	Proof	.50
	1975G	39.391	—	.10	.25
	1975G	.043	—	Proof	.50
	1975J	60.207	—	.10	.25
	1975J	.043	—	Proof	.50
	1976D	78.074	—	.10	.25
	1976D	.043	—	Proof	.50
	1976F	90.130	—	.10	.25
	1976F	.043	—	Proof	.50
	1976G	51.988	—	.10	.25
	1976G	.043	—	Proof	.50
	1976J	80.145	—	.10	.25
	1976J	.043	—	Proof	.50
	1977D	84.516	—	.10	.20
	1977D	.051	—	Proof	.40
	1977F	97.504	—	.10	.20
	1977F	.051	—	Proof	.40
	1977G	56.276	—	.10	.20
	1977G	.051	—	Proof	.40
	1977J	86.888	—	.10	.20
	1977J	.051	—	Proof	.40
	1978D	84.500	—	.10	.20
	1978D	.054	—	Proof	.40
	1978F	97.500	—	.10	.20
	1978F	.054	—	Proof	.40
	1978G	56.225	—	.10	.20
	1978G	.054	—	Proof	.40
	1978J	86.775	—	.10	.20
	1978J	.054	—	Proof	.40
	1979D	91.000	—	.10	.20
	1979D	.089	—	Proof	.40
	1979F	105.000	—	.10	.20
	1979F	.089	—	Proof	.40
	1979G	60.550	—	.10	.20
	1979G	.089	—	Proof	.40
	1979J	93.480	—	.10	.20
	1979J	.089	—	Proof	.40
	1980D	93.360	—	.10	.20
	1980D	.110	—	Proof	.40
	1980F	120.360	—	.10	.20
	1980F	.110	—	Proof	.40
	1980G	50.830	—	.10	.20
	1980G	.110	—	Proof	.40
	1980J	102.260	—	.10	.20
	1980J	.110	—	Proof	.40
	1981D	93.910	—	.10	.20

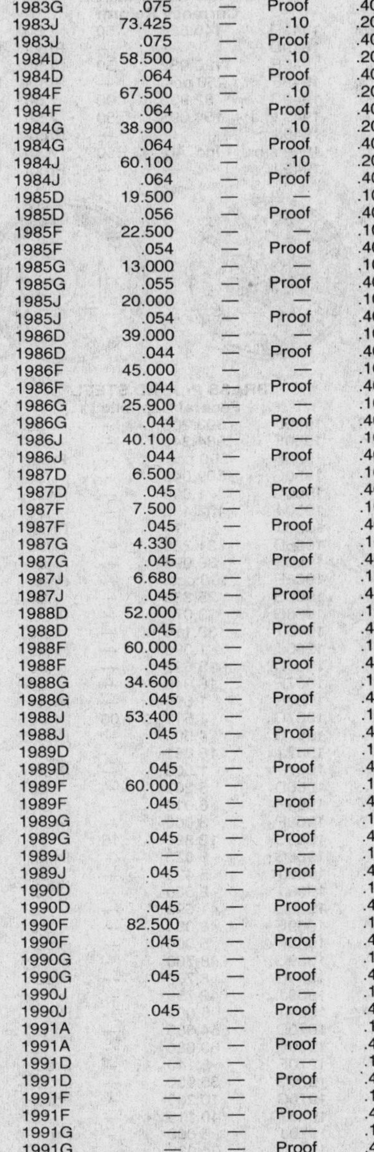

KM#	Date	Mintage	VF	XF	Unc
106a	1981D	.091	—	Proof	.40
	1981F	83.710	—	.10	.20
	1981F	.091	—	Proof	.40
	1981G	89.850	—	.10	.20
	1981G	.091	—	Proof	.40
	1981J	87.250	—	.10	.20
	1981J	.091	—	Proof	.40
	1982D	64.390	—	.10	.20
	1982D	.078	—	Proof	.40
	1982F	36.870	—	.10	.20
	1982F	.078	—	Proof	.40
	1982G	58.590	—	.10	.20
	1982G	.078	—	Proof	.40
	1982J	57.690	—	.10	.20
	1982J	.078	—	Proof	.40
	1983D	71.500	—	.10	.20
	1983D	.075	—	Proof	.40
	1983F	82.500	—	.10	.20
	1983F	.075	—	Proof	.40
	1983G	47.575	—	.10	.20
	1983G	.075	—	Proof	.40
	1983J	73.425	—	.10	.20
	1983J	.075	—	Proof	.40
	1984D	58.500	—	.10	.20
	1984D	.064	—	Proof	.40
	1984F	67.500	—	.10	.20
	1984F	.064	—	Proof	.40
	1984G	38.900	—	.10	.20
	1984G	.064	—	Proof	.40
	1984J	60.100	—	.10	.20
	1984J	.064	—	Proof	.40
	1985D	19.500	—	—	.10
	1985D	.056	—	Proof	.40
	1985F	22.500	—	—	.10
	1985F	.054	—	Proof	.40
	1985G	13.000	—	—	.10
	1985G	.055	—	Proof	.40
	1985J	20.000	—	—	.10
	1985J	.054	—	Proof	.40
	1986D	39.000	—	—	.10
	1986D	.044	—	Proof	.40
	1986F	45.000	—	—	.10
	1986F	.044	—	Proof	.40
	1986G	25.900	—	—	.10
	1986G	.044	—	Proof	.40
	1986J	40.100	—	—	.10
	1986J	.044	—	Proof	.40
	1987D	6.500	—	—	.10
	1987D	.045	—	Proof	.40
	1987F	7.500	—	—	.10
	1987F	.045	—	Proof	.40
	1987G	4.330	—	—	.10
	1987G	.045	—	Proof	.40
	1987J	6.680	—	—	.10
	1987J	.045	—	Proof	.40
	1988D	52.000	—	—	.10
	1988D	.045	—	Proof	.40
	1988F	60.000	—	—	.10
	1988F	.045	—	Proof	.40
	1988G	34.600	—	—	.10
	1988G	.045	—	Proof	.40
	1988J	53.400	—	—	.10
	1988J	.045	—	Proof	.40
	1989D	—	—	—	.10
	1989D	.045	—	Proof	.40
	1989F	60.000	—	—	.10
	1989F	.045	—	Proof	.40
	1989G	—	—	—	.10
	1989G	.045	—	Proof	.40
	1989J	—	—	—	.10
	1989J	.045	—	Proof	.40
	1990D	—	—	—	.10
	1990D	.045	—	Proof	.40
	1990F	82.500	—	—	.10
	1990F	.045	—	Proof	.40
	1990G	—	—	—	.10
	1990G	.045	—	Proof	.40
	1990J	—	—	—	.10
	1990J	.045	—	Proof	.40
	1991A	—	—	—	.10
	1991A	—	—	Proof	.40
	1991D	—	—	—	.10
	1991D	—	—	Proof	.40
	1991F	—	—	—	.10
	1991F	—	—	Proof	.40
	1991G	—	—	—	.10
	1991G	—	—	Proof	.40
	1991J	—	—	—	.10
	1991J	—	—	Proof	.40

5 PFENNIG

BRASS-CLAD STEEL
Currency Reform

KM#	Date	Mintage	VF	XF	Unc
102	1949D	60.026	.10	7.50	40.00
	1949D	—	—	Proof	150.00
	1949F	66.082	.10	7.50	25.00
	1949F	250 pcs.	—	Proof	75.00
	1949G	57.356	.10	7.50	45.00
	1949J	68.977	.10	7.50	35.00
	1949J	—	—	Proof	75.00

BRASS PLATED STEEL
Federal Republic

KM#	Date	Mintage	VF	XF	Unc
107	1950D	271.962	—	1.00	4.00
	1950F	362.880	—	1.00	4.00
	1950F	500 pcs.	—	Proof	55.00
	1950G	180.492	—	1.00	4.00
	1950G	1,800	—	Proof	3.00
	1950J lg.J	285.283	—	1.00	4.00
	1950J	—	—	Proof	12.00
	1950J sm.J	Inc. Ab.	—	1.00	4.00
	1950J	—	—	Proof	12.00
	1966D	26.036	—	1.00	7.50
	1966F	30.047	—	1.00	7.50
	1966F	100 pcs.	—	Proof	50.00
	1966G	17.333	—	1.00	7.50
	1966G	3,070	—	Proof	6.50
	1966J	26.741	—	1.00	7.50
	1966J	1,000	—	Proof	15.00
	1967D	10.418	—	1.00	7.50
	1967F	12.012	—	1.00	7.50
	1967F	1,500	—	Proof	12.50
	1967G	1.736	2.50	5.00	30.00
	1967G	4,500	—	Proof	6.00
	1967J	10.706	—	1.00	7.50
	1967J	1,500	—	Proof	15.00
	1968D	13.047	—	.25	4.00
	1968F	15.026	—	.25	4.00
	1968F	3,000	—	Proof	8.00
	1968G	13.855	—	.25	4.00
	1968G	6,023	—	Proof	5.00
	1968J	13.362	—	.25	4.00
	1968J	2,000	—	Proof	12.50
	1969D	23.488	—	.10	1.00
	1969F	27.046	—	.10	1.00
	1969F	5,000	—	Proof	2.00
	1969G	15.631	—	.10	1.00
	1969G	8,700	—	Proof	1.50
	1969J	24.120	—	.10	1.00
	1969J	5,000	—	Proof	2.00
	1970D	39.940	—	.10	.25
	1970F	45.517	—	.10	.25
	1970F	5,140	—	Proof	2.00
	1970G	27.638	—	.10	.25
	1970G	10,200	—	Proof	1.50
	1970J	40.873	—	.10	.25
	1970J	5,000	—	Proof	2.00
	1971D	57.345	—	.10	.25
	1971D	8,000	—	Proof	1.50
	1971F	66.426	—	.10	.25
	1971F	8,000	—	Proof	1.50
	1971G	38.284	—	.10	.25
	1971G	10,000	—	Proof	1.50
	1971J	58.566	—	.10	.25
	1971J	8,000	—	Proof	1.50
	1972D	52.325	—	.10	.25
	1972D	8,000	—	Proof	1.50
	1972F	60.292	—	.10	.25
	1972F	8,000	—	Proof	1.50
	1972G	34.719	—	.10	.25
	1972G	10,000	—	Proof	1.50
	1972J	54.218	—	.10	.25
	1972J	8,000	—	Proof	1.50
	1973D	15.596	—	.10	.25
	1973D	9,000	—	Proof	1.50
	1973F	18.039	—	.10	.25
	1973F	9,000	—	Proof	1.50
	1973G	10.391	—	.10	.25
	1973G	9,000	—	Proof	1.50
	1973J	16.035	—	.10	.25
	1973J	9,000	—	Proof	1.50
	1974D	15.769	—	.10	.25
	1974D	.035	—	Proof	.50
	1974F	18.143	—	.10	.25
	1974F	.035	—	Proof	.50
	1974G	10.508	—	.10	.25
	1974G	.035	—	Proof	.50
	1974J	16.055	—	.10	.25
	1974J	.035	—	Proof	.50
	1975D	15.715	—	.10	.25
	1975D	.043	—	Proof	.50
	1975F	18.013	—	.10	.25
	1975F	.043	—	Proof	.50
	1975G	10.466	—	.10	.25
	1975G	.043	—	Proof	.50
	1975J	16.201	—	.10	.25
	1975J	.043	—	Proof	.50
	1976D	47.091	—	.10	.25
	1976D	.043	—	Proof	.50
	1976F	54.370	—	.10	.25
	1976F	.043	—	Proof	.50
	1976G	31.367	—	.10	.25
	1976G	.043	—	Proof	.50
	1976J	48.321	—	.10	.25
	1976J	.043	—	Proof	.50
	1977D	52.159	—	.10	.20
	1977D	.051	—	Proof	.40
	1977F	60.124	—	.10	.20
	1977F	.051	—	Proof	.40
	1977G	34.600	—	.10	.20
	1977G	.051	—	Proof	.40
	1977J	53.481	—	.10	.20

KM#	Date	Mintage	VF	XF	Unc
107	1977J	.051	—	Proof	.40
	1978D	41.600	—	.10	.20
	1978D	.054	—	Proof	.40
	1978F	48.000	—	.10	.20
	1978F	.054	—	Proof	.40
	1978G	27.680	—	.10	.20
	1978G	.054	—	Proof	.40
	1978J	42.720	—	.10	.20
	1978J	.054	—	Proof	.40
	1979D	41.600	—	.10	.20
	1979D	.089	—	Proof	.40
	1979F	48.000	—	.10	.20
	1979F	.089	—	Proof	.40
	1979G	27.680	—	.10	.20
	1979G	.089	—	Proof	.40
	1979J	42.711	—	.10	.20
	1979J	.089	—	Proof	.40
	1980D	39.880	—	.10	.20
	1980D	.110	—	Proof	.40
	1980F	53.270	—	.10	.20
	1980F	.110	—	Proof	.40
	1980G	43.070	—	.10	.20
	1980G	.110	—	Proof	.40
	1980J	59.130	—	.10	.20
	1980J	.110	—	Proof	.40
	1981D	82.250	—	.10	.20
	1981D	.091	—	Proof	.40
	1981F	84.910	—	.10	.20
	1981F	.091	—	Proof	.40
	1981G	41.910	—	.10	.20
	1981G	.091	—	Proof	.40
	1981J	49.290	—	.10	.20
	1981J	.091	—	Proof	.40
	1982D	57.500	—	.10	.20
	1982D	.078	—	Proof	.40
	1982F	53.290	—	.10	.20
	1982F	.078	—	Proof	.40
	1982G	23.750	—	.10	.20
	1982G	.078	—	Proof	.40
	1982J	62.000	—	.10	.20
	1982J	.078	—	Proof	.40
	1983D	46.800	—	.10	.20
	1983D	.075	—	Proof	.40
	1983F	54.000	—	.10	.20
	1983F	.075	—	Proof	.40
	1983G	31.140	—	.10	.20
	1983G	.075	—	Proof	.40
	1983J	48.060	—	.10	.20
	1983J	.075	—	Proof	.40
	1984D	36.400	—	.10	.20
	1984D	.064	—	Proof	.40
	1984F	42.000	—	.10	.20
	1984F	.064	—	Proof	.40
	1984G	24.200	—	.10	.20
	1984G	.064	—	Proof	.40
	1984J	37.400	—	.10	.20
	1984J	.064	—	Proof	.40
	1985D	15.600	—	—	.10
	1985D	.056	—	Proof	.40
	1985F	18.000	—	—	.10
	1985F	.054	—	Proof	.40
	1985G	10.400	—	—	.10
	1985G	.055	—	Proof	.40
	1985J	16.000	—	—	.10
	1985J	.054	—	Proof	.40
	1986D	36.400	—	—	.10
	1986D	.044	—	Proof	.40
	1986F	42.000	—	—	.10
	1986F	.044	—	Proof	.40
	1986G	24.200	—	—	.10
	1986G	.044	—	Proof	.40
	1986J	37.400	—	—	.10
	1986J	.044	—	Proof	.40
	1987D	52.000	—	—	.10
	1987D	.045	—	Proof	.40
	1987F	60.000	—	—	.10
	1987F	.045	—	Proof	.40
	1987G	34.600	—	—	.10
	1987G	.045	—	Proof	.40
	1987J	53.400	—	—	.10
	1987J	.045	—	Proof	.40
	1988D	52.400	—	—	.10
	1988D	.045	—	Proof	.40
	1988F	72.000	—	—	.10
	1988F	.045	—	Proof	.40
	1988G	41.500	—	—	.10
	1988G	.045	—	Proof	.40
	1988J	64.100	—	—	.10
	1988J	.045	—	Proof	.40
	1989D	—	—	—	.10
	1989D	.045	—	Proof	.40
	1989F	108.000	—	—	.10
	1989F	.045	—	Proof	.40
	1989G	—	—	—	.10
	1989G	.045	—	Proof	.40
	1989J	—	—	—	.10
	1989J	.045	—	Proof	.40
	1990A	70.000	—	—	.10
	1990D	—	—	—	.10
	1990D	.045	—	Proof	.40
	1990F	108.000	—	—	.10
	1990F	.045	—	Proof	.40
	1990G	—	—	—	.10
	1990G	.045	—	Proof	.40
	1990J	—	—	—	.10
	1990J	.045	—	Proof	.40
	1991A	—	—	—	.10
	1991A	—	—	Proof	.40
	1991D	—	—	—	.10
	1991D	—	—	Proof	.40
107	1991F	—	—	—	.10
	1991F	—	—	Proof	.40
	1991G	—	—	—	.10
	1991G	—	—	Proof	.40
	1991J	—	—	—	.10
	1991J	—	—	Proof	.40

10 PFENNIG

BRASS-CLAD STEEL
Currency Reform

KM#	Date	Mintage	VF	XF	Unc
103	1949D	140.558	.50	7.50	22.50
	1949D	—	—	Proof	140.00
	1949F	120.932	.50	7.50	22.50
	1949F	250 pcs.	—	Proof	130.00
	1949G	82.933	1.00	7.50	30.00
	1949 lg.J	154.095	.50	7.50	22.50
	1949J	—	—	Proof	50.00
	1949 sm.J	Inc. Ab.	.50	7.50	22.50
	1949J	—	—	Proof	50.00

BRASS PLATED STEEL
Federal Republic

KM#	Date	Mintage	VF	XF	Unc
108	1950D	393.209	—	.20	3.00
	1950F	584.340	—	.20	3.00
	1950F	500 pcs.	—	Proof	42.50
	1950G	309.045	—	.20	3.00
	1950G	1,800	—	Proof	3.00
	1950J	402.452	—	.20	3.00
	1950J	—	—	Proof	17.50
	1966D	31.220	—	.20	3.00
	1966F	36.097	—	.20	3.00
	1966F	100 pcs.	—	Proof	75.00
	1966G	25.338	—	.20	3.00
	1966G	3,070	—	Proof	7.50
	1966J	32.116	—	.20	3.00
	1966J	1,000	—	Proof	12.50
	1967D	15.632	—	.20	4.00
	1967F	18.049	—	.20	4.00
	1967F	1,500	—	Proof	15.00
	1967G	1.518	1.00	4.00	15.00
	1967G	4,500	—	Proof	7.50
	1967J	16.051	—	.20	4.00
	1967J	1,500	—	Proof	12.50
	1968D	5.207	—	.20	3.00
	1968F	6.010	—	.20	3.00
	1968F	3,000	—	Proof	10.00
	1968G	12.384	.15	.50	3.00
	1968G	6,023	—	Proof	5.00
	1968J	5.422	—	.20	3.50
	1968J	2,000	—	Proof	10.00
	1969D	41.693	—	.15	2.00
	1969F	48.084	—	.15	.25
	1969F	5,000	—	Proof	3.00
	1969G	48.760	—	.15	.25
	1969G	8,700	—	Proof	2.50
	1969J	42.756	—	.15	.25
	1969J	5,000	—	Proof	2.50
	1970D	54.085	—	.15	.25
	1970F	60.086	—	.15	.25
	1970F	5,140	—	Proof	3.00
	1970G	35.900	—	.15	.25
	1970G	10,200	—	Proof	2.00
	1970J	40.115	—	.15	.25
	1970J	5,000	—	Proof	2.50
	1971D	54.022	—	.15	.25
	1971D	8,000	—	Proof	2.50
	1971F	92.534	—	.15	.25
	1971F	8,000	—	Proof	2.50
	1971G	88.614	—	.15	.25
	1971G	.010	—	Proof	2.00
	1971 sm.J	65.622	—	.15	.25
	1971 lg.J	Inc. Ab.	—	.15	.25
	1971J	8,000	—	Proof	1.50
	1972D	104.345	—	.15	.25
	1972D	8,000	—	Proof	1.50
	1972F	110.177	—	.15	.25
	1972F	8,000	—	Proof	1.50
	1972G	71.766	—	.15	.25
	1972G	10,000	—	Proof	1.50
	1972J	96.991	—	.15	.25
	1972J	8,000	—	Proof	1.50
	1973D	26.052	—	.15	.25
	1973D	9,000	—	Proof	1.50
	1973F	30.070	—	.15	.25
	1973F	9,000	—	Proof	1.50
	1973G	17.294	—	.15	.25
	1973G	9,000	—	Proof	1.50
	1973J	26.774	—	.15	.25
	1973J	9,000	—	Proof	1.50

KM#	Date	Mintage	VF	XF	Unc
108	1974D	15.707	—	.15	.25
	1974D	.035	—	Proof	.75
	1974F	18.135	—	.15	.25
	1974F	.035	—	Proof	.75
	1974G	10.450	—	.15	.25
	1974G	.035	—	Proof	.75
	1974J	16.056	—	.15	.25
	1974J	.035	—	Proof	.75
	1975D	15.654	—	.15	.25
	1975D	.043	—	Proof	.75
	1975F	18.043	—	.15	.25
	1975F	.043	—	Proof	.75
	1975G	10.403	—	.15	.25
	1975G	.043	—	Proof	.75
	1975J	16.111	—	.15	.25
	1975J	.043	—	Proof	.75
	1976D	65.200	—	.15	.25
	1976D	.043	—	Proof	.75
	1976F	75.282	—	.15	.25
	1976F	.043	—	Proof	.75
	1976G	43.372	—	.15	.25
	1976G	.043	—	Proof	.75
	1976J	66.930	—	.15	.25
	1976J	.043	—	Proof	.75
	1977D	64.989	—	.10	.20
	1977D	.051	—	Proof	.50
	1977F	75.052	—	.10	.20
	1977F	.051	—	Proof	.50
	1977G	43.300	—	.10	.20
	1977G	.051	—	Proof	.50
	1977J	66.800	—	.10	.20
	1977J	.051	—	Proof	.50
	1978D	91.000	—	.10	.20
	1978D	.054	—	Proof	.50
	1978F	105.000	—	.10	.20
	1978F	.054	—	Proof	.50
	1978G	60.590	—	.10	.20
	1978G	.054	—	Proof	.50
	1978J	93.490	—	.10	.20
	1978J	.054	—	Proof	.50
	1979D	104.000	—	.10	.20
	1979D	.089	—	Proof	.50
	1979F	120.000	—	.10	.20
	1979F	.089	—	Proof	.50
	1979G	69.200	—	.10	.20
	1979G	.089	—	Proof	.50
	1979J	106.800	—	.10	.20
	1979J	.089	—	Proof	.50
	1980D	65.450	—	.10	.20
	1980D	.110	—	Proof	.50
	1980F	122.780	—	.10	.20
	1980F	.110	—	Proof	.50
	1980G	75.410	—	.10	.20
	1980G	.110	—	Proof	.50
	1980J	70.960	—	.10	.20
	1980J	.110	—	Proof	.50
	1981D	135.200	—	.10	.20
	1981D	.091	—	Proof	.50
	1981F	117.410	—	.10	.20
	1981F	.091	—	Proof	.50
	1981G	69.440	—	.10	.20
	1981G	.091	—	Proof	.50
	1981J	138.360	—	.10	.20
	1981J	.091	—	Proof	.50
	1982D	74.690	—	.10	.20
	1982D	.078	—	Proof	.50
	1982F	85.140	—	.10	.20
	1982F	.078	—	Proof	.50
	1982G	50.840	—	.10	.20
	1982G	.078	—	Proof	.50
	1982J	80.620	—	.10	.20
	1982J	.078	—	Proof	.50
	1983D	33.800	—	.10	.20
	1983D	.075	—	Proof	.50
	1983F	39.000	—	.10	.20
	1983F	.075	—	Proof	.50
	1983G	22.490	—	.10	.20
	1983G	.075	—	Proof	.50
	1983J	34.710	—	.10	.20
	1983J	.075	—	Proof	.50
	1984D	52.000	—	.10	.20
	1984D	.064	—	Proof	.50
	1984F	60.000	—	.10	.20
	1984F	.064	—	Proof	.50
	1984G	34.600	—	.10	.20
	1984G	.064	—	Proof	.50
	1984J	53.400	—	.10	.20
	1984J	.064	—	Proof	.50
	1985D	78.000	—	—	.15
	1985D	.056	—	Proof	.50
	1985F	90.000	—	—	.15
	1985F	.054	—	Proof	.50
	1985G	51.900	—	—	.15
	1985G	.055	—	Proof	.50
	1985J	80.100	—	—	.15
	1985J	.054	—	Proof	.50
	1986D	41.600	—	—	.15
	1986D	.044	—	Proof	.50
	1986F	48.000	—	—	.15
	1986F	.044	—	Proof	.50
	1986G	27.700	—	—	.15
	1986G	.044	—	Proof	.50
	1986J	42.700	—	—	.15
	1986J	.044	—	Proof	.15
	1987D	58.500	—	—	.10
	1987D	.045	—	Proof	.15
	1987F	67.500	—	—	.10
	1987F	.045	—	Proof	.15
	1987G	38.900	—	—	.10
	1987G	.045	—	Proof	.50

KM#	Date	Mintage	VF	XF	Unc
108	1987J	60.100	—	—	.15
	1987J	.045	—	Proof	.50
	1988D	109.200	—	—	.15
	1988D	.045	—	Proof	.50
	1988F	126.000	—	—	.15
	1988F	.045	—	Proof	.50
	1988G	72.700	—	—	.15
	1988G	.045	—	Proof	.50
	1988J	112.100	—	—	.15
	1988J	.045	—	Proof	.50
	1989D	—	—	—	.15
	1989D	.045	—	Proof	.50
	1989F	138.000	—	—	.15
	1989F	.045	—	Proof	.50
	1989G	—	—	—	.15
	1989G	.045	—	Proof	.50
	1989J	—	—	—	.15
	1989J	.045	—	Proof	.50
	1990A	100.000	—	—	.15
	1990D	—	—	—	.15
	1990D	.045	—	Proof	.50
	1990F	180.000	—	—	.15
	1990F	.045	—	Proof	.50
	1990G	—	—	—	.15
	1990G	.045	—	Proof	.50
	1990J	—	—	—	.15
	1990J	.045	—	Proof	.50
	1991A	—	—	—	.15
	1991A	—	—	Proof	.40
	1991D	—	—	—	.15
	1991D	—	—	Proof	.40
	1991F	—	—	—	.15
	1991F	—	—	Proof	.40
	1991G	—	—	—	.15
	1991G	—	—	Proof	.40
	1991J	—	—	—	.15
	1991J	—	—	Proof	.40

50 PFENNIG

COPPER-NICKEL
Currency Reform

KM#	Date	Mintage	VF	XF	Unc
104	1949D	39.108	.75	3.50	35.00
	1949F	45.118	.75	3.50	35.00
	1949F	200 pcs.	—	Proof	125.00
	1949G	25.924	.75	4.00	45.00
	1949J	42.303	.75	3.50	45.00
	1949J	—	—	Proof	150.00
	1950G	.030	175.00	250.00	350.00

NOTE: The 1950G dated coin was restruck without authorization by a mint official using genuine dies - quantity unknown.

Federal Republic
Reeded edge

KM#	Date	Mintage	VF	XF	Unc
109.1	1950D	100.735	.50	.75	7.50
	1950F	143.510	.50	.75	7.50
	1950F	450 pcs.	—	Proof	85.00
	1950G	66.421	.50	.75	8.50
	1950G	1,800	—	Proof	3.50
	1950J	102.736	.50	.75	7.50
	1950J	—	—	Proof	22.50
	1966D	8.328	.50	.75	12.50
	1966F	9.605	.50	.75	12.50
	1966F	100 pcs.	—	Proof	125.00
	1966G	5.543	.50	.65	12.50
	1966G	3,070	—	Proof	8.50
	1966J	8.569	.50	.65	12.50
	1966J	1,000	—	Proof	18.00
	1967D	5.207	.50	.65	12.50
	1967F	6.005	.50	.65	12.50
	1967F	1,500	—	Proof	15.00
	1967G	1.843	.50	1.00	15.00
	1967G	4,500	—	Proof	10.00
	1967J	10.684	.50	.65	12.50
	1967J	1,500	—	Proof	15.00
	1968D	7.809	.50	.60	10.00
	1968F	3.000	.50	.60	10.00
	1968F	3,000	—	Proof	12.00
	1968G	6.818	.50	.60	10.00
	1968G	6,023	—	Proof	6.50
	1968J	2.672	.50	.65	15.00
	1968J	2,000	—	Proof	12.50
	1969D	14.561	.45	.55	2.00
	1969F	16.804	.45	.55	2.00
	1969F	5,000	—	Proof	3.50
	1969G	9.704	.45	.55	2.00
	1969G	8,700	—	Proof	3.00
	1969J	14.969	.45	.55	2.00
	1969J	5,000	—	Proof	10.00
	1970D	25.294	.45	.55	1.00
	1970F	26.455	.45	.55	1.00
109.1	1970F	5,140	—	Proof	3.50
	1970G	11.955	.45	.55	1.00
	1970G	10,200	—	Proof	3.00
	1970J	10.683	.45	.55	1.00
	1970J	5,000	—	Proof	3.50
	1971D	23.393	.45	.55	.75
	1971D	8,000	—	Proof	3.00
	1971F	29.746	.45	.55	.75
	1971F	8,000	—	Proof	3.00
	1971G	15.556	.45	.55	.75
	1971G	.010	—	Proof	3.00
	1971 lg.J	24.044	.45	.55	.75
	1971 sm.J	Inc. Ab.	.45	.55	.75
	1971J	8,000	—	Proof	3.00

Plain edge

KM#	Date	Mintage	VF	XF	Unc
109.2	1972D	26.008	—	.45	.60
	1972D	8,000	—	Proof	2.00
	1972F	30.043	—	.45	.60
	1972F	8,000	—	Proof	2.00
	1972G	17.337	—	.45	.60
	1972G	10,000	—	Proof	2.00
	1972J	26.707	—	.45	.60
	1972J	8,000	—	Proof	2.00
	1973D	7.810	—	.45	1.00
	1973D	9,000	—	Proof	2.00
	1973F	8.994	—	.45	.60
	1973F	9,000	—	Proof	2.00
	1973G	5.201	—	.45	.60
	1973G	9,000	—	Proof	2.00
	1973J	8.011	—	.45	.60
	1973J	9,000	—	Proof	2.00
	1974D	18.264	—	.45	1.00
	1974D	.035	—	Proof	1.00
	1974 lg.F	21.036	—	.45	.60
	1974 sm.F	Inc. Ab.	—	.45	1.00
	1974F	.035	—	Proof	1.00
	1974G	12.159	—	.45	.60
	1974G	.035	—	Proof	1.00
	1974J	18.752	—	.45	.60
	1974J	.035	—	Proof	1.00
	1975D	13.055	—	.45	1.00
	1975D	.043	—	Proof	1.00
	1975F	15.003	—	.45	.60
	1975F	.043	—	Proof	1.00
	1975G	8.675	—	.45	.60
	1975G	.043	—	Proof	1.00
	1975J	13.379	—	.45	.60
	1975J	.043	—	Proof	1.00
	1976D	10.411	—	.45	1.00
	1976D	.043	—	Proof	1.00
	1976F	12.048	—	.45	.60
	1976F	.043	—	Proof	1.00
	1976G	6.653	—	.45	.60
	1976G	.043	—	Proof	1.00
	1976J	10.716	—	.45	.60
	1976J	.043	—	Proof	1.00
	1977D	10.400	—	.45	1.00
	1977D	.051	—	Proof	.75
	1977F	12.000	—	.45	.60
	1977F	.051	—	Proof	.75
	1977G	6.921	—	.45	.60
	1977G	.051	—	Proof	.75
	1977J	10.708	—	.45	.60
	1977J	.051	—	Proof	.75
	1978D	10.400	—	.45	.60
	1978D	.054	—	Proof	.75
	1978F	12.000	—	.45	.60
	1978F	.054	—	Proof	.75
	1978G	6.640	—	.45	.60
	1978G	.054	—	Proof	.75
	1978J	10.680	—	.45	.60
	1978J	.054	—	Proof	.75
	1979D	10.400	—	.45	.60
	1979D	.089	—	Proof	.75
	1979F	12.000	—	.45	.60
	1979F	.089	—	Proof	.75
	1979G	6.920	—	.45	.60
	1979G	.089	—	Proof	.75
	1979J	10.680	—	.45	.60
	1979J	.089	—	Proof	.75
	1980D	23.250	—	.45	.60
	1980D	.110	—	Proof	.75
	1980F	17.440	—	.45	.60
	1980F	.110	—	Proof	.75
	1980G	22.460	—	.45	.60
	1980G	.110	—	Proof	.75
	1980J	24.030	—	.45	.60
	1980J	.110	—	Proof	.75
	1981D	17.900	—	.45	.60
	1981D	.091	—	Proof	.75
	1981F	29.810	—	.45	.60
	1981F	.091	—	Proof	.75
	1981G	10.880	—	.45	.60
	1981G	.091	—	Proof	.75
	1981J	24.140	—	.45	.60
	1981J	.091	—	Proof	.75
	1982D	21.540	—	.45	.60
	1982D	.078	—	Proof	.75
	1982F	28.900	—	.45	.60
	1982F	.078	—	Proof	.75
	1982G	19.710	—	.45	.60
	1982G	.078	—	Proof	.75
	1982J	17.210	—	.45	.60
	1982J	.078	—	Proof	.75
	1983D	20.800	—	.45	.60
	1983D	.075	—	Proof	.75
	1983F	24.000	—	.45	.60
	1983F	.075	—	Proof	.75
	1983G	13.840	—	.45	.60
109.2	1983G	.075	—	Proof	.75
	1983J	21.360	—	.45	.60
	1983J	.075	—	Proof	.75
	1984D	11.700	—	.45	.60
	1984D	.064	—	Proof	.75
	1984F	13.500	—	.45	.60
	1984F	.064	—	Proof	.75
	1984G	7.800	—	.45	.60
	1984G	.064	—	Proof	.75
	1984J	12.000	—	.45	.60
	1984J	.064	—	Proof	.75
	1985D	15.700	—	—	.50
	1985D	.056	—	Proof	.75
	1985F	18.000	—	—	.50
	1985F	.054	—	Proof	.75
	1985G	10.400	—	—	.50
	1985G	.055	—	Proof	.75
	1985J	16.100	—	—	.50
	1985J	.054	—	Proof	.75
	1986D	2.100	—	—	.50
	1986D	.044	—	Proof	.75
	1986F	2.400	—	—	.50
	1986F	.044	—	Proof	.75
	1986G	1.400	—	—	.50
	1986G	.044	—	Proof	.75
	1986J	2.100	—	—	.50
	1986J	.044	—	Proof	.75
	1987D	.520	—	—	.50
	1987D	.045	—	Proof	.75
	1987F	.600	—	—	.50
	1987F	.045	—	Proof	.75
	1987G	.350	—	—	.50
	1987G	.045	—	Proof	.75
	1987J	.530	—	—	.50
	1987J	.045	—	Proof	.75
	1988D	4.160	—	—	.50
	1988D	.045	—	Proof	.75
	1988F	4.800	—	—	.50
	1988F	.045	—	Proof	.75
	1988G	2.770	—	—	.50
	1988G	.045	—	Proof	.75
	1988J	4.300	—	—	.50
	1988J	.045	—	Proof	.75
	1989D	—	—	—	.50
	1989D	.045	—	Proof	.75
	1989F	42.000	—	—	.50
	1989F	.045	—	Proof	.75
	1989G	—	—	—	.50
	1989G	.045	—	Proof	.75
	1989J	—	—	—	.50
	1989J	.045	—	Proof	.75
	1990A	150.000	—	—	1.00
	1990D	—	—	—	.50
	1990D	.045	—	Proof	.75
	1990F	67.500	—	—	.50
	1990F	.045	—	Proof	.75
	1990G	—	—	—	.50
	1990G	.045	—	Proof	.75
	1990J	—	—	—	.50
	1990J	.045	—	Proof	.75
	1991A	—	—	—	.50
	1991A	—	—	Proof	.75
	1991D	—	—	—	.50
	1991D	—	—	Proof	.75
	1991F	—	—	—	.50
	1991F	—	—	Proof	.75
	1991G	—	—	—	.50
	1991G	—	—	Proof	.75
	1991J	—	—	—	.50
	1991J	—	—	Proof	.75

MARK

COPPER-NICKEL
Federal Republic

KM#	Date	Mintage	VF	XF	Unc
110	1950D	60.467	.75	2.50	40.00
	1950D	—	—	Proof	150.00
	1950F	69.183	.75	2.50	40.00
	1950F	150 pcs.	—	Proof	400.00
	1950G	39.826	.75	2.50	60.00
	1950G	*200 pcs.	—	Proof	325.00
	1950J	61.483	.75	2.50	45.00
	1950J	—	—	Proof	125.00
	1954D	5.202	1.00	7.50	165.00
	1954F	6.000	1.00	7.50	150.00
	1954F	175 pcs.	—	Proof	325.00
	1954G	3.459	1.00	70.00	800.00
	1954G	15 pcs.	—	Proof	1500.
	1954J	5.341	1.00	7.50	175.00
	1954J	—	—	Proof	200.00
	1955D	3.093	1.00	7.50	175.00
	1955F	4.909	1.00	7.50	300.00
	1955F	*20 pcs.	—	Proof	1000.
	1955G	2.500	15.00	90.00	1000.
	1955J	5.294	1.00	7.50	175.00
	1956D	13.231	1.00	5.00	150.00
	1956F	14.700	1.00	5.00	150.00
	1956F	100 pcs.	—	Proof	300.00
	1956G	8.362	1.00	5.00	250.00
	1956J	11.478	1.00	7.50	200.00

KM#	Date	Mintage	VF	XF	Unc
110	1957D	6.820	1.00	7.50	150.00
	1957D	100 pcs.	—	Proof	300.00
	1957F	6.390	1.00	7.50	150.00
	1957F	100 pcs.	—	Proof	350.00
	1957G	3.841	1.00	7.50	120.00
	1957J	6.632	1.00	7.50	150.00
	1957J	—	—	Proof	550.00
	1958D	4.150	1.00	5.00	150.00
	1958D	—	—	Proof	300.00
	1958F	4.109	1.00	5.00	200.00
	1958F	100 pcs.	—	Proof	550.00
	1958G	3.460	1.00	5.00	175.00
	1958J	4.656	1.00	5.00	175.00
	1959D	10.409	.85	2.50	60.00
	1959F	11.972	.85	2.50	60.00
	1959F	100 pcs.	—	Proof	—
	1959G	6.921	.85	2.50	70.00
	1959G	*16 pcs.	—	Proof	2100.
	1959J	10.691	.85	2.50	60.00
	1960D	5.453	.85	2.50	60.00
	1960F	5.709	.85	2.50	60.00
	1960F	100 pcs.	—	Proof	250.00
	1960G	3.632	.85	2.50	60.00
	1960G	—	—	Proof	150.00
	1960J	5.612	.85	2.50	50.00
	1961D	7.536	.85	2.50	50.00
	1961F	6.029	.85	2.50	50.00
	1961G	4.843	.85	2.50	55.00
	1961G	20 pcs.	—	Proof	1150.
	1961J	7.483	.85	2.50	50.00
	1962D	10.327	.85	2.50	30.00
	1962F	11.122	.85	2.50	30.00
	1962G	6.054	.85	2.50	25.00
	1962G	*100 pcs.	—	Proof	250.00
	1962J	10.822	.85	2.50	25.00
	1963D	12.624	.85	2.50	25.00
	1963F	18.292	.85	2.50	25.00
	1963G	11.253	.85	2.50	25.00
	1963G	*600 pcs.	—	Proof	—
	1963J	15.906	.85	2.50	25.00
	1964D	8.048	.85	2.50	25.00
	1964F	12.796	.85	2.50	25.00
	1964G	3.465	.85	2.50	25.00
	1964G	*600 pcs.	—	Proof	40.00
	1964J	6.958	.85	2.50	25.00
	1965D	9.388	.75	2.00	20.00
	1965F	9.013	.75	2.00	20.00
	1965F	*80 pcs.	—	Proof	175.00
	1965G	6.232	.75	2.00	20.00
	1965G	1,200	—	Proof	10.00
	1965J	8.024	.75	2.00	20.00
	1966D	11.717	.75	2.00	15.00
	1966F	11.368	.75	2.00	15.00
	1966F	100 pcs.	—	Proof	150.00
	1966G	7.799	.75	2.00	15.00
	1966G	3,070	—	Proof	12.50
	1966J	12.030	.75	2.00	15.00
	1966J	1,000	—	Proof	25.00
	1967D	13.017	.75	2.00	12.50
	1967F	7.500	.75	2.00	12.50
	1967F	1,500	—	Proof	20.00
	1967G	4.324	.75	2.00	12.50
	1967G	4,500	—	Proof	15.00
	1967J	13.357	.75	2.00	12.50
	1967J	1,500	—	Proof	20.00
	1968D	1.303	.75	4.00	20.00
	1968F	1.500	.75	4.00	20.00
	1968F	3,000	—	Proof	15.00
	1968G	5.198	.75	3.00	20.00
	1968G	6,023	—	Proof	7.50
	1968J	1.338	.75	4.00	25.00
	1968J	2,000	—	Proof	15.00
	1969D	13.025	.75	1.50	10.00
	1969F	15.021	.75	1.50	10.00
	1969F	5,000	—	Proof	6.00
	1969G	8.665	.75	1.50	10.00
	1969G	8,700	—	Proof	5.00
	1969J	13.370	.75	1.50	10.00
	1969J	5,000	—	Proof	5.00
	1970D	17.928	.75	1.00	8.00
	1970F	19.408	.75	1.00	8.00
	1970F	5,140	—	Proof	6.00
	1970G	20.386	.75	1.00	8.00
	1970G	10,200	—	Proof	5.00
	1970J	10.707	.75	1.00	8.00
	1970J	5,000	—	Proof	5.00
	1971D	24.513	.75	1.00	3.00
	1971D	8,000	—	Proof	5.00
	1971F	28.275	.75	1.00	3.00
	1971F	8,000	—	Proof	5.00
	1971G	16.375	.75	1.00	3.00
	1971G	.010	—	Proof	5.00
	1971J	25.214	.75	1.00	3.00
	1971J	8,000	—	Proof	5.00
	1972D	20.904	.75	1.00	2.00
	1972D	8,000	—	Proof	4.00
	1972F	24.086	.75	1.00	2.00
	1972F	8,000	—	Proof	4.00
	1972G	13.868	.75	1.00	2.00
	1972G	.010	—	Proof	4.00
	1972J	21.360	.75	1.00	2.00
	1972J	8,000	—	Proof	4.00
	1973D	14.327	.75	1.00	2.00
	1973D	9,000	—	Proof	4.00
	1973F	16.592	.75	1.00	2.00
	1973F	9,000	—	Proof	4.00
	1973G	10.409	.75	1.00	2.00
	1973G	9,000	—	Proof	4.00
	1973J	14.704	.75	1.00	2.00
	1973J	9,000	—	Proof	4.00

KM#	Date	Mintage	VF	XF	Unc
110	1974D	20.876	.75	1.00	2.00
	1974D	.035	—	Proof	2.00
	1974F	24.057	.75	1.00	2.00
	1974F	.035	—	Proof	2.00
	1974G	13.931	.75	1.00	2.00
	1974G	.035	—	Proof	2.00
	1974J	21.440	.75	1.00	2.00
	1974J	.035	—	Proof	2.00
	1975D	18.241	.75	1.00	1.50
	1975D	.043	—	Proof	2.00
	1975F	21.059	.75	1.00	1.50
	1975F	.043	—	Proof	2.00
	1975G	12.142	.75	1.00	1.50
	1975G	.043	—	Proof	2.00
	1975J	18.770	.75	1.00	1.50
	1975J	.043	—	Proof	2.00
	1976D	15.670	.75	1.00	1.50
	1976D	.043	—	Proof	2.00
	1976F	18.105	.75	1.00	1.50
	1976F	.043	—	Proof	2.00
	1976G	10.382	.75	1.00	1.50
	1976G	.043	—	Proof	2.00
	1976J	16.046	.75	1.00	1.50
	1976J	.043	—	Proof	2.00
	1977D	20.801	.75	.85	1.00
	1977D	.051	—	Proof	1.25
	1977F	24.026	.75	.85	1.00
	1977F	.051	—	Proof	1.25
	1977G	13.849	.75	.85	1.00
	1977G	.051	—	Proof	1.25
	1977J	21.416	.75	.85	1.00
	1977J	.051	—	Proof	1.25
	1978D	15.600	.75	.85	1.00
	1978D	.054	—	Proof	1.25
	1978F	18.000	.75	.85	1.00
	1978F	.054	—	Proof	1.25
	1978G	10.380	.75	.85	1.00
	1978G	.054	—	Proof	1.25
	1978J	16.020	.75	.85	1.00
	1978J	.054	—	Proof	1.25
	1979D	18.200	.75	.85	1.00
	1979D	.089	—	Proof	1.25
	1979F	21.000	.75	.85	1.00
	1979F	.089	—	Proof	1.25
	1979G	12.110	.75	.85	1.00
	1979G	.089	—	Proof	1.25
	1979J	18.690	.75	.85	1.00
	1979J	.089	—	Proof	1.25
	1980D	24.330	—	.75	.90
	1980D	.110	—	Proof	1.00
	1980F	9.670	—	.75	.90
	1980F	.110	—	Proof	1.00
	1980G	8.540	—	.75	.90
	1980G	.110	—	Proof	1.00
	1980J	16.010	—	.75	.90
	1980J	.110	—	Proof	1.00
	1981D	21.150	—	.75	.90
	1981D	.091	—	Proof	1.00
	1981F	25.910	—	.75	.90
	1981F	.091	—	Proof	1.00
	1981G	14.090	—	.75	.90
	1981G	.091	—	Proof	1.00
	1981J	18.800	—	.75	.90
	1981J	.091	—	Proof	1.00
	1982D	20.590	—	.75	.90
	1982D	.078	—	Proof	1.00
	1982F	22.990	—	.75	.90
	1982F	.078	—	Proof	1.00
	1982G	14.900	—	.75	.90
	1982G	.078	—	Proof	1.00
	1982J	11.520	—	.75	.90
	1982J	.078	—	Proof	1.00
	1983D	18.200	—	.75	.90
	1983D	.075	—	Proof	1.00
	1983F	21.000	—	.75	.90
	1983F	.075	—	Proof	1.00
	1983G	12.100	—	.75	.90
	1983G	.075	—	Proof	1.00
	1983J	18.690	—	.75	.90
	1983J	.075	—	Proof	1.00
	1984D	8.400	—	.75	.90
	1984D	.064	—	Proof	1.50
	1984F	9.700	—	.75	.90
	1984F	.064	—	Proof	1.50
	1984G	5.600	—	.75	.90
	1984G	.064	—	Proof	1.50
	1984J	8.700	—	.75	.90
	1984J	.064	—	Proof	1.50
	1985D	11.700	—	—	.85
	1985D	.056	—	Proof	1.50
	1985F	13.500	—	—	.85
	1985F	.054	—	Proof	1.50
	1985G	7.800	—	—	.85
	1985G	.055	—	Proof	1.50
	1985J	12.000	—	—	.85
	1985J	.054	—	Proof	1.50
	1986D	10.400	—	—	.85
	1986D	.044	—	Proof	1.50
	1986F	12.000	—	—	.85
	1986F	.044	—	Proof	1.50
	1986G	6.900	—	—	.85
	1986G	.044	—	Proof	1.50
	1986J	10.700	—	—	.85
	1986J	.044	—	Proof	1.50
	1987D	3.120	—	—	.85
	1987D	.045	—	Proof	1.50
	1987F	3.600	—	—	.85
	1987F	.045	—	Proof	1.50
	1987G	2.080	—	—	.85
	1987G	.045	—	Proof	1.50

KM#	Date	Mintage	VF	XF	Unc
110	1987J	3.200	—	—	.85
	1987J	.045	—	Proof	1.50
	1988D	20.800	—	—	.85
	1988D	.045	—	Proof	1.50
	1988F	24.000	—	—	.85
	1988F	.045	—	Proof	1.50
	1988G	13.800	—	—	.85
	1988G	.045	—	Proof	1.50
	1988J	21.400	—	—	.85
	1988J	.045	—	Proof	1.50
	1989D	—	—	—	.85
	1989D	.045	—	Proof	1.50
	1989F	45.000	—	—	.85
	1989F	.045	—	Proof	1.50
	1989G	—	—	—	.85
	1989G	.045	—	Proof	1.50
	1989J	—	—	—	.85
	1989J	.045	—	Proof	1.50
	1990A	55.000	—	—	2.00
	1990D	—	—	—	.85
	1990D	.045	—	Proof	1.50
	1990F	89.700	—	—	.85
	1990F	.045	—	Proof	1.50
	1990G	—	—	—	.85
	1990G	.045	—	Proof	1.50
	1990J	—	—	—	.85
	1990J	.045	—	Proof	1.50
	1991A	—	—	—	.85
	1991A	—	—	Proof	1.50
	1991D	—	—	—	.85
	1991D	—	—	Proof	1.50
	1991F	—	—	—	.85
	1991F	—	—	Proof	1.50
	1991G	—	—	—	.85
	1991G	—	—	Proof	1.50
	1991J	—	—	—	.85
	1991J	—	—	Proof	1.50

2 MARK

COPPER-NICKEL
Federal Republic

KM#	Date	Mintage	VF	XF	Unc
111	1951D	19.564	22.50	40.00	100.00
	1951D	—	—	Proof	300.00
	1951F	22.609	20.00	30.00	85.00
	1951F	150 pcs.	—	Proof	300.00
	1951G	*13.012	30.00	80.00	185.00
	1951G	—	—	Proof	300.00
	1951J	20.104	20.00	30.00	85.00
	1951J	—	—	Proof	300.00

***NOTE:** The 1951G dated coin was restruck without authorization by a mint official using genuine dies - quantity unknown.

Max Planck

KM#	Date	Mintage	VF	XF	Unc
116	1957D	7.452	2.00	5.00	35.00
	1957D	—	—	Proof	85.00
	1957F	6.337	2.00	5.00	35.00
	1957F	100 pcs.	—	Proof	85.00
	1957G	2.598	3.00	7.50	110.00
	1957J	11.210	2.00	5.00	30.00
	1957J	—	—	Proof	80.00
	1958D	12.623	1.50	4.00	35.00
	1958D	—	—	Proof	135.00
	1958F	16.825	1.50	4.00	35.00
	1958F	300 pcs.	—	Proof	75.00
	1958G	10.744	1.50	4.00	35.00
	1958J	9.408	1.50	4.00	35.00
	1959D	1.020	4.00	10.00	200.00
	1959D	—	—	Proof	—
	1959F	.203	15.00	60.00	350.00
	1960D	3.535	1.50	4.00	25.00
	1960D	—	—	Proof	60.00
	1960F	3.692	1.50	4.00	25.00
	1960F	50 pcs.	—	Proof	—
	1960G	2.695	2.00	4.00	25.00
	1960J	4.676	1.50	4.00	25.00
	1961D	3.918	1.50	4.00	20.00
	1961F	3.872	1.50	4.00	20.00
	1961G	2.776	2.00	4.00	25.00
	1961G	20 pcs.	—	Proof	1150.
	1961J	2.940	1.50	4.00	25.00
	1962D	4.105	2.00	6.00	20.00
	1962F	3.344	2.00	6.00	20.00
	1962G	1.800	2.00	6.00	25.00
	1962G	—	—	Proof	60.00
	1962J	3.609	2.00	6.00	17.50

KM#	Date	Mintage	VF	XF	Unc
116	1963D	4.411	1.50	4.00	17.50
	1963F	3.752	1.50	4.00	17.50
	1963G	3.448	1.50	4.00	17.50
	1963G	*600 pcs.	—	Proof	55.00
	1963J	7.348	1.50	4.00	17.50
	1964D	5.205	1.50	4.00	12.50
	1964F	4.834	1.50	4.00	12.50
	1964G	3.044	1.50	4.00	12.50
	1964G	600 pcs.		Proof	55.00
	1964J	2.681	1.50	4.00	12.50
	1965D	3.903	1.50	2.50	10.00
	1965F	4.045	1.50	2.50	10.00
	1965F	300 pcs.	—	Proof	200.00
	1965G	2.599	1.50	2.50	10.00
	1965G	1,200	—	Proof	5.00
	1965J	4.007	1.50	2.50	10.00
	1966D	5.855	1.50	2.50	7.00
	1966F	3.750	1.50	2.50	7.00
	1966F	100 pcs.	—	Proof	200.00
	1966G	3.895	1.50	2.50	7.00
	1966G	3,070	—	Proof	12.50
	1966J	6.014	1.50	2.50	7.00
	1966J	1,000	—	Proof	25.00
	1967D	3.254	1.50	2.50	7.00
	1967F	3.758	1.50	2.50	7.00
	1967F	1,500	—	Proof	20.00
	1967G	1.878	1.50	4.00	12.50
	1967G	4,500	—	Proof	15.00
	1967J	6.684	1.25	2.50	7.00
	1967J	1,500	—	Proof	22.00
	1968D	4.166	1.50	2.50	10.00
	1968F	1.050	2.00	5.00	15.00
	1968F	3,000	—	Proof	15.00
	1968G	3.060	2.00	2.50	8.00
	1968G	6,023	—	Proof	10.00
	1968J	.939	2.00	4.00	15.00
	1968J	2,000	—	Proof	18.00
	1969D	2.602	2.00	2.50	10.00
	1969F	3.005	2.00	2.50	10.00
	1969F	5,100	—	Proof	6.00
	1969G	1.754	2.00	2.50	12.50
	1969G	8,700	—	Proof	6.00
	1969J	2.680	2.00	2.50	8.00
	1969J	5,000	—	Proof	6.00
	1970D	5.203	1.50	2.00	4.00
	1970F	6.018	1.50	2.00	4.00
	1970F	5,140	—	Proof	7.50
	1970G	3.461	1.50	2.00	4.00
	1970G	.010	—	Proof	5.00
	1970J	5.691	1.50	2.00	4.00
	1970J	5,000	—	Proof	6.00
	1971D	8.451	1.00	1.25	3.00
	1971D	8,000	—	Proof	5.00
	1971F	10.017	1.00	1.25	3.00
	1971F	8,000	—	Proof	5.00
	1971G	5.631	1.00	1.25	3.00
	1971G	.010	—	Proof	5.00
	1971J	8.786	1.00	1.25	3.00
	1971J	8,000	—	Proof	6.00

COPPER-NICKEL CLAD NICKEL
Konrad Adenauer

KM#	Date	Mintage	VF	XF	Unc
124	1969D	7.001	—	1.50	3.00
	1969F	7.006	—	1.50	3.00
	1969G	7.010	—	1.50	3.00
	1969J	7.000	—	1.50	3.00
	1970D	7.318	—	1.50	3.00
	1970F	8.422	—	1.50	3.00
	1970G	4.844	—	1.50	3.00
	1970J	7.476	—	1.50	3.00
	1971D	7.287	—	1.50	3.00
	1971F	8.400	—	1.50	3.00
	1971G	4.848	—	1.50	3.00
	1971J	7.476	—	1.50	3.00
	1972D	7.286	—	1.50	3.00
	1972D	8,000	—	Proof	4.50
	1972F	8.392	—	1.50	3.00
	1972F	8,000	—	Proof	4.50
	1972G	4.848	—	1.50	3.00
	1972G	.010	—	Proof	4.50
	1972J	7.476	—	1.50	3.00
	1972J	8,000	—	Proof	4.50
	1973D	10.393	—	1.50	3.00
	1973D	9,000	—	Proof	4.50
	1973F	11.015	—	1.50	3.00
	1973F	9,000	—	Proof	4.50
	1973G	9.022	—	1.50	3.00
	1973G	9,000	—	Proof	4.50
	1973J	12.272	—	1.50	3.00
	1973J	9,000	—	Proof	4.50
	1974D	5.151	—	1.50	3.00
	1974D	.035	—	Proof	2.25
	1974F	5.894	—	1.50	3.00
	1974F	.035	—	Proof	2.25
	1974G	3.790	—	1.50	3.00
	1974G	.035	—	Proof	2.25
	1974J	5.282	—	1.50	3.00
	1974J	.035	—	Proof	2.25
124	1975D	4.553	—	1.50	2.50
	1975D	.043	—	Proof	2.25
	1975F	5.270	—	1.50	2.50
	1975F	.043	—	Proof	2.25
	1975G	3.035	—	1.50	2.50
	1975G	.043	—	Proof	2.25
	1975J	4.673	—	1.50	2.50
	1975J	.043	—	Proof	2.25
	1976D	4.576	—	1.50	2.50
	1976D	.043	—	Proof	2.25
	1976F	5.257	—	1.50	2.50
	1976F	.043	—	Proof	2.25
	1976G	3.028	—	1.50	2.50
	1976G	.043	—	Proof	2.25
	1976J	4.673	—	1.50	2.50
	1976J	.043	—	Proof	2.25
	1977D	5.906	—	1.50	2.50
	1977D	.051	—	Proof	2.00
	1977F	6.765	—	1.50	2.50
	1977F	.051	—	Proof	2.00
	1977G	3.892	—	1.50	2.50
	1977G	.051	—	Proof	2.00
	1977J	6.007	—	1.50	2.50
	1977J	.051	—	Proof	2.00
	1978D	3.304	—	1.50	2.50
	1978D	.054	—	Proof	2.00
	1978F	3,804	—	1.50	2.50
	1978F	.054	—	Proof	2.00
	1978G	2.217	—	1.50	2.50
	1978G	.054	—	Proof	2.00
	1978J	3.392	—	1.50	2.50
	1978J	.054	—	Proof	2.00
	1979D	3.209	—	1.50	2.50
	1979D	.089	—	Proof	2.00
	1979F	3.689	—	1.50	2.50
	1979F	.089	—	Proof	2.00
	1979G	2.165	—	1.50	2.50
	1979G	.089	—	Proof	2.00
	1979J	3.293	—	1.50	2.50
	1979J	.089	—	Proof	2.00
	1980D	10.810	—	1.50	2.00
	1980D	.110	—	Proof	2.00
	1980F	8.910	—	1.50	2.00
	1980F	.110	—	Proof	2.00
	1980G	1.170	—	1.50	2.00
	1980G	.110	—	Proof	2.00
	1980J	4.670	—	1.50	2.00
	1980J	.110	—	Proof	2.00
	1981D	8.180	—	1.50	2.00
	1981D	.091	—	Proof	2.00
	1981F	7.690	—	1.50	2.00
	1981F	.091	—	Proof	2.00
	1981G	7.070	—	1.50	2.00
	1981G	.091	—	Proof	2.00
	1981J	8.290	—	1.50	2.00
	1981J	.091	—	Proof	2.00
	1982D	9.220	—	1.50	2.00
	1982D	.078	—	Proof	2.00
	1982F	11.260	—	1.50	2.00
	1982F	.078	—	Proof	2.00
	1982G	6.640	—	1.50	2.00
	1982G	.078	—	Proof	2.00
	1982J	9.790	—	1.50	2.00
	1982J	.078	—	Proof	2.00
	1983D	1.560	—	1.50	2.00
	1983D	.075	—	Proof	2.00
	1983F	1.800	—	1.50	2.00
	1983F	.075	—	Proof	2.00
	1983G	1.030	—	1.50	2.00
	1983G	.075	—	Proof	2.00
	1983J	1.600	—	1.50	2.00
	1983J	.075	—	Proof	2.00
	1984D	.052	—	1.50	2.00
	1984D	.064	—	Proof	2.00
	1984F	.060	—	1.50	2.00
	1984F	.064	—	Proof	2.00
	1984G	.035	—	1.50	2.00
	1984G	.064	—	Proof	2.00
	1984J	.053	—	1.50	2.00
	1984J	.064	—	Proof	2.00
	1985D	2.600	—	—	2.00
	1985D	.056	—	Proof	2.25
	1985F	3.000	—	—	1.75
	1985F	.054	—	Proof	2.25
	1985G	1.730	—	—	1.75
	1985G	.055	—	Proof	2.25
	1985J	2.670	—	—	1.75
	1985J	.054	—	Proof	2.25
	1986D	2.600	—	—	1.75
	1986D	.044	—	Proof	2.25
	1986F	3.000	—	—	1.75
	1986F	.044	—	Proof	2.25
	1986G	1.730	—	—	1.75
	1986G	.044	—	Proof	2.25
	1986J	2.670	—	—	1.75
	1986J	.044	—	Proof	2.25
	1987D	4.420	—	—	1.75
	1987D	.045	—	Proof	2.25
	1987F	5.100	—	—	1.75
	1987F	.045	—	Proof	2.25
	1987G	2.940	—	—	1.75
	1987G	.045	—	Proof	2.25
	1987J	4.540	—	—	1.75
	1987J	.045	—	Proof	2.25

Theodor Heuss

KM#	Date	Mintage	VF	XF	Unc
A127 (127)	1970D	7.317	—	1.50	3.00
	1970F	8.426	—	1.50	3.00
	1970G	4.844	—	1.50	3.00
	1970J	7.476	—	1.50	3.00
	1971D	7.280	—	1.50	3.00
	1971F	8.403	—	1.50	3.00
	1971G	4.841	—	1.50	3.00
	1971J	7.476	—	1.50	3.00
	1972D	7.288	—	1.50	3.00
	1972D	8,000	—	Proof	4.50
	1972F	8.401	—	1.50	3.00
	1972F	8,000	—	Proof	4.50
	1972G	4.859	—	1.50	3.00
	1972G	.010	—	Proof	4.50
	1972J	7.476	—	1.50	3.00
	1972J	8,000	—	Proof	4.50
	1973D	10.379	—	1.50	3.00
	1973D	9,000	—	Proof	4.50
	1973F	11.018	—	1.50	3.00
	1973F	9,000	—	Proof	4.50
	1973G	8.975	—	1.50	3.00
	1973G	9,000	—	Proof	4.50
	1973J	12.360	—	1.50	3.00
	1973J	9,000	—	Proof	4.50
	1974D	5.147	—	1.50	3.00
	1974D	.035	—	Proof	2.00
	1974F	5.899	—	1.50	3.00
	1974F	.035	—	Proof	2.00
	1974G	3.820	—	1.50	3.00
	1974G	.035	—	Proof	2.00
	1974J	5.280	—	1.50	3.00
	1974J	.035	—	Proof	2.00
	1975D	4.623	—	1.50	2.00
	1975D	.043	—	Proof	2.00
	1975F	5.251	—	1.50	2.00
	1975F	.043	—	Proof	2.00
	1975G	3.034	—	1.50	2.00
	1975G	.043	—	Proof	2.00
	1975J	4.675	—	1.50	2.00
	1975J	.043	—	Proof	2.00
	1976D	4.546	—	1.50	2.00
	1976D	.043	—	Proof	2.00
	1976F	5.259	—	1.50	2.00
	1976F	.043	—	Proof	2.00
	1976G	3.028	—	1.50	2.00
	1976G	.043	—	Proof	2.00
	1976J	4.681	—	1.50	2.00
	1976J	.043	—	Proof	2.00
	1977D	5.857	—	1.50	2.00
	1977D	.051	—	Proof	1.75
	1977F	6.752	—	1.50	2.00
	1977F	.051	—	Proof	1.75
	1977G	3.892	—	1.50	2.00
	1977G	.051	—	Proof	1.75
	1977J	6.009	—	1.50	2.00
	1977J	.051	—	Proof	1.75
	1978D	3.804	—	1.50	2.00
	1978D	.054	—	Proof	1.75
	1978F	3.804	—	1.50	2.00
	1978F	.054	—	Proof	1.75
	1978G	2.217	—	1.50	2.00
	1978G	.054	—	Proof	1.75
	1978J	3.392	—	1.50	2.00
	1978J	.054	—	Proof	1.75
	1979D	3.209	—	1.50	2.00
	1979D	.089	—	Proof	1.75
	1979F	3.689	—	1.50	2.00
	1979F	.089	—	Proof	1.75
	1979G	2.165	—	1.50	2.00
	1979G	.089	—	Proof	1.75
	1979J	3.293	—	1.50	2.00
	1979J	.089	—	Proof	1.75
	1980D	2.000	—	1.50	1.75
	1980D	.110	—	Proof	1.75
	1980F	2.300	—	1.50	1.75
	1980F	.110	—	Proof	1.75
	1980G	1.300	—	1.50	1.75
	1980G	.110	—	Proof	1.75
	1980J	2.000	—	1.50	1.75
	1980J	.110	—	Proof	1.75
	1981D	2.000	—	1.50	1.75
	1981D	.091	—	Proof	1.75
	1981F	2.300	—	1.50	1.75
	1981F	.091	—	Proof	1.75
	1981G	1.300	—	1.50	1.75
	1981G	.091	—	Proof	1.75
	1981J	2.000	—	1.50	1.75
	1981J	.091	—	Proof	1.75
	1982D	3.100	—	1.50	1.75
	1982D	.078	—	Proof	1.75
	1982F	3.600	—	1.50	1.75
	1982F	.078	—	Proof	1.75
	1982G	2.100	—	1.50	1.75
	1982G	.078	—	Proof	1.75
	1982J	3.200	—	1.50	1.75
	1982J	.078	—	Proof	1.75

KM#	Date	Mintage	VF	XF	Unc
(127)	1983D	1.560	—	1.50	1.75
	1983D	.075	—	Proof	1.75
	1983F	1.800	—	1.50	1.75
	1983F	.075	—	Proof	1.75
	1983G	1.030	—	1.50	1.75
	1983G	.075	—	Proof	1.75
	1983J	1.600	—	1.50	1.75
	1983J	.075	—	Proof	1.75
	1984D	.052	—	1.50	1.75
	1984D	.064	—	Proof	2.00
	1984F	.060	—	1.50	1.75
	1984F	.064	—	Proof	2.00
	1984G	.035	—	1.50	1.75
	1984G	.064	—	Proof	2.00
	1984J	.053	—	1.50	1.75
	1984J	.064	—	Proof	2.00
	1985D	2.600	—	—	1.75
	1985D	.056	—	Proof	2.25
	1985F	3.000	—	—	1.75
	1985F	.054	—	Proof	2.25
	1985G	1.730	—	—	1.75
	1985G	.055	—	Proof	2.25
	1985J	2.670	—	—	1.75
	1985J	.054	—	Proof	2.25
	1986D	2.600	—	—	1.75
	1986D	.044	—	Proof	2.25
	1986F	3.000	—	—	1.75
	1986F	.044	—	Proof	2.25
	1986G	1.730	—	—	1.75
	1986G	.044	—	Proof	2.25
	1986J	2.670	—	—	1.75
	1986J	.044	—	Proof	2.25
	1987D	4.420	—	—	1.75
	1987D	.045	—	Proof	2.25
	1987F	5.100	—	—	1.75
	1987F	.045	—	Proof	2.25
	1987G	2.940	—	—	1.75
	1987G	.045	—	Proof	2.25
	1987J	4.540	—	—	1.75
	1987J	.045	—	Proof	2.25

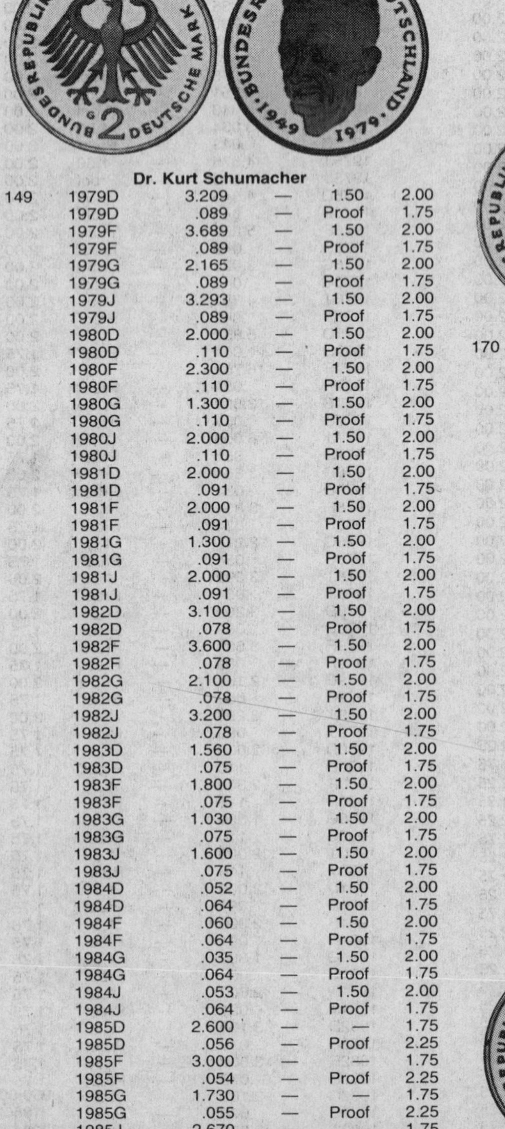

Dr. Kurt Schumacher

KM#	Date	Mintage	VF	XF	Unc
149	1979D	3.209	—	1.50	2.00
	1979D	.089	—	Proof	1.75
	1979F	3.689	—	1.50	2.00
	1979F	.089	—	Proof	1.75
	1979G	2.165	—	1.50	2.00
	1979G	.089	—	Proof	1.75
	1979J	3.293	—	1.50	2.00
	1979J	.089	—	Proof	1.75
	1980D	2.000	—	1.50	2.00
	1980D	.110	—	Proof	1.75
	1980F	2.300	—	1.50	2.00
	1980F	.110	—	Proof	1.75
	1980G	1.300	—	1.50	2.00
	1980G	.110	—	Proof	1.75
	1980J	2.000	—	1.50	2.00
	1980J	.110	—	Proof	1.75
	1981D	2.000	—	1.50	2.00
	1981D	.091	—	Proof	1.75
	1981F	2.000	—	1.50	2.00
	1981F	.091	—	Proof	1.75
	1981G	1.300	—	1.50	2.00
	1981G	.091	—	Proof	1.75
	1981J	2.000	—	1.50	2.00
	1981J	.091	—	Proof	1.75
	1982D	3.100	—	1.50	2.00
	1982D	.078	—	Proof	1.75
	1982F	3.600	—	1.50	2.00
	1982F	.078	—	Proof	1.75
	1982G	2.100	—	1.50	2.00
	1982G	.078	—	Proof	1.75
	1982J	3.200	—	1.50	2.00
	1982J	.078	—	Proof	1.75
	1983D	1.560	—	1.50	2.00
	1983D	.075	—	Proof	1.75
	1983F	1.800	—	1.50	2.00
	1983F	.075	—	Proof	1.75
	1983G	1.030	—	1.50	2.00
	1983G	.075	—	Proof	1.75
	1983J	1.600	—	1.50	2.00
	1983J	.075	—	Proof	1.75
	1984D	.052	—	1.50	2.00
	1984D	.064	—	Proof	1.75
	1984F	.060	—	1.50	2.00
	1984F	.064	—	Proof	1.75
	1984G	.035	—	1.50	2.00
	1984G	.064	—	Proof	1.75
	1984J	.053	—	1.50	2.00
	1984J	.064	—	Proof	1.75
	1985D	2.600	—	—	1.75
	1985D	.056	—	Proof	2.25
	1985F	3.000	—	—	1.75
	1985F	.054	—	Proof	2.25
	1985G	1.730	—	—	1.75
	1985G	.055	—	Proof	2.25
	1985J	2.670	—	—	1.75
	1985J	.054	—	Proof	2.25

KM#	Date	Mintage	VF	XF	Unc
149	1986D	2.600	—	—	1.75
	1986D	.044	—	Proof	2.25
	1986F	3.000	—	—	1.75
	1986F	.044	—	Proof	2.25
	1986G	1.730	—	—	1.75
	1986G	.044	—	Proof	2.25
	1986J	2.670	—	—	1.75
	1986J	.044	—	Proof	2.25
	1987D	4.420	—	—	1.75
	1987D	.045	—	Proof	2.25
	1987F	5.100	—	—	1.75
	1987F	.045	—	Proof	2.25
	1987G	2.940	—	—	1.75
	1987G	.045	—	Proof	2.25
	1987J	4.540	—	—	1.75
	1987J	.045	—	Proof	2.25
	1988D	5.850	—	—	1.75
	1988D	.045	—	Proof	2.25
	1988F	6.750	—	—	1.75
	1988F	.045	—	Proof	2.25
	1988G	3.890	—	—	1.75
	1988G	.045	—	Proof	2.25
	1988J	6.010	—	—	1.75
	1988J	.045	—	Proof	2.25
	1989D	—	—	—	1.75
	1989D	.045	—	Proof	2.25
	1989F	12.000	—	—	1.75
	1989F	.045	—	Proof	2.25
	1989G	—	—	—	1.75
	1989G	.045	—	Proof	2.25
	1989J	—	—	—	1.75
	1989J	.045	—	Proof	2.25
	1990D	—	—	—	1.75
	1990D	.045	—	Proof	2.25
	1990F	21.200	—	—	1.75
	1990F	.045	—	Proof	2.25
	1990G	—	—	—	1.75
	1990G	.045	—	Proof	2.25
	1990J	—	—	—	1.75
	1990J	.045	—	Proof	2.25
	1991A	—	—	—	1.75
	1991A	—	—	Proof	2.25
	1991D	—	—	—	1.75
	1991D	—	—	Proof	2.25
	1991F	—	—	—	1.75
	1991F	—	—	Proof	2.25
	1991G	—	—	—	1.75
	1991G	—	—	Proof	2.25
	1991J	—	—	—	1.75
	1991J	—	—	Proof	2.25

Ludwig Erhard

KM#	Date	Mintage	VF	XF	Unc
170	1988D	5.850	—	—	1.65
	1988D	.045	—	Proof	2.00
	1988F	6.750	—	—	1.65
	1988F	.045	—	Proof	2.00
	1988G	3.890	—	—	1.65
	1988G	.045	—	Proof	2.00
	1988J	6.010	—	—	1.65
	1988J	.045	—	Proof	2.00
	1989D	—	—	—	1.65
	1989D	.045	—	Proof	2.00
	1989F	12.000	—	—	1.65
	1989F	.045	—	Proof	2.00
	1989G	—	—	—	1.65
	1989G	.045	—	Proof	2.00
	1989J	—	—	—	1.65
	1989J	.045	—	Proof	2.00
	1990D	—	—	—	1.65
	1990D	.045	—	Proof	2.00
	1990F	21.200	—	—	1.65
	1990F	.045	—	Proof	2.00
	1990G	—	—	—	1.65
	1990G	.045	—	Proof	2.00
	1990J	—	—	—	1.65
	1990J	.045	—	Proof	2.00
	1991A	—	—	—	1.65
	1991A	—	—	Proof	2.00
	1991D	—	—	—	1.65
	1991D	—	—	Proof	2.00
	1991F	—	—	—	1.65
	1991F	—	—	Proof	2.00
	1991G	—	—	—	1.65
	1991G	—	—	Proof	2.00
	1991J	—	—	—	1.65
	1991J	—	—	Proof	2.00

Franz Joseph Strauss

KM#	Date	Mintage	VF	XF	Unc
175	1990D	—	—	—	1.75
	1990D	.045	—	Proof	2.25
	1990F	21.200	—	—	1.75
	1990F	.045	—	Proof	2.25
	1990G	—	—	—	1.75
	1990G	.045	—	Proof	2.25
	1990J	—	—	—	1.75
	1990J	.045	—	Proof	2.25
	1991A	—	—	—	1.75
	1991A	—	—	Proof	2.25
	1991D	—	—	—	1.75
	1991D	—	—	Proof	2.25
	1991F	—	—	—	1.75
	1991F	—	—	Proof	2.25
	1991G	—	—	—	1.75
	1991G	—	—	Proof	2.25
	1991J	—	—	—	1.75
	1991J	—	—	Proof	2.25

5 MARK

11.2000 g, .625 SILVER, .2250 oz ASW
Federal Republic

KM#	Date	Mintage	VF	XF	Unc
112.1	1951D	20.600	4.00	15.00	55.00
	1951D	—	—	Proof	250.00
	1951F	24.000	4.00	15.00	65.00
	1951F	280 pcs.	—	Proof	250.00
	1951G	13.840	4.00	15.00	65.00
	1951G	—	—	Proof	450.00
	1951J	21.360	4.00	15.00	55.00
	1951J	—	—	Proof	225.00
	1956D	1.092	10.00	45.00	135.00
	1956D	—	—	Proof	400.00
	1956F	1.200	10.00	45.00	160.00
	1956F	23 pcs.	—	Proof	900.00
	1956J	1.068	10.00	45.00	135.00
	1956J	—	—	Proof	400.00
	1957D	.566	10.00	50.00	200.00
	1957D	—	—	Proof	275.00
	1957F	2.100	7.50	45.00	175.00
	1957F	—	—	Proof	500.00
	1957G	.692	10.00	45.00	200.00
	1957G	—	—	Proof	300.00
	1957J	1.630	6.00	25.00	145.00
	1957J	—	—	Proof	250.00
	1958D	1.226	7.50	25.00	110.00
	1958D	—	—	Proof	300.00
	1958F	.600	20.00	100.00	550.00
	1958F	100 pcs.	—	Proof	750.00
	1958G	1.557	7.50	25.00	100.00
	1958G	—	—	Proof	400.00
	1958J	.060	700.00	1350.	2850.
	1958J	—	—	Proof	2850.
	1959D	.496	10.00	40.00	235.00
	1959D	—	—	Proof	400.00
	1959G	.692	12.50	40.00	200.00
	1959G	—	—	Proof	500.00
	1959J	.713	8.00	30.00	200.00
	1959J	—	—	Proof	375.00
	1960D	1.040	7.00	18.00	90.00
	1960D	—	—	Proof	300.00
	1960F	1.576	7.00	18.00	90.00
	1960F	50 pcs.	—	Proof	300.00
	1960G	.692	7.00	18.00	90.00
	1960G	—	—	Proof	250.00
	1960J	1.618	7.00	18.00	55.00
	1960J	—	—	Proof	400.00
	1961D	1.040	4.50	15.00	55.00
	1961D	—	—	Proof	225.00
	1961F	.824	4.50	18.00	110.00
	1961F	—	—	Proof	450.00
	1961J	.518	6.00	28.00	110.00
	1961J	—	—	Proof	550.00
	1963D	2.080	4.50	15.00	50.00
	1963D	—	—	Proof	350.00
	1963F	1.254	4.50	15.00	60.00
	1963F	—	—	Proof	350.00
	1963G	.600	4.50	18.00	75.00
	1963G	*100 pcs.	—	Proof	450.00
	1963J	2.136	4.50	15.00	45.00
	1963J	—	—	Proof	350.00
	1964D	.456	8.00	30.00	135.00
	1964D	—	—	Proof	375.00
	1964F	2.646	4.50	12.50	55.00
	1964F	—	—	Proof	350.00
	1964G	1.649	4.50	12.50	35.00
	1964G	*600 pcs.	—	Proof	80.00
	1964J	1.335	4.00	12.50	35.00
	1964J	—	—	Proof	200.00
	1965D	4.354	4.00	12.50	30.00
	1965D	—	—	Proof	175.00
	1965F	4.050	4.00	8.00	30.00
	1965F	*80 pcs.	—	Proof	425.00
	1965G	2.335	4.00	8.00	22.50
	1965G	8,233	—	Proof	20.00
	1965J	3.605	4.00	8.00	20.00

KM#	Date	Mintage	VF	XF	Unc
112.1	1965J	—	—	Proof	250.00
	1966D	5.200	4.00	8.00	20.00
	1966D	—	—	Proof	250.00
	1966F	6.000	4.00	8.00	20.00
	1966F	100 pcs.	—	Proof	425.00
	1966G	3.460	4.00	8.00	20.00
	1966G	3,070	—	Proof	45.00
	1966J	5.340	4.00	8.00	22.50
	1966J	1.000	—	Proof	110.00
	1967D	3.120	4.00	8.00	20.00
	1967D	—	—	Proof	200.00
	1967F	3.598	4.00	8.00	25.00
	1967F	1,500	—	Proof	75.00
	1967G	1.406	4.00	8.00	30.00
	1967G	4,500	—	Proof	35.00
	1967J	3.204	4.00	8.00	25.00
	1967J	1,500	—	Proof	90.00
	1968D	1.300	4.00	8.00	20.00
	1968D	—	—	Proof	60.00
	1968F	1.497	4.00	8.00	20.00
	1968F	3,000	—	Proof	75.00
	1968G	1.535	4.00	8.00	20.00
	1968G	6,023	—	Proof	35.00
	1968J	1.335	4.00	8.00	25.00
	1968J	2,000	—	Proof	70.00
	1969D	2.080	4.00	8.00	15.00
	1969D	—	—	Proof	20.00
	1969F	2.395	4.00	8.00	17.50
	1969F	5,000	—	Proof	18.00
	1969G	3.484	4.00	8.00	15.00
	1969G	8,700	—	Proof	17.50
	1969J	2.136	4.00	8.00	15.00
	1969J	5,000	—	Proof	20.00
	1970D	2.000	4.00	8.00	15.00
	1970D	—	—	Proof	17.50
	1970F	1.995	4.00	8.00	15.00
	1970F	5,140	—	Proof	20.00
	1970G	6.000	3.50	4.50	7.50
	1970G	10,200	—	Proof	15.00
	1970J	4.000	3.50	4.50	7.50
	1970J	5,000	—	Proof	18.00
	1971D	4.000	3.50	4.50	7.50
	1971D	8,000	—	Proof	15.00
	1971F	3.993	3.50	4.50	7.50
	1971F	8,000	—	Proof	15.00
	1971G	6.010	3.50	4.50	7.50
	1971G	.010	—	Proof	15.00
	1971J	6.000	3.50	4.50	7.50
	1971J	8,000	—	Proof	18.00
	1972D	3.000	3.50	4.50	7.50
	1972D	8,000	—	Proof	15.00
	1972F	8.992	3.50	4.50	7.50
	1972F	8,100	—	Proof	15.00
	1972G	4.999	3.50	4.50	7.50
	1972G	.010	—	Proof	15.00
	1972J	6.000	3.50	4.50	6.50
	1972J	8,000	—	Proof	15.00
	1973D	3.380	3.50	4.50	6.50
	1973D	9,000	—	Proof	15.00
	1973F	3.891	3.50	4.50	6.50
	1973F	9,100	—	Proof	15.00
	1973G	2.240	3.50	4.50	6.50
	1973G	9,000	—	Proof	15.00
	1973J	5.571	3.50	4.50	6.50
	1973J	9,000	—	Proof	15.00
	1974D	4.594	3.50	4.50	6.50
	1974D	.035	—	Proof	12.00
	1974F	6.514	3.50	4.50	6.50
	1974F	.035	—	Proof	12.00
	1974G	3.708	3.50	4.50	6.50
	1974G	.035	—	Proof	12.00
	1974J	2.968	3.50	4.50	6.50
	1974J	.035	—	Proof	12.00
	Uninscribed plain edge errors				
112.2	1959D	Inc. Ab.	25.00	55.00	75.00
	1959J	Inc. Ab.	25.00	55.00	75.00
	1963J	Inc. Ab.	25.00	55.00	75.00
	1964F	Inc. Ab.	25.00	55.00	75.00
	1965F	Inc. Ab.	25.00	55.00	75.00
	1965G	Inc. Ab.	25.00	55.00	75.00
	1966G	Inc. Ab.	25.00	55.00	75.00
	1967G	Inc. Ab.	25.00	55.00	75.00
	Error. W/edge lettering: "GRUSS DICH DEUTSCH LAND AUS HERZENSGRUND"				
112.3	1957	Inc. Ab.	800.00	1000.	1400.
	COPPER-NICKEL CLAD NICKEL, 10.00 g				
140.1	1975D	65.663	—	3.50	4.50
	1975D	.043	—	Proof	7.00
	1975F	75.002	—	3.50	4.50
	1975F	.043	—	Proof	7.00
	1975G	43.297	—	3.50	4.50
	1975G	.043	—	Proof	7.00
	1975J	67.372	—	3.50	4.50
	1975J	.043	—	Proof	7.00
	1976D	7.821	—	3.50	5.00
140.1	1976D	.043	—	Proof	7.00
	1976F	9.072	—	3.50	5.00
	1976F	.043	—	Proof	7.00
	1976G	5.784	—	3.50	5.00
	1976G	.043	—	Proof	7.00
	1976J	8.068	—	3.50	5.00
	1976J	.043	—	Proof	7.00
	1977D	8.321	—	3.50	5.00
	1977D	.051	—	Proof	6.00
	1977F	9.612	—	3.50	5.00
	1977F	.051	—	Proof	6.00
	1977G	5.746	—	3.50	5.00
	1977G	.051	—	Proof	6.00
	1977J	8.577	—	3.50	5.00
	1977J	.051	—	Proof	6.00
	1978D	7.854	—	3.50	5.00
	1978D	.054	—	Proof	6.00
	1978F	9.054	—	3.50	5.00
	1978F	.054	—	Proof	6.00
	1978G	5.244	—	3.50	5.00
	1978G	.054	—	Proof	6.00
	1978J	8.064	—	3.50	5.00
	1978J	.054	—	Proof	6.00
	1979D	7.889	—	3.50	5.00
	1979D	.089	—	Proof	6.00
	1979F	9.089	—	3.50	5.00
	1979F	.089	—	Proof	6.00
	1979G	5.279	—	3.50	5.00
	1979G	.089	—	Proof	6.00
	1979J	8.099	—	3.50	5.00
	1979J	.089	—	Proof	6.00
	1980D	8.300	—	3.50	5.00
	1980D	.110	—	Proof	6.00
	1980F	9.640	—	3.50	5.00
	1980F	.110	—	Proof	6.00
	1980G	5.500	—	3.50	5.00
	1980G	.110	—	Proof	6.00
	1980J	8.500	—	3.50	5.00
	1980J	.110	—	Proof	6.00
	1981D	8.300	—	3.50	5.00
	1981D	.091	—	Proof	6.00
	1981F	9.600	—	3.50	5.00
	1981F	.091	—	Proof	6.00
	1981G	5.500	—	3.50	5.00
	1981G	.091	—	Proof	6.00
	1981J	8.500	—	3.50	5.00
	1981J	.091	—	Proof	6.00
	1982D	8.900	—	3.50	5.00
	1982D	.078	—	Proof	6.00
	1982F	10.300	—	3.50	5.00
	1982F	.078	—	Proof	6.00
	1982G	5.990	—	3.50	5.00
	1982G	.078	—	Proof	6.00
	1982J	9.100	—	3.50	5.00
	1982J	.078	—	Proof	6.00
	1983D	6.240	—	3.50	5.00
	1983D	.075	—	Proof	6.00
	1983F	7.200	—	3.50	5.00
	1983F	.075	—	Proof	6.00
	1983G	4.152	—	3.50	5.00
	1983G	.075	—	Proof	6.00
	1983J	6.408	—	3.50	5.00
	1983J	.075	—	Proof	6.00
	1984D	6.000	—	3.50	5.00
	1984D	.064	—	Proof	6.00
	1984F	6.900	—	3.50	5.00
	1984F	.064	—	Proof	6.00
	1984G	4.000	—	3.50	5.00
	1984G	.064	—	Proof	6.00
	1984J	6.100	—	3.50	5.00
	1984J	.064	—	Proof	6.00
	1985D	4.900	—	3.50	5.00
	1985D	.056	—	Proof	6.00
	1985F	5.700	—	3.50	5.00
	1985F	.054	—	Proof	6.00
	1985G	3.300	—	3.50	5.00
	1985G	.055	—	Proof	6.00
	1985J	5.100	—	3.50	5.00
	1985J	.054	—	Proof	6.00
	1986D	4.900	—	3.50	5.00
	1986D	.044	—	Proof	6.00
	1986F	5.700	—	3.50	5.00
	1986F	.044	—	Proof	6.00
	1986G	3.300	—	3.50	5.00
	1986G	.044	—	Proof	6.00
	1986J	5.100	—	3.50	5.00
	1986J	.044	—	Proof	6.00
	1987D	6.760	—	3.50	5.00
	1987D	.045	—	Proof	6.00
	1987F	7.800	—	3.50	5.00
	1987F	.045	—	Proof	6.00
	1987G	4.500	—	3.50	5.00
	1987G	.045	—	Proof	6.00
	1987J	6.940	—	3.50	5.00
	1987J	.045	—	Proof	6.00
	1988D	11.960	—	—	4.00
	1988D	.045	—	Proof	5.00
	1988F	13.800	—	—	4.00
	1988F	.045	—	Proof	5.00
	1988G	7.960	—	—	4.00
	1988G	.045	—	Proof	5.00
	1988J	12.280	—	—	4.00
	1988J	.045	—	Proof	5.00
	1989D	—	—	—	4.00
	1989D	.045	—	Proof	5.00
	1989F	19.800	—	—	4.00
	1989F	.045	—	Proof	5.00
	1989G	—	—	—	4.00
	1989G	.045	—	Proof	5.00
	1989J	—	—	—	4.00
140.1	1989J	.045	—	Proof	5.00
	1990D	—	—	—	4.00
	1990D	.045	—	Proof	5.00
	1990F	24.120	—	—	4.00
	1990F	.045	—	Proof	5.00
	1990G	—	—	—	4.00
	1990G	.045	—	Proof	5.00
	1990J	—	—	—	4.00
	1990J	.045	—	Proof	5.00
	1991A	—	—	—	4.00
	1991A	—	—	Proof	5.00
	1991D	—	—	—	4.00
	1991D	—	—	Proof	5.00
	1991F	—	—	—	4.00
	1991F	—	—	Proof	5.00
	1991G	—	—	—	4.00
	1991G	—	—	Proof	5.00
	1991J	—	—	—	4.00
	1991J	—	—	Proof	5.00
	5.00 g, thin variety				
140.2	1975	—	—	3.50	5.00

NOTE: Illegally produced by a German Mint official.

COMMEMORATIVE 5 MARK

11.2000 g, .625 SILVER, .2250 oz ASW
Centenary - Nurnberg Museum

KM#	Date	Mintage	VF	XF	Unc
113	1952D	.199	600.00	1200.	1600.
	1952D	1,345	—	Proof	3000.

150th Anniversary - Death of Friedrich von Schiller

KM#	Date	Mintage	VF	XF	Unc
114	1955F	.199	300.00	850.00	1150.
	1955F	1,217	—	Proof	1650.

300th Anniversary - Birth of Ludwig von Baden

KM#	Date	Mintage	VF	XF	Unc
115	1955G	.198	300.00	800.00	1050.
	1955G	*2,000	—	Proof	2000.

***NOTE:** This coin was restruck without authorization by a mint official using genuine dies - quantity unknown.

Centenary - Death of Joseph Freiherr von Eichendorff

KM#	Date	Mintage	VF	XF	Unc
117	1957J	.198	300.00	750.00	950.00
	1957J	*2,000	—	Proof	1850.

***NOTE:** This coin was restruck without authorization by a mint official using genuine dies - quantity unknown.

150th Anniversary - Death of Johann Gottlieb Fichte

KM#	Date	Mintage	VF	XF	Unc
118	1964J	.495	150.00	300.00	425.00
	1964J	5,000	—	Proof	900.00

250th Anniversary - Death of Gottfried Wilhelm Leibniz

KM#	Date	Mintage	VF	XF	Unc
119	1966D	1.940	25.00	45.00	60.00
	1966D	.060	—	Proof	125.00

Wilhelm & Alexander von Humboldt

KM#	Date	Mintage	VF	XF	Unc
120	1967F	2.000	27.50	50.00	65.00
	1967F	.060	—	Proof	225.00

150th Anniversary - Birth of Friedrich Raiffeisen

KM#	Date	Mintage	VF	XF	Unc
121	1968J	3.860	3.50	5.00	10.00
	1968J	.140	—	Proof	40.00

500th Anniversary - Death of Johannes Gutenberg

KM#	Date	Mintage	VF	XF	Unc
122	1968G	2.900	10.00	18.50	30.00
	1968G	.100	—	Proof	80.00

150th Anniversary - Birth of Max von Pettenkoffer

KM#	Date	Mintage	VF	XF	Unc
123	1968D	2.900	5.00	12.50	17.50
	1968D	.100	—	Proof	55.00

NOTE: Varieties with normal and frosted devices. Normal variety being scarcer.

150th Anniversary - Birth of Theodor Fontane

KM#	Date	Mintage	VF	XF	Unc
125	1969G	2.830	8.00	15.00	25.00
	1969G	.170	—	Proof	35.00

375th Anniversary - Death of Gerhard Mercator

KM#	Date	Mintage	VF	XF	Unc
126	1969F	5.004	3.50	4.50	6.00
	1969F	.200	—	Proof	16.50

200th Anniversary - Birth of Ludwig van Beethoven

KM#	Date	Mintage	VF	XF	Unc
127	1970F	5.000	3.50	4.50	8.00
	1970F	.200	—	Proof	17.50

German Unification

KM#	Date	Mintage	VF	XF	Unc
128	1971G	5.000	5.00	7.50	12.50
	1971G	.200	—	Proof	20.00

500th Anniversary - Birth of Albrecht Durer

KM#	Date	Mintage	VF	XF	Unc
129	1971D	8.000	3.50	4.00	5.00
	1971D	.200	—	Proof	27.50

500th Anniversary - Birth of Nicholas Copernicus

KM#	Date	Mintage	VF	XF	Unc
136	1973J	8.000	3.50	4.00	5.00
	1973J	.250	—	Proof	11.00

125th Anniversary - Frankfurt Parliament

KM#	Date	Mintage	VF	XF	Unc
137	1973G	8.000	3.50	4.00	5.00
	1973G	.250	—	Proof	11.00

25th Anniversary - Constitutional Law

KM#	Date	Mintage	VF	XF	Unc
138	1974F	8.000	3.50	4.00	5.00
	1974F	.250	—	Proof	10.00

250th Anniversary - Birth of Immanuel Kant

KM#	Date	Mintage	VF	XF	Unc
139	1974D	8.000	3.50	4.00	5.00
	1974D	.250	—	Proof	15.00

50th Anniversary - Death of Friedrich Ebert

KM#	Date	Mintage	VF	XF	Unc
141	1975J	8.000	3.50	4.00	5.00
	1975J	.250	—	Proof	12.00

European Monument Protection Year

11.2 g, 2.1mm thick

KM#	Date	Mintage	VF	XF	Unc
142.1	1975F	8.000	3.50	4.00	5.00
	1975F	.250	—	Proof	10.00

5.3 g, 1.4mm thick

KM#	Date	Mintage	VF	XF	Unc
142.2	1975F	Inc. Ab.	3.50	4.00	5.00

Centenary - Birth of Albert Schweitzer

KM#	Date	Mintage	VF	XF	Unc
143	1975G	8.000	3.50	4.00	5.00
	1975G	.250	—	Proof	12.50

300th Anniversary - Death of von Grimmelshausen

KM#	Date	Mintage	VF	XF	Unc
144	1976D	8.000	3.50	4.00	5.00
	1976D	.250	—	Proof	20.00

200th Anniversary - Birth of Carl Friedrich Gauss

KM#	Date	Mintage	VF	XF	Unc
145	1977J	8.000	3.50	4.00	5.00
	1977J	.250	—	Proof	17.50

200th Anniversary - Birth of Heinrich von Kleist

KM#	Date	Mintage	VF	XF	Unc
146	1977G	8.000	3.50	4.00	5.00
	1977G	.250	—	Proof	15.00

100th Anniversary - Birth of Gustav Stresemann

KM#	Date	Mintage	VF	XF	Unc
147	1978D	8.000	3.50	4.00	5.00
	1978D	.250	—	Proof	12.50

275th Anniversary - Death of Balthasar Neumann

KM#	Date	Mintage	VF	XF	Unc
148	1978F	8.000	3.50	4.00	5.00
	1978F	.259	—	Proof	8.00

150th Anniversary - German Archeological Institute

KM#	Date	Mintage	VF	XF	Unc
150	1979J	8.000	3.50	4.50	6.50
	1979J	.250	—	Proof	13.50

COPPER-NICKEL CLAD NICKEL

100th Anniversary - Birth of Otto Hahn

KM#	Date	Mintage	VF	XF	Unc
151	1979G	5.000	3.50	4.50	7.00
	1979G	.350	—	Proof	10.00

11.2000 g, .625 SILVER, .2250 oz ASW

KM#	Date	Mintage	VF	XF	Unc
151a	1979G	18 pcs.	—	—	22,500.

COPPER-NICKEL CLAD NICKEL

750th Anniversary - Death of von der Vogelweide

KM#	Date	Mintage	VF	XF	Unc
152	1980D	5.000	3.50	4.50	6.50
	1980D	.350	—	Proof	10.00

100th Anniversary - Cologne Cathedral

KM#	Date	Mintage	VF	XF	Unc
153	1980F	5.000	3.50	6.50	8.50
	1980F	.350	—	Proof	14.50

200th Anniversary - Death of Gotthold Ephraim Lessing

KM#	Date	Mintage	VF	XF	Unc
154	1981J	6.500	3.50	4.00	6.00
	1981J	.350	—	Proof	8.00

150th Anniversary - Death of Carl von Stein

KM#	Date	Mintage	VF	XF	Unc
155	1981G	6.500	3.50	4.00	5.00
	1981G	.350	—	Proof	8.00

150th Anniversary - Death of Johann Wolfgang von Goethe

KM#	Date	Mintage	VF	XF	Unc
156	1982D	8.000	3.50	4.00	5.00
	1982D	.350	—	Proof	8.00

10th Anniversary - U.N. Environmental Conference

KM#	Date	Mintage	VF	XF	Unc
157	1982F	8.000	3.50	4.00	5.00
	1982F	.350	—	Proof	8.50

100th Anniversary - Death of Karl Marx

KM#	Date	Mintage	VF	XF	Unc
158	1983J	8.000	3.50	4.00	5.00
	1983J	.350	—	Proof	8.00

500th Anniversary - Birth of Martin Luther

KM#	Date	Mintage	VF	XF	Unc
159	1983G	8.000	3.50	4.00	5.00
	1983G	.350	—	Proof	15.00

150th Anniversary - German Customs Union

KM#	Date	Mintage	VF	XF	Unc
160	1984D	8.000	3.50	4.00	5.00
	1984D	.350	—	Proof	8.00

175th Anniversary - Birth of Felix Bartholdy

KM#	Date	Mintage	VF	XF	Unc
161	1984J	8.000	3.50	4.00	5.00
	1984J	.350	—	Proof	8.00

European Year of Music

KM#	Date	Mintage	VF	XF	Unc
162	1985F	8.000	3.50	4.00	5.00
	1985F	.350	—	Proof	8.00

150th Anniversary - German Railroad

KM#	Date	Mintage	VF	XF	Unc
163	1985G	8.000	3.50	4.00	5.00
	1985G	.350	—	Proof	8.00

600th Anniversary - Heidelberg University

KM#	Date	Mintage	VF	XF	Unc
164	1986D	8.000	3.50	4.00	5.00
	1986D	.350	—	Proof	8.00

200th Anniversary - Death of Frederick the Great

KM#	Date	Mintage	VF	XF	Unc
165	1986F	8.000	3.50	4.00	5.00
	1986F	.350	—	Proof	8.00

COMMEMORATIVE 10 MARK

15.5000 g, .625 SILVER, .3115 oz ASW
Munich Olympics - 'In Deutschland'

KM#	Date	Mintage	VF	XF	Unc
130	1972D	2.500	—	7.00	9.00
	1972D	.125	—	Proof	25.00
	1972F	2.375	—	7.00	9.00
	1972F	.125	—	Proof	25.00
	1972G	2.500	—	7.00	9.00
	1972G	.125	—	Proof	25.00
	1972J	2.500	—	7.00	9.00
	1972J	.125	—	Proof	25.00

Munich Olympics Symbol: 'Schleife' (knot).

KM#	Date	Mintage	VF	XF	Unc
131	1972D	5.000	—	6.50	7.50
	1972D	.125	—	Proof	12.50
	1972F	4.875	—	6.50	7.50
	1972F	.125	—	Proof	12.50
	1972G	5.000	—	6.50	7.50
	1972G	.125	—	Proof	12.50
	1972J	5.000	—	6.50	7.50
	1972J	.125	—	Proof	12.50

Munich Olympics - 'Athletes'

KM#	Date	Mintage	VF	XF	Unc
132	1972D	5.000	—	6.50	7.50
	1972D	.150	—	Proof	12.00
	1972F	4.850	—	6.50	7.50
	1972F	.150	—	Proof	12.00
	1972G	5.000	—	6.50	7.50
	1972G	.150	—	Proof	12.00
	1972J	5.000	—	6.50	7.50
	1972J	.150	—	Proof	12.00

Munich Olympics - 'Stadium'

KM#	Date	Mintage	VF	XF	Unc
133	1972D	5.000	—	6.50	7.50
	1972D	.150	—	Proof	12.00
	1972F	4.850	—	6.50	7.50
	1972F	.150	—	Proof	12.00
	1972G	5.000	—	6.50	7.50
	1972G	.150	—	Proof	12.00
	1972J	5.000	—	6.50	7.50
	1972J	.150	—	Proof	12.00

Munich Olympics - 'In Munchen'

KM#	Date	Mintage	VF	XF	Unc
134	1972D	2.500	—	7.00	9.00
	1972D	.150	—	Proof	12.50
	1972F	2.350	—	7.00	9.00
	1972F	.150	—	Proof	12.50
	1972G	2.500	—	7.00	9.00
	1972G	.150	—	Proof	12.50
	1972J	2.500	—	7.00	9.00
	1972J	.150	—	Proof	12.50

Munich Olympics 'Olympic Flame'

KM#	Date	Mintage	VF	XF	Unc
135	1972D	5.000	—	6.50	7.50
	1972D	.150	—	Proof	12.00
	1972F	4.850	—	6.50	7.50
	1972F	.150	—	Proof	12.00
	1972G	5.000	—	6.50	7.50
	1972G	.150	—	Proof	12.00
	1972J	5.000	—	6.50	7.50
	1972J	.150	—	Proof	12.00

750th Anniversary - Berlin

KM#	Date	Mintage	VF	XF	Unc
166	1987J	8.000	—	—	12.50
	1987J	.350	—	Proof	165.00

European Unity

KM#	Date	Mintage	VF	XF	Unc
167	1987G	8.000	—	—	10.00
	1987G	.350	—	Proof	100.00

200th Anniversary - Birth of Arthur Schopenhauer

KM#	Date	Mintage	VF	XF	Unc
168	1988D	8.000	—	—	10.00
	1988D	.350	—	Proof	35.00

100th Anniversary - Death of Carl Zeiss

KM#	Date	Mintage	VF	XF	Unc
169	1988F	8.000	—	—	10.00
	1988F	.350	—	Proof	25.00

800th Year - Port of Hamburg

KM#	Date	Mintage	VF	XF	Unc
171	1989J	8.000	—	—	10.00
	1989J	.350	—	Proof	25.00

2000th Anniversary - City of Bonn

KM#	Date	Mintage	VF	XF	Unc
172	1989D	8.000	—	—	10.00
	1989D	.350	—	Proof	25.00

40th Anniversary - Republic

KM#	Date	Mintage	VF	XF	Unc
173	1989G	8.000	—	—	10.00
	1989G	.350	—	Proof	40.00

Death of Kaiser Friedrich Barbarossa

KM#	Date	Mintage	VF	XF	Unc
174	1990F	7.450	—	—	10.00
	1990F	.400	—	Proof	25.00

800th Anniversary - the Teutonic Order

KM#	Date	Mintage	VF	XF	Unc
176	1990J	8.850	—	—	10.00
	1990J	—	—	Proof	25.00

German Unity - Brandenburg Gate

KM#	Date	Mintage	VF	XF	Unc
177	1991A	—	—	—	12.50
	1991A	—	—	Proof	25.00

Kathe Kollwitz - Artist

KM#	Date	Mintage	VF	XF	Unc
178	1992G	—	—	—	12.50
	1992G	—	—	Proof	25.00

Civil Pour-le-Merite Order

KM#	Date	Mintage	VF	XF	Unc
179	1992D	—	—	—	12.50
	1992D	—	—	Proof	25.00

1000 Anniversary - Potsdam

KM#	Date	Mintage	VF	XF	Unc
180	1993F	—	—	—	12.50
	1993F	—	—	Proof	25.00

MINT SETS (MS)

KM#	Date	Mintage	Identification	Issue Price	Mkt. Val.
MS1	1974D(9)	.020	KM105,106a,107-108,109.2, 110,112.1,124,127,A127	—	40.00
MS2	1974F(9)	.020	KM105,106a,107-108,109.2, 110,112.1,124,127,A127	—	40.00
MS3	1974G(9)	.020	KM105,106a,107-108,109.2, 110,112.1,124,127,A127	—	40.00
MS4	1974J(9)	.020	KM105,106a,107-108,109.2, 110,112.1,124,127,A127	—	40.00
MS5	1975D(9)	26,000	KM105,106a,107-108,109.2, 110,124,A127,140.1	—	20.00
MS6	1975F(9)	.026	KM105,106a,107-108,109.2, 110,124,A127,140.1	—	20.00
MS7	1975G(9)	.026	KM105,106a,107-108,109.2, 110,124,A127,140.1	—	20.00
MS8	1975J(9)	.026	KM105,106a,107-108,109.2, 110,124,A127,140.1	—	20.00
MS9	1976D(9)	.026	KM105,106a,107-108,109.2, 110,124,A127,140.1	—	17.50
MS10	1976F(9)	.026	KM105,106a,107-108,109.2, 110,124,A127,140.1	—	17.50
MS11	1976G(9)	.026	KM105,106a,107-108,109.2, 110,124,A127,140.1	—	17.50
MS12	1976J(9)	.026	KM105,106a,107-108,109.2, 110,124,A127,140.1	—	17.50
MS13	1977D(9)	.029	KM105,106a,107-108,109.2, 110,124,A127,140.1	—	15.00
MS14	1977F(9)	.029	KM105,106a,107-108,109.2, 110,124,A127,140.1	—	15.00
MS15	1977G(9)	.029	KM105,106a,107-108,109.2, 110,124,A127,140.1	—	15.00
MS16	1977J(9)	.029	KM105,106a,107-108,109.2, 110,124,A127,140.1	—	15.00
MS17	1978D(9)	.030	KM105,106a,107-108,109.2, 110,124,A127,140.1	—	12.50
MS18	1978F(9)	.030	KM105,106a,107-108,109.2, 110,124,A127,140.1	—	12.50
MS19	1978G(9)	.030	KM105,106a,107-108,109.2, 110,124,A127,140.1	—	12.50
MS20	1978J(9)	.030	KM105,106a,107-108,109.2, 110,124,A127,140.1	—	12.50
MS21	1979D(10)	.034	KM105,106a,107-108, 109.2,110,124,A127, 140.1,149	11.00	12.50
MS22	1979F(10)	.034	KM105,106a,107-108, 109.2,110,124,A127, 140.1,149	11.00	12.50
MS23	1979G(10)	.034	KM105,106a,107-108, 109.2,110,124,A127, 140.1,149	11.00	12.50
MS24	1979J(10)	.034	KM105,106a,107-108, 109.2,110,124,A127, 140.1,149	11.00	12.50
MS25	1980D(10)	.036	KM105,106a,107-108, 109.2,110,124,A127, 140.1,149	11.00	12.50
MS26	1980F(10)	.036	KM105,106a,107-108, 109.2,110,124,A127, 140.1,149	11.00	12.50
MS27	1980G(10)	.036	KM105,106a,107-108, 109.2,110,124,A127, 140.1,149	11.00	12.50
MS28	1980J(10)	.036	KM105,106a,107-108, 109.2,110,124,A127, 140.1,149	11.00	12.50
MS29	1981D(10)	.038	KM105,106a,107-108, 109.2,110,124,A127, 140.1,149	11.00	12.50
MS30	1981F(10)	.038	KM105,106a,107-108, 109.2,110,124,A127, 140.1,149	11.00	12.50
MS31	1981G(10)	.038	KM105,106a,107-108, 109.2,110,124,A127, 140.1,149	11.00	12.50
MS32	1981J(10)	.038	KM105,106a,107-108, 109.2,110,124,A127, 140.1,149	11.00	12.50
MS33	1982D(10)	—	KM105,106a,107-108, 109.2,110,124,A127, 140.1,149	11.00	12.50
MS34	1982F(10)	—	KM105,106a,107-108, 109.2,110,124,A127, 140.1,149	11.00	12.50
MS35	1982G(10)	—	KM105,106a,107-108, 109.2,110,124,A127, 140.1,149	11.00	12.50
MS36	1982J(10)	—	KM105,106a,107-108, 109.2,110,124,A127, 140.1,149	11.00	12.50
MS37	1983D(10)	—	KM105,106a,107-108, 109.2,110,124,A127, 140.1,149	11.00	12.50
MS38	1983F(10)	—	KM105,106a,107-108, 109.2,110,124,A127, 140.1,149	11.00	12.50
MS39	1983G(10)	—	KM105,106a,107-108, 109.2,110,124,A127, 140.1,149	11.00	12.50
MS40	1983J(10)	—	KM105,106a,107-108, 109.2,110,124,A127, 140.1,149	11.00	12.50
MS41	1984D(10)	—	KM105,106a,107-108, 109.2,110,124,A127, 140.1,149	11.00	12.50
MS42	1984F(10)	—	KM105,106a,107-108, 109.2,110,124,A127, 140.1,149	11.00	12.50
MS43	1984G(10)	—	KM105,106a,107-108, 109.2,110,124,A127, 140.1,149	11.00	12.50
MS44	1984J(10)	—	KM105,106a,107-108, 109.2,110,124,A127, 140.1,149	11.00	12.50
MS45	1985D(10)	—	KM105,106a,107-108, 109.2,110,124,A127, 140.1,149	11.00	12.50
MS46	1985F(10)	—	KM105,106a,107-108, 109.2,110,124,A127, 140.1,149	11.00	12.50
MS47	1985G(10)	—	KM105,106a,107-108, 109.2,110,124,A127, 140.1,149	11.00	12.50
MS48	1985J(10)	—	KM105,106a,107-108, 109.2,110,124,A127, 140.1,149	11.00	12.50
MS49	1986D(10)	—	KM105,106a,107-108, 109.2,110,124,A127, 140.1,149	11.00	12.50
MS50	1986F(10)	—	KM105,106a,107-108, 109.2,110,124,A127, 140.1,149	11.00	12.50
MS51	1986G(10)	—	KM105,106a,107-108, 109.2,110,124,A127, 140.1,149	11.00	12.50
MS52	1986J(10)	—	KM105,106a,107-108, 109.2,110,124,A127, 140.1,149	11.00	12.50
MS53	1987D(10)	—	KM105,106a,107-108, 109.2,110,124,A127, 140.1,149	11.00	12.50
MS54	1987F(10)	—	KM105,106a,107-108, 109.2,110,124,A127, 140.1,149	11.00	12.50
MS55	1987G(10)	—	KM105,106a,107-108, 109.2,110,124,A127, 140.1,149	11.00	12.50
MS56	1987J(10)	—	KM105,106a,107-108, 109.2,110,124,A127, 140.1,149	11.00	12.50
MS57	1988D(9)	—	KM105,106a,107-108,109.2, 110,140.1,149,170	—	10.00
MS58	1988F(9)	—	KM105,106a,107-108,109.2, 110,140.1,149,170	—	10.00
MS59	1988G(9)	—	KM105,106a,107-108,109.2, 110,140.1,149,170	—	10.00
MS60	1988J(9)	—	KM105,106a,107-108,109.2, 110,140.1,149,170	—	10.00
MS61	1989D(9)	—	KM105,106a,107-108,109.2, 110,140.1,149,170	—	10.00
MS62	1989F(9)	—	KM105,106a,107-108,109.2, 110,140.1,149,170	—	10.00
MS63	1989G(9)	—	KM105,106a,107-108,109.2, 110,140.1,149,170	—	10.00
MS64	1989J(9)	—	KM105,106a,107-108,109.2, 110,140.1,149,170	—	10.00
MS65	1990D(10)	—	KM105,106a,107-108,109.2, 110,140.1,149,170,175	—	12.00
MS66	1990F(10)	—	KM105,106a,107-108,109.2, 110,140.1,149,170,175	—	12.00
MS67	1990G(10)	—	KM105,106a,107-108,109.2, 110,140.1,149,170,175	—	12.00
MS68	1990J(10)	—	KM105,106a,107-108,109.2, 110,140.1,149,170,175	—	12.00
MS69	1991A(10)	—	KM105,106a,107-108,109.2, 110,140.1,149,170,175	—	12.00
MS70	1991D(10)	—	KM105,106a,107-108,109.2, 110,140.1,149,170,175	—	12.00
MS71	1991F(10)	—	KM105,106a,107-108,109.2, 110,140.1,149,170,175	—	12.00
MS72	1991G(10)	—	KM105,106a,107-108,109.2, 110,140.1,149,170,175	—	12.00
MS73	1991J(10)	—	KM105,106a,107-108,109.2, 110,140.1,149,170,175	—	12.00

NOTE: Mint sets are issued in pliable plastic.

PROOF SETS (PS)

NOTE: 1964 and 1965 proof sets contained 1 Pfennig, 5 pf., 10 pf., 50 Pfennig coins dated 1950. The 8 pieces dated 1963G were issued as individual coins. Since the early 1970's proof sets are issued in stiff plastic cases.

KM#	Date	Mintage	Identification	Issue Price	Mkt. Val.
PS1	1950-64G(8)	*600	KM105-108,109.1,110, 112.1,116	—	200.00
PS2	1950-65F(8)	—	KM105-108,109.1,110, 112.1,116	—	900.00
PS3	1950-65G(8)	1,200	KM105-108,109.1,110, 112.1,116	—	50.00
PS4	1966F(8)	100	KM105-108,109.1,110, 112.1,116	—	900.00
PS5	1966G(8)	3,070	KM105-108,109.1,110,		

KM#	Date	Mintage	Identification	Issue Price	Mkt. Val.
PS5			112.1,116	—	100.00
PS6	1966J(8)	1,000	KM105-108,109.1,110, 112.1,116	—	225.00
PS7	1967F(8)	1,500	KM105-108,109.1,110, 112.1,116	—	170.00
PS8	1967G(8)	4,150	KM105-108,109.1,110, 112.1,116	—	90.00
PS9	1967G(8)	550	KM105,106a*,107-108, 109.1,110,112.1,116	—	750.00

***NOTE:** "2 PFG Magnetic" This coin was restruck without authorization by a German mint official using genuine dies. Quantity unknown.

KM#	Date	Mintage	Identification	Issue Price	Mkt. Val.
PS10	1967J(8)	1,500	KM105,106a,107-108, 109.1,110,112.1,116	—	190.00
PS11	1968F(8)	3,000	KM105,106a,107-108, 109.1,110,112.1,116	—	110.00
PS12	1968G(8)	6,023	KM105,106a,107-108, 109.1,110,112.1,116	—	90.00
PS13	1968J(8)	2,000	KM105,106a,107-108, 109.1,110,112.1,116	—	165.00
PS14	1969F(8)	5,000	KM105,106a,107-108, 109.1,110,112.1,116	—	40.00
PS15	1969G(8)	8,700	KM105,106a,107-108, 109.1,110,112.1,116	—	50.00
PS16	1969J(8)	5,000	KM105,106a,107-108, 109.1,110,112.1,116	—	40.00
PS17	1970F(8)	5,140	KM105,106a,107-108, 109.1,110,112.1,116	—	40.00
PS18	1970G(8)	10,200	KM105,106a,107-108, 109.1,110,112.1,116	—	40.00
PS19	1970J(8)	5,000	KM105,106a,107-108, 109.1,110,112.1,116	—	40.00
PS20	1971D(8)	8,000	KM105,106a,107-108, 109.1,110,112.1,116	—	35.00
PS21	1971F(8)	8,000	KM105,106a,107-108, 109.1,110,112.1,116	—	35.00
PS22	1971G(8)	10,200	KM105,106a,107-108, 109.1,110,112.1,116	—	30.00
PS23	1971J(8)	8,000	KM105,106a,107-108, 109.1,110,112.1,116	—	35.00
PS24	1972D(9)	8,000	KM105,106a,107-108, 109.2,110,112.1,124, A127	—	35.00
PS25	1972F(9)	8,000	KM105,106a,107-108, 109.2,110,112.1,124, A127	—	35.00
PS26	1972G(9)	10,000	KM105,106a,107-108, 109.2,110,112.1,124, A127	—	35.00
PS27	1972J(9)	8,000	KM105,106a,107-108, 109.2,110,112.1,124, A127	—	35.00
PS28	1973D(9)	9,000	KM105,106a,107-108, 109.2,110,112.1,124, A127	—	35.00
PS29	1973F(9)	9,000	KM105,106a,107-108, 109.2,110,112.1,124, A127	—	35.00
PS30	1973G(9)	9,000	KM105,106a,107-108, 109.2,110,112.1,124, A127	—	35.00
PS31	1973J(9)	9,000	KM105,106a,107-108, 109.2,110,112.1,124, A127	—	35.00
PS32	1974D(9)	35,000	KM105,106a,107-108, 109.2,110,112.1,124, A127	10.00	25.00
PS33	1974F(9)	35,000	KM105,106a,107-108, 109.2,110,112.1,124, A127	10.00	25.00
PS34	1974G(9)	35,000	KM105,106a,107-108, 109.2,110,112.1,124, A127	10.00	25.00
PS35	1974J(9)	35,000	KM105,106a,107-108, 109.2,110,112.1,124, A127	10.00	25.00
PS36	1975D(9)	43,120	KM105,106a,107-108, 109.2,110,124,A127, 140.1	10.00	15.00
PS37	1975F(9)	43,100	KM105,106a,107-108, 109.2,110,124,A127, 140.1	10.00	15.00
PS38	1975G(9)	43,100	KM105,106a,107-108, 109.2,110,124,A127, 140.1	10.00	15.00
PS39	1975J(9)	43,120	KM105,106a,107-108, 109.2,110,124,A127, 140.1	10.00	15.00
PS40	1976D(9)	43,120	KM105,106a,107-108, 109.2,110,124,A127, 140.1	10.00	14.00
PS41	1976F(9)	43,100	KM105,106a,107-108, 109.2,110,124,A127, 140.1	10.00	14.00
PS42	1976G(9)	43,100	KM105,106a,107-108, 109.2,110,124,A127, 140.1	10.00	14.00
PS43	1976J(9)	43,120	KM105,106a,107-108, 109.2,110,124,A127, 140.1	10.00	14.00
PS44	1977D(9)	50,620	KM105,106a,107-108, 109.2,110,124,A127, 140.1	12.50	10.00
PS45	1977F(9)	50,600	KM105,106a,107-108, 109.2,110,124,A127, 140.1	12.50	10.00
PS46	1977G(9)	50,600	KM105,106a,107-108, 109.2,110,124,A127, 140.1	12.50	10.00
PS47	1977J(9)	50,620	KM105,106a,107-108, 109.2,110,124,A127, 140.1	12.50	10.00
PS48	1978D(9)	.054	KM105,106a,107-108, 109.2,110,124,A127, 140.1	13.00	10.00
PS49	1978F(9)	.054	KM105,106a,107-108, 109.2,110,124,A127,1 140.1	13.00	10.00
PS50	1978G(9)	.054	KM105,106a,107-108, 109.2,110,124,A127, 140.1	13.00	10.00
PS51	1978J(9)	.054	KM105,106a,107-108, 109.2,110,124,A127, 140.1	13.00	10.00
PS52	1979D(10)	.089	KM105,106a,107-108, 109.2,110,124,A127, 140.1,149	15.00	12.00
PS53	1979F(10)	.089	KM105,106a,107-108, 109.2,110,124,A127, 140.1,149	15.00	12.00
PS54	1979G(10)	.089	KM105,106a,107-108, 109.2,110,124,A127, 140.1,149	15.00	12.00
PS55	1979J(10)	.089	KM105,106a,107-108, 109.2,110,124,A127, 140.1,149	15.00	12.00
PS56	1980D(10)	.060	KM105,106a,107-108, 109.2,110,124,A127, 140.1,149	15.00	12.00
PS57	1980F(10)	.060	KM105,106a,107-108, 109.2,110,124,A127, 140.1,149	15.00	12.00
PS58	1980G(10)	.060	KM105,106a,107-108, 109.2,110,124,A127, 140.1,149	15.00	12.00
PS59	1980J(10)	.060	KM105,106a,107-108, 109.2,110,124,A127, 140.1,149	15.00	12.00
PS60	1981D(10)	.091	KM105,106a,107-108, 109.2,110,124,A127, 140.1,149	15.00	12.00
PS61	1981F(10)	.091	KM105,106a,107-108, 109.2,110,124,A127, 140.1,149	15.00	12.00
PS62	1981G(10)	.091	KM105,106a,107-108, 109.2,110,124,A127, 140.1,149	15.00	12.00
PS63	1981J(10)	.091	KM105,106a,107-108, 109.2,110,124,A127, 140.1,149	15.00	12.00
PS64	1982D(10)	.078	KM105,106a,107-108, 109.2,110,124,A127, 140.1,149	15.00	12.00
PS65	1982F(10)	.078	KM105,106a,107-108, 109.2,110,124,A127, 140.1,149	15.00	12.00
PS66	1982G(10)	.078	KM105,106a,107-108, 109.2,110,124,A127, 140.1,149	15.00	12.00
PS67	1982J(10)	.078	KM105,106a,107-108, 109.2,110,124,A127, 140.1,149	15.00	12.00
PS68	1983D(10)	.075	KM105,106a,107-108, 109.2,110,124,A127, 140.1,149	15.00	12.00
PS69	1983F(10)	.075	KM105,106a,107-108, 109.2,110,124,A127, 140.1,149	15.00	12.00
PS70	1983G(10)	.075	KM105,106a,107-108, 109.2,110,124,A127, 140.1,149	15.00	12.00
PS71	1983J(10)	.075	KM105,106a,107-108, 109.2,110,124,A127, 140.1,149	15.00	12.00
PS72	1984D(10)	.064	KM105,106a,107-108, 109.2,110,124,A127, 140.1,149	15.00	14.50
PS73	1984F(10)	.064	KM105,106a,107-108, 109.2,110,124,A127, 140.1,149	15.00	14.50
PS74	1984G(10)	.064	KM105,106a,107-108, 109.2,110,124,A127, 140.1,149	15.00	14.50
PS75	1984J(10)	.064	KM105,106a,107-108, 109.2,110,124,A127, 140.1,149	15.00	14.50
PS76	1985D(10)	.056	KM105,106a,107-108, 109.2,110,124,A127, 140.1,149	15.00	16.50
PS77	1985F(10)	.054	KM105,106a,107-108, 109.2,110,124,A127, 140.1,149	15.00	16.50
PS78	1985G(10)	.055	KM105,106a,107-108, 109.2,110,124,A127, 140.1,149	15.00	16.50
PS79	1985J(10)	.054	KM105,106a,107-108, 109.2,110,124,A127, 140.1,149	15.00	16.50
PS80	1986D(10)	.044	KM105,106a,107-108, 109.2,110,124,A127, 140.1,149	15.00	16.50
PS81	1986F(10)	.044	KM105,106a,107-108, 109.2,110,124,A127, 140.1,149	15.00	16.50
PS82	1986G(10)	.044	KM105,106a,107-108, 109.2,110,124,A127, 140.1,149	15.00	16.50
PS83	1986J(10)	.044	KM105,106a,107-108, 109.2,110,124,A127, 140.1,149	15.00	16.50
PS84	1987D(10)	.045	KM105,106a,107-108, 109.2,110,124,A127, 140.1,149	15.00	16.50
PS85	1987F(10)	.045	KM105,106a,107-108, 109.2,110,124,A127, 140.1,149	15.00	16.50
PS86	1987G(10)	.045	KM105,106a,107-108, 109.2,110,124,A127, 140.1,149	15.00	16.50
PS87	1987J(10)	.045	KM105,106a,107-108, 109.2,110,124,A127, 140.1,149	15.00	16.50
PS88	1988D(9)	.045	KM105,106a,107-108, 109.2,110,140.1,149, 170	—	13.50
PS89	1988F(9)	.045	KM105,106a,107-108, 109.2,110,140.1,149, 170	—	13.50
PS90	1988G(9)	.045	KM105,106a,107-108, 109.2,110,140.1,149, 170	—	13.50
PS91	1988J(9)	.045	KM105,106a,107-108, 109.2,110,140.1,149, 170	—	13.50
PS92	1989D(9)	.045	KM105,106a,107-108, 109.2,110,140.1,149, 170	—	13.50
PS93	1989F(9)	.045	KM105,106a,107-108, 109.2,110,140.1,149, 170	—	13.50
PS94	1989G(9)	.045	KM105,106a,107-108, 109.2,110,140.1,149, 170	—	13.50
PS95	1989J(9)	.045	KM105,106a,107-108, 109.2,110,140.1,149, 170	—	13.50
PS96	1990D(10)	.045	KM105,106a,107-108, 109.2,110,140.1,149, 170,175	—	16.50
PS97	1990F(10)	.045	KM105,106a,107-108, 109.2,110,140.1,149, 170,175	—	16.50
PS98	1990G(10)	.045	KM105,106a,107-108, 109.2,110,140.1,149, 170,175	—	16.50
PS99	1990J(10)	.045	KM105,106a,107-108, 109.2,110,140.1,149, 170,175	—	16.50
PS100	1991A(10)	—	KM105,106a,107-108, 109.2,110,140.1,149, 170,175	—	16.50
PS101	1991D(10)	—	KM105,106a,107-108, 109.2,110,140.1,149, 170,175	—	16.50
PS102	1991F(10)	—	KM105,106a,107-108, 109.2,110,140.1,149, 170,175	—	16.50
PS103	1991G(10)	—	KM105,106a,107-108, 109.2,110,140.1,149, 170,175	—	16.50
PS104	1991J(10)	—	KM105,106a,107-108, 109.2,110,140.1,149, 170,175	—	16.50

SAARLAND

The Saar, the 10th state of the German Federal Republic, is located in the coal-rich Saar basin on the Franco-German frontier, and has an area of 991 sq. mi. and a population of 1.2 million. Capital: Saarbrucken. It is an important center of mining and heavy industry.

MINT MARKS

(a) - Paris - privy marks only

10 FRANKEN

ALUMINUM-BRONZE

KM#	Date	Mintage	Fine	VF	XF	Unc
1	1954(a)	11.000	.75	1.50	2.50	5.00

20 FRANKEN

ALUMINUM-BRONZE

KM#	Date	Mintage	Fine	VF	XF	Unc
2	1954(a)	12.950	.75	1.50	3.00	7.00

50 FRANKEN

ALUMINUM-BRONZE

KM#	Date	Mintage	Fine	VF	XF	Unc
3	1954(a)	5.300	3.00	5.00	10.00	20.00

100 FRANKEN

COPPER-NICKEL

KM#	Date	Mintage	Fine	VF	XF	Unc
4	1955(a)	11.000	2.50	4.00	7.50	15.00

GERMANY–DEMOCRATIC REP.

The German Democratic Republic, located on the great north European plain, had an area of 41,768 sq. mi. (108,330 sq. km.) and a population of 16.6 million. The figures included East Berlin which had been incorporated into the G.D.R. Capital: East Berlin. The economy was highly industrialized. Machinery, transport equipment chemicals, and lignite were exported.

During the closing days of World War II in Europe, Soviet troops advancing into Germany from the east occupied the German provinces of Mecklenburg, Brandenburg, Lusatia, Saxony and Thuringia. These five provinces comprised the occupation zone administered by the Soviet Union after the cessation of hostilities. The other three zones were administered by the U.S., Great Britain and France. Under the Potsdam agreement, questions affecting Germany as a whole were to be settled by the commanders of the occupation zones acting jointly and by unanimous decision. When Soviet intransigence rendered the quadripartite commission inoperable, the three western zones were united to form the Federal Republic of Germany, May 23, 1949. Thereupon the Soviet Union dissolved its occupation zone and established it as the Democratic Republic of Germany, Oct. 7, 1949.

The post-WW II division of Germany was ended Oct. 3, 1990, when the German Democratic Republic (East Germany) ceased to exist and its five constituent provinces were formally admitted to the Federal Republic of Germany. An election Dec. 2, 1990, chose representatives to the united federal parliament (Bundestag), which then conducted its opening session in Berlin in the old Reichstag building. Although Berlin technically is the capital of the newly reunited Germany, the actual seat of government remains for the time being in Bonn.

MINT MARKS

A - Berlin
E - Muldenhutten

MONETARY SYSTEM

100 Pfennig = 1 Mark

PFENNIG

ALUMINUM

KM#	Date	Mintage	VF	XF	Unc
1	1948A	243.000	.20	4.00	17.50
	1949A	Inc. Ab.	.20	4.00	17.50
	1949E	55.200	5.00	35.00	100.00
	1950A	Inc. 1948A	.20	3.00	17.50
	1950E	Inc. 1949E	1.00	25.00	50.00

KM#	Date	Mintage	VF	XF	Unc
5	1952A	297.213	.30	2.00	8.50
	1952E	49.296	.40	8.50	22.50
	1953A	114.002	.30	2.00	8.50
	1953E	50.876	.40	7.50	18.50

KM#	Date	Mintage	VF	XF	Unc
8.1	1960A	101.808	.10	.25	3.00
	1961A	101.776	.10	.25	3.00
	1962A	81.459	.10	.25	3.00
	1963A	101.402	.10	.25	3.00
	1964A	98.967	.10	.25	3.00
	1965A	38.585	3.00	15.00	35.00
	1968A	813.680	.10	.25	.50
	1972A	4.801	2.00	10.00	25.00
	1973A	5.518	1.50	8.00	22.50
	1975A	202.752	.10	.25	.50

Rev: Smaller design features.

KM#	Date	Mintage	VF	XF	Unc
8.2	1977A	61.560	.10	.25	2.00
8.2	1978A	200.050	.10	.20	.50
	1979A	100.640	.10	.20	.50
	1979A	—	—	Proof	—
	1980A	153.000	.10	.20	.50
	1980A	—	—	Proof	—
	1981A	200.436	.10	.20	.50
	1981A	40 pcs.	—	Proof	—
	1982A	99.200	.10	.20	.50
	1982A	2,500	—	Proof	10.00
	1983A	150.000	.10	.20	.50
	1983A	2,550	—	Proof	20.00
	1984A	137.600	.10	.20	.50
	1984A	3,015	—	Proof	4.50
	1985A	125.060	.10	.20	.50
	1985A	2,816	—	Proof	4.50
	1986A	73.900	.10	.20	.50
	1986A	2,800	—	Proof	4.50
	1987A	50.015	.10	.20	.50
	1987A	2,345	—	Proof	4.50
	1988A	75.450	.10	.20	.50
	1988A	2,300	—	Proof	4.50
	1989A	84.410	.10	.20	.50
	1989A	2,300	—	Proof	4.50
	1990A	15.670	.10	.20	2.00

5 PFENNIG

ALUMINUM

KM#	Date	Mintage	VF	XF	Unc
2	1948A	205.072	.50	1.00	7.50
	1949A	Inc. Ab.	.50	1.00	7.50
	1950A	Inc. Ab.	.50	6.00	17.50

KM#	Date	Mintage	VF	XF	Unc
6	1952A	113.397	.30	.75	8.50
	1952E	24.024	.50	7.50	27.50
	1953A	40.994	.40	.60	8.50
	1953E	28.665	.50	7.50	25.00

KM#	Date	Mintage	VF	XF	Unc
9.1	1968A	282.303	.25	.35	.75
	1972A	51.462	.25	.35	1.50
	1975A	84.710	.25	.35	.75

Obv. and rev: Smaller design features.

KM#	Date	Mintage	VF	XF	Unc
9.2	1978A	43.257	.15	.25	.50
	1979A	46.194	.15	.25	.50
	1979A	—	—	Proof	—
	1980A	31.977	.15	.25	.50
	1980A	—	—	Proof	—
	1981A	33.102	.15	.25	.50
	1981A	40 pcs.	—	Proof	—
	1982A	.916	1.75	7.50	22.50
	1982A	2,500	—	Proof	10.00
	1983A	100.890	.15	.25	.50
	1983A	2,550	—	Proof	20.00
	1984A	*6,000	—	—	30.00
	1984A	3,015	—	Proof	4.50
	1985A	1.000	1.50	6.50	18.50
	1985A	2,816	—	Proof	4.50
	1986A	1.000	1.50	6.50	18.50
	1986A	2,800	—	Proof	4.50
	1987A	*.020	—	—	12.50
	1987A	2,345	—	Proof	4.50
	1988A	35.930	.15	.25	.50
	1988A	2,300	—	Proof	4.50
	1989A	21.550	.15	.25	.50
	1989A	2,300	—	Proof	4.50
	1990A	50.640	.15	.25	.50

NOTE: Varieties exist.

10 PFENNIG

ALUMINUM

KM#	Date	Mintage	VF	XF	Unc
3	1948A	216.537	.50	8.50	14.50
	1949A	Inc. Ab.	.50	8.50	14.50
	1950A	Inc. Ab.	.50	6.00	12.50
	1950E	16.000	1.00	15.00	30.00

KM#	Date	Mintage	VF	XF	Unc
7	1952A	70.427	.25	.50	8.50
	1952E	21.498	.50	15.00	30.00
	1953A	18.611	.50	.75	8.50
	1953E	11.500	.75	15.00	27.50

KM#	Date	Mintage	VF	XF	Unc
10.1	1963A	21.063	2.00	10.00	35.00
	1965A	55.313	.15	.25	3.00
	1967A	96.955	.15	.25	3.00
	1968A	207.461	.15	.25	.75
	1970A	13.387	.15	.25	1.00
	1971A	66.618	.15	.25	.75
	1972A	5.702	.50	3.00	12.00
	1973A	11.257	.15	.25	1.50
	1978A	40.000	.15	.25	1.50
	1979A	54.665	.15	.25	.50
	1979A	—	—	Proof	—
	1980A	20.664	.15	.25	.50
	1980A	—	—	Proof	—
	1981A	40.704	.15	.25	.50
	1981A	40 pcs.	—	Proof	—
	1982A	40.212	.15	.25	1.50
	1982A	2,500	—	Proof	10.00
	1983A	40.699	.15	.25	.50
	1983A	2,550	—	Proof	20.00
	1984A	*.012	—	—	25.00
	1984A	3,015	—	Proof	4.50
	1985A	1.010	.35	4.50	17.50
	1985A	2,816	—	Proof	4.50
	1986A	1.000	.35	4.50	17.50
	1986A	2,800	—	Proof	4.50
	1987A	*.020	—	—	12.00
	1987A	2,345	—	Proof	4.50
	1988A	10.705	.15	.25	.75
	1988A	2,300	—	Proof	4.50
	1989A	37.640	.15	.25	.50
	1989A	2,300	—	Proof	4.50
	1990A	*.014	—	—	15.00

***NOTE:** Issued in sets only, remainder unaccountable.

NOTE: Inscription varieties exist.

20 PFENNIG

BRASS

KM#	Date	Mintage	VF	XF	Unc
11	1969	167.168	.20	.35	2.50
	1971	24.563	.20	.35	3.50
	1972A	5.007	.20	2.50	10.00
	1973A	2.524	.20	4.50	20.00
	1974A	7.458	.20	2.50	10.00
	1979A	.293	.20	1.50	7.50
	1979A	—	—	Proof	—
	1980A	2.190	.20	.35	5.00
	1980A	—	—	Proof	—
	1981A	.983	.20	.50	7.50
	1981A	40 pcs.	—	Proof	—
	1982A	10.458	.20	2.50	8.50
	1982A	2,500	—	Proof	12.50
	1983A	25.809	.20	.35	3.00
	1983A	2,550	—	Proof	25.00
	1984A	25.009	.20	.35	3.00
	1984A	3,015	—	Proof	5.50
	1985A	1.559	.20	.35	4.00
	1985A	2,816	—	Proof	5.50
	1986A	1.147	.20	.35	4.00
	1986A	2,800	—	Proof	5.50
	1987A	*.020	—	—	8.00
	1987A	2,345	—	Proof	5.50
	1988A	*.015	—	—	10.00
	1988A	2,300	—	Proof	5.50
	1989A	14.690	.20	.35	2.00
	1989A	2,300	—	Proof	5.50
	1990A	*.014	—	—	15.00

***NOTE:** Issued in sets only, remainder unaccountable.

NOTE: Ribbon width varieties exist.

50 PFENNIG

ALUMINUM-BRONZE

KM#	Date	Mintage	VF	XF	Unc
4	1949A	Inc. Be.	—	5000.	—
	1950A	67.703	2.00	6.00	35.00

NOTE: Some authorities believe the 1949 dated piece is a pattern.

ALUMINUM

Obv: Small coat of arms.

KM#	Date	Mintage	VF	XF	Unc
12.1	1958A	101.606	.25	.45	6.50

Obv: Larger coat of arms.

KM#	Date	Mintage	VF	XF	Unc
12.2	1968A	19.860	.25	.45	4.00
	1971A	35.829	.25	.45	1.00
	1972A	8.117	.25	.45	2.00
	1973A	6.530	.25	.45	6.50
	1979A	1.027	.25	.45	6.50
	1979A	—	—	Proof	—
	1980A	1.118	.25	.45	6.50
	1980A	—	—	Proof	—
	1981A	10.546	.25	.45	1.00
	1981A	40 pcs.	—	Proof	—
	1982A	79.832	.25	.45	1.00
	1982A	2,500	—	Proof	12.50
	1983A	1.309	.25	.45	6.50
	1983A	2,550	—	Proof	25.00
	1984A	*5,000	—	—	30.00
	1984A	3,015	—	Proof	5.50
	1985A	1.565	.25	.45	6.50
	1985A	2,816	—	Proof	5.50
	1986A	.776	.25	.45	6.50
	1986A	2,800	—	Proof	5.50
	1987A	*.021	—	—	12.00
	1987A	2,345	—	Proof	5.50
	1988A	*.015	—	—	14.00
	1988A	2,300	—	Proof	5.50
	1989A	.031	.25	.45	6.50
	1989A	2,300	—	Proof	5.50
	1990A	*.014	—	—	15.00

***NOTE:** Issued in sets only, remainder unaccountable.

NOTE: Inscription varieties exist.

MARK

ALUMINUM

KM#	Date	Mintage	VF	XF	Unc
13	1956A	112.108	.50	1.00	7.50
	1962A	45.920	.50	1.00	7.50
	1963A	31.910	.50	1.00	7.50

Rev: Small 1.

KM#	Date	Mintage	VF	XF	Unc
35.1	1972A	30.288	.50	1.00	5.00

Rev: Large 1.

KM#	Date	Mintage	VF	XF	Unc
35.2	1973A	6.972	.50	2.00	10.00
	1975A	32.094	.50	1.00	6.50
	1977A	119.813	.50	.75	1.25
	1978A	18.824	.50	.75	1.25
	1979A	1.003	.50	1.00	7.50
	1979A	—	—	Proof	—
	1980A	1.069	.50	1.00	7.50
	1980A	—	—	Proof	—
	1981A	1.006	.50	1.00	7.50
	1981A	40 pcs.	—	Proof	—
	1982A	51.619	.50	.75	1.25
	1982A	2,500	—	Proof	25.00
	1983A	1.065	.50	1.00	7.50
	1983A	2,550	—	Proof	30.00
	1984A	*5,000	—	—	65.00
	1984A	3,015	—	Proof	7.50
35.2	1985A	1.128	—	1.00	7.50
	1985A	2,816	—	Proof	7.50
	1986A	1.000	.50	1.00	7.50
	1986A	2,800	—	Proof	7.50
	1987A	*.021	—	—	5.50
	1987A	2,345	—	Proof	7.50
	1988A	*.015	—	—	7.50
	1988A	2,300	—	Proof	7.50
	1989A	.033	.50	.75	5.00
	1989A	2,300	—	Proof	7.50
	1990A	*.014	—	—	20.00

***NOTE:** Issued in sets only, remainder unaccountable.

2 MARK

ALUMINUM

KM#	Date	Mintage	VF	XF	Unc
14	1957A	77.961	.90	1.25	5.00

KM#	Date	Mintage	VF	XF	Unc
48	1974A	5.790	.90	2.00	12.00
	1975A	32.464	.90	1.50	10.00
	1977A	27.859	.90	1.50	10.00
	1978A	23.415	.90	1.50	10.00
	1979A	.985	.90	1.25	7.50
	1979A	—	—	Proof	—
	1980A	1.019	.90	1.25	7.50
	1980A	—	—	Proof	—
	1981A	.939	.90	1.25	7.50
	1981A	40 pcs.	—	Proof	—
	1982A	60.488	.90	1.00	2.00
	1982A	2,500	—	Proof	55.00
	1983A	1.030	.90	1.00	5.00
	1983A	2,550	—	Proof	75.00
	1984A	*6,000	—	—	30.00
	1984A	3,015	—	Proof	20.00
	1985A	1.310	.90	1.00	5.00
	1985A	2,816	—	Proof	20.00
	1986A	1.000	.90	1.00	6.00
	1986A	2,800	—	Proof	20.00
	1987A	*.030	—	—	6.00
	1987A	2,345	—	Proof	20.00
	1988A	*.015	—	—	6.50
	1988A	2,300	—	Proof	20.00
	1989A	.046	.90	1.00	6.50
	1989A	2,300	—	Proof	20.00
	1990A	*.014	—	—	20.00

***NOTE:** Issued in sets only, remainder unaccountable.

5 MARK

COPPER-NICKEL

125th Anniversary of Birth of Robert Koch

KM#	Date	Mintage	XF	Unc	BU
19.1	1968A	.100	—	—	50.00

Error: Plain edge.

KM#	Date	Mintage	XF	Unc	BU
19.2	1968A	—	—	—	—

20th Anniversary D.D.R.

KM#	Date	Mintage	XF	Unc	BU
22.1	1969	50.220	—	—	5.00

Error: Plain edge.

KM#	Date	Mintage	XF	Unc	BU
22.2	1969	—	—	—	—

Error: Mongolian inscription and dates on edge.

KM#	Date	Mintage	XF	Unc	BU
22.3	1969	—	—	—	—

NICKEL

KM#	Date	Mintage	XF	Unc	BU
22.1a	1969	12,741	—	220.00	—

Heinrich Hertz

KM#	Date	Mintage	XF	Unc	BU
23	1969A	.100	—	—	40.00

Wilhelm Conrad Rontgen

KM#	Date	Mintage	XF	Unc	BU
26	1970A	.100	—	—	45.00

Brandenburg Gate

KM#	Date	Mintage	XF	Unc	BU
29	1971A	4.000	—	—	5.00
	1979A	.032	—	—	20.00
	1979A	2,500	—	Proof	—
	1980A	.030	—	—	25.00
	1980A	2,500	—	Proof	—
	1981A	.030	—	—	25.00
	1981A	2,500	—	Proof	—
	1982A	.028	—	—	25.00
	1982A	2,500	—	Proof	100.00
	1983A	3,000	—	—	450.00
	1984A	.028	—	—	30.00
	1984A	3,015	—	Proof	80.00
	1985A	3,000	—	—	450.00
	1986A	.028	—	—	30.00
	1986A	2,800	—	Proof	70.00
	1987A	.220	—	—	10.00
	1987A	6,424	—	Proof	60.00
	1988A	.028	—	—	25.00
	1988A	2,300	—	Proof	70.00
	1989A	.028	—	—	25.00
	1989A	2,405	—	Proof	70.00
	1990A	.050	—	—	35.00

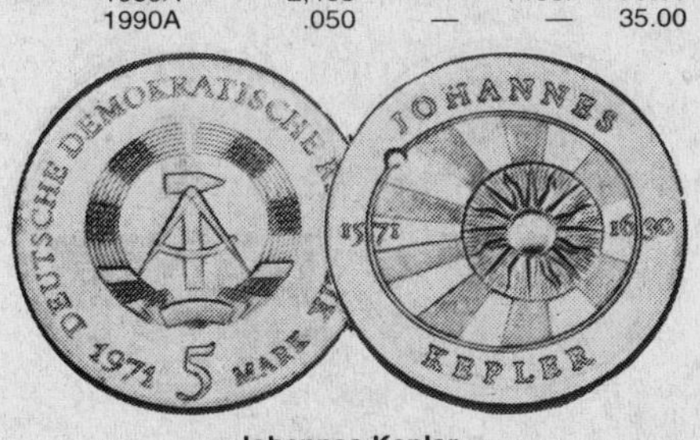

Johannes Kepler

KM#	Date	Mintage	XF	Unc	BU
30	1971A	.100	—	—	40.00

75th Anniversary - Death of Johannes Brahms

KM#	Date	Mintage	XF	Unc	BU
36.1	1972A	.055	—	—	50.00

Error: Double edge inscription.

KM#	Date	Mintage	XF	Unc	BU
36.2	1972A	—	—	—	—

City of Meissen

KM#	Date	Mintage	XF	Unc	BU
37	1972A	3.500	—	—	5.00
	1981A	40 pcs.	—	Proof	2500.
	1983A	.028	—	—	85.00
	1983A	2,550	—	Proof	160.00

125th Anniversary - Birth of Otto Lilienthal

KM#	Date	Mintage	XF	Unc	BU
43	1973A	.100	—	—	55.00

Centenary - Death of Philipp Reis

KM#	Date	Mintage	XF	Unc	BU
49	1974A	.100	—	—	35.00

100th Anniversary - Birth of Thomas Mann

KM#	Date	Mintage	XF	Unc	BU
54	1975A	.100	—	—	40.00

International Women's Year

KM#	Date	Mintage	XF	Unc	BU
55	1975A	.250	—	—	35.00

200th Anniversary - Birth of Ferdinand von Schill

KM#	Date	Mintage	XF	Unc	BU
60	1976A	.100	—	—	45.00

125th Anniversary - Death of Friedrich Ludwig Jahn

KM#	Date	Mintage	XF	Unc	BU
64	1977A	.090	—	—	75.00
	1977A	.010	—	Proof	125.00

175th Anniversary - Death of Friedrich Klopstock

KM#	Date	Mintage	XF	Unc	BU
67	1978A	.096	—	—	65.00
	1978A	4,500	—	Proof	120.00

Anti-Apartheid Year

KM#	Date	Mintage	XF	Unc	BU
68	1978A	.196	—	—	20.00
	1978A	4,000	—	Proof	100.00

100th Anniversary - Birth of Albert Einstein

KM#	Date	Mintage	XF	Unc	BU
72	1979A	.056	—	—	75.00
	1979A	4,500	—	Proof	110.00

75th Anniversary - Death of Adolph von Menzel

KM#	Date	Mintage	XF	Unc	BU
76	1980A	.055	—	—	90.00
	1980A	5,500	—	Proof	125.00

450th Anniversary - Death of Tilman Riemenschneider

KM#	Date	Mintage	XF	Unc	BU
79	1981A	.055	—	—	145.00
	1981A	5,500	—	Proof	160.00

200th Anniversary - Birth of Friedrich Frobel

KM#	Date	Mintage	XF	Unc	BU
84	1982A	.055	—	—	120.00
	1982A	5,500	—	Proof	150.00

COPPER-NICKEL-ZINC
Goethe's Weimar Cottage

KM#	Date	Mintage	XF	Unc	BU
85	1982A	.245	—	—	30.00
	1982A	5,500	—	Proof	70.00
	1982A	210 pcs.		Matte Proof	3000.

Wartburg Castle

KM#	Date	Mintage	XF	Unc	BU
86	1982A	.245	—	—	30.00
	1982A	5,500	—	Proof	70.00
	1983A	.010	—	—	275.00

COPPER-NICKEL
Wittenberg Church

KM#	Date	Mintage	XF	Unc	BU
89	1983A	.245	—	—	27.50
	1983A	5,500	—	Proof	70.00

Martin Luther's Birth Place

KM#	Date	Mintage	XF	Unc	BU
90	1983A	.245	—	—	27.50
	1983A	5,500	—	Proof	70.00

COPPER-NICKEL-ZINC
125th Anniversary - Birth of Max Planck

KM#	Date	Mintage	XF	Unc	BU
91	1983A	.056	—	—	60.00
	1983A	4,200	—	Proof	100.00

COPPER-NICKEL
Leipzig Old City Hall

KM#	Date	Mintage	XF	Unc	BU
96	1984A	.245	—	—	27.50
	1984A	5,500	—	Proof	55.00

Thomas Church of Leipzig

KM#	Date	Mintage	XF	Unc	BU
97	1984A	.245	—	—	27.50
	1984A	5,500	—	Proof	55.00

150th Anniversary - Death of Adolf Freiherr von Lutzow

KM#	Date	Mintage	XF	Unc	BU
98	1984A	.055	—	—	60.00
	1984A	5,000	—	Proof	85.00

Restoration of Dresden Women's Church

KM#	Date	Mintage	XF	Unc	BU
102	1985A	.245	—	—	25.00
	1985A	8,476	—	Proof	40.00

Restoration of Dresden Zwinger

KM#	Date	Mintage	XF	Unc	BU
103	1985A	.245	—	—	30.00
	1985A	5,500	—	Proof	45.00

225th Anniversary - Death of Caroline Neuber

KM#	Date	Mintage	XF	Unc	BU
104	1985A	.056	—	—	70.00
	1985A	4,000	—	Proof	90.00

Potsdam - Sanssouci Palace

KM#	Date	Mintage	XF	Unc	BU
110	1986A	.296	—	—	20.00
	1986A	4,200	—	Proof	50.00

Potsdam - New Palace

KM#	Date	Mintage	XF	Unc	BU
111	1986A	.296	—	—	20.00
	1986A	4,200	—	Proof	50.00

175th Anniversary - Death of Heinrich von Kleist

KM#	Date	Mintage	XF	Unc	BU
112	1986A	.056	—	—	135.00
	1986A	4,000	—	Proof	150.00

COPPER-ZINC-NICKEL
Berlin - Nikolai Quarter

KM#	Date	Mintage	XF	Unc	BU
114	1987A	.496	—	—	12.00
	1987A	4,200	—	Proof	50.00

Berlin - Red City Hall

KM#	Date	Mintage	XF	Unc	BU
115	1987A	.496	—	—	12.00
	1987A	4,200	—	Proof	50.00

Berlin - Universal Time Clock

KM#	Date	Mintage	XF	Unc	BU
116	1987A	.496	—	—	12.00
	1987A	4,200	—	Proof	50.00

COPPER-NICKEL
Germany's First Railroad

KM#	Date	Mintage	XF	Unc	BU
120	1988A	.496	—	—	15.00
	1988A	4,200	—	Proof	100.00

Port City of Rostock

KM#	Date	Mintage	XF	Unc	BU
121	1988A	.496	—	—	12.00
	1988A	4,200	—	Proof	50.00

50th Anniversary - Death of Ernst Barlach

KM#	Date	Mintage	XF	Unc	BU
122	1988A	.056	—	—	50.00
	1988A	4,000	—	Proof	75.00

COPPER-ZINC-NICKEL
Katharinen Kirche in Zwickau

KM#	Date	Mintage	XF	Unc	BU
129	1989A	.496	—	—	12.00
	1989A	4,200	—	Proof	50.00

Marien Kirche in Muhlhausen

KM#	Date	Mintage	XF	Unc	BU
130	1989A	.496	—	—	12.00
	1989A	4,200	—	Proof	50.00

100th Anniversary - Birth of Carl von Ossietzky

KM#	Date	Mintage	XF	Unc	BU
131	1989A	.056	—	—	45.00
	1989A	4,000	—	Proof	65.00

100th Anniversary - Birth of Kurt Tucholsky

KM#	Date	Mintage	XF	Unc	BU
133	1990A	.051	—	—	45.00
	1990A	4,000	—	Proof	65.00

500 Years of Postal Service

KM#	Date	Mintage	XF	Unc	BU
134	1990A	.496	—	—	10.00
	1990A	4,200	—	Proof	45.00

Zeughaus Museum

KM#	Date	Mintage	XF	Unc	BU
135	1990A	.496	—	—	10.00
	1990A	4,200	—	Proof	45.00

10 MARK

17.0000 g, .800 SILVER, .4373 oz ASW
125th Annivesary - Death of Karl Friedrich Schinkel
Edge: 10 MARK DER DEUTSCHEN NOTEN BANK

KM#	Date	Mintage	XF	Unc	BU
15.1	1966A	.050	—	—	325.00

Error: Plain edge

KM#	Date	Mintage	XF	Unc	BU
15.2	1966A	—	—	—	—

100th Anniversary - Birth of Kathe Kollwitz

KM#	Date	Mintage	XF	Unc	BU
17.1	1967A	.097	—	—	75.00

Error, edge: 10 MARK*10 MARK*10 MARK*

KM#	Date	Mintage	XF	Unc	BU
17.2	1967A	3,000	—	—	150.00

17.0000 g, .625 SILVER, .3416 oz ASW
500th Anniversary - Death of Johann Gutenberg

KM#	Date	Mintage	XF	Unc	BU
20	1968A	.100	—	—	65.00

250th Anniversary - Death of
Johann Friedrich Bottger

KM#	Date	Mintage	XF	Unc	BU
24	1969A	.100	—	—	55.00

Ludwig van Beethoven

KM#	Date	Mintage	XF	Unc	BU
27.1	1970A	.100	—	—	70.00

Error: Plain edge.

KM#	Date	Mintage	XF	Unc	BU
27.2	1970A	—	—	—	—

Albrecht Durer

KM#	Date	Mintage	XF	Unc	BU
31	1971A	.100	—	—	65.00

COPPER-NICKEL
Buchenwald Memorial

KM#	Date	Mintage	XF	Unc	BU
38	1972A	2.500	—	—	7.00

17.0000 g, .625 SILVER, .3416 oz ASW
175th Anniversary - Birth of Heinrich Heine

KM#	Date	Mintage	XF	Unc	BU
39	1972A	.100	—	—	60.00

COPPER-NICKEL
10th Youth Festival Games

KM#	Date	Mintage	XF	Unc	BU
44	1973A	1.500	—	—	7.00

17.0000 g, .625 SILVER, .3416 oz ASW
75th Anniversary - Birth of Bertolt Brecht

KM#	Date	Mintage	XF	Unc	BU
45	1973A	.100	—	—	60.00

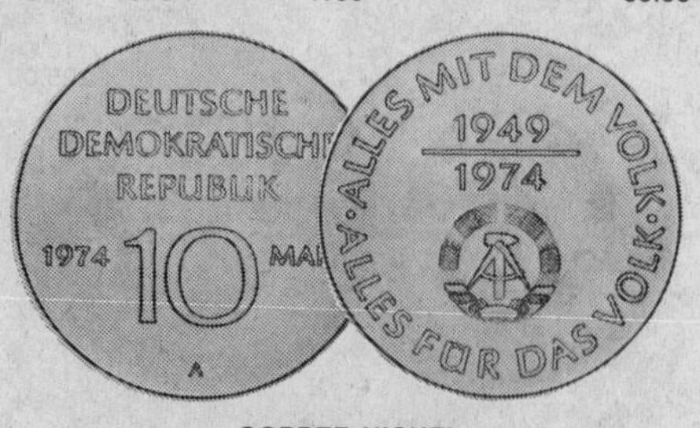

COPPER-NICKEL
25th Anniversary, with state motto

KM#	Date	Mintage	XF	Unc	BU
50	1974A	3.000	—	—	7.00

17.0000 g, .625 SILVER, .3416 oz ASW
25th Anniversary D.D.R.

KM#	Date	Mintage	XF	Unc	BU
51	1974A	.070	—	—	65.00
	1974A	200 pcs.	—	Proof	2200.

200th Anniversary - Birth of Caspar David Friedrich

KM#	Date	Mintage	XF	Unc	BU
52	1974A	.075	—	—	60.00

Centenary - Birth of Albert Schweitzer

KM#	Date	Mintage	XF	Unc	BU
56	1975A	.099	—	—	55.00
	1975A	1,040	—	Proof	1750.

17.0000 g, .500 SILVER, .2733 oz ASW
Plain edge
Mule. Obv: KM#58. Rev: KM#56.

KM#	Date	Mintage	XF	Unc	BU
57	1975A	6,700	—	—	125.00

COPPER-NICKEL
20th Anniversary - Warsaw Pact

KM#	Date	Mintage	XF	Unc	BU
58	1975A	2.500	—	—	7.00

20th Anniversary - National People's Army

KM#	Date	Mintage	XF	Unc	BU
61	1976A	.750	—	—	12.00

17.0000 g, .500 SILVER, .2733 oz ASW
150th Anniversary - Death of Carl Maria von Weber

KM#	Date	Mintage	XF	Unc	BU
62	1976A	.094	—	—	65.00
	1976A	6,037	—	Proof	90.00

375th Anniversary Birth of Otto von Guericke

KM#	Date	Mintage	XF	Unc	BU
65	1977A	.069	—	—	75.00
	1977A	6,000	—	Proof	100.00

175th Anniversary - Birth of Justus von Liebig

KM#	Date	Mintage	XF	Unc	BU
69	1978A	.071	—	—	75.00
	1978A	4,500	—	Proof	110.00

COPPER-NICKEL
Joint USSR-DDR Orbital Flight

KM#	Date	Mintage	XF	Unc	BU
70	1978A	.748	—	—	22.50
	1978A	2,200	—	Proof	450.00

17.0000 g, .500 SILVER, .2733 oz ASW
175th Anniversary - Birth of Ludwig Feuerbach

KM#	Date	Mintage	XF	Unc	BU
73	1979A	.051	—	—	65.00
	1979A	4,500	—	Proof	90.00

225th Anniversary - Birth of
Gerhard von Scharnhorst

KM#	Date	Mintage	XF	Unc	BU
77	1980A	.055	—	—	65.00
	1980A	5,500	—	Proof	90.00

COPPER-NICKEL
25th Anniversary - National People's Army

KM#	Date	Mintage	XF	Unc	BU
80	1981A	.745	—	—	10.00
	1981A	5,500	—	Proof	75.00

17.0000 g, .500 SILVER, .2733 oz ASW
150th Anniversary - Death of Georg Hegel

KM#	Date	Mintage	XF	Unc	BU
81	1981A	.050	—	—	60.00
	1981A	5,500	—	Proof	85.00

COPPER-NICKEL
700th Anniversary - Berlin Mint

KM#	Date	Mintage	XF	Unc	BU
82	1981A	.055	—	—	35.00
	1981A	5,500	—	Proof	90.00

17.0000 g, .500 SILVER, .2733 oz ASW
Leipzig Gewandhaus

KM#	Date	Mintage	XF	Unc	BU
87	1982A	.050	—	—	80.00
	1982A	5,500	—	Proof	100.00

17.1100 g, .500 SILVER, .2751 oz ASW
100th Anniversary - Death of Richard Wagner

KM#	Date	Mintage	XF	Unc	BU
92	1983A	.044	—	—	60.00
	1983A	5,500	—	Proof	85.00

COPPER-NICKEL-ZINC
30th Anniversary - Workers Militia

KM#	Date	Mintage	XF	Unc	BU
93	1983A	.495	—	—	12.00
	1983A	5,000	—	Proof	55.00

17.0000 g, .500 SILVER, .2733 oz ASW
100th Anniversary - Death of Alfred Brehm

KM#	Date	Mintage	XF	Unc	BU
99	1984A	.050	—	—	60.00
	1984A	5,000	—	Proof	90.00

Restoration of Semper Opera in Dresden

KM#	Date	Mintage	XF	Unc	BU
101	1985A	.050	—	—	70.00
	1985A	5,000	—	Proof	100.00

COPPER-NICKEL-ZINC
40th Anniversary - Liberation from Fascism

KM#	Date	Mintage	XF	Unc	BU
106	1985A	.745	—	—	10.00
	1985A	5,500	—	Proof	50.00

17.0000 g, .500 SILVER, .2733 oz ASW

KM#	Date	Mintage	XF	Unc	BU
106a	1985A	—	—	Proof	2450.

175th Anniversary - Humboldt University

KM#	Date	Mintage	XF	Unc	BU
107	1985A	.051	—	—	75.00
	1985A	4,000	—	Proof	100.00

COPPER-NICKEL
100th Anniversary - Birth of Ernst Thalmann

KM#	Date	Mintage	XF	Unc	BU
109	1986A	.746	—	—	12.00
	1986A	4,000	—	Proof	65.00

17.0000 g, .500 SILVER, .2733 oz ASW
Charite - Berlin

KM#	Date	Mintage	XF	Unc	BU
113	1986A	.051	—	—	65.00
	1986A	4,000	—	Proof	90.00

Berlin - Theater

KM#	Date	Mintage	XF	Unc	BU
118	1987A	.051	—	—	65.00
	1987A	4,000	—	Proof	90.00

500th Anniversary - Birth of Ulrich von Hutton

KM#	Date	Mintage	XF	Unc	BU
123	1988A	.052	—	—	90.00
	1988A	3,500	—	Proof	170.00

COPPER-NICKEL
East German Sports

KM#	Date	Mintage	XF	Unc	BU
125	1988A	.747	—	—	10.00
	1988A	3,200	—	Proof	90.00

Council of Mutual Economic Aid

KM#	Date	Mintage	XF	Unc	BU
126	1989A	—	—	—	50.00
	1989A	3,000	—	Proof	90.00

17.0000 g, .500 SILVER, .2733 oz ASW
200th Anniversary - Birth of Johann Gottfried Schadow

KM#	Date	Mintage	XF	Unc	BU
128	1989A	.051	—	—	110.00
	1989A	4,000	—	Proof	225.00

COPPER-NICKEL-ZINC
40th Anniversary - East German Government

KM#	Date	Mintage	XF	Unc	BU
132	1989A	.746	—	—	10.00
	1989A	3,080	—	Proof	85.00

International Labor Day

KM#	Date	Mintage	XF	Unc	BU
136	1990A	.747	—	—	10.00
	1990A	4,367	—	Proof	65.00

17.0000 g, .500 SILVER, .2733 oz ASW
Johann Gottlieb Fichte

KM#	Date	Mintage	XF	Unc	BU
137	1990A	.037	—	—	100.00
	1990A	4,900	—	Proof	225.00

20 MARK

20.9000 g, .800 SILVER, .5376 oz ASW
250th Anniversary - Death of Gottfried Wilhelm Leibniz
Edge: 20 MARK DER DEUTSCHEN NOTEN BANK

KM#	Date	Mintage	XF	Unc	BU
16.1	1966A	.050	—	—	225.00

Edge: (error) 10 MARK DER DEUTSCHEN NOTEN BANK

KM#	Date	Mintage	XF	Unc	BU
16.2	1966A	—	—	—	—

200th Anniversary - Birth of Wilhelm von Humboldt

KM#	Date	Mintage	XF	Unc	BU
18.1	1967A	.097	—	—	155.00

Edge: (error) 20 MARK* 20 MARK*20 MARK*20 MARK*

KM#	Date	Mintage	XF	Unc	BU
18.2	1967A	3,000	—	—	550.00

150th Anniversary - Birth of Karl Marx

KM#	Date	Mintage	XF	Unc	BU
21	1968A	.100	—	—	140.00

20.9000 g, .625 SILVER, .4200 oz ASW
Johann Wolfgang von Goethe

KM#	Date	Mintage	XF	Unc	BU
25	1969A	.100	—	—	155.00
	1969A	—	—	Proof	Rare

150th Anniversary - Birth of Friedrich Engels

KM#	Date	Mintage	XF	Unc	BU
28	1970A	.100	—	—	130.00
	1970A	—	—	Proof	Rare

Karl Liebknecht-Rosa Luxemburg

KM#	Date	Mintage	XF	Unc	BU
32	1971A	.100	—	—	85.00

COPPER-NICKEL
100th Anniversary - Birth of Heinrich Mann

KM#	Date	Mintage	XF	Unc	BU
33	1971	2.000	—	—	10.00

85th Birthday of Ernst Thalmann

KM#	Date	Mintage	XF	Unc	BU
34	1971A	2.500	—	—	10.00

NOTE: Edge varieties exist.

Friedrich von Schiller

KM#	Date	Mintage	XF	Unc	BU
40	1972A	3.000	—	—	10.00

20.9000 g, .625 SILVER, .4200 oz ASW
500th Anniversary - Birth of Lucas Cranach

KM#	Date	Mintage	XF	Unc	BU
41	1972A	.100	—	—	75.00

COPPER-NICKEL
Wilhelm Pieck

KM#	Date	Mintage	XF	Unc	BU
42	1972A	2.500	—	—	10.00

20.9000 g, .625 SILVER, .4200 oz ASW
60th Anniversary - Death of August Bebel

KM#	Date	Mintage	XF	Unc	BU
46	1973A	.100	—	—	75.00

COPPER-NICKEL
Otto Grotewohl

KM#	Date	Mintage	XF	Unc	BU
47	1973A	2.500	—	—	10.00

20.9000 g, .625 SILVER, .4200 oz ASW
250th Anniversary - Death of Immanuel Kant

KM#	Date	Mintage	XF	Unc	BU
53	1974A	.096	—	—	90.00
	1974A	4,221	—	Proof	130.00

225th Anniversary - Death of Johann Sebastian Bach

KM#	Date	Mintage	XF	Unc	BU
59	1975A	.100	—	—	100.00
	1975A	Inc. Ab.	—	Proof	3500.

150th Anniversary - Birth of Wilhelm Liebknecht

KM#	Date	Mintage	XF	Unc	BU
63	1976A	.096	—	—	80.00
	1976A	4,000	—	Proof	150.00

20.9000 g, .500 SILVER, .3360 oz ASW
200th Anniversary - Birth of Carl Friedrich Gauss

KM#	Date	Mintage	XF	Unc	BU
66	1977A	.055	—	—	85.00

175th Anniversary - Death of Johann von Herder

KM#	Date	Mintage	XF	Unc	BU
71	1978A	.051	—	—	80.00
	1978A	4,500	—	Proof	150.00

250th Anniversary - Birth of Gotthold Ephraim Lessing

KM#	Date	Mintage	XF	Unc	BU
74	1979A	.041	—	—	85.00
	1979A	4,500	—	Proof	100.00

COPPER-NICKEL
30th Anniversary - East German Regime

KM#	Date	Mintage	XF	Unc	BU
75	1979A	1.000	—	—	18.00

20.9200 g, .500 SILVER, .3360 oz ASW
75th Anniversary - Death of Ernst Abbe

KM#	Date	Mintage	XF	Unc	BU
78	1980A	.040	—	—	75.00
	1980A	5,500	—	Proof	100.00

150th Anniversary - Death of vom Stein

KM#	Date	Mintage	XF	Unc	BU
83	1981A	.040	—	—	75.00
	1981A	5,500	—	Proof	120.00

125th Anniversary - Birth of Clara Zetkin

KM#	Date	Mintage	XF	Unc	BU
88	1982A	.040	—	—	70.00
	1982A	5,500	—	Proof	100.00

500th Anniversary - Birth of Martin Luther

KM#	Date	Mintage	XF	Unc	BU
94	1983A	.045	—	—	465.00
	1983A	5,000	—	Proof	485.00

COPPER-NICKEL

100th Anniversary - Death of Karl Marx

KM#	Date	Mintage	XF	Unc	BU
95	1983A	.995	—	—	18.00
	1983A	5,000	—	Proof	80.00

20.9200 g, .500 SILVER, .3360 oz ASW
225th Anniversary - Death of
Georg Friedrich Handel

KM#	Date	Mintage	XF	Unc	BU
100	1984A	.041	—	—	130.00
	1984A	4,500	—	Proof	150.00

125th Anniversary - Death of Ernst Moritz Arndt

KM#	Date	Mintage	XF	Unc	BU
105	1985A	.041	—	—	70.00
	1985A	4,000	—	Proof	100.00

20.9000 g, .625 SILVER, .4200 oz ASW
200th Anniversary - Birth of
Jacob and Wilhelm Grimm

KM#	Date	Mintage	XF	Unc	BU
108	1986A	.037	—	—	245.00
	1986A	3,500	—	Proof	275.00

Berlin - City Seal

KM#	Date	Mintage	XF	Unc	BU
119.1	1987A	.042	—	—	450.00
	1987A	2,100	—	Proof	1700.

NOTE: Seal on reverse totally frosted on proof coins.

Rev: Fields in seal polished.

KM#	Date	Mintage	XF	Unc	BU
119.2	1987A	2,100	—	Proof	1700.

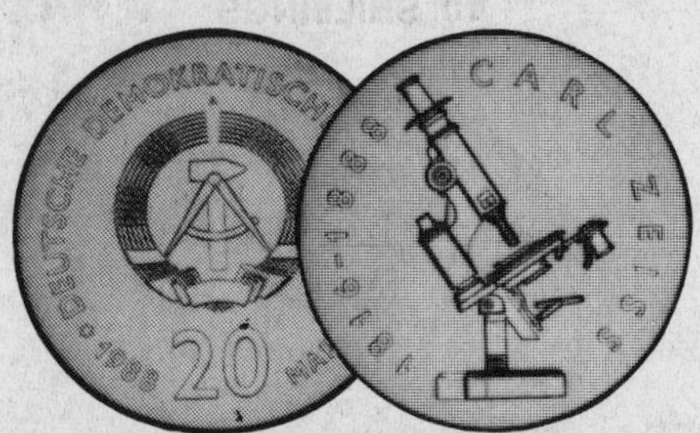

100th Anniversary - Death of Carl Zeiss

KM#	Date	Mintage	XF	Unc	BU
124	1988A	.037	—	—	110.00
	1988A	3,500	—	Proof	150.00

500th Anniversary - Birth of Thomas Muntzer

KM#	Date	Mintage	XF	Unc	BU
127	1989A	.037	—	—	100.00
	1989A	3,500	—	Proof	220.00

Andreas Schluter

KM#	Date	Mintage	XF	Unc	BU
138	1990A	.037	—	—	90.00
	1990A	3,500	—	Proof	230.00

COPPER-NICKEL
Opening of Brandenburg Gate
Obv: State emblem, value and legend.

KM#	Date	Mintage	XF	Unc	BU
139	1990A	.300	—	—	25.00

18.2000 g, .999 SILVER, .5852 oz ASW

KM#	Date	Mintage	XF	Unc	BU
139a	1990A	.145	—	—	55.00
	1990A	5,000	—	Proof	200.00

MINT SETS (MS)

NOTE: Issue date of mint sets from 1979-1989 are determined by the five mark coin. The minors in these sets are of mixed dates.

KM#	Date	Mintage	Identification	Issue Price	Mkt. Val.
MS1	1979A(8)	26,000	KM8.2-10.2,11-12,29,35,48	—	75.00
MS2	1980A(8)	25,000	KM8.2-10.2,11-12,29,35,48	—	100.00
MS3	1981(8)	25,000	KM8.2-10.2,11-12,29,35,48	—	85.00
MS4	1982(8)	21,000	KM8.2-10.2,11-12,29,35,48	—	100.00
MS5	1982(7)	4,500	KM8.2-10.2,11-12,35,48	—	12.00
MS6	1983(8)	19,000	KM8.2-10.2,11-12,35,37,48	—	250.00
MS7	1983(7)	4,500	KM8.2-10.2,11-12,35,48	—	12.00
MS8	1984(8)	19,000	KM8.2-10.2,11-12,29,35,48	—	225.00
MS9	1984(7)	4,500	KM8.2-10.2,11-12,35,48	—	12.00
MS10	1985(8)	6,000	KM8.2-10.2,11-12,35,48,102	—	85.00
MS11	1985(7)	4,500	KM8.2-10.2,11-12,35,48	—	12.00
MS12	1986(8)	7,000	KM8.2-10.2,11-12,29,35,48	—	85.00
MS13	1986(7)	4,500	KM8.2-10.2,11-12,35,48	—	10.00
MS14	1987(8)	8,000	KM8.2-10.2,11-12,29,35,48	—	60.00
MS15	1987(7)	4,500	KM8.2-10.2,11-12,35,48	—	10.00
MS16	1988(8)	11,000	KM8.2-10.2,11-12,29,35,48	—	100.00
MS17	1988(7)	4,500	KM8.2-10.2,11-12,35,48	—	10.00
MS18	1989(8)	11,000	KM8.2-10.2,11-12,29,35,48	—	100.00
MS19	1989(7)	4,500	KM8.2-10.2,11-12,35,48	—	10.00
MS20	1990(8)	11,000	KM8.2-10.2,11-12,29,35,48	—	125.00

NOTE: The 7 pc. sets contain a plaque depicting Von Schadow's art as displayed on the walls of the Berlin Mint.

PROOF SETS (PS)

KM#	Date	Mintage	Identification	Issue Price	Mkt. Val.
PS1	1981(8)	20	KM8.2-10.2,11-12,35,48,79	—	1000.
PS2	1981(8)	20	KM8.2-10.2,11-12,35,37,48	—	6000.
PS3	1982(8)	2,500	KM8.2-10.2,11-12,29,35,48	—	250.00
PS4	1983(8)	2,550	KM8.2-10.2,11-12,35,37,48	—	375.00
PS5	1984(8)	3,015	KM8.2-10.2,11-12,29,35,48	—	135.00
PS6	1985(8)	2,816	KM8.2-10.2,11-12,35,48,102	—	115.00
PS7	1986(8)	2,800	KM8.2-10.2,11-12,29,35,48	—	125.00
PS8	1987(8)	2,345	KM8.2-10.2,11-12,29,35,48	—	115.00
PS9	1988(8)	2,300	KM8.2-10.2,11-12,29,35,48	—	125.00
PS10	1989(8)	2,300	KM8.2-10.2,11-12,29,35,48	—	125.00

GHANA

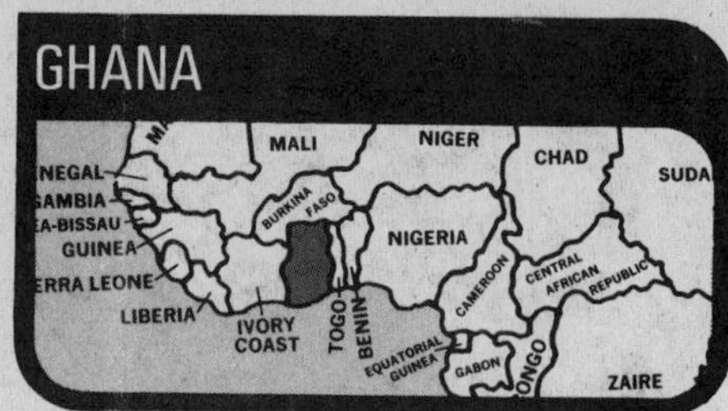

The Republic of Ghana, a member of the British Commonwealth situated on the West Coast of Africa between Ivory Coast and Togo, has an area of 92,100 sq. mi. (238,540 sq. km.) and a population of 14 million, almost entirely African. Capital: Accra. Cocoa (the major crop), coconuts, palm kernels and coffee are exported. Mining, second in importance to agriculture, is concentrated on gold, manganese and industrial diamonds.

First visited by Portuguese traders in 1470, and through the 17th century was used by various European powers -England, Denmark, Holland, Germany -as a center for their slave trade. Britain achieved control of the Gold Coast in 1821, and established the colony of Gold Coast in 1874. In 1901 Britain annexed the neighboring Ashanti Kingdom in the same year a northern region known as the Northern Territories became a British protectorate. Part of the former German colony of Togoland was mandated to Britain by the League of Nations and administered as part of the Gold Coast. The state of Ghana, comprising the Gold Coast and British Togoland, obtained independence on March 6, 1957, becoming the first Negro African colony to do so. On July I, 1960, Ghana adopted a republican constitution, changing from a ministerial to a presidential form of government. The government was overthrown, the constitution suspended and the National Assembly dissolved by the Ghanaian army and police on Feb. 24, 1966. The government was returned to civilian authority in Oct. 1969, but was again seized by military officers in a bloodless coup on Jan. 13, 1972. Ghana remains a member of the Commonwealth of Nations, with executive authority vested in the Supreme Military council.

Ghana's monetary denomination of 'Cedi' is derived from the word 'sedie' meaning cowrie, a shell money commonly employed by coastal tribes.

GOLD COAST

RULERS

British

MONETARY SYSTEM

8 Tackoe = 1 Ackey

1/2 ACKEY

7.0900 g, .925 SILVER, .2108 oz ASW

KM#	Date	Mintage	Fine	VF	XF	Unc
8	1818	*2,170	50.00	125.00	200.00	—
	1818	—	—	—	Proof	320.00

ACKEY

14.1300 g, .925 SILVER, .4202 oz ASW

KM#	Date	Mintage	Fine	VF	XF	Unc
9	1818	*1,085	150.00	300.00	450.00	—
	1818	—	—	—	Proof	750.00

NOTE: For later issues see British West Africa.

GHANA

MONETARY SYSTEM

12 Pence = 1 Shilling

1/2 PENNY

BRONZE

Dr. Kwame Nkrumah

KM#	Date	Mintage	VF	XF	Unc
1	1958	32.200	—	.10	.25
	1958	.020	—	Proof	.50

PENNY

BRONZE

Dr. Kwame Nkrumah

KM#	Date	Mintage	VF	XF	Unc
2	1958	60.000	—	.15	.35
	1958	.020	—	Proof	.75

3 PENCE

COPPER-NICKEL

Dr. Kwame Nkrumah

KM#	Date	Mintage	VF	XF	Unc
3	1958	25.200	.10	.25	.50
	1958	.020	—	Proof	1.00

6 PENCE

COPPER-NICKEL

Dr. Kwame Nkrumah

KM#	Date	Mintage	VF	XF	Unc
4	1958	15.200	.10	.25	.65
	1958	—	—	Proof	1.25

SHILLING

COPPER-NICKEL

Dr. Kwame Nkrumah

KM#	Date	Mintage	VF	XF	Unc
5	1958	34.400	.15	.35	1.25
	1958	.020	—	Proof	1.75

2 SHILLINGS

COPPER-NICKEL

Dr. Kwame Nkrumah

KM#	Date	Mintage	VF	XF	Unc
6	1958	72.700	.25	.65	2.00
	1958	.020	—	Proof	2.50

10 SHILLINGS

28.2800 g, .925 SILVER, .8411 oz ASW

Dr. Kwame Nkrumah

KM#	Date	Mintage	VF	XF	Unc
7	1958	.011	—	Proof	10.00

DECIMAL COINAGE

100 Pesewas = 1 Cedi

1/2 PESEWA

BRONZE

Bush Drums

KM#	Date	Mintage	VF	XF	Unc
12	1967	30.000	—	.10	.25
	1967	2,000	—	Proof	.75

PESEWA

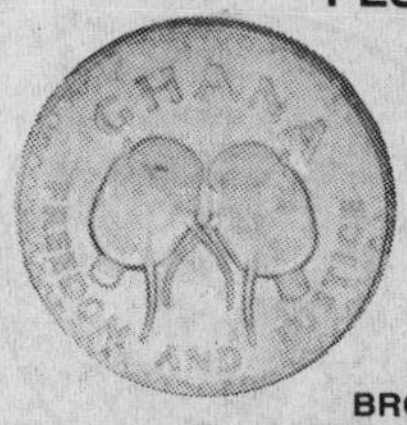

BRONZE

Bush Drums

KM#	Date	Mintage	VF	XF	Unc
13	1967	30.000	—	.15	.30
	1967	2,000	—	Proof	1.00
	1975	50.250	—	.10	.25
	1979	5.000	—	.10	.25

2-1/2 PESEWAS

COPPER-NICKEL

Cocoa Beans

KM#	Date	Mintage	VF	XF	Unc
14	1967	6.000	—	.10	.35
	1967	2,000	—	Proof	1.25

5 PESEWAS

COPPER-NICKEL

Dr. Kwame Nkrumah

KM#	Date	Mintage	VF	XF	Unc
8	1965	30.000	.10	.20	.50

Cocoa Beans

KM#	Date	Mintage	VF	XF	Unc
15	1967	30.000	.10	.15	.40
	1967	2,000	—	Proof	1.50
	1973	8.000	.10	.15	.40
	1975	20.000	.10	.15	.35

10 PESEWAS

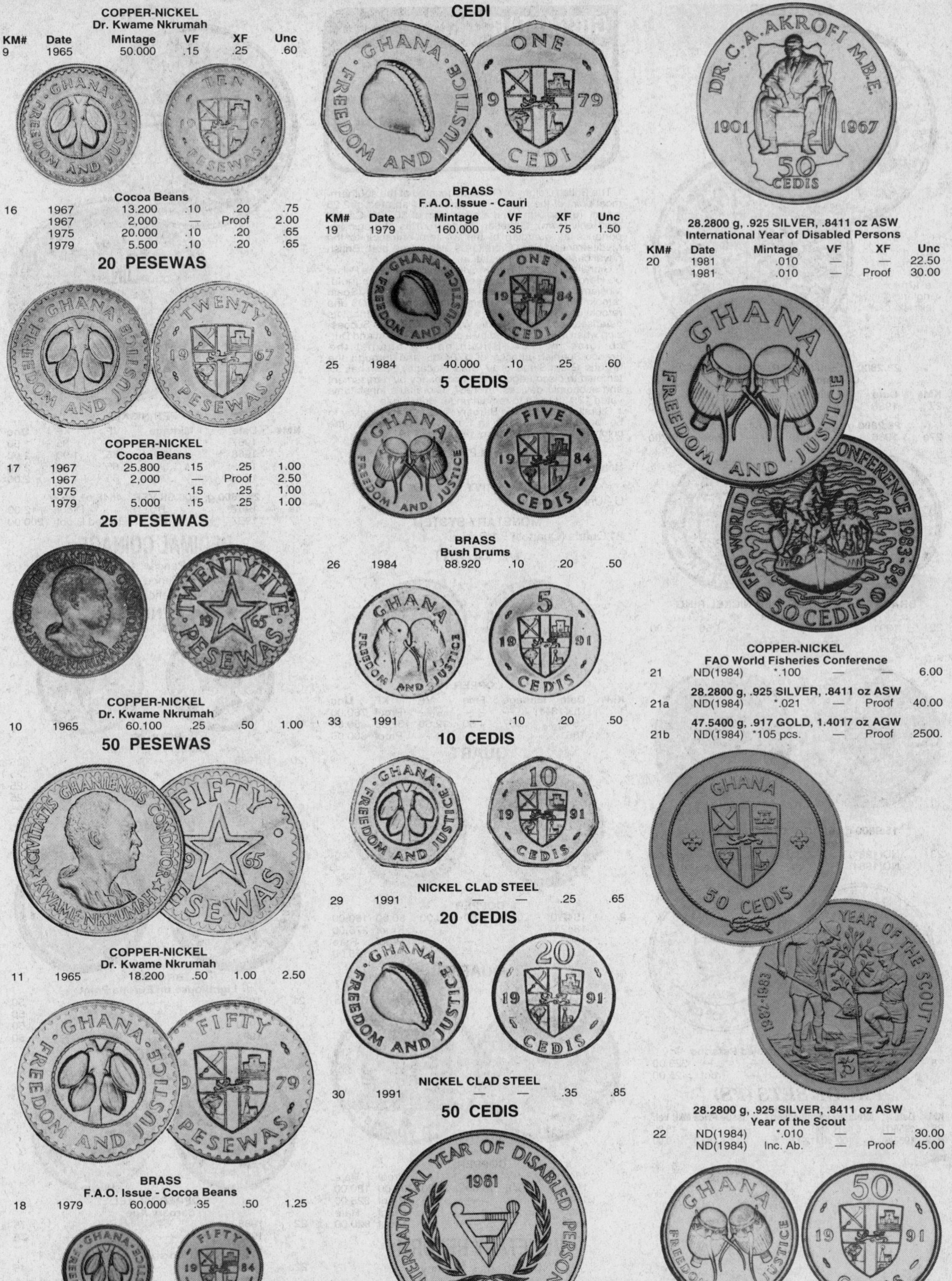

COPPER-NICKEL
Dr. Kwame Nkrumah

KM#	Date	Mintage	VF	XF	Unc
9	1965	50.000	.15	.25	.60

Cocoa Beans

KM#	Date	Mintage	VF	XF	Unc
16	1967	13.200	.10	.20	.75
	1967	2,000	—	Proof	2.00
	1975	20.000	.10	.20	.65
	1979	5.500	.10	.20	.65

20 PESEWAS

COPPER-NICKEL
Cocoa Beans

KM#	Date	Mintage	VF	XF	Unc
17	1967	25.800	.15	.25	1.00
	1967	2,000	—	Proof	2.50
	1975	—	.15	.25	1.00
	1979	5.000	.15	.25	1.00

25 PESEWAS

COPPER-NICKEL
Dr. Kwame Nkrumah

KM#	Date	Mintage	VF	XF	Unc
10	1965	60.100	.25	.50	1.00

50 PESEWAS

COPPER-NICKEL
Dr. Kwame Nkrumah

KM#	Date	Mintage	VF	XF	Unc
11	1965	18.200	.50	1.00	2.50

BRASS
F.A.O. Issue - Cocoa Beans

KM#	Date	Mintage	VF	XF	Unc
18	1979	60.000	.35	.50	1.25
24	1984	10.000	.10	.25	.60

CEDI

BRASS
F.A.O. Issue - Cauri

KM#	Date	Mintage	VF	XF	Unc
19	1979	160.000	.35	.75	1.50
25	1984	40.000	.10	.25	.60

5 CEDIS

BRASS
Bush Drums

KM#	Date	Mintage	VF	XF	Unc
26	1984	88.920	.10	.20	.50
33	1991	—	.10	.20	.50

10 CEDIS

NICKEL CLAD STEEL

KM#	Date	Mintage	VF	XF	Unc
29	1991	—	—	.25	.65

20 CEDIS

NICKEL CLAD STEEL

KM#	Date	Mintage	VF	XF	Unc
30	1991	—	—	.35	.85

50 CEDIS

28.2800 g, .925 SILVER, .8411 oz ASW
International Year of Disabled Persons

KM#	Date	Mintage	VF	XF	Unc
20	1981	.010	—	—	22.50
	1981	.010	—	Proof	30.00

COPPER-NICKEL
FAO World Fisheries Conference

KM#	Date	Mintage	VF	XF	Unc
21	ND(1984)	*.100	—	—	6.00

28.2800 g, .925 SILVER, .8411 oz ASW

KM#	Date	Mintage	VF	XF	Unc
21a	ND(1984)	*.021	—	Proof	40.00

47.5400 g, .917 GOLD, 1.4017 oz AGW

KM#	Date	Mintage	VF	XF	Unc
21b	ND(1984)	*105 pcs.	—	Proof	2500.

28.2800 g, .925 SILVER, .8411 oz ASW
Year of the Scout

KM#	Date	Mintage	VF	XF	Unc
22	ND(1984)	*.010	—	—	30.00
	ND(1984)	Inc. Ab.	—	Proof	45.00

COPPER-NICKEL

KM#	Date	Mintage	VF	XF	Unc
31	1991	—	—	1.00	2.00

100 CEDIS

28.2800 g, .500 SILVER, .4546 oz ASW
Commonwealth Games

KM#	Date	Mintage	VF	XF	Unc
27	1986	*.050	—	—	15.00

28.2800 g, .925 SILVER, .8411 oz ASW

KM#	Date	Mintage	VF	XF	Unc
27a	1986	*.020	—	Proof	25.00

BRASS CENTER IN COPPER-NICKEL RING
Colda Beans

KM#	Date	Mintage	VF	XF	Unc
32	1991	—	—	1.50	3.00

500 CEDIS

15.9800 g, .917 GOLD, .4711 oz AGW
Year of the Scout

KM#	Date	Mintage	VF	XF	Unc
23	ND(1984)	2,000	—	—	325.00
	ND(1984)	2,000	—	Proof	425.00

International Year of Disabled Persons

KM#	Date	Mintage	VF	XF	Unc
28	1981	—	—	—	325.00
	1981	—	—	Proof	425.00

PROOF SETS (PS)

KM#	Date	Mintage	Identification	Issue Price	Mkt. Val.
PS1	1958(7)	6,431	KM1-7	—	15.00
PS2	1967(6)	100	KM12-17	8.53	9.00

Listings For

GHURFAH: refer to Yemen Republic

GIBRALTAR

The British Colony of Gibraltar, located at the southernmost point of the Iberian Peninsula, has an area of 2.25 sq. mi. (6.5 sq. km.) and a population of 30,000. Capital (and only town): Gibraltar. Aside from its strategic importance as guardian of the western entrance to the Mediterranean Sea, Gibraltar is also a free port, British naval base, and coaling station.

Gibraltar, rooted in Greek mythology as one of the Pillars of Hercules, has long been a coveted stronghold. Moslems took it from Spain and fortified it in 711. Spain retook it in 1309, lost it again to the Moors in 1333 and retook it in 1462. After 1540 Spain strengthened its defenses and held it until the War of the Spanish Succession when it was captured by a combined British and Dutch force in 1704. Britain held it against the Franco-Spanish attacks of 1704-05 and through the historic 'Great Siege' of 1779-83. Recently Spain has attempted to discourage British occupancy by harassment and economic devices. In 1967, Gibraltar's inhabitants voted 12,138 to 44 to remain under British rule.

Gibraltar's celebrated Barbary Ape, the last monkey to be found in a wild state in Europe, is featured on the colony's first decimal crown, released in 1972.

RULERS

British

MINT PRIVY MARKS

U - Unc finish

MONETARY SYSTEM

24 Quarts (Quartos) = 1 Real

1/2 QUART

COPPER

KM#	Date	Mintage	Fine	VF	XF	Unc
1	ND(1841)	—	—	—	Proof	760.00
	1842	.387	4.50	12.50	32.50	80.00
	1861	—	—	—	Proof	800.00

QUART

COPPER

KM#	Date	Mintage	Fine	VF	XF	Unc
2	1842/0	.097	9.00	30.00	80.00	160.00
	1842/0	—	—	—	Proof	275.00
	1860	—	—	—	Proof	Rare
	1861	—	—	—	Proof	725.00

2 QUARTS

COPPER

KM#	Date	Mintage	Fine	VF	XF	Unc
3	1841	—	—	—	Proof	Rare
	1842/1	.048	15.00	40.00	90.00	180.00
	1842/1	—	—	—	Proof	325.00
	1860	—	—	—	Proof	Rare
	1861	—	—	—	Proof	820.00

MONETARY REFORM

4 Farthings = 1 Penny
12 Pence = 1 Shilling
2 Shillings = 1 Florin
5 Shillings = 1 Crown
20 Shillings = 1 Pound

CROWN

COPPER-NICKEL

KM#	Date	Mintage	VF	XF	Unc
4	1967	.125	.50	.85	1.50
	1968	.040	.65	1.00	2.00
	1969	.040	.65	1.00	2.00
	1970	.045	.65	1.00	2.00

28.2800 g, .500 SILVER, .4546 oz ASW

KM#	Date	Mintage	VF	XF	Unc
4a	1967	.010	—	Proof	12.00
	1967	50 pcs.		Frosted Proof	200.00

DECIMAL COINAGE

5 New Pence = 1 Shilling
25 New Pence = 1 Crown
100 New Pence = 1 Pound

PENNY

BRONZE
Barbary Partridge

KM#	Date	Mintage	VF	XF	Unc
20	1988	—	—	—	.25
	1989	—	—	—	.25
	1990	—	—	—	.25
	1992	—	—	—	.25
	1993	—	—	—	.25

2 PENCE

BRONZE
Lighthouse on Europa Point

KM#	Date	Mintage	VF	XF	Unc
21	1988	—	—	—	.50
	1989	—	—	—	.50
	1990	—	—	—	.50
	1991	—	—	—	.50

5 PENCE

COPPER-NICKEL
Barbary Ape

KM#	Date	Mintage	VF	XF	Unc
22	1988	—	—	—	.75
	1989	—	—	—	.75

Reduced size, 18mm

KM#	Date	Mintage	VF	XF	Unc
22a	1990	—	—	—	.45

3.2500 g, .925 SILVER, .0966 oz ASW

KM#	Date	Mintage	VF	XF	Unc
22b	1990	—	—	Proof	25.00

3.2500 g, .917 GOLD, .0958 oz AGW

KM#	Date	Mintage	VF	XF	Unc
22c	1990	—	—	Proof	125.00

3.2500 g, .950 PLATINUM, .0993 oz APW

KM#	Date	Mintage	VF	XF	Unc
22d	1990	—	—	Proof	150.00

10 PENCE

COPPER-NICKEL
Moorish Castle

KM#	Date	Mintage	VF	XF	Unc
23	1988	—	—	—	1.00
	1989	—	—	—	1.00
	1990	—	—	—	1.00
	1991	—	—	—	1.00

Euro-Port

KM#	Date	Mintage	VF	XF	Unc
112	1992	—	—	—	1.00

6.5000 g, .925 SILVER, .1933 oz ASW

KM#	Date	Mintage	VF	XF	Unc
112a	1992	—	—	—	27.50

6.5000 g, .917 GOLD, .1914 oz AGW

KM#	Date	Mintage	VF	XF	Unc
112b	1992	—	—	—	—

6.5000 g, .950 PLATINUM, .1985 oz APW

KM#	Date	Mintage	VF	XF	Unc
112c	1992	—	—	—	—

20 PENCE

COPPER-NICKEL
Our Lady of Europe

KM#	Date	Mintage	VF	XF	Unc
16	1988	—	—	—	1.50
	1989	—	—	—	1.50
	1990	—	—	—	1.50

25 NEW PENCE

COPPER-NICKEL
Magot

KM#	Date	Mintage	VF	XF	Unc
5	1971	.075	—	1.00	2.00

28.2800 g, .500 SILVER, .4546 oz ASW

KM#	Date	Mintage	VF	XF	Unc
5a	1971	.020	—	Proof	12.00
	1971	50 pcs.	Frosted Proof		200.00

COPPER-NICKEL
25th Wedding Anniversary

KM#	Date	Mintage	VF	XF	Unc
6	1972	.070	—	1.00	2.50

28.2800 g, .925 SILVER, .8411 oz ASW

KM#	Date	Mintage	VF	XF	Unc
6a	1972	.015	—	Proof	12.50

COPPER-NICKEL
Queen's Silver Jubilee

KM#	Date	Mintage	VF	XF	Unc
10	1977	.065	—	1.00	2.50

28.2800 g, .925 SILVER, .8411 oz ASW

KM#	Date	Mintage	VF	XF	Unc
10a	1977	.024	—	Proof	12.50

50 PENCE

COPPER-NICKEL

KM#	Date	Mintage	VF	XF	Unc
17	1988	—	—	—	2.00
	1989	—	—	—	2.00

Christmas

KM#	Date	Mintage	VF	XF	Unc
19	1988	—	—	—	4.00
	1988	—	—	Proof	15.00

15.5000 g, .925 SILVER, .4610 oz ASW

KM#	Date	Mintage	VF	XF	Unc
19a	1988	—	—	Proof	15.00

26.0000 g, .917 GOLD, .7666 oz AGW

KM#	Date	Mintage	VF	XF	Unc
19b	1988	—	—	Proof	450.00

30.4000 g, .950 PLATINUM, .9286 oz APW

KM#	Date	Mintage	VF	XF	Unc
19c	1988	—	—	Proof	700.00

COPPER-NICKEL
Christmas

KM#	Date	Mintage	VF	XF	Unc
31	1989	—	—	—	4.00
	1989	*.030	—	Proof	8.00

15.5000 g, .925 SILVER, .4610 oz ASW

KM#	Date	Mintage	VF	XF	Unc
31a	1989	*5,000	—	Proof	45.00

26.0000 g, .917 GOLD, .7666 oz AGW

KM#	Date	Mintage	VF	XF	Unc
31b	1989	*250 pcs.	—	Proof	750.00

30.4000 g, .950 PLATINUM, .9286 oz APW

KM#	Date	Mintage	VF	XF	Unc
31c	1989	*50 pcs.	—	Proof	1000.

COPPER-NICKEL
Dolphins

KM#	Date	Mintage	VF	XF	Unc
39	1990	—	—	—	2.75
	1993	—	—	—	2.75

15.5000 g, .925 SILVER, .4610 oz ASW

KM#	Date	Mintage	VF	XF	Unc
39a	1990	—	—	Proof	45.00

26.0000 g, .917 GOLD, .7666 oz AGW

KM#	Date	Mintage	VF	XF	Unc
39b	1990	—	—	Proof	800.00

30.4000 g, .950 PLATINUM, .9286 oz APW

KM#	Date	Mintage	VF	XF	Unc
39c	1990	—	—	Proof	1100.

COPPER-NICKEL
Christmas

KM#	Date	Mintage	VF	XF	Unc
47	1990	—	—	—	4.00
	1990	.030	—	Proof	8.00

15.5000 g, .925 SILVER, .4610 oz ASW

KM#	Date	Mintage	VF	XF	Unc
47a	1990	5,000	—	Proof	45.00

26.0000 g, .917 GOLD, .7666 oz AGW

KM#	Date	Mintage	VF	XF	Unc
47b	1990	250 pcs.	—	Proof	700.00

30.4000 g, .950 PLATINUM, .9286 oz APW

KM#	Date	Mintage	VF	XF	Unc
47c	1990	50 pcs.	—	Proof	1000.

COPPER-NICKEL
Christmas

KM#	Date	Mintage	VF	XF	Unc
83	1991	—	—	—	4.00
	1991	.030	—	Proof	8.00

15.5000 g, .925 SILVER, .4610 oz ASW

KM#	Date	Mintage	VF	XF	Unc
83a	1991	5,000	—	Proof	40.00

26.0000 g, .917 GOLD, .7666 oz AGW

KM#	Date	Mintage	VF	XF	Unc
83b	1991	250 pcs.	—	Proof	685.00

30.4000 g, .950 PLATINUM, .9286 oz APW

KM#	Date	Mintage	VF	XF	Unc
83c	1991	50 pcs.	—	Proof	860.00

COPPER-NICKEL
Christmas

KM#	Date	Mintage	VF	XF	Unc
108	1992	—	—	—	3.50

15.5000 g, .925 SILVER, .4610 oz ASW

KM#	Date	Mintage	VF	XF	Unc
108a	1992	5,000	—	Proof	40.00

COPPER-NICKEL
Christmas - Santa in Automobile

KM#	Date	Mintage	VF	XF	Unc
190	1993	—	—	—	3.50
	1993	*.030	—	Proof	8.00

15.5000g, .925 SILVER, .4610 oz ASW

KM#	Date	Mintage	VF	XF	Unc
190a	1993	*5,000	—	Proof	40.00

26.0000 g, .917 GOLD, .7666 oz AGW

KM#	Date	Mintage	VF	XF	Unc
190b	1993	*250 pcs.	—	Proof	685.00

30.4000 g, .950 PLATINUM, .9286 oz APW

KM#	Date	Mintage	VF	XF	Unc
190c	1993	*50 pcs.	—	Proof	860.00

1/25 CROWN

1.2440 g, .999 GOLD, .0400 oz AGW
Japanese Royal Wedding
Similar to 1/2 Crown, KM#127.

KM#	Date	Mintage	VF	XF	Unc
124	1993	*.025	—	Proof	—

International Friendship - Stylized Panda
Similar to 1 Crown, KM#180.

KM#	Date	Mintage	VF	XF	Unc
183	1993	*.025	—	Proof	45.00

International Friendship - Natural Panda
Similar to 1 Crown, KM#184.

KM#	Date	Mintage	VF	XF	Unc
187	1993	*5,000	—	Proof	45.00

1/10 CROWN

3.1100 g, .999 GOLD, .1000 oz AGW
Barcelona Olympics - Discus Thrower
Similar to 1 Crown, KM#66.

KM#	Date	Mintage	VF	XF	Unc
50	1991	*.020	—	Proof	80.00
	1992	—	—	Proof	80.00

Barcelona Olympics - Chariot Racing
Similar to 1 Crown, KM#67.

KM#	Date	Mintage	VF	XF	Unc
51	1991	*.020	—	Proof	80.00
	1992	—	—	Proof	80.00

Barcelona Olympics - Runners
Similar to 1 Crown, KM#68.

KM#	Date	Mintage	VF	XF	Unc
52	1991	*.020	—	Proof	80.00
	1992	—	—	Proof	80.00

Barcelona Olympics - Javelin Thrower
Similar to 1 Crown, KM#69.

KM#	Date	Mintage	VF	XF	Unc
53	1991	*.020	—	Proof	80.00
	1992	—	—	Proof	80.00

Barcelona Olympics - Wrestlers
Similar to 1 Crown, KM#70.

KM#	Date	Mintage	VF	XF	Unc
54	1991	*.020	—	Proof	80.00
	1992	—	—	Proof	80.00

Barcelona Olympics - Boxers
Similar to 1 Crown, KM#71.

KM#	Date	Mintage	VF	XF	Unc
55	1991	*.020	—	Proof	80.00
	1992	—	—	Proof	80.00

Barcelona Olympics - Long Jumper
Similar to 1 Crown, KM#72.

KM#	Date	Mintage	VF	XF	Unc
56	1991	*.020	—	Proof	80.00
	1992	—	—	Proof	80.00

Barcelona Olympics - Olympic Victor
Similar to 1 Crown, KM#73.

KM#	Date	Mintage	VF	XF	Unc
57	1991	*.020	—	Proof	80.00
	1992	—	—	Proof	80.00

Japanese Royal Wedding
Similar to 1/2 Crown, KM#127.

KM#	Date	Mintage	VF	XF	Unc
125	1993	*.010	—	Proof	—

International Friendship - Stylized Panda
Similar to 1 Crown, KM#180.

KM#	Date	Mintage	VF	XF	Unc
182	1993	*.020	—	Proof	85.00

International Friendship - Natural Panda
Similar to 1 Crown, KM#184.

KM#	Date	Mintage	VF	XF	Unc
186	1993	*.020	—	Proof	85.00

1/5 CROWN

6.2200 g, .999 GOLD, .2000 oz AGW
Penny Black Stamp
Similar to 1 Crown, KM#49.

KM#	Date	Mintage	VF	XF	Unc
48	1990	*5,000	—	Proof	240.00

Barcelona Olympics - Discus Thrower
Similar to 1 Crown, KM#66.

KM#	Date	Mintage	VF	XF	Unc
58	1991	*5,000	—	Proof	160.00
	1992	—	—	Proof	160.00

6.2200 g, .999 PLATINUM, .2000 oz APW

KM#	Date	Mintage	VF	XF	Unc
58a	1991	*1,000	—	Proof	210.00
	1992	—	—	Proof	210.00

6.2200 g, .999 GOLD, .2000 oz AGW
Barcelona Olympics - Chariot Racing
Similar to 1 Crown, KM#67.

KM#	Date	Mintage	VF	XF	Unc
59	1991	*5,000	—	Proof	160.00
	1992	—	—	Proof	160.00

6.2200 g, .999 PLATINUM, .2000 oz APW

KM#	Date	Mintage	VF	XF	Unc
59a	1991	*1,000	—	Proof	210.00
	1992	—	—	Proof	210.00

6.2200 g, .999 GOLD, .2000 oz AGW
Barcelona Olympics - Runners
Similar to 1 Crown, KM#68.

KM#	Date	Mintage	VF	XF	Unc
60	1991	*5,000	—	Proof	160.00
	1992	—	—	Proof	160.00

6.2200 g, .999 PLATINUM, .2000 oz APW

KM#	Date	Mintage	VF	XF	Unc
60a	1991	*1,000	—	Proof	210.00
	1992	—	—	Proof	210.00

6.2200 g, .999 GOLD, .2000 oz AGW
Barcelona Olympics - Javelin Thrower
Similar to 1 Crown, KM#69.

KM#	Date	Mintage	VF	XF	Unc
61	1991	*5,000	—	Proof	160.00
	1992	—	—	Proof	160.00

6.2200 g, .999 PLATINUM, .2000 oz APW

KM#	Date	Mintage	VF	XF	Unc
61a	1991	*1,000	—	Proof	210.00
	1992	—	—	Proof	210.00

6.2200 g, .999 GOLD, .2000 oz AGW
Barcelona Olympics - Wrestlers
Similar to 1 Crown, KM#70.

KM#	Date	Mintage	VF	XF	Unc
62	1991	*5,000	—	Proof	160.00
	1992	—	—	Proof	160.00

6.2200 g, .999 PLATINUM, .2000 oz APW

KM#	Date	Mintage	VF	XF	Unc
62a	1991	*1,000	—	Proof	210.00
	1992	—	—	Proof	210.00

6.2200 g, .999 GOLD, .2000 oz AGW
Barcelona Olympics - Boxers
Similar to 1 Crown, KM#71.

KM#	Date	Mintage	VF	XF	Unc
63	1991	*5,000	—	Proof	160.00
	1992	—	—	Proof	160.00

6.2200 g, .999 PLATINUM, .2000 oz APW

KM#	Date	Mintage	VF	XF	Unc
63a	1991	*1,000	—	Proof	210.00
	1992	—	—	Proof	210.00

6.2200 g, .999 GOLD, .2000 oz AGW
Barcelona Olympics - Long Jumper
Similar to 1 Crown, KM#72.

KM#	Date	Mintage	VF	XF	Unc
64	1991	*5,000	—	Proof	160.00
	1992	—	—	Proof	160.00

6.2200 g, .999 PLATINUM, .2000 oz APW

KM#	Date	Mintage	VF	XF	Unc
64a	1991	*1,000	—	Proof	210.00
	1992	—	—	Proof	210.00

6.2200 g, .999 GOLD, .2000 oz AGW
Barcelona Olympics - Olympic Victor
Similar to 1 Crown, KM#73.

KM#	Date	Mintage	VF	XF	Unc
65	1991	*5,000	—	Proof	160.00
	1992	—	—	Proof	160.00

6.2200 g, .999 PLATINUM, .2000 oz APW

KM#	Date	Mintage	VF	XF	Unc
65a	1991	*1,000	—	Proof	210.00
	1992	—	—	Proof	210.00

6.2200 g, .999 GOLD, .2000 oz AGW
World Cup Soccer - Italian Flag
Similar to 1 Crown, KM#33.

KM#	Date	Mintage	VF	XF	Unc
76	1990	500 pcs.	—	Proof	250.00

6.2200 g, .999 PLATINUM, .2000 oz APW

KM#	Date	Mintage	VF	XF	Unc
76a	1990	250 pcs.	—	Proof	350.00

6.2200 g, .999 GOLD, .2000 oz AGW
World Cup Soccer - Map of Italy
Similar to 1 Crown, KM#34.

KM#	Date	Mintage	VF	XF	Unc
77	1990	500 pcs.	—	Proof	250.00

6.2200 g, .999 PLATINUM, .2000 oz APW

KM#	Date	Mintage	VF	XF	Unc
77a	1990	250 pcs.	—	Proof	350.00

6.2200 g, .999 GOLD, .2000 oz AGW
World Cup Soccer - Goalie Catching Ball
Similar to 1 Crown, KM#35.

KM#	Date	Mintage	VF	XF	Unc
78	1990	500 pcs.	—	Proof	250.00

6.2200 g, .999 PLATINUM, .2000 oz APW

KM#	Date	Mintage	VF	XF	Unc
78a	1990	250 pcs.	—	Proof	350.00

6.2200 g, .999 GOLD, .2000 oz AGW
World Cup Soccer - 1 Player
Similar to 1 Crown, KM#36.

KM#	Date	Mintage	VF	XF	Unc
79	1990	500 pcs.	—	Proof	250.00

6.2200 g, .999 PLATINUM, .2000 oz APW

KM#	Date	Mintage	VF	XF	Unc
79a	1990	250 pcs.	—	Proof	350.00

6.2200 g, .999 GOLD, .2000 oz AGW
World Cup Soccer - 2 Players
Similar to 1 Crown, KM#37.

KM#	Date	Mintage	VF	XF	Unc
80	1990	500 pcs.	—	Proof	250.00

6.2200 g, .999 PLATINUM, .2000 oz APW

KM#	Date	Mintage	VF	XF	Unc
80a	1990	250 pcs.	—	Proof	350.00

6.2200 g, .999 GOLD, .2000 oz AGW
World Cup Soccer - 3 Players
Similar to 1 Crown, KM#38.

KM#	Date	Mintage	VF	XF	Unc
81	1990	500 pcs.	—	Proof	250.00

6.2200 g, .999 PLATINUM, .2000 oz APW

KM#	Date	Mintage	VF	XF	Unc
81a	1990	250 pcs.	—	Proof	350.00

6.2200 g, .999 GOLD, .2000 oz AGW
Japanese Royal Wedding
Similar to 1/2 Crown, KM#126.

KM#	Date	Mintage	VF	XF	Unc
126	1993	*5,000	—	Proof	—

WWII Warships - USS Philadelphia

KM#	Date	Mintage	VF	XF	Unc
153	1993	*5,000	—	Proof	175.00

WWII Warships - USS McLanahan

KM#	Date	Mintage	VF	XF	Unc
154	1993	*5,000	—	Proof	175.00

WWII Warships - HNLMS Isaac Sweers

KM#	Date	Mintage	VF	XF	Unc
155	1993	*5,000	—	Proof	175.00

WWII Warships - USS Weehawken

KM#	Date	Mintage	VF	XF	Unc
156	1993	*5,000	—	Proof	175.00

WWII Warships - HMS Warspite

KM#	Date	Mintage	VF	XF	Unc
157	1993	*5,000	—	Proof	175.00

WWII Warships - HMS Hood

KM#	Date	Mintage	VF	XF	Unc
158	1993	*5,000	—	Proof	175.00

WWII Warships - HMS Penelope

KM#	Date	Mintage	VF	XF	Unc
159	1993	*5,000	—	Proof	175.00

WWII Warships - HMCS Prescott

KM#	Date	Mintage	VF	XF	Unc
160	1993	*5,000	—	Proof	175.00

WWII Warships - HMS Ark Royal

KM#	Date	Mintage	VF	XF	Unc
161	1993	*5,000	—	Proof	175.00

WWII Warships - USS Gleaves

KM#	Date	Mintage	VF	XF	Unc
162	1993	*5,000	—	Proof	175.00

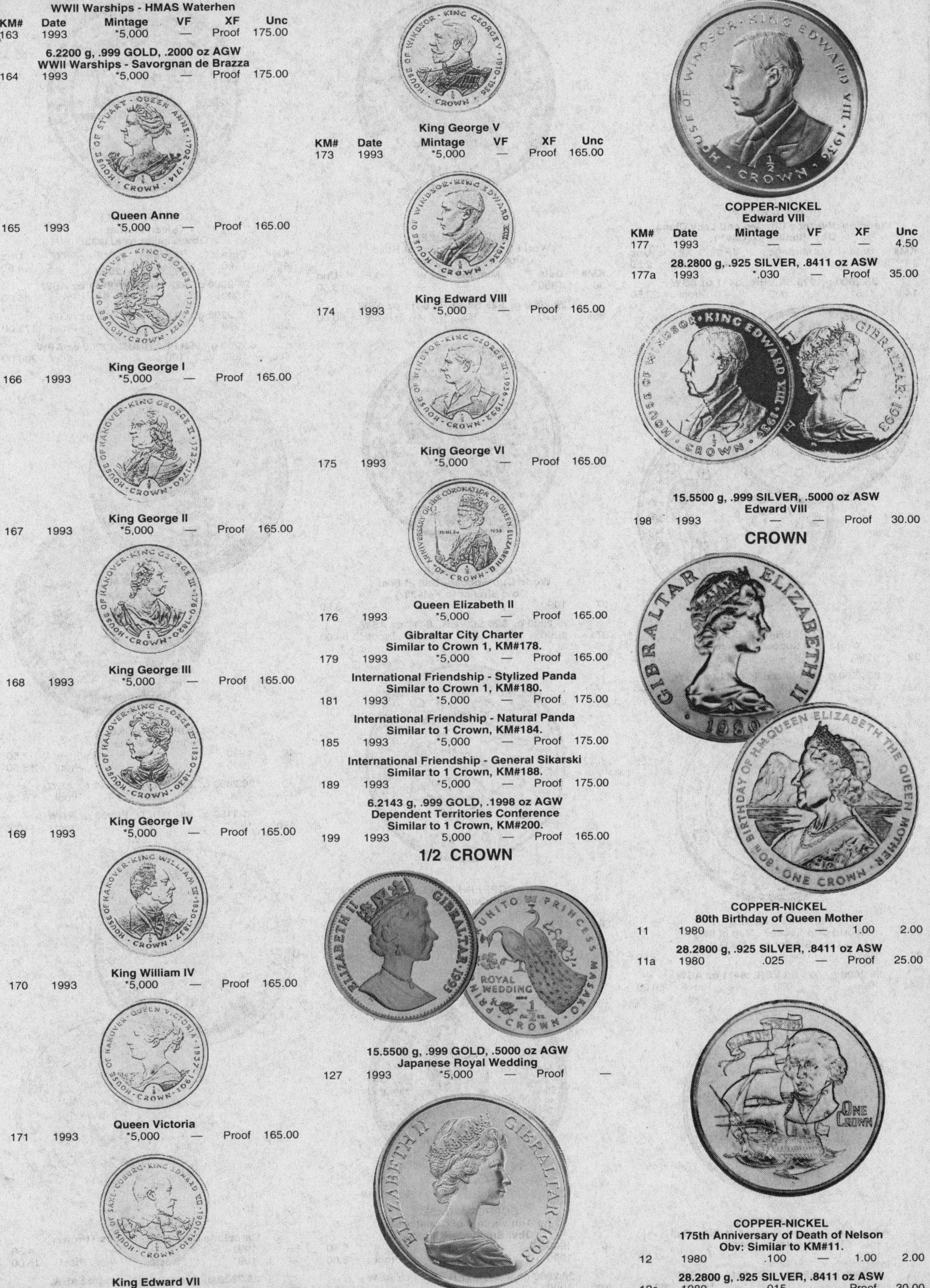

WWII Warships - HMAS Waterhen

KM#	Date	Mintage	VF	XF	Unc
163	1993	*5,000	—	Proof	175.00

6.2200 g, .999 GOLD, .2000 oz AGW
WWII Warships - Savorgnan de Brazza

KM#	Date	Mintage	VF	XF	Unc
164	1993	*5,000	—	Proof	175.00

Queen Anne

KM#	Date	Mintage	VF	XF	Unc
165	1993	*5,000	—	Proof	165.00

King George I

KM#	Date	Mintage	VF	XF	Unc
166	1993	*5,000	—	Proof	165.00

King George II

KM#	Date	Mintage	VF	XF	Unc
167	1993	*5,000	—	Proof	165.00

King George III

KM#	Date	Mintage	VF	XF	Unc
168	1993	*5,000	—	Proof	165.00

King George IV

KM#	Date	Mintage	VF	XF	Unc
169	1993	*5,000	—	Proof	165.00

King William IV

KM#	Date	Mintage	VF	XF	Unc
170	1993	*5,000	—	Proof	165.00

Queen Victoria

KM#	Date	Mintage	VF	XF	Unc
171	1993	*5,000	—	Proof	165.00

King Edward VII

KM#	Date	Mintage	VF	XF	Unc
172	1993	*5,000	—	Proof	165.00

King George V

KM#	Date	Mintage	VF	XF	Unc
173	1993	*5,000	—	Proof	165.00

King Edward VIII

KM#	Date	Mintage	VF	XF	Unc
174	1993	*5,000	—	Proof	165.00

King George VI

KM#	Date	Mintage	VF	XF	Unc
175	1993	*5,000	—	Proof	165.00

Queen Elizabeth II

KM#	Date	Mintage	VF	XF	Unc
176	1993	*5,000	—	Proof	165.00

Gibraltar City Charter
Similar to Crown 1, KM#178.

KM#	Date	Mintage	VF	XF	Unc
179	1993	*5,000	—	Proof	165.00

International Friendship - Stylized Panda
Similar to Crown 1, KM#180.

KM#	Date	Mintage	VF	XF	Unc
181	1993	*5,000	—	Proof	175.00

International Friendship - Natural Panda
Similar to 1 Crown, KM#184.

KM#	Date	Mintage	VF	XF	Unc
185	1993	*5,000	—	Proof	175.00

International Friendship - General Sikarski
Similar to 1 Crown, KM#188.

KM#	Date	Mintage	VF	XF	Unc
189	1993	*5,000	—	Proof	175.00

6.2143 g, .999 GOLD, .1998 oz AGW
Dependent Territories Conference
Similar to 1 Crown, KM#200.

KM#	Date	Mintage	VF	XF	Unc
199	1993	5,000	—	Proof	165.00

1/2 CROWN

15.5500 g, .999 GOLD, .5000 oz AGW
Japanese Royal Wedding

KM#	Date	Mintage	VF	XF	Unc
127	1993	*5,000	—	Proof	—

COPPER-NICKEL
Edward VIII

KM#	Date	Mintage	VF	XF	Unc
177	1993	—	—	—	4.50

28.2800 g, .925 SILVER, .8411 oz ASW

KM#	Date	Mintage	VF	XF	Unc
177a	1993	*.030	—	Proof	35.00

15.5500 g, .999 SILVER, .5000 oz ASW
Edward VIII

KM#	Date	Mintage	VF	XF	Unc
198	1993	—	—	Proof	30.00

CROWN

COPPER-NICKEL
80th Birthday of Queen Mother

KM#	Date	Mintage	VF	XF	Unc
11	1980	—	—	1.00	2.00

28.2800 g, .925 SILVER, .8411 oz ASW

KM#	Date	Mintage	VF	XF	Unc
11a	1980	.025	—	Proof	25.00

COPPER-NICKEL
175th Anniversary of Death of Nelson
Obv: Similar to KM#11.

KM#	Date	Mintage	VF	XF	Unc
12	1980	.100	—	1.00	2.00

28.2800 g, .925 SILVER, .8411 oz ASW

KM#	Date	Mintage	VF	XF	Unc
12a	1980	.015	—	Proof	30.00

COPPER-NICKEL
Wedding of Prince Charles and Lady Diana
Obv: Similar to KM#11.

KM#	Date	Mintage	VF	XF	Unc
14	1981	—	—	1.00	2.50
	28.2800 g, .925 SILVER, .8411 oz ASW				
14a	1981	.030	—	Proof	22.50

COPPER-NICKEL
World Cup Soccer - Italian Flag

KM#	Date	Mintage	VF	XF	Unc
33	1990	—	—	—	3.50
	28.2800 g, .925 SILVER, .8411 oz ASW				
33a	1990	.030	—	Proof	60.00

COPPER-NICKEL
World Cup Soccer - Map of Italy
Obv: Similar to KM#33.

KM#	Date	Mintage	VF	XF	Unc
34	1990	—	—	—	3.50
	28.2800 g, .925 SILVER, .8411 oz ASW				
34a	1990	.030	—	Proof	60.00

COPPER-NICKEL
World Cup Soccer - Goalie Catching Ball
Obv: Similar to KM#33.

KM#	Date	Mintage	VF	XF	Unc
35	1990	—	—	—	3.50
	28.2800 g, .925 SILVER, .8411 oz ASW				
35a	1990	.030	—	Proof	60.00

COPPER-NICKEL
World Cup Soccer - Ball at Head
Obv: Similar to KM#33.

KM#	Date	Mintage	VF	XF	Unc
36	1990	—	—	—	3.50
	28.2800 g, .925 SILVER, .8411 oz ASW				
36a	1990	.030	—	Proof	60.00

COPPER-NICKEL
World Cup Soccer - Ball at Feet
Obv: Similar to KM#33.

KM#	Date	Mintage	VF	XF	Unc
37	1990	—	—	—	3.50
	28.2800 g, .925 SILVER, .8411 oz ASW				
37a	1990	.030	—	Proof	60.00

COPPER-NICKEL
World Cup Soccer - 3 Players
Obv: Similar to KM#33.

KM#	Date	Mintage	VF	XF	Unc
38	1990	—	—	—	3.50
	28.2800 g, .925 SILVER, .8411 oz ASW				
38a	1990	.030	—	Proof	60.00

COPPER-NICKEL
21st Anniversary of Constitution
Obv: Similar to KM#33.

KM#	Date	Mintage	VF	XF	Unc
40	1990	—	—	—	6.50
	1990	.050	—	Proof	8.00
	28.2800 g, .925 SILVER, .8411 oz ASW				
40a	1990	.030	—	Proof	50.00

COPPER-NICKEL
Queen Mother
Obv: Similar to KM#33.

KM#	Date	Mintage	VF	XF	Unc
46	1990	—	—	—	4.50
	28.2800 g, .925 SILVER, .8411 oz ASW				
46a	1990	.025	—	Proof	35.00
	6.2200 g, .999 GOLD, .2000 oz AGW				
46b	1990	500 pcs.	—	Proof	175.00
	6.2200 g, .999 PLATINUM, .2000 oz APW				
46c	1990	100 pcs.	—	Proof	200.00

COPPER-NICKEL
Penny Black Stamp

KM#	Date	Mintage	VF	XF	Unc
49	1990	—	—	—	7.50
	1990	—	—	Proof	16.50
	28.2800 g, .925 SILVER, .8411 oz ASW				
49a	1990	*.030	—	Proof	50.00
	31.1190 g, .999 GOLD, 1.0006 oz AGW				
49b	1990	*1,000	—	Proof	1100.

COPPER-NICKEL
Barcelona Olympics - Discus Thrower

KM#	Date	Mintage	VF	XF	Unc
66	1991	—	—	—	4.50
	1991	50 pcs.	—	Proof	15.00
	28.2800 g, .925 SILVER, .8411 oz ASW				
66a	1992	*.030	—	Proof	55.00

COPPER-NICKEL
Barcelona Olympics - Chariot Racing
Obv: Similar to KM#66.

KM#	Date	Mintage	VF	XF	Unc
67	1991	—	—	—	4.50
	1991	50 pcs.	—	Proof	15.00

28.2800 g, .925 SILVER, .8411 oz ASW

KM#	Date	Mintage	VF	XF	Unc
67a	1992	*.030	—	Proof	55.00

COPPER-NICKEL
Barcelona Olympics - Runners
Obv: Similar to KM#66.

KM#	Date	Mintage	VF	XF	Unc
68	1991	—	—	—	4.50
	1991	50 pcs.	—	Proof	15.00

28.2800 g, .925 SILVER, .8411 oz ASW

KM#	Date	Mintage	VF	XF	Unc
68a	1992	*.030	—	Proof	55.00

COPPER-NICKEL
Barcelona Olympics - Javelin Thrower
Obv: Similar to KM#66.

KM#	Date	Mintage	VF	XF	Unc
69	1991	—	—	—	4.50
	1991	50 pcs.	—	Proof	15.00

28.2800 g, .925 SILVER, .8411 oz ASW

KM#	Date	Mintage	VF	XF	Unc
69a	1992	*.030	—	Proof	55.00

COPPER-NICKEL
Barcelona Olympics - Wrestlers
Obv: Similar to KM#66.

KM#	Date	Mintage	VF	XF	Unc
70	1991	—	—	—	4.50
	1991	50 pcs.	—	Proof	15.00

28.2800 g, .925 SILVER, .8411 oz ASW

KM#	Date	Mintage	VF	XF	Unc
70a	1992	*.030	—	Proof	55.00

COPPER-NICKEL
Barcelona Olympics - Boxers
Obv: Similar to KM#66.

KM#	Date	Mintage	VF	XF	Unc
71	1991	—	—	—	4.50
	1991	50 pcs.	—	Proof	15.00

28.2800 g, .925 SILVER, .8411 oz ASW

KM#	Date	Mintage	VF	XF	Unc
71a	1992	*.030	—	Proof	55.00

COPPER-NICKEL
Barcelona Olympics - Long Jumper
Obv: Similar to KM#66.

KM#	Date	Mintage	VF	XF	Unc
72	1991	—	—	—	4.50
	1991	50 pcs.	—	Proof	15.00

28.2800 g, .925 SILVER, .8411 oz ASW

KM#	Date	Mintage	VF	XF	Unc
72a	1992	*.030	—	Proof	55.00

COPPER-NICKEL
Barcelona Olympics - Olympic Victor
Obv: Similar to KM#66.

KM#	Date	Mintage	VF	XF	Unc
73	1991	—	—	—	4.50
	1991	50 pcs.	—	Proof	15.00

28.2800 g, .925 SILVER, .8411 oz ASW

KM#	Date	Mintage	VF	XF	Unc
73a	1992	*.030	—	Proof	55.00

28.2800 g, .925 SILVER, .8411 oz ASW
Rotary Club of Gibraltar

KM#	Date	Mintage	VF	XF	Unc
74a	1991	*.030	—	Proof	110.00

15.5500 g, .999 GOLD, .5000 oz AGW

KM#	Date	Mintage	VF	XF	Unc
74b	1991	*5,000	—	Proof	650.00

COPPER-NICKEL
10th Wedding Anniversary - Prince Charles

KM#	Date	Mintage	VF	XF	Unc
84	1991	—	—	—	4.00

28.2800 g, .925 SILVER, .8411 oz ASW

KM#	Date	Mintage	VF	XF	Unc
84a	1991	—	—	Proof	35.00

6.2200 g, .999 GOLD, .2000 oz AGW

KM#	Date	Mintage	VF	XF	Unc
84b	1991	—	—	Proof	200.00

COPPER-NICKEL
10th Wedding Anniversary - Princess Diana
Obv: Similar to KM#84.

KM#	Date	Mintage	VF	XF	Unc
85	1991	—	—	—	4.00

28.2800 g, .925 SILVER, .8411 oz ASW

KM#	Date	Mintage	VF	XF	Unc
85a	1991	—	—	Proof	35.00

6.2200 g, .999 GOLD, .2000 oz AGW

KM#	Date	Mintage	VF	XF	Unc
85b	1991	—	—	Proof	200.00

COPPER-NICKEL
10th Wedding Anniversary - Royal Yacht
Obv: Similar to KM#84.

KM#	Date	Mintage	VF	XF	Unc
86	1991	—	—	—	4.00

28.2800 g, .925 SILVER, .8411 oz ASW

KM#	Date	Mintage	VF	XF	Unc
86a	1991	—	—	Proof	35.00

6.2200 g, .999 GOLD, .2000 oz AGW

KM#	Date	Mintage	VF	XF	Unc
86b	1991	—	—	Proof	200.00

COPPER-NICKEL

Corgi Dog

KM#	Date	Mintage	VF	XF	Unc
95	1991	—	—	—	6.00
	31.1030 g, .999 SILVER, 1.0000 oz ASW				
95a	1991	.050	—	Proof	35.00

Cocker Spaniel
Obv: Similar to KM#95.

KM#	Date	Mintage	VF	XF	Unc
103	1992	—	—	—	6.00

WWII Warships - USS Philadelphia

KM#	Date	Mintage	VF	XF	Unc
113	1993	—	—	—	4.00
	28.2800 g, .925 SILVER, .8411 oz ASW				
113a	1993	*.030	—	Proof	35.00

COPPER-NICKEL
WWII Warships - USS McLanahan

KM#	Date	Mintage	VF	XF	Unc
114	1993	—	—	—	4.00
	28.2800 g, .925 SILVER, .8411 oz ASW				
114a	1993	*.030	—	Proof	35.00

COPPER-NICKEL
WWII Warships HNLMS Isaac Sweers

KM#	Date	Mintage	VF	XF	Unc
115	1993	—	—	—	4.00
	28.2800 g, .925 SILVER, .8411 oz ASW				
115a	1993	*.030	—	Proof	35.00

COPPER-NICKEL
WWII Warships - USS Weehawken

KM#	Date	Mintage	VF	XF	Unc
116	1993	—	—	—	4.00
	28.2800 g, .925 SILVER, .8411 oz ASW				
116a	1993	*.030	—	Proof	35.00

COPPER-NICKEL
WWII Warships - HMS Warspite

KM#	Date	Mintage	VF	XF	Unc
117	1993	—	—	—	4.00
	28.2800 g, .925 SILVER, .8411 oz ASW				
117a	1993	*.030	—	Proof	35.00

COPPER-NICKEL
WWII Warships - HMS Hood

KM#	Date	Mintage	VF	XF	Unc
118	1993	—	—	—	4.00
	28.2800 g, .925 SILVER, .8411 oz ASW				
118a	1993	*.030	—	Proof	35.00

COPPER-NICKEL
WWII Warships - HMS Penelope

KM#	Date	Mintage	VF	XF	Unc
119	1993	—	—	—	4.00
	28.2800 g, .925 SILVER, .8411 oz ASW				
119a	1993	*.030	—	Proof	35.00

COPPER-NICKEL
WWII Warships - HMCS Prescott

KM#	Date	Mintage	VF	XF	Unc
120	1993	—	—	—	4.00
	28.2800 g, .925 SILVER, .8411 oz ASW				
120a	1993	*.030	—	Proof	35.00

COPPER-NICKEL
WWII Warships - HMS Ark Royal

KM#	Date	Mintage	VF	XF	Unc
121	1993	—	—	—	4.00
	28.2800 g, .925 SILVER, .8411 oz ASW				
121a	1993	*.030	—	Proof	35.00

COPPER-NICKEL
WWII Warships - USS Gleaves

KM#	Date	Mintage	VF	XF	Unc
122	1993	—	—	—	4.00
	28.2800 g, .925 SILVER, .8411 oz ASW				
122a	1993	*.030	—	Proof	35.00

COPPER-NICKEL
WWII Warships - HMAS Waterhen

KM#	Date	Mintage	VF	XF	Unc
123	1993	—	—	—	4.00
	28.2800 g, .925 SILVER, .8411 oz ASW				
123a	1993	*.030	—	Proof	35.00

COPPER-NICKEL
WWII Warships - Savorgnan de Brazza

KM#	Date	Mintage	VF	XF	Unc
144	1993	—	—	—	4.00

28.2800 g, .925 SILVER, .8411 oz ASW

KM#	Date	Mintage	VF	XF	Unc
144a	1993	*.030	—	Proof	35.00

Queen Anne - 1702-1714

KM#	Date	Mintage	VF	XF	Unc
132	1993	—	—	P/L	4.00

28.2800 g, .925 SILVER, .8411 oz ASW

KM#	Date	Mintage	VF	XF	Unc
132a	1993	*.030	—	Proof	35.00

COPPER-NICKEL
King George I - 1714-1727

KM#	Date	Mintage	VF	XF	Unc
133	1993	—	—	P/L	4.00

28.2800 g, .925 SILVER, .8411 oz ASW

KM#	Date	Mintage	VF	XF	Unc
133a	1993	*.030	—	Proof	35.00

COPPER-NICKEL
King George II - 1727-1760

KM#	Date	Mintage	VF	XF	Unc
134	1993	—	—	P/L	4.00

28.2800 g, .925 SILVER, .8411 oz ASW

KM#	Date	Mintage	VF	XF	Unc
134a	1993	*.030	—	Proof	35.00

COPPER-NICKEL
King George III - 1760-1820

KM#	Date	Mintage	VF	XF	Unc
135	1993	—	—	P/L	4.00

28.2800 g, .925 SILVER, .8411 oz ASW

KM#	Date	Mintage	VF	XF	Unc
135a	1993	*.030	—	Proof	35.00

COPPER-NICKEL
King George IV - 1820-1830

KM#	Date	Mintage	VF	XF	Unc
136	1993	—	—	P/L	4.00

28.2800 g, .925 SILVER, .8411 oz ASW

KM#	Date	Mintage	VF	XF	Unc
136a	1993	*.030	—	Proof	35.00

COPPER-NICKEL
King William IV - 1830-1837

KM#	Date	Mintage	VF	XF	Unc
137	1993	—	—	P/L	4.00

28.2800 g, .925 SILVER, .8411 oz ASW

KM#	Date	Mintage	VF	XF	Unc
137a	1993	*.030	—	Proof	35.00

COPPER-NICKEL
Queen Victoria - 1837-1901

KM#	Date	Mintage	VF	XF	Unc
138	1993	—	—	P/L	4.00

28.2800 g, .925 SILVER, .8411 oz ASW

KM#	Date	Mintage	VF	XF	Unc
138a	1993	*.030	—	Proof	35.00

COPPER-NICKEL
King Edward VII - 1901-1910

KM#	Date	Mintage	VF	XF	Unc
139	1993	—	—	P/L	4.00

28.2800 g, .925 SILVER, .8411 oz ASW

KM#	Date	Mintage	VF	XF	Unc
139a	1993	*.030	—	Proof	35.00

COPPER-NICKEL
King George V - 1910-1936

KM#	Date	Mintage	VF	XF	Unc
140	1993	—	—	P/L	4.00

28.2800 g, .925 SILVER, .8411 oz ASW

KM#	Date	Mintage	VF	XF	Unc
140a	1993	*.030	—	Proof	35.00

COPPER-NICKEL
King Edward VIII - 1936

KM#	Date	Mintage	VF	XF	Unc
141	1993	—	—	P/L	4.00

28.2800 g, .925 SILVER, .8411 oz ASW

KM#	Date	Mintage	VF	XF	Unc
141a	1993	*.030	—	Proof	35.00

COPPER-NICKEL
King George VI - 1936-1952

KM#	Date	Mintage	VF	XF	Unc
142	1993	—	—	P/L	4.00

28.2800 g, .925 SILVER, .8411 oz ASW

KM#	Date	Mintage	VF	XF	Unc
142a	1993	*.030	—	Proof	35.00

COPPER-NICKEL
Coronation of Queen Elizabeth II

KM#	Date	Mintage	VF	XF	Unc
143	1993	—	—	P/L	4.00
	28.2800 g, .925 SILVER, .8411 oz ASW				
143a	1993	*.030	—	Proof	35.00

COPPER-NICKEL
XVII Winter Olympics - Skaters

KM#	Date	Mintage	VF	XF	Unc
145	1993	—	—	Proof	4.00
	28.2800 g, .925 SILVER, .8411 oz ASW				
145a	1993	*.030	—	Proof	35.00
	6.2200 g, .999 GOLD, .2000 oz AGW				
145b	1993	*5,000	—	Proof	200.00

COPPER-NICKEL
XVII Winter Olympics - Ice Hockey

KM#	Date	Mintage	VF	XF	Unc
146	1993	—	—	Proof	4.00
	28.2800 g, .925 SILVER, .8411 oz ASW				
146a	1993	*.030	—	Proof	35.00
	6.2200 g, .999 GOLD, .2000 oz AGW				
146b	1993	*5,000	—	Proof	200.00

COPPER-NICKEL
XVII Winter Olympics - Bobsledding

KM#	Date	Mintage	VF	XF	Unc
147	1993	—	—	Proof	4.00
	28.2800 g, .925 SILVER, .8411 oz ASW				
147a	1993	*.030	—	Proof	35.00
	6.2200 g, .999 GOLD, .2000 oz AGW				
147b	1993	*5,000	—	Proof	200.00

COPPER-NICKEL
XVII Winter Olympics - Skiers

KM#	Date	Mintage	VF	XF	Unc
148	1993	—	—	Proof	4.00
	28.2800 g, .925 SILVER, .8411 oz ASW				
148a	1993	*.030	—	Proof	35.00
	6.2200 g, .999 GOLD, .2000 oz AGW				
148b	1993	*5,000	—	Proof	200.00

COPPER-NICKEL
Preserve Planet Earth - Cetiosaurus

KM#	Date	Mintage	VF	XF	Unc
149	1993	—	—	—	6.50
	28.2800 g, .925 SILVER, .8411 oz ASW				
149a	1993	*.030	—	Proof	35.00
	6.2200 g, .999 GOLD, .2000 oz AGW				
150	1993	*5,000	—	Proof	165.00

COPPER-NICKEL
Preserve Planet Earth - Stegosaurus

KM#	Date	Mintage	VF	XF	Unc
151	1993	—	—	—	6.50
	28.2800 g, .925 SILVER, .8411 oz ASW				
151a	1993	*.030	—	Proof	35.00
	6.2200 g, .999 GOLD, .2000 oz AGW				
152	1993	*5,000	—	Proof	165.00

28.2800 g, .925 SILVER, .8411 oz ASW
Gibraltar City Charter

KM#	Date	Mintage	VF	XF	Unc
178	1992	*.030	—	Proof	35.00

COPPER-NICKEL
International Friendship - Stylized Panda
Obv: Similar to KM#178.

KM#	Date	Mintage	VF	XF	Unc
180	1993	—	—	—	4.50
	28.2800 g, .925 SILVER, .8411 oz ASW				
180a	1993	*.030	—	Proof	35.00

COPPER-NICKEL
International Friendship - Natural Panda

KM#	Date	Mintage	VF	XF	Unc
184	1993	—	—	—	4.50
	28.2800 g, .925 SILVER, .8411 oz ASW				
184a	1993	*.030	—	Proof	35.00

COPPER-NICKEL
International Friendship - General Sikorski

KM#	Date	Mintage	VF	XF	Unc
188	1993	—	—	—	5.00
	28.2800 g, .925 SILVER, .8411 oz ASW				
188a	1993	*.030	—	Proof	35.00

COPPER-NICKEL
Dachshund

KM#	Date	Mintage	VF	XF	Unc
192	1993	—	—	—	5.50
	31.1030 g, .925 SILVER, 1.0000 oz ASW				
192a	1993	—	—	Proof	42.50

COPPER-NICKEL
Dependent Territories Conference

KM#	Date	Mintage	VF	XF	Unc
200	1993	—	—	—	6.50
	28.2800 g, .925 SILVER, .8411 oz ASW				
200a	1993	*.030	—	Proof	35.00

2 CROWN

62.2070 g, .999 SILVER, 2.0000 oz ASW
Japanese Royal Wedding
Obv: Similar to 5 Crown, KM#106.

KM#	Date	Mintage	VF	XF	Unc
128	1993	*.020	—	Proof	—
	62.2070 g, .999 GOLD, 2.0000 oz AGW Japanese Royal Wedding Obv: Portrait of Queen Elizabeth II.				
129	1993	*500 pcs.	—	Proof	—

5 CROWN

155.9230 g, .999 SILVER, 5.0000 oz ASW
Illustration reduced. Actual size: 65mm.
Olympics - Discus Thrower

KM#	Date	Mintage	VF	XF	Unc
106	1991	1,000	—	Proof	275.00

10 CROWN

311.8460 g, .999 SILVER, 10.0000 oz ASW
Illustration reduced. Actual size: 73mm.
Olympics - Ancient Runners
Obv: Portrait of Queen Elizabeth II.

KM#	Date	Mintage	VF	XF	Unc
107	1991	—	—	Proof	400.00
	Japanese Royal Wedding Obv: Similar to 5 Crown, KM#106. Rev: Similar to 2 Crown, KM#128.				
130	1993	*5,000	—	Proof	—

32 CROWN

1,000.0000 g, .999 SILVER, 32.1543 oz ASW
Japanese Royal Wedding
Obv: Similar to 5 Crown, KM#106.
Rev: Similar to 2 Crown, KM#128.

KM#	Date	Mintage	VF	XF	Unc
131	1993	*1,000	—	Proof	—

POUND

NICKEL-BRASS

KM#	Date	Mintage	VF	XF	Unc
18	1988	—	—	—	3.50
	1990	—	—	—	3.50
	9.5000 g, .925 SILVER, .2825 oz ASW				
18a	1988	—	—	Proof	15.00
	9.5000 g, .917 GOLD, .2800 oz AGW				
18b	1988	—	—	Proof	350.00

NICKEL-BRASS
150th Anniversary of Gibraltar Coinage

KM#	Date	Mintage	VF	XF	Unc
32	1989	—	—	—	4.00
	9.5000 g, .925 SILVER, .2826 oz ASW				
32a	1989	*2,500	—	Proof	35.00
	9.5000 g, .917 GOLD, .2800 oz AGW				
32b	1989	150 pcs.	—	Proof	350.00
	9.0000 g, .950 PLATINUM, .2749 oz APW				
32c	1989	100 pcs.	—	Proof	375.00

NICKEL-BRASS
Referendum of 1967

KM#	Date	Mintage	VF	XF	Unc
191	1993	—	—	—	4.50
	9.5000 g, .925 SILVER, .2825 oz ASW				
191a	1993	*5,000	—	Proof	35.00
	9.5000 g, .917 GOLD, .2800 oz AGW				
191b	1993	*3,500	—	Proof	350.00

2 POUNDS

VIRENIUM
Cannon In Tunnel of Fortress

KM#	Date	Mintage	VF	XF	Unc
24	1988	—	—	—	7.50
	1989	—	—	—	7.50
	1990	—	—	—	7.50

Columbus and Ship

KM#	Date	Mintage	VF	XF	Unc
98	1992	—	—	—	6.50
	9.3000 g, .925 SILVER, .2766 oz ASW				
98a	1992	*5,000	—	Proof	35.00
	15.9400 g, .917 GOLD, .4730 oz AGW				
98b	1992	*5,000	—	Proof	—
	18.0000 g, .950 PLATINUM, .5498 oz APW				
98c	1992	*1,000	—	Proof	—

5 POUNDS

VIRENIUM
Hercules

KM#	Date	Mintage	VF	XF	Unc
25	1988	—	—	—	15.00
	1989	—	—	—	15.00
	1990	—	—	—	15.00

25 POUNDS

7.7700 g, .917 GOLD, .2291 oz AGW
250th Anniversary Introduction of British Sterling

KM#	Date	Mintage	VF	XF	Unc
7	1975	2,395	—	—	125.00
	1975	750 pcs.	—	Proof	200.00

50 POUNDS

15.5500 g, .917 GOLD, .4585 oz AGW
250th Anniversary Introduction of British Sterling
Obv: Similar to 25 Pounds, KM#7.

KM#	Date	Mintage	VF	XF	Unc
8	1975	1,625	—	—	250.00
	1975	750 pcs.	—	Proof	350.00

15.9760 g, .917 GOLD, .4711 oz AGW
175th Anniversary of Death of Nelson

KM#	Date	Mintage	VF	XF	Unc
13	1980	7,500	—	—	235.00
	1980	5,000	—	Proof	275.00

Wedding of Prince Charles and Lady Diana

KM#	Date	Mintage	VF	XF	Unc
15	1981	—	—	—	250.00
	1981	2,500	—	Proof	300.00

100 POUNDS

31.1000 g, .917 GOLD, .9170 oz AGW
250th Anniversary Introduction of British Sterling
Obv: Similar to 25 Pounds, KM#7.

KM#	Date	Mintage	VF	XF	Unc
9	1975	1,625	—	—	500.00
	1975	750 pcs.	—	Proof	600.00

SOVEREIGN SERIES

1/4 SOVEREIGN

1.9900 g, .917 GOLD, .0586 oz AGW
150th Anniversary of Regal Coinage
Similar to 5 Sovereigns, KM#30.2.

KM#	Date	Mintage	VF	XF	Unc
26	1989 U	—	—	—	—
	1989	*1,989	—	Proof	70.00

Constitution
Obv: Similar to 5 Sovereigns, KM#30.1.
Rev: Similar to 5 Sovereigns, KM#45.

KM#	Date	Mintage	VF	XF	Unc
41	1990	1,000	—	Proof	65.00

1/2 SOVEREIGN

3.9800 g, .917 GOLD, .1173 oz AGW
150th Anniversary of Regal Coinage
Similar to 5 Sovereigns, KM#30.2.

KM#	Date	Mintage	VF	XF	Unc
27	1989 U	—	—	—	—
	1989	*1,989	—	Proof	135.00

Constitution
Obv: Similar to 5 Sovereigns, KM#30.1.
Rev: Similar to 5 Sovereigns, KM#45.

KM#	Date	Mintage	VF	XF	Unc
42	1990	1,000	—	Proof	125.00

SOVEREIGN

7.9600 g, .917 GOLD, .2346 oz AGW
150th Anniversary of Regal Coinage
Similar to 5 Sovereigns, KM#30.2.

KM#	Date	Mintage	VF	XF	Unc
28	1989 U	—	—	—	—
	1989	*1,989	—	Proof	275.00

Constitution
Obv: Similar to 5 Sovereigns, KM#30.1.
Rev: Similar to 5 Sovereigns, KM#45.

KM#	Date	Mintage	VF	XF	Unc
43	1990	1,000	—	Proof	250.00

2 SOVEREIGNS

15.9400 g, .917 GOLD, .4698 oz AGW
150th Anniversary of Regal Coinage
Similar to 5 Sovereigns, KM#30.2.

KM#	Date	Mintage	VF	XF	Unc
29	1989	*1,989	—	Proof	550.00

Constitution
Obv: Similar to 5 Sovereigns, KM#30.1.
Rev: Similar to 5 Sovereigns, KM#45.

KM#	Date	Mintage	VF	XF	Unc
44	1990	1,000	—	Proof	500.00

5 SOVEREIGNS

39.8300 g, .917 GOLD, 1.1740 oz AGW
150th Anniversary of Regal Coinage

KM#	Date	Mintage	VF	XF	Unc
30	1989	*1,989	—	Proof	1100.

Constitution
Obv: Similar to KM#30.

KM#	Date	Mintage	VF	XF	Unc
45	1990	1,000	—	Proof	950.00

ROYAL SERIES

1/25 ROYAL

1.2400 g, .999 GOLD, .0400 oz AGW
Corgi Dog
Similar to 1 Royal, KM#97.

KM#	Date	Mintage	VF	XF	Unc
91	1991	—	—		*BV + 25%*
	1991	5,000	—	Proof	50.00

Cocker Spaniel
Similar to 1 Royal, KM#105.

KM#	Date	Mintage	VF	XF	Unc
99	1992	—	—		*BV + 25%*
	1992	—	—	Proof	50.00

Dachshund

KM#	Date	Mintage	VF	XF	Unc
193	1993	—	—		*BV + 25%*
	1993	—	—	Proof	50.00

1/10 ROYAL

3.1100 g, .999 GOLD, .1000 oz AGW
Corgi Dog
Similar to 1 Royal, KM#97.

KM#	Date	Mintage	VF	XF	Unc
92	1991	—	—		*BV + 20%*
	1991	6,000	—	Proof	100.00

Cocker Spaniel
Similar to 1 Royal, KM#105.

KM#	Date	Mintage	VF	XF	Unc
100	1992	—	—		*BV + 20%*
	1992	—	—	Proof	100.00

Dachshund

KM#	Date	Mintage	VF	XF	Unc
194	1993	—	—		*BV + 20%*
	1993	—	—	Proof	100.00

1/5 ROYAL

6.2200 g, .999 GOLD, .2000 oz AGW
Corgi Dog
Similar to 1 Royal, KM#97.

KM#	Date	Mintage	VF	XF	Unc
93	1991	—	—		*BV + 15%*
	1991	—	—	Proof	185.00

Cocker Spaniel
Similar to 1 Royal, KM#105.

KM#	Date	Mintage	VF	XF	Unc
101	1992	—	—		*BV + 15%*
	1992	—	—	Proof	185.00

Dachshund

KM#	Date	Mintage	VF	XF	Unc
195	1993	—	—		*BV + 15%*
	1993	—	—	Proof	185.00

1/2 ROYAL

15.5500 g, .999 SILVER, .5000 oz ASW
Corgi Dog
Similar to 1 Royal, KM#97.

KM#	Date	Mintage	VF	XF	Unc
94	1991	—	—		*BV + 10%*
	1991	—	—	Proof	365.00

Cocker Spaniel
Similar to 1 Royal, KM#105.

KM#	Date	Mintage	VF	XF	Unc
102	1992	—	—		*BV + 10%*
	1992	—	—	Proof	365.00

Dachshund

KM#	Date	Mintage	VF	XF	Unc
196	1993	—	—		*BV + 10%*
	1993	—	—	Proof	365.00

ROYAL

31.1030 g, .999 GOLD, 1.0000 oz AGW
Corgi Dog

KM#	Date	Mintage	VF	XF	Unc
97	1991	—	—		*BV + 5%*
	1991	—	—	Proof	750.00

31.1030 g, .999 SILVER, 1.0000 oz ASW
Cocker Spaniel
Similar to KM#105.

KM#	Date	Mintage	VF	XF	Unc
104	1992	.050	—	Proof	35.00

31.1030 g, .999 GOLD, 1.0000 oz AGW

KM#	Date	Mintage	VF	XF	Unc
105	1992	—	—		*BV + 5%*
	1992	—	—	Proof	750.00

Dachshund

KM#	Date	Mintage	VF	XF	Unc
197	1993	—	—	*BV + 5%*	
	1993	—	—	Proof	750.00

EUROPEAN CURRENCY UNITS

10 POUNDS - 14 ECUS

10.0000 g, .925 SILVER, .2974 oz ASW
European Currency Unit
Obv: Uncouped portrait.

KM#	Date	Mintage	VF	XF	Unc
87	1991	*.010	—	Proof	50.00
	1992	—	—	—	20.00

Obv: Couped portrait.

KM#	Date	Mintage	VF	XF	Unc
89	1991	—	—	—	20.00
	1992	—	—	—	20.00

Obv: Uncouped portrait.

KM#	Date	Mintage	VF	XF	Unc
109	1992	—	—	Proof	50.00
	1993	—	—	Proof	50.00

25 POUNDS - 35 ECUS

28.2800 g, .925 SILVER, .8411 oz ASW
European Currency Unit
Similar to 10 Pounds - 14 Ecus, KM#87.
Obv: Uncouped portrait. Rev: Knight left.

KM#	Date	Mintage	VF	XF	Unc
88	1991	*.010	—	Proof	100.00
	1992	—	—	—	50.00

Obv: Couped portrait.

KM#	Date	Mintage	VF	XF	Unc
90	1991	—	—	—	50.00
	1992	—	—	—	50.00

Obv: Uncouped portrait. Rev: Knight right.

KM#	Date	Mintage	VF	XF	Unc
110	1992	—	—	Proof	100.00
	1993	—	—	Proof	100.00

50 POUNDS - 70 ECUS

6.1200 g, .500 GOLD, .1000 oz AGW
Obv: Couped portrait.

KM#	Date	Mintage	VF	XF	Unc
75	1991	—	—	—	125.00
	1992	—	—	—	125.00

6.2210 g, .999 GOLD, .2000 oz AGW
Obv: Uncouped portrait.

KM#	Date	Mintage	VF	XF	Unc
82	1991	5,000	—	Proof	250.00
	1992	—	—	Proof	250.00

Obv: Uncouped portrait.

KM#	Date	Mintage	VF	XF	Unc
111	1992	—	—	Proof	250.00
	1993	1,000	—	Proof	250.00

MINT SETS (MS)

KM#	Date	Mintage	Identification	Issue Price	Mkt. Val.
MS1	1975(3)	1,625	KM7-9	—	925.00
MS2	1988(9)	—	KM16-18,20-25	21.00	30.00
MS3	1990(9)	—	KM16,18,20-21, 22a,23-25,39	25.00	25.00

PROOF SETS (PS)

KM#	Date	Mintage	Identification	Issue Price	Mkt. Val.
PS1	1975(3)	750	KM7-9	875.00	1250.
PS2	1989(5)	—	KM26-30	—	2130.
PS3	1989(2)	—	KM29-30	—	1650.
PS4	1990(6)	*500	KM76-81	—	1500.
PS5	1990(6)	*250	KM76a-81a	—	2100.
PS6	1990(5)	1,000	KM41-45	1800.	1900.
PS7	1991(8)	*20,000	KM50-57	—	640.00
PS8	1991(8)	*5,000	KM58-65	—	1280.
PS9	1991(8)	*1,000	KM58a-65a	—	1680.
PS10	1991(8)	50	KM66-73	120.00	120.00
PS11	1991(5)	1,000	KM91-94,97	—	1450.
PS12	1992(5)	1,000	KM99-102,105	—	1450.

Listings For

GOLD COAST: refer to Ghana

GREAT BRITAIN

The United Kingdom of Great Britain and Northern Ireland, located off the northwest coast of the European continent, has an area of 94,227 sq. mi. (244,820 sq. km.) and a population of 56.4 million. Capital: London. The economy is based on industrial activity and trading. Machinery, motor vehicles, chemicals, and textile yarns and fabrics are exported.

After the departure of the Romans, who brought Britain into a more active relationship with Europe, it fell prey to invaders from Scandinavia and the Low Countries who drove the original Britons into Scotland and Wales, and established a profusion of kingdoms that finally united in the 11th century under the Danish King Canute. Norman rule, following the conquest of 1066, stimulated the development of those institutions which have since distinguished British life. Henry VIII (1509-47) turned Britain from continental adventuring and faced it to the sea - a decision that made Britain a world power during the reign of Elizabeth I (1558-1603). Strengthened by the Industrial Revolution and the defeat of Napoleon, 19th century Britain turned to the remote parts of the world and established a colonial empire of such extent and prosperity that the world has never seen its like. World Wars I and II sealed the fate of the Empire and relegated Britain to a lesser role in world affairs by draining her resources and inaugurating a world-wide movement toward national self-determination in her former colonies.

By the mid-20th century, most of the territories formerly comprising the British Empire had gained independence, and the empire had evolved into the Commonwealth of Nations, an association of equal and autonomous states which enjoy special trade interests. The Commonwealth is presently composed of 50 member nations, including the United Kingdom. All recognize the British monarch as head of the Commonwealth. Sixteen continue to recognize the British monarch as Head of State. They are: United Kingdom, Antigua and Barbuda, Australia, Bahamas, Barbados, Canada, Grenada, Jamaica, New Zealand, Papua New Guinea, St. Christopher & Nevis, Saint Lucia, Saint Vincent and the Grenadines, Solomon Islands, and Tuvalu.

RULERS

George III, 1760-1820
George IV, 1820-1830
William IV, 1830-1837
Victoria, 1837-1901
Edward VII, 1901-1910
George V, 1910-1936
Edward VIII, 1936
George VI, 1936-1952
Elizabeth II, 1952

MINT MARKS

Commencing 1837

H - Heaton
KN - King's Norton

MONETARY SYSTEM

4 Farthings = 1 Penny
12 Pence = 1 Shilling
2 Shillings = 1 Florin
5 Shillings = 1 Crown
20 Shillings = 1 Pound (Sovereign)
21 Shillings = 1 Guinea

NOTE: Proofs exist for many dates of British coins in the 19th and early 20th centuries and for virtually all coins between 1926 and 1964. Those not specifically listed here are extremely rare.

1/4 FARTHING

COPPER

KM#	Date	Mintage	Fine	VF	XF	Unc
737	1839	3.840	18.00	35.00	75.00	150.00
	1839	—	—	—	Proof	—
	1851	2.215	18.00	35.00	80.00	175.00
	1851	—	—	—	Proof	—
	1852	Inc. Ab.	18.00	35.00	75.00	160.00
	1853	Inc. Ab.	18.00	35.00	80.00	175.00
	1853	—	—	—	Proof	450.00

BRONZED COPPER

KM#	Date	Mintage	Fine	VF	XF	Unc
737a	1852	—	—	—	Proof	600.00
	1853	*10-15	—	—	Proof	450.00
	1868	—	—	—	Proof	450.00

***NOTE:** Although the design of the above series is of the homeland type, the issues were struck for Ceylon.

1/3 FARTHING

COPPER

KM#	Date	Mintage	Fine	VF	XF	Unc
703	1827	—	10.00	20.00	45.00	150.00
	1827	—	—	—	Proof	350.00

KM#	Date	Mintage	Fine	VF	XF	Unc
721	1835	—	10.00	20.00	45.00	150.00
	1835	—	—	—	Proof	350.00

KM#	Date	Mintage	Fine	VF	XF	Unc
743	1844	1.301	25.00	45.00	120.00	250.00
	1844 (error) RE for REG.					
		Inc. Ab.	35.00	60.00	150.00	325.00

BRONZE

KM#	Date	Mintage	Fine	VF	XF	Unc
750	1866	.576	4.50	9.00	18.00	50.00
	1866	—	—	—	Proof	350.00
	1868	.144	5.00	10.00	20.00	50.00
	1868	—	—	—	Proof	300.00
	1876	.162	5.00	10.00	20.00	75.00
	1878	.288	5.00	10.00	20.00	75.00
	1878	—	—	—	Proof	—
	1881	.144	5.00	10.00	20.00	75.00
	1881	—	—	—	Proof	300.00
	1884	.144	5.00	10.00	20.00	50.00
	1885	.288	4.50	9.00	18.00	50.00

KM#	Date	Mintage	Fine	VF	XF	Unc
791	1902	.288	3.50	6.00	10.00	25.00

KM#	Date	Mintage	Fine	VF	XF	Unc
823	1913	.288	3.50	6.00	10.00	25.00

***NOTE:** Although the designs of the above types are in the homeland style, the issues were struck for Malta.

1/2 FARTHING

COPPER

Rev: Britannia's head breaks legend.

KM#	Date	Mintage	Fine	VF	XF	Unc
704.1	1828	7.680	10.00	25.00	65.00	180.00
	1828	—	—	—	Proof	350.00
	1830	—	—	—	Proof	350.00

Rev: Britannia's head below legend.

KM#	Date	Mintage	Fine	VF	XF	Unc
704.2	1828	Inc. Ab.	10.00	25.00	65.00	180.00
	1830 large date					
		8.776	10.00	25.00	65.00	170.00
	1830 small date					
		Inc. Ab.	12.00	35.00	85.00	190.00
	1830	—	—	—	Proof	350.00

BRONZED COPPER

KM#	Date	Mintage	Fine	VF	XF	Unc
704.1a	1828	—	—	—	Proof	300.00

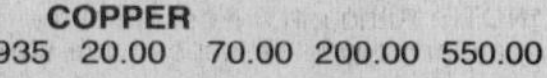

COPPER

KM#	Date	Mintage	Fine	VF	XF	Unc
724	1837	1.935	20.00	70.00	200.00	550.00

KM#	Date	Mintage	Fine	VF	XF	Unc
738	1839	2.043	4.00	10.00	25.00	70.00
	1842	—	3.00	7.00	20.00	50.00
	1843	3.441	2.50	6.00	12.00	35.00
	1844	6.451	2.50	5.00	10.00	30.00
	1844 E of REGINA over N					
		Inc. Ab.	8.50	25.00	80.00	200.00
	1847	3.011	4.00	8.00	20.00	70.00
	1851/5851	—	6.00	15.00	35.00	90.00
	1851	—	4.00	10.00	25.00	75.00
	1852	.989	5.00	12.00	30.00	75.00
	1853	.955	6.50	15.00	40.00	100.00
	1853	—	—	—	Proof	300.00
	1854	.677	6.50	15.00	40.00	120.00
	1856 small date					
		.914	8.00	18.00	45.00	130.00
	1856 large date					
		Inc. Ab.	17.00	40.00	80.00	150.00

***NOTE:** Although the design of the above series is of the homeland type, the issues were originally struck for Ceylon. The issue was made current also in the United Kingdom by proclamation in 1842.

FARTHING

COPPER

KM#	Date	Mintage	Fine	VF	XF	Unc
661	1806	—	2.00	5.00	20.00	65.00
	1806	—	—	—	Proof	225.00
	1807	—	3.00	7.50	25.00	70.00

GILT COPPER

KM#	Date	Mintage	Fine	VF	XF	Unc
661a	1806	—	—	—	Proof	325.00

BRONZED COPPER

KM#	Date	Mintage	Fine	VF	XF	Unc
661b	1806	—	—	—	Proof	225.00

COPPER

KM#	Date	Mintage	Fine	VF	XF	Unc
677	1821	2.688	1.75	4.00	25.00	85.00
	1821	—	—	—	Proof	300.00
	1822	5.924	1.75	4.00	20.00	70.00
	1822	—	—	—	Proof	300.00
	1823	2.365	2.00	5.00	22.00	75.00
	1823 letter I for 1 in date					
		Inc. Ab.	6.00	15.00	30.00	125.00
	1825	4.300	1.75	4.00	22.00	75.00
	1826	6.666	3.00	6.00	25.00	85.00

KM#	Date	Mintage	Fine	VF	XF	Unc
697	1826	Inc. Ab.	2.50	5.00	30.00	80.00
	1826	—	—	—	Proof	200.00
	1827	2.365	3.00	8.00	30.00	85.00
	1828	2.365	2.50	5.50	30.00	100.00
	1829	1.505	4.00	9.00	35.00	125.00
	1830	2.365	2.50	5.00	30.00	80.00
	1831	—	—	—	Proof	300.00

BRONZED COPPER

KM#	Date	Mintage	Fine	VF	XF	Unc
697a	1826	*150 pcs.	—	—	Proof	185.00

COPPER

KM#	Date	Mintage	Fine	VF	XF	Unc
705	1831	2.688	3.00	8.00	30.00	120.00
	1831	—	—	—	Proof	200.00
	1834	1.935	3.00	8.00	30.00	120.00
	1835	1.720	3.00	8.00	35.00	125.00
	1836	1.290	3.50	9.00	35.00	125.00
	1837	3.011	3.00	8.00	30.00	120.00

KM#	Date	Mintage	Fine	VF	XF	Unc
725	1838	.591	3.00	7.50	20.00	55.00
	1839	4.301	2.00	5.00	15.00	50.00
	1839	—	—	—	Proof	200.00
	1840	3.011	2.00	5.00	17.50	55.00
	1841	1.720	2.00	5.00	17.50	45.00
	1841*	—	—	—	Proof	175.00
	1842	1.290	4.50	14.00	30.00	70.00
	1842 4 over inverted 4					
		—	—	—	Rare	—
	1843	4.086	2.00	4.00	15.00	45.00
	1843 letter I for 1 in date					
		Inc. Ab.	3.50	8.50	32.50	125.00
	1844	.430	27.50	60.00	225.00	475.00
	1845	3.226	2.00	7.00	18.00	65.00
	1846	2.580	4.50	15.00	35.00	90.00
	1847	3.880	2.00	5.00	15.00	60.00
	1848	1.290	2.25	8.00	22.50	75.00
	1849	.645	10.00	27.50	65.00	250.00
	1850/70	.430	10.00	30.00	60.00	175.00
	1850	Inc. Ab.	3.00	6.00	15.00	65.00
	1851	1.935	6.00	15.00	40.00	130.00
	1851 D of DEI/tipped D					
		Inc. Ab.	50.00	150.00	400.00	700.00
	1852	.823	6.00	17.50	40.00	135.00
	1853/2	1.028	75.00	125.00	200.00	350.00
	1853 WW designers initials raised					
		Inc. Ab.	1.50	4.00	12.50	40.00
	1853	—	—	—	Proof	350.00
	1853 WW designers initials incuse					
		Inc. Ab.	7.50	15.00	30.00	55.00
	1853	—	—	—	Proof	350.00
	1854	4.946	1.25	4.00	14.00	50.00
	1855 WW designers initials raised					
		3.441	4.00	15.00	30.00	75.00
	1855 WW designers initials incuse					
		Inc. Ab.	3.00	12.50	27.50	70.00
	1856	1.771	3.00	10.00	32.50	80.00
	1856 R of Victoria over E					
		Inc. Ab.	25.00	60.00	150.00	300.00
	1857	1.075	1.25	3.50	12.50	35.00
	1858	1.720	1.25	3.50	12.50	35.00
	1859	1.290	10.00	20.00	60.00	120.00
	1860/59	—	—	—	—	—
	1860	—	800.00	1500.	3000.	5500.
	1864	—	—	—	Rare	—

NOTE: Proofs dated 1841 were probably restruck at a later date.

BRONZED COPPER

KM#	Date	Mintage	Fine	VF	XF	Unc
725a	1839	*300 pcs.	—	—	Proof	Rare
	1853					
		*10-15 pcs.	—	—	Proof	Rare

BRONZE

Beaded border.

KM#	Date	Mintage	Fine	VF	XF	Unc
747.1	1860	2.867	2.00	4.00	10.00	30.00
	1860	—	—	—	Proof	300.00

Toothed border.

KM#	Date	Mintage	Fine	VF	XF	Unc
747.2	1860	Inc. Ab.	1.00	2.50	8.00	27.50
	1860 toothed/beaded border					
		Inc. Ab.	70.00	150.00	250.00	650.00
	1861	8.602	1.00	2.00	6.00	27.50
	1861	—	—	—	Proof	350.00
	1862 small 8					
		14.336	1.00	2.00	5.00	25.00
	1862 lg.8	I.A.	1.50	3.75	9.00	30.00
	1862	—	—	—	Proof	350.00
	1863	1.434	25.00	50.00	110.00	300.00
	1863	—	—	—	Proof	700.00
	1864	2.509	1.50	3.00	12.00	35.00
	1865/2	4.659	2.00	4.50	12.00	35.00
	1865/3	Inc. Ab.	2.50	5.00	15.00	40.00
	1865 lg.8	I.A.	1.50	2.50	7.00	30.00
	1865 sm.8	I.A.	1.50	2.50	6.00	30.00
	1866	3.584	1.00	2.00	6.00	30.00
	1866	—	—	—	Proof	350.00
	1867	5.018	1.50	3.00	10.00	30.00
	1867	—	—	—	Proof	350.00
	1868	4.851	1.50	3.00	10.00	30.00
	1868	—	—	—	Proof	200.00
	1869	3.226	3.00	7.50	25.00	60.00
	1872	2.150	1.50	3.50	9.00	35.00
	1873	3.226	1.25	2.75	7.00	27.50

Obv: Mature bust.

KM#	Date	Mintage	Fine	VF	XF	Unc
753	1874H	3.584	1.50	3.00	8.00	27.50
	1874H	—	—	—	Proof	200.00
	1874H normal G's over horizontal G's					
		Inc. Ab.	75.00	175.00	300.00	—
	1875 large date, 5 berries					
		.713	9.00	20.00	40.00	120.00
	1875 small date, 5 berries					
		Inc. Ab.	15.00	25.00	50.00	175.00
	1875 small date, 4 berries					
		Inc. Ab.	12.00	22.00	45.00	165.00
	1875H	6.093	1.00	2.00	5.00	17.50
	1875H	—	—	—	Proof	200.00
	1876H	1.075	6.00	15.00	30.00	75.00
	1877	—	—	—	Proof	2500.
	1878	4.009	1.00	2.00	5.00	25.00
	1878	—	—	—	Proof	350.00
	1879	3.977	1.00	2.00	5.00	25.00
	1879 large 9					
		Inc. Ab.	1.50	3.00	8.00	35.00
	1880 3 berries in wreath					
		1.843	3.75	7.50	17.50	55.00
	1880 4 berries in wreath					
		Inc. Ab.	1.25	2.50	5.00	25.00
	1881 3 berries in wreath					
		3.495	1.50	3.00	6.00	25.00
	1881 4 berries in wreath					
		Inc. Ab.	3.50	7.50	20.00	55.00
	1881 shield heraldically colored					
		—	—	—	Proof	800.00
	1881H	1.792	1.50	3.50	6.00	25.00
	1882H	1.792	1.50	3.50	6.00	25.00
	1882H	—	—	—	Proof	400.00
	1883	1.129	2.00	7.50	20.00	45.00
	1883	—	—	—	Proof	400.00
	1884	5.782	.75	1.50	3.50	20.00
	1884	—	—	—	Proof	400.00
	1885	5.442	1.00	2.00	3.50	20.00
	1885	—	—	—	Prcof	400.00
	1886	7.708	.75	1.50	3.00	18.00
	1886	—	—	—	Proof	400.00
	1887	1.341	2.00	4.00	9.00	30.00
	1888	1.887	1.50	3.00	5.00	22.50
	1890	2.133	1.50	2.50	4.00	22.00
	1890	—	—	—	Proof	400.00
	1891	4.960	.75	1.50	3.00	20.00
	1891	—	—	—	Proof	350.00
	1892	.887	3.00	7.50	15.00	40.00
	1892	—	—	—	Proof	400.00
	1893	3.904	.75	1.50	3.00	20.00
	1894	2.397	.75	1.50	3.50	22.00
	1895	2.853	10.00	20.00	50.00	120.00
788.1	1895	Inc. Ab.	.50	1.25	3.50	9.50
	1896	3.669	.35	1.00	3.00	9.00
	1896	—	—	—	Proof	300.00
	1897	4.580	.75	2.00	5.00	17.50

Blackened finish

KM#	Date	Mintage	Fine	VF	XF	Unc
788.2	1897	Inc. Ab.	.45	1.25	3.00	10.00
	1898	4.010	.60	1.50	3.50	14.00
	1899	3.865	.35	.75	2.00	10.00
	1900	5.969	.35	.75	2.00	9.00
	1901	8.016	.30	.65	2.00	9.00

KM#	Date	Mintage	Fine	VF	XF	Unc
792	1902	5.125	.60	1.50	3.00	10.00
	1903	5.331	.75	1.75	4.00	17.00
	1903 shield heraldically colored					
		—	—	—	Proof	675.00
	1904	3.629	1.50	3.00	6.50	18.50
	1905	4.077	.60	1.75	4.00	17.00
	1906	5.340	.50	1.50	3.50	15.00
	1907	4.399	.75	1.50	4.00	16.00
	1908	4.265	.75	1.50	4.00	16.00
	1909	8.852	.50	1.50	3.50	15.00
	1910	2.598	1.75	4.00	8.00	20.00

KM#	Date	Mintage	Fine	VF	XF	Unc
808.1	1911	5.197	.60	1.00	3.00	7.00
	1912	7.670	.35	.75	2.50	7.00
	1913	4.184	.50	.75	2.50	7.00
	1914	6.127	.35	.75	2.50	7.00
	1915	7.129	.50	.75	2.50	7.00
	1916	10.993	.35	.75	1.50	6.00
	1917	21.435	.15	.35	1.50	6.00
	1918	19.363	.75	1.50	4.00	12.00

Bright finish

KM#	Date	Mintage	Fine	VF	XF	Unc
808.2	1918	Inc. Ab.	.20	.40	1.00	4.00
	1919	15.089	.20	.40	1.00	4.00
	1920	11.481	.20	.40	1.00	4.00
	1921	9.469	.20	.40	1.00	5.00
	1922	9.957	.20	.40	1.00	5.00
	1923	8.034	.20	.40	1.00	6.00
	1924	8.733	.20	.40	1.00	6.00
	1925	12.635	.20	.40	1.00	4.00

Obv: Smaller head.

KM#	Date	Mintage	Fine	VF	XF	Unc
825	1926	9.792	.15	.40	1.00	6.00
	1926	—	—	—	Proof	—
	1927	7.868	.15	.40	1.00	5.00
	1927	—	—	—	Proof	—
	1928	11.626	.15	.35	.75	3.50
	1928	—	—	—	Proof	125.00
	1929	8.419	.15	.35	.75	3.50
	1929	—	—	—	Proof	125.00
	1930	4.195	.25	.50	1.00	5.00
	1930	—	—	—	Proof	125.00
	1931	6.595	.15	.35	.75	3.50
	1931	—	—	—	Proof	125.00
	1932	9.293	.15	.35	.75	3.50
	1932	—	—	—	Proof	125.00
	1933	4.560	.15	.35	.75	3.50
	1933	—	—	—	Proof	125.00
	1934	3.053	.35	.75	1.75	6.00
	1934	—	—	—	Proof	125.00
	1935	2.227	1.00	2.00	3.50	9.00
	1935	—	—	—	Proof	150.00
	1936	9.734	.15	.35	.75	3.00
	1936	—	—	—	Proof	150.00

KM#	Date	Mintage	Fine	VF	XF	Unc
843	1937	8.131	.15	.25	.40	1.50
	1937	.026	—	—	Proof	4.00
	1938	7.450	.15	.30	.60	3.50
	1938	—	—	—	Proof	125.00
	1939	31.440	.10	.25	.40	1.50
	1939	—	—	—	Proof	125.00
	1940	18.360	.10	.25	.50	3.50
	1940	—	—	—	Proof	—
	1941	27.312	.10	.25	.40	1.50
	1941	—	—	—	Proof	—
	1942	28.858	.10	.20	.35	1.50
	1942	—	—	—	Proof	—
	1943	33.346	.10	.15	.30	1.50
	1943	—	—	—	Proof	—
	1944	25.138	.10	.15	.30	1.50
	1944	—	—	—	Proof	—
	1945	23.736	.10	.20	.35	1.50
	1945	—	—	—	Proof	—
	1946	24.365	.10	.20	.35	1.50
	1946	—	—	—	Proof	—
	1947	14.746	.10	.20	.35	1.50
	1947	—	—	—	Proof	—
	1948	16.622	.10	.20	.35	1.50
	1948	—	—	—	Proof	—

Obv. leg: W/o IND IMP.

KM#	Date	Mintage	Fine	VF	XF	Unc
867	1949	8.424	.10	.20	.35	1.50
	1949	—	—	—	Proof	—
	1950	10.325	.10	.20	.35	1.50
	1950	.018	—	—	Proof	3.00
	1951	14.016	.10	.20	.35	1.75
	1951	.020	—	—	Proof	3.00
	1952	5.251	.10	.20	.35	1.75
	1952	—	—	—	Proof	125.00

KM#	Date	Mintage	Fine	VF	XF	Unc
881	1953	6.131	.15	.25	.35	2.00
	1953	.040	—	—	Proof	5.00

Obv. leg: W/o BRITT OMN.

KM#	Date	Mintage	Fine	VF	XF	Unc
895	1954	6.566	.10	.15	.30	1.75
	1954	—	—	—	Proof	125.00
	1955	5.779	.10	.15	.30	1.75
	1955	—	—	—	Proof	—
895	1956	1.997	.25	.50	.75	3.50
	1956	—	—	—	Proof	—

1/2 PENNY

COPPER

KM#	Date	Mintage	Fine	VF	XF	Unc
662	1806 w/o berries					
		—	2.00	5.00	20.00	90.00
	1806 3 berries					
		—	2.00	4.50	18.00	90.00
	1806 w/o berries					
		—	—	—	Proof	250.00
	1806 2 berries					
		—	—	—	Proof	250.00
	1806 3 berries					
		—	—	—	Proof	250.00
	1807	—	2.50	5.50	20.00	100.00

BRONZED COPPER

KM#	Date	Mintage	Fine	VF	XF	Unc
662a	1806	—	—	—	Proof	275.0

COPPER

KM#	Date	Mintage	Fine	VF	XF	Unc
692	1825	.215	7.50	15.00	50.00	145.00
	1825	—	—	—	Proof	275.00
	1826/5	9.032	3.00	10.00	50.00	200.00
	1826	Inc. Ab.	2.00	7.00	35.00	125.00
	1826	—	—	—	Proof	200.00
	1827	5.376	2.50	7.50	45.00	140.00

BRONZED COPPER

KM#	Date	Mintage	Fine	VF	XF	Unc
692a	1826	*150	—	—	Proof	250.00

COPPER

KM#	Date	Mintage	Fine	VF	XF	Unc
706	1831	.806	4.50	9.00	45.00	170.00
	1834	.538	5.00	10.00	50.00	175.00
	1837	.349	4.00	8.00	40.00	160.00

BRONZED COPPER

KM#	Date	Mintage	Fine	VF	XF	Unc
706a	1831	—	—	—	Proof	200.00

COPPER

KM#	Date	Mintage	Fine	VF	XF	Unc
726	1838	.457	2.00	4.00	15.00	85.00
	1841	1.075	2.00	4.00	15.00	85.00
	1843	.968	6.00	15.00	45.00	150.00
	1844	1.075	3.50	8.00	35.00	115.00
	1845	1.075	30.00	70.00	275.00	800.00
	1846	.860	5.00	10.00	30.00	110.00
	1847	.725	6.00	10.00	30.00	110.00
	1848/7	.323	2.00	5.00	15.00	100.00
	1848	Inc. Ab.	2.50	6.00	22.50	110.00
	1851	.215	2.00	5.00	15.00	100.00
	1852	.637	2.00	5.00	15.00	100.00
	1853/2	1.559	6.00	15.00	45.00	150.00
	1853	Inc. Ab.	1.25	3.00	12.00	70.00
	1853	—	—	—	Proof	175.00
	1854	12.257	1.25	3.00	10.00	70.00
	1855	7.456	1.25	3.00	10.00	70.00
	1856	1.942	2.00	5.00	20.00	100.00
	1857	1.183	1.25	4.00	15.00	75.00
	1857 dots on shield					
		Inc. Ab.	1.25	4.00	12.00	75.00
	1858/6	2.473	5.00	12.00	37.50	110.00
	1858/7	Inc. Ab.	2.00	6.00	18.00	75.00
	1858	Inc. Ab.	1.50	4.50	15.00	70.00
	1858 sm.dt.	I.A.	2.00	5.50	18.00	70.00

KM#	Date	Mintage	Fine	VF	XF	Unc
726	1859/8	1.290	4.50	12.00	40.00	115.00
	1859	Inc. Ab.	2.50	6.00	18.00	70.00
	1860	—	200.00	500.00	2250.	4500.
	1860	—	—	—	Proof	5000.

BRONZED COPPER

KM#	Date	Mintage	Fine	VF	XF	Unc
726a	1839 normal alignment	*300 pcs.	—	—	Proof	225.00
	1839 coin alignment	Inc. Ab.	—	—	Proof	300.00
	1841	—	—	—	Proof	—
	1853	*10-15 pcs.	—	—	Proof	Rare

BRONZE

Beaded border

KM#	Date	Mintage	Fine	VF	XF	Unc
748.1	1860	6.630	1.50	4.00	12.00	50.00
	1860	—	—	—	Proof	400.00

Toothed border

KM#	Date	Mintage	Fine	VF	XF	Unc
748.2	1860	Inc. Ab.	1.50	4.00	12.00	50.00
	1860 toothed/beaded border	—	—	—	—	—
	1860 w/7 berries in wreath	Inc. Ab.	1.50	4.00	12.00	45.00
	1860 w/7 berries in wreath	—	—	—	Proof	400.00
	1860 w/7 berries in wreath; rd.top lighthouse	Inc. Ab.	4.25	15.00	70.00	225.00
	1860 w/5 berries in wreath	Inc. Ab.	2.00	7.25	35.00	70.00
	1860 w/4 berries in wreath	Inc. Ab.	1.50	4.00	12.00	45.00
	1860 w/4 berries in wreath; rd.top lighthouse	Inc. Ab.	2.25	7.25	40.00	70.00
	1861/81	54.118	—	—	Rare	—
	1861	Inc. Ab.	1.50	4.00	10.00	40.00
	1861	—	—	—	Proof	300.00
	1861 w/5 berries in wreath L.C.W. on rock	Inc. Ab.	10.00	25.00	75.00	300.00
	1861 w/4 berries in wreath L.C.W. on rock	Inc. Ab.	2.00	3.00	12.50	90.00
	1861 w/4 berries in wreath L.C.W. on rock	—	—	—	Proof	550.00
	1861 w/4 berries in wreath	Inc. Ab.	2.00	4.00	10.00	40.00
	1861 L.C.W. on rock	Inc. Ab.	2.50	7.00	15.00	45.00
	1861 HALF over HALP	Inc. Ab.	20.00	60.00	175.00	450.00
	1862 L.C.W. on rock, B to left of lighthouse	61.107	50.00	150.00	600.00	1200.
	1862 C to left of lighthouse	Inc. Ab.	50.00	150.00	600.00	1200.
	1862 A to left of lighthouse	Inc. Ab.	50.00	150.00	600.00	1200.
	1862	—	—	—	Proof	300.00
	1862	Inc. Ab.	1.25	3.00	12.00	45.00
	1862L.C.W.	I.A.	7.00	15.00	40.00	90.00
	1863 sm.3	15.949	1.50	5.00	20.00	50.00
	1863 sm.3	—	—	—	Proof	300.00
	1863 lg.3	I.A.	1.50	5.00	20.00	50.00
	1864	.538	3.50	8.00	25.00	85.00
	1865/3	8.064	30.00	85.00	270.00	600.00
	1865	Inc. Ab.	4.00	12.00	30.00	75.00
	1866	2.509	2.50	7.50	20.00	50.00
	1866	—	—	—	Proof	300.00
	1867	2.509	4.00	10.00	27.50	70.00
	1867	—	—	—	Proof	300.00
	1868	3.046	2.50	7.50	20.00	65.00
	1868	—	—	—	Proof	250.00
	1869	3.226	7.50	25.00	75.00	175.00
	1870	4.351	2.50	7.50	20.00	65.00
	1871	1.075	22.50	60.00	150.00	450.00
	1872	4.659	3.00	7.50	20.00	50.00
	1873	3.405	4.50	10.00	25.00	70.00
	1874 w/5 berries in wreath	Inc. Ab.	5.00	15.00	40.00	100.00

Obv: Mature bust.

KM#	Date	Mintage	Fine	VF	XF	Unc
754	1874 w/6 berries in wreath; large date	1.348	4.50	12.00	30.00	80.00
	1874 w/6 berries in wreath; small date	Inc. Ab.	—	12.00	30.00	80.00
	1874 w/4 berries in wreath; large date	Inc. Ab.	3.50	15.00	40.00	120.00
	1874H w/6 berries in wreath; small date	5.018	3.00	8.00	20.00	50.00
754	1874H	—	—	—	Proof	300.00
	1874H w/6 berries in wr.;sm.dt. hvy.plan.	—	—	—	—	—
	1875	5.431	1.75	4.50	12.50	40.00
	1875H	1.254	7.00	15.00	35.00	85.00
	1875H	—	—	—	Proof	350.00
	1876H lg.date	6.810	3.00	7.50	20.00	60.00
	1876H small date	Inc. Ab.	2.00	5.00	15.00	50.00
	1876H sm.dt.	—	—	—	Proof	350.00
	1876H sm.date heavy planchet	—	15.00	50.00	150.00	400.00
	1877	5.210	2.00	5.00	15.00	50.00
	1877	—	—	—	Proof	300.00
	1878 small date	1.426	8.00	25.00	50.00	200.00
	1878 sm.dt.	—	—	—	Proof	400.00
	1878 lg.date	I.A.	25.00	85.00	275.00	800.00
	1878 lg.date	—	—	—	Proof	850.00
	1879	3.583	1.50	4.00	12.00	40.00
	1880	2.423	2.50	6.50	15.00	45.00
	1880	—	—	—	Proof	400.00
	1881	2.008	2.50	7.50	20.00	50.00
	1881 shield heraldically colored	—	—	—	Proof	600.00
	1881 shield heraldically colored, broach on bust	2 known	—	—	Proof	1250.
	1881H	1.792	2.50	7.50	20.00	50.00
	1882H	4.480	1.15	4.50	15.00	45.00
	1882H different dies	—	—	—	Proof	700.00
	1883 rose on front of dress	3.001	5.00	10.00	20.00	50.00
	1883 rose on front of dress	—	—	—	Proof	400.00
	1883 broach on front of dress	Inc. Ab.	3.50	6.00	15.00	40.00
	1884	6.990	1.15	3.00	12.50	40.00
	1884	—	—	—	Proof	350.00
	1885	8.601	1.15	3.00	12.50	40.00
	1885	—	—	—	Proof	350.00
	1886	8.586	1.00	2.75	12.50	40.00
	1886	—	—	—	Proof	175.00
	1887	10.701	1.00	2.75	10.00	35.00
	1888	6.815	1.25	3.25	11.50	37.50
	1889/8	7.748	35.00	60.00	120.00	275.00
	1889/8	1 known	—	—	Proof	—
	1889	Inc. Ab.	1.00	2.75	11.50	35.00
	1890	11.254	1.00	2.75	9.00	35.00
	1890	—	—	—	Proof	400.00
	1891	13.192	1.00	2.50	9.00	35.00
	1891	—	—	—	Proof	400.00
	1892	2.478	1.15	2.75	9.00	35.00
	1892	—	—	—	Proof	400.00
	1893	7.229	.80	2.25	9.00	35.00
	1894	1.768	3.00	7.00	25.00	60.00

KM#	Date	Mintage	Fine	VF	XF	Unc
789	1895	3.032	.75	1.50	4.00	18.00
	1895	—	—	—	Proof	400.00
	1896	9.143	.75	1.50	3.50	15.00
	1896	—	—	—	Proof	400.00
	1897	8.690	.50	1.25	4.50	20.00
	1897 high sea level	Inc. Ab.	.60	1.50	3.50	15.00
	1898	8.595	1.00	3.00	7.50	20.00
	1899	12.108	.75	2.00	4.50	15.00
	1900	13.805	.50	1.00	2.75	9.00
	1901	11.127	.40	.75	2.00	8.00
	1901	—	—	—	Proof	400.00

Rev: Low horizon.

KM#	Date	Mintage	Fine	VF	XF	Unc
793.1	1902	13.673	8.00	22.50	60.00	120.00

Rev: High horizon.

KM#	Date	Mintage	Fine	VF	XF	Unc
793.2	1902	Inc. Ab.	.50	2.00	5.00	15.00
	1903	11.451	.75	2.50	7.50	30.00
	1904	8.131	1.50	3.50	12.00	40.00
	1905	10.125	1.00	3.00	8.00	25.00
	1906	11.101	.75	2.00	6.00	25.00
	1907	16.849	.75	2.00	6.00	25.00
	1908	16.621	.75	2.00	6.00	25.00
	1909	8.279	1.00	3.00	8.00	30.00
	1910	10.770	1.00	2.50	7.00	25.00

KM#	Date	Mintage	Fine	VF	XF	Unc
809	1911	12.571	.75	1.75	4.50	13.50
	1912	21.186	.50	1.25	4.00	12.50
	1913	17.476	.75	2.25	8.00	25.00
	1914	20.289	.75	1.75	5.00	16.50
	1915	21.563	.75	1.75	5.00	16.50
	1916	39.386	.75	1.50	3.50	12.00
	1917	38.245	.75	1.25	3.50	12.00
	1918	22.321	.75	1.50	3.50	12.00
	1919	28.104	.50	1.50	3.50	12.00
	1920	35.147	.50	1.50	3.50	12.00
	1921	28.027	.75	1.50	3.50	12.00
	1922	10.735	1.00	2.25	5.00	15.00
	1923	12.266	.50	1.50	3.50	12.00
	1924	13.971	.75	2.00	5.00	15.00
	1925 obv. of 1924	12.216	1.00	2.50	7.00	17.50

Obv: Modified effigy.

KM#	Date	Mintage	Fine	VF	XF	Unc
824	1925 obv. of 1926	Inc. Ab.	1.50	5.00	10.00	25.00
	1926	6.712	1.50	3.00	6.00	16.50
	1926	—	—	—	Proof	325.00
	1927	15.590	.75	1.25	3.50	11.50
	1927	—	—	—	Proof	275.00

Obv: Smaller head.

KM#	Date	Mintage	Fine	VF	XF	Unc
837	1928	20.935	.25	.75	3.00	11.00
	1928	—	—	—	Proof	250.00
	1929	25.680	.25	.75	3.00	11.00
	1929	—	—	—	Proof	250.00
	1930	12.533	.25	.75	3.00	11.00
	1930	—	—	—	Proof	250.00
	1931	16.138	.25	.75	3.00	11.00
	1931	—	—	—	Proof	250.00
	1932	14.448	.25	.75	3.25	12.00
	1932	—	—	—	Proof	250.00
	1933	10.560	.25	.75	3.25	12.50
	1933	—	—	—	Proof	250.00
	1934	7.704	.50	1.00	3.50	14.00
	1934	—	—	—	Proof	250.00
	1935	12.180	.25	.75	2.50	10.00
	1935	—	—	—	Proof	225.00
	1936	23.009	.25	.65	2.00	5.50
	1936	—	—	—	Proof	225.00

KM#	Date	Mintage	Fine	VF	XF	Unc
844	1937	24.504	.25	.35	.50	1.50
	1937	.026	—	—	Proof	5.00
	1938	40.320	.25	.50	1.25	3.75
	1938	—	—	—	Proof	225.00
	1939	28.925	.25	.50	1.25	3.50
	1939	—	—	—	Proof	225.00
	1940	32.162	.25	.50	2.00	5.00
	1940	—	—	—	Proof	275.00
	1941	45.120	.20	.50	1.50	5.00
	1941	—	—	—	Proof	275.00
	1942	71.909	.10	.20	.60	2.25
	1942	—	—	—	Proof	200.00
	1943	76.200	.10	.25	1.00	2.25
	1943	—	—	—	Proof	200.00
	1944	81.840	.10	.25	1.00	3.00
	1944	—	—	—	Proof	200.00
	1945	57.000	.10	.25	.90	2.00
	1945	—	—	—	Proof	200.00
	1946	22.726	.20	.50	2.75	7.00
	1946	—	—	—	Proof	200.00
	1947	21.266	.10	.25	2.00	5.00
	1947	—	—	—	Proof	200.00
	1948	26.947	.10	.25	.90	2.25
	1948	—	—	—	Proof	200.00

Obv. leg: W/o IND IMP.

KM#	Date	Mintage	Fine	VF	XF	Unc
868	1949	24.744	.10	.25	1.25	4.00
	1949	—	—	—	Proof	200.00
	1950	24.154	.10	.25	1.50	4.50
	1950	.018	—	—	Proof	5.00
	1951	14.868	.25	.50	1.50	6.00
	1951	.020	—	—	Proof	6.00
	1952	33.278	.10	.25	1.00	2.25
	1952	—	—	—	Proof	200.00

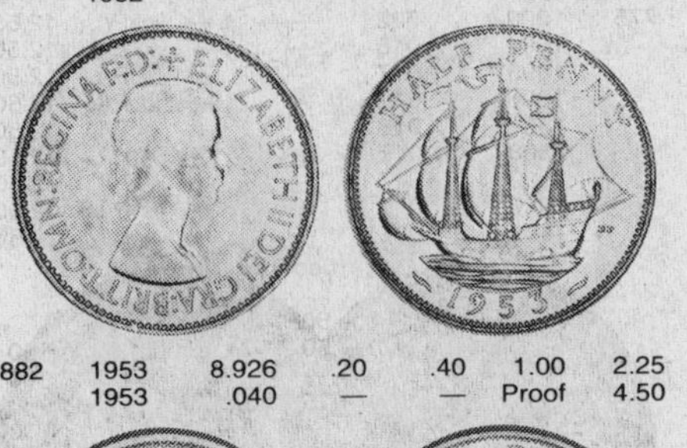

KM#	Date	Mintage	Fine	VF	XF	Unc
882	1953	8.926	.20	.40	1.00	2.25
	1953	.040	—	—	Proof	4.50

Obv. leg: W/o BRITT OMN.

KM#	Date	Mintage	Fine	VF	XF	Unc
896	1954	19.375	.10	.25	1.50	4.50
	1954	—	—	—	Proof	225.00
	1955	18.799	.10	.25	1.50	5.00
	1955	—	—	—	Proof	225.00
	1956	21.799	.15	.50	1.50	5.00
	1956	—	—	—	Proof	225.00
	1957	43.684	.10	.25	.50	1.50
	1957	—	—	—	Proof	225.00
	1958	62.318	—	.10	.20	.75
	1958	—	—	—	Proof	225.00
	1959	79.176	—	.10	.15	.40
	1959	—	—	—	Proof	225.00
	1960	41.340	—	.10	.15	.30
	1960	—	—	—	Proof	225.00
	1961	—	—	—	Proof	225.00
	1962	41.779	—	—	.10	.20
	1962	—	—	—	Proof	225.00
	1963	45.036	—	—	.10	.20
	1963	—	—	—	Proof	200.00
	1964	78.583	—	—	.10	.15
	1964	—	—	—	Proof	200.00
	1965	98.083	—	—	—	.10
	1966	95.289	—	—	—	.10
	1967	146.491	—	—	—	.10
	1970	.750	—	—	Proof	1.50

PENNY

COPPER

KM#	Date	Mintage	Fine	VF	XF	Unc
663	1806	—	5.00	10.00	50.00	165.00
	1806	—	—	—	Proof	300.00
	1807	—	6.00	12.00	55.00	180.00
	1808	Unique	—	—	—	—

BRONZED COPPER

KM#	Date	Mintage	Fine	VF	XF	Unc
663a	1806	—	—	—	Proof	300.00

GILT COPPER

KM#	Date	Mintage	Fine	VF	XF	Unc
663b	1806	—	—	—	Proof	500.00

.4713 g, .925 SILVER, .0140 oz ASW

KM#	Date	Mintage	Fine	VF	XF	Unc
668	1817	—	5.00	8.00	15.00	30.00
	1817	.010	—	—	P/L	35.00
	1818	—	5.00	8.00	15.00	30.00
	1818	9,504	—	—	P/L	35.00
	1820	—	5.00	8.00	15.00	30.00
	1820	7,920	—	—	P/L	35.00

KM#	Date	Mintage	Fine	VF	XF	Unc
683	1822	.012	—	—	P/L	35.00
	1823	.013	—	—	P/L	30.00
	1824	9,504	—	—	P/L	35.00
	1825	8,712	—	—	P/L	30.00
	1826	8,712	—	—	P/L	30.00
	1827	7,920	—	—	P/L	30.00
	1828	7,920	—	—	P/L	30.00
	1829	7,920	—	—	P/L	30.00
	1830	7,920	—	—	P/L	30.00

COPPER

KM#	Date	Mintage	Fine	VF	XF	Unc
693	1825	1.075	6.00	20.00	80.00	235.00
	1825	—	—	—	Proof	500.00
	1826	5.914	4.50	18.00	60.00	200.00
	1826	—	—	—	Proof	400.00
	1827	1.452	80.00	250.00	1600.	2500.

BRONZED COPPER

KM#	Date	Mintage	Fine	VF	XF	Unc
693a	1826	—	—	—	Proof	300.00

COPPER

KM#	Date	Mintage	Fine	VF	XF	Unc
707	1831	.806	8.50	35.00	120.00	425.00
	1831 .W.W incuse on truncation	Inc. Ab.	10.00	40.00	130.00	460.00
	1831 W.W incuse on truncation	Inc. Ab.	12.00	45.00	140.00	500.00
	1834	.323	12.00	50.00	140.00	500.00
	1837	.175	15.00	65.00	150.00	575.00

BRONZED COPPER

KM#	Date	Mintage	Fine	VF	XF	Unc
707a	1831	—	—	—	Proof	400.00

.4713 g, .925 SILVER, .0140 oz ASW

KM#	Date	Mintage	Fine	VF	XF	Unc
708	1831	.010	—	—	P/L	22.50
	1832	8,712	—	—	P/L	22.50
	1833	8,712	—	—	P/L	22.50
	1834	8,712	—	—	P/L	22.50
	1835	8,712	—	—	P/L	22.50
	1836	8,712	—	—	P/L	22.50
	1837	8,712	—	—	P/L	22.50

KM#	Date	Mintage	Fine	VF	XF	Unc
727	1838	8,976	—	—	P/L	15.00
	1839	8,976	—	—	P/L	15.00
	1840	8,976	—	—	P/L	15.00
	1841	7,920	—	—	P/L	15.00
	1842	8,896	—	—	P/L	15.00
	1843	7,920	—	—	P/L	15.00
	1844	7,920	—	—	P/L	15.00
	1845	7,920	—	—	P/L	15.00
	1846	7,920	—	—	P/L	15.00
	1847	7,920	—	—	P/L	15.00
	1848	7,920	—	—	P/L	15.00
	1849	7,920	—	—	P/L	15.00
	1850	7,920	—	—	P/L	15.00
	1851	7,128	—	—	P/L	15.00
	1852	7,920	—	—	P/L	15.00
	1853	7,920	—	—	P/L	15.00
	1854	7,920	—	—	P/L	15.00
	1855	7,920	—	—	P/L	15.00
	1856	7,920	—	—	P/L	15.00
	1857	7,920	—	—	P/L	15.00
	1858	7,920	—	—	P/L	15.00
	1859	7,920	—	—	P/L	15.00
	1860	7,920	—	—	P/L	15.00
	1861	7,920	—	—	P/L	15.00
	1862	7,920	—	—	P/L	15.00
	1863	7,920	—	—	P/L	15.00
	1864	7,920	—	—	P/L	15.00
	1865	7,920	—	—	P/L	15.00
	1866	7,920	—	—	P/L	15.00
	1867	7,920	—	—	P/L	15.00
	1868	7,920	—	—	P/L	15.00
	1869	7,920	—	—	P/L	15.00
	1870	9,002	—	—	P/L	15.00
	1871	9,286	—	—	P/L	15.00
	1872	8,956	—	—	P/L	15.00
	1873	7,932	—	—	P/L	15.00
	1874	8,741	—	—	P/L	15.00
	1875	8,459	—	—	P/L	15.00
	1876	.010	—	—	P/L	15.00
	1877	8,936	—	—	P/L	15.00
	1878	9,903	—	—	P/L	15.00
	1879	.011	—	—	P/L	15.00
	1880	.011	—	—	P/L	15.00
	1881	9,017	—	—	P/L	15.00
	1882	.011	—	—	P/L	15.00
	1883	.012	—	—	P/L	15.00
	1884	.014	—	—	P/L	15.00
	1885	.012	—	—	P/L	15.00
	1886	.016	—	—	P/L	15.00
	1887	.018	—	—	P/L	20.00

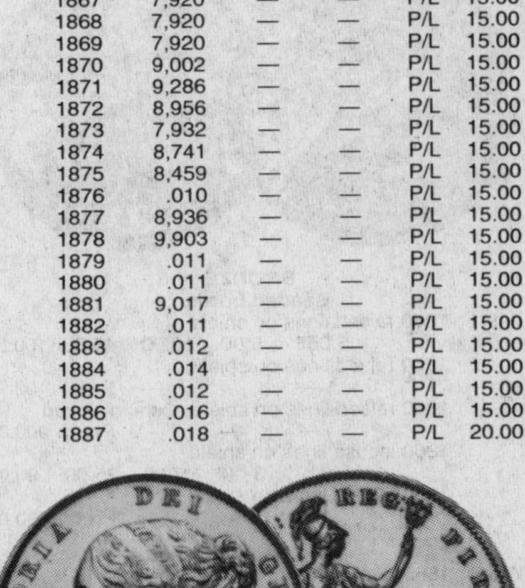

COPPER

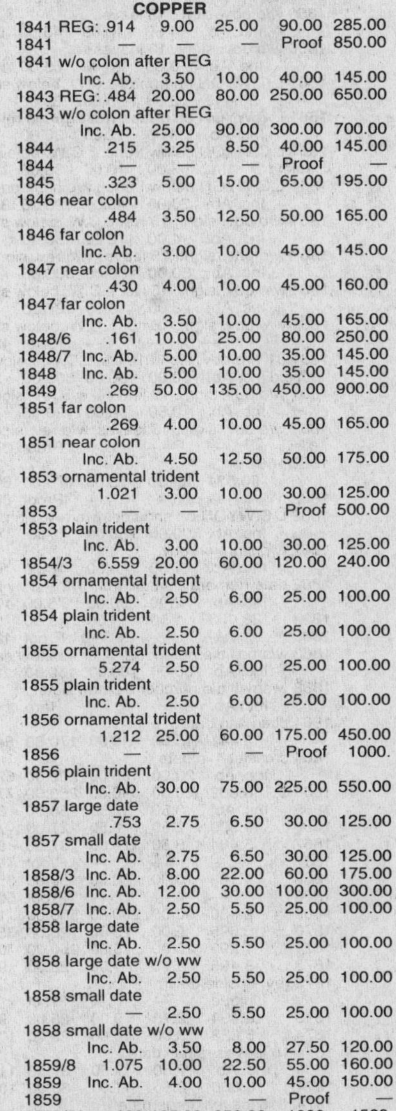

KM#	Date	Mintage	Fine	VF	XF	Unc
739	1841 REG:	.914	9.00	25.00	90.00	285.00
	1841	—	—	—	Proof	850.00
	1841 w/o colon after REG	Inc. Ab.	3.50	10.00	40.00	145.00
	1843 REG:	.484	20.00	80.00	250.00	650.00
	1843 w/o colon after REG	Inc. Ab.	25.00	90.00	300.00	700.00
	1844	.215	3.25	8.50	40.00	145.00
	1844	—	—	—	Proof	—
	1845	.323	5.00	15.00	65.00	195.00
	1846 near colon	.484	3.50	12.50	50.00	165.00
	1846 far colon	Inc. Ab.	3.00	10.00	45.00	145.00
	1847 near colon	.430	4.00	10.00	45.00	160.00
	1847 far colon	Inc. Ab.	3.50	10.00	45.00	165.00
	1848/6	.161	10.00	25.00	80.00	250.00
	1848/7	Inc. Ab.	5.00	10.00	35.00	145.00
	1848	Inc. Ab.	5.00	10.00	35.00	145.00
	1849	.269	50.00	135.00	450.00	900.00
	1851 far colon	.269	4.00	10.00	45.00	165.00
	1851 near colon	Inc. Ab.	4.50	12.50	50.00	175.00
	1853 ornamental trident	1.021	3.00	10.00	30.00	125.00
	1853	—	—	—	Proof	500.00
	1853 plain trident	Inc. Ab.	3.00	10.00	30.00	125.00
	1854/3	6.559	20.00	60.00	120.00	240.00
	1854 ornamental trident	Inc. Ab.	2.50	6.00	25.00	100.00
	1854 plain trident	Inc. Ab.	2.50	6.00	25.00	100.00
	1855 ornamental trident	5.274	2.50	6.00	25.00	100.00
	1855 plain trident	Inc. Ab.	2.50	6.00	25.00	100.00
	1856 ornamental trident	1.212	25.00	60.00	175.00	450.00
	1856	—	—	—	Proof	1000.
	1856 plain trident	Inc. Ab.	30.00	75.00	225.00	550.00
	1857 large date	.753	2.75	6.50	30.00	125.00
	1857 small date	Inc. Ab.	2.75	6.50	30.00	125.00
	1858/3	Inc. Ab.	8.00	22.00	60.00	175.00
	1858/6	Inc. Ab.	12.00	30.00	100.00	300.00
	1858/7	Inc. Ab.	2.50	5.50	25.00	100.00
	1858 large date	Inc. Ab.	2.50	5.50	25.00	100.00
	1858 large date w/o ww	Inc. Ab.	2.50	5.50	25.00	100.00
	1858 small date	—	2.50	5.50	25.00	100.00
	1858 small date w/o ww	Inc. Ab.	3.50	8.00	27.50	120.00
	1859/8	1.075	10.00	22.50	55.00	160.00
	1859	Inc. Ab.	4.00	10.00	45.00	150.00
	1859	—	—	—	Proof	—
	1860/59	.032	125.00	350.00	1000.	1500.

BRONZED COPPER

KM#	Date	Mintage	Fine	VF	XF	Unc
739a	1839	*300 pcs.	—	—	Proof	500.00
	1841	—	—	—	Proof	1000.
	1853	*10-15 pcs.	—	—	Proof	700.00

BRONZE

Beaded border.

KM#	Date	Mintage	Fine	VF	XF	Unc
749.1	1860 raised lines on shield	5.053	5.00	10.00	45.00	100.00
	1860 raised lines on shield	—	—	—	Proof	400.00
	1860 raised lines on shield, extra thick flan	—	—	—	Proof	900.00
	1860 incuse lines on shield	Inc. Ab.	3.00	7.00	35.00	90.00
	1860 incuse lines on shield	—	—	—	Proof	800.00

Toothed border.

KM#	Date	Mintage	Fine	VF	XF	Unc
749.2	1860 beaded border/toothed border	Inc. Ab.	55.00	145.00	630.00	2700.
	1860 toothed border/beaded border	Inc. Ab.	50.00	120.00	550.00	
	1860 L.C.W. below foot, L.C.WYON on shoulder	Inc. Ab.	15.00	45.00	100.00	250.00
	1860 L.C.W. below shield,L.C.WYON below shoulder	I.A.	3.00	7.50	30.00	80.00
	1860 L.C.WYON on shoulder,L.C.W. below shield	I.A.	3.00	7.50	30.00	100.00
	1860 L.C.WYON on shoulder,L.C.W. below shield	—	—	—	Proof	400.00
	1860 w/o obv. sign., 15 leaves	Inc. Ab.	4.50	10.00	45.00	100.00
	1860 w/o obv. sign., 16 leaves	Inc. Ab.	8.00	20.00	65.00	175.00
	1861 L.C.WYON on trunc.; L.C.W. below shield	36.449	2.00	5.00	25.00	75.00
	1861 L.C.WYON on trunc., w/o sign. on rev.	Inc. Ab.	3.00	12.00	30.00	80.00
	1861 L.C.WYON below trunc. L.C.W. below shield	I.A.	3.00	10.00	30.00	75.00
	1861 L.C.WYON below trunc., w/o sign. on rev.	Inc. Ab.	20.00	45.00	120.00	350.00
	1861 w/o obv. sign., 15 lvs. L.C.W. below shield	Inc. Ab.	4.00	12.00	30.00	75.00
	1861 w/o obv. sign., 15 leaves w/o rev. sign.	Inc. Ab.	50.00	150.00	300.00	1000.
	1861 w/o obv. sign., 16 lvs. L.C.W. below shield	Inc. Ab.	3.00	5.00	27.50	75.00
	1861 w/o obv. sign., 16 lvs. L.C.W. below shield	—	—	—	Proof	425.00
	1861/81 w/o obv. sign., 16 lvs. L.C.W. below shield	Inc. Ab.	50.00	150.00	300.00	1000.
	1861 w/o obv. sign., 16 leaves, w/o rev. sign.	Inc. Ab.	2.50	8.00	20.00	75.00
	1861 w/o obv. sign., 16 leaves, w/o rev. sign.	—	—	—	Proof	375.00
	1862/1662	50.534	22.50	75.00	175.00	600.00
	1862	—	—	—	Proof	800.00
	1862 L.C.WYON on shoulder w/o rev. sign.	Inc. Ab.	300.00	750.00	1750.	4000.
	1862 w/o sign. on obv.	Inc. Ab.	1.50	4.50	18.00	65.00
	1862 date numerals small, from 1/2 Penny Die	Inc. Ab.	12.00	30.00	75.00	175.00
	1863	28.063	1.50	4.50	18.00	55.00
	1863	—	—	—	Proof	425.00
	1863 w/small die number 2, 3, or 4 below date	Inc. Ab.	100.00	180.00	450.00	1200.
	1863 w/small die number 5 below date	Inc. Ab.	—	—	Rare	—
	1864 plain 4 in date	3.441	15.00	40.00	170.00	540.00
	1864 crosslet 4 in date	Inc. Ab.	20.00	65.00	200.00	625.00
	1865/3	8.602	30.00	90.00	250.00	775.00
	1865	Inc. Ab.	3.50	12.50	35.00	80.00
	1866	9.999	2.50	8.50	27.00	70.00
	1867	5.484	3.50	10.00	37.50	90.00
	1867	—	—	—	Proof	700.00
	1868	1.183	10.00	30.00	120.00	355.00
	1868	—	—	—	Proof	500.00
	1869	2.580	50.00	200.00	500.00	1350.
	1870	5.695	5.00	25.00	120.00	355.00
	1871	1.290	25.00	75.00	250.00	700.00
	1872	8.495	2.75	9.00	25.00	90.00
	1872 rev. upside down	Unique	—	—	Proof	—
	1873	8.494	2.75	9.00	25.00	90.00
	1874	5.622	3.00	10.00	25.00	100.00
	1874 16 leaves, small date	Inc. Ab.	7.50	17.50	37.50	110.00
	1874H	6.666	3.50	11.00	30.00	100.00
	1874H 16 leaves, large date	Inc. Ab.	3.00	7.50	35.00	100.00

Obv: Mature bust.

KM#	Date	Mintage	Fine	VF	XF	Unc
755	1874 17 leaves, thin ribbons	Inc. Ab.	3.00	10.00	30.00	100.00
	1874 17 leaves, thin ribbons, small date	Inc. Ab.	3.00	10.00	30.00	100.00
	1874 17 leaves, thick ribbons	Inc. Ab.	7.50	30.00	100.00	300.00
	1874 17 leaves, thick ribbons, small date	Inc. Ab.	3.00	10.00	30.00	100.00
	1874H 17 leaves, thin ribbons	Inc. Ab.	4.00	12.00	30.00	75.00
	1874H 17 leaves, thin ribbons, small date	Inc. Ab.	4.00	12.00	30.00	75.00
	1874H 17 leaves, thin ribbons, small date	—	—	—	Proof	300.00
	1874H 17 leaves, thin ribbons, large date	Inc. Ab.	15.00	50.00	250.00	700.00
	1875	10.691	3.00	9.00	22.50	65.00
	1875 small date	Inc. Ab.	3.00	9.00	22.50	65.00
	1875 large date	Inc. Ab.	3.00	9.00	22.50	65.00
	1875 large date, heavy planchet	Unique	—	—	Proof	—
	1875H small date	.753	150.00	300.00	900.00	2500.
	1875H large date	Inc. Ab.	25.00	90.00	250.00	650.00
	1875H large date	—	—	—	Proof	800.00
	1876H large date	11.075	3.00	8.50	17.50	50.00
	1876H large date	Inc. Ab.	—	—	Proof	500.00
	1876H small date	Inc. Ab.	3.00	8.50	17.50	50.00
	1877 small date	9.625	100.00	300.00	1000.	2000.
	1877 large date	Inc. Ab.	3.25	9.50	20.00	55.00
	1877 large date	—	—	—	Proof	500.00
	1878	2.764	4.00	12.00	30.00	65.00
	1878	—	—	—	Proof	500.00
	1879 large date; raised lines on wreath	7.666	15.00	40.00	125.00	250.00
	1879 large date; incuse lines in wreath	Inc. Ab.	2.50	8.50	18.00	55.00
	1879 large date; incuse lines in wreath	Unique	—	—	Proof	—
	1879 sm.dt.	I.A.	7.50	25.00	100.00	300.00
	1880	3.001	5.00	13.50	35.00	100.00
	1880	—	—	—	Proof	500.00
	1880 rock to left of lighthouse	Inc. Ab.	5.00	13.50	35.00	100.00
	1880 obv. 15 leaves as 1881	—	—	—	Proof	Rare
	1881	2.302	4.00	12.00	30.00	70.00
	1881	—	—	—	Proof	450.00
	1881 obv. as 1880; shield heraldically colored	I.A.	100.00	300.00	750.00	2250.
	1881 obv. as 1880; shield heraldically colored	I.A.	—	—	Proof	—
	1881 obv. and rev. as 1880	Inc. Ab.	6.00	18.00	50.00	130.00
	1881 shield heraldically colored	—	—	—	Proof	1100.
	1881H obv: 15 leaves in wreath	3.763	2.50	7.00	17.50	65.00
	1881H obv: 15 leaves in wreath	—	—	—	Proof	600.00
	1882H convex shield	7.526	2.75	10.00	50.00	100.00
	1882H flat shield	Inc. Ab.	2.75	8.00	20.00	65.00
	1882H	—	—	—	Proof	1000.
	1882	Inc. Ab.	75.00	225.00	725.00	1750.
	1883	6.237	2.00	6.50	17.50	70.00
	1883	—	—	—	Proof	450.00
	1884	11.703	1.50	5.00	15.00	55.00
	1884	—	—	—	Proof	500.00
	1885	7.146	1.50	5.00	15.00	55.00
	1885	—	—	—	Proof	500.00
	1886	6.088	1.25	4.00	12.50	50.00
	1886	—	—	—	Proof	700.00
	1887	5.315	1.25	4.00	15.00	50.00
	1888	5.125	1.25	4.00	15.00	50.00
	1889	12.560	1.25	4.50	15.00	55.00
	1889 14 leaves in wreath	Inc. Ab.	1.25	4.50	15.00	55.00
	1889 14 leaves in wreath	—	—	—	Proof	500.00
	1890	15.331	1.00	3.00	12.00	40.00
	1890	—	—	—	Proof	450.00
	1891	17.886	1.00	3.00	12.00	40.00
	1891	—	—	—	Proof	450.00
755	1892	10.502	1.00	3.00	12.00	45.00
	1892	—	—	—	Proof	450.00
	1893	8.162	1.00	3.00	12.00	45.00
	1893	—	—	—	Proof	500.00
	1894	3.883	3.00	8.00	20.00	65.00

.4713 g, .925 SILVER, .0140 oz ASW

KM#	Date	Mintage	Fine	VF	XF	Unc
770	1888	.014	—	—	P/L	15.00
	1889	.014	—	—	P/L	15.00
	1890	.013	—	—	P/L	15.00
	1891	.022	—	—	P/L	15.00
	1892	.016	—	—	P/L	15.00

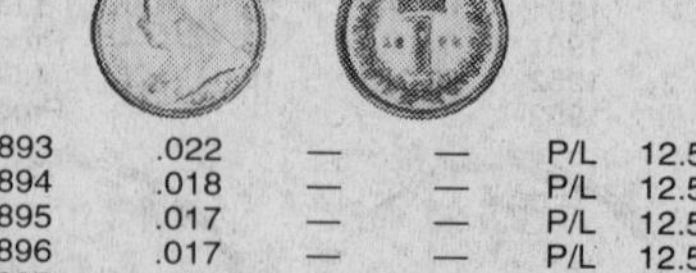

KM#	Date	Mintage	Fine	VF	XF	Unc
775	1893	.022	—	—	P/L	12.50
	1894	.018	—	—	P/L	12.50
	1895	.017	—	—	P/L	12.50
	1896	.017	—	—	P/L	12.50
	1897	.016	—	—	P/L	12.50
	1898	.017	—	—	P/L	12.50
	1899	.017	—	—	P/L	12.50
	1900	.017	—	—	P/L	12.50
	1901	.018	—	—	P/L	12.50

BRONZE

KM#	Date	Mintage	Fine	VF	XF	Unc
790	1895 P 2mm. from trident	5.396	15.00	40.00	120.00	275.00
	1895 P 2mm. from trident	Inc. Ab.	—	—	Proof	450.00
	1895 P 1mm. from trident	Inc. Ab.	.50	1.75	7.50	35.00
	1895 P 1mm. from trident	—	—	—	Proof	350.00
	1896	24.147	.40	1.25	4.50	30.00
	1896	—	—	—	Proof	325.00
	1897 normal sea level	20.757	.35	1.00	3.75	22.00
	1897 normal sea level	—	—	—	Proof	375.00
	1897 high sea level	Inc. Ab.	15.00	40.00	120.00	275.00
	1898	14.297	1.00	3.00	10.00	35.00
	1899	26.441	.40	1.50	5.25	22.00
	1900	31.778	.35	1.00	3.75	16.50
	1901	22.206	.30	.75	2.00	12.00
	1901	—	—	—	Proof	250.00

Rev: Low sea level.

KM#	Date	Mintage	Fine	VF	XF	Unc
794.1	1902	26.977	4.00	9.00	22.50	65.00

Rev: High sea level.

KM#	Date	Mintage	Fine	VF	XF	Unc
794.2	1902	Inc. Ab.	.60	2.00	4.50	15.00
	1903	21.415	.65	2.50	6.50	22.50
	1904	12.913	1.00	3.00	10.00	35.00
	1905	17.784	.70	2.50	9.00	30.00
	1906	37.990	.60	2.00	6.00	25.00
	1907	47.322	.60	2.00	7.00	25.00
	1908	31.506	.75	2.50	7.50	35.00
	1908	—	—	—	Proof	Rare
	1909	19.617	.65	2.25	7.00	35.00
	1910	29.549	.50	1.75	5.00	25.00

.4713 g, .925 SILVER, .0140 oz ASW

KM#	Date	Mintage	Fine	VF	XF	Unc
795	1902	.021	—	—	P/L	12.50
	1903	.017	—	—	P/L	12.50
	1904	.019	—	—	P/L	12.50
	1905	.018	—	—	P/L	12.50
	1906	.019	—	—	P/L	12.50
	1907	.018	—	—	P/L	12.50
	1908	.018	—	—	P/L	12.50
	1909	2,948	—	—	P/L	15.00
	1910	3,392	—	—	P/L	20.00

BRONZE

KM#	Date	Mintage	Fine	VF	XF	Unc
810	1911	23.079	.50	1.25	5.00	18.00
	1912	48.306	.35	1.00	5.00	18.00
	1912H	16.800	1.00	5.00	25.00	85.00
	1913	65.497	.40	1.25	8.00	35.00
	1914	50.821	.35	1.00	5.00	20.00
	1915	47.311	.50	1.25	6.00	22.00
	1916	86.411	.35	1.00	4.50	20.00
	1917	107.905	.35	1.00	4.50	20.00
	1918	84.227	.35	1.00	4.50	20.00
	1918H	2.573	2.00	20.00	100.00	200.00
	1918KN	I.A.	3.25	30.00	125.00	300.00
	1919	113.761	.35	1.00	4.50	22.00
	1919H	4.526	1.25	6.50	60.00	200.00
	1919KN	I.A.	5.00	35.00	150.00	425.00
	1920	124.693	.35	1.00	4.00	16.50
	1921	129.718	.30	.75	3.00	12.00
	1922	16.347	.75	2.50	10.00	25.00
	1926	4.499	1.50	5.00	15.00	35.00
	1926	—	—	—	Proof	800.00

.4713 g, .925 SILVER, .0140 oz ASW

KM#	Date	Mintage	Fine	VF	XF	Unc
811	1911	1,913	—	—	P/L	15.00
	1912	1,616	—	—	P/L	15.00
	1913	1,590	—	—	P/L	15.00
	1914	1,818	—	—	P/L	15.00
	1915	2,072	—	—	P/L	15.00
	1916	1,647	—	—	P/L	15.00
	1917	1,820	—	—	P/L	15.00
	1918	1,911	—	—	P/L	15.00
	1919	1,699	—	—	P/L	15.00
	1920	1,715	—	—	P/L	15.00

.4713 g, .500 SILVER, .0076 oz ASW

KM#	Date	Mintage	Fine	VF	XF	Unc
811a	1921	1,847	—	—	P/L	15.00
	1922	1,758	—	—	P/L	15.00
	1923	1,840	—	—	P/L	15.00
	1924	1,619	—	—	P/L	15.00
	1925	1,890	—	—	P/L	15.00
	1926	2,180	—	—	P/L	15.00
	1927	1,647	—	—	P/L	15.00

BRONZE

Obv: Modified head.

KM#	Date	Mintage	Fine	VF	XF	Unc
826	1926	Inc. Ab.	10.00	35.00	250.00	850.00
	1926	—	—	—	Proof	—
	1927	60.990	.35	1.00	4.50	10.00
	1927	—	—	—	Proof	600.00

Obv: Smaller head.

KM#	Date	Mintage	Fine	VF	XF	Unc
838	1928	50.178	.25	.50	2.25	7.00
	1928	—	—	—	Proof	250.00
	1929	49.133	.25	.50	2.25	8.00
	1929	—	—	—	Proof	250.00
	1930	29.098	.35	1.00	4.50	14.00
	1930	—	—	—	Proof	250.00
	1931	19.843	.35	1.00	4.50	14.00
	1931	—	—	—	Proof	250.00
	1932	8.278	1.50	3.50	15.00	40.00
	1932	—	—	—	Proof	250.00
	1933	—	—	—	Rare	—
	1934	13.966	.50	2.00	9.00	27.50
	1934	—	—	—	Proof	250.00
	1935	56.070	.25	.50	1.75	4.50

KM#	Date	Mintage	Fine	VF	XF	Unc
838	1935	—	—	—	Proof	225.00
	1936	154.296	.20	.35	1.00	3.50
	1936	—	—	—	Proof	225.00

.4713 g, .500 SILVER, .0076 oz ASW

Obv: Modified effigy.

KM#	Date	Mintage	Fine	VF	XF	Unc
839	1928	1,846	—	—	P/L	15.00
	1929	1,837	—	—	P/L	15.00
	1930	1,724	—	—	P/L	15.00
	1931	1,759	—	—	P/L	15.00
	1932	1,835	—	—	P/L	15.00
	1933	1,872	—	—	P/L	15.00
	1934	1,919	—	—	P/L	15.00
	1935	1,975	—	—	P/L	15.00
	1936	1,329	—	—	P/L	15.00

BRONZE

KM#	Date	Mintage	Fine	VF	XF	Unc
845	1937	88.896	.20	.35	1.25	2.25
	1937	.026	—	—	Proof	9.00
	1938	121.560	.20	.35	1.25	2.25
	1938	—	—	—	Proof	225.00
	1939	55.560	.20	.35	1.25	3.50
	1939	—	—	—	Proof	225.00
	1940	42.284	.25	.50	2.25	8.00
	1940	—	—	—	Proof	—
	1944	42.600	.25	.50	2.25	7.00
	1944	—	—	—	Proof	—
	1945	79.531	.20	.35	1.50	5.00
	1945	—	—	—	Proof	—
	1946	66.856	.15	.25	.75	3.00
	1946	—	—	—	Proof	—
	1947	52.220	.15	.25	.75	2.25
	1947	—	—	—	Proof	—
	1948	63.961	.15	.25	.75	3.00
	1948	—	—	—	Proof	—

.4713 g, .500 SILVER, .0076 oz ASW

KM#	Date	Mintage	Fine	VF	XF	Unc
846	1937	1,329	—	—	P/L	15.00
	1938	1,275	—	—	P/L	15.00
	1939	1,253	—	—	P/L	15.00
	1940	1,375	—	—	P/L	15.00
	1941	1,255	—	—	P/L	15.00
	1942	1,243	—	—	P/L	15.00
	1943	1,347	—	—	P/L	15.00
	1944	1,259	—	—	P/L	15.00
	1945	1,367	—	—	P/L	15.00
	1946	1,479	—	—	P/L	15.00

.4713 g, .925 SILVER, .0140 oz ASW

KM#	Date	Mintage	Fine	VF	XF	Unc
846a	1947	1,387	—	—	P/L	15.00
	1948	1,397	—	—	P/L	15.00

BRONZE

Obv. leg: W/o IND IMP.

KM#	Date	Mintage	Fine	VF	XF	Unc
869	1949	14.324	.15	.25	.75	3.00
	1949	—	—	—	Proof	—
	1950	.240	2.50	8.00	15.00	30.00
	1950	.018	—	—	Proof	30.00
	1951	.120	3.50	9.00	17.50	32.50
	1951	.020	—	—	Proof	30.00

.4713 g, .925 SILVER, .0140 oz ASW

KM#	Date	Mintage	Fine	VF	XF	Unc
870	1949	1,407	—	—	P/L	15.00
	1950	1,527	—	—	P/L	15.00
	1951	1,480	—	—	P/L	15.00
	1952	1,024	—	—	P/L	15.00

BRONZE

KM#	Date	Mintage	Fine	VF	XF	Unc
883	1953	1.308	.75	1.50	2.50	4.50
	1953	.040	—	—	Proof	9.00

.4713 g, .925 SILVER, .0140 oz ASW

KM#	Date	Mintage	Fine	VF	XF	Unc
884	1953	1,050	—	—	P/L	95.00

BRONZE

Obv. leg: W/o BRITT OMN.

KM#	Date	Mintage	Fine	VF	XF	Unc
897	1954	1 known	—	—	—	—
	1961	48.313	—	.10	.15	.80
	1961	—	—	—	Proof	—
	1962	143.309	—	—	.10	.15
	1962	—	—	—	Proof	—
	1963	125.236	—	—	.10	.15
	1963	—	—	—	Proof	—
	1964	153.294	—	—	—	.10
	1964	—	—	—	Proof	—
	1965	121.310	—	—	—	.10
	1966	165.739	—	—	—	.10
	1967	654.564	—	—	—	.10
	1970	.750	—	—	Proof	2.50

.4713 g, .925 SILVER, .0140 oz ASW

KM#	Date	Mintage	Fine	VF	XF	Unc
898	1954	1,088	—	—	P/L	15.00
	1955	1,036	—	—	P/L	15.00
	1956	1,100	—	—	P/L	15.00
	1957	1,168	—	—	P/L	15.00
	1958	1,112	—	—	P/L	15.00
	1959	1,118	—	—	P/L	15.00
	1960	1,124	—	—	P/L	15.00
	1961	1,200	—	—	P/L	15.00
	1962	1,127	—	—	P/L	15.00
	1963	1,133	—	—	P/L	15.00
	1964	1,215	—	—	P/L	15.00
	1965	1,143	—	—	P/L	15.00
	1966	1,206	—	—	P/L	15.00
	1967	1,068	—	—	P/L	15.00
	1968	964 pcs.	—	—	P/L	15.00
	1969	1,002	—	—	P/L	15.00
	1970	980 pcs.	—	—	P/L	15.00
	1971	1,108	—	—	P/L	15.00
	1972	1,026	—	—	P/L	15.00
	1973	1,004	—	—	P/L	15.00
	1974	1,138	—	—	P/L	15.00
	1975	1,050	—	—	P/L	15.00
	1976	1,158	—	—	P/L	15.00
	1977	1,240	—	—	P/L	17.50
	1978	1,178	—	—	P/L	17.50
	1979	1,188	—	—	P/L	17.50
	1980	1,198	—	—	P/L	17.50
	1981	1,288	—	—	P/L	17.50
	1982	1,218	—	—	P/L	17.50
	1983	1,228	—	—	P/L	17.50
	1984	1,354	—	—	P/L	17.50
	1985	1,248	—	—	P/L	17.50
	1986	1,378	—	—	P/L	17.50
	1987	1,512	—	—	P/L	17.50
	1988	1,402	—	—	P/L	17.50
	1989	1,353	—	—	P/L	17.50
	1990	1,523	—	—	P/L	17.50
	1991	1,514	—	—	P/L	17.50
	1992	—	—	—	P/L	17.50
	1993	—	—	—	P/L	17.50
	1994	—	—	—	P/L	17.50

1-1/2 PENCE

.7069 g, .925 SILVER, .0210 oz ASW

KM#	Date	Mintage	Fine	VF	XF	Unc
719	1834	.800	2.75	6.25	22.00	60.00
	1835/4	.634	12.00	30.00	45.00	150.00
	1835	Inc. Ab.	2.75	6.25	22.00	60.00
	1836	.158	2.75	6.25	22.00	60.00
	1837	.031	12.00	25.00	60.00	175.00

KM#	Date	Mintage	Fine	VF	XF	Unc
728	1838	.539	2.75	6.00	15.00	40.00
	1839	.760	2.50	6.00	17.50	40.00
	1840	.095	6.00	15.00	30.00	70.00
	1841	.158	3.00	7.00	20.00	40.00
	1842	1.869	3.00	7.00	20.00	40.00

KM#	Date	Mintage	Fine	VF	XF	Unc
728	1843/34	.475	8.00	20.00	35.00	90.00
	1843	Inc. Ab.	2.00	5.00	15.00	35.00
	1860	.160	3.50	10.00	25.00	50.00
	1862	.256	3.50	10.00	25.00	50.00
	1870	—	—	—	Proof	900.00

***NOTE:** Although the design of the above series is of the homeland type, the issues were struck for Ceylon and Jamaica.

2 PENCE

.9426 g, .925 SILVER, .0280 oz ASW

KM#	Date	Mintage	Fine	VF	XF	Unc
669	1817	—	6.00	11.00	20.00	45.00
	1817	2,376	—	—	P/L	30.00
	1818	—	6.00	11.00	20.00	45.00
	1818	2,376	—	—	P/L	30.00
	1820	—	6.00	11.00	20.00	45.00
	1820	1,584	—	—	P/L	30.00
684	1822	5,940	—	—	P/L	30.00
	1823	3,960	—	—	P/L	35.00
	1824	3,168	—	—	P/L	40.00
	1825	3,960	—	—	P/L	35.00
	1826	3,960	—	—	P/L	35.00
	1827	3,960	—	—	P/L	35.00
	1828	3,960	—	—	P/L	35.00
	1829	3,960	—	—	P/L	35.00
	1830	3,960	—	—	P/L	35.00
709	1831	4,752	—	—	P/L	22.50
	1832	3,564	—	—	P/L	22.50
	1833	3,564	—	—	P/L	22.50
	1834	3,564	—	—	P/L	22.50
	1835	3,564	—	—	P/L	22.50
	1836	3,564	—	—	P/L	22.50
	1837	3,564	—	—	P/L	22.50
729	1838	*1.045	2.00	4.00	8.00	15.00
	1838	4,488	—	—	P/L	15.00
	1839	4,488	—	—	P/L	15.00
	1840	4,488	—	—	P/L	15.00
	1841	3,960	—	—	P/L	15.00
	1842	4,488	—	—	P/L	15.00
	1843	*.903	2.00	4.00	8.00	15.00
	1843	4,752	—	—	P/L	15.00
	1844	4,752	—	—	P/L	15.00
	1845	4,752	—	—	P/L	15.00
	1846	4,752	—	—	P/L	15.00
	1847	4,752	—	—	P/L	15.00
	1848	*.261	2.00	4.00	8.00	15.00
	1848	4,752	—	—	P/L	15.00
	1849	4,752	—	—	P/L	15.00
	1850	4,752	—	—	P/L	15.00
	1851	4,752	—	—	P/L	15.00
	1852	4,752	—	—	P/L	15.00
	1853	4,752	—	—	P/L	15.00
	1854	4,752	—	—	P/L	15.00
	1855	4,752	—	—	P/L	15.00
	1856	4,752	—	—	P/L	15.00
	1857	4,752	—	—	P/L	15.00
	1858	4,752	—	—	P/L	15.00
	1859	4,752	—	—	P/L	15.00
	1860	4,752	—	—	P/L	15.00
	1861	4,752	—	—	P/L	15.00
	1862	4,752	—	—	P/L	15.00
	1863	4,752	—	—	P/L	15.00
	1864	4,752	—	—	P/L	15.00
	1865	4,752	—	—	P/L	15.00
	1866	4,752	—	—	P/L	15.00
	1867	4,752	—	—	P/L	15.00
	1868	4,752	—	—	P/L	15.00
	1869	4,752	—	—	P/L	15.00
	1870	5,347	—	—	P/L	15.00
	1871	4,753	—	—	P/L	15.00
	1872	4,719	—	—	P/L	15.00
	1873	4,756	—	—	P/L	15.00
	1874	5,578	—	—	P/L	15.00
	1875	5,745	—	—	P/L	15.00
	1876	6,655	—	—	P/L	15.00
	1877	7,189	—	—	P/L	15.00
	1878	6,709	—	—	P/L	15.00
	1879	6,925	—	—	P/L	15.00
	1880	6,247	—	—	P/L	15.00
	1881	6,001	—	—	P/L	15.00
	1882	7,264	—	—	P/L	15.00

KM#	Date	Mintage	Fine	VF	XF	Unc
729	1883	7,232	—	—	P/L	15.00
	1884	6,042	—	—	P/L	15.00
	1885	5,958	—	—	P/L	15.00
	1886	9,167	—	—	P/L	15.00
	1887	8,296	—	—	P/L	20.00

***NOTE:** Struck for use in British Guyana and the West Indies. Other dates included in Maundy sets.

KM#	Date	Mintage	Fine	VF	XF	Unc
771	1888	9,528	—	—	P/L	15.00
	1889	6,727	—	—	P/L	15.00
	1890	8,613	—	—	P/L	15.00
	1891	.010	—	—	P/L	15.00
	1892	.012	—	—	P/L	15.00
776	1893	.014	—	—	P/L	12.50
	1894	.012	—	—	P/L	12.50
	1895	.011	—	—	P/L	12.50
	1896	.011	—	—	P/L	12.50
	1897	.011	—	—	P/L	12.50
	1898	.012	—	—	P/L	12.50
	1899	.015	—	—	P/L	12.50
	1900	.011	—	—	P/L	12.50
	1901	.014	—	—	P/L	12.50
796	1902	.014	—	—	P/L	12.50
	1903	.013	—	—	P/L	12.50
	1904	.014	—	—	P/L	12.50
	1905	.011	—	—	P/L	12.50
	1906	.011	—	—	P/L	12.50
	1907	8,760	—	—	P/L	12.50
	1908	.015	—	—	P/L	12.50
	1909	2,695	—	—	P/L	15.00
	1910	2,998	—	—	P/L	20.00
812	1911	1,635	—	—	P/L	17.50
	1912	1,678	—	—	P/L	17.50
	1913	1,880	—	—	P/L	17.50
	1914	1,659	—	—	P/L	17.50
	1915	1,465	—	—	P/L	17.50
	1916	1,509	—	—	P/L	17.50
	1917	1,506	—	—	P/L	17.50
	1918	1,547	—	—	P/L	17.50
	1919	1,567	—	—	P/L	17.50
	1920	1,630	—	—	P/L	17.50

.9426 g, .500 SILVER, .0152 oz ASW

KM#	Date	Mintage	Fine	VF	XF	Unc
812a	1921	1,794	—	—	P/L	20.00
	1922	3,074	—	—	P/L	20.00
	1923	1,527	—	—	P/L	20.00
	1924	1,602	—	—	P/L	20.00
	1925	1,670	—	—	P/L	20.00
	1926	1,902	—	—	P/L	20.00
	1927	1,766	—	—	P/L	20.00

Obv: Modified effigy.

KM#	Date	Mintage	Fine	VF	XF	Unc
840	1928	1,706	—	—	P/L	17.50
	1929	1,862	—	—	P/L	17.50
	1930	1,901	—	—	P/L	17.50
	1931	1,897	—	—	P/L	17.50
	1932	1,960	—	—	P/L	17.50
	1933	2,066	—	—	P/L	17.50
	1934	1,927	—	—	P/L	17.50
	1935	1,928	—	—	P/L	17.50
	1936	1,365	—	—	P/L	20.00
847	1937	1,472	—	—	P/L	17.50
	1938	1,374	—	—	P/L	17.50
	1939	1,436	—	—	P/L	17.50
	1940	1,277	—	—	P/L	17.50
	1941	1,345	—	—	P/L	17.50
	1942	1,231	—	—	P/L	17.50
	1943	1,239	—	—	P/L	17.50
	1944	1,345	—	—	P/L	17.50
	1945	1,355	—	—	P/L	17.50
	1946	1,365	—	—	P/L	17.50

.9426 g, .925 SILVER, .0280 oz ASW

KM#	Date	Mintage	Fine	VF	XF	Unc
847a	1947	1,479	—	—	P/L	17.50
	1948	1,385	—	—	P/L	17.50

Obv. leg: W/o IND IMP.

KM#	Date	Mintage	Fine	VF	XF	Unc
871	1949	1,395	—	—	P/L	17.50
	1950	1,405	—	—	P/L	17.50
	1951	1,580	—	—	P/L	17.50
	1952	1,064	—	—	P/L	17.50
885	1953	1,025	—	—	P/L	85.00

Obv. leg: W/o BRITT OMN.

KM#	Date	Mintage	Fine	VF	XF	Unc
899	1954	1,020	—	—	P/L	20.00
	1955	1,082	—	—	P/L	20.00
	1956	1,088	—	—	P/L	20.00
	1957	1,094	—	—	P/L	20.00
	1958	1,164	—	—	P/L	20.00
	1959	1,106	—	—	P/L	20.00
	1960	1,112	—	—	P/L	20.00
	1961	1,118	—	—	P/L	20.00
	1962	1,197	—	—	P/L	20.00
	1963	1,131	—	—	P/L	20.00
	1964	1,137	—	—	P/L	20.00
	1965	1,221	—	—	P/L	20.00
	1966	1,206	—	—	P/L	20.00
	1967	986 pcs.	—	—	P/L	20.00
	1968	1,048	—	—	P/L	20.00
	1969	1,002	—	—	P/L	20.00
	1970	980 pcs.	—	—	P/L	20.00
	1971	1,018	—	—	P/L	20.00
	1972	1,026	—	—	P/L	20.00
	1973	1,004	—	—	P/L	20.00
	1974	1,042	—	—	P/L	20.00
	1975	1,148	—	—	P/L	20.00
	1976	1,158	—	—	P/L	20.00
	1977	1,138	—	—	P/L	22.00
	1978	1,282	—	—	P/L	22.00
	1979	1,188	—	—	P/L	22.00
	1980	1,198	—	—	P/L	22.00
	1981	1,178	—	—	P/L	22.00
	1982	1,330	—	—	P/L	22.00
	1983	1,228	—	—	P/L	22.00
	1984	1,238	—	—	P/L	22.00
	1985	1,366	—	—	P/L	22.00
	1986	1,378	—	—	P/L	22.00
	1987	1,390	—	—	P/L	22.00
	1988	1,526	—	—	P/L	22.00
	1989	1,353	—	—	P/L	22.00
	1990	1,523	—	—	P/L	22.00
	1991	1,384	—	—	P/L	22.00
	1992	—	—	—	P/L	22.00
	1993	—	—	—	P/L	22.00
	1994	—	—	—	P/L	22.00

3 PENCE

1.4138 g, .925 SILVER, .0420 oz ASW
Obv: George III bust right. Rev: Value.

KM#	Date	Mintage	Fine	VF	XF	Unc
670	1817	—	7.00	15.00	30.00	70.00
	1817	1,584	—	—	P/L	70.00
	1818	—	7.00	15.00	30.00	70.00
	1818	1,584	—	—	P/L	70.00
	1820	—	7.00	15.00	30.00	70.00
	1820	1,320	—	—	P/L	70.00

Obv: Small head.

KM#	Date	Mintage	Fine	VF	XF	Unc
685.1	1822	3,960	—	—	P/L	80.00
	1822	—	—	—	Proof	—

Obv: Large head.

KM#	Date	Mintage	Fine	VF	XF	Unc
685.2	1823	2,640	—	—	P/L	55.00
	1824	2,112	—	—	P/L	65.00
	1825	3,432	—	—	P/L	55.00
	1826	3,432	—	—	P/L	55.00
	1827	3,168	—	—	P/L	55.00
	1828	3,168	—	—	P/L	55.00
	1829	3,168	—	—	P/L	55.00
	1830	3,168	—	—	P/L	55.00
710	1831	3,960	—	—	P/L	80.00
	1832	2,904	—	—	P/L	70.00
	1833	2,904	—	—	P/L	70.00
	1834	.400	3.00	8.00	25.00	110.00
	1834	2,904	—	—	P/L	70.00
	1835	.491	3.00	8.00	25.00	110.00
	1835	2,904	—	—	P/L	70.00
	1836	.411	3.00	8.00	25.00	90.00
	1836	2,904	—	—	P/L	70.00

KM#	Date	Mintage	Fine	VF	XF	Unc
710	1837	.430	5.00	12.00	30.00	120.00
	1837	2,904	—	—	P/L	70.00
730	1838	1.200	2.50	6.00	30.00	72.00
	1838	4,312	—	—	P/L	40.00
	1839	.570	6.00	12.00	45.00	110.00
	1839	4,356	—	—	P/L	40.00
	1840	.630	2.50	7.50	36.00	80.00
	1840	4,356	—	—	P/L	40.00
	1841	.440	3.00	7.50	36.00	80.00
	1841	2,904	—	—	P/L	45.00
	1842	—	4.00	10.00	40.00	80.00
	1842	4,356	—	—	P/L	45.00
	1843	2.030	2.50	7.50	35.00	75.00
	1843	4,488	—	—	P/L	45.00
	1844	1.050	2.50	9.00	45.00	90.00
	1844	4,488	—	—	P/L	45.00
	1845	1.319	2.50	5.00	20.00	50.00
	1845	4,488	—	—	P/L	45.00
	1846	.052	5.00	12.50	45.00	95.00
	1846	4,488	—	—	P/L	45.00
	1847	4,488	—	—	P/L	45.00
	1848	4,488	—	—	P/L	45.00
	1849	.131	10.00	20.00	50.00	100.00
	1849	4,488	—	—	P/L	45.00
	1850	.955	2.50	5.00	30.00	60.00
	1850	4,488	—	—	P/L	45.00
	1851	.484	3.00	6.00	30.00	60.00
	1851	4,488	—	—	P/L	45.00
	1852	4,488	—	—	P/L	45.00
	1853	.036	7.50	15.00	55.00	120.00
	1853	4,488	—	—	P/L	45.00
	1854	1.472	2.50	5.00	30.00	60.00
	1854	4,488	—	—	P/L	45.00
	1855	.388	3.00	8.00	32.00	65.00
	1855	4,488	—	—	P/L	45.00
	1856	1.018	2.50	4.50	25.00	50.00
	1856	4,488	—	—	P/L	45.00
	1857	1.767	2.75	7.50	30.00	60.00
	1857	4,488	—	—	P/L	45.00
	1858	1.446	2.50	5.00	25.00	55.00
	1858	4,488	—	—	P/L	45.00
	1859	3.584	2.50	5.00	20.00	40.00
	1859	4,488	—	—	P/L	45.00
	1860	3.410	2.50	5.00	20.00	40.00
	1860	4,488	—	—	P/L	45.00
	1861	3.299	2.50	5.00	20.00	40.00
	1861	4,488	—	—	P/L	45.00
	1862	1.161	2.50	5.00	25.00	50.00
	1862	4,488	—	—	P/L	45.00
	1863	.954	4.00	9.00	40.00	75.00
	1863	4,488	—	—	P/L	45.00
	1864	1.335	2.50	5.00	30.00	60.00
	1864	4,488	—	—	P/L	45.00
	1865	1.747	3.00	9.00	40.00	75.00
	1865	4,488	—	—	P/L	45.00
	1866	1.905	2.50	5.00	30.00	65.00
	1866	4,488	—	—	P/L	45.00
	1867	.717	3.00	6.00	40.00	75.00
	1867	4,488	—	—	P/L	45.00
	1868	1.462	2.50	5.00	30.00	65.00
	1868	4,488	—	—	P/L	45.00
	1868 (error) RRITANIAR					
		Inc. Ab.	22.50	55.00	225.00	450.00
	1869	—	40.00	100.00	225.00	450.00
	1869	4,488	—	—	P/L	45.00
	1870	1.288	2.50	4.50	25.00	50.00
	1870	4,488	—	—	P/L	45.00
	1871	1.004	2.50	4.50	25.00	50.00
	1871	4,488	—	—	P/L	45.00
	1872	1.298	1.75	4.00	22.50	45.00
	1872	4,488	—	—	P/L	45.00
	1873	4.060	1.60	3.25	20.00	40.00
	1873	4,488	—	—	P/L	45.00
	1874	4.432	1.60	3.25	20.00	40.00
	1874	4,488	—	—	P/L	45.00
	1875	3.311	1.60	3.25	18.00	35.00
	1875	4,488	—	—	P/L	45.00
	1876	1.839	1.60	3.25	18.00	35.00
	1876	4,488	—	—	P/L	45.00
	1877	2.627	1.60	3.25	18.00	35.00
	1877	4,488	—	—	P/L	45.00
	1878	2.424	1.60	3.25	18.00	35.00
	1878	4,488	—	—	P/L	45.00
	1879	3.145	1.60	3.25	18.00	35.00
	1879	4,488	—	—	P/L	45.00
	1879	—	—	—	Proof	150.00
	1880	1.615	1.50	3.00	18.00	35.00
	1880	4,488	—	—	P/L	45.00
	1881	3.253	1.40	2.75	15.00	30.00
	1881	4,488	—	—	P/L	45.00
	1882	.447	3.00	6.00	22.50	50.00
	1882	4,488	—	—	P/L	45.00
	1883	4.374	1.45	2.75	15.00	30.00
	1883	4,488	—	—	P/L	45.00
	1884	3.327	1.45	2.75	15.00	30.00
	1884	4,488	—	—	P/L	45.00
	1885	5.188	1.45	2.75	15.00	30.00
	1885	4,488	—	—	P/L	45.00
	1886	6.157	1.45	2.75	15.00	30.00
	1886	4,488	—	—	P/L	45.00
	1887	2.785	3.50	8.50	25.00	55.00
	1887	4,488	—	—	P/L	45.00
	1887	—	—	—	Proof	100.00

KM#	Date	Mintage	Fine	VF	XF	Unc
758	1887	Inc. Ab.	1.25	2.25	4.50	12.00
	1887	Inc. Ab.	—	—	Proof	70.00
	1888	.523	3.00	6.00	15.00	30.00
	1888	4,488	—	—	P/L	40.00
	1889	4.591	1.50	2.75	12.50	25.00
	1889	4,488	—	—	P/L	40.00
	1890	4.470	1.50	2.75	12.50	25.00
	1890	4,488	—	—	P/L	40.00
	1891	6.328	1.50	2.75	12.50	25.00
	1891	4,488	—	—	P/L	40.00
	1892	2.583	3.00	6.00	15.00	27.50
	1892	4,488	—	—	P/L	40.00
	1893 open 3					
		3.076	20.00	40.00	120.00	225.00
	1893 closed 3					
		Inc. Ab.	18.00	35.00	95.00	200.00
777	1893	Inc. Ab.	1.00	2.00	5.00	20.00
	1893	8,976	—	—	P/L	30.00
	1893	1,312	—	—	Proof	75.00
	1894	1.618	1.00	2.00	8.00	25.00
	1894	8,976	—	—	P/L	30.00
	1895	4.798	.75	2.00	8.00	25.00
	1895	8,976	—	—	P/L	30.00
	1896	4.607	.75	1.75	7.00	20.00
	1896	8,976	—	—	P/L	30.00
	1897	4.550	.75	1.75	5.00	20.00
	1897	8,976	—	—	P/L	30.00
	1898	4.576	.75	1.75	5.00	20.00
	1898	8,976	—	—	P/L	30.00
	1899	6.253	.75	1.75	5.00	20.00
	1899	8,976	—	—	P/L	30.00
	1900	10.661	.75	1.50	4.50	20.00
	1900	8,976	—	—	P/L	30.00
	1901	6.100	.75	1.50	4.50	20.00
	1901	8,976	—	—	P/L	30.00
797.1	1902	8.287	1.00	2.00	6.00	15.00
	1902	8,976	—	—	P/L	22.50
	1902	.015	—	—	Proof	20.00
	1903	5.235	1.00	3.00	10.00	30.00
	1903	8,976	—	—	P/L	22.50
	1904 type of 1903 w/small ball on 3					
		3.630	6.00	12.50	35.00	70.00
	1904	8,876	—	—	P/L	22.50
797.2	1904 type of 1905 w/large ball on 3					
		Inc. Ab.	4.50	10.00	30.00	60.00
	1905	3.563	4.50	9.00	25.00	50.00
	1905	8,976	—	—	P/L	22.50
	1906	3.174	4.00	8.00	20.00	40.00
	1906	8,800	—	—	P/L	22.50
	1907	4.841	.75	2.50	9.00	25.00
	1907	.011	—	—	P/L	22.50
	1908	8.176	.75	2.25	9.00	30.00
	1908	8,760	—	—	P/L	22.50
	1909	4.055	2.00	5.00	10.00	30.00
	1909	1,983	—	—	P/L	22.50
	1910	4.565	.75	2.00	7.50	25.00
	1910	1,140	—	—	P/L	25.00
813	1911	5.843	1.00	2.00	4.00	16.50
	1911	1,991	—	—	P/L	27.50
	1911	6,007	—	—	Proof	35.00
	1912	8.934	.60	1.00	4.00	16.50
	1912	1,246	—	—	P/L	27.50
	1913	7.144	.60	1.00	5.00	18.00
	1913	1,228	—	—	P/L	27.50
	1914	6.735	.50	.85	3.50	14.00
	1914	982 pcs.	—	—	P/L	27.50
	1915	5.452	1.00	2.00	4.00	16.50
	1915	1,293	—	—	P/L	27.50
	1916	18.556	.50	.75	3.00	10.00
	1916	1,128	—	—	P/L	27.50
	1917	21.664	.50	.75	3.00	10.00
	1917	1,237	—	—	P/L	27.50
	1918	20.632	.50	.75	3.00	10.00

KM#	Date	Mintage	Fine	VF	XF	Unc
813	1918	1,375	—	—	P/L	27.50
	1919	16.846	.50	.75	3.00	10.00
	1919	1,258	—	—	P/L	27.50
	1920	16.705	.50	.75	3.50	10.00
	1920	1,399	—	—	P/L	27.50

1.4138 g, .500 SILVER, .0227 oz ASW

KM#	Date	Mintage	Fine	VF	XF	Unc
813a	1920	Inc. Ab.	BV	.65	3.00	10.00
	1921	8.751	BV	1.50	3.00	14.00
	1921	1,386	—	—	P/L	25.00
	1922	7.981	BV	1.50	3.00	14.00
	1922	1,373	—	—	P/L	25.00
	1923	1,430	—	—	P/L	25.00
	1924	1,515	—	—	P/L	25.00
	1925	3.733	1.25	2.50	9.00	20.00
	1925	1,438	—	—	P/L	25.00
	1926	4.109	2.50	6.00	16.50	35.00
	1926	1,504	—	—	P/L	25.00
	1927	1,690	—	—	P/L	25.00

Obv: Modified effigy.

KM#	Date	Mintage	Fine	VF	XF	Unc
827	1926	Inc. Ab.	1.00	2.50	10.00	25.00
	1928	1,835	—	—	P/L	22.50
	1929	1,761	—	—	P/L	22.50
	1930	1,948	—	—	P/L	22.50
	1931	1,818	—	—	P/L	22.50
	1932	2,042	—	—	P/L	22.50
	1933	1,920	—	—	P/L	22.50
	1934	1,887	—	—	P/L	22.50
	1935	2,007	—	—	P/L	22.50
	1936	1,307	—	—	P/L	25.00

Rev: Oak sprigs w/acorns.

KM#	Date	Mintage	Fine	VF	XF	Unc
831	1927	.015	—	—	Proof	60.00
	1928	1.302	2.50	5.00	10.00	25.00
	1928	—	—	—	Proof	250.00
	1930	1.319	1.50	3.00	7.50	15.00
	1930	—	—	—	Proof	200.00
	1931	6.252	BV	.50	1.50	7.50
	1931	—	—	—	Proof	200.00
	1932	5.887	BV	.50	1.50	7.50
	1932	—	—	—	Proof	200.00
	1933	5.579	BV	.50	1.50	7.50
	1933	—	—	—	Proof	200.00
	1934	7.406	BV	.50	1.50	7.50
	1934	—	—	—	Proof	200.00
	1935	7.028	BV	.50	1.50	7.50
	1935	—	—	—	Proof	175.00
	1936	3.239	BV	.50	1.50	7.50
	1936	—	—	—	Proof	175.00
848	1937	8.148	BV	.50	1.50	5.00
	1937	.026	—	—	Proof	10.00
	1938	6.402	BV	.50	2.50	8.00
	1938	—	—	—	Proof	175.00
	1939	1.356	.75	1.25	2.50	12.00
	1939	—	—	—	Proof	175.00
	1940	7.914	BV	.50	1.00	5.00
	1940	—	—	—	Proof	—
	1941	7.979	BV	.50	1.00	5.00
	1941	—	—	—	Proof	—
	1942	4.144	1.00	2.00	4 00	20.00
	1943	1.379	2.00	4.50	8.00	25.00
	1944	2.006	3.25	8.50	17.50	50.00
	1945	.320*	—	—	2000.	—

***NOTE:** Issue melted, one known.

NICKEL-BRASS

KM#	Date	Mintage	Fine	VF	XF	Unc
849	1937	45.708	.25	40	1.00	3.00
	1937	.026	—	—	Proof	7.50
	1938	14.532	.40	.80	4.00	12.00
	1938	—	—	—	Proof	—
	1939	5.603	.70	2.00	6.00	27.50
	1939	—	—	—	Proof	—
	1940	12.636	.25	80	2.50	7.00
	1940	—	—	—	Proof	—
	1941	60.239	.25	.40	1.00	5.00
	1941	—	—	—	Proof	—
	1942	103.214	.20	.30	1.00	3.00
	1942	—	—	—	Proof	—
	1943	101.702	.20	.30	1.00	3.00

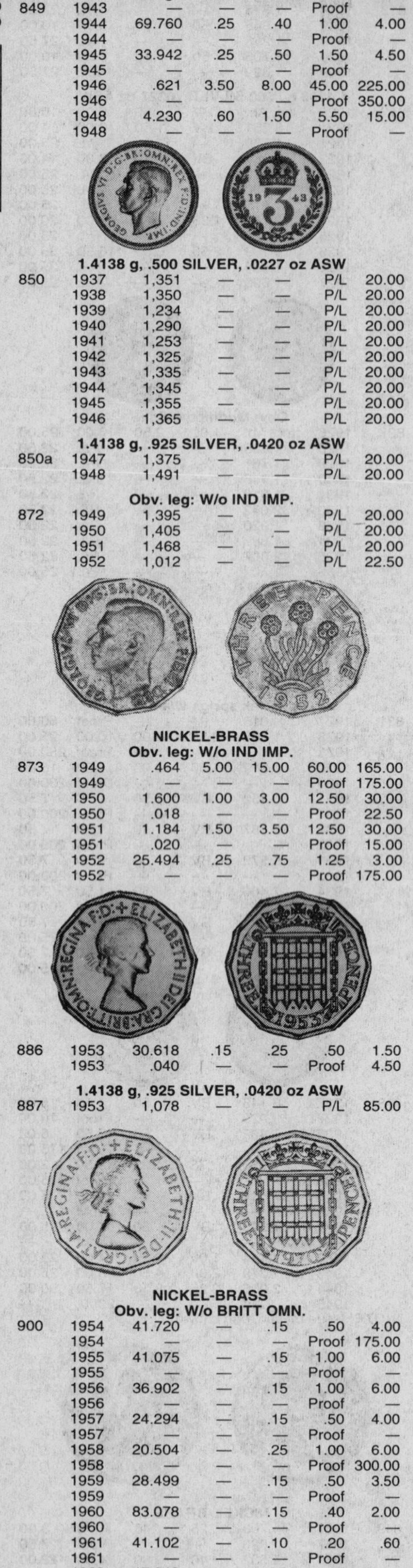

KM#	Date	Mintage	Fine	VF	XF	Unc
849	1943	—	—	—	Proof	—
	1944	69.760	.25	.40	1.00	4.00
	1944	—	—	—	Proof	—
	1945	33.942	.25	.50	1.50	4.50
	1945	—	—	—	Proof	—
	1946	.621	3.50	8.00	45.00	225.00
	1946	—	—	—	Proof	350.00
	1948	4.230	.60	1.50	5.50	15.00
	1948	—	—	—	Proof	—

1.4138 g, .500 SILVER, .0227 oz ASW

KM#	Date	Mintage	Fine	VF	XF	Unc
850	1937	1,351	—	—	P/L	20.00
	1938	1,350	—	—	P/L	20.00
	1939	1,234	—	—	P/L	20.00
	1940	1,290	—	—	P/L	20.00
	1941	1,253	—	—	P/L	20.00
	1942	1,325	—	—	P/L	20.00
	1943	1,335	—	—	P/L	20.00
	1944	1,345	—	—	P/L	20.00
	1945	1,355	—	—	P/L	20.00
	1946	1,365	—	—	P/L	20.00

1.4138 g, .925 SILVER, .0420 oz ASW

KM#	Date	Mintage	Fine	VF	XF	Unc
850a	1947	1,375	—	—	P/L	20.00
	1948	1,491	—	—	P/L	20.00

Obv. leg: W/o IND IMP.

KM#	Date	Mintage	Fine	VF	XF	Unc
872	1949	1,395	—	—	P/L	20.00
	1950	1,405	—	—	P/L	20.00
	1951	1,468	—	—	P/L	20.00
	1952	1,012	—	—	P/L	22.50

NICKEL-BRASS
Obv. leg: W/o IND IMP.

KM#	Date	Mintage	Fine	VF	XF	Unc
873	1949	.464	5.00	15.00	60.00	165.00
	1949	—	—	—	Proof	175.00
	1950	1.600	1.00	3.00	12.50	30.00
	1950	.018	—	—	Proof	22.50
	1951	1.184	1.50	3.50	12.50	30.00
	1951	.020	—	—	Proof	15.00
	1952	25.494	.25	.75	1.25	3.00
	1952	—	—	—	Proof	175.00
886	1953	30.618	.15	.25	.50	1.50
	1953	.040	—	—	Proof	4.50

1.4138 g, .925 SILVER, .0420 oz ASW

KM#	Date	Mintage	Fine	VF	XF	Unc
887	1953	1,078	—	—	P/L	85.00

NICKEL-BRASS
Obv. leg: W/o BRITT OMN.

KM#	Date	Mintage	Fine	VF	XF	Unc
900	1954	41.720	—	.15	.50	4.00
	1954	—	—	—	Proof	175.00
	1955	41.075	—	.15	1.00	6.00
	1955	—	—	—	Proof	—
	1956	36.902	—	.15	1.00	6.00
	1956	—	—	—	Proof	—
	1957	24.294	—	.15	.50	4.00
	1957	—	—	—	Proof	—
	1958	20.504	—	.25	1.00	6.00
	1958	—	—	—	Proof	300.00
	1959	28.499	—	.15	.50	3.50
	1959	—	—	—	Proof	—
	1960	83.078	—	.15	.40	2.00
	1960	—	—	—	Proof	—
	1961	41.102	—	.10	.20	.60
	1961	—	—	—	Proof	—
	1962	47.242	—	.10	.20	.40
	1962	—	—	—	Proof	—
	1963	35.280	—	.10	.15	.25
	1963	—	—	—	Proof	—
	1964	47.440	—	.10	.15	.25
	1964	—	—	—	Proof	—
	1965	23.907	—	.10	.15	.25
	1966	55.320	—	.10	.15	.25
	1967	49.000	—	.10	.15	.25
	1970	.750	—	—	Proof	2.50

1.4138 g, .925 SILVER, .0420 oz ASW
Obv. leg: W/o BRITT OMN.

KM#	Date	Mintage	Fine	VF	XF	Unc
901	1954	1,076	—	—	P/L	20.00
	1955	1,082	—	—	P/L	20.00
	1956	1,088	—	—	P/L	20.00
	1957	1,094	—	—	P/L	20.00
	1958	1,100	—	—	P/L	20.00
	1959	1,172	—	—	P/L	20.00
	1960	1,112	—	—	P/L	20.00
	1961	1,118	—	—	P/L	20.00
	1962	1,125	—	—	P/L	20.00
	1963	1,205	—	—	P/L	20.00
	1964	1,213	—	—	P/L	20.00
	1965	1,221	—	—	P/L	20.00
	1966	1,206	—	—	P/L	20.00
	1967	986 pcs.	—	—	P/L	20.00
	1968	964 pcs.	—	—	P/L	20.00
	1969	1,088	—	—	P/L	20.00
	1970	980 pcs.	—	—	P/L	20.00
	1971	1,018	—	—	P/L	20.00
	1972	1,026	—	—	P/L	20.00
	1973	1,098	—	—	P/L	20.00
	1974	1,138	—	—	P/L	20.00
	1975	1,148	—	—	P/L	20.00
	1976	1,158	—	—	P/L	20.00
	1977	1,138	—	—	P/L	22.00
	1978	1,178	—	—	P/L	22.00
	1979	1,294	—	—	P/L	22.00
	1980	1,198	—	—	P/L	22.00
	1981	1,178	—	—	P/L	22.00
	1982	1,218	—	—	P/L	22.00
	1983	1,342	—	—	P/L	22.00
	1984	1,354	—	—	P/L	22.00
	1985	1,366	—	—	P/L	22.00
	1986	1,378	—	—	P/L	22.00
	1987	1,390	—	—	P/L	22.00
	1988	1,528	—	—	P/L	22.00
	1989	1,353	—	—	P/L	22.00
	1990	1,523	—	—	P/L	22.00
	1991	1,384	—	—	P/L	22.00
	1992	—	—	—	P/L	22.00
	1993	—	—	—	P/L	22.00
	1994	—	—	—	P/L	22.00

4 PENCE (GROAT)

1.8851 g, .925 SILVER, .0561 oz ASW
Obv: Old head of George III. Rev: Value.

KM#	Date	Mintage	Fine	VF	XF	Unc
671	1817	—	10.00	22.50	40.00	90.00
	1817	1,386	—	—	P/L	70.00
	1818	—	10.00	22.50	40.00	90.00
	1818	1,188	—	—	P/L	70.00
	1820	—	10.00	22.50	40.00	90.00
	1820	990 pcs.	—	—	P/L	70.00

KM#	Date	Mintage	Fine	VF	XF	Unc
686	1822	—	9.00	15.00	25.00	50.00
	1822	2,970	—	—	P/L	70.00
	1823	—	9.00	15.00	25.00	50.00
	1823	1,980	—	—	P/L	60.00
	1824	—	9.00	15.00	25.00	50.00
	1824	1,584	—	—	P/L	65.00
	1825	—	9.00	15.00	25.00	50.00
	1825	2,376	—	—	P/L	60.00
	1826	—	9.00	15.00	25.00	50.00
	1826	2,376	—	—	P/L	60.00
	1827	—	9.00	15.00	25.00	50.00
	1827	2,772	—	—	P/L	60.00
	1828	—	9.00	15.00	25.00	50.00
	1828	2,772	—	—	P/L	60.00
	1829	—	9.00	15.00	25.00	50.00
	1829	2,772	—	—	P/L	60.00
	1830	—	9.00	15.00	25.00	50.00
	1830	2,772	—	—	P/L	60.00

KM#	Date	Mintage	Fine	VF	XF	Unc
711	1831	—	5.00	12.00	22.50	45.00
	1831	3,564	—	—	P/L	55.00
	1832	—	5.00	12.00	22.50	45.00
	1832	2,574	—	—	P/L	40.00
	1833	—	5.00	12.00	22.50	45.00
	1833	2,574	—	—	P/L	40.00
	1834	—	5.00	12.00	22.50	45.00
	1834	2,574	—	—	P/L	40.00
	1835	—	5.00	12.00	22.50	45.00
	1835	2,574	—	—	P/L	40.00
	1836	—	5.00	12.00	22.50	45.00
	1836	2,574	—	—	P/L	40.00
	1837	—	6.00	12.00	22.50	45.00
	1837	2,574	—	—	P/L	40.00

KM#	Date	Mintage	Fine	VF	XF	Unc
723	1836	4.253	2.25	4.50	17.50	45.00
	1836 reeded edge		—	—	Proof	600.00
	1836 plain edge		—	—	Proof	300.00
	1837	.962	4.00	8.00	20.00	60.00
	1837	—	—	—	Proof	225.00

***NOTE:** Although the design of the above coin is of the homeland type, the issues were primarily used for circulation in British Guiana.

KM#	Date	Mintage	Fine	VF	XF	Unc
731.1	1838	2.150	2.25	4.50	17.50	40.00
	1838/8 second 8 over horizontal 8					
		Inc. Ab.	6.00	12.50	45.00	100.00
	1839	1.461	3.00	8.00	25.00	60.00
	1840	1.497	2.75	6.00	22.50	50.00
	1841	.345	4.50	13.00	35.00	75.00
	1842/1	.725	6.00	15.00	37.50	90.00
	1842	Inc. Ab.	4.00	8.00	27.50	70.00
	1842	—	—	—	Proof	500.00
	1843	1.818	3.00	8.00	27.50	70.00
	1844	.855	5.00	13.00	35.00	75.00
	1845	.915	3.00	8.00	27.50	60.00
	1846	1.366	3.00	8.00	27.50	60.00
	1847/6	.226	30.00	55.00	120.00	220.00
	1848/6	.713	3.50	10.00	32.50	70.00
	1848/7	Inc. Ab.	3.50	10.00	32.50	70.00
	1848	Inc. Ab.	3.00	6.00	22.50	50.00
	1849/8	.380	6.00	15.00	55.00	125.00
	1849	Inc. Ab.	3.50	10.00	32.50	70.00
	1851	.031	9.00	20.00	60.00	150.00
	1852	—	70.00	135.00	325.00	700.00
	1853	.012	65.00	125.00	300.00	650.00
	1854	1.097	2.75	6.00	22.50	50.00
	1855	.646	4.00	8.00	22.50	50.00
	1857 3-4 known		—	—	Proof	1400.
	1862	—	—	—	Proof	800.00

NOTE: The above issue was produced for circulation in both Great Britain and British Guiana.

Plain edge.

KM#	Date	Mintage	Fine	VF	XF	Unc
731.2	1838	—	—	—	Proof	200.00
	1839	—	—	—	Proof	200.00
	1853					
		*10-15 pcs.	—	—	Proof	Rare

KM#	Date	Mintage	Fine	VF	XF	Unc
732	1838	4,158	—	—	P/L	17.50
	1839	4,125	—	—	P/L	17.50
	1840	4,125	—	—	P/L	17.50
	1841	2,574	—	—	P/L	20.00
	1842	4,125	—	—	P/L	17.50
	1843	4,158	—	—	P/L	17.50
	1844	4,158	—	—	P/L	17.50
	1845	4,158	—	—	P/L	17.50
	1846	4,158	—	—	P/L	17.50
	1847	4,158	—	—	P/L	17.50
	1848	4,158	—	—	P/L	17.50
	1849	4,158	—	—	P/L	17.50
	1850	4,158	—	—	P/L	17.50
	1851	4,158	—	—	P/L	17.50
	1852	4,158	—	—	P/L	17.50
	1853	4,158	—	—	P/L	17.50
	1854	4,158	—	—	P/L	17.50
	1855	4,158	—	—	P/L	17.50
	1856	4,158	—	—	P/L	17.50
	1857	4,158	—	—	P/L	17.50
	1858	4,158	—	—	P/L	17.50
	1859	4,158	—	—	P/L	17.50
	1860	4,158	—	—	P/L	17.50
	1861	4,158	—	—	P/L	17.50
	1862	4,158	—	—	P/L	17.50
	1863	4,158	—	—	P/L	17.50
	1864	4,158	—	—	P/L	17.50
	1865	4,158	—	—	P/L	17.50
	1866	4,158	—	—	P/L	17.50
	1867	4,158	—	—	P/L	17.50
	1868	4,158	—	—	P/L	17.50
	1869	4,158	—	—	P/L	17.50
	1870	4,569	—	—	P/L	17.50
	1871	4,627	—	—	P/L	17.50
	1872	4,328	—	—	P/L	17.50
	1873	4,162	—	—	P/L	17.50
	1874	5,937	—	—	P/L	17.50
	1875	4,154	—	—	P/L	17.50
	1876	4,862	—	—	P/L	17.50
	1877	4,850	—	—	P/L	17.50
	1878	5,735	—	—	P/L	17.50
	1879	5,202	—	—	P/L	17.50
	1880	5,199	—	—	P/L	17.50
	1881	6,203	—	—	P/L	17.50

KM#	Date	Mintage	Fine	VF	XF	Unc
732	1882	4,146	—	—	P/L	17.50
	1883	5,096	—	—	P/L	17.50
	1884	5,353	—	—	P/L	17.50
	1885	5,791	—	—	P/L	17.50
	1886	6,785	—	—	P/L	17.50
	1887	5,292	—	—	P/L	17.50
772	1888	.120	4.00	10.00	25.00	55.00
	1888	—	—	—	Proof	125.00

NOTE: The above piece was exclusively for use in British Guiana and the West Indies.

KM#	Date	Mintage	Fine	VF	XF	Unc
773	1888	9,583	—	—	P/L	20.00
	1889	6,088	—	—	P/L	20.00
	1890	9,087	—	—	P/L	20.00
	1891	.011	—	—	P/L	20.00
	1892	8,524	—	—	P/L	20.00
778	1893	.011	—	—	P/L	15.00
	1894	9,385	—	—	P/L	15.00
	1895	8,877	—	—	P/L	15.00
	1896	8,476	—	—	P/L	15.00
	1897	9,388	—	—	P/L	15.00
	1898	9,147	—	—	P/L	15.00
	1899	.014	—	—	P/L	15.00
	1900	9,571	—	—	P/L	15.00
	1901	.012	—	—	P/L	15.00
798	1902	.010	—	—	P/L	15.00
	1903	9,729	—	—	P/L	15.00
	1904	.012	—	—	P/L	15.00
	1905	.011	—	—	P/L	15.00
	1906	.011	—	—	P/L	15.00
	1907	.011	—	—	P/L	15.00
	1908	9,929	—	—	P/L	15.00
	1909	2,428	—	—	P/L	20.00
	1910	2,755	—	—	P/L	22.50
814	1911	1,768	—	—	P/L	17.50
	1912	1,700	—	—	P/L	17.50
	1913	1,798	—	—	P/L	17.50
	1914	1,651	—	—	P/L	17.50
	1915	1,441	—	—	P/L	17.50
	1916	1,499	—	—	P/L	17.50
	1917	1,478	—	—	P/L	17.50
	1918	1,479	—	—	P/L	17.50
	1919	1,524	—	—	P/L	17.50
	1920	1,460	—	—	P/L	17.50

1.8851 g, .500 SILVER, .0303 oz ASW

KM#	Date	Mintage	Fine	VF	XF	Unc
814a	1921	1,542	—	—	P/L	17.50
	1922	1,609	—	—	P/L	17.50
	1923	1,635	—	—	P/L	17.50
	1924	1,665	—	—	P/L	17.50
	1925	1,786	—	—	P/L	17.50
	1926	1,762	—	—	P/L	17.50
	1927	1,681	—	—	P/L	17.50

Obv: Modified effigy.

KM#	Date	Mintage	Fine	VF	XF	Unc
841	1928	1,642	—	—	P/L	20.00
	1929	1,969	—	—	P/L	20.00
	1930	1,744	—	—	P/L	20.00
	1931	1,915	—	—	P/L	20.00
	1932	1,937	—	—	P/L	20.00
	1933	1,931	—	—	P/L	20.00
	1934	1,893	—	—	P/L	20.00
	1935	1,995	—	—	P/L	20.00
	1936	1,323	—	—	P/L	22.50
851	1937	1,325	—	—	P/L	20.00
	1938	1,424	—	—	P/L	20.00
	1939	1,332	—	—	P/L	20.00
	1940	1,367	—	—	P/L	20.00
	1941	1,345	—	—	P/L	20.00
	1942	1,325	—	—	P/L	20.00

KM#	Date	Mintage	Fine	VF	XF	Unc
851	1943	1,335	—	—	P/L	20.00
	1944	1,345	—	—	P/L	20.00
	1945	1,355	—	—	P/L	20.00
	1946	1,365	—	—	P/L	20.00

1.8851 g, .925 SILVER, .0561 oz ASW

KM#	Date	Mintage	Fine	VF	XF	Unc
851a	1947	1,375	—	—	P/L	20.00
	1948	1,385	—	—	P/L	20.00

Obv. leg: W/o IND IMP.

KM#	Date	Mintage	Fine	VF	XF	Unc
874	1949	1,503	—	—	P/L	20.00
	1950	1,515	—	—	P/L	20.00
	1951	1,580	—	—	P/L	20.00
	1952	1,064	—	—	P/L	22.50
888	1953	1,078	—	—	P/L	85.00

Obv. leg: W/o BRITT OMN.

KM#	Date	Mintage	Fine	VF	XF	Unc
902	1954	1,076	—	—	P/L	20.00
	1955	1,082	—	—	P/L	20.00
	1956	1,088	—	—	P/L	20.00
	1957	1,094	—	—	P/L	20.00
	1958	1,100	—	—	P/L	20.00
	1959	1,106	—	—	P/L	20.00
	1960	1,180	—	—	P/L	20.00
	1961	1,118	—	—	P/L	20.00
	1962	1,197	—	—	P/L	20.00
	1963	1,205	—	—	P/L	20.00
	1964	1,213	—	—	P/L	20.00
	1965	1,221	—	—	P/L	20.00
	1966	1,206	—	—	P/L	20.00
	1967	986 pcs.	—	—	P/L	20.00
	1968	964 pcs.	—	—	P/L	20.00
	1969	1,002	—	—	P/L	20.00
	1970	1,068	—	—	P/L	20.00
	1971	1,108	—	—	P/L	20.00
	1972	1,118	—	—	P/L	20.00
	1973	1,098	—	—	P/L	20.00
	1974	1,138	—	—	P/L	20.00
	1975	1,148	—	—	P/L	20.00
	1976	1,158	—	—	P/L	20.00
	1977	1,138	—	—	P/L	22.00
	1978	1,178	—	—	P/L	22.00
	1979	1,188	—	—	P/L	22.00
	1980	1,306	—	—	P/L	22.00
	1981	1,288	—	—	P/L	22.00
	1982	1,330	—	—	P/L	22.00
	1983	1,342	—	—	P/L	22.00
	1984	1,354	—	—	P/L	22.00
	1985	1,366	—	—	P/L	22.00
	1986	1,378	—	—	P/L	22.00
	1987	1,390	—	—	P/L	22.00
	1988	1,402	—	—	P/L	22.00
	1989	1,353	—	—	P/L	22.00
	1990	1,523	—	—	P/L	22.00
	1991	1,514	—	—	P/L	22.00
	1992	—	—	—	P/L	22.00
	1993	—	—	—	P/L	22.00
	1994	—	—	—	P/L	22.00

6 PENCE

2.8276 g, .925 SILVER, .0841 oz ASW

KM#	Date	Mintage	Fine	VF	XF	Unc
665	1816	—	3.50	8.50	30.00	75.00
	1816	—	—	—	Proof	750.00
	1817	10.922	3.00	8.00	30.00	75.00
	1817	—	—	—	Proof	500.00
	1817 plain edge		—	—	Proof	500.00
	1818	4.285	8.00	17.50	60.00	150.00
	1818	—	—	—	Proof	700.00
	1819/8	—	6.00	15.00	50.00	160.00
	1819/8	—	—	—	Proof	750.00
	1819	4.712	4.00	9.00	32.00	75.00
	1819	1.489	—	—	Proof	1000.
	1820 inverted 1	1.489	25.00	85.00	275.00	500.00
	1820	Inc. Ab.	4.00	9.00	32.00	80.00
	1820	—	—	—	Proof	—
678	1821	.863	8.00	18.00	75.00	200.00
678	1821	—	—	—	Proof	500.00
	1821 (error) BBITANNIAR	—	45.00	120.00	450.00	900.00
691	1824	.634	8.00	18.00	70.00	190.00
	1824	—	—	—	Proof	750.00
	1825	.483	6.00	14.00	60.00	160.00
	1825	—	—	—	Proof	300.00
	1826	.689	20.00	60.00	220.00	500.00
	1826	—	—	—	Proof	400.00
698	1826	Inc. Ab.	5.00	12.00	55.00	145.00
	1826	Inc. Ab.	—	—	Proof	250.00
	1827	.166	15.00	45.00	115.00	300.00
	1828	.016	8.00	25.00	85.00	225.00
	1829	.404	6.00	20.00	75.00	175.00
	1829	—	—	—	Proof	—
712	1831	1.340	4.50	17.50	65.00	155.00
	1831	Inc. Ab.	—	—	Proof	250.00
	1831 plain edge		—	—	Proof	250.00
	1834	5.892	4.50	15.00	55.00	135.00
	1834	—	—	—	Proof	—
	1834 round-topped 3	Inc. Ab.	—	—	Proof	—
	1835	1.555	6.00	20.00	60.00	140.00
	1835 round-topped 3	Inc. Ab.	—	—	Proof	—
	1836	1.988	11.00	37.50	120.00	240.00
	1836 round-topped 3	Inc. Ab.	—	—	Proof	—
	1837	.507	7.50	22.50	115.00	200.00
	1837	—	—	—	Proof	—

PALLADIUM

KM#	Date	Mintage	Fine	VF	XF	Unc
712a	1831	—	—	—	Proof	—

3.0100 g, .925 SILVER, .0895 oz ASW
Rev: W/o die numbers.

KM#	Date	Mintage	Fine	VF	XF	Unc
733.1	1838	1.608	3.50	12.00	50.00	125.00
	1838	—	—	—	Proof	200.00
	1839	3.311	3.50	12.00	50.00	125.00
	1839	Inc. Ab.	—	—	Proof	300.00
	1840	2.099	4.00	12.00	65.00	140.00
	1841	1.386	4.00	15.00	70.00	145.00
	1842	.602	5.00	15.00	80.00	180.00
	1843	3.160	3.50	12.00	65.00	150.00
	1844	3.976	3.50	12.00	50.00	130.00
	1844 large 44	Inc. Ab.	4.00	15.00	60.00	150.00
	1845	3.714	3.50	12.00	50.00	120.00
	1846	4.267	3.50	12.00	50.00	120.00
	1848/6	.586	20.00	60.00	220.00	525.00
	1848/7	Inc. Ab.	20.00	60.00	220.00	525.00
	1848	Inc. Ab.	18.00	55.00	220.00	525.00
	1849	.210	—	None reported		—
	1850/30	.499	7.50	25.00	90.00	—
	1850	Inc. Ab.	5.00	20.00	75.00	180.00
	1851	2.288	4.00	15.00	50.00	125.00
	1852	.905	5.00	15.00	50.00	130.00
	1853	3.838	3.50	12.00	45.00	120.00
	1853	*40 pcs.	—	—	Proof	450.00
	1854	.840	35.00	65.00	225.00	450.00
	1855	1.129	3.50	12.00	50.00	125.00
	1855	—	—	—	Proof	—
	1856	2.780	3.50	12.00	50.00	125.00
	1857	2.233	4.00	12.00	65.00	135.00
	1858	1.932	4.00	12.00	65.00	135.00
	1858	—	—	—	Proof	600.00
	1859/8	4.689	4.00	15.00	60.00	145.00
	1859	Inc. Ab.	4.00	12.00	50.00	135.00
	1860	1.101	4.00	12.00	60.00	145.00
	1861	.600	—	Reported, not confirmed		
	1862	.990	15.00	35.00	185.00	400.00
	1863	.491	10.00	30.00	120.00	240.00
	1866	5.140	22.50	45.00	100.00	220.00

Rev: W/die numbers.

KM#	Date	Mintage	Fine	VF	XF	Unc
733.2	1864	4.253	3.50	12.00	50.00	125.00
	1865	1.632	4.00	14.00	55.00	135.00
	1866	Inc.Ab.	3.50	12.00	50.00	125.00

Obv: New portrait. Rev: W/die numbers.

KM#	Date	Mintage	Fine	VF	XF	Unc
751.1	1867	1.362	6.00	20.00	70.00	175.00
	1867	—	—	—	Proof	1000.
	1868	1.069	6.00	20.00	70.00	175.00
	1869	.388	7.50	22.50	75.00	200.00
	1869	—	—	—	Proof	1000.
	1870	.480	8.00	20.00	75.00	200.00
	1870	—	—	—	Proof	1000.
	1870 plain edge		—	—	Proof	1000.
	1871	3.663	3.50	12.50	45.00	100.00
	1871	—	—	—	Proof	1000.
	1871 plain edge		—	—	Proof	1000.
	1872	3.382	3.50	12.50	45.00	100.00
	1873	4.595	3.00	11.00	40.00	90.00
	1874	4.226	2.75	9.00	40.00	90.00
	1875	3.257	2.75	9.00	40.00	90.00
	1876	.841	8.00	20.00	65.00	150.00
	1877	4.066	3.00	11.00	40.00	95.00
	1878/7	2.625	25.00	75.00	175.00	350.00
	1878	—	—	—	Proof	1000.
	1878 (error) DRITANNIAR	Inc. Ab.	22.50	60.00	350.00	900.00
	1879	3.326	7.00	20.00	70.00	175.00
	1879	—	—	—	Proof	1000.

Rev: W/o die numbers.

KM#	Date	Mintage	Fine	VF	XF	Unc
751.2	1871	Inc. Ab.	8.00	20.00	50.00	125.00
	1877	Inc. Ab.	3.00	11.00	40.00	90.00
	1878	Inc. Ab.	3.00	11.00	40.00	90.00
	1879	Inc. Ab.	4.00	12.00	40.00	90.00
	1880 obverse of 1879	3.892	5.00	15.00	50.00	110.00

Obv: New portrait, longer hair waves.

KM#	Date	Mintage	Fine	VF	XF	Unc
757	1880	Inc. Ab.	2.50	10.00	30.00	70.00
	1880	—	—	—	Proof	1000.
	1881	6.239	2.25	8.00	25.00	50.00
	1881	—	—	—	Proof	1000.
	1881 plain edge		—	—	Proof	1000.
	1882	.760	7.00	20.00	60.00	130.00
	1883	4.987	2.25	8.00	25.00	50.00
	1884	3.423	2.25	8.00	25.00	50.00
	1885	4.653	2.25	8.00	25.00	50.00
	1885	—	—	—	Proof	800.00
	1886	2.728	2.25	8.00	25.00	50.00
	1886	—	—	—	Proof	800.00
	1887	3.676	2.25	7.00	22.50	50.00
	1887	—	—	—	Proof	800.00

KM#	Date	Mintage	Fine	VF	XF	Unc
759	1887	Inc.KM757	1.50	3.00	6.00	12.00
	1887	—	—	—	Proof	225.00

KM#	Date	Mintage	Fine	VF	XF	Unc
760	1887	Inc.KM757	2.00	3.50	6.00	15.00
	1887	Inc.KM757	—	—	Proof	225.00
	1888	4.198	2.00	6.00	17.50	45.00
	1888	—	—	—	Proof	1500.
	1889	8.739	2.00	5.00	15.00	45.00
	1890	9.387	2.00	6.00	17.50	45.00
	1890	—	—	—	Proof	700.00
	1891	7.023	2.00	6.00	17.50	45.00
	1892	6.246	2.00	6.00	17.50	45.00
	1893	7.351	150.00	300.00	750.00	1800.

KM#	Date	Mintage	Fine	VF	XF	Unc
779	1893	Inc. Ab.	1.50	3.75	15.00	35.00
	1893	1,312	—	—	Proof	150.00
	1894	3.468	1.75	4.50	17.50	45.00
	1895	7.025	1.50	3.75	15.00	35.00
	1896	6.652	1.50	3.75	15.00	35.00
	1897	5.031	1.50	3.50	12.50	35.00
	1898	5.914	1.50	3.50	12.50	35.00
	1899	7.997	1.50	3.75	15.00	37.50
	1900	8.980	1.50	3.50	12.50	35.00
	1901	5.109	1.50	3.50	12.50	35.00

KM#	Date	Mintage	Fine	VF	XF	Unc
799	1902	6.356	2.00	4.00	15.00	35.00
	1902	.015	—	Matte Proof		35.00
	1903	5.411	2.75	9.00	30.00	70.00
	1904	4.487	3.50	10.00	32.50	90.00
	1905	4.236	3.50	10.00	32.50	80.00
	1906	7.641	2.50	5.00	20.00	60.00
	1907	8.734	2.50	8.00	20.00	60.00
	1908	6.739	3.50	12.00	30.00	85.00
	1909	6.584	2.75	7.50	25.00	70.00
	1910	12.491	2.25	7.00	16.00	40.00

KM#	Date	Mintage	Fine	VF	XF	Unc
815	1911	9.165	1.00	2.00	7.50	25.00
	1911	6,007	—	—	Proof	50.00
	1912	10.984	1.00	3.00	15.00	50.00
	1913	7.500	1.50	4.50	20.00	55.00
	1914	22.715	1.00	2.00	5.00	17.50
	1915	15.695	1.00	2.00	5.00	17.50
	1916	22.207	1.00	2.00	5.00	17.50
	1917	7.725	1.50	3.00	12.50	40.00
	1918	27.559	1.00	1.75	6.00	17.50
	1919	13.375	1.00	2.00	12.00	35.00
	1920	14.136	1.00	2.00	12.00	35.00

2.8276 g, .500 SILVER, .0455 oz ASW
Narrow rim

KM#	Date	Mintage	Fine	VF	XF	Unc
815a.1	1920	Inc. Ab.	.75	2.00	12.50	35.00
	1921	30.340	.75	2.00	9.00	30.00
	1922	16.879	.75	2.00	9.00	30.00
	1923	6.383	1.25	3.00	11.50	45.00
	1924	17.444	.75	1.50	9.00	32.50
	1925	12.721	.75	2.50	10.00	35.00

Wide rim

KM#	Date	Mintage	Fine	VF	XF	Unc
815a.2	1925	Inc. Ab.	.75	1.50	9.00	22.50
	1926	21.810	.75	1.50	9.00	22.50

Obv: Modified effigy, slightly smaller bust.

KM#	Date	Mintage	Fine	VF	XF	Unc
828	1926	Inc. Ab.	BV	1.50	7.50	22.50
	1927	8.925	BV	1.50	7.50	25.00
	1927	—	—	—	Proof	250.00

Rev: Oak sprigs w/acorns.

KM#	Date	Mintage	Fine	VF	XF	Unc
832	1927	.015	—	—	Proof	30.00
	1928	23.123	BV	.75	2.75	12.00
	1928	—	—	—	Proof	—
	1929	28.319	BV	.75	2.75	12.00
	1929	—	—	—	Proof	—
	1930	16.990	BV	.75	3.00	13.00
	1930	—	—	—	Proof	250.00
	1931	16.873	BV	.75	3.00	13.00
	1931	—	—	—	Proof	250.00
	1932	9.406	.75	1.50	4.50	22.50
	1932	—	—	—	Proof	250.00
	1933	22.185	BV	.75	2.75	12.00
	1933	—	—	—	Proof	250.00
	1934	9.304	.75	1.50	4.50	17.50
	1934	—	—	—	Proof	225.00
	1935	13.996	BV	.75	2.25	12.00
	1935	—	—	—	Proof	225.00
	1936	24.380	BV	.75	2.25	10.00
	1936	—	—	—	Proof	250.00

NOTE: Varieties in edge milling exist.

KM#	Date	Mintage	Fine	VF	XF	Unc
852	1937	22.303	—	BV	1.00	3.00
	1937	.026	—	—	Proof	9.00
	1938	13.403	.75	1.00	3.00	9.00
	1938	—	—	—	Proof	225.00
	1939	28.670	BV	.75	1.50	4.50
	1939	—	—	—	Proof	225.00
	1940	20.875	BV	.75	1.50	4.50
	1940	—	—	—	Proof	275.00
	1941	23.087	BV	.75	1.50	4.50
	1941	—	—	—	Proof	275.00
	1942	44.943	BV	.75	1.50	2.50
	1943	46.927	—	BV	1.00	2.50
	1943	—	—	—	Proof	200.00
	1944	36.953	—	BV	1.00	2.00
	1944	—	—	—	Proof	200.00
	1945	39.939	—	BV	1.00	2.00
	1945	—	—	—	Proof	200.00
	1946	43.466	—	BV	1.00	2.00
	1946	—	—	—	Proof	200.00

COPPER-NICKEL

KM#	Date	Mintage	Fine	VF	XF	Unc
862	1947	29.993	—	.15	.50	2.00
	1947	—	—	—	Proof	250.00
	1948	88.324	—	.15	.50	2.00
	1948	—	—	—	Proof	250.00

Rev. leg: W/o IND IMP.

KM#	Date	Mintage	Fine	VF	XF	Unc
875	1949	41.336	—	.15	.50	3.50
	1949	—	—	—	Proof	225.00
	1950	32.742	—	.15	.50	3.50
	1950	.018	—	—	Proof	6.00
	1951	40.399	—	.15	.50	3.50
	1951	.020	—	—	Proof	6.00
	1952	1.013	1.00	2.75	12.50	32.50
	1952	—	—	—	Proof	225.00

KM#	Date	Mintage	Fine	VF	XF	Unc
889	1953	70.324	—	.10	.40	1.50
	1953	.040	—	—	Proof	3.50

Obv. leg: W/o BRITT OMN.

KM#	Date	Mintage	Fine	VF	XF	Unc
903	1954	105.241	—	.10	.50	3.50
	1954	—	—	—	Proof	150.00
	1955	109.930	—	.10	.15	1.00
	1955	—	—	—	Proof	150.00
	1956	109.842	—	.10	.15	1.00
	1956	—	—	—	Proof	—
	1957	105.654	—	.10	.15	.50
	1957	—	—	—	Proof	150.00
	1958	123.519	—	.10	.50	3.50
	1958	—	—	—	Proof	150.00
	1959	93.089	—	.10	.15	.35
	1959	—	—	—	Proof	150.00
	1960	103.283	—	.10	.30	2.50
	1960	—	—	—	Proof	150.00
	1961	115.052	—	.10	.30	2.50
	1961	—	—	—	Proof	150.00
	1962	166.484	—	.10	.15	.40
	1962	—	—	—	Proof	150.00
	1963	120.056	—	.10	.15	.25
	1963	—	—	—	Proof	150.00
	1964	152.336	—	.10	.15	.25
	1964	—	—	—	Proof	150.00
	1965	129.644	—	—	.10	.20
	1966	175.676	—	—	.10	.20
	1967	240.788	—	—	.10	.20
	1970	.750	—	—	Proof	2.00

SHILLING

5.6552 g, .925 SILVER, .1682 oz ASW

KM#	Date	Mintage	Fine	VF	XF	Unc
666	1816	—	3.50	8.50	30.00	125.00
	1816	—	—	—	Proof	750.00
	1816 plain edge		—	—	Proof	750.00
	1817	23.031	4.00	10.00	35.00	130.00
	1817 plain edge		—	—	Proof	650.00
	1818	1.342	12.50	35.00	75.00	250.00
	1818 (error) GEOR/E	Inc. Ab.	—	—	—	—
	1819/8	7.595	9.00	25.00	100.00	300.00
	1819	Inc. Ab.	4.00	10.00	45.00	200.00
	1820	7.975	4.00	10.00	45.00	200.00
	1820	—	—	—	Proof	650.00

KM#	Date	Mintage	Fine	VF	XF	Unc
679	1821	2.463	7.50	15.00	100.00	200.00
	1821	—	—	—	Proof	650.00

KM#	Date	Mintage	Fine	VF	XF	Unc
687	1823	.693	15.00	45.00	125.00	275.00
	1823	—	—	—	Proof	1000.
	1824	4.158	5.50	15.00	75.00	175.00
	1824	—	—	—	Proof	1000.
	1825/3	2.459	5.50	15.00	90.00	200.00
	1825	Inc. Ab.	5.50	15.00	90.00	200.00
	1825	—	—	—	Proof	750.00

KM#	Date	Mintage	Fine	VF	XF	Unc
694	1825	Inc. Ab.	5.00	10.00	90.00	200.00
	1825	—	—	—	Proof	275.00
	1825 plain edge		—	—	Proof	325.00
	1826/2	6.352	—	—	—	—
	1826	Inc.Ab.	5.00	10.00	90.00	200.00
	1826	—	—	—	Proof	275.00
	1827	.574	10.00	30.00	150.00	300.00
	1828	—	10.00	30.00	150.00	300.00
	1829	.879	8.00	22.50	110.00	240.00
	1829	—	—	—	Proof	750.00

KM#	Date	Mintage	Fine	VF	XF	Unc
713	1831 plain edge		—	—	Proof	675.00
	1831 milled edge		—	—	Proof	750.00
	1834	3.223	5.00	22.50	90.00	200.00
	1834	—	—	—	Proof	1200.
	1835	1.449	6.75	30.00	110.00	240.00
	1835	—	—	—	Proof	1200.
	1836	3.568	5.00	20.00	90.00	200.00
	1836	—	—	—	Proof	1400.
	1837	.479	7.50	27.50	125.00	300.00
	1837	—	—	—	Proof	1400.

High relief. W/o die numbers.

KM#	Date	Mintage	Fine	VF	XF	Unc
734.1	1838WW	1.956	6.50	20.00	50.00	160.00
	1838	Inc. Ab.	—	—	Proof	700.00
	1839WW	5.667	6.50	20.00	50.00	160.00
	1839WW	—	—	—	Proof	325.00
	1839	Inc. Ab.	6.00	17.50	45.00	150.00
	1839	Inc. Ab.	—	—	Proof	325.00
	1840	1.639	20.00	60.00	150.00	350.00
	1840	—	—	—	Proof	500.00
	1841	.875	8.50	30.00	80.00	270.00
	1842	2.095	4.50	17.50	50.00	150.00
	1842	—	—	—	Proof	1500.
	1843	1.465	9.00	30.00	80.00	240.00
	1844	4.467	4.50	17.50	50.00	150.00
	1845	4.083	6.00	20.00	65.00	175.00
	1846	4.031	4.50	17.50	60.00	175.00
	1848/6	1.041	25.00	75.00	200.00	350.00
	1849	.645	7.50	20.00	70.00	170.00
	1850/46	.685	175.00	525.00	1600.	3600.
	1850	Inc. Ab.	175.00	525.00	1600.	3600.
	1851	.470	60.00	145.00	550.00	1600.
	1851	—	—	—	Proof	2000.
	1852	1.307	4.50	17.50	50.00	145.00
	1853	4.256	4.50	17.50	50.00	145.00
	1853	—	—	—	Proof	600.00
	1854	.552	40.00	150.00	450.00	1100.

KM#	Date	Mintage	Fine	VF	XF	Unc
734.1	1855	1.368	4.50	17.50	60.00	150.00
	1856	3.168	4.50	17.50	60.00	150.00
	1857	2.562	4.50	17.50	60.00	150.00
	1858	3.109	4.50	17.50	60.00	150.00
	1858	—	—	—	Proof	1200.
	1859	4.562	4.50	17.50	60.00	150.00
	1860	1.671	6.00	22.50	85.00	200.00
	1861	1.382	6.00	22.50	85.00	200.00
	1862	.954	20.00	70.00	125.00	300.00
	1863	.859	20.00	75.00	150.00	375.00

W/die numbers.

KM#	Date	Mintage	Fine	VF	XF	Unc
734.3	1864	4.519	4.50	15.00	50.00	135.00
	1865	5.619	4.50	15.00	50.00	135.00
	1866	4.990	4.50	15.00	50.00	135.00
	1867	2.166	5.00	17.50	60.00	165.00
	1867 (error) 'BBITANNIAR'	—	—	—	—	—
	1867	—	—	—	Proof	1000.
	1867 plain edge		—	—	Proof	—

Low relief, w/die numbers.

KM#	Date	Mintage	Fine	VF	XF	Unc
734.2	1867	—	30.00	80.00	225.00	550.00
	1868	3.330	5.00	18.00	65.00	165.00
	1869	.737	7.00	25.00	85.00	190.00
	1870	1.467	6.00	20.00	80.00	175.00
	1871	4.910	4.00	12.50	45.00	110.00
	1871	—	—	—	Proof	—
	1871 plain edge			—	Proof	1000.
	1872	8.898	4.00	12.50	45.00	110.00
	1873	6.590	4.00	12.50	45.00	110.00
	1874	5.504	4.00	12.50	45.00	110.00
	1875	4.354	4.00	12.50	45.00	110.00
	1876	1.057	6.00	15.00	65.00	160.00
	1877	2.981	3.50	12.00	40.00	90.00
	1878	3.127	3.50	12.00	40.00	90.00
	1878	—	—	—	Proof	1200.
	1879	3.611	5.00	20.00	90.00	175.00

W/o die numbers.

KM#	Date	Mintage	Fine	VF	XF	Unc
734.4	1879	Inc. Ab.	5.00	15.00	65.00	160.00
	1880	4.843	3.00	9.00	35.00	85.00
	1880	—	—	—	Proof	1000.
	1880 plain edge		—	—	Proof	1200.
	1881	5.255	3.00	9.00	35.00	85.00
	1881	—	—	—	Proof	1200.
	1881 plain edge		—	—	Proof	1500.
	1882	1.612	10.00	20.00	75.00	190.00
	1883	7.281	3.00	8.00	30.00	85.00
	1884	3.924	3.00	8.00	30.00	85.00
	1884	—	—	—	Proof	1000.
	1885	3.337	3.00	8.00	30.00	85.00
	1885	—	—	—	Proof	1000.
	1886	2.087	3.00	8.00	30.00	85.00
	1886	—	—	—	Proof	1000.
	1887	4.034	4.50	10.00	50.00	165.00
	1887	—	—	—	Proof	1000.

Small bust

KM#	Date	Mintage	Fine	VF	XF	Unc
761	1887	Inc. Ab.	2.00	3.00	6.00	25.00
	1887	1,084	—	—	Proof	125.00
	1888/7	4.527	3.00	6.00	20.00	55.00
	1888	Inc. Ab.	3.00	6.00	20.00	55.00
	1889	7.040	20.00	50.00	300.00	700.00
	1889	—	—	—	Proof	1250.

Large bust

KM#	Date	Mintage	Fine	VF	XF	Unc
774	1889	—	2.50	5.00	15.00	75.00
	1890	8.794	3.00	7.50	22.50	95.00
	1891	5.665	3.00	7.50	25.00	100.00
	1891	—	—	—	Proof	1250.
	1892	4.592	3.50	7.50	25.00	120.00

KM#	Date	Mintage	Fine	VF	XF	Unc
780	1893	7.039	2.00	4.00	20.00	45.00
	1893	1,312	—	—	Proof	125.00
	1894	5.953	2.50	6.00	20.00	60.00
	1895	8.800	2.00	5.00	20.00	50.00
	1896	9.265	2.00	5.00	20.00	50.00

KM#	Date	Mintage	Fine	VF	XF	Unc
780	1897	6.270	2.00	5.00	20.00	50.00
	1898	9.769	2.00	5.00	20.00	50.00
	1899	10.965	2.00	5.00	20.00	50.00
	1900	10.938	2.00	5.00	20.00	50.00
	1901	3.426	3.00	6.00	20.00	50.00

KM#	Date	Mintage	Fine	VF	XF	Unc
800	1902	7.890	2.50	7.00	20.00	50.00
	1902	.015	—		Matte Proof	50.00
	1903	2.062	4.00	15.00	60.00	110.00
	1904	2.040	4.00	15.00	60.00	115.00
	1905	.488	32.50	70.00	350.00	900.00
	1906	10.791	2.75	8.00	25.00	60.00
	1907	14.083	3.00	10.00	30.00	70.00
	1908	3.807	9.00	20.00	65.00	150.00
	1909	5.665	4.00	15.00	65.00	130.00
	1910	26.547	2.00	7.00	20.00	50.00

KM#	Date	Mintage	Fine	VF	XF	Unc
816	1911	20.066	2.00	3.00	10.00	35.00
	1911	6,007	—	—	Proof	65.00
	1912	15.594	2.00	2.50	8.50	55.00
	1913	9.002	3.00	6.00	30.00	75.00
	1914	23.416	2.00	2.50	5.00	25.00
	1915	39.279	2.00	2.50	5.00	25.00
	1916	35.862	2.00	2.50	5.00	25.00
	1917	22.203	2.00	2.50	5.00	30.00
	1918	34.916	2.00	2.50	5.00	30.00
	1919	10.824	2.25	3.50	9.00	35.00

5.6552 g, .500 SILVER, .0909 oz ASW

KM#	Date	Mintage	Fine	VF	XF	Unc
816a	1920	22.825	BV	2.50	10.00	32.50
	1921	22.649	BV	2.50	10.00	45.00
	1922	27.216	BV	3.00	15.00	42.50
	1923	14.575	BV	2.50	10.00	42.50
	1924	9.250	BV	2.50	10.00	45.00
	1925	5.419	2.50	7.50	18.00	70.00
	1926	22.516	BV	5.00	12.00	45.00

Obv: Modified effigy, slightly smaller bust.

KM#	Date	Mintage	Fine	VF	XF	Unc
829	1926	Inc. Ab.	BV	2.00	6.00	35.00
	1927	9.262	BV	2.00	7.50	40.00

Rev: Larger lion and crown.

KM#	Date	Mintage	Fine	VF	XF	Unc
833	1927	Inc. Ab.	BV	2.00	6.00	40.00
	1927	.015	—	—	Proof	35.00
	1928	18.137	—	BV	3.00	12.00
	1928	—	—	—	Proof	425.00
	1929	19.343	—	BV	3.00	15.00
	1929	—	—	—	Proof	—
	1930	3.137	1.50	3.50	12.00	42.50
	1930	—	—	—	Proof	500.00
	1931	6.994	BV	2.00	4.50	15.00
	1931	—	—	—	Proof	425.00
	1932	12.168	BV	2.00	4.50	15.00
	1932	—	—	—	Proof	425.00
	1933	11.512	BV	2.00	4.50	15.00
	1933	—	—	—	Proof	425.00
	1934	6.138	BV	3.00	10.00	35.00
	1934	—	—	—	Proof	425.00
	1935	9.183	—	BV	2.25	10.00
	1935	—	—	—	Proof	400.00
	1936	11.911	—	BV	2.25	10.00
	1936	—	—	—	Proof	400.00

Rev: English crest.

KM#	Date	Mintage	Fine	VF	XF	Unc
853	1937	8.359	—	BV	2.00	7.50
	1937	.026	—	—	Proof	11.00
	1938	4.833	—	BV	3.00	19.00
	1938	—	—	—	Proof	400.00
	1939	11.053	—	BV	2.00	6.00
	1939	—	—	—	Proof	400.00
	1940	11.099	—	BV	2.00	6.00
	1940	—	—	—	Proof	—
	1941	11.392	—	BV	2.00	6.00
	1941	—	—	—	Proof	—
	1942	17.454	—	BV	2.00	4.50
	1943	11.404	—	BV	2.00	4.50
	1944	11.587	—	BV	2.00	4.50
	1945	15.143	—	BV	2.00	4.50
	1945	—	—	—	Proof	—
	1946	18.664	—	BV	1.50	3.50
	1946	—	—	—	Proof	—

Rev: Scottish crest.

KM#	Date	Mintage	Fine	VF	XF	Unc
854	1937	6.749	—	BV	2.00	7.50
	1937	.026	—	—	Proof	9.00
	1938	4.798	—	BV	4.00	15.00
	1938	—	—	—	Proof	400.00
	1939	10.264	—	BV	2.50	6.00
	1939	—	—	—	Proof	400.00
	1940	9.913	—	BV	2.50	6.00
	1940	—	—	—	Proof	—
	1941	8.086	—	BV	3.00	12.50
	1941	—	—	—	Proof	—
	1942	13.677	—	BV	2.50	6.00
	1943	9.824	—	BV	2.50	6.00
	1944	10.990	—	BV	2.50	7.50
	1945	15.106	—	BV	1.50	3.50
	1945	—	—	—	Proof	—
	1946	16.382	—	BV	1.50	3.50
	1946	—	—	—	Proof	—

COPPER-NICKEL

Rev: English crest.

KM#	Date	Mintage	Fine	VF	XF	Unc
863	1947	12.121	.10	.25	1.00	6.00
	1947	—	—	—	Proof	400.00
	1948	45.577	.10	.15	.50	4.00
	1948	—	—	—	Proof	200.00

Rev: Scottish crest.

KM#	Date	Mintage	Fine	VF	XF	Unc
864	1947	12.283	.10	.25	1.00	6.00
	1947	—	—	—	Proof	—
	1948	45.352	.10	.15	.50	4.00
	1948	—	—	—	Proof	200.00

Rev: English crest, leg: W/o IND IMP.

KM#	Date	Mintage	Fine	VF	XF	Unc
876	1949	19.328	.10	.25	1.25	6.50
	1949	—	—	—	Proof	—
	1950	19.244	.10	.25	1.50	8.00
	1950	.018	—	—	Proof	9.00
	1951	9.957	.10	.25	1.50	8.00
	1951	.020	—	—	Proof	9.00

Rev: Scottish crest.

KM#	Date	Mintage	Fine	VF	XF	Unc
877	1949	21.243	.10	.25	1.25	6.50
	1949	—	—	—	Proof	—
	1950	14.300	.10	.25	1.50	8.00
	1950	.018	—	—	Proof	9.00
	1951	10.961	.10	.25	1.50	8.00
	1951	.020	—	—	Proof	9.00

Rev: English arms.

KM#	Date	Mintage	Fine	VF	XF	Unc
890	1953	41.943	—	.10	.25	1.75
	1953	.040	—	—	Proof	7.50

Rev: Scottish arms.

KM#	Date	Mintage	Fine	VF	XF	Unc
891	1953	20.664	—	.10	.25	1.75
	1953	.040	—	—	Proof	7.50

Obv. leg: W/o BRITT OMN. Rev: English arms.

KM#	Date	Mintage	Fine	VF	XF	Unc
904	1954	30.162	—	.10	.25	1.75
	1954	—	—	—	Proof	200.00
	1955	45.260	—	.10	.25	1.75
	1955	—	—	—	Proof	—
	1956	44.970	—	.10	.50	5.00
	1956	—	—	—	Proof	—
	1957	42.774	—	.10	.25	1.50
	1957	—	—	—	Proof	—
	1958	14.392	.25	.75	2.50	10.00
	1958	—	—	—	Proof	—
	1959	19.443	—	.10	.25	1.50
	1959	—	—	—	Proof	—
	1960	27.028	—	.10	.25	1.50
	1960	—	—	—	Proof	—
	1961	39.817	—	.10	.25	1.25
	1961	—	—	—	Proof	—
	1962	36.704	—	.10	.15	.50
	1962	—	—	—	Proof	—
	1963	49.434	—	—	.10	.25
	1963	—	—	—	Proof	—
	1964	8.591	—	—	.10	.25
	1964	—	—	—	Proof	—
	1965	9.216	—	—	.10	.25
	1966	15.002	—	—	.10	.25
	1970	.750	—	—	Proof	3.00

Rev: Scottish arms.

KM#	Date	Mintage	Fine	VF	XF	Unc
905	1954	26.772	—	.10	.25	1.75
	1954	—	—	—	Proof	150.00
	1955	27.951	—	.10	.25	1.75
	1955	—	—	—	Proof	—
	1956	42.854	—	.10	1.00	10.00
	1956	—	—	—	Proof	—
	1957	17.960	—	.10	1.00	10.00
	1957	—	—	—	Proof	—
	1958	40.823	—	.10	.25	1.75
	1958	—	—	—	Proof	—
	1959	1.013	1.00	3.00	6.00	20.00
	1959	—	—	—	Proof	—
	1960	14.376	—	.10	.50	3.50
	1960	—	—	—	Proof	—
	1961	2.763	.25	.50	1.25	6.00
	1961	—	—	—	Proof	—
	1962	17.475	—	.10	.15	.50
	1962	—	—	—	Proof	—
	1963	32.300	—	—	.10	.25
	1963	—	—	—	Proof	—
	1964	5.239	—	—	.10	.25
	1965	2.774	—	—	.10	.25
	1966	15.604	—	—	.10	.25
	1970	.750	—	—	Proof	2.50

FLORIN

(2 Shillings)

11.3104 g, .925 SILVER, .3364 oz ASW

KM#	Date	Mintage	Fine	VF	XF	Unc
745	1848	—	—	—	Proof	3500.
	1848 plain edge		—	—	Proof	1250.
	1849	.414	12.50	30.00	75.00	275.00

Gothic type. Obv. leg: BRIT. . . .

W/o die numbers.

KM#	Date	Mintage	Fine	VF	XF	Unc
746.1	1851	1,540	—	—	—	—
	1851	—	25.00	—	Proof	8000.
	1852	1.015	8.50	32.00	90.00	240.00
	1852	—	—	—	Proof	1500.
	1853	3.920	8.75	35.00	100.00	300.00
	1853	—	—	—	Proof	1750.
	1854	.550	350.00	700.00	1500.	—
	1855	.831	8.50	32.00	110.00	350.00
	1856	2.202	8.75	35.00	110.00	325.00
	1857	1.671	8.00	32.00	110.00	300.00
	1857	—	—	—	Proof	2000.
	1858	2.239	8.00	32.00	110.00	300.00
	1858	—	—	—	Proof	3000.
	1859	2.568	8.00	32.00	110.00	300.00
	1860	1.475	13.00	40.00	150.00	450.00
	1862	.594	25.00	100.00	400.00	900.00
	1862 plain edge		—	—	Proof	4000.
	1863	.939	25.00	100.00	400.00	900.00
	1863 plain edge		—	—	Proof	3000.

W/die numbers.

KM#	Date	Mintage	Fine	VF	XF	Unc
746.3	1864	1.861	8.00	32.00	110.00	350.00
	1864	—	—	—	Proof	3000.
	1865	1.580	8.50	32.00	110.00	325.00
	1866	.915	8.50	32.00	110.00	400.00
	1867	.424	20.00	60.00	250.00	700.00
	1867 plain edge		—	—	Proof	4000.

Obv. leg: BRITT. . . . w/die number.

KM#	Date	Mintage	Fine	VF	XF	Unc
746.2	1868	.870	8.50	32.00	110.00	400.00
	1869	.297	8.50	32.00	95.00	275.00
	1869	—	—	—	Proof	2000.
	1870	1.081	8.00	32.00	110.00	325.00
	1871	3.426	8.00	32.00	110.00	325.00
	1871	—	—	—	Proof	2250.
	1871 plain edge		—	—	Proof	2250.
	1872	7.200	7.50	30.00	90.00	240.00
	1873	5.922	8.00	32.00	90.00	240.00
	1873	—	—	—	Proof	2500.
	1874	1.643	8.00	32.00	95.00	275.00
	1875	1.117	8.00	32.00	95.00	275.00
	1876	.580	8.00	32.00	100.00	300.00
	1877	.682	8.00	32.00	100.00	300.00
	1878	1.787	8.00	32.00	100.00	325.00
	1878	—	—	—	Proof	2750.
	1879	1.512	15.00	50.00	150.00	375.00

W/o die numbers.

KM#	Date	Mintage	Fine	VF	XF	Unc
746.4	1877	Inc. Ab.	25.00	70.00	300.00	650.00
	1878	Inc. Ab.	8.00	32.00	100.00	325.00
	1878	—	—	—	Proof	4500.
	1879	Inc. Ab.	12.50	35.00	125.00	350.00
	1879	—	—	—	Proof	2250.
	1880	2.161	7.50	30.00	85.00	275.00
	1880	—	—	—	Proof	4000.
	1881	2.576	7.50	30.00	85.00	275.00
	1881	—	—	—	Proof	2250.
	1881 plain edge		—	—	Proof	2500.
	1881 (error) MDCCCLXXRI					
		Inc. Ab.	12.00	40.00	120.00	300.00
	1883	3.556	7.50	30.00	90.00	240.00
	1884	1.447	7.50	30.00	90.00	275.00
	1885	1.758	7.50	30.00	80.00	240.00
	1885	—	—	—	Proof	2000.
	1886	.592	8.50	32.00	100.00	300.00
	1886	—	—	—	Proof	2000.

KM#	Date	Mintage	Fine	VF	XF	Unc
46.4	1887	1.777	10.00	40.00	120.00	375.00
	1887	—	—	—	Proof	2000.

NOTE: Varieties exist.

KM#	Date	Mintage	Fine	VF	XF	Unc
762	1887	Inc. Ab.	3.00	6.00	16.00	38.00
	1887	1,084	—	—	Proof	150.00
	1888	1.548	4.00	8.00	25.00	65.00
	1889	2.974	4.00	8.00	25.00	65.00
	1890	1.685	6.50	30.00	95.00	200.00
	1891	.836	15.00	55.00	165.00	300.00
	1892	.283	17.50	60.00	200.00	400.00
	1892	—	—	—	Proof	1500.

KM#	Date	Mintage	Fine	VF	XF	Unc
781	1893	1.666	3.50	10.00	25.00	65.00
	1893	1.312	—	—	Proof	150.00
	1894	1.953	3.50	10.00	35.00	75.00
	1895	2.183	3.50	10.00	30.00	70.00
	1896	2.944	3.50	10.00	35.00	75.00
	1897	1.700	3.50	10.00	30.00	70.00
	1898	3.061	3.50	10.00	35.00	70.00
	1899	3.970	3.50	10.00	30.00	70.00
	1900	5.529	3.50	10.00	30.00	70.00
	1901	2.649	3.50	10.00	25.00	65.00

KM#	Date	Mintage	Fine	VF	XF	Unc
801	1902	2.190	7.50	15.00	30.00	70.00
	1902	.015	—	Matte Proof		75.00
	1903	.995	12.00	45.00	100.00	120.00
	1904	2.770	10.00	40.00	100.00	200.00
	1905	1.188	25.00	75.00	175.00	475.00
	1906	6.910	8.00	25.00	55.00	130.00
	1907	5.948	8.00	25.00	70.00	175.00
	1908	3.280	9.00	27.50	110.00	240.00
	1909	3.483	10.00	37.50	125.00	275.00
	1910	5.651	6.00	14.00	40.00	90.00

KM#	Date	Mintage	Fine	VF	XF	Unc
817	1911	5.951	4.00	7.50	30.00	75.00
	1911	6.007	—	—	Proof	90.00
	1912	8.572	4.50	9.00	45.00	90.00
	1913	4.545	6.00	12.00	50.00	100.00
	1914	21.253	3.00	5.00	15.00	40.00
	1915	12.358	3.00	4.00	10.00	40.00
	1916	21.064	3.00	4.00	10.00	40.00
	1917	11.182	3.00	6.00	12.50	60.00
	1918	29.212	3.00	4.00	10.00	40.00
	1919	9.469	3.50	5.00	10.00	50.00

11.3104 g, .500 SILVER, .1818 oz ASW

KM#	Date	Mintage	Fine	VF	XF	Unc
817a	1920	15.388	1.75	4.50	13.50	55.00
	1921	34.864	1.75	3.00	12.00	37.50
	1922	23.861	1.75	3.00	13.50	50.00
	1923	21.547	1.75	3.00	13.50	37.50
	1924	4.582	2.00	5.00	15.00	65.00
	1925	1.404	10.00	40.00	95.00	200.00
	1926	5.125	3.50	8.00	30.00	90.00

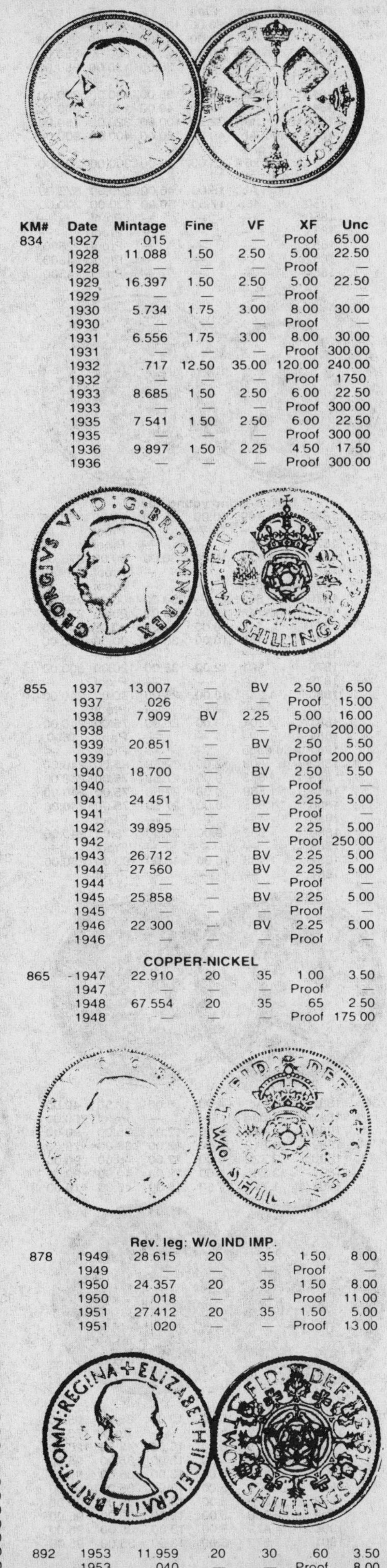

KM#	Date	Mintage	Fine	VF	XF	Unc
834	1927	.015	—	—	Proof	65.00
	1928	11.088	1.50	2.50	5.00	22.50
	1928	—	—	—	Proof	—
	1929	16.397	1.50	2.50	5.00	22.50
	1929	—	—	—	Proof	—
	1930	5.734	1.75	3.00	8.00	30.00
	1930	—	—	—	Proof	—
	1931	6.556	1.75	3.00	8.00	30.00
	1931	—	—	—	Proof	300.00
	1932	.717	12.50	35.00	120.00	240.00
	1932	—	—	—	Proof	1750.
	1933	8.685	1.50	2.50	6.00	22.50
	1933	—	—	—	Proof	300.00
	1935	7.541	1.50	2.50	6.00	22.50
	1935	—	—	—	Proof	300.00
	1936	9.897	1.50	2.25	4.50	17.50
	1936	—	—	—	Proof	300.00

KM#	Date	Mintage	Fine	VF	XF	Unc
855	1937	13.007	—	BV	2.50	6.50
	1937	.026	—	—	Proof	15.00
	1938	7.909	BV	2.25	5.00	16.00
	1938	—	—	—	Proof	200.00
	1939	20.851	—	BV	2.50	5.50
	1939	—	—	—	Proof	200.00
	1940	18.700	—	BV	2.50	5.50
	1940	—	—	—	Proof	—
	1941	24.451	—	BV	2.25	5.00
	1941	—	—	—	Proof	—
	1942	39.895	—	BV	2.25	5.00
	1942	—	—	—	Proof	250.00
	1943	26.712	—	BV	2.25	5.00
	1944	27.560	—	BV	2.25	5.00
	1944	—	—	—	Proof	—
	1945	25.858	—	BV	2.25	5.00
	1945	—	—	—	Proof	—
	1946	22.300	—	BV	2.25	5.00
	1946	—	—	—	Proof	—

COPPER-NICKEL

KM#	Date	Mintage	Fine	VF	XF	Unc
865	1947	22.910	.20	.35	1.00	3.50
	1947	—	—	—	Proof	—
	1948	67.554	.20	.35	.65	2.50
	1948	—	—	—	Proof	175.00

Rev. leg: W/o IND IMP.

KM#	Date	Mintage	Fine	VF	XF	Unc
878	1949	28.615	.20	.35	1.50	8.00
	1949	—	—	—	Proof	—
	1950	24.357	.20	.35	1.50	8.00
	1950	.018	—	—	Proof	11.00
	1951	27.412	.20	.35	1.50	5.00
	1951	.020	—	—	Proof	13.00

KM#	Date	Mintage	Fine	VF	XF	Unc
892	1953	11.959	.20	.30	.60	3.50
	1953	.040	—	—	Proof	8.00

Obv. leg: W/o BRITT OMN.

KM#	Date	Mintage	Fine	VF	XF	Unc
906	1954	13.085	.20	.50	3.50	18.00
	1954	—	—	—	Proof	250.00
	1955	25.887	.20	.30	.50	1.75
	1955	—	—	—	Proof	—
	1956	47.824	.20	.30	.50	2.50
	1956	—	—	—	Proof	200.00
	1957	33.071	.20	.35	1.75	16.00
	1957	—	—	—	Proof	—
	1958	9.565	.25	.50	.75	8.00
	1958	—	—	—	Proof	325.00
	1959	14.080	.25	.50	3.50	20.00
	1959	—	—	—	Proof	—
	1960	13.832	—	.20	.30	1.75
	1960	—	—	—	Proof	—
	1961	37.735	—	.20	.40	2.00
	1961	—	—	—	Proof	—
	1962	35.148	—	.20	.30	1.50
	1962	—	—	—	Proof	—
	1963	26.471	—	.20	.25	1.00
	1963	—	—	—	Proof	—
	1964	16.539	—	.20	.25	1.00
	1965	48.163	—	.20	.25	.75
	1966	83.999	—	.20	.25	.75
	1967	39.718	—	.20	.25	.75
	1970	.750	—	—	Proof	3.00

1/2 CROWN

14.1380 g, .925 SILVER, .4205 oz ASW

Obv: Large bust.

KM#	Date	Mintage	Fine	VF	XF	Unc
667	1816	—	12.00	40.00	175.00	550.00
	1816 reeded edge		—	—	Proof	1250
	1816 plain edge		—	—	Proof	1250
	1817	8.093	10.00	35.00	130.00	225.00
	1817 reeded edge		—	—	Proof	1250
	1817 plain edge		—	—	Proof	1250

Obv: Small head.

KM#	Date	Mintage	Fine	VF	XF	Unc
672	1817	Inc. Ab.	10.00	35.00	130.00	225.00
	1817	—	—	—	Proof	1250.
	1817 plain edge		—	—	Proof	1500.
	1818	2.905	15.00	40.00	150.00	350.00
	1818	—	—	—	Proof	1000.
	1819	4.790	10.00	35.00	135.00	325.00
	1819	—	—	—	Proof	1000.
	1820	2.397	15.00	50.00	175.00	375.00
	1820	—	—	—	Proof	1000.
	1820 plain edge		—	—	Proof	1250.

KM#	Date	Mintage	Fine	VF	XF	Unc
676	1820	Inc. Ab.	12.00	30.00	135.00	300.00
	1820	—	—	—	Proof	900.00
	1820 plain edge		—	—	Proof	1200.
	1821	1.435	15.00	35.00	145.00	300.00

KM#	Date	Mintage	Fine	VF	XF	Unc
676	1821	—	—	—	Proof	950.00
	1823	2.004	225.00	675.00	3250.	5500.

KM#	Date	Mintage	Fine	VF	XF	Unc
688	1823	Inc. Ab.	14.00	35.00	160.00	400.00
	1823	—	—	—	Proof	1250.
	1824	.466	17.50	45.00	190.00	600.00
	1824	—	—	—	Proof	1250.

KM#	Date	Mintage	Fine	VF	XF	Unc
695	1824	—	—	—	Proof	4500.
	1825	2.259	12.00	37.50	135.00	300.00
	1825	—	—	—	Proof	1000.
	1825 plain edge		—	—	Proof	1200.
	1826	2.189	10.00	30.00	115.00	250.00
	1826	—	—	—	Proof	725.00
	1828	.050	17.50	55.00	250.00	600.00
	1829	.508	15.00	55.00	160.00	425.00

KM#	Date	Mintage	Fine	VF	XF	Unc
714.1	1831	—	—	—	Proof	1000.
	1831 plain edge		—	—	Proof	750.00

Obv: Larger, modified bust.

KM#	Date	Mintage	Fine	VF	XF	Unc
714.2	1834 W.W. in caps					
		.993	20.00	60.00	200.00	350.00
	1834	—	—	—	Proof	1500.
	1834 W.W. in script					
		Inc. Ab.	15.00	40.00	150.00	300.00
	1834	—	—	—	Proof	1500.
	1834 plain edge		—	—	Proof	2000.
	1835	.282	25.00	60.00	200.00	400.00
	1836/5	1.589	30.00	65.00	225.00	500.00
	1836	Inc. Ab.	15.00	40.00	150.00	300.00
	1836 plain edge		—	—	Proof	1800.
	1837	.151	25.00	60.00	200.00	400.00

KM#	Date	Mintage	Fine	VF	XF	Unc
740	1839 W.W. in relief					
		—	200.00	750.00	2750.	4250.
	1839 plain edge		—	—	Proof	1100.
	1840 W.W. incuse					
		.386	25.00	75.00	185.00	400.00

KM#	Date	Mintage	Fine	VF	XF	Unc
740	1841	.043	30.00	100.00	450.00	1100.
	1842	.486	10.00	35.00	150.00	350.00
	1843	.455	20.00	70.00	300.00	650.00
	1844	1.999	10.00	35.00	150.00	350.00
	1845/3	2.232	—	—	—	—
	1845	Inc. Ab.	10.00	35.00	130.00	300.00
	1846	1.540	10.00	40.00	140.00	300.00
	1848/6	.367	32.50	100.00	320.00	750.00
	1848	Inc. Ab.	40.00	120.00	400.00	900.00
	1849 large date					
		.261	15.00	45.00	300.00	700.00
	1849 small date					
		Inc. Ab.	15.00	40.00	280.00	675.00
	1850	.485	17.50	50.00	320.00	700.00
	1850	—	—	—	Proof	—
	1851	—	—	—	Proof	—
	1853	—	—	—	Proof	2500.
	1862	—	—	—	Proof	4500.
	1864	—	—	—	Proof	4500.

Obv: Second young head.

KM#	Date	Mintage	Fine	VF	XF	Unc
756	1874	2.189	10.00	25.00	80.00	250.00
	1874	—	—	—	Proof	—
	1874 plain edge		—	—	Proof	—
	1875	1.113	10.00	30.00	90.00	275.00
	1875	—	—	—	Proof	—
	1875 plain edge		—	—	Proof	—
	1876/5	.633	—	200.00	400.00	950.00
	1876	Inc. Ab.	10.00	30.00	90.00	275.00
	1877	.447	10.00	30.00	90.00	240.00
	1878	1.466	10.00	30.00	90.00	240.00
	1878	—	—	—	Proof	—
	1879	.901	12.00	35.00	120.00	300.00
	1879	—	—	—	Proof	—
	1880	1.346	10.00	25.00	80.00	240.00
	1880	—	—	—	Proof	—
	1881	2.301	9.00	25.00	75.00	240.00
	1881	—	—	—	Proof	1500.
	1881 plain edge		—	—	Proof	—
	1882	.808	12.00	32.50	85.00	240.00
	1883	2.983	9.00	27.50	75.00	240.00
	1884	1.569	9.00	27.50	75.00	240.00
	1885	1.628	9.00	27.50	75.00	240.00
	1885	—	—	—	Proof	—
	1886	.892	9.00	27.50	75.00	240.00
	1886	—	—	—	Proof	—
	1887	1.438	10.00	40.00	100.00	250.00
	1887	—	—	—	Proof	—

KM#	Date	Mintage	Fine	VF	XF	Unc
764	1887	Inc. Ab.	4.00	8.00	12.50	40.00
	1887	1,084	—	—	Proof	200.00
	1888	1.429	6.00	12.00	35.00	90.00
	1889	4.812	6.00	12.00	30.00	75.00
	1890	3.228	6.00	12.00	40.00	90.00
	1891	2.285	6.00	12.00	40.00	90.00
	1892	1.711	7.50	15.00	45.00	110.00

KM#	Date	Mintage	Fine	VF	XF	Unc
782	1893	1.793	5.00	13.00	35.00	95.00
	1893	1,312	—	—	Proof	175.00
	1894	1.525	6.00	16.00	45.00	120.00
	1895	1.773	5.00	13.00	35.00	95.00
	1896	2.149	5.00	13.00	35.00	95.00
	1897	1.679	5.00	13.00	35.00	95.00
	1898	1.870	5.00	13.00	35.00	95.00
	1899	2.866	5.00	13.00	35.00	95.00
	1900	4.479	5.00	13.00	35.00	95.00
	1901	1.577	5.00	13.00	35.00	95.00

KM#	Date	Mintage	Fine	VF	XF	Unc
802	1902	1.316	10.00	20.00	40.00	100.00
	1902	.015	—		Matte Proof	100.00
	1903	.275	22.50	75.00	300.00	850.00
	1904	.710	15.00	45.00	175.00	500.00
	1905	.166	100.00	300.00	1000.	1750.
	1906	2.886	9.00	25.00	55.00	200.00
	1907	3.694	10.00	27.50	55.00	210.00
	1908	1.759	12.00	30.00	80.00	265.00
	1909	3.052	10.00	22.50	60.00	175.00
	1910	2.558	8.50	20.00	40.00	120.00

KM#	Date	Mintage	Fine	VF	XF	Unc
818.1	1911	2.915	5.00	12.00	40.00	120.00
	1911	6,007	—	—	Proof	130.00
	1912	4.701	5.00	12.00	40.00	100.00
	1913	4.090	6.50	15.00	50.00	140.00
	1914	18.333	4.00	7.00	12.50	45.00
	1915	32.433	4.00	6.00	12.50	40.00
	1916	29.530	4.00	6.00	12.50	40.00
	1917	11.172	4.50	7.00	15.00	50.00
	1918	29.080	4.00	6.00	12.50	40.00
	1919	10.267	4.50	8.00	17.50	55.00

14.1380 g, .500 SILVER, .2273 oz ASW
Rev: Crown touches shield.

KM#	Date	Mintage	Fine	VF	XF	Unc
818.1a	1920	17.983	2.25	5.00	17.50	75.00
	1921	23.678	2.25	5.00	20.00	85.00
	1922	16.397	2.25	5.00	20.00	85.00

Rev: Groove between crown and shield.

KM#	Date	Mintage	Fine	VF	XF	Unc
818.2	1922	Inc. Ab.	2.50	5.00	17.50	70.00
	1923	26.309	2.00	4.50	12.50	40.00
	1924	5.866	3.00	7.50	20.00	80.00
	1925	1.413	12.50	30.00	150.00	400.00
	1926	4.474	3.00	10.00	35.00	95.00

Obv: Modified effigy; larger beads.

KM#	Date	Mintage	Fine	VF	XF	Unc
830	1926	Inc. Ab.	3.00	10.00	50.00	135.00
	1927	6.838	2.50	6.00	15.00	50.00

KM#	Date	Mintage	Fine	VF	XF	Unc
835	1927	.015	—	—	Proof	50.00
	1928	18.763	2.00	3.00	7.50	22.50
	1928	—	—	—	Proof	—
	1929	17.633	2.00	3.00	7.50	22.50
	1929	—	—	—	Proof	—
	1930	.810	10.00	25.00	130.00	275.00
	1930	—	—	—	Proof	1000.
	1931	11.264	2.00	4.00	8.00	22.50
	1931	—	—	—	Proof	600.00
	1932	4.794	3.50	8.00	17.50	45.00
	1932	—	—	—	Proof	600.00
	1933	10.311	2.00	4.00	8.00	22.50
	1933	—	—	—	Proof	600.00
	1934	2.422	3.25	7.00	25.00	85.00
	1934	—	—	—	Proof	600.00
	1935	7.022	2.00	3.00	6.50	20.00
	1935	—	—	—	Proof	600.00
	1936	7.039	2.00	3.00	6.00	17.50
	1936	—	—	—	Proof	600.00

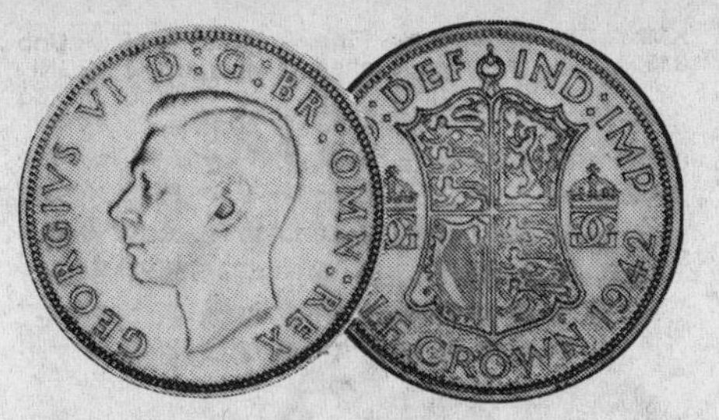

KM#	Date	Mintage	Fine	VF	XF	Unc
856	1937	9.106	BV	2.00	3.50	11.00
	1937	.026	—	—	Proof	16.00
	1938	6.426	BV	2.50	7.50	25.00
	1938	—	—	—	Proof	400.00
	1939	15.479	BV	2.00	3.50	11.00
	1939	—	—	—	Proof	400.00
	1940	17.948	BV	2.00	3.00	8.00
	1940	—	—	—	Proof	—
	1941	15.774	BV	1.75	2.75	6.50
	1941	—	—	—	Proof	—
	1942	31.220	BV	1.75	2.75	6.25
	1943	15.463	BV	1.75	2.75	6.25
	1943	—	—	—	Proof	—
	1944	15.255	BV	1.75	2.75	6.25
	1945	19.849	BV	1.75	2.75	6.25
	1945	—	—	—	Proof	—
	1946	22.725	BV	1.75	2.75	6.25
	1946	—	—	—	Proof	—

COPPER-NICKEL

KM#	Date	Mintage	Fine	VF	XF	Unc
866	1947	21.910	.25	.50	1.25	5.00
	1947	—	—	—	Proof	400.00
	1948	71.165	.25	.50	1.25	5.00
	1948	—	—	—	Proof	350.00

Rev. leg: W/o IND IMP.

KM#	Date	Mintage	Fine	VF	XF	Unc
879	1949	28.273	.25	.50	1.25	10.00
	1949	—	—	—	Proof	—
	1950	28.336	.25	.50	1.50	10.00
	1950	.018	—	—	Proof	12.50
	1951	9.004	.50	.75	1.50	10.00
	1951	.020	—	—	Proof	12.50
	1952	1 known	—	11,000.	—	—

KM#	Date	Mintage	Fine	VF	XF	Unc
893	1953	4.333	.50	.75	1.50	3.50
	1953	.040	—	—	Proof	12.00

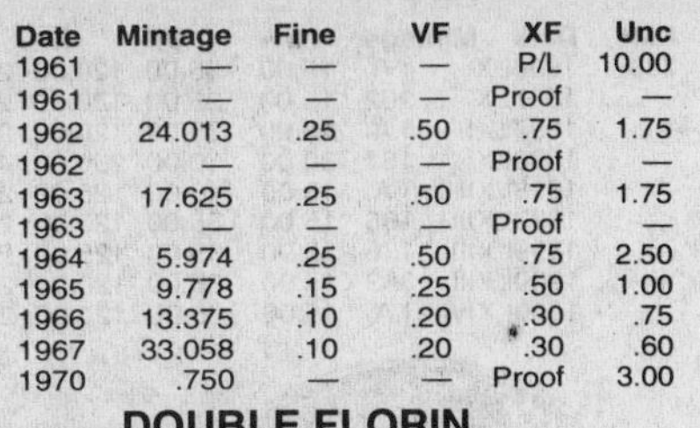

Obv. leg: W/o BRITT OMN.

KM#	Date	Mintage	Fine	VF	XF	Unc
907	1954	11.615	.50	1.00	5.00	20.00
	1954	—	—	—	Proof	400.00
	1955	23.629	.25	.50	1.00	5.00
	1955	—	—	—	Proof	—
	1956	33.935	.25	.50	1.00	5.00
	1956	—	—	—	Proof	—
	1957	34.201	.25	.50	.75	3.50
	1957	—	—	—	Proof	—
	1958	15.746	.25	.75	4.00	12.50
	1958	—	—	—	Proof	—
	1959	9.029	1.00	1.50	6.50	28.00
	1959	—	—	—	Proof	—
	1960	19.929	.25	.50	.75	5.00
	1960	—	—	—	Proof	—
	1961	25.888	.25	.50	.75	1.75

KM#	Date	Mintage	Fine	VF	XF	Unc
907	1961	—	—	—	P/L	10.00
	1961	—	—	—	Proof	—
	1962	24.013	.25	.50	.75	1.75
	1962	—	—	—	Proof	—
	1963	17.625	.25	.50	.75	1.75
	1963	—	—	—	Proof	—
	1964	5.974	.25	.50	.75	2.50
	1965	9.778	.15	.25	.50	1.00
	1966	13.375	.10	.20	.30	.75
	1967	33.058	.10	.20	.30	.60
	1970	.750	—	—	Proof	3.00

DOUBLE FLORIN

22.6207 g, .925 SILVER, .6727 oz ASW

KM#	Date	Mintage	Fine	VF	XF	Unc
763	1887 Roman I	.483	10.00	17.50	35.00	100.00
	1887 Roman I	1,084	—	—	Proof	950.00
	1887 Arabic 1	Inc. Ab.	10.00	17.50	35.00	100.00
	1887 Arabic 1	*2,916	—	—	Proof	350.00
	1888	.243	10.00	22.00	55.00	180.00
	1888 2nd I in VICTORIA, inverted 1	Inc. Ab.	20.00	35.00	120.00	325.00
	1889	1.185	10.00	17.50	40.00	100.00
	1889 2nd I in VICTORIA, inverted 1	Inc. Ab.	20.00	35.00	150.00	500.00
	1890	.782	10.00	20.00	50.00	175.00

CROWN

28.2759 g, .925 SILVER, .8409 oz ASW

KM#	Date	Mintage	Fine	VF	XF	Unc
675	1818 LVIII	.155	25.00	60.00	180.00	550.00
	1818 LIX	I.A.	25.00	60.00	180.00	500.00
	1819/8 LIX	.683	32.50	100.00	350.00	900.00
	1819 LIX	I.A.	25.00	60.00	180.00	550.00
	1819 LX	I.A.	25.00	60.00	180.00	500.00
	1819 plain edge	—	—	—	Proof	—
	1820/19 LX	—	32.50	100.00	350.00	800.00
	1820 LX	.448	25.00	60.00	200.00	650.00

SECUNDO on edge

KM#	Date	Mintage	Fine	VF	XF	Unc
680.1	1821	.438	30.00	65.00	300.00	950.00
	1821	—	—	—	Proof	2500.
	1822	.125	35.00	80.00	450.00	1200.
	1822	—	—	—	Proof	3000.

TERTIO on edge

KM#	Date	Mintage	Fine	VF	XF	Unc
680.2	1821	—	—	—	Proof	3500.
	1822	—	30.00	65.00	300.00	950.00
	1822	—	—	—	Proof	5000.

KM#	Date	Mintage	Fine	VF	XF	Unc
699	1826 plain edge	—	Reported, not confirmed			
	1826 SEPTIMO on edge	150 pcs.	—	—	Proof	4000.
	1826 LVIII on edge	—	—	—	Proof	Rare

KM#	Date	Mintage	Fine	VF	XF	Unc
715	1831	100 pcs.	—	—	Proof	8000.

KM#	Date	Mintage	Fine	VF	XF	Unc
741	1839	—	—	—	Proof	4500.
	1844	.094	25.00	75.00	450.00	2250.
	1844	—	—	—	Proof	12,000.
	1845	.159	25.00	75.00	450.00	2250.
	1845	—	—	—	Proof	11,000.
	1847	.141	30.00	90.00	600.00	3900.
	1847	—	—	—	Proof	—

KM#	Date	Mintage	Fine	VF	XF	Unc
744	1847 UN DECIMO on edge	8,000	—	—	Proof	2500.
	Impaired Proof		300.00	475.00	700.00	—
	1847 SEPTIMO on edge	—	—	—	Proof	9000.
	1847 plain edge	—			Proof	2400.
	Impaired Proof		300.00	575.00	900.00	—
	1853 SEPTIMO on edge	460 pcs.	—	—	Proof	7000.
	1853 plain edge		—	—	Proof	8000.

KM#	Date	Mintage	Fine	VF	XF	Unc
765	1887	.173	13.50	27.50	55.00	110.00
	1887	1,084	—	—	Proof	500.00
	1888	.132	16.00	35.00	65.00	250.00
	1889	1.807	13.50	27.50	55.00	150.00
	1890	.998	14.50	30.00	60.00	220.00
	1891	.566	16.00	35.00	65.00	225.00
	1892	.451	18.00	40.00	75.00	300.00

KM#	Date	Mintage	Fine	VF	XF	Unc
783	1893LVI	.498	15.00	35.00	95.00	240.00
	1893LVI	1,312	—	—	Proof	650.00
	1893LVII	I.A.	30.00	110.00	300.00	600.00
	1894LVII	.145	15.00	50.00	140.00	280.00
	1894LVIII	I.A.	15.00	35.00	125.00	275.00
	1895LVIII	.253	15.00	35.00	125.00	275.00
	1895LIX	I.A.	15.00	35.00	120.00	260.00
	1896LIX	.318	25.00	50.00	250.00	500.00

KM#	Date	Mintage	Fine	VF	XF	Unc
783	1896LX	I.A.	15.00	35.00	120.00	260.00
	1897LX	.262	15.00	35.00	120.00	260.00
	1897LXI	I.A.	15.00	35.00	120.00	260.00
	1898LXI	.161	30.00	60.00	250.00	400.00
	1898LXII	I.A.	15.00	40.00	125.00	275.00
	1899LXII	.166	15.00	35.00	125.00	275.00
	1899LXIII	I.A.	15.00	35.00	125.00	275.00
	1900LXIII	.353	15.00	35.00	120.00	260.00
	1900LXIV	I.A.	15.00	35.00	120.00	260.00

KM#	Date	Mintage	Fine	VF	XF	Unc
803	1902	.256	25.00	50.00	90.00	175.00
	1902	.015	—		Matte Proof	200.00

28.2759 g, .500 SILVER, .4546 oz ASW

KM#	Date	Mintage	Fine	VF	XF	Unc
836	1927	.015	—	—	Proof	200.00
	1928	9,034	60.00	95.00	150.00	325.00
	1928	—	—	—	Proof	1200.
	1929	4,994	65.00	100.00	165.00	350.00
	1929	—	—	—	Proof	1500.
	1930	4,847	65.00	100.00	165.00	350.00
	1930	—	—	—	Proof	1500.
	1931	4,056	70.00	125.00	200.00	400.00
	1931	—	—	—	Proof	—
	1932	2,395	85.00	175.00	250.00	600.00
	1932	—	—	—	Proof	2500.
	1933	7,132	65.00	100.00	165.00	350.00
	1933	—	—	—	Proof	—
	1934	932 pcs.	450.00	750.00	1500.	2500.
	1934	—	—	—	Proof	3200.
	1936	2,473	90.00	180.00	250.00	550.00
	1936	—	—	—	Proof	1500.

George V Silver Jubilee

KM#	Date	Mintage	Fine	VF	XF	Unc
842	1935 incused edge lettering	.715	6.00	8.00	12.50	25.00
	1935 specimen in box of issue	—	—	—	—	75.00
	1935 (error) edge lettering: MEN.ANNO-REGNI XXV.	Inc. Ab.	—	—	Proof	900.00

.925 SILVER

KM#	Date	Mintage	Fine	VF	XF	Unc
842a	1935 raised edge lettering	2,500	—	—	Proof	400.00

47.8300 g, .917 GOLD, 1.4096 oz AGW

KM#	Date	Mintage	Fine	VF	XF	Unc
842b	1935	28 pcs.	—	—	Proof	—

KM#	Date	Mintage	Fine	VF	XF	Unc
857	1937	.419	8.00	12.00	18.50	35.00
	1937	.026	—	—	Proof	60.00
	1937	—	—	V.I.P. Proof		350.00

COPPER-NICKEL
Festival of Britain

KM#	Date	Mintage	Fine	VF	XF	Unc
880	1951	2.004	—	—	P/L	10.00
	1951	—	—	—	Proof	—
	1951	30-50 pcs.	—	V.I.P. Proof		300.00

Coronation of Queen Elizabeth II

KM#	Date	Mintage	Fine	VF	XF	Unc
894	1953	5.963	—	—	2.25	4.00
	1953	.040	—	—	Proof	25.00
	1953	20-30 pcs.	—	V.I.P. Proof		300.00

British Exhibition in New York

KM#	Date	Mintage	Fine	VF	XF	Unc
909	1960	1.024	—	—	4.00	6.00
	1960	.070	—	—	P/L	12.50
	1960	30-50 pcs.	—	V.I.P. Proof		300.00

Winston Churchill

KM#	Date	Mintage	Fine	VF	XF	Unc
910	1965	9.640	—	—	.60	.80
	1965	—	—		Specimen	325.00

NOTE: The Specimen is struck with satin-finish.

GUINEA SERIES

1/3 GUINEA

2.7834 g, .917 GOLD, .0820 oz AGW

KM#	Date	Mintage	Fine	VF	XF	Unc
648	1801	—	60.00	90.00	150.00	225.00
	1802	—	60.00	90.00	150.00	225.00
	1803	—	60.00	90.00	150.00	225.00

KM#	Date	Mintage	Fine	VF	XF	Unc
650	1804	—	60.00	90.00	150.00	250.00
	1806	—	60.00	90.00	150.00	250.00
	1808	—	60.00	90.00	150.00	250.00
	1809	—	60.00	90.00	150.00	250.00
	1810	—	60.00	90.00	150.00	250.00
	1811	—	125.00	300.00	800.00	1100.
	1813	—	65.00	100.00	325.00	550.00
	1813	—	—	—	Proof	3000.

1/2 GUINEA

4.1750 g, .917 GOLD, .1230 oz AGW

KM#	Date	Mintage	Fine	VF	XF	Unc
649	1801	—	100.00	125.00	200.00	525.00
	1802	—	100.00	125.00	200.00	525.00
	1803	—	100.00	125.00	200.00	525.00

KM#	Date	Mintage	Fine	VF	XF	Unc
651	1804	—	100.00	125.00	200.00	525.00
	1806	—	100.00	125.00	200.00	525.00
	1808	—	100.00	125.00	200.00	525.00
	1809	—	100.00	125.00	200.00	525.00
	1810	—	100.00	125.00	200.00	525.00
	1811	—	100.00	150.00	300.00	650.00
	1813	—	100.00	125.00	275.00	600.00

GUINEA

8.3500 g, .917 GOLD, .2461 oz AGW

KM#	Date	Mintage	Fine	VF	XF	Unc
664	1813	—	250.00	500.00	850.00	1750.
	1813	—	—	—	Proof	5000.

SOVEREIGN SERIES

1/2 SOVEREIGN

MINT MARKS

C - Ottawa, Canada
I - Bombay, India
M - Melbourne, Australia
P - Perth, Australia
S - Sydney, Australia
SA - Pretoria, South Africa

NOTE: 1/2 Sovereigns were struck at various foreign mints. The mint mark on the St. George/dragon type is usually found on the base below the right rear hoof of the horse. On shield type reverse the mint mark is found below the shield. Refer to appropriate country listings elsewhere in this catalog for coins having mint marks.

3.9940 g, .917 GOLD, .1177 oz AGW

KM#	Date	Mintage	Fine	VF	XF	Unc
673	1817	2.080	70.00	150.00	325.00	550.00
	1817	—	—	—	Proof	3500.
	1818/7	1.030	—	—	Rare	—
	1818	Inc. Ab.	75.00	150.00	350.00	650.00
	1818	—	—	—	Proof	5000.
	1820	.035	90.00	175.00	400.00	700.00

KM#	Date	Mintage	Fine	VF	XF	Unc
681	1821	.231	225.00	600.00	1700.	2700.
	1821	—	—	—	Proof	5000.

KM#	Date	Mintage	Fine	VF	XF	Unc
689	1823	.224	100.00	225.00	525.00	800.00
	1823	—	—	—	Proof	5500.
	1824	.592	90.00	200.00	450.00	800.00
	1825	.761	90.00	200.00	450.00	800.00
	1825	—	—	—	Proof	2000.

Obv: Bare head.

KM#	Date	Mintage	Fine	VF	XF	Unc
700	1826	.345	80.00	180.00	450.00	800.00
	1826	—	—	—	Proof	1750.
	1827	.492	85.00	200.00	475.00	1000.
	1828	1.225	80.00	190.00	450.00	900.00

KM#	Date	Mintage	Fine	VF	XF	Unc
716	1831	—	—	—	Proof	2000.

18mm

KM#	Date	Mintage	Fine	VF	XF	Unc
720	1834	.134	115.00	250.00	600.00	1400.

19mm

KM#	Date	Mintage	Fine	VF	XF	Unc
722	1835	.773	95.00	225.00	600.00	1200.
	1836	.147	250.00	500.00	1500.	3500.
	1837	.160	95.00	250.00	550.00	1000.

Rev: W/o die number.

KM#	Date	Mintage	Fine	VF	XF	Unc
735.1	1838	.273	75.00	90.00	225.00	625.00
	1839	1,230	—	—	Proof	3000.
	1841	.509	75.00	90.00	225.00	625.00
	1842	2.223	75.00	90.00	200.00	550.00
	1843	1.252	75.00	90.00	200.00	625.00
	1844	1.127	75.00	90.00	200.00	550.00
	1845	.888	75.00	220.00	325.00	750.00
	1846	1.064	75.00	100.00	225.00	625.00
	1847	.983	75.00	90.00	200.00	550.00
	1848	.411	75.00	150.00	250.00	800.00
	1849	.845	75.00	100.00	200.00	550.00
	1850	.180	180.00	275.00	900.00	1625.
	1851	.774	70.00	100.00	225.00	625.00
	1852	1.378	70.00	100.00	200.00	550.00
	1853	2.709	70.00	100.00	200.00	550.00
	1853	—	—	—	Proof	5000.
	1854	1.125	225.00	350.00	650.00	1500.
	1855	1.120	70.00	100.00	200.00	550.00
	1856	2.392	70.00	100.00	200.00	550.00
	1857	.728	70.00	100.00	150.00	450.00
	1858	.856	70.00	100.00	175.00	495.00
	1859	2.204	70.00	90.00	175.00	495.00
	1860	1.132	70.00	90.00	175.00	495.00
	1861	1.131	70.00	100.00	200.00	575.00
	1862	—	350.00	600.00	2700.	6500.
	1863	1.572	70.00	90.00	150.00	450.00
	1880	1.009	60.00	75.00	125.00	325.00
	1883	2.870	60.00	90.00	150.00	325.00
	1884	1.114	60.00	90.00	150.00	325.00
	1885/3	4.469	80.00	110.00	180.00	375.00
	1885	Inc. Ab.	60.00	90.00	100.00	290.00

NOTE: 1854 is much rarer than the mintage figure indicates.

Rev: W/die number.

KM#	Date	Mintage	Fine	VF	XF	Unc
735.2	1863	Inc. Ab.	60.00	85.00	180.00	400.00
	1864	1.758	60.00	85.00	180.00	400.00
	1865	1.835	60.00	85.00	180.00	400.00
	1866	2.059	60.00	85.00	180.00	400.00
	1867	.993	60.00	85.00	180.00	400.00
	1869	1.862	60.00	85.00	200.00	400.00
	1870	.160	60.00	85.00	200.00	400.00
	1871	2.063	60.00	85.00	200.00	400.00
	1871 plain edge		—	—	Proof	4000.
	1872	3.249	60.00	85.00	150.00	400.00
	1873	1.927	60.00	85.00	150.00	400.00
	1874	1.884	60.00	85.00	150.00	400.00
	1875	.516	60.00	85.00	150.00	400.00
	1876	2.785	60.00	85.00	150.00	400.00
	1877	2.197	60.00	75.00	125.00	325.00
	1878	2.082	60.00	75.00	125.00	325.00
	1879	.035	75.00	125.00	200.00	300.00
	1880	Inc. Ab.	60.00	75.00	125.00	325.00

KM#	Date	Mintage	Fine	VF	XF	Unc
766	1887	.872	BV	65.00	100.00	125.00
	1887	797 pcs.	—	—	Proof	500.00
	1890	2.266	BV	65.00	100.00	150.00
	1891	1.079	BV	65.00	100.00	150.00
	1892	13.680	BV	65.00	100.00	150.00
	1893	4.427	BV	65.00	100.00	150.00

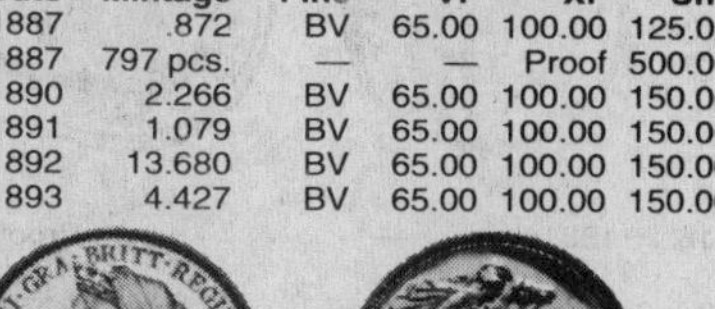

KM#	Date	Mintage	Fine	VF	XF	Unc
784	1893	Inc. Ab.	BV	65.00	85.00	115.00
	1893	773 pcs.	—	—	Proof	500.00
	1894	3.795	BV	60.00	75.00	125.00
	1895	2.869	BV	60.00	75.00	125.00
	1896	2.947	BV	60.00	75.00	125.00
	1897	3.568	BV	60.00	75.00	125.00
	1898	2.869	BV	60.00	75.00	125.00
	1899	3.362	BV	60.00	75.00	125.00
	1900	4.307	BV	60.00	75.00	125.00
	1901	2.038	BV	60.00	75.00	125.00

KM#	Date	Mintage	Fine	VF	XF	Unc
804	1902	4.244	BV	60.00	75.00	100.00
	1902	.015	—	—	Proof	225.00
	1903	2.522	BV	60.00	70.00	100.00
	1904	1.717	BV	60.00	70.00	100.00
	1905	3.024	BV	60.00	70.00	100.00
	1906	4.245	BV	60.00	70.00	100.00
	1907	4.233	BV	60.00	70.00	100.00
	1908	3.997	BV	60.00	70.00	100.00
	1909	4.011	BV	60.00	70.00	100.00
	1910	5.024	BV	60.00	70.00	100.00

KM#	Date	Mintage	Fine	VF	XF	Unc
819	1911	6.104	BV	60.00	70.00	100.00
	1911	3,764	—	—	Proof	325.00
	1912	6.224	BV	60.00	70.00	100.00
	1913	6.094	BV	60.00	70.00	100.00
	1914	7.251	BV	60.00	70.00	100.00
	1915	2.043	BV	60.00	70.00	100.00

KM#	Date	Mintage	Fine	VF	XF	Unc
858	1937	5,500	—	—	Proof	275.00
	1937	1 pc.	—		Matte Proof	Unique

3.9900 g, .917 GOLD, .1176 oz AGW

KM#	Date	Mintage	Fine	VF	XF	Unc
922	1980	.010	—	—	Proof	60.00
	1982	2.500	—	—	—	50.00
	1982	.023	—	—	Proof	60.00
	1983	.022	—	—	Proof	60.00
	1984	.022	—	—	Proof	60.00

Obv: New portrait of Elizabeth II.

KM#	Date	Mintage	Fine	VF	XF	Unc
942	1985	.025	—	—	Proof	60.00
	1986	.025	—	—	Proof	60.00
	1987	.023	—	—	Proof	60.00
	1988	*.023	—	—	Proof	60.00

KM#	Date	Mintage	Fine	VF	XF	Unc
942	1990	*.020	—	—	Proof	60.00
	1991	*9,000	—	—	Proof	150.00
	1992	7,500	—	—	Proof	155.00
	1993	7,500	—	—	Proof	145.00

500th Anniversary of the Gold Sovereign

KM#	Date	Mintage	Fine	VF	XF	Unc
955	1989	*.025	—	—	Proof	85.00

SOVEREIGN

MINT MARKS

C - Ottawa, Canada
I - Bombay, India
M - Melbourne, Australia
P - Perth, Australia
S - Sydney, Australia
SA - Pretoria, South Africa

NOTE: Sovereigns were struck at various colonial mints. The mint mark on the St. George/dragon type is usually found on the base below the right rear hoof of the horse. On shield type reverse the mint mark is found below the shield or on the obverse below the truncation. Refer to appropriate country listings elsewhere in this catalog for coins having these mint marks.

7.9881 g, .917 GOLD, .2354 oz AGW

KM#	Date	Mintage	Fine	VF	XF	Unc
674	1817	3.235	150.00	225.00	525.00	1000.
	1817	—	—	—	Proof	8000.
	1818	2.347	150.00	275.00	625.00	1200.
	1819	3,574	—	—	Rare	—
	1820	.932	150.00	225.00	525.00	1000.
	1820	—	—	—	Proof	—

KM#	Date	Mintage	Fine	VF	XF	Unc
682	1821	9.405	150.00	225.00	675.00	1250.
	1821	—	—	—	Proof	4500.
	1822	5.357	160.00	225.00	725.00	1100.
	1823	.617	225.00	500.00	1400.	—
	1824	3.768	175.00	225.00	800.00	1200.
	1825	4.200	225.00	500.00	1200.	3000.

KM#	Date	Mintage	Fine	VF	XF	Unc
696	1825	Inc. Ab.	125.00	225.00	675.00	1200.
	1825	—	—	—	Proof	3500.
	1825 plain edge		—	—	Proof	5000.
	1826	5.724	125.00	200.00	675.00	1100.
	1826	—	—	—	Proof	3500.
	1827	2.267	125.00	225.00	725.00	1200.
	1828 only 6 or 7 known					
		.386	800.00	2500.	6500.	—
	1829	2.445	125.00	225.00	675.00	1200.
	1830	2.388	125.00	225.00	675.00	1200.
	1830	—	—	—	Proof	—
	1830 plain edge		—	—	Proof	10,000.

KM#	Date	Mintage	Fine	VF	XF	Unc
717	1831	.599	150.00	300.00	800.00	1500.
	1831	—	—	—	Proof	5500.
	1832	3.737	125.00	200.00	625.00	1200.
	1833	1.225	125.00	225.00	725.00	1300.
	1835	.723	125.00	225.00	725.00	1300.
	1836	1.714	125.00	225.00	725.00	1300.
	1837	1.173	125.00	225.00	725.00	1300.

Rev: W/o die number.

KM#	Date	Mintage	Fine	VF	XF	Unc
736.1	1838	2.719	BV	160.00	275.00	725.00
	1838	—	—	—	Proof	4000.
	1839	.504	175.00	350.00	1000.	2000.
	1839	—	—	—	Proof	5000.
	1841	.124	1100.	1800.	5500.	—
	1842	4.865	—	BV	275.00	725.00
	1843/2	5.982	500.00	—	—	—
	1843	Inc. Ab.	—	BV	225.00	625.00
	1843 narrow shield					
		Inc. Ab.	4000.	6500.	—	—
	1844	3.000	—	BV	225.00	525.00
	1845	3.801	—	BV	225.00	475.00
	1846	3.803	—	BV	200.00	525.00
	1847	4.667	—	BV	200.00	525.00
	1848	2.247	—	BV	225.00	525.00
	1849	1.755	—	BV	225.00	575.00
	1850	1.402	—	BV	175.00	475.00
	1851	4.014	—	BV	175.00	475.00
	1852	8.053	—	BV	175.00	475.00
	1853	—	—	—	Proof	7200.
	1853 WW raised					
		10.598	—	BV	175.00	475.00
	1853 WW incuse					
		Inc. Ab.	—	BV	175.00	475.00
	1854 WW raised					
		3.590	—	BV	175.00	525.00
	1854 WW incuse					
		Inc. Ab.	—	BV	175.00	525.00
	1855 WW raised				175.00	450.00
		8.448	—	BV	175.00	450.00
	1855 WW incuse					
		Inc. Ab.	—	BV	175.00	450.00
	1856	4.806	—	BV	175.00	450.00
	1856 sm.dt. I.A.		—	BV	175.00	450.00
	1857	4.496	—	BV	175.00	450.00
	1858	.803	BV	125.00	200.00	1000.
	1859	1.548	—	BV	175.00	525.00
	1859 sm.dt. I.A.		—	BV	175.00	525.00
	1860	2.556	—	BV	350.00	900.00
	1861	7.623	—	BV	200.00	450.00
	1862/1	—	—	—	—	—
	1862	7.836	—	BV	175.00	400.00
	1863	5.922	—	BV	150.00	450.00
	1872	13.487	—	BV	150.00	300.00

Rev: Die number below wreath.

KM#	Date	Mintage	Fine	VF	XF	Unc
736.2	1863	Inc. Ab.	—	BV	150.00	400.00
	1864	8.656	—	BV	150.00	400.00
	1865	1.450	—	BV	150.00	400.00
	1866	4.047	—	BV	150.00	400.00
	1868	1.653	—	BV	150.00	400.00
	1869	6.441	—	BV	150.00	400.00
	1869	—	—	—	Proof	4000.
	1870	2.190	—	BV	150.00	400.00
	1871	8.767	—	BV	150.00	275.00
	1872	Inc. Ab.	—	BV	150.00	300.00
	1873	2.368	—	BV	150.00	300.00
	1874	.521	800.00	1800.	—	—

Ansell Variety
Obv: Additional line on lower edge of ribbon.

KM#	Date	Mintage	Fine	VF	XF	Unc
736.3	1859	.168	900.00	1600.	2500.	—

KM#	Date	Mintage	Fine	VF	XF	Unc
752	1871	Inc. Ab.	—	BV	150.00	350.00
	1871	—	—	—	Proof	3500.
	1872	Inc. Ab.	—	BV	120.00	290.00
	1873	Inc. Ab.	—	BV	160.00	350.00
	1874	Inc. Ab.	125.00	150.00	350.00	550.00
	1876	3.319	—	BV	135.00	350.00
	1876	Inc. Ab.	—	—	Proof	6500.
	1878	1.091	—	BV	135.00	350.00
	1879	.020	180.00	450.00	1350.	4000.
	1880	3.650	—	BV	135.00	350.00
	1880 w/o designers initials on rev.					
		—	—	BV	135.00	350.00
	1884	1.770	—	BV	135.00	300.00
	1885	.718	—	BV	135.00	300.00

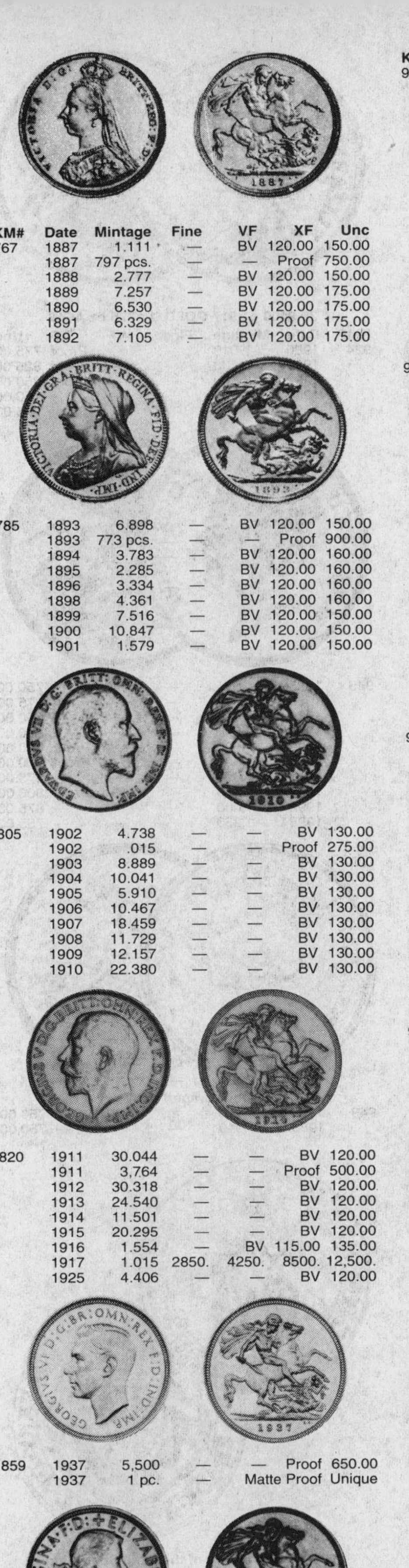

KM#	Date	Mintage	Fine	VF	XF	Unc
767	1887	1.111	—	BV	120.00	150.00
	1887	797 pcs.		—	Proof	750.00
	1888	2.777	—	BV	120.00	150.00
	1889	7.257	—	BV	120.00	175.00
	1890	6.530	—	BV	120.00	175.00
	1891	6.329	—	BV	120.00	175.00
	1892	7.105	—	BV	120.00	175.00

KM#	Date	Mintage	Fine	VF	XF	Unc
785	1893	6.898	—	BV	120.00	150.00
	1893	773 pcs.	—	—	Proof	900.00
	1894	3.783	—	BV	120.00	160.00
	1895	2.285	—	BV	120.00	160.00
	1896	3.334	—	BV	120.00	160.00
	1898	4.361	—	BV	120.00	160.00
	1899	7.516	—	BV	120.00	150.00
	1900	10.847	—	BV	120.00	150.00
	1901	1.579	—	BV	120.00	150.00

KM#	Date	Mintage	Fine	VF	XF	Unc
805	1902	4.738	—	—	BV	130.00
	1902	.015	—	—	Proof	275.00
	1903	8.889	—	—	BV	130.00
	1904	10.041	—	—	BV	130.00
	1905	5.910	—	—	BV	130.00
	1906	10.467	—	—	BV	130.00
	1907	18.459	—	—	BV	130.00
	1908	11.729	—	—	BV	130.00
	1909	12.157	—	—	BV	130.00
	1910	22.380	—	—	BV	130.00

KM#	Date	Mintage	Fine	VF	XF	Unc
820	1911	30.044	—	—	BV	120.00
	1911	3,764	—	—	Proof	500.00
	1912	30.318	—	—	BV	120.00
	1913	24.540	—	—	BV	120.00
	1914	11.501	—	—	BV	120.00
	1915	20.295	—	—	BV	120.00
	1916	1.554	—	BV	115.00	135.00
	1917	1.015	2850.	4250.	8500.	12,500.
	1925	4.406	—	—	BV	120.00

KM#	Date	Mintage	Fine	VF	XF	Unc
859	1937	5,500	—	—	Proof	650.00
	1937	1 pc.	—		Matte Proof	Unique

KM#	Date	Mintage	Fine	VF	XF	Unc
908	1957	2.072	—	—	BV	125.00
	1957	—	—	—	Proof	—
	1958	8.700	—	—	BV	115.00
	1958	—	—	—	Proof	—
	1959	1.358	—	—	BV	120.00
	1959	—	—	—	Proof	—

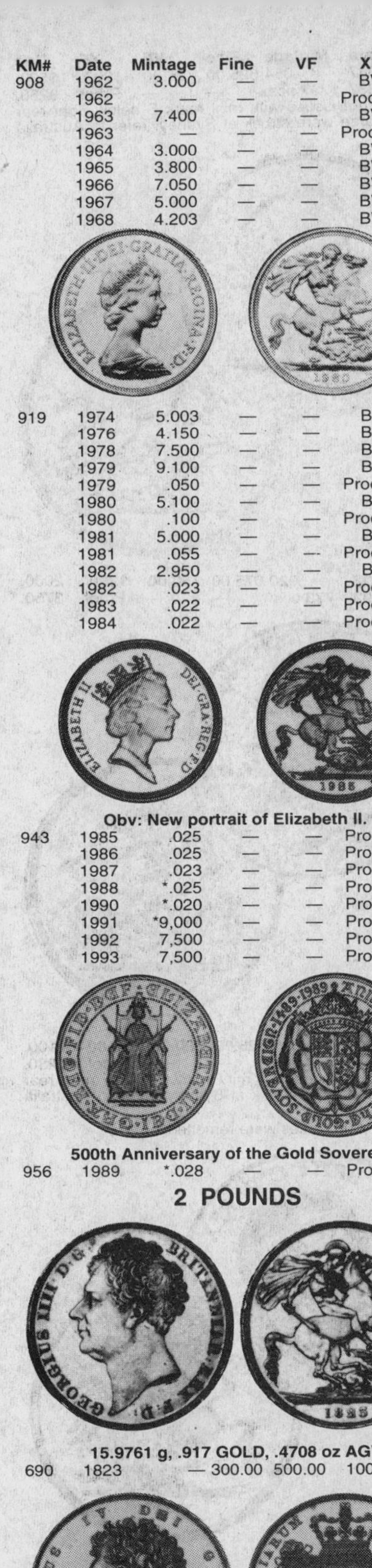

KM#	Date	Mintage	Fine	VF	XF	Unc
908	1962	3.000	—	—	BV	115.00
	1962	—	—	—	Proof	—
	1963	7.400	—	—	BV	115.00
	1963	—	—	—	Proof	—
	1964	3.000	—	—	BV	115.00
	1965	3.800	—	—	BV	115.00
	1966	7.050	—	—	BV	115.00
	1967	5.000	—	—	BV	115.00
	1968	4.203	—	—	BV	115.00

KM#	Date	Mintage	Fine	VF	XF	Unc
919	1974	5.003	—	—	BV	115.00
	1976	4.150	—	—	BV	115.00
	1978	7.500	—	—	BV	115.00
	1979	9.100	—	—	BV	115.00
	1979	.050	—	—	Proof	120.00
	1980	5.100	—	—	BV	115.00
	1980	.100	—	—	Proof	120.00
	1981	5.000	—	—	BV	115.00
	1981	.055	—	—	Proof	120.00
	1982	2.950	—	—	BV	115.00
	1982	.023	—	—	Proof	125.00
	1983	.022	—	—	Proof	125.00
	1984	.022	—	—	Proof	125.00

Obv: New portrait of Elizabeth II.

KM#	Date	Mintage	Fine	VF	XF	Unc
943	1985	.025	—	—	Proof	150.00
	1986	.025	—	—	Proof	150.00
	1987	.023	—	—	Proof	150.00
	1988	*.025	—	—	Proof	150.00
	1990	*.020	—	—	Proof	150.00
	1991	*9,000	—	—	Proof	275.00
	1992	7,500	—	—	Proof	275.00
	1993	7,500	—	—	Proof	250.00

500th Anniversary of the Gold Sovereign

KM#	Date	Mintage	Fine	VF	XF	Unc
956	1989	*.028	—	—	Proof	175.00

2 POUNDS

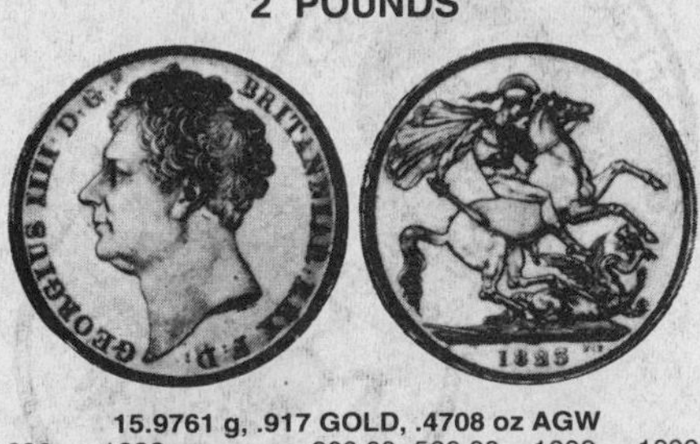

15.9761 g, .917 GOLD, .4708 oz AGW

KM#	Date	Mintage	Fine	VF	XF	Unc
690	1823	—	300.00	500.00	1000.	1800.

KM#	Date	Mintage	Fine	VF	XF	Unc
701	1826	450 pcs.	—	—	Proof	6000.

KM#	Date	Mintage	Fine	VF	XF	Unc
718	1831	225 pcs.	—	—	Proof	7500.

KM#	Date	Mintage	Fine	VF	XF	Unc
768	1887	.091	250.00	300.00	400.00	550.00
	1887	797 pcs.	—	—	Proof	1200.

NOTE: Proof issues with mint mark S below right rear hoof of horse were struck at Sydney, refer to Australia listings.

KM#	Date	Mintage	Fine	VF	XF	Unc
786	1893	.052	250.00	325.00	675.00	900.00
	1893	773 pcs.	—	—	Proof	1750.

KM#	Date	Mintage	Fine	VF	XF	Unc
806	1902	.046	250.00	300.00	475.00	575.00
	1902	8,066	—	—	Proof	650.00

NOTE: Proof issues with mint mark S below right rear hoof of horse were struck at Sydney, refer to Australia listings.

KM#	Date	Mintage	Fine	VF	XF	Unc
821	1911	2,812	—	—	Proof	1300.

KM#	Date	Mintage	Fine	VF	XF	Unc
860	1937	5,500	—	—	Proof	750.00
	1937	1 pc.	—		Matte Proof	Unique

15.9200 g, .917 GOLD, .4694 oz AGW

KM#	Date	Mintage	Fine	VF	XF	Unc
923	1980	.010	—	—	Proof	300.00
	1982	2,500	—	—	Proof	550.00
	1983	.013	—	—	Proof	300.00

Obv: New portrait of Elizabeth II.

KM#	Date	Mintage	Fine	VF	XF	Unc
944	1985	.013	—	—	Proof	300.00
	1987	.015	—	—	Proof	320.00
	1988	*.015	—	—	Proof	320.00
	1990	*.012	—	—	Proof	320.00
	1991	*5,000	—	—	Proof	530.00
	1992	3,000	—	—	Proof	530.00
	1993	3,000	—	—	Proof	475.00

15.9800 g, .917 GOLD, .4708 oz AGW
500th Anniversary of the Gold Sovereign

KM#	Date	Mintage	Fine	VF	XF	Unc
957	1989	*.017	—	—	Proof	350.00

5 POUNDS

39.9403 g, .917 GOLD, 1.1773 oz AGW
Lettered Edge

KM#	Date	Mintage	Fine	VF	XF	Unc
702	1826	150 pcs.	—	—	Proof	12,500.

NOTE: Includes lettered edge patterns KM#Pn96.

KM#	Date	Mintage	Fine	VF	XF	Unc
742	1839	400 pcs.	—	—	Proof	28,000.

KM#	Date	Mintage	Fine	VF	XF	Unc
769	1887	.054	625.00	725.00	1000.	1500.
	1887	797 pcs.	—	—	Proof	3250.

NOTE: Proof issues with mint mark S below right rear hoof of horse were struck at Sydney, refer to Australia listings.

KM#	Date	Mintage	Fine	VF	XF	Unc
787	1893	.020	675.00	750.00	1200.	2000.
	1893	773 pcs.	—	—	Proof	3750.

KM#	Date	Mintage	Fine	VF	XF	Unc
807	1902	*.035	625.00	700.00	850.00	1100.
	1902	8,066	—	—	Proof	1250.

NOTE: Proof issues with mint mark S below right rear hoof of horse were struck at Sydney, refer to Australia listings.
***NOTE:** 27,000 pieces were remelted.

KM#	Date	Mintage	Fine	VF	XF	Unc
822	1911	2,812	—	—	Proof	2250.

KM#	Date	Mintage	Fine	VF	XF	Unc
861	1937	5,500	—	—	Proof	1250.
	1937	1 pc.	—		Matte Proof	Unique

39.9400 g, .917 GOLD, 1.1775 oz AGW

KM#	Date	Mintage	Fine	VF	XF	Unc
924	1980	.010	—	—	Proof	775.00
	1981	5,400	—	—	Proof	825.00
	1982	2,500	—	—	Proof	850.00
	1984 U	.025	—	—	—	750.00
	1984	8,000	—	—	Proof	775.00

KM#	Date	Mintage	Fine	VF	XF	Unc
945	1985 U	.025	—	—	—	750.00
	1985	.013	—	—	Proof	775.00
	1986 U	.018	—	—	—	750.00
	1990 U	*3,500	—	—	—	800.00
	1990	*2,500	—	—	Proof	800.00
	1991	*1,500	—	—	Proof	800.00
	1991 U	1,500	—	—	—	875.00
	1992	1,250	—	—	Proof	800.00
	1992 U	*1,000	—	—	—	875.00
	1993 U	1,250	—	—	—	755.00

Obv: Draped bust

KM#	Date	Mintage	Fine	VF	XF	Unc
949	1987 U	.010	—	—	—	750.00
	1988 U	*.010	—	—	—	750.00

500th Anniversary of the Gold Sovereign

KM#	Date	Mintage	Fine	VF	XF	Unc
958	1989	.010	—	—	—	750.00
	1989	*5,000	—	—	Proof	800.00

DECIMAL COINAGE

1971-1981
5 New Pence = 1 Shilling
25 New Pence = 1 Crown
100 New Pence = 1 Pound
1982—
100 Pence = 1 Pound

1/2 NEW PENNY

BRONZE

KM#	Date	Mintage	Fine	VF	XF	Unc
914	1971	1,394.188	—	—	.10	.20
	1971	.350	—	—	Proof	1.00
	1972	.150	—	—	Proof	3.00
	1973	365.680	—	—	.10	.40
	1973	.100	—	—	Proof	1.00
	1974	365.448	—	—	.10	.35
	1974	.100	—	—	Proof	1.00
	1975	197.600	—	—	.10	.45
	1975	.100	—	—	Proof	1.00
	1976	412.172	—	—	.10	.35
	1976	.100	—	—	Proof	1.00
	1977	66.368	—	—	.10	.20
	1977	.194	—	—	Proof	1.00
	1978	59.532	—	—	.10	2.00
	1978	.088	—	—	Proof	1.00
	1979	219.132	—	—	.10	.20
	1979	.081	—	—	Proof	1.00
	1980	202.788	—	—	.10	.20
	1980	.143	—	—	Proof	1.00
	1981	32.484	—	—	.10	.45
	1981	.100	—	—	Proof	1.00

1/2 PENNY

BRONZE
Rev: HALF PENNY above crown and fraction.

KM#	Date	Mintage	Fine	VF	XF	Unc
926	1982	190.752	—	—	.10	.15
	1982	.107	—	—	Proof	1.00
	1983	7.600	—	—	.10	1.00
	1983	.108	—	—	Proof	1.50
	1984	*.159	—	—	—	2.00
	1984	.107	—	—	Proof	2.50

*NOTE: Issued in sets only.

NEW PENNY

BRONZE

KM#	Date	Mintage	Fine	VF	XF	Unc
915	1971	1,521.666	—	—	.10	.20
	1971	.350	—	—	Proof	1.25
	1972	.150	—	—	Proof	3.00
	1973	280.196	—	—	.10	.55
	1973	.100	—	—	Proof	1.25
	1974	330.892	—	—	.10	.55
	1974	.100	—	—	Proof	1.25
	1975	221.604	—	—	.10	.55
	1975	.100	—	—	Proof	1.25
	1976	241.800	—	—	—	.25
	1976	.100	—	—	Proof	1.25
	1977	285.430	—	—	.10	.25
	1977	.194	—	—	Proof	1.25
	1978	292.770	—	—	.10	.60
	1978	.088	—	—	Proof	1.25
	1979	459.000	—	—	.10	.20
	1979	.081	—	—	Proof	1.25
	1980	416.304	—	—	.10	.20
	1980	.143	—	—	Proof	1.25
	1981	301.800	—	—	.10	.20
	1981	.100	—	—	Proof	1.25

PENNY

BRONZE
Rev: ONE PENNY above portcullis and chains and 1.

KM#	Date	Mintage	Fine	VF	XF	Unc
927	1982	121.429	—	—	.10	.40
	1982	.107	—	—	Proof	1.25
	1983	243.002	—	—	.10	.30
	1983	.108	—	—	Proof	1.25
	1984	154.760	—	—	.10	.15
	1984	.107	—	—	Proof	1.25

KM#	Date	Mintage	Fine	VF	XF	Unc
935	1985	200.605	—	—	.10	.15
	1985	.102	—	—	Proof	1.25
	1986	369.989	—	—	.10	.30
	1986	.125	—	—	Proof	1.25
	1987	499.946	—	—	.10	.15
	1987	.089	—	—	Proof	1.25
	1988	793.492	—	—	.10	.15
	1988	*.125	—	—	Proof	1.25
	1989	658.142	—	—	.10	.15
	1989	.100	—	—	Proof	1.25
	1990	458.750	—	—	.10	.15
	1990	*.100	—	—	Proof	1.25
	1991	—	—	—	.10	.15
	1991	—	—	—	Proof	1.25

*NOTE: Issued in sets only.

COPPER PLATED STEEL

KM#	Date	Mintage	Fine	VF	XF	Unc
935a	1992	251.000	—	—	.10	.15
	1992	—	—	—	Proof	1.25
	1993	107.000	—	—	.10	.15
	1993	—	—	—	Proof	1.25
	1994	—	—	—	.10	.15
	1994	—	—	—	Proof	1.25

2 NEW PENCE

BRONZE

KM#	Date	Mintage	Fine	VF	XF	Unc
916	1971	1,454.856	—	—	.10	.20
	1971	.350	—	—	Proof	1.50
	1972	.150	—	—	Proof	3.50
	1973	.100	—	—	Proof	3.50
	1974	.100	—	—	Proof	3.50
	1975	145.545	—	—	.10	.40
	1975	.100	—	—	Proof	1.50
	1976	181.379	—	—	.10	.30
	1976	.100	—	—	Proof	1.50
	1977	109.281	—	—	.10	.30
	1977	.194	—	—	Proof	1.50
	1978	189.658	—	—	.10	.40
	1978	.088	—	—	Proof	1.50
	1979	268.300	—	—	.10	.20
	1979	.081	—	—	Proof	1.50
	1980	408.527	—	—	.10	.20
	1980	.143	—	—	Proof	1.50
	1981	353.191	—	—	.10	.20
	1981	.100	—	—	Proof	1.50
	1983	*	—	—	—	.30

*NOTE: Issued in sets only.

2 PENCE

BRONZE
Rev: TWO PENCE above plumes of Prince of Wales and 2.

KM#	Date	Mintage	Fine	VF	XF	Unc
928	1982	*.205	—	—	—	1.00
	1982	*.107	—	—	Proof	1.50
	1983	*.631	—	—	—	1.00
	1983	*.108	—	—	Proof	1.50
	1984	*.159	—	—	—	.75
	1984	*.107	—	—	Proof	1.50

*NOTE: Issued in sets only.

KM#	Date	Mintage	Fine	VF	XF	Unc
936	1985	107.113	—	—	.10	.25
	1985	*.102	—	—	Proof	1.50
	1986	168.968	—	—	.10	.50
	1986	*.125	—	—	Proof	1.50
	1987	218.101	—	—	.10	.25
	1987	.089	—	—	Proof	1.50
	1988	419.889	—	—	.10	.25
	1988	*.125	—	—	Proof	1.50
	1989	359.226	—	—	.10	.25
	1989	.100	—	—	Proof	1.50
	1990	147.968	—	—	.10	.25
	1990	*.100	—	—	Proof	1.50
	1991	—	—	—	.10	.25
	1991	—	—	—	Proof	1.50

*NOTE: Issued in sets only.

COPPER PLATED STEEL

KM#	Date	Mintage	Fine	VF	XF	Unc
936a	1992	96.000	—	—	.10	.15
	1992	—	—	—	Proof	1.50
	1993	—	—	—	.10	.15
	1993	—	—	—	Proof	1.50
	1994	—	—	—	.10	.15
	1994	—	—	—	Proof	1.50

5 NEW PENCE

COPPER-NICKEL

KM#	Date	Mintage	Fine	VF	XF	Unc
911	1968	98.868	—	—	.15	.30
	1969	119.270	—	—	.15	.40
	1970	225.948	—	—	.15	.40
	1971	81.783	—	—	.15	.50
	1971	.350	—	—	Proof	1.50
	1972	.150	—	—	Proof	3.50
	1973	.100	—	—	Proof	3.50
	1974	.100	—	—	Proof	3.50
	1975	116.906	—	—	.15	.30
	1975	.100	—	—	Proof	1.50
	1976	.100	—	—	Proof	3.50
	1977	24.308	—	—	.15	.35
	1977	.194	—	—	Proof	1.50
	1978	61.094	—	—	.15	2.50
	1978	.088	—	—	Proof	1.50
	1979	155.456	—	—	.15	.30
	1979	.081	—	—	Proof	1.50
	1980	203.020	—	—	.15	.30
	1980	.143	—	—	Proof	1.50
	1981	.100	—	—	Proof	1.50

5 PENCE

COPPER-NICKEL
Rev: FIVE PENCE above Scottish thistle and 5.

KM#	Date	Mintage	Fine	VF	XF	Unc
929	1982	*.205	—	—	—	2.25
	1982	*.107	—	—	Proof	1.50
	1983	*.637	—	—	—	1.25
	1983	*.108	—	—	Proof	1.50
	1984	*.159	—	—	—	1.00
	1984	*.107	—	—	Proof	1.50

*NOTE: Issued in sets only.

KM#	Date	Mintage	Fine	VF	XF	Unc
937	1985	*178	—	—	—	2.00
	1985	*102	—	—	Proof	1.50
	1986	*.167	—	—	—	1.00
	1986	*.125	—	—	Proof	1.50
	1987	48.220	—	—	.15	.30
	1987	*.089	—	—	Proof	1.50
	1988	120.775	—	—	.15	.30
	1988	*.125	—	—	Proof	1.50
	1989	101.406	—	—	.15	.30
	1989	.100	—	—	Proof	1.50
	1990	*	—	—	—	.50
	1990	—	—	—	Proof	1.50

*NOTE: Issued in sets only.

6.5000 g, .925 SILVER, .1933 oz ASW

KM#	Date	Mintage	Fine	VF	XF	Unc
937a	1990	.035	—	—	Proof	25.00

COPPER-NICKEL

Reduced size.

KM#	Date	Mintage	Fine	VF	XF	Unc
937b	1990	1,634.840	—	—	—	.35
	1990	—	—	—	Proof	1.50
	1991	591.615	—	—	—	.35
	1991	—	—	—	Proof	1.50
	1992	—	—	—	—	.35
	1992	—	—	—	Proof	1.50
	1993	—	—	—	—	.35
	1993	—	—	—	Proof	1.50
	1994	—	—	—	—	.35
	1994	—	—	—	Proof	1.50

3.7400 g, .925 SILVER, .1112 oz ASW

KM#	Date	Mintage	Fine	VF	XF	Unc
937c	1990	*.035	—	—	Proof	22.50

*NOTE: Issued in sets only.

7.4800 g, .925 SILVER, .2224 oz ASW

KM#	Date	Mintage	Fine	VF	XF	Unc
937d	1990	.020	—	—	Proof	60.00

10 NEW PENCE

COPPER-NICKEL

KM#	Date	Mintage	Fine	VF	XF	Unc
912	1968	336.143	—	—	.25	.50
	1969	314.008	—	—	.25	.60
	1970	133.571	—	—	.25	1.00
	1971	63.205	—	—	.25	1.00
	1971	.350	—	—	Proof	1.75
	1972	.150	—	—	Proof	3.75
	1973	152.174	—	—	.25	.50
	1973	.100	—	—	Proof	1.75
	1974	92.741	—	—	.25	.50
	1974	.100	—	—	Proof	1.75
	1975	181.559	—	—	.25	.50
	1975	.100	—	—	Proof	1.75
	1976	228.220	—	—	.25	.50
	1976	.100	—	—	Proof	1.75
	1977	59.323	—	—	.25	.60
	1977	.194	—	—	Proof	1.75
	1978	.088	—	—	Proof	1.75
	1979	115.457	—	—	.25	.60
	1979	.081	—	—	Proof	1.75
	1980	88.650	—	—	.25	.60
	1980	.143	—	—	Proof	1.75
	1981	3.433	—	.25	.50	4.00
	1981	.100	—	—	Proof	1.75

10 PENCE

COPPER-NICKEL
Rev: TEN PENCE above crowned lion and 10.

KM#	Date	Mintage	Fine	VF	XF	Unc
930	1982	*.205	—	—	—	2.00
	1982	*.107	—	—	Proof	1.75
	1983	*.637	—	—	—	2.00
	1983	*.108	—	—	Proof	1.75
	1984	*.159	—	—	—	1.25
	1984	*.107	—	—	Proof	1.75

*NOTE: Issued in sets only.

KM#	Date	Mintage	Fine	VF	XF	Unc
938	1985	*.178	—	—	—	1.00
	1985	*.102	—	—	Proof	1.75
	1986	*.167	—	—	—	.80
	1986	*.125	—	—	Proof	1.75
	1987	*.172	—	—	—	.50
	1987	*.089	—	—	Proof	1.75
	1988	*.134	—	—	—	.50
	1988	*.125	—	—	Proof	1.75
	1989	*.078	—	—	—	.50
	1989	.100	—	—	Proof	1.75
	1990	*	—	—	—	.50
	1990	.100	—	—	Proof	1.75
	1991	*	—	—	—	.50
	1991	—	—	—	Proof	1.75
	1992	*	—	—	—	.50
	1992	*	—	—	Proof	1.75

*NOTE: Issued in sets only.

Reduced size.

KM#	Date	Mintage	Fine	VF	XF	Unc
938a	1992	—	—	—	—	.50
	1992	—	—	—	Proof	1.75
	1993	—	—	—	—	.50
	1993	—	—	—	Proof	1.75
	1994	—	—	—	—	.50
	1994	—	—	—	Proof	1.75

6.5000 g, .925 SILVER, .1933 oz ASW

KM#	Date	Mintage	Fine	VF	XF	Unc
938c	1992	.035	—	—	Proof	20.00

11.3100 g, .925 SILVER, .3363 oz ASW

KM#	Date	Mintage	Fine	VF	XF	Unc
938b	1992	.035	—	—	Proof	30.00

20 PENCE

COPPER-NICKEL

KM#	Date	Mintage	Fine	VF	XF	Unc
931	1982	740.815	—	—	.45	.65
	1982	.107	—	—	Proof	5.00
	1983	158.463	—	—	.45	.65
	1983	.108	—	—	Proof	5.00
	1984	65.351	—	—	.45	.65
	1984	.107	—	—	Proof	5.00

KM#	Date	Mintage	Fine	VF	XF	Unc
939	1985	74.274	—	—	.45	.75
	1985	*.102	—	—	Proof	5.00
	1986	*.167	—	—	—	.60
	1986	*.125	—	—	Proof	5.00
	1987	137.450	—	—	.45	.75
	1987	.089	—	—	Proof	5.00
	1988	38.038	—	—	.45	.75
	1988	*.125	—	—	Proof	5.00
	1989	132.014	—	—	.45	.75
	1989	.100	—	—	Proof	5.00
	1990	75.001	—	—	.45	.75
	1990	.100	—	—	Proof	5.00
	1991	**	—	—	—	—
	1991	—	—	—	Proof	5.00
	1992	—	—	—	.45	.75
	1992	—	—	—	Proof	5.00
	1993	—	—	—	.45	.75
	1993	—	—	—	Proof	5.00
	1994	—	—	—	.45	.75
	1994	—	—	—	Proof	5.00

*NOTE: Issued in sets only.
**NOTE: Not released into circulation.

25 NEW PENCE

COPPER-NICKEL
Royal Silver Wedding Anniversary

KM#	Date	Mintage	Fine	VF	XF	Unc
917	1972	7.452	—	—	.60	1.50
	1972	.150	—	—	Proof	7.50

28.2759 g, .925 SILVER, .8409 oz ASW

KM#	Date	Mintage	Fine	VF	XF	Unc
917a	1972	.100	—	—	Proof	25.00

COPPER-NICKEL
Silver Jubilee of Reign

KM#	Date	Mintage	Fine	VF	XF	Unc
920	1977	36.989	—	—	.60	1.25
	1977	.194	—	—	Proof	6.00
	1977(RMF)*	—	—	—	—	4.00

*NOTE: Sealed in Royal Mint Folder and First Day Covers.

28.2759 g, .925 SILVER, .8409 oz ASW

KM#	Date	Mintage	Fine	VF	XF	Unc
920a	1977	.377	—	—	Proof	20.00

COPPER-NICKEL
80th Birthday of Queen Mother

KM#	Date	Mintage	Fine	VF	XF	Unc
921	1980	9.478	—	—	.60	1.50

28.2759 g, .925 SILVER, .8409 oz ASW

KM#	Date	Mintage	Fine	VF	XF	Unc
921a	1980	.084	—	—	Proof	40.00

CROWN

COPPER-NICKEL
Wedding of Prince Charles and Lady Diana
Obv: Similar to 25 New Pence, KM#917.

KM#	Date	Mintage	Fine	VF	XF	Unc
925	1981	27.360	—	—	.60	1.50

28.2759 g, .925 SILVER, .8409 oz ASW

KM#	Date	Mintage	Fine	VF	XF	Unc
925a	1981	.218	—	—	Proof	35.00

50 NEW PENCE

COPPER-NICKEL

KM#	Date	Mintage	Fine	VF	XF	Unc
913	1969	188.400	—	—	1.25	2.50
	1970	19.461	—	—	1.25	2.50
	1971	.350	—	—	Proof	3.00
	1972	.150	—	—	Proof	4.00
	1974	.100	—	—	Proof	3.00
	1975	.100	—	—	Proof	3.00
	1976	43.747	—	—	1.75	3.50
	1976	.100	—	—	Proof	2.50
	1977	49.536	—	—	1.75	3.50
	1977	.194	—	—	Proof	2.50
	1978	72.005	—	—	1.75	3.50
	1978	.088	—	—	Proof	2.50
	1979	58.680	—	—	1.75	2.25
	1979	.081	—	—	Proof	2.50
	1980	89.086	—	—	1.75	2.25
	1980	.143	—	—	Proof	2.50
	1981	74.003	—	—	1.75	2.25
	1981	.100	—	—	Proof	2.50

50 PENCE

COPPER-NICKEL
Entry Into E.E.C.

KM#	Date	Mintage	Fine	VF	XF	Unc
918	1973	89.775	—	—	1.25	2.00
	1973	.357	—	—	Proof	6.00

Rev: FIFTY PENCE above seated Britannia and 50.

KM#	Date	Mintage	Fine	VF	XF	Unc
932	1982	51.312	—	—	1.25	1.75
	1982	.107	—	—	Proof	2.50
	1983	23.436	—	—	1.25	2.00
	1983	.125	—	—	Proof	2.50
	1984	*.107	—	—	—	2.25
	1984	.125	—	—	Proof	2.50

***NOTE:** Issued in sets only.

KM#	Date	Mintage	Fine	VF	XF	Unc
940	1985	.680	—	—	1.25	1.65
	1985	.102	—	—	Proof	2.50
	1986	*.167	—	—	—	1.75
	1986	.125	—	—	Proof	2.50
	1987	*.172	—	—	—	1.75
	1987	.089	—	—	Proof	2.50
	1988	*.134	—	—	—	1.75
	1988	*.125	—	—	Proof	2.50
	1989	*.078	—	—	—	1.75
	1989	.100	—	—	Proof	2.50
	1990	*	—	—	—	1.75
	1990	.100	—	—	Proof	2.50
	1991	*	—	—	—	1.75
	1991	*	—	—	Proof	2.50
	1992	*	—	—	—	1.75
	1992	*	—	—	Proof	2.50
	1993	—	—	—	1.25	1.65
	1993	—	—	—	Proof	2.50

***NOTE:** Issued in sets only.

British Presidency of European Council of Ministers

KM#	Date	Mintage	Fine	VF	XF	Unc
963	1992	—	—	—	—	2.75
963	1992	*.100	—	—	Proof	18.00
	1993	—	—	—	—	2.75
	1993	—	—	—	Proof	18.00

13.5000 g, .925 SILVER, .4014 oz ASW

KM#	Date	Mintage	Fine	VF	XF	Unc
963a	1992	*.035	—	—	Proof	45.00

26.3200 g, .917 GOLD, .7757 oz AGW

KM#	Date	Mintage	Fine	VF	XF	Unc
963b	1992	*2,500	—	—	Proof	675.00

COPPER-NICKEL
50th Anniversary of Normandy Invasion

KM#	Date	Mintage	Fine	VF	XF	Unc
966	1994	—	—	—	—	2.75
	1994	—	—	—	Proof	18.00

POUND

NICKEL-BRASS

KM#	Date	Mintage	Fine	VF	XF	Unc
933	1983	443.054	—	—	2.25	3.50
	1983	.108	—	—	Proof	6.00

9.5000 g, .925 SILVER, .2825 oz ASW

KM#	Date	Mintage	Fine	VF	XF	Unc
933a	1983	.050	—	—	Proof	22.00

19.0000 g, .925 SILVER, .5651 oz ASW

KM#	Date	Mintage	Fine	VF	XF	Unc
933b	1983	.010	—	—	Proof	125.00

NICKEL-BRASS
Rev: Scottish thistle.

KM#	Date	Mintage	Fine	VF	XF	Unc
934	1984	146.257	—	—	2.25	3.50
	1984	.107	—	—	Proof	6.00

9.5000 g, .925 SILVER, .2825 oz ASW

KM#	Date	Mintage	Fine	VF	XF	Unc
934a	1984	.045	—	—	Proof	18.00

19.0000 g, .925 SILVER, .5651 oz ASW

KM#	Date	Mintage	Fine	VF	XF	Unc
934b	1984	.015	—	—	Proof	65.00

NICKEL-BRASS
Rev: Welsh leek.

KM#	Date	Mintage	Fine	VF	XF	Unc
941	1985	228.431	—	—	2.00	3.50
	1985	.102	—	—	Proof	6.00
	1990	97.123	—	—	2.00	3.50
	1990	.100	—	—	Proof	6.00

9.5000 g, .925 SILVER, .2825 oz ASW

KM#	Date	Mintage	Fine	VF	XF	Unc
941a	1985	.050	—	—	Proof	18.00
	1990	*.025	—	—	Proof	22.50

19.0000 g, .925 SILVER, .5651 oz ASW

KM#	Date	Mintage	Fine	VF	XF	Unc
941b	1985	.015	—	—	Proof	45.00

NICKEL-BRASS
Northern Ireland - Blooming Flax

KM#	Date	Mintage	Fine	VF	XF	Unc
946	1986	10.410	—	—	2.00	3.50
	1986	.125	—	—	Proof	6.00
	1991	—	—	—	2.00	3.50
	1991	—	—	—	Proof	6.00

9.5000 g, .925 SILVER, .2825 oz ASW

KM#	Date	Mintage	Fine	VF	XF	Unc
946a	1986	.050	—	—	Proof	18.00
	1991	*.025	—	—	Proof	25.00

19.0000 g, .925 SILVER, .5651 oz ASW

KM#	Date	Mintage	Fine	VF	XF	Unc
946b	1986	.015	—	—	Proof	35.00

NICKEL-BRASS
Oak Tree

KM#	Date	Mintage	Fine	VF	XF	Unc
948	1987	39.299	—	—	—	3.50
	1987	.125	—	—	Proof	6.00
	1992	—	—	—	—	3.50
	1992	—	—	—	Proof	6.00

9.5000 g, .925 SILVER, .2825 oz ASW

KM#	Date	Mintage	Fine	VF	XF	Unc
948a	1987	.050	—	—	Proof	18.00
	1992	*.025	—	—	Proof	35.00

19.0000 g, .925 SILVER, .5651 oz ASW

KM#	Date	Mintage	Fine	VF	XF	Unc
948b	1987	.015	—	—	Proof	35.00

COPPER-ZINC-NICKEL

KM#	Date	Mintage	Fine	VF	XF	Unc
954	1988	7.119	—	—	—	3.50
	1988	*.125	—	—	Proof	6.00

9.5000 g, .925 SILVER, .2826 oz ASW

KM#	Date	Mintage	Fine	VF	XF	Unc
954a	1988	*.050	—	—	Proof	18.00

19.0000 g, .925 SILVER, .5651 oz ASW

KM#	Date	Mintage	Fine	VF	XF	Unc
954b	1988	.015	—	—	Proof	35.00

NICKEL-BRASS
Scottish Flora
Obv: Queen's portrait. Rev: Scottish thistle.

KM#	Date	Mintage	Fine	VF	XF	Unc
959	1989	70.533	—	—	—	3.50
	1989	.100	—	—	Proof	6.00

9.5000 g, .925 SILVER, .2826 oz ASW

KM#	Date	Mintage	Fine	VF	XF	Unc
959a	1989	*.025	—	—	Proof	22.50

19.0000 g, .925 SILVER, .5652 oz ASW

KM#	Date	Mintage	Fine	VF	XF	Unc
959b	1989	*.010	—	—	Proof	35.00

NICKEL-BRASS
Royal Coat of Arms

KM#	Date	Mintage	Fine	VF	XF	Unc
964	1993	—	—	—	—	3.50
	1993	—	—	—	Proof	6.00

9.5000 g, .925 SILVER, .2826 oz ASW

KM#	Date	Mintage	Fine	VF	XF	Unc
964a	1993	*.025	—	—	Proof	35.00

19.0000 g, .925 SILVER, .5652 oz ASW

KM#	Date	Mintage	Fine	VF	XF	Unc
964b	1993	*.013	—	—	Proof	85.00

NICKEL-BRASS
Scotland

KM#	Date	Mintage	Fine	VF	XF	Unc
967	1994	—	—	—	—	3.50
	1994	—	—	—	Proof	6.00

2 POUNDS

NICKEL-BRASS
Commonwealth Games

KM#	Date	Mintage	Fine	VF	XF	Unc
947	1986	8.212	—	—	4.50	6.50
	1986	.125	—	—	Proof	12.00

15.9800 g, .500 SILVER, .2569 oz ASW

KM#	Date	Mintage	Fine	VF	XF	Unc
947a	1986	.125	—	—	—	10.00

15.9800 g, .925 SILVER, .4752 oz ASW

KM#	Date	Mintage	Fine	VF	XF	Unc
947b	1986	.075	—	—	Proof	20.00

15.9800 g, .917 GOLD, .4710 oz AGW

KM#	Date	Mintage	Fine	VF	XF	Unc
947c	1986	.018	—	—	Proof	200.00

NICKEL-BRASS
Tercentenary of Bill of Rights

KM#	Date	Mintage	Fine	VF	XF	Unc
960	1989	4.397	—	—	—	6.00
	1989	.100	—	—	Proof	8.00

15.9800 g, .925 SILVER, .4752 oz ASW

KM#	Date	Mintage	Fine	VF	XF	Unc
960a	1989	.025	—	—	Proof	20.00

31.9600 g, .925 SILVER, .9506 oz ASW

KM#	Date	Mintage	Fine	VF	XF	Unc
960b	1989	.010	—	—	Proof	30.00

NICKEL-BRASS
Tercentenary of Claim of Right

KM#	Date	Mintage	Fine	VF	XF	Unc
961	1989	.346	—	—	—	6.00
	1989	.100	—	—	Proof	8.00

15.9800 g, .925 SILVER, .4752 oz ASW

KM#	Date	Mintage	Fine	VF	XF	Unc
961a	1989	.025	—	—	Proof	20.00

31.9600 g, .925 SILVER, .9506 oz ASW

KM#	Date	Mintage	Fine	VF	XF	Unc
961b	1989	.010	—	—	Proof	30.00

NICKEL-BRASS
300th Anniversary of Bank of England

KM#	Date	Mintage	Fine	VF	XF	Unc
968	1994	—	—	—	—	6.00
	1994	—	—	—	Proof	9.00

5 POUNDS

COPPER-NICKEL
90th Birthday of Queen Mother

KM#	Date	Mintage	Fine	VF	XF	Unc
962	1990	—	—	—	—	12.50

28.2800 g, .925 SILVER, .8411 oz ASW

KM#	Date	Mintage	Fine	VF	XF	Unc
962a	1990	*.150	—	—	Proof	30.00

39.9400 g, .917 GOLD, 1.1775 oz AGW

KM#	Date	Mintage	Fine	VF	XF	Unc
962b	1990	*2,500	—	—	Proof	650.00

COPPER-NICKEL
40th Anniversary of Reign

KM#	Date	Mintage	Fine	VF	XF	Unc
965	1993	—	—	—	—	12.50
	1993	*.100	—	—	Proof	25.00

28.2800 g, .925 SILVER, .8411 oz ASW

KM#	Date	Mintage	Fine	VF	XF	Unc
965a	1993	*.100	—	—	Proof	45.00

39.9400 g, .917 GOLD, 1.1175 oz AGW
40th Anniversary of Reign

KM#	Date	Mintage	Fine	VF	XF	Unc
965b	1993	*2,500	—	—	Proof	950.00

BULLION ISSUES

Until 1990, .917 Gold was commonly alloyed with copper by the British Royal Mint.

All proof issues have designers name as P. Nathan. The uncirculated issues use only Nathan.

10 POUNDS

(1/10 Ounce - Britannia)

3.4120 g, .917 GOLD, .1000 oz AGW

KM#	Date	Mintage	Fine	VF	XF	Unc
950	1987	—	—	—		*BV + 16%*
	1987	.026	—	—	Proof	60.00
	1988	—	—	—		*BV + 16%*
	1988	*.019	—	—	Proof	60.00
	1989	—	—	—		*BV + 16%*
	1989	*6,500	—	—	Proof	60.00

3.4120 g, .917 GOLD/.999 SILVER, .1000 oz AGW

KM#	Date	Mintage	Fine	VF	XF	Unc
950a	1990	*5,000	—	—	Proof	60.00
	1991	2,750	—	—	Proof	110.00
	1992	1,500	—	—	Proof	110.00
	1993	*1,000	—	—	Proof	110.00

25 POUNDS

(1/4 Ounce - Britannia)

8.5130 g, .917 GOLD, .2500 oz AGW

KM#	Date	Mintage	Fine	VF	XF	Unc
951	1987	—	—	—		*BV + 8%*
	1987	.026	—	—	Proof	125.00
	1988	—	—	—		*BV + 8%*
	1988	*.014	—	—	Proof	125.00
	1989	—	—	—		*BV + 8%*
	1989	*4,000	—	—	Proof	125.00

8.5130 g, .917 GOLD/.999 SILVER, .2500 oz AGW

KM#	Date	Mintage	Fine	VF	XF	Unc
951a	1990	*2,500	—	—	Proof	125.00
	1991	750 pcs.	—	—	Proof	250.00
	1992	500 pcs.	—	—	Proof	250.00
	1993	*500 pcs.	—	—	Proof	—

50 POUNDS

(1/2 Ounce - Britannia)

17.0250 g, .917 GOLD, .5000 oz AGW

KM#	Date	Mintage	Fine	VF	XF	Unc
952	1987	—	—	—		*BV + 6%*
	1987	.013	—	—	Proof	250.00
	1988	—	—	—		*BV + 6%*
	1988	*6,500	—	—	Proof	250.00
	1989	—	—	—		*BV + 6%*
	1989	*2,500	—	—	Proof	250.00

17.0250 g, .917 GOLD/.999 SILVER, .5000 oz AGW

KM#	Date	Mintage	Fine	VF	XF	Unc
952a	1990	*2,500	—	—	Proof	250.00
	1991	750 pcs.	—	—	Proof	475.00
	1992	500 pcs.	—	—	Proof	475.00
	1993	*500 pcs.	—	—	Proof	—

100 POUNDS

(1 Ounce - Britannia)

34.0500 g, .917 GOLD, 1.0000 oz AGW

KM#	Date	Mintage	Fine	VF	XF	Unc
953	1987	—	—	—		*BV + 4%*
	1987	.013	—	—	Proof	500.00
	1988	—	—	—		*BV + 4%*
	1988	*8,500	—	—	Proof	500.00
	1989	—	—	—		*BV + 4%*
	1989	*2,600	—	—	Proof	500.00

34.0500 g, .917 GOLD/.999 SILVER, 1.0000 oz AGW

KM#	Date	Mintage	Fine	VF	XF	Unc
953a	1990	*3,500	—	—	Proof	500.00
	1991	1,250	—	—	Proof	925.00
	1992	500 pcs.	—	—	Proof	925.00
	1993	*500 pcs.	—	—	Proof	1660.

COUNTERMARKED COINAGE

BANK OF ENGLAND

Emergency issue foreign silver coins, usually Spanish Colonial, having a bust of George III within an oval (1797) or octagonal (1804) frame. Countermarked 8 Reales circulated at 4 Shillings 9 Pence in 1797 and 5 Shillings in 1804. The puncheons used for countermarking foreign coins for this series were available for many years afterward, especially the oval die and apparently a number of foreign coins other than Spanish or Spanish Colonial 8 Reales were countermarked for collectors.

Type II

1804
Head of George III in octagon.

NOTE: Coins other than 8 Reales bearing this cmk. are considered spurious by some authorities.

DOLLAR

SILVER

c/m: Type II on Bolivia (Potosi) 8 Reales, KM#55.

KM#	Date	Year	VG	Fine	VF	XF
652	ND	(1773-89)	75.00	125.00	250.00	400.00

c/m: Type II on Bolivia (Potosi) 8 Reales, KM#73.1.

KM#	Date	Year	VG	Fine	VF	XF
653	ND	(1791-1808)	75.00	125.00	250.00	400.00

c/m: Type II on France 1 Ecu, C#78.

KM#	Date	Year	VG	Fine	VF	XF
654	ND	(1774-92)	—	—	Rare	—

c/m: Type II on Mexico 8 Reales, KM#106.

KM#	Date	Year	VG	Fine	VF	XF
655	ND	(1772-89)	65.00	100.00	200.00	325.00

c/m: Type II on Mexico 8 Reales, KM#109.

KM#	Date	Year	VG	Fine	VF	XF
656	ND	(1791-1808)	65.00	100.00	200.00	325.00

c/m: Type II on Peru (Lima) 8 Reales, KM#78.

KM#	Date	Year	VG	Fine	VF	XF
657	ND	(1772-89)	—	—	Rare	—

c/m: Type II on Peru (Lima) 8 Reales, KM#97.

KM#	Date	Year	VG	Fine	VF	XF
658	ND	(1791-1808)	—	—	Rare	—

c/m: Type II on Spanish (Seville) 8 Reales, C#71.

KM#	Date	Year	VG	Fine	VF	XF
659	ND	(1788-1808)	—	—	Rare	—

c/m: Type II on United States 1 Dollar, C#34.

KM#	Date	Year	VG	Fine	VF	XF
660	ND	(1795-98)	—	—	Rare	—

c/m: Type II on United States 1 Dollar, C#34a.

KM#	Date	Year	VG	Fine	VF	XF
660a	ND	(1798-1803)	—	—	Rare	—

TRADE COINAGE

KINGDOM

Britannia Series

Issued to facilitate British trade in the Orient, the reverse design incorporates the denomination in Chinese characters and Malay script.

This issue was struck at the Bombay (B) and Calcutta (C) Mints in India, except for 1925 and 1930 issues which were struck at London, although through error the mint marks did not appear on some early issues as indicated.

DOLLAR

26.9568 g, .900 SILVER, .7800 oz ASW

KM#	Date	Mintage	Fine	VF	XF	Unc
T5	1895B	3.316	30.00	50.00	75.00	200.00
(T2)	1895B	Inc. Ab.	—	—	Proof	850.00
(T2)	1895	Inc. Ab.	40.00	70.00	100.00	250.00
	1895	Inc. Ab.	—	—	Proof	800.00
	1896B	6.136	60.00	90.00	150.00	350.00
	1896B	Inc. Ab.	—	—	Proof	800.00
	1897/6B	21.286	40.00	60.00	100.00	150.00
	1897B	Inc. Ab.	15.00	20.00	28.00	60.00
	1897B	Inc. Ab.	—	—	Proof	800.00
	1897	Inc. Ab.	15.00	20.00	28.00	60.00
	1897	Inc. Ab.	—	—	Proof	800.00
	1898B	21.546	15.00	20.00	28.00	60.00
	1898B	Inc. Ab.	—	—	Proof	800.00
	1898	Inc. Ab.	15.00	20.00	28.00	60.00
	1899B	30.743	15.00	20.00	28.00	60.00
	1899B	Inc. Ab.	—	—	Proof	800.00
	1900/1000B	9.107	40.00	60.00	100.00	150.00
	1900/890B	I.A.	40.00	60.00	100.00	150.00
	1900	—	100.00	175.00	250.00	600.00
	1900B	Inc. Ab.	15.00	20.00	28.00	60.00
	1900B	Inc. Ab.	—	—	Proof	800.00
	1900B (restrike)	25 known	—	—	Proof	1000.
	1900C	.363	90.00	150.00	250.00	500.00
	1901/0B	25.680	40.00	60.00	100.00	200.00
	1901B	Inc. Ab.	15.00	20.00	28.00	60.00
	1901B	Inc. Ab.	—	—	Proof	800.00
	1901C	1.514	25.00	45.00	100.00	175.00
	1902B	30.404	15.00	20.00	28.00	60.00
	1902B	Inc. Ab.	—	—	Proof	800.00
	1902C	1.267	25.00	45.00	80.00	150.00
	1902C	Inc. Ab.	—	—	Proof	800.00
	1903/2B	3.956	15.00	25.00	40.00	75.00
	1903B	Inc. Ab.	15.00	20.00	28.00	60.00
	1903B	Inc. Ab.	—	—	Proof	800.00
	1904/898B	.649	50.00	80.00	125.00	200.00
	1904/3B	I.A.	30.00	50.00	100.00	225.00
	1904/0B	I.A.	80.00	125.00	175.00	300.00
	1904B	Inc. Ab.	40.00	60.00	100.00	250.00
	1904B	Inc. Ab.	—	—	Proof	700.00
	1907B	1.946	15.00	20.00	28.00	60.00
	1908/3B	6.871	40.00	60.00	100.00	175.00
	1908/7B	I.A.	35.00	50.00	90.00	125.00
	1908B	Inc. Ab.	15.00	20.00	28.00	60.00
	1908B	Inc. Ab.	—	—	Proof	700.00
	1909/8B	5.954	30.00	45.00	80.00	125.00
	1909B	Inc. Ab.	15.00	20.00	28.00	60.00
	1910/00B	5.553	40.00	60.00	100.00	175.00
	1910B	Inc. Ab.	15.00	20.00	28.00	60.00
	1911/00 B	—	30.00	50.00	100.00	150.00
	1911B	37.471	15.00	20.00	25.00	50.00
	1912B	5.672	15.00	20.00	25.00	50.00
	1912B	Inc. Ab.	—	—	Proof	800.00
	1913/2 B	—	100.00	150.00	250.00	700.00
	1913B	1.567	30.00	60.00	125.00	300.00
	1913B	Inc. Ab.	—	—	Proof	800.00
	1921B	*5 known	—	—	—	15,000.
	1921B (restrike)		—	—	Proof	4500.
	1925	6.870	15.00	20.00	28.00	60.00
	1929/1B	5.100	30.00	50.00	80.00	150.00
	1929B	Inc. Ab.	15.00	20.00	28.00	60.00
	1929B	Inc. Ab.	—	—	Proof	800.00
	1930B	10.400	15.00	20.00	25.00	50.00
	1930B	Inc. Ab.	—	—	Proof	800.00
	1930	6.660	15.00	20.00	25.00	50.00
	1934B	17.335	75.00	125.00	200.00	400.00
	1934B	Inc. Ab.	—	—	Proof	3500.
	1934B (restrike)	20 known	—	—	Proof	3000.
	1935B	**15 known	1000.	1500.	2500.	5000.
	1935B	—	—	—	Proof	7500.
	1935B (restrike)	20 known	—	—	Proof	4000.

***NOTE:** Original mintage 50,211.
****NOTE:** Original mintage 6,811,995.

GOLD

KM#	Date	Mintage	Fine	VF	XF	Unc
T5a	1895B (restrike)		—	—	Proof	7500.
(T2a)	1895 (restrike)		—	—	Proof	7500.
	1896B (restrike)		—	—	Proof	7500.
	1897B (restrike)		—	—	Proof	7500.
	1897 (restrike)		—	—	Proof	7500.
	1898B (restrike)		—	—	Proof	7500.
	1899B (restrike)		—	—	Proof	7500.
	1900B (restrike)		—	—	Proof	7500.
	1901B (restrike)		—	—	Proof	7500.
	1902B (restrike)		—	—	Proof	7500.

TOKEN ISSUES (Tn)

Bank of England

1 SHILLING 6 PENCE

(18 Pence)

.925 SILVER

KM#	Date	Mintage	Fine	VF	XF	Unc
Tn2	1811	—	5.00	16.00	45.00	90.00
	1811	—	—	—	Proof	800.00
	1812	—	5.00	17.00	50.00	100.00
	1812	—	—	—	Proof	800.00

KM#	Date	Mintage	Fine	VF	XF	Unc
Tn3	1812	—	4.50	15.00	40.00	85.00
	1813	—	4.50	15.00	40.00	85.00
	1814	—	4.50	15.00	40.00	85.00
	1815	—	4.50	15.00	40.00	85.00
	1816	—	8.00	20.00	50.00	100.00

3 SHILLINGS

.925 SILVER

KM#	Date	Mintage	Fine	VF	XF	Unc
Tn4	1811	—	10.00	25.00	65.00	150.00
	1811	—	—	—	Proof	1000.
	1812	—	10.00	30.00	70.00	160.00

KM#	Date	Mintage	Fine	VF	XF	Unc
Tn5	1812	—	10.00	25.00	60.00	145.00
	1812	—	—	—	Proof	1000.
	1813	—	10.00	25.00	60.00	145.00
	1814	—	10.00	25.00	60.00	155.00
	1815	—	10.00	25.00	60.00	155.00
	1816	—	150.00	300.00	600.00	1000.

DOLLAR

.903 SILVER
Bank of England

KM#	Date	Mintage	Fine	VF	XF	Unc
Tn1	1804	—	55.00	120.00	320.00	600.00
	1804	—	—	—	Proof	1500.

COPPER

KM#	Date	Mintage	Fine	VF	XF	Unc
Tn1a	1804	—	—	—	Proof	900.00

NOTE: The silver proofs were struck on specially prepared flans while circulation strikes were struck over Spanish and Spanish Colonial 8 Reales.

MAUNDY SETS (MDS)

These small silver coins are a special ceremonial issue struck each year for use at the traditional ceremony on Maundy Thursday when the reigning monarch (or a representative) distributes them to a selected group of elderly men and women. The amount distributed to each person (in pence) is equal to the present age of the monarch. The issue has consisted of silver 1, 2, 3 and 4 penny pieces since the reign of Charles II.

KM#	Date	Mintage	Identification	Mkt. Val.
MDS63	1817	1,584	KM668-671	*XF* 150.00
MDS64	1818	1,188	KM668-671	*XF* 150.00
MDS65	1820	1,584	KM668-671	*XF* 150.00
MDS66	1822	2,970	KM683,684,685.1,686	*XF* 150.00
MDS67	1822	—	KM683,684,685.1,686	*Proof* 345.00
MDS68	1823	1,980	KM683,684,685.2,686	*XF* 150.00
MDS69	1824	1,584	KM683,684,685.2,686	*XF* 150.00
MDS70	1825	2,376	KM683,684,685.2,686	*XF* 150.00
MDS71	1826	2,376	KM683,684,685.2,686	*XF* 150.00
MDS72	1826	—	KM683,684,685.2,686	*Proof* 345.00
MDS73	1827	2,772	KM683,684,685.2,686	*XF* 150.00
MDS74	1828	2,772	KM683,684,685.2,686	*XF* 150.00
MDS75	1828	—	KM683,684,685.2,686	*Proof* 345.00
MDS76	1829	2,772	KM683,684,685.2,686	*XF* 150.00
MDS77	1830	2,772	KM683,684,685.2,686	*XF* 150.00
MDS78	1831	3,564	KM708-711	*XF* 150.00
MDS79	1831	—	KM708-711	*Proof* 500.00
MDS80	1832	2,574	KM708-711	*XF* 125.00
MDS81	1833	2,574	KM708-711	*XF* 125.00
MDS82	1834	2,574	KM708-711	*XF* 125.00
MDS83	1835	2,574	KM708-711	*XF* 125.00
MDS84	1836	2,574	KM708-711	*XF* 125.00
MDS85	1837	2,574	KM708-711	*XF* 125.00
MDS86	1838	4,158	KM727,729-730,732	100.00
MDS87	1838	—	KM727,729-730,732	200.00
MDS88	1839	4,125	KM727,729-730,732	100.00
MDS89	1839	300	KM727,729-730,732	*Proof* 400.00
MDS90	1840	4,125	KM727,729-730,732	110.00
MDS91	1841	2,574	KM727,729-730,732	110.00
MDS92	1842	4,125	KM727,729-730,732	100.00
MDS93	1843	4,158	KM727,729-730,732	100.00
MDS94	1844	4,158	KM727,729-730,732	100.00
MDS95	1845	4,158	KM727,729-730,732	100.00
MDS96	1846	4,158	KM727,729-730,732	100.00
MDS97	1847	4,158	KM727,729-730,732	100.00
MDS98	1848	4,158	KM727,729-730,732	100.00
MDS99	1849	4,158	KM727,729-730,732	100.00
MDS100	1850	4,158	KM727,729-730,732	100.00
MDS101	1851	4,158	KM727,729-730,732	100.00
MDS102	1852	4,158	KM727,729-730,732	100.00
MDS103	1853	4,158	KM727,729-730,732	100.00
MDS104	1853	—	KM727,729-730,732	*Proof* 750.00
MDS105	1854	4,158	KM727,729-730,732	100.00
MDS106	1855	4,158	KM727,729-730,732	100.00
MDS107	1856	4,158	KM727,729-730,732	100.00
MDS108	1857	4,158	KM727,729-730,732	100.00
MDS109	1858	4,158	KM727,729-730,732	100.00
MDS110	1859	4,158	KM727,729-730,732	100.00
MDS111	1860	4,158	KM727,729-730,732	100.00
MDS112	1861	4,158	KM727,729-730,732	100.00
MDS113	1862	4,158	KM727,729-730,732	100.00
MDS114	1863	4,158	KM727,729-730,732	100.00
MDS115	1864	4,158	KM727,729-730,732	100.00
MDS116	1865	4,158	KM727,729-730,732	100.00
MDS117	1866	4,158	KM727,729-730,732	100.00
MDS118	1867	4,158	KM727,729-730,732	100.00
MDS119	1867	—	KM727,729-730,732	*Proof* 300.00
MDS120	1868	4,158	KM727,729-730,732	100.00
MDS121	1869	4,158	KM727,729-730,732	125.00
MDS122	1870	4,488	KM727,729-730,732	100.00
MDS123	1871	4,488	KM727,729-730,732	100.00
MDS124	1871	—	KM727,729-730,732	*Proof* 300.00
MDS125	1872	4,328	KM727,729-730,732	100.00
MDS126	1873	4,162	KM727,729-730,732	100.00
MDS127	1874	4,488	KM727,729-730,732	100.00
MDS128	1875	4,154	KM727,729-730,732	100.00
MDS129	1876	4,488	KM727,729-730,732	100.00
MDS130	1877	4,488	KM727,729-730,732	100.00
MDS131	1878	4,488	KM727,729-730,732	100.00
MDS132	1878	—	KM727,729-730,732	*Proof* 300.00
MDS133	1879	4,488	KM727,729-730,732	100.00
MDS134	1880	4,488	KM727,729-730,732	100.00
MDS135	1881	4,488	KM727,729-730,732	100.00
MDS136	1881	—	KM727,729-730,732	*Proof* 350.00
MDS137	1882	4,488	KM727,729-730,732	100.00
MDS138	1883	4,488	KM727,729-730,732	100.00
MDS139	1884	4,488	KM727,729-730,732	100.00
MDS140	1885	4,488	KM727,729-730,732	100.00
MDS141	1886	4,488	KM727,729-730,732	100.00
MDS142	1887	4,488	KM727,729-730,732	100.00
MDS143	1888	4,488	KM758,770-771,773	105.00
MDS144	1889	4,488	KM758,770-771,773	105.00
MDS145	1888	—	KM758,770-771,773	*Proof* 200.00
MDS146	1890	4,488	KM758,770-771,773	105.00
MDS147	1891	4,488	KM758,770-771,773	105.00
MDS148	1892	4,488	KM758,770-771,773	105.00
MDS149	1893	8,976	KM775-778	80.00
MDS150	1894	8,976	KM775-778	80.00
MDS151	1895	8,877	KM775-778	80.00
MDS152	1896	8,476	KM775-778	80.00
MDS153	1897	9,388	KM775-778	80.00
MDS154	1898	9,147	KM775-778	80.00
MDS155	1899	8,976	KM775-778	80.00
MDS156	1900	8,976	KM775-778	80.00
MDS157	1901	8,976	KM775-778	80.00
MDS158	1902	8,976	KM795-798	60.00
MDS159	1902	—	KM795-798	*Proof* 80.00
MDS160	1903	8,976	KM795-798	60.00
MDS161	1904	8,976	KM795-798	60.00
MDS162	1905	8,976	KM795-798	60.00
MDS163	1906	8,800	KM795-798	60.00
MDS164	1907	8,760	KM795-798	60.00
MDS165	1908	8,760	KM795-798	60.00
MDS166	1909	1,983	KM795-798	85.00
MDS167	1910	1,440	KM795-798	100.00
MDS168	1911	1,768	KM811-814	75.00
MDS169	1911	6,007	KM811-814	*Proof* 100.00
MDS170	1912	1,246	KM811-814	75.00
MDS171	1913	1,228	KM811-814	75.00
MDS172	1914	982	KM811-814	75.00
MDS173	1915	1,293	KM811-814	75.00
MDS174	1916	1,128	KM811-814	75.00
MDS175	1917	1,237	KM811-814	75.00
MDS176	1918	1,375	KM811-814	75.00
MDS177	1919	1,258	KM811-814	75.00
MDS178	1920	1,399	KM811-814	75.00
MDS179	1921	1,386	KM811a-814a	75.00
MDS180	1922	1,373	KM811a-814a	75.00
MDS181	1923	1,430	KM811a-814a	75.00
MDS182	1924	1,515	KM811a-814a	75.00
MDS183	1925	1,438	KM811a-814a	75.00
MDS184	1926	1,504	KM811a-814a	75.00
MDS185	1927	1,647	KM811a-814a	75.00
MDS186	1928	1,642	KM827,839-841	75.00
MDS187	1929	1,761	KM827,839-841	75.00
MDS188	1930	1,724	KM827,839-841	75.00
MDS189	1931	1,759	KM827,839-841	75.00
MDS190	1932	1,835	KM827,839-841	75.00
MDS191	1933	1,872	KM827,839-841	75.00
MDS192	1934	1,887	KM827,839-841	75.00
MDS193	1935	1,926	KM827,839-841	75.00
MDS194	1936	1,323	KM827,839-841	180.00
MDS195	1937	1,325	KM846-847,850-851	75.00
MDS196	1937	.026	KM846-847,850-851	*Proof* 75.00
MDS197	1938	1,275	KM846-847,850-851	75.00
MDS198	1939	1,234	KM846-847,850-851	75.00
MDS199	1940	1,277	KM846-847,850-851	75.00
MDS200	1941	1,253	KM846-847,850-851	75.00
MDS201	1942	1,231	KM846-847,850-851	75.00
MDS202	1943	1,239	KM846-847,850-851	75.00
MDS203	1944	1,259	KM846-847,850-851	75.00
MDS204	1945	1,355	KM846-847,850-851	75.00
MDS205	1946	1,365	KM846-847,850-851	75.00
MDS206	1947	1,375	KM846a-847a,850a-851a	75.00
MDS207	1948	1,385	KM846a-847a,850a-851a	75.00
MDS208	1949	1,395	KM870-872,874	80.00
MDS209	1950	1,405	KM870-872,874	80.00
MDS210	1951	1,468	KM870-872,874	80.00
MDS211	1952	1,012	KM870-872,874	90.00
MDS212	1953	1,025	KM884-885,887-888	450.00
MDS213	1954	1,020	KM898-899,901-902	75.00
MDS214	1955	1,036	KM898-899,901-902	75.00
MDS215	1956	1,088	KM898-899,901-902	75.00
MDS216	1957	1,094	KM898-899,901-902	75.00
MDS217	1958	1,100	KM898-899,901-902	75.00
MDS218	1959	1,106	KM898-899,901-902	75.00
MDS219	1960	1,112	KM898-899,901-902	75.00
MDS220	1961	1,118	KM898-899,901-902	75.00
MDS221	1962	1,125	KM898-899,901-902	75.00
MDS222	1963	1,131	KM898-899,901-902	75.00
MDS223	1964	1,137	KM898-899,901-902	75.00
MDS224	1965	1,143	KM898-899,901-902	75.00
MDS225	1966	1,206	KM898-899,901-902	75.00
MDS226	1967	986	KM898-899,901-902	75.00
MDS227	1968	964	KM898-899,901-902	75.00
MDS228	1969	1,002	KM898-899,901-902	75.00
MDS229	1970	980	KM898-899,901-902	75.00
MDS230	1971	1,018	KM898-899,901-902	75.00
MDS231	1972	1,026	KM898-899,901-902	75.00
MDS232	1973	1,004	KM898-899,901-902	75.00
MDS233	1974	1,042	KM898-899,901-902	75.00
MDS234	1975	1,050	KM898-899,901-902	75.00
MDS235	1976	1,257	KM898-899,901-902	75.00
MDS236	1977	1,248	KM898-899,901-902	85.00
MDS237	1978	1,179	KM898-899,901-902	85.00
MDS238	1979	1,180	KM898-899,901-902	85.00
MDS239	1980	1,148	KM898-899,901-902	85.00
MDS240	1981	1,398	KM898-899,901-902	85.00
MDS241	1982	1,220	KM898-899,901-902	85.00
MDS242	1983	1,228	KM898-899,901-902	85.00
MDS243	1984	1,238	KM898-899,901-902	85.00
MDS244	1985	1,248	KM898-899,901-902	85.00
MDS245	1986	1,378	KM898-899,901-902	85.00
MDS246	1987	1,390	KM898-899,901-902	85.00
MDS247	1988	1,402	KM898-899,901-902	85.00
MDS248	1989	1,353	KM898-899,901-902	85.00
MDS249	1990	1,523	KM898-899,901-902	85.00
MDS250	1991	1,384	KM898-899,901-902	85.00
MD251	1992	—	KM898-899,901-902	—
MD252	1993	—	KM898-899,901-902	—
MD253	1994	—	KM898-899,901-902	—

NOTE: The mintage figures above represent the maximum number of complete sets possible.

MINT SETS (MS)

KM#	Date	Mintage	Identification	Issue Price	Mkt. Val.
MS101	1953(9)	—	KM881-883,886,889-893	1.25	12.00
MS102	1968/71(5)	—	KM911-912,914-916. 10P and 5P dated 1968. 2P, 1P, 1/2P dated 1971. Blue wallet.	.50	2.00
MS103	1982(7)	205,000	KM926-932	6.00	6.50
MS104	1983(8)	637,100	KM926-933	8.75	9.00
MS105	1984(8)	158,820	KM926-932,934	8.75	7.00
MS106	1985(7)	178,375	KM935-941	8.75	6.00
MS107	1986(8)	167,224	KM935-940,946-947	9.75	10.00
MS108	1987(7)	172,425	KM935-940,948	9.00	7.50
MS109	1988(7)	134,067	KM935-940,954	9.00	7.50
MS110	1989(7)	77,569	KM935-940,959	10.00	10.00
MS111	1989(2)	—	KM960-961	11.00	11.00
MS112	1990(7)	—	KM935-936,937B,938 941	15.00	10.00
MS113	1991(7)	—	KM935-936,937b,938 940,946	15.00	10.00
MS114	1991(7)	—	KM935-936,937b,938 940, 946 baby pack	18.50	18.50
MS115	1992(9)	—	KM935-938,938a,939 940,948,963	17.50	15.00
			baby pack	22.50	22.50
MS116	1992(9)	—	KM935-938,938a,939 940,948,963 baby pack	22.50	22.50
MS117	1993(8)	—	KM935a-936a,937b,938a, 939-940,963-964	22.50	22.50
MS118	1994(7)	—	KM935a-936a,937b, 938a,966-968	22.50	22.50

PROOF SETS (PS)

KM#	Date	Mintage	Identification	Issue Price	Mkt. Val.
PS1	1821(6)	*2-5	KM677-682	—	Rare
PS2	1826(15)	*150	KM683-686,691,692a 693a,694-695,697a, 699-702	—	35,000.
PS3	1826(11)	Inc. Ab.	KM691,692a-693a,694 696,697a,700-702	—	30,000.
PS4	1831(14)	*225	KM705,706a-707a,709 714,716-718,720 835	—	26,500.
PS5	1839(15)	300	KM725a-726a,727,729 730,731.2,732-736, 739a,740-742	—	47,000.
PS6	1839/48(16)	Inc. Ab.	KM725a-726a,727,729 730,731.2,732-736, 739a,740-742,745	—	47,000.
PS7	1853(17)	—	KM725a-726a,727,729 730,731.2,732-736, 737a-739a,740a,744, 746	—	35,000.
PS8	1853(16)	Inc. Ab.	KM725a-726a,727,729 730,731.2,732-736, 738a-739a,740a,744, 746	—	33,500.
PS9	1887(11)	797	KM758-759,761-769	—	10,000.
PS10	1887(11)	Inc. Ab.	KM758-762,764-769	—	10,000.
PS11	1887(7)	287	KM758-759,761-765	—	1500.
PS12	1887(7)	Inc. Ab.	KM758-762,764-765	—	1500.
PS13	1893(10)	773	KM777,779,787	—	10,000.
PS14	1893(6)	556	KM777,779-783	—	1800.
PS15	1902(13)	8,066	KM795-807	—	2500.
PS16	1902(11)	7,057	KM795-805	—	600.00
PS17	1911(12)	2,812	KM811-822	—	5250.
PS18	1911(10)	952	KM811-820	—	1100.
PS19	1911(8)	2,241	KM811-818	—	425.00
PS20	1927(6)	15,030	KM831-836	—	400.00
PS21	1937(15)	26,402	KM843-857	—	175.00
PS-A22	1937(4)	1	KM858-861 Matte Proof	—	Unique
PS22	1937(4)	5,500	KM858-861	—	2600.
PS23	1950(9)	17,513	KM867-869,873,875 879	2.50	60.00
PS24	1951(10)	20,000	KM867-869,873,875 880	2.80	80.00
PS25	1953(10)	40,000	KM881-883,886,889 894	3.50	50.00
PS26	1970(8)	750,000	KM896-897,900,903 907 (Issued 1971)	8.75	8.00
PS27	1971(6)	350,000	KM911-916 (Issued 1973)	8.85	12.50
PS28	1972(7)	150,000	KM911-917 (Issued 1976)	13.00	8.00
PS29	1973(6)	100,000	KM911-912,914-916, 918 (Issued 1976)	13.00	8.00
PS30	1974(6)	100,000	KM911-916 (Issued 1976)	13.00	8.00
PS31	1975(6)	100,000	KM911-916 (Issued 1976)	13.00	8.00
PS32	1976(6)	100,000	KM911-916	13.00	8.00
PS33	1977(7)	193,800	KM911-916,920	17.00	12.50
PS34	1978(6)	88,100	KM911-916	15.00	10.00
PS35	1979(6)	81,000	KM911-916	15.00	10.00
PS36	1980(6)	143,400	KM911-916	23.00	8.00
PS37	1980(4)	10,000	KM919,922-924	2650.	1250.
PS38	1981(2)	2,500	KM919,925a	—	160.00
PS39	1981(6)	—	KM911-916	26.00	8.00
PS40	1981(9)	5,000	KM911-916,919,924, 925a	—	1000.
PS41	1982(7)	—	KM926-932	21.60	8.00
PS42	1982(4)	2,500	KM919,922-924	—	1600.
PS43	1983(8)	125,000	KM926-933	29.95	12.00
PS44	1983(3)	—	KM919,922-923	775.00	600.00
PS45	1984(8)	125,000	KM926-932,934	29.95	10.00
PS46	1984(3)	—	KM919,922,924	1275.	950.00
PS47	1985(7)	125,000	KM935-941	29.75	10.00
PS48	1985(4)	12,500	KM942-945	1395.	1250.
PS49	1986(8)	125,000	KM935-940,946-947	29.75	15.00
PS50	1986(3)	12,500	KM942-943,947c	675.00	675.00
PS51	1987(7)	125,000	KM935-940,948	29.75	15.00
PS52	1987(4)	10,000	KM950-953	1595.	1000.
PS53	1987(3)	12,500	KM942-944	675.00	600.00
PS54	1987(2)	12,500	KM950-951	325.00	200.00
PS55	1988(7)	*125,000	KM935-940,954	29.75	15.00
PS56	1988(4)	6,500	KM950-953	1595.	1000.
PS57	1988(3)	—	KM942-944	775.00	550.00
PS58	1988(2)	7,500	KM950-951	340.00	200.00
PS59	1989(9)	*100,000	KM935-940,959-961	34.95	20.00
PS60	1989(4)	*2,500	KM950-953	1595.	1000.

KM#	Date	Mintage	Identification	Issue Price	Mkt. Val.
PS61	1989(4)	*5,000	KM955-958	1595.	1600.
PS62	1989(3)	*15,000	KM955-957	775.00	700.00
PS63	1989(2)	*1,500	KM950-951	340.00	200.00
PS64	1989(2)	—	KM960a-961a	—	90.00
PS65	1989(2)	—	KM960b-961b	—	250.00
PS66	1990(8)	*100,000	KM935-937,937b,938 941, leatherette case	35.00	25.00
PS67	1990(8)	Inc. Ab.	KM935-937,937b,938 941, leather case	45.00	35.00
PS68	1990(4)	*2,500	KM942-944,949	1595.	1400.
PS69	1990(4)	*2,500	KM950a-953a	1595.	1000.
PS70	1990(3)	*7,500	KM942-944	775.00	600.00
PS71	1990(3)	*35,000	KM937a-937c	47.50	47.50
PS72	1991(7)	*10,000	KM935-936,937b,938 940,946, leatherette case	38.50	22.50
PS73	1991(7)	*10,000	KM935-936,937b,938 940,946, leather case	48.50	27.50
PS74	1991(4)	*1,500	KM942-944,949	1750.	1750.
PS75	1991(4)	750	KM950a-953a	1750.	1750.
PS76	1991(3)	*2,500	KM942-944	895.00	900.00
PS77	1992(9)	*100,000	KM935-938,938a,939 940,948,963, leatherette case	44.50	40.00
PS78	1992(9)	*100,000	KM935-938,938a,939 940,948,963, leather case	44.50	40.00
PS79	1992(4)	1,250	KM942-945	1750.	1750.
PS80	1992(4)	*1,000	KM938b,938c,948a,963a	122.00	—
PS81	1992(3)	1,250	KM942-944	895.00	895.00
PS82	1992(2)	—	KM938b-938c	59.45	60.00
PS83	1993(8)	*100,000	KM935a-936a,937b,938a, 939-940,964-965, standard case	50.00	50.00
PS84	1993(8)	Inc. Ab.	KM935a-936a,937b,938a, 939-940,964-965, deluxe case	60.00	60.00
PS85	1993(4)	500	KM950a-953a	1755.	1755.
PS86	1993(4)	1,250	KM942-945	1560.	—
PS87	1993(3)	1,250	KM942-944	800.00	—
PS88	1994(7)	*100,000	KM935a-936a,937b,938a, 966-968, standard case	45.00	45.00
PS89	1994(7)	Inc. Ab.	KM935a-936a,937b,938a, 966-968, deluxe case	55.00	55.00

***NOTE:** Estimated mintage figures.

The Hellenic Republic of Greece is situated in southeastern Europe on the southern tip of the Balkan Peninsula. The republic includes many islands, the most important of which are Crete and the Ionian Islands. Greece (including islands) has an area of 50,944 sq. mi. (131,940 sq. km.) and a population of 10 million. Capital: Athens. Greece is still largely agricultural. Tobacco, cotton, fruit and wool are exported.

Greece, the Mother of Western civilization, attained the peak of its culture in the 5th century B.C., when it contributed more to government, drama, art and architecture than any other people to this time. Greece fell under Roman domination in the 2nd and 1st centuries B.C., becoming part of the Byzantine Empire until Constantinople fell to the Crusaders in 1202. With the fall of Constantinople to the Turks in 1453, Greece became part of the Ottoman Empire. Independence from Turkey was won with the revolution of 1821-27. In 1833, Greece was established as a monarchy, with sovereignty guaranteed by Britain, France and Russia. After a lengthy power struggle between the monarchist forces and democratic factions, Greece was proclaimed a republic in 1925. The monarchy was restored in 1935 and reconfirmed by a plebiscite in 1946. The Italians invaded Greece via Albania on Oct. 28, 1940 but were driven back well within the Albanian border. Germany began their invasion in April 1941 and quickly overran the entire country and drove off a British Expeditionary force by the end of April. King George II and his new government went into exile. The GermanItalian occupation of Greece lasted until Oct. 1944 and German for the last year. On April 21, 1967, a military junta took control of the government and suspended the constitution, King Constantine II made an unsuccessful attempt against the junta in the fall of 1968 and consequently fled to Italy. The monarchy was formally abolished by plebiscite, Dec. 8, 1974, and Greece established as the 'Hellenic Republic,' the third republic in Greek history.

RULERS

John Capodistrias, 1828-1831
King Otto, 1832-1862
George I, 1863-1913
Constantine I, 1913-1917, 1920-1922
Alexander I, 1917-1920
George II, 1922-1923, 1935-1947
Paul I, 1947-1964
Constantine II, 1964-1973

MINT MARKS

(a) - Paris, privy marks only
A - Paris
B - Vienna
BB - Strassburg
(c) - Aegina (1828-1832), Chain and anchor
H - Heaton, Birmingham
K - Bordeaux
KN - King's Norton
(o) - Athens (1838-1855), Owl
(p) - Poissy - Thunderbolt

MONETARY SYSTEM

Until 1831
100 Lepta = 1 Phoenix
Commencing 1831
100 Lepta = 1 Drachma

KINGDOM

1828-1925

LEPTON

COPPER, 17mm
Obv: Phoenix in solid circle.

KM#	Date	Mintage	Fine	VF	XF	Unc
1	1828	.480	45.00	70.00	120.00	260.00
	1830	.026	50.00	100.00	150.00	350.00

Obv: Phoenix in pearl circle, 17mm.

KM#	Date	Mintage	Fine	VF	XF	Unc
5	1830	.400	40.00	80.00	125.00	275.00

Obv: W/o circle, 16mm.

KM#	Date	Mintage	Fine	VF	XF	Unc
9	1831	.612	40.00	80.00	125.00	300.00

Type 1 — ΒΑΣΙΛΕΙΑ

KM#	Date	Mintage	Fine	VF	XF	Unc
13	1832	2.200	20.00	40.00	80.00	200.00
	1833	Inc. Ab.	15.00	25.00	50.00	90.00
	1834	Inc. Ab.	60.00	100.00	200.00	600.00
	1837	.160	20.00	40.00	100.00	250.00
	1838	.270	20.00	40.00	100.00	250.00
	1839	.150	20.00	40.00	100.00	250.00
	1840	.700	20.00	40.00	80.00	200.00
	1841	.370	20.00	40.00	100.00	250.00
	1842	.120	20.00	40.00	100.00	250.00
	1843	.630	20.00	40.00	100.00	250.00

Type 2 — ΒΑΣΙΛΕΙΟΝ

KM#	Date	Mintage	Fine	VF	XF	Unc
22	1844	.151	25.00	70.00	200.00	450.00
	1845	.160	20.00	65.00	160.00	400.00
	1846	.141	20.00	60.00	140.00	300.00

Obv: Smaller crowned arms.
Rev: Redesigned wreath.

KM#	Date	Mintage	Fine	VF	XF	Unc
26	1847	.273	40.00	80.00	200.00	450.00
	1848	.084	20.00	40.00	100.00	300.00
	1849	.090	20.00	40.00	100.00	300.00

Size reduced to 15mm

KM#	Date	Mintage	Fine	VF	XF	Unc
30	1851	.400	20.00	40.00	85.00	200.00
	1857	.243	20.00	40.00	90.00	250.00

KM#	Date	Mintage	Fine	VF	XF	Unc
40	1869BB	14.976	2.00	4.00	12.50	40.00
	1870BB	Inc. Ab.	10.00	25.00	75.00	150.00

KM#	Date	Mintage	Fine	VF	XF	Unc
52	1878K	7.132	2.00	5.00	12.50	40.00
	1879A	.398	3.50	7.50	20.00	70.00

2 LEPTA

COPPER
Type 1 — ΒΑΣΙΛΕΙΑ

KM#	Date	Mintage	Fine	VF	XF	Unc
14	1832	2.475	20.00	40.00	100.00	230.00
	1833	Inc. Ab.	12.50	20.00	40.00	85.00
	1834	Inc. Ab.	40.00	80.00	125.00	250.00
	1836	.049	75.00	125.00	225.00	500.00
	1837	.222	20.00	40.00	100.00	200.00
	1838	.701	20.00	40.00	80.00	175.00
	1839	.661	20.00	40.00	80.00	175.00
	1840	.520	20.00	40.00	80.00	175.00
	1842	.470	20.00	40.00	80.00	175.00

Type 2 — ΒΑΣΙΛΕΙΟΝ

KM#	Date	Mintage	Fine	VF	XF	Unc
23	1844	.206	40.00	75.00	125.00	250.00
	1845	.242	40.00	75.00	125.00	250.00

Obv: Smaller crowned arms.
Rev: Redesigned wreath.

KM#	Date	Mintage	Fine	VF	XF	Unc
27	1847	.082	40.00	100.00	175.00	375.00
	1848	.258	20.00	40.00	100.00	220.00
	1849	.146	20.00	40.00	100.00	220.00

Size reduced to 17mm.

KM#	Date	Mintage	Fine	VF	XF	Unc
31	1851	.388	20.00	40.00	85.00	220.00
	1857	.544	20.00	40.00	80.00	200.00

KM#	Date	Mintage	Fine	VF	XF	Unc
41	1869BB	7.482	2.00	4.00	12.00	60.00
	1869BB	—	—	—	Proof	220.00

KM#	Date	Mintage	Fine	VF	XF	Unc
53	1878K large anchor					
		3.750	1.00	3.00	10.00	50.00
	1878K small anchor					
		Inc. Ab.	10.00	25.00	40.00	80.00
	1878K	—	—	—	Proof	220.00

5 LEPTA

COPPER, 28mm
Obv: Phoenix in solid circle.

KM#	Date	Mintage	Fine	VF	XF	Unc
2	1828	.400	40.00	80.00	125.00	325.00
	1830	.022	40.00	100.00	175.00	500.00

Obv: Phoenix in pearl circle.

KM#	Date	Mintage	Fine	VF	XF	Unc
6	1830	.150	40.00	80.00	150.00	400.00

Obv: W/o circle.

KM#	Date	Mintage	Fine	VF	XF	Unc
10	1831	.230	40.00	60.00	120.00	300.00

Type 1 — ΒΑΣΙΛΕΙΑ

KM#	Date	Mintage	Fine	VF	XF	Unc
16	1833	2.500	10.00	20.00	40.00	90.00
	1834	Inc. Ab.	40.00	80.00	150.00	400.00
	1836	1,000	200.00	400.00	1000.	2000.
	1837	.116	40.00	60.00	125.00	300.00
	1838/7	1.472	20.00	50.00	100.00	250.00
	1838	Inc. Ab.	20.00	40.00	80.00	200.00
	1839	1.186	20.00	40.00	80.00	200.00
	1840	.417	20.00	40.00	80.00	200.00
	1841	.864	20.00	40.00	80.00	200.00
	1842	.682	20.00	40.00	80.00	200.00

Type 2 — ΒΑΣΙΛΕΙΟΝ

KM#	Date	Mintage	Fine	VF	XF	Unc
24	1844	.089	40.00	80.00	150.00	300.00
	1845	.316	40.00	80.00	150.00	300.00
	1846	.190	40.00	60.00	125.00	250.00

KM#	Date	Mintage	Fine	VF	XF	Unc
28	1847	.270	40.00	80.00	150.00	350.00
	1848	.394	40.00	80.00	150.00	300.00
	1849	.374	40.00	60.00	125.00	250.00

KM#	Date	Mintage	Fine	VF	XF	Unc
32	1851	.620	20.00	40.00	85.00	230.00
	1857	.350	20.00	45.00	90.00	240.00

KM#	Date	Mintage	Fine	VF	XF	Unc
42	1869BB	23.945	1.00	3.50	8.00	40.00
	1870BB	Inc. Ab.	15.00	30.00	60.00	150.00

KM#	Date	Mintage	Fine	VF	XF	Unc
54	1878K	11.528	1.00	3.00	10.00	50.00
	1879A	.470	20.00	40.00	80.00	300.00
	1882A	14.400	2.00	5.00	12.50	50.00

COPPER-NICKEL

KM#	Date	Mintage	Fine	VF	XF	Unc
58	1894A	4.000	1.00	2.50	7.00	25.00
	1895A	4.000	1.00	2.50	7.00	25.00

NICKEL

KM#	Date	Mintage	Fine	VF	XF	Unc
62	1912(a)	25.053	.50	1.00	2.50	12.00

10 LEPTA

COPPER, 35mm.
Obv: Phoenix in solid circle.

KM#	Date	Mintage	Fine	VF	XF	Unc
3	1828	.450	40.00	75.00	150.00	350.00
	1830	.034	50.00	100.00	200.00	500.00

Obv: Phoenix in pearl circle, 33mm.

KM#	Date	Mintage	Fine	VF	XF	Unc
8	1830	1.200	40.00	75.00	150.00	350.00

NOTE: Varieties exist.

Obv: Phoenix w/o circle.

KM#	Date	Mintage	Fine	VF	XF	Unc
12	1831	1.223	40.00	60.00	100.00	200.00

Type 1 — ΒΑΣΙΛΕΙΑ

KM#	Date	Mintage	Fine	VF	XF	Unc
17	1833	.520	20.00	40.00	50.00	125.00
	1836	.919	30.00	50.00	125.00	225.00
	1837	2.660	30.00	50.00	125.00	200.00
	1838	.918	30.00	50.00	125.00	250.00
	1843	.700	30.00	50.00	125.00	250.00
	1844	1.064	75.00	125.00	250.00	550.00

Type 2 — ΒΑΣΙΛΕΙΟΝ

KM#	Date	Mintage	Fine	VF	XF	Unc
25	1844	Inc. Ab.	30.00	50.00	125.00	275.00
	1845	.985	30.00	50.00	200.00	350.00
	1846/45	1.275	30.00	50.00	125.00	250.00
	1846	Inc. Ab.	30.00	50.00	125.00	275.00

KM#	Date	Mintage	Fine	VF	XF	Unc
29	1847	.740	50.00	80.00	225.00	450.00
	1848	1.174	30.00	60.00	150.00	300.00
	1849/8 small crown					
		1.160	30.00	50.00	125.00	220.00
	1849 small crown					
		Inc. Ab.	30.00	50.00	125.00	200.00
	1849 large crown					
		Inc. Ab.	200.00	400.00	700.00	1000.
	1850	1.282	30.00	50.00	125.00	200.00
	1851	.587	30.00	50.00	125.00	250.00
	1857	.883	30.00	50.00	125.00	220.00

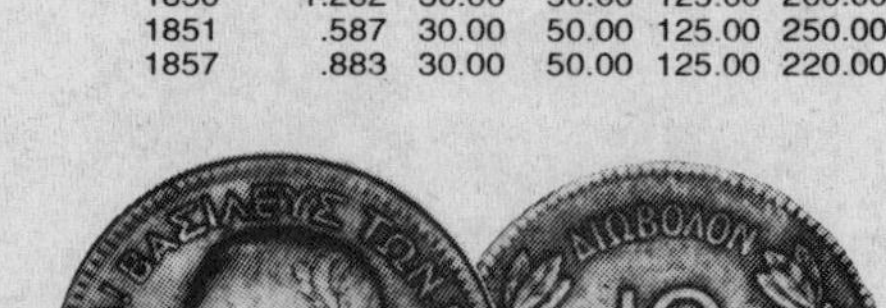

KM#	Date	Mintage	Fine	VF	XF	Unc
43	1869BB	14.994	2.00	4.00	8.00	40.00
	1869BB	—	—	—	Proof	250.00
	1870BB	Inc. Ab.	15.00	30.00	60.00	200.00

KM#	Date	Mintage	Fine	VF	XF	Unc
55	1878K	7.140	1.00	3.00	7.50	50.00
	1879A	.358	20.00	40.00	90.00	325.00
	1882A	16.000	1.00	3.00	7.00	45.00

COPPER-NICKEL

KM#	Date	Mintage	Fine	VF	XF	Unc
59	1894A	3.000	1.00	2.50	5.50	25.00
	1895A	3.000	1.00	2.50	5.50	25.00

NICKEL

KM#	Date	Mintage	Fine	VF	XF	Unc
63	1912(a)	28.973	.25	.50	2.50	15.00

1.5200 g, ALUMINUM
1.7mm thick

KM#	Date	Mintage	Fine	VF	XF	Unc
66.1	1922(p)	120.00	1.00	2.00	5.00	20.00

1.6500 g, 2.2mm thick

KM#	Date	Mintage	Fine	VF	XF	Unc
66.2	1922(p)	—	—	—	—	—

20 LEPTA

COPPER

KM#	Date	Mintage	Fine	VF	XF	Unc
11	1831	2.273	25.00	50.00	150.00	450.00

1.0000 g, .835 SILVER, .0268 oz ASW

KM#	Date	Mintage	Fine	VF	XF	Unc
44	1874A	2.223	3.00	5.00	15.00	35.00
	1874A	—	—	—	Proof	400.00
	1883A	1.000	3.50	8.00	30.00	85.00

COPPER-NICKEL

KM#	Date	Mintage	Fine	VF	XF	Unc
57	1893A	.248	5.00	25.00	75.00	400.00
	1894A	4.752	1.00	2.00	6.00	30.00
	1895A	5.000	1.00	2.00	6.00	30.00

NICKEL

KM#	Date	Mintage	Fine	VF	XF	Unc
64	1912(a)	10.145	.50	1.00	4.00	15.00

1/4 DRACHMA

1.2500 g, .900 SILVER, .0361 oz ASW
Obv: Young head.

KM#	Date	Mintage	Fine	VF	XF	Unc
18	1833	.780	25.00	50.00	80.00	175.00
	1834A	—	25.00	50.00	125.00	225.00
	1845	—	300.00	500.00	1500.	3000.
	1846	—	400.00	800.00	2000.	4000.

Obv: Old head, 15mm.

KM#	Date	Mintage	Fine	VF	XF	Unc
33	1851	—	300.00	600.00	1250.	2750.
	1855	—	100.00	200.00	500.00	1000.

1/2 DRACHMA

2.5000 g, .900 SILVER, .0723 oz ASW

KM#	Date	Mintage	Fine	VF	XF	Unc
19	1833	.900	25.00	50.00	80.00	175.00
	1834A	—	30.00	80.00	125.00	250.00
	1842(o)	—	150.00	350.00	800.00	2000.
	1843(o)	—	200.00	500.00	1000.	2500.
	1846	—	100.00	350.00	800.00	2000.
	1847	—	200.00	500.00	1000.	2500.

KM#	Date	Mintage	Fine	VF	XF	Unc
34	1851	—	200.00	500.00	1000.	2500.
	1855	—	100.00	200.00	500.00	1000.

50 LEPTA

2.5000 g, .835 SILVER, .0671 oz ASW

KM#	Date	Mintage	Fine	VF	XF	Unc
37	1868A	60 pcs.	—	—	—	5000.
	1874A	4.501	2.50	5.50	15.00	35.00
	1874A	—	—	—	Proof	400.00
	1883A	.600	4.00	10.00	30.00	90.00

COPPER-NICKEL

KM#	Date	Mintage	Fine	VF	XF	Unc
65	1921H	1.000	300.00	600.00	1250.	2250.
	1921KN	1.524	500.00	900.00	1750.	3250.

PHOENIX

3.8700 g, .943 SILVER, .1173 oz ASW

KM#	Date	Mintage	Fine	VF	XF	Unc
4	1828(Aegina)	.012	150.00	300.00	750.00	1500.

DRACHMA

4.5000 g, .900 SILVER, .1446 oz ASW
Obv: Young head.

KM#	Date	Mintage	Fine	VF	XF	Unc
15	1832	1.125	30.00	60.00	100.00	350.00
	1833	Inc. Ab.	25.00	50.00	75.00	200.00
	1833	—	—	—	Proof	1000.
	1833A	—	30.00	65.00	140.00	400.00
	1833A	—	—	—	Proof	1000.
	1834A	—	50.00	100.00	300.00	800.00
	1845(o)	—	500.00	1000.	2000.	4000.
	1846	—	125.00	250.00	750.00	1500.
	1847	—	400.00	900.00	1800.	3750.

Obv: Old head.

KM#	Date	Mintage	Fine	VF	XF	Unc
35	1851	—	250.00	500.00	1200.	3000.

5.0000 g, .835 SILVER, .1342 oz ASW

KM#	Date	Mintage	Fine	VF	XF	Unc
38	1868A	.480	10.00	25.00	60.00	175.00
	1873A	1.802	10.00	20.00	50.00	150.00
	1873A	—	—	—	Proof	500.00
	1874A	2.249	15.00	30.00	85.00	225.00
	1883A	.800	20.00	50.00	150.00	400.00

KM#	Date	Mintage	Fine	VF	XF	Unc
60	1910(a)	4.570	4.00	8.00	20.00	40.00
	1911(a)	1.881	5.00	10.00	25.00	55.00

2 DRACHMAI

10.0000 g, .835 SILVER, .2684 oz ASW

KM#	Date	Mintage	Fine	VF	XF	Unc
39	1868A	.047	25.00	55.00	175.00	750.00
	1873A	.839	25.00	50.00	150.00	650.00
	1873A	—	—	—	Proof	1000.
	1883A	.250	25.00	55.00	225.00	800.00

KM#	Date	Mintage	Fine	VF	XF	Unc
61	1911(a)	1.500	5.00	20.00	50.00	100.00

5 DRACHMAI

22.5000 g, .900 SILVER, .6511 oz ASW

KM#	Date	Mintage	Fine	VF	XF	Unc
20	1833	.378	100.00	200.00	500.00	1000.
	1833	—	—	—	Proof	3000.
	1833A	—	100.00	200.00	500.00	1000.
	1833A	—	—	—	Proof	3000.
	1833(o)	—	1200.	2400.	6000.	10,000.
	1844(o)	—	300.00	600.00	1200.	2400.
	1845	—	3000.	4800.	6500.	10,500.

Rev: Similar to KM#20.

KM#	Date	Mintage	Fine	VF	XF	Unc
36	1851	—	500.00	800.00	2250.	6000.
	1851	—	—	—	Proof	—

25.0000 g, .900 SILVER, .7234 oz ASW

KM#	Date	Mintage	Fine	VF	XF	Unc
46	1875A	1.000	25.00	60.00	175.00	500.00
	1875A reversed anchor					
		—	150.00	200.00	500.00	2500.
	1875A	—	—	—	Proof	2000.
	1876A	2.092	25.00	60.00	175.00	500.00
	1876A	—	—	—	Proof	2000.

1.6129 g, .900 GOLD, .0467 oz AGW

KM#	Date	Mintage	Fine	VF	XF	Unc
47	1876A	9,294	250.00	450.00	850.00	1750.

10 DRACHMAI

3.2258 g, .900 GOLD, .0933 oz AGW

KM#	Date	Mintage	Fine	VF	XF	Unc
48	1876A	.019	200.00	350.00	550.00	1500.

20 DRACHMAI

5.7760 g, .900 GOLD, .1672 oz AGW

KM#	Date	Mintage	Fine	VF	XF	Unc
21	1833	.018	250.00	650.00	1150.	2500.

6.4516 g, .900 GOLD, .1867 oz AGW

KM#	Date	Mintage	Fine	VF	XF	Unc
49	1876A	.037	125.00	225.00	350.00	750.00
	1876A 1 known	—		—	Proof	*12,000.

*NOTE: Spink Coin Auctions no. 10 9-80 Brilliant F.D.C. realized $12,000.

KM#	Date	Mintage	Fine	VF	XF	Unc
56	1884A	.550	90.00	120.00	160.00	250.00
	1884A	—	—	—	Proof	3500.

50 DRACHMAI

16.1290 g, .900 GOLD, .4667 oz AGW

KM#	Date	Mintage	Fine	VF	XF	Unc
50	1876A	182 pcs.	2000.	3000.	5000.	9000.

100 DRACHMAI

32.2580 g, .900 GOLD, .9335 oz AGW

KM#	Date	Mintage	Fine	VF	XF	Unc
51	1876A	76 pcs.	5000.	8000.	13,000.	20,000.
	1876A	—	—	—	Proof	25,000.

REPUBLIC

1925-1935

20 LEPTA

COPPER-NICKEL

KM#	Date	Mintage	Fine	VF	XF	Unc
67	1926	20.000	.50	1.00	3.00	8.00

50 LEPTA

COPPER-NICKEL

KM#	Date	Mintage	Fine	VF	XF	Unc
68	1926	20.000	.20	.50	2.00	5.00
	1926B (1930)					
		20.000	.20	.50	2.00	5.00

DRACHMA

COPPER-NICKEL

KM#	Date	Mintage	Fine	VF	XF	Unc
69	1926	15.000	.20	.50	2.00	5.00
	1926B (1930)					
		20.000	.20	.50	2.00	5.00

2 DRACHMAI

COPPER-NICKEL

KM#	Date	Mintage	Fine	VF	XF	Unc
70	1926	22.000	.50	1.00	3.00	10.00

5 DRACHMAI

NICKEL

LONDON MINT: In second set of berries on left only 1 berry will have a dot on it.

KM#	Date	Mintage	Fine	VF	XF	Unc
71.1	1930	23.500	.50	1.00	3.50	20.00
	1930	—	—	—	Proof	—

BRUSSELS MINT: 2 berries will have dots.

KM#	Date	Mintage	Fine	VF	XF	Unc
71.2	1930	1.500	1.00	3.00	9.00	45.00

10 DRACHMAI

7.0000 g, .500 SILVER, .1125 oz ASW

KM#	Date	Mintage	Fine	VF	XF	Unc
72	1930	7.500	2.50	5.00	12.50	50.00
	1930	—	—	—	Proof	—

20 DRACHMAI

11.3100 g, .500 SILVER, .1818 oz ASW

KM#	Date	Mintage	Fine	VF	XF	Unc
73	1930	11.500	4.00	6.00	12.50	40.00
	1930	—	—	—	Proof	—

KINGDOM

1935-1973

5 LEPTA

ALUMINUM

KM#	Date	Mintage	Fine	VF	XF	Unc
77	1954	15.000	—	.10	.50	1.50
	1971	1.002	.20	.50	1.50	6.00

NOTE: 1971 dated coins have smaller hole at center.

10 LEPTA

ALUMINUM

KM#	Date	Mintage	Fine	VF	XF	Unc
78	1954	48.000	—	.10	.35	1.75
	1959	20.000	—	.10	.35	1.75
	1964	12.000	—	.10	.35	1.75
	1965*	—	—	—	—	3.00
	1965*	4,987	—	—	Proof	4.50
	1966	20.000	—	.10	.35	1.75
	1969	20.000	—	.10	.35	1.75
	1971	5.922	—	.25	1.50	6.50

***NOTE:** Only sold in sets.
NOTE: 1971 dated coins have smaller hole at center.

20 LEPTA

ALUMINUM

KM#	Date	Mintage	Fine	VF	XF	Unc
79	1954	24.000	—	.10	.50	2.00
	1959	20.000	—	.10	.50	2.00
	1964	8.000	—	.10	.50	2.00
	1966	15.000	—	.10	.50	2.00
	1969	20.000	—	.10	.50	2.00
	1971	4.108	—	.20	1.00	2.50

NOTE: 1971 dated coins have smaller hole at center.

50 LEPTA

COPPER-NICKEL

KM#	Date	Mintage	Fine	VF	XF	Unc
80	1954	37.228	.15	.25	.75	1.50
	1957	5.108	.15	.50	2.00	10.00
	1957	—	—	—	Proof	150.00
	1959	10.160	.15	.25	.75	1.50
	1962 plain edge					
		20.500	.15	.25	.75	1.50
	1962 serrated edge					
		Inc. Ab.	.15	.25	.75	1.50
	1964	20.000	.15	.25	.75	1.50
	1965*	—	—	—	—	3.00
	1965*	4,987	—	—	Proof	4.50

***NOTE:** Only sold in sets.

KM#	Date	Mintage	Fine	VF	XF	Unc
88	1966	30.000	.20	.50	1.00	3.50
	1970	10.160	.30	.60	1.50	4.50

DRACHMA

COPPER-NICKEL

KM#	Date	Mintage	Fine	VF	XF	Unc
81	1954	24.091	.15	.25	.75	2.50
	1957	8.151	.15	.25	2.00	10.00
	1957	—	—	—	Proof	200.00
	1959	10.180	.15	.25	2.00	10.00
	1962	20.060	.15	.25	.75	2.50
	1965*	—	—	—	—	3.00
	1965*	4,987	—	—	Proof	4.50

***NOTE:** Only sold in sets.

KM#	Date	Mintage	Fine	VF	XF	Unc
89	1966	20.000	—	.15	.45	1.50
	1967	20.000	—	.15	.45	1.50
	1970	7.001	—	.50	1.00	3.00

2 DRACHMAI

COPPER-NICKEL

KM#	Date	Mintage	Fine	VF	XF	Unc
82	1954	12.609	.50	.75	1.50	5.00
	1957	10.171	.50	.75	2.50	10.00
	1957	—	—	—	Proof	300.00
	1959	5.000	.50	.75	2.50	10.00
	1962	10.096	.50	.75	1.50	5.00
	1965*	—	—	—	—	3.00
	1965*	4,987	—	—	Proof	4.50

***NOTE:** Only sold in sets.

KM#	Date	Mintage	Fine	VF	XF	Unc
90	1966	10.000	.15	.25	.50	1.50
	1967	10.000	.15	.25	.50	1.50
	1970	7.000	.50	1.00	2.00	4.00

5 DRACHMAI

COPPER-NICKEL

KM#	Date	Mintage	Fine	VF	XF	Unc
83	1954	21.000	.25	.50	1.00	5.00
	1965*	—	—	—	—	4.00
	1965*	4,987	—	—	Proof	6.00

***NOTE:** Only sold in sets.

KM#	Date	Mintage	Fine	VF	XF	Unc
91	1966	12.000	.15	.25	1.00	5.00
	1970	5.000	.50	1.00	3.00	6.00

10 DRACHMAI

NICKEL

KM#	Date	Mintage	Fine	VF	XF	Unc
84	1959	20.000	.30	.50	1.50	5.00
	1959	—	—	—	Proof	200.00
	1965*	—	—	—	—	4.00
	1965*	4,987	—	—	Proof	6.00

***NOTE:** Only sold in sets.

COPPER-NICKEL

KM#	Date	Mintage	Fine	VF	XF	Unc
96	1968	40.000	.25	.50	.75	3.50

20 DRACHMAI

6.4516 g, .900 GOLD, .1867 oz AGW
5th Anniversary Restoration of Monarchy

KM#	Date	Mintage	Fine	VF	XF	Unc
74	ND(1940)					
		200 pcs.	—	—	Proof	4000.

7.5000 g, .835 SILVER, .2013 oz ASW

KM#	Date	Mintage	Fine	VF	XF	Unc
85	1960	20.000	—	BV	2.50	4.00
	1960	—	—	—	Proof	350.00
	1965*	—	—	—	—	5.00
	1965*	4,987	—	—	Proof	7.00

***NOTE:** Only sold in sets.

30 DRACHMAI

18.0000 g, .835 SILVER, .4832 oz ASW
Centennial of Royal Greek Dynasty

KM#	Date	Mintage	Fine	VF	XF	Unc
86	1963	3.000	—	BV	4.00	7.00

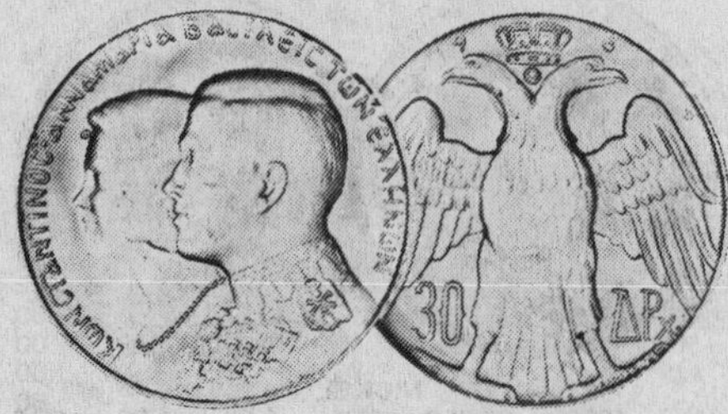

12.0000 g, .835 SILVER, .3221 oz ASW
Constantine and Anne-Marie Wedding

KM#	Date	Mintage	Fine	VF	XF	Unc
87	1964 (Berne)	1.000	—	BV	3.50	5.00
	1964 (Kongsberg)	1.000	—	BV	3.50	5.00

100 DRACHMAI

25.0000 g, .900 SILVER, .7235 oz ASW
5th Anniversary Restoration of Monarchy

KM#	Date	Mintage	Fine	VF	XF	Unc
75	ND(1940)	500 pcs.	—	—	Proof	800.00

32.2580 g, .900 GOLD, .9335 oz AGW

KM#	Date	Mintage	Fine	VF	XF	Unc
76	ND(1940)	140 pcs.	—	—	Proof	9500.

TRANSITION COINAGE

10 LEPTA

ALUMINUM
Obv: Soldier and Phoenix.

KM#	Date	Mintage	Fine	VF	XF	Unc
102	1973	2.742	—	.10	1.00	4.00

20 LEPTA

ALUMINUM

KM#	Date	Mintage	Fine	VF	XF	Unc
104	1973	2.718	—	.20	.60	4.00

50 LEPTA

COPPER-NICKEL
Obv: Small head.

KM#	Date	Mintage	Fine	VF	XF	Unc
97.1	1971	10.999	—	.10	.15	1.00
	1973	9.342	—	.20	.50	2.00

Obv: Large head.

KM#	Date	Mintage	Fine	VF	XF	Unc
97.2	1973	Inc. Ab.	—	.20	.50	2.00

DRACHMA

COPPER-NICKEL

KM#	Date	Mintage	Fine	VF	XF	Unc
98	1971	11.985	—	.20	.75	2.00
	1973	8.196	—	.25	1.00	3.00

2 DRACHMAI

COPPER-NICKEL

KM#	Date	Mintage	Fine	VF	XF	Unc
99	1971	9.998	.15	.25	.75	2.00
	1973	7.972	.20	.50	1.50	3.50

5 DRACHMAI

COPPER-NICKEL

KM#	Date	Mintage	Fine	VF	XF	Unc
100	1971	4.014	.25	.50	2.00	5.00
	1973	3.166	.25	.50	1.50	3.00

10 DRACHMAI

COPPER-NICKEL
Rev. Phoenix

KM#	Date	Mintage	Fine	VF	XF	Unc
101	1971	.502	.25	.50	1.00	5.00
	1973	.541	.50	1.00	2.50	5.00

20 DRACHMAI

6.4516 g, .900 GOLD, .1867 oz AGW
1967 Revolution

KM#	Date	Mintage	Fine	VF	XF	Unc
92	1967(1970)	.020	—	—	—	300.00

COPPER-NICKEL
Rev: Narrow rim w/faint veil or no veil.

KM#	Date	Mintage	Fine	VF	XF	Unc
111.1	1973	3.092	.25	.50	1.50	6.00

Rev: Wide rim w/heavy veil and broken wave design at rear hoof.

KM#	Date	Mintage	Fine	VF	XF	Unc
111.2	1973	Inc. Ab.	1.00	2.00	4.00	12.00

Rev: Wide rim w/continuous wave design at rear hoof.

KM#	Date	Mintage	Fine	VF	XF	Unc
111.3	1973	Inc. Ab.	.25	.50	1.00	5.00

50 DRACHMAI

12.5000 g, .835 SILVER, .3355 oz ASW
1967 Revolution

KM#	Date	Mintage	Fine	VF	XF	Unc
93	1967(1970)	.100	—	—	25.00	30.00

100 DRACHMAI

25.0000 g, .835 SILVER, .6712 oz ASW, 38mm
1967 Revolution

KM#	Date	Mintage	Fine	VF	XF	Unc
94	1967(1970)	.030	—	—	35.00	60.00

32.2580 g, .900 GOLD, .9335 oz AGW, 34mm

KM#	Date	Mintage	Fine	VF	XF	Unc
95	1967(1970)	.010	—	—	—	1000.

DEMOCRATIC REPUBLIC

1973 —

10 LEPTA

ALUMINUM
Obv: Modified design; soldier omitted.

KM#	Date	Mintage	Fine	VF	XF	Unc
103	1973	4.110	—	.10	.50	2.00

KM#	Date	Mintage	Fine	VF	XF	Unc
113	1976	2.043	—	.10	.30	1.50
	1978	.797	.50	1.00	4.00	12.50
	1978	.020	—	—	Proof	5.00

20 LEPTA

ALUMINUM

KM#	Date	Mintage	Fine	VF	XF	Unc
105	1973	5.246	—	.20	.50	3.00

KM#	Date	Mintage	Fine	VF	XF	Unc
114	1976	2.506	—	.20	.40	3.00
	1978	.803	.50	1.00	3.00	10.00
	1978	.020	—	—	Proof	4.50

50 LEPTA

NICKEL-BRASS

KM#	Date	Mintage	Fine	VF	XF	Unc
106	1973	19.512	—	.10	.15	1.00

Markos Botsaris

KM#	Date	Mintage	Fine	VF	XF	Unc
115	1976	55.646	—	.10	.15	1.25
	1978	12.010	—	.10	.15	1.50
	1978	.020	—	—	Proof	3.00
	1980	6.682	—	.10	.15	2.00
	1982	3.365	—	.10	.15	2.00
	1984	1.208	—	.10	.15	2.00
	1986	—	—	.10	.15	1.50

DRACHMA

NICKEL-BRASS

KM#	Date	Mintage	Fine	VF	XF	Unc
107	1973	12.842	—	.10	.30	1.50

Konstantinos Kanaris

KM#	Date	Mintage	Fine	VF	XF	Unc
116	1976	133.560	—	.10	.15	1.00
	1978	21.200	—	.10	.15	1.25
	1978	.020	—	—	Proof	2.50
	1980	52.503	—	.10	.15	1.25
	1982	54.186	—	.10	.15	1.25
	1984	33.665	—	.10	.15	1.25
	1986	17.901	—	.10	.15	1.25

NOTE: Varieties exist for the 1976 dated coins.

COPPER
Bouboulina - Heroine

KM#	Date	Mintage	Fine	VF	XF	Unc
150	1988	36.707	—	—	—	.20
	1990	—	—	—	—	.20
	1993	—	—	—	—	.20
	1993	—	—	—	Proof	3.50

2 DRACHMAI

NICKEL-BRASS

KM#	Date	Mintage	Fine	VF	XF	Unc
108	1973	10.935	.10	.20	.40	1.50

Georgios Karaiskakis

KM#	Date	Mintage	Fine	VF	XF	Unc
117	1976	115.801	—	.15	.25	1.25
	1978	16.772	—	.15	.25	1.25
	1978	.020	—	—	Proof	2.50
	1980	45.955	—	.15	.25	1.25

2 DRACHMES

NICKEL-BRASS

KM#	Date	Mintage	Fine	VF	XF	Unc
130	1982	64.414	—	.10	.20	1.00
	1984	31.861	—	.10	.20	1.00
	1986	21.019	—	.10	.20	1.00

COPPER
Manto Mavrogenous

KM#	Date	Mintage	Fine	VF	XF	Unc
151	1988	30.273	—	—	—	.30
	1990	—	—	—	—	.30
	1993	—	—	—	—	.30
	1993	—	—	—	Proof	4.50

5 DRACHMAI

COPPER-NICKEL
Denomination spelling ends with I.

KM#	Date	Mintage	Fine	VF	XF	Unc
109.1	1973	13.931	.25	.50	1.00	1.75

Denomination spelling ends with A.

KM#	Date	Mintage	Fine	VF	XF	Unc
109.2	1973	Inc. Ab.	1.00	2.00	4.00	10.00

Aristotle

KM#	Date	Mintage	Fine	VF	XF	Unc
118	1976	104.133	.10	.20	.35	1.00
	1978	17.404	.10	.20	.35	1.00
	1978	.020	—	—	Proof	2.00
	1980	33.701	.10	.20	.35	1.00

5 DRACHMES

COPPER-NICKEL

KM#	Date	Mintage	Fine	VF	XF	Unc
131	1982	42.647	.10	.20	.35	1.00
	1984	29.778	.10	.20	.35	1.00
	1986	16.730	.10	.20	.35	1.00
	1988	19.671	—	—	.30	.50
	1990	—	—	—	.30	.50
	1992	—	—	—	.30	.50
	1993	—	—	—	.30	.50
	1993	—	—	—	Proof	4.50

10 DRACHMAI

COPPER-NICKEL

KM#	Date	Mintage	Fine	VF	XF	Unc
110	1973	8.456	.25	.50	1.25	3.00

Democritus

KM#	Date	Mintage	Fine	VF	XF	Unc
119	1976	83.445	.15	.25	.50	1.00
	1978	14.637	.15	.25	.50	1.25
	1978	.020	—	—	Proof	2.50
	1980	28.733	.15	.25	.50	1.25

10 DRACHMES

COPPER-NICKEL

KM#	Date	Mintage	Fine	VF	XF	Unc
132	1982	33.539	.15	.25	.50	1.00
	1984	23.802	.15	.25	.50	1.00
	1986	24.441	.15	.25	.50	1.00
	1988	16.869	—	—	.35	.65
	1990	—	—	—	.35	.65
	1992	—	—	—	.35	.65
	1993	—	—	—	.35	.65
	1993	—	—	—	Proof	5.00

20 DRACHMAI

COPPER-NICKEL

KM#	Date	Mintage	Fine	VF	XF	Unc
112	1973	10.079	.20	.30	.50	1.50

Pericles

KM#	Date	Mintage	Fine	VF	XF	Unc
120	1976	65.353	.20	.30	.50	1.25
	1978	8.808	.20	.30	.50	1.50
	1978	.020	—	—	Proof	3.00
	1980	17.562	.20	.30	.50	1.25

20 DRACHMES

COPPER-NICKEL

KM#	Date	Mintage	Fine	VF	XF	Unc
133	1982	24.299	.20	.30	.50	1.00
	1984	13.412	.20	.30	.50	1.25
	1986	10.553	.20	.30	.50	1.00
	1988	16.196	—	—	.50	1.00

NICKEL-BRONZE
Dionysus Solomos - Composer of National Anthem

KM#	Date	Mintage	Fine	VF	XF	Unc
154	1990	—	—	—	—	1.00
	1992	—	—	—	—	1.00
	1993	—	—	—	—	1.00
	1993	—	—	—	Proof	6.50

50 DRACHMAI

COPPER-NICKEL
Solon the Archon of Athens

KM#	Date	Mintage	Fine	VF	XF	Unc
124	1980	32.251	.40	.60	1.00	2.50

50 DRACHMES

COPPER-NICKEL
Obv: Denomination in modern Greek.

KM#	Date	Mintage	Fine	VF	XF	Unc
134	1982	18.899	.40	.60	1.00	1.50
	1984	11.411	.40	.60	1.00	1.50

NICKEL-BRASS
Homer

KM#	Date	Mintage	Fine	VF	XF	Unc
147	1986	12.078	—	.50	1.00	2.50
	1988	23.589	—	—	.75	1.50
	1990	—	—	—	.75	1.75
	1992	—	—	—	.75	1.75
	1993	—	—	—	.75	1.75
	1993	—	—	—	Proof	7.50

100 DRACHMAI

13.0000 g, .650 SILVER, .2717 oz ASW
50th Anniversary of Bank of Greece

KM#	Date	Mintage	Fine	VF	XF	Unc
121	1978	.020	—	—	Proof	70.00

5.7800 g, .900 SILVER, .1672 oz ASW
Pan-European Games
Ancient Olympic Broad Jump

KM#	Date	Mintage	Fine	VF	XF	Unc
125	1981	.150	—	—	—	7.00
	1981	.150	—	—	Proof	10.00

Pan-European Games - 1896 Olympic High Jump

KM#	Date	Mintage	Fine	VF	XF	Unc
135	1982	.150	—	—	—	7.00
	1982	Inc. Ab.	—	—	Proof	10.00

Pan-European Games - Pole Vault

KM#	Date	Mintage	Fine	VF	XF	Unc
136	1982	.150	—	—	—	7.00
	1982	Inc. Ab.	—	—	Proof	10.00

100 DRACHMES

COPPER-NICKEL
28th Chess Olympics

KM#	Date	Mintage	Fine	VF	XF	Unc
152	1988	—	—	—	—	6.00

BRASS
Macedonia - Alexander the Great

KM#	Date	Mintage	Fine	VF	XF	Unc
159	1990	—	—	—	—	3.00
	1991	—	—	—	—	3.00
	1992	—	—	—	—	3.00
	1993	—	—	—	—	3.00
	1993	—	—	—	Proof	8.50

250 DRACHMAI

14.4400 g, .900 SILVER, .4178 oz ASW
Pan-European Games
Ancient Olympic Javelin Throwing

KM#	Date	Mintage	Fine	VF	XF	Unc
126	1981	.150	—	—	—	12.50
	1981	.150	—	—	Proof	15.00

Pan-European Games
1896 Olympic Discus Throwing

KM#	Date	Mintage	Fine	VF	XF	Unc
137	1982	.150	—	—	—	12.50
	1982	Inc. Ab.	—	—	Proof	15.00

Pan-European Games - Shot Put

KM#	Date	Mintage	Fine	VF	XF	Unc
138	1982	.150	—	—	—	12.50
	1982	Inc. Ab.	—	—	Proof	15.00

500 DRACHMES

13.0000 g, .900 SILVER, .3762 oz ASW
Common Market Membership

KM#	Date	Mintage	Fine	VF	XF	Unc
122	1979	.018	—	—	Proof	135.00

500 DRACHMAI

28.8800 g, .900 SILVER, .8357 oz ASW
Pan-European Games - Ancient Olympic Relay Race

KM#	Date	Mintage	Fine	VF	XF	Unc
127	1981	.150	—	—	—	20.00
	1981	.150	—	—	Proof	24.00

Pan-European Games - 1896 Olympic Racers at Starting Blocks

KM#	Date	Mintage	Fine	VF	XF	Unc
139	1982	.150	—	—	—	20.00
	1982	Inc. Ab.	—	—	Proof	24.00

Pan-European Games - Racers

KM#	Date	Mintage	Fine	VF	XF	Unc
140	1982	.150	—	—	—	20.00
	1982	Inc. Ab.	—	—	Proof	24.00

500 DRACHMES

18.0000 g, .900 SILVER, .5209 oz ASW
Olympics - Torch

KM#	Date	Mintage	Fine	VF	XF	Unc
145	1984	.025	—	—	—	45.00
	1984	.025	—	—	Proof	60.00

18.1100 g, .900 SILVER, .5240 oz ASW
28th Chess Olympics

KM#	Date	Mintage	Fine	VF	XF	Unc
153	1988	3,000	—	—	Proof	100.00

18.0000 g, .900 SILVER, .5208 oz ASW
XI Mediterranean Games

KM#	Date	Mintage	Fine	VF	XF	Unc
157	1991	.010	—	—	Proof	25.00

17.0000 g, .925 SILVER, .5056 oz ASW
2500th Anniversary of Democracy

KM#	Date	Mintage	Fine	VF	XF	Unc
160	1993	*.030	—	—	Proof	35.00

1000 DRACHMES

23.3300 g, .925 SILVER, .6939 oz ASW
Decade For Women

KM#	Date	Mintage	Fine	VF	XF	Unc
148	1985	.020	—	—	Proof	52.50

18.0000 g, .900 SILVER, .5208 oz ASW
50th Anniversary of Italian Invasion of Greece

KM#	Date	Mintage	Fine	VF	XF	Unc
155	1990	.010	—	—	Proof	55.00

2500 DRACHMAI

6.4500 g, .900 GOLD, .1866 oz AGW
Pan-European Games - Ancient Olympics

KM#	Date	Mintage	Fine	VF	XF	Unc
128	1981	.075	—	—	Proof	110.00

Pan-European Games - 1896 Olympics

KM#	Date	Mintage	Fine	VF	XF	Unc
141	1982	.050	—	—	Proof	120.00

Pan-European Games

KM#	Date	Mintage	Fine	VF	XF	Unc
142	1982	.050	—	—	Proof	120.00

5000 DRACHMAI

12.5000 g, .900 GOLD, .3617 oz AGW
Pan-European Games - Ancient Olympics

KM#	Date	Mintage	Fine	VF	XF	Unc
129	1981	.075	—	—	Proof	210.00

Pan-European Games - 1896 Olympics
Obv: Similar to KM#129.

KM#	Date	Mintage	Fine	VF	XF	Unc
143	1982	.050	—	—	Proof	220.00

Pan-European Games

KM#	Date	Mintage	Fine	VF	XF	Unc
144	1982	.050	—	—	Proof	220.00

5000 DRACHMES

8.0000 g, .900 GOLD, .2315 oz AGW
Olympics - Apollo
Obv: Similar to 500 Drachmai, KM#145. Rev: Apollo.

KM#	Date	Mintage	Fine	VF	XF	Unc
146	1984	.015	—	—	Proof	425.00

10,000 DRACHMES

20.0000 g, .900 GOLD, .5787 oz AGW
Common Market Membership

KM#	Date	Mintage	Fine	VF	XF	Unc
123	1979	—	—	—	—	520.00

7.1300 g, .900 GOLD, .2063 oz AGW
Decade For Women

KM#	Date	Mintage	Fine	VF	XF	Unc
149	1985	2,835	—	—	Proof	300.00

8.0000 g, .900 GOLD, .2315 oz AGW
XI Mediterranean Games

KM#	Date	Mintage	Fine	VF	XF	Unc
158	1991	2,000	—	—	Proof	300.00

8.5000 g, .917 GOLD, .2506 oz AGW
2500th Anniversary of Democracy

KM#	Date	Mintage	Fine	VF	XF	Unc
161	1993	*.010	—	—	Proof	275.00

20,000 DRACHMES

8.0000 g, .900 GOLD, .2315 oz AGW
50th Anniversary of Italian Invasion of Greece

KM#	Date	Mintage	Fine	VF	XF	Unc
156	1990	1,000	—	—	Proof	520.00

MINT SETS (MS)

KM#	Date	Mintage	Identification	Issue Price	Mkt. Val.
MS1	1965(7)	—	KM78,80-85	—	22.00

NOTE: These coins were sold at the mint in Greece as a set; they have never been released for circulation. Mintages of the various coins vary from 170,000 to 190,000 pieces.

KM#	Date	Mintage	Identification	Issue Price	Mkt. Val.
MS2	1978	50,000	—	—	15.00
MS3	1982(7)	—	KM115-116,130-134	—	5.00
MS4	1993(7)	—	KM131-132,147,150-151, 154,159	—	20.00

PROOF SETS (PS)

KM#	Date	Mintage	Identification	Issue Price	Mkt. Val.
PS1	1965(7)	4,987	KM78,80-85	10.25	35.00
PS2	1978(8)	20,000	KM113-120	—	25.00
PS3	1993(8)	—	KM131-132,147,150-151, 154,159-160	—	75.00

CRETE

The island of Crete (Kreti), located 60 miles southeast of the Peloponnesus, was the center of a brilliant civilization that flourished before the advent of Greek culture. After being conquered by the Romans, Byzantines, Moslems and Venetians, Crete became part of the Turkish Empire in 1669. As a consequence of the Greek Revolution of the 1820s, it was ceded to Egypt. Egypt returned the island to the Turks in 1840, and they ceded it to Greece in 1913, after the Second Balkan War.

RULERS

Prince George, 1898-1906

MINT MARKS

A - Paris
(a) - Paris (privy marks only)

LEPTON

BRONZE, 15mm

KM#	Date	Mintage	Fine	VF	XF	Unc
1.1	1900A	.289	3.00	7.00	15.00	40.00
	1901A	1.711	2.00	5.00	12.00	30.00

16mm

KM#	Date	Mintage	Fine	VF	XF	Unc
1.2	1901A	Inc. Ab.	3.00	6.00	12.50	32.50

2 LEPTA

BRONZE

KM#	Date	Mintage	Fine	VF	XF	Unc
2	1900A	.793	3.00	6.00	12.50	32.50
	1901A	.707	4.00	8.00	15.00	35.00

5 LEPTA

COPPER-NICKEL

KM#	Date	Mintage	Fine	VF	XF	Unc
3	1900A	4.000	2.00	4.00	18.00	75.00

10 LEPTA

COPPER-NICKEL

KM#	Date	Mintage	Fine	VF	XF	Unc
4.1	1900A	2.000	2.00	6.00	20.00	85.00

Medal strike

KM#	Date	Mintage	Fine	VF	XF	Unc
4.2	1900A	—	7.50	20.00	55.00	200.00

20 LEPTA

COPPER-NICKEL

KM#	Date	Mintage	Fine	VF	XF	Unc
5	1900A	1.250	3.00	6.00	25.00	100.00

NOTE: For coins similar to the five listings above, but dated 1893-95, see Greece.

50 LEPTA

2.5000 g, .835 SILVER, .0671 oz ASW

KM#	Date	Mintage	Fine	VF	XF	Unc
6	1901(a)	.600	12.00	50.00	110.00	250.00

DRACHMA

5.0000 g, .835 SILVER, .1342 oz ASW

KM#	Date	Mintage	Fine	VF	XF	Unc
7	1901(a)	.500	25.00	50.00	160.00	400.00

2 DRACHMAI

10.0000 g, .835 SILVER, .2685 oz ASW

KM#	Date	Mintage	Fine	VF	XF	Unc
8	1901(a)	.175	30.00	80.00	280.00	800.00

5 DRACHMAI

25.0000 g, .900 SILVER, .7234 oz ASW

KM#	Date	Mintage	Fine	VF	XF	Unc
9	1901(a)	.150	35.00	120.00	450.00	1750.

IONIAN ISLANDS

The Ionian Islands, situated in the Ionian Sea to the west of Greece, is the collective name for the islands of Corfu, Cephalonia, Zante, Santa Maura, Ithaca, Cythera and Paxo, with their minor dependencies. Before Britain acquired the islands, 1809-14, they were at various times subject to the authority of Venice, France, Russia and Turkey. They remained under British control until their cession to Greece on March 29, 1864.

(1799-1807)

MONETARY SYSTEM

2 Soldi = 1 Gazetta

GAZETTA

COPPER
Similar to 5 Gazettae, KM#2.

KM#	Date	Mintage	VG	Fine	VF	XF
1	1801	—	75.00	150.00	350.00	750.00

5 GAZETTAE

COPPER
Rev: Denomination in Greek.

KM#	Date	Mintage	VG	Fine	VF	XF
2	1801	—	100.00	250.00	500.00	1000.

Rev: Denomination in Italian.

KM#	Date	Mintage	VG	Fine	VF	XF
3	1801	—	100.00	250.00	500.00	1000.

10 GAZETTAE

COPPER
Obv. leg:ΣΠΤΑΝΗΣΟΣ ΠΟΛΙΤΣΙΑ
Rev: Denomination in Greek.

KM#	Date	Mintage	VG	Fine	VF	XF
4	1801	—	125.00	300.00	600.00	1250.

Obv. leg:ΣΠΤΑΝΗΣΟΣ ΠΟΛΙΤΣΙΑ
Rev: Denomination in Italian.

KM#	Date	Mintage	VG	Fine	VF	XF
5	1801	—	—	—	Rare	—

COUNTERMARKED COINAGE

BRITISH ADMINISTRATION

(1809-1863)

The British military forces under General Campbell were headquartered on the island of Zacynthos (Zante). A shortage of small silver coinage resulted in the countermarking of circulated coins of the Two Sicilies of 10 and 20 Grani denominations and worn Spanish and Spanish Colonial silver 1 and 2 reales coinage.

The Type I countermarks of 1813 were raised numerals 25, 30, 50 and 60 in rectangular indent. These being easily counterfeited lead to the 1814 Type II oval indent with a crudely executed bust of King George III over raised numerals. The Type II countermark was applied to existing Type I countermarked coinage and other coins found in circulation. No single countermarked Type I pieces are known to have survived.

MONETARY SYSTEM
40 Paras = 1 Piastre
220 Paras = 1 Spanish Dollar (8 Reales)

TYPE I

Raised 25, 30, 50 or 60 in rectangular indent.

TYPE II

Portrait of King George III over 25, 30, 50 or 60 in oval indent.

25 PARAS

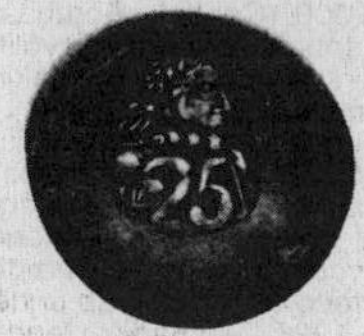
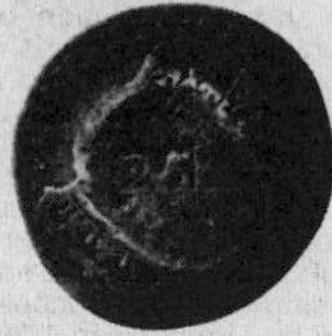

SILVER
c/m: Type I and II on Naples and Sicily 10 Grani of Charles II.

KM#	Date	Mintage	Good	VG	Fine	VF
18	ND(1814)	—	150.00	250.00	425.00	750.00

c/m: Type II on Spanish or Spanish Colonial 1 Real.

KM#	Date	Mintage	Good	VG	Fine	VF
19	ND(1814)	—	150.00	200.00	325.00	550.00

30 PARAS

SILVER
c/m: Type II on Naples and Sicily 10 Grani.

KM#	Date	Mintage	Good	VG	Fine	VF
20	ND(1814)	—	—	—	Rare	—

c/m: Type II on Spanish or Spanish Colonial 1 Real.

KM#	Date	Mintage	Good	VG	Fine	VF
21	ND(1814)	—	—	—	Rare	—

NOTE: One unusual piece exists with only one countermark on a French coin of Louis XIV. It is considered by some experts to be a contemporary counterfeit, since the authorization for these coins mentions only Spanish and Two Sicilies coinage. However, it may be that the islanders were permitted to present any silver coins in their possession for countermarking.

50 PARAS

SILVER
c/m: Type II on Naples & Sicily 20 Grani of Charles II.

KM#	Date	Mintage	Good	VG	Fine	VF
22.1	ND(1814)	—	150.00	225.00	400.00	700.00

c/m: Type II on Naples & Sicily 20 Grani of Ferdinando IV.

KM#	Date	Mintage	Good	VG	Fine	VF
22.2	ND(1814)	—	150.00	225.00	400.00	700.00

c/m: Type I and II on Spanish or Spanish Colonial 2 Reales.

KM#	Date	Mintage	Good	VG	Fine	VF
23.1	ND(1814)	—	150.00	225.00	400.00	700.00

c/m: Type I and II on worn disc.

KM#	Date	Mintage	Good	VG	Fine	VF
23.2	ND(1814)	—	125.00	200.00	300.00	550.00

60 PARAS

SILVER
c/m: Type II on Naples and Sicily 20 Grani.

KM#	Date	Mintage	Good	VG	Fine	VF
24	ND(1814)	—	275.00	400.00	650.00	1000.

c/m: Type I and II on Spanish 2 Reales of Philip V.

KM#	Date	Mintage	Good	VG	Fine	VF
25	ND(1814)	—	275.00	400.00	650.00	1000.

DECIMAL COINAGE

MONETARY SYSTEM
(Until 1835)
4 Lepta = Obol
100 Oboli = 1 Dollar
(Commencing 1835)
5 Lepta = Obol
100 Oboli = 1 Dollar

LEPTON

COPPER
Obv: Winged lion above date.
Rev: Seated Britannia above 4 (= 1/4 Obol).

KM#	Date	Mintage	Fine	VF	XF	Unc
30	1821	—	100.00	250.00	500.00	1000.

NOTE: Most of these coins are overstruck on Venetian coins by native craftsmen, and are very crude.

KM#	Date	Mintage	Fine	VF	XF	Unc
34	1834.	—	1.00	5.00	10.00	35.00
	1834.	—	—	—	Proof	200.00
	1835.	—	1.00	5.00	10.00	35.00
	1835	—	1.00	5.00	10.00	35.00
	1848.	13.483	3.00	10.00	25.00	75.00
	1848	Inc. Ab.	3.00	10.00	25.00	75.00
	1849.	Inc. Ab.	1.00	5.00	10.00	35.00
	1849	—	—	—	Proof	200.00
	1851.	Inc. Ab.	1.00	5.00	10.00	35.00
	1851.	—	—	—	Proof	200.00
	1853.	1.344	1.00	5.00	10.00	35.00
	1853	—	—	—	Proof	200.00
	1857.	Inc. Ab.	1.00	5.00	10.00	35.00
	1857	Inc. Ab.	1.00	5.00	10.00	35.00
	1862.	Inc. Ab.	1.00	5.00	10.00	35.00
	1862	—	—	—	Proof	200.00

2 LEPTA

COPPER

KM#	Date	Mintage	Fine	VF	XF	Unc
31	1819.	9.462	10.00	25.00	50.00	100.00
	1819	—	—	—	Proof	250.00
	1820.	Inc. Ab.	10.00	25.00	50.00	100.00
	1820	—	—	—	Proof	250.00

OBOL

COPPER

KM#	Date	Mintage	Fine	VF	XF	Unc
32	1819.	8.279	25.00	50.00	75.00	150.00
	1819	—	—	—	Proof	450.00
	1819 medal strike					
		—	—	—	Proof	500.00

2 OBOLI

COPPER

KM#	Date	Mintage	Fine	VF	XF	Unc
33	1819	4.140	25.00	50.00	100.00	200.00
	1819	—	—	—	Proof	550.00
	1819 medal strike					
		—	—	—	Proof	600.00

30 LEPTA

1.4100 g, .925 SILVER, .0419 oz ASW

KM#	Date	Mintage	Fine	VF	XF	Unc
35	1834	—	25.00	50.00	75.00	150.00
	1834	—	—	—	Proof	350.00
	1834.	—	25.00	50.00	75.00	200.00
	1848.	.331	65.00	125.00	325.00	750.00
	1849	Inc. Ab.	25.00	50.00	75.00	200.00
	1849	—	—	—	Proof	350.00
	1849.	Inc. Ab.	25.00	50.00	75.00	200.00
	1851	Inc. Ab.	25.00	50.00	75.00	200.00
	1851	—	—	—	Proof	350.00
	1852	Inc. Ab.	25.00	50.00	75.00	200.00
	1852	—	—	—	Proof	350.00
	1857	Inc. Ab.	25.00	50.00	75.00	200.00
	1857.	Inc. Ab.	25.00	50.00	75.00	200.00
	1862	Inc. Ab.	10.00	25.00	50.00	100.00

GREENLAND

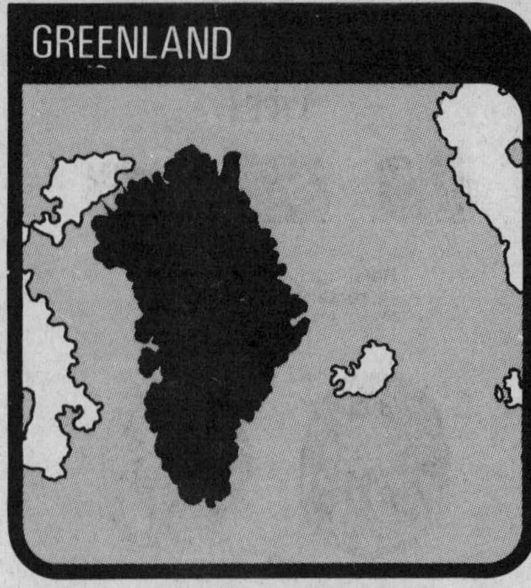

Greenland, an integral part of the Danish realm, is a huge island situated between the North Atlantic Ocean and the Polar Sea, almost entirely within the Arctic Circle. It has an area of 840,000 sq. mi. (2,175,600 sq. km.) and a population of 48,000. Capital: Godthaab. Greenland is the world's only source of natural cryolite, a fluoride of sodium and aluminum important in making aluminum. Fish products and minerals are exported.

Eric the Red discovered Greenland in 982 and established the first settlement in 986. Greenland was a republic until 1261, when the sovereignty of Norway was extended to the island. The original colony was abandoned about 1400 when increasing cold interfered with the breeding of cattle. Successful recolonization was undertaken by Denmark in 1721. In 1921 Denmark extended its claim to include the entire island, and made it a colony of the crown in 1924. The island's colonial status was abolished by amendment to the Danish constitution on June 5, 1953, and Greenland became an integral part of the Kingdom of Denmark. It has been an autonomous state since May 1, 1979.

RULERS

Danish

MINT MARKS

Heart (h) Copenhagen

MINTMASTERS INITIALS

HCN - Hans Christian Nielsen, 1919-1927

C - Alfred Frederik Christiansen, 1956-1971

MONEYERS INITIALS

GI, GJ - Knud Gunnar Jensen, 1901-1933

HS, S - Harald Salomon, 1933-1968

MONETARY SYSTEM

100 Ore = 1 Krone

25 ORE

COPPER-NICKEL

KM#	Date	Mintage	Fine	VF	XF	Unc
5	1926HCN(h)GJ					
		.310	1.50	3.00	5.00	10.00

Center hole added to KM#5.

KM#	Date	Mintage	Fine	VF	XF	Unc
6	1926HCN(h)GJ					
		.060	10.00	20.00	40.00	—

NOTE: KM#5 was withdrawn from circulation and hole added in the USA.

50 ORE

ALUMINUM-BRONZE

KM#	Date	Mintage	Fine	VF	XF	Unc
7	1926HCN(h)GJ					
		.196	2.50	5.00	7.50	12.50

KRONE

ALUMINUM-BRONZE

KM#	Date	Mintage	Fine	VF	XF	Unc
8	1926HCN(h)GJ					
		.287	2.00	4.00	8.50	22.50

KM#	Date	Mintage	Fine	VF	XF	Unc
10	1957C(h)S	.100	3.50	6.50	10.00	18.00
	COPPER-NICKEL					
10a	1960C(h)S	.109	2.00	4.00	5.50	8.50
	1964C(h)S	.110	2.25	4.50	5.50	7.00

5 KRONER

BRASS

KM#	Date	Mintage	Fine	VF	XF	Unc
9	1944	.100	20.00	30.00	45.00	80.00

GRENADA

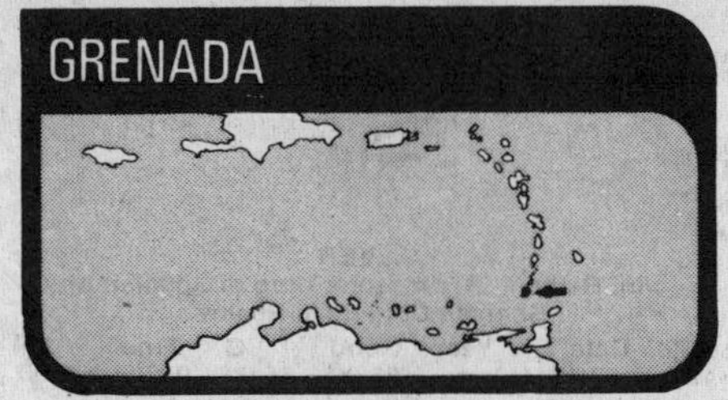

Grenada, located in the Windward Islands of the Caribbean Sea 90 miles (145 km.) north of Trinidad, has (with Carriacou and Petit Martinique) an area of 133 sq. mi. (344 sq. km.) and a population of 110,000. Capital: St. George's. Grenada is the smallest independent nation in the Western Hemisphere. The economy is based on agriculture and tourism. Sugar, coconuts, nutmeg, cocoa and bananas are exported.

Columbus discovered Grenada in 1498 during his third voyage to the Americas. Spain failed to colonize the island, and in 1627 granted it to the British who sold it to the French who colonized it in 1650. Grenada was captured by the British in 1763, retaken by the French in 1779, and finally ceded to the British in 1783. In 1958 Grenada joined the Federation of the West Indies, which was dissolved in 1962. In 1967 it became an internally self-governing British associated state. Full independence was attained on Feb. 4, 1974. Grenada is a member of the Commonwealth of Nations. The prime minister is the Head of Government.

The early coinage of Grenada consists of cut and counterstamped pieces of Spanish or Spanish Colonial Reales, which were valued at 11 Bits. In 1787 8 Reales coins were cut into 11 triangular pieces and counterstamped with an incuse G. Later in 1814 large denomination cut pieces were issued being 1/2, 1/3 or 1/6 cuts and counterstamped with a 'TR', incuse 'G' and a number 6, 4, 2, or 1 indicating the value in bitts.

RULERS

British

MONETARY SYSTEM

1798-1840

12 Bits = 9 Shillings = 1 Dollar

NECESSITY COINAGE

BIT
(9 Pence)

SILVER
c/m: 'TR', 'G', '1' on 1/3 cut of Spanish or Spanish Colonial 2 Reales.

KM#	Date	Mintage	Good	VG	Fine	VF
11	ND (ca.1818)	—	75.00	125.00	200.00	300.00

c/m: 'GS', 'G', '1' on 1/3 cut of Spanish or Spanish Colonial 2 Reales.

KM#	Date	Mintage	Good	VG	Fine	VF
12	ND (ca.1818)	—	75.00	125.00	200.00	300.00

2 BITS
(1 Shilling 6 Pence)

SILVER
c/m: 'TR', 'G', '2' on 1/6 cut of Spanish or Spanish Colonial 8 Reales.

KM#	Date	Mintage	Good	VG	Fine	VF
5	ND(1814)	*9,000	75.00	125.00	200.00	300.00

c/m: 'GS', 'G', '2' on 1/6 cut of Spanish or Spanish Colonial 8 Reales.

KM#	Date	Mintage	Good	VG	Fine	VF
6	ND(1814)	—	75.00	125.00	200.00	300.00

4 BITS
(3 Shillings)

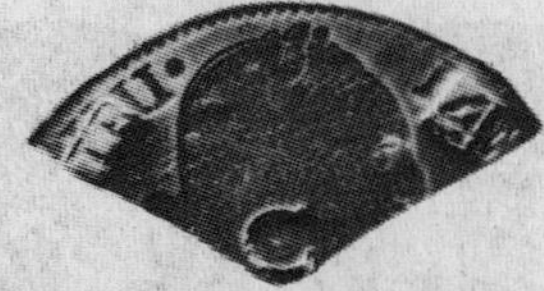

SILVER
c/m: 'TR', 'G', '4' on 1/3 cut of Spanish or Spanish Colonial 8 Reales.

KM#	Date	Mintage	Good	VG	Fine	VF
7	ND(1814)	*9,000	125.00	200.00	300.00	500.00

c/m: 'GS', 'G', '4' on 1/3 cut of Spanish or Spanish Colonial 8 Reales.

KM#	Date	Mintage	Good	VG	Fine	VF
8	ND(1814)	—	125.00	200.00	300.00	500.00

6 BITS
(4 Shillings 6 Pence)

SILVER
c/m: 'TR', 'G', '6' on 1/2 cut of Spanish or Spanish Colonial 8 Reales.

KM#	Date	Mintage	Good	VG	Fine	VF
9	ND(1814)	*.012	400.00	700.00	1200.	1750.

c/m: 'GS', 'G', '6' on 1/2 cut of Spanish or Spanish Colonial 8 Reales.

KM#	Date	Mintage	Good	VG	Fine	VF
10	ND(1814)	—	400.00	700.00	1200.	1750.

MODERN COINAGE

4 DOLLARS

COPPER-NICKEL
F.A.O. Issue

KM#	Date	Mintage	VF	XF	Unc
15	1970	.013	—	5.00	10.00
	1970	2,000	—	Proof	25.00

10 DOLLARS

COPPER-NICKEL
Royal Visit

KM#	Date	Mintage	VF	XF	Unc
16	1985	*.100	—	2.50	3.50
	28.2800 g, .925 SILVER, .8411 oz ASW				
16a	1985	*5,000	—	Proof	30.00
	47.5400 g, .917 GOLD, 1.4013 oz AGW				
16b	1985	*250 pcs.	—	Proof	1200.

100 DOLLARS

129.5900 g, .925 SILVER, 3.8543 oz ASW
Illustration reduced. Actual size: 63mm
Tropical Birds - Dove
Obv: Arms in circle, country name above, date below.

KM#	Date	Mintage	VF	XF	Unc
17	1988	*.010	—	Proof	120.00

GUADELOUPE

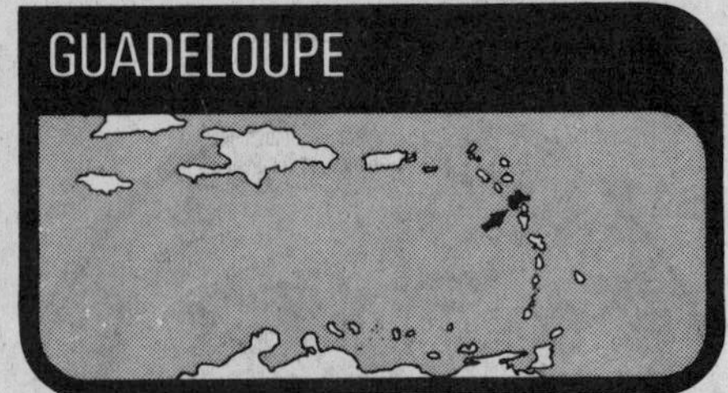

The French Overseas Department of Guadeloupe, located in the Leeward Islands of the West Indies about 300 miles (493 km.) southeast of Puerto Rico, has an area of 687 sq. mi. (1,780 sq. km.) and a population of 306,000. Actually it is two islands separated by a narrow salt water stream: volcanic Basse-Terre to the west and the flatter limestone formation of Grande-Terre to the east. Capital: Basse-Terre, on the island of that name. The principal industries are agriculture, the distillation of liquors, and tourism. Sugar, bananas, and rum are exported.

Guadeloupe was discovered by Columbus in 1493 and settled in 1635 by two Frenchmen, L'Olive and Duplessis, who took possession in the name of the French Company of the Islands of America. When repeated efforts by private companies to colonize the island failed, it was relinquished to the French crown in 1674, and established as a dependency of Martinique. The British occupied the island on two occasions, 1759-63 and 1810-16, before it passed permanently to France. A colony until 1946 Guadeloupe was then made an overseas territory of the French Union. In 1958 it voted to become an Overseas Department within the new French Community.

The well-known R.F. in garland oval countermark of the French Government is only legitimate if on a French Colonies 12 deniers 1767 C#4. Two other similar but incuse RF countermarks are on cut pieces in the values of 1 and 4 escalins.

RULERS

French, until 1759, 1763-1810, 1816 -
British, 1759-1763, 1810-1816

MONETARY SYSTEM

3 Deniers = 1 Liard
4 Liards = 1 Sol (Sous)
20 Sols = 1 Livre
6 Livres = 1 Ecu

NOTE: During the British Occupation period the Spanish and Spanish Colonial 8 Reales equalled 10 Livres.

CUT & COUNTERMARKED COINAGE

French Occupation

Until 1810

ESCALIN

SILVER
c/m: 'R.F.' on cut from outside ring of a center cut Spanish or Spanish Colonial 8 Reales.

KM#	Date	Year	Good	VG	Fine	VF
2	ND(1802)	—	25.00	50.00	100.00	225.00

4 E (ESCALINS)

SILVER
c/m: '4E RF' on center plug of Spanish or Spanish Colonial 8 Reales.

KM#	Date	Year	Good	VG	Fine	VF
3	ND(1802)	—	175.00	300.00	500.00	1200.

20 LIVRES

.917 GOLD
c/m: '20 w/small horse's head' on false Brazil 6400 Reis, type of KM#172.2.

KM#	Date	Year	Good	VG	Fine	VF
4.1	ND(1803)	(1751-77)	—	—	5500.	7500.

c/m: '20 w/small horse's head' on false Brazil 6400 Reis, type of KM#199.2.

KM#	Date	Year	Good	VG	Fine	VF
4.2	ND(1803)	(1777-86)	—	—	5500.	7500.

22 LIVRES

GOLD
c/m: '22 w/small bearded human face' on Brazil 6400 Reis, KM#199.2.

KM#	Date	Year	Good	VG	Fine	VF
5	ND(1803)	(1777-86)	—	—	Rare	—

NOTE: The previously listed Brazil 6400 Reis with large 'G' in 15 pointed sunburst indent countermark are considered incorrectly attributed and possibly spurious by some authorities. Refer to "Unusual World Coins" 3rd edition c.1992.

British Occupation

1810-1816

10 SOUS

SILVER
c/m: Crowned 'G' on France 6 Sols, C#38.

KM#	Date	Year	Good	VG	Fine	VF
13	ND(1811)	(1726-40)	30.00	50.00	80.00	160.00

c/m: Crowned 'G' on France 6 Sols, C#43.

KM#	Date	Year	Good	VG	Fine	VF
14	ND(1811)	(1743-70)	30.00	50.00	80.00	160.00

c/m: Crowned 'G' on Great Britain 3 Pence, KM#591.

KM#	Date	Year	Good	VG	Fine	VF
12	ND(1811)	(1762-86)	30.00	50.00	80.00	160.00

c/m: Crowned 'G' on Spanish or Spanish Colonial 1/2 Real.

KM#	Date	Year	Good	VG	Fine	VF
11	ND(1811)	—	30.00	50.00	80.00	160.00

20 SOUS

(Livre)

SILVER
c/m: Radiant 'G' on center plug of Spanish or Spanish Colonial 8 Reales.

KM#	Date	Year	Good	VG	Fine	VF
19	ND(1811)	—	35.00	65.00	90.00	175.00

c/m: Crowned 'G' on France 12 Sols, C#39.

KM#	Date	Year	Good	VG	Fine	VF
18	ND(1811)	(1726-32)	40.00	70.00	100.00	185.00

c/m: Crowned 'G' on France 12 Sols, C#44.

KM#	Date	Year	Good	VG	Fine	VF
16	ND(1811)	(1743-70)	40.00	70.00	100.00	185.00

c/m: Crowned 'G' on France 12 Sols, C#75.

KM#	Date	Year	Good	VG	Fine	VF
31	ND(1811)	(1775-89)	40.00	70.00	100.00	185.00

c/m: Crowned 'G' on Great Britain 6 Pence, KM#582.

KM#	Date	Year	Good	VG	Fine	VF
17	ND(1811)	(1743-58)	40.00	70.00	100.00	185.00

c/m: Crowned 'G' on Spanish or Spanish Colonial 1 Real.

KM#	Date	Year	Good	VG	Fine	VF
15	ND(1811)	—	40.00	70.00	100.00	185.00

40 SOUS

(2 Livres)

SILVER
c/m: Crowned 'G' on France 1/3 Ecu, C#30.

KM#	Date	Year	Good	VG	Fine	VF
20	ND(1811)	(1720-23)	45.00	85.00	120.00	200.00

c/m: Crowned 'G' on France 24 Sols, C#40.

KM#	Date	Year	Good	VG	Fine	VF
23	ND(1811)	(1726-37)	45.50	85.00	120.00	200.00

c/m: Crowned 'G' on France 24 Sols, C#45.

KM#	Date	Year	Good	VG	Fine	VF
32	ND(1811)	(1741-70)	50.00	90.00	120.00	200.00

c/m: Crowned 'G' on France 24 Sols, C#45a.

KM#	Date	Year	Good	VG	Fine	VF
33	ND(1811)	(1771-74)	55.00	100.00	130.00	225.00

c/m: Crowned 'G' on France 24 Sols, C#76.

KM#	Date	Year	Good	VG	Fine	VF
21	ND(1811)	(1774-90)	45.00	85.00	120.00	200.00

c/m: Crowned 'G' on Great Britain 1 Shilling, KM#607.

KM#	Date	Good	VG	Fine	VF
22	ND(1811)(1787)	40.00	80.00	110.00	190.00

2 LIVRES 5 SOUS

SILVER
c/m: Crowned 'G' on quarter segment of 9 Livres, KM#24-26, 35-36.

KM#	Date	Year	Good	VG	Fine	VF
34	ND(1811)	—	60.00	150.00	225.00	425.00

2 LIVRES 10 SOUS

SILVER
c/m: Crowned 'G' on quarter segment of Spanish or Spanish Colonial 8 Reales.

KM#	Date	Year	Good	VG	Fine	VF
30	ND(1813)	—	40.00	80.00	165.00	300.00

9 LIVRES

SILVER
c/m: Crowned 'G' on obv. and rev. of Mexico 8 Reales, KM#106 w/crenated square hole.

KM#	Date	Year	Good	VG	Fine	VF
24	ND(1811)	(1772-89)	200.00	250.00	350.00	550.00

c/m: Crowned 'G' on obv. and rev. of Mexico 8 Reales, KM#109 w/crenated square hole.

KM#	Date	Year	Good	VG	Fine	VF
25	ND(1811)	(1791-1808)	200.00	250.00	350.00	550.00

c/m: Crowned 'G' on obv. and rev. of Mexico 8 Reales, KM#110 w/crenated square hole.

KM#	Date	Year	Good	VG	Fine	VF
26	ND(1811)	(1808-10)	200.00	250.00	350.00	550.00

c/m: Crowned 'G' on obv. and rev. of Peru (Lima) 8 Reales, KM#97 w/crenated square hole.

KM#	Date	Year	Good	VG	Fine	VF
35	ND(1811)	(1791-1808)	225.00	275.00	375.00	600.00

c/m: Crowned 'G' on obv. and rev. of Peru (Lima) 8 Reales, KM#106.2 w/crenated square hole.

KM#	Date	Year	Good	VG	Fine	VF
36	ND(1811)	(1809-11)	250.00	350.00	650.00	950.00

NOTE: The square plug was used in making 20 Sous, KM#19.

82 LIVRES, 10 SOLS

.917 GOLD
c/m: Crowned 'G' and 82.10 on Brazil 6400 Reis, KM#172.

KM#	Date	Year	Good	VG	Fine	VF
27	ND(1811)	(1751-77)	2150.	3250.	5000.	8500.

c/m: Crowned 'G' and 82.10 on Brazil 6400

Reis, KM#199.

KM#	Date	Year	Good	VG	Fine	VF
28	ND(1811)					
		(1777-86)	1250.	2000.	3000.	5000.

c/m: Crowned 'G' and 82.10 on Brazil 6400 Reis, KM#226.

KM#	Date	Year	Good	VG	Fine	VF
29	ND(1811)					
		(1789-1805)	2000.	3000.	4500.	7500.

NOTE: Spurious countermarks on KM#27-29 lack the raised decimal point between "82" and "10".

MODERN COINAGE

MONETARY SYSTEM

100 Centimes = 1 Franc

50 CENTIMES

COPPER-NICKEL

KM#	Date	Mintage	Fine	VF	XF	Unc
45	1903	.600	5.00	9.00	25.00	100.00
(35)	1921	.600	4.00	8.00	20.00	85.00

FRANC

COPPER-NICKEL

KM#	Date	Mintage	Fine	VF	XF	Unc
46	1903	.700	6.00	12.00	35.00	125.00
(36)	1921	.700	5.00	10.00	30.00	110.00

GUATEMALA

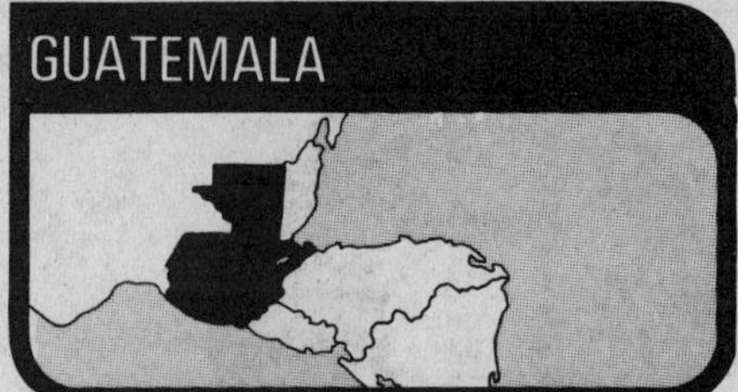

The Republic of Guatemala, the northernmost of the five Central American republics, has an area of 42,042 sq. mi. (108,890 sq. km.) and a population of 8 million. Capital: Guatemala City. The economy of Guatemala is heavily dependent on agriculture, however, the country is rich in nickel resources which are being developed. Coffee, cotton and bananas are exported.

Guatemala, once the site of an ancient Mayan civilization, was conquered by Pedro de Alvarado, the resourceful lieutenant of Cortes who undertook the conquest from Mexico. Cruel but strategically skillful, he progressed rapidly along the Pacific coastal lowlands to the highland plain of Quetzaltenango where the decisive battle for Guatemala was fought. After routing the Indian forces, he established the city of Guatemala, 1524. The Spanish Captaincy-General of Guatemala included all Central America but Panama. Guatemala declared its independence of Spain in 1821 and was absorbed into the Mexican empire of Augustin Iturbide, 1822-23. From 1823 to 1839 Guatemala was a constituent state of the Central American Republic. Upon dissolution of the federation, Guatemala became an independent republic.

RULERS

Spanish until 1821

MINT MARKS

Antigua, the old capital city of Santiago delos Caballeros including the mint facility was destroyed by a volcanic eruption and earthquake in 1773. A new mint and capital city was established in Guatemala City. Coin production recommenced in late 1776 using dies with the plain G mint mark.

H - Heaton, Birmingham

NG - Nueva Guatemala - 1777 onward

ASSAYERS INITIALS

Letter	Date	Name
M	1785-1822	Manuel Eusebio Sanchez

COLONIAL MILLED COINAGE

1/4 REAL

.8460 g, .896 SILVER, .0243 oz ASW
Mint mark: G
Obv: Castle. Rev: Lion.

KM#	Date	Mintage	VG	Fine	VF	XF
59	1801	—	4.00	9.00	15.00	50.00
	1802	—	4.00	9.00	15.00	50.00
	1803	—	4.00	9.00	15.00	50.00
	1804	—	4.00	9.00	15.00	50.00
	1805	—	12.50	25.00	35.00	100.00
	1806	—	10.00	20.00	30.00	90.00
	1807	—	4.00	9.00	15.00	50.00

NOTE: Earlier dates (1796-1800) exist for this type.

KM#	Date	Mintage	VG	Fine	VF	XF
72	1808	—	4.00	9.00	15.00	50.00
	1809	—	4.00	9.00	25.00	60.00
	1810	—	4.00	9.00	20.00	50.00
	1811	—	12.50	25.00	40.00	100.00
	1812	—	12.50	25.00	40.00	100.00
	1813	—	4.00	9.00	20.00	60.00
	1814	—	4.00	9.00	20.00	60.00
	1815	—	4.00	9.00	20.00	60.00
	1816	—	4.00	9.00	20.00	50.00
	1817	—	4.00	9.00	20.00	60.00
	1818	—	4.00	9.00	20.00	60.00
	1819	—	4.00	9.00	20.00	60.00
	1820	—	4.00	9.00	20.00	50.00
	1821	—	3.00	7.00	12.50	35.00
	1822	—	300.00	600.00	1000.	2000.

1/2 REAL

1.6921 g, .896 SILVER, .0487 oz ASW
Mint mark: NG
Obv: Bust of Charles IV, leg: CAROLUS IIII. . . . .
Rev: Arms, pillar.

KM#	Date	Mintage	VG	Fine	VF	XF
50	1801 M	—	6.00	10.00	18.00	55.00
	1802 M	—	6.00	10.00	18.00	55.00
	1803 M	—	6.00	12.00	25.00	65.00
	1804 M	—	6.00	12.00	25.00	65.00
	1805 M	—	6.00	12.00	25.00	65.00
	1806 M	—	6.00	12.00	25.00	65.00
	1807 M	—	6.00	12.00	25.00	65.00

NOTE: Earlier dates (1790-1800) exist for this type.

Obv. leg: FERDIND VII. . . ., bust of Charles IV.

KM#	Date	Mintage	VG	Fine	VF	XF
60	1808 M	—	15.00	30.00	60.00	125.00
	1809 M	—	4.50	9.00	20.00	40.00
	1810 M	—	5.00	10.00	20.00	45.00

Ferdinand VII

KM#	Date	Mintage	VG	Fine	VF	XF
65	1808 M	—	20.00	40.00	80.00	125.00
	1811 M	—	100.00	—	—	—
	1812 M	—	10.00	18.00	35.00	90.00
	1813 M	—	10.00	18.00	35.00	100.00
	1814 M	—	4.00	7.00	15.00	40.00
	1815 M	—	4.00	7.00	15.00	40.00
	1816 M	—	3.00	5.00	10.00	25.00
	1817 M	—	5.00	10.00	25.00	65.00
	1818 M	—	6.00	12.00	25.00	65.00
	1819 M	—	5.00	10.00	25.00	65.00
	1820 M	—	3.00	5.00	10.00	20.00
	1821 M	—	5.00	12.00	20.00	60.00

REAL

3.3841 g, .896 SILVER, .0975 oz ASW
Mint mark: NG
Obv: Bust of Charles IIII.
Rev: Arms, pillars.

KM#	Date	Mintage	VG	Fine	VF	XF
54	1801 M	—	6.00	12.00	30.00	70.00
	1802/1 M	—	6.00	12.00	30.00	70.00
	1802 M	—	6.00	12.00	30.00	70.00
	1803 M	—	6.00	12.00	30.00	70.00
	1804 M	—	6.00	12.00	30.00	70.00
	1805 M	—	6.00	12.00	30.00	70.00
	1806 M	—	6.00	12.00	30.00	70.00
	1807 M	—	6.00	12.00	30.00	70.00

NOTE: Earlier dates (1791-1800) exist for this type.

Obv. leg: FERDIND VII. . ., bust of Charles IV.

KM#	Date	Mintage	VG	Fine	VF	XF
61	1808 M	—	5.00	9.00	17.50	60.00
	1809 M	—	4.00	8.50	15.00	40.00
	1810 M	—	6.00	12.00	20.00	55.00

Ferdinand VII

KM#	Date	Mintage	VG	Fine	VF	XF
66	1808 M	—	—	—	Rare	—
	1811 M	—	4.00	8.00	15.00	30.00
	1812 M	—	4.00	8.00	15.00	30.00
	1813 M	—	10.00	17.50	35.00	60.00
	1814 M	—	4.00	9.00	17.50	35.00
	1815 M	—	3.00	6.00	12.00	25.00
	1816 M	—	4.00	9.00	17.50	40.00
	1817 M	—	3.00	6.00	12.00	25.00
	1818 M	—	3.00	6.00	10.00	22.50
	1819 M	—	4.00	7.50	15.00	35.00
	1820 M	—	3.00	6.00	10.00	22.50
	1821 M	—	3.00	6.00	10.00	22.50

2 REALES

6.7682 g, .896 SILVER, .1950 oz ASW
Mint mark: NG
Obv: Bust of Charles IIII.
Rev: Arms, pillars.

KM#	Date	Mintage	VG	Fine	VF	XF
51	1801 M	—	4.00	7.00	15.00	55.00
	1802 M	—	6.00	12.00	30.00	65.00
	1803 M	—	12.00	25.00	55.00	100.00
	1804 M	—	4.00	7.00	15.00	55.00
	1805 M	—	4.00	7.00	15.00	55.00
	1806 M	—	18.00	35.00	65.00	125.00
	1807 M	—	18.00	35.00	65.00	125.00

NOTE: Earlier dates (1791-1800) exist for this type.

Obv. leg: FERDIND VII. . ., bust of Charles IV.

KM#	Date	Mintage	VG	Fine	VF	XF
62	1808 M	—	10.00	20.00	40.00	90.00
	1809 M	—	5.00	10.00	25.00	55.00
	1810 M	—	4.00	8.00	22.50	48.00

Ferdinand VII

KM#	Date	Mintage	VG	Fine	VF	XF
67	1808 M	—	20.00	40.00	80.00	160.00
	1811 M	—	12.00	18.00	30.00	60.00
	1812 M	—	5.00	9.00	22.50	50.00
	1813 M	—	12.00	25.00	80.00	160.00
	1814 M	—	12.00	25.00	80.00	160.00
	1815 M	—	5.00	9.00	22.50	50.00
	1816 M	—	6.00	10.00	25.00	60.00
	1817 M	—	5.00	9.00	22.50	50.00
	1818 M	—	5.00	9.00	22.50	50.00
	1819 M	—	5.00	9.00	22.50	50.00

KM#	Date	Mintage	VG	Fine	VF	XF
67	1820 M	—	5.00	9.00	22.50	50.00
	1821 M	—	4.00	7.00	20.00	45.00

4 REALES

13.5365 g, .896 SILVER, .3900 oz ASW
Mint mark: NG
Charles IIII

KM#	Date	Mintage	VG	Fine	VF	XF
52	1801 M	—	35.00	75.00	150.00	250.00
	1802 M	—	50.00	100.00	175.00	250.00
	1803 M	—	50.00	100.00	175.00	275.00
	1804 M	—	50.00	100.00	175.00	350.00
	1805 M	—	50.00	100.00	175.00	300.00
	1806/5 M	—	40.00	85.00	165.00	275.00
	1806 M	—	35.00	75.00	150.00	250.00
	1807 M	—	35.00	75.00	125.00	200.00

NOTE: Earlier dates (1790-1800) exist for this type.

Obv. leg: FERDIND VII. . ., bust of Charles IV.

KM#	Date	Mintage	VG	Fine	VF	XF
63	1808 M	—	100.00	200.00	350.00	550.00
	1809 M	—	65.00	125.00	250.00	400.00
	1810 M	—	65.00	125.00	250.00	400.00

Ferdinand VII

KM#	Date	Mintage	VG	Fine	VF	XF
68	1808 M	—	150.00	300.00	500.00	800.00
	1811 M	—	50.00	100.00	200.00	325.00
	1812 M	—	50.00	100.00	200.00	325.00
	1813 M	—	50.00	100.00	200.00	325.00
	1814 M	—	30.00	75.00	125.00	200.00
	1815/4 M	—	50.00	100.00	175.00	275.00
	1815 M	—	35.00	85.00	125.00	200.00
	1816 M	—	50.00	100.00	175.00	250.00
	1817 M	—	50.00	100.00	175.00	250.00
	1818 M	—	35.00	85.00	150.00	225.00
	1819 M	—	35.00	85.00	150.00	225.00
	1820 M	—	50.00	100.00	175.00	365.00
	1821 M	—	35.00	85.00	150.00	225.00

8 REALES

27.0730 g, .896 SILVER, .7799 oz ASW
Mint mark: NG
Obv: Bust of Charles IIII right. Rev: Arms, pillars.

KM#	Date	Mintage	VG	Fine	VF	XF
53	1801 obv. leg: inverted "JJJJ"					
		—	60.00	150.00	225.00	375.00
	1801 obv. leg: "IIII"					
		—	55.00	100.00	200.00	350.00
	1802 M	—	60.00	150.00	225.00	375.00
	1803 M	—	55.00	100.00	200.00	350.00
	1804 M	—	55.00	100.00	200.00	350.00
	1805 M	—	55.00	100.00	200.00	350.00
	1806/5 M	—	75.00	200.00	325.00	425.00
	1807 M	—	55.00	100.00	200.00	350.00

NOTE: Earlier dates (1790-1800) exist for this type.

Obv. leg: FERDIND VII. . . ., bust of Charles IIII.

KM#	Date	Mintage	VG	Fine	VF	XF
64	1808 M	—	110.00	260.00	450.00	825.00
	1809/8 M	—	85.00	200.00	350.00	675.00
	1809 M	—	75.00	175.00	250.00	600.00
	1810 M	—	75.00	175.00	250.00	525.00

Ferdinand VII

KM#	Date	Mintage	VG	Fine	VF	XF
69	1808 M	—	—	—	—	*Rare	—
	1811 M	—	100.00	200.00	400.00	750.00
	1812 M	—	25.00	40.00	75.00	150.00
	1813 M	—	25.00	40.00	75.00	150.00
	1814 M	—	25.00	40.00	75.00	150.00
	1815 M	—	25.00	40.00	75.00	150.00
	1816 M	—	25.00	40.00	75.00	150.00
	1817 M	—	25.00	40.00	75.00	150.00
	1818 M	—	25.00	40.00	75.00	150.00
	1819 M	—	25.00	40.00	75.00	150.00
	1820 M	—	25.00	40.00	75.00	150.00
	1821 M	—	25.00	40.00	75.00	150.00

***NOTE:** Superior Dec. 1990 sale choice VF realized $14,300.

ESCUDO

3.3841 g, .875 GOLD, .0952 oz AGW
Mint mark: NG
Charles IIII

KM#	Date	Mintage	VG	Fine	VF	XF
55	1801 M	—	600.00	1200.	1800.	3000.

NOTE: Earlier dates (1794 and 1797) exist for this type.

Ferdinand VII

KM#	Date	Mintage	VG	Fine	VF	XF
74	1817 M	—	700.00	1500.	2000.	3500.

2 ESCUDOS

6.7682 g, .875 GOLD, .1904 oz AGW
Mint mark: NG
Obv: Bust of Charles IIII.

KM#	Date	Mintage	VG	Fine	VF	XF
56	1801 M	—	1000.	2000.	3500.	6000.

NOTE: Earlier dates (1794 and 1797) exist for this type.

KM#	Date	Mintage	VG	Fine	VF	XF
70	1808 M	—	600.00	1250.	2000.	3250.
	1811 M	—	600.00	1250.	2000.	3250.
	1817 M	—	300.00	600.00	1000.	1500.

4 ESCUDOS

13.5365 g, .875 GOLD, .3808 oz AGW
Mint mark: NG
Charles IIII

KM#	Date	Mintage	VG	Fine	VF	XF
57	1801 M	—	—	—	Rare	—

NOTE: Earlier dates (1794 and 1797) exist for this type.

Ferdinand VII

KM#	Date	Mintage	VG	Fine	VF	XF
73	1813 M	—	— Reported, not confirmed			
	1817 M	—	1000.	2000.	3500.	6000.

8 ESCUDOS

27.0730 g, .875 GOLD, .7616 oz AGW
Mint mark: NG
Charles IIII

KM#	Date	Mintage	VG	Fine	VF	XF
58	1801 M	—	—	—	Rare	—

NOTE: Earlier dates (1794 and 1797) exist for this type.
***NOTE:** Sotheby's Geneva sale 5-90 VF realized $19,360.

Ferdinand VII

KM#	Date	Mintage	VG	Fine	VF	XF
71	1808 M	—	—	—	*Rare	—
	1811 M	—	—	6000.	10,000.	17,500.
	1817 M	—	—	4000.	6500.	11,000.

***NOTE:** Sotheby's Geneva sale 5-90 VF realized $74,800.

PROVISIONAL COINAGE

(Under Central American Republic)

REAL

.903 SILVER
Mint mark: NG
Obv. leg: ESTADO DE GUATEMALA

KM#	Date	Mintage	VG	Fine	VF	XF
75	1829 M	—	50.00	110.00	225.00	400.00

COUNTERMARKED COINAGE

1838-1841

TYPE I
Sun at left behind volcano under long cloud.

2 REALES

SILVER
c/m: Type I on Peru (Lima) 'cob' 2 Reales, KM#16.

KM#	Date	Good	VG	Fine	VF
78	ND(1659-60)	—	—	Rare	—

4 REALES

SILVER

c/m: Type I on Boliva 'cob' 4 Reales, KM#30a.

KM#	Date	Good	VG	Fine	VF
76.3	ND(1729-47)	150.00	225.00	300.00	—

c/m: Type I on Bolivia 'cob' 4 Reales, KM#44.

KM#	Date	Good	VG	Fine	VF
76.4	ND(1760-77)	150.00	225.00	300.00	—

c/m: Type I on 'cob' 4 Reales, KM#11.

KM#	Date	Good	VG	Fine	VF
76.1	ND(1747-53) •	225.00	325.00	450.00	—

c/m: Type I on Mexico 'cob' 4 Reales, KM#40a.

KM#	Date	Good	VG	Fine	VF
76.5	ND(1729-34)	500.00	700.00	1000.	—

c/m: Type I on Mexico-Sombrerete
4 Reales, KM#175.

KM#	Date	Good	VG	Fine	VF
76.2	ND(1811-12)	500.00	—	—	—

8 REALES

SILVER
c/m: Type I on Bolivia (Potosi) 'Royal'
8 Reales, KM#21.

KM#	Date	Good	VG	Fine	VF
77.10	ND(1621-65)	—	—	—	—

c/m: Type I on Bolivia (Potosi) 'cob'
8 Reales, KM#31a.

KM#	Date	Good	VG	Fine	VF
77.11	ND(1729-47)	225.00	325.00	450.00	—

c/m: Type I on Bolivia (Potosi) 'cob'
8 Reales, KM#40.

KM#	Date	Good	VG	Fine	VF
77.12	ND(1747-60)	225.00	325.00	450.00	—

c/m: Type I on Bolivia (Potosi) 'cob'
8 Reales, KM#45.

KM#	Date	Good	VG	Fine	VF
77.5	ND(1760-73)	225.00	325.00	450.00	—

c/m: Type I on 'cob' 8 Reales, KM#6.

KM#	Date	Good	VG	Fine	VF
77.1	ND(1733-46)	200.00	300.00	400.00	550.00

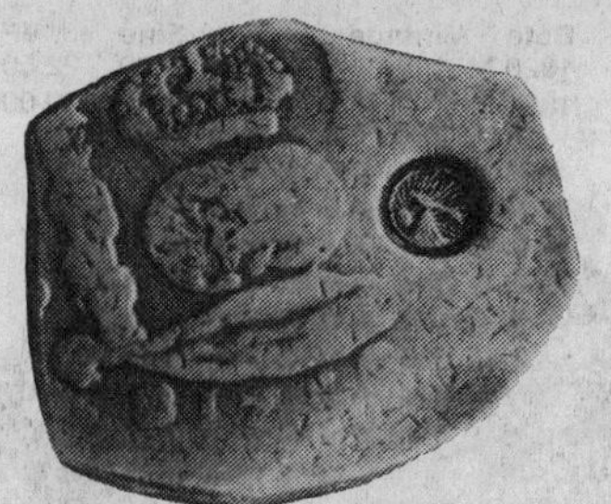

c/m: Type I on 'cob' 8 Reales, KM#12.

KM#	Date	Good	VG	Fine	VF
77.2	ND(1747-53)	200.00	300.00	400.00	550.00

c/m: Type I on Mexico 'cob' 8 Reales, KM#46.

KM#	Date	Good	VG	Fine	VF
77.6	ND(1668-1701)	225.00	325.00	450.00	—

c/m: Type I on Mexico 'cob' 8 Reales, KM#47a.

KM#	Date	Good	VG	Fine	VF
77.7	ND(1729-33)	225.00	325.00	450.00	—

c/m: Type I on Mexico 'klippe' 8 Reales, KM#48.

KM#	Date	Good	VG	Fine	VF
77.8	ND(1733-34)	225.00	325.00	450.00	—

c/m: Type I on Peru (Lima) 'cob' 8 Reales, KM#24.

KM#	Date	Good	VG	Fine	VF
77.13	ND(1684-1701)	200.00	300.00	400.00	550.00

c/m: Type I on Peru (Lima) 'cob'
8 Reales of Philip V.

KM#	Date	Good	VG	Fine	VF
77.3	ND(1700-46)	200.00	300.00	400.00	550.00

c/m: Type I on Peru 8 Reales, KM#130.

KM#	Date	Good	VG	Fine	VF
77.9	ND(1824)	150.00	220.00	300.00	400.00

c/m: Type I on Peru 8 Reales, KM#142.1.

KM#	Date	Good	VG	Fine	VF
77.14	ND(1825-28)	150.00	220.00	300.00	400.00

c/m: Type I on Peru 8 Reales, KM#142.3.

KM#	Date	Good	VG	Fine	VF
77.4	ND(1828-?)	150.00	220.00	300.00	400.00

Type II
Sun above a row of volcanos in 6.5mm circle.

2 REALES

SILVER

c/m: Type II on Bolivia 2 Soles, KM#95.

KM#	Date	Good	VG	Fine	VF
81	ND(1827-30)	55.00	85.00	110.00	150.00

c/m: Type II on Peru 2 Reales, KM#141.1.

KM#	Date	Good	VG	Fine	VF
82	ND(1825-40)	55.00	85.00	110.00	150.00

4 REALES

SILVER

c/m: Type II on Bolivia (Potosi) 'cob'
4 Reales of Philip II.

KM#	Date	Good	VG	Fine	VF
85.1	ND(1556-98)	125.00	185.00	260.00	350.00

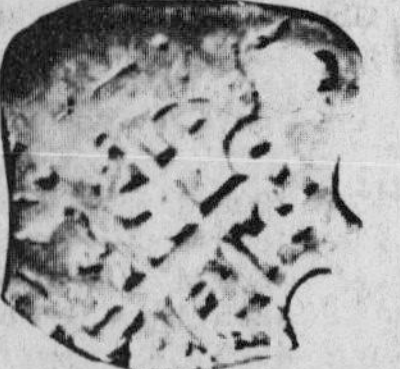

c/m: Type II on Bolivia (Potosi) 'cob'

4 Reales, KM#39.

KM#	Date	Good	VG	Fine	VF
85.5	ND(1746-59)	80.00	125.00	165.00	225.00

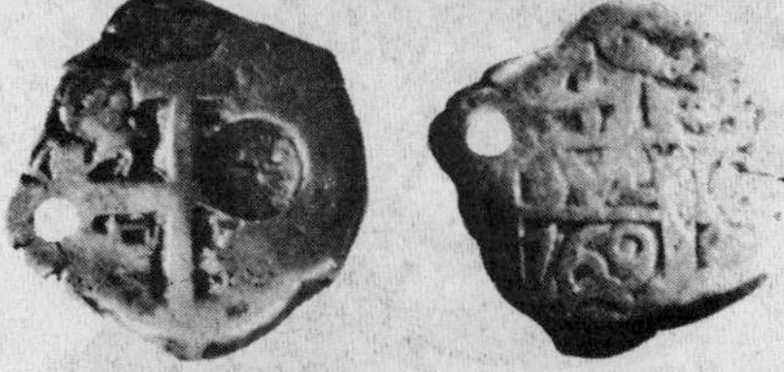

c/m: Type II on Bolivia (Potosi) 'cob' 4 Reales, KM#44.

85.6 ND(1759-88) 80.00 125.00 165.00 225.00

c/m: Type II on Bolivia 4 Soles, KM#96.

92 ND(1827-30) 60.00 110.00 175.00 250.00

c/m: Type II on Guatemala 'cob' 4 Reales, KM#5.

87.1 ND(1733-46) 110.00 165.00 225.00 300.00

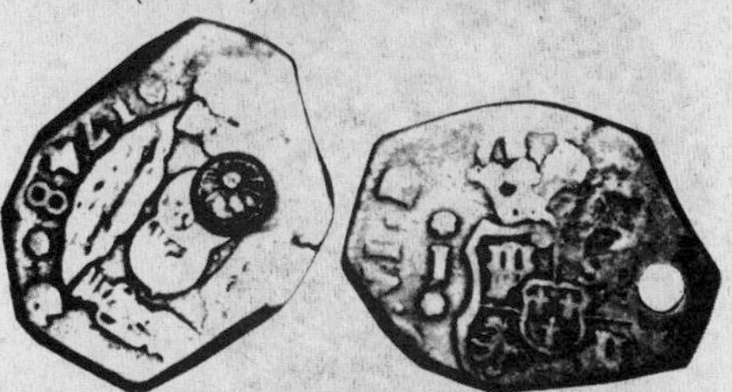

c/m: Type II on Guatemala 'cob' 4 Reales, KM#11.

87.2 ND(1747-53) 110.00 165.00 225.00 300.00
(88)

c/m: Type II on Honduras 'cob' 4 Reales, KM#16.1.

88 ND(1823-24) — — — —

c/m: Type II on Mexico 4 Reales of Carlos and Johanna, (late type).

89.1 ND — — — —

c/m: Type II on Mexico 'cob' 4 Reales of Philip II.

89.2 ND(1556-98) 125.00 185.00 260.00 350.00

c/m: Type II on Mexico 'klippe' 4 Reales, KM#41.

89.5 ND(1733-34) 225.00 300.00 375.00 500.00

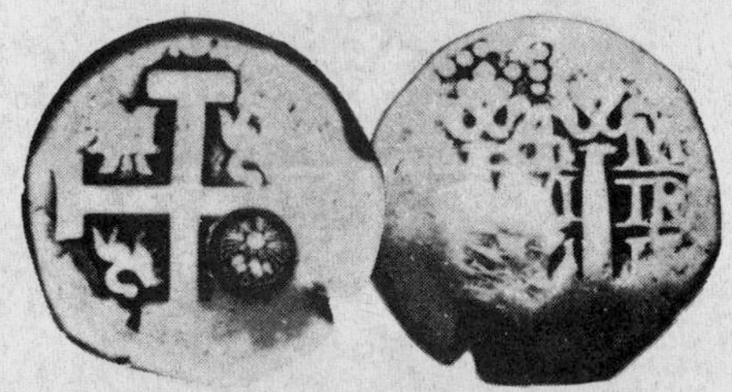

c/m: Type II on Peru (Lima) 'cob' 4 Reales of Charles II.

90.1 ND(1665-1700) 80.00 125.00 165.00 225.00

c/m: Type II on Peru (Lima) 'cob' 4 Reales, KM#33.

KM#	Date	Good	VG	Fine	VF
90.2	ND(1700-46)	80.00	125.00	165.00	225.00

c/m: Type II on Peru (Lima) 'Royal' 4 Reales, KM#33.

90.3 ND(1700-46) — — — —

c/m: Type II on Peru (Cuzco) 4 Reales, KM#151.1.

91 ND(1835-36) 60.00 110.00 175.00 250.00

8 REALES

SILVER

c/m: Type II on Bolivia (Potosi) 'cob' 8 Reales, KM#5.

94.1 ND(1556-98) 80.00 125.00 165.00 225.00

c/m: Type II on Bolivia (Potosi) 'Royal' 8 Reales, KM#5.

94.2 ND(1621-65) 750.00 1100. 1500. 2000.

c/m: Type II on Bolivia (Potosi) 'cob' 8 Reales, KM#19.

95 ND(1621-65) 80.00 125.00 165.00 225.00

c/m: Type II on Bolivia (Potosi) 'Royal' 8 Reales, KM#26.

KM#	Date	Good	VG	Fine	VF
96.1	ND(1665-1700)	750.00	1100.	1500.	2000.

c/m: Type II on Bolivia (Potosi) 'cob' 8 Reales, KM#26.

96.2 ND(1665-1700) 125.00 185.00 250.00 350.00

c/m: Type II on Bolivia (Potosi) 'cob' 8 Reales, KM#31.

97 ND(1700-46) 110.00 165.00 225.00 300.00

c/m: Type II on Bolivia (Potosi) 'cob' 8 Reales, KM#35.

98 ND(1725-27) 250.00 450.00 550.00 950.00

c/m: Type II on Bolivia (Potosi) 'cob' 8 Reales, KM#40.

99 ND(1746-59) 80.00 125.00 165.00 225.00

c/m: Type II on Bolivia (Potosi) 'cob' 8 Reales, KM#45.

100 ND(1759-88) 80.00 125.00 165.00 225.00

c/m: Type II on Bolivia 8 Soles, KM#97.

106 ND(1838-41) 50.00 90.00 135.00 200.00

c/m: Type II on Guatemala 'cob' 8 Reales, KM#6.

KM#	Date	Good	VG	Fine	VF
101	ND(1733-46)	125.00	185.00	250.00	350.00

c/m: Type II on Guatemala 'cob' 8 Reales, KM#12.

KM#	Date	Good	VG	Fine	VF
102	ND(1747-53)	110.00	165.00	225.00	300.00

c/m: Type II on Mexico 'cob' 8 Reales, KM#45.

KM#	Date	Good	VG	Fine	VF
104	ND(1621-67)	110.00	165.00	225.00	300.00

c/m: Type II on Mexico 'Royal' 8 Reales, KM#47.

KM#	Date	Good	VG	Fine	VF
105.1	ND(1701-28)	—	—	Rare	—

c/m: Type II on Mexico 'cob' 8 Reales, KM#47a.

KM#	Date	Good	VG	Fine	VF
105.2	ND(1729-33)	85.00	130.00	180.00	240.00

c/m: Type II on Mexico 'Klippe' 8 Reales, KM#48.

KM#	Date	Good	VG	Fine	VF
107	ND(1733-34)	185.00	275.00	375.00	500.00

c/m: Type II on Peru (Lima) 'Royal' 8 Reales of Philip II.

KM#	Date	Good	VG	Fine	VF
108	ND(1555-58)	675.00	1000.	1350.	1800.

c/m: Type II on Peru (Star of Lima) 'cob' 8 Reales of Philip IV, KM#18.

KM#	Date	Good	VG	Fine	VF
109	ND(1659-60)	—	—	Rare	—

c/m: Type II on Peru (Lima) 'cob' 8 Reales, KM#24.

KM#	Date	Good	VG	Fine	VF
110.1	ND(1684-1701)	85.00	130.00	180.00	240.00

c/m: Type II on Peru (Lima) 'Royal' 8 Reales, KM#24.

KM#	Date	Good	VG	Fine	VF
110.2	ND(1684-1701)	550.00	825.00	1125.	1500.

c/m: Type II on Peru (Lima) 'cob' 8 Reales, KM#34.

KM#	Date	Good	VG	Fine	VF
111.1	ND(1701-23)	80.00	125.00	165.00	225.00

c/m: Type II on Peru (Lima) 'cob' 8 Reales, KM#39.

KM#	Date	Good	VG	Fine	VF
111.2	ND(1725-26)	300.00	575.00	800.00	1100.

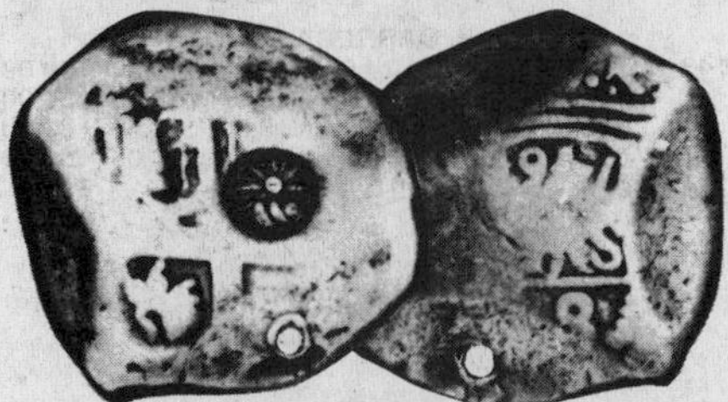

c/m: Type II on Peru (Lima) 'cob' 8 Reales, KM#41.

KM#	Date	Good	VG	Fine	VF
111.3	ND(1727-46)	80.00	125.00	165.00	225.00

c/m: Type II on Peru (Lima) 8 Reales, KM#142.3.

KM#	Date	Good	VG	Fine	VF
111.5	ND(1828-?)	80.00	125.00	165.00	225.00

Type III

Obv: Sun above 3 volcanos in 6.5mm circle.
Rev: Sunface in star, bow and arrow in 7mm circle.

8 REALES

SILVER

c/m: Type III on Bolivia 8 Soles, KM#97.

KM#	Date	Good	VG	Fine	VF
112.1	ND(1827-40)	110.00	165.00	225.00	325.00

c/m: Type III on Chile (Santiago) 8 Reales, KM#96.1.

KM#	Date	Good	VG	Fine	VF
112.2	ND(1837-40)	125.00	185.00	250.00	350.00

c/m: Type III on Peru (Lima) 8 Reales, KM#136.

KM#	Date	Good	VG	Fine	VF
120.1	ND(1822-23)	150.00	225.00	300.00	400.00

c/m: Type III on Peru (Lima) 8 Reales, KM#142.1.

KM#	Date	Good	VG	Fine	VF
120.2	ND(1825-28)	45.00	75.00	120.00	175.00

c/m: Type III on Peru (Lima) 8 Reales, KM#142.3.

KM#	Date	Good	VG	Fine	VF
120.3	ND(1828-40)	40.00	65.00	100.00	150.00

c/m: Type III on Peru (Cuzco) 8 Reales, KM#142.2.

KM#	Date	Good	VG	Fine	VF
120.4	ND(1826-36)	45.00	75.00	120.00	175.00

c/m: Type III on Peru (North) 8 Reales, KM#155.

KM#	Date	Good	VG	Fine	VF
120.5	ND(1836-39)	45.00	75.00	120.00	175.00

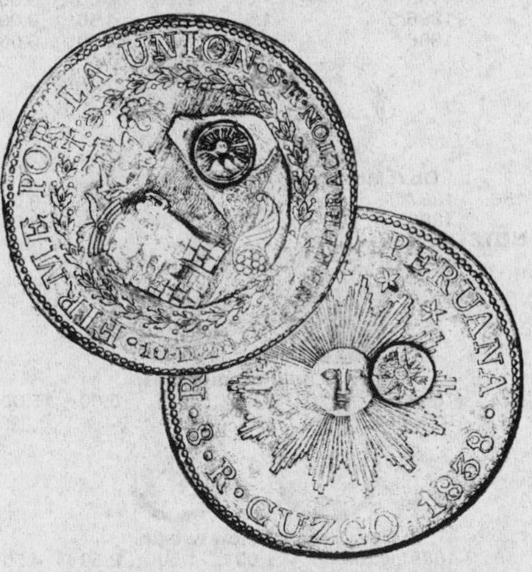

c/s: Type III on Peru (South) 8 Reales, KM#170.4.

KM#	Date	Good	VG	Fine	VF
120.6	ND(1837-39)	375.00	550.00	750.00	1000.

NOTE: Coins dated after 1841 with the Type III c/m are believed to be counterfeit by some authorities.

COUNTERSTAMPED COINAGE

Type IV

NOTE: Similar dies as used for Type III but instead of being applied as individual countermarks they were paired in hinged dies and counterstamped in one application. This was done without respect to the host coins obverse or reverse.

8 REALES

SILVER

c/s: Type IV on Argentina (Potosi) 8 Reales, KM#14.

KM#	Date	Good	VG	Fine	VF
113	ND(1815)	225.00	330.00	450.00	600.00

c/s: Type IV on Bolivia 8 Soles, KM#97.

KM#	Date	Good	VG	Fine	VF
114	ND(1827-40)	45.00	75.00	120.00	175.00

c/s: Type IV on Chile (Santiago) 8 Reales, KM#96.1.

KM#	Date	Good	VG	Fine	VF
115	ND(1837-40)	125.00	185.00	250.00	350.00

c/s: Type IV on Peru (Lima) 8 Reales, KM#136.

KM#	Date	Good	VG	Fine	VF
116	ND(1822-23)	150.00	225.00	300.00	400.00

c/s: Type IV on Peru (Lima) 8 Reales, KM#142.1.

KM#	Date	Good	VG	Fine	VF
117	ND(1825-28)	45.00	75.00	120.00	175.00

c/s: Type IV on Peru (Lima) 8 Reales, KM#142.3.

KM#	Date	Good	VG	Fine	VF
118	ND(1828-41)	40.00	65.00	100.00	150.00

c/s: Type IV on Peru (Cuzco) 8 Reales, KM#142.2.

KM#	Date	Good	VG	Fine	VF
119	ND(1826-36)	45.00	75.00	120.00	175.00

c/s: Type IV on Peru (North) 8 Reales, KM#155.

KM#	Date	Good	VG	Fine	VF
121	ND(1836-39)	45.00	75.00	120.00	175.00

NOTE: Coins dated after 1841 with the Type IV c/s are believed to be counterfeit by some authorities.

REPUBLIC

MONETARY SYSTEM

8 Reales = 1 Peso

1/4 REAL

.7600 g, .903 SILVER, .0220 oz ASW

KM#	Date	Mintage	Fine	VF	XF	Unc
130	1859	—	200.00	300.00	500.00	—
	1860	.116	6.00	10.00	20.00	35.00
	1861	—	7.00	12.50	17.50	27.50
	1862	—	6.50	10.00	15.00	25.00
	1863	—	7.00	12.50	17.50	30.00
	1864	—	7.00	12.50	17.50	30.00
	1865	.023	22.50	45.00	75.00	150.00
	1866	.205	5.00	8.50	12.50	22.50
	1867	.169	5.00	8.50	12.50	22.50
	1868	.148	5.00	8.50	12.50	22.50
	1869	.242	5.00	8.50	12.50	22.50

.7700 g, .900 SILVER, .0222 oz ASW
Rev: 0.900 below wreath.

KM#	Date	Mintage	Fine	VF	XF	Unc
146	1872 P	—	2.00	3.50	5.50	9.00
	1873/2 P	.308	5.00	10.00	15.00	25.00
	1873 P	Inc. Ab.	1.00	1.75	3.00	5.00
	1874 P	—	7.50	12.50	20.00	35.00
	1875/3 P	—	—	—	—	—
	1875 P	—	1.00	1.75	3.00	12.50
	1876 P	—	10.00	15.00	25.00	40.00
	1878 P	2 known	175.00	250.00	—	—
	1878 F	.680	1.00	1.75	3.00	8.00

NOTE: Varieties exist.

.7700 g, .835 SILVER, .0206 oz ASW
Rev: 0.835 below small wreath.

KM#	Date	Mintage	Fine	VF	XF	Unc
146a.1	1878	Inc.KM146	2.00	3.50	6.50	12.50

Rev: 0.835 below large wreath.

KM#	Date	Mintage	Fine	VF	XF	Unc
146a.2	1878	Inc.KM146	1.50	2.50	4.00	8.00
	1879	.171	1.50	2.50	4.00	8.00

Rev: W/o fineness.

KM#	Date	Mintage	Fine	VF	XF	Unc
146a.3	1878 large G					
		Inc. KM146	2.75	4.50	9.00	15.00
	1878 medium G					
		Inc. KM146	2.25	3.50	7.50	14.00
	1878 small G					
		Inc. KM146	2.75	4.50	10.00	17.50
	1879 large G					
		Inc. KM146a.2	5.50	9.00	15.00	25.00

Obv: Long-rayed sun. Rev: 0.835 added.

KM#	Date	Mintage	Fine	VF	XF	Unc
151	1879					
		Inc. KM146a.2	1.50	2.00	3.00	6.50
	1880	.115	1.00	1.75	3.00	6.50
	1881/79	.073	5.00	10.00	15.00	25.00
	1881	Inc. Ab.	3.00	4.50	8.00	13.50
	1882	—	1.00	1.50	2.50	5.00
	1883	.195	15.00	25.00	40.00	70.00
	1884	.100	1.00	1.50	2.50	5.00
	1885	—	7.50	12.50	20.00	35.00
	1886/5	—	1.50	2.50	4.50	8.00
	1886	—	1.25	2.00	3.50	6.50

Obv: Mountains w/short-rayed sun.

KM#	Date	Mintage	Fine	VF	XF	Unc
156	1887	—	1.50	2.50	4.00	8.00
	1888	—	1.00	1.50	2.25	3.50

NOTE: Varieties exist.

Obv: G below mountains.

KM#	Date	Mintage	Fine	VF	XF	Unc
157	1889	.870	2.00	3.00	5.00	15.00

Rev: 5 stars below wreath.

KM#	Date	Mintage	Fine	VF	XF	Unc
158	1889	Inc.KM157	1.00	1.50	2.50	4.50
	1890	—	1.00	1.50	2.50	4.50
	1891	—	1.50	2.50	4.00	6.50
	1893	—	—	—	—	—

NOTE: Varieties exist.

Obv: Mountains w/long-rayed sun.

KM#	Date	Mintage	Fine	VF	XF	Unc
159	1892	.512	20.00	35.00	90.00	180.00
	1893/2	.749	2.00	4.00	8.00	15.00
	1893 lg. dt.	I.A.	1.00	1.50	2.00	3.00
	1893 sm. dt.	I.A.	1.00	1.50	2.00	3.00

Rev: 3 stars below thin wreath.

KM#	Date	Mintage	Fine	VF	XF	Unc
161	1893	Inc.KM159	1.00	1.50	2.00	3.00
	1894	.059	6.50	10.00	15.00	25.00

Rev: 5 stars below full wreath.

KM#	Date	Mintage	Fine	VF	XF	Unc
162	1894	—	.50	.75	1.25	2.00
	1894H	.800	.50	.75	1.50	2.50
	1894H	—	—	—	Proof	100.00
	1895	1.482	.50	.75	1.25	2.00
	1896	2.071	.50	.75	1.25	2.00
	1897	.989	.50	.75	1.50	2.25
	1898	.384	.50	1.00	1.75	3.00
	1899	.080	1.50	2.50	4.50	8.00

COPPER-NICKEL

KM#	Date	Mintage	Fine	VF	XF	Unc
175	1900H	2.944	.15	.35	1.00	2.50
	1901H	5.056	.15	.35	.75	2.00

MEDIO (1/2) REAL

1.5500 g, .903 SILVER, .0449 oz ASW
Rev: MED: REAL

KM#	Date	Mintage	Fine	VF	XF	Unc
131	1859	—	15.00	30.00	60.00	125.00
	1860 R	.191	6.00	10.00	18.50	45.00
	1861	—	15.00	30.00	60.00	125.00
	1861 R	—	6.00	10.00	18.50	45.00

Obv. leg: RAFAEL CARRERA PTE.
Rev: MED. RL

KM#	Date	Mintage	Fine	VF	XF	Unc
138	1862 R	—	3.50	6.00	12.00	30.00
	1863/2 R	—	6.00	10.00	18.50	45.00
	1863 R	—	4.50	9.00	13.50	30.00
	1865/3 R	.057	4.50	9.00	13.50	30.00
	1865 R	Inc. Ab.	3.25	6.00	10.00	22.50

Obv. leg: R. CARRERA FUNDADOR

KM#	Date	Mintage	Fine	VF	XF	Unc
143	1867 R	.092	4.00	8.50	13.50	30.00
	1868 R	.102	4.00	8.50	13.50	30.00
	1869	.117	4.00	8.50	13.50	30.00
	1869 R	—	4.25	9.00	16.00	35.00

1.5000 g, .900 SILVER, .0435 oz ASW

KM#	Date	Mintage	Fine	VF	XF	Unc
147	1872 P	—	4.25	9.00	18.50	45.00
	1873 P	.035	5.00	10.00	20.00	50.00

1.5000 g, .835 SILVER, .0402 oz ASW

KM#	Date	Mintage	Fine	VF	XF	Unc
147a.1	1878	—	2.25	4.50	7.50	22.50
	1879	Inc.KM152	3.50	6.50	9.50	25.00

NOTE: Wide and narrow dates exist for 1879. Large and small dates and letters exist for 1878.

Rev: W/o fineness.

KM#	Date	Mintage	Fine	VF	XF	Unc
147a.2	1878 lg. date	—	2.25	4.25	7.50	18.50
	1878 sm. date	—	2.25	4.25	7.50	18.50
	1893	Inc.KM163	5.00	8.50	12.00	27.50

Obv: 1/2 RL.

KM#	Date	Mintage	Fine	VF	XF	Unc
152	1879 D	1.683	2.00	4.00	6.00	10.00
	1880/79 D					
		2.715	3.00	6.00	9.00	17.50
	1880 D	Inc. Ab.	.75	1.25	2.50	5.00
	1880/70 E	I.A.	—	—	—	—
	1880 E	Inc. Ab.	6.00	10.00	15.00	22.50

NOTE: Varieties exist.

Obv: MEDIO REAL.

KM#	Date	Mintage	Fine	VF	XF	Unc
155.1	1880/770 E					
		Inc. KM152	3.00	4.50	7.50	12.50
	1880/790 E					
		Inc. KM152	3.00	4.50	7.50	12.50
	1880/79 E					
		Inc. KM152	3.00	4.50	7.50	12.50
	1880 E					
		Inc. KM152	.75	1.50	2.50	4.00
	1881 E	—	.75	2.00	3.00	4.50
	1883/1 E	.046	8.00	12.50	28.00	50.00
	1883 E	Inc. Ab.	4.50	8.50	15.00	22.50

NOTE: Varieties exist.

Rev: Star between fineness and date.

KM#	Date	Mintage	Fine	VF	XF	Unc
155.2	1889/779	.481	1.25	2.00	4.50	10.00
	1889	Inc. Ab.	1.25	2.00	4.50	10.00
	1890/89	—	2.00	4.50	8.50	15.00
	1890	—	1.25	2.00	4.50	10.00

Rev: W/o fineness, small wreath.

KM#	Date	Mintage	Fine	VF	XF	Unc
163	1893/2	.360	13.50	30.00	70.00	120.00
	1893	Inc. Ab.	12.00	25.00	50.00	90.00

Rev: Large wreath.

KM#	Date	Mintage	Fine	VF	XF	Unc
164	1893 large date, blundered flat top 3					
		Inc. KM163	4.00	7.50	16.50	30.00
	1893 small date, round top 3					
		Inc. KM163	4.00	7.50	16.50	30.00

KM#	Date	Mintage	Fine	VF	XF	Unc
165	1894	.619	.65	1.25	2.25	4.00
	1894H	.900	.65	1.25	2.00	3.00
	1894H	—	—	—	Proof	100.00
	1895	.819	.65	1.25	2.00	3.00
	1895H	.300	1.25	2.25	3.75	5.50
	1896	1.062	.65	1.25	2.00	3.00
	1897	.528	.65	1.25	2.00	3.00

NOTE: Varieties exist.

1.5500 g, .600 SILVER, .0299 oz ASW

KM#	Date	Mintage	Fine	VF	XF	Unc
170	1899	.486	.75	1.25	2.50	3.50

COPPER-NICKEL

KM#	Date	Mintage	Fine	VF	XF	Unc
176	1900	5.348	.25	.50	.60	2.25
	1901	6.652	.25	.50	.60	2.25

UN (1) REAL

3.0000 g, .903 SILVER, .0870 oz ASW
Rev: UN REAL.

KM#	Date	Mintage	Fine	VF	XF	Unc
132	1859	—	60.00	100.00	—	—
	1859/95 R	—	—	—	—	—
	1859 R	—	10.00	18.00	30.00	75.00
	1860 R	.177	5.00	9.00	15.00	35.00

Obv. leg: RAFAEL CARRERA PTE. . . .w/FRENER F. below truncation. Rev: UN RL.

KM#	Date	Mintage	Fine	VF	XF	Unc
137.1	1861 R	—	4.00	7.50	12.50	30.00
	1862 R	—	3.00	6.00	10.00	25.00
	1863 R	—	5.00	9.00	15.00	35.00
	1864 R	—	3.00	5.50	11.50	25.00
	1865 R	—	5.25	9.50	16.50	40.00

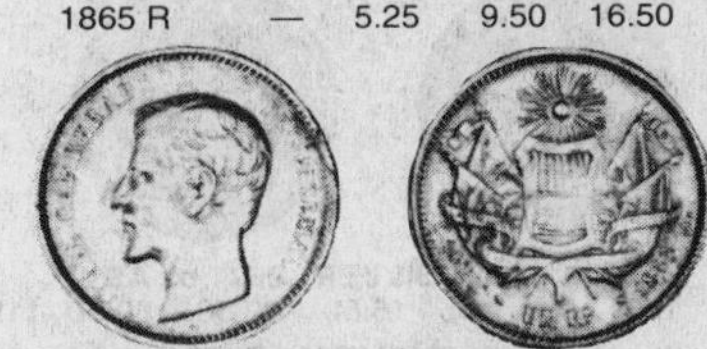

W/o Frener F below bust.

KM#	Date	Mintage	Fine	VF	XF	Unc
137.2	1865 R	—	3.00	5.50	10.00	22.50

NOTE: Varieties exist.

Obv. leg: R. CARRERA FUNDADOR. . . .
Rev: 1 RL.

KM#	Date	Mintage	Fine	VF	XF	Unc
141	1866 R	.385	4.00	9.00	16.00	35.00
	1867 R	.199	4.00	9.00	16.00	35.00

Rev: UN REAL.

KM#	Date	Mintage	Fine	VF	XF	Unc
145	1868 R	.335	4.00	9.00	16.00	35.00
	1869 R	.131	4.00	9.00	16.00	35.00

3.1500 g, .900 SILVER, .0911 oz ASW

KM#	Date	Mintage	Fine	VF	XF	Unc
148.1	1872 P	3,816	12.50	27.50	45.00	115.00
	1874 P	—	7.50	16.50	27.50	65.00
	1878 F	.159	7.50	17.50	30.00	75.00

Obv: W/o fineness.

KM#	Date	Mintage	Fine	VF	XF	Unc
148.2	1878	Inc. Ab.	15.00	30.00	50.00	120.00

NOTE: Wide and narrow dates exist.

KM#	Date	Mintage	Fine	VF	XF	Unc
153	1879 D	.037	10.00	22.50	37.50	60.00

3.2500 g, .835 SILVER, .0872 oz ASW

KM#	Date	Mintage	Fine	VF	XF	Unc
153a.1	1883	.046	3.50	6.00	12.00	17.50

Rev: Star between fineness and date.

KM#	Date	Mintage	Fine	VF	XF	Unc
153a.2	1889	.332	1.50	2.75	3.50	6.00
	1890/89	—	2.00	4.50	6.50	12.50
	1890	—	1.50	2.75	3.50	6.00
	1891	—	1.50	2.75	3.50	6.00
	1893	.293	2.00	4.00	5.00	8.00

NOTE: Wide and narrow dates exist on 1893 dated coins.

KM#	Date	Mintage	Fine	VF	XF	Unc
166	1894	.326	2.00	3.00	4.25	6.50
	1894H	.600	2.00	3.00	4.00	5.50
	1894H	—	—	—	Proof	100.00
	1895H	.200	3.00	6.00	9.00	15.00
	1896	.203	2.00	3.00	4.25	6.50
	1897	.701	2.00	3.00	4.00	5.50
	1898	.040	6.50	11.50	20.00	32.50

Rev: W/o fineness.

KM#	Date	Mintage	Fine	VF	XF	Unc
171	1899	—	6.50	10.00	20.00	32.50

3.1500 g, .750 SILVER, .0759 oz ASW

KM#	Date	Mintage	Fine	VF	XF	Unc
172	1899	—	100.00	150.00	250.00	—

3.1000 g, .600 SILVER, .0598 oz ASW

KM#	Date	Mintage	Fine	VF	XF	Unc
173	1899	—	2.00	2.50	5.00	12.50

3.1500 g, .500 SILVER, .0506 oz ASW

KM#	Date	Mintage	Fine	VF	XF	Unc
174	1899	—	1.25	2.75	6.00	12.50
	1900	1.874	1.25	2.75	7.00	15.00

NOTE: Varieties exist.

.500/.550 SILVER

KM#	Date	Mintage	Fine	VF	XF	Unc
174a	1899	—	—	—	—	—

COPPER-NICKEL

KM#	Date	Mintage	Fine	VF	XF	Unc
177	1900	4.612	—	.30	.75	1.50
	1901	7.388	—	.25	.75	1.25
	1910	4.000	—	.30	.75	1.50
	1911	2.000	—	.35	1.00	2.00
	1912	8.000	—	.25	.75	1.25

DOS (2) REALES

6.3000 g, .903 SILVER, .1829 oz ASW, 27.5mm
Obv. leg: RAFAEL CARRERA PE., thick letters.

KM#	Date	Mintage	VG	Fine	VF	XF
133	1859	—	175.00	275.00	375.00	600.00

NOTE: Often holed; beware of repaired specimens.

6.2000 g, .903 SILVER, .1800 oz ASW, 26mm
Obv: Thin letters.

KM#	Date	Mintage	VG	Fine	VF	XF
134	1860 R	—	2.50	7.50	12.50	40.00
	1861 R	—	3.50	10.00	17.50	45.00

6.1000 g, .903 SILVER, .1770 oz ASW, 24mm
Rev: Narrower shield.

KM#	Date	Mintage	Fine	VF	XF	Unc
139	1862 R	—	6.00	10.00	16.00	40.00
	1863 R	—	6.00	10.00	16.00	40.00
	1864 R	—	6.00	10.00	16.00	40.00
	1865 R	.410	6.00	10.00	16.00	40.00

KM#	Date	Mintage	Fine	VF	XF	Unc
139	1865 R w/o period after date					
		Inc. Ab.	6.00	10.00	16.00	40.00

NOTE: Wide and narrow dates exist on 1863 dated coins.

Obv. leg: R. CARRERA FUNDADOR. . . .

KM#	Date	Mintage	Fine	VF	XF	Unc
142	1866 R	.334	4.00	8.50	14.00	35.00
	1867 R	.293	4.00	8.50	14.00	35.00
	1868 R	.267	4.50	8.50	14.00	35.00
	1869 R	.124	6.50	12.00	18.00	45.00

6.1000 g, .900 SILVER, .1765 oz ASW

KM#	Date	Mintage	Fine	VF	XF	Unc
149	1872 P	—	6.50	13.50	23.50	47.50
	1873 P	.610	4.00	8.00	18.00	38.00

KM#	Date	Mintage	Fine	VF	XF	Unc
154	1879 D	.101	6.50	12.00	18.00	50.00

0.835/0.900 SILVER

KM#	Date	Mintage	Fine	VF	XF	Unc
154a	1881 E	2.975	7.50	10.00	12.50	15.00

.835 SILVER

KM#	Date	Mintage	Fine	VF	XF	Unc
154c	1881 E	—	—	—	—	—

6.2000 g, .835 SILVER, .1664 oz ASW
Rev: Star between fineness and date.

KM#	Date	Mintage	VG	Fine	VF	XF
154b.1	1892	—	70.00	170.00	280.00	400.00

Rev: W/o star.

KM#	Date	Mintage	VG	Fine	VF	XF
154b.2	1892	—	70.00	170.00	280.00	400.00

KM#	Date	Mintage	Fine	VF	XF	Unc
167	1894	1.094	2.25	4.50	7.00	12.50
	1894H	.900	2.25	4.50	7.00	12.50
	1894H	—	—	—	Proof	300.00
	1895	2.783	2.25	4.50	7.00	12.50
	1895H	.300	3.75	6.00	9.00	15.00

KM#	Date	Mintage	Fine	VF	XF	Unc
167	1896	.605	2.25	4.50	7.00	12.50
	1897	1.041	2.25	4.50	7.00	12.50
	1898	5.172	1.75	3.25	6.50	12.00
	1899	.040	10.00	17.50	25.00	50.00

CUATRO (4) REALES

0.8065 g, .875 GOLD, .0226 oz AGW

KM#	Date	Mintage	Fine	VF	XF	Unc
135	1860 R	—	20.00	35.00	50.00	90.00
	1861 R	.277	17.50	30.00	40.00	75.00
	1864 R	—	25.00	60.00	100.00	150.00

12.5000 g, .903 SILVER, .3629 oz ASW
Obv. leg: RAFAEL CARRERA PTE. . . .

KM#	Date	Mintage	VG	Fine	VF	XF
136	1860 R	4,760	6.50	20.00	32.50	60.00
	1861 R	—	5.00	18.00	30.00	50.00

Rev: Shield narrowed.

KM#	Date	Mintage	Fine	VF	XF	Unc
140	1863 R	—	10.00	17.50	25.00	200.00
	1865/55 R	.082	—	—	—	—
	1865/3 R	I.A.	18.00	30.00	45.00	350.00
	1865 R	Inc. Ab.	10.00	16.50	22.50	200.00

Obv. leg: R. CARRERA FUNDADOR. . . .

KM#	Date	Mintage	VG	Fine	VF	XF
144	1867 R	.054	5.00	15.00	18.00	25.00
	1868 R	.036	5.00	15.00	20.00	30.00
	1869 R	—	—	—	Rare	—

12.5000 g, .900 SILVER, .3617 oz ASW

KM#	Date	Mintage	Fine	VF	XF	Unc
150	1873 P	.024	18.50	40.00	100.00	200.00
	1878 D	.010	27.50	60.00	125.00	250.00
	1879 D	7,664	27.50	60.00	125.00	250.00
	1879 P	—	45.00	85.00	145.00	290.00
	1892 R.G.	—	60.00	135.00	275.00	550.00
	1893	—	100.00	225.00	550.00	875.00
	1893 R.G.	—	100.00	225.00	550.00	875.00

12.5000 g, .835 SILVER, .3356 oz ASW

KM#	Date	Mintage	Fine	VF	XF	Unc
160	1892	2,600	275.00	500.00	1000.	2500.

12.5000 g, .900 SILVER, .3617 oz ASW

KM#	Date	Mintage	Fine	VF	XF	Unc
168.1	1894H	.500	6.00	12.50	18.50	32.50
	1894H	—	—	—	Proof	400.00

Obv. and rev: H mint mark.

KM#	Date	Mintage	Fine	VF	XF	Unc
168.2	1894H	Inc. Ab.	80.00	120.00	250.00	500.00

DECIMAL COINAGE

100 Centavos (Centimos) = 1 Peso

CENTAVO

BRONZE

KM#	Date	Mintage	Fine	VF	XF	Unc
196	1871	—	2.00	5.00	10.00	27.50

KM#	Date	Mintage	Fine	VF	XF	Unc
202.1	1881	—	3.50	7.50	12.00	40.00

Die breaks in 1881 have the appearance of 1884.

KM#	Date	Mintage	Fine	VF	XF	Unc
202.2	1881	—	5.00	10.00	15.00	45.00

5 CENTAVOS

1.2500 g, .835 SILVER, .0335 oz ASW

KM#	Date	Mintage	Fine	VF	XF	Unc
203	1881	.118	10.00	25.00	40.00	80.00

10 CENTAVOS

2.5000 g, .835 SILVER, .0671 oz ASW

KM#	Date	Mintage	Fine	VF	XF	Unc
204	1881	.056	16.50	32.50	50.00	115.00

25 CENTIMOS

6.2500 g, .900 SILVER, .1808 oz ASW

KM#	Date	Mintage	Fine	VF	XF	Unc
189	1869 R	.181	6.00	13.50	25.00	70.00
	1870 R	.180	4.50	9.00	20.00	60.00

25 CENTAVOS

6.2500 g, .835 SILVER, .1677 oz ASW

KM#	Date	Mintage	Fine	VF	XF	Unc
205.1	1881 E	5.044	2.50	4.50	6.00	10.00
	1882 E	—	2.50	4.50	6.00	10.00
	1885 E	—	2.50	4.50	6.00	10.00
	1888 E	—	4.00	6.00	8.50	12.00
	1888	—	7.00	12.00	20.00	30.00
	1888 G	—	2.50	4.50	6.00	10.00
	1889 G	.496	2.50	4.50	6.00	10.00
	1889 G medal rotation	Inc. Ab.	—	—	—	—

NOTE: Varieties exist.

Star replaces assayers initial

KM#	Date	Mintage	Fine	VF	XF	Unc
205.2	1889	Inc. Ab.	2.50	4.50	6.00	15.00
	1890	—	2.75	5.00	7.50	15.00
	1891	—	6.00	12.00	20.00	30.00

KM#	Date	Mintage	VG	Fine	VF	XF
206	1882	—	125.00	225.00	325.00	450.00

Rev: W/o star.

KM#	Date	Mintage	Fine	VF	XF	Unc
209.1	1892	—	30.00	50.00	75.00	100.00

Rev: Star between fineness and date.

KM#	Date	Mintage	Fine	VF	XF	Unc
209.2	1890	—	6.00	12.00	22.50	35.00
	1892	—	2.50	5.00	8.00	15.00
	1893	—	2.25	4.50	7.00	12.00

NOTE: Varieties exist.

50 CENTAVOS

12.5000 g., .835 SILVER, .3356 oz ASW

KM#	Date	Mintage	VG	Fine	VF	XF
195	1870 R	.140	5.00	10.00	18.50	50.00

PESO

25.0000 g, .903 SILVER, .7258 oz ASW

KM#	Date	Mintage	VG	Fine	VF	XF
178	1859	—	40.00	200.00	350.00	600.00
	1859 R	—	75.00	350.00	550.00	900.00

1.6129 g, .875 GOLD, .0454 oz AGW

KM#	Date	Mintage	VG	Fine	VF	XF
179	1859 R	—	25.00	35.00	50.00	75.00
	1860 R	.037	25.00	35.00	50.00	75.00

27.0000 g, .903 SILVER, .7839 oz ASW

KM#	Date	Mintage	VG	Fine	VF	XF
182	1862 R	—	15.00	25.00	80.00	125.00
	1863 R	—	12.00	20.00	40.00	80.00
	1864 R	—	6.00	10.00	17.50	37.50
	1864.R	—	6.00	10.00	17.50	37.50
	1865 sm.R	.119	7.00	12.00	20.00	40.00
	1865 lg.R	I.A.	15.00	25.00	80.00	125.00

Rev: L10D.20G

KM#	Date	Mintage	VG	Fine	VF	XF
186.1	1866 R	.109	7.00	12.00	20.00	40.00
	1867 R	.173	6.00	10.00	17.50	37.50
	1868 R	.060	8.00	15.00	25.00	50.00

Rev: W/o 'L' before 10Ds.20Gs.

KM#	Date	Mintage	VG	Fine	VF	XF
186.2	1869 R	.186	40.00	80.00	150.00	275.00

25.0000 g, .900 SILVER, .7234 oz ASW
Rev: L0.900

KM#	Date	Mintage	VG	Fine	VF	XF
190.1	1869/99 R	Inc. KM186	10.00	17.50	25.00	75.00
	1869 R	Inc.KM186	6.00	10.00	17.50	37.50
	1870 R	.283	6.00	10.00	15.00	35.00
	1871 R	—	6.00	10.00	15.00	30.00

Rev: W/o 'L' before 0.900.

KM#	Date	Mintage	VG	Fine	VF	XF
190.2	1869 R	Inc.KM186	8.00	15.00	25.00	45.00

Rev: W/o L and 0.900.

KM#	Date	Mintage	VG	Fine	VF	XF
190.3	1869 R	Inc. KM186	30.00	50.00	80.00	120.00
	1869	Inc. KM186	—	—	—	—

Rev: Date and fineness at bottom.

KM#	Date	Mintage	Fine	VF	XF	Unc
197.1	1872 P	.014	30.00	60.00	100.00	500.00
	1872 R	—	—	—	Rare	—
	1873 P	.078	20.00	40.00	80.00	300.00
	1873 P (error fineness 0900)	—	30.00	50.00	90.00	250.00

Rev: Quetzal w/short tail.

KM#	Date	Mintage	Fine	VF	XF	Unc
197.2	1873 P	—	30.00	50.00	90.00	250.00

Rev: Date and fineness at top.

KM#	Date	Mintage	VG	Fine	VF	XF
200	1878 D	1,076	300.00	600.00	1200.	2000.
	1879 D	.010	100.00	200.00	300.00	600.00

Rev: Full spray design.

KM#	Date	Mintage	VG	Fine	VF	XF
201	1879 D	Inc. KM200	125.00	250.00	350.00	500.00
	1893 G	—	800.00	—	—	—
	1893 RG	1,119	550.00	1000.	1700.	2750.

Obv: Modified Liberty design.

KM#	Date	Mintage	Fine	VF	XF	Unc
207	1882/1 E	—	—	—	Rare	—
	1888 G	—	350.00	600.00	1100.	2000.
	1889 G	—	350.00	600.00	1100.	2000.

KM#	Date	Mintage	VG	Fine	VF	XF
208	1882 A.E.	—	20.00	30.00	70.00	225.00
	1889 MG	6,794	125.00	200.00	350.00	600.00

KM#	Date	Mintage	Fine	VF	XF	Unc
210	1894	1.696	7.00	12.50	17.50	45.00
	1894H	.875	7.00	12.50	17.50	55.00
	1894H	—	—	—	Proof	800.00
	1895	1.415	7.00	12.50	17.50	50.00
	1895H	.375	8.00	15.00	22.00	75.00
	1895H	—	—	—	Proof	—
	1896/5	1.403	10.00	17.50	25.00	85.00
	1896	Inc. Ab.	7.00	12.50	17.50	50.00
	1897	—	12.00	20.00	30.00	100.00

2 PESOS

3.2258 g, .875 GOLD, .0907 oz AGW

KM#	Date	Mintage	VG	Fine	VF	XF
180	1859 R	—	50.00	65.00	125.00	200.00

4 PESOS

6.4516 g, .875 GOLD, .1815 oz AGW

KM#	Date	Mintage	VG	Fine	VF	XF
181	1861 R	—	175.00	250.00	400.00	550.00
	1862 R	—	175.00	250.00	400.00	550.00

KM#	Date	Mintage	VG	Fine	VF	XF
187	1868 R	561 pcs.	250.00	500.00	700.00	950.00
	1868 R	778 pcs.	250.00	500.00	700.00	950.00
	1869 R	.020	100.00	175.00	250.00	375.00

5 PESOS

8.0645 g, .900 GOLD, .2333 oz AGW

KM#	Date	Mintage	VG	Fine	VF	XF
191	1869 R	.049	110.00	125.00	175.00	250.00

KM#	Date	Mintage	VG	Fine	VF	XF
198	1872 P	—	125.00	200.00	350.00	550.00
	1873 P	—	—	—	Rare	—
	1874 P	—	125.00	200.00	350.00	550.00
	1875 P	—	—	—	Rare	—
	1876 F	—	—	—	Rare	—
	1877 F	—	125.00	200.00	350.00	550.00
	1878 D	—	125.00	200.00	350.00	550.00

8 PESOS

12.9039 g, .875 GOLD, .3630 oz AGW

KM#	Date	Mintage	VG	Fine	VF	XF
184	1864 R	—	300.00	450.00	750.00	1200.

Similar to 4 Pesos, KM#187.

KM#	Date	Mintage	VG	Fine	VF	XF
192	1869 R	—	500.00	650.00	2000.	3000.

10 PESOS

16.1290 g, .900 GOLD, .4667 oz AGW

KM#	Date	Mintage	VG	Fine	VF	XF
193	1869 R	.020	225.00	300.00	450.00	700.00

16 PESOS

25.8078 g, .875 GOLD, .7259 oz AGW

KM#	Date	Mintage	VG	Fine	VF	XF
183	1863 R	—	—	—	3500.	5500.
	1864 R	—	—	—	Rare	—
	1865 R	—	—	—	Rare	—

NOTE: A few AU-Unc specimens of the 1863R were found in a box shook loose from its hiding place during the 1977 Guatemala earthquake.

Reduced size

KM#	Date	Mintage	VG	Fine	VF	XF
185	1865 R	190 pcs.	1000.	2000.	4000.	6000.

KM#	Date	Mintage	VG	Fine	VF	XF
188	1867 R	467 pcs.	850.00	1750.	3500.	5000.
	1869 R	3,465	400.00	600.00	800.00	1500.

20 PESOS

32.2580 g, .900 GOLD, .9334 oz AGW

KM#	Date	Mintage	VG	Fine	VF	XF
194	1869 R	.016	450.00	550.00	700.00	950.00

KM#	Date	Mintage	VG	Fine	VF	XF
199	1877 F	—	1000.	2000.	5000.	8000.
	1878 F	—	1000.	2000.	5000.	8000.

COUNTERSTAMPED COINAGE

By 1894, foreign coins had become so prevalent that on August 10 the government authorized their counterstamping at the mint, with official 1/2 Real dies of 1894, to legitimize their circulation.

(PESO)

.917 SILVER
c/s: On Brazil 2000 Reis, KM#475.

KM#	Date	Year	Mintage	Fine	VF	XF
213	1894	1875	—	—	Rare	—

25.0000 g, .900 SILVER, .7234 oz ASW
c/s: On Chile 8 Reales, KM#96.2.

KM#	Date	Year	Mintage	Fine	VF	XF
214	1894	1848 JM	—	—	Rare	—
	1894	1849 ML	— Reported, not confirmed			

c/s: On Chile Peso, KM#129.

KM#	Date	Year	Mintage	Fine	VF	XF
215	1894	1853	550.00	1200.	2000.	—
		1854	350.00	750.00	1250.	—
		1855	350.00	750.00	1250.	—

c/s: On Chile Peso, KM#142.1.

KM#	Date	Year	Mintage	Fine	VF	XF
216	1894	1867	—	125.00	200.00	300.00
		1868	—	125.00	200.00	300.00
		1869	—	50.00	75.00	125.00
		1870/69	—	50.00	75.00	125.00
		1870	—	50.00	75.00	125.00
		1871	—	75.00	125.00	200.00
		1872	—	20.00	30.00	50.00
		1873/2	—	20.00	30.00	50.00
		1873	—	20.00	30.00	50.00
		1874	—	20.00	30.00	50.00
		1875	—	20.00	30.00	50.00
		1876	—	20.00	30.00	50.00
		1877	—	20.00	30.00	50.00
		1878	—	20.00	30.00	50.00
		1879	—	20.00	30.00	50.00
		1880	—	20.00	30.00	50.00
		1881	—	20.00	30.00	50.00
		1882/1	—	20.00	30.00	50.00
		1882	—	20.00	30.00	50.00
		1883	—	20.00	30.00	50.00
		1884	—	20.00	30.00	50.00
		1885/3	—	20.00	30.00	50.00
		1885	—	20.00	30.00	50.00
		1886	—	20.00	30.00	50.00
		1887	— Reported, not confirmed			
		1889	—	50.00	75.00	125.00
		1890/89	—	150.00	225.00	300.00
		1890	—	150.00	225.00	300.00
		1891	— Reported, not confirmed			

c/s: Off center on Chile Peso, KM#142.1.

KM#	Date	Year	Mintage	Fine	VF	XF
217	1894	1880	—	—	—	—

.903 SILVER
c/s: On Guatemala Peso, KM#178.

KM#	Date	Year	Mintage	Fine	VF	XF
218	1894	1859	— Reported, not confirmed			

c/s: On Guatemala Peso, KM#190.1.

KM#	Date	Year	Mintage	Fine	VF	XF
219	1894	1869	—	—	Rare	—

c/s: On Guatemala Peso, KM#208.

KM#	Date	Year	Mintage	Fine	VF	XF
220	1894	1882AE	—	—	Rare	—

c/s: On Guatemala Peso, KM#210.

KM#	Date	Year	Mintage	Fine	VF	XF
221	1894	1894	— Reported, not confirmed			
		1894 H	—	—	Rare	—

c/s: On Honduras Peso, KM#47.

KM#	Date	Year	Mintage	Fine	VF	XF
222	1894	1882	—	—	Rare	—

c/s: On Honduras Peso, KM#52.

KM#	Date	Year	Mintage	Fine	VF	XF
223	1894	1890	—	850.00	1350.	—
		1891	—	850.00	1350.	—

c/s: On Peru Un Sol, KM#196.

KM#	Date	Year	Mintage	Fine	VF	XF
224	1894	1864 Y.B.	—	15.00	25.00	35.00
		1864 Y.B. Deteano	—	—	Rare	—
		1865 Y.B.	—	50.00	100.00	175.00
		1866 Y.B.	—	20.00	30.00	40.00
		1867 Y.B.	—	20.00	30.00	40.00
		1868 Y.B.	—	20.00	30.00	40.00
		1869 Y.B.	—	20.00	30.00	40.00
		1870 Y.J.	—	20.00	30.00	40.00
		1871 Y.J.	—	20.00	30.00	40.00
		1872 Y.J.	—	20.00	30.00	40.00
		1873 Y.J.	—	50.00	100.00	175.00
		1873 L.D.	—	50.00	100.00	175.00
		1874 Y.J.	—	20.00	30.00	40.00
		1875 Y.J.	—	20.00	30.00	40.00
		1879 Y.J.	—	25.00	45.00	65.00
		1880 Y.J.	—	40.00	60.00	100.00
		1881 B.F.	—	30.00	50.00	75.00

KM#	Date	Year	Mintage	Fine	VF	XF
224		1882 B.F.	—	40.00	60.00	100.00
		1882 F.N.	—	50.00	100.00	175.00
		1883 F.N.	—	100.00	165.00	250.00
		1884 B.D.	—	40.00	60.00	100.00
		1884 R.D.	—	20.00	30.00	40.00
		1885 R.D.	—	20.00	30.00	40.00
		1885 T.D.	—	20.00	30.00	40.00
		1886 R.D.	—	100.00	165.00	250.00
		1886 T.F.	—	25.00	45.00	65.00
		1887 T.F.	—	15.00	22.50	30.00
		1888 T.F.	—	15.00	22.50	30.00
		1889 T.F.	—	15.00	22.50	30.00
		1890/80 T.F.	—	30.00	50.00	75.00
		1890 T.F.	—	15.00	22.50	30.00
		1891 T.F.	—	15.00	22.50	30.00
		1892 T.F.	—	15.00	22.50	30.00
		1893 T.F.	—	15.00	22.50	30.00
		1393 T.F. (error)	—	450.00	600.00	900.00
		1894 T.F.	—	20.00	30.00	40.00

c/s: On Peru 5 Pesetas, KM#201.1.

KM#	Date	Year	Mintage	Fine	VF	XF
225	1894	1880 B.F. w/B below wreath w/o dot	—	80.00	110.00	160.00
		1880 B.F. w/B. below wreath	—	80.00	110.00	160.00

c/s: On Peru 5 Pesetas, KM#201.3.

KM#	Date	Year	Mintage	Fine	VF	XF
226	1894	1881 B	—	Reported, not confirmed		
		1882 LM	—	300.00	500.00	800.00

c/s: On Salvador Peso, KM#115.1.

KM#	Date	Year	Mintage	Fine	VF	XF
227	1894	1892	—	1000.	1400.	2000.
		1893	—	1000.	1400.	2000.
		1894	—	Reported, not confirmed		

PROVISIONAL COINAGE

12-1/2 CENTAVOS

BRONZE

KM#	Date	Mintage	Fine	VF	XF	Unc
230	1915	6.000	.75	1.25	3.00	8.00

25 CENTAVOS

BRONZE

KM#	Date	Mintage	Fine	VF	XF	Unc
231	1915	4.000	.75	1.25	2.50	6.50

50 CENTAVOS

ALUMINUM-BRONZE
Thin numerals in denomination.

KM#	Date	Mintage	Fine	VF	XF	Unc
232.1	1922	3.803	.65	1.00	3.00	8.50

Thick numerals in denomination.

KM#	Date	Mintage	Fine	VF	XF	Unc
232.2	1922	Inc. Ab.	.65	1.00	3.00	8.50

PESO

ALUMINUM-BRONZE

KM#	Date	Mintage	Fine	VF	XF	Unc
233	1923	1.477	1.00	1.50	3.50	12.50

5 PESOS

ALUMINUM-BRONZE

KM#	Date	Mintage	Fine	VF	XF	Unc
234	1923	.440	1.50	2.75	6.50	22.50

MONETARY REFORM

100 Centavos = 1 Quetzal

MEDIO (1/2) CENTAVO

BRASS

KM#	Date	Mintage	Fine	VF	XF	Unc
248	1932	6.000	.15	.50	1.00	4.00
	1932	—	—	—	Proof	—
	1946	.640	.50	1.00	2.50	10.00

UN (1) CENTAVO

COPPER
Obv: Incuse legend on scroll.

KM#	Date	Mintage	Fine	VF	XF	Unc
237	1925	.357	3.50	6.50	13.50	32.50

BRONZE

KM#	Date	Mintage	Fine	VF	XF	Unc
237a	1925	Inc. Ab.	5.00	8.00	15.00	42.50

KM#	Date	Mintage	Fine	VF	XF	Unc
247	1929	.500	2.00	3.00	6.00	22.50
	1929	—	—	—	Proof	—

BRASS

KM#	Date	Mintage	Fine	VF	XF	Unc
249	1932	3.000	.40	1.00	3.00	10.00
	1932	—	—	—	Proof	—
	1933	1.500	.60	1.50	4.50	12.00
	1933	—	—	—	Proof	—
	1934	1.000	.50	1.25	4.50	12.00
	1934	—	—	—	Proof	—
	1936	1.500	.40	1.00	4.50	12.00
	1936	—	—	—	Proof	—
	1938/7	1.000	.40	1.00	5.00	12.50
	1938	Inc. Ab.	.40	1.00	4.50	12.00
	1938	—	—	—	Proof	—
	1939	1.500	.50	1.25	4.50	9.50
	1939	—	—	—	Proof	—
	1946	.539	—	.10	.50	4.50
	1947	1.121	—	.10	.25	2.50
	1948	1.651	—	.10	.25	3.50
	1949	1.022	—	.10	.35	3.50

KM#	Date	Mintage	Fine	VF	XF	Unc
251	1943	.450	3.00	6.00	10.00	20.00
	1944	2.050	.50	1.25	2.50	8.00

KM#	Date	Mintage	Fine	VF	XF	Unc
254	1949	1.091	—	.10	.25	3.50
	1950	3.663	—	.10	.20	1.75
	1951	3.586	—	.10	.40	1.00
	1952	1.445	—	.10	.20	1.00
	1953	2.214	—	.10	.20	1.00
	1954	1.455	—	.10	.25	2.25

NICKEL-BRASS
Obv: Larger bust.

KM#	Date	Mintage	Fine	VF	XF	Unc
259	1954	10.000	—	—	.10	.50
	1957	1.600	—	.10	.15	.75
	1958	2.000	—	.10	.15	.60

BRASS
Obv: Larger legend.

KM#	Date	Mintage	Fine	VF	XF	Unc
260	1958	10.001	—	—	.10	.35
	1961	1.826	—	—	.10	.20
	1963	4.926	—	—	.10	.20
	1964	4.280	—	—	.10	.20

Size reduced, 19mm.

KM#	Date	Mintage	Fine	VF	XF	Unc
265	1965	3.845	—	—	.10	.15
	1966	6.100	—	—	.10	.15
	1967	6.400	—	—	.10	.15
	1968	2.590	—	—	.10	.15
	1969	13.780	—	—	.10	.15
	1970	10.511	—	—	.10	.15

NOTE: Varieties in size and style of date exist.

KM#	Date	Mintage	Fine	VF	XF	Unc
273	1972	11.500	—	—	.10	.15
	1973	12.000	—	—	.10	.15

Obv: Incuse legend on scroll. Rev: Large head.

KM#	Date	Mintage	Fine	VF	XF	Unc
275.1	1974	10.000	—	—	.10	.15
	1975	15.000	—	—	.10	.15
	1976	15.230	—	—	.10	.15
	1977	30.000	—	—	.10	.15
	1978	30.000	—	—	.10	.15
	1979	30.000	—	—	.10	.15

Rev: Small head.

KM#	Date	Mintage	Fine	VF	XF	Unc
275.2	1979	Inc. Ab.	—	—	.10	.15
	1980	20.000	—	—	.10	.15
	1984	20.000	—	—	.10	.15
	1985	—	—	—	.10	.15
	1986	—	—	—	.10	.15
	1987	50.000	—	—	.10	.15
	1988	51.400	—	—	.10	.15
	1989	—	—	—	.10	.15
	1990	—	—	—	.10	.15
	1991	—	—	—	.10	.15
	1992	—	—	—	.10	.15

Obv: Legend on scroll in relief.

KM#	Date	Mintage	Fine	VF	XF	Unc
275.3	1981	30.000	—	—	.10	.15
	1982	30.000	—	—	.10	.15

NOTE: Varieties exist.

Rev: New portrait of Las Casas.

KM#	Date	Mintage	Fine	VF	XF	Unc
275.4	1993	—	—	—	.10	.15

DOS (2) CENTAVOS

BRASS

KM#	Date	Mintage	Fine	VF	XF	Unc
250	1932	3.000	.50	1.25	3.50	17.50
	1932	—	—	—	Proof	—

KM#	Date	Mintage	Fine	VF	XF	Unc
252	1943	.150	3.00	7.50	12.00	30.00
	1944	1.100	.60	2.00	3.75	10.00

5 CENTAVOS

1.6667 g, .720 SILVER, .0386 oz ASW
Obv: Long-tailed quetzal.

KM#	Date	Mintage	Fine	VF	XF	Unc
238.1	1925	.573	3.00	5.75	11.50	25.00
	1944	1.026	BV	1.00	2.00	10.00
	1945	4.026	BV	.75	1.50	7.50
	1947	1.834	BV	1.00	1.50	4.50
	1948	1.103	BV	1.00	1.50	9.00
	1949	.551	.50	1.50	2.50	11.00

2.5000 g, .900 GOLD, .0723 oz AGW

KM#	Date	Mintage	Fine	VF	XF	Unc
238.1a	1925	8 pcs.	—	—	750.00	950.00

1.6667 g, .720 SILVER, .0386 oz ASW
Obv: Short-tailed quetzal.

KM#	Date	Mintage	Fine	VF	XF	Unc
238.2	1928	1.000	BV	1.00	2.00	7.50
	1928	—	—	—	Proof	—
	1929	1.000	BV	1.00	2.00	7.50
	1929	—	—	—	Proof	—
	1932	2.000	BV	1.00	1.50	6.50
	1932	—	—	—	Proof	—
	1933	.600	BV	1.00	2.50	9.00
	1933	—	—	—	Proof	—
	1934	1.200	BV	1.00	2.00	7.50
	1934	—	—	—	Proof	—
	1937	.400	BV	1.00	1.50	7.50
	1937	—	—	—	Proof	—
	1938	.300	.50	1.50	2.50	9.00
	1938	—	—	—	Proof	—
	1943	.900	BV	.75	1.50	5.00

Mule. Obv: KM238.1. Rev: KM255.

KM#	Date	Mintage	Fine	VF	XF	Unc
A255	1949	Inc.KM255	65.00	125.00	200.00	375.00

KM#	Date	Mintage	Fine	VF	XF	Unc
255	1949	.305	.50	1.50	3.50	12.50

NOTE: Varieties exist.

KM#	Date	Mintage	Fine	VF	XF	Unc
257.1	1950	.453	BV	1.00	2.00	9.00
	1951	1.032	BV	1.00	1.50	5.00
	1952	.913	BV	1.00	1.50	4.00
	1953	.447	BV	1.00	2.50	4.00
	1954	.520	BV	1.00	1.50	8.00
	1955	2.062	BV	1.00	1.50	3.00
	1956	1.301	BV	1.00	1.50	3.00
	1957	2.941	BV	1.00	1.50	2.50

2.7300 g, .620 GOLD, .0544 oz AGW

KM#	Date	Mintage	Fine	VF	XF	Unc
257.1a	1953	25 pcs.	—	—	—	550.00

NOTE: Distributed amongst delegates.

Small crude date **Large crude date**

1.6667 g, .720 SILVER, .0386 oz ASW
Obv: Short-tailed quetzal.

KM#	Date	Mintage	Fine	VF	XF	Unc
257.2	1958 small date					
		3.025	BV	.75	1.00	1.50
	1958 large date					
		Inc. Ab.	BV	1.00	1.50	3.00

Obv: Long-tailed quetzal.

KM#	Date	Mintage	Fine	VF	XF	Unc
257.3	1958 small date					
		Inc. Ab.	BV	1.00	1.50	3.00
	1959	.232	BV	1.00	1.50	2.00

Rev: Level ground at tree.

KM#	Date	Mintage	Fine	VF	XF	Unc
261	1960	4.770	—	BV	.50	1.00
	1961	6.756	—	BV	.50	1.00
	1964	1.529	—	BV	.50	1.00

COPPER-NICKEL

KM#	Date	Mintage	Fine	VF	XF	Unc
266	1965	1.642	—	.10	.50	2.00
	1966	3.600	—	—	.10	.25
	1967	2.800	—	—	.10	.25
	1968	4.030	—	—	.10	.25
	1969	7.210	—	—	.10	.25
	1970	8.121	—	—	.10	.25

NOTE: Varieties exist.

KM#	Date	Mintage	Fine	VF	XF	Unc
270	1971	8.270	—	—	.10	.25
	1974	10.575	—	—	.10	.25
	1975	10.000	—	—	.10	.25
	1976	6.000	—	—	.10	.25
	1977	20.000	—	—	.10	.25

Obv: Legend on scroll incuse.

KM#	Date	Mintage	Fine	VF	XF	Unc
276.1	1977	Inc. Ab.	—	—	.10	.25
	1978	15.000	—	—	.10	.20
	1979	12.000	—	—	.10	.20

Obv: Legend on scroll in relief.

KM#	Date	Mintage	Fine	VF	XF	Unc
276.2	1980	8.000	—	—	.10	.20

Rev: Different tree.

KM#	Date	Mintage	Fine	VF	XF	Unc
276.3	1981	8.000	—	—	.10	.20
	1985	—	—	—	.10	.20

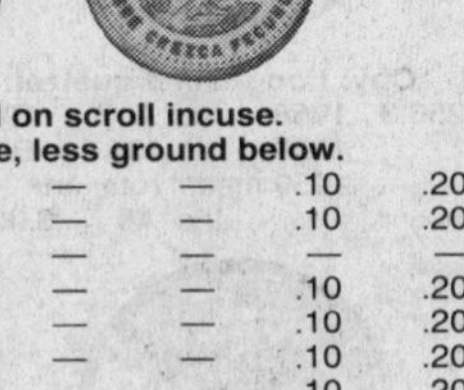

Obv: Legend on scroll incuse.
Rev: Smaller tree, less ground below.

KM#	Date	Mintage	Fine	VF	XF	Unc
276.4	1985	—	—	—	.10	.20
	1986 lg. date	—	—	—	.10	.20
	1986 sm. date	—	—	—	—	—
	1987	25.000	—	—	.10	.20
	1988	21.800	—	—	.10	.20
	1989	—	—	—	.10	.20
	1990	—	—	—	.10	.20
	1991	—	—	—	.10	.20
	1992	—	—	—	.10	.20
	1993	—	—	—	.10	.20

NOTE: Varieties exist.

10 CENTAVOS

3.3333 g, .720 SILVER, .0772 oz ASW
Obv: Long-tailed quetzal.

KM#	Date	Mintage	Fine	VF	XF	Unc
239.1	1925	.573	3.50	6.50	13.50	30.00
	1944	.155	1.00	2.75	5.75	15.00
	1945	1.499	BV	1.25	2.00	4.00
	1947	.471	BV	1.50	2.50	7.50
	1948	.324	BV	1.50	2.50	4.50
	1949	.145	BV	2.00	3.50	10.00

NOTE: Varieties exist.

.900 GOLD

KM#	Date	Mintage	Fine	VF	XF	Unc
239.1a	1925	8 pcs.	—	—	Rare	—

3.3333 g, .720 SILVER, .0772 oz ASW
Obv: Short-tailed quetzal.

KM#	Date	Mintage	Fine	VF	XF	Unc
239.2	1928	.500	BV	2.50	5.00	10.00
	1928	—	—	—	Proof	—
	1929	.500	BV	2.00	3.50	12.50
	1929	—	—	—	Proof	—
	1932	.500	BV	2.00	3.50	10.00
	1932	—	—	—	Proof	—
	1933	.650	BV	1.75	3.00	10.00
	1933	—	—	—	Proof	—
	1934	.300	BV	1.75	3.00	15.00
	1934	—	—	—	Proof	—
	1936	.200	BV	2.50	4.50	17.50
	1936	—	—	—	Proof	—
	1938	.150	1.00	3.00	5.00	12.50
	1938	—	—	—	Proof	—
	1943	.600	BV	1.25	2.50	7.50
	1947					
		Inc.KM239.1	BV	2.50	3.00	7.50

Rev: Small monolith.

KM#	Date	Mintage	Fine	VF	XF	Unc
256.1	1949	.281	BV	2.50	3.50	10.00
	1950	.550	BV	1.50	2.50	5.00
	1951	.263	BV	2.50	4.50	12.00
	1952	.307	BV	1.50	2.50	5.00
	1953	.388	BV	1.50	2.50	5.00
	1955	.896	BV	1.50	2.50	5.00
	1956	.501	BV	1.50	2.50	7.50
	1958	1.528	BV	1.50	2.50	6.00

Rev: Larger monolith.

KM#	Date	Mintage	Fine	VF	XF	Unc
256.2	1957	1.123	BV	1.25	2.00	3.00
	1958	Inc. Ab.	BV	1.50	2.50	5.00
	1958 medal rotation					
		Inc. Ab.	6.00	12.00	22.50	40.00

Obv: Long-tailed quetzal. Rev: Small monolith.

KM#	Date	Mintage	Fine	VF	XF	Unc
256.3	1958	Inc. Ab.	BV	1.25	2.00	3.00
	1959	.461	BV	1.25	2.00	3.00
	1959 medal rotation					
		Inc. Ab.	6.00	12.00	22.50	37.50

KM#	Date	Mintage	Fine	VF	XF	Unc
262	1960	1.743	BV	1.50	2.00	2.50
	1961	2.647	BV	1.50	2.00	2.50
	1964	.965	BV	1.50	2.00	2.50

COPPER-NICKEL

KM#	Date	Mintage	Fine	VF	XF	Unc
267	1965	2.227	—	.10	.20	.60
	1966	1.550	—	.10	.25	.70
	1967	3.120	—	.10	.20	.50
	1968	3.220	—	.10	.20	.50
	1969	3.530	—	.10	.20	.50
	1970	4.153	—	.10	.20	.50

NOTE: Varieties exist.

KM#	Date	Mintage	Fine	VF	XF	Unc
271	1971	4.580	—	.10	.20	.50
	1973	1.100	—	.10	.25	.70

KM#	Date	Mintage	Fine	VF	XF	Unc
274	1974	3.500	—	.10	.20	.50
	1975 dots flank date					
		6.000	—	.10	.20	.50

Wide rim toothed border.

KM#	Date	Mintage	Fine	VF	XF	Unc
277.1	1976	2.000	—	.10	.20	.50

Obv: Legend on scroll incuse.

KM#	Date	Mintage	Fine	VF	XF	Unc
277.2	1977	5.000	—	.10	.20	.35

Round beads instead of toothed border.

KM#	Date	Mintage	Fine	VF	XF	Unc
277.3	1978	8.500	—	.10	.20	.35
	1979	11.000	—	.10	.20	.35

Rev: Larger 10.

KM#	Date	Mintage	Fine	VF	XF	Unc
277.6	1986	—	—	.10	.20	.35
	1987	17.000	—	.10	.20	.35
	1988	13.250	—	.10	.20	.35
	1989	—	—	.10	.20	.35
	1990	—	—	.10	.20	.35
	1991	—	—	.10	.20	.35
	1992	—	—	.10	.20	.35

Obv: Legend on scroll in relief, quetzal in silhouette. Rev: Different design.

KM#	Date	Mintage	Fine	VF	XF	Unc
277.4	1980	5.000	—	.10	.20	.35
	1981	4.000	—	.10	.20	.35

Obv: Quetzal is solid, larger monolith.

KM#	Date	Mintage	Fine	VF	XF	Unc
277.5	1983	20.000	—	.10	.20	.35
	1986	—	—	.10	.20	.35

1/4 QUETZAL

8.3333 g, .720 SILVER, .1929 oz ASW
Lettered edge

KM#	Date	Mintage	Fine	VF	XF	Unc
240.1	1925	1.160	3.75	7.50	22.50	55.00

Obv: W/o NOBLE below scroll.

KM#	Date	Mintage	Fine	VF	XF	Unc
240.2	1925	Inc. Ab.	37.50	75.00	185.00	425.00

.900 GOLD

KM#	Date	Mintage	Fine	VF	XF	Unc
240a	1925	8 pcs.	—	—	Rare	—

8.3333 g, .720 SILVER, .1929 oz ASW
Rev: Larger design.

KM#	Date	Mintage	Fine	VF	XF	Unc
243.1	1926	2.000	2.00	4.00	10.00	30.00
	1928	.400	2.50	4.50	10.00	32.50
	1928	—	—	—	Proof	—
	1929	.400	2.50	5.00	12.50	35.00
	1929	—	—	—	Proof	—

Reeded edge

KM#	Date	Mintage	Fine	VF	XF	Unc
243.2	1946	.203	3.00	6.50	13.50	20.00
	1947	.134	3.50	7.00	12.00	16.50
	1948	.129	3.50	6.50	11.50	16.00
	1949/8	.025	5.50	8.50	15.00	25.00
	1949	Inc. Ab.	20.00	50.00	100.00	175.00

25 CENTAVOS

8.3333 g, .720 SILVER, .1929 oz ASW

KM#	Date	Mintage	Fine	VF	XF	Unc
253	1943	.900	2.25	5.50	10.00	40.00
A258	1949	—	60.00	120.00	200.00	375.00

KM#	Date	Mintage	Fine	VF	XF	Unc
258	1950	.081	2.00	4.00	8.00	17.50
	1951	.011	6.00	15.00	25.00	75.00
	1952	.112	BV	2.50	6.00	10.00
	1954	.246	BV	2.50	5.00	8.00
	1955	.409	BV	2.50	5.00	8.00
	1956	.342	BV	2.50	5.00	8.00
	1957	.257	BV	2.50	5.00	8.00
	1958	.394	BV	2.50	5.00	8.00
	1959/8	.277	BV	2.50	6.00	10.00
	1959	Inc. Ab.	BV	2.50	5.00	8.00

KM#	Date	Mintage	Fine	VF	XF	Unc
263	1960	.560	BV	2.25	3.25	6.00
	1960 medal rotation					
		Inc. Ab.	20.00	50.00	100.00	175.00
	1961	.750	BV	2.25	3.25	6.00
	1963	1.100	BV	2.00	3.00	5.50
	1964	.299	BV	2.25	3.25	6.00

COPPER-NICKEL

KM#	Date	Mintage	Fine	VF	XF	Unc
268	1965	1.178	.10	.15	.50	1.75
	1966	.910	.10	.15	.50	1.75

Rev: Modified design.

KM#	Date	Mintage	Fine	VF	XF	Unc
269	1967	1.140	.10	.15	.50	1.75
	1968	1.540	.10	.15	.50	1.50
	1969	2.070	.10	.15	.50	1.50
	1970	2.501	.10	.15	.50	1.50

KM#	Date	Mintage	Fine	VF	XF	Unc
272	1971	2.850	.10	.15	.40	1.00
	1975	1.592	.10	.15	.40	1.00
	1976	2.000	.10	.15	.40	1.00

Obv: Legend on scroll incuse. Rev: Large head.

KM#	Date	Mintage	Fine	VF	XF	Unc
278.1	1977	2.000	.10	.15	.40	1.00
	1978	4.400	.10	.15	.30	.75
	1979	5.400	.10	.15	.30	.75

Obv: Legend on scroll in relief. Rev: Small head. Wide rim.

KM#	Date	Mintage	Fine	VF	XF	Unc
278.2	1981	1.600	.10	.15	.40	1.00

Obv: Quetzal is solid. Narrow rim.

KM#	Date	Mintage	Fine	VF	XF	Unc
278.4	1982	2.000	.10	.15	.40	1.00

Obv: Legend on scroll incuse.

KM#	Date	Mintage	Fine	VF	XF	Unc
278.3	1984	2.000	.10	.15	.40	1.00
	1985	—	.10	.15	.30	.75
	1986	—	.10	.15	.30	.75
	1987	13.316	.10	.15	.30	.75
	1988	6.600	.10	.15	.30	.75
	1989	—	.10	.15	.30	.75
	1990	—	.10	.15	.30	.75
	1991	—	.10	.15	.30	.75
	1992	—	.10	.15	.30	.75
	1993	—	.10	.15	.30	.75

NOTE: Varieties exist in number of wing feathers, details on head and style of 25.

1/2 QUETZAL

16.6667 g, .720 SILVER, .3858 oz ASW

KM#	Date	Mintage	Fine	VF	XF	Unc
241.1	1925	.400	17.50	27.50	60.00	175.00

Obv: W/o NOBLE below scroll.

KM#	Date	Mintage	Fine	VF	XF	Unc
241.2	1925	Inc. Ab.	70.00	100.00	200.00	700.00

50 CENTAVOS

12.0000 g, .720 SILVER, .2777 oz ASW

KM#	Date	Mintage	Fine	VF	XF	Unc
264	1962	1.983	—	BV	2.50	5.00
	1963/2	.350	3.50	7.50	12.50	20.00
	1963	Inc. Ab.	—	BV	2.50	5.00

QUETZAL

33.3333 g, .720 SILVER, .7716 oz ASW

KM#	Date	Mintage	Fine	VF	XF	Unc
242	1925	*.010	475.00	650.00	950.00	2000.

***NOTE:** 7,000 pcs. were withdrawn and remelted soon after issue and more met with the same fate in 1932.

27.0000 g, .925 SILVER, .8030 oz ASW
Carlos Merida

KM#	Date	Mintage	Fine	VF	XF	Unc
279	1992	—	—	—	Proof	50.00

5 QUETZALES

8.3592 g, .900 GOLD, .2419 oz AGW

KM#	Date	Mintage	Fine	VF	XF	Unc
244	1926	.048	150.00	200.00	250.00	350.00

10 QUETZALES

16.7185 g, .900 GOLD, .4838 oz AGW

KM#	Date	Mintage	Fine	VF	XF	Unc
245	1926	.018	275.00	350.00	425.00	750.00

20 QUETZALES

33.4370 g, .900 GOLD, .9676 oz AGW

KM#	Date	Mintage	Fine	VF	XF	Unc
246	1926	.049	450.00	550.00	750.00	1000.

PROOF SETS (PS)

KM#	Date	Mintage	Identification	Issue Price	Mkt. Val.
PS1	1894H(6)	—	KM162,165-167,168.1,210	—	1800.
PS2	1895/1896(6)	—	KM162,165-167,210, 4 Reales 1895 Pn9	—	Rare

GUERNSEY

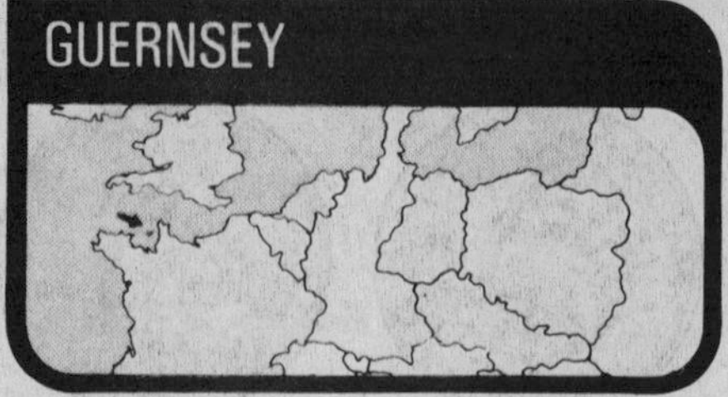

The Bailiwick of Guernsey, a British crown dependency located in the English Channel 30 miles (48 km.) west of Normandy, France, has an area of 30 sq. mi. (194 sq. km.) (including the isles of Alderney, Jethou, Herm, Brechou, and Sark), and a population of 54,000. Capital: St. Peter Port. Agriculture and cattle breeding are the main occupations.

Militant monks from the duchy of Normandy established the first permanent settlements on Guernsey prior to the Norman invasion of England, but the prevalence of prehistoric monuments suggests an earlier occupancy. The island, the only part of the duchy of Normandy belonging to the British crown, has been a possession of Britain since the Norman Conquest of 1066. During the Anglo-French wars, the harbors of Guernsey were employed in the building and outfitting of ships for the English privateers preying on French shipping. Guernsey is administered by its own laws and customs. Acts passed by the British Parliament are not applicable to Guernsey unless the island is specifically mentioned. During World War II, German troops occupied the island from June 30, 1940 till May 9, 1945.

RULERS

British

MINT MARKS

H - Heaton, Birmingham

MONETARY SYSTEM

8 Doubles = 1 Penny
12 Pence = 1 Shilling
5 Shillings = 1 Crown
20 Shillings = 1 Pound

1 Stem

3 Stems

DOUBLE

COPPER

KM#	Date	Mintage	Fine	VF	XF	Unc
1	1830	1.649	1.00	3.00	8.50	25.00
	.1830	Inc. Ab.	5.00	15.00	30.00	45.00
	1868/30	.064	1.50	4.50	12.50	30.00
	1868	Inc. Ab.	2.00	6.00	18.00	37.50

BRONZED COPPER

KM#	Date	Mintage	Fine	VF	XF	Unc
1a	1830	—	—	—	Proof	250.00

BRONZE

KM#	Date	Mintage	Fine	VF	XF	Unc
10	1885H	.056	.50	1.50	4.50	12.50
	1885H	—	—	—	Proof	175.00
	1889H	.112	.30	.85	3.00	7.50
	1889H	—	—	—	Proof	200.00
	1893H	.056	.50	1.50	4.50	12.50
	1899H	.056	.25	.75	3.00	8.50
	1902H	.084	.20	.60	2.25	4.00
	1902H	—	—	—	Proof	250.00
	1903H	.112	.15	.30	1.25	2.50
	1911H	.045	.50	1.50	4.00	12.00

BRONZED COPPER

KM#	Date	Mintage	Fine	VF	XF	Unc
10a	1885H	—	—	—	Proof	275.00

BRONZE

KM#	Date	Mintage	Fine	VF	XF	Unc
11	1911H	.090	.30	1.20	3.00	6.00
	1914H	.045	1.50	3.00	6.00	12.00
	1929H	.079	.30	.85	2.50	5.50
	1933H	.096	.30	.85	2.50	5.50
	1938H	.096	.30	.85	2.50	5.50

2 DOUBLES

COPPER

KM#	Date	Mintage	Fine	VF	XF	Unc
4	1858	.056	6.00	18.00	55.00	125.00

BRONZE

Obv: Leaves w/1 stem.

KM#	Date	Mintage	Fine	VF	XF	Unc
8	1868	.035	7.50	13.50	35.00	70.00
	1874	.045	4.50	9.00	25.00	50.00
	1885H	.071	1.25	2.75	6.00	12.00
	1885H	—	—	—	Proof	175.00
	1889H	.036	.85	3.00	8.00	15.00
	1889H	—	—	—	Proof	200.00
	1899H	.036	.85	3.00	9.00	18.50
	1902H	.018	4.50	9.00	21.00	32.50
	1902H	—	—	—	Proof	250.00
	1903H	.018	6.00	12.50	25.00	37.50
	1906H	.018	6.00	12.50	25.00	37.50
	1908H	.018	6.00	12.50	25.00	37.50
	1911H	.029	4.50	9.00	15.00	27.50

BRONZED COPPER

KM#	Date	Mintage	Fine	VF	XF	Unc
8a	1885H	—	—	—	Proof	275.00

BRONZE

Obv: Leaves w/3 stems.

KM#	Date	Mintage	Fine	VF	XF	Unc
9	1868	Inc. KM8	7.50	13.50	35.00	70.00

KM#	Date	Mintage	Fine	VF	XF	Unc
12	1914H	.029	4.50	9.00	18.50	27.50
	1914H	—	—	—	Proof	125.00
	1917H	.015	20.00	40.00	80.00	175.00
	1918H	.057	1.25	2.50	9.00	15.00
	1920H	.057	1.25	2.50	9.00	15.00
	1929H	.079	.35	1.25	6.00	10.00

4 DOUBLES

COPPER

KM#	Date	Mintage	Fine	VF	XF	Unc
2	1830	.655	2.25	7.50	30.00	60.00
	1830	—	—	—	Proof	275.00
	1858	.114	3.00	15.00	30.00	60.00

NOTE: A rare mule restrike exists of the St. Helena obv. 1/2 Penny 1821 and rev. of Guernsey 4 Doubles dated 1830. Market valuation $600.00 (VF).

BRONZED COPPER

KM#	Date	Mintage	Fine	VF	XF	Unc
2a	1830	—	—	—	Proof	350.00

BRONZE

Obv: Leaves w/3 stems.

KM#	Date	Mintage	Fine	VF	XF	Unc
5	1864/54	.213	.85	1.75	9.00	18.50
	1868	.058	2.25	4.00	12.50	25.00
	1874	.069	1.50	3.00	11.50	22.50
	1885H	.070	1.25	2.25	7.50	20.00
	1885H	—	—	—	Proof	175.00
	1889H	.104	.75	1.25	6.00	15.00
	1889H	—	—	—	Proof	200.00
	1893H	.052	1.50	3.00	7.50	20.00
	1902H	.105	.85	1.75	3.00	7.50
	1902H	—	—	—	Proof	250.00
	1903H	.052	1.50	3.00	9.00	25.00
	1906H	.052	1.50	3.00	9.00	25.00
	1908H	.026	3.00	7.50	15.00	30.00
	1910H	.052	1.50	3.00	9.00	25.00
	1910H	—	—	—	Proof	250.00
	1911H	.052	2.25	4.50	13.50	27.50

NOTE: Varieties exist.

BRONZED COPPER

KM#	Date	Mintage	Fine	VF	XF	Unc
5a	1885H	—	—	—	Proof	275.00

BRONZE

Obv: Leaves w/1 stem.

KM#	Date	Mintage	Fine	VF	XF	Unc
6	1864	Inc. KM5	1.25	2.25	9.00	18.50

KM#	Date	Mintage	Fine	VF	XF	Unc
13	1914H	.209	.75	1.50	4.50	12.50
	1918H	.157	.75	1.50	6.00	17.50
	1920H	.157	.45	1.25	4.50	10.00
	1945H	.096	.45	1.25	4.50	10.00
	1949H	.019	1.50	3.00	12.00	20.00

Guernsey Lily

KM#	Date	Mintage	Fine	VF	XF	Unc
15	1956	.240	.25	.50	.75	2.25
	1956	2,100	—	—	Proof	5.00
	1966	.010	—	—	Proof	2.00

8 DOUBLES

COPPER

KM#	Date	Mintage	Fine	VF	XF	Unc
3	1834	.222	4.00	10.00	25.00	75.00
	1834	—	—	—	Proof	350.00
	1858	.111	5.00	12.50	25.00	65.00
	1858	—	—	—	Proof	375.00

BRONZED COPPER

KM#	Date	Mintage	Fine	VF	XF	Unc
3a	1834	—	—	—	Proof	550.00

BRONZE

KM#	Date	Mintage	Fine	VF	XF	Unc
7	1864	.280	1.25	3.00	9.00	27.50
	1864	—	—	—	Proof	175.00
	1868	.060	4.00	9.00	27.50	55.00
	1874	.070	2.25	4.50	9.00	20.00
	1885H	.070	1.50	3.00	9.00	20.00
	1885H	—	—	—	Proof	200.00
	1889H	.222	.75	2.25	6.00	12.50
	1889H	—	—	—	Proof	175.00
	1893H	.118	1.50	3.00	6.00	15.00
	1893H large date and denomination					
		Inc. Ab.	1.50	3.00	6.00	15.00
	1902H	.235	1.25	2.25	6.00	12.50
	1902H	—	—	—	Proof	250.00
	1903H	.118	.50	1.75	4.50	10.00

KM#	Date	Mintage	Fine	VF	XF	Unc
7	1910H	.091	1.25	2.50	12.50	25.00
	1910H	—	—	—	Proof	250.00
	1911H	.078	3.00	8.50	15.00	30.00

BRONZED COPPER

KM#	Date	Mintage	Fine	VF	XF	Unc
7a	1885H	—	—	—	Proof	325.00

BRONZE

KM#	Date	Mintage	Fine	VF	XF	Unc
14	1914H	.157	.65	1.75	4.50	10.00
	1914H	—	—	—	Proof	150.00
	1918H	.157	.65	1.75	4.50	10.00
	1920H	.157	.50	1.50	4.00	9.00
	1920H	—	—	—	Proof	150.00
	1934H	.124	.50	1.50	4.00	9.00
	1934H	500 pcs.	—	—	Proof	175.00
	1938H	.120	.50	1.50	4.00	9.00
	1938H	—	—	—	Proof	250.00
	1945H	.192	.40	.85	2.00	5.50
	1947H	.240	.30	.60	2.25	5.00
	1949H	.230	.30	.60	2.25	5.00

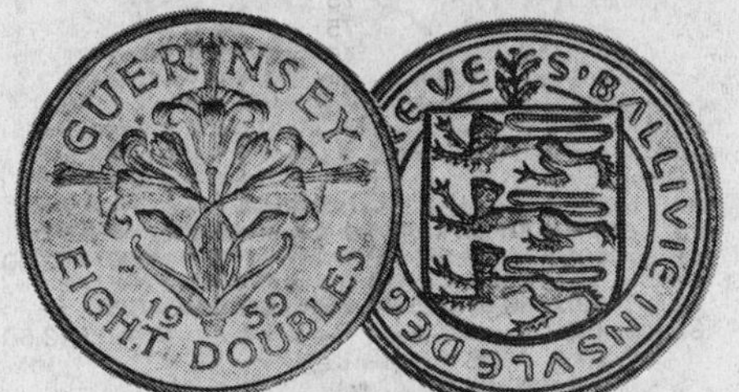

3 Flowered Lily

KM#	Date	Mintage	Fine	VF	XF	Unc
16	1956	.500	.10	.20	.50	1.50
	1956	2,100	—	—	Proof	5.00
	1959	.500	.10	.20	.50	1.50
	1959	—	—	—	Proof	—
	1966	.010	—	—	Proof	2.00

3 PENCE

COPPER-NICKEL
Guernsey Cow
Thin flan

KM#	Date	Mintage	Fine	VF	XF	Unc
17	1956	.500	.10	.20	.50	1.25
	1956	2,100	—	—	Proof	5.00

Thick flan

KM#	Date	Mintage	Fine	VF	XF	Unc
18	1959	.500	.10	.20	.50	1.00
	1959	—	—	—	Proof	150.00
	1966	.010	—	—	Proof	2.00

10 SHILLINGS

COPPER-NICKEL
900th Anniversary Norman Conquest

KM#	Date	Mintage	Fine	VF	XF	Unc
19	1966	.300	—	1.00	1.25	1.75
	1966	.010	—	—	Proof	4.00

DECIMAL COINAGE

100 Pence = 1 Pound

1/2 NEW PENNY

BRONZE

KM#	Date	Mintage	Fine	VF	XF	Unc
20	1971	2.066	—	—	.10	.25
	1971	.010	—	—	Proof	1.00

1/2 PENNY

BRONZE

KM#	Date	Mintage	Fine	VF	XF	Unc
33	1979	.020	—	—	Proof	1.00

NEW PENNY

BRONZE
Gannet

KM#	Date	Mintage	Fine	VF	XF	Unc
21	1971	1.922	—	—	.10	.20
	1971	.010	—	—	Proof	1.00

PENNY

BRONZE
Gannet

KM#	Date	Mintage	Fine	VF	XF	Unc
27	1977	.640	—	—	.10	.20
	1979	2.400	—	—	.10	.20
	1979	.020	—	—	Proof	1.00
	1981	.010	—	—	Proof	2.00

KM#	Date	Mintage	Fine	VF	XF	Unc
40	1985	.060	—	—	.10	.20
	1985	2,500	—	—	Proof	2.00
	1986	1.010	—	—	.10	.20
	1986	2,500	—	—	Proof	2.00
	1987	5,000	—	—	.10	.20
	1987	*2,500	—	—	Proof	2.00
	1988	.500	—	—	.10	.20
	1988	2,500	—	—	Proof	2.00
	1989	1.000	—	—	.10	.20
	1989	*2,500	—	—	Proof	2.00
	1990	5,000	—	—	.10	.20
	1990	700 pcs.	—	—	Proof	4.00

COPPER PLATED STEEL

KM#	Date	Mintage	Fine	VF	XF	Unc
40a	1992	*	—	—	—	.30
	1992	*	—	—	Proof	5.00

***NOTE:** In sets only.

2 NEW PENCE

BRONZE
Windmill From Sark

KM#	Date	Mintage	Fine	VF	XF	Unc
22	1971	1.680	—	—	.10	.30
	1971	.010	—	—	Proof	1.00

2 PENCE

BRONZE
Windmill From Sark

KM#	Date	Mintage	Fine	VF	XF	Unc
28	1977	.700	—	—	.10	.20
	1979	2.400	—	—	.10	.25
	1979	.020	—	—	Proof	1.00
	1981	.010	—	—	Proof	2.00

Guernsey Cow

KM#	Date	Mintage	Fine	VF	XF	Unc
41	1985	.060	—	—	.10	.20
	1985	2,500	—	—	Proof	2.00
	1986	.510	—	—	.10	.20
	1986	2,500	—	—	Proof	2.00
	1987	5,000	—	—	.10	.20
	1987	*2,500	—	—	Proof	2.00
	1988	.500	—	—	.10	.20
	1988	2,500	—	—	Proof	2.00
	1989	.500	—	—	.10	.20
	1989	*2,500	—	—	Proof	2.00
	1990	.380	—	—	.10	.20
	1990	700 pcs.	—	—	Proof	4.00

COPPER PLATED STEEL

KM#	Date	Mintage	Fine	VF	XF	Unc
41a	1992	*	—	—	—	.30
	1992	*	—	—	Proof	5.00

***NOTE:** In sets only.

5 NEW PENCE

COPPER-NICKEL
Guernsey Lily

KM#	Date	Mintage	Fine	VF	XF	Unc
23	1968	.800	—	.10	.15	.35
	1971	.010	—	—	Proof	2.00

5 PENCE

COPPER-NICKEL
Guernsey Lily

KM#	Date	Mintage	Fine	VF	XF	Unc
29	1977	.250	—	—	.15	.35
	1979	.200	—	—	.15	.40
	1979	.020	—	—	Proof	2.00
	1981	.010	—	—	Proof	3.00
	1982	.200	—	—	.15	.40

KM#	Date	Mintage	Fine	VF	XF	Unc
42.1	1985	.035	—	—	.15	.40
	1985	2,500	—	—	Proof	2.50
	1986	.100	—	—	.15	.40
	1986	2,500	—	—	Proof	2.50
	1987	.300	—	—	.15	.40
	1987	*2,500	—	—	Proof	2.50
	1988	.405	—	—	.15	.40
	1988	2,500	—	—	Proof	2.50
	1989	5,000	—	—	.15	.40
	1989	*2,500	—	—	Proof	2.50
	1990	*2,520	—	—	.15	.50
	1990	700 pcs.	—	—	Proof	5.00

Reduced size

KM#	Date	Mintage	Fine	VF	XF	Unc
42.2	1990	2.400	—	—	.15	.40
	1990	700 pcs.	—	—	Proof	5.00
	1992	.400	—	—	—	.50
	1992	*	—	—	Proof	6.00

***NOTE:** In sets only.

10 NEW PENCE

COPPER-NICKEL
Guernsey Cow

KM#	Date	Mintage	Fine	VF	XF	Unc
24	1968	.600	—	.20	.35	.75
	1970	.300	—	.20	.35	.75
	1971	.010	—	—	Proof	2.00

10 PENCE

COPPER-NICKEL
Guernsey Cow

KM#	Date	Mintage	Fine	VF	XF	Unc
30	1977	.480	—	—	.20	.50
	1979	.659	—	—	.20	.50
	1979	.020	—	—	Proof	3.00
	1981	.010	—	—	Proof	3.00
	1982	.200	—	—	.20	.60
	1984	.400	—	—	.20	.60

Tomato Plant

KM#	Date	Mintage	Fine	VF	XF	Unc
43.1	1985	.110	—	—	.20	.50
	1985	2,500	—	—	Proof	2.50
	1986	.300	—	—	.20	.50
	1986	2,500	—	—	Proof	6.00
	1987	.250	—	—	.20	.50
	1987	*2,500	—	—	Proof	2.50
	1988	.300	—	—	.20	.50
	1988	2,500	—	—	Proof	2.50
	1989	.200	—	—	.20	.50
	1989	*2,500	—	—	Proof	2.50
	1990	3,500	—	—	.20	.50
	1990	700 pcs.	—	—	Proof	5.00

Reduced size, 24.5mm.

KM#	Date	Mintage	Fine	VF	XF	Unc
43.2	1992	3.500	—	—	—	.50
	1992	*	—	—	Proof	6.00

***NOTE**: In sets only.

20 PENCE

COPPER-NICKEL
Guernsey Milk Can

KM#	Date	Mintage	Fine	VF	XF	Unc
38	1982	.500	—	—	.40	.75
	1983	.500	—	—	.40	.75

KM#	Date	Mintage	Fine	VF	XF	Unc
44	1985	.035	—	—	.40	.75
	1985	2,500	—	—	Proof	3.00
	1986	.010	—	—	.40	.75
	1986	2,500	—	—	Proof	3.00
	1987	5,000	—	—	.40	.75
	1987	*2,500	—	—	Proof	3.00
	1988	5,000	—	—	.40	.75
	1988	2,500	—	—	Proof	3.00
	1989	.093	—	—	.40	.75
	1989	*2,500	—	—	Proof	3.00
44	1990	.113	—	—	.40	.75
	1990	700 pcs.	—	—	Proof	6.00
	1992	.550	—	—	—	1.00
	1992	*	—	—	Proof	7.00

***NOTE**: In sets only.

25 PENCE

COPPER-NICKEL
25th Wedding Anniversary

KM#	Date	Mintage	Fine	VF	XF	Unc
26	1972	.056	—	—	3.00	6.50

28.2759 g, .925 SILVER, .8410 oz ASW

KM#	Date	Mintage	Fine	VF	XF	Unc
26a	1972	.015	—	—	Proof	15.00

COPPER-NICKEL
Queen's Silver Jubilee

KM#	Date	Mintage	Fine	VF	XF	Unc
31	1977	.207	—	—	1.00	2.00

28.2759 g, .925 SILVER, .8410 oz ASW

KM#	Date	Mintage	Fine	VF	XF	Unc
31a	1977	.025	—	—	Proof	12.50

COPPER-NICKEL
Royal Visit

KM#	Date	Mintage	Fine	VF	XF	Unc
32	1978	.105	—	—	1.00	2.00

28.2759 g, .925 SILVER, .8410 oz ASW

KM#	Date	Mintage	Fine	VF	XF	Unc
32a	1978	.025	—	—	Proof	12.50

COPPER-NICKEL
80th Birthday of Queen Mother

KM#	Date	Mintage	Fine	VF	XF	Unc
35	1980	.150	—	—	1.00	2.00

28.2759 g, .925 SILVER, .8410 oz ASW

KM#	Date	Mintage	Fine	VF	XF	Unc
35a	1980	.025	—	—	Proof	13.50

COPPER-NICKEL
Wedding of Prince Charles and Lady Diana
Obv: Similar to 25 New Pence, KM#35.

KM#	Date	Mintage	Fine	VF	XF	Unc
36	1981	.114	—	—	1.25	2.75

28.2759 g, .925 SILVER, .8410 oz ASW

KM#	Date	Mintage	Fine	VF	XF	Unc
36a	1981	.012	—	—	Proof	25.00

50 NEW PENCE

COPPER-NICKEL
Ducal Cap of Duke of Normandy

KM#	Date	Mintage	Fine	VF	XF	Unc
25	1969	.200	—	1.00	1.50	2.50
	1970	.200	—	1.00	1.50	2.50
	1971	.010	—	—	Proof	3.00

50 PENCE

COPPER-NICKEL
Ducal Cap of Duke of Normandy

KM#	Date	Mintage	Fine	VF	XF	Unc
34	1979	.020	—	—	Proof	4.50
	1981	.200	—	.90	1.10	1.60
	1981	.010	—	—	Proof	5.50
	1982	.150	—	.90	1.10	1.60

KM#	Date	Mintage	Fine	VF	XF	Unc
34	1983	.200	—	.90	1.10	1.60
	1984	.200	—	.90	1.10	1.60

KM#	Date	Mintage	Fine	VF	XF	Unc
45	1985	.035	—	.90	1.10	1.60
	1985	2,500	—	—	Proof	4.00
	1986	.010	—	.90	1.10	1.60
	1986	2,500	—	—	Proof	4.00
	1987	5,000	—	.90	1.10	1.60
	1987	*2,500	—	—	Proof	4.50
	1988	6,000	—	.90	1.10	1.60
	1988	2,500	—	—	Proof	4.50
	1989	.055	—	.90	1.10	1.60
	1989	*2,500	—	—	Proof	4.50
	1990	.080	—	.90	1.10	1.60
	1990	700 pcs.	—	—	Proof	7.50
	1992	.065	—	—	—	2.00
	1992	*	—	—	Proof	10.00

***NOTE:** In sets only.

POUND

COPPER-NICKEL-ZINC
Guernsey Lily

KM#	Date	Mintage	Fine	VF	XF	Unc
37	1981	.200	—	1.80	2.00	2.75
	1981	.010	—	—	Proof	4.50
	8.0000 g, .917 GOLD, .2358 oz AGW					
37a	1981	4,500	—	—	Proof	175.00

ALUMINUM-BRONZE
H.M.S. Crescent

KM#	Date	Mintage	Fine	VF	XF	Unc
39	1983	.269	—	1.80	2.00	2.75

COPPER-NICKEL-ZINC

KM#	Date	Mintage	Fine	VF	XF	Unc
46	1985	.035	—	—	1.75	2.50
	1985	2,500	—	—	Proof	6.50
	1986	.010	—	—	1.75	2.50
	1986	2,500	—	—	Proof	6.50
	1987	5,000	—	—	1.75	2.50
	1987	*2,500	—	—	Proof	6.50
	1988	5,000	—	—	1.75	2.50
	1988	2,500	—	—	Proof	6.50
	1989	5,000	—	—	1.75	2.50
	1989	*2,500	—	—	Proof	6.50
	1990	3,500	—	—	1.75	2.50
	1990	700 pcs.	—	—	Proof	10.00
	1992	*	—	—	—	3.50
	1992	*	—	—	Proof	12.50

***NOTE:** In sets only.

2 POUNDS

COPPER-NICKEL
40th Anniversary of Liberation from Germans

KM#	Date	Mintage	Fine	VF	XF	Unc
47	1985	.075	—	—	3.50	5.50
	1985	2,500	—	—	Proof	8.00
	28.2800 g, .925 SILVER, .8411 oz ASW					
47a	1985	2,500	—	—	Proof	35.00

COPPER-NICKEL
Commonwealth Games

KM#	Date	Mintage	Fine	VF	XF	Unc
48	1986	.010	—	—	—	6.00
	1986	—	—	—	Proof	10.00
	28.2800 g, .500 SILVER, .4547 oz ASW					
48a	1986	*.050	—	—	—	15.00
	28.2800 g, .925 SILVER, .8411 oz ASW					
48b	1986	*.020	—	—	Proof	30.00

COPPER-NICKEL
900th Anniversary - Death of
William The Conqueror

KM#	Date	Mintage	Fine	VF	XF	Unc
49	1987	.018	—	—	—	7.00
	1987	*2,500	—	—	Proof	10.00
	28.2800 g, .925 SILVER, .8411 oz ASW					
49a	1987	2,500	—	—	Proof	35.00
	47.5400 g, .917 GOLD, 1.4012 oz AGW					
49b	1987	90 pcs.	—	—	Proof	1550.

COPPER-NICKEL
William II

KM#	Date	Mintage	Fine	VF	XF	Unc
50	1988	7,500	—	—	—	6.50
	1988	2,500	—	—	Proof	10.00

28.2800 g, .925 SILVER, .8411 oz ASW

KM#	Date	Mintage	Fine	VF	XF	Unc
50a	1988	2,500	—	—	Proof	40.00

COPPER-NICKEL
Henry I

KM#	Date	Mintage	Fine	VF	XF	Unc
51	1989	.010	—	—	—	6.50
	1989	*2,500	—	—	Proof	10.00
	28.2800 g, .925 SILVER, .8411 oz ASW					
51a	1989	*2,500	—	—	Proof	45.00

COPPER-NICKEL
Royal Visit

KM#	Date	Mintage	Fine	VF	XF	Unc
52	1989	5,000	—	—	—	8.00
	28.2800 g, .925 SILVER, .8411 oz ASW					
52a	1989	5,000	—	—	Proof	45.00

COPPER-NICKEL
90th Birthday of Queen Mother

KM#	Date	Mintage	Fine	VF	XF	Unc
53	1990	9,000	—	—	—	8.00
	28.2800 g, .925 SILVER, .8411 oz ASW					
53a	1990	1,302	—	—	Proof	60.00

COPPER-NICKEL
Henry II

KM#	Date	Mintage	Fine	VF	XF	Unc
54	1991	—	—	—	—	7.50

28.2800 g, .925 SILVER, .8411 oz ASW

KM#	Date	Mintage	Fine	VF	XF	Unc
54a	1991	*2,500	—	—	Proof	60.00

COPPER-NICKEL
40th Anniversary of Coronation

KM#	Date	Mintage	Fine	VF	XF	Unc
55	ND(1993)	—	—	—	—	6.50

28.2800 g, .925 SILVER, .8411 oz ASW

KM#	Date	Mintage	Fine	VF	XF	Unc
55a	ND(1993)	*.010	—	—	Proof	55.00

TOKEN ISSUES (Tn)
Bishop de Jersey & Co./ Bank of Guernsey
5 SHILLINGS

.892 SILVER

KM#	Date	Mintage	VG	Fine	VF	XF
Tn1	1809	*7 known	—	—	Rare	—

NOTE: Spink R.J. Ford sale 10-90 good XF realized $19,380.

NOTE: The above issue was struck over Spanish or Spanish Colonial 8 Reales. They were forbidden by the Guernsey legislation to circulate in 1809.

MINT SETS (MS)

KM#	Date	Mintage	Identification	Issue Price	Mkt. Val.
MS1	1985(8)	10,000	KM40-41,42.1,43-47	8.75	11.25
MS2	1985(7)	—	KM40-41,42.1,43-46	—	—
MS3	1986(7)	5,000	KM40-46	8.75	5.75
MS4	1987(7)	7,500	KM40-46	11.00	5.75
MS5	1988(7)	5,000	KM40-46	13.00	14.00
MS6	1989(7)	*5,000	KM40-46	17.00	15.00
MS7	1990(8)	2,520	KM40-41,42.1-42.2,43-46	16.00	16.00
MS8	1992(7)	—	KM40-41,42.2,43-46	22.50	18.00

PROOF SETS (PS)

KM#	Date	Mintage	Identification	Issue Price	Mkt. Val.
PS1	1885H(4)	—	KM5,7,8,10	—	725.00
PS2	1885H(4)	—	KM5a,7a,8a,10a	—	1150.
PS3	1902H(4)	—	KM5,7-8,10	—	1000.
PS4	1910H(2)	—	KM5,7	—	500.00
PS5	1956(6)	1,050	KM15-17 double set	—	27.50
PS6	1966(4)	10,000	KM15-16,18,19	—	10.00
PS7	1971(6)	10,000	KM20-25	16.00	10.00
PS8	1979(6)	4,963	KM27-30,33-34	25.00	12.50
PS9	1981(6)	10,000	KM27-30,34,37	29.00	20.00
PS10	1985(8)	2,500	KM40-47	29.75	30.00
PS11	1986(8)	2,500	KM40-46,48	35.00	32.00
PS12	1987(8)	*2,500	KM40-46,49	33.00	32.00
PS13	1988(8)	2,500	KM40-46,50	45.00	32.00
PS14	1989(8)	*2,500	KM40-46,51	45.00	32.00
PS15	1990(8)	700	KM40-41,42.1-42.2,43-46	46.00	46.00
PS16	1992(7)	—	KM40-41,42.2,43.2,44-46	52.50	52.50

GUINEA

The Republic of Guinea, situated on the Atlantic Coast of Africa between Sierra Leone and Guinea-Bissau, has an area of 94,964 sq. mi. (245,860 sq. km.) and a population of 6.4 million. Capital: Conakry. Although Guinea contains one-third of the world's reserves of bauxite and significant deposits of iron ore, gold and diamonds, the economy is still dependent on argiculture. Aluminum, bananas, copra and coffee are exported.

The coast of Guinea was known to Portuguese navigators of the 15th century but was seldom visited by European traders of the 16th-18th centuries because of its dangerous coastal waters. French penetration of the area began in the mid-19th century with the entering into of protectorate treaties with several of the coastal chiefs. After a long struggle with Guinea's native leader Samory Toure, France secured the area and until 1890 administered it as a part of Senegal. In 1895 the colony (-Guinee Francais) became an autonomous part of the federation of French West Africa. The inhabitants were extended French citizenship in 1946 when the colony became an overseas territory of the French Union. Guinea became an independent republic on Oct. 2, 1958, when it declined to enter the new French Community.

MONETARY SYSTEM

100 Centimes = 1 Franc

FRANC

COPPER-NICKEL
Ahmed Sekou Toure

KM#	Date	Mintage	Fine	VF	XF	Unc
4	1962	—	1.00	1.75	3.00	6.50
	1962	—	—	—	Proof	50.00

5 FRANCS

ALUMINUM-BRONZE
Ahmed Sekou Toure

KM#	Date	Mintage	Fine	VF	XF	Unc
1	1959	—	2.50	4.00	8.00	20.00

COPPER-NICKEL

KM#	Date	Mintage	Fine	VF	XF	Unc
5	1962	—	1.00	1.50	2.50	5.00
	1962	—	—	—	Proof	70.00

10 FRANCS

ALUMINUM-BRONZE
Ahmed Sekou Toure

KM#	Date	Mintage	Fine	VF	XF	Unc
2	1959	—	5.00	8.00	16.00	35.00

COPPER-NICKEL

KM#	Date	Mintage	Fine	VF	XF	Unc
6	1962	—	1.50	2.50	4.50	9.00
	1962	—	—	—	Proof	85.00

25 FRANCS

ALUMINUM-BRONZE
Ahmed Sekou Toure

KM#	Date	Mintage	Fine	VF	XF	Unc
3	1959	—	9.00	15.00	25.00	75.00

COPPER-NICKEL

KM#	Date	Mintage	Fine	VF	XF	Unc
7	1962	—	2.50	4.00	7.50	14.00
	1962	—	—	—	Proof	120.00

50 FRANCS

COPPER-NICKEL
Ahmed Sekou Toure

KM#	Date	Mintage	Fine	VF	XF	Unc
8	1969	4.000	10.00	20.00	35.00	55.00

NOTE: Not released into circulation.

100 FRANCS

5.6500 g, .999 SILVER, .1816 oz ASW
10th Anniversary of Independence
Dr. Martin Luther King

KM#	Date	Mintage	Fine	VF	XF	Unc
9	1969	9,700	—	—	Proof	8.00
	1970	Inc. Ab.	—	—	Proof	8.00

COPPER-NICKEL
Ahmed Sekou Toure

KM#	Date	Mintage	Fine	VF	XF	Unc
41	1971	2.585	9.00	18.00	30.00	45.00

NOTE: Not released into circulation.

200 FRANCS

11.7000 g, .999 SILVER, .3761 oz ASW
10th Anniversary of Independence
John and Robert Kennedy

KM#	Date	Mintage	Fine	VF	XF	Unc
10	1969	.010	—	—	Proof	10.00
	1970	Inc. Ab.	—	—	Proof	10.00

10th Anniversary of Independence - Almany Toure

KM#	Date	Mintage	Fine	VF	XF	Unc
11	1969	6,100	—	—	Proof	12.50
	1970	Inc. Ab.	—	—	Proof	12.50

250 FRANCS

14.5300 g, .999 SILVER, .4671 oz ASW
10th Anniversary of Independence - Lunar Landing

KM#	Date	Mintage	Fine	VF	XF	Unc
12	1969	.026	—	—	Proof	15.00
	1970	Inc. Ab.	—	—	Proof	15.00

10th Anniversary of Independence -
Alpha Yaya Diallo

KM#	Date	Mintage	Fine	VF	XF	Unc
13	1969	6,100	—	—	Proof	16.50
	1970	Inc. Ab.	—	—	Proof	16.50

Apollo XIII

KM#	Date	Mintage	Fine	VF	XF	Unc
14	1969	4,450	—	—	Proof	17.50
	1970	Inc. Ab.	—	—	Proof	17.50

Spacecraft Sojuz

KM#	Date	Mintage	Fine	VF	XF	Unc
21	1970	3,500	—	—	Proof	22.00

500 FRANCS

29.0800 g, .999 SILVER, .9349 oz ASW
10th Anniversary of Independence -
Munich Olympics

KM#	Date	Mintage	Fine	VF	XF	Unc
15	1969	7,200	—	—	Proof	27.50
	1970	1,900	—	—	Proof	45.00

10th Anniversary of Independence -
Oiseaux Dancers
Rev: Similar to KM#15.

KM#	Date	Mintage	Fine	VF	XF	Unc
16	1969	7,150	—	—	Proof	27.50
	1970	—	—	—	Proof	45.00

Ikhnaton
Rev: Similar to KM#15.

KM#	Date	Mintage	Fine	VF	XF	Unc
22	1970	4,180	—	—	Proof	35.00

Chephren
Rev: Similar to KM#15.

KM#	Date	Mintage	Fine	VF	XF	Unc
23	1970	4,150	—	—	Proof	35.00

Cleopatra
Rev: Similar to KM#15.

KM#	Date	Mintage	Fine	VF	XF	Unc
24	1970	5,250	—	—	Proof	35.00

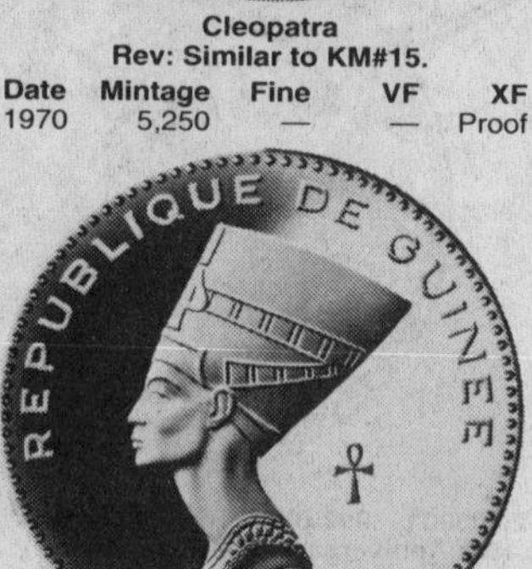

Queen Nefertiti
Rev: Similar to KM#15.

KM#	Date	Mintage	Fine	VF	XF	Unc
25	1970	4,610	—	—	Proof	35.00

Rameses III
Rev: Similar to KM#15.

KM#	Date	Mintage	Fine	VF	XF	Unc
26	1970	4,330	—	—	Proof	35.00

Tutankhamen
Rev: Similar to KM#15.

KM#	Date	Mintage	Fine	VF	XF	Unc
27	1970	4,280	—	—	Proof	37.50

Queen Teyi
Rev: Similar to KM#15.

KM#	Date	Mintage	Fine	VF	XF	Unc
28	1970	4,120	—	—	Proof	35.00

Gamal Abdel Nasser
Rev: Similar to KM#15.

KM#	Date	Mintage	Fine	VF	XF	Unc
29	1970	950	—	—	Proof	55.00

1000 FRANCS

4.0000 g, .900 GOLD, .1157 oz AGW
10th Anniversary of Independence
John and Robert Kennedy

KM#	Date	Mintage	Fine	VF	XF	Unc
17	1969	6,600	—	—	Proof	100.00
	1970	Inc. Ab.	—	—	Proof	100.00

2000 FRANCS

8.0000 g., .900 GOLD, .2315 oz AGW
10th Anniversary of Independence - Lunar Landing

KM#	Date	Mintage	Fine	VF	XF	Unc
18	1969	.015	—	—	Proof	140.00

Apollo XIII
Obv: Similar to 250 Francs, KM#14.

KM#	Date	Mintage	Fine	VF	XF	Unc
30	1970	1,775	—	—	Proof	165.00

Spacecraft Sojuz
Obv: Similar to 250 Francs, KM#21.

KM#	Date	Mintage	Fine	VF	XF	Unc
31	1970	2,840	—	—	Proof	150.00

5000 FRANCS

20.0000 g, .900 GOLD, .5787 oz AGW
Gamal Abdel Nasser

KM#	Date	Mintage	Fine	VF	XF	Unc
19	1970	4,000	—	—	Proof	325.00

10th Anniversary of Independence -
Munich Olympics

KM#	Date	Mintage	Fine	VF	XF	Unc
32	1969	2,740	—	—	Proof	350.00
	1970	500 pcs.	—	—	Proof	400.00

Ikhnaton
Obv: Similar to 500 Francs, KM#22.

KM#	Date	Mintage	Fine	VF	XF	Unc
33	1970	685 pcs.	—	—	Proof	475.00

Chephren
Obv: Similar to 500 Francs, KM#23.

KM#	Date	Mintage	Fine	VF	XF	Unc
34	1970	675 pcs.	—	—	Proof	475.00

Cleopatra
Obv: Similar to 500 Francs, KM#24.

KM#	Date	Mintage	Fine	VF	XF	Unc
35	1970	789 pcs.	—	—	Proof	475.00

Queen Nefertiti
Obv: Similar to 500 Francs, KM#25.

KM#	Date	Mintage	Fine	VF	XF	Unc
36	1970	774 pcs.	—	—	Proof	475.00

Ramses III
Obv: Similar to 500 Francs, KM#26.

KM#	Date	Mintage	Fine	VF	XF	Unc
37	1970	695 pcs.	—	—	Proof	475.00

Tutankhamen
Obv: Similar to 500 Francs, KM#27.

KM#	Date	Mintage	Fine	VF	XF	Unc
38	1970	675 pcs.	—	—	Proof	475.00

Queen Teyi
Obv: Similar to 500 Francs, KM#28.

KM#	Date	Mintage	Fine	VF	XF	Unc
39	1970	685 pcs.	—	—	Proof	475.00

Gamal Abdel Nasser
Obv: Similar to 500 Francs, KM#29.

KM#	Date	Mintage	Fine	VF	XF	Unc
40	1970	185 pcs.	—	—	Proof	600.00

10,000 FRANCS

40.0000 g, .900 GOLD, 1.1575 oz AGW
10th Anniversary of Independence - Sekou Toure
Rev: Similar to 5000 Francs, KM#19.

KM#	Date	Mintage	Fine	VF	XF	Unc
20	1969	2,300	—	—	Proof	750.00
	1970	—	—	—	Proof	950.00

DECIMAL COINAGE

100 Cauris = 1 Syli

50 CAURIS

ALUMINUM

KM#	Date	Mintage	Fine	VF	XF	Unc
42	1971	—	1.50	2.50	5.00	10.00

SYLI

ALUMINUM

KM#	Date	Mintage	Fine	VF	XF	Unc
43	1971	—	2.50	3.50	6.50	14.00

2 SYLIS

ALUMINUM

KM#	Date	Mintage	Fine	VF	XF	Unc
44	1971	—	1.50	2.50	4.50	9.00

5 SYLIS

ALUMINUM

KM#	Date	Mintage	Fine	VF	XF	Unc
45	1971	—	2.00	3.00	5.00	10.00

500 SYLIS

40.0000 g, .925 SILVER, 1.1897 oz ASW
Miriam Makeba

KM#	Date	Mintage	Fine	VF	XF	Unc
46	1977	500 pcs.	—	—	—	100.00
	1977	500 pcs.	—	—	Proof	125.00

Patrice Lumumba
Rev: Similar to KM#46.

KM#	Date	Mintage	Fine	VF	XF	Unc
47	1977	250 pcs.	—	—	—	150.00
	1977	150 pcs.	—	—	Proof	200.00

1000 SYLIS

2.9300 g, .900 GOLD, .0847 oz AGW
Miriam Makeba
Rev: Similar to 2000 Sylis, KM#50.

KM#	Date	Mintage	Fine	VF	XF	Unc
48	1977	300 pcs.	—	—	—	90.00
	1977	250 pcs.	—	—	Proof	100.00

Nkrumah
Rev: Similar to 2000 Sylis, KM#50.

KM#	Date	Mintage	Fine	VF	XF	Unc
49	1977	150 pcs.	—	—	—	150.00
	1977	150 pcs.	—	—	Proof	150.00

2000 SYLIS

5.8700 g, .900 GOLD, .1698 oz AGW
Mao Tse Tung

KM#	Date	Mintage	Fine	VF	XF	Unc
50	1977	200 pcs.	—	—	—	200.00
	1977	200 pcs.	—	—	Proof	200.00

Sekou Toure

KM#	Date	Mintage	Fine	VF	XF	Unc
51	1977	100 pcs.	—	—	—	175.00
	1977	50 pcs.	—	—	Proof	225.00

MONETARY REFORM

FRANC

BRASS CLAD STEEL

KM#	Date	Mintage	Fine	VF	XF	Unc
56	1985	—	.10	.20	.40	1.00

5 FRANCS

BRASS CLAD STEEL

KM#	Date	Mintage	Fine	VF	XF	Unc
53	1985	—	.10	.20	.40	1.00

10 FRANCS

BRASS CLAD STEEL

KM#	Date	Mintage	Fine	VF	XF	Unc
52	1985	—	.20	.40	.80	1.25

25 FRANCS

BRASS

KM#	Date	Mintage	Fine	VF	XF	Unc
60	1987	—	.20	.40	.85	1.75

100 FRANCS

16.0000 g, .999 SILVER, .5144 oz ASW
1992 Olympics - Discus Thrower

KM#	Date	Mintage	Fine	VF	XF	Unc
57	1988	*5,000	—	—	—	65.00

200 FRANCS

16.0000 g, .999 SILVER, .5144 oz ASW
1992 Olympics - Basketball Players

KM#	Date	Mintage	Fine	VF	XF	Unc
58	1988	*5,000	—	—	—	65.00

300 FRANCS

16.0000 g, .999 SILVER, .5144 oz ASW
1992 Olympics - Stadium

KM#	Date	Mintage	Fine	VF	XF	Unc
59	1988	*5,000	—	—	—	65.00

10,000 FRANCS

25.0000 g, .999 SILVER, .8038 oz ASW
30th Anniversary of Coinage
Rev: Palm branches and denomination.

KM#	Date	Mintage	Fine	VF	XF	Unc
61	1990	1,000	—	—	Proof	85.00

15.9760 g, .917 GOLD, .4708 oz AGW
30th Anniversary of the Currency
Obv: Arms w/dates on each side.
Rev: Palm branches and denomination.

KM#	Date	Mintage	Fine	VF	XF	Unc
62	1990	*200 pcs.	—	—	Proof	—

MINT SETS (MS)

KM#	Date	Mintage	Identification	Issue Price	Mkt. Val.
MS1	1977(6)	—	KM46-51	—	785.00
MS2	1988(3)	*5,000	KM57-59	150.00	200.00

PROOF SETS (PS)

KM#	Date	Mintage	Identification	Issue Price	Mkt. Val.
PS1	1962(4)	—	KM4-7	—	325.00
PS2	1969(7)	—	KM9-13,15-16	62.50	115.00
PS3	1969(4)	—	KM17-20	236.50	1300.
PS4	1970(7)	—	KM9-13,15-16	62.50	140.00
PS5	1970(7)	—	KM22-28	85.00	250.00
PS6	1970(7)	—	KM33-39	440.00	3300.
PS7	1970(3)	—	KM12,14,21	29.95	55.00
PS8	1977(6)	—	KM46-51	—	900.00

NOTE: Coins were issued in sets made per order containing from 1 to 11 different coins.

GUINEA-BISSAU

The Republic of Guinea-Bissau, formerly Portuguese Guinea, an overseas province on the west coast of Africa between Senegal and Guinea, has an area of 13,948 sq. mi. (36,120 sq. km.) and a population of *929,000. Capital: Bissau. The country has undeveloped deposits of oil and bauxite. Peanuts, oil-palm kernels and hides are exported.

Portuguese Guinea was discovered by Portuguese navigator Nuno Tristao in 1446. Trading rights in the area were granted to Cape Verde islanders but few prominent posts were established before 1851, and they were principally coastal installations. The chief export of this colony's early period was slaves for South America, a practice that adversely affected trade with the native people and retarded subjection of the interior. Territorial disputes with France delayed final demarcation of the colony's frontiers until 1905.

The African Party for the Independence of GuineaBissau was founded in 1956, and several years later began a guerrilla warfare that grew in effectiveness until 1974, when the rebels controlled most of the colony. Portugal's costly overseas wars in her African territories resulted in a military coup in Portugal in April 1974, that appreciably brightened the prospects for freedom for Guinea-Bissau. In August, 1974, the Lisbon government signed an agreement granting independence to Portuguese Guinea effective Sept. 10, 1974. The new republic took the name of Guinea-Bissau.

RULERS

Portuguese until 1974

PORTUGUESE GUINEA

MONETARY SYSTEM

100 Centavos = 1 Escudo

5 CENTAVOS

BRONZE

KM#	Date	Mintage	Fine	VF	XF	Unc
1	1933	.100	2.00	4.00	8.00	15.00

10 CENTAVOS

BRONZE

KM#	Date	Mintage	Fine	VF	XF	Unc
2	1933	.250	5.50	12.50	45.00	220.00

ALUMINUM

KM#	Date	Mintage	Fine	VF	XF	Unc
12	1973	.100	1.00	2.00	3.50	7.00

20 CENTAVOS

BRONZE

KM#	Date	Mintage	Fine	VF	XF	Unc
3	1933	.350	1.00	4.00	10.00	25.00

KM#	Date	Mintage	Fine	VF	XF	Unc
13	1973	.100	1.00	2.00	3.50	7.00

50 CENTAVOS

NICKEL-BRONZE

KM#	Date	Mintage	Fine	VF	XF	Unc
4	1933	.600	2.00	7.50	20.00	150.00

BRONZE
500th Anniversary of Discovery

KM#	Date	Mintage	Fine	VF	XF	Unc
6	1946	2.000	.50	1.50	3.50	12.00

KM#	Date	Mintage	Fine	VF	XF	Unc
8	1952	10.000	.20	.50	1.00	3.00

ESCUDO

NICKEL-BRONZE

KM#	Date	Mintage	Fine	VF	XF	Unc
5	1933	.800	4.50	10.00	40.00	200.00

BRONZE
500th Anniversary of Discovery

KM#	Date	Mintage	Fine	VF	XF	Unc
7	1946	2.000	1.00	1.25	2.50	7.00

KM#	Date	Mintage	Fine	VF	XF	Unc
14	1973	.250	1.00	2.00	3.50	8.00

2-1/2 ESCUDOS

COPPER-NICKEL

KM#	Date	Mintage	Fine	VF	XF	Unc
9	1952	3.010	.50	1.00	1.75	4.00

5 ESCUDOS

COPPER-NICKEL

KM#	Date	Mintage	Fine	VF	XF	Unc
15	1973	.800	1.00	1.50	2.50	7.50

10 ESCUDOS

5.0000 g, .720 SILVER, .1157 oz ASW

KM#	Date	Mintage	Fine	VF	XF	Unc
10	1952	1.200	BV	2.50	8.50	20.00

COPPER-NICKEL

KM#	Date	Mintage	Fine	VF	XF	Unc
16	1973	1.700	1.00	1.50	2.50	8.50

20 ESCUDOS

10.0000 g, .720 SILVER, .2315 oz ASW

KM#	Date	Mintage	Fine	VF	XF	Unc
11	1952	.750	BV	4.00	10.00	25.00

GUINEA-BISSAU

MONETARY SYSTEM

100 Centavos = 1 Peso

50 CENTAVOS

ALUMINUM
F.A.O. Issue

KM#	Date	Mintage	Fine	VF	XF	Unc
17	1977	6.000	.50	1.00	1.75	3.00

PESO

ALUMINUM-BRONZE
F.A.O. Issue

KM#	Date	Mintage	Fine	VF	XF	Unc
18	1977	7.000	.50	1.00	1.75	3.00

2-1/2 PESOS

ALUMINUM-BRONZE
F.A.O. Issue

KM#	Date	Mintage	Fine	VF	XF	Unc
19	1977	4.000	.65	1.25	2.25	4.00
	ALUMINUM					
19a	1977	—	.65	1.25	2.25	4.00

5 PESOS

COPPER-NICKEL
F.A.O. Issue

KM#	Date	Mintage	Fine	VF	XF	Unc
20	1977	6.000	1.00	2.00	4.00	8.00

20 PESOS

COPPER-NICKEL
F.A.O. Issue

KM#	Date	Mintage	Fine	VF	XF	Unc
21	1977	2.500	1.50	3.50	7.50	15.00

2000 PESOS

NICKEL PLATED STEEL
Olympics - Hand Ball Player

KM#	Date	Mintage	Fine	VF	XF	Unc
28	1991	—	—	—	—	15.00

10,000 PESOS

16.0000 g, .999 SILVER, .5144 oz ASW
Nuno Tristad - Discovery of Guinea-Bissau

KM#	Date	Mintage	VF	XF	Unc
27	1991	—	—	Proof	47.50

11.9700 g, .999 SILVER, .3848 oz ASW
Soccer Player

KM#	Date	Mintage	VF	XF	Unc
29	1991	—	—	—	42.50

19.6700 g, .999 SILVER, .6324 oz ASW
XXV Olympics - Floor Exercise

KM#	Date	Mintage	VF	XF	Unc
30	1992	*5,000	—	Proof	45.00

15.0000 g, .999 SILVER, .4823 oz ASW
Elephant Standing on Africa

KM#	Date	Mintage	VF	XF	Unc
31	1993	—	—	Proof	32.50

Prehistoric Life - Stegosaurus

KM#	Date	Mintage	VF	XF	Unc
32	1993	—	—	Proof	32.50

20,000 PESOS

25.0000 g, .999 SILVER, .8039 oz ASW
II Extraordinary Congress

KM#	Date	Mintage	VF	XF	Unc
25	1990	2,000	—	—	42.50

10th Anniversary

KM#	Date	Mintage	VF	XF	Unc
26	1990	*2,500	—	Proof	47.50

20.0000 g, .999 SILVER, .6430 oz ASW
Defense of Nature - Elephant

KM#	Date	Mintage	VF	XF	Unc
33	1993	—	—	Proof	40.00

20.1000 g, .999 SILVER, .6456 oz ASW
Sailing Ship - Passat

KM#	Date	Mintage	VF	XF	Unc
34	1993	—	—	Proof	40.00

GUYANA

The Cooperative Republic of Guyana, an independent member of the British Commonwealth situated on the northeast coast of South America, has an area of 83,000 sq. mi. (214,970 sq. km.) and a population of 955,000. Capital: Georgetown. The economy is basically agrarian. Sugar, rice and bauxite are exported.

The original area of Essequibo and Demerary, which included present-day Surinam, French Guiana, and parts of Brazil and Venezuela was sighted by Columbus in 1498. The first European settlement was made late in the 16th century by the Dutch, however; the region was claimed for the British by Sir Walter Raleigh during the reign of Elizabeth I. For the next 150 years, possession alternated between the Dutch and the British, with a short interval of French control. The British exercised de facto control after 1796, although the area, which included the Dutch colonies of Essequibo, Demerary and Berbice, was not ceded to them by the Dutch until 1814. From 1803 to 1831, Essequibo and Demerary were administered separately from Berbice. The three colonies were united in the British Crown Colony of British Guiana in 1831. British Guiana won internal self-government in 1952 and full independence, under the traditional name of Guyana, on May 26, 1966. Guyana became a republic on Feb. 23, 1970. It is a member of the Commonwealth of Nations. The president is the Chief of State. The prime minister is the Head of Government.

RULERS

British, until 1966

MONETARY SYSTEM

(Until 1839)

20 Stiver = 1 Guilder (Gulden)
3 Guilders = 12 Bits = 5 Shillings
= 1 Dollar

(Commencing 1839)

3-1/8 Guilders = 50 Pence

ESSEQUIBO & DEMERARY

NECESSITY COINAGE

1808 EMERGENCY ISSUES

During the time of the countermarked coins of the Bank og England for George III, Spanish or Spanish Colonial 8 Reales were punched to form two new denominations. The plug or center was countermarked 3 Bits while the holed 8 Reales was countermarked 3 Guilders.

3 BITS

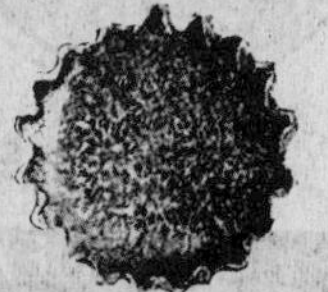

.903 SILVER
c/m: E & D 3 Bt on serrated center plug from 8 Reales.

KM#	Date	Year	VG	Fine	VF	XF
1	ND(1808)	—	950.00	1600.	2650.	3350.

3 GUILDERS

.903 SILVER
c/m: E & D 3 G D in dotted oval on Mexico City. 8 Reales, KM#109.

KM#	Date	Year	VG	Fine	VF	XF
2	ND(1808)	1791	1550.	2550.	4250.	5000.
		1796	1550.	2550.	4250.	5000.
		1803	1550.	2550.	4250.	5000.

COLONIAL COINAGE

1/2 STIVER

COPPER

KM#	Date	Mintage	Fine	VF	XF	Unc
9	1813	.215	1.50	5.50	45.00	100.00
	1813	—	—	—	Proof	350.00

COPPER-GILT

KM#	Date	Mintage	Fine	VF	XF	Unc
9a	1813	—	—	—	Proof	650.00

STIVER

COPPER

KM#	Date	Mintage	Fine	VF	XF	Unc
10	1813	.215	2.25	7.50	50.00	100.00
	1813	—	—	—	Proof	400.00

COPPER-GILT

KM#	Date	Mintage	Fine	VF	XF	Unc
10a	1813	—	—	—	Proof	600.00

1/8 GUILDER

0.9700 g, .816 SILVER, .0255 oz ASW

KM#	Date	Mintage	Fine	VF	XF	Unc
16	1832	.098	6.00	12.00	35.00	75.00
	1832	—	—	—	Proof	250.00
	1835/1	.071	10.00	19.00	37.50	95.00
	1835/3	I.A.	10.00	19.00	37.50	95.00
	1835	Inc. Ab.	7.50	17.00	30.00	70.00
	1835 plain edge	—	—	—	Proof	300.00
	1835 reeded edge	—	—	—	Proof	400.00

1/4 GUILDER

1.9400 g, .816 SILVER, .0510 oz ASW
Similar to 2 Guilders, KM#7.

KM#	Date	Mintage	Fine	VF	XF	Unc
4	1809	.124	12.50	25.00	65.00	150.00

NOTE: Flan size varies.

Similar to 1 Guilder, KM#13.

KM#	Date	Mintage	Fine	VF	XF	Unc
11	1816	.043	12.50	25.00	65.00	150.00
	1816	—	—	—	Proof	350.00

KM#	Date	Mintage	Fine	VF	XF	Unc
17	1832	.039	12.50	22.50	50.00	150.00
	1833	.097	9.00	17.50	40.00	125.00
	1833	—	—	—	Proof	575.00
	1835/3	.073	9.00	17.50	40.00	125.00
	1835	Inc. Ab.	7.00	12.00	27.50	100.00
	1835 plain edge	—	—	—	Proof	450.00
	1835 reeded edge	—	—	—	Proof	500.00

1/2 GUILDER

3.8800 g, .816 SILVER, .1020 oz ASW
Similar to 2 Guilders, KM#7.

KM#	Date	Mintage	Fine	VF	XF	Unc
5	1809	.064	15.00	37.50	110.00	225.00

KM#	Date	Mintage	Fine	VF	XF	Unc
12	1816	.034	12.50	27.50	100.00	200.00
	1816	—	—	—	Proof	350.00

KM#	Date	Mintage	Fine	VF	XF	Unc
18	1832	.087	11.00	22.50	95.00	200.00
	1832	—	—	—	Proof	350.00
	1835/5	.036	12.50	25.00	95.00	200.00
	1835	Inc. Ab.	19.00	27.50	50.00	125.00
	1835 plain edge	—	—	—	Proof	400.00
	1835 reeded edge	—	—	—	Proof	500.00

GUILDER

7.7700 g, .816 SILVER, .2040 oz ASW

KM#	Date	Mintage	Fine	VF	XF	Unc
6	1809	.032	20.00	40.00	125.00	350.00

KM#	Date	Mintage	Fine	VF	XF	Unc
13	1816	.034	15.00	30.00	100.00	300.00
	1816	—	—	—	Proof	400.00

KM#	Date	Mintage	Fine	VF	XF	Unc
19	1832	.047	10.00	25.00	60.00	200.00
	1832	—	—	—	Proof	425.00
	1835	.022	15.00	30.00	75.00	250.00
	1835 plain edge	—	—	—	Proof	550.00
	1835 reeded edge	—	—	—	Proof	600.00

NOTE: 1832 dated coins exist w/flat and round top 3.

2 GUILDERS

15.5500 g, .816 SILVER, .4079 oz ASW

KM#	Date	Mintage	Fine	VF	XF	Unc
7	1809	.016	75.00	175.00	400.00	2250.

KM#	Date	Mintage	Fine	VF	XF	Unc
14	1816	.015	50.00	125.00	250.00	700.00
	1816	—	—	—	Proof	Rare

KM#	Date	Mintage	Fine	VF	XF	Unc
20	1832	.014	60.00	150.00	400.00	1500.
	1832	—	—	—	Proof	Rare

3 GUILDERS

23.3200 g, .816 SILVER, .6118 oz ASW

KM#	Date	Mintage	Fine	VF	XF	Unc
8	1809	.021	175.00	350.00	700.00	2750.

KM#	Date	Mintage	Fine	VF	XF	Unc
15	1816	.010	150.00	300.00	600.00	1750.
	1816	—	—	—	Proof	Rare

Rev: Similar to 2 Guilders, KM#20.

KM#	Date	Mintage	Fine	VF	XF	Unc
21	1832	7,156	250.00	550.00	1500.	4500.
	1832	—	—	—	Proof	Rare

BRITISH GUIANA

In October, 1835, the minting of currency two pence pieces was approved by the Treasury. These coins, identical to those in the Maundy sets, were circulated in British Guiana with dates of 1838, 1843 and 1848. Groats of the Victorian era and the seated Britannia type were also circulated in this colony. See homeland types in Great Britain.

1/8 GUILDER

0.9700 g, .816 SILVER, .0127 oz ASW

KM#	Date	Mintage	Fine	VF	XF	Unc
22	1836	.180	8.50	15.00	40.00	90.00
	1836	—	—	—	Proof	125.00

1/4 GUILDER

1.9400 g, .816 SILVER, .0255 oz ASW

KM#	Date	Mintage	Fine	VF	XF	Unc
23	1836	.216	12.50	25.00	50.00	125.00
	1836	—	—	—	Proof	225.00

1/2 GUILDER

3.8800 g, .816 SILVER, .0510 oz ASW

KM#	Date	Mintage	Fine	VF	XF	Unc
24	1836	.118	12.50	30.00	70.00	150.00
	1836	—	—	—	Proof	300.00

GUILDER

7.7700 g, .816 SILVER, .1020 oz ASW

KM#	Date	Mintage	Fine	VF	XF	Unc
25	1836	.057	15.00	35.00	95.00	200.00
	1836 plain edge	—		—	Proof	400.00
	1836 reeded edge	—		—	Proof	1250.

BRITISH GUIANA AND WEST INDIES

From 1836 through 1888 regular issue 4 Pence (Groats) as well as general issue strikes of the Maundy type 2 Pence (1838, 1843 & 1848) of Great Britain were circulated in British Guiana and the West Indies. These are listed under Great Britain.

MONETARY SYSTEM

12 Pence = 1 Shilling
4 Shillings 2 Pence = 1 Dollar

4 PENCE

1.8851 g, .925 SILVER, .0560 oz ASW

KM#	Date	Mintage	Fine	VF	XF	Unc
26	1891	.336	1.75	4.50	8.00	30.00
	1894	.120	2.75	6.50	12.50	45.00
	1900	.045	3.25	10.00	20.00	70.00
	1901	.060	3.00	7.50	12.50	50.00

KM#	Date	Mintage	Fine	VF	XF	Unc
27	1903	.060	3.00	7.50	17.50	50.00
	1903	—	—		Matte Proof	450.00
	1908	.030	5.00	12.50	25.00	85.00
	1909	.036	5.00	12.50	25.00	85.00
	1910	.066	3.00	10.00	22.50	75.00

KM#	Date	Mintage	Fine	VF	XF	Unc
28	1911	.030	5.00	12.50	35.00	110.00
	1913	.030	5.00	12.50	35.00	110.00
	1916	.030	5.00	12.50	35.00	110.00

BRITISH GUIANA

4 PENCE

1.8851 g, .925 SILVER, .0560 oz ASW

KM#	Date	Mintage	Fine	VF	XF	Unc
29	1917	.072	3.00	7.50	22.50	90.00
	1917	—	—		Matte Proof	450.00
	1918	.210	1.25	3.50	15.00	55.00
	1921	.090	3.00	7.50	17.50	70.00
	1923	.012	20.00	45.00	85.00	160.00
	1925	.030	3.50	8.50	32.50	100.00
	1926	.030	3.50	8.50	25.00	65.00
	1931	.015	10.00	25.00	60.00	120.00
	1931	—	—	—	Proof	175.00
	1935	.036	3.00	7.50	20.00	55.00
	1935	—	—	—	Proof	175.00
	1936	.063	1.75	2.50	10.00	30.00
	1936	—	—	—	Proof	225.00

KM#	Date	Mintage	Fine	VF	XF	Unc
30	1938	.030	1.75	2.50	10.00	25.00
	1938	—	—	—	Proof	175.00
	1939	.048	1.75	2.50	7.50	20.00
	1939	—	—	—	Proof	175.00
	1940	.090	1.25	2.00	3.50	18.50
	1940	—	—	—	Proof	175.00
	1941	.120	1.25	1.75	3.00	12.50
	1941	—	—	—	Proof	175.00
	1942	.180	1.25	1.75	3.00	12.50
	1942	—	—	—	Proof	175.00
	1943	.240	1.25	1.75	2.50	8.00
	1943	—	—	—	Proof	400.00

1.8851 g, .500 SILVER, .0303 oz ASW

KM#	Date	Mintage	Fine	VF	XF	Unc
30a	1944	.090	.75	1.25	2.50	8.00
	1945	.120	.50	1.00	2.00	7.00
	1945	—	—	—	Proof	200.00

GUYANA

MONETARY SYSTEM

100 Cents = 1 Dollar

MINT MARKS

FM - Franklin Mint, U.S.A.*

NOTE: From 1975 the Franklin Mint has produced coinage in up to 3 different qualities. Qualities of issue are designated in ( ) after each date and are defined as follows:

(M) MATTE - Normal circulation strike or a dull finish produced by sandblasting special uncirculated (polish finish) or proof quality dies.

(U) SPECIAL UNCIRCULATED - Polished or proof-like in appearance without any frosted features.

(P) PROOF - The highest quality obtainable having mirror-like fields and frosted features.

CENT

NICKEL-BRASS
Stylized Lotus Flower

KM#	Date	Mintage	VF	XF	Unc
31	1967	6.000	—	.10	.25
31	1967	5,100	—	Proof	2.00
	1969	4.000	—	.10	.25
	1970	6.000	—	.10	.25
	1971	4.000	—	.10	.25
	1972	4.000	—	.10	.25
	1973	4.000	—	.10	.25
	1974	11.000	—	.10	.20
	1975	—	—	.10	.25
	1976	—	—	.10	.25
	1977	16.000	—	.10	.20
	1978	10.450	—	.10	.20
	1979	—	—	.10	.20
	1980	12.000	—	.10	.20
	1981	10.000	—	.10	.20
	1982	8.000	—	.10	.20
	1983	12.000	—	.10	.20
	1985	8.000	—	.10	.20
	1987	6.000	—	.10	.20
	1988	.080	—	.10	.20
	1989	—	—	.10	.20

BRONZE
10th Anniversary of Independence - Manatee

KM#	Date	Mintage	VF	XF	Unc
37	1976FM(M)	.015	—	.10	.30
	1976FM(U)	50 pcs.	—	—	—
	1976FM(P)	.028	—	Proof	.50
	1977FM(U)	.015	—	.10	.30
	1977FM(P)	7,215	—	Proof	.50
	1978FM(U)	.015	—	.10	.30
	1978FM(P)	5,044	—	Proof	.50
	1979FM(U)	.015	—	.10	.30
	1979FM(P)	3,547	—	Proof	.50
	1980FM(U)	.030	—	.10	.30
	1980FM(P)	863 pcs.	—	Proof	.60

5 CENTS

NICKEL-BRASS
Stylized Lotus Flower

KM#	Date	Mintage	VF	XF	Unc
32	1967	4.600	—	.10	.25
	1967	5,100	—	Proof	2.25
	1972	1.200	—	.10	.30
	1974	3.000	—	.10	.30
	1975	—	—	.10	.30
	1976	—	—	.10	.30
	1977	1.500	—	.10	.20
	1978	2,000	—	.50	4.00
	1979	—	—	—	—
	1980	1.000	—	.10	.20
	1981	1.000	—	.10	.20
	1982	2.000	—	.10	.20
	1985	3.000	—	.10	.20
	1986	4.000	—	.10	.20
	1987	3.000	—	.10	.20
	1988	2.000	—	.10	.20
	1989	—	—	.10	.20
	1991	—	—	.10	.20

NOTE: Varieties exist.

BRASS
10th Anniversary of Independence - Jaguar

KM#	Date	Mintage	VF	XF	Unc
38	1976FM(M)	.015	—	.10	.40
	1976FM(U)	50 pcs.	—	—	—
	1976FM(P)	.028	—	Proof	.75
	1977FM(U)	.015	—	.10	.40
	1977FM(P)	7,215	—	Proof	.75
	1978FM(U)	.015	—	.10	.40
	1978FM(P)	5,044	—	Proof	.75
	1979FM(U)	.015	—	.10	.40
	1979FM(P)	3,547	—	Proof	.75
	1980FM(U)	.030	—	.10	.40
	1980FM(P)	863 pcs.	—	Proof	.90

10 CENTS

COPPER-NICKEL

KM#	Date	Mintage	VF	XF	Unc
33	1967	4.000	.10	.20	.35
	1967	5,100	—	Proof	2.50
	1973	1.500	.10	.20	.35

KM#	Date	Mintage	VF	XF	Unc
33	1974	1.700	.10	.20	.35
	1976	—	.10	.20	.35
	1977	4.000	.10	.20	.35
	1978	2.010	.10	.20	.35
	1979	—	.10	.20	.35
	1980	1.000	.10	.20	.35
	1981	1.000	.10	.20	.35
	1982	2.000	.10	.20	.35
	1985	3.000	.10	.20	.35
	1986	4.000	.10	.20	.35
	1987	3.000	.10	.20	.35
	1988	2.000	.10	.20	.35
	1989	—	.10	.20	.35
	1990	—	.10	.20	.35

10th Anniversary of Independence - Sakiwinki

KM#	Date	Mintage	VF	XF	Unc
39	1976	2.006	—	.15	.50
	1976FM(M)	.010	—	.15	.60
	1976FM(U)	50 pcs.	—	—	—
	1976FM(P)	.028	—	Proof	1.00
	1977	1.500	—	.15	.50
	1977FM(U)	.010	—	.15	.60
	1977FM(P)	7,215	—	Proof	1.00
	1978FM(U)	.010	—	.15	.60
	1978FM(P)	5,044	—	Proof	1.00
	1979FM(U)	.010	—	.15	.60
	1979FM(P)	3,547	—	Proof	1.00
	1980FM(U)	.020	—	.15	.60
	1980FM(P)	863 pcs.	—	Proof	1.25

25 CENTS

COPPER-NICKEL

KM#	Date	Mintage	VF	XF	Unc
34	1967	3.500	.15	.25	.65
	1967	5,100	—	Proof	3.00
	1972	1.000	.15	.25	.65
	1974	4.000	.15	.25	.65
	1975	—	.15	.25	.65
	1976	—	.15	.25	.65
	1977	4.000	.15	.25	.65
	1978	2.006	.15	.25	.65
	1981	1.000	.15	.25	.65
	1982	1.500	.15	.25	.65
	1984	1.000	.15	.25	.65
	1985	2.000	.15	.25	.65
	1986	4.000	.15	.25	.65
	1987	3.000	.15	.25	.65
	1988	4.000	.15	.25	.65
	1989	—	.15	.25	.65
	1990	—	.15	.25	.65

10th Anniversary of Independence - Harpy Eagle

KM#	Date	Mintage	VF	XF	Unc
40	1976FM(M)	4,000	—	.30	2.00
	1976FM(U)	50 pcs.	—	—	—
	1976FM(P)	.028	—	Proof	1.50
	1977	2.000	.15	.25	1.00
	1977FM(U)	4,000	—	.30	4.00
	1977FM(P)	7,215	—	Proof	1.50
	1978FM(U)	4,000	—	.30	4.00
	1978FM(P)	5,044	—	Proof	1.50
	1979FM(U)	4,000	—	.30	4.00
	1979FM(P)	3,547	—	Proof	1.50
	1980FM(U)	8,437	—	.30	4.00
	1980FM(P)	863 pcs.	—	Proof	1.75

50 CENTS

COPPER-NICKEL

KM#	Date	Mintage	VF	XF	Unc
35	1967	1.000	.25	.35	.75
	1967	5,100	—	Proof	3.50

10th Anniversary of Independence - Conje Pheasant

KM#	Date	Mintage	VF	XF	Unc
41	1976FM(M)	2,000	—	.40	5.00
	1976FM(U)	50 pcs.	—	—	—
	1976FM(P)	.028	—	Proof	2.00
	1977FM(U)	2,000	—	.40	5.00
	1977FM(P)	7,215	—	Proof	2.00
	1978FM(U)	2,000	—	.40	5.00
	1978FM(P)	5,044	—	Proof	2.00
	1979FM(U)	2,000	—	.40	5.00
	1979FM(P)	3,547	—	Proof	2.00
	1980FM(U)	4,437	—	.40	3.50
	1980FM(P)	863 pcs.	—	Proof	2.50

DOLLAR

COPPER-NICKEL
F.A.O. Issue

KM#	Date	Mintage	VF	XF	Unc
36	1970	.500	.50	1.00	2.50
	1970	5,000	—	Proof	4.00

10th Anniversary of Independence - Caiman

KM#	Date	Mintage	VF	XF	Unc
42	1976FM(M)	600 pcs.	—	.50	4.00
	1976FM(U)	50 pcs.	—	—	—
	1976FM(P)	.028	—	Proof	5.00
	1977FM(U)	500 pcs.	—	.50	4.00
	1977FM(P)	7,215	—	Proof	5.00
	1978FM(U)	500 pcs.	—	.50	4.00
	1978FM(P)	5,044	—	Proof	5.00
	1979FM(U)	500 pcs.	—	.50	4.00
	1979FM(P)	3,547	—	Proof	5.00
	1980FM(U)	1,437	—	.50	4.00
	1980FM(P)	863 pcs.	—	Proof	6.00

5 DOLLARS

COPPER-NICKEL
10th Anniversary of Independence
Obv: Similar to 1 Dollar, KM#42.

KM#	Date	Mintage	VF	XF	Unc
43	1976FM(M)	400 pcs.	—	—	12.50
	1976FM(U)	150 pcs.	—	—	17.50
	1977FM(U)	100 pcs.	—	—	25.00
	1978FM(U)	100 pcs.	—	—	25.00
	1979FM(U)	100 pcs.	—	—	25.00
	1980FM(U)	547 pcs.	—	—	15.00

37.3000 g, .500 SILVER, .5996 oz ASW

KM#	Date	Mintage	VF	XF	Unc
43a	1976FM(P)	.018	—	Proof	8.00
	1977FM(P)	5,685	—	Proof	10.00
	1978FM(P)	3,825	—	Proof	12.00
	1979FM(P)	2,665	—	Proof	12.00
	1980FM(P)	347 pcs.	—	Proof	17.50

10 DOLLARS

COPPER-NICKEL
10th Anniversary of Independence
Obv: Similar to 1 Dollar, KM#42.

KM#	Date	Mintage	VF	XF	Unc
44	1976FM(M)	300 pcs.	—	—	35.00
	1976FM(U)	300 pcs.	—	—	35.00
	1977FM(U)	100 pcs.	—	—	50.00
	1978FM(U)	100 pcs.	—	—	50.00
	1979FM(U)	100 pcs.	—	—	50.00
	1980FM(U)	247 pcs.	—	—	40.00

43.2300 g, .925 SILVER, 1.2856 oz ASW

KM#	Date	Mintage	VF	XF	Unc
44a	1976FM(P)	.018	—	Proof	15.00
	1977FM(P)	5,685	—	Proof	17.50
	1978FM(P)	3,825	—	Proof	20.00
	1979FM(P)	2,665	—	Proof	20.00
	1980FM(P)	347 pcs.	—	Proof	25.00

50 DOLLARS

48.3000 g, .925 SILVER, 1.4365 oz ASW
10th Anniversary of Independence - Enmore Martyrs

KM#	Date	Mintage	VF	XF	Unc
45	1976FM(U)	100 pcs.	—	—	135.00
	1976FM(P)	1,001	—	Proof	110.00

100 DOLLARS

5.7400 g, .500 GOLD, .0923 oz AGW
10th Anniversary of Independence - Arawak Indian

KM#	Date	Mintage	VF	XF	Unc
46	1976FM(U)	100 pcs.	—	—	120.00
	1976FM(P)	.021	—	Proof	60.00

5.5800 g, .500 GOLD, .0897 oz AGW

Legendary Golden Man

KM#	Date	Mintage	VF	XF	Unc
47	1977FM(U)	100 pcs.	—	—	120.00
	1977FM(P)	7,635	—	Proof	65.00

PROOF SETS (PS)

KM#	Date	Mintage	Identification	Issue Price	Mkt. Val.
PS1	1967(5)	5,100	KM31-35	10.50	10.00
PS2	1976FM(8)	17,536	KM37-42,43a,44a	45.00	32.50
PS3	1976FM(6)	10,302	KM37-42	15.00	10.00
PS4	1977FM(8)	5,685	KM37-42,43a,44a	45.00	37.50
PS5	1977FM(6)	1,530	KM37-42	15.00	15.00
PS6	1978FM(8)	3,825	KM37-42,43a,44a	47.50	40.00
PS7	1978FM(6)	1,219	KM37-42	16.00	15.00
PS8	1979FM(8)	2,665	KM37-42,43a,44a	47.50	42.50
PS9	1979FM(6)	882	KM37-42	16.00	15.00
PS10	1980FM(8)	1,900	KM37-42,43a,44a	100.00	55.00
PS11	1980FM(6)	863	KM37-42	19.00	15.00

HAITI

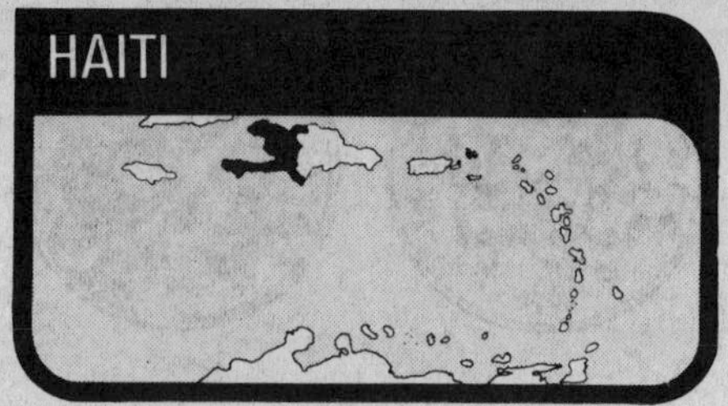

The Republic of Haiti, which occupies the western onethird of the island of Hispaniola in the Caribbean Sea between Puerto Rico and Cuba, has an area of 10,714 sq. mi.(27,750 sq. km.) and a population of 5.4 million. Capital: Port-au-Prince. The economy is based on agriculture; but light manufacturing and tourism are increasingly important. Coffee, bauxite, sugar, essential oils and handicrafts are exported.

Columbus discovered Hispaniola in 1492. Spain colonized the island, making Santo Domingo the base for exploration of the Western Hemisphere. The area that is now Haiti was ceded to France by Spain in 1697. Slaves brought from Africa to work the coffee and sugar cane plantations made it one of the richest colonies of the French Empire. A slave revolt in the 1790's led to the establishment of the Republic of Haiti in 1804, making it the oldest black republic in the world and the second oldest republic (after the United States) in the Western Hemisphere.

The French language is used on Haitian coins although it is spoken by only about 10 percent of the populace. A form of Creole serves as the language of most of the Haitians.

Two dating systems are used on Haiti's 19th century coins. One is Christian, the other Revolutionary -dating from 1803 when the French were permanently ousted by a native revolt. Thus, a date of AN30, (i.e., year 30) is equivalent to 1833 A.D. Some coins carry both date forms. In the listings which follow only coins dated only in the Revolutionary system are listed by AN years in the date column.

RULERS

French, until 1804

MINT MARKS

A - Paris
(a) - Paris, privy marks only
HEATON - Birmingham

MONETARY SYSTEM

12 Deniers = 1 Sol
20 Sols = 1 Livre
100 Centimes = 1 Gourde

HISPANIOLA

TOWN OF LE CAP

(Old Cap Francois)

Port city on the northern coast of Haiti.Under a French edict of July 13, 1781 various Spanish-American and other circulating silver coins were to be counterstamped with a crowned anchor and C for the island. These were made at the capitol and the pieces given values of 1 Escalin and 1/2 Escalin. Copper coins were counterstamped L.C. and S.D.

MONETARY SYSTEM

15 Sols = 1 Escalin (1 Real)

COUNTERMARKED COINAGE

SOL

BRONZE
c/m: L.C. in rectangle on English 1/2 Penny token of 1792.

KM#	Date	Mintage	Good	VG	Fine	VF
5	ND(1802-09)	—	100.00	175.00	275.00	500.00

1/2 ESCALIN

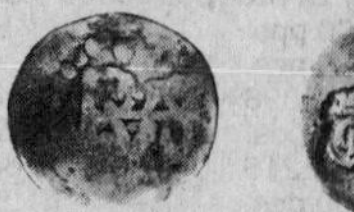

SILVER, 0.93 g
c/m: Crowned C and anchor on Potosi 1/2 Real size cob.

KM#	Date	Mintage	Good	VG	Fine	VF
7.1	ND(1780-1802)		150.00	275.00	400.00	650.00

SILVER, 1.07 g
c/m: Crowned C and anchor on center cut of Potosi 1 Real size cob.

KM#	Date	Mintage	Good	VG	Fine	VF
7.2	ND(1780-1802)		200.00	375.00	550.00	850.00

SILVER
Ring substituted for crown on anchor.

KM#	Date	Mintage	Good	VG	Fine	VF
6	ND	—	150.00	275.00	400.00	650.00

ESCALIN

SILVER, 2.36 g
c/m: Crowned C and anchor on center cut of Lima or Potosi 2 Real size cob.

KM#	Date	Mintage	Good	VG	Fine	VF
8.1	ND(1780-1802)		175.00	300.00	450.00	700.00

SILVER, 2.80 g
c/m: Crowned C and anchor on Angola 2 Macutas.

KM#	Date	Mintage	Good	VG	Fine	VF
8.2	ND(1780-1802)		185.00	325.00	500.00	800.00

SILVER
Ring substituted for crown on anchor

KM#	Date	Mintage	Good	VG	Fine	VF
9	ND	—	175.00	300.00	450.00	700.00

FRENCH OCCUPATION COINAGE

SOL

BRONZE
c/m: S:D. in rectangle on French Sol, C#73.

KM#	Date	Mintage	Good	VG	Fine	VF
13	ND(1802-09)	—	90.00	180.00	300.00	525.00

c/m: ND over S:D. on French copper coin.

KM#	Date	Mintage	Good	VG	Fine	VF
14	ND(1802-09)	—	80.00	160.00	275.00	475.00

c/m: Crowned N on English 1/2 Penny, KM#392.

KM#	Date	Mintage	Good	VG	Fine	VF
15	ND(1802-09)	—	90.00	180.00	300.00	525.00

REPUBLICAN COINAGE

RULERS

Toussaint L'Ouverture, 1798-1802

MONETARY SYSTEM

15 Sols (Sous) = 1 Escalin (Real)

DEMY (1/2) ESCALIN

SILVER

KM#	Date	Mintage	VG	Fine	VF	XF
21	ND(1802)	—	125.00	250.00	500.00	750.00

UN (1) ESCALIN

SILVER

KM#	Date	Mintage	VG	Fine	VF	XF
22	ND(1802)	—	100.00	200.00	400.00	600.00

DEUX (2) ESCALIN

SILVER

KM#	Date	Mintage	VG	Fine	VF	XF
23	ND(1802)	—	200.00	300.00	550.00	800.00

HAITI

7 SOLS 6 DENIERS

SILVER
Similar to 15 Sols, KM#6.

KM#	Date	Mintage	Good	VG	Fine	VF
3	1807	—	45.00	100.00	225.00	500.00
	1808	—	35.00	60.00	90.00	160.00
	1809	—	28.50	50.00	75.00	140.00

15 SOLS

SILVER

KM#	Date	Mintage	Good	VG	Fine	VF
6	1807	—	20.00	35.00	65.00	125.00
	1808	—	22.00	40.00	85.00	150.00
	1809	—	22.00	40.00	85.00	150.00

30 SOLS

SILVER

KM#	Date	Mintage	Good	VG	Fine	VF
8	1807	2 known	—	—	—	—

NOTE: Christie's Norweb sale 5-85 VF realized $7150. Bank Leu Bostonian sale 10-90 VF realized $4110.

DECIMAL COINAGE

100 Centimes = 1 Gourde

UNE (1) CENTIME

COPPER

KM#	Date	Year	VG	Fine	VF	XF
21	1828	AN 25	6.50	17.50	32.50	50.00
	1829	AN 26	4.00	8.00	17.50	37.50
	1830	AN 27	3.50	7.50	11.50	30.00
	1830	AN 28	18.00	30.00	75.00	150.00
	1830	AN 29	75.00	150.00	250.00	425.00
	1831	AN 28	2.00	4.00	9.00	27.50
	1832	AN 28	22.50	32.50	75.00	150.00
	1832	AN 29	1.75	3.50	9.00	27.50
	1834	AN 31	2.00	4.00	9.00	27.50
	1840	AN 37	2.00	4.00	8.00	22.50
	1841	AN 38	2.50	6.00	10.00	30.00
	1842	AN 39	1.75	3.25	7.50	22.50

NOTE: Die varieties exist and both diework and striking become progressively cruder throughout this series.

22mm

KM#	Date	Year	VG	Fine	VF	XF
24	1846	AN 43	.75	2.25	4.50	10.00

Reduced size, 21mm
Obv: Leaves point inward.
Rev: W/large star after legend.

KM#	Date	Year	VG	Fine	VF	XF
25.1	1846	AN 43	.65	2.00	3.00	7.50

Rev: Large Phrygian cap.

KM#	Date	Year	VG	Fine	VF	XF
25.2	1846	.AN 43	1.00	2.50	4.00	10.00

NOTE: Varieties exist in style of wreath and legend.

Similar to KM#25.2 but stop after legend.

KM#	Date	Year	VG	Fine	VF	XF
30	1849	AN 46	80.00	160.00	275.00	350.00

Similar to KM#25.2 but leg: EMPIRE D'HAITI.

KM#	Date	Year	VG	Fine	VF	XF
33	1850	AN 47	40.00	95.00	180.00	300.00

KM#	Date	Year	VG	Fine	VF	XF
34	1850	—	2.50	5.00	8.00	20.00

BRONZE

KM#	Date	Mintage	Fine	VF	XF	Unc
42	1881	.830	2.00	3.50	5.50	20.00
	1881	—	—	—	Proof	200.00

KM#	Date	Mintage	Fine	VF	XF	Unc
48	1886A	2.500	1.75	3.00	5.00	15.00
	1894A	2.070	1.75	3.00	5.00	20.00
	1895A	5.420	1.75	3.00	5.00	30.00

DEUX (2) CENTIMES

COPPER

KM#	Date	Year	VG	Fine	VF	XF
22	1828	AN 25	12.00	30.00	75.00	150.00
	1828	AN 26	10.00	28.00	65.00	135.00
	1829	AN 26	3.00	6.00	10.00	28.00
	1830	AN 26	12.50	30.00	65.00	120.00
	1830	AN 27	10.00	28.00	10.00	25.00
	1831	AN 28	2.50	5.00	8.00	20.00
	1840	AN 37	2.50	5.00	8.00	20.00
	1840 backwards 4					
		AN 37	3.00	6.00	10.00	25.00
	1841	AN 38	2.50	5.00	8.00	20.00
	1842	AN 39	2.50	5.00	8.00	20.00

NOTE: Die varieties exist and became progressively cruder throughout this series.

26mm

KM#	Date	Year	VG	Fine	VF	XF
26	1846	AN 43	1.25	3.00	4.75	9.00
	1846	AN 43	—	—	Proof	300.00
	1846	AN 43/2	2.00	4.00	5.75	11.00

Reduced size, 24mm
Obv: Leaves point inward.
Rev: W/large star after legend.

KM#	Date	Year	VG	Fine	VF	XF
27.1	1846	AN 43	1.75	3.50	5.00	9.50

Rev: Large Phrygian cap.

KM#	Date	Year	VG	Fine	VF	XF
27.2 (27.1)	1846	AN 43	2.25	4.00	5.00	10.00

NOTE: Varieties exist w/o accents on E's, date as AN 43 and AN.43.

KM#	Date	Year	VG	Fine	VF	XF
31	1849	AN 46	27.50	42.50	80.00	150.00

Obv. leg: EMPIRE D'HAITI.

KM#	Date	Year	VG	Fine	VF	XF
35	1850	AN 47	40.00	75.00	125.00	250.00

KM#	Date	Mintage	VG	Fine	VF	XF
36	1850	—	1.75	4.75	10.00	20.00

BRONZE

KM#	Date	Mintage	Fine	VF	XF	Unc
43	1881	.830	2.75	4.50	8.00	20.00
	1881	—	—	—	Proof	150.00

KM#	Date	Mintage	Fine	VF	XF	Unc
49	1886A	1.250	1.50	2.50	5.00	35.00
	1894A	3.750	1.50	2.50	5.00	50.00

CINQ (5) CENTIMES

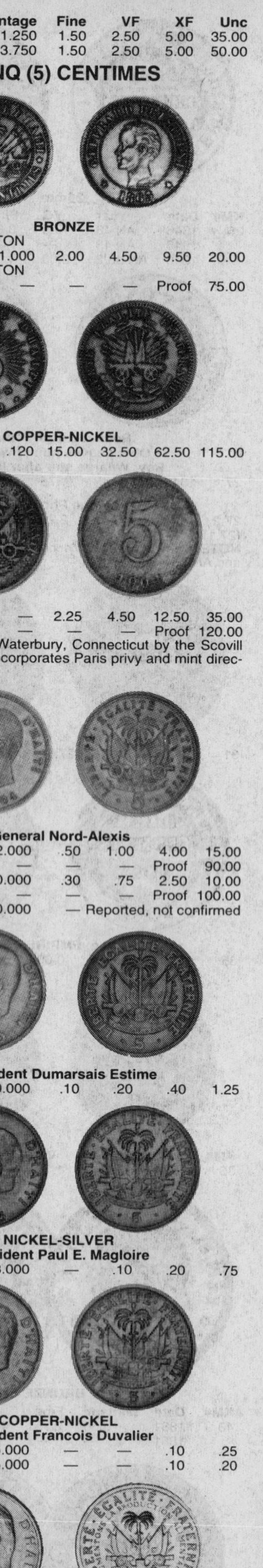

BRONZE

KM#	Date	Mintage	Fine	VF	XF	Unc
39	1863HEATON	1.000	2.00	4.50	9.50	20.00
	1863HEATON	—	—	—	Proof	75.00

COPPER-NICKEL

KM#	Date	Mintage	Fine	VF	XF	Unc
50	1889	.120	15.00	32.50	62.50	115.00
52	1904 (a)	—	2.25	4.50	12.50	35.00
	1904 (a)	—	—	—	Proof	120.00

NOTE: Struck at Waterbury, Connecticut by the Scovill Mfg. Co. Design incorporates Paris privy and mint director's marks.

General Nord-Alexis

KM#	Date	Mintage	Fine	VF	XF	Unc
53	1904	2.000	.50	1.00	4.00	15.00
	1904	—	—	—	Proof	90.00
	1905	20.000	.30	.75	2.50	10.00
	1905	—	—	—	Proof	100.00
	1906	10.000	— Reported, not confirmed			

President Dumarsais Estime

KM#	Date	Mintage	Fine	VF	XF	Unc
57	1949	10.000	.10	.20	.40	1.25

NICKEL-SILVER
President Paul E. Magloire

KM#	Date	Mintage	Fine	VF	XF	Unc
59	1953	3.000	—	.10	.20	.75

COPPER-NICKEL
President Francois Duvalier

KM#	Date	Mintage	Fine	VF	XF	Unc
62	1958	15.000	—	—	.10	.25
	1970	5.000	—	—	.10	.20

F.A.O. Issue - President Jean-Claude Duvalier

KM#	Date	Mintage	Fine	VF	XF	Unc
119	1975	16.000	—	—	.10	.20

F.A.O. Issue

KM#	Date	Mintage	Fine	VF	XF	Unc
145	1981	.015	—	.10	.25	1.00

6 CENTIMES

.835 SILVER
Obv: Arms/snake type.

KM#	Date	Year	VG	Fine	VF	XF
10	1813	AN 10	75.00	125.00	200.00	400.00
		Rev: Boyer bust.				
17	1818	AN 15	10.00	20.00	30.00	60.00

COPPER

KM#	Date	Year	VG	Fine	VF	XF
28	1846	AN 43	3.00	6.50	10.00	20.00

KM#	Date	Year	VG	Fine	VF	XF
32	1849	AN 46	22.50	37.50	55.00	100.00

KM#	Date	Year	VG	Fine	VF	XF
37	1850	AN 47	100.00	215.00	375.00	600.00

6-1/4 CENTIMES

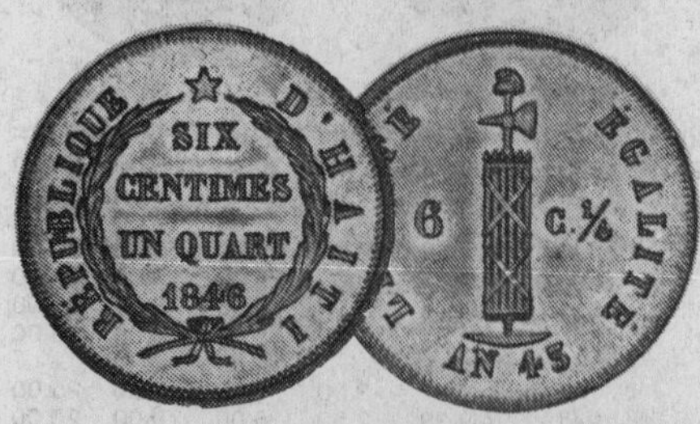

COPPER

KM#	Date	Year	VG	Fine	VF	XF
29	1846	AN 43	3.75	8.50	15.00	25.00

KM#	Date	Mintage	VG	Fine	VF	XF
38	1850	—	2.75	5.00	7.50	20.00

DIX (10) CENTIMES

BRONZE
Mint mark: HEATON

KM#	Date	Mintage	Fine	VF	XF	Unc
40	1863	1.000	2.25	4.50	7.50	22.50
	1863	—	—	—	Proof	80.00

2.5000 g, .835 SILVER, .0671 oz ASW

KM#	Date	Mintage	Fine	VF	XF	Unc
44	1881(a)	1.500	1.50	3.00	8.00	25.00
	1881(a)	—	—	—	Proof	450.00
	1882(a)	1.800	1.25	2.25	8.00	25.00
	1882(a)	—	—	—	Proof	400.00
	1886(a)	1.500	2.00	4.00	15.00	40.00
	1886(a)	—	—	—	Proof	550.00
	1887(a)	1.050	1.25	2.25	10.00	30.00
	1887(a)	—	—	—	Proof	350.00
	1890(a)	1.000	1.75	3.50	15.00	40.00
	1890(a)	—	—	—	Proof	550.00
	1894(a)	3.720	1.25	2.25	8.00	25.00
	1894(a)	—	—	—	Proof	400.00

COPPER-NICKEL
General Nord-Alexis

KM#	Date	Mintage	Fine	VF	XF	Unc
54	1906	10.000	.50	1.00	3.00	15.00
	1906	—	—	—	Proof	100.00

President Dumarsais Estime

KM#	Date	Mintage	Fine	VF	XF	Unc
58	1949	5.000	.15	.25	.50	1.50

NICKEL-SILVER
President Paul E. Magloire

KM#	Date	Mintage	Fine	VF	XF	Unc
60	1953	1.500	—	.10	.25	1.25

COPPER-NICKEL

President Francois Duvalier

KM#	Date	Mintage	Fine	VF	XF	Unc
63	1958	7.500	—	.10	.15	.35
	1970	2.500	—	—	.10	.20

F.A.O. Issue - President Jean-Claude Duvalier

KM#	Date	Mintage	Fine	VF	XF	Unc
120	1975	12.000	—	—	.10	.20
	1983	2.000	—	—	.10	.30

F.A.O. Issue

KM#	Date	Mintage	Fine	VF	XF	Unc
146	1981	.015	—	.10	.25	1.00

12 CENTIMES

SILVER
Obv: Arms type.

KM#	Date	Year	Good	VG	Fine	VF
11	(1813)	AN 10	18.00	40.00	90.00	160.00
	(1814)	AN XI	3.75	8.00	15.00	30.00
	(1815)	AN 12	6.50	15.00	30.00	60.00

Rev: Petion type, large head.

KM#	Date	Year	Good	VG	Fine	VF
13	(1817)	AN 14	2.50	6.00	13.50	28.50

Rev: Petion type, small head.

KM#	Date	Year	Good	VG	Fine	VF
14	(1817)	AN 14	2.50	6.00	13.50	28.50

Rev: Boyer type.

KM#	Date	Year	Good	VG	Fine	VF
19	(1827)	AN 24	4.00	9.00	20.00	40.00
	(1828)	AN 25	9.00	18.00	50.00	100.00
	(1829)	AN 26	20.00	45.00	100.00	200.00

VINGT (20) CENTIMES

BRONZE
Mint mark: HEATON

KM#	Date	Mintage	Fine	VF	XF	Unc
41	1863	1.000	2.00	5.00	9.50	35.00
	1863	—	—	—	Proof	80.00

5.0000 g, .835 SILVER, .1342 oz ASW

KM#	Date	Mintage	Fine	VF	XF	Unc
45	1881(a)	1.250	2.50	4.50	8.00	40.00
	1881(a)	—	—	—	Proof	450.00
	1882(a)	1.250	2.50	4.50	8.00	40.00
	1882(a)	—	—	—	Proof	450.00
	1887(a)	.350	3.00	5.00	10.00	50.00
	1887(a)	—	—	—	Proof	600.00
	1890(a)	.070	4.50	9.00	15.00	75.00
	1890(a)	—	—	—	Proof	800.00
	1894(a)	1.850	2.50	4.50	8.00	50.00
	1894(a)	—	—	—	Proof	450.00
	1895(a)	1.270	2.50	4.50	8.00	50.00
	1895(a)	—	—	—	Proof	450.00

COPPER-NICKEL
General Pedro Nord-Alexis

KM#	Date	Mintage	Fine	VF	XF	Unc
55	1907	5.000	1.00	2.00	4.50	15.00
	1907	—	—	—	Proof	125.00
	1908	—	—	— Reported, not confirmed		

NICKEL-SILVER
President Paul E. Magloire

KM#	Date	Mintage	Fine	VF	XF	Unc
61	1956	2.500	.20	.35	.75	2.50

President Francois Duvalier

KM#	Date	Mintage	Fine	VF	XF	Unc
77	1970	1.000	—	—	.10	.50

COPPER-NICKEL
F.A.O. Issue - President Jean-Claude Duvalier

KM#	Date	Mintage	Fine	VF	XF	Unc
100	1972	1.500	—	.10	.25	1.00
	1975	4.000	—	—	.10	.50
	1983	1.500	—	—	.10	.50

F.A.O. Issue

KM#	Date	Mintage	Fine	VF	XF	Unc
147	1981	.015	—	.10	.25	1.25

KM#	Date	Mintage	Fine	VF	XF	Unc
152	1986	2.500	—	—	.10	.50
	1989	—	—	—	.10	.50
	1991	—	—	—	.10	.50

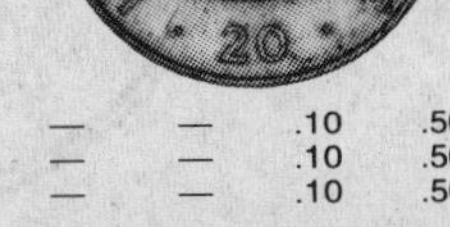

25 CENTIMES

SILVER, 22-25mm
Arms type

KM#	Date	Year	Good	VG	Fine	VF
12.1	(1813)	AN 10	6.00	16.50	30.00	70.00

20-21mm

KM#	Date	Year	Good	VG	Fine	VF
12.2	(1814)	AN XI	3.75	7.00	12.50	25.00
	(1815)	AN 12	3.00	4.50	10.00	20.00
	(1816)	AN 13	3.50	5.50	11.50	22.50

NOTE: The above coins exist w/solid and dotted spear shafts, and other minor die-cutting differences.

Rev: Petion type.

KM#	Date	Year	Good	VG	Fine	VF
15.1	(1817)	AN 14	1.75	3.75	7.50	16.50
15.2	(1817)	AN 14P	8.00	16.00	32.50	65.00

Rev: Boyer type.

KM#	Date	Year	Good	VG	Fine	VF
18	(1818)	AN 15	6.00	15.00	32.50	65.00
	(1825)	AN 22	— Reported, not confirmed			
	(1827)	AN 24	1.75	3.75	7.00	15.00
	(1828)	AN 25	2.00	4.00	8.00	16.50
	(1829)	AN 26	3.25	7.50	16.50	37.50
	(1831)	AN 28	2.00	4.50	11.50	27.50
	(1834)	AN 31	2.00	4.50	11.50	27.50

50 CENTIMES

SILVER

KM#	Date	Year	Good	VG	Fine	VF
20	(1827)	AN 24	6.50	17.50	37.50	75.00
	(1828)	AN 25	2.75	6.00	12.00	20.00
	(1829)	AN 26	2.75	6.50	14.00	30.00
	(1830)	AN 27	6.50	17.50	35.00	75.00
	(1831)	AN 28	2.75	6.00	11.00	18.00
	(1832)	AN 29	2.75	6.50	12.00	20.00
	(1833)	AN 30	5.50	13.50	30.00	60.00

12.5000 g, .835 SILVER, .3356 oz ASW

KM#	Date	Mintage	Fine	VF	XF	Unc
47	1882(a)	.440	3.00	6.00	12.00	60.00
	1882(a)	—	—	—	Proof	600.00
	1883(a)	.400	3.00	6.00	12.00	100.00
	1883(a)	—	—	—	Proof	600.00
	1887(a)	.250	3.00	6.00	12.00	60.00
	1887(a)	—	—	—	Proof	800.00
	1890(a)	.100	4.00	8.00	15.00	100.00
	1890(a)	—	—	—	Proof	1000.
	1895(a)	.900	3.00	6.00	12.00	75.00
	1895(a)	—	—	—	Proof	600.00

COPPER-NICKEL
General Nord-Alexis

KM#	Date	Mintage	Fine	VF	XF	Unc
56	1907	2.000	.90	1.75	5.50	15.00
	1907	—	—	—	Proof	175.00
	1908	.800	1.00	2.50	8.50	20.00
	1908	—	—	—	Proof	200.00

F.A.O. Issue - President Jean-Claude Duvalier

KM#	Date	Mintage	Fine	VF	XF	Unc
101	1972	.600	—	.10	.25	1.50
	1975	1.200	—	.10	.15	.80
	1979	2.000	—	.10	.15	.80
	1983	1.000	—	.10	.15	.80
	1985	—	—	—	—	.75

F.A.O. Issue

KM#	Date	Mintage	Fine	VF	XF	Unc
148	1981	.015	—	.10	.50	2.00

Similar to 20 Centimes, KM#152.

KM#	Date	Mintage	Fine	VF	XF	Unc
153	1986	2.000	—	.10	.15	.80
	1989	—	—	.10	.15	.80
	1991	—	—	.10	.15	.80

100 CENTIMES

SILVER

KM#	Date	Year	VG	Fine	VF	XF
23	(1829)	AN 26	6.00	12.00	20.00	45.00
	(1830)	AN 27	7.00	15.00	25.00	50.00
	(1833)	AN 30	10.00	20.00	35.00	75.00

GOURDE

25.0000 g, .900 SILVER, .7234 oz ASW

KM#	Date	Mintage	Fine	VF	XF	Unc
46	1881(a)	.200	20.00	35.00	75.00	300.00
	1881(a)	—	—	—	Proof	2000.
	1882(a)	.500	15.00	25.00	62.50	250.00
	1882(a)	—	—	—	Proof	2000.
	1887(a)	.200	15.00	25.00	62.50	250.00
	1887(a)	—	—	—	Proof	2500.
	1895(a)	.100	20.00	35.00	85.00	350.00
	1895(a)	—	—	—	Proof	3250.

5 GOURDES

23.5200 g, .999 SILVER, .7555 oz ASW
10th Aniversary of Revolution
Columbus Discovers America

KM#	Date	Mintage	VF	XF	Unc
64	1967IC	4,650	—	Proof	14.00
	1968IC	5,750	—	Proof	14.00
	1969IC	1,175	—	Proof	18.00
	1970IC	2,060	—	Proof	18.00

Haitienne Paradise
Rev: Similar to KM#64.

KM#	Date	Mintage	VF	XF	Unc
78	1971IC	1,585	—	Proof	35.00

10 GOURDES

47.0500 g, .999 SILVER, 1.5113 oz ASW
10th Anniversary of Revolution - Gen. Louverture

KM#	Date	Mintage	VF	XF	Unc
65	1967IC	6,750	—	Proof	25.00
	1968IC	5,725	—	Proof	25.00
	1969IC	1,100	—	Proof	35.00
	1970IC	1,500	—	Proof	35.00

Seminole Indian Chief - Osceola
Rev: Similar to KM#65.

KM#	Date	Mintage	VF	XF	Unc
79	1971IC	3,535	—	Proof	45.00

Sioux Indian Chief - Sitting Bull
Rev: Similar to KM#65.

KM#	Date	Mintage	VF	XF	Unc
80	1971IC	3,185	—	Proof	45.00

Fox Indian Chief - Playing Fox
Rev: Similar to KM#65.

KM#	Date	Mintage	VF	XF	Unc
81	1971IC	3,035	—	Proof	45.00

Chiricahua Indian Chief - Geronimo
Rev: Similar to KM#65.

KM#	Date	Mintage	VF	XF	Unc
82	1971IC	3,285	—	Proof	45.00

Seminole Indian Chief - Billy Bowlegs
Rev: Similar to KM#65.

KM#	Date	Mintage	VF	XF	Unc
83	1971IC	3,735	—	Proof	45.00

Nez Perce Indian Chief - Joseph
Rev: Similar to KM#65.

KM#	Date	Mintage	VF	XF	Unc
84	1971IC	3,235	—	Proof	45.00

Yankton Sioux Indian Chief - War Eagle
Rev: Similar to KM#65.

KM#	Date	Mintage	VF	XF	Unc
85	1971IC	3,135	—	Proof	45.00

Oglala Sioux Indian Chief - Red Cloud
Rev: Similar to KM#65.

KM#	Date	Mintage	VF	XF	Unc
86	1971IC	3,235	—	Proof	45.00

Cherokee Indian Chief - Stalking Turkey
Rev: Similar to KM#65.

KM#	Date	Mintage	VF	XF	Unc
87	1971IC	3,185	—	Proof	45.00

20 GOURDES

3.9500 g, .900 GOLD, .1143 oz AGW
10th Anniversary of Revolution - Mackandal

KM#	Date	Mintage	VF	XF	Unc
66	1967IC	*10,351	—	Proof	55.00
	1968IC	—	—	Proof	55.00
	1969IC	—	—	Proof	65.00
	1970IC	—	—	Proof	75.00

25 GOURDES

117.6000 g, .999 SILVER, 3.7809 oz ASW
10th Anniversary of Revolution - Art Objects
Illustration reduced. Actual size: 60mm.
Rev: Similar to 5 Gourdes, KM#64.

KM#	Date	Mintage	VF	XF	Unc
67	1967IC	4,650	—	Proof	75.00
	1968IC	5,810	—	Proof	75.00
	1969IC	1,115	—	Proof	90.00
	1970IC	1,000	—	Proof	90.00

International Airport
Rev: Similar to 5 Gourdes, KM#64.
Illustration reduced. Actual size: 60mm.

KM#	Date	Mintage	VF	XF	Unc
88	1971IC	1,935	—	—	150.00

10.0000 g, .925 SILVER, .2973 oz ASW

KM#	Date	Mintage	VF	XF	Unc
102	1973	6,100	—	—	7.50
	1973	5,470	—	Proof	10.00
	1974	—	—	Proof	30.00

World Soccer Championship Games

KM#	Date	Mintage	VF	XF	Unc
103	1973	.057	—	—	5.00
	1973	6,430	—	Proof	10.00

8.3750 g, .925 SILVER, .2491 oz ASW
United States Bicentennial

KM#	Date	Mintage	VF	XF	Unc
112	1974	.025	—	—	6.00
	1974	600 pcs.	—	Proof	20.00
	1975	—	—	Proof	25.00
	1976	.010	—	Proof	12.50

International Women's Year
Rev: Similar to KM#67.

KM#	Date	Mintage	VF	XF	Unc
121	1975	7,180	—	—	15.00
	1975	1,440	—	Proof	25.00

30 GOURDES

9.1100 g, .585 GOLD, .1713 oz AGW
10th Anniversary of Revolution
Citadel of St. Christopher

KM#	Date	Mintage	VF	XF	Unc
72	1969IC	1,185	—	Proof	125.00
	1970IC	Inc. Ab.	—	Proof	150.00

40 GOURDES

12.1500 g, .585 GOLD, .2285 oz AGW
10th Anniversary of Revolution - J. J. Dessalines

KM#	Date	Mintage	VF	XF	Unc
73	1969IC	1,005	—	Proof	200.00
	1970IC	Inc. Ab.	—	Proof	220.00

50 GOURDES

9.8700 g, .900 GOLD, .2856 oz AGW
10th Anniversary of Revolution - Dancer

KM#	Date	Mintage	VF	XF	Unc
68	1967IC	*8,681	—	Proof	150.00
	1968IC	—	—	Proof	180.00
	1969IC	—	—	Proof	210.00
	1970IC	—	—	Proof	235.00

Heros de Vertieres
Rev: Similar to KM#68.

KM#	Date	Mintage	VF	XF	Unc
89	1971IC	485 pcs.	—	Proof	300.00

20.1000 g, .925 SILVER, .5978 oz ASW
Woman on the Beach

KM#	Date	Mintage	VF	XF	Unc
104	1973	8,685	—	—	17.50
	1973	5,973	—	Proof	20.00
	1974	—	—	Proof	45.00

Woman and Child

KM#	Date	Mintage	VF	XF	Unc
105	1973	7,300	—	—	12.50
	1973	5,853	—	Proof	17.50
	1974	—	—	—	35.00
	1974	—	—	Proof	45.00

16.9000 g, .925 SILVER, .5026 oz ASW
World Soccer Championship Games

KM#	Date	Mintage	VF	XF	Unc
106	1973	.012	—	Proof	15.00

1976 Montreal Olympiad

KM#	Date	Mintage	VF	XF	Unc
113	1974	.021	—	—	15.00
	1974	2,358	—	Proof	22.00
	1975	—	—	Proof	27.50
	1976	8,000	—	Proof	20.00

Rev: Smaller 4 in date.

KM#	Date	Mintage	VF	XF	Unc
114	1974	—	—	Proof	16.00

Holy Year

KM#	Date	Mintage	VF	XF	Unc
123	1974	—	—	—	12.50
	1974	960 pcs.	—	Proof	18.00
	1975	—	—	—	25.00
	1976	6,000	—	Proof	22.50

21.3000 g, .925 SILVER, .6334 oz ASW
World Soccer Championship Games
Rev: Similar to KM#104.

KM#	Date	Mintage	VF	XF	Unc
127	1977	.011	—	—	20.00
	1977	9,000	—	Proof	25.00

Human Rights
Rev: Similar to KM#104.

KM#	Date	Mintage	VF	XF	Unc
128	1977	800 pcs.	—	—	22.50
	1977	545 pcs.	—	Proof	30.00

1980 Moscow Olympics

KM#	Date	Mintage	VF	XF	Unc
129	1977	3,969	—	—	20.00
	1977	3,720	—	Proof	30.00
	1978	*350 pcs.	—	Proof	85.00

20th Anniversary of European Market

KM#	Date	Mintage	VF	XF	Unc
130.1	1977	421 pcs.	—	—	30.00
	1977	364 pcs.	—	Proof	50.00

Obv: Entire area within circle frosted.
Rev: Date added below arms.

KM#	Date	Mintage	VF	XF	Unc
130.2	1978	—	—	Proof	65.00

Queen of the Sugar
Rev: Similar to KM#104.

KM#	Date	Mintage	VF	XF	Unc
131	1977	321 pcs.	—	—	27.50
	1977	602 pcs.	—	Proof	35.00

20.0000 g, .925 SILVER, .5948 oz ASW
F.A.O. Issue

KM#	Date	Mintage	VF	XF	Unc
149	1981	.014	—	—	18.00

Papal Visit

KM#	Date	Mintage	VF	XF	Unc
150	1983	1,000	—	Proof	30.00

60 GOURDES

18.2200 g, .585 GOLD,.3427 oz AGW
10th Anniversary of Revolution - Alexandre Petion

KM#	Date	Mintage	VF	XF	Unc
74	1969IC	935 pcs.	—	Proof	275.00
	1970IC	Inc. Ab.	—	Proof	375.00

100 GOURDES

19.7500 g, .900 GOLD, .5715 oz AGW
10th Anniversary of Revolution - Marie Jeanne

KM#	Date	Mintage	VF	XF	Unc
69	1967IC	*8,682	—	Proof	300.00
	1968IC	—	—	Proof	325.00
	1969IC	—	—	Proof	325.00
	1970IC	—	—	Proof	350.00

Seminole Indian Chief - Osceola
Rev: Similar to KM#69.

KM#	Date	Mintage	VF	XF	Unc
90	1971IC	435 pcs.	—	Proof	400.00

Sioux Indian Chief - Sitting Bull
Rev: Similar to KM#69.

KM#	Date	Mintage	VF	XF	Unc
91	1971IC	475 pcs.	—	Proof	400.00

Fox Indian Chief - Playing Fox
Rev: Similar to KM#69.

KM#	Date	Mintage	VF	XF	Unc
92	1971IC	425 pcs.	—	Proof	400.00

Chiricahua Indian Chief - Geronimo
Rev: Similar to KM#69.

KM#	Date	Mintage	VF	XF	Unc
93	1971IC	520 pcs.	—	Proof	400.00

Seminole Indian Chief - Billy Bowlegs
Rev: Similar to KM#69.

KM#	Date	Mintage	VF	XF	Unc
94	1971IC	425 pcs.	—	Proof	400.00

Nez Perce Indian Chief - Joseph
Rev: Similar to KM#69.

KM#	Date	Mintage	VF	XF	Unc
95	1971IC	455 pcs.	—	Proof	400.00

Yankton Sioux Indian Chief - War Eagle
Rev: Similar to KM#69.

KM#	Date	Mintage	VF	XF	Unc
96	1971IC	455 pcs.	—	Proof	400.00

Oglala Sioux Indian Chief - Red Cloud
Rev: Similar to KM#69.

KM#	Date	Mintage	VF	XF	Unc
97	1971IC	455 pcs.	—	Proof	400.00

Cherokee Indian Chief - Stalking Turkey
Rev: Similar to KM#69.

KM#	Date	Mintage	VF	XF	Unc
98	1971IC	425 pcs.	—	Proof	400.00

1.4500 g, .900 GOLD, .0419 oz AGW
Christopher Columbus

KM#	Date	Mintage	VF	XF	Unc
107	1973	3,233	—	—	40.00
	1973	915 pcs.	—	Proof	75.00

43.0000 g, .925 SILVER, 1.2789 oz ASW
Sadat and Begin
Rev: Similar to KM#69.

KM#	Date	Mintage	VF	XF	Unc
132	1977	550 pcs.	—	—	60.00
	1977	500 pcs.	—	Proof	80.00

20th Anniversary of European Market
Rev: Similar to KM#69.

KM#	Date	Mintage	VF	XF	Unc
133	1977	321 pcs.	—	—	75.00
	1977	214 pcs.	—	Proof	100.00

50th Anniversary of Lindbergh's New York to Paris Flight
Rev: Similar to KM#69.

KM#	Date	Mintage	VF	XF	Unc
134	1977	321 pcs.	—	—	75.00
	1977	214 pcs.	—	Proof	125.00

Statue of Liberty
Rev: Similar to KM#69.

KM#	Date	Mintage	VF	XF	Unc
135	1977	321 pcs.	—	—	75.00
	1977	214 pcs.	—	Proof	125.00

200 GOURDES

39.4900 g, .900 GOLD, 1.1427oz AGW
10th Anniversary of Revolution
Revolt of Santo Domingo

KM#	Date	Mintage	VF	XF	Unc
70	1967IC	*4,199	—	Proof	500.00
	1968IC	—	—	Proof	525.00
	1969IC	—	—	Proof	525.00
	1970IC	—	—	Proof	550.00

Revolutionist From St. Dominique
Rev: Similar to 100 Gourdes, KM#69.

KM#	Date	Mintage	VF	XF	Unc
99	1971IC	235 pcs.	—	Proof	800.00

2.9100 g, .900 GOLD, .0842 oz AGW
World Soccer Championship Games

KM#	Date	Mintage	VF	XF	Unc
108	1973	5,167	—	—	60.00
	1973	915 pcs.	—	Proof	100.00

Holy Year
Rev: Fineness stamped on hexagonal mound, spears w/spearheads.

KM#	Date	Mintage	VF	XF	Unc
115	1974	4,965	—	—	60.00
	1974	660 pcs.	—	Proof	80.00

Holy Year
Rev: Fineness stamped on oval mound, spears w/arrowheads.

KM#	Date	Mintage	VF	XF	Unc
124	1975	—	—	Proof	80.00

International Women's Year
Rev: Similar to KM#124.

KM#	Date	Mintage	VF	XF	Unc
125	1975	2,260	—	—	60.00
	1975	840 pcs.	—	Proof	125.00

250 GOURDES

75.9500 g, .585 GOLD, 1.4286oz AGW
10th Anniversary of Revolution - King H. Christophe
Rev: Similar to KM#136.

KM#	Date	Mintage	VF	XF	Unc
75	1969IC	470 pcs.	—	Proof	1200.
	1970IC	—	—	—	—

4.2500 g, .900 GOLD, .1229oz AGW
Human Rights

KM#	Date	Mintage	VF	XF	Unc
136	1977	282 pcs.	—	—	125.00
	1977	288 pcs.	—	Proof	145.00

Sadat and Begin

KM#	Date	Mintage	VF	XF	Unc
137	1977	270 pcs.	—	—	125.00
	1977	520 pcs.	—	Proof	145.00

20th Anniversary of European Market

KM#	Date	Mintage	VF	XF	Unc
138	1977	107 pcs.	—	—	190.00
	1977	107 pcs.	—	Proof	200.00

50th Anniversary of Lindbergh's
New York to Paris Flight
Obv: Portrait of Lindbergh in flier's cap above Spirit of St. Louis. Rev: Similar to KM#137.

KM#	Date	Mintage	VF	XF	Unc
139	1977	107 pcs.	—	—	215.00
	1977	107 pcs.	—	Proof	225.00

500 GOURDES

151.9000 g, .585 GOLD, 2.8572 oz AGW
10th Anniversary of Revolution - Haitian Native Art
Illustration reduced. Actual size: 68mm.
Rev: Similar to KM#141.

KM#	Date	Mintage	VF	XF	Unc
76	1969IC	435 pcs.	—	Proof	2000.
	1970IC	—	—	—	—

7.2800 g, .900 GOLD, .2106 oz AGW

KM#	Date	Mintage	VF	XF	Unc
109	1973	2,380	—	—	150.00
	1973	915 pcs.	—	Proof	175.00

KM#	Date	Mintage	VF	XF	Unc
110	1973	2,265	—	—	125.00
	1973	915 pcs.	—	Proof	145.00

6.5000 g, .900 GOLD, .1881 oz AGW
Obv: Same as 1000 Gourdes, KM#118.
Rev: Similar to KM#141.

KM#	Date	Mintage	VF	XF	Unc
116	1974	—	—	Proof	150.00

1976 Montreal Olympiad
Rev: Fineness stamped on hexagonal mound, spears w/spearheads.

KM#	Date	Mintage	VF	XF	Unc
117	1974	3,489	—	—	125.00
	1974	1,140	—	Proof	145.00

1976 Montreal Olympiad
Rev: Fineness stamped on hexagonal mound, spears w/arrowheads.

KM#	Date	Mintage	VF	XF	Unc
126	1975	120 pcs.	—	—	350.00

8.5000 g, .900 GOLD, .2459 oz AGW
World Soccer Championship Games

KM#	Date	Mintage	VF	XF	Unc
140	1977	450 pcs.	—	—	220.00
	1977	200 pcs.	—	Proof	325.00

1980 Moscow Olympics

KM#	Date	Mintage	VF	XF	Unc
141	1977	695 pcs.	—	—	225.00
	1977	504 pcs.	—	Proof	250.00
	1978	*350 pcs.	—	Proof	550.00

20th Anniversary of European Common Market
Obv: Map of Europe. Rev: Similar to KM#141.

KM#	Date	Mintage	VF	XF	Unc
142	1977	207 pcs.	—	—	225.00
	1977	257 pcs.	—	Proof	275.00
	1978	—	—	—	275.00
	1978	—	—	Proof	425.00

Economic Connections

KM#	Date	Mintage	VF	XF	Unc
143	1977	107 pcs.	—	—	250.00
	1977	107 pcs.	—	Proof	300.00

Duvalier

KM#	Date	Mintage	VF	XF	Unc
144	1977	107 pcs.	—	—	250.00
	1977	328 pcs.	—	Proof	250.00

10.5000 g, .900 GOLD, .3038 oz AGW
Papal Visit

KM#	Date	Mintage	VF	XF	Unc
151	1983	1,000	—	Proof	200.00

1000 GOURDES

197.4800 g, .900 GOLD, 5.7148 oz AGW
10th Anniversary of Revolution - Dr. Francois Duvalier
Rev: Similar to KM#118.

KM#	Date	Mintage	VF	XF	Unc
71	1967IC	*2,950	—	Proof	2500.
	1968IC	—	—	Proof	2750.
	1969IC	—	—	Proof	3000.
	1970IC	—	—	Proof	3250.

14.5600 g, .900 GOLD, .4213 oz AGW
Jean Claude Duvalier

KM#	Date	Mintage	VF	XF	Unc
111	1973	—	—	—	200.00
	1973	915 pcs.	—	Proof	250.00

13.0000 g, .900 GOLD, .3762 oz AGW
United States Bicentennial

KM#	Date	Mintage	VF	XF	Unc
118	1974	3,040	—	—	190.00
	1974	480 pcs.	—	Proof	275.00
	1975	—	—	Proof	600.00

INSURRECTION ISSUE

Issued c. 1889 by General Florvil Hippolyte who became President from 1889-1896.

GOURDE

B.P.1.G. = Bon Pour 1 Gourde

BRONZE, uniface
c/m: B.P.1G/GL.H

KM#	Date	Mintage	Fine	VF	XF	Unc
51	ND(1889)	.100	50.00	125.00	350.00	600.00

NOTE: An 1881 dated 2 Centime with this c/m was reported in the Medina collection.

MINT SETS (MS)

KM#	Date	Mintage	Identification	Issue Price	Mkt. Val.
MS1	1973(9)	8,000	KM102-105,107-109(2), 111	490.00	625.00
MS2	1973(4)	—	KM102-105	60.00	37.50
MS3	1975(2)	—	KM121,125	50.25	65.00

PROOF SETS (PS)

KM#	Date	Mintage	Identification	Issue Price	Mkt. Val.
PS1	1967(5)	2,525	KM66,68-71	722.00	3550.
PS2	1967(3)	4,650	KM64,65,67	47.00	125.00
PS3	1968(5)	475	KM66,68-71	823.00	3875.
PS4	1968(3)	5,725	KM64,65,67	53.50	125.00
PS5	1969(5)	435	KM72-76	475.00	3800.
PS6	1969(5)	140	KM66,68-71	823.00	4150.
PS7	1969(3)	1,100	KM64,65,67	53.50	150.00
PS8	1970(5)	—	KM66,68-71	823.00	4500.
PS9	1970(3)	1,000	KM64,65,67	53.50	150.00
PS10	1971(9)	—	KM79-87	135.00	360.00
PS11	1971(9)	—	KM90-98	—	3600.
PS12	1973(8)	1,250	KM102-105,107-109,111	830.00	575.00
PS13	1973(4)	3,500	KM102-105	60.00	50.00
PS14	1975(2)	—	KM121,125	67.25	150.00
PS17	1976(3)	*—	KM112,113,123	—	55.00
PS18	1978(2)	350	KM129,141	—	650.00
PS19	1978(2)	—	KM130.2,142	—	500.00

***NOTE:** Although the insert information card in #PS17 states B.U., this issue is considered to be of proof quality.

Listings For

HAWAII: refer to United States

HEJAZ: refer to Saudi Arabia

HONDURAS

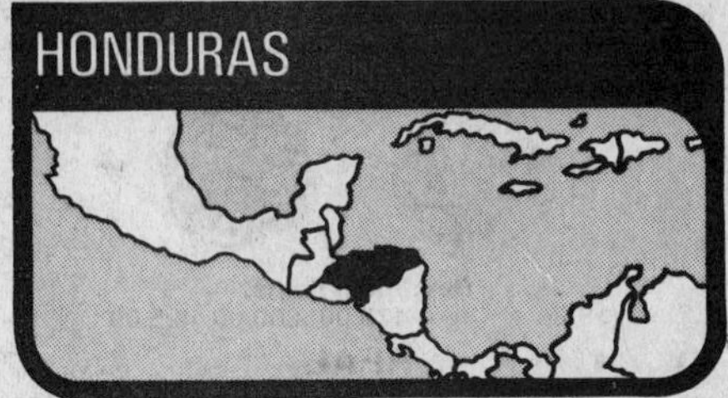

The Republic of Honduras, situated in Central America between Nicaragua and Guatemala, has an area of 43,277 sq. mi. (112,090 sq. km.) and a population of 4.5 million. Capital: Tegucigalpa. Agriculture, mining (gold and silver), and logging are the major economic activities. Bananas, timber and coffee are exported.

The eastern part of Honduras was part of the ancient Mayan Empire; however, the largest Indian community in Honduras was the not too well known Lencas. Honduras was claimed for Spain by Columbus in 1502, during his last voyage to the Americas. The first settlement was made by Cristobal de Olid under orders from Hernando Cortes, then in Mexico. The area, regarded as one of the most promising sources of gold and silver in the New World, was a part of the Captaincy General of Guatemala throughout the colonial period. After declaring its independence from Spain in 1821, Honduras fell briefly to the Mexican empire of Augustin de Iturbide, and then joined the Central American Republic (1823-39). Upon dissolution of that federation, Honduras became an independent republic.

RULERS

Spanish, until 1821

Augustin Iturbide (Emperor of Mexico), 1822-1823

MINT MARKS

A - Paris, 1869-1871

P-Y - Provincia Yoro (?)

T - Tegucigalpa, 1825-1862

T.G. - Yoro

T.L. - Comayagua

NOTE: Extensive die varieties exist for coins struck in Honduras with almost endless date and overdate varieties. Federation style coinage continued to be issued until 1861. (See Central American Republic listings.)

MONETARY SYSTEM

16 Reales = 1 Escudo

COLONIAL COINAGE

8 REALES

SILVER, crude
Obv: Bust of Fernando VII.
Rev: Arms within legends.

KM#	Date	Mintage	Good	VG	Fine	VF
3	1813	—	— Reported, not confirmed			

EMPIRE OF MEXICO

2 REALES

SILVER
Obv: Iturbide. Rev: Eagle on cactus.

KM#	Date	Mintage	Good	VG	Fine	VF
6	1823	—	—	—	Rare	—

PROVISIONAL GOVERNMENT

(1823)

1/2 REAL

SILVER

KM#	Date	Mintage	Good	VG	Fine	VF
9	1823TL	—	—	—	Rare	—

KM#	Date	Mintage	Good	VG	Fine	VF
10	1823	—	—	—	Rare	—

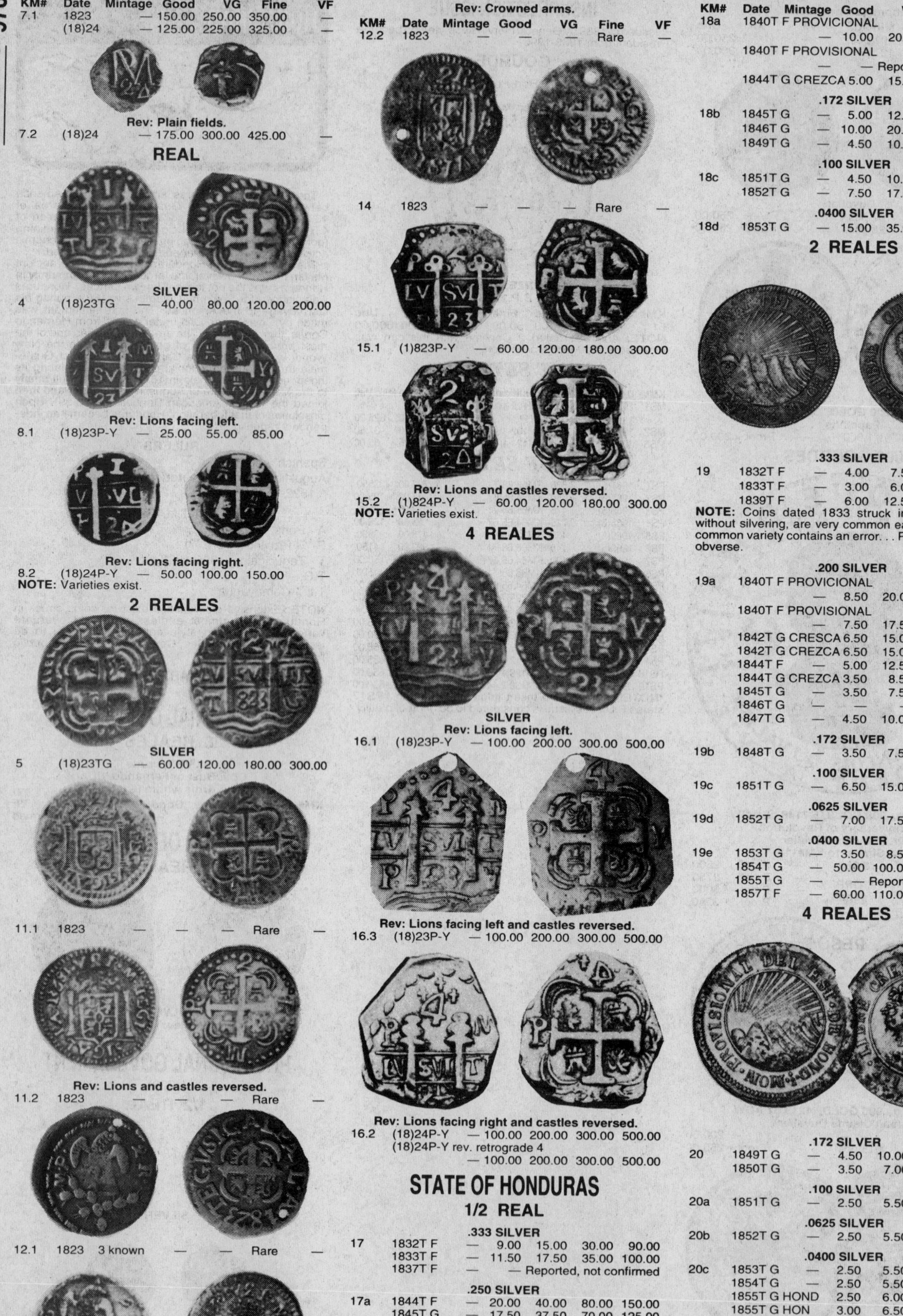

KM#	Date	Mintage	Good	VG	Fine	VF
7.1	1823	—	150.00	250.00	350.00	—
	(18)24	—	125.00	225.00	325.00	—

Rev: Plain fields.

KM#	Date	Mintage	Good	VG	Fine	VF
7.2	(18)24	—	175.00	300.00	425.00	—

REAL

SILVER

KM#	Date	Mintage	Good	VG	Fine	VF
4	(18)23TG	—	40.00	80.00	120.00	200.00

Rev: Lions facing left.

KM#	Date	Mintage	Good	VG	Fine	VF
8.1	(18)23P-Y	—	25.00	55.00	85.00	—

Rev: Lions facing right.

KM#	Date	Mintage	Good	VG	Fine	VF
8.2	(18)24P-Y	—	50.00	100.00	150.00	—

NOTE: Varieties exist.

2 REALES

SILVER

KM#	Date	Mintage	Good	VG	Fine	VF
5	(18)23TG	—	60.00	120.00	180.00	300.00
11.1	1823	—	—	—	Rare	—

Rev: Lions and castles reversed.

KM#	Date	Mintage	Good	VG	Fine	VF
11.2	1823	—	—	—	Rare	—
12.1	1823	3 known	—	—	Rare	—

Rev: Crowned arms.

KM#	Date	Mintage	Good	VG	Fine	VF
12.2	1823	—	—	—	Rare	—
14	1823	—	—	—	Rare	—
15.1	(1)823P-Y	—	60.00	120.00	180.00	300.00

Rev: Lions and castles reversed.

KM#	Date	Mintage	Good	VG	Fine	VF
15.2	(1)824P-Y	—	60.00	120.00	180.00	300.00

NOTE: Varieties exist.

4 REALES

SILVER

Rev: Lions facing left.

KM#	Date	Mintage	Good	VG	Fine	VF
16.1	(18)23P-Y	—	100.00	200.00	300.00	500.00

Rev: Lions facing left and castles reversed.

KM#	Date	Mintage	Good	VG	Fine	VF
16.3	(18)23P-Y	—	100.00	200.00	300.00	500.00

Rev: Lions facing right and castles reversed.

KM#	Date	Mintage	Good	VG	Fine	VF
16.2	(18)24P-Y	—	100.00	200.00	300.00	500.00
	(18)24P-Y rev. retrograde 4	—	100.00	200.00	300.00	500.00

STATE OF HONDURAS

1/2 REAL

.333 SILVER

KM#	Date	Mintage	Good	VG	Fine	VF
17	1832T F	—	9.00	15.00	30.00	90.00
	1833T F	—	11.50	17.50	35.00	100.00
	1837T F	—	— Reported, not confirmed			

.250 SILVER

KM#	Date	Mintage	Good	VG	Fine	VF
17a	1844T F	—	20.00	40.00	80.00	150.00
	1845T G	—	17.50	37.50	70.00	125.00

REAL

.333 SILVER

KM#	Date	Mintage	Good	VG	Fine	VF
18	1832T F	—	4.50	10.00	20.00	40.00
	1839T F	—	10.00	20.00	35.00	75.00

.200 SILVER

KM#	Date	Mintage	Good	VG	Fine	VF
18a	1840T F PROVICIONAL	—	10.00	20.00	35.00	75.00
	1840T F PROVISIONAL	—	— Reported, not confirmed			
	1844T G CREZCA	5.00	15.00	30.00	60.00	

.172 SILVER

KM#	Date	Mintage	Good	VG	Fine	VF
18b	1845T G	—	5.00	12.00	22.50	40.00
	1846T G	—	10.00	20.00	35.00	75.00
	1849T G	—	4.50	10.00	20.00	32.50

.100 SILVER

KM#	Date	Mintage	Good	VG	Fine	VF
18c	1851T G	—	4.50	10.00	20.00	32.50
	1852T G	—	7.50	17.50	30.00	60.00

.0400 SILVER

KM#	Date	Mintage	Good	VG	Fine	VF
18d	1853T G	—	15.00	35.00	60.00	150.00

2 REALES

.333 SILVER

KM#	Date	Mintage	Good	VG	Fine	VF
19	1832T F	—	4.00	7.50	15.00	25.00
	1833T F	—	3.00	6.00	10.00	15.00
	1839T F	—	6.00	12.50	25.00	50.00

NOTE: Coins dated 1833 struck in copper, with or without silvering, are very common early counterfeits. A common variety contains an error. . . PROVISINAL. . . on obverse.

.200 SILVER

KM#	Date	Mintage	Good	VG	Fine	VF
19a	1840T F PROVICIONAL	—	8.50	20.00	35.00	75.00
	1840T F PROVISIONAL	—	7.50	17.50	32.50	65.00
	1842T G CRESCA	6.50	15.00	30.00	60.00	
	1842T G CREZCA	6.50	15.00	30.00	60.00	
	1844T F	—	5.00	12.50	27.50	55.00
	1844T G CREZCA	3.50	8.50	17.50	27.50	
	1845T G	—	3.50	7.50	15.00	25.00
	1846T G	—	—	—	Rare	—
	1847T G	—	4.50	10.00	20.00	30.00

.172 SILVER

KM#	Date	Mintage	Good	VG	Fine	VF
19b	1848T G	—	3.50	7.50	15.00	25.00

.100 SILVER

KM#	Date	Mintage	Good	VG	Fine	VF
19c	1851T G	—	6.50	15.00	30.00	60.00

.0625 SILVER

KM#	Date	Mintage	Good	VG	Fine	VF
19d	1852T G	—	7.00	17.50	35.00	75.00

.0400 SILVER

KM#	Date	Mintage	Good	VG	Fine	VF
19e	1853T G	—	3.50	8.50	20.00	40.00
	1854T G	—	50.00	100.00	200.00	—
	1855T G	—	— Reported, not confirmed			
	1857T F	—	60.00	110.00	220.00	—

4 REALES

.172 SILVER

KM#	Date	Mintage	Good	VG	Fine	VF
20	1849T G	—	4.50	10.00	17.50	27.50
	1850T G	—	3.50	7.00	12.50	22.50

.100 SILVER

KM#	Date	Mintage	Good	VG	Fine	VF
20a	1851T G	—	2.50	5.50	10.00	20.00

.0625 SILVER

KM#	Date	Mintage	Good	VG	Fine	VF
20b	1852T G	—	2.50	5.50	10.00	20.00

.0400 SILVER

KM#	Date	Mintage	Good	VG	Fine	VF
20c	1853T G	—	2.50	5.50	10.00	20.00
	1854T G	—	2.50	5.50	10.00	20.00
	1855T G HOND	2.50	6.00	12.00	22.00	
	1855T G HON	3.00	6.50	15.00	27.50	

COPPER

KM#	Date	Mintage	Good	VG	Fine	VF
20d	1856T G	—	4.50	9.00	18.50	35.00
	1856T F	—	—	—	Rare	—

COPPER-LEAD ALLOY

KM#	Date	Mintage	Good	VG	Fine	VF
20e	1857T F	—	6.00	12.00	22.50	45.00
	1857/2T F/G	—	—	—	—	—

8 REALES

COPPER

KM#	Date	Mintage	Good	VG	Fine	VF
21	1856T G	—	6.50	12.50	30.00	60.00
	1856T FL	—	—	—	—	—

COPPER-LEAD ALLOY

KM#	Date	Mintage	Good	VG	Fine	VF
21a	1857T FL	—	4.50	8.00	12.50	25.00
	1858T FL w/HON	—	6.00	12.00	20.00	35.00
	1858T FL w/HOND	—	6.00	12.00	20.00	35.00
	1859T FL w/PROVISIONAL	—	6.50	12.50	25.00	45.00
	1859T FL w/PROVICIONAL (error)	—	10.00	18.50	30.00	50.00
	1860T FL	2 known	—	—	—	—
	1861T FL	—	8.50	15.00	35.00	75.00

PROVISIONAL COINAGE

NOTE: Similar coins, with rosettes instead of dots separating their legends, are patterns or trial strikes which were struck in England.

PESO

COPPER
Rev: Dots separate legends.

KM#	Date	Mintage	VG	Fine	VF	XF
24	1862T A	—	2.75	7.50	15.00	27.50

2 PESOS

COPPER
Rev: Dots separate legends.

KM#	Date	Mintage	VG	Fine	VF	XF
25	1862T A	—	2.75	7.50	17.50	37.50

4 PESOS

COPPER
Rev: Dots separate legends.

KM#	Date	Mintage	VG	Fine	VF	XF
26	1862T A	—	4.00	12.50	30.00	60.00

8 PESOS

COPPER
Rev: Dots separate legends; curved base 2 in date.

KM#	Date	Mintage	VG	Fine	VF	XF
27	1862T A	—	8.50	25.00	50.00	100.00

REPUBLIC

1/8 REAL

COPPER-NICKEL

KM#	Date	Mintage	Fine	VF	XF	Unc
30	1869A	—	3.50	8.00	12.50	25.00
	1870A	—	3.00	7.00	10.00	17.50

1/4 REAL

COPPER-NICKEL

KM#	Date	Mintage	Fine	VF	XF	Unc
31	1869A	—	1.25	2.75	7.00	14.00
	1870A	—	2.50	5.50	15.00	30.00

1/2 REAL

COPPER-NICKEL

KM#	Date	Mintage	Fine	VF	XF	Unc
32	1869A	—	1.25	3.00	7.00	17.50
	1870A	—	10.00	22.50	40.00	100.00
	1871A	—	—	—	90.00	175.00

REAL

COPPER-NICKEL

KM#	Date	Mintage	Fine	VF	XF	Unc
33	1869A	—	7.50	18.00	32.50	70.00
	1870A	—	5.00	12.00	17.50	40.00

NOTE: Varieties exist.

PESO SERIES

100 Centavos = 1 Peso

1/2 CENTAVO

BRONZE

KM#	Date	Mintage	VG	Fine	VF	XF
45	1881	—	16.00	30.00	60.00	125.00
	1883	—	15.00	27.50	42.50	80.00
	1885	—	12.50	22.50	30.00	50.00
	1886	—	12.50	22.50	30.00	60.00
	1889	—	15.00	27.50	40.00	70.00
	1891	—	250.00	350.00	500.00	—

UN (1) CENTAVO

BRONZE

KM#	Date	Mintage	VG	Fine	VF	XF
40	1878	.346	37.50	70.00	150.00	250.00
	1879	Inc. Ab.	13.50	27.50	50.00	100.00
	1880	Inc. Ab.	12.00	22.50	45.00	100.00

Plain and reeded edges

KM#	Date	Mintage	VG	Fine	VF	XF
46	1881	.132	5.00	12.50	22.50	45.00
	1884	.022	3.00	7.50	15.00	35.00
	1885	—	2.50	6.50	12.50	30.00
	1886	—	3.00	7.50	15.00	30.00
	1889/5	—	7.00	15.00	27.50	50.00
	1889 medal rotation	—	7.00	15.00	27.50	50.00
	1890	—	2.50	7.50	15.00	35.00
	1896	.061	5.00	12.50	22.00	40.00
	1898/88	.054	8.00	20.00	35.00	60.00
	1898	Inc. Ab.	5.00	12.50	22.00	40.00
	1899 small 99	.180	6.00	14.00	25.00	45.00
	1899 lg.99	I.A.	6.00	14.00	25.00	45.00
	1900	.029	5.00	12.50	22.00	40.00
	1901/0	.098	7.00	12.50	22.00	37.50
	1901	Inc. Ab.	7.00	12.50	22.00	37.50
	1902	—	4.00	8.00	15.00	35.00
	1903/2/0	—	7.00	15.00	25.00	45.00
	1903/2/1	—	7.00	15.00	25.00	45.00
	1904	—	5.00	12.50	22.00	40.00
	1907/4	.234	5.00	12.50	22.00	40.00
	1907	Inc. Ab.	5.00	12.50	22.00	40.00

NOTE: Varieties exist.

Obv: KM#46. Rev: Altered KM#49.

KM#	Date	Mintage	VG	Fine	VF	XF
59	1890	—	10.00	20.00	45.00	100.00
	1893	—	12.50	25.00	40.00	75.00
	1895	.045	10.00	20.00	45.00	100.00
	1907 large UN	Inc. KM46	.50	1.75	4.00	9.00
	1907 small UN	Inc. KM46	.50	1.75	4.00	9.00
	1908	.263	7.50	16.50	32.50	50.00

NOTE: Varieties exist.

Mule. Obv: KM#46. Rev: KM#40.

KM#	Date	Mintage	VG	Fine	VF	XF
60	ND	—	125.00	250.00	400.00	600.00

Obv: KM#49. Rev: Altered KM#49.

KM#	Date	Mintage	VG	Fine	VF	XF
61	1890*	—	12.00	25.00	45.00	75.00
	1891*	—	2.00	5.00	10.00	22.50
	1892	—	—	—	Rare	—
	1893/83	—	—	—	—	—
	1893*	—	2.00	5.00	10.00	22.50
	1895	—	10.00	25.00	45.00	75.00
	1908*	Inc. KM59	5.00	10.00	20.00	30.00

***NOTE:** These dates found with die-cutting error or broken die that reads REPLBLICA.
NOTE: Varieties exist.

Mule. Obv: KM#59. Rev: KM#40.

KM#	Date	Mintage	VG	Fine	VF	XF
A63	ND(c.1895)	—	—	—	—	—

Mule. Obv: Pattern 5 Peso of 1871.

KM#	Date	Mintage	VG	Fine	VF	XF
63	1895	—	150.00	300.00	500.00	750.00

Obv: KM#45. Rev: Altered KM#45.

KM#	Date	Mintage	VG	Fine	VF	XF
65	1910/5	.410	10.00	22.00	35.00	60.00
	1910	.410	8.50	20.00	32.50	50.00
	1911/811	.062	10.00	22.00	35.00	60.00
	1911/885	I.A.	10.00	22.00	35.00	60.00
	1911	Inc. Ab.	6.00	15.00	25.00	40.00

NOTE: Varieties exist.

Obv: KM#48. Rev: Altered KM#45.

KM#	Date	Mintage	VG	Fine	VF	XF
66	1910	Inc. Ab.	8.00	22.50	37.50	60.00
	1610 (error) inverted 9	Inc. Ab.	16.50	40.00	65.00	100.00
	1910 (error) second 1 inverted	Inc. Ab.	12.00	25.00	40.00	65.00
	1911 CENTAVOS	Inc. Ab.	—	—	Rare	—

Obv: KM#48. Rev: Altered KM#48.

KM#	Date	Mintage	VG	Fine	VF	XF
67	1910	Inc. Ab.	3.75	8.00	15.00	25.00
	1911	Inc. Ab.	—	Reported, not confirmed		

Obv: KM#45. Rev: Altered KM#48.

KM#	Date	Mintage	VG	Fine	VF	XF
68	1910	Inc. Ab.	17.50	40.00	65.00	125.00

Similar to KM#65, CENTAVO omitted.

KM#	Date	Mintage	VG	Fine	VF	XF
70	1919	.168	1.75	3.50	6.00	20.00
	1920	.030	2.75	5.00	9.50	25.00

2 CENTAVOS

BRONZE
Rev: Altered KM#49.

KM#	Date	Mintage	VG	Fine	VF	XF
64	1907	Inc. Be.	—	—	Rare	—
	1908	Inc. Be.	35.00	75.00	150.00	300.00

Obv: KM#46. Rev: Altered KM#46.

KM#	Date	Mintage	VG	Fine	VF	XF
69	1910	.435	1.00	2.50	4.50	12.00
	1911	.068	2.50	6.00	10.00	25.00
	1912 CENTAVOS	.088	.75	2.50	4.00	12.00
	1912 CENTAVO	Inc. Ab.	1.50	3.75	7.00	20.00
	1913	.258	.75	2.50	4.50	15.00

NOTE: Reverse dies often very crudely recut, especially 1910 and 1911. Some coins of 1910 appear to be struck over earlier 1 or 2 Centavos, probably 1907 or 1908.

Rev: CENTAVOS omitted.

KM#	Date	Mintage	VG	Fine	VF	XF
71	1919	.117	1.25	3.00	5.00	15.00
	1920	.283	.50	1.25	2.75	10.00
	1920 dot	I.A.	.65	1.50	3.00	10.00

NOTE: Varieties exist.

5 CENTAVOS

1.2500 g, .835 SILVER, .0336 oz ASW
Obv: Arms. Rev: Tree.

KM#	Date	Mintage	VG	Fine	VF	XF
34	1871	2,056	75.00	165.00	300.00	650.00
	1871	—	—	—	Proof	—

NOTE: The above coin reads "0.900" but is actually 0.835 fine and was struck in 1879 and 1880.

Obv: Eagle. Rev: Standing Liberty.

KM#	Date	Mintage	VG	Fine	VF	XF
43	1879	—	—	—	Rare	—

KM#	Date	Mintage	VG	Fine	VF	XF
48	1884	—	10.00	22.50	37.50	65.00
	1885	—	12.50	25.00	40.00	75.00
	1886	—	12.50	25.00	40.00	75.00
	1890	—	—	Reported, not confirmed		
	1902	—	25.00	50.00	100.00	150.00

KM#	Date	Mintage	VG	Fine	VF	XF
54	1886	—	5.00	12.00	18.00	35.00
	6188 (error)	2 known	—	—	Rare	—
	1895/85	—	—	—	Rare	—
	1895	—	—	—	Rare	—
	1896/85	.035	2.50	5.00	12.50	20.00
	1896/86	I.A.	2.50	5.00	12.50	20.00
	1896	Inc. Ab.	3.50	7.00	15.00	25.00

NOTE: Varieties exist.

10 CENTAVOS

2.5000 g, .835 SILVER, .0671 oz ASW

KM#	Date	Mintage	VG	Fine	VF	XF
35	1871	.017	12.00	25.00	45.00	85.00

NOTE: The above coin reads "0.900" but is actually 0.835 fine.

Obv: Eagle. Rev: Standing Liberty.

KM#	Date	Mintage	VG	Fine	VF	XF
41	1878	—	—	—	Rare	—
	1879	—	—	—	Rare	—

Mule. Obv: KM#41. Rev: KM#35.

KM#	Date	Mintage	VG	Fine	VF	XF
42	1878	—	—	—	Rare	—

KM#	Date	Mintage	VG	Fine	VF	XF
49	1884	—	7.50	22.50	35.00	60.00
	1885	—	6.00	17.50	27.50	50.00
	1886	—	7.50	22.50	35.00	60.00
	1889	—	22.50	50.00	85.00	130.00
	1891	—	—	Reported, not confirmed		
	1893*	—	7.50	22.50	37.50	65.00
	1895*	.053	6.00	18.50	40.00	100.00
	1900*	5,300	30.00	60.00	100.00	200.00

***NOTE:** These dates found with die-cutting error or broken die that reads REPLBLICA.

Mule. Obv: KM#35. Rev: KM#49.
P on reverse.

KM#	Date	Mintage	VG	Fine	VF	XF
55.1	1886	—	18.50	37.50	70.00	—
	1895/71	—	—	—	—	—
	1895	—	16.50	30.00	55.00	—

1-P replaces date.

KM#	Date	Mintage	VG	Fine	VF	XF
55.2	ND	—	30.00	70.00	120.00	—

Rev: Without P.

KM#	Date	Mintage	VG	Fine	VF	XF
55.3	1895 lg.dt.	—	—	—	—	—
	1895 sm.dt.	—	—	—	—	—

25 CENTAVOS

6.2500 g, .900 SILVER, .1808 oz ASW

KM#	Date	Mintage	VG	Fine	VF	XF
36	1871	.177	2.50	5.50	13.50	37.50

KM#	Date	Mintage	VG	Fine	VF	XF
50	1883	—	2.75	6.50	11.00	23.50
	1884	—	2.00	5.00	9.00	20.00
	1885/4	—	—	—	—	—
	1885	—	2.25	6.00	10.00	22.50
	1886/1	—	2.75	6.50	11.00	23.50
	1887	—	—	Reported, not confirmed		
	1888/7	—	5.00	12.00	22.50	42.50
	1888	—	2.25	5.00	10.00	22.50
	1890/85	—	3.50	7.50	15.00	27.50
	1890/88	—	3.50	7.50	15.00	27.50
	1890/89	—	3.50	7.50	15.00	27.50
	1891/181	—	3.50	7.50	15.00	27.50
	1891/81	—	3.50	7.50	15.00	27.50
	1891	—	3.00	6.75	12.50	25.00
	1892/81	—	2.25	5.00	10.00	20.00
	1892/1	—	2.25	5.00	10.00	20.00
	1893/83	—	2.75	6.00	11.00	22.50
	1893/88	—	2.75	6.00	11.00	22.50
	1895/83	.012	3.50	7.50	15.00	27.50
	1895	Inc. Ab.	2.25	5.00	10.00	20.00
	1896	.274	3.50	7.00	12.50	22.50
	1898	.190	—	Reported, not confirmed		
	1899/88	.030	10.00	20.00	40.00	65.00

NOTE: Varieties exist.

6.2500 g, .835 SILVER, .1678 oz ASW

KM#	Date	Mintage	VG	Fine	VF	XF
50a	1899/88 .835/.900 medal rotation	I.A.	7.00	15.00	25.00	40.00
	1899	I.A.	5.00	11.00	17.50	30.00
	1900/800 .835/.900	.039	2.25	5.00	11.00	22.50
	1900/891	I.A.	2.25	5.00	11.00	22.50
	1900	Inc. Ab.	2.25	5.00	11.00	22.50
	1901/801	—	4.00	7.50	15.00	28.00
	1901	.054	2.25	5.00	10.00	20.00
	1902/802	—	4.00	7.50	15.00	28.00
	1902/812	—	4.00	7.50	15.00	28.00
	1902/891	—	4.00	7.50	15.00	28.00
	1902/1F	—	2.25	5.00	10.00	20.00
	1902F	—	3.75	7.50	15.00	27.50
	1904	—	11.00	22.50	37.50	67.50
	1907/4	.014	4.50	7.50	15.00	28.00
	1907	Inc. Ab.	6.00	12.00	22.50	37.50
	1910	745 pcs.	—	Reported, not confirmed		
	1912 .835/.900	7,168	10.00	17.50	35.00	60.00
	1913/0	.052	—	—	—	—
	1913/2	I.A.	—	—	—	—
	1913	Inc. Ab.	5.00	10.00	17.50	32.50

NOTE: Varieties exist.

50 CENTAVOS

12.5000 g, .900 SILVER, .3617 oz ASW

KM#	Date	Mintage	VG	Fine	VF	XF
37	1871	.040	3.75	11.00	18.50	45.00

KM#	Date	Mintage	VG	Fine	VF	XF
44	1879	—	165.00	350.00	650.00	1250.

KM#	Date	Mintage	VG	Fine	VF	XF
51	1883	—	5.50	11.00	25.00	50.00
	1883P	—	8.00	16.00	27.50	55.00
	1884	—	5.00	10.00	20.00	40.00
	1885 medal rotation	—	5.00	10.00	22.50	45.00
	1885 coin rotation	—	5.00	10.00	22.50	45.00
	1886/5	—	7.00	15.00	30.00	60.00
	1886	—	5.50	12.50	27.50	55.00
	1887/5	—	7.00	15.00	30.00	60.00
	1887	—	7.00	15.00	30.00	60.00
	1896/86	—	175.00	350.00	650.00	—
	1897	.037	37.50	67.50	110.00	—
	1910	602 pcs.	500.00	900.00	—	—
	12.5000 g, .835 SILVER, .3355 oz ASW					
51a	1908/897	447 pcs.	42.50	90.00	150.00	225.00
	1908 .835/.900	Inc. Ab.	28.50	60.00	90.00	150.00
	1911	90 pcs.	—	Reported, not confirmed		

PESO

1.6120 g, .900 GOLD, .0467 oz AGW
Similar to 5 Centavos, KM#34.

KM#	Date	Mintage	Fine	VF	XF	Unc
38	1871	—	—	—	Rare	—

Mule. Obv: KM#38. Rev: KM#56.

KM#	Date	Mintage	Fine	VF	XF	Unc
39	1871	—	325.00	550.00	825.00	1700.

25.0000 g, .900 SILVER, .7234 oz ASW
Rev: Small CENTRO-AMERICA.

KM#	Date	Mintage	VG	Fine	VF	XF
47	1881	.026	15.00	32.50	55.00	120.00
	1882 medal rotation	.076	15.00	27.50	45.00	100.00
	1882 coin rotation	Inc. Ab.	15.00	27.50	45.00	100.00
	1883	—	15.00	30.00	50.00	110.00

Rev: Large CENTRO-AMERICA.

KM#	Date	Mintage	VG	Fine	VF	XF
52	1883/1	—	50.00	100.00	200.00	400.00
	1884	—	12.50	27.50	45.00	85.00
	1885	—	12.50	25.00	40.00	75.00
	1886	—	12.50	27.50	45.00	85.00
	1887	—	12.50	27.50	45.00	85.00
	1888	—	12.50	25.00	40.00	75.00
	1889/8	—	12.50	25.00	40.00	75.00
	1889	—	12.50	25.00	40.00	75.00
	1890	—	12.50	25.00	40.00	75.00
	1891/88	—	12.50	25.00	40.00	75.00
	1891/89	—	12.50	25.00	40.00	75.00
	1892/0	—	12.50	25.00	40.00	75.00
	1892/1	—	12.50	25.00	40.00	75.00
	1893/1	—	200.00	500.00	950.00	1600.
	1895/0	.080	15.00	30.00	60.00	110.00
	1895	Inc. Ab.	15.00	30.00	60.00	110.00
	1899/87P		400.00	800.00	1500.	—
	1902	—	17.50	40.00	70.00	120.00
	1903 flat top 3	—	17.50	35.00	60.00	100.00
	1903 round top 3	—	22.50	45.00	85.00	150.00
	1904	.020	22.50	45.00	85.00	150.00
	1914	—	200.00	500.00	900.00	1500.

NOTE: Overdates and recut dies are prevalent.

Mule. Obv: KM#47, w/o 25 GMOS above UN PESO.
Rev: KM#52.

KM#	Date	Mintage	VG	Fine	VF	XF
62	1894/82	—	15.00	30.00	50.00	100.00
	1894/2 closed 4	—	20.00	37.50	60.00	125.00
	1894/2 open 4	—	20.00	37.50	60.00	125.00
	1895/85	I.A.	15.00	30.00	50.00	100.00
	1895/3	I.A.	15.00	30.00	50.00	100.00
	1895/4	I.A.	15.00	30.00	50.00	100.00
	1896/4	.021	25.00	55.00	90.00	—

1.6120 g, .900 GOLD, .0467 oz AGW

KM#	Date	Mintage	Fine	VF	XF	Unc
56	1887	—	—	Reported, not confirmed		
	1888	—	125.00	250.00	375.00	650.00
	1889	—	—	Reported, not confirmed		
	1890	—	—	Reported, not confirmed		
	1895	43 pcs.	125.00	250.00	375.00	650.00
	1896	—	125.00	250.00	375.00	650.00
	1899	—	—	Reported, not confirmed		
	1901	—	150.00	300.00	600.00	900.00
	1902	—	140.00	300.00	500.00	800.00
	1907	—	140.00	250.00	450.00	700.00
	1912	350 pcs.	—	Reported, not confirmed		
	1913	6,000	—	Reported, not confirmed		
	1914/882	—	275.00	450.00	600.00	900.00
	1914/03	—	275.00	450.00	600.00	900.00
	1919	—	150.00	300.00	550.00	800.00
	1920	—	150.00	300.00	550.00	800.00
	1922	—	140.00	250.00	450.00	650.00
	ND	—	—	—	—	—

5 PESOS

8.0645 g, .900 GOLD, .2333 oz AGW

KM#	Date	Mintage	Fine	VF	XF	Unc
53	1883	—	450.00	650.00	1000.	1500.
	1888/3	—	450.00	650.00	1000.	1500.
	1889	—	—	Reported, not confirmed		
	1890	—	600.00	750.00	1100.	1750.
	1895	20 pcs.	600.00	900.00	1350.	2000.
	1896	55 pcs.	600.00	900.00	1350.	2000.
	1897	—	450.00	650.00	1000.	1500.
	1900	—	450.00	650.00	1000.	1500.
	1902	—	450.00	650.00	1000.	1500.
	1908/888	—	450.00	650.00	1000.	1500.
	1913	1,200	450.00	650.00	1000.	1500.

10 PESOS

16.1290 g, .900 GOLD, .4667 oz AGW

KM#	Date	Mintage	Fine	VF	XF	Unc
58	1889	25 pcs.	5000.	6000.	7500.	10,000.
	1895	10 pcs.	—	Reported, not confirmed		

20 PESOS

32.2580 g, .900 GOLD, .9335 oz AGW

KM#	Date	Mintage	Fine	VF	XF	Unc
57	1888	—	3500.	5000.	8000.	15,000.
	1895/88	—	—	—	Rare	—
	1895	—	—	—	Rare	—
	1908/888	—	5000.	7500.	15,000.	—
	1908/897	—	—	—	*Rare	—
	1908	—	5000.	7500.	15,000.	—

***NOTE:** Stack's Hammel sale 9-82 VF realized $12,000.

Ponterio & Associates NYINC. sale 12-86 choice XF realized $30,800.

Superior Casterline sale 5-89 choice XF realized $28,600.

MONETARY REFORM

100 Centavos = 1 Lempira

CENTAVO

BRONZE, thick planchet, 2.00 g

77.1	1935	2.000	.25	.75	2.00	7.50
	1939	2.000	.25	.50	1.50	6.00
	1949	4.000	.10	.30	.75	2.50
	Thin planchet, 1.50 g					
77.2	1954	3.500	.10	.15	.25	1.00
	1956	2.000	.10	.15	.25	.50
	1957/6	28.000	—	—	—	—
	1957	Inc. Ab.	—	.10	.15	.30
	COPPER-CLAD STEEL					
77a.1	1974	—	—	.10	.15	.25
	1985	—	—	.10	.15	.25
	1992	—	—	.10	.15	.25

BRONZE
Obv: Modified arms, clouds behind pyramid.

77a.2	1988	50.000	—	.10	.15	.25
	1992	—	—	.10	.15	.25

2 CENTAVOS

BRONZE

78	1939	2.000	.25	.50	1.50	6.00
	1949	3.000	.10	.25	1.00	4.00
	1954	2.000	.10	.25	1.00	3.00
	1956	20.000	—	.10	.15	.40

BRONZE-CLAD STEEL

78a	1974	—	—	.10	.15	.25

5 CENTAVOS

COPPER-NICKEL

Dentilated border.

KM#	Date	Mintage	Fine	VF	XF	Unc
72.1	1931	2.000	.50	1.50	2.50	15.00
	1932	1.000	.35	.75	1.50	10.00
	1949	2.000	.20	.50	1.00	4.00
	1972	5.000	—	.10	.15	.25

Beaded border.

KM#	Date	Mintage	Fine	VF	XF	Unc
72.2	1954	1.400	.15	.25	.60	3.00
	1956	10.070	—	.10	.15	.50
	1980	20.000	—	.10	.15	.25

BRASS

KM#	Date	Mintage	Fine	VF	XF	Unc
72.2a	1975	20.000	—	.10	.15	.25
	1989	—	—	.10	.15	.25
	1993	—	—	.10	.15	.25

NOTE: Varieties exist.

10 CENTAVOS

COPPER-NICKEL
Dentilated border.

KM#	Date	Mintage	Fine	VF	XF	Unc
76.1	1932	1.500	.75	1.50	4.00	25.00
	1951	1.000	.25	.75	1.50	4.00
	1956	7.560	.10	.15	.25	.75

Beaded border.

KM#	Date	Mintage	Fine	VF	XF	Unc
76.2	1954	1.200	.10	.20	.35	1.00
	1967	—	.10	.25	.50	2.00
	1980	15.000	.10	.25	.50	2.00

BRASS

KM#	Date	Mintage	Fine	VF	XF	Unc
76.1a	1976	—	—	—	.10	.25
	1989	—	—	—	.10	.25
	1993	—	—	—	.10	.25

NOTE: Varieties exist.

20 CENTAVOS

2.5000 g, .900 SILVER, .0723 oz ASW
Chief Lempira

KM#	Date	Mintage	Fine	VF	XF	Unc
73	1931	1.000	1.00	3.00	6.00	17.50
	1932	.750	1.25	3.25	7.00	17.50
	1951	1.500	BV	1.25	2.50	7.00
	1952	2.500	BV	1.25	2.00	6.00
	1958	2.000	BV	1.25	2.00	5.00

COPPER-NICKEL

KM#	Date	Mintage	Fine	VF	XF	Unc
79	1967	12.000	—	.10	.15	.50

Different style lettering.

KM#	Date	Mintage	Fine	VF	XF	Unc
81	1973	15.000	—	.10	.15	.50

KM#	Date	Mintage	Fine	VF	XF	Unc
83	1978	30.000	—	.10	.15	.50
	1990	—	—	.10	.15	.50

NICKEL PLATED STEEL

KM#	Date	Mintage	Fine	VF	XF	Unc
83a	1991	—	—	.10	.15	.50
	1993	—	—	.10	.15	.50

50 CENTAVOS

6.2500 g, .900 SILVER, .1808 oz ASW
Chief Lempira

KM#	Date	Mintage	Fine	VF	XF	Unc
74	1931	.500	1.00	3.00	6.00	30.00
	1932	1.100	1.00	2.00	5.00	25.00
	1937	1.000	1.00	2.00	5.00	25.00
	1951	.500	1.00	2.00	4.00	20.00

COPPER-NICKEL

KM#	Date	Mintage	Fine	VF	XF	Unc
80	1967	4.800	—	.25	.35	1.00

F.A.O. Issue

KM#	Date	Mintage	Fine	VF	XF	Unc
82	1973	4.400	—	.25	.35	1.00

KM#	Date	Mintage	Fine	VF	XF	Unc
84	1978	12.000	—	.25	.35	1.00
	1990	—	—	.25	.35	1.00

NICKEL PLATED STEEL

KM#	Date	Mintage	Fine	VF	XF	Unc
84a	1991	—	—	.25	.35	1.00

LEMPIRA

12.5000 g, .900 SILVER, .3617 oz ASW
Chief Lempira

KM#	Date	Mintage	Fine	VF	XF	Unc
75	1931	.550	BV	3.50	7.00	30.00
	1932	1.000	—	BV	6.00	25.00
	1933	.400	BV	3.50	7.00	30.00
	1934	.600	BV	3.50	7.00	25.00
	1935	1.000	—	BV	6.00	25.00
	1937	4.000	—	BV	5.00	17.50

MEDALLIC PROCLAMATION ISSUES (M)

Vice-Royalty of New Spain

A proclamation issue was struck for Ferdinand VII as the new King of Spain while he was under Napoleonic French guard.

TRUXILLO

(Trujillo)

2 REALES

SILVER
Ferdinand VII

KM#	Date	Mintage	Fine	VF	XF	Unc
M1	1808	—	125.00	250.00	425.00	750.00

HONG KONG

The colony of Hong Kong, a British colony situated at the mouth of the Canton or Pearl River 90 miles (145 km.) southeast of Canton, has an area of 403 sq. mi. (1,040 sq. km.) and a population of 5.2 million. Capital: Victoria. The free port of Hong Kong, the commercial center of the Far East, is a trans-shipment point for goods destined for China and the countries of the Western Pacific. Light manufacturing and tourism are important components of the economy.

Long a haven for fishermen-pirates and opium smugglers, the island of Hong Kong was ceded to Britain at the conclusion of the first Opium War, 1839-1842. At the time, the acquisition of a 'barren rock' was ridiculed by both London and English merchants operating in the Far East. The Kowloon Peninsula and Stonecutter's Island were ceded in 1860, and the so-called New Territories, comprising most of the mainland of the colony, were leased to Britain for 99 years in 1898.

The legends on Hong Kong coinage are bilingual: English and Chinese. The rare 1941 cent was dispatched to Hong Kong in several shipments. One fell into Japanese hands while another was melted down by the British and a third was sunk during enemy action.

RULERS

British

MINT MARKS

H - Heaton

KN - King's Norton

MONETARY SYSTEM

10 Mils (Wen, Ch'ien) = 1 Cent (Hsien)

10 Cents = 1 Chiao

100 Cents = 10 Chiao = 1 Dollar (Yuan)

MIL

BRONZE

Obv: Chinese value: *1 Wen*.

KM#	Date	Mintage	Fine	VF	XF	Unc
1	1863	19.000	1.00	2.00	4.00	15.00
	1863	—	—	—	Proof	250.00
	1864	—	500.00	600.00	800.00	1800.
	1864	—	—	—	Proof	—
	1865	40.000	—	—	1000.	1500.

Rev: W/o Hyphen between HONG KONG.

KM#	Date	Mintage	Fine	VF	XF	Unc
2	1865	Inc. Ab.	1.00	2.00	4.00	15.00

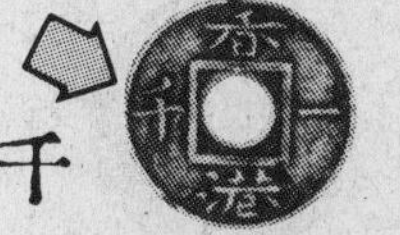

Obv: Chinese value: *1 Ch'ien*.

KM#	Date	Mintage	Fine	VF	XF	Unc
3	1866	20.000	1.00	2.00	5.00	15.00

CENT

BRONZE

Obv: 14 pearls in left arch of crown.

KM#	Date	Mintage	Fine	VF	XF	Unc
4.1	1863	1.000	1.00	3.50	7.50	40.00
	1863	—	—	—	Proof	270.00
	1863 dot on reverse			—	Proof	350.00
	1865/3	1.000	1.50	7.50	15.00	40.00
	1865	Inc. Ab.	1.00	3.50	7.50	35.00
	1865	—	—	—	Proof	270.00
	1866	1.000	1.00	3.50	7.50	35.00
	1866	—	—	—	Proof	275.00
	1875	1.000	1.00	3.50	7.50	35.00
	1875	—	—	—	Proof	275.00
	1876	1.000	1.00	3.50	7.50	35.00
	1876	—	—	—	Proof	275.00
	1877	2.000	1.50	4.50	9.00	45.00
	1877	—	—	—	Proof	275.00

Obv: 15 pearls in left arch of crown.

KM#	Date	Mintage	Fine	VF	XF	Unc
4.2	1877	2.000	1.00	3.50	7.50	35.00
	1877	—	—	—	Proof	275.00
	1879	Inc. Be.	1.00	3.50	7.50	35.00
	1879	—	—	—	Proof	275.00

Obv: 5 pearls in center of crown.

KM#	Date	Mintage	Fine	VF	XF	Unc
4.3	1879	1.000	1.50	7.00	15.00	45.00
	1879	—	—	—	Proof	275.00
	1880	1.000	1.00	3.50	12.50	40.00
	1880	—	—	—	Proof	275.00
	1881	1.000	1.00	3.50	12.50	40.00
	1881	—	—	—	Proof	250.00
	1899	1.000	1.00	3.00	7.50	35.00
	1899	—	—	—	Proof	200.00
	1900H	1.000	1.00	2.00	6.00	25.00
	1900H	—	—	—	Proof	200.00
	1901	5.000	.75	2.00	4.00	20.00
	1901H	10.000	.75	2.00	4.00	15.00

KM#	Date	Mintage	Fine	VF	XF	Unc
11	1902	5.000	.75	2.00	3.50	15.00
	1903	5.000	.75	2.00	3.50	15.00
	1904H	10.000	.75	2.00	3.50	15.00
	1905	2.500	1.00	2.50	5.00	20.00
	1905H	12.500	.75	2.00	3.50	15.00

KM#	Date	Mintage	Fine	VF	XF	Unc
16	1919H	2.500	.50	1.00	2.00	8.00
	1923	2.500	.50	1.00	2.00	10.00
	1924	5.000	.50	1.00	2.00	7.50
	1925	2.500	.50	1.00	2.00	9.00
	1926	2.500	.50	1.00	2.00	9.00
	1926	—	—	—	Proof	140.00

KM#	Date	Mintage	Fine	VF	XF	Unc
17	1931	5.000	.25	.35	.75	2.00
	1931	—	—	—	Proof	90.00
	1933	6.500	.25	.35	.75	2.00
	1933	—	—	—	Proof	90.00
	1934	5.000	.25	.35	.75	2.00
	1934	—	—	—	Proof	90.00

KM#	Date	Mintage	Fine	VF	XF	Unc
24	1941	5.000	400.00	1000.	1500.	2000.
	1941	—	—	—	Proof	4500.

5 CENTS

1.3577 g, .800 SILVER, .0349 oz ASW

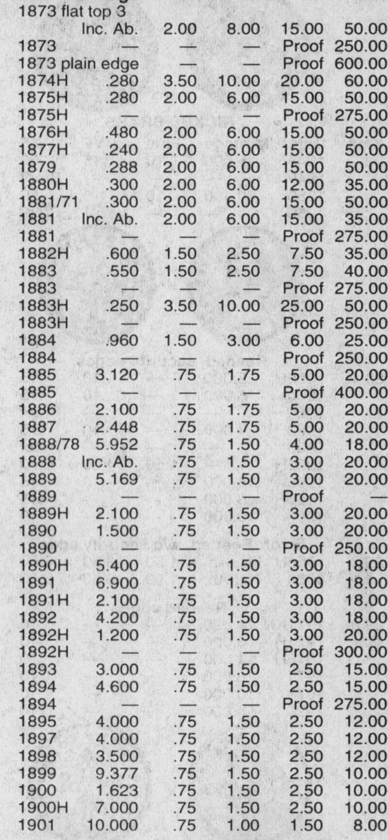

KM#	Date	Mintage	Fine	VF	XF	Unc
5	1866	1.313	2.50	4.00	8.00	45.00
	1866 milled edge	—	—	—	Proof	250.00
	1866 plain edge	—	—	—	Proof	275.00
	1867	Inc. Ab.	3.50	7.50	12.00	45.00
	1867	—	—	—	Proof	250.00
	1868	Inc. Ab.	2.00	5.00	10.00	35.00
	1872/68H	.136	2.50	6.00	15.00	60.00
	1872H Arabic 1	Inc. Ab.	2.50	6.00	15.00	45.00
	1872H Roman I	Inc. Ab.	3.50	10.00	15.00	60.00
	1873/63	.387	2.50	8.00	17.50	50.00
	1873/63H	.256	2.50	5.00	8.00	35.00
	1873H round top 3	Inc. Ab.	2.00	8.00	15.00	50.00
	1873 flat top 3	Inc. Ab.	2.00	8.00	15.00	50.00
	1873	—	—	—	Proof	250.00
	1873 plain edge	—	—	—	Proof	600.00
	1874H	.280	3.50	10.00	20.00	60.00
	1875H	.280	2.00	6.00	15.00	50.00
	1875H	—	—	—	Proof	275.00
	1876H	.480	2.00	6.00	15.00	50.00
	1877H	.240	2.00	6.00	15.00	50.00
	1879	.288	2.00	6.00	15.00	50.00
	1880H	.300	2.00	6.00	12.00	35.00
	1881/71	.300	2.00	6.00	15.00	50.00
	1881	Inc. Ab.	2.00	6.00	15.00	35.00
	1881	—	—	—	Proof	275.00
	1882H	.600	1.50	2.50	7.50	35.00
	1883	.550	1.50	2.50	7.50	40.00
	1883	—	—	—	Proof	275.00
	1883H	.250	3.50	10.00	25.00	50.00
	1883H	—	—	—	Proof	250.00
	1884	.960	1.50	3.00	6.00	25.00
	1884	—	—	—	Proof	250.00
	1885	3.120	.75	1.75	5.00	20.00
	1885	—	—	—	Proof	400.00
	1886	2.100	.75	1.75	5.00	20.00
	1887	2.448	.75	1.75	5.00	20.00
	1888/78	5.952	.75	1.50	4.00	18.00
	1888	Inc. Ab.	.75	1.50	3.00	20.00
	1889	5.169	.75	1.50	3.00	20.00
	1889	—	—	—	Proof	—
	1889H	2.100	.75	1.50	3.00	20.00
	1890	1.500	.75	1.50	3.00	20.00
	1890	—	—	—	Proof	250.00
	1890H	5.400	.75	1.50	3.00	18.00
	1891	6.900	.75	1.50	3.00	18.00
	1891H	2.100	.75	1.50	3.00	18.00
	1892	4.200	.75	1.50	3.00	18.00
	1892H	1.200	.75	1.50	3.00	20.00
	1892H	—	—	—	Proof	300.00
	1893	3.000	.75	1.50	2.50	15.00
	1894	4.600	.75	1.50	2.50	15.00
	1894	—	—	—	Proof	275.00
	1895	4.000	.75	1.50	2.50	12.00
	1897	4.000	.75	1.50	2.50	12.00
	1898	3.500	.75	1.50	2.50	12.00
	1899	9.377	.75	1.50	2.50	10.00
	1900	1.623	.75	1.50	2.50	10.00
	1900H	7.000	.75	1.50	2.50	10.00
	1901	10.000	.75	1.00	1.50	8.00

KM#	Date	Mintage	Fine	VF	XF	Unc
12	1903	6.000	.75	1.50	2.50	8.00
	1903	—	—	—	Proof	200.00
	1904	8.000	.75	1.50	2.50	8.00
	1904	—	—	—	Proof	175.00
	1905	1.000	.65	1.25	2.25	4.50
	1905H	7.000	.65	1.25	2.25	4.00

KM#	Date	Mintage	Fine	VF	XF	Unc
18	1932	3.000	.50	.75	1.75	3.50
	1932	—	—	—	Proof	150.00
	1933	2.000	.50	.75	1.75	3.50
	1933	—	—	—	Proof	150.00

COPPER-NICKEL

KM#	Date	Mintage	Fine	VF	XF	Unc
18a	1935	1.000	.75	1.50	3.00	6.00
	1935	—	—	—	Proof	100.00

NICKEL

KM#	Date	Mintage	Fine	VF	XF	Unc
20	1937	3.000	.50	1.00	1.50	3.00
	1937	—	—	—	Proof	60.00

KM#	Date	Mintage	Fine	VF	XF	Unc
22	1938	3.000	.20	.35	.85	2.00
	1938	—	—	—	Proof	125.00
	1939H	3.090	.20	.35	.85	2.00
	1939H	—	—	—	Proof	125.00
	1939KN	4.710	.20	.35	.65	2.00
	1941H	.777	125.00	150.00	250.00	325.00
	1941KN	1.075	65.00	85.00	125.00	275.00

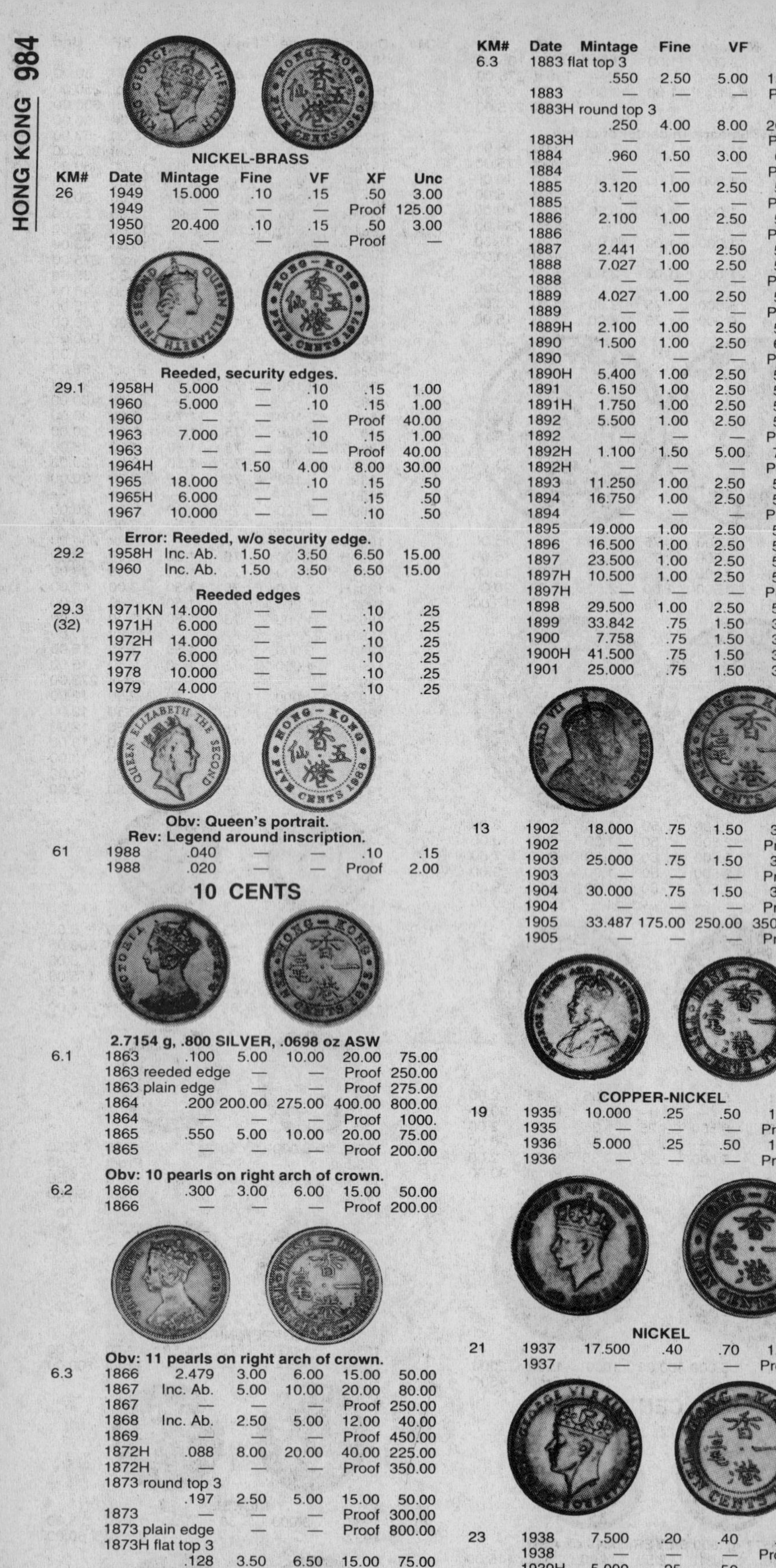

NICKEL-BRASS

KM#	Date	Mintage	Fine	VF	XF	Unc
26	1949	15.000	.10	.15	.50	3.00
	1949	—	—	—	Proof	125.00
	1950	20.400	.10	.15	.50	3.00
	1950	—	—	—	Proof	—

Reeded, security edges.

KM#	Date	Mintage	Fine	VF	XF	Unc
29.1	1958H	5.000	—	.10	.15	1.00
	1960	5.000	—	.10	.15	1.00
	1960	—	—	—	Proof	40.00
	1963	7.000	—	.10	.15	1.00
	1963	—	—	—	Proof	40.00
	1964H	—	1.50	4.00	8.00	30.00
	1965	18.000	—	.10	.15	.50
	1965H	6.000	—	—	.15	.50
	1967	10.000	—	—	.10	.50

Error: Reeded, w/o security edge.

KM#	Date	Mintage	Fine	VF	XF	Unc
29.2	1958H	Inc. Ab.	1.50	3.50	6.50	15.00
	1960	Inc. Ab.	1.50	3.50	6.50	15.00

Reeded edges

KM#	Date	Mintage	Fine	VF	XF	Unc
29.3	1971KN	14.000	—	—	.10	.25
(32)	1971H	6.000	—	—	.10	.25
	1972H	14.000	—	—	.10	.25
	1977	6.000	—	—	.10	.25
	1978	10.000	—	—	.10	.25
	1979	4.000	—	—	.10	.25

Obv: Queen's portrait.
Rev: Legend around inscription.

KM#	Date	Mintage	Fine	VF	XF	Unc
61	1988	.040	—	—	.10	.15
	1988	.020	—	—	Proof	2.00

10 CENTS

2.7154 g, .800 SILVER, .0698 oz ASW

KM#	Date	Mintage	Fine	VF	XF	Unc
6.1	1863	.100	5.00	10.00	20.00	75.00
	1863 reeded edge	—		—	Proof	250.00
	1863 plain edge	—		—	Proof	275.00
	1864	.200	200.00	275.00	400.00	800.00
	1864	—	—	—	Proof	1000.
	1865	.550	5.00	10.00	20.00	75.00
	1865	—	—	—	Proof	200.00

Obv: 10 pearls on right arch of crown.

KM#	Date	Mintage	Fine	VF	XF	Unc
6.2	1866	.300	3.00	6.00	15.00	50.00
	1866	—	—	—	Proof	200.00

Obv: 11 pearls on right arch of crown.

KM#	Date	Mintage	Fine	VF	XF	Unc
6.3	1866	2.479	3.00	6.00	15.00	50.00
	1867	Inc. Ab.	5.00	10.00	20.00	80.00
	1867	—	—	—	Proof	250.00
	1868	Inc. Ab.	2.50	5.00	12.00	40.00
	1869	—	—	—	Proof	450.00
	1872H	.088	8.00	20.00	40.00	225.00
	1872H	—	—	—	Proof	350.00
	1873 round top 3					
		.197	2.50	5.00	15.00	50.00
	1873	—	—	—	Proof	300.00
	1873 plain edge	—		—	Proof	800.00
	1873H flat top 3					
		.128	3.50	6.50	15.00	75.00
	1874H	.200	2.50	5.00	15.00	60.00
	1875H	.200	2.50	5.00	15.00	75.00
	1875H	—	—	—	Proof	300.00
	1876H	.480	2.50	5.00	15.00	50.00
	1877H	.240	2.50	5.00	15.00	50.00
	1877H	—	—	—	Proof	350.00
	1879	.288	2.50	5.00	15.00	50.00
	1879	—	—	—	Proof	300.00
	1880H	.300	2.50	5.00	15.00	50.00
	1880H	—	—	—	Proof	300.00
	1881	.300	2.50	5.00	15.00	50.00
	1881	—	—	—	Proof	300.00
	1882H	.500	2.50	5.00	15.00	50.00
	1882H	—	—	—	Proof	400.00

KM#	Date	Mintage	Fine	VF	XF	Unc
6.3	1883 flat top 3					
		.550	2.50	5.00	15.00	40.00
	1883	—	—	—	Proof	300.00
	1883H round top 3					
		.250	4.00	8.00	20.00	65.00
	1883H	—	—	—	Proof	300.00
	1884	.960	1.50	3.00	6.50	25.00
	1884	—	—	—	Proof	250.00
	1885	3.120	1.00	2.50	5.00	20.00
	1885	—	—	—	Proof	700.00
	1886	2.100	1.00	2.50	5.00	20.00
	1886	—	—	—	Proof	200.00
	1887	2.441	1.00	2.50	5.00	20.00
	1888	7.027	1.00	2.50	5.00	20.00
	1888	—	—	—	Proof	200.00
	1889	4.027	1.00	2.50	5.00	20.00
	1889	—	—	—	Proof	200.00
	1889H	2.100	1.00	2.50	5.00	20.00
	1890	1.500	1.00	2.50	6.00	35.00
	1890	—	—	—	Proof	250.00
	1890H	5.400	1.00	2.50	5.00	20.00
	1891	6.150	1.00	2.50	5.00	20.00
	1891H	1.750	1.00	2.50	5.00	35.00
	1892	5.500	1.00	2.50	5.00	20.00
	1892	—	—	—	Proof	200.00
	1892H	1.100	1.50	5.00	7.50	40.00
	1892H	—	—	—	Proof	200.00
	1893	11.250	1.00	2.50	5.00	20.00
	1894	16.750	1.00	2.50	5.00	20.00
	1894	—	—	—	Proof	225.00
	1895	19.000	1.00	2.50	5.00	20.00
	1896	16.500	1.00	2.50	5.00	20.00
	1897	23.500	1.00	2.50	5.00	18.00
	1897H	10.500	1.00	2.50	5.00	18.00
	1897H	—	—	—	Proof	400.00
	1898	29.500	1.00	2.50	5.00	18.00
	1899	33.842	.75	1.50	3.00	18.00
	1900	7.758	.75	1.50	3.00	18.00
	1900H	41.500	.75	1.50	3.00	18.00
	1901	25.000	.75	1.50	3.00	18.00

KM#	Date	Mintage	Fine	VF	XF	Unc
13	1902	18.000	.75	1.50	3.00	12.50
	1902	—	—	—	Proof	150.00
	1903	25.000	.75	1.50	3.00	12.50
	1903	—	—	—	Proof	150.00
	1904	30.000	.75	1.50	3.00	12.50
	1904	—	—	—	Proof	150.00
	1905	33.487	175.00	250.00	350.00	625.00
	1905	—	—	—	Proof	1100.

COPPER-NICKEL

KM#	Date	Mintage	Fine	VF	XF	Unc
19	1935	10.000	.25	.50	1.00	5.00
	1935	—	—	—	Proof	60.00
	1936	5.000	.25	.50	1.00	5.00
	1936	—	—	—	Proof	60.00

NICKEL

KM#	Date	Mintage	Fine	VF	XF	Unc
21	1937	17.500	.40	.70	1.00	2.50
	1937	—	—	—	Proof	60.00

KM#	Date	Mintage	Fine	VF	XF	Unc
23	1938	7.500	.20	.40	.60	2.50
	1938	—	—	—	Proof	50.00
	1939H	5.000	.25	.50	.75	2.50
	1939KN	5.000	.15	.30	.50	2.50
	1939KN	—	—	—	Proof	50.00

NICKEL-BRASS

Reeded, security edge.

KM#	Date	Mintage	Fine	VF	XF	Unc
25	1948	30.000	.15	.25	.40	2.00
	1948	—	—	—	Proof	50.00
	1949	35.000	.15	.25	.40	2.00
	1949	—	—	—	Proof	50.00
	1950	20.000	.15	.25	.35	2.00
	1950	—	—	—	Proof	50.00
	1951	5.000	.15	.25	.40	4.00
	1951	—	—	—	Proof	50.00

Error: Reeded, w/o security edge.

KM#	Date	Mintage	Fine	VF	XF	Unc
25a	1950	Inc. Ab.	2.00	3.75	5.50	15.00

Reeded, w/security edges.

KM#	Date	Mintage	Fine	VF	XF	Unc
28.1	1955	10.000	.10	.15	.35	1.00
	1955	—	—	—	Proof	40.00
	1956	3.110	.10	.20	.50	10.00
	1956	—	—	—	Proof	40.00
	1956H	4.488	.10	.15	.35	2.00
	1956KN	2.500	.25	.50	2.00	10.00
	1957H	5.250	.10	.15	.30	1.00
	1957KN	2.800	.10	.15	.30	1.50
	1958KN	10.000	.10	.15	.25	1.00
	1959H	20.000	.10	.15	.20	.50
	1960	12.500	.10	.15	.20	.50
	1960	—	—	—	Proof	40.00
	1960H	10.000	.10	.15	.20	.75
	1961	20.000	.10	.15	.20	.50
	1961	—	—	—	Proof	40.00
	1961H	5.000	.10	.15	.20	4.00
	1961KN	5.000	.10	.15	.20	.75
	1963	27.000	.10	.15	.20	4.00
	1963	—	—	—	Proof	40.00
	1963H	3.000	.20	.30	.50	1.00
	1963KN	I.A.	.10	.15	.20	.50
	1964	9.000	.10	.15	.20	.50
	1964H	21.000	.10	.15	.20	.50
	1965	40.000	.10	.15	.20	.50
	1965H	8.000	.10	.15	.20	.50
	1965KN	I.A.	.10	.15	.20	.50
	1967	10.000	.10	.15	.20	.50
	1968H	15.000	.10	.15	.20	.50

Error: Reeded, w/o security edge.

KM#	Date	Mintage	Fine	VF	XF	Unc
28.2	1956H	Inc. Ab.	2.25	4.50	8.50	17.50
	1963	—	2.25	4.50	8.50	17.50

Reeded edges

KM#	Date	Mintage	Fine	VF	XF	Unc
28.3	1971H	22.000	—	.10	.15	.35
(33)	1972KN	20.000	—	.10	.15	.35
	1973	2.250	.10	.20	.50	1.00
	1974	4.600	—	.10	.15	.35
	1975	44.840	—	.10	.15	.35
	1978	57.500	—	.10	.15	.35
	1979	101.500	—	.10	.15	.35
	1980	*24.000	—	225.00	450.00	900.00

***NOTE:** Very few pieces released for circulation. At this time approximately 40 are known to exist within the numismatic community.

KM#	Date	Mintage	Fine	VF	XF	Unc
49	1982	—	—	.10	.15	.20
	1983	110.016	—	.10	.15	.20
	1984	30.016	—	.10	.15	.20

KM#	Date	Mintage	Fine	VF	XF	Unc
55	1985	34.016	—	—	.10	.20
	1986	40.000	—	—	.10	.20
	1987	—	—	—	.10	.20
	1988	30.000	—	—	.10	.20
	1988	.020	—	—	Proof	2.00
	1989	40.000	—	—	.10	.20
	1990	—	—	—	.10	.20
	1991	—	—	—	.10	.20
	1992	24.000	—	—	.10	.20

BRASS PLATED STEEL
Bauhinia Flower

KM#	Date	Mintage	Fine	VF	XF	Unc
66	1993	—	—	—	.10	.20
	1993	—	—	—	Proof	2.00

20 CENTS

5.4308 g, .800 SILVER, .1397 oz ASW

KM#	Date	Mintage	Fine	VF	XF	Unc
7	1866	.445	7.00	20.00	40.00	225.00
	1866 reeded edge		—	—	Proof	450.00
	1866 plain edge		—	—	Proof	475.00
	1867	Inc. Ab.	9.00	25.00	50.00	225.00
	1867	—	—	—	Proof	450.00
	1868	Inc. Ab.	7.00	20.00	40.00	225.00
	1868	—	—	—	Proof	450.00
	1872/68H	.064	9.00	25.00	50.00	275.00
	1872H	Inc. Ab.	7.00	20.00	40.00	225.00
	1872H	—	—	—	Proof	500.00
	1873	.096	7.00	20.00	40.00	225.00
	1873 plain edge		—	—	Proof	1200.
	1873H	.064	7.00	20.00	40.00	225.00
	1874H	.070	7.00	20.00	40.00	225.00
	1875H	.070	7.00	20.00	40.00	225.00
	1875H	—	—	—	Proof	450.00
	1876H	.120	7.00	20.00	40.00	225.00
	1877H	.060	7.00	20.00	40.00	250.00
	1879	.020	150.00	350.00	550.00	1200.
	1879	—	—	—	Proof	2000.
	1880H	.025	50.00	75.00	175.00	400.00
	1881	.030	100.00	150.00	325.00	900.00
	1881	—	—	—	Proof	1200.
	1882H	.100	7.00	20.00	40.00	225.00
	1882H	—	—	—	Proof	550.00
	1883	.138	7.00	20.00	40.00	225.00
	1883	—	—	—	Proof	400.00
	1883H	.063	7.00	20.00	40.00	225.00
	1883H	—	—	—	Proof	400.00
	1884	.080	7.00	20.00	40.00	225.00
	1884	—	—	—	Proof	400.00
	1885	.260	5.00	12.00	30.00	200.00
	1885	—	—	—	Proof	1000.
	1886	.175	5.00	12.00	30.00	225.00
	1887	.200	5.00	12.00	30.00	200.00
	1888	.500	5.00	12.00	30.00	200.00
	1888	—	—	—	Proof	500.00
	1889	.440	5.00	12.00	30.00	200.00
	1889	—	—	—	Proof	500.00
	1889H	.175	5.00	12.00	30.00	200.00
	1890	.125	5.00	12.00	30.00	175.00
	1890H	.450	5.00	12.00	30.00	175.00
	1891	.575	5.00	12.00	30.00	175.00
	1891H	.175	7.00	15.00	35.00	240.00
	1892	.450	5.00	12.00	30.00	150.00
	1892H	.100	8.00	16.00	40.00	250.00
	1893	.750	5.00	12.00	25.00	150.00
	1894	.650	5.00	12.00	25.00	150.00
	1894	—	—	—	Proof	500.00
	1895	.500	5.00	12.00	25.00	150.00
	1896	.250	5.00	12.00	25.00	150.00
	1898	.125	5.00	12.00	25.00	175.00

KM#	Date	Mintage	Fine	VF	XF	Unc
14	1902	.250	10.00	25.00	45.00	185.00
	1902	—	—	—	Proof	500.00
	1904	.250	10.00	25.00	45.00	185.00
	1905	.750	300.00	500.00	625.00	1150.
	1905	—	—	—	Proof	1600.

NICKEL-BRASS

KM#	Date	Mintage	Fine	VF	XF	Unc
36	1975	71.000	—	.10	.15	.25
	1976	42.000	—	.10	.15	.25
	1977	Inc. Ab.	—	.10	.15	.25
	1978	86.000	—	.10	.15	.25
	1979	94.500	—	.10	.15	.25
	1980	65.000	—	.10	.15	.25
	1982	30.000	—	.10	.15	.25
	1983	15.000	—	.10	.15	.25

BRASS

Obv: Mature Queen's portrait.

KM#	Date	Mintage	Fine	VF	XF	Unc
59	1985	10.000	—	.10	.15	.25
	1988	*.040	—	.10	.15	.25
	1988	*.020	—	—	Proof	2.00
	1989	17.000	—	.10	.15	.25
	1990	—	—	.10	.15	.25
	1991	—	—	.10	.15	.25
	1992	131.000	—	.10	.15	.25

NICKEL-BRASS
Bauhinia Flower

KM#	Date	Mintage	Fine	VF	XF	Unc
67	1993	—	—	—	.15	.25
	1993	—	—	—	Proof	2.00

1/2 DOLLAR

13.478 g, .900 SILVER, .3900 oz ASW

KM#	Date	Mintage	Fine	VF	XF	Unc
8	1866	.059	150.00	250.00	450.00	1250.
	1866 reeded edge		—	—	Proof	2250.
	1866 plain edge		—	—	Proof	Rare
	1867	Inc. Ab.	225.00	400.00	800.00	2400.
	1867	—	—	—	Proof	3000.
	1868	—	—	—	Proof	3000.

50 CENTS

13.5769 g, .800 SILVER, .3492 oz ASW, 31mm
Obv: W/o mint mark.

KM#	Date	Mintage	Fine	VF	XF	Unc
9.1	1890	.050	18.00	30.00	60.00	300.00
	1890	—	—	—	Proof	600.00
	1891	.150	15.00	25.00	45.00	300.00
	1891	—	—	—	Proof	600.00
	1892	.090	15.00	25.00	45.00	300.00
	1892	—	—	—	Proof	600.00
	1893	.150	15.00	25.00	45.00	300.00
	1894	.130	15.00	25.00	45.00	300.00
	1894	—	—	—	Proof	600.00

32mm
Obv: Mint mark below bust.

KM#	Date	Mintage	Fine	VF	XF	Unc
9.2	1891H	.070	20.00	30.00	50.00	300.00
	1892H	.020	25.00	60.00	125.00	450.00
	1892H	—	—	—	Proof	600.00

KM#	Date	Mintage	Fine	VF	XF	Unc
15	1902	.100	12.00	20.00	35.00	85.00
	1902	—	—	—	Proof	500.00
	1904	.100	12.00	20.00	35.00	85.00
	1904	—	—	—	Proof	500.00
	1905	.300	10.00	15.00	25.00	60.00
	1905	—	—	—	Proof	500.00

COPPER-NICKEL

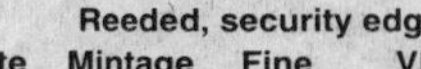

Reeded, security edge.

KM#	Date	Mintage	Fine	VF	XF	Unc
27.1	1951	15.000	.25	.50	1.00	5.00
	1951	—	—	—	Proof	125.00

Error: Reeded, w/o security edge.

KM#	Date	Mintage	Fine	VF	XF	Unc
27.2	1951	Inc. Ab.	2.00	4.00	8.00	20.00

Reeded, security edge.

KM#	Date	Mintage	Fine	VF	XF	Unc
30.1	1958H	4.000	—	.20	.40	1.00
	1960	4.000	—	.20	.40	1.00
	1960	—	—	—	Proof	—
	1961	6.000	—	.20	.40	1.00
	1961	—	—	—	Proof	—
	1963H	10.000	—	.20	.40	1.00
	1964	5.000	—	.20	.40	1.00
	1965KN	8.000	—	.20	.40	1.00
	1966	5.000	—	.20	.40	1.00
	1967	12.000	—	.20	.40	1.00
	1968H	12.000	—	.20	.40	1.00
	1970H	4.600	—	.20	.40	1.00

Error: Reeded, w/o security edge.

KM#	Date	Mintage	Fine	VF	XF	Unc
30.2	1958H	Inc. Ab.	2.00	4.00	8.00	20.00

Reeded edge

KM#	Date	Mintage	Fine	VF	XF	Unc
34	1971KN	—	—	.20	.40	1.00
	1972	30.000	—	.20	.40	1.00
	1973	36.800	—	.20	.40	1.00
	1974	6.000	—	.20	.40	1.00
	1975	8.000	—	.20	.40	1.00

NICKEL-BRASS

KM#	Date	Mintage	Fine	VF	XF	Unc
41	1977	60.001	—	.20	.30	.75
	1978	70.000	—	.20	.30	.75
	1979	60.640	—	.20	.30	.75
	1980	120.000	—	.20	.30	.75

Obv: Mature Queen's portrait.

KM#	Date	Mintage	Fine	VF	XF	Unc
62	1988	*.040	—	.20	.30	.75
	1988	*.020	—	—	Proof	4.00
	1990	27,000	—	.20	.30	.75

BRASS PLATED STEEL
Bauhinia Flower

KM#	Date	Mintage	Fine	VF	XF	Unc
68	1993	—	—	.20	.30	.75
	1993	—	—	—	Proof	4.00

DOLLAR

26.9568 g, .900 SILVER, .7800 oz ASW

KM#	Date	Mintage	Fine	VF	XF	Unc
10	1866	2.109	60.00	110.00	175.00	500.00
	1866 reeded edge		—	—	Proof	1000.
	1866 plain edge		—	—	Proof	2500.
	1867/6	Inc. Ab.	70.00	125.00	200.00	550.00
	1867	Inc. Ab.	60.00	110.00	175.00	500.00
	1867	—	—	—	Proof	3000.
	1868	Inc. Ab.	60.00	110.00	175.00	500.00
	1868	—	—	—	Proof	2500.

COPPER-NICKEL
Reeded, security edge.

KM#	Date	Mintage	Fine	VF	XF	Unc
31.1	1960H	40.000	—	.40	.75	2.00
	1960KN	40.000	—	.40	.75	2.00
	1970H	15.000	—	.40	.75	2.00

NOTE: Mint mark is below "LL" of "DOLLAR".

Error: Reeded, w/o security edge.

KM#	Date	Mintage	Fine	VF	XF	Unc
31.2	1960H	Inc. Ab.	3.00	6.00	11.50	22.50

Reeded edge

KM#	Date	Mintage	Fine	VF	XF	Unc
35	1971H	8.000	—	.40	.70	2.00
	1972	20.000	—	.40	.70	1.50
	1973	8.125	—	.40	.70	2.00
	1974	26.000	—	.40	.70	1.50
	1975	22.500	—	.40	.70	1.50

KM#	Date	Mintage	Fine	VF	XF	Unc
43	1978	120.000	—	.40	.70	1.00
	1979	104.908	—	.40	.70	1.00
	1980	100.000	—	.40	.70	1.00

Obv: Mature Queen's portrait.
Rev: Lion within legend.

KM#	Date	Mintage	Fine	VF	XF	Unc
63	1987	—	—	.30	.50	.75
	1988	20.000	—	.30	.50	.75
	1988	.020	—	—	Proof	7.50
	1989	20.000	—	.30	.50	.75
	1990	—	—	.30	.50	.75
	1991	—	—	.30	.50	.75
	1992	25.000	—	.30	.50	.75

NICKEL PLATED STEEL
Bauhinia Flower

KM#	Date	Mintage	Fine	VF	XF	Unc
69	1993	—	—	.30	.50	.75
	1993	—	—	—	Proof	7.50

2 DOLLARS

COPPER-NICKEL

KM#	Date	Mintage	Fine	VF	XF	Unc
37	1975	60.000	—	.45	.85	1.50
	1978	.504	—	.45	1.00	2.00
	1979	9.032	—	.45	.85	1.50
	1980	30.000	—	.45	.85	1.50
	1981	30.000	—	.45	.85	1.50
	1982	30.000	—	.45	.85	1.50
	1983	7.002	—	.45	.85	1.50
	1984	22.002	—	.45	.85	1.50

Obv: Mature Queen's portrait.

KM#	Date	Mintage	Fine	VF	XF	Unc
60	1985	10.002	—	—	.50	1.00
	1986	15.000	—	—	.50	1.00
	1987	—	—	—	.50	1.00
	1988	5.000	—	—	.50	1.00
	1988	.020	—	—	Proof	10.00
	1989	33.000	—	—	.50	1.00
	1990	—	—	—	.50	1.00
	1991	—	—	—	.50	1.00
	1992	4.370	—	—	.50	1.00

Bauhinia Flower

KM#	Date	Mintage	Fine	VF	XF	Unc
64	1993	—	—	—	—	1.00
	1993	—	—	—	Proof	10.00

5 DOLLARS

COPPER-NICKEL

KM#	Date	Mintage	Fine	VF	XF	Unc
39	1976	30.000	—	1.00	1.50	2.50
	1978	10.000	—	1.00	1.50	3.00
	1979	12.000	—	1.00	1.50	2.50

KM#	Date	Mintage	Fine	VF	XF	Unc
46	1980	40.000	—	1.00	1.50	2.50
	1981	20.000	—	1.00	1.50	2.50
	1982	10.000	—	1.00	1.50	2.50
	1983	4.000	—	1.00	1.50	2.50
	1984	4.500	—	1.00	1.50	2.50

KM#	Date	Mintage	Fine	VF	XF	Unc
56	1985	6.000	—	—	.75	1.75
	1986	8.000	—	—	.75	1.75
	1987	—	—	—	.75	1.75
	1988	16.000	—	—	.75	1.75
	1988	.020	—	—	Proof	15.00
	1989	37.000	—	—	.75	1.75
	1991	—	—	—	.75	1.75

Bauhinia Flower

KM#	Date	Mintage	Fine	VF	XF	Unc
65	1993	—	—	—	—	1.75
	1993	—	—	—	Proof	15.00

10 DOLLARS

NICKEL-BRASS Ring COPPER-NICKEL Center
Bauhinia Flower

KM#	Date	Mintage	Fine	VF	XF	Unc
70	1993	—	—	—	—	2.75
	1993	*.030	—	—	Proof	15.00

18.3000 g, .375 Ring, .917 Center GOLD, .3826 oz AGW

KM#	Date	Mintage	Fine	VF	XF	Unc
70a	1994	.020	—	—	Proof	375.00

1000 DOLLARS

15.9700 g, .917 GOLD, .4708 oz AGW
Visit of Queen Elizabeth

KM#	Date	Mintage	Fine	VF	XF	Unc
38	1975	.015	—	—	—	250.00
	1975	5,005	—	—	Proof	950.00

Year of the Dragon

KM#	Date	Mintage	Fine	VF	XF	Unc
40	1976	.020	—	—	—	400.00
	1976	6,911	—	—	Proof	1000.

Year of the Snake

KM#	Date	Mintage	Fine	VF	XF	Unc
42	1977	.020	—	—	—	300.00
	1977	.010	—	—	Proof	525.00

Year of the Horse

KM#	Date	Mintage	Fine	VF	XF	Unc
44	1978	.020	—	—	—	300.00
	1978	.010	—	—	Proof	500.00

Year of the Goat

KM#	Date	Mintage	Fine	VF	XF	Unc
45	1979	.030	—	—	—	250.00
	1979	.015	—	—	Proof	325.00

Year of the Monkey

KM#	Date	Mintage	Fine	VF	XF	Unc
47	1980	.031	—	—	—	225.00
	1980	.018	—	—	Proof	300.00

Year of the Cockerel

KM#	Date	Mintage	Fine	VF	XF	Unc
48	1981	.033	—	—	—	225.00
	1981	.022	—	—	Proof	300.00

Year of the Dog

KM#	Date	Mintage	Fine	VF	XF	Unc
50	1982	.033	—	—	—	225.00
	1982	.022	—	—	Proof	350.00

Year of the Pig

KM#	Date	Mintage	Fine	VF	XF	Unc
51	1983	.033	—	—	—	400.00
	1983	.022	—	—	Proof	650.00

Year of the Rat

KM#	Date	Mintage	Fine	VF	XF	Unc
52	1984	.020	—	—	—	300.00
	1984	.010	—	—	Proof	425.00

Year of the Ox

KM#	Date	Mintage	Fine	VF	XF	Unc
53	1985	.030	—	—	—	350.00
	1985	.010	—	—	Proof	550.00

Year of the Tiger

KM#	Date	Mintage	Fine	VF	XF	Unc
54	1986	.020	—	—	—	325.00
	1986	.010	—	—	Proof	450.00

Royal Visit of Queen Elizabeth II

KM#	Date	Mintage	Fine	VF	XF	Unc
57	1986	.020	—	—	—	225.00
	1986	.012	—	—	Proof	325.00

Year of the Rabbit

KM#	Date	Mintage	Fine	VF	XF	Unc
58	1987	.020	—	—	—	225.00
	1987	.012	—	—	Proof	325.00

MINT SETS (MS)

KM#	Date	Mintage	Identification	Issue Price	Mkt. Val.
MS1	1988(7)	—	KM55-56,59-63	13.00	15.00
MS2	1993(7)	—	KM64-70	20.00	22.50

PROOF SETS (PS)

KM#	Date	Mintage	Identification	Issue Price	Mkt. Val.
PS1	1866(5)	—	KM5,6.1,7-8,10	—	3000.
PS2	1873(3)	1 known	KM5,6.3,7	—	4500.
PS3	1885(3)	1 known	KM5,6.3,7	—	3000.
PS4	1988(7)	*25,000	KM55-56,59-63	39.75	42.50
PS5	1993(7)	*30,000	KM64-70	50.00	55.00

HUNGARY

The Republic of Hungary, located in central Europe, has an area of 35,929 sq. mi. (93,030 sq. km.) and a population of 10.7 million. Capital: Budapest. The economy is based on agriculture, bauxite and a rapidly expanding industrial sector. Machinery, chemicals, iron and steel, and fruits and vegetables are exported.

The ancient kingdom of Hungary, founded by the Magyars in the 9th century, achieved its greatest extension in in the mid-14th century when its dominions touched the Baltic, Black and Mediterranean seas. After suffering repeated Turkish invasions, Hungary accepted Habsburg rule to escape Turkish occupation, regaining independence in 1867 with the Emperor of Austria as king of a dual Austro-Hungarian Monarchy. After World War I, Hungary lost 2/3 of its territory and 1/2 of its population and underwent a period of drastic political revision. The short-lived republic of 1918 was followed by a chaotic interval of communist rule, 1919, and the restoration of the monarchy in 1920 with Admiral Horthy as regent of the kingdom. Although a German ally in World War II, Hungary was occupied by German troops who imposed a pro-Nazi dictatorship, 1944. Soviet armies drove out the Germans in 1945 and assisted the communist minority in seizing power. A revised constitution published on Aug. 20, 1949, established Hungary as a 'People's Republic' of the Soviet type. On October 23, 1989, Hungary was proclaimed the Republic of Hungary.

RULERS

Austrian until 1918

MINT MARKS

A, CA, WI - Vienna (Becs)
B, K, KB - Kremnitz (Kormoczbanya)
BP - Budapest
CH - Pressburg (Pozsony)
CM - Kaschau (Kassa)
G, GN, NB - Nagybanya
GYF - Karlsburg (Gyulafehervar)
HA - Hall
S - Schmollnitz (Szomolnok)

LEGEND VARIETIES

X: After 1750, during the reign of Maria Theresa, crossed staves which appear as an "X" were placed after the date denoting her reign over the Austrian Netherlands.

MONETARY SYSTEM

Until 1857

2 Poltura = 3 Krajczar
60 Krajczar = 1 Forint (Gulden)
2 Forint = 1 Convention Thaler

1857-1891

100 Krajczar = 1 Forint

1892-1925

100 Filler = 1 Korona

1926-1945

100 Filler = 1 Pengo

Commencing 1946

100 Filler = 1 Forint

NOTE: Many coins of Hungary through 1948, especially 1925-1945, have been restruck in recent times. These may be identified by a rosette in the vicinity of the mint mark. Restrike mintages for KM#440-449, 451-458, 468-469, 475-477, 480-483, 494, 496-498 are usually about 1000 pieces, later date mintages are not known.

5/10 KRAJCZAR

COPPER
Mint mark: KB

KM#	Date	Mintage	Fine	VF	XF	Unc
468	1882	2.400	2.50	4.00	5.50	9.00
	1882	(restrike)	—	—	Proof	8.00

KRAJCZAR

COPPER
Mint mark: KB

KM#	Date	Mintage	Fine	VF	XF	Unc
441.1	1868	12.530	.50	1.00	2.00	4.50
	1868	(restrike)	—	—	Proof	10.00
	1869	5.070	.50	1.25	3.00	8.50
	1872	—	.50	1.50	3.00	7.50
	1873	—	35.00	65.00	100.00	150.00

Mint mark: GYF

KM#	Date	Mintage	Fine	VF	XF	Unc
441.2	1868	—	—	—	Rare	—

Mint mark: KB

KM#	Date	Mintage	Fine	VF	XF	Unc
458	1878	4.480	12.00	18.00	30.00	45.00
	1879	10.101	3.00	7.50	12.00	17.50
	1881	12.233	3.00	7.50	12.00	17.50
	1882	19.800	5.00	11.00	17.50	27.50
	1883	8.535	9.00	15.00	27.50	35.00
	1885	26.606	1.25	3.50	7.50	12.00
	1886	17.671	2.00	5.50	9.00	15.00
	1887	11.989	2.50	6.00	12.00	18.00
	1888	10.334	3.50	7.00	12.00	18.00

NOTE: Wreath varieties exist for 1878 dated coins.

Mule. Obv: KM#441. Rev: KM#458.

KM#	Date	Mintage	Fine	VF	XF	Unc
459	1878	—	25.00	35.00	60.00	85.00

KM#	Date	Mintage	Fine	VF	XF	Unc
478	1891*	16.272	2.50	5.00	8.00	14.50
	1892	5.871	7.00	15.00	22.50	32.50

***NOTE:** Variations in thickness of planchet exist.

4 KRAJCZAR

COPPER
Mint mark: KB

KM#	Date	Mintage	Fine	VF	XF	Unc
442	1868	3.100	3.00	7.50	15.00	30.00
	1868	(restrike)	—	—	Proof	18.00

NOTE: Wreath varieties exist.

10 KRAJCZAR

3.8900 g, .500 SILVER, .0625 oz ASW

KM#	Date	Mintage	Fine	VF	XF	Unc
421	1837	—	100.00	175.00	300.00	475.00
	1838	—	50.00	90.00	140.00	240.00
	1839	—	4.00	10.00	20.00	35.00
	1840	—	5.00	12.00	24.00	50.00
	1841	—	4.50	10.00	20.00	35.00
	1842	—	4.50	10.00	20.00	35.00
	1843	—	5.00	12.00	24.00	50.00
	1844	—	5.00	9.00	17.50	32.50
	1845	—	5.00	9.00	17.50	32.50
	1846	—	4.00	8.00	15.00	27.00
	1847	—	2.50	4.00	9.00	18.00
	1848	—	2.50	4.00	9.00	18.00

2.0000 g, .500 SILVER, .0321 oz ASW
Mint mark: KB
Obv. leg: . . . . .AP.KIRALYA. Rev. leg: VALTO PENZ.

KM#	Date	Mintage	Fine	VF	XF	Unc
440.1	1867	c.1,000	—	—	—	—
	1868	—	15.00	35.00	60.00	120.00
	1868	(restrike)	—	—	Proof	20.00

Mint mark: GYF

KM#	Date	Mintage	Fine	VF	XF	Unc
440.2	1868	—	15.00	35.00	60.00	120.00

1.6600 g, .400 SILVER, .0213 oz ASW
Rev. leg: MAGYAR KIRALYI VALTO PENZ.

KM#	Date	Mintage	Fine	VF	XF	Unc
443.1	1868	3.250	12.00	25.00	40.00	65.00
	1868	(restrike)	—	—	Proof	22.50
	1869	12.747	6.00	22.50	40.00	65.00

Mint mark: GYF

KM#	Date	Mintage	Fine	VF	XF	Unc
443.2	1868	1.012	20.00	40.00	85.00	175.00
	1869	2.747	12.00	25.00	40.00	70.00

NOTE: Varieties exist.

Mint mark: KB
Obv. leg: AP.KIR. Rev. leg: VALTO PENZ.

KM#	Date	Mintage	Fine	VF	XF	Unc
451.1	1870	21.933	3.50	7.50	18.00	35.00
	1870	(restrike)	—	—	Proof	17.50
	1871	(restrike from 1885)			Rare	—
	1872	1.154	7.50	15.00	30.00	50.00
	1873	1.066	7.50	15.00	30.00	50.00
	1874	1.324	9.00	18.00	35.00	55.00
	1875	.425	18.00	27.50	55.00	80.00
	1876	.518	10.00	27.50	55.00	80.00
	1877	.460	15.00	32.00	58.00	85.00
	1887	.025	80.00	135.00	190.00	275.00
	1888	.358	9.00	18.00	35.00	65.00
	1889	—	—	Reported, not confirmed		

Mint mark: GYF

KM#	Date	Mintage	Fine	VF	XF	Unc
451.2	1870	3.032	7.50	15.00	30.00	50.00
	1871	3.383	7.50	15.00	30.00	50.00

Mint mark: KB
Mule. Obv: KM#451.1. Rev. KM#440.

KM#	Date	Mintage	Fine	VF	XF	Unc
444	1868	—	—	—	Rare	—
	1868	(restrike)	—	—	Proof	20.00

20 KRAJCZAR

SILVER
Mint mark: A
Obv: Ribbons on wreath forward across neck.
Rev: Madonna with child.

KM#	Date	Mintage	Fine	VF	XF	Unc
415.1	1830	—	55.00	110.00	220.00	400.00

Obv: Left ribbon on wreath behind neck

KM#	Date	Mintage	Fine	VF	XF	Unc
415.2	1830	—	100.00	200.00	350.00	600.00
	1831	—	—	Reported, not confirmed		

Mint mark: B
Obv: Both ribbons on wreath behind neck

KM#	Date	Mintage	Fine	VF	XF	Unc
415.3	1832	—	40.00	80.00	160.00	325.00
	1833	—	12.50	25.00	50.00	100.00
	1834	—	5.00	10.00	25.00	50.00
	1835	—	10.00	20.00	40.00	80.00

6.6800 g, .583 SILVER, .1252 oz ASW
Obv. leg: FERD. I. Rev. leg: S. MARIA. . .

KM#	Date	Mintage	Fine	VF	XF	Unc
422	1837	—	4.00	7.50	15.00	35.00
	1838	—	4.00	7.50	15.00	35.00
	1839	—	3.50	5.00	7.50	20.00
	1840	—	3.50	5.00	7.50	20.00
	1841	—	3.50	5.00	7.50	20.00
	1842	—	4.00	7.50	15.00	30.00
	1843	—	3.50	5.00	7.50	20.00
	1844	—	3.50	5.00	7.50	20.00
	1845	—	3.50	5.00	7.50	20.00
	1846	—	3.50	5.00	7.50	20.00
	1847	—	3.50	5.00	7.50	20.00
	1848	—	3.50	5.00	7.50	20.00

2.6600 g, .500 SILVER, .0427 oz ASW
Mint mark: KB
Obv. leg: . . . .AP.KIRALYA. Rev. leg: VALTO PENZ.

KM#	Date	Mintage	Fine	VF	XF	Unc
445.1	1868	—	15.00	40.00	70.00	150.00
	1868	(restrike)	—	—	Proof	20.00

Mint mark: GYF

KM#	Date	Mintage	Fine	VF	XF	Unc
445.2	1868	—	35.00	80.00	120.00	170.00

Mint mark: KB
Rev. leg: MAGYAR KIRALYI VALTO PENZ.

KM#	Date	Mintage	Fine	VF	XF	Unc
446.1	1868	3.224	7.50	17.50	32.50	60.00
	1868	(restrike)	—	—	Proof	20.00
	1869	9.487	5.00	14.00	24.00	50.00

Mint mark: GYF

KM#	Date	Mintage	Fine	VF	XF	Unc
446.2	1868	1.039	9.50	20.00	42.00	80.00
	1869	2.299	9.00	17.50	35.00	65.00

Mint mark: KB
Rev. leg: VALTO PENZ.

KM#	Date	Mintage	Fine	VF	XF	Unc
452.1	1870	4.427	12.50	27.50	65.00	110.00
	1870	(restrike)	—	—	Proof	20.00
	1871	25 pcs. (restrike from 1855)			Proof	—
	1872	1.286	27.50	55.00	110.00	160.00

Mint mark: GYF

KM#	Date	Mintage	Fine	VF	XF	Unc
452.2	1870	7.213	30.00	65.00	110.00	150.00

Mint mark: KB
Mule. Obv: KM#452.1. Rev: KM#445.1.

KM#	Date	Mintage	Fine	VF	XF	Unc
447	1868	—	—	—	Rare	—
	1868	(restrike)	—	—	Proof	20.00

FORINT

12.3457 g, .900 SILVER, .3572 oz ASW
Mint mark: KB

KM#	Date	Mintage	Fine	VF	XF	Unc
449.1	1868	.570	11.00	17.50	35.00	70.00
	1868	(restrike)	—	—	Proof	40.00
	1869	.490	10.00	20.00	27.50	45.00
	1869 plain edge	—	—	—	—	—

Mint mark: GYF

KM#	Date	Mintage	Fine	VF	XF	Unc
449.2	1868	.270	11.00	22.50	30.00	60.00
	1869	.360	7.50	15.00	30.00	45.00

Mint mark: KB

KM#	Date	Mintage	Fine	VF	XF	Unc
453.1	1870	1.250	15.00	32.50	62.50	110.00
	1871	2.440	12.00	25.00	45.00	90.00
	1872	3.456	7.00	15.00	30.00	60.00
	1873	2.338	12.00	25.00	50.00	90.00
	1874	2.082	12.00	25.00	50.00	90.00
	1875	2.074	8.00	16.00	32.50	55.00
	1876	4.136	5.00	8.00	12.50	22.50
	1877	2.241	5.00	8.00	12.50	22.50
	1878	5.717	5.00	8.00	12.50	22.50
	1879	25.756	5.00	8.00	12.50	22.50

Mint mark: GYF

KM#	Date	Mintage	Fine	VF	XF	Unc
453.2	1870	.570	80.00	150.00	225.00	500.00
	1871	.240	300.00	425.00	625.00	1100.

Mint mark: KB
Obv: Larger head and legends.

KM#	Date	Mintage	Fine	VF	XF	Unc
465	1880	3.815	5.00	8.00	12.00	22.50
	1881	15.495	4.50	6.00	9.00	15.00

NOTE: Varieties exist.

KM#	Date	Mintage	Fine	VF	XF	Unc
469	1882	1.897	7.00	12.50	25.00	50.00
	1883	7.041	5.00	8.00	12.50	22.50
	1884	1.722	5.00	10.00	20.00	40.00
	1885	1.672	5.00	10.00	20.00	40.00
	1886	1.566	7.00	12.50	25.00	50.00
	1887	2.022	5.00	10.00	20.00	40.00
	1888	1.841	5.00	10.00	18.00	35.00
	1889	1.974	5.00	10.00	18.00	35.00
	1890	2.022	6.50	12.50	25.00	50.00

NOTE: Variety exists for 1882 date w/larger mint mark.

KM#	Date	Mintage	Fine	VF	XF	Unc
475	1890	Inc. Ab.	10.00	20.00	35.00	55.00
	1891	1.470	7.50	15.00	22.50	45.00
	1892	1.607	7.00	15.00	22.50	45.00
	1892	(restrike)	—	—	Proof	25.00

1/2 THALER

14.0300 g, .833 SILVER, .3757 oz ASW
Mint mark: A

KM#	Date	Mintage	Fine	VF	XF	Unc
416	1830	—	100.00	170.00	250.00	400.00

Mint mark: B

KM#	Date	Mintage	Fine	VF	XF	Unc
420	1831	*	125.00	225.00	475.00	725.00
	1833	*	70.00	180.00	320.00	550.00
	1834	—	275.00	450.00	600.00	1000.

NOTE: 1831 and 1833 dated coins are restrikes from 1841.

KM#	Date	Mintage	Fine	VF	XF	Unc
423	1837	—	300.00	550.00	900.00	1250.
	1839	—	450.00	800.00	1350.	1800.

THALER

.833 SILVER
Obv: Head right, ribbons on wreath forward across neck. Rev: Madonna w/child.

KM#	Date	Mintage	Fine	VF	XF	Unc
417.1	1830	—	65.00	140.00	275.00	525.00

Mint mark: B

KM#	Date	Mintage	Fine	VF	XF	Unc
417.2	1830	—	275.00	550.00	900.00	1350.

Obv: Ribbons on wreath behind neck.

KM#	Date	Mintage	Fine	VF	XF	Unc
418	1830	—	—	Reported, not confirmed		
	1831	—	95.00	160.00	400.00	725.00
	1833	—	80.00	120.00	325.00	475.00

NOTE: 1831 and 1833 dated coins are restrikes from 1841.

Obv: Head right, leg: FERD I. D.G. . . . .

KM#	Date	Mintage	Fine	VF	XF	Unc
424	1837	—	400.00	700.00	1000.	1400.
	1839	—	—	—	Rare	—

WAR OF INDEPENDENCE

1848-1849

EGY (1) KRAJCZAR

COPPER
Mint: Kremnitz

KM#	Date	Mintage	Fine	VF	XF	Unc
430.1	1848	—	2.00	6.00	12.50	25.00

Mint mark: NB

KM#	Date	Mintage	Fine	VF	XF	Unc
430.2	1849	—	20.00	40.00	60.00	100.00

HAROM (3) KRAJCZAR

COPPER
Mint mark: NB

KM#	Date	Mintage	Fine	VF	XF	Unc
434	1849	—	10.00	20.00	40.00	80.00

NOTE: Varieties exist overstruck w/figure of Madonna.

HAT (6) KRAJCZAR

.220 SILVER
Mint mark: NB

KM#	Date	Mintage	Fine	VF	XF	Unc
435	1849	—	5.00	10.00	20.00	35.00

10 KRAJCZAR

3.8900 g, .500 SILVER, .0625 oz ASW
Mint mark: KB
Rev. leg: SZ. MARIA. . . . .

KM#	Date	Mintage	Fine	VF	XF	Unc
431	1848	—	15.00	30.00	65.00	125.00

20 KRAJCZAR

6.6800 g, .583 SILVER, .1252 oz ASW
Mint mark: KB
Rev. leg: SZ. MARIA. . .

KM#	Date	Mintage	Fine	VF	XF	Unc
432	1848	—	2.50	5.00	10.00	25.00

MONETARY REFORM

1892-1925
100 Filler = 1 Korona

FILLER

BRONZE
Mint mark: KB

KM#	Date	Mintage	Fine	VF	XF	Unc
480	1892	8.153	17.50	32.50	60.00	95.00
	1892	(restrike w/rosette)				
		—	—	—	Proof	10.00
	1893	Inc. Ab.	1.75	3.00	5.50	16.00
	1894	8.642	.50	1.00	1.75	6.00
	1895	9.121	.50	1.00	1.75	6.00
	1896	5.397	1.25	3.00	6.00	15.00
	1897	5.157	4.50	7.50	15.00	30.00
	1898	1.419	5.00	10.00	20.00	40.00
	1899	5.066	1.75	3.50	7.00	17.50
	1900	10.461	1.00	2.00	4.00	11.50
	1901	5.994	4.00	8.00	17.00	32.50
	1902	16.299	.20	.50	1.25	4.00
	1903	2.291	9.00	20.00	35.00	55.00
	1906	.061	65.00	120.00	180.00	275.00
	1914	—	65.00	90.00	135.00	210.00
	1914	—	—	—	Proof	400.00

2 FILLER

BRONZE
Mint mark: KB

KM#	Date	Mintage	Fine	VF	XF	Unc
481	1892	17.176	40.00	60.00	95.00	150.00
	1893	Inc. Ab.	1.75	4.00	6.50	9.00
	1894	39.150	.25	.50	1.50	3.00
	1895	65.017	.25	.50	1.50	3.00
	1896	53.716	.25	.50	1.50	3.00
	1897	37.297	.25	.50	1.50	3.00
	1898	14.073	2.25	4.50	8.50	12.50
	1899	21.570	2.25	4.50	8.50	12.50
	1900	.584	70.00	125.00	200.00	250.00
	1901	25.805	.25	.50	1.50	3.00
	1902	6.937	5.50	8.50	13.50	20.00
	1903	4.052	17.50	25.00	35.00	50.00
	1904	4.203	6.00	12.00	27.50	40.00
	1905	9.335	.50	1.00	1.75	3.00
	1906	3.140	1.75	2.50	5.00	7.50
	1907	9.943	5.50	9.00	12.00	17.50
	1908	16.486	.35	.50	1.25	3.00
	1909	19.075	.35	.50	1.25	3.00
	1910	5.338	4.50	7.50	10.00	15.00
	1910	(restrike w/rosette)				
		—	—	—	Proof	10.00
	1914	4.106	.35	.50	1.00	3.00
	1915	1.294	1.00	1.50	3.00	5.00

IRON

KM#	Date	Mintage	Fine	VF	XF	Unc
497	1916	—	4.50	9.00	13.00	18.00
	1917	—	1.00	2.50	6.00	12.00
	1918	—	2.00	4.50	9.00	15.00

NOTE: Varieties in planchet thickness exist for 1917.

10 FILLER

NICKEL
Mint mark: KB

KM#	Date	Mintage	Fine	VF	XF	Unc
482	1892	15.753	3.00	6.00	17.50	27.50
	1893	Inc. Ab.	.25	.50	1.50	4.00
	1894	39.463	.25	.50	1.50	4.00
	1895	16.804	.25	.50	1.50	4.00
	1896	—	—	Reported, not confirmed		
	1906	.056	75.00	175.00	250.00	325.00
	1908	6.819	.25	.50	1.50	4.00
	1909	17.204	.30	.60	2.00	4.00
	1914	—	175.00	275.00	550.00	900.00

NOTE: Edge varieties exist.

COPPER-NICKEL-ZINC

KM#	Date	Mintage	Fine	VF	XF	Unc
494	1914	4.400	200.00	300.00	500.00	900.00
	1915	Inc. Ab.	.30	.60	1.50	4.00
	1915	(restrike w/rosette)				
		Inc. Ab.	—	—	Proof	4.00
	1916	Inc. Ab.	.50	1.25	2.50	5.00

IRON

KM#	Date	Mintage	Fine	VF	XF	Unc
496	1915	11.500	9.00	20.00	32.50	55.00
	1916	Inc. Ab.	—	—	—	—
	1918	Inc. Ab.	15.00	30.00	55.00	85.00
	1918	(restrike)	—	—	Proof	12.00
	1920	3.275	2.50	5.00	10.00	18.00
	1920	(restrike)	—	—	Proof	12.00

NOTE: Varieties exist.

20 FILLER

NICKEL
Mint mark: KB

KM#	Date	Mintage	Fine	VF	XF	Unc
483	1892	.696	2.00	4.00	8.00	12.00
	1893	27.187	.50	1.25	2.50	6.00
	1894	26.117	.50	1.25	2.50	6.00
	1906	.067	275.00	400.00	600.00	1250.
	1907	1.248	2.50	5.00	8.00	11.00
	1908	10.770	.75	1.75	3.75	7.50
	1914	5.387	3.75	6.50	9.00	13.50
	1914	(restrike)	—	—	Proof	12.50

NOTE: Edge varieties exist.

IRON

KM#	Date	Mintage	Fine	VF	XF	Unc
498	1914	18.826	18.00	32.50	45.00	70.00
	1916	Inc. Ab.	.50	1.25	2.50	7.00
	1917	Inc. Ab.	.75	1.75	3.50	8.00
	1918	Inc. Ab.	.75	1.75	3.50	8.00
	1918	(restrike)	—	—	Proof	7.00
	1920	12.000	2.25	4.50	8.00	15.00
	1921	Inc. Ab.	18.00	32.50	45.00	70.00
	1921	(restrike)	—	—	Proof	10.00
	1922	—	—	—	Rare	—

NOTE: Edge varieties exist.

BRASS

KM#	Date	Mintage	Fine	VF	XF	Unc
498a	1922	(restrike)	—	—	Proof	15.00

KORONA

5.0000 g, .835 SILVER, .1342 oz ASW
Mint mark: KB

KM#	Date	Mintage	Fine	VF	XF	Unc
484	1892	.015	4.00	8.00	40.00	150.00
	1893	24.385	BV	3.50	5.00	12.50
	1894	12.077	BV	3.25	4.50	10.00
	1895	18.544	BV	3.25	4.50	10.00
	1896	3.983	3.50	6.00	8.50	13.50
	1906	.024	150.00	200.00	300.00	425.00

NOTE: Obverse varieties exist.

Millennium Commemorative

KM#	Date	Mintage	Fine	VF	XF	Unc
487	1896	1.000	2.25	3.25	5.50	15.00
	1896	(restrike)	—	—	Proof	17.50

NOTE: The above issue has been restruck in proof several times, both with and without edge inscriptions.

KM#	Date	Mintage	Fine	VF	XF	Unc
492	1912	4.004	2.50	5.00	10.00	15.00
	1913	5,214	50.00	80.00	140.00	190.00
	1914	5.886	BV	3.75	7.00	11.00
	1915	3.934	BV	3.00	4.50	6.00
	1916	—	BV	3.50	6.00	8.00

2 KORONA

10.0000 g, .835 SILVER, .2685 oz ASW
Mint mark: KB

KM#	Date	Mintage	Fine	VF	XF	Unc
493	1912	4.000	BV	4.50	6.50	15.00
	1913	3.000	BV	4.50	6.50	15.00
	1914	.500	20.00	30.00	50.00	80.00

5 KORONA

24.0000 g, .900 SILVER, .6944 oz ASW
Mint mark: KB

KM#	Date	Mintage	Fine	VF	XF	Unc
488	1900	3.840	10.00	18.00	40.00	80.00
	1900	(restrike w/rosette)		—	Proof	40.00
	1900	(restrike w/o rosette)		—	Proof	40.00
	1906	1,263	1000.	1500.	2000.	2500.
	1907	.500	12.00	20.00	40.00	85.00
	1908	1.742	10.00	18.00	40.00	75.00
	1909	1.299	10.00	18.00	40.00	90.00
	1909 U.P.	(restrike)		—	Proof	30.00

40th Anniversary of Coronation of Franz Josef

KM#	Date	Mintage	Fine	VF	XF	Unc
489	1907	.300	15.00	22.00	35.00	55.00
	1907	(restrike)		—	Proof	30.00
	1907 U.P.	(restrike)		—	Proof	30.00

10 KORONA

3.3875 g, .900 GOLD, .0980 oz AGW
Mint mark: KB

KM#	Date	Mintage	Fine	VF	XF	Unc
485	1892	1.087	BV	45.00	55.00	65.00
	1892	(restrike)	—	—	Proof	45.00
	1893	Inc. Ab.	BV	45.00	55.00	65.00
	1894	.986	BV	45.00	55.00	65.00
	1895	—	1500.	2500.	3500.	4500.
	1895	(restrike)	—	—	Proof	50.00
	1896	.032	60.00	85.00	100.00	125.00
	1897	.259	BV	45.00	55.00	65.00
	1898	.218	BV	45.00	55.00	65.00
	1899	.231	BV	45.00	55.00	65.00
	1900	.228	BV	45.00	55.00	65.00
	1901	.230	BV	45.00	55.00	65.00
	1902	.243	BV	45.00	55.00	65.00
	1903	.228	BV	45.00	55.00	65.00
	1904	1.531	BV	45.00	55.00	65.00
	1905	.869	BV	45.00	55.00	65.00
	1906	.748	BV	45.00	55.00	65.00
	1907	.752	BV	45.00	55.00	65.00
	1908	.509	BV	45.00	55.00	65.00
	1909	.574	BV	45.00	55.00	65.00
	1910	1.362	BV	45.00	55.00	65.00
	1911	1.828	BV	45.00	55.00	65.00
	1912	.739	50.00	60.00	70.00	85.00
	1913	.137	50.00	75.00	100.00	125.00
	1914	.115	50.00	80.00	135.00	160.00
	1915	.054	1000.	2000.	3000.	4000.

20 KORONA

6.7750 g, .900 GOLD, .1960 oz AGW
Mint mark: KB

KM#	Date	Mintage	Fine	VF	XF	Unc
486	1892	1.779	BV	80.00	90.00	115.00
	1892	(restrike)	—	—	Proof	100.00
	1893	5.089	BV	80.00	90.00	115.00
	1894	2.526	BV	80.00	90.00	115.00
	1895	1.935	BV	80.00	90.00	115.00
	1895	(restrike)	—	—	Proof	100.00
	1896	1.023	BV	80.00	90.00	115.00
	1897	1.819	BV	80.00	90.00	115.00
	1898	1.281	BV	80.00	90.00	115.00
	1899	.712	BV	80.00	90.00	115.00
	1900	.435	BV	80.00	90.00	115.00
	1901	.510	BV	80.00	90.00	115.00
	1902	.523	BV	80.00	90.00	115.00
	1903	.505	BV	80.00	90.00	115.00
	1904	.572	BV	80.00	90.00	115.00
	1905	.526	BV	80.00	90.00	115.00
	1906	.353	BV	80.00	90.00	115.00
	1907	.194	100.00	150.00	175.00	200.00
	1908	.138	BV	80.00	90.00	115.00
	1909	.459	BV	80.00	90.00	115.00
	1910	.085	125.00	175.00	250.00	300.00
	1911	.063	BV	80.00	90.00	115.00
	1912	.211	BV	80.00	90.00	115.00
	1913	.320	110.00	140.00	165.00	200.00
	1914	.176	BV	80.00	90.00	115.00
	1915	.690	110.00	140.00	165.00	200.00

Rev: Bosnian arms added.

KM#	Date	Mintage	Fine	VF	XF	Unc
495	1914	—	BV	90.00	100.00	135.00
	1915	—	—	—	—	—
	1916	—	125.00	175.00	275.00	400.00

Obv. leg: KAROLY. . . . .

KM#	Date	Mintage	Fine	VF	XF	Unc
500	1918	—	—	—	Rare	—

100 KORONA

33.8753 g, .900 GOLD, .9802 oz AGW
Mint mark: KB
40th Anniversary of Coronation of Franz Josef

KM#	Date	Mintage	Fine	VF	XF	Unc
490	1907	.011	500.00	650.00	900.00	1200.
	1907	(restrike)	—	—	Proof	800.00
	1907 U.P.	(restrike)	—	—	Proof	800.00

KM#	Date	Mintage	Fine	VF	XF	Unc
491	1907	1,088	600.00	1200.	1500.	1800.
	1908	4,038	550.00	850.00	1250.	1750.
	1908	(restrike)	—	—	Proof	450.00

REGENCY

1926-1945

MONETARY SYSTEM
100 Filler = 1 Pengo

FILLER

BRONZE
Mint mark: BP

KM#	Date	Mintage	Fine	VF	XF	Unc
505	1926	6.471	.15	.30	1.00	3.50
	1927	16.529	.10	.20	.50	3.00
	1928	7.000	.10	.25	.75	3.50
	1929	.418	5.00	10.00	20.00	35.00
	1930	3.734	.15	.30	1.00	5.00
	1931	10.849	.10	.20	.60	3.00
	1932	5.000	.10	.25	.75	4.00
	1932	(restrike)	—	—	Proof	3.75
	1933	5.000	.10	.25	.75	4.50
	1934	3.111	.15	.30	1.00	3.50
	1935	6.889	.10	.25	.75	4.00
	1936	10.000	.10	.20	.60	2.50
	1938	10.575	.10	.20	.60	2.50
	1939	10.425	.10	.20	.60	2.50

2 FILLER

BRONZE
Mint mark: BP

KM#	Date	Mintage	Fine	VF	XF	Unc
506	1926	17.777	.10	.20	.40	2.00
	1927	44.836	.10	.20	.40	2.00
	1928	11.448	.10	.20	.40	2.00
	1929	8.995	.10	.25	.50	2.50
	1930	6.943	.10	.25	.50	2.50
	1931	.826	.40	.90	2.50	6.50
	1932	4.174	2.00	4.00	9.00	18.00
	1933	.501	1.50	3.00	7.50	15.00
	1934	9.499	.10	.20	.40	2.00
	1935	10.000	.10	.20	.40	2.00
	1936	2.049	.15	.30	.75	4.00
	1937	7.951	.10	.25	.50	2.00
	1938	14.125	.10	.20	.40	1.50
	1939	16.875	.10	.20	.40	1.50
	1940	7.000	.10	.25	.50	1.50

STEEL

KM#	Date	Mintage	Fine	VF	XF	Unc
518.1	1940	64.500	.50	1.25	3.50	6.00

KM#	Date	Mintage	Fine	VF	XF	Unc
518.2	1940	78.000	.15	.30	1.00	3.00
	1941	12.000	10.00	25.00	50.00	90.00
	1942	13.000	.15	.30	1.00	3.50
	1942	(restrike)	—	—	Proof	6.50

ZINC

KM#	Date	Mintage	Fine	VF	XF	Unc
519	1943	37.000	.10	.20	.70	3.00
	1943	(restrike)	—	—	Proof	6.50
	1944	55.159	.10	.20	.70	2.50

NOTE: Variations in planchets exist.

10 FILLER

COPPER-NICKEL
Mint mark: BP

KM#	Date	Mintage	Fine	VF	XF	Unc
507	1926	20.001	.50	1.50	3.00	7.00
	1927	12.255	.50	1.50	3.00	7.00
	1935	4.740	.50	1.50	3.00	4.50
	1936	3.005	.50	1.50	3.00	4.50
	1938	6.700	.50	1.50	3.00	4.50
	1939	4.460	1.50	3.50	7.00	12.00
	1940	.960	5.00	10.00	20.00	35.00

STEEL

KM#	Date	Mintage	Fine	VF	XF	Unc
507a	1940	45.927	.10	.20	.80	3.50
	1941	24.963	.10	.20	.80	3.50
	1942	44.110	.10	.20	.80	3.50

20 FILLER

COPPER-NICKEL
Mint mark: BP

KM#	Date	Mintage	Fine	VF	XF	Unc
508	1926	25.000	.75	2.00	3.50	6.00
	1927	.830	5.00	15.00	30.00	50.00
	1938	20.150	.10	.25	1.00	2.50
	1939	2.020	1.50	3.50	6.50	10.00
	1940	2.470	1.50	3.50	6.50	10.00

STEEL

KM#	Date	Mintage	Fine	VF	XF	Unc
520	1941	75.007	.10	.20	.90	4.00
	1943	7.500	.10	.20	.90	4.00
	1944	25.000	.10	.20	.90	4.00
	1944	(restrike)	—	—	Proof	7.00

50 FILLER

COPPER-NICKEL
Mint mark: BP

KM#	Date	Mintage	Fine	VF	XF	Unc
509	1926	14.921	.75	2.00	3.50	6.00
	1938	20.079	.20	.40	1.00	3.00
	1939	2.770	1.50	3.50	7.50	12.00
	1939	(restrike)	—	—	Proof	16.50
	1940	6.230	1.00	3.00	6.00	10.00

PENGO

5.0000 g, .640 SILVER, .1029 oz ASW
Mint mark: BP

KM#	Date	Mintage	Fine	VF	XF	Unc
510	1926	15.000	BV	1.50	3.00	6.00
	1927	18.000	BV	1.50	3.00	6.00
	1937	4.000	BV	1.50	2.50	6.00

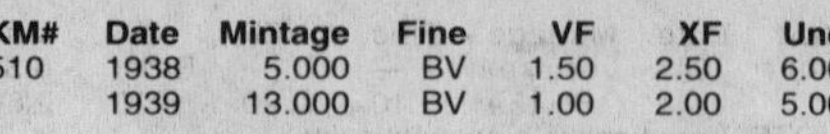

KM#	Date	Mintage	Fine	VF	XF	Unc
510	1938	5.000	BV	1.50	2.50	6.00
	1939	13.000	BV	1.00	2.00	5.00

ALUMINUM

KM#	Date	Mintage	Fine	VF	XF	Unc
521	1941	80.000	.10	.20	.50	1.00
	1942	19.000	.10	.20	.50	1.00
	1943	2.000	.50	1.50	3.00	8.00
	1944	16.000	.10	.20	.50	1.00

2 PENGO

10.0000 g, .640 SILVER, .2058 oz ASW
Mint mark: BP

KM#	Date	Mintage	Fine	VF	XF	Unc
511	1929	5.000	1.25	3.00	4.75	8.50
	1931	.110	10.00	20.00	40.00	65.00
	1932	.602	1.50	4.00	8.00	12.00
	1933	1.051	1.25	3.00	6.00	9.00
	1935	.050	25.00	65.00	120.00	250.00
	1936	.711	2.00	5.00	10.00	15.00
	1937	1.500	1.25	3.00	4.75	8.50
	1938	6.417	1.25	3.00	4.75	8.50
	1939	2.103	1.25	3.00	4.75	8.50

Founding of Pazmany University Tercentenary

KM#	Date	Mintage	Fine	VF	XF	Unc
513	1935	.050	2.00	5.00	8.00	12.50
	1935	(restrike not marked)			Proof	22.50

Death of Rakoczi Bicentennial

KM#	Date	Mintage	Fine	VF	XF	Unc
514	1935	.100	2.00	4.00	6.00	10.00
	1935	(restrike not marked)			Proof	22.50

50th Anniversary Death of Liszt

KM#	Date	Mintage	Fine	VF	XF	Unc
515	1936	.200	1.50	2.50	4.50	8.00
	1936	(restrike not marked)			Proof	18.00

ALUMINUM

KM#	Date	Mintage	Fine	VF	XF	Unc
522.1	1941	24.000	.15	.30	.50	.80
	1942	8.000	.15	.30	.50	.80
	1943	10.000	.15	.30	.50	.80

Rev: Base of 2 is wavy.

KM#	Date	Mintage	Fine	VF	XF	Unc
522.2	1941	.040	6.00	12.00	22.00	40.00

5 PENGO

25.0000 g, .640 SILVER, .5145 oz ASW
Mint mark: BP
10th Anniversary of Regency of Admiral Horthy
Raised, sharp edge reeding.

KM#	Date	Mintage	Fine	VF	XF	Unc
512.1	1930	3.650	4.50	9.00	12.00	17.50

25.3300 g, .640 SILVER, .5213 oz ASW, 36.1mm

KM#	Date	Mintage	Fine	VF	XF	Unc
512.2	1930	(restrike)	—	—	Proof	18.50

25.0000 g, .640 SILVER, .5145 oz ASW, 36.1mm
900th Anniversary of Death of St. Stephan

KM#	Date	Mintage	Fine	VF	XF	Unc
516	1938	.600	4.50	9.00	14.00	25.00
	1938	(restrike not marked)			Proof	27.50

Admiral Miklos Horthy
Smooth, ornamented edge.

KM#	Date	Mintage	Fine	VF	XF	Unc
517	1938	60 pcs.	—	—	Rare	—
	1939	.408	4.50	9.00	14.00	25.00

ALUMINUM
75th Birthday of Admiral Horthy

KM#	Date	Mintage	Fine	VF	XF	Unc
523	1943	2.000	.50	1.00	2.00	4.00
	1943	(restrike)	—	—	Proof	6.00

PROVISIONAL GOVERNMENT

1944-1946

5 PENGO

ALUMINUM
Mint mark: BP

KM#	Date	Mintage	Fine	VF	XF	Unc
525	1945	5.002	.50	1.00	2.00	4.00
	1945 PROBAVERET (restrike)		—	—	Proof	10.00

REPUBLIC

1946-1949

MONETARY SYSTEM
100 Filler = 1 Forint

2 FILLER

BRONZE
Mint mark: BP

KM#	Date	Mintage	Fine	VF	XF	Unc
529	1946	13.665	.10	.15	.30	.50
	1947	23.865	.10	.15	.30	.50
	1947	(restrike)	—	—	Proof	3.00

5 FILLER

ALUMINUM
Mint mark: BP

KM#	Date	Mintage	Fine	VF	XF	Unc
535	1948	24.000	.20	.40	.60	1.00
	1951	15.000	.15	.25	.40	.60

10 FILLER

ALUMINUM-BRONZE
Mint mark: BP

KM#	Date	Mintage	Fine	VF	XF	Unc
530	1946	23.565	.10	.20	.40	.80
	1947	29.580	.10	.20	.40	.90
	1947	(restrike)	—	—	Proof	3.00
	1948	4.885	.50	1.00	2.00	4.50
	1950	8.000	.30	.70	2.00	4.00

ALUMINUM

KM#	Date	Mintage	Fine	VF	XF	Unc
530a	1950	2,000	—	—	10.00	20.00

20 FILLER

ALUMINUM-BRONZE
Mint mark: BP

KM#	Date	Mintage	Fine	VF	XF	Unc
531	1946	16.560	.15	.30	.50	1.00
	1946	(restrike)	—	—	Proof	5.00
	1947	18.260	.15	.30	.75	1.25
	1948	5.180	.50	1.00	3.00	6.00
	1950	5.000	.50	1.00	2.50	5.00

50 FILLER

ALUMINUM
Mint mark: BP

KM#	Date	Mintage	Fine	VF	XF	Unc
536	1948	15.000	.50	1.00	3.00	5.00
	1948	(restrike)	—	—	Proof	6.00

FORINT

ALUMINUM
Mint mark: BP

KM#	Date	Mintage	Fine	VF	XF	Unc
532	1946	38.900	.75	1.25	2.00	4.50
	1947	2.600	2.00	4.00	6.00	12.00
	1949	17.000	1.50	2.00	4.00	8.00

2 FORINT

ALUMINUM
Mint mark: BP

KM#	Date	Mintage	Fine	VF	XF	Unc
533	1946	10.000	1.25	2.75	5.00	10.00
	1947	3.500	2.00	4.00	8.00	15.00

5 FORINT

20.0000 g, .835 SILVER, .5369 oz ASW
Mint mark: BP
Lajos Kossuth
Thick planchet

KM#	Date	Mintage	Fine	VF	XF	Unc
534	1946	.040	3.50	6.50	12.50	20.00

12.0000 g, .500 SILVER, .1929 oz ASW
1.7mm thin planchet

KM#	Date	Mintage	Fine	VF	XF	Unc
534a	1946	—	—	—	—	—
	1947	10.004	BV	1.75	2.50	4.00
	1947	(restrike)	—	—	Proof	6.50

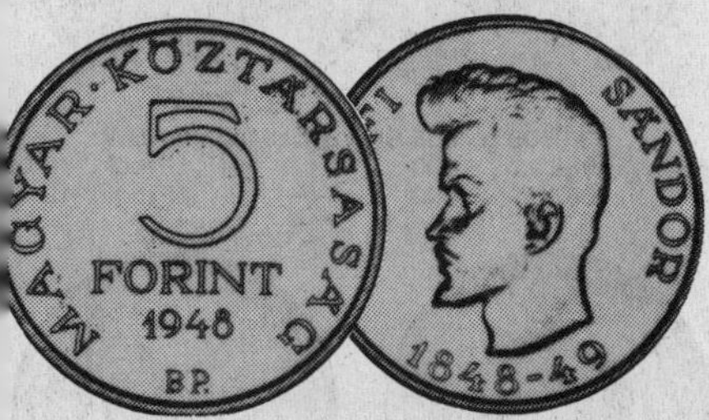

12.0000 g, .500 SILVER, .1929 oz ASW
Centenary of 1848 Revolution - Petofi

KM#	Date	Mintage	Fine	VF	XF	Unc
537	1948	.100	BV	2.00	3.00	6.00
	1948	(restrike)	—	—	Proof	20.00

10 FORINT

20.0000 g, .500 SILVER, .3215 oz ASW
Mint mark: BP
Centenary of 1848 Revolution - Szechenyi

KM#	Date	Mintage	Fine	VF	XF	Unc
538	1948	.100	2.50	3.50	6.50	10.00
	1948	(restrike)	—	—	Proof	15.00

20 FORINT

28.0000 g, .500 SILVER, .4501 oz ASW
Mint mark: BP
Centenary of 1848 Revolution - Tancsics

KM#	Date	Mintage	Fine	VF	XF	Unc
539	1948	.050	5.00	8.00	10.00	16.00
	1948	(restrike)	—	—	Proof	25.00

PEOPLES REPUBLIC

1949-1989

MONETARY SYSTEM
100 Filler = 1 Forint

2 FILLER

ALUMINUM
Mint mark: BP

KM#	Date	Mintage	Fine	VF	XF	Unc
546	1950	24.990	—	—	—	.20
	1952	5.600	—	—	.15	.35
	1953	9.400	—	—	—	.20
	1954	10.000	—	—	—	.20
	1955	6.029	—	—	—	.25
	1956	4.000	—	—	—	.25
	1957	5.000	—	—	—	.25
	1960	3.000	—	—	—	.25
	1961	2.000	—	—	—	.25
	1962	3.000	—	—	—	.25
	1963	2.082	—	—	—	.25
	1965	.540	.25	1.00	3.00	7.00
	1971	1.035	—	—	—	.25
	1972	1.000	—	—	—	.25
	1973	2.826	—	—	—	.25
	1974	.050	—	—	—	.25
	1975	.050	—	—	—	.25
	1976	.050	—	—	—	.25
	1977	.050	—	—	—	.25
	1978	.050	—	—	—	.25
	1979	.030	—	—	—	.25
	1980	.030	—	—	—	.25
546	1981	.030	—	—	—	.25
	1982	.030	—	—	—	.25
	1983	.030	—	—	—	.25
	1984	.030	—	—	—	.25
	1985	.030	—	—	—	.25
	1986	.030	—	—	—	.25
	1987	.030	—	—	—	.25
	1988	.030	—	—	—	.25
	1989	.030	—	—	—	.25

COPPER-NICKEL

KM#	Date	Mintage	Fine	VF	XF	Unc
546a	1966	5,000		—	Proof	1.50
	1967	5,000		—	Proof	1.50

5 FILLER

ALUMINUM
Mint mark: BP

KM#	Date	Mintage	Fine	VF	XF	Unc
549	1953	10.000	—	—	.10	.25
	1955	6.005	—	—	.10	.25
	1956	6.012	—	—	.10	.25
	1957	5.000	—	—	.10	.25
	1959	8.000	—	—	.10	.25
	1960	7.000	—	—	.10	.25
	1961	4.410	—	—	.10	.25
	1962	5.590	—	—	.10	.25
	1963	4.020	—	—	.10	.25
	1964	3.600	—	—	.10	.25
	1965	6.000	—	—	.10	.25
	1970	3.900	.10	.20	.50	2.00
	1971	.100	—	—	.10	.20
	1972	.050	—	—	.10	.20
	1973	.105	—	—	.10	.20
	1974	.060	—	—	.10	.20
	1975	.060	—	—	.10	.20
	1976	.050	—	—	.10	.20
	1977	.050	—	—	.10	.20
	1978	.050	—	—	.10	.20
	1979	.030	—	—	.10	.20
	1980	.030	—	—	.10	.20
	1981	.030	—	—	.10	.20
	1982	.030	—	—	.10	.20
	1983	.030	—	—	.10	.20
	1984	.030	—	—	.10	.20
	1985	.030	—	—	.10	.20
	1986	.030	—	—	.10	.20
	1987	.030	—	—	.10	.20
	1988	.030	—	—	.10	.20
	1989	.030	—	—	.10	.20

COPPER-NICKEL

KM#	Date	Mintage	Fine	VF	XF	Unc
549a	1966	5,000	—	—	Proof	2.00
	1967	5,000	—	—	Proof	2.00

10 FILLER

ALUMINUM
Mint mark: BP

KM#	Date	Mintage	Fine	VF	XF	Unc
547	1950	5.040	5.00	10.00	20.00	30.00
	1951	80.950	.10	.20	.50	1.50
	1955	10.019	.10	.20	.50	1.50
	1957	13.000	.10	.20	.50	1.50
	1958	12.015	.10	.20	.50	1.50
	1959	15.000	.10	.20	.50	1.50
	1960	5.000	.20	.40	1.00	2.50
	1961	13.000	.10	.20	.50	1.50
	1962	4.000	.20	.40	1.00	2.50
	1963	8.000	.15	.30	.75	2.00
	1964	17.000	.10	.20	.50	1.50
	1965	21.880	.10	.20	.50	1.50
	1966	8.120	.15	.30	.75	2.00

COPPER-NICKEL

KM#	Date	Mintage	Fine	VF	XF	Unc
547a	1966	5,000	—	—	Proof	3.00
	1967	5,000	—	—	Proof	3.00

ALUMINUM, reduced size

KM#	Date	Mintage	Fine	VF	XF	Unc
572	1967	5,000	1.00	2.00	10.00	20.00
	1968	16.086	—	.10	.20	.40
	1969	50.760	—	.10	.20	.40
	1970	28.399	—	.10	.20	.40
	1971	28.800	—	—	.10	.25
	1972	17.220	—	—	.10	.25
	1973	33.720	—	—	.10	.25
	1974	24.930	—	—	.10	.25
	1975	30.000	—	—	.10	.25
	1976	20.025	—	—	.10	.25
	1977	30.075	—	—	.10	.25

KM#	Date	Mintage	Fine	VF	XF	Unc
572	1978	36.005	—	—	.10	.20
	1979	36.060	—	—	.10	.20
	1980	36.000	—	—	.10	.20
	1981	36.000	—	—	.10	.20
	1982	45.015	—	—	.10	.20
	1983	45.030	—	—	.10	.20
	1984	42.075	—	—	.10	.20
	1985	40.035	—	—	.10	.20
	1986	48.075	—	—	.10	.20
	1987	45.000	—	—	.10	.20
	1988	48.015	—	—	.10	.20
	1989	79.440	—	—	—	.15

20 FILLER

ALUMINUM
Mint mark: BP

KM#	Date	Mintage	Fine	VF	XF	Unc
550	1953	45.000	.10	.20	.50	1.25
	1955	10.023	.10	.20	.50	1.25
	1957	5.000	.20	.40	1.00	3.50
	1958	10.000	.10	.20	.50	1.25
	1959	13.000	.10	.20	.50	1.25
	1961	9.000	.15	.30	.70	1.75
	1963	7.000	.20	.40	1.00	2.25
	1964	10.400	.10	.20	.50	1.00
	1965	15.000	.10	.20	.50	1.00
	1966	5.000	.20	.40	1.00	2.25

COPPER-NICKEL

KM#	Date	Mintage	Fine	VF	XF	Unc
550a	1966	5,000	—	—	Proof	4.00
	1967	5,000	—	—	Proof	4.00

ALUMINUM
Reduced size

KM#	Date	Mintage	Fine	VF	XF	Unc
573	1967	10.000	—	.15	.30	.60
	1968	57.990	—	.15	.30	.60
	1969	25.510	—	.15	.30	.60
	1970	19.960	—	.15	.30	.60
	1971	20.109	—	—	.10	.40
	7971(error)	.011	1.50	3.00	5.50	10.00
	1972	29.610	—	—	.10	.40
	1973	25.400	—	—	.10	.40
	1974	35.010	—	—	.10	.40
	1975	30.010	—	—	.10	.30
	1976	30.010	—	—	.10	.30
	1977	30.050	—	—	.10	.30
	1978	30.140	—	—	.10	.30
	1979	32.010	—	—	.10	.30
	1980	45.010	—	—	.10	.30
	1981	34.020	—	—	.10	.30
	1982	35.010	—	—	.10	.30
	1983	43.210	—	—	.10	.30
	1984	42.270	—	—	.10	.30
	1985	40.440	—	—	.10	.30
	1986	48.000	—	—	.10	.30
	1987	55.000	—	—	.10	.30
	1988	48.010	—	—	.10	.30
	1989	90.810	—	—	—	.25

F.A.O. Issue

KM#	Date	Mintage	Fine	VF	XF	Unc
627	1983	.050	—	.10	.20	.60

50 FILLER

ALUMINUM
Mint mark: BP

KM#	Date	Mintage	Fine	VF	XF	Unc
551	1953	10.017	.30	.75	1.50	3.00
	1965	3.005	.20	.50	1.00	2.50
	1966	1.500	.20	.50	1.00	2.50

COPPER-NICKEL

KM#	Date	Mintage	Fine	VF	XF	Unc
551a	1966	5,000	—	—	Proof	5.00
	1967	5,000	—	—	Proof	5.00

ALUMINUM

KM#	Date	Mintage	Fine	VF	XF	Unc
574	1967	20.000	—	.15	.30	.60
	1968	13.830	—	.15	.30	.60
	1969	10.085	—	.15	.30	.60
	1971	.050	—	.10	.25	.50
	1972	.520	—	.10	.20	.40
	1973	7.600	—	—	.10	.30
	1974	5.000	—	—	.10	.30
	1975	10.160	—	—	.10	.30
	1976	15.130	—	—	.10	.30
	1977	10.050	—	—	.10	.30
	1978	10.110	—	—	.10	.30
	1979	10.060	—	—	.10	.30
	1980	15.000	—	—	.10	.30
	1981	10.000	—	—	.10	.30
	1982	10.000	—	—	.10	.30
	1983	10.070	—	—	.10	.30
	1984	14.060	—	—	.10	.30
	1985	12.020	—	—	.10	.30
	1986	17.140	—	—	.10	.30
	1987	23.000	—	—	.10	.30
	1988	18.050	—	—	.10	.30
	1989	28.590	—	—	.10	.30

FORINT

ALUMINUM
Mint mark: BP

KM#	Date	Mintage	Fine	VF	XF	Unc
545	1949	19.440	.40	1.00	2.00	4.00
	1950	39.060	.40	1.00	2.00	4.00
	1952	63.018	.50	1.25	2.50	5.00

KM#	Date	Mintage	Fine	VF	XF	Unc
555	1957	7.500	.30	.70	1.80	3.50
	1958	5.070	.30	.70	1.80	4.00
	1960	5.000	.15	.45	.85	1.75
	1961	5.000	.15	.45	.85	1.75
	1963	3.000	.30	.70	1.80	3.50
	1964	6.080	.15	.45	.85	1.75
	1965	9.810	.15	.45	.85	1.75
	1966	5.680	.50	1.25	2.50	4.50

5.8500 g, .835 SILVER, .1570 oz ASW

KM#	Date	Mintage	Fine	VF	XF	Unc
555a	1966	5,000	—	—	Proof	7.00
	1967	5,000	—	—	Proof	7.00

ALUMINUM
Reduced size, 22.8mm

KM#	Date	Mintage	Fine	VF	XF	Unc
575	1967	60.000	.10	.20	.40	1.25
	1968	51.430	.10	.20	.40	1.25
	1969	26.120	.10	.20	.40	1.25
	1970	10.000	.10	.20	.40	1.25
	1971	1.390	—	.10	.20	.50
	1972	.110	—	.10	.20	.60
	1973	1.990	—	.10	.20	.50
	1974	4.990	—	.10	.20	.50
	1975	10.000	—	.10	.20	.50
	1976	15.000	—	.10	.20	.50
	1977	10.050	—	.10	.20	.50
	1978	.050	—	.10	.20	.60
	1979	10.070	—	.10	.20	.50
	1980	20.040	—	.10	.20	.50
	1981	25.040	—	.10	.20	.50
	1982	10.000	—	.10	.20	.50
	1983	20.140	—	.10	.20	.50
	1984	6.010	—	.10	.20	.50
	1985	.030	—	.10	.20	.50
	1986	.030	—	.10	.20	.50
	1987	13.000	—	.10	.20	.50
	1988	20.080	—	.10	.20	.50
	1989	—	—	.10	.20	.50

2 FORINT

COPPER-NICKEL
Mint mark: BP

KM#	Date	Mintage	Fine	VF	XF	Unc
548	1950	18.500	.50	1.00	2.00	5.00
	1951	4.000	.60	1.25	2.50	5.50
	1952	4.540	.60	1.25	2.50	5.50

KM#	Date	Mintage	Fine	VF	XF	Unc
556	1957	5.000	.25	.75	1.50	3.25
	1958	1.033	.50	1.00	2.00	4.50
	1960	4.000	.25	.75	1.50	3.25
	1961	.690	.60	1.25	2.50	6.00
	1962	1.190	.25	.75	1.50	3.25

COPPER-NICKEL-ZINC

KM#	Date	Mintage	Fine	VF	XF	Unc
556a	1962	1.210	.10	.25	.75	1.75
	1963	3.100	.10	.25	.75	1.75
	1964	3.250	.10	.25	.75	1.75
	1965	4.395	.10	.25	.75	1.75
	1966	6.630	.10	.25	.75	1.75

6.1200 g, .835 SILVER, .1643 oz ASW

KM#	Date	Mintage	Fine	VF	XF	Unc
556b	1966	5,000	—	—	Proof	9.00
	1967	5,000	—	—	Proof	9.00

BRASS

KM#	Date	Mintage	Fine	VF	XF	Unc
591	1970	50.000	.10	.20	.40	1.75
	1971	10.025	—	.15	.35	.85
	1972	10.015	—	.15	.35	.85
	1973	.820	.10	.25	.50	2.00
	1974	10.000	—	.15	.35	.85
	1975	20.030	—	.15	.35	.85
	1976	15.000	—	.15	.35	.85
	1977	10.115	—	.15	.35	.85
	1978	12.000	—	.15	.35	.85
	1979	10.005	—	.15	.35	.85
	1980	12.005	—	.15	.35	.85
	1981	10.035	—	.15	.35	.85
	1982	10.005	—	.15	.35	.85
	1983	20.160	—	.15	.35	.85
	1984	5.000	—	.15	.35	.85
	1985	10.675	—	.15	.35	.85
	1986	.030	—	.15	.35	1.25
	1987	5.030	—	.15	.35	.85
	1988	5.035	—	.15	.35	.85
	1989	—	—	.15	.35	.85

5 FORINT

13.0000 g, .835 SILVER, .3490 oz ASW

KM#	Date	Mintage	Fine	VF	XF	Unc
534b	1966	5,000	—	—	Proof	12.00
	1967	5,000	—	—	Proof	12.00

COPPER-NICKEL
Mint mark: BP
Lajos Kossuth

KM#	Date	Mintage	Fine	VF	XF	Unc
576	1967	20.000	.20	.50	.75	1.25
	1968	.029	3.50	7.50	12.50	25.00

NICKEL

KM#	Date	Mintage	Fine	VF	XF	Unc
594	1971	20.004	.15	.30	.50	1.00
	1972	5.000	.15	.30	.50	1.00
	1973	.100	.15	.30	.50	1.00
	1974	.050	.15	.30	.50	1.00
	1975	.050	.15	.30	.50	1.00
	1976	5.090	.15	.30	.50	1.00
	1977	.050	.15	.30	.50	1.00
	1978	6.000	.15	.30	.50	1.00
	1979	10.000	.15	.30	.50	1.00
	1980	6.002	.15	.30	.50	1.00
	1981	5.002	.15	.30	.50	1.00
	1982	.936	.15	.30	.50	1.00

F.A.O. Issue

KM#	Date	Mintage	Fine	VF	XF	Unc
628	1983	.050	.10	.20	.50	1.25

COPPER-NICKEL
Lajos Kossuth

KM#	Date	Mintage	Fine	VF	XF	Unc
635	1983	15.240	—	.15	.25	.50
	1984	25.018	—	.15	.25	.50
	1985	25.286	—	.15	.25	.50
	1986	1.030	—	.15	.25	.50
	1987	.030	—	.15	.25	.50
	1988	4.050	—	.15	.25	.50
	1989	—	—	.15	.25	.50

10 FORINT

12.5000 g, .800 SILVER, .3215 oz ASW
Mint mark: BP
10th Anniversary of Forint

KM#	Date	Mintage	Fine	VF	XF	Unc
552	1956	.022	3.00	5.00	8.00	16.00

NICKEL

KM#	Date	Mintage	Fine	VF	XF	Unc
595	1971	24.998	.20	.50	.80	1.50
	1972	25.000	.20	.50	.80	1.50
	1973	.078	.20	.50	.80	1.50
	1974	.050	.20	.50	.80	1.50
	1975	.050	.20	.50	.80	1.50
	1976	3.568	.20	.50	.80	1.50
	1977	4.618	.20	.50	.80	1.50
	1978	.050	.20	.50	.80	2.00
	1979	5.000	.20	.50	.80	1.50
	1980	2.550	.20	.50	.80	1.50
	1982	.030	.20	.50	.80	2.00

F.A.O. Issue

KM#	Date	Mintage	Fine	VF	XF	Unc
620	1981	.060	—	—	1.25	2.50

F.A.O. Issue

KM#	Date	Mintage	Fine	VF	XF	Unc
629	1983	.050	—	—	1.25	2.50

ALUMINUM-BRONZE
Circulation Coinage

KM#	Date	Mintage	Fine	VF	XF	Unc
636	1983	11.004	.10	.25	.40	1.00
	1984	7.578	.10	.25	.40	1.00
	1985	27.648	.10	.25	.40	1.00
	1986	15.000	.10	.25	.40	1.00
	1987	10.000	.10	.25	.40	1.00
	1988	5.000	.10	.25	.40	1.00
	1989	—	.10	.25	.40	1.00

20 FORINT

17.5000 g, .800 SILVER, .4501 oz ASW
Mint mark: BP
10th Anniversary of Forint

KM#	Date	Mintage	Fine	VF	XF	Unc
553	1956	.022	4.50	8.00	12.00	20.00

COPPER-NICKEL
Dozsa - Circulation Coinage

KM#	Date	Mintage	Fine	VF	XF	Unc
630	1982	12.814	.20	.50	.75	1.25
	1983	18.596	.20	.50	.75	1.25
	1984	31.016	.20	.50	.75	1.25
	1985	20.122	.20	.50	.75	1.25
	1986	6.000	.20	.50	.75	1.25
	1987	.030	.20	.50	.75	1.25
	1988	.030	.20	.50	.75	1.25
	1989	—	.20	.50	.75	1.25

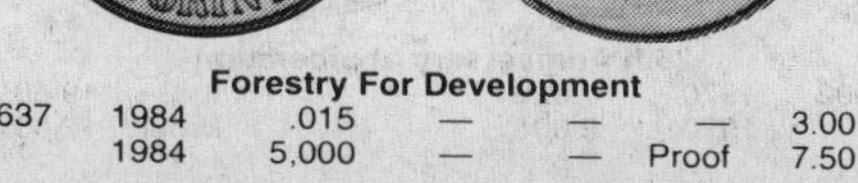

Forestry For Development

KM#	Date	Mintage	Fine	VF	XF	Unc
637	1984	.015	—	—	—	3.00
	1984	5,000	—	—	Proof	7.50

F.A.O. Issue

KM#	Date	Mintage	Fine	VF	XF	Unc
653	1985	.025	—	—	—	2.00
	1985	—	—	—	Proof	6.00

25 (HUSZONOT) FORINT

20.0000 g, .800 SILVER, .5144 oz ASW
Mint mark: BP
10th Anniversary of Forint

KM#	Date	Mintage	Fine	VF	XF	Unc
554	1956	.022	5.00	10.00	15.00	22.50

17.5000 g, .750 SILVER, .4220 oz ASW
150th Anniversary of Birth of Liszt

KM#	Date	Mintage	Fine	VF	XF	Unc
557	1961	.015	—	—	Proof	20.00

80th Anniversary of Birth of Bartok

KM#	Date	Mintage	Fine	VF	XF	Unc
558	1961	.015	—	—	Proof	20.00

12.0000 g, .640 SILVER, .2469 oz ASW
400th Anniversary of Death of Zrinyi

KM#	Date	Mintage	Fine	VF	XF	Unc
567	1966	.011	—	—	Proof	20.00

12.0000 g, .750 SILVER, .2893 oz ASW
85th Birthday of Kodaly

KM#	Date	Mintage	Fine	VF	XF	Unc
577	1967	.015	—	—	—	10.00
	1967	—	—	—	Proof	12.50

50 (OTVEN) FORINT

20.0000 g, .750 SILVER, .4822 oz ASW
Mint mark: BP
150th Anniversary of Birth of Liszt

KM#	Date	Mintage	Fine	VF	XF	Unc
559	1961	.015	—	—	Proof	20.00

3.8380 g, .986 GOLD, .1217 oz AGW

KM#	Date	Mintage	Fine	VF	XF	Unc
560	1961	2,503	—	—	Proof	125.00

20.0000 g, .750 SILVER, .4822 oz ASW
80th Anniversary of Birth of Bartok

KM#	Date	Mintage	Fine	VF	XF	Unc
561	1961	.015	—	—	Proof	20.00

3.8380 g, .986 GOLD, .1217 oz AGW

KM#	Date	Mintage	Fine	VF	XF	Unc
562	1961	2,503	—	—	Proof	125.00

20.0000 g, .640 SILVER, .4115 oz ASW
400th Anniversary of Death of Zrinyi

KM#	Date	Mintage	Fine	VF	XF	Unc
568	1966	.011	—	—	Proof	25.00

20.0000 g, .750 SILVER, .4822 oz ASW
85th Birthday of Kodaly

KM#	Date	Mintage	Fine	VF	XF	Unc
578	1967	.015	—	—	—	10.00
	1967	—	—	—	Proof	12.50

20.0000 g, .640 SILVER, .4115 oz ASW
150th Anniversary of Birth of Semmelweis

KM#	Date	Mintage	Fine	VF	XF	Unc
582	1968	.020	—	—	—	10.00
	1968	4,750	—	—	Proof	12.50

4.2050 g, .900 GOLD, .1217 oz AGW

KM#	Date	Mintage	Fine	VF	XF	Unc
583	1968	.025	—	—	Proof	125.00

16.0000 g, .640 SILVER, .3292 oz ASW
50th Anniversary Republic of Councils

KM#	Date	Mintage	Fine	VF	XF	Unc
589	1969	.012	—	—	—	10.00
	1969	3,000	—	—	Proof	12.50

25th Anniversary of Liberation

KM#	Date	Mintage	Fine	VF	XF	Unc
592	1970	.020	—	—	—	9.00
	1970	5,000	—	—	Proof	12.00

1000th Anniversary of Birth of St. Stephen

KM#	Date	Mintage	Fine	VF	XF	Unc
596	1972	.024	—	—	—	12.00
	1972	6,000	—	—	Proof	15.00

150th Anniversary of Birth of Sandor Petofi

KM#	Date	Mintage	Fine	VF	XF	Unc
599	1973	.024	—	—	—	8.00
	1973	6,000	—	—	Proof	10.00

50th Anniversary of National Bank

KM#	Date	Mintage	Fine	VF	XF	Unc
601	1974	.024	—	—	—	8.00
	1974	6,000	—	—	Proof	10.00

COPPER-NICKEL
25th Anniversary of
World Wildlife Foundation - Falcon

KM#	Date	Mintage	Fine	VF	XF	Unc
663	1988	.045	—	—	—	5.00

100 (SZAZ) FORINT

7.6760 g, .986 GOLD, .2431 oz AGW
Mint mark: BP
150th Anniversary of Birth of Liszt

KM#	Date	Mintage	Fine	VF	XF	Unc
563	1961	2,500	—	—	Proof	175.00

80th Anniversary of Birth of Bartok

KM#	Date	Mintage	Fine	VF	XF	Unc
564	1961	2,500	—	—	Proof	175.00

8.4100 g, .900 GOLD, .2433 oz AGW
400th Anniversary of Death of Zrinyi

KM#	Date	Mintage	Fine	VF	XF	Unc
569	1966	3,300	—	—	Proof	175.00

28.0000 g, .750 SILVER, .6752 oz ASW
85th Birthday of Kodaly

KM#	Date	Mintage	Fine	VF	XF	Unc
579	1967	.010	—	—	—	35.00
	1967	—	—	—	Proof	40.00

28.0000 g, .640 SILVER, .5762 oz ASW
150th Anniversary of Birth of Semmelweis

KM#	Date	Mintage	Fine	VF	XF	Unc
584	1968	.020	—	—	—	10.00
	1968	4,750	—	—	Proof	17.50

8.4100 g, .900 GOLD, .2433 oz AGW

KM#	Date	Mintage	Fine	VF	XF	Unc
585	1968	.023	—	—	Proof	175.00

22.0000 g, .640 SILVER, .4527 oz ASW
50th Anniversary of Republic of Councils

KM#	Date	Mintage	Fine	VF	XF	Unc
590	1969	.012	—	—	—	12.00
	1969	3,000	—	—	Proof	15.00

25th Anniversary of Liberation

KM#	Date	Mintage	Fine	VF	XF	Unc
593	1970	.020	—	—	—	10.00
	1970	5,000	—	—	Proof	12.00

1000th Anniversary of Birth of St. Stephen

KM#	Date	Mintage	Fine	VF	XF	Unc
597	1972	.024	—	—	—	14.00
	1972	6,000	—	—	Proof	18.00

Buda and Pest Union Centennial

KM#	Date	Mintage	Fine	VF	XF	Unc
598	1972	.025	—	—	—	10.00
	1972	6,000	—	—	Proof	16.00

150th Anniversary of Birth of Sandor Petofi

KM#	Date	Mintage	Fine	VF	XF	Unc
600	1973	.024	—	—	—	10.00
	1973	6,000	—	—	Proof	16.00

25th Anniversary of KGST

KM#	Date	Mintage	Fine	VF	XF	Unc
602	1974	.020	—	—	—	10.00
	1974	5,000	—	—	Proof	16.00

50th Anniversary of National Bank

KM#	Date	Mintage	Fine	VF	XF	Unc
603	1974	.024	—	—	—	10.00
	1974	6,000	—	—	Proof	16.00

NICKEL
1st Soviet-Hungarian Space Flight

KM#	Date	Mintage	Fine	VF	XF	Unc
617	1980	.180	—	—	—	4.00
	1980	.020	—	—	Proof	8.00

World Food Day

KM#	Date	Mintage	Fine	VF	XF	Unc
621	1981	.080	—	—	—	5.00
	1981	.020	—	—	Proof	10.00

COPPER-NICKEL-ZINC
1300th Anniversary of Bulgarian Statehood

KM#	Date	Mintage	Fine	VF	XF	Unc
622	1981	.050	—	—	Proof	8.00

COPPER-NICKEL
World Football Championship

KM#	Date	Mintage	Fine	VF	XF	Unc
626	1982	.150	—	—	—	2.50

F.A.O. Issue

KM#	Date	Mintage	Fine	VF	XF	Unc
631	1983	.050	—	—	—	3.50
	1983	.010	—	—	Proof	10.00

COPPER-NICKEL-ZINC
200th Anniversary of Birth of Simon Bolivar

KM#	Date	Mintage	Fine	VF	XF	Unc
632	1983	.020	—	—	—	5.00
	1983	.010	—	—	Proof	10.00

Count Istvan Szechenyi

KM#	Date	Mintage	Fine	VF	XF	Unc
633	1983	.030	—	—	—	6.00
	1983	.020	—	—	Proof	8.00

100th Anniversary of Birth of Bela Czobel - Painter

KM#	Date	Mintage	Fine	VF	XF	Unc
634	1983	.020	—	—	—	6.00
	1983	.010	—	—	Proof	10.00

200th Anniversary of Birth of Sandor Korosi Csoma

KM#	Date	Mintage	Fine	VF	XF	Unc
638	1984	.020	—	—	—	6.00
	1984	.010	—	—	Proof	10.00

Forestry For Development

KM#	Date	Mintage	Fine	VF	XF	Unc
639	1984	.015	—	—	—	6.00
	1984	5,000	—	—	Proof	12.00

Wildlife Preservation - Turtle

KM#	Date	Mintage	Fine	VF	XF	Unc
644	1985	.020	—	—	—	7.00

Wildlife Preservation - Otter

KM#	Date	Mintage	Fine	VF	XF	Unc
645	1985	.020	—	—	—	7.00

Wildlife Preservation - Wildcat

KM#	Date	Mintage	Fine	VF	XF	Unc
646	1985	.020	—	—	—	7.00

World Football - Map of Mexico

KM#	Date	Mintage	Fine	VF	XF	Unc
647	1985	.030	—	—	—	6.00
	1985	7,500	—	—	Proof	10.00

World Football - Indian Artifacts

KM#	Date	Mintage	Fine	VF	XF	Unc
648	1985	.030	—	—	—	6.00
	1985	7,500	—	—	Proof	10.00

Budapest Cultural Forum

KM#	Date	Mintage	Fine	VF	XF	Unc
651	1985	.040	—	—	—	6.00
	1985	—	—	—	Proof	9.00

F.A.O. Issue

KM#	Date	Mintage	Fine	VF	XF	Unc
654	1985	.020	—	—	—	6.00
	1985	5,000	—	—	Proof	9.00

200th Anniversary of Birth of Andras Fay

KM#	Date	Mintage	Fine	VF	XF	Unc
655	1986	.042	—	—	—	6.00
	1986	8,000	—	—	Proof	9.00

Europe Football Championship

KM#	Date	Mintage	Fine	VF	XF	Unc
665	1988	.020	—	—	—	17.50

COPPER-NICKEL
1990 World Cup Soccer

KM#	Date	Mintage	Fine	VF	XF	Unc
664	1988	.023	—	—	—	17.50

1990 World Cup Soccer

KM#	Date	Mintage	Fine	VF	XF	Unc
668	1989	.023	—	—	—	17.50

200 (KETSZAZ) FORINT

16.8210 g, .900 GOLD, .4867 oz AGW
Mint mark: BP
150th Anniversary of Birth of Ignac Semmelweis

KM#	Date	Mintage	Fine	VF	XF	Unc
586	1968	.014	—	—	Proof	300.00

28.0000 g, .640 SILVER, .5762 oz ASW
Mint mark: BP
30th Anniversary of Liberation

KM#	Date	Mintage	Fine	VF	XF	Unc
604	1975	.020	—	—	—	18.00
	1975	.010	—	—	Proof	20.00

150th Anniversary Academy of Science

KM#	Date	Mintage	Fine	VF	XF	Unc
605	1975	.020	—	—	—	18.00
	1975	.010	—	—	Proof	20.00

300th Anniversary of Birth of Ferencz Rakoczi II

KM#	Date	Mintage	Fine	VF	XF	Unc
606	1976	.025	—	—	—	16.50
	1976	5,000	—	—	Proof	22.50

Mihaly M. Unkacsy

KM#	Date	Mintage	Fine	VF	XF	Unc
607	1976	.025	—	—	—	16.50
	1976	5,000	—	—	Proof	22.50

Pal Szinyei Merse

KM#	Date	Mintage	Fine	VF	XF	Unc
608	1976	.025	—	—	—	16.50
	1976	5,000	—	—	Proof	22.50

Gyula Derkovits

KM#	Date	Mintage	Fine	VF	XF	Unc
609	1976	.025	—	—	—	16.50
	1976	5,000	—	—	Proof	22.50

Adam Manyoki

KM#	Date	Mintage	Fine	VF	XF	Unc
610	1977	.025	—	—	—	16.50
	1977	5,000	—	—	Proof	22.50

Tivadar CS. Kosztka

KM#	Date	Mintage	Fine	VF	XF	Unc
611	1977	.025	—	—	—	16.50
	1977	5,000	—	—	Proof	22.50

Jozsef Rippl-Ronai

KM#	Date	Mintage	Fine	VF	XF	Unc
612	1977	.025	—	—	—	16.50
	1977	5,000	—	—	Proof	20.00

175th Anniversary of National Museum

KM#	Date	Mintage	Fine	VF	XF	Unc
613	1977	.025	—	—	—	16.50
	1977	5,000	—	—	Proof	20.00

First Hungarian Gold Forint

KM#	Date	Mintage	Fine	VF	XF	Unc
614	1978	.025	—	—	—	18.00
	1978	5,000	—	—	Proof	22.00

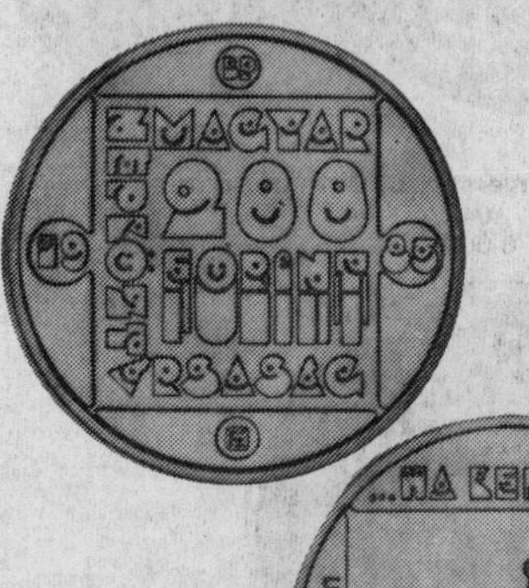

International Year of the Child

KM#	Date	Mintage	Fine	VF	XF	Unc
615	1979	9,000	—	—	—	18.00
	1979	.021	—	—	Proof	20.00

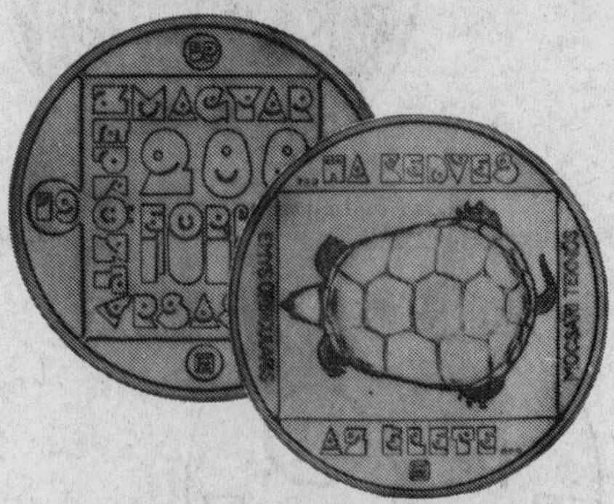

22.0000 g, .640 SILVER, .4527 oz ASW
350th Anniversary of Death of Gabor Bethlen

KM#	Date	Mintage	Fine	VF	XF	Unc
616	1979	.015	—	—	—	18.00
	1979	5,000	—	—	Proof	25.00

16.0000 g, .640 SILVER, .3292 oz ASW
XIII Winter Olympics - Lake Placid

KM#	Date	Mintage	Fine	VF	XF	Unc
618	1980	.015	—	—	Proof	20.00

Wildlife Preservation - Otter

KM#	Date	Mintage	Fine	VF	XF	Unc
643	1985	.013	—	—	—	18.00
	1985	2,000	—	—	Proof	28.00

Wildlife Preservation - Turtle

KM#	Date	Mintage	Fine	VF	XF	Unc
649	1985	.013	—	—	—	18.00
	1985	2,000	—	—	Proof	28.00

Wildlife Preservation - Wildcat

KM#	Date	Mintage	Fine	VF	XF	Unc
650	1985	.013	—	—	—	18.00
	1985	2,000	—	—	Proof	28.00

500 (OTSZAZ) FORINT

38.3800 g, .986 GOLD, 1.2168 oz AGW
Mint mark: BP
150th Anniversary of Birth of Liszt

KM#	Date	Mintage	Fine	VF	XF	Unc
565	1961	2,503	—	—	P/L	750.00

80th Anniversary of Birth of Bela Bartok

KM#	Date	Mintage	Fine	VF	XF	Unc
566	1961	2,503	—	—	P/L	750.00

42.0522 g, .900 GOLD, 1.2169 oz AGW
400th Anniversary of Death of Zrinyi

KM#	Date	Mintage	Fine	VF	XF	Unc
570	1966	1,100	—	—	Proof	750.00

85th Birthday of Kodaly

KM#	Date	Mintage	Fine	VF	XF	Unc
580	1967	—	—	—	—	625.00
	1967	1,000	—	—	Proof	750.00

150th Anniversary of Birth of Ignacz Semmelweis
Rev: Similar to 50 Forint, KM#583.

KM#	Date	Mintage	Fine	VF	XF	Unc
587	1968	9,000	—	—	Proof	750.00

39.0000 g, .640 SILVER, .8025 oz ASW
XIII Winter Olympics - Lake Placid
Mint mark: BP
Rev: Similar to 200 Forint, KM#618.

KM#	Date	Mintage	Fine	VF	XF	Unc
619	1980	.013	—	—	Proof	75.00

25.0000 g, .640 SILVER, .5144 oz ASW
Centennial of Birth of Bela Bartok

KM#	Date	Mintage	Fine	VF	XF	Unc
623	1981	.013	—	—	—	27.50
	1981	.013	—	—	Proof	32.50

28.0000 g, .640 SILVER, .5762 oz ASW
World Football Championship

KM#	Date	Mintage	Fine	VF	XF	Unc
624	1981	6,000	—	—	—	25.00
	1981	.040	—	—	Proof	30.00

World Football Championship

KM#	Date	Mintage	Fine	VF	XF	Unc
625	1981	6,000	—	—	—	25.00
	1981	.040	—	—	Proof	30.00

Decade for Women

KM#	Date	Mintage	Fine	VF	XF	Unc
640	1984	8,000	—	—	—	23.00
	1984	.020	—	—	Proof	30.00

Winter Olympics - Cross Country Skiers

KM#	Date	Mintage	Fine	VF	XF	Unc
641	1984	8,000	—	—	—	23.00
	1984	.012	—	—	Proof	30.00

Los Angeles Olympics - Gymnast

KM#	Date	Mintage	Fine	VF	XF	Unc
642	1984	8,000	—	—	—	23.00
	1984	.012	—	—	Proof	30.00

Budapest Cultural Forum

KM#	Date	Mintage	Fine	VF	XF	Unc
652	1985	.015	—	—	—	18.00
	1985	.010	—	—	Proof	20.00

World Football Championship - Players

KM#	Date	Mintage	Fine	VF	XF	Unc
656	1986	8,000	—	—	—	22.00
	1986	.017	—	—	Proof	27.00

World Football Championship - Stadium

KM#	Date	Mintage	Fine	VF	XF	Unc
657	1986	8,000	—	—	—	22.00
	1986	.017	—	—	Proof	27.00

28.0000 g, .900 SILVER, .8102 oz ASW
300th Anniversary of Repossession of Buda From the Turks

KM#	Date	Mintage	Fine	VF	XF	Unc
658	1986	.020	—	—	—	22.00
	1986	.010	—	—	Proof	27.00

Winter Olympics - Speed Skating

KM#	Date	Mintage	Fine	VF	XF	Unc
659	1986	.015	—	—	—	22.00
	1986	.015	—	—	Proof	27.00

Seoul Olympics - Wrestlers

KM#	Date	Mintage	Fine	VF	XF	Unc
660	1987	.015	—	—	—	22.00
	1987	.015	—	—	Proof	27.00

World Wildlife Fund - Bird of Prey

KM#	Date	Mintage	Fine	VF	XF	Unc
661	1988	.010	—	—	—	22.00
	1988	.025	—	—	Proof	27.00

950th Anniversary of Death of St. Stephan

KM#	Date	Mintage	Fine	VF	XF	Unc
662	1988	5,000	—	—	—	45.00
	1988	.015	—	—	Proof	40.00

Europe Football Championship

KM#	Date	Mintage	Fine	VF	XF	Unc
666	1988	8,000	—	—	—	50.00
	1988	.012	—	—	Proof	45.00

World Football Championship

KM#	Date	Mintage	Fine	VF	XF	Unc
667	1988	7,000	—	—	—	50.00
	1988	.015	—	—	Proof	45.00

World Football Championship - 2 Players

KM#	Date	Mintage	Fine	VF	XF	Unc
669	1989	7,000	—	—	—	50.00
	1989	.015	—	—	Proof	45.00

Save The Children Fund

KM#	Date	Mintage	Fine	VF	XF	Unc
670	1989	.010	—	—	—	45.00
	1989	.020	—	—	Proof	50.00

1992 Barcelona Olympics - Flame

KM#	Date	Mintage	Fine	VF	XF	Unc
671	1989	.015	—	—	—	45.00
	1989	.015	—	—	Proof	50.00

1000 (EZER) FORINT

84.1040 g, .900 GOLD, 2.4339 oz AGW
Mint mark: BP
400th Anniversary of Death of Miklos Zrinyi
Obv: Similar to 500 Forint, KM#570.

KM#	Date	Mintage	Fine	VF	XF	Unc
571	1966	330 pcs.	—	—	Proof	1750.

85th Birthday of Zoltan Kodaly
Obv: Similar to 500 Forint, KM#580.

KM#	Date	Mintage	Fine	VF	XF	Unc
581	1967	500 pcs.	—	—	Proof	1500.

150th Anniversary of Birth of Ignacz Semmelweis
Rev: Similar to 500 Forint, KM#587.

KM#	Date	Mintage	Fine	VF	XF	Unc
588	1968	1,570	—	—	Proof	1250.

REPUBLIC

1989—

MONETARY SYSTEM

100 Filler = 1 Forint

2 FILLER

ALUMINUM
Mint mark: BP

KM#	Date	Mintage	Fine	VF	XF	Unc
673	1990	.030	—	—	—	.25
	1991	—	—	—	—	.25
	1992	—	—	—	—	.25
	1993	—	—	—	—	.25

5 FILLER

ALUMINUM
Mint mark: BP

KM#	Date	Mintage	Fine	VF	XF	Unc
674	1990	.030	—	—	—	.25
	1991	—	—	—	—	.25
	1992	—	—	—	—	.25

10 FILLER

ALUMINUM
Mint mark: BP

KM#	Date	Mintage	Fine	VF	XF	Unc
675	1990	.660	—	—	—	.25
	1991	—	—	—	—	.25
	1992	—	—	—	—	.25
	1993	—	—	—	—	.25

20 FILLER

ALUMINUM
Mint mark: BP

KM#	Date	Mintage	Fine	VF	XF	Unc
676	1990	1.300	—	—	—	.25
	1991	—	—	—	—	.25
	1992	—	—	—	—	.25
	1993	—	—	—	—	.25

50 FILLER

ALUMINUM
Mint mark: BP

KM#	Date	Mintage	Fine	VF	XF	Unc
677	1990	5.740	—	—	—	.25
	1991	—	—	—	—	.25
	1992	—	—	—	—	.25
	1993	—	—	—	—	.25

FORINT

BRASS

KM#	Date	Mintage	Fine	VF	XF	Unc
692	1992	—	—	—	—	.25
	1993	—	—	—	—	.25

2 FORINT

COPPER-NICKEL

KM#	Date	Mintage	Fine	VF	XF	Unc
693	1992	—	—	—	—	.35
	1993	—	—	—	—	.35

5 FORINT

BRASS
Egret

KM#	Date	Mintage	Fine	VF	XF	Unc
694	1992	—	—	—	—	.65
	1993	—	—	—	—	.65

10 FORINT

COPPER-NICKEL CLAD BRASS

KM#	Date	Mintage	Fine	VF	XF	Unc
695	1992	—	—	—	—	1.00
	1993	—	—	—	—	1.00

20 FORINT

NICKEL-BRASS

KM#	Date	Mintage	Fine	VF	XF	Unc
696	1992	—	—	—	—	1.50
	1993	—	—	—	—	1.50

50 FORINT

COPPER-NICKEL CLAD BRASS

KM#	Date	Mintage	Fine	VF	XF	Unc
697	1992	—	—	—	—	2.25
	1993	—	—	—	—	2.25

100 (SZAZ) FORINT

COPPER-NICKEL-ZINC
Mint mark: BP
Andras Fay

KM#	Date	Mintage	Fine	VF	XF	Unc
678	1990	.020	—	—	—	6.00
	1990	.010	—	—	Proof	8.00

Papal Visit

KM#	Date	Mintage	Fine	VF	XF	Unc
682	1991	.030	—	—	—	3.00
	1991	.030	—	—	Proof	6.00

BRASS

KM#	Date	Mintage	Fine	VF	XF	Unc
698	1993	—	—	—	—	3.75

200 FORINT

9.9400 g, .500 SILVER, .1598 oz ASW
Mint mark: BP
Storks

KM#	Date	Mintage	Fine	VF	XF	Unc
688	1992	.020	—	—	—	10.00
	1992	.080	—	—	Proof	18.00

11.9700 g, .900 SILVER, .3463 oz ASW
National Bank

KM#	Date	Mintage	Fine	VF	XF	Unc
689	1992	—	—	—	—	10.00
	1992	.080	—	—	Proof	20.00
	1993	—	—	—	—	10.00
	1993	—	—	—	Proof	20.00

500 (OTSZAZ) FORINT

28.0000 g, .900 SILVER, .8102 oz ASW
Mint mark: BP
Albertville Olympics 1992

KM#	Date	Mintage	Fine	VF	XF	Unc
672	1989	.015	—	—	—	45.00
	1989	.015	—	—	Proof	50.00

King Mathias and Queen Beatrix

KM#	Date	Mintage	Fine	VF	XF	Unc
679	1990	.015	—	—	—	40.00
	1990	.015	—	—	Proof	45.00

2 Capital Cities of King Mathias

KM#	Date	Mintage	Fine	VF	XF	Unc
680	1990	.015	—	—	—	40.00
	1990	.015	—	—	Proof	45.00

Papal Visit

KM#	Date	Mintage	Fine	VF	XF	Unc
683	1991	.010	—	—	—	40.00
	1991	.020	—	—	Proof	45.00

200th Anniversary of Birth of Count Szechenyi

KM#	Date	Mintage	Fine	VF	XF	Unc
685	1991	.015	—	—	—	40.00
	1991	.015	—	—	Proof	45.00

Karoly Robert Emlekere

KM#	Date	Mintage	Fine	VF	XF	Unc
686	1992	1,000	—	—	—	50.00
	1992	.020	—	—	Proof	40.00

Canonization of King Ladislaus

KM#	Date	Mintage	Fine	VF	XF	Unc
687	1992	.010	—	—	—	35.00
	1992	.020	—	—	Proof	40.00

Telstar 1

KM#	Date	Mintage	Fine	VF	XF	Unc
690	1992	*5,000	—	—	—	60.00
	1992	*.015	—	—	Proof	55.00

31.4600 g, .925 SILVER, .9357 oz ASW
River Steamship - Arpad

KM#	Date	Mintage	Fine	VF	XF	Unc
702	1993	.010	—	—	—	45.00
	1993	.015	—	—	Proof	55.00

European Currency Union

KM#	Date	Mintage	Fine	VF	XF	Unc
704	1993	.010	—	—	—	35.00
	1993	.030	—	—	Proof	40.00

Expo 96

KM#	Date	Mintage	Fine	VF	XF	Unc
705	1993	.020	—	—	—	35.00
	1993	.080	—	—	Proof	40.00

5000 FORINT

6.9820 g, .986 GOLD, .2213 oz AGW
500th Anniversary of Death of Matthias I

KM#	Date	Mintage	Fine	VF	XF	Unc
681	1990	.010	—	—	Proof	175.00

10000 (TIZEZER) FORINT

6.9820 g, .986 GOLD, .2213 oz AGW
Mint mark: BP
Papal Visit

KM#	Date	Mintage	Fine	VF	XF	Unc
684	1991	.010	—	—	Proof	275.00

Karoly Robert

KM#	Date	Mintage	Fine	VF	XF	Unc
691	1992	.010	—	—	Proof	275.00

Erkel Ferenc

KM#	Date	Mintage	Fine	VF	XF	Unc
703	1993	5,000	—	—	Proof	275.00

TRADE COINAGE

DUCAT

3.4900 g, .986 GOLD, .1106 oz AGW
Obv. leg: FRANC I.D.G. . . .

KM#	Date	Mintage	Fine	VF	XF	Unc
419	1830	—	175.00	250.00	325.00	500.00
	1832	—	200.00	300.00	400.00	550.00
	1833	—	150.00	225.00	300.00	450.00
	1834	—	150.00	225.00	300.00	450.00
	1835	—	150.00	225.00	300.00	450.00

Obv. leg: FERD. I.D.G. . . .

KM#	Date	Mintage	Fine	VF	XF	Unc
425	1837	—	175.00	350.00	500.00	750.00
	1838	—	175.00	350.00	500.00	750.00
	1839	—	150.00	225.00	300.00	500.00
	1840	—	150.00	225.00	300.00	500.00
	1841	—	150.00	225.00	300.00	500.00
	1842	—	150.00	225.00	300.00	500.00
	1843	—	175.00	350.00	450.00	650.00
	1844	—	150.00	225.00	300.00	500.00
	1845	—	175.00	300.00	450.00	650.00
	1846	—	150.00	225.00	300.00	500.00
	1847	—	150.00	225.00	300.00	500.00
	1848	—	150.00	225.00	300.00	500.00

Rev. leg: SZ. MARIA. . . .

KM#	Date	Mintage	Fine	VF	XF	Unc
433	1848	—	100.00	175.00	250.00	350.00

Mint mark: KB

KM#	Date	Mintage	Fine	VF	XF	Unc
448.1	1868	.128	100.00	200.00	275.00	400.00
	1869	.090	90.00	150.00	200.00	300.00

Mint mark: GYF

KM#	Date	Mintage	Fine	VF	XF	Unc
448.2	1868	.400	85.00	140.00	200.00	300.00
	1869	.270	90.00	150.00	200.00	300.00

Mint mark: KB
Obv: Similar to KM#448.1.
Rev: Similar to 8 Forint, KM#477.

KM#	Date	Mintage	Fine	VF	XF	Unc
456	1870	.017	—	—	—	—
	1870	(restrike)	—	—	Proof	100.00

KM#	Date	Mintage	Fine	VF	XF	Unc
457	1877	456 pcs.	800.00	1250.	1500.	2000.
	1879	3,651	500.00	900.00	1500.	2000.
	1880	5,075	600.00	1000.	1500.	1750.
	1880	(restrike)	—	—	Proof	—
	1881	*43 pcs.	1250.	2000.	2500.	3000.

4 FORINT/10 FRANCS

3.2258 g, .900 GOLD, .0934 oz AGW
Mint mark: GYF

KM#	Date	Mintage	Fine	VF	XF	Unc
454.1	1870	.049	55.00	70.00	90.00	125.00

Mint mark: KB

KM#	Date	Mintage	Fine	VF	XF	Unc
454.2	1870	.102	55.00	70.00	90.00	125.00
	1870 UP	(restrike)		—	Proof	70.00
	1871	.090	55.00	80.00	100.00	130.00
	1872	.053	55.00	65.00	85.00	125.00
	1873	.013	80.00	115.00	175.00	200.00
	1874	8,228	80.00	115.00	175.00	210.00
	1875	.011	85.00	125.00	175.00	225.00
	1876	.024	55.00	80.00	110.00	130.00
	1877	.024	55.00	75.00	100.00	125.00
	1878	.015	55.00	80.00	110.00	130.00
	1879	.012	55.00	80.00	110.00	130.00

NOTE: Semi official restrikes have the letters UP below the bust.

Older head

KM#	Date	Mintage	Fine	VF	XF	Unc
466	1880	.013	55.00	80.00	110.00	130.00
	1881	.012	55.00	80.00	110.00	130.00
	1882	.013	55.00	80.00	110.00	125.00
	1883	.012	55.00	80.00	110.00	125.00
	1884	.054	55.00	65.00	95.00	125.00
	1885	.064	55.00	70.00	100.00	125.00
	1886	.039	55.00	65.00	80.00	125.00
	1887	.039	55.00	65.00	95.00	125.00
	1888	.049	55.00	65.00	95.00	125.00
	1889	.019	100.00	150.00	225.00	300.00
	1890	Inc.Y19	95.00	140.00	200.00	275.00

Rev: Fiume arms.

KM#	Date	Mintage	Fine	VF	XF	Unc
476.1	1890	.029	200.00	300.00	375.00	500.00
	1891	.032	60.00	75.00	100.00	150.00

Mint: Unknown

KM#	Date	Mintage	Fine	VF	XF	Unc
476.2	1892	20 pcs.	800.00	1100.	1800.	3000.

8 FORINT/20 FRANCS

6.4516 g, .900 GOLD, .1867 oz AGW

KM#	Date	Mintage	Fine	VF	XF	Unc
455.1	1870	.046	BV	110.00	135.00	165.00
	1871	.076	BV	100.00	120.00	140.00
	1872	.273	BV	100.00	120.00	140.00
	1873	.245	BV	100.00	120.00	140.00
	1874	.237	BV	100.00	120.00	160.00
	1875	.261	BV	100.00	120.00	160.00
	1876	.314	BV	100.00	120.00	140.00
	1877	.303	BV	100.00	120.00	140.00
	1878	.308	BV	110.00	130.00	160.00
	1879	.306	BV	100.00	120.00	140.00
	1880	.301	90.00	120.00	150.00	200.00

Mint mark: GYF

KM#	Date	Mintage	Fine	VF	XF	Unc
455.2	1870	.125	BV	100.00	130.00	150.00
	1871	.177	BV	100.00	120.00	140.00

Mint mark: KB
Obv: Larger head.

KM#	Date	Mintage	Fine	VF	XF	Unc
467	1880	Inc. Ab.	BV	100.00	110.00	140.00
	1881	.309	BV	100.00	120.00	140.00
	1882	.304	BV	100.00	120.00	140.00
	1883	.300	BV	100.00	120.00	140.00
	1884	.284	BV	100.00	120.00	140.00
	1885	.267	BV	100.00	120.00	140.00
	1886	.313	BV	100.00	120.00	140.00
	1887	.294	BV	100.00	120.00	140.00
	1888	.296	BV	100.00	120.00	140.00
	1889	.351	BV	100.00	120.00	140.00
	1890	Inc. Be.	BV	100.00	110.00	140.00

Rev: Fiume arms.

KM#	Date	Mintage	Fine	VF	XF	Unc
477	1890	.329	BV	100.00	125.00	175.00
	1891	.378	BV	100.00	130.00	160.00
	1892	.231	BV	120.00	160.00	200.00

MINT SETS (MS)

KM#	Date	Mintage	Identification	Issue Price	Mkt. Val.
MS1	1971(9)	—	KM546,549,572-575, 591,594-595	—	5.00
MS2	1972(9)	—	KM546,549,572-575, 591,594-595	—	5.00
MS3	1973(9)	—	KM546,549,572-575, 591,594-595	—	5.00
MS4	1974(9)	—	KM546,549,572-575, 591,594-595	—	5.00
MS5	1975(9)	—	KM546,549,572-575, 591,594-595	—	5.00
MS6	1976(9)	—	KM546,549,572-575, 591,594-595	—	5.00
MS7	1977(9)	—	KM546,549,572-575, 591,594-595	—	5.00
MS8	1978(9)	—	KM546,549,572-575, 591,594-595	—	5.00
MS9	1979(9)	—	KM546,549,572-575, 591,594-595	—	5.00
MS10	1980(9)	—	KM546,549,572-575, 591,594-595	—	5.00
MS11	1981(9)	—	KM546,549,572-575, 591,594-595	—	5.00
MS12	1982(9)	—	KM546,549,572-575, 591,594-595	—	5.00
MS13	1983(10)	—	KM546,549,572-575, 591,630,635-636	—	5.50
MS14	1984(10)	—	KM546,549,572-575, 591,630,635-636	—	5.50
MS15	1985(10)	—	KM546,549,572-575, 591,630,635-636	—	5.50
MS16	1986(10)	—	KM546,549,572-575, 591,630,635-636	—	5.50
MS17	1987(10)	—	KM546,549,572-575, 591,630,635-636	—	5.50
MS18	1988(10)	—	KM546,549,572-575, 591,630,635-636	—	5.50
MS19	1989(10)	—	KM546,549,572-575, 591,630,635-636	—	5.50
MS20	1990(5)	—	KM673-677	—	4.50
MS21	1991(5)	—	KM673-677	—	4.50
MS22	1992(5)	—	KM673-677	—	4.50
MS23	1993(11)	—	KM675-677,689,692-698	—	6.00

SPECIMEN SETS (SS)

KM#	Date	Mintage	Identification	Issue Price	Mkt. Val.
SS1	1977(9)	—	KM546,549,572-575, 591,594-595	—	5.00
SS2	1978(9)	—	KM546,549,572-575, 591,594-595	—	5.00
SS3	1979(9)	—	KM546,549,572-575, 591,594-595	—	5.00
SS4	1981(9)	—	KM546,549,572-575, 591,594-595	—	5.00
SS5	1989(10)	—	KM546,549,572-575, 591,630,635-636	—	5.50

PROOF SETS (PS)

KM#	Date	Mintage	Identification	Issue Price	Mkt. Val.
PS1	1961(6)	2,500	KM560,562-566	—	2100.
PS2	1961(4)	—	KM557-559,561	—	120.00
PS3	1966(8)	2,000	KM534b,546a-547a, 549a-551a,555a, 556b	15.00	30.00
PS4	1966(3)	330	KM569-571	430.00	2675.
PS5	1966(2)	11,000	KM567-568	7.50	55.00
PS6	1967(8)	5,000	KM534b,546a-547a, 549a-551a,555a, 556b	15.00	30.00
PS7	1967(2)	500	KM580-581	—	2250.
PS8	1968(5)	7,000	KM583,585-588	—	2850.
PS9	1968(2)	4,750	KM582,584	35.00	27.50
PS10	1969(2)	3,000	KM589-590	35.00	27.50
PS11	1970(2)	4,000	KM592-593	25.00	25.00
PS12	1972(2)	6,000	KM596-597	25.00	37.50
PS13	1973(2)	6,000	KM599-600	—	27.50
PS14	1974(2)	—	KM601,603	—	27.50
PS15	1976(3)	5,000	KM607-609	—	90.00
PS16	1977(3)	—	KM610-612	—	65.00

ICELAND

The Republic of Iceland, an island of recent volcanic origin in the North Atlantic east of Greenland and immediately south of the Arctic Circle, has an area of 39,768 sq. mi. (103,000 sq. km.) and a population of 262,193. Capital: Reykjavik. Fishing is the chief industry and accounts for more than 70 percent of the exports.

Iceland was settled by Norwegians in the 9th century and established as an independent republic in 930. The Icelandic assembly called the 'Althing', also established in 930, is the oldest parliament in the world. Iceland came under Norwegian sovereignty in 1262, and passed to Denmark when Norway and Denmark were united under the Danish crown in 1380. In 1918 it was established as a virtually independent kingdom in union with Denmark. On June 17, 1944, while Denmark was still under occupation by troops of the Third Reich, Iceland was established by plebiscite as an independent republic.

RULERS

Christian X, 1912-1944

MINT MARKS

Heart (h) - Copenhagen

MINTMASTERS INITIALS

HCN - Hans Christian Nielsen, 1919-1927
N - Niels Peter Nielsen, 1927-1955

MONEYERS INITIALS

GI, GJ - Knud Gunnar Jensen, 1901-1933

MONETARY SYSTEM

100 Aurar = 1 Krona

KINGDOM

EYRIR

BRONZE
Mint mark: Heart

KM#	Date	Mintage	Fine	VF	XF	Unc
5.1	1926 HCN-GJ	.405	1.50	3.00	6.50	17.50
	1931 N-GJ	.462	1.00	2.50	5.50	15.00
	1937 N-GJ wide date	.211	2.00	4.00	7.50	20.00
	1937 N-GJ narrow date	Inc. Ab.	2.00	4.00	7.50	20.00
	1938 N-GJ	.279	1.00	2.00	3.50	10.00
	1939 N-GJ large 3	.305	1.00	2.00	3.50	10.00
	1939 N-GJ small 3	Inc. Ab.	1.00	2.00	3.50	10.00
	Mint: London					
5.2	1940	1.000	.25	.50	1.00	2.50
	1940	—	—	—	Proof	165.00
	1942	2.000	.25	.40	.75	2.00

2 AURAR

BRONZE
Mint mark: Heart

KM#	Date	Mintage	Fine	VF	XF	Unc
6.1	1926 HCN-GJ	.498	1.50	3.00	8.00	20.00
	1931 N-GJ	.446	1.00	2.50	7.00	16.00
	1938 N-GJ	.206	6.00	12.00	17.50	28.00
	1940 N-GJ	.257	5.00	10.00	15.00	25.00

NOTE: Varieties exist in the appearance of the numeral 8 in 1938 dated coins. As the die slowly deteriorated 'globs' were added into the upper loop and also later on in the lower loop.

Mint: London

KM#	Date	Mintage	Fine	VF	XF	Unc
6.2	1940	1.000	.40	.75	1.50	3.00
	1940	—	—	—	Proof	220.00
	1942	2.000	.20	.50	1.00	2.00

5 AURAR

BRONZE
Mint mark: Heart

KM#	Date	Mintage	Fine	VF	XF	Unc
7.1	1926 HCN-GJ	.355	5.00	10.00	25.00	65.00
	1931 N-GJ	.311	5.00	10.00	25.00	65.00

Mint: London

KM#	Date	Mintage	Fine	VF	XF	Unc
7.2	1940	1.000	.60	1.25	2.50	5.00
	1940	—	—	—	Proof	250.00
	1942	2.000	.35	.85	1.50	3.00

10 AURAR

COPPER-NICKEL
Mint mark: Heart

KM#	Date	Mintage	Fine	VF	XF	Unc
1.1	1922HCN GJ	.300	2.00	3.50	7.00	20.00
	1923HCN GJ	.302	3.00	4.50	9.00	22.50
	1925HCN GJ	.321	15.00	25.00	40.00	70.00
	1929 N-GJ	.176	15.00	25.00	45.00	75.00
	1933 N-GJ	.157	10.00	20.00	30.00	55.00
	1936 N-GJ	.213	3.00	6.00	10.00	20.00
	1939/6 N-GJ	.208	5.00	10.00	15.00	30.00
	1939 N-GJ	I.A.	4.00	8.00	12.00	20.00
	Mint: London					
1.2	1940	1.500	.35	.75	1.50	4.50
	1940	—	—	—	Proof	165.00
	ZINC					
1a	1942	2.000	1.50	3.00	6.00	22.50

25 AURAR

COPPER-NICKEL
Mint mark: Heart

KM#	Date	Mintage	Fine	VF	XF	Unc
2.1	1922HCN GJ	.300	1.00	2.50	4.00	20.00
	1923HCN GJ	.304	1.00	2.50	4.00	20.00
	1925HCN GJ	.207	2.50	4.50	8.00	25.00
	1933 N-GJ	.104	10.00	15.00	25.00	55.00
	1937 N-GJ near 7	.201	3.00	5.00	9.00	25.00
	1937 N-GJ far 7	I.A.	3.00	5.00	9.00	25.00
	Mint: London					
2.2	1940	1.500	.25	.50	1.00	2.50
	1940	—	—	—	Proof	200.00
	ZINC					
2a	1942	2.000	1.00	2.50	5.00	20.00

KRONA

ALUMINUM-BRONZE
Mint mark: Heart

KM#	Date	Mintage	Fine	VF	XF	Unc
3.1	1925HCN GJ	.252	3.00	6.00	25.00	85.00
	1929 N-GJ	.154	5.00	10.00	30.00	100.00
	1940 N-GJ	.209	1.50	2.50	5.00	15.00
	Mint: London					
3.2	1940	.715	1.00	2.00	4.00	10.00

2 KRONUR

ALUMINUM-BRONZE
Mint mark: Heart

KM#	Date	Mintage	Fine	VF	XF	Unc
4.1	1925HCN GJ	.126	7.50	12.50	40.00	110.00
	1929 N-GJ	.077	10.00	20.00	60.00	200.00
	Mint: London					
4.2	1940	.546	.75	1.50	3.50	10.00

REPUBLIC

EYRIR

BRONZE

KM#	Date	Mintage	Fine	VF	XF	Unc
8	1946	4.000	.10	.15	.50	1.00
	1946	—	—	—	Proof	170.00
	1953	4.000	.10	.15	.40	.75
	1953	—	—	—	Proof	45.00
	1956	2.000	.10	.15	.40	.75
	1956	—	—	—	Proof	45.00
	1957	2.000	.10	.15	.40	.75
	1957	—	—	—	Proof	45.00
	1958	2.000	.10	.15	.40	.75
	1958	—	—	—	Proof	45.00
	1959	1.600	.10	.15	.40	.75
	1959	—	—	—	Proof	45.00
	1966	1.000	.10	.15	.40	.75
	1966	.015	—	—	Proof	3.25

NOTE: Values for the 1953-59 proof issues are for impaired proofs. Brilliant proofs may bring 3 to 4 times these figures.

5 AURAR

BRONZE

KM#	Date	Mintage	Fine	VF	XF	Unc
9	1946	4.000	.10	.25	.50	1.25
	1946	—	—	—	Proof	190.00
	1958	.400	.50	2.00	3.50	5.00
	1958	—	—	—	Proof	70.00
	1959	.600	.50	2.00	3.00	4.50
	1959	—	—	—	Proof	70.00
	1960	1.200	.15	.40	1.00	1.75
	1960	—	—	—	Proof	70.00
	1961	1.200	.15	.40	1.00	1.75
	1961	—	—	—	Proof	70.00
	1963	1.200	.10	.30	.75	1.50
	1963	—	—	—	Proof	70.00
	1965	.800	.10	.20	.50	1.00
	1966	1.000	.10	.20	.50	1.00
	1966	.015	—	—	Proof	3.25

NOTE: Values for the 1958-63 proof issues are for impaired proofs. Brilliant proofs may bring 3 to 4 times these figures.

10 AURAR

COPPER-NICKEL

KM#	Date	Mintage	Fine	VF	XF	Unc
10	1946	4.000	—	.10	.20	.60
	1946	—	—	—	Proof	180.00
	1953	4.000	—	.10	.20	.50
	1953	—	—	—	Proof	45.00
	1957	1.200	.25	.75	2.00	5.00
	1957	—	—	—	Proof	45.00
	1958	.500	.20	.50	1.00	2.00
	1958	—	—	—	Proof	45.00
	1959	3.000	.20	.50	1.50	4.00
	1959	—	—	—	Proof	45.00
	1960	1.000	.10	.20	.40	1.00
	1960	—	—	—	Proof	45.00
	1961	2.000	—	—	.10	.30
	1961	—	—	—	Proof	45.00
	1962	3.000	—	—	.10	.20
	1962	—	—	—	Proof	45.00
	1963	4.000	—	—	.10	.20
	1963	—	—	—	Proof	45.00
	1965	2.000	—	—	.10	.20

KM#	Date	Mintage	Fine	VF	XF	Unc
10	1966	4.000	—	—	.10	.20
	1967	2.000	—	—	.10	.20
	1969 coarse edge reeding					
		3.200	—	—	.10	.20
	1969 fine edge reeding					
		Inc. Ab.	—	—	.10	.20

NOTE: Values for the 1953-63 proof issues are for impaired proofs. Brilliant proofs may bring 3 to 4 times these figures.

ALUMINUM

KM#	Date	Mintage	Fine	VF	XF	Unc
10a	1970	4.800	—		.10	.20
	1971	11.200	—	—	.10	.20
	1973	4.800	—	—	.10	.20
	1974	4.800	—	—	.10	.20
	1974	.015	—	—	Proof	3.25

25 AURAR

COPPER-NICKEL

KM#	Date	Mintage	Fine	VF	XF	Unc
11	1946	2.000	.10	.15	.35	1.25
	1946	—	—	—	Proof	180.00
	1951	2.000	.10	.15	.35	.75
	1951	—	—	—	Proof	50.00
	1954	2.000	.10	.15	.35	.75
	1954	—	—	—	Proof	50.00
	1957	1.000	.20	.50	1.50	3.50
	1957	—	—	—	Proof	50.00
	1958	.500	.20	.40	.60	1.00
	1958	—	—	—	Proof	50.00
	1959	2.000	.20	.50	1.50	3.00
	1959	—	—	—	Proof	50.00
	1960	1.000	—	—	.10	.30
	1960	—	—	—	Proof	50.00
	1961	1.200	—	—	.10	.30
	1961	—	—	—	Proof	50.00
	1962	2.000	—	—	.10	.25
	1962	—	—	—	Proof	50.00
	1963	3.000	—	—	.10	.25
	1963	—	—	—	Proof	50.00
	1965	4.000	—	—	.10	.25
	1966	2.000	—	—	.10	.25
	1967	3.000	—	—	.10	.25
	1967	.015	—	—	Proof	3.25

NOTE: Values for the 1951-63 proof issues are for impaired proofs. Brilliant proofs may bring 3 to 4 times these figures.

50 AURAR

NICKEL-BRASS

KM#	Date	Mintage	Fine	VF	XF	Unc
17	1969	1.000	—	—	.10	.30
	1970	2.000	—	—	.10	.30
	1971	2.000	—	—	.10	.30
	1973	1.000	—	—	.10	.30
	1974	2.000	—	—	.10	.30
	1974	.015	—	—	Proof	3.25

KRONA

ALUMINUM-BRONZE

KM#	Date	Mintage	Fine	VF	XF	Unc
12	1946	2.175	—	.10	.40	1.50

NICKEL-BRASS

KM#	Date	Mintage	Fine	VF	XF	Unc
12a	1957	1.000	.10	.15	.40	1.50
	1957	—	—	—	Proof	60.00
	1959	.500	.10	.20	.75	2.00
	1959	—	—	—	Proof	60.00
	1961	.500	.10	.20	.75	2.00
	1961	—	—	—	Proof	60.00
	1962	1.000	.10	.15	.20	.60
	1962	—	—	—	Proof	60.00
	1963	1.500	—	.10	.15	.50
	1963	—	—	—	Proof	60.00
	1965	2.000	—	—	.10	.50
	1966	2.000	—	—	.10	.50
	1969	2.000	—	—	.10	.25
	1970	3.000	—	—	.10	.25
	1971	2.500	—	—	.10	.25

Large Date, Royal Mint **Thin Date, Ottawa Mint**

KM#	Date	Mintage	Fine	VF	XF	Unc
12a	1973 large round knob 3					
		2.500	—	—	.10	.50
	1973 thin, sharp end 3					
		3.500	—	—	.10	.25
	1974	5.000	—	—	.10	.25
	1975	10.500	—	—	.10	.25
	1975	.015	—	—	Proof	3.25

NOTE: Values for the 1957-1963 proof issues are for impaired proofs. Brilliant proofs may bring 3 to 4 times these figures.

ALUMINUM

KM#	Date	Mintage	Fine	VF	XF	Unc
23	1976	10.000	—	—	.10	.20
	1977	10.000	—	—	.10	.20
	1978	13.000	—	—	.10	.20
	1980	7.225	—	—	.10	.20
	1980	.015	—	—	Proof	3.25

2 KRONUR

ALUMINUM-BRONZE
Republic

KM#	Date	Mintage	Fine	VF	XF	Unc
13	1946	1.086	.20	.40	.80	3.50

NICKEL-BRASS

KM#	Date	Mintage	Fine	VF	XF	Unc
13a.1	1958	.500	.20	.50	1.00	3.00
	1958	—	—	—	Proof	70.00
	1962	.500	.20	.50	1.00	3.00
	1962	—	—	—	Proof	70.00
	1963	.750	.15	.30	.60	2.00
	1963	—	—	—	Proof	70.00
	1966	1.000	.10	.20	.40	1.50
	1966	.015	—	—	Proof	3.25

NOTE: Values for the 1958-63 proof issues are for impaired proofs. Brilliant proofs may bring 3 to 4 times these figures.

Thick planchet, 11.50 g

KM#	Date	Mintage	Fine	VF	XF	Unc
13a.2	1966	300 pcs.	—	—	225.00	300.00

5 KRONUR

COPPER-NICKEL

KM#	Date	Mintage	Fine	VF	XF	Unc
18	1969	1.000	—	.15	.25	.50
	1970	1.000	—	.15	.25	.50
	1971	.500	.10	.20	.50	1.00
	1973	1.100	—	.10	.20	.40
	1974	1.200	—	.10	.15	.25
	1975	1.500	—	.10	.15	.25
	1976	.500	—	.10	.20	.40
	1977	1.000	—	.10	.15	.25
	1978	4.672	—	.10	.15	.25
	1980	2.400	—	.10	.15	.25
	1980	.015	—	—	Proof	3.25

10 KRONUR

COPPER-NICKEL

KM#	Date	Mintage	Fine	VF	XF	Unc
15	1967	1.000	.15	.25	.50	1.50
	1969	.500	.15	.30	.75	2.00
	1970	1.000	—	.15	.30	.75
15	1971	1.500	—	.15	.30	.75
	1973	1.500	—	.15	.30	.75
	1974	2.000	—	.10	.25	.60
	1975	2.500	—	.10	.25	.60
	1976	2.500	—	.10	.25	.60
	1977	2.000	—	.10	.25	.60
	1978	10.500	—	.10	.25	.60
	1980	4.600	—	.10	.25	.60
	1980	.015	—	—	Proof	3.25

50 KRONUR

NICKEL
50th Anniversary of Sovereignty

KM#	Date	Mintage	Fine	VF	XF	Unc
16	1968	.100	1.50	2.50	4.00	7.00

COPPER-NICKEL
Parliament Building

KM#	Date	Mintage	Fine	VF	XF	Unc
19	1970	.800	.25	.50	1.00	2.00
	1971	.500	.25	.50	1.00	2.50
	1973	.050	1.00	1.50	2.50	4.00
	1974	.200	.25	.50	1.00	2.00
	1975	.500	.20	.35	.75	1.50
	1976	.500	.20	.35	.75	1.50
	1977	.200	.20	.35	.75	1.50
	1978	2.040	.20	.35	.50	1.00
	1980	1.500	.20	.35	.50	1.00
	1980	.015	—	—	Proof	3.25

500 KRONUR

8.9604 g, .900 GOLD, .2593 oz AGW
Jon Sigurdsson Sesquicentennial

KM#	Date	Mintage	Fine	VF	XF	Unc
14	1961	.010	—	—	—	200.00
	1961	—	—	—	Proof	700.00

20.0000 g, .925 SILVER, .5968 oz ASW
1100th Anniversary 1st Settlement

KM#	Date	Mintage	Fine	VF	XF	Unc
20	1974	.070	—	—	—	8.00
	1974	*.058	—	—	Proof	12.50

NOTE: 17,000 proof coins were remelted.

1000 KRONUR

30.0000 g, .925 SILVER, .8923 oz ASW
1100th Anniversary 1st Settlement

KM#	Date	Mintage	Fine	VF	XF	Unc
21	1974	.070	—	—	—	12.00
	1974	*.058	—	—	Proof	17.50

NOTE: 17,000 proof coins were remelted.

10,000 KRONUR

15.5000 g, .900 GOLD, .4485 oz AGW
1100th Anniversary 1st Settlement

KM#	Date	Mintage	Fine	VF	XF	Unc
22	1974	.012	—	—	—	225.00
	1974	8,000	—	—	Proof	275.00

MONETARY REFORM

100 Old Kronur = 1 New Krona

5 AURAR

BRONZE
Skate

KM#	Date	Mintage	Fine	VF	XF	Unc
24	1981	15.000	—	—	—	.10
	1981	.015	—	—	Proof	3.50
	1982	—	—	—	—	.10
	1984	—	—	—	—	.10

10 AURAR

BRONZE
Cuttle-Fish

KM#	Date	Mintage	Fine	VF	XF	Unc
25	1981	50.000	—	—	—	.10
	1981	.015	—	—	Proof	5.00
	1982	—	—	—	—	.10
	1984	—	—	—	—	.10

50 AURAR

BRONZE
Shrimp

KM#	Date	Mintage	Fine	VF	XF	Unc
26	1981	10.000	—	—	.10	.30
	1981	.015	—	—	Proof	6.00
	1982	—	—	—	.10	.30
	1984	—	—	—	.10	.30

BRONZE COATED STEEL

KM#	Date	Mintage	Fine	VF	XF	Unc
26a	1986	2.000	—	—	—	.30

KRONA

COPPER-NICKEL
Cod

KM#	Date	Mintage	Fine	VF	XF	Unc
27	1981	18.000	—	—	.10	.25
	1981	.015	—	—	Proof	8.00
	1984	7.000	—	—	.10	.30
	1987	7.500	—	—	.10	.30

NICKEL COATED STEEL

KM#	Date	Mintage	Fine	VF	XF	Unc
27a	1989	5.000	—	—	—	.35
	1991	5.180	—	—	—	.35
	1992	5.000	—	—	—	.35

5 KRONUR

Dolphins

KM#	Date	Mintage	Fine	VF	XF	Unc
28	1981	4.350	—	—	.15	.85
	1981	.015	—	—	Proof	10.00
	1984	1.000	—	—	.15	1.00
	1987	3.000	—	—	.15	1.00
	1992	2.000	—	—	.15	1.00

10 KRONUR

COPPER-NICKEL
4 Capelins

KM#	Date	Mintage	Fine	VF	XF	Unc
29	1984	10.000	—	—	.25	1.50
	1987	7.500	—	—	.25	1.50

50 KRONUR

NICKEL-BRASS
Crab

KM#	Date	Mintage	Fine	VF	XF	Unc
31	1987	4.000	—	—	—	3.00
	1992	2.000	—	—	—	4.00

500 KRONUR

20.0000 g, .500 SILVER, .3215 oz ASW
100th Anniversary of Icelandic Banknotes

KM#	Date	Mintage	Fine	VF	XF	Unc
30	1986	.015	—	—	—	40.00

20.0000 g, .925 SILVER, .5968 oz ASW

KM#	Date	Mintage	Fine	VF	XF	Unc
30a	1986	5,000	—	—	Proof	60.00

MINT SETS (MS)

KM#	Date	Mintage	Identification	Issue Price	Mkt. Val.
MS1	1930(3)	10,000	KM-M1-M3	—	295.00
MS2	1970(6)	—	KM10a,12a,15,17-19	—	5.00
MS3	1971(6)	—	KM10a,12a,15,17-19	—	6.00
MS4	1973(6)	—	KM10a,12a,15,17-19	3.25	5.25
MS5	1974(6)	—	KM10a,12a,15,17-19	3.25	3.50
MS6	1974(2)	70,000	KM20,21	30.00	20.00
MS7	1975(4)	—	KM12a,15,18-19	—	3.50
MS8	1976(4)	—	KM15,18-19,23	—	3.50
MS9	1977(4)	—	KM15,18-19,23	—	3.50
MS10	1978(4)	—	KM15,18,19,23	—	3.50
MS11	1980(4)	—	KM15,18,19,23	—	3.50
MS12	1981(5)	—	KM24-28	—	3.50

PROOF SETS (PS)

KM#	Date	Mintage	Identification	Issue Price	Mkt. Val.
PS1	1940(5)	—	KM1.2-2.2,5.2-7.2	—	1000.
PS2	1946(4)	—	KM8-11	—	725.00
PS3	1974(3)	8,000	KM20-22	272.00	280.00
PS4	1974(2)	58,000	KM20,21	38.00	30.00
PS5	1980(11)	15,000	(Mixed dates) 1966: KM-9,13a.1; 1967: KM11; 1974: KM10a,17; 1975: KM12a; 1980: KM15,18,19,23	40.00	35.00
PS6	1981(5)	15,000	KM24-28	32.00	32.50

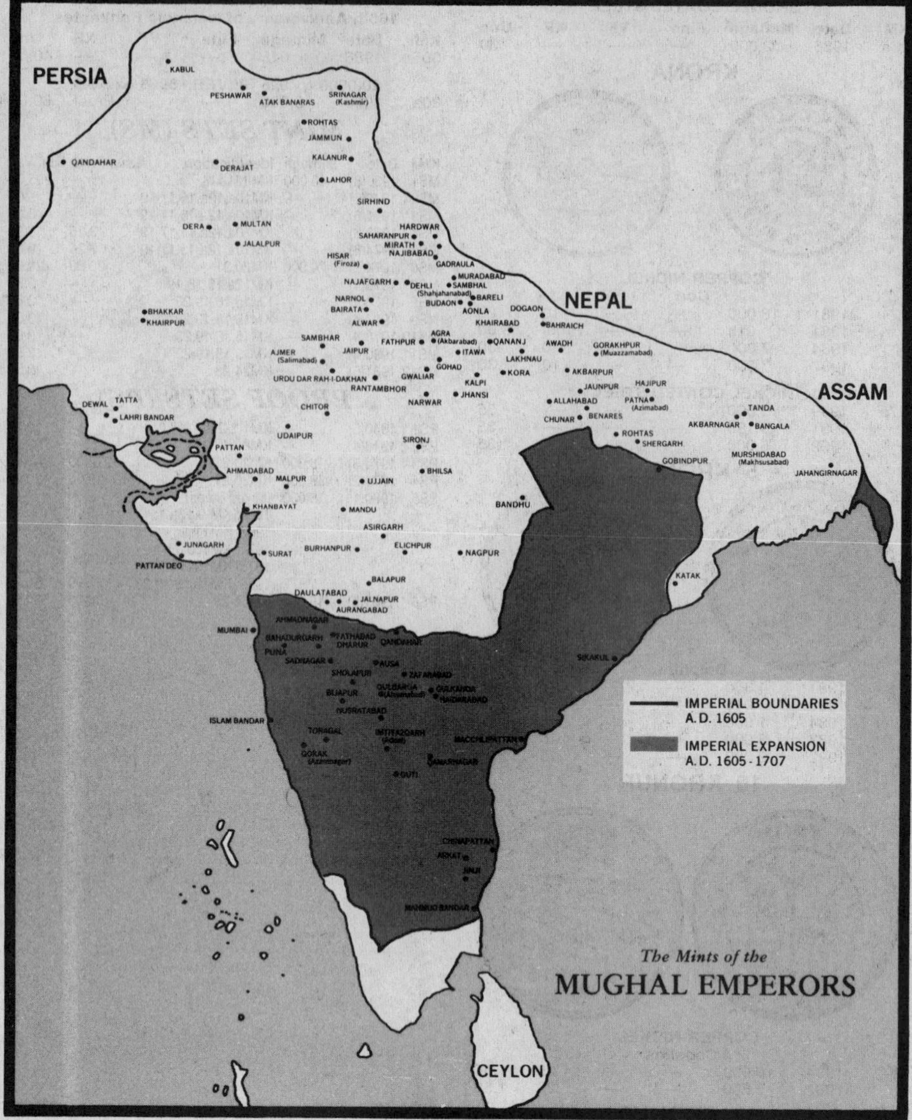

The Lodi Sultanate of Delhi was conquered by Zahir-uddin Muhammad Babur, a Chagatai Mongol descended from Tamerlane, in 1525AD. His son, Nasir-ud-din Muhammad Humayun, lost the new empire in a series of battles with the Bihari Afghan Sher Shah, who founded the shortlived Suri dynasty. Humayun, with the assistance of the Emperor of Persia, recovered his kingdom from Sher Shah's successors in 1555AD. He did not long enjoy the fruits of victory for his fatal fall down his library steps brought his teenage son Jalal-ud-din Muhammad Akbar to the throne in the following year. During Akbar's long reign of a half century the Mughal Empire was firmly established throughout much of North India. Under Akbar's son and grandson, the emperors Nur-ud-din Muhammad Jahangir and Shihab-ud-din Muhammad Shah Jahan, the state reached its apogee and art, culture and commerce flourished.

One of the major achievements of the Mughal government was the establishment of a universal silver currency, based on the rupee, a coin of 11.6 grams and as close to pure silver content as the metallurgy of the time was capable of attaining. Supplementary coins were the gold mohur and copper dam. The values of these coin denominations were nominally fixed at 8 rupees to 1 mohur, and 40 dams to 1 rupee, but market forces determined actual exchange rates which were different.

The maximum expansion of the geographical area under direct Mughal rule was achieved during the reign of Aurangzeb Alamgir. By his death in 1707AD, the whole peninsula, indeed the whole subcontinent of India, with minor exceptions owed fealty to the Mughal emperor.

Aurangzeb's wars, lasting decades, upset the stability and prosperity of the kingdom. The internal dissention and rebellion which resulted brought the eclipse of the empire in succeeding reigns. The Mughal monetary system, especially the silver rupee, supplanted most local currencies throughout India. The number of Mughal mints rose sharply and direct central control declined, so that by the time of the emperor Shah Alam II, many nominally Mugal mints served independent states. The common element in all these coinage issues was the presence of the Mugal emperor's name and titles on the obverse. In the following catalog no attempt has been made to solve the problem of separating Mughal from Princely State coins by historical criteria: all Mughal-style coins are considered products of the Mughal empire until the death of muhammad Shah in 1784AD; thereafter all coins are considered Princely State issues unless there is evidence of the mint being under ever-diminishing Imperial control.

EMPERORS

محمد اکبر

Muhammad Akbar II,
AH1221-1253/1806-1837AD

سراج الدین محمد بہادر شاہ

Bahadur Shah II, Suraj-ud-din Muhammad
AH1253-1273/1837-1858AD

MINTNAMES

Ahmadabad	احمد اباد
Akbarabad (Agra)	اکبر آباد
Gokulgarh	گوکل گره
Hardwar (Tirath)	هاردوار
Saharanpur	سهارنپور
Shahjahanabad (Dehli)	شاه جهان آباد

DATING

The Mughal coins were dated both in the Hejira era and in the regnal era of each emperor. The four-digit Hejira year usually was shown on the obverse, with the one or two-digit regnal (jalus) year on the reverse. Since the regnal and calendar years did not coincide, it was common for two different regnal years to appear on the coins produced during any calendar year. The first jalus year of each reign was usually written as a word, *ahd,* rather than as a numeral.

SHAH ALAM II

AH1173-1221/1759-1806AD

Except for the Delhi Mint, most of the later coins struck in the name of this Emperor were Princely State issues, and can be found in their appropriate place under the States. Earlier issues come from nearly 100 mints, and it is always a problem to determine in what year coins of a particular mint cease to be Mughal and become State issues.

The following mints, for the most part in the Delhi (Shahjahanabad) area, may be considered the nucleus of Mughal mints during Shah Alam's reign. They were located in provinces governed by Mughal functionaries, whose increasing independence is reflected in the growing eccentricity of coin design.

In some cases the distinctive geometric designs and floral devices found on the coins were true mint marks, representative of a single mint. In other instances the '-mint marks' listed below were temporary privy marks or simply decoration.

Shah Alam II legends were used in some states long after his death, until AH1314/1879AD at Ujjain, for example. This is not the case with true Mughal issues.

NOTICE

Unlike the previous listings by ruler, denomination and mint the following are by ruler, mint and denomination.

MUGHAL GOVERNOR ISSUES

Daulat Rao Sindhia
AH1209-1218/1794-1803AD

PAISA

COPPER
Rev: JWH.

KM#	Date	Year	Good	VG	Fine	VF
549.1	AH1216	42	12.50	25.00	42.00	60.00
	—	43	12.50	25.00	42.00	60.00

NOTE: J.W.H. - John William Hessing, Governor of Agra.
NOTE: Earlier date (AH1215) exists for this type.

Rev: Spearhead.

549.2	AH1217	(43)	12.50	25.00	42.00	60.00

Obv: Katar.

549.3	AH121x	—	12.50	25.00	42.00	60.00

Rev: Pistol.

550	AH1216	43	6.00	12.00	20.00	32.00
	1217	44	6.00	12.00	20.00	32.00
	1218	44	6.00	12.00	20.00	32.00

Rev: Pistol and fish.

KM#	Date	Year	Good	VG	Fine	VF
551	AH1216	43	5.50	11.00	17.50	25.00
	1217	—	5.50	11.00	17.50	25.00
	1220	—	5.50	11.00	17.50	25.00

RUPEE

SILVER, 11.444 g
Rev: Fish.

KM#	Date	Year	VG	Fine	VF	XF
554	AH1217	44	7.50	15.00	25.00	35.00
	—	45	7.50	15.00	25.00	35.00

NOTE: Earlier dates (Yr.38-43, AH1215) exist for this type.

EAST INDIA COMPANY

From October 18, 1803 (AH1218)

RUPEE

SILVER, 11.444 g
Rev: Fish.

KM#	Date	Year	VG	Fine	VF	XF
560	AH1219	47	10.00	20.00	32.50	45.00
	1220	47	10.00	20.00	32.50	45.00

Gokulgarh Mint

Mint mark: 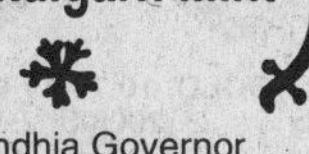
Sindhia Governor

RUPEE

SILVER, 11.444 g

KM#	Date	VG	Fine	VF	XF
624	AH1216-1218/46	7.50	15.00	25.00	35.00

NOTE: Earlier dates (AH1202-1215) exist for this type.

Hardwar Mint

A mint of the Mughal governor of Saharanpur.

RUPEE

SILVER, 11.444 g

KM#	Date	Year	VG	Fine	VF	XF
630	AH1219	46	15.00	30.00	42.50	60.00

NOTE: Earlier dates (AH1205/31-1214/41) exist for this type.

Saharanpur Mint

LOCAL GOVERNOR ISSUES

General Perron (for Sindhia)
AH1215-1218/1800-1803

Mint mark:  **stylized dagger**

PAISA

COPPER
Rev: Additional symbols chakra and hexfoil.

KM#	Date	Year	Good	VG	Fine	VF
673	AH1217	44	4.00	6.50	10.00	15.00
673	1218	45	4.00	6.50	10.00	15.00

NOTE: Earlier dates (AH1206-1215) exist for this type.

RUPEE

SILVER, 11.444 g

KM#	Date	Year	VG	Fine	VF	XF
675	AH1216	43	9.00	18.00	30.00	45.00
	1217	44	9.00	18.00	30.00	45.00
	1218/7	43	9.00	18.00	30.00	45.00
	1218	45	9.00	18.00	30.00	45.00

NOTE: Earlier dates (AH1204-1215) exist for this type.

Rev: Circled dot additional symbol.

KM#	Date	Year	VG	Fine	VF	XF
676	AH1216	43	10.00	20.00	35.00	50.00
	1217	44	10.00	20.00	35.00	50.00

EAST INDIA COMPANY

PAISA

COPPER
Rev: St. Stephen's cross.

KM#	Date	Year	Good	VG	Fine	VF
690	AH1218	45	5.00	9.00	13.00	20.00

RUPEE

SILVER, 11.444 g
Rev: St. Stephen's cross.

KM#	Date	Year	VG	Fine	VF	XF
692	AH1218	45	12.50	25.00	42.00	60.00

Rev: Vertical spray.

KM#	Date	Year	VG	Fine	VF	XF
693	AH1217	44	9.00	18.00	30.00	45.00
	18/x (error for 1218)					
		45	9.00	18.00	30.00	45.00
	1219	46	9.00	18.00	30.00	45.00

Rev: W/o symbol.

KM#	Date	Year	VG	Fine	VF	XF
694	AH1220	47	9.00	18.00	30.00	45.00
	1220	49	9.00	18.00	30.00	45.00

Shahjahanabad Mint

Mint marks:
(silver and gold)

Obverse: 

Reverse: 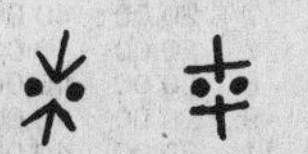

PAISA

COPPER

KM#	Date	Year	Good	VG	Fine	VF
700	AH1219	46	2.00	3.25	5.00	8.50
	1219	47	2.00	3.25	5.00	8.50
	1220	48	2.00	3.25	5.00	8.50

NOTE: Earlier dates (AH1185-1214) exist for this type.

1/4 RUPEE

SILVER, 14mm, 2.861 g
Obv: Additional činquefoil symbol.

KM#	Date	Year	VG	Fine	VF	XF
704	AH1220	48	14.00	28.00	47.50	65.00

1/2 RUPEE

SILVER, 18mm
Obv: Additional cinquefoil symbol.

KM#	Date	Year	VG	Fine	VF	XF
707	AH1220	47	27.50	45.00	62.50	85.00

RUPEE

NOTE: The size of the Shahjahanabad rupees of Shah Alam II was subject to a wide variance. The early issues tended to be normal size for the hammered coinage (about 22mm). As the power of the emperor waned, the flan size of the Shahjahanabad rupees waxed, reflecting the increasingly ceremonial role of the coinage. The later coins should not be confused with the Nazarana (presentation) coins, which always show a full border design around the legend.

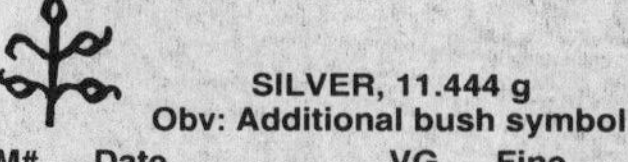

SILVER, 11.444 g
Obv: Additional bush symbol.

KM#	Date	VG	Fine	VF	XF
711	AH1216/44-1218/45	10.00	20.00	35.00	50.00

Obv: Additional lion symbol.

KM#	Date	Year	VG	Fine	VF	XF
712	AH1218	46	25.00	50.00	85.00	120.00

Obv: Additional cinquefoil symbol.

KM#	Date	Year	VG	Fine	VF	XF
713	AH1218	46	32.50	65.00	110.00	160.00

NAZARANA RUPEE

SILVER, 29-36mm, 11.444 g
Obv: Additional bush symbol.

KM#	Date	Year	VG	Fine	VF	XF
718	AH1218	46	55.00	90.00	130.00	175.00

Obv: Additional cinquefoil symbol.

KM#	Date	Year	VG	Fine	VF	XF
B719	AH1218	46	85.00	140.00	200.00	285.00

Obv. and rev. leg: Within wreath of roses, thistles and shamrocks.

KM#	Date	Year	VG	Fine	VF	XF
714	AH1219	47	37.50	62.50	85.00	120.00
	1220	47	37.50	62.50	85.00	120.00
	1220	48	37.50	62.50	85.00	120.00
	1221	48	37.50	62.50	85.00	120.00

Obv: Additional cinquefoil symbol.

KM#	Date	Year	VG	Fine	VF	XF
C719	AH1221	49	45.00	75.00	110.00	150.00

NAZARANA MOHUR

GOLD, 10.70-11.40 g
Obv: Additional bush symbol.

KM#	Date	Year	VG	Fine	VF	XF
721	AH1217	45	300.00	500.00	700.00	1000.
	1218	46	300.00	500.00	700.00	1000.

Obv. and rev. leg: Within wreath of roses, thistles and shamrocks.

KM#	Date	Year	VG	Fine	VF	XF
722	AH1219	47	250.00	400.00	600.00	750.00
	1221	48	250.00	400.00	600.00	750.00

Surat Mint

The Nawab of Surat continued to issue coins in the name of his nominal Mughal suzerain Shah Alam II until the British took over Surat and its mint in 1800AD (AH1214/5), Shah Alam's 43rd regnal year. These coin types of the Nawab of Surat were replicated by the British East India Company in Surat using privy mark #1 and the frozen regnal year 46 of Shah Alam II, see Bombay Presidency types KM#209.1, 210.1, 211.1, 212.1 and 214.

1/2 RUPEE

SILVER, 5.40-5.80 g

Obv: Surat privy mark #1.

KM#	Date	Year	VG	Fine	VF	XF
723	AH—	31	5.50	11.00	17.50	25.00

RUPEE

SILVER, 10.70-11.60 g
Obv: Surat privy mark #1.

KM#	Date	Year	VG	Fine	VF	XF
724	AH—	44	8.00	16.00	28.00	40.00

MUHAMMAD AKBAR II

AH1221-1253/1806-1837AD

Shahjahanabad Mint

The mint of the walled city of Delhi produced a limited number of coins each year with which the East India Company's resident paid a pension to the Mughal Emperor. KM#777 was struck for this purpose until 1818, when the mint was closed for regular coinage. Thereafter, only a few presentation coins (KM#779.1) were struck annually on the occasion of the king's accession.

PAISA

COPPER

KM#	Date	Year	Good	VG	Fine	VF
770	AH1222	1	2.00	3.25	5.00	8.50
	1222	2	2.00	3.25	5.00	8.50

Rev: Letter "S" by regnal year.

KM#	Date	Year	Good	VG	Fine	VF
771	AH1225	4	2.00	3.25	5.00	8.50
	1225	5	2.00	3.25	5.00	8.50
	1226	5	2.00	3.25	5.00	8.50
	1226	6	2.00	3.25	5.00	8.50
	1230	9	2.00	3.25	5.00	8.50
	1231	10	2.00	3.25	5.00	8.50
	1233	12	2.00	3.25	5.00	8.50

1/4 RUPEE

SILVER, 2.861 g

KM#	Date	Year	VG	Fine	VF	XF
773	AH122x	7	12.50	25.00	42.00	60.00

1/2 RUPEE

SILVER, 5.722 g

KM#	Date	Year	VG	Fine	VF	XF
775	AH1221	1	25.00	50.00	85.00	120.00
	1225	4	25.00	50.00	85.00	120.00

RUPEE

SILVER, 11.444 g

KM#	Date	Year	VG	Fine	VF	XF
776	AH1202	1	20.00	40.00	65.00	95.00

KM#	Date	Year	VG	Fine	VF	XF
777	AH1221	1	20.00	40.00	65.00	95.00
	1222	1	20.00	40.00	65.00	95.00
	1222	2	20.00	40.00	65.00	95.00
	1223	2	20.00	40.00	65.00	95.00
	1223	3	20.00	40.00	65.00	95.00
	1224	3	20.00	40.00	65.00	95.00
	1225	4	20.00	40.00	65.00	95.00
	1226	5	20.00	40.00	65.00	95.00
	1226	6	20.00	40.00	65.00	95.00
	1227	6	20.00	40.00	65.00	95.00
	1227	7	20.00	40.00	65.00	95.00
	1228	7	20.00	40.00	65.00	95.00
	1228	8	20.00	40.00	65.00	95.00
	1229	9	20.00	40.00	65.00	95.00
	12xx	11	20.00	40.00	65.00	95.00

NAZARANA RUPEE

SILVER

KM#	Date	Year	VG	Fine	VF	XF
779.1	AH1223	3	110.00	185.00	250.00	350.00
	1224	3	110.00	185.00	250.00	350.00
	1225	4	110.00	185.00	250.00	350.00
	1226	5	110.00	185.00	250.00	350.00
	1227	7	110.00	185.00	250.00	350.00
	1235	15	110.00	185.00	250.00	350.00
	1237	17	110.00	185.00	250.00	350.00
	1239	19	110.00	185.00	250.00	350.00
	1240	20	110.00	185.00	250.00	350.00
	1241	21	110.00	185.00	250.00	350.00
	1242	22	110.00	185.00	250.00	350.00
	1248	28	110.00	185.00	250.00	350.00
	1249	29	110.00	185.00	250.00	350.00

SILVER, 11.444 g

KM#	Date	Year	VG	Fine	VF	XF
779.2	AH1251	31	—	—	Rare	—
	1252	32	—	—	Rare	—

MOHUR

GOLD, 10.70-11.40 g

KM#	Date	Year	VG	Fine	VF	XF
781	AH122x	2	200.00	350.00	500.00	700.00
	1223	6	200.00	350.00	500.00	700.00
	122x	6	200.00	350.00	500.00	700.00

NAZARANA MOHUR

GOLD, 10.70-11.40 g

KM#	Date	Year	VG	Fine	VF	XF
783	AH1221	1	—	—	Rare	—
	1234	12	—	—	Rare	—

SURAJ-UD-DIN MUHAMMAD BAHADUR SHAH II

AH1253-1273/1837-1857AD

Shahjahanabad Mint

NAZARANA RUPEE

SILVER, 11.444 g

KM#	Date	Year	VG	Fine	VF	XF
790	AH1253	1	500.00	850.00	1200.	1700.
	1254	2	500.00	850.00	1200.	1700.
	1255	3	500.00	850.00	1200.	1700.
	1256	4	500.00	850.00	1200.	1700.
	1257	5	500.00	850.00	1200.	1700.
	1258	6	500.00	850.00	1200.	1700.

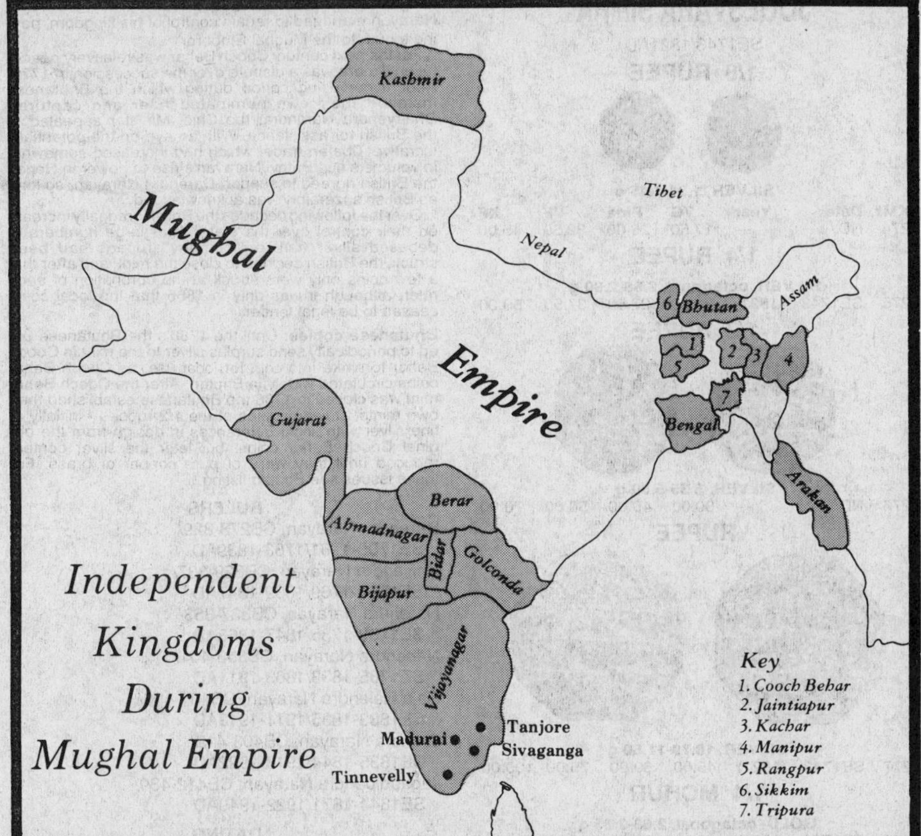

ASSAM

AHOM KINGDOM

It was in the 13th century that a tribal leader called Sukapha, with about 9,000 followers, left their traditional home in the Shan States of Northern Burma, and carved out the Ahom Kingdom in upper Assam.

The Ahom Kingdom gradually increased in power and extent over the following centuries, particularly during the reign of King Suhungmung (1497-1539). This king also took on a Hindu title, Svarga Narayan, which shows the increasing influence of the Brahmins over the court. Although several of the other Hindu states in north-east India started a silver coinage during the 16th century, it was not until the mid-17th century that the Ahoms first struck coin.

From the time of Kusain Shah's invasion of Cooch Behar in 1494AD the Muslims had cast acquisitive eyes towards the valley of the Brahmaputra, but the Ahoms managed to preserve their independence. In 1661 Aurangzeb's governor in Bengal, Mir Jumla, made a determined effort to bring Assam under Mughal rule. Cooch Behar was annexed without difficulty, and in March 1662 Mir Jumla occupied Gargaon, the Ahom capital, without opposition. However, during the rainy season the Muslim forces suffered severely from disease, lack of food and from the occasional attacks from the Ahom forces, who had tactically withdrawn from the capital together with the king. After the end of the monsoon a supply line was opened with Bengal again, but morale in the Muslim army was low, so Mir Jumla was forced to agree to peace terms somewhat less onerous than the Mughals liked to impose on subjugated states. The Ahoms agreed to pay tribute, but the Ahom kingdom remained entirely independent of Mughal control, and never again did a Muslim army venture into upper Assam.

During the eighteenth century the Kingdom became weakened with civil war, culminating in the expulsion of Gaurinatha Simha from his capital in 1787 by the Moamarias. The British helped Gaurinatha regain his kingdom in 1794, but otherwise took little interest in the affairs of Assam. The end of the Ahom Kingdom was not due to intervention from Bengal, but from Burma. After initial invasions commencing in 1816, the Burmese conquered the whole of Assam in 1821/2, and seemed bent on expanding their Kingdom even further. The British in Bengal were quick to retaliate and drove the Burmese from Assam in 1824, and from then on Assam became firmly under British control with no further independent coinage.

RULERS

Ruler's names, where present on the coins, usually appear on the obverse (dated) side, starting either at the end of the first line, after Shri, or in the second line. Most of the Ahom rulers after the adoption of Hinduism in about 1500AD had both an Ahom and a Hindu name.

HINDU NAME	AHOM NAME
Kamalesvara Simha	Suklingpha

কমলেশ্বৰসিংহ

SE1717-1733/1795-1811AD

Chandrakanta Simha — **Sudingpha**

চন্দ্রকান্তসিংহ

SE1733-1740/1811-1818AD

Brajanatha Simha

ব্রজনাথসিংহ

SE1740-1741/1818-1819AD

Chandrakanta Simha — **Sudingpha**

চন্দ্রকান্তসিংহ

SE1741-1743/1819-1821AD

Jogesvara Simha

যোগেশ্বরসিংহ

SE1743-1746/1821-1824AD

COINAGE

It is frequently stated that coins were first struck in Assam during the reign of King Suklenmung (1539-1552), but this is merely due to a misreading of the Ahom legend on the coins of King Supungmung (1663-70). The earliest Ahom coins known, therefore, were struck during the reign of King Jayadhvaja Simha (1648-1663).

Although the inscription and general design of these first coins of the Ahom Kingdom were copied from the coins of Cooch Behar, the octagonal shape was entirely Ahom, and according to tradition was chosen because of the belief that the Ahom country was eight sided. Apart from the unique shape, the coins were of similar fabric and weight standard to the Moghul rupee.

The earliest coins had inscriptions in Sanskrit using the Bengali script, but the retreat of the Moghul army under Mir Jumla in 1663 seems to have led to a revival of Ahom nationalism that may account for the fact that most of the coins struck between 1663 and 1696 had inscriptions in the old Ahom script, with invocations to Ahom deities.

Up to this time all the coins, following normal practice in North-East India, were merely dated to the coronation year of the ruler, but Rudra Simha (1696-1714) instituted the practice of dating coins to the year of issue. This ruler was a fervent Hindu, and reinstated Sanskrit inscriptions on the coins. After this the Ahom script was used on a few rare ceremonial issues.

The majority of coins issued were of silver, with binary subdivions down to a fraction of 1/32nd rupee. Cowrie shells were used for small change. Gold coins were struck throughout the period, often using the same dies as were used for the silver coins. A few copper coins were struck during the reign of Brajanatha Simha (1818-19), but these are very rare.

MINTNAMES

Rangpur

CHANDRAKANTA SIMHA

SE1732-39,41,42/1810-17,19,20AD

1/32 RUPEE

SILVER, oval, 0.34-0.36 g

KM#	Date	Year	VG	Fine	VF	XF
245	ND	—	15.00	20.00	26.50	35.00

1/16 RUPEE

SILVER, 7mm, octagonal, 0.67-0.72 g

KM#	Date	Year	VG	Fine	VF	XF
246	ND	—	15.00	20.00	26.50	35.00

1/8 RUPEE

SILVER, 1.34-1.45 g

KM#	Date	Year	VG	Fine	VF	XF
247	ND	—	15.00	20.00	26.50	35.00

1/4 RUPEE

SILVER, 2.68-2.90 g

KM#	Date	Year	VG	Fine	VF	XF
248	SE1741	(1819)	25.00	35.00	45.00	60.00
	1742	(1820)	25.00	35.00	45.00	60.00

1/2 RUPEE

SILVER, 5.35-5.80 g

KM#	Date	Year	VG	Fine	VF	XF
249	ND	—	25.00	35.00	45.00	60.00

RUPEE

SILVER, 10.70-11.60 g

KM#	Date	Year	VG	Fine	VF	XF
250	SE1741	(1819)	30.00	40.00	50.00	70.00
	1742	(1820)	30.00	40.00	50.00	70.00

KM#	Date	Year	VG	Fine	VF	XF
251	SE1742	(1820)	30.00	40.00	50.00	70.00

1/32 MOHUR

GOLD, 0.34-0.36 g

KM#	Date	Year	VG	Fine	VF	XF
252	ND	—	20.00	35.00	50.00	75.00

1/16 MOHUR

GOLD, 0.67-0.72 g

KM#	Date	Year	VG	Fine	VF	XF
253	ND	—	30.00	45.00	70.00	100.00

MOHUR

GOLD, 10.70-11.40 g

KM#	Date	Year	VG	Fine	VF	XF
257	SE1741	(1819)	165.00	210.00	300.00	425.00

BRAJANATHA SIMHA

SE1739-1740/1818-1819AD

PANA

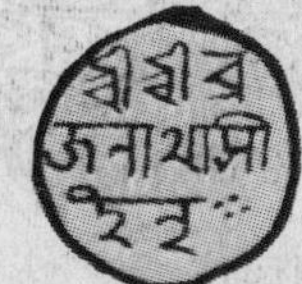

COPPER, 5.60 g

KM#	Date	Year	VG	Fine	VF	XF
258	ND	—	12.50	21.50	35.00	50.00

2 PANA

COPPER, 11.00 g

KM#	Date	Year	VG	Fine	VF	XF
259	SE1739	(1817)	16.50	27.50	45.00	65.00

1/32 RUPEE

SILVER, 6mm, round, 0.34-0.36 g

KM#	Date	Year	VG	Fine	VF	XF
260	ND	—	15.00	20.00	26.50	35.00

1/16 RUPEE

SILVER, 0.67-0.72 g

KM#	Date	Year	VG	Fine	VF	XF
261	ND	—	15.00	20.00	26.50	35.00

1/8 RUPEE

SILVER, 1.34-1.45 g

KM#	Date	Year	VG	Fine	VF	XF
262	ND	—	15.00	20.00	26.50	35.00

1/4 RUPEE

SILVER, 2.68-2.90 g

KM#	Date	Year	VG	Fine	VF	XF
263	SE1739	(1817)	16.50	27.50	40.00	55.00
	1740	(1818)	16.50	27.50	40.00	55.00

1/2 RUPEE

SILVER, 5.35-5.80 g

KM#	Date	Year	VG	Fine	VF	XF
264	ND	7	16.50	27.50	40.00	55.00

RUPEE

SILVER, 10.70-11.60 g

KM#	Date	Year	VG	Fine	VF	XF
265	SE1739	(1817)	18.50	30.00	50.00	70.00
	1740	(1818)	18.50	30.00	50.00	70.00

1/32 MOHUR

GOLD, 0.34-0.36 g

KM#	Date	Year	VG	Fine	VF	XF
266	ND	—	20.00	30.00	50.00	75.00

1/8 MOHUR

GOLD, octagonal, 1.34-1.42 g

KM#	Date	Year	VG	Fine	VF	XF
268	ND	—	35.00	50.00	75.00	100.00

1/4 MOHUR

GOLD, octagonal, 2.68-2.85 g

KM#	Date	Year	VG	Fine	VF	XF
269	SE1739	(1817)	50.00	65.00	85.00	125.00

MOHUR

GOLD, 10.70-11.40 g

KM#	Date	Year	VG	Fine	VF	XF
271	SE1739	(1817)	150.00	185.00	265.00	375.00
	1740	(1818)	150.00	185.00	265.00	375.00

JOGESVARA SIMHA

SE1743/1821AD

1/8 RUPEE

SILVER, 1.34-1.45 g

KM#	Date	Year	VG	Fine	VF	XF
274	ND	—	17.50	25.00	32.50	45.00

1/4 RUPEE

SILVER, octagonal, 2.68-2.90 g

KM#	Date	Year	VG	Fine	VF	XF
275	SE1743	(1821)	20.00	27.50	37.50	50.00

1/2 RUPEE

SILVER, 5.35-5.80 g

KM#	Date	Year	VG	Fine	VF	XF
276	ND	—	30.00	40.00	50.00	70.00

RUPEE

SILVER, 10.70-11.60 g

KM#	Date	Year	VG	Fine	VF	XF
277	SE1743	(1821)	45.00	60.00	75.00	100.00

1/4 MOHUR

GOLD, octagonal, 2.68-2.85 g

KM#	Date	Year	VG	Fine	VF	XF
281	SE1743	(1821)	150.00	185.00	265.00	375.00

COOCH BEHAR

During the 15th century, the area that was to become Cooch Behar was ruled by the powerful Hindu kings of Kamata, who were defeated by Sultan 'Ala al din Husain Shah of Bengal in 1494AD. In 1511AD the kingdom of Cooch Behar was established by Chandan, a chieftain of the Koch tribe.

Chandan was succeeded about 1522 by Visvasimha, who consolidated the kingdom, and set up his capital at the present town of Cooch Behar. It was he who laid the foundations of the prosperity of the area by developing the Tibetan trade routes through Bhutan. Visvasimha is said to have abdicated about 1555AD to become an ascetic, and was succeeded by his son Nara Narayan, under whose reign the state reached the zenith of its power.

From the solid basis set up by his father, Nara Narayan set out, assisted by his brother Sukladhvaja, to extend the borders of his kingdom. Over the next quarter century he proceeded to subdue part of the Assam Valley, Kachar, Manipur, the Khasi and Jaintia Hills and part of Tripura and Sylhet. Nara Narayan was the first king of Cooch Behar to strike coins, and the varied style may indicate that he set up several mints over his empire. The style of one piece is very similar to that of later pieces struck by the Rajas of Jaintiapur, which suggests Jaintiapur as the mint for this variety, but no other varieties have been assigned to specific mints.

After the death of Sukladhvaja, who was a great general, the military strength of the kingdom waned. Nara Narayan quarrelled with Sukladhvaja's son Raghu Deva, and the latter set himself up as ruler of the eastern part of the kingdom in 1581, initially under the suzerainty of his uncle, but after Nara Narayan's death, as full independent ruler.

Nara Narayan's son, Lakshmi Narayan inherited the western part of the kingdom, but no attempt was made to consolidate the conquests made by his father, and Kachar, Tripura and other states reverted to their former fully independent state. Lakshmi Narayan was a weak, peaceloving king, who preferred to declare himself a vassal of the Mughal Emperor in 1596, rather than make any attempt to preserve his independence. In accepting Mughal suzerainty, he gravely offended his subjects, who rose in revolt. The Mughals assisted Lakshmi Narayan quell the rebellion, and in 1603 a treaty was signed under which Lakshmi Narayan agreed never again to strike full rupees and to abandon certain other royal prerogatives. The Eastern Kingdom under Raghu Deva and his son Parikshit refused to bow to Mughal domination in the same way, and in 1612 the Mughals invaded and destroyed their kingdom.

After Lakshmi Narayan's death in 1627, the new ruler Vira Narayan exhibited a certain degree of independence by striking full rupees and retaking the former Eastern Cooch Behar Kingdom from the Mughals. By this time, however, a powerful leader had emerged in Bhutan, and trade was disrupted by wars between Bhutan and Tibet, causing a reduction in the number of coins struck.

The Mughals soon recaptured the eastern territories, but the next ruler, Prana Narayan, was able to reopen trade links with Tibet through Bhutan. In 1661 Prana Narayan was expelled from his capital by the Mughal governor of Bengal, Mir Jumla, and sought refuge in Bhutan. At this time Mir Jumla struck coins in Cooch Behar in the name of the Mughal Emperor Aurangzeb, but while Mir Jumla was stuck in Assam during the monsoon of 1663, Prana Narayan managed to regain control of his kingdom, paying tribute to the Mughal Emperor.

For the next century Cooch Behar was relatively peaceful until there was a dispute over the succession in 1772. After a confusing period during which the Bhutanese installed their own nominated ruler and captured Dhairyendra Narandra, the Chief Minister appealed to the British for assistance. With an eye on the potentially lucrative Tibetan trade, which had increased somewhat in volume since Prithvi Narayan's rise to power in Nepal, the British agreed to support Darendra Narayan, so long as British suzerainty was acknowledged.

Over the following decades the British gradually increased their control over the state. After large numbers of debased silver half, or "Narainy" rupees had been struck, the British decided to close the mint, and after that a few coins only were struck at the coronation of each ruler, although it was only in 1866 that the local coins ceased to be legal tender.

Bhutanese copies: Until the 1780's the Bhutanese used to periodically send surplus silver to the mint in Cooch Behar to strike into coin for local use, as Cooch Behar coins circulated widely in Bhutan. After the Cooch Behar mint was closed in 1788 the Bhutanese established their own mints, striking copies of the 1/2 rupees - initially of fine silver with slight differences in design from the original Cooch Behar coins, but later the silver content reduced until they were of pure copper or brass. For these issues see Bhutan listing.

RULERS

Harendra Narayan, CB273-329/ SE1705-1761/1783-1839AD
Shivendra Narayan, CB329-337/ SE1761-1769/1839-1847AD
Narendra Narayan, CB337-353/ SE1769-1785/1847-1863AD
Nripendra Narayan, CB353-401/ SE1785-1833/1863-1911AD
Raja Rajendra Narayan, CB401-403/ SE1833-1835/1911-1913AD
Jitendra Narayan, CB403-412/ SE1835-1844/1913-1922AD
Jagaddipendra Narayan, CB412-439/ SE1844-1871/1922-1949AD

DATING

The coins are dated in either the Saka era (Saka yr. + 78 = AD year) or the Cooch Behar era (CB yr. + 1510 = AD year) calculated from the year of the founding of the kingdom by Chandan in 1511AD. Some coins have dates in both eras, but as the Saka always refers back to the accession year, and the Cooch Behar year seems to show the actual date of striking, the two years do not necessarily correspond to the same AD year.

Unfortunately the dies for the half rupees were usually rather broader than the flans, so the year is only rarely visible.

HARENDRA NARAYAN

CB273-329/SE1705-1761/1783-1839AD

These names usually cannot be differentiated.

'rendra' center left on obverse

1/2 RUPEE

SILVER, 4.70 g

KM#	Date	Year	VG	Fine	VF	XF
141	ND	—	5.00	8.00	11.00	15.00

KACHAR

The Kacharis are probably the original inhabitants of the Assam Valley, and in the 13th century ruled much of the south bank of the Brahmaputra from their capital at Dimapur.

Around 1530 the Ahoms inflicted several crushing defeats on the Kacharis, Dimapur was sacked, and the Kacharis were forced to retreat further south and set up a new capital at Maibong.

Very little is known about this obscure state, and the only time that coins were struck in any quantity was during the late 16th and early 17th centuries. One coin, indeed, proudly announces the conquest of Sylhet, but this military prowess seems to have been short lived, and the small kingdom was only saved from Muslim domination by its isolation and lack of economic worth.

A few coins were struck during the 18th and 19th centuries, but this was probably merely as a demonstration of independence, rather than for any economic reason.

In 1819, the last Kachari ruler, Govind Chandra was ousted by the Manipuri ruler Chaurajit Simha, and during the Burmese occupation of Manipur and Assam, the Manipuris remained in control of Kachar. In 1824, Govind Chandra was restored to his throne by the British, and ruled under British suzerainty. By all accounts his administration was not a success, and in 1832, soon after Govind Chandra had been murdered, the British took over the administration of the State in "compliance with the frequent and earnestly expressed wishes of the people".

The earliest coins of Kachar were clearly copied from the contemporary coins of Cooch Behar, with weight standard also copied from the Bengali standard. The flans are, however, even broader than those of the Cooch Behar coins, making the coins very distinctive.

A number of spectacular gold and silver coins, purporting to come from Kachar, appeared in Calcutta during the 1960's, but as their authenticity has been doubted, they have been omitted from this listing.

RULERS

A list of the Kings of Kachar has been preserved in local traditions, but is rather unreliable. The following list has been compiled from this traditional list, together with names and dates obtained from other sources, but may not be completely accurate.

Krishna Chandra Narayan, SE1712-1735/c.1790-1813AD
Govinda Chandra, SE1735-1741/1814-1819AD
Chaurajit Singh, (of Manipur), SE1741-1745/1819-1823AD
Gambhir Singh, (of Manipur), SE1745-1746/1823-1824AD
Govinda Chandra, SE1746-1752/1824-1830AD

GOVINDA CHANDRA

SE1735-1752/1813-1830AD

RUPEE

SILVER, 25mm, 10.70-11.60 g

KM#	Date	Year	VG	Fine	VF	XF
150	SE1736	(1814)	100.00	150.00	225.00	325.00

MANIPUR

Although the Manipuri traditions preserve a long list of kings which purports to go back to the early years of the Christian era, the first ruler whose existence can be verified from more tangible sources was a Naga called Panheiba, who adopted the Hindu religion and took the name of Gharib Niwaz about 1714AD.

Gharib Niwaz seems to have been a powerful ruler, who was successful in the frequent wars with Burma, and hence raised the country from obscurity. He was murdered in 1750, together with his eldest son, and it was during the reign of the latter's son, Gaura Singh, that the British first came into contact with Manipur. After the death of Gharib Niwaz the Burmese had more success with their incursions into Manipur, and by 1761 there was a danger that the capital would be captured, so the Manipuris appealed to the British for military assistance. This was granted, and in 1762 British troops helped the Manipuris drive out the Burmese, and a treaty of alliance was signed. On this occasion 500 meklee gold rupees were sent to the British as part payment for the expenses of this assistance.

Gaura Singh died in 1764 and from then until 1798 his brother Jai Singh heroically defended his country against the Burmese. In the early years of his reign he suffered many setbacks, but for the last ten years of his reign his position was fairly secure. In 1798 Jai Singh abdicated and died the following year. The next 35 years were to see five of his eight sons on the throne, plotting against each other and enlisting Burmese support for their internecine rivalry. After 1812 the Manipuri King was little more than a puppet in the hands of the Burmese, and when the Kings tried to assert their independence they were ousted to become Kings of Kachar.

In 1824, after the 1st Burma war, the Burmese were finally driven out of Manipur and Gambhir Singh, one of the younger sons of Jai Singh, asked for British assistance to regain control of his kingdom. This was granted, and from 1825 until his death in 1834 Gambhir Singh ruled well and restored an element of prosperity to his kingdom. A British resident was stationed in Manipur, but the King ruled his country independently. The British stayed aloof from several palace intrigues and revolutions, and it was only in 1891, after several British Officials had been killed, that the administration was brought under the control of a British Political Agent.

RULERS

Madhu Chandra, SE1723-1728/1801-1806AD
Chaurajit Singh, SE1728-1734/1806-1812AD
Marjit Singh, under Burmese suzerainty, SE1734-1741/1812-1819AD
Huidromba Subol, SE1741-1742/1819-1820AD
Gambhir Singh, SE1742-1743/1820-1821AD
Jadu Singh, SE1743-1745/1821-1823AD
Raghab Singh, SE1745-1746/1823-1824AD
Bhadra Singh, SE1746-1747/1824-1825AD
Gambhir Singh, restored by the British, SE1747-1756/1825-1834AD
Chandra Kirti, SE1756-1765/1834-1843AD
Nar Singh, SE1765-1771/1843-1849AD
Chandra Kirti, SE1771-1808/1849-1886AD
Sura Chandra Singh, SE1808-1812/1886-1890AD
Kula Chandra Singh, SE1812-1813/1890-1891AD
Chura Chandra, SE1813-1862/1891-1941AD
Bodh Chandra, SE1862-1870/1941-1949AD

COINAGE

The only coins struck in quantity for circulation in Manipur were small bell-metal (circa 74 percent copper, 23 percent tin, 3 percent zinc) coins called "sel". According to local tradition these coins were first struck in the 17th century, but this is doubtful, and it seems likely that the sels were first struck in the second half of the 18th century. Unfortunately few of the sels can be attributed to any particular ruler, as they merely bear a Nagari letter deemed auspicious for the particular reign, and it has not been recorded which letter was deemed auspicious for which ruler.

The value of the sel functioned relative to the rupees which also circulated in Manipur for making large purchases, although Government accounts were kept in sel until 1891. Prior to 1838 the sel was valued at about 900 to the rupee, but after that date it fell in value to around 480 to the rupee, although there were occasional fluctuations. About 1878, speculative hoarding of sel forced the value up to 240 to the rupee, but large numbers of sel were struck at this time, and from then until 1891, when the sel were withdrawn from circulation, their value remained fairly stable at about 400 to the rupee.

During the years after 1714AD some square gold and silver coins were struck, but as few have survived, they were probably only struck in small quantities for ceremonial rather than monetary use.

Apart from the coins mentioned above, some larger bell-metal coins have been attributed to Manipur, but the attribution is still somewhat tentative. Also several other gold coins, two with an image of Krishna playing the flute, have been discovered in Calcutta in recent years, but as their authenticity has been queried, they have not been included in the following listing.

DATING

Most of the silver and gold coins of Manipur are dated in the Saka era (Sake date + 78 = AD date), but at least one coin is dated in the Manipuri "Chandrabda" era, which may be converted to the AD year by adding 788 to the Chandrabda date.

MONETARY SYSTEM

(Until 1838AD)
880 to 960 Sel = 1 Rupee
(Commencing 1838AD)
420-480 Sel = 1 Rupee

CHAURAJIT SINGH

SE1725-1734/1803-1812AD

1/4 RUPEE

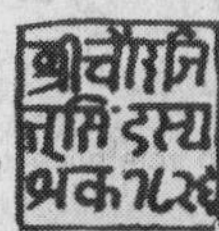

SILVER, 2.68-2.90 g

C#	Date	Year	VG	Fine	VF	XF
55	SE1726	(1804)	42.00	85.00	140.00	200.00
	1729	(1807)	42.00	85.00	140.00	200.00

1/2 RUPEE

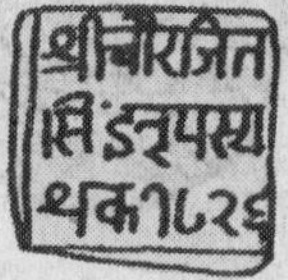
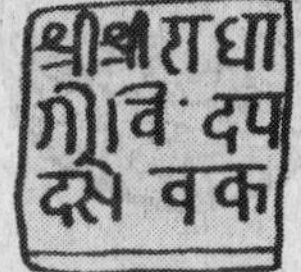

SILVER, 5.35-5.80 g

C#	Date	Year	VG	Fine	VF	XF
56	SE1726	(1804)	50.00	100.00	175.00	250.00

RUPEE

SILVER, 10.70-11.60 g

C#	Date	Year	VG	Fine	VF	XF
57	SE1728	(1806)	90.00	180.00	300.00	450.00
	1729	(1807)	90.00	180.00	300.00	450.00
	1732	(1810)	90.00	180.00	300.00	450.00
	1734	(1812)	60.00	120.00	200.00	300.00

MOHUR

GOLD, 11.20-12.50 g

C#	Date	Year	VG	Fine	VF	XF
61	SE1731	(1809)	225.00	375.00	625.00	875.00

MARJIT SINGH

SE1734-1741/1812-1819AD

RUPEE

SILVER, 11.50 g

C#	Date	Year	VG	Fine	VF	XF
71	SE1736	(1814)	50.00	100.00	175.00	250.00

MOHUR

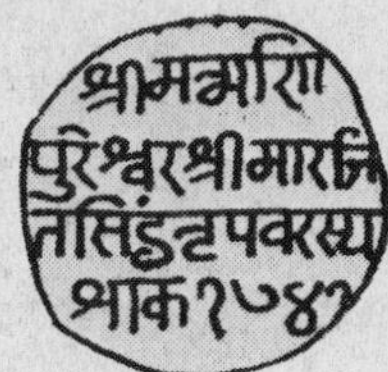

GOLD, 10.70-11.40 g

C#	Date	Year	VG	Fine	VF	XF
75	SE1741	(1819)	375.00	625.00	875.00	1150.

GAMBHIR SINGH

SE1748-1756/1826-1834AD

MOHUR

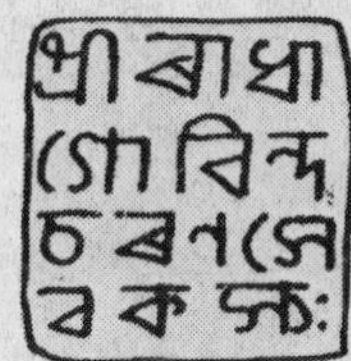
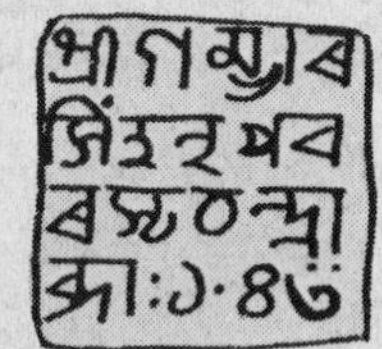

GOLD, 10.70-11.40 g

C#	Date	Year	VG	Fine	VF	XF
85	1043*	(1831)	375.00	625.00	875.00	1150.

***NOTE:** Chandrabdah 1043 (a local date system).

ANONYMOUS ISSUES

These bear a single Bengali character, of uncertain significance, and cannot be assigned to particular rulers. All are uniface.

SEL

BRONZE BELL-METAL, uniface

Sri

C#	Date	Good	VG	Fine	VF
1	ND	3.50	6.00	8.00	10.00

NOTE: Many variations in style exist, 2 varieties are illustrated above.

Ma

C#	Date	Good	VG	Fine	VF
2	ND	5.00	8.00	11.50	15.00

Ra

C#	Date	Good	VG	Fine	VF
3	ND	6.00	10.00	15.00	20.00

(Said to be on issue of Nara Singh, 1843-50)

Ka

C#	Date	Good	VG	Fine	VF
4	ND	6.00	10.00	15.00	20.00

(Struck before 1820)

La

C#	Date	Good	VG	Fine	VF
5	ND	6.00	10.00	15.00	20.00

(Perhaps an issue of Sura Chandra, 1886-90)

Ku

C#	Date	Good	VG	Fine	VF
6	ND	6.00	10.00	15.00	20.00

(Probably an issue of Kula Chandra Singh, 1890-91)

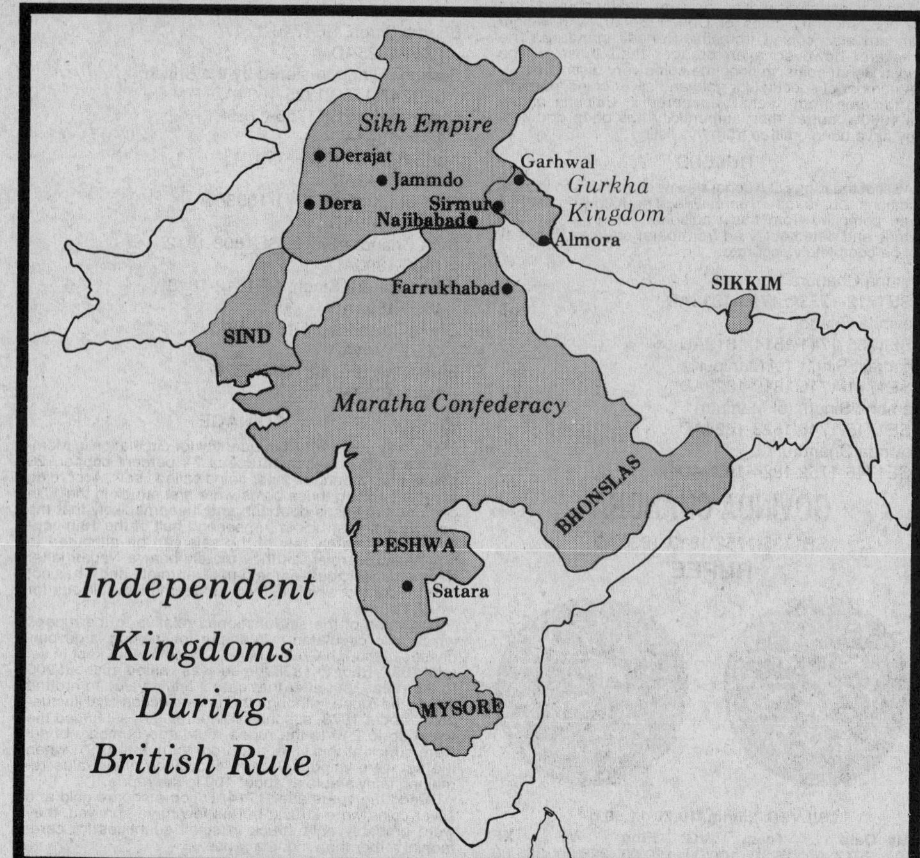

Independent Kingdoms During British Rule

FARRUKHABAD

Farrukhabad a district in north India was founded early in the eighteenth century by the Afghan, Mohammed Khan (d.1743), who was governor first of Allahabad and later of Malwa. The subsequent struggles of his sons with Awadh, with the Rohillas and with the Marathas, culminated in Farrukhabad becoming a tributary to Awadh, by which state Farrukhabad was entirely surrounded. In 1801 Farrukhabad was ceded to the British by the Nawab Vizier of Awadh.

For similar coins struck in the name of Ahmad Shah (Durrani) dated AH1174, 1176 refer to Afghanistan, Durrani listings. For later issues with fixed regnal year 45 refer to India-British/Bengal Presidency listings.

MINTNAME

Commencing AH1167

احمدنكر فرخ اباد

Ahmadnagar-Farrukhabad

NOTE: Catalog numbers are in reference to Craig's Mughal listings.

AHMADNAGAR - FARRUKHABAD MINT

In the name of Shah Alam II
AH1173-1221/1759-1806AD

FALUS

COPPER

C#	Date	Year	Good	VG	Fine	VF
71.5	AH1219	39	4.50	8.50	13.50	20.00

In the name of Muhammad Akbar II
AH1221-1253/1806-1837AD

1/2 ANNA

COPPER

C#	Date	Year	Good	VG	Fine	VF
123.5	AH1226	6	5.00	10.00	15.00	22.50
	1233	12	4.50	8.50	13.50	20.00

In the name of Shah Alam II
AH1173-1221/1759-1806AD

RUPEE

SILVER, 10.70-11.60 g

C#	Date	Year	VG	Fine	VF	XF
86.2	AH1216	39	8.50	13.50	20.00	35.00
	1217	39	8.50	13.50	20.00	35.00
	1218	39	8.50	13.50	20.00	35.00
	1219	39	8.50	13.50	20.00	35.00
	1220	39	8.50	13.50	20.00	35.00
	1224	39	8.50	13.50	20.00	35.00
	1225	39	8.50	13.50	20.00	35.00
	1227	39	8.50	13.50	20.00	35.00
	1228	39	8.50	13.50	20.00	35.00

NOTE: Earlier dates (AH1175-1215) exist for this type.

NAZARANA RUPEE

Issued after cession to the British

SILVER, 10.70-11.60 g

C#	Date	Year	VG	Fine	VF	XF
86.2a	AH1228	39	35.00	65.00	100.00	150.00

GURKHA KINGDOM

GARHWAL

RULERS

Girvan Yuddha, of Nepal
VS1860-1872/1803-1815AD

SRINAGAR MINT

In the names of Shah Alam II and Girvan Yuddha, of Nepal
VS1860-1863/1803-1806AD

TIMASHA

SILVER

C#	Date		VG	Fine	VF	XF
35	VS(18)65	(1808)	6.50	10.00	15.00	22.50
	(18)66	(1809)	6.50	10.00	15.00	22.50
	Date off flan		4.00	6.50	10.00	15.00

In the names of Muhammad Akbar II and Girvan Yuddha, of Nepal
VS1863-1870/1806-1813AD

TIMASHA

SILVER

C#	Date		VG	Fine	VF	XF
36	VS(18)66	(1809)	6.50	10.00	15.00	22.50
	(18)67	(1810)	6.50	10.00	15.00	22.50
	(18)68	(1811)	6.50	10.00	15.00	22.50
	(18)69	(1812)	6.50	10.00	15.00	22.50
	(18)70	(1813)	6.50	10.00	15.00	22.50

In the name of Girvan Yuddha
VS1860-1873/1803-1816AD

PAISA

COPPER

C#	Date	Year	Good	VG	Fine	VF
30	VS1859	(1802)	4.00	6.00	8.00	12.50
	1872	(1815)	3.00	4.50	7.00	10.00
	1873	(1816)	4.00	6.00	8.00	12.50

TIMASHA

SILVER

C#	Date	Year	VG	Fine	VF	XF
37	ND	—	6.50	10.00	15.00	22.50

KUMAON

RULER

Girvan Yuddha, of Nepal
VS1860-1873/1803-1816AD

Almora Mint

PAISA

COPPER

C#	Date	Year	Good	VG	Fine	VF
10	VS(18)66 (1809)		3.00	5.00	8.00	12.50

SIRMUR

RULER

Girvan Yuddha, of Nepal
VS1860-1873/1803-1816AD

NAHAN MINT

1/2 PAISA

COPPER

C#	Date	Year	Good	VG	Fine	VF
20	AH1227	—	3.00	5.00	8.00	12.50

PAISA

COPPER

C#	Date	Year	Good	VG	Fine	VF
21	AH1227	—	4.00	6.00	9.00	13.50

MARATHA CONFEDERACY

The origins of the Marathas are lost in the early history of the remote hill country of the Western Ghats in present-day Maharashtra. By the fifteenth century they had come into occasional prominence for their resistance to Muslim incursions into their homelands. They were a rugged wiry people who, by the seventeenth century, had accomodated themselves to the political realities of their times by becoming feudatories, or mercenaries, to the sultans of Bijapur. It is not clear exactly what happened to suddenly thrust the Marathas into the limelight of Indian history in the seventeenth century. The most likely explanation seems to be that the broad sweep of Aurangzeb's campaigns across the Deccan, his insensitivity towards Hindu sentiment, and the pre-eminence he gave to Islam, all served to politicize a hitherto politically quiescent people. And just as Aurangzeb supplied the occasion, the Marathas found in Sivaji the man.

In the seventeenth century Shahji, the father of Sivaji, was holder of a small fiefdom under the Bijapur sultans. His son, taking advantage of the declining authority of his overlords, seized some of the surrounding territory. Bijapur proved incapable of quelling his insurrection. Drawing encouragement from this experience, Sivaji's forces sacked and plundered the Mughal port of Surat in 1664. From this point until his death in 1680 Sivaji maintained a sort of running guerilla war with Aurangzeb. There were no decisive victories for either side but Sivaji left behind him a cohesive and well organized regional alliance in the Western Deccan, a small isolated kingdom in Tanjore and a few pockets of territory on the west coast.

After Sivaji's death the struggle was renewed as Aurangzeb advanced into the Deccan. It was the years after Aurangzeb's death in 1707 which really saw revival as the Maratha confederacy gained a new cohesiveness and its military successes began to make it look as if the Marathas might even become the new masters of India. The revenues of much of the Deccan now flowed into (finished up in) Maratha pockets. Baji Rao I, the Peshwa, pressed as far north as the gates of Delhi and in 1738 he gained control of Malwa. Parts of Gujarat also were in confederacy hands. Bengal was invaded, Orissa annexed (1751), and the territories of the Nizam of Hyderabad and the Carnatic appeared at risk. It was during this period that some of the great Maratha families gained prominence - the Holkars, the Sindhias, the Gaekwars and the Bhonslas - families who later, as the confederacy began to disintegrate and give way to rivalry, would assert their own regional interests at the expense of the alliance.

The turning point for Maratha fortunes was the battle of Panipat on January 14th 1761. Intending to stop the Afghan, Ahmad Shah Abdali (Durrani), in his tracks, the Marathas assembled the greatest army in their history and placed it under the unified command of the Peshwa of Poona. By nightfall the Peshwa's son and heir, Bhao Sahib, and all the leading chiefs, were dead. Maratha losses were said to have been in excess of a hundred thousand men. The Marathas would still remain a force to be reckoned with, they would again cross the Chambel (1767), and they would still give the Nizam's forces a thrashing (1795), but from 1761 onwards internal dissension grew rife and the Maratha Confederacy would never again exhibit sufficient cohesion to be considered a serious contender for the crown of India.

This powerful alliance of Marathi warriors owed nominal allegiance to the Rajas of Satara (descendents of Shivaji) and drew their unity from the leadership of the Peshwa, the hereditary prime minister of the confederation. In the mid-eighteenth century the Marathas were at the apogee of their influence, having hastened the end of effective Mughal power in the Deccan and western India. They successfully checked the intrusions of the Durranis into north India, although the experience left them so militarily exhausted that the dominance in Hindustan passed to other hands.

The great families of the lieutenants of the Peshwa gradually carved out regional power bases and became progressively less responsive to the authority of their formal superiors. The Maratha power as such was broken in a series of wars with the East India Company, bitterly fought and very close contests which settled the fate of large sections of India. Broadly speaking the Marathas may for convenience sake be listed in two categories, the lines which became extinct through British action and those which accomodated the English after defeat and survived to become Princely States. The latter will be found elsewhere in the catalogue; the non-surviving political units are catalogued below.

BHONSLAS

RULERS

Raghoji II, 1788-1816AD
Raghoji III, 1816-1853AD

MINTS

Cuttack 

Most coins are imitations of Mughal coins of Ahmad Shah (1748-54AD), more or less barbarized. The Bhonslas mints were closed when the state was abolished in 1854.

Cuttack Mint

PAISA

Rev. symbols ۳ and ɘ

"Zareepathka" flag added after 1825.

COPPER

KM#	Date	Year	Good	VG	Fine	VF
A11	ND	—	2.00	3.00	4.00	7.00

1/16 RUPEE

SILVER, 0.61-0.72 g

KM#	Date	Year	VG	Fine	VF	XF
11	ND	—	7.50	15.00	25.00	35.00

1/8 RUPEE

SILVER, 1.33-1.45 g

KM#	Date	Year	VG	Fine	VF	XF
12	ND	—	7.50	15.00	25.00	35.00

1/4 RUPEE

SILVER, 2.67-2.90 g
Rev: Flag only.

KM#	Date	Year	VG	Fine	VF	XF
13	ND	—	6.50	13.00	21.00	30.00

Rev: Both symbols.

KM#	Date	Year	VG	Fine	VF	XF
14	ND	—	6.50	13.00	21.00	30.00

1/2 RUPEE

SILVER, 5.35-5.80 g
Rev: Both symbols.

KM#	Date	Year	VG	Fine	VF	XF
15	ND	—	7.50	15.00	21.50	35.00

RUPEE

SILVER, 10.70-11.60 g
W/o mint marks. Mintname: Katak
Pseudo regnal year

KM#	Date	Year	VG	Fine	VF	XF
16	ND	52	12.50	25.00	42.00	60.00
		57	12.50	25.00	42.00	60.00
		512	12.50	25.00	42.00	60.00

Rev: Flag only, pseudo regnal years.

KM#	Date	Year	VG	Fine	VF	XF
17	ND	5	10.00	20.00	35.00	50.00
		51	10.00	20.00	35.00	50.00
		52	10.00	20.00	35.00	50.00
		511	10.00	20.00	35.00	50.00
		512	10.00	20.00	35.00	50.00
		521	10.00	20.00	35.00	50.00

Rev: Both symbols.

KM#	Date	Year	VG	Fine	VF	XF
18	ND	5	12.50	25.00	42.00	60.00

NAZARANA RUPEE

SILVER

KM#	Date	Year	VG	Fine	VF	XF
19	—	22	—	—	—	—

PESHWAS

RULERS

Baji Rao, 1796-1818AD

MINTS

Ahmadabad احمد اباد

Bagalkot بگلكوت

Gulshanabad (Nasik)

گلشن آباد

Jalaun جلوت

بلونت نگر

Jhansi
Mintname: Balwantnagar

Kunch كونچ

Poona پونہ

روش نگرساگر

Saugor
Mintname: Ravishnagar Saugar

Ahmadabad Mint

One of Maratha Mints from 1757-1800, it was leased to Baroda from 1800-1804, returned during 1804-1806, released to Baroda in 1806, and ceded to Baroda in 1817 (1232AH). In 1818, it was annexed by the East India Company finally closed in 1835.

MINT MARKS

Obv: Ankus  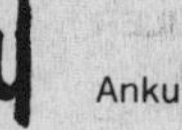 Ankus w/pennant 

Mint symbol on rev. at lower left: 

NOTE: Baroda coins of this mint have the Nagari initial of the ruler. British coins have the following mark on rev:

In the name of Muhammad Akbar II
AH1221-1253/1806-1837AD

PAISA

COPPER

KM#	Date	Year	VG	Fine	VF	XF
53	AH1232	10	3.00	4.00	6.50	9.00

1/2 RUPEE

SILVER, 18mm, 5.35-5.80 g
Mint mark: Ankus.

KM#	Date	Year	VG	Fine	VF	XF
54	AH—	—	6.00	9.00	14.00	20.00

Mint mark: Ankus w/pennant.

KM#	Date	Year	VG	Fine	VF	XF
55	AHxxxx	10	6.00	9.00	14.00	20.00

RUPEE

SILVER, 10.70-11.60 g
Mint mark: Ankus and scissors.

KM#	Date	Year	VG	Fine	VF	XF
56	AH1230	8	12.50	18.50	25.00	35.00

Mint mark: Ankus.

KM#	Date	Year	VG	Fine	VF	XF
57	AH122x	8	7.50	12.50	18.50	27.50
		9	7.50	12.50	18.50	27.50

Mint mark: Ankus w/pennant.

KM#	Date	Year	VG	Fine	VF	XF
58	AH1231	9	8.50	13.50	20.00	30.00
	1231	10	8.50	13.50	20.00	30.00

Gulshanabad Mint

Nasik

In the name of Shah Alam II
AH1173-1221/1759-1806AD

1/4 RUPEE

SILVER, 2.68-2.90 g

KM#	Date	Year	VG	Fine	VF	XF
107	AH1236	—	10.00	12.50	16.50	21.50

1/2 RUPEE

SILVER, 5.35-5.80 g

KM#	Date	Year	VG	Fine	VF	XF
108	AH1229	—	10.00	16.50	21.50	30.00
	1235	—	10.00	16.50	21.50	30.00

NOTE: Earlier date (AH1207) exists for this type.

RUPEE

SILVER, 10.70-11.60 g

KM#	Date	Year	VG	Fine	VF	XF
109	AH1219	—	12.50	18.50	25.00	35.00
	1227	—	12.50	18.50	25.00	35.00
	1229	—	12.50	18.50	25.00	35.00
	1232	—	12.50	18.50	25.00	35.00
	1234	—	12.50	18.50	25.00	35.00
	1235	—	12.50	18.50	25.00	35.00
	1236	—	12.50	18.50	25.00	35.00
	1251	—	12.50	18.50	25.00	35.00

NOTE: Earlier date (AH1206) exists for this type.

Jalaun Mint

Obv. symbols:  and

Rev:  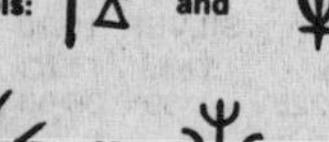 or

In the name of Shah Alam II
AH1173-1221/1759-1806AD

RUPEE

Mintname: 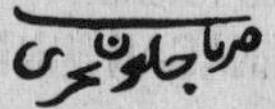

Zarb ba Jalaun Hijri

SILVER, 10.70-11.60 g
Crude fabric, narrow flan.

KM#	Date	Year	VG	Fine	VF	XF
124	AH1224	49	12.50	18.50	25.00	35.00
	1222	55	12.50	18.50	25.00	35.00

Mintname: 

Zarb Ku(nch), Kuna(r), Jalaun

Fine fabric, normal flan.

KM#	Date	Year	VG	Fine	VF	XF
125	AH—	49	15.00	21.50	33.50	45.00

Crude fabric, narrow flan.

KM#	Date	Year	VG	Fine	VF	XF
126	AH1222	17 (error)	6.50	10.00	15.00	22.50
	1223	17 (error)	6.50	10.00	15.00	22.50
	—	21	6.50	10.00	15.00	22.50
	1222	51	6.50	10.00	15.00	22.50
	1222	52	6.50	10.00	15.00	22.50
	1222	53	6.50	10.00	15.00	22.50
	1222	55	6.50	10.00	15.00	22.50
	1222	57	6.50	10.00	15.00	22.50

In the names of Shah Alam II
AH1173-1221/1759-1806AD
and Latif Khan

KM#	Date	Year	VG	Fine	VF	XF
128	AH—	53	30.00	40.00	55.00	75.00

Jhansi Mint

Mint mark: 

on reverse

Mintname: 

Balwantnagar

In the name of Shah Alam II

AH1173-1221/1759-1806AD

RUPEE

SILVER, 10.70-11.60 g
Obv: 99111 added.

KM#	Date	Year	VG	Fine	VF	XF
144	AH1220	47	10.00	15.00	20.00	27.50
	1221	48	10.00	15.00	20.00	27.50
	1223	50	10.00	15.00	20.00	27.50
	1224	52	10.00	15.00	20.00	27.50
	1234	—	10.00	15.00	20.00	27.50

Rev: Lily.

KM#	Date	Year	VG	Fine	VF	XF
145	AH—	3	11.50	17.50	23.50	33.50
	—	4	11.50	17.50	23.50	33.50

Kunch Mint

Mint marks: 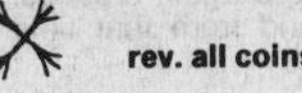 **rev. all coins**

 **#1 obv.**  **#2, obv.**

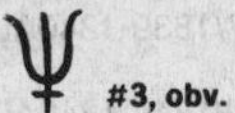 **#3, obv.**

 **#4, rev.** 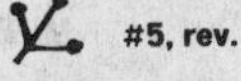 **#5, rev.**

Mintname:

Kunch Hijri

EAST INDIA COMPANY

As administrator of Kunch for Holkar from AH1220R.Y.47/1805AD.

RUPEE

SILVER, 10.70-11.60 g
Obv: Symbols #1, #2, #3.
Rev: Symbol #4.

KM#	Date	Year	VG	Fine	VF	XF
178	AH1220	47	16.00	22.50	35.00	50.00
	1221	47	16.00	22.50	35.00	50.00

Poona Mint

"Muhiabad Poona" Mint opened in 1750 and closed between 1834-1835.

In the name of Ali Gauhar, the name of Shah Alam II before his accession

NOTE: On Feb. 10, 1818AD (AH1233, Falsi Era 1128) the British East India Company took over Poona, so all coins of that date or later are British Colonial issues.

Mint marks:

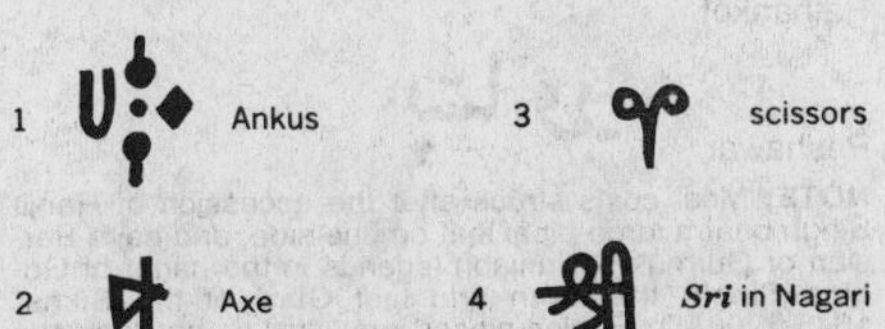

1 Ankus 3 scissors
2 Axe 4 *Sri* in Nagari

1/8 RUPEE

SILVER, 1.34-1.45 g
Rev: Mint mark #1 w/regnal year in Persian numerals.

KM#	Date	Year	VG	Fine	VF	XF
207	—	—	10.00	16.50	21.50	30.00

NOTE: This coin was copied by the local rulers at Alibagh Wai and Wadgaon.

1/4 RUPEE

SILVER, 2.68-2.90 g
Rev: Mint mark #1 w/regnal year in Persian numerals.

208 — — — Reported, not confirmed

NOTE: This coin was copied by the local rulers at Alibagh Wai and Wadgaon.

Rev: Mint mark #1 w/Fasli date in Nagari numerals.

KM#	Date	Year	VG	Fine	VF	XF
209	FE1238	(1828)	8.50	13.50	20.00	28.50

Rev: Mint mark: #2.

KM#	Date	Year	VG	Fine	VF	XF
210	FE1242	—	16.00	22.50	35.00	50.00

1/2 RUPEE

SILVER, 5.35-5.80 g
Rev: Mint mark #1 w/regnal year in Persian numerals.

KM#	Date	Year	VG	Fine	VF	XF
211	—	—	13.50	20.00	27.50	37.50

NOTE: This coin was copied by the local rulers at Alibagh Wai and Wadgaon.

Rev: Mint mark #1 w/Fasli date in Nagari numerals.

KM#	Date	Year	VG	Fine	VF	XF
212	FE1233	(1823)	10.00	16.50	21.50	30.00
	1236	(1826)	10.00	16.50	21.50	30.00
	1240	(1830)	10.00	16.50	21.50	30.00

RUPEE

SILVER, 10.70-11.60 g
Ankusi Rupee
Rev: Mint mark #1 w/regnal year in Persian numerals.

KM#	Date	Year	VG	Fine	VF	XF
213	—	11	7.00	11.00	16.50	25.00
	—	12	7.00	11.00	16.50	25.00
	—	15	7.00	11.00	16.50	25.00
	AH1225	—	7.50	12.50	18.50	27.50
	1229	—	7.50	12.50	18.50	27.50

NOTE: This coin was copied by the local rulers at Alibagh Wai and Wadgaon.

Rev: Mint mark #1, Fasli date in Nagari numerals

KM#	Date	Year	VG	Fine	VF	XF
214	FE1232	(1822)	6.50	10.00	15.00	22.50
	1233	(1823)	6.50	10.00	15.00	22.50
	1234	(1824)	6.50	10.00	15.00	22.50
	1235	(1825)	6.50	10.00	15.00	22.50
	1236	(1826)	6.50	10.00	15.00	22.50
	1237	(1827)	6.50	10.00	15.00	22.50
	1238	(1828)	6.50	10.00	15.00	22.50
	1239	(1829)	6.50	10.00	15.00	22.50
	1240	(1830)	6.50	10.00	15.00	22.50
	1241	(1831)	6.50	10.00	15.00	22.50
	1242	(1832)	6.50	10.00	15.00	22.50
	1243	(1833)	6.50	10.00	15.00	22.50
	1244	(1834)	6.50	10.00	15.00	22.50

Rev: Mint mark #3, Fasli date in Nagari numerals.

KM#	Date	Year	VG	Fine	VF	XF
217	AH1230	—	10.00	16.50	21.50	30.00
	1231	—	10.00	16.50	21.50	30.00
	1232	—	10.00	16.50	21.50	30.00
	1234	—	10.00	16.50	21.50	30.00
	1236	—	10.00	16.50	21.50	30.00
	1238	—	10.00	16.50	21.50	30.00
	1239	—	10.00	16.50	21.50	30.00
	1240	—	10.00	16.50	21.50	30.00
	1241	—	10.00	16.50	21.50	30.00
	1242	—	10.00	16.50	21.50	30.00
	1243	—	10.00	16.50	21.50	30.00
	1244	—	10.00	16.50	21.50	30.00
	ND	30	11.50	17.50	23.50	33.50

NOTE: Earlier date (AH1207) exists for this type.

Saugor Mint

Mint marks:  **obv.**

rev.

Pataka First type **Trisul First type**

Second type **Second type**

Mintname: Ravishnagar Sagar

In the name of Shah Alam II

AH1173-1221/1759-1806AD

Symbol  **on obv.**

KM#	Date	Year	Good	VG	Fine	VF
236	—	55	2.00	3.50	5.00	7.50

NOTE: Earlier date (Yr. 38) exists for this type.

1/2 RUPEE

SILVER, 5.35-5.80 g

KM#	Date	Year	VG	Fine	VF	XF
237	AH—	51	10.00	16.50	21.50	30.00

RUPEE

SILVER, 10.70-11.60 g

KM#	Date	Year	VG	Fine	VF	XF
240	AH1216	42	7.00	11.50	16.50	25.00
	1218	43	7.00	11.50	16.50	25.00
	1218	44	7.00	11.50	16.50	25.00
	1219	44	7.00	11.50	16.50	25.00
	1220	45	7.00	11.50	16.50	25.00
	1222	47	7.00	11.50	16.50	25.00
	122x	48	7.00	11.50	16.50	25.00
	1224	49	7.00	11.50	16.50	25.00

NOTE: Earlier dates (Yr.31-41) exist for this type.

Similar to KM#240 but very crude.

KM#	Date	Year	VG	Fine	VF	XF
241	AH—	52	7.00	11.50	16.50	25.00
	—	55	7.00	11.50	16.50	25.00

EAST INDIA COMPANY

Local issues post 1818-1819AD

PAISA

COPPER

KM#	Date	Year	Good	VG	Fine	VF
270	FE1230	(1820)	3.50	5.00	7.00	10.00
	1231	(1821)	3.50	5.00	7.00	10.00
	1232	(1822)	3.50	5.00	7.00	10.00
	1233	(1823)	3.50	5.00	7.00	10.00
	1234	(1824)	3.50	5.00	7.00	10.00
	1235	(1825)	3.50	5.00	7.00	10.00
	1237	(1827)	3.50	5.00	7.00	10.00
	1238	(1828)	3.50	5.00	7.00	10.00
	1240	(1830)	3.50	5.00	7.00	10.00

Bagalkot Mint

RUPEE

SILVER, 10.70-11.60 g

KM#	Date	Year	VG	Fine	VF	XF
271	1819	—	25.00	33.50	50.00	70.00

PUDUKKOTTAI

Pudukota

Pudukkottai was founded by Raghunatha Raya Tondaiman in 1686 when he defeated the Pallavaraya chiefs of the area. The family came from Tondaimandalam, a small village near Tirupathi, and belonged to the Kallen (or robber) caste. In the late eighteenth century the Tondaimans aided the British in their struggles against the French in the Carnatic. With British ascendancy, the Pudukkottai rulers were confirmed in their control of the region. This was regularized in 1806 when, subject to a yearly tribute of one elephant, the rajas of Pudukkottai were guaranteed their position. In 1948 the State was merged into the Trichinopoly District.

RULERS

Martanda Bhairava, 1886-1928AD

Rajagopala, 1928-1947AD

DUMP COINAGE

AMMAN CASH

COPPER, 1.30 g

Obv: Goddess Brihadamba. Rev. Telugu: *Vijaya.*

KM#	Date	Mintage	VG	Fine	VF	XF
3	ND	—	.90	1.50	2.50	4.00

HEAVY AMMAN CASH

COPPER, 1.65 g

KM#	Date	Mintage	VG	Fine	VF	XF
4	ND	—	—	—	Rare	—

MILLED COINAGE

AMMAN CASH

COPPER, 1.25 g

KM#	Date	Mintage	Fine	VF	XF	Unc
6	ND(1889)	*5.000	.20	.50	.85	1.50

NOTE: Struck by the Birmingham Mint between 18891906. Later contracts were produced by the Calcutta Mint.

ROHILKHAND

The nawabs of Rohilkhand were Rohillas who traced their origins to Sardar Daud Khan (d. 1749), an Afghan adventurer. Daud Khan's adopted son, Ali Muhammed, annexed a huge tract of land north of the Ganges between Itawa and the Himalayas, and received the title of nawab from the Mughal emperor.

In 1754 this territory was partitioned among his many sons, who thereafter formed a loose confederacy, alternately given to feuding internally and uniting to meet aggression by the Marathas, Awadh, and Imperial forces in turn. By the end of the century Rohilla power had been crushed by the combined forces of Awadh and the British, leaving only Rampur in Rohilla hands under the sovereignty of Nawab Faizullah Khan. In 1801 Rampur was ceded to the East India Company and in 1950 it was absorbed into Uttar Pradesh.

MINT

Mintname: Bareli بريلي

BARELI MINT

REVOLT OF 1857

The Mutiny

During the mutiny of 1857-58AD, Khan Bahadur Khan, a descendent of Hafiz Rahmat Khan, declared himself Subahdar of Rohilkhand under the Mughal Emperor Bahadur Shah Zafar. The independent government sat at Bareli, issuing rupees on the Mughal pattern of Shah Alam II, with current Hijri year and a regnal year dating from AH1202/1788AD, the year Rohilla power ended with the death of Ghulam Qadir.

RUPEE

SILVER, 10.70-11.60 g

KM#	Date	Year	VG	Fine	VF	XF
46	AH1274	72	—	—	Rare	—

SIKH EMPIRE

The father of Sikhism, Guru Nanak (1469-1539), was distinguished from almost all others who founded states or empires in India by being a purely religious teacher. Deeply Indian in the basic premises which underlay even those aspects of his theology which differed from the mainstream, he stressed the unity of God and the universal brotherhood of man. He was totally opposed to the divisions of the caste system and his teaching struggled to attain a practical balance between Hinduism and Islam. His message was a message of reconciliation, first with God, then with man. He exhibited no political ambition.

Guru Nanak was succeeded by 9 other gurus of Sikhism. Together they laid the foundations of a religious community in the Punjab which would, much later, transform itself into the Sikh Empire. Gradually this gentle religion of reconciliation became transformed into a formidable, aggressive military power. It was a metamorphosis which was, at least partly, thrust upon the Sikh community by Mughal oppression. The fifth guru of Sikhism, Arjun, was executed in 1606 on the order of Jahangir. His successor, Hargobind, was to spend his years in constant struggle against the Mughals, first against Jahangir and later against Shah Jahan. The ninth guru, Tegh Bahadur, was executed by Aurangzeb for refusing to embrace Islam. The stage had been set for a full confrontation with Mughal authority. It was against such a background that Sikhism's tenth guru, Guru Govind Singh (1675-1708), set about organizing the Sikhs into a military power. He gave new discipline to Sikhism. Its adherents were forbidden wine and tobacco and they were required to conform to the 5 outward signs of allegiance - to keep their hair unshaven and to wear short drawers (kuchcha), a comb (kungha), an iron bangle (kara) and a dagger (kirpan).

With Govind Singh's death the Khalsa, the Sikh brotherhood, emerged as the controlling body of Sikhism and the Granth, the official compilation of Govind Singh's teaching, became the "Bible" of Sikhism. At this point the Sikhs took to the hills. It was here, constantly harassed by Mughal forces, that Sikh militarism was forged into an effective weapon and tempered by fire. Gradually the Sikhs emerged from their safe forts in the hills and made their presence felt in the plains of the Punjab. As Nadir Shah retired from Delhi laden with the prizes of war in 1739, the stragglers of his Persian army were cut down by the Sikhs. Similarly, Ahmad Shah Durrani's first intrusion into India (1747-1748) was made the more lively by Sikh sorties into his rearguard. Gradually the Sikhs became both more confident and more effective, and their quite frequent military reversals served only to strengthen their determination and to deepen their sense of identity. Their first notable success came about 1756 when the Sikhs temporarily occupied Lahore and used the Mughal mint to strike their own rupee bearing the inscription, *Coined by the grace of the Khalsa in the country of Ahmad, conquered by Jessa the Kalal.* But the Sikhs were, as yet, most effective as guerrilla bands operating out of the hill country. On Ahmad Shah's fifth expedition into India (1759-1761) the Sikhs reverted to their well-tried role of forming tight mobile units which could choose both the time and the place of their attacks on the Durrani army. In spite of a serious reverse at Ludhiana in 1762 at the hands of Ahmad Shah, the Sikhs once again regrouped. In December 1763 they decisively defeated the Durrani governor of Sirhind and occupied the area.

The Sikhs now swept all before them, recapturing Lahore in 1764. The whole tract of land between the Jhelum and the Sutlej was now divided among the Sikh chieftains. At Lahore, and later at Amritsar, the Govind Shahi rupee proclaiming that Guru Govind Singh had received *Deg, Tegh and Fath* (Grace, Power and Victory) from Nanak, was struck. The name of the Mughal emperor was pointedly omitted. The Sikhs now subdivided into twelve *misls* "equals", each responsible for its own fate and each conducting its own military adventures into surrounding areas. By 1792 the most prominent chief in the Punjab was Mahan Singh of the Sukerchakia *misl.* His death that same year left the boy destined to become Sikhism's best-known statesman, Ranjit Singh, as his successor. A year later Shah Zaman, King of Kabul, recognized (confirmed) him as the possessor of Lahore.

For the next forty years Ranjit Singh dominated Sikh affairs. In 1802 he seized Amritsar and followed this by capturing Ludhiana (1806), Multan (1818), Kashmir (1819), Ladakh (1833) and Peshawar (1834). By the time of his death in June 1839 Ranjit was the only leader in India capable of offering a serious challenge to the East India Company.

By a treaty concluded in 1809 with the British, Ranjit had been confirmed as ruler of the tracts he had occupied south of the Sutlej, but the agreement had restricted him from seeking any further expansion to the north or west of the river. In spite of the terms of the treaty, the British remained suspicious of Ranjit's ultimate intentions. His steady policy of expansion frequently left apprehensions in the minds of the British - with whose interests Ranjit's own often clashed - that the Sikhs had secret ambitions against Company controlled territory. But it was to Ranjit's credit that he welded the Sikhs of the Punjab into an effective and unified fighting force, capable of resisting both the Afghans and the Marathas and able to stand up to British pressures. He inherited a loose alliance of fiercely independent chiefs, he left a disciplined and well equipped army of over fifty thousand men. He also left a well consolidated regional empire in the extreme northwest of India, roughly extending over the northern half of present-day Pakistan.

After the death of Ranjit the Sikh empire began to disintegrate as power passed from chief to chief in murderous rivalry. At the same time relationships with the British began to deteriorate. The treaty of 1809 no longer proved able to hold the peace, and the Sikh army attacked the British (1845-1846) only to be badly beaten in a series of confrontations. The Treaty of Lahore which followed this first Anglo-Sikh war reduced the Sikh army to a maximum of twenty thousand men and twelve thousand cavalry. It obliged the Sikhs to cede the Jallandar Doab and Kashmir to the British, and required them to pay an indemnity of fifty thousand pounds and accept a British resident at their court. In 1848 the Sikhs again revolted, and were again crushed. In 1849 the Punjab was annexed and from that time onward they came under British rule.

RULERS

Ranjit Singh
VS1856-1896/1799-1839AD

Kurruk Singh
VS1896-1897/1839-1840AD

Sher Singh
VS1897-1900/1840-1843AD

Dulip Singh
VS1900-1906/1843-1849AD

MINTS

Amritsar (Ambratsar) امبرت سر

Dera ديره

Derajat ديره جات

Kashmir كشمير or ਕਸਮੀਰ

Lahore لاهور

Multan ملتان

Nimak نمک

Pathankot

Peshawar پشاور

NOTE: Most coins struck after the accession of Ranjit Singh bear a large pipal leaf on one side, and have Persian or Gurmukhi (Punjabi) legends in the name of Gobind Singh, the tenth and last Guru of the Sikhs, 1675-1708AD. Earlier pieces are similar, but lack the pipal leaf. There is a great variety of coppers, and only representative types are catalogued here; many crude pieces were struck at the official and at unofficial mints, and bear illegible or semi-literate inscriptions. None of the coins bear the name of the Sikh ruler.

AMRITSAR MINT

First Copper Series

Persian legends. Various types.

1/2 PAISA

COPPER

KM#	Date	Year	Good	VG	Fine	VF
3	VS1897	(1840)	3.00	5.00	8.00	12.50

HEAVY PAISA

COPPER, 11.00-12.00 g
Rev: Pipal leaf and date.

KM#	Date	Year	Good	VG	Fine	VF
4	VS1880	(1823)	2.00	3.25	5.00	8.50
(4.1)	1881	(1824)	2.00	3.25	5.00	8.50
	1882	(1825)	2.00	3.25	5.00	8.50

1/4 ANNA

COPPER, 8.00-9.00 g
Obv: Date.
Rev: *Nanak Shahi*, denomination and date.

KM#	Date	Year	Good	VG	Fine	VF
5	VS1896	(1839)	3.00	5.00	8.00	12.50
(4.2)	1897	(1840)	3.00	5.00	8.00	12.50

2 PAISE

COPPER

KM#	Date	Year	Good	VG	Fine	VF
6	VS1880	(1823)	4.00	7.50	12.50	20.00

Second Copper Series

Gurmukhi legends. Obv: Pipal leaf in center.

HEAVY PAISA

COPPER, 11.00-12.00 g
Obv: Date in bottom line.

KM#	Date	Year	Good	VG	Fine	VF
7.1	VS1885	(1828)	1.50	3.00	5.00	8.00

NOTE: Date often off flan on normal strikes.

Rev: Cross.

KM#	Date	Year	Good	VG	Fine	VF
7.4	VS188x	(18xx)	1.50	3.00	5.00	8.00

Obv: Pipal leaf spray, mintname. Rev: Pipal leaf.

KM#	Date	Year	Good	VG	Fine	VF
7.12	ND	—	2.50	5.00	9.00	15.00

Obv: Pipal leaf spray, mintname. Rev: Quatrefoil.

KM#	Date	Year	Good	VG	Fine	VF
7.13	ND	—	2.50	5.00	9.00	15.00

Obv: Pipal leaf spray, mintname.
Rev: No control mark.

KM#	Date	Year	Good	VG	Fine	VF
7.14	ND	—	2.50	5.00	9.00	15.00

LIGHT PAISA

COPPER, 7.00-10.00 g
Similar to KM#7.1 but cruder, undated.

KM#	Date	Year	Good	VG	Fine	VF
7.1a	ND	—	1.00	2.00	3.50	6.00

Obv: Cross. Rev: Double line.

KM#	Date	Year	Good	VG	Fine	VF
7.10	ND	—	1.50	3.00	5.00	8.00

Rev: Banner w/tail end down.

KM#	Date	Year	Good	VG	Fine	VF
7.2	ND	—	1.75	3.50	6.00	10.00

Rev: Banner w/tail end up.

KM#	Date	Year	Good	VG	Fine	VF
7.9	ND	—	2.25	4.50	7.50	12.50

Rev: Flower.

KM#	Date	Year	Good	VG	Fine	VF
7.3	ND	—	1.50	3.00	5.00	8.00

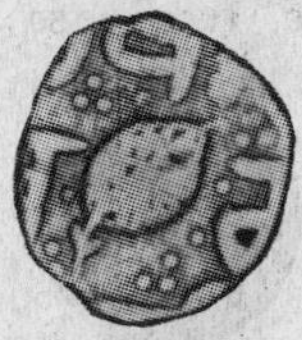

Rev: Trident.

KM#	Date	Year	Good	VG	Fine	VF
7.5	ND	—	1.50	3.00	5.00	8.00

Rev: Katar right.

KM#	Date	Year	Good	VG	Fine	VF
7.6	ND	—	1.75	3.50	6.00	10.00

Rev: Katar left.

KM#	Date	Year	Good	VG	Fine	VF
7.11	ND	—	1.75	3.50	6.00	10.00

Rev: Lion.

KM#	Date	Year	Good	VG	Fine	VF
7.7	ND	—	3.00	6.00	10.00	17.50

Rev: Pipal leaf spray.

KM#	Date	Year	Good	VG	Fine	VF
7.8	ND	—	2.25	4.50	7.50	12.50

2 PAISE

COPPER

KM#	Date	Year	Good	VG	Fine	VF
8.1	VS1876	(1819)	12.50	25.00	40.00	65.00

KM#	Date	Year	Good	VG	Fine	VF
8.2	VS—	—	6.00	12.00	20.00	35.00

KM#	Date	Year	Good	VG	Fine	VF
8.3	VS188x	(18xx)	3.75	7.50	12.00	20.00

MULTIPLE PAISAS

(Not struck for general circulation)

COPPER, 38.00-40.00 g

KM#	Date	Year	Good	VG	Fine	VF
9.1	VS1885	(1828)	—	—	Rare	—

Rev: Banner.

KM#	Date	Year	Good	VG	Fine	VF
9.2	—	—	—	—	Rare	—

Rev: Cross.

KM#	Date	Year	Good	VG	Fine	VF
9.3	—	—	—	—	Rare	—

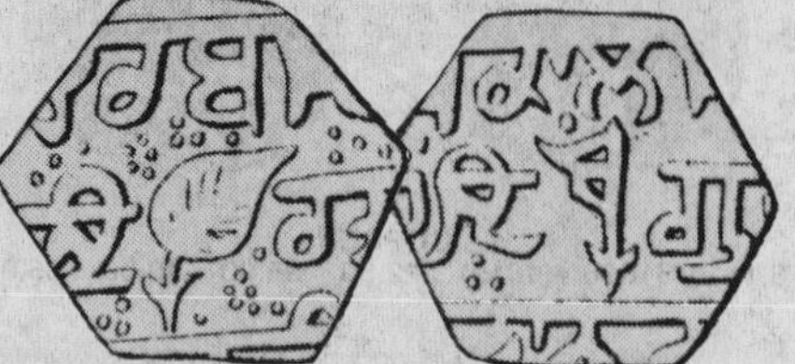

Rev: Banner ?

KM#	Date	Year	Good	VG	Fine	VF
9.4	—	—	—	—	Rare	—

Third Copper Series

Persian and Gurmukhi legends.

FALUS

COPPER

KM#	Date	Year	Good	VG	Fine	VF
10.1	—	—	6.00	10.00	15.00	25.00

KM#	Date	Year	Good	VG	Fine	VF
10.2	VS1900	(1843)	2.75	5.00	7.50	12.50
	1901	(1844)	2.75	5.00	7.50	12.50
	ND	—	2.75	5.00	7.50	12.50

KM#	Date	Year	Good	VG	Fine	VF
10.3	—	—	6.00	10.00	15.00	25.00

KM#	Date	Year	Good	VG	Fine	VF
10.4	—	—	6.00	10.00	15.00	25.00

Silver Series

1/8 RUPEE

SILVER, 1.34-1.45 g
Rev: Dated VS1884.

KM#	Date	Year	VG	Fine	VF	XF
17.1	VS(18)95	(1838)	10.00	16.00	21.50	30.00

Rev: Dated VS1885.

KM#	Date	Year	VG	Fine	VF	XF
17.2	VS(18)99	(1842)	10.00	16.00	21.50	30.00
	1900	(1843)	10.00	16.00	21.50	30.00
	1903	(1846)	10.00	16.00	21.50	30.00

1/4 RUPEE

SILVER, 15mm, 2.68-2.90 g

KM#	Date	Year	VG	Fine	VF	XF
18.1	VS(18)80	(1823)	10.00	16.00	21.50	30.00

Rev: Dated VS1884.

KM#	Date	Year	VG	Fine	VF	XF
18.2	VS(18)85	(1828)	8.50	13.50	20.00	28.50
	(18)86	(1829)	8.50	13.50	20.00	28.50
	(18)89	(1832)	8.50	13.50	20.00	28.50
	(18)95	(1838)	8.50	13.50	20.00	28.50

Rev: Dated VS1885.

KM#	Date	Year	VG	Fine	VF	XF
18.3	VS(18)93	(1836)	8.50	13.50	20.00	28.50
	(18)94	(1837)	8.50	13.50	20.00	27.50
	(18)95	(1838)	8.50	13.50	20.00	27.50
	(18)97	(1840)	8.50	13.50	20.00	27.50
	(18)98	(1841)	8.50	13.50	20.00	27.50
	(18)99	(1842)	8.50	13.50	20.00	27.50
	1900	(1843)	8.50	13.50	20.00	27.50
	1901	(1844)	8.50	13.50	20.00	27.50
	1902	(1845)	8.50	13.50	20.00	27.50
	1903	(1846)	8.50	13.50	20.00	27.50

Obv. leg: Gurmukhi *Sate* below chhatra.

KM#	Date	Year	VG	Fine	VF	XF
18.4	VS1903	(1846)	8.50	13.50	20.00	27.50
	VS1904	(1847)	8.50	13.50	20.00	27.50

1/2 RUPEE

 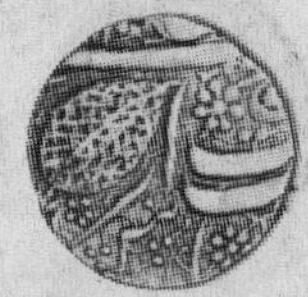

SILVER, 5.35-5.80 g
Rev: Actual date.

KM#	Date	Year	VG	Fine	VF	XF
19.1	VS1880	(1823)	7.00	11.00	16.50	25.00

Rev: Dated VS1884.

KM#	Date	Year	VG	Fine	VF	XF
19.2	VS(18)85	(1828)	7.00	11.00	16.50	25.00
	(18)92	(1835)	7.00	11.00	16.50	25.00
	(18)93	(1836)	7.00	11.00	16.50	25.00
	(18)95	(1838)	7.00	11.00	16.50	25.00
	(18)99	(1842)	7.00	11.00	16.50	25.00

Rev: Dated VS1885.

KM#	Date	Year	VG	Fine	VF	XF
19.3	VS(18)93	(1836)	7.00	11.00	16.50	25.00
	(18)97	(1840)	7.00	11.00	16.50	25.00
	(18)98	(1841)	7.00	11.00	16.50	25.00
	(18)99	(1842)	7.00	11.00	16.50	25.00
	1900	(1843)	7.00	11.00	16.50	25.00
	1901	(1844)	7.00	11.00	16.50	25.00
	1902	(1845)	7.00	11.00	16.50	25.00
	1903	(1846)	7.00	11.00	16.50	25.00
	1904	(1847)	7.00	11.00	16.50	25.00
	1905	(1848)	7.00	11.00	16.50	25.00

NOTE: Some specimens dated 1903 have SATE.

Obv. leg: Gurmukri *Om*.

KM#	Date	Year	VG	Fine	VF	XF
19.4	VS(18)97	—	8.50	13.50	20.00	27.50

KM#	Date	Year	VG	Fine	VF	XF
19.5	VS1902	—	10.00	16.00	21.50	30.00

RUPEE

SILVER, 10.70-11.60 g
Obv: Second legend arrangement.
Rev: Katar.

KM#	Date	Year	VG	Fine	VF	XF
A20.2	VS1859	(1802)	16.50	23.50	32.50	45.00
	1862	(1805)	16.50	23.50	32.50	45.00
	1863	(1806)	16.50	23.50	32.50	45.00
	1864	(1807)	16.50	23.50	32.50	45.00
	1865	(1808)	16.50	23.50	32.50	45.00

NOTE: Earlier dates (VS1841-1854) exist for this type.

Rev: Mintname and date.

KM#	Date	Year	VG	Fine	VF	XF
20.1	VS1858	(1801)	10.00	16.00	21.50	30.00
	1859	(1802)	10.00	16.00	21.50	30.00
	1860	(1803)	7.00	11.00	16.50	25.00
	1861	(1804)	7.00	11.00	16.50	25.00
	1863	(1806)	7.00	11.00	16.50	25.00
	1864	(1807)	7.00	11.00	16.50	25.00
	1865	(1808)	6.50	10.00	15.00	22.50
	1866	(1809)	6.50	10.00	15.00	22.50
	1867	(1810)	6.50	10.00	15.00	22.50
	1868	(1811)	6.50	10.00	15.00	22.50
	1869	(1812)	6.50	10.00	15.00	22.50
	1870	(1813)	6.50	10.00	15.00	22.50
	1871	(1814)	6.50	10.00	15.00	22.50
	1872	(1815)	6.50	10.00	15.00	22.50
	1873	(1816)	6.50	10.00	15.00	22.50
	1874	(1817)	6.50	10.00	15.00	22.50
	1875	(1818)	6.50	10.00	15.00	22.50
	1876	(1819)	6.50	10.00	15.00	22.50
	1877	(1820)	6.50	10.00	15.00	22.50
	1878	(1821)	6.50	10.00	15.00	22.50
	1879	(1822)	6.50	10.00	15.00	22.50

NOTE: Earlier dates (VS1848-1857) exist for this type.
NOTE: Double lines below dates exist for some 1869, 1870 and 1871 coins and are considered rare.

Larger flan

KM#	Date	Year	VG	Fine	VF	XF
20.5	VS1880	(1823)	6.50	10.00	15.00	22.50
	1881	(1824)	6.50	10.00	15.00	22.50
	1882	(1825)	6.50	10.00	15.00	22.50
	1883	(1826)	6.50	10.00	15.00	22.50
	1884	(1827)	6.50	10.00	15.00	22.50
	1885	(1828)	—	—	Rare	—
	1888	(1831)	—	—	Rare	—
	1889	(1832)	—	—	Rare	—

NOTE: The mint symbols appear to change frequently in the above series.

Obv: Hand. Rev: Dotted leaf.

KM#	Date	Year	VG	Fine	VF	XF
20.2	VS1859	(1802)	11.50	17.50	23.50	33.50

Obv: Double oval. Rev: Dotted leaf.

KM#	Date	Year	VG	Fine	VF	XF
20.3	VS1858	(1801)	11.50	17.50	23.50	33.50
	1859	(1802)	11.50	17.50	23.50	33.50

NOTE: Also exists without special mark on obv.

The "Mora" Rupee
Rev: Branches w/berries.

KM#	Date	Year	VG	Fine	VF	XF
20.4	VS1858	(1801)	17.50	25.00	35.00	50.00
(YB20)	1859	(1802)	17.50	25.00	35.00	50.00
	1860	(1803)	17.50	25.00	35.00	50.00
	1861	(1804)	17.50	25.00	35.00	50.00
	1862	(1805)	17.50	25.00	35.00	50.00

KM#	Date	Year	VG	Fine	VF	XF
20.5	1862	(1805)	17.50	25.00	35.00	50.00
(YD20)	1863	(1806)	17.50	25.00	35.00	50.00

The "Arisi" Rupee
Rev: Symbol said to be mirror.

KM#	Date	Year	VG	Fine	VF	XF
20.6	VS1862	(1805)	17.50	25.00	35.00	50.00
(YC20)	1863	(1806)	17.50	25.00	35.00	50.00

Obv: Partial or full actual dates.
Rev: VS1884 fixed.

KM#	Date	Year	VG	Fine	VF	XF
21	VS(18)85	(1828)	7.00	11.00	16.50	25.00
	(18)86	(1829)	7.00	11.00	16.50	25.00
	(18)87	(1830)	7.00	11.00	16.50	25.00
	(18)88	(1831)	7.00	11.00	16.50	25.00
	(18)89	(1832)	7.00	11.00	16.50	25.00
	(18)90	(1833)	7.00	11.00	16.50	25.00
	(18)91	(1834)	7.00	11.00	16.50	25.00
	(18)92	(1835)	7.00	11.00	16.50	25.00
	(18)93	(1836)	7.00	11.00	16.50	25.00
	(18)94	(1837)	— Reported, not confirmed			
	(18)95	(1838)	7.00	11.00	16.50	25.00
	(18)96	(1839)	7.00	11.00	16.50	25.00
	(18)97	(1840)	7.00	11.00	16.50	25.00
	(18)98/7	(1841)	7.00	11.50	16.50	25.00
	(18)98	(1841)	7.00	11.50	16.50	25.00
	(18)99	(1842)	7.00	11.50	16.50	25.00
	1900	(1843)	7.00	11.50	16.50	25.00
	1901	(1844)	7.00	11.50	16.50	25.00
	1903	(1846)	7.00	11.50	16.50	25.00
	1904	(1847)	7.00	11.50	16.50	25.00

Obv: Partial actual dates.
Rev: VS1885 fixed.

KM#	Date	Year	VG	Fine	VF	XF
22.1	VS(18)93	(1836)	7.50	12.50	18.50	27.50
(22.3)	VS(18)94	(1837)	7.50	12.50	18.50	27.50

KM#	Date	Year	VG	Fine	VF	XF
(22.3)	(18)95	(1838)	6.00	9.00	13.50	20.00
	(18)96	(1839)	6.00	9.00	13.50	20.00
	(18)97	(1840)	6.00	9.00	13.50	20.00

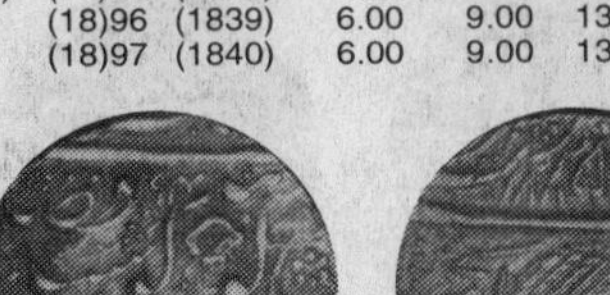 

Rev: Katar.

KM#	Date	Year	VG	Fine	VF	XF
22.2	VS(18)94	(1837)	8.50	13.50	20.00	28.50
	(18)98	(1841)	6.00	9.00	13.50	20.00

Obv. Nagari: *Om.*

KM#	Date	Year	VG	Fine	VF	XF
22.4	VS(18)97	(1840)	10.00	16.00	21.50	30.00

Obv: Trisul (trident).

KM#	Date	Year	VG	Fine	VF	XF
22.5	VS(18)98	(1841)	10.00	16.00	21.50	30.00
	(18)99	(1842)	10.00	16.00	21.50	30.00

Obv: Chhatra (umbrella).

KM#	Date	Year	VG	Fine	VF	XF
22.6	VS(18)99	(1842)	6.50	10.00	15.00	22.50
	1900	(1843)	6.50	10.00	15.00	22.50
	1901	(1844)	6.50	10.00	15.00	22.50

Obv: 3-lobed leaf.
Similar to 1/2 Rupee, KM#19.5.

KM#	Date	Year	VG	Fine	VF	XF
22.7	VS1902	(1845)	8.50	13.50	20.00	28.50

Obv: Pataka (banner).

KM#	Date	Year	VG	Fine	VF	XF
22.8	VS1902	(1845)	8.50	13.50	20.00	28.50
	1903	(1846)	8.50	13.50	20.00	28.50

Obv: Gurmukhi *Sate* beneath chhatra.

KM#	Date	Year	VG	Fine	VF	XF
22.9	VS1903	(1846)	8.50	13.50	20.00	28.50
	1904	(1847)	8.50	13.50	20.00	28.50

Obv: Lazy W beneath chhatra.

KM#	Date	Year	VG	Fine	VF	XF
22.10	VS1905	(1848)	7.50	12.50	18.50	27.50
	1906	(1849)	21.50	35.00	50.00	75.00

Obv: Nagari *Shiva.*

KM#	Date	Year	VG	Fine	VF	XF
22.11	VS1905	(1848)	10.00	16.00	21.50	30.00

Mule. Obv: Dot cluster. Rev: KM#21.

KM#	Date	Year	VG	Fine	VF	XF
22.12	VS1905	VS1884	12.50	20.00	27.50	37.50

NAZARANA RUPEE

SILVER, 10.70-11.60 g

KM#	Date	Year	VG	Fine	VF	XF
20.1a	VS1873	(1816)	1000.	1600.	2300.	—

1/4 MOHUR

GOLD

KM#	Date	Year	VG	Fine	VF	XF
27	VS(18)95	(1838)	—	—	Rare	—
	(18)97	(1840)	—	—	Rare	—

1/2 MOHUR

GOLD

KM#	Date	Year	VG	Fine	VF	XF
A25	VS1877	(1820)	—	—	Rare	—

MOHUR

GOLD, 10.70-11.40 g
Rev: W/pipal leaf.

KM#	Date	Year	VG	Fine	VF	XF
24.1	VS1858	(1801)	185.00	250.00	350.00	475.00
	1861	(1804)	185.00	250.00	350.00	475.00
	1882	(1825)	185.00	250.00	350.00	475.00

Rev: W/o pipal leaf.

KM#	Date	Year	VG	Fine	VF	XF
24.2	VS1868	(1811)	185.00	250.00	350.00	475.00
	1901	(1844)	185.00	250.00	350.00	475.00

"Mora" type similar to 1 Rupee, KM#20.4.

KM#	Date	Year	VG	Fine	VF	XF
23	VS1862	(1805)	—	—	Rare	—

"Arisi" type similar to 1 Rupee, KM#20.5.

KM#	Date	Year	VG	Fine	VF	XF
26	VS1862	(1805)	—	—	Rare	—
	1863	(1806)	—	—	Rare	—

DOUBLE MOHUR

GOLD

KM#	Date	Year	VG	Fine	VF	XF
25	VS1884	(18)85	—		Rare	—

KASHMIR MINT

PAISA

COPPER
Gurmukhi and Persian legends

KM#	Date	Year	Good	VG	Fine	VF
40.1	VS2078 (sic)	—	4.50	7.50	12.50	20.00

Persian and Gurmukhi legends.

KM#	Date	Year	Good	VG	Fine	VF
40.2	ND	—	4.00	5.00	10.00	16.50

KM#	Date	Year	Good	VG	Fine	VF
40.3	VS188x	(18xx)	4.00	6.50	10.00	16.50

Persian legends, sword.

KM#	Date	Year	Good	VG	Fine	VF
41.1	VS1894	(1837)	3.00	5.00	8.00	15.00

Persian legends, rosette.

KM#	Date	Year	Good	VG	Fine	VF
41.2	ND	—	3.50	5.50	9.00	15.00

KM#	Date	Year	Good	VG	Fine	VF
41.3	VS1895	(1838)	4.00	6.50	10.00	16.50

KM#	Date	Year	Good	VG	Fine	VF
42	VS189x	(18xx)	4.00	6.50	10.00	16.50

1/4 RUPEE

SILVER, 2.75 g

KM#	Date	Year	VG	Fine	VF	XF
43	VS1898	(1841)	—	—	Rare	—

1/2 RUPEE

SILVER, 5.50 g

KM#	Date	Year	VG	Fine	VF	XF
44	ND	—	—	—	Rare	—

RUPEE

SILVER, 7.60 g
Gurmukhi legends

KM#	Date	Year	VG	Fine	VF	XF
45	VS1892	(1835)	—	—	Rare	—

NOTE: KM#45 is of light weight.

SILVER, 10.70-11.60 g
Obv: Flower spray. Rev: Date to right.

KM#	Date	Year	VG	Fine	VF	XF
46.1	VS1876	(1819)	7.50	12.50	18.50	27.50

Obv: Flower spray. Rev: Date divided horizontally.

KM#	Date	Year	VG	Fine	VF	XF
46.2	VS1876	(1819)	7.50	12.50	18.50	27.50

Obv: Flower spray.
Rev: Legend divided vertically, date at top.

KM#	Date	Year	VG	Fine	VF	XF
46.3	VS1877	(1820)	7.50	12.50	18.50	27.50
	1878	(1821)	7.50	12.50	18.50	27.50

Obv: Gurmukhi *Hara*.

KM#	Date	Year	VG	Fine	VF	XF
46.4	VS1878	(1821)	7.50	12.50	18.50	27.50
	1879	(1822)	7.50	12.50	18.50	27.50

Obv: Nagari *Om Sri*.

KM#	Date	Year	VG	Fine	VF	XF
46.5	VS1879	(1822)	10.00	15.00	21.50	30.00

Obv: Nagari *Haraji* or *Hara*.

KM#	Date	Year	VG	Fine	VF	XF
46.6	VS1879	(1822)	10.00	15.00	21.50	30.00

Rev: Sword across leaf stem.

KM#	Date	Year	VG	Fine	VF	XF
46.14	VS1880	(1823)	—	—	Rare	—

Obv: Floral symbol, 4-pointed star.

KM#	Date	Year	VG	Fine	VF	XF
46.7	VS1881	(1824)	7.50	12.50	18.50	27.50

Obv: Banner.

KM#	Date	Year	VG	Fine	VF	XF
46.8	VS1881	(1824)	7.50	12.50	18.50	27.50
	1882	(1825)	7.50	12.50	18.50	27.50
	1883	(1826)	7.50	12.50	18.50	27.50

Obv: Dotted chakra.

KM#	Date	Year	VG	Fine	VF	XF
46.9	VS1883	(1826)	7.50	12.50	18.50	27.50

NOTE: Some also have Persian *Kaf*.

Obv: Persian *Ram* and *Kaf*.

KM#	Date	Year	VG	Fine	VF	XF
46.10	VS—	—	7.50	12.50	18.50	27.50

Obv: Persian letter.

KM#	Date	Year	VG	Fine	VF	XF
46.11	VS1885	(1828)	7.50	12.50	18.50	27.50
	1887	(1830)	7.50	12.50	18.50	27.50

Rev: Cross and letter form "I".

KM#	Date	Year	VG	Fine	VF	XF
46.12	VS1886	(1829)	7.50	12.50	18.50	27.50

Obv: Sprig

KM#	Date	Year	VG	Fine	VF	XF
46.15	VS1887	(1830)	15.00	21.50	30.00	40.00

Rev: Letter in field, *Bha*.

KM#	Date	Year	VG	Fine	VF	XF
46.13	VS1887	(1830)	7.50	12.50	18.50	27.50
	1888	(1831)	7.50	12.50	18.50	27.50

Rev: Sprig

KM#	Date	Year	VG	Fine	VF	XF
46.16	VS1887	(1830)	7.50	12.50	18.50	27.50

Rev: Circled date.

KM#	Date	Year	VG	Fine	VF	XF
48	VS1884	(1827)	15.00	21.50	30.00	40.00

Obv: Date.

KM#	Date	Year	VG	Fine	VF	XF
49	VS1889	(1832)	10.00	15.00	21.50	30.00
	1890	(1833)	10.00	15.00	21.50	30.00
	Rev: Lion to right of leaf.					
A50	VS1890	(1833)	—	—	Rare	—
	Rev: Date at top.					
B50	VS1891	(1834)	17.50	25.00	35.00	50.00

Obv: Sword through circle.

KM#	Date	Year	VG	Fine	VF	XF
50	VS1892	(1835)	10.00	15.00	21.50	30.00
	1893	(1836)	10.00	15.00	21.50	30.00
	1894	(1837)	10.00	15.00	21.50	30.00
	1895	(1838)	10.00	15.00	21.50	30.00
	1896	(1839)	10.00	15.00	21.50	30.00
	1897	(1840)	10.00	15.00	21.50	30.00
	1898	(1841)	10.00	15.00	21.50	30.00

Rev: Outlined leaf.

KM#	Date	Year	VG	Fine	VF	XF
51	VS1894	(1837)	22.50	35.00	47.50	65.00
	1895	(1838)	22.50	35.00	47.50	65.00
	1896	(1839)	22.50	35.00	47.50	65.00
	1897	(1840)	22.50	35.00	47.50	65.00

19mm
Obv: Persian letter *Sin* in place of sword.
Rev: Regular pipal leaf.

KM#	Date	Year	VG	Fine	VF	XF
52	VS1898	(1841)	12.50	18.50	25.00	35.00
	1899	(1842)	12.50	18.50	25.00	35.00
	1900	(1843)	12.50	18.50	25.00	35.00
	1901	(1844)	12.50	18.50	25.00	35.00
	1902	(1845)	12.50	18.50	25.00	35.00
	1903	(1846)	12.50	18.50	25.00	35.00

LAHORE MINT

Dar-us-Sultanat

PAISA

COPPER

KM#	Date	Year	Good	VG	Fine	VF
60	VS1880	(1823)	4.00	6.50	10.00	15.00
	1881	(1824)	4.00	6.50	10.00	15.00
	1888	(1831)	4.00	6.50	10.00	15.00

1/2 RUPEE

SILVER, 18mm, 5.35-5.80 g

KM#	Date	Year	VG	Fine	VF	XF
62	VS1864	(1807)	16.50	23.50	32.50	45.00
	1889	(1832)	16.50	23.50	32.50	45.00

NOTE: Earlier dates (VS1828-1847) exist for this type.

In the name of Guru Gobind Singh

RUPEE

SILVER, 10.70-11.60 g
Actual VS years.

KM#	Date	Year	VG	Fine	VF	XF
66.1	VS1858	(1801)	10.00	15.00	21.50	30.00
	1859	(1802)	10.00	15.00	21.50	30.00
	1860	(1803)	10.00	15.00	21.50	30.00
	1861	(1804)	10.00	15.00	21.50	30.00
	1862	(1805)	10.00	15.00	21.50	30.00
	1863	(1806)	10.00	15.00	21.50	30.00
	1864	(1807)	10.00	15.00	21.50	30.00
	1865	(1808)	10.00	15.00	21.50	30.00
	1866	(1809)	10.00	15.00	21.50	30.00
	1867	(1810)	10.00	15.00	21.50	30.00
	1868	(1811)	10.00	15.00	21.50	30.00
	1869	(1812)	10.00	15.00	21.50	30.00
	1870	(1813)	10.00	15.00	21.50	30.00
	1871	(1814)	10.00	15.00	21.50	30.00
	1872	(1815)	10.00	15.00	21.50	30.00
	1873	(1816)	10.00	15.00	21.50	30.00
	1874	(1817)	10.00	15.00	21.50	30.00
	1875	(1818)	10.00	15.00	21.50	30.00
	1876	(1819)	10.00	15.00	21.50	30.00
	1877	(1820)	10.00	15.00	21.50	30.00
	1878	(1821)	10.00	15.00	21.50	30.00
	1879	(1822)	10.00	15.00	21.50	30.00
	1880	(1823)	10.00	15.00	21.50	30.00
	1881	(1824)	10.00	15.00	21.50	30.00
	1882	(1825)	10.00	15.00	21.50	30.00
	1883	(1826)	10.00	15.00	21.50	30.00
	1884	(1827)	10.00	15.00	21.50	30.00
	1885	(1828)	10.00	15.00	21.50	30.00
	1887	(1830)	10.00	15.00	21.50	30.00

NOTE: Earlier dates (VS1856-1857) exist for this type.

Obv: Actual date. Rev: VS1884.

KM#	Date	Year	VG	Fine	VF	XF
66.2	VS18(87)	(1831)	10.00	15.00	21.50	30.00
	18(88)	(1831)	10.00	15.00	21.50	30.00
	(18)89	(1832)	10.00	15.00	21.50	30.00
	(18)90	(1833)	10.00	15.00	21.50	30.00
	(18)91	(1834)	10.00	15.00	21.50	30.00
	(18)92	(1835)	10.00	15.00	21.50	30.00
	(18)93	(1836)	10.00	15.00	21.50	30.00
	(18)94	(1837)	10.00	15.00	21.50	30.00

Rev: VS1885

KM#	Date	Year	VG	Fine	VF	XF
67	VS(18)93	(1836)	10.00	15.00	21.50	30.00
	VS(18)94	(1837)	10.00	15.00	21.50	30.00
	(18)95	(1838)	10.00	15.00	21.50	30.00
	(18)96	(1839)	10.00	15.00	21.50	30.00
	1902	(1845)	10.00	15.00	21.50	30.00
	1903	(1846)	10.00	15.00	21.50	30.00

Rev: Ranjit Singh, Guru Nanak, date VS1885.

KM#	Date	Year	VG	Fine	VF	XF
68	VS(18)93	(1836)	—	—	Rare	—

MOHUR

GOLD, 10.85 g

KM#	Date	Year	VG	Fine	VF	XF
69	VS1884	(1827)	—	—	Rare	—

MULTAN MINT

PAISA

COPPER

KM#	Date	Year	Good	VG	Fine	VF
77	VS1875	(1818)	3.50	6.00	10.00	17.50
	1878	(1821)	3.50	6.00	10.00	17.50

NOTE: Also found with botched or fictitious dates.

DOUBLE PAISA

COPPER

KM#	Date	Year	Good	VG	Fine	VF
78	VS1904	(1847)	35.00	50.00	70.00	100.00

1/2 RUPEE

SILVER

KM#	Date	Year	VG	Fine	VF	XF
81	VS1880	(1823)	20.00	32.00	45.00	60.00

RUPEE

SILVER, 10.70-11.60 g
Obv: Plain. Rev: Pipal leaf.

KM#	Date	Year	VG	Fine	VF	XF
84	VS1875	(1818)	15.00	21.50	30.00	40.00
	1876	(1819)	15.00	21.50	30.00	40.00
	1877	(1820)	15.00	21.50	30.00	40.00
	1878	(1821)	15.00	21.50	30.00	40.00
	1879	(1822)	15.00	21.50	30.00	40.00

Obv: Trident. Rev: Pipal leaf.

KM#	Date	Year	VG	Fine	VF	XF
85	VS1880	(1823)	15.00	21.50	30.00	40.00
	1881	(1824)	15.00	21.50	30.00	40.00
	1882	(1825)	15.00	21.50	30.00	40.00
	1883	(1826)	15.00	21.50	30.00	40.00
	1884	(1827)	15.00	21.50	30.00	40.00

Obv: Flower. Rev: Pipal leaf.

KM#	Date	Year	VG	Fine	VF	XF
86.1	VS1885	(1828)	12.50	18.50	25.00	35.00
	1886	(1829)	12.50	18.50	25.00	35.00
	1887	(1830)	12.50	18.50	25.00	35.00
	1888	(1831)	12.50	18.50	25.00	35.00
	1890	(1832)	12.50	18.50	25.00	35.00
	1891	(1834)	12.50	18.50	25.00	35.00
	1892	(1835)	12.50	18.50	25.00	35.00
	1893	(1836)	12.50	18.50	25.00	35.00
	1894	(1837)	12.50	18.50	25.00	35.00
	1895	(1838)	12.50	18.50	25.00	35.00
	1896	(1839)	12.50	18.50	25.00	35.00
	1897	(1840)	12.50	18.50	25.00	35.00
	1898	(1841)	12.50	18.50	25.00	35.00
	1899	(1842)	12.50	18.50	25.00	35.00
	1900	(1843)	12.50	18.50	25.00	35.00
	1901	(1844)	12.50	18.50	25.00	35.00
	1902	(1845)	12.50	18.50	25.00	35.00
	1904	(1847)	12.50	18.50	25.00	35.00
	1905	(1848)	12.50	18.50	25.00	35.00

NAZARANA RUPEE

SILVER, 10.70-11.60 g

KM#	Date	Year	VG	Fine	VF	XF
86.2	VS1896	(1839)	50.00	75.00	110.00	150.00

GOLD RUPEE

GOLD, 0.57 g

KM#	Date	Year	VG	Fine	VF	XF
87	VS1905	(1848)	17.50	25.00	35.00	50.00

NOTE: Struck by Diwan Mulraj (April 1848 - Jan. 1849/ VS1905).

1/5 MOHUR

GOLD, 2.21 g

KM#	Date	Year	VG	Fine	VF	XF
A87	VS1885/96	(1839)	—	—	Rare	—

NIMAK MINT

(Pind Dadan Khan)

RUPEE

SILVER, 10.70-11.60 g

KM#	Date	Year	VG	Fine	VF	XF
88	VS1904	(1847)	85.00	140.00	220.00	325.00
	1905	(1848)	85.00	140.00	220.00	325.00

Obv: Nagari *Ram Jim*.

KM#	Date	Year	VG	Fine	VF	XF
89	VS1905	(1848)	—	—	Rare	—

PESHAWAR MINT

FALUS

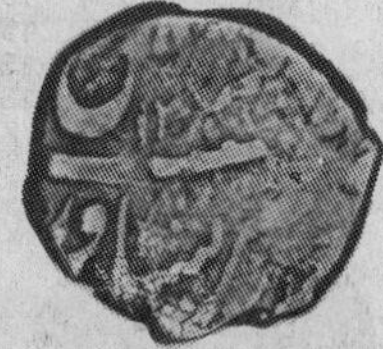

COPPER
Rev: Persian leg.

KM#	Date	Year	Good	VG	Fine	VF
93.1	AH1248	—	3.00	5.00	7.50	12.50
	1249	—	3.00	5.00	7.50	12.50

Obv: Pipal leaf, mintname. Rev. leg: *Shah*.

KM#	Date	Year	Good	VG	Fine	VF
93.2	—	—	4.00	6.00	9.00	14.00

Rev: Gurmukhi leg. & Nagari date.

KM#	Date	Year	Good	VG	Fine	VF
94	VS1891	(1834)	6.00	10.00	15.00	22.50

KM#	Date	Year	Good	VG	Fine	VF
95	ND or date off flan	—	3.00	5.00	7.50	12.50

KM#	Date	Year	Good	VG	Fine	VF
96	AH126x	—	3.00	5.00	7.50	12.50

COPPER

KM#	Date	Year	Good	VG	Fine	VF
97 (90)	VS1894	(1837)	7.50	12.50	20.00	35.00

RUPEE

SILVER, 8.50 g
Rev: Plain pipal leaf.

KM#	Date	Year	VG	Fine	VF	XF
98.1	VS1891	(1834)	13.50	23.50	32.50	45.00

Rev: Dotted outline around pipal leaf.

KM#	Date	Year	VG	Fine	VF	XF
98.2	VS1892	(1835)	13.00	22.00	30.00	42.50
	1893	(1836)	13.00	22.00	30.00	42.50
	1894	(1837)	13.00	22.00	30.00	42.50

NOTE: Some specimens dated VS1894 weigh 10.50-11.00 g.

UNCERTAIN MINTS

RUPEE

SILVER, 10.70-11.60 g
Obv: Trident. Rev: Lion.
Bearing name of "Fateh Singh Ahluwalia"

KM#	Date	Year	VG	Fine	VF	XF
99	VS1862	(1805)	100.00	150.00	200.00	275.00

KM#	Date	Year	VG	Fine	VF	XF
72	VS1880	(1823)	—	—	Rare	—

SIKH FEUDATORY STATES

DERA

Sikh Protectorate, 1819-1847AD

Dera is known more fully as Dera Ghazi Khan, as distinguished from Dera Ismail Khan (Derajat).

PAISA

COPPER, 7.00-8.00 g
Obv: Flower and pipal leaf, mintname, date above.

KM#	Date	Year	Good	VG	Fine	VF
100	VS1892	(1835)	4.00	6.00	9.00	14.00

KM#	Date	Year	Good	VG	Fine	VF
101	VS1896	(1839)	3.00	5.00	7.50	11.50
	1898	(1841)	3.00	5.00	7.50	11.50
	ND	—	2.75	4.00	5.50	8.00

RUPEE

SILVER, 10.70-11.60 g

KM#	Date	Year	VG	Fine	VF	XF
102	VS1884/904	—	—	—	Rare	—

DERAJAT

Sikh Protectorate, 1819-1847AD

Derajat was the region centered about Dera Ismail Khan where the mint was presumably located.

NOTE: There are many varieties of copper coins, only a sample of which are listed below.

PAISA

COPPER
Obv: *Rayij*. Mintname: *Derajat*.

KM#	Date	Year	Good	VG	Fine	VF
105	AH1241	—	3.25	5.00	8.50	13.50
	1242	—	3.25	5.00	8.50	13.50

Obv: *Rayij*. Rev: *Samadi* monogram.

KM#	Date	Year	Good	VG	Fine	VF
106	AH124x	—	4.00	6.25	10.00	16.50

Obv: *Sahih*. Rev: Mintname & date.

KM#	Date	Year	Good	VG	Fine	VF
108	AH1252	—	3.50	5.50	9.00	15.00

Obv: Funny lion right, AH date.

KM#	Date	Year	Good	VG	Fine	VF
110	AH1254	—	—	—	—	—

Obv: Lion left, AH date.

KM#	Date	Year	Good	VG	Fine	VF
111.1	AH1246	—	2.25	4.00	6.50	10.00
	1247	—	2.25	4.00	6.50	10.00
	1249	—	2.25	4.00	6.50	10.00
	1254	—	2.25	4.00	6.50	10.00
	1261	—	2.25	4.00	6.50	10.00
	1262	—	2.25	4.00	6.50	10.00
	1265	—	2.25	4.00	6.50	10.00
	1267	—	2.25	4.00	6.50	10.00
	1276	—	2.25	4.00	6.50	10.00

Obv: Lion right, AH date

KM#	Date	Year	Good	VG	Fine	VF
111.2	AH1254	—	3.50	5.00	9.00	13.50

Obv: Horse, AH date

KM#	Date	Year	Good	VG	Fine	VF
111.3	AH1252	—	5.00	7.50	11.00	16.00

Obv: *Fath*. Rev: Leaf.

KM#	Date	Year	Good	VG	Fine	VF
112	—	—	2.75	4.50	7.50	11.50

Obv: Lion right.

KM#	Date	Year	Good	VG	Fine	VF
113	VS1793 (error, for 1893)	(1836)	3.25	5.00	8.00	13.50

Similar to 1 Rupee, KM#120.

KM#	Date	Year	Good	VG	Fine	VF
114	VS189x	(18xx)	4.00	6.00	10.00	15.00

RUPEE

SILVER, 10.70-11.60 g
Obv: Date below Gurmukhi letter.
Rev: Neat leaf.

KM#	Date	Year	VG	Fine	VF	XF
119	VS1892	(1835)	25.00	37.50	50.00	70.00
	1893	(1836)	25.00	37.50	50.00	70.00
	1894	(1837)	25.00	37.50	50.00	70.00

Obv: Date above Gurmukhi letter.
Rev: Crude leaf.

KM#	Date	Year	VG	Fine	VF	XF
120	VS1892	(1835)	20.00	31.50	42.50	60.00
	1893	(1836)	20.00	31.50	42.50	60.00
	1894	(1837)	20.00	31.50	42.50	60.00
	1895	(1838)	20.00	31.50	42.50	60.00
	1896	(1839)	20.00	31.50	42.50	60.00
	1897	(1840)	20.00	31.50	42.50	60.00
	1898	(1841)	20.00	31.50	42.50	60.00
	1899	(1842)	20.00	31.50	42.50	60.00
	1900	(1843)	20.00	31.50	42.50	60.00
	1901	(1844)	20.00	31.50	42.50	60.00
	1902	(1845)	20.00	31.50	42.50	60.00
	1905	(1848)	20.00	31.50	42.50	60.00

NAJIBABAD

Symbols: on obv. and on rev.

PAISA

 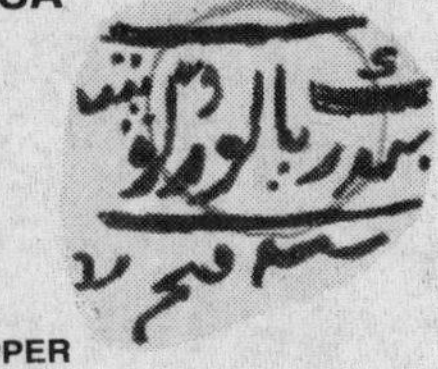

COPPER
Obv: Date.

KM#	Date	Year	Good	VG	Fine	VF
131	AH—	40	4.00	7.50	12.50	20.00
	124(3)	41	4.00	7.50	12.50	20.00

Legend of Shah Alam II

Obv:  Rev: 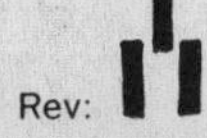

KM#	Date	Year	Good	VG	Fine	VF
132	AH1221	47	5.00	8.50	15.00	25.00

SIKKIM

A Kingdom located above northeast India between China, Bhutan and Nepal. In 1890 it became a British protectorate and later in 1949 it became a protectorate of India and in 1975, a state.

The Kingdom of Sikkim covers an area of some 2,800 sq. mi., and is situated on the southern slopes of the Himalayas, sandwiched between India to the south, Tibet to the north, Nepal to the west and Bhutan to the east. On its border with Nepal is the third highest mountain in the world, Kanchenjunga.

The Kingdom was founded in 1642 when Phuntsog Namgyal was proclaimed Chogyal or King. His ancestors had come to the Sikkim area about 150 years earlier from Eastern Tibet and, over the years had gained the confidence and respect of the indigenous inhabitants, the Lapchas. The descendents of Phuntsog Namgyal have ruled Sikkim ever since.

In the latter part of the eighteenth century Sikkim was subject to a number of Gurkha incursions, the impact of which was to place Sikkim on the British side in the Nepal War of 1815-1816. At the conclusion of this campaign Sikkim received certain tracts of land relinquished by Nepal and, in return, was obliged to accept British protection and control.

Initially Sikkim covered an area at least twice as large as it is now, but annexations by neighbouring powers reduced its size until in 1835 it reached its present area after the Chogyal "presented" the hills of Darjeeling to the British "out of friendship". In 1861 Sikkim became a protectorate of British India with the British exercising complete control over foreign affairs and defense and the Chogyal being in charge of all other internal matters.

India's independence brought little change to this situation until April 1973 when there was an uprising during which the Chogyal asked for the assistance of the Indian Government. An agreement has now been reached under which the Chogyal's powers are to be greatly reduced and the administration of Sikkim is to be headed by a "chief nomination of the Government of India."

For practically the entire period of its history, Sikkim had no coinage of its own and until the last century, trade was carried out by barter with taxes paid in kind. On the few occasions when inhabitants needed money, Tibetan coins, silver or gold bullion, or later, Indian coins were used. For only three or four years in the 1800's coins struck in Sikkim, and then they were struck by Nepalese immigrants. Since the beginning of the twentieth century Indian currency has circulated widely and exclusively.

Since the late 18th century the Nepalese have exhibited a strong urge to leave the overcrowded hills of Nepal and seek their fortunes elsewhere. Sikkim, being so close, was an obvious target for settlement and in order to prevent this, the seventh ruler of Sikkim, Tsugphud Namgyal (1793-1864) prohibited the settlement of Nepalese in Sikkim. This ban was effective until the early years of the reign of Thutob Namgyal (1874-1914) when certain powerful landowners realized that it was profitable to allow Nepalese to settle and work the land. Foremost of these were the brothers Kangsa Dewan and Phodong Lama. These two brothers struck a deal with two rich Nepalese traders, the brothers Lachmidas and Chandrabir Pradhan, under which a large tract of land which had recently been confiscated from a Sikkimese nobleman who had been convicted of embezzlement, was made over to the Nepalese brothers. This deal was strongly criticized by the Sikkimese people, but was supported by the British and finally the Kangsa brothers persuaded the Chogyal in 1878 to allow Nepalese settlement in "uninhabited and waste lands of Sikkim". Since then Nepalese immigrants have flooded into Sikkim and now comprise a majority of the population of the country.

It was the Pradhan brothers who were responsible for the Sikkim coinage. Soon after acquiring their lands they obtained licences to mine copper in a number of places, most important of which were Tuk Khani, Bhotan Khani near Rangpo and Pachay Khani. Some of this copper was sold in Nepal and Darjeeling, but some remained unsold, so in 1882 the brothers sought and obtained the permission of the Chogyal to strike copper coins. The minting was done in two places near the mines of Tuk Khani and Pachay Khani. Unfortunately for the Pradhan brothers, the Deputy Commissioner of Darjeeling forbade circulation of the Sikkim coins in the Darjeeling district and this made the coins unpopular among the people. The minting was not profitable and was discontinued in 1885.

The coins themselves are, except for the inscription, exact copies of the Nepalese paisa of Surendra Vira Vikrama Shah. They are very poorly struck and very few specimens have all the details of the design visible. The date is only very rarely legible. Three major types are known, but there is no indication of the mint of origin and die-links exist between the types. The coins are all intended to be the same denomination, one paisa, although the weights of individual specimens vary within the range 6.00 g to 4.00 g around a mean of about 5.20 g.

RULERS

Thutab Namgyel
VS1931-1968/1874-1911AD

THUTAB NAMGYEL

VS1931-1968/1874-1911AD

PAISA

COPPER, 20-22mm, 4.00-6.00 g
Obv: Leg. in 3 lines within square, date below.
Rev: Leg. in 3 lines within square.

KM#	Date	Year	Good	VG	Fine	VF
1	VS1940	(1883)	10.00	17.50	25.00	35.00
	1941	(1884)	5.00	8.50	12.50	17.50

Obv: Leg. in 4 lines within square, date below.

KM#	Date	Year	Good	VG	Fine	VF
2	VS1941	(1884)	10.00	17.50	25.00	35.00

Obv: Leg. in 3 lines within square, date below, w/*Ti* of *Sikimpati* on third line.

KM#	Date	Year	Good	VG	Fine	VF
3.1	VS1941	(1884)	5.00	8.50	12.50	17.50
	1942	(1885)	5.00	8.50	12.50	17.50

Rev. leg: *Sarkar* spelled incorrectly *Sakar*.

KM#	Date	Year	Good	VG	Fine	VF
3.2	VS1941	(1884)	5.00	8.50	12.50	17.50
	1942	(1885)	5.00	8.50	12.50	17.50

Rev. leg: *Sarkar* spelled incorrectly *Sikar*.

KM#	Date	Year	Good	VG	Fine	VF
3.3	VS1941	(1884)	5.00	8.50	12.50	17.50
	1942	(1885)	5.00	8.50	12.50	17.50

SIND

Sind has an extremely ancient historical record having been successively occupied and governed by the Indus Valley civilization (ca. 1500 BC), Alexander the Great (325BC) Chandragupta Maurya (ca.305BC), Asoka (274232BC) and others until the first Muslim inroads into Sind after 712AD. For almost the next three hundred years Sind was subject to Arab caliphs, after which it was conquered by Sultan Mahmud of Ghazni who conducted annual raids into India after 1000AD. Even then it remained semi-independent under local dynasties until, under Akbar (who was himself born at Umarkot in Sind), Sind became part of the Mughal empire.

The amirs of Hyderabad and Khairpur came into existence after the Mughal empire had started to disintegrate. Khairpur had been governed by the Kalhoras but in the 1780s they were overthrown by the Talpurs, a Baluchi family. Khairpur State was founded by Mir Sohrab Khan Talpur. In 1813 Khairpur ceased to pay tribute to Afghanistan and, in 1832(1247/48AH), it was recognized by the British as a separate state within Sind. In 1843, when the rest of Sind was annexed by the British in the aftermath of the Anglo-Sikh War, Khairpur remained separate and was only merged into the neighboring territory by its accession in 1947 to Pakistan.

AMIRS of HYDERABAD
Haidarabad Sind Mint

حیدرآباد سند

Mintname: Haidarabad Sind

In the name of Taimur Shah Durrani

RUPEE

SILVER, 10.70-11.60 g

KM#	Date	Year	VG	Fine	VF	XF
18	ND	—	17.50	25.00	35.00	50.00

SIND MINT

سند

RUPEE

SILVER, 11.00-11.50 g

KM#	Date	Year	VG	Fine	VF	XF
19	AH1239	—	12.00	20.00	28.00	40.00
	1240	—	12.00	20.00	28.00	40.00
	1241	—	12.00	20.00	28.00	40.00
	1242	—	12.00	20.00	28.00	40.00
	1245	—	12.00	20.00	28.00	40.00

KM#	Date	Year	VG	Fine	VF	XF
	Rev. mint mark: Star below *Sana*.					
19.2	ND	—	8.50	13.50	20.00	28.50
	Mint mark: Group of 6 dots.					
19.1	ND	—	8.50	13.50	20.00	28.50
	7.50-7.80 g					
20	AH1252	—	8.50	14.00	20.00	28.50
	1255	—	8.50	14.00	20.00	28.50
	1256	—	8.50	14.00	20.00	28.50
	1257	—	8.50	14.00	20.00	28.50
	Mint mark: 6-petal flower.					
20.1	ND	—	7.50	12.50	18.50	27.50
	Mint mark: Rosette of 6 dots.					
20.2	ND	—	7.50	12.50	18.50	27.50
	Mint mark: Cross.					
20.3	ND	—	8.50	14.00	20.00	28.50
	Mint mark: Sprig w/3 berries.					
20.4	ND	—	8.50	14.00	20.00	28.50
	Rev: W/o mark, w/Fath (Victory).					
21	ND	—	12.00	20.00	28.00	40.00

It is not known to which victory the reference is made.

AMIRS of KHAIRPUR

Formally independent
After AH1248/1832AD

RULERS

Nasir al-Din Muhammad
AH1239-1260/1823-1843 AD

Bhakhar Mint

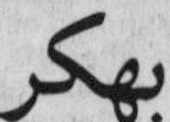
بهکر

Mintname: Bhakhar, Bakhar, or Bakkar

All Rupees bear 2 mint marks, one on the obverse at the top of the central cartouche, one on the reverse, usually to the upper right of the *J* of *Julus*.

In the name of Mahmud Shah Durrani

RUPEE

SILVER, 11.00-11.50 g
Obv. and rev: W/o mint marks.

C#	Date	Year	VG	Fine	VF	XF
10	AH1240	—	12.50	21.00	30.50	45.00
	1245	—	9.00	15.00	21.50	30.00

C#	Date	Year	VG	Fine	VF	XF
	Obv. and rev: Star.					
10.1	AH1252	—	9.00	15.00	21.50	30.00
	1254	—	9.00	15.00	21.50	30.00
	1255	—	9.00	15.00	21.50	30.00
	Obv: Star. Rev: Branch.					
10.2	AH1255	—	9.00	15.00	21.50	30.00

C#	Date	Year	VG	Fine	VF	XF
	Obv: Branch. Rev: Star.					
10.2a	AH1225 (error) for 1252		10.00	16.00	22.50	32.50

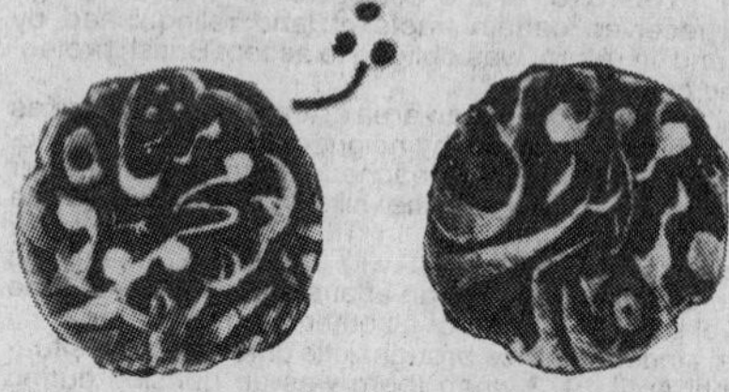

C#	Date	Year	VG	Fine	VF	XF
	Obv. and rev: Branch.					
10.3	AH1256	—	9.00	15.00	21.50	30.00
	1258	—	9.00	15.00	21.50	30.00
	Obv: Pigeon. Rev: Plume.					
10.4	AH1256	—	9.00	15.00	21.50	30.00
	Obv: Pigeon. Rev: Peacock.					
10.5	AH1258	—	10.00	17.50	25.00	35.00

C#	Date	Year	VG	Fine	VF	XF
	Obv: Pigeon. Rev: Leaf.					
10.8	AH1258	—	10.00	17.50	25.00	35.00
	Obv: Hare. Rev: Peacock.					
10.6	AH1258	—	10.00	17.50	25.00	35.00

C#	Date	Year	VG	Fine	VF	XF
	Rev: Date in *S* of *Julus*.					
10.7	AH1259	—	10.00	17.50	25.00	35.00

BRITISH OCCUPATION

After AH1259/1843AD

RUPEE

SILVER
Obv: Hare. Rev: British lion.

C#	Date	Year	VG	Fine	VF	XF
11	AH1259	—	15.00	25.00	35.00	50.00
	1261	—	15.00	25.00	35.00	50.00

Obv: Hare.
Obv. and rev: Floral mint marks of various kinds.

C#	Date	Year	VG	Fine	VF	XF
12	AH1262	—	8.50	14.00	20.00	28.50
	1263	—	8.50	14.00	20.00	28.50
	1264	—	8.50	14.00	20.00	28.50
	1265	—	8.50	14.00	20.00	28.50
	1266	—	8.50	14.00	20.00	28.50
	1267	—	8.50	14.00	20.00	28.50
	1268	—	8.50	14.00	20.00	28.50
	1269	—	8.50	14.00	20.00	28.50
	Obv: Hare. Rev: Peacock					
13	AH1259	—	16.50	23.50	32.50	45.00

LOCAL ISSUES

Shikarpur Mint

شکارپور

Mintname: Shikarpur

Anonymous

FALUS

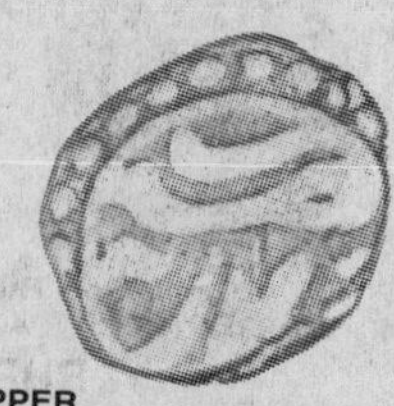

COPPER

C#	Date	Year	Good	VG	Fine	VF
30.1	AH1255	—	3.00	5.00	7.50	12.50

C#	Date	Year	Good	VG	Fine	VF
	Rev: Star at top.					
30.2	AH1255	—	3.00	5.00	7.50	12.50

Tatta Mint

تته

Mintname: Tatta

In the name of Taimur Shah Durrani

RUPEE

SILVER, 10.70-11.60 g

C#	Date	Year	VG	Fine	VF	XF
45	ND	—	8.50	13.50	20.00	28.50

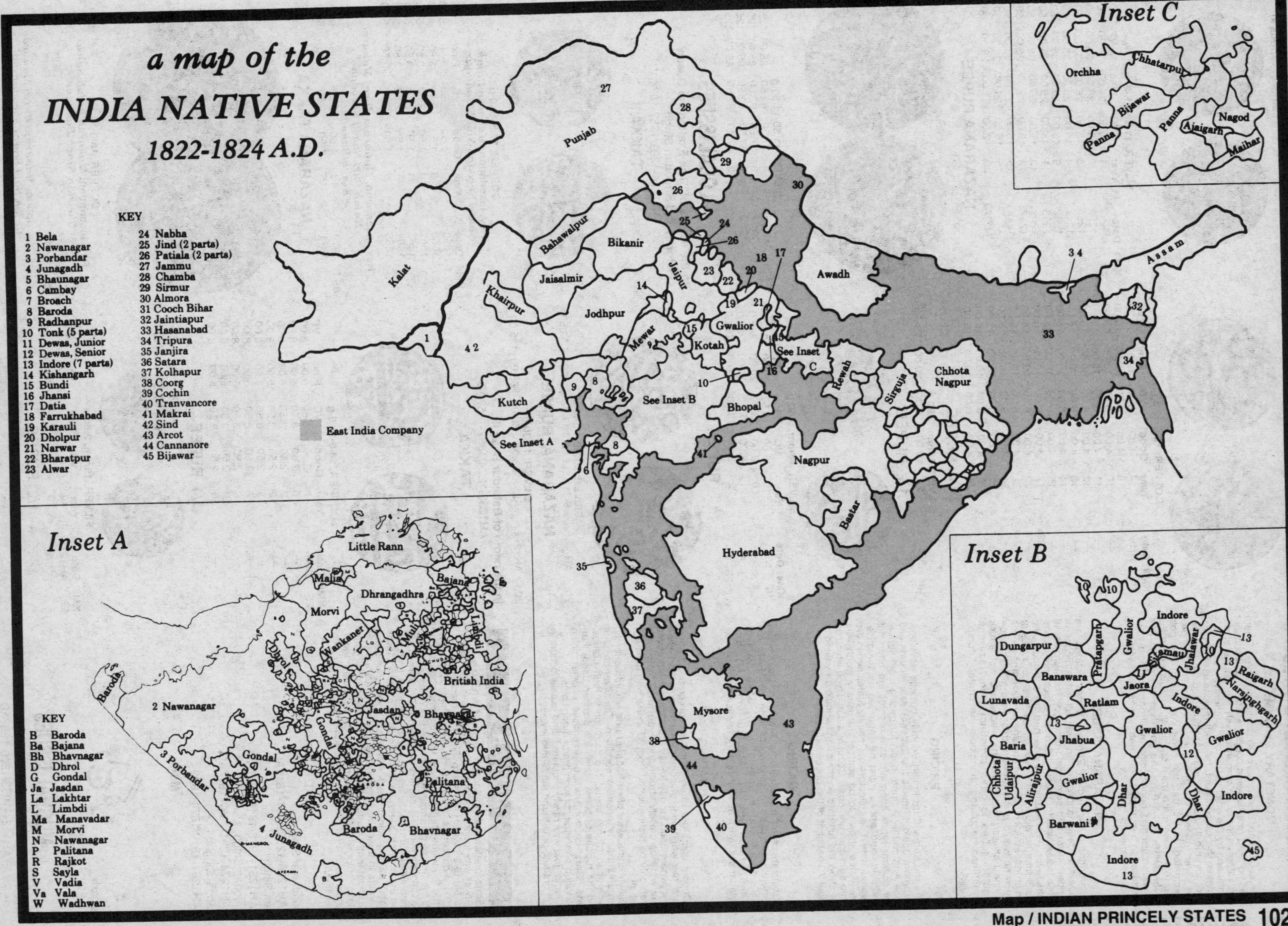

a map of the INDIA NATIVE STATES 1822-1824 A.D.

KEY

1 Bela
2 Nawanagar
3 Porbandar
4 Junagadh
5 Bhaunagar
6 Cambay
7 Broach
8 Baroda
9 Radhanpur
10 Tonk (5 parts)
11 Dewas, Junior
12 Dewas, Senior
13 Indore (7 parts)
14 Kishangarh
15 Bundi
16 Jhansi
17 Datia
18 Farrukhabad
19 Karauli
20 Dholpur
21 Narwar
22 Bharatpur
23 Alwar
24 Nabha
25 Jind (2 parts)
26 Patiala (2 parts)
27 Jammu
28 Chamba
29 Sirmur
30 Almora
31 Cooch Bihar
32 Jaintiapur
33 Hasanabad
34 Tripura
35 Janjira
36 Satara
37 Kolhapur
38 Coorg
39 Cochin
40 Tranvancore
41 Makrai
42 Sind
43 Arcot
44 Cannanore
45 Bijawar

East India Company

Inset A

KEY

B Baroda
Ba Bajana
Bh Bhavnagar
D Dhrol
G Gondal
Ja Jasdan
La Lakhtar
L Limbdi
Ma Manavadar
M Morvi
N Nawanagar
P Palitana
R Rajkot
S Sayla
V Vadia
Va Vala
W Wadhwan

Inset B

Inset C

INDIAN PRINCELY STATES

MONETARY SYSTEMS

In each state, local rates of exchange prevailed. There was no fixed rate between copper, silver or gold coin but the rates varied in accordance with the values of the metal and by the edict of the local authority.

Within the subcontinent, different regions used distinctive coinage standards. In North India and the Deccan, the silver rupee (11.6 g) and gold mohur (11.0 g) predominated. In Gujarat, the silver kori (4.7 g) and gold kori (6.4 g) were the main currency. In South India the silver fanam (0.7-1.0 g) and gold hun or Pagoda (3.4 g) were current. Copper coins in all parts of India were produced to a myriad of local metrologies with seemingly endless varieties.

NAZARANA ISSUES

Throughout the Indian Princely States listings are Nazarana designations for special full flan strikings of copper, silver and some gold coinage. The purpose of these issues was for presentation to the local monarch to gain favor. For example if one had an audience with one's ruler he would exchange goods, currency notes or the cruder struck circulating coinage for Nazarana pieces which he would present to the ruler as a gift. The borderline between true Nazarana pieces and well struck regular issues is often indistinct. The Nazarans sometimes circulated alongside the cruder "dump" issues.

PRICING

As the demand for Indian Princely coinage develops, and more dealers handle the material, sale records and price lists enable a firmer basis for pricing most series. For scarcer types adequate sale records are often not available, and prices must be regarded as tentative. Inasmuch as date collectors of Princely States series are few, dates known to be scarce are usually worth little more than common ones. Coins of a dated type which do not show the full date on their flans should be valued at about 70 per cent of the prices indicated.

DATING

Coins are dated in several eras. Arabic and Devanagari numerals are used in conjunction with the Hejira era (AH), the Vikrama Samvat (VS), Saka Samvat (Saka), Fasli era (FE) Mauludi era (AM), and Malabar era (ME), as well as the Christian era (AD).

GRADING

Copper coins are rarely found in high grade, as they were the workhorse of coinage circulation, and were everywhere used for day-to-day transactions. Moreover, they were carelessly struck and even when 'new', can often only be distinguished from VF coins with difficulty, if at all.

Silver coins were often hoarded and not infrequently, turn up in nearly as-struck condition. The silver coins of Hyderabad (dump coins) are common in high grades, and the rupees of some states are scarcer 'used' than 'new'. Great caution must be exercised in determining the value or scarcity of high grade dump coins.

Dump gold was rarely circulated, and usually occurs in high grades, or is found made into jewelry.

ALWAR

State located in Rajputana in northwestern India.

Alwar was founded about 1722 by a Rajput chieftain of the Naruka clan, Rao Pratap Singh of Macheri (1740-1791), a descendant of the family which had ruled Jaipur in the fourteenth century. Alwar was distinguished by being the first of the Princely States to use coins struck at the Calcutta Mint. These, first issued in 1877, were of the same weight and assay as the Imperial Rupee, and carried the bust of Queen Victoria, Empress of India. Alwar State, having allied itself with East India Company interests in their struggles against the Marathas early in the nineteenth century, continued to maintain a good relationship with the British right up to Indian Independence in 1947. In May 1949, Alwar was merged into Rajasthan.

LOCAL RULERS

Bakhtawar Singh
AH1206-1230/1791-1815AD

Bani Singh
AH1231-1273/1815-1857AD

Sheodan Singh
AH1274-1291/1857-1874AD

Mangal Singh
AH1291-1310/1874-1892

MINT

Rajgarh راج گره

MUGHAL ISSUES

In the name of Muhammad Akbar II
AH1221-1253/1806-1837AD

TAKKA

COPPER, 18.0-18.5 g

KM#	Date	Year	Good	VG	Fine	VF
15	AH—	4	4.00	6.00	10.00	15.00
	—	6	4.00	6.00	10.00	15.00
	—	10	4.00	6.00	10.00	15.00
	—	11	4.00	6.00	10.00	15.00
	—	12	4.00	6.00	10.00	15.00
	—	13	4.00	6.00	10.00	15.00
	—	14	4.00	6.00	10.00	15.00
	—	16	4.00	6.00	10.00	15.00
	122x	17	4.00	6.00	10.00	15.00
	—	20	4.00	6.00	10.00	15.00
	12xx	21	4.00	6.00	10.00	15.00
	—	24	4.00	6.00	10.00	15.00
	—	25	4.00	6.00	10.00	15.00
	—	26	4.00	6.00	10.00	15.00
	—	28	4.00	6.00	10.00	15.00

1/4 RUPEE

SILVER, 13mm, 2.80 g

KM#	Date	Year	VG	Fine	VF	XF
18	ND	22	10.00	15.00	20.00	27.50

1/2 RUPEE

SILVER, 18mm, 5.60 g

KM#	Date	Year	VG	Fine	VF	XF
19	ND	19	8.00	13.50	20.00	28.50
	—	20	8.00	13.50	20.00	28.50
	—	21	8.00	13.50	20.00	28.50
	—	22	8.00	13.50	20.00	28.50

RUPEE

SILVER, 11.20-11.40 g

KM#	Date	Year	VG	Fine	VF	XF
20	AH—	6-31	11.00	17.50	24.00	32.50

NAZARANA RUPEE

SILVER, 11.30 g

KM#	Date	Year	VG	Fine	VF	XF
20a	AH12xx	26	35.00	60.00	85.00	125.00

In the name of Bahadur Shah II
AH1253-1274/1837-1857AD

TAKKA

COPPER, 18.0-18.5 g

KM#	Date	Year	Good	VG	Fine	VF
25	AH—	2	2.50	3.50	5.00	8.00
	—	6	2.50	3.50	5.00	8.00
	—	9	2.50	3.50	5.00	8.00
	—	12	2.50	3.50	5.00	8.00
	—	15	2.50	3.50	5.00	8.00
	—	17	2.50	3.50	5.00	8.00
	—	18	2.50	3.50	5.00	8.00
	—	19	2.50	3.50	5.00	8.00
	—	20	2.50	3.50	5.00	8.00

1/4 RUPEE

SILVER, 16mm, 2.80 g

KM#	Date	Year	VG	Fine	VF	XF
28	AH127x	1x	—	—	—	—
	AH—	20	—	—	Rare	—

1/2 RUPEE

SILVER, 18mm, 5.65 g

KM#	Date	Year	VG	Fine	VF	XF
29	AH—	17	—	—	Rare	—

RUPEE

SILVER, 11.30-11.40 g

KM#	Date	Year	VG	Fine	VF	XF
30	AH—	1	12.50	21.00	28.50	40.00
	1255	2	15.00	25.00	35.00	50.00
	1255	3	15.00	25.00	35.00	50.00
	12xx	4	15.00	25.00	35.00	50.00
	1262	9	15.00	25.00	35.00	50.00
	1263	11	15.00	25.00	35.00	50.00
	126x	12	15.00	25.00	35.00	50.00
	1267	13	15.00	25.00	35.00	50.00
	12xx	15	15.00	25.00	35.00	50.00
	—	16	15.00	25.00	35.00	50.00
	(12)73	20	12.50	21.00	28.50	40.00

NAZARANA RUPEE

SILVER, 11.30-11.50 g

KM#	Date	Year	VG	Fine	VF	XF
30a	AH125x	1	37.50	62.50	85.00	125.00
	1261	8	37.50	62.50	85.00	125.00
	1262	9	37.50	62.50	85.00	125.00
	1267	13	37.50	62.50	85.00	125.00

LOCAL ISSUES

In the names of "The Exalted the Queen" (Victoria) and Sheodan Singh
AH1274-1291/1857-1874AD

TAKKA

COPPER, 18.5-19.0 g
Rev. inscription: *Maharao Rajah Sawai Sheodan Singh Bahadur.*

KM#	Date	Year	Good	VG	Fine	VF
35.1	1859	—	1.50	2.50	3.50	5.00
	1860	3	1.50	2.50	3.50	5.00
	1861	4	1.50	2.50	3.50	5.00
	1862	4	1.50	2.50	3.50	5.00
	1864	—	1.50	2.50	3.50	5.00
	1865	9	1.50	2.50	3.50	5.00

Rev. inscription: *Maharaja di-raj Maharao Rajah Shri Sawai Sheodan Singh Bahadur.*

KM#	Date	Year	Good	VG	Fine	VF
35.2	1870	13	1.50	2.50	3.50	5.00
	1871	15	1.50	2.50	3.50	5.00

NAZARANA TAKKA

COPPER, 18.5-19.1 g
Rev. inscription: *Maharao Rajah Sawai Sheodan Singh Bahadur.*

KM#	Date	Year	Good	VG	Fine	VF
35a.1	1865	9	—	—	Rare	—
	1866	9	—	—	Rare	—

Rev. inscription: *Maharaja di-raj Maharao Rajah Shri Sawai Sheodan Singh Bahadur.*

KM#	Date	Year	Good	VG	Fine	VF
35a.2	1871	15	11.50	18.50	25.00	35.00

RUPEE

SILVER, 11.20-11.30 g

KM#	Date	Year	VG	Fine	VF	XF
37	1859	2	12.50	21.50	30.00	40.00
	1860	3	12.50	21.50	30.00	40.00
	1860	4	12.50	21.50	30.00	40.00
	1861	4	12.50	21.50	30.00	40.00
	1863	6	12.50	21.50	30.00	40.00
	1864	7	12.50	21.50	30.00	40.00
	1865	8	15.00	21.50	30.00	40.00
	1865	9	15.00	21.50	30.00	40.00
	—	10	15.00	21.50	30.00	40.00

NAZARANA RUPEE

SILVER, 10.70-11.60 g
Rev. inscription: *Maharao Rajah Sawai Sheodan Singh Bahadur.*

KM#	Date	Year	VG	Fine	VF	XF
37a.1	1859	3	— Reported, not confirmed			
	1865	9	37.50	62.50	85.00	125.00
	1867	10	37.50	62.50	85.00	125.00

Rev. inscription: *Maharaja di-raj Maharao Rajah Shri Sawai Sheodan Singh Bahadur.*

KM#	Date	Year	VG	Fine	VF	XF
37a.2	1870	15	37.50	62.50	85.00	125.00
	(1874)	18	— Reported, not confirmed			

PRESENTATION ISSUES

In the name of Mangal Singh
AH1291-1310/1874-1892AD

Only a few each of KM#40 and 41 were struck at the Rajgarh Mint each year for presentation purposes.

NAZARANA TAKKA

COPPER, 18.5 g
Similar to Nazarana Rupee, KM#41.

KM#	Date	Year	VG	Fine	VF	XF
40	1874	—	8.50	15.00	25.00	40.00
	1891	—	8.50	15.00	25.00	40.00

RUPEE

SILVER, dump, 11.3 g

KM#	Date	Year	VG	Fine	VF	XF
42	—	2	—	—	—	—
	1876	3	—	—	—	—
	1877	4	—	—	—	—

NAZARANA RUPEE

SILVER, 11.30-11.35 g

KM#	Date	Year	VG	Fine	VF	XF
41	1876	3	30.00	50.00	70.00	100.00
	1877	4	30.00	50.00	70.00	100.00
	188x	—	30.00	50.00	70.00	100.00

MILLED COINAGE

RUPEE

11.6600 g, .917 SILVER, .3438 oz ASW

KM#	Date	Mintage	Fine	VF	XF	Unc
45	1788(error)	.200	7.00	12.00	20.00	35.00
	1877	.200	6.00	10.00	17.50	30.00
	1877	—	—	—	Proof	250.00
	1878	.206	7.00	12.00	20.00	35.00
45	1880	.196	6.00	10.00	17.50	30.00
	1882	.206	6.00	10.00	17.50	30.00
	1882	—	—	—	Proof	250.00

KM#	Date	Mintage	Fine	VF	XF	Unc
46	1891	160	6.00	10.00	16.50	27.50
	1891	—	—	—	Proof	250.00

GOLD

KM#	Date	Mintage	Fine	VF	XF	Unc
46a	1891	(restrike)	—	—	Proof	750.00

ASSAM

Refer to Independent Kingdoms during the Mughal Empire.

AWADH

Oudh

Kingdom located in northeastern India. The Nawabs of Awadh traced their origins to Muhammed Amin, a Persian adventurer who had attached himself to the court of Muhammed Shah, the Mughal Emperor, early in the eighteenth century. In 1720 Muhammed Amin was appointed Mughal Subahdar of Awadh, in which capacity he soon exhibited a considerable measure of independence. Until 1819, after Ghazi-ud-din had been encouraged by the Governor-General, Lord Hastings, to accept the title of King, Muhammed Amim's successors were known simply as the Nawabs of Awadh. The British offer, and Ghaziud-din's acceptance of it provided a clear indication of just how far Mughal decline had proceeded. The Mughal Emperor was now little more than a pensioner of the East India Company. Yet the coinage of Ghazi-ud-din immediately after 1819 marks also the hesitation he felt in taking so dramatic, and in the eyes of some of the princes of India, so ungrateful a step.

In 1856 Awadh was annexed by the British on the grounds of internal misrule. The king makers were now also seen as the king breakers. In setting aside the royal house of Awadh, the Muslim princes of India were added to that growing list of those who had come to fear the outcome of British hegemony. And it was here, in Awadh, that the Great Revolt of 1857 found its most fertile soil.

In 1877, Awadh along with Agra was placed under one administrator. It was made part of the United Provinces in 1902.

RULERS

Sa'adat Ali,
AH1213-1230/1798-1814AD
Ghazi-ud-Din Haidar, as Nawab,
AH1230-1234/1814-1819AD
as King, AH1234-1243/1819-1827AD
Nasir-ud-Din Haidar,
AH1243-1253/1827-1837AD
Muhammad Ali Shah,
AH1253-1258/1837-1842AD
Amjad Ali Shah,
AH1258-1263/1842-1847AD
Wajid Ali Shah,
AH1263-1272/1847-1856AD
Brijis Qadr,
AH1273-1274/1857-1858AD

MINTS

Allahabad الله اباد

Asafabad (Bareli) آصف اباد

Asafnagar آصف نگر

Awadh اوده

Banaras بنارس

Bareli بريلي

Hathras هاتهرسا

Itawa اتاوا

Kanauj قنوج

Kora كورا

Lucknow لكهو

Muhammadabad Banaras محمد اباد بنارس

Muradabad مراد اباد

Najibabad نجيب اباد

Shahabad شاه اباد

Tanda تانده

BARELI MINT

EAST INDIA COMPANY

In the name of Shah Alam II
AH1173-1221/1759-1806AD

RUPEE

SILVER, 10.70-11.60 g
Obv. leg: *Sahib Qirani*, cross.
Rev: Fish, star-shaped flower, Persian letter *Alif*.

KM#	Date	Year	VG	Fine	VF	XF
52.1	AH1216	37	15.00	21.50	31.50	40.00

Rev: Fish, star-shaped flower, Persian letter *He*.

KM#	Date	Year	VG	Fine	VF	XF
52.2	AH1216	37	15.00	21.50	31.50	40.00

Rev: Fish, star-shaped flower, Persian letter *Wa*.

KM#	Date	Year	VG	Fine	VF	XF
52.3	AH1216	37	12.50	17.50	25.00	35.00
	1217	37	12.50	17.50	25.00	35.00
	1218	37	12.50	17.50	25.00	35.00
	1219	37	12.50	17.50	25.00	35.00
	1220	37	12.50	17.50	25.00	35.00

NOTE: The letter *Wa* on East India Company issues was reputedly the initial of the surname of the new settlement officer for Bareli, Henry Wellesley. The earlier issue, with letter *He*, may have been a less majestic initial of his personal name.

LUCKNOW MINT

Mintname: Muhammadabad Banaras

The issues of the Nawab-Wazir in this mintname are distinguished from East India Company issues on the basis of distinctive fabric and fixed regnal year: 26 for Awadh, 17 for East India Company.

In the name of Shah Alam II
AH1173-1221/1759-1806AD

FALUS

COPPER, irregular flan

KM#	Date	Year	Good	VG	Fine	VF
97	AH1217	26	.75	1.50	2.50	4.00
	1218	26	.75	1.50	2.50	4.00
	1219	26	.75	1.50	2.50	4.00
	1222	26	.75	1.50	2.50	4.00
	1224	26	.75	1.50	2.50	4.00
	1227	26	.75	1.50	2.50	4.00
	1229	26	.75	1.50	2.50	4.00
	1230	26	.75	1.50	2.50	4.00
	1231	26	.75	1.50	2.50	4.00
	1232	—	.75	1.50	2.50	4.00
	1233	—	.75	1.50	2.50	4.00
	1234	—	.75	1.50	2.50	4.00

COPPER, round flan

KM#	Date	Year	Good	VG	Fine	VF
98	AH1222	—	1.75	3.00	4.50	7.00
	1223	—	1.75	3.00	4.50	7.00
	1228	26	1.75	3.00	4.50	7.00
	1229	29	1.75	3.00	4.50	7.00
	1233	—	1.75	3.00	4.50	7.00

NOTE: Earlier date (AH1208) exists for this type.

1/8 RUPEE

SILVER, 1.34-1.45 g
Rev: Frozen regnal year, flag and star.

KM#	Date	Year	VG	Fine	VF	XF
100.2	AH1218	26	5.50	8.00	11.50	17.50
	1222	26	5.50	8.00	11.50	17.50
	1226	26	5.50	8.00	11.50	17.50
	1229	26	5.50	8.00	11.50	17.50
	1232	26	5.50	8.00	11.50	17.50
	1233	26	5.50	8.00	11.50	17.50

NOTE: Earlier date (AH1215) exists for this type.

1/4 RUPEE

SILVER, 2.68-2.90 g
Rev: Frozen regnal year, flag and star.

KM#	Date	Year	VG	Fine	VF	XF
101.2	AH1218	26	5.50	8.00	11.50	17.50
	1225	26	5.50	8.00	11.50	17.50
	1231	26	5.50	8.00	11.50	17.50
	1233	26	5.50	8.00	11.50	17.50

1/2 RUPEE

SILVER, 5.38-5.80 g

KM#	Date	Year	VG	Fine	VF	XF
102.2	AH1223	26	6.00	9.00	13.50	20.00

NOTE: Earlier dates (AH1207-1208) exist for this type.

Obv: W/o AH date.

KM#	Date	Year	VG	Fine	VF	XF
102.3	ND	26	6.00	9.00	13.50	20.00

RUPEE

SILVER, 10.70-11.60 g
Rev: Frozen regnal year, flag and star.

KM#	Date	Year	VG	Fine	VF	XF
103.2	AH1216	26	7.50	12.50	18.50	27.50
	1217	26	7.50	12.50	18.50	27.50
	1218	26	7.50	12.50	18.50	27.50
	1219	26	7.50	12.50	18.50	27.50
	1220	26	7.50	12.50	18.50	27.50
	1221	26	7.00	11.00	16.50	25.00
	1222	26	7.00	11.00	16.50	25.00
	1223	26	7.00	11.00	16.50	25.00
	1224	26	7.00	11.00	16.50	25.00
	1225	26	7.00	11.00	16.50	25.00
	1226	26	7.00	11.00	16.50	25.00
	1227	26	7.00	11.00	16.50	25.00
	1228	26	7.00	11.00	16.50	25.00
	1229	26	7.00	11.00	16.50	25.00
	1230	26	7.00	11.00	16.50	25.00
	1231	26	7.00	11.00	16.50	25.00
	1232	26	7.00	11.00	16.50	25.00
	1233	26	7.00	11.00	16.50	25.00
	1234	26	7.00	11.00	16.50	25.00

NOTE: Earlier dates (AH1201-1215) exist for this type.
NOTE: For similar coins also dated AH1229/R.Y. 26, see KM#386.

Obv: W/o AH date.

KM#	Date	Year	VG	Fine	VF	XF
103.3	ND	26	—	—	Rare	—

NAZARANA RUPEE

SILVER, 10.70-11.60 g, 28mm
Similar to 1 Rupee, KM#103, broad flan.
Rev: Frozen regnal year.

KM#	Date	Year	VG	Fine	VF	XF
104	AH1216	26	32.50	45.00	62.50	85.00

1/2 MOHUR

GOLD, 5.35-5.70 g
Rev: Frozen regnal year.

KM#	Date	Year	VG	Fine	VF	XF
A105	AH1224	26	150.00	250.00	350.00	500.00

MOHUR

GOLD, 10.70-11.40 g
Rev: Frozen regnal year.

KM#	Date	Year	VG	Fine	VF	XF
105	AH1218	26	185.00	225.00	265.00	350.00
	1222	26	185.00	225.00	265.00	350.00
	1229	26	185.00	225.00	265.00	350.00
	1230	26	185.00	225.00	265.00	350.00
	1231	26	185.00	225.00	265.00	350.00

NAJIBABAD MINT

To Awadh in 1774AD. For issues before AH1188/R.Y. 15, see Rohilkhand.

In the name of Shah Alam II

AH1173-1221/1759-1806AD

1/2 PAISA

COPPER, 3.60-3.80 g
Rev: Verticle fish.

KM#	Date	Year	Good	VG	Fine	VF
110	AH—	24	2.50	4.00	6.50	10.00

PAISA

Various weight standards

COPPER
Obv: Crescent. Rev: Vertical fish.

KM#	Date	Year	Good	VG	Fine	VF
111	AH1216	43	3.00	4.00	6.00	8.50
	1217	44	3.00	4.00	6.00	8.50
	1218	47	3.00	4.00	6.00	8.50
	1219	—	3.00	4.00	6.00	8.50

NOTE: Earlier dates (AH1198-1215) exist for this type.

Rev: Horizontal fish.

KM#	Date	Year	Good	VG	Fine	VF
113	AH1216	43	5.00	7.00	10.00	15.00
	1217	44	5.00	7.00	10.00	15.00

NOTE: Earlier date (AH1215) exists for this type.

INDEPENDENT KINGS

GHAZI-UD-DIN HAIDAR

King, AH1234-1243/1819-1827AD

In the name of Shah Alam II

AH1173-1221/1759-1806AD

FALUS

COPPER

KM#	Date	Year	Good	VG	Fine	VF
140	AH1234	26	1.50	2.25	2.75	4.00
	1235	26	1.50	2.25	2.75	4.00

1/8 RUPEE

SILVER, 1.34-2.45 g

KM#	Date	Year	VG	Fine	VF	XF
142	AH1234	26	12.50	18.50	25.00	35.00

1/4 RUPEE

SILVER, 2.68-2.90 g

KM#	Date	Year	VG	Fine	VF	XF
144	AH1234	26	12.50	18.50	25.00	35.00

1/2 RUPEE

SILVER

KM#	Date	Year	VG	Fine	VF	XF
145	AH1234	26	17.50	25.00	35.00	50.00

RUPEE

SILVER, 10.70-11.60 g

KM#	Date	Year	VG	Fine	VF	XF
146	AH1234	26	12.50	18.50	25.00	35.00

1/2 MOHUR

GOLD, 5.35-5.70 g

KM#	Date	Year	VG	Fine	VF	XF
148	AH1234	26	110.00	125.00	145.00	165.00

MOHUR

GOLD, 10.70-11.40 g

KM#	Date	Year	VG	Fine	VF	XF
150	AH1234	26	225.00	250.00	285.00	325.00

In his own name

NOTE: Coins dated AH1234 have regnal year 5 for Haidar as Nawab; coins dated AH1235 and later have his regnal year as king AH1235 R.Y. 1.

NOTE: The mintname comes with 2 different epithets:

VARIETY I: AH1234-1235; *Dar ul-Amaret Lakhnau Suba Awadh*

VARIETY II: AH1236-1243 *Dar us-Sultanat Lakhnau Suba Awadh*

FALUS

COPPER
Mintname: Variety I

KM#	Date	Year	Good	VG	Fine	VF
155.1	AH1234	5	1.35	2.75	4.50	7.50
	1235	1	1.00	2.00	3.50	6.00

Mintname: Variety II

KM#	Date	Year	Good	VG	Fine	VF
155.2	AH1236	2	.85	1.75	3.00	5.00
	1237	3	.85	1.75	3.00	5.00
	1238	4	.85	1.75	3.00	5.00
	1239	5	.85	1.75	3.00	5.00

24-25mm

KM#	Date	Year	Good	VG	Fine	VF
155.3	AH1240	6	7.50	12.00	20.00	35.00

NOTE: Struck with 1 Rupee dies.

1/16 RUPEE

(Anna)

SILVER, 0.67-0.72 g

KM#	Date	Year	VG	Fine	VF	XF
157	AH1235	1	15.00	21.50	30.00	40.00

1/8 RUPEE

(2 Annas)

SILVER, 12-14mm, 1.34-1.45 g

KM#	Date	Year	VG	Fine	VF	XF
159	AH1235	1	10.00	15.00	21.50	30.00
	1236	2	10.00	15.00	21.50	30.00
	—	5	10.00	15.00	21.50	30.00

1/4 RUPEE

SILVER, 15-17mm, 2.68-2.90 g

KM#	Date	Year	VG	Fine	VF	XF
161	AH1236	2	7.00	11.00	16.50	25.00
	—	4	7.00	11.00	16.50	25.00
	—	6	7.00	11.00	16.50	25.00
	124x	8	7.00	11.00	16.50	25.00

1/2 RUPEE

SILVER, 5.35-5.80 g

KM#	Date	Year	VG	Fine	VF	XF
163	AH1235	1	15.00	21.50	30.00	40.00
	1236	2	15.00	21.50	30.00	40.00
	1237	3	15.00	21.50	30.00	40.00
	1238	4	10.00	15.00	21.50	30.00
	1239	5	10.00	15.00	21.50	30.00
	1240	6	10.00	15.00	21.50	30.00
	1242	8	10.00	15.00	21.50	30.00

RUPEE

SILVER, 10.70-11.60 g
Mintname: Variety I

KM#	Date	Year	VG	Fine	VF	XF
165.1	AH1234	5	7.50	12.50	18.50	27.50
	1235	1	7.50	12.50	18.50	27.50

Mintname: Variety II

KM#	Date	Year	VG	Fine	VF	XF
165.2	AH1236	2	7.50	12.50	18.50	27.50
	1237	3	7.50	12.50	18.50	27.50
	1238	4	7.50	12.50	18.50	27.50
	1239	5	7.50	12.50	18.50	27.50
	1240	6	7.50	12.50	18.50	27.50
	1241	7	7.50	12.50	18.50	27.50
	1242	8	7.50	12.50	18.50	27.50
	1243	9	7.50	12.50	18.50	27.50

1/4 ASHRAFI

GOLD, 2.68-2.85 g

KM#	Date	Year	VG	Fine	VF	XF
168	AH1236	—	65.00	85.00	110.00	135.00
	1243	—	65.00	85.00	110.00	135.00

ASHRAFI

GOLD, 10.70-11.40 g
Mintname: Variety I

KM#	Date	Year	VG	Fine	VF	XF
170.1	AH1234	5	250.00	285.00	325.00	425.00

Mintname: Variety II

KM#	Date	Year	VG	Fine	VF	XF
170.2	AH1235	1	250.00	285.00	325.00	425.00
	1236	1	250.00	285.00	325.00	425.00
	1236	2	250.00	285.00	325.00	425.00
	1238	4	250.00	285.00	325.00	425.00
	1239	5	250.00	285.00	325.00	425.00
	1240	6	250.00	285.00	325.00	425.00
	1241	7	250.00	285.00	325.00	425.00
	1242	8	250.00	285.00	325.00	425.00

NASIR-UD-DIN HAIDAR

AH1243-1253/1827-1837AD

In the name of Sulayman Jah

FALUS

COPPER

KM#	Date	Year	Good	VG	Fine	VF
175	AH1243	1	1.25	2.00	3.50	6.00
	1244	1	1.25	2.00	3.50	6.00
	1244	2	1.25	2.00	3.50	6.00

1/8 RUPEE

SILVER, 13mm, 1.34-1.45 g

KM#	Date	Year	VG	Fine	VF	XF
180	AH1244	2	7.00	11.00	16.50	25.00
	1245	3	7.00	11.00	16.50	25.00

1/4 RUPEE

SILVER, 2.68-2.90 g

KM#	Date	Year	VG	Fine	VF	XF
182	AH1244	2	6.50	10.00	15.00	22.50
	1251	8	6.50	10.00	15.00	22.50

1/2 RUPEE

SILVER, 5.35-5.80 g

KM#	Date	Year	VG	Fine	VF	XF
184	AH1243	1	6.00	9.00	13.50	20.00
	1244	2	6.00	9.00	13.50	20.00

RUPEE

SILVER, 10.70-11.60 g

KM#	Date	Year	VG	Fine	VF	XF
186	AH1243	1	7.50	12.50	18.50	27.50
	1244	1	7.50	12.50	18.50	27.50
	1244	2	7.50	12.50	18.50	27.50
	1245	1	7.50	12.50	18.50	27.50
	1245	2	7.00	12.50	18.50	27.50

1/2 ASHRAFI

GOLD

KM#	Date	Year	VG	Fine	VF	XF
189	AH1243	1	—	—	—	—

ASHRAFI

GOLD, 10.70-11.40 g

KM#	Date	Year	VG	Fine	VF	XF
190	AH1243	1	185.00	235.00	300.00	400.00

In the name of Nasir al-Din Haidar

NOTE: This series comes in 2 major varieties, the difference being in the coat of arms and position of regnal years.

Variety I: Katar (knife) above and regnal year between fish.

Variety II: Katar between fish and regnal year now in marginal inscription.

FALUS

COPPER
Mint mark: Variety I

KM#	Date	Year	Good	VG	Fine	VF
195.1	AH1245	2	2.00	3.50	6.00	10.00
	1245	3	2.00	3.50	6.00	10.00
	1246	3	2.00	3.50	6.00	10.00
	1246	4	2.00	3.50	6.00	10.00
	1247	4	2.00	3.50	6.00	10.00
	1247	5	2.00	3.50	6.00	10.00
	1248	5	2.00	3.50	6.00	10.00
	1249	6	2.00	3.50	6.00	10.00

Mint mark: Variety II

KM#	Date	Year	Good	VG	Fine	VF
195.2	AH1249	6	2.00	3.50	6.00	10.00
	1250	7	2.00	3.50	6.00	10.00

1/16 RUPEE

(Anna)

SILVER, 9-13mm, 0.67-0.72 g
Mint mark: Variety II

KM#	Date	Year	VG	Fine	VF	XF
197	AH1250	—	7.00	11.00	16.50	25.00
	1252	—	7.00	11.00	16.50	25.00

1/8 RUPEE

SILVER, 14mm, 1.34-1.45 g
Mint mark: Variety I

KM#	Date	Year	VG	Fine	VF	XF
199.1	AH1246	3	6.50	10.00	15.00	22.50
	1248	5	6.50	10.00	15.00	22.50

Mint mark: Variety II.

KM#	Date	Year	VG	Fine	VF	XF
199.2	AH1250	—	7.00	11.00	16.50	25.00

1/4 RUPEE

SILVER, 2.68-2.90 g
Mint mark: Variety I

KM#	Date	Year	VG	Fine	VF	XF
201.1	AH1245	3	8.50	13.50	20.00	28.50
	124x	4	8.50	13.50	20.00	28.50
	1247	5	8.50	13.50	20.00	28.50
	1248	5	8.50	13.50	20.00	28.50
	—	6	8.50	13.50	20.00	28.50

Mint mark: Variety II

KM#	Date	Year	VG	Fine	VF	XF
201.2	AH1250	—	12.50	18.50	25.00	35.00
	1251	8	12.50	18.50	25.00	35.00

1/2 RUPEE

SILVER, 5.35-5.80 g
Mint mark: Variety I

KM#	Date	Year	VG	Fine	VF	XF
203	AH1243	1	12.50	18.50	25.00	35.00
	1247	5	12.50	18.50	25.00	35.00
	1248	5	12.50	18.50	25.00	35.00
	1248	6	12.50	18.50	25.00	35.00
	1250	7	12.50	18.50	25.00	35.00

RUPEE

SILVER, 10.70-11.60 g
Mint mark: Variety I

KM#	Date	Year	VG	Fine	VF	XF
205.1	AH1245	3	7.50	12.50	18.50	27.50
	1246	3	7.50	12.50	18.50	27.50
	1246	4	7.50	12.50	18.50	27.50
	1247	4	7.50	12.50	18.50	27.50
	1247	5	7.50	12.50	18.50	27.50
	1248	5	7.50	12.50	18.50	27.50
	1248	6	7.50	12.50	18.50	27.50
	1249	6	7.50	12.50	18.50	27.50

Mint mark: Variety II

KM#	Date	Year	VG	Fine	VF	XF
205.2	AH1249	7	7.00	11.50	16.50	25.00
	1250	7	7.00	11.50	16.50	25.00
	1250	8	7.00	11.50	16.50	25.00
	1251	7	7.00	11.50	16.50	25.00
	1251	8	7.00	11.50	16.50	25.00
	1252	7	7.00	11.50	16.50	25.00
	1252	8	7.00	11.50	16.50	25.00
	1252	9	7.00	11.50	16.50	25.00
	1253	9	7.00	11.50	16.50	25.00
	1253	10	7.00	11.50	16.50	25.00

Reduced size.

KM#	Date	Year	VG	Fine	VF	XF
205.3	AH1250	7	20.00	31.50	42.50	60.00

NOTE: Struck with 1/4 Rupee dies.

1/2 ASHRAFI

GOLD, 5.35-5.70 g

KM#	Date	Year	VG	Fine	VF	XF
235	AH1251	9	110.00	140.00	180.00	240.00

ASHRAFI

GOLD, 25mm, 10.70-11.40 g
Mint mark: Variety I

KM#	Date	Year	VG	Fine	VF	XF
240	AH1245	3	185.00	235.00	300.00	400.00
	1246	3	185.00	235.00	300.00	400.00
	1252	9	185.00	235.00	300.00	400.00

MUHAMMAD ALI SHAH

AH1253-1258/1837-1842AD

NOTE: Mintname comes in 2 varieties.
VARIETY AIII. *SubaaAwadhhDar-as-Sultanat Lakhnau*, on coins dated AH1253/1.
VARIETY III. *Suba Awadh Baitu-s-Sultanat Lakhnau*, on all coins dated through AH1256/Yr. 3.
VARIETY IV. *Mulk Awadh Baitu-s-Sultanat Lakhnau*, on all coins beginning with date AH1256/Yr. 3.

FALUS

COPPER

KM#	Date	Year	Good	VG	Fine	VF
305	AH1253	1	1.25	2.25	3.50	6.00
	1254	2	1.25	2.25	3.50	6.00
	1255	3	1.25	2.25	3.50	6.00

1/8 RUPEE

SILVER, 10mm, 1.34-1.45 g

KM#	Date	Year	VG	Fine	VF	XF
310	AH1253	1	5.50	8.00	12.00	18.50
	1256	(3)	5.50	8.00	12.00	18.50

1/4 RUPEE

SILVER, 2.68-2.90 g

KM#	Date	Year	VG	Fine	VF	XF
312	AH1253	—	5.50	8.00	12.00	18.50
	1254	—	5.50	8.00	12.00	18.50
	1255	—	5.50	8.00	12.00	18.50
	1256	—	5.50	8.00	12.00	18.50

1/2 RUPEE

SILVER, 5.35-5.80 g
Mintname: Variety AIII.

KM#	Date	Year	VG	Fine	VF	XF
313	AH1253	1	—	—	Rare	—

Mintname: Variety III.

KM#	Date	Year	VG	Fine	VF	XF
314.1	AH1254	—	5.50	8.00	12.00	18.50

Mintname: Variety IV.

KM#	Date	Year	VG	Fine	VF	XF
314.2	AH1256	3	5.50	8.00	12.00	18.50
	1258	—	5.50	8.00	12.00	18.50

RUPEE

SILVER, 10.70-11.60 g
Mintname: Variety III.

KM#	Date	Year	VG	Fine	VF	XF
316.1	AH1253	1	7.50	12.50	18.50	27.50
	1254	1	7.50	12.50	18.50	27.50
	1254	2	7.50	12.50	18.50	27.50
	1255	2	7.50	12.50	18.50	27.50
	1255	3	7.50	12.50	18.50	27.50
	1256	3	7.50	12.50	18.50	27.50

Mintname: Variety IV.

KM#	Date	Year	VG	Fine	VF	XF
316.2	AH1254	1	7.50	12.50	18.50	27.50
	1256	3	7.50	12.50	18.50	27.50
	1256	4	7.50	12.50	18.50	27.50
	1257	4	7.50	12.50	18.50	27.50
	1257	5	7.50	12.50	18.50	27.50
	1258	5	7.50	12.50	18.50	27.50

1/2 ASHRAFI

GOLD, 5.35-5.70 g

KM#	Date	Year	VG	Fine	VF	XF
320	AH1253	1	125.00	150.00	185.00	225.00

ASHRAFI

GOLD, 10.70-11.40 g
Mintname: Variety III.

KM#	Date	Year	VG	Fine	VF	XF
322.1	AH1253	1	175.00	225.00	275.00	375.00
	1255	3	175.00	225.00	275.00	375.00

Mintname: Variety IV.

KM#	Date	Year	VG	Fine	VF	XF
322.2	AH1258	—	175.00	225.00	275.00	375.00

AMJAD ALI SHAH

AH1258-1263/1842-1847AD

FALUS

COPPER

KM#	Date	Year	Good	VG	Fine	VF
325	AH1258	1	2.00	3.50	6.00	10.00
	1259	1	2.00	3.50	6.00	10.00
	1259	2	2.00	3.50	6.00	10.00
	1260	2	2.00	3.50	6.00	10.00
	1262	—	2.00	3.50	6.00	10.00

Finer style, 27mm

KM#	Date	Year	Good	VG	Fine	VF
326	AH1258	1	5.00	10.00	15.00	21.50

1/16 RUPEE

SILVER, 0.67-0.72 g

KM#	Date	Year	VG	Fine	VF	XF
328	AH1262	—	6.00	9.00	13.50	20.00

1/8 RUPEE

SILVER, 1.34-1.45 g

KM#	Date	Year	VG	Fine	VF	XF
330	AH1258	—	5.50	8.00	12.00	18.50
	1259	—	5.50	8.00	12.00	18.50
	1262	—	5.50	8.00	12.00	18.50

1/4 RUPEE

SILVER, 2.68-2.90 g

KM#	Date	Year	VG	Fine	VF	XF
332	AH1259	2	5.50	8.50	12.00	18.50
	1260	3	5.50	8.50	12.00	18.50

1/2 RUPEE

SILVER, 18-20mm, 5.35-5.80 g

KM#	Date	Year	VG	Fine	VF	XF
334	AH1259	2	5.50	8.50	12.00	18.50
	1260	3	5.50	8.50	12.00	18.50
	1261	—	5.50	8.50	12.00	18.50

RUPEE

SILVER, 10.70-11.60 g
Mintname: Variety IV

KM#	Date	Year	VG	Fine	VF	XF
336	AH1258	1	7.50	12.50	18.50	27.50
	1259	1	7.50	12.50	18.50	27.50
	1259	2	7.50	12.50	18.50	27.50
	1260	2	7.50	12.50	18.50	27.50
	1260	3	7.50	12.50	18.50	27.50
	1261	3	7.50	12.50	18.50	27.50
	1261	4	7.50	12.50	18.50	27.50
	1262	4	7.50	12.50	18.50	27.50
	1262	5	7.50	12.50	18.50	27.50
	1263	5	7.50	12.50	18.50	27.50

1/4 ASHRAFI

GOLD, 2.37-2.85 g

KM#	Date	Year	VG	Fine	VF	XF
339	AH1260	—	165.00	240.00	350.00	500.00

1/2 ASHRAFI

GOLD, 5.35-5.70 g

KM#	Date	Year	VG	Fine	VF	XF
340	AH1258	—	125.00	200.00	285.00	400.00
	1259	2	125.00	200.00	285.00	400.00
	1263	—	125.00	200.00	285.00	400.00

ASHRAFI

GOLD, 10.70-11.40 g

KM#	Date	Year	VG	Fine	VF	XF
342	AH1258	—	175.00	225.00	275.00	365.00
	1259	2	175.00	225.00	275.00	365.00
	1261	4	175.00	225.00	275.00	365.00
	1262	5	175.00	225.00	275.00	365.00
	1263	—	175.00	225.00	275.00	365.00

WAJID ALI SHAH

AH1263-1272/1847-1856AD

NOTE: Wajid Alis coins come in 3 varieties, depending on form of mintname:
VARIETY IV: *Mulk Awadh Baitu-s-Sultanat Lakhnau*, AH1263-1267/Yr.4.
VARIETY V: *Mulk Awadh Akhtarnagar*, AH1267/5 reported so far only for Rupees dated 1267/Yr. 5. The same date/year combination is also found in Var. VI.
VARIETY VI: *Baitus-s-Sultanat Lakhnau Mulk Awadh Akhtar-Nagar*, 1267/Yr. 5-1272.

1/8 FALUS

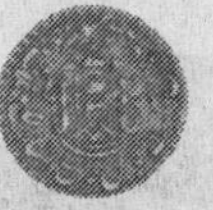

COPPER

KM#	Date	Year	Good	VG	Fine	VF
345	AH1270	7	3.50	6.00	8.00	11.50
	1270	8	3.50	6.00	8.00	11.50
	1271	—	3.00	5.00	7.00	10.00

1/4 FALUS

COPPER

KM#	Date	Year	Good	VG	Fine	VF
347	AH1270	7	3.00	5.00	7.00	10.00
	1270	8	3.50	6.00	8.50	12.00
	1272	9	3.00	5.00	7.00	10.00

1/2 FALUS

COPPER

KM#	Date	Year	Good	VG	Fine	VF
349	AH1269	—	2.75	4.50	6.00	8.50
	1270	7	2.75	4.50	6.00	8.50
	1270	8	2.75	4.50	6.00	8.50
	1271	—	2.75	4.50	6.00	8.50
	1272	—	2.75	4.50	6.00	8.50

FALUS

COPPER
Mintname: Variety IV.

KM#	Date	Year	Good	VG	Fine	VF
351.1	AH—	1	1.50	2.50	3.00	4.50
	1263	—	2.00	3.50	5.00	7.00
	1264	2	2.00	3.50	5.00	7.00

Mintname: Variety V.

KM#	Date	Year	Good	VG	Fine	VF
351.2	AH1267	4	10.00	15.00	25.00	40.00

Mintname: Variety VI.

KM#	Date	Year	Good	VG	Fine	VF
351.3	AH1270	8	2.00	3.50	5.00	7.00
	1270	9	2.00	3.50	5.00	7.00
	1271?	—	2.00	3.50	5.00	7.00
	1272	—	2.00	3.50	5.00	7.00

Rectangular, 14x18mm

KM#	Date	Year	Good	VG	Fine	VF
351.4	AH1271	—	2.00	3.50	5.00	7.00

NOTE: Barbarous versions of KM#351, without legible date or year, are common and worth half of what a legible date specimen commands.

1/16 RUPEE

SILVER, 0.67-0.72 g

KM#	Date	Year	VG	Fine	VF	XF
355	AH126x	—	5.50	8.00	10.00	15.50
	1270	8	5.50	8.00	10.00	15.50
	1270	2(sic)	5.50	8.00	10.00	15.50
	1271	—	5.50	8.00	10.00	15.50
	1272	—	5.50	8.00	10.00	15.50

1/8 RUPEE

SILVER, 1.34-1.45 g
Mintname: Variety IV.

KM#	Date	Year	VG	Fine	VF	XF
357.1	AH1264	1	5.50	8.00	12.50	18.50
	1264	2	5.50	8.00	12.50	18.50
	1265	2	5.50	8.00	12.50	18.50
	1266	—	5.50	8.00	12.50	18.50
	126x	5	5.50	8.00	12.50	18.50
	1268	—	5.50	8.00	12.50	18.50

Mintname: Variety VI.

KM#	Date	Year	VG	Fine	VF	XF
357.2	AH1268	—	5.50	8.00	12.50	18.50
	1269	—	5.50	8.00	12.50	18.50
	1270	8	5.50	8.00	12.50	18.50
	1271	9	5.50	8.00	12.50	18.50

1/4 RUPEE

SILVER, 2.68-2.90 g
Mintname: Variety IV.

KM#	Date	Year	VG	Fine	VF	XF
361.1	AH1263	1	5.50	8.00	12.50	18.50
	1265	—	5.50	8.00	12.50	18.50

Mintname: Variety VI.

KM#	Date	Year	VG	Fine	VF	XF
361.2	AH1267	5	5.50	8.00	12.50	18.50
	1268	—	5.50	8.00	12.50	18.50
	1269	6	5.50	8.00	12.50	18.50
	1271	9	5.50	8.00	12.50	18.50

1/2 RUPEE

SILVER, 5.35-5.80 g
Mintname: Variety IV.

KM#	Date	Year	VG	Fine	VF	XF
363.1	AH1263	2	6.00	9.00	13.50	20.00
	1265	2	6.00	9.00	13.50	20.00
	1266	3	6.00	9.00	13.50	20.00

Mintname: Variety VI.

KM#	Date	Year	VG	Fine	VF	XF
363.2	AH1268	5	6.00	9.00	13.50	20.00
	1269	6	6.00	9.00	13.50	20.00
	1271	8	6.00	9.00	13.50	20.00
	1271	9	6.00	9.00	13.50	20.00

RUPEE

SILVER, 10.70-11.60 g
Mintname: Variety IV.

KM#	Date	Year	VG	Fine	VF	XF
365.1	AH1263	1	7.50	11.00	16.50	25.00
	1264	1	7.50	11.00	16.50	25.00
	1264	2	7.50	11.00	16.50	25.00
	1265	1	7.50	11.00	16.50	25.00
	1265	2	7.50	11.00	16.50	25.00
	1265	3	7.50	11.00	16.50	25.00
	1266	3	7.50	11.00	16.50	25.00
	1266	4	7.50	11.00	16.50	25.00
	1267	3	7.50	11.00	16.50	25.00
	1267	4	7.50	11.00	16.50	25.00
	1268	4	7.50	11.00	16.50	25.00

Mintname: Variety V.

KM#	Date	Year	VG	Fine	VF	XF
365.2	AH1267	5	17.50	25.00	35.00	50.00

Mintname: Variety VI.

KM#	Date	Year	VG	Fine	VF	XF
365.3	AH1267	5	7.00	11.00	16.50	25.00
	1268	5	7.00	11.00	16.50	25.00
	1268	6	7.00	11.00	16.50	25.00
	1269	6	7.00	11.00	16.50	25.00
	1269	2(sic - 2 is a backwards 6)	7.00	11.00	16.50	25.00
	1269	7	7.00	11.00	16.50	25.00
	1270	7	7.00	11.00	16.50	25.00
	1270	8	7.00	11.00	16.50	25.00
	1271	8	7.00	11.00	16.50	25.00
	1271	9	7.00	11.00	16.50	25.00
	1272	9	7.00	11.00	16.50	25.00
	1272	10	7.00	11.00	16.50	25.00

1/16 ASHRAFI

GOLD, 10mm, 0.67-0.71 g

KM#	Date	Year	VG	Fine	VF	XF
370	AH1270	—	35.00	45.00	55.00	70.00

1/8 ASHRAFI

GOLD, 1.34-1.42 g

KM#	Date	Year	VG	Fine	VF	XF
372	AH1263-72	1-10	40.00	50.00	60.00	85.00

1/4 ASHRAFI

GOLD, 2.68-2.85 g

KM#	Date	Year	VG	Fine	VF	XF
374	AH1267	5	60.00	75.00	90.00	125.00
	1268	*5	60.00	75.00	90.00	125.00

1/2 ASHRAFI

GOLD, 5.35-5.70 g
Mintname: Variety IV.

KM#	Date	Year	VG	Fine	VF	XF
376	AH1265	3	110.00	125.00	150.00	185.00
	1267	4	110.00	125.00	150.00	185.00
	1267	5	110.00	125.00	150.00	185.00

ASHRAFI

GOLD, 10.70-11.40 g
Mintname: Variety IV.

KM#	Date	Year	VG	Fine	VF	XF
378.1	AH1263	1	165.00	200.00	250.00	300.00
	1263	2	165.00	200.00	250.00	300.00
	1264	2	165.00	200.00	250.00	300.00
	1265	2	165.00	200.00	250.00	300.00
	1265	3	165.00	200.00	250.00	300.00
	1266	3	165.00	200.00	250.00	300.00
	1267	4	165.00	200.00	250.00	300.00
	1268	5	165.00	200.00	250.00	300.00

Mintname: Variety VI.

KM#	Date	Year	VG	Fine	VF	XF
378.3	AH1272	9	165.00	200.00	250.00	300.00

BRIJIS QADR

1857-1858AD

Nawab-Wazir during the Indian Mutiny

NOTE: Fictitious dating in imitation of coinage before AH1234/1819. Identifiable only by style and mintname, *Awadh* at top of reverse, and *Subah* at bottom, dated only AH1229/r.y.26.

FALUS

COPPER

KM#	Date	Year	Good	VG	Fine	VF
380	AH1229	26	12.50	22.50	32.50	50.00

1/8 RUPEE

SILVER, 13-14mm, 1.34-1.45 g

KM#	Date	Year	VG	Fine	VF	XF
382	AH1229	26	50.00	75.00	110.00	150.00

1/2 RUPEE

SILVER, 2.68-2.90 g

KM#	Date	Year	VG	Fine	VF	XF
384	AH1229	26	40.00	62.50	85.00	120.00

RUPEE

SILVER, 10.70-11.60 g

KM#	Date	Year	VG	Fine	VF	XF
386	AH1229	26	45.00	70.00	100.00	140.00

ASHRAFI

GOLD, 10.70-11.40 g

KM#	Date	Year	VG	Fine	VF	XF
390	AH1229	26	350.00	500.00	700.00	1000.

BAHAWALPUR

The Amirs of Bahawalpur established their independence from Afghan control towards the close of the eighteenth century. In the 1830's the state's independence under British suzerainty became guaranteed by treaty. With the creation of Pakistan in 1947 Bahawalpur, with an area of almost 17,500 square miles, became its premier Princely State. Bahawalpur State, named after its capital, stretched for almost three hundred miles along the left bank of the Sutlej, Panjnad andIndus rivers.

For earlier issues in the names of the Durrani rulers, see Afghanistan.

RULERS

Amirs

Muhammad Bahawal Khan II
AH1186-1224/1772-1809AD

Sadiq Muhammad Khan II
AH1224-1241/1809-1825AD

Muhammad Bahawal Khan III
AH1241-1269/1825-1852AD

Sadiq Muhammad Khan III
AH1269-1270/1852-1853AD

Fateh Khan
AH1270-1275/1853-1858AD

Muhammad Bahawal Khan IV
AH1275-1283/1858-1866AD

Sir Sadiq Muhammad Khan IV
AH1283-1317/1866-1899AD

Alhaj Muhammad Bahawal Khan V
AH1317-1325/1899-1907AD

Sir Sadiq Muhammad Khan V
AH1325-1365/1907-1947AD

MINTS

Ahmadpur احمد پور

Dar al-Islam دار الالسلام

Bahawalpur بهاولپور

Khanpur خانبور

The mintnames at the bottom of the reverses of Bahawalpur State rupees are often off the flans. In most cases these rupees can be attributed to one of the three mints from other characteristics. Ahmadpur rupees weigh considerably less than those of the other two mints. Bahawalpur and Khanpur rupees can usually be differentiated by the location of their dates and other characteristics, as illustrated below (Y#4 and Y#5).

AHMADPUR MINT

In the name of Mahmud Shah
AH1216-1218/1801-1803AD

RUPEE

SILVER, 10.70-11.60 g

C#	Date	Year	VG	Fine	VF	XF
18	AH1217	48	13.50	20.00	27.50	37.50
	—	49	13.50	20.00	27.50	37.50

Anonymous

Reduced weight, 7.70-7.80 g
Dated on obverse, sometimes also on reverse.

Y#	Date	Year	VG	Fine	VF	XF
3.1	AH1246	—	9.00	18.00	28.00	40.00
	1251	—	9.00	18.00	28.00	40.00
	1252	—	9.00	18.00	28.00	40.00
	1253	—	9.00	18.00	28.00	40.00
	1254	—	9.00	18.00	28.00	40.00
	1256	—	9.00	18.00	28.00	40.00
	1257	—	9.00	18.00	28.00	40.00
	1258	—	9.00	18.00	28.00	40.00
	1259	—	9.00	18.00	28.00	40.00
	1260	—	15.00	30.00	50.00	65.00
	1261	—	9.00	18.00	28.00	40.00
	1262	—	9.00	18.00	28.00	40.00
	1263	—	9.00	18.00	28.00	40.00
	1264	—	9.00	18.00	28.00	40.00
	1265	—	9.00	18.00	28.00	40.00

Obv: Date in oval.

Y#	Date	Year	VG	Fine	VF	XF
3.2 (3.3)	AH1270	—	25.00	37.50	50.00	70.00

7.00-7.60 g
Obv: Date in center.

Y#	Date	Year	VG	Fine	VF	XF
3.3	AH1275	—	12.50	18.50	25.00	35.00
	1276	—	12.50	18.50	25.00	35.00
	1277	—	12.50	18.50	25.00	35.00
	1278	—	12.50	18.50	25.00	35.00
	1279	—	12.50	18.50	25.00	35.00
	1280	—	12.50	18.50	25.00	35.00
	1281	—	12.50	18.50	25.00	35.00
	1282	—	12.50	18.50	25.00	35.00
	1283	—	12.50	18.50	25.00	35.00
	1284	—	12.50	18.50	25.00	35.00

7.90-8.10 g
Dated on obverse and reverse.

Y#	Date	Year	VG	Fine	VF	XF
3.4	AH1285	—	20.00	30.00	45.00	65.00
	1286	—	20.00	30.00	45.00	65.00

BAHAWALPUR MINT

Anonymous

FALUS

COPPER
Square or round

Y#	Date	Year	Good	VG	Fine	VF
1	AH1225	—	3.00	5.00	7.00	10.00
	1237	13	3.00	5.00	7.00	10.00
	1244	—	3.00	5.00	7.00	10.00
	1248	—	3.00	5.00	7.00	10.00
	1249	—	3.00	5.00	7.00	10.00
	1254	—	3.00	5.00	7.00	10.00
	1259	—	3.00	5.00	7.00	10.00
	1261	—	3.00	5.00	7.00	10.00
	1269	—	3.00	5.00	7.00	10.00
	1270	—	3.00	5.00	7.00	10.00
	1271	—	3.00	5.00	7.00	10.00
	1273	—	3.00	5.00	7.00	10.00
	1276	—	3.00	5.00	7.00	10.00
	1277	—	3.00	5.00	7.00	10.00
	1281	—	3.00	5.00	7.00	10.00

NOTE: Earlier dates (AH1205-1214) exist for this type.

PAISA

COPPER

Y#	Date	Year	Good	VG	Fine	VF
2.1	AH1301	—	3.50	6.00	8.50	12.00
	1302	—	3.50	6.00	8.50	12.00
	1304	—	3.50	6.00	8.50	12.00
	1311	—	3.50	6.00	8.50	12.00
	1312	—	3.50	6.00	8.50	12.00
	1313	—	3.50	6.00	8.50	12.00
	1315	—	3.50	6.00	8.50	12.00
	1317	—	3.50	6.00	8.50	12.00
	1321	—	3.50	6.00	8.50	12.00
	1325	—	3.50	6.00	8.50	12.00

Y#	Date	Year	Good	VG	Fine	VF
2.2	ND	—	4.00	7.50	12.00	20.00

RUPEE

SILVER, 9.80-10.10 g
Obv: Lily, date in center.

Y#	Date	Year	VG	Fine	VF	XF
4.1	AH1254	—	9.00	18.00	28.00	40.00
	1255	—	9.00	18.00	28.00	40.00
	1256	—	9.00	18.00	28.00	40.00
	1258	—	9.00	18.00	28.00	40.00
	1259	—	9.00	18.00	28.00	40.00

10.40-10.50 g
Obv. and rev: Date in rectangle or cinqfoil.

Y#	Date	Year	VG	Fine	VF	XF
4.2	AH1270	—	14.00	28.00	45.00	65.00
	1272	—	14.00	28.00	45.00	65.00
	1273	—	17.50	35.00	60.00	85.00
	1274	—	14.00	28.00	45.00	65.00

10.50-10.70 g
Obv: Date in center.

Y#	Date	Year	VG	Fine	VF	XF
4.3	AH1273	—	9.00	18.00	28.00	40.00
	1274	—	9.00	18.00	28.00	40.00
	1275	—	9.00	18.00	28.00	40.00

8.50-8.80 g
Obv: Date in center.

Y#	Date	Year	VG	Fine	VF	XF
4.4	AH1278	—	9.00	18.00	28.00	40.00
	1279	—	9.00	18.00	28.00	40.00
	1280	—	9.00	18.00	28.00	40.00
	1281	—	9.00	18.00	28.00	40.00
	1282	—	9.00	18.00	28.00	40.00
	1283	—	9.00	18.00	28.00	40.00
	1283/4	—	9.00	18.00	28.00	40.00

MUHAMMAD BAHAWAL KHAN V

AH1317-1325/1899-1907AD

PAISA

COPPER

Y#	Date	Year	Good	VG	Fine	VF
6	AH1324	—	3.50	6.00	9.00	12.50
	1325	—	3.50	6.00	9.00	12.50

NOTE: For anonymous Paisas struck during the years of his reign, see Y#2.

SADIQ MUHAMMAD KHAN V

AH1325-1365/1907-47AD

PAISA

COPPER, square

Y#	Date	Year	Good	VG	Fine	VF
7.1	AH1326	—	3.50	6.00	9.00	12.50
	1327	—	3.50	6.00	9.00	12.50

Rev: W/o date.

Y#	Date	Year	Good	VG	Fine	VF
7.2	ND	—	4.00	7.50	12.50	20.00

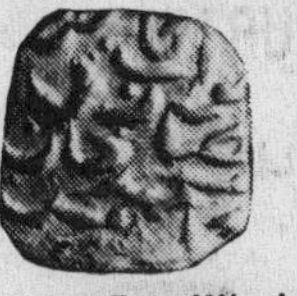

Rev: W/o date or star.

Y#	Date	Year	Good	VG	Fine	VF
7.3	ND	—	5.50	9.00	13.50	20.00
8	AH1342	—	7.50	11.00	15.00	20.00
	1343	—	7.50	11.00	15.00	20.00

Milled Coinage

1/2 PICE

COPPER

Y#	Date	Year	Fine	VF	XF	Unc
12	AH1359	1940	.35	.75	1.25	2.00
	1359	1940	—	—	Proof	—

PAISA

(1/4 Anna)

COPPER

Y#	Date	Year	Fine	VF	XF	Unc
9	AH1343	—	11.50	17.50	25.00	40.00

Y#	Date	Year	Fine	VF	XF	Unc
13	AH1359	1940	.75	1.25	2.00	3.00
	1359	1940	—	—	Proof	—

NAZARANA RUPEE

SILVER, 12.30 g

Y#	Date	Year	Fine	VF	XF	Unc
10	AH1343	—	—	250.00	325.00	400.00

ASHRAFI

GOLD, 22.5mm, 7.00 g

Y#	Date	Year	Fine	VF	XF	Unc
11	AH1343	—	—	400.00	500.00	650.00
	10.00 g					
11a	AH1343	—	—	—	Proof	2000.

NOTE: KM#10 and #11 designs prepared for the nawab by Spink & Son Ltd., London.

KHANPUR MINT

Anonymous

FALUS

COPPER

C#	Date	Year	Good	VG	Fine	VF
7	AH1197 (retrograde)					
			20.00	32.50	50.00	75.00
	Date off flan	—	10.00	15.00	22.50	35.00

RUPEE

SILVER, 9.80-10.10 g
Dated on obverse and reverse.

Y#	Date	Year	VG	Fine	VF	XF
5.1	AH1255	—	15.00	30.00	42.00	60.00
	1256	—	15.00	30.00	42.00	60.00
	1258	—	15.00	30.00	42.00	60.00
	1259	—	15.00	30.00	42.00	60.00
	1260	—	15.00	30.00	42.00	60.00
	1261	—	15.00	30.00	42.00	60.00
	1263	—	15.00	30.00	42.00	60.00
	1264	—	15.00	30.00	42.00	60.00
	1265	—	15.00	30.00	42.00	60.00
	1266	—	15.00	30.00	42.00	60.00
	1267	—	15.00	30.00	42.00	60.00
	1268/7	—	15.00	30.00	42.00	60.00
	1269	—	15.00	30.00	42.00	60.00

8.50-8.80 g
Obv: Date in center.

Y#	Date	Year	VG	Fine	VF	XF
5.2	AH1280	—	10.00	20.00	35.00	50.00
	1281	—	10.00	20.00	35.00	50.00
	1282	—	10.00	20.00	35.00	50.00

BAJRANGGARH

Bajranggarh was a small state in the district of Gwalior. The mint epithet of Bajranggarh was Jainagar. All the coins, irrespective of when they were minted, were struck in the name of Maharaja Jai Singh and bore similar legends.

RULERS

Jai Singh, 1797-1818AD

PAISA

COPPER

KM#	Date	Year	Good	VG	Fine	VF
2	—	11	4.50	8.00	12.00	17.50
	—	12	4.50	8.00	12.00	17.50

RUPEE

SILVER, 10.70-11.60 g
W/o symbols, thin flan.

KM#	Date	Year	VG	Fine	VF	XF
6	—	12	10.00	20.00	35.00	50.00
	—	13	10.00	25.00	42.00	50.00
	—	15	10.00	20.00	35.00	50.00
	—	16	10.00	20.00	35.00	50.00
	—	17	10.00	20.00	35.00	50.00
		Thick flan, 20mm				
7	—	18	10.00	20.00	35.00	50.00
	—	19	10.00	20.00	35.00	50.00
	—	20	10.00	20.00	35.00	50.00

MOHUR

GOLD, 10.70-11.40 g
Small lettering, w/o symbols.

KM#	Date	Year	VG	Fine	VF	XF
13	—	16	165.00	225.00	350.00	500.00

NOTE: For later issues bearing lotus and bow and arrow symbols (issued by Sindhia) see Gwalior.

BANSWARA

This state in southern Rajputana was founded in 1538 when the state of Dungarpur was divided between 2 sons of the Maharawal, the younger receiving the territory of Banswara with the title also of Maharawal. The rulers of Banswara were Sissodia Rajputs who claimed descent from the powerful Maharanas of Mewar-Udaipur.

Constantly harassed by the Marathas during the 18th Century, Banswara concluded an alliance in 1818 with the British who provided protection from external enemies in exchange for a portion of the state's revenues. In 1935 the state comprised 1,606 square miles with a population of 225,000, a quarter of whom were aboriginal Bhil tribal people.

During most of the 19th Century, Banswara used the "Salim Shahi" coinage of neighboring Pratapgarh State. But around 1870 Maharawal Lakshman Singh, defying a British prohibiting order of that year, introduced a series of crude coins in copper, silver and gold for use within the state. The legends on these coins are in a secret script, said to have been invented by Lakshman Singh himself. The central word in these legends has been tentatively identified as "Samsatraba" (for "Samba Satra", a designation for the Hindu deity Shiva) in the longer form, or "Samba" for the shorter form. All the gold and silver coins, and a few rare copper ones, carry the longer form. The copper coins were made for circulation, but the gold and silver were produced mainly for presentation.

RULERS

Lakshman Singh, 1844-1905AD
Shambhu Singh, 1906-1908AD
British Administration, 1908-1914AD
Pirthi Singh II, 1914-1944AD
Chandravir Singh, 1944-1949AD

LEGENDS

Samba
Samba is a name of Shiva

With *Ba* downwards is a common error of the die cutters.

Samsatraba
For *Samba Satra*

ANONYMOUS ISSUES

1/4 PAISA

COPPER, 2.40-2.60 g
Obv. and rev: *Samba* in circle, ending downward.

KM#	Date	Year	Good	VG	Fine	VF
1	ND	—	3.00	5.00	8.00	12.50

1/2 PAISA

COPPER, 4.30-5.50 g
Obv. and rev: *Samba* ends upward.

KM#	Date	Year	Good	VG	Fine	VF
3	ND	—	1.75	3.00	6.50	10.00

Obv. and rev: *Samba* ends downward.

KM#	Date	Year	Good	VG	Fine	VF
4	ND	—	1.75	3.00	6.50	10.00

Obv. and rev: *Samba* within leg. ends upwards.

KM#	Date	Year	Good	VG	Fine	VF
5	ND	—	1.00	1.75	4.00	6.50

Obv: *Samba* ends upward.
Rev: *Samba* ends downward.

KM#	Date	Year	Good	VG	Fine	VF
6	ND	—	1.75	3.00	6.50	10.00
	Obv. and rev: *Samba* ends down, in large circles.					
7	ND	—	3.00	5.00	8.00	12.50

PAISA

COPPER, 10.20-11.70 g
Obv. and rev: *Samba* within small circle ends downward. Thick flan.

KM#	Date	Year	Good	VG	Fine	VF
8	ND	—	3.00	5.00	8.00	12.00

Obv. and rev: Like KM#8. Broad, thin flan.

KM#	Date	Year	Good	VG	Fine	VF
9	ND	—	4.50	8.00	12.00	17.50

Obv. & rev: *Samba* within leg. ends upward.

KM#	Date	Year	Good	VG	Fine	VF
10	ND	—	1.00	1.75	4.00	6.50

Obv. & rev: *Samba* ends downward.

KM#	Date	Year	Good	VG	Fine	VF
11	ND	—	1.00	1.75	4.00	6.50

Obv: *Samba* ends upward.
Rev: *Samba* ends downward.

KM#	Date	Year	Good	VG	Fine	VF
12	ND	—	1.75	3.00	6.50	10.00

Obv: *Samba* within leg. ends downward.
Rev: *Samba* within large circle ends downward.

KM#	Date	Year	Good	VG	Fine	VF
13	ND	—	3.00	5.00	8.00	12.50

Samsatraba Series

Obv. and rev. leg: *Samsatraba* within circle.

KM#	Date	Year	Good	VG	Fine	VF
14	ND	—	3.00	5.00	8.00	12.50

NAZARANA 1/8 RUPEE

SILVER, 1.00 g
Obv. and rev: *Samsatraba.*

KM#	Date	Year	Fine	VF	XF	Unc
20	ND	—	11.00	17.50	23.50	32.50

NAZARANA 1/4 RUPEE

SILVER, 2.00 g
Obv. and rev. leg: *Samsatraba.*

KM#	Date	Year	Fine	VF	XF	Unc
21	ND	—	11.50	18.50	25.00	35.00

NAZARANA 1/2 RUPEE

SILVER, 4.00 g
Obv. and rev. leg: *Samsatraba.*

KM#	Date	Year	Fine	VF	XF	Unc
22	ND	—	12.50	21.50	28.50	40.00

NAZARANA RUPEE

SILVER, 8.00-8.20 g
Thick flan
Obv. and rev. leg: *Samsatraba.*

KM#	Date	Year	VG	Fine	VF	XF
16	ND	—	9.00	15.00	21.50	30.00

Broad thin flan

KM#	Date	Year	Fine	VF	XF	Unc
23	ND	—	6.50	11.00	16.50	25.00

HEAVY RUPEE

SILVER, 12.00 g
Similar to Nazarana Rupee, KM#16.

KM#	Date	Year	Fine	VF	XF	Unc
17	ND	—	—	—	Rare	—

Similar to Nazarana Rupee, KM#23.

KM#	Date	Year	Fine	VF	XF	Unc
24	ND	—	—	—	Rare	—

NAZARANA MOHUR

GOLD, 12.00 g
Thick flan.
Obv. and rev. leg: *Samsatraba.*

KM#	Date	Year	VG	Fine	VF	XF
18	ND	—	150.00	185.00	250.00	350.00

Broad, thin flan.

KM#	Date	Year	Fine	VF	XF	Unc
25	ND	—	135.00	200.00	285.00	375.00

BARODA

Maratha state located in western India. The ruling line was descended from Damaji, a Maratha soldier, who received the title of "Distinguished Swordsman" in 1721 (hence the scimitar on most Baroda coins). The Baroda title "Gaikwara" comes from "gaikwar" or cow herd, Damaji's father's occupation.

The Maratha rulers of Baroda, the Gaekwar family rose to prominence in the mid-eighteenth century by carving out for themselves a dominion from territories which were previously under the control of the Poona Marathas, and to a lesser extent, of the Raja of Jodhpur. Chronic internal disputes regarding the succession to the masnad culminated in the intervention of British troops in support of one candidate, Anand Rao Gaekwar, in 1800. Then, in 1802, an agreement with the East India Company released the Baroda princes from their fear of domination by the Maratha Peshwa of Poona but subordinated them to Company interests. Nevertheless, for almost the next century and a half Baroda maintained a good relationship with the British and continued as a major Princely State right up to 1947, when it acceded to the Indian Union.

RULERS

Gaekwars

Anand Rao
AH1215-1235/1800-1819AD
Sayaji Rao II
AH1235-1264/1819-1847AD
Ganpat Rao
AH1264-1273/1847-1856AD
Khande Rao
AH1273-1287/1856-1870AD
Malhar Rao
AH1287-1292/1870-1875AD
Sayaji Rao III
AH1292-1357/VS1932-1995/1875-1938AD
Pratap Singh
VS1995-2008/1938-1951AD

MINTS

Ahmadabad
Amreli
Baroda
Jambusar
Petlad

MINT MARKS

Ahmadabad Mint

Ankus, Maratha mark.

Nagari letters denoting Baroda ruler:

गा

Ga - Anand Rao's Shah Alam II coins, Ahmadabad Mint (with two verticle stems).

आ

A - Anand Rao's Shah Alam II coins, Petlad Mint.

म

Ma - Manaji Rao's Shah Alam II coins, Baroda Mint.

आ

A - Anand Rao's Muhammad Akbar II coins, Baroda Mint.

गा

Ga-a - Anand Rao's Muhammad Akbar II coins, Ahmadabad Mint (with three verticle stems).

सा

Sa - Sayaji Rao II, Baroda Mint.

सा गा or सा गा

(Sri) Sa Ga - Sayaji Rao II, Amreli Mint.

ग गा

Ga Ga - Ganpat Rao, Amreli Mint.

गा

Ga - Ganpat Rao, Baroda Mint.

श्री ग गा

Sri Ga Ga - Ganpat Rao, Amreli Mint.

खा

Kha - Khande Rao, Muhammad Akbar II coins, Baroda Mint.

ख·गा

Kha Ga - Khande Rao, coins in own name, Baroda Mint.

श्री ख गा

Sri Kha Ga - Khande Rao, Amreli Mint.

मा गा

Ma Ga - Malhar Rao.

सा गा

Sa Ga - Sayaji Rao III, Amreli Mint

सा ·गा

Sa Ga - Sayaji Rao III, Baroda Mint.

NOTE: The first 2 marks are found only on the coins of Ahmadabad Mint, and serve to identify it. The remaining 16 marks are used to indicate the ruler under whom the coin was struck; when no mintname is given after the ruler's name in the above list, that shows that the symbol was used at all his mints. Note the various forms of *'G'* and *'Ga'* used above.

AHMADABAD MINT

A Maratha mint from 1757-1800, Ahmadabad was leased to Baroda 1800-1804 and 1806-1817, when it was ceded to Baroda. However, in 1818 it was annexed by the British East India Company.

ANAND RAO

AH1212-1235/1800-1819AD

In the name of Shah Alam II
AH1173-1221/1759-1806AD
Nagari *Ga* and ankus

1/4 RUPEE

SILVER

C#	Date	Year	VG	Fine	VF	XF
17	—	—	7.50	15.00	25.00	35.00

1/2 RUPEE

SILVER, 5.35-5.80 g

C#	Date	Year	VG	Fine	VF	XF
18	—	4x	6.50	13.00	22.00	32.00

RUPEE

SILVER, 10.70-11.60 g

C#	Date	Year	VG	Fine	VF	XF
19	—	3x	5.50	11.00	18.00	28.00
	—	41	5.50	11.00	18.00	28.00
	—	5x	5.50	11.00	18.00	28.00

In the name of Muhammad Akbar II

AH1221-1253/1806-1837AD

Nagari *Ga* and ankus

1/2 RUPEE

SILVER, 5.35-5.80 g

A28 — — 6.50 13.00 21.00 30.00

RUPEE

SILVER, 10.70-11.60 g

C#	Date	Year	VG	Fine	VF	XF
28	AH1225	—	5.50	11.00	18.00	28.00
	1227	6	5.50	11.00	18.00	28.00
	—	6	5.50	11.00	18.00	28.00
	1229	7	5.50	11.00	18.00	28.00
	1229	8	5.50	11.00	18.00	28.00
	1231	9	5.50	11.00	18.00	28.00
	1232	10	5.50	11.00	18.00	28.00
	1233	11	5.50	11.00	18.00	28.00

NOTE: The Ahmedabad Mint was acquired by the British in 1818AD (AH1233). Refer to British India, Bombay Presidency KM#257-260.

AMRELI MINT

SAYAJI RAO II

AH1235-1264/1819-1847AD

Nagari *Sa Ga*

1/2 PAISA

COPPER

Similar to 1 Paisa, C#30.

C#	Date	Year	Good	VG	Fine	VF
A29.1	ND	—	2.50	4.50	7.00	10.00

Obv: Katar above scimatar.

A29.2 AH125x — 2.50 4.50 7.00 10.00

PAISA

COPPER, 7.00-8.00 g

Obv: Scimitar.

29.1 AH1253 — 2.50 4.50 7.00 10.00

Obv: Elephant left w/flag right.

C#	Date	Year	Good	VG	Fine	VF
29.2	AH1256	—	3.00	5.50	8.50	11.50

Obv: Elephant and flag left.

29.3 AH1256 — 2.50 4.50 7.00 10.00

Obv: Katar above scimitar.

C#	Date	Year	Good	VG	Fine	VF
29.4	AH1245	—	2.50	4.50	7.00	10.00
	1256	—	2.50	4.50	7.00	10.00
	1257	—	2.50	4.50	7.00	10.00

Obv: Elephant w/flag right. Rev: Similar to C#29.4.

29.5 ND — 5.00 6.50 10.00 15.00

Obv: Scimitar.

29.6 AH1257 — 2.50 4.50 7.00 10.00

Obv: Crescent.

29.7 AH1262 — 3.00 5.50 8.50 11.50

Obv: Crescent. Rev: Trident.

29.8 AH— — 3.00 5.50 8.50 11.50

Obv: Large *Sa*.

30.1 ND — 1.50 2.50 4.00 5.50

30.2 ND — 1.50 2.50 4.00 5.50

GANPAT RAO

AH1264-1273/1847-1856AD

Nagari *Ga Ga*

1/2 PAISA

COPPER, 14mm

A39 AH1266 — 2.50 4.50 6.00 8.50

PAISA

COPPER

Obv: Lotus at left, scimitar at right.

C#	Date	Year	Good	VG	Fine	VF
39.1	ND	—	3.00	5.50	7.00	9.00
	AH1266	3	3.00	5.50	7.00	9.00
	1272	—	3.00	5.50	7.00	9.00

Obv: Scimitar at left, lotus at right.

39.2 AH1266 — 3.00 5.50 7.00 9.00

KHANDE RAO

AH1273-1287/1856-1870AD

Nagari *Sri Kha Ga*

1/2 PAISA

COPPER

A1 AH1277 — — — — —

PAISA

COPPER, 7.00 g

Thin flan

Y#	Date	Year	Good	VG	Fine	VF
1.1	AH1277	—	2.00	3.50	5.50	8.00

Obv: Scimitar at upper left.

1.2 AH— 13 2.00 3.50 5.50 8.00

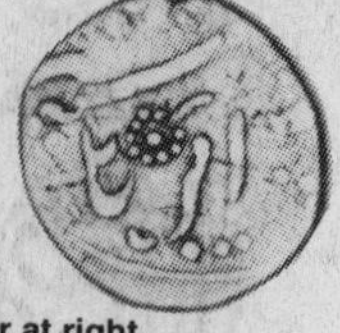

Obv: Scimitar at right.

Y#	Date	Year	Good	VG	Fine	VF
1.3	AH—	—	2.00	3.50	5.50	8.00
1.4	AH1270	—	2.00	3.50	5.50	8.00

Thick flan, cruder types.

1a ND — 2.00 3,50 5.50 8.00

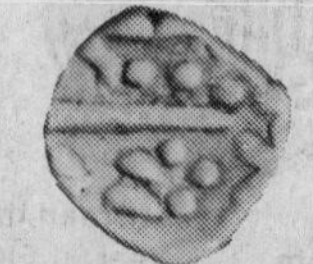

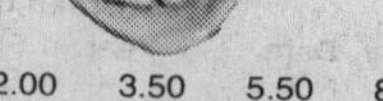

1b ND — 2.00 3.50 5.50 8.00

1/4 MOHUR

GOLD, 2.80, 15mm

Y#	Date	Year	Good	VG	Fine	VF
B13	AH127x	—	—	—	Rare	—

SAYAJI RAO III

AH1292-1357/1875-1939AD

Nagari *Sa Ga*

1/4 PAISA

COPPER

Y#	Date	Year	Good	VG	Fine	VF
A2	AH1312(retrograde)	—	5.00	8.00	12.00	18.00

1/2 PAISA

COPPER, 16mm

Y#	Date	Year	Good	VG	Fine	VF
2	AH1312	—	1.75	3.25	4.50	6.00

PAISA

COPPER

Obv and rev: Date.

Y#	Date	Year	Good	VG	Fine	VF
3	AH1312(retrograde)	—	3.00	5.00	7.50	10.00
	1313(retrograde)	—	3.00	5.00	7.50	10.00

Rev: English S with serifs to left of *Sa Ga* and sword in *S* of *Julus*.

Y#	Date	Year	Good	VG	Fine	VF
3a	ND	—	6.00	10.00	14.00	18.50

NOTE: These coins may have been issued by Sayaji Rao II w/blundered dates.

BARODA MINT

ANAND RAO

AH1215-1235/1800-1819AD

In the name of Muhammad Akbar II

AH1221-1253/1806-1837AD

Nagari *A* and scimitar

1/2 PAISA

COPPER, 14mm

C#	Date	Year	Good	VG	Fine	VF
20	AH1232	11	2.00	3.00	4.00	5.00
	123x	14	2.00	3.00	4.00	5.00

PAISA

COPPER, 9.80 g

C#	Date	Year	Good	VG	Fine	VF
21	AH1226	6	1.25	2.50	3.50	5.00
	1227	7	1.25	2.50	3.50	5.00
	122x	8	1.25	2.50	3.50	5.00
	122x	9	1.25	2.50	3.50	5.00
	1231	11	1.25	2.50	3.50	5.00
	—	13	1.25	2.50	3.50	5.00
	1234	14	1.25	2.50	3.50	5.00
	1236	16	1.25	2.50	3.50	5.00

1/8 RUPEE

SILVER, 1.34-1.45 g

C#	Date	Year	VG	Fine	VF	XF
24	AH122x	—	5.00	7.00	10.00	15.00
	1233	—	5.00	7.00	10.00	15.00
	1234	—	5.00	7.00	10.00	15.00

1/4 RUPEE

SILVER, 2.68-2.90 g

C#	Date	Year	VG	Fine	VF	XF
25	AH1228	—	5.50	8.00	12.50	18.50

1/2 RUPEE

SILVER, 5.35-5.80 g

C#	Date	Year	VG	Fine	VF	XF
26	AH1222	2	6.00	9.00	13.50	20.00
	1226	6	6.00	9.00	13.50	20.00
	1228	8	6.00	9.00	13.50	20.00
	1234	14	6.00	9.00	13.50	20.00

RUPEE

SILVER, 10.70-11.60 g

C#	Date	Year	VG	Fine	VF	XF
27	AH1222	2	7.50	12.50	18.50	27.50
	1224	4	7.50	12.50	18.50	27.50
	1225	5	7.50	12.50	18.50	27.50
	1226	6	7.50	12.50	18.50	27.50
	1227	7	7.50	12.50	18.50	27.50
	1228	8	7.50	12.50	18.50	27.50
	1229	9	7.50	12.50	18.50	27.50
	1232	12	7.50	12.50	18.50	27.50
	1233	13	7.50	12.50	18.50	27.50
	1234	14	7.50	12.50	18.50	27.50

SAYAJI RAO II

AH1235-1264/1819-1847AD

In the name of Muhammad Akbar II

AH1221-1253/1806-1837AD

Nagari *Sa* or *Sa Ga* and other symbols.

1/2 PAISA

COPPER, 14-15mm, 4.30 g

Rev: W/o symbols.

C#	Date	Year	Good	VG	Fine	VF
31.1	AH123x	—	1.25	2.50	4.00	6.00

Rev: Cross.

C#	Date	Year	Good	VG	Fine	VF
31.2	ND	—	1.25	2.50	4.00	6.00
	AH1236	16	2.00	4.00	6.00	10.00

Rev: Sun.

C#	Date	Year	Good	VG	Fine	VF
31.4	ND	—	1.25	2.50	4.00	6.00

Rev: Flag.

C#	Date	Year	Good	VG	Fine	VF
31.5	AH1251	—	2.00	4.00	6.00	10.00

Rev: Shaded ball.

C#	Date	Year	Good	VG	Fine	VF
31.8	AH1260	40	1.25	2.50	4.00	6.00

PAISA

COPPER, 18-24mm, 10.20 g

Rev: W/o symbol.

C#	Date	Year	Good	VG	Fine	VF
33.1	AH1236	16	1.25	2.00	3.00	4.50

Rev: Accented outlined cross.

C#	Date	Year	Good	VG	Fine	VF
33.2	AH1240	20	1.25	2.25	3.50	5.00
	1241	20	1.25	2.25	3.50	5.00

Rev: Simple outlined cross.

C#	Date	Year	Good	VG	Fine	VF
33.3	AH1243	23	1.25	2.25	3.50	5.00
	1244	—	1.25	2.25	3.50	5.00

Accented cross outline

C#	Date	Year	Good	VG	Fine	VF
33.14	1244	—	1.25	2.25	3.50	5.00

Rev: Rayed sun.

C#	Date	Year	Good	VG	Fine	VF
33.4	AH124x	23	1.25	2.25	3.50	5.00
	1247	27	1.25	2.25	3.50	5.00

Rev: Person.

C#	Date	Year	Good	VG	Fine	VF
33.13	AH1248	28	1.25	2.25	3.50	5.00
	1249	29	1.25	2.25	3.50	5.00

Rev: Flag.

C#	Date	Year	Good	VG	Fine	VF
33.5	AH12xx	28	1.25	2.25	3.50	5.00
	1249	29	1.25	2.25	3.50	5.00
	12xx	30	1.25	2.25	3.50	5.00
	1250	—	1.25	2.25	3.50	5.00
	1251	—	1.25	2.25	3.50	5.00
	1253	—	1.25	2.25	3.50	5.00

Rev: Upright cross.

C#	Date	Year	Good	VG	Fine	VF
33.6	AH1255	35	1.25	2.25	3.50	5.00

Rev: Tulip

C#	Date	Year	Good	VG	Fine	VF
33.9	AH1253	33	1.25	2.25	3.50	5.00
	1254	—	1.25	2.25	3.50	5.00
	1255	36	1.25	2.25	3.50	5.00

Rev: 4 petal flower.

C#	Date	Year	Good	VG	Fine	VF
33.15	AH1255	35	2.00	3.50	5.00	7.00

Rev: 5 petal flower.

C#	Date	Year	Good	VG	Fine	VF
33.7	AH—	35	1.25	2.25	3.50	5.00
	1255	36	1.25	2.25	3.50	5.00
	1256	36	1.25	2.25	3.50	5.00
	1263	—	1.25	2.25	3.50	5.00

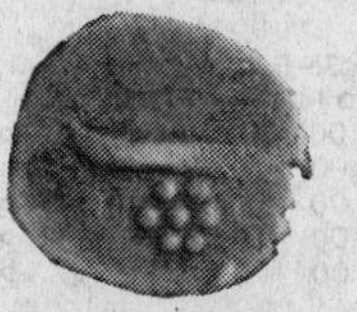

Rev: Shaded ball.

C#	Date	Year	Good	VG	Fine	VF
33.8	AH1260	40	1.00	2.00	3.00	4.00
	1261	41	1.00	2.00	3.00	4.00
	1262	—	1.00	2.00	3.00	4.00

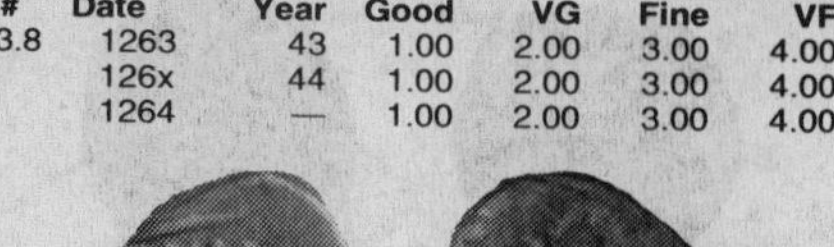

C#	Date	Year	Good	VG	Fine	VF
33.8	1263	43	1.00	2.00	3.00	4.00
	126x	44	1.00	2.00	3.00	4.00
	1264	—	1.00	2.00	3.00	4.00

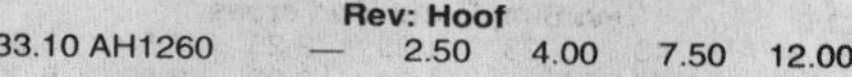

Rev: Hoof

C#	Date	Year	Good	VG	Fine	VF
33.10	AH1260	—	2.50	4.00	7.50	12.00

Rev: Flag and branch.

C#	Date	Year	Good	VG	Fine	VF
33.11	ND	—	2.00	3.50	6.00	10.00

Rev: Flower

C#	Date	Year	Good	VG	Fine	VF
33.12	AH12xx	—	2.00	3.50	6.00	10.00

1/8 RUPEE

SILVER, 11-14mm, 1.34-1.45 g
Rev: Scimitar to left of *Julus*.

C#	Date	Year	VG	Fine	VF	XF
35.1	AH—	17	5.00	7.00	10.00	15.00

Rev: Scimitar above *Julus*.

C#	Date	Year	VG	Fine	VF	XF
35.2	—	26	5.00	7.00	10.00	15.00

Rev: Scimitar to right of *Julus*.

C#	Date	Year	VG	Fine	VF	XF
35.3	AH12xx	—	5.00	7.00	10.00	15.00

1/4 RUPEE

SILVER, 2.68-2.90 g
Rev: Scimitar to left of *Julus*.

C#	Date	Year	VG	Fine	VF	XF
36.1	AH1238	18	5.50	8.00	12.50	18.50

Rev: Scimitar above *Julus*.

C#	Date	Year	VG	Fine	VF	XF
36.2	AH—	24	5.50	8.00	12.50	18.50

Rev: Scimitar to right of *Julus*.

C#	Date	Year	VG	Fine	VF	XF
36.3	AH1249	29	5.50	8.00	12.50	18.50
	1250	29	5.50	8.00	12.50	18.50
	1257	37	5.50	8.00	12.50	18.50

1/2 RUPEE

SILVER, 5.35-5.80 g
Rev: Scimitar to left of *Julus*.

C#	Date	Year	VG	Fine	VF	XF
37.1	AH1238	18	6.00	9.00	13.50	20.00
	1239	19	6.00	9.00	13.50	20.00
	12xx	20	6.00	9.00	13.50	20.00
	1241	21	6.00	9.00	13.50	20.00
	124x	27	6.00	9.00	13.50	20.00

Rev: Scimitar above *Julus*.

C#	Date	Year	VG	Fine	VF	XF
37.2	AH124x	24	6.00	9.00	13.50	20.00
	124x	26	6.00	9.00	13.50	20.00
	124x	27	6.00	9.00	13.50	20.00

Rev: Scimitar to right of *Julus*.

C#	Date	Year	VG	Fine	VF	XF
37.3	AH1254	33	6.00	9.00	13.50	20.00
	125x	35	6.00	9.00	13.50	20.00
	125x	37	6.00	9.00	13.50	20.00
	125x	38	6.00	9.00	13.50	20.00
	125x	39	6.00	9.00	13.50	20.00
	1260	40	6.00	9.00	13.50	20.00
	126x	42	6.00	9.00	13.50	20.00

RUPEE

SILVER, 10.70-11.60 g
Rev: Scimitar to left of *Julus*.

C#	Date	Year	VG	Fine	VF	XF
38.1	AH1237	17	7.50	12.50	18.50	27.50
	1238	18	7.50	12.50	18.50	27.50
	1239	19	7.50	12.50	18.50	27.50
	1240	19	7.50	12.50	18.50	27.50
	1240	20	7.50	12.50	18.50	27.50
	1241	21	7.50	12.50	18.50	27.50
	1242	22	7.50	12.50	18.50	27.50

Rev: Scimitar above *Julus*.

C#	Date	Year	VG	Fine	VF	XF
38.2	AH1244	24	7.50	12.50	18.50	27.50
	124x	25	7.50	12.50	18.50	27.50
	1248	27	7.50	12.50	18.50	27.50

Rev: Scimitar to right of *Julus*.

C#	Date	Year	VG	Fine	VF	XF
38.3	AH1247	—	7.50	12.50	18.50	27.50
	1249	29	7.50	12.50	18.50	27.50
	1250	30	7.50	12.50	18.50	27.50
	1251	32	7.50	12.50	18.50	27.50
	1253	33	7.50	12.50	18.50	27.50
	1254	33	7.50	12.50	18.50	27.50
	1255	35	7.50	12.50	18.50	27.50
	1256	36	7.50	12.50	18.50	27.50
	1257	37	7.50	12.50	18.50	27.50
	1258	38	7.50	12.50	18.50	27.50
	1259	39	7.50	12.50	18.50	27.50
	1260	40	7.50	12.50	18.50	27.50

GANPAT RAO

AH1264-1273/1847-1856AD

In the name of Muhammad Akbar II

AH1221-1253/1806-1837AD

Nagari *Ga* and scimitar.

1/2 PAISA

COPPER, 15mm, 5.00 g
Obv: Shaded ball in center.

C#	Date	Year	Good	VG	Fine	VF
41	AH1264-1272	—	1.00	2.00	3.00	4.50

PAISA

COPPER, 10.00 g

C#	Date	Year	Good	VG	Fine	VF
42	AH1263	43	2.00	3.00	4.00	5.50
	1264	44	2.00	3.00	4.00	5.50
	1265	45	2.00	3.00	4.00	5.50
	1266	46	2.00	3.00	4.00	5.50
	1272	52	2.00	3.00	4.00	5.50

Obv: Shaded ball in center.

C#	Date	Year	Good	VG	Fine	VF
43	AH1264	4x	2.00	3.00	4.00	5.50
	1266	4x	2.00	3.00	4.00	5.50
	1268	4x	2.00	3.00	4.00	5.50

1/8 RUPEE

SILVER, 11mm, 1.34-1.45 g

C#	Date	Year	VG	Fine	VF	XF
44	AH126x	—	5.50	8.00	10.00	15.00
	1269	—	5.50	8.00	10.00	15.00

1/4 RUPEE

SILVER, 2.68-2.90 g

C#	Date	Year	VG	Fine	VF	XF
45	AH126x	—	5.50	8.00	12.50	18.50
	1272	52	5.50	8.00	12.50	18.50

1/2 RUPEE

SILVER, 5.35-5.80 g

C#	Date	Year	VG	Fine	VF	XF
46	AH126x	43	6.00	9.00	13.50	20.00
	1264	44	6.00	9.00	13.50	20.00
	126x	45	6.00	9.00	13.50	20.00
	1267	46	6.00	9.00	13.50	20.00
	1268	47	6.00	9.00	13.50	20.00
	12xx	49	6.00	9.00	13.50	20.00
	1271	—	6.00	9.00	13.50	20.00
	127x	51	6.00	9.00	13.50	20.00
	1272	52	6.00	9.00	13.50	20.00

RUPEE

SILVER, 10.70-11.60 g

C#	Date	Year	VG	Fine	VF	XF
47	AH1264	43	7.00	11.00	16.50	25.00
	1265	43	7.00	11.00	16.50	25.00
	1265	44	7.00	11.00	16.50	25.00
	126x	45	7.00	11.00	16.50	25.00
	126x	46	7.00	11.00	16.50	25.00
	1268	47	7.00	11.00	16.50	25.00
	1271	50	7.00	11.00	16.50	25.00
	1272	51	7.00	11.00	16.50	25.00
	1272	52	7.00	11.00	16.50	25.00

KHANDE RAO

AH1273-1287/1856-1870AD

In the name of Muhammad Akbar II

AH1221-1253/1806-1837AD

Nagari *Kha* and scimitar.

1/2 PAISA

COPPER, 15mm, 4.20 g
Rev: Pomegranate.

Y#	Date	Year	Good	VG	Fine	VF
1	ND	—	1.25	2.00	3.00	4.00

PAISA

COPPER, 8.40 g
Rev: Pomegranate.

Y#	Date	Year	Good	VG	Fine	VF
2	AH1273	52	1.50	2.50	3.50	5.00

1/4 RUPEE

SILVER, 2.68-2.90 g

Y#	Date	Year	VG	Fine	VF	XF
3	AH1273	52	5.00	8.00	12.50	18.50
	1278	—	5.00	8.00	12.50	18.50

1/2 RUPEE

SILVER, 5.35-5.80 g

Y#	Date	Year	VG	Fine	VF	XF
4	AH1267	—	5.50	9.00	13.50	20.00
	1272	—	5.50	9.00	13.50	20.00
	127x	52	5.50	9.00	13.50	20.00
	1274	—	5.50	9.00	13.50	20.00
	1275	—	5.50	9.00	13.50	20.00
	1282	—	5.50	9.00	13.50	20.00

RUPEE

SILVER, 10.70-11.60 g

Y#	Date	Year	VG	Fine	VF	XF
5	AH1273	5x	6.50	11.00	16.50	25.00
	1274	53	6.50	11.00	16.50	25.00
	1275	—	6.50	11.00	16.50	25.00
	128x	—	6.50	11.00	16.50	25.00

In the name of the Commander of the Sovereign Band (a title of the Gaekwar, ruler of Baroda).

From AH1274 (1857AD)

Nagari *Kha Ga* and scimitar.

1/2 PAISA

COPPER, 3.40 g
Rev: Scimitar.

Y#	Date	Year	Good	VG	Fine	VF
6	AH1275	—	2.00	3.00	4.00	5.50
	1276	—	2.00	3.00	4.00	5.50
	1277	—	3.00	5.00	7.50	12.00

Rev: Scimitar and hoof.

Y#	Date	Year	Good	VG	Fine	VF
6a	AH128x	—	5.00	7.50	10.00	15.00
	1285	—	5.00	7.50	10.00	15.00

PAISA

COPPER, 7.00-8.00 g
Rev: Scimitar.

Y#	Date	Year	Good	VG	Fine	VF
7	AH1274	—	2.00	3.00	4.00	5.50
	1275	—	1.25	2.25	3.25	4.00
	1276	—	1.25	2.25	3.25	4.00
	1277	—	2.00	3.00	4.00	5.50

Rev: Scimitar and hoof.

Y#	Date	Year	Good	VG	Fine	VF
7a	AH1281	—	3.50	4.50	6.00	8.00
	1282	—	3.50	4.50	6.00	8.00
	1283	—	3.50	4.50	6.00	8.00
	1284	—	3.50	4.50	6.00	8.00
	1285	—	3.50	4.50	6.00	8.00

2 PAISA

COPPER, 15.00 g
Rev: Scimitar and hoof.

Y#	Date	Year	Good	VG	Fine	VF
8	AH1281	—	2.50	4.00	5.50	7.50
	1284	—	2.50	4.00	5.50	7.50
	1285	—	2.50	4.00	5.50	7.50

1/8 RUPEE

SILVER, 1.34-1.45 g

Y#	Date	Year	VG	Fine	VF	XF
9	AH1282	—	5.00	7.00	10.00	15.00

1/4 RUPEE

SILVER, 2.68-2.90 g

Y#	Date	Year	VG	Fine	VF	XF
10	AH1274	—	4.50	6.50	9.00	18.50
	1282	—	4.50	6.50	9.00	18.50
	1283	—	4.50	6.50	9.00	18.50
	1286	—	4.50	6.50	9.00	18.50

1/2 RUPEE

SILVER, 5.35-5.80 g

Y#	Date	Year	VG	Fine	VF	XF
11	AH1274	—	6.00	9.00	13.50	20.00
	1275	—	6.00	9.00	13.50	20.00
	1276	—	6.00	9.00	13.50	20.00
	1277	—	6.00	9.00	13.50	20.00
	1278	—	6.00	9.00	13.50	20.00
	1279	—	6.00	9.00	13.50	20.00
	1280	—	6.00	9.00	13.50	20.00
	1282	—	6.00	9.00	13.50	20.00
	1284	—	6.00	9.00	13.50	20.00
	1285	—	6.00	9.00	13.50	20.00
	1286	—	6.00	9.00	13.50	20.00

RUPEE

SILVER, 10.70-11.60 g

Y#	Date	Year	VG	Fine	VF	XF
12	AH1274	—	6.50	10.00	15.00	22.50
	1275	—	6.50	10.00	15.00	22.50
	1276	—	6.50	10.00	15.00	22.50
	1277	—	6.50	10.00	15.00	22.50
	1278	—	6.50	10.00	15.00	22.50
	1280	—	6.50	10.00	15.00	22.50
	1281	—	6.50	10.00	15.00	22.50
	1282	—	6.50	10.00	15.00	22.50
	1283	—	6.50	10.00	15.00	22.50
	1284	—	6.50	10.00	15.00	22.50
	1285	—	6.50	10.00	15.00	22.50
	1286	—	6.50	10.00	15.00	22.50
	1287	—	6.50	10.00	15.00	22.50
	(12)87	—	6.50	10.00	15.00	22.50

NAZARANA 1-1/2 RUPEES

SILVER, 18.10 g

Y#	Date	Year	VG	Fine	VF	XF
A13	AH1275	—	—	—	Rare	—

Milled Coinage

NAZARANA 1/2 RUPEE

SILVER, 5.65 g

Y#	Date	Year	VG	Fine	VF	XF
13	AH1287	—	50.00	85.00	120.00	175.00

NAZARANA RUPEE

SILVER, 11.30 g
Obv. Persian leg: ***Kahnde Rao.***

Y#	Date	Year	VG	Fine	VF	XF
14.1	AH1287	—	40.00	70.00	100.00	140.00

Obv. Persian leg: ***Khande Rao.***

Y#	Date	Year	VG	Fine	VF	XF
14.2	AH1287	—	60.00	100.00	140.00	200.00

Dump Coinage

MALHAR RAO

AH1287-1292/1870-1875AD

Nagari *Ma Ga* and scimitar.

1/2 PAISA

COPPER, 4.00 g

Y#	Date	Year	Good	VG	Fine	VF
15	AH1288	—	2.00	3.00	4.00	5.50
	1290	—	2.00	3.00	4.00	5.50

PAISA

COPPER, 7.60-8.60 g

Y#	Date	Year	Good	VG	Fine	VF
16	AH1288	—	1.25	2.50	3.50	5.00
	1289	—	1.25	2.50	3.50	5.00
	1290	—	1.25	2.50	3.50	5.00
	ND	—	1.25	2.50	3.50	5.00

2 PAISA

COPPER, 16.10 g

Y#	Date	Year	Good	VG	Fine	VF
17	AH1288	—	2.00	3.00	4.00	5.50
	1289	—	2.00	3.00	4.00	5.50
	1290	—	2.00	3.00	4.00	5.50

NAZARANA 2 PAISA

COPPER

Y#	Date	Year	Good	VG	Fine	VF
A17	AH1289	—	—	—	Rare	—

1/8 RUPEE

SILVER, 11mm, 1.34-1.45 g

Y#	Date	Year	VG	Fine	VF	XF
18	AH129x	—	4.00	6.00	9.00	13.50

1/4 RUPEE

SILVER, 13mm, 2.68-2.90 g

Y#	Date	Year	VG	Fine	VF	XF
19	AH1290	—	5.00	7.00	10.00	15.00

1/2 RUPEE

SILVER, 5.35-5.80 g

Y#	Date	Year	VG	Fine	VF	XF
20	AH1287	—	5.50	8.00	12.50	18.50
	1288	—	5.50	8.00	12.50	18.50
	1289	—	5.50	8.00	12.50	18.50
	1290	—	5.50	8.00	12.50	18.50

RUPEE

SILVER, 10.70-11.60 g

Y#	Date	Year	VG	Fine	VF	XF
21	AH1287	—	6.00	9.00	13.50	20.00
	1288	—	6.00	9.00	13.50	20.00
	1289	—	6.00	9.00	13.50	20.00
	1290	—	6.00	9.00	13.50	20.00
	—	122	6.00	9.00	13.50	20.00

NAZARANA RUPEE

SILVER, 10.70-11.60 g

Y#	Date	Year	VG	Fine	VF	XF
21a	AH1288	—	50.00	85.00	120.00	170.00

NAZARANA 2 RUPEES

SILVER, 21.40-23.20 g

Y#	Date	Year	VG	Fine	VF	XF
22	AH1288	—	—	—	Rare	—

SAYAJI RAO III

AH1292-1357/VS1932-1995/1875-1938AD

Nagari *Sa Ga* and scimitar.

1/4 PAISA

COPPER

Y#	Date	Year	Good	VG	Fine	VF
A23	VS194x	—	2.50	5.00	8.50	12.50

1/2 PAISA

COPPER

Y#	Date	Year	Good	VG	Fine	VF
23	VS1937	(1880)	1.50	2.50	4.00	5.50
	1947	(1890)	1.50	2.50	4.00	5.50
	1948	(1891)	1.50	2.50	4.00	5.50

PAISA

COPPER

Y#	Date	Year	Good	VG	Fine	VF
24	VS1937	(1880)	1.50	2.50	4.00	5.50
	1947	(1890)	1.50	2.50	4.00	5.50
	1948/7	(1890)	1.50	2.50	4.00	5.50
	1948	(1891)	1.50	2.50	4.00	5.50

Machine-punched planchets.

Y#	Date	Year	Good	VG	Fine	VF
24a	VS1949	(1892)	2.00	3.50	5.00	7.00

NOTE: Generally struck off-center.

2 PAISE

COPPER

Y#	Date	Year	Good	VG	Fine	VF
25	VS1937	(1880)	3.50	5.00	6.50	8.50
	1947	(1890)	3.50	5.00	6.50	8.50
	1948	(1891)	3.50	5.00	6.50	8.50

17.00 g
Machine-punched planchets.

Y#	Date	Year	Good	VG	Fine	VF
25a	VS1949	(1892)	3.75	5.50	7.50	10.00

NOTE: Generally struck off-center.

1/8 RUPEE

SILVER, 1.34-1.45 g

Y#	Date	Year	VG	Fine	VF	XF
26	AH1294	—	4.00	6.00	9.00	13.50
	1295	—	4.00	6.00	9.00	13.50
	1297	—	4.00	6.00	9.00	13.50
	1299	—	4.00	6.00	9.00	13.50

1/4 RUPEE

SILVER, 13mm, 2.68-2.90 g

Y#	Date	Year	VG	Fine	VF	XF
27	AH1292	—	5.00	7.00	10.00	15.00
	1299	—	5.00	7.00	10.00	15.00

1/2 RUPEE

SILVER, 5.35-5.80 g

Y#	Date	Year	VG	Fine	VF	XF
28	AH1292	—	5.50	8.00	12.50	18.50
	1293	—	5.50	8.00	12.50	18.50
	1294	—	5.50	8.00	12.50	18.50
	1295	—	5.50	8.00	12.50	18.50
	1297	—	5.50	8.00	12.50	18.50
	1298	—	5.50	8.00	12.50	18.50
	1299	—	5.50	8.00	12.50	18.50
	1300	—	5.50	8.00	12.50	18.50
	1301	—	5.50	8.00	12.50	18.50
	1302	—	5.50	8.00	12.50	18.50

RUPEE

SILVER, 10.70-11.60 g

Y#	Date	Year	VG	Fine	VF	XF
29	AH1292	—	6.00	9.00	13.50	20.00
	1293	—	6.00	9.00	13.50	20.00
	1294	—	6.00	9.00	13.50	20.00
	1295	—	6.00	9.00	13.50	20.00
	1298	—	6.00	9.00	13.50	20.00
	1299	—	6.00	9.00	13.50	20.00
	1300	—	6.00	9.00	13.50	20.00
	1301	—	6.00	9.00	13.50	20.00
	1302	—	6.00	9.00	13.50	20.00

Milled Coinage

PAI

COPPER
Obv: Annulets between letters.

Y#	Date	Year	Good	VG	Fine	VF
30.1	VS1944	(1887)	.50	1.00	1.50	2.00

Obv: Pellets between letters.

Y#	Date	Year	Good	VG	Fine	VF
30.1a	VS1944	(1887)	2.50	5.00	8.00	12.00

Obv: W/o annulets.
Thick planchet

Y#	Date	Year	VG	Fine	VF	XF
30.2	VS1944	(1887)	.75	1.50	2.00	2.50
	1945	(1888)	.35	.75	1.00	1.50
	1946	(1889)	.75	1.50	2.00	2.50
	1947	(1890)	.75	1.50	2.00	2.50

Thin planchet. Obv: Large legends.

Y#	Date	Year	VG	Fine	VF	XF
30.2a	VS1948	(1891)	.75	1.50	2.00	2.50
	1949	(1892)	.35	.75	1.00	1.50
	1950/49	(1893)	.75	1.25	1.75	2.25

Obv: Small legends.

Y#	Date	Year	VG	Fine	VF	XF
30.3	VS1950	(1893)	.35	.75	1.00	1.50

PAISA

COPPER
Obv: Inner leg. curved, long hoof.

Y#	Date	Year	VG	Fine	VF	XF
31.1	VS1940	(1883)	1.00	2.00	2.50	3.00
	1941	(1884)	1.00	2.00	2.50	3.00
	1942	(1885)	1.75	2.50	3.75	5.00

Thick planchet, 2mm, 8.00-8.30 g
Obv: Inner leg. straight, short hoof.

Y#	Date	Year	VG	Fine	VF	XF
31.2	VS1941	(1884)	.75	1.50	2.00	2.75
	1942	(1885)	.35	.75	1.25	1.75
	1943	(1886)	.35	.75	1.25	1.75
	1944	(1887)	.35	.75	1.25	1.75
	1945	(1888)	.50	1.00	1.50	2.00
	1946/3		—	—	—	—
	1946	(1889)	.50	1.00	1.50	2.00
	1947	(1890)	.35	.75	1.25	1.75

Thin planchet, 1.6mm, 6.50-6.80 g
Obv. & rev: Smaller inner circle.

Y#	Date	Year	VG	Fine	VF	XF
31.2a	AH1948	(1891)	.30	.60	1.00	1.50
	1949	(1892)	.30	.60	1.00	1.50
	1950	(1893)	.30	.60	1.00	1.50

2 PAISA

COPPER
Obv: Inner leg. curved, long hoof.
Rev: Large inner leg. and date.

Y#	Date	Year	VG	Fine	VF	XF
32.1	VS1940	(1883)	2.00	3.50	5.00	6.50
	1941	(1884)	2.00	3.50	5.00	6.50

Thick planchet, 2.9mm, 16.30-16.80 g
Obv: Inner leg. straight, short hoof.
Rev: Small inner leg. and date.

Y#	Date	Year	VG	Fine	VF	XF
32.2	VS1941	(1884)	1.00	2.00	3.00	4.50
	1942	(1885)	1.00	2.00	3.00	4.50
	1943	(1886)	.75	1.50	2.25	3.00
	1944/3	(1887)	.75	1.50	2.25	3.00
	1944	(1887)	.75	1.50	2.25	3.00
	1945/2	—	—	—	—	—
	1945	(1888)	.75	1.50	2.25	3.00
	1946	(1889)	1.25	2.50	4.00	6.00
	1947	(1890)	.75	1.50	2.25	3.00
	1948	(1891)	2.50	4.00	6.00	8.50
	1949	(1892)	— Reported, not confirmed			

Thin planchet, 2.4mm, 12.40-13.30 g

Y#	Date	Year	VG	Fine	VF	XF
32.2a	VS1948	(1891)	.50	1.00	1.50	2.25
	1949/4	(1892)	.50	1.00	1.50	2.25
	1949/8	(1892)	.75	1.50	2.25	3.00
	1949	(1892)	.75	1.50	2.25	3.00
	1950	(1893)	.65	1.25	1.75	2.50

2 ANNAS

SILVER

Y#	Date	Year	Fine	VF	XF	Unc
33	VS1949	(1892)	7.00	11.00	16.50	25.00

Y#	Date	Year	Fine	VF	XF	Unc
33a	VS1951	(1894)	6.50	10.00	15.00	22.50
	1952	(1895)	6.50	10.00	15.00	22.50

4 ANNAS

SILVER

Y#	Date	Year	Fine	VF	XF	Unc
34	VS1949	(1892)	7.00	11.00	16.00	25.00

Y#	Date	Year	Fine	VF	XF	Unc
34a	VS1951	(1894)	6.00	9.00	13.50	20.00
	1952	(1895)	6.00	9.00	13.50	20.00

1/2 RUPEE

SILVER

Y#	Date	Year	Fine	VF	XF	Unc
35	VS1948	(1891)	30.00	40.00	55.00	80.00
	1949	(1892)	30.00	40.00	55.00	80.00

Y#	Date	Year	Fine	VF	XF	Unc
35a	VS1951	(1894)	12.50	18.50	25.00	35.00
	1952	(1895)	12.50	18.50	25.00	35.00

RUPEE

SILVER

Y#	Date	Year	Fine	VF	XF	Unc
36	VS1948	(1891)	13.50	20.00	27.50	37.50
	1949	(1892)	13.50	20.00	27.50	37.50

Y#	Date	Year	Fine	VF	XF	Unc
36a	VS1951	(1894)	11.50	17.50	23.50	32.50
	1952	(1895)	11.50	17.50	23.50	32.50
	1953	(1896)	11.50	17.50	23.50	32.50
	1954	(1897)	11.50	17.50	23.50	32.50
	1955	(1898)	11.50	17.50	23.50	32.50
	1956	(1899)	11.50	17.50	23.50	32.50

1/6 MOHUR

GOLD, 14.5mm, 1.04-1.18 g

Y#	Date	Year	Fine	VF	XF	Unc
A37	VS1943	(1886)	165.00	225.00	275.00	350.00

Y#	Date	Year	Fine	VF	XF	Unc
37	1951	(1894)	165.00	225.00	275.00	350.00
	1953	(1896)	165.00	225.00	275.00	350.00
	1959	(1902)	165.00	225.00	275.00	350.00

1/3 MOHUR

GOLD, 16mm, 2.07-2.39 g

Y#	Date	Year	Fine	VF	XF	Unc
A38	VS1942	(1885)	185.00	250.00	325.00	400.00
38	1959	(1902)	185.00	250.00	325.00	400.00

MOHUR

GOLD, 21mm, 6.20-6.40 g

Y#	Date	Year	Fine	VF	XF	Unc
A39	VS1942	(1885)	265.00	350.00	500.00	750.00

Y#	Date	Year	Fine	VF	XF	Unc
39	VS1945	(1888)	250.00	325.00	450.00	650.00
	1952	(1895)	250.00	325.00	450.00	650.00
	1953	(1896)	250.00	325.00	450.00	650.00
	1959	(1902)	250.00	325.00	450.00	650.00

PRATAP SINGH

VS1995-2008/1938-1951AD

1/3 MOHUR

GOLD, 18mm, 2.07-2.13 g

Y#	Date	Year	Fine	VF	XF	Unc
40	VS1995	(1939)	—	400.00	600.00	900.00

SILVER

Y#	Date	Year	Fine	VF	XF	Unc
40a	VS1995 (restrike)	(1939)		—	75.00	100.00

MOHUR

GOLD, 21mm, 6.20-6.40 g

Y#	Date	Year	Fine	VF	XF	Unc
41	VS1995	(1939)	—	400.00	600.00	900.00

SILVER

Y#	Date	Year	Fine	VF	XF	Unc
41a	VS1995 (restrike)	(1939)		—	75.00	100.00

PETLAD MINT

ANAND RAO

AH1215-1235/1800-1819AD

In the name of Shah Alam II

AH1173-1221/1759-1806AD

and Years of Anand Rao

Regnal Years 1-7

Nagari *A*

PAISA

COPPER, 20mm

C#	Date	Year	Good	VG	Fine	VF
10	—	—	2.50	3.50	4.50	7.00

RUPEE

SILVER, 10.70-11.60 g

C#	Date	Year	VG	Fine	VF	XF
13	—	3	10.00	15.00	21.50	30.00
	—	4	10.00	15.00	21.50	30.00

BELA

Las Bela, Beylah

State located in Baluchistan.

Of very ancient origins, the later history of Las Bela was intimately associated with that of Kalat to which State it became subject in 1758. Thereafter, however, the Arab chieftains of Las Bela, known as Jams, proved capable of demonstrating a very considerable degree of independence. The State continued up to 1947, at which time it acceded to Pakistan.

RULERS

Mir Jamir Khan
AH1246-1287/1830-1869AD
Mir Ali Khan III
AH1287-1294/1869-1877AD
Mir Jamir Khan, restored
AH1294-1306/1877-1888AD

MIR JAMIR KHAN

AH1246-1287/1830-1869AD

FALUS

COPPER

C#	Date	Year	Good	VG	Fine	VF
5	AH1271	—	10.00	20.00	35.00	60.00
	1276	—	10.00	20.00	35.00	60.00
	1285	—	10.00	20.00	35.00	60.00
	1286	—	10.00	20.00	35.00	60.00

In the name of Mahmud Khan Durani

FALUS

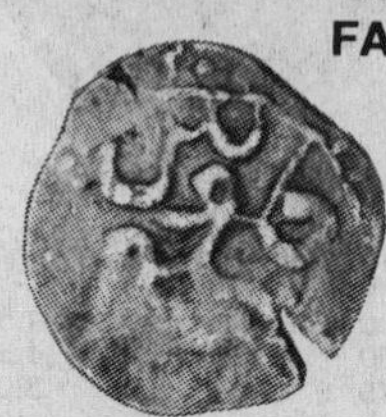

COPPER

C#	Date	Year	Good	VG	Fine	VF
10	ND	—	6.00	12.50	21.50	35.00

BHARATPUR

State located in Rajputana in northwest India.

Bharatpur was founded by Balchand, a Jat chieftain who took advantage of Mughal confusion and weakness after the death of Aurangzeb to seize the area. In 1756 the ruler at that time, Suraj Mal, received the title of Raja. Bharatpur became increasingly associated with Maratha ambitions and, in spite of treaty ties to the East India Company, assisted the Maratha Confederacy in their struggles against the British. This gained them few friends in British circles, but the early attempts by the British to force the submission of Bharatpur fortress proved abortive. In 1826 however, the British took the opportunity offered by a bitter internal feud concerning the succession finally to reduce the stronghold. The rival claimant was exiled to Allahabad and Balwant Singh, then a child of seven, was placed on the throne under the supervision of a British Political Agent. From that time onwards Bharatpur came under British control until it acceded to the Indian Union at Independence.

RULERS

Ranjit Singh
AH1190-1220/1776-1805AD
Randhir Singh
AH1220-1239/1805-1823AD
Baldeo Singh
AH1239-1241/1823-1824AD
Durjan Singh
AH1241-1242/1825-1826AD
Balwant Singh
AH1242-1269/1826-1853AD
Jaswant Singh
AH1269-1311/1853-1893AD/
VS1909-1950

MINTS

Bharatpur بهرت پور

Braj Indrapur برج اندرا پور

Mahe Indrapur مها اندر پور

BHARATPUR MINT

Mintname: Bharatpur or Braj Indrapur

Mint marks:  

In the name of Shah Alam II

AH1173-1221/1759-1806AD

TAKKA

COPPER, 17.50-18.50 g

KM#	Date	Year	Good	VG	Fine	VF
11	AH1216	50	1.25	2.50	4.00	5.50
	—	56	1.25	2.50	4.00	5.50

NOTE: Earlier dates (Yr.4-49) exist for this type.

RUPEE

SILVER, 11.00-11.10 g
Mintname: Braj Indrapur

KM#	Date	Year	VG	Fine	VF	XF
26	AH1216	44	7.00	11.00	16.50	25.00
	1217	45	7.00	11.00	16.50	25.00
	1218	46	7.00	11.00	16.50	25.00
	1219	47	7.00	11.00	16.50	25.00

NOTE: Earlier dates (AH118x-1215) exist for this type.

In the name of Muhammad Akbar II

AH1221-1253/1806-1837AD

TAKKA

COPPER, 17.50-18.50 g

KM#	Date	Year	Good	VG	Fine	VF
101	AH—	20	2.50	4.00	6.50	10.00
	—	22	2.50	4.00	6.50	10.00
	12xx	22	2.50	4.00	6.50	10.00
	1272	48	2.50	4.00	6.50	10.00
	1276	42	2.50	4.00	6.50	10.00
	1279	49	2.50	4.00	6.50	10.00

NOTE: This date is posthumous.

1/4 RUPEE

SILVER, 15mm, 2.75 g

KM#	Date	Year	VG	Fine	VF	XF
104	AH—	—	10.00	15.00	21.50	30.00

1/2 RUPEE

SILVER, 5.50 g

KM#	Date	Year	VG	Fine	VF	XF
105	AH—	22	8.50	13.50	20.00	28.50
	12xx	34	8.50	13.50	20.00	28.50
	—	35	8.50	13.50	20.00	28.50

RUPEE

SILVER, 11.00-11.10 g
Thick flan.

KM#	Date	Year	VG	Fine	VF	XF
106	AH1221	—	7.00	11.00	16.50	25.00
	1222	2	7.00	11.00	16.50	25.00
	122x	3	7.00	11.00	16.50	25.00
	1224	4	7.00	11.00	16.50	25.00
	1225	4	7.00	11.00	16.50	25.00
	1225	5	7.00	11.00	16.50	25.00
	1226	6	7.00	11.00	16.50	25.00
	1227	7	7.00	11.00	16.50	25.00
	1228	8	7.00	11.00	16.50	25.00
	1229	9	7.00	11.00	16.50	25.00
	1230	10	7.00	11.00	16.50	25.00
	1231	11	7.00	11.00	16.50	25.00
	1232	12	7.00	11.00	16.50	25.00

KM#	Date	Year	VG	Fine	VF	XF
106	1233	13	7.00	11.00	16.50	25.00
	1234	14	7.00	11.00	16.50	25.00
	xxxx	15	7.00	11.00	16.50	25.00
	1236	16	7.00	11.00	16.50	25.00
	1238	18	7.00	11.00	16.50	25.00
	1239	19	7.00	11.00	16.50	25.00
	12xx	21	7.00	11.00	16.50	25.00
	1243	22	7.00	11.00	16.50	25.00
	1244	23	7.00	11.00	16.50	25.00
	124x	24	7.00	11.00	16.50	25.00
	124x	25	7.00	11.00	16.50	25.00
	12xx	26	7.00	11.00	16.50	25.00
	1247	27	7.00	11.00	16.50	25.00
	1248	28	7.00	11.00	16.50	25.00
	1249	29	7.00	11.00	16.50	25.00
	12xx	30	7.00	11.00	16.50	25.00
	1251	31	7.00	11.00	16.50	25.00
	1252	32	7.00	11.00	16.50	25.00
	1253	34	7.00	11.00	16.50	25.00
	1252	35	7.00	11.00	16.50	25.00
	12xx	36	7.00	11.00	16.50	25.00
	1256	38	7.00	11.00	16.50	25.00
	12xx	39	7.00	11.00	16.50	25.00
	1270	40	7.00	11.00	16.50	25.00
	1270	41	7.00	11.00	16.50	25.00
	—	42	7.00	11.00	16.50	25.00
	—	45	7.00	11.00	16.50	25.00
	—	46	7.00	11.00	16.50	25.00
	12xx	47	7.00	11.00	16.50	25.00
	—	48	7.00	11.00	16.50	25.00
	12xx	49	7.00	11.00	16.50	25.00

NOTE: Regnal years 34-48 (AH1253-1278) were posthumous, being struck during the reign of the Mughal emperor Bahadur Shah Zafar.

Thin flan

KM#	Date	Year	VG	Fine	VF	XF
106a	AH1233	13	18.50	26.50	37.50	55.00
	1234	14	18.50	26.50	37.50	55.00
	1235	14	18.50	26.50	37.50	55.00
	1235	15	18.50	26.50	37.50	55.00
	1236	16	18.50	26.50	37.50	55.00
	1236	19	18.50	26.50	37.50	55.00
	1237	17	18.50	26.50	37.50	55.00
	1238	18	18.50	26.50	37.50	55.00

NAZARANA RUPEE

SILVER, 11.00-11.15 g

KM#	Date	Year	VG	Fine	VF	XF
107	AH1235	15	35.00	50.00	70.00	100.00

MOHUR

GOLD, 10.70-11.40 g

KM#	Date	Year	VG	Fine	VF	XF
110	AH12xx	1	275.00	450.00	650.00	950.00
	12xx	3	275.00	450.00	650.00	950.00
	123x	11	275.00	450.00	650.00	950.00
	12xx	14	275.00	450.00	650.00	950.00
	12xx	15	275.00	450.00	650.00	950.00

In the name of Bahadur Shah II

AH1253-1274/1837-1858AD

Mintname: Braj Indrapur

Mint marks:

Katar Star

RUPEE

SILVER, 11.00-11.10 g

KM#	Date	Year	VG	Fine	VF	XF
146	AH127x/VS1911	17	13.50	20.00	27.50	37.50
	127x/VS1912	18	13.50	20.00	27.50	37.50
	1273/VS1913	19	13.50	20.00	27.50	37.50
	-/VS1914	20	13.50	20.00	27.50	37.50

In the names of Queen Victoria کوین وکٹوریا

and Jaswant Singh

Mintnames: Bharatpur and Braj Indrapur

Mint marks:

RUPEE

SILVER, 11.00-11.10 g

Rev: Katar at left of star and date.

KM#	Date	Year	VG	Fine	VF	XF
156	VS1910	1858	50.00	70.00	100.00	150.00

Rev: Star at left of katar and date.

KM#	Date	Year	VG	Fine	VF	XF
157	VS1910	1858	40.00	60.00	85.00	120.00

MOHUR

GOLD, 10.70-11.40 g

Rev: Katar at left of star and date.

KM#	Date	Year	VG	Fine	VF	XF
160	VS1910	1858	600.00	1000.	1400.	2000.

With titles of Queen Victoria

RUPEE

SILVER, 11.00-11.10 g

KM#	Date	Year	VG	Fine	VF	XF
166	VS1914	1858	40.00	70.00	85.00	120.00
	1915	1858	40.00	70.00	85.00	120.00
	1916	1859	40.00	70.00	85.00	120.00
	1917	1861	40.00	70.00	85.00	120.00
	1917	1851 (error)	40.00	70.00	85.00	120.00
	1922	1865	40.00	70.00	85.00	120.00

MOHUR

GOLD, 10.70-11.40 g

KM#	Date	Year	VG	Fine	VF	XF
170	VS1915	1858	600.00	1000.	1400.	2000.
	1916	1859	600.00	1000.	1400.	2000.
	1918	1862	600.00	1000.	1400.	2000.
	1919	1862	600.00	1000.	1400.	2000.

NOTE: For similar coins with dagger at left and sword at right of Queen's bust, see Bindraban State.

DIG MINT

In the name of Muhammad Akbar II

AH1221-1253/1806-1837AD

Mintname: Mahe Indrapur

Mint marks:

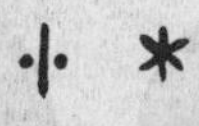

RUPEE

SILVER, 10.70-11.60 g

Narrow flan

KM#	Date	Year	VG	Fine	VF	XF
126	AH—	1	7.00	11.00	16.50	25.00
	—	3	7.00	11.00	16.50	25.00
	12xx	7	7.00	11.00	16.50	25.00
	1229	9	7.00	11.00	16.50	25.00
	—	10	7.00	11.00	16.50	25.00
	1231	11	7.00	11.00	16.50	25.00
	1232	12	7.00	11.00	16.50	25.00
	123x	13	7.00	11.00	16.50	25.00
	AH1237	18	7.00	11.00	16.50	25.00
	12xx	19	7.00	11.00	16.50	25.00
	12xx	24	7.00	11.00	16.50	25.00
	—	26	7.00	11.00	16.50	25.00
	1246	27	7.00	11.00	16.50	25.00
	12xx	28	7.00	11.00	16.50	25.00
	12xx	29	7.00	11.00	16.50	25.00
	12xx	31	7.00	11.00	16.50	25.00
	—	32	7.00	11.00	16.50	25.00
	—	36	7.00	11.00	16.50	25.00
	—	42	7.00	11.00	16.50	25.00
	—	47	7.00	11.00	16.50	25.00

NOTE: Issues with regnal years 32-47 are posthumous.

Wide flan

KM#	Date	Year	VG	Fine	VF	XF
126a	AH1234	14	22.50	35.00	47.50	65.00
	12xx	15	22.50	35.00	47.50	65.00
	123x	16	22.50	35.00	47.50	65.00
	—	17	22.50	35.00	47.50	65.00

With titles of Queen Victoria

1/4 RUPEE

SILVER, 2.68-2.90 g

KM#	Date	Year	VG	Fine	VF	XF
174	VS1910	1858	70.00	100.00	140.00	200.00

RUPEE

SILVER, 10.70-11.60 g

Rev: Katar at left of star and date.

KM#	Date	Year	VG	Fine	VF	XF
176.1	VS1910	1858	45.00	75.00	110.00	160.00

Rev: Star at left of Katar and date.

KM#	Date	Year	VG	Fine	VF	XF
176.2	VS1910	1858	45.00	75.00	110.00	160.00

KUMBER MINT

In the name of Shah Alam II
AH1173-1221/1759-1806AD

Mintname: Mahe Indrapur

Mint marks: 

RUPEE

In the name of Muhammad Akbar II
AH1221-1253/1806-1837AD

SILVER, 11.05-11.10 g
Narrow flan

KM#	Date	Year	VG	Fine	VF	XF
116	AH1222	3	7.00	11.00	16.50	25.00
	12xx	5	7.00	11.00	16.50	25.00
	12xx	6	7.00	11.00	16.50	25.00
	12xx	7	7.00	11.00	16.50	25.00
	122x	8	7.00	11.00	16.50	25.00
	1229	9	7.00	11.00	16.50	25.00
	1229	10	7.00	11.00	16.50	25.00
	—	11	7.00	11.00	16.50	25.00
	1233	13	7.00	11.00	16.50	25.00
	12xx	21	7.00	11.00	16.50	25.00
	1243	22	7.00	11.00	16.50	25.00
	12xx	23	7.00	11.00	16.50	25.00
	—	24	7.00	11.00	16.50	25.00
	124x	25	7.00	11.00	16.50	25.00
	124x	26	7.00	11.00	16.50	25.00
	12xx	27	7.00	11.00	16.50	25.00
	1248	28	7.00	11.00	16.50	25.00
	1249	29	7.00	11.00	16.50	25.00
	12xx	46	7.00	11.00	16.50	25.00
	—	47	7.00	11.00	16.50	25.00
	1262	48	7.00	11.00	16.50	25.00

NOTE: The issues of regnal years 32 and later are posthumous.

Wide flan

KM#	Date	Year	VG	Fine	VF	XF
116a	AH1234	14	20.00	31.50	42.50	60.00
	1235	15	20.00	31.50	42.50	60.00
	1238	16	20.00	31.50	42.50	60.00

UNCERTAIN MINT

Possibly the fortress of Ver (Wair).
Arabic *Wa* = ver?

Mint marks: 

In the name of Muhammad Akbar II
AH1221-1253/1806-1837AD

RUPEE

SILVER, 11.05-11.10 g

KM#	Date	Year	VG	Fine	VF	XF
136	AH12xx	3	7.00	11.00	16.50	25.00
	12xx	5	7.00	11.00	16.50	25.00
	12xx	6	7.00	11.00	16.50	25.00
	122x	7	7.00	11.00	16.50	25.00
	12xx	8	7.00	11.00	16.50	25.00
	12xx	9	7.00	11.00	16.50	25.00
	123x	11	7.00	11.00	16.50	25.00
	123x	12	7.00	11.00	16.50	25.00
	12xx	15	7.00	11.00	16.50	25.00
	1238	16	7.00	11.00	16.50	25.00
	—	19	7.00	11.00	16.50	25.00
	124x	21	7.00	11.00	16.50	25.00
	—	23	7.00	11.00	16.50	25.00
	124x	25	7.00	11.00	16.50	25.00
	12xx	26	7.00	11.00	16.50	25.00
	124x	28	7.00	11.00	16.50	25.00
	—	31	7.00	11.00	16.50	25.00
	1252	32	7.00	11.00	16.50	25.00
	12xx	41	7.00	11.00	16.50	25.00
	126x	47	7.00	11.00	16.50	25.00

BHAUNAGAR

State located in northwest India on the west shore of the Gulf of Cambay.

The Thakurs of Bhaunagar, as the rulers were titled, were Gohel Rajputs. They traced their control of the area back to the thirteenth century. Under the umbrella of British paramountcy, the Thakurs of Bhaunagar were regarded as relatively enlightened rulers. The State was absorbed into Saurashtra in February 1948.

Anonymous Types: Bearing the distinguishing Nagari legend *Bahadur* in addition to the Mughal legends.

MONETARY SYSTEM

2 Trambiyo = 1 Dokda
1-1/2 Dokda = 1 Dhingla

Mughal Issues

In the name of Shah Jahan III

DOKDO

COPPER
Rev: 1825 incuse in panel.

C#	Date	Year	Good	VG	Fine	VF
15b	1825	—	3.00	5.00	8.00	12.00

NOTE: Acutal date of striking unknown.

In the name of Muhammad Akbar II
AH1221-1253/1806-1837AD

DHINGLO

COPPER

C#	Date	Year	Good	VG	Fine	VF
30	ND	—	3.00	5.00	8.00	12.00

Anonymous Issues

DOKDA

 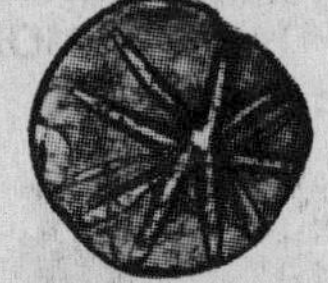

COPPER

KM#	Date	Year	Good	VG	Fine	VF
1	VS2004	(1947)	4.00	6.00	10.00	15.00

BHOPAL

Bhopal was the second largest Muslim state located in central India. It was founded in 1723 by Dost Muhammed Khan, an Afghan adventurer of the Mirazi Khel clan, who was in the service of Aurangzeb. After the Emperor's death in 1707 Dost Muhammed asserted his independence. Early in the following century his successors, threatened by the Marathas and subjected to Pindari raids into their territory, sought to cultivate a good relationship with the British. In 1817, at the time of the Maratha and Pindari War, Bhopal signed a treaty with the British East India Company which placed them squarely under imperial protection and control. After 1897 the British rupee was recognized as the only legal tender.

RULERS

Kudsia Begam
AH1235-1253/1819-1837AD
Jahangir Muhammad Khan
AH1253-1261/1837-1844AD
Sikandar Begam
AH1261-1285/1844-1868AD
Shah Jahan Begam
AH1285-1319/1868-1901AD

Mint

Bhopal

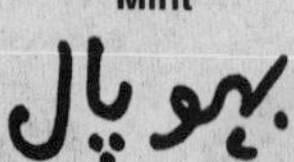

Mughal Issues

In the name of Muhammad Akbar II
AH1221-1253/1806-1837AD

1/8 RUPEE

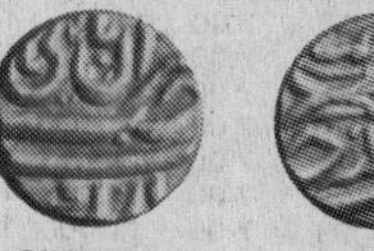

SILVER, 12mm, 1.34-1.45 g

C#	Date	Year	VG	Fine	VF	XF
24	AH—	11	7.00	11.00	16.50	25.00
	—	16	7.00	11.00	16.50	25.00
	—	29	7.00	11.00	16.50	25.00

1/4 RUPEE

SILVER, 13mm, 2.68-2.90 g

C#	Date	Year	VG	Fine	VF	XF
25	AH—	16	6.50	10.00	15.00	22.50
	—	18	6.50	10.00	15.00	22.50
	—	26	6.50	10.00	15.00	22.50
	—	29	6.50	10.00	15.00	22.50

1/2 RUPEE

SILVER, 15mm, 5.35-5.80 g

C#	Date	Year	VG	Fine	VF	XF
26	AH—	9	7.00	11.00	16.50	25.00
	—	16	7.00	11.00	16.50	25.00
	—	29	7.00	11.00	16.50	25.00

RUPEE

SILVER, 10.70-11.60 g

C#	Date	Year	VG	Fine	VF	XF
27	AH—	1	7.50	12.50	18.50	27.50
	—	4	7.50	12.50	18.50	27.50
	—	5	7.50	12.50	18.50	27.50
	—	6	7.50	12.50	18.50	27.50
	—	7	7.50	12.50	18.50	27.50
	—	8	7.50	12.50	18.50	27.50
	—	9	7.50	12.50	18.50	27.50
	—	10	7.50	12.50	18.50	27.50
	—	11	7.50	12.50	18.50	27.50
	—	12	7.50	12.50	18.50	27.50
	—	13	7.50	12.50	18.50	27.50
	—	14	7.50	12.50	18.50	27.50
	—	15	7.50	12.50	18.50	27.50
	—	16	7.50	12.50	18.50	27.50
	—	17	7.50	12.50	18.50	27.50
	—	18	7.50	12.50	18.50	27.50
	—	19	7.50	12.50	18.50	27.50
	—	20	7.50	12.50	18.50	27.50
	—	21	7.50	12.50	18.50	27.50
	—	22	7.50	12.50	18.50	27.50
	—	23	7.50	12.50	18.50	27.50
	—	25	7.50	12.50	18.50	27.50
	—	26	7.50	12.50	18.50	27.50
	—	27	7.50	12.50	18.50	27.50
	—	30	7.50	12.50	18.50	27.50
	—	31	7.50	12.50	18.50	27.50
	—	32	7.50	12.50	18.50	27.50
	—	33	7.50	12.50	18.50	27.50
	—	34	7.50	12.50	18.50	27.50
	—	35	7.50	12.50	18.50	27.50

Anonymous Issues

PAISA

COPPER, 21-22mm
Obv: ***Bhopal.*** **Rev: Year in circle.**

C#	Date	Year	Good	VG	Fine	VF
20	—	25	2.00	3.25	5.00	8.50
	—	29	2.00	3.25	5.00	8.50

Rev: Whisk

C#	Date	Year	Good	VG	Fine	VF
21	—	28	4.00	6.50	10.00	17.50

UNIFACE PAISA

COPPER
Persian ***Bhopal*** **in circular depressed area.**

C#	Date	Year	Good	VG	Fine	VF
20a	ND	—	3.00	5.00	8.00	12.50

Persian ***Sikka Bhopal*** **and date.**

C#	Date	Year	Good	VG	Fine	VF
21a	AH1255	—	3.00	5.00	8.00	12.50

Fly whisk and scimitar

C#	Date	Year	Good	VG	Fine	VF
21b	—	13	2.50	4.50	6.50	10.00
	ND	—	2.50	4.50	6.50	10.00
	ND	26	2.50	4.50	6.50	10.00

Persian *Fateh* and scimitar.

C#	Date	Year	Good	VG	Fine	VF
21c	ND	8	2.50	4.50	6.50	10.00

Persian *Jim* and year

C#	Date	Year	Good	VG	Fine	VF
21d	ND	5	2.00	3.25	5.00	8.50
		10	2.00	3.25	5.00	8.50
		11	2.00	3.25	5.00	8.50
		12	2.00	3.25	5.00	8.50
		47	2.00	3.25	5.00	8.50

Persian *Fateh* w/o scimitar.

C#	Date	Year	Good	VG	Fine	VF
21e	ND	—	—	—	—	—

1/4 ANNA

COPPER
Rev: Denomination.

Y#	Date	Year	Good	VG	Fine	VF
1	AH1266	—	1.50	2.25	3.50	6.50
	1269	—	1.50	2.25	3.50	6.50
	1272	—	1.50	2.25	3.50	6.50
	1273	—	1.50	2.25	3.50	6.50
	1276	—	1.50	2.25	3.50	6.50
	1279	—	1.50	2.25	3.50	6.50

Rev: Date and denomination.

Y#	Date	Year	Good	VG	Fine	VF
4.1	AH1285	—	1.00	1.75	2.50	4.50

Y#	Date	Year	Good	VG	Fine	VF
4.2	AH1285	—	1.00	1.75	2.50	4.50
	1286	—	1.00	1.75	2.50	4.50
	1287	—	1.00	1.75	2.50	4.50
	1288	—	1.00	1.75	2.50	4.50
	1289	—	1.00	1.75	2.50	4.50
	1292	—	1.00	1.75	2.50	4.50
	1293	—	1.00	1.75	2.50	4.50
	1296	—	1.00	1.75	2.50	4.50
	1299	—	1.00	1.75	2.50	4.50
	130x	—	1.00	1.75	2.50	4.50

NOTE: Coins dated 1286 exist w/o word *Hejira* above date on reverse, and w/split date.

1/2 ANNA

COPPER, 20-21mm
Rev: Denomination.

Y#	Date	Year	Good	VG	Fine	VF
2	AH1276	—	2.00	3.25	5.00	8.50
	1278	—	2.00	3.25	5.00	8.50

Rev: Date and denomination.

Y#	Date	Year	Good	VG	Fine	VF
5	AH1286	—	2.00	3.25	5.00	8.50
	1289	—	2.00	3.25	5.00	8.50
	1299	—	2.00	3.25	5.00	8.50
	1300	—	2.00	3.25	5.00	8.50

ANNA

COPPER
Rev: Denomination.

Y#	Date	Year	Good	VG	Fine	VF
.3	AH1276	—	3.00	5.00	8.00	12.50

27-30mm
Rev: Date and denomination.

Y#	Date	Year	Good	VG	Fine	VF
6	AH1286	—	4.00	6.50	10.00	15.00
	1288	—	4.00	6.50	10.00	15.00
	1289	—	4.00	6.50	10.00	15.00
	1300	—	4.00	6.50	10.00	15.00

1/8 RUPEE

SILVER, 1.34-1.45 g
Obv: *Zarb* above *Bhopal*.

Y#	Date	Year	VG	Fine	VF	XF
7	AH1271	5	4.50	9.00	15.00	22.00
	1275	—	4.50	9.00	15.00	22.00
	1288	7	4.50	9.00	15.00	22.00
	1289	8	4.50	9.00	15.00	22.00
	1291	8	4.50	9.00	15.00	22.00

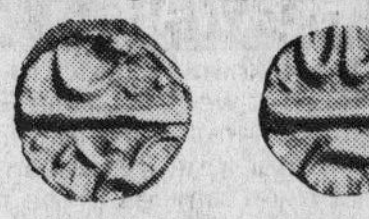

Obv: *Zarb* below *Bhopal*.

Y#	Date	Year	VG	Fine	VF	XF
11	AH129x	8	4.25	8.50	14.00	20.00
	1294	9	4.25	8.50	14.00	20.00
	1303	15	4.25	8.50	14.00	20.00
	1306	17	4.25	8.50	14.00	20.00

1/4 RUPEE

SILVER, 2.68-2.90 g
Obv: *Zarb* above *Bhopal*.

Y#	Date	Year	VG	Fine	VF	XF
8	AH1275	—	4.25	8.50	14.00	20.00
	1282	2	4.25	8.50	14.00	20.00
	1283	2	4.25	8.50	14.00	20.00
	1284	8	4.25	8.50	14.00	20.00
	1285	8	4.25	8.50	14.00	20.00
	1287	8	4.25	8.50	14.00	20.00
	1288	8	4.25	8.50	14.00	20.00

Obv: *Zarb* below *Bhopal*.

Y#	Date	Year	VG	Fine	VF	XF
12	AH1293	8	3.75	7.50	12.50	18.50
	1294	9	3.75	7.50	12.50	18.50
	1295	10	3.75	7.50	12.50	18.50
	1297	12	3.75	7.50	12.50	18.50
	1301	—	3.75	7.50	12.50	18.50
	1303	15	3.75	7.50	12.50	18.50
	1305	16	3.75	7.50	12.50	18.50

1/2 RUPEE

SILVER, 5.35-5.80 g
Obv: *Zarb* above *Bhopal*.

Y#	Date	Year	VG	Fine	VF	XF
9	AH1275	—	5.00	10.00	17.50	25.00
	1278	—	5.00	10.00	17.50	25.00
	1279	5	5.00	10.00	17.50	25.00
	1280	—	5.00	10.00	17.50	25.00
9	1281	—	5.00	10.00	17.50	25.00
	1282	2	5.00	10.00	17.50	25.00
	1283	8	4.50	9.00	15.00	22.00
	1285	5	4.50	9.00	15.00	22.00
	1287	8	4.50	9.00	15.00	22.00
	1288	7	4.50	9.00	15.00	22.00
	1288	8	4.50	9.00	15.00	22.00
	1289	8	4.50	9.00	15.00	22.00
	1291	8	4.50	9.00	15.00	22.00
	1292	8	4.50	9.00	15.00	22.00

Obv: *Zarb* below *Bhopal*.

Y#	Date	Year	VG	Fine	VF	XF
13	AH1294	4	4.25	8.50	14.00	20.00
	1294	9	4.25	8.50	14.00	20.00
	1295	—	4.25	8.50	14.00	20.00
	1296	11	4.25	8.50	14.00	20.00
	130(2)	14	4.25	8.50	14.00	20.00
	1303	15	4.25	8.50	14.00	20.00
	1306	17	4.25	8.50	14.00	20.00
	130(5)	16	4.25	8.50	14.00	20.00
	1307	19	4.25	8.50	14.00	20.00
	1308	20	4.25	8.50	14.00	20.00
	130x	24	4.25	8.50	14.00	20.00

RUPEE

SILVER, 10.70-11.60 g
Obv: *Zarb* above *Bhopal*.

Y#	Date	Year	VG	Fine	VF	XF
10	AH1271	5	6.00	12.00	20.00	28.00
	1272	—	6.00	12.00	20.00	28.00
	1275	—	6.00	12.00	20.00	28.00
	1276	—	6.00	12.00	20.00	28.00
	1277	—	6.00	12.00	20.00	28.00
	1278	2	6.00	12.00	20.00	28.00
	1279	3	6.00	12.00	20.00	28.00
	1279	4	6.00	12.00	20.00	28.00
	1279	5	6.00	12.00	20.00	28.00
	1280	5	6.00	12.00	20.00	28.00
	1281	8	6.00	12.00	20.00	28.00
	1282	2	6.00	12.00	20.00	28.00
	1282	6	6.00	12.00	20.00	28.00
	1282	8	6.00	12.00	20.00	28.00
	1283	7	6.00	12.00	20.00	28.00
	1283	8	6.00	12.00	20.00	28.00
	1284	8	6.00	12.00	20.00	28.00
	1285	5	6.00	12.00	20.00	28.00
	1285	8	6.00	12.00	20.00	28.00
	1288	7	6.00	12.00	20.00	28.00
	1288	8	6.00	12.00	20.00	28.00
	1289	8	6.00	12.00	20.00	28.00
	1289	9	6.00	12.00	20.00	28.00
	1291	8	6.00	12.00	20.00	28.00
	1292	8	6.00	12.00	20.00	28.00
	1293	8	6.00	12.00	20.00	28.00

Obv: *Zarb* below *Bhopal*.

Y#	Date	Year	VG	Fine	VF	XF
14	AH1293	8	5.00	10.00	17.50	25.00
	1294	8	5.00	10.00	17.50	25.00
	1294	9	5.00	10.00	17.50	25.00
	1295	10	5.00	10.00	17.50	25.00
	1295	11	5.00	10.00	17.50	25.00
	1296	11	5.00	10.00	17.50	25.00
	1297	12	5.00	10.00	17.50	25.00
	1298	9	5.00	10.00	17.50	25.00
	1298	10	5.00	10.00	17.50	25.00
	1298	13	5.00	10.00	17.50	25.00
	1298	15	5.00	10.00	17.50	25.00
	1302	14	5.00	10.00	17.50	25.00
	1304	15	5.00	10.00	17.50	25.00
	1305	16	5.00	10.00	17.50	25.00
	1306	17	5.00	10.00	17.50	25.00
	1308	14	5.00	10.00	17.50	25.00

NAZARANAS

NOTE: Previously listed Nazarana 1 Rupee, Y#B14 and Nazarana 2 Rupees, Y#A14 are currently being researched and now include a 1-1/2 Rupee weight for the series.

SHAH JAHAN BEGAM

AH1285-1319/1868-1901AD

PIE (or 1/2 Paisa)

COPPER

Y#	Date	Year	Good	VG	Fine	VF
15	AH1305	—	1.50	2.25	3.50	6.50

1/4 ANNA

COPPER

Y#	Date	Year	Good	VG	Fine	VF
16	AH1302	—	1.00	1.75	2.50	4.50
	1303	—	1.00	1.75	2.50	4.50
	1305	—	1.00	1.75	2.50	4.50
	1306	—	1.00	1.75	2.50	4.50

1/2 ANNA

COPPER

Y#	Date	Year	Good	VG	Fine	VF
17.1	AH1302	—	1.25	2.00	3.00	5.50
	1303	—	1.25	2.00	3.00	5.50
	1304	—	1.25	2.00	3.00	5.50
	1305	—	1.25	2.00	3.00	5.50
	1306	—	1.25	2.00	3.00	5.50

Large flan.

Y#	Date	Year	Good	VG	Fine	VF
17.2	AH1309	—	2.00	3.25	5.00	8.50

ANNA

COPPER

Y#	Date	Year	Good	VG	Fine	VF
18	AH1302	—	2.50	4.50	6.50	10.00
	1303	—	2.50	4.50	6.50	10.00
	1304	—	2.50	4.50	6.50	10.00
	1305	—	2.50	4.50	6.50	10.00
	1306	—	2.50	4.50	6.50	10.00

Struck from 1/2 Anna dies

Y#	Date	Year	Good	VG	Fine	VF
18a	—	—	2.50	4.50	6.50	10.00

NAZARANA ANNA

COPPER, 30.20 g

Y#	Date	Year	Good	VG	Fine	VF
18b	AH1303	—	—	—	Rare	—

BHOPAL FEUDATORY

NARSINGHGARH

The Rajput rulers of this feudatory traced their origins back into the fourteenth century when their ancestors migrated from Malwa through Sind before settling at Narsinghgarh.

PAISA

COPPER

Y#	Date	Year	Good	VG	Fine	VF
91	ND	—	2.50	4.50	6.50	10.00

BIJAWAR

State located in Bundelkhand District in north-central India. The rulers of Bijawar were Bundela Rajputs. They were descended from Maharaja Chhatarsal who, earlier, having ruled a much larger territory, became forebearer to a number of Rajput royal families in the region. As far as the British were concerned, the authority of the rulers of Bijawar stemmed from a mandate issued by the East India Company in 1811 which required, in return, a guarantee of allegiance. In 1866 the ruler became a maharaja.

RULERS

Lakshman Singh, 1833-1847AD

Bhau Pratap Singh, 1847-1900AD

In the Name of Shah Alam II

AH1173-1221/1759-1806AD

RUPEE

SILVER, 10.70-11.60 g

KM#	Date	Year	VG	Fine	VF	XF
15	ND	—	12.50	21.00	28.50	40.00

BIKANIR

Bikanir, located in Rajputana was established as a state sometime between 1465 and 1504 by Jodhpur Rathor Rajput named Rao Bikaji. During the period of the Great Mughals Bikanir was intimately linked to Delhi by ties of both loyalty and marriage. Both Akbar and Jahangir contracted marriages with princesses of the Bikanir Rajputs, and the Bikanir nobility rendered outstanding service in the Mughal armies. Bikanir came under British influence in 1817 and after 1947 was incorporated into Rajasthan.

RULERS

Surat Singh
AH1202-1244/1787-1828AD

Ratan Singh
AH1244-1268/1828-1851AD

Sardar Singh
AH1268-1289/1851-1872AD

Dungar Singh
AH1289-1305/1872-1887AD

Ganga Singhji
VS1944-1999/1887-1942AD

Sadul Singh
VS1999-2004/1942-1947AD

MINT

Bikanir

MINT MARKS

1. Gaj Singh, AH1159-1202
2. (")
3. Surat Singh, AH1202-1244
4. (")
5. (")
6. Ratan Singh, AH1244-1268 (2 Vars.)
7. Sardar Singh, AH1268-1289
8. Dungar Singh, AH1289-1305
9. Ganga Singh, VS1949-1999

NOTE: The above symbols normally occur in groups on the obverse or reverse of the coins; the various combinations are shown for each series.

Mughal Issues

SURAT SINGH

AH1202-1244/1787-1828AD

Regnal years of Shah Alam II

Years 28-52

RUPEE

SILVER, 10.70-11.60 g
Obv: Mark #1. Rev: Mark #3.

KM#	Date	Year	VG	Fine	VF	XF
17	AH1217	41	7.50	12.50	18.50	27.50
	1217	43	7.50	12.50	18.50	27.50
	1227	47	7.50	12.50	18.50	27.50
	1229	51	7.50	12.50	18.50	27.50
	1229	52	7.50	12.50	18.50	27.50

NOTE: Earlier dates (AH1204-1209) exist for this type.

In the name of Shah Alam II

AH1173-1221/1759-1806AD

RATAN SINGH

AH1244-1268/1828-1851AD

PAISA

COPPER, uniface round or square, 12-18mm
Symbol of Ratan Singh

KM#	Date	Year	Good	VG	Fine	VF
20	ND	—	2.00	3.25	5.00	8.50

In the name of Alamgir II

AH1167-1173/1754-1759AD

1/2 PAISA

COPPER
Rev: Mark #6.

KM#	Date	Year	Good	VG	Fine	VF
22	ND	25	.75	1.25	2.00	3.00
	—	41	.75	1.25	2.00	3.00

PAISA

COPPER
Rev: Mark #6.

KM#	Date	Year	Good	VG	Fine	VF
23	ND	41	.75	1.25	2.00	3.00

NOTE: So called year 21 is debased copy of year 41.

Regnal years of Muhammad Akbar II
Years 21-52

RUPEE

SILVER, 10.70-11.60 g
Obv: Mark #1. Rev: Marks #3 and 6.

KM#	Date	Year	VG	Fine	VF	XF
32	AH1229	21	7.00	11.00	16.50	25.00
	1229	25	7.00	11.00	16.50	25.00
	1229	31	7.00	11.00	16.50	25.00
	1229	32	7.00	11.00	16.50	25.00
	1229	41	7.00	11.00	16.50	25.00
	1229	47	7.00	11.00	16.50	25.00
	1229	52	7.00	11.00	16.50	25.00

In the name of Shah Alam II
AH1173-1221/1759-1806AD

NAZARANA RUPEE

SILVER, 10.70-11.60 g

32a	AH1229	25	25.00	37.50	50.00	70.00

SARDAR SINGH

AH1268-1289/1851-1872AD

In the Name of Alamgir II
AH1167-1173/1754-1759AD

1/2 PAISA

COPPER, 17mm

KM#	Date	Year	Good	VG	Fine	VF
34	AH1229	18	2.00	3.00	4.50	6.50

1/4 RUPEE

SILVER, 16mm, 2.68-2.90 g

KM#	Date	Year	VG	Fine	VF	XF
35	AH—	—	5.00	7.00	10.00	15.00

1/2 RUPEE

SILVER, 18mm, 5.35-5.80 g

36	AH—	—	5.50	8.00	12.50	18.50

Regnal years of Bahadur Shah II
Years 18-21

RUPEE

SILVER, 10.70-11.60 g
Rev: Marks #1, 4 (or 5), 6, and 7.
Years of Bahadur Shah II

KM#	Date	Year	VG	Fine	VF	XF
37	AH1229	18	6.00	9.00	13.50	20.00
	1229	21	6.00	9.00	13.50	20.00

NAZARANA RUPEE

SILVER, 29mm, 10.70-11.60 g

37a	AH1229	21	32.50	45.00	62.50	85.00

Regal Issues

In the Name of Queen Victoria

Beginning 1859AD

Reverse marks from left to right: #6, 7, 2, 5.

All types in this series from KM41 to KM54a carry the frozen years VS1916/1859AD. Occasionally regnal years are visible at the bottom of the reverse to the right of *Zarb* when the planchet is struck low on the die. The year 39 has been observed on KM#50.

PAISA

COPPER

KM#	Date	Year	Good	VG	Fine	VF
41	VS1916	1859	.75	1.25	2.00	3.00

1/8 RUPEE

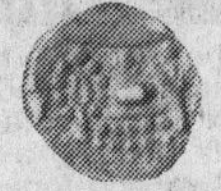

SILVER, 11-12mm, 1.34-1.45 g

KM#	Date	Year	VG	Fine	VF	XF
42	VS1916	1859	4.00	6.00	9.00	13.50

1/4 RUPEE

SILVER, 15mm, 2.68-2.90 g

43	VS1916	1859	5.00	7.00	10.00	15.00

1/2 RUPEE

SILVER, 18mm, 5.35-5.80 g

44	VS1916	1859	6.00	9.00	12.50	18.50

RUPEE

SILVER, 10.70-11.60 g

45	VS1916	1859	7.00	11.00	16.50	25.00
	1912 error for 1916		—	—	—	—

NAZARANA RUPEE

SILVER, 30mm, 10.70-11.60 g

46	VS1916	1859	37.50	52.50	75.00	110.00

Local Issues

DUNGAR SINGH

AH1289-1305/1872-1887AD

Reverse marks, left to right: #6, 7, 8, 2, 5.

PAISA

COPPER

KM#	Date	Year	Good	VG	Fine	VF
50	VS1916	1859	.75	1.25	2.00	3.00

1/8 RUPEE

SILVER, 12mm, 1.34-1.45 g

KM#	Date	Year	VG	Fine	VF	XF
51	VS1916	1859	4.00	6.00	9.00	13.50

1/4 RUPEE

SILVER, 14mm, 2.68-2.90 g

52	VS1916	1859	5.00	7.00	10.00	15.00

1/2 RUPEE

SILVER, 17mm, 5.35-5.80 g

53	VS1916	1859	6.00	9.00	12.50	18.50

RUPEE

SILVER, 10.70-11.60 g

54	VS1916	1859	7.00	11.00	16.50	25.00

NAZARANA RUPEE

SILVER, 30mm, 10.70-11.60 g

54a	VS1916	1859	37.50	52.50	75.00	110.00

GANGA SINGH

VS1944-1999/SE1965-2020/1887-1942AD

Reverse marks, left to right: #6, 7, 9, 8, 2, 5.
All dump coins w/frozen date VS1916/1859AD and actual VS date.

PAISA

COPPER, 18mm

KM#	Date	Year	Good	VG	Fine	VF
61	VS1946	(1889)	1.75	2.50	3.50	5.00

1/8 RUPEE

SILVER, 12mm, 1.34-1.45 g

KM#	Date	Year	VG	Fine	VF	XF
62	VS1944	(1887)	4.00	6.00	9.00	13.50

1/4 RUPEE

SILVER, 2.68-2.90 g

63	VS1944	(1887)	5.00	7.00	10.00	15.00

1/2 RUPEE

SILVER, 5.35-5.80 g

64	VS1944	(1887)	6.00	9.00	12.50	18.00

RUPEE

SILVER, 10.70-11.60 g

65	VS1944	(1887)	7.00	11.00	16.50	25.00

NAZARANA RUPEE

SILVER, 30mm, 10.70-11.60 g

65a	VS1944	(1887)	37.50	52.50	75.00	110.00
	1966	(1909)	37.50	52.50	75.00	110.00

Milled Coinage

1/2 PICE

COPPER

KM#	Date	Mintage	Fine	VF	XF	Unc
70	1894	.500	5.00	12.00	20.00	35.00
	1894	—	—	—	Proof	100.00
			SILVER			
70a	1894	(restrike)	—	—	Proof	125.00
			GOLD			
70b	1894	(restrike)	—	—	Proof	450.00

1/4 ANNA

COPPER

KM#	Date	Mintage	Fine	VF	XF	Unc
71	1895	6.156	4.00	10.00	17.50	30.00
	1895	—	—	—	Proof	125.00
			SILVER			
71a	1895	(restrike)	—	—	Proof	125.00
			GOLD			
71b	1895	(restrike)	—	—	Proof	650.00

RUPEE

SILVER, 11.66 g

KM#	Date	Mintage	Fine	VF	XF	Unc
72	1892	.596	7.50	12.50	18.50	27.50
	1892	—	—	—	Proof	200.00
	1897	.111	20.00	31.50	42.50	60.00
	1897	—	—	—	Proof	200.00

NAZARANA RUPEE

SILVER
50th Anniversary of Reign
Ganga Singhji

KM#	Date	Year	Fine	VF	XF	Unc
73	VS1994	(1937)	12.50	16.50	22.50	35.00
	1994	(1937)		(restrike)	P/L	16.50

NAZARANA 1/2 MOHUR

GOLD, 19mm, 4.40 g
50th Anniversary of Reign
Ganga Singhji

KM#	Date	Year	Fine	VF	XF	Unc
74	VS1994	(1937)	100.00	125.00	150.00	225.00
	1994	(1937)		(restrike)	P/L	150.00
			SILVER			
74a	VS1994	(1937)		(restrike)	P/L	50.00

NAZARANA MOHUR

GOLD, 21mm, 8.50 g
50th Anniversary of Reign
Ganga Singhji

KM#	Date	Year	Fine	VF	XF	Unc
75	VS1994	(1937)	175.00	225.00	275.00	350.00
	1994	(1937)		(restrike)	P/L	250.00
			SILVER			
75a	VS1994	(1937)	—	—	—	20.00
	1994	(1937)		(restrike)	P/L	50.00

GOLD, 21mm, 8.68 g
Sadul Singh

KM#	Date	Year	Fine	VF	XF	Unc
80	VS1999	(1942)	—	—	700.00	1000.

BINDRABAN

This city, the modern Vrindavan, was not a princely state. The area surrounding the city, including the neighboring city of Mathura, was under Jat control in the mid-eighteenth century, although nominally subject to Awadh. After varying fortunes the area passed to the East India Company in 1803-05 (i.e. AH1217-1220; VS18601862). The coins below display symbols of Awadh, Mughals, Delhi and Bhartpur, although it is clear that they were not mints of any of those authorities, especially in the British period.

MINTS AND MINTNAMES

Bindraban بندرابن

Muminabad مومن اباد

Shahjahanabad شاجهان اباد

Gokul گوكل

Mathura Islamabad اسلام اباد

BINDRABAN MINT

MINTNAMES

Muminabad مومن اباد

Shahjahanabad شاجهان اباد

Mughal Issues

In the name of Shah Alam II
AH1173-1221/1759-1806AD

PAISA

COPPER
Mintname: *Muminabad.*

KM#	Date	Year	Good	VG	Fine	VF
5	AH1216	44	1.75	2.50	4.00	6.00

NOTE: Earlier dates (AH1211-1212) exist for this type.

RUPEE

SILVER, 10.70-11.60 g
Rev: Trident and 5 trident figure.

KM#	Date	Year	VG	Fine	VF	XF
10.6	AH1217	45	11.50	17.50	23.50	32.50

Local Issues

In the name of Queen Victoria

1/4 RUPEE

SILVER, 2.68-2.90 g

KM#	Date	Year	VG	Fine	VF	XF
16	VS1915	1858	20.00	35.00	50.00	70.00
	1916	1859	20.00	35.00	50.00	70.00
	1924	1867	20.00	35.00	50.00	70.00

1/2 RUPEE

SILVER, 5.35-5.80 g

KM#	Date	Year	VG	Fine	VF	XF
17	VS1915	1858	22.50	38.50	55.00	80.00
	1916	1859	22.50	38.50	55.00	80.00
	1924	1867	22.50	38.50	55.00	80.00

RUPEE

SILVER, 10.70-11.60 g

KM#	Date	Year	VG	Fine	VF	XF
18	VS1915	1858	30.00	50.00	75.00	110.00
	1916	1859	30.00	50.00	75.00	110.00

Rev: *Fazl Hami-din*

KM#	Date	Year	VG	Fine	VF	XF
19	AD1867	12	35.00	60.00	85.00	120.00

MATHURA MINT

MINTNAME

Islamabad اسلام آباد

In the name of Muhammad Akbar II
AH1221-1253/1806-1837AD

1/2 PAISA

COPPER, 3.00 g
Similar to 1 Paisa, KM#35, but w/royal leg.

KM#	Date	Year	Good	VG	Fine	VF
51	ND	—	2.50	3.50	5.00	7.00

PAISA

COPPER, 6.00 g
Similar to 1/2 Paisa, KM#51.

KM#	Date	Year	Good	VG	Fine	VF
52	ND	—	2.25	3.25	5.00	8.50

BROACH

From very early times Broach, located on the north bank of the Narmada River 30 miles from the Gulf of Cambay, was an important port on the sea route to Europe. It was known as Barakacheva to early Chinese travellers, and as Barygaza to Ptolemy. After the Islamic invasions of India it was incorporated into the Muslim kingdom of Gujerat and remained so until 1572 when it was annexed by Akbar. During the reign of Aurangzeb, Broach first began to experience Maratha incursions. In 1772, it came briefly under British influence before being ceded to Sindhia in 1783. It was returned to the East India Company in 1803 and thereafter remained in British control.

RULERS

To British 1772-1783 and 1803 on
To Gwalior 1783-1803

MINT

Broach

Mint marks:

Cross **(Gwalior and E.I.C.)**

EAST INDIA COMPANY

1/2 RUPEE

SILVER, 5.35-5.80 g
Rev: Cross.

C#	Date	Year	VG	Fine	VF	XF
A36	ND	—	17.50	25.00	35.00	50.00

RUPEE

SILVER, 10.70-11.60 g

C#	Date	Year	VG	Fine	VF	XF
36	AH—	2x	22.50	31.50	42.50	60.00

NOTE: Other coins with cross mint mark were probably also issued under the Sindhias. For other Broach issues see Gwalior.

BUNDI

State in Rajputana in northwest India.

Bundi was founded in 1342 by a Chauhan Rajput, Rao Dewa (Deoraj). Until the Maratha defeat early in the nineteenth century, Bundi was greatly harassed by the forces of Holkar and Sindhia. In 1818 it came under British protection and control and remained so until 1947. In 1948 the State was absorbed into Rajasthan.

RULERS

Ajit Singh
VS1827-1861/1770-1804AD

Bishen Singh
VS1861-1878/1804-1821AD

Ram Singh
VS1878-1946/1824-1889AD

Raghubir Singh
VS1946-1984/1889-1927AD

Ishwari Singh
VS1984-2004/1927-1947AD

MINT

Bundi

Mintname: Bundi

All of the coins of Bundi struck prior to the Mutiny (1857) are in the name of the Mughal emperor and bear the following 2 marks on the reverse, to the left and right of the regnal year, respectively:

On all Mughal issues:

Only on Muhammad Akbar and Muhammad Bahadur issues:

The same symbols appear on the coins of Kotah, but the difference is that the Kotah pieces have the mint name *Kotahurf Nandgaon* and later issues only have *Nandgaon.*

Mughal Issues

In the name of Muhammad Akbar II
AH1221-1253/1806-1837AD

TAKKA

COPPER, 17.50-18.00 g, round
W/leg: *Shah Akbar Bahadur Badshah Ghazi.*

C#	Date	Year	Good	VG	Fine	VF
15	AH—	2	2.50	3.50	4.50	6.00
	—	3	2.50	3.50	4.50	6.00

W/leg: *Sahib Qiran Sani.*

C#	Date	Year	Good	VG	Fine	VF
17	AH—	2	1.25	2.00	3.00	4.50
	—	4	1.25	2.00	3.00	4.50
	—	6	1.25	2.00	3.00	4.50
	—	7	1.25	2.00	3.00	4.50
	—	9	1.25	2.00	3.00	4.50
	—	11	1.25	2.00	3.00	4.50
	—	12	1.25	2.00	3.00	4.50
	—	13	1.25	2.00	3.00	4.50
	—	14	1.25	2.00	3.00	4.50
	—	15	1.50	2.50	3.50	5.00
	—	16	1.50	2.50	3.50	5.00

COPPER, 17.50-18.00 g, square
W/leg: *Sahib Qiran Sani.*

C#	Date	Year	Good	VG	Fine	VF
17a	AH—	4	1.50	2.50	3.50	5.00
	—	5	1.50	2.50	3.50	5.00
	—	6	1.50	2.50	3.50	5.00
	—	11	1.50	2.50	3.50	5.00
	—	14	1.50	2.50	3.50	5.00
	—	24	1.50	2.50	3.50	5.00
	—	25	1.25	2.00	3.00	4.50
	—	26	1.25	2.00	3.00	4.50

1/2 RUPEE

SILVER, 15mm, 5.50 g
W/leg: *Bad Shah Ghazi.*

C#	Date	Year	VG	Fine	VF	XF
25	AH—	1	11.50	17.50	23.50	32.50

RUPEE

SILVER, 11.10-11.15 g
W/leg: *Bad Shah Ghazi.*

C#	Date	Year	VG	Fine	VF	XF
29	AH—	1	10.00	15.00	21.00	30.00
	1222	2	10.00	15.00	21.00	30.00
	—	3	10.00	15.00	21.00	30.00

W/leg: *Sahib Qiran Sani.*

C#	Date	Year	VG	Fine	VF	XF
30	AH—	3	8.00	13.50	20.00	28.50
	—	5	8.00	13.50	20.00	28.50
	—	6	8.00	13.50	20.00	28.50
	—	9	8.00	13.50	20.00	28.50
	—	10	8.00	13.50	20.00	28.50
	—	11	8.00	13.50	20.00	28.50
	—	12	8.00	13.50	20.00	28.50
	—	13	8.00	13.50	20.00	28.50
	—	15	8.00	13.50	20.00	28.50
	—	16	8.00	13.50	20.00	28.50
	—	17	8.00	13.50	20.00	28.50
	—	18	8.00	13.50	20.00	28.50
	—	19	8.00	13.50	20.00	28.50
	—	20	8.00	13.50	20.00	28.50
	—	21	8.00	13.50	20.00	28.50
	—	22	8.00	13.50	20.00	28.50
	—	27	8.00	13.50	20.00	28.50
	—	30	8.00	13.50	20.00	28.50
	—	31	8.00	13.50	20.00	28.50
	—	32	8.00	13.50	20.00	28.50

C#	Date	Year	VG	Fine	VF	XF
31	AH1246	25	10.00	15.00	21.00	30.00

MOHUR

GOLD, 10.70 g

C#	Date	Year	VG	Fine	VF	XF
33	AH—	15	220.00	240.00	265.00	300.00

In the name of Bahadur Shah II
AH1253-1274/1837-1858AD

TAKKA

COPPER, 20mm, 17.60-17.70 g

C#	Date	Year	Good	VG	Fine	VF
35	AH—	9	4.50	6.50	8.50	12.50
	—	11	4.50	6.50	8.50	12.50
	—	14	4.50	6.50	8.50	12.50
	—	19	4.50	6.50	8.50	12.50

RUPEE

SILVER, 19mm, 11.15-11.20 g

C#	Date	Year	VG	Fine	VF	XF
40	AH—	1	8.00	13.50	20.00	28.50
	—	2	8.00	13.50	20.00	28.50
	—	3	8.00	13.50	20.00	28.50
	—	4	8.00	13.50	20.00	28.50
	—	5	8.00	13.50	20.00	28.50
	—	6	8.00	13.50	20.00	28.50
	—	7	8.00	13.50	20.00	28.50
	—	8	8.00	13.50	20.00	28.50
	—	9	8.00	13.50	20.00	28.50
	—	10	8.00	13.50	20.00	28.50
	—	12	8.00	13.50	20.00	28.50
	—	13	8.00	13.50	20.00	28.50
	—	14	8.00	13.50	20.00	28.50
	—	15	8.00	13.50	20.00	28.50
	—	16	8.00	13.50	20.00	28.50
	—	18	8.00	13.50	20.00	28.50
	—	19	8.00	13.50	20.00	28.50
	—	21	8.00	13.50	20.00	28.50

NAZARANA RUPEE

SILVER, square

C#	Date	Year	VG	Fine	VF	XF
40a	AH	5	—	—	—	—
	—	19	—	—	—	—

Regal Issues

In the name of Queen Victoria
Obv: AD date. Rev: VS date.

1/2 PAISA

COPPER, 9-11mm, 5.50 g
Obv. leg: VICTORIA QUEEN. Rev: Date.

Y#	Date	Year	Good	VG	Fine	VF
1	VS1924	1867	.75	1.25	2.25	3.50

5.00-5.20 g

Y#	Date	Year	Good	VG	Fine	VF
Y-A2	VS1963	1906	.75	1.25	2.25	3.50
	1965	1908	.75	1.25	2.25	3.50
	1966	1909	.75	1.25	2.25	3.50
	1967	1910	.75	1.25	2.25	3.50

PAISA

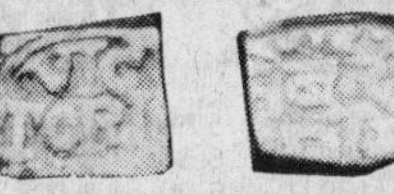

COPPER, 10.60-10.70 g

Y#	Date	Year	Good	VG	Fine	VF
2	VS1915	1858	.35	.65	1.00	1.50
	1924	1867	.25	.50	.85	1.25
	1934	1877	.25	.50	.85	1.25
	1935	1878	.25	.50	.85	1.25
	1936	1879	.25	.50	.85	1.25
	1940	1883	.25	.50	.85	1.25
	1942	1885	.25	.50	.85	1.25
	1943	1886	.25	.50	.85	1.25
	1944	1887	.25	.50	.85	1.25
	1945	1888	.25	.50	.85	1.25
	1946	1889	.25	.50	.85	1.25
	1947	—	.25	.50	.85	1.25
	1955	1898	.25	.50	.85	1.25

TAKKA

COPPER, 17.15-17.65 g

Y#	Date	Year	Good	VG	Fine	VF
3	VS1915	1858	.35	.85	1.25	1.75
	1919	1862	.35	.85	1.25	1.75
	1921	1864	.35	.85	1.25	1.75
	1922	1864	.35	.85	1.25	1.75
	1922	1865	.35	.85	1.25	1.75
	1923	1866	.35	.85	1.25	1.75
	1924	1867	.35	.85	1.25	1.75
	1925	1868	.35	.85	1.25	1.75
	1926	1869	.35	.85	1.25	1.75
	1928	1871	.35	.85	1.25	1.75
	1929	1872	.35	.85	1.25	1.75
	1932	1875	.35	.85	1.25	1.75
	1934	1877	.25	.50	.85	1.25
	1935	1878	.25	.50	.85	1.25
	1936	1879	.25	.50	.85	1.25
	1939	1882	.25	.50	.85	1.25
	1940	1883	.25	.50	.85	1.25
	1942	1885	.25	.50	.85	1.25
	1943	1886	.25	.50	.85	1.25
	1944	1887	.25	.50	.85	1.25
	1945	1888	.25	.50	.85	1.25
	1946	1889	.25	.50	.85	1.25
	1955	1898	.85	1.25	2.00	3.00
	1956	1894	.85	1.25	2.00	3.00
	1956	1898	.85	1.25	2.00	3.00
	1956	1899	1.25	2.25	3.50	5.00
	Date off flan		.65	1.10	1.75	2.50

1/4 RUPEE

SILVER, 2.80 g

Y#	Date	Year	VG	Fine	VF	XF
4	VS1915	1858	4.00	6.00	9.00	13.50
	1935	1888	4.00	6.00	9.00	13.50
	1936	1879	4.00	6.00	9.00	13.50
	Date off flan		3.00	4.50	6.50	10.00

Y#	Date	Year	VG	Fine	VF	XF
7	VS1944	(1887)	5.00	7.00	10.00	15.00
	1946	(1889)	5.00	7.00	10.00	15.00
	1947	(1890)	4.00	6.00	9.00	13.50
	1953	(1896)	4.00	6.00	9.00	13.50
	1955	(1898)	4.00	6.00	9.00	13.50
	Date off flan		3.00	4.50	6.50	10.00

1/2 RUPEE

SILVER, 5.50-5.60 g

Y#	Date	Year	VG	Fine	VF	XF
5	VS1915	1858	5.00	7.00	10.00	15.00

Y#	Date	Year	VG	Fine	VF	XF
5	1930	1873	5.00	7.00	10.00	15.00
	1933	1876	5.00	7.00	10.00	15.00
	1937	1880	5.00	7.00	10.00	15.00
	1940	1883	5.00	7.00	10.00	15.00
	1941	1884	5.00	7.00	10.00	15.00
	1943	1886	5.00	7.00	10.00	15.00
	Date off flan		3.00	4.50	6.50	10.00

Y#	Date	Year	VG	Fine	VF	XF
8	VS1945	1888	5.50	8.00	12.50	18.50
	1946	(1889)	5.50	8.00	12.50	18.50
	1948	(1891)	5.00	7.00	10.00	15.00
	1949	(1892)	5.00	7.00	10.00	15.00
	1953	(1896)	5.50	8.00	12.50	18.50
	1954	(1897)	5.00	7.00	10.00	15.00
	1955	(1898)	5.50	8.00	12.50	18.50
	Date off flan		3.00	4.50	6.50	10.00

RUPEE

SILVER, 11.00-11.15 g

Y#	Date	Year	VG	Fine	VF	XF
6	VS1915	1858	6.00	9.00	13.50	20.00
	1915	1859	6.00	9.00	13.50	20.00
	1916	1859	6.50	10.00	15.00	22.50
	1916	1860	6.50	10.00	15.00	22.50
	1917	1860	6.00	9.00	13.50	20.00
	1918	1861	6.00	9.00	13.50	20.00
	1919	1862	6.00	9.00	13.50	20.00
	1920	1863	6.00	9.00	13.50	20.00
	1921	1864	6.00	9.00	13.50	20.00
	1922	1865	6.00	9.00	13.50	20.00
	1923	1866	6.00	9.00	13.50	20.00
	1924	1867	6.00	9.00	13.50	20.00
	1925	1868	6.00	9.00	13.50	20.00
	1925 (sic)	1864	6.00	9.00	13.50	20.00
	1926	1869	6.00	9.00	13.50	20.00
	1927	1870	6.00	9.00	13.50	20.00
	1928	1871	6.00	9.00	13.50	20.00
	1929	1872	6.00	9.00	13.50	20.00
	1930	1873	6.00	9.00	13.50	20.00
	1931	1874	6.00	9.00	13.50	20.00
	1932	1875	6.00	9.00	13.50	20.00
	1933	1876	6.00	9.00	13.50	20.00
	1934	1877	6.00	9.00	13.50	20.00
	1935	1878	6.00	9.00	13.50	20.00
	1936	1879	6.00	9.00	13.50	20.00
	1937	1880	6.00	9.00	13.50	20.00
	1938	1881	6.00	9.00	13.50	20.00
	1939	1882	6.00	9.00	13.50	20.00
	1940	1883	6.00	9.00	13.50	20.00
	1941	1884	6.00	9.00	13.50	20.00
	1942	1885	6.00	9.00	13.50	20.00
	1943	1886	6.00	9.00	13.50	20.00
	Date off flan		5.00	7.00	10.00	15.00

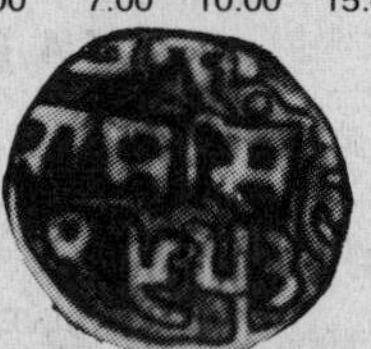

Y#	Date	Year	VG	Fine	VF	XF
9	VS1943	(1886)	6.00	9.00	13.50	20.00
	1944	(1887)	6.00	9.00	13.50	20.00
	1945	(1888)	6.00	9.00	13.50	20.00
	1946	(1889)	6.00	9.00	13.50	20.00
	1947	(1890)	6.00	9.00	13.50	20.00
	1948	(1891)	6.00	9.00	13.50	20.00
	1949	(1892)	6.00	9.00	13.50	20.00
	1950	(1893)	6.00	9.00	13.50	20.00
	1951	1894	6.00	9.00	13.50	20.00
	1953	(1894)	6.00	9.00	13.50	20.00
	1954	(1897)	6.00	9.00	13.50	20.00
	1955	(1898)	6.00	9.00	13.50	20.00
	1957	(1900)	6.00	9.00	13.50	20.00
	Date off flan		5.00	7.00	10.00	15.00

NAZARANA RUPEE

SILVER, 10.60-11.00 g

Y#	Date	Year	VG	Fine	VF	XF
6a	VS1915	1858	16.00	22.50	31.50	42.50
	1919	1862	16.00	22.50	31.50	42.50
	1925	1868	16.00	22.50	31.50	42.50
	1929	1872	16.00	22.50	31.50	42.50
	1932	1875	16.00	22.50	31.50	42.50
	1934	1877	16.00	22.50	31.50	42.50
	1935	1878	16.00	22.50	31.50	42.50
	1937	1880	16.00	22.50	31.50	42.50

Y#	Date	Year	VG	Fine	VF	XF
9a	VS1943	(1886)	35.00	50.00	70.00	110.00
	1945	(1888)	35.00	50.00	70.00	110.00
	1946	(1889)	35.00	50.00	70.00	110.00
	1947	(1890)	35.00	50.00	70.00	110.00
	1948	(1891)	35.00	50.00	70.00	110.00
	1949	(1892)	35.00	50.00	70.00	110.00
	1950	(1893)	35.00	50.00	70.00	110.00
	1951	(1894)	35.00	50.00	70.00	110.00
	1952	(1895)	35.00	50.00	70.00	110.00

Y#	Date	Year	VG	Fine	VF	XF
10	VS1958	(1901)	40.00	62.50	85.00	120.00

In the name of Edward VII

1/2 PAISA

COPPER, 4.70-5.10 g

Y#	Date	Year	Good	VG	Fine	VF
A12	VS1963	(1906)	— Reported, not confirmed			
	1965	(1908)	6.00	9.00	12.50	16.50
	1973	(1916)	6.00	9.00	12.50	16.50
	1974	(1917)	6.00	9.00	12.50	16.50
	1976	(1919)	6.00	9.00	12.50	16.50

1/4 RUPEE

SILVER, 2.65-2.70 g

Y#	Date	Year	VG	Fine	VF	XF
B11	VS1958	(1901)	15.00	21.50	30.00	40.00
	1959	(1902)	15.00	21.50	30.00	40.00
	1961	(1904)	15.00	21.50	30.00	40.00
	1962	(1905)	15.00	21.50	30.00	40.00

Y#	Date	Year	VG	Fine	VF	XF
12	VS1963	(1906)	4.00	6.00	9.00	13.50
	1964	(1907)	4.00	6.00	9.00	13.50
	1965	(1908)	4.00	6.00	9.00	13.50
	1966	(1909)	4.00	6.00	9.00	13.50

1/2 RUPEE

SILVER, 16-18mm, 5.30-5.40 g

Y#	Date	Year	VG	Fine	VF	XF
A11	VS1958	(1901)	15.00	21.50	30.00	40.00

Y#	Date	Year	VG	Fine	VF	XF
13	VS1963	(1906)	5.50	8.00	12.50	18.50
	1964	(1907)	5.00	7.00	10.00	15.00
	1965	(1908)	5.00	7.00	10.00	15.00
	1966	(1909)	5.00	7.00	10.00	15.00

RUPEE

SILVER, 10.60-11.70 g

Y#	Date	Year	VG	Fine	VF	XF
11	VS1958	(1901)	6.50	10.00	15.00	22.50
	1959	(1902)	6.50	10.00	15.00	22.50
	1960	(1903)	6.50	10.00	15.00	22.50
	1961	(1904)	6.50	10.00	15.00	22.50
	1962	(1905)	6.50	10.00	15.00	22.50
	1963	(1906)	6.50	10.00	15.00	22.50

Y#	Date	Year	VG	Fine	VF	XF
14	VS1963	(1906)	6.50	10.00	15.00	22.50
	1964	(1907)	6.50	10.00	15.00	22.50
	1965	(1908)	6.50	10.00	15.00	22.50
	1966	(1909)	6.50	10.00	15.00	22.50
	1967	(1910)	6.50	10.00	15.00	22.50
	1968	(1911)	6.50	10.00	15.00	22.50
	1969	(1912)	6.50	10.00	15.00	22.50

NAZARANA RUPEE

SILVER, 10.70-11.60 g
Broad square flan

Y#	Date	Year	VG	Fine	VF	XF
11a	VS1962	(1905)	37.50	52.50	75.00	110.00

Obv: Plain katar.

Y#	Date	Year	VG	Fine	VF	XF
14a	VS1966	(1909)	35.00	50.00	70.00	100.00
	1967	(1910)	35.00	50.00	70.00	100.00
	1968	(1911)	35.00	50.00	70.00	100.00
	1969	(1912)	35.00	50.00	70.00	100.00
	1970	(1913)	35.00	50.00	70.00	100.00

Round

Y#	Date	Year	VG	Fine	VF	XF
14b	VS1967	(1910)	15.00	21.50	30.00	40.00
	1968	(1911)	15.00	21.50	30.00	40.00
	1969	(1912)	15.00	21.50	30.00	40.00

In the name of George V

PAISA

COPPER, rectangular or square, 5.00-5.35 g

Y#	Date	Year	Good	VG	Fine	VF
15	VS1973	(1916)	1.50	2.25	3.00	4.00
	1974	(1917)	1.50	2.25	3.00	4.00
	1976	(1919)	1.50	2.25	3.00	4.00
	1977	(1920)	1.50	2.25	3.00	4.00
	1980	(1923)	1.50	2.25	3.00	4.00
	1981	(1924)	1.50	2.25	3.00	4.00
	1982	(1925)	1.50	2.25	3.00	4.00
	1983	(1926)	1.50	2.25	3.00	4.00
	1984	(1927)	1.50	2.25	3.00	4.00
	1986	(1929)	2.00	3.00	4.00	5.00
	1987	(1930)	2.00	3.00	4.00	5.00
	1988	(1931)	3.00	4.00	5.50	7.50
	1990	(1933)	3.00	4.00	5.50	7.50
	1991	(1934)	3.00	4.00	5.50	7.50
	1992	(1935)	3.00	4.00	5.50	7.50

NOTE: Size and weight vary.

1/4 RUPEE

SILVER, 2.60-2.70 g

Y#	Date	Year	VG	Fine	VF	XF
16	VS1972	(1915)	3.00	4.50	6.50	10.00
	1973	(1916)	3.00	4.50	6.50	10.00
	1974	(1917)	3.00	4.50	6.50	10.00
	1980	(1923)	3.00	4.50	6.50	10.00
	1981	(1924)	3.00	4.50	6.50	10.00
	1982	(1925)	3.00	4.50	6.50	10.00

13mm, similar to 1/2 Rupee, Y#19.

Y#	Date	Year	VG	Fine	VF	XF
A19	VS1915(sic)	1925	20.00	31.50	42.50	60.00

1/2 RUPEE

SILVER, 5.30-5.40 g

Y#	Date	Year	VG	Fine	VF	XF
17	VS1972	(1915)	5.00	7.00	10.00	15.00
	1973	(1916)	5.00	7.00	10.00	15.00
	1974	(1917)	4.00	6.00	9.00	13.50
	1979	(1922)	4.00	6.00	9.00	13.50
	1980	(1923)	4.00	6.00	9.00	13.50
	1981	(1924)	4.00	6.00	9.00	13.50
	1982	(1925)	4.00	6.00	9.00	13.50
	1983	(1926)	4.00	6.00	9.00	13.50
	1984	(1927)	4.00	6.00	9.00	13.50

Y#	Date	Year	VG	Fine	VF	XF
19	VS1915(sic)	1925	23.50	38.50	55.00	80.00

RUPEE

SILVER, 10.60-10.70 g
Obv: Plain katar.

Y#	Date	Year	VG	Fine	VF	XF
18.1	VS1972	(1915)	6.00	9.00	13.50	20.00
	1973	(1916)	6.00	9.00	13.50	20.00
	1974	(1917)	6.00	9.00	13.50	20.00
	1975	(1918)	6.00	9.00	13.50	20.00
	1979	(1922)	6.00	9.00	13.50	20.00

Obv: Fancy katar.

Y#	Date	Year	VG	Fine	VF	XF
18.2	VS1979	(1922)	6.00	9.00	13.50	20.00
	1980	(1923)	6.00	9.00	13.50	20.00
	1981	(1924)	6.00	9.00	13.50	20.00
	1982	(1925)	6.00	9.00	13.50	20.00
	1983	(1926)	6.00	9.00	13.50	20.00
	1984	(1927)	6.00	9.00	13.50	20.00
	1987	(1930)	6.00	9.00	13.50	20.00
	1989	(1932)	6.00	9.00	13.50	20.00
	Date off flan		4.00	6.00	9.00	13.50

Y#	Date	Year	VG	Fine	VF	XF
20	VS1915(sic)	1925	45.00	70.00	100.00	140.00

NAZARANA RUPEE

SILVER, square, 10.50-11.70 g

Y#	Date	Year	VG	Fine	VF	XF
18a	VS1965	(1908)	32.50	45.00	62.50	85.00
	1971	(1914)	32.50	45.00	62.50	85.00
	1974	(1917)	32.50	45.00	62.50	85.00
	1975	(1918)	32.50	45.00	62.50	85.00
	1977	(1920)	32.50	45.00	62.50	85.00
	1979	(1922)	32.50	45.00	62.50	85.00
	1980	(1923)	32.50	45.00	62.50	85.00
	1981	(1924)	32.50	45.00	62.50	85.00
18a	1983	(1926)	32.50	45.00	62.50	85.00
	1984	(1927)	32.50	45.00	62.50	85.00
	1987	(1930)	32.50	45.00	62.50	85.00
20a	VS1915(sic)	1925	45.00	75.00	110.00	150.00

CAMBAY

Khanbayat

Although of very ancient origins as a port, located at the head of the Gulf of Cambay in West India, Cambay did not come into existence as a separate state until about 1730 after the breakdown of Mughal authority in Delhi. The nawabs of Cambay traced their ancestry to Momin Khan II, the last of the Muslim governors of Gujerat. The State came under British control after two decades of Maratha rule.

RULERS

Hussain Yafar Khan
AH1257-1297/1841-1880AD
Ja'far Ali Khan
AH1297-1333/VS1937-1972/1880-1915AD

Mint: Khanbayat

HUSSAIN YAFAR KHAN

AH1257-1297/1841-1880AD

In the name of Shah Alam II

FALUS

COPPER
Obv. c/m: Persian *Shah* on irregular planchets.

Y#	Date	Year	Good	VG	Fine	VF
A1	ND	—	4.00	5.00	6.50	8.00

RUPEE

SILVER, 10.70-11.60 g

Y#	Date	Year	VG	Fine	VF	XF
1	AH1282	—	8.50	13.50	20.00	28.50
	1294	—	8.50	13.50	20.00	28.50

NOTE: Fractional denominations are reported to exist.

JA'FAR ALI KHAN

AH1297-1333/VS1937-1972/1880-1915AD

Anonymous

1/4 PAISA

COPPER
Obv. c/m: Persian *Shah*.

Y#	Date	Year	Good	VG	Fine	VF
2	ND	—	3.00	5.50	7.50	10.00

1/2 PAISA

COPPER, round
Obv. c/m: Persian *Shah*.

Y#	Date	Year	Good	VG	Fine	VF
3	VS194x	—	3.00	5.50	7.50	9.00
	(19)62	(1905)	3.00	5.50	7.50	9.00

Square

Y#	Date	Year	Good	VG	Fine	VF
3a	VS194x	—	3.00	5.50	7.50	9.00
	(19)62	(1905)	3.00	5.50	7.50	9.00

14-15mm
Rev: Denomination in words.

Y#	Date	Year	Good	VG	Fine	VF
5	VS1963	(1906)	3.50	6.50	9.00	12.50
	1964	(1907)	3.50	6.50	9.00	12.50

Rev: Denomination in numerals.

Y#	Date	Year	Good	VG	Fine	VF
5a	VS1964	(1907)	3.00	5.00	7.50	10.00
	1965	(1908)	3.00	5.00	7.50	10.00
	1966	(1909)	3.00	5.00	7.50	10.00

PAISA

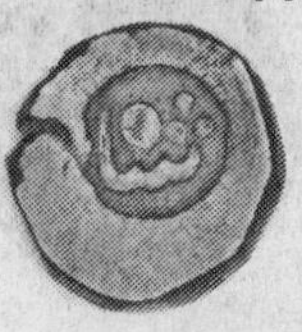

COPPER, round
Obv. c/m: Persian *Shah*.

Y#	Date	Year	Good	VG	Fine	VF
4	ND	—	1.25	2.00	3.00	4.25

Square

Y#	Date	Year	Good	VG	Fine	VF
4a	ND	—	1.50	2.25	3.25	4.50

Y#	Date	Year	Good	VG	Fine	VF
6	VS1962	(1905)	1.00	1.50	2.00	3.50
	1963	(1906)	1.00	1.50	2.00	3.50
	1964	(1907)	1.25	1.75	2.50	4.25
	1965	(1908)	1.00	1.50	2.00	3.50
	1966	(1909)	1.00	1.50	2.00	3.50
	1968	(1911)	1.00	1.50	2.00	3.50
	1970	(1913)	1.65	2.50	4.00	5.00

NOTE: Varieties exist.

In the name of Ja'far Ali Khan

1/8 RUPEE

SILVER, 11mm, 1.34-1.45 g

Y#	Date	Year	VG	Fine	VF	XF
7	AH1313	—	6.50	10.00	15.00	22.50

1/4 RUPEE

SILVER, 14mm, 2.68-2.90 g

Y#	Date	Year	VG	Fine	VF	XF
8	AH1313	—	7.00	11.00	16.50	25.00

1/2 RUPEE

SILVER, 5.35-5.80 g

Y#	Date	Year	VG	Fine	VF	XF
9	AH1313	17	10.00	15.00	21.50	30.00
	1317	—	10.00	15.00	21.50	30.00

RUPEE

SILVER, 10.70-11.60 g

Y#	Date	Year	VG	Fine	VF	XF
10	AH1311	—	15.00	21.50	30.00	40.00
	1313	17	15.00	21.50	30.00	40.00
	1317	21	15.00	21.50	30.00	40.00
	1319	23	15.00	21.50	30.00	40.00

CHAMBA

The rulers of this mountainous state in north India, the origins of which go back as far as the sixth century, were Rajputs. Although Chamba was sometimes subject to the rulers of Kashmir, and later to the Mughals, even when nominally in subjection the remoteness of the region gave its rulers a considerable degree of autonomy. In 1846 the State came under British protection and in 1948 was merged into Himachal Pradesh.

RULERS

Charhat Singh, 1808-1844AD
Lakar Shah of Basoli, rebel, 1844AD
Sri Singh, 1844-1870AD
Sham Singh, 1870-1904AD

Mint mark:

CHARHAT SINGH

1808-1844AD

PAISA

COPPER

KM#	Date	Year	Good	VG	Fine	VF
3	AH—	15	7.00	11.00	16.50	25.00
	—	16	7.00	11.00	16.50	25.00
	—	17	7.00	11.00	16.50	25.00
	ND	—	5.50	8.50	13.50	20.00

LAKAR SHAH of BASOLI

Rebel, 1844AD

PAISA

COPPER, 18-22mm
Obv: W/o trident below leg.

KM#	Date	Year	Good	VG	Fine	VF
6	ND	—	10.00	16.50	25.00	37.50

SRI SINGH

1844-1870AD

PAISA

COPPER
c/m: Trident on 1 Paisa, KM#6.

KM#	Date	Year	Good	VG	Fine	VF
9	ND	—	10.00	20.00	32.50	50.00

Crude, degenerate copy of KM#3.

KM#	Date	Year	Good	VG	Fine	VF
10	ND	—	3.50	5.50	8.00	12.50

NOTE: KM#9 was also struck during the reign of Shah Singh, 1870-1904AD. It is also found struck over KM#3.

CHHOTA UDAIPUR

Formerly one of the non-Aryan-Chota Nagpur states located in Bengal, Chhota Udaipur originated in the late fifteenth century. Its founders were Chauhan Rajputs who, having been expelled from Ajmer, finally re-established themselves in Chhota Udaipur. The rulers were known as Maharawals, and by the nineteenth century became related to the British in India by the usual treaties.

RULERS

Guman Singhji
SE1744-1773/1822-1851AD
Jitsinghji
SE1773-1803/VS1908-1938/1851-1881AD
Motisinghji
VS1938-1952/1881-1905AD

GUMAN SINGHJI

SE1744-1773/1822-1851AD

PAISA

COPPER, 7.40 g

KM#	Date	Year	Good	VG	Fine	VF
10	—	—	4.00	6.00	8.50	11.50

2 PAISA

COPPER, 13.40-14.00 g

KM#	Date	Year	Good	VG	Fine	VF
15.1	SE(1)765	(1843)	3.50	5.50	7.50	10.00
	1767	(1845)	3.50	5.50	7.50	10.00

KM#	Date	Year	Good	VG	Fine	VF
15.2	SE1797	(1875)	3.50	5.50	7.50	10.00

KM#	Date	Year	Good	VG	Fine	VF
15.3	ND	—	3.50	5.50	7.50	10.00

JITSINGHJI

SE1773-1803/VS1908-1938/1851-1881AD

PAISA

COPPER, 22mm, 7.40 g

Y#	Date	Year	Good	VG	Fine	VF
1	SE1787	(1865)	2.50	4.50	6.50	8.50

2 PAISA

COPPER, 13.40-14.00 g

Y#	Date	Year	Good	VG	Fine	VF
2	SE1787	—	5.50	7.00	9.00	12.00

Y#	Date	Year	Good	VG	Fine	VF
3	VS1919	(1862)	7.00	9.00	12.00	16.50
	1924	(1867)	7.00	9.00	12.00	16.50

MOTISINGHJI

VS1938-1952/1881-1905AD

PAISA

COPPER, 7.40 g

Y#	Date	Year	Good	VG	Fine	VF
4	VS1948	(1891)	6.00	7.50	10.00	13.50

2 PAISA

COPPER, 13.40-14.00 g

Y#	Date	Year	Good	VG	Fine	VF
5	VS1948	(1891)	5.00	6.50	8.50	11.50

CIS - SUTLEJ STATES

The name Cis-Sutlej States was applied to those states in the tract of land south of the Sutlej and to the north of the Delhi territory. Before 1846 the majority of these chieftains were substantially independent, subject only to the general oversight of an agent of the Governor-General. After the first Sikh war (1845-1846) this independence became somewhat circumscribed and in 1849 the Punjab was annexed and the Cis-Sutlej States were merged into the new province of British India. Perhaps surprisingly, most of these States distinguished themselves on the side of the British during the Great Revolt of 1857.

HANSI

RULER

Raja George Thomas

MINT

Sahibabad

RUPEE

SILVER
Obv: Umbrella. Rev: Sunface.

KM#	Date	Year	VG	Fine	VF	XF
1	AH1214	42	—	—	Rare	—

JIND

State located in the southern Punjab and north Haryana states.

The ruling princes belonged to the same Jat family as the maharajas of Patiala. Like them they traced their ancestry back to Baryam, a revenue collector under Babur (1526). The State was founded by Gajpat Singh after he took part in the Sikh uprising against the Afghan governor of Sirhind in 1763. One of Gajpat Singh's daughters became the mother of Ranjit Singh.

RULERS

Bhag Singh, 1786-1819AD
Sangat Singh, 1822-1834AD
Sarup Singh, 1834-1864AD
Raghbir Singh, 1864-1887AD
Ranbir Singh, VS1943/1887AD

RAGHBIR SINGH

1864-1887AD

RUPEE

SILVER, 18mm, 10.70-11.60 g
Rev: Similar to 1 Rupee, KM#1 but finer style.

KM#	Date	Year	VG	Fine	VF	XF
5 (Y1)	AH—	4 (frozen)	20.00	31.50	42.50	60.00

KALSIA

A Sikh state located in the Punjab.

MINT

Chhacrauli

PAISA

COPPER
Obv: Daggar mint mark. Rev: Quatrefoil and sword.

KM#	Date	Year	Good	VG	Fine	VF
32 (610)	AH1216	41	(error) 6.00	10.00	16.00	25.00
	1218	44	6.00	10.00	16.00	25.00

NOTE: Earlier dates (AH1214-1216) exist for this type.

MALER KOTLA

State located in the Punjab in northwest India, founded by the Maler Kotla family who were Sherwani Afghans who had travelled to India from Kabul in 1467 as officials of the Delhi emperors.

Coins are imitations of a rupee of Ahmad Shah Durrani, year 4, struck at the Sirhind mint, and except for the last ruler, contain the chief's initial on the reverse. The chiefs were called Ra'is until 1821, Nawabs thereafter.

For similar issues see Patiala.

RULERS

Amir Khan
AH1237-1261/1821-1845AD
Sube (Mah bub) Khan
AH1261-1276/1845-1859AD
Sikandar Ali Khan
AH1276-1288/1859-1871AD
Ibrahim Ali Khan

AH1288-1326/1871-1908AD
Ahmad Ali Khan
AH1326-/1908-AD

AMIR KHAN

AH1237-1261/1821-1845AD

Identifying Marks:

On reverse

1/4 RUPEE

SILVER, 2.68-2.90 g

C#	Date	Year	VG	Fine	VF	XF
13	AH—	4 (frozen)	9.00	15.00	21.50	30.00

1/2 RUPEE

SILVER, 16mm, 5.35-5.80 g

C#	Date	Year	VG	Fine	VF	XF
14	AH—	4 (frozen)	9.00	15.00	21.50	30.00

RUPEE

SILVER, 17mm, 10.70-11.60 g

C#	Date	Year	VG	Fine	VF	XF
15	AH—	4 (frozen)	5.50	9.00	13.50	20.00

SUBE (Mahbub) KHAN

AH1261-1276/1845-1859AD

Identifying Marks:

On reverse

1/4 RUPEE

SILVER, 2.68-2.90 g

C#	Date	Year	VG	Fine	VF	XF
18	AH—	4 (frozen)	9.00	15.00	21.50	30.00

1/2 RUPEE

SILVER, 15mm, 5.35-5.80 g

C#	Date	Year	VG	Fine	VF	XF
19	AH—	4 (frozen)	9.00	15.00	21.50	30.00

RUPEE

SILVER, 10.70-11.60 g

C#	Date	Year	VG	Fine	VF	XF
20	ND	—	5.50	9.00	13.50	20.00

SIKANDAR ALI KHAN

AH1276-1288/1859-1871AD

Identifying Marks:

On reverse

1/4 RUPEE

SILVER, 2.68-2.90 g

Y#	Date	Year	VG	Fine	VF	XF
1	ND	—	17.50	25.00	35.00	50.00

1/2 RUPEE

SILVER, 5.35-5.80 g

Y#	Date	Year	VG	Fine	VF	XF
2	ND	—	15.00	21.50	30.00	40.00

RUPEE

SILVER, 10.70-11.60 g

Y#	Date	Year	VG	Fine	VF	XF
3	AH1281	—	—	—	—	—
	ND	—	7.00	11.00	16.50	25.00

IBRAHIM ALI KHAN

AH1288-1326/1871-1908AD

Identifying Marks:

On reverse

1/4 RUPEE

SILVER, 2.68-2.90 g

Y#	Date	Year	VG	Fine	VF	XF
4	ND	—	12.50	18.50	25.00	35.00

1/2 RUPEE

SILVER, 16mm, 5.35-5.80 g

Y#	Date	Year	VG	Fine	VF	XF
5	ND	—	11.50	17.50	23.50	32.50

RUPEE

SILVER, 10.70-11.60 g

Y#	Date	Year	VG	Fine	VF	XF
6	ND	—	6.00	9.00	13.50	20.00
	AH1292	—	12.50	15.00	20.00	35.00
	1311	—	12.50	15.00	20.00	35.00

AHMAD ALI KHAN

AH1326-/1908-AD

Identifying Marks:

On reverse

1/2 PAISA

COPPER

Y#	Date	Year	Good	VG	Fine	VF
7	ND	—	7.00	11.00	16.50	25.00

PAISA

COPPER

Y#	Date	Year	Good	VG	Fine	VF
8	AH3126 (error for 1326)		17.50	25.00	35.00	50.00

RUPEE

SILVER, 10.70-11.60 g

Y#	Date	Year	VG	Fine	VF	XF
9	ND	—	6.00	9.00	13.50	20.00

NAZARANA 2 RUPEE

SILVER, 22.00 g

Y#	Date	Year	VG	Fine	VF	XF
10	AH1326	—	—	—	Rare	—

NABHA

State located in the Punjab in northwest India and founded in the 18th century.

The ancestry of these rulers was identical to that of Jind. Until 1845 Nabha's history closely paralleled that of Patiala. At this point, however, the raja sided with the Sikhs. It was left to his son to make amends to the British in 1847.

RULERS

Jaswant Singh
VS1840-1897/1783-1840AD
Bharpur Singh
VS1903-1920/1846-1863AD
Hira Singh
VS1927-1968/1870-1911AD

MINT

سرکار نابهه

Sarkar Nabha

JASWANT SINGH

VS1840-1897/1783-1840AD

Identifying Marks:

On reverse.

In the name of Ahmad Shah Durrani

RUPEE

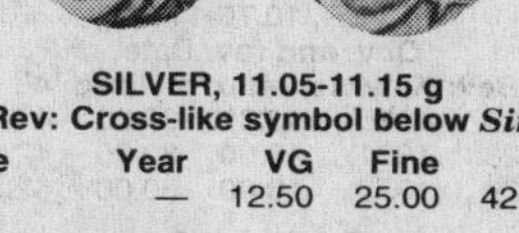

SILVER, 11.05-11.15 g
Rev: Cross-like symbol below *Sin*.

C#	Date	Year	VG	Fine	VF	XF
20.1	ND	—	12.50	25.00	42.00	60.00

Rev: Star below *Sin*.

C#	Date	Year	VG	Fine	VF	XF
20.2	VS(18)77 (1820)		12.50	25.00	42.00	60.00

Rev: Branch symbol.

C#	Date	Year	VG	Fine	VF	XF
20.3	VS(18)82	(1825)	12.50	25.00	42.00	60.00
	(18)83	(1826)	12.50	25.00	42.00	60.00
	(18)85	(1828)	12.50	25.00	42.00	60.00
	(18)93	(1836)	12.50	25.00	42.00	60.00

In the name of Guru Govind Singh

C#	Date	Year	VG	Fine	VF	XF
20.4	VS1892	(1835)	12.50	25.00	42.00	60.00
	1893	(1836)	12.50	25.00	42.00	60.00
	1895	(1838)	12.50	25.00	42.00	60.00

BHARPUR SINGH

VS1903-1920/1846-1863AD

Identifying Marks:

On reverse

In the name of Guru Govind Singh

RUPEE

SILVER, 11.00-11.10 g
Rev: Leaf to left of stylized '4'.

Y#	Date	Year	VG	Fine	VF	XF
1	VS1907	(1850)	30.00	50.00	70.00	100.00
	1908	(1851)	30.00	50.00	70.00	100.00
	1911	(1854)	30.00	50.00	70.00	100.00
	1912	(1855)	30.00	50.00	70.00	100.00
	1913	(1856)	30.00	50.00	70.00	100.00
	1916	(1859)	30.00	50.00	70.00	100.00
	1917	(1860)	30.00	50.00	70.00	100.00
	1920	(1863)	30.00	50.00	70.00	100.00

MOHUR

GOLD, 9.50-9.60 g

Y#	Date	Year	VG	Fine	VF	XF
A2	VS1907	(1850)	250.00	325.00	400.00	450.00
	1911	(1854)	250.00	325.00	400.00	450.00

HIRA SINGH

VS1927-1968/1870-1911AD

Identifying Marks:

On reverse

RUPEE

SILVER, 10.70-11.60 g
Obv. and rev: Date.
Rev: Katar to left of stylized '4'.

Y#	Date	Year	VG	Fine	VF	XF
2	VS1927	(1870)	18.00	30.00	42.50	60.00
	1928	(1871)	18.00	30.00	42.50	60.00
	1929	(1872)	18.00	30.00	42.50	60.00

PATIALA

State located in the Punjab in northwest India. In the mid-18th century the Raja was given his title and mint right by Ahmad Shah Durrani of Afghanistan, whose coin he copied.

The rulers became Maharajas in 1810AD. The maharaja of Patiala was also recognized as the leader of the Phulkean tribe. Although Patiala's ruling family were Sikhs, theyy stemmedd from thee same Jat stock as the rulers of Jind and Nabha. Unlike others, however, Patiala's Sikh rulers had never hesitated to seek British assistance at those times when they felt threatened by their co-religionist neighbors. In 1857 Patiala's forces were immediately made available on the side of the British.

RULERS

Sahib Singh
AH1196-1229/1781-1813AD
Karm Singh
AH1229-1261/1813-1845AD
Narindar Singh
VS1902-1919/1845-1862AD
Mahindar Singh
VS1919-1933/1862-1876AD
Rajindar Singh
VS1933-1957/1876-1900AD
Bhupindra Singh
VS1958-1995/1900-1937AD
Yadvindra Singh
VS1994-2005/1937-1948AD

MINT

سهرند

Sirhind

KARM SINGH

AH1229-1261/1813-1845AD

Identifying Marks:

On reverse

1/4 RUPEE

SILVER, 2.80 g

C#	Date	Year	VG	Fine	VF	XF
28	AH—	—	10.00	15.00	21.50	30.00

RUPEE

SILVER, 11.10-11.20 g
Rev: W/o symbols around.

C#	Date	Year	VG	Fine	VF	XF
30.1	AH—	—	11.50	17.50	23.50	32.50

Rev: *Alif* to left of

C#	Date	Year	VG	Fine	VF	XF
30.2	AH—	—	11.50	17.50	23.50	32.50

Rev: Crescent to right of

C#	Date	Year	VG	Fine	VF	XF
30.3	AH—	—	11.50	17.50	23.50	32.50

Rev: Three-pointed leaf to right of

C#	Date	Year	VG	Fine	VF	XF
30.4	AH—	—	11.50	17.50	23.50	32.50

Rev: Crescent to right, branch to left of

C#	Date	Year	VG	Fine	VF	XF
30.5	AH—	—	11.50	17.50	23.50	32.50

Rev: Branch to right of

C#	Date	Year	VG	Fine	VF	XF
30.6	AH—	—	11.50	17.50	23.50	32.50

Rev: Branches both sides of

C#	Date	Year	VG	Fine	VF	XF
30.7	AH—	—	11.50	17.50	23.50	32.50

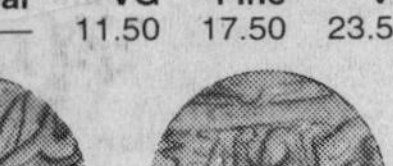

Rev: Scimitar to left of

C#	Date	Year	VG	Fine	VF	XF
31	AH—	—	16.50	23.50	32.50	45.00

NAZARANA RUPEE

SILVER, 24mm, 11.10-11.20 g

C#	Date	Year	VG	Fine	VF	XF
30a	VS1893	(1836)	—	—	Rare	—
	(18)98	(1841)	—	—	Rare	—

MOHUR

GOLD, 10.50 g
Rev: 3-pointed leaf to right of

C#	Date	Year	VG	Fine	VF	XF
35	AH—	—	200.00	250.00	300.00	375.00

NARINDAR SINGH

VS1902-1919/1845-1862AD

Identifying Marks:

On reverse

In the name of Ahmad Shah Durrani

1/4 RUPEE

SILVER, 2.75-2.80 g

Y#	Date	Year	VG	Fine	VF	XF
A1	ND	—	27.50	40.00	52.50	75.00

RUPEE

SILVER, 11.10-11.20 g

Y#	Date	Year	VG	Fine	VF	XF
1	VS1902	(1845)	15.00	27.50	40.00	55.00

In the name of Guru Govind Singh

w/Sikh leg.

Y#	Date	Year	VG	Fine	VF	XF
3	VS1906	—	37.50	52.50	75.00	110.00

MOHUR

GOLD, 17-18mm, 10.50 g

Y#	Date	Year	VG	Fine	VF	XF
2	VS190x	—	200.00	250.00	300.00	375.00

MAHINDAR SINGH

VS1919-1933/1862-1876AD

Identifying Marks:

On reverse

RUPEE

SILVER, 16-17mm, 11.10-11.20 g

Y#	Date	Year	VG	Fine	VF	XF
3	AH—	—	35.00	50.00	70.00	100.00

RAJINDAR SINGH

VS1933-1957/1876-1900AD

Identifying Marks:

On reverse

1/4 RUPEE

SILVER, 13mm, 2.75-2.80 g

Y#	Date	Year	VG	Fine	VF	XF
4	AH—	—	16.00	22.50	31.50	40.00

1/2 RUPEE

SILVER, 16mm, 5.50-5.60 g

Y#	Date	Year	VG	Fine	VF	XF
5	AH—	—	16.00	22.50	31.50	40.00

RUPEE

SILVER, 11.10-11.20 g

Y#	Date	Year	VG	Fine	VF	XF
6	VS(19)43	—	17.50	25.00	35.00	50.00
	(19)44	4	17.50	25.00	35.00	50.00
	(19)45	4	17.50	25.00	35.00	50.00
	(19)46	4	17.50	25.00	35.00	50.00
	(19)47	4	17.50	25.00	35.00	50.00
	(19)48	4	20.00	31.50	42.50	60.00

NAZARANA RUPEE

SILVER, 11.10-11.20 g

Y#	Date	Year	VG	Fine	VF	XF
6a	AH—	4 (frozen)				
			—	—	Rare	—

1/3 MOHUR

GOLD, 3.50 g
Rev: Katar at left.

Y#	Date	Fine	VF	XF	Unc
7	VS(19)50(1893)	85.00	100.00	125.00	175.00

MOHUR

GOLD, 18mm, 10.50 g

Y#	Date	Year	Fine	VF	XF	Unc
9	ND	—	200.00	250.00	300.00	375.00
	VS(19)48(1891)		200.00	250.00	300.00	375.00

BHUPINDRA SINGH

VS1958-1995/1900-1937AD

In the name of Guru Govind Singh

RUPEE

SILVER, 11.10-11.20 g

Y#	Date	Year	VG	Fine	VF	XF
A3	VS1958	(1901)	—	—	—	—

1/6 MOHUR

GOLD, 1.75 g

Y#	Date	Year	Fine	VF	XF	Unc
14	VS(19)58(1901)		85.00	100.00	125.00	175.00

1/3 MOHUR

GOLD, 3.50 g
Rev: Katar at left.

KM#	Date	Year	Fine	VF	XF	Unc
15	VS(19)58	(1901)	85.00	100.00	125.00	175.00

2/3 MOHUR

GOLD, 18mm, 7.00 g,
Rev: Katar at left.

Y#	Date	Year	Fine	VF	XF	Unc
16	VS(19)58(1901)		125.00	140.00	165.00	225.00

MOHUR

GOLD, 10.50 g
Rev: Katar at left.

Y#	Date	Year	Fine	VF	XF	Unc
17	VS(19)58(1901)		150.00	200.00	275.00	400.00

YADVINDRA SINGH

VS1994-2005/1937-1948AD

In the name of Guru Govind Singh

RUPEE

SILVER, 11.10-11.20 g

Y#	Date	Year	VG	Fine	VF	XF
A1	VS1994	(1937)	—	—	—	—

1/6 MOHUR

GOLD, 1.75 g
Rev: Bayoneted rifle at left.

Y#	Date	Year	Fine	VF	XF	Unc
19	VS(19)94(1937)		75.00	100.00	125.00	175.00

1/3 MOHUR

GOLD, 3.50 g
Rev: Bayoneted rifle at left.

KM#	Date	Year	Fine	VF	XF	Unc
20	VS(19)94	(1937)	75.00	100.00	125.00	175.00

2/3 MOHUR

GOLD, 18mm, 7.00 g
Rev: Bayoneted rifle at left.

Y#	Date	Year	Fine	VF	XF	Unc
21	VS(19)94(1937)		150.00	185.00	210.00	250.00

UNCERTAIN ISSUES

Possibly early twentieth century.

Identifying Marks:

On reverse

RUPEE

SILVER, 10.70-11.60 g

KM#	Date	Year	VG	Fine	VF	XF
1	AH—	4 (frozen)				
			12.50	18.50	25.00	35.00

DATIA

State located in north-central India, governed by Maharajas.

Datia was founded in 1735 by Bhagwan Das, son of Narsingh Dev of the Orchha royal house. In 1804 the State concluded its first treaty with the East India Company and thereafter came under British protection and control.

RULERS

Parachat
AH1217-1255/1802-1839AD
Vijaya Bahadur
AH1255-1274/1839-1857AD
Bhawani Singh
AH1274-1325/1857-1907AD
Govind Singh
AH1325-1368/1907-1948AD

MINT

Dalipnagar

Gaja Shahi Series

Struck for more than 100 years, with the AH date on the obverse and the regnal year on the reverse bearing little relationship to each other. These are close copies of Orchha C#24-32 and can only be distinguished by the symbols, which are always different from those of Orchha, except for the Gaja (mace):

Gaja always on reverse 

 On obverse (Datia Mint Symbol)

On reverse

1/2 PAISA

COPPER, 6.00 g

C#	Date	Year	Good	VG	Fine	VF
22	AH—	4x	2.50	3.50	5.00	7.50
	1320	—	3.00	4.50	6.50	10.00

PAISA

COPPER, round or squarish, 12.00-13.00 g

C#	Date	Year	Good	VG	Fine	VF
23	AH1246	24	2.50	3.25	4.00	5.50
	1248	—	2.50	3.25	4.00	5.50
	1258	—	2.50	3.25	4.00	5.50
	—	39	2.50	3.25	4.00	5.50
	1274	45	2.50	3.25	4.00	5.50
	1278	45	2.50	3.25	4.00	5.50
	1282	4x	2.50	3.25	4.00	5.50
	1283	—	2.50	3.25	4.00	5.50
	1320	46	2.50	3.25	4.00	5.50

1/8 RUPEE

SILVER, 1.34-1.45 g

C#	Date	Year	VG	Fine	VF	XF
35	AH—	22	6.00	10.00	14.00	20.00
	—	4x	6.00	10.00	14.00	20.00

1/4 RUPEE

SILVER, 2.68-2.90 g

C#	Date	Year	VG	Fine	VF	XF
36	AH1317	23	6.00	12.50	17.50	25.00

1/2 RUPEE

SILVER, 5.35-5.80 g

C#	Date	Year	VG	Fine	VF	XF
37	AH1311	19	6.00	12.50	17.50	25.00
	—	23	6.00	12.50	17.50	25.00
	1316	24	6.00	12.50	17.50	25.00
	1317	25	6.00	12.50	17.50	25.00
	—	29	6.00	12.50	17.50	25.00

RUPEE

SILVER, 10.70-11.60 g

C#	Date	Year	VG	Fine	VF	XF
38	AH1211	43	6.00	10.00	15.00	22.50
	1214	42	6.00	10.00	15.00	22.50
	1215	23	6.00	10.00	15.00	22.50
	1221	43	6.00	10.00	15.00	22.50
	1233	24	6.00	10.00	15.00	22.50
	1233	28	6.00	10.00	15.00	22.50
	1235	14	6.00	10.00	15.00	22.50
	1249	28	6.00	10.00	15.00	22.50
	1250	28	6.00	10.00	15.00	22.50
	1257	48	6.00	10.00	15.00	22.50
	1258	38	6.00	10.00	15.00	22.50
	1262	29	6.00	10.00	15.00	22.50
	1270	36	6.00	10.00	15.00	22.50
	1271	37	6.00	10.00	15.00	22.50
	1272	38	6.00	10.00	15.00	22.50
	1273	39	6.00	10.00	15.00	22.50
	1274	44	6.00	10.00	15.00	22.50
	1275	41	6.00	10.00	15.00	22.50
	1277	44	6.00	10.00	15.00	22.50
	1278	45	6.00	10.00	15.00	22.50
	1281	48	6.00	10.00	15.00	22.50
	1282	46	6.00	10.00	15.00	22.50
	1286	46	6.00	10.00	15.00	22.50
	1287	46	6.00	10.00	15.00	22.50
	1311	19	6.00	10.00	15.00	22.50
	1312	24	6.00	10.00	15.00	22.50
	1312	25	6.00	10.00	15.00	22.50
	1312	30	6.00	10.00	15.00	22.50
	1313	24	6.00	10.00	15.00	22.50
	1314	24	6.00	10.00	15.00	22.50
	1314	40	6.00	10.00	15.00	22.50
	1315	23	6.00	10.00	15.00	22.50
	—	35	6.00	10.00	15.00	22.50

In the name of Muhammad Akbar II

RUPEE

SILVER, 10.70-11.60 g

C#	Date	Year	VG	Fine	VF	XF
45	AH1270	33	15.00	25.00	35.00	50.00

DEWAS JUNIOR BRANCH

A Maratha state located in west-central India. The raja, the brother of the raja of Dewas Senior Branch had a palace in Dewas City. They descended from two brothers, Tukoji and Jiwaji who were given Dewas City in 1726 by Peshwa Baji Rao as a reward for army services.

Largely due to its geographical location Dewas suffered much at the hands of the armies of Holkar and Sindhia, and from Pindari incursions. In 1818 the State came under British protection.

LOCAL RULERS

Narayan Rao, 1864-1892

NARAYAN RAO

1864-1892AD

1/12 ANNA

COPPER

KM#	Date	Mintage	Fine	VF	XF	Unc
1	1888	.112	10.00	20.00	35.00	60.00
	1888	—	—	—	Proof	125.00

1/4 ANNA

COPPER

KM#	Date	Mintage	Fine	VF	XF	Unc
3	1888	.484	9.00	18.00	30.00	50.00
	1888	—	—	—	Proof	150.00

SILVER

KM#	Date	Mintage	Fine	VF	XF	Unc
3a	1888	(restrike)	—	—	Proof	125.00

DEWAS SENIOR BRANCH

A Maratha state located in west-central India. The raja, the brother of the raja of Dewas Junior Branch had a palace in Dewas city. They descended from two brothers, Tukoji and Jiwaji who were given Dewas City in 1726 by Peshwa Baji Rao as a reward for army services.

Largely due to its geographical location Dewas suffered much at the hands of the armies of Holkar and Sindhia, and from Pindari incursions. In 1818 the State came under British protection.

LOCAL RULERS

Krishnaji Rao, 1860-1899AD
Vikrama Simha Rao, 1937-1948AD

ALLOTE MINT

PAISA

COPPER

KM#	Date	Good	VG	Fine	VF
10	—	2.50	3.50	5.00	7.00

NOTE: Varieties exist.

REGAL ISSUES

Milled Coinage

1/12 ANNA

COPPER

KM#	Date	Mintage	Fine	VF	XF	Unc
11	1888	.112	6.00	12.00	20.00	35.00
	1888	—	—	—	Proof	125.00

SILVER

KM#	Date	Mintage	Fine	VF	XF	Unc
11a	1888	(restrike)	—	—	Proof	100.00

1/4 ANNA

COPPER

KM#	Date	Mintage	Fine	VF	XF	Unc
12	1888	.484	7.50	15.00	25.00	40.00
	1888	—	—	—	Proof	150.00

VIKRAMA SIMHA RAO

1937-1948AD

PAISA

COPPER

KM#	Date	Year	Fine	VF	XF	Unc
13	VS2000	1944	27.50	55.00	90.00	150.00
	2001	1944	22.50	45.00	75.00	125.00

DHAR

The territory in central India in which Dhar was located had been controlled by the Paramara clan of Rajputs from the ninth century to the thirteenth, after which it passed into Muslim hands. The modern Princely State of Dhar originated in the first half of the eighteenth century when the Maratha Peshwa, Baji Rao, handed over the region as a fiefdom to Anand Rao Ponwar. Anand Rao Ponwar was of the same stock as the rulers of Dewas and a descendant of the original Paramara Rajputs. Sometimes in conflict with Holkar, sometimes with Sindhia, in 1819 Dhar came under British protection. No silver or gold coinage was ever struck at Dhar. In 1895 the British silver rupee was adopted.

LOCAL RULERS

Jaswant Rao
AH1250-1274/1834-1857AD
Anand Rao III
AH1276-1316/1860-1898AD
Anand Rao IV
AH1363-1368/1943-1948AD

JASWANT RAO

AH1250-1274/1834-1857AD

PAISA

COPPER

KM#	Date	Year	Good	VG	Fine	VF
2	ND	—	2.50	4.00	6.50	10.00

Obv: Banners.

KM#	Date	Year	Good	VG	Fine	VF
1	AH1266	—	2.50	4.00	6.50	10.00

ANAND RAO III

AH1276-1316/1860-1898AD

1/2 PAISA

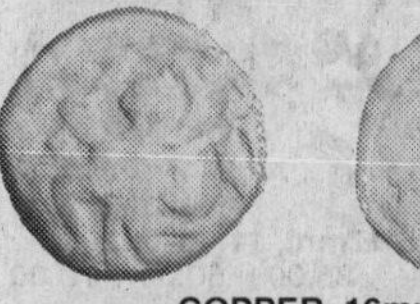

COPPER, 16mm
Obv: Hanuman w/banners.

KM#	Date	Year	Good	VG	Fine	VF
5	AH1289	—	3.00	5.00	9.00	15.00

PAISA

COPPER
Obv: Hanuman w/banners.

KM#	Date	Year	Good	VG	Fine	VF
6	AH1289	—	3.00	5.00	8.00	12.50

Milled Coinage

1/12 ANNA

COPPER

KM#	Date	Mintage	Fine	VF	XF	Unc
11	1887	—	1.35	3.50	9.00	15.00
	1887	—	—	—	Proof	125.00

SILVER

KM#	Date	Mintage	Fine	VF	XF	Unc
11a	1887	(restrike)	—	—	Proof	100.00

GOLD

KM#	Date	Mintage	Fine	VF	XF	Unc
11b	1887	(restrike)	—	—	Proof	350.00

1/2 PICE

COPPER

KM#	Date	Mintage	Fine	VF	XF	Unc
12	1887	—	2.00	5.00	12.00	20.00
	1887	—	—	—	Proof	150.00

SILVER

KM#	Date	Mintage	Fine	VF	XF	Unc
12a	1887	(restrike)	—	—	Proof	125.00

GOLD

KM#	Date	Mintage	Fine	VF	XF	Unc
12b	1887	(restrike)	—	—	Proof	450.00

1/4 ANNA

COPPER

KM#	Date	Mintage	Fine	VF	XF	Unc
13	1887	—	3.00	7.50	18.00	30.00
	1887	—	—	—	Proof	175.00

SILVER

KM#	Date	Mintage	Fine	VF	XF	Unc
13a	1887	(restrike)	—	—	Proof	150.00

GOLD

KM#	Date	Mintage	Fine	VF	XF	Unc
13b	1887	(restrike)	—	—	Proof	650.00

DHOLPUR

State located in Rajputana, northwest India.

Dholpur had a varied and turbulent history. From the eighth until the twelfth centuries it was ruled by Tonwar Rajputs. Early in the sixteenth century the entire region came under the Mughals. It was included by Akbar in Agra province. With Mughal decline after 1707, Dholpur experienced many masters until, in 1782, it fell into the hands of Sindhia. In 1803 the territory was captured by the British and in 1805 it was returned to the ranas of Gohad, Bamraolia Jats, from whom it had earlier been wrested by Sindhia. The ranas of Gohad opened the mint which operated until 1857.

RULER

Kirat Singh
AH1203-1221/1788-1806AD, in Gohad
AH1221-1251/1806-1837AD, in Dholpur

MINTS

Dholpur دہلوپور

Gohad گوهد

DHOLPUR MINT

Mint marks:

On obverse

On reverse Type 1

or Type 2

In the name of Muhammad Akbar II
AH1221-1253/1806-1837AD

RUPEE

SILVER, 10.70-11.60 g

C#	Date	Year	VG	Fine	VF	XF
12.1	AH1221	—	17.50	25.00	35.00	50.00
	1225	4	35.00	50.00	70.00	100.00

C#	Date	Year	VG	Fine	VF	XF
12.2	AH1226	5	35.00	50.00	70.00	100.00
	1228	—	17.50	25.00	35.00	50.00
	1228	17	17.50	25.00	35.00	50.00
	—	19	17.50	25.00	35.00	50.00
	—	21	17.50	25.00	35.00	50.00

GOHAD MINT

Mint marks:

On obverse

or

reverse

Pistol

Star

or

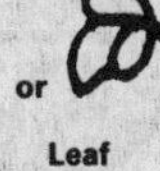

Leaf

In the name of Shah Alam II
AH1173-1221/1759-1806AD

RUPEE

SILVER, 10.70-11.60 g
Obv: Pistol.

C#	Date	Year	VG	Fine	VF	XF
5.1	AH1218	46	18.50	31.50	42.50	60.00
	1219	47	18.50	31.50	42.50	60.00

NOTE: Earlier dates (AH1185-1208) exist for this type.

Rev: Pistol.

C#	Date	Year	VG	Fine	VF	XF
6	AH1245	24	20.00	31.50	42.50	60.00

In the name of Muhammad Akbar II
AH1221-1253/1806-1837AD

1/2 RUPEE

SILVER, 5.35-5.80 g

C#	Date	Year	VG	Fine	VF	XF
11	AH—	—	15.00	25.00	35.00	50.00

RUPEE

SILVER, 10.70-11.60 g
Rev: Pistol and leaf.

C#	Date	Year	VG	Fine	VF	XF
12a.1	AH1247	26	12.50	25.00	42.00	60.00
	1249	28	12.50	25.00	42.00	60.00
	1250	29	12.50	25.00	42.00	60.00
	1251	30	12.50	25.00	42.00	60.00

Rev: Pistol and star.

C#	Date	Year	VG	Fine	VF	XF
12a.2	AH1251	30	12.50	25.00	42.00	60.00

Rev: Pistol and leaf.

C#	Date	Year	VG	Fine	VF	XF
12c	AH1252	31	12.50	25.00	42.00	60.00

***NOTE:** Actually struck in AH1274/1857AD.

NAZARANA RUPEE

SILVER, 10.70-11.60 g
Rev: Pistol and leaf.

C#	Date	Year	VG	Fine	VF	XF
12b.2	1252*	30	45.00	75.00	110.00	150.00

***NOTE:** Actually struck in AH1274/1857 AD.

MOHUR

GOLD, 10.70-11.60 g

C#	Date	Year	VG	Fine	VF	XF
15	AH1252*	—	—	—	Rare	—

***NOTE:** Actually struck in AH1274/1857 AD.

DUNGARPUR

A district in northwest India which became part of Rajasthan in 1948.

The maharawals of Dungarpur were descended from the Mewar chieftains of the twelth century. In 1527 the upper Mahi basin was bifurcated to form the Princely States of Dungarpur and Banswara. Thereafter Dungarpur came successively under Mughal and Maratha control until in 1818 it came under British protection.

RULERS

Udai Singh
VS1909-1955/1852-1898AD
Bijey Singh
VS1955-1975/1898-1918AD
Lakshman Singh
VS1975-2005/1918-1948AD

UDAI SINGH

VS1909-1955/1852-1898AD

1/4 PAISA

COPPER, 2.50 g

KM#	Date	Year	Good	VG	Fine	VF
1	VS1917	(1860)	6.00	10.00	16.00	25.00

1/2 PAISA

COPPER, 5.00 g
Obv: Dagger points left.

KM#	Date	Year	Good	VG	Fine	VF
4	VS1917	(1860)	—	—	—	—

PAISA

COPPER, 9.50-11.00 g
Obv: Dagger points right.

KM#	Date	Year	Good	VG	Fine	VF
2	VS1911	(1854)	3.00	5.00	8.00	12.50
(YA1)	1916	—	3.00	5.00	8.00	12.50
	1917	(1860)	3.00	5.00	8.00	12.50

Obv: Dagger points left.

KM#	Date	Year	Good	VG	Fine	VF
3	VS1917	(1860)	3.00	5.00	8.00	12.50

MOHUR

GOLD, 10.91 g

KM#	Date	Year	VG	Fine	VF	XF
6	VS1925	(1868)	—	—	850.00	1250.

NOTE: Authenticity being questioned by certain authorities.

LAKSHMAN SINGH

VS1975-2005/1918-1948AD

PAISA

COPPER
Rev: 2 bars above *P* of *Paisa*.

KM#	Date	Year	Good	VG	Fine	VF
7 (Y1.1)	VS2001	(1944)	18.00	30.00	50.00	75.00

Rev: One bar above *P* of *Pesa*.

KM#	Date	Year	Good	VG	Fine	VF
8 (Y1.2)	VS2001	(1944)	9.00	15.00	25.00	37.50

NAZARANA MOHUR

GOLD, 11.00 g

KM#	Date	Year	VG	Fine	VF	XF
9	VS1996	(1939)	—	—	—	—
(M1)	2001	(1944)	—	—	—	—

FARRUKHABAD

Refer to Independent Kingdoms during British rule.

GWALIOR

Sindhia

State located in central India. Capital originally was Ujjain (= Daru-l-fath), but was later transferred to Gwalior in 1810. The Gwalior ruling family, the Sindhias, were descendants of the Maratha chief Ranoji Sindhia (d.1750). His youngest son, Mahadji Sindhia (d.1794) was anxious to establish his independence from the over-lordship of the Peshwas of Poona. Unable to achieve this alone, it was the Peshwa's crushing defeat by Ahmad Shah Durrani at Panipat in 1761 which helped realize his ambitions. Largely in the interests of sustaining this autonomy, but partly as a result of a defeat at East India Company hands in 1781, Mahadji concluded an alliance with the British in 1782. In 1785, he reinstalled the fallen Mughal Emperor, Shah Alam, on the throne at Dehli. Very early in the nineteenth century, Gwalior's relationship with the British began to deteriorate, a situation which culminated in the Anglo-Maratha War of 1803. Gwalior's forces under Daulat Rao were defeated. In consequence, and by the terms of the peace treaty which followed, his territory was truncated. In 1818, Gwalior suffered a further loss of land at British hands. In the years that ensued, as the East India Company's possessions became transformed into empire and as the Pax Britannica swept across the subcontinent, the Sindhia family's relationship with their British overlords steadliy improved.

RULERS

Daulat Rao
AH1209-1243/1794-1827AD
Baija Bai, Regent,
(Widow of Daulat Rao)
AH1243-1249/1827-1833AD
Jankoji Rao
AH1243-1259/1827-1843AD
Jayaji Rao
AH1259-1304/1843-1886AD
Madho Rao
VS1943-1982/1886-1925AD
Jivaji Rao
VS1982-2005/1925-1948AD

MINTS

Bajranggarh "Jaynagar" जयनगर

Basoda بسوره

Bhilsa "Alamgirpur" عالمگیرپور

Broach بروچ

Burhanpur برہانپور

Dohad દોહદ

Garhakota "Ravishnagar Sagar" روش نگر ساگر

Gwalior Fort گواليار

Isagarh عسي گره

Jawad

Jhansi "Balwantnagar" بلونت نگر

Lashkar

Mandasor

Rajod राजोद

Rathgarh "Daulatgarh" دولت گره

Shadhorah شادہورہ

Sheopur شیوپور

Sipri "Narwar" نروار

Ujjain, dar ul Fateh دار الفتح اجين

NOTE: None of the coins of Gwalior prior to the beginning of machine-struck coinage in 1889AD bears the name of the Sindhia (ruler of Gwalior), but beginning with the reign of Baija Bao, a Nagari letter is used to indicate the ruler under whom it was struck, as follows:

Sri	श्री	Baija Bao
Jo	जे	Jankoji Rao
Ji	जी	Jayaji Rao
Ma	मा	Madho Rao

However, not all the coins bear the initial of the ruler, especially the copper.

The coinage of Gwalior is extremely complicated and not fully understood. Each mint, and there were probably more than twenty in all, maintained its own styles and types, and operated fully independently of every other mint. Hence it is most logical to list the issues of each mint together, rather than attempt to list the coins by reign or denomination. The mints are best identified by the presence of special symbols on the obverse or reverse of the coins, and those symbols are noted whenever possible. Types are listed with designation of reign only when the initial of the ruler appears on the coin; others are assigned a single number for the full duration of their issuance.

Most of the coins of Gwalior are undated, or issued over long periods of time with frozen dates, in order to discourage the nefarious practice of devaluing coins of older dates (for example, one-year old coins might be devalued 1 percent, two-year olds 2 percent, and so forth). Many of the types were struck with frozen dates for several decades, and in many other cases, the dates remained frozen while the ruler's initial changed. The frozen dates may be either AH dates or regnal years, or both.

Regularly dated series often continued over long durations, such as the Ujjain rupees (C#259); the lists of such coins are probably very fragmentary, and many unlisted dates will be discovered. In general, unlisted dates are worth no more than listed dates of the same type.

BAJRANGGARH MINT

For coins issued by Jai Singh, AH1213-1233 refer to Bajranggarh State listings.

AJIT SINGH

AH1235-1274/1819-1857AD

Mint mark: जयनगर

Types of Jai Singh with added mint marks:

Lotus

Bow and arrow

1/8 RUPEE

SILVER, 16mm, 1.34-1.45 g
Obv: Bow and arrow. Rev: Lotus.

KM#	Date	Year	VG	Fine	VF	XF
12	ND(1827-61)	NRY	10.00	15.00	21.50	30.00

1/4 RUPEE

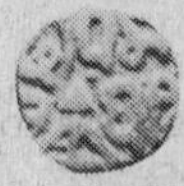

SILVER, 2.68-2.90 g
Obv: Bow and arrow. Rev: Lotus.

KM#	Date	Year	VG	Fine	VF	XF
13	ND(1827-61)	NRY	8.50	13.50	20.00	28.50

1/2 RUPEE

SILVER, 5.35-5.80 g
Obv: Bow and arrow. Rev: Lotus.

KM#	Date	Year	VG	Fine	VF	XF
14	ND(1827-61)	NRY	7.50	12.50	18.50	27.50

RUPEE

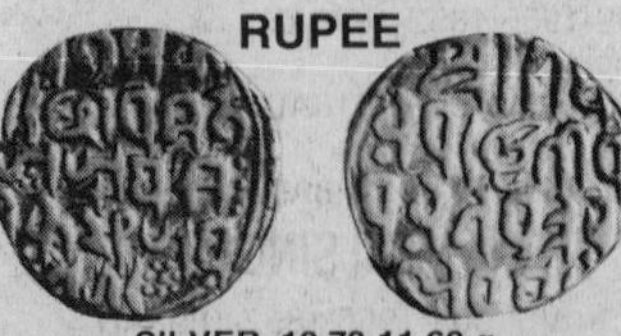

SILVER, 10.70-11.60 g

Rev: Lotus.

KM#	Date	Year	VG	Fine	VF	XF
15	ND(1819)	21	15.00	21.50	30.00	40.00
	(1820)	22	15.00	21.50	30.00	40.00

Obv: Bow and arrow. Rev: Lotus.

KM#	Date	Year	VG	Fine	VF	XF
16	ND(1821)	23	7.00	11.00	16.50	25.00
	(1822)	24	7.00	11.00	16.50	25.00
	(1823)	25	7.00	11.00	16.50	25.00
	(1824)	26	7.00	11.00	16.50	25.00
	(1825)	27	7.00	11.00	16.50	25.00
	(1826)	28	7.00	11.00	16.50	25.00
	(1827)	29	7.00	11.00	16.50	25.00

KM#	Date	Year	VG	Fine	VF	XF
17	ND(1827-61)	NRY	6.00	9.00	13.50	20.00

BASODA MINT

Daulat Rao

AH1209-1243/1794-1827AD

In the name of Muhammad Akbar II
AH1221-1253/1806-1837AD

Mint marks: 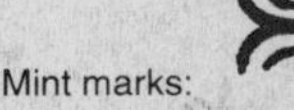 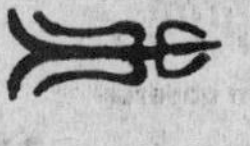 

RUPEE

SILVER, 10.70-11.60 g

KM#	Date	Year	VG	Fine	VF	XF
18	AH124x	18	25.00	37.50	50.00	70.00

JANKOJI RAO

AH1243-1259/1833-1843AD

In the name of Muhammad Akbar II
AH1221-1253/1806-1837AD
and Jankoji Rao

With additional mint mark: 

RUPEE

SILVER, 10.70-11.60 g

KM#	Date	Year	VG	Fine	VF	XF
19.1	AH1252	32	25.00	37.50	50.00	70.00
	1254	32	25.00	37.50	50.00	70.00

JAYAJI RAO

AH1259-1304/1843-1886AD

In the name of Muhammad Akbar II
AH1221-1253/1806-1837AD
and Jankoji Rao

RUPEE

SILVER, 10.70-11.60 g

KM#	Date	Year	VG	Fine	VF	XF
19.2	AH1274	3x	25.00	37.50	50.00	70.00
	1274	46	25.00	37.50	50.00	70.00

BHILSA MINT

DAULAT RAO

AH1209-1243/1794-1827AD

In the name of Muhammad Akbar II

AH1221-1253/1806-1837AD

1/8 RUPEE

SILVER

KM#	Date	Year	VG	Fine	VF	XF
A20	—	—	7.50	15.00	25.00	35.00

1/4 RUPEE

SILVER, 2.68-2.90 g

KM#	Date	Year	VG	Fine	VF	XF
20	AH—	16	8.50	17.00	28.00	40.00

1/2 RUPEE

SILVER, 5.35-5.80 g

KM#	Date	Year	VG	Fine	VF	XF
21	AH—	15	11.00	22.00	35.00	50.00

RUPEE

SILVER, 10.70-11.60 g

Obv: 3-leaf symbol. Rev: Regnal year.

KM#	Date	Year	VG	Fine	VF	XF
22	AH—	7	8.50	17.00	28.00	40.00
	—	9	8.50	17.00	28.00	40.00
	—	11	8.50	17.00	28.00	40.00
	—	13	8.50	17.00	28.00	40.00
	—	14	8.50	17.00	28.00	40.00
	—	15	8.50	17.00	28.00	40.00
	—	16	8.50	17.00	28.00	40.00
	—	17	8.50	17.00	28.00	40.00
	—	19	8.50	17.00	28.00	40.00
	—	20	8.50	17.00	28.00	40.00
	—	26	8.50	17.00	28.00	40.00
	—	51	8.50	17.00	28.00	40.00

JAYAJI RAO

AH1259-1304/1843-1886AD

NOTE: The bow & arrow and trident appear on nearly all coins of Bhilsa, Gwalior Fort, and Lashkar Mints, and cannot be used to identify any one of them.

In the name of Shah Alam II

AH1173-1221/1759-1806AD

with additional initial of Jayaji Rao जी

Frozen date AH(12)25

1/8 RUPEE

SILVER, 1.34-1.45 g

Obv: W/o sword.

KM#	Date	Year	VG	Fine	VF	XF
23.1	AH(12)25	—	7.00	11.00	16.50	25.00

Obv: W/sword.

KM#	Date	Year	VG	Fine	VF	XF
23.2	AH(12)25	—	7.00	11.00	16.50	25.00

1/4 RUPEE

SILVER, 12-14mm, 2.68-2.90 g

Obv: W/o sword.

KM#	Date	Year	VG	Fine	VF	XF
24.1	AH(12)25	—	7.00	11.00	16.50	25.00

Obv: W/sword.

KM#	Date	Year	VG	Fine	VF	XF
24.2	AH(12)25	—	7.00	11.00	16.50	25.00

1/2 RUPEE

SILVER, 5.35-5.80 g

Obv: W/o sword.

KM#	Date	Year	VG	Fine	VF	XF
25	AH(12)25	—	10.00	15.00	21.50	30.00

Obv: Sword.

KM#	Date	Year	VG	Fine	VF	XF
26	AH(12)25	—	10.00	15.00	21.50	30.00

RUPEE

SILVER, 10.70-11.60 g

Obv: W/o sword. Rev: Bow and arrow.

KM#	Date	Year	VG	Fine	VF	XF
27	AH(12)25	23	6.00	9.00	13.50	20.00

Obv: Sword. Rev: Bow and arrow.

KM#	Date	Year	VG	Fine	VF	XF
28	AH(12)25	—	5.50	8.00	12.50	18.50

With additional initial of Madho Rao II

1/8 RUPEE

SILVER, 9-10mm, 1.34-1.45 g

KM#	Date	Year	VG	Fine	VF	XF
29	AH(12)25	—	6.00	9.00	13.50	20.00

1/4 RUPEE

SILVER, 2.68-2.90 g

KM#	Date	Year	VG	Fine	VF	XF
30	AH(12)25	—	6.00	9.00	13.50	20.00

1/2 RUPEE

SILVER, 5.35-5.80 g

KM#	Date	Year	VG	Fine	VF	XF
31	AH(12)25	—	7.00	11.00	16.50	25.00

RUPEE

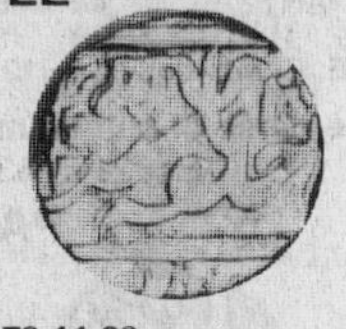

SILVER, 10.70-11.60 g

KM#	Date	Year	VG	Fine	VF	XF
32	AH(12)25	—	7.00	11.00	16.50	25.00

BROACH MINT

RUPEE

SILVER, 10.70-11.60 g

KM#	Date	Year	VG	Fine	VF	XF
34	AH—	27	5.00	10.00	17.50	25.00
	—	29	5.00	10.00	17.50	25.00
	—	32	5.00	10.00	17.50	25.00
	—	34	5.00	10.00	17.50	25.00
	—	35	5.00	10.00	17.50	25.00

BURHANPUR MINT

DAULAT RAO

AH1209-1243/1794-1827AD

In the name of Shah Alam II

AH1173-1221/1759-1806AD

PAISA

COPPER, square, 18.14 g

KM#	Date	Year	Good	VG	Fine	VF
40	AH1218	—	2.50	4.00	6.00	8.00

RUPEE

SILVER, 10.70-11.60 g

KM#	Date	Year	VG	Fine	VF	XF
38.2	AH1216	4x	6.00	12.00	20.00	28.00
	1217	45	6.00	12.00	20.00	28.00
	1218	—	6.00	12.00	20.00	28.00
	1219	4x	6.00	12.00	20.00	28.00
	1220	—	10.00	14.00	20.00	27.50
	1221	4x	6.00	12.00	20.00	28.00
	1222	—	6.00	12.00	20.00	28.00
	1223	4x	6.00	12.00	20.00	28.00
	1224	4x	6.00	12.00	20.00	28.00
	1225	—	6.00	12.00	20.00	28.00
	1227	—	6.00	12.00	20.00	28.00
	1229	—	6.00	12.00	20.00	28.00
	1230	—	6.00	12.00	20.00	28.00
	1231	—	10.00	14.00	20.00	27.50
	1232	—	6.00	12.00	20.00	28.00
	1233	—	6.00	12.00	20.00	28.00
	1234	3x	6.00	12.00	20.00	28.00
	1235	39	6.00	12.00	20.00	28.00
	1237	—	6.00	12.00	20.00	28.00
	1238	—	6.00	12.00	20.00	28.00
	1239	—	6.00	12.00	20.00	28.00
	1240	—	10.00	14.00	20.00	27.50
	1242	—	6.00	12.00	20.00	28.00
	1243	—	6.00	12.00	20.00	28.00

NOTE: Earlier dates (AH1209-1215) exist for this type.

BAIJA BAI

AH1243-1249/1827-1833AD

In the name of Shah Alam II

AH1173-1221/1759-1806AD

RUPEE

SILVER, 10.70-11.60 g

KM#	Date	Year	VG	Fine	VF	XF
38.3	AH1247	—	7.50	15.00	25.00	36.00

JANKOJI RAO

AH1243-1259/1827-1843AD

In the name of Shah Alam II

AH1173-1221/1759-1806AD

RUPEE

SILVER, 10.70-11.60 g

KM#	Date	Year	VG	Fine	VF	XF
38.4	AH1255	—	10.00	14.00	20.00	30.00

JAYAJI RAO

AH1243-1249/1827-1833AD

Mint mark:  

PAISA

COPPER, 15.23 g

KM#	Date	Year	Good	VG	Fine	VF
41	ND	—	2.50	4.50	6.50	10.00

1/4 RUPEE

SILVER, 15mm, 2.68-2.90 g

KM#	Date	Year	VG	Fine	VF	XF
42	AH1214	—	6.50	13.00	21.00	30.00

1/2 RUPEE

SILVER, 17mm, 5.35-5.70 g

KM#	Date	Year	VG	Fine	VF	XF
43	AH1214	—	10.00	20.00	32.00	45.00
	1261	—	10.00	20.00	32.00	45.00
	1274	—	10.00	20.00	32.00	45.00

RUPEE

SILVER, 10.70-11.60 g

KM#	Date	Year	VG	Fine	VF	XF
44	AH1259	—	7.50	15.00	22.00	32.00
	AH1260	—	7.50	15.00	22.00	32.00
	1261	—	7.50	15.00	22.00	32.00
	1262	—	7.50	15.00	22.00	32.00
	1266	—	7.50	15.00	22.00	32.00
	1267	—	7.50	15.00	22.00	32.00
	1268	—	7.50	15.00	22.00	32.00
	1271	—	7.50	15.00	22.00	32.00
	1272	—	7.50	15.00	22.00	32.00
	1273	—	7.50	15.00	22.00	32.00
	1274	—	7.50	15.00	22.00	32.00
	1275	—	7.50	15.00	22.00	32.00
	1276	—	7.50	15.00	22.00	32.00
	1277	—	7.50	15.00	22.00	32.00

In the name of Alyjah Bahadur

NOTE: Alyjah Bahadur was the hereditary title of the Sindhia rulers of Gwalior, and was used by all rulers of the dynasty.

Mint marks:

to right of date

PAISA

COPPER, 12.44-15.29 g
Rev: Leaf and snake.

KM#	Date	Year	Good	VG	Fine	VF
45	AH1260	—	4.50	8.00	12.00	17.50
	1273	—	4.50	8.00	12.00	17.50
	1274	—	4.50	8.00	12.00	17.50
	1275	—	4.50	8.00	12.00	17.50

DOHAD MINT

Mint mark:

JAYAJI RAO

AH1259-1304/VS1900-1943/1843-1886AD

1/3 PAISA

COPPER, 1.69-1.88 g

KM#	Date	Year	Good	VG	Fine	VF
49	VS1912	(1855)	3.00	5.00	8.00	12.50

PAISA

COPPER, thick flan, 6.00-6.20 g

KM#	Date	Year	Good	VG	Fine	VF
50.1	VS1912	(1855)	5.00	9.00	13.00	20.00

Thin flan

KM#	Date	Year	Good	VG	Fine	VF
50.2	VS1912	(1855)	5.00	9.00	13.00	20.00

GARHAKOTA MINT

Mint marks:

JAYAJI RAO

AH1259-1304/1843-1886AD

1/2 RUPEE

SILVER, 5.35-5.80 g
Similar to 1 Rupee, KM#53.

KM#	Date	Year	VG	Fine	VF	XF
51	AH—	55	6.00	9.00	13.50	20.00

RUPEE

SILVER, 10.70-11.60 g

KM#	Date	Year	VG	Fine	VF	XF
53	AH—	55	10.00	15.00	21.50	30.00

GWALIOR FORT MINT

DAULAT RAO

AH1209-1243/1794-1827AD

In the name of Shah Alam II

AH1173-1221/1759-1806AD

RUPEE

SILVER, 10.70-11.60 g

KM#	Date	Year	VG	Fine	VF	XF
57.2	AH1216	44	8.00	13.50	20.00	28.50
	1221	48	8.00	13.50	20.00	28.50

NOTE: Earlier dates (AH1210-1213) exist for this type.

In the name of Muhammad Akbar II

AH1221-1253/1806-1837AD

PAISA

COPPER

KM#	Date	Year	Good	VG	Fine	VF
59	AH1224	3	1.00	1.65	2.50	4.00
	122x	4	1.00	1.65	2.50	4.00
	1232	—	1.00	1.65	2.50	4.00
	1235	14	1.00	1.65	2.50	4.00
	1236	15	1.00	1.65	2.50	4.00
	1241	—	1.00	1.65	2.50	4.00

1/4 RUPEE

SILVER

KM#	Date	Year	VG	Fine	VF	XF
A60	AH1228	—	9.00	18.00	28.00	40.00

1/2 RUPEE

SILVER, 5.35-5.80 g
Similar to 1 Rupee, KM#61.

KM#	Date	Year	VG	Fine	VF	XF
60	AH—	—	9.00	18.00	28.00	40.00

RUPEE

Mint marks:

on obverse

on reverse

SILVER, 10.70-11.60 g

KM#	Date	Year	VG	Fine	VF	XF
61	AH1222	1	9.00	18.00	28.00	40.00

KM#	Date	Year	VG	Fine	VF	XF
62	AH1227	6	6.50	13.00	22.00	32.00
	1228	7	6.50	13.00	22.00	32.00
	1229	8	6.50	13.00	22.00	32.00
	1230	9	6.50	13.00	22.00	32.00
	1231	10	6.50	13.00	22.00	32.00
	1231	11	6.50	13.00	22.00	32.00
	1232	11	6.50	13.00	22.00	32.00
	1233	12	6.50	13.00	22.00	32.00
	1234	13	6.50	13.00	22.00	32.00
	1235	14	6.50	13.00	22.00	32.00
	1236	15	6.50	13.00	22.00	32.00
	1239	19	6.50	13.00	22.00	32.00
	1240	19	6.50	13.00	22.00	32.00
	1241	19	6.50	13.00	22.00	32.00

BAIJA BAO

AH1243-1249/1827-1833AD

In the name of Muhammad Shah
With initial *Shri*

NAZARANA 1/3 MOHUR

GOLD, 18mm, 3.57-3.80 g
Nagari *Sri* for Baija Rao

KM#	Date	Year	VG	Fine	VF	XF
63	AH1130	2 (frozen)	125.00	165.00	200.00	235.00

NOTE: Struck ca.1827AD.

In the name of Muhammad Akbar

AH1221-1253/1806-1837AD

PAISA

COPPER

KM#	Date	Year	Good	VG	Fine	VF
64	AH1244	24	3.00	5.00	8.00	12.50
	1245	25	3.00	5.00	8.00	12.50

With *Sri* for Baija Bao

RUPEE

SILVER, 10.70-11.60 g
Obv. & Rev: Five-flowered symbol.

KM#	Date	Year	VG	Fine	VF	XF
65	AH—	23	11.50	22.50	35.00	50.00

NOTE: The regnal year 23 becomes frozen with this issue on all silver coins of this mint (identified by five-flowered symbol) and of Lashkar Mint.

JANKOJI RAO

AH1243-1259/1827-1843AD

In the name of Muhammad Shah

AH1131-1161/1719-1748AD

With initial *Ja*.

NAZARANA 1/3 MOHUR

GOLD, 3.57-3.80 g
Nagari *Ja* for Jankoji

KM#	Date	Year	VG	Fine	VF	XF
66	AH1130	2 (frozen)	125.00	165.00	200.00	235.00

NOTE: Struck ca.1834AD.

In the name of Muhammad Akbar II

AH1221-1253/1806-1837AD

With additional initial of Jankoji Rao

Symbols:

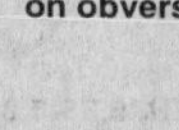

on obverse

on rev. (points up or down)

1/8 RUPEE

SILVER, 1.34-1.45 g

Similar to Rupee, KM#72.

KM#	Date	Year	VG	Fine	VF	XF
67	AH1244	23	5.00	7.00	10.00	15.00

1/4 RUPEE

SILVER, 2.68-2.90 g
Similar to Rupee, KM#72.

KM#	Date	Year	VG	Fine	VF	XF
68	AH1244	23	6.00	10.00	14.00	20.00

Similar to Rupee, KM#73.

KM#	Date	Year	VG	Fine	VF	XF
69	AH1244	23	6.00	10.00	14.00	20.00

1/2 RUPEE

SILVER, 5.35-5.70 g

KM#	Date	Year	VG	Fine	VF	XF
70	AH1244	23	7.50	12.50	17.50	25.00

KM#	Date	Year	VG	Fine	VF	XF
71	AH1244	23	7.50	12.50	17.50	25.00

RUPEE

SILVER, 10.70-11.60 g
Rev: Bow and arrow points down.

KM#	Date	Year	VG	Fine	VF	XF
72	AH1244	23	8.50	14.00	20.00	28.00

Rev: Bow and arrow points up.

KM#	Date	Year	VG	Fine	VF	XF
73	AH1244	23	8.50	14.00	20.00	28.00

JAYAJI RAO

AH1259-1304/1843-1886

In the name of Muhammad Shah
AH1131-1161/1719-1748AD

जी

With initial *Ji.*

NAZARANA 1/3 MOHUR

GOLD, 3.57-3.80 g
Nagari *Ji* for Jayaji

KM#	Date	Year	VG	Fine	VF	XF
74	AH1130	2 (frozen)	125.00	165.00	200.00	235.00

NOTE: Struck ca.1843AD.

MOHUR

GOLD

KM#	Date	Year	VG	Fine	VF	XF
A75	AH1130	2	400.00	475.00	550.00	600.00

In the name of Muhammad Akbar
AH1221-1253/1806-1837AD
With additional initial of Jayaji Rao
Symbols as on KM#69 and 70, but more stylized.

PAISA

COPPER

KM#	Date	Year	Good	VG	Fine	VF
75	AH1269	—	1.25	2.00	3.00	5.00
	127x	42	1.25	2.00	3.00	5.00
	127x	45	1.25	2.00	3.00	5.00
	127x	46	1.25	2.00	3.00	5.00
	127x	47	1.25	2.00	3.00	5.00
	1277	48	1.25	2.00	3.00	5.00
	1278	49	1.25	2.00	3.00	5.00
	1279	49	1.25	2.00	3.00	5.00
	—	54	1.25	2.00	3.00	5.00
	—	56	1.25	2.00	3.00	5.00

Obv: Trisul.

KM#	Date	Year	Good	VG	Fine	VF
76	AH—	—	1.25	2.00	3.00	5.00

1/16 RUPEE

SILVER, 9mm, 0.67-0.72 g

KM#	Date	Year	VG	Fine	VF	XF
77	AH—	23	4.00	6.00	9.00	13.50

1/8 RUPEE

SILVER, 11mm, 1.34-1.45 g

KM#	Date	Year	VG	Fine	VF	XF
78	AH—	23	5.00	7.00	10.00	15.00

1/4 RUPEE

SILVER, 13mm, 2.68-2.90 g

KM#	Date	Year	VG	Fine	VF	XF
79	AH—	23	6.00	10.00	14.00	20.00

1/2 RUPEE

SILVER, 15mm, 5.35-5.70 g
Rev: Bow and arrow points down.

KM#	Date	Year	VG	Fine	VF	XF
80	AH—	23	6.00	10.00	17.50	25.00

RUPEE

SILVER, 17-19mm, 10.70-11.60 g
Rev: Bow and arrow points up.

KM#	Date	Year	VG	Fine	VF	XF
81	AH—	23	5.50	9.00	14.00	20.00

Rev: Bow and arrow points down.

KM#	Date	Year	VG	Fine	VF	XF
82	AH—	23	5.50	9.00	14.00	20.00

NAZARANA RUPEE

SILVER, 10.70-11.60 g

KM#	Date	Year	VG	Fine	VF	XF
83	AH125x	23	60.00	100.00	140.00	200.00

MADHO RAO

AH1304-1313/1886-1925AD

In the name of Muhammad Shah
with initial of Madho Rao II

1/3 MOHUR

GOLD, 21mm, 3.57-3.80 g

KM#	Date	Year	VG	Fine	VF	XF
84	AH1130	2 (frozen)	125.00	165.00	200.00	235.00

NOTE: Struck ca.1886AD.

ISAGARH MINT

DAULAT RAO

AH1209-1243/1794-1827AD

In the name of Muhammad Akbar II
AH1221-1253/1806-1837AD

Mint marks: 

PAISA

COPPER
Obv: Cannon right. Rev: Snake.

KM#	Date	Year	VG	Fine	VF	XF
89	AH—	2x	11.50	17.50	26.50	37.50

RUPEE

SILVER, 10.70-11.60 g
Rev: Cannon left.

KM#	Date	Year	VG	Fine	VF	XF
85	AH122x	8	13.50	20.00	27.50	37.50
	1230	10	13.50	20.00	27.50	37.50
	1230	11	13.50	20.00	27.50	37.50

Obv: Cannon left. Rev: Bhilsa leaf and battle axe.

KM#	Date	Year	VG	Fine	VF	XF
86	AH—	—	13.50	20.00	27.50	37.50

Obv: Cannon right.
Rev: Bhilsa leaf, battle axe and snake.

KM#	Date	Year	VG	Fine	VF	XF
87	AH1229	8	13.50	20.00	27.50	37.50
	1230	10	13.50	20.00	27.50	37.50
	1231	11	13.50	20.00	27.50	37.50
	123x	15	13.50	20.00	27.50	37.50

Obv: Cannon right and snake.
Rev: Bhilsa leaf and battle axe.

KM#	Date	Year	VG	Fine	VF	XF
88	AH—	—	13.50	20.00	27.50	37.50

JANKOJI RAO

AH1243-1259/1827-1843AD

1/4 RUPEE

SILVER, 2.67-2.90 g
Similar to 1 Rupee, KM#92.

KM#	Date	Year	VG	Fine	VF	XF
A90	AH12xx	23	8.50	13.50	20.00	28.50

1/2 RUPEE

Mint marks: 

on reverse

SILVER, 5.35-5.80 g
Similar to 1 Rupee, KM#92.

KM#	Date	Year	VG	Fine	VF	XF
90	AH1243	23	8.50	13.50	20.00	28.50

Similar to 1 Rupee, KM#93.

KM#	Date	Year	VG	Fine	VF	XF
91	AH1223 (error 1243)	23	8.50	13.50	20.00	28.50

RUPEE

SILVER, 10.70-11.60 g

KM#	Date	Year	VG	Fine	VF	XF
92	AH1223 (error)	23	11.50	16.50	25.00	36.50
	1243	23	11.50	16.50	25.00	36.50

Mint mark:  **on obv.**

Obv: Lotus bud.

KM#	Date	Year	VG	Fine	VF	XF
93	ND	—	7.00	11.00	16.50	25.00
	AH1252	—	7.00	11.00	16.50	25.00

JAWAD MINT

JANKOJI RAO

AH1243-1259/1827-1843AD

PAISA

COPPER
Obv: Letter *Ja* and spear.

KM#	Date	Year	Good	VG	Fine	VF
103	ND	—	2.50	4.50	6.50	10.00

Obv: Letter *Ja* (retrograde) and spear.

KM#	Date	Year	Good	VG	Fine	VF
104	ND	—	2.50	4.50	6.50	10.00

Obv: Banner, letter *Ji* and snake. Rev: Trisul.

KM#	Date	Year	Good	VG	Fine	VF
105	ND	—	3.00	5.00	8.00	12.50

Obv: Letter *Ji*, scimitar and snake.
Rev: Trisul.

KM#	Date	Year	Good	VG	Fine	VF
106	ND	—	2.50	4.50	6.50	10.00

Obv: Letters *Ja*, *Ja*, *Ja?* and snake.
Rev: Trisul.

KM#	Date	Year	Good	VG	Fine	VF
107	ND	—	2.50	4.50	6.50	10.00

Obv: Snake between letters *S* and *ra*, scimitar.
Rev: Trisul.

KM#	Date	Year	Good	VG	Fine	VF
108	ND	—	2.50	4.50	6.50	7.50

MADHO RAO

AH1304-1313/1886-1925AD

PAISA

With initial of Madho Rao II

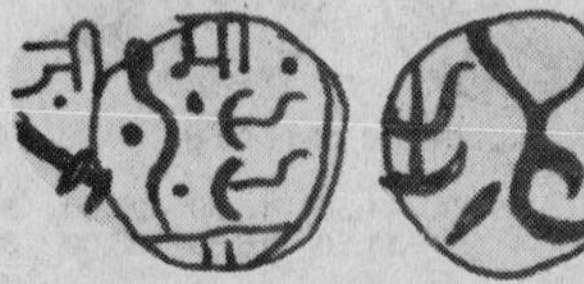

COPPER
Obv: Snake between letters *Ji* and *Ma*, scimitar.
Rev: Trisul.

KM#	Date	Year	Good	VG	Fine	VF
109	ND	—	3.00	5.00	8.00	12.50

Obv: Letters *Ji* and *Ma*, snake.
Rev: Trisul.

KM#	Date	Year	Good	VG	Fine	VF
110	ND	—	3.00	5.00	8.00	12.50

JHANSI MINT

To Gwalior 1865-1886AD

Regular Jhansi types (q.v.), identifiable as Sindhia issues only by date, and by Persian Ji for Jayaji. Similar to coins struck by the Maratha Governors of the Peshwa until 1853AD.

JAYAJI RAO

AH1259-1304/1843-1886AD

PAISA

COPPER, 11.15-15.55 g
Obv: Trisul. Rev: Persian *Ji* above leaf, flywhisk.

KM#	Date	Year	Good	VG	Fine	VF
111	ND	—	3.00	5.00	8.00	12.50

1/8 RUPEE

SILVER, 1.34-1.45 g
Rev: Persian *Ji*.

KM#	Date	Year	VG	Fine	VF	XF
112	ND	—	6.50	10.00	15.00	22.50

RUPEE

SILVER, 10.70-11.60 g
Rev: Persian *Ji*.

KM#	Date	Year	VG	Fine	VF	XF
113	AH—	48	7.00	11.00	16.50	25.00
	1282	5x	7.00	11.00	16.50	25.00
	1284	5x	7.00	11.00	16.50	25.00

LASHKAR MINT

In the name of Shah Alam II

AH1173-1221/1759-1806AD

NOTE: All the following coins of this mint are in the name of Shah Alam II, with initials and mint marks as shown.

Mint mark:

With regnal years of Shah Alam II

1/8 RUPEE

SILVER, 12mm, 1.34-1.45 g

KM#	Date	Year	VG	Fine	VF	XF
116	ND	(1811-21)	6.00	9.00	13.50	20.00

1/4 RUPEE

SILVER, 2.68-2.90 g

KM#	Date	Year	VG	Fine	VF	XF
117	ND	(1811-21)	6.00	9.00	13.50	20.00

1/2 RUPEE

SILVER, 16mm, 5.35-5.80 g

KM#	Date	Year	VG	Fine	VF	XF
118	ND	(1811-21)	7.00	11.00	16.50	25.00

RUPEE

SILVER, 10.70-11.60 g

KM#	Date	Year	VG	Fine	VF	XF
119	ND	(1811-21)	10.00	15.00	21.50	30.00

Mint marks:

With regnal years of Muhammad Akbar II

1/8 RUPEE

SILVER, 1.34-1.45 g

KM#	Date	Year	VG	Fine	VF	XF
120	AH—	—	4.00	6.00	9.00	13.50

1/4 RUPEE

SILVER, 2.68-2.90 g
Rev: W/dot in *"J"* of *Julus*.

KM#	Date	Year	VG	Fine	VF	XF
121.1	AH—	—	5.00	7.00	10.00	15.00

Rev: W/o dot in *"J"* of *Julus*.

KM#	Date	Year	VG	Fine	VF	XF
121.2	AH—	—	5.00	7.00	10.00	15.00

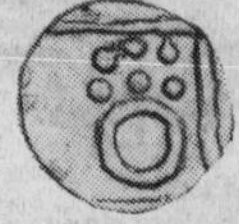

Rev: Lily in *J* of *Julus*.

KM#	Date	Year	VG	Fine	VF	XF
122	AH—	17	5.00	7.00	10.00	15.00

1/2 RUPEE

SILVER, 5.35-5.80 g
Rev: W/dot in *"J"* of *Julus*.

KM#	Date	Year	VG	Fine	VF	XF
123.1	AH—	—	6.00	9.00	13.50	20.00

Rev: W/o dot in *"J"* of *Julus*.

KM#	Date	Year	VG	Fine	VF	XF
123.2	AH—	—	6.00	9.00	13.50	20.00

Rev: Lily blossom in *J* in *Julus*.

KM#	Date	Year	VG	Fine	VF	XF
A124	AH—	17	6.00	9.00	13.50	20.00

RUPEE

SILVER, 10.70-11.60 g
Rev: W/and w/o dot in *"J"* of *Julus*.

KM#	Date	Year	VG	Fine	VF	XF
124	AH—	16	6.00	10.00	15.00	22.50
	—	17	6.00	10.00	15.00	22.50
	—	18	6.00	10.00	15.00	22.50
	—	19	6.00	10.00	15.00	22.50
	—	21	6.00	10.00	15.00	22.50
	—	22	6.00	10.00	15.00	22.50

Rev: Lily in *J* of *Julus*.

KM#	Date	Year	VG	Fine	VF	XF
125	AH—	17	6.00	10.00	15.00	22.50
	—	19	6.00	10.00	15.00	22.50

BAIJA BAI

AH1243-1249/1827-1833AD

In the name of Muhammad Shah

AH1131-1161/1719-1748AD

MOHUR

GOLD, 10.70-11.60 g
Rev: *Shri*.

KM#	Date	Year	VG	Fine	VF	XF
126	AH1130	2	220.00	240.00	265.00	300.00

In the name of Shah Alam

AH1173-1221/1759-1806AD

1/4 RUPEE

SILVER, 15mm, 2.68-2.90 g
Rev: *Shri* and trisul.

KM#	Date	Year	VG	Fine	VF	XF
127	AH—	23	5.00	7.00	10.00	15.00

1/2 RUPEE

SILVER, 17mm, 5.35-5.80 g
Rev: *Shri* and trisul.

KM#	Date	Year	VG	Fine	VF	XF
128	AH—	23	5.00	8.00	12.50	18.50

RUPEE

SILVER, 10.70-11.60 g
Rev: *Shri* and trisul.

KM#	Date	Year	VG	Fine	VF	XF
129	AH—	23	6.50	10.00	15.00	22.50

JANKOJI RAO

Struck by Jankoji Rao
AH1243-1259/1827-1843AD

Mint marks: 

PAISA

COPPER, 13.35 g
Obv: Trisul. Rev: Flywhisk and spear.

KM#	Date	Year	Good	VG	Fine	VF
131	AH—	12	1.25	2.50	3.50	5.50
	—	22	1.25	2.50	3.50	5.50
	—	23	1.25	2.50	3.50	5.50
	—	31	1.25	2.50	3.50	5.50

2 PAISA

BRONZE

KM#	Date	Year	Good	VG	Fine	VF
A132	AH—	22	—	—	—	—

In the name of Muhammad Shah
AH1131-1161/1719-1748AD

MOHUR

GOLD, 10.70-11.40 g
Rev: Bow and arrow points up, *Ja*.

KM#	Date	Year	VG	Fine	VF	XF
132	AH1130	2	220.00	240.00	265.00	300.00

Rev: Bow and arrow points down, *Ja*.

KM#	Date	Year	VG	Fine	VF	XF
133	AH1130	2	220.00	240.00	265.00	300.00

In the name of Shah Alam
AH1173-1221/1759-1806AD

1/8 RUPEE

SILVER, 1.34-1.45 g
Rev: Bow and arrow points up, *Ja* and trisul.

KM#	Date	Year	VG	Fine	VF	XF
134	AH—	23	3.00	4.50	6.50	10.00

Rev: Bow and arrow points down, *Ja* and trisul.

KM#	Date	Year	VG	Fine	VF	XF
135	AH—	23	3.00	4.50	6.50	10.00

1/4 RUPEE

SILVER, 12mm, 2.68-2.90 g
Rev: Bow and arrow points up, *Ja* and trisul.

KM#	Date	Year	VG	Fine	VF	XF
136	AH—	23	4.00	6.00	9.00	13.50

Rev: Bow and arrow points down, *Ja* and trisul.

KM#	Date	Year	VG	Fine	VF	XF
137	AH—	23	4.00	6.00	9.00	13.50

1/2 RUPEE

SILVER, 16mm, 5.35-5.80 g
Rev: Bow and arrow points up, *Ja* and trisul.

KM#	Date	Year	VG	Fine	VF	XF
138	AH—	23	5.00	7.00	10.00	15.00

Rev: Bow and arrow points down, *Ja* and trisul.

KM#	Date	Year	VG	Fine	VF	XF
139	AH—	23	5.00	7.00	10.00	15.00

RUPEE

SILVER, 10.70-11.60 g
Rev: Bow and arrow points up, *Ja* and trisul.

KM#	Date	Year	VG	Fine	VF	XF
140	AH—	23	7.00	11.00	16.50	25.00

Rev: Bow and arrow points down, *Ja* and trisul.

KM#	Date	Year	VG	Fine	VF	XF
141	AH—	23	7.00	11.00	16.50	25.00

JAYAJI RAO

AH1259-1304/1843-1886AD

Anonymous Issues

Struck by Jayaji Rao for 30 years, 1869-1899AD.

1/2 PAISA

COPPER, 12mm, 3.00 g

KM#	Date	Year	Good	VG	Fine	VF
142	VS1926	(1869)	5.00	7.00	10.00	13.50

PAISA

COPPER, 6.00 g

KM#	Date	Year	Good	VG	Fine	VF
143	VS1926	(1869)	.35	.75	1.25	2.25

Regular Coinage

In name of Shah Alam II
with initials of Jayaji Rao

Copper coins have symbols

 **or**  **on reverse**

1/2 PAISA

COPPER, 4.80-4.95 g
Obv: Trisul. Rev: Flywhisk, *Shri* and spear.

KM#	Date	Year	Good	VG	Fine	VF
130	AH—	23	1.50	3.00	5.00	7.50

PAISA

COPPER, 9.60-9.90 g

KM#	Date	Year	Good	VG	Fine	VF
145	AH—	23	1.00	1.75	3.00	5.00

2 PAISA

COPPER, 17.00-20.00 g

KM#	Date	Year	Good	VG	Fine	VF
146	AH—	23	2.00	3.75	6.00	10.00

1/16 RUPEE

SILVER, 9mm, 0.67-0.72 g
Rev: Bow and arrow points down, *Ji*.

KM#	Date	Year	VG	Fine	VF	XF
147	AH—	23	2.50	4.50	6.50	10.00

1/8 RUPEE

SILVER, 1.34-1.45 g
Rev: Bow and arrow points down, *Ji*.

KM#	Date	Year	VG	Fine	VF	XF
148.1	AH—	23	4.00	6.00	9.00	13.50
		25	4.00	6.00	9.00	13.50

Rev: + below *Ji*.

KM#	Date	Year	VG	Fine	VF	XF
148.2	AH—	—	4.00	6.00	9.00	13.50

1/4 RUPEE

SILVER, 2.68-2.90 g
Rev: Bow and arrow points down, *Ji*.

KM#	Date	Year	VG	Fine	VF	XF
149	AH—	23	4.00	6.00	9.00	13.50
	—	24	4.00	6.00	9.00	13.50
	—	25	4.00	6.00	9.00	13.50
	—	27	4.00	6.00	9.00	13.50

1/2 RUPEE

SILVER, 5.35-5.80 g
Rev: Bow and arrow points down, *Ji*.

KM#	Date	Year	VG	Fine	VF	XF
150	AH—	23	5.00	7.00	10.00	15.00
	—	25	5.00	7.00	10.00	15.00
	—	26	5.00	7.00	10.00	15.00
	—	27	5.00	7.00	10.00	15.00

Rev: Bow and arrow points up, *Ji*.

KM#	Date	Year	VG	Fine	VF	XF
151	AH—	2x	5.00	7.00	10.00	15.00

RUPEE

SILVER, 10.70-11.60 g
Rev: Bow and arrow points down, *Ji*.

KM#	Date	Year	VG	Fine	VF	XF
152	AH—	23	6.00	9.00	13.50	20.00
	—	27	6.00	9.00	13.50	20.00
	—	29	6.00	9.00	13.50	20.00

Rev: Bow and arrow points up, *Ji*.

KM#	Date	Year	VG	Fine	VF	XF
153	AH—	2x	7.00	11.00	16.50	25.00

NAZARANA RUPEE

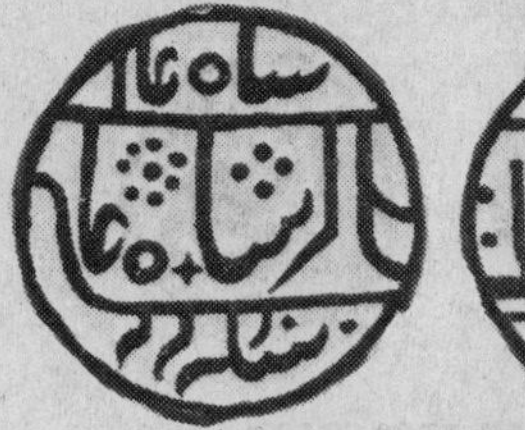

SILVER, 10.70-11.60 g
Rev: Bow and arrow points down, *Ji*, trisul.

KM#	Date	Year	VG	Fine	VF	XF
154	AH—	23	75.00	110.00	165.00	250.00

1/5 MOHUR

GOLD, 2.21 g

KM#	Date	Year	VG	Fine	VF	XF
A155	AH—	—	—	—	—	—

MOHUR

GOLD, 10.70-11.40 g
Rev: Bow and arrow points up, *Ji*.

KM#	Date	Year	VG	Fine	VF	XF
155	AH1130	2	250.00	325.00	400.00	500.00

MADHO RAO

VS1943-1982/1886-1925AD

With initial of Madho Rao II

Symbols as on previous series.

1/16 RUPEE

SILVER, 0.67-0.72 g
Rev: Bow and arrow points down *Ma*, trisul.

KM#	Date	Year	VG	Fine	VF	XF
A156	AH—	23	3.00	4.50	6.50	10.00

1/8 RUPEE

SILVER, 1.34-1.45 g
Rev: Bow and arrow points down, *Ma*, trisul.

KM#	Date	Year	VG	Fine	VF	XF
156	AH—	23	4.00	6.00	9.00	13.50

1/4 RUPEE

SILVER, 2.68-2.90 g
Rev: Bow and arrow points down, *Ma*, trisul.

KM#	Date	Year	VG	Fine	VF	XF
157	AH—	23	5.00	7.00	10.00	15.50

1/2 RUPEE

SILVER, 5.35-5.80 g
Rev: Bow and arrow points down, *Ma*, trisul.

KM#	Date	Year	VG	Fine	VF	XF
158	AH—	23	6.00	9.00	13.50	20.00

RUPEE

SILVER, 10.70-11.60 g
Rev: Bow and arrow points down, *Ma*, trisul.

KM#	Date	Year	VG	Fine	VF	XF
159	AH—	23	5.50	8.00	12.50	18.50

MOHUR

GOLD, 10.70-11.40 g
Rev: Bow and arrow points up, *Ma*, trisul.

KM#	Date	Year	VG	Fine	VF	XF
160	AH1130	2	250.00	325.00	400.00	500.00

MILLED COINAGE

PIE

COPPER

KM#	Date	Year	VG	Fine	VF	XF
A161	VS1946	(1889)	—	—	Rare	—

KM#	Date	Year	VG	Fine	VF	XF
161	VS(19)55	(1898)	—	—	Rare	—

1/2 PICE

COPPER, 20mm

KM#	Date	Year	VG	Fine	VF	XF
162	VS1946	(1889)	75.00	125.00	250.00	350.00

Punched from 1/4 Anna, KM#168.

KM#	Date	Year	VG	Fine	VF	XF
163	VS1946	(1889)	75.00	125.00	200.00	—

KM#	Date	Year	Fine	VF	XF	Unc
164	VS1956	(1899)	.65	2.00	4.00	10.00
	1957	(1900)	.65	2.00	4.00	10.00
	1958	(1901)	.65	2.00	4.00	10.00

1/4 ANNA

COPPER
Obv: 16 point star, wide nose on sun.

KM#	Date	Year	VG	Fine	VF	XF
165	VS1944	(1887)	100.00	175.00	275.00	400.00

Obv: 18 point star, wide nose on sun.

KM#	Date	Year	VG	Fine	VF	XF
166	VS1944	(1887)	100.00	175.00	275.00	400.00

Obv: 17 point star, wide nose on sun.

KM#	Date	Year	VG	Fine	VF	XF
167	VS1945	(1888)	100.00	150.00	250.00	475.00

Obv: 16 point star, narrow nose on sun.

KM#	Date	Year	VG	Fine	VF	XF
168	VS1946	(1889)	62.50	87.50	140.00	200.00

KM#	Date	Year	Fine	VF	XF	Unc
169	VS1953	(1896)	.75	2.25	4.50	11.00
	1954	(1897)	.75	2.25	4.50	11.00
	1956	(1899)	.75	2.25	4.50	11.00
	1957	(1900)	.75	2.25	4.50	11.00
	1958	(1901)	.75	2.25	4.50	11.00

2.2mm thick planchet, 6.60 g

KM#	Date	Year	Fine	VF	XF	Unc
170	VS1970	(1913)	.15	.50	.85	2.00

1.6mm thin planchet, 5.10 g

KM#	Date	Year	Fine	VF	XF	Unc
171	VS1970	(1913)	1.25	3.50	5.00	7.00
	1974	(1917)	.20	.60	1.00	1.75

Obv: Continuous legend below portrait.

KM#	Date	Year	Fine	VF	XF	Unc
172	VS1974	(1917)	4.00	6.00	9.00	12.00

1/2 ANNA

COPPER

KM#	Date	Year	VG	Fine	VF	XF
173	VS1946	(1889)	75.00	135.00	200.00	300.00

RUPEE

SILVER, 32mm

KM#	Date	Year	VG	Fine	VF	XF
174	VS1954	(1897)	75.00	135.00	200.00	300.00

1/3 MOHUR

GOLD, 3.45 g

KM#	Date	Year	Fine	VF	XF	Unc
175	VS1959	(1902)	265.00	375.00	550.00	800.00

JIVAJI RAO

1925-1948AD

1/4 ANNA

COPPER
Thick planchet, 5.10 g
Obv: Ornate robe.

176.1	VS1986	(1929)	.20	.60	1.00	2.00

Obv: Plainer robe.

176.2	VS1986	(1929)	.20	.60	1.00	2.00

Thin planchet, 3.10 g

177	VS1986	(1929)	.75	2.50	3.50	6.00
	1999	(1942)	1.00	3.50	5.00	7.50

Obv: Facing coiled cobras below bust.
Rev: W/o inscriptions on side.

178.1	VS1999	(1942)	.15	.50	.85	1.50

Obv: W/o facing coiled cobras below bust.

178.2	VS1999	(1942)	.15	.50	.85	1.50

1/2 ANNA

BRASS

179	VS1999	(1942)	.15	.50	.85	1.50
	1999	(1942)	—	—	Proof	50.00

MANDASOR MINT

JAYAJI RAO

AH1259-1304/1843-1886AD

PAISA

COPPER
Obv. leg: *Sa Ma Sa.*
Rev. leg: *A(lijah) Ba(hadur),* trisul divides date.

KM#	Date	Year	Good	VG	Fine	VF
180	VS1937	(1880)	1.25	2.75	4.00	6.00
	3791 (error-1937)	(1880)	1.25	2.75	4.00	6.00
	3711 (error-1937)	(1880)	1.25	2.75	4.00	6.00

Rev: Date to left of trisul.

181	VS1937	(1880)	1.25	2.75	4.00	6.00

Rev. leg: Retrograde.

182	VS1937	(1880)	1.25	2.75	4.00	6.00

Obv. and rev. leg: Retrograde.

183	VS1937	(1880)	1.25	2.75	4.00	6.00

NARWAR MINT

To Gwalior from 1805AD

Coins continued to be struck in the types of Narwar state with dates after AH1221/1806AD. The AH1230 date was retained for several years.

Daulat Rao

AH1209-1243/1794-1827AD

In the name of Shah Alam II
AH1173-1221/1759-1806AD

Mint marks:

Katar  on rev. (copper)

Bhilsa leaf  on rev. (silver)

1/2 PAISA

COPPER, 3.37 g
Rev: Vertical katar.

184.2	AH1216	43	1.75	3.00	5.00	8.00
	1216	44	1.75	3.00	5.00	8.00
	1216	45	1.75	3.00	5.00	8.00
	1217	44	1.75	3.00	5.00	8.00
	1217	45	1.75	3.00	5.00	8.00
	1217	46	1.75	3.00	5.00	8.00
	1219	46	1.75	3.00	5.00	8.00
	1230	7	—	—	—	—
	1230	21	1.75	3.00	5.00	8.00

NOTE: Earlier date (AH1215) exists for this type.

PAISA

COPPER

185	AH1228	7	2.00	3.50	5.00	7.50
	1230	12	2.00	3.50	5.00	7.50
	1230	21	2.00	3.50	5.00	7.50

1/16 RUPEE

SILVER, 0.67-0.72 g

KM#	Date	Year	VG	Fine	VF	XF
186	AH1230	—	3.00	4.50	6.50	10.00

1/8 RUPEE

SILVER, 1.34-1.45 g

187	AH1230	—	4.00	6.00	9.00	13.50

1/4 RUPEE

SILVER, 2.68-2.90 g

188	AH1230	15	6.50	10.00	15.00	22.50

NOTE: Earlier date (AH1207) exists for this type.

1/2 RUPEE

SILVER, 5.35-5.80 g

189	AH1230	12	6.50	10.00	15.00	22.50
	1230	21	6.50	10.00	15.00	22.50

RUPEE

SILVER, 10.70-11.60 g

190	AH1228	7	7.50	12.50	18.50	27.50
	1230	9	7.50	12.50	18.50	27.50
	1230	11	7.50	12.50	18.50	27.50
	1230	12	7.50	12.50	18.50	27.50
	1230	15	7.50	12.50	18.50	27.50
	1230	21	7.50	12.50	18.50	27.50
	—	35	7.50	12.50	18.50	27.50

RAJOD MINT

Symbol: Figure of Hanuman.

1/2 PAISA

COPPER, 7.71 g
Obv: Lingam at right.

KM#	Date	Year	Good	VG	Fine	VF
191	VS1936	(1879)	4.00	7.50	12.50	20.00

PAISA

COPPER, 17.10 g

192.1	VS1930	(1873)	7.50	12.00	20.00	35.00

Reduced weight, 11.50-12.30 g
Obv: Hanuman. Rev: 9 of date in Sanskrit.

192.2	VS1930	(1873)	7.50	12.00	20.00	35.00

Obv: Hanuman. Rev: 9 of date in Gujarati.

193	VS1930	(1873)	7.50	12.00	20.00	35.00

Obv: Lingam at right.
Rev: 9 of date in sanskrit.

KM#	Date	Year	Good	VG	Fine	VF
194	VS1936	(1879)	7.50	12.00	20.00	35.00

Rev: 9 of date in Gujarati.

KM#	Date	Year	Good	VG	Fine	VF
195	VS1936	(1879)	7.50	12.00	20.00	35.00

Obv: Snake at right.

KM#	Date	Year	Good	VG	Fine	VF
196	VS1940	(1883)	7.50	12.00	20.00	35.00

RATHGARH MINT

RUPEE

SILVER, 10.70.0011.60 G
Obv: Snake

KM#	Date	Year	VG	Fine	VF	XF
197	AH1221	1	15.00	21.00	30.00	40.00
	12xx	3	15.00	21.00	30.00	40.00
	12xx	4	15.00	21.00	30.00	40.00
	12xx	6	15.00	21.00	30.00	40.00
	12xx	7	15.00	21.00	30.00	40.00
	1232	8	15.00	21.00	30.00	40.00
	12xx	13	15.00	21.00	30.00	40.00
	123x	15	15.00	21.00	30.00	40.00
	12xx	18	15.00	21.00	30.00	40.00
	12xx	22	15.00	21.00	30.00	40.00

SHADORAH MINT

NOTE: Formerly listed as Seondha.

In the name of Muhammad Akbar II
AH1221-1253/1806-1837AD

Mint marks:

KM#199 on rev.

also has  on rev.

KM#200 obv.

on rev.

DAULAT RAO

AH1209-1243/1794-1827AD

RUPEE

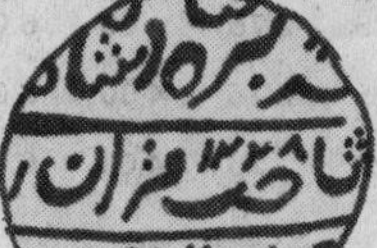

SILVER, 10.70-11.60 g
Rev: Cannon left, mintname at bottom.

KM#	Date	Year	VG	Fine	VF	XF
199	AH1228	—	—	—	Rare	—
	Obv: Cannon right, mintname at top.					
200	ND	—	—	—	Rare	—

SHEOPUR MINT

In the name of Muhammad Akbar II
AH1221-1253/1806-1837AD

Mint mark:

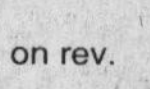

on rev.

DAULAT RAO

AH1209-1243/1794-1827AD

RUPEE

SILVER, 10.70-11.60 g
Rev: Cannon left.

KM#	Date	Year	VG	Fine	VF	XF
201	AH1228	7	6.50	13.00	22.00	32.00
	1228	8	6.50	13.00	22.00	32.00
	1228	9	6.50	13.00	22.00	32.00
	1228	10	6.50	13.00	22.00	32.00
	1228	11	6.50	13.00	22.00	32.00
	1228	12	7.50	12.50	18.50	27.50
	1228	13	6.50	13.00	22.00	32.00
	1228	15	6.50	13.00	22.00	32.00
	1228	16	6.50	13.00	22.00	32.00
	1228	17	6.50	13.00	22.00	32.00
	1228	18	6.50	13.00	22.00	32.00
	1228	19	6.50	13.00	22.00	32.00
	1228	20	6.50	13.00	22.00	32.00
	1228	21	6.50	13.00	22.00	32.00
	1228	22	6.50	13.00	22.00	32.00
	1228	27	6.50	13.00	22.00	32.00
	1228	28	6.50	13.00	22.00	32.00
	1230	—	6.50	13.00	22.00	32.00

BAIJA BAO

AH1243-1249/1827-1833AD

RUPEE

SILVER, 10.70-11.60 g
Rev: Cannon left.

KM#	Date	Year	VG	Fine	VF	XF
202	AH1248	27	9.00	18.00	28.00	40.00
	1248	28	9.00	18.00	28.00	40.00

JAYAJI RAO

AH1259-1304/1843-1886AD

1/8 RUPEE

SILVER, 1.34-1.45 g
Rev: Cannon left. *Ji.*

KM#	Date	Year	VG	Fine	VF	XF
A203	AH12xx	1	10.00	20.00	35.00	50.00

RUPEE

SILVER, 10.70-11.60 g
Rev: Cannon left, *Ji.*

KM#	Date	Year	VG	Fine	VF	XF
203	AH1270	1	9.00	18.00	28.00	40.00
	1271	1	9.00	18.00	28.00	40.00
	1272	1	9.00	18.00	28.00	40.00
	1273	1	9.00	18.00	28.00	40.00
	1274	1	9.00	18.00	28.00	40.00
	1276	1	9.00	18.00	28.00	40.00

Obv: 113. Rev: 113 and *Ji.*

KM#	Date	Year	VG	Fine	VF	XF
204	AH—	13	9.00	18.00	27.00	38.00
	—	15	9.00	18.00	27.00	38.00

SIPRI MINT

Mintname: Narwar

In the name of Shah Alam II
AH1173-1221/1759-1806AD

1/2 RUPEE

SILVER, 5.35-5.80 g

KM#	Date	Year	VG	Fine	VF	XF
A205	AH1106	47	9.00	18.00	28.00	40.00

RUPEE

SILVER, 10.70-11.60 g

KM#	Date	Year	VG	Fine	VF	XF
205	AH1106	44	7.00	14.00	24.00	35.00
	1106	46	7.00	14.00	24.00	35.00
	1106	47	7.00	14.00	24.00	35.00

NOTE: The above were struck by the Kachwaha Raja of Narwar as tributary to Sindhia.

DAULAT RAO

AH1209-1243/1794-1827AD

RUPEE

SILVER, 10.70-11.60 g
Flower in outline.

KM#	Date	Year	VG	Fine	VF	XF
206	AH1106	47	10.00	20.00	32.00	45.00

Solid flower.

KM#	Date	Year	VG	Fine	VF	XF
207	AH1106	47	10.00	20.00	32.00	45.00

With regnal years of Muhammad Akbar II
AH1221-1253/1806-1837AD

KM#	Date	Year	VG	Fine	VF	XF
208	AH1106	9	13.50	27.00	45.00	65.00

BAIJA BAI

AH1243-1249/1827-1833AD

RUPEE

SILVER, 10.70-11.60 g
Rev: *Shri.*

KM#	Date	Year	VG	Fine	VF	XF
209	AH1106	17	18.00	36.00	60.00	85.00

JANKOJI RAO

AH1243-1259/1833-1843AD

RUPEE

SILVER, 10.70-11.60 g
Rev: *Ja.*

KM#	Date	Year	VG	Fine	VF	XF
210	AH—	9	11.00	22.00	35.00	50.00

With regnal years of Muhammad Akbar II

KM#	Date	Year	VG	Fine	VF	XF
211	AH—	35	9.00	18.00	30.00	42.00

UJJAIN MINT

Mint marks:

on most issues

on many copper issues

DAULAT RAO

AH1209-1243/1794-1827

PAISA

COPPER, 12.83-14.00 g

KM#	Date	Year	Good	VG	Fine	VF
219	AH12xx	—	1.50	3.00	5.00	7.50

KM#	Date	Year	Good	VG	Fine	VF
220	AH—	—	1.50	3.00	5.00	7.50

KM#	Date	Year	Good	VG	Fine	VF
221	AH—	—	1.50	3.00	5.00	7.50

KM#	Date	Year	Good	VG	Fine	VF
222	AH1220	—	1.50	3.00	5.00	7.50

1/4 RUPEE

SILVER, 2.67-2.90 g
Obv: AH date below

KM#	Date	Year	VG	Fine	VF	XF
A223	AH—	62	5.00	7.00	10.00	15.00
	—	64	5.00	7.00	10.00	15.00

1/2 RUPEE

SILVER, 5.35-5.80 g
Obv: AH date below

KM#	Date	Year	Good	VG	Fine	VF
B223	AH—	64	5.50	8.00	12.50	18.50

RUPEE

SILVER, 10.70-11.60 g
Obv: AH date below

KM#	Date	Year	VG	Fine	VF	XF
224	AH1216	44	5.00	7.00	10.00	15.00
	12xx	44	5.00	7.00	10.00	15.00
	—	45	5.00	7.00	10.00	15.00
	—	46	5.00	7.00	10.00	15.00
	—	48	5.00	7.00	10.00	15.00
	—	51	5.00	7.00	10.00	15.00
	—	52	5.00	7.00	10.00	15.00
	—	55	5.00	7.00	10.00	15.00
	122x	57	5.00	7.00	10.00	15.00
	—	58	5.00	7.00	10.00	15.00
	—	59	5.00	7.00	10.00	15.00
	—	60	5.00	7.00	10.00	15.00
	—	61	5.00	7.00	10.00	15.00
	—	62	5.00	7.00	10.00	15.00
	—	63	5.00	7.00	10.00	15.00
	123x	64	5.00	7.00	10.00	15.00
	—	67	5.00	7.00	10.00	15.00
	—	68	5.00	7.00	10.00	15.00
	—	69	5.00	7.00	10.00	15.00

BAIJA BAI

AH1243-1249/1827-1833AD

1/2 RUPEE

SILVER, 5.35-5.80 g

KM#	Date	Year	VG	Fine	VF	XF
226	AH—	73	7.00	11.00	16.50	25.00

RUPEE

SILVER, 10.70-11.60 g

KM#	Date	Year	VG	Fine	VF	XF
227	AH—	71	6.00	9.00	13.50	20.00
	—	73	6.00	9.00	13.50	20.00

With regnal years of Mohammad Akbar

Rev: *Shri.*

KM#	Date	Year	VG	Fine	VF	XF
228	AH—	23	—	—	Rare	—

JANKOJI RAO

AH1243-1259/1827-1843AD

With regnal years of Shah Alam

1/4 RUPEE

SILVER, 2.67-2.90 g

KM#	Date	Year	VG	Fine	VF	XF
A229	AH—	80	5.00	7.00	10.00	15.00

1/2 RUPEE

SILVER, 5.35-5.80 g

KM#	Date	Year	VG	Fine	VF	XF
229	AH—	77	6.00	9.00	12.50	18.50
	—	80	6.00	9.00	12.50	18.50

RUPEE

SILVER, 10.70-11.60 g

KM#	Date	Year	VG	Fine	VF	XF
230	AH—	77	6.00	9.00	13.50	20.00
230	—	78	6.00	9.00	13.50	20.00
	—	79	6.00	9.00	13.50	20.00
	—	80	6.00	9.00	13.50	20.00
	—	83	6.00	9.00	13.50	20.00
	—	84	6.00	9.00	13.50	20.00
	—	85	6.00	9.00	13.50	20.00

JAYAJI RAO

AH1259-1304/1843-1886AD

PAISA

COPPER, round or square

KM#	Date	Year	Good	VG	Fine	VF
231	AH1262	—	2.00	3.25	5.00	8.50
	1263	—	2.00	3.25	5.00	8.50
	1266	—	2.00	3.25	5.00	8.50
	1267	—	2.00	3.25	5.00	8.50

Obv: Arrow added.

KM#	Date	Year	Good	VG	Fine	VF
232	AH1278	—	2.00	3.25	5.00	8.50
	1281	—	2.00	3.25	5.00	8.50
	1292	—	2.00	3.25	5.00	8.50
	1295	—	2.00	3.25	5.00	8.50

Obv: *Shri.*

KM#	Date	Year	Good	VG	Fine	VF
233	AH1272	—	2.00	3.25	5.00	8.50
	1278	—	2.00	3.25	5.00	8.50
	1287	—	2.00	3.25	5.00	8.50
	1292	—	2.00	3.25	5.00	8.50
	1295	—	2.00	3.25	5.00	8.50

1/8 RUPEE

SILVER, 1.34-1.45 g

KM#	Date	Year	VG	Fine	VF	XF
234	AH—	—	4.00	6.00	9.00	13.50

1/4 RUPEE

SILVER, 2.68-2.90 g

KM#	Date	Year	VG	Fine	VF	XF
235	AH—	92	5.00	7.00	10.00	15.00

1/2 RUPEE

SILVER, 5.35-5.80 g
Regnal years of Shah Alam

KM#	Date	Year	VG	Fine	VF	XF
236	AH—	98	5.50	8.00	12.50	18.50

RUPEE

SILVER, 10.70-11.60 g

KM#	Date	Year	VG	Fine	VF	XF
237	AH—	89	6.00	9.00	13.50	20.00
	—	92	6.00	9.00	13.50	20.00
	—	93	6.00	9.00	13.50	20.00
	—	94	6.00	9.00	13.50	20.00
	—	95	6.00	9.00	13.50	20.00
	—	98	6.00	9.00	13.50	20.00
	—	99	6.00	9.00	13.50	20.00
	—	100	6.00	9.00	13.50	20.00

With regnal years of the British "Raj"

These are a continuation of the thick cruder fabric rupees similar to those issued in the later period with Shah Alam II's regnal years.

1/8 RUPEE

SILVER, 1.34-1.45 g

KM#	Date	Year	VG	Fine	VF	XF
A238	AH—	26	5.00	7.00	10.00	15.00

1/2 RUPEE

SILVER, 5.35-5.80 g

KM#	Date	Year	VG	Fine	VF	XF
C238	AH—	28	7.00	11.00	16.50	25.00

RUPEE

SILVER, 10.70-11.60 g

KM#	Date	Year	VG	Fine	VF	XF
238	AH—	3	6.00	10.00	15.00	22.50
	—	4	6.00	10.00	15.00	22.50
	—	8	6.00	10.00	15.00	22.50
	—	9	6.00	10.00	15.00	22.50
	—	22	6.00	10.00	15.00	22.50
	—	25	6.00	10.00	15.00	22.50
	—	26	6.00	10.00	15.00	22.50
	—	28	6.00	10.00	15.00	22.50

MADHO RAO

AH1304-1344/1886-1925AD

With initial of Madho Rao II

Regnal years of the British Raj (Yr. 1 = AD1857)

1/16 RUPEE

SILVER, 0.67-0.72 g

KM#	Date	Year	VG	Fine	VF	XF
239	AH1312	—	4.00	6.00	9.00	13.50
	1313	37	4.00	6.00	9.00	13.50

1/8 RUPEE

SILVER, 1.34-1.45 g

KM#	Date	Year	VG	Fine	VF	XF
A240	AH—	31	5.00	7.00	10.00	15.00

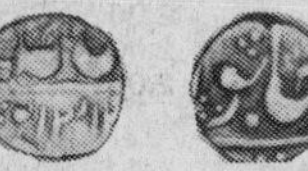

KM#	Date	Year	VG	Fine	VF	XF
240	AH13xx	33	5.00	7.00	18.00	15.00
	1310	34	5.00	7.00	10.00	15.00
	1311	35	5.00	7.00	10.00	15.00
	1312	36	5.00	7.00	10.00	15.00
	1313	37	5.00	7.00	10.00	15.00

1/4 RUPEE

SILVER, 2.68-2.90 g

KM#	Date	Year	VG	Fine	VF	XF
241	AH1310	34	5.50	8.00	12.50	18.50
	1311	35	5.50	8.00	12.50	18.50
	1312	36	5.50	8.00	12.50	18.50
	1313	37	5.50	8.00	12.50	18.50
	1314	38	5.50	8.00	12.50	18.50

1/2 RUPEE

SILVER, 14-15mm, 5.35-5.80 g

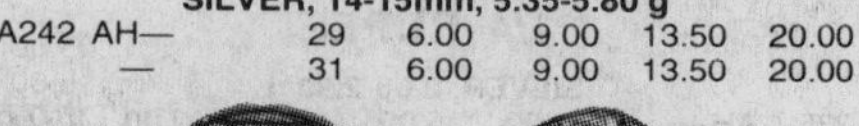

KM#	Date	Year	VG	Fine	VF	XF
A242	AH—	29	6.00	9.00	13.50	20.00
	—	31	6.00	9.00	13.50	20.00

KM#	Date	Year	VG	Fine	VF	XF
242	AH1310	34	6.00	9.00	13.50	20.00
	1311	35	6.00	9.00	13.50	20.00
	1312	36	6.00	9.00	13.50	20.00
	1313	37	6.00	9.00	13.50	20.00
	1314	38	6.00	9.00	13.50	20.00

RUPEE

SILVER, 10.70-11.60 g

KM#	Date	Year	VG	Fine	VF	XF
243	AH—	29	6.50	10.00	15.00	22.50
	—	31	6.50	10.00	15.00	22.50
	—	32	6.50	10.00	15.00	22.50

فصل

Obv: AH date below

KM#	Date	Year	VG	Fine	VF	XF
244	AH130x	33	6.50	10.00	15.00	22.50
	13xx	34	6.50	10.00	15.00	22.50

Obv: AH date in center.

KM#	Date	Year	VG	Fine	VF	XF
245	AH1310	34	5.50	8.00	12.50	18.50
	1310	35	5.50	8.00	12.50	18.50
	1311	34	5.50	8.00	12.50	18.50
	1311	35	5.50	8.00	12.50	18.50
	1311	36	5.50	8.00	12.50	18.50
	1312	34	(error)			
			6.50	10.00	15.00	22.50
	1312	36	5.50	8.00	12.50	18.50
	1313	37	5.50	8.00	12.50	18.50
	1314	38	5.50	8.00	12.50	18.50

UNCERTAIN MINT

PAISA

COPPER

Obv: Horse. Rev. leg: Retrograde.

KM#	Date	Year	Good	VG	Fine	VF
246	AH—	32	17.50	35.00	60.00	100.00

Obv: Hand.

KM#	Date	Year	Good	VG	Fine	VF
247	AH—	ND	10.00	20.00	35.00	50.00

HYDERABAD

Haidarabad

Hyderabad State, the largest Indian State and the last remnant of Mughal suzerainty in South or Central India, traced its foundation to Nizam-ul Mulk, the Mughal viceroy in the Deccan. From about 1724 the first nizam, as the rulers of Hyderabad came to be called, took advantage of Mughal decline in the North to assert an all but ceremonial independence of the emperor. The East India Company defeated Hyderabad's natural enemies, the Muslim rulers of Mysore and the Marathas, with the help of troops furnished under alliances between them and the Nizam. This formed the beginning of a relationship which persisted for a century and a half until India's Independence. Hyderabad was the premier Princely State, with a population (in 1935) of fourteen and a half million. It was not absorbed into the Indian Union until 1948. Hyderabad City is located beside Golkonda, the citadel of the Qutb Shahi sultans until they were overthrown by Aurangzeb in 1687. A beautifully located city on the bank of the Musi river, the mint epithet was appropriately Farkundah Bunyad, "of happy foundation".

Hyderabad exercised authority over a number of feudatories or samasthans. Some of these, such as Gadwal and Shorapur, paid tribute to both the Nizam and the Marathas. These feudatories were generally in the hands of local rajas whose ancestry predated the establishment of Hyderabad State. There were also many mints in the State, both private and government. There was little or no standardization of the purity of silver coinage until the twentieth century. At least one banker, Pestonji Meherji by name, was distinguished by minting his own coins.

RULERS

Nizam Ali Khan
AH1175-1218/1761-1803AD
Sikandar Jah
AH1218-1244/1803-1829AD
Nasir-ad-Daula
AH1244-1273/1829-1857AD
Afzal-ad-Daula
AH1273-1285/1857-1869AD
Mir Mahbub Ali Khan II
AH1285-1329/1869-1911AD
Mir Usman Ali Khan
AH1329-1367/1911-1948AD

MINTS

Amaravati امراوتی

Aurangabad اورنگ اباد

Mintname: Khujista Bunyad

Daulatabad دولت اباد

Haidarabad فرخنده بنیاد

Mintname: Farkhanda Bunyad

Haidarabad حیدراباد

AMARAVATI MINT

RUPEE

SILVER

KM#	Date	Year	Good	VG	Fine	VF
1	AH1240	—	—	—	Rare	—
	1241	—	—	—	Rare	—

AURANGABAD MINT

Mint marks: 

خجسته بنیاد

Mintname: Khujista Bunyad

NIZAM ALI KHAN

AH1175-1218/1761-1803AD

In the name of Shah Alam II

AH1173-1221/1759-1806AD

RUPEE

SILVER, 10.70-11.60 g

KM#	Date	Year	VG	Fine	VF	XF
5	AH1218	—	10.00	15.00	21.50	30.00

NOTE: Earlier dates (AH1176-1193) exist for this type.

In the name of Muhammad Akbar II

AH1221-1253/1806-1837AD

Obv: W/o Persian letter *S*.

KM#	Date	Year	VG	Fine	VF	XF
45	AH1227	6	7.50	12.50	18.50	27.50
	1230	9	7.50	12.50	18.50	27.50
	—	16	7.50	12.50	18.50	27.50
	1234	17	7.50	12.50	18.50	27.50
	1239	17	7.50	12.50	18.50	27.50
	1240	20	7.50	12.50	18.50	27.50
	1241	2x	7.50	12.50	18.50	27.50
	1242	—	7.50	12.50	18.50	27.50

NASIR AD-DAULA

AH1244-1273/1829-1857AD

In the name of Muhammad Akbar II

AH1221-1253/1806-1837AD

RUPEE

SILVER, 10.70-11.60 g

KM#	Date	Year	VG	Fine	VF	XF
66.1	AH1251	—	7.50	12.50	18.50	27.50

In the name of Bahadur Shah

AH1253-1274/1837-1858AD

Struck by Pestonji Meherji, a Bombay banker in the time of Nasir al-Daula, AD1829-57.

1/8 RUPEE

SILVER, 1.34-1.45 g

C#	Date	Year	VG	Fine	VF	XF
63.2 (57)	AH1256	4	6.50	10.00	15.00	22.50

1/4 RUPEE

SILVER, 2.68-2.90 g

C#	Date	Year	VG	Fine	VF	XF
64.1 (58)	AH1256	4	6.50	10.00	15.00	22.50

1/2 RUPEE

SILVER, 17mm, 5.35-5.80 g

C#	Date	Year	VG	Fine	VF	XF
65.2 (59)	AH1256	4	10.00	15.00	21.50	30.00

RUPEE

SILVER, 10.70-11.60 g

C#	Date	Year	VG	Fine	VF	XF
66.2 (60)	AH1254	2	7.50	12.50	18.50	27.50
	1256	4	7.50	12.50	18.50	27.50
	1264	—	7.50	12.50	18.50	27.50

FARKHANDA BUNYAD MINT

Hyderabad

Mint mark: 

Rev: Persian letter *N:* 

SIKANDAR JAH

AH1218-1244/1803-1829AD

In the name of Shah Alam II

AH1173-1221/1759-1806AD

PAISA

COPPER

C#	Date	Year	Good	VG	Fine	VF
40	AH1217	—	1.25	2.00	3.00	4.50
	1218	—	1.25	2.00	3.00	4.50

RUPEE

SILVER, 20-21mm, 10.70-11.60 g

C#	Date	Year	VG	Fine	VF	XF
41	AH1218	—	12.50	18.50	25.00	35.00
	1220	—	12.50	18.50	25.00	35.00

HAIDARABAD MINT

Mint mark: 

Persian letter *S.*

SIKANDAR JAH

AH1218-1244/1803-1829AD

In the name of Muhammad Akbar II

AH1221-1253/1806-1837AD

PAISA

COPPER, 17-20mm

C#	Date	Year	Good	VG	Fine	VF
44	AH1221	—	1.25	2.00	2.75	3.50
	1229	—	1.25	2.00	2.75	3.50
	1237	—	1.25	2.00	2.75	3.50

1/4 RUPEE

SILVER, 2.68-2.90 g

C#	Date	Year	VG	Fine	VF	XF
46	AH1238	—	5.50	8.00	12.50	18.50
	1239	—	5.50	8.00	12.50	18.50
	1241	—	5.50	8.00	12.50	18.50
	1242	23	5.50	8.00	12.50	18.50

1/2 RUPEE

SILVER, 5.35-5.80 g

C#	Date	Year	VG	Fine	VF	XF
47	AH1235	14	5.00	7.00	10.00	15.00
	1237	—	5.00	7.00	10.00	15.00
	1238	—	5.00	7.00	10.00	15.00
	1241	—	5.00	7.00	10.00	15.00
	1242	23	5.00	7.00	10.00	15.00

RUPEE

SILVER, 10.70-11.60 g

C#	Date	Year	VG	Fine	VF	XF
48.1	AH1222	—	6.00	9.00	13.50	20.00
	1224	—	6.00	9.00	13.50	20.00
	1225	4	6.00	9.00	13.50	20.00
	1226	4	6.00	9.00	13.50	20.00
	1227	6	6.00	9.00	13.50	20.00
	1227	7	6.00	9.00	13.50	20.00
	1228	7	6.00	9.00	13.50	20.00
	1229	8	6.00	9.00	13.50	20.00
	1230	9	6.00	9.00	13.50	20.00
	1231	10	6.00	9.00	13.50	20.00
	1232	11	6.00	9.00	13.50	20.00
	1233	12	6.00	9.00	13.50	20.00
	1234	13	6.00	9.00	13.50	20.00
	1235	15	6.00	9.00	13.50	20.00
	1236	15	6.00	9.00	13.50	20.00
	1237	16	6.00	9.00	13.50	20.00
	1239	21	6.00	9.00	13.50	20.00
	1240	21	6.00	9.00	13.50	20.00
	1240	22	6.00	9.00	13.50	20.00
	1241	22	6.00	9.00	13.50	20.00
	1242	23	6.00	9.00	13.50	20.00
	1243	24	6.00	9.00	13.50	20.00
	1244	25	6.00	9.00	13.50	20.00

Rev: Maharaja above mint.

C#	Date	Year	VG	Fine	VF	XF
48.2	AH1238	—	6.00	9.00	13.50	20.00

NAZARANA RUPEE

SILVER, 10.70-11.60 g

C#	Date	Year	VG	Fine	VF	XF
48a	AH1237	16	100.00	175.00	250.00	350.00
	1238	17	100.00	175.00	250.00	350.00

1/16 MOHUR

GOLD, 0.67-0.70 g

C#	Date	Year	VG	Fine	VF	XF
56	AH123x	—	35.00	50.00	70.00	100.00

1/8 MOHUR

GOLD, 1.34-1.42 g

C#	Date	Year	VG	Fine	VF	XF
57	AH123x	—	45.00	65.00	90.00	125.00

1/4 MOHUR

GOLD, 2.68-2.85 g

C#	Date	Year	VG	Fine	VF	XF
58	AH1236	15	60.00	90.00	120.00	160.00

NAZARANA 1/4 MOHUR

GOLD, 2.68-2.85 g

C#	Date	Year	VG	Fine	VF	XF
A58	AH1236	15	—	—	Rare	—

1/2 MOHUR

GOLD, 5.35-5.70 g

C#	Date	Year	VG	Fine	VF	XF
59	AH123x	—	90.00	135.00	185.00	225.00

MOHUR

GOLD, 10.70-11.40 g

C#	Date	Year	VG	Fine	VF	XF
60	AH1226	—	185.00	235.00	285.00	325.00
	1227	—	185.00	235.00	285.00	325.00
	1228	7	185.00	235.00	285.00	325.00
	1231	—	185.00	235.00	285.00	325.00
	1234	—	185.00	235.00	285.00	325.00
	1235	—	185.00	235.00	285.00	325.00
	1236	15	185.00	235.00	285.00	325.00
	1237	16	185.00	235.00	285.00	325.00
	1238	—	185.00	235.00	285.00	325.00
	1241	—	185.00	235.00	285.00	325.00
	1242	—	185.00	235.00	285.00	325.00
	1243	24	185.00	235.00	285.00	325.00
	1244	—	185.00	235.00	285.00	325.00

NAZARANA MOHUR

GOLD, 10.70-11.40 g

C#	Date	Year	VG	Fine	VF	XF
60a	AH1236	15	—	—	Rare	—

NASIR AD-DAULA

AH1244-1273/1829-1857AD

Mint mark: 

Rev: Persian letter *N:* 

First Series

In the name of Muhammad Akbar II to AH1252, with his regnal years.

PAISA

COPPER

C#	Date	Year	Good	VG	Fine	VF
61.3	AH1247	—	2.00	3.00	4.50	7.50
	1250	—	2.00	3.00	4.50	7.50
	Date off flan	—	1.00	2.00	3.50	5.00

1/4 RUPEE

SILVER, 2.68-2.90 g

C#	Date	Year	VG	Fine	VF	XF
64.3	AH1246	—	3.50	5.00	7.50	12.50
	1247	—	3.50	5.00	7.50	12.50
	1249	—	3.50	5.00	7.50	12.50
	1251	—	3.50	5.00	7.50	12.50

1/2 RUPEE

SILVER, 18mm, 5.35-5.80 g

C#	Date	Year	VG	Fine	VF	XF
65.3	AH1249	—	5.50	8.00	12.50	18.50
	1250	—	5.50	8.00	12.50	18.50
	1251	33	5.50	8.00	12.50	18.50

RUPEE

SILVER, 0.70-11.60 g

C#	Date	Year	VG	Fine	VF	XF
66.3	AH1245	26	7.50	10.00	15.00	20.00
	1246	—	7.50	10.00	15.00	20.00
	1248	29	7.50	10.00	15.00	20.00
	1249	—	7.50	10.00	15.00	20.00
	1250	31	7.50	10.00	15.00	20.00
	1251	33	7.50	10.00	15.00	20.00
	1252	34	7.50	10.00	15.00	20.00
	1253	35	7.50	10.00	15.00	20.00

1/16 MOHUR

GOLD, 0.67-0.71 g

C#	Date	Year	VG	Fine	VF	XF
68	AH	—	25.00	35.00	45.00	60.00

1/8 MOHUR

GOLD, 1.34-1.42 g

C#	Date	Year	VG	Fine	VF	XF
69	AH	—	35.00	50.00	70.00	100.00

1/4 MOHUR

GOLD, 2.68-2.85 g

C#	Date	Year	VG	Fine	VF	XF
70	AH	—	50.00	85.00	120.00	150.00

1/2 MOHUR

GOLD, 5.35-5.70 g

C#	Date	Year	VG	Fine	VF	XF
71	AH	—	90.00	125.00	165.00	200.00

MOHUR

GOLD, 22-23mm

C#	Date	Year	VG	Fine	VF	XF
72	AH1244	—	185.00	235.00	285.00	325.00
	1246	—	185.00	235.00	285.00	325.00
	1248	—	185.00	235.00	285.00	325.00
	1249	—	185.00	235.00	285.00	325.00
	1251	—	185.00	235.00	285.00	325.00

Second Series

In the name of Bahadur Shah

Years 1-22/AH1253-1274

PAISA

COPPER, round or square

C#	Date	Year	Good	VG	Fine	VF
73	AH1257	4	2.00	3.00	4.00	7.00

C#	Date	Year	Good	VG	Fine	VF
73	1258	—	2.00	3.00	4.00	7.00
	1262	—	2.00	3.00	4.00	7.00
	1272	—	2.00	3.00	4.00	7.00
	1273	—	2.00	3.00	4.00	7.00
	Date off flan	—	1.00	2.00	3.00	4.50

1/16 RUPEE

SILVER, 9-11mm, 0.67-0.72 g

C#	Date	Year	VG	Fine	VF	XF
75	AH1272	—	4.00	7.50	10.00	15.00

1/8 RUPEE

SILVER, 11-13mm, 1.34-1.45 g

C#	Date	Year	VG	Fine	VF	XF
76	AH1272	—	4.00	7.50	10.00	15.00

1/4 RUPEE

SILVER, 14-15mm, 2.68-2.90 g

C#	Date	Year	VG	Fine	VF	XF
77	AH1257	—	7.00	11.00	16.50	25.00
	1268	—	7.00	11.00	16.50	25.00
	1272	17	7.00	11.00	16.50	25.00
	1273	18	7.00	11.00	16.50	25.00

1/2 RUPEE

SILVER, 16-19mm, 5.35-5.80 g

C#	Date	Year	VG	Fine	VF	XF
78	AH1257	5	6.50	10.00	15.00	22.50
	1260	—	6.50	10.00	15.00	22.50

RUPEE

SILVER, 10.70-11.60 g

C#	Date	Year	VG	Fine	VF	XF
79	AH1253	1	6.00	9.00	13.50	20.00
	1258	6	6.00	9.00	13.50	20.00
	1261	8	6.00	9.00	13.50	20.00
	1262	9	6.00	9.00	13.50	20.00
	1266	11	6.00	9.00	13.50	30.00
	1267	12	6.00	9.00	13.50	20.00
	1268	12	6.00	9.00	13.50	20.00
	1268	13	6.00	9.00	13.50	20.00
	1270	15	6.00	9.00	13.50	20.00
	1270	16	6.00	9.00	13.50	20.00
	1271	16	6.00	9.00	13.50	20.00
	1271	17	6.00	9.00	13.50	20.00
	1272	17	6.00	9.00	13.50	20.00
	1273	18	6.00	9.00	13.50	20.00

1/16 MOHUR

GOLD, 0.67-0.71 g

C#	Date	Year	VG	Fine	VF	XF
80	AH	—	35.00	50.00	70.00	100.00

1/8 MOHUR

GOLD, 1.34-1.42 g

C#	Date	Year	VG	Fine	VF	XF
81	AH	—	40.00	65.00	90.00	125.00

1/4 MOHUR

GOLD, 2.68-2.85 g

C#	Date	Year	VG	Fine	VF	XF
82	AH	—	50.00	85.00	120.00	160.00

1/2 MOHUR

GOLD, 5.35-5.70 g

C#	Date	Year	VG	Fine	VF	XF
83	AH	—	80.00	130.00	185.00	225.00

MOHUR

GOLD, 22mm, 10.70-11.40 gm

C#	Date	Year	VG	Fine	VF	XF
84	AH1258	6	175.00	215.00	265.00	300.00
	1260	—	175.00	215.00	265.00	300.00
	1261	8	175.00	215.00	265.00	300.00
	1263	9	175.00	215.00	265.00	300.00
	1264	—	175.00	215.00	265.00	300.00
	1265	—	175.00	215.00	265.00	300.00
	1266	11	175.00	215.00	265.00	300.00

C#	Date	Year	VG	Fine	VF	XF
84	1267	12	175.00	215.00	265.00	300.00
	1268	—	175.00	215.00	265.00	300.00
	1269	—	175.00	215.00	265.00	300.00
	1270	—	175.00	215.00	265.00	300.00
	1271	—	175.00	215.00	265.00	300.00
	1273	17	175.00	215.00	265.00	300.00

AFZAL AD-DAULA

AH1273-1285/1857-1869AD

First Series

In the name of Bahadur Shah II

Mint marks:

#1 

#2 

#3

For his last two years, AH1274-75, regnal year 18 w/Persian letter *A* (symbol 3) above *Padishah* on obv. Copper coins have symbol #1, while silver and gold have #2.

1/2 PAISA

COPPER

C#	Date	Year	Good	VG	Fine	VF
85	AH1275	—	1.50	2.50	3.50	6.00
		19	1.50	2.50	3.50	6.00

PAISA

COPPER

C#	Date	Year	Good	VG	Fine	VF
86	AH1275	18	1.50	2.50	3.50	6.00
	1276	19	1.50	2.50	3.50	6.00
	1277	19	1.50	2.50	3.50	6.00
	Date off flan	—	1.25	2.25	3.00	4.50

1/8 RUPEE

SILVER, 13mm, 1.34-1.45 g

C#	Date	Year	VG	Fine	VF	XF
88	AH1275	—	4.00	7.50	10.00	15.00

1/4 RUPEE

SILVER, 14mm, 2.68-2.90 g

C#	Date	Year	VG	Fine	VF	XF
89	AH1274	—	4.00	7.50	10.00	15.00

1/2 RUPEE

SILVER, 17mm, 5.35-5.80 g

C#	Date	Year	VG	Fine	VF	XF
90	AH1274	—	6.50	10.00	15.00	22.50

RUPEE

SILVER, 10.70-11.60 g

C#	Date	Year	VG	Fine	VF	XF
91	AH1273	18	7.50	10.00	13.50	20.00
	1274	18	7.50	10.00	13.50	20.00
	1275	18	7.50	10.00	13.50	20.00

MOHUR

GOLD, 23mm

C#	Date	Year	VG	Fine	VF	XF
96	AH1274	—	185.00	225.00	275.00	325.00
	1275	—	185.00	225.00	275.00	325.00

Second Series

In the name of Asaf Jah, Nizam al-Mulk, Founder of the Nizami line (1713-1748AD).

Persian letter *A* for Afzal above *k* of *Mulk* on obv. All coins bear the numeral '92' on upper obverse.

PAISA

(Dub)

COPPER
Irregular and regular shapes, 16-30mm

Y#	Date	Year	Good	VG	Fine	VF
1	AH1282	—	1.75	2.50	3.50	5.00
	1283	—	1.75	2.50	3.50	5.00
	Date off flan		1.00	2.00	3.00	4.00

1/16 RUPEE

(Anna)

SILVER, 9mm, 0.67-0.72 g

Y#	Date	Year	VG	Fine	VF	XF
2	AH1275	—	2.50	4.00	6.50	10.00

1/8 RUPEE

SILVER, 11-13mm, 1.34-1.45 g

Y#	Date	Year	VG	Fine	VF	XF
3	AH1278	—	3.00	5.00	7.00	10.00
	1279	—	3.00	5.00	7.00	10.00

1/4 RUPEE

SILVER, 2.68-2.90 g

Y#	Date	Year	VG	Fine	VF	XF
4	AH1276	—	3.00	5.00	7.00	10.00
	1278	—	3.00	5.00	7.00	10.00
	1283	10	3.00	5.00	7.00	10.00

1/2 RUPEE

SILVER, 5.35-5.80 g

Y#	Date	Year	VG	Fine	VF	XF
5	AH1276	—	3.50	6.00	8.00	12.50
	1277	—	3.50	6.00	8.00	12.50
	128(4)	11	3.50	6.00	8.00	12.50

RUPEE

SILVER, 10.70-11.60 g

Y#	Date	Year	VG	Fine	VF	XF
6	AH1275	2	3.00	6.00	8.00	12.50
	1276	3	3.00	6.00	8.00	12.50
	1276	4	3.00	6.00	8.00	12.50
	1277	4	3.00	6.00	8.00	12.50
	1278	5	3.00	6.00	8.00	12.50
	1279	6	3.00	6.00	8.00	12.50
	1280	7	3.00	6.00	8.00	12.50
	1281	7	3.00	6.00	8.00	12.50
	1281	8	3.00	6.00	8.00	12.50
	1282	9	3.00	6.00	8.00	12.50
	1283	10	3.00	6.00	8.00	12.50
	1284	11	3.00	6.00	8.00	12.50
	1285	12	3.00	6.00	8.00	12.50

1/16 MOHUR

GOLD, 8-9mm, 0.67-0.71 g

Y#	Date	Year	VG	Fine	VF	XF
7	AH	—	— Reported, not confirmed			

1/8 MOHUR

GOLD, 11mm, 1.34-1.42 g

Y#	Date	Year	VG	Fine	VF	XF
8	AH1279-81		40.00	55.00	70.00	90.00

1/4 MOHUR

GOLD, 14mm, 2.68-2.85 g

Y#	Date	Year	VG	Fine	VF	XF
9	AH1281	—	50.00	75.00	110.00	140.00

1/2 MOHUR

GOLD, 16mm, 5.35-5.70 g

Y#	Date	Year	VG	Fine	VF	XF
10	AH1281	—	90.00	120.00	165.00	200.00

MOHUR

GOLD, 10.70-11.40 g

Y#	Date	Year	VG	Fine	VF	XF
11	AH1275	—	160.00	185.00	220.00	265.00
	1276	—	160.00	185.00	220.00	265.00
	1277	—	160.00	185.00	220.00	265.00
	1278	—	160.00	185.00	220.00	265.00
	1279	—	160.00	185.00	220.00	265.00
	1280	—	160.00	185.00	220.00	265.00
	1281	8	160.00	185.00	220.00	265.00
	1282	—	160.00	185.00	220.00	265.00
	1283	—	160.00	185.00	220.00	265.00
	1284	—	160.00	185.00	220.00	265.00
	1285	—	160.00	185.00	220.00	265.00

MIR MAHBUB ALI KHAN II

AH1285-1329/1868-1911AD

In the name of Asaf Jah, Nizam al-Mulk, Founder of the Nizami line (1713-1748AD).

Persian letter *M* for Mahbub above *k* of *Mulk* on obv.

1/2 PAISA

COPPER

Y#	Date	Year	Good	VG	Fine	VF
A12	ND	—	—	—	—	—

PAISA (DUB)

COPPER
Round, rectangular, irregular shape
Many sizes and weights

Y#	Date	Year	Good	VG	Fine	VF
12	AH1290	—	1.50	2.50	3.50	5.00
	1291	—	1.50	2.50	3.50	5.00
	1292	—	1.50	2.50	3.50	5.00
	1296	—	1.50	2.50	3.50	5.00
	1297	—	1.50	2.50	3.50	5.00
	1298	14	1.50	2.50	3.50	5.00
	1300	—	1.50	2.50	3.50	5.00
	1301	—	1.50	2.50	3.50	5.00
	1302	18	1.50	2.50	3.50	5.00
	1303	—	1.50	2.50	3.50	5.00
	1308	—	1.50	2.50	3.50	5.00
	1313	—	1.50	2.50	3.50	5.00

1/2 ANNA

COPPER

Y#	Date	Year	Good	VG	Fine	VF
A13	AH1311	27	—	—	—	—

1/16 RUPEE

.818 SILVER, 0.698 g

Y#	Date	Year	VG	Fine	VF	XF
13	AH1299	15	1.00	1.75	2.50	3.50
	1300	—	1.00	1.75	2.50	3.50
	1303	—	1.00	1.75	2.50	3.50
	1304	—	1.00	1.75	2.50	3.50
	1305	—	1.00	1.75	2.50	3.50
	1307	—	1.00	1.75	2.50	3.50
	1313	—	1.00	1.75	2.50	3.50
	1314	30	1.00	1.75	2.50	3.50
	1321	37	1.00	1.75	2.50	3.50

1/8 RUPEE

.818 SILVER, 1.397 g

Y#	Date	Year	VG	Fine	VF	XF
14	AH1286	—	1.75	2.25	3.00	3.75
	1287	2	1.75	2.25	3.00	3.75
	1289	—	1.75	2.25	3.00	3.75
	1290	—	1.75	2.25	3.00	3.75
	1295	11	1.75	2.25	3.00	3.75
	1297	—	1.75	2.25	3.00	3.75
	1298	14	1.75	2.25	3.00	3.75
	1299	15	1.75	2.25	3.00	3.75
	1300	—	1.75	2.25	3.00	3.75
	1301	17	1.75	2.25	3.00	3.75
	1302	17	1.75	2.25	3.00	3.75
	1302	18	1.75	2.25	3.00	3.75
	1304	20	1.75	2.25	3.00	3.75
	1305	—	1.75	2.25	3.00	3.75
	1306	—	1.75	2.25	3.00	3.75
	1307	—	1.75	2.25	3.00	3.75
	1308	24	1.75	2.25	3.00	3.75
	1309	—	1.75	2.25	3.00	3.75
	1311	—	1.75	2.25	3.00	3.75
	1316	33	1.75	2.25	3.00	3.75
	1317	33	1.75	2.25	3.00	3.75
	1318	—	1.75	2.25	3.00	3.75
	1321	37	1.75	2.25	3.00	3.75
	Date off flan		1.00	1.50	2.00	2.75

1/4 RUPEE

.818 SILVER, 2.794 g

Y#	Date	Year	VG	Fine	VF	XF
15	AH1286	—	2.00	2.75	4.50	5.50
	1287	—	2.00	2.75	4.50	5.50
	1288	—	2.00	2.75	4.50	5.50
	1289	—	2.00	2.75	4.50	5.50
	1290	—	2.00	2.75	4.50	5.50
	1291	7	2.00	2.75	4.50	5.50
	1294	—	2.00	2.75	4.50	5.50
	1295	—	2.00	2.75	4.50	5.50
	1297	—	2.00	2.75	4.50	5.50
	1298	14	2.00	2.75	4.50	5.50
	1299	15	2.00	2.75	4.50	5.50
	1300	16	2.00	2.75	4.50	5.50
	1301	17	2.00	2.75	4.50	5.50
	1302	—	2.00	2.75	4.50	5.50
	1304	—	2.00	2.75	4.50	5.50
	1305	22	2.00	2.75	4.50	5.50
	1306	22	2.00	2.75	4.50	5.50
	1307	23	2.00	2.75	4.50	5.50
	1307	24	2.00	2.75	4.50	5.50
	1308	—	2.00	2.75	4.50	5.50
	1309	—	2.00	2.75	4.50	5.50
	1310	—	2.00	2.75	4.50	5.50
	1313	29	2.00	2.75	4.50	5.50
	1314	—	2.00	2.75	4.50	5.50
	1315	31	2.00	2.75	4.50	5.50
	1316	32	2.00	2.75	4.50	5.50
	1316	33	2.00	2.75	4.50	5.50
	1317	33	2.00	2.75	4.50	5.50
	1321	37	2.00	2.75	4.50	5.50

1/2 RUPEE

.818 SILVER, 5.589 g

Y#	Date	Year	VG	Fine	VF	XF
16	AH1286	1	3.00	4.00	5.50	10.00
	1289	—	3.00	4.00	5.50	10.00
	1291	7	3.00	4.00	5.50	10.00
	1292	—	3.00	4.00	5.50	10.00
	1294	10	3.00	4.00	5.50	10.00
	1295	—	3.00	4.00	5.50	10.00
	1299	15	3.00	4.00	5.50	10.00
	1301	17	3.00	4.00	5.50	10.00
	1302	18	3.00	4.00	5.50	10.00
	1304	—	3.00	4.00	5.50	10.00
	1305	22	3.00	4.00	5.50	10.00
	1306	22	3.00	4.00	5.50	10.00
	1307	23	3.00	4.00	5.50	10.00
	1308	—	3.00	4.00	5.50	10.00
	1310	—	3.00	4.00	5.50	10.00
	1316	32	3.00	4.00	5.50	10.00
	1317	—	3.00	4.00	5.50	10.00

RUPEE

.818 SILVER, 11.178 g

Y#	Date	Year	VG	Fine	VF	XF
17	AH1286	1	4.50	5.50	6.50	9.00
	1287	—	4.50	5.50	6.50	9.00
	1288	3	4.50	5.50	6.50	9.00
	1289	4	4.50	5.50	6.50	9.00
	1293	—	4.50	5.50	6.50	9.00
	1294	10	4.50	5.50	6.50	9.00
	1295	10	4.50	5.50	6.50	9.00
	1295	11	4.50	5.50	6.50	9.00
	1298	—	4.50	5.50	6.50	9.00
	1299	15	4.50	5.50	6.50	9.00
	1299	16	4.50	5.50	6.50	9.00
	1300	16	4.50	5.50	6.50	9.00
	1301	—	4.50	5.50	6.50	9.00
	1302	18	4.50	5.50	6.50	9.00
	1305	—	4.50	5.50	6.50	9.00
	1306	22	4.50	5.50	6.50	9.00
	1307	23	4.50	5.50	6.50	9.00
	1308	24	4.50	5.50	6.50	9.00
	1308	25	4.50	5.50	6.50	9.00
	1309	25	4.50	5.50	6.50	9.00
	1310	26	4.50	5.50	6.50	9.00
	1315	32	4.50	5.50	6.50	9.00
	1316	32	4.50	5.50	6.50	9.00
	1317	33	4.50	5.50	6.50	9.00
	1317	34	4.50	5.50	6.50	9.00
	1318	34	4.50	5.50	6.50	9.00

1/16 ASHRAFI

.910 GOLD, 0.698 g

Y#	Date	Year	VG	Fine	VF	XF
18	AH1305	—	20.00	30.00	40.00	60.00
	1314	—	20.00	30.00	40.00	60.00
	1315	—	20.00	30.00	40.00	60.00
	1321	37	20.00	30.00	40.00	60.00

1/8 ASHRAFI

.910 GOLD, 1.397 g

Y#	Date	Year	VG	Fine	VF	XF
19	AH1293	—	25.00	40.00	60.00	75.00
	1302	—	25.00	40.00	60.00	75.00
	1306	—	25.00	40.00	60.00	75.00
	1309	—	25.00	40.00	60.00	75.00
	1313	—	25.00	40.00	60.00	75.00
	1316	—	25.00	40.00	60.00	75.00
	1317	33	25.00	40.00	60.00	75.00
	1318	—	25.00	40.00	60.00	75.00
	1320	—	25.00	40.00	60.00	75.00
	1321	—	25.00	40.00	60.00	75.00

1/4 ASHRAFI

.910 GOLD, 2.794 g

Y#	Date	Year	VG	Fine	VF	XF
20	AH1301	—	45.00	60.00	80.00	100.00
	1304	—	45.00	60.00	80.00	100.00
	1306	—	45.00	60.00	80.00	100.00
	1309	—	45.00	60.00	80.00	100.00
	1314	30	45.00	60.00	80.00	100.00
	1315	—	45.00	60.00	80.00	100.00
	1316	—	45.00	60.00	80.00	100.00
	1318	35	45.00	60.00	80.00	100.00
	1319	35	45.00	60.00	80.00	100.00
	1319	—	45.00	60.00	80.00	100.00

1/2 ASHRAFI

.910 GOLD, 5.589 g

Y#	Date	Year	VG	Fine	VF	XF
21	AH1316	—	75.00	90.00	110.00	140.00
	1317	—	75.00	90.00	110.00	140.00
	1320	—	75.00	90.00	110.00	140.00
	1321	—	75.00	90.00	110.00	140.00

ASHRAFI

.910 GOLD, 11.178 g

Y#	Date	Year	VG	Fine	VF	XF
22	AH1286	1	150.00	170.00	200.00	250.00
	1287	—	150.00	170.00	200.00	250.00
	1288	—	150.00	170.00	200.00	250.00
	1289	—	150.00	170.00	200.00	250.00
	1290	—	150.00	170.00	200.00	250.00
	1292	—	150.00	170.00	200.00	250.00
	1293	—	150.00	170.00	200.00	250.00
	1294	—	150.00	170.00	200.00	250.00
	1295	—	150.00	170.00	200.00	250.00
	1296	—	150.00	170.00	200.00	250.00
	1297	—	150.00	170.00	200.00	250.00
	1298	14	150.00	170.00	200.00	250.00
	1299	—	150.00	170.00	200.00	250.00
	1300	16	150.00	170.00	200.00	250.00
	1301	—	150.00	170.00	200.00	250.00
	1302	—	150.00	170.00	200.00	250.00
	1303	—	150.00	170.00	200.00	250.00
	1304	—	150.00	170.00	200.00	250.00
	1305	—	150.00	170.00	200.00	250.00
	1306	—	150.00	170.00	200.00	250.00
	1307	—	150.00	170.00	200.00	250.00
	1308	—	150.00	170.00	200.00	250.00
	1309	—	150.00	170.00	200.00	250.00
	1310	—	150.00	170.00	200.00	250.00
	1311	—	150.00	170.00	200.00	250.00
	1312	28	150.00	170.00	200.00	250.00
	1313	—	150.00	170.00	200.00	250.00
	1314	30	150.00	170.00	200.00	250.00
	1314	31	150.00	170.00	200.00	250.00
	1315	—	150.00	170.00	200.00	250.00
	1316	—	150.00	170.00	200.00	250.00
	1317	—	150.00	170.00	200.00	250.00
	1318	—	150.00	170.00	200.00	250.00
	1319	—	150.00	170.00	200.00	250.00
	1320	—	150.00	170.00	200.00	250.00
	1321	—	150.00	170.00	200.00	250.00

MILLED COINAGE

PROVISIONAL ISSUES

AH1311/27-1318/35

1/4 ANNA

COPPER

KM#	Date	Year	VG	Fine	VF	XF
27	AH1312	27	—	—	—	—
	1312	28	—	—	—	—

1/2 ANNA

COPPER

KM#	Date	Year	VG	Fine	VF	XF
28	AH1311	27	—	—	—	—

ANNA

COPPER

KM#	Date	Year	VG	Fine	VF	XF
32	AH1305	21	55.00	85.00	125.00	175.00

2 ANNAS

.818 SILVER, 1.397 g

Y#	Date	Year	VG	Fine	VF	XF
29	AH1318	35	10.00	17.50	27.50	37.50

4 ANNAS

.818 SILVER, 2.794 g

Y#	Date	Year	VG	Fine	VF	XF
30	AH1318	32	27.50	37.50	50.00	60.00
	1318	34	8.50	16.50	25.00	33.50
	1318	35	8.50	16.50	25.00	33.50

8 ANNAS

.818 SILVER, 5.589 g

Y#	Date	Year	VG	Fine	VF	XF
31	AH1312	28	10.00	20.00	30.00	40.00
	1318	34	10.00	20.00	30.00	40.00
	1318	35	10.00	20.00	30.00	40.00

RUPEE

.818 SILVER, 11.178 g

Y#	Date	Year	VG	Fine	VF	XF
32	AH1312	28	10.00	15.00	20.00	30.00
	1313	29	10.00	15.00	20.00	30.00
	1314	30	10.00	15.00	20.00	30.00
	1318	34	10.00	15.00	20.00	30.00

ASHRAFI

.910 GOLD, 24mm, 11.05-11.20 g

Y#	Date	Year	VG	Fine	VF	XF
33	AH1311	27	600.00	800.00	1000.	1250.

REGULAR COINAGE

REGNAL YEAR LOCATION

Copper and Silver Series

Year 20

Gold Series

Year 25

NOTE: The AH date exists with two different regnal years in many cases.

Type I Type II

The early renditions of the name of Asaf Jah in Type I included an accent bar at lower right. This was removed for Type II during the production year of AH1328. Numerals for 92 appear above similar to earlier coinage not to be confused with regnal years or date.

PAI

COPPER

Y#	Date	Year	Fine	VF	XF	Unc
34	AH1326	42	4.00	6.00	9.00	15.00
	1327	42	4.00	6.00	9.00	15.00
	1329	—	— Reported, not confirmed			

2 PAI

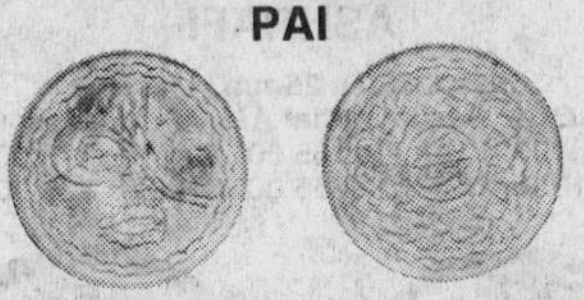

COPPER

Y#	Date	Year	Fine	VF	XF	Unc
35	AH1322	37	1.00	1.25	1.75	2.75
	1322	38	.75	1.00	1.50	2.50
	1322	39	1.00	1.25	1.75	2.75
	1323	38	1.00	1.25	1.75	2.75
	1323	39	.60	.75	1.00	1.50
	1323	40	.75	1.00	1.50	2.50
	1323	41	.75	1.00	1.50	2.50
	1324	39	1.00	1.25	1.75	2.75
	1324	40	.60	.85	1.25	1.75
	1324	41	.75	1.00	1.50	2.50
	1325	40	1.00	1.25	1.75	2.75
	1325	41	.75	1.00	1.50	2.50
	1329	43	.50	.65	1.00	1.75
	1329	44	.50	.65	1.00	1.75
	1329	45	.50	.65	1.00	1.75

1/2 ANNA

COPPER

Y#	Date	Year	Fine	VF	XF	Unc
36	AH1324	38	2.50	4.00	6.00	10.00
	1324	40	1.50	2.25	3.00	4.00
	1324	41	2.25	3.00	3.50	4.50
	1325	40	2.00	3.25	3.75	5.50
	1325	41	2.00	3.25	3.75	5.50
	1326	41	2.50	3.75	4.50	7.00
	1329	44	1.50	2.50	3.00	4.00

2 ANNAS

.818 SILVER, 1.39 g

Y#	Date	Year	Fine	VF	XF	Unc
37	AH132334(SIC)		1.50	2.50	5.00	8.00
	1323	39	.75	1.25	3.00	5.00

4 ANNAS

.818 SILVER, 2.794 g
Type I

Y#	Date	Year	Fine	VF	XF	Unc
38.1	AH1323	39	4.00	4.75	5.50	9.00
	1326	43	8.50	16.50	25.00	32.50

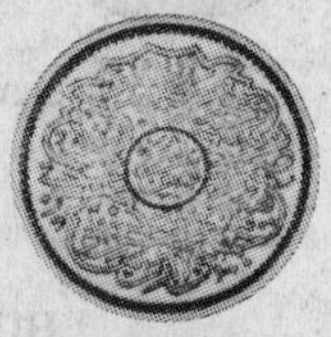

Struck with dies of 1/2 Ashrafi.

Y#	Date	Year	Fine	VF	XF	Unc
38.2	AH1324	40	—	—	—	—

Type II

Y#	Date	Year	Fine	VF	XF	Unc
38.3	AH1328	43	4.00	4.75	6.00	10.00
	1329	44	4.00	4.75	5.50	9.00

8 ANNAS

.818 SILVER, 5.589 g
Type I

Y#	Date	Year	Fine	VF	XF	Unc
39.1	AH1322	38	— Reported, not confirmed			

Type II

Y#	Date	Year	Fine	VF	XF	Unc
39.2	AH1328	43	6.50	7.50	9.00	15.00
	1329	44	6.50	7.50	9.00	15.00

RUPEE

.818 SILVER, 11.178 g
Type I

Y#	Date	Year	Fine	VF	XF	Unc
40.1	AH1319	35	11.50	13.50	16.50	27.50
	1321	37	11.50	13.50	16.50	27.50
	1321	38	11.50	13.50	15.00	25.00
	1322	38	11.50	13.50	15.00	25.00
	1322	39	11.50	13.50	15.00	25.00
	1323	39	11.50	13.50	15.00	25.00
	1324	40	11.50	13.50	15.00	25.00
	1325	41	11.50	13.50	15.00	25.00
	1326	41	11.50	13.50	15.00	25.00

Type II

Y#	Date	Year	Fine	VF	XF	Unc
40.2	AH1328	43	11.50	13.50	15.00	25.00
	1329	44	11.50	13.50	15.00	25.00

1/8 ASHRAFI

.910 GOLD, 1.394 g

Y#	Date	Year	Fine	VF	XF	Unc
41	AH1325	41	35.00	50.00	65.00	85.00
	1329	—	35.00	50.00	65.00	85.00
	1329	44	35.00	50.00	65.00	85.00

1/4 ASHRAFI

.910 GOLD, 2.794 g

Y#	Date	Year	Fine	VF	XF	Unc
42	AH1325	41	50.00	65.00	85.00	125.00
	1329	44	50.00	65.00	85.00	125.00

1/2 ASHRAFI

.910 GOLD, 5.589 g
Type I

Y#	Date	Year	Fine	VF	XF	Unc
43.1	AH1325	41	80.00	110.00	150.00	250.00
	1326	41	80.00	110.00	150.00	250.00
	1329	44	80.00	110.00	150.00	250.00

Type II

Y#	Date	Year	Fine	VF	XF	Unc
43.2	AH1328	43	80.00	110.00	150.00	250.00

ASHRAFI

.910 GOLD, 24mm, 11.178 g

Y#	Date	Year	Fine	VF	XF	Unc
44	AH1325	41	165.00	225.00	300.00	400.00
	1329	—	165.00	225.00	300.00	400.00

MIR USMAN ALI KHAN

AH1329-1368/1911-1948AD

First Coinage

AH1329-1361

PAI

BRONZE

Y#	Date	Year	Fine	VF	XF	Unc
45	AH1338	—	1.50	2.00	2.50	4.00
	1344	15	.60	.75	1.00	1.50
	1349	20	.60	.75	1.00	1.50
	1352	23	1.00	1.25	1.50	2.50
	1352	24	1.00	1.25	1.50	2.50
	1353	23	1.00	1.25	1.50	2.50
	1353	24	.70	.85	1.10	1.75

2 PAI

BRONZE
Obv: Short *Ain* in toughra.

Y#	Date	Year	Fine	VF	XF	Unc
46	AH1329	1	10.00	15.00	22.50	35.00
	1330	1	8.00	12.50	20.00	32.50

NOTE: See also 1 Rupee, Y#53 and Y#53a.

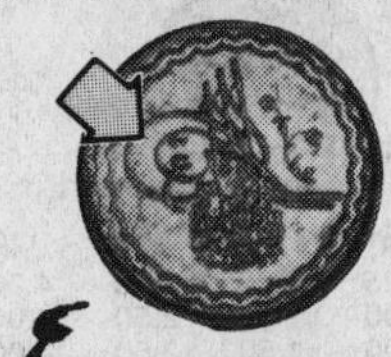

Obv: Full *Ain* in toughra.

Y#	Date	Year	Fine	VF	XF	Unc
46a	AH1330	1	1.50	2.00	2.50	3.50
	1330	2	.35	.50	.65	1.00
	1331	2	.35	.50	.65	1.00
	1331	3	.50	.65	.75	1.00
	1332	3	.35	.50	.65	1.00
	1332	4	.60	.75	1.00	1.50
	1333	3	.60	.75	1.00	1.50
	1333	4	.35	.50	.65	1.00
	1333	5	.75	1.00	1.25	2.00
	1334	3	.60	.75	1.00	1.50
	1335	6	.35	.50	.65	1.00
	1335	7	.35	.50	.65	1.00
	1336	7	.35	.50	.65	1.00
	1336	8	.50	.65	.80	1.25
	1337	7	.75	1.00	1.25	2.00
	1337	8	.60	.75	1.00	1.50
	1338	8	.75	1.00	1.25	2.00
	1338	9	.35	.50	.65	1.00
	1338	11	.50	.75	1.00	1.50
	1339	10	.75	1.00	1.25	2.00
	1339	11	.75	1.00	1.25	2.00
	1342	13	.60	.75	1.00	1.50
	1342	14	.35	.50	.65	1.00
	1343	14	.35	.50	.65	1.00
	1343	15	.40	.60	.75	1.25
	1344	15	.50	.65	.80	1.25
	1345	16	.35	.50	.65	1.00
	1347	18	.75	1.00	1.25	2.00
	1347	19	.75	1.00	1.25	2.00
	1348	19	.35	.50	.65	1.00
	1349	20	.35	.50	.65	1.00

1/2 ANNA

BRONZE

Y#	Date	Year	Fine	VF	XF	Unc
47	AH1332	2	.75	1.00	1.25	2.00
	1332	3	.75	1.00	1.25	2.00
	1334	4	1.25	1.50	2.00	3.25
	1344	15	1.25	1.50	2.00	3.25
	1348	20	1.00	1.35	1.75	2.75

ANNA

COPPER-NICKEL

Y#	Date	Year	Fine	VF	XF	Unc
48	AH1338	—	.50	.75	1.00	1.50
	1339	—	1.00	1.35	1.75	2.75
	1340	—	.60	.85	1.25	1.75
	1341	—	.75	1.00	1.35	2.00
	1344	—	.50	.75	1.00	1.50
	1347	—	.50	.75	1.00	1.50
	1348	—	.60	.85	1.25	1.75
	1349	—	.50	.75	1.00	1.50
	1351	—	.50	.75	1.00	1.50
	1352	—	1.00	1.35	1.75	2.75
	1353	—	.50	.75	1.00	1.50
	1354	—	.50	.75	1.00	1.50

Y#	Date	Year	Fine	VF	XF	Unc
49	AH1356	—	.35	.50	.65	1.00
	1357	—	.50	.65	.85	1.35
	1358	—	.35	.50	.65	1.00
	1359	—	.75	1.00	1.25	2.00
	1360	—	.75	1.00	1.25	2.00
	1361	—	.75	1.00	1.25	2.00

2 ANNAS

.818 SILVER, 1.397 g

Y#	Date	Year	Fine	VF	XF	Unc
50	AH1335	6	1.25	1.75	2.50	4.00
	1337	9	1.00	1.50	2.50	4.00
	1338	10	1.00	1.50	2.50	4.00
	1340	11	1.00	1.50	2.50	4.00
	1341	13	1.00	1.50	2.50	4.00
	1341	14	1.25	2.00	3.00	5.00
	1342	13	1.00	1.50	2.50	4.00
	1343	14	1.00	1.50	2.25	3.50
	1343	15	1.00	1.50	2.25	3.50
	1347	—	1.25	2.00	3.00	5.00
	1348	19	1.00	1.50	2.25	3.50
	1351	22	1.00	1.50	2.50	4.00
	1355	26	1.00	1.50	2.50	4.00

4 ANNAS

.818 SILVER, 2.794 g

Y#	Date	Year	Fine	VF	XF	Unc
51	AH1337	9	1.75	3.00	4.50	7.00
	1340	11	1.75	3.00	4.50	7.00
	1342	13	1.75	3.00	4.50	7.00
	1342	14	1.75	3.00	4.50	7.00
	1348	19	1.75	3.00	4.50	7.00
	1351	22	1.75	3.00	4.50	7.00
	1354	25	1.75	3.00	4.50	7.00
	1358	30	1.75	3.00	4.50	7.00

8 ANNAS

.818 SILVER, 5.589 g

Y#	Date	Year	Fine	VF	XF	Unc
52	AH1337	9	3.50	5.00	8.00	12.00
	1342	13	3.50	5.00	8.00	12.00
	1343	13	3.50	5.00	8.00	12.00
	1354	25	3.50	5.00	8.00	12.00

RUPEE

.818 SILVER, 11.178 g
Obv: Partial initial *Ain* in doorway.

Y#	Date	Year	Fine	VF	XF	Unc
53	AH1330	1	BV	7.50	10.00	25.00

Obv: Full *Ain* in doorway.

Y#	Date	Year	Fine	VF	XF	Unc
53a	AH1330	1	6.00	10.00	12.50	25.00
	1330	2	6.00	10.00	12.50	25.00
	1331	2	4.00	7.00	10.00	20.00
	1331	3	4.00	7.00	10.00	20.00
	1332	3	4.00	7.00	10.00	20.00
	1334	6	4.00	7.00	10.00	20.00
	1335	6	4.00	7.00	10.00	20.00
	1335	7	4.00	7.00	10.00	20.00
	1336	7	4.00	7.00	10.00	20.00
	1337	8	4.00	7.00	10.00	20.00
	1337	9	11.50	15.00	20.00	25.00
	1338	9	4.00	7.00	10.00	20.00
	1339	9	4.00	7.00	10.00	20.00
	1340	11	4.00	7.00	10.00	20.00
	1341	12	4.00	7.00	10.00	20.00
	1342	13	4.00	7.00	10.00	20.00
	1343	14	4.00	7.00	10.00	20.00

1/8 ASHRAFI

.910 GOLD, 11mm, 1.394 g
Obv: Partial *Ain* in doorway.

Y#	Date	Year	Fine	VF	XF	Unc
54.1	AH1329	1	—	—	Rare	—

Obv: Full *Ain* in doorway.

Y#	Date	Year	Fine	VF	XF	Unc
54.2	AH1337	8	30.00	37.50	50.00	70.00
	1340	11	30.00	37.50	50.00	70.00
	1343	—	30.00	37.50	50.00	70.00
	1344	15	30.00	37.50	50.00	70.00
	1353	—	30.00	37.50	50.00	70.00
	1354	25	30.00	37.50	50.00	70.00
	1356	27	30.00	37.50	50.00	70.00
	1360	—	30.00	37.50	50.00	70.00
	1366	37	30.00	37.50	50.00	70.00
	1368	39	30.00	37.50	50.00	70.00

1/4 ASHRAFI

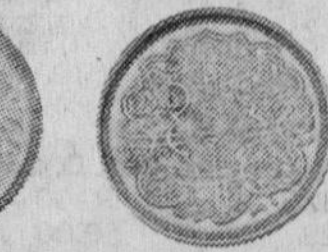

.910 GOLD, 2.794 g

Y#	Date	Year	Fine	VF	XF	Unc
55	AH1337	8	40.00	60.00	85.00	125.00
	1342	13	40.00	60.00	85.00	125.00
	1342	14	40.00	60.00	85.00	125.00
	1349	20	40.00	60.00	85.00	125.00
	1353	23	40.00	60.00	85.00	125.00
	1354	25	40.00	60.00	85.00	125.00
	1357	—	40.00	60.00	85.00	125.00
	1360	31	40.00	60.00	85.00	125.00
	1367	38	40.00	60.00	85.00	125.00

1/2 ASHRAFI

.910 GOLD, 21mm, 5.589 g
Obv: Partial *Ain* in doorway.

Y#	Date	Year	Fine	VF	XF	Unc
56.1	AH1329	1	85.00	125.00	175.00	250.00

Obv: Full *Ain* in doorway.

Y#	Date	Year	Fine	VF	XF	Unc
56.2	1337	8	75.00	100.00	140.00	200.00
	1342	14	75.00	100.00	140.00	200.00
	1343	14	75.00	100.00	140.00	200.00
	1345	16	75.00	100.00	140.00	200.00
	1349	20	75.00	100.00	140.00	200.00
	1354	25	75.00	100.00	140.00	200.00
	1357	29	75.00	100.00	140.00	200.00
	1367	38	75.00	100.00	140.00	200.00

ASHRAFI

.910 GOLD, 25mm, 11.178 g
Obv: Partial initial *Ain* in doorway.

Y#	Date	Year	Fine	VF	XF	Unc
57	AH1329	1	165.00	220.00	325.00	450.00
	1330	1	165.00	220.00	325.00	450.00

Obv: Full *Ain* in doorway.

Y#	Date	Year	Fine	VF	XF	Unc
57a	AH1331	3	140.00	160.00	240.00	350.00
	1333	4	140.00	160.00	240.00	350.00
	1337	8	140.00	160.00	240.00	350.00
	1337	9	140.00	160.00	240.00	350.00
	1338	9	140.00	160.00	240.00	350.00
	1340	11	140.00	160.00	240.00	350.00
	1342	14	140.00	165.00	240.00	350.00
	1343	14	140.00	160.00	240.00	350.00
	1344	15	140.00	160.00	240.00	350.00
	1348	19	140.00	160.00	240.00	350.00
	1349	20	140.00	160.00	240.00	350.00
	1354	25	140.00	160.00	240.00	350.00
	1358	30	140.00	160.00	240.00	350.00
	1360	31	140.00	160.00	240.00	350.00

Second Coinage

AH1361-1368

2 PAI

BRONZE

Y#	Date	Year	Fine	VF	XF	Unc
58	AH1362	33	.25	.35	.50	.75
	1363	34	.25	.35	.50	.75
	1363	35	.20	.25	.50	.75
	1364	35	.20	.25	.50	.75
	1365	36	.20	.25	.50	.75
	1366	37	.20	.25	.50	.75
	1368	39	.20	.25	.50	.75

ANNA

BRONZE

Y#	Date	Year	Fine	VF	XF	Unc
59	AH1361	—	.40	.50	.75	1.50
	1362	—	.40	.50	.75	1.50
	1364	—	.40	.50	.75	1.50
	1365	—	.40	.50	.75	1.50
	1366	—	.40	.50	.75	1.50
	1368	—	.40	.50	.75	1.50

2 ANNAS

SILVER, 1.397 g

Y#	Date	Year	Fine	VF	XF	Unc
60	AH1362	33	.40	.60	1.00	2.00

NICKEL

Y#	Date	Year	Fine	VF	XF	Unc
64	AH1366	37	.15	.25	.35	1.00
	1368	39	.25	.35	.45	1.50

4 ANNAS

SILVER, 2.794 g

Y#	Date	Year	Fine	VF	XF	Unc
61	AH1362	33	.70	.80	1.00	2.00
	1362	34	.75	.90	1.10	2.25
	1364	33	.80	1.00	1.25	2.50
	1364	35	.80	1.00	1.25	2.50
	1364	36	.80	1.00	1.25	2.50
	1365	36	.80	1.00	1.25	2.50

NICKEL

Y#	Date	Year	Fine	VF	XF	Unc
65	AH1366	37	.40	.50	.75	1.50
	1368	39	.40	.50	.75	1.50

8 ANNAS

SILVER, 5.589 g

Y#	Date	Year	Fine	VF	XF	Unc
62	AH1363	34	3.00	5.00	9.00	15.00

NICKEL

Y#	Date	Year	Fine	VF	XF	Unc
66	AH1366	37	.70	.85	1.00	2.00

RUPEE

SILVER, 11.178 g

Y#	Date	Year	Fine	VF	XF	Unc
63	AH1361	31	4.00	6.50	10.00	15.00
	1361	32	4.00	6.50	10.00	15.00
	1362	34	4.00	6.50	10.00	15.00
	1364	35	4.00	6.50	10.00	15.00
	1364	36	4.00	6.50	10.00	15.00
	1365	36	4.00	6.50	10.00	15.00

HYDERABAD FEUDATORIES

AURANGABAD

'TOKA' CASH

COPPER
Rev: Battle-axe in canopy, date below.

C#	Date	Year	Good	VG	Fine	VF
28	FE1241	—	5.00	10.00	16.50	25.00

Date in Nagari numerals.

C#	Date	Year	Good	VG	Fine	VF
30	AH1273	—	4.00	8.00	12.50	20.00

NOTE: C#28 and #30 were named after Toka Raj who operated the Aurangabad Mint under a state license from about 1830.

ELICHPUR

ANONYMOUS COINAGE

PAISA

COPPER, 18-20mm, 11.50 g
Obv: Tiger right.

C#	Date	Year	Good	VG	Fine	VF
10	AH1250	—	4.00	6.50	10.00	15.00
	1263	—	4.00	6.50	10.00	15.00
	Date off flan	—	2.50	4.00	6.50	10.00

Obv: Tiger left.

C#	Date	Year	Good	VG	Fine	VF
10a	AH1250	—	4.00	6.50	10.00	15.00
	1263	—	4.00	6.50	10.00	15.00
	1285	—	4.00	6.50	10.00	15.00
	Date off flan	—	2.50	4.00	6.50	10.00

2 PAISA

COPPER, 15.50 g
Obv: Tiger left.

C#	Date	Year	Good	VG	Fine	VF
15	AH1250	—	5.00	9.00	13.00	20.00

Obv: Tiger right.

C#	Date	Year	Good	VG	Fine	VF
15a	AH1250	—	5.00	9.00	13.00	20.00

KALAYANI

Kallian

A town located in north Mysore.

NAWAB

Mohammad Shah Khair al-Din

Mint mark:

1/8 RUPEE

SILVER, 1.34-1.45 g

KM#	Date	Year	VG	Fine	VF	XF
2	AH1226	—	7.50	12.50	18.50	27.50

RUPEE

SILVER, 10.70-11.60 g
Rev: W/o Persian *Ha* to right of tiger.

KM#	Date	Year	VG	Fine	VF	XF
5	AH1212	—	55.00	90.00	150.00	225.00

Rev: Persian *Ha* to right of tiger.

KM#	Date	Year	VG	Fine	VF	XF
6	AH1226	—	30.00	50.00	85.00	125.00
	ND	—	30.00	50.00	85.00	125.00

NOTE: Earlier dates (AH1212-1215) exist for this type.

NARAYANPETT

Local Rajas

Dilshadabad on coins.

MINT MARKS

ती *Ti* obv. dated AH1186/1186, C#40

क *K* rev. dated AH1186/1186, C#40

गो *Go* obv. dated AH1186/1252, C#37-40

ल *L* rev. dated AH1186/1252, C#37-40

In the name of Shah Alam II

AH1173-1221/1759-1806AD

PAISA

COPPER

C#	Date	Year	Good	VG	Fine	VF
34	AH1202	1252	3.50	5.50	8.00	11.50

1/8 RUPEE

SILVER, 1.34-1.45 g

C#	Date	Year	VG	Fine	VF	XF
37	AH1186	1252	4.50	7.50	10.00	15.00

1/4 RUPEE

SILVER, 13mm, 2.68-2.90 g

C#	Date	Year	VG	Fine	VF	XF
38	AH1186	1252	6.00	10.00	15.00	22.50

1/2 RUPEE

SILVER, 16mm, 5.35-5.80 g

C#	Date	Year	VG	Fine	VF	XF
39	AH1186	1252	6.50	11.50	16.50	25.00

RUPEE

SILVER, 10.70-11.60 g

C#	Date	Year	VG	Fine	VF	XF
40	AH1186	1186	9.00	15.00	21.50	30.00
	1186	1239	9.00	15.00	21.50	30.00
	1186	1245	9.00	15.00	21.50	30.00
	1186	1246	9.00	15.00	21.50	30.00
	1186	1251	9.00	15.00	21.50	30.00
	1186	1252	9.00	15.00	21.50	30.00
	1186	1254	9.00	15.00	21.50	30.00

SHORAPUR

Bahiri Feudatory

1/2 PAISA

COPPER, 14mm

C#	Date	Year	Good	VG	Fine	VF
62	ND	—	3.50	5.50	8.00	11.50

COPPER, 13mm
Similar to 1 Paisa, C#66.

C#	Date	Year	Good	VG	Fine	VF
65	AH1262	—	2.50	4.00	6.50	10.00

PAISA

COPPER

C#	Date	Year	Good	VG	Fine	VF
63	ND	—	2.00	3.25	5.00	8.50

Rev: Inscribed *Bahiri*.

C#	Date	Year	Good	VG	Fine	VF
64	ND	—	2.50	4.00	6.50	10.00

Rev: *Bahiri*, date.

C#	Date	Year	Good	VG	Fine	VF
66	AH1261	—	2.50	4.00	6.50	10.00
	1262	—	2.50	4.00	6.50	10.00

Obv: Different from C#66.

C#	Date	Year	Good	VG	Fine	VF
67	AH1262	—	2.50	4.00	6.50	10.00

WANPARTI

Bahiri Rajas

Sagur mintname on coins is Nasirabad. The latter is honorific for the Sagur Mint copied from the rupees of Dharwar.

In the name of Muhammad Akbar II
AH1221-1253/1806-1837AD

1/4 RUPEE

SILVER, 2.67-2.90 g

C#	Date	Year	VG	Fine	VF	XF
78	AH1235	14	7.50	12.50	18.50	27.50

RUPEE

SILVER, 10.70-11.60 g
Obv: 'J'. Rev: 'A' in Nagari.

C#	Date	Year	VG	Fine	VF	XF
80	AH1235	14	7.50	12.50	18.50	27.50
	1235	15	7.50	12.50	18.50	27.50

INDORE

The Holkars were one of the three dominant Maratha powers (with the Peshwas and Sindhias), with major land holdings in Central India.

Indore State originated in 1728 with a grant of land north of the Narbada river by the Maratha Peshwa of Poona to Malhar Rao Holkar, a cavalry commander in his service. After Holkar's death (ca.1765) his daughterin-law, Ahalya Bai, assumed the position of Queen Regent. Together with Tukoji Rao she effectively ruled the State until her death thirty years later. But it was left to Tukoji's son, Jaswant Rao, to challenge the dominance of the Poona Marathas in the Maratha Confederacy, eventually defeating the Peshwa's army in 1802. But at this point the fortunes of the Holkars suffered a serious reverse. Although Jaswant Rao had initially defeated a small British force under Col. William Monson, he was badly beaten by a contingent under Lord Lake. As a result Holkar was forced to cede a considerable portion of his territory and from this time until India's independence in 1947, the residual State of Indore was obliged to accept British protection.

For more detailed data on the Indore series, see *A STUDY OF HOLKAR STATE COINAGE*, by P.K. Sethi, S.K. Bhatt and R. Holkar (1976).

HOLKAR RULERS

Jaswant Rao
SE1719-1734/AH1213-1226/
1798-1811AD
Mulhar Rao II
AH1226-1248/1811-1833AD
Martand Rao
AH1249/1834AD
Hari Rao
AH1250-1260/1834-1843AD
Khande Rao
AH1260-1261/1843-1844AD
Tukoji Rao II
VS1891-1943/SE1766-1808/
AH1261-1304/1844-1886AD
Shivaji Rao
VS1943-1960/FE1296-1313/
1886-1903AD
Tukoji Rao III
VS1960-1983/1903-1926AD
Yashwant Rao
VS1983-2005/1926-1948AD

HONORIFIC TITLE

Bahadur

REGNAL YEARS

In reference to:
Alamgir II, Year 1/AH1167-1168
Shah Alam II, Year 1/AH1173-1174
Muhammad Akbar II, Year 1/AH1221-1222
Malhar Rao I, as Subehdar, Year 1/
AH1170-1171

MINTS

Chandor جانرد

Indore اندور or इंदोर

جعفرابادعرف جانرد
J'afarabad 'urf Chandor

Maheshwar (see Malharnagar)

Malharnagar ملهارنگر

Sironj سرونج

NOTE: According to Sethi, Bhatt and Holkar, the coins of both the Maheshwar and Malharnagar Mints bear the mintname "Malharnagar" in honor of Malhar Rao I, founder of the state. They can only be distinguished by their distinctive mint marks, as noted below.

MUGHAL ISSUES

In the name of Shah Alam II
AH 1173-1221/1759-1806 AD

Until AH1296/1880AD all coinage of Indore was struck in the name of Shah Alam II, with the exception of a few rare special or nazarana issues. The coinage of the individual rulers until 1880AD cannot be told apart except by the date, as no change of type was made for more than a century.

INDORE MINT

Coins issued intermittently from 1772 to 1935 A.D.

JASWANT RAO

SE1719-1734/AH1212-1226
1797-1811AD

In the name of Mughal King of Delhi and Jaswant Rao

NAZARANA RUPEE

SILVER, 10.70-11.60 g

KM#	Date	Year	VG	Fine	VF	XF
6	SE1728	(1806)	50.00	75.00	110.00	150.00

In the name of Muhammad Akbar II
AH1221-1253/1806-1837AD
and Jaswant Rao

KM#	Date	Year	VG	Fine	VF	XF
7	SE1728	(1806)	—	—	Rare	—

KM#	Date	Year	VG	Fine	VF	XF
8	AH1222	2	32.50	45.00	62.50	85.00

Presentation Issues

These "mudra" coins appear to have been machine struck although mint machines were not introduced in Indore until 1864.

TUKOJI RAO II

VS1891-1943/SE1766-1808
AH1260-1304/1844-1886AD

COPPER 1/2 MUDRA

COPPER, 4.35-5.10 g

KM#	Date	Year	Good	VG	Fine	VF
10	SE1780	(1858)	20.00	32.50	50.00	75.00
	1788	VS1923	20.00	32.50	50.00	75.00

COPPER MUDRA

COPPER, 7.80-11.00 g

KM#	Date	Year	Good	VG	Fine	VF
11	SE1780	(1858)	30.00	60.00	100.00	150.00
	1788	VS1923	—	—	Rare	—

1/2 ANNA

COPPER, 16.60 g

KM#	Date	Year	Good	VG	Fine	VF
12	VS1942	(1885)	—	—	Rare	—

13.40 g

KM#	Date	Year	Good	VG	Fine	VF
13	VS1942/SE1807/1885		25.00	45.00	65.00	100.00

SILVER MUDRA

SILVER, 11.20 g

Obv: Blank within wreath.

Obv: Two varieties of swirls.

KM#	Date	Year	VG	Fine	VF	XF
15	SE1780	(1858)	40.00	60.00	90.00	125.00
16	SE1780	(1858)	40.00	60.00	90.00	125.00
17	SE1780	(1858)	60.00	100.00	140.00	175.00
18	SE1788	VS1923	75.00	110.00	150.00	200.00
19	VS1934	FE1287	75.00	110.00	150.00	200.00
20	VS1934	FE1287	100.00	150.00	200.00	250.00

1/2 RUPEE

SILVER, 5.50 g

KM#	Date	Year	VG	Fine	VF	XF
21	AH1289	—	55.00	70.00	85.00	110.00
22	ND	—	55.00	70.00	85.00	110.00

RUPEE

SILVER, 11.20 g

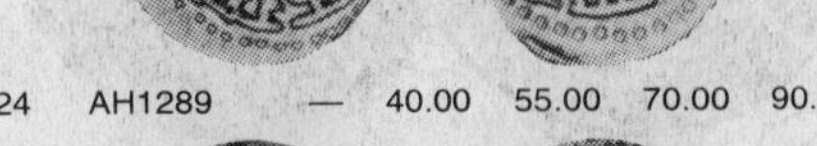

KM#	Date	Year	VG	Fine	VF	XF
23	ND	—	25.00	35.00	45.00	60.00
24	AH1289	—	40.00	55.00	70.00	90.00
25	AH1295	—	40.00	55.00	70.00	90.00

MOHUR

GOLD, 10.83 g

KM#	Date	Year	VG	Fine	VF	XF
27	VS1941	(1883)	—	—	Rare	—

Milled Coinage

SHIVAJI RAO

VS1943-1960/FE1296-1313/1886-1903AD

Without ruler's name

1/2 PAISA

COPPER

Rev: Denomination in 2 lines: *1/2 Adhela Paisa.*

Rev: Denomination in 3 lines: *1/2 Dhaleka Paisa.*

KM#	Date	Year	Good	VG	Fine	VF
30.1	VS1944	(1887)	10.00	15.00	21.50	30.00
30.2	VS1944	(1887)	10.00	15.00	21.50	30.00

In the name of Shivaji Rao

Rev: Denomination in 2 lines: *Adha Paisa.*

KM#	Date	Year	Good	VG	Fine	VF
31	VS1946	(1889)	11.50	16.50	23.50	32.50

Without ruler's name

1/4 ANNA

COPPER

Obv: Date below bull.

Rev: *Indore* below denomination.

KM#	Date	Year	Good	VG	Fine	VF
32.1	VS1943	(1886)	1.50	3.00	5.00	7.50

Rev: Retrograde.

KM#	Date	Year	Good	VG	Fine	VF
32.2	VS1943	(1886)	—	—	—	—

Obv: Continuous leg. w/*Indore* below bull.

Rev: Date below denomination.

KM#	Date	Year	Good	VG	Fine	VF
32.3	VS1943	(1886)	.35	.75	1.25	2.50
	1944	(1887)	.50	1.00	1.50	3.00
	1945	(1888)	.75	1.25	2.00	4.00

Obv: Broken leg. w/*Indore* upright below bull.

KM#	Date	Year	Good	VG	Fine	VF
32.4	VS1943	(1886)	2.00	4.00	6.50	8.50
	1944	(1887)	2.00	4.00	6.50	8.50

Obv: Cross w/dot in each quadrant flanking *Indore.*

KM#	Date	Year	Good	VG	Fine	VF
32.5	VS1943	(1886)	1.00	2.00	3.00	6.00

In the name of Sivaji Rao

Obv: Continuous leg. w/ruler's name and *Indore* .

Rev: Date below denomination.

KM#	Date	Year	Good	VG	Fine	VF
33.1	VS1944	(1887)	.85	1.75	2.50	5.00
	1945	(1888)	.75	1.50	2.00	4.00
	1946	(1889)	.85	1.75	2.50	5.00
	1947	(1890)	.75	1.50	2.00	4.00

Obv. leg: Ruler's name spelled *Sayaji Rao.*

KM#	Date	Year	Good	VG	Fine	VF
33.2	VS1944	(1887)	1.00	2.00	4.00	8.00

Obv: Continuous leg. w/ruler's name and *Bahadur*.
Rev: *Indore* above denomination and date.

KM#	Date	Year	Good	VG	Fine	VF
33.3	VS1947	(1890)	.75	1.50	2.25	4.50
	1948	(1891)	.50	1.00	1.50	3.00
	1956	(1899)	.35	.75	1.25	2.50
	1957	(1900)	.65	1.25	1.75	2.50
	1958	(1901)	.65	1.25	1.75	3.50
	1959	(1902)	.65	1.25	1.75	3.50

NOTE: Floral border varieties exist.

Rev: Date below denomination.

KM#	Date	Year	Good	VG	Fine	VF
33.4	VS1948	(1891)	1.00	2.00	4.00	6.00

Without ruler's name

1/2 ANNA

COPPER
Obv: Date below bull.
Rev: *Indore* below denomination.

KM#	Date	Year	Good	VG	Fine	VF
34.1	VS1943	(1886)	3.00	5.00	8.50	14.00

Obv: Continuous leg. w/*Indore* below bull.

KM#	Date	Year	Good	VG	Fine	VF
34.2	VS1943	(1886)	3.00	5.00	7.00	10.00
	1944	(1887)	3.00	5.00	7.00	10.00

Obv. leg: *Indore* behind bull
Rev: *Indore* above denomination and date.

KM#	Date	Year	Good	VG	Fine	VF
34.3	VS1943	(1886)	4.00	6.00	8.50	12.50

Obv: Broken leg. w/*Indore* upright below bull.

KM#	Date	Year	Good	VG	Fine	VF
34.4	VS1943	(1886)	3.00	5.00	7.00	10.00

In the name of Sivaji Rao

Obv. leg: Ruler's name and *Indore*.
Rev: Date below denomination.

KM#	Date	Year	Good	VG	Fine	VF
35.1	VS1944	(1887)	3.00	5.00	7.00	10.00
	1945	(1888)	3.00	5.00	7.00	10.00
	1947	(1890)	7.50	13.50	20.00	30.00

NOTE: Floral border varieties exist.

Obv: Broken leg. w/*Bahadur* upright below bull.
Rev: *Indore* above denomination and date.

KM#	Date	Year	Good	VG	Fine	VF
35.2	VS1943	(1886)	3.50	5.50	8.50	11.50

Obv: Continuous leg. w/ruler's name and *Bahadur*.
Rev: *Indore* above denomination and date.

KM#	Date	Year	Good	VG	Fine	VF
35.3	VS1945	(1888)	1.00	1.50	2.25	4.50
	1947	(1890)	1.00	1.50	2.00	4.00
	1948	(1891)	1.00	1.50	2.00	3.00
	1956	(1899)	1.00	1.50	2.00	3.00
	1957	(1900)	1.00	1.50	2.00	3.00
	1958	(1901)	1.00	1.50	2.00	4.00
	1959	(1902)	1.00	1.50	2.00	4.00

Dump Coinage

In the name of Shah Alam II
AH 1173-1221/1759-1806 AD

First Series

Crossed scimitar and spear below sunface w/Fasli Era and Vikrama Samvat Era dating.

1/4 RUPEE

SILVER, 2.68-2.90 g

KM#	Date	Year	VG	Fine	VF	XF
37	FE1295	VS1945	17.50	25.00	35.00	50.00

1/2 RUPEE

SILVER, 5.35-5.80 g

KM#	Date	Year	VG	Fine	VF	XF
38	FE1295	VS1947	17.50	25.00	35.00	50.00
	1296	VS1947	17.50	25.00	35.00	50.00

RUPEE

SILVER, 10.70-11.60 g
Obv: Large flames.

KM#	Date	Year	VG	Fine	VF	XF
39.1	FE1294	VS1945	16.50	23.50	32.50	45.00
	1295	VS1945	16.50	23.50	32.50	45.00
	1296	VS1945	16.50	23.50	32.50	45.00

Obv: Small flames.

KM#	Date	Year	VG	Fine	VF	XF
39.2	FE1295	R.Y.122	15.00	21.50	30.00	40.00
	1296	VS1945	15.00	21.50	30.00	40.00

Obv: W/o flames.

KM#	Date	Year	VG	Fine	VF	XF
39.3	FE1295	VS1947	16.50	23.50	32.50	45.00
	1296	1947	16.50	23.50	32.50	45.00
	1297	1947	16.50	23.50	32.50	45.00

Second Series

NOTE: There are 2 minor sub-varieties, one w/U-shaped mark on forehead of sunface and the other w/dot. Vikrama Samvat Era dating.

PAISA

COPPER

KM#	Date	Year	VG	Fine	VF	XF
40	VS1948	—	—	—	Rare	—

1/8 RUPEE

SILVER, 1.34-1.45 g

KM#	Date	Year	VG	Fine	VF	XF
41	VS1947	(1890)	3.50	5.50	7.00	10.00
	1950	(1893)	3.50	5.50	7.00	10.00
	1951	(1894)	3.50	5.50	7.00	10.00

1/4 RUPEE

SILVER, 2.68-2.90 g

KM#	Date	Year	VG	Fine	VF	XF
42	VS1947	(1890)	3.50	6.00	8.50	12.50
	1951	(1893)	3.50	6.00	8.50	12.50
	1954	(1897)	3.50	6.00	8.50	12.50
	Date off flan		2.00	3.00	4.00	7.00

1/2 RUPEE

SILVER, 5.35-5.80 g

KM#	Date	Year	VG	Fine	VF	XF
43	VS1947	(1890)	4.00	7.00	10.00	15.00
	1948	(1891)	4.00	7.00	10.00	15.00
	1949	(1892)	4.00	7.00	10.00	15.00
	1950	(1893)	4.00	7.00	10.00	15.00
	1951	(1894)	4.00	7.00	10.00	15.00
	1952	(1895)	4.00	7.00	10.00	15.00
	1953	(1896)	4.00	7.00	10.00	15.00
	1954	(1897)	4.00	7.00	10.00	15.00
	Date off flan		2.50	3.50	5.00	8.00

RUPEE

SILVER, 10.70-11.60 g

KM#	Date	Year	VG	Fine	VF	XF
44	VS1947	(1890)	5.50	8.50	12.50	18.50
	1948	(1891)	5.50	8.50	12.50	18.50
	1949	(1892)	5.50	8.50	12.50	18.50
	1950	(1893)	5.50	8.50	12.50	18.50
	1951	(1894)	5.50	8.50	12.50	18.50
	1952	(1895)	5.50	8.50	12.50	18.50
	1953	(1896)	5.50	8.50	12.50	18.50

KM#	Date	Year	VG	Fine	VF	XF
44	1954	(1897)	5.50	8.50	12.50	18.50
	1955	(1898)	5.50	8.50	12.50	18.50
	Date off flan		3.00	4.50	6.00	10.00

NAZARANA RUPEE

SILVER, 11.13-11.21 g

45	VS1947	(1890)	37.50	52.50	75.00	110.00

MILLED COINAGE

Third Series

This series was introduced in 1898 to counteract counterfeiting of the second series which had begun to proliferate as a result of a sharp fall in the price of silver. Idle minting machines were reactivated for this purpose, but the series was short-lived.

1/2 ANNA

COPPER, 10.03 g

KM#	Date	Year	Fine	VF	XF	Unc
46	VS1955	(1898)	—	—	Rare	—

RUPEE

SILVER, 11.20 g
Obv: Turban separates legend.

47.1	VS1956	(1899)	90.00	140.00	200.00	300.00

Obv: Continuous legend.

47.2	VS1958	(1901)	140.00	200.00	275.00	400.00

Yeshwant Rao

VS1983-2005/1926-1948AD

Fourth Series

1/4 ANNA

COPPER

49	VS1992	1935	1.00	2.00	3.50	6.00

1/2 ANNA

COPPER

50	VS1992	1935	1.25	2.50	4.00	7.00

MAHESHWAR MINT

In operation from 1767 to 1803.

Distinctive Marks:

Bilva Leaf
Silver

Lingam - Yoni.
Copper and Silver.

NOTE: The following copper coins are illustrative of this variegated series. Many varieties and other dates exist.

1/4 RUPEE

SILVER, 2.68-2.90 g
Rev: Bilva leaf and lingam.

KM#	Date	Year	VG	Fine	VF	XF
56.2	AH1216	—	7.00	12.00	17.50	25.00
	1217	—	7.00	12.00	17.50	25.00

NOTE: Earlier dates (AH1202-1216) exist for this type.

1/2 RUPEE

SILVER, 5.35-5.80 g
Rev: Bilva leaf and lingam.

57.2	AH1216	44	8.50	13.50	20.00	28.50
	1217	—	8.50	13.50	20.00	28.50

NOTE: Earlier dates (AH1202-1211) exist for this type.

RUPEE

SILVER, 10.70-11.60 g
Rev: Bilva leaf and lingam.

58.2	AH1216	44	6.00	10.00	14.00	20.00
	1217	46	6.00	10.00	14.00	20.00

NOTE: Earlier dates (AH1201-1215) exist for this type.

NAZARANA RUPEE

SILVER

59	AH1267	97	—	—	Rare	—

NOTE: Brief revival of this type under Tukoji Rao II for presentation.

MALHARNAGAR MINT

Located in capital, Indore City. In operation regularly from 1768 to 1878.

Mintname: Malharnagar

Distinctive Marks:

Bilva Leaf
Copper

Sunface
Copper and Silver

PAISA

COPPER, 7.15 g
Obv: Katar. Rev: Sunface and regnal year.

KM#	Date	Year	Good	VG	Fine	VF
A61	AH—	37	6.00	10.00	14.00	20.00

1/4 ANNA

COPPER, 9.60-9.70 g

61	AH1244	—	3.00	4.00	5.50	7.50
	12xx	88	3.00	4.00	5.50	7.50

COPPER, 12.20-12.40 g
Obv. leg: Hindi leg. *Pau Anna*

KM#	Date	Year	Good	VG	Fine	VF
62	AH1267	97	5.00	6.50	8.50	11.50

1/2 ANNA

COPPER, 18.70-20.00 g

63	AH1243	1251	3.00	4.00	5.50	7.50
	1244	—	3.00	4.00	5.50	7.50
	12xx	88	3.00	4.00	5.50	7.50

COPPER, 12.00-17.30 g
Obv. leg: *Hindi Adha Anna*

64	AH1261	—	2.50	3.25	4.00	6.00
	1266	—	2.50	3.25	4.00	6.00
	1267	97	2.75	3.50	4.50	6.50
	1268	—	2.50	3.25	4.00	6.00
	1269	99	3.00	3.50	4.50	6.50
	1271	—	2.50	3.25	4.00	6.00
	1285	—	1.75	2.50	3.50	5.50
	1286	113	2.25	3.00	4.00	6.00
	1286 dated both sides					
		—	3.00	3.50	4.00	6.00

NAZARANA 1/2 ANNA

COPPER

65	AH12xx	99	—	—	—	—

1/2 ANNA

COPPER

68	AH1286	—	3.00	4.00	5.00	6.50

In the name of Shah Alam II

AH1173-1221/1759-1806AD

1/16 RUPEE

SILVER

KM#	Date	Year	VG	Fine	VF	XF
70	AH1248	—	—	—	Rare	—
	1266	—	—	—	Rare	—

1/8 RUPEE

SILVER, 1.34-1.45 g

71	AH1227	—	3.50	6.00	8.50	12.50
	1236	—	3.50	6.00	8.50	12.50
	1237	—	3.50	6.00	8.50	12.50
	1248	—	2.50	4.00	6.00	8.50
	(12)55	—	2.50	4.00	6.00	8.50

KM#	Date	Year	VG	Fine	VF	XF
71	1257	—	2.50	4.00	6.00	8.50
	1262	—	2.50	4.00	6.00	8.50
	1268	—	2.50	4.00	6.00	8.50
	1269	—	2.50	4.00	6.00	8.50
	1270	—	2.50	4.00	6.00	8.50
	1271	—	2.50	4.00	6.00	8.50
	1272	—	2.50	4.00	6.00	8.50
	1278	—	2.50	4.00	6.00	8.50
	1279	—	2.50	4.00	6.00	8.50
	1282	—	2.00	4.00	6.00	8.50
	1287	—	2.50	4.00	6.00	8.50
	1289	—	2.50	4.00	6.00	8.50
	1291	—	2.50	4.00	6.00	8.50
	1292	—	2.50	4.00	6.00	8.50
	1293	—	2.50	4.00	6.00	8.50
	1294	—	2.50	4.00	6.00	8.50
	1295	—	2.50	4.00	6.00	8.50

1/4 RUPEE

SILVER, 2.68-2.90 g

KM#	Date	Year	VG	Fine	VF	XF
72	AH1231	—	3.00	5.00	7.00	10.00
	1232	—	3.00	5.00	7.00	10.00
	1233	—	3.00	5.00	7.00	10.00
	1234	—	3.00	5.00	7.00	10.00
	1235	—	3.00	5.00	7.00	10.00
	1236	—	3.00	5.00	7.00	10.00
	1237	—	3.00	5.00	7.00	10.00
	1240	—	3.00	5.00	7.00	10.00
	1241	—	3.00	5.00	7.00	10.00
	1243	—	3.00	5.00	7.00	10.00
	1244	—	3.00	5.00	7.00	10.00
	1246	—	3.00	5.00	7.00	10.00
	1249	—	3.00	5.00	7.00	10.00
	1250	—	3.00	5.00	7.00	10.00
	1251	—	3.00	5.00	7.00	10.00
	1252	—	3.00	5.00	7.00	10.00
	1253	—	3.00	5.00	7.00	10.00
	1255	—	3.00	5.00	7.00	10.00
	1256	—	3.00	5.00	7.00	10.00
	1261	—	3.00	5.00	7.00	10.00
	1263	—	3.00	5.00	7.00	10.00
	1264	—	3.00	5.00	7.00	10.00
	1265	—	3.00	5.00	7.00	10.00
	1266	—	3.00	5.00	7.00	10.00
	1267	—	3.00	5.00	7.00	10.00
	1268	—	3.00	5.00	7.00	10.00
	1269	—	3.00	5.00	7.00	10.00
	1270	—	3.00	5.00	7.00	10.00
	1272	—	3.00	5.00	7.00	10.00
	1273	—	3.00	5.00	7.00	10.00
	1275	—	3.00	5.00	7.00	10.00
	1277	—	3.00	5.00	7.00	10.00
	1278	—	3.00	5.00	7.00	10.00
	1279	—	3.00	5.00	7.00	10.00
	1282	—	3.00	5.00	7.00	10.00
	1285	—	3.00	5.00	7.00	10.00
	1286	—	3.00	5.00	7.00	10.00
	1288	—	3.00	5.00	7.00	10.00
	1289	—	3.00	5.00	7.00	10.00
	1290	—	3.00	5.00	7.00	10.00
	1291	—	3.00	5.00	7.00	10.00
	1292	—	3.00	5.00	7.00	10.00
	1293	—	3.00	5.00	7.00	10.00
	1294	—	3.00	5.00	7.00	10.00
	1295	—	3.00	5.00	7.00	10.00

NOTE: Earlier dates exist for this type.

25mm
Broad, thin planchet

KM#	Date	Year	VG	Fine	VF	XF
72a	AH1280	110	17.50	25.00	35.00	50.00

1/2 RUPEE

SILVER, 5.35-5.80 g

KM#	Date	Year	VG	Fine	VF	XF
73	AH1227	—	4.00	6.00	9.00	13.50
	1228	—	4.00	6.00	9.00	13.50
	1230	—	4.00	6.00	9.00	13.50
	1231	—	4.00	6.00	9.00	13.50
	1233	—	4.00	6.00	9.00	13.50
	1234	6x	4.00	6.00	9.00	13.50
	1237	—	4.00	6.00	9.00	13.50
	1238	—	4.00	6.00	9.00	13.50
	1240	—	4.00	6.00	9.00	13.50
	1242	—	4.00	6.00	9.00	13.50
	1244	72	4.00	6.00	9.00	13.50
	1245	—	4.00	6.00	9.00	13.50
	1246	—	4.00	6.00	9.00	13.50
	1247	—	4.00	6.00	9.00	13.50
	1248	—	4.00	6.00	9.00	13.50
	1250	—	4.00	6.00	9.00	13.50
	1251	—	4.00	6.00	9.00	13.50
	1253	—	4.00	6.00	9.00	13.50
	1255	—	4.00	6.00	9.00	13.50
	1258	—	4.00	6.00	9.00	13.50
	1260	—	4.00	6.00	9.00	13.50
	1262	—	4.00	6.00	9.00	13.50
	1263	—	4.00	6.00	9.00	13.50

KM#	Date	Year	VG	Fine	VF	XF
73	1264	—	4.00	6.00	9.00	13.50
	1265	—	4.00	6.00	9.00	13.50
	1266	—	4.00	6.00	9.00	13.50
	1267	—	4.00	6.00	9.00	13.50
	1268	—	4.00	6.00	9.00	13.50
	1270	—	4.00	6.00	9.00	13.50
	1272	—	4.00	6.00	9.00	13.50
	1273	—	4.00	6.00	9.00	13.50
	1274	—	4.00	6.00	9.00	13.50
	1275	—	4.00	6.00	9.00	13.50
	1276	—	4.00	6.00	9.00	13.50
	1277	—	4.00	6.00	9.00	13.50
	1278	—	4.00	6.00	9.00	13.50
	1279	—	4.00	6.00	9.00	13.50
	1280	—	4.00	6.00	9.00	13.50
	1281	—	4.00	6.00	9.00	13.50
	1283	—	4.00	6.00	9.00	13.50
	1286	—	4.00	6.00	9.00	13.50
	1288	—	4.00	6.00	9.00	13.50
	1289	—	4.00	6.00	9.00	13.50
	1291	—	4.00	6.00	9.00	13.50
	1292	—	4.00	6.00	9.00	13.50
	1293	—	4.00	6.00	9.00	13.50
	1294	120	4.00	6.00	9.00	13.50
	1285	—	4.00	6.00	9.00	13.50
	1295	—	4.00	6.00	9.00	13.50
	1296	—	4.00	6.00	9.00	13.50
	—	121	4.00	6.00	9.00	13.50

NAZARANA 1/2 RUPEE

SILVER, 5.35-5.80 g
Broad, thin planchet

KM#	Date	Year	VG	Fine	VF	XF
74	AH1236	69	25.00	37.50	50.00	70.00
	1280	110	25.00	37.50	50.00	70.00

RUPEE

SILVER, 10.70-11.60 g

KM#	Date	Year	VG	Fine	VF	XF
76	AH1216	—	5.00	7.00	10.00	15.00
	1217	44	5.00	7.00	10.00	15.00
	1224	—	5.00	7.00	10.00	15.00
	1225	59	5.00	7.00	10.00	15.00
	1226	60	5.00	7.00	10.00	15.00
	1228	62	5.00	7.00	10.00	15.00
	1230	61	5.00	7.00	10.00	15.00
	1230	62	5.00	7.00	10.00	15.00
	1231	63	5.00	7.00	10.00	15.00
	1231	64	5.00	7.00	10.00	15.00
	1232	65	5.00	7.00	10.00	15.00
	1233	66	5.00	7.00	10.00	15.00
	1234	67	5.00	7.00	10.00	15.00
	1235	68	5.00	7.00	10.00	15.00
	1237	67	5.00	7.00	10.00	15.00
	1237	70	5.00	7.00	10.00	15.00
	1238	70	5.00	7.00	10.00	15.00
	1240	—	5.00	7.00	10.00	15.00
	1241	—	5.00	7.00	10.00	15.00
	1242	75	5.00	7.00	10.00	15.00
	1243	76	5.00	7.00	10.00	15.00
	1244	72	5.00	7.00	10.00	15.00
	(12)44	74	5.00	7.00	10.00	15.00
	1246	76	5.00	7.00	10.00	15.00
	1248	77	5.00	7.00	10.00	15.00
	1249	—	5.00	7.00	10.00	15.00
	1251	81	5.00	7.00	10.00	15.00
	1250	79	5.00	7.00	10.00	15.00
	1255	85	5.00	7.00	10.00	15.00
	1257	87	5.00	7.00	10.00	15.00
	1258	88	5.00	7.00	10.00	15.00
	1260	9x	5.00	7.00	10.00	15.00
	1262	—	5.00	7.00	10.00	15.00
	1263	—	5.00	7.00	10.00	15.00
	1264	94	5.00	7.00	10.00	15.00
	1265	95	5.00	7.00	10.00	15.00
	1266	9x	5.00	7.00	10.00	15.00
	1266	96	5.00	7.00	10.00	15.00
	1267	97	5.00	7.00	10.00	15.00
	1268	98	5.00	7.00	10.00	15.00
	1269	9x	5.00	7.00	10.00	15.00
	1270	—	5.00	7.00	10.00	15.00
	1272	102	5.00	7.00	10.00	15.00
	1273	—	5.00	7.00	10.00	15.00
	1275	105	5.00	7.00	10.00	15.00
	1276	105	5.00	7.00	10.00	15.00
	1277	—	5.00	7.00	10.00	15.00
	1278	—	5.00	7.00	10.00	15.00
	1279	—	5.00	7.00	10.00	15.00
	1280	—	5.00	7.00	10.00	15.00

KM#	Date	Year	VG	Fine	VF	XF
76	1282	111	5.00	7.00	10.00	15.00
	1285	112	5.00	7.00	10.00	15.00
	1286	113	5.00	7.00	10.00	15.00
	1288	115	5.00	7.00	10.00	15.00
	1289	115	5.00	7.00	10.00	15.00
	1292	118	5.00	7.00	10.00	15.00
	1292	120	5.00	7.00	10.00	15.00
	1293	111	5.00	7.00	10.00	15.00
	1293	119	5.00	7.00	10.00	15.00
	1294	120	5.00	7.00	10.00	15.00
	1295	121	5.00	7.00	10.00	15.00
	1295	122	5.00	7.00	10.00	15.00
	1296	122	5.00	7.00	10.00	15.00

NOTE: Earlier dates(AH1180-1215) exist for this type.

NAZARANA RUPEE

SILVER, 10.70-11.60 g

KM#	Date	Year	VG	Fine	VF	XF
77	AH1225	59	—	—	Rare	—
	1280	110	—	—	Rare	—

UNCERTAIN MINTS

NOTE: 1/2 Paisa and 1 Paisa coins previously listedhere now are listed in Banswara-IPS.

1/2 ANNA

Symbol Series

COPPER
Obv: Mace. Rev: Branch w/3 leaves.

KM#	Date	Year	Good	VG	Fine	VF
91	AH1228	—	3.50	4.50	5.50	7.50

Obv: Katar. Rev: Axe.

KM#	Date	Year	Good	VG	Fine	VF
92	AH1230	—	3.50	4.50	5.50	7.50

Rev: Jhar and mace.

KM#	Date	Year	Good	VG	Fine	VF
93	AH1230	—	3.50	4.50	5.50	7.50

Obv: Katar. Rev: Broad axe.

KM#	Date	Year	Good	VG	Fine	VF
94	AH1230	—	3.50	4.50	5.50	7.50

Obv: Broad axe. Rev: Dagger.

KM#	Date	Year	Good	VG	Fine	VF
95	AH1233	66	3.50	4.50	5.50	7.50
	1241	—	3.50	4.50	5.50	7.50

Obv: Pinwheel. Rev: Geometric design.

KM#	Date	Year	Good	VG	Fine	VF
96	ND	—	3.50	4.50	5.50	7.50

Obv: Trisul and double pennant flags.
Rev: Broad axe.

97	AH1220	—	3.50	4.50	5.50	7.50

NOTE: These coins were struck AH1202-1244 with many minor varieties of symbols of which the above are only a sample.

JAFARABAD

Jafarabad was a tiny state of some twelve villages and fifty three square miles of territory on the southern coast of Kathiawar. The state was founded in the mideighteenth century by Sidi Hilol of the Janjira ruling house. Jafarabad was subject to the Nawab of Janjira until 1924, after which oversight was exercised by the British Agent of the Governor-General in the Western India States Agency. The coinage is anonymous and crude, and is attributed to Jaffarabad State primarily on the basis of provenance.

Anonymous Coinage

FIRST SERIES

Obv: Persian script.

3/4 KORI

BILLON, 3.40 g

KM#	Date	Year	VG	Fine	VF	XF
1	ND	—	5.50	9.00	13.50	20.00

KORI

BILLON, 4.70 g

2	ND	—	5.50	9.00	13.50	20.00

1-1/2 KORI

BILLON, 7.00 g

3	ND	—	5.50	9.00	13.50	20.00

NOTE: The attribution of these coins is very tentative. The denominations are only suggested by the average weights.

SECOND SERIES

Obv: Tree between two flags.

1/2 KORI

BILLON, 2.36-3.18 g

5	ND	—	5.00	7.00	10.00	15.00

KORI

BILLON, 3.46-3.82 g

6	ND	—	5.00	7.00	10.00	15.00

JAIPUR

Tradition has it that the region of Jaipur, located in northwest India, once belonged to an ancient Kachwaha Rajput dynasty which claimed descent from Kush, one of the sons of Rama, King of Ayodhya. But the Princely State of Jaipur originated in the twelfth century. Comparatively small in size, the State remained largely unnoticed until after the sixteenth century when the Jaipur royal house became famous for its military skills and thereafter supplied the Mughals with some of their more distinguished generals. The city of Jaipur was founded about 1728 by Maharaja Jai Singh II who was also well known for his knowledge of mathematics and astronomy. The late eighteenth and early nineteenth centuries were difficult times for Jaipur. They were marked by internal rivalry, exacerbated by Maratha or Pindari incursions. In 1818 this culminated with a treaty whereby Jaipur came under British protection and oversight.

RULERS

Pratap Singh
AH1192-1218/1778-1803AD
Jagat Singh II
AH1218-1234/1803-1818AD
Mohan Singh
AH1234-1235/1818-1819AD
Jai Singh III
AH1235-1251/1819-1835AD
Ram Singh
AH1251-1298/1835-1880AD
Madho Singh II, 1880-1922AD
Man Singh II, 1922-1949AD

All coins struck prior to AH1274/1857AD are in the name of the Mughal emperor. The corresponding AH date is listed in ( ) with each regnal year. Some overlapping of AH dates with regnal years will be found. Partial dates and recorded full dates are represented by partial ( ) or without ( ).

Beginning in 1857AD, coins were struck jointly in the names and corresponding AD dates of the British sovereign and the names and regnal years of the Maharajas of Jaipur.

The coins ordinarily bear both AH date before 1857 or the AD date after 1857 as well as the regnal year, but as it is found only at the extreme right of the obverse die, it almost never is visible on the regular coinage but generally legible on the Nazarana coins which were struck utilizing the entire dies.

The listing of regnal years is very incomplete and many more years will turn up. In general, unlisted years are usually worth no more than years listed.

MINTNAMES

Coins were struck at two mints, which bear the following characteristic marks on the reverse:

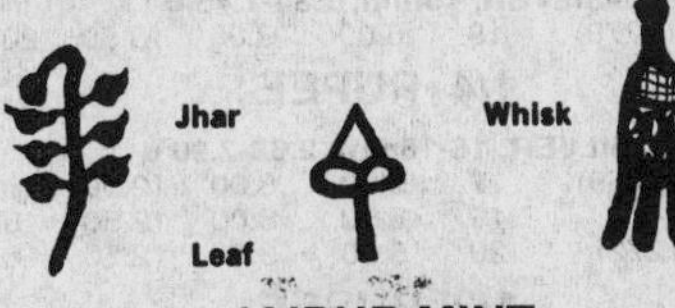

Sawai Jaipur

Sawai Madhopur

NOTE: *Sawai* is merely an honorific title accorded each of the two cities.

Mint marks:

JAIPUR MINT
Mughal Issues

In the name of Shah Alam II
AH1173-1221/1759-1806AD

PAISA

COPPER
Rev: Large Jhar.

C#	Date	Year	Good	VG	Fine	VF
35	AH—	44	2.50	4.50	6.50	10.00
	—	45	2.50	4.50	6.50	10.00

NOTE: Earlier dates (Year 35-41) exist for this type.

NAZARANA PAISA

COPPER
Rev: Large Jhar.

35a	AH—	45	15.00	27.50	40.00	60.00

NOTE: Earlier dates (Year 37-39) exist for this type.

NAZARANA 1/4 RUPEE

SILVER, 2.67-2.90 g

C#	Date	Year	VG	Fine	VF	XF
E36	AH(1216)	44	—	—	Rare	—

RUPEE

SILVER, 10.70-11.60 g
Mint mark: Jhar

C#	Date	Year	VG	Fine	VF	XF
36	AH—	44	5.50	8.00	12.50	18.50
	—	45	5.50	8.00	12.50	18.50
	(1218)	46	5.50	8.00	12.50	18.50
	(1219)	47	5.50	8.00	12.50	18.50

NOTE: Earlier dates (AH1197-1215) exist for this type.

SILVER, 10.70-11.60 g
Large flan.

36a	AH1217	43	60.00	100.00	140.00	200.00

In the name of Muhammad Akbar II
AH1221-1253/1806-1837AD

NAZARANA PAISA

COPPER
Rev: Whisk.

C#	Date	Year	Good	VG	Fine	VF
46	AH—	3	20.00	32.50	50.00	75.00
	—	8	20.00	32.50	50.00	75.00
	—	11	20.00	32.50	50.00	75.00

PAISA

COPPER, 18-20mm
Similar to Nazarana Paisa, C#47a.

47	AH—	12	2.00	3.25	5.00	7.50
	—	13	2.00	3.25	5.00	7.50
	—	17	2.00	3.25	5.00	7.50
	—	22	2.00	3.25	5.00	7.50
	—	26	2.00	3.25	5.00	7.50
	—	27	2.00	3.25	5.00	7.50
	—	29	2.00	3.25	5.00	7.50
	—	35	2.00	3.25	5.00	7.50

NAZARANA PAISA

COPPER
Rev: Jhar.

47a	AH—	4	12.50	22.00	32.50	50.00
	—	9	12.50	22.00	32.50	50.00
	—	10	12.50	22.00	32.50	50.00
	—	11	12.50	22.00	32.50	50.00
	—	15	12.50	22.00	32.50	50.00
	—	16	12.50	22.00	32.50	50.00
	—	22	12.50	22.00	32.50	50.00
	—	28	12.50	22.00	32.50	50.00

1/8 RUPEE

SILVER, 17-18mm, 1.34-1.45 g

C#	Date	Year	VG	Fine	VF	XF
52	AH(1242)	22	5.50	8.00	12.50	18.50

1/4 RUPEE

SILVER, 18-19mm, 2.68-2.90 g

53	AH(1237)	17	6.00	9.00	13.50	20.00
	—	20	6.00	9.00	13.50	20.00
	—	24	6.00	9.00	13.50	20.00
	(1248)	28	6.00	9.00	13.50	20.00

1/2 RUPEE

SILVER, 18-20mm, 5.35-5.80 g

54	AH(1236)	16	6.50	10.00	15.00	22.50
	—	23	6.50	10.00	15.00	22.50
	(1251)	31	6.50	10.00	15.00	22.50

NAZARANA 1/2 RUPEE

SILVER, 5.35-5.70 g

54a	AH—	20	—	—	—	—

RUPEE

SILVER, 10.70-11.60 g

C#	Date	Year	VG	Fine	VF	XF
55	AH1221	1	6.00	9.00	13.50	20.00
	1222	2	6.00	9.00	13.50	20.00
	122(3)	3	6.00	9.00	13.50	20.00
	1226	4	6.00	9.00	13.50	20.00
	1228	6	6.00	9.00	13.50	20.00
	1229	9	6.00	9.00	13.50	20.00
	1230	10	6.00	9.00	13.50	20.00
	1233	11	6.00	9.00	13.50	20.00
	123x	12	6.00	9.00	13.50	20.00
	1233	13	6.00	9.00	13.50	20.00
	1234	13	6.00	9.00	13.50	20.00
	1234	14	6.00	9.00	13.50	20.00
	1235	15	6.00	9.00	13.50	20.00
	1238	18	6.00	9.00	13.50	20.00
	1240	20	6.00	9.00	13.50	20.00
	1243	22	6.00	9.00	13.50	20.00
	—	24	6.00	9.00	13.50	20.00
	1246	25	6.00	9.00	13.50	20.00
	124x	26	6.00	9.00	13.50	20.00
	1249	27	6.00	9.00	13.50	20.00
	1250	30	6.00	9.00	13.50	20.00
	125x	31	6.00	9.00	13.50	20.00

Square

C#	Date	Year	VG	Fine	VF	XF
55b	AH123x	10	—	—	Rare	—

NAZARANA RUPEE

SILVER, 10.70-11.60 g

C#	Date	Year	VG	Fine	VF	XF
55a	AH1221	1	30.00	50.00	70.00	100.00
	1230	9	30.00	50.00	70.00	100.00
	1232	11	30.00	50.00	70.00	100.00
	1237	16	30.00	50.00	70.00	100.00
	1240	20	30.00	50.00	70.00	100.00
	1240	21	30.00	50.00	70.00	100.00
	1242	22	30.00	50.00	70.00	100.00
	1243	23	30.00	50.00	70.00	100.00
	1246	25	30.00	50.00	70.00	100.00
	1248	27	30.00	50.00	70.00	100.00
	1249	27	30.00	50.00	70.00	100.00
	1249	29	30.00	50.00	70.00	100.00
	1250	28	30.00	50.00	70.00	100.00
	1251	29	30.00	50.00	70.00	100.00
	125x	30	30.00	50.00	70.00	100.00

1/2 MOHUR

GOLD, 5.35-5.80 g

C#	Date	Year	VG	Fine	VF	XF
61	AH124x	25	100.00	150.00	225.00	325.00

MOHUR

GOLD, 10.70-11.60 g

C#	Date	Year	VG	Fine	VF	XF
62	AH122(1)	1	BV	160.00	225.00	300.00
	(1227)	7	BV	160.00	225.00	300.00
	(1228)	8	BV	160.00	225.00	300.00
	(1229)	9	BV	160.00	225.00	300.00
	(1231)	11	BV	160.00	225.00	300.00
	(1232)	12	BV	160.00	225.00	300.00
	(1236)	16	BV	160.00	225.00	300.00
	(1239)	19	BV	160.00	225.00	300.00
	12(44)	24	BV	160.00	225.00	300.00
	(1249)	29	BV	160.00	225.00	300.00
	(1250)	30	BV	160.00	225.00	300.00

In the name of Bahadur Shah II

AH1253-1274/1837-1858AD

PAISA

COPPER

C#	Date	Year	Good	VG	Fine	VF
85	AH—	13	3.00	5.00	8.00	12.50

NAZARANA PAISA

COPPER

C#	Date	Year	Good	VG	Fine	VF
85a	AH—	1	16.00	26.50	40.00	60.00
	—	2	16.00	26.50	40.00	60.00
	—	6	16.00	26.50	40.00	60.00
	—	10	16.00	26.50	40.00	60.00
	—	11	16.00	26.50	40.00	60.00
	—	12	16.00	26.50	40.00	60.00
	—	13	16.00	26.50	40.00	60.00
	—	14	16.00	26.50	40.00	60.00
	—	17	16.00	26.50	40.00	60.00

1/16 RUPEE

SILVER, 0.67-0.72 g

C#	Date	Year	VG	Fine	VF	XF
89	AH(1259)	7	6.50	10.00	15.00	22.50
	(1261)	9	6.50	10.00	15.00	22.50
	(1270)	18	6.50	10.00	15.00	22.50

1/8 RUPEE

SILVER, 15mm, 1.34-1.45 g

C#	Date	Year	VG	Fine	VF	XF
90	AH(1270)	18	6.00	9.00	13.50	20.00

1/4 RUPEE

SILVER, 16-18mm, 2.68-2.90 g

C#	Date	Year	VG	Fine	VF	XF
91	AH(1259)	7	5.50	8.00	12.50	18.50
	—	19	5.50	8.00	12.50	18.50
	(1272)	20	5.50	8.00	12.50	18.50

1/2 RUPEE

SILVER, 18-19mm, 5.35-5.80 g

C#	Date	Year	VG	Fine	VF	XF
92	AH(1257)	5	5.50	8.00	12.50	18.50
	—	11	5.50	8.00	12.50	18.50
	(1270)	18	5.50	8.00	12.50	18.50

RUPEE

SILVER, 10.70-11.60 g

C#	Date	Year	VG	Fine	VF	XF
93	AH1253	1	5.00	7.00	10.00	15.00
	1256	3	5.00	7.00	10.00	15.00
	1257	4	5.00	7.00	10.00	15.00
	1258	5	5.00	7.00	10.00	15.00
	1261	8	5.00	7.00	10.00	15.00
	1262	9	5.00	7.00	10.00	15.00
	1263	10	5.00	7.00	10.00	15.00
	—	11	5.00	7.00	10.00	15.00
	1265	12	5.00	7.00	10.00	15.00
	1268	14	5.00	7.00	10.00	15.00
	—	15	5.00	7.00	10.00	15.00
	1270	17	5.00	7.00	10.00	15.00
	1271	17	5.00	7.00	10.00	15.00
	—	19	5.00	7.00	10.00	15.00
	1273	20	5.00	7.00	10.00	15.00

NAZARANA RUPEE

SILVER, 32-35mm, 10.70-11.60 g

C#	Date	Year	VG	Fine	VF	XF
93a	AH1256	3	33.50	47.50	65.00	90.00
	1258	4	33.50	47.50	65.00	90.00
	1258	5	33.50	47.50	65.00	90.00
	1262	9	33.50	47.50	65.00	90.00
	1264	11	33.50	47.50	65.00	90.00
	1268	8	(error-mule)			
			33.50	47.50	65.00	90.00
	1266	13	33.50	47.50	65.00	90.00
	1271	19	33.50	47.50	65.00	90.00
	1273	20	33.50	47.50	65.00	90.00

1/4 MOHUR

GOLD, 17mm, 2.68-2.85 g

C#	Date	Year	VG	Fine	VF	XF
98	AH(1264)	12	80.00	125.00	150.00	225.00

1/2 MOHUR

GOLD, 18mm, 5.35-5.70 g

C#	Date	Year	VG	Fine	VF	XF
99	AH(1264)	12	100.00	150.00	200.00	275.00

MOHUR

GOLD, 10.70-11.40 g

C#	Date	Year	VG	Fine	VF	XF
100	AH1253	1	150.00	200.00	250.00	325.00
	(1257)	5	150.00	200.00	250.00	325.00
	12(59)	7	150.00	200.00	250.00	325.00
	1262	9	150.00	200.00	250.00	325.00
	(1262)	10	150.00	200.00	250.00	325.00
	(1263)	11	150.00	200.00	250.00	325.00
	(1264)	12	150.00	200.00	250.00	325.00
	(1265)	13	150.00	200.00	250.00	325.00
	(1266)	14	150.00	200.00	250.00	325.00
	1(267)	15	150.00	200.00	250.00	325.00
	(1271)	19	150.00	200.00	250.00	325.00
	1272	18	150.00	200.00	250.00	325.00
	(1272)	20	150.00	200.00	250.00	325.00

Regal Issues

In the names of Queen Victoria

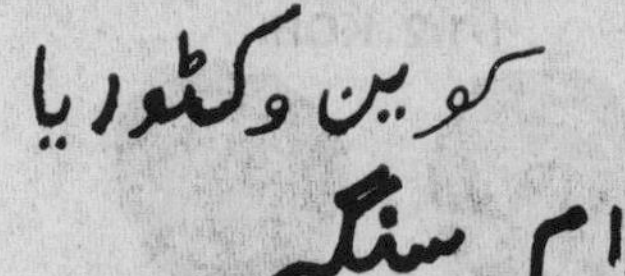

and Ram Singh

Years 22-45/1857-1880AD

NEW PAISA

COPPER

Y#	Date	Year	Good	VG	Fine	VF
1	(1871)	36	1.00	2.00	2.75	5.00
	(1872)	37	1.00	2.00	2.75	5.00
	(1873)	38	1.00	2.00	2.75	5.00
	(1874)	39	1.00	2.00	2.75	5.00
	(1875)	40	1.00	2.00	2.75	5.00
	(1876)	41	1.00	2.00	2.75	5.00
	(1877)	42	1.00	2.00	2.75	5.00
	(1880)	45	1.25	2.25	3.25	6.00

NOTE: Years 36 and 37 are struck on broader flans.

NAZARANA OLD PAISA

COPPER

Y#	Date	Year	Good	VG	Fine	VF
1a	1858	23	25.00	45.00	65.00	100.00
	1862	27	25.00	45.00	65.00	100.00

NAZARANA NEW PAISA

COPPER, 28mm

Y#	Date	Year	Good	VG	Fine	VF
1b	1862	27	12.00	18.50	30.00	45.00
	1864	29	12.00	18.50	30.00	45.00
	1865	30	12.00	18.50	30.00	45.00

Y#	Date	Year	Good	VG	Fine	VF
1b	1872	37	12.00	18.50	30.00	45.00
	1873	38	12.00	18.50	30.00	45.00
	1875	40	12.00	18.50	30.00	45.00
	1876	41	12.00	18.50	30.00	45.00
	1879	44	12.00	18.50	30.00	45.00
	1880	45	12.00	18.50	30.00	45.00

1/8 RUPEE

SILVER, 14mm, 1.34-1.45 g

Y#	Date	Year	VG	Fine	VF	XF
3	(1857)	22	3.50	5.00	7.50	12.00
	(1862)	27	3.50	5.00	7.50	12.00
	(1877)	42	3.50	5.00	7.50	12.00

1/4 RUPEE

SILVER, 2.68-2.90 g

Y#	Date	Year	VG	Fine	VF	XF
4	(1861)	26	4.00	6.00	9.00	13.50
	(1862)	27	4.00	6.00	9.00	13.50
	(1863)	28	4.00	6.00	9.00	13.50
	(1867)	32	4.00	6.00	9.00	13.50
	(1868)	33	4.00	6.00	9.00	13.50
	(1876)	41	4.00	6.00	9.00	13.50
	(1878)	43	4.00	6.00	9.00	13.50
	(1879)	44	4.00	6.00	9.00	13.50

NAZARANA 1/4 RUPEE

SILVER

Y#	Date	Year	VG	Fine	VF	XF
4a	(1879)	44	17.50	25.00	35.00	50.00

1/2 RUPEE

SILVER, 18-21mm, 5.35-5.80 g

Y#	Date	Year	VG	Fine	VF	XF
5	(1857)	22	5.00	7.00	10.00	15.00
	(1862)	27	5.00	7.00	10.00	15.00
	(1868)	33	5.00	7.00	10.00	15.00
	(1869)	35	5.00	7.00	10.00	15.00
	(1871)	36	5.00	7.00	10.00	15.00
	—	42	5.00	7.00	10.00	15.00
	(1879)	44	5.00	7.00	10.00	15.00
	(1880)	45	5.00	7.00	10.00	15.00

NAZARANA 1/2 RUPEE

SILVER

Y#	Date	Year	VG	Fine	VF	XF
5a	(1865)	30	17.50	25.00	35.00	50.00

RUPEE

SILVER, 10.70-11.60 g

Y#	Date	Year	VG	Fine	VF	XF
6	(1858)	23	5.50	8.00	12.00	18.50
	(1860)	25	5.50	8.00	12.00	18.50
	(1862)	27	5.50	8.00	12.00	18.50
	(1864)	29	5.50	8.00	12.00	18.50
	(1865)	30	5.50	8.00	12.00	18.50
	1866	31	5.50	8.00	12.00	18.50
	(1867)	32	5.50	8.00	12.00	18.50
	(1868)	33	5.50	8.00	12.00	18.50
	1869	34	5.50	8.00	12.00	18.50
	(1870)	35	5.50	8.00	12.00	18.50
	(1871)	36	5.50	8.00	12.00	18.50
	(1873)	38	5.50	8.00	12.00	18.50
	(1875)	40	5.50	8.00	12.00	18.50
	(1876)	41	5.50	8.00	12.00	18.50
	(1877)	42	5.50	8.00	12.00	18.50
	(1878)	43	5.50	8.00	12.00	18.50
	(1879)	44	5.50	8.00	12.00	18.50
	(1880)	45	5.50	8.00	12.00	18.50

NAZARANA RUPEE

SILVER, 10.70-11.60 g

Y#	Date	Year	VG	Fine	VF	XF
6a	1858	23	27.00	40.00	52.50	75.00
	1859	24	27.00	40.00	52.50	75.00
	1861	26	27.00	40.00	52.50	75.00
	1864	29	27.00	40.00	52.50	75.00
	1865	30	27.00	40.00	52.50	75.00
	1866	31	27.00	40.00	52.50	75.00
	1867	32	27.00	40.00	52.50	75.00
	1870	35	27.00	40.00	52.50	75.00
	1871	36	27.00	40.00	52.50	75.00
	1875	40	27.00	40.00	52.50	75.00

MOHUR

GOLD, 10.70-11.40 g

Y#	Date	Year	VG	Fine	VF	XF
7	(1856)	21	135.00	155.00	185.00	225.00
	(1860)	23	135.00	155.00	185.00	225.00
	(1860)	25	135.00	155.00	185.00	225.00
	18(60)	25	135.00	155.00	185.00	225.00
	1861	26	135.00	155.00	185.00	225.00
	(1864)	29	135.00	155.00	185.00	225.00
	—	31	135.00	155.00	185.00	225.00
	—	35	135.00	155.00	185.00	225.00
	(1871)	36	135.00	155.00	185.00	225.00
	(1872)	37	135.00	155.00	185.00	225.00

In the names of Queen Victoria

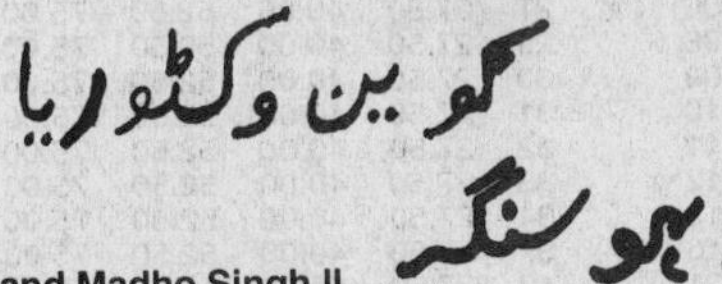

and Madho Singh II

Years 1-43/1880-1922AD

NOTE: Queen Victoria's name was retained on Madho Singh II's coinage until 1922AD. No coins were struck with Edward VII's name by Madho Singh II.

PAISA

COPPER, 6.15-6.30 g

Y#	Date	Year	Good	VG	Fine	VF
8	(1882)	3	.60	1.00	2.00	4.00
	(1883)	4	.60	1.00	2.00	4.00
	(1884)	5	.60	1.00	2.00	4.00
	(1887)	8	.60	1.00	2.00	4.00
	(1898)	19	.30	.65	1.35	2.00
	(1899)	20	.30	.65	1.35	2.00
	(1900)	21	.30	.65	1.35	2.00
	(1901)	22	.30	.65	1.35	2.00
	(1902)	23	.30	.65	1.35	2.00
	(1903)	24	.30	.65	1.35	2.00
	(1904)	25	.30	.65	1.35	2.00
	(1906)	27	.30	.65	1.35	2.00
	(1907)	28	.30	.65	1.35	2.00
	(1908)	29	.30	.65	1.35	2.00
	(1916)	37	.30	.65	1.35	2.00
	(1917)	38	.30	.65	1.35	2.00
	(1918)	39	.30	.65	1.35	2.00
	(1920)	41	.30	.65	1.35	2.00

COPPER, 13.50-16.50 g

Y#	Date	Year	Good	VG	Fine	VF
8b	1897	18	12.50	22.50	32.50	50.00

NAZARANA NEW PAISA

COPPER

Y#	Date	Year	VG	Fine	VF	XF
8a	1880	1	12.50	17.50	25.00	40.00
	1895	16	12.50	17.50	25.00	40.00
	1897	17	12.50	17.50	25.00	40.00
	1897	18	12.50	17.50	25.00	40.00
	1899	20	12.50	17.50	25.00	40.00
	1900	21	12.50	17.50	25.00	40.00
	1901	22	12.50	17.50	25.00	40.00
	1902	23	12.50	17.50	25.00	40.00
	1903	24	12.50	17.50	25.00	40.00
	1904	25	12.50	17.50	25.00	40.00
	1905	26	12.50	17.50	25.00	40.00
	1906	27	12.50	17.50	25.00	40.00
	1907	28	12.50	17.50	25.00	40.00
	1908	29	12.50	17.50	25.00	40.00
	1909	30	12.50	17.50	25.00	40.00
	1910	31	12.50	17.50	25.00	40.00
	1911	32	12.50	17.50	25.00	40.00
	1912	33	12.50	17.50	25.00	40.00
	1913	34	12.50	17.50	25.00	40.00
	1914	35	12.50	17.50	25.00	40.00
	1915	36	12.50	17.50	25.00	40.00
	1916	37	12.50	17.50	25.00	40.00
	1917	38	12.50	17.50	25.00	40.00

NOTE: Well-centered issues on thin planchets may be restrikes.

1/16 RUPEE

SILVER, 10mm, 0.67-0.72 g

Y#	Date	Year	VG	Fine	VF	XF
9	(1881)	2	5.00	7.00	10.00	15.00
	(1882)	3	5.00	7.00	10.00	15.00
	(1889)	10	5.00	7.00	10.00	15.00
	(1912)	33	5.00	7.00	10.00	15.00

1/8 RUPEE

SILVER, 1.34-1.45 g

Y#	Date	Year	VG	Fine	VF	XF
10	(1883)	4	2.50	3.50	5.00	8.00
	(1885)	6	2.50	3.50	5.00	8.00
	(1890)	11	2.50	3.50	5.00	8.00
	(1891)	12	2.50	3.50	5.00	8.00
	(1897)	18	2.50	3.50	5.00	8.00
	(1898)	19	2.50	3.50	5.00	8.00
	(1900)	21	2.50	3.50	5.00	8.00
	(1901)	22	2.50	3.50	5.00	8.00
	(1902)	23	2.50	3.50	5.00	8.00
	(1905)	26	2.50	3.50	5.00	8.00
	(1906)	27	2.50	3.50	5.00	8.00
	(1907)	28	2.50	3.50	5.00	8.00
	(1908)	29	2.50	3.50	5.00	8.00
	(1920)	41	2.50	3.50	5.00	8.00
	(1921)	42	2.50	3.50	5.00	8.00

1/4 RUPEE

SILVER, 2.68-2.90 g

Y#	Date	Year	VG	Fine	VF	XF
11	(1880)	1	3.00	4.50	6.50	10.00
	(1881)	2	3.00	4.50	6.50	10.00
	(1883)	4	3.00	4.50	6.50	10.00
	(1885)	6	3.00	4.50	6.50	10.00
	(1886)	7	3.00	4.50	6.50	10.00
	(1887)	8	3.00	4.50	6.50	10.00
	(1889)	10	3.00	4.50	6.50	10.00
	(1890)	11	3.00	4.50	6.50	10.00
	(1891)	12	3.00	4.50	6.50	10.00
	(1893)	14	3.00	4.50	6.50	10.00
	(1894)	15	3.00	4.50	6.50	10.00
	(1895)	16	3.00	4.50	6.50	10.00
	(1896)	17	3.00	4.50	6.50	10.00
	(1897)	18	3.00	4.50	6.50	10.00
	(1898)	19	3.00	4.50	6.50	10.00
	(1899)	20	3.00	4.50	6.50	10.00
	1900	21	3.00	4.50	6.50	10.00
	(1901)	22	3.00	4.50	6.50	10.00
	(1902)	23	3.00	4.50	6.50	10.00
	(1903)	24	3.00	4.50	6.50	10.00
	(1905)	26	3.00	4.50	6.50	10.00
	(1906)	27	3.00	4.50	6.50	10.00
	(1907)	28	3.00	4.50	6.50	10.00
	(1908)	29	3.00	4.50	6.50	10.00
	(1909)	30	3.00	4.50	6.50	10.00
	(1913)	34	3.00	4.50	6.50	10.00
	(1916)	37	3.00	4.50	6.50	10.00
	(1917)	38	3.00	4.50	6.50	10.00
	(1921)	42	3.00	4.50	6.50	10.00

1/2 RUPEE

SILVER, 5.35-5.80 g

Y#	Date	Year	VG	Fine	VF	XF
12	(1880)	1	3.50	5.00	7.50	12.00
	(1882)	3	3.50	5.00	7.50	12.00
	(1883)	4	3.50	5.00	7.50	12.00
	(1884)	5	3.50	5.00	7.50	12.00
	(1886)	7	3.50	5.00	7.50	12.00
	(1887)	8	3.50	5.00	7.50	12.00
	(1888)	9	3.50	5.00	7.50	12.00
	(1889)	10	3.50	5.00	7.50	12.00
	(1891)	12	3.50	5.00	7.50	12.00
	(1893)	14	3.50	5.00	7.50	12.00
	(1894)	15	3.50	5.00	7.50	12.00
	(1896)	17	3.50	5.00	7.50	12.00
	(1897)	18	3.50	5.00	7.50	12.00
	(1898)	19	3.50	5.00	7.50	12.00
	(1899)	20	3.50	5.00	7.50	12.00
	190(0)	21	3.50	5.00	7.50	12.00
	1901	22	3.50	5.00	7.50	12.00
	(1902)	23	3.50	5.00	7.50	12.00
	(1905)	26	3.50	5.00	7.50	12.00
	(1908)	29	3.50	5.00	7.50	12.00
	(1909)	30	3.50	5.00	7.50	12.00
	(1916)	37	3.50	5.00	7.50	12.00

RUPEE

SILVER, 10.70-11.60 g

Y#	Date	Year	VG	Fine	VF	XF
13	(1880)	1	4.00	6.00	9.00	13.50
	(1881)	2	4.00	6.00	9.00	13.50
	(1882)	3	4.00	6.00	9.00	13.50
	(1883)	4	4.00	6.00	9.00	13.50
	(1884)	5	4.00	6.00	9.00	13.50
	(1885)	6	4.00	6.00	9.00	13.50
	(1886)	7	4.00	6.00	9.00	13.50
	1886	8	4.00	6.00	9.00	13.50
	1887	8	4.00	6.00	9.00	13.50
	1888	9	4.00	6.00	9.00	13.50
	(1889)	10	4.00	6.00	9.00	13.50
	(1890)	11	4.00	6.00	9.00	13.50
	(1891)	12	4.00	6.00	9.00	13.50
	(1892)	13	4.00	6.00	9.00	13.50
	(1893)	14	4.00	6.00	9.00	13.50
	(1894)	15	4.00	6.00	9.00	13.50
	(1895)	16	4.00	6.00	9.00	13.50
	(1896)	17	4.00	6.00	9.00	13.50
	(1897)	18	4.00	6.00	9.00	13.50
	(1898)	19	4.00	6.00	9.00	13.50
	(1899)	20	4.00	6.00	8.50	13.50
	(1900)	21	4.00	6.00	9.00	13.50
	(1902)	23	4.00	6.00	9.00	13.50
	1903	24	4.00	6.00	9.00	13.50
	(1904)	25	4.00	6.00	9.00	13.50
	(1905)	26	4.00	6.00	9.00	13.50
	(1906)	27	4.00	6.00	9.00	13.50
	(1908)	29	4.00	6.00	9.00	13.50
	(1909)	30	4.00	6.00	9.00	13.50
	(1910)	31	4.00	6.00	9.00	13.50
	(1912)	33	4.00	6.00	9.00	13.50
	(1916)	37	4.00	6.00	9.00	13.50
	191(8)	39	4.00	6.00	9.00	13.50
	(1919)	40	4.00	6.00	9.00	13.50
	(1921)	42	4.00	6.00	9.00	13.50
	1922	43	4.00	6.00	9.00	13.50

NAZARANA RUPEE

SILVER, 30-31mm, 10.70-11.60 g

Y#	Date	Year	VG	Fine	VF	XF
13a	1880	1	35.00	50.00	70.00	100.00
	1881	2	35.00	50.00	70.00	100.00
	1882	3	35.00	50.00	70.00	100.00
	1883	4	35.00	50.00	70.00	100.00
	1884	5	35.00	50.00	70.00	100.00

36-37mm

Y#	Date	Year	VG	Fine	VF	XF
13b	1884	5	27.50	40.00	52.50	75.00
	1886	7	27.50	40.00	52.50	75.00
	1887	8	27.50	40.00	52.50	75.00
	1888	9	27.50	40.00	52.50	75.00
	1889	10	27.50	40.00	52.50	75.00
	1890	11	27.50	40.00	52.50	75.00
	1891	12	27.50	40.00	52.50	75.00
	1895	16	27.50	40.00	52.50	75.00
	1896	13	27.50	40.00	52.50	75.00
	1897	18	27.50	40.00	52.50	75.00
	1899	20	27.50	40.00	52.50	75.00
	1901	22	27.50	40.00	52.50	75.00
	1903	24	27.50	40.00	52.50	75.00
	1904	25	27.50	40.00	52.50	75.00
	1906	27	27.50	40.00	52.50	75.00
	1908	29	27.50	40.00	52.50	75.00
	1909	30	27.50	40.00	52.50	75.00
	1910	31	27.50	40.00	52.50	75.00
	1911	32	27.50	40.00	52.50	75.00
	1912	33	27.50	40.00	52.50	75.00
	1913	34	27.50	40.00	52.50	75.00
	1916	37	27.50	40.00	52.50	75.00
	1921	42	27.50	40.00	52.50	75.00

MOHUR

GOLD, 10.70-11.40 g

Y#	Date	Year	VG	Fine	VF	XF
14	(1881)	2	135.00	155.00	185.00	225.00
	(1884)	5	135.00	155.00	185.00	225.00
	(1895)	16	135.00	155.00	185.00	225.00
	(1896)	17	135.00	155.00	185.00	225.00
	(1899)	20	135.00	155.00	185.00	225.00
	(1916)	37	135.00	155.00	185.00	225.00
	(1919)	40	135.00	155.00	185.00	225.00

NAZARANA MOHUR

GOLD, 29-36mm, 10.70-11.40 g

Y#	Date	Year	VG	Fine	VF	XF
14a	1880	1	425.00	700.00	1000.	1650.
	1887	8	425.00	700.00	1000.	1650.

In the names of George V جارج

and Man Singh II مان سنگه

Years 1-14/1922-1935AD

NAZARANA PAISA

COPPER

Y#	Date	Year	VG	Fine	VF	XF
B15	1922	1	10.00	17.50	25.00	40.00
	1923	2	10.00	17.50	25.00	40.00
	1924	3	10.00	17.50	25.00	40.00
	1924	4	10.00	17.50	25.00	40.00
	1925	4	10.00	17.50	25.00	40.00
	1926	5	10.00	17.50	25.00	40.00
	1927	5	10.00	17.50	25.00	40.00
	1927	6	10.00	17.50	25.00	40.00
	1928	7	10.00	17.50	25.00	40.00
	1929	8	10.00	17.50	25.00	40.00
	1930	9	10.00	17.50	25.00	40.00
	19(30)	10	10.00	17.50	25.00	40.00
	1931	10	10.00	17.50	25.00	40.00
	1932	11	10.00	17.50	25.00	40.00
	1933	12	10.00	17.50	25.00	40.00
	1934	13	10.00	17.50	25.00	40.00
	1935	14	10.00	17.50	25.00	40.00

RUPEE

SILVER, 10.70 g

Y#	Date	Year	VG	Fine	VF	XF
15	1922	1	25.00	37.50	50.00	70.00

NAZARANA RUPEE

SILVER, 10.70 g

Y#	Date	Year	VG	Fine	VF	XF
15a	1924	3	40.00	62.50	85.00	120.00
	1928	7	40.00	62.50	85.00	120.00
	1932	11	40.00	62.50	85.00	120.00

MOHUR

GOLD, 10.70-11.40 g

Y#	Date	Year	VG	Fine	VF	XF
A15	1(924)	3	165.00	225.00	325.00	450.00

In the names of Edward VIII ایڈورڈ

and Man Singh II مان سنگه

Year 15/1936AD

NAZARANA PAISA

COPPER

Y#	Date	Year	VG	Fine	VF	XF
A16	1936	15	—	—	—	—

NAZARANA RUPEE

SILVER, 10.70 g

Y#	Date	Year	VG	Fine	VF	XF
B16	1936	15	—	—	Rare	—

In the names of George VI جارج

and Man Singh II

Years 15-28/1936-1949AD

NOTE: Refer to George V and Man Singh II legends.

1/2 PAISA

COPPER

Dump struck w/o collar.

Y#	Date	Year	VG	Fine	VF	XF
16.1	(1942)	21	1.00	1.75	2.50	4.50

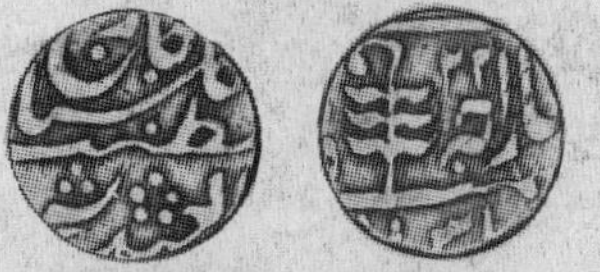

Crude struck in collar.

Y#	Date	Year	VG	Fine	VF	XF
16.2	(1943)	22	1.00	1.75	2.50	4.50
	(1944)	23	1.00	1.75	2.50	4.50

NAZARANA PAISA

COPPER

Y#	Date	Year	VG	Fine	VF	XF
17	1937	16	10.00	17.50	25.00	40.00
	1938	17	10.00	17.50	25.00	40.00
	1939	18	10.00	17.50	25.00	40.00
	1940	19	10.00	17.50	25.00	40.00
	1941	20	10.00	17.50	25.00	40.00
	1942	21	10.00	17.50	25.00	40.00
	1943	22	10.00	17.50	25.00	40.00
	19(44)	23	10.00	17.50	25.00	40.00
	1945	24	10.00	17.50	25.00	40.00
	1946	25	10.00	17.50	25.00	40.00
	1947	26	10.00	17.50	25.00	40.00
	1948	27	10.00	17.50	25.00	40.00
	1949	28	10.00	17.50	25.00	40.00

ANNA

BRASS

Y#	Date	Year	VG	Fine	VF	XF
18	1943	—	.20	.40	.60	1.00
	1944/3	—	.40	.80	1.20	2.00
	1944	—	.20	.40	.60	1.00

Y#	Date	Year	VG	Fine	VF	XF
19	1944	—	.20	.40	.60	1.00
	1944	—	—	—	Proof	—

2 ANNA

BRASS

Y#	Date	Year	VG	Fine	VF	XF
20	1942	21	3.00	4.50	6.00	10.00

NAZARANA RUPEE

SILVER, 10.70-11.60 g

Y#	Date	Year	VG	Fine	VF	XF
21	1938	17	25.00	40.00	55.00	80.00
	1938	20	30.00	50.00	70.00	100.00
	1941	20	25.00	40.00	55.00	80.00

Mule. Obv: Y#21a. Rev: Y#13a.

Y#	Date	Year	VG	Fine	VF	XF
A21	1949	3	—	—	—	—

Y#	Date	Year	VG	Fine	VF	XF
21a	1939	18	15.00	21.50	30.50	40.00
	1941	20	15.00	21.50	30.50	40.00
	1943	22	15.00	21.50	30.50	40.00
	1945	24	15.00	21.50	30.50	40.00
	1948	27	15.00	21.50	30.50	40.00
	1949	28	15.00	21.50	30.50	40.00

MOHUR

GOLD, 10.70-11.40 g

Y#	Date	Year	VG	Fine	VF	XF
22	(1941)	20	135.00	155.00	185.00	225.00
	(1943)	22	135.00	155.00	185.00	225.00
	(1949)	28	135.00	155.00	185.00	225.00

MADHOPUR MINT

In the name of Muhammad Akbar II

AH1221-1253/1806-1837AD

PAISA

COPPER

C#	Date	Year	Good	VG	Fine	VF
71	AH—	13	3.00	5.00	7.50	11.50
	—	14	3.00	5.00	7.50	11.50

1/2 NAZARANA RUPEE

SILVER, 5.30 g

C#	Date	Year	VG	Fine	VF	XF
74	AH12(21)	1	—	—	—	—

RUPEE

SILVER, 10.70-11.60 g

C#	Date	Year	VG	Fine	VF	XF
75	AH1221	1	6.00	9.00	13.00	20.00
	(1222)	2	6.00	9.00	13.00	20.00
	(1224)	4	6.00	9.00	13.00	20.00
	(1225)	5	6.00	9.00	13.00	20.00
	(1226)	6	6.00	9.00	13.00	20.00
	(1227)	7	6.00	9.00	13.00	20.00
	(1228)	8	6.00	9.00	13.00	20.00
	(1229)	9	6.00	9.00	13.00	20.00
	123(0)	10	6.00	9.00	13.00	20.00
	(1231)	11	6.00	9.00	13.00	20.00
	(1232)	12	6.00	9.00	13.00	20.00
	(1233)	13	6.00	9.00	13.00	20.00
	(1234)	14	6.00	9.00	13.00	20.00
	(1235)	15	6.00	9.00	13.00	20.00
	(1236)	16	6.00	9.00	13.00	20.00
	(1237)	17	6.00	9.00	13.00	20.00
	(1238)	18	6.00	9.00	13.00	20.00
	(1239)	20	6.00	9.00	13.00	20.00
	(1241)	21	6.00	9.00	13.00	20.00
	(1242)	22	6.00	9.00	13.00	20.00
	(1243)	23	6.00	9.00	13.00	20.00
	(1244)	24	6.00	9.00	13.00	20.00
	(1246)	26	6.00	9.00	13.00	20.00
	(1249)	29	6.00	9.00	13.00	20.00
	(1250)	30	6.00	9.00	13.00	20.00
	(1251)	31	6.00	9.00	13.00	20.00

In the name of Bahadur Shah II

AH1253-1274/1837-1857AD

RUPEE

SILVER, 10.70-11.60 g

C#	Date	Year	VG	Fine	VF	XF
96	AH(1254)	2	5.50	8.00	12.50	18.50
	125(5)	3	5.50	8.00	12.50	18.50
	(1256)	4	5.50	8.00	12.50	18.50
	(1257)	5	5.50	8.00	12.50	18.50
	(1258)	6	5.50	8.00	12.50	18.50
	(1259)	7	5.50	8.00	12.50	18.50
	1260	7	5.50	8.00	12.50	18.50
	(1260)	8	5.50	8.00	12.50	18.50
	(1263)	10	5.50	8.00	12.50	18.50
	(1264)	12	5.50	8.00	12.50	18.50
	(1267)	15	5.50	8.00	12.50	18.50

C#	Date	Year	VG	Fine	VF	XF
96	(1269)	17	5.50	8.00	12.50	18.50
	(1270)	18	5.50	8.00	12.50	18.50

JAIPUR FEUDATORY STATE

Khetri

A small state in northern Jaipur ruled by the Sadhani chieftains.

Mintname: Muzaffargarh

Mint marks: 

In the name of Shah Alam II

AH1173-1221/1759-1806AD

RUPEE

SILVER, 10.70-11.60 g
Obv. leg: ***Sahib Qiran.***

KM#	Date	Year	Good	VG	Fine	VF
2	AH12xx	44	8.50	13.50	20.00	28.50
	12xx	45	8.50	13.50	20.00	28.50
	1218	46	8.50	13.50	20.00	28.50
	12xx	47	8.50	13.50	20.00	28.50

NOTE: Earlier dates (AH1202-121x) exist for this type.

In the name of Muhammad Akbar II

KM#	Date	Year	Good	VG	Fine	VF
3	AH1221	1	22.50	35.00	47.50	65.00
	1222	2	22.50	35.00	47.50	65.00
	1223	3	22.50	35.00	47.50	65.00

JAISALMIR

Although the ruling Rajputs (or rawals) of this desert territory, located in northwest India traced their ancestry back to pre-Asokan times, the State of Jaisalmir was founded by Deoraj, the first rawal, only in the tenth century. Jaisalmir city was established by Rawal Jaisal, after whom both the city and the State were named. Like Jaipur, Jaisalmir reached its zenith in Mughal times, after being forced to acknowledge the supremacy of Delhi in the time of the Emperor Shah Jahan. With Mughal disintegration, Jaisalmir also fell upon hard times and most of its outlying provinces were lost. The state came under British protection in 1818, and on March 30th, 1949 it was merged into Rajasthan.

RULERS

Mulraj Singh
AH1176-1235/1762-1819AD
Gaj Singh
AH1235-1263/1819-1846AD
Ranjit Singh
AH1263-1281/1846-1864AD
Bairi Sal, 1865-1891AD

Anonymous Issues

MINT

Jaisalmir 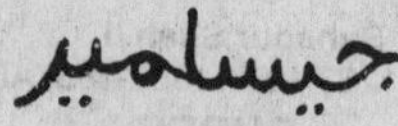

DODIA PAISA

COPPER

C#	Date	Year	Good	VG	Fine	VF
4	ND	—	2.50	4.50	6.50	10.00

NOTE: Struck 1660-1863AD with recorded weights as low as 0.75 and as high as 2.85 g.

Mughal Issues

"Akheyshahi" Series

In the name of Muhammad Shah

AH1131-1161/1719-1748AD
Struck 1756-1860AD

1/8 RUPEE

SILVER, 11-12mm, 1.35 g

C#	Date	Year	VG	Fine	VF	XF
7	AH1153	22	5.50	8.00	10.00	15.00

1/4 RUPEE

SILVER, 2.70 g

C#	Date	Year	VG	Fine	VF	XF
8	AH1153	22	4.00	6.00	9.00	13.50

1/2 RUPEE

C#	Date	Year	VG	Fine	VF	XF
	SILVER, 5.25 g					
9	AH1153	22	5.50	8.00	10.00	15.00
	Square, 5.50 g					
9a	AH1153	22	—	—	—	—

RUPEE

C#	Date	Year	VG	Fine	VF	XF
	SILVER, 10.50-11.00 g					
10	AH1153	22	9.00	15.00	21.50	30.00
	Square, 11.00 g					
10c	AH1153	22	—	—	—	—

NAZARANA RUPEE

SILVER, 11.00 g

C#	Date	Year	VG	Fine	VF	XF
10a	AH1153	22	45.00	75.00	110.00	150.00

2-1/2 RUPEE

SILVER, Square, 28.00 g

C#	Date	Year	VG	Fine	VF	XF
10b	AH1153	22	—	—	Rare	—

MOHUR

GOLD, 22mm, 10.70-10.80 g

C#	Date	Year	VG	Fine	VF	XF
15	AH1153	22	155.00	185.00	225.00	325.00

Regal Issues

In the Name of Queen Victoria

First Series: Frozen regnal year 22 w/o mint marks.

1/8 RUPEE

SILVER, 1.32 g

Y#	Date	Year	VG	Fine	VF	XF
1	AH—	22	2.50	3.50	5.00	8.00

1/4 RUPEE

SILVER, 2.65 g

Y#	Date	Year	VG	Fine	VF	XF
2	AH—	22	3.00	4.50	6.50	10.00

1/2 RUPEE

SILVER, 5.30 g

Y#	Date	Year	VG	Fine	VF	XF
3	AH—	22	5.50	8.00	10.00	15.00

RUPEE

SILVER, 10.50-10.60 g

Y#	Date	Year	VG	Fine	VF	XF
4	AH—	22	8.50	13.50	20.00	28.50

NAZARANA RUPEE

SILVER, 10.60 g

Y#	Date	Year	VG	Fine	VF	XF
4a	AH—	22	45.00	75.00	110.00	150.00

Y#	Date	Year	VG	Fine	VF	XF
4b	AH—	22	90.00	150.00	220.00	300.00

NAZARANA 1-1/2 RUPEE

SILVER, 16.00 g

Y#	Date	Year	VG	Fine	VF	XF
4c	AH—	22	120.00	200.00	275.00	400.00

NAZARANA 2 RUPEE

SILVER, 21.30 g

Y#	Date	Year	VG	Fine	VF	XF
4d	AH—	22	150.00	250.00	350.00	500.00

Second Series: Frozen regnal year 22 w/mint marks on rev.

Bird

Umbrella

1/8 RUPEE

SILVER, 1.33 g

Y#	Date	Year	VG	Fine	VF	XF
5	AH—	22	2.00	3.00	4.00	7.00

1/4 RUPEE

SILVER, 2.65 g

Y#	Date	Year	VG	Fine	VF	XF
6	AH—	22	2.50	3.50	5.00	8.00

1/2 RUPEE

SILVER, 5.30 g

Y#	Date	Year	VG	Fine	VF	XF
7	AH—	22	3.00	4.50	6.50	10.00

RUPEE

SILVER, 10.60 g

Y#	Date	Year	VG	Fine	VF	XF
8	AH—	22	5.00	7.00	10.00	15.00

NAZARANA RUPEE

SILVER, 10.60 g

Y#	Date	Year	VG	Fine	VF	XF
8a	AH—	22	60.00	80.00	100.00	150.00

Y#	Date	Year	VG	Fine	VF	XF
8b	AH—	22	140.00	200.00	275.00	400.00

NAZARANA 2 RUPEES

SILVER, 21.30 g

Y#	Date	Year	VG	Fine	VF	XF
8c	AH—	22	150.00	250.00	350.00	500.00

1/8 MOHUR

GOLD, 12mm, 1.35 g

Y#	Date	Year	VG	Fine	VF	XF
9	AH—	22	—	—	Rare	—

1/4 MOHUR

GOLD, 15mm, 2.70 g

Y#	Date	Year	VG	Fine	VF	XF
10	AH—	22	—	—	Rare	—

1/2 MOHUR

GOLD, 18mm, 5.40 g

Y#	Date	Year	VG	Fine	VF	XF
11	AH—	22	—	—	Rare	—

MOHUR

GOLD, 10.80 g

Y#	Date	Year	VG	Fine	VF	XF
12	AH—	22	165.00	210.00	300.00	425.00

JANJIRA ISLAND

Island near Bombay. Dynasty of Nawabs dates from 1489AD.

The origin of the nawabs of Janjira is obscure. They were Sidi or Abyssinian Muslims whose ancestors, serving as admirals to the Muslim rulers of the Deccan, had been granted jagirs (revenue-producing land tenures) under the Adil Shahi sultans of Bijapur. In 1870, Janjira came under direct British rule. Until 1924 the nawabs of Janjira also exercised suzerainty over Jafarabad on the Kathiawar peninsular.

RULERS

Sidi Ibrahim Khan II
AH1204-06,19-42/1789-92,1804-26AD
Sidi Muhammad Khan
AH1242-1265/1826-1848AD
Sidi Ibrahim Khan III
AH1265-1297/1848-1879AD

SIDI IBRAHIM KHAN II

AH1204-1206,1219-1242
1789-1792,1804-1826AD

PAISA

COPPER

KM#	Date	Year	Good	VG	Fine	VF
5	ND	—	5.00	9.00	13.00	20.00

SIDI MUHAMMAD KHAN

AH1242-1265/1826-1848AD

PAISA

COPPER

KM#	Date	Year	Good	VG	Fine	VF
15	ND	—	4.50	8.00	12.00	17.50

SIDI IBRAHIM KHAN III

AH1265-1297/1848-1879AD

PAISA

COPPER
Obv: Date

KM#	Date	Year	Good	VG	Fine	VF
25	AH1284	—	3.00	5.00	8.00	12.50

Rev: Date

KM#	Date	Year	Good	VG	Fine	VF
26	AH1284	—	2.50	4.00	6.50	10.00

Rev: Date

KM#	Date	Year	Good	VG	Fine	VF
28	AH1288	—	4.00	6.50	10.00	15.00

JAORA

Ghafar Khan (d. 1825), the first Nawab of Jaora, was brother-in-law to Amir Khan, the Pindari leader. Jaora was subordinate to Indore, having been granted control of the territory in central India in return for the maintenance of a body of cavalry and, later, of foot soldiers which were to be made available to Indore when required. The nawabs of Jaora maintained a good relationship with the British which, after 1818, left them in control of the area independently of Indore. In August 1948 Jaora was absorbed into Madhya Pradesh.

RULERS

Muhammad Ismail
AH1282-1313/1865-1895AD

MINT

Jaora جاورا

PAISA

COPPER
Rev: Wheel left of flag.

KM#	Date	Year	Good	VG	Fine	VF
5	AH1282	—	5.00	9.00	13.00	20.00

KM#	Date	Year	Good	VG	Fine	VF
6	AH1284	—	4.50	8.50	12.50	18.50
	1285	—	4.50	8.50	12.50	18.50

Rev: Flag only.

KM#	Date	Year	Good	VG	Fine	VF
7	AH1295	—	2.50	4.00	6.50	10.00

Milled Coinage

PAISA

COPPER

KM#	Date	Year	VG	Fine	VF	XF
10	1893/VS1950/AH1310		2.50	4.00	6.50	10.00
	1893/VS1950/AH1311		3.00	5.00	8.00	12.50
	1894/VS1950/AH1310		2.50	4.00	6.50	10.00
	1894/VS1950/AH1311		2.50	4.00	6.50	10.00
	1894/VS1951/AH1311		2.50	4.00	6.50	10.00
	1895/VS1951/AH1311		2.50	4.00	6.50	10.00
	1895/VS1952/AH1311		2.50	4.00	6.50	10.00
	1895/VS1952/AH1312		3.00	5.00	8.00	12.50
	1895/VS1952/AH1313		2.50	4.00	6.50	10.00
	1895/VS1953/AH1313		3.00	5.00	8.00	12.50
	1896/VS1953/AH1313		2.50	4.00	6.50	10.00
	1896/VS1953/ AH1331 (error for 1313 w/ second 3 retrograde)		3.00	5.00	8.00	12.50
	1896/VS1953/AH1331 (error for 1313)		4.00	6.50	10.00	15.00

2 PAISA

COPPER

KM#	Date	Year	VG	Fine	VF	XF
12	1893/VS1950/AH1310		4.50	8.00	12.00	17.50
	1894/VS1950/AH1310		5.00	9.00	13.50	20.00

JHABUA

A state located in northwest India, west of Indore.

Prior to 1818 the Raja of Jhabua was responsible for paying an annual tribute to Indore. The rajas were Rathor Rajputs who had been established in the area since the seventeenth century. They were descended from the rajas of Jodhpur. In 1818 Jhabua came under British protection and control.

RULERS

Gopal Singh
VS1897-1952/1840-1895AD

MINT

Jhabua

PAISA

COPPER
Obv. leg: Devanagari *Jabuva*.
Rev. leg: Arabic *Jabua*.

KM#	Date	Year	Good	VG	Fine	VF
1	VS(19)29	(1872)	8.50	11.50	15.00	21.50
	(19)35	(1878)	8.50	11.50	15.00	21.50
	Obv. leg: Devanagari *Jhabua*. Rev: Date.					
2	VS(19)36	(1879)	8.50	11.50	15.00	21.50
	Obv. Devanagari date: Sa(mvat) 21.					
3	VS(19)21	(1864)	7.00	10.00	13.50	17.50
	(19)22	(1865)	7.00	10.00	13.50	17.50

Obv: Trident. Rev: Date.

KM#	Date	Year	Good	VG	Fine	VF
4	VS(19)31	(1874)	3.50	5.00	6.50	8.50
	ND	—	3.50	5.00	6.50	8.50

Obv: 4 lobed flower. Rev: Date.

KM#	Date	Year	Good	VG	Fine	VF
5	VS(19)34	(1877)	3.50	5.00	6.50	8.50

Obv: Stylized leaf

KM#	Date	Year	Good	VG	Fine	VF
6	VS(19)22	(1865)	7.50	10.00	12.50	16.50
	(19)23	(1866)	5.00	7.00	10.00	14.00
	(19)24	(1867)	5.00	7.00	10.00	14.00
	(19)28	(1871)	5.00	7.00	10.00	14.00
	(19)32	(1875)	3.00	5.00	7.00	10.00
	(19)33	(1876)	3.00	5.00	7.00	10.00
	(19)35	(1878)	5.00	7.00	10.00	14.00

NOTE: Thick and thin planchets exist.

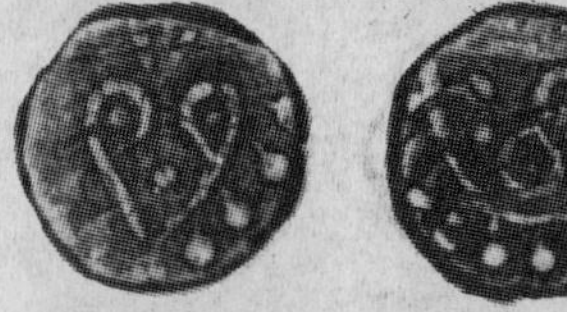

Rev: Curled branch w/berry.

KM#	Date	Good	VG	Fine	VF
7	ND	5.00	7.00	10.00	14.00

Rev: Spear point.

KM#	Date	Good	VG	Fine	VF
8	ND	3.00	5.00	7.00	10.00

Rev: Curved dagger.

KM#	Date	Good	VG	Fine	VF
9	ND	5.00	7.00	10.00	14.00

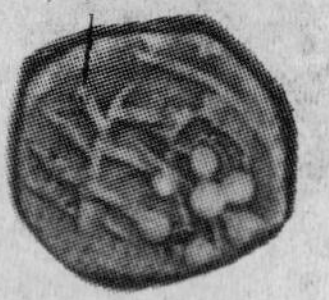

Rev: Jhar and blossom.

KM#	Date	Good	VG	Fine	VF
10	ND	4.50	6.50	9.00	13.00

Rev: 6 lobed flower.

KM#	Date	Good	VG	Fine	VF
11	ND	5.00	7.00	10.00	14.00

Rev: Tailed ball.

KM#	Date	Good	VG	Fine	VF
12	Yr. 30	4.00	6.00	8.00	12.00

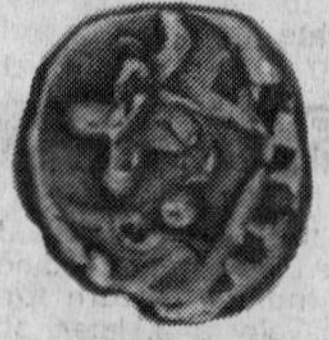

Obv: Cross. Rev: Tailed ball.

KM#	Date	Good	VG	Fine	VF
13	ND	3.00	5.00	7.00	11.00

Obv: Square. Rev: Indistinct.

KM#	Date	Good	VG	Fine	VF
14	ND	4.00	6.00	8.00	12.00

Obv: Arabic *Wa*. Rev: Groups of dots.

KM#	Date	Year	Good	VG	Fine	VF
15	ND		7.00	9.00	12.00	16.00

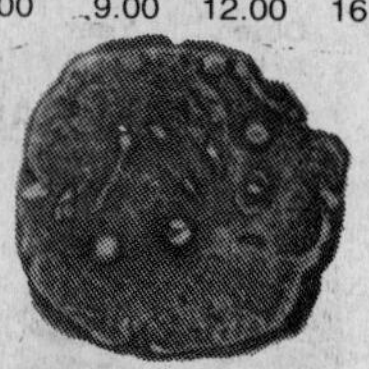

Obv: Cross and dots.

KM#	Date	Year	Good	VG	Fine	VF
16	ND	—	7.00	9.00	12.00	16.00

NOTE: In addition to the above there are other symbols, and all these occur in different combinations. The crude fabric of these coins and uncommon variety of dies indicate that they were struck by bankers, with or without official sanction. They are commonly found overstruck on earlier types or on coins of other states.

JHALAWAR

State located in Rajputana, northwest India which was originally part of Kotah. Established in memory of services to Kotah of Zalim Singh, long-time administrator of that state. His grandson was given Jhalawar in 1837AD with the title of Raj Rana.

In 1838, at a time of great internal dissention, certain districts were removed from the territory of the Princely State of Kotah to form a principality for Madan Singh, one of the contestants for power. The new state was named Jhalawar. In 1896 the ruling maharaj-rana, Zalim Singh, was deposed by the Government of India for maladministration, and much of the area that had once been ceded to Jhalawar was returned to the sovereignty of the rulers of Kotah. Madan Singh and his successors were Jhala Rajputs from Kathiawar. The residual State of Jhalawar was incorporated into Rajasthan in 1948.

RULERS

Madan Singh
AH1253-1261/1837-1845AD
Prithvi Singh
AH1261-1292/1845-1875AD
Zalim Singh
AH1294-1314/1876-1896AD
British Administration, 1896-1899

MINTNAMES

جالاوار

Jhalawar

MINT MARKS

Both marks on reverse

Mughal Issues

In the name of Muhammad Akbar
AH1221-1253/1806-1837AD

RUPEE

SILVER, 11.25 g
W/*Sahib Qiran* leg.

C#	Date	Year	Good	VG	Fine	VF
8	AH—	32	40.00	62.50	85.00	120.00

In the name of Bahadur Shah II
Years 1-22/AH1253-1274/1837-1858AD

DOUBLE PAISA

(Takka)

COPPER, square, 17.70-17.80 g

C#	Date	Year	Good	VG	Fine	VF
21	AH—	5	4.00	6.50	10.00	15.00
	—	6	4.00	6.50	10.00	15.00
	—	12	4.00	6.50	10.00	15.00
	—	21	4.00	6.50	10.00	15.00

1/8 RUPEE

SILVER, 1.40 g

C#	Date	Year	VG	Fine	VF	XF
25	AH—	11	4.00	6.00	9.00	13.50

1/4 RUPEE

SILVER, 2.80 g

C#	Date	Year	VG	Fine	VF	XF
26	AH—	—	3.50	5.00	7.50	12.00

1/2 RUPEE

SILVER, 5.60 g

C#	Date	Year	VG	Fine	VF	XF
27	AH—	—	5.50	8.00	12.50	18.50

RUPEE

SILVER, 11.15-11.25 g

C#	Date	Year	VG	Fine	VF	XF
28	AH—	1	6.50	10.00	15.00	22.50
	—	3	6.50	10.00	15.00	22.50
	1259	6	6.50	10.00	15.00	22.50
	1259	13	6.50	10.00	15.00	22.50
	—	15	6.50	10.00	15.00	22.50
	—	18	6.50	10.00	15.00	22.50
	1259	19	6.50	10.00	15.00	22.50
	1259	20	6.50	10.00	15.00	22.50
	125x	22	6.50	10.00	15.00	22.50

NAZARANA RUPEE

SILVER, 30mm, 11.00-11.20 g

C#	Date	Year	VG	Fine	VF	XF
29	AH1259	6	35.00	60.00	85.00	120.00
	—	8	35.00	60.00	85.00	120.00
	1263	10	35.00	60.00	85.00	120.00
	—	21	35.00	60.00	85.00	120.00

Regal Issues

In the name of Queen Victoria

Regnal years 1-45 = 1857-1901AD

PAISA

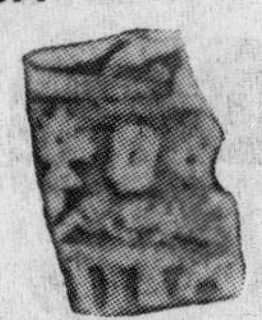

COPPER, 9.00 g

Y#	Date	Year	Good	VG	Fine	VF
1	AH—	2	2.50	4.50	7.50	12.50
	—	5	2.50	4.50	7.50	12.50

DOUBLE PAISA

COPPER, squarish, 19-21mm, 18.00 g

Y#	Date	Year	Good	VG	Fine	VF
2	AH—	1	1.25	2.25	4.00	6.50
	—	4	1.25	2.25	4.00	6.50
	—	5	1.25	2.25	4.00	6.50
	—	6	1.25	2.25	4.00	6.50
	—	7	1.25	2.25	4.00	6.50
	—	8	1.25	2.25	4.00	6.50
	—	9	1.25	2.25	4.00	6.50
	—	10	1.25	2.25	4.00	6.50
	—	11	1.25	2.25	4.00	6.50
	—	12	1.25	2.25	4.00	6.50
	—	18	1.25	2.25	4.00	6.50
	—	21	1.25	2.25	4.00	6.50
	—	22	1.25	2.25	4.00	6.50
	—	24	1.25	2.25	4.00	6.50
	—	27	1.25	2.25	4.00	6.50
	—	28	1.25	2.25	4.00	6.50
	—	29	1.25	2.25	4.00	6.50

1/8 RUPEE

SILVER, 13mm, 1.40 g

Y#	Date	Year	VG	Fine	VF	XF
3.1	AH—	5	5.00	7.00	10.00	15.00
	—	17	5.00	7.00	10.00	15.00
	—	25	5.00	7.00	10.00	15.00
	—	27	5.00	7.00	10.00	15.00
	—	28	5.00	7.00	10.00	15.00
3.2	—	37	5.00	7.00	10.00	15.00
	—	38	5.00	7.00	10.00	15.00

1/4 RUPEE

SILVER, 2.80 g

Y#	Date	Year	VG	Fine	VF	XF
4.1	AH—	7	4.00	6.00	9.00	13.50
	—	9	4.00	6.00	9.00	13.50
	—	17	4.00	6.00	9.00	13.50
	—	25	4.00	6.00	9.00	13.50
	—	28	4.00	6.00	9.00	13.50
4.2	AH—	30	4.00	6.00	9.00	13.50
	—	33	4.00	6.00	9.00	13.50
	—	36	4.00	6.00	9.00	13.50
	—	37	4.00	6.00	9.00	13.50
	—	38	4.00	6.00	9.00	13.50

1/2 RUPEE

SILVER, 5.60-5.65 g

Y#	Date	Year	VG	Fine	VF	XF
5.1	AH—	1	5.50	8.00	12.50	18.50
	—	11	5.50	8.00	12.50	18.50
	—	15	5.50	8.00	12.50	18.50
	—	22	5.50	8.00	12.50	18.50
	—	25	5.50	8.00	12.50	18.50
5.2	—	30	5.50	8.00	12.50	18.50
	—	31	5.50	8.00	12.50	18.50
	—	35	5.50	8.00	12.50	18.50
	—	36	5.50	8.00	12.50	18.50

NAZARANA 1/2 RUPEE

SILVER, 5.60-5.65 g

Y#	Date	Year	VG	Fine	VF	XF
5a	AH—	38	20.00	32.50	45.00	65.00

RUPEE

SILVER, 11.20-11.30 g

Y#	Date	Year	VG	Fine	VF	XF
6.1	AH—	1	5.50	8.00	12.50	18.50
	—	2	5.50	8.00	12.50	18.50
	—	3	5.50	8.00	12.50	18.50
	—	4	5.50	8.00	12.50	18.50
	—	5	5.50	8.00	12.50	18.50
	—	7	5.50	8.00	12.50	18.50
	—	9	5.50	8.00	12.50	18.50
	—	11	5.50	8.00	12.50	18.50
	—	12	5.50	8.00	12.50	18.50
	—	13	5.50	8.00	12.50	18.50
	—	14	5.50	8.00	12.50	18.50
	—	15	5.50	8.00	12.50	18.50
	—	16	5.50	8.00	12.50	18.50
	—	17	5.50	8.00	12.50	18.50
	—	18	5.50	8.00	12.50	18.50
	—	19	5.50	8.00	12.50	18.50
	—	20	5.50	8.00	12.50	18.50
	—	21	5.50	8.00	12.50	18.50
	—	22	5.50	8.00	12.50	18.50
	—	24	5.50	8.00	12.50	18.50
	—	25	5.50	8.00	12.50	18.50
	—	27	5.50	8.00	12.50	18.50
	—	28	5.50	8.00	12.50	18.50
	—	29	5.50	8.00	12.50	18.50
	—	30	5.50	8.00	12.50	18.50

Y#	Date	Year	VG	Fine	VF	XF
6.2	AH—	30	5.50	8.00	12.50	18.50
	—	33	5.50	8.00	12.50	18.50
	—	34	5.50	8.00	12.50	18.50
	—	35	5.50	8.00	12.50	18.50
	—	36	5.50	8.00	12.50	18.50
	—	37	5.50	8.00	12.50	18.50
	—	38	5.50	8.00	12.50	18.50
	—	41	5.50	8.00	12.50	18.50

NAZARANA RUPEE

SILVER, 11.20-11.25 g

Y#	Date	Year	VG	Fine	VF	XF
6a	VS1915	2	35.00	60.00	85.00	120.00
	1915	4	35.00	60.00	85.00	120.00
	1915	5	35.00	60.00	85.00	120.00
	1915	7	35.00	60.00	85.00	120.00
	1915	9	35.00	60.00	85.00	120.00
	1915	12	35.00	60.00	85.00	120.00
	1915	13	35.00	60.00	85.00	120.00
	1915	15	35.00	60.00	85.00	120.00
	1915	21	35.00	60.00	85.00	120.00
	1915	22	35.00	60.00	85.00	120.00
	1915	23	35.00	60.00	85.00	120.00
	1915	24	35.00	60.00	85.00	120.00
	1915	25	35.00	60.00	85.00	120.00
	1915	27	35.00	60.00	85.00	120.00
	1915	28	35.00	60.00	85.00	120.00

Y#	Date	Year	VG	Fine	VF	XF
6b	VS1915	3	52.50	87.50	125.00	165.00
	1915	15	52.50	87.50	125.00	165.00
6c	—	30	42.00	70.00	100.00	140.00
	—	31	42.00	70.00	100.00	140.00
	—	33	42.00	70.00	100.00	140.00
	—	35	42.00	70.00	100.00	140.00
	—	36	42.00	70.00	100.00	140.00
	—	37	42.00	70.00	100.00	140.00
	—	38	42.00	70.00	100.00	140.00
	—	39	42.00	70.00	100.00	140.00
	—	40	42.00	70.00	100.00	140.00

JODHPUR

Jodhpur, or Marwar, located in northwest India was the largest Princely State in the Rajputana Agency, its population in 1941 being in excess of two and a half million. The maharajadhirajas of Jodhpur were Rathor Rajputs who claimed an extremely ancient ancestry from Rama, king of Ayodhya. With the collapse of the Rathor rulers of Kanauj in 1194 the family entered Marwar, where they laid the foundation of the new state. The city of Jodhpur was built by Rao Jodha in 1459, and the city and and the state were named after him. In 1561 Akbar invaded Jodhpur, forcing its submission. In 1679 Aurangzeb sacked the city, an experience which stimulated the Rajput royal house to forge a new unity among themselves in order to extricate themselves from Mughal hegemony. Internal dissension once again asserted itself and Rajput unity, which had both benefited from and accelerated Mughal decline, fell apart before the Marathas. In 1818 Jodhpur came under British protection and control and after Indian Union the State was merged into Rajasthan. Jodhpur is best known for its particular style of riding breeches which became very popular in the West in the late nineteenth century.

RULERS

The issues of the first four rulers before 1858AD with the AH and VS dates, as well as the regnal years, are rarely actual dates and years, but were used for many years without change, and were often quite indiscriminately applied. Mismatched regnal years and dates are frequently encountered, as well as blundered dates of all sorts. Dates lying outside the reign of the rulers named on the coin (after 1858AD) were often used. Thus the date or regnal year may not represent an actual dating of the coin.

Coinage of the first four rulers (until 1858AD) is not distinguished by reign, but by type of inscription, mint, and pseudo-date.

Bhim Singh
AH1207-1218/1792-1803AD
Man Singh
AH1218-1259/1803-1843AD
Takhat Singh
AH1259-1290/VS1900-1930/
1843-1873AD
Jaswant Singh
AH1290-1313/VS1930-1952/
1873-1895AD
Sardar Singh
VS1952-1968/1895-1911AD
Sumair Singh
VS1968-1975/1911-1918AD
Umaid Singh
VS1975-2004/1918-1947AD
Hanwant Singh, as Titular Ruler
VS2004-2009/1947-1952AD

MINTNAMES

Jodhpur جودهپور

Dar-al-Mansur دارالمنصور

Nagor ناگور

Dar-al-Barkat دارالبرکات

Pali پالي

Sujat سوجت or سجت

MINT MARKS
Before 1858AD

Sujat, always on reverse. (KM#226)

Sujat, sometimes on obverse. (KM#226)

Pali, (KM#226) ला

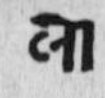

Pali, Sujat
Usually on obverse.

Jodhpur, on obverse. (KM#40) ك

Issues of 1858-1873AD

After 1858AD, the mint marks vary, and are given for each listing, wherever there is a difference.

All gold coins struck at Jodhpur Mint. All mints except Jodhpur closed by or before 1,893 AD. All copper coins were probably struck at the Jodhpur Mint, but if struck elsewhere, they bear no distinguishing marks.

In addition to the mint marks indicating the mint cities, there are also the marks of the Darogas (mint overseers), which are very useful in identifying the mints, especially when the city marks are missing or off the flan. These are given by cat.# and mint: (Only one of the marks appears on any one coin, always on the obverse.)

Jodhpur (KM#46) ग रा

Sujat (KM#237) ला

Jodhpur (KM#66) गं न श्री

Jodhpur (KM#76) ग रा रां 卐 रु

Sujat (KM#236) मा

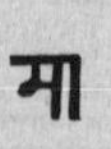

Pali (KM#197) के

Sujat (KM#246) علی

Issues of Jaswant Singh

Jodhpur (KM#76 & 81)  उ ज रू

Jodhpur (KM#76) 卐 卐 मा मा

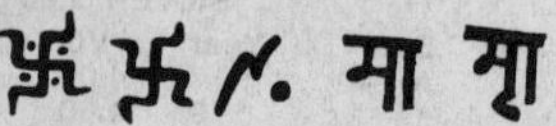

Pali (KM#206) न नँ बा बा ग भँ

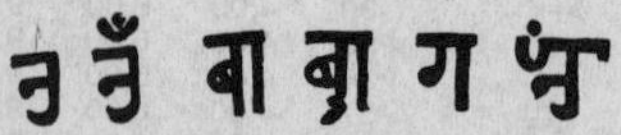

Sujat (KM#256) गा रू ज 2 ट कि रु म

Issues of Victoria and Sardar Singh

Jodhpur all न न्ना

Issues of Edward VII and George V and Sardar Singh and Sumair Singh

Jodhpur (KM#91-95, 98-100, 109, 113-115) म

Jodhpur (KM#120) द

Issues of George V and Sumair Singh

Jodhpur (KM#111-112) द

Issues of George V and Umaid Singh

Jodhpur (KM#128 & 129)  अँ

Jodhpur (KM#129) श्री

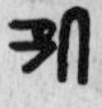

Issues of Edward VIII and Umaid Singh

Jodhpur all 

Issues of George VI and Umaid Singh

Jodhpur (KM#141-143) रं

Jodhpur (KM#144-147, 150-151) गो

Issues of George VI and Hanwant Singh

Jodhpur all 

The Daroga's marks generally consist of a symbol or a single Nagari letter, sometimes inverted, and even lying on its side. Some letters are found on more than one series, so that the mark is not a positive identification, but taken together with the city mark and the style of the coin, will provide a correct attribution.

JODHPUR MINT

Operative between AH1175/1761AD-VS2002/1945AD.

Anonymous Copper Issues With Regnal Years of Shah Alam II
Struck between 1792-1858AD

PAISA

"Bhim Shahi" Series:

COPPER, 20.00-21.00 g

KM#	Date	Year	Good	VG	Fine	VF
14	AH1227	—	2.00	3.00	4.50	7.50
	1267 (error for 1227)					
		—	2.50	4.00	6.00	10.00

NOTE: Some specimens portray a wide, floral border.
NOTE: Earlier date (AH1215) exists for this type.

"Bijy Shahi" Series:
In the names of the Mughal Emperors until 1858.

In the name of Shah Alam II
AH1173-1221/1759-1806AD

RUPEE

SILVER, 10.70-11.60 g
Obv: Sword.

KM#	Date	Year	VG	Fine	VF	XF
19	AH1218	45	6.50	10.00	15.00	22.50
	1128(error)					
		—	6.50	10.00	15.00	22.50
	1220	—	6.50	10.00	15.00	22.50
	1228(error)					
		—	6.50	10.00	15.00	22.50
	128(error)					
		—	6.50	10.00	15.00	22.50

NOTE: Earlier dates (AH1192-1215) exists for this type.

NAZARANA RUPEE

SILVER, 10.70-11.60 g
Similar to 1 Rupee, KM#19, but square.

KM#	Date	Year	VG	Fine	VF	XF
23	AH1218	45	35.00	50.00	70.00	100.00

MOHUR

GOLD, 19mm, 10.70-11.40 g

KM#	Date	Year	VG	Fine	VF	XF
26	AH1218	45	200.00	300.00	425.00	600.00

In the name of Muhammad Akbar II
AH1221-1253/1806-1837AD

PAISA

COPPER, 22.50 g

KM#	Date	Year	Good	VG	Fine	VF
32	AH—	31 on obv., 22 on rev.				
			2.50	3.50	5.50	8.00

1/4 RUPEE

SILVER, 2.67-2.90 g

KM#	Date	Year	VG	Fine	VF	XF
34	AH—	22	6.50	10.00	15.00	22.50

RUPEE

SILVER, 10.70-11.60 g

KM#	Date	Year	VG	Fine	VF	XF
36	AH—	22	7.00	11.00	16.50	25.00
	—	23	7.00	11.00	16.50	25.00

NOTE: Struck ca. 1816-1859AD.

KM#	Date	Year	VG	Fine	VF	XF
37	AH1222	—	11.50	17.50	23.50	32.50
	1227	—	11.50	17.50	23.50	32.50

MOHUR

GOLD, 20mm, 10.70-11.40 g

KM#	Date	Year	VG	Fine	VF	XF
40	AH—	22	200.00	300.00	425.00	600.00

Anonymous Issue

PAISA

COPPER, 20mm

KM#	Date	Year	Good	VG	Fine	VF
42	AH1267	—	1.75	2.50	3.50	5.00

Regal Issues

In the names of Queen Victoria and Takhat Singh

First Issue

1858-1859

RUPEE

SILVER, 10.70-11.60 g

Obv: Jhar, *Jodhpur* in Persian. Rev: Sword.

KM#	Date	Year	VG	Fine	VF	XF
46	AH—	22	7.50	12.50	18.50	27.50
	—	52	7.50	12.50	18.50	27.50

MOHUR

GOLD, 20mm, 10.70-11.40 g

KM#	Date	Year	VG	Fine	VF	XF
50	AH—	22	175.00	250.00	350.00	500.00

Second Issue

1860-1869

RUPEE

SILVER, 21mm, 10.70-11.60 g

Obv: Jhar. Rev: Sword, *Jodhpur* in Persian.

KM#	Date	Year	VG	Fine	VF	XF
56	AH—	22 & 21	7.00	11.00	16.50	25.00
	—	22 only	7.00	11.00	16.50	25.00
	—	52 & 16	7.00	11.00	16.50	25.00
	—	52 only	7.00	11.00	16.50	25.00

In the name of Takhat Singh

Queen Victoria refered to in title only as 'Queen, Ruler of India and Europe'. Actual mint names appear on this and all subsequent issues.

Third Issue

1859-1869

Nagari legend *Sri Mataji* added on reverse, referring to Kul Devi, patron goddess of the Rathor clan.

RUPEE

SILVER, 21mm, 10.70-11.60 g

Rev. leg: *Sri Mataji.*

KM#	Date	Year	VG	Fine	VF	XF
66	AH—	22 & 61	7.50	12.50	18.50	27.50
	—	22 only	7.50	12.50	18.50	27.50

NOTE: Struck ca. 1849-1862AD.

KM#	Date	Year	VG	Fine	VF	XF
67	VS1926	22	7.00	11.00	16.50	25.00
	1927	—	7.00	11.00	16.50	25.00

Reduced size

KM#	Date	Year	VG	Fine	VF	XF
68	VS1928	(1871)	20.00	31.50	42.50	60.00

MOHUR

GOLD, 10.70-11.40 g

KM#	Date	Year	VG	Fine	VF	XF
70	VS1926	(1869)	—	—	Rare	—

NOTE: Struck with rupee dies.

In the name of Queen Victoria

PAISA

COPPER, 20-25mm

KM#	Date	Year	Good	VG	Fine	VF
71	AH1293	61	1.00	2.00	2.75	3.75
	1305	65	1.25	2.25	3.00	4.00
	Date off flan	—	.50	1.00	1.50	2.25

KM#	Date	Year	Good	VG	Fine	VF
72	VS1940	(1883)	1.25	2.25	3.00	4.00
	1940 inverted	1883	2.50	4.00	6.50	9.00
	1941	(1884)	1.00	2.00	2.75	3.75
	1942	(1885)	1.25	2.25	3.00	4.00
	1943	(1886)	1.25	2.25	3.00	4.00
	1944	(1887)	1.25	2.25	3.00	4.00
	1945	(1888)	1.25	2.25	3.00	4.00
	1947	(1890)	1.25	2.25	3.00	4.00
	1948	(1891)	2.00	3.50	5.50	7.00

2 PAISA

COPPER

KM#	Date	Year	Good	VG	Fine	VF
A72	VS1943	(1886)	—	—	—	—

In the names of Queen Victoria and Jaswant Singh

1/8 RUPEE

SILVER, 1.34-1.45 g

KM#	Date	Year	VG	Fine	VF	XF
73	AH—	22	8.50	13.50	20.00	28.50

1/4 RUPEE

SILVER, 2.68-2.90 g

KM#	Date	Year	VG	Fine	VF	XF
74	AH—	22	8.50	13.50	20.00	28.50

1/2 RUPEE

SILVER, 17mm, 5.35-5.80 g

KM#	Date	Year	VG	Fine	VF	XF
75	VS1944	(1887)	15.00	25.00	35.00	50.00
	1945	(1888)	15.00	25.00	35.00	50.00

RUPEE

SILVER, 10.70-11.60 g

KM#	Date	Year	VG	Fine	VF	XF
76	AH1293	—	6.50	10.00	16.50	25.00
	1923 error for 1293	—	6.50	11.00	16.50	25.00
	Date off flan		5.00	7.00	10.00	15.00

KM#	Date	Year	VG	Fine	VF	XF
77	VS1941	(1884)	6.50	10.00	16.50	25.00
	1942	(1885)	6.50	10.00	16.50	25.00
	2491 error for 1942		6.50	10.00	16.50	25.00
	1943	(1886)	6.50	10.00	16.50	25.00
	8941 error for 1948	(1891)	6.50	10.00	16.50	25.00
	1950	(1893)	6.50	10.00	16.50	25.00
	Date off flan		5.00	7.00	10.00	15.00

1/4 MOHUR

GOLD, 13mm, 2.68-2.85 g

KM#	Date	Year	VG	Fine	VF	XF
79	—	—	60.00	85.00	110.00	165.00

1/2 MOHUR

GOLD, 18mm, 5.35-5.70 g

KM#	Date	Year	VG	Fine	VF	XF
80	—	—	100.00	150.00	210.00	300.00

MOHUR

GOLD, 20mm, 10.70-11.40 g

KM#	Date	Year	VG	Fine	VF	XF
81	VS1942	22	175.00	250.00	350.00	500.00

In the names of Queen Victoria and Sardar Singh

1/8 RUPEE

SILVER, 1.34-1.45 g

KM#	Date	Year	VG	Fine	VF	XF
83	VS—	—	8.50	13.50	20.00	28.50

1/4 RUPEE

SILVER, 2.68-2.90 g

KM#	Date	Year	VG	Fine	VF	XF
84	VS—	—	7.00	11.00	16.50	25.00

1/2 RUPEE

SILVER, 5.35-5.80 g

KM#	Date	Year	VG	Fine	VF	XF
85	VS—	—	12.50	18.50	25.00	35.00

RUPEE

SILVER, 10.70-11.60 g

KM#	Date	Year	VG	Fine	VF	XF
86	VS1955	(1898)	16.00	22.50	31.50	40.00
	1956	(1899)	16.00	22.50	31.50	40.00

1/4 MOHUR

GOLD, 15mm, 2.68-2.85 g

KM#	Date	Year	VG	Fine	VF	XF
88	VS1952	(1895)	60.00	85.00	110.00	165.00

1/2 MOHUR

GOLD, 18mm, 5.35-5.70 g

KM#	Date	Year	VG	Fine	VF	XF
89	VS1952	(1895)	100.00	150.00	210.00	300.00

MOHUR

GOLD, 21mm, 10.70-11.40 g

KM#	Date	Year	VG	Fine	VF	XF
90	VS1952	1895	175.00	250.00	350.00	500.00

In the names of Edward VII and Sardar Singh

1/4 ANNA

COPPER, 10.00-11.00 g

KM#	Date	Year	Good	VG	Fine	VF
91	1901	—	1.50	2.50	3.75	5.50
	1902	—	1.50	2.50	3.75	5.50
	1903	—	1.50	2.50	3.75	5.50
	1904	—	1.50	2.50	3.75	5.50
	1905	—	1.50	2.50	3.75	5.50
	1906	—	.50	1.00	1.75	2.50
	1609 (error)	—	1.50	2.50	3.75	5.50
	1907	—	1.00	2.00	3.25	4.50
	1908	—	1.00	2.00	3.25	4.50
	1909	—	1.00	2.00	3.25	4.50
	1910	—	1.00	2.00	3.25	4.50
	1290 (error)	—	1.25	2.25	3.00	4.00
	1291 (error)	—	.75	1.50	2.25	3.25
	1967 (error)	—	1.25	2.25	3.00	4.00
	2091 (error)	—	1.25	2.25	3.00	4.00
	5201 (error)	—	1.25	2.25	3.00	4.00

NOTE: Other blundered dates' exist.

1/2 ANNA

COPPER, 20.00-22.00 g

KM#	Date	Year	Good	VG	Fine	VF
92	1906	—	3.50	5.00	7.00	11.50
	1908	—	3.50	5.00	7.00	11.50

1/8 RUPEE

SILVER, 1.34-1.45 g

KM#	Date	Year	VG	Fine	VF	XF
93	—	—	17.50	25.00	35.00	50.00

1/4 RUPEE

SILVER, 19mm, 2.68-2.90 g

KM#	Date	Year	VG	Fine	VF	XF
94	VS1965	(1908)	18.50	26.50	37.50	55.00

1/2 RUPEE

SILVER, 5.35-5.80 g

KM#	Date	Year	VG	Fine	VF	XF
95	ND	—	20.00	31.50	42.50	60.00

1/4 MOHUR

GOLD, 13mm, 2.68-2.85 g

KM#	Date	Year	VG	Fine	VF	XF
98	1906	—	60.00	85.00	110.00	165.00

1/2 MOHUR

GOLD, 18mm, 5.35-5.70 g

KM#	Date	Year	VG	Fine	VF	XF
99	1906	—	100.00	150.00	210.00	300.00

MOHUR

GOLD, 20mm, 10.70-11.40 g

KM#	Date	Year	VG	Fine	VF	XF
100	1906	—	175.00	250.00	350.00	500.00

In the names of Edward VII and Sumair Singh

1/2 MOHUR

GOLD, 5.35-5.70 g

KM#	Date	Year	VG	Fine	VF	XF
109	(1910)	—	200.00	250.00	300.00	400.00

In the names of George V and Sumair Singh

1/4 ANNA

COPPER

KM#	Date	Year	Good	VG	Fine	VF
111	1911	—	6.50	9.00	12.50	17.50
	1914	—	6.50	9.00	12.50	17.50

1/2 ANNA

COPPER, 25mm

KM#	Date	Year	Good	VG	Fine	VF
112	1914	—	5.00	8.50	12.50	20.00
	1918	—	5.00	8.50	12.50	20.00

1/8 RUPEE

SILVER, 1.34-1.45 g

KM#	Date	Year	VG	Fine	VF	XF
113	—	—	15.00	21.50	30.00	40.00

1/4 RUPEE

SILVER, 2.68-2.90 g

KM#	Date	Year	Good	VG	Fine	VF
114	—	—	15.00	21.50	30.00	40.00

1/2 RUPEE

SILVER, 5.35-5.80 g

KM#	Date	Year	Good	VG	Fine	VF
115	—	—	15.00	21.50	30.00	40.00

RUPEE

SILVER, 21mm, 10.70-11.60 g

KM#	Date	Year	Good	VG	Fine	VF
116	—	—	18.50	26.50	37.50	55.00

MOHUR

GOLD, 10.70-11.40 g

KM#	Date	Year	VG	Fine	VF	XF
120	ND	—	175.00	250.00	350.00	500.00

In the names of George V and Umaid Singh

1/4 ANNA

NOTE: Refer to Sirohi State for previously listed 1/4 Anna, Y#34.

1/4 RUPEE

SILVER, 18mm, 2.68-2.90 g

KM#	Date	Year	VG	Fine	VF	XF
124	—	—	18.50	26.50	37.50	55.00

1/4 MOHUR

GOLD, 16mm, 2.68-2.85 g

KM#	Date	Year	VG	Fine	VF	XF
127	—	—	60.00	90.00	120.00	175.00

1/2 MOHUR

GOLD, 5.35-5.70 g

KM#	Date	Year	VG	Fine	VF	XF
128	—	—	100.00	150.00	210.00	300.00

MOHUR

GOLD, 10.70-11.60 g
Obv: *Om.*

KM#	Date	Year	VG	Fine	VF	XF
129	—	—	175.00	250.00	350.00	500.00

Obv: *Shri.*

KM#	Date	Year	VG	Fine	VF	XF
130	—	—	165.00	210.00	300.00	425.00

In the names of Edward VIII and Umaid Singh

1/4 ANNA

COPPER
Obv: W/o Persian '8' left of Daroga's mark.

KM#	Date	Year	Good	VG	Fine	VF
131	1936	—	1.75	2.75	4.00	6.50

Obv: Large Persian '8' left of Daroga's mark.

KM#	Date	Year	Good	VG	Fine	VF
132	1936	—	1.75	2.75	4.00	6.50

NOTE: Blundered legend varieties also exist.

Obv: Small Persian '8' left of Daroga's mark.

KM#	Date	Year	Good	VG	Fine	VF
133	1936	—	1.75	2.75	4.00	6.50

MOHUR

GOLD, 11.01 g

KM#	Date	Year	VG	Fine	VF	XF
140	1936	—	—	—	—	—

In the names of George VI and Umaid Singh

1/4 ANNA

COPPER, 19mm, thick, 10.00-11.00 g

KM#	Date	Year	Good	VG	Fine	VF
141.1	AH—	1937	1.25	1.75	2.50	3.50
	—	1938	1.25	1.75	2.50	3.50

Obv: Small numeral 6 left of Daroga's mark.

KM#	Date	Year	Good	VG	Fine	VF
141.2	AH—	1939	3.00	4.00	7.00	10.00

KM#	Date	Year	Good	VG	Fine	VF
142	VS1996	(1939)	2.00	3.00	4.00	6.00
143	ND	—	3.00	4.50	6.50	10.00

Thin flan, 3.00 g
Obv: W/o Persian '6' below Daroga's mark.

KM#	Date	Year	Good	VG	Fine	VF
144	VS2000	(1943)	1.75	2.75	4.00	5.50
	Date off flan		.20	.30	.50	1.00

Obv: Persian '6' below Daroga's mark.

KM#	Date	Year	Good	VG	Fine	VF
145	VS2000	(1943)	1.75	2.75	4.00	5.50
	2001	(1944)	1.75	2.75	4.00	5.50
	2002	(1945)	1.75	2.75	4.00	5.50

NOTE: Varieties exist.

Obv: Persian 2 below Daroga's mark.

KM#	Date	Year	Good	VG	Fine	VF
146	VS—	—	—	—	—	—

Obv: Cock standing left, legend around.
Rev: Date and *Rajya Narvar*.

KM#	Date	Year	Good	VG	Fine	VF
147	VS2000	—	—	—	Rare	—

MOHUR

GOLD, 10.70-11.40 g
Obv. & rev: Large leg.

KM#	Date	Year	VG	Fine	VF	XF
150	—	—	175.00	250.00	350.00	500.00

Obv. & rev: Small leg.

KM#	Date	Year	VG	Fine	VF	XF
151	—	—	175.00	250.00	350.00	500.00

In the names of George VI and Hanwant Singh

1/4 ANNA

COPPER

KM#	Date	Year	Good	VG	Fine	VF
152	—	—	12.50	20.00	32.50	50.00

1/4 MOHUR

GOLD, 2.68-2.85 g

KM#	Date	Year	VG	Fine	VF	XF
158	—	—	—	—	Rare	—

MOHUR

GOLD, 10.70-11.40 g

KM#	Date	Year	VG	Fine	VF	XF
160	—	—	250.00	350.00	500.00	650.00

NAGOR MINT

Operative until AH1289/1872AD.

In the name of Shah Alam II
AH1173-1221/1759-1806AD

RUPEE

SILVER, 11.40-11.50 g
Rev: *Nagore* at top.

KM#	Date	Year	VG	Fine	VF	XF
177	AH1218	—	12.50	21.50	28.50	40.00

NOTE: Earlier dates (AH1190-1215) exist for this type.

In the name of Takhat Singh
VS1900-1930/1843-1873AD

RUPEE

SILVER, 11.40-11.50 g

KM#	Date	Year	VG	Fine	VF	XF
182	VS1926	(1869)	7.50	12.50	18.50	27.50

PALI MINT

Operative until VS1950/1893AD.

In the names of Queen Victoria and Takhat Singh

RUPEE

SILVER, 10.70-11.60 g
Obv: Jhar and swastika.

KM#	Date	Year	VG	Fine	VF	XF
186	—	52 & 16	11.50	17.50	23.50	32.50

NAZARANA RUPEE

SILVER
Obv: Swastika. Rev: Jhar and sword.

KM#	Date	Year	VG	Fine	VF	XF
187	ND	—	20.00	31.50	42.50	60.00

In the name of Takhat Singh
VS1900-1930/1843-1873AD

RUPEE

SILVER, 10.70-11.60 g
Rev: Jhar and sword.

KM#	Date	Year	VG	Fine	VF	XF
196	VS1926	45	8.50	13.50	20.00	28.50

Rev: Swastika.

KM#	Date	Year	VG	Fine	VF	XF
197	VS1926	(1879)	12.00	20.00	27.50	37.50
	1929	(1882)	12.00	20.00	27.50	37.50

In the names of Queen Victoria and Jaswant Singh

1/8 RUPEE

SILVER, 1.34-1.45 g

KM#	Date	Year	VG	Fine	VF	XF
203	AH—	—	6.50	10.00	15.00	22.50

1/4 RUPEE

SILVER, 2.67-2.90 g

KM#	Date	Year	VG	Fine	VF	XF
204	AH—	—	7.00	11.00	16.50	25.00

1/2 RUPEE

SILVER, 5.35-5.80 g

KM#	Date	Year	VG	Fine	VF	XF
205	VS1945	(1898)	8.50	13.50	20.00	28.50

RUPEE

SILVER, 19-21mm, 10.70-11.60 g
Rev: Jhar and sword.

KM#	Date	Year	VG	Fine	VF	XF
206	VS1930	(1883)	6.00	10.00	15.00	22.50
	1931	(1884)	6.00	10.00	15.00	22.50
	1931	40	6.00	10.00	15.00	22.50
	1932	40	6.00	10.00	15.00	22.50
	1934	40	6.00	10.00	15.00	22.50
	1934	(1887)	6.00	10.00	15.00	22.50
	1935	(1888)	6.00	10.00	15.00	22.50
	1939	(1892)	6.00	10.00	15.00	22.50
	1940	(1893)	6.00	10.00	15.00	22.50
	1941	(1894)	6.00	10.00	15.00	22.50
	1943	(1896)	6.00	10.00	15.00	22.50
	1944	(1897)	6.00	10.00	15.00	22.50
	1950	(1893)	6.00	10.00	15.00	22.50
	Date off flan		5.00	7.00	10.00	15.00

In the names of Queen Victoria and Sardar Singh

RUPEE

SILVER, 10.70-11.60 g

KM#	Date	Year	VG	Fine	VF	XF
216	—	—	15.00	25.00	35.00	50.00

SUJAT MINT

Operative until AH1306/VS1945/1888AD.

In the name of Shah Alam II
AH1173-1221/1759-1806AD

RUPEE

SILVER, 10.70-11.60 g

KM#	Date	Year	VG	Fine	VF	XF
226	AH1264	—	7.50	12.50	18.50	27.50

NOTE: Struck ca. 1848-1859.

In the names of Queen Victoria and Takhat Singh

RUPEE

SILVER, 10.70-11.60 g

Rev: Katar.

KM#	Date	Year	VG	Fine	VF	XF
236	—	16	7.50	12.50	18.50	27.50
	—	22	7.50	12.50	18.50	27.50

Rev: Katar.

KM#	Date	Year	VG	Fine	VF	XF
237	—	13	8.50	13.50	20.00	28.50
	—	16	8.50	13.50	20.00	28.50

NOTE: Struck ca. 1869AD.

In the name of Takhat Singh

VS1900-1930/1843-1873AD

PAISA

COPPER

Rev: Katar.

KM#	Date	Year	VG	Fine	VF	XF
240	AH1267	—	3.50	8.50	14.00	20.00

RUPEE

SILVER, 10.70-11.60 g

KM#	Date	Year	VG	Fine	VF	XF
246	VS1926	(1869)	9.00	15.00	21.50	30.00
	1928	(1871)	9.00	15.00	21.50	30.00

In the names of Queen Victoria and Jaswant Singh

RUPEE

SILVER, 10.70-11.60 g

KM#	Date	Year	VG	Fine	VF	XF
256	AH1291	(1882)	7.00	11.00	16.50	25.00
	Date off flan		4.50	7.50	11.00	16.50
257	VS1929	22	7.00	11.00	16.50	25.00
	1933	(1876)	7.00	11.00	16.50	25.00
	1936	(1879)	7.00	11.00	16.50	25.00
	1938	(1881)	7.00	11.00	16.50	25.00
	Date off flan		4.50	7.50	11.00	16.50

Obv: Devanagari *Sri Maheshji*.

KM#	Date	Year	VG	Fine	VF	XF
258	—	22	11.50	17.50	23.50	32.50

Obv: Devanagari *Sri Ragunathji*.

KM#	Date	Year	VG	Fine	VF	XF
259	—	—	13.50	20.00	27.50	37.50

Obv: Jhar and "X".

KM#	Date	Year	VG	Fine	VF	XF
260	VS1932	22	13.50	20.00	27.50	37.50

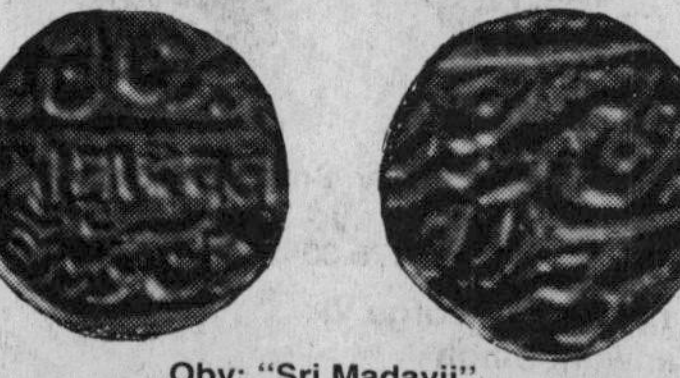

Obv: "Sri Madavji".

KM#	Date	Year	VG	Fine	VF	XF
261	—	22	15.00	22.50	30.00	40.00

JODHPUR FEUDATORY STATES

Kuchawan

Kuchawan was a semi-independent feudatory. The thakur of Kuchawan, an Udawat Rajput, was the only feudatory of Jodhpur permitted to strike his own coinage.

Refer also to Gwalior-Ajmir Mint and Maratha Confederacy-Ajmir Mint.

In the name of Queen Victoria

1/4 RUPEE

SILVER, 13mm, 2.68-2.90 g

KM#	Date	Year	VG	Fine	VF	XF
284	1863	—	11.50	18.50	25.00	35.00

1/2 RUPEE

SILVER, 15-16mm, 5.35-5.80 g

KM#	Date	Year	VG	Fine	VF	XF
285	1863	—	11.50	18.50	25.00	35.00

RUPEE

SILVER, 10.70-11.60 g

KM#	Date	Year	VG	Fine	VF	XF
286	1863	—	5.50	9.00	13.50	20.00

NAZARANA RUPEE

SILVER, 10.70-11.60 g

KM#	Date	Year	VG	Fine	VF	XF
287	1863	—	18.50	31.50	42.50	60.00

JUNAGADH

A state located in the Kathiawar peninsula of Western India was originally a petty Rajput kingdom until conquered by the Sultan of Ahmadabad in 1472. It became a Mughal dependency under the Emperor Akbar, administered by the Ahmadabad Subah. In 1735, when the empire began to disintegrate, a Mughal officer and military adventurer, Sher Khan Babi, expelled the Mughal governor and asserted his independence. From that time until Indian independence his descendents ruled the state as nawabs. In 1947 the Nawab of Junagadh tried to acceed to the new nation of Pakistan but the Hindu majority in the state objected and Junagadh was absorbed by the Republic of India.

Junagadh first entered into treaty relations with the British in 1807 and maintained a close and friendly association with the Raj. In 1924 this relationship was formalized when Junagadh was placed under an Agent to the Governor General in the western India States. In 1935 the state comprised 3,337 square miles with a population of 545,152, four-fifths of whom were Hindus.

RULERS

Bahadur Khan,
AH1226-1256/VS1868-1897/1811-1840AD
Hamid Khan II,
AH1256-1268/VS1897-1908/1840-1851AD
Mahabat Khan II,
AH1268-1300/VS1908-1939/1851-1882AD
Bahadur Khan III
AH1300-1309/VS1939-1948/1882-1891AD
Rasul Muhammad Khan
AH1309-1329/VS1948-1968/1891-1911AD
Mahabat Khan III
AH1329-1368/VS1968-2005/1911-1948AD

Mughal Issues

In the name of Muhammad Akbar II

AH1221-1253/1806-1837AD

With title *Sri Diwana* on obverse, AH and SE dates on reverse.

DOKDO

COPPER

KM#	Date	Year	Good	VG	Fine	VF
11	AH1239-48					
	VS1880-89		2.50	5.00	8.00	12.50

1/2 KORI

SILVER, 2.30 g

KM#	Date	Year	VG	Fine	VF	XF
13	AH1236	VS1877	3.00	4.50	6.50	10.00
	1245	1886	3.00	4.50	6.50	10.00
	1247	1889	3.00	4.50	6.50	10.00
	1251	1892	3.00	4.50	6.50	10.00
	1267	19xx	3.00	4.50	6.50	10.00
	1268	1909	3.00	4.50	6.50	10.00
	1270	1910	3.00	4.50	6.50	10.00
	1271	1911	3.00	4.50	6.50	10.00
	1272	1912	3.00	4.50	6.50	10.00
	1273	1913	3.00	4.50	6.50	10.00
	1274	1914	3.00	4.50	6.50	10.00
	1275	1915	3.00	4.50	6.50	10.00
	1276	1916	3.00	4.50	6.50	10.00
	1277	1917	3.00	4.50	6.50	10.00
	1278	1918	3.00	4.50	6.50	10.00
	1279	1919	3.00	4.50	6.50	10.00
	1280	1920	3.00	4.50	6.50	10.00

KORI

SILVER, 4.60 g

KM#	Date	Year	VG	Fine	VF	XF
15	AH1235	VS1875	2.50	3.50	5.00	8.00
	1235	1876	2.50	3.50	5.00	8.00
	1236	1877	2.50	3.50	5.00	8.00
	1245	1885	2.50	3.50	5.00	8.00
	1245	1886	2.50	3.50	5.00	8.00
	1246	1886	2.50	3.50	5.00	8.00
	1246	1887	2.50	3.50	5.00	8.00
	1247	1887	2.50	3.50	5.00	8.00
	1247	1888	2.50	3.50	5.00	8.00
	1249	1889	2.50	3.50	5.00	8.00
	1249	1890	2.50	3.50	5.00	8.00
	1251	1892	2.50	3.50	5.00	8.00
	1521	1892	(error)			
			2.50	3.50	5.00	8.00
	1252	1892	2.50	3.50	5.00	8.00
19	AH1263	190x	2.50	3.50	5.00	8.00
	1267	1907	2.50	3.50	5.00	8.00
	1268	1908	2.50	3.50	5.00	8.00
23	AH1270	1910	2.50	3.50	5.00	8.00
	1272	1912	2.50	3.50	5.00	8.00
	1273	1913	2.50	3.50	5.00	8.00
	1273	1914	2.50	3.50	5.00	8.00
	1274	1914	2.50	3.50	5.00	8.00
	1275	1915	2.50	3.50	5.00	8.00
	1276	1915	2.50	3.50	5.00	8.00
	1277	1917	2.50	3.50	5.00	8.00
	1278	1918	2.50	3.50	5.00	8.00
	1279	1919	2.50	3.50	5.00	8.00
	1280	1920	2.50	3.50	5.00	8.00

NOTE: After the death of the Mughal Emperor Muhammad Akbar II in AH1253/1837AD, Junagadh continued to issue its coins in his name posthumously until at least AH1280/VS1920 (1863AD), well into the reign of Nawab Mahabat Khan II.

Local Issues

MAHABAT KHAN II

AH1268-1300/VS1908-1939/1851-1882AD

DOKDO

COPPER

KM#	Date	Year	Good	VG	Fine	VF
27	VS1931	(1874)	15.00	25.00	40.00	60.00
	1935	(1878)	13.50	22.50	35.00	50.00

1/2 KORI

SILVER, 2.30 g

KM#	Date	Year	VG	Fine	VF	XF
29	AH1293	VS1934	6.00	9.00	13.50	20.00
	1299	1938	6.00	9.00	13.50	20.00

KORI

SILVER, 4.60 g

KM#	Date	Year	VG	Fine	VF	XF
30	AH1292	VS1932	2.00	3.00	4.00	7.00
	1293	1933	2.00	3.00	4.00	7.00
	1293	1934	2.00	3.00	4.00	7.00
	1297	1935	2.00	3.00	4.00	7.00
	1297	1936	2.00	3.00	4.00	7.00
	1298	1937	2.00	3.00	4.00	7.00
	1299	1938	2.00	3.00	4.00	7.00

NAZARANA KORI

SILVER, 4.60 g

KM#	Date	Year	VG	Fine	VF	XF
31	AH1297	VS1936	18.50	31.50	42.50	60.00

GOLD KORI

GOLD, 15-16mm

KM#	Date	Year	Fine	VF	XF	Unc
34	AH1292	VS1932	225.00	350.00	500.00	750.00

BAHADUR KHAN III

AH1300-1309/VS1939-1948/1882-1891AD

1/2 GOLD KORI

GOLD

KM#	Date	Year	Fine	VF	XF	Unc
39	AH1309	VS1947	150.00	225.00	375.00	550.00

GOLD KORI

GOLD, 4.61 g

KM#	Date	Year	Fine	VF	XF	Unc
41	AH1309	VS1947	225.00	350.00	500.00	750.00

RASUL MUHAMMAD KHAN

AH1309-1329/VS1948-1968/1891-1911AD

DOKDO

COPPER

KM#	Date	Year	Good	VG	Fine	VF
43	AH1325	VS1963	4.50	6.50	10.00	15.00

Rev: Date w/o rosettes.

KM#	Date	Year	Good	VG	Fine	VF
44.1	VS1963	(1906)	1.25	2.00	3.00	4.50

Rev: Date w/circles.

KM#	Date	Year	Good	VG	Fine	VF
44.2	VS1964	(1907)	1.25	2.00	3.00	4.50

Rev: Date w/solid stars.

KM#	Date	Year	Good	VG	Fine	VF
44.3	VS1964	(1907)	1.25	2.00	3.00	4.50

Rev: Date w/outlined stars.

KM#	Date	Year	Good	VG	Fine	VF
44.4	VS1964	(1907)	1.25	2.00	3.00	4.50

Rev: Date between rosettes.

KM#	Date	Year	Good	VG	Fine	VF
45	VS1964	(1907)	.50	.85	1.25	1.75
	1965	(1908)	.50	.85	1.25	1.75
	1966	(1909)	.50	.85	1.25	1.75
	1967	(1910)	1.00	1.75	2.50	3.50

KM#	Date	Year	Good	VG	Fine	VF
46.1	ND	—	1.75	2.75	4.00	5.50

Rev: Stars between inscriptions.

KM#	Date	Year	Good	VG	Fine	VF
46.2	ND	—	1.75	2.75	4.00	5.50

2 DOKDA

COPPER

KM#	Date	Year	Good	VG	Fine	VF
48	VS1964	(1907)	7.50	12.50	20.00	30.00

KORI

SILVER, 15mm, 4.6 g

KM#	Date	Year	VG	Fine	VF	XF
52	VS1966	(1909)	17.50	25.00	35.00	50.00

GOLD KORI

GOLD, 4.02-4.77 g

KM#	Date	Year	Fine	VF	XF	Unc
56	AH1309	VS1948	—	—	900.00	1300.

KM#	Date	Year	Fine	VF	XF	Unc
57	AH1318	VS1956	—	—	1100.	1600.

KM#	Date	Year	Fine	VF	XF	Unc
58	AH1325	VS1963	—	—	850.00	1250.

MOHUR

GOLD, 11.54 g

KM#	Date	Year	Fine	VF	XF	Unc
60	AH1325	VS1963	—	—	1750.	2500.

MAHABAT KHAN III

AH1329-1368/VS1968-2005/1911-1948AD

DOKDO

COPPER, 19mm

KM#	Date	Year	Good	VG	Fine	VF
63	VS1985	(1928)	10.00	16.50	25.00	40.00
	1990	(1933)	10.00	16.50	25.00	40.00

KALAT

Khelat or Kelat

A state located in Baluchistan, Pakistan.

The Khanate of Kalat had originally been a feudatory of Kabul. Its ruler, the wali, later became a trusted leader in the army of Ahmad Shah Durrani, who in 1761 invaded India and crushed both Mughal and Maratha forces at the battle of Panipat. In 1839 Kalat was taken by the British, and the wali, Mehrab Khan, was killed. The victors then installed his son, Nasir Khan, as ruler and in 1854 a formal treaty was executed. From that time Kalat came under British control, with the Government of India frequently acting as referees in disputes between the wali and his chiefs. In 1893 the wali was deposed for misrule and Kalat's mint was closed.

RULERS

Mehrab Khan,
AH1232-1255/1816-1839AD
Nasir Khan,
AH1256-1274/1841-1856AD
Khudadad Khan,
AH1274-1311/1856-1893AD

MINT

Kalat کلات

MEHRAB KHAN

AH1232-1255/1816-1839AD

FALUS

COPPER

KM#	Date	Year	Good	VG	Fine	VF
11	AH1237	—	4.00	6.00	9.00	13.50
	1238	—	4.00	6.00	9.00	13.50
	1240	—	4.00	6.00	9.00	13.50

KHUDADAD KHAN

AH1274-1311/1857-1893AD

In the name of Mahmud Khan Durrani

FALUS

COPPER

Round, irregular, or rough-cut octagonal

KM#	Date	Year	Good	VG	Fine	VF
21	AH10786 (error for 1286)	—	3.50	6.00	10.00	15.00
	AH1186(error for 1286?)	—	3.50	6.00	10.00	15.00
	1281	—	3.50	6.00	10.00	15.00
	1282	—	3.50	6.00	10.00	15.00

KM#	Date	Year	Good	VG	Fine	VF
21	1290	—	3.50	6.00	10.00	15.00
	1293	—	3.50	6.00	10.00	15.00
	1294	—	3.50	6.00	10.00	15.00
	1295	—	2.50	4.00	7.00	10.00
	1296	—	3.50	6.00	10.00	15.00
	ND	—	2.00	3.25	5.00	8.50

KARAULI

State located in Rajputana, northwest India.

Karauli was established in the eleventh century by Jadon Rajputs, of the same stock as the royal house of Jaisalmir. They are thought to have migrated to Rajasthan from the Mathura region some years earlier. The state passed successively under Mughal and Maratha suzerainty before coming under British authority in 1817.

The Maharajas of Karauli first struck coins in the reign of Manak Pal.

RULERS

Manak Pal
AH1186-1233/1772-1817AD
Harbaksh Pal
AH1233-1254/1817-1838AD
Pratap Pal
AH1255-1264/1838-1848AD
Nar Singh Pal
AH1264-1268/1848-1852AD
Madan Pal
AH1268-1286/1854-1869AD
Jai Singh Pal, 1869-1875AD
Arjun Pal, 1876-1886AD
Bhanwar Pal, 1886-1927

MINT

Karauli کرولی and करौली

MINTNAME

Sawai Jaipur سوای جی پور

MINT MARKS

Katar — Jhar on reverse

Mughal Issues

PAISA

COPPER

KM#	Date	Year	Good	VG	Fine	VF
11	AH121x	44	3.00	6.00	10.00	16.50

NOTE: Earlier dates (Yr. 25-38) exist for this type.

RUPEE

SILVER, 10.80-11.20 g

KM#	Date	Year	VG	Fine	VF	XF
16	AH1216	43	20.00	31.50	42.50	60.00
	—	44	20.00	31.50	42.50	60.00

NOTE: Earlier dates (AH1216, Yr. 43 and 44) exist for this type.

In the name of Muhammad Akbar II
AH1221-1253/1806-1837AD

TAKKA

COPPER, 17.80-17.90 g

KM#	Date	Year	Good	VG	Fine	VF
21	AH122x	4	3.00	6.00	10.00	16.50
	—	10	3.00	6.00	10.00	16.50
	—	28	3.00	6.00	10.00	16.50

RUPEE

SILVER, 10.90-11.10 g

KM#	Date	Year	VG	Fine	VF	XF
26	AH1223	2	20.00	31.50	42.50	60.00
	1227	6	20.00	31.50	42.50	60.00
	1228	7	20.00	31.50	42.50	60.00
	122x	9	20.00	31.50	42.50	60.00
	1231	10	20.00	31.50	42.50	60.00
	1232	11	20.00	31.50	42.50	60.00
	1233	12	20.00	31.50	42.50	60.00
	1233	14	20.00	31.50	42.50	60.00
	1233	15	20.00	31.50	42.50	60.00
	1237	16	20.00	31.50	42.50	60.00
	1238	16	20.00	31.50	42.50	60.00
	1239 (retrograde 9)	17	20.00	31.50	42.50	60.00
	1240	19	20.00	31.50	42.50	60.00
	1244	25	20.00	31.50	42.50	60.00
	1254(sic)	23	20.00	31.50	42.50	60.00

In the name of Bahadur Shah II
AH1253-1274/1837-1858AD

RUPEE

SILVER, 10.60-11.00 g

KM#	Date	Year	VG	Fine	VF	XF
31	AH12xx	9	17.50	25.00	35.00	50.00
	—	11	17.50	25.00	35.00	50.00
	—	12	17.50	25.00	35.00	50.00

SILVER, 10.90-11.05 g
W/o legible AH year.

KM#	Date	Year	VG	Fine	VF	XF
33	AH—	13	17.50	25.00	35.00	50.00
	—	15	17.50	25.00	35.00	50.00

Regal Issues

In the name of Queen Victoria
Years of Madan Pal
Years 1-14

NOTE: 2 types of coins exist in the name of Queen Victoria; 1859 - the year of introduction of these coins and 1852 - the official accession year of Madan Pal.

TAKKA

COPPER

KM#	Date	Year	Good	VG	Fine	VF
36	1852	13	2.50	5.00	7.50	11.50

1/4 RUPEE

SILVER, 13mm, 2.68-2.90 g

KM#	Date	Year	VG	Fine	VF	XF
42.1	1859	7	12.50	18.50	25.00	35.00
42.2	1852	13	12.50	18.50	25.00	35.00
	1852	14	12.50	18.50	25.00	35.00

1/2 RUPEE

SILVER, 18mm, 5.35-5.80 g

KM#	Date	Year	VG	Fine	VF	XF
43.1	1859	—	15.00	21.50	30.00	40.00
43.2	1852	—	15.00	21.50	30.00	40.00

RUPEE

SILVER, 10.90-11.00 g

KM#	Date	Year	VG	Fine	VF	XF
44.1	1859	7	15.00	21.50	30.00	40.00
	1859	9	15.00	21.50	30.00	40.00
44.2	1852	9	15.00	21.50	30.00	40.00
	1852	10	15.00	21.50	30.00	40.00
	1852	11	15.00	21.50	30.00	40.00
	1852	12	15.00	21.50	30.00	40.00

KM#	Date	Year	VG	Fine	VF	XF
44.2	1852	13	15.00	21.50	30.00	40.00
	1852	14	15.00	21.50	30.00	40.00

In the name of the Exalted Queen, the Emperor of India
Years of Arjun Pal
Years 1-11

1/2 PAISA

COPPER, 13mm, 4.50 g

KM#	Date	Year	Good	VG	Fine	VF
49	1886	11	4.50	6.00	10.00	15.00

PAISA

COPPER, 9.00 g

KM#	Date	Year	Good	VG	Fine	VF
50	1886	11	1.75	2.75	4.00	7.50
	188x	16	1.75	2.75	4.00	7.50

TAKKA

COPPER, 18.00 g
Rev: Katar upper right.

KM#	Date	Year	Good	VG	Fine	VF
51	1881	—	1.75	2.75	4.00	7.50
	1882 (error for 1886)	11	1.75	2.75	4.00	7.50
	1883	—	1.75	2.75	4.00	7.50
	1885	9	1.75	2.75	4.00	7.50
	1885	10	1.75	2.75	4.00	7.50
	1886	11	1.75	2.75	4.00	7.50

RUPEE

SILVER, 10.90-11.10 g

KM#	Date	Year	VG	Fine	VF	XF
56	1882	7	15.00	21.50	30.00	40.00
	1883	—	15.00	21.50	30.00	40.00
	1884	9	15.00	21.50	30.00	40.00
	1885	10	15.00	21.50	30.00	40.00
	1886	11	15.00	21.50	30.00	40.00

In the name of the Exalted Queen, the Emperor of India
Years of Bhanwal Pal
Years 1-11

1/2 PAISA

COPPER, 9.00 g

KM#	Date	Year	Good	VG	Fine	VF
61	1886	1	1.75	3.00	5.00	8.00
	1887	2	1.75	3.00	5.00	8.00
	1891	5	1.75	3.00	5.00	8.00

TAKKA

COPPER, 18.00-18.25 g

KM#	Date	Year	Good	VG	Fine	VF
62	1885	—	1.75	2.75	4.50	6.50
	1886	1	1.75	2.75	4.50	6.50
	1887	2	1.75	2.75	4.50	6.50
	1891	5	1.75	2.75	4.50	6.50
	1891	6	1.75	2.75	4.50	6.50
	1893	8	1.75	2.75	4.50	6.50

1/8 RUPEE

SILVER, 1.35 g

KM#	Date	Year	VG	Fine	VF	XF
66	—	15	—	—	—	—

1/4 RUPEE

SILVER, 2.75 g

KM#	Date	Year	VG	Fine	VF	XF
68	1891	5	10.00	15.00	21.50	30.00
	1893	8	10.00	15.00	21.50	30.00
	1896	11	10.00	15.00	21.50	30.00

1/2 RUPEE

SILVER, 18mm, 5.45-5.60 g

KM#	Date	Year	VG	Fine	VF	XF
69	—	4	—	—	—	—
	1891	5	—	—	—	—
	1893	8	12.50	18.50	25.00	35.00
	1896	10	12.50	18.50	25.00	35.00

RUPEE

SILVER, 10.90-11.15 g

KM#	Date	Year	VG	Fine	VF	XF
70	1885	1	10.00	15.00	21.50	30.00
	1886	1	10.00	15.00	21.50	30.00
	1886	2	10.00	15.00	21.50	30.00
	1888	2	10.00	15.00	21.50	30.00
	1888	3	10.00	15.00	21.50	30.00
	1889	4	10.00	15.00	21.50	30.00
	1890	4	10.00	15.00	21.50	30.00
	1890	—	10.00	15.00	21.50	30.00
	1891	6	10.00	15.00	21.50	30.00
	1892	8	10.00	15.00	21.50	30.00
	1893	8	10.00	15.00	21.50	30.00
	1894	8	10.00	15.00	21.50	30.00
	1894	9	10.00	15.00	21.50	30.00
	1895	10	10.00	15.00	21.50	30.00
	1896	11	10.00	15.00	21.50	30.00
	1897	11	10.00	15.00	21.50	30.00

Anonymous Issues

1/2 MOHUR

GOLD

KM#	Date	Year	Fine	VF	XF	Unc
75	ND	2	—	—	Rare	—

MOHUR

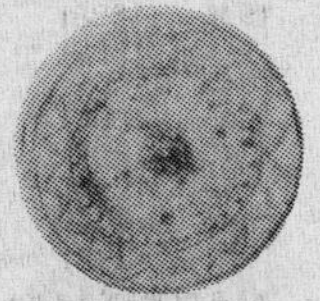

GOLD, 10.95 g

KM#	Date	Year	Fine	VF	XF	Unc
76	ND	2	—	—	Rare	—

KASHMIR

State located in extreme northern India. Part of Afghanistan Durrani Empire 1752-1819AD, under Sikhs of Punjab 1819-1846AD, locally ruled by Dogra Rajas thereafter. For earlier coinage refer to Afghanistan and Sikh Empire.

RULERS

Dogra Rajas

Gulab Singh
VS1903-1913/1846-1856AD

Ranbir Singh
VS1914-1942/1857-1885AD

Pertab Singh
VS1942-1979/1885-1925AD

MINTS

Jammu

Ladakh لداخ

Srinagar 

JAMMU MINT

Dogra Issues

Anonymous Issues

PAISA

COPPER

Obv: Persian leg. Rev: Gurmukhi leg.

Y#	Date	Year	Good	VG	Fine	VF
1	VS1914	(1857)	1.00	1.75	2.50	4.00
	1915	(1858)	1.00	1.75	2.50	4.00
	1917	(1860)	1.00	1.75	2.50	4.00
	1918	(1861)	1.00	1.75	2.50	4.00
	1919	(1862)	1.00	1.75	2.50	4.00
	1921	(1864)	1.00	1.75	2.50	4.00
	1922	(1865)	1.00	1.75	2.50	4.00
	ND	—	—	—	—	—

Rev: Takari leg.
Machine-punched planchets.

Y#	Date	Year	Good	VG	Fine	VF
2	VS1935	(1876)	5.00	9.00	12.00	20.00
	1936	(1877)	5.00	9.00	12.00	20.00

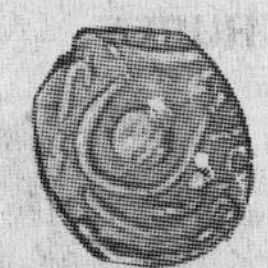

Dump style, uneven planchets.

Y#	Date	Year	Good	VG	Fine	VF
2a	VS1935	(1876)	1.00	1.75	2.50	4.00
	1937	(1878)	1.00	1.75	2.50	4.00
	1938	(1879)	1.00	1.75	2.50	4.00
	1939	(1880)	1.00	1.75	2.50	4.00
	1940	(1881)	1.00	1.75	2.50	4.00
	1942	(1883)	1.00	1.75	2.50	4.00
	1943	(1884)	1.00	1.75	2.50	4.00
	1946	(1887)	1.00	1.75	2.50	4.00
	1947	(1888)	1.00	1.75	2.50	4.00
	1948	(1889)	1.00	1.75	2.50	4.00
	1949	(1890)	1.00	1.75	2.50	4.00

Anonymous Issue

1/3 MOHUR

GOLD, 3.57-3.80 g

Y#	Date	Year	VG	Fine	VF	XF
3	VS1921	(1864)	185.00	300.00	425.00	600.00

LADAKH MINT

NOTE: For coins struck at the Ladakh Mint refer to Indian Princely State, Ladakh.

SRINAGAR MINT

First Copper Series

Many varieties exist.

PAISA

COPPER

Obv: Fancy leaf.

Y#	Date	Year	Good	VG	Fine	VF
1.1	VS1904	(1847)	2.50	4.00	6.50	10.00

Obv: Trident. Rev: Scimitar through circle.

Y#	Date	Year	Good	VG	Fine	VF
1.2	VS1908	(1851)	2.50	4.00	6.50	10.00

Rev: Fancy leaf.

Y#	Date	Year	Good	VG	Fine	VF
1.3	—	—	2.50	4.00	6.50	10.00

Second Copper Series

Obv: Fancy leaf. Rev: Scimitar through circle.

1/2 ANNA

COPPER

Y#	Date	Year	Good	VG	Fine	VF
8	VS1920	(1863)	5.00	9.00	13.00	20.00

ANNA

COPPER

Y#	Date	Year	Good	VG	Fine	VF
9	VS1920	(1863)	6.00	10.00	16.00	25.00
	1092 (error for 1920)		6.00	10.00	16.00	25.00
	1924	(1867)	6.00	10.00	16.00	25.00

Third Copper Series

Obv: Date in cartouche.

1/2 PAISA

COPPER, 2.50-3.00 g

Y#	Date	Year	Good	VG	Fine	VF
6	VS1922	(1865)	2.00	3.25	5.00	8.50
	1924	(1867)	2.00	3.25	5.00	8.50

PAISA

COPPER, 5.50-6.00 g

Y#	Date	Year	Good	VG	Fine	VF
7	VS1920	(1863)	.85	1.35	2.00	3.50
	1921	(1864)	.85	1.35	2.00	3.50
	1922	(1865)	.85	1.35	2.00	3.50
	1923	(1866)	1.00	1.75	2.50	4.00
	1926	(1869)	1.00	1.75	2.50	4.00
	1927	(1870)	.85	1.35	2.00	3.50
	1928	(1871)	.85	1.35	2.00	3.50
	1930	(1873)	1.00	1.75	2.50	3.50
	1931	(1874)	1.00	1.75	2.50	3.50

Fourth Copper Series

Obv: *JHS*. Rev: Takari leg.

1/4 PAISA

COPPER, 1.50 g

Y#	Date	Year	Good	VG	Fine	VF
17	VS1935	(1878)	3.00	5.00	8.00	12.50

Y#	Date	Year	Good	VG	Fine	VF
17	1941	(1884)	3.00	5.00	8.00	12.50
	Date off flan		1.75	2.75	4.00	7.00

1/2 PAISA

COPPER, 3.00 g

Y#	Date	Year	Good	VG	Fine	VF
18	VS1927	(1870)	1.50	2.50	4.00	6.00
	1928	(1871)	1.50	2.50	4.00	6.00
	1932	(1875)	1.00	1.75	2.50	4.00
	1933	(1876)	1.00	1.75	2.50	4.00
	1933 on obv/1934 on rev.	(1875/76)	1.25	2.25	3.50	5.50
	1934	(1877)	1.00	1.75	2.50	4.00
	1936	(1879)	1.00	1.75	2.50	4.00
	1937	(1880)	1.00	1.75	2.50	4.00
	1938	(1881)	1.00	1.75	2.50	4.00
	1939	(1882)	1.00	1.75	2.50	4.00
	1940	(1883)	1.00	1.75	2.50	4.00
	1941	(1884)	1.00	1.75	2.50	4.00

PAISA

COPPER, 6.00 g

Y#	Date	Year	Good	VG	Fine	VF
19	VS1937	(1880)	2.00	3.25	5.00	8.50
	1938	(1881)	2.00	3.25	5.00	8.50
	1939	(1882)	2.00	3.25	5.00	8.50
	1940	(1883)	2.00	3.25	5.00	8.50

First Silver Series

Rev: Leaf and date, w/o *JHS.*

NOTE: The dot for 'O' in 1903, 1904, 1905 is sometimes omitted.

1/8 RUPEE

SILVER, 1.28-1.35 g

Y#	Date	Year	VG	Fine	VF	XF
2	VS1903	(1846)	7.00	11.00	16.50	25.00
	1904	(1847)	7.00	11.00	16.50	25.00
	1905	(1848)	7.00	11.00	16.50	25.00

1/4 RUPEE

SILVER, 2.57-2.70 g

Y#	Date	Year	VG	Fine	VF	XF
3	VS1903	(1846)	6.50	10.00	15.00	22.50
	1904	(1847)	6.50	10.00	15.00	22.50

1/2 RUPEE

SILVER, 5.15-5.40 g

Y#	Date	Year	VG	Fine	VF	XF
4	VS1903	(1846)	7.50	12.50	18.50	27.50
	1904	(1847)	7.50	12.50	18.50	27.50
	1905	(1848)	7.50	12.50	18.50	27.50
	1906	(1849)	7.50	12.50	18.50	27.50

RUPEE

SILVER, 10.30-10.80 g

Y#	Date	Year	VG	Fine	VF	XF
5	VS1903	(1846)	7.00	11.00	16.50	25.00
	1904	(1847)	7.00	11.00	16.50	25.00
	1905	(1848)	7.50	12.50	18.50	27.50
	1906	(1849)	7.50	12.50	18.50	27.50

Second Silver Series

Obv. and rev: Persian leg. w/JHS added to rev.

1/16 RUPEE

SILVER, 0.64-0.67 g

Y#	Date	Year	VG	Fine	VF	XF
9	VS—	—	5.50	8.00	12.50	18.50

1/8 RUPEE

SILVER, 1.28-1.35 g

Y#	Date	Year	VG	Fine	VF	XF
10	VS1914	(1857)	5.50	8.00	12.50	18.50
	1925	(1868)	5.50	8.00	12.50	18.50

1/4 RUPEE

SILVER, 2.57-2.70 g

Y#	Date	Year	VG	Fine	VF	XF
11	VS1914	(1857)	6.00	9.00	13.50	20.00
	1922	(1865)	6.00	9.00	13.50	20.00
	1925	(1868)	6.00	9.00	13.50	20.00

1/2 RUPEE

SILVER, 5.15-5.40 g

Y#	Date	Year	VG	Fine	VF	XF
12	VS1914	(1857)	6.50	10.00	15.00	22.50
	1922	(1865)	6.50	10.00	15.00	22.50

"KHAM" RUPEE

SILVER, 10.30-10.80 g

Y#	Date	Year	VG	Fine	VF	XF
13	VS1906	(1849)	7.00	11.00	16.50	25.00
	1907	(1850)	7.00	11.00	16.50	25.00
	1908	(1851)	7.00	11.00	16.50	25.00
	1909	(1852)	7.00	11.00	16.50	25.00
	1910	(1853)	7.00	11.00	16.50	25.00
	1911	(1854)	7.00	11.00	16.50	25.00
	1912	(1855)	7.00	11.00	16.50	25.00
	1913	(1856)	7.00	11.00	16.50	25.00
	1914	(1857)	7.00	11.00	16.50	25.00
	1915	(1858)	7.00	11.00	16.50	25.00
	1916	(1859)	7.00	11.00	16.50	25.00
	1917	(1860)	7.00	11.00	16.50	25.00
	1918	(1861)	7.00	11.00	16.50	25.00
	1919	(1862)	7.00	11.00	16.50	25.00
	1920	(1863)	7.00	11.00	16.50	25.00
	1921	(1864)	7.00	11.00	16.50	25.00
	1922	(1865)	7.00	11.00	16.50	25.00
	1923	(1866)	7.00	11.00	16.50	25.00
	1924	(1867)	7.00	11.00	16.50	25.00
	1925	(1868)	7.00	11.00	16.50	25.00
	1926	(1869)	7.00	11.00	16.50	25.00
	1927	(1870)	7.00	11.00	16.50	25.00

Third Silver Series

Obv: Persian leg. w/*JHS.* Rev: Takari leg. Rupee weight Rupee weight reduced to 6.80 g from 10.30-10.80 g.

1/4 RUPEE

SILVER, 15mm, 1.65-1.70 g

Y#	Date	Year	VG	Fine	VF	XF
14	VS1928	(1871)	15.00	21.50	30.00	40.00

1/2 RUPEE

SILVER, 17mm, 3.30-3.40 g

Y#	Date	Year	VG	Fine	VF	XF
15	VS1928	(1871)	15.00	21.00	30.00	40.00

RUPEE

SILVER, 6.60-6.80 g
Machine-struck in collar.

Y#	Date	Year	VG	Fine	VF	XF
16	VS1927	(1870)	27.50	45.00	62.50	85.00
	1928	(1871)	27.50	45.00	62.50	85.00

Struck on machine punched planchets.

Y#	Date	Year	VG	Fine	VF	XF
16a	VS1927	(1870)	7.00	11.00	16.50	25.00
	1928	(1871)	7.00	11.00	16.50	25.00
	1929	(1872)	9.00	15.00	21.50	30.00

Struck on dump planchets.

Y#	Date	Year	VG	Fine	VF	XF
16b	VS1929	(1872)	7.50	12.50	18.50	27.50
	1930	(1873)	7.50	12.50	18.50	27.50
	1931	(1874)	7.50	12.50	18.50	27.50
	1932	(1875)	7.50	12.50	18.50	27.50

Fourth Silver Series ("Chilki")

Obv: Persian date in second line. Rev: Davanagari date in second line.

1/2 RUPEE

SILVER, 3.30 g

Y#	Date	Year	VG	Fine	VF	XF
20	VS1946	(1889)	7.00	11.00	16.50	25.00
	1948	(1891)	7.00	11.00	16.50	25.00
	1950	(1893)	7.00	11.00	16.50	25.00
	1951	(1894)	7.00	11.00	16.50	25.00

RUPEE

SILVER, 6.80 g

Y#	Date	Year	VG	Fine	VF	XF
21	VS1931	(1874)	12.50	18.50	25.00	35.00
	1932	(1875)	12.50	18.50	25.00	35.00
	1933	(1876)	12.50	18.50	25.00	35.00

6.65 g

Y#	Date	Year	VG	Fine	VF	XF
21a	VS1934	(1877)	5.50	8.00	12.50	18.50
	1935	(1878)	5.50	8.00	12.50	18.50
	1936	(1879)	5.50	8.00	12.50	18.50
	1937	(1880)	5.50	8.00	12.50	18.50
	1938	(1881)	5.50	8.00	12.50	18.50
	1939	(1882)	5.50	8.00	12.50	18.50
	1940	(1883)	5.50	8.00	12.50	18.50
	1941	(1884)	5.50	8.00	12.50	18.50
	1942	(1885)	5.50	8.00	12.50	18.50
	1943	(1886)	5.50	8.00	12.50	18.50
	1944	(1887)	5.50	8.00	12.50	18.50
	1945	(1888)	5.50	8.00	12.50	18.50
	1946	(1889)	5.50	8.00	12.50	18.50
	1947	(1890)	5.50	8.00	12.50	18.50
	1948	(1891)	5.50	8.00	12.50	18.50
	1949	(1892)	5.50	8.00	12.50	18.50
	1950	(1893)	5.50	8.00	12.50	18.50
	1951	(1894)	5.50	8.00	12.50	18.50
	1952	(1895)	5.50	8.00	12.50	18.50

NAZARANA 1/4 MOHUR

GOLD, 14-15mm, 2.30 g

Y#	Date	Year	VF	XF	Unc	BU
22	VS193x	—	—	500.00	700.00	1000.

KISHANGARH

The maharajas of Kishangarh, a small state in northwest India, in the vicinity of Ajmer, belonged to the Rathor Rajputs. The town of Kishangarh, which gave its name to the state, was founded in 1611 and was itself named after Kishen Singh, the first ruler. The maharajas succeeded in reaching terms with Akbar in the late sixteenth century, and again in 1818 with the British. In 1949 the state was merged into Rajasthan.

RULERS

Kalyan Singh
AH1212-1248/1797-1832AD
Mokham Singh
AH1248-1256/1832-1841AD
Prithvi Singh
AH1256-1297/1841-1879AD
Sardul Singh
AH1297-1318/1879-1900AD
Madan Singh

AH1318-1345/1900-1926AD
Yaghyanarayan Singh
AH1345-1357/1926-1938AD
Sirmer Singh
VS1995-2000/1938-1949AD

MINT

Kishangarh کشنگڑہ

Mint mark:

On reverse

Mughal Issues

In the name of Muhammad Akbar II
AH1221-1253/1806-1837AD

PAISA

COPPER, 17.25-17.50 g
Crude copy of Jaipur C#47

C#	Date	Year	Good	VG	Fine	VF
25	ND	—	1.00	1.50	2.50	5.00

TAKKA

COPPER, 17.25-17.50 g
Crude copy of Jaipur, C#35

C#	Date	Year	Good	VG	Fine	VF
5	AH—	—	1.25	1.75	2.50	5.00
	—	7	1.25	1.75	2.50	5.00
	—	7	1.25	1.75	2.50	5.00

Regal Issues

In the names of Queen Victoria and Prithvi Singh
1858-1879AD
Frozen regnal year 24 of Shah Alam II.

RUPEE

SILVER, 10.70-10.85 g

Y#	Date	Year	VG	Fine	VF	XF
1.1	1858	24	11.50	17.50	23.50	32.50

Different arrangement of inscription.

Y#	Date	Year	VG	Fine	VF	XF
1.2	1859	24	11.50	17.50	23.50	32.50

NOTE: A full size multiple rupee special strike weighing 24.33 g is known to exist.

MOHUR

GOLD, 10.9 g

Y#	Date	Year	VG	Fine	VF	XF
A1	1858	24	—	—	—	—

In the names of Queen Victoria and Sardul Singh
1879-1900AD

1/2 RUPEE

SILVER, 5.40 g

Y#	Date	Year	VG	Fine	VF	XF
A2	1880	—	11.50	18.50	25.00	35.00

RUPEE

SILVER, 10.80 g

Y#	Date	Year	VG	Fine	VF	XF
2	1880	24	15.00	25.00	35.00	50.00

MOHUR

GOLD, 10.90 g

Y#	Date	Year	VG	Fine	VF	XF
C2	ND	—	185.00	300.00	425.00	600.00

In the names of Empress Victoria and Madan Singh

1/2 RUPEE

SILVER, 5.40 g

Y#	Date	Year	VG	Fine	VF	XF
A3	ND	—	12.50	21.00	28.50	40.00

RUPEE

SILVER, 10.80 g

Y#	Date	Year	VG	Fine	VF	XF
C3	ND	—	—	—	—	—

MOHUR

GOLD, 10.90 g

Y#	Date	Year	VG	Fine	VF	XF
D3	ND	—	185.00	300.00	425.00	600.00

In the names of Edward VII and probably Madan Singh
1900-1926AD

1/4 RUPEE

SILVER, 2.70 g

Y#	Date	Year	VG	Fine	VF	XF
B3	ND	—	12.50	21.00	28.50	40.00

1/2 RUPEE

SILVER, 5.40 g

Y#	Date	Year	VG	Fine	VF	XF
3	1902	24	12.00	20.00	27.50	37.50

In the names of George V and Yaghyanarayan
1926-1938AD

1/4 RUPEE

SILVER, 15mm, 2.70 g

Y#	Date	Year	VG	Fine	VF	XF
4	—	24	12.50	20.00	27.50	37.50

1/2 RUPEE

SILVER, 5.40 g

Y#	Date	Year	VG	Fine	VF	XF
5	—	24	12.50	20.00	27.50	37.50

RUPEE

SILVER, 10.80 g

Y#	Date	Year	VG	Fine	VF	XF
6	—	24	18.50	31.50	42.50	60.00

NAZARANA RUPEE

SILVER, 10.70-10.80 g

Y#	Date	Year	VG	Fine	VF	XF
6a	—	—	60.00	100.00	140.00	200.00

1/2 MOHUR

GOLD, 18mm, ca. 5.50 g

Y#	Date	Year	VG	Fine	VF	XF
7	—	24	135.00	225.00	350.00	500.00

MOHUR

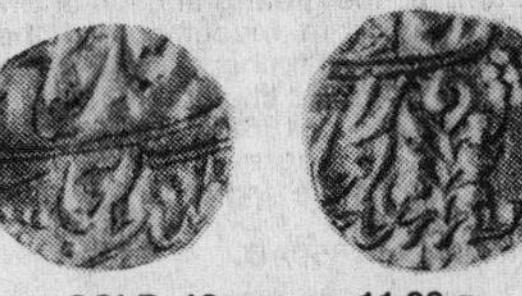

GOLD, 19mm, ca. 11.00 g

Y#	Date	Year	VG	Fine	VF	XF
8	—	24	185.00	300.00	425.00	600.00

Anonymous Issues

First Series

Obv. Nagari leg: *Chadi* (= silver).

1/8 RUPEE

SILVER, 1.35 g

Y#	Date	Year	VG	Fine	VF	XF
9	—	—	11.50	18.50	25.00	35.00

1/4 RUPEE

SILVER, 2.70 g

Y#	Date	Year	VG	Fine	VF	XF
10	—	—	11.50	18.50	25.00	35.00

1/2 RUPEE

SILVER, 5.40 g

Y#	Date	Year	VG	Fine	VF	XF
11	—	—	11.00	17.50	23.50	32.50

RUPEE

SILVER, 10.85-11.05 g

Y#	Date	Year	VG	Fine	VF	XF
12	—	—	14.00	23.50	32.50	45.00

Second Series

Obv: Denominations in Nagari, Persian and "merchants numerals", in Annas.

2 ANNAS

SILVER, 1.32 g

Y#	Date	Year	VG	Fine	VF	XF
13	—	24	12.50	21.00	28.50	40.00

4 ANNAS

SILVER, 2.62 g

Y#	Date	Year	VG	Fine	VF	XF
14	—	24	6.00	10.00	15.00	22.50

8 ANNAS

SILVER, 5.35 g

Y#	Date	Year	VG	Fine	VF	XF
15	—	24	6.50	11.00	16.50	25.00

KOLHAPUR

Maratha state in southwest India between Goa and

Bombay.

The maharajas of Kolhapur traced their origins and ancestry to Raja Ram, son of Shivaji, the founder of the Maratha kingdom, and to his courageous wife Tarabai who officiated as regent on behalf of her son after Raja Ram's death in 1698. Kolhapur's existence as a separate state dates from about 1730 when a family quarrel left Sambaji, the great-grandson of Sivaji, as the first raja of Kolhapur. In recognition of their special eminence among the Maratha chieftains the rulers of Kolhapur bore the honorific title of "Chhatrapati Maharaja". Between 1811 and 1862 Kolhapur concluded a series of treaties and agreements with the British whereby the state came increasingly under British protection and control.

The mint closed ca. 1850AD.

MINT

عظم نکر کوکاک

Mintname: A'zamnagar Gokak, Pseudo

Mughal Issues

In the name of Muhammad Shah
(struck until ca. 1850AD)

1/4 RUPEE

SILVER, 12mm, 2.68-2.90 g

C#	Date	Year	VG	Fine	VF	XF
14	ND	—	13.50	20.00	27.50	37.50

1/2 RUPEE

SILVER, 15mm, 5.35-5.80 g

C#	Date	Year	VG	Fine	VF	XF
15	ND	—	13.50	20.00	27.50	37.50

RUPEE

SILVER, 10.70-11.60 g

C#	Date	Year	VG	Fine	VF	XF
16	ND	—	6.50	11.00	16.50	25.00
	AH1132	6	6.50	11.00	16.50	25.00

Fine calligraphy

C#	Date	Year	VG	Fine	VF	XF
25	1821	—	12.50	21.00	28.50	40.00

Regal Issues

EAST INDIA COMPANY

Local issue from Shahupur.

1/2 RUPEE

SILVER, 5.35-5.80 g

C#	Date	Year	VG	Fine	VF	XF
29	1821	—	16.50	26.50	37.50	55.00

RUPEE

SILVER, 10.70-11.60 g

C#	Date	Year	VG	Fine	VF	XF
30	1821	—	16.50	26.50	37.50	55.00

KOTAH

Kotah State, located in northwest India was subdivided out of Bundi early in the seventeenth century when it was given to a younger son of the Bundi raja by the Mughal emperor. The ruler, or maharao, was a Chauhan Rajput. During the years of Maratha ascendancy Kotah fell on hard times, especially from the depredations of Holkar. In 1817 the State came under treaty with the British.

RULERS

Ram Singh II
VS1885-1923/1828-1866AD

Chattar Singh
VS1923-1946/1866-1889AD

Umed Singh II
VS1946-1992/1889-1935AD

MINT

ننرکاوت

Mintname: *Nandgaon*

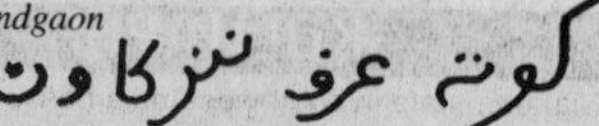

Kotah urf Nandgaon
(or Nandgaon urf Kotah)

MINT MARKS

1. 

2.

3.

4.

5. 

Mint mark #1 appears beneath #4 on all Kotah coins, and serves to distinguish coins of Kotah from similar issues of Bundi in the pre-Victoria period.

C#28 has mint mark #2 on obv., #1, 3 and 4 on rev. All later issues have #1 on obv., #1, 5 and 4 on rev.

Mughal Issues

RUPEE

SILVER, 11.05-11.20 g
Mint: Kotah urf Nandgaon
Mint: Kotah Nandgaon
Rev: Flower mint mark in front of regnal year.

C#	Date	Year	VG	Fine	VF	XF
28.3	AH—	44	8.50	13.50	20.00	28.50
	—	45	8.50	13.50	20.00	28.50
	—	46	8.50	13.50	20.00	28.50
	—	47	8.50	13.50	20.00	28.50

In the name of Muhammad Akbar II
AH1221-1253/1806-1837AD

NAZARANA RUPEE

SILVER, 11.20 g
Mint: Kotah Nandgaon

C#	Date	Year	VG	Fine	VF	XF
A28	AH1215	41	—	—	—	—

MOHUR

GOLD, 10.67 g
Mint: Kotah Nandgaon

C#	Date	Year	VG	Fine	VF	XF
B28	AH—	32	—	—	—	—

TAKKA

COPPER, square, 17.00-18.00 g

C#	Date	Year	Good	VG	Fine	VF
29	AH—	25	2.50	3.50	4.50	6.00
	—	29	2.50	3.50	4.50	6.00

Obv: W/o mint mark #1.

C#	Date	Year	Good	VG	Fine	VF
29a	AH—	4	1.50	2.50	4.50	7.00
	—	5	1.50	2.50	4.50	7.00

Obv: W/#1 mint mark.

C#	Date	Year	Good	VG	Fine	VF
29b	AH—	6	1.50	2.50	4.50	7.00
	—	7	1.50	2.50	4.50	7.00
	—	8	1.50	2.50	4.50	7.00
	—	10	1.50	2.50	4.50	7.00
	—	11	1.50	2.50	4.50	7.00
	—	12	1.50	2.50	4.50	7.00
	—	13	1.50	2.50	4.50	7.00
	—	14	1.50	2.50	4.50	7.00
	—	15	1.50	2.50	4.50	7.00
	—	16	1.50	2.50	4.50	7.00
	—	17	1.50	2.50	4.50	7.00
	—	18	1.50	2.50	4.50	7.00
	—	25	1.50	2.50	4.50	7.00
	—	26	1.50	2.50	4.50	7.00
	—	27	1.50	2.50	4.50	7.00
	—	28	1.50	2.50	4.50	7.00
	—	29	1.50	2.50	4.50	7.00
	—	30	1.50	2.50	4.50	7.00
	—	33	1.50	2.50	4.50	7.00

1/4 RUPEE

SILVER, 2.80 g
Obv: W/#1 mint mark.

C#	Date	Year	VG	Fine	VF	XF
29c	AH—	23	—	—	—	—

RUPEE

SILVER, 11.20-11.25 g
Obv: W/o mint mark #1.

C#	Date	Year	VG	Fine	VF	XF
30	AH—	1	6.50	10.00	15.00	22.50
	—	3	6.50	10.00	15.00	22.50

Obv: W/#1 mint mark.

C#	Date	Year	VG	Fine	VF	XF
30c	AH—	12	6.50	10.00	15.00	22.50
	—	15	6.50	10.00	15.00	22.50
	—	16	6.50	10.00	15.00	22.50
	—	18	6.50	10.00	15.00	22.50
	—	20	6.50	10.00	15.00	22.50
	—	22	6.50	10.00	15.00	22.50
	—	23	6.50	10.00	15.00	22.50
	—	24	6.50	10.00	15.00	22.50
	—	28	6.50	10.00	15.00	22.50
	1252	29	6.50	10.00	15.00	22.50
	—	30	6.50	10.00	15.00	22.50
	—	31	6.50	10.00	15.00	22.50
	—	32	6.50	10.00	15.00	22.50

NAZARANA RUPEE

SILVER, square, 11.20-11.30 g
Obv: W/o #1 mint mark.

C#	Date	Year	VG	Fine	VF	XF
30a	AH—	5	37.50	62.50	85.00	120.00

Obv: W/#1 mint mark.

C#	Date	Year	VG	Fine	VF	XF
30d	AH—	11	37.50	62.50	85.00	120.00
	—	16	37.50	62.50	85.00	120.00
	—	19	37.50	62.50	85.00	120.00
	—	23	37.50	62.50	85.00	120.00
	—	27	37.50	62.50	85.00	120.00

Obv: W/#1 mint mark.
Round, 27-31mm

C#	Date	Year	VG	Fine	VF	XF
30b	AH1237	16	37.50	62.50	85.00	120.00
	1239	18	37.50	62.50	85.00	120.00
	1240	19	37.50	62.50	85.00	120.00
	1242	22	37.50	62.50	85.00	120.00
	1245	24	37.50	62.50	85.00	120.00
	124x	30	37.50	62.50	85.00	120.00
	125x	32	37.50	62.50	85.00	120.00

NOTE: Formerly listed under Bundi State.

MOHUR

GOLD, 10.70 g
Obv: W/o mint mark # 1.

C#	Date	Year	VG	Fine	VF	XF
30e	AH—	2	—	—	—	—

Obv: W/#1 mint mark.

C#	Date	Year	VG	Fine	VF	XF
30f	AH—	19	—	—	—	—

In the name of Bahadur Shah II
AH1253-1274/1837-1857AD

1/8 RUPEE

SILVER, 10mm, 1.40 g

C#	Date	Year	VG	Fine	VF	XF
31	AH—	—	7.00	11.00	16.50	25.00

1/4 RUPEE

SILVER, 12mm, 2.80 g

C#	Date	Year	VG	Fine	VF	XF
A31	AH—	—	7.00	11.00	16.50	25.00

1/2 RUPEE

SILVER, 5.60 g

C#	Date	Year	VG	Fine	VF	XF
B31	AH—	—	7.50	12.50	18.50	27.50

RUPEE

SILVER, 11.00-11.25 g

C#	Date	Year	VG	Fine	VF	XF
32	AH—	4	6.00	9.00	13.50	20.00
	—	5	6.00	9.00	13.50	20.00
	—	6	6.00	9.00	13.50	20.00

C#	Date	Year	VG	Fine	VF	XF
32	—	7	6.00	9.00	13.50	20.00
	—	8	6.00	9.00	13.50	20.00
	—	9	6.00	9.00	13.50	20.00
	—	11	6.00	9.00	13.50	20.00
	—	12	6.00	9.00	13.50	20.00
	—	15	6.00	9.00	13.50	20.00
	—	16	6.00	9.00	13.50	20.00
	—	17	6.00	9.00	13.50	20.00
	—	18	6.00	9.00	13.50	20.00
	—	19	6.00	9.00	13.50	20.00
	—	20	6.00	9.00	13.50	20.00
	—	21	6.00	9.00	13.50	20.00

NAZARANA RUPEE

SILVER, 10.70-11.60 g

C#	Date	Year	VG	Fine	VF	XF
32a	AH—	1	27.50	45.00	62.50	85.00
	—	2	27.50	45.00	62.50	85.00
	—	3	27.50	45.00	62.50	85.00
	—	4	27.50	45.00	62.50	85.00
	—	5	27.50	45.00	62.50	85.00
	1205	6	27.50	45.00	62.50	85.00
	—	7	27.50	45.00	62.50	85.00
	—	8	27.50	45.00	62.50	85.00
	—	9	27.50	45.00	62.50	85.00
	—	10	27.50	45.00	62.50	85.00
	—	11	27.50	45.00	62.50	85.00
	—	12	27.50	45.00	62.50	85.00
	—	13	27.50	45.00	62.50	85.00
	—	14	27.50	45.00	62.50	85.00
	—	15	27.50	45.00	62.50	85.00
	—	16	27.50	45.00	62.50	85.00
	—	17	27.50	45.00	62.50	85.00
	—	18	27.50	45.00	62.50	85.00
	—	19	27.50	45.00	62.50	85.00
	—	20	27.50	45.00	62.50	85.00
	—	21	27.50	45.00	62.50	85.00
	—	22	27.50	45.00	62.50	85.00

NOTE: All specimens show rudimentary traces of AH dates on obverse.

MOHUR

GOLD, 19mm, 10.70-11.40 g

C#	Date	Year	VG	Fine	VF	XF
33	AH—	1	185.00	300.00	425.00	600.00
	—	19	185.00	300.00	425.00	600.00
	—	20	185.00	300.00	425.00	600.00
	—	21	185.00	300.00	425.00	600.00

Regal Issues

In the name of the Queen of England

From 1858AD

PAISA

COPPER, 12-16mm, 9.00-12.00 g

Y#	Date	Year	Good	VG	Fine	VF
1	AH—	37	1.50	2.50	3.75	6.00
	—	38	1.50	2.50	3.75	6.00
	—	39	1.50	2.50	3.75	6.00
	—	40	1.50	2.50	3.75	6.00

TAKKA

COPPER, 15-20mm, 16.80-18.00 g

Y#	Date	Year	Good	VG	Fine	VF
2	AH—	1	1.25	2.00	3.25	5.00
	—	2	1.25	2.00	3.25	5.00

Y#	Date	Year	Good	VG	Fine	VF
2	—	6	1.25	2.00	3.25	5.00
	—	8	1.25	2.00	3.25	5.00
	—	24	1.25	2.00	3.25	5.00
	—	27	1.25	2.00	3.25	5.00
	—	28	1.25	2.00	3.25	5.00
	—	29	1.25	2.00	3.25	5.00
	—	30	1.25	2.00	3.25	5.00
	—	31	1.25	2.00	3.25	5.00
	—	32	1.25	2.00	3.25	5.00
	—	35	1.25	2.00	3.25	5.00
	—	37	1.25	2.00	3.25	5.00
	—	38	1.25	2.00	3.25	5.00
	—	39	1.25	2.00	3.25	5.00
	—	40	1.25	2.00	3.25	5.00
	—	41	1.25	2.00	3.25	5.00
	—	51	1.25	2.00	3.25	5.00

1/8 RUPEE

SILVER, 1.40 g

Y#	Date	Year	VG	Fine	VF	XF
3	AH—	22	5.00	7.00	10.00	15.00
	—	27	5.00	7.00	10.00	15.00
	—	20	5.00	7.00	10.00	15.00
	—	29	5.00	7.00	10.00	15.00
	—	30	5.00	7.00	10.00	15.00
	—	31	5.00	7.00	10.00	15.00
	—	32	5.00	7.00	10.00	15.00
	—	33	5.00	7.00	10.00	15.00
	—	34	5.00	7.00	10.00	15.00
	—	36	5.00	7.00	10.00	15.00
	—	37	5.00	7.00	10.00	15.00
	—	38	5.00	7.00	10.00	15.00

1/4 RUPEE

SILVER, 2.80 g

Y#	Date	Year	VG	Fine	VF	XF
4	AH—	1	4.00	6.00	9.00	13.50
	—	2	4.00	6.00	9.00	13.50
	—	5	4.00	6.00	9.00	13.50
	—	8	4.00	6.00	9.00	13.50
	—	10	4.00	6.00	9.00	13.50
	—	22	4.00	6.00	9.00	13.50
	—	23	4.00	6.00	9.00	13.50
	—	26	4.00	6.00	9.00	13.50
	—	27	4.00	6.00	9.00	13.50
	—	29	4.00	6.00	9.00	13.50
	—	30	4.00	6.00	9.00	13.50
	—	31	4.00	6.00	9.00	13.50
	—	32	4.00	6.00	9.00	13.50
	—	33	4.00	6.00	9.00	13.50
	—	35	4.00	6.00	9.00	13.50
	—	37	4.00	6.00	9.00	13.50
	—	38	4.00	6.00	9.00	13.50

1/2 RUPEE

SILVER, 5.60 g

Y#	Date	Year	VG	Fine	VF	XF
5	AH—	1	5.50	8.00	12.50	18.50
	—	4	5.50	8.00	12.50	18.50
	—	8	5.50	8.00	12.50	18.50
	—	18	5.50	8.00	12.50	18.50
	—	22	5.50	8.00	12.50	18.50
	—	24	5.50	8.00	12.50	18.50
	—	25	5.50	8.00	12.50	18.50
	—	27	5.50	8.00	12.50	18.50
	—	28	5.50	8.00	12.50	18.50
	—	29	5.50	8.00	12.50	18.50
	—	30	5.50	8.00	12.50	18.50
	—	31	5.50	8.00	12.50	18.50
	—	32	5.50	8.00	12.50	18.50
	—	33	5.50	8.00	12.50	18.50
	—	34	5.50	8.00	12.50	18.50
	—	35	5.50	8.00	12.50	18.50
	—	36	5.50	8.00	12.50	18.50
	—	37	5.50	8.00	12.50	18.50
	—	38	5.50	8.00	12.50	18.50

RUPEE

SILVER, 11.20 g

Y#	Date	Year	VG	Fine	VF	XF
6	AH—	1	5.50	8.00	10.00	15.00
	—	2	5.50	8.00	10.00	15.00
	—	4	5.50	8.00	10.00	15.00
	—	5	5.50	8.00	10.00	15.00

Y#	Date	Year	VG	Fine	VF	XF
6	—	6	5.50	8.00	10.00	15.00
	—	7	5.50	8.00	10.00	15.00
	—	8	5.50	8.00	10.00	15.00
	—	9	5.50	8.00	10.00	15.00
	—	10	5.50	8.00	10.00	15.00
	—	11	5.50	8.00	10.00	15.00
	—	12	5.50	8.00	10.00	15.00
	—	13	5.50	8.00	10.00	15.00
	—	14	5.50	8.00	10.00	15.00
	—	15	5.50	8.00	10.00	15.00
	—	16	5.50	8.00	10.00	15.00
	—	17	5.50	8.00	10.00	15.00
	—	18	5.50	8.00	10.00	15.00
	—	19	5.50	8.00	10.00	15.00
	—	20	5.50	8.00	10.00	15.00
	—	21	5.50	8.00	10.00	15.00
	—	22	5.50	8.00	10.00	15.00
	—	24	5.50	8.00	10.00	15.00
	—	25	5.50	8.00	10.00	15.00
	—	26	5.50	8.00	10.00	15.00
	—	28	5.50	8.00	10.00	15.00
	—	29	5.50	8.00	10.00	15.00
	—	31	5.50	8.00	10.00	15.00
	—	32	5.50	8.00	10.00	15.00
	—	34	5.50	8.00	10.00	15.00
	—	35	5.50	8.00	10.00	15.00
	—	37	5.50	8.00	10.00	15.00
	—	38	5.50	8.00	10.00	15.00
	—	39	5.50	8.00	10.00	15.00
	—	40	5.50	8.00	10.00	15.00
	—	41	5.50	8.00	10.00	15.00
	—	44	5.50	8.00	10.00	15.00

10th Anniversary of Reign of Umed Singh II and 80th Birthday of Queen Victoria
Rev: Full year.

Y#	Date	Year	VG	Fine	VF	XF
7	VS1956	(1899)	17.50	25.00	35.00	50.00

NAZARANA RUPEE

SILVER, 11.20 g

Y#	Date	Year	VG	Fine	VF	XF
6a	AH—	1	32.50	45.00	62.50	85.00
	—	2	32.50	45.00	62.50	85.00
	—	3	32.50	45.00	62.50	85.00
	—	4	32.50	45.00	62.50	85.00
	—	5	32.50	45.00	62.50	85.00
	—	6	32.50	45.00	62.50	85.00
	—	7	32.50	45.00	62.50	85.00
	—	8	32.50	45.00	62.50	85.00
	—	9	32.50	45.00	62.50	85.00
	—	10	32.50	45.00	62.50	85.00
	—	11	32.50	45.00	62.50	85.00
	—	12	32.50	45.00	62.50	85.00
	—	13	32.50	45.00	62.50	85.00
	—	14	32.50	45.00	62.50	85.00
	—	15	32.50	45.00	62.50	85.00
	—	16	32.50	45.00	62.50	85.00
	—	17	32.50	45.00	62.50	85.00
	—	18	32.50	45.00	62.50	85.00
	—	19	32.50	45.00	62.50	85.00
	—	20	32.50	45.00	62.50	85.00
	—	21	32.50	45.00	62.50	85.00
	—	22	32.50	45.00	62.50	85.00
	—	23	32.50	45.00	62.50	85.00
	—	24	32.50	45.00	62.50	85.00
	—	25	32.50	45.00	62.50	85.00
	—	26	32.50	45.00	62.50	85.00
	—	27	32.50	45.00	62.50	85.00
	—	28	32.50	45.00	62.50	85.00
	—	29	32.50	45.00	62.50	85.00
	—	30	32.50	45.00	62.50	85.00
	—	31	32.50	45.00	62.50	85.00
	—	32	32.50	45.00	62.50	85.00
	—	39	32.50	45.00	62.50	85.00
	—	43	32.50	45.00	62.50	85.00
	—	44	32.50	45.00	62.50	85.00

Y#	Date	Year	VG	Fine	VF	XF
7a	VS1956	(1899)	40.00	62.50	85.00	120.00

1/8 MOHUR

GOLD, 1.34 g

Y#	Date	Year	VG	Fine	VF	XF
A8a	VS(19)56(1899)		185.00	300.00	425.00	600.00

1/2 MOHUR

GOLD, 5.35 g

Y#	Date	Year	VG	Fine	VF	XF
C8	AH—	42	185.00	300.00	425.00	600.00

MOHUR

GOLD, 10.70 g

Y#	Date	Year	VG	Fine	VF	XF
8	AH—	1	175.00	250.00	350.00	500.00
	—	6	175.00	250.00	350.00	500.00
	—	8	175.00	250.00	350.00	500.00
	—	9	175.00	250.00	350.00	500.00
	—	15	175.00	250.00	350.00	500.00
	—	31	175.00	250.00	350.00	500.00
	—	32	175.00	250.00	350.00	500.00
	—	44	175.00	250.00	350.00	500.00

KUTCH

State located in northwest India, consisting of a peninsula north of the Gulf of Kutch.

The rulers of Kutch were Jareja Rajputs who, coming from Tatta in Sind, conquered Kutch in the fourteenth or fifteenth centuries. The capital city of Bhuj is thought to date from the mid-sixteenth century. In 1617, after Akbar's conquest of Gujerat and the fall of the Gujerat sultans, the Kutch ruler, Rao Bharmal I (1586-1632) visited Jahangir and established a relationship which was sufficiently warm as to leave Kutch virtually independent throughout the Mughal period. Early in the nineteenth century internal disorder and the existence of rival claimants to the throne resulted in British intrusion into the state's affairs. Rao Bharmalji II was deposed in favor of Rao Desalji II who proved much more amenable to the Government of India's wishes. He and his successors continued to rule in a manner considered by the British to be most enlightened and, as a result, Maharao Khengarji III was created a Knight Grand Commander of the Indian Empire. In view of its geographical isolation Kutch came under the direct control of the Central Government at India's independence.

First coinage was struck in 1617AD.

RULERS

Rayadhanji II
AH1192-1230/1778-1814AD

राउ श्री रायधणजी

Ra-o Sri Ra-y(a)-dh(a)-n-ji

Bharmalji II
AH1230-1235/1814-1819AD

राउ श्री भारमलजी

Ra-o Sri Bha-r-m(a)-l-ji

Desalji II
AH1235-1277/VS1876-1917/1819-1860AD

राउ श्री देसलजी

Ra-o Sri De-s(a)-l-ji

राउ श्री देसलजी

Ra-o Sri De-sa-l-ji

Pragmalji II
VS1917-1932/1860-1875AD

राउ श्री प्रागमलजी

Ra-o Sri Pra-g-m(a)-l-ji

महाराउ श्री प्रागमलजी

M(a)-ha-ra-o Sri Pra-g-m(a)-l-ji

महाराजाधिराज मिरजा महाराउ श्री

Ma-ha-ra-ja Dhi-ra-j Mi-r-ja M(a)-ha-ra-o Sri

प्रागमलजी बहादुर

Pra-g-m(a)-l-ji B(a)-ha-du-r

Khengarji III
VS1932-1999/1875-1942AD

महाराओ श्री खेंगारजी

M(a)-ha-ra-o Sri Khen-ga-r-ji

महाराउ खेंगारजी

Ma-ha-ra-o Khen-ga-r-ji

महाराजाधिराज मिरजा महाराओ श्री

Ma-ha-ra-ja Dhi-ra-j Mi-r-ja M(a)-ha-ra-o Sri

खेंगारजी बहादुर कछभुज

Khen-ga-r-ji B(a)-ha-du-r K(a)-chh-bhu-j

मिरजां महाराओ श्री खेंगारजी

Mi-r-jan M(a)-ha-ra-o Sri Khen-ga-r-ji

महाराओ श्री खेंगारजी

M(a)-ha-ra-o Sri Khen-ga-r-ji

महाराजाधिराज मिरजां महाराउ

M(a)-ha-ra-ja Dhi-ra-j Mi-r-jan M(a)-ha-ra-o

श्री खेंगारजी बहादुर

Sri-Khen-ga-r-ji B(a)-ha-du-r

श्री खेंगारजी सवाई बहादुर

Sri Khen-ga-r-ji Sa-va-i B(a)-ha-du-r

महाराउ श्री खेंगारजी कच्छभुज

M(a)-ha-ra-o Sri Khen-ga-r-ji K(a)-chchh-bhu-j

Vijayarajji
VS1999-2004/1942-1947AD

विजयराजजी

Vi-j(a)-y(a)-ra-j-ji

M(a)-ha-ra-o Sri Vi-j(a)-y(a)-ra-j-ji K(a)-chchh 2000

Madanasinhji
VS2004/1947 AD

मदनसिंहजी

M(a)-d(a)-n(a)-sin-h-ji

MINT

भुज or بهوج

Bhuj (Devavnagri) (Persian)

MONETARY SYSTEM

2 Trambiyo = 1 Dokda
3 Trambiyo = 1 Dhingla
8 Dokda = 1 Kori

NOTE: All coins through Bharmalji II bear a common type, derived from the Gujarati coinage of Muzaffar III (late 16th century AD), and bear a stylized form of the date AH978 (1570AD). The silver issues of Bharmalji II also have the fictitious date AH1165. The rulers name appears in the Devavnagri script on the obverse.

BHARMALJI II

AH1230-1235/1814-1819AD

TRAMBIYO

COPPER, 4.00 g

C#	Date	Good	VG	Fine	VF
31	ND	2.50	4.00	5.50	7.50

DOKDO

COPPER, 16mm, 8.30 g

C#	Date	Good	VG	Fine	VF
32	ND	2.50	4.00	5.50	7.50

DHINGLO

COPPER, 17mm, 12.00 g

C#	Date	Good	VG	Fine	VF
33	ND	3.00	4.50	6.00	8.50

1/2 KORI

SILVER, 2.10 g

C#	Date	VG	Fine	VF	XF
35.1	AH1165 (fictitious)	3.50	5.00	7.50	12.00

Name of Bharmalji.

C#	Date	VG	Fine	VF	XF
35.2	AH1234	—	—	—	—

KORI

SILVER, 4.40 g

C#	Date	VG	Fine	VF	XF
36	AH1165 (fictitious)	3.00	4.50	6.50	10.00

DESALJI II

AH1235-1277/VS1875-1917/1818-1860AD

The coins of Desalji II may be divided into four basic series, which may be differentiated as follows:

FIRST SERIES: Similar to coins of Bharmalji, but w/Desalji's name in Devavnagri on rev.

SECOND SERIES: In the name of the Mughal Emperor Akbar II and of Desalji in Devavnagri on obv., mint and both dates in Persian leg. on rev. but actual SE date in Devavnagri numerals. AH date is frozen (12)34, SE dates 1875-1887.

THIRD SERIES: Obv: Persian leg., rev: in Devavnagri script Dates: AH1250-1266, VS1892-1904. Many sub-varieties of type, some w/only AH dates, some w/only SE dates, some w/both. In the name of Muhammad Akbar II.

FOURTH SERIES: Same as third series, but in the name of Bahadur II. VS1909-1916 on silver and gold issues and AH1267-1274 on copper.

NOTE: Although Muhammad Akbar II was succeeded by Bahadur II on the Mughal throne in AH1253, the change is not acknowledged on Kutch coinage until AH1263 and Bahadur Shah is honored until VS1916/1859AD, the year after he was deposed by the British following the mutiny.

First Series

TRAMBIYO

COPPER, 4.20 g

C#	Date	Good	VG	Fine	VF
38	ND	1.00	1.50	2.50	4.00

DOKDO

COPPER, 8.70 g

C#	Date	Good	VG	Fine	VF
39	ND	1.00	1.50	2.50	4.00

DHINGLO

COPPER, 18mm, 12.90 g

C#	Date	Good	VG	Fine	VF
40	ND	1.25	2.00	3.00	4.50

Second Series

Obv: Persian leg. w/Devavnagri name below. Rev: Persian leg.

In the name of Muhammad Akbar II
AH1221-1253/1806-1837AD

NOTE: The frozen date AH1234 on this series is the accession date of Desalji II.

TRAMBIYO

COPPER, 4.00 g

C#	Date	Year	Good	VG	Fine	VF
41	AH1234	VS1880	2.50	3.50	5.00	7.50

DOKDO

COPPER, 7.90 g

C#	Date	Year	Good	VG	Fine	VF
42	AH1234	VS1880	2.50	3.50	5.00	7.00

DHINGLO

COPPER, 12.30 g

C#	Date	Year	Good	VG	Fine	VF
43	AH1234	VS1880	2.75	4.00	5.50	7.50

1/2 KORI

SILVER, 2.10-2.20 g

C#	Date	Year	VG	Fine	VF	XF
52	AH1234	VS1877	4.00	6.00	9.00	13.50

KORI

SILVER, 4.40-4.50 g

C#	Date	Year	VG	Fine	VF	XF
53	AH1234	VS1875	3.00	4.50	6.50	10.00
	1234	1876	3.00	4.50	6.50	10.00
	1234	1877	3.00	4.50	6.50	10.00
	1234	1879	3.00	4.50	6.50	10.00
	1234	1880	3.00	4.50	6.50	10.00
	1234	1881	3.00	4.50	6.50	10.00
	1234	1882	3.00	4.50	6.50	10.00
	1234	1884	3.00	4.50	6.50	10.00
	1234	1885	3.00	4.50	6.50	10.00
	1234	1887	3.00	4.50	6.50	10.00

Third Series

Obv: Persian leg. Rev: Devavnagri leg. below Persian mintname on copper, date below Devavnagri leg. on silver.

In the name of Muhammad Akbar II
AH1221-1253/1806-1837AD

TRAMBIYO

COPPER, 4.10 g

C#	Date	Good	VG	Fine	VF
45	AH1255	1.00	1.50	2.50	4.00
	1256	1.00	1.50	2.50	4.00
	1257	1.00	1.50	2.50	4.00
	1258	1.00	1.50	2.50	4.00
	1259	1.00	1.50	2.50	4.00
	1260	1.00	1.50	2.50	4.00
	1261	1.00	1.50	2.50	4.00
	1262	1.00	1.50	2.50	4.00

DOKDO

COPPER, 8.10 g

C#	Date	Good	VG	Fine	VF
46	AH1259	1.00	1.50	2.50	4.00
	1261	1.00	1.50	2.50	4.00
	1262	1.00	1.50	2.50	4.00

DHINGLO

COPPER, 12.00-12.50 g

C#	Date	Good	VG	Fine	VF
47	AH1255	1.75	3.00	4.00	5.50
	1257	1.25	2.00	3.00	4.50
	1258	1.25	2.00	3.00	4.50
	1259	1.25	2.00	3.00	4.50
	1261	1.25	2.00	3.00	4.50
	1262	1.25	2.00	3.00	4.50
	1263	—	—	—	—
	1266	1.50	2.50	3.50	5.00
	1268	1.50	2.50	3.50	5.00

1/2 KORI

SILVER, 2.10-2.20 g
Rev: Katar below Devavnagri date w/Kutch *9*.

C#	Date	Year	VG	Fine	VF	XF
55	VS1891	(1834)	4.00	6.00	9.00	13.50
	1892	(1835)	3.50	5.00	7.50	12.00

Rev: Katar below date.

C#	Date	Year	VG	Fine	VF	XF
55a	AH1252	VS1893	4.00	6.00	9.00	13.50

Rev: Katar to right of Devavnagri date.

C#	Date	Year	VG	Fine	VF	XF
55b	AH1252	VS1894	4.00	6.00	9.00	13.50

Rev: Katar below Kutch date.

C#	Date	Year	VG	Fine	VF	XF
58	VS1895	(1838)	3.00	4.50	6.50	10.00

Obv: AH date at left in middle leg.

C#	Date	Year	VG	Fine	VF	XF
58a	AH1262	VS1903	3.50	5.00	7.50	12.00
	1263	1904	3.50	5.00	7.50	12.00

KORI

SILVER, 4.40-4.50 g
Rev: Katar below Devavnagri date w/Kutch *9*.

C#	Date	Year	VG	Fine	VF	XF
56	AH1250	VS1892	4.00	6.00	9.00	13.50
	1251	1892	3.00	4.50	6.50	10.00
	1252	1893	3.00	4.50	6.50	10.00

Rev: Katar to right of Devavnagri date.

C#	Date	Year	VG	Fine	VF	XF
56a	AH1252	VS1894	3.50	5.00	7.50	12.00
59	VS1895	(1838)	3.50	5.00	7.50	12.00

Rev: Katar to right of Devavnagri date.

C#	Date	Year	VG	Fine	VF	XF
59b	VS1901	(1844)	3.00	4.50	6.50	10.00
	1902	(1845)	3.00	4.50	6.50	10.00

Obv: AH date at left in middle leg.

C#	Date	Year	VG	Fine	VF	XF
59a	AH1262	VS1903	2.50	3.50	5.00	8.00

Fourth Series

In name of Bahadur Shah II
AH1253-1274/1837-1858AD

TRAMBIYO

COPPER, 14mm, 4.10 g

C#	Date	Good	VG	Fine	VF
61	AH1263	1.75	2.75	4.00	5.50
	1266	1.75	2.75	4.00	5.50
	ND	1.75	2.75	4.00	5.50

C#	Date	Good	VG	Fine	VF
61a	AH1267	1.00	1.50	2.00	3.50
	1269	1.00	1.50	2.00	3.50
	1274	1.00	1.50	2.00	3.50

DOKDO

COPPER, 17-19mm, 8.10 g

C#	Date	Good	VG	Fine	VF
62	AH1263	1.50	2.50	4.00	5.00
	1266	1.50	2.50	4.00	5.00

C#	Date	Good	VG	Fine	VF
62a	AH1267	1.50	2.50	4.00	5.00
	1269	1.00	1.50	2.00	2.50
	1274	—	Reported, not confirmed		

DHINGLO

COPPER, 18-21mm, 12.00-12.50 g

C#	Date	Good	VG	Fine	VF
63	AH1263	2.50	4.00	5.25	6.50
	1266	2.00	3.50	4.50	5.50

C#	Date	Good	VG	Fine	VF
63a	AH1267	1.25	2.00	2.50	3.00
	1268	1.25	2.00	2.50	3.00
	1269	1.25	2.00	2.50	3.00
	1270	1.50	2.75	3.25	4.00
	1271	1.50	2.75	3.25	4.00
	1272	1.25	2.00	2.50	3.00
	1273	1.50	2.75	3.25	4.00
	1274	1.50	2.75	3.25	4.00

1/2 KORI

SILVER, 2.20 g

C#	Date	Year	VG	Fine	VF	XF
65	VS1909	(1852)	2.50	3.50	5.00	8.00
	1910	(1853)	2.50	3.50	5.00	8.00
	1911	(1854)	3.00	4.50	6.50	10.00
	1912	(1855)	2.50	3.50	5.00	8.00
	1913	(1856)	2.50	3.50	5.00	8.00
	1914	(1857)	2.50	3.50	5.00	8.00

KORI

SILVER, 4.40-4.50 g

C#	Date	Year	VG	Fine	VF	XF
66	VS1909	(1852)	2.50	3.50	5.00	8.00
	1910	(1853)	2.50	3.50	5.00	8.00
	1911	(1854)	3.00	4.50	6.50	10.00
	1912	(1855)	2.50	3.50	5.00	8.00
	1913	(1856)	2.50	3.50	5.00	8.00
	1914	(1857)	2.50	3.50	5.00	8.00
	1915	(1858)	5.00	7.00	10.00	15.00
	1916	(1859)	5.50	8.00	12.50	18.50

25 KORI

.999 GOLD, 4.67 g

C#	Date	Year	Fine	VF	XF	Unc
67	VS1911	(1854)	70.00	100.00	120.00	150.00
	1912	(1855)	70.00	100.00	120.00	150.00
	1913	(1856)	70.00	100.00	120.00	150.00
	1914	(1857)	70.00	100.00	120.00	150.00
	1915	(1858)	70.00	100.00	120.00	150.00

MILLED COINAGE

Regal Issues

PRAGMALJI II

VS1917-1932/1860-1875AD

Pragmalji II is the first ruler of Kutch to pay homage to Queen Victoria. He experimented with a joint formulation his first year, VS1917/1860AD, see the rare coin type Y#A14. In VS1919/1862AD he settled on a standard type acknowledging "Queen Victoria, Mighty Queen" and himself as "Rao" or "Maharao", see types Y#13, 14 and 17.

TRAMBIYO

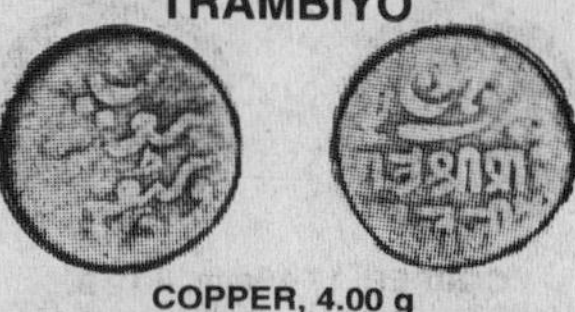

COPPER, 4.00 g

Y#	Date	Good	VG	Fine	VF
1	1865	1.25	2.00	3.00	4.50

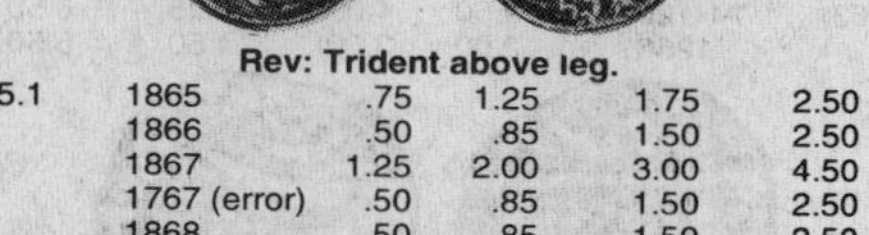

Rev: 2 characters right of trident.

Y#	Date	Good	VG	Fine	VF
5	1865	.50	.85	1.50	2.50
	1866	1.50	2.50	3.50	5.00

Rev: Trident above leg.

Y#	Date	Good	VG	Fine	VF
5.1	1865	.75	1.25	1.75	2.50
	1866	.50	.85	1.50	2.50
	1867	1.25	2.00	3.00	4.50
	1767 (error)	.50	.85	1.50	2.50
	1868	.50	.85	1.50	2.50

Obv: Persian leg. w/*Victoria* at bottom.

Y#	Date	Year	Good	VG	Fine	VF
9	1869	VS1925	1.00	1.50	2.50	3.75
	1869	1926	1.50	2.50	3.50	4.50

Obv: Persian leg. w/*Victoria* at top.

Y#	Date	Year	Good	VG	Fine	VF
9.1	1869	VS1926	.50	1.00	2.00	3.00
	1874	1930	.50	1.00	2.00	3.00

DOKDO

COPPER, 8.00 g

Y#	Date	Good	VG	Fine	VF
6	1865	1.25	2.00	2.50	3.50
	1866	1.00	1.75	2.25	3.00
	1867	.90	1.50	1.75	2.50
	1868	.60	1.00	1.50	2.75
	1869 (retrograde 9)	1.50	2.50	3.75	5.00

Obv: Persian leg. w/*Victoria* at top.

Y#	Date	Year	Good	VG	Fine	VF
10	1869	VS1925	1.25	2.00	3.00	4.50

Obv: Persian leg. w/*Victoria* at bottom.

Y#	Date	Year	Good	VG	Fine	VF
10.1	1869	VS1925	.60	1.00	1.50	2.50
	1869	1926	1.00	1.50	2.00	3.00
	1869	1927	1.50	2.50	3.50	5.00

Obv: Persian leg. w/*Victoria* right.

Y#	Date	Year	Good	VG	Fine	VF
10.2	1873	VS1930	1.00	1.50	2.00	3.00
	1874	1930	.60	1.00	1.50	2.50

1-1/2 DOKDA

COPPER, 12.00 g
Obv: Persian leg. w/*Victoria* at top.

Y#	Date	Year	Good	VG	Fine	VF
11	1869	1926	.75	1.25	1.75	2.25
	1780	1925 (error)	1.75	3.00	3.50	4.25
	1780	1926 (error)	.90	1.50	2.00	2.50
	1870	1927	.60	1.00	1.50	2.00
	1870	1928	.60	1.00	1.50	2.00
	1780	1928 (error)	.75	1.25	1.75	2.25
	1871	1928	.60	1.00	1.50	2.00
	1872	1928	.75	1.25	1.75	2.25

Obv: Persian leg. w/*Victoria* to right.

Y#	Date	Year	Good	VG	Fine	VF
11.1	1871	VS1928	.90	1.50	2.00	2.50
	1872	1928	.90	1.50	2.00	2.50
	1872	1929	.75	1.25	1.75	2.25
	1873	1929	.60	1.00	1.50	2.25
	1879	1929 (error)	.75	1.25	1.75	2.25
	1873	1930	.60	1.00	1.50	2.25
	1783	1930 (error)	.75	1.25	1.75	2.50
	1874	1930	.60	1.00	1.50	2.00
	1874	1931	.60	1.00	1.50	2.00
	1874	1932	1.25	2.00	2.75	3.50
	1875	1930	1.00	1.75	2.50	3.50
	1875	1931	.75	1.25	1.75	2.25

Obv: Persian leg. on top written differently, w/*Victoria* to right.

Y#	Date	Year	Good	VG	Fine	VF
11.2	1875	1932	.75	1.25	1.75	2.25
	1876	1933	.75	1.25	1.75	2.25

Obv: Persian leg. w/*Victoria* to left.

Y#	Date	Year	Good	VG	Fine	VF
11.3	1872	VS1928	1.50	2.50	3.75	5.00
	1872	1929	1.50	2.50	3.75	5.00

3 DOKDA

COPPER, 24.00 g
Rev: *Sa(m)vat* at upper left, date at right.

Y#	Date	Year	Good	VG	Fine	VF
8	1868	VS1925	2.50	4.00	6.00	7.50

Obv: Similar to Y#8.2.
Rev: *Sa(m)vat* and date at top.

Y#	Date	Year	Good	VG	Fine	VF
8.1	1868	VS1925	2.50	4.00	6.00	7.50

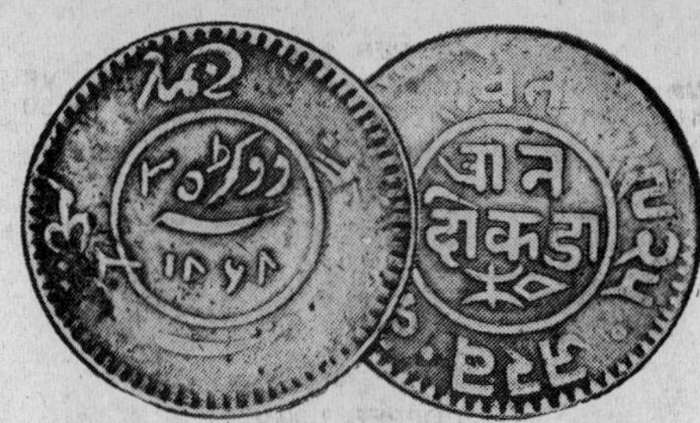

Rev: *Sa(m)vat* at top, date at right.

Y#	Date	Year	Good	VG	Fine	VF
8.2	1868	VS1925	2.50	4.00	6.00	7.50

Y#	Date	Year	Good	VG	Fine	VF
12	1868	VS1925	2.50	4.00	5.50	6.50
	1869	1925	2.00	3.50	4.50	5.75
	1869	1926	2.00	3.50	4.50	5.75

1/2 KORI

2.3500 g, .610 SILVER, .0460 oz ASW

Y#	Date	Year	VG	Fine	VF	XF
13	1862	VS1919	2.50	3.50	5.00	8.00
	1862	1920	2.00	3.00	4.00	7.00
	1863	1920	2.50	3.50	5.00	8.00
	1763	1920 (error)	2.50	3.50	5.00	8.00
	1863	1921	2.00	3.00	4.00	7.00

KORI

4.7000 g, .610 SILVER, .0921 oz ASW
Rev: Rosette after date.

Y#	Date	Year	VG	Fine	VF	XF
A14	1860	VS1917	—	—	Rare	—

Y#	Date	Year	VG	Fine	VF	XF
14	1862	VS1918	2.00	3.00	4.00	7.00
	1862	1919	2.50	3.50	5.00	8.00
	1862	1920	2.00	3.00	4.00	7.00
	1863	1920	2.00	3.00	4.00	7.00
	1863	1921	2.00	3.00	4.00	7.00

2-1/2 KORI

6.9350 g, .937 SILVER, .2089 oz ASW

Y#	Date	Year	VG	Fine	VF	XF
15	1875	VS1931	4.00	6.00	9.00	13.50
	1785	1931	5.50	8.00	12.50	18.50
	1875	1932	4.00	6.00	9.00	13.50

5 KORI

13.8700 g, .937 SILVER, .4178 oz ASW

Y#	Date	Year	VG	Fine	VF	XF
16	1863	VS1921	20.00	31.50	42.50	60.00

Obv: Leg. rearranged.

Y#	Date	Year	VG	Fine	VF	XF
16.1	1865	VS1921	8.50	13.50	20.00	28.50
	1865	1922	7.00	11.00	16.50	25.00
	1866	1922	6.50	10.00	15.00	22.50
	1866	1923	6.50	10.00	15.00	22.50
	1870	1927	7.00	11.00	16.50	25.00
	1874	1931	6.00	9.00	13.50	20.00
	1875	1931	6.00	9.00	13.50	20.00
	1875	1932	6.00	9.00	13.50	20.00

25 KORI

4.6750 g, .999 GOLD, .1501 oz AGW

Y#	Date	Year	Fine	VF	XF	Unc
17	1862	VS1919	70.00	100.00	120.00	150.00
	1863	1920	70.00	100.00	120.00	150.00
	1863	1921	70.00	100.00	120.00	150.00

Y#	Date	Year	Fine	VF	XF	Unc
17a	1870	VS1926	70.00	100.00	120.00	150.00
	1870	1927	70.00	100.00	120.00	150.00

50 KORI

9.3500 g, .906 GOLD, .2723 oz AGW

Y#	Date	Year	Fine	VF	XF	Unc
18	1668 (sic - error for 1866)	VS1923	130.00	185.00	230.00	275.00
	1866	1923	110.00	150.00	180.00	225.00
	1873	1930	110.00	150.00	180.00	225.00
	1874	1930	110.00	150.00	180.00	225.00
	1874	1931	110.00	150.00	180.00	225.00

100 KORI

18.7000 g, .906 GOLD, .5446 oz AGW

Y#	Date	Year	Fine	VF	XF	Unc
19	1866	VS1922	225.00	285.00	375.00	500.00
	1866	1923	225.00	285.00	375.00	500.00

KHENGARJI III

VS1932-1998/1875-1942AD

First Series

Obv. leg: *Queen Victoria, Mighty Queen.*

DOKDO

COPPER, 8.00 g

Y#	Date	Year	Good	VG	Fine	VF
22	1878	VS1934	10.00	17.50	20.00	25.00
	1878	1935	13.50	22.50	25.00	30.00
	(1)878	1935	15.00	25.00	27.50	32.50

1-1/2 DOKDA

COPPER, 12.00 g

Y#	Date	Year	Good	VG	Fine	VF
23	1876	VS1933	.90	1.50	2.00	2.50
	1877	1933	.90	1.50	2.00	2.50
	1877	1934	.90	1.50	2.00	2.50
	1877	1922 (error)	.90	1.50	2.00	2.50
	1878	1934	.90	1.50	2.00	2.50
	1878	1935	1.25	2.00	2.50	3.00

Obv: Similar to 1 1/2 Dokda, Y#11.

Y#	Date	Year	Good	VG	Fine	VF
23.1	1876	VS1933	1.25	2.00	2.50	3.50

KORI

2.3500 g, .610 SILVER, .0460 oz ASW

Y#	Date	Year	VG	Fine	VF	XF
26	1876	VS1932	50.00	75.00	110.00	150.00
	1876	1933	50.00	75.00	110.00	150.00

5 KORI

13.8700 g, .937 SILVER, .4178 oz ASW

Y#	Date	Year	VG	Fine	VF	XF
28	1876	VS1933	20.00	31.50	42.50	60.00

Second Series

Obv. leg: *Victoria, Empress of India.*

TRAMBIYO

COPPER, 4.00 g

Y#	Date	Year	Good	VG	Fine	VF
30	1881	VS1938	.50	.75	1.00	1.50
	1882	1938	.30	.50	.75	1.25
	1883	1939	.30	.50	.75	1.25
	1883	1940	.50	.75	1.00	1.50

Rev: *Kutch* added below date.

Y#	Date	Year	Good	VG	Fine	VF
30.1	1883	VS1940	.50	.75	1.00	1.50

DOKDO

COPPER, 8.00 g

Y#	Date	Year	Good	VG	Fine	VF
31	1882	VS1938	.50	.75	1.00	1.50
	1882	1939	.90	1.50	2.00	2.50
	1883	1939	.50	.75	1.00	1.50

Rev: *Kutch* added below date.

Y#	Date	Year	Good	VG	Fine	VF
31.1	1883	VS1940	.50	.75	1.00	1.50
	1884	1940	.50	.75	1.00	1.50

Obv: Leg. similar to Y#31.1 but spaced similar to Y#31.3.

Y#	Date	Year	Good	VG	Fine	VF
31.2	1892	VS1948	2.50	4.00	6.00	8.50

Obv: Urdu leg. *Victoria* written differently.

Y#	Date	Year	Good	VG	Fine	VF
31.3	1899	VS1956	.90	1.50	2.00	3.00

1-1/2 DOKDA

COPPER, 12.00 g

Y#	Date	Year	Good	VG	Fine	VF
32	1882	VS1938	.60	1.00	1.25	1.75
	1882	1939	.60	1.00	1.25	1.75
	1883	1939	.60	1.00	1.25	1.75
	1883	1940	.60	1.00	1.25	1.75

Rev: *Kutch* added below date.

Y#	Date	Year	Good	VG	Fine	VF
32.1	1883	VS1940	.60	1.00	1.25	1.75
	1884	1940	.60	1.00	1.25	1.75
	1884	1941	.60	1.00	1.25	1.75

Finer style

Y#	Date	Year	Good	VG	Fine	VF
32.2	1885	VS1942	.75	1.25	1.50	2.00
	1887	1944	.75	1.25	1.50	2.00
	1888	1944	.75	1.25	1.50	2.00
32.3	1892	1948	.75	1.25	1.50	2.00
	1894	1950	.75	1.25	1.50	2.00

Y#	Date	Year	Good	VG	Fine	VF
32.4	1899	VS1955	1.25	2.00	2.50	3.00
	1899	1956	1.25	2.00	2.75	3.50

3 DOKDA

COPPER, 24.00 g

Y#	Date	Year	Good	VG	Fine	VF
33	1883	VS1940	1.25	2.00	2.50	3.00
	1885	1942	.90	1.50	2.00	2.50
	1886	1942	1.35	2.25	3.00	4.00
	1887	1944	.90	1.50	2.00	2.50
	1888	1944	1.25	2.00	2.50	3.00

Y#	Date	Year	Good	VG	Fine	VF
33.1	1894	VS1951	1.50	2.50	3.00	3.50
	1899	1955	1.50	2.50	3.00	3.50

1/2 KORI

2.3500 g, .610 SILVER, .0460 oz ASW

Y#	Date	Year	VG	Fine	VF	XF
34	1898	VS1954	2.50	3.50	5.00	8.00
	1899	1955	2.50	3.50	5.00	8.00
	1899	1956	2.50	3.50	5.00	8.00
	1900	1956	2.50	3.50	5.00	8.00
	1900	1957	3.00	4.50	6.50	10.00

KORI

4.7000 g, .610 SILVER, .0921 oz ASW
Rev: Closed crescent.

Y#	Date	Year	VG	Fine	VF	XF
35	1881	VS1938	2.50	3.50	5.00	8.00
	1882	1938	2.50	3.50	5.00	8.00
	1882	1939	2.00	3.00	4.00	7.00
	1883	1939	2.00	3.00	4.00	7.00
	1883	1940.	2.00	3.00	4.00	7.00
	1884	1941	2.50	3.50	5.00	8.00
	1885	1941	2.00	3.00	4.00	7.00

Rev: Open crescent.

Y#	Date	Year	VG	Fine	VF	XF
35.1	1894	VS1950	2.50	3.50	5.00	8.00
	1896	1952	2.50	3.50	5.00	8.00
	1897	1953	2.00	3.00	4.00	7.00
	1897	1954	2.00	3.00	4.00	7.00
	1898	1954	2.00	3.00	4.00	7.00
	1898	1955	2.00	3.00	4.00	7.00
	1899	1955	2.00	3.00	4.00	7.00
	1899	1956	2.00	3.00	4.00	7.00
	1900	1956	2.00	3.00	4.00	7.00
	1900	1957	2.00	3.00	4.00	7.00
	1901	1957	3.00	4.50	6.50	10.00

2-1/2 KORI

6.9350 g, .937 SILVER, .2089 oz ASW
Rev: Closed crescent.

Y#	Date	Year	VG	Fine	VF	XF
36	1881	VS1938	5.00	7.00	10.00	15.00
	1882	1938	4.00	6.00	9.00	13.50

Rev: Open crescent.

Y#	Date	Year	VG	Fine	VF	XF
36.1	1894	VS1951	4.00	6.00	9.00	13.50
	1895	1951	3.50	5.00	7.00	12.00
	1897	1953	3.50	5.00	7.00	12.00
	1897	1954	3.50	5.00	7.00	12.00
	1898	1954	4.00	6.00	9.00	13.50
	1898	1955	4.00	6.00	9.00	13.50
	1899	1955	4.00	6.00	9.00	13.50

Y#	Date	Year	VG	Fine	VF	XF
36.2	1899	VS1955	4.00	6.00	9.00	13.50
	1899	1956	3.50	5.00	7.50	12.00

5 KORI

13.8700 g, .937 SILVER, .4178 oz ASW
Obv: Leaves of wreath point counter-clockwise.

Y#	Date	Year	VG	Fine	VF	XF
37	1880	VS1937	7.00	11.00	16.50	25.00
	1881	1937	6.50	10.00	15.00	22.50
	1881	1938	6.50	10.00	15.00	22.50

Obv: Leaves of wreath point clockwise.

Y#	Date	Year	VG	Fine	VF	XF
37.1	1881	VS1937	6.50	10.00	15.00	22.50
	1881	1938	6.50	10.00	15.00	22.50

Rev: Bars to left and right of center leg.

Y#	Date	Year	VG	Fine	VF	XF
37.2	1881	VS1937	6.50	10.00	15.00	22.50

Obv: Similar to Y#37. Rev: Similar to Y#37.2.

Y#	Date	Year	VG	Fine	VF	XF
37.3	1880	VS1937	6.50	10.00	15.00	22.50

Obv: Changed wreath. Rev: Closed crescent.

Y#	Date	Year	VG	Fine	VF	XF
37.4	1881	VS1938	6.50	10.00	15.00	22.50
	1882	1938	6.50	10.00	15.00	22.50
	1882	1939	6.50	10.00	15.00	22.50
	1883	1939	6.50	10.00	15.00	22.50
	1883	1940	6.50	10.00	15.00	22.50
	1884	1939	(error)			
			—	—	—	—
	1884	1940	6.50	10.00	15.00	22.50
	1884	1941	6.50	10.00	15.00	22.50
	1885	1941	6.50	10.00	15.00	22.50
	1885	1942	15.00	21.50	30.00	40.00
	1886	1943	15.00	21.50	30.00	40.00

Rev: Open crescent.

Y#	Date	Year	VG	Fine	VF	XF
37.5	1890	VS1947	13.50	20.00	27.50	37.50
	1893	1950	10.00	15.00	21.50	30.00
	1894	1950	6.50	10.00	15.00	22.50
	1894	1951	6.50	10.00	15.00	22.50
	1895	1951	6.50	10.00	15.00	22.50
	1895	1952	6.50	10.00	15.00	22.50
	1896	1952	6.50	10.00	15.00	22.50
	1896	1953	6.50	10.00	15.00	22.50
	1896	1954	(error)			
			13.50	20.00	27.50	37.50
	1897	1951	(error)			
			7.00	11.00	16.50	25.00
	1897	1953	6.50	10.00	15.00	22.50
	1897	1954	6.50	10.00	15.00	22.50
	1898	1951	(error)			
			12.50	18.50	25.00	35.00
	1898	1953	6.50	10.00	15.00	22.50
	1898	1954	6.50	10.00	15.00	22.50
	1898	1955	6.50	10.00	15.00	22.50
	1899	1955	7.00	11.00	16.50	25.00

Y#	Date	Year	VG	Fine	VF	XF
37.6	1899	VS1955	6.50	10.00	15.00	22.50
	1899	1956	6.50	10.00	15.00	22.50
	1901	1957	17.50	25.00	35.00	50.00

Third Series

In the name of Edward VII

TRAMBIYO

COPPER, 4.00 g

Y#	Date	Year	VG	Fine	VF	XF
38	1908	VS1965	1.50	2.50	3.50	4.50
	1909	1965	.60	1.00	1.50	2.50
	1909	1966	.60	1.00	1.50	2.00
	1910	1966	1.60	2.75	4.25	6.00

DOKDO

COPPER, 8.00 g

Y#	Date	Year	VG	Fine	VF	XF
39	1909	VS1965	.75	1.25	1.50	2.00
	1909	1966	.75	1.25	1.50	2.00

1-1/2 DOKDA

COPPER, 23mm, 12.00 g

Y#	Date	Year	VG	Fine	VF	XF
40	1909	VS1965	60.00	100.00	115.00	150.00

3 DOKDA

COPPER, 24.00 g

Y#	Date	Year	VG	Fine	VF	XF
41	1909	VS1965	60.00	100.00	115.00	150.00

5 KORI

13.8700 g, .937 SILVER, .4178 oz ASW

Y#	Date	Year	VG	Fine	VF	XF
45	1902	VS1959	120.00	185.00	250.00	365.00
	1903	1960	120.00	185.00	250.00	365.00
	1904	1961	120.00	185.00	250.00	365.00
	1905	1962	120.00	185.00	250.00	365.00
	1906	1963	120.00	185.00	250.00	365.00
	1907	1964	120.00	185.00	250.00	365.00
	1908	1965	100.00	150.00	225.00	300.00
	1909	1966	100.00	150.00	225.00	300.00

Fourth Series

In the name of George V

NOTE: New automatic minting equipment was introduced in 1928 and used to strike the finer style coins from 1928 to 1947 when the mint closed.

TRAMBIYO

COPPER, 4.00 g

Y#	Date	Year	VG	Fine	VF	XF
46	1919	VS1976	.30	.50	.75	1.00
	1920	1976	.30	.50	.75	1.50
	1920	1977	.30	.50	.75	1.50

Y#	Date	Year	VG	Fine	VF	XF
54	1928	VS1984	.60	1.00	2.00	3.00
	1928	1985	.30	.50	.75	1.00

DOKDO

COPPER, 8.00 g

Y#	Date	Year	VG	Fine	VF	XF
47	1920	VS1976	.60	1.00	1.25	2.00
	1920	1977	.60	1.00	1.25	2.00

Y#	Date	Year	VG	Fine	VF	XF
55	1922	VS1982	(error)			
			1.25	1.75	2.50	3.50
	1928	1984	.60	1.00	1.25	1.50
	1929	1985	.60	1.00	1.25	1.50

1-1/2 DOKDA

COPPER, 12.00 g

Y#	Date	Year	VG	Fine	VF	XF
48	1926	VS1982	.90	1.50	2.50	3.00

Y#	Date	Year	VG	Fine	VF	XF
56	1928	VS1985	.50	.75	1.00	1.50
	1929	1985	.50	.75	1.00	1.50
	1929	1986	.50	.75	1.00	1.50
	1931	1987	.50	.75	1.00	1.50
	1931	1988	.50	.75	1.00	1.50
	1932	1988	1.00	1.50	2.50	4.00
	1932	1989	.50	.75	1.00	1.50

3 DOKDA

COPPER, 24.00 g

Y#	Date	Year	VG	Fine	VF	XF
49	1926	VS1982	1.50	2.50	3.50	4.50

Y#	Date	Year	VG	Fine	VF	XF
57	1928	VS1985	.60	1.00	1.50	2.25
	1929	1985	.60	1.00	1.50	2.25
	1929	1986	.60	1.00	1.50	2.25
	1930	1987	.60	1.00	1.50	2.25
	1931	1987	.60	1.00	1.50	2.25
	1934	1990	.60	1.00	1.50	2.25
	1934	1991	.60	1.00	1.50	2.25
	1935	1992	.60	1.00	1.50	2.25

1/2 KORI

2.3500 g, .601 SILVER, .0460 oz ASW

Y#	Date	Year	VG	Fine	VF	XF
58	1928	VS1985	2.00	3.00	4.00	7.00

KORI

4.7000 g, .601 SILVER, .0921 oz ASW

Y#	Date	Year	Fine	VF	XF	Unc
51	1913	VS1970	2.00	3.00	4.00	7.00
	1923	1979	2.00	3.00	4.00	7.00
	1923	1980	2.00	3.00	4.00	7.00
51	1927	1984	2.50	3.50	5.00	8.00
	1927	1985	— Reported, not confirmed			

Y#	Date	Year	Fine	VF	XF	Unc
59	1928	VS1985	2.50	3.50	5.00	8.00
	1929	1985	2.50	3.50	5.00	8.00
	1931	1987	6.50	10.00	15.00	22.50
	1931	1988	2.50	3.00	5.00	8.00
	1932	1988	2.50	3.00	5.00	8.00
	1932	1989	2.50	3.00	5.00	8.00
	1933	1989	2.50	3.00	5.00	8.00
	1933	1990	2.50	3.00	5.00	8.00
	1934	1990	2.50	3.00	5.00	8.00
	1934	1991	2.50	3.00	5.00	8.00
	1935	1991	2.50	3.00	5.00	8.00
	1935	1992	2.50	3.00	5.00	8.00
	1936	1992	3.00	4.50	6.50	10.00

2-1/2 KORI

6.9350 g, .937 SILVER, .2089 oz ASW

Y#	Date	Year	Fine	VF	XF	Unc
52	1916	VS1973	4.00	6.00	9.00	13.50
	1917	1973	4.00	6.00	9.00	13.50
	1917	1974	4.00	6.00	9.00	13.50
	1918	1974	4.00	6.00	9.00	13.50
	1919	1975	4.00	6.00	9.00	13.50
	1922	1978	4.00	6.00	9.00	13.50
	1922	1979	4.00	6.00	9.00	13.50
	1924	1981	4.00	6.00	9.00	13.50
	1926	1983	4.00	6.00	9.00	13.50

Rev: Smaller leg.

Y#	Date	Year	Fine	VF	XF	Unc
52a	1927	VS1984	5.00	7.00	10.00	15.00
	1928	1985	4.00	6.00	9.00	13.50
	1930	1986	4.00	6.00	9.00	13.50
	1930	1987	4.00	6.00	9.00	13.50
	1932	1988	4.00	6.00	9.00	13.50
	1932	1989	4.00	6.00	9.00	13.50
	1933	1989	4.00	6.00	9.00	13.50
	1933	1990	4.00	6.00	9.00	13.50
	1934	1990	4.00	6.00	9.00	13.50
	1934	1991	4.00	6.00	9.00	13.50
	1935	1991	4.00	6.00	9.00	13.50
	1935	1992	4.00	6.00	9.00	13.50

5 KORI

13.8700 g, .937 SILVER, .4178 oz ASW

Y#	Date	Year	Fine	VF	XF	Unc
53	1913	VS1970	6.50	10.00	15.00	22.50
	1915	1972	6.50	10.00	15.00	22.50
	1916	1973	6.50	10.00	15.00	22.50
	1916	1975	(error)			
			12.50	18.50	25.00	35.00
	1917	1973	6.50	10.00	15.00	22.50
	1917	1974	6.50	10.00	15.00	22.50
	1918	1974	6.50	10.00	15.00	22.50
	1918	1975	6.50	10.00	15.00	22.50
	1919	1975	6.50	10.00	15.00	22.50
	1919	1976	25.00	37.50	50.00	70.00
	1920	1977	7.00	11.00	16.50	25.00
	1921	1977	6.50	10.00	15.00	22.50
	1921	1978	6.50	10.00	15.00	22.50
	1922	1974	(error)			
			—	—	—	—
	1922	1978	6.50	10.00	15.00	22.50
	1922	1979	6.50	10.00	15.00	22.50
	1922	1982	(error)			
			7.50	12.50	18.50	27.50

Y#	Date	Year	Fine	VF	XF	Unc
53	1923	1979	6.50	10.00	15.00	22.50
	1924	1978	(error)			
			20.00	31.50	42.50	60.00
	1924	1980	12.00	13.00	15.00	22.50
	1924	1981	12.00	13.00	15.00	22.50
	1925	1982	12.00	13.00	15.00	22.50
	1926	1978	(error)			
			12.50	18.50	25.00	35.00
	1926	1982	6.50	10.00	15.00	22.50
	1926	1983	6.50	10.00	15.00	22.50
	1927	1984	17.50	25.00	35.00	50.00
	1927	1984	—	—	Proof	275.00

NOTE: 5 Kori coins were issued with reeded edges until 1925AD which is when the security edge was introduced. 1924 and 1926 dates exist with lettered edges.

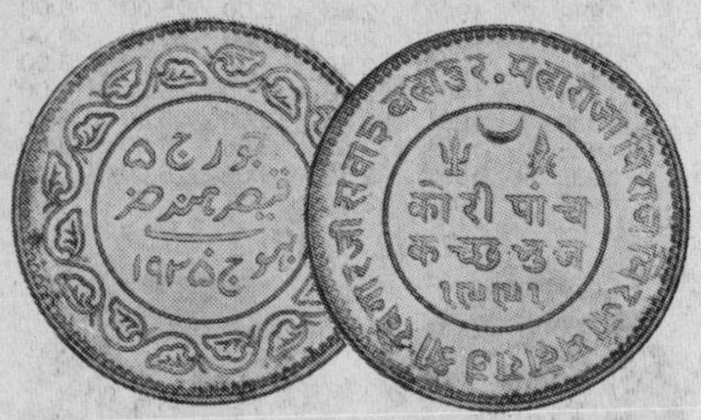

Obv. and rev: Smaller leg.

Y#	Date	Year	Fine	VF	XF	Unc
53a	1928	VS1985	15.00	21.50	30.00	40.00
	1929	1986	6.50	10.00	15.00	22.50
	1930	1986	6.50	10.00	15.00	22.50
	1930	1987	6.50	10.00	15.00	22.50
	1931	1987	6.50	10.00	15.00	22.50
	1931	1988	6.50	10.00	15.00	22.50
	1932	1988	6.50	10.00	15.00	22.50
	1932	1989	6.50	10.00	15.00	22.50
	1933	1989	6.50	10.00	15.00	22.50
	1933	1990	6.50	10.00	15.00	22.50
	1934	1990	6.50	10.00	15.00	22.50
	1934	1991	6.50	10.00	15.00	22.50
	1935	1991	6.50	10.00	15.00	22.50
	1935	1992	6.50	10.00	15.00	22.50
	1936	1992	6.50	10.00	15.00	22.50

Fifth Series

In the name of Edward VIII

3 DOKDA

COPPER, 24.00 g

Y#	Date	Year	VG	Fine	VF	XF
63	1936	VS1993	3.00	5.00	7.50	10.00

KORI

4.7000 g, .601 SILVER, .0921 oz ASW

Y#	Date	Year	Fine	VF	XF	Unc
65	1936	VS1992	3.00	4.50	6.50	10.00
	1936	1993	3.00	4.50	6.50	10.00

2-1/2 KORI

6.9350 g, .937 SILVER, .2089 oz ASW

Y#	Date	Year	Fine	VF	XF	Unc
66	1936	VS1992	11.50	17.50	23.50	32.50
	1936	1993	11.50	17.50	23.50	32.50

5 KORI

13.8700 g, .937 SILVER, .4178 oz ASW

Y#	Date	Year	Fine	VF	XF	Unc
67	1936	VS1992	5.00	7.00	10.00	15.00
	1936	1993	5.00	7.00	10.00	15.00

Sixth Series

In the name of George VI

3 DOKDA

COPPER, 24.00 g

Y#	Date	Year	VG	Fine	VF	XF
71	1937	VS1993	.90	1.50	2.00	3.00

KORI

4.7000 g, .601 SILVER, .0921 oz ASW

Y#	Date	Year	Fine	VF	XF	Unc
73	1937	VS1993	3.00	4.50	6.50	10.00
	1937	1994	3.00	4.50	6.50	10.00
	1938	1995	3.00	4.50	6.50	10.00
	1939	1995	3.00	4.50	6.50	10.00
	1939	1996	3.00	4.50	6.50	10.00
	1940	1996	3.00	4.50	6.50	10.00

2-1/2 KORI

6.9350 g, .937 SILVER, .2089 oz ASW

Y#	Date	Year	Fine	VF	XF	Unc
74	1937	VS1993	5.00	7.00	10.00	15.00

5 KORI

13.8700 g, .937 SILVER, .4178 oz ASW

Y#	Date	Year	Fine	VF	XF	Unc
75	1936	VS1993	7.00	11.00	16.50	25.00
	1937	1993	6.50	10.00	15.00	22.50
	1937	1994	6.50	10.00	15.00	22.50
	1938	1994	6.50	10.00	15.00	22.50
	1938	1995	6.50	10.00	15.00	22.50
	1941	1997	10.00	15.00	21.50	30.00
	1941	1998	6.50	10.00	15.00	22.50

VIJAYARAJJI

VS1998-2004/1942-1947AD

In the name of George VI

TRAMBIYO

COPPER

Y#	Date	Year	Fine	VF	XF	Unc
76	1943	VS2000	.25	.50	1.00	1.50
	1944	2000	.25	.50	1.00	1.50

DHINGLO

(1/16 Kori 1-1/2 Dokda)

COPPER

Y#	Date	Year	Fine	VF	XF	Unc
77	1943	VS2000	.20	.35	.60	1.00
	1944	2000	.20	.35	.60	1.00
	1947	2004	.20	.35	.60	1.00
	1948	2004	.50	1.00	2.00	3.50

DHABU

(1/8 Kori 3 Dokda)

COPPER

Y#	Date	Year	Fine	VF	XF	Unc
78	1943	VS1999	.25	.40	.65	1.00
	1943	2000	.25	.40	.65	1.00
	1944	2000	.25	.40	.65	1.00
	1947	2004	.25	.40	.65	1.00

PAYALO

(1/4 Kori)

COPPER

Y#	Date	Year	Fine	VF	XF	Unc
79	1943	VS1999	.75	1.00	1.50	2.50
	1943	2000	.75	1.00	1.50	2.50
	1944	2000	.75	1.00	1.50	2.50
	1944	2001	.75	1.00	1.50	2.50
	1945	2001	.35	.50	.75	1.25
	1945	2002	.35	.50	.75	1.25
	1946	2002	.35	.50	.75	1.25
	1946	2003	.35	.50	.75	1.25
	1947	2003	.75	1.00	1.50	2.50

ADHIO

(1/2 Kori)

COPPER

Y#	Date	Year	Fine	VF	XF	Unc
80	1943	VS1999	1.50	1.75	2.00	3.50
	1943	2000	1.50	1.75	2.00	3.50
	1944	2001	1.25	1.50	1.75	3.00
	1945	2001	1.50	1.75	2.00	3.50
	1945	2002	1.50	1.75	2.00	3.50
	1946	2002	1.50	1.75	2.00	3.50

KORI

SILVER, 4.66 g
Similar to Y#51.

A81	1942	VS1998	—	—	Rare	—

4.7000 g, .601 SILVER, .0921 oz ASW

81	1942	VS1999	2.50	3.50	5.00	8.00
	1943	1999	2.50	3.50	5.00	8.00
	1943	2000	2.50	3.50	5.00	8.00
	1944	2000	2.50	3.50	5.00	8.00
	1944	2001	2.50	3.50	5.00	8.00

5 KORI

13.8700 g, .937 SILVER, .4178 oz ASW

82	1942	VS1998	6.50	10.00	15.00	22.50
	1942	1999	6.50	10.00	15.00	22.50
	1943	1998	— Reported, not confirmed			

10 KORI

SILVER, 17.39 g

82A	1943	VS1999	—	—	Rare	—

MADANASINGHJI

VS2004-2005/1947-1948AD

DHABU

(1/8 Kori)

COPPER

83	VS2004	(1947)	.75	1.25	1.75	3.00

KORI

4.7000 g, .601 SILVER, .0921 oz ASW

84	VS2004	(1947)	5.00	7.00	10.00	15.00

5 KORI

13.8700 g, .937 SILVER, .4178 oz ASW

85	VS2004	(1947)	80.00	125.00	170.00	240.00

LADAKH

Ladakh, a district in northern India, contained the western Himalayas and the valley of the upper Indus river. Area: 45,762 sq. mi. Capital: Leh.

In 1639, the Moghuls marched on Ladakh and defeated them near Karpu. The King Sen-ge-rnam-rgyal promised to pay tribute, if allowed to return home, but never did. In 1665, the Moghul governor of Kashmir demanded the acceptance of Moghul suzerainty under threat of invasion. Knowing the strength of Aurangzeb, King Deb-Idan-rnamrgyal sent a tribute of gold ashraphis, rupees and other precious objects. It is probable that coins were struck for this occasion in the name of Aurangzeb but no such coins have yet been discovered.

For the next century no further mention is made of coins until in 1781 it is recorded that a Muslim goldsmith from Leh was hired to strike Ladakhi coins called ja'u.

The obverse of the first Ladakhi timashas or ja'u is a close copy of the Farrukhsiyar inscription of the early Garhwali timashas even including the regnal year at the bottom. The reverse has a clearly written Zarb Tibet at the bottom and dots at the top. At the center are crescents and an illegible inscription.

On some of the early Ladakh coins Hejira dates appear which coincide with the period when the Garhwal mint was closed and trade was diverted from Garhwal to Ladakh. No other Ladakh coins of this first issue have been discovered with a literate date. Between 1781 and 1803 it is likely that a considerable number of ja'u were struck. Most specimens were of good silver but later issues were very debased because of the scarcity of silver.

The next type of coin has a different obverse with the Muslim title of the King of Ladakh clearly inscribed as well as the number 14 at the lower left. This issue may have been prompted to demonstrate Ladakhi independence and is the only ja'u to bear a date.

The most remarkable of all Ladakhi coins has a fully legible inscription on the obverse in smaller writing and is enclosed in a circle with no regnal year. The reverse legend refers to the prime minister as well as the title of the king and is the only Ladakhi coin to do so and is very rare.

The appearance of Mahmud Shah on the obverse of the next type coin is thought to acknowledge suzerainty of the ruler of Kashmir. There is a plain circle surrounded by a border of dots. The reverse reverts to the earlier designs but has a finer style with thicker writing.

The next change in type took place after the conquest of Ladakh by Gulab Singh and the Dogra army in 1835. After a crushing defeat of the Dogra army in Tibet, the Ladakhis tried to shake off the Dogra supremacy but the rebellion was crushed. Ladakh was now firmly incorporated within the Empire of Jammu and the monarchy was abolished. Until 1845, Gulab Singh acknowledged Sikh suzerainty but ruled Ladakh as a part of Jammu.

After the defeat of the Sikhs by the British, Gulab Singh offered to pay the war indemnities to the British in exchange for being made independent ruler of Jammu and Kashmir.

Two types of ja'u were struck during the period of the Dogra domination. One combined the tiger knife and Mahmud Shah design and the other the tiger knife and Raja Gulab Singh in Nagari script.

Between 1867 and 1870 an issue of copper coins was made for Ladakh for local use and in 1871 a small issue of ja'u was made. Neither of these coins seemed to have much commercial impact in Ladakh and their issue was suspended after 1871. No special currency was struck in or for Ladakh after this.

RULERS

Tshe Pal Namgyal
1802-1830AD
Tshe Wan Rabtan Namgyal
1830-1837AD
Tshe Pal Namgyal, restored
1839-1840AD
Kunda Namgyal
1840-1842AD

JA'U

1815AD

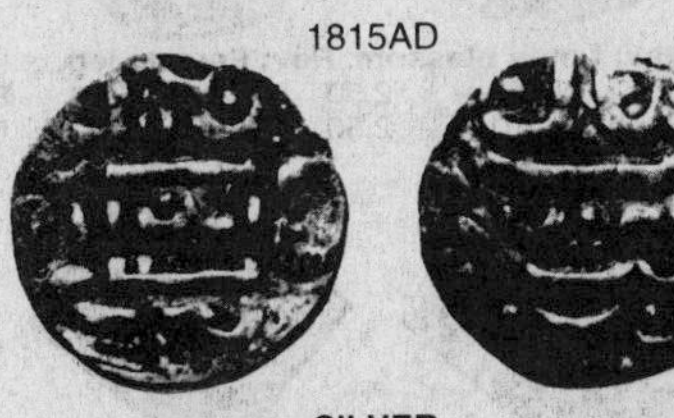

SILVER
Obv: Square around *Siyar* of Furrukhsiyar.

KM#	Date	Year	Good	VG	Fine	VF
2	ND	—	6.00	10.00	17.50	25.00

1815-1816AD

In the name of Mahmud Khan

Obv. leg: *Aqibat Mahmud Khan.*

3	ND	—	8.50	15.00	25.00	35.00

Obv. leg: *Aqibat Mahmud Khan* within circle.

Rev. leg: *Qalon Seban Tondub, Tibet.*

KM#	Date	Year	Good	VG	Fine	VF
4	ND	—	50.00	75.00	100.00	150.00

1816-1842AD

In the name of Mahmud Shah

Obv. and rev: Plain border.
Obv. leg: *Mahmud Shah.*

5.1	ND	—	10.00	14.00	18.50	25.00

Obv. and rev: Dotted border.

5.2	ND	—	10.00	14.00	18.50	25.00

Obv: Dotted border. Rev: Plain border.

5.3	ND	—	10.00	14.00	18.50	25.00

5.4	ND	—	10.00	14.00	18.50	25.00

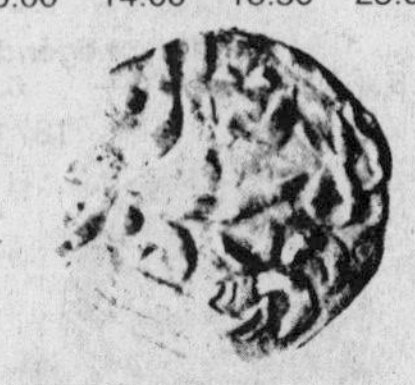

Obv: Retrograde.

5.5	ND	—	10.00	14.00	18.50	25.00

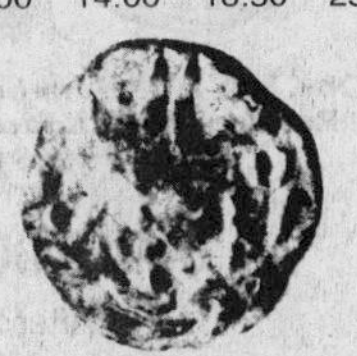

5.6	ND	—	10.00	14.00	18.50	25.00

1841AD

Obv. leg: *Mahmud Shah* within circle, dotted border. Rev: Katar pointing right, *Zarb Butan* above and below.

6	ND	—	10.00	14.00	18.50	25.00

1842-1850AD

In the name of Gulab Singh

Obv. leg: *Raja Gulab Singh*

in Nagari in 3 lines.

KM#	Date	Year	Good	VG	Fine	VF
7.1 (Y1)	ND	—	6.00	10.00	12.50	15.00

Rev: Dot on blade of Katar.

7.2 (Y1)	ND	—	6.00	10.00	12.50	15.00

Rev: Figure 8 on its side on blade of Katar.

7.3	ND	—	6.00	10.00	12.50	15.00

Obv. leg: Error, *Raja Galab Bing*.
Rev: Figure 8 on its side on blade of Katar.

7.4	ND	—	6.00	10.00	12.50	15.00

Rev: Legend blundered.

7.5	ND	—	6.00	10.00	12.50	15.00

1871AD

Obv. leg: *1928 Jam-bu'i Par* in Tibetan script.
Rev. leg: *Zarb Ladakh, Qilimrao Jamun, Sanah 1928* in Arabic script.

8	ND	—	15.00	25.00	32.50	40.00

UNDER DOGRA RULE

After 1834AD

PAISA

COPPER, 19mm

9	VS1924	(1867)	2.50	4.00	6.50	10.00
	1925	(1868)	2.50	4.00	6.50	10.00
	1926	(1869)	2.50	4.00	6.50	10.00
	1927	(1870)	2.50	4.00	6.50	10.00

LUNAVADA

This small state in the Panch Mahal district of western India was ruled by Solanki Rajputs who claimed descent from Sidraj Jaisingh, the ruler of Anhalwara Patan and Gujerat. The rulers, or maharanas, traced their sovereignty to the early decades of the fifteenth century. At different times the State was feudatory to either Baroda or Sindhia.

WAKHAT SINGHJI

VS1924-1986/1867-1929AD

1/2 PAISA

NOTE: Struck with paisa dies, either on small planchets, or paisas cut in half.

COPPER, rectangular or round, 3.50-4.00 g
Obv: Open hand.
Rev. leg: Mughal style Persian.

KM#	Date	Year	Good	VG	Fine	VF
2.1	ND	—	2.75	4.50	6.00	8.50

Obv: Crescent left and star right of hand.

2.2	ND	—	3.00	6.00	8.50	12.50

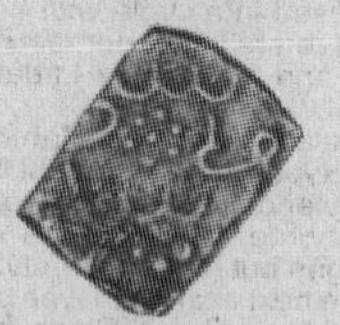

Obv: Open hand in square, *Lunavada* around clockwise. Rev: Date & Devanagari leg.

3	VS1942	(1885)	3.00	5.00	7.50	10.00

Obv: Lion right *Lunavada* and date.
Rev: Devanagari leg. w/ruler's name.

4	VS1949	(1892)	2.75	4.50	6.00	8.50

PAISA

COPPER, round or rectangular, 6.50-8.30 g
Obv: Two sabres.

5	ND	—	3.50	6.00	8.50	12.50

Obv: Cannon barrel.

6	ND	—	3.50	6.00	8.50	12.50

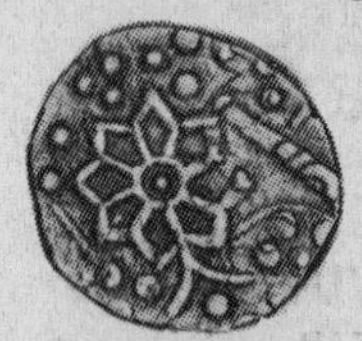

Obv: Lotus blossom. Rev: Persian leg.

7	ND	—	2.50	4.00	5.50	8.50
	VS1968	(1911)	2.50	4.00	5.50	8.50

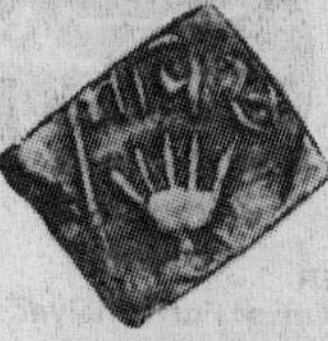

Obv: Open hand, leg. above.

8	ND	—	2.50	4.00	5.50	8.50

Obv: Katar.

11	ND	—	6.00	12.00	17.50	25.00

Obv: Open hand in square, on square planchet.

9.1	VS1942	(1885)	2.50	4.00	5.50	8.50
	1249 (error)	(1885)	2.50	4.00	5.50	8.50

Similar to KM9.1 but round planchet.

KM#	Date	Year	Good	VG	Fine	VF
9.2	VS1942	(1885)	2.50	4.00	5.50	8.50

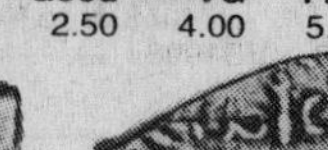

Obv: Lion, *Lunavada* and date.

10	VS1949	(1892)	2.50	4.00	5.50	8.50

NOTE: Coins of Lunavada are frequently found over struck over earlier types, and over other coins of Rampur.

MAKRAI

The rajas of Makrai belong to a very ancient Gond family whose title, Raja Hatiyarai, had been conferred upon them by the emperors of Delhi. This small state of some forty-five villages struggled with varying degrees of success against the Poona Peshwa, Sindhia and the Pindaris before passing under British protection in the nineteenth century.

RULER

Raja Bharat Shah
1886-1920AD

PAISA

COPPER

1	ND	—	2.00	3.00	4.50	7.00

Square planchet.

2	ND	—	—	—	—	—

MANIPUR

Refer to Independent Kingdoms during the Mughal Empire.

MARATHA CONFEDERACY

Refer to Independent Kingdoms during British rule.

MEWAR

State located in Rajputana, northwest India. Capital: Udaipur.

The rulers of Mewar were universally regarded as the highest ranking Rajput house in India. The maharana of Mewar was looked upon as the representative of Rama, the ancient king of Ayodhya - and the family who were Sesodia Rajputs of the Gehlot clan, traced its descent through Rama to Kanak Sen who ruled in the second century. The clan is believed to have migrated to Chitor from Gujarat sometime in the eighth century.

None of the indigenous rulers of India resisted the Muslim invasions into India with greater tenacity than the Rajputs of Mewar. It was their proud boast that they had never permitted a daughter to go into the Mughal harem. Three times the fortress and town of Chitor had fallen to Muslim invaders, to Alauddin Khilji (1303), to Bahadur Shah of Gujarat (1534) and to Akbar (1568). Each time Chitor gradually recovered but the last was the most traumatic experience of all. Rather than to submit to the Mughal onslaught, the women burned themselves on funeral pyres in a fearful rite called jauhar, and the men fell on the swords of the invaders.

After the sacking of Chitor the rana, Udai Singh, retired to the Aravali hills where he founded Udaipur, the capital after 1570. Udai Singh's son, Partab, refused to submit to the Mughal and recovered most of the territory lost in 1568. In the early nineteenth century Mewar suffered much at the hands of Marathas - Holkar, Sindhia and the Pindaris - until, in 1818, the State came under British supervision. In April 1948 Mewar was merged into Rajasthan and the maharana became governor Maharajpramukh of the new province.

RULERS

Bhim Singh,
AH1192-1244/1777-1828AD
Jawan Singh
AH1244-1254/1828-1838AD
Sirdar Singh
AH1254-1258/1838-1842AD
Swarup Singh
AH1258-1278/1842-1861AD
Shambhu Singh

AH1278-1291/1861-1874AD
Sajjan Singh
AH1291-1302/1874-1884AD
Fatteh Singh,
VS1941-1986/1884-1929AD
Bhupal Singh,
VS1987-2005/1930-1948AD

MINTS

Chitor चितोड़

Chitarkot चित्रकूट

Udaipur उदयपुर

NOTE: All Mewar coinage is struck without ruler's name, and is largely undated. certain types were generally struck over several reigns.

CHITOR MINT

Chitori Series

In the name of Alamgir II
AH1167-1173/1754/1759AD

Struck at Chitor Mint between ca 1760 and the middle of the 19th century.

Mint mark:

1/16 RUPEE

SILVER, 0.70 g

C#	Date	Year	VG	Fine	VF	XF
22	ND	—	6.00	9.00	12.50	18.50

1/8 RUPEE

SILVER, 1.30 g

C#	Date	Year	VG	Fine	VF	XF
23	ND	—	5.00	7.00	10.00	15.00

1/4 RUPEE

SILVER, 2.60-2.70 g

C#	Date	Year	VG	Fine	VF	XF
24	ND	—	4.50	6.00	9.00	13.50

1/2 RUPEE

SILVER, 5.30-5.40 g

C#	Date	Year	VG	Fine	VF	XF
25	ND	—	3.50	5.00	7.50	12.00

RUPEE

SILVER, 10.70-11.10 g

C#	Date	Year	VG	Fine	VF	XF
26	AH1180	—	15.00	20.00	30.00	45.00
	ND	—	5.00	7.00	10.00	15.00

UDAIPUR MINT

Udaipuri Series

In the name of Alamgir II
AH1167-1173/1754-1759AD

Struck at the Udaipur mint from about 1780 to the middle of the 19th century.

Mint mark: 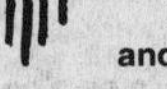 and  on obverse.

PAISA

COPPER, 10.00-10.20 g

C#	Date	Year	VG	Fine	VF	XF
27	ND	—	—	—	—	—

1/16 RUPEE

SILVER, 0.60 g

C#	Date	Year	VG	Fine	VF	XF
28	ND	—	— Reported, not confirmed			

1/8 RUPEE

SILVER, 1.35 g

C#	Date	Year	VG	Fine	VF	XF
29	ND	—	— Reported, not confirmed			

1/4 RUPEE

SILVER, 2.70 g

C#	Date	Year	VG	Fine	VF	XF
30	ND	—	5.00	7.00	10.00	15.00

1/2 RUPEE

SILVER, 5.40 g

C#	Date	Year	VG	Fine	VF	XF
31	ND	—	5.00	7.00	10.00	15.00

RUPEE

SILVER, 11.80 g

C#	Date	Year	VG	Fine	VF	XF
32	ND	—	5.50	8.00	12.50	18.50

Chandori Series

Ordered by Bhim Singh, and struck at the Udaipur Mint until 1842AD. Recalled by Swarup Shah.

Mint mark:

On obverse

On reverse

1/2 RUPEE

SILVER, 5.35-5.80 g

C#	Date	Year	VG	Fine	VF	XF
43	ND	—	7.00	11.00	16.50	25.00

RUPEE

SILVER, 10.90-11.00 g

C#	Date	Year	VG	Fine	VF	XF
44	ND	—	7.00	11.00	16.50	25.00

New Chandori Series

Struck at the Udaipur Mint between 1842-1890AD. Many die varieties exist.

Mint mark:

On obverse

1/16 RUPEE

SILVER, 9mm, 0.65 g

Y#	Date	Year	VG	Fine	VF	XF
1	ND	—	3.00	4.50	6.50	10.00

1/8 RUPEE

SILVER, 1.35 g

Y#	Date	Year	VG	Fine	VF	XF
2	ND	—	2.50	3.50	5.00	8.00

1/4 RUPEE

SILVER, 2.70 g

Y#	Date	Year	VG	Fine	VF	XF
3	ND	—	2.50	3.50	5.00	8.00

1/2 RUPEE

SILVER, 5.40 g

Y#	Date	Year	VG	Fine	VF	XF
4	ND	—	3.00	4.50	6.50	10.00

RUPEE

SILVER, 10.80-10.90 g

Y#	Date	Year	VG	Fine	VF	XF
5	ND	—	5.00	7.00	10.00	15.00

MOHUR

GOLD, 7.52 g

Y#	Date	Year	VG	Fine	VF	XF
6	ND	—	150.00	185.00	350.00	325.00

Swarupshahi Series

Struck at the Udaipur Mint between ca.1858-1920AD. Many die varieties exist.

1/16 RUPEE

SILVER, round, 0.65 g

Y#	Date	Year	VG	Fine	VF	XF
7.1	ND	—	2.50	3.50	5.00	8.00

Irregular shape, 8-10mm.

Y#	Date	Year	VG	Fine	VF	XF
7.2	ND	—	3.00	4.50	6.50	10.00

1/8 RUPEE

SILVER, 11-12mm, 1.30 g

Y#	Date	Year	VG	Fine	VF	XF
8	ND	—	3.00	4.50	6.50	10.00

1/4 RUPEE

SILVER, 2.60 g

Y#	Date	Year	VG	Fine	VF	XF
9	ND	—	2.50	3.50	5.00	8.00

1/2 RUPEE

SILVER, 5.20-5.40 g

Y#	Date	Year	VG	Fine	VF	XF
10	ND	—	3.00	4.50	6.50	10.00

RUPEE

SILVER, 10.75-10.85 g

Y#	Date	Year	VG	Fine	VF	XF
11	ND	—	4.00	6.00	9.00	13.50

1/4 MOHUR

GOLD, 2.70-2.75 g

Y#	Date	Year	VG	Fine	VF	XF
A12	ND	—	55.00	60.00	75.00	100.00

MOHUR

GOLD, 10.95 g

Y#	Date	Year	VG	Fine	VF	XF
12	ND	—	160.00	185.00	225.00	300.00

FATTEH SINGH

VS1941-1987/1884-1930AD

With names of Chitor and Udaipur.

PIE

COPPER, 2.50 g

Y#	Date	Year	Good	VG	Fine	VF
13	VS1975	(1918)	7.50	12.50	18.50	27.50

2.10 g

Y#	Date	Year	Good	VG	Fine	VF
14	VS1978	(1921)	6.00	10.00	15.00	22.50

Milled Coinage

In the name of 'A Friend of London'.

Dated VS1985 ie. 1928AD, but actually struck at the Alipore Mint in Calcutta between 1931-1932AD, the Y#22 rupee in 1931, the rest in 1932.

1/16 RUPEE

SILVER, 0.95 g

Y#	Date	Mintage	Fine	VF	XF	Unc
18	VS1985 (1928)	3.262	2.00	3.00	4.00	7.00

1/8 RUPEE

SILVER, 1.36 g

Y#	Date	Mintage	Fine	VF	XF	Unc
19	VS1985 (1928)	.800	2.50	3.50	5.00	8.00

1/4 RUPEE

SILVER, 2.72 g

Y#	Date	Mintage	Fine	VF	XF	Unc
20	VS1985 (1928)	.839	3.00	4.00	6.50	10.00

1/2 RUPEE

SILVER, 5.46 g

Y#	Date	Mintage	Fine	VF	XF	Unc
21	VS1985 (1928)	.648	4.00	6.00	9.00	13.50

GOLD, 5.35-5.70 g

Y#	Date	Mintage	Fine	VF	XF	Unc
21a	VS1985 (1928)	—	—	—	Proof	350.00

RUPEE

SILVER, 10.86 g
Obv: Thin legends.

Y#	Date	Mintage	Fine	VF	XF	Unc
22.1	VS1985 (1928)	14.906	5.00	7.00	10.00	15.00

Obv: Thick legends.

Y#	Date	Mintage	Fine	VF	XF	Unc
22.2	VS1985 (1928)	Inc. Ab.	7.00	11.00	16.50	25.00

GOLD

Y#	Date	Mintage	Fine	VF	XF	Unc
22a	VS1985 (1928)	—	—	—	Proof	450.00

BHUPAL SINGH

VS1987-2005/1930-1948AD

1/4 ANNA

COPPER, 2.20 g

Y#	Date	Year	Fine	VF	XF	Unc
15	VS1999	(1942)	.50	.85	1.25	2.00

1/2 ANNA

COPPER, 3.50 g

Y#	Date	Year	Fine	VF	XF	Unc
16	VS1999	(1942)	.50	.85	1.25	2.00

NOTE: Varieties w/large and small inscriptions exist.

ANNA

COPPER, 4.30 g

Y#	Date	Year	Fine	VF	XF	Unc
17	VS2000	(1943)	.60	1.00	1.25	2.50

LOCAL ISSUES

Umarda

1/2 PAISA

COPPER

Y#	Date	Year	Good	VG	Fine	VF
23	ND	6	.45	.75	1.00	1.50

NOTE: Varieties exist.

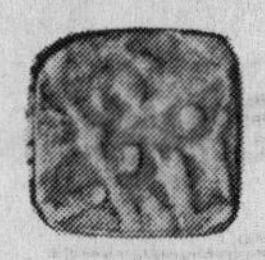

Y#	Date	Year	Good	VG	Fine	VF
24	ND(1938-41)	—	.75	1.25	1.75	2.50

NOTE: Varieties exist.

FEUDATORY STATES

Bhinda

ZURAWAR SINGH

AH1214-1243/1799-1827AD

PAISA

COPPER

C#	Date	Year	Good	VG	Fine	VF
1	ND	—	3.00	5.00	7.50	12.50

Salumba

2 PIES

COPPER

C#	Date	Year	Good	VG	Fine	VF
1	ND(1815-34)	—	3.00	5.00	7.00	11.50
	ND(1835-70)	—	3.00	5.00	7.00	11.50

Shahpur

RULERS

Jagat Singh,
AH1261-1270/1845-1853AD
Lachman Singh,
AH1270-1287/1853-1870AD
Nahat Singh,
AH1287-1351/1870-1932AD

PAISA

COPPER

C#	Date	Year	Good	VG	Fine	VF
10	ND(1827-70)	—	2.50	4.00	6.00	10.00

In the name of Alamgir II

AH1167-1173/1754-1759AD

Copy of his Dehli coin with Yr. 12 as a frozen fictitious year. Distinguished by the addition of a small trisul to lower obv.

1/4 RUPEE

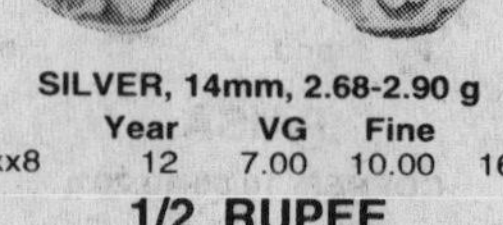

SILVER, 14mm, 2.68-2.90 g

C#	Date	Year	VG	Fine	VF	XF
20	AHxxx8	12	7.00	10.00	16.50	25.00

1/2 RUPEE

SILVER, 17mm, 5.35-5.80 g

C#	Date	Year	VG	Fine	VF	XF
21	AHxxx8	12	10.00	15.00	21.50	30.00

RUPEE

SILVER, 10.70-11.60 g

C#	Date	Year	VG	Fine	VF	XF
22	AHxxx8	12	12.50	18.50	25.00	35.00

MOHUR

GOLD, 18mm, 10.70-11.40 g

C#	Date	Year	VG	Fine	VF	XF
29	AHxxx8	12	180.00	225.00	275.00	325.00

MYSORE

Large state in Southern India. Governed until 1761AD by various Hindu dynasties, then by Haider Ali and Tipu Sultan.

In 1831, Krishnaraja being deposed for maladministration and pensioned off, the administration of Mysore State then came directly under the British. The coinage of Mysore ceased in 1843. After the Great Revolt of 1857, the policy of eliminating Indian princes was discontinued and as a result, Mysore was returned in 1881 to the control of an adopted son of Krishnaraja Wodeyar. The Wodeyars continued to hold the State until 1947 although they did not issue coins. In November 1956 modern Mysore was inaugurated as a linguistic state within the Indian Union.

NOTE: For earlier issues see Mysore, Independent Kingdoms under British rule.

RULERS

Dewan Purnaiya, regent,
AH1214-1225/1799-1810AD
Krishna Raja Wodeyar,
AH1225-1285/1810-1868AD

MINTS

Mysore مهی سور

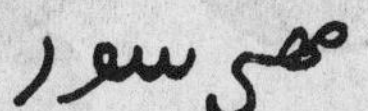

Nagar نگر or نکر

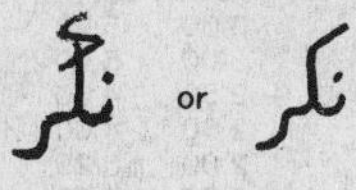

MONETARY SYSTEM

2 Fanams = 1 Anna
4 Annas = 1 Pavali
4 Pavalis = 1 Rupee

MYSORE MINT
Anonymous Issues

1/6 PAVALI

SILVER, 0.45-0.48 g

C#	Date	VG	Fine	VF	XF
199	ND	5.50	11.00	18.00	25.00

1/3 PAVALI

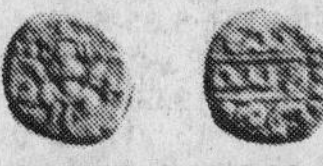

SILVER, 0.89-0.96 g
Obv: Dancing figure (Chamundi).

C#	Date	Year	VG	Fine	VF	XF
200	ND	—	12.50	25.00	42.00	70.00

2/3 PAVALI

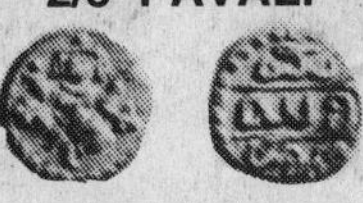

SILVER, 1.78-1.92 g
Obv: Dancing figure (Chamundi).

C#	Date	Year	VG	Fine	VF	XF
201	ND	—	12.50	25.00	42.00	70.00

In the name of Shah Alam II
AH1173-1221/1759-1806AD

1/4 RUPEE (PAVALI)

SILVER, 2.68-2.90 g
Obv: Dancing figure (Chamundi).

C#	Date	Year	VG	Fine	VF	XF
202	AH1220	—	7.50	15.00	25.00	35.00
	1221	—	7.50	15.00	25.00	35.00
	1223	—	7.50	15.00	25.00	35.00
	1226	—	7.50	15.00	25.00	35.00
	1229	—	7.50	15.00	25.00	35.00
	1243	—	7.50	15.00	25.00	35.00
	1244	—	7.50	15.00	25.00	35.00
	1245	—	7.50	15.00	25.00	35.00
	1246	—	7.50	15.00	25.00	35.00
	1247	—	7.50	15.00	25.00	35.00
	1248	—	7.50	15.00	25.00	35.00
	3421	—	7.50	15.00	25.00	35.00
	4421	—	7.50	15.00	25.00	35.00

NOTE: Earlier date (AH1214) exists for this type.

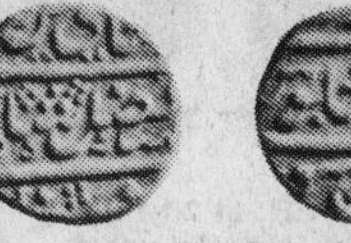

C#	Date	Year	VG	Fine	VF	XF
205	AH1220	44	6.50	13.00	22.00	32.00
	1220	45	6.50	13.00	22.00	32.00
	1221	45	6.50	13.00	22.00	32.00
	—	76	6.50	13.00	22.00	32.00
	—	84	6.50	13.00	22.00	32.00

1/2 RUPEE

SILVER, 5.35-5.80 g

C#	Date	Year	VG	Fine	VF	XF
206	—	35	7.50	15.00	25.00	35.00
	—	39	7.50	15.00	25.00	35.00
	—	76	7.50	15.00	25.00	35.00

RUPEE

SILVER, 10.70-11.60 g

C#	Date	Year	VG	Fine	VF	XF
207	AH1219	44	10.00	20.00	32.50	45.00
	1221	25	10.00	20.00	32.50	45.00
	1221	45	10.00	20.00	32.50	45.00
	1222	46	10.00	20.00	32.50	45.00
	1221	47	10.00	20.00	32.50	45.00
	1222	64	10.00	20.00	32.50	45.00
	12xx	48	10.00	20.00	32.50	45.00
	1223	64	10.00	20.00	32.50	45.00
	1224	64	10.00	20.00	32.50	45.00
	1224	74	10.00	20.00	32.50	45.00
	1225	74	10.00	20.00	32.50	45.00
	1225	94	10.00	20.00	32.50	45.00
	1226	94	10.00	20.00	32.50	45.00
	1227	95	10.00	20.00	32.50	45.00
	1228	95	10.00	20.00	32.50	45.00
	1229	96	10.00	20.00	32.50	45.00
	1230	97	10.00	20.00	32.50	45.00
	1231	98	10.00	20.00	32.50	45.00
	1232	99	10.00	20.00	32.50	45.00
	1234	98	10.00	20.00	32.50	45.00
	1234	99	10.00	20.00	32.50	45.00
	1235	98	10.00	20.00	32.50	45.00
	1236	98	10.00	20.00	32.50	45.00
	1237	37	10.00	20.00	32.50	45.00
	1238	37	10.00	20.00	32.50	45.00
	1239	3x	10.00	20.00	32.50	45.00
	1240	98	10.00	20.00	32.50	45.00
	1242	37	10.00	20.00	32.50	45.00
	1243	98	10.00	20.00	32.50	45.00
	1247	47	10.00	20.00	32.50	45.00
	1248	48	10.00	20.00	32.50	45.00
	x421	45	10.00	20.00	32.50	45.00
	x421	47	10.00	20.00	32.50	45.00

NOTE: Earlier dates (AH1214-1215) exist for this type.

FANAM

GOLD, 0.33-0.40 g
Narasimha

C#	Date	Year	VG	Fine	VF	XF
212	ND	—	7.50	10.00	13.50	20.00

PAGODA

GOLD, 3.40 g
Shiva and Parvati

C#	Date	Year	VG	Fine	VF	XF
210	ND	—	45.00	60.00	75.00	100.00

NOTE: Fanams and 1/2 Pagodas of this type are recent fabrications.

1/4 MOHUR

GOLD, 2.68-2.85 g

Mughal type

C#	Date	Year	VG	Fine	VF	XF
215	—	45	—	—	Rare	—

DEWAN PURNAIYA

Regent for Krishnaraja Wodeyar
AH1214-1225/1799-1810AD

A Sardula (mythical tiger) is illustrated on all of Dewan Purnaiya's coins.

75 CASH

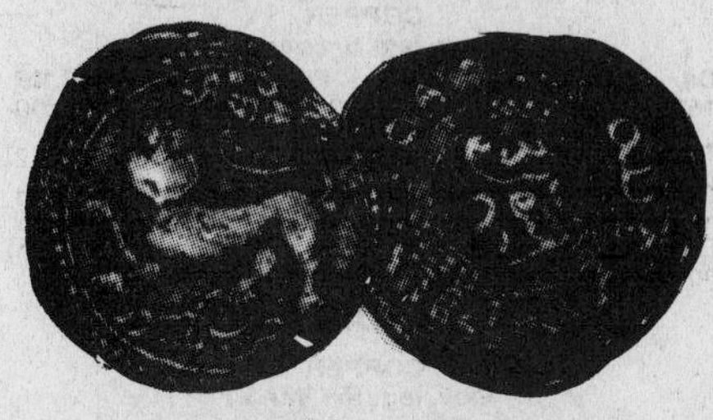

COPPER, 23.59 g

C#	Date	Good	VG	Fine	VF
189	ND(1799-1868)	—	—	—	—

KRISHNA RAJA WODEYAR

AH1225-1285/1810-1868AD
British control after 1831

(Types I-IV struck 1811-1833)

***SRI* VARIETIES**

Variety I:  

Variety II:

Type I, ca. 1811

Obv: Elephant left below sun and moon. Rev: 3 line Nagari leg.

6-1/4 CASH

COPPER

C#	Date	VG	Fine	VF	XF
170	ND	5.00	9.00	13.00	20.00

Type II

Obv: Elephant below Kanarese, *Sri* between sun and moon. Rev: 2 lines of Kanarese, denomination in English at the top on the 5 and 10 Cash, at the bottom on the 20 and 40 Cash. The English denomination is often encountered blundered.

5 CASH

COPPER
Obv. leg: *Sri* var. I.

C#	Date	VG	Fine	VF	XF
171	ND	2.00	3.25	5.00	8.50
	ND (X CASH in error)	2.50	4.50	7.00	11.00
	ND yr.2	9.00	16.00	24.00	35.00

10 CASH

COPPER
Obv. leg: *Sri* var. I.

C#	Date	VG	Fine	VF	XF
174	ND	4.50	8.00	12.00	17.50

20 CASH

COPPER
Obv. leg: *Sri* var. I.

C#	Date	VG	Fine	VF	XF
177	ND	1.25	2.25	3.50	5.50

40 CASH

COPPER
Obv. leg: ***Sri*** **var. I.**

C#	Date	VG	Fine	VF	XF
180	ND	12.50	20.00	32.50	50.00

Type III

Obv: Elephant below Kanarese, *Sri* between sun and moon. Rev: 3 line Kanarese leg., denomination in English at the bottom. The English denomination is often encountered blundered or retrograde.

5 CASH

COPPER
Obv. leg: ***Sri*** **var. I.**

C#	Date	Good	VG	Fine	VF
171a.1	ND	4.00	6.50	10.00	15.00

Obv. leg: ***Sri*** **var. II.**

C#	Date	Good	VG	Fine	VF
171a.2	ND	4.00	6.50	10.00	15.00

10 CASH

COPPER
Obv. leg: ***Sri*** **var. II.**

C#	Date	Good	VG	Fine	VF
174a	ND	3.00	5.00	8.00	12.50
	ND (X CASH retrograde)	4.00	6.50	10.00	15.00

20 CASH

COPPER
Obv. leg: ***Sri*** **var. II.**

C#	Date	Good	VG	Fine	VF
177a	ND	1.00	1.75	2.50	4.00

Type IV

Obv: Elephant below Kanarese leg. *Sri* between sun and /moon/*Chamuni*. Rev: Similar to Type III.

5 CASH

COPPER
Obv. leg: ***Sri*** **var. I.**

C#	Date	Good	VG	Fine	VF
171b	ND	2.50	4.00	6.50	10.00

10 CASH

COPPER
Obv. leg: ***Sri*** **var. I.**

C#	Date	Good	VG	Fine	VF
174b	ND	4.00	6.50	10.00	15.00

20 CASH

COPPER
Obv. leg: ***Sri*** **var. I.**

C#	Date	Good	VG	Fine	VF
177b	ND	3.00	5.00	8.00	12.50

25 CASH

COPPER, 11.20-11.40 g
Obv. leg: ***Sri*** **var. I.**

C#	Date	Good	VG	Fine	VF
179	ND	—	—	—	—

Type V

Obv: Sardula (mythical lion) below Kanarese leg. *Sri* between sun and moon/*Chamundi*. Rev. Kanarese leg. *Krishna* in center surrounded by mintname and denomination.

2-1/2 CASH

COPPER

C#	Date	Good	VG	Fine	VF
190.1	1833	4.00	6.00	9.00	13.50

5 CASH

COPPER

C#	Date	Good	VG	Fine	VF
191.1	1833	2.00	3.25	5.00	8.50
	1834	2.00	3.25	5.00	8.50
	1838	2.00	3.25	5.00	8.50

10 CASH

COPPER

C#	Date	Good	VG	Fine	VF
192.1	1833	2.50	4.00	6.50	10.00
	1834	2.50	4.00	6.50	10.00

20 CASH

COPPER

C#	Date	Good	VG	Fine	VF
193.1	1833	2.00	3.25	5.00	8.50
	1834	2.00	3.25	5.00	8.50
	1835	2.00	3.25	5.00	8.50
	1836	2.00	3.25	5.00	8.50
	1838	2.00	3.25	5.00	8.50

NOTE: The 1833 has 2 varieties: W/palm frond before Sardula and w/frond before and above.

Type VI

Obv: Lion, date below. Struck at the Bangalore subsidary mint facility.

2-1/2 CASH

COPPER

C#	Date	Good	VG	Fine	VF
190.2	1834	3.00	5.00	8.00	12.50
	1839	2.50	4.00	6.50	10.00
	1840	2.50	4.00	6.50	10.00
	1841	2.50	4.00	6.50	10.00
	1842	2.00	3.25	5.00	8.50
	1843	2.00	3.25	5.00	8.50

5 CASH

COPPER

C#	Date	Good	VG	Fine	VF
191.2	1834	1.75	2.75	4.00	7.00
	1835	1.75	2.75	4.00	7.00
	1836	1.75	2.75	4.00	7.00
	1837	1.75	2.75	4.00	7.00
	1838	1.75	2.75	4.00	7.00
	1839	1.75	2.75	4.00	7.00
	1840	1.75	2.75	4.00	7.00
	1841	1.75	2.75	4.00	7.00
	1842	1.75	2.75	4.00	7.00
	1843	1.75	2.75	4.00	7.00

10 CASH

COPPER

C#	Date	Good	VG	Fine	VF
192.2	1834/3	4.00	6.50	11.00	17.00
	1834	4.00	6.50	10.00	15.00
	1835	3.00	5.00	8.00	12.50
	1836	3.00	5.00	8.00	12.50
	1837	3.00	5.00	8.00	12.50
	1838	3.00	5.00	8.00	12.50
	1839	3.00	5.00	8.00	12.50
	1840	3.00	5.00	8.00	12.50
	1841	3.00	5.00	8.00	12.50
	1842	3.00	5.00	8.00	12.50
	1843	3.00	5.00	8.00	12.50
	1848(sic)	2.00	3.25	5.50	8.50
	1848(sic) rev. leg: MEILLEE XX CASH. . . . retrograde	2.00	3.25	5.50	8.50

20 CASH

COPPER

C#	Date	Good	VG	Fine	VF
193.2	1833	3.00	5.00	8.00	12.50
	1834	3.00	5.00	8.00	12.50
	1835	2.50	4.00	6.50	10.00
	1836	2.50	4.00	6.50	10.00
	1837	2.00	3.25	5.50	8.50
	1838	2.00	3.25	5.50	8.50
	1839	2.00	3.25	5.50	8.50
	1840	2.00	3.25	5.50	8.50
	1841	2.00	3.25	5.50	8.50
	1843	2.00	3.25	5.50	8.50

NOTE: All dates have MEILEE on rev.; some 1834 have MILAY, and some 1837 have MILEE. Some numerals are distorted.

NAGAR MINT

KRISHNA RAJA WODEYAR

AH1225-1285/1810-1868AD

1/2 RUPEE

SILVER, 5.35-5.80 g

C#	Date	Year	VG	Fine	VF	XF
206a	—	74	13.50	22.50	31.50	42.50
	—	84	13.50	22.50	31.50	42.50

RUPEE

SILVER, 10.70-11.60 g

C#	Date	Year	VG	Fine	VF	XF
207a	—	46	27.50	45.00	62.50	85.00
	AH1225	84	27.50	45.00	62.50	85.00

NARWAR

Narwar was a tiny state in western Malwa with a population of about four thousand (ca.1900). The ruling chiefs were Jhala Rajputs. In AH1220/1805AD it came under Gwalior.

For later issues see Gwalior - Narwar Mint listings.

RULERS

Daulat Rao
AH1209-1243/1759-1806AD

DAULAT RAO

AH1209-1243/1794-1827AD

In the name of Shah Alam II
AH1173-1221/1759-1806AD

RUPEE

SILVER, 10.70-11.60 g
Rev: Katar and floral spray.

KM#	Date	Year	VG	Fine	VF	XF
26	AH1216	44	15.00	25.00	35.00	50.00
	1216	45	15.00	25.00	35.00	50.00
	1217	44	15.00	25.00	35.00	50.00
	1217	48	15.00	25.00	35.00	50.00

NAWANAGAR

(Navanagar)

State located on the Kathiawar peninsula, west-central India.

The rulers, or jams, of Kutch were Jareja Rajputs who had entered the Kathiawar peninsular from Kutch and dispossessed the ancient family of Jathwas. Nawanagar was founded about 1535 by Jam Raval, who was possibly the elder brother of the Jam of Kutch. The great fort of Nawanagar was built by Jam Jasaji (d. 1814). The state became tributary to the Gaekwar family and, in the nineteenth century, also to the British. In 1948 the state was merged into Saurashtra.

RULERS

Vibhaji
VS1909-1951/1852-1894AD
Jaswant Singh
VS1951-1964/1894-1907AD

MONETARY SYSTEM

2 Trambiyo = 1 Dokda
3 Trambiyo = 1 Dhinglo
8 Dokda = 1 Kori

Early Types: Stylized imitations of the coins of Muzaffar III of Gujarat (156-173AD), dated AH978 (= 1570AD), were struck from the end of the 16th century until the early part of the reign of Vibhaji. These show a steady degradation of style over the nearly 300 years of issue, but no types can be dated to specific rulers. The former attribution of these coins to Ranmalji II (1820-1852AD) is incorrect. All are inscribed Sri Jamji, title of all rulers of Nawanager.

Varieties in this series are the rule, not the exception. These include legend style and small marks in the field such as a crescent, Katar (dagger), etc.

DUMP COINAGE

Crude style; ca. 1570-1850AD

TRAMBIYO

COPPER, 3.20-4.00 g

KM#	Date	Good	VG	Fine	VF
1	AH(9)78 (frozen)	1.25	2.00	3.00	4.50

DOKDO

COPPER, 7.00-8.00 g

KM#	Date	Good	VG	Fine	VF
2	AH(9)78 (frozen)	.40	.75	1.00	1.50

NOTE: Earlier issues weigh up to 9.30 g.

DHINGLO

(1 1/2 Dokda)

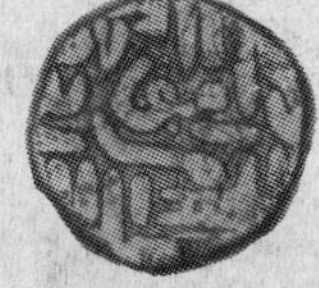

COPPER, 10.50-12.50 g

KM#	Date	Good	VG	Fine	VF
3	AH(9)78 (frozen)	1.25	2.00	3.00	4.00

1/2 KORI

SILVER, 2.30-2.40 g

KM#	Date	Good	VG	Fine	VF
4	AH(9)78 (frozen)	1.75	3.00	4.50	6.00

KORI

SILVER, 4.60-4.80 g

KM#	Date	Good	VG	Fine	VF
5	AH(9)78 (frozen)	1.50	2.50	3.25	4.00

Finer style from ca. 1850AD.

TRAMBIYO

COPPER, 3.10-3.30 g

KM#	Date	Good	VG	Fine	VF
6	AH(9)78 (frozen)	1.00	2.00	3.25	4.50

DOKDO

COPPER, 6.20-6.60 g

KM#	Date	Good	VG	Fine	VF
7	AH(9)78 (frozen)	.65	1.15	1.75	2.50

DHINGLO

(1 1/2 Dokda)

COPPER, 9.30-9.90 g

KM#	Date	Good	VG	Fine	VF
8	AH(9)78 (frozen)	1.00	1.75	2.50	3.50

1/2 KORI

SILVER, 2.30-2.40 g

KM#	Date	Good	VG	Fine	VF
9	AH(9)78 (frozen)	2.50	3.50	5.00	8.00

KORI

SILVER, 4.60-4.80 g

KM#	Date	Good	VG	Fine	VF
10	AH(9)78 (frozen)	2.00	3.00	4.00	7.00

VIBHAJI

VS1909-1951/1852-1894AD

TRAMBIYO

COPPER, 3.10-3.20 g

KM#	Date	Good	VG	Fine	VF
13	AH(9)78 (frozen)	1.00	1.75	3.00	4.00

3.30-3.50 g
Similar to Dokdo, KM#16.

KM#	Date	Good	VG	Fine	VF
15	VS1919 (1862)	3.50	6.00	7.50	10.00

DOKDO

COPPER, 6.20-6.40 g

KM#	Date	Good	VG	Fine	VF
14	AH(9)78 (frozen)	.90	1.40	2.25	3.00

6.60-7.00 g

KM#	Date	Year	Good	VG	Fine
16	VS1909	(1852)	3.50	6.00	7.50
	1917	(1860)	3.50	6.00	7.50
	1919	(1862)	3.50	6.00	7.50

2 DOKDA

COPPER, 12.40-12.80 g

KM#	Date	Year	Good	VG	Fine
18	VS1943	(1886)	4.00	7.00	10.00

3 DOKDA

COPPER, 18.00-19.60 g

KM#	Date	Year	Good	VG	Fine
17	VS1928	(1871)	3.50	5.50	7.00

KM#	Date	Year	Good	VG	Fine
19	VS1942	(1885)	3.00	4.50	6.50

KORI

SILVER, 4.60-4.80 g
Plain edge

KM#	Date	Year	VG	Fine	VF	XF
20	VS1934	(1877)	5.00	7.00	10.00	15.00
	1935	(1878)	5.00	7.00	10.00	15.00
	1936	(1879)	3.00	4.50	6.50	10.00

2-1/2 KORI

SILVER, 6.80-7.20 g
Reduced weight, milled edge

KM#	Date	Year	VG	Fine	VF	XF
21	VS1948	(1891)	6.50	10.00	15.00	22.50
	1949	(1892)	6.50	10.00	15.00	22.50
	1950	(1893)	6.50	10.00	15.00	22.50

5 KORI

SILVER, 13.60-14.40 g
Reduced weight.
Obv. and rev: Large inner circle, milled edge.

KM#	Date	Year	Fine	VF	XF	Unc
22	VS1945	(1888)	7.50	12.50	18.50	27.50
	1946	(1889)	7.50	12.50	18.50	27.50
	1947	(1890)	7.50	12.50	18.50	27.50

Obv. and rev. leg: Smaller characters.

KM#	Date	Year	Fine	VF	XF	Unc
23	VS1948	(1891)	7.50	12.50	18.50	27.50
	1949	(1892)	7.50	12.50	18.50	27.50
	1950	(1893)	7.50	12.50	18.50	27.50

1/2 GOLD KORI

GOLD, 3.20-3.30 g

KM#	Date	VG	Fine	VF	XF
11	AH978 (frozen)				
		60.00	85.00	125.00	165.00

GOLD KORI

GOLD, 6.40-6.60 g

KM#	Date	VG	Fine	VF	XF
12	AH(9)78 (frozen)				
		85.00	125.00	185.00	250.00

JASWANT SINGH

VS1951-1964/1894-1907AD

TRAMBIYO

COPPER, 3.10-3.20 g

KM#	Date	Year	Good	VG	Fine	VF
24	VS1956(1899)		10.00	16.50	25.00	40.00

DOKDO

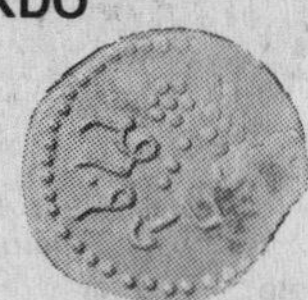

COPPER, 6.20-6.40 g

KM#	Date	Year	Good	VG	Fine	VF
25	VS1956(1899)		9.00	15.00	22.50	36.50

DHINGLO

(1 1/2 Dokda)

COPPER, 9.30-9.60 g

KM#	Date	Year	Good	VG	Fine	VF
26	VS1956(1899)		7.50	12.50	20.00	30.00

2 DOKDA

COPPER, 12.40-13.20 g

KM#	Date	Year	Good	VG	Fine	VF
27	VS1956(1899)		12.50	20.00	33.50	45.00

3 DOKDA

COPPER, 18.60-19.80 g

KM#	Date	Year	Good	VG	Fine	VF
28	VS1956(1899)		12.50	22.50	35.00	50.00

ORCHHA

State located in north-central India.

Orchha, the oldest and highest ranking of all the Bundela States, was founded by Rudra Pratap, a Garhwar Rajput, early in the sixteenth century. During the years of Mughal expansion, Orchha came under the supervision of Delhi. A few years later Jujhar Singh (1626-1635) rebelled but was defeated and dispossessed. Shah Jahan installed his brother as ruler in 1641. In the eighteenth century, as the Marathas took control of the region, only Orchha from among the Bundela States was not totally subjugated by the Peshwa. In the nineteenth century Orchha came under British protection.

The Orchha coinage was called Gaja Shahi because of the gaja or mace which was its symbol.

RULERS

Vikramajit Mahendra
AH1211-1233/1796-1817AD
Dharam Pal
AH1233-1250/1817-1834AD
Taj Singh
AH1250-1258/1834-1842AD
Surjain Singh
AH1258-1265/1842-1848AD
Hamir Singh
AH1265-1291/1848-1874AD
Pratap Singh
AH1291-1349/1874-1930AD

MINT MARKS

1 Reverse. (This is the symbol most characteristic of Orchha's coinage and is copied on the Datia imitations)

2 Obverse, most common.

3 Obverse, less common.

4 Reverse

5 Reverse

6 Reverse

7 Reverse

8 Reverse

9 Reverse

10 Reverse

Marks #4 through #10 are found in addition to Mark #1.

The Datia copies can only be distinguished by the mint marks, other than #1, which is common to both series for the list of Datia marks, see listings under that state.

There seems to be no correspondence between AH dates on the obverse and regnal years on the reverse!

In the name of Shah Alam II

AH1173-1221/1759-1806AD

PAISA

COPPER

C#	Date	Year	Good	VG	Fine	VF
25	AH1232	46	1.00	2.00	3.25	4.50
	1278	45	1.00	2.00	3.25	4.50
	1282	42	1.00	2.00	3.25	4.50

NOTE: Earlier dates (AH120x-1214) exist for this type.

1/8 RUPEE

SILVER, 1.34-1.45 g

C#	Date	Year	VG	Fine	VF	XF
29	AH1233	45	4.00	7.00	10.00	15.00

NOTE: Earlier date (AH1211) exists for this type.

1/4 RUPEE

SILVER, 12mm, 2.68-2.90 g

C#	Date	Year	VG	Fine	VF	XF
30	AH1228	40	3.50	6.00	9.00	13.50
	1233	45	3.50	6.00	9.00	13.50
	123x	46	3.50	6.00	9.00	13.50
	1233	5x	3.50	6.00	9.00	13.50
	1251	3x	3.50	6.00	9.00	13.50

NOTE: Earlier date (AH1211) exists for this type.

RUPEE

SILVER, 10.70-11.60 g

C#	Date	Year	VG	Fine	VF	XF
32	AH1216	44	6.00	10.00	14.00	20.00
	1216	46	6.00	10.00	14.00	20.00
	1218	46	6.00	10.00	14.00	20.00
	1218	47	6.00	10.00	14.00	20.00
	121x	47	6.00	10.00	14.00	20.00
	1219	48	6.00	10.00	14.00	20.00
	1221	40	6.00	10.00	14.00	20.00
	1232	40	6.00	10.00	14.00	20.00
	1233	40	6.00	10.00	14.00	20.00
	1236	15	6.00	10.00	14.00	20.00
	1245	43	6.00	10.00	14.00	20.00
	1252	32	6.00	10.00	14.00	20.00
	1257	39	6.00	10.00	14.00	20.00

NOTE: Earlier dates (AH1211-1215) exist for this type.
NOTE: Varieties exist with different variations of obverse and reverse symbols.

In the name of Muhammad Akbar II

AH1221-1253/1806-1837AD

PAISA

COPPER

C#	Date	Year	Good	VG	Fine	VF
38	AH12xx	3x	2.00	4.00	6.00	9.00
	1231	4x	—	—	—	—

RUPEE

SILVER, 20mm, 10.70-11.60 g

C#	Date	Year	VG	Fine	VF	XF
42	AH1219	2	6.00	10.00	14.00	20.00
	1321 (error for 1231)	9	7.00	11.00	16.50	25.00
	1232	10	6.00	10.00	14.00	20.00
	1257	48	6.00	10.00	14.00	20.00
	1258	38	6.00	10.00	14.00	20.00
	1270	33	6.00	10.00	14.00	20.00
	1273	39	6.00	10.00	14.00	20.00
	127x	41	6.00	10.00	14.00	20.00
	1275	4X	6.00	10.00	14.00	20.00
	1278	45	6.00	10.00	14.00	20.00

PARTABGARH

Pratapgarh

The rulers of Partabgarh, a state located in northwest India, the maharawals, were Sesodia Rajputs who are believed to have migrated in 1553 from Mewar, where their ancestors once ruled. Arriving in the area they seized control from the local Bhil chieftains but it was not until the early eighteenth century that Partabgarh town was founded by Maharawal Partab Singh. Partabgarh was tributary to Holkar until 1818 when, with the collapse of the Maratha states, the state came under British protection. The state was then managed through the Rajputana Agency until, in April 1948, it was merged into Rajasthan.

RULERS

Sawant Singh
AH1189-1241/1775-1825AD
Dulep Singh
AH1241-1281/1825-1864AD
Udaya Singh
VS1921-1947/1864-1890AD
Raganath Singh
VS1947-1986/1890-1929AD

MINT MARK

Deogarh, Deogir

SAWANT SINGH

AH1189-1241/1775-1825AD

Second Type

Frozen date AH1199/Yr. 29. The meaning of Yr. 29 is the 29th regnal year of Sawant Singh, 1804.

1/8 RUPEE

SILVER, 11mm, 1.34-1.40 g

KM#	Date	Year	VG	Fine	VF	XF
10	AH1199	29	3.50	6.00	9.00	13.50

1/4 RUPEE

SILVER, 2.68-2.70 g

KM#	Date	Year	VG	Fine	VF	XF
11	AH1199	29	5.00	7.00	10.00	15.00

1/2 RUPEE

SILVER, 5.35-5.40 g

KM#	Date	Year	VG	Fine	VF	XF
12	AH1199	29	3.50	6.00	9.00	13.50

RUPEE

SILVER, 19-20mm, 10.70-11.80 g

KM#	Date	Year	VG	Fine	VF	XF
13	AH1199	29	5.00	7.00	10.00	15.00

NAZARANA RUPEE

SILVER, square, 10.90-11.30 g

KM#	Date	Year	VG	Fine	VF	XF
14	AH1199	29	35.00	60.00	85.00	125.00

DULEP SINGH

AH1241-1281/1825-1864AD

In the name of Shah Alam II

Frozen date AH1236/Yr. 45. The meaning of Yr. 45 is not known.

1/8 RUPEE

SILVER, 1.34-1.36 g

KM#	Date	Year	VG	Fine	VF	XF
20	AH1236	45	3.50	5.50	8.00	12.50

1/4 RUPEE

SILVER, 2.68-2.72 g

KM#	Date	Year	VG	Fine	VF	XF
21	AH1236	45	3.50	6.00	9.00	13.50

1/2 RUPEE

SILVER, 5.35-5.45 g

KM#	Date	Year	VG	Fine	VF	XF
22	AH1236	45	3.50	5.50	8.50	12.50

RUPEE

SILVER, 10.70-10.90 g

KM#	Date	Year	VG	Fine	VF	XF
23	AH1236	45	4.00	6.00	9.00	13.50

KM#	Date	Year	VG	Fine	VF	XF
24	AH1236	45	37.50	62.50	85.00	120.00

NAZARANA RUPEE

SILVER, square, 10.70-10.90 g

KM#	Date	Year	VG	Fine	VF	XF
25	AH1236	45	35.00	60.00	85.00	125.00

NAZARANA 2-1/2 RUPEES

SILVER, 27.20-27.45 g

KM#	Date	Year	VG	Fine	VF	XF
26	AH1236	45	75.00	125.00	175.00	250.00

UDAYA SINGH

VS1921-1947/1864-1890AD

PAISA

COPPER, 8.00 g
Obv: 2 eyes on god.

KM#	Date	Year	Good	VG	Fine	VF
30	VS1935	(1878)	1.25	2.25	3.25	5.00

7.60-8.00 g
Obv: 1 eye on god.

KM#	Date	Year	Good	VG	Fine	VF
(31)	VS1942	(1885)	1.00	1.75	2.50	4.00

KM#	Date	Year	Good	VG	Fine	VF
32	VS1943	(1886)	1.00	1.75	2.50	4.00

In the name of the 'Shah of London' (= Queen Victoria)

Frozen date AH1236/Yr. 45, struck from 1859 to ca. 1900. Easily distinguished from the KM#21-23 series by the word London directly below the date AH1236.

1/8 RUPEE

SILVER, 1.36 g

KM#	Date	Year	VG	Fine	VF	XF
33	AH1236	45	3.00	4.50	6.50	10.00

1/4 RUPEE

SILVER, 2.68 g

KM#	Date	Year	VG	Fine	VF	XF
34	AH1236	45	3.50	5.50	8.50	12.50

1/2 RUPEE

SILVER, 5.45 g

KM#	Date	Year	VG	Fine	VF	XF
35	AH1236	45	3.00	4.50	6.50	10.00

NAZARANA 1/2 RUPEE

SILVER, 5.40 g, Square

KM#	Date	Year	VG	Fine	VF	XF
35a	AH1236	45	—	—	Rare	—

RUPEE

SILVER, 10.90 g

KM#	Date	Year	VG	Fine	VF	XF
36	AH1236	45	4.00	6.00	9.00	13.50

NAZARANA RUPEE

SILVER, square, 10.90 g

KM#	Date	Year	VG	Fine	VF	XF
37	AH1236	45	37.50	62.50	85.00	120.00

Large flan

KM#	Date	Year	VG	Fine	VF	XF
38	AH1236	45	—	—	Rare	—

RAGANATH SINGH

VS1947-1986/1890-1929AD

PAISA

COPPER, 7.50-8.40 g

KM#	Date	Year	Good	VG	Fine	VF
40	VS1953	(1896)	1.50	2.50	3.50	5.00

PORBANDAR

State located on the Kathiawar peninsula in western India. The rulers, or ranas, of Porbandar were Jethwa Rajputs of ancient Rajput lineage. They are believed to have arrived from the north and settled the area as early as the tenth century. Their seat of government was transferred to Porbandar from Chaya, the ancient capital, in 1785. The Rana of Porbandar paid an annual tribute of 30,000 rupees to the Gaekwar of Baroda. In 1807 Porbandar acceded to British control, and in February 1948 became part of Saurashtra State. The coins of Porbandar are similar to the coins of Kutch and Navanagar and derive from a prototype struck in AH978/1570AD by Muzaffar Shah III of Gujarat. They have, in Nagari, the additional inscription, *Sri Rana.*

श्रीराणा

All are dated AH(9)78. They were struck until about 1890AD, and cannot be assigned to any specific ruler.

MONETARY SYSTEM

2 Trambiyo = 1 Dokda
3 Trambiyo = 1 Dhingla
8 Dokda = 1 Kori

1/2 TRAMBIYO

COPPER

C#	Date	Year	Good	VG	Fine	VF
30	AH(9)78 (frozen)		2.00	4.00	7.50	11.50

TRAMBIYO

COPPER

C#	Date	Year	Good	VG	Fine	VF
31	AH(9)78 (frozen)		2.00	3.25	5.00	8.50

DOKDO

COPPER

C#	Date	Year	Good	VG	Fine	VF
32	AH(9)78 (frozen)		1.00	1.75	2.50	4.50

DHINGLA

COPPER, 18-19mm

C#	Date	Year	Good	VG	Fine	VF
33	AH(9)78 (frozen)		3.00	5.00	8.00	12.50

Rectangular, 20x15mm
Cruder calligraphy

C#	Date	Year	Good	VG	Fine	VF
34	AH(9)78 (frozen)		4.50	8.50	12.50	17.50

NOTE: Said to have been struck by Khimji (1813-1831AD).

1/4 KORI

SILVER, 8-9mm

C#	Date	Year	VG	Fine	VF	XF
36	AH(9)78 (frozen)		6.50	10.00	15.00	22.50

1/2 KORI

SILVER

C#	Date	Year	VG	Fine	VF	XF
37	AH(9)78 (frozen)		4.00	6.50	10.00	15.00

KORI

SILVER

C#	Date	Year	VG	Fine	VF	XF
38	AH(9)78 (frozen)		2.50	4.00	6.50	10.00

PUDUKKOTTAI

Refer to Independent Kingdoms under British rule.

RADHANPUR

State located on the Kathiawar peninsula.

The nawabs of Radhanpur were Pathans of the Babi family who rose to high office in the service of Shah Jahan and Murad Bakhsh in Gujarat. Sometime in the late seventeenth or early eighteenth centuries one of the family was appointed faujdar of Radhanpur and the surrounding area. After Aurangzeb's death, Kamal-ud-din Khan Babi seized the governorship of Ahmadabad, but this was relinquished in 1753 to the forces of the Peshwa of Poona and the Gaekwar of Baroda. Radhanpur, however, remained in Babi control as a Maratha Jagir until 1820 when the State came under British protection.

All silver coins of Radhanpur appear to be nazarana issues.

RULERS

Zorawar Khan
AH1241-1291/1825-1874AD
Bismilla Khan
AH1291-1313/1874-1895AD

MINT

رادهنپور

Radhanpur

ZORAWAR KHAN

AH1241-1291/1825-1874AD

In the name of Queen Victoria

کوین وکٹوریا

and Zorawar Khan

PAISA

Jo 

COPPER or BRONZE, uniface

KM#	Date	Year	Good	VG	Fine	VF
3	ND	—	1.00	1.75	2.50	4.00

2 ANNAS

SILVER, 1.34-1.45 g

KM#	Date	Year	VG	Fine	VF	XF
8	AH1288	1871	15.00	25.00	35.00	50.00

4 ANNAS

SILVER, 2.68-2.90 g

KM#	Date	Year	VG	Fine	VF	XF
9	AH1287	1869	14.00	23.50	32.50	45.00
	1287	1871	14.00	23.50	32.50	45.00
	1288	1871	14.00	23.50	32.50	45.00
	1288	1872	14.00	23.50	32.50	45.00

8 ANNAS

SILVER, 5.35-5.80 g

KM#	Date	Year	VG	Fine	VF	XF
10	AH1284	1869	15.00	25.00	35.00	50.00
	1286	1869	15.00	25.00	35.00	50.00
	1287	1869	15.00	25.00	35.00	50.00
	1287	1870	15.00	25.00	35.00	50.00
	1288	1871	15.00	25.00	35.00	50.00
	1289	1871	15.00	25.00	35.00	50.00

50 FALUS

SILVER

KM#	Date	Year	VG	Fine	VF	XF
5	AH1284	1867	18.50	31.50	42.50	60.00

RUPEE

SILVER, 10.70-11.60 g

KM#	Date	Year	VG	Fine	VF	XF
11	AH1287	1870	14.00	23.50	32.50	45.00
	1287	1871	14.00	23.50	32.50	45.00
	1288	1871	14.00	23.50	32.50	45.00
	1288	1872	14.00	23.50	32.50	45.00
	1289	1872	14.00	23.50	32.50	45.00

100 FALUS

SILVER

KM#	Date	Year	VG	Fine	VF	XF
6	AH1284	1867	18.00	30.00	45.00	65.00
	1286	1868	18.00	30.00	45.00	65.00
	1286	1869	18.00	30.00	45.00	65.00
	1287	1870	18.00	30.00	45.00	65.00
	1287	18771 (error for 1871)				
			18.00	30.00	45.00	65.00

MOHUR

GOLD, 27mm, 10.70-11.40 g

KM#	Date	Year	VG	Fine	VF	XF
15	AH1277	1860	175.00	225.00	275.00	400.00

BISMILLA KHAN

AH1291-1313/1874-1895AD

In the name of Queen Victoria

کوین وکٹوریا

and Bismillah Khan

PAISA

Ji 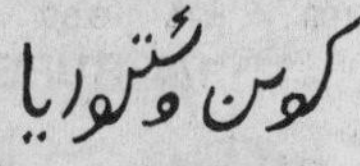

COPPER or BRONZE, uniface, 8.39 g

KM#	Date	Year	Good	VG	Fine	VF
16	ND	—	1.75	2.25	3.00	4.50

2 ANNAS

SILVER, 15mm, 1.34-1.45 g

KM#	Date	Year	VG	Fine	VF	XF
18	AH—	1880	18.00	30.00	42.50	60.00

4 ANNAS

SILVER, 2.68-2.90 g
Obv. leg: Field divided twice, Nawab's name at top. Rev. leg: Field divided once, Queen's name upper left.

KM#	Date	Year	VG	Fine	VF	XF
19	AH—	1880	15.00	25.00	35.00	50.00

In the name of Empress Victoria and Bismillah Khan

8 ANNAS

SILVER, 5.35-5.80 g

KM#	Date	Year	VG	Fine	VF	XF
21	AH1291	1875	12.00	20.00	30.00	45.00

In the name of Queen Victoria and Bismillah Khan

Obv. leg: Field divided twice, Nawab's name at top. Rev. leg: 2 field dividers, Queen's name center left, center line three words.

KM#	Date	Year	VG	Fine	VF	XF
22	AH1297	1880	12.00	20.00	30.00	45.00

Rev. leg: W/o field dividers, Queen's name lower left.

23	AH1297	1881	12.00	20.00	30.00	45.00

Rev. leg: 2 field dividers, Queen's name center left, center line 3 words.

24	AH1299	1881	12.00	20.00	30.00	45.00

Obv. leg: 2 field dividers, Nawab's name center in one line. Rev. leg: W/o field dividers, Queen's name lower left.

25	AH1299	1881	12.00	20.00	30.00	45.00

RUPEE

SILVER, 10.70-11.60 g
Obv. leg: 2 field dividers, Nawab's name center in one line. Rev. leg: Field divided once above *Dak*.

27	AH1297	1880	18.00	30.00	42.50	60.00
	1298	1880	18.00	30.00	45.00	65.00

Obv. leg: Field divided twice, Nawab's name at top. Rev. leg: 2 field dividers, Queen's name center left, center line 3 words.

28	AH1299	1881	16.50	26.50	37.50	55.00

Obv. leg: 2 field dividers, Nawab's name center in one line. Rev. leg: Field divided once w/ Queen's titles in different order.

KM#	Date	Year	VG	Fine	VF	XF
29	AH1297	1881	18.00	30.00	45.00	65.00
	1298	1881	16.50	26.50	37.50	55.00

Rev. leg: 1 field divider, w/o Queen's name, mint name above.

30	AH1311	1894	18.00	30.00	42.50	60.00

Obv. leg: 1 field divider, Nawab's name above. Rev. leg: W/o Queen's name, mint name below.

31	AH1311	1894	18.00	30.00	42.50	60.00

RAMPUR

This tiny estate of four and a half square miles was held by Chauda Rajputs in the old Gujerat States Agency Area. It was feudatory to Lunavada and the estate was controlled by a thakur or, latterly, by four shareholders.

Anonymous Issues

The following listings may be from Lunavada or from Rampur. They are often found overstruck on coins of Lunavada, and over other states, including Sailana.

1/2 PAISA

COPPER, 3.00-4.00 g
Obv: Open hand in square.
Rev. leg: *Rampar*.

KM#	Date	Year	Good	VG	Fine	VF
1	ND	—	4.00	6.50	10.00	15.00

Obv: Sunbursts. Rev. leg: *Rampar*.

2	ND	—	5.00	9.00	13.00	20.00

PAISA

COPPER, 1.90-4.30 g
Obv: Sunbursts. Rev. leg: *Rampar*.

3	ND	—	2.00	3.25	5.00	8.50

Obv: Spears. Rev: Spears.

4	ND	—	2.00	3.25	5.00	8.50

Round or square, 8.50 g
Obv: Spears. Rev: *Rampar*.

5	ND	—	2.00	3.25	5.00	8.50

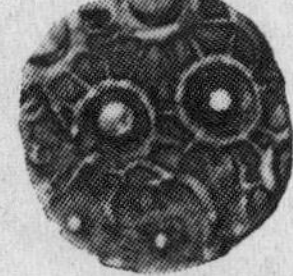

Round or square, 7.50-8.30 g
Obv: Sunbursts. Rev. leg: *Rampar*.

6	ND	—	2.00	3.25	5.00	8.50

Square, 7.50-8.30 g
Obv: Solar symbol. Rev. leg: *Rampar*.

KM#	Date	Year	Good	VG	Fine	VF
7	ND	—	4.00	6.00	9.00	13.50

Obv: Spears. Rev: Persian legend.

8	ND	—	2.00	3.25	5.00	8.50

PIE

COPPER, 2.30 g

12	ND	—	—	—	—	—

RATLAM

State located northwest of Indore in Madhya Pradesh.

The rajas of Ratlam were Rathor Rajputs, descendants of the younger branch of the Jodhpur ruling family. Ratlam became the premier Rajput state in western Malwa. The founder, Ratan Singh, received the territory as a grant from Shah Jahan in 1631. Before Maratha collapse some fifteen percent of the state's annual revenue went to Sindhia as tribute. Under British protection it was supervised by the Central India Agency and in 1948 Ratlam became a district of Madhya Bharat.

RULERS

Ranjit Singh
VS1921-1950/1864-1893AD

NOTE: 1 Paisa previously listed here now is listed in Banswara-IPS.

RANJIT SINGH

VS1921-1950/1864-1893AD

PAISA

COPPER, 22mm

21	VS1921	(1864)	6.00	9.00	12.50	18.50

Obv: Katar.

22	VS1927	(1870)	3.00	5.00	8.00	12.50
	1928	(1871)	2.00	3.25	5.00	8.50

23	1885	—	3.00	5.00	8.00	12.50

Milled Coinage

PAISA

COPPER
Obv: Hanuman.
Thick planchet

KM#	Date	Year	Fine	VF	XF	Unc
24	VS1945	(1888)	4.00	6.00	9.00	13.50
	1947	(1890)	4.50	8.00	12.00	17.50
	1948	(1891)	1.00	1.75	2.50	4.50

Thin, crude restrike of KM#24.

25	VS1947	(1890)	.40	.65	1.00	1.75

NOTE: KM#25 was struck c.1942-1945AD using the same dies as for KM#25.

REWA

State located in eastern north-central India.

The rulers of Rewa were Baghela Rajputs of the Solanki

clan who probably migrated from Anhilwara Patan in Gujarat about the eleventh century. Arriving in Bundelkhand they carved out for themselves a substantial kingdom which remained independent until 1597, when they were obliged to become Mughal tributaries under Akbar. With Mughal decline Rewa began to move once more towards independence, this time under the nominal suzerainty of the Peshwa. In 1812 the raja of Rewa, Jai Singh Deo was coerced into a treaty with the British and, failing to observe its conditions, was forced to yield to British control in 1813-1814. In 1948 Rewa was merged into Vindhya Pradesh.

RULERS

Jai Singh Deo
VS1866-1892/1809-1835AD
Vishvanath Singh
VS1892-1900/1835-1843AD
Raghuraj Singh
VS1900-1937/1843-1880AD
Gulab Singh
VS1975-2003/1918-1946AD

JAI SINGH DEO

VS1866-1892/1809-1835AD

PAISA

COPPER, 6.80 g

KM#	Date	Year	Good	VG	Fine	VF
11	VS1890	(1823)	2.00	3.00	4.50	7.00

8.80-12.60 g

KM#	Date	Year	Good	VG	Fine	VF
12	ND	—	1.75	2.75	4.00	6.00

2 PAISA

COPPER

KM#	Date	Year	Good	VG	Fine	VF
14	ND	—	2.50	4.00	7.00	11.00

VISHVANATH SINGH

VS1892-1900/1835-1843AD

PAISA

COPPER, 7.80 g

KM#	Date	Year	Good	VG	Fine	VF
16	ND	—	2.50	3.50	5.00	8.50

2 PAISA

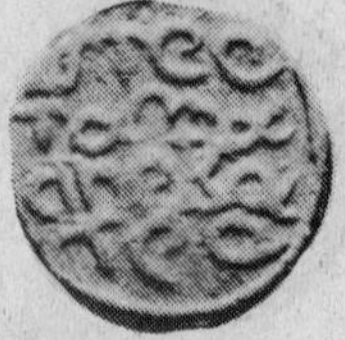

COPPER, 16.80 g

KM#	Date	Year	Good	VG	Fine	VF
18	ND	—	2.50	3.50	5.00	8.50

MOHUR

GOLD, 9.75 g

KM#	Date	Year	VG	Fine	VF	XF
22	ND	—	250.00	425.00	600.00	850.00

RAGHURAJ SINGH

VS1900-1937/1843-1880AD

In the name of Agent Bushby Saheb

PAISA

COPPER

KM#	Date	Year	Good	VG	Fine	VF
24	VS1906	(1849)	2.75	4.50	6.50	10.00

2 PAISE

COPPER
Obv: Lion left.

KM#	Date	Year	Good	VG	Fine	VF
26	VS1906	(1849)	2.75	4.50	6.50	10.00

Obv: Lion right.

KM#	Date	Year	Good	VG	Fine	VF
27	VS1906	(1849)	5.00	7.00	9.00	13.50

GULAB SINGH

VS1975-2003/1918-1946AD

1/2 RUPEE

SILVER, thin flan
Accession Commemorative

KM#	Date	Year	VG	Fine	VF	XF
29	VS1975	(1918)	18.50	31.50	42.50	60.00

RUPEE

SILVER, thick flan
Accession Commemorative

KM#	Date	Year	VG	Fine	VF	XF
31	VS1975	(1918)	18.50	31.50	42.50	60.00

1/2 MOHUR

GOLD, 4.40-5.40 g
Accession Commemorative

KM#	Date	Year	VG	Fine	VF	XF
33	VS1975	(1918)	200.00	300.00	425.00	600.00

MOHUR

GOLD, 10.70-11.71 g
Accession Commemorative

KM#	Date	Year	VG	Fine	VF	XF
35	VS1975	(1918)	165.00	225.00	325.00	450.00

KM#	Date	Year	VG	Fine	VF	XF
36	VS1975	(1918)	165.00	225.00	325.00	450.00

11.36 g
Obv: Plain border banner below supporters.

KM#	Date	Year	VG	Fine	VF	XF
38	VS1976	(1919)	225.00	385.00	550.00	800.00

Reduced weight, 8.80 g

KM#	Date	Year	VG	Fine	VF	XF
40	VS1977	(1920)	175.00	265.00	385.00	550.00

ROHILKHAND

Refer to Independent Kingdoms during British rule.

SAILANA

This small state in west-central India, of slightly over one hundred square miles had once been part of Ratlam, but about 1709 it asserted its independence under the leadership of Pratab Singh, the second son of Chhatrasal. The town of Sailana was founded in 1730 by Jai Singh's successor, and from that date the state was named after it. Due to its small size and vulnerability, Sailana was obliged to become tributary to Sindhia to ensure its survival. In 1819 this payment was limited to one-third of the state's revenues. Later, under agreements of 1840 and 1860, the tribute went to the British for the support of British Indian troops in the region. Barmawal was feudatory to Sailana.

LOCAL RULERS

Dule Singh
VS1907-1952/1850-1895AD
Jaswant Singh, 1895-1919AD
Dilip Singh Bahadur, 1919-1948

ANONYMOUS COINAGE

KM#4-6 are believed to be 1 Paisa struck to progressively lighter weights in later periods.

(1/2) PAISA

COPPER, 4.80-5.80 g

KM#	Date	Year	Good	VG	Fine	VF
4	ND	—	1.50	2.25	3.50	5.00

PAISA

COPPER, 7.50-9.70 g
Obv: Pennant points either up or down.

KM#	Date	Year	Good	VG	Fine	VF
5	ND	—	.50	.85	1.25	2.00

NOTE: KM#5 is known struck over an Egyptian 20 Para KM#244 or #246, cut down to an irregular shape. Other combinations could exist.

(2) PAISA

COPPER, 11.60-12.30 g

KM#	Date	Year	Good	VG	Fine	VF
6	ND	—	2.00	3.25	5.00	8.50

DULE SINGH

VS1907-1952/1850-1895AD

1/2 PAISA

COPPER, 5.20 g
Obv: Pennant points left.

KM#	Date	Year	Good	VG	Fine	VF
10	VS1944	(1887)	2.00	3.25	5.00	8.00

KM#	Date	Year	Good	VG	Fine	VF
11	VS1937	(1880)	1.25	2.25	3.50	5.50
	7391 (retrograde)	(1880)	1.25	2.25	3.50	5.50

11.80 g
Rev: Sprig, Nagari date.

KM#	Date	Year	Good	VG	Fine	VF
12	VS1940	(1883)	1.75	2.75	4.00	7.00

10.90 g
Rev: Arabic numerals in Samvat date.

KM#	Date	Year	Good	VG	Fine	VF
13	1921	(1884)	1.75	2.75	4.00	7.00

PAISA

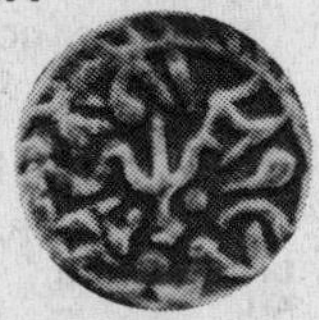

COPPER, 10.80-11.00 g
Obv: Pennant points right.
Rev: Trident.

KM#	Date	Year	Good	VG	Fine	VF
14	VS1944	(1887)	1.75	2.75	4.00	7.00

REGAL ISSUES

JASWANT SINGH

1890-1919AD

1/4 ANNA

COPPER

KM#	Date	Mintage	Fine	VF	XF	Unc
15	1908	.224	6.50	11.50	18.50	30.00
	1908	—	—	—	Proof	185.00

KM#	Date	Mintage	Fine	VF	XF	Unc
16	1912	.224	4.50	7.50	12.50	20.00
	1912	—	—	—	Proof	175.00

SAILANA FEUDATORY STATE

BARMAWAL

RULER

Raja Handa Singh

PAISA

COPPER
Obv: Hanuman.

KM#	Date	Year	Good	VG	Fine	VF
1	ND	—	6.00	10.00	14.00	20.00

NOTE: KM#1 was struck prior to 1881AD.

SIKHS

Refer to Sikh Empire, Independent Kingdom during British rule.

SIKKIM

Refer to Independent Kingdom during British rule.

SIND

Refer to Independent Kingdom during British rule.

SIRMUR

Sirmur Nahan

The ruling Rajput family of this Himalayan principality claimed descent from the Jaisalmir royal house and had ruled the region, located in north India, since the end of the eleventh century. From 1803 to 1815, Sirmur came under Gurkha control but on their expulsion by the British during the Nepal War, the original Rajput family was restored to their ancestral dominions as a British feudatory.

NOTE: For earlier issues, see Gurkhas.

RULERS

Fath Prakash, restored
VS1872-1890/1815-1833AD

PAISA

COPPER

KM#	Date	Year	Good	VG	Fine	VF
11	VS1877	(1820)	6.50	11.50	18.50	30.00

SIROHI

Formerly Rajputana States Agency; merged in Rajasthan State, except for the tehsils (districts) of Abu Road and Dilawara which were merged with Bombay. Bordered on the north, northeast and west by Jodhpur, on the south by Palanpur, Danta and Idar; and on the east by Mewar.

While the ruling family claims descent from Prithwiraj, the Chauhan King of Delhi, the actual founder of the Sirohi house was one Deoraj, a 13th century figure who was the progenitor of the Deora clan of Rajputs. The present capital, Sirohi, was founded in 1425, about which time the Rana of Chitor is said to have taken refuge at Mount Abu from the army of Kutb-ud-din of Gujarat. The British entered by treaty in 1823, disallowed the claims of Jodhpur to Sirohi lands, ultimately bringing the Minas to submission and the straying thakurs back into line.

RULER

Sheo Singh, VS1873-1919/1816-1862AD

1/4 ANNA

COPPER, 9.75-10.90 g
Rev. leg: *Zarb Raj Sirohi*, scimitar.

KM#	Date	Year	Good	VG	Fine	VF
11	VS1910	(1853)	3.50	5.50	8.50	12.50

NOTE: Previously listed under Jodhpur State.

SITAMAU

Sitamau, in western Malwa, was founded in 1695 by Raja Kesho Das, a scion of the Rathor rulers of Ratlam. Sitamau was tributary to Sindhia before passing under British protection and control in the nineteenth century.

RULERS

Raja Ram Singh
VS1859-1924/1802-1867AD
Bahadur Singh
VS1942-1956/1885-1899AD
Shardul Singh
VS1956-1957/1899-1900AD

RAJA RAM SINGH

VS1859-1924/1802-1867AD

PAISA

COPPER, 18-20mm

KM#	Date	Year	Good	VG	Fine	VF
1	1844	—	4.00	6.00	9.00	13.50

BAHADUR SINGH

VS1942-1956/1885-1899AD

1/2 PAISA

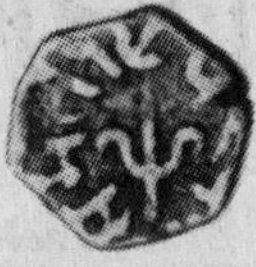

COPPER

KM#	Date	Year	Good	VG	Fine	VF
3	ND	—	4.00	6.00	9.00	13.50

PAISA

COPPER

KM#	Date	Year	Good	VG	Fine	VF
4	VS1948	(1891)	2.50	4.50	7.00	11.00

SHARDUL SINGH

VS1956-1957/1899-1900AD

1/2 PAISA

COPPER, 16-18mm

KM#	Date	Year	Good	VG	Fine	VF
5	VS1956	(1899)	4.00	6.00	9.00	13.50

NOTE: Varieties exist.

TONK

Tunk

State located partially in Rajputana and in central India. Tonk was founded in 1806 by Amir Khan (d. 1834), the Pathan Pindari leader, who received the territory from Holkar. Amir Khan caused great havoc in Central India by his lightning raids into neighboring states. In 1817 he was forced into submission by the East India Company and remained under British control until India's independence. In March 1948 Tonk was incorporated into Rajasthan.

RULERS

Amir Khan
AH1213-1250/1798-1834AD
Wazir Muhammad Khan
AH1250-1281/1834-1864AD
Muhammad Ali Khan
AH1280-1284/1864-1867AD
Muhammad Ibrahim Ali Khan
AH1284-1349/1868-1930AD
Muhammad Sa'adat Ali Khan
AH1349-1368/1930-1949AD

MINT MARKS

Sironj سرونج

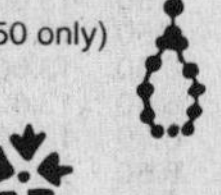

Tonk تونک

Necklace (on C#50 only)

Flower (on all)

Leaf (several forms)

Beginning with the reign of Muhammad Ibrahim Ali Khan, most coins have both AD and AH dates. Circulation with both dates fully legible are worth about 20 per cent more than listed prices. Coins with one date fully legible are worth prices shown. Coins with both dates off are of little value.

There are many minor and major variations of type, varying with location of date, orientation of leaf, arrangement of legend. Although these fall into easily distinguished patterns, they are strictly for the specialist and are omitted here.

SIRONJ MINT

Mughal Issues

In the name of Muhammad Akbar II
AH1221-1253/1806-1837AD

PAISA

COPPER, 23mm
Rev: Jhar.

C#	Date	Year	Good	VG	Fine	VF
45	AH1225	—	4.00	10.00	15.00	25.00

Rev: Horse.

C#	Date	Year	Good	VG	Fine	VF
45a	AH1226	—	5.00	12.50	20.00	30.00

Rev: Uncertain symbols.

C#	Date	Year	Good	VG	Fine	VF
45c	AH1247	—	3.50	7.00	12.00	20.00

Rev: Rosette & katar.

C#	Date	Year	Good	VG	Fine	VF
45d	AH1250	—	4.00	10.00	15.00	25.00

20-21mm
Rev: Rosette & necklace.

C#	Date	Year	Good	VG	Fine	VF
50	AH1252	—	3.00	7.00	12.00	20.00
	1253	—	3.00	7.00	12.00	20.00
	1269	—	3.00	7.00	12.00	20.00

1/4 RUPEE

SILVER, 13mm, 2.68-2.90 g

C#	Date	Year	VG	Fine	VF	XF
58	AH1253	—	7.50	13.00	22.00	32.00

1/2 RUPEE

SILVER, 5.35-5.80 g

C#	Date	Year	VG	Fine	VF	XF
59	AH1253	—	6.50	13.00	22.00	32.00
	1256	—	6.50	13.00	22.00	32.00
	1267	—	6.50	13.00	22.00	32.00

RUPEE

SILVER, 10.70-11.60 g

C#	Date	Year	VG	Fine	VF	XF
60	AH1219	—	6.50	13.00	21.00	30.00
	1221	—	6.50	13.00	21.00	30.00
	1228	—	6.50	13.00	21.00	30.00
	1233	—	6.50	13.00	21.00	30.00
	1235	—	6.50	13.00	21.00	30.00
	1243	—	6.50	13.00	21.00	30.00
	1245	—	6.50	13.00	21.00	30.00
	1252	—	6.50	13.00	21.00	30.00
	1253	31	6.50	13.00	21.00	30.00
	1264	—	6.50	13.00	21.00	30.00
	1269	—	6.50	13.00	21.00	30.00

Regal Issues

In the names of Queen Victoria and Wazir Muhammad Khan
AH1250-1281/1834-1864AD

PAISA

COPPER, 18-20mm

Y#	Date	Year	Good	VG	Fine	VF
1	AH1278	—	4.00	6.25	10.00	16.50

RUPEE

SILVER, 10.70-11.60 g

Y#	Date	Year	VG	Fine	VF	XF
2	AH1276	—	12.50	18.50	25.00	35.00
	1277	—	12.50	18.50	25.00	35.00
	1280	—	12.50	18.50	25.00	35.00

In the names of Queen Victoria and Muhammad Ali Khan
AH1281-1285/1864-1867AD

PAISA

COPPER, 23-24mm

Y#	Date	Year	Good	VG	Fine	VF
3	AH1283	—	3.00	5.00	7.50	12.50
	1285	—	3.00	5.00	7.50	12.50
	1286	—	3.00	5.00	7.50	12.50
	1288	—	3.00	5.00	7.50	12.50
	1289	—	3.00	5.00	7.50	12.50

1/8 RUPEE

SILVER, 12mm, 1.34-1.45 g

Y#	Date	Year	VG	Fine	VF	XF
4	ND (off flan)	—	6.50	13.00	22.00	32.00
	AH(12)8x	—	6.50	13.00	22.00	32.00

1/4 RUPEE

SILVER, 15mm, 2.68-2.90 g

Y#	Date	Year	VG	Fine	VF	XF
5	AH1289	—	6.00	12.00	21.00	30.00

1/2 RUPEE

SILVER, 16-17mm, 5.35-5.80 g

Y#	Date	Year	VG	Fine	VF	XF
6	AH1289	—	6.50	13.00	22.00	32.00

RUPEE

SILVER, 10.70-11.60 g

Y#	Date	Year	VG	Fine	VF	XF
7	AH1282	—	9.00	18.00	28.00	40.00
	1286	—	9.00	18.00	28.00	40.00
	1288	—	9.00	18.00	28.00	40.00
	1289	—	9.00	18.00	28.00	40.00
	1292	—	9.00	18.00	28.00	40.00
	1296	—	9.00	18.00	28.00	40.00
	—	1891	9.00	18.00	28.00	40.00

In the names of Victoria Empress and Muhammad Ibrahim Ali Khan
AH1285-1348/1867-1930AD

PIE

COPPER, 16mm

Y#	Date	Year	Good	VG	Fine	VF
11	AH1314	—	4.50	8.00	12.00	17.50

PAISA

COPPER, 23mm

Y#	Date	Year	Good	VG	Fine	VF
12	AH1298	—	4.00	6.50	10.00	15.00
	1299	—	4.00	6.50	10.00	15.00
	1302	—	4.00	6.50	10.00	15.00
	1308	—	4.00	6.50	10.00	15.00

1/8 RUPEE

SILVER, 1.34-1.45 g

Y#	Date	Year	VG	Fine	VF	XF
A13	AH(13)10					
A13		(1893)	9.00	18.00	28.00	40.00

1/4 RUPEE

SILVER, about 12mm, 2.68-2.90 g

Y#	Date	Year	VG	Fine	VF	XF
13	AH(13)10	(1893)	7.50	15.00	25.00	35.00
	(13)14	(1896)	7.50	15.00	25.00	35.00

1/2 RUPEE

SILVER, 5.35-5.80 g

Y#	Date	Year	VG	Fine	VF	XF
14	AH1306	—	7.50	15.00	25.00	35.00
	1310	1893	7.50	15.00	25.00	35.00
	1314	1896	7.50	15.00	25.00	35.00

RUPEE

SILVER, 10.70-11.60 g

Y#	Date	Year	VG	Fine	VF	XF
15	AH1299	—	9.00	18.00	28.00	40.00
	1303	—	9.00	18.00	28.00	40.00
	1304	23	9.00	18.00	28.00	40.00
	1306	—	9.00	18.00	28.00	40.00
	1309	1892	9.00	18.00	28.00	40.00
	1310	1893	9.00	18.00	28.00	40.00

In the name of Queen Victoria and Muhammad Ibrahim Ali Khan

TONK MINT

NOTE: All coins with both AH and AD dates clearly readable command about a 50 per cent premium.

PAISA

COPPER

Y#	Date	Year	Good	VG	Fine	VF
8	AH1290	—	3.50	6.00	10.00	17.50

1/8 RUPEE

SILVER, 1.34-1.45 g

Y#	Date	Year	VG	Fine	VF	XF
9	AH	—	10.00	15.00	21.50	30.00

RUPEE

SILVER, 10.70-11.60 g

Y#	Date	Year	VG	Fine	VF	XF
10	—	1873	10.00	15.00	21.50	30.00
	AH1290	1873	10.00	15.00	21.50	30.00
	1290	187x	10.00	15.00	21.50	30.00
	1292	187x	10.00	15.00	21.50	30.00
	1293	187x	10.00	15.00	21.50	30.00
	1294	187x	10.00	15.00	21.50	30.00
	1293	1876	10.00	15.00	21.50	30.00
	1294	1877	10.00	15.00	21.50	30.00

NOTE: Var. 1, illustrated above, has no leaf, but a branch on obverse. All others have the leaf, as on the 1 Paisa, Y#8. Six varieties are known.

In the names of Victoria Empress and Muhammad Ibrahim Ali Khan

PAISA

COPPER
Obv: AH date in exergue.

Y#	Date	Year	Good	VG	Fine	VF
16	AH1290	187x	1.75	3.25	5.00	8.00
	1292	1876	1.75	3.25	5.00	8.00

Y#	Date	Year	Good	VG	Fine	VF
16	1294	1877	1.75	3.25	5.00	8.00
	1295	187x	1.50	3.00	4.00	6.50
	1298	1880	1.50	3.00	4.00	6.50
	1298	1881	1.50	3.00	4.00	6.50
	1302	1885	1.00	2.50	3.50	5.50
	1303	1885	1.00	2.50	3.50	5.50
	1303	1886	1.00	2.50	3.50	5.50

NOTE: 4 varieties are known.

1/8 RUPEE

SILVER, 1.34-1.45 g

Y#	Date	Year	VG	Fine	VF	XF
17	AH1309	1892	6.00	9.00	13.50	20.00
	1317	1899	6.00	9.00	13.50	20.00

1/4 RUPEE

SILVER, 14-15mm, 2.68-2.90 g

Y#	Date	Year	VG	Fine	VF	XF
18	AH1305	1888	6.00	9.00	13.50	20.00
	1309	1892	6.00	9.00	13.50	20.00
	1316	189x	6.00	9.00	13.50	20.00
	1317	1899	6.00	9.00	13.50	20.00
	1318	1xxx	6.00	9.00	13.50	20.00

1/2 RUPEE

SILVER, 5.35-5.80 g

Y#	Date	Year	VG	Fine	VF	XF
19	AH129x	1882	6.50	10.00	15.00	22.50
	1305	1888	6.50	10.00	15.00	22.50
	1209	1892	6.50	10.00	15.00	22.50
	1309	1892	6.50	10.00	15.00	22.50
	1317	1899	6.50	10.00	15.00	22.50

RUPEE

SILVER, 10.70-11.60 g

Y#	Date	Year	VG	Fine	VF	XF
20	AH1293	1876	6.50	10.00	15.00	22.50
	1294	187x	6.50	10.00	15.00	22.50
	1295	187x	6.50	10.00	15.00	22.50
	1295	1878	6.50	10.00	15.00	22.50
	1296	1879	6.50	10.00	15.00	22.50
	1297	1879	6.50	10.00	15.00	22.50
	1297	1880	6.50	10.00	15.00	22.50
	1298	1881	6.50	10.00	15.00	22.50
	1299	1879	6.50	10.00	15.00	22.50
	1301	1884	6.50	10.00	15.00	22.50
	1302	1884	6.50	10.00	15.00	22.50
	1304	1887	6.50	10.00	15.00	22.50
	1305	1888	6.50	10.00	15.00	22.50
	1307	18xx	6.50	10.00	15.00	22.50
	1308	1890	6.50	10.00	15.00	22.50
	1308	1891	6.50	10.00	15.00	22.50
	1309	1891	6.50	10.00	15.00	22.50
	1309	1892	6.50	10.00	15.00	22.50
	1310	1893	6.50	10.00	15.00	22.50
	1311	—	6.50	10.00	15.00	22.50
	1312	189x	6.50	10.00	15.00	22.50
	1313	1895	6.50	10.00	15.00	22.50
	1315	1897	6.50	10.00	15.00	22.50

NAZARANA RUPEE

SILVER, 10.70-11.60 g

Y#	Date	Year	VG	Fine	VF	XF
20a	AH1297	1880	—	Rare	—	

NAZARANA 2 RUPEES

SILVER, 32mm, 21.40-23.20 g

Y#	Date	Year	VG	Fine	VF	XF
21	AH1297	1880	125.00	150.00	225.00	300.00
	1298	1881	125.00	150.00	225.00	300.00

MOHUR

GOLD, 19mm, 10.70-11.40 g

Y#	Date	Year	VG	Fine	VF	XF
22	AH1297	1880	200.00	250.00	325.00	400.00
	1298	188x	200.00	250.00	325.00	400.00

NAZARANA 2 MOHURS

GOLD, 21.40-22.80 g

Y#	Date	Year	VG	Fine	VF	XF
23	AH1297	1880	350.00	600.00	800.00	1000.

In the names of George V and Muhammad Ibrahim Ali Khan

PAISA

COPPER, 7.30 g

Y#	Date	Year	Good	VG	Fine	VF
24.1	AH1329	1911	1.25	2.25	3.50	5.50
	1329 (sic) 1329		1.25	2.25	3.50	5.50
	1911 (sic) 1911		1.25	2.25	3.50	5.50
	1329 (sic) 1917		1.25	2.25	3.50	5.50
	1330	1911	1.25	2.25	3.50	5.50

Reduced weight, 5.00 g

Y#	Date	Year	Good	VG	Fine	VF
24.2	AH1335	1917	1.25	2.25	3.50	5.50
	(13)38	192x	1.25	2.25	3.50	5.50
	1342	1924	1.00	1.75	2.50	4.50
	1344	1925	1.00	1.75	2.50	4.50
	1344	1926	1.00	1.75	2.50	4.50
	1345	1927	1.00	1.75	2.50	4.50
	134x	1928	1.00	1.75	2.50	4.50

1/4 ANNA

COPPER, 8.30 g

Y#	Date	Year	Good	VG	Fine	VF
A25.1	AH1335	1917	1.25	2.25	3.50	5.50
	1336	1917	1.25	2.25	3.50	5.50

Reduced weight, 5.40 g

Y#	Date	Year	Good	VG	Fine	VF
A25.2	AH1336	1917	1.00	1.75	2.50	4.50

1/8 RUPEE

SILVER, 11mm, 1.34-1.45 g

Y#	Date	Year	VG	Fine	VF	XF
25	AH1346	1928	6.50	10.00	15.00	22.50

1/4 RUPEE

SILVER, 2.68-2.90 g

Y#	Date	Year	VG	Fine	VF	XF
26	AH1346	1928	6.50	10.00	15.00	22.50

1/2 RUPEE

SILVER, 16mm, 5.35-5.80 g

Y#	Date	Year	VG	Fine	VF	XF
27	AH1346	1928	11.50	17.50	23.50	32.50

RUPEE

SILVER, 10.70-11.60 g

Y#	Date	Year	VG	Fine	VF	XF
28	AH1329	—	5.50	8.00	12.50	18.50
	1330	1912	5.50	8.00	12.50	18.50
	1341	1923	5.50	8.00	12.50	18.50
	1342	1924	5.50	8.00	12.50	18.50
	1343	1925	5.50	8.00	12.50	18.50
	1344	1925	5.50	8.00	12.50	18.50
	1344	1926	5.50	8.00	12.50	18.50
	1345	1926	5.50	8.00	12.50	18.50
	1346	1926	5.50	8.00	12.50	18.50
	1346	1927	5.50	8.00	12.50	18.50
	1347	1928	5.50	8.00	12.50	18.50
	1348	1928	5.50	8.00	12.50	18.50
	1348	1929	5.50	8.00	12.50	18.50
	134x	1930	5.50	8.00	12.50	18.50

In the names of George V and Muhammad Sa'adat Ali Khan
AH1348-1368/1930-1949AD

1/8 RUPEE

SILVER, 1.34-1.45 g

Y#	Date	Year	VG	Fine	VF	XF
30	AH1351	—	4.00	6.50	10.00	15.00
	1352	—	4.00	6.50	10.00	15.00
	1353	1934	4.00	6.50	10.00	15.00

Milled Coinage

PICE

(Paisa)

COPPER, 26mm

KM#	Date	Mintage	Fine	VF	XF	Unc
29	AH1350//1932	.640	.50	1.00	2.00	3.50

KM#	Date	Mintage	Fine	VF	XF	Unc
29a	AH1350//1932	.640	.25	.50	1.00	1.75

NOTE: Struck 1934.

TRAVANCORE

State located in extreme southwest India. A mint was established in ME965/1789-1790AD.

The region of Travancore had a lengthy history before being annexed by the Vijayanagar kingdom. With Vijayanagar's defeat at the battle of Talikota in 1565, Travancore passed under Muslim control until the late eighteenth century, when it merged as a state in its own right under Raja Martanda Varma. At this time the raja allied himself with British interests as a protection against the Muslim dynasty of Mysore. In 1795 the raja of Travancore officially accepted a subsidiary alliance with the East India Company, and remained within the orbit of British influence from then until India's independence.

RULERS

Bala Rama Varma I
ME973-986/1798-1810AD
Rani Parvathi Bai, regent
ME990-1004/1815-1829AD
Rama Varma III
ME1004-1022/1829-1847AD
Martanda Varma II
ME1022-1035/1847-1860AD
Rama Varma IV
ME1035-1055/1860-1880AD
Rama Varma V
ME1057-1062/1880-1885AD
Rama Varma VI
ME1062-1101/1885-1924AD

Bala Rama Varma II
ME1101-1126/1924-1949AD

MONETARY SYSTEM

16 Cash (Kasu) = 1 Chuckram
4 Chuckram = 1 Fanam
2 Fanams = 1 Anantaraya
7 Fanams = 1 Rupee
52-1/2 Fanam = 1 Pagoda

DATING

ME dates are of the Malabar Era. Add 824 or 825 to the ME date for the AD date. (e.g., ME1112 plus 824-825 = 1936-1937AD).

BALA RAMA VARMA I

ME973-986/1798-1810AD

1/2 CHUCKRAM

COPPER

KM#	Date	Year	VG	Fine	VF	XF
5 (1)	ND	—	4.00	7.50	12.00	20.00

SILVER

KM#	Date	Year	VG	Fine	VF	XF
7 (C10)	ND	(1809-10)	2.00	3.75	5.50	8.00

CHUCKRAM

SILVER

KM#	Date	Year	VG	Fine	VF	XF
1 (C11)	ND	(1600-1860)	.60	1.00	1.50	2.00

2 CHUCKRAMS

SILVER

KM#	Date	Year	VG	Fine	VF	XF
8 (C12)	ND	(1809-10)	5.00	8.50	12.50	18.50

1/2 ANANTARAYA

(Fanam)

GOLD

KM#	Date	Year	VG	Fine	VF	XF
2 (C19)	ND	(1790-1830)	6.00	9.00	14.00	20.00

ANANTARAYA

(2 Fanam)

GOLD

KM#	Date	Year	VG	Fine	VF	XF
3 (C22)	ND	(1790-1860)	10.00	15.00	21.50	30.00

NOTE: For similar coins with leaf sprays on the obverse see KM#23.

RANI PARVATHI BAI

Regent, ME990-1004/1815-1829AD

CASH

COPPER

KM#	Date	Year	VG	Fine	VF	XF
9 (C25)	ME991-7	(1815-21)	3.00	5.00	8.50	12.50

2 CASH

COPPER

KM#	Date	Year	VG	Fine	VF	XF
10 (C26)	ME991	(1815)	4.00	7.00	10.00	15.00
	ME997	(1821)	4.00	7.00	10.00	15.00

4 CASH

COPPER

KM#	Date	Year	VG	Fine	VF	XF
11 (C27)	ME991	(1815)	6.00	10.00	14.00	20.00

8 CASH

COPPER

KM#	Date	Year	VG	Fine	VF	XF
12 (C28)	ME991	(1814)	10.00	17.50	25.00	35.00

RAMA VARMA III

ME1004-1022/1829-1847AD

CASH

COPPER

KM#	Date	Year	VG	Fine	VF	XF
14 (C36)	ME1005	(1830)	2.25	3.50	5.00	7.50

KM#	Date	Year	VG	Fine	VF	XF
15 (C38)	ND	(1830-39)	1.50	2.25	3.50	5.00

MARTANDA VARMA II

ME1004-1022/1847-1860AD

CASH

COPPER

KM#	Date	Year	VG	Fine	VF	XF
16 (Y1)	ND	(1848-60)	1.00	1.75	2.50	3.50

2 CASH

COPPER

KM#	Date	Year	VG	Fine	VF	XF
17 (Y2)	ND	(1848-49)	3.00	5.00	7.00	10.00

4 CASH

COPPER

KM#	Date	Year	VG	Fine	VF	XF
18 (Y3)	ND		4.00	7.00	10.00	15.00

8 CASH

COPPER

KM#	Date	Year	VG	Fine	VF	XF
19 (YA4)	ND		7.50	12.50	17.50	25.00

RAMA VARMA IV

ME1035-1055/1860-1880AD

CASH

COPPER, 8-10mm

KM#	Date	Year	VG	Fine	VF	XF
20 (Y1a)	ND	(1860-85)	.60	1.00	1.50	2.00

CHUCKRAM

SILVER

KM#	Date	Year	VG	Fine	VF	XF
21 (Y8)	ND	(1860-1901)	.85	1.40	2.00	3.00

VELLI FANAM

DUMP SILVER

KM#	Date	Year	VG	Fine	VF	XF
22 (Y9)	ND	(1860-61)	3.00	5.00	17.00	10.00

Machine-struck

KM#	Date	Year	VG	Fine	VF	XF
24.1 (Y10)	ND	(1864)	1.00	1.75	2.75	4.00

Rev: W/o 2 upper dots.

KM#	Date	Year	VG	Fine	VF	XF
24.2	ND	(1864)	1.00	1.75	2.75	4.00

ANATARAYA

(Fanam)

GOLD

KM#	Date	Year	Fine	VF	XF	Unc
23 (Y11)	ND	(1860-90)	7.50	12.50	18.50	28.50

1/2 PAGODA

GOLD, 1.28 g
Similar to 1 Pagoda, KM#16.

KM#	Date	Year	Fine	VF	XF	Unc
25 (Y15)	1877		65.00	100.00	140.00	200.00

PAGODA

GOLD, 2.55 g

KM#	Date	Year	Fine	VF	XF	Unc
26 (Y16)	1877		110.00	175.00	250.00	350.00

2 PAGODA

GOLD, 5.10 g

KM#	Date	Year	Fine	VF	XF	Unc
27 (Y17)	1877		160.00	265.00	375.00	550.00

RAMA VARMA V

ME1057-1062/1880-1885AD

VIRARAYA FANAM

SILVER

KM#	Date	Year	VG	Fine	VF	XF
29	ND	(1881)	1.00	1.75	2.50	3.50

GOLD

KM#	Date	Year	VG	Fine	VF	XF
30 (Y19)	ND	(1881)	6.00	10.00	15.00	22.50

1/2 SOVEREIGN

3.9940 g, .917 GOLD, .1177 oz AGW

KM#	Date	Mintage	Fine	VF	XF	Unc
31 (Y20)	ME1057//1881	2,000	300.00	500.00	700.00	1000.

SOVEREIGN

7.9881 g, .917 GOLD, .2354 oz AGW

KM#	Date	Mintage	Fine	VF	XF	Unc
32 (Y21)	ME1057//1881	1,000	200.00	350.00	500.00	700.00

RAMA VARMA VI

ME1062-1101/1885-1924AD

Dump Coinage

CASH

COPPER

KM#	Date	Year	VG	Fine	VF	XF
34 (Y1b)	ND	(1885-95)	.60	1.00	1.50	2.25

NOTE: KM#34 is a rather degenerated copy of KM#16.

1/4 CHUCKRAM

COPPER

KM#	Date	Year	VG	Fine	VF	XF
35 (Y22)	ND	(1888-89)	3.00	5.00	7.00	10.00

1/2 CHUCKRAM

COPPER

KM#	Date	Year	VG	Fine	VF	XF
36 (Y23)	ND(1888-89)		4.00	6.50	9.00	15.00

KALI FANAM

GOLD

KM#	Date	Year	Fine	VF	XF	Unc
39 (Y24)	ND	(1890-95)	5.00	8.50	12.50	17.50

Milled Coinage

CASH

COPPER, 0.65 g
Obv. leg: CASH 1

KM#	Date	Year	Fine	VF	XF	Unc
40 (Y29)	ND	(1901)	9.00	15.00	22.50	35.00

COPPER, thick, 0.65g

KM#	Date	Year	Fine	VF	XF	Unc
46 (Y41.1)	ND	—	.50	.70	1.00	1.50

NOTE: Refer to Bala Rama Varma II listings for thin variety, KM#57.

4 CASH

COPPER
Obv. leg: CASH FOUR

KM#	Date	Year	Fine	VF	XF	Unc
41 (Y30)	ND	(1901-10)	3.00	5.00	7.00	10.00

Obv. leg: FOUR CASH

KM#	Date	Year	Fine	VF	XF	Unc
47 (Y30a)	ND	(1906-35)	1.00	1.75	2.50	3.50
	ND	(1906-35)	—	—	Proof	50.00

8 CASH

COPPER
Obv. leg: CASH EIGHT

KM#	Date	Year	Fine	VF	XF	Unc
42 (Y31)	ND	(1901-10)	4.50	7.00	10.00	15.00

Obv. leg: EIGHT CASH

KM#	Date	Year	Fine	VF	XF	Unc
48 (Y31a)	ND	(1906-35)	1.35	2.25	3.00	5.00
	ND	(1906-35)	—	—	Proof	60.00

CHUCKRAM

COPPER
Obv. leg: CHUCKRAM ONE

KM#	Date	Year	Fine	VF	XF	Unc
43 (Y32)	ND	(1901-10)	4.50	7.00	10.00	15.00

Obv. leg: ONE CHUCKRAM

KM#	Date	Year	Fine	VF	XF	Unc
49 (Y32a)	ND	(1906-35)	1.35	2.25	3.00	4.50

2 CHUCKRAMS

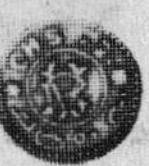

SILVER
Obv. leg: CHS. 2

KM#	Date	Year	Fine	VF	XF	Unc
44 (Y33)	ND	(1901)	4.50	7.00	10.00	15.00

Obv. leg: 2 CHS.

KM#	Date	Year	Fine	VF	XF	Unc
50 (Y33a)	ND	(1906-28)	2.00	3.50	5.00	7.00

FANAM

SILVER
Obv. leg: FANAM ONE. Plain edge.

KM#	Date	Year	Fine	VF	XF	Unc
45 (Y34a.1)	ND	(1901)	3.50	6.00	8.50	12.00

NOTE: Edge varieties exist.

Obv. leg: ONE FANAM

KM#	Date	Year	Fine	VF	XF	Unc
54 (Y34)	ND	(1911)	10.00	17.50	25.00	35.00

Obv. leg: FANAM ONE. Reeded edge.

KM#	Date	Year	Fine	VF	XF	Unc
55 (Y34a.2)	ND	(1911)	3.00	5.00	7.00	10.00

.950 SILVER

KM#	Date	Mintage	Fine	VF	XF	Unc
51 (Y34b)	ME1087(1910)	1.100	3.00	5.00	7.00	10.00
	ME1096(1919)	.350	3.50	6.00	8.50	12.00
	ME1099(1922)	.350	3.50	6.00	8.50	12.00
	ME1100(1923)	.700	3.50	6.00	8.50	12.00
	ME1103(1926)	.700	3.50	6.00	8.50	12.00
	ME1106(1929)	.700	3.50	6.00	8.50	12.00

1/4 RUPEE

SILVER, 2.72 g

KM#	Date	Year	Fine	VF	XF	Unc
37 (Y35.1)	1889	—	7.50	12.50	17.50	25.00

2.7200 g, .950 SILVER, .0831 oz ASW

KM#	Date	Mintage	Fine	VF	XF	Unc
52 (Y35.2)	ME1082(1905)	—	6.00	10.00	14.00	20.00
	ME1083(1906)	—	6.00	10.00	14.00	20.00
	ME1085(1908)	—	6.00	10.00	14.00	20.00
	ME1086(1909)	—	6.00	10.00	14.00	20.00
	ME1087(1911)	.400	4.50	7.00	10.00	15.00
	ME1096(1919)	—	3.00	5.00	7.00	10.00
	ME1099(1922)	—	3.00	5.00	7.00	10.00
	ME1100(1923)	—	3.00	5.00	7.00	10.00
	ME1103(1926)	.200	3.00	5.00	7.00	10.00
	ME1106(1929)	.200	3.00	5.00	7.00	10.00

1/2 RUPEE

SILVER, 5.44 g

KM#	Date	Year	Fine	VF	XF	Unc
38 (Y36.1)	1889	—	12.00	20.00	28.00	40.00

5.4400 g, .950 SILVER, .1662 oz ASW
Rev. leg: Shorter on bottom.

KM#	Date	Mintage	Fine	VF	XF	Unc
53 (Y36.2)	ME1084(1907)	—	8.50	14.00	20.00	28.00
	ME1085(1908)	—	8.50	14.00	20.00	28.00
	ME1086(1909)	—	8.50	14.00	20.00	28.00
	ME1087(1910)	.300	6.00	10.00	14.00	20.00

KM#	Date	Mintage	Fine	VF	XF	Unc
(Y36.2)	ME1103(1926)	.100	7.50	12.50	17.50	25.00
	ME1106(1929)	.100	7.50	12.50	17.50	25.00
	ME1107(1930)	.800	6.00	10.00	14.00	20.00

BALA RAMA VARMA II

ME1101-1126/1924-1949AD

CASH

COPPER, thin, 0.48 g

KM#	Date	Year	Fine	VF	XF	Unc
57	ND	(1938-49)	.15	.25	.35	.50
(Y41.2)	ND	(1938-49)	—	—	Proof	35.00

NOTE: Refer to Rama Varma VI listings for thick variety, KM#46.

4 CASH

BRONZE
Obv: BRV monogram.

KM#	Date	Year	Fine	VF	XF	Unc
58 (Y42)	ND	(1938-49)	.60	1.00	1.50	2.25

8 CASH

BRONZE
Obv. monogram: BRV

KM#	Date	Year	Fine	VF	XF	Unc
59 (Y43)	ND	(1938-49)	.85	1.50	2.25	3.00

CHUCKRAM

BRONZE

KM#	Date	Year	Fine	VF	XF	Unc
60 (Y44)	ME1114	(1938)	1.25	2.25	3.50	5.00
	ND	(1939-49)	.60	1.00	1.50	2.50

FANAM

SILVER

KM#	Date	Mintage	Fine	VF	XF	Unc
61 (Y45)	ME1112(1937)	.350	3.00	5.00	7.00	10.00

.500 SILVER

KM#	Date	Mintage	Fine	VF	XF	Unc
65 (Y45a)	ME1116(1941)	2.096	.90	1.50	2.00	3.00
	1116(1941)	—	—	—	Proof	50.00
	1118(1942)	4.157	.90	1.50	2.00	3.00
	1118(1942)	—	—	—	Proof	50.00
	1121(1946)	1.925	1.25	2.25	3.50	5.00

1/4 RUPEE

SILVER

KM#	Date	Mintage	Fine	VF	XF	Unc
62 (Y46)	ME1112(1937)	.200	4.50	7.00	10.00	15.00

.500 SILVER

KM#	Date	Mintage	Fine	VF	XF	Unc
66 (Y46a)	ME1116(1941)	.126	2.25	3.75	5.50	8.00
	1116(1941)	—	—	—	Proof	65.00
	1118(1942)	—	4.00	7.00	10.00	15.00

1/2 RUPEE

SILVER

KM#	Date	Mintage	Fine	VF	XF	Unc
63 (Y47)	ME1112(1937)	.200	8.50	14.00	20.00	28.50

1/2 CHITRA RUPEE

SILVER, reeded edge

KM#	Date	Mintage	Fine	VF	XF	Unc
64 (Y47a)	ME1114(1938/9)	—	6.00	10.00	14.00	20.00

.500 SILVER, Security edge

KM#	Date	Mintage	Fine	VF	XF	Unc
67 (Y47b)	ME1116(1941)	1.600	3.00	5.00	7.00	10.00
	1118/6(1942)	1.111	4.00	7.00	10.00	15.00
	1118(1942)	Inc. Ab.	3.00	5.00	7.00	10.00
	1118(1942)	—	—	—	Proof	85.00
	1121(1946)	.200	3.00	5.00	7.00	10.00

TULABHARAM MEDALLIC ISSUES (M)

These presentation coins were struck prior to the weighing in ceremony of the Maharajah. The balance of his weight in these gold coins were distributed amongst the learned Brahmins and are referred to as Tulabhara Kasu. The legend reads *Sri Patmanabha,* the National Deity.

1/4 PAGODA

GOLD, uniface, 8.8mm, 0.63 g
Tamil leg. in 3 lines.

KM#	Date	Year	Fine	VF	XF	Unc
M1	ND	(1829,47)	50.00	70.00	100.00	150.00

Uniface, 12.7mm, 0.63 g
Tamil leg. in 3 lines.

KM#	Date	Year	Fine	VF	XF	Unc
M5	ND	(1850,55)	50.00	70.00	100.00	150.00

10.9-12.7mm, 0.64 g
Obv: Conch shell within wreath.
Rev: Tamil leg. in 3 lines within wreath.

KM#	Date	Year	Fine	VF	XF	Unc
M9	ND	(1870-1931)	45.00	65.00	90.00	135.00

1/2 PAGODA

GOLD, uniface, 10.9mm, 1.27 g
Tamil leg. in 3 lines.

KM#	Date	Year	Fine	VF	XF	Unc
M2	ND	(1829,47)	60.00	80.00	110.00	165.00

Uniface, 14.5mm, 1.27 g
Tamil leg. in 3 lines.

KM#	Date	Year	Fine	VF	XF	Unc
M6	ND	(1850,55)	60.00	80.00	110.00	165.00

1.28 g

KM#	Date	Year	Fine	VF	XF	Unc
M10	ND	(1870-1931)	55.00	85.00	120.00	175.00

PAGODA

GOLD, uniface, 13mm, 2.54 g
Tamil leg. in 3 lines.

KM#	Date	Year	Fine	VF	XF	Unc
M3	ND	(1829,47)	100.00	135.00	175.00	250.00

Uniface, 17mm, 2.54 g
Tamil leg. in 3 lines.

KM#	Date	Year	Fine	VF	XF	Unc
M7	ND	(1850,55)	100.00	135.00	175.00	250.00

2.54 g

KM#	Date	Year	Fine	VF	XF	Unc
M11	ND	(1870-1931)	85.00	140.00	200.00	285.00

2 PAGODAS

GOLD, uniface, 15.4mm, 5.06 g
Tamil leg. in 3 lines.

KM#	Date	Year	Fine	VF	XF	Unc
M4	ND	(1829,47)	120.00	200.00	275.00	400.00

Uniface, 20.3mm, 5.06 g
Tamil leg. in 3 lines.

KM#	Date	Year	Fine	VF	XF	Unc
M8	ND	(1850,55)	120.00	200.00	275.00	400.00

20.0-23.9mm, 5.09 g
Obv: Conch shell within wreath.
Rev: Tamil leg. in 3 lines within wreath.

KM#	Date	Year	Fine	VF	XF	Unc
M12	ND	(1870-1931)	125.00	210.00	300.00	425.00

TRIPURA

Hill Tipperah

Tripura was a Hindu Kingdom consisting of a strip of the fertile plains east of Bengal, and a large tract of hill territory beyond, which had a reputation for providing wild elephants.

At times when Bengal was weak, Tripura rose to prominence and extended its rule into the plains, but when Bengal was strong the kingdom consisted purely of the hill area, which was virtually impregnable and not of enough economic worth to encourage the Muslims to conquer it. In this way Tripura was able to maintain its full independence until the 19th century.

The origins of the Kingdom are veiled in legend, but the first coins were struck during the reign of Ratna Manikya (1464-89) and copied the weight and fabric of the contemporary issues of the Sultans of Bengal. He also copied the lion design that had appeared on certain rare tangkas of Nasir-ud-din Mahmud Shah I dated AH849 (1445AD). In other respects the designs were purely Hindu, and the lion was retained on most of the later issues as a national emblem.

Tripura rose to a political zenith during the 16th century, while Muslim rule in Bengal was weak, and several coins were struck to commemorate successful military campaigns from Chittagong in the south to Sylhet in the north. These conquests were not sustained, and in the early 17th century the Mughal army was able to inflict severe defeats on Tripura, which was forced to pay tribute.

In about 1733AD all the territory in the plains was annexed by the Mughals, and the Raja merely managed his estate there as a zemindar, although he still retained control as independent King of his hill territory.

The situation remained unchanged when the British took over the administration of Bengal in 1765, and it was only in 1871 that the British appointed an agent in the hills, and began to assist the Maharaja in the administration of his hill territory, which became known as the State of Hill Tipperah.

After the middle of the 18th century, coins were not struck for monetary reasons, but merely for ceremonial use at coronations and other ceremonies, and to keep up the treasured right of coinage.

The coins of Tripura are unusual in that the majority have the name of the King together with that of his Queen, and is the only coinage in the world where this was done consistently.

In common with most other Hindu coinages of northeast India, the coins bear fixed dates. Usually the date used was that of the coronation ceremony, but during the 16th century, coins which were struck with a design commemorating a particular event, bore the date of that event, which can be useful as a historical source, where other written evidence is virtually non-existent.

All modern Tripura coins were presentation pieces, more medallic than monetary in nature. They were struck in very limited numbers and although not intended for local circulation, they are often found in worn condition.

RULERS

Rajadhara Manikya
SE1707-1726/1785-1804AD

Rama Ganga Manikya

রাম গঙ্গা মানিক্য

SE1728-1731,1735-1748/
1806-1809,1813-1826AD

Queens of Rama Ganga Manikya
Queen Tara
Queen Chandra Tara

চন্দ্র তারা

Durga Manikya

দুর্গা মানিক্য

SE1731-1735/1809-1813AD

Queen of Durga Manikya
Queen Sumitra

সুমিত্রা

Kashi Chandra Manikya
SE1748-1752/1826-1830AD

Queens of Kashi Chandra Manikya
Queen Chandraveth
Queen Kirti Lakshmi

Krishna Kishore Manikya

কৃষ্ণ কিশোর মানিক্য

SE1752-1772/1830-1850AD

Queens of Krishna Kishore
Queen Bidumukhi
Queen Ratna Mala

রত্ন মালা

Queen Purnakala
Queen Sudhakshina

Ishana Chandra Manikya
SE1772-1784/1850-1862AD

Queens of Ishana Chandra Manikya
Queen Chandresvari
Queen Muktabani
Queen Rajalakshmi

Vira Chandra Manikya

বীর চন্দ্র মানিক্য

SE1784-1818/TE1272-1306/1862-1896AD

Queens of Vira Chandra Manikya
Queen Bhanumati

ভানুমতী

Queen Rajesvari

রাজেশ্বরী

Queen Manmohini

Radha Kishore Manikya
TE1306-1319/1896-1909AD

Queens of Radha Kishore
Queen Ratnaman Zari
Queen Tulsivati

Virendra Kishore Manikya
TE1319-1333/1909-1923AD

Queen of Virendra Kishore
Queen Prabhavati

Vira Vikrama Kishore Manikya

বীর বিক্রম কিশোর মানিক্য

TE1333-1357/1923-1947AD

Queens of Vira Vikrama Kishore Manikya
Queen Kanchan Prabha

কাঞ্চন প্রভা

Queen Kirti Mani

DATING

While the early coinage is dated in the Saka Era (SE) the later issues are dated in the Tripurabda era (TE). To convert, TE date plus 590 = AD date. The dates appear to be accession years.

RAMA GANGA MANIKYA

SE1728-1731/1806-1809AD

RUPEE

SILVER, plain edge, 10.30-10.70 g
Rev. leg: W/*Queen Tara.*

KM#	Date	Year	VG	Fine	VF	XF
259	SE1728	(1806)	40.00	65.00	90.00	200.00

Oblique edge milling

KM#	Date	Year	VG	Fine	VF	XF
260	SE1728	(1806)	60.00	90.00	125.00	240.00

MOHUR

GOLD

KM#	Date	Year	VG	Fine	VF	XF
265	SE1728	(1806)	300.00	500.00	700.00	1000.

DURGA MANIKYA

SE1731-1735/1809-1813AD

RUPEE

SILVER, 10.30-10.70 g
Rev. leg: W/*Srimati Sumitra Maha Devah.*

KM#	Date	Year	VG	Fine	VF	XF
275	SE1731	(1809)	40.00	65.00	90.00	200.00

MOHUR

GOLD, 10.94 g

KM#	Date	Year	VG	Fine	VF	XF
280	SE1731	(1809)	300.00	500.00	700.00	1000.

RAMA GANGA MANIKYA

SE1735-1748/1813-1826AD

RUPEE

SILVER, 10.30-10.70 g
Rev. leg: W/*Sri Srimati Chandra Tara Maha Devi.*

KM#	Date	Year	VG	Fine	VF	XF
290	SE1743	(1821)	40.00	65.00	90.00	200.00

MOHUR

GOLD

KM#	Date	Year	VG	Fine	VF	XF
295	SE1743	(1821)	300.00	500.00	700.00	1000.

KASHI CHANDRA MANIKYA

SE1748-1752/1826-1830AD

RUPEE

SILVER, 10.30-10.70 g
Rev. leg: W/*Queen Chandravethi.*

KM#	Date	Year	VG	Fine	VF	XF
305	SE1748	(1826)	60.00	90.00	125.00	200.00

Rev. leg: W/*Queen Kirti Lakshmi.*

KM#	Date	Year	VG	Fine	VF	XF
306	SE1748	(1826)	60.00	90.00	125.00	200.00

MOHUR

GOLD
Rev. leg: W/*Queen Kirti Lakshimi.*

KM#	Date	Year	VG	Fine	VF	XF
308	SE1748	(1826)	70.00	100.00	150.00	250.00

KRISHNA KISHORA MANIKYA

SE1752-1772/1830-1850AD

RUPEE

SILVER, 10.30-10.70 g
Rev. leg: W/*Queen Bidhukala.*

KM#	Date	Year	VG	Fine	VF	XF
315	SE1752	(1830)	60.00	90.00	135.00	225.00

Rev. leg: W/*Queen Bidumukhi* added.

KM#	Date	Year	VG	Fine	VF	XF
316	SE1752	(1830)	60.00	90.00	135.00	225.00

Rev. leg: W/*Queen Purnakala* added.

KM#	Date	Year	VG	Fine	VF	XF
317	SE1752	(1830)	60.00	90.00	135.00	225.00

Rev. leg: W/*Sri Srimati Ratna Mala Maha Deva.*

KM#	Date	Year	VG	Fine	VF	XF
318	SE1752	(1830)	45.00	70.00	100.00	175.00

MOHUR

GOLD, 11.59 g
Rev. leg: W/*Queen Akhilesvari.*

KM#	Date	Year	VG	Fine	VF	XF
323	SE1752	(1830)	300.00	500.00	700.00	1000.

Rev. leg: W/*Sri Srimati Ratna Mala Maha Deva.*

KM#	Date	Year	VG	Fine	VF	XF
324	SE1752	(1830)	300.00	500.00	700.00	1000.

Rev. leg: W/*Queen Sudakshina* added.

KM#	Date	Year	VG	Fine	VF	XF
325	SE1752	(1830)	300.00	500.00	700.00	1000.

ISHANA CHANDRA MANIKYA

SE1772-1784/1850-1862AD

RUPEE

SILVER, 10.30-10.70 g
Rev. leg: W/*Queen Chandresvari.*

KM#	Date	Year	VG	Fine	VF	XF
335	SE1771	(1849)	45.00	70.00	100.00	160.00

Rev. leg: W/*Queen Muktavali.*

336 SE1771 (1849) 45.00 70.00 100.00 160.00

Rev. leg: W/*Queen Raja Lakshmi.*

337 SE1771 (1849) 45.00 70.00 100.00 160.00

MOHUR

GOLD
Rev. leg: W/*Queen Chandresvari.*

342 SE1771 (1849) 250.00 400.00 550.00 800.00

Rev. leg: W/*Queen Muktauali.*

343 SE1771 (1849) 275.00 450.00 650.00 1000.

Rev. leg: W/*Queen Raja Lakshmi.*

344 SE1771 (1849) 275.00 450.00 650.00 1000.

VIRA CHANDRA MANIKYA

SE1784-1818/TE1272-1306/1862-1896AD

RUPEE

SILVER, plain edge, 10.30-10.70 g
Rev. leg: W/*Sri Srimati Bhanumati Maha Devi.*

354 SE1791 (1869) 40.00 65.00 90.00 160.00

Machine struck, milled edge

355 TE1279 (1869) 40.00 65.00 90.00 160.00

Rev. leg: W/*Queen Manamohini.*

KM#	Date	Year	VG	Fine	VF	XF
356	TE1279	(1869)	40.00	65.00	90.00	160.00

Rev. leg: W/*Sri Srimati Rajesvari Maha Devi.*
Hand struck

357 SE1791 (1869) 50.00 80.00 120.00 200.00

Machine struck

358 TE1279 (1869) 40.00 65.00 90.00 160.00

MOHUR

GOLD
Similar to 1 Rupee, KM#354.

360 SE1791 (1869) 225.00 385.00 550.00 800.00

Similar to 1 Rupee, KM#356.

363 TE1279 (1869) 225.00 385.00 550.00 800.00

Similar to 1 Rupee, KM#357.
Rev. leg: W/*Srimati Rajesvari Maha Devah.*

364 SE1791 (1869) 250.00 425.00 600.00 850.00

RADHA KISHORE MANIKYA

TE1306-1319/1896-1909AD

1/2 RUPEE

SILVER
Rev. leg: W/*Queen Tulsiwati*

373 TE1306 (1896) 50.00 80.00 120.00 200.00

RUPEE

SILVER, 11.30-11.90 g
Mule. Obv: KM#375. Rev: KM#356.

374 TE1306 (1896) 60.00 90.00 125.00 200.00

Rev. leg: W/*Queen Ratna Manjari.*

375 TE1306 (1896) 45.00 70.00 100.00 160.00

8.80 g
Rev. leg: W/*Queen Tulsiwati.*

376 TE1306 (1896) 40.00 65.00 90.00 150.00

MOHUR

GOLD
Rev. leg: W/*Queen Ratna Manjari.*

KM#	Date	Year	VG	Fine	VF	XF
381	TE1306	(1896)	250.00	425.00	600.00	850.00

VIRENDRA KISHORE MANIKYA

TE1319-1333/1909-1923AD

MOHUR

GOLD
Rev. leg: W/*Queen Prabhavati.*

396 TE1319 (1909) 300.00 500.00 750.00 1150.

VIRA VIKRAMA KISHORE MANIKYA

TE1333-1357/1923-1947AD

RUPEE

SILVER, milled edge, 11.30-11.90 g

406 TE1337 (1930) 20.00 30.00 45.00 65.00

NOTE: Varieties exist.

Security edge

407 TE1337 (1930) 45.00 70.00 100.00 140.00

Rev. leg: W/*Queen Kirti Mani.*

408 TE1341 (1934) 40.00 62.50 85.00 120.00

Rev. leg: W/*Sri Srimati Maharani Kanchan Prabha Maha Devi.*

KM#	Date	Year	VG	Fine	VF	XF
409	TE1338	(1931)	17.50	27.50	37.50	55.00
	1341	(1934)	17.50	27.50	37.50	55.00

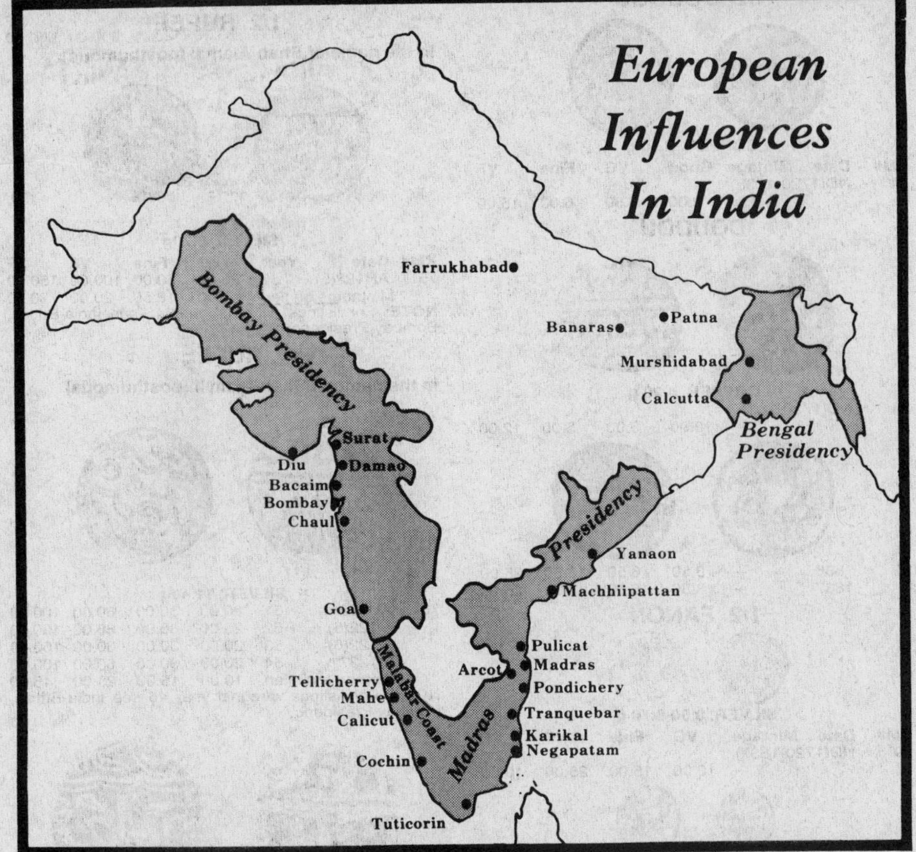

INDIA-DANISH

TRANQUEBAR

Danish India or Tranquebar is a town and former Danish colony on the southeast coast of India. In Danish times, 1620-1845, it was a factory site and seaport operated by the Danish Asiatic Company. Tranquebar and the other Danish settlements in India were sold to the British East India Company in 1845.

RULERS

Danish until 1845

MONETARY SYSTEM

80 Kas (Cash) = Royaliner (Fano or Fanam)
8 Royaliner=1 Rupee
18 Royaliner=1 Speciesdaler

DANISH ROYAL COLONY

KAS

COPPER, 0.52 g
Obv: Crowned FVIR monogram.
Rev: Value, date below.

KM#	Date	Mintage	Good	VG	Fine	VF
151	1816	—	—	—	Rare	—
	1819	—	15.00	25.00	40.00	65.00

IV KAS

COPPER, 2.75 g
Obv: Crowned C7 monogram.

KM#	Date	Mintage	Good	VG	Fine	VF
155	1807	—	6.50	11.50	21.50	33.50

NOTE: Earlier dates (1782-1797) exist for this type.

Obv: Crowned FR, VI below.

KM#	Date	Mintage	Good	VG	Fine	VF
158	1815	—	6.50	10.00	17.50	27.50
	1816	—	6.00	9.00	16.50	26.50
	1817	—	7.00	11.00	18.50	28.50
	1820	—	6.00	9.00	16.50	26.50
	1821	—	20.00	32.50	50.00	80.00
	1822	—	6.00	9.00	16.50	26.50
	1823	—	5.50	8.50	15.00	25.00
	1824	—	5.50	8.50	15.00	25.00

Obv: Crown design standardized.

KM#	Date	Mintage	Good	VG	Fine	VF
159.1	1824	—	6.00	9.00	16.00	27.50
	1825	—	7.50	12.50	20.00	35.00
	1830	—	6.50	10.00	18.50	30.00
	1831	—	5.50	8.50	15.00	25.00
	1832	—	5.50	8.50	15.00	25.00
	1833	—	5.50	8.50	15.00	25.00
	1834	—	5.50	8.50	15.00	25.00
	1837	—	3.00	6.00	15.00	25.00
	1838	—	3.00	6.00	15.00	25.00
	1839	—	3.00	6.00	15.00	25.00

Rev: Retrograde S in KAS.

KM#	Date	Mintage	Good	VG	Fine	VF
159.2	1817	—	6.00	9.00	15.00	25.00
	1831	—	12.50	20.00	32.50	50.00

KM#	Date	Mintage	Good	VG	Fine	VF
160	1824	—	25.00	35.00	60.00	100.00

Obv: Crowned C VIII R monogram.

KM#	Date	Mintage	Good	VG	Fine	VF
161	1840	—	3.50	7.00	17.50	27.50
	1841	—	3.50	7.00	17.50	27.50
	1842	—	3.50	7.00	17.50	27.50
	1843	—	3.50	7.00	17.50	27.50
	1844	—	5.00	9.00	22.50	33.50

Obv: Crowned CR monogram.

KM#	Date	Mintage	Good	VG	Fine	VF
162	1844	—	3.00	7.00	15.00	25.00
	1845	—	4.00	9.00	20.00	35.00

10 KAS

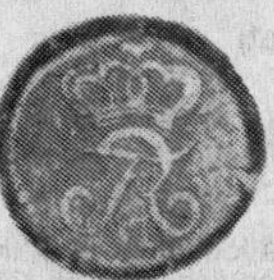

COPPER
Obv: Crowned FR, VI between and below.

KM#	Date	Mintage	Good	VG	Fine	VF
166	1816	—	15.00	25.00	40.00	65.00
	1822	—	15.00	25.00	40.00	65.00
	1838	—	15.00	25.00	40.00	65.00
	1839	—	13.50	22.50	37.50	60.00

Obv: Crowned CR, VIII between and below.

KM#	Date	Mintage	Good	VG	Fine	VF
167	1842	—	25.00	40.00	65.00	100.00

ROYALIN

SILVER
Obv: Crowned C7 monogram.
Rev: Value, arms w/lion between date.

KM#	Date	Mintage	VG	Fine	VF	XF
168	1807	—	20.00	35.00	65.00	100.00

NOTE: Earlier dates (1767-1799) exist for this type.

FANO

(Royalin, Fanam)

SILVER
Obv: Crowned FR, VI between and below.

KM#	Date	Mintage	VG	Fine	VF	XF
170	1816	—	35.00	60.00	100.00	165.00
	1818	—	35.00	60.00	100.00	165.00

2 ROYALINER

SILVER
Obv: Crowned C7 monogram.

KM#	Date	Mintage	VG	Fine	VF	XF
171	1807	—	25.00	40.00	75.00	125.00

NOTE: Earlier dates (1767-1799) exist for this type.

2 FANO

(2 Royaliner, 2 Fanams)

SILVER
Obv: Crowned FR, VI between and below.

KM#	Date	Mintage	VG	Fine	VF	XF
173	1816	—	50.00	80.00	125.00	200.00
	1818	—	50.00	80.00	125.00	200.00

INDIA-FRENCH

It was not until 1664, during the reign of Louis XIV, that the Compagnie des Indes Orientales was formed for the purpose of obtaining holdings on the subcontinent of India. Between 1666 and 1721, French settlements were established at Arcot, Mahe, Surat, Pondichery, Masulipatam, Karikal, Yanam, Murshidabad, Chandernagore, Balasore and Calicut. War with Britain reduced the French holdings to Chandernagore, Pondichery, Karikal, Yanam and Mahe. Chandernagore voted in 1949 to join India and became part of the Republic of India in 1950. Pondichery, Karikal, Yanam and Mahe formed the Pondichery union territory and joined the republic of India in 1954.

RULERS

French until 1945

MINTS

Arcot (Arkat) اركات

Pondichery پهلجري

Surat سورت

MONETARY SYSTEM

Cache Kas or Cash
Doudou = 4 Caches
Biche = 1 Pice
2 Royalins = 1 Fanon Pondichery
5 Heavy Fanons = 1 Rupee Mahe
64 Biches = 1 Rupee

NOTE: The undated coinage was struck ca. 1720 well into the early 19th century.

ARCOT MINT

(Arkat)

Mint mark:

Crescent

A crescent moon mint mark is found to left of the regnal year for those struck at the Pondichery Mint. For listings of similar coins with lotus mint mark refer to India-British-Madras Presidency.

In the name of Shah Alam II

AH1173-1221/1759-1806AD

1/4 RUPEE

SILVER, 2.80 g

KM#	Date	Year	VG	Fine	VF	XF
13	AH1216	45	35.00	70.00	100.00	160.00
	1221	49	21.50	42.00	85.00	120.00
	1222	49	35.00	70.00	100.00	160.00

NOTE: Earlier date (AH1184) exists for this type.

1/2 RUPEE

SILVER, 5.70 g

KM#	Date	Year	VG	Fine	VF	XF
14	AH1221	49	31.50	63.00	90.00	130.00

NOTE: Earlier dates (AH1184-1205) exist for this type.

RUPEE

SILVER, 11.40 g

KM#	Date	Year	VG	Fine	VF	XF
15	AH1218	43	12.50	25.00	30.00	50.00
	1218	44	12.50	25.00	30.00	50.00
	1219/8	44	12.50	25.00	30.00	50.00
	1219	44	12.50	25.00	30.00	50.00
	1219	45	12.50	25.00	30.00	50.00
	1220	43	12.50	25.00	30.00	50.00
	1220	45	12.50	25.00	30.00	50.00
	1221	43	12.50	25.00	30.00	50.00
	1221	45	12.50	25.00	30.00	50.00
	1222	43	12.50	25.00	30.00	50.00

NOTE: Earlier dates (AH1177-1208) exist for this type.

NAZARANA RUPEE

SILVER, 32-33mm, 11.40 g

KM#	Date	Year	VG	Fine	VF	XF
16	AH1218	43(sic)	—	—	450.00	700.00
	1218	58	—	—	450.00	700.00
	1233	58(sic)	—	—	450.00	700.00

PONDICHERY MINT

A city south of Madras on the southeast coast which became the site of the French Mint from 1700 to 1841. Pondichery was settled by the French in 1683. It became their main Indian possession even though it was occupied by the Dutch in 1693-1698 and several times by the British from 1761-1816.

CACHE

BRONZE

KM#	Date	Mintage	Good	VG	Fine	VF
33	ND(1720-1835)	—	3.50	6.50	13.50	25.00

1/2 DOUDOU

COPPER, 2.10 g

KM#	Date	Mintage	Good	VG	Fine	VF
34	ND(1720-1835)	—	2.00	3.00	6.00	15.00

DOUDOU

COPPER, 4.20 g

KM#	Date	Mintage	Good	VG	Fine	VF
35	ND(1720-1835)	—	2.00	3.00	5.00	12.00

KM#	Date	Mintage	Good	VG	Fine	VF
52	1836	—	3.50	6.50	13.50	25.00
	1837	—	3.50	6.50	13.50	25.00

1/2 FANON

SILVER, 0.50-0.70 g

KM#	Date	Mintage	VG	Fine	VF	XF
39	ND(1720-1837)	—	10.00	15.00	25.00	40.00

KM#	Date	Mintage	VG	Fine	VF	XF
53	1837	—	16.50	28.50	45.00	75.00

FANON

SILVER, 1.500-1.593 g
Similar to 2 Fanon KM #49.

KM#	Date	Mintage	VG	Fine	VF	XF
45	ND	—	12.50	20.00	35.00	60.00

KM#	Date	Mintage	VG	Fine	VF	XF
54	1837	—	16.50	28.50	45.00	75.00

2 FANON

SILVER, 2.20-2.76 g
Obv: Pearled crown.

KM#	Date	Mintage	VG	Fine	VF	XF
48	ND(1720-1837)	—	16.50	28.50	45.00	75.00

Obv: Flowered crown.

KM#	Date	Mintage	VG	Fine	VF	XF
49	ND(1720-1837)	—	16.50	28.50	45.00	75.00

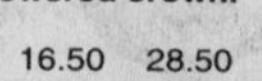

KM#	Date	Mintage	VG	Fine	VF	XF
55	1837	—	20.00	32.50	55.00	90.00

PAGODA

GOLD, 3.40 g
Obv: Flowered crown.

KM#	Date	Mintage	VG	Fine	VF	XF
51	ND(1830-48)	—	—	—	450.00	600.00

SURAT MINT

The French silver coins struck similar to late Mughal issues in two different periods. See also India-British, Bombay Presidency.

1/2 RUPEE

In the name of Shah Alam II (posthumous)

SILVER, 5.70g

KM#	Date	Year	VG	Fine	VF	XF
75	AH122(5)	52	25.00	50.00	100.00	150.00
	Mintname off flan		7.50	12.50	20.00	30.00

NOTE: For listings w/regnal year 46 see India-British, Bombay Presidency.

RUPEE

In the name of Shah Alam II (posthumous)

SILVER, 11.40g

KM#	Date	Year	VG	Fine	VF	XF
76	AH122(4)	51	20.00	30.00	60.00	100.00
	122(5)	52	20.00	30.00	60.00	100.00
	122(6)	53	20.00	30.00	60.00	100.00
	1227	54	20.00	30.00	60.00	100.00
	Mintname off flan		10.00	15.00	25.00	45.00

NOTE: For listings w/regnal year 46 see India-British, Bombay Presidency.

Rev: W/symbol.

KM#	Date	Year	VG	Fine	VF	XF
77 (76.2)	AH122x	5x	25.00	40.00	75.00	125.00

INDIA-PORTUGUESE

Vasco da Gama, the Portuguese explorer, first visited India in 1498. Portugal seized control of a number of islands and small enclaves on the west coast of India, and for the next hundred years enjoyed a monopoly on trade. With the arrival of powerful Dutch and English fleets in the first half of the 17th century, Portuguese power in the area declined until virtually all of India that remained under Portuguese control were the west coast enclaves of Goa, Damao and Diu. They were forcibly annexed by India in 1962.

RULERS

Portuguese until 1961

IDENTIFICATION

The undated coppers are best identified by the shape of the coat of arms.

Maria I-Somewhat triangular shield (baroque style)
Joao VI, as Regent: oval shield
Joao VI, as King: square shield superimposed on globe
Maria II: square shield on plain background

DENOMINATION

The denomination of most copper coins appears in numerals on the reverse, though 30 Reis is often given as "1/2 T", and 60 Reis as "T" (T = Tanga). The silver coins have the denomination in words, usually on the obverse until 1850, then on the reverse.

DAMAO

(Daman)

A city located 100 miles north of Bombay. It was captured by the Portuguese in 1559. A mint was opened in Damao in 1611. This mint continued in operation until 1854. While important to early Portuguese trade, Damao dwindled as time passed. It was annexed to India in 1962.

MONETARY SYSTEM

375 Bazacucos = 300 Reis
300 Reis = 1 Pardao
60 Reis = 1 Tanga
2 Pardao (Xerafins) = 1 Rupia

15 REIS

COPPER
Maria II

KM#	Date	Mintage	Good	VG	Fine	VF
25	1843	—	8.50	16.50	30.00	50.00

Pedro V

KM#	Date	Mintage	Good	VG	Fine	VF
26	1854	—	7.00	15.00	25.00	45.00

30 REIS

COPPER
Maria II

KM#	Date	Mintage	Good	VG	Fine	VF
23	1840	—	6.00	12.00	20.00	37.50

Pedro V
Similar to KM#23.

KM#	Date	Mintage	Good	VG	Fine	VF
27	1854	—	7.00	15.00	22.00	40.00

60 REIS

COPPER
Maria II

KM#	Date	Mintage	Good	VG	Fine	VF
24	1840	—	10.00	20.00	35.00	60.00

Pedro V
Similar to KM#24.

KM#	Date	Mintage	Good	VG	Fine	VF
28	1854	—	15.00	30.00	50.00	90.00

DIU

A district in Western India formerly belonging to Portugal. It is 170 miles northwest of Bombay on the Kathiawar peninsula. The Portuguese settled here and built a fort in 1535. A mint was opened in 1685 and was closed in 1859. As with Damao, the importance of Diu diminished with the passage of time. It was annexed to India in 1962.

MONETARY SYSTEM

750 Bazarucos = 600 Reis
40 Atia = 10 Tanga = 1 Rupia

5 BAZARUCOS

LEAD or TIN, 20-23mm
Joao
Obv: Crude crowned arms.
Rev: Date in angles of cross.

KM#	Date	Mintage	Good	VG	Fine	VF
44	1801	—	6.50	12.50	17.50	27.50

NOTE: Earlier dates (1799-1800) exist for this type.

21mm
Similar to 20 Bazarucos, KM#47.

KM#	Date	Mintage	Good	VG	Fine	VF
52	1807	—	12.50	25.00	35.00	50.00

Pedro IV
20-22mm

KM#	Date	Mintage	Good	VG	Fine	VF
56	1827	—	5.00	10.00	15.00	25.00
	1828	—	5.00	10.00	15.00	25.00

10 BAZARUCOS

LEAD or TIN, 27mm
Pedro IV

KM#	Date	Mintage	Good	VG	Fine	VF
57	1827	—	5.00	10.00	18.00	30.00
	1828	—	5.00	10.00	18.00	30.00

20 BAZARUCOS

TIN, 14.00-16.50 g
Joao

KM#	Date	Mintage	Good	VG	Fine	VF
47	1801	—	6.00	12.00	20.00	30.00

NOTE: Earlier dates (1799-1800) exist for this type.

33-36mm
Similar to KM#47.

KM#	Date	Mintage	Good	VG	Fine	VF
53	1807	—	15.00	27.50	40.00	60.00

Pedro IV

KM#	Date	Mintage	Good	VG	Fine	VF
58	1827	—	6.00	12.00	20.00	35.00
	1828	—	6.00	12.00	20.00	35.00

30 REIS

COPPER
Joao

KM#	Date	Mintage	Good	VG	Fine	VF
54	1818	—	6.00	11.00	18.00	40.00

60 REIS

COPPER
Joao
Similar to 30 Reis, KM#54.

KM#	Date	Mintage	Good	VG	Fine	VF
55	1818	—	7.50	15.00	23.50	50.00

150 REIS

SILVER
Joao
Obv: Crowned arms. Rev: Date in angles of cross.

KM#	Date	Mintage	Good	VG	Fine	VF
50	1806	—	30.00	50.00	110.00	225.00

Pedro V

KM#	Date	Mintage	Good	VG	Fine	VF
60	1859	—	20.00	35.00	70.00	150.00

300 REIS

SILVER
Joao

KM#	Date	Mintage	Good	VG	Fine	VF
51	1806	—	25.00	40.00	100.00	200.00

Pedro V

KM#	Date	Mintage	Good	VG	Fine	VF
61	1859	—	25.00	40.00	100.00	200.00

RUPIA

(600 Reis)

SILVER, 10.63 g
Joao
Obv: Crowned arms.
Rev: Date in angles of cross.

KM#	Date	Mintage	Good	VG	Fine	VF
49	1804	—	75.00	125.00	250.00	500.00
	1805	—	75.00	125.00	250.00	500.00
	1806	—	75.00	125.00	250.00	500.00

Maria II

KM#	Date	Mintage	Good	VG	Fine	VF
59	1841	—	100.00	150.00	300.00	600.00

GOA

Goa was the capitol of Portuguese India and is located 250 miles south of Bombay on the west coast of India. It was taken by Albuquerque in 1510. A mint was established immediately and operated until closed by the British in 1869. Later coins were struck at Calcutta and Bombay. Goa was annexed by India in 1962.

MONETARY SYSTEM

375 Bazarucos = 300 Reis
240 Reis = 1 Pardao
2 Xerafim = 1 Rupia

NOTE: The silver Xerafim was equal to the silver Pardao, but the gold Xerafim varied according to fluctuations in the gold/silver ratio.

BASTARDO

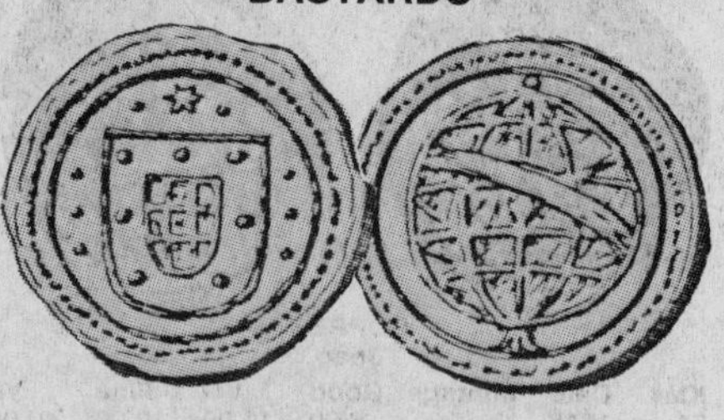

TIN, 9.30 g
Maria II
Obv: Arms; dots at sides; star and dots at top in circle. Rev: Astrolabe in circle.

KM#	Date	Mintage	Good	VG	Fine	VF
18	1845	—	4.00	7.00	12.50	25.00

3 REIS

COPPER
Joao
Similar to 6 Reis, KM#211.

KM#	Date	Mintage	Good	VG	Fine	VF
209	ND	—	6.00	10.00	20.00	35.00

Similar to 4-1/2 Reis, KM#225.

KM#	Date	Mintage	Good	VG	Fine	VF
224	ND	—	6.00	10.00	20.00	35.00

Maria II

KM#	Date	Mintage	Good	VG	Fine	VF
257	ND	—	5.00	8.00	15.00	25.00
	1842	—	5.00	8.00	15.00	25.00
	1844	—	5.00	8.00	15.00	25.00
	1845	—	5.00	8.00	15.00	25.00
	1846	—	5.00	8.00	15.00	25.00
	1848	—	5.00	8.00	15.00	25.00

4-1/2 REIS

COPPER
Joao
Similar to 6 Reis, KM#211.

KM#	Date	Mintage	Good	VG	Fine	VF
210	ND	—	6.00	10.00	20.00	35.00

KM#	Date	Mintage	Good	VG	Fine	VF
225	ND	—	6.00	10.00	20.00	35.00

Maria II

KM#	Date	Mintage	Good	VG	Fine	VF
258	ND	—	4.00	6.00	10.00	18.00
	1845	—	4.00	7.00	12.00	20.00
	1846	—	4.00	7.00	12.00	20.00
	1847	—	4.00	7.00	12.00	20.00
	1848	—	4.00	7.00	12.00	20.00

6 REIS

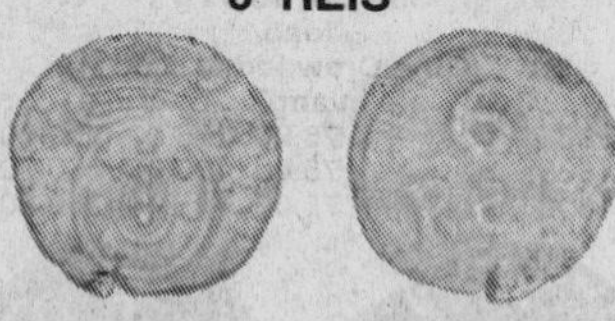

COPPER, 3.70-4.30 g
Joao

KM#	Date	Mintage	Good	VG	Fine	VF
211	ND	—	6.00	10.00	15.00	25.00

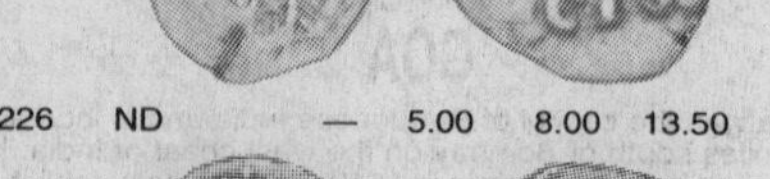

KM#	Date	Mintage	Good	VG	Fine	VF
226	ND	—	5.00	8.00	13.50	22.00

Maria II

KM#	Date	Mintage	Good	VG	Fine	VF
259	ND	—	4.00	7.00	12.00	20.00
	1845	—	4.00	7.00	12.00	20.00
	1846	—	4.00	7.00	12.00	20.00
	1847	—	4.00	7.00	12.00	20.00
	1848	—	4.00	7.00	12.00	20.00

7-1/2 REIS

COPPER, 4.80 g
Joao
Obv: Similar to 6 Reis, KM#211.
Rev. denomination: 7-1/2 REIS

KM#	Date	Mintage	Good	VG	Fine	VF
212	ND	—	6.50	12.50	17.50	35.00

Rev. denomination: 7-2/4 REIS

KM#	Date	Mintage	Good	VG	Fine	VF
213	ND	—	12.50	25.00	35.00	70.00

Obv: Similar to 6 Reis, KM#226.
Rev. denomination: 7-1/2 REIS

KM#	Date	Mintage	Good	VG	Fine	VF
227	ND	—	6.00	11.50	17.50	35.00

Maria II

KM#	Date	Mintage	Good	VG	Fine	VF
260	ND	—	4.00	7.00	12.00	20.00
	1845	—	4.00	7.00	12.00	20.00
	1846	—	4.00	7.00	12.00	20.00
	1847	—	4.50	7.50	12.50	25.00
	1848	—	4.50	7.50	12.50	25.00
	1849	—	4.50	7.50	12.50	25.00

9 REIS

COPPER
Joao
Obv: Similar to 6 Reis, KM#226.
Rev. denomination: 9 REIS

KM#	Date	Mintage	Good	VG	Fine	VF
228	ND	—	10.00	15.00	20.00	40.00

Rev. denomination: NOVE REIS

KM#	Date	Mintage	Good	VG	Fine	VF
229	ND	—	7.50	12.50	25.00	50.00

10 REIS

COPPER
Joao
Rev: Retrograde S.

KM#	Date	Mintage	Good	VG	Fine	VF
214	ND	—	6.00	11.00	17.50	35.00

Similar to 6 Reis, KM#226.

KM#	Date	Mintage	Good	VG	Fine	VF
230	ND	—	5.00	10.00	15.00	30.00

Maria II

KM#	Date	Mintage	Good	VG	Fine	VF
261	ND	—	2.00	4.00	8.50	15.00
	1845	—	1.75	3.50	7.50	12.50

12 REIS

COPPER
Joao

KM#	Date	Mintage	Good	VG	Fine	VF
215	ND	—	7.00	12.50	20.00	40.00

Similar to 6 Reis, KM#226.

KM#	Date	Mintage	Good	VG	Fine	VF
231	ND	—	6.00	11.50	17.50	35.00

Maria II

KM#	Date	Mintage	Good	VG	Fine	VF
262	ND	—	7.00	12.50	20.00	40.00
	1848	—	7.00	12.50	20.00	40.00

15 REIS

COPPER, 9.30 g
Joao

KM#	Date	Mintage	Good	VG	Fine	VF
216	ND	—	6.00	11.50	17.50	35.00

KM#	Date	Mintage	Good	VG	Fine	VF
232	ND	—	4.00	7.50	12.50	25.00

Maria II

KM#	Date	Mintage	Good	VG	Fine	VF
263	ND	—	2.00	4.00	8.50	16.50

c/m: 15 in circle on earlier coins.

KM#	Date	Mintage	Good	VG	Fine	VF
264	ND(1846)	—	1.75	3.50	7.50	15.00

1/2 TANGA

(30 Reis)

COPPER
Joao
Similar to 15 Reis, KM#216.

KM#	Date	Mintage	Good	VG	Fine	VF
217	ND	—	7.50	15.00	20.00	37.50

KM#	Date	Mintage	Good	VG	Fine	VF
233	ND	—	7.50	15.00	20.00	37.50

Miguel

KM#	Date	Mintage	Good	VG	Fine	VF
249	ND	—	6.50	12.00	18.00	35.00

c/m: PR 809 in dentilated circle on earlier coins.

KM#	Date	Mintage	Good	VG	Fine	VF
250	ND	—	6.50	12.00	18.00	35.00

Maria II

KM#	Date	Mintage	Good	VG	Fine	VF
265	ND	—	6.50	12.00	18.00	35.00

c/m: 30 in circle over earlier coins.

KM#	Date	Mintage	Good	VG	Fine	VF
274	ND(1846)	—	10.00	15.00	25.00	50.00

TANGA

(60 Reis)

COPPER

Joao

Obv: Head right. Rev: Crowned arms.

KM#	Date	Mintage	Good	VG	Fine	VF
208	1802	—	17.50	35.00	60.00	120.00
	1803	—	17.50	35.00	60.00	120.00

Obv: Crowned arms. Rev: Value.

KM#	Date	Mintage	Good	VG	Fine	VF
218	ND	—	5.50	10.00	16.50	28.50

KM#	Date	Mintage	Good	VG	Fine	VF
234	ND	—	12.50	20.00	30.00	60.00

SILVER, 1.10 g

KM#	Date	Mintage	Good	VG	Fine	VF
240	1819	—	35.00	45.00	60.00	85.00
	1823	—	35.00	45.00	60.00	85.00

COPPER

Miguel

KM#	Date	Mintage	Good	VG	Fine	VF
251	ND	—	8.50	16.50	27.50	45.00

c/m: PR 809 in dentilated circle on earlier coins.

KM#	Date	Mintage	Good	VG	Fine	VF
253	ND	—	7.50	15.00	25.00	40.00

Maria II

KM#	Date	Mintage	Good	VG	Fine	VF
266	ND	—	7.50	15.00	25.00	40.00

c/m: 60 in circle over earlier coins.

KM#	Date	Mintage	Good	VG	Fine	VF
267	ND(1846)	—	7.50	15.00	25.00	40.00

SILVER, 1.03-1.25 g

Pedro V

KM#	Date	Mintage	Good	VG	Fine	VF
277	1856	—	25.00	35.00	50.00	75.00
	1858	—	25.00	35.00	50.00	75.00
	1859	—	25.00	35.00	50.00	75.00

1/2 XERAFIM

SILVER, 2.67-2.71 g

Joao

KM#	Date	Mintage	Good	VG	Fine	VF
235	1818	—	35.00	45.00	60.00	85.00
	1819	—	35.00	45.00	60.00	85.00

KM#	Date	Mintage	Good	VG	Fine	VF
236	1818	—	25.00	35.00	45.00	75.00
	1819/8	—	35.00	45.00	60.00	85.00
	1819	—	25.00	35.00	45.00	75.00
	1820	—	25.00	35.00	45.00	75.00
	1823	—	25.00	35.00	45.00	75.00

Miguel

KM#	Date	Mintage	Good	VG	Fine	VF
255	1831	—	40.00	65.00	100.00	200.00

1/2 PARDAO

(150 Reis)

SILVER, 2.80-2.95 g

Joao

Obv: Head right, value: 150 RES.

Rev: Crowned arms.

KM#	Date	Mintage	Good	VG	Fine	VF
206	1802	—	10.00	20.00	45.00	75.00
	1803	—	10.00	20.00	45.00	75.00

KM#	Date	Mintage	Good	VG	Fine	VF
206	1804	—	10.00	20.00	45.00	75.00
	1806	—	10.00	20.00	45.00	75.00

NOTE: Earlier dates (1798-1799) exist for this type.

Maria II

KM#	Date	Mintage	Good	VG	Fine	VF
271	1845	—	20.00	30.00	40.00	70.00
	1846	—	20.00	30.00	40.00	70.00
	1846/5	—	25.00	35.00	50.00	90.00
	1849	—	20.00	30.00	40.00	70.00

Pedro V

KM#	Date	Mintage	Good	VG	Fine	VF
280	1857	—	25.00	35.00	50.00	80.00
	1860	—	25.00	35.00	50.00	80.00
	1861	—	25.00	35.00	50.00	80.00

PARDAO

(300 Reis)

SILVER, 5.84-5.95 g

Obv: Head right. Rev: Crowned arms.

KM#	Date	Mintage	Good	VG	Fine	VF
204	1801	—	10.00	20.00	40.00	80.00
	1802	—	10.00	20.00	40.00	80.00
	1803	—	10.00	20.00	40.00	80.00
	1804	—	10.00	20.00	40.00	80.00
	1805	—	10.00	20.00	40.00	80.00
	1806	—	10.00	20.00	40.00	80.00

NOTE: Earlier dates (1796-1800) exist for this type.

Joao

KM#	Date	Mintage	Good	VG	Fine	VF
221	1808	—	17.50	27.50	37.50	75.00
	1809	—	17.50	27.50	37.50	75.00
	1810	—	17.50	27.50	37.50	75.00
	1811	—	17.50	27.50	37.50	75.00
	1812/09	—	35.00	60.00	100.00	225.00
	1815/09	—	35.00	60.00	100.00	225.00
	1815	—	17.50	27.50	37.50	75.00
	1816	—	17.50	27.50	37.50	75.00
	1817	—	17.50	27.50	37.50	75.00
	1818	—	17.50	27.50	37.50	75.00

KM#	Date	Mintage	Good	VG	Fine	VF
237	1818	—	20.00	30.00	50.00	80.00
	1819	—	20.00	30.00	50.00	80.00
	1820	—	20.00	30.00	50.00	80.00
	1821	—	20.00	30.00	50.00	80.00
	1822	—	20.00	30.00	50.00	80.00
	1823	—	20.00	30.00	50.00	80.00
	1824	—	20.00	30.00	50.00	80.00
	1825	—	20.00	30.00	50.00	80.00

Obv: Diademed head.

KM#	Date	Mintage	Good	VG	Fine	VF
238	ND	—	20.00	30.00	40.00	80.00

Pedro IV

KM#	Date	Mintage	Good	VG	Fine	VF
247	ND	—	40.00	55.00	70.00	140.00
	1827	—	40.00	55.00	70.00	140.00

Miguel

KM#	Date	Mintage	Good	VG	Fine	VF
256	1831	—	35.00	50.00	65.00	130.00
	1833	—	35.00	50.00	65.00	130.00

Maria II

KM#	Date	Mintage	Good	VG	Fine	VF
268	1839	—	32.50	45.00	60.00	120.00
	1840	—	32.50	45.00	60.00	120.00
	1841	—	32.50	45.00	60.00	120.00

KM#	Date	Mintage	Good	VG	Fine	VF
272	1845	—	20.00	30.00	40.00	80.00
	1846	—	20.00	30.00	40.00	80.00
	1847	—	20.00	30.00	40.00	80.00
	1848	—	20.00	30.00	40.00	80.00

Rev: Value and arms.

KM#	Date	Mintage	Good	VG	Fine	VF
276	1851	—	30.00	37.50	50.00	100.00

Pedro V

KM#	Date	Mintage	Good	VG	Fine	VF
278	1856	—	30.00	40.00	55.00	110.00
	1857	—	30.00	40.00	55.00	110.00
	1860	—	30.00	40.00	55.00	110.00
	1861	—	30.00	40.00	55.00	110.00

Luis I

KM#	Date	Mintage	Good	VG	Fine	VF
281	1866	—	30.00	40.00	55.00	110.00
	1868	—	30.00	40.00	55.00	110.00
	1869	—	30.00	40.00	55.00	110.00

XERAFIM

GOLD, 0.40-0.41 g
Joao
Obv: Arms on crowned globe.
Rev: Value and date in angles of cross.

KM#	Date	Mintage	Good	VG	Fine	VF
241	1819	—	350.00	750.00	1250.	2000.

RUPIA

SILVER, 11.80 g

KM#	Date	Mintage	Good	VG	Fine	VF
205	1801	—	11.50	18.50	30.00	45.00
	1802	—	11.50	18.50	30.00	45.00
	1803	—	11.50	18.50	30.00	45.00
	1804	—	11.50	18.50	30.00	45.00
	1805	—	11.50	18.50	30.00	45.00
	1806	—	11.50	18.50	30.00	45.00
	1807	—	11.50	18.50	30.00	45.00

NOTE: Several varieties exist.
NOTE: Earlier dates (1796-1800) exist for this type.

Joao

KM#	Date	Mintage	Good	VG	Fine	VF
219	1807 inverted "A" for "V" in "Rupia"	—	40.00	55.00	70.00	140.00
	1808	—	40.00	55.00	70.00	140.00
	1809	—	40.00	55.00	70.00	140.00
	1810	—	40.00	55.00	70.00	140.00
	1811	—	40.00	55.00	70.00	140.00
	1812	—	40.00	55.00	70.00	140.00
	1813	—	40.00	60.00	80.00	160.00
	1814	—	40.00	60.00	80.00	160.00
	1815	—	40.00	60.00	80.00	160.00
	1816	—	40.00	55.00	70.00	140.00
	1817	—	40.00	55.00	70.00	140.00

Mule. Obv: KM#219. Rev: KM#205.

KM#	Date	Mintage	Good	VG	Fine	VF
220	1807	—	40.00	55.00	70.00	140.00

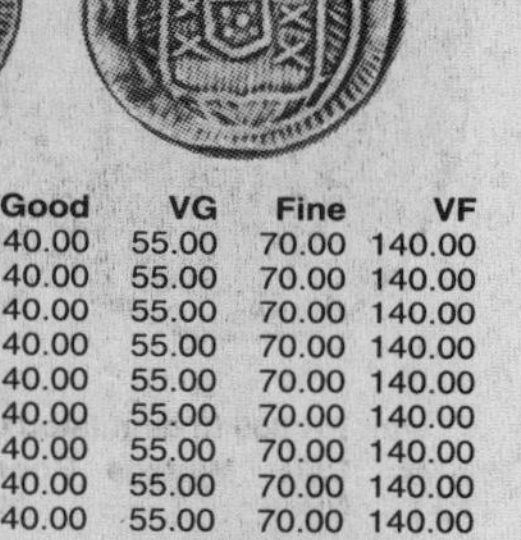

KM#	Date	Mintage	Good	VG	Fine	VF
239	1818	—	40.00	55.00	70.00	140.00
	1819	—	40.00	55.00	70.00	140.00
	1820	—	40.00	55.00	70.00	140.00
	1821	—	40.00	55.00	70.00	140.00
	1822	—	40.00	55.00	70.00	140.00
	1823	—	40.00	55.00	70.00	140.00
	1824	—	40.00	55.00	70.00	140.00
	1825	—	40.00	55.00	70.00	140.00
	1826	—	40.00	55.00	70.00	140.00

Pedro IV

KM#	Date	Mintage	Good	VG	Fine	VF
248	1827	—	80.00	100.00	125.00	250.00
	1828	—	80.00	100.00	125.00	250.00

Miguel

KM#	Date	Mintage	Good	VG	Fine	VF
254	1829	—	70.00	85.00	110.00	225.00
	1830	—	60.00	75.00	90.00	180.00
	1831	—	55.00	65.00	80.00	160.00
	1832	—	55.00	65.00	80.00	160.00
	1833	—	55.00	65.00	80.00	160.00

Maria II

KM#	Date	Mintage	Good	VG	Fine	VF
269	1839	—	22.50	45.00	60.00	75.00
	1840	—	22.50	45.00	60.00	75.00
	1841	—	22.50	45.00	60.00	75.00

KM#	Date	Mintage	Good	VG	Fine	VF
273	1845	—	20.00	40.00	55.00	70.00
	1846	—	20.00	40.00	55.00	70.00
	1847	—	20.00	40.00	55.00	70.00
	1848	—	20.00	40.00	55.00	70.00
	1849	—	20.00	40.00	55.00	70.00

KM#	Date	Mintage	Good	VG	Fine	VF
275	1850	—	25.00	50.00	70.00	90.00
	1851	—	25.00	50.00	70.00	90.00

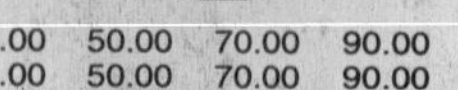

Pedro V

KM#	Date	Mintage	Good	VG	Fine	VF
279	1856	—	20.00	40.00	55.00	70.00
279	1857	—	20.00	40.00	55.00	70.00
	1858	—	20.00	40.00	55.00	70.00
	1859	—	20.00	40.00	55.00	70.00
	1860	—	20.00	40.00	55.00	70.00
	1861	—	20.00	40.00	55.00	70.00

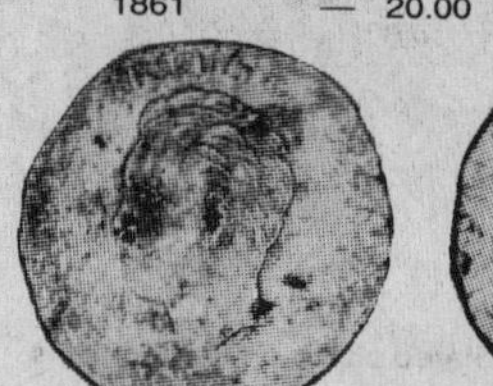

Luiz I

KM#	Date	Mintage	Good	VG	Fine	VF
282	1866	—	25.00	50.00	65.00	80.00
	1867	—	25.00	50.00	65.00	80.00
	1868	—	25.00	50.00	65.00	80.00
	1869	—	25.00	50.00	65.00	80.00

2 XERAFINS

GOLD, 0.81 g
Joao

KM#	Date	Mintage	Good	VG	Fine	VF
223	1815	—	— Reported, not confirmed			
242	1819	—	— Reported, not confirmed			

4 XERAFINS

GOLD, 1.63 g
Maria I

KM#	Date	Mintage	Good	VG	Fine	VF
202	1803	—	275.00	500.00	850.00	1400.

NOTE: Earlier dates (1791-1795) exist for this type.

Joao

KM#	Date	Mintage	Good	VG	Fine	VF
243	1819	—	450.00	900.00	1500.	2500.

8 XERAFINS

GOLD, 3.25 g
Maria I

KM#	Date	Mintage	Good	VG	Fine	VF
192	1804	—	500.00	850.00	1250.	1850.
	1805	—	500.00	850.00	1250.	1850.

NOTE: Earlier dates (1782-1795) exist for this type.

Joao
Obv: Crowned oval arms.

KM#	Date	Mintage	Good	VG	Fine	VF
244	1819	—	600.00	1000.	1650.	2750.

Obv: Similar to 1 Rupia, KM#239.

KM#	Date	Mintage	Good	VG	Fine	VF
245	1819	—	— Reported, not confirmed			

12 XERAFINS

GOLD, 4.87 g
Maria I

KM#	Date	Mintage	Good	VG	Fine	VF
187	1801	—	250.00	500.00	850.00	1450.
	1802	—	250.00	500.00	850.00	1450.
	1803	—	250.00	450.00	750.00	1250.
	1804	—	250.00	450.00	750.00	1250.
	1806	—	250.00	450.00	750.00	1250.
	1809	—	250.00	450.00	750.00	1250.

NOTE: Earlier dates (1781-1800) exist for this type.

Joao

KM#	Date	Mintage	Good	VG	Fine	VF
222	1808	—	450.00	750.00	1250.	1850.
	1811	—	450.00	750.00	1250.	1850.
	1812	—	450.00	750.00	1250.	1850.
	1813	—	450.00	750.00	1250.	1850.
	1814	—	450.00	750.00	1250.	1850.
	1815	—	450.00	750.00	1250.	1850.
	1816	—	450.00	750.00	1250.	1850.

KM#	Date	Mintage	Good	VG	Fine	VF
246	1819	—	500.00	900.00	1500.	2000.
	1820	—	500.00	900.00	1500.	2000.
	1822	—	500.00	900.00	1500.	2000.
	1824	—	500.00	900.00	1500.	2000.
	1825	—	500.00	900.00	1500.	2000.

Maria II

KM#	Date	Mintage	Good	VG	Fine	VF
270	1840	—	550.00	1000.	1650.	2250.
	1841	—	550.00	1000.	1650.	2250.

COLONIAL COINAGE

MONETARY SYSTEM

960 Reis = 16 Tanga = 1 Rupia

3 REIS

COPPER

KM#	Date	Mintage	Fine	VF	XF	Unc
1	1871	.052	3.00	7.00	12.00	28.00

5 REIS

COPPER

KM#	Date	Mintage	Fine	VF	XF	Unc
2	1871	.051	4.00	8.00	15.00	40.00

1/12 TANGA

BRONZE
Carlos I
Roman numeral dating

KM#	Date	Mintage	Fine	VF	XF	Unc
13	1901	.960	1.50	3.50	7.00	15.00
	1901	—	—	—	P/L	125.00
	1903	.960	1.75	3.75	7.50	18.00

OITAVO (1/8) TANGA

COPPER
Luiz I

KM#	Date	Mintage	Fine	VF	XF	Unc
7	1881	12.397	1.50	3.50	8.00	18.00
	1884	Inc. Ab.	1.50	3.50	9.00	20.00
	1886	Inc. Ab.	2.00	4.00	10.00	22.00

BRONZE
Carlos I
Roman numeral dating

KM#	Date	Mintage	Fine	VF	XF	Unc
14	1901	.960	1.00	3.00	8.00	18.00
	1901	—	—	—	P/L	150.00
	1903	.960	2.00	4.00	10.00	22.00

10 REIS

COPPER

KM#	Date	Mintage	Fine	VF	XF	Unc
3	1871	.051	5.00	10.00	16.50	45.00

QUARTO (1/4) TANGA

(15 Reis)

COPPER

KM#	Date	Mintage	Fine	VF	XF	Unc
4	1871	.051	10.00	15.00	25.00	65.00

Luiz I

KM#	Date	Mintage	Fine	VF	XF	Unc
8	1881	7.242	2.75	5.50	11.50	27.50
	1884	Inc. Ab.	3.25	6.50	12.50	30.00
	1886	Inc. Ab.	2.25	4.50	8.50	22.50
	1888	Inc. Ab.	30.00	50.00	90.00	900.00

BRONZE
Carlos I
Roman numeral dating

KM#	Date	Mintage	Fine	VF	XF	Unc
15	1901	.800	1.50	3.00	9.00	20.00
	1901	—	—	—	P/L	175.00
	1903	.800	1.75	3.75	10.00	22.00

1/2 TANGA

(30 Reis)

COPPER

KM#	Date	Mintage	Fine	VF	XF	Unc
5	1871	.050	12.00	18.00	30.00	70.00

BRONZE
Carlos I
Roman numeral dating

KM#	Date	Mintage	Fine	VF	XF	Unc
16	1901	.800	2.00	4.00	12.00	35.00
	1901	—	—	—	P/L	200.00
	1903	.800	3.00	6.00	15.00	40.00

TANGA

(60 Reis)

COPPER

KM#	Date	Mintage	Fine	VF	XF	Unc
6	1871	.050	15.00	25.00	40.00	135.00

BRONZE

KM#	Date	Mintage	Fine	VF	XF	Unc
19	1934	.100	2.50	5.00	15.00	30.00

KM#	Date	Mintage	Fine	VF	XF	Unc
24	1947	1.000	.50	1.00	2.00	5.00

KM#	Date	Mintage	Fine	VF	XF	Unc
28	1952	9.600	.35	.65	1.25	3.50

OITAVO DE (1/8) RUPIA

1.4600 g, .917 SILVER, .0430 oz ASW
Luiz I

KM#	Date	Mintage	Fine	VF	XF	Unc
9	1881	.902	3.00	6.00	12.00	35.00

2 TANGAS

COPPER-NICKEL

KM#	Date	Mintage	Fine	VF	XF	Unc
20	1934	.150	2.50	5.00	15.00	35.00

QUARTO DE (1/4) RUPIA

2.9200 g, .917 SILVER, .0860 oz ASW
Luiz I

KM#	Date	Mintage	Fine	VF	XF	Unc
10	1881	.471	5.00	8.00	16.00	40.00

COPPER-NICKEL

KM#	Date	Mintage	Fine	VF	XF	Unc
25	1947	.800	1.00	2.00	3.50	9.00
	1952	4.000	.50	1.00	2.00	5.00

4 TANGAS

COPPER-NICKEL

KM#	Date	Mintage	Fine	VF	XF	Unc
21	1934	.100	3.00	6.00	18.00	40.00

MEIA (1/2) RUPIA

5.8300 g, .917 SILVER, .1719 oz ASW
Luiz I

KM#	Date	Mintage	Fine	VF	XF	Unc
11	1881	.357	4.00	8.00	15.00	45.00
	1882	Inc. Ab.	5.00	10.00	20.00	50.00

6.0000 g, .835 SILVER, .1610 oz ASW

KM#	Date	Mintage	Fine	VF	XF	Unc
23	1936	.100	3.50	7.50	10.00	25.00

COPPER-NICKEL

KM#	Date	Mintage	Fine	VF	XF	Unc
26	1947	.600	1.00	2.00	4.00	10.00
	1952	2.000	.50	1.00	2.50	4.50

UMA (1) RUPIA

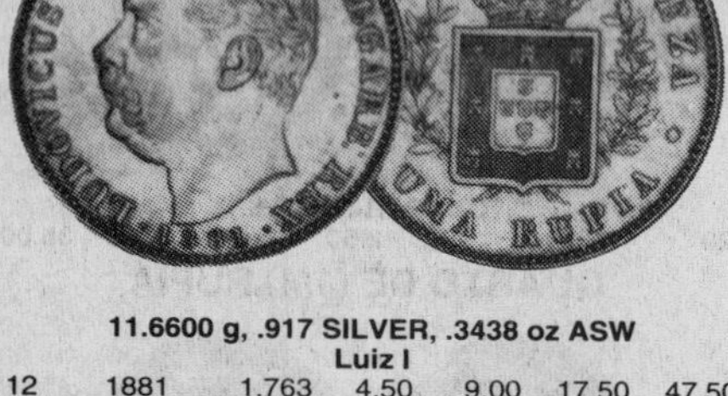

11.6600 g, .917 SILVER, .3438 oz ASW
Luiz I

KM#	Date	Mintage	Fine	VF	XF	Unc
12	1881	1.763	4.50	9.00	17.50	47.50
	1882	Inc. Ab.	4.00	8.00	16.00	45.00

Carlos I

KM#	Date	Mintage	Fine	VF	XF	Unc
17	1903	.200	4.00	7.50	14.50	40.00
	1904	.100	5.00	10.00	20.00	55.00

KM#	Date	Mintage	Fine	VF	XF	Unc
18	1912	.300	12.00	25.00	50.00	100.00

12.0000 g, .917 SILVER, .3536 oz ASW

KM#	Date	Mintage	Fine	VF	XF	Unc
22	1935	.300	5.00	8.00	12.00	25.00

12.0000 g, .500 SILVER, .1929 oz ASW

KM#	Date	Mintage	Fine	VF	XF	Unc
27	1947	.900	2.00	4.00	8.50	22.00

COPPER-NICKEL

KM#	Date	Mintage	Fine	VF	XF	Unc
29	1952	1.000	1.50	3.00	6.50	15.00
	1954	—	25.00	50.00	100.00	200.00

DECIMAL COINAGE

100 Centavos = 1 Escudo

10 CENTAVOS

BRONZE

KM#	Date	Mintage	Fine	VF	XF	Unc
30	1958	5.000	.20	.40	.85	2.00
	1959	Inc. Ab.	.20	.35	.75	1.50
	1961	1.000	.20	.35	.75	1.50

30 CENTAVOS

BRONZE

KM#	Date	Mintage	Fine	VF	XF	Unc
31	1958	5.000	.35	.75	1.25	4.00
	1959	Inc. Ab.	.75	1.50	3.00	7.50

60 CENTAVOS

COPPER-NICKEL

KM#	Date	Mintage	Fine	VF	XF	Unc
32	1958	5.000	.75	1.50	3.00	6.00
	1959	Inc. Ab.	.65	1.25	2.50	5.00

ESCUDO

COPPER-NICKEL

KM#	Date	Mintage	Fine	VF	XF	Unc
33	1958	6.000	.45	.85	1.50	4.00
	1959	Inc. Ab.	.45	.85	1.50	4.00

3 ESCUDOS

COPPER-NICKEL

KM#	Date	Mintage	Fine	VF	XF	Unc
34	1958	5.000	.65	1.25	2.50	5.50
	1959	Inc. Ab.	.65	1.25	2.50	5.50

6 ESCUDOS

COPPER-NICKEL

KM#	Date	Mintage	Fine	VF	XF	Unc
35	1959	4.000	1.25	2.50	3.50	9.00

INDIA-BRITISH

The civilization of India, which began about 2500 B.C., flourished under a succession of empires - notably those of Chandragupta, Asoka and the Mughals - until undermined in the 18th and 19th centuries by European Colonial powers.

The Portuguese were the first to arrive, off Calicut in May 1498. It wasn't until 1612, after the Portuguese and Spanish power had begun to wane, that the British East India Company established its initial settlement at Surat. Britain could not have chosen a more propitious time as the central girdle of petty states, and the southern Vijayanagar Empire were crumbling and ripe for foreign exploitation. By the end of the century, English traders were firmly established in Bombay, Madras, Calcutta and lesser places elsewhere, and Britain was implementing its announced policy to create such civil and military institutions 'as may be the foundation of secure English domination for all time'. By 1757, following the successful conclusion of a war of colonial rivalry with France during which the military victories of Robert Clive, a young officer with the British East India Company, made him a powerful man in India, the British were firmly settled in India as not only traders but as conquerors. During the next 60 years, the British East India Company acquired dominion over most of India by bribery and force, and governed it directly or through puppet princelings.

Because of the Sepoy Mutiny of 1857-58, a large scale mutiny among Indian soldiers of the Bengal army, control of the government of India was transferred from the East India Company to the British Crown. At this point in world history, India was the brightest jewel in the imperial diadem of the British lords of the earth, but even then a movement for greater Indian representation in government presaged the Indian Empire's twilight hour less than a century hence - it would pass into history on Aug. 15, 1947.

BENGAL PRESIDENCY

East India Company

(Until 1835)

In 1633 a group of 8 Englishmen obtained a permit to trade in Bengal from the Nawab of Orissa. Shortly thereafter trading factories were established at Balasore and Hariharpur. Although greater trading privileges were granted to the East India Company by the Emperor Shah Jahan in 1634, by 1642 the 2 original factories were abandoned.

In 1651, through an English surgeon named Broughton, a permit was acquired to trade at Bengal. Hugli was the first location, followed by Kasimbazar, Balasore and Patna (the last 3 in 1653). Calcutta became of increasing importance in this area and on December 20, 1699 Calcutta was declared a presidency and renamed Fort p9=9

During these times there were many conflicts with the Nawab, both diplomatic and military, and the ultimate outcome was the intervention of Clive and the restoration of Calcutta as an important trading center.

During the earlier trading times in Bengal most of the monies used were imported rupees from the Madras factory. These were primarily of the Arcot type. After Clive's victory one of the concessions in the peace treaty was the right to make Mughal type coinage. The Nawab gave specific details as to what form the coinage should take.

In 1765 Emperor Shah Alam gave the East India Company possessions in Bengal, Orissa and Bihar. This made the company nominally responsible only to the Emperor.

In 1777 the "Frozen Year 19" (of Shah Alam) rupees were made at Calcutta and were continued until 1835. The Arcot rupees were discontinued at Calcutta about 1777.

MINTS

علي نكر كلكته

Alinagar Kalkatah

بنارس

Banaras

كلكته

Calcutta (Kalkatah)

فرخ اباد

Farrukhabad

ساكر

Sagar

BANARAS

(Banares, Varanasi)

NOTE: Coins of similar dates with different legends are listed under Indian Princely States, Awadh.

PICE

In the name of Shah Alam II

COPPER, dump, 11.40 g
Mint: Banares
Obv. and rev: Trisul (trident) symbols added.

KM#	Date	Year	Good	VG	Fine	VF
16	(1802-3)	45	2.00	5.00	10.00	20.00
	(1806-7)	49	2.00	5.00	10.00	20.00

NOTE: Earlier dates (Year 28-42) exist for this type.

COPPER, dump, 23.5mm, 6.23 g

KM#	Date	Year	VG	Fine	VF	XF
27	(1815-21)	37	2.00	3.00	6.00	10.00

Reduced weight, 6.15 g

KM#	Date	Year	VG	Fine	VF	XF
28	(1821-7)	37	1.75	3.75	7.50	12.50

Large flan, 24.5-26.5mm.

KM#	Date	Year	VG	Fine	VF	XF
29	(1827-9)	37	2.50	4.50	8.50	13.50

Obv. and rev: Crossbar on trisuls, 21-24.5mm.

KM#	Date	Year	VG	Fine	VF	XF
30	(1827-9)	37	2.50	4.50	8.50	13.50
	(1827-9)	37	—	—	Proof	75.00

1/16 RUPEE

In the name of Shah Alam II

SILVER, dump, 0.67-0.73 g
Mint: Banaras

KM#	Date	Year	VG	Fine	VF	XF
32	AH1226	17/49	12.50	25.00	50.00	100.00

NOTE: Earlier dates (AH1193-1215) exist for this type.

1/8 RUPEE

In the name of Shah Alam II

SILVER, dump, 1.34-1.45 g
Mint: Banaras

KM#	Date	Year	VG	Fine	VF	XF
33	AH1221	17/48	7.50	15.00	37.50	75.00
	122x	17/48	7.50	15.00	37.50	75.00
	1225	17/49	7.50	15.00	37.50	75.00
	1226	17/49	7.50	15.00	37.50	75.00

NOTE: Earlier dates (AH1193-1215) exist for this type.

1/4 RUPEE

In the name of Shah Alam II

SILVER, dump, 2.68-2.91 g
Mint: Banaras

KM#	Date	Year	VG	Fine	VF	XF
34 (24)	AH122x	17/46	12.50	25.00	50.00	100.00
	1225	17/49	12.50	25.00	50.00	100.00
	1226	17/49	12.50	25.00	50.00	100.00

NOTE: Earlier dates (AH1193-1215) exist for this type.

Struck w/o Darogah's marks

KM#	Date	Year	VG	Fine	VF	XF
35	AH1229	17/49	8.00	20.00	45.00	75.00

Machine struck, broad flan, w/oblique milling.

KM#	Date	Year	VG	Fine	VF	XF
36	AH1229	17/49	— Reported, not confirmed			

1/2 RUPEE

In the name of Shah Alam II

SILVER, dump, 5.35-5.82 g
Mint: Banaras

KM#	Date	Year	VG	Fine	VF	XF
37	1225	17/49	75.00	150.00	225.00	300.00
	1226	17/49	75.00	150.00	225.00	300.00

NOTE: Earlier date (AH1193) exists for this type.

Mint: Calcutta
Struck w/o Darogah's marks.

KM#	Date	Year	VG	Fine	VF	XF
38	AH1229	17/49	20.00	45.00	100.00	150.00

Machine struck, broad flan w/oblique milling.

KM#	Date	Year	Fine	VF	XF	Unc
39	AH1229	17/49	15.00	37.50	75.00	150.00

RUPEE

In the name of Shah Alam II

SILVER, dump, 10.70-11.60 g
Mint: Banaras

KM#	Date	Year	VG	Fine	VF	XF
40	AH1216	17/43	14.00	23.50	25.00	45.00
	1216	17/44	14.00	23.50	25.00	45.00
	1217	17/44	14.00	23.50	25.00	45.00
	1217	17/45	14.00	23.50	25.00	45.00
	1218	17/45	14.00	23.50	25.00	45.00
	1218	17/46	14.00	23.50	25.00	45.00
	1219	17/46	14.00	23.50	25.00	45.00
	1219	17/47	14.00	23.50	25.00	45.00
	1220	17/47	14.00	23.50	25.00	45.00
	1220	17/48	14.00	23.50	25.00	45.00
	1221	17/48	14.00	23.50	25.00	45.00
	1221	17/49	14.00	23.50	25.00	45.00
	1222	17/49	14.00	23.50	25.00	45.00
	1223	17/49	14.00	23.50	25.00	45.00
	1224	17/49	14.00	23.50	25.00	45.00
	1225	17/49	14.00	23.50	25.00	45.00
	1226	17/49	14.00	23.50	25.00	45.00
	1227	17/49	25.00	40.00	52.50	75.00

NOTE: Earlier dates (AH1190-1215) exist for this type.

W/o Darogah's marks.

KM#	Date	Year	VG	Fine	VF	XF
41	AH1228	17/49	25.00	40.00	52.50	75.00
	1229	17/49	25.00	40.00	52.50	75.00

Machine struck, broad flan w/oblique milling.

KM#	Date	Year	Fine	VF	XF	Unc
42	AH1229	17/49	32.00	53.00	75.00	110.00

NAZARANA RUPEE

SILVER, 11.64 g
Mint: Banaras
Large flan

KM#	Date	Year	VG	Fine	VF	XF
44	AH1217	17/45	85.00	165.00	275.00	450.00

Large full flan

45	AH1219	17/47	—	—	500.00	850.00

CALCUTTA

PIE

COPPER

KM#	Date	Year	Fine	VF	XF	Unc
58	(1831)	—	.35	1.00	8.00	20.00
	(1831)	—	—	—	Proof	85.00

1/2 PICE

COPPER, 3.11 g
Mint: Calcutta

KM#	Date	Year	VG	Fine	VF	XF
A54	(1809)	37	2.50	5.00	10.00	15.00
(24)	(c.1820)	37		(restrike)	Proof	65.00

PICE

COPPER, 6.54 g.

54	(1809)	37	.40	1.00	8.00	45.00
	(c.1820)	37		(restrike)	Proof	80.00

Reduced weight, 6.46 g, 27.2mm

55	(1817)	37	.40	1.00	8.00	45.00

26mm

56	(1829)	37	1.25	3.00	6.00	35.00
	(1829)	37	—	—	Proof	200.00

Reduced weight, 6.13 g, 23mm

KM#	Date	Year	VG	Fine	VF	XF
57	(1831)	37	.50	1.50	3.00	25.00
	(1831)	37	—	—	Proof	200.00

2 PICE

In the name of Shah Alam II

COPPER, 12.33 g
Mint: Calcutta

A55	(1809)	37	10.00	20.00	35.00	50.00
(26)	(c.1820)	37		(restrike)	Proof	100.00

1/2 ANNA

COPPER

KM#	Date	Year	Fine	VF	XF	Unc
59	(1831-35)	—	1.00	3.00	15.00	40.00
	(1831-35)	—	—	—	Proof	150.00

FARRUKHABAD

PICE

COPPER

KM#	Date	Year	Good	VG	Fine	VF
64	—	45	35.00	75.00	120.00	200.00

TRISUL PICE

COPPER, 6.20 g
Mint: Farrukhabad
Obv: 6-pointed stars.

KM#	Date	Year	VG	Fine	VF	XF
A65	—	45	—	—	—	—

Obv: Trident replaces stars.

65	(1820)	45	1.50	3.00	10.00	45.00

Mint: Sagar
Obv. & rev: Trident

KM#	Date	Year	VG	Fine	VF	XF
71	(1826)	45	1.50	3.00	10.00	45.00

Obv: 6-petalled rosette replaces trident

72	(1833)	45	1.50	3.00	10.00	45.00

2 PICE

COPPER
Similar to 1 Pice, KM#64.

KM#	Date	Year	Good	VG	Fine	VF
63	—	45	—	—	—	—

1/4 RUPEE

.955 SILVER, 2.80 g
Mint: Farrukhabad
Oblique milling (1806-1819)

KM#	Date	Year	Fine	VF	XF	Unc
66	AH—	45	4.00	8.00	20.00	50.00

.909 SILVER, 2.92 g
Vertical milling (1820-1831)

67	AH—	45	4.00	8.00	20.00	50.00

Mints: Calcutta and Banaras

73	AH1204	45	4.00	8.00	20.00	50.00

Mint: Calcutta
Plain edge (1831-1833)

75	AH1204	45	3.00	6.00	15.00	35.00
	1204	45	—	—	Proof	250.00

1/2 RUPEE

.955 SILVER, 5.60 g
Mint: Farrukhabad
Oblique milling (1806-1819)

68	—	45	7.50	15.00	35.00	75.00

.909 SILVER, 5.80 g
Mints: Calcutta and Banaras
Vertical milling (1820-1831)

74	—	45	7.50	15.00	35.00	75.00

Mint: Calcutta
Plain edge (1831-1833)

76	—	45	5.00	10.00	25.00	50.00
	—	45	—	—	Proof	300.00

RUPEE

.955 SILVER, 11.21 g
Mints: Farrukhabad and Calcutta
Oblique milling (1806-1819)

69	—	45	5.00	10.00	30.00	75.00

.909 SILVER, 11.68 g
Mints: Farrukhabad, Calcutta, Banaras, Sagar
Vertical milling (1820-1831)

KM#	Date	Year	Fine	VF	XF	Unc
70	—	45	5.00	10.00	30.00	75.00

Mint: Calcutta, mm: Crescent.
Obv. and rev: Thin rim; plain edge (1831-1833).

KM#	Date	Year	Fine	VF	XF	Unc
77	—	45	4.00	8.00	25.00	50.00
	—	45	—	—	Proof	400.00

W/o mint mark.
Obv. and rev: Broad rim; plain edge (1833-1835).

KM#	Date	Year	Fine	VF	XF	Unc
78	—	45	4.00	8.00	25.00	50.00
	—	45	—	—	Proof	400.00

MURSHIDABAD

1/4 RUPEE

SILVER, 2.90 g
Mints: Calcutta, Dacca, Patna
Oblique milling (1793-1818).

KM#	Date	Year	Fine	VF	XF	Unc
96	AH1204	19	1.50	5.00	15.00	25.00
	1204	19	—	—	Proof	300.00

Vertical milling (1819-1829)

KM#	Date	Year	Fine	VF	XF	Unc
104	AH1204	19	1.50	5.00	15.00	25.00

Mint: New Calcutta
Plain edge (1830-1833)

KM#	Date	Year	Fine	VF	XF	Unc
115	AH1204	19	1.50	5.00	15.00	25.00

1/2 RUPEE

SILVER, 5.80 g
Mints: Calcutta, Dacca, Murshidabad, Patna
Oblique milling (1793-1818)

KM#	Date	Year	Fine	VF	XF	Unc
97	—	19	2.50	8.50	25.00	50.00
	—	19	—	—	Proof	400.00

Vertical milling (1819-1829)

KM#	Date	Year	Fine	VF	XF	Unc
105	—	19	3.50	10.00	30.00	50.00
	—	19	—	—	Proof	300.00

Mint: New Calcutta
Plain edge (1830-1833)
Rev: Crescent at upper left.

KM#	Date	Year	Fine	VF	XF	Unc
116	—	19	3.50	10.00	30.00	50.00
	—	19	—	—	Proof	300.00

RUPEE

SILVER, 11.60 g
Mints: Calcutta, Dacca, Murshidabad, Patna
Machine struck, oblique milling (1793-1818)

KM#	Date	Year	Fine	VF	XF	Unc
99	—	19	5.00	8.50	15.00	30.00

Obv: Star added.
Vertical milling (1819-1832)

KM#	Date	Year	Fine	VF	XF	Unc
108	—	19	5.00	8.50	15.00	25.00

Rev: Privy mark 'S' at upper left.

KM#	Date	Year	Fine	VF	XF	Unc
109	—	19	15.00	25.00	60.00	100.00

Mint: New Calcutta
Plain edge (1830-1833)
Rev: Crescent at upper left.

KM#	Date	Year	Fine	VF	XF	Unc
117	—	19	5.50	11.50	22.50	45.00
	—	19	—	—	Proof	350.00

1/4 MOHUR

.996 GOLD, 3.09 g
Mints: Calcutta, Murshidabad
Mintname: Murshidabad
Oblique milling (1793-1818)

KM#	Date	Year	VG	Fine	VF	XF
100	AH1204	19	BV	45.00	75.00	150.00

.917 GOLD, 3.31 g
Vertical milling (1819-1832)

KM#	Date	Year	VG	Fine	VF	XF
110	AH1204	19	BV	50.00	100.00	175.00
	1204	19	—	—	Proof	1250.

1/2 MOHUR

.996 GOLD, 6.18 g
Mint: Calcutta
Machine struck, oblique milling (1793-1818)

KM#	Date	Year	VG	Fine	VF	XF
101	AH1202	19	BV	100.00	200.00	350.00

.917 GOLD, 6.63 gm.
Vertical milling (1819-1832)

KM#	Date	Year	VG	Fine	VF	XF
111	AH1202	19	BV	100.00	200.00	350.00
	1202	19	—	—	Proof	1500.

MOHUR

.996 GOLD, 12.36 g
Mints: Calcutta, Murshidabad
Machine struck, oblique milling (1793-1818)

KM#	Date	Year	VG	Fine	VF	XF
103	AH1202	19	BV	150.00	200.00	300.00

.917 GOLD, 13.26 g
Mint: Calcutta
Vertical milling (1819-1825)

KM#	Date	Year	VG	Fine	VF	XF
112	AH1202	19	BV	175.00	250.00	350.00
	1202	19	—	—	Proof	1650.

.996 GOLD, 12.36 g
Low relief, oblique left milling (1825)

KM#	Date	Year	VG	Fine	VF	XF
113	AH1202	19	BV	150.00	200.00	350.00

Similar to KM#113 w/crescent added (1830) on rev.

KM#	Date	Year	VG	Fine	VF	XF
114	AH1202	19	BV	175.00	300.00	400.00
	1202	19	—	—	Proof	1750.

BOMBAY PRESIDENCY

Following a naval victory over the Portuguese on December 24, 1612 negotiations were started that developed into the opening of the first East India Company factory in Surat in 1613. Silver coins for the New World as well as various other foreign coins were used in early trade. Within the decade the Mughal mint at Surat was melting all of these foreign coins and re-minting them as various denominations of Mughal coinage.

Bombay became an English holding as part of the dowry of Catherine of Braganza, Princess of Portugal when she was betrothed to Charles II of England. Also included in the dowry was Tangier and $500,000. With this acquisition the trading center of the Indian West Coast moved from Surat to Bombay.

Possession of Bombay Island took place on February 8, 1665 and by 1672 the East India Company had a mint in Bombay to serve their trading interests. European designed coins were struck here until 1717. Experimental issues of Mughal style rupees with regnal years pertaining to the reigns of James II and William and Mary made in 1693-94.

From 1717 to 1778 the Mughal style Bombay rupee was the principal coin of the West India trade, although bulk foreign coins were used for striking rupees at Surat.

After the East India Company took over the city of Surat in 1800 they slowed the mint production and finally transferred all activity to Bombay in 1815.

MINTS

Ahmadabad احمد اباد

Bombay (Munbai) منبى

COPPER COINAGE

1/4 PICE

COPPER, dump, 2.65 g

KM#	Date	Year	Good	VG	Fine	VF
219	1816	—	6.00	15.00	45.00	75.00
	1821	—	6.00	15.00	45.00	75.00
	1825	—	6.00	15.00	45.00	75.00

PIE

COPPER, 2.16 g
Mint: Bombay
Obv: Center lion on helmet above shield.

KM#	Date	Year	Fine	VF	XF	Unc
230	AH1246	1830	—	—	Proof	300.00
	1246	1831	.75	2.00	25.00	60.00
	1246	1831	—	—	Proof	175.00

Mint: Calcutta
Rev: Tall Persian legend.

KM#	Date	Year	Fine	VF	XF	Unc
261	AH1248	1833	.40	1.00	12.00	45.00
	1248	1833	—	—	Proof	100.00

Rev: Short Persian legend.

KM#	Date	Year	Fine	VF	XF	Unc
262	AH1248	1833	.40	1.00	12.00	45.00

Mule. Obv: KM#261. Rev: KM#230.

KM#	Date	Year	Fine	VF	XF	Unc
263	AH1246	1833	—	—	—	—

Mule. Obv: KM#230. Rev: KM#261.

KM#	Date	Year	Fine	VF	XF	Unc
264	AH1248	1831	—	—	—	—

1/2 PICE

COPPER, dump, 5.31 g

KM#	Date	Year	Good	VG	Fine	VF
197	1802	—	3.00	10.00	30.00	75.00
	1803	—	— Reported, not confirmed			
	1808	—	3.00	10.00	30.00	75.00
	1810	—	3.00	10.00	30.00	75.00
	1813	—	3.00	10.00	30.00	75.00
	1815	—	3.00	10.00	30.00	75.00
	1816	—	3.00	10.00	30.00	75.00
	1818	—	3.00	10.00	30.00	75.00
	1819	—	3.00	10.00	30.00	75.00
	1825	—	3.00	10.00	30.00	75.00
	1826	—	3.00	10.00	30.00	75.00
	1827	—	3.00	10.00	30.00	75.00
	1829	—	3.00	10.00	30.00	75.00

COPPER, 9mm, 0.90-1.20 g
Obv: Bale mark. Rev: Date.

KM#	Date	Year	Good	VG	Fine	VF
202	(1)803	—	3.00	10.00	30.00	75.00

COPPER, 3.23 g
Obv: Center lion on helmet above shield.

KM#	Date	Year	VG	Fine	VF	XF
204	AH1219	1804	.40	1.00	8.00	40.00
	1219	1804	—	—	Proof	50.00

COPPER, machine struck, 3.83 g
Mint: Ahmadabad
Similar to 1 Pice, KM#226.

KM#	Date	Year	VG	Fine	VF	XF
255	AH1234	13	—	—	—	—

COPPER, dump, 17-18mm, 3.76 g
Mint: Local Southern Concan

KM#	Date	Year	Good	VG	Fine	VF
225	1820	—	3.00	10.00	35.00	100.00
	1821	—	3.00	10.00	35.00	100.00

PICE

COPPER, dump, 10.62 g

KM#	Date	Year	Good	VG	Fine	VF
198	1802	—	2.00	5.00	12.00	40.00
	1803	—	2.00	5.00	12.00	40.00
	1804	—	2.00	5.00	12.00	40.00
	1808	—	2.00	5.00	12.00	40.00
	1809	—	2.00	5.00	12.00	40.00
	1810	—	2.00	5.00	12.00	40.00
	1813	—	2.00	5.00	12.00	40.00
	1815	—	2.00	5.00	12.00	40.00
	1816	—	2.00	5.00	12.00	40.00
	1818	—	2.00	5.00	12.00	40.00
	1819	—	2.00	5.00	12.00	40.00
	1825	—	2.00	5.00	12.00	40.00
	1826	—	2.00	5.00	12.00	40.00
	1827	—	2.00	5.00	12.00	40.00
	1828	—	2.00	5.00	12.00	40.00
	1829	—	2.00	5.00	12.00	40.00

COPPER, 2.20-2.85 g

KM#	Date	Year	Good	VG	Fine	VF
203	1803	—	3.00	10.00	30.00	75.00
	1807	—	3.00	10.00	30.00	75.00

COPPER, dump, 6.47 g

KM#	Date	Year	VG	Fine	VF	XF
205	AH1219	1804	.40	1.00	10.00	50.00
	1219	1804	—	—	Proof	65.00

Mint: Ahmadabad
19-20mm, 7.53 g

KM#	Date	Year	Good	VG	Fine	VF
226	AH1232	—	—	—	—	—
	1233	12	—	—	—	—
	1234	12	—	—	Rare	—
	1236	(14)	5.00	15.00	45.00	125.00

20mm, 6.70 g

KM#	Date	Year	Good	VG	Fine	VF
227	1829	—	5.00	15.00	45.00	125.00

1/4 ANNA

(Paisa)

COPPER, 6.47 g
Mint: Bombay
Obv. leg: EAST INDIA COMPANY

KM#	Date	Year	Fine	VF	XF	Unc
231.1	AH1246	1830	1.25	3.00	35.00	75.00
	1246	1830	—	—	Proof	250.00
	1246	1832	1.25	3.00	35.00	75.00

Rev: Arabic in different style, medium English letters.

KM#	Date	Year	Fine	VF	XF	Unc
231.2	AH1247	1832	1.25	3.00	35.00	75.00

Mint: Calcutta
Obv: Flat shield, w/o E.I.C. leg.
Rev: Large English letters.

KM#	Date	Year	Fine	VF	XF	Unc
232	AH1249	1833	.75	2.00	30.00	75.00
	1249	1833	—	—	Proof	200.00

Mule. Obv: KM#232. Rev: KM#231.2.

KM#	Date	Year	Fine	VF	XF	Unc
233	AH1247	1833	15.00	50.00	150.00	350.00

Obv. Convex shield w/o E.I.C. leg.
Rev: Small English letters

KM#	Date	Year	Fine	VF	XF	Unc
234	AH1249	1833	.75	2.00	30.00	75.00
	1249	1833	—	—	Proof	200.00

Mule. Obv: KM#231. Rev: KM#232.

KM#	Date	Year	Fine	VF	XF	Unc
235	AH1249	1832	9.00	27.50	80.00	200.00

2 PICE

COPPER, dump, 21.25 g
Rev: Value '2' above *Adil*.

KM#	Date	Year	Good	VG	Fine	VF
199	1802	—	1.50	4.00	7.50	15.00
	1803	—	1.50	4.00	7.50	15.00
	1804	—	1.50	4.00	7.50	15.00
	1808	—	2.00	5.50	10.00	20.00

Rev: W/o value '2' above *Adil*.

KM#	Date	Year	Good	VG	Fine	VF
200	1808	—	1.00	3.00	15.00	45.00
	1809	—	1.00	3.00	15.00	45.00
	1810	—	1.00	3.00	15.00	45.00
	1812	—	— Reported, not confirmed			
	1813	—	1.00	3.00	15.00	45.00
	1816	—	1.00	3.00	15.00	45.00
	1818	—	1.00	3.00	15.00	45.00
	1819	—	1.00	3.00	15.00	45.00
	1825	—	1.00	3.00	15.00	45.00
	1826	—	1.00	3.00	15.00	45.00
	1827	—	— Reported, not confirmed			
	1828	—	1.00	3.00	15.00	45.00
	1829	—	1.00	3.00	15.00	45.00

COPPER, 12.95 g

KM#	Date	Year	VG	Fine	VF	XF
206	AH1219	1804	.40	1.00	10.00	50.00
	1219	1804	—	—	Proof	120.00

Mule. Obv: KM#206. Rev: Madras 20 Cash, KM#321.

KM#	Date	Year	VG	Fine	VF	XF
207	—	1804	—	—	Proof	175.00

1/2 ANNA

COPPER, 30.5mm, 12.95 g

KM#	Date	Year	Fine	VF	XF	Unc
250	AH1246	1832	—	—	Proof	500.00

Rev: English letters, 2mm.

KM#	Date	Year	Fine	VF	XF	Unc
251	AH1249	1834	2.00	5.00	65.00	125.00
	1249	1834	—	—	Proof	350.00

Rev: English letters, 2.5mm.

KM#	Date	Year	Fine	VF	XF	Unc
252	AH1249	1834	2.00	5.00	65.00	125.00

Rev: English letters, 1mm.

KM#	Date	Year	Fine	VF	XF	Unc
253	AH1249	1834	2.00	5.00	65.00	125.00

COPPER, dump, 23-24mm, 15.60 gm.
Mint: Local Southern Concan
Rev: W/Nagari value and date.

KM#	Date	Year	VG	Fine	VF	XF
228	1820	—	5.00	10.00	35.00	100.00
	1821	—	5.00	10.00	35.00	100.00

22.5mm, 13.60 gm.
Rev: Western date.

KM#	Date	Year	VG	Fine	VF	XF
229	1828	—	7.50	15.00	45.00	125.00
	1829	—	7.50	15.00	45.00	125.00

4 PICE

COPPER, 42.51 gm.
Rev: Value '4' above *Adil*.

KM#	Date	Year	VG	Fine	VF	XF
201	1802	—	10.00	20.00	60.00	150.00
	1803	—	10.00	20.00	60.00	150.00
	1804	—	10.00	20.00	60.00	150.00
	1816	—	15.00	30.00	90.00	225.00

SILVER COINAGE

PRIVY MARKS

Mint privy marks on dump issues often were intended tobe "secret" (= privy marks), indicating changes instandards as well as mint of origin. The following chart isderived from IV Pridmore:

Privy marks involve the 3 diamonds and 4 dots in center line of obverse.

No.	Mint
1	Surat 1800-15
2	Bombay 1801-02
3	Bombay 1802
4*	Bombay 1803-24
4b	Bombay 1803-24
5*	Bombay 1825-31
5b	Bombay 1825-31
6	Bombay 1800-24
7	and 1825 Bombay 1825
8	on rev. Bombay 1825-31
9	Unknown

***NOTE:** Crown also may be inverted.

1/16 RUPEE

In the name of Shah Alam II

SILVER, 0.72 g
Mint: Surat

KM#	Date	Year	VG	Fine	VF	XF
208	(1800-1815)	46	8.50	20.00	50.00	100.00

In the name of Muhammad Akbar II

Mint: Ahmadabad

KM#	Date	Year	VG	Fine	VF	XF
256	AH1234	12	4.50	6.50	9.00	12.50

See note after Rupee, KM#260.

1/8 RUPEE

In the name of Shah Alam II

SILVER, dump, 1.44 g
Mint: Surat, privy mark #1

KM#	Date	Year	VG	Fine	VF	XF
209.1	(1800-1815)	46	1.50	5.00	12.50	30.00

Mint: Bombay, privy mark #6

KM#	Date	Year	VG	Fine	VF	XF
209.2	(1800-1824)	46	1.50	5.00	12.50	30.00

SILVER, dump, 1.46 g
Mint: Bombay, privy mark #8

KM#	Date	Year	VG	Fine	VF	XF
215	1825	46	1.50	5.00	12.50	30.00

Mint: Bombay, privy mark #9

A215 — — — Reported, not confirmed

In the name of Muhammad Akbar II

11-14mm
Mint: Ahmadabad

KM#	Date	Year	VG	Fine	VF	XF
257	AH1234	12	3.00	4.50	6.50	8.50
	1248	—	3.00	4.50	6.50	8.50

See note after Rupee, KM#260.

1/4 RUPEE

In the name of Shah Alam II

SILVER, dump, 2.88 g
Mint: Surat, privy mark #1

KM#	Date	Year	VG	Fine	VF	XF
210.1	(1800-1815)	46	1.50	5.00	10.00	15.00

Mint: Bombay, privy mark #6

KM#	Date	Year	VG	Fine	VF	XF
210.2	(1800-1824)	46	1.50	5.00	10.00	15.00

Mint: Bombay, privy mark #7

KM#	Date	Year	VG	Fine	VF	XF
210.3	(1825)	46	—	—	—	—

SILVER, dump, 2.91 g
Mint: Bombay, privy mark #8

KM#	Date	Year	VG	Fine	VF	XF
216	1825	46	7.50	12.50	20.00	35.00

SILVER, dump, 2.91 g
Machine struck, plain edge.

KM#	Date	Year	Fine	VF	XF	Unc
220	AH1215	46	1.25	3.00	15.00	25.00
	1215	46	—	—	Proof	275.00

In the name of Muhammad Akbar II

Dump
Mint: Ahmadabad

KM#	Date	Year	VG	Fine	VF	XF
258	AH1234	12	2.50	4.00	6.00	10.00

See note after Rupee, KM#260.

1/2 RUPEE

In the name of Shah Alam II

SILVER, dump, 5.76 g
Mint: Surat, privy mark #1

KM#	Date	Year	VG	Fine	VF	XF
211.1	(1800-1815)	46	3.50	7.50	15.00	25.00

Mint: Bombay, privy mark #6

KM#	Date	Year	VG	Fine	VF	XF
211.2	(1800-1824)	46	3.50	7.50	15.00	25.00

NOTE: For listings of coins w/regnal year 52 see India-French.

5.83 g
Mint: Bombay, privy mark #7

KM#	Date	Year	VG	Fine	VF	XF
217.1	1825	46	5.00	10.00	20.00	35.00

Mint: Bombay, privy mark #8

KM#	Date	Year	VG	Fine	VF	XF
217.2	1825-1831	46	5.00	10.00	20.00	35.00

Mint: Bombay, privy mark #9

KM#	Date	Year	VG	Fine	VF	XF
217.3	—	46	10.00	20.00	45.00	—

Mint: Surat

Machine struck, plain edge.

KM#	Date	Year	Fine	VF	XF	Unc
221	AH1215	46	2.50	7.50	20.00	35.00
	1215	46	—	—	Proof	350.00

In the name of Muhammad Akbar II

Dump
Mint: Ahmadabad

KM#	Date	Year	VG	Fine	VF	XF
259	AH1239	15	3.50	5.50	8.50	15.00
	1242	—	3.50	5.50	8.50	15.00
	1243	—	3.50	5.50	8.50	15.00
	1248	—	3.50	5.50	8.50	15.00

NOTE: See note after Rupee, KM#260.

RUPEE

In the name of Shah Alam II

SILVER, dump, 11.59 g
Mint: Calcutta, 1810-1813
Obv: Inverted crescent privy mark.
Machine struck, plain edge.

KM#	Date	Mintage	VG	Fine	VF	XF
224	—	2.037	15.00	35.00	75.00	125.00

Mint: Surat, privy mark #1

KM#	Date	Year	VG	Fine	VF	XF
212.1	(1800-1815)	46	7.00	10.00	15.00	25.00

Mint: Bombay, privy mark #6

KM#	Date	Year	VG	Fine	VF	XF
212.2	(1800-1824)	46	7.00	10.00	15.00	25.00

NOTE: For listings of coins w/regnal years 51-54 see IndiaFrench.

11.66 g
Mint: Bombay, privy mark #7

KM#	Date	Year	VG	Fine	VF	XF
218.1	1825	46	7.50	12.50	20.00	35.00

Mint: Bombay, privy mark #8

KM#	Date	Year	VG	Fine	VF	XF
218.2	1825-1831	—	7.50	12.50	20.00	35.00

Mint: Bombay, privy mark #9

KM#	Date	Year	VG	Fine	VF	XF
218.3	—	46	15.00	25.00	50.00	—

Mint: Calcutta
Machine struck, vertical milling.

KM#	Date	Year	Fine	VF	XF	Unc
222	AH1215	46	5.00	15.00	50.00	100.00
	1215	46	—	—	Proof	400.00

Mint: Bombay
Plain edge

KM#	Date	Year	Fine	VF	XF	Unc
223	AH1215	46	3.00	5.00	20.00	50.00
	1215	46	—	—	Proof	400.00

In the name of Muhammad Akbar II

Dump
Mint: Ahmadabad

KM#	Date	Year	VG	Fine	VF	XF
260	AH1233	11	6.00	10.00	13.50	20.00
	1233	12	6.00	10.00	13.50	20.00
	1234	12	6.00	10.00	13.50	20.00
	1234	13	6.00	10.00	13.50	20.00
	1235	13	6.00	10.00	13.50	20.00
	1235	14	6.00	10.00	13.50	20.00
	1236	13	6.00	10.00	13.50	20.00
	1236	14	6.00	10.00	13.50	20.00
	1239	15	6.00	10.00	13.50	20.00
	1241	16	6.00	10.00	13.50	20.00
	1242	—	6.00	10.00	13.50	20.00
	1243	—	6.00	10.00	13.50	20.00
	1244	—	6.00	10.00	13.50	20.00
	1248	—	6.00	10.00	13.50	20.00
	1249	—	6.00	10.00	13.50	20.00
	1250	—	6.00	10.00	13.50	20.00
	1251	—	6.00	10.00	13.50	20.00

NOTE: Ahmadabad Mint was acquired by the British in 1818AD/AH1233 and finally closed in 1835AD. For other issues, see Mughals, Baroda, and Ahmadabad. Symbols as on Ahmadabad State Issues (q.v.), struck in the name of Muhammad Akbar II.

1/15 MOHUR

In the name of Shah Alam II

GOLD, dump, 7-8mm, 0.77 g
Mint: Surat (1800-1815)

KM#	Date	Year	VG	Fine	VF	XF
213	—	46	27.50	45.00	75.00	125.00

Mint: Bombay
Privy mark: Crescent.

KM#	Date	Year	VG	Fine	VF	XF
236	ND(1801-2)	46	60.00	100.00	250.00	350.00

Privy mark #4b

KM#	Date	Year	VG	Fine	VF	XF
237.1	ND(1803-24)	46	27.50	45.00	75.00	125.00

Privy mark #5b

KM#	Date	Year	VG	Fine	VF	XF
237.2	ND(1803-24)	46	27.50	45.00	75.00	125.00

PANCHIA

(1/3 Mohur)

GOLD, dump, 3.86 g
Mint: Surat

KM#	Date	Year	VG	Fine	VF	XF
239	—	46	45.00	75.00	125.00	250.00

Privy mark: Crescent.

KM#	Date	Year	VG	Fine	VF	XF
240	ND(1801-2)	46	90.00	150.00	250.00	375.00

Privy mark: Inverted date.

KM#	Date	Year	VG	Fine	VF	XF
241	1802	46	120.00	200.00	350.00	500.00

Privy mark: Normal crown.

KM#	Date	Year	VG	Fine	VF	XF
243	ND(1803-24)	46	45.00	75.00	125.00	250.00

Privy mark: Inverted crown.

KM#	Date	Year	VG	Fine	VF	XF
245	—	46	45.00	75.00	125.00	250.00

Privy marks: Normal crown and 6 petal rosette.

KM#	Date	Year	VG	Fine	VF	XF
247	ND(1825-31)	46	45.00	75.00	125.00	250.00

Privy marks: Inverted crown and 6 petal rosette.

KM#	Date	Year	VG	Fine	VF	XF
249	—	46	45.00	75.00	125.00	250.00

MOHUR

(15 Rupees)

In the name of Shah Alam II

GOLD, dump, 16-19mm, 11.59 g
Mint: Surat

KM#	Date	Year	VG	Fine	VF	XF
214	ND(1801-15)	46	BV	175.00	250.00	350.00

Mint: Bombay
Privy mark: Crescent.

KM#	Date	Year	VG	Fine	VF	XF
242	ND(1801-02)	46	150.00	250.00	450.00	650.00

Privy mark: Normal crown.

KM#	Date	Year	VG	Fine	VF	XF
244	ND(1803-24)	46	BV	175.00	250.00	350.00

Privy mark: Inverted crown.

KM#	Date	Year	VG	Fine	VF	XF
246	ND(1803-24)	46	BV	175.00	250.00	350.00

Privy marks: Normal crown and 6 petal rosette.

KM#	Date	Year	VG	Fine	VF	XF
248	ND(1825-31)	46	BV	175.00	250.00	350.00

MALABAR COAST

Tellicherry

MINT

Mintname: Mumbai (Bombay)

1/5 RUPEE

KM#	Date	Year	VG	Fine	VF	XF
271	AH1131	1	3.50	7.50	15.00	35.00
269	AH—	2	—	—	—	—

SILVER, dump, 2.32 g

KM#	Date	Year	VG	Fine	VF	XF
277	1805	—	1.00	2.00	5.00	15.00

PAGODA

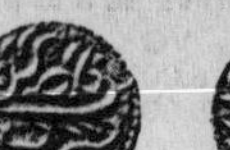

GOLD, dump, 3.00 g

KM#	Date	Year	VG	Fine	VF	XF
278	1809	—	75.00	100.00	250.00	400.00

MADRAS PRESIDENCY

English trade was begun on the east coast of India in 1611. The first factory was at Mazulipatam and was maintained intermittently until modern times.

Madras was founded in 1639 and Fort St. George was made the chief factory on the east coast in 1641. A mint was established at Fort St. George where coins of the style of Vijayanagar were struck.

The Madras mint began minting copper coins after the renovation. In 1689 silver fanams were authorized to be struck by the new Board of Directors.

In 1692 the Mughal Emperor Aurangzeb gave permission for Mughal type rupees to be struck at Madras. These circulated locally and were also sent to Bengal. The chief competition for the Madras coins were the Arcot rupees. Some of the bulk coins from Madras were sent to the Nawabs mint to be made into Arcot rupees. In 1742 the East India Company applied for and received permission to make their own Arcot rupees. Coining operations ceased in Madras in 1869.

MONETARY SYSTEM

1 Dudu = 10 Cash
8 Dudu = 1 Fanam
36 Fanam = 1 Pagoda (1688-1802)
42 Fanam = 1 Pagoda (1802-1817)
45 Fanam = 1 Pagoda (1817-1835)
3-1/2 Rupees = 1 Pagoda

MINTS

Arcot 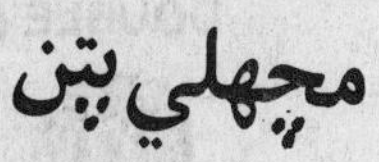

Masulipatnarn (Machilipatnam)

Pagoda Series

CASH

COPPER, 1.10 g
Obv: Bale mark. Rev: Date.

KM#	Date	Mintage	Good	VG	Fine	VF
314	1803	—	1.75	3.00	12.00	50.00

Machine struck, 11.5mm, 0.64 g

KM#	Date	Mintage	Fine	VF	XF	Unc
315	1803	—	.50	2.00	10.00	25.00
	1803	—	—	—	Proof	35.00

NOTE: Similar pieces weighing 1.27 g are modern fantasies. Refer to *Unusual World Coins*, 3rd edition, c.1992.

		SILVER				
315a	1803	—	—	—	Proof	75.00
		GILT GOLD				
315b	1803	—	—	—	Proof	350.00
		GOLD				
315c	1803	—	—	—	Proof	—

1/2 DUDU
(5 Cash)

COPPER, 4.43 g

KM#	Date	Mintage	Good	VG	Fine	VF
305	1802	—	— Reported, not confirmed			
	1804	—	— Reported, not confirmed			

NOTE: Earlier dates (1755-1791) exist for this type.

V (5) CASH

COPPER, 16mm, 1.21 g
Obv: Line of dots above denomination.

KM#	Date	Mintage	VG	Fine	VF	XF
324	ND(1807)	—	4.00	15.00	50.00	175.00

21mm, 3.23 g
Obv: Large lettering.

KM#	Date	Mintage	Fine	VF	XF	Unc
316	1803	—	2.00	4.00	35.00	175.00

Obv: Small lettering.

KM#	Date	Mintage	Fine	VF	XF	Unc
317	1803	—	2.00	4.00	35.00	175.00
		Modified design				
318	1803	—	—	—	Proof	70.00
		SILVER				
318a	1803	—	—	—	Proof	125.00
		GILT GOLD				
318b	1803	—	—	—	Proof	—
		GOLD				
318c	1803	—	—	—	Proof	—

1/4 DUB
(5 Cash)

COPPER, 16.5mm, 2.57 g

KM#	Date	Mintage	VG	Fine	VF	XF
325	ND(1807)	—	25.00	75.00	150.00	250.00

DUDU

COPPER, 6.30 g

KM#	Date	Mintage	Good	VG	Fine	VF
306	1801	—	2.00	5.00	15.00	70.00
	1805	—	2.00	5.00	15.00	70.00
	1806	—	— Reported, not confirmed			

NOTE: Earlier dates (1755-1800) exist for this type.

X (10) CASH

COPPER, 23.5mm, 4.83 g

KM#	Date	Mintage	VG	Fine	VF	XF
326	ND(1807)	—	5.00	20.00	100.00	250.00

NOTE: Seven varieties exist; i.e. dividing lines, dots and star, etc. Also exists struck on a XX Cash planchet.

Heavy issue, 25.8mm, 6.47 g

KM#	Date	Mintage	Fine	VF	XF	Unc
319	1803	—	1.75	6.00	45.00	250.00
	1803	—	—	—	Proof	90.00
	1808	—	1.75	6.00	45.00	250.00
	1808	—	—	—	Proof	90.00
		SILVER				
319a	1808	—	—	—	Proof	150.00
		GILT GOLD				
319b	1808	—	—	—	Proof	600.00
		GOLD				
319c	1808	—	—	—	Proof	—
		COPPER, 25.8mm, 4.66 g				
320	1808	—	1.75	6.00	45.00	250.00
	1808	—	—	—	Proof	90.00

NOTE: Nice salvaged (and cleaned) examples from the Admiral Gardner are very common.

1/2 DUB
(10 Cash)

COPPER, 22.7mm, 5.15 g

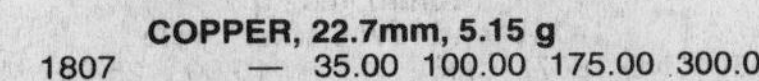

KM#	Date	Mintage	VG	Fine	VF	XF
327	1807	—	35.00	100.00	175.00	300.00

 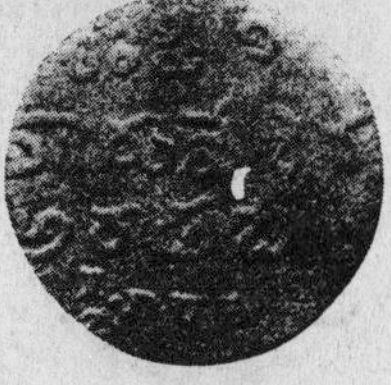

26mm, 4.75 g

KM#	Date	Mintage	Good	VG	Fine	VF
345	1808	—	5.00	10.00	20.00	50.00

XX (20) CASH

COPPER, 26.5mm, 9.65 g

KM#	Date	Mintage	VG	Fine	VF	XF
328	ND(1807)	—	6.50	25.00	125.00	350.00

NOTE: Five varieties exist; i.e. dividing lines, dots and star.

Heavy issue, 30.7mm, 12.95 g

KM#	Date	Mintage	Fine	VF	XF	Unc
321	1803	—	2.50	8.00	60.00	300.00
	1803	—	—	—	Proof	120.00
	1808	—	2.50	8.00	60.00	300.00
	1808	—	—	—	Proof	120.00

NOTE: For 1804 date see Bombay 2 Pice Mule, KM#207.

		SILVER				
321a	1808	—	—	—	Proof	150.00
		GILT GOLD				
321b	1808	—	—	—	Proof	750.00
		GOLD				
321c	1808	—	—	—	Proof	—
		COPPER, 30.7mm, 9.33 g				
322	1808	—	2.00	8.00	60.00	300.00
	1808	—	—	—	Proof	120.00

NOTE: Nice salvaged (and cleaned) examples from the Admiral Gardner exist, trading near XF.

Mule. Obv: KM#321. Rev: 1/48 Rupee, KM#394.

KM#	Date	Mintage	Fine	VF	XF	Unc
323	180x	—	—	—	—	—

DUB
(20 Cash)

COPPER, 27.2mm, 7.56 g

KM#	Date	Mintage	VG	Fine	VF	XF
329	1807	—	15.00	75.00	150.00	200.00
	1808	—	15.00	75.00	150.00	200.00

NOTE: An unusual issue referred to as a 'Regulating Dub'. The translation is 'This and three new Dubs are one small Fanam'.

26.5mm, 10.31 g

KM#	Date	Mintage	Fine	VF	XF	Unc
330	(1807)	—	50.00	125.00	200.00	350.00

26.8mm, 10.00 g

KM#	Date	Mintage	Good	VG	Fine	VF
346	1808	—	7.50	15.00	35.00	75.00

24.3mm, 9.90 g

KM#	Date	Mintage	Good	VG	Fine	VF
347	1808	—	7.50	15.00	35.00	75.00

XL (40) CASH

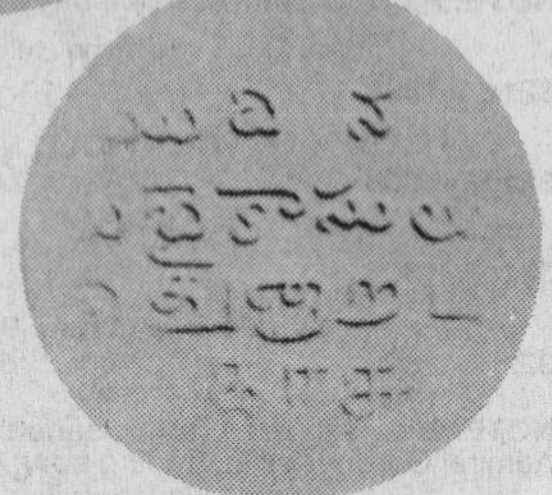

COPPER, 36mm, 19.31 g
Obv: Large Persian legend.
Rev: Large legends.

KM#	Date	Mintage	VG	Fine	VF	XF
331	ND(1807)	—	12.50	50.00	200.00	500.00

Obv: Small Persian legend.
Rev: Small legends.

KM#	Date	Mintage	VG	Fine	VF	XF
332	ND(1807)	—	12.50	50.00	200.00	500.00

Obv: Dots below "XL CASH".

KM#	Date	Mintage	VG	Fine	VF	XF
333	ND(1807)	—	12.50	50.00	200.00	500.00

2 DUBS

(40 Cash)

COPPER, 39.2mm, 20.61 g

KM#	Date	Mintage	VG	Fine	VF	XF
334	ND(1807)	—	50.00	150.00	250.00	600.00

36mm, 19.69 gm.

KM#	Date	Mintage	Good	VG	Fine	VF
348	ND(1808)	—	8.00	20.00	75.00	150.00

FANAM

Reduced weight, 0.91 g
Rev: W/o bead at left and right.

KM#	Date	Mintage	VG	Fine	VF	XF
307	ND(1765-1807)		3.25	8.00	20.00	40.00

10mm, 0.92 g
Obv. and rev: Center circle

KM#	Date	Mintage	VG	Fine	VF	XF
335	ND(1807)	.386	4.00	10.00	25.00	45.00

Obv: W/o center circle.

KM#	Date	Mintage	VG	Fine	VF	XF
336	ND(1807)	I.A.	4.00	10.00	25.00	45.00

Obv: W/o branches below star.

KM#	Date	Mintage	VG	Fine	VF	XF
337	ND(1807)	I.A.	4.00	10.00	25.00	45.00

11-11.5mm

KM#	Date	Mintage	VG	Fine	VF	XF
349	ND(1808)	1.545	1.00	2.00	5.00	12.00

NOTE: Two varieties exist of the buckle at the bottom of the obverse.

DOUBLE (2) FANAM

Reduced weight, 1.83 g

KM#	Date	Mintage	VG	Fine	VF	XF
308	ND(1765-1807)		4.00	10.00	25.00	50.00

12.5mm, 1.85 g
Obv: Center circle. Rev: W/o center circle.

KM#	Date	Mintage	VG	Fine	VF	XF
338	ND(1807)	1.511	2.00	5.00	15.00	35.00

Obv. and rev: W/o center circle.

KM#	Date	Mintage	VG	Fine	VF	XF
339	ND(1807)	I.A.	2.00	5.00	15.00	35.00

Obv. and rev: Center circles.

KM#	Date	Mintage	VG	Fine	VF	XF
340	ND(1807)	I.A.	2.00	5.00	15.00	35.00

Obv: W/o center circle. Rev: W/center circle.

KM#	Date	Mintage	VG	Fine	VF	XF
341	ND(1807)	I.A.	2.00	5.00	15.00	35.00

KM#	Date	Mintage	VG	Fine	VF	XF
350	ND(1808)	6.044	1.50	3.00	9.00	15.00

NOTE: Four varieties exist of the buckle at the bottom of the obverse.

5 FANAMS

SILVER, 17.3mm, 4.65 g

KM#	Date	Mintage	VG	Fine	VF	XF
342	ND(1807)	.988	4.00	10.00	25.00	75.00

21-22mm

KM#	Date	Mintage	VG	Fine	VF	XF
351	ND(1808)	3.954	2.00	5.00	15.00	35.00

NOTE: Eight varieties exist of the buckle at lower left of the obverse.

1/4 PAGODA

GOLD, 0.837 g
Obv: Single diety.

KM#	Date	Mintage	VG	Fine	VF	XF
A280	ND(c.1800)	—	—	—	—	—

SILVER, 27.2mm, 10.58 g

KM#	Date	Mintage	VG	Fine	VF	XF
343	ND(1807)	1.773	13.50	35.00	125.00	300.00

NOTE: Two varieties exist, one with 9 stars to each side of the Gopuram, the other having 13 stars.

25.5mm

KM#	Date	Mintage	VG	Fine	VF	XF
352.1	ND(1808)	7.092	4.00	10.00	25.00	75.00

Obv: Small English lettering.

352.2	ND(1808)	I.A.	4.00	10.00	25.00	75.00

NOTE: Five varieties exist of the buckle at lower left of the obverse.

1/2 PAGODA

.903 SILVER, 36.5mm, 21.17 g

344	ND(1807)	.501	100.00	225.00	550.00	1000.

NOTE: Four varieties exist; 12, 14, 15 or 18 stars in the field at left and right of the Gopuram. KM#344 can be found overstruck on large plugs made from Spanish or Spanish Colonial 8 reales.

35.5mm
Obv: Large English lettering.

353	ND(1808-11)	2.000	35.00	85.00	225.00	400.00

NOTE: KM#353 can be found overstruck on large plugs made from Spanish or Spanish Colonial 8 reales.

Obv: Small English lettering.

KM#	Date	Mintage	VG	Fine	VF	XF
354	ND(1808-11)	I.A.	35.00	85.00	225.00	400.00

NOTE: KM#353 can be found overstruck on large plugs made from Spanish or Spanish Colonial 8 reales.

Obv: Error "HALF PGODA"

355	ND(1808-11)	I.A.	35.00	85.00	225.00	400.00

NOTE: KM#353 can be found overstruck on large plugs made from Spanish or Spanish Colonial 8 reales.

PAGODA

GOLD, 10-11mm
Star Pagoda

303	ND(1740-1807)	—	50.00	125.00	175.00	275.00

12-14mm, 3.43 g
Obv: Three Swami Pagoda

304	ND(1740-1807)	—	50.00	125.00	175.00	275.00

16.9-17.5mm, 2.97 g

KM#	Date	Mintage	Fine	VF	XF	Unc
356	ND(1808-15)	1.382	50.00	125.00	175.00	275.00

2 PAGODAS

GOLD, 20.5-22.0mm, 5.94 g
Obv: 14 stars.

357	ND(1808-15)	1.064	100.00	250.00	425.00	550.00

21.0-22.2mm
Obv: 18 stars.

358.1	ND (1808-15)	Inc. Ab.	100.00	250.00	425.00	550.00

Obv: Small letters.

KM#	Date	Mintage	Fine	VF	XF	Unc
358.2	ND(1808-15)	Inc. Ab.	100.00	250.00	425.00	550.00

TEGNAPATAM

Fort St. David

Rupee Series

1/2 DUB

COPPER, dump, 16mm, 6.60-6.90 g
Obv: Persian *Struck at Machhlipatanbandar*.
Rev: Date, legend.

KM#	Date	Mintage	Good	VG	Fine	VF
385	AH1175-1222	—	5.00	9.00	13.50	20.00

PIE

COPPER

KM#	Date	Year	Mintage	VF	XF	Unc
428	AH1240	1825	4.741	1.00	4.00	15.00
	1240	1825	Inc. Ab.	—	Proof	80.00
	1248	1833	—	10.00	20.00	50.00

DUB

COPPER, dump, 20mm, 13.00-14.00 g
Obv: Persian *Struck at Machhlipatanbandar*.
Rev: Date, legend.

KM#	Date	Mintage	Good	VG	Fine	VF
386	AH1175-1222	—	5.50	11.50	21.50	35.00

Similar to KM#386 but w/English M on rev.

387	AH1218	—	7.50	15.00	22.50	40.00

2 PIES

COPPER

KM#	Date	Year	Mintage	VF	XF	Unc
429	AH1240	1825	7.126	2.00	6.00	20.00
	1240	1825	Inc. Ab.	—	Proof	100.00

4 PIES

COPPER
Rev: Right wreath tip points up.

430	AH1240	1824	7.136	3.00	8.00	25.00
	1240	1824	Inc. Ab.	—	Proof	150.00

Rev: Right wreath tip points down.

431	AH1240	1825	Inc. Ab.	3.00	8.00	25.00
	1240	1825	Inc. Ab.	—	Proof	150.00

Rev: Right wreath tip points up.

432	AH1240	1825	Inc. Ab.	3.00	8.00	25.00

Rev: Right wreath tip in straight line.

433	AH1240	1825	Inc. Ab.	3.00	8.00	25.00

1/16 RUPEE

In the name of Alamgir II

SILVER, 10.5mm
Mint: Madras
(mm: Lotus, 1817-1835)

Oblique milling.

KM#	Date	Year	Fine	VF	XF	Unc
411	AH1172	6	1.00	2.00	10.00	20.00

Mint: Calcutta
(mm: Rose 1823-1825)
Oblique milling

KM#	Date	Year	Fine	VF	XF	Unc
423	AH1172	6	1.00	2.00	8.00	15.00

2 ANNAS

SILVER, 16.4mm, 1.48 g

KM#	Date	Mintage	VG	Fine	VF	XF
405	ND(1808)	.065	100.00	250.00	500.00	650.00

Rev: W/o star.

KM#	Date	Mintage	VG	Fine	VF	XF
406	ND(1808)	I. A.	100.00	250.00	500.00	650.00

1/8 RUPEE

In the name of Alamgir II

SILVER, 16.5mm, 1.51 g
Mint: Calcutta
(mm: Lotus 1807)
Oblique milling

KM#	Date	Mintage	Fine	VF	XF	Unc
399	AH1172//6	.020	15.00	45.00	100.00	175.00

13.5mm, 1.46 g
Mint: Madras
(mm: Lotus 1812-1817)
Oblique milling

KM#	Date	Mintage	Fine	VF	XF	Unc
408	AH1172//6	.104	1.20	2.00	8.00	20.00

(mm: Closed form lotus 1817-1835)
Oblique milling

KM#	Date	Mintage	Fine	VF	XF	Unc
412	AH1172//6	10.790	1.20	2.00	8.00	20.00

Mint: Calcutta
(mm: Rose 1823-1825)
Oblique milling

KM#	Date	Mintage	Fine	VF	XF	Unc
424	AH1172//6	—	1.20	2.00	10.00	20.00

4 ANNAS

SILVER, 17mm, 2.97 g

KM#	Date	Mintage	VG	Fine	VF	XF
407	ND(1808)	.044	125.00	300.00	600.00	750.00

1/4 RUPEE

In the name of Alamgir II

SILVER, 15.5mm, 2.81-2.86 g
Mint: Calcutta
(mm: Lotus 1807)
16.5mm, 3.02 g
Oblique milling.

KM#	Date	Year	Mintage	VF	XF	Unc
400	AH1172	6	.018	25.00	100.00	175.00

SILVER, 17.4mm, 2.91 g
Mint: Madras
(mm: Lotus 1812-1817)
Indented cord milling

KM#	Date	Mintage	Fine	VF	XF	Unc
409	AH1172//6	.784	1.75	3.00	10.00	25.00
	1176//6	Inc. Ab.	1.75	3.00	10.00	25.00

(mm: Closed form lotus 1817-1835)
Indented cord milling.

KM#	Date	Mintage	Fine	VF	XF	Unc
413	AH1172//6	5.227	3.00	5.00	15.00	35.00

Mint: Calcutta
(mm: Rose 1823-1825)
Vertical milling.

KM#	Date	Mintage	Fine	VF	XF	Unc
425	AH1172//6	—	2.50	4.00	10.00	20.00

(mm: Rose, crescent added 1830-1835)
Vertical milling.

KM#	Date	Mintage	Fine	VF	XF	Unc
434	AH1172//6	—	3.00	5.00	25.00	50.00
	1172//6	—	—	—	Proof	300.00

1/2 RUPEE

In the name of Alamgir II

SILVER, 22mm, 6.05 g
Mint: Calcutta, mintname: Madras.
(mm: Lotus 1807). Oblique milling.

KM#	Date	Mintage	Fine	VF	XF	Unc
401	AH1172//6	.108	17.50	30.00	75.00	150.00

21.7mm, 5.83 g
Indented cord milling.

KM#	Date	Mintage	Fine	VF	XF	Unc
402	AH1172//6	3.392	3.00	5.00	15.00	30.00
	1176//6	Inc. Ab.	3.00	5.00	15.00	30.00

Mint: Madras
(mm: Closed formed lotus 1817-1835)
Indented cord milling.

KM#	Date	Mintage	Fine	VF	XF	Unc
414	AH1172//6	10.674	1.75	3.00	15.00	25.00

Mint: Calcutta
(mm: Rose 1823-1825)
Vertical milling

KM#	Date	Mintage	Fine	VF	XF	Unc
426	AH1172//6	—	3.00	5.00	25.00	50.00

(mm: Rose, crescent added 1830-1835)
Vertical milling.

KM#	Date	Mintage	Fine	VF	XF	Unc
435	AH1172//6	—	6.00	10.00	35.00	65.00
	1172//6	—	—	—	Proof	350.00

RUPEE

SILVER, 28mm, 12.1 g
Mint: Madras. (mm: Lotus 1807).
Oblique milling

KM#	Date	Mintage	Fine	VF	XF	Unc
403	AH1172//6	2.145	9.00	15.00	50.00	100.00

27.8mm, 11.66 g
(mm: Lotus 1812-1817)
Indented cord milling

KM#	Date	Mintage	Fine	VF	XF	Unc
410	AH1172//6	10.939	1.75	3.00	10.00	25.00
	1176//6	Inc. Ab.	1.75	3.00	10.00	25.00

(mm: Closed form lotus 1817-1835)
Indented cord milling

KM#	Date	Mintage	Fine	VF	XF	Unc
415	AH1172//6	63.116	1.75	3.00	15.00	25.00

Mint: Calcutta
(mm: Rose 1823-1825)
Vertical milling

KM#	Date	Mintage	Fine	VF	XF	Unc
427	AH1172//6	—	1.75	3.00	20.00	35.00

(mm: Rose, crescent added 1830-1835)
Vertical milling.

KM#	Date	Mintage	Fine	VF	XF	Unc
436	AH1172//6	—	1.75	3.00	20.00	35.00
	1172//6	—	—	—	Proof	400.00

NOTE: Dump rupees in the name of Alamgir, with a small crescent to left of regnal year and mint name "Arcot", were struck by the French (see India-French) as were Arcot rupees in the names of other Mughal emperors.

2 RUPEES

SILVER, 39.5mm, 24.19 g
Mint: Madras. (mm: Lotus 1807).

KM#	Date	Mintage	VG	Fine	VF	XF
404.1	AH1172//2					
		.165	120.00	200.00	350.00	550.00

KM#	Date	Mintage	VG	Fine	VF	XF
404.2	AH1172//6					
		Inc. Ab.	120.00	200.00	350.00	550.00

NOTE: Struck over Spanish or Spanish Colonial 8 Reales.

1/4 MOHUR

GOLD, 17.4mm, 2.91 g
Mint: Madras. (mm: Lotus 1817).

KM#	Date	Mintage	VG	Fine	VF	XF
416	AH1172//6					
		2,000	300.00	500.00	850.00	1250.

GOLD, 17mm
Mint: Madras.

KM#	Date	Mintage	Fine	VF	XF	Unc
419	ND(1819)	.092	125.00	250.00	350.00	600.00

5 RUPEES

GOLD, 19.5mm, 3.88 g

KM#	Date	Mintage	Fine	VF	XF	Unc
422	ND(1820)	2.180	45.00	75.00	125.00	175.00

1/2 MOHUR

GOLD, 21.7mm, 5.83 g
Mint: Madras. (mm: Lotus 1817).

KM#	Date	Mintage	VG	Fine	VF	XF
417	AH1172//6					
		7,500	450.00	750.00	1250.	2000.

GOLD, 21.2mm

KM#	Date	Mintage	Fine	VF	XF	Unc
420	ND(1819)	.213	150.00	350.00	550.00	750.00

MOHUR

GOLD, 27.8mm, 11.66 g
Mint: Madras. (mm: Lotus 1817).

KM#	Date	Mintage	VG	Fine	VF	XF
418	AH1172//6					
		.059	200.00	350.00	750.00	1000.

KM#	Date	Mintage	Fine	VF	XF	Unc
421.1	ND(1819)	1.118	175.00	200.00	425.00	600.00

Obv: Large letters.

KM#	Date	Mintage	Fine	VF	XF	Unc
421.2	ND(1819)	I.A.	175.00	200.00	425.00	600.00

COLONIAL COINAGE

This section lists the coins of British India from reign of William IV (1835) to the reign of George VI (1947). The issues are divided into two main parts:

Coins struck under the authority of the East India Company (E.I.C.) from 1835 until the trading monopoly of the E.I.C. was abolished in 1853. From August 2, 1858 the property and powers of the Company were transferred to the British Crown. From November 1, 1858 to November 1, 1862 the coins continued to bear the design and inscription of the Company.

Coins struck under the authority of the Crown (Regal issues) from 1862 until 1947.

The first regal issues bear the date 1862 and were struck with the date 1862 unchanged until 1874. From then onward all coins bear the year date. The copper coins dated 1862 have not yet been fully attributed and therefore are not listed by the mint of issue.

In 1877 Queen Victoria was proclaimed Empress of India and the title of the obverse legend was changed accordingly.

For a detailed account of the work of the various mints and the numerous die varieties the general collector and specialist should refer to "THE COINS OF THE BRITISH COMMONWEALTH OF NATIONS to the end of the reign of King George VI - 1952", Part 4, India, Vol. 1 and 2, by F. Pridmore, Spink, 1980.

RULERS

British until 1947

MINT MARKS

The coins of British India were struck at the following mints, indicated in the catalogue by either capital letters after the date when the actual letter appears on the coins or small letters in ( ) designating the mint of issue. Plain dates indicate Royal Mint strikes.

B-Bombay, 1835-1947
C or CM-Calcutta, 1835-1947
H - Ralph Heaton & Sons, Birmingham (1857-1858)
I-Bombay, 1918-1919
L-Lahore, 1943-1945
M-Madras, 1869 (closed Sept. 1869)
P-Pretoria, South Africa, 1943-1944
W - J. Watt & Sons, Birmingham (1860)

In 1947 British rule came to an end and India was divided into two self-governing countries, India and Pakistan. In 1971 Bangladash seceded from Pakistan. All are now independent republics and although they are still members of the British Commonwealth of Nations, their coinages do not belong to the British India series.

MONETARY SYSTEM

3 Pies = 1 Pice
4 Pice = 1 Anna
16 Annas = 1 Rupee
15 Rupees = 1 Mohur

The transition from the coins of the Moslem monetary system began with the silver pattern Rupees of William IV, 1834, issued by the East India Company, with the value on the reverse, given in English, Bengali, Persian and Nagari characters. This coinage was struck for several years, as dated, except for the currency Rupee which was struck from 1835 to 1840, all dated 1835.

The portrait coins issued by the East India Company for Victoria show two different head designs on the obverse, which are called Type I and Type II. The coins with Type I head have a continuous obverse legend and were struck from 1840 to 1851. The coins with the Type II head have a divided obverse legend and were struck from 1850 (Calcutta) until 1862. The date on the coins remained unchanged: the Rupee, 1/2 Rupee and 1/4 Rupee are dated 1840, the 2 Annas and the Mohur are dated 1841. Both issues were struck at the Calcutta, Bombay and Madras Mints. Numerous varieties exist in the rupee series of 1840. Noticable differences in the ribbon designs of the English vs. Indian obverses exist.

Type I coins have on the reverse a dot after the date, those of Type II have no dot, except for some rare 1/4 Rupees and 2 Annas. The latter are mules, struck from reverse dies of the preceding issue.

ENGRAVER INITIALS

The following initials appear on the obverse on the truncation:

F - William N. Forbes, Calcutta, 1836-1855
R.S. - Robert Saunders, Calcutta, 1826-1836
S Incuse (Type I)
WW raised or incuse (Type II)
WWS or SWW (Type II)
WWB raised (Type II)

On both issues, the "S" is the initial of Major, later Lt. Col. J. T. Smith, mintmaster at Madras from February 1840 to September 1855.

The 'B' which occurs only on Rupees of Type II, is the initial of Major, later Lt. Col. J. H. Bell (mintmaster at Madras, 1855-1859).

The initials WW which appear on all coins of Type II, are those of William Wyon, Chief Engraver of the Royal Mint, London, who prepared this obverse design in 1849.

Proof and Proof-like restrikes

Original proofs are similar to early English Specimen strikes with wire edges and matte finish busts, arms, etc. Restrikes of most of the coins minted from the period 1835 were regularly supplied until this practice was discontinued on July 1, 1970.

Early proof restrikes are found with slight hairlining from polishing of the old dies. Bust, field, arms etc. are of even smoothness and exhibit a small raised diamond on obverse field behind head.

Modern proof-like (P/L) restrikes are usually heavily hairlined from excessive polishing of the old dies and have a glassy, varnished or proof-like appearance. Many are common while some are quite scarce including some unusual mulings.

East India Company

1/12 ANNA

(1 Pie)

COPPER
Calcutta: 17.5mm; Bombay: 18.0mm; Madras: 17.7-17.9mm

KM#	Date	Mintage	Fine	VF	XF	Unc
445	1835(b)	72.313	1.00	2.50	4.00	8.00
	1835(m)	133.788	.75	2.00	3.00	6.00
	1835(c)	—	—	—	Proof	75.00
	1848(c)	14.380	1.25	3.00	5.00	10.00

1/2 PICE

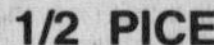

COPPER

KM#	Date	Mintage	Fine	VF	XF	Unc
464	1853(c)	62.408	1.75	3.50	8.00	20.00
	1853(c)	—	—	—	Proof	100.00
	1853(c) (restrike)		—	—	P/L	25.00

1/4 ANNA

COPPER
Obv: Small shield.
Rev. large leg: ONE QUARTER ANNA.

KM#	Date	Mintage	Fine	VF	XF	Unc
446.1	1833(b)	—	—	—	Proof	175.00
	1835(b)	36.767	1.00	2.00	4.00	10.00
	1835(m)	186.530	1.00	2.00	4.00	10.00

NOTE: The 1835 dated coins exist in both medal and coin rotations.

Obv: Small shield.
Rev. small leg: ONE QUARTER ANNA.
Calcutta: 26.2mm; Bombay: 25.2mm; Madras: 25.5mm.

KM#	Date	Mintage	Fine	VF	XF	Unc
446.2	1835(b)	I.A.	1.00	2.00	4.00	10.00
	1835(c)	755.059	1.00	2.00	4.00	10.00
	1835(c)	—	—	—	Proof	75.00
	1835(m)	I.A.	1.00	2.00	4.00	10.00
	1849	—	—	—	Proof	250.00

NOTE: 6 varieties for Madras, 2 varieties for Calcutta.

Obv: Large shield.
Rev: Wreath tips are single leaves.

KM#	Date	Mintage	Fine	VF	XF	Unc
463.1	1857(h)	47.040	1.00	2.00	10.00	45.00
	1858(w)	62.720	.85	1.50	2.50	10.00
	1858(w)	—	—	—	Proof	125.00

Rev: Wreath tips are double leaves.

KM#	Date	Mintage	Fine	VF	XF	Unc
463.2	1857(h)	Inc. Ab.	.85	2.00	10.00	45.00
	1857(h)	—	—	—	Proof	125.00
	1858(h)	172.480	1.00	2.00	4.00	10.00
	1858(h)	—	—	—	Proof	125.00

1/2 ANNA

COPPER
Mule. Obv. Bombay KM#251. Rev: KM#447.

KM#	Date	Mintage	Fine	VF	XF	Unc
	1834	—	—	—	275.00	450.00

Bombay: 29.7mm; Madras: 30.8mm.

KM#	Date	Mintage	Fine	VF	XF	Unc
447.1	1835(b)	8.658	2.00	4.00	10.00	50.00
	1835(b)	—	—	—	Proof	100.00
	1835(b) (restrike)		—	—	P/L	35.00
	1835(m)	95.203	2.00	4.00	10.00	50.00
	1835(m)	—	—	—	Proof	100.00
	1845C	17.160	2.00	4.00	12.50	65.00

Beaded rim w/milled edge.

KM#	Date	Mintage	Fine	VF	XF	Unc
447.2	1835(c)	—	—	—	Proof	300.00

SILVER

KM#	Date	Mintage	Fine	VF	XF	Unc
447.2a	1835(c)	—	—	—	Proof	550.00

2 ANNAS

1.4600 g, .917 SILVER, .0430 oz ASW
Type I: Obv. leg. continuous.
Mint: Bombay, 15.8mm

KM#	Date	Mintage	Fine	VF	XF	Unc
459.1	1841(b)	11.431	2.00	4.00	8.50	20.00

Mint: Calcutta, 15.4-15.5mm
Rev: W/crescent on left ribbon bow.

KM#	Date	Mintage	Fine	VF	XF	Unc
459.2	1841(c)	8.385	2.00	4.00	8.50	20.00
	1841(c) (restrike)	—	—	—	P/L	25.00
	1841(c)	—	—	—	Proof	50.00

Obv: S incuse on truncation, small "v" on right tie of wreath.

KM#	Date	Mintage	Fine	VF	XF	Unc
459.3	1841(m)	10.503	3.50	6.50	12.50	25.00
	1841(b) (restrike)		—	—	P/L	25.00

Type II: Obv. leg. divided.
Rev: Type I, dot after date.

KM#	Date	Mintage	Fine	VF	XF	Unc
460.1	1841.(c)	43.002	7.50	12.50	25.00	50.00
	1841.(c) (early restrike)			—	Proof	150.00

Obv: W.W. raised on truncation.

KM#	Date	Mintage	Fine	VF	XF	Unc
460.2	1841(c)	Inc. Ab.	1.50	3.00	7.50	15.00
	1841(c)	—	—	—	Proof	150.00

Obv: W.W raised on truncation.

KM#	Date	Mintage	Fine	VF	XF	Unc
460.3	1841(b)	8.427	1.50	3.00	7.50	15.00

Obv: S incuse, W.W. raised.

KM#	Date	Mintage	Fine	VF	XF	Unc
460.4	1841(m)	26.930	2.00	4.00	8.50	17.50
	1841(m)	—	—	—	Proof	150.00

Obv: WW raised.

KM#	Date	Mintage	Fine	VF	XF	Unc
460.5	1849	(early restrike)		—	Proof	250.00
	1849	(restrike)	—	—	P/L	25.00

1/4 RUPEE

2.9200 g, .917 SILVER, .0860 oz ASW
Obv: F in relief on truncation.

آنہ

Rev: "*ana*" in Persian:

KM#	Date	Mintage	Fine	VF	XF	Unc
448.1	1835.(c)	.922	3.50	6.50	12.50	30.00
	1835.(c)	—	—	—	Proof	600.00
	1835.(c) (restrike)		—	—	P/L	30.00

Obv: F incuse on truncation.

KM#	Date	Mintage	Fine	VF	XF	Unc
448.2	1835.(c)	Inc. Ab.	4.50	7.50	15.00	40.00
	1835(c)	Inc. Ab.	3.50	6.50	12.50	35.00

Obv: W/o initial on truncation.

KM#	Date	Mintage	Fine	VF	XF	Unc
448.3	1835(b)	5.760	5.00	10.00	20.00	40.00
	1835(b)	—	—	—	Proof	600.00
	1835(b) (early restrike)			—	P/L	30.00

Obv: RS incuse on truncation.

KM#	Date	Mintage	Fine	VF	XF	Unc
448.4	1835(c)	—	5.00	10.00	20.00	40.00

आना

Obv: RS incuse. Rev: "*ana*" in Hindi:

KM#	Date	Mintage	Fine	VF	XF	Unc
448.5	1835(c)	Inc. Ab.	11.50	22.50	45.00	90.00
	1835(c)	—	—	—	Proof	600.00

GOLD

KM#	Date	Mintage	Fine	VF	XF	Unc
448a	1835(c)	—	—	—	—	—

2.9200 g, .917 SILVER, .0860 oz AGW
Type I: Obv. leg. continuous.
Mint: Bombay, 19.7mm
Obv: "Plump" head.

KM#	Date	Mintage	Fine	VF	XF	Unc
453.1	1840(b)	10.617	2.50	5.00	10.00	25.00
	1840(b) (restrike)	—	—	—	P/L	30.00

Mint: Calcutta, 19.5mm.
Rev: W/crescent on left ribbon bow.
First rev: 20 berries.

KM#	Date	Mintage	Fine	VF	XF	Unc
453.2	1840(c)	12.994	2.50	5.00	10.00	20.00
	1840(c)	—	—	—	Proof	200.00

Obv: S incuse on truncation.
Rev: W/v on right ribbon bow.
First rev: S incuse on truncation.

KM#	Date	Mintage	Fine	VF	XF	Unc
453.3	1840(m)	6.450	3.75	7.50	15.00	30.00

Obv: "Indian" head w/thinner features.
Second rev: 34 berries.

KM#	Date	Mintage	Fine	VF	XF	Unc
453.4	1840(c)	Inc. Ab.	2.50	5.00	10.00	20.00
	1840(c)	—	—	—	Proof	200.00

Type II. Obv. leg. divided.
Mule. Rev. KM#453.4.

KM#	Date	Mintage	Fine	VF	XF	Unc
454.1	1840.(c)	32.012	10.00	20.00	40.00	80.00
	1840.(c)	—	—	—	Proof	200.00

Obv: W.W. raised on truncation.

KM#	Date	Mintage	Fine	VF	XF	Unc
454.2	1840(c)	Inc. Ab.	2.50	5.00	10.00	20.00
	1840(c)	—	—	—	Proof	200.00

Obv: W.W. and B raised on truncation.

KM#	Date	Mintage	Fine	VF	XF	Unc
454.3	1840(m)	13.664	4.00	6.00	12.00	30.00

Obv: W.W. S raised on truncation.

KM#	Date	Mintage	Fine	VF	XF	Unc
454.4	1840(m)	Inc. Ab.	4.00	8.00	15.00	30.00

Obv: W.W. on truncation. Plain edge.

KM#	Date	Mintage	Fine	VF	XF	Unc
454.5	1849	(early restrike)		—	Proof	300.00
	1849	(restrike)	—	—	P/L	45.00

Milled edge.

KM#	Date	Mintage	Fine	VF	XF	Unc
454.6	1849	(early restrike)		—	Proof	300.00
	1849	(restrike)	—	—	P/L	45.00

1/2 RUPEE

5.8300 g, .917 SILVER, .1719 oz ASW
Obv: W/o initial on truncation.

KM#	Date	Mintage	Fine	VF	XF	Unc
449.1	1835.(b)	3.573	7.50	15.00	30.00	60.00
	1835.(b)(restrike)		—	—	P/L	60.00

Obv: F raised on truncation.

KM#	Date	Mintage	Fine	VF	XF	Unc
449.2	1835.(c)	6.700	7.50	15.00	30.00	60.00
	1835(c) (restrike)		—	—	P/L	60.00

Obv: F incuse.

KM#	Date	Mintage	Fine	VF	XF	Unc
449.3	1835.(c)	—	7.50	15.00	30.00	60.00
	1835.(c) (early restrike)			—	Proof	250.00

Obv: RS incuse.

KM#	Date	Mintage	Fine	VF	XF	Unc
449.4	1835.(c)	.521	10.00	20.00	40.00	80.00
	1835.(c)	—	—	—	Proof	700.00

GOLD

KM#	Date	Mintage	Fine	VF	XF	Unc
449a	1835(c)	—	—	—	—	—

5.8300 g, .917 SILVER, .1719 oz ASW
Type I: Obv. leg. continuous.
Mint: Bombay, 24.5-24.6mm
Obv: "Plump" head.

KM#	Date	Mintage	Fine	VF	XF	Unc
455.1	1840.(b)	9.844	5.00	10.00	20.00	45.00
	1840.(b) (restrike)		—	—	P/L	35.00
Mint: Calcutta: 24.2-24.4mm Rev: W/crescent on left ribbon bow.						
455.2	1840.(c)	8.049	5.00	10.00	20.00	45.00
	1840.(c)		—	—	Proof	250.00
	1840.(c)(restrike)		—	—	P/L	35.00
Obv: S incuse on truncation.						
455.3	1840.(m)	1.874	—	—	Rare	—
Obv: "Indian" head w/thinner features. Rev: W/mm, crescent, on left ribbon bow.						
455.4	1840.(c)	I.A.	5.00	10.00	20.00	45.00
	1840.(c)	I.A.	—	—	Proof	250.00
	1840.(c) (restrike)		—	—	P/L	35.00
Mule. Obv: KM#455.1. Rev: KM#456.1.						
A455	1840(c)	—	4.50	8.50	17.50	40.00

Type II: Obv. leg. divided.
Obv: .W.W incuse.

KM#	Date	Mintage	Fine	VF	XF	Unc
456.1	1840(b & c)	18.551	4.00	8.00	15.00	35.00
Obv: W.W. incuse and S.						
456.2	1840(m)	2.507	5.00	10.00	20.00	40.00
Obv:. W.W incuse. Milled edge.						
456.3	1849 (early restrike)			—	Proof	400.00
	1849 (restrike)		—	—	P/L	50.00
Plain edge.						
456.4	1849 (early restrike)			—	Proof	400.00
	1849 (restrike)		—	—	P/L	50.00
Mule. Obv: KM#456.1. Rev: KM#455.4.						
A456	1840.	—	4.50	8.50	17.50	40.00

RUPEE

11.6600 g, .917 SILVER, .3438 oz ASW
Obv. leg: Thick lettering. W/o initial on truncation.

KM#	Date	Mintage	Fine	VF	XF	Unc
450.1	1835.(b)	53.713	8.50	12.50	25.00	50.00
	1835.(b)	—	—	—	Proof	500.00
	1835.(b) (restrike)	—	—	—	P/L	40.00
Obv: F raised on truncation.						
450.2	1835.(c)	—	8.50	15.00	30.00	60.00
	1835.(c)	—	—	—	Proof	500.00
	1835.(c)	—	—	—	P/L	60.00
Obv: F incuse on truncation.						
450.3	1835.(c)	—	8.50	15.00	30.00	60.00
	1835.(c)	—	—	—	Proof	750.00
	1835.(c) (restrike)		—	—	P/L	60.00
Obv: RS incuse on truncation.						
450.4	1835.(c)	15.759	10.00	20.00	40.00	85.00
	1835.(c)	—	—	—	Proof	750.00

KM#	Date	Mintage	Fine	VF	XF	Unc
450.5	1840/35.(c)	—	90.00	175.00	300.00	600.00
450.6	1835.(c)	—	—	—	Rare	—

KM#	Date	Mintage	Fine	VF	XF	Unc
Obv. leg: Thin lettering. RS incuse on truncation.						
450.7	1835.(c)	—	35.00	60.00	100.00	250.00
GOLD						
450a	1835.(c)	—	—	—	—	—

11.6600 g, .917 SILVER, .3438 oz ASW
Type I: Obv. leg. continuous.

The major reverse varieties occur on the Type I Rupees of all three mints. The first reverse has 19 berries in the wreath, the second reverse has 34 and 35 berries (Calcutta) and 35 berries (Bombay and Madras). There are several minor varieties of the first reverse, but these are not listed. Madras specimens of Type I with the 1st reverse also have a small, raised "V" on the lower part of the right ribbon bow.

Mint: Calcutta, 1st rev. 31.5mm, 2nd rev. 31.1-31.3mm
Obv: "Plump" head.
Rev: 19 berries w/crescent on left ribbon bow.

KM#	Date	Mintage	Fine	VF	XF	Unc
457.1	1840.(c)	179.935	6.00	10.00	17.50	40.00
	1840.(c)	—	—	—	Proof	325.00
Mint: Bombay, 31.6-31.8mm Rev: 35 berries.						
457.2	1840.(b)	109.838	7.00	10.00	17.50	40.00
Rev: 19 berries, small diamonds.						
457.3	1840.(b)	I.A.	7.00	10.00	17.50	40.00
Rev: 19 berries, large diamonds.						
457.4	1840.(b)	I.A.	7.00	10.00	17.50	40.00
Mint: Madras, 31.9-32.2mm Obv: S incuse on truncation. Rev: 19 berries, small diamonds, w/V on right ribbon bow.						
457.5	1840.(m)	21.898	9.00	18.50	37.50	75.00
Rev: 19 berries, large diamonds.						
457.6	1840.(m)	I.A.	9.00	18.50	37.50	75.00
Obv: W/o S. Rev: 19 berries, w/v on left ribbon bow.						
457.7	1840.(m)	I.A.	9.00	18.50	37.50	75.00
Obv: S incuse. Rev: 20 berries, w/o small v.						
457.8	1840.(m)	I.A.	8.00	12.50	20.00	40.00
Obv: S incuse. Rev: 35 berries, w/o small v.						
457.9	1840.(m)	I.A.	10.00	15.00	30.00	60.00
Obv: "Indian" head w/thinner features. Rev: 35 berries w/crescent on left ribbon bow.						
457.10	1840.(c)	I.A.	9.00	18.50	37.50	75.00
	1840.(c)	—	—	—	Proof	350.00
Rev: 34 berries.						
457.11	1840.(c)	—	—	—	Proof	350.00
Rev: 34 berries , small "m" on left ribbon end, dot after date.						
457.12	1840.(m)	—	—	—	—	—

Type II: Obv. leg. divided.
Mint: Calcutta, 30.5mm.

KM#	Date	Mintage	Fine	VF	XF	Unc
Obv: W.W. raised. Rev: 28 berries, small diamonds.						
458.1	1840(c)	398.554	2.50	5.00	10.00	20.00
Obv: W.W. raised. Rev: 28 berries, large diamonds.						
458.2	1840(c)	Inc. Ab.	2.50	5.00	10.00	20.00
Mint: Bombay, 30.8mm Obv: W.W. raised. Rev: 27 berries.						
458.3	1840(b)	312.598	2.50	5.00	10.00	20.00
	1840(b)	—	—	—	Proof	325.00
Obv: W.W.B raised, small B. Rev: 28 berries.						
458.4	1840(m)	55.049	2.50	5.00	10.00	20.00
Obv: W.W.B raised, large B. Rev: 28 berries.						
458.5	1840(m)	I.A.	2.50	5.00	10.00	20.00
Obv: W.W.B raised, small letters. Rev: 28 berries.						
458.6	1840(m)	I.A.	2.50	5.00	10.00	20.00
Obv: W.W.S raised. Rev: 28 berries.						
458.7	1840(m)	—	2.50	5.00	10.00	20.00

Obv: W.W. Rev: 25 berries.
Milled edge.

KM#	Date	Mintage	Fine	VF	XF	Unc
458.8	1849 (early restrike)			—	Proof	500.00
	1849 (restrike)		—	—	P/L	100.00
Plain edge						
458.9	1849 (early restrike)			—	Proof	500.00
	1849 (restrike)		—	—	P/L	100.00
Mule. Obv: KM#458.1. Rev: 25 berries.						
458.10	1840		—	—	Rare	—
COPPER Obv: W.W.B						
458a	1840(m)	—	—	—	Rare	—

MOHUR

11.6600 g, .917 GOLD, .3437 oz AGW
Obv: W/o initials.
Milled edge.

KM#	Date	Mintage	Fine	VF	XF	Unc
451.1	1835(b)	—	200.00	350.00	500.00	850.00
	1835(b) (restrike)		—	—	P/L	275.00
Obv: RS incuse on truncation.						
451.2	1835(c)	.029	275.00	450.00	650.00	1000.
	1835(c)	—	—	—	Proof	—
	1835(c) (restrike)		—	—	P/L	400.00
Obv: F incuse on truncation.						
451.3	1835(c)	.111	250.00	375.00	500.00	800.00
	1835(c) (restrike)		—	—	P/L	500.00
Plain edge. Obv: RS incuse on truncation.						
451.4	1835(c)	—	—	—	Proof	Rare
Obv: F incuse on truncation.						
451.5	1835(c)	—	—	—	Proof	Rare
SILVER						
451a	1835(c)	—	—	—	Proof	Rare
COPPER						
451b	1835(c)	—	—	—	Proof	650.00

11.6600 g, .917 GOLD, .3437 oz AGW
Type I: Obv. leg. continuous.
Obv: Dot on truncation.

KM#	Date	Mintage	Fine	VF	XF	Unc
461.1	1841.(b)	5,960	—	—	650.00	1000.
461.2	1841.(c)	.601	175.00	225.00	300.00	400.00
	1841.(c)	—	—	—	Proof	1500.
Obv: S incuse on truncation.						
461.3	1841.(m)	.032	250.00	325.00	450.00	600.00
	1841.(m)	—	—	—	Proof	1500.

Type II. Obv. leg. divided.

Lg. date normal 4 Lg. date crosslet 4

KM#	Date	Mintage	Fine	VF	XF	Unc
Obv: W.W. incuse; lg. leg. and lg. date w/normal 4.						
462.1	1841.(c)	.442	150.00	200.00	300.00	400.00
	1841.(c) (restrike)		—	—	P/L	450.00
Obv: W.W. incuse; lg. leg. and lg. date w/crosslet 4.						
462.2	1841.(c)	—	175.00	225.00	300.00	400.00

Small date

Obv: W.W. incuse; sm. leg. and sm. date w/normal 4.

KM#	Date	Mintage	Fine	VF	XF	Unc
462.3	1841.	—	200.00	325.00	450.00	600.00

Mule. Obv: KM#462. Rev: KM#451.

KM#	Date	Mintage	Fine	VF	XF	Unc
A462	1841.(c) (restrike)		—	—	P/L	450.00

2 MOHURS

23.3200 g, .917 GOLD, .6873 oz AGW
RS incuse on truncation.

Milled edge.

KM#	Date	Mintage	Fine	VF	XF	Unc
452.1	1835.(c)	1,170	850.00	1250.	1750.	3000.
	1835.(c)	—	—	—	Proof	3500.
	1835.(c) (restrike)		—	—	P/L	1350.

Plain edge.

KM#	Date	Mintage	Fine	VF	XF	Unc
452.2	1835.(c)	—	—	—	Rare	—

SILVER

KM#	Date	Mintage	Fine	VF	XF	Unc
452a	1835.(c)	—	—	—	Proof	1500.

COPPER

KM#	Date	Mintage	Fine	VF	XF	Unc
452b	1835.(c)	—	—	—	Proof	750.00

REGAL COINAGE

1/12 ANNA

NOTE: The coins dated 1862 were struck at Calcutta, Bombay and Madras but have not yet been attributed to the mint of issue.

Calcutta Mint issues 1874-76 are 17.3mm in diameter. From 1877 the coins have a diameter of 17.5mm and the obverse legend at the lower right is distant from the bust. The issues dated 1882 and 1886 have a small incuse "C" on a bead of the circle below the date. Bombay issues 1874-76 have a diameter of 17.9mm. From 1877 the obverse legend at the lower right is close to the bust.

COPPER

KM#	Date	Mintage	Fine	VF	XF	Unc
465	1862(c) 17.4-17.5mm	2.502	1.25	2.50	5.00	10.00
	1862(b) 17.9-18.0mm	2.999	1.25	2.50	5.00	10.00
	1862(m) 17.6-17.7mm	40.487	.75	1.25	2.50	7.50
	1862(c)	—	—	—	Proof	50.00
	1862(c) (restrike)		—	—	P/L	35.00
	1874(c)	4.819	1.25	2.50	5.00	10.00
	1874(b)	2.960	1.25	2.50	5.00	10.00
	1875(c)	4.646	1.25	2.50	5.00	10.00
	1875(c)	—	—	—	Proof	65.00
	1875(b)	3.068	1.25	2.50	5.00	10.00
	1876(c)	20.318	1.00	1.50	2.50	7.50
	1876(b)	Inc. 1875(b)	1.25	2.50	5.00	10.00

GOLD

KM#	Date	Mintage	Fine	VF	XF	Unc
465b	1862(c) (restrike)		—	—	P/L	250.00

COPPER

KM#	Date	Mintage	Fine	VF	XF	Unc
483	1877(b)	1.551	.50	1.00	2.50	6.00
	1877(b)	—	—	—	Proof	50.00
	1877(c)	5.880	.50	1.00	2.50	6.00
	1877(c)	—	—	—	Proof	50.00
	1877(c) (restrike)		—	—	P/L	25.00
	1878(c)	5.525	.50	1.00	2.50	6.00
	1878(c)	—	—	—	Proof	50.00
	1881(b)	2.954	.50	1.00	2.50	6.00
	1882(c)	4.344	.50	1.00	2.00	5.00
	1883(c)	9.840	.50	1.00	2.00	5.00
	1883(b)	4.794	.35	.75	1.75	4.00
	1883(b)	—	—	—	Proof	50.00
	1884(b)	8.074	.50	1.00	2.50	6.00
	1884(b)	—	—	—	Proof	50.00
	1885(c)	4.783	.50	1.00	2.00	5.00
	1886(c)	18.663	.35	.75	1.75	4.00
	1886(b)	5.783	.50	1.00	2.50	6.00
	1886(b)	—	—	—	Proof	50.00
	1887(c)	8.724	.50	1.00	2.00	5.00
	1887(b)	8.242	.50	1.00	2.50	6.00
	1888(c)	4.662	.50	1.00	2.00	5.00
	1888(b)	2.143	.50	1.00	2.50	6.00
	1889(c)	7.602	.50	1.00	2.00	5.00
	1889(b)	5.660	.50	1.00	2.50	6.00
	1890(b)	—	—	—	Proof	50.00
	1890(c)	21.732	.35	.75	1.75	4.00
	1890 (restrike)		—	—	P/L	20.00
	1891(c)	17.306	.35	.75	1.75	4.00
	1891(c)	—	—	—	Proof	50.00
	1891(c) (restrike)		—	—	P/L	20.00
	1892(c)	13.793	.35	.75	1.75	4.00
	1892(c)	—	—	—	Proof	50.00
	1892(c) (restrike)		—	—	P/L	20.00
	1893(c)	10.034	.35	.75	1.75	4.00
	1893(c)	—	—	—	Proof	50.00
	1893(b) (restrike)		—	—	P/L	20.00
	1894(c)	18.392	.35	.75	1.75	4.00
	1894(c)	—	—	—	Proof	50.00
	1894(c) (restrike)		—	—	P/L	20.00
	1895(c)	15.208	.35	.75	1.75	4.00
	1895(c)	—	—	—	Proof	50.00
	1896(c)	.922	.50	1.25	2.50	6.00
	1896(c)	—	—	—	Proof	50.00
	1896(c) (restrike)		—	—	P/L	20.00
	1897(c)	20.822	.35	.75	1.75	4.00
	1897(c)	—	—	—	Proof	50.00
	1897(c) (restrike)		—	—	P/L	20.00
	1898(c)	13.882	.35	.75	1.75	4.00
	1898(c)	—	—	—	Proof	50.00
	1898(c) (restrike)		—	—	P/L	20.00
	1899(c)	10.056	.35	.75	1.75	4.50
	1899(c)	—	—	—	Proof	50.00
	1899(c) (restrike)		—	—	P/L	20.00
	1901(c)	21.345	.35	.75	1.75	4.00
	1901(c)	—	—	—	Proof	50.00
	1901(c) (restrike)		—	—	P/L	20.00

NOTE: On come Calcutta issues between 1882-1886 a small 'c' can be found on one of the beads of the inner circle on the rev.

ALUMINUM

KM#	Date	Mintage	Fine	VF	XF	Unc
483a	1891(b)	—	—	—	Proof	100.00

SILVER

KM#	Date	Mintage	Fine	VF	XF	Unc
483b	1892(c) (restrike)		—	—	P/L	75.00
	1893(c) (restrike)		—	—	P/L	75.00
	1894(c) (restrike)		—	—	P/L	75.00
	1895(c) (restrike)		—	—	P/L	75.00
	1896(c) (restrike)		—	—	P/L	75.00
	1897(c) (restrike)		—	—	P/L	75.00
	1898(c) (restrike)		—	—	P/L	75.00
	1899(c) (restrike)		—	—	P/L	75.00
	1901(c) (restrike)		—	—	P/L	75.00

GOLD

KM#	Date	Mintage	Fine	VF	XF	Unc
483c	1891(c) (restrike)		—	—	P/L	250.00
	1892(c) (restrike)		—	—	P/L	250.00
	1893(c) (restrike)		—	—	P/L	250.00
	1895(c) (restrike)		—	—	P/L	250.00
	1896(c) (restrike)		—	—	P/L	250.00
	1897(c) (restrike)		—	—	P/L	250.00
	1898(c) (restrike)		—	—	P/L	250.00
	1899(c) (restrike)		—	—	P/L	250.00
	1901(c) (restrike)		—	—	P/L	250.00

COPPER
Thick planchets

KM#	Date	Mintage	Fine	VF	XF	Unc
497	1903(c)	7.883	.35	1.25	6.00	15.00
	1903(c)	—	—	—	Proof	60.00
	1903(c) (restrike)		—	—	P/L	20.00
	1904(c)	16.506	.25	1.00	4.00	12.00
	1904(c)	—	—	—	Proof	60.00
	1904(c) (restrike)		—	—	P/L	20.00
	1905(c)	13.060	.25	1.00	4.00	12.00
	1905(c) (restrike)		—	—	P/L	20.00
	1906(c)	9.072	.25	1.00	4.00	12.00
	1906(c)	—	—	—	Proof	60.00
	1906(c) (restrike)		—	—	P/L	20.00

SILVER

KM#	Date	Mintage	Fine	VF	XF	Unc
497a	1904(c) (restrike)		—	—	P/L	75.00
	1905(c) (restrike)		—	—	P/L	75.00

BRONZE
Thin planchets

KM#	Date	Mintage	Fine	VF	XF	Unc
498	1906(c)	2.184	.35	.75	5.00	15.00
	1906(c)	—	—	—	Proof	50.00
	1907(c)	20.985	.25	.50	3.00	9.00
	1907(c)	—	—	—	Proof	50.00
	1907(c) (restrike)		—	—	P/L	20.00
	1908(c)	22.036	.25	.50	3.00	9.00
	1908(c)	—	—	—	Proof	50.00
	1908(c) (restrike)		—	—	P/L	20.00
	1909(c)	12.316	.25	.50	3.00	9.00
	1909(c) (restrike)		—	—	P/L	20.00
	1910(c)	23.520	.25	.50	3.00	9.00
	1910(c) (restrike)		—	—	P/L	20.00

ALUMINUM

KM#	Date	Mintage	Fine	VF	XF	Unc
498a	1909(c)	—	—	—	Proof	75.00

BRONZE

NOTE: Calcutta Mint issues have no mint mark. Bombay Mint issues have a small raised bead or dot below the center of the date.

KM#	Date	Mintage	Fine	VF	XF	Unc
509	1912(c)	—	.50	.75	1.50	4.50
	1912(c)	—	—	—	Proof	50.00
	1912(c) (restrike)		—	—	P/L	20.00
	1913(c)	25.937	.25	.50	1.00	3.00
	1913(c)	—	—	—	Proof	40.00
	1913(c) (restrike)		—	—	P/L	20.00
	1914(c)	29.184	.25	.50	.75	1.50
	1914(c)	—	—	—	Proof	40.00
	1914(c) (restrike)		—	—	P/L	20.00
	1915(c)	20.563	.25	.50	.75	1.50
	1915(c)	—	—	—	Proof	40.00
	1915(c) (restrike)		—	—	P/L	20.00
	1916(c)	12.230	.25	.50	.75	1.50
	1916(c)	—	—	—	Proof	40.00
	1916(c) (restrike)		—	—	P/L	20.00
	1917(c)	26.880	.25	.50	.75	1.50
	1917(c)	—	—	—	Proof	40.00
	1917(c) (restrike)		—	—	P/L	20.00
	1918(c)	29.088	.25	.50	.75	1.50
	1918(c)	—	—	—	Proof	40.00
	1918(c) (restrike)		—	—	P/L	20.00
	1919(c)	20.686	.25	.50	.75	1.50
	1919(c)	—	—	—	Proof	40.00
	1919(c) (restrike)		—	—	P/L	20.00
	1920(c)	42.221	.25	.50	.75	1.50
	1920(c)	—	—	—	Proof	40.00
	1920(c) (restrike)		—	—	P/L	20.00
	1921(c)	19.334	.25	.50	.75	1.50
	1921(c)	—	—	—	Proof	40.00
	1921(c) (restrike)		—	—	P/L	20.00
	1923(c)	6.662	.25	.50	.75	1.50
	1923(c)	—	—	—	Proof	40.00
	1923(b)	4.877	.25	.50	.75	1.50
	1923(b)	—	—	—	Proof	40.00
	1923(b) (restrike)		—	—	P/L	20.00
	1924(c)	2.515	.25	.50	.75	1.50
	1924(c)	—	—	—	Proof	40.00
	1924(b)	11.711	.25	.50	.75	1.50
	1924(b)	—	—	—	Proof	40.00
	1924(b) (restrike)		—	—	P/L	20.00
	1925(c)	6.106	.25	.50	.75	1.50
	1925(c)	—	—	—	Proof	40.00
	1925(b)	5.871	.25	.50	.75	1.50
	1925(b)	—	—	—	Proof	40.00
	1925(b) (restrike)		—	—	P/L	20.00
	1926(c)	4.147	.25	.50	.75	1.50
	1926(c)	—	—	—	Proof	40.00
	1926(b)	18.406	.25	.50	.75	1.50
	1926(b)	—	—	—	Proof	40.00
	1926(b) (restrike)		—	—	P/L	20.00
	1927(c)	2.880	.25	.50	.75	1.50
	1927(c)	—	—	—	Proof	40.00
	1927(b)	4.846	.25	.50	.75	1.50
	1927(b)	—	—	—	Proof	40.00
	1927(b) (restrike)		—	—	P/L	20.00
	1928(c)	11.846	.25	.50	.75	1.50
	1928(c)	—	—	—	Proof	40.00
	1928(b)	8.077	.25	.50	.75	1.50
	1928(b)	—	—	—	Proof	40.00
	1928 (restrike)		—	—	P/L	20.00
	1929(c)	15.130	.25	.50	.75	1.50
	1929(c)	—	—	—	Proof	40.00
	1929(c) (restrike)		—	—	P/L	20.00
	1930(c)	13.498	.25	.50	.75	1.50
	1930(c)	—	—	—	Proof	40.00
	1930(c) (restrike)		—	—	P/L	20.00
	1931(c)	18.278	.25	.50	.75	1.50
	1931(c)	—	—	—	Proof	40.00
	1931(c) (restrike)		—	—	P/L	20.00
	1932(c)	23.213	.25	.50	.75	1.50
	1932(c)	—	—	—	Proof	40.00
	1932(c) (restrike)		—	—	P/L	20.00
	1933(c)	16.896	.25	.50	.75	1.50
	1933(c)	—	—	—	Proof	40.00
	1933(c) (restrike)		—	—	P/L	20.00
	1934(c)	17.146	.25	.50	.75	1.50
	1934(c)	—	—	—	Proof	40.00
	1934(c) (restrike)		—	—	P/L	20.00
	1935(c)	19.142	.25	.50	.75	1.50
	1935(c)	—	—	—	Proof	40.00
	1935(c) (restrike)		—	—	P/L	20.00
	1936(c)	23.213	.25	.50	.75	1.50
	1936(b)	12.887	.25	.50	.75	1.50
	1936(b) (restrike)		—	—	P/L	20.00

First head

NOTE: Calcutta Mint issues have no mint mark. Bombay Mint issues have a small dot below the date except for those dated 1942 which have a dot on either side of ANNA and the date, and one dot after "INDIA".

KM#	Date	Mintage	Fine	VF	XF	Unc
526	1938(c)	—	—	—	Proof	35.00

KM#	Date	Mintage	Fine	VF	XF	Unc
526	1939(c)	3.571	.25	.50	1.00	2.50
	1939(b)	17.407	.25	.50	1.00	2.50

Second head

KM#	Date	Mintage	Fine	VF	XF	Unc
527	1938(c) (restrike)		—	—	P/L	20.00
	1939(c)	5.245	.25	.50	1.00	2.50
	1939(c)	—	—	—	Proof	35.00
	1939(b)	31.306	.25	.50	1.00	2.00
	1939(b)	—	—	—	Proof	35.00
	1939(b) (restrike)		—	—	P/L	20.00
	1941(b)	6.137	.25	.50	.75	1.50
	1942(b)	6.124	1.00	2.25	3.50	7.00
	1942(b)	—	—	—	Proof	35.00
	1942(b) (restrike)		—	—	P/L	20.00

1/2 PICE

NOTE: The 1/2 Pice dated 1862 was struck at all three Indian Government Mints i.e. Calcutta, Bombay and Madras but a correct attribution to the mint of issue has not yet been possible. Two different busts and two reverses have been noted so far.

COPPER

KM#	Date	Mintage	Fine	VF	XF	Unc
466	1862(c) (21.25mm)	96.843	1.25	2.50	5.00	15.00
	1862(m) (21.4mm)	6.400	1.50	3.50	6.50	20.00
	1862(c)	—	—	—	Proof	50.00
	1862(c) (restrike)		—	—	P/L	25.00
	1875(c)	—	—	—	Proof	75.00
	1875(c) (restrike)		—	—	P/L	25.00

GOLD

KM#	Date	Mintage	Fine	VF	XF	Unc
466b	1862(c)	—	—	—	Proof	250.00

COPPER

KM#	Date	Mintage	Fine	VF	XF	Unc
484	1877(c)	—	—	—	Proof	75.00
	1877(c) (restrike)		—	—	P/L	25.00
	1878(c)	—	—	—	Proof	75.00
	1885(c)	6.206	1.25	2.50	4.00	10.00
	1886(c)	7.733	1.25	2.50	4.00	10.00
	1887(c)	6.464	1.25	2.50	4.00	10.00
	1888(c)	3.190	1.25	2.50	4.00	10.00
	1889(c)	7.587	1.25	2.50	4.00	10.00
	1890(c)	3.504	1.25	2.50	4.00	10.00
	1890(c)	—	—	—	Proof	50.00
	1890(c) (restrike)		—	—	P/L	20.00
	1891(c)	5.139	1.25	2.50	4.00	10.00
	1891(c)	—	—	—	Proof	50.00
	1891(c) (restrike)		—	—	P/L	20.00
	1892(c)	4.774	1.25	2.50	4.00	10.00
	1892(c)	—	—	—	Proof	50.00
	1892(c) (restrike)		—	—	P/L	20.00
	1893(c)	7.005	1.25	2.50	4.00	10.00
	1893(c)	—	—	—	Proof	50.00
	1893(c) (restrike)		—	—	P/L	20.00
	1894(c)	7.777	1.25	2.50	4.00	10.00
	1894(c)	—	—	—	Proof	50.00
	1894(c) (restrike)		—	—	P/L	20.00
	1895(c)	9.874	1.00	1.75	3.50	8.50
	1895(c)	—	—	—	Proof	50.00
	1896(c)	6.113	1.25	2.50	4.00	10.00
	1896(c)	—	—	—	Proof	50.00
	1897(c)	8.484	1.25	2.50	4.00	10.00
	1897(c)	—	—	—	Proof	35.00
	1897(c) (restrike)		—	—	P/L	20.00
	1898(c)	12.940	1.00	1.75	3.50	8.50
	1898(c)	—	—	—	Proof	50.00
	1898(c) (restrike)		—	—	P/L	20.00
	1899(c)	7.936	1.25	2.50	4.00	10.00
	1899(c)	—	—	—	Proof	50.00
	1899(c) (restrike)		—	—	P/L	20.00
	1900(c)	5.219	1.25	2.50	4.00	10.00
	1900(c) (restrike)		—	—	P/L	20.00
	1901(c)	16.057	1.00	1.75	3.50	8.50
	1901(c)	Inc. Ab.	—	—	Proof	50.00
	1901(c) (restrike)		—	—	P/L	20.00

ALUMINUM

KM#	Date	Mintage	Fine	VF	XF	Unc
484a	1891(b)	—	—	—	Proof	85.00

SILVER

KM#	Date	Mintage	Fine	VF	XF	Unc
484b	1892(c) (restrike)		—	—	P/L	75.00
	1893(c) (restrike)		—	—	P/L	75.00
	1894(c) (restrike)		—	—	P/L	75.00
	1895(c) (restrike)		—	—	P/L	75.00
	1896(c) (restrike)		—	—	P/L	75.00
484b	1897(c) (restrike)		—	—	P/L	75.00
	1898(c) (restrike)		—	—	P/L	75.00
	1899(c) (restrike)		—	—	P/L	75.00
	1900(c) (restrike)		—	—	P/L	75.00
	1901(c) (restrike)		—	—	P/L	75.00

GOLD

KM#	Date	Mintage	Fine	VF	XF	Unc
484c	1891(c) (restrike)		—	—	P/L	450.00
	1892(c) (restrike)		—	—	P/L	450.00
	1893(c) (restrike)		—	—	P/L	450.00
	1895(c) (restrike)		—	—	P/L	450.00
	1896(c) (restrike)		—	—	P/L	450.00
	1897(c) (restrike)		—	—	P/L	450.00
	1898(c) (restrike)		—	—	P/L	450.00
	1899(c) (restrike)		—	—	P/L	450.00
	1901(c) (restrike)		—	—	P/L	450.00

COPPER

KM#	Date	Mintage	Fine	VF	XF	Unc
499	1903(c)	5.376	.75	1.50	5.00	15.00
	1903(c)	—	—	—	Proof	45.00
	1903(c) (restrike)		—	—	P/L	20.00
	1904(c)	8.464	.75	1.50	5.00	15.00
	1904(c)	—	—	—	Proof	45.00
	1904(c) (restrike)		—	—	P/L	20.00
	1905(c)	—	.75	1.50	5.00	15.00
	1905(c) (restrike)		—	—	P/L	20.00
	1906(c)	—	.75	1.50	5.00	15.00
	1906(c)	—	—	—	Proof	45.00
	1906(c) (restrike)		—	—	P/L	20.00

BRONZE
Thinner planchets

KM#	Date	Mintage	Fine	VF	XF	Unc
500	1904(c)	—	—	—	Proof	45.00
	1906(c)	—	.75	1.50	4.50	12.50
	1906(c)	—	—	—	Proof	45.00
	1907(c)	—	.75	1.50	4.50	12.50
	1907(c)	—	—	—	Proof	45.00
	1907(c) (restrike)		—	—	P/L	20.00
	1908(c)	—	.75	1.50	4.50	12.50
	1908(c)	—	—	—	Proof	45.00
	1908(c) (restrike)		—	—	P/L	20.00
	1909(c)	—	.50	1.00	4.00	10.00
	1909(c) (restrike)		—	—	P/L	20.00
	1910(c)	—	.75	1.50	4.50	12.50

ALUMINUM

KM#	Date	Mintage	Fine	VF	XF	Unc
500a	1909(c)	—	—	—	Proof	100.00

NICKEL

KM#	Date	Mintage	Fine	VF	XF	Unc
500b	1904(c)	—	—	—	Proof	100.00

SILVER

KM#	Date	Mintage	Fine	VF	XF	Unc
500c	1903(c) (restrike)		—	—	P/L	75.00
	1904(c) (restrike)		—	—	P/L	75.00
	1905(c) (restrike)		—	—	P/L	75.00

BRONZE

KM#	Date	Mintage	Fine	VF	XF	Unc
510	1912(c)	—	.25	.50	.75	3.00
	1912(c)	—	—	—	Proof	40.00
	1912(c) (restrike)		—	—	P/L	20.00
	1913(c)	12.912	.25	.50	.75	3.00
	1913(c)	—	—	—	Proof	40.00
	1913(c) (restrike)		—	—	P/L	20.00
	1914(c)	10.022	.15	.30	.50	2.50
	1914(c)	—	—	—	Proof	40.00
	1914(c) (restrike)		—	—	P/L	20.00
	1915(c)	8.653	.15	.30	.50	2.50
	1915(c)	—	—	—	Proof	40.00
	1915(c) (restrike)		—	—	P/L	20.00
	1916(c)	5.875	.15	.30	.50	2.50
	1916(c)	—	—	—	Proof	40.00
	1916(c) (restrike)		—	—	P/L	20.00
	1917(c)	13.094	.15	.30	.50	2.50
	1917(c)	—	—	—	Proof	40.00
	1917(c) (restrike)		—	—	P/L	20.00
	1918(c)	4.608	.15	.30	.50	2.50
	1918(c)	—	—	—	Proof	40.00
	1918(c) (restrike)		—	—	P/L	20.00
	1919(c)	13.516	.15	.30	.50	2.50
	1919(c)	—	—	—	Proof	40.00
	1919(c) (restrike)		—	—	P/L	20.00
	1920(c)	7.437	.15	.30	.50	2.50
	1920(c)	—	—	—	Proof	40.00
	1920(c) (restrike)		—	—	P/L	20.00
	1921(c)	6.131	.15	.30	.50	2.50
	1921(c)	—	—	—	Proof	40.00
	1921(c) (restrike)		—	—	P/L	20.00
	1922(c)	4.941	.15	.30	.50	2.50
	1922(c)	—	—	—	Proof	40.00
	1922(c) (restrike)		—	—	P/L	20.00
	1923(c)	6.272	.15	.30	.50	2.50
	1923(c)	—	—	—	Proof	40.00
	1923(c) (restrike)		—	—	P/L	20.00
	1924(c)	10.624	.15	.30	.50	2.50
510	1924(c)	—	—	—	Proof	40.00
	1924(c) (restrike)		—	—	P/L	20.00
	1925(c)	3.622	.15	.30	.50	2.50
	1925(c)	—	—	—	Proof	40.00
	1925(c) (restrike)		—	—	P/L	20.00
	1926(c)	6.528	.15	.30	.50	2.50
	1926(c)	—	—	—	Proof	40.00
	1926(c) (restrike)		—	—	P/L	20.00
	1927(c)	6.528	.15	.30	.50	2.50
	1927(c)	—	—	—	Proof	40.00
	1927(c) (restrike)		—	—	P/L	20.00
	1928(c)	7.332	.15	.30	.50	2.50
	1928(c)	—	—	—	Proof	40.00
	1928(c) (restrike)		—	—	P/L	20.00
	1929(c)	7.654	.15	.30	.50	2.50
	1929(c)	—	—	—	Proof	40.00
	1929(c) (restrike)		—	—	P/L	20.00
	1930(c)	7.181	.15	.30	.50	2.50
	1930(c)	—	—	—	Proof	40.00
	1930(c) (restrike)		—	—	P/L	20.00
	1931(c)	8.794	.15	.30	.50	2.50
	1931(c)	—	—	—	Proof	40.00
	1931(c) (restrike)		—	—	P/L	20.00
	1932(c)	5.440	.15	.30	.50	2.50
	1932(c)	—	—	—	Proof	40.00
	1932(c) (restrike)		—	—	P/L	20.00
	1933(c)	9.242	.15	.30	.50	2.50
	1933(c)	—	—	—	Proof	40.00
	1933(c) (restrike)		—	—	P/L	20.00
	1934(c)	8.947	.15	.30	.50	2.50
	1934(c)	—	—	—	Proof	40.00
	1934(c) (restrike)		—	—	P/L	20.00
	1935(c)	15.501	.15	.30	.50	2.00
	1935(c)	—	—	—	Proof	40.00
	1935(c) (restrike)		—	—	P/L	20.00
	1936(c)	26.726	.10	.25	.40	1.25
	1936(c) (restrike)		—	—	P/L	20.00

Obv: First head, high relief.

NOTE: Calcutta Mint issues have no mint mark. Bombay Mint issues have a small dot below the date.

KM#	Date	Mintage	Fine	VF	XF	Unc
528	1938(c)	—	—	—	Proof	30.00
	1938(c) (restrike)		—	—	P/L	25.00
	1939(c)	17.357	.15	.40	.65	1.75
	1939(c)	—	—	—	Proof	30.00
	1939(b)	9.343	.15	.40	.65	1.75
	1939(b)	—	—	—	Proof	30.00
	1939(b) (restrike)		—	—	P/L	25.00
	1940(c)	23.770	.15	.40	.65	1.75
	1940(c)	—	—	—	Proof	30.00
	1940(c) (restrike)		—	—	P/L	25.00

NOTE: Calcutta Mint reported 11,161,600 mintage for 1938 but only proof and modern P/L restrikes are known.

Obv: Second head, low relief.

KM#	Date	Mintage	Fine	VF	XF	Unc
529	1942(b)	—	—	—	Proof	50.00
	1942(b) (restrike)		—	—	P/L	35.00

1/4 ANNA

NOTE: The one quarter Anna dated 1862 was struck at Calcutta, Bombay and Madras. From 1874 onward the issues from Calcutta and Bombay have a distinctive type of reverse and the coins are identified as follows.

On Calcutta Mint issues the floral design has a leaf below the center of the date. Some specimens dated 1879-1887 have also as a mint mark, a tiny incuse "C" on a bead of the beaded circle, below the center of the date.

On Bombay Mint issues the floral design has a leaf below the first and the last numeral of the date.

COPPER

KM#	Date	Mintage	Fine	VF	XF	Unc
467	1862(c)	99.504	.75	1.50	3.00	9.00
	1862(c) w/V in bottom of bust	10.654	1.25	2.50	5.00	15.00
	1862(c)	—	—	—	Proof	100.00
	1862(c) (restrike)		—	—	P/L	30.00
	1862(b) w/V in point of shoulder	32.149	1.00	2.00	4.00	12.00
	1862(b) w/dot below date	2.366	2.50	5.00	10.00	25.00
	1862(m) 25.5mm	186.227	.75	1.50	3.00	9.00

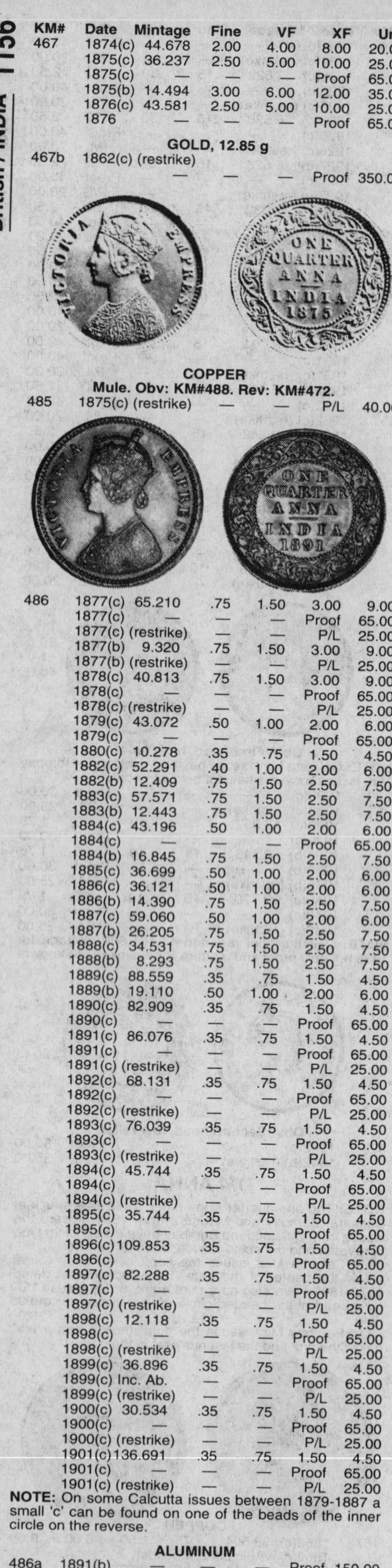

KM#	Date	Mintage	Fine	VF	XF	Unc
467	1874(c)	44.678	2.00	4.00	8.00	20.00
	1875(c)	36.237	2.50	5.00	10.00	25.00
	1875(c)	—	—	—	Proof	65.00
	1875(b)	14.494	3.00	6.00	12.00	35.00
	1876(c)	43.581	2.50	5.00	10.00	25.00
	1876	—	—	—	Proof	65.00

GOLD, 12.85 g

KM#	Date	Mintage	Fine	VF	XF	Unc
467b	1862(c) (restrike)	—	—	—	Proof	350.00

COPPER

Mule. Obv: KM#488. Rev: KM#472.

KM#	Date	Mintage	Fine	VF	XF	Unc
485	1875(c) (restrike)	—	—	—	P/L	40.00

KM#	Date	Mintage	Fine	VF	XF	Unc
486	1877(c)	65.210	.75	1.50	3.00	9.00
	1877(c)	—	—	—	Proof	65.00
	1877(c) (restrike)	—	—	—	P/L	25.00
	1877(b)	9.320	.75	1.50	3.00	9.00
	1877(b) (restrike)	—	—	—	P/L	25.00
	1878(c)	40.813	.75	1.50	3.00	9.00
	1878(c)	—	—	—	Proof	65.00
	1878(c) (restrike)	—	—	—	P/L	25.00
	1879(c)	43.072	.50	1.00	2.00	6.00
	1879(c)	—	—	—	Proof	65.00
	1880(c)	10.278	.35	.75	1.50	4.50
	1882(c)	52.291	.40	1.00	2.00	6.00
	1882(b)	12.409	.75	1.50	2.50	7.50
	1883(c)	57.571	.75	1.50	2.50	7.50
	1883(b)	12.443	.75	1.50	2.50	7.50
	1884(c)	43.196	.50	1.00	2.00	6.00
	1884(c)	—	—	—	Proof	65.00
	1884(b)	16.845	.75	1.50	2.50	7.50
	1885(c)	36.699	.50	1.00	2.00	6.00
	1886(c)	36.121	.50	1.00	2.00	6.00
	1886(b)	14.390	.75	1.50	2.50	7.50
	1887(c)	59.060	.50	1.00	2.00	6.00
	1887(b)	26.205	.75	1.50	2.50	7.50
	1888(c)	34.531	.75	1.50	2.50	7.50
	1888(b)	8.293	.75	1.50	2.50	7.50
	1889(c)	88.559	.35	.75	1.50	4.50
	1889(b)	19.110	.50	1.00	2.00	6.00
	1890(c)	82.909	.35	.75	1.50	4.50
	1890(c)	—	—	—	Proof	65.00
	1891(c)	86.076	.35	.75	1.50	4.50
	1891(c)	—	—	—	Proof	65.00
	1891(c) (restrike)	—	—	—	P/L	25.00
	1892(c)	68.131	.35	.75	1.50	4.50
	1892(c)	—	—	—	Proof	65.00
	1892(c) (restrike)	—	—	—	P/L	25.00
	1893(c)	76.039	.35	.75	1.50	4.50
	1893(c)	—	—	—	Proof	65.00
	1893(c) (restrike)	—	—	—	P/L	25.00
	1894(c)	45.744	.35	.75	1.50	4.50
	1894(c)	—	—	—	Proof	65.00
	1894(c) (restrike)	—	—	—	P/L	25.00
	1895(c)	35.744	.35	.75	1.50	4.50
	1895(c)	—	—	—	Proof	65.00
	1896(c)	109.853	.35	.75	1.50	4.50
	1896(c)	—	—	—	Proof	65.00
	1897(c)	82.288	.35	.75	1.50	4.50
	1897(c)	—	—	—	Proof	65.00
	1897(c) (restrike)	—	—	—	P/L	25.00
	1898(c)	12.118	.35	.75	1.50	4.50
	1898(c)	—	—	—	Proof	65.00
	1898(c) (restrike)	—	—	—	P/L	25.00
	1899(c)	36.896	.35	.75	1.50	4.50
	1899(c)	Inc. Ab.	—	—	Proof	65.00
	1899(c) (restrike)	—	—	—	P/L	25.00
	1900(c)	30.534	.35	.75	1.50	4.50
	1900(c)	—	—	—	Proof	65.00
	1900(c) (restrike)	—	—	—	P/L	25.00
	1901(c)	136.691	.35	.75	1.50	4.50
	1901(c)	—	—	—	Proof	65.00
	1901(c) (restrike)	—	—	—	P/L	25.00

NOTE: On some Calcutta issues between 1879-1887 a small 'c' can be found on one of the beads of the inner circle on the reverse.

ALUMINUM

KM#	Date	Mintage	Fine	VF	XF	Unc
486a	1891(b)	—	—	—	Proof	150.00

SILVER

KM#	Date	Mintage	Fine	VF	XF	Unc
486b	1891(c) (restrike)	—	—	—	P/L	75.00
	1892(c) (restrike)	—	—	—	P/L	75.00
	1893(c) (restrike)	—	—	—	P/L	75.00
	1894(c) (restrike)	—	—	—	P/L	75.00
	1895(c) (restrike)	—	—	—	P/L	75.00
	1896(c) (restrike)	—	—	—	P/L	75.00
	1897(c) (restrike)	—	—	—	P/L	75.00
486b	1898(c) (restrike)	—	—	—	P/L	75.00
	1899(c) (restrike)	—	—	—	P/L	75.00
	1900(c) (restrike)	—	—	—	P/L	75.00
	1901(c) (restrike)	—	—	—	P/L	75.00

GOLD

KM#	Date	Mintage	Fine	VF	XF	Unc
486c	1891(c) (restrike)	—	—	—	P/L	400.00
	1892(c) (restrike)	—	—	—	P/L	400.00
	1893(c) (restrike)	—	—	—	P/L	400.00
	1895(c) (restrike)	—	—	—	P/L	400.00
	1896(c) (restrike)	—	—	—	P/L	400.00
	1897(c) (restrike)	—	—	—	P/L	400.00
	1898(c) (restrike)	—	—	—	P/L	400.00
	1899(c) (restrike)	—	—	—	P/L	400.00
	1900(c) (restrike)	—	—	—	P/L	400.00
	1901(c) (restrike)	—	—	—	P/L	400.00

COPPER

KM#	Date	Mintage	Fine	VF	XF	Unc
501	1903(c)	105.974	.35	1.75	7.50	35.00
	1903(c)	—	—	—	Proof	50.00
	1903(c) (restrike)	—	—	—	P/L	25.00
	1904(c)	104.595	.35	1.75	7.50	35.00
	1904(c)	—	—	—	Proof	50.00
	1904(c) (restrike)	—	—	—	P/L	25.00
	1905(c)	130.058	.35	1.75	7.50	35.00
	1905(c)	—	—	—	Proof	50.00
	1905(c) (restrike)	—	—	—	P/L	25.00
	1906(c)	47.229	.35	1.75	7.50	35.00
	1906(c)	—	—	—	Proof	50.00

NICKEL

KM#	Date	Mintage	Fine	VF	XF	Unc
501a	1906(c)	—	—	—	Proof	150.00

SILVER

KM#	Date	Mintage	Fine	VF	XF	Unc
501b	1903(c) (restrike)	—	—	—	P/L	100.00
	1904(c) (restrike)	—	—	—	P/L	100.00
	1905(c) (restrike)	—	—	—	P/L	100.00

BRONZE

Thinner planchet

KM#	Date	Mintage	Fine	VF	XF	Unc
502	1906(c)	115.786	.35	1.25	6.50	30.00
	1906(c)	—	—	—	Proof	40.00
	1907(c)	234.682	.35	1.25	6.50	30.00
	1907(c)	—	—	—	Proof	40.00
	1907(c) (restrike)	—	—	—	P/L	20.00
	1908(c)	58.066	.35	1.25	6.50	30.00
	1908(c)	—	—	—	Proof	40.00
	1908(c) (restrike)	—	—	—	P/L	20.00
	1909(c)	29.966	.35	1.25	6.50	30.00
	1909(c)	—	—	—	Proof	40.00
	1909(c) (restrike)	—	—	—	P/L	20.00
	1910(c)	47.265	.35	1.25	6.50	30.00
	1910(c) (restrike)	—	—	—	P/L	20.00

ALUMINUM

KM#	Date	Mintage	Fine	VF	XF	Unc
502a	1908(c)	—	—	—	Proof	150.00

BRONZE

NOTE: Calcutta Mint issues have no mint mark. Bombay Mint issues have a small dot below the date. The pieces dated 1911, like the other coins with that date, show the "Pig" elephant.

KM#	Date	Mintage	Fine	VF	XF	Unc
511	1911(c)	55.918	.75	2.00	5.00	20.00
	1911(c)	—	—	—	Proof	55.00
	1911(c) (restrike)	—	—	—	P/L	20.00
512	1912(c)	107.456	.20	.40	.75	3.00
	1912(c)	—	—	—	Proof	35.00
	1912(c) (restrike)	—	—	—	P/L	20.00
	1913(c)	82.061	.25	.50	.85	3.00
	1913(c)	—	—	—	Proof	35.00
	1913(c) (restrike)	—	—	—	P/L	20.00
	1914(c)	40.576	.20	.40	.75	2.50
	1914(c)	—	—	—	Proof	35.00
	1914(c) (restrike)	—	—	—	P/L	20.00
	1915(c)	—	—	Reported, not confirmed		
	1916(c)	1.632	3.50	7.00	12.00	25.00
	1916(c)	—	—	—	Proof	50.00
	1917(c)	69.370	.20	.40	.75	2.50
	1917(c)	—	—	—	Proof	35.00
	1917(c) (restrike)	—	—	—	P/L	20.00
	1918(c)	84.045	.20	.40	.75	2.50
	1918(c)	—	—	—	Proof	35.00
	1918(c) (restrike)	—	—	—	P/L	20.00
	1919(c)	212.467	.20	.40	.75	2.50
	1919(c)	—	—	—	Proof	35.00
	1919(c) (restrike)	—	—	—	P/L	20.00
	1920(c)	96.019	.20	.40	.75	2.50
	1920(c)	—	—	—	Proof	35.00
	1920(c) (restrike)	—	—	—	P/L	20.00
	1921(c)	—	—	—	Proof	35.00

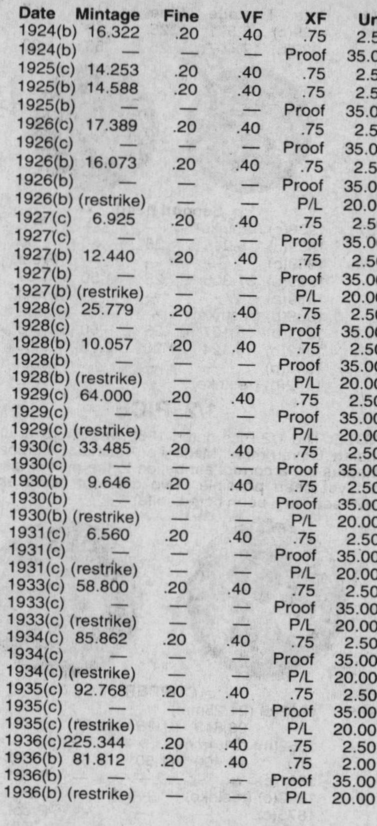

KM#	Date	Mintage	Fine	VF	XF	Unc
512	1924(b)	16.322	.20	.40	.75	2.50
	1924(b)	—	—	—	Proof	35.00
	1925(c)	14.253	.20	.40	.75	2.50
	1925(b)	14.588	.20	.40	.75	2.50
	1925(b)	—	—	—	Proof	35.00
	1926(c)	17.389	.20	.40	.75	2.50
	1926(c)	—	—	—	Proof	35.00
	1926(b)	16.073	.20	.40	.75	2.50
	1926(b)	—	—	—	Proof	35.00
	1926(b) (restrike)	—	—	—	P/L	20.00
	1927(c)	6.925	.20	.40	.75	2.50
	1927(c)	—	—	—	Proof	35.00
	1927(b)	12.440	.20	.40	.75	2.50
	1927(b)	—	—	—	Proof	35.00
	1927(b) (restrike)	—	—	—	P/L	20.00
	1928(c)	25.779	.20	.40	.75	2.50
	1928(c)	—	—	—	Proof	35.00
	1928(b)	10.057	.20	.40	.75	2.50
	1928(b)	—	—	—	Proof	35.00
	1928(b) (restrike)	—	—	—	P/L	20.00
	1929(c)	64.000	.20	.40	.75	2.50
	1929(c)	—	—	—	Proof	35.00
	1929(c) (restrike)	—	—	—	P/L	20.00
	1930(c)	33.485	.20	.40	.75	2.50
	1930(c)	—	—	—	Proof	35.00
	1930(b)	9.646	.20	.40	.75	2.50
	1930(b)	—	—	—	Proof	35.00
	1930(b) (restrike)	—	—	—	P/L	20.00
	1931(c)	6.560	.20	.40	.75	2.50
	1931(c)	—	—	—	Proof	35.00
	1931(c) (restrike)	—	—	—	P/L	20.00
	1933(c)	58.800	.20	.40	.75	2.50
	1933(c)	—	—	—	Proof	35.00
	1933(c) (restrike)	—	—	—	P/L	20.00
	1934(c)	85.862	.20	.40	.75	2.50
	1934(c)	—	—	—	Proof	35.00
	1934(c) (restrike)	—	—	—	P/L	20.00
	1935(c)	92.768	.20	.40	.75	2.50
	1935(c)	—	—	—	Proof	35.00
	1935(c) (restrike)	—	—	—	P/L	20.00
	1936(c)	225.344	.20	.40	.75	2.50
	1936(b)	81.812	.20	.40	.75	2.00
	1936(b)	—	—	—	Proof	35.00
	1936(b) (restrike)	—	—	—	P/L	20.00

Obv: First head, high relief.

NOTE: Calcutta Mint issues have no mint mark. Bombay Mint issues have a small dot above N of "ONE".

KM#	Date	Mintage	Fine	VF	XF	Unc
530	1938(c)	33.792	.25	.40	.75	1.50
	1938(c)	—	—	—	Proof	35.00
	1938(b)	16.796	.25	.40	.75	1.50
	1938(b) (restrike)	—	—	—	P/L	30.00
	1939(c)	78.279	.30	.50	1.00	2.00
	1939(c)	—	—	—	Proof	35.00
	1939(b)	60.171	.30	.50	1.00	3.00
	1939(b)	—	—	—	Proof	35.00
	1939(b) (restrike)	—	—	—	P/L	30.00
	1940(b)	116.721	.35	.75	1.50	3.00

Obv: Second head, low relief.

KM#	Date	Mintage	Fine	VF	XF	Unc
531	1940(c)	140.410	.15	.35	.65	1.00
	1940(c)	—	—	—	Proof	35.00
	1940(b)	Inc. KM530	.15	.35	.65	1.00
	1940(b) (restrike)	—	—	—	P/L	25.00
	1941(c)	121.107	.15	.35	.65	1.00
	1941(c) (restrike)	—	—	—	P/L	25.00
	1941(b)	1.446	—	.60	1.50	5.00
	1942(c)	34.298	.15	.35	.65	1.00
	1942(b)	8.768	.15	.35	.65	1.00
	1942(b) (restrike)	—	—	—	P/L	25.00

PICE

NOTE: There are three types of the crown, which is on the obverse at the top. These are shown below and are designated as (RC) Round Crown, (HC) High Crown, and (FC) Flat Crown. Calcutta Mint issues have no mint mark. The issues from the other mints have the mint mark below the date as following: Lahore, raised "L"; Pretoria, small round dot; Bombay, diamond dot or "large" round dot. On the Bombay issues dated 1944 the mint mark appears to be a large dot over a diamond.

Round Crown (RC)

High Crown (HC) **Flat Crown (FC)**

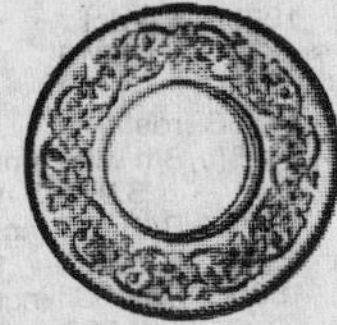

BRONZE

Obv: Small date, small legends.

KM#	Date	Mintage	Fine	VF	XF	Unc
532	1943(b) (RC) diamond					
		164.659	.25	.40	.85	2.75

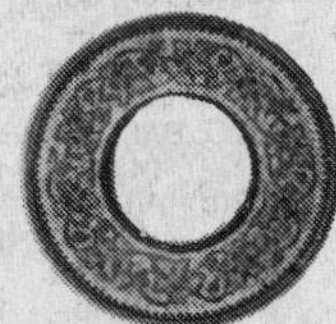

Obv: Large date, large legends.

KM#	Date	Mintage	Fine	VF	XF	Unc
533	1943(b) (HC) large dot					
		—	.15	.35	.65	1.00
	1943(p) (HC) small dot					
		98.997	.15	.35	.65	1.00
	1944(c) (HC)	—	.15	.35	.65	1.00
	1944(c) (HC)	—	—	—	Proof	25.00
	1944(b) (HC) large dot					
		195.354	.15	.35	.65	1.00
	1944(b) (HC) diamond					
		—	.20	.40	.75	1.75
	1944(b) (FC) large dot					
		—	.20	.40	.75	1.75
	1944(b) (restrike)		—	—	P/L	20.00
	1944(p) (HC) small dot					
		141.003	.20	.40	.75	1.75
	1944L (HC)					
		29.802	.15	.35	.65	1.00
	1945(c) (FC)					
		156.322	.15	.35	.65	1.00
	1945(b) (FC) diamond					
		237.197	.15	.35	.65	1.00
	1945(b) (FC) large dot					
		Inc. Ab.	.15	.35	.65	1.00
	1945(b) (restrike)		—	—	P/L	20.00
	1945L (FC)					
		238.825	.15	.35	.65	1.00
	1947(c) (HC)					
		153.702	.15	.35	.65	1.00
	1947(b) (HC) diamond					
		43.654	.15	.35	.65	1.00
	1947(b)	—	—	—	Proof	25.00
	1947 (restrike)		—	—	P/L	20.00

1/2 ANNA

NOTE: The half Anna dated 1862 was struck at all three Indian Government Mints, i.e. Calcutta, Bombay and Madras but a correct attribution to the mint of issue has not yet been possible.

The coins dated 1875-76 were struck at the Calcutta Mint, those dated 1877 were struck at Calcutta and Bombay. Two different busts occur on the 1877 issue.

BUST A - The bottom section of the front dress panel has a small flower in the upper left corner and a large flower at right of center.

BUST C - The bottom section of the front dress panel has a five-dotted flower at right of center.

NOTE: Bust B is the common obverse on 1862 issues and is not described here.

The Bombay issue dated 1877 was identified by the type of the date figure "7" which has a short horizontal stroke and a long downstroke. This type of "7" appears on most Bombay issues but not on any denomination of the Calcutta Mint.

COPPER

KM#	Date	Mintage	Fine	VF	XF	Unc
468	1862(c) 31.3mm					
		7.235	10.00	20.00	30.00	75.00
	1862(c)	—	—	—	Proof	125.00
	1862(c) (restrike)		—	—	P/L	50.00
	1862(b) 30.5mm					
		4.802	10.00	20.00	30.00	75.00
	1862(m) 30.7mm					
		66.515	5.00	10.00	18.50	60.00
	1862(c) 30.9mm w/v in bottom of bust					
		7.399	10.00	20.00	30.00	75.00
	1862(c)	—	—	—	Proof	125.00
	1862(c) (restrike)		—	—	P/L	35.00
	1875(c), bust A					
		—	12.50	25.00	50.00	100.00
	1875(c)	—	—	—	Proof	150.00
	1875(c) (restrike)		—	—	P/L	50.00
	1876(c), bust A					
		3.437	12.50	25.00	50.00	100.00

GOLD

KM#	Date	Mintage	Fine	VF	XF	Unc
468b	1862(c)	—	—	—	Proof	650.00

COPPER

KM#	Date	Mintage	Fine	VF	XF	Unc
487	1877(c), bust C, wide short 7's in date					
		3.584	10.00	20.00	40.00	100.00
	1877(c) Inc. Ab.		—	—	Proof	100.00
	1877(c) (restrike)		—	—	P/L	40.00
	1877(b), bust A, narrow tall 7's in date					
		3.454	12.00	20.00	40.00	100.00
	1878(c)	—	—	—	Proof	100.00
	1878(c) (restrike)		—	—	P/L	65.00
	1879(c)	—	—	—	Proof	100.00
	1879(c) (restrike)		—	—	P/L	75.00
	1884(b)	—	—	—	Proof	100.00
	1884(b) (restrike)		—	—	P/L	75.00
	1890(c)	—	—	—	Proof	100.00
	1890(c) (restrike)		—	—	P/L	65.00
	1891(c)	86.077	—	—	Proof	100.00
	1891(c) (restrike)		—	—	P/L	65.00
	1892(c)	—	—	—	Proof	100.00
	1892(c) (restrike)		—	—	P/L	65.00
	1893(c)	76.038	—	—	Proof	100.00
	1893(c) (restrike)		—	—	P/L	65.00
	1894	—	—	— Reported, not confirmed		

NOTE: On Calcutta issue 1879 a small incuse 'c' can be found on one of the beads at the inner circle on the rev.

ALUMINUM

KM#	Date	Mintage	Fine	VF	XF	Unc
487a	1891(b)	—	—	—	Proof	100.00

SILVER

KM#	Date	Mintage	Fine	VF	XF	Unc
487b	1892(c) (restrike)		—	—	P/L	150.00
	1893(c) (restrike)		—	—	P/L	150.00

GOLD

KM#	Date	Mintage	Fine	VF	XF	Unc
487c	1891(c) (restrike)		—	—	P/L	500.00
	1892(c) (restrike)		—	—	P/L	500.00
	1893(c) (restrike)		—	—	P/L	500.00

COPPER

Obv: Head of Edward VII. Rev: Similar to KM#487.

KM#	Date	Mintage	Fine	VF	XF	Unc
503	1904(c)	—	—	—	Proof	2000.

COPPER-NICKEL

Rev. leg: /INDIA/

KM#	Date	Mintage	Fine	VF	XF	Unc
534	1940(c)	—	—	—	Proof	325.00
	1940(c) (restrike)		—	—	P/L	50.00

GOLD

KM#	Date	Mintage	Fine	VF	XF	Unc
534a	1940(c) (restrike)		—	—	P/L	250.00

NICKEL-BRASS

NOTE: Calcutta Mint struck this denomination each year 1942-1945, denoted by a dot before and after the word INDIA on the reverse. Bombay Mint struck only with the dates 1942 and 1945, denoted by INDIA without dots before and after. Calcutta also issued proof coins each year while Bombay issued none. However, Bombay later produced proof-like restrikes using old dies from both Bombay and Calcutta indiscriminately; they are all attributed here to Bombay. Source: Pridmore.

Obv: Second head.

Rev. leg: INDIA (w/o dots).

NOTE: Bombay Mint issues dated 1942-1945 are without a dot before and after India.

KM#	Date	Mintage	Fine	VF	XF	Unc
534b.1	1942(b)	7.945	.15	.35	.65	1.25
	1942(b) (restrike)		—	—	P/L	40.00
	1943(b) (restrike)		—	—	P/L	40.00
	1944(b) (restrike)		—	—	P/L	40.00
	1945(b)	6.264	— Reported, not confirmed			
	1945(b) (restrike)		—	—	P/L	25.00

Rev. leg: /INDIA/

KM#	Date	Mintage	Fine	VF	XF	Unc
534b.2	1942(c)	159.000	.10	.15	.35	1.00
	1942(c)	—	—	—	Proof	30.00
	1943(c)	437.760	.10	.15	.35	1.00
	1943(c)	—	—	—	Proof	40.00
	1944(c)	514.800	.10	.15	.35	1.00
	1944(c)	—	—	—	Proof	40.00
	1945(c)	215.732	.10	.15	.35	1.00
	1945(c)	—	—	—	Proof	40.00

COPPER-NICKEL

NOTE: Calcutta Mint continued to issue this denomination with the dot before and after INDIA in 1946 and 1947. Bombay also struck in 1946 and 1947, the 1946 issue denoted by a small dot in the center of the dashes before and after the date on the reverse (as well as a dot before and after INDIA, like Calcutta); the characteristics of the 1947 Bombay issue have not been determined but are thought also to resemble the 1946 issue. This denomination is also reported to have been struck in a quantity of 50,829 pieces in 1946 at the new Lahore Mint but no way of distinguishing this issue has been found. The proof issue in 1946 was struck by Bombay, not Calcutta. Source: Pridmore.

KM#	Date	Mintage	Fine	VF	XF	Unc
535.1	1946(b)	48.744	.10	.15	.35	1.00
	1946(b)	—	—	—	Proof	30.00
	1946(b) (restrike)		—	—	P/L	25.00
	1947(b)	24.144	— Reported, not confirmed			
	1947(b) (restrike)		—	—	P/L	50.00

KM#	Date	Mintage	Fine	VF	XF	Unc
535.2	1946(c)	75.159	.10	.15	.35	1.00
	1947(c)	126.392	.10	.15	.35	1.00
	1947(c)	—	—	—	Proof	40.00
	1947(c) (restrike)		—	—	P/L	25.00

ANNA

NOTE: Struck only at the Bombay Mint, the pieces have as mint mark a small incuse "B" in the space below the cross pattee of the crown on the obverse.

COPPER-NICKEL

KM#	Date	Mintage	Fine	VF	XF	Unc
504	1906B	.200	20.00	50.00	125.00	300.00
	1907B	37.256	.50	1.25	2.00	5.00
	1907B	—	—	—	Proof	60.00
	1908B	22.536	.50	1.25	2.00	5.00
	1908B	—	—	—	Proof	60.00
	1909B	24.800	.50	1.25	2.00	5.00
	1909B	—	—	—	Proof	60.00
	1910B	40.200	.50	1.25	2.00	5.00
	1910B	—	—	—	Proof	60.00

NOTE: Until 1920 all were struck at the Bombay Mint without mint mark. From 1923 on the Bombay Mint issues have a small raised bead or dot below the date. Calcutta Mint issues have no mint mark.

KM#	Date	Mintage	Fine	VF	XF	Unc
513	1912(b)	39.400	.40	1.00	2.50	6.00
	1912	—	—	—	Proof	50.00
	1913(b)	39.776	.40	1.00	2.50	6.00
	1913	—	—	—	Proof	50.00
	1914(b)	48.000	.25	.50	1.75	3.50
	1914	—	—	—	Proof	50.00
	1915(b)	12.470	.25	.50	1.75	3.50
	1915	—	—	—	Proof	50.00
	1916(b)	26.738	.25	.50	1.75	3.50
	1917(b)	50.136	.25	.50	1.75	3.50
	1917	—	—	—	Proof	50.00
	1918(b)	80.360	.25	.50	1.75	3.50
	1918(b)	—	—	—	Proof	50.00
	1919(b)	141.000	.25	.35	1.75	3.00
	1919(b)	—	—	—	Proof	50.00
	1919(c)	—	—	—	Proof	50.00
	1920(b)	11.671	.25	.50	1.50	4.00
	1920(b)	—	—	—	Proof	50.00
	1923(b)	6.438	.25	.50	1.50	4.00
	1923(b)	—	—	—	Proof	50.00
	1924(c)	13.536	.25	.50	1.75	3.00
	1924(c)	—	—	—	Proof	50.00
	1924(b)	—	.25	.50	2.00	5.00
	1924(b)	—	—	—	Proof	50.00
	1924(b) (restrike)	—	—	—	P/L	20.00
	1925(c)	19.832	.25	.50	2.00	5.00
	1925(c)	—	—	—	Proof	50.00
	1925(b)	—	.25	.50	2.00	5.00
	1925(b)	—	—	—	Proof	50.00
	1925(b) (restrike)	—	—	—	P/L	20.00
	1926(c)	14.216	.25	.50	2.00	5.00
	1926(c)	—	—	—	Proof	50.00
	1926(b)	8.988	.25	.50	2.00	5.00
	1926(b)	—	—	—	Proof	50.00
	1926(b) (restrike)	—	—	—	P/L	20.00
	1927(c)	11.080	.25	.50	2.00	5.00
	1927(c)	—	—	—	Proof	50.00
	1927(b)	6.444	.25	.50	2.00	5.00
	1927(b)	—	—	—	Proof	50.00
	1927(b) (restrike)	—	—	—	P/L	20.00
	1928(c)	23.432	.25	.50	2.00	5.00
	1928(c)	—	—	—	Proof	50.00
	1928(b)	11.340	.25	.50	2.00	5.00
	1928(b)	—	—	—	Proof	50.00
	1928(b) (restrike)	—	—	—	P/L	20.00
	1929(c)	43.184	.25	.50	2.00	5.00
	1929(c)	—	—	—	Proof	50.00
	1929(c) (restrike)	—	—	—	P/L	20.00
	1930(c)	27.978	.25	.50	2.00	5.00
	1930(c)	—	—	—	Proof	50.00
	1930(c) (restrike)	—	—	—	P/L	20.00
	1933(c)	8.968	.25	.50	2.00	5.00
	1933(c)	—	—	—	Proof	50.00
	1933(c) (restrike)	—	—	—	P/L	20.00
	1934(c)	37.248	.25	.40	1.50	4.00
	1934(c)	—	—	—	Proof	50.00
	1934(c) (restrike)	—	—	—	P/L	20.00
	1935(c)	18.384	.25	.40	1.50	4.00
	1935(c)	—	—	—	Proof	50.00
	1935(b)	29.221	.25	.40	1.50	4.00
	1935(b)	—	—	—	Proof	50.00
	1935(b) (restrike)	—	—	—	P/L	20.00
	1936(c)	4.008	.25	.40	1.50	4.00
	1936(b)	91.689	.20	.35	1.25	3.00
	1936(b)	—	—	—	Proof	50.00

Obv: First Head, High Relief.

NOTE: Calcutta Mint issues have no mint mark. Bombay Mint issues have a small dot below the date.

KM#	Date	Mintage	Fine	VF	XF	Unc
536	1938(c)	7.128	.30	.75	1.50	5.00
	1938(c)	—	—	—	Proof	40.00
	1938(b)	3.126	.30	.75	1.50	3.00
	1938(b) (restrike)	—	—	—	P/L	20.00
	1939(c)	18.192	.15	.40	.75	2.25
	1939(b)	36.157	.15	.40	.75	2.25
	1939(b) (restrike)	—	—	—	P/L	20.00
	1940(c) (restrike)	—	—	—	P/L	20.00

Obv: Second head, low relief, large crown.

Rev: Large "I".

KM#	Date	Mintage	Fine	VF	XF	Unc
537	1940(c)	76.392	.10	.25	.50	1.50
	1940(b)	144.712	.10	.25	.50	1.50
	1940(b) (restrike)	—	—	—	P/L	20.00
	1941(c)	62.480	.10	.15	.25	.75
	1941(b)	40.170	.10	.15	.25	.75
	1941(b) (restrike)	—	—	—	P/L	25.00

NICKEL-BRASS

KM#	Date	Mintage	Fine	VF	XF	Unc
537a	1942(c)	194.056	.10	.25	.50	1.50
	1942(c)	—	—	—	Proof	35.00
	1942(b)	103.240	.10	.25	.50	1.50
	1942(b) (restrike)	—	—	—	P/L	20.00
	1943(c)	352.256	.10	.25	.50	1.50
	1943(c)	—	—	—	Proof	35.00
	1943(b)	134.500	.10	.25	.50	1.50
	1943(b) (restrike)	—	—	—	P/L	20.00
	1944(c)	457.608	.10	.25	.50	1.50
	1944(c)	—	—	—	Proof	35.00
	1944(b)	175.208	.10	.25	.50	1.50
	1944(b) (restrike)	—	—	—	P/L	20.00

COPPER-NICKEL
Obv: Second head, low relief, small crown.
Rev: Small "I".

KM#	Date	Mintage	Fine	VF	XF	Unc
538	1945(c)	278.360	.10	.25	.50	1.50
	1945(b)	61.228	.10	.25	.50	1.50
	1946(c)	100.820	.10	.15	.35	1.00
	1946(b)	82.052	.10	.15	.35	1.00
	1946(b)	—	—	—	Proof	40.00
	1946(b) (restrike)	—	—	—	P/L	25.00
	1947(c)	148.656	.10	.25	.35	1.00
	1947(c)	—	—	—	Proof	40.00
	1947(b)	50.096	.10	.15	.35	1.00
	1947(b)	—	—	—	Proof	40.00

NICKEL-BRASS
Obv: Second head, low relief, large crown.
Rev: Small "I".

KM#	Date	Mintage	Fine	VF	XF	Unc
539	1945(c)	278.360	.10	.25	.75	1.50
	1945(c)	—	—	—	Proof	35.00
	1945(b)	61.228	.10	.25	.75	1.50
	1945(b) (restrike)	—	—	—	P/L	25.00

2 ANNAS

NOTE: The distinguishing features of the 2 busts and 2 reverses are:
BUST A-The front dress panel has 4 sections. The last section has at left, 3 leaves, and a small indistinct flower in the upper right corner.
BUST B-The front dress panel has 3 1/2 sections. The last, incomplete section shows only 3 small leaf tops.
REVERSE I-Large top flower; the 2 large petals above the whorl are long and curved downward.
REVERSE II-Small top flower; the 2 large petals above the whorl are short and horizontal.

The 2 Annas dated 1862-76 have been re-attributed as a result of latest studies. The 2 Annas, dated 1877 having a bead in the tip of the top flower is now attributed to Calcutta.

Calcutta issues dated 1862-78 have no mint mark. The diameter of the coins is 15.25mm, except for the 1877 issue with the bead in the top flower which is 15.4mm. From 1879 the mint mark is a small incuse "C" in the whorl below the center of the bottom flower. Calcutta coins dated 1874 have not yet been verified.

Bombay issues until 1877 are without mint mark and have a diameter of 15.8mm. From 1877-1883 the mint mark is a small raised bead directly above the bottom flower. From 1884 the coins have a small B raised or incuse, above the whorl of the top flower. Madras issues (1862 only) are 16mm diameter.

1.4600 g, .917 SILVER, .0430 oz ASW
Obv: Bust "A".

KM#	Date	Mintage	Fine	VF	XF	Unc
469	1862(c) 15.3-15.4mm	29.653	1.75	3.50	7.50	15.00
	1862(c)	—	—	—	Proof	100.00
	1862(b) 15.7-15.9mm	21.037	2.50	5.00	10.00	20.00
	1862(b) (restrike)	—	—	—	P/L	35.00
	1862(m) 16.0mm	4.202	2.75	5.50	11.00	22.00
	1874(c)	5.690	1.75	3.50	7.50	15.00
	1874(b)	9.508	1.50	3.00	6.00	12.00

KM#	Date	Mintage	Fine	VF	XF	Unc
469	1874(b) dot I.A.	2.50	5.00	10.00	20.00	
	1875(c)	6.512	1.50	3.00	6.00	12.00
	1875(c)	—	—	—	Proof	100.00
	1875(b)	1.712	2.50	5.00	10.00	20.00
	1876(c)	10.504	1.00	2.00	4.00	8.00
	1876(b)	3.911	2.00	4.00	8.00	16.00

GOLD

KM#	Date	Mintage	Fine	VF	XF	Unc
469a	1862	—	—	—	Proof	350.00

1.4600 g, .917 SILVER, .0430 oz ASW

KM#	Date	Mintage	Fine	VF	XF	Unc
488	1877(c)A/I, w/o mm.	3.575	1.25	2.50	5.00	10.00
	1877(c) A/I, dot below	Inc. Ab.	1.75	3.50	7.00	14.00
	1877(c)	—	—	—	Proof	100.00
	1877(c)B/II, w/o mm.	Inc. Ab	1.75	3.50	7.00	14.00
	1877(c) (restrike)	—	—	—	P/L	30.00
	1877(c) B/II, dot in top flower	Inc. Ab.	1.25	2.50	5.00	10.00
	1877(b) A/I dot above lower flower	2.215	1.25	2.50	5.00	10.00
	1878B A.I, dot	2.215	1.25	2.50	5.00	10.00
	1878B	—	—	—	Proof	100.00
	1878B (restrike)	—	—	—	P/L	30.00
	1878(c)B/II w/o mm.	3.994	1.25	2.50	5.00	10.00
	1879C B/II, "C" incuse	3.541	1.25	2.50	5.00	10.00
	1880C B/II, "C" incuse	2.539	1.25	2.50	5.00	10.00
	1881C B/II, "C" incuse	4.400	1.25	2.50	5.00	10.00
	1881C	—	—	—	Proof	100.00
	1881(b) A/I, dot	2.449	1.25	2.50	5.00	10.00
	1881(b) A/II, dot	—	1.75	3.50	7.00	14.00
	1881(b) B/II, dot	Inc. Ab.	1.25	2.50	5.00	10.00
	1882C B/II, "C" incuse	14.360	1.25	2.50	5.00	10.00
	1882(b) A/I, dot	2.629	1.25	2.50	5.00	10.00
	1882(b) B/II, dot	Inc. Ab.	1.25	2.50	5.00	10.00
	1882	—	—	—	Proof	100.00
	1883C B/II, "C" incuse	2.736	1.25	2.50	5.00	10.00
	1883(b)A/I, w/o mm.	Inc. Ab.	1.25	2.50	5.00	10.00
	1883(b) A/I, dot	4.416	1.25	2.50	5.00	10.00
	1883(b) B/II, dot	Inc. Ab.	1.25	2.50	5.00	10.00
	1884C B/II, "C" incuse	7.200	1.25	2.50	5.00	10.00
	1884(b) A/I, w/o mm.	1.638	1.25	2.50	5.00	10.00
	1884(b) A/I, dot	Inc. Ab.	1.25	2.50	5.00	10.00
	1884B A/I, "B" raised	Inc. Ab.	1.25	2.50	5.00	10.00
	1884B A/I, dot, "B" raised	Inc. Ab.	1.25	2.50	5.00	10.00
	1884B B/II, "B" incuse	Inc. Ab.	1.25	2.50	5.00	10.00
	1885C B/II, "C" incuse	1.335	1.25	2.50	5.00	10.00
	1885B A/I, "B" raised	—	1.75	3.50	7.00	14.00
	1885B B/II, "B" raised	2.262	1.25	2.50	5.00	10.00
	1886C B/II, "C" incuse	10.346	1.25	2.50	5.00	10.00
	1886B B/II, "B" incuse	3.155	1.25	2.50	5.00	10.00
	1887C B/II, "C" incuse	13.927	1.25	2.50	5.00	10.00
	1887B B/II, "B" incuse	3.283	1.25	2.50	5.00	10.00
	1888(c)B/II, w/o mm.	9.307	1.25	2.50	5.00	10.00
	1888B B/II, "B" incuse	8.039	1.25	2.50	5.00	10.00
	1888B	—	—	—	Proof	100.00
	1889C B/II, "C" incuse	.135	1.75	3.50	7.00	14.00
	1889B B/II, "B" incuse	5.895	1.25	2.50	5.00	10.00
	1890C B/II, "C" incuse	9.836	1.25	2.50	5.00	10.00
	1890C	—	—	—	Proof	100.00
	1890B B/II, "B" raised	7.790	1.25	2.50	5.00	10.00
	1890B B/II, "B" incuse	Inc. Ab.	1.25	2.50	5.00	10.00
	1890B (restrike)	—	—	—	P/L	30.00
	1891C B/II, "C" incuse	8.621	1.25	2.50	5.00	10.00
	1891C	—	—	—	Proof	100.00
	1891B B/II, "B" incuse					

KM#	Date	Mintage	Fine	VF	XF	Unc
488		4.230	1.25	2.50	5.00	10.00
	1891B (restrike)		—	—	P/L	30.00
	1892C B/II, "C" incuse	6.971	1.25	2.50	5.00	10.00
	1892C	—	—	—	Proof	100.00
	1892B B/II, "B" incuse	9.347	1.25	2.50	5.00	10.00
	1892B (restrike)		—	—	P/L	30.00
	1893C B/II, "C" incuse	8.003	1.25	2.50	5.00	10.00
	1893C	—	—	—	Proof	100.00
	1893B B/II, "B" incuse	10.716	1.25	2.50	5.00	10.00
	1893B (restrike)		—	—	P/L	30.00
	1894C B/II, "C" incuse	2.461	1.25	2.50	5.00	10.00
	1894C	—	—	—	Proof	100.00
	1894B B/II, "B" incuse	Inc. Ab.	1.25	2.50	5.00	10.00
	1894B (restrike)		—	—	P/L	30.00
	1895C B/II, "C" incuse	9.668	1.25	2.50	5.00	10.00
	1896C B/II, "C" incuse	6.616	1.25	2.50	5.00	10.00
	1896C	—	—	—	Proof	100.00
	1896B B/II, "B" incuse	8.235	1.25	2.50	5.00	10.00
	1897C B/II, "C" incuse	12.103	1.25	2.50	5.00	10.00
	1897C	—	—	—	Proof	100.00
	1897B B/II, "B" incuse	8.041	1.25	2.50	5.00	10.00
	1897B	—	—	—	Proof	100.00
	1897B (restrike)		—	—	P/L	30.00
	1898C B/II, "C" incuse	4.011	1.25	2.50	5.00	10.00
	1898B B/II, "B" incuse	3.250	1.25	2.50	5.00	10.00
	1898B	—	—	—	Proof	100.00
	1898B (restrike)		—	—	P/L	30.00
	1899	—	—	—	Proof	100.00
	1900C B/II, "C" incuse	1.705	1.25	2.50	5.00	10.00
	1900	—	—	—	Proof	—
	1900B B/I "B" raised	—	2.50	5.00	10.00	20.00
	1900B B/II, "B" raised	4.439	1.25	2.50	5.00	10.00
	1900B	—	—	—	Proof	100.00
	1900B (restrike)		—	—	P/L	30.00
	1901C B/II, "C" incuse	8.944	1.25	2.50	5.00	10.00
	1901C	Inc. Ab.	—	—	Proof	35.00
	1901B B/I "B" incuse	—	2.50	5.00	10.00	20.00
	1901B B/II, "B" incuse	1.706	1.25	2.50	5.00	10.00
	1901B	—	—	—	Proof	100.00
	1901B (restrike)		—	—	P/L	30.00
	1901B B/I "B" raised	—	2.50	5.00	10.00	20.00
	1901B B/II, "B" raised	Inc. Ab.	1.25	2.50	5.00	10.00

COPPER OR BRONZE

KM#	Date	Mintage	Fine	VF	XF	Unc
488b	1884	—	—	—	Proof	75.00
	1891	—	—	—	Proof	75.00
	1892	—	—	—	Proof	75.00

GOLD

KM#	Date	Mintage	Fine	VF	XF	Unc
488c	1891 (restrike)		—	—	P/L	250.00
	1892 (restrike)		—	—	P/L	250.00
	1893 (restrike)		—	—	P/L	250.00
	1896 (restrike)		—	—	P/L	250.00
	1897 (restrike)		—	—	P/L	250.00
	1898 (restrike)		—	—	P/L	250.00
	1900 (restrike)		—	—	P/L	250.00

1.4600 g, .917 SILVER, .0430 oz ASW
Mule. Obv: KM#469. Rev: KM#488.

KM#	Date	Mintage	Fine	VF	XF	Unc
489	1877 (restrike)		—	—	P/L	20.00

KM#	Date	Mintage	Fine	VF	XF	Unc
505	1903(c)	4.434	1.50	3.00	6.00	12.00
	1903(c)	—	—	—	Proof	65.00
	1903(c) (restrike)		—	—	P/L	25.00
	1904(c)	14.632	1.50	3.00	6.00	12.00
	1904(c)	—	—	—	Proof	65.00
	1904(c) (restrike)		—	—	P/L	25.00
	1905(c)	19.303	1.50	3.00	6.00	12.00
	1905(c) (restrike)		—	—	P/L	25.00
	1906(c)	1.629	1.50	3.00	6.00	12.00
	1906(c) (restrike)		—	—	P/L	25.00
	1907(c)	22.145	1.50	3.00	6.00	12.00
	1907(c)	—	—	—	Proof	65.00
	1908(c)	21.600	1.50	3.00	6.00	12.00
	1908(c)	—	—	—	Proof	65.00
	1908(c) (restrike)		—	—	P/L	25.00
	1909(c)	6.769	1.75	3.50	7.00	14.00
	1909(c)	—	—	—	Proof	65.00
	1909(c) (restrike)		—	—	P/L	25.00
	1910(c)	1.604	1.25	2.50	5.00	10.00
	1910(c)	—	—	—	Proof	65.00
	1910(c) (restrike)		—	—	P/L	25.00

GOLD

KM#	Date	Mintage	Fine	VF	XF	Unc
505a	1904(c) (restrike)		—	—	P/L	250.00
	1906(c) (restrike)		—	—	P/L	250.00
	1910(c) (restrike)		—	—	P/L	250.00

1.4600 g, .917 SILVER, .0430 oz ASW

NOTE: Calcutta Mint issues have no mint mark. Bombay Mint issues have a small raised bead or dot below the lotus flower at the bottom of the reverse. The 2 Annas dated 1911, like the other coins with the same date, has the "Pig" elephant. On these pieces like on the 1/4 Rupee, the King's bust is slightly smaller and has a higher relief than the later issues with the redesigned elephant.

KM#	Date	Mintage	Fine	VF	XF	Unc
514	1911(c)	16.760	1.50	3.00	6.00	12.00
	1911(c)	—	—	—	Proof	75.00
	1911(c) (restrike)		—	—	P/L	50.00
515	1912(c)	7.724	1.25	2.50	5.00	10.00
	1912(c)	—	—	—	Proof	50.00
	1912(b)	2.462	1.25	2.50	5.00	10.00
	1912(b)	—	—	—	Proof	50.00
	1912(b) (restrike)		—	—	P/L	25.00
	1913(c)	13.959	1.25	2.50	5.00	10.00
	1913(c)	—	—	—	Proof	50.00
	1913(b)	5.461	1.25	2.50	5.00	10.00
	1913(b)	—	—	—	Proof	50.00
	1913(b) (restrike)		—	—	P/L	25.00
	1914(c)	8.861	1.25	2.50	5.00	10.00
	1914(c)	—	—	—	Proof	50.00
	1914(b)	3.231	1.25	2.50	5.00	10.00
	1914(b) (restrike)		—	—	P/L	25.00
	1915(c)	1.620	1.25	2.50	5.00	10.00
	1915(c)	—	—	—	Proof	50.00
	1915(b)	2.711	1.25	2.50	5.00	10.00
	1915(b) (restrike)		—	—	P/L	25.00
	1916(c)	9.849	1.25	2.00	4.00	8.00
	1916(c)	—	—	—	Proof	50.00
	1916(c) (restrike)		—	—	P/L	25.00
	1917(c)	35.491	1.25	2.00	4.00	8.00
	1917(c)	—	—	—	Proof	50.00
	1917(c) (restrike)		—	—	P/L	25.00

COPPER-NICKEL

NOTE: Calcutta Mint issues have no mint mark. Bombay Mint issues have a small raised dot on the reverse at the bottom near the rim.

KM#	Date	Mintage	Fine	VF	XF	Unc
516	1918(c)	53.412	1.25	1.75	4.00	10.00
	1918(c)	—	—	—	Proof	50.00
	1918(b)	9.191	1.25	1.75	4.00	10.00
	1918(b)	—	—	—	Proof	50.00
	1918(b) (restrike)		—	—	P/L	20.00
	1919(c)	8.904	1.25	1.75	4.00	10.00
	1919(c)	—	—	—	Proof	50.00
	1919(c) (restrike)		—	—	P/L	20.00
	1920(b)	—	—	—	Proof	125.00
	1920(c)	13.520	1.25	1.75	4.00	10.00
	1920(c)	—	—	—	Proof	50.00
	1923(c)	7.656	1.25	1.75	4.00	10.00
	1923(c)	—	—	—	Proof	50.00
	1923(b)	6.431	1.25	1.75	4.00	10.00
	1923(b)	—	—	—	Proof	50.00
	1923(b) (restrike)		—	—	P/L	20.00
	1924(c)	8.384	1.25	1.75	4.00	10.00
	1924(c)	—	—	—	Proof	50.00
	1924(b)	4.818	1.25	1.75	4.00	10.00
	1924(b)	—	—	—	Proof	50.00
	1924(b) (restrike)		—	—	P/L	20.00
	1925(c)	10.848	1.25	1.75	4.00	10.00
	1925(c)	—	—	—	Proof	50.00
	1925(b)	8.348	1.25	1.75	4.00	10.00
	1925(b)	—	—	—	Proof	50.00
	1925(b) (restrike)		—	—	P/L	20.00
	1926(c)	8.352	1.25	1.75	4.00	10.00
	1926(c)	—	—	—	Proof	50.00
	1926(b)	2.927	1.25	1.75	4.00	10.00
	1926(b)	—	—	—	Proof	50.00
	1926(b) (restrike)		—	—	P/L	20.00
	1927(c)	6.424	1.25	1.75	4.00	10.00
	1927(c)	—	—	—	Proof	50.00
	1927(b)	4.835	1.25	1.75	4.00	10.00
	1927(b)	—	—	—	Proof	50.00
	1927(b) (restrike)		—	—	P/L	20.00
	1928(c)	7.352	1.25	1.75	4.00	10.00
	1928(c)	—	—	—	Proof	50.00
	1928(b)	4.876	1.25	1.75	4.00	10.00
	1928(b)	—	—	—	Proof	50.00
	1928(b) (restrike)		—	—	P/L	20.00
	1929(c)	13.408	1.25	1.75	4.00	10.00
	1929(c)	—	—	—	Proof	50.00
	1929(c) (restrike)		—	—	P/L	20.00
	1930(c)	8.888	1.25	1.75	4.00	10.00
	1930(c)	—	—	—	Proof	50.00
	1930(c) (restrike)		—	—	P/L	20.00
	1930(b)	—	1.25	1.75	4.00	10.00
	1933(c)	4.300	1.25	1.75	4.00	10.00

KM#	Date	Mintage	Fine	VF	XF	Unc
516	1933(c)	—	—	—	Proof	50.00
	1933(c) (restrike)		—	—	P/L	20.00
	1934(c)	7.016	1.25	1.75	4.00	10.00
	1934(c)	—	—	—	Proof	50.00
	1934(c) (restrike)		—	—	P/L	20.00
	1935(c)	12.354	1.25	1.75	4.00	10.00
	1935(b)	21.017	1.00	1.50	3.00	8.00
	1935(b)	—	—	—	Proof	50.00
	1935(b) (restrike)		—	—	P/L	20.00
	1936(b)	36.295	1.00	1.50	3.00	8.00
	1936(b)	—	—	—	Proof	50.00

Obv: First head, high relief.

NOTE: Calcutta Mint issues have no mint mark. Bombay Mint issues have a small dot before and after the date.

KM#	Date	Mintage	Fine	VF	XF	Unc
540	1939(c)	4.148	1.25	3.00	6.00	15.00
	1939(b)	3.392	2.00	5.00	10.00	25.00

Obv: Second head, low relief, large crown.
Rev: Large "2".

KM#	Date	Mintage	Fine	VF	XF	Unc
541	1939(c)	Inc. Ab.	1.25	2.00	2.50	4.00
	1939(c)	—	—	—	Proof	40.00
	1939(b)	Inc. Ab.	.20	.30	.50	1.00
	1939(b)	—	—	—	Proof	40.00
	1939(b) (restrike)		—	—	P/L	25.00
	1940(c)	37.636	.20	.30	.50	2.00
	1940(c)	—	—	—	Proof	40.00
	1940(b)	50.599	.20	.30	.50	2.00
	1940(b) (restrike)		—	—	P/L	25.00
	1941(c)	63.456	.20	.30	.50	1.00
	1941(b)	10.760	.20	.30	.75	2.50
	1941(b)	—	—	—	Proof	40.00
	1941(b) (restrike)		—	—	P/L	25.00

NICKEL-BRASS

KM#	Date	Mintage	Fine	VF	XF	Unc
541a	1942(b) small 4	133.000	.25	.35	.50	2.00
	1942(b) large 4	Inc. Ab.	.20	.35	.50	2.00
	1943(b)	343.680	.25	.35	.50	2.00
	1944L	6.352	.50	1.25	2.00	5.00
	1944(b) small 4	219.700	.25	.35	.50	2.00
	1944(b) large 4	Inc. Ab.	.25	.35	.50	2.00

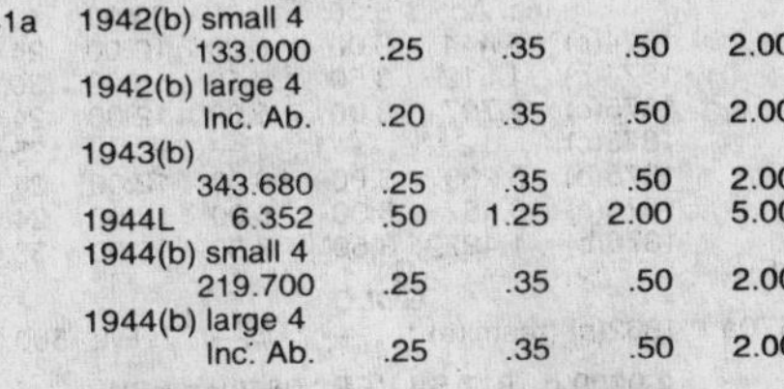

COPPER-NICKEL
Obv: Second head, low relief, small crown.
Rev: Small "2".

KM#	Date	Mintage	Fine	VF	XF	Unc
542	1946(c)	67.276	.20	.30	.50	2.00
	1946(b)	52.500	.20	.30	.50	2.00
	1946(b)	—	—	—	Proof	40.00
	1946(b) (restrike)		—	—	P/L	25.00
	1946(l)	*25.480	.20	.30	.50	2.00
	1947(c)	57.428	.20	.30	.50	2.00
	1947(b)	38.908	.20	.30	.50	2.00
	1947(b)	—	—	—	Proof	40.00
	1947(b) (restrike)		—	—	P/L	25.00

NOTE: W/o L mint mark but w/small diamond-shaped mark left of "1" on rev.

NICKEL-BRASS
Obv: Second head, low relief, large crown.
Rev: Small "2".

KM#	Date	Mintage	Fine	VF	XF	Unc
543	1945(c)	24.260	.25	.75	1.25	2.75

KM#	Date	Mintage	Fine	VF	XF	Unc
543	1945(c)	—	—	—	Proof	40.00
	1945(b)	136.688	.25	.35	.50	1.50
	1945(b) (restrike)		—	—	P/L	25.00

1/4 RUPEE

NOTE: The distinguishing features of the 3 busts and 2 reverses are as following:

BUST A-The front dress panel is divided into 4 sections. The last section has a 5-dotted flower at right.

BUST B-The front dress panel is divided into 4 sections. The last section, which is incomplete has a 5-petalled flower in the center.

BUST C-The front dress panel is divided into 3 sections. The last section has a 5-dotted flower at left.

REVERSE I-The 2 large petals above the base of the top flower are long and curved downward; long stroke between "1/4".

REVERSE II-The 2 large petals above the base of the top flower are short and horizontal; short stroke between "1/4".

As a result of recent studies, the 1/4 Rupees dated 1862-1876 have been re-attributed.

CALCUTTA issues dated 1862-1878 have no mint mark. The diameter of the coins is 19-19.2mm and the milling is coarse. From 1879 the mint mark is a small incuse "C" which is in the whorl below the center of the bottom flower.

BOMBAY issues dated 1862, 1875 and 1876 have no mint mark. These have a diameter of 19.7-8mm and the milling is narrow. The coins dated 1874, 1877-1883 have as mint mark a small bead directly above the bottom flower. From 1884 the mint mark is a small "B" raised or incuse, which is above the whorl, in the top flower.

MADRAS issues (1862 only) have a diameter of 20mm.

2.9200 g, .917 SILVER, .0860 oz ASW
Obv: Bust A. Rev: I.

KM#	Date	Mintage	Fine	VF	XF	Unc
470	1862(c) 19.3-19.4mm	19.412	2.50	5.00	10.00	20.00
	1862(c)	—	—	—	Proof	125.00
	1862(b) 19.7-19.8mm	11.390	2.50	5.00	10.00	20.00
	1862(b) (restrike)		—	—	P/L	35.00
	1862(m) 19.9-20.0mm	5.049	5.00	10.00	20.00	40.00
	1862(m) V1(I)CTORIA (error)	Inc. Ab.	5.00	10.00	20.00	40.00
	1874(c)	5.444	3.00	6.00	12.00	24.00
	1874(b)	1.612	3.50	7.50	15.00	30.00
	1875(c)	2.797	3.00	6.00	12.00	24.00
	1875(c)	—	—	—	Proof	125.00
	1875(b)	5.239	3.00	6.00	12.00	24.00
	1876(c)	6.457	3.00	6.00	12.00	24.00
	1876(b)	1.427	3.50	7.50	15.00	30.00

GOLD

KM#	Date	Mintage	Fine	VF	XF	Unc
470a	1862(c) (restrike)		—	—	P/L	500.00

2.9200 g, .917 SILVER, .0860 oz ASW.
Mule. Obv: 5 Rupee, KM#474.
Rev: 1/4 Rupee, KM#470.

KM#	Date	Mintage	Fine	VF	XF	Unc
471	1862(c) (restrike)		—	—	P/L	50.00

KM#	Date	Mintage	Fine	VF	XF	Unc
490	1877(c) B/I, no mm.	3.440	2.50	5.00	10.00	20.00
	1877(c)	—	—	—	Proof	125.00
	1877(b) A/I, dot	.884	3.50	7.50	15.00	30.00
	1877(b) B/I, dot	Inc. Ab.	3.50	7.50	15.00	30.00
	1877(b)	—	—	—	Proof	125.00
	1877(b) (restrike)		—	—	P/L	30.00
	1878C	3.284	2.00	3.50	7.50	15.00
	1878(c) C/II, w/o mm.	.044	2.00	3.50	8.00	20.00
	1878(c)	—	—	—	Proof	125.00
	1878(c) (restrike)		—	—	P/L	30.00
	1879C C/II, "C" incuse	Inc. Ab.	2.00	3.50	8.00	20.00
	1879(b)	—	—	—	Proof	125.00
	1880C C/II, "C" incuse	Inc. Be.	2.00	3.50	8.00	20.00
	1881C C/II, "C" incuse	3.244	2.00	3.75	8.00	20.00
	1881C	—	—	—	Proof	125.00
	1881(b) A/II, dot	1.444	2.00	3.75	8.00	20.00
	1881(b) B/I, dot	Inc. Ab.	4.00	7.50	15.00	30.00
	1882C C/II, "C" incuse	.612	2.00	3.50	8.00	20.00
	1882C	—	—	—	Proof	125.00
490	1882(b) A/II, dot	2.775	2.00	3.75	8.00	20.00
	1882(b) B/I, dot	Inc. Ab.	3.00	6.00	12.00	25.00
	1882(b) C/II, dot	Inc. Ab.	2.25	4.00	8.00	20.00
	1883C C/II, "C" incuse	2.871	4.00	7.50	15.00	30.00
	1883(b) B/I, dot	.184	2.25	4.00	8.00	20.00
	1884C C/II "C" incuse	3.596	3.75	7.50	15.00	30.00
	1884B B/I, "B" raised	1.709	3.75	7.50	15.00	30.00
	1884B C/II, "B" raised	Inc. Ab.	3.75	7.50	15.00	30.00
	1884B	—	—	—	Proof	125.00
	1885C C/II, "C" incuse	1.024	3.75	7.50	15.00	30.00
	1885B B/I, "B" raised	1.118	3.75	7.50	15.00	30.00
	1886C C/II, "C" incuse	7.087	2.25	4.00	8.00	20.00
	1886B C/II, "B" raised	1.684	3.75	7.50	15.00	30.00
	1887C C/II, "C" incuse	6.494	2.25	4.00	8.00	20.00
	1887B C/II, "B" raised	4.422	2.50	5.00	10.00	20.00
	1888(c) C/II, no mm.	4.945	2.50	5.00	10.00	20.00
	1888B C/II, "B" raised	2.278	3.00	6.00	12.00	25.00
	1888B C/II, "B" incuse	Inc. Ab.	3.75	7.50	15.00	30.00
	1889C C/II, "C" incuse	8.075	2.25	4.00	8.00	20.00
	1889B C/II, "B" incuse	4.298	2.50	5.00	10.00	20.00
	1889	—	—	—	Proof	125.00
	1890C C/II, "C" incuse	Inc. 1891	2.50	5.00	10.00	20.00
	1890C	—	—	—	Proof	125.00
	1890B C/I, "B" incuse	—	4.00	7.50	15.00	30.00
	1890B C/II, "B" incuse	.459	4.50	8.50	16.50	32.50
	1890B (restrike)		—	—	P/L	30.00
	1891C C/II, "C" incuse	13.770	2.25	4.00	8.00	20.00
	1891B C/I, "B" incuse	.883	3.75	7.50	15.00	30.00
	1892C	—	2.50	5.00	10.00	20.00
	1892C	—	—	—	Proof	125.00
	1892B C/I, "B" incuse	4.059	2.00	3.00	6.00	15.00
	1892B	—	—	—	Proof	125.00
	1893C C/II, "C" incuse	6.435	2.00	3.00	6.00	15.00
	1893C	—	—	—	Proof	125.00
	1893B C/I, "B" incuse	6.137	2.00	3.00	6.00	15.00
	1893B (restrike)		—	—	P/L	30.00
	1894C C/II, "C" incuse	2.653	2.00	3.00	6.00	15.00
	1894C	—	—	—	Proof	125.00
	1894B C/I, "B" incuse	2.385	2.00	3.00	6.00	15.00
	1894B	—	—	—	Proof	125.00
	1894B (restrike)		—	—	P/L	30.00
	1896C C/II, "C" incuse	6.811	2.00	3.00	6.00	15.00
	1896C	—	—	—	Proof	125.00
	1897C C/II, "C" incuse	5.884	2.00	3.00	6.00	15.00
	1897C	—	—	—	Proof	125.00
	1897B C/I, "B" incuse	2.893	2.00	3.00	6.00	15.00
	1897B	—	—	—	Proof	125.00
	1897B (restrike)		—	—	P/L	30.00
	1898C C/II, "C" incuse	1.330	2.00	3.00	6.00	15.00
	1898C	—	—	—	Proof	125.00
	1898B C/I, "B" incuse	2.056	2.00	3.00	6.00	15.00
	1898B	—	—	—	Proof	125.00
	1898B (restrike)		—	—	P/L	30.00
	1900C C/II, "C" incuse	1.606	2.00	3.00	6.00	15.00
	1900C	—	—	—	Proof	125.00
	1900C (restrike)		—	—	P/L	30.00
	1901C C/II, "C" incuse	4.476	2.00	3.00	6.00	15.00
	1901C	—	—	—	Proof	125.00
	1901C (restrike)		—	—	P/L	30.00

COPPER OR BRONZE

KM#	Date	Mintage	Fine	VF	XF	Unc
490b	1884	—	—	—	Proof	100.00
	1891	—	—	—	Proof	100.00
	1892	—	—	—	Proof	100.00

GOLD

KM#	Date	Mintage	Fine	VF	XF	Unc
490c	1891 (restrike)		—	—	P/L	350.00
	1892 (restrike)		—	—	P/L	350.00
	1893 (restrike)		—	—	P/L	350.00
	1896 (restrike)		—	—	P/L	350.00
	1897 (restrike)		—	—	P/L	350.00
	1898 (restrike)		—	—	P/L	350.00
	1900 (restrike)		—	—	P/L	350.00

2.9200 g, .917 SILVER, .0860 oz ASW

KM#	Date	Mintage	Fine	VF	XF	Unc
506	1903(c)	2.472	1.50	3.00	8.00	20.00
	1903(c)	—	—	—	Proof	100.00
	1903(c) (restrike)		—	—	P/L	30.00
	1904(c)	28.241	1.50	3.00	8.00	20.00
	1904(c)	—	—	—	Proof	100.00
	1904(c) (restrike)		—	—	P/L	30.00
	1905(c)	10.026	1.50	3.00	8.00	20.00
	1905(c)	—	—	—	Proof	100.00
	1905(c) (restrike)		—	—	P/L	30.00
	1906(c)	16.300	1.50	3.00	8.00	20.00
	1906(c) (restrike)		—	—	P/L	30.00
	1907(c)	10.672	1.50	3.00	8.00	20.00
	1907(c)	—	—	—	Proof	100.00
	1907(c) (restrike)		—	—	P/L	30.00
	1908(c)	11.464	1.50	3.00	8.00	20.00
	1908(c)	—	—	—	Proof	100.00
	1908(c) (restrike)		—	—	P/L	30.00
	1909(c)	—	—	—	Proof	125.00
	1909(c) (restrike)		—	—	P/L	30.00
	1910(c)	.802	1.50	3.00	8.00	20.00
	1910(c)	—	—	—	Proof	100.00
	1910(c) (restrike)		—	—	P/L	30.00

GOLD

KM#	Date	Mintage	Fine	VF	XF	Unc
506a	1910(c) (restrike)		—	—	P/L	500.00

2.9200 g, .917 SILVER, .0860 oz ASW

NOTE: Calcutta Mint issues have no mint mark. Bombay Mint issues have a small raised bead or dot in the space below the lotus flower at the bottom of the reverse. The 1/4 Rupee dated 1911, like the other coins with the same date, has the "Pig" elephant. On these pieces the King's bust is slightly smaller and has a higher relief than later issues with the re-designed elephant.

KM#	Date	Mintage	Fine	VF	XF	Unc
517	1911(c)	8.024	2.00	4.00	8.00	20.00
	1911(c)	—	—	—	Proof	90.00
	1911(c) (restrike)		—	—	P/L	60.00
518	1912(c)	2.245	2.00	2.75	5.00	15.00
	1912(c)	—	—	—	Proof	65.00
	1912(b)	1.168	2.00	2.75	5.00	15.00
	1912(b)	—	—	—	Proof	65.00
	1912(b) (restrike)		—	—	P/L	25.00
	1913(c)	9.587	2.00	2.75	5.00	15.00
	1913(c)	—	—	—	Proof	65.00
	1913(b)	2.276	2.00	2.75	5.00	15.00
	1913(b)	—	—	—	Proof	65.00
	1913(b) (restrike)		—	—	P/L	25.00
	1914(c)	6.014	2.00	2.75	5.00	10.00
	1914(c)	—	—	—	Proof	65.00
	1914(b)	3.967	2.00	2.75	5.00	10.00
	1914(b) (restrike)		—	—	P/L	25.00
	1915(c)	.851	2.25	4.00	10.00	35.00
	1915(c)	—	—	—	Proof	65.00
	1915(b)	2.096	2.00	2.75	5.00	15.00
	1915(b) (restrike)		—	—	P/L	25.00
	1916(c)	10.716	2.00	2.75	5.00	15.00
	1916(c)	—	—	—	Proof	65.00
	1916(c) (restrike)		—	—	P/L	25.00
	1917(c)	21.380	2.00	2.75	5.00	15.00
	1917(c)	—	—	—	Proof	65.00
	1917(c) (restrike)		—	—	P/L	25.00
	1918(c)	43.306	2.00	2.75	5.00	15.00
	1918(c)	—	—	—	Proof	65.00
	1919(b)	—	3.50	7.50	15.00	30.00
	1919(c)	35.557	2.00	2.75	5.00	15.00
	1919(c)	—	—	—	Proof	65.00
	1920(b)	—	3.25	6.50	12.50	25.00
	1925(b)	2.003	2.00	2.75	5.00	15.00
	1925(b)	—	—	—	Proof	65.00
	1925(b) (restrike)		—	—	P/L	25.00
	1926(c)	6.117	2.00	2.75	5.00	15.00
	1926(c)	—	—	—	Proof	65.00
	1926(c) (restrike)		—	—	P/L	25.00
	1928(b)	4.023	2.00	2.75	5.00	15.00
	1928(b)	—	—	—	Proof	65.00
	1929(c)	4.013	2.00	2.75	5.00	15.00
	1929(c)	—	—	—	Proof	65.00
	1929(c) (restrike)		—	—	P/L	25.00
	1930(c)	3.942	2.00	2.75	5.00	15.00
	1930(c)	—	—	—	Proof	65.00
	1930(c) (restrike)		—	—	P/L	25.00
	1934(c)	3.947	2.00	2.75	5.00	10.00
	1936(c)	21.771	1.25	2.25	4.00	8.00
	1936(b)	7.142	1.25	2.25	4.00	8.00
	1936(b) (restrike)		—	—	P/L	25.00

NOTE: The silver coinage of George VI is a very complex series with numerous obverse and reverse die varieties. Two different designs of the head appear on the obverse of most denominations struck for George VI. The "First Head" shows the Kings effigy in high relief; the "Second Head" in low relief. In 1941-42 The "Second Head" was slightly reduced in size and this type continued to be used on the silver coins and on some of the smaller denominations.

First Head

Second Head (small) Second Head (large)

From 1942 to 1945 the reverse designs of the silver coins change slightly every year. However, a distinct reverse variety occurs on Rupees and 1/4 Rupees dated 1943-44 and on the half Rupee dated 1944, all struck at Bombay. This variety may be distinguished from the other coins by the design of the center bottom flower as illustrated, and is designated as Reverse B.

On the normal common varieties dated 1943-44 the three "scalloped circles" are not connected to each other and the bead in the center is not attached to the nearest circle.

Obv: First head, reeded edge.

NOTE: Calcutta Mint issues have no mint mark. Bombay coins have a small bead below the lotus flower at the bottom on the reverse, except those dated 1943-1944 with reverse B which have a diamond. Lahore Mint issues have a small "L" in the same position. The nickel coins have a diamond below the date on the reverse.

KM#	Date	Mintage	Fine	VF	XF	Unc
544	1938(c)	—	—	—	Proof	65.00
	1938(c) (restrike)		—	—	P/L	25.00
	1939(c)	3.072	2.00	3.50	6.00	12.00
	1939(c)	—	—	—	Proof	65.00
	1939(b)	6.770	2.00	3.50	5.00	10.00
	1939(b) (restrike)		—	—	P/L	25.00

2.9200 g, .500 SILVER, .0469 oz ASW

KM#	Date	Mintage	Fine	VF	XF	Unc
544a	1940(b)	24.635	2.00	3.50	5.00	10.00

Obv: Small second head, low relief, large crown.
Rev: Reeded edge.

KM#	Date	Mintage	Fine	VF	XF	Unc
545	1940(c)	68.675	BV	1.50	2.50	6.00
	1940(c)	—	—	—	Proof	65.00
	1940(b)	28.947	BV	1.50	2.50	6.00

Obv: Small second head, low relief, small crown.
Reeded edge.

KM#	Date	Mintage	Fine	VF	XF	Unc
546	1942(c)	88.096	BV	1.50	2.25	4.50
	1943(c)	90.994	BV	1.50	2.25	4.50

Obv: Small second head, low relief, small crown.
Security edge.

KM#	Date	Mintage	Fine	VF	XF	Unc
547	1943B	95.200	BV	1.50	2.25	4.50
	1943B	—	—	—	Proof	60.00
	1943B reverse B	Inc. Ab.	BV	1.50	2.25	4.50
	1943L	23.700	BV	1.50	2.25	4.50
	1944B	170.504	BV	1.50	2.25	4.50
	1944B reverse B	Inc. Ab.	BV	1.50	2.25	4.50
	1944L	86.400	BV	1.50	2.25	4.50
	1945(b) small 5	181.648	BV	1.50	2.25	4.50
	1945(b) large 5	Inc. Ab.	BV	.85	1.75	4.00
	1945L small 5	29.751	BV	1.50	2.25	4.50
	1945L large 5	Inc. Ab.	BV	1.00	2.00	5.00

NICKEL
Reeded edge.

KM#	Date	Mintage	Fine	VF	XF	Unc
548	1946(b)	83.600	.30	.60	1.00	2.75
	1947(b)	109.948	.40	.75	1.50	3.50
	1947(b)	—	—	—	Proof	50.00

4 ANNAS

NOTE: Calcutta Mint issues have no mint mark. Bombay Mint issues have a small raised dot on the reverse at the bottom near the rim.

COPPER-NICKEL

KM#	Date	Mintage	Fine	VF	XF	Unc
519	1919(c)	18.632	2.50	5.00	10.00	20.00
	1919(c)	—	—	—	Proof	150.00
	1919(b)	7.672	3.25	6.50	12.50	25.00
	1919 (restrike)		—	—	P/L	25.00
	1920(c)	18.191	2.50	5.00	10.00	20.00
	1920(c)	—	—	—	Proof	150.00
	1920(b)	1.666	2.50	5.00	10.00	20.00
	1920(b)	—	—	—	Proof	150.00
	1920(b) (restrike)		—	—	P/L	25.00
	1921(c)	—	—	—	Proof	150.00
	1921(c) (restrike)		—	—	P/L	75.00
	1921(b)	1.219	3.00	6.50	12.50	25.00
	1921(b)	—	—	—	Proof	150.00
	1921 (restrike)		—	—	P/L	25.00

8 ANNAS

NOTE: Calcutta Mint issues have no mint mark. Bombay Mint issues have a small raised dot on the reverse at the bottom near the rim.

COPPER-NICKEL

KM#	Date	Mintage	Fine	VF	XF	Unc
520	1919(c)	2.980	3.75	7.50	15.00	30.00
	1919(c)	—	—	—	Proof	150.00
	1919(b)	1.400	4.00	8.50	17.50	35.00
	1919(b) (restrike)		—	—	P/L	30.00
	1920(c)	—	—	—	Proof	150.00
	1920(c) (restrike)		—	—	P/L	75.00
	1920(b)	1.000	12.50	25.00	50.00	100.00
	1920(b)	—	—	—	Proof	150.00
	1920(b) (restrike)		—	—	P/L	30.00

1/2 RUPEE

Distinguishing Features

BUST A-The front dress panel has 4 sections. The last section has a round flower at left and right.

BUST B-The dress panel has 4-1/2 or 4-2/3 sections. The last, incomplete section has a 5-petalled flower at left of center.

BUST C-The dress panel is the same as on Bust B but the floral design of the dress differs.

Bust B Bust C

REVERSE I-The top flower is open and the 2 large petals above the whorl are short and horizontal.

REVERSE II-The top flower is closed and the 2 petals above the whorl are long and curved downward.

CALCUTTA issues have Bust A/Reverse I and Bust C/Reverse II dated 1862-1878 have no mint mark. From 1879 the mint mark is a small incuse "C" located in the whorl, below the center of the bottom flower.

BOMBAY and MADRAS issues dated 1862 have no mint mark. From 1874-1884 the mint mark is a small bead directly above the center of the bottom flower. From 1885 the mint mark is a "B" raised or incuse, in the top flower.

5.8300 g, .917 SILVER, .1719 oz ASW

KM#	Date	Mintage	Fine	VF	XF	Unc
472	1862(c) A/I	7.649	5.00	10.00	20.00	50.00
	1862(c)	—	—	—	Proof	175.00
	1862(c) A/II w/V in bottom of bust	.736	7.50	15.00	30.00	60.00
	1862(c)	—	—	—	Proof	175.00
	1862(b & m) B/II	7.122	5.00	10.00	20.00	40.00
	1862(b) (restrike)		—	—	P/L	35.00
	1862(c) C/II	1.623	5.00	10.00	20.00	40.00
	1874(b) B/II, dot	1.654	7.50	15.00	30.00	65.00
	1875(c) A/I	2.257	5.00	10.00	20.00	50.00
	1875(c)	—	—	—	Proof	175.00
	1875(b) B/II, dot	1.023	7.50	15.00	30.00	65.00
	1876(b) B/II, dot	.966	7.50	15.00	30.00	65.00
	GOLD					
472a	1862(c) (restrike)		—	—	P/L	600.00

5.8300 g, .917 SILVER, .1719 oz ASW

KM#	Date	Mintage	Fine	VF	XF	Unc
491	1877(c) A/I	.858	5.00	10.00	20.00	45.00
	1877(c)	—	—	—	Proof	175.00
	1877(b) B/II, dot	.214	7.50	15.00	30.00	60.00
	1887(b) (restrike)		—	—	P/L	30.00
	1878(c) A/I	1.390	5.00	10.00	20.00	45.00
	1878(c)	—	—	—	Proof	175.00
	1878(c) (restrike)		—	—	P/L	30.00
	1879C A/I, "C" incuse	1.008	5.00	10.00	20.00	45.00
	1879(b)	—	—	—	Proof	175.00
	1880C A/I, "C" incuse	.180	7.50	15.00	30.00	60.00
	1881C A/I, "C" incuse	.921	5.00	10.00	20.00	45.00
	1881C	—	—	—	Proof	175.00
	1881(b) B/II, dot	1.591	5.00	10.00	20.00	45.00
	1882C A/I, "C" incuse	1.161	5.00	10.00	20.00	45.00
	1882C	—	—	—	Proof	175.00
	1882(b) B/II, dot	.308	8.00	17.50	35.00	70.00
	1882(b) A/II, dot	Inc. Ab.	8.00	17.50	35.00	70.00
	1883C A/I, "C" incuse	1.036	5.00	10.00	20.00	45.00
	1884C A/I, "C" incuse	—	5.00	10.00	20.00	45.00
	1884(b) A/II, dot	1.110	5.00	10.00	20.00	45.00
	1884(b) A/II, no mm.	Inc. Ab.	5.00	10.00	20.00	45.00
	1884	—	—	—	Proof	175.00
	1885C A/I, "C" incuse	1.408	3.75	7.50	15.00	40.00
	1885B A/II, "B" raised	.390	5.00	10.00	20.00	45.00
	1886C A/I, "C" incuse					

KM#	Date	Mintage	Fine	VF	XF	Unc
491		2.645	3.75	7.50	15.00	40.00
	1886B A/II, "B" raised	1.116	3.75	7.50	15.00	40.00
	1887C A/I, "C" incuse	2.275	3.75	7.50	15.00	40.00
	1887B A/II, "B" raised	.407	5.00	10.00	20.00	45.00
	1888C A/I, "C" incuse	1.100	3.75	7.50	15.00	40.00
	1888B A/II, "B" raised	1.748	5.00	10.00	20.00	45.00
	1888(b) A/II, no mm.	Inc. Ab.	5.00	10.00	20.00	45.00
	1889C A/I, "C" incuse	2.331	3.75	7.50	15.00	40.00
	1889B A/II, "B" raised	1.083	3.75	7.50	15.00	40.00
	1889B A/I, "B" incuse	Inc. Ab.	3.75	7.50	15.00	40.00
	1890C	—	—	—	Proof	175.00
	1890C (restrike)		—	—	P/L	30.00
	1891C	—	—	—	Proof	175.00
	1891B A/I, "B" incuse	—	—	—	Proof	175.00
	1891B	—	—	—	Proof	175.00
	1891 (restrike)		—	—	P/L	30.00
	1892C A/I, "C" incuse	1.761	3.75	7.50	15.00	40.00
	1892C	—	—	—	Proof	175.00
	1892B A/I, "B" incuse	1.104	3.75	7.50	15.00	40.00
	1892B	—	—	—	Proof	175.00
	1893C A/I, "C" incuse	—	3.75	7.50	15.00	40.00
	1893C	—	—	—	Proof	175.00
	1893B A/I, "B" incuse	2.462	3.75	7.50	15.00	40.00
	1893B (restrike)		—	—	P/L	40.00
	1894C A/I, "C" incuse	1.277	3.75	7.50	15.00	40.00
	1894C	—	—	—	Proof	175.00
	1894B A/I, "B" incuse	—	4.00	10.00	20.00	50.00
	1894B (restrike)		—	—	P/L	40.00
	1896C A/I, "C" incuse	2.114	3.75	7.50	15.00	40.00
	1896C	—	—	—	Proof	175.00
	1897C A/I, "C" incuse	—	3.75	7.50	15.00	40.00
	1897C	—	—	—	Proof	175.00
	1897B A/I, "B" incuse	.560	3.75	7.50	15.00	40.00
	1897B	—	—	—	Proof	175.00
	1897B (restrike)		—	—	P/L	35.00
	1898C A/I, "C" incuse	2.057	3.75	7.50	15.00	40.00
	1898C	—	—	—	Proof	175.00
	1898B A/I, "B" incuse	.458	5.00	10.00	20.00	45.00
	1898B	—	—	—	Proof	175.00
	1898B (restrike)		—	—	P/L	35.00
	1899C A/I, "C" incuse	6.893	3.75	7.50	15.00	40.00
	1899C	—	—	—	Proof	175.00
	1899B A/I, "B" incuse	11.174	2.50	5.00	10.00	30.00
	1899B A/I, "B" incuse, inverted B	—	5.00	10.00	30.00	60.00
	1899B	Inc. Ab.	—	—	Proof	175.00
	1899B (restrike)		—	—	P/L	35.00
	1900C A/I (restrike)			—	P/L	35.00

ALUMINUM

KM#	Date	Mintage	Fine	VF	XF	Unc
491a	1891	—	—	—	Proof	—

COPPER OR BRONZE

KM#	Date	Mintage	Fine	VF	XF	Unc
491b	1884	—	—	—	Proof	100.00
	1891	—	—	—	Proof	100.00
	1892	—	—	—	Proof	100.00

GOLD

KM#	Date	Mintage	Fine	VF	XF	Unc
491c	1891 (restrike)		—	—	P/L	450.00
	1892 (restrike)		—	—	P/L	450.00
	1893 (restrike)		—	—	P/L	450.00
	1896 (restrike)		—	—	P/L	450.00
	1897 (restrike)		—	—	P/L	450.00
	1898 (restrike)		—	—	P/L	450.00
	1899 (restrike)		—	—	P/L	450.00

5.8300 g, .917 SILVER, .1719 oz ASW

NOTE: Calcutta Mint issues have no mint mark. Bombay Mint issues have a small incuse "B" in the space below the cross pattee of the crown on the reverse.

KM#	Date	Mintage	Fine	VF	XF	Unc
507	1904(c)	—	—	—	Proof	175.00
	1904(c) (restrike)		—	—	P/L	40.00
	1905(c)	.823	3.50	10.00	25.00	50.00
	1905(c) (restrike)		—	—	P/L	40.00
	1906(c)	3.036	3.50	10.00	25.00	50.00
	1906B	.400	3.75	12.50	30.00	60.00
	1906B (restrike)		—	—	P/L	40.00
	1907(c)	2.786	3.50	10.00	25.00	50.00

KM#	Date	Mintage	Fine	VF	XF	Unc
507	1907(c)	—	—	—	Proof	150.00
	1907B	1.856	3.50	10.00	25.00	50.00
	1907B	—	—	—	Proof	150.00
	1907B (restrike)		—	—	P/L	40.00
	1908(c)	1.577	3.50	10.00	25.00	50.00
	1908(c)	—	—	—	Proof	150.00
	1908(c) (restrike)		—	—	P/L	40.00
	1909(c)	1.569	3.50	10.00	25.00	50.00
	1909(c)	—	—	—	Proof	150.00
	1909(c) (restrike)		—	—	P/L	40.00
	1909B	—	—	—	Proof	450.00
	1909B (restrike)		—	—	P/L	90.00
	1910(c)	3.413	3.50	10.00	25.00	50.00
	1910(c)	—	—	—	Proof	150.00
	1910B	.809	3.50	10.00	25.00	50.00
	1910B	—	—	—	Proof	150.00
	1910B (restrike)		—	—	P/L	40.00

NOTE: Calcutta Mint issues have no mint marks. Bombay Mint issues have a small raised bead or dot in the space below the lotus flower at the bottom of the reverse. The half Rupee dated 1911 like the Rupee and all other issues of that year has the "Pig" elephant. It was struck only at the Calcutta Mint.

KM#	Date	Mintage	Fine	VF	XF	Unc
521	1911(c)	2.293	2.00	6.00	12.50	30.00
	1911(c)	—	—	—	Proof	175.00
	1911(c) (restrike)		—	—	P/L	75.00
522	1912(c)	3.390	2.00	6.00	12.50	30.00
	1912(c)	—	—	—	Proof	125.00
	1912(b)	1.505	2.00	6.00	12.50	30.00
	1912(b)	—	—	—	Proof	125.00
	1912(b) (restrike)		—	—	P/L	25.00
	1913(c)	Inc. Ab.	2.00	6.00	12.50	30.00
	1913(c)	—	—	—	Proof	125.00
	1913(b)	Inc. Ab.	2.00	6.00	12.50	30.00
	1913(b)	—	—	—	Proof	125.00
	1913(b) (restrike)		—	—	P/L	25.00
	1914(c)	1.639	2.00	6.00	12.50	30.00
	1914(c)	—	—	—	Proof	125.00
	1914(b)	1.919	2.00	6.00	12.50	30.00
	1914(b) (restrike)		—	—	P/L	25.00
	1915(c)	1.600	2.00	6.00	12.50	30.00
	1915(c)	—	—	—	Proof	125.00
	1916(c)	1.402	2.00	6.00	12.50	30.00
	1916(c)	—	—	—	Proof	125.00
	1916(b)	4.615	2.00	6.00	12.50	30.00
	1917(c)	—	—	—	Proof	125.00
	1917(b)	8.422	2.00	6.00	12.50	30.00
	1917(b)	—	—	—	Proof	125.00
	1918(c) (restrike)		—	—	P/L	25.00
	1918(b)	8.768	2.00	6.00	12.50	30.00
	1918(b) (restrike)		—	—	P/L	25.00
	1919(b)	12.180	2.00	6.00	12.50	30.00
	1919(b)	—	—	—	Proof	125.00
	1919(b) (restrike)		—	—	P/L	25.00
	1919(c)	—	4.00	8.00	17.50	40.00
	1921(c)	5.804	2.00	6.00	12.50	30.00
	1921(c)	—	—	—	Proof	125.00
	1921(c) (restrike)		—	—	P/L	25.00
	1922(c)	4.405	2.00	6.00	12.50	30.00
	1922(c)	—	—	—	Proof	125.00
	1922(b)	1.037	2.00	6.00	12.50	30.00
	1922(b)	—	—	—	Proof	125.00
	1922(b) (restrike)		—	—	P/L	25.00
	1923(c)	—	2.00	6.00	12.50	30.00
	1923(c) (restrike)		—	—	P/L	25.00
	1923(b)	1.005	2.00	6.00	12.50	30.00
	1923(b)	—	—	—	Proof	125.00
	1923(b) (restrike)		—	—	P/L	25.00
	1924(c)	3.646	2.00	6.00	12.50	30.00
	1924(c)	—	—	—	Proof	125.00
	1924(b)	2.089	2.00	6.00	12.50	30.00
	1924(b)	—	—	—	Proof	125.00
	1924(b) (restrike)		—	—	P/L	25.00
	1925(c)	3.975	2.00	6.00	12.50	30.00
	1925(c)	—	—	—	Proof	125.00
	1925(b)	1.627	2.00	6.00	12.50	30.00
	1925(b)	—	—	—	Proof	125.00
	1925(b) (restrike)		—	—	P/L	25.00
	1926(c)	6.139	2.00	6.00	12.50	30.00
	1926(c)	—	—	—	Proof	125.00
	1926(b)	2.011	2.00	6.00	12.50	30.00
	1926(b)	—	—	—	Proof	125.00
	1926(b) (restrike)		—	—	P/L	25.00
	1927(c)	2.032	2.00	6.00	12.50	30.00
	1927(c)	—	—	—	Proof	125.00
	1927(c) (restrike)		—	—	P/L	25.00
	1928(b)	2.466	2.00	6.00	12.50	30.00
	1928(b)	—	—	—	Proof	125.00
	1929(c)	4.050	2.00	6.00	12.50	30.00
	1929(c)	—	—	—	Proof	125.00
	1929(c) (restrike)		—	—	P/L	25.00
	1930(c)	2.036	2.00	6.00	12.50	30.00
	1930(c)	—	—	—	Proof	125.00
	1930(c) (restrike)		—	—	P/L	25.00
	1933/2(c)	4.056	5.00	10.00	25.00	50.00
	1933(c)	Inc. Ab.	2.00	6.00	12.50	30.00
	1933(c)	—	—	—	Proof	75.00

KM#	Date	Mintage	Fine	VF	XF	Unc
522	1933(c) (restrike)		—	—	P/L	25.00
	1934(c)	4.056	2.00	6.00	12.50	30.00
	1934(c)	—	—	—	Proof	125.00
	1934(c) (restrike)		—	—	P/L	25.00
	1936(c)	16.919	2.00	6.00	12.50	30.00
	1936(b)	6.693	2.00	6.00	12.50	30.00
	1936(b) (restrike)		—	—	P/L	25.00

Obv: First head, reeded edge.

NOTE: Calcutta Mint issues have no mint mark. Bombay coins dated 1938-43 and 1945 have a bead below the lotus flower at the bottom of the reverse. Specimens dated 1944 with Reverse B have a diamond in the same position. Those dated 1944 with the normal common reverse have either a bead or a diamond. Lahore Mint issues have a small raised "L" in the same position as the Bombay coins. Bombay Mint 1943 coins have either large or small denticles on obverse. The nickel pieces of the last issue have a diamond below the date on the reverse.

KM#	Date	Mintage	Fine	VF	XF	Unc
549	1938(c)	—	—	—	Proof	100.00
	1938(b)	2.200	BV	3.00	7.50	15.00
	1938(b) (restrike)		—	—	P/L	25.00
	1939(c)	3.300	BV	3.00	7.50	15.00
	1939(c)	—	—	—	Proof	75.00
	1939(b)	10.096	BV	3.00	7.50	15.00
	1939(b)	—	—	—	Proof	75.00
	1939(b) (restrike)		—	—	P/L	25.00

Obv: Large second head, reeded edge.

KM#	Date	Mintage	Fine	VF	XF	Unc
550	1939(c)	Inc. Ab.	BV	3.00	6.50	15.00
	1939(b)	Inc. Ab.	BV	3.00	6.50	13.50

5.8300 g, .500 SILVER, .0937 oz ASW

KM#	Date	Mintage	Fine	VF	XF	Unc
550a	1940(c)	32.898	BV	3.00	6.00	12.00
	1940(c)	—	—	—	Proof	75.00
	1940(b)	17.811	BV	3.00	6.50	13.50
	1940(b) (restrike)		—	—	P/L	25.00

Obv: Large second head, security edge.

KM#	Date	Mintage	Fine	VF	XF	Unc
551	1941(b)	26.100	BV	2.00	5.00	12.50
	1942(b)	61.600	BV	2.00	5.00	12.50

Obv: Small second head, security edge.
Rev: Denomination and inner circle smaller.

KM#	Date	Mintage	Fine	VF	XF	Unc
552	1942(b)	Inc. Ab.	BV	2.00	4.50	9.00
	1943(b)	90.400	BV	2.00	4.50	9.00
	1943(b)	—	—	—	Proof	75.00
	1943B reverse B	—	BV	2.00	4.50	9.00
	1943L	9.000	BV	2.00	4.50	9.00
	1943L	—	—	—	Proof	75.00
	1944(b)	46.200	BV	2.00	4.50	9.00
	1944B reverse B	Inc. Ab.	BV	2.00	4.50	9.00
	1944L	79.100	BV	2.00	4.50	9.00
	1945(b)	32.722	BV	2.00	4.50	9.00
	1945L small date	79.192	BV	2.00	4.50	9.00
	1945L large date	Inc. Ab.	2.50	5.00	10.00	20.00

NICKEL
Mule. Obv: KM#552. Rev: KM#549.

KM#	Date	Mintage	Fine	VF	XF	Unc
A553	1938(c) (restrike)		—	—	P/L	—

KM#	Date	Mintage	Fine	VF	XF	Unc
553	1946(b)	47.500	.50	1.00	2.25	4.50
	1947(b)	62.724	.50	1.00	2.00	4.00
	1947(b)	—	—	—	Proof	65.00

RUPEE

NOTE: The Rupees dated 1862 were struck with the date unchanged until 1874. However, in 1863 Bombay Mint adopted a method of adding dots or beads to its dies to indicate the exact year of minting.

The beads occur in the following positions:

1. Below the base or whorl of the top flower.
2. Above or around the top of the bottom flower.
3. In both positions together.

The different busts are identified as follows:

BUST A-The front dress panel has 3-3/4 sections with 2 dividing lines below the lowest string of pearls.

BUST B-The front dress panel has 4-1/4 sections with 3 dividing lines below the lowest string of pearls.

BUST C-Like Bust A, but shorter at the bottom. The front panel has only 3-1/3 sections.

The reverses are identified by the design of the top center flower as illustrated.

I

II

III

A variety of Reverse II, designated as IIa, shows the flower buds with a pineapple like pattern above "ONE" and above right of the second "E" of "RUPEE". In the listing of 1862 Rupees, the date column indicates the year in which the coins are believed to have been struck. The variety column lists the Obverse/reverse combination and the bead position. For example, A/I 0/0 means Bust A, Reverse I and no beads. A II 1/2 means Bust A, Reverse II, and 1 bead at the top and 2 beads at the bottom.

Mintage for 1862 Rupees

Calcutta	269,427,222
Bombay	408,003,034
Madras	29,481,923

NOTE: The B/II 0/0 coins are attributed to the mint of issues as follows:

CALCUTTA, 30.3mm, round pearls in crown arch.
BOMBAY, 30.5mm, elongated pearls in crown arch. The scroll like floral design of the dress is in flat relief and has a depression around it.
MADRAS, 30.55mm, elongated pearls in crown arch. The floral design is in high relief and shows no depression.

11.6600 g, .917 SILVER, .3438 oz ASW
Common date: 1862

KM#	Date	Year	Fine	VF	XF	Unc
473.1	A/I, 0/0	1862-63(m)	5.00	7.50	12.50	25.00
	A/II, 0/0 (30.7mm)	1862-63(b)	12.50	20.00	32.50	60.00
	A/IIa, 0/0	1862-63(c)	7.50	12.50	16.50	35.00
	B/II, 0/0	1862-63(c)	6.50	11.50	15.00	30.00
	B/II, 0/0	1862-63(b)	5.00	7.50	12.50	25.00
	B/II, 0/0	1862-63(m)	5.00	7.50	12.50	25.00
	B/IIa, 0/0	1862-63(b) or (m)	12.50	20.00	30.00	60.00
	A/III, 0/0	1862-63(c)	12.50	20.00	30.00	60.00
	B/III, 0/0	1862-63(c)	12.50	20.00	30.00	60.00
	B/II, 1/0	1863(b)	7.50	12.50	16.50	35.00
	A/II, 0/2	1864(b)	12.50	20.00	40.00	80.00
	B/II, 2/0	1864(b)	12.50	20.00	40.00	80.00
	B/II, 3/0	1864(b)	12.50	20.00	40.00	80.00
	A/II, 2/0	1864(b)	—	—	Rare	—
	B/II, 0/3	1865(b)	5.00	7.50	12.50	30.00
	B/II, 2/3	1865(b)	12.50	20.00	40.00	80.00
	A/I, 0/4	1866(b)	12.50	20.00	40.00	80.00
	B/I, 0/4	1866(b)	12.50	20.00	40.00	80.00
	A/II, 0/4	1866(b)	8.00	15.00	30.00	60.00
	A/II, 2/4	1866(b)	15.00	30.00	50.00	90.00
	B/II, 0/4	1866(b)	8.00	15.00	30.00	60.00
	A/II, 0/5	1867(b)	5.00	7.50	13.50	30.00
	A/II, 0/6	1868(b)	5.00	7.50	13.50	30.00
	A/II, 0/7	1869(b)	5.00	7.50	13.50	30.00
	B/II, 0/6	1869(b)	—	—	Rare	—
	B/II, 0/7	1869(b)	12.50	20.00	32.50	60.00
	A/II, 1/7 (top dot in top flower)	1869-70(b)	—	—	Rare	—
	A/II, 1/7 (top dot in normal position)	1872(b)	12.50	20.00	40.00	80.00
	A/II, 0/8	1870(b)	12.50	20.00	40.00	80.00
	A/II, 0/9	1871(b)	12.50	20.00	40.00	80.00
	A/II, 0/10	1872(b)	7.50	12.50	16.50	35.00
	A/II, 1/10 (top dot in top flower)	1872-73(b)	12.50	20.00	40.00	80.00
	A/II, 1/10 (top dot in normal position)	1873(b)	12.50	20.00	40.00	80.00
	A/I, 1/11	1873(b)	7.50	12.50	16.50	35.00
	A/II, 0/1	1873(b)	12.50	20.00	40.00	80.00
	A/II, 1/1	1873(b)	12.50	20.00	40.00	80.00
	A/II, 0/12	1874(b)	12.50	20.00	40.00	80.00
	A/II, 1/2	1874(b)	10.00	17.50	27.50	50.00
	A/I, 1/2	1874(b)	12.50	20.00	40.00	80.00
	C/I, 1/2	1874(b)	12.50	20.00	40.00	80.00
	C/II, 1/2	1874(b)	10.00	17.50	27.50	50.00
	1862(c)	—	—	—	Proof	200.00
	1862(c) (restrike)		—	—	P/L	55.00

GOLD

KM#	Date	Mintage	Fine	VF	XF	Unc
473.1a	1862(c) (restrike)		—	—	P/L	—

From 1874 onward the coins show the year date. The designs are similar to those on the 1862 Rupees but only Bust "A" and the Reverse I and II were used.

CALCUTTA Mint issues dated 1874-78 have no mint mark. From 1879 the mint mark is a small incuse "C" on the whorl below the center of the bottom lotus flower on the reverse. All Calcutta issues have Reverse I.
BOMBAY Mint issues dated 1875-83 have as mint mark a small bead directly above the center of the bottom lotus flower. From 1883 the mint mark is a small "B" raised or incuse above the whorl or base of the top flower. Both mint marks occur on the coins dated 1883. The issues dated 1874-76 have Reverse II only, those dated 1877-85 have both Reverses I and II. Reverse II distinguishes the 1874 coins which have no mint mark from those of Calcutta.

NOTE: There are reverse varieties in most of the following Rupees. Reverse II flowers are found in various sizes. Two bottom rosettes are found rotated, i.e., 1 petal up or down.

11.6600 g, .917 SILVER, .3438 oz ASW

KM#	Date	Mintage	Fine	VF	XF	Unc
473.2	1874(c) Rev.I	15.014	2.50	8.00	12.00	25.00
	1874(b) Rev.II	25.509	2.50	8.00	12.00	25.00
	1874(b) Rev. II, dot	Inc. Ab.	3.00	10.00	15.00	30.00
	1874(b)	—	—	—	Proof	175.00
	1874(b) (restrike)		—	—	P/L	35.00
	1875(c) Rev.I	11.632	2.50	8.00	12.00	25.00
	1875(c) Rev.II	—	2.50	8.00	12.00	25.00
	1875(c)	—	—	—	Proof	175.00
	1875(b) Rev.II, dot below	19.360	2.50	8.00	12.00	25.00
	1875(b)	—	—	—	Proof	175.00
	1875(b) (restrike)		—	—	P/L	35.00
	1875(b) C/II, dot below	Inc. Ab.	—	—	—	—
	1876(c) Rev.I	12.001	2.50	8.00	12.00	25.00
	1876(b) Rev.II, dot	28.950	2.50	8.00	12.00	25.00
	1876(b)	—	—	—	Proof	175.00
	1876(b) (restrike)		—	—	P/L	35.00

KM#	Date	Mintage	Fine	VF	XF	Unc
492	1877(c) Rev.I	39.252	2.50	8.00	12.00	25.00
	1877(c)	—	—	—	Proof	175.00
	1877(b) Rev.I, dot	95.554	2.50	8.00	12.00	25.00
	1877(b) Rev.II, dot	Inc. Ab.	2.50	8.00	12.00	25.00
	1877(b)	—	—	—	Proof	175.00
	1877(b) (restrike)		—	—	P/L	75.00
	1878(c) Rev.I	32.653	2.50	8.00	12.00	25.00
	1878(c)	—	—	—	Proof	175.00
	1878(b) Rev.I, dot	63.927	2.50	8.00	12.00	25.00
	1878(b) Rev.II, dot	Inc. Ab.	2.50	8.00	12.00	25.00
	1878(b)	—	—	—	Proof	175.00
	1878(b) (restrike)		—	—	P/L	35.00
	1879C Rev.I, "C" incuse	15.928	2.50	8.00	12.00	25.00
	1879(b) Rev.I, dot	72.800	6.50	17.50	27.50	50.00
	1879(b) Rev.II, dot	Inc. Ab.	2.50	8.00	12.00	25.00
	1879(b) Rev.II, dot (rosette var.)	Inc. Ab.	2.50	8.00	12.00	25.00
	1879(b)	—	—	—	Proof	175.00
	1879(b) (restrike)		—	—	P/L	35.00
	1880C Rev.I, "C" incuse	18.400	3.00	10.00	15.00	30.00
	1880(b) Rev.I, dot	53.786	2.50	8.00	12.00	25.00
	1880(b) Rev.II, dot	Inc. Ab.	2.50	8.00	12.00	25.00
	1880(b) (restrike)		—	—	P/L	35.00
	1881C Rev.I, "C" incuse	2.436	3.00	10.00	15.00	35.00
	1881C	—	—	—	Proof	175.00
	1881(b) Rev.I, dot	3.162	6.50	17.50	27.50	50.00
	1881(b) Rev.II, dot	Inc. Ab.	6.50	17.50	27.50	50.00
	1881(b) (restrike)		—	—	P/L	35.00
	1882C Rev.I, "C" incuse	15.090	2.50	8.00	12.00	25.00
	1882C	—	—	—	Proof	175.00
	1882(b) Rev.I, dot	56.397	2.50	8.00	12.00	25.00
	1882(b) (restrike)		—	—	P/L	35.00
	1882 Rev. II, dot	—	—	—	—	—
	1883C Rev.I, "C" incuse	5.123	3.00	10.00	15.00	30.00
	1883(c) Rev.I, no mm.	Inc. Ab.	7.50	20.00	37.50	70.00
	1883(b) Rev.I, dot	18.023	6.50	17.50	27.50	50.00
	1883B Rev.I, "B" raised	Inc. Ab.	6.50	17.50	27.50	50.00
	1883B Rev.I, dot, "B" raised	Inc. Ab.	7.50	20.00	37.50	70.00
	1883B (restrike)		—	—	P/L	35.00
	1884C Rev.I, "C" incuse	11.642	2.50	8.00	12.00	25.00
	1884B Rev.I, "B" raised	35.847	3.00	10.00	17.50	35.00
	1884B Rev. II, "B" raised on whorl below bottom flower	I.A.	6.50	17.50	27.50	50.00
	1884B (restrike)		—	—	P/L	35.00
	1885C Rev.I, "C" incuse	34.152	2.50	8.00	12.00	25.00
	1885C	—	—	—	Proof	175.00
	1885B Rev.I, "B" raised	64.878	2.50	8.00	12.00	25.00
	1885B Rev.II, "B" raised	Inc. Ab.	2.50	8.00	12.00	25.00
	1885B Rev.I, "B" incuse	Inc. Ab	2.50	8.00	12.00	25.00

KM#	Date	Mintage	Fine	VF	XF	Unc
492		Inc. Ab.	6.50	17.50	27.50	50.00
	1885B (restrike)		—	—	P/L	35.00
	1886C Rev.I, "C" incuse	10.878	2.50	8.00	12.00	25.00
	1886C	—	—	—	Proof	175.00
	1886B Rev.I, "B" incuse	41.146	2.50	8.00	12.00	25.00
	1886B (restrike)		—	—	P/L	35.00
	1887C Rev.I, "C" incuse	40.200	2.50	8.00	12.00	25.00
	1887B Rev.I, "B" raised	48.400	2.50	8.00	12.00	25.00
	1887B Rev.I, "B" incuse	Inc. Ab.	2.50	8.00	12.00	25.00
	1887B Rev.I, "B" incuse, inverted B	Inc. Ab.	3.00	10.00	15.00	30.00
	1887B (restrike)		—	—	P/L	35.00
	1888C Rev.I, "C" incuse	7.568	2.50	8.00	12.00	25.00
	1888B Rev.I, "B" raised	63.200	2.50	8.00	12.00	25.00
	1888B Rev.I, "B" incuse	Inc. Ab.	2.50	8.00	12.00	25.00
	1888B (restrike)		—	—	P/L	35.00
	1889C Rev.I, "C" incuse	9.368	2.50	8.00	12.00	25.00
	1889B Rev.I, "B" raised	65.300	2.50	8.00	12.00	30.00
	1889B Rev.I, "B" incuse	Inc. Ab.	2.50	8.00	12.00	25.00
	1889B (restrike)		—	—	P/L	35.00
	1890C Rev.I, "C" incuse	24.742	2.50	8.00	12.00	25.00
	1890C	—	—	—	Proof	175.00
	1890B Rev.I, "B" incuse	92.900	2.50	8.00	12.00	25.00
	1890B (restrike)		—	—	P/L	35.00
	1891C Rev.I, "C" incuse	14.670	2.50	8.00	12.00	25.00
	1891C	—	—	—	Proof	175.00
	1891B Rev.I, "B" incuse	49.500	2.50	8.00	12.00	25.00
	1891B	—	—	—	Proof	175.00
	1892C Rev.I, "C" incuse	32.455	2.50	8.00	12.00	25.00
	1892C	—	—	—	Proof	175.00
	1892B Rev.I, "B" raised	72.200	2.50	8.00	12.00	25.00
	1892B Rev.I, "B" incuse	Inc. Ab.	2.50	8.00	12.00	25.00
	1892B	—	—	—	Proof	175.00
	1892B (restrike)		—	—	P/L	35.00
	1893C Rev.I, "C" incuse	9.140	2.50	8.00	12.00	25.00
	1893C	—	—	—	Proof	175.00
	1893B Rev.I, "B" incuse	69.590	2.50	8.00	12.00	25.00
	1893B	—	—	—	Proof	175.00
	1893B (restrike)		—	—	P/L	35.00
	1894C	—	—	—	Proof	200.00
	1897C Rev.I, "C" incuse	.470	15.00	35.00	70.00	175.00
	1897C	—	—	—	Proof	225.00
	1897B Rev.I, "B" incuse	1.055	6.50	17.50	27.50	50.00
	1897B	—	—	—	Proof	175.00
	1897B (restrike)		—	—	P/L	35.00
	1898C Rev.I, "C" incuse	1.251	4.00	12.50	22.50	40.00
	1898C	—	—	—	Proof	175.00
	1898B Rev.I, "B" incuse	6.268	2.50	8.00	12.00	25.00
	1898B	—	—	—	Proof	175.00
	1898B (restrike)		—	—	P/L	35.00
	1900C Rev.I, "C" incuse	5.291	2.50	8.00	12.00	25.00
	1900C	—	—	—	Proof	175.00
	1900B Rev.I, "B" incuse	65.237	BV	6.00	12.00	25.00
	1900B	—	—	—	Proof	175.00
	1900B (restrike)		—	—	P/L	35.00
	1901C Rev.I, "C" incuse	72.017	BV	6.00	12.00	25.00
	1901C	Inc. Ab.	—	—	Proof	175.00
	1901B Rev.I, "B" incuse	103.258	BV	6.00	12.00	25.00
	1901B	—	—	—	Proof	175.00
	1901B (restrike)		—	—	P/L	35.00

ALUMINUM

KM#	Date	Mintage	Fine	VF	XF	Unc
492a	1891B	—	—	—	Proof	—

COPPER OR BRONZE

KM#	Date	Mintage	Fine	VF	XF	Unc
492b	1884	—	—	—	Proof	100.00
	1885	—	—	—	Proof	100.00
	1887	—	—	—	Proof	100.00
	1891	—	—	—	Proof	100.00
	1892	—	—	—	Proof	100.00

GOLD

KM#	Date	Mintage	Fine	VF	XF	Unc
492c	1891	(restrike)	—	—	P/L	500.00
	1892	(restrike)	—	—	P/L	500.00
	1893	(restrike)	—	—	P/L	500.00
	1898	(restrike)	—	—	P/L	500.00
	1900B	(restrike)	—	—	P/L	500.00

11.6600 g, .917 SILVER, .3438 oz ASW

NOTE: Calcutta Mint issues have no mint mark. Bombay Mint issues have a small incuse "B" in the space below the cross pattee of the crown on the reverse.

KM#	Date	Mintage	Fine	VF	XF	Unc
508	1903(c)	49.403	BV	6.00	12.00	25.00
	1903(c)	—	—	—	Proof	350.00
	1903B (in relief)	52.969	BV	6.00	12.00	25.00
	1903B	—	—	—	Proof	350.00
	1903B (incuse)	Inc. Ab.	BV	6.00	12.00	25.00
	1903B (restrike)		—	—	P/L	30.00
	1904(c)	58.339	BV	6.00	12.00	25.00
	1904(c)	—	—	—	Proof	350.00
	1904B	101.949	BV	6.00	12.00	25.00
	1904B	—	—	—	Proof	350.00
	1904B (restrike)		—	—	P/L	30.00
	1905(c)	51.258	BV	6.00	12.00	25.00
	1905(c)	—	—	—	Proof	350.00
	1905B	76.202	BV	6.00	12.00	25.00
	1905B	—	—	—	Proof	350.00
	1905B (restrike)		—	—	P/L	30.00
	1906(c)	104.797	BV	6.00	15.00	30.00
	1906B	158.953	BV	6.00	15.00	30.00
	1906B	—	—	—	Proof	350.00
	1906B (restrike)		—	—	P/L	30.00
	1907(c)	81.338	BV	6.00	15.00	30.00
	1907(c)	—	—	—	Proof	350.00
	1907B	170.912	BV	6.00	15.00	30.00
	1907B	—	—	—	Proof	350.00
	1907B (restrike)		—	—	P/L	30.00
	1908(c)	20.218	BV	6.00	15.00	30.00
	1908(c)	—	—	—	Proof	350.00
	1908B	10.715	5.00	15.00	30.00	60.00
	1908B	—	—	—	Proof	350.00
	1908B (restrike)		—	—	P/L	30.00
	1909(c)	12.759	BV	6.00	15.00	30.00
	1909(c)	—	—	—	Proof	350.00
	1909B	9.539	5.00	15.00	30.00	60.00
	1909B	—	—	—	Proof	350.00
	1909B (restrike)		—	—	P/L	30.00
	1910(c)	12.627	BV	6.00	12.00	25.00
	1910(c)	—	—	—	Proof	350.00
	1910B	10.885	BV	6.00	12.00	25.00
	1910B	—	—	—	Proof	350.00
	1910B (restrike)		—	—	P/L	30.00

NOTE: Calcutta Mint issues have no mint mark. Bombay Mint issues have a small raised bead or dot in the space below the lotus flower at the bottom of the reverse.

Obverse Dies

Type I

Type II

Type I - Obv. die w/elephant with piglike feet and short tail. Nicknamed "pig rupee".

Type II - Obv. die w/redesigned elephant with outlined ear, heavy feet and long tail.

The Rupees dated 1911 were rejected by the public because the elephant, on the Order of the Indian Empire shown on the King's robe, was thought to resemble a pig, an animal considered unclean by most Indians. Out of a total of 9.4 million pieces struck at both mints, only 700,000 were issued, and many of these were withdrawn and melted with unissued pieces. The issues dated 1912 and later have a re-designed elephant.

KM#	Date	Mintage	Fine	VF	XF	Unc
523	1911(c)	4.300	10.00	20.00	40.00	100.00
	1911(c)	—	—	—	Proof	600.00
	1911(b)	5.143	10.00	20.00	40.00	100.00
	1911(b) (restrike)		—	—	P/L	75.00

Redesigned elephant.

KM#	Date	Mintage	Fine	VF	XF	Unc
524	1912(c)	45.122	2.50	7.50	15.00	35.00
	1912(c)	—	—	—	Proof	500.00
	1912(b)	79.067	BV	6.00	12.50	25.00
	1912(b)	—	—	—	Proof	500.00
	1912B (restrike)		—	—	P/L	30.00
	1913(c)	75.800	BV	6.00	12.50	25.00
524	1913(c)	—	—	—	Proof	500.00
	1913(b)	87.466	BV	6.00	12.50	25.00
	1913(b)	—	—	—	Proof	500.00
	1913(b) (restrike)		—	—	P/L	30.00
	1914(c)	33.100	BV	6.00	12.50	25.00
	1914(c)	—	—	—	Proof	500.00
	1914(b)	15.270	BV	6.00	12.50	25.00
	1914(b)	—	—	—	Proof	500.00
	1914(b) (restrike)		—	—	P/L	30.00
	1915(c)	9.900	5.00	15.00	30.00	60.00
	1915(c)	—	—	—	Proof	500.00
	1915(b)	5.372	7.50	20.00	40.00	80.00
	1915(b)	—	—	—	Proof	500.00
	1915(b) (restrike)		—	—	P/L	30.00
	1916(c)	115.000	BV	6.00	12.50	20.00
	1916(c)	—	—	—	Proof	500.00
	1916(b)	97.900	BV	6.00	12.50	20.00
	1916(b)	—	—	—	Proof	500.00
	1916(b) (restrike)		—	—	P/L	30.00
	1917(c)	114.974	BV	6.00	12.50	20.00
	1917(c)	—	—	—	Proof	500.00
	1917(b)	151.583	BV	6.00	12.50	20.00
	1917(b)	—	—	—	Proof	500.00
	1917(b) (restrike)		—	—	P/L	30.00
	1918(c)	205.420	BV	6.00	12.50	20.00
	1918(c)	—	—	—	Proof	500.00
	1918(b)	210.550	BV	6.00	12.50	20.00
	1918(b)	—	—	—	Proof	500.00
	1918(b) (restrike)		—	—	P/L	30.00
	1919(c)	211.206	BV	6.00	12.50	20.00
	1919(c)	—	—	—	Proof	500.00
	1919(b)	226.706	BV	6.00	12.50	20.00
	1919(b)	—	—	—	Proof	500.00
	1919(b) (restrike)		—	—	P/L	30.00
	1920(c)	50.500	BV	6.00	12.50	20.00
	1920(c)	—	—	—	Proof	500.00
	1920(b)	55.937	BV	6.00	12.50	20.00
	1920(b)	—	—	—	Proof	500.00
	1920B (restrike)		—	—	P/L	30.00
	1921(b)	5.115	12.50	37.50	75.00	125.00
	1921(b)	—	—	—	Proof	500.00
	1922(b)	2.051	12.50	37.50	75.00	125.00
	1922(b)	—	—	—	Proof	500.00
	1935(c)	—	—	—	Proof	500.00
	1935(c) (restrike)		—	—	P/L	125.00
	1936(c)	—		—	Proof	500.00

Obv: "First Head", reeded edge.

KM#	Date	Mintage	Fine	VF	XF	Unc
554	1938(c)	—	—	—	Proof	275.00
	1939(c)	—	—	—	Proof	350.00

NOTE: No rupees with the "First Head" were struck for circulation. Those dated 1938-39 were struck in 1940 before the fineness of the silver coins was reduced to .500.

The pieces struck at Calcutta have no mint mark. Bombay issues dated 1938-41 and 1944-45 have a bead below the lotus flower at the bottom of the reverse while those dated 1942-44 have a small diamond mark in the same position. On the specimens dated 1944 with Reverse B the mint mark appears to be a "bead over a diamond". Lahore Mint issues have a small raised "L" in the same position as the Bombay coins. The last issue nickel rupees struck at Bombay have a small diamond below the date on the reverse. The rupees dated 1943 occur with large and small "Second Head" and with large and small date figure "3".

Obv: Large "Second Head", reeded edge.

KM#	Date	Mintage	Fine	VF	XF	Unc
555	1938(b) w/o dot	7.352	7.50	11.50	16.50	27.50
	1938(b) dot	I.A.	7.50	11.50	16.50	27.50
	1938(b) (restrike)		—	—	P/L	50.00
	1939(b) dot	2.450	150.00	300.00	600.00	1200.

11.6600 g, .500 SILVER, .1874 oz ASW
Security edge

KM#	Date	Mintage	Fine	VF	XF	Unc
556	1939(b)	—	200.00	400.00	800.00	1500.
	1940(b)	153.120	BV	4.00	10.00	20.00
	1941(b)	111.480	BV	4.00	10.00	20.00
	1943(b)	Inc. Be.	BV	4.00	10.00	20.00

Obv: Small "Second Head", security edge.

KM#	Date	Mintage	Fine	VF	XF	Unc
557	1942(b)	244.500	BV	4.00	10.00	20.00
	1943(b)	65.995	BV	4.00	10.00	20.00
	1943(b) Rev. B	Inc. Ab.	BV	4.00	10.00	20.00
	1944(b) Rev. B	146.206	BV	4.00	10.00	20.00
	1944(b)	Inc. Ab.	BV	4.00	10.00	20.00
	1944L small L	91.400	BV	4.00	10.00	20.00
	1944L large L	Inc. Ab.	BV	4.00	10.00	20.00
	1945(b) small date	142.666	BV	3.00	6.00	12.50
	1945(b) large date	Inc. Ab.	BV	3.00	7.50	15.00
	1945(b)	—	—	—	Proof	—
	1945L	118.126	BV	3.00	6.00	12.50

Reeded edge (error)

KM#	Date	Mintage	Fine	VF	XF	Unc
558	1944(b)	—	—	—	—	—
	1945(b)	—	—	—	—	—

NICKEL

Mule. Obv: KM#557. Rev: KM#555.

KM#	Date	Mintage	Fine	VF	XF	Unc
A559	1938(c) (restrike)		—	—	P/L	125.00

Rev: New design, security edge.

KM#	Date	Mintage	Fine	VF	XF	Unc
559	1947(b)	118.128	1.50	2.50	5.00	10.00
	1947B	—	—	—	Proof	75.00
	1947(I)	41.911	1.50	3.00	6.00	12.00

NOTE: Bombay issue has diamond mark below date, Lahore w/o privy mark.

5 RUPEES

3.8870 g, .917 GOLD, .1146 oz AGW
Obv: Young bust.
Reeded edge

KM#	Date	Year	Fine	VF	XF	Unc
474	1870CM	—	125.00	175.00	300.00	400.00
	1875	—	—	—	Proof	850.00

Plain edge

KM#	Date	Year	Fine	VF	XF	Unc
475	1870	—	—	—	Proof	850.00

SILVER

KM#	Date	Year	Fine	VF	XF	Unc
475a	1870	—	—	—	Proof	—

3.8870 g, .917 GOLD, .1146 oz AGW
Obv: Mature bust.
Reeded edge

KM#	Date	Mintage	Fine	VF	XF	Unc
476	1870(c)	.013	125.00	175.00	300.00	400.00
	1870(c)	—	—	—	Proof	450.00
	1870(c) (restrike)		—	—	P/L	400.00

Mule. Obv: 1/4 Rupee, Bust A, KM#490.
Rev: KM#476.
Obv: Young bust.

KM#	Date	Year	Fine	VF	XF	Unc
493.1	1879(b) (restrike)		—	—	P/L	400.00

Mule. Obv: 1/4 Rupee, Bust B. Rev: KM#476.

KM#	Date	Year	Fine	VF	XF	Unc
493.2	1879(b) (restrike)		—	—	P/L	400.00

Mule. Obv: 1/4 Rupee, Bust C. Rev: KM#476.

KM#	Date	Year	Fine	VF	XF	Unc
493.3	1879(b) (restrike)		—	—	P/L	400.00

Obv: Mature bust.

KM#	Date	Year	Fine	VF	XF	Unc
494	1879(b) (restrike)		—	—	P/L	275.00

10 RUPEES

7.7740 g, .917 GOLD, .2292 oz AGW
Obv: Young bust.
Reeded edge

KM#	Date	Mintage	Fine	VF	XF	Unc
477	1870CM		—	—	Proof	500.00
	1870CM (restrike)		—	—	P/L	500.00
	1875		—	—	Proof	1250.

Plain edge

KM#	Date	Mintage	Fine	VF	XF	Unc
478	1870	—	—	—	Proof	1250.

SILVER

KM#	Date	Mintage	Fine	VF	XF	Unc
478a	1870	—	—	—	Proof	—

7.7740 g, .917 GOLD, .2292 oz AGW
Obv: Mature bust.
Reeded edge

KM#	Date	Mintage	Fine	VF	XF	Unc
479	1870(c)	7,932	150.00	275.00	400.00	500.00
	1870(c)	—	—	—	Proof	500.00
	1870(c) (restrike)	—	—	—	P/L	500.00

KM#	Date	Mintage	Fine	VF	XF	Unc
495	1878(b)	—	—	—	Proof	1250.
	1878(b) (restrike)	—	—	—	P/L	500.00
	1879(b)	—	—	—	Proof	1250.
	1879(b) (restrike)	—	—	—	P/L	500.00

15 RUPEES

7.9881 g, .917 GOLD, .2354 oz AGW

KM#	Date	Mintage	Fine	VF	XF	Unc
525	1918(b)	2.110	120.00	165.00	225.00	325.00
	1918(b)	12 pcs.	—	—	Proof	1250.
	1918(b) (restrike)		—	—	P/L	300.00

NOTE: The above issue was equal in weight and fineness to the British sovereign.

MOHUR

11.6600 g, .917 GOLD, .3437 oz AGW
Obv: Young bust.

KM#	Date	Mintage	Fine	VF	XF	Unc
480	1862(c)	.153	200.00	275.00	350.00	450.00
	1862(c)	Inc. Ab.	—	—	Proof	850.00
	1862(c) (restrike)		—	—	P/L	350.00

KM#	Date	Mintage	Fine	VF	XF	Unc
480	1862(c) w/V on bust	Inc. Ab.	200.00	275.00	350.00	450.00
	1862(c) w/V on rev. in design below date	Inc. Ab.	200.00	275.00	350.00	450.00
	1862(c) w/V on bust and on rev.	—	200.00	275.00	350.00	450.00
	1862(c) w/V on bust and 2 flowers in bottom panel	I.A.	200.00	275.00	350.00	450.00
	1870(c)	—	—	—	Proof	750.00
	1870(c) (restrike)		—	—	P/L	400.00
	1875(c) w/V on bust	.011	225.00	300.00	500.00	750.00
	1875(c)	—	—	—	Proof	2500.
	1875(c) (restrike)		—	—	P/L	400.00

COPPER OR BRONZE

KM#	Date	Mintage	Fine	VF	XF	Unc
480a	1862(c)	—	—	—	350.00	—

Mule. Obv: KM#481. Rev: KM#480.

KM#	Date	Mintage	Fine	VF	XF	Unc
A481	1862(c)	—	—	—	—	—

11.6600 g, .917 GOLD, .3437 oz AGW
Obv: Mature bust.

KM#	Date	Mintage	Fine	VF	XF	Unc
481	1870(c)	—	—	—	Proof	2500.
	1870(c) (restrike)		—	—	P/L	400.00

Mule. Obv: KM#496. Rev: KM#481.

KM#	Date	Mintage	Fine	VF	XF	Unc
482	1870(c)	—	—	—	P/L	650.00

Obv: Young bust.

KM#	Date	Mintage	Fine	VF	XF	Unc
496	1877(c)	.010	175.00	200.00	275.00	425.00
	1878(c) (restrike)		—	—	P/L	400.00
	1879C	.019	175.00	200.00	275.00	425.00
	1879(b) modified rev.	—	—	—	Proof	2500.
	1879(b) (restrike)		—	—	P/L	400.00
	1881	.023	175.00	200.00	275.00	425.00
	1882C	.012	175.00	200.00	275.00	425.00
	1882(b) w/o C mm (restrike)			—	P/L	400.00
	1884(c)	8,643	185.00	275.00	375.00	500.00
	1885(c)	.015	175.00	200.00	275.00	425.00
	1888(c)	.015	175.00	250.00	325.00	425.00
	1889(c)	.015	175.00	200.00	275.00	425.00
	1889(c) (restrike)		—	—	P/L	400.00
	1891(c)	.017	175.00	200.00	275.00	425.00

COPPER OR BRONZE

KM#	Date	Mintage	Fine	VF	XF	Unc
496a	1878(b)	—	—	—	350.00	—

TRADE COINAGE

SOVEREIGN

7.9881 g, .917 GOLD, .2354 oz AGW

KM#	Date	Mintage	Fine	VF	XF	Unc
525A	1918I	1.295	120.00	135.00	165.00	200.00
	1918I	—	—	—	Proof	—
	1918I (restrike)	—	—	—	P/L	175.00

NOTE: The Mansfield Commission of 1868 allowed for the admission of British and Australian sovereigns (see Australian section; sovereigns with shield reverse were struck for export to India) as payment for sums due.

The fifth branch of the Royal Mint was established in a section of the Bombay Mint as from December 21, 1917. This was a war-time measure, its purpose being to strike into sovereigns the gold blanks supplied by the Bombay and other Indian mints. The Bombay sovereigns bear the mint mark I and were struck from August 15, 1918 to April 22, 1919. The branch-mint was closed in May, 1919.

MINT SETS (MS)

KM#	Date	Mintage	Identification	Mkt.Val.
MS1	1835c(3)	—	KM448a-450a	—

PROOF SETS (PS)

KM#	Date	Mintage	Identification	Mkt.Val.
PS1	1835c(3)	—	KM445-447	500.00
PS2	1875(3)	—	KM474,477,480	4500.
PS3	1904(5)	—	KM497,499,503,Pn70(2)	3000.
PS4	1904(3)	—	KM497,499,501(bronze) w/'1' c/m on rev.	3000.
PS5	1911c(4)	—	KM514,517,521,523	400.00
PS6	1919c(8)	—	KM513,516,519-520 (2 each—V.I.P.)	1500.
PS7	1938c(6)	—	KM527-528,530,536,544,555	350.00
PS8	1947b(7)	—	KM533,535,538,542,548, 553,559	300.00

ANDAMAN ISLANDS

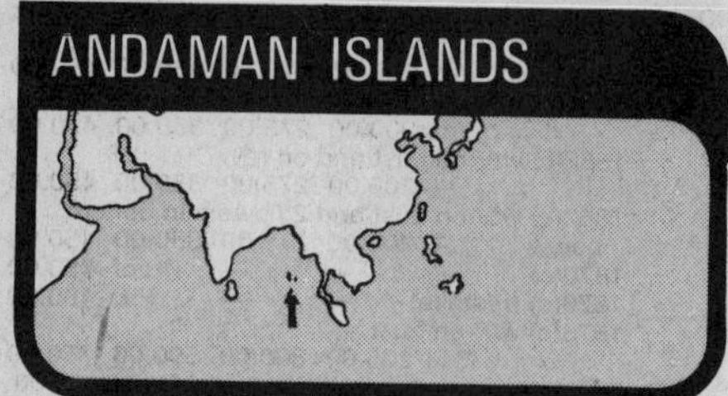

The Andaman Islands are the northern group of 204 volcanic and coral isles in the east part of the Bay of Bengal about 400 miles directly west of the coast of lower Burma has an area of 2,508 sq. mi. and a population of 65,000. Capital: Port Blair. Chief exports are timber and coconut.

In 1789 the first British settlement was established at Port Blair. It was relocated at Port Cornwallis on North Andaman in 1791 and abandoned in 1796. A penal colony on South Andaman was re-established at the place now known as Port Blair. In 1872 the islands were merged with the nearby Nicobar Islands to form a single administrative unit. No prisoners were sent here after 1921 and the penal colony was closed just after World War II. These islands were occupied by the Japanese in World War II and were for a time handed over to the "Provisional Government of Azad Hind" (Free India) to administer until August 1947. Although the islands are geographically remote from India, and their people ethnically distinct, their previous association with British India resulted in their incorporation into the Indian Republic at Independence in 1947.

RULERS

British, until 1947

TOKEN ISSUES (Tn)

RUPEE

COPPER

KM#	Date	Mintage	VG	Fine	VF	XF
Tn1	1861	*.020	1250.	1750.	2250.	3250.
	W/o center hole.					
Tn1a	1861	—	—	—	Unc.	3500.
	Mule w/o center hole. Obv: KM#Tn2. Rev: KM#Tn1.					
Tn1b	1861	—	—	—	Proof	Rare
	Mule w/center hole. Obv: KM#Tn2. Rev: KM#Tn1.					
Tn1c	1861	—	1500.	2000.	2500.	3500.

KM#	Date	Mintage	VG	Fine	VF	XF
Tn2	1866	*.021	1750.	2250.	2750.	4000.

***NOTE:** Recalled from circulation in 1870 with 17,788 pcs. outstanding for both types.

INDIA

The Republic of India, a subcontinent jutting southward from the mainland of Asia, has an area of 1,269,346 sq. mi. (3,287,590 sq. km.) and a population of 766.1 million, second only to that of the People's Republic of China. Capital: New Delhi. India's economy is based on agriculture and industrial activity. Engineering goods, cotton apparel and fabrics, handicrafts, tea, iron and steel are exported.

The people of India have had a continuous civilization since about 2,500 B.C., when an urban culture based on commerce and trade, and to a lesser extent, agriculture, was developed by the inhabitants of the Indus River Valley. The origins of this civilization are uncertain, but it declined about 1,500 B.C., when the region was conquered by the Aryans. Over the following 2,000 years, the Aryans developed a Brahmanic civilization and introduced the caste system. Several successive empires flourished in India over the following centuries, notably those of the Mauryans, Guptas, and Mughals. In the 8th centuries A.D., the Arabs expanded into western India, bringing with them the Islamic faith. A Muslim dynasty (the Mughal Empire) controlled virtually the entire subcontinent during the period preceding the arrival of the Europeans; an Indo-Islamic style of art and architecture evolved, of which the Taj Mahal is a splendid example.

The Portuguese were the first Europeans to arrive, off Calicut in May 1498. It wasn't until 1612, after Portuguese and Spanish power began to wane, that the British East India Company established its initial settlement at Surat. By the end of the century, English traders were firmly established in Bombay, Madras, and Calcutta, as well as in some parts of the interior, and Britain was implementing a policy to create the civil and military institutions that would insure British dominion over the country. By 1757, following the successful conclusion of a war of colonial rivalry with France, the British were firmly established in India as not only traders, but as conquerors. During the next 60 years, the British East India Company acquired dominion over most of India by intrigue and force, and ruled directly, or through puppet princelings.

The Indian Mutiny (called the first War of Independence by Indian Nationalists) of 1857-58, begun by Indian troops in the service of the British East India Company, revealed the intensity of the growing resentment against British domination. The widespread rebellion against British rule was unsuccessful, but resulted in the transfer of government from the company to the British crown, and was a source of inspiration, to later Indian nationalists. Agitation for representation in the government continued.

Following World War I, in which India sent six million troops to fight at the side of the Allies, Indian nationalism intensified under the banner of the Indian National Congress and the leadership of Mohandas Karamchand Gandhi, who called for non-violent revolt against British authority. The Government of India Act of 1935 proposed a federal status linking the British Indian provinces with the many princely states; in addition, provincial legislatures were to be created. The federal status was never implemented, but the legislatures were created after the election of 1937, with the National Congress winning majorities in most of the provinces.

When Britain declared war on Germany in Sept. 1939, the viceroy declared India also to be at war with a common enemy. The Congress, however, demanded independence as a condition for cooperation; Britain refused. But as the Japanese advanced into Asia, Britain offered to transfer to Indians power over all but military affairs during the war, and set forth a plan for postwar independence. Congress was willing to accept the wartime transfer of power, but both Congress and the Muslim League rejected Britain's plan for independence; Congress because it did not sufficiently safeguard Indian unity, the Muslims (who wanted a separate Muslim state) because of fears of what would happen to Muslims within a united India.

Early in 1947, Prime Minister Clement Attlee announced that Britain would leave India "by a date not later than June 1948," even though the Hindus and Muslims could not agree among themselves on a plan for selfgovernment. The National Congress, aware that the Muslim League would revolt rather than accept an all-India government, reluctantly agreed to the formation of a separate Muslim state. The Muslim-majority provinces of the North West Frontier. Sindh and West Punjab in the west, and East Bengal in the east were separated from India to form the Muslim state of Pakistan, which became independent on Aug. 14, 1947. India became independent on the following day.

The Republic of India is a member of the Commonwealth of Nations. The president is the Chief of State. The prime minister is the Head of Government.

MINT MARKS

(Most mint marks appear directly below the date.)

B - Bombay, proof issues only
(B) - Bombay, diamond or dot
C - Canadian, Ottawa
(C) - Calcutta, no mint mark
H - Heaton Mint, Birmingham
(H) - Hyderabad, star
(Hd) - Hyderabad, split diamond
(Hy) - Hyderabad, dot in diamond
(L) - London, diamond below first date digit
(N) - Noida, dot
(S) - Seoul, star below first date digit

All Republic of India proof coins were struck in the Bombay Mint. From 1950 through 1964 they carry the regular diamond mint mark and can be distinguished from circulation issues only by their proof-like finish. From 1969 proofs carry the capital "B" mint mark. Some Bombay issues after 1969 have a "proof-like" appearance although bearing the diamond mint mark of circulation issues. Beginning in 1972 proofs of the larger denominations - 10, 20 and 100 rupees - were partly frosted on their main features, including numerals. From 1975 all proofs were similarly frosted, from the 1 paisa to 100 rupees. Proof-like issues are often erroneously offered as proofs.

MONETARY SYSTEM

(Until 1957)

4 Pice = 1 Anna
16 Annas = 1 Rupee

PICE

BRONZE

KM#	Date	Mintage	VF	XF	Unc
	Var. 1: 1.6mm thick, 0.3mm edge rim				
565.1	1950(B)	32.080	.35	.60	1.25
	Var. 2: 1.6mm thick, 1.0mm edge rim				
565.2	1950(B)	Inc. Ab.	.20	.30	.60
	1950(B)	—	—	Proof	1.50
	1950(C)	14.000	.20	.30	.60
	Var. 3: 1.2mm thick, 0.8mm edge rim				
566	1951(B)	104.626	.10	.15	.35
	1951(C)	127.300	.10	.15	.35
	1952(B)	213.830	.10	.15	.35
	1953(B)	242.358	.10	.15	.35
	1953(C)	111.000	.10	.15	.35
	1953(Hd)	Inc. Ab.	10.00	15.00	20.00
	1954(B)	136.758	.10	.15	.35
	1954(B)	—	—	Proof	1.50
	1954(C)	52.600	.10	.15	.35
	1954(Hd)	Inc. Ab.	5.00	8.00	12.00
	1955(B)	24.423	.15	.25	.50
	1955(Hd)	Inc. Ab.	6.00	10.00	15.00

NOTE: A variety of 1954Hd exists with mint mark split horizontally, instead of vertically.

1/2 ANNA

COPPER-NICKEL

KM#	Date	Mintage	VF	XF	Unc
567	1950(B)	26.076	.10	.25	.35
	1950(B)	—	—	Proof	1.50
	1950(C)	3.100	.50	.75	1.50
	1954(B)	14.000	.10	.25	.40
	1954(B)	—	—	Proof	1.50
	1954(C)	20.800	.10	.25	.40
	1955(B)	22.488	.10	.25	.35

NOTE: Varieties of date size exist.

ANNA

COPPER-NICKEL

KM#	Date	Mintage	VF	XF	Unc
568	1950(B)	9.944	.25	.50	1.00
	1950(B)	—	—	Proof	1.50
	1954(B)	20.388	.10	.25	.50
	1954(B)	—	—	Proof	1.50
	1955(B)	—	4.00	6.00	8.00

2 ANNAS

COPPER-NICKEL

KM#	Date	Mintage	VF	XF	Unc
569	1950(B)	7.536	.25	.50	1.50
	1950(B)	—	—	Proof	1.50
	1954(B)	10.548	.25	.50	1.25
	1954(B)	—	—	Proof	1.50
	1955(B)	—	4.00	6.00	8.00

1/4 RUPEE

NICKEL
Var. 1: Large lion

KM#	Date	Mintage	VF	XF	Unc
570	1950(B)	7.650	.30	.60	1.50
	1950(B)	—	—	Proof	1.50
	1950(C)	7.800	.30	.60	1.50
	1951(B)	41.439	.25	.50	1.00
	1951(C)	13.500	.25	.50	1.00
	1954(B)	—	—	Proof	1.50
	1954(C)	58.300	.25	.50	1.25
	1955(B)	57.936	.50	1.00	2.50

Var. 2: Small lion

KM#	Date	Mintage	VF	XF	Unc
571	1954(C)	Inc. Ab.	.25	.40	.75
	1955(C)	28.900	.25	.40	.75
	1956(C)	22.000	.25	.50	1.00

1/2 RUPEE

NICKEL
Var. 1: Large lion

KM#	Date	Mintage	VF	XF	Unc
572	1950(B)	12.352	.50	1.00	1.50
	1950(B)	—	—	Proof	2.00
	1950(C)	1.100	.75	1.50	3.00
	1951(B)	9.239	.75	1.50	2.50
	1954(B)	—	—	Proof	2.00
	1954(C)	36.300	.40	1.00	1.50
	1955(B)	18.977	.75	1.50	2.50

Var. 2: Small lion
Obv: Dots missing between words.

KM#	Date	Mintage	VF	XF	Unc
573	1956(C)	24.900	.25	.40	1.00

RUPEE

NICKEL

KM#	Date	Mintage	VF	XF	Unc
574	1950(B)	19.412	1.25	2.00	4.00
	1950(B)	—	—	Proof	3.00
	1954(B)	Inc. Ab.	2.00	3.00	5.00
	1954(B)	—	—	Proof	3.00

DECIMAL COINAGE

100 Naye Paise = 1 Rupee (1957-63)
100 Paise = 1 Rupee (1964)

NOTE: The Paisa was at first called "Naya Paisa" (= New Paisa), so that people would distinguish from the old non-decimal Paisa (or Pice, equal to 1/64 Rupee). After 7 years, the word 'new' was dropped, and the coin was simply called a "Paisa".

NOTE: Many of the Paisa standard types come with two obverse varieties: (three varieties for 25 Paise).

OBV. I: Asoka lion pedestal small. Short, squat 'D' in 'INDIA'.

OBV. II: Asoka lion pedestal larger. Lettering closer to rim. Tall, more elegant "D" in "INDIA". The shape of the "D" in INDIA is the easiest way to distinguish the 2 obverses.

Obv I

Obv II

NOTE: Paisa standard pieces with mint mark B, 1969 to date, were struck only in proof.

NOTE: Indian mintage figures are not divided by mint, and often include dates other than the year in which struck. They should be regarded with reserve.

NAYA PAISA

BRONZE

KM#	Date	Mintage	VF	XF	Unc
575	1957(B)	618.630	—	.10	.25
	1957(C)	Inc. Ab.	—	.10	.25
	1957(Hd)	Inc. Ab.	.10	.20	.35
	1958(B)	468.630	.20	.30	.50
	1958(Hd)	Inc. Ab.	.10	.20	.35
	1959(B)	351.120	.10	.20	.35
	1959(C)	Inc. Ab.	.10	.15	.25
	1959(Hd)	Inc. Ab.	.10	.20	.35
	1960(B)	357.940	—	.10	.20
	1960(B)	—	—	Proof	1.00
	1960(C)	Inc. Ab.	.80	1.50	2.50
	1960(Hd)	Inc. Ab.	3.25	4.00	5.00
	1961(B)	573.170	—	.10	.20
	1961(B)	—	—	Proof	1.00
	1961(C)	Inc. Ab.	.10	.15	.25
	1961(Hy)	Inc. Ab.	.50	.75	1.25
	1962(B)	—	5.00	6.50	8.00

NOTE: 1962(B) has only been found in some of the 1962 uncirculated mint sets.

NOTE: Varieties of the split diamond have been reported.

NICKEL-BRASS

KM#	Date	Mintage	VF	XF	Unc
575a	1962(B)	235.103	.10	.15	.25
	1962(B)	—	—	Proof	1.00
	1962(C)	Inc. Ab.	.10	.15	.30
	1962(Hy)	Inc. Ab.	.50	.75	1.25
	1963(B)	343.313	.10	.15	.25
	1963(B)	—	—	Proof	1.00
	1963(C)	Inc. Ab.	.25	.50	1.00
	1963(H)	Inc. Ab.	.10	.25	.40

PAISA

NICKEL-BRASS
Obverse 1

KM#	Date	Mintage	VF	XF	Unc
582	1964(B)	539.068	—	.10	.25
	1964(C)	Inc. Ab.	—	.10	.20
	1964(H)	Inc. Ab.	—	.10	.25

BRONZE

KM#	Date	Mintage	VF	XF	Unc
582a	1964(H)	Inc. Ab.	.35	.50	1.00

ALUMINUM
Obverse 1

KM#	Date	Mintage	VF	XF	Unc
592	1965(B)	223.480	.20	.35	.60
	1965(Hy)	Inc. Ab.	.15	.25	.40
	1966(B)	404.200	.10	.20	.30
	1966(C)	Inc. Ab.	.15	.30	.50
	1966(Hy)	Inc. Ab.	—	.10	.15
	1967(B)	450.433	—	.10	.25
	1967(C)	Inc. Ab.	—	.10	.20
	1967(Hy)	Inc. Ab.	—	.10	.15
	1968(B)	302.720	—	—	.10
	1968(C)	Inc. Ab.	—	.10	.20
	1968(Hy)	Inc. Ab.	—	—	.10
	1969(B)	125.930	.30	.50	.80
	1969B	9,147	—	Proof	.25
	1969(H)	Inc. Ab.	.30	.50	.80
	1970(B)	15.800	—	.10	.25
	1970B	3,046	—	Proof	.25
	1971B	4,375	—	Proof	.25
	1971(H)	112.100	—	—	.10
	1972(B)	62.090	—	—	.10
	1972B	7,895	—	Proof	.25
	1972(H)	Inc. Ab.	—	—	.10
	1973B	7,562	—	Proof	.10
	1974B	—	—	Proof	.10
	1975B	—	—	Proof	.10
	1976B	—	—	Proof	.10
	1977B	—	—	Proof	.10
	1978B	—	—	Proof	.10
	1979B	—	—	Proof	.10
	1980B	—	—	Proof	.10
	1981B	—	—	Proof	.10

NOTE: 1970(B) is found only in the uncirculated sets of that year. It has a mirrorlike surface.

Obverse 2

KM#	Date	Mintage	VF	XF	Unc
606	1969(C)	Inc. Ab.	.20	.25	.40
	1970(C)	Inc. Ab.	—	—	.10

2 NAYE PAISE

COPPER-NICKEL

KM#	Date	Mintage	VF	XF	Unc
576	1957(B)	406.230	—	.10	.25
	1957(C)	Inc. Ab.	—	.10	.25
	1958(B)	245.660	—	.10	.25
	1958(C)	Inc. Ab.	.10	.15	.30
	1959(B)	171.445	—	.10	.20
	1959(C)	Inc. Ab.	.25	.40	.80
	1960(B)	121.820	—	.10	.25
	1960(B)	—	—	Proof	1.00
	1960(C)	Inc. Ab.	.10	.15	.25
	1961(B)	190.610	—	.10	.20
	1961(B)	—	—	Proof	1.00
	1961(C)	Inc. Ab.	.10	.15	.20
	1962(B)	318.181	—	.10	.20
	1962(B)	—	—	Proof	1.00
	1962(C)	Inc. Ab.	—	.10	.20
	1963(B)	372.380	—	.10	.20
	1963(B)	—	—	Proof	1.00
	1963(C)	Inc. Ab.	—	.10	.20

2 PAISE

COPPER-NICKEL
Obverse 1

KM#	Date	Mintage	VF	XF	Unc
583	1964(B)	323.504	—	.10	.15
	1964(C)	Inc. Ab.	—	.10	.15

ALUMINUM
Obverse 1. Rev: 10mm '2'.

KM#	Date	Mintage	VF	XF	Unc
593	1965(B)	175.770	—	.10	.20
	1965(C)	Inc. Ab.	.10	.20	.35
	1966(B)	386.795	—	.10	.15
	1966(C)	Inc. Ab.	—	.10	.15
	1967(B)	454.593	—	.10	.25

Obverse 1. Rev: 10-1/2mm '2'.

KM#	Date	Mintage	VF	XF	Unc
595	1967(C)	Inc. Ab.	—	.10	.15

Obverse 2. Rev: 10mm '2'.

KM#	Date	Mintage	VF	XF	Unc
596	1967(B)		.50	1.00	1.50

Obverse 1. Rev: 11mm '2'.

KM#	Date	Mintage	VF	XF	Unc
602	1968(C)	—	.50	1.25	2.50
	1977(B)	—	—	.10	.15
	1978(B)	—	—	.15	.30

Obverse 2. Rev: 11mm '2'.

KM#	Date	Mintage	VF	XF	Unc
603	1968(B)	305.205	—	—	.10
	1968(C)	Inc. Ab.	—	.10	.25
	1969(B)	5.335	1.00	1.50	2.00
	1969B	9,147	—	Proof	.25
	1970(B)	—	.50	1.00	1.50
	1970B	3,046	—	Proof	.25
	1970(C)	79.100	—	—	.10
	1971B	4,375	—	Proof	.25

KM#	Date	Mintage	VF	XF	Unc
603	1971(C)	207.900	—	—	.10
	1972B	7,895	—	Proof	.25
	1972(C)	261.270	—	.10	.15
	1972(H)	Inc. Ab.	—	—	.10
	1973B	7,562	—	Proof	.15
	1973(C)	—	—	.10	.20
	1973(H)	—	—	—	.10
	1974B	—	—	Proof	.15
	1974(C)	—	—	—	.10
	1974(H)	—	—	—	.10
	1975B	—	—	Proof	.15
	1975(C)	184.500	—	—	.10
	1975(H)	Inc. Ab.	—	—	.10
	1976(B)	68.140	—	—	.10
	1976B	—	—	Proof	.15
	1976(H)	—	—	—	.10
	1977(B)	251.955	—	—	.10
	1977B	—	—	Proof	.15
	1977(H)	Inc. Ab.	—	—	.10
	1978(B)	144.010	—	—	.10
	1978B	—	—	Proof	.10
	1978(H)	Inc. Ab.	—	—	.10
	1979B	—	—	Proof	.10
	1980B	—	—	Proof	.10
	1981B	—	—	Proof	.10

NOTE: Varieties of date size exist.
NOTE: 1970(B) is found only in the uncirculated sets of that year. It has a mirrorlike surface.

3 PAISE

ALUMINUM
Obverse 1

KM#	Date	Mintage	VF	XF	Unc
584	1964(B)	138.890	—	.10	.15
	1964(C)	Inc. Ab.	—	.10	.20
	1965(B)	459.825	—	.10	.15
	1965(C)	Inc. Ab.	.10	.20	.35
	1966(B)	390.440	—	.10	.15
	1966(C)	Inc. Ab.	—	.10	.15
	1966(Hy)	Inc. Ab.	.20	.35	.50
	1967(B)	167.018	—	.10	.35
	1967(C)	Inc. Ab.	—	.10	.15
	1967(H)	Inc. Ab.	.30	.50	.75
	1968(B)	—	.30	.50	1.00

Obverse 2

KM#	Date	Mintage	VF	XF	Unc
597	1967(C)	—	.30	.75	1.25
	1967(H)	Inc. Ab.	.30	.75	1.25
	1968(B)	246.390	—	.10	.20
	1968(C)	Inc. Ab.	.30	.45	.70
	1968(H)	Inc. Ab.	—	.10	.20
	1969B	9,147	—	Proof	.25
	1969(C)	7.025	—	.10	.20
	1969(H)	Inc. Ab.	.40	.60	1.00
	1970(B)	—	1.00	1.50	2.50
	1970B	3,046	—	Proof	.25
	1970(C)	15.300	—	.10	.15
	1971B	4,375	—	Proof	.25
	1971(C)	203.100	—	.10	.15
	1971(H)	Inc. Ab.	—	.10	.15

NOTE: 1970(B) is found only in the uncirculated sets of that year. It has a mirrorlike surface.

Obverse 2

KM#	Date	Mintage	VF	XF	Unc
617	1972B	7,895	—	Proof	.25
	1973B	7,562	—	Proof	.20
	1974B	—	—	Proof	.20
	1975B	—	—	Proof	.20
	1976B	—	—	Proof	.20
	1977B	—	—	Proof	.20
	1978B	—	—	Proof	.20
	1979B	—	—	Proof	.20
	1980B	—	—	Proof	.20
	1981B	—	—	Proof	.20

5 NAYE PAISE

COPPER-NICKEL

KM#	Date	Mintage	VF	XF	Unc
577	1957(B)	227.210	.10	.20	.40
	1957(C)	Inc. Ab.	.10	.20	.40
	1958(B)	214.320	.10	.20	.40
	1958(C)	Inc. Ab.	.10	.20	.40
	1959(B)	137.105	.10	.20	.40
	1959(C)	Inc. Ab.	.15	.40	.90
	1960(B)	93.345	.10	.25	.60
	1960(B)	—	—	Proof	1.50
	1960(C)	Inc. Ab.	.10	.30	.75
	1960(Hy)	Inc. Ab.	.50	1.00	2.00
	1961(B)	197.620	.10	.15	.30
	1961(B)	—	—	Proof	1.50
	1961(C)	Inc. Ab.	.25	.50	1.00
	1961(Hy)	Inc. Ab.	1.00	2.00	3.00
	1962(B)	224.277	.10	.15	.35
	1962(B)	—	—	Proof	1.50
	1962(C)	Inc. Ab.	.10	.15	.35
	1962(Hy)	Inc. Ab.	.50	1.00	2.00
	1963(B)	332.600	.10	.15	.30
	1963(B)	—	—	Proof	1.50
	1963(C)	Inc. Ab.	.15	.45	.70
	1963(H)	Inc. Ab.	.75	1.50	2.50

5 PAISE

COPPER-NICKEL
Obverse 1

KM#	Date	Mintage	VF	XF	Unc
585	1964(B)	156.000	.40	.60	1.00
	1964(C)	Inc. Ab.	.25	.45	.70
	1964(H)	Inc. Ab.	.75	1.50	2.50
	1965(B)	203.855	.10	.20	.35
	1965(C)	Inc. Ab.	.25	.45	.70
	1965(H)	Inc. Ab.	1.25	2.00	3.00
	1966(B)	101.395	.40	.60	1.00
	1966(C)	Inc. Ab.	.25	.45	.70

6mm Short 5 7mm Tall 5
6.5mm Medium 5

ALUMINUM
Obverse 1
Rev: Short 5.

KM#	Date	Mintage	VF	XF	Unc
598.1	1967(B)	608.533	.10	.15	.50
	Rev: Medium 5.				
598.2	1967(B)	Inc.Ab.	.15	.25	.75
	1967(c)	Inc.Ab.	.15	.25	.75
	Rev: Tall 5.				
598.3	1967(B)	Inc.Ab.	.25	.50	1.00
	1967(c)	Inc.Ab.	.25	.50	1.00
	1967(H)	Inc.Ab.	—	.10	.25
	1968(B)	—	2.00	3.00	4.00
	1968(C)	—	.75	1.50	3.00
	1968(H)	666.750	.70	1.00	1.50
	1971(H)	499.200	—	.10	.15

Obverse 2

KM#	Date	Mintage	VF	XF	Unc
599	1967(H)	—	1.25	1.75	2.75
	1968(B)	Inc. KM598	—	.10	.15
	1968(C)	Inc. KM598	—	.10	.15
	1968(H)	Inc. KM598	.10	.15	.40
	1969(B)	3.740	.75	1.50	2.50
	1969B	9,147	—	Proof	.25
	1970(B)	39.900	.15	.25	.50
	1970B	3,046	—	Proof	.25
	1970(C)	Inc. Ab.	.15	.25	.40
	1970(H)	Inc. Ab.	.20	.40	.60
	1971(B)	Inc. w/1971(H) of KM598			
			—	.10	.15
	1971B	4,375	—	Proof	.25
	1971(C)	Inc. Ab.	—	.10	.15
	1971(H)	—	—	.10	.15

Obverse 1

KM#	Date	Mintage	VF	XF	Unc
618	1972(H)	512.430	—	.10	.15
	Rev: Larger 5.				
626	1973(H)	—	1.50	2.00	3.00
	1977(B)	—	—	—	.10
	1978(B)	—	—	—	.10

Obverse 2. Rev: 11mm 5.

KM#	Date	Mintage	VF	XF	Unc
619	1972(B)	Inc. KM618	—	.10	.15
	1972B	7,895	—	Proof	.25
	1972(C)	Inc. KM618	—	.10	.15
	1972(H)	—	1.00	2.00	3.00
	1973(B)	—	—	.10	.15
	1973B	7,562	—	Proof	.25
	1973(C)	—	—	.10	.15
	1974B	—	—	Proof	.25
	1974(C)	—	—	.10	.15
	1975(B)	—	—	.10	.15
	1976(B)	53.205	—	.10	.20
	1976(H)	—	—	.10	.15
	1979(H)	—	—	.10	.20

Rev: Larger 5 11.5mm.

KM#	Date	Mintage	VF	XF	Unc
627	1973(H)	—	—	.10	.15
	1974(B)	—	—	.10	.15
	1974(H)	—	—	.10	.15
	1974B	—	—	Proof	.25
	1975(B)	—	—	.10	.15
	1975B	—	—	Proof	.25
	1975(C)	289.080	—	.10	.15
	1975(H)	Inc. Ab.	—	.10	.15
	1976(C)	—	—	.10	.15
	1977(B)	257.900	—	.10	.15
	1977(C)	Inc. Ab.	—	.10	.20
	1977(H)	Inc. Ab.	—	.10	.20
	1978(C)	—	—	.10	.20
	1978(H)	—	—	.10	.20
	1979(B)	—	—	.10	.20
	1980(B)	21.440	—	.10	.20
	1980B	—	—	Proof	.20
	1980(C)	Inc. Ab.	—	.10	.20
	1980(H)	Inc. Ab.	—	.10	.20
	1981B	—	—	Proof	.20
	1981(C)	4.365	—	.10	.20
	1981(H)	Inc. Ab.	—	.10	.20
	1982B	3.499	—	Proof	.20
	1982(C)	Inc. Ab.	—	.10	.20
	1982(H)	Inc. Ab.	—	.10	.20
	1983(B)	3.110	—	.10	.20
	1983(C)	Inc. Ab.	—	.10	.20
	1983(H)	Inc. Ab.	—	.10	.20
	1984(B)	28.265	—	.10	.20
	1984(C)	—	—	.20	.40
	1984(H)	Inc. Ab.	—	.10	.20

NOTE: Due to faulty dies, 1981(H) often resembles the non-existant 1981(B).

F.A.O. Issue, FOOD & WORK FOR ALL

KM#	Date	Mintage	VF	XF	Unc
640	1976(B)	34.680	—	.10	.20
	1976B	—	—	Proof	.20
	1976(C)	60.040	—	.10	.20
	1976(H)	60.290	—	.10	.20

F.A.O. Issue, SAVE FOR DEVELOPMENT

KM#	Date	Mintage	VF	XF	Unc
644	1977(B)	20.100	—	.10	.20
	1977B	2,224	—	Proof	.25
	1977(C)	40.470	—	.10	.20
	1977(H)	—	—	.10	.20

F.A.O. Issue, FOOD & SHELTER FOR ALL

KM#	Date	Mintage	VF	XF	Unc
648	1978(B)	17.440	—	.10	.20
	1978B	—	—	Proof	.25
	1978(C)	30.870	—	.10	.20
	1978(H)	—	—	.10	.20

International Year of the Child

KM#	Date	Mintage	VF	XF	Unc
652	1979(B)	—	—	.10	.15
	1979B	—	—	Proof	.25
	1979(C)	—	—	.10	.15
	1979(H)	—	—	.10	.15

KM#	Date	Mintage	VF	XF	Unc
691	1984(C)	—	—	1.00	2.00
	1985(B)	54.860	—	.15	.20
	1985(C)	Inc. Ab.	—	1.00	2.00
	1985(H)	Inc. Ab.	—	.10	.15
	1986(B)	—	—	.10	.15
	1986(C)	—	—	.15	.20
	1986(H)	—	—	.10	.15
	1987(C)	—	—	.10	.15
	1987(H)	—	—	.10	.15
	1988(C)	—	—	.10	.15
	1988(H)	—	—	.10	.15
	1989(H)	—	—	.10	.15
	1990(C)	—	—	.10	.15
	1990(C)	—	—	.10	.15
	1991(C)	—	—	.10	.15
	1991(H)	—	—	.10	.15
	1992(B)	—	—	.10	.15
	1992(H)	—	—	.10	.15

10 NAYE PAISE

COPPER-NICKEL
Rev: 6.5mm "10".

KM#	Date	Mintage	VF	XF	Unc
578.1	1957(B)	139.655	.15	.30	.50
	1957(C)	Inc. Ab.	.15	.30	.50

Rev: 7mm "10".

KM#	Date	Mintage	VF	XF	Unc
578.2	1958(B)	123.160	.15	.30	.50
	1958(C)	Inc. Ab.	.25	.50	1.00
	1959(B)	148.570	.15	.30	.50
	1959(C)	Inc. Ab.	.15	.30	.50
	1960(B)	52.335	.15	.30	.50
	1960(B)	—	—	Proof	1.50
	1961(B)	172.545	.15	.30	.50
	1961(B)	—	—	Proof	1.50
	1961(C)	Inc. Ab.	.15	.30	.50
	1961(Hy)	Inc. Ab.	1.75	2.50	4.00
	1962(B)	172.777	.15	.30	.50
	1962(B)	—	—	Proof	1.50
	1962(C)	Inc. Ab.	.15	.30	.50
	1962(Hy)	Inc. Ab.	1.00	1.50	2.50
	1963(B)	182.834	.10	.20	.45
	1963(B)	—	—	Proof	1.50
	1963(C)	Inc. Ab.	.10	.20	.45
	1963(H)	Inc. Ab.	.60	1.00	2.00

10 PAISE

COPPER-NICKEL
Obverse 1. Rev: 6.5mm '10'.

KM#	Date	Mintage	VF	XF	Unc
586	1964(B) open 4	84.112	.10	.20	.45
	1964(B) closed 4	Inc. Ab.	1.50	2.00	3.00
	1964(C)	Inc. Ab.	.15	.30	.60
	1964(H)	Inc. Ab.	1.00	1.50	2.50
	1965(B)	253.430	—	.10	.40
	1965(C)	Inc. Ab.	—	.10	.40
	1965(Hy)	Inc. Ab.	1.00	1.50	2.50
	1965(H)	Inc. Ab.	.75	1.25	2.00
	1966(B)	326.990	—	.10	.40
	1966(C)	Inc. Ab.	—	.10	.40
	1966(Hy)	Inc. Ab.	.20	.35	.65
	1967(B)	59.443	.30	.50	.75
	1967(C)	Inc. Ab.	.30	.50	.75
	1967(H)	Inc. Ab.	.40	.75	1.25

NICKEL-BRASS
Obverse 1

KM#	Date	Mintage	VF	XF	Unc
604	1968(H)	55.940	2.00	3.00	4.00

Obverse 2. Rev: 6.5mm '10'.

KM#	Date	Mintage	VF	XF	Unc
605	1968(B)	Inc. KM604	.10	.20	.35
	1968(C)	Inc. KM604	.10	.15	.25
	1968(H)	Inc. KM604	.10	.20	.35

Obverse 2. Rev: 7mm '10'.

KM#	Date	Mintage	VF	XF	Unc
607	1969(B)	65.405	.10	.15	.25
	1969B	9,147	—	Proof	.25
	1969(C)	Inc. Ab.	.10	.30	.50
	1969(H)	Inc. Ab.	.10	.15	.25
	1970(B)	48.400	.10	.15	.50
	1970B	3,046	—	Proof	.25
	1970(C)	Inc. Ab.	.10	.20	.35
	1971(B)	88.800	.10	.15	.25
	1971B	4,375	—	Proof	.25

ALUMINUM
Obverse 2. Rev: 9mm 10.

KM#	Date	Mintage	VF	XF	Unc
615.1	1971(B)	146.100	—	.10	.20
	1971(C)	Inc. Ab.	—	.10	.20
	1971(H)	Inc. Ab.	.15	.30	.50
	1972(B)	735.090	—	.10	.20
	1972B	7,895	—	Proof	.75
	1972(C)	Inc. Ab.	—	.10	.20
	1973(B)	—	—	.10	.20
	1973B	7,567	—	Proof	.75
	1973(C)	—	—	.10	.20
	1973(H)	—	.10	.15	.30
	1974(B)	—	—	.10	.20
	1974(C)	—	—	.10	.20
	1974(H)	—	.10	.25	.50
	1975(B)	—	.10	.15	.25
	1975(C)	298.830	—	.10	.15
	1976(C)	Inc. Ab.	.25	.50	1.00
	1977(B)	25.288	—	.10	.15
	1977(C)	Inc. Ab.	—	.10	.15
	1978(B)	48.215	—	.10	.15
	1978(C)	Inc. Ab.	—	.10	.15
	1978(H)	Inc. Ab.	—	.10	.15

Rev: 8mm 10.

KM#	Date	Mintage	VF	XF	Unc
615.2	1979(B)	—	—	.10	.15
	1979(C)	—	—	.10	.15
	1979(H)	—	—	.10	.15
	1980(B)	—	—	.10	.15
	1980(C)	—	—	.10	.15
	1980(H)	—	—	.10	.15
	1981(B)	—	—	.10	.15
	1981(C)	—	—	.10	.15
	1982(C)	—	—	.10	.15
	1982(H)	—	—	.10	.15

F.A.O. Issue

KM#	Date	Mintage	VF	XF	Unc
631	1974(B)	146.070	—	.10	.15
	1974B	—	—	Proof	.25
	1974(C)	168.500	—	.10	.20
	1974(H)	10.010	.15	.25	.50

F.A.O. Issue - Women's Year

KM#	Date	Mintage	VF	XF	Unc
635	1975(B)	69.160	—	.10	.15
	1975B	—	—	Proof	.25
	1975(C)	84.820	—	.10	.15

NOTE: Mint mark is below wheat stalk.

F.A.O. Issue, FOOD & WORK FOR ALL

KM#	Date	Mintage	VF	XF	Unc
641	1976(B)	36.040	—	.10	.15
	1976B	—	—	Proof	.25
	1976(C)	26.180	—	.10	.15

F.A.O. Issue, SAVE FOR DEVELOPMENT

KM#	Date	Mintage	VF	XF	Unc
645	1977(B)	17.040	—	.10	.15
	1977B	2,224	—	Proof	.25
	1977(C)	8.020	—	.10	.15

F.A.O. Issue, FOOD & SHELTER FOR ALL

KM#	Date	Mintage	VF	XF	Unc
649	1978(B)	24.470	—	.10	.15
	1978B	—	—	Proof	.25
	1978(C)	26.160	.25	.50	2.00
	1978(H)	Inc. Ab.	—	.10	.15

International Year of the Child

KM#	Date	Mintage	VF	XF	Unc
653	1979(B)	—	—	.10	.15
	1979B	—	—	Proof	.25
	1979(C)	—	—	.10	.15
	1979(H)	—	.20	.40	.60

Mule. Obv: KM#649. Rev: KM#653.

KM#	Date	Mintage	VF	XF	Unc
654	1979(B)	—	5.00	7.50	10.00

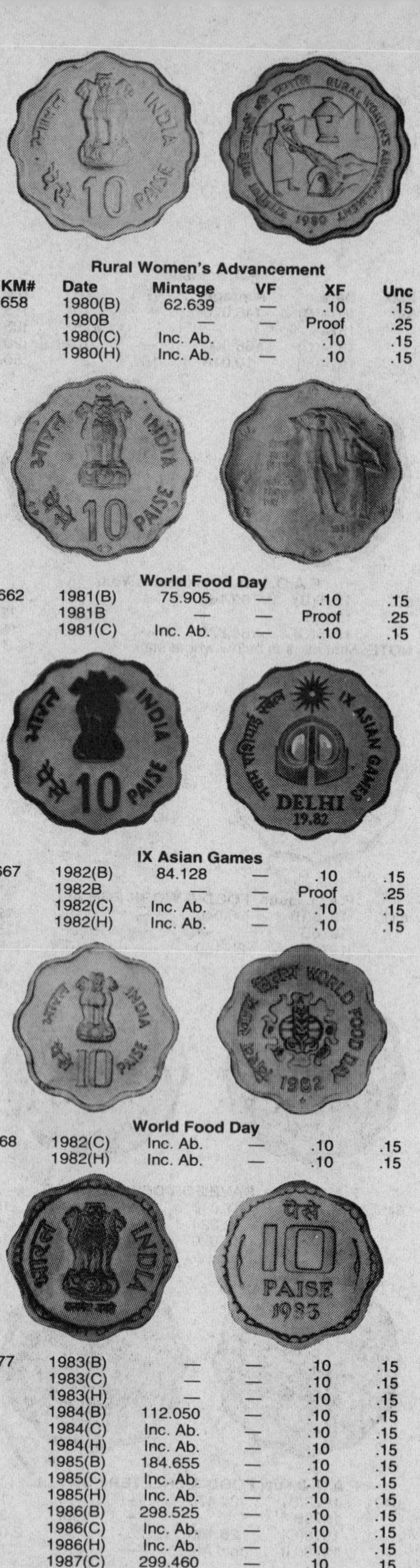

Rural Women's Advancement

KM#	Date	Mintage	VF	XF	Unc
658	1980(B)	62.639	—	.10	.15
	1980B	—	—	Proof	.25
	1980(C)	Inc. Ab.	—	.10	.15
	1980(H)	Inc. Ab.	—	.10	.15

World Food Day

KM#	Date	Mintage	VF	XF	Unc
662	1981(B)	75.905	—	.10	.15
	1981B	—	—	Proof	.25
	1981(C)	Inc. Ab.	—	.10	.15

IX Asian Games

KM#	Date	Mintage	VF	XF	Unc
667	1982(B)	84.128	—	.10	.15
	1982B	—	—	Proof	.25
	1982(C)	Inc. Ab.	—	.10	.15
	1982(H)	Inc. Ab.	—	.10	.15

World Food Day

KM#	Date	Mintage	VF	XF	Unc
668	1982(C)	Inc. Ab.	—	.10	.15
	1982(H)	Inc. Ab.	—	.10	.15

KM#	Date	Mintage	VF	XF	Unc
677	1983(B)	—	—	.10	.15
	1983(C)	—	—	.10	.15
	1983(H)	—	—	.10	.15
	1984(B)	112.050	—	.10	.15
	1984(C)	Inc. Ab.	—	.10	.15
	1984(H)	Inc. Ab.	—	.10	.15
	1985(B)	184.655	—	.10	.15
	1985(C)	Inc. Ab.	—	.10	.15
	1985(H)	Inc. Ab.	—	.10	.15
	1986(B)	298.525	—	.10	.15
	1986(C)	Inc. Ab.	—	.10	.15
	1986(H)	Inc. Ab.	—	.10	.15
	1987(C)	299.460	—	.10	.15
	1987(H)	Inc. Ab.	—	.10	.15
	1988(B)	264.510	—	.10	.15
	1988(C)	Inc. Ab.	—	.10	.15
	1988(H)	Inc. Ab.	—	.10	.15
	1989(B)	—	—	.10	.15
	1989(C)	—	—	.10	.15
	1989(H)	—	—	.10	.15
	1990(B)	—	—	.15	.25
	1991(B)	—	—	.15	.25
	1991(C)	—	—	.15	.25
	1991(H)	—	—	.15	.25
	1993(C)	—	—	.15	.25

STAINLESS STEEL

KM#	Date	Mintage	VF	XF	Unc
702	1988C	183.040	—	.10	.25
	1988(B)	4.040	—	.10	.25
	1988(C)	—	—	.10	.25
	1988(H)	Inc. Ab.	—	.10	.25
	1988(N)	—	—	.10	.25
	1989(B)	—	—	.10	.25
	1989(C)	—	—	.10	.25
	1989(H)	—	—	.10	.25
	1989(N)	—	—	.10	.25
	1990(B)	—	—	.10	.25
	1990(H)	—	—	.10	.25
	1990(N)	—	—	.10	.25
	1991(C)	—	—	.10	.25
	1991(H)	—	—	.10	.25
	1991(N)	—	—	.10	.25

NOTE: Varieties of date size exist.

20 PAISE

NICKEL-BRASS
Lotus Blossom

KM#	Date	Mintage	VF	XF	Unc
564 (605)	1968(B)	10.585	.15	.25	.50
	1968(C)	Inc. Ab.	.20	.40	.75
	1969(B)	197.940	.10	.15	.35
	1969(C)	—	.10	.15	.35
	1970(B)	Inc. Ab.	.10	.15	.35
	1970(C)	Inc. Ab.	.10	.15	.35
	1970(H)	Inc. Ab.	.10	.15	.35
	1971(B)	124.200	.10	.15	.35

ALUMINUM-BRONZE
Mahatma Gandhi Centennial of Birth

KM#	Date	Mintage	VF	XF	Unc
608	ND(1969)(B)	45,010	.10	.15	.75
	ND(1969)B	9,147	—	Proof	.25
	ND(1969)(C)	45.070	.10	.15	.75
	ND(1969)(H)	3.000	.25	.50	1.00

NOTE: Struck during 1969 and 1970.

F.A.O. Issue, FOOD FOR ALL
Wide rims.

KM#	Date	Mintage	VF	XF	Unc
612	1970(B)	5.160	.15	.30	.60
	1970B	3,046	—	Proof	1.85
	1970(C)	5.010	.15	.30	.60

Narrow rims.

KM#	Date	Mintage	VF	XF	Unc
616	1971(B)	.060	.15	.30	.60
	1971B	4,375	—	Proof	1.85

ALUMINUM

KM#	Date	Mintage	VF	XF	Unc
669	1982(B)	—	—	.10	.20
	1982(H)	—	—	.10	.20
	1983(C)	28.505	—	.10	.20
	1983(H)	Inc. Ab.	—	.10	.20
	1984(B)	72.163	—	.10	.20
	1984(C)	Inc. Ab.	—	.10	.20
	1984(H)	Inc. Ab.	—	.10	.20
	1985(B)	84.495	—	.10	.20
	1985(C)	Inc. Ab.	—	.10	.20
	1985(H)	Inc. Ab.	—	.10	.20

KM#	Date	Mintage	VF	XF	Unc
669	1986(B)	155.610	—	.10	.20
	1986(C)	Inc. Ab.	—	.10	.20
	1986(H)	Inc. Ab.	—	.10	.20
	1987(C)	—	Reported, not confirmed		
	1987(H)	153.073	—	.10	.20
	1988(B)	125.048	—	.10	.20
	1988(C)	Inc. Ab.	—	.10	.20
	1988(H)	Inc. Ab.	—	.10	.20
	1989(C)	—	—	.10	.15
	1989(H)	—	—	.10	.15
	1990(C)	—	—	.10	.15
	1990(H)	—	—	.10	.15
	1991(C)	—	—	.10	.15
	1991(H)	—	—	.10	.15

F.A.O. Issue
Similar to 10 Paise, KM#668.

KM#	Date	Mintage	VF	XF	Unc
685	1982(B)	—	.10	.20	.50
	1982(C)	—	.10	.20	.50
	1982(H)	—	.10	.20	.50

FAO - Fisheries

KM#	Date	Mintage	VF	XF	Unc
678	1983(B)	Inc. KM669	.10	.20	.50
	1983(C)	Inc. KM669	.10	.20	.50
	1983(H)	Inc. KM669	.10	.20	.50

25 NAYE PAISE

NICKEL
Rev: Small 25.

KM#	Date	Mintage	VF	XF	Unc
579.1	1957(B)	5.640	.40	.75	1.50
	1957(C)	Inc. Ab.	.40	.75	1.50
	1959(B)	43.080	.20	.40	.75
	1959(C)	Inc. Ab.	.15	.30	.50
	1960(B)	115.320	.15	.30	.50
	1960(B)	—	—	Proof	2.00
	1960(C)	Inc. Ab.	.15	.30	.50

Rev: Large 25.

KM#	Date	Mintage	VF	XF	Unc
579.2	1961(B)	109.008	.15	.30	.50
	1961(B)	—	.15	Proof	2.00
	1961(C)	Inc. Ab.	.15	.30	.50
	1962(B)	79.242	.15	.30	.50
	1962(B)	—	.15	Proof	2.00
	1962(C)	Inc. Ab.	.15	.30	.50
	1963(B)	101.565	.15	.30	.50
	1963(B)	—	.15	Proof	2.00
	1963(C)	Inc. Ab.	.15	.30	.50

25 PAISE

NICKEL
Obverse 1, Reverse 1

KM#	Date	Mintage	VF	XF	Unc
587	1964(B)	85.321	.10	.25	.50
	1964(C)	Inc. Ab.	.10	.25	.50

Obverse 1, Reverse 2

KM#	Date	Mintage	VF	XF	Unc
594	1965(B)	143.662	.10	.20	.40
	1965(C)	Inc. Ab.	.10	.20	.40
	1966(B)	59.040	.10	.20	.40
	1966(C)	Inc. Ab.	.15	.30	.60
	1967(B)	30.027	2.00	3.00	4.00

Obverse 2, Reverse 2

KM#	Date	Mintage	VF	XF	Unc
600	1967(C)	Inc. KM594	.15	.30	.60
	1968(C)	Inc. KM594	.20	.40	.80

COPPER-NICKEL

Obverse 1

KM#	Date	Mintage	VF	XF	Unc
620	1972(B)	367.640	—	.10	.30
	1972B	7,895	—	Proof	.35
	1972(H)	Inc. Ab.	—	.10	.40
	1973(B)	—	—	.10	.30
	1973B	7,567	—	Proof	.35
	1973(H)	—	—	.10	.30
	1974(B)	—	—	.10	.25
	1974B	—	—	Proof	.35
	1974(H)	—	—	.10	.35
	1975(B)	559.980	—	.10	.25
	1975B	—	—	Proof	.35
	1975(H)	Inc. Ab.	—	.10	.25
	1976(B)	30.016	—	.10	.25
	1976B	Inc. Ab.	—	Proof	.35
	1976(H)	Inc. Ab.	—	.10	.25
	1977(B)	270.520	—	.10	.25
	1977(C)	Inc. Ab.	—	.10	.40
	1977(H)	Inc. Ab.	—	.10	.25
	1978(B)	131.632	—	.10	.25
	1978B	Inc. Ab.	—	Proof	.35
	1978(C)	—	—	.10	.25
	1978(H)	—	—	.10	.25
	1979(B)	—	—	.10	.25
	1979(C)	—	—	.10	.25
	1979(H)	—	.20	.35	.75
	1980(B)	6.175	—	.10	.25
	1980(C)	Inc. Ab.	—	.10	.25
	1980(H)	Inc. Ab.	—	.10	.30
	1981(B)	11.048	—	.10	.30
	1981(C)	Inc. Ab.	.50	.75	1.50
	1981(H)	Inc. Ab.	—	.10	.25
	1982(C)	38.288	—	.10	.25
	1983(C)	137.488	—	.10	.20
	1984(B) rounded edge	98.740	—	.10	.20
	1984(B) sharp straight edge	Inc. Ab.	—	.10	.20
	1984(C) rounded edge	Inc. Ab.	—	.10	.20
	1984(C) sharp straight edge	Inc. Ab.	—	.10	.20
	1985(B)	113.872	—	.10	.20
	1985C	Inc. Ab.	—	.10	.20
	1985(C) rounded edge	Inc. Ab.	—	.10	.20
	1985(C) sharp straight edge	Inc. Ab.	—	.10	.20
	1985(H)	Inc. Ab.	—	.10	.20
	1986(B)	362.624	—	.10	.20
	1986(C)	Inc. Ab.	—	.10	.20
	1986(H)	Inc. Ab.	—	.10	.20
	1987(B)	341.160	—	.10	.20
	1987(C)	Inc. Ab.	—	.10	.20
	1987(H)	Inc. Ab.	—	.10	.20
	1988(B)	303.252	—	.10	.20
	1988(C)	Inc. Ab.	—	.10	.20
	1988(H)	Inc. Ab.	—	.10	.20
	1989(B)	—	—	.10	.20
	1989(C)	—	—	.10	.20
	1990(B)	—	—	.10	.20
	1993(N)	—	—	.10	.20

NOTE: Two varieties exist of 1985(B), 1986(C) and 1987(C): 1) 9mm wide Ashoka capital, 2) 8 1/2 mm wide Ashoka capital and varieties of fur on the lion.

Obverse 2
9mm between lion nosetips, 15mm across field.

KM#	Date	Mintage	VF	XF	Unc
621	1972(C)	—	—	.10	.25
	1977(B)	Inc. KM620	—	.10	.25
	1977B	Inc. KM620	—	Proof	.35
	1978(B)	Inc. KM620	.50	1.00	2.00
	1979B	—	—	Proof	.35

Obverse 2
10mm between lion nosetips, 16-16.3mm across field.

KM#	Date	Mintage	VF	XF	Unc
622	1972(C)	Inc. KM620	1.00	1.40	2.00
	1973(C)	—	.10	.15	.30
	1974(C)	—	.10	.15	.30
	1975(C)	Inc. KM620	.10	.15	.30
	1976(C)	—	.25	.50	1.00

Rural Women's Advancement

KM#	Date	Mintage	VF	XF	Unc
659	1980(B)	Inc. KM620	.10	.15	.30
	1980B	—	—	Proof	.30
	1980(C)	Inc. KM620	.10	.15	.30
	1980(H)	Inc. KM620	.10	.25	.50

World Food Day

KM#	Date	Mintage	VF	XF	Unc
663	1981(B)	Inc. KM620	.10	.15	.30
	1981B	—	—	Proof	.35
	1981(C)	Inc. KM620	.10	.20	.40
	1981(H)	Inc. KM620	.10	.25	.50

IX Asian Games

KM#	Date	Mintage	VF	XF	Unc
670	1982(B)	Inc. KM620	.10	.15	.35
	1982B	—	—	Proof	.50
	1982(C)	Inc.KM620	.10	.15	.35
	1982(H)	Inc.KM620	.10	.15	.35

Forestry

KM#	Date	Mintage	VF	XF	Unc
692	1985(B)	Inc.KM620	.10	.20	.60
	1985(H)	Inc.KM620	.10	.20	.60

STAINLESS STEEL
Rhinoceros

KM#	Date	Mintage	VF	XF	Unc
703	1988C	305.280	.10	.15	.30
	1988(B)	—	.10	.15	.30
	1988(C)	18.920	.10	.15	.50
	1988(H)	—	.10	.15	.30
	1988(N)	Inc. Ab.	.10	.15	.30
	1989(B)	—	.10	.15	.30
	1989(C)	—	.10	.15	.30
	1989(H)	—	.10	.15	.30
	1989(N)	—	.10	.15	.30
	1990(B)	—	.10	.15	.30
	1990(C)	—	.10	.15	.30
	1990(H)	—	.10	.15	.30
	1990(N)	—	.10	.15	.30
	1991(B)	—	.10	.15	.25
	1991(C)	—	.10	.15	.25
	1991(H)	—	.10	.15	.25
	1991(N)	—	.10	.15	.25
	1992(B)	—	.10	.15	.25
	1992(N)	—	.10	.15	.25
	1993(B)	—	.10	.15	.25
	1993(N)	—	.10	.15	.25

50 NAYE PAISE

NICKEL

KM#	Date	Mintage	VF	XF	Unc
580	1960(B)	11.224	.40	.75	1.50
	1960(B)	—	—	Proof	3.00
	1960(C)	Inc. Ab.	.30	.50	1.25
	1961(B)	45.992	.25	.40	.75
	1961(B)	—	—	Proof	3.00
	1961(C)	Inc. Ab.	.25	.40	.75
	1962(B)	64.228	.25	.40	.75
	1962(B)	—	—	Proof	3.00
	1962(C)	Inc. Ab.	.25	.40	.75
	1963(B)	58.168	.25	.40	.75
	1963(B)	—	—	Proof	3.00
	1963(C)	Inc. Ab.	.25	.50	1.00

50 PAISE

NICKEL
Death of Jawaharlal Nehru
Rev. leg: English.

KM#	Date	Mintage	VF	XF	Unc
588	ND(1964)(B)	21.900	.30	.65	1.00
	ND(1964)B	—	—	Proof	2.50
	ND(1964)(C)	7.160	.50	1.00	2.00

Rev. leg: Hindi.

KM#	Date	Mintage	VF	XF	Unc
589	ND(1964)(B)	36.190	.30	.65	1.00
	ND(1964)(C)	28.350	.50	.75	1.25

NOTE: Nehru commemorative issues were struck until 1967.

Obverse 1, Reverse 1

KM#	Date	Mintage	VF	XF	Unc
590	1964(C)	23.361	.35	.60	1.00
	1967(B)	19.267	.25	.45	.75

Obverse 2, Reverse 2

KM#	Date	Mintage	VF	XF	Unc
601	1967(C)	—	.40	.75	1.25
	1968(B)	28.076	.20	.30	.60
	1968(C)	Inc. Ab.	.20	.30	.60
	1969(B)	59.388	.20	.30	.60
	1969(C)	Inc. Ab.	.25	.50	1.00
	1970(B)	Inc. Ab.	.20	.30	.50
	1970(C)	Inc. Ab.	.20	.30	.60
	1971(C)	57.900	.20	.30	.50

Obverse 1, Reverse 2

KM#	Date	Mintage	VF	XF	Unc
613	1970(B)	Inc. 1969	.20	.30	.75
	1970B	3,046	—	Proof	.60
	1971B	4,375	—	Proof	.60

Mahatma Gandhi Centennial of Birth

KM#	Date	Mintage	VF	XF	Unc
609	ND(1969)(B)	10.260	.20	.30	.60
	ND(1969)B	9,147	—	Proof	.60
	ND(1969)(C)	12.100	.20	.30	.60

NOTE: Struck during 1969 and 1970.

COPPER-NICKEL
25th Anniversary of Independence

KM#	Date	Mintage	VF	XF	Unc
623	ND(1972)(B)	43.800	.10	.20	.50
	ND(1972)B	7,895	—	Proof	.75
	ND(1972)(C)	40.080	.10	.20	.50

Obverse 2. Rev: Lettering spaced out.

KM#	Date	Mintage	VF	XF	Unc
624	1972(B)	—	.10	.20	.50
	1972(C)	—	.10	.20	.50
	1973(B)	—	.10	.20	.50
	1973(C)	—	.40	.75	1.25

F.A.O. Issue - Grow More Food

KM#	Date	Mintage	VF	XF	Unc
628	1973(B)	28.720	.15	.20	.60
	1973B	.011	—	Proof	.60
	1973(C)	40.100	.15	.25	.60

Obverse 2, Rev. Lettering close.

KM#	Date	Mintage	VF	XF	Unc
632	1974(B)	—	.10	.20	.40
	1974B	—	—	Proof	.50
	1974(C)	—	.10	.20	.40
	1975(B)	225.880	.10	.20	.40
	1975B	—	—	Proof	.50
	1975(C)	Inc. Ab.	.10	.20	.40
	1975(H)	—	—	.35	.60
	1976(B)	99.564	.10	.15	.40
	1976B	Inc. Ab.	—	Proof	.50
	1976(C)	Inc. Ab.	.10	.20	.45
	1976(H)	Inc. Ab.	.10	.20	.45
	1977(B)	97.272	.10	.15	.40
	1977B	Inc. Ab.	—	Proof	.50
	1977(C)	Inc. Ab.	.10	.20	.45
	1977(H)	Inc. Ab.	.10	.15	.40
	1978B	25.648	—	Proof	.50
	1978(C)	—	.10	.15	.50
	1979B	—	—	Proof	.50
	1980(B)	—	.10	.15	.50
	1980B	—	—	Proof	.50
	1980(C)	—	.10	.15	.50
	1981B	—	—	Proof	.50
	1983(C)	62.634	.10	.15	.50

National Integration

KM#	Date	Mintage	VF	XF	Unc
671	1982(B)	9.804	.15	.25	.65
	1982(C)	Inc. Ab.	.35	.55	1.00

Circulation Coinage

KM#	Date	Mintage	VF	XF	Unc
680	1984(B)	61.548	.10	.15	.40
	1984(C)	Inc. Ab.	.10	.15	.40
	1984(H)	—	.10	.15	.40
	1985(B)	210.964	.10	.15	.40
	1985(C)	Inc. Ab.	.10	.15	.40
	1985(H)	Inc. Ab.	.10	.15	.40
	1985(S)	Inc. Ab.	.10	.15	.40
	1986(C)	117.576	.10	.15	.40
	1987(B)	—	.10	.15	.35
	1987(C)	145.140	.10	.15	.35
	1987(H)	Inc. Ab.	.10	.15	.35
	1988(B)	149.092	.10	.15	.35
	1988(C)	Inc. Ab.	.10	.15	.35
	1988(H)	Inc. Ab.	.10	.15	.35

KM#	Date	Mintage	VF	XF	Unc
680	1989(B)	—	.10	.15	.35
	1989(C)	—	.10	.15	.35
	1989(H)	—	Reported, not confirmed		
	1990(B)	—	.10	.15	.35

Golden Jubilee of Reserve Bank of India

KM#	Date	Mintage	VF	XF	Unc
681	1985(B)	Inc.KM680	.25	.40	.85
	1985B	Inc.KM680	—	Proof	15.00
	1985(H)	Inc.KM680	.25	.40	.85

Death of Indira Gandhi

KM#	Date	Mintage	VF	XF	Unc
686	ND(1985)(B)	Inc.KM680	.15	.30	.70
	ND(1985)B	Inc.KM680	—	Proof	15.00
	ND(1985)(C)	Inc.KM680	.15	.30	.70
	ND(1985)(H)	Inc.KM680	.15	.30	.70

F.A.O. Fisheries

KM#	Date	Mintage	VF	XF	Unc
696	1986(B)	Inc.KM680	—	.35	.75
	1986B	Inc.KM680	—	Proof	15.00
	1986(H)	Inc.KM680	—	.35	.75

STAINLESS STEEL
Parliament Building in New Delhi

KM#	Date	Mintage	VF	XF	Unc
704	1988C	272.160	.10	.20	.40
	1988(B)	—	.10	.20	.50
	1988(C)	2.195	.10	.20	.50
	1988(H)	Inc. Ab.	.10	.20	.50
	1988(N)	—	.10	.20	.50
	1989(B)	—	.10	.20	.35
	1989(C)	—	.10	.20	.35
	1989(H)	—	.10	.20	.35
	1989(N)	—	.10	.20	.35
	1990(B)	—	.10	.20	.35
	1990(C)	—	.10	.20	.35
	1990(H)	—	.10	.20	.50
	1990(N)	—	.10	.20	.35
	1991(B)	—	.10	.15	.25
	1991(C)	—	.10	.15	.25
	1991(H)	—	.10	.15	.25
	1991(N)	—	.10	.15	.25
	1992(B)	—	.10	.15	.25
	1992(N)	—	.10	.15	.25

RUPEE

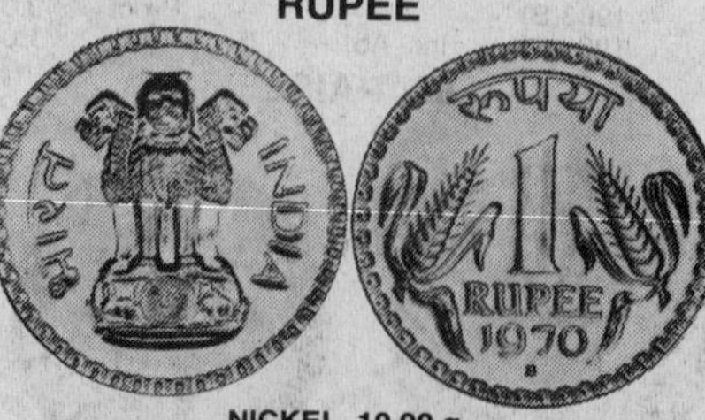

NICKEL, 10.00 g
Obverse 1

KM#	Date	Mintage	VF	XF	Unc
581	1962B	—	—	Proof	4.00
	1962(C)	3.689	.50	1.00	2.00
	1970(B)	Inc. Ab.	2.00	3.00	4.00
	1970B	3,046	—	Proof	1.50
	1971B	4,375	—	Proof	1.50
	1972B	7,895	—	Proof	1.50
	1973B	7,567	—	Proof	1.50
	1974B	—	—	Proof	1.50

Death of Jawaharlal Nehru

KM#	Date	Mintage	VF	XF	Unc
591	ND(1964)(B)	10.010	.65	1.00	1.75
	ND(1964)B	—	—	Proof	5.00
	ND(1964)(C)	10.020	.65	1.00	1.75

NOTE: Nehru commemorative issues were struck until 1967.

Mahatma Gandhi Centennial of Birth

KM#	Date	Mintage	VF	XF	Unc
610	ND(1969)(B)	5.180	.25	.40	2.00
	ND(1969)B	9,147	—	Proof	1.00
	ND(1969)(C)	6.690	.50	1.25	2.50

NOTE: Struck during 1969 and 1970.

COPPER-NICKEL, 8.00 g

KM#	Date	Mintage	VF	XF	Unc
636	1975(B)	98.850	.20	.35	.75
	1975B	—	—	Proof	1.00
	1975(C)	—	2.00	4.00	7.00
	1976(B)	161.895	.20	.35	.75
	1976B	Inc. Ab.	—	Proof	1.00
	1977(B)	177.105	.20	.35	.75
	1977B	Inc. Ab.	—	Proof	1.00
	1978(B)	127.348	.20	.35	.75
	1978B	Inc. Ab.	—	Proof	1.00
	1978(C)	Inc. Ab.	.20	.35	.75
	1979(C)	—	5.00	6.00	7.50

Obverse 2

KM#	Date	Mintage	VF	XF	Unc
637	1975(C)	Inc. 636	.25	.50	1.00
	1976(C)	Inc. 636	.25	.50	1.00

Obv: Letter "I" INDIA has serifs.

KM#	Date	Mintage	VF	XF	Unc
655	1979(B)	—	.20	.35	.75
	1979B	—	—	Proof	1.00
	1979(C)	—	1.50	3.00	6.00
	1980(B)	84.768	.20	.35	.75
	1980B	—	—	Proof	1.00
	1980(C)	Inc. Ab.	.25	.40	.85
	1981(B) short tooth border	82.458	.20	.35	.75
	1981(B) long tooth border	Inc. Ab.	.20	.35	.75
	1981B	—	—	Proof	1.00
	1981(C)	Inc. Ab.	.20	.35	.75
	1982(B) short tooth border	116.811	.20	.35	.75
	1982(B) long tooth border	Inc. Ab.	.20	.35	.75
	1983(B)	71.552	.20	.35	.75
	1983(C)	Inc. Ab.	.20	.35	.75
	1984(B)	34.935	.20	.35	.75
	1984(C)	Inc. Ab.	.20	.35	.75

COPPER-NICKEL
Security edge

KM#	Date	Mintage	VF	XF	Unc
679.1	1983(B)	32.490	.20	.35	.65
	1983(C)	Inc. Ab.	.20	.35	.65
	1984(B)	152.378	.20	.35	.65
	1984(C)	Inc. Ab.	.20	.35	.65
	1984(H)	Inc. Ab.	.20	.35	.65
	1984(L)	—	.20	.35	.65
	1985(B)	444.516	.20	.35	.65
	1985(C)	Inc. Ab.	.20	.35	.65
	1985(H)	Inc. Ab.	.20	.35	.65
	1985(L)	Inc. Ab.	.20	.35	.65
	1985(S)	Inc. Ab.	.20	.35	.65
	1986(B)	1,396.074	.20	.35	.65
	1986(C)	Inc. Ab.	.20	.35	.65
	1986(H)	Inc. Ab.	.20	.35	.65
	1987(B)	685.502	.20	.35	.65
	1987(C)	Inc. Ab.	.20	.35	.65
	1987(H)	Inc. Ab.	.20	.35	.65
	1988(B)	240.447	.20	.35	.65
	1988(C)	Inc. Ab.	.20	.35	.65
	1988(H)	Inc. Ab.	.20	.35	.65
	1989(B)	—	.20	.35	.65
	1989(C)	—	.20	.30	.50
	1989(H)	—	.20	.30	.50
	1989(N)	—	—	—	—
	1990(B)	—	.15	.25	.45
	1990(C)	—	.15	.25	.45
	1990(H)	—	.15	.25	.45
	1990(N)	—	.15	.25	.45

Milled edge

KM#	Date	Mintage	VF	XF	Unc
679.2	1990(B)	—	.15	.25	.45
	1990(C)	—	.15	.25	.45
	1990(H)	—	.15	.25	.45
	1991(B)	—	.15	.25	.45
	1991(C)	—	.15	.25	.45
	1991(H)	—	.15	.25	.45
	1991(N)	—	Reported, not confirmed		

Youth Year

KM#	Date	Mintage	VF	XF	Unc
693	1985(B)	Inc.KM679	.15	.35	1.25
	1985(C)	Inc.KM679	.15	.35	1.25
	1985(C)	Inc.KM679	—	Proof	5.00

F.A.O. - Small Farmers

KM#	Date	Mintage	VF	XF	Unc
699	1987(B)	234.223	.20	.35	1.00
	1987B	—	—	Proof	5.00
	1987(C)	Inc. Ab.	.20	.35	.75
	1987(H)	191.120	.20	.35	.75
	1987(L)	260.160	.20	.35	.75

F.A.O. - Rainfed Farming

KM#	Date	Mintage	VF	XF	Unc
710	1988(B)	Inc.KM679	.15	.25	.50
	1988(C)	—	.15	.25	.50

100th Anniversary of Nehru's Birth

KM#	Date	Mintage	VF	XF	Unc
705	1989(B)	—	.20	.40	.75
	1989B	—	—	Proof	5.00
	1989(H)	—	.20	.40	.75

F.A.O. - Food & Environment

KM#	Date	Mintage	VF	XF	Unc
709	1989(B)	—	.20	.40	.75
	1989(H)	—	.20	.40	.75

Dr. Ambedkar

KM#	Date	Mintage	VF	XF	Unc
711	1990(B)	—	—	.30	.60
	1990(H)	—	—	.35	.75

15th Anniversary of I.C.D.S.

KM#	Date	Mintage	VF	XF	Unc
712	1990(B)	—	—	.30	.75
	1990(H)	—	—	.30	.75

SAARC Year - Care For the Girl Child

KM#	Date	Mintage	VF	XF	Unc
713	1990(B)	—	—	.30	.75
	1990(H)	—	—	.30	.75

NOTE: Edge varieties exist for coins minted at Bombay Mint.

F.A.O. - Farming Scene

KM#	Date	Mintage	VF	XF	Unc
714	1990(H)	—	—	.30	.75

Rajiv Ghandi

KM#	Date	Mintage	VF	XF	Unc
715	1991(B)	—	—	.30	.75
	1991(H)	—	—	.30	.75
	1991(N)	—	—	.30	.75

Commonwealth Parliamentary Conference

KM#	Date	Mintage	VF	XF	Unc
716	1991(B)	—	—	.30	.75

Tourism Year

KM#	Date	Mintage	VF	XF	Unc
717	1991(B)	—	—	.30	.75
	1991(H)	—	—	.30	.75

STAINLESS STEEL

KM#	Date	Mintage	VF	XF	Unc
718	1992(B)	—	.10	.20	.35
	1992(H)	—	.10	.20	.35
	1993(C)	—	.10	.20	.35
	1993(H)	—	.10	.20	.35
	1993(N)	—	.10	.20	.35

Quit India

KM#	Date	Mintage	VF	XF	Unc
719	1992(B)	—	—	.30	.75

World Food Day

KM#	Date	Mintage	VF	XF	Unc
720	1992(C)	—	—	.30	.75

Inter Parliamentary Union Conference

KM#	Date	Mintage	VF	XF	Unc
722	1993(B)	—	—	.30	.75

2 RUPEES

COPPER-NICKEL
IX Asian Games

KM#	Date	Mintage	VF	XF	Unc
672	1982(B)	12.720	.25	.50	1.00
	1982B	Inc. Ab.	—	Proof	2.00
	1982(C)	Inc. Ab.	.25	.50	1.00

National Integration

KM#	Date	Mintage	VF	XF	Unc
673.1	1982(B)	Inc. KM672	.25	.50	1.00
	1982(C)	Inc. KM672	.25	.50	1.00
	1990(B)	—	.20	.40	.75
	1990(C)	—	.25	.50	1.00
	1990(H)	—	.30	.60	1.25

Reduced size: 26mm

KM#	Date	Mintage	VF	XF	Unc
673.2	1992(B)	—	.20	.40	.75
	1992(C)	—	.20	.40	.75
	1992(H)	—	.20	.40	.75
	1993(B)	—	.20	.40	.75
	1993(H)	—	.20	.40	.75

Golden Jubilee of Reserve Bank of India

KM#	Date	Mintage	VF	XF	Unc
682	1985B	—	—	Proof	25.00

Small Family Happy Family

KM#	Date	Mintage	VF	XF	Unc
723	1993(B)	—	—	.50	1.00

5 RUPEES

COPPER-NICKEL
Death of Indira Gandhi

KM#	Date	Mintage	VF	XF	Unc
687	ND(1985)(B)	59.288	.50	1.00	3.00
	ND(1985)B	Inc. Ab.	—	Proof	25.00
	ND(1985)(H)	Inc. Ab.	.80	1.50	4.00

100th Anniversary of Nehru's Birth

KM#	Date	Mintage	VF	XF	Unc
706	1989(B)	—	—	—	3.00
	1989B	—	—	Proof	25.00

NOTE: Varieties of size of mint marks and legends exist.

KM#	Date	Mintage	VF	XF	Unc
721	1992(C)	—	.25	.40	.75
	1992(H)	—	.25	.40	.75
	1993(B)	—	.25	.40	.75

10 RUPEES

15.0000 g, .800 SILVER, .3858 oz ASW
Mahatma Gandhi Centennial of Birth

KM#	Date	Mintage	VF	XF	Unc
611	ND(1969)(B)	3.160	—	—	6.00
	ND(1969)B	9,147	—	Proof	7.50
	ND(1969)(C)	.100	—	—	7.50

NOTE: Struck during 1969 and 1970.

F.A.O. Issue

KM#	Date	Mintage	VF	XF	Unc
614	1970(B)	.300	—	—	5.00
	1970B	3,046	—	Proof	10.00
	1970(C)	.100	—	—	7.00
	1971(B)	—	—	—	7.00
	1971B	1,594	—	Proof	10.00

22.3000 g, .500 SILVER, .3585 oz ASW
25th Anniversary of Independence

KM#	Date	Mintage	VF	XF	Unc
625	1972(B)	1.000	—	—	5.00
	1972B	7,895	—	Proof	6.50
	1972(C)	1.000	—	—	5.00

F.A.O. Issue

KM#	Date	Mintage	VF	XF	Unc
629	1973(B)	.064	—	—	5.00
	1973B	.015	—	Proof	6.50

COPPER-NICKEL
F.A.O. Issue

KM#	Date	Mintage	VF	XF	Unc
633	1974(B)	.065	—	1.50	2.50
	1974B	.012	—	Proof	3.50

F.A.O. - Women's Year

KM#	Date	Mintage	VF	XF	Unc
638	1975(B)	.049	—	1.50	2.50
	1975B	2,531	—	Proof	5.00

F.A.O. Issue, FOOD & WORK FOR ALL

KM#	Date	Mintage	VF	XF	Unc
642	1976(B)	.049	—	1.50	2.50
	1976B	3,400	—	Proof	5.00

F.A.O. Issue, SAVE FOR DEVELOPMENT

KM#	Date	Mintage	VF	XF	Unc
646	1977(B)	.020	—	1.50	2.50
	1977B	5,969	—	Proof	5.00

F.A.O. Issue, FOOD & SHELTER FOR ALL

KM#	Date	Mintage	VF	XF	Unc
650	1978(B)	.025	—	1.50	2.50
	1978B	—	—	Proof	5.00

International Year of the Child

KM#	Date	Mintage	VF	XF	Unc
656	1979(B)	—	—	2.00	3.50
	1979B	—	—	Proof	6.00

Rural Women's Advancement

KM#	Date	Mintage	VF	XF	Unc
660	1980(B)	—	—	2.00	4.00
	1980B	—	—	Proof	6.00

World Food Day

KM#	Date	Mintage	VF	XF	Unc
664	1981(B)	—	—	2.00	4.00
	1981B	—	—	Proof	6.00

IX Asian Games

KM#	Date	Mintage	VF	XF	Unc
674	1982(B)	—	—	2.00	4.00
	1982B	—	—	Proof	6.00

National Integration

KM#	Date	Mintage	VF	XF	Unc
676	1982(B)	—	—	—	6.00

Golden Jubilee of Reserve Bank of India

KM#	Date	Mintage	VF	XF	Unc
683	1985(B)	—	—	—	18.00
	1985B	—	—	Proof	20.00

Youth Year
Similar to 1 Rupee, KM#693

KM#	Date	Mintage	VF	XF	Unc
694	1985(C)	—	—	—	10.00
	1985(C)	—	—	Proof	15.00

20 RUPEES

30.0000 g, .500 SILVER, .4823 oz ASW
F.A.O. Issue

KM#	Date	Mintage	VF	XF	Unc
630	1973(B)	.064	—	—	7.50
	1973B	.012	—	Proof	10.00

COPPER-NICKEL
Death of Indira Gandhi

KM#	Date	Mintage	VF	XF	Unc
688	ND(1985)(B)	—	—	—	10.00
	ND(1985)B	—	—	Proof	15.00

F.A.O. Fisheries

KM#	Date	Mintage	VF	XF	Unc
697	1986(B)	—	—	—	10.00
	1986B	—	—	Proof	15.00

F.A.O. - Small Farmers

KM#	Date	Mintage	VF	XF	Unc
700	1987(B)	—	—	—	10.00
	1987B	—	—	Proof	15.00

100th Anniversary of Nehru's Birth

KM#	Date	Mintage	VF	XF	Unc
707	1989(B)	—	—	—	10.00
	1989B	—	—	Proof	15.00

50 RUPEES

34.7000 g, .500 SILVER, .5578 oz ASW
F.A.O. Issue

KM#	Date	Mintage	VF	XF	Unc
634	1974(B)	.082	—	—	7.50
	1974B	.013	—	Proof	9.00

F.A.O. - Women's Year

KM#	Date	Mintage	VF	XF	Unc
639	1975(B)	.065	—	—	8.50
	1975B	2,691	—	Proof	15.00

F.A.O Issue, FOOD & WORK FOR ALL

KM#	Date	Mintage	VF	XF	Unc
643	1976(B)	.042	—	—	10.00
	1976B	3,385	—	Proof	12.50

F.A.O. Issue, SAVE FOR DEVELOPMENT

KM#	Date	Mintage	VF	XF	Unc
647	1977(B)	.026	—	—	10.00
	1977B	2,544	—	Proof	15.00

F.A.O. Issue, FOOD & SHELTER FOR ALL

KM#	Date	Mintage	VF	XF	Unc
651	1978(B)	.025	—	—	10.00
	1978B	—	—	Proof	12.50

World Food Day

KM#	Date	Mintage	VF	XF	Unc
665	1981(B)	.022	—	—	17.50
	1981B	2,950	—	Proof	22.50

National Integration

KM#	Date	Mintage	VF	XF	Unc
690	1982(B)	—	—	—	25.00
	1982B	—	—	Proof	35.00

International Year of the Child

657	1979(B)	—	—	—	10.00
	1979B	—	—	Proof	15.00

29.1600 g, .925 SILVER, .8673 oz ASW
International Year of the Child

666	1981(1983)B	—	—	Proof	22.50

Golden Jubilee of Reserve Bank of India

684	1985(B)	—	—	—	30.00
	1985B	—	—	Proof	38.00

100 RUPEES

35.0000 g, .500 SILVER, .5627 oz ASW
Rural Women's Advancement

661	1980(B)	.021	—	—	17.50
	1980B	5,811	—	Proof	22.50

35.0000 g, .500 SILVER, .5627 oz AGW
IX Asian Games

675	1982(B)	—	—	—	17.50
	1982B	—	—	Proof	22.50

Death of Indira Gandhi

689	ND(1985)(B)	—	—	—	25.00
	ND(1985)B	—	—	Proof	35.00

Youth Year
Similar to 1 Rupee, KM#693

695	1985(C)	.016	—	—	30.00
	1985(C)	6,267	—	Proof	40.00

F.A.O. Fisheries

KM#	Date	Mintage	VF	XF	Unc
698	1986(B)	—	—	—	30.00
	1986B	—	—	Proof	40.00

F.A.O. - Small Farmers

KM#	Date	Mintage	VF	XF	Unc
701	1987(B)	—	—	—	30.00
	1987B	—	—	Proof	50.00

100th Anniversary of Nehru's Birth

KM#	Date	Mintage	VF	XF	Unc
708	1989(B)	—	—	—	30.00
	1989B	—	—	Proof	50.00

MINT SETS (MS)

KM#	Date	Mintage	Identification	Issue Price	Mkt. Val.
MS1	1950(7)	—	—	3.60	10.00
MS2	1954(7)	—	—	3.60	10.00
MS3	1962(6)	—	KM575a,576-580	1.50	3.00
MS4	1962(7)	—	KM575a,576-581	3.60	3.50
MS5	ND(1964)(B)(2)		KM588,591	1.00	3.75
MS6	1967(8)	—	KM581,584-587,590, 592-593 (1962 dated Rupee)	1.00	7.00
MS7	1969B(4)	25,281	KM608-611, blue plastic case	2.50	10.00
MS8	1970(B)(8)	—	KM581,584,592-593, 599,601,605,607, brown vinyl case, diamond below date	1.00	10.00
MS9	1970(B)(2)	22,999	KM612,614	2.00	9.00
MS10	1971(B)(2)	9,987	KM614,616	—	8.50
MS11	1972(B)(2)	43,121	KM623,625	2.00	6.50
MS12	1973(B)(2)	48,670	KM629-630	—	13.50
MS13	1974(B)(2)	50,219	KM633-634	10.00	12.50
MS14	1975(B)(2)	40,279	KM638-639	12.00	12.50
MS15	1976(B)(2)	25,105	KM642-643	12.00	12.50
MS16	1977(B)(2)	17,071	KM646-647	12.00	12.50
MS17	1978(B)(2)	15,041	KM650-651	10.00	12.50
MS18	1979(B)(2)	—	KM656-657	—	13.00
MS19	1980(B)(2)	—	KM660-661	—	21.00
MS20	1981(B)(2)	—	KM664-665	—	21.00
MS21	1982(B)(2)	—	KM674-675	—	21.00
MS22	1985(B)(2)	—	KM683-684	48.00	48.00
MS23	ND(1985)(B)(2)	—	KM688-689	43.00	55.00
MS24	ND(1985)(C)(2)	—	KM694-695	—	25.00
MS25	1986(2)	—	KM697-698	45.00	35.00
MS26	1987B(2)	—	KM700-701	45.00	55.00
MS27	1989(2)	—	KM707-708	40.00	40.00
MS28	1989(4)	—	KM705-708	50.00	50.00

PROOF SETS (PS)

NOTE: Beginning in 1969, all proof coins have B beneath date for Bombay Mint. Non-proof Bombay coins have diamond mint mark.

KM#	Date	Mintage	Identification	Issue Price	Mkt. Val.
PS1	1950B(7)	-*	KM565.1,567-570,572, 574	8.40	30.00
PS2	1954B(7)	-*	KM566-570,572,574	8.40	50.00
PS3	1960B(6)	-*	KM575-580	7.00	30.00
PS4	1961B(6)	-*	KM575-580	7.00	40.00
PS5	1962B(7)	-*	KM575a,576-581, (1960 dated 1-50 New Paisa)	8.40	40.00
PS6	1962B(7)	-*	KM575a,576-581	8.40	35.00
PS7	1963B(6)	-*	KM575a,576-580 (1961 dated 1-50 New Paisa	7.00	30.00
PS8	1963B(7)	-*	KM575a,576-581 (1962 Rupee)	8.40	25.00
PS9	ND(1964)B(2)	-*	KM588,591	5.00	7.50
PS10	1969B(9)	9,097	KM592,597,599,603, 607,608-611	15.25	10.00
PS11	1970B(9)	2,900	KM581,584,590,592, 603,598,605,612, 614	15.25	14.00
PS12	1971B(9)	4,161	KM581,592,603,615, 617,619-620,623, 625	15.25	13.00
PS13	1972B(9)	7,701	KM581,592,603,615, 617-618,620,623, 625	15.25	10.00
PS14	1973B(10)	7,563	KM581,592,603,615, 617,620,626,628 630	26.00	20.00
PS15	1973B(9)	3,326	KM581,592,603,615, 617,620,626,628 629	15.25	10.00
PS16	1973B(2)	2,408	KM629-630	17.50	17.50
PS17	1974B(10)	9,138	KM581,592,603,617, 620,626,631-634	29.00	18.00
PS18	1974B(2)	1,712	KM633-634	7.50	16.00
PS19	1975B(10)	2,370	KM592,603,617,620, 626,632,635-636, 638-639	35.00	22.50
PS20	1975B(2)	160	KM638-639	22.00	20.00
PS21	1976B(10)	3,209	KM581,592,603,617, 620,632,640-643	35.00	20.00
PS22	1976B(2)	190	KM642-643	22.00	17.50
PS23	1977B(10)	2,222	KM592,603,617,621, 632,636,644-647	35.00	22.50
PS24	1977B(2)	—	KM646-647	—	20.00
PS25	1978B(10)	1,390	KM592,603,617,620, 632,636,648-651	35.00	20.00
PS26	1978B(2)	—	KM650-651	—	17.50
PS27	1979B(9)?	—	KM592,603,617,621, 632,636,652-653, 656-657	—	25.00
PS28	1979B(2)	—	KM656-657	—	20.00
PS29	1980B(10)?	—	KM592,603,617,626, 632,636,658-661	—	32.50
PS30	1980B(2)	—	KM660-661	—	29.00
PS31	1981B(10)?	—	KM592,603,617,626, 632,636,662-665	—	32.50
PS-A32	1981B(4)	—	KM662-665	—	50.00
PS32	1981B(2)	—	KM664-665	—	29.00
PS33	1982B(4)	—	KM670,672,674-675	48.00	32.50
PS34	1982B(2)	—	KM674-675	38.00	29.00
PS35	1985B(4)	—	KM681-684	98.00	98.00
PS36	1985B(2)	—	KM683-684	58.00	58.00
PS37	ND(1985)B(4)	—	KM686-689	88.00	105.00
PS38	ND(1985)B(2)	—	KM688-689	48.00	65.00
PS39	1985(C)(3)	—	KM693-695	—	36.00
PS40	1986B(3)	—	KM696-698	70.00	60.00
PS41	1986B(2)	—	KM697-698	50.00	45.00
PS42	1987B(3)	—	KM699-701	65.00	70.00
PS43	1987B(2)	—	KM700-701	60.00	65.00
PS44	1989B(4)	—	KM705-708	90.00	90.00
PS45	1989B(2)	—	KM707-708	65.00	65.00

Listings For

INDO-CHINA: refer to French Indo-China

INDONESIA

The Republic of Indonesia, the world's largest archipelago, extends for more than 3,000 miles (4,827 km.) along the equator from the mainland of southeast Asia to Australia. The 17,508 islands comprising the archipelago have a combined area of 788,425 sq. mi. (1,919,440 sq. km.) and a population of 187.7 million, including East Timor. Capital: Djakarta. Petroleum, timber, rubber, and coffee are exported.

Had Columbus succeeded in reaching the fabled Spice Islands, he would have found advanced civilizations a millennium old, and temples still ranked among the finest examples of ancient art. During the opening centuries of the Christian era, the islands were influenced by Hindu priests and traders who spread their culture and religion. Moslem invasions began in the 13th century, fragmenting the island kingdoms into small states which were unable to resist Western colonial infiltration. Portuguese traders established posts in the 16th century, but they were soon outnumbered by the Dutch who arrived in 1596 and gradually asserted control over the islands comprising present-day Indonesia. Dutch dominance, interrupted by British incursions during the Napoleonic Wars, established the Netherlands East Indies as one of the richest colonial possessions in the world.

The Indonesian independence movement, which began between the two world wars, was encouraged by the Japanese during their 3 1/2-year occupation during World War II. Indonesia proclaimed its independence on Aug. 17, 1945, three days after the surrender of Japan, and established it on Dec. 27, 1949, after four years of guerilla warfare including two large scale campaigns by the Dutch in an effort to reassert control. Further rebellions led by the Netherlands Indies army occurred in 1950. Through the efforts of President Mohammad Achmad Sukarno (1950-67) the new Republic not only held together but developed within intellectually. West Irian, formerly Netherlands New Guinea, came under the administration of Indonesia on May 1, 1963.

On November 28, 1975 the Portuguese Province of Timor, an overseas province occupying the eastern half of the East Indian island of Timor, attained independence as the People's Democratic Republic of East Timor. On December 5, 1975 the government of the People's Democratic Republic was seized by a guerrilla faction sympathetic to the Indonesian territorial claim to East Timor which ousted the constitutional government and replaced it with the Provisional Government of East Timor. On July 17, 1976, the Provisional Government enacted a law that dissolved the free republic and made East Timor the 27th province of Indonesia.

Coinage for the Indonesian Archipelago is varied and extensive. The Dutch struck coins for the islands at various mints in the Netherlands and the islands under the auspices of the VOC (United East India Company), the Batavian Republic and the Kingdom of the Netherlands. The British issued a coinage during the various occupations by the British East Indian Company, 1811-24. Modern coinage issued by the Republic of Indonesia includes separate series for West Irian and for the Riau Archipelago, an area of small islands between Singapore and Sumatra.

NETHERLANDS EAST INDIES

RULERS

Batavian Republic 1799-1806
Louis Napoleon, King of Holland, 1806-1811
Dutch, 1816-1942

MINT MARKS

H - Amsterdam (H)
Hk - Harderwijk (star, rosette, cock, cross, Z)
Hn - Hoorn (star)
E - Einkhuizen (star)
Dt - Dordrecht (rosette)
K - Kampen (eagle)
S - Utrecht
Sa - Surabaya (Sa)

MONETARY SYSTEM

120 Duits=120 Cents
1 Gulden=1 Java Rupee
16 Silver Rupees=1 Gold Mohur

BONKS: Because of the slow delivery of coins from the Netherlands, the government in the East Indies often resorted to the manufacture of "Bonks". These were simply lumps cut from the copper (or tin) rods used for coining. This eliminated the problems inherent in casting round coins and allowed the production of large quantities of legal tender very quickly. The thicker rods were used for the 2 and 8 Stiver Bonks and the thinner rod for the smaller denominations.

DUITS: On many of the Duit and 1/2 Duit coins of the East Indies dated 1802-1826, the value appears as 5-1/32-G (1/2 Duit) and 5-1/16-G (Duit). This is interpreted as; 5 of the pieces equal 1/16 Guilder or 5 equal

1/32 Guilder. However, in 1802 the rate of exchange was set so that 6 Duits should equal 1/16 Guilder which would mean the Duit actually equaled 1/96 Guilder and the 1/2 Duit equaled 1/192 Guilder, but because of the perennial shortage of small coins, the error was ignored and the coins released to circulation.

CENTS: Although some coins in 1833-1841 appear with value as 1 CT (1 Cent) and 2 CT (2 Cent) they are considered Duits and Double Duits and were exchanged at the rate of 1 Duit = 1/96 Guilder, not on a decimal system.

COLONIAL COINAGE

GELDERLAND

MINTMASTER PRIVY MARKS

Privy Mark	Date	Name
Ear of corn	1782-1809	Martin Hendrik Lohse

MONETARY SYSTEM

4 Duits = 1 Stuiver
20 Stuivers = 1 Gulden

DUIT

COPPER
Obv: Crowned arms of Gelderland, leg: IN DEO-SP.NOS.

KM#	Date	Mintage	VG	Fine	VF	XF
50.2	1802	—	2.00	3.00	5.00	7.50
	1803	—	2.00	3.00	5.00	7.50
	1804	—	3.50	6.50	12.50	20.00
	1805	—	2.00	3.00	5.00	7.50
	1085 (error)	—	—	—	—	—
	1806	—	2.00	3.00	5.00	7.50

NOTE: Varieties exist.
NOTE: Earlier dates (1771-1794) exist for this type.

HOLLAND

MINT MARKS

H - Heus, Amsterdam
Rosette - Dordrecht, 1601-1806
Star - Enkhuisen, 1796-1803
Star - Hoorn, 1803-1809

DUIT

COPPER
Obv: Crowned arms of Holland.
Rev: VOC monogram above date.

KM#	Date	Mintage	VG	Fine	VF	XF
70	1802 star	—	6.00	12.00	20.00	30.00
	1802 rosette	—	7.50	15.00	25.00	50.00
	1803	—	6.00	12.00	20.00	30.00
	1804	—	10.00	20.00	30.00	60.00

NOTE: 3 varieties exist.
NOTE: Earlier dates (1726-1793) exist for this type.

Batavian Republic

1799-1806

1/2 DUIT

(1/) 5 (of) 1/32 G = 1/160 G

COPPER

KM#	Date	Mintage	VG	Fine	VF	XF
75	1802	.157	2.50	6.00	10.00	17.50
	1803	—	4.00	9.00	15.00	25.00
	1804	—	4.00	9.00	15.00	25.00
	1805	—	2.00	5.00	8.00	15.00
	1806	—	2.00	5.00	8.00	15.00
	1807	—	.30	.75	1.25	3.00
	1808	—	.30	.75	1.25	3.00
	1809	—	.60	1.00	3.00	5.00

NOTE: Many varieties exist.

DUIT

(1/) 5 (of) 1/16 G = 1/80 G

COPPER

Obv: Holland Arms.

KM#	Date	Mintage	VG	Fine	VF	XF
76	1802	.358	4.00	8.00	12.00	18.00
	1803	—	2.50	4.00	6.00	9.00
	1804	—	2.50	4.00	6.00	9.00
	1805	—	2.50	4.00	6.00	9.00
	1806	—	2.50	4.00	6.00	9.00
	1807	—	.75	1.25	2.00	3.00
	1808/6	—	10.00	17.50	30.00	50.00
	1808	—	.75	1.25	2.00	3.00
	1809/6	—	10.00	17.50	30.00	50.00
	1809/8	—	10.00	17.50	30.00	50.00
	1809	—	4.00	8.00	12.00	18.00

NOTE: Varieties exist.

BRASS

KM#	Date	Mintage	VG	Fine	VF	XF
76a	1808	—	—	—	—	—

SILVER

KM#	Date	Mintage	VG	Fine	VF	XF
76b	1802	—	40.00	60.00	90.00	150.00

NOTE: Special presentation strikes produced by the mintmaster on demand.

1/16 GULDEN

0.6600 g, .916 SILVER, .0194 oz ASW, 15mm

KM#	Date	Mintage	Fine	VF	XF	Unc
77	1802	—	20.00	30.00	50.00	85.00

NOTE: 4 varieties exist.

16mm
Rev: W/o inner circle.

KM#	Date	Mintage	Fine	VF	XF	Unc
78	1802	—	20.00	30.00	45.00	75.00

NOTE: 3 varieties exist.

1/8 GULDEN

1.3250 g, .916 SILVER, .0390 oz ASW, 19mm

KM#	Date	Mintage	Fine	VF	XF	Unc
79	1802	—	30.00	40.00	60.00	100.00

NOTE: 4 varieties exist.

18mm
Rev: W/o inner circle.

KM#	Date	Mintage	Fine	VF	XF	Unc
80	1802	—	20.00	30.00	45.00	75.00

NOTE: 3 varieties exist.

1/4 GULDEN

2.6500 g, .916 SILVER, .0781 oz ASW

KM#	Date	Mintage	Fine	VF	XF	Unc
81	1802	—	30.00	40.00	60.00	100.00

NOTE: 6 varieties exist.

GOLD

KM#	Date	Mintage	Fine	VF	XF	Unc
81a	1802	—	—	—	Proof	Rare

1/2 GULDEN

5.3800 g, .916 SILVER, .1561 oz ASW
Rev: Ship w/INDIAE BATAV, date around.

KM#	Date	Mintage	Fine	VF	XF	Unc
82	1802	—	30.00	45.00	70.00	125.00

NOTE: 2 varieties exist.

GOLD

KM#	Date	Mintage	Fine	VF	XF	Unc
82a	1802	—	—	—	Proof	Rare

GULDEN

10.6160 g, .916 SILVER, .3127 oz ASW

KM#	Date	Mintage	Fine	VF	XF	Unc
83	1802	—	30.00	50.00	100.00	175.00

NOTE: 5 varieties exist.

GOLD

KM#	Date	Mintage	Fine	VF	XF	Unc
83a	1802	—	—	—	Proof	Rare

OVERYSSEL

MINTMASTER PRIVY MARKS

Privy Mark	Date	Name
Heraldic eagle	1763-1807	Nicolaas Wonneman

Batavian Republic

1799-1806

DUIT

COPPER
Obv: Overyssel arms.

KM#	Date	Mintage	VG	Fine	VF	XF
100	1803	—	1.75	3.00	5.00	9.00
	1804	—	1.75	3.00	5.00	9.00
	1805	—	1.75	3.00	5.00	9.00
	1806	—	4.50	8.00	13.50	23.50
	1807	—	4.50	11.00	18.00	30.00

NOTE: Varieties exist.

SILVER

KM#	Date	Mintage	VG	Fine	VF	XF
100a	1804	—	—	—	Proof	Unique
	1807 plain edge	—	—	—	Proof	—
	1807 milled edge	—	—	—	Proof	—

KINGDOM OF THE NETHERLANDS

DECIMAL COINAGE

100 Cents = 1 Gulden

MINT MARKS

D - Denver, U.S.A.
P - Philadelphia, U.S.A.
S - San Francisco, U.S.A.
(U) Caduceus, Utrecht

PRIVY MARKS

Date	Privy Mark
1818-1840	Torch
1839-1846	Fleur de lis
1846-1874	Sword
1874	Sword in scabbard
1875-1887	Broad axe
1887	Broad axe and star
1888-1909	Halberd
1909	Halberd and star
1909-1933	Sea Horse
1933-1942	Grapes
1940-1945	Palm Tree

1/4 CENT

COPPER
Similar to 1 Cent, KM#317

KM#	Date	Mintage	Fine	VF	XF	Unc
320	1934	—	—	—	Proof	—

1/2 CENT

COPPER

KM#	Date	Mintage	Fine	VF	XF	Unc
306	1855(u)	—	—	—	Proof	180.00
	1856(u)	10.800	15.00	35.00	60.00	100.00
	1857(u)	36.800	6.00	15.00	25.00	45.00

KM#	Date	Mintage	Fine	VF	XF	Unc
306	1858(u)	53.588	5.00	10.00	20.00	55.00
	1859(u)	219.600	2.00	3.50	7.00	12.50
	1860(u)	107.124	2.00	3.50	7.00	12.50
	1902(u)	20.000	2.00	5.00	12.00	32.50
	1908(u)	10.600	3.00	7.00	15.00	35.00
	1908(u)	—	—	—	Proof	50.00
	1909(u)	4.400	6.00	15.00	25.00	50.00

BRONZE

Mintmasters mark: Sea horse

KM#	Date	Mintage	Fine	VF	XF	Unc
314.1	1914(u)	50.000	1.00	2.00	4.00	6.00
	1916(u)	10.000	2.00	5.00	10.00	20.00
	1921(u)	4.000	5.00	10.00	20.00	35.00
	1932(u)	10.000	2.00	4.00	8.00	15.00
	1933(u)	15.000	2.00	3.00	6.00	12.50

Mintmasters mark: Grapes

KM#	Date	Mintage	Fine	VF	XF	Unc
314.2	1933(u)	5.000	10.00	20.00	35.00	65.00
	1934(u)	30.000	1.50	2.50	5.00	7.00
	1935(u)	14.000	1.50	2.50	5.00	7.00
	1936(u)	12.000	1.50	2.50	5.00	7.00
	1936(u)	—	—	—	Proof	40.00
	1937(u)	8.400	1.50	2.50	5.00	7.00
	1937(u)	—	—	—	Proof	40.00
	1938(u)	3.600	3.50	7.50	15.00	30.00
	1939(u)	2.000	5.00	10.00	20.00	40.00
	1945P	400.000	.25	.50	1.00	2.00

CENT

COPPER

Obv: Legend begins and ends above date.

KM#	Date	Mintage	Fine	VF	XF	Unc
307.1	1855(u)	.100	30.00	50.00	65.00	85.00
	1855(u)	—	—	—	Proof	150.00
	1856(u)	67.900	3.50	6.00	10.00	20.00
	1856(u)	—	—	—	Proof	100.00

Obv: Legend begins and ends beside date.

KM#	Date	Mintage	Fine	VF	XF	Unc
307.2	1856(u)	Inc. Ab.	3.50	6.00	10.00	20.00
	1856(u)	—	—	—	Proof	100.00
	1857(u)	162.000	2.00	4.00	7.50	15.00
	1858(u)	119.431	2.00	4.00	7.50	15.00
	1859(u)	40.800	5.00	10.00	20.00	40.00
	1860(u)	14.455	7.50	15.00	30.00	60.00
	1896(u)	60.400	5.00	10.00	20.00	40.00
	1896(u)	—	—	—	Proof	120.00
	1897(u)	69.600	5.00	10.00	20.00	40.00
	1897(u)	—	—	—	Proof	120.00
	1898(u)	36.600	5.00	10.00	20.00	40.00
	1899(u)	18.400	6.00	12.50	25.00	50.00
	1899(u)	—	—	—	Proof	70.00
	1901(u)	15.000	6.00	12.50	25.00	50.00
	1901(u)	—	—	—	Proof	70.00
	1902(u)	10.000	5.00	10.00	20.00	40.00
	1907(u)	7.500	5.00	10.00	20.00	40.00
	1907(u)	—	—	—	Proof	100.00
	1908(u)	12.500	4.50	9.00	17.50	35.00
	1908(u)	—	—	—	Proof	80.00
	1909(u)	7.500	5.00	10.00	20.00	40.00
	1912(u)	25.000	4.50	9.00	17.50	35.00

BRONZE

KM#	Date	Mintage	Fine	VF	XF	Unc
315	1914(u)	85.000	1.25	2.50	5.00	10.00
	1914(u)	—	—	—	Proof	120.00
	1916(u)	16.440	2.50	5.00	10.00	20.00
	1919(u)	20.000	2.50	5.00	10.00	20.00
	1920(u)	120.000	1.25	2.50	5.00	10.00
	1926(u)	10.000	3.50	7.50	15.00	30.00
	1929(u)	50.000	1.25	2.50	5.00	10.00
	1929(u)	—	—	—	Proof	120.00

KM#	Date	Mintage	Fine	VF	XF	Unc
317	1936(u)	52.000	.50	1.25	2.50	5.00
	1937(u)	120.400	.30	1.00	2.00	4.00
	1937(u)	—	—	—	Proof	85.00
	1938(u)	150.000	.30	1.00	2.00	4.00
	1939(u)	81.400	.50	1.25	2.50	5.00
	1942P	100.000	.25	.50	1.00	2.00
	1945P	335.000	.10	.25	.50	1.00
	1945D	133.800	.50	1.00	2.00	3.00
	1945S	102.568	.10	.25	.50	1.00

2-1/2 CENTS

COPPER

KM#	Date	Mintage	Fine	VF	XF	Unc
308	1856(u)	2.480	15.00	30.00	50.00	85.00
	1856(u)	—	—	—	Proof	130.00
	1857(u)	36.560	8.50	15.00	25.00	45.00
	1857(u)	—	—	—	Proof	130.00
	1858(u)	40.990	10.00	17.50	30.00	50.00
	1896(u)	1.120	15.00	30.00	50.00	80.00
	1897(u)	18.105	5.00	10.00	20.00	40.00
	1898(u)	7.600	5.00	10.00	22.00	45.00
	1899(u)	10.400	5.00	10.00	20.00	40.00
	1902(u)	6.000	7.00	15.00	30.00	55.00
	1907(u)	3.000	8.00	17.50	35.00	45.00
	1908(u)	5.940	5.00	10.00	22.00	45.00
	1908(u)	—	—	—	Proof	130.00
	1909(u)	3.060	8.00	17.50	35.00	65.00
	1913(u)	4.000	8.00	17.50	35.00	65.00
	1913(u)	—	—	—	Proof	130.00

BRONZE

KM#	Date	Mintage	Fine	VF	XF	Unc
316	1914(u)	22.000	3.00	6.00	12.00	25.00
	1914(u)	—	—	—	Proof	160.00
	1915(u)	6.000	5.00	10.00	20.00	40.00
	1920(u)	48.000	1.50	2.50	4.50	9.00
	1920(u)	—	—	—	Proof	160.00
	1945P	200.000	.30	.60	1.25	2.50

1/20 GULDEN

.6100 g, .720 SILVER, .0141 oz ASW

KM#	Date	Mintage	Fine	VF	XF	Unc
303	1854(u)	—	65.00	125.00	200.00	350.00
	1854(u)	—	—	—	Proof	—
	1855(u)	.492	3.00	6.00	12.50	25.00

5 CENTS

COPPER-NICKEL

KM#	Date	Mintage	Fine	VF	XF	Unc
313	1913(u)	60.000	1.00	2.00	4.00	10.00
	1913(u)	—	—	—	Proof	220.00
	1921(u)	40.000	1.25	3.00	6.00	15.00
	1921(u)	—	—	—	Proof	250.00
	1922(u)	20.000	3.00	7.00	15.00	30.00

1/10 GULDEN

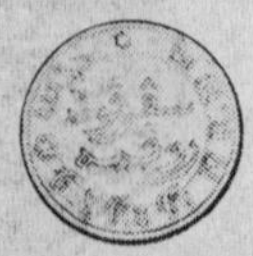

1.2500 g, .720 SILVER, .0289 oz ASW

KM#	Date	Mintage	Fine	VF	XF	Unc
304	1854(u)	3.550	3.00	6.00	12.50	25.00
	1854(u)	—	—	—	Proof	130.00
	1855(u)	6.452	2.00	4.00	10.00	20.00
	1855(u)	—	—	—	Proof	—
	1856(u)	3.000	3.50	6.00	15.00	30.00
	1857(u)	11.000	2.00	4.00	8.00	15.00
	1858(u)	14.000	1.50	3.00	6.00	12.50

KM#	Date	Mintage	Fine	VF	XF	Unc
304	1882(u)	7.500	2.00	4.00	8.00	15.00
	1884(u)	3.550	2.00	4.00	8.00	15.00
	1884(u)	—	—	—	Proof	100.00
	1885(u)	.825	15.00	30.00	50.00	80.00
	1891(u)	5.000	1.50	3.00	6.00	12.00
	1891(u)	—	—	—	Proof	85.00
	1893(u)	5.000	1.50	3.00	6.00	12.00
	1893(u)	—	—	—	Proof	85.00
	1896(u)	3.075	3.00	6.00	12.50	25.00
	1896(u)	—	—	—	Proof	100.00
	1898(u)	2.500	6.00	12.50	25.00	50.00
	1898(u)	—	—	—	Proof	120.00
	1900(u)	6.850	2.00	4.00	8.00	15.00
	1901(u)	5.000	2.00	4.00	10.00	20.00
	1901(u)	—	—	—	Proof	120.00

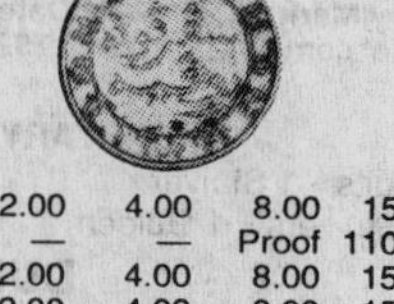

KM#	Date	Mintage	Fine	VF	XF	Unc
309	1903(u)	5.000	2.00	4.00	8.00	15.00
	1903(u)	—	—	—	Proof	110.00
	1904(u)	5.000	2.00	4.00	8.00	15.00
	1905(u)	5.000	2.00	4.00	8.00	15.00
	1906(u)	7.500	1.50	3.50	7.50	15.00
	1907(u)	14.000	1.50	3.00	6.00	12.50
	1907(u)	—	—	—	Proof	60.00
	1908(u)	3.000	3.00	6.00	12.50	25.00
	1909(u)	10.000	1.50	3.00	6.00	12.50
	1909(u)	—	—	—	Proof	110.00

Obv. & rev: Wide rims and small leg.

KM#	Date	Mintage	Fine	VF	XF	Unc
311	1910(u)	15.000	3.00	6.00	12.50	20.00
	1910(u)	—	—	—	Proof	140.00
	1911(u)	10.000	5.00	10.00	20.00	40.00
	1912(u)	25.000	1.00	2.50	5.00	10.00
	1913(u)	15.000	1.00	2.50	5.00	10.00
	1914(u)	25.000	1.00	2.50	5.00	10.00
	1915(u)	15.000	1.00	2.50	5.00	10.00
	1918(u)	30.000	1.00	2.50	5.00	10.00
	1919(u)	20.000	1.00	2.50	4.50	9.00
	1920(u)	8.500	2.00	4.00	7.50	15.00
	1928(u)	30.000	1.00	1.50	2.00	4.00
	1930(u)	15.000	1.00	1.75	2.50	5.00

Obv. & rev: Narrow rims and large leg.

KM#	Date	Mintage	Fine	VF	XF	Unc
318	1937(u)	20.000	.40	.75	1.50	3.00
	1937(u)	—	—	—	Proof	130.00
	1938(u)	30.000	.40	.75	1.50	3.00
	1939(u)	5.400	1.25	2.50	5.00	10.00
	1940(u)	10.000	1.00	1.75	3.75	7.50
	1941P	41.850	.25	.50	1.00	1.75
	1941S	58.150	.35	.65	1.25	2.25
	1942S	75.000	.25	.50	.75	1.75
	1945P	100.720	.25	.50	.75	1.75
	1945S	19.280	.40	.75	1.50	3.00

1/4 GULDEN

4.0610 g, .568 SILVER, .0742 oz ASW

KM#	Date	Mintage	VG	Fine	VF	XF
301.1	1826(u)	1.238	6.50	12.50	20.00	45.00
	1826(u)	—	—	—	Proof	120.00
	1827(u)	1.003	6.50	12.50	20.00	45.00
	1834/27(u)	1.002	12.00	25.00	40.00	80.00
	1834(u)	Inc. Ab.	6.50	12.50	20.00	45.00
	1840(u)	.973	6.50	12.50	20.00	45.00

Coarse milling

KM#	Date	Mintage	VG	Fine	VF	XF
301.2	1826(u)	Inc. Ab.	15.00	30.00	45.00	85.00

3.1800 g, .720 SILVER, .0736 oz ASW

KM#	Date	Mintage	Fine	VF	XF	Unc
305	1854(u)	11.460	5.00	10.00	20.00	40.00
	1854(u)	—	—	—	Proof	110.00
	1855(u)	4.541	5.00	10.00	20.00	45.00

KM#	Date	Mintage	Fine	VF	XF	Unc
305	1855(u)	—	—	—	Proof	100.00
	1857(u)	2.400	7.50	15.00	30.00	60.00
	1858(u)	4.800	5.00	10.00	20.00	45.00
	1858(u)	—	—	—	Proof	80.00
	1882(u)	2.200	10.00	20.00	40.00	80.00
	1883(u)	.800	25.00	50.00	85.00	150.00
	1883(u)	—	—	—	Proof	175.00
	1885(u)	1.750	10.00	20.00	40.00	80.00
	1890(u)	1.140	10.00	20.00	40.00	80.00
	1891(u)	.860	20.00	40.00	60.00	120.00
	1893(u)	2.000	7.50	15.00	30.00	60.00
	1893(u)	—	—	—	Proof	175.00
	1896(u)	1.230	10.00	20.00	40.00	80.00
	1898(u)	3.000	5.00	10.00	20.00	45.00
	1898(u)	—	—	—	Proof	120.00
	1900(u)	2.800	5.00	10.00	20.00	45.00
	1901(u)	2.000	6.00	12.50	25.00	50.00
	1901(u)	—	—	—	Proof	100.00

KM#	Date	Mintage	Fine	VF	XF	Unc
310	1903(u)	2.000	4.00	8.00	17.50	35.00
	1903(u)	—	—	—	Proof	100.00
	1904(u)	2.000	4.00	8.00	17.50	35.00
	1904(u)	—	—	—	Proof	100.00
	1905(u)	2.000	4.00	8.00	17.50	35.00
	1905(u)	—	—	—	Proof	170.00
	1906(u)	4.000	3.50	7.50	15.00	30.00
	1907(u)	4.400	3.50	7.50	15.00	30.00
	1907(u)	—	—	—	Proof	100.00
	1908(u)	2.000	4.00	8.00	17.50	35.00
	1909(u)	4.000	3.50	7.50	15.00	30.00

Obv. & rev: Wide rims and small leg.

KM#	Date	Mintage	Fine	VF	XF	Unc
312	1910(u)	6.000	7.50	15.00	30.00	60.00
	1911(u)	4.000	7.50	15.00	30.00	60.00
	1912(u)	10.000	3.50	7.50	15.00	30.00
	1913(u)	6.000	6.50	12.50	25.00	50.00
	1914(u)	10.000	3.50	7.50	15.00	30.00
	1915(u)	6.000	6.00	10.00	20.00	40.00
	1917(u)	12.000	2.00	4.00	10.00	20.00
	1919(u)	6.000	6.00	10.00	20.00	35.00
	1920(u)	20.000	1.50	3.00	7.50	15.00
	1921(u)	24.000	1.50	3.00	7.50	15.00
	1929(u)	5.000	3.00	5.00	15.00	25.00
	1930(u)	7.000	1.00	2.00	4.00	7.50
	1930(u)	—	—	—	Proof	160.00

Obv. & rev: Narrow rims and large leg.

KM#	Date	Mintage	Fine	VF	XF	Unc
319	1937(u)	8.000	1.25	2.00	4.00	7.50
	1938(u)	12.000	1.00	1.50	2.25	5.00
	1939(u)	10.400	1.00	1.50	2.25	5.00
	1941P	34.947	.25	.65	1.25	2.00
	1941S	5.053	1.50	2.50	5.00	10.00
	1942S	32.000	.25	.65	1.25	2.00
	1945S	56.000	.25	.65	1.25	2.00

1/2 GULDEN

5.3830 g, .893 SILVER
Similar to 1/4 Gulden, KM#301.1.

KM#	Date	Mintage	VG	Fine	VF	XF
302	1826(u)	.517	15.00	25.00	45.00	100.00
	1827(u)	.037	75.00	150.00	250.00	450.00
	1834/27(u)	.501	20.00	35.00	65.00	150.00
	1834(u)	Inc. Ab.	15.00	25.00	45.00	100.00

GULDEN

10.7700 g, .893 SILVER, .3092 oz ASW

KM#	Date	Mintage	VG	Fine	VF	XF
300	1821(u)	.099	45.00	80.00	175.00	350.00

10.0000 g, .945 SILVER, .3038 oz ASW

KM#	Date	Mintage	VG	Fine	VF	XF
300a	1839(u)	2.217	10.00	20.00	40.00	80.00
	1840(u)	1.981	12.50	25.00	45.00	85.00

TRADE COINAGE

DUCAT

.986 GOLD

These gold coins, intended primarily for circulation in the Netherlands East Indies will be found listed as KM#83 in the Netherlands section.

WORLD WAR II COINAGE

Netherlands and Netherlands East Indies coins of the 1941-45 period were struck at U.S. Mints (P-Philadelphia, D-Denver, S-San Francisco and bear the mint mark and a palm tree (acorn on Homeland issues) flanking the date. The following issues - KM330 and KM331 are of the usual Netherlands types, being distinguished from similar 1944-45 issues produced in the name of the Homeland by the presence of the palm tree, but were produced for release in the colony. See other related issues under Curacao and Surinam.

HOMELAND COINAGE

GULDEN

10.0000 g, .720 SILVER, .2315 oz ASW

KM#	Date	Mintage	Fine	VF	XF	Unc
330	1943D	20.000	2.50	4.50	8.00	15.00

2 1/2 GULDEN

25.0000 g, .720 SILVER, .5787 oz ASW

KM#	Date	Mintage	Fine	VF	XF	Unc
331	1943D	2.000	6.00	12.00	17.50	30.00

JAPANESE OCCUPATION

10 SEN

TIN ALLOY

Three coins were struck primarily for circulation in the East Indies. The Sen, 5 Sen and 10 Sen are inscribed DAI NIHON (Great Japan) and are found listed under Japan - Occupation Issues as Y#22, Y#24 and Pn48.

PROOF SETS (PS)

KM#	Date	Mintage	Identification	Issue Price	Mkt. Val.
PS1	1854/58(12)	—	KM303 (2 pcs. 1854), KM304 (2 pcs. 1855), KM305 (1855 & 1858), KM306 (2 pcs. 1855), KM307 (2 pcs. 1856), KM308 (2 pcs. 1857)	—	—

Batavian Republic

1799-1806

MINTMASTERS INITIALS

Z - J.A. Zwekkert

1/2 STUIVER

COPPER BONK, 7.72 g
Value and date each in pearled rectangle.

KM#	Date	Mintage	Good	VG	Fine	VF
213	1804	—	20.00	35.00	60.00	100.00
	1805	*.545	—	—	Rare	—

NOTE: 3 varieties exist for 1804 while most of 1805 dated coins were recalled and melted down.

STUIVER

COPPER BONK, 23.16 g

KM#	Date	Mintage	Good	VG	Fine	VF
206	1801	—	8.50	15.00	25.00	45.00
	1802	—	6.00	10.00	20.00	35.00
	1803	—	7.50	12.50	25.00	40.00

NOTE: Roman I in date of 1802 issues.
NOTE: Earlier date (1800) exists for this type.

Reduced weight, 19.30 g
Value and date each in pearl rectangle.

KM#	Date	Mintage	Good	VG	Fine	VF
210	1803	—	4.25	7.50	13.00	25.00
	1804	—	6.00	11.00	20.00	35.00
	1805	—	5.00	10.00	15.00	30.00
	1806	—	6.00	11.00	20.00	35.00

NOTE: Varieties exist.

2 STUIVER

COPPER BONK, 46.32 g

KM#	Date	Mintage	Good	VG	Fine	VF
207	1801	—	10.00	17.50	30.00	55.00
	1802	—	6.00	10.00	18.00	45.00
	1803	—	6.00	10.00	18.00	45.00

NOTE: Roman I in date of 1802 issues.
NOTE: Earlier date (1800) exists for this type.

Reduced weight, 38.60 g

KM#	Date	Mintage	Good	VG	Fine	VF
211	1803	—	8.50	15.00	25.00	45.00
	1804	—	8.50	15.00	25.00	45.00
	1805	—	8.50	15.00	25.00	45.00
	1806	—	8.50	15.00	25.00	45.00

NOTE: Varieties exist.

8 STUIVER

COPPER BONK, 154.40 g
Illustration reduced. Actual size: 74 mm.
Value and date in pearl circles.

KM#	Date	Mintage	VG	Fine	VF	XF
212	1803	.395	225.00	325.00	450.00	575.00

1/2 RUPEE

6.5750 g, .792 SILVER, .1674 oz ASW

KM#	Date	Mintage	VG	Fine	VF	XF
215	1805 Z	—	25.00	45.00	80.00	145.00
	1806 Z	—	25.00	45.00	80.00	145.00

NOTE: 12 varieties exist.

RUPEE

13.1500 g, .792 SILVER, .3349 oz ASW
Thick planchet.

KM#	Date	Mintage	VG	Fine	VF	XF
208	1801 Z	—	20.00	30.00	50.00	85.00
	1802 Z	—	30.00	50.00	100.00	150.00
	1803 Z	—	20.00	30.00	50.00	85.00

NOTE: Varieties exist.
NOTE: Earlier date (1800) exists for this type.

Thin planchet.

KM#	Date	Mintage	VG	Fine	VF	XF
214	1804 Z	—	25.00	45.00	80.00	135.00
	1805 Z	—	25.00	45.00	80.00	135.00
	1806 Z	—	20.00	35.00	60.00	100.00
	1808 Z	—	45.00	75.00	125.00	200.00

NOTE: Varieties exist.

1/2 GOLD RUPEE

8.0000 g, .750 GOLD, .1929 oz AGW
Obv. Arabic leg., AD date.

KM#	Date	Mintage	VG	Fine	VF	XF
209	1801 Z	—	300.00	500.00	750.00	1250.
	1802 Z	—	300.00	500.00	750.00	1250.
	1803 Z	—	—	—	Unique	—
	1807 Z	—	600.00	1100.	1600.	2400.

NOTE: Earlier date (1800) exists for this type.

Kingdom of Holland

DUIT

COPPER
Obv: VOC and star above. Rev: JAVA/date.

KM#	Date	Mintage	VG	Fine	VF	XF
220	1806	—	10.00	15.00	25.00	50.00
	1807	—	4.00	6.00	12.00	25.00
	1808	—	4.00	6.00	12.00	25.00
	1809	—	3.00	5.00	10.00	20.00
	1810	—	—	—	Rare	—

NOTE: Varieties exist.

Obv: Block LN. Rev: JAVA/date.

KM#	Date	Mintage	VG	Fine	VF	XF
223	1808	—	3.00	6.00	10.00	20.00
	1809	—	2.50	5.00	8.00	18.00
	1810	—	2.50	5.00	8.00	18.00

NOTE: Varieties exist.

KM#	Date	Mintage	VG	Fine	VF	XF
225	1810 Z	—	2.50	4.00	7.00	11.50
	1811 Z	—	1.50	2.50	3.50	6.00

NOTE: Several varieties of above 2 coins exist.

Obv. and rev: Ornate borders.

KM#	Date	Mintage	VG	Fine	VF	XF
226	1810 Z	—	15.00	25.00	40.00	65.00

1/2 STUIVER

COPPER
Obv: Ornate LN below value.

KM#	Date	Mintage	VG	Fine	VF	XF
227	1810 Z	—	70.00	130.00	235.00	430.00

NOTE: 3 varieties exist.

KM#	Date	Mintage	VG	Fine	VF	XF
228	1810 Z	—	2.75	5.00	9.00	16.00
	1811 Z	—	2.75	5.00	9.00	16.00

NOTE: Several varieties exist.

STUIVER

COPPER BONK, 19.30 g

KM#	Date	Mintage	Good	VG	Fine	VF
221	1807	—	15.00	25.00	50.00	85.00
	1808	—	—	—	Rare	—
	1809	—	7.00	12.50	22.50	40.00
	1810	—	5.00	10.00	17.50	30.00

NOTE: Varieties exist. Considerable depreciation in weight as dates progressed.

11.58 g., retrograde S.

KM#	Date	Mintage	Good	VG	Fine	VF
229	1809	—	22.50	45.00	65.00	90.00
	1810	—	22.50	45.00	65.00	90.00

COPPER

Obv: Ornate LN, value. Rev: JAVA/date.

KM#	Date	Mintage	VG	Fine	VF	XF
230	1810 Z	—	80.00	200.00	300.00	450.00

NOTE: 2 varieties exist.

2 STUIVER

COPPER BONK, 38.60 g

KM#	Date	Mintage	Good	VG	Fine	VF
222	1807	—	12.00	25.00	45.00	90.00
	1808	—	12.00	25.00	45.00	90.00

Reduced weight, 23.16 g

KM#	Date	Mintage	Good	VG	Fine	VF
224.1	1809	—	7.50	12.50	20.00	35.00
	1810	—	7.50	12.50	20.00	35.00

NOTE: Varieties exist.

15.0-25.0 g
Obv: Retrograde S.

KM#	Date	Mintage	Good	VG	Fine	VF
224.2	1809	—	—	—	—	—
	1810	—	3.50	7.50	12.50	20.00

NOTE: Varieties exist. Light weight coins (6.0-10 g) are contemporary forgeries.

Kingdom of the Netherlands

1/2 STUIVER

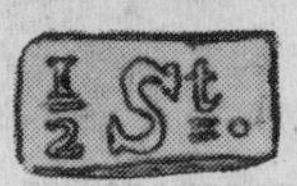

COPPER BONK, 7.72 g
Value and date in lined rectangle.

KM#	Date	Mintage	VG	Fine	VF	XF
216	1818	—	15.00	25.00	45.00	80.00

STUIVER

COPPER BONK, 15.44 g
Value and date each in rectangle.

KM#	Date	Mintage	VG	Fine	VF	XF
235	1818	—	12.50	25.00	40.00	75.00

NOTE: Varieties exist.

2 STUIVER

COPPER BONK, 30.88 g
Value and date each in rectangle.

KM#	Date	Mintage	VG	Fine	VF	XF
236	1818	—	10.00	20.00	35.00	60.00
	1819	—	15.00	25.00	45.00	80.00

NOTE: Varieties exist.

BRITISH OCCUPATION

1811-1816

DUIT

COPPER

KM#	Date	Mintage	VG	Fine	VF	XF
240	1811	—	6.50	12.50	20.00	36.50
	1812	—	5.00	8.00	15.00	25.00

NOTE: At least 5 varieties exist of each date.

BRASS

KM#	Date	Mintage	VG	Fine	VF	XF
240a	1812	—	7.50	15.00	25.00	45.00

TIN

KM#	Date	Mintage	VG	Fine	VF	XF
244	1813	16.747	20.00	30.00	65.00	120.00
	1814	33.656	20.00	30.00	55.00	100.00

1/2 STIVER

COPPER

KM#	Date	Mintage	VG	Fine	VF	XF
241	1811 Z	—	6.50	10.00	18.00	30.00
	1812 Z	—	5.50	7.50	15.00	25.00
	1813 Z	—	5.50	7.50	15.00	25.00
	1814 Z	—	7.50	12.50	20.00	35.00
	1815 Z	—	7.50	12.50	25.00	45.00

NOTE: At least 3 varieties exist of each date.

STIVER

COPPER

KM#	Date	Mintage	VG	Fine	VF	XF
243	1812 Z	—	—	—	Rare	—
	1814 Z	—	20.00	35.00	60.00	100.00
	1815 Z	—	45.00	90.00	140.00	250.00

NOTE: 3 varieties exist of 1814.

1/2 RUPEE

6.5700 g, .792 SILVER, .1673 oz ASW
Obv: Javanese leg. and date.
Rev: Arabic leg. and date.

KM#	Date	Year	VG	Fine	VF	XF
246	AH1668					
	AS1740	(1813)(error = AH1228)				
	3 or 4 known		—	—	Rare	—
	1229					
		1741 (1814)	175.00	225.00	300.00	400.00

NOTE: The 1/2 Rupee struck in silver is similar to the 1/2 Mohur struck in gold except a five-petaled flower replaces the Christian date on the silver coins.

RUPEE

13.1500 g, .792 SILVER, .3349 oz ASW
Error date AH1668

KM#	Date	Year	VG	Fine	VF	XF
247	AH1668					
	AS1740		(error = AH1228) 3 var.			
			20.00	35.00	65.00	120.00
	1228	1740	(error w/Y's for Arabic 2's)			
			20.00	35.00	65.00	120.00
	1229	1741	150.00	225.00	325.00	475.00
	1230	1743	w/OZ			
			25.00	45.00	85.00	150.00
	1230	1743	w/.Z			
			30.00	60.00	100.00	180.00
	1231	1743	—	—	Unique	—
	1232	1743	35.00	70.00	125.00	200.00
	1232	1744/3	40.00	80.00	135.00	225.00
	1232	1744	30.00	55.00	90.00	160.00

NOTE: Many varieties and overstrikes exist of the above.

1/2 MOHUR

8.0060 g, .750 GOLD, .1931 oz AGW

KM#	Date	Year				
248	AH1668					
	AS1740	1813 (error = AH1228)				
			—	—	Rare	—
	1229	1743	1814			
			—	2000.	2250.	2750.

NOTE: Varieties exist.

8.0060 g, .833 GOLD, .2144 oz AGW

KM#	Date	Year				
248a	AH1230					
	AS1743	1815	w/OZ			
			1750.	2250.	2500.	3000.
	1230	1743	1815	w/Z		
			1750.	2250.	2500.	3000.
	1230	1743	1816 (error = AH1231)			
			1250.	1750.	2000.	2500.
	1231/0	1743	1816			
			1250.	1750.	2000.	2500.
	1231	1743	1816			
			1250.	1750.	2000.	2500.

Obv: Numerals in date reversed. Rev: M added.

249	1231	1743	1816	—	Rare	—

MADURA ISLAND

SUMENEP

Sumenep is a sultanate on the island of Madura.

TITLES

سمنف

Sumenep

RULERS

Sultan Paku Nata Ningrat, 1811-1854

COUNTERMARKED COINAGE

Madura Star

RUPEE

SILVER
c/m: 'Madura Star' on Java 1 Rupee, KM#175.

KM#	Date	Year	Good	VG	Fine	VF
191.1	ND	(1764-89)	35.00	55.00	85.00	125.00

c/m: 'Madura Star' on Java 1 Rupee, KM#175a.

KM#	Date	Year	Good	VG	Fine	VF
191.2	ND	(1795-99)	35.00	55.00	80.00	120.00

c/m: 'Madura Star' on Java 1 Rupee, KM#247.

KM#	Date	Year	Good	VG	Fine	VF
191.3	ND	(AS1740-44)	35.00	55.00	80.00	120.00

c/m: 'Madura Star' on India-Bombay 1 Rupee, KM#260.

KM#	Date	Year	Good	VG	Fine	VF
191.4	ND	(AH1233-51)	—	—	—	—

GULDEN

SILVER
c/m: 'Madura Star' on Netherlands Gelderland 1 Gulden, KM#100.1.

KM#	Date	Year	Good	VG	Fine	VF
193.1	ND	(1760-95)	25.00	40.00	65.00	100.00

c/m: 'Madura Star' on Netherlands Holland 1 Gulden, KM#73.

KM#	Date	Year	Good	VG	Fine	VF
193.2	ND	(1734-94)	25.00	40.00	65.00	100.00

c/m: 'Madura Star' on Netherlands Utrecht 1 Gulden, KM#102.

KM#	Date	Year	Good	VG	Fine	VF
193.3	ND	(1748-94)	25.00	40.00	65.00	100.00

c/m: 'Madura Star' on Holland 1 Gulden, KM#83.

KM#	Date	Year	Good	VG	Fine	VF
193.4	ND	(1802)	30.00	50.00	80.00	120.00

DUCATON

(Thaler, Daalder)

SILVER
c/m: 'Madura Star' in shield on Austria Burgau Thaler, KM#15.

KM#	Date	Year	Good	VG	Fine	VF
199.1	ND	(1764-65)	30.00	55.00	100.00	175.00

c/m: 'Madura Star' in shield on Austria Tyrol Thaler, KM#745.

KM#	Date	Year	Good	VG	Fine	VF
199.2	ND	(1754-65)	80.00	140.00	245.00	425.00

c/m: 'Madura Star' in shield on Mexico City Mint 8 Reales, KM#104.1.

KM#	Date	Year	Good	VG	Fine	VF
201.1	ND	(1747-60)	90.00	120.00	180.00	300.00

c/m: 'Madura Star' in shield on Mexico City Mint 8 Reales, KM#105.

KM#	Date	Year	Good	VG	Fine	VF
201.5	ND	1771	100.00	200.00	325.00	500.00

c/m: 'Madura Star' in shield on Mexico City Mint 8 Reales, KM#107.

KM#	Date	Year	Good	VG	Fine	VF
201.2	ND	1789	70.00	100.00	150.00	250.00
		1790	60.00	90.00	130.00	200.00

c/m: 'Madura Star' in shield on Mexico City Mint 8 Reales, KM#109.

KM#	Date	Year	Good	VG	Fine	VF
201.3	ND	(1790-1808)	40.00	60.00	90.00	150.00

c/m: 'Madura Star' in shield on Potosi Mint 8 Reales, KM#73.1.

KM#	Date	Year	Good	VG	Fine	VF
201.4	ND	(1791-1808)	50.00	70.00	100.00	160.00

c/m: 'Madura star' in shield on Netherlands West Friesland Ducation, KM#127.

KM#	Date	Year	Good	VG	Fine	VF
203.1	ND	(1742-93)	55.00	90.00	135.00	200.00

c/m: 'Madura Star' in shield on Netherlands Holland Ducaton, KM#90.

KM#	Date	Year	Good	VG	Fine	VF
203.2	ND	(1734-93)	60.00	100.00	140.00	210.00

Sumenep* and *(1)230

1/2 REAL BATU

SILVER
c/m: *Sumenep* and 5-petaled flower on Mexico City Mint 'cob' 4 Reales, KM#40.

KM#	Date	Year	Good	VG	Fine	VF
196.1	ND or AH(1)230	17xx J	150.00	200.00	300.00	500.00

c/m: *Sumenep* and 5-petaled flower on Mexico City Mint 'cob' 4 Reales, KM#40a.

KM#	Date	Year	Good	VG	Fine	VF
196.2	ND or AH(1)230	1730 R	100.00	150.00	225.00	375.00
		1731 F	100.00	150.00	225.00	375.00
		1732/1 MF	120.00	180.00	260.00	425.00

NOTE: Also known w/an additional c/m 5-pointed star w/circular center.

REAL BATU

SILVER
c/m: *Sumenep* and *(1)230* in Arabic on Mexico City Mint 'cob' 8 Reales, KM#47a.

KM#	Date	Year	Good	VG	Fine	VF
197	ND or AH(1)230	1729 R	70.00	100.00	150.00	250.00
		1730 R	70.00	100.00	150.00	250.00
		1731 F	70.00	100.00	150.00	250.00
		1732 F	70.00	100.00	150.00	250.00

NOTE: Also known w/an additional c/m 5-pointed star w/circular center.

GOLD RUPEE

GOLD
c/m: *Sumenep* and *(1)230* in Arabic on Spanish Colonial 2 Escudos.

KM#	Date	Year	Good	VG	Fine	VF
205	AH(1)230	—	—	—	Rare	—

SUMATRA, Island of

An island, south of the Malay peninsula, was first reached by Europeans for trade in 1599. Competition between European powers for trading rights continued until 1824 at which time it became a Dutch possession. British coins for the island were struck at the Birmingham Mint by Matthew Boulton in 1786 and other issues were struck at Indian mints.

TITLES

Pulu Percha

MONETARY SYSTEM

100 Kepings = 1 Suku
4 Suku = 1 Dollar (Spanish)

DENOMINATIONS

The following Arabic legends appear for the denomination with an Arabic number above.

(1) Keping

Sakeping

Satu Keping

(2) Dua Keping

(3) Tiga Keping

(4) Ampat Keping

EAST INDIA COMPANY

1685 - 1824

KEPING

COPPER
Thick planchet, 3.476 g

KM#	Date	Year	Fine	VF	XF	Unc
262	AH1219	1804	2.50	5.00	10.00	20.00
	1219	1804	—	—	Proof	65.00
	1219	1804	—		Gilt Proof	85.00

Thin planchet, 2.050 g

KM#	Date	Year	Fine	VF	XF	Unc
263	AH1219	1804	2.50	5.00	12.50	25.00

2 KEPINGS

COPPER
Thick planchet, 6.47 g

KM#	Date	Year	Fine	VF	XF	Unc
264	AH1219	1804	3.00	6.00	16.50	25.00
		1804	—	—	Proof	75.00
		1804	—		Gilt Proof	125.00

Thin planchet, 4.40 g

KM#	Date	Year	Fine	VF	XF	Unc
265	AH1219	1804	2.50	5.00	12.50	20.00

4 KEPINGS

COPPER

Thick planchet, 12.80 g

KM#	Date	Year	Fine	VF	XF	Unc
266	AH1219	1804	3.75	7.50	20.00	45.00
	1219	1804	—	—	Proof	85.00
	1219	1804	—		Gilt Proof	200.00

Thin planchet, 8.50 g

KM#	Date	Year	Fine	VF	XF	Unc
267	AH1219	1804	3.75	7.50	20.00	45.00

KINGDOM OF THE NETHERLANDS

MINTMASTER INITIALS

D - Demmenie
H H. de Heus (Amsterdam)
J - L.J. Jeekel
S - J.D.C. Suermondt (Utrecht)
V - K.J. de Vogel
W - C.H. Williams

1/2 DUIT

(1/) 5 (of) 1/32 G. = 1/160 G.

COPPER

Mint: Amsterdam

KM#	Date	Mintage	VG	Fine	VF	XF
280.3	1814 H	—	—	—	Rare	—
(85)	1815 H	—	1.00	2.00	5.00	12.50
	1816 H	—	1.00	2.00	5.00	12.50

NOTE: Varieties exist.

Mint: Utrecht

KM#	Date	Mintage	VG	Fine	VF	XF
280.1	1816 S	23.818	.80	2.00	4.00	7.50

NOTE: Actually minted 1820-22.

Mint: Sourabaya

KM#	Date	Mintage	VG	Fine	VF	XF
280.2	1816	—	2.00	5.00	10.00	18.50
	1818	—	.80	2.00	4.00	7.50
	1821	—	.80	2.00	4.00	7.50
	1822	—	2.00	5.00	10.00	17.50

NOTE: Varieties exist.

1/8 STUIVER

(1/2 Duit)

COPPER

Mint: Utrecht

KM#	Date	Mintage	VG	Fine	VF	XF
286	1822 S	1.300	2.00	4.50	9.00	15.00
	1823 S	33.000	1.00	2.50	4.50	7.50
	1824 S	21.000	1.00	2.50	4.50	7.50
	1825 S	44.000	1.00	2.50	4.50	7.50
	1826 S	69.000	.75	1.50	3.50	6.50

NOTE: Varieties exist. Date 1826 with lion of 1822-1825 with a thick, bushy tail are very rare.

DUIT

(1/) 5 (of) 1/16 G. = 1/80 G.

COPPER

Mint: Amsterdam

KM#	Date	Mintage	VG	Fine	VF	XF
279	1814 H	—	—	—	Rare	—
(86)	1814 w/o H	—	—	—	—	—
	1815 H	—	2.50	4.50	9.00	16.00
	1816 H	—	2.50	4.50	9.00	16.00

NOTE: Varieties exist. 1814 dated coins were struck on larger planchets.

Mint: Utrecht

KM#	Date	Mintage	VG	Fine	VF	XF
281	1816 S	64.562	.75	1.50	3.00	6.00

NOTE: Actually minted 1820-22.

Mint: Sourabaya

Obv: Double lined shield.

KM#	Date	Mintage	VG	Fine	VF	XF
282.1	1816	—	5.00	8.00	15.00	25.00
	1818	—	1.50	2.50	4.00	7.50
	1819	—	2.50	4.50	7.50	15.00
	1820	—	1.50	2.50	4.00	7.50
	1821	—	1.75	3.25	5.75	10.00
	1822	—	3.50	5.50	10.00	18.00

NOTE: 1816 dated coins were actually struck in 1820.

Obv: Single lined shield.

KM#	Date	Mintage	VG	Fine	VF	XF
282.2	1821	—	1.75	3.25	5.75	10.00
	1822	—	1.50	2.50	4.00	7.50
	1823	—	1.75	3.25	5.75	10.00
	1824	—	2.50	4.50	7.50	15.00
	1825	—	1.50	2.50	4.00	7.50
	1826	—	5.00	8.00	14.00	25.00

1/4 STUIVER

(Duit)

COPPER

Mint: Utrecht

KM#	Date	Mintage	VG	Fine	VF	XF
287	1822 S	30.000	1.00	2.50	5.00	10.00
	1823 S	29.000	1.00	2.50	5.00	10.00
	1824 S	26.000	1.00	2.50	5.00	10.00
	1825 S	125.000	.75	2.00	4.00	7.50
	1826 S	208.000	.50	1.50	3.00	5.00
	1836 S	33.453	1.00	2.50	5.00	10.00

NOTE: 2 varieties known. Counterfeits w/border of dots, and very thin planchets exist.

1/2 STUIVER

COPPER

Obv: G. below shield.

KM#	Date	Mintage	VG	Fine	VF	XF
283	1818	—	2.00	3.00	6.50	12.50
	1819	—	2.00	3.00	6.50	12.50
	1820	—	2.00	3.00	6.50	12.50

NOTE: Varieties exist.

Obv: G. removed, double lined shield.

KM#	Date	Mintage	VG	Fine	VF	XF
284.1	1820	—	2.00	4.00	6.00	17.50
	1821	—	2.00	4.00	6.00	17.50

Obv: Single lined shield.

KM#	Date	Mintage	VG	Fine	VF	XF
284.2	1821	—	2.00	4.00	6.00	17.50
	1822	—	1.50	2.25	4.00	12.50
	1823	—	1.50	2.25	4.00	12.50
	1824	—	1.50	2.25	4.00	12.50
	1825	—	1.50	2.25	4.00	12.50
	1826	—	2.00	4.00	6.00	17.50

KM#	Date	Mintage	VG	Fine	VF	XF
285	1821S	10.000	.75	1.50	2.50	5.00
	1822S	7.000	.75	1.50	2.50	5.00
	1823S	19.000	.75	1.50	2.50	5.00
	1824S	5.500	1.00	2.50	4.50	9.00
	1825S	42.000	.75	1.50	2.50	5.00
	1826S	66.000	.75	1.50	2.50	5.00

DECIMAL COINAGE

100 Cents = 1 Gulden

CENT

(Duit)

COPPER

KM#	Date	Mintage	VG	Fine	VF	XF
290	1833D	21.778	15.00	30.00	50.00	100.00
	1833V	Inc. Ab.	2.00	3.00	7.00	12.50
	1834V	66.237	1.50	2.50	5.00	10.00
	1835V	48.674	1.50	2.50	5.00	10.00
	1836V	94.825	1.50	2.50	5.00	10.00
	1837V	182.888	1.50	2.50	5.00	10.00
	1837C	Inc. Ab.	—	—	Rare	—
	1837J	Inc. Ab.	1.25	2.50	4.50	8.00
	1838J	235.524	1.25	2.50	4.50	8.00
	1839J	314.953	1.25	2.50	4.50	8.00
	1839W	Inc. Ab.	.75	1.25	2.50	5.00
	1840W	461.726	.75	1.25	2.50	5.00

NOTE: Varieties exist. Mintage figures for 1839 and 1840 include KM#111.4 and KM#111.5.

2 CENTS

(Double Duit)

COPPER

KM#	Date	Mintage	VG	Fine	VF	XF
291	1833D	11.305*	15.00	25.00	50.00	100.00
	1833V	Inc. Ab.	2.50	4.00	8.00	15.00
	1834V	32.997	1.50	2.50	4.50	8.00
	1835V	24.627	1.50	2.50	4.50	8.00
	1836V	48.612	1.50	2.50	4.50	8.00
	1837J	54.812	1.50	2.50	5.00	10.00
	1837V	Inc. Ab.	1.50	2.50	4.50	8.00
	1838J	93.809	1.50	2.50	5.00	10.00
	1839J	90.964	1.50	2.50	5.00	10.00
	1839W	Inc. Ab.	2.50	4.00	8.00	15.00
	1840W	98.086	2.50	4.00	8.00	15.00
	1841W	115.321	2.50	4.00	8.00	15.00

NOTE: Varieties exist. Mintage figures for 1840 and 1841 include KM#118.

INDONESIA

MONETARY SYSTEM

100 Sen = 1 Rupiah

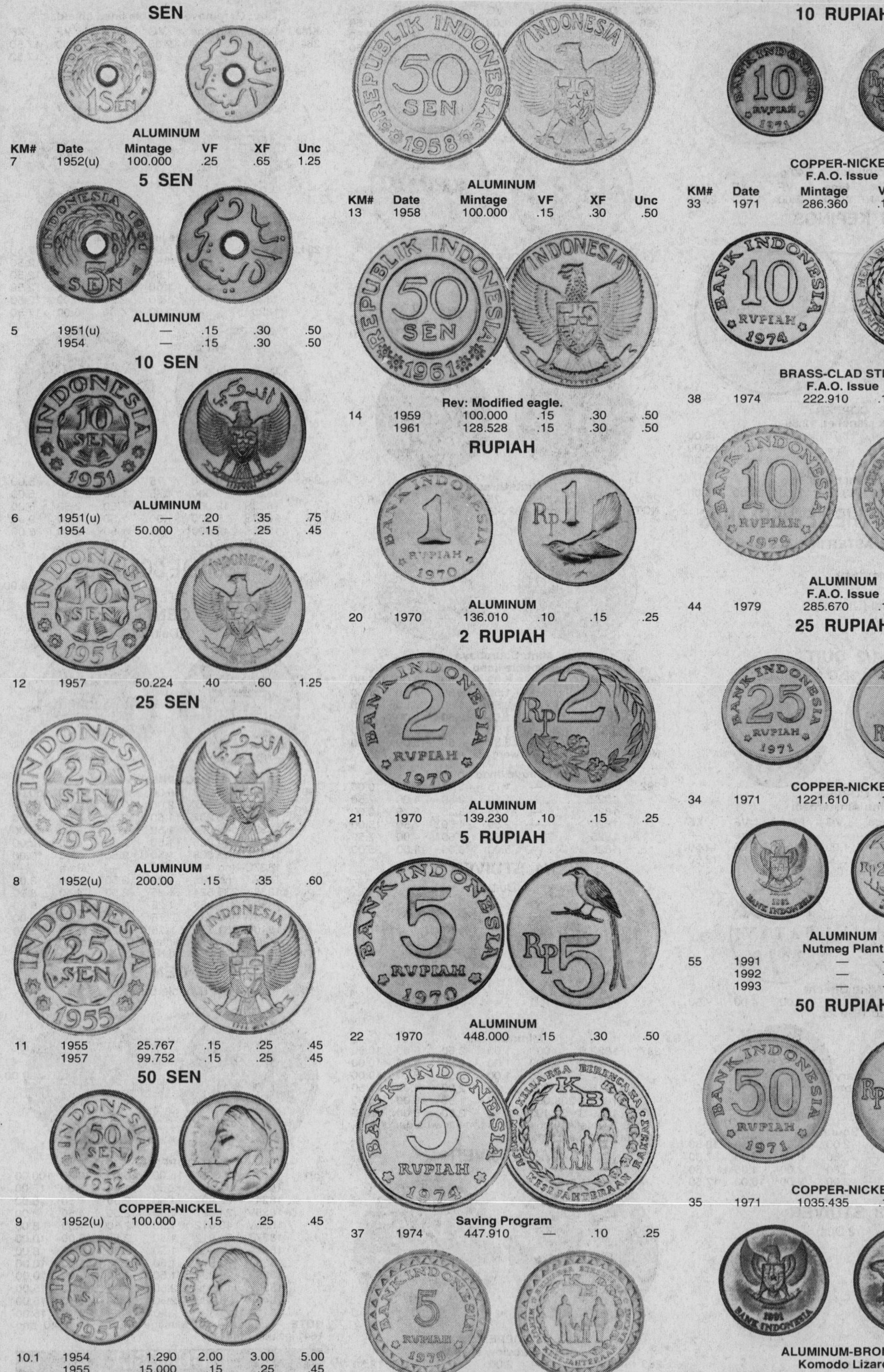

SEN

ALUMINUM

KM#	Date	Mintage	VF	XF	Unc
7	1952(u)	100.000	.25	.65	1.25

5 SEN

ALUMINUM

KM#	Date	Mintage	VF	XF	Unc
5	1951(u)	—	.15	.30	.50
	1954	—	.15	.30	.50

10 SEN

ALUMINUM

KM#	Date	Mintage	VF	XF	Unc
6	1951(u)	—	.20	.35	.75
	1954	50.000	.15	.25	.45
12	1957	50.224	.40	.60	1.25

25 SEN

ALUMINUM

KM#	Date	Mintage	VF	XF	Unc
8	1952(u)	200.00	.15	.35	.60
11	1955	25.767	.15	.25	.45
	1957	99.752	.15	.25	.45

50 SEN

COPPER-NICKEL

KM#	Date	Mintage	VF	XF	Unc
9	1952(u)	100.000	.15	.25	.45
10.1	1954	1.290	2.00	3.00	5.00
	1955	15.000	.15	.25	.45

Rev: Different head, larger lettering.

KM#	Date	Mintage	VF	XF	Unc
10.2	1957	24.977	.15	.25	.45

ALUMINUM

KM#	Date	Mintage	VF	XF	Unc
13	1958	100.000	.15	.30	.50

Rev: Modified eagle.

KM#	Date	Mintage	VF	XF	Unc
14	1959	100.000	.15	.30	.50
	1961	128.528	.15	.30	.50

RUPIAH

ALUMINUM

KM#	Date	Mintage	VF	XF	Unc
20	1970	136.010	.10	.15	.25

2 RUPIAH

ALUMINUM

KM#	Date	Mintage	VF	XF	Unc
21	1970	139.230	.10	.15	.25

5 RUPIAH

ALUMINUM

KM#	Date	Mintage	VF	XF	Unc
22	1970	448.000	.15	.30	.50

Saving Program

KM#	Date	Mintage	VF	XF	Unc
37	1974	447.910	—	.10	.25

Saving Program

KM#	Date	Mintage	VF	XF	Unc
43	1979	413.200	.10	.15	.30

10 RUPIAH

COPPER-NICKEL
F.A.O. Issue

KM#	Date	Mintage	VF	XF	Unc
33	1971	286.360	.10	.15	.30

BRASS-CLAD STEEL
F.A.O. Issue

KM#	Date	Mintage	VF	XF	Unc
38	1974	222.910	.10	.25	.50

ALUMINUM
F.A.O. Issue

KM#	Date	Mintage	VF	XF	Unc
44	1979	285.670	.10	.15	.45

25 RUPIAH

COPPER-NICKEL

KM#	Date	Mintage	VF	XF	Unc
34	1971	1221.610	.15	.25	.50

ALUMINUM
Nutmeg Plant

KM#	Date	Mintage	VF	XF	Unc
55	1991	—	—	—	.75
	1992	—	—	—	.75
	1993	—	—	—	.75

50 RUPIAH

COPPER-NICKEL

KM#	Date	Mintage	VF	XF	Unc
35	1971	1035.435	.15	.25	.55

ALUMINUM-BRONZE
Komodo Lizard

KM#	Date	Mintage	VF	XF	Unc
52	1991	—	—	—	.50
	1992	—	—	—	.50
	1993	—	—	—	.50

100 RUPIAH

COPPER-NICKEL

KM#	Date	Mintage	VF	XF	Unc
36	1973	252.868	.25	.50	1.25

Forestry For Prosperity

KM#	Date	Mintage	VF	XF	Unc
42	1978	907.773	.30	.60	1.50

ALUMUNIM-BRONZE
Cow Racing

KM#	Date	Mintage	VF	XF	Unc
53	1991	—	—	—	.75
	1992	—	—	—	.75
	1993	—	—	—	.75

200 RUPIAH

8.0000 g, .999 SILVER, .2569 oz ASW
25th Anniversary of Independence
Great Bird of Paradise

KM#	Date	Mintage	VF	XF	Unc
23	1970	5,100	—	Proof	15.00

250 RUPIAH

10.0000 g, .999 SILVER, .3212 oz ASW
25th Anniversary of Independence
Manjusri Statue from Temple of Tumpang

KM#	Date	Mintage	VF	XF	Unc
24	1970	5,000	—	Proof	20.00

500 RUPIAH

20.0000 g, .999 SILVER, .6424 oz ASW
25th Anniversary of Independence
Wayang Dancer
Obv: Similar to 10,000 Rupiah, KM#30.

KM#	Date	Mintage	VF	XF	Unc
25	1970	4,800	—	Proof	30.00

ALUMINUM-BRONZE
Stick of Jasmine.

KM#	Date	Mintage	VF	XF	Unc
54	1991	—	—	—	2.50
	1992	—	—	—	3.00

750 RUPIAH

30.0000 g, .999 SILVER, .9636 oz ASW
25th Anniversary of Independence
Garuda Bird
Obv: Similar to 20,000 Rupiah, KM#31.

KM#	Date	Mintage	VF	XF	Unc
26	1970	4,950	—	Proof	60.00

1000 RUPIAH

40.0000 g, .999 SILVER, 1.2848 oz ASW
25th Anniversary of Independence
General Sudirman
Obv: Similar to 25,000 Rupiah, KM#32.
Rev: Similar to 750 Rupiah, KM#26.

KM#	Date	Mintage	VF	XF	Unc
27	1970	4,250	—	Proof	70.00

COPPER-NICKEL RING BRASS CENTER
Palm Tree

KM#	Date	Mintage	VF	XF	Unc
56	1993	—	—	—	1.00

2000 RUPIAH

4.9300 g, .900 GOLD, .1426 oz AGW
25th Anniversary of Independence
Great Bird of Paradise

KM#	Date	Mintage	VF	XF	Unc
28	1970	2,970	—	Proof	110.00

25.6500 g, .500 SILVER, .4123 oz ASW
Conservation Series - Javan Tiger

KM#	Date	Mintage	VF	XF	Unc
39	1974	.043	—	—	12.00

28.2800 g, .925 SILVER, .8411 oz ASW

KM#	Date	Mintage	VF	XF	Unc
39a	1974	.018	—	Proof	18.50

5000 RUPIAH

12.3400 g, .900 GOLD, .3571 oz AGW
25th Anniversary of Independence
Manjusri Statue from Temple of Tumpang
Rev: Similar to 2000 Rupiah, KM#28.

KM#	Date	Mintage	VF	XF	Unc
29	1970	2,150	—	Proof	235.00

32.0000 g, .500 SILVER, .5144 oz ASW
Conservation Series - Orangutan

KM#	Date	Mintage	VF	XF	Unc
40	1974	.043	—	—	15.00

35.0000 g, .925 SILVER, 1.0409 oz ASW

KM#	Date	Mintage	VF	XF	Unc
40a	1974	.017	—	Proof	20.00

10000 RUPIAH

24.6800 g, .900 GOLD, .7142 oz AGW
25th Anniversary of Independence
Wayang Dancer
Rev: Similar to 2000 Rupiah, KM#28.

KM#	Date	Mintage	VF	XF	Unc
30	1970	1,440	—	Proof	475.00

19.4400 g, .925 SILVER, .5782 oz ASW
Wildlife - Babi Rusa (Wild Pig)

KM#	Date	Mintage	VF	XF	Unc
45	1987	.025	—	Proof	40.00

Save The Children - Playing Badminton

KM#	Date	Mintage	VF	XF	Unc
50	1990	.020	—	Proof	50.00

20000 RUPIAH

49.3700 g, .900 GOLD, 1.4391 oz AGW
25th Anniversary of Independence
Garuda Bird
Rev: Similar to 2000 Rupiah, KM#28.

KM#	Date	Mintage	VF	XF	Unc
31	1970	1,285	—	Proof	975.00

25000 RUPIAH

61.7100 g, .900 GOLD, 1.7858 oz AGW
25th Anniversary of Independence
General Sudirman
Rev: Similar to 20,000 Rupiah, KM#31.

KM#	Date	Mintage	VF	XF	Unc
32	1970	970 pcs.	—	Proof	1200.

100000 RUPIAH

33.4370 g, .900 GOLD, .9676 oz AGW
Conservation Series - Komodo Lizard

KM#	Date	Mintage	VF	XF	Unc
41	1974	5,333	—	—	475.00
	1974	1,369	—	Proof	600.00

125000 RUPIAH

8.0000 g, .958 GOLD, .2465 oz AGW
45 years of Independence - Graha Museum

KM#	Date	Mintage	VF	XF	Unc
47	1990	—	—	Proof	250.00

200000 RUPIAH

10.0000 g, .917 GOLD, .2947 oz AGW
Wildlife - Javan Rhinoceros

KM#	Date	Mintage	VF	XF	Unc
46	1987	5,000	—	Proof	400.00

Save The Children - Balinese Dancer

KM#	Date	Mintage	VF	XF	Unc
51	1990	3,000	—	Proof	300.00

250000 RUPIAH

17.0000 g, .958 GOLD, .5238 oz AGW
45 Years of Independence - Archipelago
Obv: Similar to 125,000 Rupiah, KM#47.

KM#	Date	Mintage	VF	XF	Unc
48	1990	—	—	Proof	450.00

750000 RUPIAH

45.0000 g, .958 GOLD, 1.3866 oz AGW
45 Years of Independence - Arms of Generation
Obv: Similar to 125,000 Rupiah, KM#47.

KM#	Date	Mintage	VF	XF	Unc
49	1990	—	—	Proof	1400.

MINT SETS (MS)

KM#	Date	Mintage	Identification	Issue Price	Mkt. Val.
MS1	Mixed dates(14)	—	KM5-6(1951 & 1954), 7-9 (1952), 10.1(1955), 10.2(1957), 11(1955, 1957), 12(1957), 14(1961)	—	18.00
MS2	1970(3)	—	KM20-22	—	1.50
MS3	1971(3)	—	KM33-35	—	1.50

PROOF SETS (PS)

KM#	Date	Mintage	Identification	Issue Price	Mkt. Val.
PS1	1970(10)	970	KM23-32	490.00	3150.
PS2	1970(5)	4,250	KM23-27	50.00	165.00
PS3	1974(2)	30,000	KM39a-40a	50.00	40.00
PS4	1990(3)	—	KM47-49	2000.	2100.
PS5	1990(2)	—	KM50-51	—	350.00

RIAU ARCHIPELAGO

A group of islands off the tip of the Malay Peninsula. Coins were issued near the end of 1963 (although dated 1962) and recalled as worthless on Sept. 30, 1964. They were legal tender from Oct. 15, 1963 to July 1, 1964.

INSCRIPTION ON EDGE
KEPULAUAN RIAU

SEN

ALUMINUM

KM#	Date	Mintage	Fine	VF	XF	Unc
5	1962	—	.35	.75	1.50	2.50

5 SEN

ALUMINUM

KM#	Date	Mintage	Fine	VF	XF	Unc
6	1962	—	.25	.50	1.00	2.00

10 SEN

ALUMINUM

KM#	Date	Mintage	Fine	VF	XF	Unc
7	1962	—	.25	.50	1.00	2.25

25 SEN

ALUMINUM
Similar to Irian Barat, KM#8.1.

KM#	Date	Mintage	Fine	VF	XF	Unc
8.1	1962	—	— Reported, not confirmed			

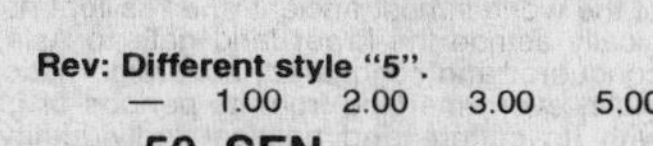

Rev: Different style "5".

KM#	Date	Mintage	Fine	VF	XF	Unc
8.2	1962	—	1.00	2.00	3.00	5.00

50 SEN

ALUMINUM
Rev: 17 laurel leaves.

KM#	Date	Mintage	Fine	VF	XF	Unc
9.1	1962	—	.75	1.50	2.50	5.00

Rev: 16 laurel leaves.

KM#	Date	Mintage	Fine	VF	XF	Unc
9.2	1962	—	—	—	—	—

IRIAN BARAT

(West Irian, Irian Jaya, Netherlands New Guinea)

A province of Indonesia comprising the western half of the island of New Guinea. A special set of coins dated 1962 were issued in 1964 and were recalled December 31, 1971 and are no longer legal tender.

NO INSCRIPTION ON EDGE

SEN

ALUMINUM
Plain edge

KM#	Date	Mintage	Fine	VF	XF	Unc
5	1962	—	.25	.50	1.00	1.75

5 SEN

ALUMINUM
Plain edge

KM#	Date	Mintage	Fine	VF	XF	Unc
6	1962	—	.50	1.00	1.50	2.00

10 SEN

ALUMINUM
Plain edge

KM#	Date	Mintage	Fine	VF	XF	Unc
7	1962	—	.50	1.00	1.50	2.25

25 SEN

ALUMINUM
Reeded edge

KM#	Date	Mintage	Fine	VF	XF	Unc
8.1	1962	—	—	—	—	—

Rev: Different style "5".

KM#	Date	Mintage	Fine	VF	XF	Unc
8.2	1962	—	.75	1.50	2.50	4.50

50 SEN

ALUMINUM
Reeded edge

KM#	Date	Mintage	Fine	VF	XF	Unc
9	1962	—	.75	1.50	2.50	5.00

TIMOR

(East Timor)

An island in the Lesser Sunda group, presently part of Indonesia but formerly divided between Portugal and the Netherlands. Portugal discovered and owned the eastern half of the island since 1512 and made coins for this colony. Made part of Indonesia in 1975.

MONETARY SYSTEM
100 Avos = 1 Pataca

COUNTERMARKED COINAGE

June 13, 1900

(8 REALES)

SILVER
c/m: Maltese cross on Mexico, Chihuahua 8 Reales, KM#377.2.

KM#	Date	Mintage	Fine	VF	XF	Unc
8	1890 MM	—	—	—	—	—

NOTE: Other dates, 1886, 1891, 1893, 1894 and 1896 are reported but mints are unknown.

COLONIAL COINAGE

10 AVOS

BRONZE

KM#	Date	Mintage	Fine	VF	XF	Unc
5	1945	.050	20.00	45.00	75.00	140.00
	1948	.500	.60	1.00	2.00	5.00
	1951	6.250	.50	.75	1.50	3.00

20 AVOS

NICKEL-BRONZE

KM#	Date	Mintage	Fine	VF	XF	Unc
6	1945	.050	7.50	12.50	25.00	65.00

50 AVOS

3.5000 g, .650 SILVER, .0731 oz ASW

KM#	Date	Mintage	Fine	VF	XF	Unc
7	1945	.100	20.00	37.50	55.00	90.00
	1948	.500	2.50	5.00	8.50	20.00
	1951	6.250	1.50	3.00	5.50	12.00

MONETARY REFORM

100 Centavos = 1 Escudo

10 CENTAVOS

BRONZE

KM#	Date	Mintage	Fine	VF	XF	Unc
10	1958	1.000	.50	1.00	2.00	6.50

20 CENTAVOS

BRONZE

KM#	Date	Mintage	Fine	VF	XF	Unc
17	1970	1.000	.15	.25	.50	1.50

30 CENTAVOS

BRONZE

KM#	Date	Mintage	Fine	VF	XF	Unc
11	1958	2.000	.50	1.00	1.50	4.00

50 CENTAVOS

BRONZE

KM#	Date	Mintage	Fine	VF	XF	Unc
18	1970	1.000	.15	.25	.50	1.50

60 CENTAVOS

COPPER-ZINC-NICKEL

KM#	Date	Mintage	Fine	VF	XF	Unc
12	1958	1.000	.50	1.50	3.00	7.50

ESCUDO

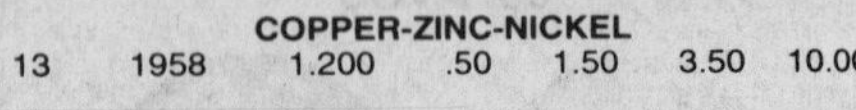

COPPER-ZINC-NICKEL

KM#	Date	Mintage	Fine	VF	XF	Unc
13	1958	1.200	.50	1.50	3.50	10.00

BRONZE

KM#	Date	Mintage	Fine	VF	XF	Unc
19	1970	1.200	.15	.35	1.00	2.00

2-1/2 ESCUDOS

COPPER-NICKEL

KM#	Date	Mintage	Fine	VF	XF	Unc
20	1970	1.000	.25	.50	1.25	2.50

3 ESCUDOS

3.5000 g, .650 SILVER, .0731 oz ASW

KM#	Date	Mintage	Fine	VF	XF	Unc
14	1958	1.000	2.00	2.50	4.00	8.00

5 ESCUDOS

COPPER-NICKEL

KM#	Date	Mintage	Fine	VF	XF	Unc
21	1970	1.200	.50	.75	1.50	4.00

6 ESCUDOS

7.0000 g, .650 SILVER, .1463 oz ASW

KM#	Date	Mintage	Fine	VF	XF	Unc
15	1958	1.000	3.50	5.50	9.00	15.00

10 ESCUDOS

7.0000 g, .650 SILVER, .1463 oz ASW

KM#	Date	Mintage	Fine	VF	XF	Unc
16	1964	.600	3.50	5.50	9.00	15.00

COPPER-NICKEL

KM#	Date	Mintage	Fine	VF	XF	Unc
22	1970	.700	1.00	1.50	2.50	7.00

IRAN

The Islamic Republic of Iran, located between the Caspian Sea and the Persian Gulf in southwestern Asia, has an area of 636,296 sq. mi. (1,648,000 sq. km.) and a population of 40 million. Capital: Tehran. Although predominantly an agricultural state, Iran depends heavily on oil for foreign exchange. Crude oil, carpets and agricultural products are exported.

Iran (historically known as Persia until 1931AD) is one of the world's most ancient and resilient nations. Strategically astride the lower land gate to Asia, it has been conqueror and conquered, sovereign nation and vassal state, ever emerging from its periods of glory or travail with its culture and political individuality intact. Iran (Persia) was a powerful empire under Cyrus the Great (600-529 B.C.), its borders extending from the Indus to the Nile. It has also been conquered by the predatory empires of antique and recent times - Assyrian, Medean, Macedonian, Seljuq, Turk, Mongol - and more recently been coveted by Russia, the Third Reich and Great Britain. Revolts against the absolute power of the Persian shahs resulted in the establishment of a constitutional monarchy in 1906.

With 4,000 troops, Reza Khan marched on the capital arriving in Tehran in the early morning of Feb. 22, 1921. The government was taken over with hardly a shot and Zia ad-Din was set up as premier, but the real power was with Reza Khan, although he was officially only the minister of war. In 1923, Reza Khan appointed himself prime minister and summoned the "majlis." Who eventually gave him military powers and he became independent of the shah's authority. In 1925 Reza Khan Pahlavi was elected Shah of Persia. A few weeks later his eldest son, Shahpur Mohammed Reza was appointed Crown Prince and was crowned on April 25, 1926.

In 1931 the Kingdom of Persia became known as the Kingdom of Iran. In 1979, the monarchy was toppled and an Islamic Republic proclaimed.

TITLES

Dar al-Khilafat

RULERS

Qajar Dynasty

Fath'ali Shah,
AH1212-1250/1797-1834AD
Sultan Ali Shah, in Tehran
AH1250/1834AD (30 days)
Husayn Ali Shah,
AH1250/1834AD (6 months)
(in Southern Iran only)
Muhammad Shah,
AH1250-1264/1834-1848AD
Nasir al-Din Shah,
AH1264-1313/1848-1896AD
Muzaffar al-Din Shah,
AH1313-1324/1896-1907AD
Muhammad Ali Shah,
AH1324-1327/1907-1909AD
Sultan Ahmad Shah,
AH1327-1344/1909-1925AD

Pahlavi Dynasty

Reza Shah, as prime minister,
SH1302-1304/1923-1925AD
as Shah,
SH1304-1320/1925-1941AD
Mohammad Reza Pahlavi, Shah
SH1320-1358/1941-1979AD

Islamic Republic, SH1358-/1979-AD

MINTNAMES

Abushahr (Bushire) ابو شهر

Ardebil اردبيل

Astarabad استراباد

Bandar Abbas بندر عباس

Bandar Abushahr بندر ابو شهر

Mint	Arabic
Basra (al-Basrah, Iraq)	البصره
Behbehan	بهبهان
Bhakkar	بهكر
Borujerd	بروجرد
Darband	دربند
Dezful	دزفول
Eravan (Iravan)	ايروان
Fouman	فومان
Ganjah (Ganja)	كنجه
Gilan	كيلان
Hamadan	همدان
Herat	هرات
Huwayza	حويزه
Isfahan	اصفهان
Jelou (Army Mint)	جلو
Kashan	كاشان
Kerman	كرمان
Kermanshahan (Kermanshah)	كرمانشاهان
Khoy (Khoi)	خوى
Lahijan	لاهيجان
Lahore	لاهور
Maragheh	مراغه
Mashad	مشهد
Mazandaran	مازندران
Nakhchawan	نخجوان
Naseri	ناصرى
Nihawand	نهاوند
Nukhwi	نخوى
Panahabad	پناه آباد
Peshawar (Pakistan)	بشاور
Qazvin	قزوين
Qomm (Kumm)	قم
Ra'nash	رعنش
Rasht	رشت
Rekab (Rikab)	ركاب
Reza'iyeh	رضائيه
Sarakhs	سرخس
Sari	ساري
Sa'uj Bulagh	ساوج بلاق
Shamakha (Shemakhi - Azerbaijan)	شماخه
Shiraz	شيراز
Shushtar	شوشتر
Simnan	سمنان
Sind	سند
Sirvan (Azerbaijan)	
Sultanabad	سلطان آباد
Tabaristan	طبرستان
Tabriz	تبريز
Tehran	طهران
Tiflis (Georgia)	تفليس
Tuyserkan	توى سركان
Urumi (Reza'iyeh)	ارومى
Yazd	يزد
Zanjan	زنجان

COIN DATING

Iranian coins were dated according to the Moslem lunar calendar until March 21, 1925 (AD), when dating was switched to a new calendar based on the solar year, indicated by the notation SH. The monarchial calender system was adopted in 1976 = MS2535 and was abandoned in 1978 = MS2537. The previously used solar year calendar was restored at that time.

MONETARY SYSTEM

1798-1825 (AH 1212-1241)

1250 Dinars = 1 Riyal
8 Riyals = 1 Toman

1825-1931 (AH1241-1344, SH1304-09)

50 Dinars = 1 Shahi
20 Shahis = 1 Kran (Qiran)
10 Krans = 1 Toman

NOTE: From AD1830-34 (AH1245-50) the gold Toman was known as a 'Keshwarsetan.'

1932-Date (SH1310-Date)

5 Dinars = 1 Shahi
20 Shahis = 1 Rial (100 Dinars)
10 Rials = 1 Toman

NOTE: The Toman ceased to be an official unit in 1932, but continues to be applied in popular usage. Thus, '135 Rials' is always expressed as '13 Toman, 5 Rials'. The term 'Rial' is often used in conversation, as well as either 'Kran' or 'Ezar' (short for Hazar = 1000) is used.

NOTE: The Law of 18 March 1930 fixed the gold Pahlavi at 20 Rials. No gold coins were struck. The Law of 13 March 1932 divided the Pahlavi into 100 Rials, instead of 20. The Rial's weight was reduced from 0.3661 grams of pure gold to 0.0732. Since 1937 gold has been allowed to float and the Pahlavi is quoted daily in Rials in the marketplaces.

HAMMERED 'DUMP' COINAGE

Copper Coinage

During the nineteenth century, copper coins (falus, flus) were issued at some 40 or more local mints, each of which coined falus for local use only. Copper coins did not circulate generally, but were restricted to the city of their origin and its immediate environs. The local mintmaster, often in collaboration with the local governor, determined the type, design, and weight of the coinage, and regulated its circulation.

In theory, copper coins were recalled and changed about every year, with a substantial fee payable to the mintmaster for the exchange of old coin for new. To discourage further use the old coin was either demonetized or tariffed at a lower value, usually about half its original.

In order to facilitate the recognition of new and old coin, the type was changed annually, the type being the obverse pictorial design, so that illiterate shopkeepers could tell the difference and not be deceived by obsolete coins. However, after a number of years, the same types would be reinstated for another year. In practice, the system worked more informally, and surviving coins show that at some mints, identical types were struck for several years running and were not recalled annually.

The metrology of the copper Falus is uncertain. While it seems that Falus were intended to follow an assigned weight standard, great tolerance was permitted. The weight standard was frequently changed (or the mintmaster issued lighter coins and pocketed the difference), and each mint city maintained its own standard and copper currency policies.

As a result of the frequent recoinage of copper and its frequent demonetization, copper coins were not hoarded or saved, and are consequently quite scarce today. Annual change meant that each mint had a multiplicity of types and varieties, most of which are uncommon today. The following listings are not an attempt at completeness, but give a representative selection of the products of each mint.

IMPORTANT: Most types were used at many different mints. The type can therefore not be used to attribute a coin to the mint of its issue. The ONLY certain way of attributing the coin is to read the mint name on the reverse. Well struck copper falus with clear mintname and date are worth a premium.

LOCAL COPPER FALUS

Mint: Abushahr
Obv: Lion.

KM#	Date	Mintage	Good	VG	Fine	VF
2	AH1270	—	4.50	7.50	12.50	20.00
	Obv: 2 lions facing.					
56	AHxxxx	—	—	—	—	—

Obv: Bale mark.

KM#	Date	Mintage	Good	VG	Fine	VF
3	AH1234	—	7.50	12.50	20.00	32.50

Obv: Peacock.

KM#	Date	Mintage	Good	VG	Fine	VF
4	AH1239	—	5.50	9.00	15.00	25.00

Obv: 2 peacocks facing left and right.

KM#	Date	Mintage	Good	VG	Fine	VF
57	AH1257	—	—	—	—	—

Obv: Fish.

KM#	Date	Mintage	Good	VG	Fine	VF
5	AH1221	—	—	—	—	—
	1231	—	5.50	9.00	15.00	25.00

Mint: Ardebil
Obv: Peacock holding snake in beak.

KM#	Date	Mintage	Good	VG	Fine	VF
6	AH1232	—	6.00	10.00	17.50	30.00

Mint: Astarabad
Obv: 2 Ibexes.

KM#	Date	Mintage	Good	VG	Fine	VF
7	ND	—	6.00	10.00	17.50	30.00

Obv: Man on horseback.

KM#	Date	Mintage	Good	VG	Fine	VF
A7	AH1259	—	6.00	10.00	17.50	30.00

Obv: Sun above lion facing right.

KM#	Date	Mintage	Good	VG	Fine	VF
58	ND	—	6.00	10.00	17.50	30.00

Mint: Borujerd
Obv: Soldier leaning on his rifle.

KM#	Date	Mintage	Good	VG	Fine	VF
10	AH124x	—	8.00	13.50	21.50	35.00
	1261	—	—	—	—	—

Obv: Small bird.

KM#	Date	Mintage	Good	VG	Fine	VF
11	ND	—	5.50	9.00	15.00	25.00

Mint: Darband
Obv: Peacock right.

KM#	Date	Mintage	Good	VG	Fine	VF
59	AH1228	—	—	—	—	—

Mint: Ganjah
Obv: Goose.

KM#	Date	Mintage	Good	VG	Fine	VF
15	AH1257	—	8.00	13.50	21.50	35.00

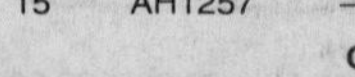

Obv: Horse.

KM#	Date	Mintage	Good	VG	Fine	VF
60	AH1220	—	—	—	—	—

Mint: Hamadan

KM#	Date	Mintage	Good	VG	Fine	VF
18	AH1254	—	6.00	10.00	16.50	27.50

Mint: Eravan
Obv: Camel.

KM#	Date	Mintage	Good	VG	Fine	VF
19	AH1223	—	8.00	13.50	21.50	35.00

Mint: Isfahan
Obv: Scales.

KM#	Date	Mintage	Good	VG	Fine	VF
21	AH1242	—	3.50	6.00	10.00	16.50

Mint: Kashan
Obv: Lion and sun in wreath.
Denomination: 50 Dinars

KM#	Date	Mintage	Good	VG	Fine	VF
24	AH1293	—	6.00	10.00	17.50	30.00

NOTE: This type was an attempt to reform the copper coinage by Nasir al-Din Shah, and was also struck at Isfahan, Tehran, Tabriz and Shiraz in AH1293 and 1294. Kashan is the rarest mint, Tehran and Isfahan the most plentiful.

Mint: Kerman
Obv: Lion in wreath.

KM#	Date	Mintage	Good	VG	Fine	VF
27	AH1287	—	4.50	7.50	12.50	20.00

Mint: Kermanshahan
Obv: Sunface.

KM#	Date	Mintage	Good	VG	Fine	VF
28	AH1245	—	4.50	7.50	12.50	20.00

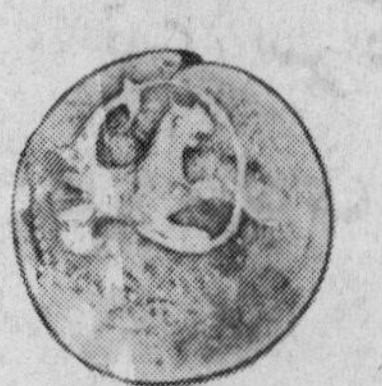

Obv: Lion.

KM#	Date	Mintage	Good	VG	Fine	VF
29	ND	—	6.00	10.00	16.50	27.50

Obv: Camel and rider.

KM#	Date	Mintage	Good	VG	Fine	VF
16	AH1244	—	5.50	9.00	15.00	25.00

Obv: Horseman riding left. Rev: Lion and sun.

KM#	Date	Mintage	Good	VG	Fine	VF
62	AH1231	—	—	—	—	—

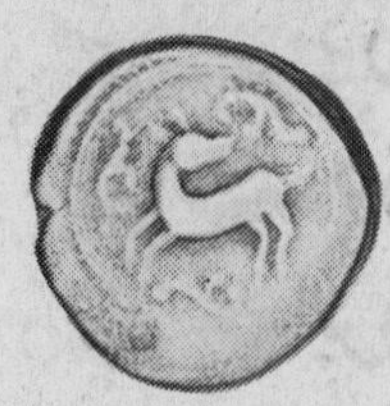

Mint: Khoy
Obv: Gazelle.

KM#	Date	Mintage	Good	VG	Fine	VF
26	AH1230	—	5.50	9.00	15.00	25.00

Mint: Lenjeh - Bandar Lengeh

KM#	Date	Mintage	Good	VG	Fine	VF
B30	AH1247	—	25.00	45.00	75.00	125.00
	1259	—	40.00	75.00	110.00	150.00

Mint: Maragheh
Obv: Peacock.

KM#	Date	Mintage	Good	VG	Fine	VF
31	AH1270	—	7.50	12.50	20.00	32.50

Mint: Mashad
Obv: Elephant and rider.

KM#	Date	Mintage	Good	VG	Fine	VF
32	AH1246	—	2.50	4.50	9.00	14.50

Obv: Sunface.

KM#	Date	Mintage	Good	VG	Fine	VF
63	AH1237	—	—	—	—	—

Obv: Lion and sun.

KM#	Date	Mintage	Good	VG	Fine	VF
64	AH1258	—	—	—	—	—
	1261	—	—	—	—	—

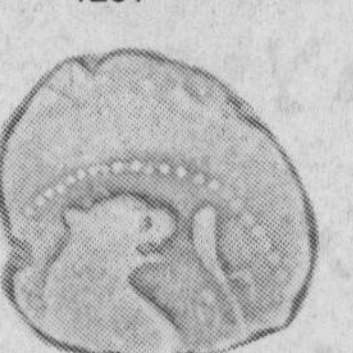

Mint: Nihawand
Obv: Lion sitting.

KM#	Date	Mintage	Good	VG	Fine	VF
34	AH1240	—	9.00	15.00	25.00	40.00

Mint: Qazwin
Obv: Lion and sun.

KM#	Date	Mintage	Good	VG	Fine	VF
35	ND	—	4.50	7.50	12.50	20.00

Obv: Lion and sun in wreath.

KM#	Date	Mintage	Good	VG	Fine	VF
A35	AH129x	—	4.50	7.50	12.50	20.00

Mint: Rasht
Obv: Lion and sun.

KM#	Date	Mintage	Good	VG	Fine	VF
36	AH1246	—	4.50	7.50	12.50	20.00

Obv: Lion.

KM#	Date	Mintage	Good	VG	Fine	VF
37	AH1233	—	4.50	8.00	13.50	22.50

Obv: Sunface.

KM#	Date	Mintage	Good	VG	Fine	VF
A37	AH1247	—	4.50	7.50	12.50	20.00

Mint: Sa'ujbulagh
Obv: 2 Guinea hens.

KM#	Date	Mintage	Good	VG	Fine	VF
39	ND	—	4.50	7.50	12.50	20.00

Obv: Lion and sun, stylized.

KM#	Date	Mintage	Good	VG	Fine	VF
40	AH1230	—	5.50	9.00	15.00	25.00

Mint: Shiraz
Obv: Scales.

KM#	Date	Mintage	Good	VG	Fine	VF
41	AH126x	—	4.50	7.50	12.50	20.00

Mint: Tabriz
Obv: Lion and sun.

KM#	Date	Mintage	Good	VG	Fine	VF
45	AH1235	—	3.50	6.00	10.00	16.50
	1236	—	3.50	6.00	10.00	16.50

Obv: Lion passant.

KM#	Date	Mintage	Good	VG	Fine	VF
47	AH125x	—	3.50	6.00	10.00	16.50

Oblique edge milling
Obv: Radiant sunface within wreath.

KM#	Date	Mintage	Good	VG	Fine	VF
A47	AH1229	—	3.50	7.50	12.50	20.00
	1230	—	3.50	7.50	12.50	20.00

Mint: Tehran
Obv: Peacock.

KM#	Date	Mintage	Good	VG	Fine	VF
48	AH1222	—	3.50	6.00	10.00	16.50

Obv: Russian eagle.

KM#	Date	Mintage	Good	VG	Fine	VF
49	ND	—	6.00	10.00	17.50	30.00

Obv: Lion and sun in wreath.

KM#	Date	Mintage	Good	VG	Fine	VF
A49	AH1293	—	4.50	7.50	12.50	20.00

NOTE: Other mints also produced local Falus, for which examples were not available to illustrate. Still other mints operated only or largely at earlier dates. These include Damavand, Damghan, Darabjird, Ja'farafad, Kangan, Ra'nash, Semnan, Tuy, Tus and more.

SILVER AND GOLD COINAGE

The precious metal monetary system of Qajar Persia prior to the reforms of 1878 was the direct descendant of the Mongol system introduced by Ghazan Mahmud in 1297AD, and was the last example of a medieval Islamic coinage. It is not a modern system, and cannot be understood as such. It is not possible to list types, dates, and mints as for other countries, both because of the nature of the coinage, and because very little research has been done on the series. The following comments should help elucidate its nature.

STANDARDS: The weight of the primary silver and gold coins was set by law and was expressed in terms of the Mesqal (about 4.61 g) and the Nokhod (24 Nokhod = 1 Mesqal). The primary silver coin was the Rupee from AH1211-1212, the Riyal from AH1212-1241, and the Gheran from AH1241-1344. The standard gold coin was the Toman. Currently the price of gold is quoted in Mesqals.

DENOMINATIONS: In addition to the primary denominations, noted in the last paragraph, fractional pieces were coined, valued at one-eighth, one-fourth, and one-half the primary denomination, usually in much smaller quantities. These were ordinarily struck from the same dies as the larger pieces, sometimes on broad, thin flans, sometimes on thick, dumpy flans. On the smaller coins, the denomination can best be determined only by weighing the coin. The denomination is almost never expressed on the coin!

DEVALUATIONS: From time to time, the standard for silver and gold was reduced, and the old coin recalled and replaced with lighter coin, the difference going to the government coffers. The effect was that of a devaluation of the primary silver and gold coins, or inversely regarded, an increase in the price of silver and gold. The durations of each standard varied from about 2 to 20 years. The standards are given for each ruler, as the denomination can only be determined when the standard is known.

LIGHTWEIGHT AND ALLOYED PIECES: Most of the smaller denomination coins were issued at lighter weights than those prescribed by law, with the difference going to the pockets of the mintmasters. Other mints, notably Hamadan, added excessive amounts of alloy to the coins, and some mintmasters lost their heads as a result. Discrepancies in weight of as much as 15 percent and more are observed, with the result that it is often quite impossible to determine the denomination of a coin!

OVERSIZE COINS: Occasionally, multiples of the primary denominations were produced, usually on special occasions for presentation by the Shah to his favorites. These 'coins' did not circulate (except as bullion), and were usually worn as ornaments. They were the 'NCLT's' of their day.

MINTS & EPITHETS: Qajar coinage was struck at 34 mints (plus at least a dozen others striking only copper Falus), which are listed previously, with drawings of the mint names in Persian, as they appear on the coins. However, the Persian script admits of infinite variation and stylistic whimsy, so the forms given are only guides, and not absolute. Only a knowledge of the script will assure correct reading. In addition to the city name, most mint names were given identifying epithets, which occasionally appear in lieu of the mint name, particularly at Iravan and Mashhad.

TYPES: There were no types in the modern sense, but the arrangement of the legends and the ornamental borders were frequently changed. These changes do not coincide with changes in standards, and cannot be used to determine the mint, which must be found by actually reading the reverse inscriptions.

ARRANGEMENT

The following listings are arranged by ruler, first, the various standards are explained. Then, the coins are listed by denomination within each reign. For each denomination, one or more pieces, when available, are illustrated, with the mint and date noted beneath each photo. For each type, a date range is given, but this range indicates the years during which the particular type was current, and does not imply that every year of the interval is known on actual coins. Because dates were carelessly engraved, and old dies were used until they wore out or broke, we occasionally find coins of a particular type dated before or after the indicated interval. Such coins command no premium. No attempt has been made to determine which mints actually exist for which types.

NADIR MIRZA AFSHAR

in Mashhad AH1210-1218/1795-1803

Type for this reign:

Name of ruler within central cartouche with blank margins around, *al-Sultan Nadir*. Reverse, mint and date below, benediction above, *Edama Allah Daulatahu*, "may God prolong his reign."

SHAHI

SILVER, 11.50 g

KM#	Date	Mint	Fine	VF	XF
671	AH1216	Mashhad	75.00	125.00	200.00

RUPI

SILVER, 11.50 g

KM#	Date	Mint	Fine	VF	XF
672	AH1216	Mashhad	100.00	160.00	250.00

HUSAIN QULI KHAN OAJAR

Rebel in Isfahan, AH1216/1801

Description not available.

RIYAL

SILVER, 10.40 g

KM#	Date	Mint	Fine	VF	XF
676	AH1216	Isfahan	125.00	200.00	300.00

MINTS FOR SILVER AND GOLD

The following mints struck silver and/or gold coins during the period AD1796-1878 (AH1211-1296). All except the Central Mint at Tehran were suppressed by order of Nasir al-Din Shah in AH1295/1878.

The first column lists the mint name and the following three columns provide valuation adjustments for silver coins of each mint for each reign. Special premiums are not applicable to gold coins from the rarer mints. A dash (-) means that no coins are known from the mint for the respective reign.

Relative Scarcity

(For silver coins only)
(plus percent premium)

Mint	Fath'Ali	Muhammad	Nasir Al-din
Ardabil	100	—	—
Astarabad	25	25	None
Borujerd	50	—	—
Ganja	150	—	—
Hamadan	50	None	None
Herat	—	—	100
Iravan	50	—	—
Isfahan	None	None	None
Kashan	None	—	25
Khoy	50	—	50
Kerman	25	50	50
Kirmanshahan	None	None	25
Lahijan	50	—	—
Maragheh	150	—	—
Mashad	None	None	None
Mazandaran	25	—	—
Nihavand	150	—	—
Nukhwi	200	—	—

Mint	Fath'Ali	Muhammad	Nasir Al-din
Qazvin	None	—	25
Qum	75	—	—
Rasht	None	25	25
Rekab	75	—	—
Sarakhs	—	—	200
Shiraz	None	25	25
Shushtar	150	—	See Note
Simnan	100	—	—
Tabaristan	50	25	None
Tabriz	None	None	None
Tehran	None	None	None
Tuyserkan	100	—	—
Urumi	25	—	—
Yazd	None	25	25
Zanjan	75	—	—

NOTE: A coin of Shushtar is reported for Nasir al-Din Shah, but not confirmed.

None = No premium. A dash means coins of that mint for that ruler are unknown.

FATH'ALI SHAH

AH1212-1250/1797-1834AD

Coinage Standards of Fath'Ali Shah

SILVER COINAGE

I. Rupee Standard, used only for coronation piece (C#188) AH1212. 1 Rupee = 60 Nokhod.

1 Rupee	**11.50 g**

II. First Riyal Standard, AH1212-1232, 1 Riyal = 54 Nokhod.

1/8 Riyal	**1.30 g**
1/4 Riyal	**2.60 g**
1/2 Riyal	**5.20 g**
1 Riyal	**10.40 g**

III. Second Riyal Standard, AH1232-1241, 1 Riyal = 2 Mesqal = 48 Nokhod.

1/8 Riyal	**1.15 g**
1/4 Riyal	**2.30 g**
1/2 Riyal	**4.60 g**
1 Riyal	**9.20 g**

IV. Kran Standard, AH1241-1250, 1 Kran = 1-1/2 Mesqal 36 Nokhod.

1/8 Kran	**0.90 g**
1/4 Kran	**1.70 g**
1/2 Kran	**3.50 g**
1 Kran	**6.90 g**

GOLD COINAGE

I. First Standard, AH1213-?? (after 1214), 1 Toman = 32 Nokhod.

1/2 Toman	**3.10 g**
1 Toman	**6.10 g**

II. Second Standard, AH1220-1224, 1 Toman = 30 Nokhod.

1/4 Toman	**1.50 g**
1/2 Toman	**2.90 g**
1 Toman	**5.80 g**

III. Third Standard, AH1224-1227, 1 Toman = 28 Nokhod.

1/2 Toman	**2.70 g**
1 Toman	**5.40 g**

IV. Fourth Standard, AH1227-1229, 1 Toman = 25 Nokhod.

1/2 Toman	**2.40 g**
1 Toman	**4.80 g**

V. Fifth Standard, AH1230-1244, 1 Toman = 24 Nokhod = 1 Mesqal.

1/4 Toman	**1.15 g**
1/2 Toman	**2.30 g**
1 Toman	**4.60 g**

NOTE: Some mints were using this standard as early as AH1228 if the dates on the coins are correct. However, the similarity of the '2' and '3' in Persian may have led to 1232 being read as 1222, etc.

VI. Sixth Standard, AH1246-1250, 1 Toman = 18 Nokhod.

1/2 Toman	**1.70 g**
1 Toman (Keshvarsetan)	**3.50 g**

NOTE: It is probable that all fractions exist for each standard.

TYPES

Although there are no clearly distinguishable 'types' in the European sense, changes in the obverse legend and calligraphic style enable us to divide the coinage into a sequence of five basic 'types'. Since the same dies, or similar dies, were used for all denominations, gold and silver, the following division applies to all.

TYPE I: With title 'Sultan' and thick, interlaced, coarse calligraphy. Used AH1213-1218.

TYPE II: With title 'Sultan, Son of the Sultan' and thick, coarse calligraphy, but letters separate and flowing (script known as Nasta'liq). Plain background. Used AH1218-22.

TYPE III: As last, but background filled with dots, vines, and tendrils. Used AH1222-1241.

TYPE IV: Style as Type III, but with title 'Sahibqiran' (literally, a title for a person born under an auspicious conjunction of the planets. After the title was assumed by Timor Lang in the 14th century, it lost its astrological meaning and came to denote 'Conqueror'). The coins of this type were named 'Sahibqiran' on account of this title, which was shortened in the popular idiom to 'Ghiran' (Kran). Used AH1241-1245 (but the fifth type never caught on, and most coins dated AH1246-1250 are of the fourth type).

TYPE V: As the third, but with title 'Keshvarsetan' (Conqueror of Nations). Used AH1245-1250.

NOTE: Due to mint carelessness, the use of old dies, and the whims of mintmasters, the above types are found dated before and after their 'official' spans of existence.

NOTE: Type I normally bears dates on obverse and reverse, quite frequently mismatched (no premium for such coins: they are almost as common as those with matched dates!). All other types are normally dated only on the reverse.

NOTE: The obverse is the side bearing the king's name and titles. The reverse is the side with the mint.

All silver coins of the first and second types are on the first Riyal Standard. The third type is divided into two subtypes: III A on the first Riyal Standard (AH1222-1232), III B on the reduced second Riyal Standard (AH1232-41). Types IV and V are on the Kran Standard.

Riyal Standard

1/6 RIYAL

SILVER
Mint: Yazd

C#	Date	Mintage	Good	VG	Fine	VF
189	AH1235	—	—	—	—	—

1/5 RIYAL

SILVER
Mint: Yazd

C#	Date	Mintage	Good	VG	Fine	VF
190	AH1233	—	—	—	—	—

1/8 RIYAL

SILVER, 1.30 g
Mint: Iravan

C#	Date	Mintage	Good	VG	Fine	VF
TYPE III A.						
191b	AH1222-32	—	4.00	7.50	12.00	25.00

SILVER, 1.15 g

C#	Date	Mintage	Good	VG	Fine	VF
TYPE III B.						
191c	AH1232-41	—	4.00	7.50	12.00	25.00

1/4 RIYAL

SILVER, 2.60 g
Mint: Tabriz

C#	Date	Mintage	Good	VG	Fine	VF
TYPE III A.						
192b	AH1222-32	—	4.00	7.50	12.00	20.00

SILVER, 2.60 g
Mint: Tabriz

Mint: Borujerd, 2.30 g

C#	Date	Mintage	Good	VG	Fine	VF
TYPE III B.						
192c	AH1232-41	—	3.00	5.50	9.00	15.00

1/2 RIYAL

SILVER, 5.20 g
Mint: Isfahan

C#	Date	Mintage	Good	VG	Fine	VF
TYPE I						
193	AH1213-17	—	7.50	12.50	20.00	30.00

W/o date.

C#	Date	Mintage	Good	VG	Fine	VF
TYPE II						
193a	AH1217-22	—	5.50	9.00	12.50	18.50

Mint: Yazd

C#	Date	Mintage	Good	VG	Fine	VF
TYPE III.A						
193b	AH1222-32	—	5.00	8.00	12.50	20.00

Mint: Kashan, 4.50 g

C#	Date	Mintage	Good	VG	Fine	VF
193c.3	AH123x	—	6.00	10.00	15.00	25.00

Mint: Tehran, 4.60 g

C#	Date	Mintage	Good	VG	Fine	VF
TYPE III.B						
193c.2	AH1232-41	—	5.00	8.00	11.00	16.50

RIYAL

SILVER, 10.40 g
Mint: Tehran

C#	Date	Mintage	Good	VG	Fine	VF
TYPE I						
194	AH1212-17	—	10.00	12.50	15.00	20.00

Mint: Khoy

C#	Date	Mintage	Good	VG	Fine	VF
TYPE II						
194a	AH1217-22	—	10.00	12.00	15.00	35.00

Mint: Isfahan

C#	Date	Mintage	Good	VG	Fine	VF
TYPE III.A						
194b	AH1222-32	—	10.00	11.50	13.50	17.50

SILVER, 9.20 g

C#	Date	Mintage	Good	VG	Fine	VF
TYPE III.B						
194c	AH1232-41	—	10.00	11.50	13.50	17.50

Kran Standard

1/8 KRAN

SILVER, 0.90 g
Mint: Khoy

TYPE IV

C#	Date	Mintage	Good	VG	Fine	VF
200	AH1241-45	—	4.00	7.00	12.00	25.00

Found both uniface and with two faces.

Mint: Isfahan

TYPE V

C#	Date	Mintage	Good	VG	Fine	VF
200a	AH1246-50	—	7.50	15.00	25.00	40.00

NOTE: Use of obsolete dated reverse die.

1/4 KRAN

SILVER, 1.70 g

TYPE IV

C#	Date	Mintage	Good	VG	Fine	VF
201	AH1241-45	—	5.00	10.00	16.50	26.50

1/2 KRAN

SILVER, 3.50 g
Mint: Kashan

TYPE IV

C#	Date	Mintage	Good	VG	Fine	VF
202	AH1241-45	—	5.00	8.00	15.00	25.00

KRAN

SILVER, 6.90 g
Mint: Hamadan

Mint: Mashad

TYPE IV

C#	Date	Mintage	Good	VG	Fine	VF
203	AH1241-45	—	7.00	9.00	11.50	17.50

Mint: Tabaristan

TYPE V

C#	Date	Mintage	Good	VG	Fine	VF
203a	AH1246-50	—	8.50	15.00	25.00	50.00

GOLD COINAGE

At present, it is not yet possible to determine which types were used with which standard. Until more research is done, and more coins are brought to light, we shall list the gold by standard. The fifth standard comes in two varieties, without *Sahibaqiran* AH1230-1241 and with *Sahibqiran* (AH1241-1245), referred to as standards 5A and 5B, respectively.

1/4 TOMAN

GOLD, 1.50 g

SECOND STANDARD

C#	Date	Mintage	VG	Fine	VF	XF
204a	AH1220-24	—	35.00	55.00	85.00	125.00

FOURTH STANDARD, Isfahan

C#	Date	Mintage	VG	Fine	VF	XF
204c	AH1228	—	35.00	55.00	85.00	125.00

GOLD, 1.15 g

FIFTH STANDARD, w/o *'Sahibqeran'* (5A)

C#	Date	Mintage	VG	Fine	VF	XF
204d.1	AH1230-41	—	35.00	55.00	85.00	125.00

FIFTH STANDARD, *'Sahibqeran'* (5B)

C#	Date	Mintage	VG	Fine	VF	XF
204d.2	AH1241-45	—	30.00	50.00	70.00	100.00

1/2 TOMAN

GOLD, 3.10 g

FIRST STANDARD

C#	Date	Mintage	VG	Fine	VF	XF
205	AH1213-17	—	65.00	80.00	100.00	125.00

2.90 g

SECOND STANDARD

C#	Date	Mintage	VG	Fine	VF	XF
205a	AH1220-24	—	65.00	80.00	100.00	125.00

2.70 g

THIRD STANDARD

C#	Date	Mintage	VG	Fine	VF	XF
205b	AH1224-27	—	70.00	85.00	110.00	140.00

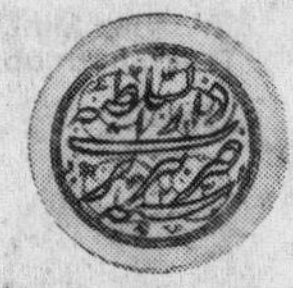

GOLD, 2.30 g
Mint: Tabriz

FIFTH STANDARD, w/o *'Sahibqiran'* (5A)

C#	Date	Mintage	VG	Fine	VF	XF
205d.1	AH1230-41	—	65.00	80.00	100.00	125.00

GOLD, 2.20 g

FIFTH STANDARD, *'Sahibqiran'* (5B)

C#	Date	Mintage	VG	Fine	VF	XF
205d.2	AH1241-45	—	70.00	85.00	110.00	140.00

1.75 g

SIXTH STANDARD, (Keshvarestan)

C#	Date	Mintage	VG	Fine	VF	XF
205e	AH1246-50	—	75.00	100.00	135.00	175.00

TOMAN

GOLD, 6.10 g
Mint: Isfahan

FIRST STANDARD

C#	Date	Mintage	VG	Fine	VF	XF
206.1	AH1213-17	—	125.00	145.00	175.00	200.00

Mint: Tehran

C#	Date	Mintage	VG	Fine	VF	XF
206.2	AH1216	—	125.00	145.00	175.00	200.00

Mint: Isfahan, 5.80 g

SECOND STANDARD

C#	Date	Mintage	VG	Fine	VF	XF
206a	AH1220-24	—	BV	90.00	100.00	150.00

5.40 g

THIRD STANDARD

C#	Date	Mintage	VG	Fine	VF	XF
206b	AH1224-27	—	BV	90.00	100.00	150.00

4.80 g

FOURTH STANDARD

C#	Date	Mintage	VG	Fine	VF	XF
206c	AH1227-29	—	BV	85.00	100.00	150.00

GOLD, 4.60 g
Mint: Borujerd

FIFTH STANDARD, w/o *'Sahibqiran'* (5A)

C#	Date	Mintage	VG	Fine	VF	XF
206d.1	AH1236	—	175.00	265.00	350.00	450.00

Mint: Eravan

C#	Date	Mintage	VG	Fine	VF	XF
206d.2	AH1230-41	—	BV	80.00	100.00	150.00

Mint: Rasht

C#	Date	Mintage	VG	Fine	VF	XF
206d.3	AH1232	—	BV	80.00	100.00	150.00

Mint: Tabriz

FIFTH STANDARD, w/o Sahibqiram (5A)

C#	Date	Mintage	VG	Fine	VF	XF
206d.4	AH1230-41	—	BV	80.00	100.00	150.00

Mint: Isfahan

FIFTH STANDARD, *'Sahibqiran'* (5B)

C#	Date	Mintage	VG	Fine	VF	XF
206d.5	AH1241-45	—	BV	80.00	100.00	150.00

Mint: Tehran, 3.50 g

SIXTH STANDARD (Keshvarsetan)

C#	Date	Mintage	VG	Fine	VF	XF
206e	AH1246-50	—	BV	75.00	100.00	150.00

Mint: Zanjan, 4.50-4.60 g

SPECIAL ISSUE: King on horseback

C#	Date	Mintage	VG	Fine	VF	XF
207	AH1236	—	650.00	1000.	1500.	2500.

Mint: Isfahan, 3.34-3.50 g

C#	Date	Mintage	VG	Fine	VF	XF
208.1	AH1245	—	1100.	1800.	2700.	4000.

C#	Date	Mintage	VG	Fine	VF	XF
208.2	AH1245	—	550.00	900.00	1350.	2000.

C#	Date	Mintage	VG	Fine	VF	XF
208.3	AH1248	—	550.00	900.00	1350.	2000.

C#	Date	Mintage	VG	Fine	VF	XF
208.4 (208.3)	AH1249	—	550.00	900.00	1350.	2000.

MINTS OF FATH'ALI SHAH

The following illustrations are of coins, mostly Riyals and Krans, for each of Fath Ali's mints. Usually only one example is shown but considerable variation exists, as die cutters emphasized artistic stylization of legends rather than standardization. In each case, the mint name, date and C# are indicated below the illustration.

Ardebil Mint, AH1245, C#203

Borujerd Mint, AH1244, C#203

Hamadan Mint, AH1250, C#203
NOTE: This AH1250 date is an example of C#203 struck five years after the introduction of C#203a.

Iravan Mint, AH1216, C#194

Isfahan Mint, AH1225, C#194b

Kashan Mint, AH1233, C#194c

Kerman Mint, AH1238, C#193c

Kermanshahan Mint, AH1233, C#194c

Lahijan Mint, AH1219, C#194a

Mashad Mint, AH1222, C#194a
Dated both obverse and reverse

Mazandaran Mint, AH1218, C#194a

Nihawand Mint, AH1242, C#203

Qazwin Mint, AH1227, C#194b

Qum Mint, AH1246, C#203

 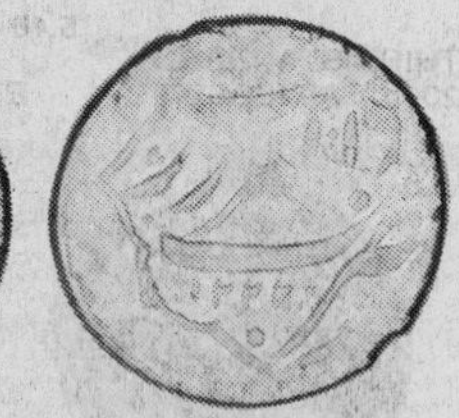
Rasht Mint, AH1222, C#194a

Shushtar Mint, AH1243, C#203

Tabaristan Mint, AH1246, C#203a

Tabriz Mint, AH1221, C#193a

Tehran Mint, AH1217, C#194a

Tuyserkan Mint, AH1241, C#203

Urumi Mint, AH1233, C#194c

Yazd Mint, AH1222, C#194b

Zanjan Mint, AH1244, C#203

For coins of Panahabad struck in the name of Fath'ali Shah, see listings under Russian Caucasia, Khanate of Karabagh.

SULTAN ALI SHAH

AH1250/1834AD
Ruled only 30 days

Silver and gold struck to Fath'ali Shah's Kran and Sixth Gold Standard, respectively. Known only from Mint of Tehran.

KRAN

SILVER, 6.90 g
Mint: Tehran

C#	Date	Mintage	VG	Fine	VF	XF
215	AH1250	—	100.00	150.00	250.00	400.00

TOMAN

GOLD, 3.50 g
Mint: Tehran

C#	Date	Mintage	VG	Fine	VF	XF
216	AH1250	—	160.00	260.00	425.00	650.00

HUSAIN ALI SHAH

AH1250/1834AD
For six months in southern Iran

Standards as for Sultan Ali mints of Kerman, Shiraz and Yazd struck silver coins. The mint at Shiraz also struck gold coins.

KRAN

SILVER, 6.90 g

C#	Date	Mintage	VG	Fine	VF	XF
219	AH1250	—	100.00	150.00	250.00	400.00

MUHAMMAD SHAH

AH1250-1264/1834-1848AD

Coinage Standards of Muhammad Shah

SILVER COINAGE

I. FIRST STANDARD AH1250-1251:
1 Kran = 1-1/2 Mesqal = 36 Nokhod
1/4 Kran 1.72 g
1/2 Kran 3.45 g
1 Kran 6.90 g

II. SECOND STANDARD, AH1252-1255:
1 Kran = 30 Nokhod
1/8 Kran 0.72 g
1/4 Kran 1.50 g
1/2 Kran 2.90 g
1 Kran 5.80 g

III. THIRD STANDARD, AH1254-1264:
1 Kran = 28 Nokhod
1/8 Kran 0.68 g
1/4 Kran 1.35 g
1/2 Kran 2.70 g
1 Kran 5.40 g
Krans 10.80 g

GOLD COINAGE

Only one standard
1 Toman = 18 Nokhod
1/4 Toman 0.90 g
1/2 Toman 1.70 g
1 Toman 3.50 g

NOTE: All coins of Muhammad Shah are essentially of a single type, with the ruler's name on the obverse, the mint & date on the reverse. The exception is the lion & sun type (C#228 below).

1/8 KRAN

SILVER, 0.72 g
Mint: Shiraz

SECOND STANDARD

C#	Date	Mintage	Good	VG	Fine	VF
224a	AH1252-55	—	4.50	8.50	15.00	25.00

0.68 g

THIRD STANDARD

C#	Date	Mintage	Good	VG	Fine	VF
224b	AH1255-64	—	4.00	8.00	13.50	22.50

1/4 KRAN

SILVER, 1.70 g
Mint: Tabriz

FIRST STANDARD

C#	Date	Mintage	Good	VG	Fine	VF
225	AH1250-51	—	5.00	10.00	17.50	27.50

1.50 g

SECOND STANDARD

C#	Date	Mintage	Good	VG	Fine	VF
225a	AH1252-55	—	4.00	8.00	13.50	22.50

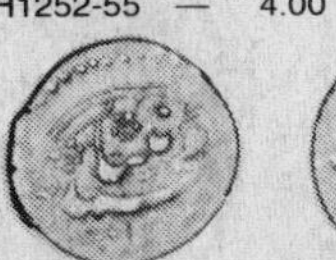

Mint: Kerman, 1.35 g

THIRD STANDARD

C#	Date	Mintage	Good	VG	Fine	VF
225b	AH1255-64	—	3.00	6.00	12.00	17.50

1/2 KRAN

SILVER, 3.50 g
Mint: Tehran

FIRST STANDARD

C#	Date	Mintage	Good	VG	Fine	VF
226	AH1250-51	—	5.00	10.00	17.50	27.50

Mint: Tabriz, 2.90 g

SECOND STANDARD

C#	Date	Mintage	Good	VG	Fine	VF
226a	AH1252-54	—	4.00	8.00	13.50	22.50

Mint: Tabaristan, 2.70 g

THIRD STANDARD

C#	Date	Mintage	Good	VG	Fine	VF
226b	AH1254-64	—	3.00	6.00	11.00	16.50

KRAN

SILVER, 6.90 g
Mint: Tabriz

FIRST STANDARD

C#	Date	Mintage	Good	VG	Fine	VF
227	AH1250-51	—	7.50	10.00	15.00	20.00

Mint: Mashad, 5.80 g

SECOND STANDARD

C#	Date	Mintage	Good	VG	Fine	VF
227a	AH1252-55	—	7.00	8.00	9.00	14.00

Mint: Isfahan, 5.40 g

THIRD STANDARD

C#	Date	Mintage	Good	VG	Fine	VF
227b	AH1254-64	—	7.00	8.00	9.00	14.00

Mint: Tehran

NOTE: Machine-milled w/obliquely reeded edge. A pattern but found circulated.

C#	Date	Mintage	Good	VG	Fine	VF
227r	AH1255	—	8.50	13.50	25.00	40.00

Lion and sun type

C#	Date	Mintage	Good	VG	Fine	VF
228	AH1258-63	—	7.50	12.50	20.00	32.50

2 KRANS

SILVER, 10.80 g
Mint: Tehran
Lion and sun type

C#	Date	Mintage	Good	VG	Fine	VF
229	AH1263	—	30.00	50.00	100.00	165.00

1/4 TOMAN

GOLD, 0.90 g

C#	Date	Mintage	VG	Fine	VF	XF
231	AH1250-64	—	45.00	70.00	100.00	135.00

1/2 TOMAN

GOLD, 1.70 g

C#	Date	Mintage	VG	Fine	VF	XF
232	AH1250-64	—	80.00	110.00	140.00	185.00

TOMAN

GOLD, 3.50 g
Mint: Mashad

C#	Date	Mintage	VG	Fine	VF	XF
233.1	AH1250-64	—	80.00	100.00	130.00	185.00

Mint: Rasht

C#	Date	Mintage	VG	Fine	VF	XF
233.2	AH1251	—	80.00	100.00	130.00	185.00

Mint: Tehran
Lion and sun type

C#	Date	Mintage	VG	Fine	VF	XF
234	AH1260-64	—	85.00	110.00	150.00	235.00

HASAN KHAN SALAR

Rebel, AH1264-1266/1848-1850AD

No coins known. Former C#241 is a coin of Muhammad Shah, dated AH1265 postumously (or error for AH1260).

NASIR AL-DIN SHAH

AH1264-1313/1848-1896AD

Coinage Standards of Nasir Al-din Shah

Hammered Coinage
AH1264-1296

SILVER COINAGE

FIRST STANDARD, AH1264-1273:
1 Kran = 28 Nokhod
1/8 Kran 0.68 g
1/4 Kran 1.35 g
1/2 Kran 2.70 g
1 Kran 5.40 g

SECOND STANDARD, AH1273-1296:
1 Kran = 26 Nokhod
1/8 Kran 0.63 g
1/4 Kran 1.30 g
1/2 Kran 2.50 g
1 Kran 5.00 g

With the introduction of machine-made coinage in AH1296/1879AD, the Kran was reduced to 24 Nokhod (4.60 g).

GOLD COINAGE

Only one standard
1 Toman = 18 Nokhod
1/4 Toman 0.86 g
1/2 Toman 1.72 g
1 Toman 3.45 g
2 Tomans 6.90 g

25 DINARS

COPPER

C#	Date	Mintage	Good	VG	Fine	VF
249	AH1271-73	—	2.00	3.00	6.00	17.00

NOTE: W/mint name. Several variations of type.

50 DINARS

(1 Shahi)

COPPER

C#	Date	Mintage	Good	VG	Fine	VF
250	AH1270-86	—	2.00	3.00	6.00	20.00

NOTE: W/o mint name.

1/8 KRAN

SILVER, uniface, 0.68 g
Mint: Rasht

FIRST STANDARD

C#	Date	Mintage	VG	Fine	VF	XF
260	AH1264-73	—	4.00	7.00	12.00	25.00

Uniface, 0.68 g
Mint: Tehran

SECOND STANDARD

C#	Date	Mintage	VG	Fine	VF	XF
260a	AH1273-94	—	3.00	6.00	10.00	17.50

1/4 KRAN

SILVER, 1.35 g
Mint: Tabriz

FIRST STANDARD

C#	Date	Mintage	VG	Fine	VF	XF
261	AH1264-73	—	3.00	6.00	9.00	15.00

Mint: Tehran

Mint: Tehran, 1.30 g

SECOND STANDARD

C#	Date	Mintage	VG	Fine	VF	XF
261a	AH1273-94	—	2.50	5.00	8.00	15.00

1/2 KRAN

SILVER
Mint: Isfahan

Mint: Khoy

Mint: Tabaristan, 2.70 g

FIRST STANDARD

C#	Date	Mintage	VG	Fine	VF	XF
262	AH1264-73	—	4.00	6.00	9.00	22.00

Mint: Astarabad

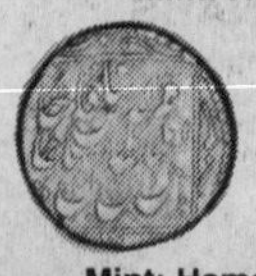 

Mint: Hamadan, 2.50 g

SECOND STANDARD

C#	Date	Mintage	VG	Fine	VF	XF
262a	AH1273-95	—	3.00	4.50	6.50	14.00

Mint: Tehran

Portrait type, 2.50 g

C#	Date	Mintage	VG	Fine	VF	XF
265	AH1273-75	—	5.00	10.00	20.00	35.00

KRAN

SILVER
Mint: Astarabad

Mint: Kerman

Mint: Astarabad

Mint: Herat, 5.40 g

FIRST STANDARD

C#	Date	Mintage	VG	Fine	VF	XF
263	AH1264-73	—	6.50	8.00	12.50	20.00

Mint: Herat

Mint: Astarabad

Mint: Hamadan

Mint: Tabriz

Mint: Tabriz, 5.00 g

SECOND STANDARD

C#	Date	Mintage	VG	Fine	VF	XF
263a	AH1273-96	—	6.50	8.00	14.00	28.00

Mint: Mashad
Toughra in wreath, 5.00 g

C#	Date	Mintage	VG	Fine	VF	XF
264.1	AH1286	—	10.00	20.00	35.00	65.00

Mashad Mint only

Plain toughra, 5.00 g

C#	Date	Mintage	VG	Fine	VF	XF
264.2	AH1287	—	10.00	20.00	35.00	65.00

Mashad Mint only

Mint: Tehran

C#	Date	Mintage	VG	Fine	VF	XF
A265.1	AH1272	—	—	—	—	—

Mint: Mashad

C#	Date	Mintage	VG	Fine	VF	XF
A265.2	AH1279	—	200.00	350.00	500.00	—

Transitional Coinage

KRAN

SILVER
Mint: Tehran
Obv: Shah's portrait facing left above wreath between Arabic leg.
Rev: Arabic leg. within wreath.

C#	Date	Mintage	VG	Fine	VF	XF
266.1	AH1272	—	100.00	250.00	400.00	650.00

Mint: Kerman
Machine-made planchet, reeded edge, 5.00 g

C#	Date	Mintage	VG	Fine	VF	XF
266.2	AH1282	—	9.00	15.00	27.50	48.00

Mint: Kermanshah, 4.60 g
Broad flan, machine-made planchet, plain edge.

C#	Date	Mintage	VG	Fine	VF	XF
266.3	AH1294	—	12.50	20.00	35.00	60.00

Mint: Yazd
Title Sahibqiran, 5.00 g

C#	Date	Mintage	VG	Fine	VF	XF
267	AH1294//1289	—	12.50	20.00	35.00	65.00

NOTE: Known only from Yazd, muled w/AH1289-dated rev.

Mint: Tehran, 5.00 g
Machine-struck (?), but crude.

C#	Date	Mintage	VG	Fine	VF	XF
268.1	AH1295	—	10.00	20.00	40.00	85.00

Rev: Crowned lion and sun, date beneath lion.

C#	Date	Mintage	VG	Fine	VF	XF
268.2	AH1295	—	10.00	20.00	40.00	85.00

Obv: Date beneath wreath.

C#	Date	Mintage	VG	Fine	VF	XF
268.3	AH1296	—	10.00	20.00	40.00	85.00

Obv: Date within wreath.

C#	Date	Mintage	VG	Fine	VF	XF
268.5	AH1295	—	10.00	20.00	40.00	85.00

Rev: Crowned mint name.

C#	Date	Mintage	VG	Fine	VF	XF
268.4	AH1296	—	20.00	35.00	50.00	95.00

NOTE: All varieties C#268 from Tehran Mint only.

1/4 TOMAN

.900 GOLD, 0.90 g

C#	Date	Mintage	VG	Fine	VF	XF
270	AH1264-93	—	50.00	80.00	110.00	150.00

1/2 TOMAN

.900 GOLD, 1.70 g
Mint: Tehran

C#	Date	Mintage	VG	Fine	VF	XF
271	AH1264-93	—	40.00	65.00	90.00	120.00

TOMAN

.900 GOLD, 3.50 g
Mint: Mashad

C#	Date	Mintage	VG	Fine	VF	XF
272.1	AH1266	—	75.00	85.00	100.00	135.00

Mint: Qazwin

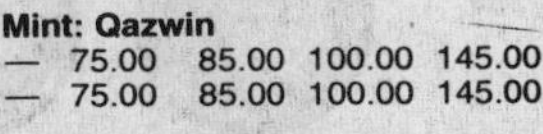

C#	Date	Mintage	VG	Fine	VF	XF
272.2	AH1267	—	75.00	85.00	100.00	145.00
	1269	—	75.00	85.00	100.00	145.00

Mint: Rasht

C#	Date	Mintage	VG	Fine	VF	XF
272.3	AH1269	—	75.00	80.00	90.00	120.00
	1277	—	75.00	80.00	90.00	120.00

Mint: Sarakhs

C#	Date	Mintage	VG	Fine	VF	XF
272.4	AH1264-94	—	75.00	80.00	90.00	120.00

Mint: Shiraz

C#	Date	Mintage	VG	Fine	VF	XF
272.5	AH1269	—	75.00	80.00	90.00	120.00

Mint: Tabriz

C#	Date	Mintage	VG	Fine	VF	XF
272.6	AH1272	—	75.00	80.00	90.00	120.00

Mint: Tehran
Obv: Facing portrait.

C#	Date	Mintage	VG	Fine	VF	XF
275.1	AH1271	—	175.00	275.00	485.00	925.00

Mint: Astarabad
Obv: Portrait left.

C#	Date	Mintage	VG	Fine	VF	XF
275.4	AH1279	—	250.00	400.00	800.00	1250.

Mint: Tehran
Obv: Portrait left.

C#	Date	Mintage	VG	Fine	VF	XF
275.2	AH1272-91	—	200.00	325.00	600.00	1100.

Mint: Isfahan

C#	Date	Mintage	VG	Fine	VF	XF
275.3	AH1274	—	250.00	400.00	800.00	1250.

2 TOMANS

.900 GOLD, 6.90 g
Mint: Kermanshah
Obv: Portrait facing.

C#	Date	Mintage	VG	Fine	VF	XF
276	AH1271	—	250.00	425.00	850.00	1700.

Mint: Mashad
Obv: Toughra.

C#	Date	Mintage	VG	Fine	VF	XF
273	AH1281	—	200.00	325.00	475.00	850.00

NOTE: This type struck at Mashad mint only.

Milled Coinage

KRAN STANDARD
AH1293-1344, SH1304-1309,
1876-1931AD

12 DINARS

(1/4 Shahi)

COPPER

Y#	Date	Mintage	Good	VG	Fine	VF
1	AH1301	—	20.00	30.00	65.00	85.00
	1303	—	30.00	40.00	75.00	100.00
	130x	—	20.00	30.00	65.00	80.00
	ND	—	15.00	25.00	35.00	60.00

25 DINARS

(1/2 Shahi)

COPPER

Y#	Date	Mintage	VG	Fine	VF	XF
2	AH1294 FP	—	10.00	15.00	30.00	50.00
	1294 w/o FP on rev.					
		—	—	25.00	40.00	75.00
	1295 FP	—	4.00	7.50	20.00	42.00
	1296	—	5.00	10.00	25.00	50.00
	1297	—	7.50	15.00	30.00	60.00
	1298	—	7.50	15.00	30.00	60.00
	1299	—	5.00	10.00	25.00	50.00
	129x	—	5.00	10.00	25.00	50.00
	1300	—	5.00	10.00	25.00	50.00
	1303	—	10.00	20.00	35.00	75.00
	ND	—	3.00	7.00	18.00	40.00

50 DINARS

(1 Shahi)

COPPER

Y#	Date	Mintage	VG	Fine	VF	XF
4	AH1293	—	30.00	45.00	70.00	125.00
	1294 FP	—	4.00	15.00	25.00	75.00
	1295 FP	—	2.00	6.00	15.00	40.00
	1296	—	2.00	6.00	15.00	40.00
	1297	—	2.00	6.00	18.00	50.00
	1298	—	8.00	15.00	35.00	75.00
	1299	—	7.00	12.00	30.00	65.00
	1300	—	2.00	6.00	15.00	40.00
	1301	—	2.00	6.00	15.00	40.00
	1302	—	8.00	15.00	35.00	75.00
	1303	—	2.00	6.00	15.00	40.00
	1304	—	8.00	15.00	35.00	75.00
	1305	—	6.00	10.00	25.00	65.00
	3301 (error) for 1303					
		—	6.00	10.00	25.00	65.00
	1330 (error) for 1303					
		—	10.00	20.00	35.00	75.00
	1792 (error) for 1297					
		—	15.00	25.00	50.00	100.00
	ND	—	4.00	10.00	25.00	50.00

NOTE: AH1293 is probably a mispunched date.

SHAHI

COPPER

Y#	Date	Mintage	Good	VG	Fine	VF
4a	AH1305	—	40.00	60.00	75.00	145.00
	ND	—	30.00	45.00	60.00	100.00

50 DINARS

COPPER-NICKEL

Y#	Date	Mintage	Fine	VF	XF	Unc
23	AH1318	10.000	.75	1.50	4.00	8.00
	1319	12.000	.75	1.50	4.00	8.00
	1321	10.000	.75	1.50	4.00	8.00
	1326	8.000	1.00	2.00	8.00	16.00
	1332	6.000	1.00	4.00	8.00	16.00
	1337	7.000	1.00	2.00	6.00	16.00

Y#	Date	Mintage	Fine	VF	XF	Unc
95	SH1305	11.000	.80	2.00	6.00	17.50
	1307	2.500	.80	2.00	6.00	17.50

100 DINARS

(2 Shahis)

صد دینار

COPPER

Y#	Date	Mintage	VG	Fine	VF	XF
5	AH1297	—	10.00	20.00	40.00	85.00
	1298	—	15.00	30.00	50.00	100.00
	1299	—	15.00	30.00	50.00	100.00
	1300	—	10.00	20.00	40.00	80.00
	1301	—	10.00	20.00	40.00	80.00
	1302	—	20.00	40.00	60.00	125.00
	1303	—	7.50	15.00	40.00	70.00
	1304	—	20.00	40.00	60.00	125.00
	1305	—	10.00	20.00	35.00	75.00
	1307	—	30.00	50.00	75.00	150.00
	1308	—	30.00	50.00	75.00	150.00
	1313	—	50.00	100.00	200.00	300.00
	1330 (error) for 1303					
		—	10.00	20.00	35.00	75.00
	ND	—	7.50	15.00	30.00	60.00

2 SHAHIS

دو شاهی

COPPER

Y#	Date	Mintage	Good	VG	Fine	VF
5a	AH1305	—	30.00	55.00	100.00	175.00
	ND	—	20.00	40.00	70.00	120.00

100 DINARS

COPPER-NICKEL

Y#	Date	Mintage	Fine	VF	XF	Unc
24	AH1318	10.000	1.75	3.00	5.00	10.00
	1319	9.000	1.00	2.50	4.00	8.00
	1321/19					
		5.000	2.50	6.00	10.00	20.00
	1321	Inc. Ab.	1.00	3.00	6.00	15.00
	1326	6.000	1.00	1.50	6.00	15.00
	1332	5.000	1.00	3.00	6.00	15.00
	1337	6.500	1.00	3.00	6.00	10.00

Y#	Date	Mintage	Fine	VF	XF	Unc
96	SH1305	4.500	1.00	2.00	5.00	20.00
	1307	3.750	1.00	2.00	5.00	25.00

200 DINARS

۲۰۰ دینار

COPPER

Y#	Date	Mintage	VG	Fine	VF	XF
6	AH1300	—	50.00	125.00	200.00	350.00
	1301	—	20.00	35.00	90.00	140.00

SHAHI SEFID

(White Shahi)

Called the White (i.e., silver) Shahi to distinguish it from the Black or Copper Shahi, the Shahi Sefid was actually worth 3 Shahis. It was used primarily for distribution on New Year's day (Now-Ruz) as good-luck gifts. Since 1926 special privately struck tokens, having no monetary value, have been used instead of coins.

The Shahi Sefid, worth 150 Dinars, was broader, but much thinner, than the 1/4 Kran (Rob'i), worth 250 Dinars.

شاهی

0.6908 g, .900 SILVER, .0200 oz ASW

Y#	Date	Mintage	VG	Fine	VF	XF
7	AH1296	—	25.00	40.00	75.00	160.00

NOTE: Date below lion instead of denomination, which is omitted.

Rev: Date below wreath.

Y#	Date	Mintage	VG	Fine	VF	XF
7a	AH1297	—	3.00	7.50	15.00	28.00
	1298	—	3.00	6.00	12.50	25.00
	1299	—	4.00	8.00	15.00	35.00
	1300	—	3.00	6.00	12.50	25.00
	1301	—	2.00	4.50	9.00	15.00
	1302	—	7.50	12.50	25.00	50.00
	1303	—	2.00	4.50	9.00	15.00
	1304	—	10.00	15.00	30.00	65.00
	1305	—	3.00	6.00	15.00	30.00
	1307/1	—	7.50	15.00	30.00	60.00
	1307	—	7.50	15.00	30.00	60.00
	1308	—	10.00	15.00	30.00	60.00
	1309/01	—	6.00	15.00	30.00	60.00
	1309	—	6.00	15.00	30.00	60.00
	'13' only	—	10.00	20.00	40.00	90.00
	ND	—	2.00	5.00	10.00	30.00

Rev: Date amidst lion's legs.
(Variations exist)

Y#	Date	Mintage	VG	Fine	VF	XF
7b	AH1313	—	20.00	35.00	60.00	100.00
	1--3	—	20.00	35.00	60.00	100.00

Obv. leg: *Nasir al-din* (Y#7a).
Rev. leg: *Sahib al-zaman* (Obv. of Y#B44).

Y#	Date	Mintage	VG	Fine	VF	XF
8	ND	—	25.00	50.00	75.00	125.00

Obv. leg: *Muzaffar al-din Shah*.

Y#	Date	Mintage	VG	Fine	VF	XF
25	AH1313	—	—	—	Rare	—
	1314	—	10.00	20.00	40.00	75.00
	1315	—	10.00	20.00	40.00	75.00
	1316	—	10.00	20.00	40.00	75.00
	1317	—	15.00	25.00	50.00	100.00
	1318	—	8.00	15.00	30.00	60.00
	1319	—	8.00	15.00	30.00	60.00
	1320	.150	8.00	15.00	30.00	60.00
	8310 (error)		8.00	15.00	30.00	60.00
	1039 (error)		15.00	25.00	50.00	100.00
	ND	—	4.00	8.00	20.00	40.00

Mule. Obv: Y#25. Rev: Y#7b.

Y#	Date	Mintage	VG	Fine	VF	XF
25.1	AH1313	—	20.00	40.00	75.00	165.00

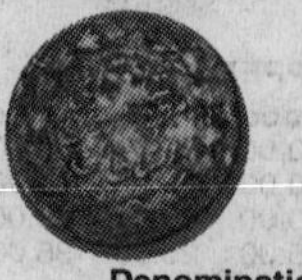

Denomination omitted

Y#	Date	Mintage	VG	Fine	VF	XF
25a	AH1319	—	—	—	Rare	—
	ND	—	25.00	50.00	80.00	165.00

NOTE: A number of varieties and mulings of Y#25 and Y#25a with other denominations, esp. 1/4 Krans and 500 Dinar pieces, are reported. These command a premium over others of the same types.

NOTE: Many Shahis of Muzaffar al-din are muled with reverses of Nasir al-din, especially with date 1301 and 1303. Worth $15 in Fine, $25.00 in VF. Many also have the Mouzaffer date of issue engraved amid the legs of old Nasir dies from which the date beneath the wreath wasn't removed. No premium for those showing old Nasir dates.

NOTE: A total of 58,000 pieces were reported struck in AH1322, 1323 and 1324, but none are known with those dates. The specimens were either struck from old dies or were undated types.

Obv. leg: *Muzaftar al-din Shah.*
Rev. leg: *Sahib al-Zaman.*

Y#	Date	Mintage	VG	Fine	VF	XF
A25	ND	—	25.00	50.00	85.00	165.00

NOTE: Two varieties are known with thick and thin script lettering.

Obv. leg: *Muhammad Ali Shah.*

Y#	Date	Mintage	VG	Fine	VF	XF
44	AH1325	—	15.00	30.00	60.00	110.00
	1326	—	10.00	16.00	32.00	65.00
	1327	—	8.00	12.00	25.00	52.00

Obv. leg: *Sahib al-Zaman.*

Y#	Date	Mintage	VG	Fine	VF	XF
B44	AH1326	—	40.00	60.00	125.00	175.00

Obv. Y#44. Rev: Obv. of Y#B44.

Y#	Date	Mintage	VG	Fine	VF	XF
A44	ND	—	30.00	50.00	80.00	150.00

Obv. leg: *Ahmad Shah.*
Rev: Date below wreath.

Y#	Date	Mintage	VG	Fine	VF	XF
64	AH1328	—	3.00	5.00	10.00	20.00
	1329	—	3.00	6.00	12.00	25.00
	1330	.189	2.00	4.00	10.00	20.00

Rev: Date amidst lion's legs.

Y#	Date	Mintage	VG	Fine	VF	XF
A64	AH1332	.010	20.00	30.00	50.00	85.00

Obv. leg: *Ahmad Shah.*
Rev. leg: *Sahib-al-Zaman.*

Y#	Date	Mintage	VG	Fine	VF	XF
B64	ND	—	40.00	60.00	125.00	200.00

Y#	Date	Mintage	VG	Fine	VF	XF
A70	AH1333	.078	2.00	5.00	10.00	20.00
	1334	.006	4.00	12.00	20.00	40.00
	1335	.073	3.00	8.00	15.00	30.00
	1335 dated 1337 on rev. amid legs					
		Inc. Ab.	20.00	40.00	80.00	165.00
	1337	.076	3.00	8.00	15.00	30.00
	1337 also dated on rev.					
		—	20.00	40.00	75.00	150.00
	1339	.010	4.00	12.00	20.00	40.00
	1342	.020	4.00	12.00	20.00	40.00

NOTE: Varieties exist.

Obv: Y#A70. Rev. leg: *Sahib-al-Zaman.*

Y#	Date	Mintage	VG	Fine	VF	XF
A70a	AH1335	—	30.00	50.00	80.00	150.00

NOTE: Mintage included in Y#A70 of AH1335.

Obv. leg: ***Sahib al-Zaman.***

Y#	Date	Mintage	VG	Fine	VF	XF
B70	AH1332	Inc. Y#A64	5.00	10.00	18.00	35.00
	1333	Inc. Y#A70	5.00	10.00	20.00	40.00
	1337	Inc. Y#A70	5.00	10.00	20.00	40.00
	1341	.003	10.00	15.00	25.00	50.00
	1342	Inc. Y#A70	10.00	15.00	25.00	50.00
	ND	—	5.00	10.00	20.00	40.00

Obv: Y#A70 dated AH1339. Rev: Similar to Y#B70 w/AH1341 between lions legs, AH1327 below wreath.

Y#	Date	Mintage	VG	Fine	VF	XF
D70	AH1339//1341-1327	—	30.00	50.00	80.00	150.00

NOTE: Numerous silver Now Ruz tokens, some with dates 1329-1331, are available in Tehran for a fraction of the price of true Shahis.

1/4 KRAN

(Rob'i = 5 Shahis)

ربعی

1.1513 g, .900 SILVER, 15mm, .0333 oz ASW
Rev: Date below wreath.

Y#	Date	Mintage	VG	Fine	VF	XF
9	AH1294	—	30.00	50.00	100.00	175.00
	1296	—	4.00	7.00	15.00	30.00
	1297	—	10.00	20.00	40.00	75.00
	1298	—	10.00	20.00	30.00	50.00
	1299	—	5.00	8.00	20.00	40.00
	1300	—	4.00	7.00	15.00	30.00
	1301	—	3.00	6.00	14.00	30.00
	1303	—	3.00	6.00	14.00	30.00
	1304	—	20.00	40.00	60.00	125.00
	1305	—	8.00	15.00	25.00	50.00
	1306	—	7.00	12.50	20.00	50.00
	1307	—	20.00	40.00	60.00	135.00
	1308	—	20.00	40.00	60.00	135.00
	1309	—	15.00	25.00	50.00	100.00
	1310	—	— Reported, not confirmed			
	1311	—	20.00	40.00	60.00	135.00
	ND	—	3.00	6.00	15.00	25.00

NOTE: Many examples of Y#9 bear broken or partial dates. These command no premium.

Rev: Date amidst legs.

Y#	Date	Mintage	VG	Fine	VF	XF
9d	AH1311	—	20.00	40.00	75.00	160.00
	1312	—	20.00	40.00	75.00	160.00
	1313	—	25.00	50.00	100.00	185.00

Obv. leg: ***Muzaffar al-din Shah.***

Y#	Date	Mintage	VG	Fine	VF	XF
26	AH1314	—	30.00	50.00	100.00	200.00
	1316	—	6.00	12.50	20.00	35.00
	1318	—	15.00	25.00	50.00	85.00
	1319	—	12.50	20.00	35.00	65.00
	ND	—	3.00	8.00	15.00	28.00

NOTE: 300 specimens reportedly struck in AH1322, but none known to exist.

Obv. leg: ***Muhammad Ali Shah.***

Y#	Date	Mintage	VG	Fine	VF	XF
45	AH1325	—	20.00	30.00	50.00	100.00
	1326	—	7.50	15.00	27.50	40.00
	1327	—	5.00	10.00	20.00	35.00

Obv. leg: ***Ahmad Shah.***

Y#	Date	Mintage	VG	Fine	VF	XF
65	AH1327	—	3.00	5.00	10.00	20.00
	1328	—	2.00	4.00	7.50	15.00
	1329	.130	7.50	12.50	20.00	40.00
	1330	.156	2.00	4.00	7.50	15.00
	1331	.030	—	—	—	—
	1313 (error for 1331)	Inc. Ab.	—	—	—	—

Rev: Date amidst legs.

Y#	Date	Mintage	VG	Fine	VF	XF
C70.1	AH1332	.252	2.00	5.00	10.00	20.00
(Y-C70)	1333	Inc. Ab.	3.00	6.00	12.00	25.00
	1334	.070	5.00	10.00	20.00	50.00
	1335	.260	2.00	4.00	8.00	15.00
	1336	.160	2.00	4.00	8.00	15.00
	1337	.080	3.00	6.00	12.00	25.00
	1339	.028	4.00	9.00	15.00	30.00
	1341	.022	5.00	12.00	20.00	40.00
	1342	.110	3.00	6.00	12.00	25.00
	1343	.186	2.00	4.00	8.00	15.00

Mule. Obv: Y#C70.1. Rev: Y#45.

Y#	Date	Mintage	VG	Fine	VF	XF
C70.2	AH1327	—	30.00	60.00	125.00	175.00
	ND	—	20.00	40.00	60.00	115.00

Obv: Y#C70, date below wreath.

Y#	Date	Mintage	VG	Fine	VF	XF
C70.3	AH1334					
(Y-C70a)		Inc. Y#C70.1	40.00	75.00	150.00	250.00

Y#	Date	Mintage	VG	Fine	VF	XF
100	SH1304	*.024	7.50	20.00	50.00	85.00
	1315	.600	1.00	2.00	3.00	6.00

NOTE: 8,000 reported struck in 1305, but that year not yet found and presumed not to exist. It seems certain that the 1315 dated coins with a short second 1 is in fact the missing 1305 date.

500 DINARS

(10 Shahis = 1/2 Kran)

First Nasir al-din legend Second Nasir al-din legend with ***Sahibqiran*** **added**

Forms of the denomination:

500 DINARS: ۵۰۰ دینار

or

پانصد دینار

10 SHAHIS: ده شاهی

2.3025 g, .900 SILVER, .0666 oz ASW
First leg: ***500 Dinars***

Y#	Date	Mintage	VG	Fine	VF	XF
10	AH1296	—	— Reported, not confirmed			
	1297	—	8.00	15.00	30.00	70.00
	1298	—	8.00	15.00	30.00	70.00
	1299	—	— Reported, not confirmed			
	1301	—	7.00	25.00	55.00	120.00
	1306	—	7.00	15.00	35.00	100.00
	1307	—	50.00	85.00	175.00	350.00
	1311	—	25.00	40.00	75.00	140.00
	ND	—	4.00	7.50	15.00	30.00

NOTE: The undated issue is often found in higher grades than dated coins.

First leg: ***10 Shahis***
Rev: Date amid legs.

Y#	Date	Mintage	VG	Fine	VF	XF
10b	AH1310	—	40.00	75.00	150.00	275.00

Second leg: ***10 Shahis***
Obv: Crown added above leg.
Rev: Date amid legs.

Y#	Date	Mintage	VG	Fine	VF	XF
10c	AH1310	—	30.00	60.00	125.00	200.00
	1311	—	30.00	60.00	125.00	200.00

First leg: ***500 Dinars***
Rev: Date amid legs.

Y#	Date	Mintage	VG	Fine	VF	XF
10d	AH1311	—	25.00	50.00	80.00	160.00
	1312	—	20.00	40.00	65.00	110.00
	1313	—	25.00	50.00	80.00	160.00

Second leg: ***500 Dinars***
Nasir al-din's Return From Europe

Y#	Date	Mintage	VG	Fine	VF	XF
A15	AH1307	—	50.00	100.00	215.00	325.00
	1307 w/1306 on rev.	—	100.00	200.00	300.00	525.00

Obv. leg: ***Muzaffar al-din, 500 Dinars.***
Rev: Date amid legs, arranged variously.

Y#	Date	Mintage	VG	Fine	VF	XF
27.1	AH1313	—	25.00	40.00	75.00	150.00
(Y27)	1314	—	10.00	20.00	40.00	100.00
	1315	—	25.00	40.00	75.00	150.00
	1316	—	25.00	40.00	75.00	150.00
	1317	—	— Reported, not confirmed			
	1318	—	15.00	30.00	50.00	125.00
	1319	—	12.50	20.00	40.00	100.00
	1322	—	10.00	20.00	30.00	50.00
	ND	—	5.00	10.00	20.00	35.00

Mule. Obv: Y#27.1. Rev: Y#10.

Y#	Date	Mintage	VG	Fine	VF	XF
27.2	AH1298	—	50.00	100.00	150.00	250.00

Y#	Date	Mintage	VG	Fine	VF	XF
30	AH1323	.130	22.50	35.00	50.00	125.00

Obv. leg: ***Muhammad Ali Shah.***

Y#	Date	Mintage	VG	Fine	VF	XF
46	AH1325	.218	20.00	40.00	75.00	160.00
	1326	.218	15.00	25.00	50.00	110.00
	1336 (error for 1326)	Inc. Ab.	20.00	35.00	60.00	125.00

Obv: Date.

Y#	Date	Mintage	VG	Fine	VF	XF
48	AH1326	Inc. Y46	20.00	40.00	85.00	150.00
	1327	—	20.00	40.00	85.00	150.00

Obv: Y#48. Rev: Y#46.
Obv. and rev: Date.

Y#	Date	Mintage	VG	Fine	VF	XF
48a	AH1325	—	75.00	125.00	175.00	320.00
	1326	—	60.00	100.00	150.00	240.00

Obv. leg: *Ahmad Shah.*

Y#	Date	Mintage	VG	Fine	VF	XF
66	AH1327	—	5.00	10.00	20.00	35.00
	1328	—	5.00	10.00	15.00	30.00
	1329	.044	10.00	15.00	25.00	50.00
	1330	.627	5.00	10.00	20.00	35.00

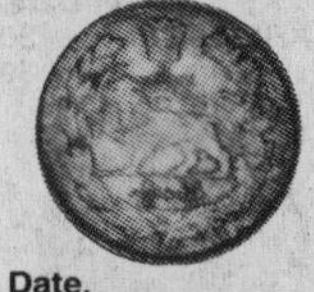

Obv: Date.

Y#	Date	Mintage	VG	Fine	VF	XF
70	AH1331	Inc. 1330	1.50	3.00	6.00	15.00
	1332	.560	1.00	2.00	5.00	10.00
	1333	.292	1.00	2.00	5.00	10.00
	1334	.065	1.50	3.00	6.00	12.00
	1335	.150	4.00	8.00	15.00	30.00
	1336	.240	2.50	4.00	8.00	20.00
	1339	—	10.00	17.50	25.00	40.00
	1343	.160	3.00	6.00	10.00	25.00

NOTE: 10,000 reported struck in AH1337 probably dated AH1336.

Obv. and rev: Date.

Y#	Date	Mintage	VG	Fine	VF	XF
70a	AH1332	Inc. Y70	15.00	30.00	50.00	90.00

Y#	Date	Mintage	Fine	VF	XF	Unc
A101	SH1304	—	130.00	180.00	375.00	675.00

Obv. leg: *Reza Shah.*

Y#	Date	Mintage	Fine	VF	XF	Unc
105	SH1305	.010	45.00	75.00	150.00	250.00

Y#	Date	Mintage	Fine	VF	XF	Unc
A109	SH1306	.005	40.00	60.00	85.00	120.00
	1307	.046	7.50	15.00	20.00	35.00
	1308	.464	7.50	15.00	20.00	35.00

NOTE: Some of the coins reported in AH1308 were dated 1307.

1000 DINARS

(Kran)

Forms of the denomination:

1000 DINARS: يكهزار دينار

1 KRAN: يكقران

4.6050 g, .900 SILVER, .1332 oz ASW
Obv. leg: *Nasir al-din Shah*, first leg.,

1000 Dinars

Y#	Date	Mintage	Fine	VF	XF	Unc
11	AH1295	—	—	—	300.00	400.00
	1296	—	4.00	8.00	20.00	55.00
	1297	—	5.00	10.00	25.00	60.00
	1298/7	—	10.00	20.00	40.00	80.00
	1298	—	10.00	20.00	40.00	80.00
	12—	—	4.00	8.00	25.00	60.00
	129x	—	4.00	8.00	25.00	60.00
	ND	—	4.00	10.00	25.00	60.00

Obv: Second leg, *1000 Dinars*

Y#	Date	Mintage	Fine	VF	XF	Unc
11a	AH1298	—	5.00	10.00	25.00	60.00
	1299	—	10.00	20.00	50.00	90.00
	129x	—	10.00	20.00	50.00	90.00
	1301	—	—	—	—	—
	1303	—	150.00	250.00	500.00	600.00
	ND	—	5.00	10.00	25.00	45.00

Obv: Second leg, *1 Kran*, crown above.

Y#	Date	Mintage	Fine	VF	XF	Unc
11c	AH1310	—	100.00	150.00	250.00	425.00
	1311	—	60.00	125.00	225.00	375.00

Obv: Second leg, *1 Kran*, w/o crown.

Y#	Date	Mintage	Fine	VF	XF	Unc
11b	AH1311	—	100.00	150.00	250.00	—

Obv: Second leg., *1000 Dinars*, w/o crown.

Y#	Date	Mintage	Fine	VF	XF	Unc
11d	AH1311	—	90.00	135.00	225.00	—
	1312	—	100.00	150.00	250.00	—

Obv. leg: *Muzaffar al-din Shah*, w/o crown.

Y#	Date	Mintage	Fine	VF	XF	Unc
A27	AH1314	—	125.00	200.00	400.00	—

Obv: Crown added above leg.

Y#	Date	Mintage	Fine	VF	XF	Unc
A27a	AH1317	—	100.00	175.00	250.00	—
	1318	—	100.00	175.00	250.00	—
	1319	—	150.00	225.00	350.00	—
	1322	—	75.00	150.00	225.00	—

Mule. Obv: Y#A27a. Rev: Y#11a.

Y#	Date	Mintage	Fine	VF	XF	Unc
B27a	AH1303	—	—	—	Rare	—

Mule. Obv: Y#A27a. Rev: Y#11d.

Y#	Date	Mintage	Fine	VF	XF	Unc
B27b	AH1312	—	—	—	Rare	—

Y#	Date	Mintage	Fine	VF	XF	Unc
31	AH1323	.125	20.00	30.00	65.00	125.00

Obv. leg: *Muhammad Ali Shah.*

Y#	Date	Mintage	Fine	VF	XF	Unc
A47	AH1325	.289	150.00	300.00	600.00	—
	1326	.289	150.00	300.00	600.00	—

Obv: Date.

Y#	Date	Mintage	Fine	VF	XF	Unc
49	AH1326	Inc. Y-A47	50.00	100.00	175.00	450.00
	1327	—	50.00	100.00	175.00	450.00

Obv: Y#49. Rev: Y#47.
Obv. and rev: Date.

Y#	Date	Mintage	Fine	VF	XF	Unc
49a	AH1326	Inc.Y47	125.00	200.00	350.00	—

Transitional Issue
Obv: Y#67. Rev: Y#49a.

Y#	Date	Mintage	Fine	VF	XF	Unc
A71	AH1326	—	—	—	Rare	—

Obv. leg: *Ahmad Shah.*

Y#	Date	Mintage	Fine	VF	XF	Unc
67	AH1327	—	15.00	25.00	40.00	70.00
	1328	—	4.00	8.00	25.00	65.00
	1329	3.000	4.00	8.00	25.00	65.00
	1330	—	4.00	8.00	25.00	65.00

24mm

Y#	Date	Mintage	Fine	VF	XF	Unc
67a	AH1330	—	3.50	7.00	18.00	30.00
	1330	—	—	Proof	Rare	

NOTE: Y#67a differs from Y#67 in that it is about 1mm broader and has a much thicker rim and more clearly defined denticles. Struck in Germany, without Iranian authorization, for circulation in western Iran during World War I.) Also, the lion lacks the triangular face & fierce expression of Y#67 and the point of the Talwar (scimitar) does not touch the sunburst as it does on Tehran issues.

23mm

Y#	Date	Mintage	Fine	VF	XF	Unc
71	AH1330 (error) for 1340	—	30.00	65.00	125.00	175.00
	1331	1.310	5.00	8.00	25.00	40.00
	1332	1.891	3.00	5.00	12.50	30.00
	1333	2.179	7.50	12.00	25.00	40.00
	1334	1.273	3.00	5.00	12.50	25.00
	1335	2.162	3.00	5.00	12.50	25.00
	1336	1.412	3.50	6.00	15.00	30.00
	1337	3.330	3.00	5.00	12.50	25.00
	1339	.035	12.50	25.00	55.00	90.00
	1340	.028	15.00	30.00	60.00	100.00
	1341	.170	8.00	15.00	35.00	60.00
	1342	.255	3.00	6.00	20.00	30.00
	1343	1.345	3.00	6.00	20.00	30.00
	1344	2.978	4.00	6.00	20.00	35.00

10th Year of Reign

Y#	Date	Mintage	Fine	VF	XF	Unc
73	AH1337	.975	40.00	65.00	130.00	210.00

Y#	Date	Mintage	Fine	VF	XF	Unc
101	SH1304	2.573	3.00	5.00	10.00	20.00
	1305	2.265	4.00	7.00	12.50	25.00

Obv. leg: *Reza Shah.*

Y#	Date	Mintage	Fine	VF	XF	Unc
106	SH1305	Inc.Y101	3.00	5.00	10.00	20.00
	1306/5	3.130	5.00	8.00	15.00	25.00
	1306	Inc. Ab.	3.00	5.00	10.00	20.00

Y#	Date	Mintage	Fine	VF	XF	Unc
109	SH1306	Inc.Y106	4.00	8.00	15.00	30.00
	1307	4.300	4.00	6.00	10.00	20.00
	1308	.603	4.00	6.00	10.00	20.00

2000 DINARS

(2 Krans)

Forms of the denomination:

2 KRANS: دو قران

2000 DINARS: دو هزار دینار

9.2100 g, .900 SILVER, .2665 oz ASW
Obv. leg: *Nasir al-din Shah*, first leg., *2000 Dinars*

Y#	Date	Mintage	Fine	VF	XF	Unc
12	AH1296	—	10.00	20.00	50.00	120.00
	1297	—	8.00	15.00	35.00	95.00
	1298/7	—	15.00	30.00	60.00	110.00
	1298	—	15.00	30.00	60.00	110.00
	ND	—	7.00	15.00	35.00	85.00

Obv: Second leg., *2000 Dinars*

Y#	Date	Mintage	Fine	VF	XF	Unc
12a	AH1298	—	10.00	20.00	50.00	110.00
	1299	—	12.50	25.00	60.00	120.00
	1299 B on rev.	—	—	—	Rare	—
	1300	—	10.00	20.00	50.00	110.00
	1301	—	12.50	25.00	60.00	120.00
	1302	—	20.00	40.00	75.00	140.00
	1303	—	20.00	40.00	75.00	140.00
	1304	—	20.00	40.00	75.00	140.00
	1305	—	10.00	20.00	50.00	110.00
	1306	—	20.00	40.00	75.00	140.00
	1307	—	25.00	50.00	100.00	—
	1308	—	25.00	50.00	100.00	—
	ND	—	10.00	20.00	50.00	110.00

NOTE: All dates after AH1301 were struck from worn dies and hence incomplete even in high grades.

NOTE: Coins dated AH1300-1305 show a 'b' to the lower left obv., often missing on poorly struck specimens or specimens from filled dies.

Obv: Second leg., *2 Krans*.
Rev: Crown above date below wreath.

Y#	Date	Mintage	Fine	VF	XF	Unc
12b.1	AH1310 (in blundered form as 13010)	—	100.00	150.00	300.00	—

Obv: W/o crown above *2 Krans*.

Y#	Date	Mintage	Fine	VF	XF	Unc
12b.2	AH1310 (in blundered form as 13010)	—	100.00	150.00	300.00	—

Obv: Second leg., *2 Krans*, w/o crown.

Rev: Date amid legs.

Y#	Date	Mintage	Fine	VF	XF	Unc
12c.1	AH1311	—	100.00	150.00	300.00	—

Obv: Crown.

Y#	Date	Mintage	Fine	VF	XF	Unc
12c.2	AH1310	—	40.00	75.00	125.00	—
	1311	—	30.00	60.00	100.00	—

Obv: W/o crown above *2000 Dinars*.

Y#	Date	Mintage	Fine	VF	XF	Unc
12d	AH1311	—	40.00	75.00	150.00	—
	1312	—	40.00	75.00	150.00	—

50th Year of Reign
Special leg: *Dhu'l-Qarneyn*.

Y#	Date	Mintage	Fine	VF	XF	Unc
C15	AH1313	—	1150.	2250.	5000.	—

NOTE: This coin was struck in quantity and was due to be released at Nasir's 50th anniversary as a largesse piece. A number of specimens were passed out to persons close to the royal court before the celebration which accounts for the few known today. Nasir al-din was assassinated just before the fiftieth year of his reign began and the balance of the issue was melted.

Mule. Obv: Y#C15. Rev: Y#12d.

Y#	Date	Mintage	Fine	VF	XF	Unc
12e	AH1313/1312	2 known	—	2500.	—	—

Obv. leg: *Muzaffar al-din Shah*, w/o crown, leg: *2000 Dinars*.

Y#	Date	Mintage	Fine	VF	XF	Unc
28	AH1313	—	100.00	150.00	250.00	—
	1314	—	75.00	125.00	225.00	—

Obv: Crown added, leg: *2000 Dinars*.
Rev: Position of date amid legs varies.

Y#	Date	Mintage	Fine	VF	XF	Unc
28a	AH1314	—	30.00	50.00	125.00	225.00
	1315	—	20.00	35.00	75.00	150.00
	1316	—	15.00	25.00	65.00	130.00
	1317	—	15.00	25.00	65.00	130.00
	1318	—	15.00	25.00	60.00	120.00
	1319	—	15.00	25.00	60.00	120.00
	1320	13.959	12.00	20.00	45.00	110.00

NOTE: Blundered dates exist.

Mule. Obv: Y#28a. Rev: Y#12d.

Y#	Date	Mintage	Fine	VF	XF	Unc
28c	AH1312	—	—	—	Rare	—

Obv. leg: *2 Krans*.

Y#	Date	Mintage	Fine	VF	XF	Unc
28b	AH1320	Inc. Ab.	15.00	25.00	50.00	100.00
	1321 (always '13201')	18.108	15.00	25.00	50.00	100.00
	1322	8.640	8.00	15.00	30.00	80.00

Y#	Date	Mintage	Fine	VF	XF	Unc
32	AH1323	Inc. 1322	15.00	30.00	60.00	120.00
	'13'*	—	60.00	100.00	200.00	—

*23 of 1323 filled in or never punched

Obv. leg: *Muhammad Ali Shah*, *2 Krans*

Y#	Date	Mintage	Fine	VF	XF	Unc
47	AH1325	3.076	15.00	25.00	50.00	100.00
	1326	3.069	7.50	11.50	20.00	50.00
	1327	—	7.50	11.50	20.00	50.00

Portrait of Shah.

Y#	Date	Mintage	Fine	VF	XF	Unc
50	AH1326	Inc. Y47	1200.	1600.	2000.	—

Obv. leg: *Ahmad Shah*, date below wreath, *2 Krans*.

Y#	Date	Mintage	Fine	VF	XF	Unc
68	AH1327	Inc. 1328	3.00	5.00	10.00	30.00
	1328	30.000	3.00	5.00	10.00	20.00
	1329	29.250	3.00	5.00	10.00	20.00

Obv: Date below wreath, *2000 Dinars*, Tehran Mint. Rev: Fierce, triangular face on lion.

Y#	Date	Mintage	Fine	VF	XF	Unc
68a.1	AH1330	2.901	5.00	8.00	15.00	35.00

Berlin Mint. Rev: Lion's face has friendly expression.

Y#	Date	Mintage	Fine	VF	XF	Unc
68a.2	AH1330	—	4.00	7.00	10.00	27.00

Rev: Date amid legs, *2000 Dinars*.

Y#	Date	Mintage	Fine	VF	XF	Unc
68b	AH1330	Inc.Y68a	4.00	7.00	10.00	30.00
	1331	13.412	5.00	10.00	17.00	40.00

Y#	Date	Mintage	Fine	VF	XF	Unc
72	AH1330 (error) for 1340	Inc. Y68a	50.00	100.00	150.00	250.00
	1331	Inc. Y68b	6.00	12.50	25.00	50.00
	1332	12.926	5.00	10.00	16.00	32.00
	1333	Inc. Ab.	5.00	7.50	15.00	30.00

Y#	Date	Mintage	Fine	VF	XF	Unc
72	1334	4.299	5.00	7.50	15.00	30.00
	1335	9.777	5.00	7.50	15.00	30.00
	1336	5.401	5.00	7.50	15.00	30.00
	1337	2.951	5.00	7.50	15.00	30.00
	1339	1.085	6.00	12.50	25.00	50.00
	1340	.254	9.00	15.00	30.00	65.00
	1341	4.460	5.00	7.50	15.00	30.00
	1342	2.245	5.00	8.00	20.00	35.00
	1343	5.205	5.00	8.00	20.00	35.00
	1344/34	12,354	—	—	—	—
	1344	Inc. Ab.	6.00	10.00	20.00	40.00

GOLD, 14.00 g

Y#	Date	Mintage	Fine	VF	XF	Unc
72a	AH1337	—	—	600.00	850.00	1200.

9.2100 g, .900 SILVER, .2665 oz ASW
10th Anniversary of Reign

Y#	Date	Mintage	Fine	VF	XF	Unc
74	AH1337	3.503	30.00	50.00	150.00	285.00

Y#	Date	Mintage	Fine	VF	XF	Unc
102	SH1304	11.920	5.00	8.00	12.00	25.00
	1305	9.785	5.00	8.00	12.00	25.00

Rev: Date below bow.

Y#	Date	Mintage	Fine	VF	XF	Unc
107	SH1305	Inc.Y102	5.00	10.00	20.00	30.00
	1306	9.380	4.00	6.00	12.50	25.00

Mule. Obv: Y#110. Rev: Y#72.

Y#	Date	Mintage	Fine	VF	XF	Unc
A110	SH1306	—	—	—	Rare	—

Y#	Date	Mintage	Fine	VF	XF	Unc
110	SH1306	Inc.Y107	4.00	6.00	12.50	22.00
	1306	—	—	—	Proof	375.00
	1306H	11.714	3.00	5.00	10.00	20.00
	1306L	7.500	3.00	5.00	8.00	15.00
	1307	11.146	3.00	6.00	15.00	25.00
	1308	1.611	4.00	10.00	20.00	30.00

5000 DINARS

(5 Krans)

23.0251 g, .900 SILVER, .6662 oz ASW
Nasir al-Din Shah

Y#	Date	Mintage	Fine	VF	XF	Unc
13	AH1296	—	100.00	150.00	275.00	425.00
	1297	—	90.00	110.00	250.00	400.00

Obv: Crown above leg., value: *5 Krans*.

Y#	Date	Mintage	Fine	VF	XF	Unc
13c	AH1311	—	1500.	2500.	5000.	—

Muzaffar al-din Shah

Y#	Date	Mintage	Fine	VF	XF	Unc
29	AH1320	.250	8.00	14.00	20.00	25.00

NOTE: Actual mintage must be considerably greater. Struck in Leningrad.

Royal Birthday

Y#	Date	Mintage	Fine	VF	XF	Unc
A40	AH1322	—	350.00	750.00	1150.	—

Obv: W/o additional inscriptions flanking head.

Y#	Date	Mintage	Fine	VF	XF	Unc
33	AH1324	3,000	650.00	1400.	2250.	—

Muhammad Ali Shah

Y#	Date	Mintage	Fine	VF	XF	Unc
A50	AH1327	—	600.00	1350.	2000.	—

Ahmad Shah

Y#	Date	Mintage	Fine	VF	XF	Unc
69	AH1331	—	60.00	150.00	250.00	500.00
	1332	3.000	8.00	12.00	30.00	85.00
	1333	.667	10.00	15.00	35.00	90.00
	1334	.443	10.00	15.00	35.00	90.00
	1335	1.884	10.00	15.00	35.00	90.00
	1337	.165	12.00	25.00	55.00	110.00
	1339	.090	12.00	25.00	55.00	110.00
	1340	.303	12.00	25.00	55.00	110.00
	1341	.757	10.00	15.00	35.00	90.00
	1342/32	.546	10.00	15.00	35.00	90.00
	1342	Inc. Ab.	10.00	15.00	35.00	90.00
	1343	.935	10.00	15.00	35.00	90.00
	1344/34	2.284	10.00	15.00	30.00	85.00
	1344	Inc. Ab.	15.00	20.00	40.00	95.00

NOTE: Beware of altered date 1331 specimens. Specimens are known dated AH1338 but are believed to be 1337 dated with the 7 inverted. (9000 reported minted in AH1336, but probably dated earlier).

Reza Shah Pahlavi

Y#	Date	Mintage	Fine	VF	XF	Unc
103	SH1304	.500	15.00	25.00	40.00	80.00
	1305	1.363	20.00	30.00	50.00	90.00

Y#	Date	Mintage	Fine	VF	XF	Unc
108	SH1305	Inc.Y103	15.00	25.00	50.00	100.00
	1306	3.186	15.00	25.00	40.00	85.00

Mule. Obv: Y#111. Rev: Y#69.

Y#	Date	Mintage	Fine	VF	XF	Unc
A111	SH1306	—	—	—	Rare	—

Y#	Date	Mintage	Fine	VF	XF	Unc
111	SH1306	Inc.Y108	9.00	12.50	20.00	37.50
	1306	—	—	—	Proof	400.00
	1306H	4.711	6.00	10.00	17.50	32.50
	1306L	3.000	6.00	7.50	30.00	45.00
	1307	3.928	6.00	7.50	15.00	30.00
	1308	.584	20.00	30.00	50.00	100.00

NOTE: Mint marks located as on 2000 Dinars Y#110.

GOLD COINAGE

NOTE: Modern imitations exist of many types, particularly the small 1/5, 1/2 and 1 Toman coins. These are usually underweight (or rarely overweight), and are sold in the bazaars at a small premium over bullion. They are usually crude and probably not intended to deceive collectors, but as a convenient form of bullion. Some are dated outside the reign of the ruler whose name or portrait they bear.

A few deceptive counterfeits are known of the large 10 Toman pieces. Many of the larger pieces are medals, which have been mistaken for coins.

2000 DINARS

(1/5 Toman)

.6520 g, .900 GOLD, .0188 oz AGW
Obv. leg: First Nasir type. Rev: Lion and sun.

Y#	Date	Mintage	Fine	VF	XF	Unc
A16	AH1295	—	125.00	175.00	350.00	425.00

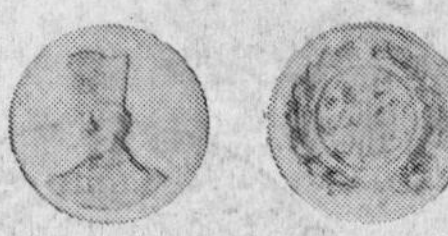

.5749 g, .900 GOLD, .0166 oz AGW
Obv: Bust of Nasir al-din Shah, AH1292-1305.

Y#	Date	Mintage	Fine	VF	XF	Unc
16	AH1297	—	20.00	40.00	75.00	125.00
	1298	—	22.50	45.00	100.00	150.00
	1299	—	20.00	40.00	75.00	125.00
	1300	—	20.00	40.00	75.00	135.00
	1301	—	20.00	40.00	75.00	135.00

Obv. leg: *Muzaffar-al-din Shah.*
Rev: Lion and sun.

Y#	Date	Mintage	Fine	VF	XF	Unc
A38	AH9301 (error for 1309)					
			125.00	175.00	275.00	400.00
	AH1305 (error)	—	— Reported, not confirmed			

Y#	Date	Mintage	Fine	VF	XF	Unc
A34	ND	—	40.00	75.00	150.00	250.00

Obv: Date and denomination added.

Y#	Date	Mintage	Fine	VF	XF	Unc
A34a	AH1319	—	60.00	125.00	185.00	320.00
	1322	—	60.00	125.00	185.00	320.00
	1323	—	60.00	125.00	185.00	320.00
	1324	—	60.00	125.00	185.00	320.00

Obv: Bust of Muhammad Ali-Shah, AH1326 turned half-left, divided date.
Rev: Leg. in closed wreath.

Y#	Date	Mintage	Fine	VF	XF	Unc
52	AH1326	—	100.00	190.00	270.00	475.00
	1327	—	100.00	190.00	270.00	475.00

Obv. leg: *Ahmad Shah,* AH1328-1332.
Rev: Lion and sun.

Y#	Date	Mintage	Fine	VF	XF	Unc
75	AH1328	—	75.00	250.00	400.00	700.00
	1329	—	65.00	125.00	250.00	350.00
	1330	—	—	—	—	—

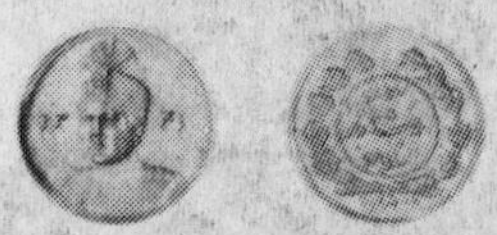

Obv: Portrait type of Ahmad Shah, AH1332-1343.
Rev: Legend.

Y#	Date	Mintage	Fine	VF	XF	Unc
79	AH1332	—	20.00	35.00	60.00	130.00
	1333	—	15.00	30.00	55.00	115.00
	1334	—	15.00	30.00	40.00	75.00
	1335	—	12.50	25.00	35.00	50.00
	1337	—	12.50	25.00	35.00	50.00
	1339	—	15.00	30.00	40.00	75.00
	1340	—	17.00	35.00	50.00	90.00
	1341	—	15.00	30.00	40.00	75.00
	1342	—	15.00	30.00	40.00	75.00
	1343	—	15.00	30.00	40.00	60.00

5000 DINARS

(1/2 Toman)

1.4372 g, .900 GOLD, .0416 oz AGW
Nasir al-din Shah, AH1292-1298

Y#	Date	Mintage	Fine	VF	XF	Unc
C16	AH1294	—	200.00	400.00	750.00	1250.
	1296	—	100.00	200.00	300.00	400.00
	1298	—	— Reported, not confirmed			
	1309	—	200.00	400.00	750.00	1250.

Obv: First Nasir portrait type.

Y#	Date	Mintage	Fine	VF	XF	Unc
17	AH1297	—	50.00	90.00	150.00	250.00
	1299	—	50.00	90.00	150.00	250.00
	1300	—	—	—	—	—
	1301	—	65.00	150.00	250.00	350.00
	1303	—	65.00	150.00	250.00	350.00
	1305	—	65.00	150.00	250.00	350.00
	13(0)5	—	65.00	150.00	250.00	350.00
	1307	—	125.00	300.00	500.00	750.00
	1213 (error) for 1312					
		—	100.00	200.00	300.00	450.00
	1313	—	150.00	300.00	500.00	750.00

Obv. leg: *Nasir Dhu'l Garneyn.*

Y#	Date	Mintage	Fine	VF	XF	Unc
—	AH1313	—	—	—	Rare	—

Obv. leg: *Muzaffar al-din Shah.*

Y#	Date	Mintage	Fine	VF	XF	Unc
38	AH1314	—	125.00	250.00	350.00	500.00
	1315	—	150.00	300.00	500.00	750.00

Y#	Date	Mintage	Fine	VF	XF	Unc
35	AH1316	—	25.00	50.00	70.00	135.00
	1318	—	25.00	50.00	75.00	150.00
	1319	—	30.00	60.00	100.00	200.00
	1320	—	30.00	60.00	100.00	200.00
	1321	—	30.00	60.00	100.00	200.00
	1322	—	30.00	60.00	100.00	200.00
	1323	—	25.00	50.00	75.00	150.00
	1324	—	25.00	50.00	75.00	150.00

Obv. leg: *Muhammad ali Shah.*
Rev: Lion and sun.

Y#	Date	Mintage	Fine	VF	XF	Unc
56	AH1324	—	125.00	200.00	325.00	450.00
	1325	—	150.00	250.00	400.00	550.00

Y#	Date	Mintage	Fine	VF	XF	Unc
53	AH1326	—	125.00	250.00	450.00	750.00
	1362 (error)		150.00	350.00	550.00	850.00
	1327	—	125.00	250.00	450.00	750.00

Obv. leg: *Ahmad Shah.*

Y#	Date	Mintage	Fine	VF	XF	Unc
76	AH1328	—	85.00	150.00	250.00	350.00
	1329	—	75.00	125.00	175.00	250.00
	1330	—	85.00	135.00	190.00	250.00

Rev. leg: Ahmad type.

Y#	Date	Mintage	Fine	VF	XF	Unc
80	AH1331	—	50.00	100.00	150.00	300.00
80	1332	—	40.00	60.00	100.00	150.00
	1333	—	25.00	40.00	75.00	125.00
	1334	—	25.00	30.00	40.00	70.00
	1335	—	25.00	30.00	40.00	70.00
	1336	—	25.00	35.00	50.00	90.00
	1337	—	25.00	30.00	40.00	70.00
	1339	—	25.00	35.00	60.00	110.00
	1340	—	25.00	35.00	60.00	110.00
	1341	—	25.00	30.00	45.00	90.00
	1342	—	25.00	30.00	45.00	90.00
	1343	—	25.00	30.00	45.00	90.00

Mule. Obv: Ahmed portrait.
Rev. leg: *Sahib al-Zaman.*

Y#	Date	Mintage	Fine	VF	XF	Unc
80a	AH1340	—	100.00	150.00	250.00	400.00

TOMAN

3.4525 g, .900 GOLD, .0988 oz AGW
30th Year of Reign
Obv: Leg. Rev: Lion and sun.

Y#	Date	Mintage	Fine	VF	XF	Unc
—	AH1293	—	200.00	300.00	450.00	600.00

3.2570 g, .900 GOLD, .0943 oz AGW
Obv. leg: First Nasir type. Rev: Lion and sun.

Y#	Date	Mintage	Fine	VF	XF	Unc
B16	AH1294	—	—	—	—	—

2.8744 g, .900 GOLD, .0832 oz AGW
Obv. leg: First Nasir type.
Rev: Lion and sun.

Y#	Date	Mintage	Fine	VF	XF	Unc
D16	AH1296	—	— Reported, not confirmed			

Obv: First portrait, w/o leg.
Rev. leg: First Nasir type.

Y#	Date	Mintage	Fine	VF	XF	Unc
A18	ND	—	100.00	185.00	250.00	350.00
	AH1297	—	110.00	200.00	300.00	450.00

Accession date: AH1294
Rev. leg: First Nasir type.

Y#	Date	Mintage	Fine	VF	XF	Unc
18	AH1297	—	50.00	70.00	140.00	275.00
	1298	—	75.00	200.00	350.00	600.00
	1299	—	50.00	75.00	150.00	300.00
	1300	—	75.00	200.00	350.00	600.00
	1301	—	50.00	100.00	200.00	350.00
	1303	—	50.00	125.00	225.00	400.00
	1304	—	70.00	200.00	350.00	600.00
	1305	—	50.00	100.00	200.00	350.00
	1306	—	70.00	200.00	350.00	600.00
	1307	—	60.00	150.00	250.00	450.00
	1309	—	70.00	175.00	300.00	550.00
	1311	—	75.00	200.00	350.00	600.00
	1312	—	75.00	200.00	350.00	600.00
	1313	—	— Reported, not confirmed			

Shah's return from Europe, AH1307.

Y#	Date	Mintage	Fine	VF	XF	Unc
D15	AH1307	—	400.00	750.00	1250.	1750.

Obv: Second portrait.
Rev. leg: First Nasir type, date added.

Y#	Date	Mintage	Fine	VF	XF	Unc
22	AH1310	—	300.00	550.00	1000.	1500.

Rev. leg: Second Nasir type.

Y#	Date	Mintage	Fine	VF	XF	Unc
22a	AH1311	—	125.00	225.00	350.00	500.00

Mule. Obv. Y#18. Rev: Y#22.

Y#	Date	Mintage	Fine	VF	XF	Unc
A22	AH1313//1310					
		—	300.00	500.00	800.00	1250.

Obv. leg: *Muzaffar al-din Shah,* AH1313-1314. Rev: Lion and sun.

Y#	Date	Mintage	Fine	VF	XF	Unc
39	AH1314	—	200.00	300.00	500.00	750.00

Obv: Muzaffar bust 1/2 right, accession date, AH1314, above left, AH1316-1324.

Y#	Date	Mintage	Fine	VF	XF	Unc
36	AH1316	—	45.00	95.00	175.00	300.00
	1318	—	45.00	80.00	150.00	275.00
	1319	—	50.00	100.00	200.00	325.00
	1321	—	50.00	100.00	200.00	325.00

Obv. leg: *Muhammad Ali Shah*, AH1324.
Rev: Lion and sun.

Y#	Date	Mintage	Fine	VF	XF	Unc
A56	AH1324	—	350.00	750.00	1000.	1500.

Obv: Mohammad Ali portrait half-left, AH1326.
Rev: Leg. in closed wreath.

Y#	Date	Mintage	Fine	VF	XF	Unc
54	AH1327	—	200.00	350.00	500.00	750.00

Obv. leg: *Ahmad Shah*, AH1328-1332.
Rev: Lion and sun.

Y#	Date	Mintage	Fine	VF	XF	Unc
77	AH1329	—	200.00	300.00	500.00	750.00

Mule. Obv: Y#81.
Rev: Ahmad Shah Pattern 2 Toman.

Y#	Date	Mintage	Fine	VF	XF	Unc
A81	AH1332	—	300.00	600.00	900.00	1500.
(A41)	1333	—	300.00	600.00	900.00	1500.

NOTE: The reverse die used was of an unadopted pattern.

Obv: Portrait, AH1332-1344
Rev. leg: Ahmad Shah type.

Y#	Date	Mintage	Fine	VF	XF	Unc
81	AH1334	—	45.00	60.00	110.00	230.00
	1335	—	45.00	70.00	110.00	230.00
	1337	—	45.00	60.00	110.00	230.00
	1339	—	45.00	70.00	110.00	230.00
	1340	—	45.00	70.00	110.00	230.00
	1341	—	40.00	50.00	100.00	200.00
	1342	—	40.00	50.00	100.00	200.00
	1343	—	40.00	50.00	100.00	200.00

Reza's First New Year Celebration
Obv. leg: Reza type. Rev: Lion and sun.

Y#	Date	Mintage	Fine	VF	XF	Unc
119	SH1305	—	125.00	200.00	300.00	450.00

2 TOMANS

6.5150 g, .900 GOLD, .1885 oz AGW
Discovery of Gold in Kurdistan
Obv: Leg. within wreath, crown above.
Rev: Leg. within wreath.

Y#	Date	Mintage	Fine	VF	XF	Unc
—	AH1295	—	—	—	Rare	—

7th Iman Commemorative
Obv: First Nasir portrait. Rev: Leg. and crown.

Y#	Date	Mintage	Fine	VF	XF	Unc
—	AH1295	—	—	—	Rare	—

5.7488 g, .900 GOLD, .1663 oz AGW
Accession date: AH1264
Obv: First Nasir portrait. Rev. leg: First Nasir type.

Y#	Date	Mintage	Fine	VF	XF	Unc
19	AH1297	—	125.00	200.00	275.00	550.00
	1298	—	250.00	400.00	750.00	1250.
	1299	—	100.00	150.00	200.00	425.00
	1309	—	—	Reported, not confirmed		

Shah's return from Europe

Y#	Date	Mintage	Fine	VF	XF	Unc
B15	AH1299//1307	—	525.00	850.00	1400.	2350.

Shah's visit to Tehran Mint

Y#	Date	Mintage	Fine	VF	XF	Unc
E15	AH1308	—	—	—	Rare	—

Rev: Lion and sun.

Y#	Date	Mintage	Fine	VF	XF	Unc
A39	AH1311	—	550.00	900.00	1500.	2500.

NOTE: Struck on 1 Toman planchet.

5.63 g

Y#	Date	Mintage	Fine	VF	XF	Unc
40	AH1322	—	150.00	250.00	400.00	750.00

5.71 g
Royal Birthday

Y#	Date	Mintage	Fine	VF	XF	Unc
41	AH1322	—	150.00	250.00	400.00	750.00

Similar to 5 Tomans, Y#88.

Y#	Date	Mintage	Fine	VF	XF	Unc
85	AH1337	—	—	—	Rare	—

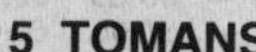

5 TOMANS

14.3720 g, .900 GOLD, .4159 oz AGW

Y#	Date	Mintage	Fine	VF	XF	Unc
78	AH1332/1	—	600.00	1000.	1700.	2700.
	1334/2/1	—	600.00	1000.	1700.	2700.

Y#	Date	Mintage	Fine	VF	XF	Unc
88	AH1337	—	—	—	Rare	—

10 TOMANS

28.7440 g, .900 GOLD, .8317 oz AGW
Obv: First portrait of Nasir al-din Shah, AH1296-97.

Y#	Date	Mintage	Fine	VF	XF	Unc
21	AH1297 H	—	1750.	2250.	3500.	5000.
	1311 H	—	—	—	7000.	10,000.

Obv: Second portrait of Nasir al-din Shah, w/medals on chest, AH1311.

Y#	Date	Mintage	Fine	VF	XF	Unc
A23	AH1311	—	2000.	3000.	5000.	7500.

Y#	Date	Mintage	Fine	VF	XF	Unc
B23	AH1311	—	2150.	3850.	5800.	9500.

Rev: Denomination at bottom.

Y#	Date	Mintage	Fine	VF	XF	Unc
B34.1	AH1314	—	3000.	6500.	9500.	12,000.

Rev: Second date replaces denomination at bottom.

Y#	Date	Mintage	Fine	VF	XF	Unc
B34.2	AH1314	—	2750.	6000.	9000.	11,500.

Obv: Date stamped. Rev: W/denomination.

Y#	Date	Mintage	Fine	VF	XF	Unc
B34.3	AH1314	—	3500.	6500.	9500.	12,000.

Y#	Date	Mintage	Fine	VF	XF	Unc
83	AH1331	—	2400.	4350.	6500.	8500.
	1334	—	—	—	Rare	—
	1337//1334*	—	—	—	6500.	8500.

***NOTE:** The date on the reverse die was not changed until it was used for striking 5 Tomans, Y#88.

Similar to 5 Tomans, Y#88.

Y#	Date	Mintage	Fine	VF	XF	Unc
91	AH1337	—	—	—	Rare	—

MEDALLIC ISSUES (M)

Earlier coins previously mentioned are now published in *UNUSUAL WORLD COINS*, 3rd edition, Krause Publications, 1988. The following items struck in gold (and silver) are all believed to be various commemorative medals.

Y#82 Ahmad Shah, AH1333 - not seen - Fifth Year of Reign.

Y#86 Ahmad Shah, AH1332 - Obv: Bust w/date AH1337. Rev: Crown in open wreath, dated AH1332. Weight fit for a 5 Toman piece.

Y#87 Ahmad Shah, AH1334 & 1337 - These are medals w/o denomination.

Y#88 Ahmad Shah, AH1337 - Pattern.

Y#89 Ahmad Shah, AH1337 - This is an off-metal strike of the 2000 Dinar coin of Y#74.

MONETARY REFORM

5 Dinars = 1 Shahi
100 Dinars = 1 Rial
100 Rials = 1 Pahlavi

DINAR

BRONZE

Y#	Date	Mintage	Fine	VF	XF	Unc
93	SH1310	10.000	8.00	15.00	30.00	60.00

2 DINARS

BRONZE

Y#	Date	Mintage	Fine	VF	XF	Unc
94	SH1310	5.000	7.00	15.00	35.00	70.00

5 DINARS

COPPER-NICKEL

Y#	Date	Mintage	Fine	VF	XF	Unc
97	SH1310	3.750	8.00	15.00	40.00	125.00

COPPER

Y#	Date	Mintage	Fine	VF	XF	Unc
97a	SH1314	.480	75.00	125.00	350.00	500.00

ALUMINUM-BRONZE

Y#	Date	Mintage	Fine	VF	XF	Unc
125	SH1315	5.665	3.00	6.00	13.50	20.00
	1316	Inc. Ab.	.50	1.00	2.50	6.00
	1317	13.025	.50	1.00	2.50	5.00
	1318	—	.50	1.00	2.50	5.00
	1319	—	.50	1.00	2.50	5.00
	1320	—	.50	1.00	2.50	5.00
	1321	—	.50	1.00	2.50	5.00

10 DINARS

COPPER-NICKEL

Y#	Date	Mintage	Fine	VF	XF	Unc
98	SH1310	3.750	8.00	20.00	50.00	150.00

COPPER

Y#	Date	Mintage	Fine	VF	XF	Unc
98a	SH1314	11.350	10.00	30.00	60.00	200.00

ALUMINUM-BRONZE

Y#	Date	Mintage	Fine	VF	XF	Unc
126	SH1315	6.195	2.00	5.00	15.00	25.00
	1316	Inc. Ab.	1.00	3.00	6.00	10.00
	1317	17.120	.50	1.00	3.00	8.00
	1318	—	.50	1.00	2.50	7.50
	1319	—	.50	1.00	3.00	8.00
	1320	—	.50	1.00	3.00	8.00
	1321	—	.50	1.00	3.00	8.00

25 DINARS

COPPER-NICKEL

Y#	Date	Mintage	Fine	VF	XF	Unc
99	SH1310	.750	15.00	30.00	60.00	175.00

COPPER

Y#	Date	Mintage	Fine	VF	XF	Unc
99a	SH1314	1.152	30.00	60.00	85.00	250.00

ALUMINUM-BRONZE

Y#	Date	Mintage	Fine	VF	XF	Unc
127	SH1326	—	3.00	6.00	15.00	30.00
	1327	—	10.00	15.00	30.00	60.00
	1329	—	4.00	7.00	20.00	40.00

Mule. Obv: 25 Dinars, Y#127. Rev: 1 Rial, Y#129.

Y#	Date	Mintage	Fine	VF	XF	Unc
127a	1329	—	50.00	100.00	150.00	250.00

1/4 RIAL

1.2500 g, .828 SILVER, .0332 oz ASW

Y#	Date	Mintage	Fine	VF	XF	Unc
104	SH1315	.600	1.00	2.00	3.00	6.00

NOTE: The second '1' is often short, so that the date looks like 1305.

1/2 RIAL

2.5000 g, .828 SILVER, .0665 oz ASW

Y#	Date	Mintage	Fine	VF	XF	Unc
112	SH1310	2.000	1.00	3.00	6.00	15.00
	1311	—	10.00	20.00	40.00	90.00
	1312	—	1.00	3.00	5.00	14.00
	1313	1.945	1.50	3.00	6.00	15.00
	1314	.100	3.00	9.00	20.00	40.00
	1315	.800	2.00	4.00	9.00	20.00

NOTE: All 1/2 Rials dated SH1311-1315 are recut dies, usually from SH1310.

10 SHAHIS

COPPER

Y#	Date	Mintage	Fine	VF	XF	Unc
92	SH1314 small date, reeded edge	15.714	4.50	8.00	22.00	48.00
	1314 lg. dt. I.A.		4.50	8.00	22.00	48.00
	1314 plain edge	Inc. Ab.	6.00	10.00	27.00	55.00

50 DINARS

ALUMINUM-BRONZE

Y#	Date	Mintage	Fine	VF	XF	Unc
128	SH1315	15.968	2.00	5.00	12.00	35.00
	1316	34.200	1.00	4.00	9.00	25.00
	1317	17.314	.50	2.00	6.00	20.00
	1318	—	.25	2.00	5.00	15.00
	1319	—	2.00	4.00	10.00	22.50
	1320	—	.25	2.00	5.00	15.00
	1321/0	—	.25	2.00	6.00	18.00
	1322/10	—	—	—	—	—
	1322/12	—	.25	1.50	3.00	10.00
	1322/0	—	.25	1.50	3.00	10.00
	1322/1	—	.25	1.50	3.00	10.00
	1331	8.162	2.00	5.00	10.00	25.00
	1332	22.892	.25	1.50	3.00	12.00

COPPER

Y#	Date	Mintage	Fine	VF	XF	Unc
128a	SH1322	—	2.00	4.00	7.00	12.00
	1322/0	—	2.00	6.00	9.00	15.00

ALUMINUM-BRONZE
Reduced thickness

Y#	Date	Mintage	Fine	VF	XF	Unc
137	SH1332	—	10.00	15.00	25.00	40.00
	1333	4.036	.25	1.00	2.50	8.00
	1334	1.370	.25	1.00	3.00	10.00
	1335	.926	.10	.50	2.00	8.00
	1336	-*	.10	.50	2.00	8.00
	1342	.800	.10	.50	2.00	8.00
	1343	1.400	.10	.50	2.00	8.00
	1344	1.600	.10	.25	1.00	6.00
	1345	1.690	.10	.25	1.00	6.00
	1346	153.648**	.10	.25	2.00	4.00
	1347	2.000	.10	.25	2.00	4.00
	1348	1.500	.10	.20	.50	3.00
	1349	.360	1.00	2.00	5.00	12.50
	1350	—	.10	.20	.50	3.00
	1351	—	.10	.20	.50	3.00
	1353	.060	.10	.20	.50	3.00
	1354	.016	.10	.50	2.00	6.00

***NOTE:** Mint reports record 126,500 in SH1337 & 20,000 in SH1338; these were probably dated SH1336.

****NOTE:** Mintage report seems excessive for this and all SH1346 coinage.

BRASS-COATED STEEL

Y#	Date	Mintage	Fine	VF	XF	Unc
137a	MS2535	.027	.25	.50	1.50	5.00
	2536	—	.25	1.00	3.50	5.00
	2537	—	.10	.75	1.25	4.00
	SH1357	—	.10	1.00	1.75	4.00
	1358	—	.10	1.00	2.00	4.00

RIAL

5.0000 g, .828 SILVER, .1331 oz ASW

Y#	Date	Mintage	Fine	VF	XF	Unc
113	SH1310	2.190	1.00	3.00	7.00	25.00
	1311	10.256	1.00	2.00	5.00	20.00
	1312	25.768	1.00	2.00	5.00	15.00
	1313	6.670	1.00	3.00	6.00	20.00

NOTE: All coins dated SH1311-13 cut or punched over SH1310.

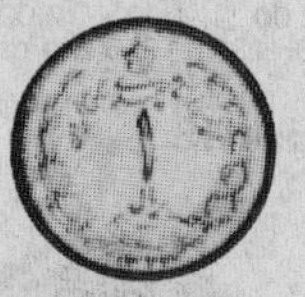
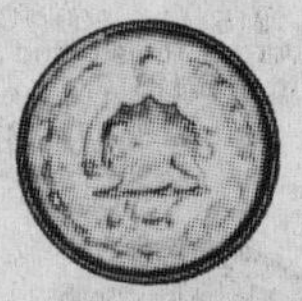

1.6000 g, .600 SILVER, .0308 oz ASW

Y#	Date	Mintage	Fine	VF	XF	Unc
129	SH1322	—	.50	1.00	2.00	5.00
	1323	—	.50	1.00	2.00	5.00
	1324/3	—	—	—	—	—
	1324	—	.50	1.00	2.00	5.00
	1325	—	.75	1.50	2.00	5.00
	1326	.567	15.00	25.00	50.00	75.00
	1327	5.795	.75	1.25	2.00	5.00
	1328	1.565	1.00	2.50	4.00	7.50
	1329	.144	22.00	35.00	65.00	100.00
	1330	—	2.00	5.00	10.00	20.00
	1424 (error for 1324)		—	—	—	—

COPPER-NICKEL

Y#	Date	Mintage	Fine	VF	XF	Unc
138	SH13(31)	4.735	.50	2.00	5.00	15.00
	13(32)	*3.320	4.00	8.00	15.00	30.00
	13(33)	16.405	.60	1.00	2.00	5.00
	13(34)	8.980	.60	1.00	2.00	5.00
	13(35)	8.910	.10	.50	2.00	5.00
	13(36)	4.450	.50	2.00	8.00	20.00

***NOTE:** Much rarer than mintage would indicate.

2.00 g

Y#	Date	Mintage	Fine	VF	XF	Unc
A140	SH1337	8.005	.50	1.00	2.00	5.00

1.75 g

Y#	Date	Mintage	Fine	VF	XF	Unc
A140a	SH1338	14.940	.10	.20	.40	3.00
	1339	8.400	.25	.50	1.00	4.00
	1340	8.490	.25	.50	1.00	4.00
	1341	8.680	.25	.50	1.00	4.00
	1342	13.332	.10	.20	.40	3.00
	1343	14.746	.10	.15	.25	2.00
	1344	12.050	.10	.20	.50	3.50
	1345	13.786	.10	.15	.20	2.00
	1346	155.321	.10	.15	.20	2.00
	1347	20.664	.10	.15	.25	3.00
	1348	22.960	.10	.15	.20	2.00
	1349	19.918	.10	.15	.20	2.00
	1350	24.248	.10	.20	.65	2.00
	1351/0	21.825	.10	.25	.40	3.00
	1351	Inc. Ab.	.10	.15	.20	2.00
	1352	31.449	.10	.15	.20	2.00
	1353 large date	33.700	.10	.20	.25	3.00
	1353 sm.dt.	I.A.	.10	.15	.20	2.00
	1354	—	.10	.15	.20	2.00
	MS2536		.10	.15	.25	3.00

NOTE: Date varieties exist.

F.A.O. Issue

Y#	Date	Mintage	Fine	VF	XF	Unc
152	SH1350	2.770	.10	.15	.25	1.00
	1351	8.605	.10	.15	.25	1.00
	1353	2.000	.10	.15	.25	1.00
	1354	1.000	.20	.30	.75	2.00

50th Anniversary of Pahlavi Rule

Y#	Date	Mintage	Fine	VF	XF	Unc
154	MS2535	61.945	.50	1.00	1.50	2.50

Obv: *Aryamehr* added to legend.

Y#	Date	Mintage	Fine	VF	XF	Unc
154a	MS2536	71.150	.10	.15	.25	2.00
	2537	—	.10	.15	.25	2.00
	2537/6537 (error 2/6)	—	—	—	—	6.00
	SH1357/6	—	.25	.50	.75	5.00
	1357	—	.25	.50	.75	3.00

2 RIALS

10.0000 g, .828 SILVER, .2662 oz ASW

Y#	Date	Mintage	Fine	VF	XF	Unc
114	SH1310	6.145	2.00	5.00	10.00	25.00
	1311	8.838	2.00	5.00	10.00	22.00
	1312	19.175	2.00	5.00	10.00	20.00
	1313	4.015	2.00	7.00	15.00	32.00

NOTE: All coins dated SH1311-13 cut or punched over SH1310.

3.2000 g, .600 SILVER, .0617 oz ASW

Y#	Date	Mintage	Fine	VF	XF	Unc
130	SH1322	—	.50	1.00	3.50	7.00
	1323/2	—	10.00	20.00	30.00	50.00
	1323	—	.50	1.00	3.00	6.00
	1324	—	.50	1.00	3.00	6.00
	1325	—	1.25	3.00	5.00	11.00
	1326	.187	15.00	30.00	50.00	90.00
	1327	3.140	.75	2.00	4.00	10.00
	1328	1.198	2.50	5.00	8.00	16.00
	1329	—	20.00	35.00	65.00	120.00
	1330	—	2.50	5.00	9.00	25.00

COPPER-NICKEL

Y#	Date	Mintage	Fine	VF	XF	Unc
139	SH1331	5.335	1.25	3.00	7.00	20.00
	1332	6.870	1.00	2.00	4.00	8.00
	1333	13.668	.15	.75	2.00	7.00
	1334	7.185	.15	.75	2.00	7.00
	1335	2.400	.15	.75	3.00	12.50
	1336	.325	15.00	25.00	40.00	75.00

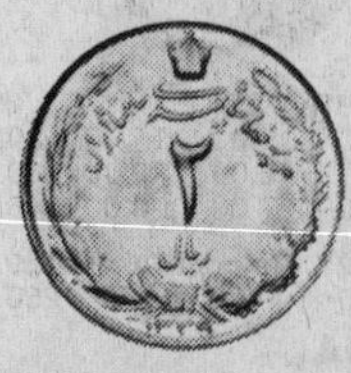

Y#	Date	Mintage	Fine	VF	XF	Unc
B140	SH1338	17.610	.10	.25	.75	4.00
	1339	8.575	.10	.25	.50	4.00
	1340	5.668	.10	.25	.50	4.00
	1341	5.820	.10	.25	.75	4.00
	1342	8.570	.10	.25	.50	4.00
	1343	11.250	.10	.25	.50	3.00
	1344	5.155	.10	.25	.50	4.00
	1345	2.267	.15	.30	1.00	5.00
	1346	92.792	—	.10	.20	4.00
	1347	10.300	—	.10	1.00	6.00
	1348	9.319	.20	.45	1.10	4.00
B140	1349	9.895	.20	.40	1.00	4.00
	1350	9.545	.15	.35	1.00	4.00
	1351	13.305	.15	.35	1.00	3.00
	1352	15.910	—	.10	.20	3.00
	1353	28.477	—	.10	.20	3.00
	1354/3	—	.20	.40	1.00	5.00
	1354	41.700	—	.10	.20	3.00
	MS2536	54.725	—	.10	.20	3.00

Obv: *Aryamehr* added to legend.

Y#	Date	Mintage	Fine	VF	XF	Unc
B140a	MS2536	I.A.	.25	.50	1.00	4.00
	2537	—	.25	.50	1.00	4.00
	SH1357	—	.25	.50	1.00	4.00

50th Anniversary of Pahlavi Rule

Y#	Date	Mintage	Fine	VF	XF	Unc
155	MS2535	59.568	—	.10	.30	2.50

5 RIALS

25.0000 g, .828 SILVER, .6655 oz ASW

Y#	Date	Mintage	Fine	VF	XF	Unc
115	SH1310	5.471	5.00	10.00	15.00	25.00
	1311	4.527	5.00	10.00	15.00	25.00
	1312/0	5.502	5.00	8.00	12.00	—
	1312	Inc. Ab.	5.00	10.00	15.00	25.00
	1313	1.208	5.00	12.00	17.50	30.00

NOTE: Most coins dated SH1311-13 are cut or punched over SH1310.

8.0000 g, .600 SILVER, .1543 oz ASW

Y#	Date	Mintage	Fine	VF	XF	Unc
131	SH1322	—	1.00	2.00	3.50	6.00
	1323	—	1.00	2.50	3.50	6.00
	1324	—	1.00	2.00	4.50	10.00
	1325	—	1.00	2.00	3.50	6.00
	1326	.061	30.00	50.00	75.00	125.00
	1327	.836	2.00	5.00	7.50	20.00
	1328	.282	2.50	10.00	20.00	40.00
	1329	—	35.00	60.00	90.00	175.00

COPPER-NICKEL

Y#	Date	Mintage	Fine	VF	XF	Unc
140	SH1331	3.660	.50	2.00	5.00	20.00

Y#	Date	Mintage	Fine	VF	XF	Unc
140	1332	16.350	.25	1.00	3.00	10.00
	1333	6.582	.25	1.00	3.00	10.00
	1334	.300	10.00	15.00	25.00	50.00
	1336	1.410	.50	2.00	5.00	20.00

7.00 g, 26mm

Y#	Date	Mintage	Fine	VF	XF	Unc
C140	SH1337	3.660	1.00	2.50	7.50	22.50
	1338	10.467	.50	2.50	8.00	20.00

5.00 g

Y#	Date	Mintage	Fine	VF	XF	Unc
C140a	SH1338	I.A.	.25	.40	2.00	6.00
	1339	3.980	.25	.40	2.00	6.00
	1340	3.814	.25	.40	2.00	6.00
	1341	2.332	.25	.40	2.00	6.00
	1342	7.838	.25	.40	1.00	4.00
	1343	9.484	.25	.40	1.00	4.00
	1344	3.468	.25	.40	1.00	4.00
	1345	6.092	.25	.40	1.00	4.00
	1346/36	74.781	.25	.40	1.50	5.00
	1346	Inc. Ab.	.25	.40	1.00	4.00

4.60 g, 24.5mm
Obv. leg: *Aryamehr* added.

Y#	Date	Mintage	Fine	VF	XF	Unc
C140b	SH1347	7.745	.50	.85	1.50	4.00
	1348	9.193	.50	.75	1.00	4.00
	1349	7.300	.50	.75	1.00	4.00
	1350	10.160	.35	.75	1.00	3.00
	1351	20.582	.25	.75	1.00	3.00
	1352	23.590	.25	.75	1.00	3.00
	1353	28.367	.25	.75	1.00	3.00
	1353 large date	Inc. Ab.	.25	.75	1.00	3.00
	1354	27.294	.25	.75	1.00	3.00
	MS2536	47.906	.20	.50	1.00	3.00
	2537	—	.35	.65	1.00	3.00
	SH1357	—	.50	.75	1.00	3.00

50th Anniversary of Pahlavi Rule

Y#	Date	Mintage	Fine	VF	XF	Unc
156	MS2535	37.144	.10	.40	.75	3.00

10 RIALS

16.0000 g, .600 SILVER, .3086 oz ASW

Y#	Date	Mintage	Fine	VF	XF	Unc
132	SH1323/2	—	2.00	3.50	7.00	20.00
	1323	—	2.00	3.00	5.00	12.00
	1324	—	2.00	3.00	5.00	15.00
	1325	—	2.00	3.00	6.00	17.50
	1326	—	40.00	75.00	100.00	160.00

NOTE: Counterfeits are known dated SH1322.

COPPER-NICKEL, 12.00 g

Y#	Date	Mintage	Fine	VF	XF	Unc
D140	SH1335	6.225	.50	2.00	4.00	10.00
	1336	4.415	1.00	3.00	7.50	15.00
	1337	.715	3.00	6.00	9.00	20.00
	1338	1.210	.50	2.00	6.00	14.00
	1339	2.775	.50	2.00	4.00	10.00
	1340	3.660	.50	2.00	4.00	10.00
	1341	.744	20.00	35.00	50.00	75.00
	1343	6.874	.50	2.00	4.00	10.00

Thin flan, 9.00 g

Y#	Date	Mintage	Fine	VF	XF	Unc
D140a	SH1341	Inc. Y#D140	.35	1.00	2.50	5.00
	1342	3.763	.35	1.00	2.00	4.00
	1343	Inc. Y#D140	.35	.75	1.50	2.50
	1344	1.627	.35	.75	1.50	2.50

Rev: Value in words.

Y#	Date	Mintage	Fine	VF	XF	Unc
149	SH1345	1.699	.50	.60	2.00	5.00
	1346	38.897	.40	.50	1.00	4.00
	1347	8.220	.40	.65	1.50	8.00
	1348	7.156	.40	.50	1.00	4.00
	1349	7.397	.40	.50	1.00	4.00
	1350	8.972	.40	.50	1.00	4.00
	1351	9.912	.40	.50	1.00	4.00
	1352	28.776	.50	2.00	4.50	7.00

Rev: Value in numerals.

Y#	Date	Mintage	Fine	VF	XF	Unc
149a	SH1352	Inc. Ab.	.30	.60	1.00	4.00
	1353	22.234	.30	.60	1.00	3.00
	1354	23.482	.30	.60	1.00	4.00
	MS2536	24.324	.30	.60	1.00	3.00
	2537	—	.30	.60	1.00	4.00
	SH1357	—	.30	1.00	1.50	4.00

F.A.O. Issue

Y#	Date	Mintage	Fine	VF	XF	Unc
150	SH1348	.150	.25	.50	1.00	3.00

50th Anniversary of Pahlavi Rule

Y#	Date	Mintage	Fine	VF	XF	Unc
157	MS2535	29.859	.25	.50	.75	3.00

20 RIALS

COPPER-NICKEL
Rev: Value in words.

Y#	Date	Mintage	Fine	VF	XF	Unc
151	SH1350	2.349	.25	1.00	3.00	6.00
151	1351	11.416	.25	.85	1.00	3.00
	1352	7.172	.25	.85	1.25	5.00

Rev: Value in numerals.

Y#	Date	Mintage	Fine	VF	XF	Unc
151a	SH1352	Inc.Y151	.25	.75	1.00	3.50
	1353	12.601	.25	.75	1.00	3.75
	1354	16.246	.25	.75	1.00	4.00
	MS2536	—	.40	.75	1.00	4.00
	2537	—	.50	.75	1.00	4.00
	SH1357	—	.50	1.00	1.50	5.00

NOTE: Varieties exist in date size.

7th Asian Games

Y#	Date	Mintage	Fine	VF	XF	Unc
153	SH1353	Inc. Ab.	1.00	2.00	3.00	5.00

50th Anniversary of Pahlavi Rule

Y#	Date	Mintage	Fine	VF	XF	Unc
158	MS2535	—	.50	1.00	2.00	4.00

F.A.O. Issue

Y#	Date	Mintage	Fine	VF	XF	Unc
160	MS2535	10.000	1.00	2.00	3.00	5.00
	2536	23.370	1.00	2.50	4.00	6.00

50th Anniversary of Bank Melli

Y#	Date	Mintage	Fine	VF	XF	Unc
162	SH1357	—	2.00	3.00	6.00	12.00

F.A.O. Issue

Y#	Date	Mintage	Fine	VF	XF	Unc
163	SH1357	5.000	.50	.75	2.00	6.00

25 RIALS

7.5000 g, .999 SILVER, .2409 oz ASW
2500th Anniversary of Persian Empire
Column Head From Artaxerxes Palace in Susa

KM#	Date	Year	Mintage	VF	XF	Unc
2	SH1350	1971	.018	—	Proof	12.00

50 RIALS

15.0000 g, .999 SILVER, .4818 oz ASW
2500th Anniversary of Persian Empire
Walking Griffin with Ram Antlers

KM#	Date	Year	Mintage	VF	XF	Unc
3	SH1350	1971	.018	—	Proof	20.00

75 RIALS

22.5000 g, .999 SILVER, .7227 oz ASW
2500th Anniversary of Persian Empire
Stone of Cyrus II
Obv: Similar to 200 Rials, KM#6.

KM#	Date	Year	Mintage	VF	XF	Unc
4	SH1350	1971	.018	—	Proof	25.00

100 RIALS

30.0000 g, .999 SILVER, .9636 oz ASW
2500th Anniversary of Persian Empire
Palace of Darius I and Pillars of Reception Hall in Persepolis. Obv: Similar to 200 Rials, KM#6.

KM#	Date	Year	Mintage	VF	XF	Unc
5	SH1350	1971	.018	—	Proof	30.00

200 RIALS

60.0000 g, .999 SILVER, 1.9273 oz ASW
2500th Anniversary of Persian Empire
Imperial Couple
Obv: Conjoined bust of royal couple left.

KM#	Date	Year	Mintage	VF	XF	Unc
6	SH1350	1971	.023	—	Proof	55.00

500 RIALS

6.5100 g, .900 GOLD, .1883 oz AGW
2500th Anniversary of Persian Empire
Walking Griffin with Ram Antlers

KM#	Date	Year	Mintage	VF	XF	Unc
8	SH1350	1971	.011	—	Proof	140.00

750 RIALS

9.7700 g, .900 GOLD, .2827 oz AGW
2500th Anniversary of Persian Empire
Stone of Cyrus II

KM#	Date	Year	Mintage	VF	XF	Unc
9	SH1350	1971	.010	—	Proof	175.00

1000 RIALS

13.0300 g, .900 GOLD, .3770 oz AGW
2500th Anniversary of Persian Empire
Palace of Darius I and Pillars of Reception Hall in Persepolis. Polished fields below ruins.

KM#	Date	Year	Mintage	VF	XF	Unc
10.1	SH1350	1971	.010	—	Proof	225.00

Frosted fields below ruins.

KM#	Date	Year	Mintage	VF	XF	Unc
10.2	SH1350	1971	Inc. Ab.	—	Proof	225.00

2000 RIALS

26.0600 g, .900 GOLD, .7541 oz AGW
2500th Anniversary of Persian Empire
Imperial Couple

KM#	Date	Year	Mintage	VF	XF	Unc
11	SH1350	1971	9,805	—	Proof	465.00

1/4 PAHLAVI

2.0340 g, .900 GOLD, 14mm, .0589 oz AGW

Y#	Date	Mintage	Fine	VF	XF	Unc
141	SH1332	.041	BV	35.00	45.00	60.00
	1333	.007	35.00	45.00	100.00	150.00
	1334	—	BV	35.00	60.00	100.00
	1335	.041	BV	35.00	45.00	60.00
	1336	—	—	—	Rare	—

Thinner & broader, 16mm

Y#	Date	Mintage	Fine	VF	XF	Unc
141a	SH1336	.007	40.00	60.00	80.00	140.00
	1337	.033	—	BV	35.00	45.00
	1338	.136	—	BV	35.00	45.00
	1339	.156	—	BV	35.00	45.00
	1340	.060	—	BV	35.00	45.00
	1342	.080	—	BV	35.00	45.00
	1343	.040	— Reported, not confirmed			
	1344	.030	—	35.00	40.00	65.00
	1345	.040	—	BV	35.00	45.00
	1346	.030	—	BV	35.00	45.00
	1347	.060	—	BV	35.00	45.00
	1348	.060	—	BV	35.00	45.00
	1349	.080	—	BV	35.00	45.00
	1350	.080	—	BV	35.00	45.00
	1351	.103	—	BV	35.00	45.00
	1352	.050	—	BV	35.00	45.00
	1353	—	—	BV	35.00	45.00

Obv. leg: *Aryamehr* added.

Y#	Date	Mintage	Fine	VF	XF	Unc
141b	SH1354	.106	—	BV	30.00	40.00
	1355	.186	—	BV	30.00	40.00
	MS2536	—	—	BV	30.00	40.00
	2537	—	—	BV	30.00	40.00
	SH1358	—	BV	35.00	75.00	115.00

1/2 PAHLAVI

4.0680 g, .900 GOLD, .1177 oz AGW

Y#	Date	Mintage	Fine	VF	XF	Unc
123	SH1310	696 pcs.	75.00	150.00	275.00	375.00
	1311	286 pcs.	75.00	175.00	300.00	400.00
	1312	892 pcs.	75.00	150.00	250.00	350.00
	1313	531 pcs.	75.00	175.00	300.00	400.00
	1314	—	75.00	175.00	300.00	400.00
	1315	1,042	75.00	175.00	275.00	375.00

Y#	Date	Mintage	Fine	VF	XF	Unc
133	SH1320	—	60.00	120.00	200.00	300.00
	1321	—	BV	60.00	100.00	150.00
	1322	—	—	BV	60.00	75.00
	1323	.076	—	BV	60.00	75.00
	1324	—	— Reported, not confirmed			

Obv: High relief head.

Y#	Date	Mintage	Fine	VF	XF	Unc
135	SH1324	—	BV	60.00	70.00	100.00
	1325	—	BV	60.00	70.00	100.00
	1326	.036	BV	60.00	75.00	125.00
	1327	.036	BV	60.00	75.00	125.00
	1328	—	BV	70.00	85.00	150.00
	1329	75 pcs.	75.00	150.00	250.00	500.00
	1330	.098	—	—	—	1350.

Obv: Low relief head.

Y#	Date	Mintage	Fine	VF	XF	Unc
142	SH1330	Inc.Y135	BV	55.00	65.00	80.00
	1332	—	125.00	200.00	350.00	500.00
	1333	—	BV	65.00	80.00	110.00
	1334	—	—	65.00	80.00	110.00
	1335	—	—	BV	60.00	80.00
	1336	.132	—	BV	60.00	80.00
	1337	.102	—	BV	60.00	70.00
	1338	.140	—	BV	60.00	70.00
	1339	.142	—	BV	60.00	70.00
	1340	.439	—	BV	60.00	70.00
	1342	.040	—	BV	60.00	75.00
	1343	—	— Reported, not confirmed			
	1344	.030	BV	75.00	90.00	125.00
	1345	.040	—	BV	60.00	72.50
	1346	.040	—	BV	60.00	72.50
	1347	.050	—	BV	60.00	65.00
	1348	.040	—	BV	60.00	70.00
	1349	.080	—	BV	60.00	70.00
	1350	.080	—	BV	60.00	70.00
	1351	.103	—	BV	60.00	70.00
	1352	.067	—	BV	60.00	70.00
	1353	—	—	BV	60.00	70.00

Obv. leg: ***Aryamehr*** **added.**

Y#	Date	Mintage	Fine	VF	XF	Unc
142a	SH1354	.037	—	BV	60.00	70.00
	1355	.153	—	BV	60.00	70.00
	MS2536	—	—	BV	60.00	70.00
	2537	—	—	BV	60.00	70.00
	SH1358	—	—	—	275.00	375.00

PAHLAVI

1.9180 g, .900 GOLD, .0555 oz AGW

Y#	Date	Mintage	Fine	VF	XF	Unc
116	SH1305	5,000	100.00	150.00	250.00	350.00

NOTE: A similar piece previously listed as Y#19 w/o crown and sprays on obv. is a medal.

Y#	Date	Mintage	Fine	VF	XF	Unc
120	SH1306	.021	45.00	65.00	85.00	125.00
	1307	5,000	60.00	85.00	120.00	180.00
	1308	989 pcs.	80.00	100.00	160.00	275.00

8.1360 g, .900 GOLD, .2354 oz AGW

Y#	Date	Mintage	Fine	VF	XF	Unc
124	SH1310	304 pcs.	300.00	500.00	850.00	1200.

Y#	Date	Mintage	Fine	VF	XF	Unc
134	SH1320*	—	—	250.00	400.00	500.00
	1322	—	—	BV	115.00	130.00
	1323	.311	—	BV	115.00	130.00
	1324	—	—	BV	115.00	130.00

***NOTE:** Possibly a pattern.

Obv: High relief head.

Y#	Date	Mintage	Fine	VF	XF	Unc
136	SH1324	—	BV	115.00	125.00	150.00
	1325	—	BV	115.00	135.00	190.00
	1326	.151	BV	115.00	150.00	190.00
	1327	.020	BV	130.00	150.00	190.00
	1328	4,000	BV	140.00	195.00	265.00
	1329	4,000	BV	140.00	195.00	265.00
	1330	.048	BV	140.00	195.00	265.00

Obv: Low relief head.

Y#	Date	Mintage	Fine	VF	XF	Unc
143	SH1330	—	—	BV	120.00	145.00
	1331	—	—	525.00	850.00	1200.
	1332	—	—	425.00	700.00	1000.
	1333	—	BV	120.00	140.00	190.00
	1334	—	BV	120.00	140.00	190.00
	1335	—	—	BV	115.00	140.00
	1336	.453	—	BV	115.00	140.00
	1337	.665	—	BV	115.00	120.00
	1338	.776	—	BV	115.00	120.00
	1339	.847	—	BV	115.00	120.00
	1340	.528	—	BV	115.00	120.00
	1342	.020	—	BV	115.00	140.00
	1343	.010	—	Reported, not confirmed		
	1344	—	BV	110.00	130.00	190.00
	1345	.020	—	BV	115.00	140.00
	1346	.030	—	BV	115.00	140.00
	1347	.040	—	BV	115.00	120.00
	1348	.070	—	BV	115.00	120.00
	1349	.070	—	BV	115.00	120.00
	1350	.060	—	BV	115.00	120.00
	1351	.100	—	BV	115.00	120.00
	1352	.320	—	BV	115.00	120.00
	1353	—	—	BV	115.00	120.00

Obv. leg: ***Aryamehr*** **added.**

Y#	Date	Mintage	Fine	VF	XF	Unc
143a	SH1354	.021	—	BV	115.00	120.00
	1355	.203	—	BV	115.00	120.00
	MS2536	—	—	BV	115.00	120.00
	2537	—	—	BV	115.00	120.00
	SH1358	—	—	125.00	200.00	300.00

2 PAHLAVI

3.8360 g, .900 GOLD, .1110 oz AGW

Y#	Date	Mintage	Fine	VF	XF	Unc
117	SH1305	1,134	200.00	330.00	500.00	975.00

Y#	Date	Mintage	Fine	VF	XF	Unc
121	SH1306	2,494	60.00	90.00	150.00	250.00
	1307	7,000	60.00	90.00	150.00	230.00
	1308	789 pcs.	75.00	115.00	200.00	285.00

2-1/2 PAHLAVI

20.3400 g, .900 GOLD, .5885 oz AGW

Y#	Date	Mintage	Fine	VF	XF	Unc
144	SH1339	1,682	BV	260.00	290.00	335.00
	1340	2,788	BV	260.00	290.00	335.00
	1342	30 pcs.	—	—	Rare	—
	1347	2,000	— Reported, not confirmed			
	1348	3,000	BV	260.00	290.00	335.00
	1349	3,000	— Reported, not confirmed			
	1350	2,000	BV	260.00	290.00	335.00
	1351	2,500	BV	260.00	290.00	335.00
	1352	3,000	BV	260.00	290.00	335.00
	1353	—	BV	260.00	290.00	335.00

Obv. leg: ***Aryamehr*** **added.**

Y#	Date	Mintage	Fine	VF	XF	Unc
144a	SH1354	.018	—	BV	260.00	300.00
	1355	.016	—	BV	260.00	300.00
	MS2536	—	—	BV	260.00	300.00
	2537	—	—	BV	260.00	300.00
	SH1358	—	—	—	Rare	—

5 PAHLAVI

9.5900 g, .900 GOLD, .2775 oz AGW

Y#	Date	Mintage	Fine	VF	XF	Unc
118	SH1305	271 pcs.	500.00	700.00	950.00	2000.

Y#	Date	Mintage	Fine	VF	XF	Unc
122	SH1306	909 pcs.	300.00	500.00	700.00	1150.
	1307	785 pcs.	300.00	500.00	850.00	1350.
	1308	121 pcs.	400.00	600.00	1400.	2200.

40.6799 g, .900 GOLD, 1.1772 oz AGW

Y#	Date	Mintage	Fine	VF	XF	Unc
145	SH1339	2,225	—	BV	550.00	600.00
	1340	2,430	—	BV	550.00	600.00
	1342	20 pcs.	—	—	Rare	—
	1347	500 pcs.	— Reported, not confirmed			
	1348	2,000	—	BV	550.00	600.00
	1349	700 pcs.	— Reported, not confirmed			
	1350	2,000	—	BV	550.00	600.00
	1351	2,500	—	BV	550.00	600.00
	1352	2,100	—	BV	550.00	600.00
	1353	—	—	BV	550.00	600.00

Obv. leg: ***Aryamehr*** **added.**

Y#	Date	Mintage	Fine	VF	XF	Unc
145a	SH1354	.010	—	BV	550.00	600.00
	1355	.017	—	BV	550.00	600.00
	MS2536	—	—	BV	550.00	600.00
	2537	—	—	BV	550.00	600.00
	SH1358	—	—	550.00	700.00	900.00

10 PAHLAVI

81.3598 g, .900 GOLD, 2.3544 oz AGW
50th Anniversary of Pahlavi Rule

Y#	Date	Mintage	Fine	VF	XF	Unc
159	MS2535	—	—	—	1200.	1550.

Centenary of Reza Shah's Birth
Obv: Similar to Y#159.

Y#	Date	Mintage	Fine	VF	XF	Unc
A159	MS2536	—	—	—	1200.	1600.

Y#	Date	Mintage	Fine	VF	XF	Unc
161	SH1358	—	—	—	1500.	2000.
	MS2537	—	—	—	1300.	1600.

MINT SETS (MS)

KM#	Date	Mintage	Identification	Issue Price	Mkt. Val.
MS1	SH1342(4)	—	YA140a,B140,C140a, D140a	2.00	15.00
MS2	SH1343(4)	—	YA140a,B140,C140a, D140a	2.00	11.50
MS3	SH1348(5)	—	Y137,A140a,B140,C140b, 149	2.00	17.00
MS4	SH1350(5)	—	Y137,A140a,B140,C140b, 149	2.00	17.00
MS5	SH1353(6)	—	Y137,A140a,B140, C140b,149a,151a	2.00	19.00
MS6	SH1354(6)	—	Y137,A140a,B140,C140b, 149a,151a,	2.00	22.00
MS7	MS2535(6)	—	Y137a,154-158	2.50	21.50
MS8	MS2536(6)	—	Y137a,B140,C140b,149a, 151a,154a	2.50	20.00

PROOF SETS (PS)

KM#	Date	Mintage	Identification	Issue Price	Mkt. Val.
PS1	SH1306	20	Y110,111*	—	1700.
*Two each type.					
PS2	1971(9)	9,805	KM2-6, 8-11	261.50	1150.
PS3	1971(5)	18,100	KM2-6	59.50	145.00

ISLAMIC REPUBLIC

50 DINARS

BRASS CLAD STEEL

Y#	Date	Mintage	Fine	VF	XF	Unc
176	SH1358	—	—	5.00	8.00	12.00

RIAL

COPPER-NICKEL

Y#	Date	Mintage	Fine	VF	XF	Unc
164	SH1358	—	—	.25	.75	2.00
	1359	—	—	.25	.75	1.75
	1360	—	—	.25	.75	1.75
	1361	—	—	.25	.75	1.75
	1362	—	—	.25	.75	1.75
	1363	—	—	—	—	—
	1364	—	—	.25	.75	1.75
	1365	—	—	.15	.65	1.25
	1366	—	—	.15	.65	1.25
	1367	—	—	.15	.65	1.25

BRONZE CLAD STEEL
Mosque of Omar

Y#	Date	Mintage	Fine	VF	XF	Unc
171	SH1359	—	—	.50	1.75	2.50

2 RIALS

COPPER-NICKEL

Y#	Date	Mintage	Fine	VF	XF	Unc
165	SH1358	—	—	.60	1.00	3.00
	1359	—	—	.50	1.00	3.00
	1360	—	—	.50	1.00	3.00
	1361	—	—	.50	.75	2.75
	1362	—	—	.35	.50	2.50
	1364	—	—	.35	.50	2.50
	1365	—	—	.25	.50	2.00
	1366	—	—	.25	.50	2.00
	1367	—	—	.25	.50	2.00

5 RIALS

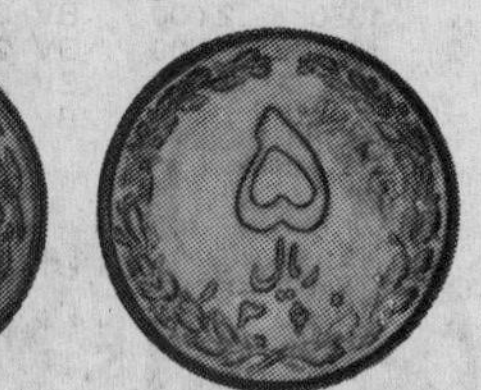

COPPER-NICKEL

Y#	Date	Mintage	Fine	VF	XF	Unc
166	SH1358	—	—	.75	1.00	3.00
	1359	—	—	.75	1.00	3.00
	1360	—	—	.75	1.00	3.00
	1361	—	—	.75	1.00	3.00
	1362	—	—	.75	1.00	3.00
	1363	—	—	.75	1.00	3.00
	1364	—	—	.75	1.00	3.00
	1365	—	—	.75	1.00	3.00
	1366	—	—	.75	1.00	3.00
	1367	—	—	.75	1.00	3.00
	1368	—	—	.75	1.00	3.00

NOTE: Date varieties exist.

BRASS
Mausoleum

Y#	Date	Mintage	Fine	VF	XF	Unc
182	SH1371	—	—	—	—	2.50

10 RIALS

COPPER-NICKEL

Y#	Date	Mintage	Fine	VF	XF	Unc
167.1	SH1358	—	—	1.00	2.50	4.50
	1359	—	—	1.00	2.50	4.50
	1360	—	—	1.00	2.50	4.50
	1361	—	—	1.00	2.00	4.00
	1364	—	—	1.00	2.00	4.00
	1365	—	—	.75	1.50	3.00
	1366	—	—	.75	1.50	3.00

Rev: Redesigned wreath.

Y#	Date	Mintage	Fine	VF	XF	Unc
167.2	SH1361	—	—	1.00	2.00	4.00
	1362	—	—	1.00	2.00	4.00
	1363	—	—	1.00	2.00	4.00
	1367	—	—	.65	1.50	3.00

NOTE: Date varieties exist.

1st Anniversary of Revolution

Y#	Date	Mintage	Fine	VF	XF	Unc
169	SH1358	—	—	1.50	2.50	4.50

Moslem Unity
Reeded edge, 6.97 g

Y#	Date	Mintage	Fine	VF	XF	Unc
175.1	SH1361	—	—	1.50	2.50	4.50

Plain edge, 3.02 g

Y#	Date	Mintage	Fine	VF	XF	Unc
175.2	SH1368	—	—	1.00	2.00	4.00

ALUMINUM-BRONZE
Mausoleum

Y#	Date	Mintage	Fine	VF	XF	Unc
180	SH1371	—	—	1.00	2.00	4.00
	1372	—	—	1.00	2.00	4.00

20 RIALS

COPPER-NICKEL

Y#	Date	Mintage	Fine	VF	XF	Unc
168	SH1358	—	—	1.75	3.00	6.00
	1359	—	—	1.75	3.00	6.00
	1360	—	—	1.25	2.50	5.00
	1361	—	—	1.25	2.50	5.00
	1362	—	—	1.25	2.50	5.00
	1363	—	—	1.00	2.50	4.00

Y#	Date	Mintage	Fine	VF	XF	Unc
168	1364	—	—	1.00	2.50	4.00
	1365	—	—	1.25	2.50	5.00
	1366	—	—	1.25	2.50	5.00
	1367	—	—	1.25	2.50	5.00

NOTE: Date varieties exist.

1400th Anniversary of Mohammed's Flight

170	SH1358	—	—	2.50	3.50	5.00

2nd Anniversary of Islamic Revolution

174	SH1359	—	—	2.50	3.50	5.00

3rd Anniversary of Islamic Revolution

173	SH1360	—	—	2.50	3.50	5.00

National Bank

177	SH1367	—	—	2.50	3.50	5.00

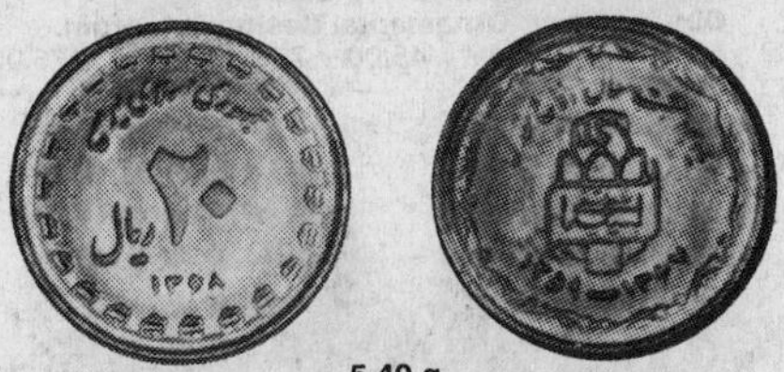

5.40 g
Islamic Republic

178.1	SH1368	—	—	2.50	3.50	5.00

4.58 g

178.2	SH1368	—	—	2.50	3.50	5.00

50 RIALS

ALUMINUM-BRONZE
Oil and Agriculture
Lettered edge

172	SH1359	—	—	5.00	7.00	10.00
	1360	—	—	5.00	7.00	10.00
	1361	—	—	5.00	7.00	10.00
	1364	—	—	5.00	7.00	10.00
	1365	—	—	5.00	7.00	10.00
	1367	—	—	—	6.00	9.00

COPPER-NICKEL
Lettered edge

Y#	Date	Mintage	Fine	VF	XF	Unc
172a	SH1368	—	—	3.50	5.50	8.00
	1369	—	—	3.50	5.50	8.00
	1370	—	—	3.50	5.50	8.00

NOTE: Edge inscription varieties exist.

10th Anniversary of Revolution

179	SH1367	—	—	3.50	5.50	8.00

Mosque

181	SH1371	—	—	3.50	5.50	8.00
	1372	—	—	3.50	5.50	8.00

100 RIALS

COPPER-NICKEL
Mosque

183	SH1372	—	—	—	—	6.50

TRADE COINAGE

1/4 AZADI

2.0339 g, .900 GOLD, .0588 oz AGW
1st Anniversary of Revolution
Obv. leg: *1st Spring Freedom.*

C163	SH1358	—	—	—	—	165.00

1/2 AZADI

4.0680 g, .900 GOLD, .1177 oz AGW
1st Anniversary of Revolution
Obv. leg: *1st Spring Freedom.*

A163	SH1358	—	—	—	—	100.00

AZADI

8.1360 g, .900 GOLD, .2354 oz AGW
1st Anniversary of Revolution

Obv. leg: *1st Spring Freedom.*

Y#	Date	Mintage	Fine	VF	XF	Unc
B163.1	SH1358	—	—	—	—	150.00

Obv. leg. shortened: *Spring Freedom.*

B163.2	SH1363	—	—	—	—	140.00

Obv. leg. larger: *Spring Freedom.*

B163.3	SH1364	—	—	—	—	140.00
	1365	—	—	—	—	140.00
	1366	—	—	—	—	140.00
	1367	—	—	—	—	140.00

2-1/2 AZADI

20.3400 g, .900 GOLD, .5885 oz AGW
1st Anniversary of Revolution
Obv. leg: *1st Spring Freedom.*

D163	SH1358	6 pcs.	—	—	—	1500.

5 AZADI

40.6800 g, .900 GOLD, 1.1770 oz AGW
1st Anniversary of Revolution
Obv. leg: *1st Spring Freedom.*

E163	SH1358	—	—	—	—	2500.

The Republic of Iraq, historically known as Mesopotamia, is located in the Near East and is bordered by Kuwait, Iran, Turkey, Syria, Jordan and Saudi Arabia. It has an area of 167,925 sq. mi. (434,920 sq. km.) and a population of 14 million. Capital: Baghdad. The economy of Iraq is based on agriculture and petroleum. Crude oil accounted for 94 percent of the exports before the war with Iran began in 1980.

Mesopotamia was the site of a number of flourishing civilizations of antiquity - Sumerian, Assyrian, Babylonian, Parthian, Persian - and of the Biblical cities of Ur, Nineveh and Babylon. Desired because of its favored location which embraced the fertile alluvial plains of the Tigris and Euphrates Rivers, Mesopotamia - 'land between the rivers' - was conquered by Cyrus the Great of Persia, Alexander of Macedonia and by Arabs who made the legendary city of Baghdad the capital of the ruling caliphate. Suleiman the Magnificent conquered Mesopotamia for Turkey in 1534, and it formed part of the Ottoman Empire until 1623, and from 1638 to 1917. Great Britain, given a League of Nations mandate over the territory in 1920, recognized Iraq as a kingdom in 1922. Iraq became an independent constitutional monarchy presided over by the Hashemite family, direct descendants of the prophet Mohammed, in 1932. In 1958, the army-led revolution of July 14 overthrew the monarchy and proclaimed a republic.

NOTE: The 'I' mint mark on 1938 and 1943 issues appears on the obverse near the point of the bust. Some of the issues of 1938 have a dot to denote a composition change from nickel to copper-nickel.

RULERS

Turkish, until 1917
British, 1921-1922
Faisal I, 1921-1933
Ghazi I, 1933-1939
Faisal II,
  Regency, 1939-1953
  King, 1953-1958

MESOPOTAMIA

MONETARY SYSTEM

40 Para = 1 Piastre (Kurus)

MINTNAME

Baghdad بغداد

al-Basrah (Basra) البصرة

al-Hille الحله

MAHMUD II

AH1223-1255/1808-1839AD

NOTE: The denominations of the following coins are tentative, and all authorities are not in agreement of the classification. Until a better system is available, that of C. Olcer will be followed. Most types are similar to Turkish coins, but with mintname Baghdad.

PARA

COPPER

KM#	Date	Year	Good	VG	Fine	VF
75	AH1223	—	—	—	—	—

2 PARA

COPPER, 16-19mm

KM#	Date	Year	Good	VG	Fine	VF
80	AH1240	—	—	—	—	—
	1241	16	— Reported, not confirmed			

5 PARA

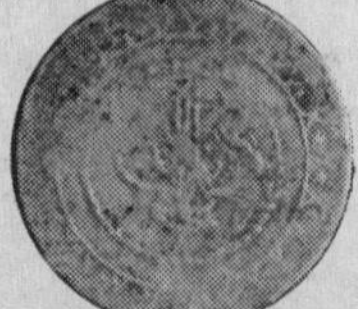

BILLON

KM#	Date	Year	Good	VG	Fine	VF
50	AH1223	12	12.00	20.00	35.00	50.00

COPPER, 1.24 g

KM#	Date	Year	Good	VG	Fine	VF
54	AH1238	—	10.00	17.00	28.00	40.00
	1240	—	10.00	17.00	28.00	40.00
	1241	—	10.00	17.00	28.00	40.00
	1244	—	10.00	17.00	28.00	40.00

Obv. and rev: Narrow floral borders.

KM#	Date	Year	Good	VG	Fine	VF
58	AH1240	—	8.00	13.00	22.50	33.50

Rev: Year above mintname.

KM#	Date	Year	Good	VG	Fine	VF
63	AH1223	18	—	—	—	—

17-25mm

KM#	Date	Year	Good	VG	Fine	VF
69	AH1223	23	12.00	20.00	35.00	50.00
	1223	25	12.00	20.00	35.00	50.00

Rev: Year above mintname.

KM#	Date	Year	Good	VG	Fine	VF
70	AH1223	25	—	—	—	—

Obv: Star of David. Rev: Similar to KM#70.

KM#	Date	Year	Good	VG	Fine	VF
71	AH1223	25	—	—	—	—

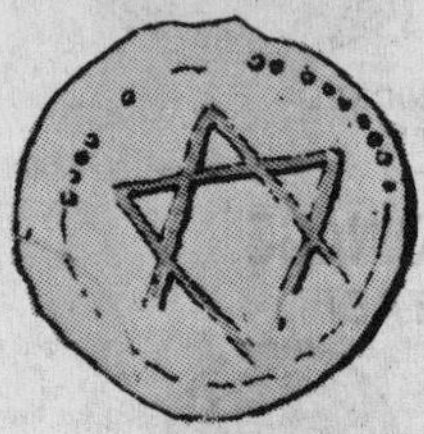

Obv: Star of David only, 29mm.

KM#	Date	Year	Good	VG	Fine	VF
72	AH1248	—	15.00	25.00	42.00	60.00

Obv: Star and crescent only, 21-25mm.

KM#	Date	Year	Good	VG	Fine	VF
73	AH1223	25	12.00	20.00	35.00	50.00
	1223	26	10.00	18.50	32.00	45.00

20-22mm

KM#	Date	Year	Good	VG	Fine	VF
79	AH1223	28	10.00	16.50	28.00	40.00
	1223	29	Reported, not confirmed			

BILLON, 0.80 g, 18mm

KM#	Date	Year	Good	VG	Fine	VF
59	AH1223	17	16.00	27.00	45.00	65.00

10 PARA

BILLON, 24mm, 2.10 g

Obv: Toughra. Rev: Mint and date within beaded borders.

KM#	Date	Year	Good	VG	Fine	VF
51	AH1223	13	50.00	85.00	140.00	200.00
	1223	15	—	—	Rare	—

26mm, 1.60-1.80 g
Obv: Toughra, mint and date. Rev. leg: 4 lines.

KM#	Date	Year	Good	VG	Fine	VF
55	AH1223	15	50.00	85.00	140.00	200.00
	1223	17	50.00	85.00	140.00	200.00

Similar to KM#55 w/ornamental borders added.

KM#	Date	Year	Good	VG	Fine	VF
60	AH1223	17	30.00	50.00	85.00	125.00

22mm, 1.40 g
Similar to KM#51, but floral borders.

KM#	Date	Year	Good	VG	Fine	VF
61	AH1223	17	30.00	50.00	85.00	125.00

20 PARA

BILLON, 28mm, 3.50-4.20 g

KM#	Date	Year	Good	VG	Fine	VF
52	AH1223	13	50.00	85.00	140.00	200.00

27mm, 3.20 g
Obv: Toughra, mint and date. Rev: 4-line leg.

KM#	Date	Year	Good	VG	Fine	VF
56	AH1223	15	50.00	85.00	140.00	200.00
	1223	17	50.00	85.00	140.00	200.00

28mm, 2.933-3.00 g
Obv. and rev: Ornamental design in margin.

KM#	Date	Year	Good	VG	Fine	VF
62	AH1223	17	45.00	75.00	125.00	175.00
	1223	21	—	—	Rare	—

Obv. and rev: Legend in margin.

KM#	Date	Year	Good	VG	Fine	VF
A63	AH1223	21	—	—	—	—

Reduced weight; 22mm, 1.20-1.60 g

KM#	Date	Year	Good	VG	Fine	VF
64	AH1223	21	32.00	55.00	90.00	130.00

22mm, 1.80-2.00 g
Similar to KM#52, but extra leg. around central design.

KM#	Date	Year	Good	VG	Fine	VF
65	AH1223	21	32.00	55.00	90.00	130.00

Similar to KM#56, 26mm, 2.00 g.

KM#	Date	Year	Good	VG	Fine	VF
68	AH1223	17	32.00	55.00	90.00	130.00
	1223	22	32.00	55.00	90.00	130.00

22-24mm
Similar to 5 Para, KM#59.

KM#	Date	Year	Good	VG	Fine	VF
75	AH1223	26	15.00	25.00	35.00	50.00
	1223	28	15.00	25.00	35.00	50.00
	1223	29	15.00	25.00	35.00	50.00

30 PARA

(Zolota)

BILLON, 31mm, 4.50 g

KM#	Date	Year	Good	VG	Fine	VF
57	AH1223	15	50.00	85.00	140.00	200.00

PIASTRE
(40 Para)

BILLON, 31mm, 3.20-4.00 g

53	AH1223	13	75.00	125.00	200.00	300.00

29mm

66	AH1223	21	50.00	85.00	140.00	200.00

Extra leg. added around central device.

67	AH1223	21	50.00	85.00	140.00	200.00

100 PARA

BILLON, 31mm, 3.00-3.20 g

76	AH1223	26	50.00	85.00	140.00	200.00

Rev: Arabic legend.

77	AH1223	26	—	—	—	—
	1223	27	—	—	—	—

5 PIASTRES

BILLON, 36mm, 5.50-6.90 g

78		21 (date error)	—	Rare	—	

KM#	Date	Year	Good	VG	Fine	VF
78	AH1223	26	18.00	30.00	50.00	75.00
	—	27	18.00	30.00	50.00	75.00

HAYRIYE ALTIN

GOLD, 20-21mm, 1.40 g

KM#	Date	Year	VG	Fine	VF	XF
74	AH1223	25	120.00	200.00	275.00	400.00

GOVERNOR SAIT PASA

Coins without name or toughra of Mahmud II

2 PARA

COPPER, 15-18mm

KM#	Date	Year	Good	VG	Fine	VF
82	AH1230	—	20.00	32.00	55.00	80.00

5 PARA

COPPER, 27mm

Obv: *Sait Pasa* within octagram.

85	AH1231	—	35.00	60.00	100.00	150.00

NOTE: This is the only Ottoman coin ever struck with a governor's name. Sait Pasa was beheaded for this infringement of tradition.

Obv: *Tamgha* within octagram.
Rev: Similar to KM#85.

88	AH1231	—	25.00	42.00	70.00	100.00

NOTE: The Tamgha was originally a sheep and cattle brand, later seal or brand. Each Turkish clan formerly kept its own Tamgha, to use both as a brand and as a seal on documents.

ABDUL MEJID

AH1255-1277/1839-1861AD

5 PARA

BILLON, 19-21mm

91	AH1255	1	100.00	150.00	250.00	350.00

IRAQ

MINT MARKS

I - Bombay

MONETARY SYSTEM

Falus, Fulus *Fals, Fils* *Falsan*

50 Fils = 1 Dirham
200 Fils = 1 Riyal
1000 Fils = 1 Dinar (Pound)

TITLES

العراق
al-Iraq

المملكة العراقية
al-Mamlakat al-Iraqiya(t)

الجمهورية العرقية
al-Jumhuriya(t) al-Iraqiya(t)

KINGDOM

FILS

BRONZE
Faisal I

KM#	Date	Mintage	Fine	VF	XF	Unc
95	1931	4.000	1.00	3.00	10.00	25.00
	1931	—	—	—	Proof	—
	1933	6.000	1.00	3.00	10.00	25.00
	1933	—	—	—	Proof	—

Ghazi I

102	1936	3.000	1.25	4.00	10.00	25.00
	1936	—	—	—	Proof	—
	1938	36.000	.25	.50	2.00	4.00
	1938	—	—	—	Proof	—
	1938-I	3.000	.50	2.00	5.00	15.00

Faisal II

109	1953	41.000	.25	.40	.60	1.00
	1953	200 pcs.	—	—	Proof	75.00

2 FILS

BRONZE
Faisal I

96	1931	2.500	1.25	4.00	10.00	25.00
	1931	—	—	—	Proof	—
	1933	1.000	1.50	5.00	15.00	35.00
	1933	—	—	—	Proof	—

Faisal II

110	1953	.500	.50	1.00	3.00	12.50
	1953	200 pcs.	—	—	Proof	100.00

4 FILS

NICKEL
Faisal I

KM#	Date	Mintage	Fine	VF	XF	Unc
97	1931	4.500	1.50	5.00	15.00	50.00
	1931	—	—	—	Proof	—
	1933	6.500	1.50	5.00	15.00	50.00
	1933	—	—	—	Proof	—

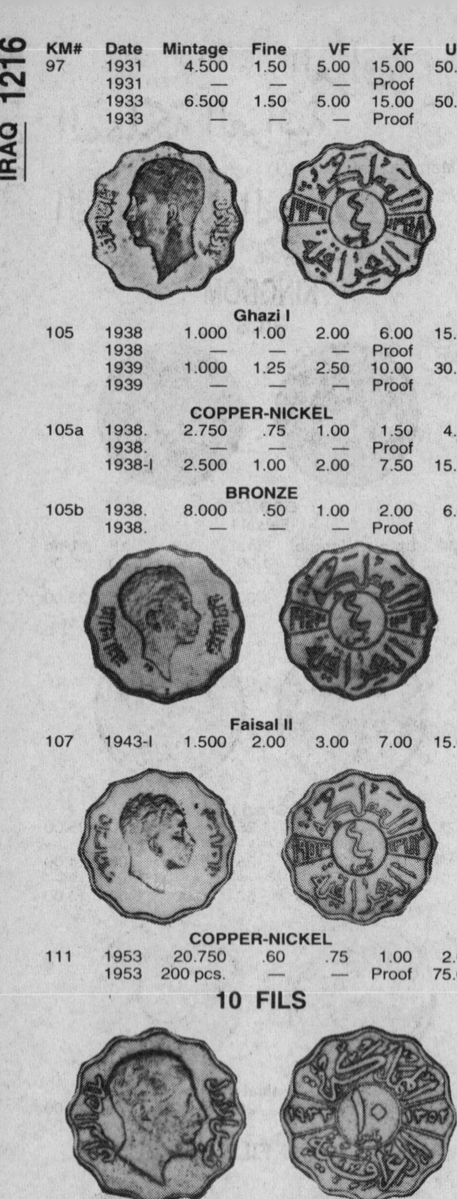

Ghazi I

KM#	Date	Mintage	Fine	VF	XF	Unc
105	1938	1.000	1.00	2.00	6.00	15.00
	1938	—	—	—	Proof	—
	1939	1.000	1.25	2.50	10.00	30.00
	1939	—	—	—	Proof	—

COPPER-NICKEL

KM#	Date	Mintage	Fine	VF	XF	Unc
105a	1938.	2.750	.75	1.00	1.50	4.00
	1938.	—	—	—	Proof	—
	1938-I	2.500	1.00	2.00	7.50	15.00

BRONZE

KM#	Date	Mintage	Fine	VF	XF	Unc
105b	1938.	8.000	.50	1.00	2.00	6.00
	1938.	—	—	—	Proof	—

Faisal II

KM#	Date	Mintage	Fine	VF	XF	Unc
107	1943-I	1.500	2.00	3.00	7.00	15.00

COPPER-NICKEL

KM#	Date	Mintage	Fine	VF	XF	Unc
111	1953	20.750	.60	.75	1.00	2.00
	1953	200 pcs.	—	—	Proof	75.00

10 FILS

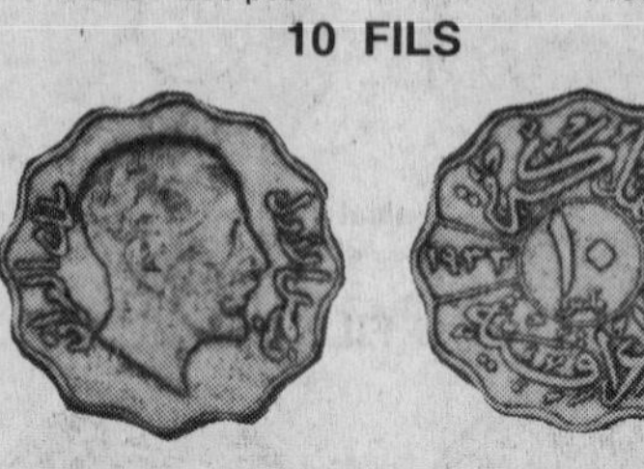

NICKEL
Faisal I

KM#	Date	Mintage	Fine	VF	XF	Unc
98	1931	2.400	2.00	6.00	15.00	50.00
	1931	—	—	—	Proof	—
	1933	2.200	2.00	6.00	15.00	50.00
	1933	—	—	—	Proof	—

Ghazi I

KM#	Date	Mintage	Fine	VF	XF	Unc
103	1937	.400	3.00	5.00	15.00	50.00
	1937	—	—	—	Proof	—
	1938	.600	2.50	4.00	10.00	35.00
	1938	—	—	—	Proof	—

COPPER-NICKEL

KM#	Date	Mintage	Fine	VF	XF	Unc
103a	1938.	1.100	1.00	2.00	4.00	10.00
	1938.	—	—	—	Proof	—
	1938-I	1.500	1.50	2.50	6.00	15.00

BRONZE

KM#	Date	Mintage	Fine	VF	XF	Unc
103b	1938.	8.250	.50	1.00	3.00	7.00
	1938.	—	—	—	Proof	—

Faisal II

KM#	Date	Mintage	Fine	VF	XF	Unc
108	1943-I	1.500	3.00	7.00	20.00	50.00

COPPER-NICKEL

KM#	Date	Mintage	Fine	VF	XF	Unc
112	1953	11.400	.50	.75	1.00	2.00
	1953	200 pcs.	—	—	Proof	75.00

20 FILS

3.6000 g, .500 SILVER, .0579 oz ASW
Faisal I

KM#	Date	Mintage	Fine	VF	XF	Unc
99	1931	1.500	4.00	10.00	25.00	75.00
	1931	—	—	—	Proof	—
	1933	1.100	4.00	10.00	25.00	75.00
	1933	—	—	—	Proof	—
	1933 (error) 1252					
		Inc. Ab.	20.00	60.00	100.00	200.00

Ghazi I

KM#	Date	Mintage	Fine	VF	XF	Unc
106	1938	1.200	1.50	3.00	7.00	20.00
	1938-I	1.350	1.50	3.50	8.00	25.00

Faisal II

KM#	Date	Mintage	Fine	VF	XF	Unc
113	1953	.250	25.00	50.00	75.00	150.00
	1953	200 pcs.	—	—	Proof	400.00

2.8000 g, .500 SILVER, .0450 oz ASW

KM#	Date	Mintage	Fine	VF	XF	Unc
116	1955	4.000	1.50	3.00	5.00	10.00
	1955	—	—	—	Proof	80.00

50 FILS

9.0000 g, .500 SILVER, .1447 oz ASW
Faisal I

KM#	Date	Mintage	Fine	VF	XF	Unc
100	1931	8.800	3.00	10.00	25.00	75.00
	1931	—	—	—	Proof	—
	1933	.800	6.00	15.00	35.00	100.00
	1933	—	—	—	Proof	—

Ghazi I

KM#	Date	Mintage	Fine	VF	XF	Unc
104	1937	1.200	2.50	7.00	10.00	30.00
	1937	—	—	—	Proof	—
	1938	5.300	2.00	4.00	6.00	25.00
	1938	—	—	—	Proof	—
	1938-I	7.500	2.00	4.00	6.00	25.00

Faisal II

KM#	Date	Mintage	Fine	VF	XF	Unc
114	1953	.560	50.00	100.00	150.00	250.00
	1953	200 pcs.	—	—	Proof	600.00

7.0000 g, .500 SILVER, .1126 oz ASW

KM#	Date	Mintage	Fine	VF	XF	Unc
117	1955	12.000	2.50	4.00	6.00	12.50
	1955	—	—	—	Proof	80.00

100 FILS

10.0000 g, .900 SILVER, .2893 oz ASW
Faisal II

KM#	Date	Mintage	Fine	VF	XF	Unc
115	1953	1.200	5.00	7.50	20.00	50.00
	1953	200 pcs.	—	—	Proof	250.00

10.0000 g, .500 SILVER, .1607 oz ASW

KM#	Date	Mintage	Fine	VF	XF	Unc
118	1955	1.000	—	—	Rare	—
	1955	—	—	—	Proof	300.00

RIYAL
(200 Fils)

20.0000 g, .500 SILVER, .3215 oz ASW
Faisal I

KM#	Date	Mintage	Fine	VF	XF	Unc
101	1932	.500	7.50	15.00	32.50	250.00
	1932	—	—	—	Proof	1000.

REPUBLIC

FILS

BRONZE

KM#	Date	Mintage	Fine	VF	XF	Unc
119	1959	72.000	.15	.25	.40	.75
	1959	400 pcs.	—	—	Proof	30.00

5 FILS

COPPER-NICKEL

KM#	Date	Mintage	Fine	VF	XF	Unc
120	1959	30.000	.15	.25	.50	1.00
	1959	400 pcs.	—	—	Proof	30.00

KM#	Date	Mintage	Fine	VF	XF	Unc
125	1967	17.000	.15	.25	.35	.50
	1971	15.000	.15	.25	.35	.50

STAINLESS STEEL

KM#	Date	Mintage	Fine	VF	XF	Unc
125a	1971	2.000	.20	.30	.50	.75
	1974	15.000	.10	.15	.25	.35
	1975	94.800	.10	.15	.25	.35
	1980	20.160	.10	.15	.25	.35
	1981	29.840	.10	.15	.25	.35

F.A.O. Issue

KM#	Date	Mintage	Fine	VF	XF	Unc
141	1975	2.000	.10	.15	.25	.50

Babylon - Ruins

KM#	Date	Mintage	Fine	VF	XF	Unc
159	1982	—	.10	.15	.25	.50

COPPER-NICKEL

KM#	Date	Mintage	Fine	VF	XF	Unc
159a	1982	—	—	—	Proof	3.00

10 FILS

COPPER-NICKEL

KM#	Date	Mintage	Fine	VF	XF	Unc
121	1959	24.000	.20	.30	.50	1.00
	1959	400 pcs.	—	—	Proof	30.00

KM#	Date	Mintage	Fine	VF	XF	Unc
126	1967	13.400	.15	.25	.35	.60
	1971	12.000	.15	.25	.35	.60

STAINLESS STEEL

KM#	Date	Mintage	Fine	VF	XF	Unc
126a	1971	1.550	.15	.25	.50	.75
	1974	12.000	.15	.25	.35	.50
	1975	52.456	.15	.25	.35	.50
	1979	13.800	.15	.25	.35	.50
	1980	11.264	.15	.25	.35	.50
	1981	63.736	.15	.25	.35	.50

F.A.O. Issue

KM#	Date	Mintage	Fine	VF	XF	Unc
142	1975	1.000	.15	.25	.50	.75

Babylon - Ishtar Gate

KM#	Date	Mintage	Fine	VF	XF	Unc
160	1982	—	—	—	—	.75

COPPER-NICKEL

KM#	Date	Mintage	Fine	VF	XF	Unc
160a	1982	—	—	—	Proof	3.00

25 FILS

2.5000 g, .500 SILVER, .0401 oz ASW

KM#	Date	Mintage	Fine	VF	XF	Unc
122	1959	12.000	.50	.75	1.50	3.00
	1959	400 pcs.	—	—	Proof	40.00

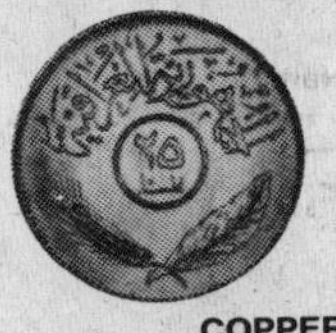

COPPER-NICKEL

KM#	Date	Mintage	Fine	VF	XF	Unc
127	1969	6.000	.15	.25	.35	.50
	1970	6.000	.15	.25	.35	.50
	1972	12.000	.15	.25	.35	.50
	1975	48.000	.15	.25	.35	.50
	1981	60.000	.15	.25	.35	.50

Babylon - Lion

KM#	Date	Mintage	Fine	VF	XF	Unc
161	1982	—	—	—	—	1.00
	1982	—	—	—	Proof	4.00

50 FILS

5.0000 g, .500 SILVER, .0803 oz ASW

KM#	Date	Mintage	Fine	VF	XF	Unc
123	1959	24.000	.75	1.25	2.00	4.50
	1959	400 pcs.	—	—	Proof	80.00

COPPER-NICKEL

KM#	Date	Mintage	Fine	VF	XF	Unc
128	1969	12.000	.20	.30	.50	.75
	1970	12.000	.20	.30	.50	.75
	1972	12.000	.20	.30	.50	.75
	1975	36.000	.20	.30	.50	.75
	1979	1.500	.20	.30	.50	.75
	1980	23.520	.20	.30	.50	.75
	1981	138.995	.20	.30	.50	.75
	1990	—	.20	.30	.50	.75

Babylon - Bull

KM#	Date	Mintage	Fine	VF	XF	Unc
162	1982	—	.25	.50	.75	2.00
	1982	—	—	—	Proof	6.00

100 FILS

10.0000 g, .500 SILVER, .1607 oz ASW

KM#	Date	Mintage	Fine	VF	XF	Unc
124	1959	6.000	2.00	3.25	4.50	8.50
	1959	400 pcs.	—	—	Proof	150.00

COPPER-NICKEL

KM#	Date	Mintage	Fine	VF	XF	Unc
129	1970	6.000	.35	.50	.75	1.25
	1972	6.000	.35	.50	.75	1.25
	1975	12.000	.35	.50	.75	1.25
	1979	1.000	.35	.75	1.50	3.00

250 FILS

NICKEL

F.A.O. Issue - Agrarian Reform Day

KM#	Date	Mintage	Fine	VF	XF	Unc
130	1970	.500	—	1.00	2.00	5.00
	1970	1,000	—	—	Proof	15.00

NOTE: Edge inscription w/FAO-250-repeated three times, relief and incuse varieties reported.

1st Anniversary Peace with Kurds

KM#	Date	Mintage	Fine	VF	XF	Unc
131	1971	.500	—	1.50	3.00	6.50
	1971	1,000	—	—	Proof	15.00

Silver Jubilee of Al Baath Party

KM#	Date	Mintage	Fine	VF	XF	Unc
135	1972	.250	—	1.50	3.00	6.50

25th Anniversary of Central Bank

KM#	Date	Mintage	Fine	VF	XF	Unc
136	1972	.250	—	1.50	3.00	6.50

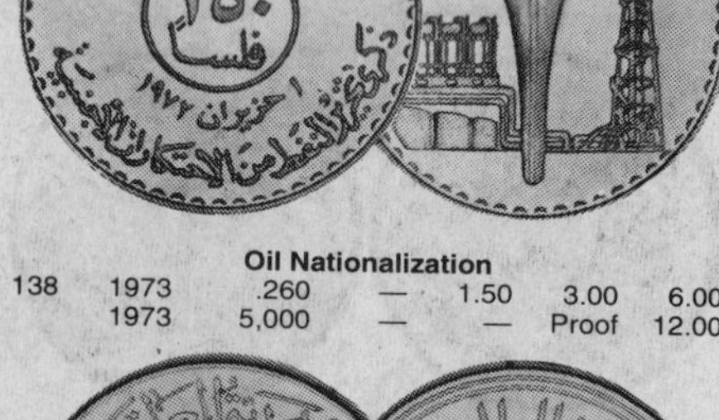

Oil Nationalization

KM#	Date	Mintage	Fine	VF	XF	Unc
138	1973	.260	—	1.50	3.00	6.00
	1973	5,000	—	—	Proof	12.00

International Year of the Child

KM#	Date	Mintage	Fine	VF	XF	Unc
144	1979	.010	—	—	Proof	7.00

COPPER-NICKEL

1st Anniversary of Hussein as President

KM#	Date	Mintage	Fine	VF	XF	Unc
146	1980	—	—	1.00	2.00	4.00

KM#	Date	Mintage	Fine	VF	XF	Unc
147	1980	—	—	1.00	2.00	4.00
	1981	25.568	—	1.00	2.00	4.00
	1990	—	—	1.00	2.00	4.00

World Food Day

KM#	Date	Mintage	Fine	VF	XF	Unc
152	1981	46.432	—	1.00	2.00	4.00

Nonaligned Nations Baghdad Conference

KM#	Date	Mintage	Fine	VF	XF	Unc
155	1982	—	—	1.00	2.00	4.50

Babylon - Top of Hammurabi Stele

KM#	Date	Mintage	Fine	VF	XF	Unc
163	1982	—	—	1.00	1.50	3.50
	1982	—	—	—	Proof	8.00

500 FILS

NICKEL

50th Anniversary of Iraqi Army

KM#	Date	Mintage	Fine	VF	XF	Unc
132	1971	.100	—	2.00	4.00	12.00
	1971	5,000	—	—	Proof	15.00

Oil Nationalization

KM#	Date	Mintage	Fine	VF	XF	Unc
139	1973	.260	—	2.00	4.00	10.00
	1973	5,000	—		Proof	15.00

9.08 g

Obv. denomination: *500 Fals*

KM#	Date	Mintage	Fine	VF	XF	Unc
165	1982	—	—	2.00	3.00	5.00

Reduced weight, 8.98 g

Obv. denomination: *500 Falsin*

KM#	Date	Mintage	Fine	VF	XF	Unc
165a	1982	—	—	20.00	35.00	85.00

9.08 g

Babylon - Lion of Babylon

Obv. denomination: *500 Fals*

KM#	Date	Mintage	Fine	VF	XF	Unc
168	1982	—	—	2.00	3.50	8.50
	1982	—	—	—	Proof	12.50

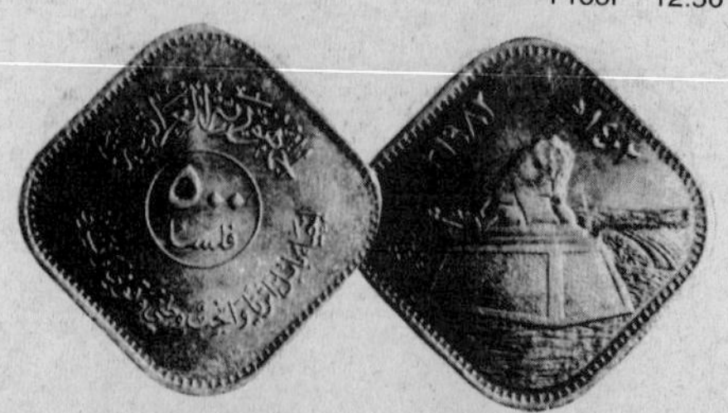

Obv. denomination: *500 Falsin*

KM#	Date	Mintage	Fine	VF	XF	Unc
168a	1982	—	—	18.00	30.00	75.00

DINAR

31.0000 g, .900 SILVER, .8971 oz ASW
50th Anniversary of Iraqi Army

KM#	Date	Mintage	Fine	VF	XF	Unc
133	1971	.020	—	—	—	18.00
	1971	—	—	—	Proof	28.00

31.0000 g, .500 SILVER, .4983 oz ASW
25th Anniversary of Central Bank

KM#	Date	Mintage	Fine	VF	XF	Unc
137	1972	.050	—	—	—	18.00
	1972	—	—	—	Proof	28.00

Oil Nationalization

KM#	Date	Mintage	Fine	VF	XF	Unc
140	1973	.060	—	—	—	18.00
	1973	5,000	—	—	Proof	35.00

31.0000 g, .900 SILVER, .8971 oz ASW
Inauguration of Tharthat-Euphrates Canal

KM#	Date	Mintage	Fine	VF	XF	Unc
143	1977	7,000	—	—	Proof	25.00

International Year of the Child

KM#	Date	Mintage	Fine	VF	XF	Unc
145	1979	5,000	—	—	Proof	45.00

30.5300 g, .900 SILVER, .8835 oz ASW
15th Century of Hegira

KM#	Date	Mintage	Fine	VF	XF	Unc
148	1980	.025	—	—	Proof	40.00

NICKEL
Battle of Qadissyiat - Saddam

KM#	Date	Mintage	Fine	VF	XF	Unc
149	1980	—	—	—	3.50	9.00
	1980	—	—	—	Proof	12.50

50th Anniversary of Iraq Air Force

KM#	Date	Mintage	Fine	VF	XF	Unc
153	1981	—	—	—	3.50	9.00

Circulation Coinage

KM#	Date	Mintage	Fine	VF	XF	Unc
170	1981	—	—	—	—	3.50

Nonaligned Nations Baghdad Conference

KM#	Date	Mintage	Fine	VF	XF	Unc
156	1982	—	—	—	3.50	9.00

Tower of Babylon

KM#	Date	Mintage	Fine	VF	XF	Unc
164	1982	—	—	—	3.50	9.00
	1982	—	—	—	Proof	12.50

5 DINARS

13.5700gm., .917 GOLD, .4001oz AGW
50th Anniversary of Iraqi Army

KM#	Date	Mintage	Fine	VF	XF	Unc
134	1971	.020	—	—	—	225.00
	1971	—	—	—	Proof	250.00

50 DINARS

13.7000 g, .917 GOLD, .4037 oz AGW
International Year of the Child

KM#	Date	Mintage	Fine	VF	XF	Unc
166	1979	.010	—	—	Proof	280.00

13.0000 g, .917 GOLD, .3832 oz AGW
15th Century of Hegira

KM#	Date	Mintage	Fine	VF	XF	Unc
150	1980	.013	—	—	Proof	225.00

13.7000 g, .917 GOLD, .4040 oz AGW
Nonaligned Nations Baghdad Conference

KM#	Date	Mintage	Fine	VF	XF	Unc
157	1982	.010	—	—	Proof	225.00

100 DINARS

26.0000 g, .917 GOLD, .7665 oz AGW
International Year of the Child

KM#	Date	Mintage	Fine	VF	XF	Unc
167	1979	.010	—	—	Proof	500.00

15th Century of Hegira

KM#	Date	Mintage	Fine	VF	XF	Unc
151	1980	.014	—	—	Proof	450.00

Nonaligned Nations Baghdad Conference

KM#	Date	Mintage	Fine	VF	XF	Unc
158	1982	.010	—	—	Proof	400.00

PROOF SETS (PS)

KM#	Date	Mintage	Identification	Issue Price	Mkt. Val.
PS1	1953(7)	200	KM109-115	—	1500.
PS2	1955(3)	—	KM116-118	—	500.00
PS3	1959(6)	400	KM119-124	—	360.00
PS4	1959(7)	—	KM119-124, plus medallic crown (M1)	—	400.00
PS5	1973(3)	5,000	KM138-140	—	60.00
PS6	1982(7)	—	KM159a-160a,161-164,168	—	50.00

IRELAND

Ireland, the island located in the Atlantic Ocean west of Great Britain, was settled by a race of tall, red-haired Celts from Gaul about 400 BC. They assimilated the native Erainn and Picts and established a Gaelic civilization. After the arrival of St. Patrick in 432 AD, Ireland evolved into a center of Latin learning which sent missionaries to Europe and possibly North America. In 1154, Pope Adrian IV gave all of Ireland to English King Henry II to administer as a Papal fief. Because of the enactment of anti-Catholic laws and the awarding of vast tracts of Irish land to Protestant absentee land-owners, English control did not become reasonably absolute until 1800 when England and Ireland became the "United Kingdom of Great Britain and Ireland". Religious freedom was restored to the Irish in 1829, but agitation for political autonomy continued until the Irish Free State was established as a Dominion on Dec. 6, 1921 while Northern Ireland remained under the British rule.

RULERS

British to 1921

MONETARY SYSTEM

4 Farthings = 1 Penny
12 Pence = 1 Shilling
5 Shillings = 1 Crown

FARTHING

KM#	Date	Mintage	Fine	VF	XF	Unc
		COPPER				
146	1806	—	4.00	9.00	40.00	120.00
	1806	—	—	—	Proof	150.00
		COPPER GILT				
146a	1805	—	—	—	Proof	250.00
	1806	—	—	—	Proof	250.00
		COPPER BRONZED				
146b	1805	—	—	—	Proof	175.00
		SILVER				
146c	1805	—	—	—	Proof	1500.
		GOLD				
146d	1805	—	—	—	Proof	Rare

KM#	Date	Mintage	Fine	VF	XF	Unc
		COPPER				
152	1822	6 known	—	—	Proof	1750.

1/2 PENNY

KM#	Date	Mintage	Fine	VF	XF	Unc
		COPPER				
147	1805	—	6.00	12.00	60.00	180.00
	1805	—	—	—	Proof	225.00
		COPPER GILT				
147a	1805	—	—	—	Proof	275.00
		COPPER BRONZED				
147b	1805	—	—	—	Proof	175.00
		SILVER				
147c	1805	—	—	—	Proof	1500.

KM#	Date	Mintage	Fine	VF	XF	Unc
		COPPER				
150	1822	—	8.00	20.00	85.00	200.00
	1822	—	—	—	Proof	300.00
	1823	—	8.00	20.00	85.00	200.00
	1823	—	—	—	Proof	300.00

PENNY

KM#	Date	Mintage	Fine	VF	XF	Unc
		COPPER				
148	1805	—	10.00	20.00	75.00	200.00
	1805	—	—	—	Proof	300.00
		COPPER GILT				
148a	1805	—	—	—	Proof	350.00
		COPPER BRONZED				
148b	1805	—	—	—	Proof	225.00
		SILVER				
148c	1805	—	—	—	Proof	1650.
		GOLD				
148d	1805	—	—	—	Proof	3500.

KM#	Date	Mintage	Fine	VF	XF	Unc
		COPPER				
151	1822	—	10.00	25.00	100.00	200.00
	1822	—	—	—	Proof	400.00
	1823	—	10.00	25.00	100.00	200.00
	1823	—	—	—	Proof	400.00

NOTE: For mule obv. KM#151 and rev. Ionian Islands 2 Oboli, KM#33 refer to Greece pattern listings.

NOTE: Similar pieces exist as 3 Shillings and 40 Pence. Refer to *Unusual World Coins*, 3rd edition, Krause Publications, Inc., c.1992.

TOKEN ISSUES (Tn)

Bank of Ireland

5 PENCE TOKEN

KM#	Date	Mintage	Fine	VF	XF	Unc
		SILVER				
Tn2	1805	—	7.50	25.00	60.00	150.00
	1806	—	15.00	50.00	125.00	225.00
	1806/5	5 known	50.00	150.00	350.00	750.00

10 PENCE TOKEN

KM#	Date	Mintage	Fine	VF	XF	Unc
		SILVER				
Tn3	1805	—	15.00	50.00	150.00	400.00
	1806	—	12.50	35.00	85.00	275.00

KM#	Date	Mintage	Fine	VF	XF	Unc
Tn5	1813	—	7.50	25.00	60.00	200.00
	1813	—	—	—	Proof	400.00

30 PENCE TOKEN

SILVER

KM#	Date	Mintage	Fine	VF	XF	Unc
Tn4	1808	—	17.50	85.00	275.00	500.00

6 SHILLINGS TOKEN

SILVER

KM#	Date	Mintage	Fine	VF	XF	Unc
Tn1	1804	—	125.00	250.00	600.00	1200.
	1804	—	—	—	Proof	1450.

NOTE: The silver proofs were struck on specially prepared plain edge polished planchets while circulation strikes were struck over Spanish and Spanish Colonial 8 Reales, that had been planed (removing 15 grains).

IRELAND REPUBLIC

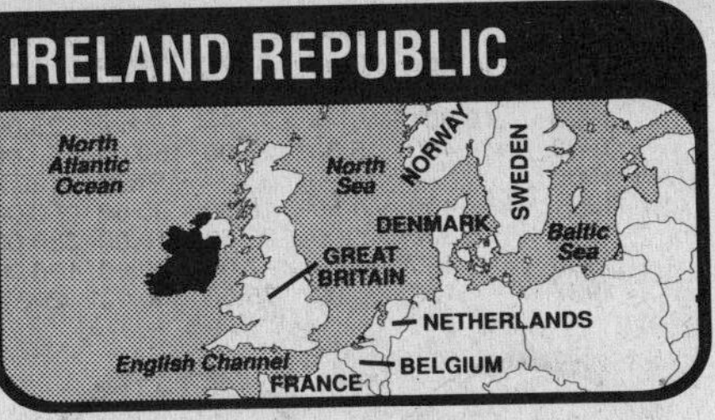

Ireland, which occupies five-sixths of the island of Ireland located in the Atlantic Ocean west of Great Britain, has an area of 27,136 sq. mi. (70,280 sq. km.) and a population of 4.3 million. Capital: Dublin. Agriculture and dairy farming are the principal industries. Meat, livestock, dairy products and textiles are exported.

A race of tall, red-haired Celts from Gaul arrived in Ireland about 400 B.C., assimilated the native Erainn and Picts, and established a Gaelic civilization. After the arrival of St. Patrick in 432AD, Ireland evolved into a center of Latin learning which sent missionaries to Europe and possibly North America. In 1154, Pope Adrian IV gave all of Ireland to English King Henry II to administer as a Papal fief. Because of the enactment of anti-Catholic laws and the awarding of vast tracts of Irish land to Protestant absentee landowners, English control did not become reasonably absolute until 1800 when England and Ireland became the 'United Kingdom of Great Britain and Ireland'. Religious freedom was restored to the Irish in 1829, but agitation for political autonomy continued until the Irish Free State was established as a dominion on Dec. 6, 1921. Ireland proclaimed itself a republic on April 18, 1949. The government, however, does not use the term "Republic of Ireland", which tacitly acknowledges the partitioning of the island into Ireland and Northern Ireland, but refers to the country simply as "Ireland".

RULERS

British, until 1921

MONETARY SYSTEM

4 Farthings = 1 Penny
12 Pence = 1 Shilling
2 Shillings = 1 Florin
20 Shillings = 1 Pound

FARTHING

BRONZE
European Woodcock

KM#	Date	Mintage	Fine	VF	XF	Unc
1	1928	.300	.50	1.50	4.50	10.00
	1928	6,001	—	—	Proof	15.00
	1930	.288	.75	1.50	4.50	20.00
	1931	.192	4.50	8.00	15.00	35.00
	1931	—	—	—	Proof	—
	1932	.192	5.00	10.00	18.00	45.00
	1933	.480	.75	1.50	4.00	20.00
	1935	.192	5.00	8.00	15.00	35.00
	1936	.192	5.00	8.00	16.50	37.50
	1937	.480	.50	1.50	3.00	15.00

KM#	Date	Mintage	Fine	VF	XF	Unc
9	1939	.768	.50	1.00	2.00	8.00
	1939	—	—	—	Proof	815.00
	1940	.192	2.00	4.00	8.00	22.50
	1941	.480	.50	.75	2.00	6.50
	1943	.480	.50	.75	2.00	6.50
	1944	.480	.75	1.25	3.00	12.00
	1946	.480	.50	.75	2.00	6.00
	1946	—	—	—	Proof	—
	1949	.192	.75	3.00	6.00	20.00
	1949	—	—	—	Proof	300.00
	1953	.192	.25	.50	1.25	3.50
	1953	—	—	—	Proof	300.00
	1959	.192	.25	.50	1.25	3.00
	1966	.096	.50	1.00	2.00	5.00

1/2 PENNY

BRONZE
Sow with Piglets

KM#	Date	Mintage	Fine	VF	XF	Unc
2	1928	2.880	.75	2.00	5.00	15.00
	1928	6,001	—	—	Proof	15.00
	1933	.720	5.00	15.00	80.00	750.00
	1935	.960	2.00	6.00	50.00	275.00
	1937	.960	1.00	3.00	15.00	40.00

KM#	Date	Mintage	Fine	VF	XF	Unc
10	1939	.240	10.00	17.50	60.00	225.00
	1939	—	—	—	Proof	1000.
	1940	1.680	1.00	4.50	40.00	180.00
	1941	2.400	.20	.50	2.50	25.00
	1942	6.931	.10	.25	1.50	8.00
	1943	2.669	.20	.50	3.00	25.00
	1946	.720	1.00	2.50	15.00	80.00
	1949	1.344	.10	.25	1.50	15.00
	1949	—	—	—	Proof	—
	1953	2.400	.10	.15	.50	2.00
	1953				Proof	400.00
	1964	2.160	.10	.15	.25	1.00
	1965	1.440	.10	.15	.75	2.00
	1966	1.680	.10	.15	.50	1.00
	1967	1.200	.10	.15	.50	1.00

PENNY

BRONZE
Hen with Chicks

KM#	Date	Mintage	Fine	VF	XF	Unc
3	1928	9.000	.75	1.50	5.00	25.00
	1928	6,001	—	—	Proof	17.50
	1931	2.400	1.00	2.00	12.00	70.00
	1931				Proof	1500.
	1933	1.680	1.00	2.50	25.00	140.00
	1935	5.472	.50	1.00	8.00	40.00
	1937	5.400	.50	1.00	15.00	75.00
	1937				Proof	1500.

KM#	Date	Mintage	Fine	VF	XF	Unc
11	1938	—	—	—	Unique	15,000.
	1940	.312	3.00	10.00	75.00	—
	1941	4.680	.25	.50	8.00	50.00
	1942	17.520	.25	.50	1.50	10.00
	1943	3.360	.75	1.50	7.50	45.00
	1946	4.800	.25	.50	3.00	20.00
	1948	4.800	.25	.50	3.00	10.00
	1949	4.080	.25	.50	3.00	10.00
	1949	—	—	—	Proof	600.00
	1950	2.400	.25	.50	4.50	15.00
	1950	—	—	—	Proof	600.00
	1952	2.400	.25	.50	2.00	12.00
	1962	1.200	.75	2.50	4.50	15.00
	1962	—	—	—	Proof	175.00
	1963	9.600	.20	.40	.75	2.00
	1963	—	—	—	Proof	175.00
	1964	6.000	.20	.40	.75	1.00
	1964	—	—	—	Proof	—
	1965	11.160	.20	.40	.75	1.00
	1966	6.000	.20	.40	.75	1.00
	1967	2.400	.20	.40	.75	1.00
	1968	21.000	.20	.40	.75	1.00
	1968	—	—	—	Proof	350.00

NOTE: Varieties exist.

3 PENCE

NICKEL

Blue Hare

KM#	Date	Mintage	Fine	VF	XF	Unc
4	1928	1.500	.50	1.00	3.50	10.00
	1928	6,001	—	—	Proof	20.00
	1933	.320	3.00	10.00	90.00	425.00
	1934	.800	1.00	2.00	12.50	70.00
	1935	.240	3.00	8.00	40.00	225.00

KM#	Date	Mintage	Fine	VF	XF	Unc
12	1939	.064	12.00	25.00	125.00	550.00
	1939	—	—	—	Proof	1500.
	1940	.720	1.50	3.00	12.50	50.00

COPPER-NICKEL

KM#	Date	Mintage	Fine	VF	XF	Unc
12a	1942	4.000	.25	.75	6.00	35.00
	1942				Proof	500.00
	1943	1.360	.50	2.00	15.00	90.00
	1943	—	—	—	Proof	—
	1946	.800	1.00	2.00	10.00	45.00
	1946	—	—	—	Proof	200.00
	1948	1.600	1.00	2.00	35.00	125.00
	1949	1.200	.25	.50	3.00	25.00
	1949	—	—	—	Proof	200.00
	1950	1.600	.25	.50	3.00	20.00
	1950	—	—	—	Proof	500.00
	1953	1.600	.25	.50	2.00	10.00
	1956	1.200	.25	.50	2.00	7.50
	1961	2.400	.15	.25	.50	5.00
	1962	3.200	.15	.25	.50	7.50
	1963	4.000	.15	.25	.50	1.50
	1964	4.000	.10	.15	.25	1.00
	1965	3.600	.10	.15	.25	1.00
	1966	4.000	.10	.15	.25	.75
	1967	2.400	.10	.15	.25	.75
	1968	4.000	.10	.15	.25	.75
	1968	—	—	—	Proof	—

6 PENCE

NICKEL
Irish Wolfhound

KM#	Date	Mintage	Fine	VF	XF	Unc
5	1928	3.201	.50	1.00	5.00	17.50
	1928	6,001	—	—	Proof	25.00
	1934	.600	1.00	2.00	17.50	125.00
	1935	.520	1.00	3.00	30.00	320.00

KM#	Date	Mintage	Fine	VF	XF	Unc
13	1939	.876	.75	2.00	8.00	55.00
	1939	—	—	—	Proof	1150.
	1940	1.120	.75	2.00	6.00	50.00

COPPER-NICKEL

KM#	Date	Mintage	Fine	VF	XF	Unc
13a	1942	1.320	.50	1.00	5.00	45.00
	1945	.400	2.00	8.00	60.00	175.00
	1946	.720	2.00	10.00	150.00	600.00
	1947	.800	1.00	12.00	30.00	80.00
	1948	.800	1.00	1.50	10.00	60.00
	1949	.600	1.50	3.50	10.00	70.00
	1950	.800	1.00	6.00	70.00	150.00
	1952	.800	.50	1.00	5.00	30.00
	1952	—	—	—	Proof	175.00
	1953	.800	.50	1.00	5.00	30.00
	1955	.600	1.00	2.50	8.00	30.00
	1956	.600	.75	2.00	4.00	20.00
	1958	.600	1.00	2.50	6.00	75.00
	1958	—	—	—	Proof	350.00
	1959	2.000	.25	.50	3.00	17.50
	1960	2.020	.25	.50	2.00	12.50
	1961	3.000	.25	.25	1.00	7.50
	1962	4.000	.25	.75	4.00	75.00
	1963	4.000	.15	.25	.50	1.50
	1964	6.000	.15	.25	.50	2.00
	1966	2.000	.15	.25	.50	1.00
	1967	4.000	.15	.25	.50	1.00
	1968	8.000	.15	.25	.50	1.00
	1969	2.000	.15	.25	.50	1.00

SHILLING

5.6552 g, .750 SILVER, .1364 oz ASW

Bull

KM#	Date	Mintage	Fine	VF	XF	Unc
6	1928	2.700	1.50	5.00	10.00	25.00
	1928	6,001	—	—	Proof	25.00
	1930	.460	5.00	25.00	150.00	550.00
	1930	—	—	—	Proof	1200.
	1931	.400	4.50	18.00	90.00	250.00
	1933	.300	5.00	22.50	110.00	350.00
	1935	.400	2.00	7.00	30.00	100.00
	1937	.100	15.00	75.00	500.00	2000.

KM#	Date	Mintage	Fine	VF	XF	Unc
14	1939	1.140	2.50	4.50	12.50	35.00
	1939	—	—	—	Proof	775.00
	1940	.580	3.00	5.00	15.00	45.00
	1941	.300	4.00	12.50	25.00	50.00
	1942	.286	4.00	7.50	15.00	40.00

COPPER-NICKEL

KM#	Date	Mintage	Fine	VF	XF	Unc
14a	1951	2.000	.25	.50	2.50	15.00
	1951	—	—	—	Proof	500.00
	1954	3.000	.25	.50	2.50	12.50
	1954	—	—	—	Proof	—
	1955	1.000	1.00	2.00	5.00	15.00
	1955	—	—	—	Proof	—
	1959	2.000	.25	.50	4.00	35.00
	1962	4.000	.25	.50	1.00	7.00
	1963	4.000	.25	.50	1.00	3.00
	1964	4.000	.25	.50	1.00	2.00
	1966	3.000	.25	.50	1.00	2.00
	1968	4.000	.25	.50	1.00	3.00

FLORIN

11.3104 g, .750 SILVER, .2727 oz ASW
Atlantic Salmon

KM#	Date	Mintage	Fine	VF	XF	Unc
7	1928	2.025	3.00	7.00	15.00	40.00
	1928	6,001	—	—	Proof	40.00
	1930	.330	6.50	25.00	150.00	500.00
	1931	.200	8.00	35.00	225.00	600.00
	1933	.300	5.00	25.00	195.00	575.00
	1934	.150	10.00	60.00	325.00	750.00
	1934	—	—	—	Proof	2750.
	1935	.390	5.00	17.50	90.00	225.00
	1937	.150	10.00	35.00	225.00	750.00

KM#	Date	Mintage	Fine	VF	XF	Unc
15	1939	1.080	2.00	5.00	20.00	45.00
	1939	—	—	—	Proof	800.00
	1940	.670	3.00	6.00	20.00	50.00
	1941	.400	3.00	10.00	25.00	60.00
	1941	—	—	—	Proof	800.00
	1942	.109	5.00	15.00	25.00	55.00
	1943	* 900.00	1600.	3500.	7500.	

***NOTE:** Approximately 35 known.

COPPER-NICKEL

KM#	Date	Mintage	Fine	VF	XF	Unc
15a	1951	1.000	1.00	2.00	6.00	17.50
	1951	—	—	—	Proof	600.00
	1954	1.000	1.00	2.00	6.00	20.00
	1954	—	—	—	Proof	450.00
	1955	1.000	1.00	2.00	5.00	17.50
	1955	—	—	—	Proof	450.00
	1959	2.000	.50	1.00	2.50	12.00
	1961	2.000	.50	1.00	7.00	40.00
	1962	2.400	.50	1.00	2.00	12.00
	1963	3.000	.25	.50	.75	7.00
	1964	4.000	.25	.50	.75	3.00
	1965	2.000	.25	.50	.75	3.00
	1966	3.625	.25	.50	.75	3.00
	1968	1.000	.25	.35	1.00	4.50

1/2 CROWN

14.1380 g, .750 SILVER, .3409 oz ASW
Irish Hunter
Rev: Close O and I in COROIN, 8 tufts in horse's tail, w/156 beads in border.

KM#	Date	Mintage	Fine	VF	XF	Unc
8	1928	2.160	3.50	10.00	20.00	50.00
	1928	6,001	—	—	Proof	45.00
	1930	.352	4.50	20.00	175.00	500.00
	1931	.160	8.50	30.00	250.00	700.00
	1933	.336	4.50	20.00	175.00	500.00
	1934	.480	4.00	15.00	40.00	150.00
	1937	.040	65.00	150.00	750.00	1750.

Rev: Normal spacing between O and I in COROIN, 7 tufts in horse's tail, w/151 beads in border.

KM#	Date	Mintage	Fine	VF	XF	Unc
16	1939	.888	3.00	8.00	17.50	55.00
	1939	—	—	—	Proof	800.00
	1940	.752	3.00	8.00	15.00	50.00
	1941	.320	4.00	12.50	30.00	75.00
	1942	.286	4.00	12.50	25.00	50.00
	1943	* 100.00	400.00	1250.	2250.	

***NOTE :** Approximately 500 known.

COPPER-NICKEL

KM#	Date	Mintage	Fine	VF	XF	Unc
16a	1951	.800	1.50	3.00	10.00	40.00
	1951	—	—	—	Proof	600.00
	1954	.400	2.00	4.00	15.00	50.00
	1954	—	—	—	Proof	500.00
	1955	1.080	1.00	2.00	6.00	30.00
	1955	—	—	—	Proof	200.00
	1959	1.600	1.00	1.75	3.00	15.00
	1961	1.600	1.00	1.75	3.50	25.00
	1961	—	—	—	Proof	—
	1962	3.200	.50	1.00	2.50	15.00
	1962	—	—	—	Proof	—
	1963	2.400	.50	1.00	2.00	7.50
	1964	3.200	.50	1.00	2.00	5.00
	1966	.700	.75	1.50	3.00	6.00
	1967	2.000	.50	1.00	2.00	6.00

NOTE: 1967 exists struck with a polished reverse die. Estimated value is $15.00 in uncirculated.

KM#8 long base 2 **KM#16-16a short base 2**
Mule. Obv: KM#16a. Rev: KM#8.

KM#	Date	Mintage	VG	Fine	VF	XF
17	1961	Inc. Ab.	—	5.00	12.00	200.00

10 SHILLINGS

18.1400 g, .833 SILVER, .4858 oz ASW
50th Anniversary of Easter Uprising

KM#	Date	Mintage	Fine	VF	XF	Unc
18	1966	*2.000	BV	3.00	7.00	12.00

KM#	Date	Mintage	Fine	VF	XF	Unc
18	1966	.020	—	—	Proof	15.00

NOTE: *Approximately 1.270 melted down.

DECIMAL COINAGE

100 Pence = 1 Pound

1/2 PENNY

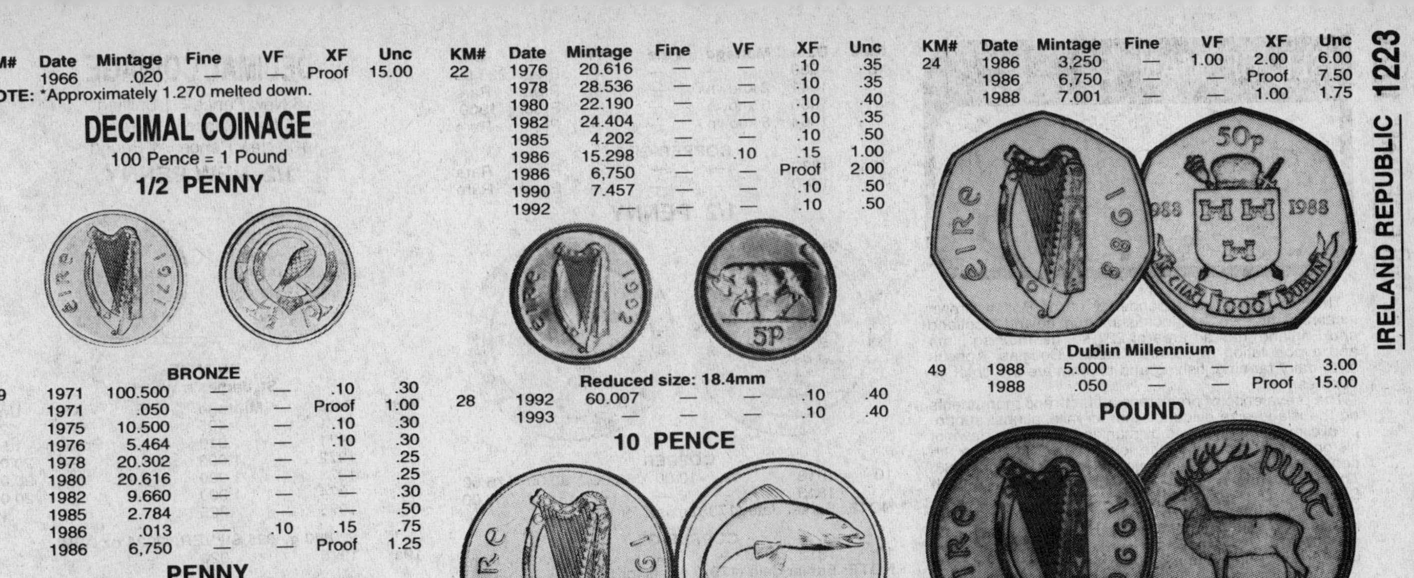

BRONZE

KM#	Date	Mintage	Fine	VF	XF	Unc
19	1971	100.500	—	—	.10	.30
	1971	.050	—	—	Proof	1.00
	1975	10.500	—	—	.10	.30
	1976	5.464	—	—	.10	.30
	1978	20.302	—	—	—	.25
	1980	20.616	—	—	—	.25
	1982	9.660	—	—	—	.30
	1985	2.784	—	—	—	.50
	1986	.013	—	.10	.15	.75
	1986	6,750	—	—	Proof	1.25

PENNY

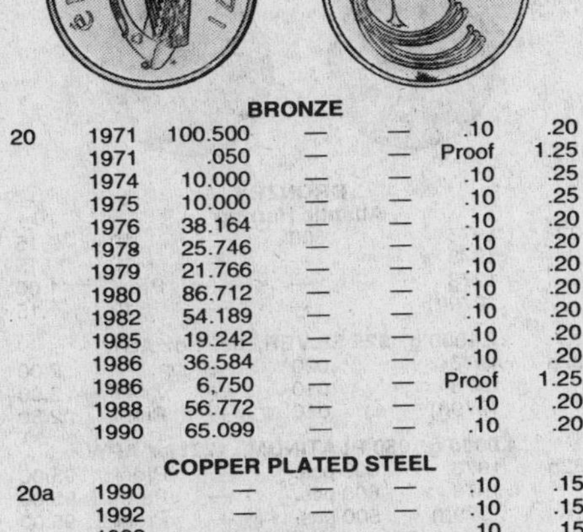

BRONZE

KM#	Date	Mintage	Fine	VF	XF	Unc
20	1971	100.500	—	—	.10	.20
	1971	.050	—	—	Proof	1.25
	1974	10.000	—	—	.10	.25
	1975	10.000	—	—	.10	.25
	1976	38.164	—	—	.10	.20
	1978	25.746	—	—	.10	.20
	1979	21.766	—	—	.10	.20
	1980	86.712	—	—	.10	.20
	1982	54.189	—	—	.10	.20
	1985	19.242	—	—	.10	.20
	1986	36.584	—	—	.10	.20
	1986	6,750	—	—	Proof	1.25
	1988	56.772	—	—	.10	.20
	1990	65.099	—	—	.10	.20

COPPER PLATED STEEL

KM#	Date	Mintage	Fine	VF	XF	Unc
20a	1990	—	—	—	.10	.15
	1992	—	—	—	.10	.15
	1993	—	—	—	.10	.15

2 PENCE

BRONZE

KM#	Date	Mintage	Fine	VF	XF	Unc
21	1971	75.500	—	—	.10	1.00
	1971	.050	—	—	Proof	1.50
	1975	20.010	—	—	.10	.30
	1976	5.414	—	—	.10	.50
	1978	12.000	—	—	.10	.30
	1979	32.373	—	—	.10	.30
	1980	59.828	—	—	.10	.30
	1982	30.435	—	—	.10	.30
	1985	14.469	—	—	.10	.30
	1986	23.865	—	—	.10	.30
	1986	6,750	—	—	Proof	1.50
	1988	35.868	—	—	.10	.30
	1990	34.284	—	—	.10	.30

COPPER PLATED STEEL

KM#	Date	Mintage	Fine	VF	XF	Unc
21a	1988	—	—	—	.10	.25
	1992	—	—	—	.10	.25

5 PENCE

COPPER-NICKEL

KM#	Date	Mintage	Fine	VF	XF	Unc
22	1969	5.000	—	.10	.15	1.00
	1970	10.000	—	—	.10	.50
	1971	8.000	—	—	.10	.45
	1971	.050	—	—	Proof	2.00
	1974	7.000	—	—	.10	.50
	1975	10.000	—	—	.10	.40
	1976	20.616	—	—	.10	.35
	1978	28.536	—	—	.10	.35
	1980	22.190	—	—	.10	.40
	1982	24.404	—	—	.10	.35
	1985	4.202	—	—	.10	.50
	1986	15.298	—	.10	.15	1.00
	1986	6,750	—	—	Proof	2.00
	1990	7.457	—	—	.10	.50
	1992		—	—	.10	.50

Reduced size: 18.4mm

KM#	Date	Mintage	Fine	VF	XF	Unc
28	1992	60.007	—	—	.10	.40
	1993	—	—	—	.10	.40

10 PENCE

COPPER-NICKEL

KM#	Date	Mintage	Fine	VF	XF	Unc
23	1969	27.000	—	—	.40	1.00
	1971	4.000	—	—	.40	1.00
	1971	.050	—	—	Proof	2.50
	1973	2.500	—	—	.40	1.50
	1974	7.500	—	—	.35	1.00
	1975	15.000	—	—	.35	.75
	1976	9.433	—	—	.35	1.00
	1978	30.905	—	—	.25	.50
	1980	44.605	—	—	.25	.50
	1982	7.374	—	—	.25	.50
	1985	4.100	—	—	.25	1.00
	1986	4,530	—	.20	.50	2.25
	1986	6,750	—	—	Proof	2.50

KM#	Date	Mintage	Fine	VF	XF	Unc
29	1993	—	—	—	—	.75

20 PENCE

NICKEL-BRONZE

KM#	Date	Mintage	Fine	VF	XF	Unc
25	1986	50.430	—	—	.50	1.50
	1986	6,750	—	—	Proof	3.50
	1988	20.661	—	—	.50	1.50
	1990	—	—	—	.50	1.50
	1992	—	—	—	.50	1.50

50 PENCE

COPPER-NICKEL

KM#	Date	Mintage	Fine	VF	XF	Unc
24	1970	9.000	—	—	1.50	5.00
	1971	.600	—	1.00	2.00	6.50
	1971	.050	—	—	Proof	3.50
	1974	1.000	—	1.00	2.00	7.50
	1975	2.000	—	—	1.50	4.00
	1976	3.000	—	—	1.25	3.00
	1977	4.800	—	—	1.25	3.00
	1978	4.500	—	—	1.25	3.00
	1979	4.000	—	—	1.25	3.00
	1981	6.000	—	—	1.00	2.00
	1982	2.000	—	—	1.25	3.00
	1983	7.000	—	—	1.00	1.75
	1986	3,250	—	1.00	2.00	6.00
	1986	6,750	—	—	Proof	7.50
	1988	7.001	—	—	1.00	1.75

Dublin Millennium

KM#	Date	Mintage	Fine	VF	XF	Unc
49	1988	5.000	—	—	—	3.00
	1988	.050	—	—	Proof	15.00

POUND

COPPER-NICKEL

KM#	Date	Mintage	Fine	VF	XF	Unc
50	1990	62.292	—	—	—	4.50
	1990	.050	—	—	Proof	27.50

MINT SETS (MS)

KM#	Date	Mintage	Identification	Issue Price	Mkt. Val.
MS1	1966(8)	96,000	KM9-11,12a-16a	—	20.00
MS2	1971(6)	—	KM19-24	1.50	9.00
MS3	Various dates (6)	—	KM19-24	—	6.50
MS4	1978(6)	—	KM19-24	—	5.00

PROOF SETS (PS)

KM#	Date	Mintage	Identification	Issue Price	Mkt. Val.
PS1	1928(8)	6,001	KM1-8	—	187.50
PS2	1966(2)	—	KM18(2)	—	35.00
PS3	1971(6)	50,000	KM19-24	4.40	12.00
PS4	1986(7)	*6,750	KM19-25	—	20.00

Listings For

IRIAN BARAT: refer to Indonesia

The Isle of Man, a dependency of the British Crown located in the Irish Sea equidistant from Ireland, Scotland and England, has an area of 227 sq. mi. (588 sq. km.) and a population of 68,000. Capital: Douglas. Agriculture, dairy farming, fishing and tourism are the chief industries.

The prevalence of prehistoric artifacts and monuments on the island give evidence that its mild, almost subtropical climate was enjoyed by mankind before the dawn of history. Vikings came to the Isle of Man during the 9th century and remained until ejected by Scotland in 1266. The island came under the protection of the British Crown in 1288, and in 1406 was granted, in perpetuity, to the earls of Derby, from whom it was inherited, 1736, by the Duke of Atholl. Rights and title were purchased from the Duke of Atholl in 1765 by the British Crown; the remaining privileges of the Atholl family were transferred to the crown in 1829. The Isle of Man is ruled by its own legislative council and the House of Keys, one of the oldest legislative assemblies in the world. Acts of Parliament passed in London do not affect the island unless it is specifically mentioned.

RULERS

(Commencing 1765)

British

MINT MARKS

PM - Pobjoy Mint

PRIVY MARKS

(a) - Big Apple
(b) - Baby Crib - 1982 dates only
(ba) - Basel Bugle
(bb) - Big Ben
(br) - Brooklyn Bridge
(c) - Chicago Water Tower CICF
(cc) - Christmas cracker
(d) - Dome
(f) - FUN logo
(fr) - Frauenkirche - Munich Numismata
(h) - Horse - Hong Kong Int.
(l) - Statue of Liberty
(m) - Queen mother's portrait
(ma) - Maple leaf - CNA
(mt) - Mistletoe - Christmas
(p) - Carrier Pigeon - Basel
(pi) - Pine tree
(pt) - Partridge in a pear tree
(s) - Bridge - SINPEX
(sg) - Sleigh - Christmas
(SL) - St. Louis arch
(ss) - Sailing Ship - Sydney
(t) - Stylized triskelion
(ti) - TICC logo - Tokyo
(v) - Viking ship

PRIVY LETTERS

A - ANA
C - Coinex, London
F - FUN
H - Hong Kong Expo
L - Long Beach
T - Torex, Toronto
U - Uncirculated
X - Ameripex

MONETARY SYSTEM

14 Pence (Manx) = 1 Shilling (Br.)
5 Shillings = 1 Crown
20 Shillings = 1 Pound

FARTHING

COPPER

KM#	Date	Mintage	Fine	VF	XF	Unc
12	1839	.213	3.00	9.00	30.00	60.00
	1839	—	—	—	Proof	225.00
	1841	2 known	—	—	Proof	Rare
	1860	6 known	—	—	Proof	1900.
	1864	3 known	—	—	Proof	Rare

COPPER-GILT

KM#	Date	Mintage	Fine	VF	XF	Unc
12a	1839	—	—	—	Proof	Rare
	1860	—	—	—	Proof	Rare

1/2 PENNY

COPPER

KM#	Date	Mintage	Fine	VF	XF	Unc
10	1813	—	10.00	35.00	80.00	175.00
	1813	—	—	—	Proof	300.00

NOTE: Earlier date (1798) exists for this type.

COPPER-GILT

KM#	Date	Mintage	Fine	VF	XF	Unc
10a	1813	—	—	—	Proof	Rare

NOTE: Earlier date (1798) exists for this type.

BRONZE

KM#	Date	Mintage	Fine	VF	XF	Unc
10b	1813	—	—	—	Proof	300.00

NOTE: Earlier date (1798) exists for this type.

COPPER

KM#	Date	Mintage	Fine	VF	XF	Unc
13	1839	.214	2.50	7.50	40.00	100.00
	1839	—	—	—	Proof	Rare
	1841	2 known	—	—	Proof	Rare
	1860	7 known	—	—	Proof	2500.

PENNY

COPPER

KM#	Date	Mintage	Fine	VF	XF	Unc
11	1813	—	7.50	35.00	100.00	225.00
	1813	—	—	—	Proof	350.00

NOTE: Earlier date (1798) exists for this type.

BRONZE GILT

KM#	Date	Mintage	Fine	VF	XF	Unc
11a	1813	—	—	—	Proof	Rare

NOTE: Earlier date (1798) exists for this type.

COPPER

KM#	Date	Mintage	Fine	VF	XF	Unc
14	1839	.081	10.00	25.00	70.00	150.00
	1839	—	—	—	Proof	Rare
	1841	2 known	—	—	Proof	Rare
	1859	7 known	—	—	Proof	1750.

DECIMAL COINAGE

5 New Pence = 1 Shilling
25 New Pence = 1 Crown
100 New Pence = 1 Pound

1/2 NEW PENNY

BRONZE
St. James's Weed

KM#	Date	Mintage	VF	XF	Unc
19	1971	.495	—	.10	.25
	1971	.010	—	Proof	1.50
	1972	1,000	—	—	20.00
	1973	1,000	—	—	20.00
	1974	1,000	—	—	20.00
	1975	.825	—	.10	.15

2.1000 g, .925 SILVER, .0624 oz ASW

KM#	Date	Mintage	VF	XF	Unc
19a	1975	.020	—	—	2.50

4.0000 g, .950 PLATINUM, .1221 oz APW

KM#	Date	Mintage	VF	XF	Unc
19b	1975	600 pcs.	—	Proof	95.00

1/2 PENNY

BRONZE
Atlantic Herring

KM#	Date	Mintage	VF	XF	Unc
32	1976	.600	—	.10	.15
	1978	—	—	.10	.15
	1978	—	—	Proof	1.00
	1979(t)	—	—	.10	.15

2.1000 g, .925 SILVER, .0624 oz ASW

KM#	Date	Mintage	VF	XF	Unc
32a	1976	.020	—	—	2.00
	1978	.010	—	—	2.00
	1979(t)	.010	—	Proof	2.50

4.0000 g, .950 PLATINUM, .1221 oz APW

KM#	Date	Mintage	VF	XF	Unc
32b	1976	600 pcs.	—	Proof	95.00
	1978	600 pcs.	—	Proof	95.00
	1979(t)	500 pcs.	—	Proof	95.00

BRONZE
F.A.O. Issue

KM#	Date	Mintage	VF	XF	Unc
40	1977 PM on rev.	.700	—	.10	.25
	1977 w/o PM on rev.	Inc. Ab.	—	—	5.00

2.1000 g, .925 SILVER, .0624 oz ASW

KM#	Date	Mintage	VF	XF	Unc
40a	1977	.010	—	Proof	2.50

BRONZE
Atlantic Herring

KM#	Date	Mintage	VF	XF	Unc
58	1980	—	—	.10	.20
	1980	—	—	Proof	1.00
	1981	—	—	.10	.20
	1982	—	—	.10	.20
	1982(b)	—	—	.10	.20
	1982(b)	.025	—	Proof	1.00
	1983	—	—	.10	.20

2.1000 g, .500 SILVER, .0337 oz ASW

KM#	Date	Mintage	VF	XF	Unc
58a	1980	.010	—	Proof	4.00

2.1000 g, .925 SILVER, .0624 oz ASW

KM#	Date	Mintage	VF	XF	Unc
58b	1982(b)	.010	—	Proof	4.00
	1983	5,000	—	Proof	5.00

3.5500 g, .917 GOLD, .1046 oz AGW

KM#	Date	Mintage	VF	XF	Unc
58c	1980	—	—	Proof	65.00
	1982(b)	500 pcs.	—	Proof	65.00
	1983	—	—	Proof	65.00

4.0000 g, .950 PLATINUM, .1221 oz APW

KM#	Date	Mintage	VF	XF	Unc
58d	1980	500 pcs.	—	Proof	95.00
	1982(b)	500 pcs.	—	Proof	95.00
	1983	—	—	Proof	95.00

BRONZE
F.A.O. Issue

KM#	Date	Mintage	VF	XF	Unc
72.1	1981	—	—	—	.10
	Rev: World Food Day added.				
72.2	1981	—	—	—	.10

Fuchsia Blossom

KM#	Date	Mintage	VF	XF	Unc
111	1984	—	—	—	.10
	2.1000 g, .925 SILVER, .0625 oz ASW				
111a	1984	—	—	Proof	5.00
	3.5500 g, .917 GOLD, .1046 oz AGW				
111b	1984	150 pcs.	—	Proof	125.00

BRONZE

KM#	Date	Mintage	VF	XF	Unc
142	1985	—	—	—	.10
	1985	.050	—	Proof	2.00
	2.1000 g, .925 SILVER, .0625 oz ASW				
142a	1985	.010	—	Proof	3.00
	3.5500 g, .917 GOLD, .1046 oz AGW				
142b	1985	300 pcs.	—	Proof	85.00
	4.0000 g, .950 PLATINUM, .1221 oz APW				
142c	1985	200 pcs.	—	Proof	95.00

NEW PENNY

BRONZE
Celtic Cross

KM#	Date	Mintage	VF	XF	Unc
20	1971	.100	—	.10	.35
	1971	.010	—	Proof	2.00
	1972	1,000	—	—	20.00
	1973	1,000	—	—	20.00
	1974	1,000	—	—	20.00
	1975	.855	—	.10	.20
	4.2000 g, .925 SILVER, .1249 oz ASW				
20a	1975	.020	—	—	5.00
	8.0000 g, .950 PLATINUM, .2443 oz APW				
20b	1975	600 pcs.	—	Proof	200.00

PENNY

BRONZE
Loaghtyn Sheep

KM#	Date	Mintage	VF	XF	Unc
33	1976	.900	—	.10	.30
	1977	1.000	—	.10	.30
	1978	—	—	.10	.30
	1978	—	—	Proof	1.25
	1979(t)	—	—	.10	.30
	4.2000 g, .925 SILVER, .1249 oz ASW				
33a	1976	.020	—	—	4.00
	1977	.010	—	Proof	5.00
	1978	.010	—	—	4.00
	1979(t)	.010	—	Proof	5.00
	8.0000 g, .950 PLATINUM, .2443 oz APW				
33b	1976	600 pcs.	—	Proof	200.00
	1978	600 pcs.	—	Proof	200.00
	1979(t)	500 pcs.	—	Proof	200.00

BRONZE
Manx Cat

KM#	Date	Mintage	VF	XF	Unc
59	1980	—	—	.10	.30
	1980	—	—	Proof	1.50
	1981	—	—	.10	.30
	1982	—	—	.10	.30
	1982(b)	—	—	.10	.30
	1982(b)	.025	—	Proof	1.50
	1983	—	—	.10	.30
	4.2000 g, .500 SILVER, .0675 oz ASW				
59a	1980	.010	—	Proof	5.00
	4.2000 g, .925 SILVER, .0675 oz ASW				
59b	1982(b)	.010	—	Proof	5.00
	1983	5,000	—	Proof	5.00
	7.1000 g, .917 GOLD, .2093 oz AGW				
59c	1980	300 pcs.	—	Proof	135.00
	1982(b)	500 pcs.	—	Proof	135.00
	1983	—	—	Proof	135.00
	8.0000 g, .950 PLATINUM, .2443 oz APW				
59d	1980	500 pcs.	—	Proof	200.00
	1982(b)	500 pcs.	—	Proof	200.00
	1983	—	—	Proof	200.00

BRONZE
Puffin

KM#	Date	Mintage	VF	XF	Unc
112	1984	—	—	.10	.20
	4.2000 g, .925 SILVER, .0675 oz ASW				
112a	1984	—	—	Proof	5.00
	7.1000 g, .917 GOLD, .2093 oz AGW				
112b	1984	150 pcs.	—	Proof	250.00

BRONZE

KM#	Date	Mintage	VF	XF	Unc
143	1985	—	—	.10	.20
	1985	.050	—	Proof	2.00
	1986	—	—	.10	.20
	1987	—	—	.10	.20
	4.2000 g, .925 SILVER, .0675 oz ASW				
143a	1985	.010	—	Proof	3.00
	7.1000 g, .917 GOLD, .2093 oz AGW				
143b	1985	300 pcs.	—	Proof	175.00
	8.0000 g, .950 PLATINUM, .2443 oz APW				
143c	1985	200 pcs.	—	Proof	200.00

BRONZE
Precision Tools

KM#	Date	Mintage	VF	XF	Unc
207	1988	—	—	—	.20
	1989	—	—	—	.20
	1990	—	—	—	.20
	1992	—	—	—	.20

2 NEW PENCE

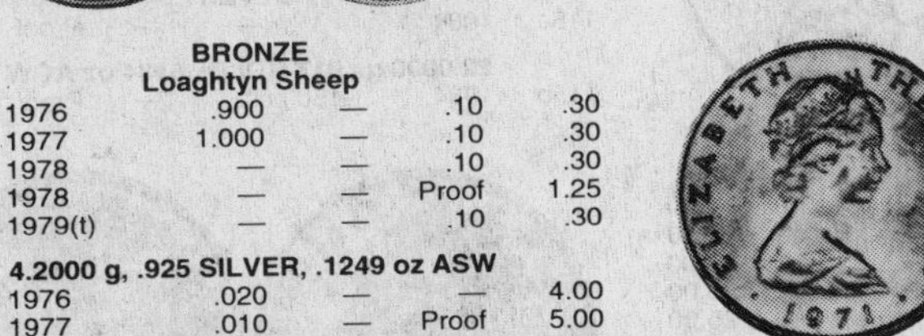

BRONZE
Falcons

KM#	Date	Mintage	VF	XF	Unc
21	1971	.100	—	.10	.50
	1971	.010	—	Proof	2.50
	1972	1,000	—	—	20.00
	1973	1,000	—	—	20.00
	1974	1,000	—	—	20.00
	1975	.725	—	.10	.25
	8.4000 g, .925 SILVER, .2498 oz ASW				
21a	1975	.020	—	—	5.00
	16.0000 g, .950 PLATINUM, .4887 oz APW				
21b	1975	600 pcs.	—	Proof	375.00

2 PENCE

BRONZE
Manx Shearwater

KM#	Date	Mintage	VF	XF	Unc
34	1976	.800	—	.10	.40
	1977	1.000	—	.10	.40
	1978	—	—	—	.40
	1978	—	—	Proof	1.25
	1979(t)	.010	—	.10	.40
	8.4000 g, .925 SILVER, .2498 oz ASW				
34a	1976	.020	—	—	5.00
	1977	.010	—	Proof	6.00
	1978	.010	—	—	6.00
	1979(t)	.010	—	Proof	6.00
	16.0000 g, .950 PLATINUM, .4887 oz APW				
34b	1976	600 pcs.	—	Proof	375.00
	1977	600 pcs.	—	Proof	375.00
	1979(t)	500 pcs.	—	Proof	375.00

BRONZE
Manx Shearwater

KM#	Date	Mintage	VF	XF	Unc
60	1980	—	—	.10	.40
	1980	—	—	Proof	1.25
	1981	—	—	.10	.40
	1982	—	—	.10	.40
	1982(b)	—	—	.10	.40
	1982(b)	.025	—	Proof	1.25
	1983	—	—	.10	.40
	8.4000 g, .500 SILVER, .1350 oz ASW				
60a	1980	.010	—	Proof	5.00
	8.4000 g, .925 SILVER, .2498 oz ASW				
60b	1982(b)	.010	—	Proof	5.00
	1983	5,000	—	Proof	6.00
	14.2000 g, .917 GOLD, .4186 oz AGW				
60c	1980	300 pcs.	—	Proof	250.00
	1982(b)	500 pcs.	—	Proof	250.00
	1983	—	—	Proof	250.00
	16.0000 g, .950 PLATINUM, .4887 oz APW				
60d	1980	500 pcs.	—	Proof	375.00
	1982(b)	500 pcs.	—	Proof	375.00
	1983	—	—	Proof	375.00

BRONZE
Falcon

KM#	Date	Mintage	VF	XF	Unc
113	1984	—	—	.10	.30
	8.4000 g, .925 SILVER, .2498 oz ASW				
113a	1984	—	—	Proof	6.00
	14.2000 g, .917 GOLD, .4185 oz AGW				
113b	1984	150 pcs.	—	Proof	450.00

BRONZE

KM#	Date	Mintage	VF	XF	Unc
144	1985	—	—	.10	.30
	1985	.050	—	Proof	3.00
	1986	—	—	.10	.30
	1987	—	—	.10	.30

8.4000 g, .925 SILVER, .2498 oz ASW

KM#	Date	Mintage	VF	XF	Unc
144a	1985	.010	—	Proof	12.00

14.2000 g, .917 GOLD, .4185 oz AGW

KM#	Date	Mintage	VF	XF	Unc
144b	1985	300 pcs.	—	Proof	350.00

16.0000 g, .950 PLATINUM, .4887 oz APW

KM#	Date	Mintage	VF	XF	Unc
144c	1985	200 pcs.	—	Proof	375.00

BRONZE
Stone Cross With Handworking Tools

KM#	Date	Mintage	VF	XF	Unc
208	1988	—	—	—	.30
	1989	—	—	—	.30
	1990	—	—	—	.30
	1992	—	—	—	.30

5 NEW PENCE

COPPER-NICKEL
Tower of Refuge

KM#	Date	Mintage	VF	XF	Unc
22	1971	.100	—	.10	.50
	1971	.010	—	Proof	2.50
	1972	1,000	—	—	25.00
	1973	1,000	—	—	25.00
	1974	1,000	—	—	25.00
	1975	1.400	—	.10	.25

6.5000 g, .925 SILVER, .1933 oz ASW

KM#	Date	Mintage	VF	XF	Unc
22a	1975	.020	—	—	5.00

12.5000 g, .950 PLATINUM, .3818 oz APW

KM#	Date	Mintage	VF	XF	Unc
22b	1975	600 pcs.	—	Proof	300.00

5 PENCE

COPPER-NICKEL
Laxey Wheel
Mint mark: PM on obverse and reverse.

KM#	Date	Mintage	VF	XF	Unc
35.1	1976	.800	—	.10	.60
	1977	—	—	.10	.60
	1978	—	—	.10	.60
	1978	—	—	Proof	1.50
	1979(t)	—	—	.10	.60

6.5000 g, .925 SILVER, .1933 oz ASW

KM#	Date	Mintage	VF	XF	Unc
35.1a	1976	.020	—	—	5.50
	1977	.010	—	Proof	5.50
	1978	.010	—	—	5.50
	1979(t)	.010	—	Proof	5.50

12.5000 g, .950 PLATINUM, .3818 oz APW

KM#	Date	Mintage	VF	XF	Unc
35.1b	1976	600 pcs.	—	Proof	300.00
	1978	600 pcs.	—	Proof	300.00
	1979(t)	500 pcs.	—	Proof	300.00

COPPER-NICKEL
Mint mark: PM on obverse only.

KM#	Date	Mintage	VF	XF	Unc
35.2	1976PM	Inc. Ab.	—	.10	.75

Loagthyn Sheep

KM#	Date	Mintage	VF	XF	Unc
61	1980	—	—	.10	.60
	1980	—	—	Proof	1.50
	1981	—	—	.10	.60
	1982	—	—	.10	.60

KM#	Date	Mintage	VF	XF	Unc
61	1982(b)	—	—	.10	.60
	1982(b)	.025	—	Proof	1.50
	1983	—	—	.10	.60

6.5000 g, .500 SILVER, .1045 oz ASW

KM#	Date	Mintage	VF	XF	Unc
61a	1980	.010	—	Proof	5.00

6.5000 g, .925 SILVER, .1933 oz ASW

KM#	Date	Mintage	VF	XF	Unc
61b	1982(b)	.010	—	Proof	5.00
	1983	5,000	—	Proof	5.00

11.0000 g, .917 GOLD, .3243 oz AGW

KM#	Date	Mintage	VF	XF	Unc
61c	1980	300 pcs.	—	Proof	200.00
	1982(b)	500 pcs.	—	Proof	200.00
	1983	—	—	Proof	200.00

12.5000 g, .950 PLATINUM, .3818 oz APW

KM#	Date	Mintage	VF	XF	Unc
61d	1980	500 pcs.	—	Proof	300.00
	1982(b)	500 pcs.	—	Proof	300.00
	1983	—	—	Proof	300.00

COPPER-NICKEL
Cushag

KM#	Date	Mintage	VF	XF	Unc
114	1984	—	—	.10	.50

6.5000 g, .925 SILVER, .1933 oz ASW

KM#	Date	Mintage	VF	XF	Unc
114a	1984	—	—	Proof	5.00

11.0000 g, .917 GOLD, .3242 oz AGW

KM#	Date	Mintage	VF	XF	Unc
114b	1984	150 pcs.	—	Proof	400.00

COPPER-NICKEL

KM#	Date	Mintage	VF	XF	Unc
145	1985	—	—	.10	.50
	1985	.050	—	Proof	3.00
	1986	—	—	.10	.50
	1987	—	—	.10	.50

6.5000 g, .925 SILVER, .1933 oz ASW

KM#	Date	Mintage	VF	XF	Unc
145a	1985	.010	—	Proof	8.00

11.0000 g, .917 GOLD, .3242 oz AGW

KM#	Date	Mintage	VF	XF	Unc
145b	1985	300 pcs.	—	Proof	200.00

12.5000 g, .950 PLATINUM, .3818 oz APW

KM#	Date	Mintage	VF	XF	Unc
145c	1985	200 pcs.	—	Proof	300.00

COPPER-NICKEL
Windsurfing

KM#	Date	Mintage	VF	XF	Unc
209.1	1988	—	—	—	.50
	1989	—	—	—	.50
	1990	—	—	—	.50

Reduced size: 18mm

KM#	Date	Mintage	VF	XF	Unc
209.2	1990	—	—	—	.50
	1990	—	—	—	.50
	1992	—	—	—	.50

10 NEW PENCE

COPPER-NICKEL
Triskelion

KM#	Date	Mintage	VF	XF	Unc
23	1971	.100	—	.20	.50
	1971	.010	—	Proof	3.50
	1972	1,000	—	—	25.00
	1973	1,000	—	—	25.00
	1974	1,000	—	—	25.00
	1975	1.500	—	.20	.40

13.0000 g, .925 SILVER, .3866 oz ASW

KM#	Date	Mintage	VF	XF	Unc
23a	1975	.020	—	—	10.00

25.0000 g, .950 PLATINUM, .7636 oz APW

KM#	Date	Mintage	VF	XF	Unc
23b	1975	600 pcs.	—	Proof	575.00

10 PENCE

COPPER-NICKEL
Triskelion
Mint mark: PM on obverse and reverse.

KM#	Date	Mintage	VF	XF	Unc
36.1	1976	2.800	—	.20	.80
	1977	—	—	.20	.80
	1978	—	—	.20	.80
	1978	—	—	Proof	2.00
	1979(t)	—	—	.20	.80

13.0000 g, .925 SILVER, .3866 oz ASW

KM#	Date	Mintage	VF	XF	Unc
36.1a	1976	.020	—	—	10.00
	1977	.010	—	Proof	10.00
	1978	.010	—	—	10.00
	1979(t)	.010	—	Proof	10.00

25.0000 g, .950 PLATINUM, .7636 oz APW

KM#	Date	Mintage	VF	XF	Unc
36.1b	1976	600 pcs.	—	Proof	575.00
	1978	600 pcs.	—	Proof	575.00
	1979(t)	500 pcs.	—	Proof	575.00

COPPER-NICKEL
Mint mark: PM on obverse only.

KM#	Date	Mintage	VF	XF	Unc
36.2	1976	Inc. Ab.	—	.20	1.00

Falcon

KM#	Date	Mintage	VF	XF	Unc
62	1980	—	—	.20	.80
	1980	—	—	Proof	2.00
	1981	—	—	.20	.80
	1982	—	—	.20	.80
	1982(b)	—	—	.20	.80
	1982(b)	.025	—	Proof	2.00
	1983	—	—	.20	.80

13.0000 g, .500 SILVER, .2090 oz ASW

KM#	Date	Mintage	VF	XF	Unc
62a	1980	.010	—	Proof	10.00

13.0000 g, .925 SILVER, .3866 oz ASW

KM#	Date	Mintage	VF	XF	Unc
62b	1982(b)	.010	—	Proof	10.00
	1983	5,000	—	Proof	12.50

22.0000 g, .917 GOLD, .6486 oz AGW

KM#	Date	Mintage	VF	XF	Unc
62c	1980	300 pcs.	—	Proof	375.00
	1982(b)	500 pcs.	—	Proof	375.00
	1983	—	—	Proof	375.00

25.0000 g, .950 PLATINUM, .7636 oz APW

KM#	Date	Mintage	VF	XF	Unc
62d	1980	500 pcs.	—	Proof	575.00
	1982(b)	500 pcs.	—	Proof	575.00
	1983	—	—	Proof	575.00

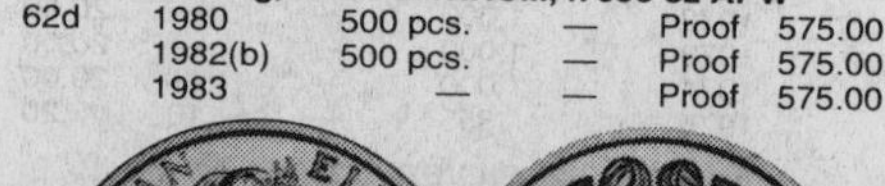

COPPER-NICKEL
Loagthyn Ram

KM#	Date	Mintage	VF	XF	Unc
115	1984	—	—	.20	.75

SILVER

KM#	Date	Mintage	VF	XF	Unc
115a	1984	—	—	Proof	10.00

22.0000 g, .917 GOLD, .6484 oz AGW

KM#	Date	Mintage	VF	XF	Unc
115b	1984	150 pcs.	—	Proof	700.00

COPPER-NICKEL

KM#	Date	Mintage	VF	XF	Unc
146	1985	—	—	.20	.75
	1985	.050	—	Proof	3.00
	1986	—	—	.20	.75
	1987	—	—	.20	.75
	13.0000 g, .925 SILVER, .3866 oz ASW				
146a	1985	.010	—	Proof	18.00
	22.0000 g, .917 GOLD, .6484 oz AGW				
146b	1985	300 pcs.	—	Proof	500.00
	25.0000 g, .950 PLATINUM, .7636 oz APW				
146c	1985	200 pcs.	—	Proof	600.00

COPPER-NICKEL
Island and Portcullis on Globe

KM#	Date	Mintage	VF	XF	Unc
210	1988	—	—	—	.75
	1989	—	—	—	.75
	1990	—	—	—	.75
	1992	—	—	—	.75

Triskeles Symbol

KM#	Date	Mintage	VF	XF	Unc
337	1992	—	—	—	.75
	8.0457 g, .925 SILVER, .2392 oz ASW				
337a	1992	—	—	Proof	12.50
	13.6158 g, .917 GOLD, .4013 oz AGW				
337b	1992	—	—	Proof	300.00
	15.4725 g, .950 PLATINUM, .4725 oz APW				
337c	1992	—	—	Proof	400.00

20 PENCE

COPPER-NICKEL
Medieval Norse History

KM#	Date	Mintage	VF	XF	Unc
90	1982	.030	—	.35	1.00
	1982(b)	—	.50	1.00	5.00
	1982(b)	.025	—	Proof	6.00
	1983	—	—	.35	1.00
	6.0000 g, .925 SILVER, .1784 oz ASW				
90a	1982	.015	—	Proof	10.00
	1982(b)	.010	—	Proof	10.00
	1983	5,000	—	Proof	15.00
	10.0000 g, .917 GOLD, .2948 oz AGW				
90b	1982	1,500	—	Proof	200.00
	1982(b)	500 pcs.	—	Proof	200.00
	1983	—	—	Proof	200.00
	11.3000 g, .950 PLATINUM, .3452 oz APW				
90c	1982	250 pcs.	—	Proof	275.00
	1982(b)	500 pcs.	—	Proof	275.00
	1983	—	—	Proof	275.00

COPPER-NICKEL
Atlantic Herring

KM#	Date	Mintage	VF	XF	Unc
116	1984	—	—	.35	1.00
	SILVER				
116a	1984	—	—	Proof	20.00
	5.0000 g, .917 GOLD, .1474 oz AGW				
116b	1984	150 pcs.	—	Proof	175.00

COPPER-NICKEL

KM#	Date	Mintage	VF	XF	Unc
147	1985	—	—	.35	1.00
	1985	.050	—	Proof	3.00
	1986	—	—	.35	1.00
	1987	—	—	.35	1.00
	5.0000 g, .925 SILVER, .1487 oz ASW				
147a	1985	.010	—	Proof	8.00
	5.0000 g, .917 GOLD, .1474 oz AGW				
147b	1985	300 pcs.	—	Proof	125.00
	5.0000 g, .950 PLATINUM, .1527 oz APW				
147c	1985	200 pcs.	—	Proof	120.00

COPPER-NICKEL
Harvest Machine

KM#	Date	Mintage	VF	XF	Unc
211	1988	—	—	—	1.00
	1989	—	—	—	1.00
	1990	—	—	—	1.00
	1992	—	—	—	1.00

CROWN
(25 Pence)

COPPER-NICKEL
Manx Cat

KM#	Date	Mintage	VF	XF	Unc
18	1970	.150	—	—	5.00
	28.2800 g, .925 SILVER, .8411 oz ASW				
18a	1970	.011	—	Proof	20.00

COPPER-NICKEL
25th Wedding Anniversary

KM#	Date	Mintage	VF	XF	Unc
25	1972	.070	—	—	5.00
	28.2800 g, .925 SILVER, .8411 oz ASW				
25a	1972	.015	—	Proof	15.00

COPPER-NICKEL
Birth of Winston Churchill Centenary

KM#	Date	Mintage	VF	XF	Unc
30	1974	.045	—	—	2.00
	28.2800 g, .925 SILVER, .8411 oz ASW				
30a	1974	—	—	—	12.50
	1974	.030	—	Proof	14.00

COPPER-NICKEL
Manx Cat

KM#	Date	Mintage	VF	XF	Unc
31	1975	.035	—	—	2.50
	28.2800 g, .925 SILVER, .8411 oz ASW				
31a	1975	—	—	—	12.50
	1975	.030	—	Proof	17.50

COPPER-NICKEL
Bicentenary of American Independence
Obv: Similar to KM#25.

KM#	Date	Mintage	VF	XF	Unc
37	1976	.050	—	—	2.00
	28.2800 g, .925 SILVER, .8411 oz ASW				
37a	1976	—	—	—	12.50
	1976	.030	—	Proof	14.00

COPPER-NICKEL
Centenary of Horse Drawn Tram
Obv: Similar to KM#25.

KM#	Date	Mintage	VF	XF	Unc
38	1976	.050	—	—	2.00
	28.2800 g, .925 SILVER, .8411 oz ASW				
38a	1976	—	—	—	12.50
	1976	.030	—	Proof	15.00

COPPER-NICKEL
Silver Jubilee
Obv: Similar to KM#31.

KM#	Date	Mintage	VF	XF	Unc
41	1977	—	—	—	3.00
	28.2800 g, .925 SILVER, .8411 oz ASW				
41a	1977	—	—	—	12.50
	1977	.030	—	Proof	15.00

COPPER-NICKEL
Queen's Jubilee Appeal
Obv: Similar to KM#25.

KM#	Date	Mintage	VF	XF	Unc
42	1977	—	—	—	2.00
	28.2800 g, .925 SILVER, .8411 oz ASW				
42a	1977	.070	—	—	12.50
	1977	.030	—	Proof	15.00

COPPER-NICKEL
25th Anniversary of Coronation
Obv: Similar to KM#31.

KM#	Date	Mintage	VF	XF	Unc
43	1978	—	—	—	2.00
	1978	—	—	Proof	7.50
	28.2800 g, .925 SILVER, .8411 oz ASW				
43a	1978	.070	—	—	12.50
	1978	.030	—	Proof	15.00

NOTE: For mule of Isle of Man KM#43 obv. with Ascension Island KM#1 rev., refer to Ascension Island listings.

COPPER-NICKEL
300th Anniversary of Manx Coinage
Obv: Similar to KM#25.

KM#	Date	Mintage	VF	XF	Unc
45	1979	—	—	—	2.50
	1979	—	—	Proof	7.50
	28.2800 g, .925 SILVER, .8411 oz ASW				
45a	1979	.070	—	—	12.50
	1979	.030	—	Proof	15.00

COPPER-NICKEL
Millenium of Tynwald - Viking Longship
Rev: Viking longship.

KM#	Date	Mintage	VF	XF	Unc
46	1979	.100	—	—	2.50
	28.2800 g, .925 SILVER, .8411 oz ASW				
46a	1979	.025	—	—	15.00
	1979	.010	—	Proof	17.50
	43.0000 g, .917 GOLD, 1.2678 oz AGW				
46b	1979	300 pcs.	—	Proof	700.00
	52.0000 g, .950 PLATINUM, 1.5884 oz APW				
46c	1979	100 pcs.	—	Proof	1200.

COPPER-NICKEL
Millenium of Tynwald - English Cog
Obv: Similar to KM#25.

KM#	Date	Mintage	VF	XF	Unc
47	1979	.100	—	—	2.50
	28.2800 g, .925 SILVER, .8411 oz ASW				
47a	1979	.025	—	—	15.00
	1979	.010	—	Proof	17.50
	43.0000 g, .917 GOLD, 1.2678 oz AGW				
47b	1979	300 pcs.	—	Proof	700.00
	52.0000 g, .950 PLATINUM, 1.5884 oz APW				
47c	1979	100 pcs.	—	Proof	1200.

COPPER-NICKEL
Millenium of Tynwald - Flemish Carrack
Obv: Similar to KM#25.

KM#	Date	Mintage	VF	XF	Unc
48	1979	.100	—	—	2.50
	28.2800 g, .925 SILVER, .8411 oz ASW				
48a	1979	.025	—	—	15.00
	1979	.010	—	Proof	17.50
	43.0000 g, .917 GOLD, 1.2678 oz AGW				
48b	1979	300 pcs.	—	Proof	700.00
	52.0000 g, .950 PLATINUM, 1.5884 oz APW				
48c	1979	100 pcs.	—	Proof	1200.

COPPER-NICKEL
Millenium of Tynwald
Obv: Similar to KM#25.
Rev: Royalist Soldier and English Man-of-War.

KM#	Date	Mintage	VF	XF	Unc
49	1979	.100	—	—	2.50
	28.2800 g, .925 SILVER, .8411 oz ASW				
49a	1979	.025	—	—	15.00
	1979	.010	—	Proof	17.50
	43.0000 g, .917 GOLD, 1.2678 oz AGW				
49b	1979	300 pcs.	—	Proof	700.00
	52.0000 g, .950 PLATINUM, 1.5884 oz APW				
49c	1979	100 pcs.	—	Proof	1200.

COPPER-NICKEL
Millenium of Tynwald
Obv: Similar to KM#25.
Rev: Lifeboat and Sir Hillary portrait.

KM#	Date	Mintage	VF	XF	Unc
50	1979	.100	—	—	2.50
	28.2800 g, .925 SILVER, .8411 oz ASW				
50a	1979	.025	—	—	15.00
	1979	.010	—	Proof	17.50
	43.0000 g, .917 GOLD, 1.2678 oz AGW				
50b	1979	300 pcs.	—	Proof	700.00
	52.0000 g, .950 PLATINUM, 1.5884 oz APW				
50c	1979	100 pcs.	—	Proof	1200.

COPPER-NICKEL
Derby Bicentennial
Obv: Similar to KM#25.

KM#	Date	Mintage	VF	XF	Unc
63	1980	.100	—	—	3.00
	28.2800 g, .925 SILVER, .8411 oz ASW				
63a	1980	.035	—	—	15.00
	1980	.020	—	Proof	20.00
	43.0000 g, .917 GOLD, 1.2678 oz AGW				
63c	1980	—	—	Proof	700.00
	52.0000 g, .950 PLATINUM, 1.5884 oz APW				
63b	1980	500 pcs.	—	Proof	1000.

COPPER-NICKEL
1980 Winter Olympics - Lake Placid
Obv: Similar to KM#25.

KM#	Date	Mintage	VF	XF	Unc
64	1980	.100	—	—	2.50
	1980	—	—	P/L	5.00

28.2800 g, .925 SILVER, .8411 oz ASW

KM#	Date	Mintage	VF	XF	Unc
64a	1980	—	—	Matte	—
	1980	.010	—	Proof	20.00

39.8000 g, .917 GOLD, 1.1735 oz AGW

KM#	Date	Mintage	VF	XF	Unc
64b	1980	1,500	—	—	650.00
	1980	500 pcs.	—	Proof	675.00

52.0000 g, .950 PLATINUM, 1.5884 oz APW

KM#	Date	Mintage	VF	XF	Unc
64c	1980	100 pcs.	—	Proof	1200.

COPPER-NICKEL
22nd Olympiad Moscow
Obv: Similar to KM#25. Rev: Runner at top.

KM#	Date	Mintage	VF	XF	Unc
65	1980	.030	—	—	2.50
	1980	—	—	P/L	5.00

28.2800 g, .925 SILVER, .8411 oz ASW

KM#	Date	Mintage	VF	XF	Unc
65a	1980	—	—	Matte	—
	1980	.010	—	Proof	20.00

39.8000 g, .917 GOLD, 1.1735 oz AGW

KM#	Date	Mintage	VF	XF	Unc
65b	1980	1,500	—	—	650.00

52.0000 g, .950 PLATINUM, 1.5884 oz APW

KM#	Date	Mintage	VF	XF	Unc
65c	1980	100 pcs.	—	Proof	1200.

COPPER-NICKEL
22nd Olympiad Moscow
Obv: Similar to KM#25. Rev: Javelin thrower at top.

KM#	Date	Mintage	VF	XF	Unc
66	1980	.030	—	—	2.50
	1980	—	—	P/L	5.00

28.2800 g, .925 SILVER, .8411 oz ASW

KM#	Date	Mintage	VF	XF	Unc
66a	1980	—	—	Matte	—
	1980	.010	—	Proof	20.00

39.8000 g, .917 GOLD, 1.1735 oz AGW

KM#	Date	Mintage	VF	XF	Unc
66b	1980	1,500	—	—	650.00

52.0000 g, .950 PLATINUM, 1.5884 oz APW

KM#	Date	Mintage	VF	XF	Unc
66c	1980	100 pcs.	—	Proof	1200.

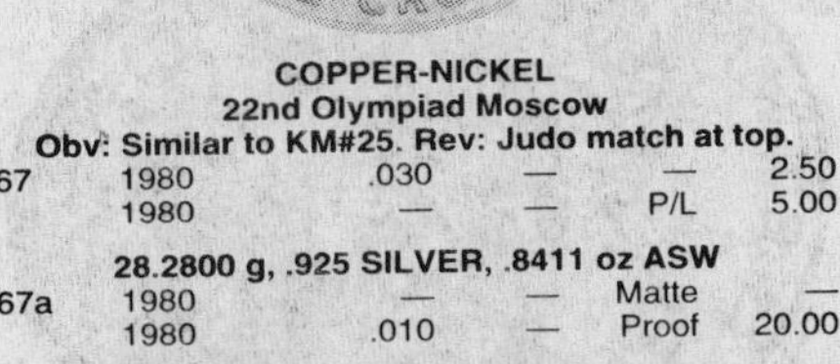

COPPER-NICKEL
22nd Olympiad Moscow
Obv: Similar to KM#25. Rev: Judo match at top.

KM#	Date	Mintage	VF	XF	Unc
67	1980	.030	—	—	2.50
	1980	—	—	P/L	5.00

28.2800 g, .925 SILVER, .8411 oz ASW

KM#	Date	Mintage	VF	XF	Unc
67a	1980	—	—	Matte	—
	1980	.010	—	Proof	20.00

39.8000 g, .917 GOLD, 1.1735 oz AGW

KM#	Date	Mintage	VF	XF	Unc
67b	1980	1,500	—	—	650.00

52.0000 g, .950 PLATINUM, 1.5884 oz APW

KM#	Date	Mintage	VF	XF	Unc
67c	1980	100 pcs.	—	Proof	1200.

COPPER-NICKEL, 37mm

80th Birthday of Queen Mother

KM#	Date	Mintage	VF	XF	Unc
68	1980	.100	—	—	3.50

28.2800 g, .500 SILVER, .4546 oz ASW

KM#	Date	Mintage	VF	XF	Unc
68a	1980	.050	—	—	15.00

28.2800 g, .925 SILVER, .8411 oz ASW

KM#	Date	Mintage	VF	XF	Unc
68b	1980	.030	—	Proof	25.00

5.0000 g, .374 GOLD, .0601 oz AGW

KM#	Date	Mintage	VF	XF	Unc
68c	1980	.050	—	—	75.00

7.9600 g, .917 GOLD, .2347 oz AGW

KM#	Date	Mintage	VF	XF	Unc
68d	1980	1,000	—	—	150.00

COPPER-NICKEL, 37mm
Duke of Edinburgh Award Scheme - Portrait

KM#	Date	Mintage	VF	XF	Unc
73	1981	.050	—	—	4.00

28.2800 g, .925 SILVER, .8411 oz ASW

KM#	Date	Mintage	VF	XF	Unc
73a	1981	.020	—	—	15.00
	1981	.015	—	Proof	20.00

52.0000 g, .950 PLATINUM, 1.5884 oz APW

KM#	Date	Mintage	VF	XF	Unc
73b	1981	100 pcs.	—	Proof	1100.

5.1000 g, .374 GOLD, .0613 oz AGW

KM#	Date	Mintage	VF	XF	Unc
73c	1981	.010	—	Proof	75.00

7.9600 g, .917 GOLD, .2347 oz AGW

KM#	Date	Mintage	VF	XF	Unc
73d	1981	1,000	—	Proof	150.00

COPPER-NICKEL, 37mm
Duke of Edinburgh Award Scheme - Monogram

KM#	Date	Mintage	VF	XF	Unc
74	1981	.050	—	—	4.00

28.2800 g, .925 SILVER, .8411 oz ASW

KM#	Date	Mintage	VF	XF	Unc
74a	1981	.020	—	—	15.00
	1981	.015	—	Proof	20.00

52.0000 g, .950 PLATINUM, 1.5884 oz APW

KM#	Date	Mintage	VF	XF	Unc
74b	1981	100 pcs.	—	Proof	1150.

5.1000 g, .374 GOLD, .0613 oz AGW

KM#	Date	Mintage	VF	XF	Unc
74c	1981	.010	—	Proof	75.00

7.9600 g, .917 GOLD, .2347 oz AGW

KM#	Date	Mintage	VF	XF	Unc
74d	1981	1,000	—	Proof	150.00

COPPER-NICKEL, 37mm
Duke of Edinburgh Award Scheme

KM#	Date	Mintage	VF	XF	Unc
75	1981	.050	—	—	4.00

28.2800 g, .925 SILVER, .8411 oz ASW

KM#	Date	Mintage	VF	XF	Unc
75a	1981	.020	—	—	15.00
	1981	.015	—	Proof	20.00

52.0000 g, .950 PLATINUM, 1.5884 oz APW

KM#	Date	Mintage	VF	XF	Unc
75b	1981	100 pcs.	—	Proof	1100.

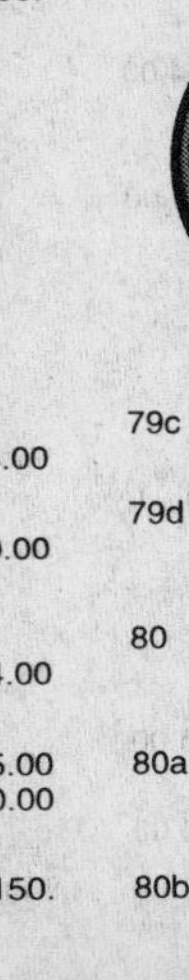

5.1000 g, .374 GOLD, .0613 oz AGW

KM#	Date	Mintage	VF	XF	Unc
75c	1981	.010	—	Proof	75.00

7.9600 g, .917 GOLD, .2347 oz AGW

KM#	Date	Mintage	VF	XF	Unc
75d	1981	1,000	—	Proof	150.00

COPPER-NICKEL, 37mm
Duke of Edinburgh Award Scheme

KM#	Date	Mintage	VF	XF	Unc
76	1981	.050	—	—	4.00

28.2800 g, .925 SILVER, .8411 oz ASW

KM#	Date	Mintage	VF	XF	Unc
76a	1981	.020	—	—	15.00
	1981	.015	—	Proof	20.00

52.0000 g, .950 PLATINUM, 1.5884 oz APW

KM#	Date	Mintage	VF	XF	Unc
76b	1981	100 pcs.	—	Proof	1150.

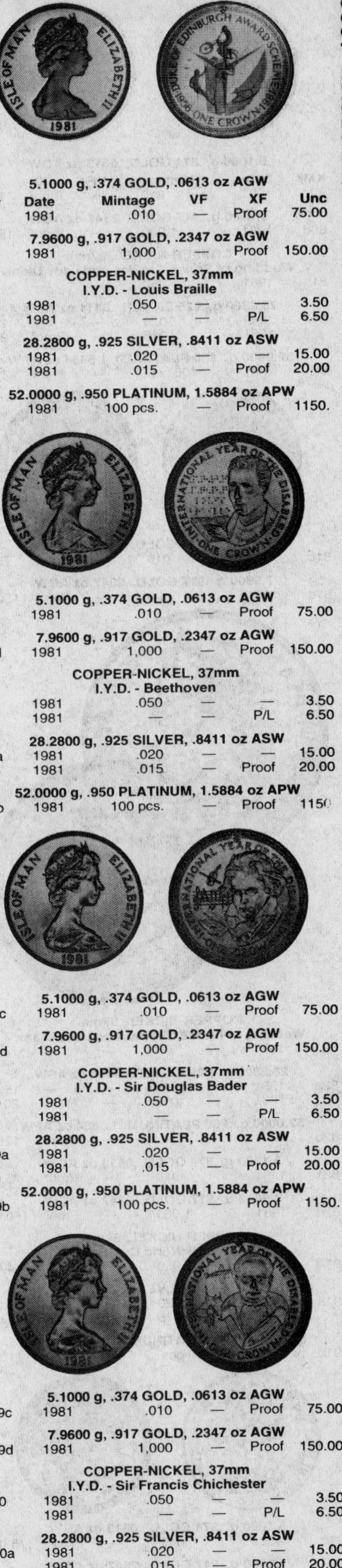

5.1000 g, .374 GOLD, .0613 oz AGW

KM#	Date	Mintage	VF	XF	Unc
76c	1981	.010	—	Proof	75.00

7.9600 g, .917 GOLD, .2347 oz AGW

KM#	Date	Mintage	VF	XF	Unc
76d	1981	1,000	—	Proof	150.00

COPPER-NICKEL, 37mm
I.Y.D. - Louis Braille

KM#	Date	Mintage	VF	XF	Unc
77	1981	.050	—	—	3.50
	1981	—	—	P/L	6.50

28.2800 g, .925 SILVER, .8411 oz ASW

KM#	Date	Mintage	VF	XF	Unc
77a	1981	.020	—	—	15.00
	1981	.015	—	Proof	20.00

52.0000 g, .950 PLATINUM, 1.5884 oz APW

KM#	Date	Mintage	VF	XF	Unc
77b	1981	100 pcs.	—	Proof	1150.

5.1000 g, .374 GOLD, .0613 oz AGW

KM#	Date	Mintage	VF	XF	Unc
77c	1981	.010	—	Proof	75.00

7.9600 g, .917 GOLD, .2347 oz AGW

KM#	Date	Mintage	VF	XF	Unc
77d	1981	1,000	—	Proof	150.00

COPPER-NICKEL, 37mm
I.Y.D. - Beethoven

KM#	Date	Mintage	VF	XF	Unc
78	1981	.050	—	—	3.50
	1981	—	—	P/L	6.50

28.2800 g, .925 SILVER, .8411 oz ASW

KM#	Date	Mintage	VF	XF	Unc
78a	1981	.020	—	—	15.00
	1981	.015	—	Proof	20.00

52.0000 g, .950 PLATINUM, 1.5884 oz APW

KM#	Date	Mintage	VF	XF	Unc
78b	1981	100 pcs.	—	Proof	1150

5.1000 g, .374 GOLD, .0613 oz AGW

KM#	Date	Mintage	VF	XF	Unc
78c	1981	.010	—	Proof	75.00

7.9600 g, .917 GOLD, .2347 oz AGW

KM#	Date	Mintage	VF	XF	Unc
78d	1981	1,000	—	Proof	150.00

COPPER-NICKEL, 37mm
I.Y.D. - Sir Douglas Bader

KM#	Date	Mintage	VF	XF	Unc
79	1981	.050	—	—	3.50
	1981	—	—	P/L	6.50

28.2800 g, .925 SILVER, .8411 oz ASW

KM#	Date	Mintage	VF	XF	Unc
79a	1981	.020	—	—	15.00
	1981	.015	—	Proof	20.00

52.0000 g, .950 PLATINUM, 1.5884 oz APW

KM#	Date	Mintage	VF	XF	Unc
79b	1981	100 pcs.	—	Proof	1150.

5.1000 g, .374 GOLD, .0613 oz AGW

KM#	Date	Mintage	VF	XF	Unc
79c	1981	.010	—	Proof	75.00

7.9600 g, .917 GOLD, .2347 oz AGW

KM#	Date	Mintage	VF	XF	Unc
79d	1981	1,000	—	Proof	150.00

COPPER-NICKEL, 37mm
I.Y.D. - Sir Francis Chichester

KM#	Date	Mintage	VF	XF	Unc
80	1981	.050	—	—	3.50
	1981	—	—	P/L	6.50

28.2800 g, .925 SILVER, .8411 oz ASW

KM#	Date	Mintage	VF	XF	Unc
80a	1981	.020	—	—	15.00
	1981	.015	—	Proof	20.00

52.0000 g, .950 PLATINUM, 1.5884 oz APW

KM#	Date	Mintage	VF	XF	Unc
80b	1981	100 pcs.	—	Proof	1150.

5.1000 g, .374 GOLD, .0613 oz AGW

KM#	Date	Mintage	VF	XF	Unc
80c	1981	.010	—	Proof	75.00

7.9600 g, .917 GOLD, .2347 oz AGW

KM#	Date	Mintage	VF	XF	Unc
80d	1981	1,000	—	Proof	150.00

COPPER-NICKEL, 37mm
Wedding of Prince Charles and Lady Diana

KM#	Date	Mintage	VF	XF	Unc
81	1981	.050	—	—	4.00
28.2800 g, .925 SILVER, .8411 oz ASW					
81a	1981	.020	—	—	20.00
	1981	.015	—	Proof	25.00
52.0000 g, .950 PLATINUM, 1.5884 oz APW					
81b	1981	100 pcs.	—	Proof	1150.

5.1000 g, .374 GOLD, .0613 oz AGW

KM#	Date	Mintage	VF	XF	Unc
81c	1981	.010	—	Proof	75.00
7.9600 g, .917 GOLD, .2347 oz AGW					
81d	1981	1,000	—	Proof	150.00

COPPER-NICKEL, 37mm
Wedding of Prince Charles and Lady Diana

KM#	Date	Mintage	VF	XF	Unc
82	1981	.050	—	—	4.00
28.2800 g, .925 SILVER, .8411 oz ASW					
82a	1981	.020	—	—	15.00
	1981	.015	—	Proof	20.00
52.0000 g, .950 PLATINUM, 1.5884 oz APW					
82b	1981	—	—	Proof	1250.
5.1000 g, .374 GOLD, .0613 oz AGW					
82c	1981	.010	—	Proof	75.00
7.9600 g, .917 GOLD, .2347 oz AGW					
82d	1981	1,000	—	Proof	150.00

COPPER-NICKEL, 37mm
Soccer-XII World Cup-Spain

KM#	Date	Mintage	VF	XF	Unc
91	1982	.050	—	—	4.00
28.2800 g, .925 SILVER, .8411 oz ASW					
91a	1982	.020	—	—	20.00
	1982	.015	—	Proof	25.00
52.0000 g, .950 PLATINUM, 1.5884 oz APW					
91b	1982	100 pcs.	—	Proof	1100.

5.1000 g, .374 GOLD, .0613 oz AGW

KM#	Date	Mintage	VF	XF	Unc
91c	1982	.040	—	Proof	75.00
7.9600 g, .917 GOLD, .2347 oz AGW					
91d	1982	4,000	—	Proof	150.00

COPPER-NICKEL, 37mm
Country Shields-XII World Cup-Spain

KM#	Date	Mintage	VF	XF	Unc
92	1982	.050	—	—	4.00
28.2800 g, .925 SILVER, .8411 oz ASW					
92a	1982	.020	—	—	20.00
	1982	.015	—	Proof	25.00
52.0000 g, .950 PLATINUM, 1.5884 oz APW					
92b	1982	100 pcs.	—	Proof	1350.

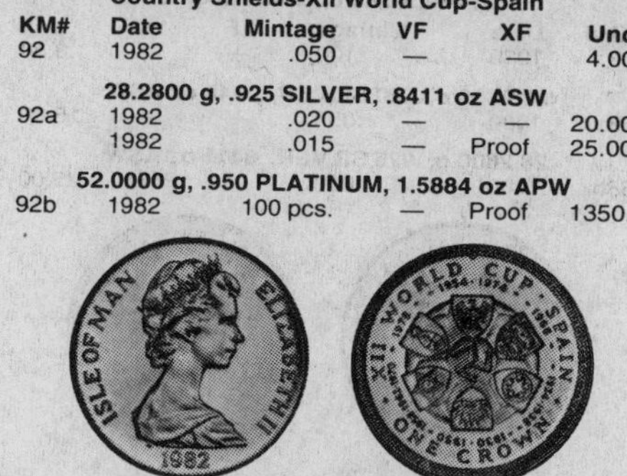

5.1000 g, .374 GOLD, .0613 oz AGW

KM#	Date	Mintage	VF	XF	Unc
92c	1982	.040	—	Proof	75.00
7.9600 g, .917 GOLD, .2347 oz AGW					
92d	1982	4,000	—	Proof	150.00

COPPER-NICKEL, 37mm
XII World Cup-Spain

KM#	Date	Mintage	VF	XF	Unc
93	1982	.050	—	—	4.00
28.2800 g, .925 SILVER, .8411 oz ASW					
93a	1982	.020	—	—	20.00
	1982	.015	—	Proof	25.00
52.0000 g, .950 PLATINUM, 1.5884 oz APW					
93b	1982	100 pcs.	—	Proof	1100.

5.1000 g, .374 GOLD, .0613 oz AGW

KM#	Date	Mintage	VF	XF	Unc
93c	1982	.040	—	Proof	75.00
7.9600 g, .917 GOLD, .2347 oz AGW					
93d	1982	4,000	—	Proof	150.00

COPPER-NICKEL, 37mm
XII World Cup-Spain

KM#	Date	Mintage	VF	XF	Unc
94	1982	.050	—	—	4.00
28.2800 g, .925 SILVER, .8411 oz ASW					
94a	1982	.020	—	—	20.00
	1982	.015	—	Proof	25.00
52.0000 g, .950 PLATINUM, 1.5884 oz APW					
94b	1982	100 pcs.	—	Proof	1100.

5.1000 g, .374 GOLD, .0613 oz AGW

KM#	Date	Mintage	VF	XF	Unc
94c	1982	.040	—	Proof	75.00
7.9600 g, .917 GOLD, .2347 oz AGW					
94d	1982	4,000	—	Proof	150.00

COPPER-NICKEL, 37mm
XII World Cup - Spain
Rev: Similar to KM#92 but 1982 above Italian shield.

KM#	Date	Mintage	VF	XF	Unc
95	1982	—	—	—	4.00
28.2800 g, .925 SILVER, .8411 oz ASW					
95a	1982	—	—	Proof	25.00
52.0000 g, .950 PLATINUM, 1.5884 oz APW					
95b	1982	—	Reported, not confirmed		

5.1000 g, .374 GOLD, .0613 oz AGW

KM#	Date	Mintage	VF	XF	Unc
95c	1982	3,000	Reported, not confirmed		
7.9600 g, .917 GOLD, .2347 oz AGW					
95d	1982	—	Reported, not confirmed		

COPPER-NICKEL, 37mm
Maritime Heritage - Mayflower

KM#	Date	Mintage	VF	XF	Unc
96	1982	.050	—	—	3.00
28.2800 g, .925 SILVER, .8411 oz ASW					
96a	1982	.015	—	—	20.00
	1982	.010	—	Proof	25.00
52.0000 g, .950 PLATINUM, 1.5884 oz APW					
96b	1982	50 pcs.	—	Proof	1250.

5.1000 g, .374 GOLD, .0613 oz AGW

KM#	Date	Mintage	VF	XF	Unc
96c	1982	.022	—	Proof	75.00
7.9600 g, .917 GOLD, .2347 oz AGW					
96d	1982	2,000	—	Proof	150.00

COPPER-NICKEL, 37mm
Maritime Heritage - H.M.S. Bounty

KM#	Date	Mintage	VF	XF	Unc
97	1982	.050	—	—	3.00
28.2800 g, .925 SILVER, .8411 oz ASW					
97a	1982	.015	—	—	20.00
	1982	.010	—	Proof	25.00
52.0000 g, .950 PLATINUM, 1.5884 oz APW					
97b	1982	50 pcs.	—	Proof	1100.

5.1000 g, .374 GOLD, .0613 oz AGW

KM#	Date	Mintage	VF	XF	Unc
97c	1982	.022	—	Proof	75.00
7.9600 g, .917 GOLD, .2347 oz AGW					
97d	1982	2,000	—	Proof	150.00

COPPER-NICKEL, 37mm
Maritime Heritage - H.M.S. Victory

KM#	Date	Mintage	VF	XF	Unc
98	1982	.050	—	—	3.00
28.2800 g, .925 SILVER, .8411 oz ASW					
98a	1982	.015	—	—	20.00
	1982	.010	—	Proof	25.00
52.0000 g, .950 PLATINUM, 1.5884 oz APW					
98b	1982	50 pcs.	—	Proof	1200.

5.1000 g, .374 GOLD, .0613 oz AGW

KM#	Date	Mintage	VF	XF	Unc
98c	1982	.022	—	Proof	75.00
7.9600 g, .917 GOLD, .2347 oz AGW					
98d	1982	2,000	—	Proof	150.00

COPPER-NICKEL, 37mm
Maritime Heritage - P.S. Mona's Queen II

KM#	Date	Mintage	VF	XF	Unc
99	1982	.050	—	—	3.00
28.2800 g, .925 SILVER, .8411 oz ASW					
99a	1982	.015	—	—	20.00
	1982	.010	—	Proof	25.00
52.0000 g, .950 PLATINUM, 1.5884 oz APW					
99b	1982	50 pcs.	—	Proof	1100.

5.1000 g, .374 GOLD, .0613 oz AGW

KM#	Date	Mintage	VF	XF	Unc
99c	1982	.022	—	Proof	75.00
7.9600 g, .917 GOLD, .2347 oz AGW					
99d	1982	2,000	—	Proof	150.00

COPPER-NICKEL, 37mm
World Cup Soccer - Spain

Rev: Similar to KM#93 w/soccer ball added in upper left field.

KM#	Date	Mintage	VF	XF	Unc
100	1982	—	—	—	4.00

Manned Flight - Balloon

KM#	Date	Mintage	VF	XF	Unc
103	1983	.050	—	—	4.00

28.2800 g, .925 SILVER, .8411 oz ASW

KM#	Date	Mintage	VF	XF	Unc
103a	1983	.015	—	—	20.00
	1983	.011	—	Proof	25.00

52.0000 g, .950 PLATINUM, 1.5884 oz APW

KM#	Date	Mintage	VF	XF	Unc
103b	1983	50 pcs.	—	Proof	1250.

5.1000 g, .374 GOLD, .0613 oz AGW

KM#	Date	Mintage	VF	XF	Unc
103c	1983	5,500	—	Proof	75.00

7.9600 g, .917 GOLD, .2347 oz AGW

KM#	Date	Mintage	VF	XF	Unc
103d	1983	500 pcs.	—	Proof	150.00

COPPER-NICKEL, 37mm
Manned Flight - Biplane

KM#	Date	Mintage	VF	XF	Unc
104	1983	.050	—	—	4.00

28.2800 g, .925 SILVER, .8411 oz ASW

KM#	Date	Mintage	VF	XF	Unc
104a	1983	.015	—	—	20.00
	1983	.011	—	Proof	25.00

52.0000 g, .950 PLATINUM, 1.5884 oz APW

KM#	Date	Mintage	VF	XF	Unc
104b	1983	50 pcs.	—	Proof	1500.

5.1000 g, .374 GOLD, .0613 oz AGW

KM#	Date	Mintage	VF	XF	Unc
104c	1983	5,500	—	Proof	75.00

7.9600 g, .917 GOLD, .2347 oz AGW

KM#	Date	Mintage	VF	XF	Unc
104d	1983	500 pcs.	—	Proof	150.00

COPPER-NICKEL, 37mm
Manned Flight - Jet

KM#	Date	Mintage	VF	XF	Unc
105	1983	.050	—	—	4.00

28.2800 g, .925 SILVER, .8411 oz ASW

KM#	Date	Mintage	VF	XF	Unc
105a	1983	.015	—	—	20.00
	1983	.011	—	Proof	25.00

52.0000 g, .950 PLATINUM, 1.5884 oz APW

KM#	Date	Mintage	VF	XF	Unc
105b	1983	50 pcs.	—	Proof	1500.

5.1000 g, .374 GOLD, .0613 oz AGW

KM#	Date	Mintage	VF	XF	Unc
105c	1983	5,500	—	Proof	75.00

7.9600 g, .917 GOLD, .2347 oz AGW

KM#	Date	Mintage	VF	XF	Unc
105d	1983	500 pcs.	—	Proof	150.00

COPPER-NICKEL, 37mm
Manned Flight - Space Shuttle

KM#	Date	Mintage	VF	XF	Unc
106	1983	.050	—	—	4.00

28.2800 g, .925 SILVER, .8411 oz ASW

KM#	Date	Mintage	VF	XF	Unc
106a	1983	.015	—	—	20.00
	1983	.011	—	Proof	25.00

52.0000 g, .950 PLATINUM, 1.5884 oz APW

KM#	Date	Mintage	VF	XF	Unc
106b	1983	50 pcs.	—	Proof	1500.

5.1000 g, .374 GOLD, .0613 oz AGW

KM#	Date	Mintage	VF	XF	Unc
106c	1983	5,500	—	Proof	75.00

7.9600 g, .917 GOLD, .2347 oz AGW

KM#	Date	Mintage	VF	XF	Unc
106d	1983	500 pcs.	—	Proof	150.00

COPPER-NICKEL, 37mm
1984 Olympics - Figure Skating

KM#	Date	Mintage	VF	XF	Unc
117	1984	.050	—	—	4.00

SILVER CLAD COPPER-NICKEL

KM#	Date	Mintage	VF	XF	Unc
117e	1984	.020	—	—	15.00

28.2800 g, .925 SILVER, .8411 oz ASW

KM#	Date	Mintage	VF	XF	Unc
117a	1984	.015	—	Proof	25.00

5.1000 g, .374 GOLD, .0613 oz AGW

KM#	Date	Mintage	VF	XF	Unc
117b	1984	.010	—	Proof	75.00

7.9600 g, .917 GOLD, .2347 oz AGW

KM#	Date	Mintage	VF	XF	Unc
117c	1984	1,000	—	Proof	150.00

52.0000 g, .950 PLATINUM, 1.5884 oz APW

KM#	Date	Mintage	VF	XF	Unc
117d	1984	100 pcs.	—	Proof	1500.

COPPER-NICKEL, 37mm
1984 Olympics - Runners

KM#	Date	Mintage	VF	XF	Unc
118	1984	.050	—	—	4.00

SILVER CLAD COPPER-NICKEL

KM#	Date	Mintage	VF	XF	Unc
118e	1984	.020	—	—	15.00

28.2800 g, .925 SILVER, .8411 oz ASW

KM#	Date	Mintage	VF	XF	Unc
118a	1984	.015	—	Proof	25.00

5.1000 g, .374 GOLD, .0613 oz AGW

KM#	Date	Mintage	VF	XF	Unc
118b	1984	.010	—	Proof	75.00

7.9600 g, .917 GOLD, .2347 oz AGW

KM#	Date	Mintage	VF	XF	Unc
118c	1984	1,000	—	Proof	150.00

52.0000 g, .950 PLATINUM, 1.5884 oz APW

KM#	Date	Mintage	VF	XF	Unc
118d	1984	100 pcs.	—	Proof	1500.

COPPER-NICKEL, 37mm
1984 Olympics - Gymnastics

KM#	Date	Mintage	VF	XF	Unc
119	1984	.050	—	—	4.00

SILVER CLAD COPPER-NICKEL

KM#	Date	Mintage	VF	XF	Unc
119e	1984	.020	—	—	15.00

28.2800 g, .925 SILVER, .8411 oz ASW

KM#	Date	Mintage	VF	XF	Unc
119a	1984	.015	—	Proof	25.00

5.1000 g, .374 GOLD, .0613 oz AGW

KM#	Date	Mintage	VF	XF	Unc
119b	1984	.010	—	Proof	75.00

7.9600 g, .917 GOLD, .2347 oz AGW

KM#	Date	Mintage	VF	XF	Unc
119c	1984	1,000	—	Proof	150.00

52.0000 g, .950 PLATINUM, 1.5884 oz APW

KM#	Date	Mintage	VF	XF	Unc
119d	1984	100 pcs.	—	Proof	1500.

COPPER-NICKEL, 37mm
1984 Olympics-Equestrian

KM#	Date	Mintage	VF	XF	Unc
120	1984	.050	—	—	4.00

SILVER CLAD COPPER-NICKEL

KM#	Date	Mintage	VF	XF	Unc
120e	1984	.020	—	—	15.00

28.2800 g, .925 SILVER, .8411 oz ASW

KM#	Date	Mintage	VF	XF	Unc
120a	1984	.015	—	Proof	25.00

5.1000 g, .374 GOLD, .0613 oz AGW

KM#	Date	Mintage	VF	XF	Unc
120b	1984	.010	—	Proof	75.00

7.9600 g, .917 GOLD, .2347 oz AGW

KM#	Date	Mintage	VF	XF	Unc
120c	1984	1,000	—	Proof	150.00

52.0000 g, .950 PLATINUM, 1.5884 oz APW

KM#	Date	Mintage	VF	XF	Unc
120d	1984	100 pcs.	—	Proof	1500.

COPPER-NICKEL, 37mm
Quincentenary of the College of Arms

KM#	Date	Mintage	VF	XF	Unc
121	1984	—	—	—	2.50
	1984	—	—	P/L	5.00

28.2800 g, .925 SILVER, .8411 oz ASW

KM#	Date	Mintage	VF	XF	Unc
121a	1984	—	—	—	20.00
	1984	—	—	Proof	25.00

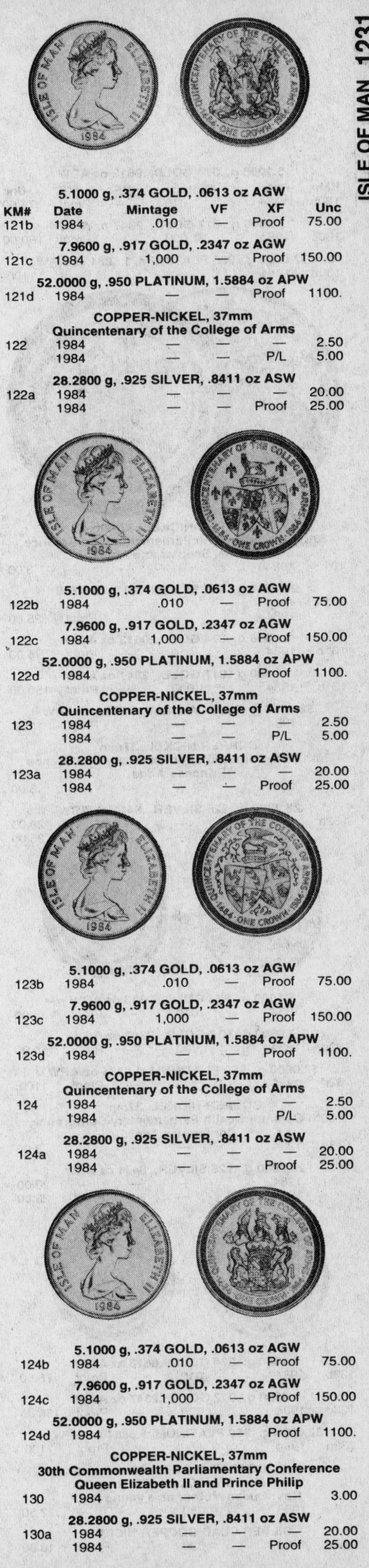

5.1000 g, .374 GOLD, .0613 oz AGW

KM#	Date	Mintage	VF	XF	Unc
121b	1984	.010	—	Proof	75.00

7.9600 g, .917 GOLD, .2347 oz AGW

KM#	Date	Mintage	VF	XF	Unc
121c	1984	1,000	—	Proof	150.00

52.0000 g, .950 PLATINUM, 1.5884 oz APW

KM#	Date	Mintage	VF	XF	Unc
121d	1984	—	—	Proof	1100.

COPPER-NICKEL, 37mm
Quincentenary of the College of Arms

KM#	Date	Mintage	VF	XF	Unc
122	1984	—	—	—	2.50
	1984	—	—	P/L	5.00

28.2800 g, .925 SILVER, .8411 oz ASW

KM#	Date	Mintage	VF	XF	Unc
122a	1984	—	—	—	20.00
	1984	—	—	Proof	25.00

5.1000 g, .374 GOLD, .0613 oz AGW

KM#	Date	Mintage	VF	XF	Unc
122b	1984	.010	—	Proof	75.00

7.9600 g, .917 GOLD, .2347 oz AGW

KM#	Date	Mintage	VF	XF	Unc
122c	1984	1,000	—	Proof	150.00

52.0000 g, .950 PLATINUM, 1.5884 oz APW

KM#	Date	Mintage	VF	XF	Unc
122d	1984	—	—	Proof	1100.

COPPER-NICKEL, 37mm
Quincentenary of the College of Arms

KM#	Date	Mintage	VF	XF	Unc
123	1984	—	—	—	2.50
	1984	—	—	P/L	5.00

28.2800 g, .925 SILVER, .8411 oz ASW

KM#	Date	Mintage	VF	XF	Unc
123a	1984	—	—	—	20.00
	1984	—	—	Proof	25.00

5.1000 g, .374 GOLD, .0613 oz AGW

KM#	Date	Mintage	VF	XF	Unc
123b	1984	.010	—	Proof	75.00

7.9600 g, .917 GOLD, .2347 oz AGW

KM#	Date	Mintage	VF	XF	Unc
123c	1984	1,000	—	Proof	150.00

52.0000 g, .950 PLATINUM, 1.5884 oz APW

KM#	Date	Mintage	VF	XF	Unc
123d	1984	—	—	Proof	1100.

COPPER-NICKEL, 37mm
Quincentenary of the College of Arms

KM#	Date	Mintage	VF	XF	Unc
124	1984	—	—	—	2.50
	1984	—	—	P/L	5.00

28.2800 g, .925 SILVER, .8411 oz ASW

KM#	Date	Mintage	VF	XF	Unc
124a	1984	—	—	—	20.00
	1984	—	—	Proof	25.00

5.1000 g, .374 GOLD, .0613 oz AGW

KM#	Date	Mintage	VF	XF	Unc
124b	1984	.010	—	Proof	75.00

7.9600 g, .917 GOLD, .2347 oz AGW

KM#	Date	Mintage	VF	XF	Unc
124c	1984	1,000	—	Proof	150.00

52.0000 g, .950 PLATINUM, 1.5884 oz APW

KM#	Date	Mintage	VF	XF	Unc
124d	1984	—	—	Proof	1100.

COPPER-NICKEL, 37mm
30th Commonwealth Parliamentary Conference
Queen Elizabeth II and Prince Philip

KM#	Date	Mintage	VF	XF	Unc
130	1984	—	—	—	3.00

28.2800 g, .925 SILVER, .8411 oz ASW

KM#	Date	Mintage	VF	XF	Unc
130a	1984	—	—	—	20.00
	1984	—	—	Proof	25.00

5.1000 g, .374 GOLD, .0613 oz AGW

KM# | Date | Mintage | VF | XF | Unc

130b 1984 .010 — Proof 75.00

7.9600 g, .917 GOLD, .2347 oz AGW

130c 1984 1,000 — Proof 150.00

52.0000 g, .950 PLATINUM, 1.5884 oz APW

130d 1984 — — Proof 1100.

COPPER-NICKEL, 37mm
30th Commonwealth Parliamentary Conference
Throne, Scepter and Shield

131 1984 — — — 3.00

28.2800 g, .925 SILVER, .8411 oz ASW

131a 1984 — — — 20.00
1984 — — Proof 25.00

5.1000 g, .374 GOLD, .0613 oz AGW

131b 1984 .010 — Proof 75.00

7.9600 g, .917 GOLD, .2347 oz AGW

131c 1984 1,000 — Proof 150.00

52.0000 g, .950 PLATINUM, 1.5884 oz APW

131d 1984 — — Proof 1100.

COPPER-NICKEL, 37mm
30th Commonwealth Parliamentary Conference
Princess Anne

132 1984 — — — 3.00

28.2800 g, .925 SILVER, .8411 oz ASW

132a 1984 — — — 20.00
1984 — — Proof 25.00

5.1000 g, .374 GOLD, .0613 oz AGW

132b 1984 .010 — Proof 75.00

7.9600 g, .917 GOLD, .2347 oz AGW

132c 1984 1,000 — Proof 150.00

52.0000 g, .950 PLATINUM, 1.5884 oz APW

132d 1984 — — Proof 1100.

COPPER-NICKEL, 37mm
30th Commonwealth Parliamentary Conference
Conference Tent

133 1984 — — — 3.00

28.2800 g, .925 SILVER, .8411 oz ASW

133a 1984 — — — 20.00
1984 — — Proof 25.00

5.1000 g, .374 GOLD, .0613 oz AGW

133b 1984 .010 — Proof 75.00

7.9600 g, .917 GOLD, .2347 oz AGW

133c 1984 1,000 — Proof 150.00

52.0000 g, .950 PLATINUM, 1.5884 oz APW

133d 1984 — — Proof 1100.

COPPER-NICKEL, 37mm
Obv: Portrait of Queen Elizabeth II.
Rev: Queen Mother as a young girl.

216 1985 *.050 — — 2.50

SILVER CLAD COPPER-NICKEL

216a 1985 *.020 — Proof 10.00

28.2800 g, .925 SILVER, .8411 oz ASW

KM# | Date | Mintage | VF | XF | Unc

216b 1985 *.015 — Proof 25.00

5.1000 g, .374 GOLD, .0613 oz AGW, 21mm

216c 1985 *.010 — Proof 75.00

7.9600 g, .917 GOLD, .2347 oz AGW

216d 1985 *1,000 — Proof 150.00

52.0000 g, .950 PLATINUM, 1.5884 oz APW, 37mm

216e 1985 *100 pcs. — Proof 1100.

COPPER-NICKEL
Rev: Portrait of King George VI and Elizabeth

217 1985 *.050 — — 2.50

SILVER CLAD COPPER-NICKEL

217a 1985 *.020 — Proof 10.00

28.2800 g, .925 SILVER, .8411 oz ASW

217b 1985 *.015 — Proof 25.00

5.1000 g, .374 GOLD, .0613 oz AGW, 21mm

217c 1985 *.010 — Proof 75.00

7.9600 g, .917 GOLD, .2347 oz AGW

217d 1985 *1,000 — Proof 150.00

52.0000 g, .950 PLATINUM, 1.5884 oz APW, 37mm

217e 1985 *100 pcs. — Proof 1100.

COPPER-NICKEL
Rev: Wedding portrait of
King George VI and Elizabeth.

218 1985 *.050 — — 2.50

SILVER CLAD COPPER-NICKEL

218a 1985 *.020 — Proof 10.00

28.2800 g, .925 SILVER, .8411 oz ASW

218b 1985 *.015 — Proof 25.00

5.1000 g, .374 GOLD, .0613 oz AGW, 21mm

218c 1985 *.010 — Proof 75.00

7.9600 g, .917 GOLD, .2347 oz AGW

218d 1985 *1,000 — Proof 150.00

52.0000 g, .950 PLATINUM, 1.5884 oz APW, 37mm

218e 1985 *100 pcs. — Proof 1100.

COPPER-NICKEL
Rev: Queen Mother and child.

219 1985 *.050 — — 2.50

SILVER CLAD COPPER-NICKEL

219a 1985 *.020 — Proof 10.00

28.2800 g, .925 SILVER, .8411 oz ASW

219b 1985 *.015 — Proof 25.00

5.1000 g, .374 GOLD, .0613 oz AGW, 21mm

219c 1985 *.010 — Proof 75.00

7.9600 g, .917 GOLD, .2347 oz AGW

219d 1985 *1,000 — Proof 150.00

52.0000 g, .950 PLATINUM, 1.5884 oz APW, 37mm

219e 1985 *100 pcs. — Proof 1100.

COPPER-NICKEL
Rev: Queen Mother and 2 daughters.

220 1985 *.050 — — 2.50
1990 — — — 4.00
1990 — — Proof 8.00

SILVER CLAD COPPER-NICKEL

220a 1985 *.020 — Proof 10.00

28.2800 g, .925 SILVER, .8411 oz ASW

220b 1985 *.015 — Proof 25.00
1990 — — Proof 20.00

5.1000 g, .374 GOLD, .0613 oz AGW, 21mm

220c 1985 *.010 — Proof 75.00

7.9600 g, .917 GOLD, .2347 oz AGW

220d 1985 *1,000 — Proof 150.00

52.0000 g, .950 PLATINUM, 1.5884 oz APW, 37mm

220e 1985 *100 pcs. — Proof 1100.

COPPER-NICKEL
Rev: Queen Mother on 80th Birthday

221 1985 *.050 — — 2.50

SILVER CLAD COPPER-NICKEL

221a 1985 *.020 — Proof 10.00

28.2800 g, .925 SILVER, .8411 oz ASW

221b 1985 *.015 — Proof 25.00

5.1000 g, .374 GOLD, .0613 oz AGW, 21mm

221c 1985 *.010 — Proof 75.00

7.9600 g, .917 GOLD, .2347 oz AGW

221d 1985 *1,000 — Proof 150.00

52.0000 g, .950 PLATINUM, 1.5884 oz APW, 37mm

221e 1985 *100 pcs. — Proof 1100.

COPPER-NICKEL
World Cup Soccer - Mexico

KM# | Date | Mintage | VF | XF | Unc

160 1986 *.050 — — 2.50

SILVER CLAD COPPER-NICKEL

160a 1986 *.020 — Proof 5.00

28.2800 g, .925 SILVER, .8411 oz ASW

160b 1986 *.015 — Proof 25.00

5.1000 g, .374 GOLD, .0613 oz AGW

160c 1986 *.010 — Proof 75.00

7.9600 g, .917 GOLD, .2347 oz AGW

160d 1986 *1,000 — Proof 150.00

52.0000 g, .950 PLATINUM, 1.5884 oz APW, 37mm

160e 1986 *200 pcs. — Proof 1100.

COPPER-NICKEL
World Cup Soccer - Mexico

161 1986 *.050 — — 2.50

SILVER CLAD COPPER-NICKEL

161a 1986 *.020 — Proof 5.00

28.2800 g, .925 SILVER, .8411 oz ASW

161b 1986 *.015 — Proof 25.00

5.1000 g, .374 GOLD, .0613 oz AGW

161c 1986 *.010 — Proof 75.00

7.9600 g, .917 GOLD, .2347 oz AGW

161d 1986 *1,000 — Proof 150.00

52.0000 g, .950 PLATINUM, 1.5884 oz APW, 37mm

161e 1986 *200 pcs. — Proof 1100.

COPPER-NICKEL
World Cup Soccer - Mexico

162 1986 *.050 — — 2.50

SILVER CLAD COPPER-NICKEL

162a 1986 *.020 — Proof 5.00

28.2800 g, .925 SILVER, .8411 oz ASW

162b 1986 *.015 — Proof 25.00

5.1000 g, .374 GOLD, .0613 oz AGW

162c 1986 *.010 — Proof 75.00

7.9600 g, .917 GOLD, .2347 oz AGW

162d 1986 *1,000 — Proof 150.00

52.0000 g, .950 PLATINUM, 1.5884 oz APW, 37mm

162e 1986 *200 pcs. — Proof 1100.

COPPER-NICKEL
World Cup Soccer - Mexico

163 1986 *.050 — — 2.50

SILVER CLAD COPPER-NICKEL

163a 1986 *.020 — Proof 5.00

28.2800 g, .925 SILVER, .8411 oz ASW

163b 1986 *.015 — Proof 25.00

5.1000 g, .374 GOLD, .0613 oz AGW

KM#	Date	Mintage	VF	XF	Unc
163c	1986	*.010	—	Proof	75.00

7.9600 g, .917 GOLD, .2347 oz AGW

KM#	Date	Mintage	VF	XF	Unc
163d	1986	*1,000	—	Proof	150.00

52.0000 g, .950 PLATINUM, 1.5884 oz APW, 37mm

KM#	Date	Mintage	VF	XF	Unc
163e	1986	*200 pcs.	—	Proof	1100.

COPPER-NICKEL
World Cup Soccer - Mexico - Map

KM#	Date	Mintage	VF	XF	Unc
164	1986	*.050	—	—	2.50

SILVER CLAD COPPER-NICKEL

KM#	Date	Mintage	VF	XF	Unc
164a	1986	*.020	—	Proof	5.00

28.2800 g, .925 SILVER, .8411 oz ASW

KM#	Date	Mintage	VF	XF	Unc
164b	1986	*.015	—	Proof	25.00

5.1000 g, .374 GOLD, .0613 oz AGW

KM#	Date	Mintage	VF	XF	Unc
164c	1986	*.010	—	Proof	75.00

7.9600 g, .917 GOLD, .2347 oz AGW

KM#	Date	Mintage	VF	XF	Unc
164d	1986	*1,000	—	Proof	150.00

52.0000 g, .950 PLATINUM, 1.5884 oz APW, 37mm

KM#	Date	Mintage	VF	XF	Unc
164e	1986	*200 pcs.	—	Proof	1100.

COPPER-NICKEL
World Cup Soccer - Mexico - Flags

KM#	Date	Mintage	VF	XF	Unc
165	1986	*.050	—	—	2.50

SILVER CLAD COPPER-NICKEL

KM#	Date	Mintage	VF	XF	Unc
165a	1986	*.020	—	Proof	5.00

28.2800 g, .925 SILVER, .8411 oz ASW

KM#	Date	Mintage	VF	XF	Unc
165b	1986	*.015	—	Proof	25.00

5.1000 g, .374 GOLD, .0613 oz AGW

KM#	Date	Mintage	VF	XF	Unc
165c	1986	*.010	—	Proof	75.00

7.9600 g, .917 GOLD, .2347 oz AGW

KM#	Date	Mintage	VF	XF	Unc
165d	1986	*1,000	—	Proof	150.00

52.0000 g, .950 PLATINUM, 1.5884 oz APW, 37mm

KM#	Date	Mintage	VF	XF	Unc
165e	1986	*200 pcs.	—	Proof	1100.

COPPER-NICKEL
Prince Andrew's Wedding - Portraits

KM#	Date	Mintage	VF	XF	Unc
173	1986	*.050	—	—	6.00
	1986	—	—	P/L	8.00

SILVER CLAD COPPER-NICKEL

KM#	Date	Mintage	VF	XF	Unc
173a	1986	*.020	—	Proof	12.00

28.2800 g, .925 SILVER, .8411 oz ASW

KM#	Date	Mintage	VF	XF	Unc
173b	1986	*.020	—	—	25.00
	1986	*.015	—	Proof	35.00

5.1000 g, .374 GOLD, .0613 oz AGW

KM#	Date	Mintage	VF	XF	Unc
173c	1986	*.010	—	Proof	75.00

7.9600 g, .917 GOLD, .2347 oz AGW

KM#	Date	Mintage	VF	XF	Unc
173d	1986	*1,000	—	Proof	150.00

52.0000 g, .950 PLATINUM, 1.5884 oz APW, 37mm

KM#	Date	Mintage	VF	XF	Unc
173e	1986	*100 pcs.	—	Proof	1200.

COPPER-NICKEL
Prince Andrew's Wedding - Coat of Arms

KM#	Date	Mintage	VF	XF	Unc
174	1986	*.050	—	—	6.00
	1986	—	—	P/L	8.00

SILVER CLAD COPPER-NICKEL

KM#	Date	Mintage	VF	XF	Unc
174a	1986	*.020	—	Proof	12.00

28.2800 g, .925 SILVER, .8411 oz ASW

KM#	Date	Mintage	VF	XF	Unc
174b	1986	*.020	—	—	25.00
	1986	*.015	—	Proof	35.00

5.1000 g, .374 GOLD, .0613 oz AGW

KM#	Date	Mintage	VF	XF	Unc
174c	1986	*.010	—	Proof	75.00

7.9600 g, .917 GOLD, .2347 oz AGW

KM#	Date	Mintage	VF	XF	Unc
174d	1986	*1,000	—	Proof	150.00

52.0000 g, .950 PLATINUM, 1.5884 oz APW, 37mm

KM#	Date	Mintage	VF	XF	Unc
174e	1986	*100 pcs.	—	Proof	1200.

COPPER-NICKEL
United States Constitution
Obv: Similar to KM#179.

KM#	Date	Mintage	VF	XF	Unc
176	1987	—	—	—	7.00

31.1000 g, .999 PALLADIUM, 1.0000 oz APW

KM#	Date	Mintage	VF	XF	Unc
176a	1987	*.028	—	Proof	300.00

31.1000 g, .995 PLATINUM, 1.0000 oz APW

KM#	Date	Mintage	VF	XF	Unc
176b	1987	*1,000	—	Proof	800.00

COPPER-NICKEL
America's Cup - Sailboats and Map

KM#	Date	Mintage	VF	XF	Unc
179	1987	—	—	—	3.00

28.2800 g, .925 SILVER, .8411 oz ASW

KM#	Date	Mintage	VF	XF	Unc
179b	1987	*.020	—	—	26.50
	1987	*.015	—	Proof	40.00

31.1030 g, .999 PALLADIUM, 1.0000 oz APW

KM#	Date	Mintage	VF	XF	Unc
179c	1987	*.025	—	Proof	250.00

COPPER-NICKEL
America's Cup - Sailboats and Cup
Obv: Similar to KM#179.

KM#	Date	Mintage	VF	XF	Unc
183	1987	—	—	—	3.00

28.2800 g, .925 SILVER, .8411 oz ASW

KM#	Date	Mintage	VF	XF	Unc
183b	1987	*.020	—	—	26.50
	1987	*.015	—	Proof	40.00

COPPER-NICKEL
America's Cup - Sailboats - Statue of Liberty
Obv: Similar to KM#179.

KM#	Date	Mintage	VF	XF	Unc
184	1987	—	—	—	3.00

28.2800 g, .925 SILVER, .8411 oz ASW

KM#	Date	Mintage	VF	XF	Unc
184b	1987	*.020	—	—	26.50
	1987	*.015	—	Proof	40.00

COPPER-NICKEL
America's Cup - George Steers
Obv: Similar to KM#179.

KM#	Date	Mintage	VF	XF	Unc
185	1987	—	—	—	3.00

28.2800 g, .925 SILVER, .8411 oz ASW

KM#	Date	Mintage	VF	XF	Unc
185b	1987	*.020	—	—	26.50
	1987	*.015	—	Proof	40.00

COPPER-NICKEL
America's Cup - Sir Thomas Lipton
Obv: Similar to KM#179.

KM#	Date	Mintage	VF	XF	Unc
186	1987	—	—	—	3.00

28.2800 g, .925 SILVER, .8411 oz ASW

KM#	Date	Mintage	VF	XF	Unc
186b	1987	*.020	—	—	26.50
	1987	*.015	—	Proof	40.00

COPPER-NICKEL
Australian Bicentennial - Cockatoo

KM#	Date	Mintage	VF	XF	Unc
222	1988	—	—	—	3.00
	1988	500 pcs.	—	Proof	6.00

Australian Bicentennial - Koala

KM#	Date	Mintage	VF	XF	Unc
223	1988	—	—	—	3.00
	1988	500 pcs.	—	Proof	6.00

Australian Bicentennial - Platypus Duckbill

KM#	Date	Mintage	VF	XF	Unc
224	1988	—	—	—	3.00
	1988	500 pcs.	—	Proof	6.00

Australian Bicentennial - Kangaroo

KM#	Date	Mintage	VF	XF	Unc
225	1988	—	—	—	3.00
	1988	500 pcs.	—	Proof	6.00

Australian Bicentennial - Dingo Dog

KM#	Date	Mintage	VF	XF	Unc
226	1988	—	—	—	3.00

Australian Bicentennial - Tasmanian Devil

KM#	Date	Mintage	VF	XF	Unc
227	1988	—	—	—	3.00

Steam Navigation - Patrick Miller's Number One

KM#	Date	Mintage	VF	XF	Unc
228	1988	—	—	—	3.00

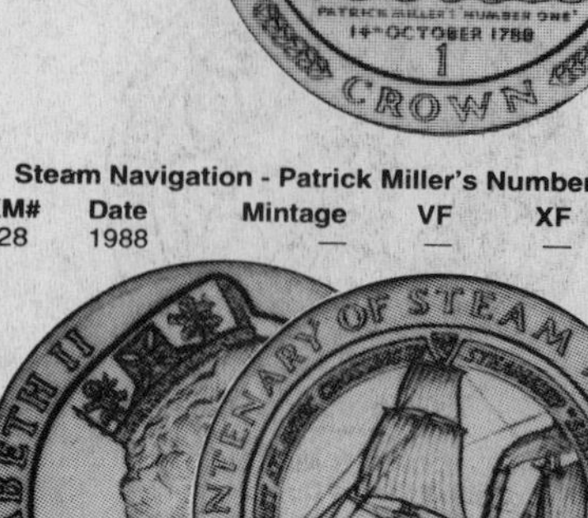

Steam Navigation - Sirius

KM#	Date	Mintage	VF	XF	Unc
229	1988	—	—	—	3.00

Steam Navigation - Chaperon

KM#	Date	Mintage	VF	XF	Unc
230	1988	—	—	—	3.00

Steam Navigation - Mauretania

KM#	Date	Mintage	VF	XF	Unc
231	1988	—	—	—	3.00

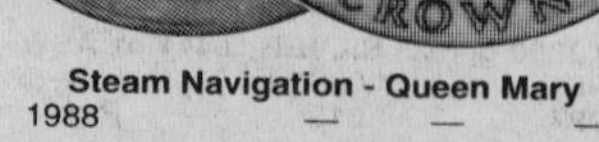

Steam Navigation - Queen Mary

KM#	Date	Mintage	VF	XF	Unc
232	1988	—	—	—	3.00

Steam Navigation - Queen Elizabeth II

KM#	Date	Mintage	VF	XF	Unc
233	1988	—	—	—	3.00

COPPER-NICKEL
Manx Cat

KM#	Date	Mintage	VF	XF	Unc
245	1988	—	—	—	7.00
	1988	250 pcs.	—	Proof	30.00

Mutiny on the Bounty - Captain Bligh and Elizabeth Betham

KM#	Date	Mintage	VF	XF	Unc
240	1989	—	—	—	3.25

28.2800 g, .925 SILVER, .8411 oz ASW

KM#	Date	Mintage	VF	XF	Unc
240a	1989	—	—	Proof	45.00

COPPER-NICKEL
Mutiny on the Bounty - H.M.S. Bounty

KM#	Date	Mintage	VF	XF	Unc
241	1989	—	—	—	3.25

28.2800 g, .925 SILVER, .8411 oz ASW

KM#	Date	Mintage	VF	XF	Unc
241a	1989	—	—	Proof	45.00

COPPER-NICKEL
Mutiny on the Bounty
Capt. Bligh and crew set afloat

KM#	Date	Mintage	VF	XF	Unc
242	1989	—	—	—	3.25
	28.2800 g, .925 SILVER, .8411 oz ASW				
242a	1989	—	—	Proof	45.00

COPPER-NICKEL
Mutiny on the Bounty - Pitcairn Island

KM#	Date	Mintage	VF	XF	Unc
243	1989	—	—	—	3.25
	28.2800 g, .925 SILVER, .8411 oz ASW				
243a	1989	—	—	Proof	45.00

COPPER-NICKEL
Washington Crossing the Delaware

KM#	Date	Mintage	VF	XF	Unc
246	1989	—	—	—	3.75
	1989	—	—	Proof	9.00
	28.2800 g, .925 SILVER, .8411 oz ASW				
246a	1989	—	—	Proof	35.00

COPPER-NICKEL
George Washington Inauguration - Portrait

KM#	Date	Mintage	VF	XF	Unc
247	1989	—	—	—	3.75
	1989	—	—	Proof	9.00
	28.2800 g, .925 SILVER, .8411 oz ASW				
247a	1989	—	—	Proof	35.00

COPPER-NICKEL
George Washington Inauguration - Portrait in frame

KM#	Date	Mintage	VF	XF	Unc
248	1989	—	—	—	3.75
	1989	—	—	Proof	9.00
	28.2800 g, .925 SILVER, .8411 oz ASW				
248a	1989	—	—	Proof	35.00

COPPER-NICKEL
George Washington Taking Oath

KM#	Date	Mintage	VF	XF	Unc
249	1989	—	—	—	3.75
	1989	—	—	Proof	9.00
	28.2800 g, .925 SILVER, .8411 oz ASW				
249a	1989	—	—	Proof	35.00

COPPER-NICKEL
Persian Cat

KM#	Date	Mintage	VF	XF	Unc
250	1989	—	—	—	10.00
	1989	250 pcs.	—	Proof	30.00

Royal Visit

KM#	Date	Mintage	VF	XF	Unc
273	1989	*.050	—	—	4.00
	31.1000 g, .999 SILVER, 1.0000 oz ASW				
273a	1989	*.020	—	Proof	35.00
	31.1000 g, .999 GOLD, 1.0000 oz AGW				
273b	1989	*7,500	—	Proof	700.00

COPPER-NICKEL
150th Anniversary of "Penny Black" Stamp

KM#	Date	Mintage	VF	XF	Unc
267	1990	—	—	—	7.50
	1990	.050	—	Proof	16.50
	28.2800 g, .925 SILVER, .8411 oz ASW				
267a	1990	.030	—	Proof	50.00
	34.0000 g, .917 GOLD, 1.0000 oz AGW				
267b	1990	*1,000	—	Proof	1100.
	52.0000 g, .950 PLATINUM, 1.5884 oz APW				
267c	1990	*50 pcs.	—	Proof	—

COPPER-NICKEL
Soccer - Milano

KM#	Date	Mintage	VF	XF	Unc
269	1990	—	—	—	3.25
	28.2800 g, .925 SILVER, .8411 oz ASW				
269a	1990	*.030	—	Proof	30.00

KM#	Date	Mintage	VF	XF	Unc
	6.2200 g, .999 GOLD, .2000 oz AGW				
269b	1990	*500 pcs.	—	Proof	125.00
	6.2200 g, .999 PLATINUM, .2000 oz APW				
269c	1990	*250 pcs.	—	Proof	150.00

COPPER-NICKEL
Soccer - Torino

KM#	Date	Mintage	VF	XF	Unc
270	1990	—	—	—	3.25
	28.2800 g, .925 SILVER, .8411 oz ASW				
270a	1990	*.030	—	Proof	30.00

KM#	Date	Mintage	VF	XF	Unc
	6.2200 g, .999 GOLD, .2000 oz AGW				
270b	1990	*500 pcs.	—	Proof	125.00
	6.2200 g, .999 PLATINUM, .2000 oz APW				
270c	1990	*250 pcs.	—	Proof	150.00

COPPER-NICKEL
Soccer - Bologna

KM#	Date	Mintage	VF	XF	Unc
271	1990	—	—	—	3.25
	28.2800 g, .925 SILVER, .8411 oz ASW				
271a	1990	*.030	—	Proof	30.00

KM#	Date	Mintage	VF	XF	Unc
	6.2200 g, .999 GOLD, .2000 oz AGW				
271b	1990	*500 pcs.	—	Proof	125.00
	6.2200 g, .999 PLATINUM, .2000 oz APW				
271c	1990	*250 pcs.	—	Proof	150.00

COPPER-NICKEL
Soccer - Palermo

KM#	Date	Mintage	VF	XF	Unc
272	1990	—	—	—	3.25
	28.2800 g, .925 SILVER, .8411 oz ASW				
272a	1990	*.030	—	Proof	30.00

6.2200 g, .999 GOLD, .2000 oz AGW

KM#	Date	Mintage	VF	XF	Unc
272b	1990	*500 pcs.	—	Proof	125.00

6.2200 g, .999 PLATINUM, .2000 oz APW

KM#	Date	Mintage	VF	XF	Unc
272c	1990	*250 pcs.	—	Proof	150.00

COPPER-NICKEL
Alley Cat

KM#	Date	Mintage	VF	XF	Unc
275	1990	—	—	—	5.00
	1990	250 pcs.	—	Proof	30.00

Sir Winston Churchill

KM#	Date	Mintage	VF	XF	Unc
283	1990	—	—	—	4.00

28.2800 g, .925 SILVER, .8411 oz ASW

KM#	Date	Mintage	VF	XF	Unc
283a	1990	*.025	—	Proof	50.00

6.2230 g, .999 GOLD, .2000 oz AGW

KM#	Date	Mintage	VF	XF	Unc
283b	1990	*500 pcs.	—	Proof	200.00

6.2230 g, .999 PLATINUM, .2000 oz APW

KM#	Date	Mintage	VF	XF	Unc
283c	1990	*100 pcs.	—	Proof	250.00

COPPER-NICKEL
Sir Winston Churchill

KM#	Date	Mintage	VF	XF	Unc
284	1990	—	—	—	4.00

28.2800 g, .925 SILVER, .8411 oz ASW

KM#	Date	Mintage	VF	XF	Unc
284a	1990	*.025	—	Proof	50.00

6.2230 g, .999 GOLD, .2000 oz AGW

KM#	Date	Mintage	VF	XF	Unc
284b	1990	*500 pcs.	—	Proof	200.00

6.2230 g, .999 PLATINUM, .2000 oz APW

KM#	Date	Mintage	VF	XF	Unc
284c	1990	*100 pcs.	—	Proof	250.00

COPPER-NICKEL
Queen Mother

KM#	Date	Mintage	VF	XF	Unc
307	1990	—	—	—	4.00
	1990	—	—	Proof	8.00

28.2800 g, .925 SILVER, .8411 oz ASW

KM#	Date	Mintage	VF	XF	Unc
307a	1990	—	—	Proof	28.00

COPPER-NICKEL
American Numismatic Association

KM#	Date	Mintage	VF	XF	Unc
291	1991	—	—	—	4.50

28.2800 g, .925 SILVER, .8411 oz ASW

KM#	Date	Mintage	VF	XF	Unc
291a	1991	—	—	Proof	45.00

COPPER-NICKEL
Norwegian Cat

KM#	Date	Mintage	VF	XF	Unc
292	1991	—	—	—	6.00
	1991	15 pcs.	—	Proof	—

10th Wedding Anniversary - Prince Charles
Similar to KM#304b.

KM#	Date	Mintage	VF	XF	Unc
304	1991	—	—	—	3.50

28.2800 g, .925 SILVER, .8411 oz ASW
Similar to KM#304b.

KM#	Date	Mintage	VF	XF	Unc
304a	1991	—	—	Proof	40.00

6.2200 g, .999 GOLD, .2000 oz AGW

KM#	Date	Mintage	VF	XF	Unc
304b	1991	—	—	Proof	165.00

COPPER-NICKEL
10th Wedding Anniversary - Princess Diana
Similar to KM#305b.

KM#	Date	Mintage	VF	XF	Unc
305	1991	—	—	—	3.50

28.2800 g, .925 SILVER, .8411 oz ASW
Similar to KM#305b.

KM#	Date	Mintage	VF	XF	Unc
305a	1991	—	—	Proof	35.00

6.2200 g, .999 GOLD, .2000 oz AGW

KM#	Date	Mintage	VF	XF	Unc
305b	1991	—	—	Proof	165.00

COPPER-NICKEL
Discovery of America - John Casement

KM#	Date	Mintage	VF	XF	Unc
310	1992	—	—	—	4.00
	1992	—	—	Proof	12.00

28.2800 g, .925 SILVER, .8411 oz ASW

KM#	Date	Mintage	VF	XF	Unc
310a	1992	—	—	Proof	55.00

COPPER-NICKEL
Discovery of America - Dan Casement

KM#	Date	Mintage	VF	XF	Unc
311	1992	—	—	—	4.00
	1992	—	—	Proof	12.00

28.2800 g, .925 SILVER, .8411 oz ASW

KM#	Date	Mintage	VF	XF	Unc
311a	1992	—	—	Proof	55.00

COPPER-NICKEL
Discovery of America - Promontory Point, Utah

KM#	Date	Mintage	VF	XF	Unc
312	1992	—	—	—	4.00
	1992	—	—	Proof	10.00

28.2800 g, .925 SILVER, .8411 oz ASW

KM#	Date	Mintage	VF	XF	Unc
312a	1992	—	—	Proof	55.00

COPPER-NICKEL
Discovery of America - Flags of United States and Isle of Man

KM#	Date	Mintage	VF	XF	Unc
313	1992	—	—	—	4.00
	1992	—	—	Proof	10.00

28.2800 g, .925 SILVER, .8411 oz ASW

KM#	Date	Mintage	VF	XF	Unc
313a	1992	—	—	Proof	55.00

COPPER-NICKEL
America's Cup
Obv: Portrait of Queen Elizabeth II.
Rev: Cameo of sailing ship above 2 modern sailboats.

KM#	Date	Mintage	VF	XF	Unc
320	1991	*125 pcs.	—	—	—

America's Cup - San Diego

KM#	Date	Mintage	VF	XF	Unc
326	1992	—	—	—	4.75
	1992	—	—	Proof	10.00

28.2800 g, .925 SILVER, .8411 oz ASW

KM#	Date	Mintage	VF	XF	Unc
326a	1992	.025	—	P/L	60.00

31.0300 g, .999 GOLD, 1.0000 oz AGW

KM#	Date	Mintage	VF	XF	Unc
326b	1992	—	—	—	800.00

COPPER-NICKEL
Siamese Cat
Obv: Portrait of Queen Elizabeth II. Rev: Seated cat.

KM#	Date	Mintage	VF	XF	Unc
332	1992	—	—	—	5.00

Maine Coon Cat
Rev: Furry cat.

KM#	Date	Mintage	VF	XF	Unc
353	1993	—	—	—	5.00

Preserve Planet Earth - Iguanodon

KM#	Date	Mintage	VF	XF	Unc
357	1993	—	—	—	6.50

Preserve Planet Earth - Diplodocus

KM#	Date	Mintage	VF	XF	Unc
358	1993	—	—	—	6.50

50 NEW PENCE

COPPER-NICKEL
Viking Ship

KM#	Date	Mintage	VF	XF	Unc
24	1971	.100	—	.75	1.50
	1971	.010	—	Proof	7.50
	1972	1,000	—	—	30.00
	1973	1,000	—	—	30.00
	1974	1,000	—	—	30.00
	1975	.227	—	.75	1.50

15.5000 g, .925 SILVER, .4610 oz ASW

KM#	Date	Mintage	VF	XF	Unc
24a	1975	.020	—	—	12.50

30.4000 g, .950 PLATINUM, .9286 oz APW

KM#	Date	Mintage	VF	XF	Unc
24b	1975	600 pcs.	—	Proof	625.00

50 PENCE

COPPER-NICKEL
Viking Ship

KM#	Date	Mintage	VF	XF	Unc
39	1976	.250	—	.75	2.00
	1977	.050	—	.75	2.50
	1978	.025	—	.75	2.50
	1978	—	—	Proof	3.50
	1979(t)	—	—	.75	3.00

15.5000 g, .925 SILVER, .4610 oz ASW

KM#	Date	Mintage	VF	XF	Unc
39a	1976	.020	—	—	12.50
	1977	.010	—	Proof	12.50
	1978	.010	—	—	12.50
	1979(t)	.010	—	Proof	12.50

30.4000 g, .950 PLATINUM, .9286 oz APW

KM#	Date	Mintage	VF	XF	Unc
39b	1976	600 pcs.	—	Proof	625.00
	1978	600 pcs.	—	Proof	625.00
	1979(t)	500 pcs.	—	Proof	625.00

COPPER-NICKEL
Manx Millenium of Tynwald
Edge inscription: H.M.Q.E.II ROYAL VISIT I.O.M. JULY 1979

KM#	Date	Mintage	VF	XF	Unc
51	1979 PM	.050	—	—	5.00

15.5000 g, .925 SILVER, .4610 oz ASW

KM#	Date	Mintage	VF	XF	Unc
51a	1979	.010	—	—	10.00
	1979	5,000	—	Proof	15.00

30.4000 g, .950 PLATINUM, .9286 oz APW

KM#	Date	Mintage	VF	XF	Unc
51b	1979	500 pcs.	—	Proof	625.00

COPPER-NICKEL
Plain edge

KM#	Date	Mintage	VF	XF	Unc
53	1979	—	—	—	3.00

15.5000 g, .925 SILVER, .4610 oz ASW

KM#	Date	Mintage	VF	XF	Unc
53a	1979	—	—	—	10.00
	1979	—	—	Proof	15.00

COPPER-NICKEL
Edge inscription: ODINS RAVEN VIKING EXHIBN NEW YORK 1980

KM#	Date	Mintage	VF	XF	Unc
69	1980	.020	—	—	4.00

15.5000 g, .925 SILVER, .4610 oz ASW

KM#	Date	Mintage	VF	XF	Unc
69a	1980	—	—	—	15.00
	1980	5,000	—	Proof	20.00

26.0000 g, .917 GOLD, .7666 oz AGW

KM#	Date	Mintage	VF	XF	Unc
69b	1980	250 pcs.	—	—	550.00

30.4000 g, .950 PLATINUM, .9286 oz APW

KM#	Date	Mintage	VF	XF	Unc
69c	1980	50 pcs.	—	Proof	775.00

COPPER-NICKEL
Viking Longship

KM#	Date	Mintage	VF	XF	Unc
70	1980	.010	—	.75	2.00
	1980	—	—	Proof	2.50
	1981	—	—	.75	2.00
	1982	—	—	.75	2.00
	1982(b)	—	—	.75	2.00
	1982(b)	.025	—	Proof	2.50
	1983	—	—	.75	2.00

15.5000 g, .500 SILVER, .2491 oz ASW

KM#	Date	Mintage	VF	XF	Unc
70a	1980	.010	—	Proof	10.00
	1982(b)	.010	—	Proof	15.00

15.5000 g, .925 SILVER, .4610 oz ASW

KM#	Date	Mintage	VF	XF	Unc
70b	1983	5,000	—	Proof	17.50

26.0000 g, .917 GOLD, .7666 oz AGW

KM#	Date	Mintage	VF	XF	Unc
70c	1980	300 pcs.	—	Proof	550.00
	1982(b)	500 pcs.	—	Proof	550.00
	1983	—	—	Proof	550.00

30.4000 g, .950 PLATINUM, .9286 oz APW

KM#	Date	Mintage	VF	XF	Unc
70d	1980	500 pcs.	—	Proof	750.00
	1982(b)	500 pcs.	—	Proof	750.00
	1983	—	—	Proof	750.00

COPPER-NICKEL
Mule. Obv: KM#69. Rev: KM#71.

KM#	Date	Mintage	VF	XF	Unc
57	1980	—	—	—	—

Christmas 1980

KM#	Date	Mintage	VF	XF	Unc
71	1980	.030	—	—	2.50

15.5000 g, .925 SILVER, .4610 oz ASW

KM#	Date	Mintage	VF	XF	Unc
71a	1980	5,000	—	Proof	15.00

26.0000 g, .917 GOLD, .7666 oz AGW

KM#	Date	Mintage	VF	XF	Unc
71b	1980	250 pcs.	—	Proof	550.00

KM#	Date	Mintage	VF	XF	Unc
30.4000 g, .950 PLATINUM, .9286 oz APW					
71c	1980	50 pcs.	—	Proof	750.00

COPPER-NICKEL
Tourist Trophy Motorcycle Races

KM#	Date	Mintage	VF	XF	Unc
83	1981	.030	—	—	2.25
15.5000 g, .925 SILVER, .4610 oz ASW					
83a	1981	5,000	—	Proof	15.00
26.0000 g, .917 GOLD, .7666 oz AGW					
83b	1981	250 pcs.	—	Proof	550.00
30.4000 g, .950 PLATINUM, .9286 oz APW					
83c	1981	50 pcs.	—	Proof	775.00

COPPER-NICKEL
Christmas 1981

KM#	Date	Mintage	VF	XF	Unc
84	1981	.030	—	—	2.50
	1981	—	—	Proof	7.50
15.5000 g, .925 SILVER, .4610 oz ASW					
84a	1981	5,000	—	Proof	15.00
26.0000 g, .917 GOLD, .7666 oz AGW					
84b	1981	250 pcs.	—	Proof	550.00
30.4000 g, .950 PLATINUM, .9286 oz APW					
84c	1981	—	—	Proof	775.00

COPPER-NICKEL
Tourist Trophy Motorcycle Races

KM#	Date	Mintage	VF	XF	Unc
101	1982	.030	—	—	2.50
	1982	—	—	Proof	7.50
15.5000 g, .925 SILVER, .4610 oz ASW					
101a	1982	5,000	—	Proof	15.00
26.0000 g, .917 GOLD, .7666 oz AGW					
101b	1982	250 pcs.	—	Proof	550.00
30.4000 g, .950 PLATINUM, .9286 oz APW					
101c	1982	50 pcs.	—	Proof	775.00

COPPER-NICKEL
Christmas 1982

KM#	Date	Mintage	VF	XF	Unc
102	1982	.030	—	—	2.50
	1982	250 pcs.	—	Proof	7.50
15.0000 g, .925 SILVER, .4610 oz ASW					
102a	1982	5,000	—	Proof	15.00
26.0000 g, .917 GOLD, .7666 oz AGW					
102b	1982	250 pcs.	—	Proof	550.00
30.4000 g, .950 PLATINUM, .9286 oz APW					
102c	1982	50 pcs.	—	Proof	750.00

COPPER-NICKEL
Christmas 1983

KM#	Date	Mintage	VF	XF	Unc
107	1983	.030	—	—	2.50
15.5000 g, .925 SILVER, .4610 oz ASW					
107a	1983	5,000	—	Proof	15.00
26.000 g, .917 GOLD, .7666 oz AGW					
107b	1983	250 pcs.	—	Proof	550.00
30.4000 g, .950 PLATINUM, .9286 oz APW					
107c	1983	50 pcs.	—	Proof	750.00

COPPER-NICKEL
Tourist Trophy Motorcycle Races

KM#	Date	Mintage	VF	XF	Unc
108	1983	.030	—	—	2.25
15.5000 g, .925 SILVER, .4610 oz ASW					
108a	1983	5,000	—	Proof	15.00
26.0000 g, .917 GOLD, .7666 oz AGW					
108b	1983	250 pcs.	—	Proof	550.00
30.4000 g, .950 PLATINUM, .9286 oz APW					
108c	1983	50 pcs.	—	Proof	775.00

COPPER-NICKEL
Viking Longship

KM#	Date	Mintage	VF	XF	Unc
125	1984	—	—	—	2.00
15.5000 g, .925 SILVER, .4610 oz ASW					
125a	1984	—	—	Proof	15.00
26.0000 g, .917 GOLD, .7666 oz AGW					
125b	1984	150 pcs.	—	Proof	550.00

COPPER-NICKEL
Tourist Trophy Motorcycle Races

KM#	Date	Mintage	VF	XF	Unc
126	1984	.030	—	—	2.25
15.5000 g, .925 SILVER, .4610 oz ASW					
126a	1984	5,000	—	Proof	15.00
26.0000 g, .917 GOLD, .7666oz AGW					
126b	1984	250 pcs.	—	Proof	550.00
30.4000 g, .950 PLATINUM, .9286 oz APW					
126c	1984	50 pcs.	—	Proof	775.00

COPPER-NICKEL
Christmas 1984

KM#	Date	Mintage	VF	XF	Unc
127	1984	—	—	—	2.50
	1984	—	—	Proof	7.50
15.5000 g, .925 SILVER, .4610 oz ASW					
127a	1984	—	—	Proof	25.00
26.0000 g, .917 GOLD, .7666 oz AGW					
127b	1984	250 pcs.	—	Proof	550.00
30.4000 g, .950 PLATINUM, .9286 oz APW					
127c	1984	—	—	Proof	750.00

COPPER-NICKEL

KM#	Date	Mintage	VF	XF	Unc
148	1985	—	—	—	2.00
	1985	*.050	—	Proof	4.00
	1986	—	—	—	2.00
	1987	—	—	—	2.00
15.5000 g, .925 SILVER, .4610 oz ASW					
148a	1985	*.010	—	Proof	15.00
26.0000 g, .917 GOLD, .7666 oz AGW					
148b	1985	*300 pcs.	—	Proof	550.00
30.4000 g, .950 PLATINUM, .9286 oz APW					
148c	1985	*200 pcs.	—	Proof	750.00

COPPER-NICKEL
Christmas 1985

KM#	Date	Mintage	VF	XF	Unc
158	1985	—	—	—	3.50
	1985	—	—	Proof	9.50
15.5000 g, .925 SILVER, .4610 oz ASW					
158a	1985	*5,000	—	Proof	20.00
26.0000 g, .917 GOLD, .7666 oz AGW					
158b	1985	*250 pcs.	—	Proof	550.00
30.4000 g, .950 PLATINUM, .9286 oz APW					
158c	1985	—	—	Proof	700.00

COPPER-NICKEL
Christmas 1986

KM#	Date	Mintage	VF	XF	Unc
172	1986	—	—	—	3.50
	1986	—	—	Proof	9.50
15.5000 g, .925 SILVER, .4610 oz ASW					
172a	1986	*5,000	—	Proof	20.00
26.0000 g, .917 GOLD, .7666 oz AGW					
172b	1986	—	—	Proof	550.00

COPPER-NICKEL
Christmas 1987

KM#	Date	Mintage	VF	XF	Unc
190	1987	*.030	—	—	2.50
	1987	—	—	Proof	7.50
	15.5000 g, .925 SILVER, .4610 oz ASW				
190a	1987	*5,000	—	Proof	20.00
	26.0000 g, .917 GOLD, .7666 oz AGW				
190b	1987	*250 pcs.	—	Proof	500.00
	30.4000 g, .950 PLATINUM, .9286 oz APW				
190c	1987	*50 pcs.	—	Proof	775.00

COPPER-NICKEL
Computer

KM#	Date	Mintage	VF	XF	Unc
212	1988	—	—	—	2.50
	1989	—	—	—	2.50
	1990	—	—	—	2.50
	1992	—	—	—	2.50

Christmas 1988

KM#	Date	Mintage	VF	XF	Unc
244	1988	—	—	—	2.50
	1988	—	—	Proof	7.50
	15.5000 g, .925 SILVER, .4610 oz ASW				
244a	1988	—	—	Proof	20.00
	26.0000 g, .917 GOLD, .7666 oz AGW				
244b	1988	—	—	Proof	500.00
	30.4000 g, .950 PLATINUM, .9286 oz APW				
244c	1988	—	—	Proof	800.00

COPPER-NICKEL
Christmas 1989

KM#	Date	Mintage	VF	XF	Unc
259	1989	—	—	—	2.50
	1989	—	—	Proof	7.50
	15.5000 g, .925 SILVER, .4610 oz ASW				
259a	1989	—	—	Proof	40.00
	26.0000 g, .917 GOLD, .7666 oz AGW				
259b	1989	—	—	Proof	835.00
	30.4000 g, .950 PLATINUM, .9286 oz APW				
259c	1989	—	—	Proof	1170.

COPPER-NICKEL
Christmas 1990

KM#	Date	Mintage	VF	XF	Unc
282	1990	—	—	—	2.50
	1990	*.030	—	Proof	7.50
	15.5000 g, .925 SILVER, .4610 oz ASW				
282a	1990	5,000	—	Proof	40.00
	26.0000 g, .917 GOLD, .7666 oz AGW				
282b	1990	250 pcs.	—	Proof	800.00
	30.4000 g, .950 PLATINUM, .9286 oz APW				
282c	1990	50 pcs.	—	Proof	1100.

COPPER-NICKEL
Christmas 1991

KM#	Date	Mintage	VF	XF	Unc
303	1991	—	—	—	2.50
	1991	.030	—	Proof	7.50
	15.5000 g, .925 SILVER, .4610 oz ASW				
303a	1991	5,000	—	Proof	40.00
	26.0000 g, .917 GOLD, .7666 oz AGW				
303b	1991	250 pcs.	—	Proof	685.00
	30.4000 g, .950 PLATINUM, .9286 oz APW				
303c	1991	50 pcs.	—	Proof	860.00

COPPER-NICKEL
Christmas 1992

KM#	Date	Mintage	VF	XF	Unc
335	1992	—	—	—	2.50
	15.5000 g, .925 SILVER, .4610 oz ASW				
335a	1992	5,000	—	Proof	40.00

COPPER-NICKEL
Christmas - Nativity Scene

KM#	Date	Mintage	VF	XF	Unc
356	1993	—	—	—	2.50
	1993	*.030	—	Proof	7.50
	15.5000 g, .925 SILVER, .4610 oz ASW				
356a	1993	*5,000	—	Proof	40.00
	26.0000 g, .917 GOLD, .7666 oz AGW				
356b	1993	*250 pcs.	—	Proof	685.00
	30.4000 g, .950 PLATINUM, .9286 oz APW				
356c	1993	*50 pcs.	—	Proof	860.00

1/2 SOVEREIGN (1/2 POUND)

3.9940 g, .917 GOLD, .1177 oz AGW
200th Anniversary of Acquisition

KM#	Date	Mintage	VF	XF	Unc
15	1965	1,500	—	—	55.00
	4.0000 g, .980 GOLD, .1260 oz AGW				
15a	1965	1,000	—	Proof	60.00

3.9813 g, .917 GOLD, .1173 oz AGW

KM#	Date	Mintage	VF	XF	Unc
26	1973	.014	—	—	65.00
	1973	1,250	—	Proof	65.00
	1974	6,566	—	—	65.00
	1974	2,500	—	Proof	70.00
	1975	1,956	—	—	65.00
	1975	—	—	Proof	70.00
	1976	2,558	—	—	65.00
	1976	—	—	Proof	70.00
	1977	—	—	—	65.00
	1977	1,250	—	Proof	70.00
	1978	1,250	—	Proof	70.00
	1979(t)	8,000	—	—	65.00
	1979(t)	.030	—	Proof	70.00
	1980(m)	7,500	—	Proof	70.00
	1980(v)	—	—	Proof	70.00
	1982(b)	.040	—	—	65.00
	1982(b)	.030	—	Proof	70.00

Wedding of Prince Charles and Lady Diana
Obv: Similar to KM#26.
Rev: Portraits of Royal Couple, joined shields.

KM#	Date	Mintage	VF	XF	Unc
85	1981	.030	—	Proof	70.00
	Similar to 5 Pounds, KM#263.				
260	1984	20 pcs.	—	—	200.00
	1984	20 pcs.	—	Proof	250.00
	Similar to 1 Pound, KM#265.				
264	1988	5,879	—	Proof	70.00

SOVEREIGN (POUND)

7.9881 g, .917 GOLD, .2355 oz AGW
200th Anniversary of Acquisition

KM#	Date	Mintage	VF	XF	Unc
16	1965	2,000	—	—	110.00
	8.0000 g, .980 GOLD, .2520 oz AGW				
16a	1965	1,000	—	Proof	120.00

7.9627 g, .917 GOLD, .2347 oz AGW

KM#	Date	Mintage	VF	XF	Unc
27	1973	.040	—	—	125.00
	1973	1,250	—	Proof	135.00
	1974	8,604	—	—	125.00
	1974	2,500	—	Proof	135.00
	1975	956 pcs.	—	—	150.00
	1975	—	—	Proof	125.00
	1976	1,238	—	—	135.00
	1976	—	—	Proof	135.00
	1977	—	—	—	135.00
	1977	1,250	—	Proof	135.00
	1978	1,250	—	Proof	135.00
	1979(t)	.010	—	—	125.00
	1979(t)	.030	—	Proof	135.00
	1980(m)	5,000	—	Proof	125.00
	1980(v)	—	—	Proof	125.00
	1982(b)	.030	—	—	125.00
	1982(b)	.040	—	Proof	125.00

VIRENIUM

KM#	Date	Mintage	VF	XF	Unc
44	1978-'A.A'	—	—	—	3.00
	1978-'A.B'	—	—	—	3.00
	1978-'A.C.'	—	—	—	2.50
	1978-'A.D'	3,780	—	—	7.50
	1978	.150	—	Proof	5.00
	1979-'A.A'	—	—	—	2.50
	1979-'A.A.'(t)	—	—	—	2.50
	1979-'A.B'	—	—	—	2.50
	1979-'A.B.'(t)	—	—	—	2.50
	1979-'A.C'	—	—	—	2.50
	1979-'A.C.'(t)	—	—	—	2.50
	1979 B.B.	—	—	Proof	5.00
	1979 crossed oars	—	—	—	2.50
	1980-'A.A.'D.M.I.H.E.	*.030	—	—	2.50
	1980-'A.A.'D.M.I.H.E.N.	—	—	—	2.50
	1980-'A.A.'T.T.	—	—	—	2.50
	1980-'A.B.'D.M.I.H.E.	—	—	—	2.50
	1980-'A.B.'D.M.I.H.E.N.				

KM#	Date	Mintage	VF	XF	Unc
		—	—	—	2.50
	1980-'A.B.'T.T.	—	—	—	2.50
	1980-'A.C.'D.M.I.H.E.	.100	—	—	2.50
	1980	5,000	—	Proof	10.00
	1981-'A.A.'	—	—	—	2.50

4.6000 g, .925 SILVER, .1368 oz ASW

KM#	Date	Mintage	VF	XF	Unc
44a	1978	—	—	—	10.00
	1978	.100	—	Proof	10.00
	1979	.075	—	Proof	10.00
	1979 D	—	—	Proof	15.00
	1980	.075	—	Proof	10.00
	1982(b)	1,000	—	Proof	35.00

9.0000 g, .950 PLATINUM, .2749 oz APW

KM#	Date	Mintage	VF	XF	Unc
44b	1978	1,000	—	Proof	200.00
	1979	—	—	Proof	200.00
	1980	1,000	—	Proof	200.00
	1982(b)	100 pcs.	—	Proof	250.00

7.9627 g, .917 GOLD, .2347 oz AGW

KM#	Date	Mintage	VF	XF	Unc
44c	1980	5,000	—	Proof	125.00
	1980T.T.	300 pcs.	—	Proof	225.00
	1982(b)	250 pcs.	—	—	225.00
	1982(b)	750 pcs.	—	Proof	200.00

• 4.6000 g, .500 SILVER, .0739 oz ASW

KM#	Date	Mintage	VF	XF	Unc
44d	1980	.010	—	Proof	15.00

7.9627 g, .917 GOLD, .2347 oz AGW
Wedding of Prince Charles and Lady Diana
Obv: Similar to KM#27.
Rev: Portraits of Royal Couple, joined shields.

KM#	Date	Mintage	VF	XF	Unc
86	1981	.040	—	Proof	150.00

VIRENIUM
Peel

KM#	Date	Mintage	VF	XF	Unc
109	1983	—	—	—	2.50

4.6000 g, .925 SILVER, .1368 oz ASW

KM#	Date	Mintage	VF	XF	Unc
109a	1983	—	—	Proof	15.00

9.5000 g, .374 GOLD, .1142 oz AGW

KM#	Date	Mintage	VF	XF	Unc
109b	1983	—	—	Proof	75.00

7.9627 g, .917 GOLD, .2347 oz AGW

KM#	Date	Mintage	VF	XF	Unc
109c	1983	—	—	Proof	150.00

9.0000 g, .950 PLATINUM, .2749 oz APW

KM#	Date	Mintage	VF	XF	Unc
109d	1983	—	—	Proof	200.00

VIRENIUM
Castletown

KM#	Date	Mintage	VF	XF	Unc
128	1984	—	—	—	3.00

4.6000 g, .925 SILVER, .1368 oz ASW

KM#	Date	Mintage	VF	XF	Unc
128a	1984	—	—	—	8.00
	1984	—	—	Proof	8.00

9.5000 g, .374 GOLD, .1142 oz AGW

KM#	Date	Mintage	VF	XF	Unc
128b	1984	4,950	—	Proof	75.00

7.9627 g, .917 GOLD, .2347 oz AGW

KM#	Date	Mintage	VF	XF	Unc
128c	1984	950 pcs.	—	Proof	150.00

9.0000 g, .950 PLATINUM, .2749 oz APW

KM#	Date	Mintage	VF	XF	Unc
128d	1984	—	—	Proof	200.00

7.9627 g, .917 GOLD, .2347 oz AGW

KM#	Date	Mintage	VF	XF	Unc
261	1984	20 pcs.	—	—	350.00
	1984	20 pcs.	—	Proof	450.00

4.6000 g, .925 SILVER, .1368 oz ASW
Ramsey

KM#	Date	Mintage	VF	XF	Unc
135	1985	—	—	—	10.00
	1985	*5,000	—	Proof	10.00

7.9627 g, .917 GOLD, .2347 oz AGW

KM#	Date	Mintage	VF	XF	Unc
135b	1985	*150 pcs.	—	Proof	175.00

9.0000 g, .950 PLATINUM, .2749 oz APW

KM#	Date	Mintage	VF	XF	Unc
135c	1985	*550 pcs.	—	Proof	200.00

VIRENIUM
Ramsey

KM#	Date	Mintage	VF	XF	Unc
151	1985(t)	—	—	—	2.50
	1985	*.025	—	Proof	5.00

4.6000 g, .925 SILVER, .1368 oz ASW
Douglas
Obv: Similar to KM#109.

KM#	Date	Mintage	VF	XF	Unc
136	1986	—	—	—	10.00
	1986	—	—	Proof	15.00

7.9627 g, .917 GOLD, .2347 oz AGW

KM#	Date	Mintage	VF	XF	Unc
136b	1986	—	—	Proof	150.00

9.0000 g, .950 PLATINUM, .2749 oz APW

KM#	Date	Mintage	VF	XF	Unc
136c	1986	—	—	Proof	200.00

VIRENIUM
Douglas

KM#	Date	Mintage	VF	XF	Unc
175	1986	—	—	—	2.50
	1986	*.025	—	Proof	5.00

KM#	Date	Mintage	VF	XF	Unc
182	1987	—	—	—	3.50

Telecommunicator

KM#	Date	Mintage	VF	XF	Unc
213	1988	—	—	—	3.50
	1989	—	—	—	3.50
	1990	—	—	—	3.50
	1992	—	—	—	3.50

7.9627 g, .917 GOLD, .2347 oz AGW

KM#	Date	Mintage	VF	XF	Unc
265	1988	—	—	—	135.00
	1988	1,600	—	Proof	150.00

2 POUNDS

15.9253 g, .917 GOLD, .4695 oz AGW

KM#	Date	Mintage	VF	XF	Unc
28	1973	3,612	—	—	235.00
	1973	1,250	—	Proof	250.00
	1974	1,257	—	—	250.00
	1974	2,500	—	Proof	235.00
	1975	456 pcs.	—	—	250.00
	1975	—	—	Proof	250.00
	1976	578 pcs.	—	—	250.00
	1976	—	—	Proof	250.00
	1977	—	—	—	250.00
	1977	1,250	—	Proof	235.00
	1978	1,250	—	Proof	250.00
	1979(t)	2,000	—	—	235.00
	1979(t)	.030	—	Proof	250.00
	1980(m)	2,000	—	Proof	235.00
	1982(b)	.015	—	—	235.00
	• 1982(b)	5,000	—	Proof	235.00

Wedding of Prince Charles and Lady Diana
Obv: Similar to KM#28.
Rev: Portraits of Royal Couple, joined shields.

KM#	Date	Mintage	VF	XF	Unc
87	1981	5,000	—	Proof	275.00

VIRENIUM
Obv: Similar to KM#28. Rev: Tower of Refuge and Manx Shearwater in flight.

KM#	Date	Mintage	VF	XF	Unc
129	1984PM	—	Reported, not confirmed		

SILVER

KM#	Date	Mintage	VF	XF	Unc
129a	1984PM	—	Reported, not confirmed		

15.9200 g, .917 GOLD, .4695 oz AGW
Similar to 5 Pounds, KM#263.

KM#	Date	Mintage	VF	XF	Unc
262	1984	20 pcs.	—	—	650.00
	1984	20 pcs.	—	Proof	800.00

VIRENIUM
Obv: Similar to 50 Pence, KM#148. Rev: Tower of Refuge and Manx Shearwater in flight.

KM#	Date	Mintage	VF	XF	Unc
149	1985	—	Reported, not confirmed		

SILVER

KM#	Date	Mintage	VF	XF	Unc
149a	1985	—	Reported, not confirmed		

VIRENIUM
Tower of Refuge

KM#	Date	Mintage	VF	XF	Unc
167	1986	—	—	—	6.50
	1986	—	—	Proof	8.50

Manx Airlines

KM#	Date	Mintage	VF	XF	Unc
214	1988	—	—	—	6.50
	1989	—	—	—	6.50
	1990	—	—	—	6.50
	1992	—	—	—	6.50

Manx Airlines Dirigible

KM#	Date	Mintage	VF	XF	Unc
257	1989	*	—	—	7.50

9.3000 g, .925 SILVER, .2766 oz ASW

KM#	Date	Mintage	VF	XF	Unc
257a	1989	—	—	—	25.00

15.9400 g, .917 GOLD, .4730 oz AGW

KM#	Date	Mintage	VF	XF	Unc
257b	1989	—	—	—	300.00

18.0000 g, .950 PLATINUM, .5498 oz APW

KM#	Date	Mintage	VF	XF	Unc
257c	1989	—	—	—	400.00

***NOTE:** Most recalled by government. Few actually issued.

VIRENIUM
Nigel Mansell - Race Driver
Similar to 5 Pounds, KM#336.

KM#	Date	Mintage	VF	XF	Unc
344	1993	—	—	—	6.50

5 POUNDS

39.9403 g, .917 GOLD, 1.1776 oz AGW
200th Anniversary of Acquisition

KM#	Date	Mintage	VF	XF	Unc
17	1965	500 pcs.	—	—	540.00

39.9500 g, .980 GOLD, 1.2588 oz AGW

KM#	Date	Mintage	VF	XF	Unc
17a	1965	1,000	—	Proof	575.00

39.8134 g, .917 GOLD, 1.1739 oz AGW

KM#	Date	Mintage	VF	XF	Unc
29	1973	3,035	—	—	600.00
	1973	1,250	—	Proof	625.00
	1974	481 pcs.	—	—	650.00
	1974	2,500	—	Proof	600.00
	1975	306 pcs.	—	—	650.00
	1975	—	—	Proof	650.00
	1976	370 pcs.	—	—	650.00
	1976	—	—	Proof	650.00
	1977	—	—	—	650.00
	1977	1,250	—	Proof	625.00
	1978	1,250	—	Proof	625.00
	1979(t)	1,000	—	—	625.00
	1979(t)	1,000	—	Proof	625.00
	1980(m)	250 pcs.	—	—	650.00
	1982(b)	.010	—	—	600.00
	1982(b)	500 pcs.	—	Proof	625.00

VIRENIUM

KM#	Date	Mintage	VF	XF	Unc
88	1981	.030	—	Proof	10.00
	1983	—	—	—	20.00

23.5000 g, .925 SILVER, .6989 oz ASW

KM#	Date	Mintage	VF	XF	Unc
88a	1981	500 pcs.	—	Proof	40.00
	1982(b)	1,000	—	Proof	35.00
	1983	5,000	—	Proof	25.00

39.9000 g, .917 GOLD, 1.1764 oz AGW

KM#	Date	Mintage	VF	XF	Unc
88b	1981	1,000	—	Proof	625.00
	1982(b)	250 pcs.	—	Proof	650.00
	1982(b)	750 pcs.	—	Proof	650.00
	1983	—	—	Proof	650.00

45.5000 g, .950 PLATINUM, 1.3898 oz APW

KM#	Date	Mintage	VF	XF	Unc
88c	1981	500 pcs.	—	Proof	800.00
	1982(b)	100 pcs.	—	Proof	1100.
	1983	—	—	Proof	1000.

39.8134 g, .917 GOLD, 1.1739 oz AGW
Wedding of Prince Charles and Lady Diana
Obv: Similar to KM#29.
Rev: Portraits of Royal Couple, joined shields.

KM#	Date	Mintage	VF	XF	Unc
89	1981	1,000	—	Proof	650.00

VIRENIUM

KM#	Date	Mintage	VF	XF	Unc
134	1984	—	—	—	10.00

23.5000 g, .925 SILVER, .6989 oz ASW

KM#	Date	Mintage	VF	XF	Unc
134a	1984	—	—	Proof	40.00

39.9000 g, .917 GOLD, 1.1759 oz AGW

KM#	Date	Mintage	VF	XF	Unc
134b	1984	150 pcs.	—	Proof	750.00

45.5000 g, .950 PLATINUM, 1.3898 oz APW

KM#	Date	Mintage	VF	XF	Unc
134c	1984	—	—	Proof	1100.

39.8300 g, .917 GOLD, 1.1740 oz AGW

KM#	Date	Mintage	VF	XF	Unc
263	1984	20 pcs.	—	—	1250.
	1984	20 pcs.	—	Proof	1650.

VIRENIUM
Obv: Similar to 50 Pence, KM#148.

KM#	Date	Mintage	VF	XF	Unc
150	1985	—	—	—	10.00
	1985	*.025	—	Proof	10.00

23.5000 g, .925 SILVER, .6989 oz ASW

KM#	Date	Mintage	VF	XF	Unc
150a	1985	*5,000	—	Proof	40.00

39.9000 g, .917 GOLD, 1.1759 oz AGW

KM#	Date	Mintage	VF	XF	Unc
150b	1985	*150 pcs.	—	Proof	750.00

45.5000 g, .950 PLATINUM, 1.3898 oz APW

KM#	Date	Mintage	VF	XF	Unc
150c	1985	*100 pcs.	—	Proof	1200.

VIRENIUM
Fishing Boat

KM#	Date	Mintage	VF	XF	Unc
215	1988	—	—	—	10.00
	1989	—	—	—	10.00
	1990	—	—	—	10.00
	1992	—	—	—	10.00

Nigel Mansell - Race Driver

KM#	Date	Mintage	VF	XF	Unc
336	1993	—	—	—	15.00

10 POUNDS

10.0000 g, .925 SILVER, .2973 oz ASW
Nigel Mansell - Race Driver
Similar to 5 Pounds, KM#336.

KM#	Date	Mintage	VF	XF	Unc
345	1993	*.020	—	Proof	35.00

25 POUNDS

28.2800 g, .925 SILVER, .8411 oz ASW
Nigel Mansell - Race Driver

KM#	Date	Mintage	VF	XF	Unc
346	1993	*.015	—	Proof	50.00

50 POUNDS

6.2200 g, .999 GOLD, .2000 oz AGW
Nigel Mansel - Race Driver
Similar to 5 Pounds, KM#336.

KM#	Date	Mintage	VF	XF	Unc
347	1993	*5,000	—	Proof	180.00

BULLION ISSUES

POBJOY MINT

(M) MATTE - Normal circulation strike.

(U) SPECIAL UNCIRCULATED - Polished or proof-like in appearance, slightly frosted features.
(P) PROOF - The highest quality obtainable having mirror-like fields and frosted features.

SILVER BULLION ISSUES

CROWN

31.1000 g, .999 SILVER, 1.0000 oz ASW
Manx Cat

KM#	Date	Mintage	VF	XF	Unc
234	1988	.015	—	Proof	40.00

Australian Bicentennial - Cockatoo
Similar to KM#222.

KM#	Date	Mintage	VF	XF	Unc
314	1988	—	—	Proof	175.00

Australian Bicentennial - Koala
Similar to KM#223.

KM#	Date	Mintage	VF	XF	Unc
315	1988	—	—	Proof	175.00

Australian Bicentennial - Platypus Duckbill
Similar to KM#224.

KM#	Date	Mintage	VF	XF	Unc
316	1988	—	—	Proof	175.00

Australian Bicentennial - Kangaroo
Similar to KM#225.

KM#	Date	Mintage	VF	XF	Unc
317	1988	—	—	Proof	175.00

Australian Bicentennial - Dingo Dog
Similar to KM#226.

KM#	Date	Mintage	VF	XF	Unc
318	1988	—	—	Proof	175.00

Australian Bicentennial - Tasmanian Devil
Similar to KM#227.

KM#	Date	Mintage	VF	XF	Unc
319	1988	—	—	Proof	175.00

Persian Cat

KM#	Date	Mintage	VF	XF	Unc
251	1989	—	—	Proof	32.50

Alley Cat
Similar to KM#281.

KM#	Date	Mintage	VF	XF	Unc
276	1990	—	—	Proof	32.50

Norwegian Cat
Similar to KM#292.

KM#	Date	Mintage	VF	XF	Unc
293	1991	.050	—	Proof	32.50

Siamese Cat

KM#	Date	Mintage	VF	XF	Unc
333	1992	.050	—	Proof	32.50

Maine Coon Cat

KM#	Date	Mintage	VF	XF	Unc
354	1993	.050	—	Proof	32.50

5 CROWNS

155.5500 g, .999 SILVER, 5.0000 oz ASW
Illustration reduced. Actual size: 65.1mm
Bicentennial of U.S.A. Constitution
Obv: Similar to 1 Crown, KM#176.

KM#	Date	Mintage	VF	XF	Unc
177	1987	.012	—	—	175.00

Illustration reduced. Actual size: 65mm
America's Cup - Sailboats and Trophy
Obv: Similar to 1 Crown, KM#179.

KM#	Date	Mintage	VF	XF	Unc
180	1987	6,000	—	Proof	175.00

Illustration reduced. Actual size: 65mm
America's Cup - Sailboats & Statue of Liberty

KM#	Date	Mintage	VF	XF	Unc
299	1987	200 pcs.	—	Proof	400.00

Illustration reduced. Actual size: 65mm
America's Cup - 3 Sailboats & Map
Obv: Similar to 10 Crowns, KM#258.

KM#	Date	Mintage	VF	XF	Unc
308	1987	—	—	Proof	275.00

Illustration reduced. Actual size: 65mm
Steam Navigation - Queen Mary
Obv: Similar to 5 Pounds, KM#215.

KM#	Date	Mintage	VF	XF	Unc
206	1988	—	—	—	175.00

Australian Bicentennial - Koala
Similar to 10 Crowns, KM#258.

KM#	Date	Mintage	VF	XF	Unc
285	1988	—	—	Proof	175.00

America's Cup
Obv: Portrait of Queen Elizabeth II.
Rev: Cameo of sailing ship above
2 modern sailboats.

KM#	Date	Mintage	VF	XF	Unc
321	1991	*15 pcs.	—	Proof	—

America's Cup
Rev: Similar to 1 Crown, KM#326.

KM#	Date	Mintage	VF	XF	Unc
327	1992	—	—	—	175.00

Illustration reduced. Actual size: 65mm.
Siamese Cat

KM#	Date	Mintage	VF	XF	Unc
348	1992	—	—	Proof	200.00

10 CROWNS

311.0350 g, .999 SILVER, 10.0000 oz ASW
Illustration reduced. Actual size: 75mm
America's Cup - Sailboats & Statue of Liberty
Obv: Similar to 1 Crown, KM#179.

KM#	Date	Mintage	VF	XF	Unc
181	1987	2,000	—	Proof	275.00

U.S. Constitution

KM#	Date	Mintage	VF	XF	Unc
188	1987	9,000	—	Proof	275.00

Illustration reduced. Actual size: 75mm
America's Cup - Sailboats and Trophy

KM#	Date	Mintage	VF	XF	Unc
300	1987	69 pcs.	—	Proof	625.00

Illustration reduced. Actual size: 75mm
America's Cup - 3 Sailboats & Map

KM#	Date	Mintage	VF	XF	Unc
309	1987	—	—	Proof	425.00

Illustration reduced. Actual size: 75mm
Australian Bicentennial - Koala

KM#	Date	Mintage	VF	XF	Unc
258	1988	*.013	—	Proof	275.00

GOLD BULLION ISSUES

Angel Series

1/20 ANGEL

1.6970 g, .917 GOLD, .0500 oz AGW
Archangel Michael

KM#	Date	Mintage	VF	XF	Unc
166	1986(pi)	—	—	—	40.00
	1986(pi)	5,000	—	Proof	50.00
	1987	—	—	—	40.00
	1987	—	—	Proof	50.00

Obv: Similar to 1 Noble, KM#205.

KM#	Date	Mintage	VF	XF	Unc
193	1988	—	—		35.00
	1988(pt)	—	—		45.00
	1989(h)	*5,000	—	Proof	50.00
	1989(mt)	3,000	—	Proof	50.00
	1990(sg)	*3,000	—	Proof	50.00
	1991(cc)	1,000	—	Proof	70.00

1/10 ANGEL

3.3900 g, .917 GOLD, .1000 oz AGW
Archangel Michael
Similar to 1 Angel, KM#139.

KM#	Date	Mintage	VF	XF	Unc
138	1984	5,000	—	Proof	160.00

KM#	Date	Mintage	VF	XF	Unc
140	1985	8,000	—	—	60.00
	1985	3,000	—	Proof	115.00
	1986	—	—	—	60.00
	1986	—	—	Proof	115.00
	1987	—	—	—	60.00
	1987	—	—	Proof	115.00

KM#	Date	Mintage	VF	XF	Unc
159	1985	5,000	—	—	60.00
	1985 A	1,000	—	—	110.00
	1985 C	1,000	—	—	125.00
	1985 H	1,000	—	—	110.00
	1985 L	1,000	—	—	100.00
	1986 A	1,000	—	—	100.00
	1986 T	1,000	—	—	110.00
	1986 X	1,000	—	—	90.00
	1987 A	1,000	—	—	90.00
	1987 F	1,000	—	Proof	115.00
	1987 L	1,000	—	—	90.00
	1987(mt)	3,000	—	Proof	100.00
	1988 A	1,000	—	Proof	85.00

Obv: Similar to 1 Noble, KM#205.

KM#	Date	Mintage	VF	XF	Unc
194	1988	—	—	—	60.00
	1989 A	250 pcs.	—	Proof	125.00
	1990 A	1,000	—	Proof	70.00
	1991 A	1,000	—	Proof	70.00

1/4 ANGEL

8.4830 g, .917 GOLD, .2500 oz AGW
Archangel Michael

KM#	Date	Mintage	VF	XF	Unc
152	1985	2,117	—	—	320.00
	1985	51 pcs.	—	Proof	450.00
	1986 L	1,000	—	—	200.00
	1986	—	—	Proof	175.00
	1987	—	—	—	150.00
	1987	—	—	Proof	200.00
	1987(s)	1,000	—	Proof	225.00
	1987(SL)	568 pcs.	—	Proof	180.00
	1987(bb)	1,000	—	Proof	200.00

KM#	Date	Mintage	VF	XF	Unc
195	1988	—	—	—	150.00
	1988(f)	1,000	—	Proof	215.00
	1988(p)	1,000	—	Proof	215.00
	1988(ss)	1,000	—	Proof	215.00
	1989 C (d)	1,000	—	Proof	200.00
	1989(p)	500 pcs.	—	Proof	200.00
	1989(hk)	1,000	—	Proof	215.00
	1990(ba)	1,000	—	Proof	200.00
	1990(c)	250 pcs.	—	Proof	220.00
	1990(h)	1,000	—	Proof	130.00
	1990(ma)	1,000	—	Proof	130.00
	1991(c)	1,000	—	Proof	150.00
	1991(fr)	500 pcs.	—	Proof	200.00

1/2 ANGEL

16.9380 g, .917 GOLD, .5000 oz AGW
Archangel Michael
Similar to 1 Angel, KM#141.

KM#	Date	Mintage	VF	XF	Unc
155	1985	1,776	—	—	270.00
	1985	51 pcs.	—	Proof	520.00
	1986	—	—	—	250.00
	1986	3,000	—	Proof	350.00
	1987	—	—	—	250.00
	1987	—	—	Proof	350.00

Obv: Similar to 1 Noble, KM#205.

KM#	Date	Mintage	VF	XF	Unc
196	1988	—	—	—	250.00

ANGEL

33.9300 g, .917 GOLD, 1.0000 oz AGW
Archangel Michael

KM#	Date	Mintage	VF	XF	Unc
139	1984	3,000	—	Proof	1050.

KM#	Date	Mintage	VF	XF	Unc
141	1985	.028	—	—	450.00
	1985	—	—	P/L	450.00
	1985	3,000	—	Proof	925.00
	1986	—	—	—	450.00
	1986	—	—	Proof	925.00
	1987	—	—	—	450.00
	1987	—	—	Proof	925.00

Hong Kong Coin Show

KM#	Date	Mintage	VF	XF	Unc
191	1987	1,000	—	Proof	800.00

KM#	Date	Mintage	VF	XF	Unc
197	1988	—	—	—	450.00
	1988(ss)	1,000	—	Proof	600.00

5 ANGEL

169.6680 g, .917 GOLD, 5.0000 oz AGW
Archangel Michael

KM#	Date	Mintage	VF	XF	Unc
156	1985	104 pcs.	—	—	3500.
	1985	90 pcs.	—	Proof	4000.
	1986	89 pcs.	—	—	3000.
	1986	250 pcs.	—	Proof	4000.
	1987	150 pcs.	—	—	3000.
	1987	27 pcs.	—	Proof	4000.

Obv: Similar to 1 Noble, KM#205.

KM#	Date	Mintage	VF	XF	Unc
198	1988	250 pcs.	—	—	2750.

10 ANGEL

339.3350 g, .917 GOLD, 10.0000 oz AGW
Archangel Michael

KM#	Date	Mintage	VF	XF	Unc
157	1985	79 pcs.	—	—	5500.
	1985	68 pcs.	—	Proof	8600.
	1986	47 pcs.	—	—	6000.
	1986	250 pcs.	—	Proof	8600.
	1987	150 pcs.	—	—	6000.
	1987	30 pcs.	—	Proof	8600.

Obv: Similar to 1 Noble, KM#205.

KM#	Date	Mintage	VF	XF	Unc
199	1988	250 pcs.	—	Proof	5500.

15 ANGEL

508.9575 g, .917 GOLD, 15.0000 oz AGW

KM#	Date	Mintage	VF	XF	Unc
189	1987	150 pcs.	—	—	9000.
	1987	18 pcs.	—	Proof	12,500.

Obv: Similar to 1 Noble, KM#205.

KM#	Date	Mintage	VF	XF	Unc
200	1988	—	—	Proof	12,500.

20 ANGEL

678.6720 g, .917 GOLD, 20.0000 oz AGW
Illustration reduced. Actual size: 75.2mm.

KM#	Date	Mintage	VF	XF	Unc
201	1988	250 pcs.	—	—	12,500.
	1988	100 pcs.	—	Proof	16,000.

GILT SILVER

KM#	Date	Mintage	VF	XF	Unc
201a	1988	—	—	—	—

25 ANGEL

848.2750 g, .917 GOLD, 25.0000 oz AGW
Obv: Queen Elizabeth II.
Rev: Michael slaying the dragon.

KM#	Date	Mintage	VF	XF	Unc
301 (249)	1989	—	—	—	18,500.

Crown Series

1/25 CROWN

1.2441 g, .999 GOLD, .0400 oz AGW
Manx Cat
Similar to 1 Crown, KM#239.

KM#	Date	Mintage	VF	XF	Unc
235	1988 U	.040	—		*BV + 20%*
	1988	5,000	—	Proof	50.00

Persian Cat
Similar to 1 Crown, KM#256.

KM#	Date	Mintage	VF	XF	Unc
252	1989	—	—		*BV + 20%*
	1989	—	—	Proof	50.00

Alley Cat
Similar to 1 Crown, KM#281.

KM#	Date	Mintage	VF	XF	Unc
277	1990	—	—		*BV + 20%*
	1990	—	—	Proof	50.00

Norwegian Cat
Similar to 1 Crown, KM#292.

KM#	Date	Mintage	VF	XF	Unc
294	1991	—	—		*BV + 20%*
	1991	—	—	Proof	50.00

America's Cup
Similar to 1 Crown, KM#326b.

KM#	Date	Mintage	VF	XF	Unc
322	1992	.050	—	P/L	45.00

Siamese Cat
Similar to 1 Crown, KM#334.

KM#	Date	Mintage	VF	XF	Unc
328	1992	—	—		*BV + 20%*
	1992	—	—	Proof	50.00

Year of the Rooster
Similar to 1 Crown, KM#342.

KM#	Date	Mintage	VF	XF	Unc
338	1993	*.025	—	Proof	50.00

Maine Coon Cat
Similar to 1 Crown, KM#355.

KM#	Date	Mintage	VF	XF	Unc
349	1993	—	—		*BV + 20%*
	1993	—	—	Proof	50.00

1/10 CROWN

3.1100 g, .999 GOLD, .1000 oz AGW
Manx Cat
Similar to 1 Crown, KM#239.

KM#	Date	Mintage	VF	XF	Unc
236	1988 U	.012	—		*BV + 15%*
	1988	5,000	—	Proof	100.00

Persian Cat
Similar to 1 Crown, KM#256.

KM#	Date	Mintage	VF	XF	Unc
253	1989	—	—		*BV + 15%*
	1989	—	—	Proof	100.00

Alley Cat
Similar to 1 Crown, KM#281.

KM#	Date	Mintage	VF	XF	Unc
278	1990	—	—		*BV + 15%*
	1990	—	—	Proof	100.00

Norwegian Cat
Similar to 1 Crown, KM#292.

KM#	Date	Mintage	VF	XF	Unc
295	1991	—	—		*BV + 15%*
	1991	—	—	Proof	100.00

America's Cup
Similar to 1 Crown, KM#326b.

KM#	Date	Mintage	VF	XF	Unc
323	1992	.025	—	P/L	90.00

Siamese Cat
Similar to 1 Crown, KM#334.

KM#	Date	Mintage	VF	XF	Unc
329	1992	—	—		*BV + 15%*
	1992	—	—	Proof	100.00

Year of the Rooster
Similar to 1 Crown, KM#342.

KM#	Date	Mintage	VF	XF	Unc
339	1993	*.020	—	Proof	100.00

Maine Coon Cat
Similar to 1 Crown, KM#355.

KM#	Date	Mintage	VF	XF	Unc
350	1993	—	—		*BV + 15%*
	1993	—	—	Proof	100.00

1/5 CROWN

6.2200 g, .999 GOLD, .2000 oz AGW
Manx Cat
Similar to 1 Crown, KM#239.

KM#	Date	Mintage	VF	XF	Unc
237	1988 U	6,750	—		*BV + 10%*
	1988	5,000	—	Proof	185.00

Persian Cat
Similar to 1 Crown, KM#256.

KM#	Date	Mintage	VF	XF	Unc
254	1989	—	—		*BV + 10%*
	1989	—	—	Proof	185.00

George Washington

KM#	Date	Mintage	VF	XF	Unc
274	1989	*5,000	—	Proof	200.00

150th Anniversary of "Penny Black" Stamp
Similar to 1 Crown, KM#267.

KM#	Date	Mintage	VF	XF	Unc
268	1990	*5,000	—	Proof	240.00

Alley Cat

KM#	Date	Mintage	VF	XF	Unc
279.1	1990	—	—		*BV + 10%*
	1990	—	—	Proof	185.00

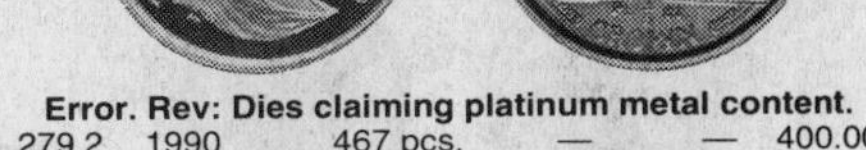

Error. Rev: Dies claiming platinum metal content.

KM#	Date	Mintage	VF	XF	Unc
279.2	1990	467 pcs.	—	—	400.00

Queen Mother
Obv: Queen Elizabeth II.
Rev: Queen Mother w/2 daughters.

KM#	Date	Mintage	VF	XF	Unc
306	1990	—	—	Proof	200.00

6.2200 g, .999 GOLD, .2000 oz AGW
American Numismatic Association

KM#	Date	Mintage	VF	XF	Unc
290	1991	100 pcs.	—	Proof	195.00

Norwegian Cat
Obv: Queen Elizabeth. Rev: Cat with bushy tail.

KM#	Date	Mintage	VF	XF	Unc
296	1991	—	—		*BV + 10%*
	1991	—	—	Proof	185.00

America's Cup - Sail Boats

KM#	Date	Mintage	VF	XF	Unc
302	1991	*250 pcs.	—	Proof	200.00

America's Cup
Similar to 1 Crown, KM#326b.

KM#	Date	Mintage	VF	XF	Unc
324	1992	.010	—	P/L	150.00

Siamese Cat
Similar to 1 Crown, KM#330.

KM#	Date	Mintage	VF	XF	Unc
330	1992	—	—		*BV + 10%*
	1992	—	—	Proof	200.00

Year of the Rooster
Similar to 1 Crown, KM#342.

KM#	Date	Mintage	VF	XF	Unc
340	1993	*.010	—	Proof	175.00

Maine Coon Cat
Similar to 1 Crown, KM#355.

KM#	Date	Mintage	VF	XF	Unc
351	1993	—	—		*BV + 10%*
	1993	—	—	Proof	200.00

1/2 CROWN

15.5500 g, .999 GOLD, .5000 oz AGW
U.S. Constitution

KM#	Date	Mintage	VF	XF	Unc
187	1987	.012	—	Proof	400.00

PLATINUM

KM#	Date	Mintage	VF	XF	Unc
187a	1987	250 pcs.	—	Proof	600.00

15.5500 g, .999 GOLD, .5000 oz AGW
Manx Cat
Similar to 1 Crown, KM#239.

KM#	Date	Mintage	VF	XF	Unc
238	1988 U	6,375	—		*BV + 7%*
	1988	5,000	—	Proof	365.00

16.4000 g, .948 GOLD, .5000 oz AGW
Australian Bicentennial - Cockatoo

KM#	Date	Mintage	VF	XF	Unc
286	1988	*7,500	—	Proof	375.00

Australian Bicentennial - Koala

KM#	Date	Mintage	VF	XF	Unc
287	1988	*7,500	—	Proof	375.00

Australian Bicentennial - Platypus Duckbill

KM#	Date	Mintage	VF	XF	Unc
288	1988	*7,500	—	Proof	375.00

Australian Bicentennial - Kangaroo

KM#	Date	Mintage	VF	XF	Unc
289	1988	*7,500	—	Proof	375.00

Persian Cat
Similar to 1 Crown, KM#256.

KM#	Date	Mintage	VF	XF	Unc
255	1989	—	—		*BV + 7%*
	1989	—	—	Proof	365.00

Alley Cat
Similar to 1 Crown, KM#281.

KM#	Date	Mintage	VF	XF	Unc
280	1990	—	—		*BV + 7%*
	1990	—	—	Proof	365.00

15.5500 g, .999 GOLD, .5000 oz AGW
Norwegian Cat

Similar to 1 Crown, KM#292.

KM#	Date	Mintage	VF	XF	Unc
297	1991	—	—		BV + 7%
	1991	—	—	Proof	365.00

America's Cup
Similar to 1 Crown, KM#326b.

KM#	Date	Mintage	VF	XF	Unc
325	1992	2,000	—	P/L	350.00

Siamese Cat
Similar to 1 Crown, KM#334.

KM#	Date	Mintage	VF	XF	Unc
331	1992	—	—		BV + 7%
	1992	—	—	Proof	365.00

Year of the Rooster
Similar to 1 Crown, KM#342.

KM#	Date	Mintage	VF	XF	Unc
341	1993	*5,000	—	Proof	375.00

Maine Coon Cat
Similar to 1 Crown, KM#355.

KM#	Date	Mintage	VF	XF	Unc
352	1993	—	—		BV + 7%
	1993	—	—	Proof	365.00

CROWN

31.1000 g, .999 GOLD, 1.0000 oz AGW
Manx Cat

KM#	Date	Mintage	VF	XF	Unc
239	1988 U	4,300	—		BV + 4%
	1988	5,000	—	Proof	750.00

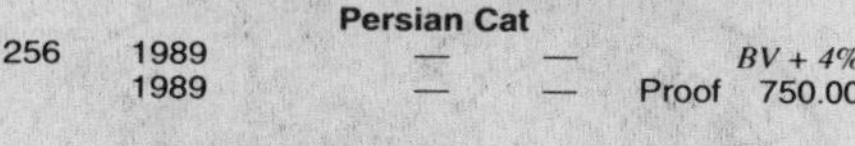

Persian Cat

KM#	Date	Mintage	VF	XF	Unc
256	1989	—	—		BV + 4%
	1989	—	—	Proof	750.00

Alley Cat

KM#	Date	Mintage	VF	XF	Unc
281	1990	—	—		BV+4%
	1990	—	—	Proof	750.00

Norwegian Cat
Similar to KM#292.

KM#	Date	Mintage	VF	XF	Unc
298	1991	—	—		BV + 4%
	1991	—	—	Proof	750.00

Siamese Cat

KM#	Date	Mintage	VF	XF	Unc
334	1992	—	—		BV + 4%
	1992	—	—	Proof	750.00

Year of the Rooster

KM#	Date	Mintage	VF	XF	Unc
342	1993	*2,500	—	Proof	750.00

Maine Coon Cat

KM#	Date	Mintage	VF	XF	Unc
355	1993	—	—		BV + 4%
	1993	—	—	Proof	750.00

PLATINUM BULLION ISSUES
NOBLE SERIES

1/20 NOBLE

1.5551 g, .999 PLATINUM, .0500 oz APW

KM#	Date	Mintage	VF	XF	Unc
266	1989	.010	—	Proof	45.00

1/10 NOBLE

3.1100 g, .999 PLATINUM, .1000 oz APW

KM#	Date	Mintage	VF	XF	Unc
137	1984	—	—	—	75.00
	1984	5,000	—	Proof	150.00

KM#	Date	Mintage	VF	XF	Unc
153	1985	.099	—	—	85.00
	1985	5,000	—	Proof	115.00
	1986	—	—	—	85.00
	1986	5,000	—	Proof	80.00
	1987	—	—	—	85.00
	1987	5,000	—	Proof	125.00

Obv: Similar to 1 Noble, KM#205.

KM#	Date	Mintage	VF	XF	Unc
202	1988	5,000	—	—	80.00
	1989	5,000	—	—	80.00

1/4 NOBLE

7.7757 g, .999 PLATINUM, .2500 oz APW

KM#	Date	Mintage	VF	XF	Unc
168	1986	2,015	—	Proof	165.00
	1987	3,250	—	Proof	250.00
	1987(l)	750 pcs.	—	Proof	165.00

Similar to 1 Noble, KM#205.

KM#	Date	Mintage	VF	XF	Unc
203	1988	—	—	—	165.00
	1988(a)	100 pcs.	—	—	185.00
	1988(p)	1,000	—	Proof	165.00
	1988(bb)	1,000	—	Proof	165.00
	1989(br)	250 pcs.	—	Proof	250.00
	1989(p)	500 pcs.	—	Proof	200.00
	1990(ba)	1,000	—	Proof	165.00
	1990(ti)	*1,000	—	Proof	165.00

1/2 NOBLE

15.5514 g, .999 PLATINUM, .5000 oz APW

KM#	Date	Mintage	VF	XF	Unc
169	1986	15 pcs.	—	Proof	500.00
	1987	3,000	—	Proof	350.00

Obv: Similar to 1 Noble, KM#205.

KM#	Date	Mintage	VF	XF	Unc
204	1988	3,000	—	Proof	350.00
	1989	3,000	—	Proof	350.00

NOBLE

31.1030 g, .999 PLATINUM, .9991 oz APW

KM#	Date	Mintage	VF	XF	Unc
110	1983	1,700	—	—	650.00
	1983	94 pcs.	—	Proof	2150.
	1984	—	—	—	650.00
	1984	2,000	—	Proof	1250.

KM#	Date	Mintage	VF	XF	Unc
154	1985	—	—	—	650.00
	1985	3,000	—	Proof	800.00
	1986	—	—	—	625.00
	1986	3,000	—	Proof	675.00
	1987	—	—	—	625.00
	1987	3,000	—	Proof	800.00

KM#	Date	Mintage	VF	XF	Unc
205	1988	3,000	—	Proof	675.00
	1989	3,000	—	Proof	675.00

5 NOBLE

155.5140 g, .999 PLATINUM, 5.0000 oz APW

KM#	Date	Mintage	VF	XF	Unc
170	1986	15 pcs.	—	Proof	4000.
	1987	11 pcs.	—	Proof	3500.
	1988	—	—	Proof	5400.

10 NOBLE

311.0280 g, .999 PLATINUM, 10.0000 oz APW
Similar to 5 Noble, KM#170.

KM#	Date	Mintage	VF	XF	Unc
171	1986	15 pcs.	—	Proof	8000.
	1987	11 pcs.	—	Proof	7500.
	1988	—	—	Proof	10,000.

CROWN SERIES

1/10 CROWN

3.1100 g, .9995 PLATINUM, .1000 oz APW
America's Cup
Similar to 1 Crown, KM#326b.

KM#	Date	Mintage	VF	XF	Unc
323a	1992	5,000	—	P/L	100.00

1/5 CROWN

6.2200 g, .999 PLATINUM, .2000 oz APW
Queen Mother
Obv: Queen Elizabeth II.
Rev: Queen Mother w/2 daughters.

KM#	Date	Mintage	VF	XF	Unc
306a	1990	—	—	Proof	300.00

1/2 CROWN

15.5500 g, .999 PLATINUM, .5000 oz APW
Australian Bicentennial - Cockatoo
Similar to KM#286.

KM#	Date	Mintage	VF	XF	Unc
359	1988	—	—	Proof	475.00

Australian Bicentennial - Koala
Similar to KM#287.

KM#	Date	Mintage	VF	XF	Unc
360	1988	—	—	Proof	475.00

Australian Bicentennial - Platypus
Similar to KM#288.

KM#	Date	Mintage	VF	XF	Unc
361	1988	—	—	Proof	475.00

Australian Bicentennial - Kangaroo
Similar to KM#289.

KM#	Date	Mintage	VF	XF	Unc
362	1988	—	—	Proof	475.00

Australian Bicentennial - Dingo Dog
Similar to KM#226.

KM#	Date	Mintage	VF	XF	Unc
363	1988	—	—	Proof	475.00

BANK TOKEN ISSUES (Tn)

1/2 PENNY

COPPER
Obv: Peel Castle.
Rev. large leg: DOUGLAS BANK TOKEN.

KM#	Date	Mintage	Fine	VF	XF	Unc
Tn1	1811	—	25.00	75.00	200.00	400.00

Rev. small leg: DOUGLAS BANK TOKEN.

KM#	Date	Mintage	Fine	VF	XF	Unc
Tn2	1811	—	30.00	100.00	325.00	500.00
	1811	—	—	—	Proof	650.00

KM#	Date	Mintage	Fine	VF	XF	Unc
Tn3	1811	—	4.00	10.00	40.00	75.00

BRONZE

KM#	Date	Mintage	Fine	VF	XF	Unc
Tn3a	1811	—	—	—	Proof	—

BRASS

KM#	Date	Mintage	Fine	VF	XF	Unc
Tn3b	1811	—	10.00	25.00	100.00	175.00

KM#	Date	Mintage	Fine	VF	XF	Unc
Tn21	1831	—	12.00	35.00	100.00	—

BRASS

KM#	Date	Mintage	Fine	VF	XF	Unc
Tn21a	1831	—	—	—	Rare	—

PENNY

COPPER, normal flan
Rev. leg: DOUGLAS BANK TOKEN. . . . .

KM#	Date	Mintage	Fine	VF	XF	Unc
Tn6	1811	—	20.00	65.00	200.00	450.00
	1811	—	—	—	Proof	650.00

COPPER, thin flan

KM#	Date	Mintage	Fine	VF	XF	Unc
Tn7	1811	—	—	—	Proof	850.00

Normal flan.
Obv: Similar to KM#Tn6.
Rev. leg: DOUGLAS TOKEN. . . .

KM#	Date	Mintage	Fine	VF	XF	Unc
Tn8	1811	—	20.00	60.00	200.00	400.00
	1811	—	—	—	Proof	600.00

Thin flan.

KM#	Date	Mintage	Fine	VF	XF	Unc
Tn9	1811	—	—	—	Proof	—

KM#	Date	Mintage	Fine	VF	XF	Unc
Tn10	1811	—	5.00	15.00	65.00	100.00
	1811	—	—	—	Proof	—

SHILLING

SILVER

KM#	Date	Mintage	Fine	VF	XF	Unc
Tn12	1811	—	175.00	375.00	750.00	1200.
	1811	—	—	—	Proof	1500.

2 SHILLINGS 6 PENCE

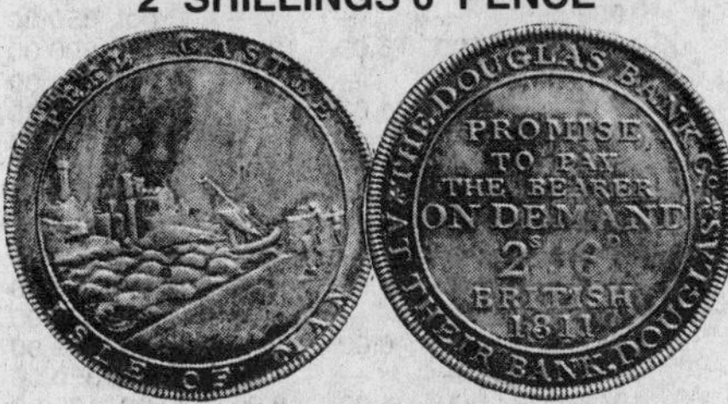

SILVER

KM#	Date	Mintage	Fine	VF	XF	Unc
Tn13	1811	—	300.00	600.00	1200.	2000.

COPPER

KM#	Date	Mintage	Fine	VF	XF	Unc
Tn13a	1811	—	—	—	Proof	Rare

5 SHILLINGS

SILVER

KM#	Date	Mintage	Fine	VF	XF	Unc
Tn14	1811	—	350.00	700.00	1500.	2500.
	1811	—	—	—	Proof	3000.

MINT SETS (MS)

KM#	Date	Mintage	Identification	Issue Price	Mkt. Val.
MS1	1965(3)	1,500	KM15-17	—	700.00
MS2	1971(6)	50,000	KM19-24	3.00	3.00
MS3	1973(4)	2,500	KM26-29	760.00	950.00
MS4	1974(4)	250	KM26-29	—	1100.
MS5	1975(6)	20,000	KM19-24	—	3.00
MS6	1975(6)	20,000	KM19a-24a	56.50	40.00
MS7	1975(4)	200	KM26-29	—	1100.
MS8	1976(6)	20,000	KM32-34,35.1,36.2,39	—	4.00
MS9	1976(6)	20,000	KM32a-36a,39a	—	37.50
MS10	1976(4)	—	KM26-29	—	1100.
MS11	1977(6)	50,000	KM33-34,35.1,36.2,39-40	—	4.00
MS12	1977(4)	180	KM26-29	—	1100.
MS13	1978(6)	10,000	KM32a-36a,39a	—	50.00
MS14	1978(6)	—	KM32-34,35.1,36.2,39	—	4.00
MS15	1979(6)	—	KM32-34,35.1-36.1,39	—	5.00
MS16	1979(4)	—	KM26-29	—	1000.
MS17	1980(6)	30,000	KM58-62,70	—	5.00
MS18	1981(6)	—	KM58-62,70	—	5.00
MS19	1982(6)	—	—	—	6.00
MS20	1983(9)	—	KM58-62,70,88,90,109	—	27.50
MS21	1983(6)	—	KM58-62,70	—	5.00
MS22	1989(9)	—	KM207-215	—	25.00
MS23	1990(9)	—	KM207-215	25.00	25.00
MS24	1992(9)	—	KM207-215	25.00	25.00

PROOF-LIKE SETS (P/L)

KM#	Date	Mintage	Identification	Issue Price	Mkt. Val.
P/L1	1980(4)	—	KM64-67, Olympics	—	20.00
P/L2	1981(4)	—	KM77-80, I.Y.D.	—	25.00
P/L3	1984(4)	—	KM121-124, College of Arms	—	20.00
P/L4	1986(2)	—	KM173-174, Andrew & Sarah Wedding	—	16.00

PROOF SETS (PS)

KM#	Date	Mintage	Identification	Issue Price	Mkt. Val.
PS1	1965(3)	1,000	KM15a-17a	—	750.00
PS2	1971(6)	10,000	KM19-24	20.00	20.00
PS3	1973(4)	1,250	KM26-29	950.00	1075.
PS4	1974(4)	2,500	KM26-29	900.00	1050.
PS5	1975(6)	600	KM19b-24b	1175.	2175.
PS6	1975(4)	—	KM26-29	—	1100.
PS7	1976(6)	600	KM32b-34b,35.1b,36b,39b	—	2175.
PS8	1976(4)	—	KM26-29	—	1100.
PS9	1977(6)	10,000	KM33a-36a,39a,40a	—	45.00
PS10	1977(4)	1,250	KM26-29	—	1100.
PS11	1978(7)	—	KM32-36,39,44	—	15.00
PS12	1978(7)	600	KM32b-34b,35.1b,36b, 39b,44b	—	2375.
PS13	1979(7)	10,000	KM32a-36a,39a,44a	110.00	50.00
PS14	1979(7)	500	KM32b-34b,35.1b,36b, 39b,44b	2765.	2375.
PS15	1979(4)	1,000	KM26-29	—	1100.
PSA16	1980(7)	—	KM44,58-62,70	—	20.00
PS16	1980(7)	10,000	KM44d,58a-62a,70a	—	50.00
PS17	1980(7)	—	KM44c,58b-62b,70b	—	170.00
PS18	1980(7)	300	KM44c,58c-62c,70c	—	1825.
PS19	1982(9)	1,000	KM44a,58a-62a,88a,90a	—	130.00
PS20	1982(9)	250	KM44c,58b-62b,88b,90b	—	1075.
PS21	1982(9)	100	KM44b,58c-62c,88c,90c	—	2650.
PS22	1982(7)	25,000	KM58-62,70,90	—	15.00
PS23	1982(7)	9,000	KM58a-62a,70a,90a	—	60.00
PS24	1982(7)	250	KM58b-62b,70b,90b	—	245.00
PS25	1982(7)	400	KM58c-62c,70c,90c	—	1900.
PS26	1983(9)	—	KM58d-62d,90a,109a	—	1575.
PS27	1983(9)	—	KM58b-62b,90b,109b	—	300.00
PS28	1983(9)	—	KM58c-62c,90c,109c	—	1450.
PS29	1985(9)	25,000	KM142-148,150-151	36.00	36.00
PS30	1985(9)	5,000	KM135,142a-148a,150a	120.00	120.00
PS31	1985(9)	150	KM135b,142b-148b,150b	3240.	3500.
PS32	1985(9)	100	KM135c,142c-148c,150c	3600.	3850.
PS33	1985(7)	25,000	KM142-148	20.00	20.00
PS34	1985(7)	5,000	KM142a-148a	72.00	72.00
PS35	1985(7)	150	KM142b-148b	2160.	2200.
PS36	1985(7)	100	KM142c-148c	2400.	2450.
PS37	1985(6)	51	KM140-141,152,155-157	—	11,000.
PS38	1986(7)	17	KM140-141,152,155-157, 166	—	12,000.
PS39	1986(6)	15	KM153-154,168-171	—	16,000.
PS40	1986(4)	2,000	KM153-154,168-169	1950.	2000.
PS41	1986(5)	2,500	KM140-141,152,166	—	16.50
PS42	1987(4)	—	KM176a,177,187-188	—	1125.
PS43	1987(6)	30	KM140-141,152,155-157	—	13,000.
PS44	1987(5)	—	KM140-141,152,155,166	—	1800.
PS45	1987(4)	3,000	KM140-141,152,155	—	1750.
PS46	1987(6)	11 pcs.	KM153-154,168-169, 170-171	—	16,000.
PS47	1987(4)	2,500	KM153-154,168-169	—	2000.
PS48	1988(5)	611	KM235-239	—	1450.
PS49	1988(4)	500	KM222-225	—	35.00
PS50	1988(4)	7,500	KM286-289, medal	—	1500.

ISRAEL

The state of Israel, a Middle Eastern republic at the eastern end of the Mediterranean Sea, bounded by Lebanon on the north, Syria on the northeast, Jordan on the east, and Egypt on the southwest, has an area of 9,000 sq. mi. (20,770 sq. km.) and a population of 4.9 million. Capital: Jerusalem. Finished diamonds, chemicals, citrus, textiles, and minerals are exported.

Palestine, which corresponds to Canaan of the Bible, was settled by the Philistines about the 12th century B.C. and shortly thereafter was invaded by the Jews who established the kingdoms of Israel and Judah. Because of its position as part of the land bridge connecting Asia and Africa, Palestine was invaded and conquered by nearly all of the historic empires of ancient Europe and Asia. In the 16th century it became a part of the Ottoman Empire. After falling to the British in World War I, it, together with Transjordan, was mandated to Great Britain by the League of Nations, 1922.

For more than half a century prior to the termination of the British mandate over Palestine, 1948, Zionist leaders had sought to create a Jewish homeland for Jews who were dispersed throughout the world. For almost as long, Jews fleeing persecution had immigrated to Palestine. The Nazi persecutions of the 1930s and 1940s increased the Jewish movement to Palestine and generated international support for the creation of a Jewish state, first promulgated by the Balfour Declaration of 1917 which asserted British support for the endeavor. The dream of a Jewish homeland was realized on May 14, 1948 when Palestine was proclaimed the State of Israel.

TITLES

Filastin فلسطين

Paleshtina (E.I.)

MONETARY SYSTEM

1000 Mils = 1 Pound

PALESTINE

MIL

BRONZE

KM#	Date	Mintage	Fine	VF	XF	Unc
1	1927	10.000	.50	1.00	2.00	15.00
	1927	66 pcs.	—	—	Proof	425.00
	1935	.704	1.00	2.50	6.00	25.00
	1937	1.200	1.50	3.00	10.00	60.00
	1939	3.700	.50	1.50	5.00	25.00
	1939	—	—	—	Proof	400.00
	1940	.396	6.50	12.50	50.00	120.00
	1941	1.920	.75	2.00	5.00	20.00
	1942	4.480	.50	1.50	4.50	19.00
	1943	2.800	.50	1.50	4.50	19.00
	1944	1.400	.75	2.00	5.00	20.00
	1946	1.632	1.50	3.50	7.00	30.00
	1946	—	—	—	Proof	450.00
	1947	*2.880	—	—	—	10,500.

***NOTE:** Only 5 known. The entire issue was to be melted down.

2 MILS

BRONZE

KM#	Date	Mintage	Fine	VF	XF	Unc
2	1927	5.000	.50	1.50	6.50	20.00
	1927	66 pcs.	—	—	Proof	425.00
	1941	1.600	1.00	2.50	10.00	30.00
	1941	—	—	—	Proof	400.00
	1942	2.400	1.00	2.50	10.00	30.00
	1945	.960	2.00	7.00	18.00	90.00
	1946	.960	4.00	8.00	20.00	100.00
	1947	*.480	—	—	—	—

***NOTE:** The entire issue was melted down.

5 MILS

COPPER-NICKEL

KM#	Date	Mintage	Fine	VF	XF	Unc
3	1927	10.000	.75	1.50	6.50	25.00
	1927	66 pcs.	—	—	Proof	425.00
	1934	.500	6.50	12.50	50.00	200.00
	1935	2.700	.75	2.00	9.00	45.00
	1939	2.000	.75	2.00	5.00	30.00
	1939	—	—	—	Proof	425.00
	1941	.400	5.00	10.00	25.00	150.00
	1941	—	—	—	Proof	375.00
	1946	1.000	1.50	3.00	8.00	25.00
	1946	—	—	—	Proof	375.00
	1947	*1.000	—	—	—	—

***NOTE:** The entire issue was melted down.

BRONZE

KM#	Date	Mintage	Fine	VF	XF	Unc
3a	1942	2.700	1.50	2.50	10.00	40.00
	1944	1.000	1.00	2.00	10.00	35.00

10 MILS

COPPER-NICKEL

KM#	Date	Mintage	Fine	VF	XF	Unc
4	1927	5.000	1.00	2.00	8.00	45.00
	1927	66 pcs.	—	—	Proof	350.00
	1933	.500	5.00	10.00	75.00	250.00
	1933	—	—	—	Proof	350.00
	1934	.500	5.00	12.00	75.00	300.00
	1934	—	—	—	Proof	375.00
	1935	1.150	1.00	3.00	20.00	225.00
	1935	—	—	—	Proof	425.00
	1937	.750	2.00	5.00	20.00	200.00
	1937	—	—	—	Proof	425.00
	1939	1.000	1.00	2.00	10.00	75.00
	1939	—	—	—	Proof	350.00
	1940	1.500	1.00	2.00	10.00	75.00
	1940	—	—	—	Proof	350.00
	1941	.400	6.00	12.00	40.00	200.00
	1941	—	—	—	Proof	350.00
	1942	.600	4.00	8.00	30.00	125.00
	1946	1.000	2.00	5.00	20.00	60.00
	1946	—	—	—	Proof	300.00
	1947	*1.000	—	—	—	—

***NOTE:** The entire issue was melted down.

BRONZE

KM#	Date	Mintage	Fine	VF	XF	Unc
4a	1942	1.000	2.50	5.00	20.00	100.00
	1943	1.000	5.00	10.00	40.00	150.00

20 MILS

COPPER-NICKEL

KM#	Date	Mintage	Fine	VF	XF	Unc
5	1927	1.500	5.00	12.00	35.00	100.00
	1927	66 pcs.	—	—	Proof	450.00
	1933	.250	10.00	20.00	50.00	350.00
	1934	.125	40.00	70.00	175.00	500.00
	1934	—	—	—	Proof	—
	1935	.575	3.00	10.00	50.00	225.00
	1940	.200	8.00	15.00	50.00	350.00
	1940	—	—	—	Proof	500.00
	1941	.100	50.00	75.00	175.00	700.00
	1941	—	—	—	Proof	1100.

BRONZE

KM#	Date	Mintage	Fine	VF	XF	Unc
5a	1942	1.100	5.00	10.00	25.00	100.00
	1944	1.000	20.00	50.00	110.00	350.00

50 MILS

5.8319 g, .720 SILVER, .1350 oz ASW

KM#	Date	Mintage	Fine	VF	XF	Unc
6	1927	8.000	3.50	6.00	12.00	60.00
	1927	66 pcs.	—	—	Proof	450.00
	1931	.500	12.00	25.00	100.00	350.00
	1933	1.000	5.00	12.00	25.00	90.00
	1934	.399	10.00	25.00	50.00	125.00
	1935	5.600	3.50	6.00	12.00	40.00
	1939	3.000	3.00	5.00	10.00	20.00
	1939	—	—	—	Proof	275.00
	1940	2.000	5.00	10.00	20.00	60.00
	1940	—	—	—	Proof	150.00
	1942	5.000	3.00	5.00	10.00	35.00

100 MILS

11.6638 g, .720 SILVER, .2700 oz ASW

KM#	Date	Mintage	Fine	VF	XF	Unc
7	1927	2.000	5.00	10.00	20.00	100.00
	1927	66 pcs.	—	—	Proof	500.00
	1931	.250	45.00	100.00	300.00	1000.
	1931	—	—	—	Proof	1250.
	1933	.500	15.00	30.00	100.00	450.00
	1934	.200	60.00	120.00	250.00	700.00
	1935	2.850	5.00	10.00	20.00	60.00
	1939	1.500	6.00	12.00	25.00	65.00
	1939	—	—	—	Proof	250.00
	1940	1.000	8.50	15.00	25.00	75.00
	1942	2.500	8.50	15.00	25.00	75.00

MINT SETS (MS)

KM#	Date	Mintage	Identification	Issue Price	Mkt. Val.
MS1	1927(14)	—	KM1-7, two each	—	1650.

PROOF SETS (PS)

KM#	Date	Mintage	Identification	Issue Price	Mkt. Val.
PS1	1927(14)	34	KM1-7, two each, original case	—	6500.
PS2	1927(7)	4	KM1-7, original case	—	4000.

ISRAEL

HEBREW COIN DATING

Modern Israel's coins carry Hebrew dating formed from a combination of the 22 consonant letters of the Hebrew alphabet and read from right to left. The Jewish calendar dates back more than 5700 years, but only five milleniums are assumed in the dating of coins. Thus, the year 5735 (1975AD) appears as 735, with the first two characters from the right indicating the number of years in hundreds; tav (400), plus shin (300). The next is lamedh (30), followed by a separation mark which has the appearance of double quotation marks, then heh (5).

The separation mark - generally similar to a single quotation mark through 5718 (1958 AD), and like a double quotation mark thereafter - serves the purpose of indicating that the letters form a number, not a word, and on some issues can be confused with the character yodh (10), which in a stylized rendering can appear quite similar, although slightly larger and thicker. The separation mark does not appear in either form on a few commemorative issues.

The Jewish New Year falls in September or October by Christian calendar reckoning. Where dual dating is encountered, with but a few exceptions the Hebrew dating on the coins of modern Israel is 3760 years greater than the Christian dating; 5735 is equivalent to 1975AD, with the 5000 assumed until 1981, when full dates appear on the coins. These exceptions are most of the Hanukka coins, (Feast of Lights), the Bank of Israel gold 50 Pound commemorative of 5725 (1964AD) and others. In such special instances the differential from Christian dating is 3761 years, except in the instance of the 5720 Chanuka Pound, which is dated 1960AD, as is the issue of 5721, an arrangement which reflects the fact that the events fall early in the Jewish year and late in the Christian.

The Star of David is not a mint mark. It appears only on some coins sold by the Government Coin and Medal Co. for collectors. It was first used in 1971 on the science coin to signify that it was minted in Jerusalem, but was later used by different mint facilities.

1957	תש"ז	(5)717
1958	תש"ח	(5)718
1958	תש"ח	(5)718
1959	תשט	(5)719
1959	תש"ט	(5)719
1960	תש"ך	(5)720
1960	תשך	(5)720
1961	תשכ"א	(5)721
1962	תשכ"ב	(5)722
1963	תשכ"ג	(5)723
1964	תשכ"ד	(5)724
1965	תשכ"ה	(5)725
1966	תשכ"ו	(5)726
1967	תשכ"ז	(5)727
1968	תשכ"ח	(5)728
1969	תשכ"ט	(5)729
1970	תש"ל	(5)730
1971	תשל"א	(5)731
1972	תשל"ב	(5)732
1973	תשל"ג	(5)733
1974	תשל"ד	(5)734
1975	תשל"ה	(5)735
1976	תשל"ו	(5)736
1977	תשל"ז	(5)737
1978	תשל"ח	(5)738
1979	תשל"ט	(5)739
1980	תש"ם	(5)740
1981	תשמ"א	(5)741
1981	התשמ"א	5741
1982	התשמ"ב	5742
1983	התשמ"ג	5743
1984	התשמ"ד	5744
1985	התשמ"ה	5745
1986	התשמ"ו	5746
1987	התשמ"ז	5747
1988	התשמ"ח	5748
1989	התשמ"ט	5749
1990	התש"ן	5750
1991	התשנ"א	5751
1992	התשנ"ב	5752
1993	התשנ"ג	5753
1994	התשנ"ד	5754

MINT MARKS

(o) - Ottawa
(s) - San Francisco
None - Jerusalem

(M) MATTE - Normal circulation strike or a dull finish produced by sandblasting special uncirculated (polish finish) or proof quality dies.

(U) SPECIAL UNCIRCULATED - Polished or proof-like in appearance without any frosted features.

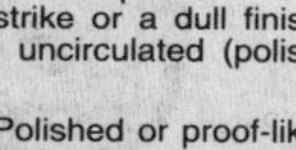

(P) PROOF - The highest quality obtainable having mirror-like fields and frosted features.

MONETARY SYSTEM

1000 Mils = 1 Pound

25 MILS

ALUMINUM

KM#	Date	Year	Mintage	VF	XF	Unc
8	5708	(1948)	.043	100.00	200.00	850.00
	5709	(1949)	open link			
			.650	25.00	50.00	100.00
	5709	(1949)	closed link			
			—	12.50	20.00	35.00

NOTE: Above 3 coins were issued April 6, 1949.

MONETARY REFORM

1000 Prutah = 1 Lirah

NOTE: The 1949 Prutah coins, except for the 100 and 500 Prutah values, occur with and without a small pearl under the bar connecting the wreath on the reverse. Only the 50 and 100 Prutah coins were issued in 5709. All later coins were struck with frozen dates.

PRUTA

ALUMINUM
Anchor

KM#	Date	Year	Mintage	VF	XF	Unc
9	5709	(1949)	w/pearl			
			2.685	.50	1.00	2.00
	5709	(1949)	w/o pearl			
			2.500	1.00	2.50	10.00
	5709	(1949)	.020	—	Proof	500.00

5 PRUTAH

BRONZE
4-Stringed Lyre

KM#	Date	Year	Mintage	VF	XF	Unc
10	5709	(1949)	w/pearl			
			5.045	.50	1.00	2.00
	5709	(1949)	.025	—	Proof	500.00
	5709	(1949)	w/o pearl			
			5.000	.50	2.00	10.00

10 PRUTAH

BRONZE
Amphora

KM#	Date	Year	Mintage	VF	XF	Unc
11	5709	(1949)	w/pearl			
			7.448	.75	2.50	30.00
	5709	(1949)	w/o pearl			
			7.500	.50	1.00	4.00
	5709	(1949)	.020	—	Proof	500.00

ALUMINUM
Ceremonial Jug

KM#	Date	Year	Mintage	VF	XF	Unc
17	5712	(1952)	26.042	.35	.75	2.00

KM#	Date	Year	Mintage	VF	XF	Unc
20	5717	(1957)	1.000	.35	.75	2.00

COPPER ELECTROPLATED ALUMINUM

KM#	Date	Year	Mintage	VF	XF	Unc
20a	5717	(1957)	1.088	.35	.75	2.00

25 PRUTAH

COPPER-NICKEL
Grapes

KM#	Date	Year	Mintage	VF	XF	Unc
12	5709	(1949)	w/pearl			
			10.520	.50	.75	2.00
	5709	(1949)	.020	—	Proof	500.00
	5709	(1949)	w/o pearl			
			2.500	10.00	20.00	50.00

NICKEL-CLAD STEEL

KM#	Date	Year	Mintage	VF	XF	Unc
12a	5714	(1954)	3.697	.50	1.00	2.00

50 PRUTAH

COPPER-NICKEL
Grape Leaves
Reeded edge

KM#	Date	Year	Mintage	VF	XF	Unc
13.1	5709	(1949)	w/pearl			
			12.040	5.00	10.00	25.00
	5709	(1949)	w/o pearl			
			Inc. Ab.	1.00	2.00	3.50
	5709	(1949)	.020	—	Proof	500.00
	5714	(1954)	.250	10.00	17.50	35.00

Plain edge

KM#	Date	Year	Mintage	VF	XF	Unc
13.2	5714	(1954)	4.500	.50	1.00	2.00

NICKEL-CLAD STEEL

KM#	Date	Year	Mintage	VF	XF	Unc
13.2a	5714	(1954)	17.774	.50	1.00	2.00

100 PRUTAH

COPPER-NICKEL
Date Palm

KM#	Date	Year	Mintage	VF	XF	Unc
14	5709	(1949)	6.062	.75	1.25	2.50
	5709	(1949)	.020	—	Proof	500.00
	5715	(1955)	5.868	1.00	1.50	3.00

NICKEL-CLAD STEEL
Reduced size, 25.6mm -Bern die
Rev: Large wreath, close to edge.

KM#	Date	Year	Mintage	VF	XF	Unc
18	5714	(1954)	.700	1.00	1.50	3.00

Utrecht die. Rev: Small wreath, away from edge.

KM#	Date	Year	Mintage	VF	XF	Unc
19	5714	(1954)	.020	300.00	450.00	1000.

250 PRUTAH

COPPER-NICKEL
Barley Spears

KM#	Date	Year	Mintage	VF	XF	Unc
15	5709	(1949)	w/pearl			
			1.496	2.50	10.00	20.00
	5709	(1949)	w/o pearl			
			.524	1.00	2.00	5.00

14.4000 g, .500 SILVER, .2315 oz ASW

KM#	Date	Year	Mintage	VF	XF	Unc
15a	5709H	(1949)	.044	5.00	7.50	12.00

NOTE: Not placed into circulation.

500 PRUTAH

25.5000 g, .500 SILVER, .4099 oz ASW
Pomegranates

KM#	Date	Year	Mintage	VF	XF	Unc
16	5709	(1949)	.034	10.00	15.00	25.00

NOTE: Not placed into circulation.

LIRAH

COPPER-NICKEL
Hanukka - Law Is Light

KM#	Date	Year	Mintage	VF	XF	Unc
22	5719	1958	.150	—	—	3.00
	5719	1958	5,000	—	Proof	55.00

MONETARY REFORM

Commencing January 1, 1960
100 Agorot = 1 Lirah

AGORAH

1960 normal date

1960 large date

1961 thick date

1961 wide date

1962 large date

1962 small date

ALUMINUM

KM#	Date	Year	Mintage	VF	XF	Unc
24.1	5720	(1960)	"Lamed" w/serif			
			12.768	5.00	10.00	20.00
	5720	(1960)	"Lamed" w/o lower serif			
			Inc. Ab.	10.00	20.00	100.00
	5720	(1960)	large date			
			300 pcs.	150.00	300.00	750.00
	5721	(1961)	19.262	.50	2.00	5.00
	5721	(1961)	thick date			
			Inc. Ab.	5.00	15.00	100.00
	5721	(1961)	wide date			
			Inc. Ab.	5.00	15.00	100.00
	5722	(1962)	large date			
			14.500	.10	.40	.75
	5722	(1962)	small date, small serifs			
			Inc. Ab.	5.00	10.00	20.00
	5723	(1963)	14.804	.10	.40	.75
	5723	(1963)	inverted reverse			
			.010	4.00	8.00	15.00
	5724	(1964)	27.552	—	—	.75
	5725	(1965)	20.708	—	—	.25
	5726	(1966)	10.165	—	—	.25
	5727	(1967)	6.781	—	—	.25
	5728	(1968)	20.899	—	—	.25
	5729	(1969)	22.120	—	—	.25
	5730	(1970)	17.748	—	—	.25
	5731	(1971)	10.290	—	—	.25
	5732	(1972)	24.512	—	—	.25
	5733	(1973)	20.496	—	—	.25
	5734	(1974)	42.080	—	—	.25
	5735	(1975)	1.574	—	—	.25
	5736	(1976)	4.512	—	—	.25
	5737	(1977)	9.680	—	—	.25
	5738	(1978)	8.864	—	—	.25
	5739	(1979)	4.048	—	—	.25
	5740	(1980)	2.600	—	—	1.00

Obv: Star of David in field.

KM#	Date	Year	Mintage	VF	XF	Unc
24.2	5731	(1971)	.175	—	—	.25
	5732	(1972)	.100	—	—	.25
	5734	(1974)	.100	—	—	.25
	5735	(1975)	.100	—	—	.25
	5736	(1976)	.070	—	—	.25
	5737	(1977)	.060	—	—	.25
	5738	(1978)	.057	—	—	.25
	5739	(1979)	.050	—	—	.25

25th Anniversary of Independence

KM#	Date	Year	Mintage	VF	XF	Unc
63	5733	(1973)	.100	In sets only		.25

NICKEL
25th Anniversary of Bank of Israel

KM#	Date	Year	Mintage	VF	XF	Unc
96	5740	(1980)	.035	In sets only		1.00

5 AGOROT

1961 normal 1961 I.C.I.

ALUMINUM-BRONZE

KM#	Date	Year	Mintage	VF	XF	Unc
25	5720	(1960)	8.019	5.00	10.00	25.00
	5721	(1961)	sharp, flat date			
			15.090	.25	.50	1.50
	5721	(1961)	I.C.I. issue w/high date w/serifs			
			5.000	10.00	20.00	75.00
	5722	(1962)	large date			
			11.198	.25	.50	1.00
	5722	(1962)	small date			
			Inc. Ab.	5.00	10.00	25.00
	5723	(1963)	1.429	.25	.50	1.25
	5724	(1964)	.021	12.00	145.00	350.00
	5725	(1965)	.201	—	.10	.25
	5726	(1966)	.291	—	.10	.25
	5727	(1967)	2.195	—	.10	.25
	5728	(1968)	4.020	—	.10	.25
	5729	(1969)	2.200	—	.10	.25
	5730	(1970)	4.004	—	.10	.25
	5731	(1971)	14.010	—	.10	.25
	5732	(1972)	9.005	—	.10	.25
	5733	(1973)	25.720	—	.10	.25
	5734	(1974)	10.470	—	.10	.25
	5735	(1975)	10.232	—	.10	.25

Obv: Star of David in field.

KM#	Date	Year	Mintage	VF	XF	Unc
25a	5731	(1971)	.126	—	—	.25
	5732	(1972)	.069	—	—	.25

COPPER-NICKEL

KM#	Date	Year	Mintage	VF	XF	Unc
25c	5734	(1974)	.093	In sets only		.25
	5735	(1975)	.062	In sets only		.25
	5736	(1976)	—	In sets only		.25
	5737	(1977)	.060	In sets only		.25
	5738	(1978)	128 pcs.	—	—	.50
	5739	(1979)	.018	—	—	.25

ALUMINUM

KM#	Date	Year	Mintage	VF	XF	Unc
25b	5736(M)	(1976)	13.156	—	.10	.25
	5737(M)	(1977)	16.800	—	.10	.25
	5737(o)	(1977)	15.000	—	.10	.25
	5738(M)	(1978)	21.480	—	.10	.25
	5738(o)(U)					
		(1978)	38.760	—	.10	.25
	5739(M)	(1979)	12.836	—	.10	.25

COPPER-NICKEL
25th Anniversary of Independence

KM#	Date	Year	Mintage	VF	XF	Unc
64	5733	(1973)	.100	In sets only		.50

NICKEL
25th Anniversary of Bank of Israel

KM#	Date	Year	Mintage	VF	XF	Unc
97	5740	(1980)	.035	In sets only		1.00

10 AGOROT

ALUMINUM-BRONZE

KM#	Date	Year	Mintage	VF	XF	Unc
26	5720	(1960)	14.397	.50	1.00	10.00
	5721	(1961)	12.821	.50	1.00	6.00
	5721	(1961)	*"Fatha"* in Arabic, leg: "Israel" Inc. Ab.	25.00	80.00	325.00

Large date-thick letters Small date-thin letters

KM#	Date	Year	Mintage	VF	XF	Unc
	5722	(1962)	large date, thick letters 8.845	.25	.50	1.00
	5722	(1962)	small date, thin letters Inc. Ab.	5.00	10.00	20.00
	5723	(1963)	3.931	.25	.50	1.00
	5724	(1964)	large date 3.612	.25	.50	1.00
	5724	(1964)	small date Inc. Ab.	10.00	20.00	50.00
	5725	(1965)	.201	—	.20	.25
	5726	(1966)	7.276	—	.10	.25
	5727	(1967)	6.426	—	.10	.25
	5728	(1968)	4.825	—	.10	.25
	5729	(1969)	6.810	—	.10	.25
	5730	(1970)	6.131	—	.10	.25
	5731	(1971)	6.810	—	.10	.25
	5732	(1972)	19.653	—	.10	.25
	5733	(1973)	16.205	—	.10	.25
	5734	(1974)	22.040	—	.10	.25
	5735	(1975)	25.135	—	.10	.25
	5736	(1976)	54.870	—	.10	.25
	5737	(1977)	27.886	—	.10	.25

Obv: Star of David in field.

KM#	Date	Year	Mintage	VF	XF	Unc
26a	5731	(1971)	.175	—	—	.25
	5732	(1972)	.100	—	—	.25

COPPER-NICKEL

KM#	Date	Year	Mintage	VF	XF	Unc
26c	5734	(1974)	.100	In sets only		.25
	5735	(1975)	.100	In sets only		.25
	5736	(1976)	.070	In sets only		.25
	5737	(1977)	.060	In sets only		.25
	5738	(1978)	.057	In sets only		.25
	5739	(1979)	—	In sets only		.25

ALUMINUM

KM#	Date	Year	Mintage	VF	XF	Unc
26b	5737(o)(U)	(1977)	30.100	—	.10	.25
	5738(M)	(1978)	24.050	—	.10	.25
	5738(o)(U)	(1978)	104.336	—	.10	.25
	5739	(1979)	22.201	—	.10	.25
	5740	(1980)	4.752	—	.10	.25

NOTE: Most of the 5740 dated coins were melted down before being issued.

COPPER-NICKEL
25th Anniversary of Independence

KM#	Date	Year	Mintage	VF	XF	Unc
65	5733	(1973)	.100	In sets only		.75

NICKEL
25th Anniversary of Bank of Israel

KM#	Date	Year	Mintage	VF	XF	Unc
98	5740	(1980)	.035	In sets only		1.00

25 AGOROT

ALUMINUM-BRONZE

KM#	Date	Year	Mintage	VF	XF	Unc
27	5720	(1960)	4.391	.25	.50	3.00
	5721	(1961)	5.009	.10	.20	1.00
	5722	(1962)	.882	.15	.30	1.00
	5723	(1963)	.194	.50	1.00	5.00
	5724	(1964)	Five trial pieces only			
	5725	(1965)	.187	.10	.20	.50
	5726	(1966)	.320	—	.10	.40
	5727	(1967)	.325	—	.10	.40
	5728	(1968)	.445	—	.10	.40
	5729	(1969)	.432	—	.10	.40
	5730	(1970)	.417	—	.10	.40
	5731	(1971)	.500	—	.10	.40
	5732	(1972)	1.883	—	.10	.40
	5733	(1973)	3.370	—	.10	.40
	5734	(1974)	2.320	—	.10	.40
	5735	(1975)	3.968	—	.10	.40
	5736	(1976)	3.901	—	.10	.40
	5737	(1977)	1.832	—	.10	.40
	5738	(1978)	12.200	—	.10	.40
	5739	(1979)	10.842	—	.10	.40

Obv: Star of David in field.

KM#	Date	Year	Mintage	VF	XF	Unc
27a	5731	(1971)	.126	—	—	.40
	5732	(1972)	.069	—	—	.40

COPPER-NICKEL

KM#	Date	Year	Mintage	VF	XF	Unc
27b	5734	(1974)	.093	In sets only		.40
	5735	(1975)	.062	In sets only		.40
	5736	(1976)	—	In sets only		.40
	5737	(1977)	.060	In sets only		.40
	5738	(1978)	.057	In sets only		.40
	5739	(1979)	.032	In sets only		.40

25th Anniversary of Independence

KM#	Date	Year	Mintage	VF	XF	Unc
66	5733	(1973)	.100	In sets only		.75

NICKEL
25th Anniversary of Bank of Israel

KM#	Date	Year	Mintage	VF	XF	Unc
99	5740	(1980)	.035	In sets only		1.00

1/2 LIRAH

COPPER-NICKEL

KM#	Date	Year	Mintage	VF	XF	Unc
36.1	5723	(1963)	large animals 5.607	.50	2.00	5.00
	5723	(1963)	small animals Inc. Ab.	3.00	15.00	30.00
	5724	(1964)	3.762	.10	.75	2.00
	5725	(1965)	1.551	.10	.15	1.00
	5726	(1966)	2.139	.10	.15	.50
	5727	(1967)	1.942	.10	.15	.50
	5728	(1968)	1.183	.10	.15	.50
	5729	(1969)	.450	.10	.20	.60
	5730	(1970)	1.001	.10	.20	.60
	5731	(1971)	.500	.10	.20	.60
	5732	(1972)	.421	.10	.20	.60
	5733	(1973)	3.225	.10	.15	.50
	5734	(1974)	4.275	.10	.15	.50
	5735	(1975)	11.066	.10	.15	.50
	5736	(1976)	4.959	.10	.15	.50
	5737	(1977)	4.983	.10	.15	.50
	5738	(1978)	14.325	.10	.15	.50
	5739	(1979)	21.391	.10	.15	.50

Obv: Star of David in field.

KM#	Date	Year	Mintage	VF	XF	Unc
36.2	5731	(1971)	.175	In sets only		.50
	5732	(1972)	.100	In sets only		.50
	5734	(1974)	.100	In sets only		.50
	5735	(1975)	.100	In sets only		.50
	5736	(1976)	.070	In sets only		.50
	5737	(1977)	.060	In sets only		.50
	5738	(1978)	.057	In sets only		.50
	5739	(1979)	.050	In sets only		.50

25th Anniversary of Independence

KM#	Date	Year	Mintage	VF	XF	Unc
67	5733	(1973)	.100	In sets only		.75

NICKEL
25th Anniversary of Bank of Israel

KM#	Date	Year	Mintage	VF	XF	Unc
100	5740	(1980)	.035	In sets only		2.00

LIRAH

COPPER-NICKEL

KM#	Date	Year	Mintage	VF	XF	Unc
37	5723	(1963)	large animals 4.212	.50	1.50	3.00
	5723	(1963)	small animals Inc. Ab.	1.00	10.00	20.00
	5724	(1964)	Only ten trial pieces struck			
	5725	(1965)	.166	.25	.50	1.25
	5726	(1966)	.290	.25	.50	1.25
	5727	(1967)	.180	.25	.50	1.25

KM#	Date	Year	Mintage	VF	XF	Unc
47.1	5727	(1967)	3.830	.10	.25	1.00
	5728	(1968)	3.932	.10	.25	1.00
	5729	(1969)	12.484	.10	.25	.75
	5730	(1970)	4.794	.10	.25	.75
	5731	(1971)	2.993	.10	.25	.75
	5732	(1972)	2.489	.10	.25	.75
	5733	(1973)	10.265	.10	.25	.75
	5734	(1974)	6.287	.10	.25	.75
	5735	(1975)	13.225	.10	.25	.75
	5736	(1976)	4.268	.10	.25	.75
	5737	(1977)	11.129	.10	.25	.75
	5738	(1978)	61.752	.10	.25	.75
	5739	(1979)	34.815	.10	.25	.75
	5740	(1980)	10.840	.10	.25	.75

NOTE: Most of the 5740 dated coins were melted down before being issued.

Obv: Star of David in field.

KM#	Date	Year	Mintage	VF	XF	Unc
47.2	5731	(1971)	.126	In sets only		.75
	5732	(1972)	.069	In sets only		.75
	5734	(1974)	.093	In sets only		.75
	5735	(1975)	.062	In sets only		.75
	5736	(1976)	—	In sets only		.75
	5737	(1977)	Inc. Ab.	In sets only		.75
	5738	(1978)	Inc. Ab.	In sets only		.75
	5739	(1979)	—	In sets only		.75

5 LIROT

COPPER-NICKEL

KM#	Date	Year	Mintage	VF	XF	Unc
90	5738	(1978)	8.350	.35	.60	1.25
	5739	(1979)	37.646	.35	.50	1.00

Obv: Star of David in field.

KM#	Date	Year	Mintage	VF	XF	Unc
90a	5739	(1979)	—	In sets only		1.00

COMMEMORATIVE COINAGE

NOTE: All proof commemoratives with the exception of the 1 and 5 Lirot issues of 1958 and the gold 100 Lirot Jerusalem 1968 issues are distinguished from the uncirculated editions by the presence of the Hebrew letter "mem".

1/2 LIRAH

COPPER-NICKEL
Feast Of Purim

KM#	Date	Year	Mintage	VF	XF	Unc
31	5721	(1961)	.020	—	—	10.00
	5721	(1961)	4,901	—	Proof	20.00
	5722	(1962)	.020	—	—	7.00
	5722	(1962)	9,894	—	Proof	12.00

LIRAH

COPPER-NICKEL
Hanukka - 50th Anniversary of Deganya

KM#	Date	Year	Mintage	VF	XF	Unc
28	5720	1960	.049	—	—	4.50
	5720	1960	4,702	—	Proof	35.00

Hanukka - Henrietta Szold

KM#	Date	Year	Mintage	VF	XF	Unc
32	5721	1960	.017	—	—	30.00
	5721	1960	3,000	—	Proof	125.00

Hanukka - Death of a Hasmonean Hero

KM#	Date	Year	Mintage	VF	XF	Unc
34	5722	1961	.019	—	—	10.00
	5722	1961	9,324	—	Proof	20.00

Hanukka - Italian Lamp

KM#	Date	Year	Mintage	VF	XF	Unc
38	5723	1962	9,560	—	—	27.50
	5723	1962	5,941	—	Proof	47.50

18th Century
Hanukka - North Africa Lamp

KM#	Date	Year	Mintage	VF	XF	Unc
42	5724	1963	9,928	—	—	27.50
	5724	1963	5,412	—	Proof	47.50

25th Anniversary of Independence

KM#	Date	Year	Mintage	VF	XF	Unc
68	5733	(1973)	.100	In sets only		1.00

NICKEL
25th Anniversary of Bank of Israel

KM#	Date	Year	Mintage	VF	XF	Unc
101	5740	(1980)	.035	In sets only		4.00

5 LIROT

25.0000 g, .900 SILVER, .7234 oz ASW
10th Anniversary-Menora

KM#	Date	Year	Mintage	VF	XF	Unc
21	5718	1958	.098	—	—	15.00
	5718	1958	2,000	—	Proof	450.00

11th Anniversary
Ingathering Of The Exiles

KM#	Date	Year	Mintage	VF	XF	Unc
23	5719	1959	.027	—	—	25.00
	5719	1959	4,682	—	Proof	70.00

5 LIROT

25.0000 g, .900 SILVER, .7234 oz ASW
12th Anniversary-Dr. Theodor Herzl

KM#	Date	Year	Mintage	VF	XF	Unc
29	5720	1960	.034	—	—	25.00
	5720	1960	4,827	—	Proof	50.00

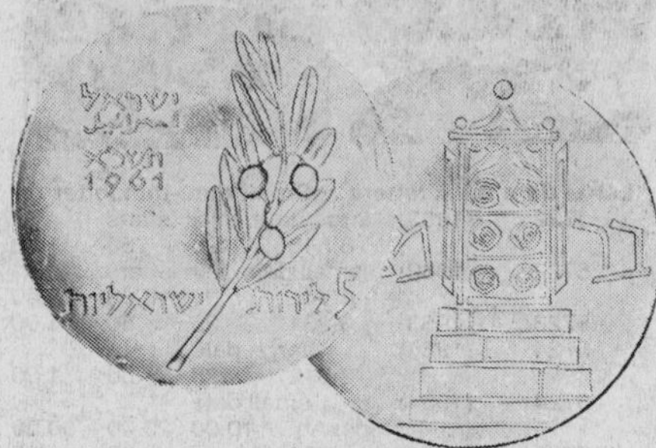

13th Anniversary-Bar Mitzvah

KM#	Date	Year	Mintage	VF	XF	Unc
33	5721	1961	.019	—	—	50.00
	5721	1961	4,455	—	Proof	80.00

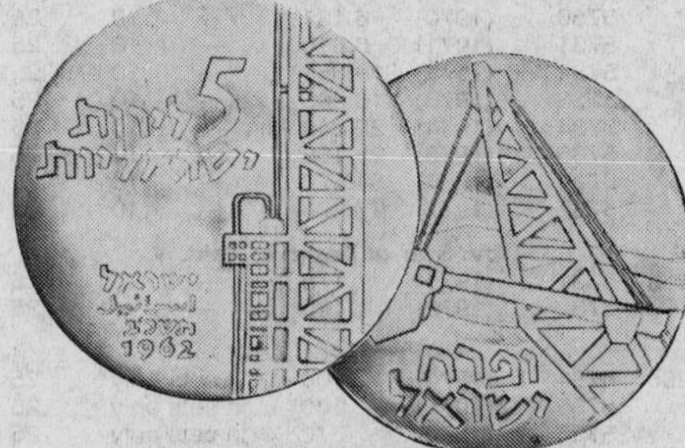

14th Anniversary
Negev Industrialization

KM#	Date	Year	Mintage	VF	XF	Unc
35	5722	1962	.010	—	—	40.00
	5722	1962	4,960	—	Proof	60.00

15th Anniversary-Seafaring

KM#	Date	Year	Mintage	VF	XF	Unc
39	5723	1963	5,960	—	—	300.00
	5723	1963	4,495	—	Proof	350.00

16th Anniversary-Israel Museum

KM#	Date	Year	Mintage	VF	XF	Unc
43	5724	1964	.011	—	—	50.00
	5724	1964	4,421	—	Proof	75.00

17th Anniversary-Knesset Building

KM#	Date	Year	Mintage	VF	XF	Unc
45	5725	1965	.025	—	—	18.00
	5725	1965	7,537	—	Proof	22.00

18th Anniversary-Israel Lives On

KM#	Date	Year	Mintage	VF	XF	Unc
46	5726	1966	.032	—	—	12.00
	5726	1966	.010	—	Proof	15.00

19th Anniversary-Port of Eilat

KM#	Date	Year	Mintage	VF	XF	Unc
48	5727	1967	.030	—	—	20.00
	5727	1967	7,680	—	Proof	25.00

20.0000 g, .750 SILVER, .4823 oz ASW
Hanukka - Russian Lamp
Plain edge.

KM#	Date	Year	Mintage	VF	XF	Unc
69.1	5733	1972	.075	—	—	7.00

Reeded edge.

KM#	Date	Year	Mintage	VF	XF	Unc
69.2	5733	1972	.022	—	Proof	10.00

20.0000 g, .500 SILVER, .3215 oz ASW
Hanukka - Babylonian Lamp
Plain edge.

KM#	Date	Year	Mintage	VF	XF	Unc
75.1	5734	1973	.095	—	—	8.00

Reeded edge.

KM#	Date	Year	Mintage	VF	XF	Unc
75.2	5734	1973	.045	—	Proof	10.00

NICKEL
25th Anniversary of Bank of Israel

KM#	Date	Year	Mintage	VF	XF	Unc
102	5740	(1980)	.035	In sets only		6.00

10 LIROT

26.0000 g, .900 SILVER, .7524 oz ASW
Victory Commemorative

KM#	Date	Year	Mintage	VF	XF	Unc
49	5727	1967	.234	—	—	10.00

26.0000 g, .935 SILVER, .7816 oz ASW

KM#	Date	Year	Mintage	VF	XF	Unc
49a	5727	1967	.050	—	Proof	14.00

26.0000 g, .900 SILVER, .7524 oz ASW
20th Anniversary - Jerusalem Reunification

KM#	Date	Year	Mintage	VF	XF	Unc
51	5728	1968	.050	—	—	12.00
	5728	1968	.020	—	Proof	14.00

21st Anniversary-Shalom

KM#	Date	Year	Mintage	VF	XF	Unc
53.1	5729	1969	.040	U. S. Mint(s)		
				—	—	12.00

Rev: K A F below helmet.

KM#	Date	Year	Mintage	VF	XF	Unc
53.2	5729	1969	.020	Jerusalem Mint		
				—	—	12.00
	5729	1969	.020	U. S. Mint(s)		
				—	Proof	12.50

22nd Anniversary - Mikveh Israel Centenary

KM#	Date	Year	Mintage	VF	XF	Unc
55	5730	1970	.048	—	—	10.00
	5730	1970	.022	—	Proof	12.00

Pidyon Haben
Plain edge.

KM#	Date	Year	Mintage	VF	XF	Unc
56.1	5730	1970	.049	—	—	10.00

Reeded edge.

KM#	Date	Year	Mintage	VF	XF	Unc
56.2	5730	1970	.015	—	Proof	12.00

NOTE: Struck at the San Francisco Mint.

Pidyon Haben
Plain edge.

KM#	Date	Year	Mintage	VF	XF	Unc
57.1	5731	1971	.030	—	—	10.00

Reeded edge.

KM#	Date	Year	Mintage	VF	XF	Unc
57.2	5731	1971	.014	—	Proof	12.00

Star of David
Jerusalem Mint

23rd Anniversary-Science and Industry

KM#	Date	Year	Mintage	VF	XF	Unc
58	5731	1971	.030 Utrecht Mint	—	—	10.00
	5731	1971	star .023 Jerusalem Mint	—	—	12.50
	5731	1971	.018	—	Proof	15.00

Let My People Go
Obv: Legend on rim, closed *Mem*.

KM#	Date	Year	Mintage	VF	XF	Unc
59.1	5731	1971	.073	—	—	10.00
	5731	1971	.020	—	Proof	12.00

Obv: Legend away from rim, open *Mem* (Berne die).

KM#	Date	Year	Mintage	VF	XF	Unc
59.2	5731	1971	80 pcs.	—	Proof	650.00

Pidyon Haben
Plain edge.

KM#	Date	Year	Mintage	VF	XF	Unc
61.1	5732	1972	star .030	—	—	10.00
	5732	1972	w/o star .015	—	—	15.00

Reeded edge.

KM#	Date	Year	Mintage	VF	XF	Unc
61.2	5732	1972	.012	—	Proof	14.00

24th Anniversary-Aviation
Lettered edge.

KM#	Date	Year	Mintage	VF	XF	Unc
62	5732	1972	.050	—	—	12.50
	5732	1972	.015	—	Proof	25.00

Pidyon Haben
Plain edge.

KM#	Date	Year	Mintage	VF	XF	Unc
70.1	5733	1973	.101	—	—	10.00

Reeded edge.

KM#	Date	Year	Mintage	VF	XF	Unc
70.2	5733	1973	.015	—	Proof	12.50

25th Anniversary of Independence
Lettered edge.

KM#	Date	Year	Mintage	VF	XF	Unc
71	5733	1973	.124	—	—	10.00
	5733	1973	.041	—	Proof	12.00

Pidyon Haben
Plain edge.

KM#	Date	Year	Mintage	VF	XF	Unc
76.1	5734	1974	.109	—	—	10.00

Reeded edge.

KM#	Date	Year	Mintage	VF	XF	Unc
76.2	5734	1974	.044	—	Proof	12.00

26th Anniversary of Independence
Lettered edge.

KM#	Date	Year	Mintage	VF	XF	Unc
77	5734	1974	.127	—	—	10.00
	5734	1974	.050	—	Proof	12.00

20.0000 g, .500 SILVER, .3215 oz ASW
Damascus Hanukka Lamp
Plain edge.

KM#	Date	Year	Mintage	VF	XF	Unc
78.1	5735	1974	.074	—	—	7.00

Reeded edge.

KM#	Date	Year	Mintage	VF	XF	Unc
78.2	5735	1974	.059	—	Proof	9.00

Holland Hanukka Lamp
Plain edge.

KM#	Date	Year	Mintage	VF	XF	Unc
84.1	5736	1975	.044	—	—	8.00

Reeded edge.

KM#	Date	Year	Mintage	VF	XF	Unc
84.2	5736	1975	.034	—	Proof	10.00

U.S. Hanukka Lamp
American Independence Bicentennial
Plain edge.

KM#	Date	Year	Mintage	VF	XF	Unc
87.1	5737	1976	.025	—	—	17.50

Reeded edge.

KM#	Date	Year	Mintage	VF	XF	Unc
87.2	5737	1976	.020	—	Proof	22.50

COPPER-NICKEL
Jerusalem Hanukka Lamp
Plain edge.

KM#	Date	Year	Mintage	VF	XF	Unc
91.1	5738	1977	.046	—	—	5.00

Reeded edge. Open style "mem".

KM#	Date	Year	Mintage	VF	XF	Unc
91.2	5738	1977	.030	—	Proof	7.00

Closed style "mem"

KM#	Date	Year	Mintage	VF	XF	Unc
91.3	5738	1977	Inc. Ab.	—	Proof	10.00

20 LIROT

7.9880 g, .917 GOLD, .2355 oz AGW
100th Anniversary of Birth of Dr. Theodor Herzl

KM#	Date	Year	Mintage	VF	XF	Unc
30	5720	1960	.010	—	—	220.00

25 LIROT

26.0000 g, .935 SILVER, .7816 oz ASW
1st Anniversary of Death of David Ben Gurion
Plain edge.

KM#	Date	Year	Mintage	VF	XF	Unc
79.1	5735	1974	.099	—	—	10.00

Reeded edge.

KM#	Date	Year	Mintage	VF	XF	Unc
79.2	5735	1974	.064	—	Proof	12.00

26.0000 g, .900 SILVER, .7524 oz ASW
Pidyon Haben
Plain edge.

KM#	Date	Year	Mintage	VF	XF	Unc
80.1	5735	1975	.062	—	—	10.00

Reeded edge.

KM#	Date	Year	Mintage	VF	XF	Unc
80.2	5735	1975	.049	—	Proof	12.00

30.0000 g, .800 SILVER, .7717 oz ASW
25th Anniversary of Israel Bond Program
Lettered edge.

KM#	Date	Year	Mintage	VF	XF	Unc
81	5735	1975	.049	—	—	11.50
	5735	1975	.040	—	Proof	12.50

26.0000 g, .900 SILVER, .7524 oz ASW
28th Anniversary of Independence - Strength
Lettered edge.

KM#	Date	Year	Mintage	VF	XF	Unc
85	5736	1976	.038	—	—	10.00
	5736	1976	.027	—	Proof	14.00

30.0000 g, .800 SILVER, .7717 oz ASW
Pidyon Haben
Plain edge.

KM#	Date	Year	Mintage	VF	XF	Unc
86.1	5736	1976	.037	—	—	10.00

Reeded edge.

KM#	Date	Year	Mintage	VF	XF	Unc
86.2	5736	1976	.029	—	Proof	12.00

20.0000 g, .500 SILVER, .3215 oz ASW
29th Anniversary of Independence - Brotherhood
Lettered edge.

KM#	Date	Year	Mintage	VF	XF	Unc
88	5737	1977	.037	—	—	10.00
	5737	1977	.027	—	Proof	12.00

26.0000 g, .900 SILVER, .7524 oz ASW
Pidyon Haben
Plain edge.

KM#	Date	Year	Mintage	VF	XF	Unc
89.1	5737	1977	.032	—	—	12.00

Reeded edge.

KM#	Date	Year	Mintage	VF	XF	Unc
89.2	5737	1977	.019	—	Proof	15.00

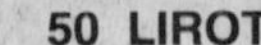

COPPER-NICKEL
French Hanukka Lamp
Plain edge.

KM#	Date	Year	Mintage	VF	XF	Unc
94.1	5739	1978	.036	—	—	5.00

Reeded edge.

KM#	Date	Year	Mintage	VF	XF	Unc
94.2	5739	1978	.022	—	Proof	10.00

50 LIROT

13.3400 g, .917 GOLD, .3933 oz AGW
10th Anniversary of Death of Weizmann

KM#	Date	Year	Mintage	VF	XF	Unc
40	5723	1962	6,202	—	Proof	300.00
	5723	1962	w/o mem 10 pcs.	—	Proof	—

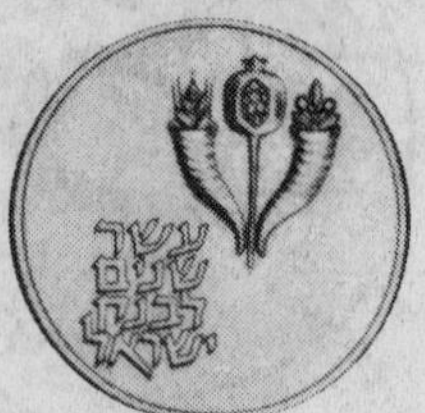

10th Anniversary of Bank of Israel

KM#	Date	Year	Mintage	VF	XF	Unc
44	5724	1964	6,014	—	—	375.00
	5724	1964	1,502	—	Proof	2500.

7.0000 g, .900 GOLD, .2025 oz AGW
25th Anniversary of Independence

KM#	Date	Year	Mintage	VF	XF	Unc
72	5733	1973	.028	—	Proof	100.00

20.0000 g, .500 SILVER, .3215 oz ASW
30th Anniversary of Independence - Loyalty
Plain edge.

KM#	Date	Year	Mintage	VF	XF	Unc
92.1	5738	1978	.040	—	—	10.00

Reeded edge.

KM#	Date	Year	Mintage	VF	XF	Unc
92.2	5738	1978	.022	—	Proof	12.50

31st Anniversary of Independence - Motherhood
Lettered edge.

KM#	Date	Year	Mintage	VF	XF	Unc
95	5739	1979	.024	—	—	12.00
	5739	1979	.016	—	Proof	14.00

100 LIROT

26.6800 g, .917 GOLD, .7866 oz AGW
10th Anniversary of Death of Weizmann

KM#	Date	Year	Mintage	VF	XF	Unc
41	5723	1962	6,203	—	Proof	425.00
	5723	1962	w/o mem 10 pcs.	—	Proof	—

Victory Commemorative

KM#	Date	Year	Mintage	VF	XF	Unc
50	5727	1967	9,004	—	Proof	425.00

25.0000 g, .800 GOLD, .6430 oz AGW
20th Anniversary - Jerusalem Reunification

KM#	Date	Year	Mintage	VF	XF	Unc
52	5728	1968	.013	—	Proof	320.00

21st Anniversary - Shalom

KM#	Date	Year	Mintage	VF	XF	Unc
54	5729	1969	.013	—	Proof	320.00

22.0000 g, .900 GOLD, .6366 oz AGW
Let My People Go

KM#	Date	Year	Mintage	VF	XF	Unc
60	5731	1971	9,956	—	Proof	320.00

13.5000 g, .900 GOLD, .3906 oz AGW
25th Anniversary of Independence

KM#	Date	Year	Mintage	VF	XF	Unc
73	5733	1973	.028	—	Proof	175.00

20.0000 g, .500 SILVER, .3215 oz ASW
Hanukka - Egyption Lamp
Plain edge.

KM#	Date	Year	Mintage	VF	XF	Unc
103.1	5740	1979	.032	—	—	12.00

Reeded edge.

KM#	Date	Year	Mintage	VF	XF	Unc
103.2	5740	1979	.019	—	Proof	20.00

200 LIROT

27.0000 g, .900 GOLD, .7813 oz AGW
25th Anniversary of Independence

KM#	Date	Year	Mintage	VF	XF	Unc
74	5733	1973	.018	—	Proof	375.00

26.0000 g, .900 SILVER, .7524 oz ASW
32nd Anniversary - Egyptian & Israeli Peace Treaty
Lettered edge.

KM#	Date	Year	Mintage	VF	XF	Unc
104	5740	1980	.020	—	—	18.00
	5740	1980	.013	—	Proof	28.00

500 LIROT

28.0000 g, .900 GOLD, .8102 oz AGW
1st Anniversary of Death of David Ben Gurion

KM#	Date	Year	Mintage	VF	XF	Unc
82	5735	1974	.048	—	Proof	370.00

20.0000 g, .900 GOLD, .5787 oz AGW
25th Anniversary of Israel Bond Program

KM#	Date	Year	Mintage	VF	XF	Unc
83	5735	1975	.031	—	Proof	275.00

1000 LIROT

12.0000 g , .900 GOLD, .3473 oz AGW
30th Anniversary of Independence

KM#	Date	Year	Mintage	VF	XF	Unc
93	5738	1978	.012	—	Proof	200.00

5000 LIROT

17.2800 g, .900 GOLD, .5000 oz AGW
32nd Anniversary - Egyptian & Israeli Peace Treaty

KM#	Date	Year	Mintage	VF	XF	Unc
105	5740	1980	6,382	—	Proof	300.00

MONETARY REFORM

Commencing February 24, 1980

10 Old Agorot = 1 New Agorah
100 New Agorot = 1 Sheqel

NEW AGORAH

ALUMINUM
Date Palm

KM#	Date	Year	Mintage	VF	XF	Unc
106	5740	(1980)	*200.000	—	—	.10
	5741	(1981)	1.000	—	.10	.20
	5742	(1982)	1.000	—	.10	.20

*NOTE: 110 million coins were reportedly melted down.

5 NEW AGOROT

ALUMINUM
Menorah

KM#	Date	Year	Mintage	VF	XF	Unc
107	5740	(1980)	69.532	—	—	.10
	5741	(1981)	1.000	—	.10	.20
	5742	(1982)	5.000	—	—	.10

10 NEW AGOROT

COPPER-NICKEL
Pomegranate

KM#	Date	Year	Mintage	VF	XF	Unc
108	5740	(1980)	*167.932	—	—	.10
	5741	(1981)	241.160	—	—	.10
	5742	(1982)	23.000	—	—	.10
	5743	(1983)	2.500	—	.10	.15
	5744	(1984)	.500	—	.10	.20

*NOTE: 70.200 million coins were reportedly melted down.

1/2 SHEQEL

COPPER-NICKEL

KM#	Date	Year	Mintage	VF	XF	Unc
109	5740	(1980)	52.308	—	.25	.50
	5741	(1981)	53.272	—	.25	.50
	5742	(1982)	18.808	—	.25	.50
	5743	(1983)	.250	—	.35	.70
	5744	(1984)	.250	—	.35	.70

7.2000 g, .850 SILVER, .1967 oz ASW
Holyland Sites - Qumran Caves

KM#	Date	Year	Mintage	VF	XF	Unc
121	5743	1982	.015	—	—	16.50

Holyland Sites - Herodion Ruins

KM#	Date	Year	Mintage	VF	XF	Unc
126	5744	1983	.011	—	—	17.50

Holyland Sites - Kidron Valley

KM#	Date	Year	Mintage	VF	XF	Unc
140	5745	1984	7,538	—	—	20.00

Holyland Sites - Capernaum

KM#	Date	Year	Mintage	VF	XF	Unc
152	5746	1985	6,010	—	—	16.50

SHEQEL

14.4000 g, .850 SILVER, .3935 oz ASW
Hanukka Corfu Lamp
Plain edge.

KM#	Date	Year	Mintage	VF	XF	Unc
110.1	5741	1980	.024	—	—	15.00

Reeded edge.

KM#	Date	Year	Mintage	VF	XF	Unc
110.2	5741	1980	.015	—	Proof	20.00

COPPER-NICKEL
Chalice

KM#	Date	Year	Mintage	VF	XF	Unc
111	5741	(1981)	154.540	—	.65	.85
	5742	(1982)	15.850	—	.65	.85
	5743	(1983)	26.360	—	.65	.85
	5744	(1984)	32.205	—	.65	.85
	5745	(1985)	.500	—	.65	1.00

14.4000 g, .850 SILVER, .3935 oz ASW
Hanukka Polish Lamp
Plain edge.

KM#	Date	Year	Mintage	VF	XF	Unc
116.1	5742	1981	.016	—	—	20.00

Reeded edge.

KM#	Date	Year	Mintage	VF	XF	Unc
116.2	5742	1981	.011	—	Proof	25.00

Holyland Sites - Qumran Caves

KM#	Date	Year	Mintage	VF	XF	Unc
122	5743	1982	9,000	—	Proof	35.00

Hanukka Yemen Lamp

KM#	Date	Year	Mintage	VF	XF	Unc
123	5743	1982	.014	—	—	20.00

35th Anniversary of the State of Israel-Valour

KM#	Date	Year	Mintage	VF	XF	Unc
127	5743	1983	.015	—	—	25.00

Holyland Sites - Herodion Ruins

KM#	Date	Year	Mintage	VF	XF	Unc
128	5744	1983	.010	—	Proof	35.00

Hanukka Prague Lamp

KM#	Date	Year	Mintage	VF	XF	Unc
129	5744	1983	.013	—	—	22.00

36th Anniversary of the State of Israel - Kinsmen

KM#	Date	Year	Mintage	VF	XF	Unc
135	5744	1984	.018	—	—	20.00

Holyland Sites - Kidron Valley

KM#	Date	Year	Mintage	VF	XF	Unc
141	5745	1984	6,798	—	Proof	45.00

Hanukka Theresianstadt Lamp

KM#	Date	Year	Mintage	VF	XF	Unc
144	5745	1984	.011	—	—	25.00

36th Anniversary and Scientific Achievement

KM#	Date	Year	Mintage	VF	XF	Unc
148	5745	1985	8,520	—	—	25.00

Holyland Sites - Capernaum

KM#	Date	Year	Mintage	VF	XF	Unc
153	5746	1985	6,010	—	Proof	40.00

Ancient Ship

KM#	Date	Year	Mintage	VF	XF	Unc
155	5745	1985	.013	—	P/L	25.00

2 SHEQALIM

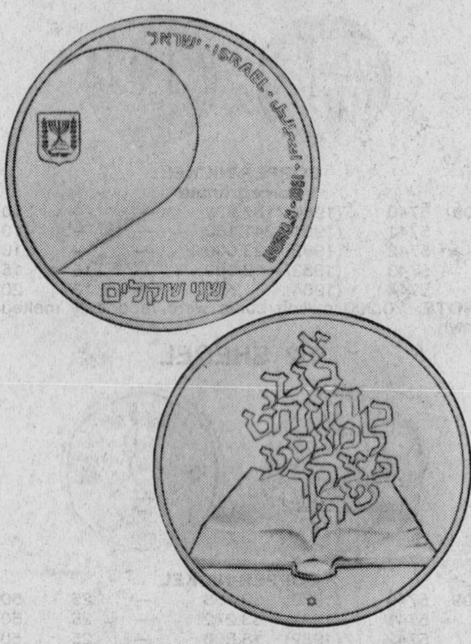

28.8000 g, .825 SILVER, .7639 oz ASW
33rd Anniversary of State of Israel
People of the Book
Lettered edge.

KM#	Date	Year	Mintage	VF	XF	Unc
112	5741	1981	.016	—	—	20.00
	5741	1981	.011	—	Proof	32.50

28.8000 g, .850 SILVER, .7871 oz ASW
34th Anniversary - Baron Edmond de Rothschild
Lettered edge.

KM#	Date	Year	Mintage	VF	XF	Unc
117	5742	1982	.013	—	—	20.00
	5742	1982	9,506	—	Proof	32.50

Hanukka Yemen Lamp

KM#	Date	Year	Mintage	VF	XF	Unc
124	5743	1982	8,996	—	Proof	45.00

35th Anniversary of the State of Israel - Valour
Rev: Similar to 1 Shequel, KM#127.

KM#	Date	Year	Mintage	VF	XF	Unc
130	5743	1983	.010	—	Proof	35.00

Hanukka Prague Lamp

KM#	Date	Year	Mintage	VF	XF	Unc
131	5744	1983	.011	—	Proof	30.00

36th Anniversary of the State of Israel - Kinsmen

KM#	Date	Year	Mintage	VF	XF	Unc
136	5744	1984	8,526	—	Proof	32.50

Hanukka Theresianstadt Lamp

KM#	Date	Year	Mintage	VF	XF	Unc
145	5745	1984	.010	—	Proof	40.00

37th Anniversary and Scientific Achievement

KM#	Date	Year	Mintage	VF	XF	Unc
149	5745	1985	8,330	—	Proof	37.50

5 SHEQALIM

ALUMINUM-BRONZE

KM#	Date	Year	Mintage	VF	XF	Unc
118	5742	(1982)	30.000	—	.75	1.25
	5743	(1983)	.994	—	1.00	2.00
	5744	(1984)	17.389	—	.75	1.25
	5745	(1985)	.250	—	1.00	2.50

8.6300 g, .900 GOLD, .2497 oz AGW
Holyland Sites - Qumran Caves

KM#	Date	Year	Mintage	VF	XF	Unc
125	5743	1982	4,927	—	Proof	200.00

Holyland Sites - Herodion Ruins

KM#	Date	Year	Mintage	VF	XF	Unc
132	5744	1983	4,346	—	Proof	200.00

Holyland Sites - Kidron Valley
Rev: View of Kidron Valley.

KM#	Date	Year	Mintage	VF	XF	Unc
142	5745	1984	2,601	—	Proof	600.00

Holyland Sites - Capernaum

KM#	Date	Year	Mintage	VF	XF	Unc
154	5746	1985	2,633	—	Proof	450.00

10 SHEQALIM

17.2800 g, .900 GOLD, .5000 oz AGW
33rd Anniversary of State of Israel
People of the Book

KM#	Date	Year	Mintage	VF	XF	Unc
113	5741	1981	5,673	—	Proof	350.00

COPPER-NICKEL
Ancient Galley

KM#	Date	Year	Mintage	VF	XF	Unc
119	5742	(1982)	36.084	—	.75	1.25
	5743	(1983)	17.851	—	.75	1.25
	5744	(1984)	31.950	—	.75	1.25
	5745	(1985)	25.864	—	.50	.75

17.2800 g, .900 GOLD, .5000 oz AGW
34th Anniversary - Baron Edmond de Rothschild

KM#	Date	Year	Mintage	VF	XF	Unc
120	5742	1982	4,875	—	Proof	325.00

35th Anniversary of the State of Israel - Valour

KM#	Date	Year	Mintage	VF	XF	Unc
133	5743	1983	3,650	—	Proof	500.00

COPPER-NICKEL
Hanukka - Trade Coin

KM#	Date	Year	Mintage	VF	XF	Unc
134	5744	(1983)	2.000	—	1.00	1.50

Theodor Herzl

KM#	Date	Year	Mintage	VF	XF	Unc
137	5744	(1984)	2.003	—	1.00	1.50

17.2800 g, .900 GOLD, .5000 oz AGW
36th Anniversary of the State of Israel - Kinsmen

KM#	Date	Year	Mintage	VF	XF	Unc
138	5744	1984	3,798	—	Proof	400.00

37th Anniversary and Scientific Achievement

KM#	Date	Year	Mintage	VF	XF	Unc
150	5745	1985	3,240	—	Proof	500.00

25 SHEQEL

26.0000 g, .900 SILVER, .7524 oz ASW
100th Anniversary of Birth of Zeev Jabotinsky
Plain edge

KM#	Date	Year	Mintage	VF	XF	Unc
114.1	5741	1980	.014	—	—	20.00

Reeded edge

KM#	Date	Year	Mintage	VF	XF	Unc
114.2	5741	1980	.012	—	Proof	32.50

50 SHEQALIM

ALUMINUM-BRONZE
Circulation Coins

KM#	Date	Year	Mintage	VF	XF	Unc
139	5744	(1984)	13.994	—	.50	1.00
	5745	(1985)	1.000	—	.75	1.50

David Ben Gurion

KM#	Date	Year	Mintage	VF	XF	Unc
147	5745	(1985)	1.000	—	1.00	1.50

100 SHEQALIM

COPPER-NICKEL
Circulation Coins

KM#	Date	Year	Mintage	VF	XF	Unc
143	5744	(1984)	30.028	—	1.00	2.00
	5745	(1985)	19.638	—	1.00	2.00

Hanukka

KM#	Date	Year	Mintage	VF	XF	Unc
146	5745	(1984)	2.000	—	1.25	2.25

Zeev Jabotinsky

KM#	Date	Year	Mintage	VF	XF	Unc
151	5745	(1985)	2.000	—	1.25	2.25

500 SHEQEL

17.2800 g, .900 GOLD, .5000 oz AGW
100th Anniversary of Birth of Zeev Jabotinsky

KM#	Date	Year	Mintage	VF	XF	Unc
115	5741	1980	7,471	—	Proof	300.00

MONETARY REFORM

September 4, 1985
10 Sheqalim = 1 Agorah
1000 Sheqalim = 1 New Sheqel

AGORAH

ALUMINUM-BRONZE

KM#	Date	Year	Mintage	VF	XF	Unc
156	5745	(1985)	58.144	—	—	.10
	5746	(1986)	95.272	—	—	.10
	5747	(1987)	1.080	—	—	.10
	5748	(1988)	15.768	—	—	.10
	5749	(1989)	10.801	—	—	.10
	5750	(1990)	4.968	—	—	.10
	5751	(1991)	.010	In sets only		.10

Hanukka

KM#	Date	Year	Mintage	VF	XF	Unc
171	5747	(1986)	1.004	—	.10	.20
	5748	(1987)	.540	—	.10	.20
	5748	(1988)	.504	—	.10	.20
	5749	(1988)	Inc. Ab	—	.10	.20
	5750	(1989)	2.160	—	.10	.20
	5751	(1990)	4.968	—	.10	.20

40th Anniversary of Israel

KM#	Date	Year	Mintage	VF	XF	Unc
193	5748	(1988)	.504	—	—	.20

5 AGOROT

ALUMINUM-BRONZE

KM#	Date	Year	Mintage	VF	XF	Unc
157	5745	(1985)	34.504	—	.10	.15
	5746	(1986)	12.384	—	.10	.15
	5747	(1987)	14.257	—	.10	.15
	5748	(1988)	9.360	—	.10	.15
	5749	(1989)	4.896	—	.10	.15
	5750	(1990)	.576	—	.10	.15
	5751	(1991)	4.464	—	.10	.15
	5752	(1992)	—	—	.10	.15

Hanukka

KM#	Date	Year	Mintage	VF	XF	Unc
172	5747	(1986)	1.004	—	.10	.30
	5748	(1987)	.536	—	.10	.30
	5749	(1988)	.504	—	.10	.30
	5750	(1989)	2.016	—	.10	.30
	5751	(1990)	1.488	—	.10	.30
	5752	(1991)	—	—	.10	.30
	5753	(1992)	.960	—	.10	.30

40th Anniversary of Israel

KM#	Date	Year	Mintage	VF	XF	Unc
194	5748	(1988)	.504	—	—	.30

10 AGOROT

ALUMINUM-BRONZE

KM#	Date	Year	Mintage	VF	XF	Unc
158	5745	(1985)	45.000	—	.10	.20
	5746	(1986)	92.754	—	.10	.20
	5747	(1987)	19.351	—	.10	.20
	5748	(1988)	8.640	—	.10	.20
	5749	(1989)	.420	—	.10	.20
	5750	(1990)	2.376	—	.10	.20
	5751	(1991)	59.425	—	.10	.20
	5752	(1992)	—	—	.10	.20
	5753	(1993)	25.920	—	.10	.20

NOTE: Coins dated 5751 (1991) exist with 6mm and 7mm long date and thick and thin letters and 7mm and 7.5mm 10.

Hanukka

KM#	Date	Year	Mintage	VF	XF	Unc
173	5747	(1986)	1.004	—	.10	.40
	5748	(1987)	.834	—	.10	.40
	5749	(1988)	.798	—	.10	.40
	5750	(1989)	2.052	—	.10	.40
	5751	(1990)	1.488	—	.10	.40
	5752	(1991)	—	—	.10	.40
	5753	(1992)	1.404	—	.10	.40

40th Anniversary of Israel

KM#	Date	Year	Mintage	VF	XF	Unc
195	5748	(1988)	.504	—	—	.40

1/2 NEW SHEQEL

ALUMINUM-BRONZE

KM#	Date	Year	Mintage	VF	XF	Unc
159	5745	(1985)	20.328	—	.35	.75
	5746	(1986)	4.392	—	.35	.75
	5747	(1987)	.144	—	.35	2.00
	5748	(1988)	.020	In sets only		3.00
	5749	(1989)	.756	—	.35	.75
	5750	(1990)	.648	—	.35	.75
	5751	(1991)	.288	—	.35	.75
	5752	(1992)	—	—	.35	.75
	5753	(1992)	5.184	—	.35	.75

Baron Edmund de Rothschild

KM#	Date	Year	Mintage	VF	XF	Unc
167	5746	(1986)	2.000	—	.50	1.50

7.2000 g, .850 SILVER, .1967 oz ASW
Holyland Sites - Akko

KM#	Date	Year	Mintage	VF	XF	Unc
168	5747	1986	6,224		—	20.00

ALUMINUM-BRONZE
Hanukka

KM#	Date	Year	Mintage	VF	XF	Unc
174	5747	(1986)	1.004	—	.35	.85
	5748	(1987)	.532	—	.35	.85
	5749	(1988)	.504	—	.35	.85
	5750	(1989)	2.016	—	.35	.85
	5751	(1990)	.960	—	.35	.85
	5752	(1991)	—	—	.35	.85
	5753	(1992)	.304	—	.35	.85

7.2000 g, .850 SILVER, .1967 oz ASW
Holyland Sites - Jericho

KM#	Date	Year	Mintage	VF	XF	Unc
180	5748	1987	7,590	—	—	20.00

Holyland Sites - Caesarea

KM#	Date	Year	Mintage	VF	XF	Unc
188	5749	1988	5,865	—	—	22.00

ALUMINUM-BRONZE
40th Anniversary of Israel

KM#	Date	Year	Mintage	VF	XF	Unc
196	5748	(1988)	.500	—	—	.50

7.2000 g, .850 SILVER, .1967 oz ASW
Jaffa Harbor

KM#	Date	Year	Mintage	VF	XF	Unc
202	5750	1989	4,940	—	—	20.00

Sea of Galilee Sites - Map

KM#	Date	Year	Mintage	VF	XF	Unc
209	5751	1990	4,346	—	—	25.00

NEW SHEQEL

COPPER-NICKEL

KM#	Date	Year	Mintage	VF	XF	Unc
160	5745	(1985)	29.088	—	.65	1.50
	5746	(1986)	20.960	—	.65	1.50
	5747	(1987)	.216	—	.65	3.00
	5748	(1988)	20.376	—	.65	1.50
	5749	(1989)	8.706	—	.65	1.50
	5750	(1990)	.756	—	.65	1.50
	5751	(1991)	1.152	—	.65	1.50
	5752	(1992)	—	—	.65	1.50
	5753	(1993)	8.640	—	.65	1.50

14.4000 g, .850 SILVER, .3935 oz ASW
Ashkenaz Hanukka Lamp

KM#	Date	Year	Mintage	VF	XF	Unc
161	5746	1985	9,460	—	—	20.00

COPPER-NICKEL
Hanukka

KM#	Date	Year	Mintage	VF	XF	Unc
163	5746	(1985)	1.056	—	.65	1.50
	5747	(1986)	1.004	—	.65	1.50
	5748	(1987)	.534	—	.65	1.50
	5749	(1988)	.504	—	.65	1.50
	5750	(1989)	2.052	—	.65	1.50
	5751	(1990)	1.104	—	.65	1.50
	5752	(1991)	—	—	.65	1.50
	5753	(1992)	.922	—	.65	1.50

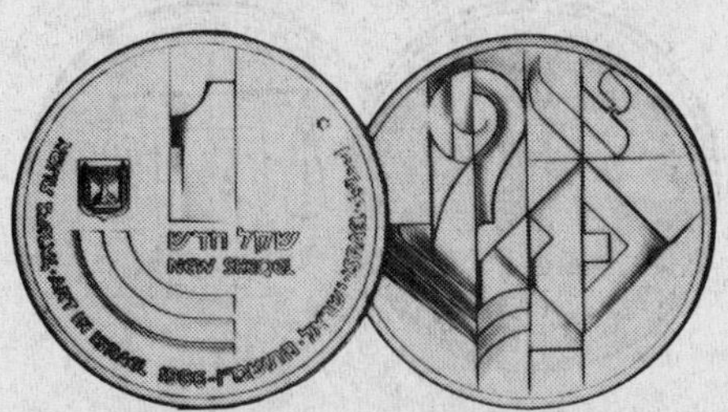

14.4000 g, .850 SILVER, .3935 oz ASW
38th Independence Day Tribute to the Arts

KM#	Date	Year	Mintage	VF	XF	Unc
164	5746	1986	8,010	—	—	25.00

Holyland Sites - Akko

KM#	Date	Year	Mintage	VF	XF	Unc
169	5747	1986	6,117	—	Proof	35.00

Algerian Hanukka Lamp

KM#	Date	Year	Mintage	VF	XF	Unc
175	5747	1986	8,227	—	—	22.00

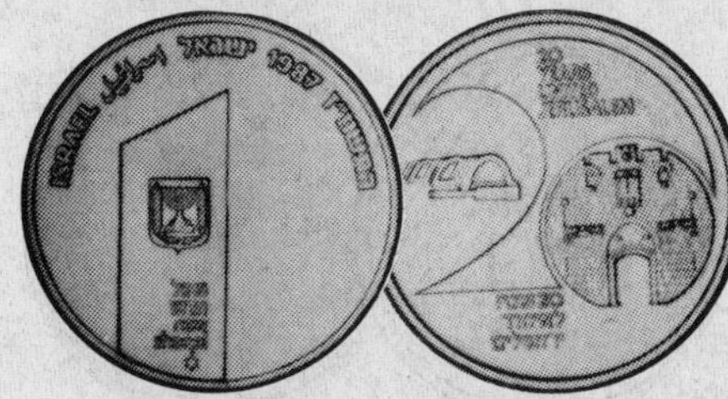

39th Anniversary - United Jerusalem

KM#	Date	Year	Mintage	VF	XF	Unc
177	5747	1987	8,107	—	—	25.00

Holyland Sites - Jericho

KM#	Date	Year	Mintage	VF	XF	Unc
181	5748	1987	8,196	—	Proof	35.00

English Hanukka Lamp

KM#	Date	Year	Mintage	VF	XF	Unc
183	5748	1987	7,810	—	—	25.00

40th Anniversary of Israel

KM#	Date	Year	Mintage	VF	XF	Unc
185	5748	1988	8,990	—	—	22.50

Holyland Sites - Caesarea

KM#	Date	Year	Mintage	VF	XF	Unc
189	5749	1988	6,560	—	Proof	45.00

Hanukka - Tunisian Lamp

KM#	Date	Year	Mintage	VF	XF	Unc
191	5749	1988	6,688	—	—	25.00

COPPER-NICKEL
40th Anniversary of Israel

KM#	Date	Year	Mintage	VF	XF	Unc
197	5748	(1988)	.504	—	—	1.75

Maimonides

KM#	Date	Year	Mintage	VF	XF	Unc
198	5748	(1988)	.980	—	—	1.75

14.4000 g, .850 SILVER, .3935 oz ASW
41st Anniversary of Independence

KM#	Date	Year	Mintage	VF	XF	Unc
199	5749	1989	6,249	—	—	22.50

Jaffa Harbor

KM#	Date	Year	Mintage	VF	XF	Unc
203	5750	1989	5,844	—	Proof	35.00

Hanukka - Persian Lamp

KM#	Date	Year	Mintage	VF	XF	Unc
205	5750	1989	6,171	—	—	22.50

Sea of Galilee Sites - Map

KM#	Date	Year	Mintage	VF	XF	Unc
210	5751	1990	4,735	—	Proof	45.00

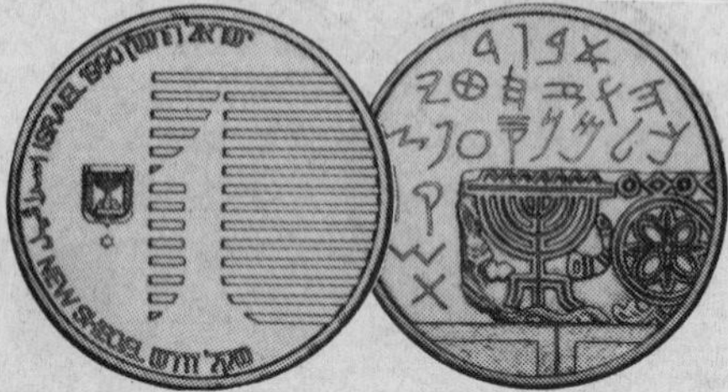

42nd Anniversary - Archaeology

KM#	Date	Year	Mintage	VF	XF	Unc
212	5750	1990	5,509	—	—	35.00

Hanukka - Cochin Lamp

KM#	Date	Year	Mintage	VF	XF	Unc
215	5751	1990	*8,000	—	—	25.00

14.4000 g, .925 SILVER, .4282 oz ASW
43rd Anniversary - Immigration to Israel

KM#	Date	Year	Mintage	VF	XF	Unc
218	5751	1991	*.015	—	—	17.50

Flora and Fauna - Cedar Trees and Dove
Similar to 2 New Sheqalim, KM#221.

KM#	Date	Year	Mintage	VF	XF	Unc
220	5751	1991	4,125	—	—	17.50

3.4600 g, .900 GOLD, .1001 oz AGW

KM#	Date	Year	Mintage	VF	XF	Unc
220a	5751	1991	2,515	—	Proof	165.00

14.4000 g, .925 SILVER, .4282 oz ASW
Hannukka Art - Kiddush Cup

KM#	Date	Year	Mintage	VF	XF	Unc
223	5751	1991	*.010	—	—	20.00

44th Anniversary - Israeli Law

KM#	Date	Year	Mintage	VF	XF	Unc
225	5752	1992	4,047	—	—	20.00

Wildlife - Roe and Lily

KM#	Date	Year	Mintage	VF	XF	Unc
231	5752	1992	*.010	—	—	30.00

3.4600 g, .900 GOLD, .1001 oz AGW

KM#	Date	Year	Mintage	VF	XF	Unc
231a	5752	1992	*4,500	—	Proof	100.00

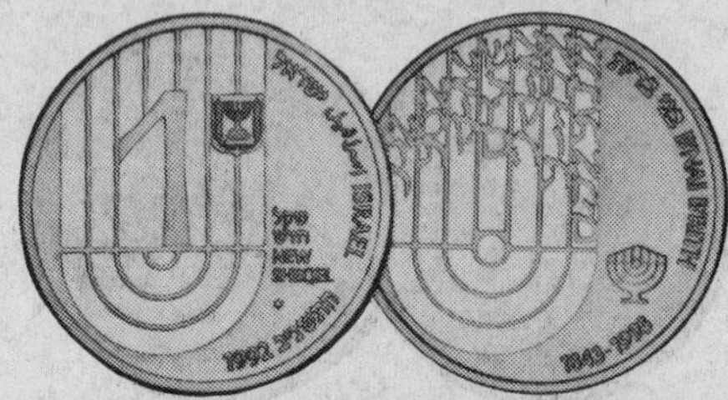

14.4000 g, .925 SILVER, .4282 oz ASW
B'nai B'rith

KM#	Date	Year	Mintage	VF	XF	Unc
234	5752	1992	*.012	—	—	25.00

Shabbat Candles

KM#	Date	Year	Mintage	VF	XF	Unc
238	5752	1992	*.010	—	—	20.00

45th Anniversary and Tourism

KM#	Date	Year	Mintage	VF	XF	Unc
240	5753	1993	*7,000	—	—	25.00

A Young Hart

KM#	Date	Year	Mintage	VF	XF	Unc
243	5753	1993	*.010	—	—	30.00

3.4600 g, .900 GOLD, .1001 oz AGW

KM#	Date	Year	Mintage	VF	XF	Unc
244	5753	1993	*4,500	—	Proof	110.00

14.4000 g, .925 SILVER, .4282 oz ASW
Revolt and Heroism

KM#	Date	Year	Mintage	VF	XF	Unc
247	5753	1993	*8,000	—	—	20.00

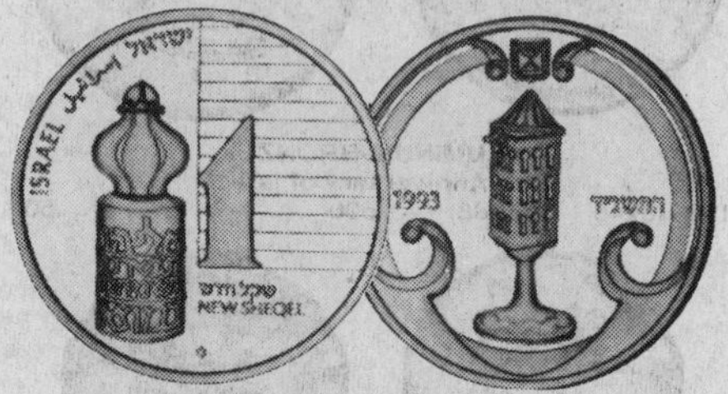

Havdalah Spicebox

KM#	Date	Year	Mintage	VF	XF	Unc
250	5753	1993	*8,000	—	—	20.00

2 NEW SHEQALIM

28.8000 g, .850 SILVER, .7871 oz ASW
Ashkanaz Hanukka Lamp

KM#	Date	Year	Mintage	VF	XF	Unc
162	5746	1985	9,225	—	Proof	30.00

38th Anniversary of Independence Day
Tribute to the Arts

KM#	Date	Year	Mintage	VF	XF	Unc
165	5746	1986	7,344	—	Proof	40.00

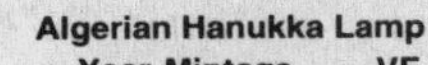

Algerian Hanukka Lamp

KM#	Date	Year	Mintage	VF	XF	Unc
176	5747	1986	8,343	—	Proof	35.00

40th Anniversary of Israel

KM#	Date	Year	Mintage	VF	XF	Unc
186	5748	1988	9,100	—	Proof	35.00

Hanukka - Persian Lamp

KM#	Date	Year	Mintage	VF	XF	Unc
206	5749	1989	6,282	—	Proof	40.00

35th Anniversary - United Jerusalem

KM#	Date	Year	Mintage	VF	XF	Unc
178	5747	1987	7,788	—	Proof	35.00

Hanukka - Tunisian Lamp

KM#	Date	Year	Mintage	VF	XF	Unc
192	5749	1988	7,110	—	Proof	35.00

42nd Anniversary - Archaeology

KM#	Date	Year	Mintage	VF	XF	Unc
213	5750	1990	5,457	—	Proof	45.00

English Hanukka Lamp

KM#	Date	Year	Mintage	VF	XF	Unc
184	5748	1987	8,039	—	Proof	35.00

41st Anniversary of Independence

KM#	Date	Year	Mintage	VF	XF	Unc
200	5749	1989	7,061	—	Proof	35.00

Hanukka - Cochin Lamp

KM#	Date	Year	Mintage	VF	XF	Unc
216	5751	1990	*8,000	—	Proof	35.00

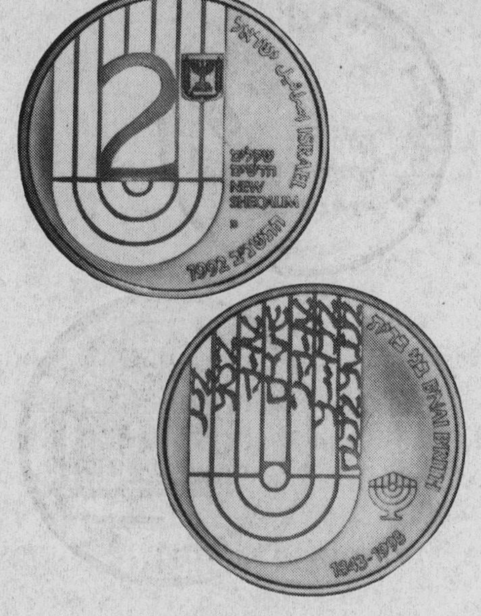

28.8000 g, .925 SILVER, .8565 oz ASW
43rd Anniversary - Immigration to Israel

KM#	Date	Year	Mintage	VF	XF	Unc
219	5751	1991	*.015	—	Proof	30.00

44th Anniversary - Israeli Law

KM#	Date	Year	Mintage	VF	XF	Unc
226	5752	1992	4,486	—	Proof	40.00

B'nai B'rith

KM#	Date	Year	Mintage	VF	XF	Unc
235	5752	1992	*.012	—	Proof	35.00

Flora and Fauna Cedar Trees and Dove

221	5752	1991	5,005	—	Proof	35.00

IX Paralympic Games

228	5752	1992	3,718	—	Proof	42.50

Shabbat Candles

239	5752	1992	*.010	—	Proof	30.00

Hannukka Art - Kiddush Cup

224	5752	1991	*.010	—	Proof	30.00

Wildlife - Roe and Lily

232	5752	1992	*.010	—	Proof	40.00

45th Anniversary and Tourism

241	5753	1993	*7,000	—	Proof	42.50

A Young Hart

KM#	Date	Year	Mintage	VF	XF	Unc
245	5753	1993	*.010	—	Proof	40.00

Revolt and Heroism

KM#	Date	Year	Mintage	VF	XF	Unc
248	5753	1993	*8,000	—	Proof	45.00

Havdalah Spicebox

KM#	Date	Year	Mintage	VF	XF	Unc
251	5753	1993	*8,000	—	Proof	40.00

5 NEW SHEQALIM

8.6300 g, .900 GOLD, .2497 oz AGW
Holyland Sites - Akko
Rev: Similar to 1 New Sheqel, KM#169.

KM#	Date	Year	Mintage	VF	XF	Unc
170	5747	1986	2,800	—	Proof	325.00

Holyland Sites - Jericho

KM#	Date	Year	Mintage	VF	XF	Unc
182	5748	1987	4,000	—	Proof	250.00

Holyland Sites - Caesarea

KM#	Date	Year	Mintage	VF	XF	Unc
190	5749	1988	3,454	—	Proof	300.00

Holyland Sites - Jaffa Harbor

KM#	Date	Year	Mintage	VF	XF	Unc
204	5750	1989	2,402	—	Proof	350.00

COPPER-NICKEL

KM#	Date	Year	Mintage	VF	XF	Unc
207	5750	(1990)	15.000	—	—	3.75
	5751	(1991)	.324	—	—	3.75
	5752	(1992)	—	—	—	3.75

Levi Eshkol

KM#	Date	Year	Mintage	VF	XF	Unc
208	5750	(1990)	1.500	—	—	5.00

8.6300 g, .900 GOLD, .2497 oz AGW
Holyland Sites - Sea of Galilee Map

KM#	Date	Year	Mintage	VF	XF	Unc
211	5751	1990	1,935	—	Proof	550.00

COPPER-NICKEL
Hanukka - Ancient Column

KM#	Date	Year	Mintage	VF	XF	Unc
217	5751	(1990)	.500	—	—	3.75
	5752	(1991)	—	—	—	3.75
	5753	(1992)	.501	—	—	3.75

8.6300 g, .900 GOLD, .2497 oz AGW

Flora and Fauna - Cedar Trees and Dove
Similar to 2 New Sheqalim, KM#221.

KM#	Date	Year	Mintage	VF	XF	Unc
222	5752	1991	2,000	—	Proof	275.00

IX Paralympic Games

KM#	Date	Year	Mintage	VF	XF	Unc
229	5752	1992	1,629	—	Proof	230.00

Wildlife - Roe and Lily

KM#	Date	Year	Mintage	VF	XF	Unc
233	5752	1992	*3,000	—	Proof	225.00

B'nai B'rith
Rev: Similar to 2 New Sheqalim, KM#235.

KM#	Date	Year	Mintage	VF	XF	Unc
236	5752	1992	*5,000	—	Proof	325.00

COPPER-NICKEL
Chaim Weizmann

KM#	Date	Year	Mintage	VF	XF	Unc
237	5752	1992	1.501	—	—	5.00

8.6300 g, .900 GOLD, .2497 oz AGW
A Young Hart

KM#	Date	Year	Mintage	VF	XF	Unc
246	5753	1993	*3,000	—	Proof	280.00

10 NEW SHEQALIM

17.2800 g, .900 GOLD, .5000 oz AGW
38th Independence Day Tribute to the Arts

KM#	Date	Year	Mintage	VF	XF	Unc
166	5746	1986	2,485	—	Proof	625.00

39th Anniversary - United Jerusalem

KM#	Date	Year	Mintage	VF	XF	Unc
179	5747	1987	3,200	—	Proof	460.00

40th Anniversary of Israel

KM#	Date	Year	Mintage	VF	XF	Unc
187	5748	1988	*4,575	—	Proof	300.00

41st Anniversary of Independence
Rev: Gazelle in forest, legend at left.

KM#	Date	Year	Mintage	VF	XF	Unc
201	5749	1989	2,743	—	Proof	450.00

42nd Anniversary - Archaeology

KM#	Date	Year	Mintage	VF	XF	Unc
214	5750	1990	1,815	—	Proof	750.00

43rd Anniversary - Immigration to Israel

KM#	Date	Year	Mintage	VF	XF	Unc
230	5751	1991	*6,000	—	Proof	400.00

44th Anniversary - Israeli Law

KM#	Date	Year	Mintage	VF	XF	Unc
227	5752	1992	2,125	—	Proof	450.00

45th Anniversary and Tourism

KM#	Date	Year	Mintage	VF	XF	Unc
242	5753	1993	*2,750	—	Proof	400.00

Revolt and Heroism
Obv: State emblem, denomination and legend.

KM#	Date	Year	Mintage	VF	XF	Unc
249	5753	1993	*3,000	—	Proof	340.00

MINT SETS (MS)

KM#	Date	Mintage	Identification	Issue Price	Mkt. Val.
MS1	1949(10)	—	KM8-12,13.1,14-15, 15a,16	—	200.00
MS2	1962(16)	4,000	KM12a,13.2a,17-20, 20a,24.1,25-27	18.50	70.00
MS3	1963(18)	7,000	As above w/KM36.1 37 in presentation holder	22.50	50.00

Trade coin sets as above, and six coin sets of 1964 and 1965 often contained circulated and cleaned coins, thus do not qualify as Mint Sets as usually defined.

KM#	Date	Mintage	Identification	Issue Price	Mkt. Val.
MS4	1963(6)	*200	KM24.1,25-26(1962), 27,36.1,37 (white folder)	2.50	150.00

KM#	Date	Mintage	Identification	Issue Price	Mkt. Val.
MS5	1963(6)	2,000	KM24.1,25-27,36.1,37 (plain white card)	2.50	125.00

KM#	Date	Mintage	Identification	Issue Price	Mkt. Val.
MS6	1963(6)	10,000	KM24.1 w/Inv. rev., 25-27, 36.1,37 (card w/map)	2.60	15.00
MS7	1963(6)*	10,544	KM24.1,25-27,36.1,37 (card w/map)	2.60	12.00

NOTE: #S7 was issued in 1964.

KM#	Date	Mintage	Identification	Issue Price	Mkt. Val.
MS8	1965(6)	153,424	KM24.1,25-27,36.1,37	3.50	2.00
MS9	1966(6)	114,714	As above	3.50	2.00
MS10	1967(6)	128,124	As above (card)	3.50	2.00
MS11	1968(6)	184,552	KM24.1,25-27,36.1, 47.1(card)	3.50	2.00
MS12	1969(6)	158,052	As above(card)	3.50	2.00
MS13	1970(6)	60,045	As above, in red wallet	3.75	3.00
MS13a	1970(6)	64,800	As above (card)	3.75	4.00
MS14	1971(6)	32,543	As above, in blue wallet	3.50	4.00
MS14a	1971(6)	**125,921	As above, in pink plastic case	3.00	3.00
MS15	1972(6)	21,486	As above, in violet wallet	3.00	5.00
MS15a	1972(6)	**68,513	As above, in violet plastic case	3.50	3.00
MS16	1973(6)	98,107	KM63-68, in blue plastic case	3.50	4.00

**W/Star of David

NON STANDARD METALS

KM#	Date	Mintage	Identification	Issue Price	Mkt. Val.
MS17	1974(6)	92,868	KM24.1,25a-27a,36.1, 47.1 in brown plastic case	3.50	3.00
MS18	1975(6)	61,686	KM24.1,25a-27a,36.2, 47.2 in brown plastic case	3.50	5.00
MS19	1976(6)	64,654	KM84-89, in green plastic case	3.50	3.00
MS20	1977(6)	37,208	KM24.1,25a-27a,36.2, 47.2	3.50	4.00
MS21	1978(6)	57,200	As above	—	5.00
MS22	1979(7)	31,590	KM24.1,25b-26b,27, 36.1,47.1,90 plastic booklet	1.80	4.00
MS23	1979(7)	—	KM24.2-25c-26c,27b, 36.2,47.2,90a	—	4.00
MS-A24	Mixed date (7)	—	KM24.1,25-27,36.1, 47.1,90	—	4.00
MS24	1980(7)	—	KM24.1,26b,47.1,106 109	3.50	10.00
MS26	1982(7)	30,000	KM106-109,111,118 119	3.50	6.00
MS27	1982(6)	18,735	KM106-109,111,118 piefort	11.00	15.00
MS28	1983(7)	17,177	KM106-109,111,118 119 piefort	11.00	14.00
MS28a	1983(5)	17,478	KM108-109,111,118 119	3.50	4.00
MS29	1984(9)	13,403	KM108-109,111,118 119,134,137,143	4.50	10.00
MS29a	1984(7)	15,572	KM106-109,111,118 119 piefort	10.00	15.00
MS30	1985(8)	15,224	KM111,118-119,139 140,143,146,151	4.50	7.00
MS31	1985(5)	14,768	KM106-109,111,118 139,143 piefort	10.00	15.00
MS32	1985(5)	7,760	KM156-160	10.00	25.00
MS33	1986(5)	12,665	KM156-160, piefort	12.00	25.00
MS34	1986(12) 5746/5747	14,305	KM156-160,163,167, 171-174 mixed dates	9.00	9.00
MS35	1986(5)	—	KM163,171-174	—	3.50
MS36	1987(10) 5747/5748	11,094	KM156-160,163,171 174 mixed dates	10.00	—
MS37	1987(5)	30,000	KM163,171-174	—	3.00
MS38	1987(5)	11,529	KM156-160, piefort	18.00	25.00
MS39	1988(6)	—	KM156-160,198 green holder	6.50	7.50
MS40	1988(4)	12,027	KM194-197, piefort	—	25.00
MS41	1988(5)	15,000—	KM193-197, blue holder	7.50	8.50
MS42	1988(5)	20,000	KM163,171-174	8.00	10.00
MS43	1989(10)	9,716	KM156-160,163,171 174	7.00	10.00
MS44	1989(5)	*15,000	KM156-160, piefort	15.00	20.00
MS45	1989(5)	7,562	KM163,171-174	—	3.00
MS46	1990(6)	12,000	KM156-160,207	8.00	10.00
MS47	1990(6)	*10,000	KM156-160,207, piefort	15.00	20.00
MS48	1990(6)	7,929	KM163,171-174,217	—	8.00
MS49	1991(7)	6,746	KM208(5750),156-160, 207(5751)	—	20.00
MS50	1991(6)	6,617	KM156-160,207, piefort	15.00	17.00
MS51	1991(5)	*6,886	KM163,172-174,217	8.00	8.00
MS52	1992(6)	*8,000	KM156-160,207	15.00	15.00
MS53	Mixed date (7)	*8,000	KM134,147,151,167 198,208,237	15.00	15.00
MS54	1992(5)	*8,000	KM157-160,207	—	10.00
MS55	1992(5)	*8,000	KM163,172-174,217	—	8.00
MS56	1993(6)	—	KM156-160,207, piefort	18.00	18.00

PROOF SETS (PS)

KM#	Date	Mintage	Identification	Issue Price	Mkt. Val.
			olive wood box	385.00	700.00
PS1	1973(3)	17,889	KM72-74,		
PS2	1980(7)	31,348	KM96-102	13.00	15.00
PS3	1981(5)	30,217	KM106-109,111, piefort	10.00	30.00

SPECIAL SELECT SETS (SS)

KM#	Date	Mintage	Identification	Issue Price	Mkt. Val.
SS1	1949(10)	300 est.	KM8-13.1 w/pearl, 14, 15 w/pearl 15 w/o pearl, 16 in two piece heavy plastic case (light blue molded bottom and a clear swivel top)	—	225.00

Listings For

Italian Somaliland: refer to Somalia

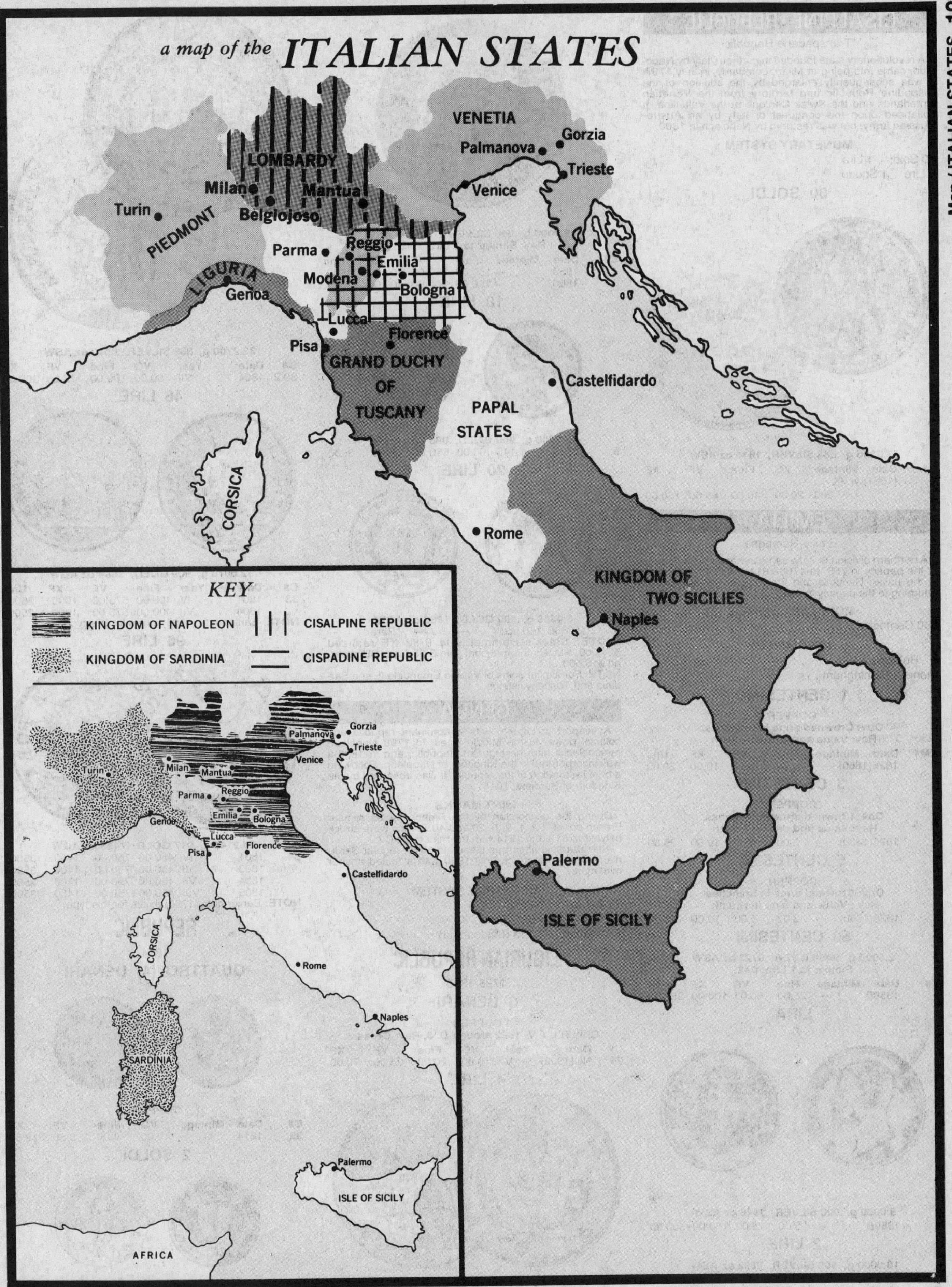
a map of the ITALIAN STATES
VENETIA
Gorzia
Palmanova
Trieste
Venice
LOMBARDY
Milan
Mantua
Belgiojoso
Turin
PIEDMONT
Parma
Reggio
Emilia
Modena
Bologna
LIGURIA
Genoa
Lucca
Florence
Pisa
GRAND DUCHY OF TUSCANY
Castelfidardo
PAPAL STATES
CORSICA
Rome
KINGDOM OF TWO SICILIES
Naples
Palermo
ISLE OF SICILY
KEY
KINGDOM OF NAPOLEON
CISALPINE REPUBLIC
KINGDOM OF SARDINIA
CISPADINE REPUBLIC
Gorzia
Palmanova
Trieste
Turin
Milan
Mantua
Venice
Parma
Reggio
Genoa
Emilia
Bologna
Lucca
Pisa
Florence
Castelfidardo
CORSICA
Rome
Naples
SARDINIA
Palermo
ISLE OF SICILY
AFRICA

ITALIAN STATES

CISALPINE REPUBLIC

Transpadane Republic

A revolutionary state founded in northern Italy by Napoleon, came into being at Milan, Lombardy, in July 1797. It was subsequently enlarged by the addition of the Cispadine Republic and territory from the Venetian hinterlands and the Swiss Cantons of the Valtellina. It collapsed upon the conquest of Italy by an Austro-Russian army, but was restored by Napoleon in 1800.

MONETARY SYSTEM

20 Soldi 1 Lira
6 Lire 1 Scudo

30 SOLDI

7.3300 g, .684 SILVER, .1612 oz ASW

C#	Date	Mintage	VG	Fine	VF	XF
1	(1801) yr. IX	.300	20.00	40.00	65.00	130.00

EMILIA

Emilia-Romagna

A northern division of Italy, came under nominal control of the papacy in 755. In 1796-1814 it was incorporated in the Italian Republic and the Kingdom of Napoleon, returning to the papacy in 1815.

MONETARY SYSTEM

100 Centesimi = 1 Lira

MINT MARKS

B - Bologna
(none) - Birmingham

1 CENTESIMO

COPPER
Obv: Crowned arms in branches.
Rev: Value and date in wreath.

KM#	Date	Mintage	Fine	VF	XF	Unc
1	1826(1860)	—	3.00	5.00	10.00	20.00

3 CENTESIMI

COPPER
Obv: Crowned arms in branches.
Rev: Value and date in wreath.

KM#	Date	Mintage	Fine	VF	XF	Unc
2	1826(1860)	—	3.00	5.00	10.00	25.00

5 CENTESIMI

COPPER
Obv: Crowned arms in branches.
Rev.: Value and date in wreath.

KM#	Date	Mintage	Fine	VF	XF	Unc
3	1826(1860)	—	3.00	5.00	10.00	30.00

50 CENTESIMI

2.5000 g, .900 SILVER, .0723 oz ASW
Similar to 1 Lira, C#2.

C#	Date	Mintage	Fine	VF	XF	Unc
1	1859B	—	25.00	50.00	100.00	250.00

LIRA

5.0000 g, .900 SILVER, .1446 oz ASW

C#	Date	Mintage	Fine	VF	XF	Unc
2	1859B	—	35.00	75.00	150.00	500.00

2 LIRE

10.0000 g, .900 SILVER, .2892 oz ASW
Similar to 1 Lira, C#2.

C#	Date	Mintage	Fine	VF	XF	Unc
3	1859B	—	200.00	350.00	450.00	1100.
	1860B	.013	150.00	250.00	400.00	1100.

5 LIRE

25.0000 g, .900 SILVER, .7320 oz ASW
Rev: Similar to 1 Lira, C#2.

C#	Date	Mintage	Fine	VF	XF	Unc
4	1859	—	150.00	250.00	500.00	2500.
	1860	—	150.00	200.00	400.00	2000.

10 LIRE

3.2200 g, .900 GOLD, .0931 oz AGW

C#	Date	Mintage	Fine	VF	XF	Unc
5	1860B	1,145	400.00	850.00	2000.	3600.

20 LIRE

6.4500 g, .900 GOLD, .1866 oz AGW

C#	Date	Mintage	Fine	VF	XF	Unc
6	1860B	150 pcs.	—	—	*Rare	—

***NOTE:** Stack's Hammel sale 9-82 XF realized $24,000. Stack's International sale 3-88 Gem BU realized $16,500.

NOTE: For similar coins of Vittorio Emanuele II, see Sardinia and Tuscany listings.

GENOA

A seaport in Liguria, was a dominant republic and colonial power in the Middle Ages. In 1798 Napoleon remodeled it into the Ligurian Republic, and in 1805 it was incorporated in the Kingdom of Napoleon. Following a brief restoration of the republic, it was absorbed by the Kingdom of Sardinia, 1815.

MINT MARKS

During the occupation by the French forces regular French coins, 1/2, 1, 2, 5, 20 and 40 Francs were struck between 1813 and 1814 with the mint mark C.L.

After Sardinia absorbed Genoa in 1815, regular Sardinian coins were struck until 1860 with a fouled anchor mint mark.

MONETARY SYSTEM

12 Denari 1 Soldo
20 Soldi 10 Parpagliola
5 Cavallotti 1 Lira (Madonnina)

LIGURIAN REPUBLIC

1798-1805

3 DENARI

COPPER
Obv: R.L.A.V. 1802 around D. 3, Rev: Cross.

C#	Date	Year	VG	Fine	VF	XF
25	ND(1802)	V	10.00	20.00	35.00	70.00

4 LIRE

16.6400 g, .889 SILVER, .4756 oz ASW

C#	Date	Year	VG	Fine	VF	XF
29	1804	VII	25.00	50.00	100.00	200.00

NOTE: Earlier dates (1798-1799) exist for this type.

8 LIRE

33.2700 g, .889 SILVER, .9510 oz ASW

C#	Date	Year	VG	Fine	VF	XF
30.2	1804	VII	60.00	100.00	175.00	300.00

48 LIRE

12.6070 g, .909 GOLD, .3684 oz AGW

C#	Date	Year	Fine	VF	XF	Unc
33	1801	IV	400.00	575.00	1000.	2500.
	1804	VII	400.00	575.00	1000.	2500.

NOTE: Earlier date (1798) exists for this type.

96 LIRE

25.2140 g, .917 GOLD, .7435 oz AGW

C#	Date	Year	Fine	VF	XF	Unc
34	1801	IV	450.00	750.00	1400.	3500.
	1803	VI	450.00	750.00	1400.	3500.
	1804	VII	450.00	750.00	1400.	3500.
	1805	VIII	450.00	750.00	1400.	3500.

NOTE: Earlier date (1798) exists for this type.

REPUBLIC

1814

QUATTRO (4) DENARI

COPPER

C#	Date	Mintage	VG	Fine	VF	XF
35	1814	—	2.00	4.00	6.50	12.50

2 SOLDI

BILLON
Rev. leg: . . . . .PRESIDIUM.

C#	Date	Mintage	VG	Fine	VF	XF
36.1	1814	—	2.50	5.50	9.00	20.00

Rev. leg: . . . . .PRAESIDIUM.

C#	Date	Mintage	VG	Fine	VF	XF
36.2	1814	—	2.50	5.50	9.00	20.00

4 SOLDI

BILLON

C#	Date	Mintage	VG	Fine	VF	XF
37	1814	—	4.00	8.00	12.00	22.50

10 SOLDI

2.1000 g, .889 SILVER, .0600 oz ASW
Obv: Crowned shield, leg: GENUENSIS.
Rev: John The Baptist standing.

C#	Date	Mintage	VG	Fine	VF	XF
38	1814	—	4.00	10.00	14.00	25.00

Obv. leg: JANUENSIS

C#	Date	Mintage	VG	Fine	VF	XF
38a	1814	—	4.00	10.00	14.00	25.00

GORIZIA

Goricia, Gorz

A city in Venetia, passed to Maximilian I of Austria in 1500, and became the holding of Charles, son of Austrian emperor Ferdinand I in 1564.

RULERS

Franz II (Austria) 1792-1835

MINT MARKS

A, W - Wien - Vienna
F, H, HA - Hall
G - Graz
G - Nagybanya
H - Gunzburg
K - Kremnitz
O - Oravitza
S - Schmollnitz

MONETARY SYSTEM

20 Soldi = 1 Lira

SOLDO

COPPER
Mint mark: F
Obv: Crowned arms. Rev: Value, date.

C#	Date	Mintage	VG	Fine	VF	XF
8.1	1801	—	—	—	Rare	—

NOTE: Earlier dates (1792-1800) exist for this type.

Mint mark: H

C#	Date	Mintage	VG	Fine	VF	XF
8.4	1801	—	3.00	6.00	12.50	30.00
	1802	—	—	—	Rare	—

NOTE: Earlier dates (1798-1800) exist for this type.

2 SOLDI

COPPER
Mint mark: F
Obv: Crowned arms. Rev: Value, date.

C#	Date	Mintage	VG	Fine	VF	XF
9.2	1801	—	—	—	Rare	—

NOTE: Earlier date (1799) exists for this type.

Mint mark: H

C#	Date	Mintage	VG	Fine	VF	XF
9.3	1801	—	2.50	5.00	10.00	25.00
	1802	—	2.50	5.00	10.00	25.00

NOTE: Earlier date (1799) exists for this type.

15 SOLDI

(8-1/2 Kreuzer)

BILLON
Mint mark: A

C#	Date	Mintage	VG	Fine	VF	XF
10.1	1802	—	5.00	10.00	20.00	50.00

Mint mark: F

C#	Date	Mintage	VG	Fine	VF	XF
10.2	1802	—	5.00	10.00	20.00	40.00

Mint mark: H

C#	Date	Mintage	VG	Fine	VF	XF
10.3	1802	—	7.50	15.00	35.00	75.00

KINGDOM OF NAPOLEON

Came into being shortly after the first French empire was proclaimed on May 18, 1804; Napoleon's Italian coronation took place at Naples on May 26, 1805.

French rule

RULERS

Napoleon I,1804-1814

MINT MARKS

B - Bologna
M - Milan
V - Venice

MONETARY SYSTEM

100 Centesimi 20 Soldi
20 Soldi 1 Lira

CENTESIMO

COPPER
Mint mark: B

C#	Date	Mintage	VG	Fine	VF	XF
1.1	1807	.092	2.00	4.00	7.50	15.00
	1808	2.270	2.00	4.00	7.50	15.00
	1809	4.413	2.00	4.00	7.50	15.00
	1810	3.813	2.00	4.00	7.50	15.00
	1811	1.335	2.00	4.00	7.50	15.00
	1812	4.813	2.00	4.00	7.50	15.00

Mint mark: M

C#	Date	Mintage	VG	Fine	VF	XF
1.2	1807	.097	3.75	7.50	12.50	30.00
	1808	3.372	2.00	4.00	7.50	15.00
	1808 (error) IMPERAPORE					
		.020	6.50	12.50	20.00	42.50
	1809	2.244	2.00	4.00	7.50	15.00
	1810/09	2.244	2.50	5.00	10.00	25.00
	1810	Inc. Ab.	2.00	4.00	7.50	15.00
	1811	1.944	2.00	4.00	7.50	15.00
	1812	2.744	2.00	4.00	7.50	15.00
	1813	3.724	2.00	4.00	7.50	15.00

NOTE: Varieties exist.

Mint mark: V

C#	Date	Mintage	VG	Fine	VF	XF
1.3	1807	.124	3.75	7.50	12.50	27.50
	1808V/M	.347	3.75	7.50	12.50	27.50
	1808	Inc. Ab.	3.75	7.50	12.50	27.50
	1809	3.017	3.00	6.00	7.50	15.00
	1810	.267	3.75	7.50	12.50	25.00
	1811	7.873	2.00	4.00	7.50	15.00
	1812	1.424	2.00	4.00	7.50	15.00
	1813	4.424	2.00	4.00	7.50	15.00

NOTE: Varieties exist.

3 CENTESIMI

COPPER
Mint mark: B

C#	Date	Mintage	VG	Fine	VF	XF
2.1	1807	.063	3.00	8.00	15.00	25.00
	1808	.215	2.00	4.00	7.50	15.00
	1810/9	1.845	4.00	8.00	15.00	30.00
	1810	Inc. Ab.	2.00	4.00	7.50	15.00
	1813/08	.845	2.50	5.00	10.00	20.00
	1813	Inc. Ab.	2.00	4.00	7.50	15.00

Mint mark: M

C#	Date	Mintage	VG	Fine	VF	XF
2.2	1807	.212	2.00	4.00	7.50	15.00
	1808	1.878	2.00	4.00	7.50	15.00
	1809	2.098	2.00	4.00	7.50	15.00
	1810/09	2.798	2.50	5.00	10.00	17.50
	1810	Inc. Ab.	2.00	4.00	7.50	15.00
	1811	2.798	2.00	4.00	7.50	15.00
	1812	3.012	2.00	4.00	7.50	15.00
	1813	2.598	2.00	4.00	7.50	15.00

NOTE: Varieties exist.

Mint mark: V

C#	Date	Mintage	VG	Fine	VF	XF
2.3	1807	.117	7.50	12.50	20.00	30.00
	1808	.527	2.00	4.00	8.00	16.00
	1809	.127	2.00	4.00	8.00	16.00
	1810/00	—	2.50	5.00	10.00	20.00
	1810	—	2.00	4.00	8.00	16.00

SOLDO

COPPER
Mint mark: B

C#	Date	Mintage	VG	Fine	VF	XF
3.1	1807	.345	5.00	10.00	20.00	35.00
	1808	.300	2.00	4.00	7.50	15.00
	1809	1.340	2.00	4.00	7.50	15.00

Mint mark: M

C#	Date	Mintage	VG	Fine	VF	XF
3.2	1807	.105	2.50	6.00	12.50	20.00
	1808	1.454	2.00	4.00	7.50	15.00
	1809	1.350	2.00	4.00	7.50	15.00
	1810	1.450	2.00	4.00	7.50	15.00
	1811	2.390	2.00	4.00	7.50	15.00
	1812	2.260	2.00	4.00	7.50	15.00
	1813	2.897	2.00	4.00	7.50	15.00

NOTE: Varieties exist.

Mint mark: V

C#	Date	Mintage	VG	Fine	VF	XF
3.3	1807	.265	2.50	5.00	15.00	35.00
	1808	.300	2.50	5.00	10.00	20.00
	1812	1.196	2.50	5.00	15.00	25.00

10 CENTESIMI

2.0000 g, .200 SILVER, .0128 oz ASW
Mint mark: M

C#	Date	Mintage	VG	Fine	VF	XF
4	1808	.012	8.50	17.50	27.50	60.00
	1809	.875	2.00	4.00	7.50	15.00
	1810	.760	2.00	4.00	7.50	15.00
	1811	1.540	2.00	4.00	7.50	15.00
	1812	.740	2.00	4.00	7.50	15.00
	1813	2.670	2.00	4.00	7.50	15.00

5 SOLDI

1.2500 g, .900 SILVER, .0361 oz ASW
Mint mark: M

C#	Date	Mintage	VG	Fine	VF	XF
5.1	1808 stars in relief on edge					
		.130	12.50	25.00	55.00	80.00
	1808 stars incuse on edge					
		Inc. Ab.	4.00	6.00	10.00	20.00
	1809	.600	4.00	6.00	10.00	20.00
	1810	1.050	4.00	6.00	10.00	20.00
	1811/0	3.000	4.50	7.00	13.00	25.00
	1811	Inc. Ab.	4.00	6.00	10.00	20.00
	1812	1.700	4.00	6.00	10.00	20.00
	1813	2.800	4.00	6.00	10.00	20.00
	1814	.700	4.00	6.00	10.00	20.00
	1814 (error) IMPERARORE					
		Inc. Ab.	15.00	30.00	45.00	80.00

NOTE: Varieties exist.

Mint mark: V

C#	Date	Mintage	VG	Fine	VF	XF
5.2	1812	.110	5.00	10.00	20.00	40.00

NOTE: Varieties exist.

Mint mark: B

C#	Date	Mintage	VG	Fine	VF	XF
5.3	1812	.330	4.50	7.00	11.00	22.50
	1812B/M	.390	4.50	7.00	11.00	22.50
	1813	2.800	4.00	6.50	10.00	20.00
	1813B/M	.320	4.50	7.00	11.00	22.50

10 SOLDI

2.5000 g, .900 SILVER, .0722 oz ASW
Mint mark: M

C#	Date	Mintage	VG	Fine	VF	XF
6.1	1808 stars in relief on edge					
		.175	8.50	17.50	35.00	70.00
	1808 stars incuse on edge					
		Inc. Ab.	4.50	6.50	10.00	20.00
	1809	.430	4.50	6.50	10.00	20.00
	1810	.550	4.50	6.50	10.00	20.00
	1811	2.050	4.50	6.50	10.00	20.00
	1812	.600	4.50	6.50	10.00	20.00
	1813	.490	4.50	6.50	10.00	20.00
	1814	.450	4.50	6.50	10.00	20.00

Mint mark: V

C#	Date	Mintage	VG	Fine	VF	XF
6.2	1811	.310	10.00	15.00	25.00	50.00
	1812	.160	4.50	7.00	12.50	25.00
	1813	.332	4.50	6.50	10.00	20.00

NOTE: Varieties exist.

Mint mark: B

C#	Date	Mintage	VG	Fine	VF	XF
6.3	1812	.018	5.00	10.00	15.00	30.00
	1812B/M	.015	5.00	10.00	15.00	30.00
	1813	.350	4.00	6.00	10.00	20.00

15 SOLDI

3.7500 g, .900 SILVER, .1083 oz ASW
Mint mark: M

C#	Date	Mintage	VG	Fine	VF	XF
7	1808	.038	22.50	40.00	65.00	140.00
	1809	.015	22.50	50.00	100.00	200.00
	1810	9,000	45.00	80.00	200.00	400.00
	1814	370 pcs.	45.00	80.00	150.00	325.00

LIRA

5.0000 g, .900 SILVER, .1444 oz ASW
Mint mark: M

C#	Date	Mintage	VG	Fine	VF	XF
8.1	1808 stars in relief on edge					
		.495	10.00	20.00	30.00	70.00
	1808 stars incuse on edge					
		Inc. Ab.	10.00	20.00	30.00	70.00
	1809	.025	5.00	10.00	20.00	40.00
	1810	.495	5.00	10.00	20.00	40.00
	1810 (error) NATOLEON					
		Inc. Ab.	20.00	45.00	70.00	150.00
	1811	1.185	5.00	10.00	20.00	40.00
	1811/08	I.A.	25.00	50.00	85.00	175.00
	1812	.340	5.00	10.00	20.00	40.00
	1813	.230	5.00	10.00	20.00	40.00
	1814	.275	5.00	10.00	20.00	40.00
	1814M/V	I.A.	10.00	25.00	50.00	100.00

Mint mark: B

C#	Date	Mintage	VG	Fine	VF	XF
8.2	1808	.103	6.50	11.50	27.50	55.00
	1810 stars in relief on edge					
		.336	6.50	11.50	27.50	55.00
	1810 stars incuse on edge					
		.310	6.50	11.50	27.50	55.00
	1811	.310	6.50	11.50	27.50	55.00
	1812	.310	6.50	11.50	27.50	55.00
	1813	.220	6.50	11.50	27.50	55.00

Mint mark: V

C#	Date	Mintage	VG	Fine	VF	XF
8.3	1811	.045	13.50	22.50	35.00	70.00
	1812	.090	13.50	22.50	35.00	70.00
	1813	.310	12.50	20.00	32.50	65.00

NOTE: Varieties exist.

2 LIRE

10.0000 g, .900 SILVER, .2888 oz ASW
Mint mark: M

C#	Date	Mintage	VG	Fine	VF	XF
9.1	1807	.010	20.00	40.00	125.00	250.00
	1808 edge inscription in relief					
		—	125.00	250.00	300.00	450.00
	1808 edge inscription incuse					
		.311	17.50	35.00	70.00	125.00
	1809	.332	15.00	30.00	50.00	90.00
	1810	.370	15.00	30.00	50.00	90.00
	1811	.513	15.00	30.00	50.00	90.00
	1812	.334	15.00	30.00	50.00	90.00
	1813	.223	15.00	30.00	50.00	90.00
	1814	3,100	35.00	60.00	75.00	150.00

NOTE: Varieties exist.

Mint mark: B

C#	Date	Mintage	VG	Fine	VF	XF
9.2	1808	2,200	25.00	50.00	200.00	400.00
	1812	.044	10.00	15.00	35.00	60.00
	1813	.348	10.00	15.00	30.00	55.00

Mint mark: V

C#	Date	Mintage	VG	Fine	VF	XF
9.3	1811	.010	15.00	30.00	60.00	125.00
	1812	.239	10.00	20.00	40.00	80.00
	1813	.213	10.00	20.00	40.00	80.00

NOTE: Varieties exist.

5 LIRE

25.0000 g, .900 SILVER, .7234 oz ASW
Mint mark: M
DIO PROTEGGE L'ITALIA on edge in relief

C#	Date	Mintage	VG	Fine	VF	XF
10.1	1807	.039	50.00	75.00	150.00	350.00
	1808	3.278	25.00	40.00	60.00	140.00
	1809	2.480	30.00	50.00	80.00	165.00
	1810	.263	35.00	60.00	100.00	200.00

NOTE: Varieties exist.

Mint mark: V

C#	Date	Mintage	VG	Fine	VF	XF
10.2	1807	610 pcs.	—	—	Rare	—
	1808	204 pcs.	—	—	Rare	—

Mint mark: B

C#	Date	Mintage	VG	Fine	VF	XF
10.3	1808	.023	30.00	50.00	80.00	165.00
	1809	.221	25.00	40.00	65.00	100.00
	1810	.317	25.00	40.00	65.00	100.00
	1811	—	22.50	35.00	60.00	100.00

Mint mark: M
Edge inscription incuse.

C#	Date	Mintage	VG	Fine	VF	XF
10.4	1809	—	27.50	40.00	80.00	165.00
	1810	—	27.50	40.00	80.00	165.00
	1811	—	27.50	40.00	80.00	165.00
	1812	1.848	27.50	40.00	80.00	165.00
	1813	.772	27.50	40.00	80.00	165.00
	1814	.102	35.00	75.00	150.00	300.00

NOTE: Varieties exist.

Mint mark: B

C#	Date	Mintage	VG	Fine	VF	XF
10.5	1810	—	22.50	35.00	50.00	125.00

Mint mark: V

C#	Date	Mintage	VG	Fine	VF	XF
10.6	1810	—	—	—	—	—
	1811	.367	35.00	65.00	125.00	300.00
	1812	.207	27.50	40.00	80.00	165.00
	1813	.071	30.00	60.00	100.00	225.00

NOTE: Varieties exist.

Mint mark: M
Letters in legend smaller, edge inscription incuse.

C#	Date	Mintage	VG	Fine	VF	XF
10.7	1808	—	27.50	40.00	80.00	165.00
	1811	2.820	27.50	40.00	80.00	165.00

Mint mark: V

C#	Date	Mintage	VG	Fine	VF	XF
10.8	1810	.014	27.50	40.00	80.00	165.00

Mint mark: B

C#	Date	Mintage	VG	Fine	VF	XF
10.9	1811	.451	22.50	35.00	50.00	125.00
	1812	.210	22.50	35.00	50.00	125.00
	1813	.110	22.50	35.00	50.00	125.00

20 LIRE

6.4510 g, .900 GOLD, .1866 oz AGW
Mint mark: M

C#	Date	Mintage	VG	Fine	VF	XF
11	1808	.087	100.00	125.00	150.00	375.00
	1809	.053	100.00	125.00	150.00	375.00
	1810	.114	100.00	125.00	150.00	325.00
	1811	.055	100.00	125.00	150.00	325.00
	1812	.045	100.00	125.00	150.00	325.00
	1813	.039	100.00	125.00	150.00	300.00
	1814	.057	100.00	125.00	150.00	300.00

40 LIRE

12.9030 g, .900 GOLD, .3733 oz AGW
Mint mark: M

C#	Date	Mintage	VG	Fine	VF	XF
12	1807	3,430	250.00	350.00	500.00	800.00
	1808 w/o mint mark					
		.352	175.00	200.00	225.00	300.00
	1808 edge inscription in relief					
		Inc. Ab.	175.00	200.00	225.00	300.00
	1808 edge inscription incuse					
		.213	175.00	200.00	225.00	300.00
	1809	.038	175.00	200.00	250.00	450.00
	1810	.158	175.00	200.00	225.00	300.00
	1811	.106	175.00	200.00	225.00	300.00
	1812	.056	175.00	200.00	225.00	400.00
	1813	.041	175.00	200.00	250.00	450.00
	1814	.264	175.00	200.00	225.00	300.00

NOTE: Varieties exist.

LOMBARDY - VENETIA

Comprised the northern Italian duchies of Milan and Mantua and the Venetian Republic which were absorbed by the Kingdom of Napoleon in 1805. After Napoleon's fall they were awarded to Austria and incorporated in the Hapsburg monarchy as the Kingdom of Lombardy-Venetia.

The Lombard campaign of 1859 restored rule under the Kingdom of Italy for Lombard in 1859 and Venetia in 1866.

RULERS

French, until 1814
Austrian, until 1859 and 1866
Italian, until 1946

MINT MARKS

A, W - Vienna
B - Kremnitz
M - Milan
S - Schmollnitz
V - Venice

MONETARY SYSTEM

(Until 1857)

100 Centesimi   20 Soldi   1 Lira
6 Lire   1 Scudo
14 Lire   1 Ducato
40 Lire   1 Sovrano

AUSTRIAN ADMINISTRATION

CENTESIMO

COPPER
Mint mark: A

C#	Date	Mintage	Fine	VF	XF	Unc
1.1	1822	—	—	—	—	250.00

Mint mark: M

C#	Date	Mintage	Fine	VF	XF	Unc
1.2	1822	—	3.00	5.00	10.00	30.00
	1834	—	3.00	5.00	8.00	25.00

NOTE: Varieties exist.

Mint mark: V

C#	Date	Mintage	Fine	VF	XF	Unc
1.3	1822	—	3.00	5.00	10.00	30.00
	1834	—	3.00	5.00	8.00	25.00

NOTE: Varieties exist.

Mint mark: M

C#	Date	Mintage	Fine	VF	XF	Unc
12.1	1839	—	3.00	5.00	8.00	25.00
	1843	—	5.00	8.00	12.00	35.00
	1846	—	3.00	5.00	8.00	25.00

Mint mark: V

C#	Date	Mintage	Fine	VF	XF	Unc
12.2	1839	—	3.00	5.00	8.00	25.00
	1843	—	3.00	5.00	8.00	25.00
	1846	—	3.00	5.00	8.00	25.00

Mint mark: M

C#	Date	Mintage	Fine	VF	XF	Unc
25	1849	—	5.00	8.00	12.00	28.00
	1850	—	5.00	8.00	12.00	28.00
	1852	—	5.00	8.00	12.00	28.00

C#	Date	Mintage	Fine	VF	XF	Unc
29.1	1852	—	7.00	10.00	15.00	30.00
	Mint mark: V					
29.2	1852	—	3.00	5.00	8.00	22.50

5/10 SOLDO

COPPER

C#	Date	Mintage	Fine	VF	XF	Unc
	Mint mark: A					
34.1	1862	12.495	2.00	3.50	6.00	15.00
	Mint mark: B					
34.2	1862	5.970	3.50	6.00	10.00	20.00
	Mint mark: V					
34.3	1862	1.915	3.50	6.00	12.00	25.00

3 CENTESIMI

COPPER

C#	Date	Mintage	Fine	VF	XF	Unc
	Mint mark: A					
2.1	1822	—	—	—	Rare	—
	Mint mark: M					
2.2	1822	—	4.00	6.00	12.00	30.00
	1834	—	6.00	10.00	18.00	40.00

NOTE: Varieties exist.

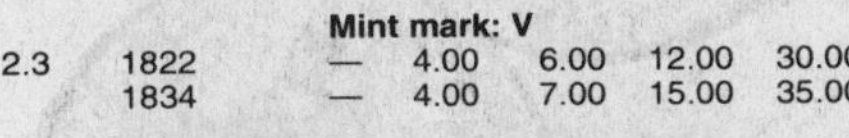

C#	Date	Mintage	Fine	VF	XF	Unc
	Mint mark: V					
2.3	1822	—	4.00	6.00	12.00	30.00
	1834	—	4.00	7.00	15.00	35.00

C#	Date	Mintage	Fine	VF	XF	Unc
	Mint mark: M					
13.1	1839	—	4.00	7.00	13.00	30.00
	1843	—	5.00	8.00	15.00	35.00
	1846	—	3.00	5.00	10.00	22.50
	Mint mark: V					
13.2	1839	—	3.00	5.00	10.00	22.50
	1843	—	3.00	5.00	10.00	22.50
	1846	—	3.00	5.00	10.00	22.50

C#	Date	Mintage	Fine	VF	XF	Unc
	Mint mark: M					
26	1849	—	3.50	6.00	12.00	25.00
	1850	—	3.50	6.00	12.00	25.00
	1852	—	3.50	6.00	12.00	25.00

C#	Date	Mintage	Fine	VF	XF	Unc
30.1	1852	—	3.00	5.00	10.00	20.00
	Mint mark: V					
30.2	1852	—	3.00	6.00	12.00	25.00

5 CENTESIMI

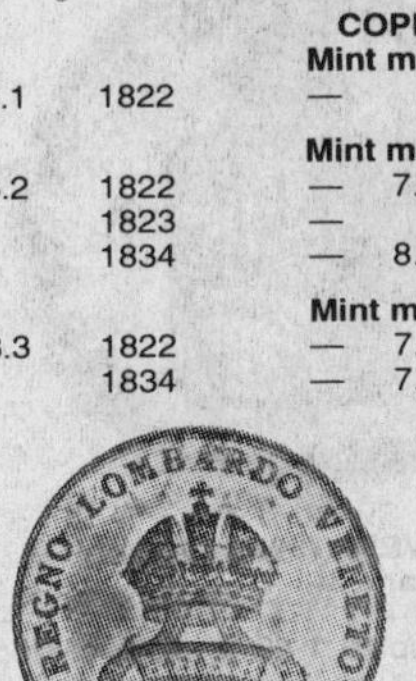

COPPER

C#	Date	Mintage	Fine	VF	XF	Unc
	Mint mark: A					
3.1	1822	—		—	Rare	—
	Mint mark: M					
3.2	1822	—	7.00	12.00	25.00	60.00
	1823	—	— Reported, not confirmed			
	1834	—	8.00	14.00	27.50	65.00
	Mint mark: V					
3.3	1822	—	7.00	12.00	25.00	60.00
	1834	—	7.00	12.00	25.00	60.00

C#	Date	Mintage	Fine	VF	XF	Unc
	Mint mark: M					
14.1	1839	—	6.00	10.00	17.50	40.00
	1843	—	5.00	8.00	15.00	35.00
	1846	—	5.00	8.00	15.00	35.00
	Mint mark: V					
14.2	1839	—	6.00	10.00	20.00	50.00
	1843	—	10.00	20.00	60.00	150.00
	1846	—	5.00	8.00	15.00	35.00

C#	Date	Mintage	Fine	VF	XF	Unc
	Mint mark: M					
27	1849	—	5.00	8.00	15.00	27.50
	1850	—	5.00	8.00	15.00	27.50

C#	Date	Mintage	Fine	VF	XF	Unc
31.1	1852	—	5.00	8.00	15.00	27.50
	Mint mark: V					
31.2	1852	—	4.00	7.00	12.00	25.00

SOLDO

COPPER

C#	Date	Mintage	Fine	VF	XF	Unc
	Mint mark: A					
35.1	1862	22.275	1.50	3.00	5.00	10.00
	Mint mark: B					
35.2	1862	8.971	2.00	3.00	6.00	12.00
	Mint mark: V					
35.3	1862	9.395	2.50	4.00	10.00	20.00

10 CENTESIMI

COPPER

Mint mark: M

Similar to 5 Centesimi, C#3.

C#	Date	Mintage	Fine	VF	XF	Unc
28	1849	—	30.00	40.00	80.00	250.00

C#	Date	Mintage	Fine	VF	XF	Unc
	Mint mark: V					
32	1852	—	8.00	15.00	30.00	75.00

15 CENTESIMI

COPPER

Similar to 10 Centesimi, C#32.

C#	Date	Mintage	Fine	VF	XF	Unc
	Mint mark: V					
33	1852	—	50.00	80.00	200.00	450.00

1/4 LIRA

1.6200 g, .600 SILVER, .0312 oz ASW

C#	Date	Mintage	Fine	VF	XF	Unc
	Mint mark: A					
4.1	1822	—	35.00	50.00	85.00	220.00
	1823	—	150.00	250.00	350.00	800.00
	Mint mark: M					
4.2	1822	—	15.00	25.00	40.00	120.00
	1823/2	—	15.00	25.00	40.00	120.00
	1823	—	15.00	25.00	40.00	120.00
	1824	—	15.00	25.00	40.00	120.00
	Mint mark: V					
4.3	1822	—	15.00	25.00	40.00	120.00
	1823	—	15.00	25.00	40.00	120.00
	1824	—	15.00	25.00	40.00	120.00
	Mint mark: A					
15.1	1835	—	— Reported, not confirmed			
	1837	—	— Reported, not confirmed			
	Mint mark: V					
15.2	1837	—	75.00	100.00	150.00	250.00
	1838	—	75.00	100.00	150.00	300.00
	1839	—	75.00	100.00	150.00	300.00
	1840	—	75.00	100.00	150.00	300.00
	1841	—	75.00	100.00	150.00	300.00
	1842	—	75.00	100.00	150.00	250.00
	1843	—	75.00	100.00	150.00	300.00
	1844	—	75.00	100.00	150.00	300.00
	Obv: Bust of Franz I. Rev: Arms.					
4a	1843	—	— Reported, not confirmed			

1/2 LIRA

2.1650 g, .900 SILVER, .0626 oz ASW

C#	Date	Mintage	Fine	VF	XF	Unc
	Mint mark: A					
5.1	1822	—	60.00	125.00	250.00	375.00
	1823	—	50.00	100.00	200.00	325.00
	1835	—	— Reported, not confirmed			
	Mint mark: M					
5.2	1822	—	12.50	20.00	40.00	100.00
	1823	—	12.50	20.00	40.00	100.00
	1824/2	—	12.50	20.00	40.00	100.00
	1824	—	12.50	20.00	40.00	100.00
	Mint mark: V					
5.3	1821	—	— Reported, not confirmed			
	1822	—	10.00	25.00	40.00	100.00
	1823/2	—	10.00	25.00	40.00	100.00
	1823	—	10.00	25.00	40.00	100.00
	1824	—	— Reported, not confirmed			
	Mint mark: A					
16.1	1835	—	— Reported, not confirmed			
	1837	—	— Reported, not confirmed			
	Mint mark: V					
16.2	1837	—	35.00	65.00	125.00	250.00
	1838	—	35.00	65.00	125.00	250.00
	1839	—	50.00	80.00	175.00	350.00
	1840	—	50.00	80.00	175.00	350.00
	1841	—	50.00	80.00	175.00	350.00
	1842	—	50.00	80.00	175.00	350.00
	1843	—	50.00	80.00	175.00	350.00
	1844	—	50.00	80.00	175.00	350.00
36	1854	—	30.00	50.00	100.00	200.00
	1855	—	35.00	75.00	150.00	300.00

LIRA

4.3300 g, .900 SILVER, .1253 oz ASW
Mint mark: A

C#	Date	Mintage	Fine	VF	XF	Unc
6.1	1822	—	75.00	150.00	250.00	550.00
	1823	—	25.00	50.00	100.00	250.00
	1835	—	—	Reported, not confirmed		

Mint mark: M

C#	Date	Mintage	Fine	VF	XF	Unc
6.2	1822	—	20.00	40.00	80.00	200.00
	1823	—	20.00	40.00	80.00	200.00
	1824/3	—	20.00	40.00	80.00	200.00
	1824	—	20.00	40.00	80.00	200.00
	1825	—	20.00	50.00	90.00	220.00

Mint mark: V

C#	Date	Mintage	Fine	VF	XF	Unc
6.3	1822	—	20.00	40.00	80.00	200.00
	1823	—	25.00	50.00	100.00	250.00

Mint mark: A

C#	Date	Mintage	Fine	VF	XF	Unc
17.1	1835	—	—	Reported, not confirmed		
	1837	—	—	Reported, not confirmed		

Mint mark: V

C#	Date	Mintage	Fine	VF	XF	Unc
17.2	1837	—	50.00	80.00	175.00	375.00
	1838	—	50.00	80.00	175.00	400.00
	1839	—	50.00	80.00	200.00	400.00
	1840	—	50.00	80.00	200.00	450.00
	1841	—	50.00	80.00	200.00	450.00
	1842	—	50.00	80.00	200.00	450.00
	1843	—	50.00	80.00	200.00	450.00
	1844	—	50.00	80.00	200.00	450.00
37.1	1852	—	40.00	65.00	125.00	250.00

Mint mark: M

C#	Date	Mintage	Fine	VF	XF	Unc
37.2	1853	—	40.00	65.00	150.00	300.00
	1854	—	50.00	80.00	175.00	400.00
	1855	—	60.00	90.00	225.00	500.00
	1856	—	50.00	80.00	175.00	400.00
	1858	—	75.00	150.00	325.00	700.00

1/2 SCUDO

12.3450 g, .900 SILVER, .3527 oz ASW
Mint mark: A

C#	Date	Mintage	Fine	VF	XF	Unc
7.1	1822	—	35.00	65.00	125.00	350.00
	1823	—	30.00	55.00	110.00	225.00
	1825	—	—	Reported, not confirmed		
	1835	—	—	Reported, not confirmed		

Mint mark: M

C#	Date	Mintage	Fine	VF	XF	Unc
7.2	1822	—	30.00	55.00	100.00	180.00
	1823	—	30.00	55.00	110.00	225.00
	1824	—	30.00	55.00	100.00	200.00
	1825	—	—	—	Rare	—
	1827	—	—	—	Rare	—

Mint mark: V

C#	Date	Mintage	Fine	VF	XF	Unc
7.3	1822	—	25.00	35.00	60.00	150.00
	1823	—	60.00	90.00	150.00	400.00
	1824	—	25.00	35.00	65.00	160.00
	1825	—	25.00	35.00	65.00	160.00
	1827	—	30.00	55.00	100.00	200.00

Mint mark: A

C#	Date	Mintage	Fine	VF	XF	Unc
18.1	1835	—	—	Reported, not confirmed		
	1837	—	—	Reported, not confirmed		

Mint mark: V

C#	Date	Mintage	Fine	VF	XF	Unc
18.2	1837	—	75.00	125.00	250.00	500.00
18.2	1838	—	75.00	125.00	250.00	500.00
	1839	—	75.00	125.00	250.00	500.00
	1840	—	75.00	125.00	250.00	500.00
	1841	—	75.00	125.00	250.00	500.00
	1842	—	75.00	125.00	250.00	500.00
	1843	—	75.00	125.00	250.00	500.00
	1844	—	75.00	125.00	250.00	500.00
	1845	—	75.00	125.00	250.00	500.00
	1846	—	75.00	125.00	250.00	500.00

W/o value

C#	Date	Mintage	Fine	VF	XF	Unc
38	1853	—	150.00	200.00	300.00	800.00

6 LIRE

26.0000 g, .900 SILVER, .7524 oz ASW
Mint mark: M

C#	Date	Mintage	Fine	VF	XF	Unc
A1	1816	—	—	—	*Rare	—

***NOTE:** Swiss Bank sale No.19 1-88 XF-FDCrealized $10,500.

SCUDO

C#	Date	Mintage	Fine	VF	XF	Unc
8.1	1822	—	25.00	45.00	100.00	250.00
	1823	—	35.00	65.00	125.00	275.00
	1824	—	35.00	65.00	135.00	325.00
	1825	—	30.00	50.00	125.00	325.00
	1826	—	30.00	50.00	125.00	325.00
	1827	—	50.00	90.00	175.00	400.00
	1828	—	125.00	200.00	300.00	700.00
	1829	—	45.00	80.00	150.00	350.00
	1830	—	45.00	80.00	150.00	350.00
	1831	—	30.00	55.00	125.00	275.00

Mint mark: A

C#	Date	Mintage	Fine	VF	XF	Unc
8.2	1821	—	—	—	Proof	—
	1822	—	50.00	90.00	185.00	400.00
	1823	—	50.00	80.00	175.00	350.00
	1824	—	65.00	100.00	200.00	500.00
	1825	—	—	Reported, not confirmed		
	1835	—	—	Reported, not confirmed		

Mint mark: V

C#	Date	Mintage	Fine	VF	XF	Unc
8.3	1822	—	35.00	75.00	100.00	225.00
	1823	—	100.00	150.00	275.00	675.00
	1824	—	30.00	50.00	125.00	325.00
	1825	—	30.00	65.00	100.00	225.00
	1826	—	30.00	50.00	110.00	200.00
	1827	—	50.00	80.00	140.00	350.00
	1828	—	90.00	140.00	250.00	650.00
	1829	—	90.00	140.00	250.00	650.00
	1830	—	50.00	75.00	125.00	325.00
	1831	—	35.00	65.00	115.00	300.00
	1832	—	35.00	65.00	115.00	300.00

Mint mark: A

C#	Date	Mintage	Fine	VF	XF	Unc
19.1	1835	—	—	Reported, not confirmed		
	1837	—	—	Reported, not confirmed		

Mint mark: M

C#	Date	Mintage	Fine	VF	XF	Unc
19.2	1837	—	100.00	175.00	400.00	1000.

Mint mark: V

C#	Date	Mintage	Fine	VF	XF	Unc
19.3	1837	—	90.00	150.00	300.00	750.00
	1838	—	100.00	160.00	350.00	850.00
	1839	—	90.00	150.00	300.00	775.00
	1840	—	70.00	140.00	250.00	700.00
	1841	—	100.00	160.00	325.00	800.00
	1842	—	90.00	150.00	300.00	750.00
	1843	—	100.00	160.00	325.00	800.00
	1844	—	100.00	160.00	325.00	800.00
	1845	—	100.00	160.00	325.00	800.00
	1846	—	90.00	150.00	300.00	750.00

W/o value

C#	Date	Mintage	Fine	VF	XF	Unc
39	1853	—	150.00	200.00	350.00	900.00

REVOLUTIONARY PROVISIONAL GOVERNMENT

5 LIRE

25.0000 g, .900 SILVER, .7234 oz ASW
Mint mark: M
Obv: Short stems above date.

C#	Date	Mintage	Fine	VF	XF	Unc
22.1	1848	.120	30.00	45.00	135.00	300.00

Obv: Long stems extend beyond date.

C#	Date	Mintage	Fine	VF	XF	Unc
22.2	1848	Inc. Ab.	50.00	120.00	300.00	700.00

Obv: Short stems end above date.
Rev: Star near crown.

C#	Date	Mintage	Fine	VF	XF	Unc
22.3	1848	Inc. Ab.	30.00	45.00	135.00	300.00

20 LIRE

6.4500 g, .900 GOLD, .1866 oz AGW
Mint mark: M

C#	Date	Mintage	Fine	VF	XF	Unc
23	1848	4,593	300.00	500.00	800.00	1600.

40 LIRE

12.9000 g, .900 GOLD, .3733 oz AGW
Mint mark: M

C#	Date	Mintage	Fine	VF	XF	Unc
24	1848	5,875	400.00	600.00	900.00	2000.

TRADE COINAGE

ZECCHINO

3.5000 g, .900 GOLD, .1012 oz AGW
Obv: Doge kneeling before St. Mark, leg: FRANC. I. . . . .
Rev: Christ standing.

C#	Date	Mintage	Fine	VF	XF	Unc
9	ND(1815)	—	750.00	1500.	2000.	2500.

NOTE: Varieties exist.

1/2 SOVRANO

5.6700 g, .900 GOLD, .1640 oz AGW

C#	Date	Mintage	Fine	VF	XF	Unc
	Mint mark: M					
10.1	1820	—	275.00	450.00	950.00	1800.
	1822	—	150.00	200.00	500.00	1000.
	1831	—	125.00	200.00	450.00	900.00
	Mint mark: A					
10.2	1822	—	125.00	200.00	400.00	850.00
	1823	—	125.00	200.00	400.00	900.00
	1831	—	125.00	200.00	400.00	900.00
	Mint mark: V					
10.3	1822	—	250.00	450.00	700.00	1700.
	1823	—	150.00	250.00	550.00	1200.

C#	Date	Mintage	Fine	VF	XF	Unc
	Mint mark: A					
10a.1	1835	—	—	Reported, not confirmed		
	Mint mark: M					
10a.2	1835	—	150.00	225.00	550.00	1100.
	1835 (AVSIRIAE error)	—	—	—	—	—

NOTE: Varieties exist.

C#	Date	Mintage	Fine	VF	XF	Unc
	Mint mark: A					
20.1	1837	—	—	Reported, not confirmed		
	1839	—	200.00	400.00	900.00	1800.
	Mint mark: M					
20.2	1837	—	500.00	750.00	1350.	2250.
	1838	—	200.00	350.00	500.00	800.00
	1839	—	200.00	350.00	500.00	800.00
	1841	—	200.00	350.00	500.00	800.00
	1842	—	225.00	450.00	700.00	1100.
	1843	—	400.00	600.00	1000.	1500.
	1844	—	225.00	450.00	700.00	1200.
	1845	—	225.00	450.00	700.00	1200.
	1846	—	225.00	450.00	700.00	1200.
	1847	—	225.00	450.00	700.00	1200.
	1848	—	200.00	450.00	700.00	1100.
	Mint mark: V					
20.3	1837	—	200.00	400.00	600.00	1000.
	1838	—	200.00	400.00	600.00	1000.
	1839	—	200.00	400.00	600.00	1000.
	1840	—	200.00	400.00	600.00	1000.
	1841	—	200.00	400.00	600.00	1000.
	1842	—	500.00	700.00	1250.	1800.
	1843	—	200.00	400.00	600.00	1000.
	1844	—	200.00	400.00	600.00	1000.
	1845	—	200.00	400.00	600.00	1000.
	1846	—	500.00	750.00	1500.	2200.
	1847	—	500.00	750.00	1500.	2200.

C#	Date	Mintage	Fine	VF	XF	Unc
	Mint mark: M					
20a	1849	—	250.00	400.00	800.00	1650.

C#	Date	Mintage	Fine	VF	XF	Unc
40.1	1854	—	350.00	550.00	1000.	2000.
	1855	—	350.00	550.00	1000.	2000.
	1856	—	350.00	550.00	1000.	2000.
	Mint mark: V					
40.2	1854	—	350.00	550.00	1000.	2000.
	1855	—	350.00	550.00	1000.	2000.
	1856	—	350.00	550.00	1000.	2000.

SOVRANO

11.3300 g, .900 GOLD, .3278 oz AGW

C#	Date	Mintage	Fine	VF	XF	Unc
	Mint mark: M					
11.1	1820	—	700.00	1100.	2000.	5000.
	1822	—	250.00	400.00	600.00	1450.
	1823	—	250.00	400.00	600.00	1450.
	1824	—	250.00	400.00	600.00	1450.
	1826	—	400.00	600.00	900.00	1550.
	1827	—	350.00	550.00	850.00	1500.
	1828	—	350.00	550.00	850.00	1500.
	1829	—	250.00	400.00	600.00	1450.
	1830/20	—	—	—	—	—
	1830	—	250.00	400.00	600.00	1450.
	1831/21	—	350.00	550.00	850.00	1500.
	1831	—	250.00	350.00	500.00	1000.
	Mint mark: A					
11.2	1822	—	250.00	350.00	500.00	1000.
	1823	—	250.00	350.00	500.00	1250.
	1831	—	200.00	300.00	450.00	900.00
	Mint mark: V					
11.3	1822	—	350.00	500.00	800.00	1500.
	Mint mark: A					
11a.1	1835	—	—	Reported, not confirmed		

C#	Date	Mintage	Fine	VF	XF	Unc
	Mint mark: M					
11a.2	1835	—	500.00	850.00	1500.	3500.

C#	Date	Mintage	Fine	VF	XF	Unc
	Mint mark: A					
21.1	1837	—	500.00	700.00	1100.	2400.
	1838	—	—	—	Rare	—
	1839	—	500.00	700.00	1100.	2400.
	1840	—	—	—	Rare	—
	1841	—	600.00	850.00	1250.	2600.
	1842	—	—	—	Rare	—
	1843	—	—	—	Rare	—
	1845	—	—	—	Rare	—
	1847	—	850.00	1500.	2700.	5000.
	Mint mark: M					
21.2	1837	—	700.00	1300.	2500.	4500.
	1838	—	350.00	500.00	1050.	2000.
	1840	—	350.00	500.00	1050.	2000.
	1841	—	700.00	1300.	2500.	4500.
	1848	—	350.00	500.00	1050.	2000.
	Mint mark: V					
21.3	1837	—	300.00	450.00	950.00	2000.
	1838	—	300.00	450.00	900.00	1700.
	1839	—	400.00	650.00	1100.	2600.
	1840	—	300.00	450.00	950.00	2000.
	1841	—	300.00	450.00	900.00	1700.
	1842	—	300.00	450.00	950.00	2000.
	1843	—	400.00	650.00	1100.	2500.
	1844	—	400.00	650.00	1100.	2500.

C#	Date	Mintage	Fine	VF	XF	Unc
21.3	1845	—	400.00	650.00	1100.	2500.
	1846	—	300.00	450.00	950.00	2000.
	1847	—	300.00	450.00	950.00	2000.

C#	Date	Mintage	Fine	VF	XF	Unc
	Mint mark: M					
41.1	1853	—	600.00	950.00	1700.	3500.
	1855	—	600.00	950.00	1700.	3500.
	1856	—	600.00	950.00	1700.	3500.
	Mint mark: V					
41.2	1854	—	800.00	1200.	2200.	4500.
	1855	—	600.00	1000.	2000.	4000.
	1856	—	550.00	900.00	1800.	3750.

LUCCA

Luca, Lucensis
Lucca and Piombino

A town in Tuscany and the residence of a marquis, was nominally a fief but managed to maintain a de facto independence until awarded by Napoleon to his sister Elisa in 1805. In 1814 it was occupied by the Neapolitans, and from 1817 to 1847 was a duchy of the queen of Etruria, after which it became a division of Tuscany.

Principality, 1805-1814
Lucca, Duchy, 1817-1847

RULERS

Felix and Elisa (Bonaparte), 1805-1814
Maria Luisa di Borbone
Duchess, 1817-1824
Carlo Lodovico di Borbone
Duke, 1824-1847

MONETARY SYSTEM

100 Centesimi = 1 Franco

3 CENTESIMI

COPPER

KM#	Date	Mintage	VG	Fine	VF	XF
21	1806	—	6.00	15.00	25.00	60.00

5 CENTESIMI

COPPER

KM#	Date	Mintage	VG	Fine	VF	XF
22	1806	—	10.00	20.00	40.00	85.00

FRANCO

5.0000 g, .900 SILVER, .1446 oz ASW

KM#	Date	Mintage	VG	Fine	VF	XF
23	1805	—	—	—	Rare	—
	1806	—	12.50	30.00	50.00	110.00
	1807	—	12.50	30.00	50.00	110.00
	1808	—	12.50	30.00	50.00	110.00

5 FRANCHI

24.8400 g, .900 SILVER, .7188 oz ASW

KM#	Date	Mintage	VG	Fine	VF	XF
24	1805	—	30.00	50.00	100.00	250.00
	1806	—	30.00	50.00	75.00	200.00
	1807	—	30.00	50.00	75.00	200.00
	1808/7	—	30.00	50.00	75.00	200.00
	1808	—	30.00	50.00	75.00	200.00

MONETARY REFORM

4 Denari = 1 Quattrino
3 Quattrini = 1 Soldo
20 Soldi = 1 Lira

QUATTRINO

COPPER
Obv. leg: DUCATO DI LUCCA. Rev: Value, date.

KM#	Date	Mintage	VG	Fine	VF	XF
31	1826	—	3.00	6.00	12.00	25.00

MEZZO (1/2) SOLDO

COPPER
Obv. leg: DUCATO DI LUCCA, crown.
Rev: Value, date.

KM#	Date	Mintage	VG	Fine	VF	XF
32	1826	—	3.00	6.00	12.00	25.00
	1835	—	3.00	6.00	12.00	25.00

2 QUATTRINI

COPPER

KM#	Date	Mintage	VG	Fine	VF	XF
33	1826	—	3.00	6.00	12.00	20.00

SOLDO

COPPER
Obv. leg: CARLO L. D. B. I. D. S. DUCA DI LUCCA

KM#	Date	Mintage	VG	Fine	VF	XF
34	1826	—	3.00	6.00	12.00	25.00

KM#	Date	Mintage	VG	Fine	VF	XF
34a	1841	—	7.50	15.00	25.00	40.00

5 QUATTRINI

COPPER
Obv: Crowned arms. Rev: Value, date.

KM#	Date	Mintage	VG	Fine	VF	XF
35	1826	—	3.00	6.00	12.00	25.00

NOTE: Varieties exist.

2 SOLDI

1.4000 g, .200 SILVER, .0090 oz ASW
Obv: Crowned arms. Rev: Value, date.

KM#	Date	Mintage	VG	Fine	VF	XF
36	1835	—	7.50	12.50	20.00	35.00

BOLOGNINO

(2 Soldi)

3.0700 g, .200 SILVER, .0197 oz ASW
Obv: Branch w/6 leaves.

C#	Date	Year	VG	Fine	VF	XF
4a	1790	(1835)		(restrike)		
			10.00	20.00	30.00	50.00

3 SOLDI

1.6000 g, .200 SILVER, .0102 oz ASW
Obv: Crowned CL monogram.

KM#	Date	Mintage	VG	Fine	VF	XF
37	1835	—	15.00	25.00	50.00	100.00

5 SOLDI

3.0000 g, .200 SILVER, .0192 oz ASW

KM#	Date	Mintage	VG	Fine	VF	XF
38	1833 flat top 3's					
		—	6.00	10.00	25.00	50.00
	1833 round top 3's					
		—	6.00	10.00	25.00	50.00
	1838	—	6.00	10.00	25.00	50.00

10 SOLDI

2.3600 g, .666 SILVER, .0505 oz ASW

C#	Date	Mintage	Fine	VF	XF	Unc
39	1833	—	10.00	18.00	30.00	75.00
	1838	—	10.00	18.00	30.00	75.00

LIRA

4.7200 g, .666 SILVER, .1010 oz ASW

C#	Date	Mintage	Fine	VF	XF	Unc
40	1834	—	10.00	20.00	40.00	100.00
	1837	—	20.00	40.00	100.00	200.00
	1838	—	10.00	20.00	40.00	100.00

2 LIRE

9.4300 g, .666 SILVER, .2019 oz ASW

C#	Date	Mintage	Fine	VF	XF	Unc
41	1837	—	35.00	60.00	150.00	250.00

NAPLES & SICILY

Two Sicilies

Consists of Sicily and the south of Italy which came into being in 1130. It passed under Spanish control in 1502; Naples was conquered by Austria in 1707. In 1733 Don Carlos of Spain was recognized as king. From then until becoming part of the united Kingdom of Italy, Naples and Sicily, together and separately, were contested for by Spain, Austria, France, and the republican and monarchial factions of Italy.

RULERS

Ferdinando IV
1799-1805 (2nd reign)
1815-1816 (restored in Naples)
1816-1825 (as King of the Two Sicilies)
Joseph Napoleon, 1806-1808
Joachim Murat, 1808-1815
(Gioacchino Napoleone)

Two Sicilies

Francesco I, 1825-1830
Ferdinand II, 1830-1859
Francesco II, 1859-1869

MONETARY SYSTEM

(Until 1813)

6 Cavalli = 1 Tornese
240 Tornese = 120 Grana = 12 Carlini
= 6 Tari = 1 Piastra
5 Grana = 1 Cinquina
100 Grana = 1 Ducato (Tallero)

KINGDOM OF NAPLES

3 CAVALLI

COPPER

C#	Date	Mintage	VG	Fine	VF	XF
91	1804	—	2.50	7.50	15.00	30.00

4 CAVALLI

COPPER

C#	Date	Mintage	VG	Fine	VF	XF
92	1804 LD	—	2.50	7.50	15.00	30.00

TORNESE

(6 Cavalli)

COPPER
Obv: Head right. Rev: Value within wreath.

C#	Date	Mintage	VG	Fine	VF	XF
93	1804 LD	—	5.00	10.00	20.00	40.00

9 CAVALLI

COPPER
Obv: Head right. Rev: Castle.

C#	Date	Mintage	VG	Fine	VF	XF
94	1801	—	15.00	35.00	60.00	100.00
	1804	—	5.00	10.00	20.00	40.00
	1804 LD	—	5.00	10.00	20.00	40.00

2 GRANA

COPPER

C#	Date	Mintage	VG	Fine	VF	XF
101	1810	—	15.00	35.00	85.00	400.00

6 TORNESI

COPPER

C#	Date	Mintage	VG	Fine	VF	XF
96	1801 A P	—	5.00	10.00	20.00	40.00
	1802 A P	—	5.00	10.00	20.00	40.00
	1803 A P	—	5.00	10.00	20.00	40.00
	1803 R C	—	6.00	12.50	25.00	45.00

NOTE: Earlier dates (1799-1800) exist for this type.

3 GRANA

COPPER

C#	Date	Mintage	VG	Fine	VF	XF
102	1810	—	15.00	30.00	60.00	250.00

Rev: Date below wreath.

C#	Date	Mintage	VG	Fine	VF	XF
102a	1810	—	15.00	30.00	60.00	250.00

60 GRANA

13.7500 g, .833 SILVER, .3682 oz ASW

C#	Date	Mintage	VG	Fine	VF	XF
97	1805 LD	—	25.00	40.00	75.00	150.00

120 GRANA

27.5000 g, .833 SILVER, .7365 oz ASW

C#	Date	Mintage	VG	Fine	VF	XF
98	1802 A P	—	25.00	40.00	75.00	150.00
	1802 P-AP	—	25.00	40.00	75.00	150.00

NOTE: Earlier dates (1799-1800) exist for this type.

Obv: Head right w/smooth hair.
Rev: Crown above small shield.

C#	Date	Mintage	VG	Fine	VF	XF
99.1	1805 LD	—	25.00	40.00	85.00	200.00

Plain edge

C#	Date	Mintage	VG	Fine	VF	XF
99.2	1805 LD	—	22.50	30.00	85.00	200.00

Obv: Head right w/curly hair.

C#	Date	Mintage	VG	Fine	VF	XF
99.3	1805 LD	—	30.00	65.00	135.00	265.00

NOTE: Varieties exist.

C#	Date	Mintage	VG	Fine	VF	XF
100	1806	—	100.00	175.00	350.00	600.00
	1807/6	—	100.00	175.00	350.00	700.00
	1807	—	80.00	150.00	275.00	450.00
	1808	—	80.00	150.00	275.00	450.00

DODICI (12) CARLINI

27.5300 g, .833 SILVER, .7373 oz ASW

C#	Date	Mintage	VG	Fine	VF	XF
103	1809	—	80.00	150.00	300.00	650.00
	1810	—	80.00	150.00	325.00	700.00

NOTE: Many varieties including mulings exist.

MONETARY REFORM

100 Centesimi = 1 Franco = 1 Lira

3 CENTESIMI

BRONZE
Obv: Head left. Rev: Value.

C#	Date	Mintage	Fine	VF	XF	Unc
105	1813	1.350	500.00	1100.	1500.	3750.

5 CENTESIMI

BRONZE

C#	Date	Mintage	Fine	VF	XF	Unc
106	1813	1.280	750.00	1250.	1750.	5250.

10 CENTESIMI

BRONZE
Obv: Head left. Rev: Value.

C#	Date	Mintage	Fine	VF	XF	Unc
107	1813	.450	750.00	1100.	1500.	2000.

MEZZA (1/2) LIRA

2.5000 g, .900 SILVER, .0723 oz ASW

C#	Date	Mintage	Fine	VF	XF	Unc
108	1813	.166	50.00	75.00	250.00	500.00

LIRA

5.0000 g, .900 SILVER, .1446 oz ASW

C#	Date	Mintage	Fine	VF	XF	Unc
109	1812	.027	50.00	150.00	300.00	500.00
	1813	.199	30.00	75.00	150.00	250.00

2 LIRE

10.0000 g, .900 SILVER, .2892 oz ASW

C#	Date	Mintage	Fine	VF	XF	Unc
110	1812	.028	100.00	200.00	350.00	700.00
	1813	.220	50.00	75.00	175.00	400.00

5 LIRE

25.0000 g, .900 SILVER, .7234 oz ASW

C#	Date	Mintage	Fine	VF	XF	Unc
111	1812	2,921	600.00	1200.	2500.	5250.
	1813	.037	100.00	300.00	600.00	1200.

20 LIRE

6.4500 g, .900 GOLD, .1866 oz AGW

C#	Date	Mintage	Fine	VF	XF	Unc
112	1813	.042	200.00	350.00	550.00	1200.
	1813 N	—	1000.	2500.	3500.	—

40 FRANCHI

12.9000 g, .900 GOLD, .3732 oz AGW

C#	Date	Mintage	Fine	VF	XF	Unc
104	1810	18 pcs.	—	—	*Rare	—

NOTE: Bowers and Merena Guia sale 3-88 VF realized $19,800. Superior Pipito sale 12-87 about XF realized $30,250.

40 LIRE

12.9000 g, .900 GOLD, .3732 oz AGW

C#	Date	Mintage	Fine	VF	XF	Unc
113	1813	.024	300.00	500.00	900.00	1900.

TWO SICILIES

NOTE: Coins bearing legends FERDINANDO IV were issued for circulation in Naples while those with FERDINANDO I were struck for Two Sicilies.

MONETARY SYSTEM

6 Cavalli = 1 Tornese
240 Tornese = 120 Grana = 12 Carlini
= 6 Tari (Naples) = 1 Piastra
5 Grana = 1 Cinquina
100 Grana = 1 Ducato (Tallero)

MEZZO (1/2) TORNESE

COPPER

C#	Date	Mintage	Fine	VF	XF	Unc
142	1832	—	3.00	6.00	15.00	30.00
	1833	—	3.00	6.00	15.00	30.00
	1835	—	3.00	6.00	15.00	30.00
	1836	—	3.00	6.00	15.00	30.00
	1838	—	3.00	6.00	15.00	30.00
	1839	—	3.00	6.00	15.00	30.00
	1840	—	6.00	9.00	20.00	35.00
	1844	—	3.00	5.50	10.00	25.00
	1845	—	3.00	5.50	10.00	25.00
	1846	—	3.00	5.50	10.00	25.00
	1847	—	3.00	5.50	10.00	25.00

C#	Date	Mintage	Fine	VF	XF	Unc
142a	1848	—	4.00	7.50	12.50	25.00
	1849	—	4.00	7.50	12.50	25.00
	1850	—	4.00	7.50	12.50	25.00
	1851	—	4.00	7.50	12.50	25.00
	1852	—	4.00	7.50	12.50	25.00
	1853	—	4.00	7.50	12.50	25.00
	1854	—	4.00	7.50	12.50	25.00

UNO (1) TORNESE

COPPER

C#	Date	Mintage	VG	Fine	VF	XF
119	1817	—	7.50	15.00	25.00	50.00

C#	Date	Mintage	VG	Fine	VF	XF
130	1827	—	4.00	8.00	15.00	30.00

Obv: Young head w/o beard, large letters.

C#	Date	Mintage	Fine	VF	XF	Unc
143	1832	—	3.00	6.00	15.00	35.00
	1833	—	3.00	6.00	15.00	35.00
	1835	—	3.50	6.00	15.00	35.00
	1836	—	10.00	17.50	25.00	45.00

Obv: Legend w/small letters.

C#	Date	Mintage	Fine	VF	XF	Unc
143a	1838	—	3.00	6.00	15.00	35.00
	1839	—	3.00	6.00	15.00	35.00
	1840	—	3.00	6.00	15.00	35.00
	1843	—	10.00	15.00	20.00	45.00
	1844	—	3.00	6.00	11.00	30.00
	1845	—	3.00	6.00	11.00	30.00
	1846	—	3.00	6.00	11.00	30.00
	1847	—	3.00	6.00	11.00	30.00
	1848	—	10.00	15.00	20.00	45.00

Obv: Older head w/beard.

C#	Date	Mintage	Fine	VF	XF	Unc
143b	1845	—	2.50	5.50	10.00	30.00
	1849	—	2.50	5.50	10.00	30.00
	1851	—	2.50	5.50	10.00	30.00
	1852	—	2.50	5.50	10.00	30.00
	1853	—	2.50	5.50	10.00	30.00
	1854	—	2.50	5.50	10.00	30.00
	1855	—	10.00	15.00	20.00	45.00
	1857	—	2.50	5.50	10.00	30.00
	1858	—	2.50	5.50	10.00	30.00
	1859	—	2.50	5.50	10.00	30.00

UNO E MEZZO (1-1/2) TORNESE

COPPER
Obv: Young head w/o beard.

C#	Date	Mintage	Fine	VF	XF	Unc
144	1832	—	7.50	15.00	30.00	75.00
	1835	—	7.50	15.00	30.00	75.00
	1836	—	7.50	15.00	30.00	75.00
	1838	—	5.00	12.50	40.00	75.00
	1839	—	7.50	15.00	30.00	75.00
	1840	—	7.50	15.00	30.00	75.00

Obv: Young head w/beard.

C#	Date	Mintage	Fine	VF	XF	Unc
144a	1844	—	5.00	12.50	25.00	65.00
	1847	—	5.00	12.50	25.00	65.00
	1848	—	5.00	12.50	25.00	65.00

Obv: Older head w/beard.

C#	Date	Mintage	Fine	VF	XF	Unc
144b	1849	—	5.00	12.50	25.00	60.00
	1850	—	5.00	12.50	25.00	60.00
	1851	—	5.00	12.50	25.00	60.00
	1853	—	5.00	12.50	25.00	60.00
	1854	—	5.00	12.50	25.00	60.00

DUE (2) TORNESI

COPPER

C#	Date	Mintage	VG	Fine	VF	XF
131	1825	—	3.00	6.50	12.50	25.00
	1826	—	3.00	6.50	12.50	25.00

Obv: Young head w/o beard.

C#	Date	Mintage	Fine	VF	XF	Unc
145	1832	—	12.00	30.00	75.00	125.00
	1835	—	12.00	30.00	75.00	125.00

Obv: Young head w/beard.

C#	Date	Mintage	Fine	VF	XF	Unc
145a	1838	—	4.00	13.50	20.00	45.00
	1839	—	3.00	8.50	20.00	40.00
	1842	—	3.00	8.50	20.00	40.00
	1843	—	3.00	8.50	20.00	40.00
	1847	—	3.00	8.50	20.00	40.00
	1848	—	3.00	8.50	20.00	40.00
	1849	—	3.00	8.50	20.00	40.00
	1851	—	3.00	8.50	20.00	40.00
	1852	—	3.00	8.50	20.00	40.00
	1853	—	3.00	8.50	20.00	40.00
	1854	—	3.00	8.50	20.00	40.00
	1855	—	3.00	8.50	20.00	40.00
	1856	—	3.00	8.50	20.00	40.00

C#	Date	Mintage	Fine	VF	XF	Unc
145b	1857	—	2.50	7.00	20.00	40.00
	1858	—	2.50	7.00	20.00	40.00
	1859	—	2.50	7.00	20.00	40.00

NOTE: Many minor varieties exist such as position of the obverse legend, placement of dots in the legend, large and small dates, etc.

C#	Date	Mintage	Fine	VF	XF	Unc
158	1859	—	2.50	7.50	20.00	45.00

TRE (3) TORNESI

COPPER
Obv: Young head w/o beard.

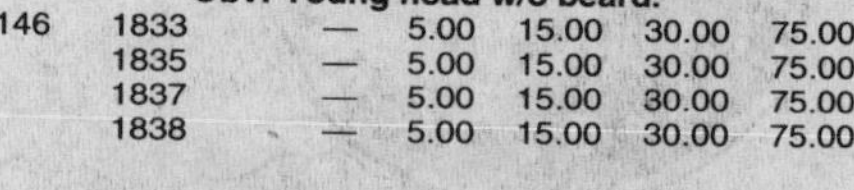

C#	Date	Mintage	Fine	VF	XF	Unc
146	1833	—	5.00	15.00	30.00	75.00
	1835	—	5.00	15.00	30.00	75.00
	1837	—	5.00	15.00	30.00	75.00
	1838	—	5.00	15.00	30.00	75.00

Obv: Young head w/beard.

C#	Date	Mintage	Fine	VF	XF	Unc
146a	1839	—	5.00	15.00	30.00	75.00
	1842	—	5.00	15.00	30.00	75.00
	1847	—	5.00	15.00	30.00	75.00
	1848	—	5.00	15.00	30.00	60.00
	1849	—	5.00	15.00	30.00	60.00
	1851	—	5.00	15.00	30.00	60.00
	1852	—	5.00	15.00	30.00	60.00
	1854	—	5.00	15.00	30.00	60.00
	1858	—	5.00	15.00	30.00	60.00

QUATTRO (4) TORNESI

COPPER

C#	Date	Mintage	VG	Fine	VF	XF
120	1817	—	15.00	30.00	45.00	90.00

CINQUE (5) TORNESI

COPPER
Obv. leg: FERDINANDVS IV. D. G. . . . .

C#	Date	Mintage	VG	Fine	VF	XF
114	1816	—	10.00	25.00	35.00	70.00

Obv. leg: FERD. I.D.G. . . . .

C#	Date	Mintage	VG	Fine	VF	XF
121	1816	—	9.00	25.00	45.00	80.00
	1817	—	5.00	10.00	20.00	40.00
	1818	—	5.00	10.00	20.00	40.00

C#	Date	Mintage	VG	Fine	VF	XF
121a	1819	—	7.50	15.00	30.00	55.00

C#	Date	Mintage	VG	Fine	VF	XF
132	1826	—	—	—	Rare	—
	1827	—	7.50	15.00	30.00	55.00

NOTE: Many varieties exist of 1827.

Obv: Young head w/o beard.

C#	Date	Mintage	Fine	VF	XF	Unc
147	1831	—	6.00	12.50	25.00	75.00
	1832	—	6.00	12.50	25.00	75.00
	1833	—	6.00	12.50	25.00	75.00
	1838	—	6.00	12.50	25.00	75.00
	1839	—	6.00	12.50	25.00	75.00
	1840	—	6.00	12.50	25.00	75.00
	1841	—	6.00	12.50	25.00	75.00

Obv: Young head w/beard.

C#	Date	Mintage	Fine	VF	XF	Unc
147a	1841	—	5.00	10.00	25.00	75.00
	1842	—	5.00	10.00	25.00	75.00
	1843	—	5.00	10.00	25.00	75.00
	1845	—	5.00	10.00	25.00	75.00

Obv: Older head w/beard.

C#	Date	Mintage	Fine	VF	XF	Unc
147b	1846	—	5.00	10.00	25.00	75.00
	1847	—	5.00	10.00	25.00	75.00
	1848	—	10.00	20.00	50.00	175.00
	1849	—	5.00	10.00	25.00	75.00
	1851	—	5.00	10.00	25.00	75.00
	1853	—	5.00	10.00	25.00	75.00
	1854	—	5.00	10.00	25.00	75.00
	1857	—	5.00	10.00	25.00	75.00
	1858	—	7.50	15.00	30.00	80.00
	1859	—	5.00	10.00	25.00	75.00

6 TORNESI

BRONZE
Overstruck on 10 Centesimi, 1813, C#107.

C#	Date	Mintage				
107a	ND	—	650.00	900.00	1500.	2500.

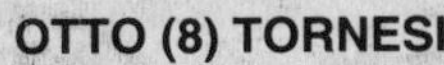

OTTO (8) TORNESI

COPPER
Obv: FERDINANDUS IV D. G., etc.
Rev: Similar to C#122

C#	Date	Mintage	VG	Fine	VF	XF
115	1816	—	10.00	20.00	40.00	100.00

Obv: FERD. I. D. G. . . . .

C#	Date	Mintage	VG	Fine	VF	XF
122	1816	—	10.00	20.00	35.00	75.00
	1817	—	10.00	20.00	35.00	75.00
	1818	—	10.00	20.00	35.00	75.00

DIECI (10) TORNESI

COPPER
Rev: Similar to 5 Tornesi, C#121a.

C#	Date	Mintage	VG	Fine	VF	XF
123	1819	—	5.00	10.00	30.00	75.00

Rev: Similar to C#148.

C#	Date	Mintage	VG	Fine	VF	XF
133	1825	—	5.00	10.00	30.00	75.00

Obv: Large head w/o beard.

C#	Date	Mintage	Fine	VF	XF	Unc
148	1831	—	15.00	35.00	75.00	175.00
	1832	—	7.50	17.50	30.00	150.00
	1833	—	7.50	17.50	30.00	150.00
	1834	—	25.00	50.00	100.00	250.00
	1835	—	7.50	17.50	30.00	90.00
	1836	—	16.00	35.00	60.00	160.00
	1837	—	10.00	20.00	40.00	150.00
	1838	—	10.00	20.00	40.00	150.00
	1839	—	10.00	20.00	40.00	100.00

Obv: Medium head w/beard.

C#	Date	Mintage	Fine	VF	XF	Unc
148a	1839	—	7.50	17.50	30.00	90.00
	1840	—	12.50	25.00	40.00	95.00
	1841	—	7.50	17.50	30.00	90.00
	1844	—	7.50	17.50	30.00	90.00
	1846	—	7.50	17.50	30.00	90.00
	1847	—	10.00	25.00	50.00	150.00
	1848	—	7.50	17.50	30.00	90.00
	1849	—	7.50	17.50	30.00	90.00
	1851	—	16.00	35.00	60.00	160.00

Obv: Older head w/beard.

C#	Date	Mintage	Fine	VF	XF	Unc
148b	1851	—	7.00	15.00	30.00	80.00
	1852	—	7.00	15.00	30.00	80.00
	1853	—	7.00	15.00	30.00	80.00
	1854	—	7.00	15.00	30.00	80.00
	1855	—	7.00	15.00	30.00	80.00
	1856	—	7.00	15.00	30.00	80.00
	1857	—	10.00	20.00	50.00	150.00
	1858	—	7.00	15.00	30.00	80.00
	1859	—	7.00	15.00	30.00	80.00

NOTE: Minor varieties exist, i.e., leg. size, location.

C#	Date	Mintage	Fine	VF	XF	Unc
159	1859	—	12.50	25.00	50.00	125.00

CINQUE (5) GRANA

1.1500 g, .833 SILVER, .0308 oz ASW
Obv: Young head right w/o beard.

C#	Date	Mintage	Fine	VF	XF	Unc
149	1836	—	3.50	6.00	15.00	50.00
	1838	—	3.50	6.00	15.00	50.00
	1844	—	3.50	6.00	15.00	50.00
	1845	—	3.50	6.00	15.00	50.00
	1846	—	3.50	6.00	15.00	50.00
	1847	—	3.50	6.00	15.00	50.00

Obv: Young head w/beard.

C#	Date	Mintage	Fine	VF	XF	Unc
149a	1848	—	7.50	12.50	20.00	50.00
	1851	—	3.50	6.00	15.00	50.00
	1853	—	3.50	6.00	15.00	50.00

10 GRANA

2.2900 g, .833 SILVER, .0613 oz ASW
Obv: Head right. Rev: Arms.

C#	Date	Mintage	VG	Fine	VF	XF
116	1815	—	7.50	15.00	35.00	65.00
	1816	—	7.50	15.00	35.00	65.00

C#	Date	Mintage	VG	Fine	VF	XF
124	1818	—	5.00	10.00	20.00	50.00

Obv: Head right.

C#	Date	Mintage	VG	Fine	VF	XF
134	1826	—	5.00	10.00	15.00	35.00

Obv: Young head w/o beard, continuous leg.

C#	Date	Mintage	Fine	VF	XF	Unc
150	1832	—	7.50	15.00	30.00	60.00
	1833	—	7.50	12.50	25.00	45.00
	1834	—	7.50	15.00	30.00	60.00
	1835	—	7.50	15.00	30.00	60.00

Obv: Leg. divided over young head w/o beard.

C#	Date	Mintage	Fine	VF	XF	Unc
150a	1835	—	6.00	12.50	20.00	50.00
	1836	—	6.00	12.50	20.00	50.00
	1837	—	6.00	12.50	20.00	50.00
	1838	—	6.00	12.50	20.00	50.00
	1839	—	6.00	12.50	20.00	50.00

Obv: Young head w/beard.

C#	Date	Mintage	Fine	VF	XF	Unc
150b	1838	—	10.00	18.00	25.00	60.00
	1839	—	6.00	12.50	20.00	50.00
	1840	—	6.00	12.50	20.00	50.00
	1841	—	6.00	12.50	20.00	50.00
	1842	—	6.00	12.50	20.00	50.00
	1843	—	15.00	25.00	40.00	70.00
	1844	—	6.00	12.50	20.00	50.00
	1845	—	6.00	12.50	20.00	50.00
	1846	—	6.00	12.50	20.00	50.00

Obv: Older head w/beard.

C#	Date	Mintage	Fine	VF	XF	Unc
150c	1847	—	5.00	7.50	15.00	40.00
	1848	—	5.00	7.50	15.00	40.00
	1849	—	10.00	20.00	40.00	100.00
	1850	—	6.00	12.50	20.00	50.00
	1851	—	6.00	12.50	20.00	50.00
	1853	—	5.00	7.50	15.00	40.00
	1854	—	5.00	7.50	15.00	40.00
	1855	—	5.00	7.50	15.00	40.00
	1856	—	5.00	7.50	15.00	40.00
	1859	—	5.00	7.50	15.00	40.00

20 GRANA

4.5900 g, .833 SILVER, .1229 oz ASW

C#	Date	Mintage	VG	Fine	VF	XF
135	1826	—	10.00	20.00	40.00	80.00

Obv: Young head w/o beard.

C#	Date	Mintage	Fine	VF	XF	Unc
151	1831	—	10.00	20.00	40.00	150.00
	1832	—	10.00	20.00	40.00	150.00
	1833	—	10.00	20.00	40.00	150.00
	1834	—	10.00	20.00	40.00	150.00
	1835	—	10.00	20.00	40.00	150.00
	1836	—	10.00	20.00	40.00	150.00
	1837	—	10.00	20.00	40.00	150.00
	1838	—	10.00	20.00	40.00	150.00
	1839	—	10.00	20.00	40.00	150.00

Obv: Young head w/beard.

C#	Date	Mintage	Fine	VF	XF	Unc
151a	1839	—	10.00	20.00	40.00	150.00
	1840	—	10.00	20.00	40.00	150.00
	1841	—	10.00	20.00	40.00	150.00
	1842	—	10.00	20.00	35.00	145.00
	1843	—	10.00	20.00	40.00	150.00
	1844	—	10.00	20.00	40.00	150.00
	1845	—	10.00	20.00	40.00	150.00
	1846	—	15.00	30.00	60.00	175.00
	1847	—	10.00	20.00	40.00	150.00
	1848	—	10.00	20.00	40.00	150.00
	1850	—	10.00	20.00	40.00	150.00
	1851	—	10.00	20.00	40.00	150.00
	1852	—	10.00	20.00	40.00	150.00
	1853	—	10.00	20.00	40.00	150.00
	1854	—	10.00	20.00	40.00	150.00
	1855	—	10.00	20.00	40.00	150.00
	1856	—	10.00	20.00	40.00	150.00
	1857	—	10.00	20.00	40.00	150.00
	1858	—	10.00	20.00	40.00	150.00
	1859/8	—	12.50	25.00	50.00	175.00
	1859	—	10.00	20.00	40.00	150.00

C#	Date	Mintage	Fine	VF	XF	Unc
160	1859	—	12.50	25.00	50.00	175.00

60 GRANA

13.7500 g, .833 SILVER, .3682 oz ASW
Obv: Head right, FERD IV. D. G., etc.

C#	Date	Mintage	VG	Fine	VF	XF
117	1816	—	15.00	25.00	75.00	175.00

Obv: Crowned head right, FERD I D. G., etc.

C#	Date	Mintage	VG	Fine	VF	XF
125	1818	—	20.00	35.00	65.00	150.00

Obv: Head right. Rev: Arms within wreath.

C#	Date	Mintage	VG	Fine	VF	XF
136	1826	—	25.00	45.00	90.00	250.00

Obv: Young head w/o beard, leg. continuous.

C#	Date	Mintage	Fine	VF	XF	Unc
152	1831	—	20.00	35.00	75.00	300.00
	1832	—	20.00	35.00	75.00	300.00
	1833	—	20.00	35.00	75.00	300.00
	1834	—	20.00	35.00	75.00	300.00

Obv: Leg. divided.

C#	Date	Mintage	Fine	VF	XF	Unc
152a	1835	—	20.00	40.00	80.00	350.00
	1836	—	20.00	35.00	75.00	300.00
	1837	—	50.00	90.00	125.00	600.00
	1838	—	20.00	35.00	75.00	300.00
	1839	—	35.00	60.00	100.00	350.00

Obv: Young head w/beard.

C#	Date	Mintage	Fine	VF	XF	Unc
152b	1841	—	35.00	65.00	115.00	300.00
	1842	—	35.00	65.00	115.00	300.00
	1845	—	35.00	65.00	115.00	300.00

Obv: Older head w/beard.

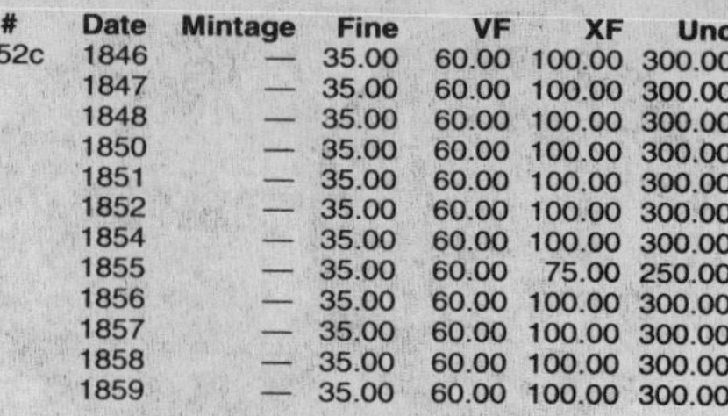

C#	Date	Mintage	Fine	VF	XF	Unc
152c	1846	—	35.00	60.00	100.00	300.00
	1847	—	35.00	60.00	100.00	300.00
	1848	—	35.00	60.00	100.00	300.00
	1850	—	35.00	60.00	100.00	300.00
	1851	—	35.00	60.00	100.00	300.00
	1852	—	35.00	60.00	100.00	300.00
	1854	—	35.00	60.00	100.00	300.00
	1855	—	35.00	60.00	75.00	250.00
	1856	—	35.00	60.00	100.00	300.00
	1857	—	35.00	60.00	100.00	300.00
	1858	—	35.00	60.00	100.00	300.00
	1859	—	35.00	60.00	100.00	300.00

120 GRANA

27.5300 g, .833 SILVER, .7373 oz ASW

C#	Date	Mintage	VG	Fine	VF	XF
118	1815	—	45.00	70.00	100.00	200.00
	1816	—	50.00	80.00	125.00	225.00
	1816R	*	55.00	90.00	140.00	275.00

***NOTE:** The R(istampato) issues were struck over the coins of Joseph Napoleon and Joachim Murat.

Obv: Large crowned head.

C#	Date	Mintage	VG	Fine	VF	XF
126	1817	—	30.00	50.00	90.00	165.00
	1818	—	20.00	30.00	50.00	145.00

Obv: Small crowned head.

C#	Date	Mintage	VG	Fine	VF	XF
126a	1818	—	25.00	35.00	75.00	200.00

27.5300 g, .833 SILVER, .7373 oz ASW

C#	Date	Mintage	Fine	VF	XF	Unc
137	1825	—	35.00	75.00	200.00	600.00
	1825R	—	45.00	90.00	250.00	800.00
	1826	—	35.00	75.00	200.00	600.00
	1826 R	—	45.00	90.00	250.00	800.00
	1828	—	55.00	100.00	275.00	900.00

Rev: Similar to C#153a.

C#	Date	Mintage	Fine	VF	XF	Unc
153	1831	—	22.50	30.00	75.00	200.00
	1832	—	22.50	30.00	75.00	200.00
	1833	—	30.00	50.00	90.00	225.00
	1834	—	30.00	50.00	90.00	225.00
	1835	—	22.50	30.00	75.00	200.00

C#	Date	Mintage	Fine	VF	XF	Unc
153a	1835	—	27.50	40.00	90.00	225.00
	1836	—	22.50	30.00	75.00	200.00
	1837	—	30.00	60.00	100.00	300.00
	1838	—	22.50	30.00	75.00	200.00
	1839	—	30.00	60.00	100.00	300.00

Rev: Similar to C#153a.

C#	Date	Mintage	Fine	VF	XF	Unc
153b	1840	—	22.50	30.00	70.00	175.00
	1841	—	22.50	30.00	70.00	175.00
	1842	—	22.50	30.00	70.00	175.00
	1843	—	22.50	30.00	70.00	175.00
	1844	—	22.50	30.00	70.00	175.00
	1845	—	22.50	30.00	70.00	175.00
	1846	—	22.50	30.00	70.00	175.00
	1847	—	25.00	50.00	100.00	200.00
	1848	—	25.00	50.00	100.00	200.00
	1849	—	100.00	150.00	500.00	1000.
	1850	—	22.50	30.00	50.00	175.00
	1851	—	22.50	30.00	70.00	175.00

NOTE: Many varieties exist.

Rev: Similar to C#153a.

C#	Date	Mintage	Fine	VF	XF	Unc
153c	1851	—	22.50	30.00	60.00	125.00
	1852	—	22.50	30.00	60.00	125.00
	1853	—	22.50	30.00	60.00	125.00
	1854	—	22.50	30.00	60.00	125.00
	1855	—	22.50	30.00	60.00	125.00
	1856	—	22.50	30.00	60.00	125.00
	1857	—	22.50	30.00	60.00	125.00
	1858	—	22.50	30.00	60.00	125.00
	1859	—	22.50	30.00	60.00	125.00

Rev: Similar to C#153a.

C#	Date	Mintage	Fine	VF	XF	Unc
161	1859	—	30.00	50.00	125.00	250.00

3 DUCATI

3.7900 g, .996 GOLD, .1213 oz AGW

C#	Date	Mintage	VG	Fine	VF	XF
127	1818	—	150.00	225.00	400.00	800.00

Obv: Head right. Rev: Winged Genius.

C#	Date	Mintage	VG	Fine	VF	XF
138	1826	—	300.00	450.00	900.00	1800.

Obv: Young head w/o beard.

C#	Date	Mintage	Fine	VF	XF	Unc
154	1831	—	200.00	250.00	350.00	800.00
	1832	—	200.00	250.00	350.00	800.00
	1835	—	200.00	250.00	350.00	800.00
154a	1837	—	200.00	250.00	350.00	800.00

Obv: Young head w/beard.

C#	Date	Mintage	Fine	VF	XF	Unc
154b	1839	—	200.00	250.00	325.00	700.00
	1840	—	200.00	250.00	350.00	750.00

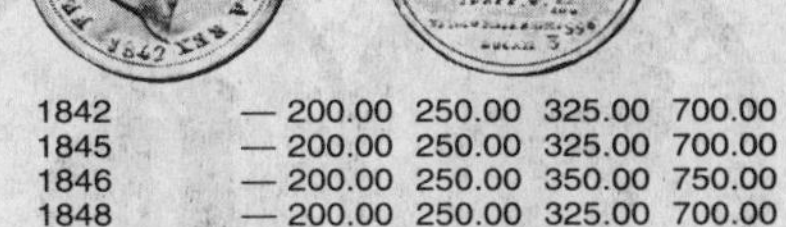

C#	Date	Mintage	Fine	VF	XF	Unc
154c	1842	—	200.00	250.00	325.00	700.00
	1845	—	200.00	250.00	325.00	700.00
	1846	—	200.00	250.00	350.00	750.00
	1848	—	200.00	250.00	325.00	700.00

Obv: Older head w/beard.

C#	Date	Mintage	Fine	VF	XF	Unc
154d	1850	—	175.00	225.00	300.00	500.00
	1851	—	175.00	225.00	300.00	500.00
	1852	—	175.00	225.00	300.00	500.00
	1854	—	125.00	175.00	250.00	450.00
	1856	—	175.00	225.00	300.00	500.00

6 DUCATI

7.5700 g, .996 GOLD, .2424 oz AGW

C#	Date	Mintage	VG	Fine	VF	XF
139	1826	—	200.00	400.00	650.00	1750.

Obv: Young head w/o beard. Rev: Winged Genius.

C#	Date	Mintage	Fine	VF	XF	Unc
155	1831	—	200.00	350.00	525.00	1300.
	1833	—	200.00	350.00	525.00	1300.
	1835	—	250.00	450.00	600.00	1650.

Obv: Young head w/beard.

C#	Date	Mintage	Fine	VF	XF	Unc
155b	1840	—	200.00	350.00	525.00	1300.

Obv: Older head w/beard.

C#	Date	Mintage	Fine	VF	XF	Unc
155c	1842	—	200.00	350.00	525.00	1300.
	1845	—	200.00	350.00	525.00	1300.
	1847	—	200.00	350.00	525.00	1300.
	1848	—	200.00	350.00	525.00	1300.
	1850	—	200.00	350.00	525.00	1300.
	1851	—	200.00	350.00	525.00	1300.
	1852	—	200.00	350.00	525.00	1300.
	1854	—	200.00	350.00	525.00	1300.
	1856	—	200.00	350.00	525.00	1300.

15 DUCATI

18.9300 g, .996 GOLD, .6062 oz AGW

C#	Date	Mintage	VG	Fine	VF	XF
128	1818	—	300.00	550.00	750.00	1300.

C#	Date	Mintage	Fine	VF	XF	Unc
140	1825	—	—	—	Rare	—

NOTE: Bowers and Merena Guia sale 3-88 XF realized $26,400.

C#	Date	Mintage	Fine	VF	XF	Unc
156	1831	—	500.00	800.00	1250.	2750.

Obv: Young head w/beard. Rev: Winged Genius.

C#	Date	Mintage	Fine	VF	XF	Unc
156c	1842	—	500.00	800.00	1250.	2750.
	1844	—	450.00	700.00	850.00	1750.
	1845	—	450.00	700.00	850.00	1750.
	1847	—	450.00	700.00	850.00	1750.

Obv: Older head w/beard.

C#	Date	Mintage	Fine	VF	XF	Unc
156d	1848	—	500.00	800.00	1250.	2750.
	1850	—	400.00	675.00	800.00	1750.
	1851	—	400.00	675.00	800.00	1750.
	1852	—	400.00	675.00	800.00	1750.
	1854	—	400.00	675.00	800.00	1750.
	1856	—	400.00	675.00	800.00	1750.

30 DUCATI

37.8700 g, .996 GOLD, 1.2128 oz AGW

C#	Date	Mintage	VG	Fine	VF	XF
129	1818	—	600.00	750.00	1400.	2000.

C#	Date	Mintage	Fine	VF	XF	Unc
141	1825	—	600.00	750.00	1500.	3000.
	1826	—	600.00	750.00	1500.	3000.

C#	Date	Mintage	Fine	VF	XF	Unc
157	1831	—	500.00	800.00	1500.	2500.
	1833	—	550.00	850.00	1600.	3000.
	1835	—	550.00	850.00	1600.	3000.

C#	Date	Mintage	Fine	VF	XF	Unc
157b	1839	—	550.00	850.00	1600.	3000.
	1840	—	550.00	850.00	1600.	3000.

C#	Date	Mintage	Fine	VF	XF	Unc
157c	1842	—	—	—	Rare	—
	1844	—	550.00	850.00	1600.	3000.
	1845	—	550.00	850.00	1600.	3000.
	1847	—	550.00	850.00	1600.	3000.
	1848	—	550.00	850.00	1600.	3000.
	1851	—	550.00	850.00	1600.	3000.
	1854	—	550.00	850.00	1600.	3000.

C#	Date	Mintage	Fine	VF	XF	Unc
157e	1850	—	500.00	800.00	1500.	2500.
	1851	—	550.00	850.00	1600.	3000.
	1852	—	550.00	850.00	1600.	3000.

Obv: Small older head w/beard.

C#	Date	Mintage	Fine	VF	XF	Unc
157d	1854	—	550.00	850.00	1600.	3000.
	1856	—	550.00	850.00	1600.	3000.

PARMA

A town in Emillia which was a papal possession from 1512 to 1545, was seized by France in 1796, and was attached to the Napoleonic empire in 1808. In 1814 Parma was assigned to Marie Louise, empress of Napoleon I. It was annexed to Sardinia in 1860.

RULERS

Ferdinando di Borbone, 1765-1802
Maria Luigia, Duchess, 1815-1847
Carlo II di Borbone, 1847-1849
Carlo III di Borbone, 1849-1854
Roberto di Borbone, 1854-1858

MONETARY SYSTEM

100 Centesimi = 20 Soldi = 1 Lira

CENTESIMO

COPPER
Similar to 5 Centesimi, C#25.

C#	Date	Mintage	Fine	VF	XF	Unc
23	1830	2.029	4.00	7.50	12.50	40.00

Obv: Head of Carlo III left. Rev: Oval arms.

C#	Date	Mintage	Fine	VF	XF	Unc
33	1854	—	200.00	300.00	375.00	500.00

3 CENTESIMI

COPPER
Similar to 5 Centesimi, C#25.

C#	Date	Mintage	Fine	VF	XF	Unc
24	1830	.511	20.00	30.00	50.00	100.00

Obv: Head of Carlo III left. Rev: Oval arms.

C#	Date	Mintage	Fine	VF	XF	Unc
34	1854	—	350.00	500.00	600.00	1000.

5 CENTESIMI

COPPER

C#	Date	Mintage	Fine	VF	XF	Unc
25	1830	1.506	5.00	10.00	20.00	60.00

Obv: Head of Carlo III left. Rev: Oval arms.

C#	Date	Mintage	Fine	VF	XF	Unc
35	1854	—	700.00	1000.	1400.	2000.

5 SOLDI

1.2500 g, .900 SILVER, .0361 oz ASW

C#	Date	Mintage	Fine	VF	XF	Unc
26	1815/3	.682	9.00	15.00	25.00	75.00
	1815	Inc. Ab.	7.50	12.50	20.00	50.00
	1830	—	10.00	15.00	25.00	50.00

10 SOLDI

2.5000 g, .900 SILVER, .0722 oz ASW

C#	Date	Mintage	Fine	VF	XF	Unc
27	1815	.530	12.00	20.00	30.00	85.00
	1830	—	25.00	50.00	100.00	200.00

LIRA

5.0000 g, .900 SILVER, .1444 oz ASW

C#	Date	Mintage	Fine	VF	XF	Unc
28	1815	.066	20.00	40.00	80.00	200.00

2 LIRE

10.0000 g, .900 SILVER, .2888 oz ASW

C#	Date	Mintage	Fine	VF	XF	Unc
29	1815	.022	50.00	100.00	200.00	500.00

5 LIRE

25.0000 g, .900 SILVER, .7234 oz ASW

C#	Date	Mintage	Fine	VF	XF	Unc
30	1815	.093	100.00	150.00	300.00	750.00
	1821	—	—	—	Rare	—
	1832	.044	125.00	200.00	400.00	1000.

C#	Date	Mintage	Fine	VF	XF	Unc
36	1858	1,000	350.00	500.00	850.00	1500.

20 LIRE

6.4500 g, .900 GOLD, .1866 oz AGW

C#	Date	Mintage	Fine	VF	XF	Unc
31	1815	.012	250.00	375.00	575.00	1000.
	1832	1,550	1000.	1500.	2000.	3000.

40 LIRE

12.9000 g, .900 GOLD, .3733 oz AGW

C#	Date	Mintage	Fine	VF	XF	Unc
32	1815	.220	175.00	275.00	375.00	625.00
	1821	.037	250.00	400.00	600.00	1400.

PIEDMONT REPUBLIC

Established by Napoleon in 1798 in the Piedmont area of northwest Italy which was the mainland possession of the kingdom of Sardinia, the republic was overthrown by Austro-Russian forces in 1799.

SUBALPINE REPUBLIC

1800-1801

5 FRANCS

25.0000 g, .900 SILVER, .7234 oz ASW

C#	Date	Mintage	VG	Fine	VF	XF
4	L'AN 10(1801)	.033	40.00	60.00	90.00	200.00

NOTE: Earlier date L'AN 9 (1800) exists for this type.

20 FRANCS

6.4500 g, .900 GOLD, .1866 oz AGW

C#	Date	Mintage	VG	Fine	VF	XF
5	L'AN 10(1801)	1,492	275.00	475.00	750.00	1200.

NOTE: Earlier date L'AN 9 (1800) exists for this type.

SARDINIA

A Roman see in the 11th century occupied by the competitive cities of Pisa and Genoa. In 1297 it was granted to James II of Aragon, and remained under Spanish control until passing to the house of Savoy in 1720. In 1861 it became the nucleus about which the United Kingdom of Italy was formed.

RULERS

Vittorio Emanuele I 1802-1821
Carlo Felice 1821-1831
Carlo Alberto 1831-1849
Vittorio Emanuele II 1849-1878

M = Milan
(t) after 1802 - Eagles head = Turin (Torino)

MONETARY SYSTEM

12 Denari = 6 Cagliarese = 1 Soldo
50 Soldi = 10 Reales = 21/2 Lire = 1 Scudo Sardo
2 Scudi Sardi = 1 Doppietta
Commencing 1816
100 Centesimi = 1 Lira

ISLAND COINAGE

TRE (3) CAGLIARESE

COPPER
Obv: Cross on arms. Rev: Value.

C#	Date	Mintage	Fine	VF	XF	Unc
88	ND(1813)	—	40.00	60.00	90.00	150.00

REALE

3.1800 g, .500 SILVER, .0551 oz ASW
Obv: Head right, leg: VIC.EM.D.G.REX. SAR.CYP.ET.IER. around, date.
Rev: Eagle on shield w/head to right, crown above.

C#	Date	Mintage	Fine	VF	XF	Unc
89.1	1812	—	60.00	90.00	125.00	250.00

Rev: Eagle's head to left.

C#	Date	Mintage	Fine	VF	XF	Unc
89.2	1812	—	60.00	90.00	125.00	250.00

MONETARY REFORM

100 Centesimi = 1 Lira

CENTESIMO

COPPER
Mint mark: Eagle head

C#	Date	Mintage	Fine	VF	XF	Unc
118	1842	1.933	40.00	60.00	75.00	140.00

3 CENTESIMI

COPPER
Mint mark: Eagle head
Obv: Arms. Rev: Value and date.

C#	Date	Mintage	Fine	VF	XF	Unc
119	1842	2.169	10.00	20.00	40.00	75.00

5 CENTESIMI

COPPER
Mint mark: Eagle head
Obv: Arms. Rev: Value and date.

C#	Date	Mintage	Fine	VF	XF	Unc
120	1842	1.845	10.00	25.00	50.00	90.00

MAINLAND COINAGE

2.6 SOLDI

BILLON
Obv: Head right, VICTORIVS EMANVEL around, date. Rev: Crowned displayed eagle w/arms of Savoy on breast.

C#	Date	Mintage	Fine	VF	XF	Unc
90	1814	—	4.00	8.00	20.00	50.00
	1815	—	4.00	8.00	20.00	50.00

1/2 SCUDO

17.5820 g, .905 SILVER, .5116 oz ASW

C#	Date	Mintage	Fine	VF	XF	Unc
91	1814	—	400.00	600.00	700.00	1500.
	1815	—	600.00	900.00	1250.	2500.

DOPPIA

9.1160 g, .905 GOLD, .2652 oz AGW
Obv. leg: VICTORIVS EMANVEL.
Rev. leg: D.G.REX.SAR. . . . .

C#	Date	Mintage	VG	Fine	VF	XF
94	1814	—	—	—	8500.	12,000.

Obv. leg: VIC.EM.D.G.REX.SAR. . . . .
Rev. leg: MONTISF.PR.PED.&. . . . .

C#	Date	Mintage	VG	Fine	VF	XF
94a	1815	—	—	—	13,000.	15,000.

NOTE: Superior Pipito sale 12-87 choice VF realized $13,750. Stack's International sale 3-88 XF realized $11,550.

MONETARY REFORM

100 Centesimi = 1 Lira

CENTESIMO

COPPER
Mint mark: Anchor

C#	Date	Mintage	Fine	VF	XF	Unc
98.1	1826 P	11.485	5.00	10.00	15.00	40.00

Mint mark: Eagle head

C#	Date	Mintage	Fine	VF	XF	Unc
98.2	1826 L	—	3.00	5.00	12.00	40.00
	1826 P	4.812	3.00	5.00	12.00	40.00

3 CENTESIMI

COPPER
Mint mark: Anchor

C#	Date	Mintage	Fine	VF	XF	Unc
99.1	1826 P	.844	3.00	5.00	12.00	40.00

Mint mark: Eagle head

C#	Date	Mintage	Fine	VF	XF	Unc
99.2	1826 L	5.778	3.00	5.00	12.00	40.00

5 CENTESIMI

COPPER
Mint mark: Anchor

C#	Date	Mintage	Fine	VF	XF	Unc
100.1	1826 P	10.514	3.00	5.00	12.00	40.00

Mint mark: Eagle head

C#	Date	Mintage	Fine	VF	XF	Unc
100.2	1826 L	32.177	3.00	5.00	12.00	40.00
	1826 P	Inc. Ab.	3.00	5.00	12.00	40.00

NOTE: C#98, 99, 100 were struck w/o mint mark at Bologna in 1860. See Emilia 1,2,3.

25 CENTESIMI

1.2500 g, .900 SILVER, .0361 oz ASW
Mint mark: Anchor
Obv: Head right. Rev: Arms.

C#	Date	Mintage	Fine	VF	XF	Unc
101.1	1829 P	.450	15.00	25.00	40.00	90.00
	1830 P	.143	15.00	25.00	40.00	90.00

Mint mark: Eagle head

C#	Date	Mintage	Fine	VF	XF	Unc
101.2	1829 L	.110	17.50	30.00	50.00	100.00
	1830 L	.234	15.00	25.00	40.00	90.00
	1830 P	Inc. Ab.	20.00	35.00	60.00	150.00

C#	Date	Mintage	Fine	VF	XF	Unc
109.1	1832 P	.120	75.00	150.00	300.00	600.00
	1833 P	—	20.00	35.00	60.00	150.00
	1837 P	.230	75.00	150.00	300.00	600.00

Mint mark: Anchor

C#	Date	Mintage	Fine	VF	XF	Unc
109.2	1833 P	7,921	25.00	40.00	60.00	120.00

50 CENTESIMI

2.5000 g, .900 SILVER, .0722 oz ASW
Mint mark: Eagle head

C#	Date	Mintage	Fine	VF	XF	Unc
102.1	1823 L	—	—	—	Rare	—
	1824 L	—	—	—	Rare	—
	1825 L	.492	12.50	25.00	50.00	150.00
	1826 L	.640	12.50	25.00	50.00	150.00
	1827 L	.401	12.50	25.00	50.00	150.00
	1828 L	.611	12.50	25.00	50.00	150.00
	1828 P	Inc. Ab.	12.50	25.00	50.00	150.00
	1829 P	.255	35.00	75.00	125.00	200.00
	1830 L	.456	12.50	25.00	50.00	150.00
	1830 P	Inc. Ab.	100.00	150.00	200.00	300.00
	1831 L	.143	12.50	25.00	50.00	150.00
	1831 P	Inc. Ab.	50.00	80.00	150.00	400.00

Mint mark: Anchor

C#	Date	Mintage	Fine	VF	XF	Unc
102.2	1826 P	.079	20.00	40.00	75.00	150.00
	1827 P	.143	15.00	30.00	60.00	125.00
	1828 P	.194	35.00	75.00	100.00	175.00
	1829 P	.107	15.00	30.00	60.00	125.00

Mint mark: Eagle head
Obv: Head right. Rev: Arms.

C#	Date	Mintage	Fine	VF	XF	Unc
110.1	1832 P	—	—	—	Rare	—
	1833 P	.062	20.00	40.00	75.00	200.00
	1834 P	.061	40.00	80.00	200.00	600.00
	1835 P	—	40.00	80.00	200.00	400.00
	1836 P	.022	40.00	80.00	200.00	600.00
	1837 P	.012	40.00	80.00	200.00	600.00
	1841 P	6,600	40.00	80.00	200.00	600.00
	1842 P	.010	20.00	35.00	75.00	200.00
	1843 P	.014	20.00	35.00	75.00	200.00
	1844 P	9,100	50.00	100.00	300.00	800.00
	1845 P	.016	40.00	75.00	125.00	250.00
	1846 P	.023	50.00	100.00	300.00	800.00
	1847 P	.011	50.00	100.00	200.00	400.00

Mint mark: Anchor

C#	Date	Mintage	Fine	VF	XF	Unc
110.2	1833 P	136 pcs.	50.00	100.00	200.00	400.00
	1844 P	.023	50.00	100.00	300.00	800.00

Obv: Head w/beard.

C#	Date	Mintage	Fine	VF	XF	Unc
121.1	1850 P	9,268	30.00	60.00	100.00	200.00
	1860 P	15 pcs.	—	—	Rare	—

Mint mark: Eagle head

C#	Date	Mintage	Fine	VF	XF	Unc
121.2	1850 B	—	12.50	25.00	50.00	150.00
	1852 B	.055	12.50	25.00	50.00	150.00
	1853 B	.021	12.50	25.00	50.00	150.00
	1855 B	—	30.00	60.00	150.00	300.00
	1856 B	9,754	12.50	25.00	50.00	150.00
	1857 B	.015	12.50	25.00	50.00	150.00
	1858 B	8,114	12.50	25.00	50.00	150.00
	1860 B	6,484	12.50	25.00	50.00	150.00

Mint mark: M

C#	Date	Mintage	Fine	VF	XF	Unc
121.3	1860	.982	15.00	30.00	65.00	175.00
	1861	—	50.00	100.00	200.00	500.00

LIRA

5.0000 g, .900 SILVER, .1444 oz ASW
Mint mark: Eagle head

C#	Date	Mintage	Fine	VF	XF	Unc
103.1	1823 L	—	—	—	Rare	—
	1824 L	.092	25.00	50.00	100.00	300.00
	1825 L	—	50.00	100.00	200.00	600.00
	1826 L	.547	20.00	40.00	75.00	200.00
	1827 L	.836	20.00	40.00	75.00	200.00
	1828 L	.345	20.00	40.00	75.00	200.00
	1828 P	Inc. Ab.	20.00	40.00	75.00	200.00
	1829 L	.111	20.00	50.00	100.00	400.00
	1830 L	.313	20.00	40.00	75.00	200.00

Mint mark: Anchor

C#	Date	Mintage	Fine	VF	XF	Unc
103.2	1824 P	5,670	25.00	50.00	100.00	400.00
	1825 P	—	20.00	40.00	75.00	200.00
	1826 P	.154	20.00	40.00	75.00	200.00
	1827 P	.251	20.00	40.00	75.00	200.00
	1828 P	.388	20.00	40.00	75.00	200.00
	1829 P	.159	20.00	40.00	75.00	200.00
	1830 P	.060	20.00	40.00	75.00	400.00

Obv: Head right. Rev: Arms.

C#	Date	Mintage	Fine	VF	XF	Unc
111.1	1831 P	.019	50.00	100.00	200.00	700.00
	1832 P	.035	35.00	75.00	200.00	600.00
	1833 P	7,620	50.00	100.00	200.00	700.00
	1834 P	.040	—	—	Rare	—
	1835 P	.023	25.00	50.00	100.00	300.00
	1837 P	.018	—	—	Rare	—
	1838 P	—	25.00	50.00	100.00	250.00
	1841 P	.011	—	—	Rare	—
	1844 P	.033	—	—	Rare	—

Mint mark: Eagle head

C#	Date	Mintage	Fine	VF	XF	Unc
111.2	1831 P	5,000	50.00	100.00	200.00	600.00
	1832 P	.030	50.00	100.00	200.00	600.00
	1833 P	85 pcs.	50.00	100.00	200.00	750.00
	1835 P	—	50.00	100.00	200.00	750.00
	1837 P	.028	50.00	100.00	200.00	600.00
	1838 P	.011	50.00	100.00	200.00	600.00
	1839 P	8,558	—	—	Rare	—
	1841 P	.020	—	—	Rare	—
	1842 P	5,184	—	—	Rare	—
	1843 P	.015	20.00	40.00	100.00	300.00
	1844 P	.015	—	—	Rare	—
	1845 P	.010	20.00	40.00	100.00	300.00
	1846 P	.019	—	—	Rare	—
	1847 P	.011	20.00	40.00	100.00	300.00
	1848 P	8,110	175.00	300.00	500.00	1000.
	1849 P	3,037	—	—	Rare	—

Mint mark: Anchor

C#	Date	Mintage	Fine	VF	XF	Unc
122.1	1850 P	—	50.00	75.00	125.00	400.00
	1853 P	7,051	50.00	75.00	150.00	600.00
	1859 P	.012	40.00	75.00	125.00	400.00
	1860 P	—	—	—	Rare	—

Mint mark: Eagle head

C#	Date	Mintage	Fine	VF	XF	Unc
122.2	1850 B	.092	25.00	50.00	150.00	400.00
122.2	1851 B	—	—	—	Rare	—
	1852 B	—	—	—	Rare	—
	1853 B	.022	25.00	50.00	150.00	400.00
	1854 B	—	—	—	Rare	—
	1855 B	.016	25.00	50.00	150.00	400.00
	1856 B	.058	20.00	40.00	100.00	300.00
	1857 B	.031	20.00	40.00	100.00	300.00
	1858 B	—	—	—	Rare	—
	1859 B	5,150	20.00	40.00	100.00	250.00
	1860 B	4,752	40.00	80.00	100.00	300.00

Mint mark: M

C#	Date	Mintage	Fine	VF	XF	Unc
122.3	1859	—	50.00	100.00	200.00	600.00
	1860	.603	50.00	100.00	200.00	600.00

2 LIRE

10.0000 g, .900 SILVER, .2888 oz ASW
Mint mark: Eagle head

C#	Date	Mintage	Fine	VF	XF	Unc
104.1	1823 L	—	—	—	Rare	—
	1825 L	.261	25.00	50.00	100.00	300.00
	1826 L	.235	25.00	50.00	100.00	350.00
	1827 L	.170	25.00	50.00	100.00	350.00
	1828 L	.102	25.00	50.00	200.00	400.00
	1829 L	—	—	—	Rare	—
	1830 L	.049	25.00	50.00	100.00	350.00
	1830 P	Inc. Ab.	25.00	50.00	150.00	400.00

Mint mark: Anchor

C#	Date	Mintage	Fine	VF	XF	Unc
104.2	1825 P	—	25.00	50.00	100.00	400.00
	1826 P	.157	25.00	50.00	100.00	350.00
	1827 P	.366	25.00	50.00	100.00	350.00
	1830 P	.115	25.00	50.00	100.00	350.00
	1831 P	.072	25.00	50.00	100.00	350.00

Obv: Younger head right.

C#	Date	Mintage	Fine	VF	XF	Unc
112.1	1832 P	.035	25.00	50.00	150.00	600.00
	1833 P	187 pcs.	50.00	100.00	200.00	1000.
	1835 P	5,142	50.00	100.00	200.00	1000.
	1836 P	.030	50.00	100.00	200.00	1000.
	1844 P	.030	25.00	50.00	100.00	500.00
	1845 P	.052	50.00	100.00	200.00	750.00
	1847 P	—	50.00	100.00	200.00	750.00

Mint mark: Eagle head

C#	Date	Mintage	Fine	VF	XF	Unc
112.2	1833 P	287 pcs.	250.00	500.00	1000.	2000.
	1834 P	—	250.00	500.00	750.00	1000.
	1835 P	.024	35.00	75.00	150.00	500.00
	1836 P	—	35.00	75.00	150.00	500.00
	1838 P	.020	—	—	Rare	—
	1839 P	.014	—	—	Rare	—
	1841 P	4,259	150.00	250.00	350.00	800.00
	1842 P	.010	35.00	75.00	150.00	500.00
	1843 P	.012	35.00	75.00	150.00	500.00
	1844 P	.012	35.00	75.00	150.00	500.00
	1845 P	.015	35.00	75.00	150.00	500.00
	1846 P	.015	35.00	75.00	150.00	500.00
	1847 P	.015	—	—	Rare	—
	1848 P	.013	—	—	Rare	—
	1849 P	3,159	—	—	Rare	—

Mint mark: Anchor
Obv: Head w/beard right.

C#	Date	Mintage	Fine	VF	XF	Unc
123.1	1850 P	—	100.00	200.00	400.00	1000.
	1853 P	5,401	—	—	Rare	—
	1854 P	2,748	60.00	125.00	300.00	900.00

Mint mark: Eagle head

C#	Date	Mintage	Fine	VF	XF	Unc
123.2	1850 B	.018	60.00	125.00	300.00	900.00
	1852 B	.023	60.00	125.00	300.00	900.00
	1853 B	4,859	60.00	125.00	300.00	900.00
	1854 B	.018	60.00	125.00	300.00	900.00
	1855 B	9,414	60.00	125.00	300.00	900.00
	1856 B	.011	60.00	125.00	300.00	900.00
	1860 B	8,963	60.00	125.00	300.00	900.00

5 LIRE

25.0000 g, .900 SILVER, .7234 oz ASW
Mint mark: Eagle head
Obv: Similar to C#93.

C#	Date	Mintage	Fine	VF	XF	Unc
92	1816 L	.023	75.00	175.00	325.00	850.00
	1817 L	.044	60.00	125.00	275.00	650.00
	1818 L	.055	60.00	125.00	275.00	650.00
	1819 L	.035	60.00	125.00	275.00	650.00
	1820 L	.101	60.00	125.00	275.00	650.00

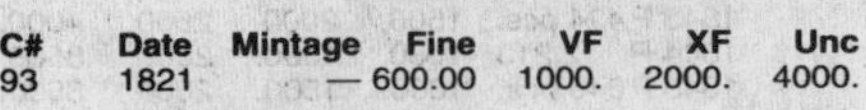

C#	Date	Mintage	Fine	VF	XF	Unc
93	1821	—	600.00	1000.	2000.	4000.

C#	Date	Mintage	Fine	VF	XF	Unc
105.1	1821 L	.035	75.00	150.00	200.00	1200.
	1822 L	.037	60.00	110.00	200.00	700.00
	1823 L	.035	60.00	110.00	200.00	500.00
	1824 L	.162	60.00	110.00	200.00	350.00
	1825 L	.395	15.00	30.00	125.00	275.00
	1826 L	.907	30.00	50.00	125.00	275.00
	1827 L	.724	15.00	30.00	125.00	275.00
	1828 L	.253	30.00	50.00	125.00	275.00
	1829 L	.312	30.00	50.00	125.00	275.00
	1830 L	.913	30.00	50.00	125.00	300.00
	1830 P	Inc. Ab.	30.00	50.00	125.00	275.00
	1831 P	.049	60.00	110.00	200.00	500.00

Mint mark: Anchor

C#	Date	Mintage	Fine	VF	XF	Unc
105.2	1824 P	.016	60.00	125.00	250.00	650.00
	1825 P	.017	75.00	150.00	300.00	800.00
	1826 P	.489	30.00	50.00	125.00	275.00
	1827 P	2.137	30.00	50.00	125.00	275.00
	1828 P	1.149	30.00	50.00	125.00	275.00
	1829 P	.597	30.00	50.00	125.00	275.00
	1830 P	1.122	30.00	50.00	125.00	275.00
	1831 P	.451	100.00	175.00	300.00	800.00

Obv: F on truncation. Rev: Arms.

C#	Date	Mintage	Fine	VF	XF	Unc
113.1	1831 P	.451	40.00	60.00	150.00	350.00

Mint mark: Eagle head

C#	Date	Mintage	Fine	VF	XF	Unc
113.2	1831 P	.049	50.00	90.00	200.00	450.00

Mint mark: Anchor
Obv: FERRARIS on truncation.

C#	Date	Mintage	Fine	VF	XF	Unc
113.3	1831 P	Inc. w/113.1	25.00	35.00	100.00	300.00
	1832 P	.317	25.00	35.00	100.00	300.00
	1833 P	.275	25.00	35.00	100.00	300.00
	1834 P	.154	25.00	35.00	100.00	300.00
	1835 P	.336	25.00	35.00	100.00	300.00
	1836 P	.595	25.00	35.00	100.00	300.00
	1837 P	.359	25.00	35.00	100.00	300.00
	1838 P	.307	25.00	35.00	100.00	300.00
	1839 P	.141	25.00	35.00	100.00	300.00
	1840 P	.193	25.00	35.00	100.00	300.00
	1841 P	.313	25.00	35.00	100.00	300.00
	1842 P	.396	25.00	35.00	100.00	300.00
	1843 P	.787	25.00	35.00	100.00	300.00
	1844 P	1.043	25.00	35.00	100.00	300.00
	1845 P	.302	25.00	35.00	100.00	300.00
	1846 P	.264	25.00	35.00	100.00	300.00
	1847 P	.142	25.00	35.00	100.00	300.00
	1848 P	.778	25.00	35.00	100.00	300.00
	1849 P	.739	25.00	35.00	100.00	300.00

Mint mark: Eagle head

C#	Date	Mintage	Fine	VF	XF	Unc
113.4	1831 P	Inc. w/113.2	50.00	90.00	200.00	450.00
	1832 P	.095	25.00	35.00	100.00	300.00
	1833 P	.060	25.00	35.00	100.00	300.00
	1834 P	.037	25.00	35.00	100.00	300.00
	1835 P	.069	25.00	35.00	100.00	300.00
	1836 P	.051	25.00	35.00	100.00	300.00
	1837 P	.036	25.00	35.00	100.00	300.00
	1838 P	.042	25.00	35.00	100.00	300.00
	1839 P	.205	25.00	35.00	100.00	300.00
	1840 P	.050	25.00	35.00	100.00	300.00
	1841 P	.015	25.00	35.00	125.00	500.00
	1842 P	.042	25.00	35.00	100.00	300.00
	1843 P	.037	25.00	35.00	100.00	300.00
	1844 P	.171	25.00	35.00	100.00	300.00
	1845 P	.042	25.00	35.00	100.00	300.00
	1846 P	.046	25.00	35.00	100.00	300.00
	1847 P	.037	25.00	35.00	100.00	300.00
	1848 P	.079	25.00	35.00	100.00	300.00
	1849 P	.104	150.00	350.00	600.00	800.00

Mint mark: Anchor

C#	Date	Mintage	Fine	VF	XF	Unc
124.1	1850 P	.721	50.00	100.00	200.00	500.00
	1851 P	.316	50.00	100.00	200.00	500.00
	1852 P	.391	50.00	100.00	200.00	500.00
	1853 P	.167	50.00	100.00	200.00	500.00
	1854 P	.284	50.00	100.00	200.00	500.00
	1855 P	.084	50.00	100.00	200.00	500.00
	1856 P	.058	50.00	100.00	200.00	500.00
	1857 P	.035	50.00	100.00	200.00	500.00
	1858 P	.030	50.00	100.00	200.00	500.00
	1859 P	.049	50.00	100.00	200.00	500.00

Mint mark: Eagle head

C#	Date	Mintage	Fine	VF	XF	Unc
124.2	1850 B	.058	50.00	100.00	200.00	500.00
	1851 B	.049	50.00	100.00	200.00	500.00
	1852 B	.097	50.00	100.00	200.00	500.00
	1854 B	.074	50.00	100.00	200.00	500.00
	1855 B	.052	50.00	100.00	200.00	500.00
	1856 B	.037	50.00	100.00	200.00	500.00
	1857 B	.019	50.00	100.00	200.00	500.00
	1858 B	.011	50.00	100.00	200.00	500.00
	1859 B	.012	50.00	100.00	200.00	500.00
	1860 B	5,044	50.00	100.00	200.00	500.00
	1861 B	.012	50.00	100.00	200.00	500.00

10 LIRE

3.2200 g, .900 GOLD, .0931 oz AGW
Mint mark: Eagle head

C#	Date	Mintage	Fine	VF	XF	Unc
114.1	1832 P	—	—	—	Rare	—
	1833 P	5,004	125.00	300.00	450.00	1000.
	1835 P	5,118	225.00	375.00	550.00	1200.
	1838 P	2,826	250.00	400.00	575.00	1250.
	1839 P	2,237	175.00	350.00	500.00	1100.
	1841 P	1,583	175.00	350.00	500.00	1100.
	1842 P	759 pcs.	250.00	475.00	650.00	1800.
	1843 P	950 pcs.	250.00	475.00	650.00	1800.
	1845 P	3,009	225.00	450.00	600.00	1500.
	1846 P	970 pcs.	250.00	475.00	650.00	1800.
	1847 P	405 pcs.	250.00	500.00	750.00	2000.

Mint mark: Anchor

C#	Date	Mintage	Fine	VF	XF	Unc
114.2	1833 P	1,550	200.00	375.00	750.00	1200.
	1835 P	—	—	—	Rare	—
	1841 P	2,809	225.00	425.00	850.00	1250.
	1843 P	4,566	225.00	425.00	850.00	1250.
	1844 P	.011	175.00	325.00	450.00	1000.
	1845 P	1,535	225.00	425.00	850.00	1250.
	1846 P	3,373	225.00	425.00	850.00	1250.
	1847 P	—	—	—	Rare	—
125.1	1850 P	4,141	300.00	750.00	1250.	1800.

Mint mark: Eagle head

C#	Date	Mintage	Fine	VF	XF	Unc
125.2	1850 B	2,326	225.00	400.00	600.00	1000.
	1852 B	—	500.00	1000.	1500.	2000.
	1853 B	—	225.00	400.00	600.00	1000.
	1854 B	1,833	225.00	400.00	600.00	1000.
	1855 B	2,566	225.00	400.00	600.00	1000.
	1856 B	2,526	225.00	400.00	600.00	1000.
	1857 B	7,193	225.00	400.00	600.00	1000.
	1858 B	2,931	225.00	400.00	600.00	1000.
	1859 B	1 known	—	—	7040.	—
	1860 B	6,036	225.00	400.00	600.00	1000.

20 LIRE

6.4500 g, .900 GOLD, .1866 oz AGW
Mint mark: Eagle head

C#	Date	Mintage	Fine	VF	XF	Unc
95	1816	.019	225.00	350.00	450.00	750.00
	1817	.040	125.00	225.00	350.00	600.00
	1818	.035	125.00	225.00	350.00	600.00
	1819	.022	125.00	225.00	350.00	600.00
	1820	.033	125.00	225.00	350.00	600.00

C#	Date	Mintage	Fine	VF	XF	Unc
96	1821	—	1500.	2500.	3750.	6000.

C#	Date	Mintage	Fine	VF	XF	Unc
106.1	1821 L	.018	175.00	225.00	300.00	475.00
	1822 L	7,460	175.00	225.00	325.00	500.00
	1823 L	.022	175.00	225.00	300.00	475.00
	1824 L	2,381	200.00	275.00	375.00	650.00
	1825 L	.028	175.00	225.00	300.00	475.00
	1826 L	.144	150.00	200.00	275.00	475.00
	1827 L	.150	150.00	200.00	275.00	475.00
	1828 L	.095	150.00	200.00	275.00	475.00
	1828 P	—	225.00	300.00	400.00	650.00
	1829 L	.061	225.00	300.00	400.00	650.00
	1829 P	—	225.00	300.00	400.00	650.00
	1830 L	—	225.00	300.00	400.00	650.00
	1830 P	.035	200.00	275.00	375.00	600.00
	1831 P	.042	125.00	200.00	300.00	475.00

Mint mark: Anchor

C#	Date	Mintage	Fine	VF	XF	Unc
106.2	1824 P	2,394	125.00	150.00	200.00	375.00

C#	Date	Mintage	Fine	VF	XF	Unc
106.2	1825 P	313 pcs.	375.00	500.00	600.00	1500.
	1827 P	1,766	225.00	300.00	400.00	500.00
	1828 P	—	—	—	Rare	—
	1829 P	—	225.00	300.00	400.00	500.00
	1830 P	3,270	375.00	500.00	600.00	800.00
	1831 P	16,189	—	—	Rare	—

C#	Date	Mintage	Fine	VF	XF	Unc
115.1	1831 P	—	100.00	125.00	150.00	275.00
	1832 P	.074	100.00	125.00	150.00	275.00
	1833 P	.080	—	—	Rare	—
	1834 P	.133	100.00	125.00	150.00	275.00
	1835 P	.052	100.00	125.00	150.00	275.00
	1836 P	.090	100.00	125.00	150.00	275.00
	1837 P	.056	—	—	Rare	—
	1838 P	.120	100.00	125.00	150.00	275.00
	1839 P	.074	—	—	Rare	—
	1840 P	.176	100.00	125.00	150.00	275.00
	1841 P	.206	125.00	175.00	250.00	375.00
	1842 P	.066	100.00	125.00	150.00	275.00
	1843 P	.045	—	—	Rare	—
	1844 P	.034	—	—	Rare	—
	1845 P	.043	100.00	125.00	150.00	275.00
	1846 P	.043	—	—	Rare	—
	1847 P	.052	100.00	125.00	150.00	275.00
	1848 P	.059	125.00	150.00	175.00	275.00
	1849 P	.111	100.00	125.00	150.00	250.00

Mint mark: Eagle head

C#	Date	Mintage	Fine	VF	XF	Unc
115.2	1831 P	—	100.00	125.00	150.00	275.00
	1832 P	.053	100.00	125.00	150.00	275.00
	1833 P	.016	100.00	125.00	150.00	275.00
	1834 P	.261	100.00	125.00	150.00	275.00
	1836 P	.014	—	—	Rare	—
	1837 P	.015	—	—	Rare	—
	1838 P	.031	100.00	125.00	150.00	275.00
	1839 P	.070	100.00	125.00	150.00	275.00
	1840 P	.028	100.00	125.00	150.00	275.00
	1841 P	.031	—	—	Rare	—
	1842 P	.026	100.00	125.00	150.00	275.00
	1843 P	.024	—	—	Rare	—
	1844 P	.030	100.00	125.00	150.00	275.00
	1845 P	.035	100.00	125.00	150.00	275.00
	1846 P	.030	100.00	125.00	150.00	275.00
	1847 P	.033	100.00	125.00	150.00	275.00
	1848 P	.059	100.00	—	Rare	—
	1849 P	.058	100.00	125.00	150.00	275.00

Unknown Mint

C#	Date	Mintage	Fine	VF	XF	Unc
115.3	1834	—	100.00	125.00	150.00	275.00
	1847	—	100.00	125.00	150.00	275.00

Mint mark: Anchor

C#	Date	Mintage	Fine	VF	XF	Unc
126.1	1850 B	.139	100.00	125.00	150.00	275.00
	1851 B	.296	100.00	125.00	150.00	275.00
	1852 B	.103	100.00	125.00	150.00	275.00
	1853 B	.137	100.00	125.00	150.00	275.00
	1854 B	.142	100.00	125.00	150.00	275.00
	1855 B	.148	100.00	125.00	150.00	275.00
	1856 B	.113	100.00	125.00	150.00	275.00
	1857 B	.059	100.00	125.00	150.00	275.00
	1858 B	.176	100.00	125.00	150.00	275.00
	1859 B	.436	100.00	125.00	150.00	275.00
	1860 B	.163	100.00	125.00	150.00	275.00

Mint mark: Eagle head

C#	Date	Mintage	Fine	VF	XF	Unc
126.2	1850 P	.066	100.00	125.00	150.00	275.00
	1851 P	.163	100.00	125.00	150.00	275.00
	1852 P	.046	100.00	125.00	150.00	275.00
	1853 P	.041	—	—	Rare	—
	1855 P	.041	100.00	125.00	150.00	275.00
	1855 P (error) EMMANVEL H for II					
		—	100.00	125.00	150.00	275.00
	1856 P	.061	375.00	500.00	750.00	1200.
	1857 P	.067	100.00	125.00	150.00	275.00
	1858 P	.103	150.00	250.00	400.00	600.00
	1859 P	.187	100.00	125.00	150.00	275.00
	1860 P	.111	100.00	150.00	175.00	375.00
	1861 P	.156	100.00	150.00	175.00	375.00

Mint mark: M

C#	Date	Mintage	Fine	VF	XF	Unc
126.3	1860	.023	125.00	200.00	300.00	500.00

40 LIRE

12.9000 g, .900 GOLD, .3733 oz AGW
Mint mark: Eagle head

C#	Date	Mintage	Fine	VF	XF	Unc
107.1	1822 L	5,011	300.00	400.00	600.00	1350.
	1823 L	—	—	—	Rare	—
	1825 L	.039	300.00	400.00	500.00	1150.
	1831 L	—	300.00	400.00	500.00	1150.
	1831 P	7,711	300.00	400.00	500.00	1150.

Mint mark: Anchor

C#	Date	Mintage	Fine	VF	XF	Unc
107.2	1825 P	3,994	300.00	400.00	650.00	1650.
	1826 P	2,844	500.00	600.00	900.00	1850.

50 LIRE

16.1200 g, .900 GOLD, .4664 oz AGW
Mint mark: Eagle head

C#	Date	Mintage	Fine	VF	XF	Unc
116.1	1832 P	93 pcs.	—	—	Rare	—
	1833 P	1,773	750.00	1000.	1500.	2500.
	1834 P	657 pcs.	—	—	Rare	—
	1835 P	1,296	—	—	Rare	—
	1836 P	385 pcs.	900.00	1250.	1750.	2750.
	1838 P	992 pcs.	—	—	Rare	—
	1839 P	553 pcs.	—	—	Rare	—
	1840 P	1,402	—	—	Rare	—
	1841 P	2,753	—	—	Rare	—
	1843 P	586 pcs.	—	—	Rare	—

Mint mark: Anchor

C#	Date	Mintage	Fine	VF	XF	Unc
116.2	1833 P	92 pcs.	4000.	5000.	6000.	7500.
	1835 P	—	—	—	Rare	—
	1841 P	562 pcs.	—	—	Rare	—

80 LIRE

25.8000 g, .900 GOLD, .7466 oz AGW
Mint mark: Eagle head

C#	Date	Mintage	Fine	VF	XF	Unc
97	1821	965 pcs.	4000.	7000.	10,000.	20,000.

C#	Date	Mintage	Fine	VF	XF	Unc
108.1	1823 L	—	—	—	Rare	—
	1824 L	5,919	450.00	550.00	650.00	1000.
	1825 L	.014	400.00	500.00	600.00	900.00
	1826 L	.076	400.00	500.00	600.00	900.00
	1827 L	.038	400.00	500.00	600.00	900.00
	1828 L	.023	400.00	500.00	600.00	900.00
	1828 P	Inc. Ab.	600.00	750.00	1000.	1500.
	1829 P	8,181	400.00	500.00	600.00	900.00
	1830 P	5,972	400.00	500.00	600.00	900.00
	1831 P	740 pcs.	800.00	1000.	1250.	2000.

Mint mark: Anchor

C#	Date	Mintage	Fine	VF	XF	Unc
108.2	1824 P	3,904	500.00	700.00	900.00	1500.
	1825 P	8,465	400.00	550.00	725.00	1200.
	1826 P	2,305	700.00	900.00	1100.	1750.
	1827 P	.015	400.00	500.00	600.00	1100.
	1828 P	8,961	400.00	500.00	600.00	1100.
	1829 P	7,436	400.00	500.00	600.00	1100.
	1830 P	.026	400.00	500.00	600.00	1100.
	1831 P	.021	600.00	800.00	1250.	2000.

100 LIRE

32.2500 g, .900 GOLD, .9332 oz AGW
Mint mark: Anchor

C#	Date	Mintage	Fine	VF	XF	Unc
117.1	1832 P	—	500.00	600.00	850.00	1800.
	1833 P	2,587	600.00	700.00	800.00	1750.
	1834 P	.012	500.00	575.00	700.00	1400.
	1835 P	8,513	500.00	600.00	850.00	1500.
	1836 P	703 pcs.	700.00	900.00	1100.	2250.
	1837 P	250 pcs.	900.00	1100.	1350.	2750.
	1838 P	4,774	—	—	Rare	—
	1839 P	2,922	—	—	Rare	—
	1840 P	1,003	700.00	900.00	1100.	2250.
	1841 P	8,889	475.00	600.00	850.00	1750.
	1842 P	3,606	700.00	900.00	1100.	2250.
	1843 P	424 pcs.	1500.	2000.	2500.	4000.
	1844 P	2,213	1000.	1500.	2000.	3500.
	1845 P	646 pcs.	1000.	1500.	2000.	3500.

Mint mark: Eagle head

C#	Date	Mintage	Fine	VF	XF	Unc
117.2	1832 P	—	475.00	550.00	750.00	1500.
	1833 P	6,769	475.00	550.00	750.00	1500.
	1834 P	.037	475.00	525.00	650.00	1350.
	1835 P	.026	475.00	525.00	650.00	1350.
	1836 P	6,236	475.00	525.00	650.00	1350.
	1837 P	3,885	475.00	550.00	750.00	1500.
	1838 P	3,916	—	—	Rare	—
	1840 P	2,898	475.00	550.00	750.00	1500.
	1841 P	1,207	700.00	1000.	1300.	2000.
	1842 P	864 pcs.	700.00	1000.	1300.	2000.
	1843 P	827 pcs.	700.00	900.00	1100.	2250.
	1844 P	91 pcs.	—	—	Rare	—

SICILY

Has a history of occupation extending back to the ancient Phoenicians. In more recent times it was part of the Kingdom of Naples and Sicily.

RULERS

Ferdinando III, 1759-1825
(became Ferdinando I in 1816
as King of Two Sicilies)
Ferdinando II, 1830-1859

MINTMASTERS INITIALS

Palermo Mint

Letter	Date	Name
JVI	1798-1807	Guiseppe Ugo
VB	1810-1816	Vicenzo Beninati

MONETARY SYSTEM

6 Cavalli = 1 Grano
20 Grani = 2 Carlini = 1 Tari
12 Tari = 1 Piastra
15 Tari = 1 Scudo
2 Scudi = 1 Oncia

MEZZO (1/2) GRANO

COPPER
Obv: Head right. Rev: Value, SICILIANO, date.

C#	Date	Mintage	VG	Fine	VF	XF
52	1836	—	10.00	25.00	60.00	125.00

UN (1) GRANO

COPPER
Obv: Eagle, leg. Rev: Value, date within wreath.

C#	Date	Mintage	VG	Fine	VF	XF
41	1801 JVI	—	6.00	10.00	20.00	35.00
	1802 JVI	—	9.00	15.00	25.00	50.00
	1803 JVI	—	20.00	30.00	50.00	100.00

C#	Date	Mintage	VG	Fine	VF	XF
42	ND(1814) VB	—	20.00	30.00	50.00	100.00
	1814 VB	—	5.00	10.00	20.00	35.00
	1815 VB	—	5.00	10.00	20.00	35.00

NOTE: Varieties exist.

Obv: Head right. Rev: SICILIANO, value, date.

C#	Date	Mintage	VG	Fine	VF	XF
53	1836	—	50.00	100.00	200.00	300.00

DUE (2) GRANI

COPPER
Obv: Eagle, leg. Rev: Value, date within wreath.

C#	Date	Mintage	VG	Fine	VF	XF
43	1801 JVI	—	20.00	30.00	50.00	100.00
	1802 JVI	—	6.00	10.00	20.00	40.00
	1803 JVI	—	6.00	10.00	20.00	40.00
	1804 JVI	—	6.00	10.00	20.00	40.00

C#	Date	Mintage	VG	Fine	VF	XF
44	1814 VB	—	10.00	15.00	25.00	50.00
	1815 VB	—	6.00	10.00	20.00	40.00

NOTE: 1814 exists w/large and small G.2.

Obv: Head right. Rev: SICILIANI, value, date.

C#	Date	Mintage	VG	Fine	VF	XF
54	1836	—	50.00	100.00	200.00	300.00

CINQUE (5) GRANI

COPPER
Obv: Eagle, leg. Rev: Value, date within wreath.

C#	Date	Mintage	VG	Fine	VF	XF
45	1801 JVI	—	30.00	45.00	75.00	150.00
	1802 JVI	—	15.00	22.50	50.00	125.00
	1803 JVI	—	15.00	22.50	50.00	125.00
	1804 JVI	—	15.00	22.50	50.00	125.00

Obv: Large head.

C#	Date	Mintage	VG	Fine	VF	XF
46	ND(1814) VB	—	30.00	45.00	75.00	150.00
	1814 VB	—	12.00	20.00	40.00	90.00
	1815 VB	—	12.00	20.00	40.00	90.00

NOTE: Varieties exist of 1815.

Obv: Small head.

C#	Date	Mintage	VG	Fine	VF	XF
46a	1815 VB	—	12.00	20.00	40.00	90.00
	1816 VB	—	20.00	30.00	50.00	100.00

Obv: Head right. Rev: SICILIANI, crown, value, date.

C#	Date	Mintage	VG	Fine	VF	XF
55	1836	—	100.00	150.00	250.00	400.00

DIECI (10) GRANI

COPPER
Obv: Eagle, leg. Rev: Value, date within wreath.

C#	Date	Mintage	VG	Fine	VF	XF
47	1801 JVI	—	20.00	30.00	50.00	125.00
	1802 JVI	—	20.00	30.00	50.00	125.00
	1803 JVI	—	20.00	30.00	50.00	125.00
	1804 JVI	—	20.00	30.00	50.00	125.00

C#	Date	Mintage	VG	Fine	VF	XF
48	ND(1814) VB	—	30.00	50.00	100.00	200.00
	1814 VB	—	20.00	30.00	50.00	150.00
	1815 VB	—	20.00	30.00	60.00	180.00

NOTE: 1815 exists with G.10. and G.10, and w/lower right tip of bust pointing to E in REX ; also tip of bust pointing to X in REX.

Obv: Head right. Rev: SICILIANI, crown, value, date.

C#	Date	Mintage	VG	Fine	VF	XF
56	1835	—	400.00	500.00	750.00	1000.
	1836	—	100.00	150.00	300.00	500.00

6 TARI

13.6600 g, .854 SILVER, .3751 oz ASW
Obv: Head right. Rev: Eagle.

C#	Date	Mintage	VG	Fine	VF	XF
48.5	1801 JVI	—	12.50	22.50	40.00	125.00

NOTE: Earlier dates (1799-1800) exist for this type.

12 TARI

27.5330 g, .883 SILVER, .7817 oz ASW
Obv: Bust right, FERDINAN.D.G.SICIL. . . .
Rev: Eagle, date.

C#	Date	Mintage	VG	Fine	VF	XF
49	1801 JVI	—	40.00	75.00	125.00	200.00
	1803 JVI	—	40.00	75.00	125.00	200.00

NOTE: 1801 exists w/REX. and REX
NOTE: Earlier dates (1799-1800) exist for this type.

Obv. leg: FERDINAN. III. D.G.SICIL. . . .

C#	Date	Mintage	VG	Fine	VF	XF
49a	1801 JVI	—	40.00	75.00	125.00	200.00
	1802 JVI	—	40.00	75.00	125.00	200.00
	1803 JVI	—	40.00	75.00	125.00	200.00
	1804 JVI	—	40.00	75.00	125.00	200.00

NOTE: Earlier dates (1799-1800) exist for this type.

Rev: J.V.I. above eagle within wreath.

C#	Date	Mintage	VG	Fine	VF	XF
50	1805 JVI	—	50.00	100.00	200.00	400.00
	1806 JVI	—	50.00	100.00	200.00	400.00
	1807 JVI	—	50.00	100.00	200.00	400.00

Rev: Eagle between V. and B. within wreath.

C#	Date	Mintage	VG	Fine	VF	XF
50a	1810 VB	—	50.00	100.00	150.00	350.00

NOTE: Seven varieties exist.

2 ONCIE

8.8150 g, .906 GOLD, .2567 oz AGW
Ferdinand III

C#	Date	Mintage	Fine	VF	XF	Unc
51	1814 VB	—	3000.	5000.	8000.	12,000.

TUSCANY

Etruria

An Italian territorial division on the west-central peninsula, belonged to the Medici from 1530 to 1737, when it was given to Francis, duke of Lorraine. In 1800 the French established it as part of the Spanish dominions; from 1807 to 1809 it was a French department. After the fall of Napoleon it reverted to its pre-Napoleonic owner, Ferdinand III.

RULERS

Louis I, 1801-1803
Charles Louis, under regency of his mother Maria Louisa, 1803-1807
Annexed To France 1807-1814
Ferdinando III Restored 1814-1824
Leopold II 1824-1848, 1849-1859
Provisional Government 1859
United to Italian Provisional Government 1859-1861

MINT MARKS

FIRENZE - Florence
LEGHORN - Livorno
PISIS - Pisa

MONETARY SYSTEM

Until 1826

12 Denari = 3 Quattrini = 1 Soldo
20 Soldi = 1 Lira
10 Lire = 1 Dena
40 Quattrini = 1 Paolo
1-1/2 Paoli = 1 Lira
10 Paoli = 1 Francescone, Scudo, Tallero
3 Zecchini = 1 Ruspone = 40 Lire

1826-1859

100 Quattrini = 1 Fiorino
4 Fiorini = 10 Paoli

1859

100 Centesimi = 1 Lira

QUATTRINO

COPPER
Obv: Square arms. Rev: Value and date.

C#	Date	Mintage	VG	Fine	VF	XF
30	1801	—	3.00	5.00	9.00	25.00

Obv: Crowned arms. Rev: Value.

C#	Date	Mintage	VG	Fine	VF	XF
40	1802	—	12.00	20.00	80.00	125.00
	1803	—	5.00	8.00	35.00	60.00
	1805 (error date)		5.50	8.50	36.50	65.00
44	1803	—	5.00	8.00	40.00	80.00
	1804	—	5.00	8.00	40.00	80.00
	1805	—	5.00	8.00	40.00	80.00
	1806	—	5.00	8.00	40.00	80.00
	1807	—	5.00	8.00	40.00	80.00

Obv: Arms, leg: FERD.III. . . . Rev: Value.

C#	Date	Mintage	VG	Fine	VF	XF
53	1819	—	2.75	4.00	15.00	30.00
	1820	—	2.75	4.00	15.00	30.00
	1821	—	2.75	4.00	15.00	30.00
	1822	—	2.75	4.00	15.00	30.00
	1824	—	2.75	4.00	15.00	30.00

Obv. leg: LEOP. II A.D.'A. GRAND. DI TOSC.

C#	Date	Mintage	VG	Fine	VF	XF
62	1827	—	2.75	4.00	12.00	25.00
	1828	—	2.75	4.00	12.00	25.00
	1829	—	2.75	4.00	12.00	25.00
	1830	—	2.75	4.00	12.00	25.00
	1831	—	2.75	4.00	12.00	25.00
	1832	—	2.75	4.00	12.00	25.00
	1833	—	2.75	4.00	12.00	25.00
	1834	—	2.75	4.00	12.00	25.00
	1835	—	2.75	4.00	12.00	25.00
	1836	—	2.75	4.00	12.00	25.00
	1837	—	2.75	4.00	12.00	25.00
	1838	—	2.75	4.00	12.00	25.00
	1840	—	2.75	4.00	12.00	25.00
	1841	—	5.00	7.50	35.00	60.00
	1843	—	5.00	7.50	35.00	60.00

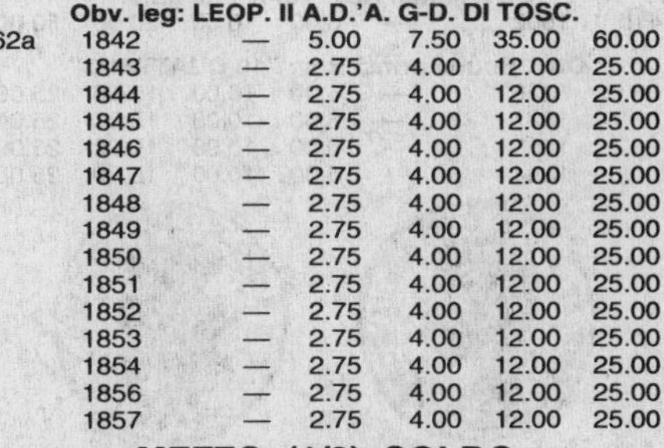

Obv. leg: LEOP. II A.D.'A. G-D. DI TOSC.

C#	Date	Mintage	VG	Fine	VF	XF
62a	1842	—	5.00	7.50	35.00	60.00
	1843	—	2.75	4.00	12.00	25.00
	1844	—	2.75	4.00	12.00	25.00
	1845	—	2.75	4.00	12.00	25.00
	1846	—	2.75	4.00	12.00	25.00
	1847	—	2.75	4.00	12.00	25.00
	1848	—	2.75	4.00	12.00	25.00
	1849	—	2.75	4.00	12.00	25.00
	1850	—	2.75	4.00	12.00	25.00
	1851	—	2.75	4.00	12.00	25.00
	1852	—	2.75	4.00	12.00	25.00
	1853	—	2.75	4.00	12.00	25.00
	1854	—	2.75	4.00	12.00	25.00
	1856	—	2.75	4.00	12.00	25.00
	1857	—	2.75	4.00	12.00	25.00

MEZZO (1/2) SOLDO

COPPER

C#	Date	Mintage	VG	Fine	VF	XF
45	ND(1804)	—	3.50	5.00	40.00	65.00

3 QUATTRINI

COPPER

C#	Date	Mintage	VG	Fine	VF	XF
64	1826	—	2.75	4.00	10.00	30.00
	1827	—	2.75	4.00	10.00	30.00
	1828	—	2.75	4.00	10.00	30.00
	1829	—	4.50	9.00	35.00	60.00
	1830	—	2.75	4.00	10.00	30.00
	1832	—	2.75	4.00	10.00	30.00
	1833	—	2.75	4.00	10.00	30.00
	1834	—	2.75	4.00	10.00	30.00
	1835	—	2.75	4.00	10.00	30.00

C#	Date	Mintage	VG	Fine	VF	XF
64	1836	—	2.75	4.00	10.00	30.00
	1838	—	2.75	4.00	10.00	30.00
	1839	—	2.75	4.00	10.00	30.00
	1840	—	2.75	4.00	10.00	30.00
	1843	—	2.75	4.00	10.00	30.00
	1845	—	2.75	4.00	10.00	30.00
	1846	—	2.75	4.00	10.00	30.00
	1851	—	2.75	4.00	10.00	30.00
	1853	—	2.75	4.00	10.00	30.00
	1854	—	4.50	9.00	35.00	60.00

SOLDO

COPPER
Obv: Arms, leg: FERD.III. . . . . Rev: Value.

C#	Date	Mintage	VG	Fine	VF	XF
54	1822	—	2.00	4.00	10.00	30.00
	1823	—	2.00	4.00	10.00	30.00

Obv: Arms, leg: LEOP.II. . . . . Rev: Value.

C#	Date	Mintage	VG	Fine	VF	XF
63	1824	—	15.00	30.00	50.00	100.00

5 QUATTRINI

BILLON

C#	Date	Mintage	VG	Fine	VF	XF
65	1826	—	3.50	7.00	30.00	40.00
	1828	—	5.00	10.00	35.00	45.00
	1829	—	3.50	7.00	30.00	40.00
	1830	—	3.50	7.00	30.00	40.00

2 SOLDI

COPPER
Obv: Arms, leg. Rev: Value.

C#	Date	Mintage	VG	Fine	VF	XF
46	1804	—	6.00	12.00	50.00	75.00
	1805	—	6.00	12.00	50.00	75.00

Obv: Arms, leg: FERDINANDUS III. . . . . Rev: Value.

C#	Date	Mintage	VG	Fine	VF	XF
55	1818	—	2.00	4.00	10.00	30.00
	1822	—	2.00	4.00	10.00	30.00

DIECI (10) QUATTRINI

BILLON

C#	Date	Mintage	VG	Fine	VF	XF
32	1801	—	4.50	6.50	10.00	30.00

Obv: Squarish arms. Rev: Value.

C#	Date	Mintage	VG	Fine	VF	XF
41	1801	—	6.00	10.00	35.00	75.00
	1802	—	6.00	10.00	35.00	75.00

Obv: Arms and date. Rev: Value in field.

C#	Date	Mintage	VG	Fine	VF	XF
41a	1802	—	12.00	20.00	50.00	100.00

Obv: Arms. Rev: Value and date.

C#	Date	Mintage	VG	Fine	VF	XF
41b	1802	—	6.00	10.00	20.00	50.00

Obv: Round arms. Rev: "10 QUATTRINI"

C#	Date	Mintage	VG	Fine	VF	XF
66	1826	—	6.00	10.00	15.00	25.00
	1827	—	6.00	10.00	15.00	25.00
	1853	—	6.00	10.00	15.00	25.00
	1854	—	6.00	10.00	15.00	25.00

C#	Date	Mintage	VG	Fine	VF	XF
67	1858	—	12.00	20.00	30.00	50.00

1/2 PAOLO

1.3700 g, .920 SILVER, .0405 oz ASW

C#	Date	Mintage	VG	Fine	VF	XF
68	1832	—	7.50	15.00	35.00	65.00
	1839	—	7.50	15.00	25.00	40.00

C#	Date	Mintage	VG	Fine	VF	XF
68a	1853	—	7.50	15.00	35.00	65.00
	1856	—	7.50	15.00	35.00	65.00
	1857	—	7.50	15.00	35.00	65.00
	1859	—	7.50	15.00	35.00	65.00

1/4 DI FIORINO

1.7190 g, .916 SILVER, .0506 oz ASW
Obv: Arms. Rev: Value.

C#	Date	Mintage	VG	Fine	VF	XF
69	1827	—	12.00	20.00	50.00	100.00

10 SOLDI

2.5100 g, .913 SILVER, .0736 oz ASW
Obv: Arms. Rev: Value.

C#	Date	Mintage	VG	Fine	VF	XF
56	1821	—	6.00	10.00	15.00	25.00
	1823	—	6.00	10.00	15.00	25.00

PAOLO

2.7400 g, .920 SILVER, .0810 oz ASW

C#	Date	Mintage	VG	Fine	VF	XF
70	1831	—	7.50	15.00	30.00	50.00
	1832	—	7.50	15.00	30.00	50.00
	1838	—	7.50	15.00	30.00	50.00

C#	Date	Mintage	VG	Fine	VF	XF
70a	1842	—	7.50	15.00	30.00	50.00
	1843	—	7.50	15.00	30.00	50.00
	1845	—	7.50	15.00	30.00	50.00
	1846	—	7.50	15.00	30.00	50.00
	1856	—	7.50	15.00	30.00	50.00
	1857	—	7.50	15.00	30.00	50.00
	1858	—	7.50	15.00	30.00	50.00

LIRA

3.9000 g, .920 SILVER, .1153 oz ASW

C#	Date	Mintage	VG	Fine	VF	XF
47	1803	—	10.00	15.00	30.00	75.00
	1806	—	10.00	15.00	30.00	75.00

4.1030 g, .913 SILVER, .1204 oz ASW
Obv: Head right. Rev: Value.

C#	Date	Mintage	VG	Fine	VF	XF
57	1821	—	12.00	20.00	50.00	100.00
	1822	—	12.00	20.00	50.00	100.00
	1823	—	12.00	20.00	50.00	100.00

1/2 FIORINO

3.4380 g, .916 SILVER, .1012 oz ASW
Obv: Arms. Rev: Value.

C#	Date	Mintage	VG	Fine	VF	XF
71	1827	—	10.00	17.50	35.00	75.00

FIORINO

6.8760 g, .916 SILVER, .2025 oz ASW

C#	Date	Mintage	VG	Fine	VF	XF
72	1826	—	10.00	15.00	25.00	75.00
	1828	—	10.00	15.00	25.00	75.00
	1830	—	10.00	15.00	25.00	75.00
	1840	—	10.00	15.00	25.00	75.00
	1842	—	10.00	15.00	25.00	75.00

C#	Date	Mintage	VG	Fine	VF	XF
72a	1843	—	10.00	15.00	25.00	50.00
	1844	—	10.00	15.00	25.00	50.00
	1847	—	10.00	15.00	25.00	50.00
	1848	—	10.00	15.00	25.00	50.00
	1856	—	10.00	15.00	25.00	50.00
	1857	—	10.00	15.00	25.00	50.00
	1858	—	10.00	15.00	25.00	50.00

5 PAOLI

13.7500 g, .913 SILVER, .4036 oz ASW

C#	Date	Mintage	VG	Fine	VF	XF
58	1819	—	30.00	50.00	200.00	350.00
	1820	—	30.00	50.00	100.00	200.00

Obv: Longer hair.

C#	Date	Mintage	VG	Fine	VF	XF
58a	1823	—	60.00	100.00	250.00	500.00

13.7500 g, .916 SILVER, .4049 oz ASW

C#	Date	Mintage	VG	Fine	VF	XF
73	1827	—	25.00	40.00	80.00	200.00
	1828	—	25.00	40.00	80.00	200.00
	1829 PC	—	25.00	40.00	80.00	200.00

C#	Date	Mintage	VG	Fine	VF	XF
73a	1834	—	125.00	150.00	250.00	600.00

FRANCESCONE

(10 Paoli)

27.5000 g, .917 SILVER, .8108 oz ASW
Obv: Bust right. Rev: Crowned arms.

C#	Date	Mintage	VG	Fine	VF	XF
37	1801	—	25.00	50.00	100.00	200.00

NOTE: Earlier dates (1791-1800) exist for this type.

27.5000 g, .934 SILVER, .8258 oz ASW

C#	Date	Mintage	VG	Fine	VF	XF
42.1	1801	—	200.00	400.00	800.00	1500.
	1802	—	200.00	400.00	800.00	1500.

Obv. and rev: Small legends.

C#	Date	Mintage	VG	Fine	VF	XF
42.2	1803	—	65.00	100.00	150.00	300.00

Rev: Modified order chain.

C#	Date	Mintage	VG	Fine	VF	XF
42.3	1803	—	65.00	100.00	150.00	300.00

27.5000 g, .913 SILVER, .8073 oz ASW
Obv. leg: CAROLVS LVD. . . .

C#	Date	Mintage	VG	Fine	VF	XF
50.1	1803	—	50.00	75.00	125.00	300.00
	1806	—	50.00	75.00	125.00	300.00
	1807	—	45.00	65.00	110.00	250.00

Obv. leg: CAROLUS LUD. . . . .

C#	Date	Mintage	VG	Fine	VF	XF
50.2	1806	—	45.00	65.00	110.00	250.00

C#	Date	Mintage	VG	Fine	VF	XF
59	1814	—	50.00	75.00	125.00	275.00
	1815	—	50.00	75.00	125.00	250.00
	1819	—	50.00	75.00	125.00	250.00
	1820	—	50.00	75.00	125.00	250.00
	1824	—	50.00	75.00	125.00	250.00

QUATTRO (4) FIORINI

27.5000 g, .916 SILVER, .8099 oz ASW

C#	Date	Mintage	VG	Fine	VF	XF
74	1826	—	50.00	100.00	200.00	500.00

C#	Date	Mintage	VG	Fine	VF	XF
75	1830	—	100.00	300.00	500.00	1450.

C#	Date	Mintage	VG	Fine	VF	XF
75a	1833	—	35.00	80.00	125.00	200.00
	1834	—	35.00	80.00	125.00	200.00
	1836	—	35.00	80.00	125.00	200.00
	1839	—	50.00	100.00	250.00	635.00
	1840	—	35.00	80.00	125.00	200.00
	1841	—	35.00	80.00	125.00	200.00

C#	Date	Mintage	VG	Fine	VF	XF
75b	1845	—	35.00	70.00	100.00	200.00
	1846	—	35.00	70.00	100.00	200.00
	1856	—	35.00	70.00	100.00	200.00
	1858	—	35.00	70.00	100.00	200.00
	1859	—	35.00	70.00	100.00	200.00

5 LIRE

19.7230 g, .958 SILVER, .6075 oz ASW

C#	Date	Mintage	VG	Fine	VF	XF
48	1803	—	25.00	40.00	125.00	250.00
	1804	—	25.00	40.00	100.00	200.00

10 LIRE

39.4470 g, .958 SILVER, 1.2151 oz ASW
Rev. leg: FLORENTIAE - date.

C#	Date	Mintage	VG	Fine	VF	XF
49.1	1803	—	50.00	90.00	150.00	350.00
	1804	—	50.00	90.00	150.00	350.00
	1805	—	50.00	90.00	150.00	350.00
	1806	—	60.00	100.00	175.00	400.00

NOTE: Legend varieties exist.

Rev. leg: FLOR - date.

C#	Date	Mintage	VG	Fine	VF	XF
49.2	1807	—	40.00	75.00	135.00	300.00

ZECCHINO

For Levant Trade

3.4900 g, .998 GOLD, .1119 oz AGW
Obv: St. Zenobio kneeling before Christ.
Rev: St. John.

C#	Date	Mintage	VG	Fine	VF	XF
51	ND(1805)	—	1500.	3000.	5000.	7000.

C#	Date	Mintage	VG	Fine	VF	XF
60	1816	—	175.00	225.00	300.00	500.00
	1821	—	175.00	225.00	300.00	500.00

3.4520 g, .998 GOLD, .1107 oz AGW

C#	Date	Mintage	VG	Fine	VF	XF
76	1824	—	100.00	150.00	200.00	400.00
	1826	—	100.00	150.00	200.00	400.00
	1829	—	100.00	150.00	200.00	400.00
	1832	—	100.00	150.00	200.00	400.00
	1853	—	100.00	150.00	200.00	400.00

RUSPONE

(3 Zecchini)

10.4610 g, .999 GOLD, .3360 oz AGW
Obv. leg: FERDINANDUS III. . . .

C#	Date	Mintage	VG	Fine	VF	XF
39	1801	—	300.00	475.00	650.00	1000.

NOTE: Earlier dates (1791-1800) exist for this type.

10.4110 g, .998 GOLD, .3340 oz AGW
Obv. leg: LUD.D.G. . . .

C#	Date	Mintage	VG	Fine	VF	XF
43	1801	—	500.00	800.00	1600.	3000.
	1803	—	400.00	650.00	1200.	2000.

C#	Date	Mintage	VG	Fine	VF	XF
52	1803	—	375.00	600.00	800.00	1250.
	1804	—	375.00	600.00	800.00	1250.
	1805	—	300.00	400.00	650.00	1000.
	1806	—	300.00	400.00	650.00	1000.
	1807	—	300.00	400.00	650.00	1000.

C#	Date	Mintage	VG	Fine	VF	XF
61	1815	—	350.00	550.00	800.00	1250.
	1816	—	350.00	550.00	800.00	1250.
	1818	—	350.00	550.00	800.00	1250.
	1820	—	350.00	550.00	800.00	1250.
	1823	—	350.00	550.00	800.00	1250.

C#	Date	Mintage	VG	Fine	VF	XF
77	1824	—	250.00	400.00	650.00	1000.
	1825	—	250.00	400.00	650.00	1000.
	1829	—	250.00	400.00	650.00	1000.
	1834	—	250.00	400.00	650.00	1000.
	1836	—	250.00	400.00	650.00	1000.

OTTANTA (80) FIORINI

32.6500 g, .999 GOLD, 1.0487 oz AGW

C#	Date	Mintage	VG	Fine	VF	XF
78	1827	—	400.00	550.00	1000.	2250.
	1828	—	400.00	550.00	1000.	2250.

1ST PROVISIONAL GOV'T.

(1859)

FIORINO

6.8800 g, .917 SILVER, .2028 oz ASW

C#	Date	Mintage	VG	Fine	VF	XF
79	1859	—	12.50	25.00	50.00	100.00

RUSPONE

10.4700 g, .998 GOLD, .3359 oz AGW

C#	Date	Mintage	Fine	VF	XF	Unc
80	1859	—	3000.	4000.	6000.	10,000.

2ND PROVISIONAL GOV'T.

(Italian 1859-1861)

CENTESIMO

COPPER

C#	Date	Mintage	VG	Fine	VF	XF
81	1859	25.000	4.00	8.00	17.50	40.00

2 CENTESIMI

COPPER

C#	Date	Mintage	VG	Fine	VF	XF
82	1859	12.500	4.00	8.00	17.50	40.00

5 CENTESIMI

COPPER

C#	Date	Mintage	VG	Fine	VF	XF
83	1859	10.000	4.00	8.00	17.50	40.00

CINQUANTA (50) CENTESIMI

2.5000 g, .900 SILVER, .0723 oz ASW
Mint mark: FIRENZE

C#	Date	Mintage	Fine	VF	XF	Unc
84	1860	2.430	5.00	10.00	25.00	75.00
	1861	1.222	100.00	200.00	400.00	1000.

LIRA

5.0000 g, .900 SILVER, .1446 oz ASW
Mint mark: FIRENZE
Rev: W/o dash between FIRENZE and date.

C#	Date	Mintage	Fine	VF	XF	Unc
85.1	1859	.061	15.00	30.00	75.00	200.00
	1860/59	1.655	12.50	22.50	55.00	110.00
	1860	Inc. Ab.	10.00	20.00	50.00	100.00

Rev: FIRENZE - 1860.

C#	Date	Mintage	Fine	VF	XF	Unc
85.2	1860	Inc. Ab.	7.50	15.00	30.00	80.00

2 LIRE

10.0000 g, .900 SILVER, .2892 oz ASW
Mint mark: FIRENZE

C#	Date	Mintage	Fine	VF	XF	Unc
86	1860	.559	30.00	60.00	100.00	300.00
	1861	.164	200.00	400.00	1000.	3000.

VENICE

Venezia

A seaport of Venetia was founded by refugees from the Hun invasions. From that time until the arrival of Napoleon in 1797, it maintained an enormous foreign trade involving the possession of many islands in the Mediterranean while keeping a state of quasi-independence despite the antagonism of jealous Italian states and the Ottoman Turks. During the French Occupation Napoleon handed it over to Austria. Later, upon the defeat of the Austrians by Prussia in 1860, Venice then became a part of the United Kingdom of Italy.

RULERS

Franz II (of Austria) 1798-1806

MINT MARKS

A - Vienna
F - Hall
V - Venice
ZV - Zecca Venezia - Venice
None - Venice

AUSTRIAN OCCUPATION

MEZZA (1/2) LIRA

4.5000 g, .250 SILVER, .0361 oz ASW
Mint mark: V
Obv: Similar to 1 Lira, KM#164.1.
Rev: Value, date within ornate border.

C#	Date	Mintage	VG	Fine	VF	XF
163.1	1802	—	15.00	25.00	75.00	175.00

Mint mark: A

C#	Date	Mintage	VG	Fine	VF	XF
163.2	1802	—	— Reported, not confirmed			

Mint mark: F

C#	Date	Mintage	VG	Fine	VF	XF
163.3	1802	—	— Reported, not confirmed			

UNA (1) LIRA

11.3600 g, .250 SILVER, .0913 oz ASW

C#	Date	Mintage	VG	Fine	VF	XF
164.1	1802	—	15.00	25.00	75.00	175.00

Mint mark: A

C#	Date	Mintage	VG	Fine	VF	XF
164.2	1802	—	— Reported, not confirmed			

Mint mark: F

C#	Date	Mintage	VG	Fine	VF	XF
164.3	1802	—	— Reported, not confirmed			

1-1/2 LIRE

8.4900 g, .250 SILVER, .0682 oz ASW
Mint mark: A
Obv: Imperial eagle. Rev: Value, date within ornate border.

C#	Date	Mintage	VG	Fine	VF	XF
165.1	1802	—	10.00	15.00	35.00	75.00

Mint mark: F

C#	Date	Mintage	VG	Fine	VF	XF
165.2	1802	—	15.00	30.00	60.00	140.00

DUE (2) LIRE

.250 SILVER, 7.95-9.46 g
Mint mark: V
Obv: Large imperial eagle.
Rev: Value, date within wreath.

C#	Date	Mintage	VG	Fine	VF	XF
162	1801	—	25.00	40.00	80.00	200.00

NOTE: Three varieties exist.

Obv: Smaller imperial eagle, uncollared strike.

C#	Date	Mintage	VG	Fine	VF	XF
162a	1801	—	20.00	50.00	100.00	250.00

NOTE: Overstruck on Austria, KM#2148.

REVOLUTIONARY ISSUES

(1848-1849)

MONETARY SYSTEM

100 Centesimi = 1 Lire

CENTESIMO

COPPER
Mint mark: ZV

C#	Date	Mintage	Fine	VF	XF	Unc
181	1849	2.761	3.00	7.00	15.00	30.00

3 CENTESIMI

COPPER
Mint mark: ZV

C#	Date	Mintage	Fine	VF	XF	Unc
182	1849	1.044	3.00	6.00	10.00	25.00

5 CENTESIMI

COPPER
Mint mark: ZV

C#	Date	Mintage	Fine	VF	XF	Unc
183	1849	1.187	3.00	6.00	12.00	30.00

15 CENTESIMI

1.2600 g, .229 SILVER, .0092 oz ASW
Mint mark: ZV

C#	Date	Mintage	Fine	VF	XF	Unc
184	1848	.155	10.00	15.00	25.00	50.00

25 CENTESIMI

1.2500 g, .900 SILVER, .0361 oz ASW
Mint mark: V

C#	Date	Mintage	Fine	VF	XF	Unc
A184	1848	—	75.00	150.00	400.00	1000.

5 LIRE

25.0000 g, .900 SILVER, .7234 oz ASW

C#	Date	Mintage	Fine	VF	XF	Unc
185	1848	6,011	75.00	125.00	200.00	375.00

Mint mark: V
Edge inscription: DIO BENEDITE L'ITALIA.

C#	Date	Mintage	Fine	VF	XF	Unc
186	1848	.011	75.00	125.00	225.00	450.00

Edge inscription error: DIO BENEDETE L'ITALIA.

C#	Date	Mintage	Fine	VF	XF	Unc
186a	1848	Inc. Ab.	100.00	200.00	325.00	650.00

20 LIRE

6.4500 g, .900 GOLD, .1866 oz AGW

C#	Date	Mintage	Fine	VF	XF	Unc
187	1848	5,210	350.00	700.00	1500.	2400.

PALMA NOVA

(In Venetia)

Was ceded to France by Austria in 1806 and was returned to Austria in 1814. In 1860 it was incorporated in the United Kingdom of Italy.

SIEGE COINAGE

Issues of French defenders in 1814

50 CENTESIMI

BILLON

C#	Date	Mintage	VG	Fine	VF	XF
2	1814	—	100.00	150.00	250.00	450.00

NOTE: Presentation pieces struck in a collar exhibit a raised rim and carry a premium.

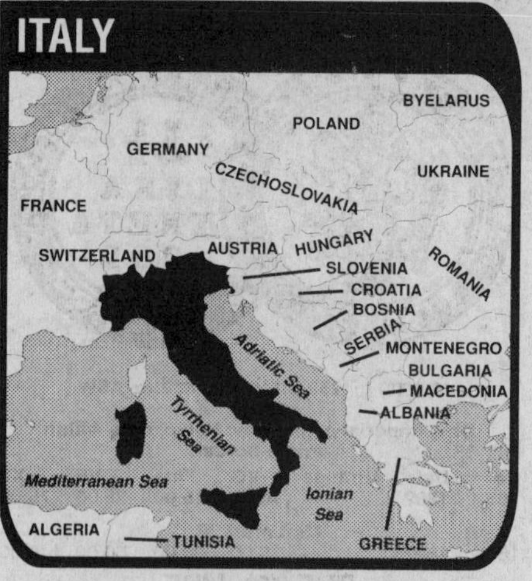

The Italian Republic, a 700-mile-long peninsula extending into the heart of the Mediterranean Sea, has an area of 116,304 sq. mi. (301,230 sq. km.) and a population of 60 million. Capital: Rome. The economy centers about agriculture, manufacturing, forestry and fishing. Machinery, textiles, clothing and motor vehicles are exported.

From the fall of Rome until modern times, 'Italy' was little more than a geographical expression. Although nominally included in the Empire of Charlemagne and the Holy Roman Empire, it was in reality divided into a number of independent states and kingdoms presided over by wealthy families, soldiers of fortune or hereditary rulers. The 19th century unification movement fostered by Mazzini, Garibaldi and Cavour attained fruition in 1860-70 with the creation of the Kingdom of Italy and the installation of Victor Emmanuel, king of Sardinia, as king of Italy. Benito Mussolini came to power during the postWorld War I period of economic and political unrest, installed a Fascist dictatorship with a figurehead king as titular Head of State, and allied with Germany for the pursuit of World War II. Following the defeat of the Axis powers, the Italian monarchy was dissolved by plebiscite, and the Italian Republic proclaimed.

KINGDOM

RULERS

Vittorio Emanuele II, 1861-1878
Umberto I, 1878-1900
Vittorio Emanuele III, 1900-1946
Umberto II, 1946
Republic, 1946—

MINT MARKS

B - Bologna (1861)
B/I - Birmingham (1893-1894)
FIRENZE - Florence (1861)
H - Birmingham (1866-1867)
KB - Berlin (1894)
M - Milan (1861-1887)
N - Naples (1861-1867)
OM - Strasbourg (1866-1867)
R - Rome (All coins from 1878 have R except where noted).
T - Turin (1861-1867)
No MM - Paris (1862-1866)

MONETARY SYSTEM

100 Centesimi = 1 Lira

CENTESIMO

COPPER

Mint mark: M

KM#	Date	Mintage	Fine	VF	XF	Unc
1.1	1861	75.000	.75	1.50	3.00	10.00
	1861 inverted M	Inc. Ab.	15.00	30.00	60.00	200.00
	1867	72.759	.75	1.50	3.00	10.00

Mint mark: N

KM#	Date	Mintage	Fine	VF	XF	Unc
1.2	1861	48.280	3.75	8.00	15.00	30.00
	1862/1	37.500	6.00	12.00	20.00	35.00
	1862	Inc. Ab.	1.25	2.00	4.00	15.00

Mint mark: T

KM#	Date	Mintage	Fine	VF	XF	Unc
1.3	1867	5.000	5.00	12.50	22.50	45.00

Mint mark: R

KM#	Date	Mintage	Fine	VF	XF	Unc
29	1895/8	13.860	1.50	3.00	7.00	22.50
	1895	Inc. Ab.	1.00	2.00	4.00	10.00
	1896	3.730	1.00	2.00	4.00	10.00
	1897	1.845	10.00	17.50	25.00	40.00
	1899	1.287	1.25	2.00	4.00	10.00
	1900	10.000	1.00	2.00	4.00	10.00

KM#	Date	Mintage	Fine	VF	XF	Unc
35	1902	.026	165.00	450.00	850.00	1500.
	1903	5.655	1.00	2.00	4.00	15.00
	1904/0	14.626	2.00	3.00	7.50	20.00
	1904	Inc. Ab.	1.00	2.00	4.00	10.00
	1905/0	8.531	2.00	3.00	7.50	20.00
	1905	Inc. Ab.	1.00	2.00	4.00	10.00
	1908	3.859	1.00	2.00	4.00	10.00

KM#	Date	Mintage	Fine	VF	XF	Unc
40	1908	.057	150.00	225.00	450.00	800.00
	1909	3.539	1.00	2.00	4.00	10.00
	1910	3.599	1.00	2.00	4.00	10.00
	1911	.700	5.00	10.00	15.00	25.00
	1912	3.995	1.00	2.00	4.00	10.00
	1913	3.200	1.00	2.00	4.00	10.00
	1914	11.585	1.00	2.00	4.00	10.00
	1915	9.757	1.00	2.00	4.00	10.00
	1916	9.845	1.00	2.00	4.00	10.00
	1917	2.400	1.00	2.00	4.00	10.00
	1918	2.710	5.00	10.00	15.00	25.00

2 CENTESIMI

COPPER

Mint mark: M

KM#	Date	Mintage	Fine	VF	XF	Unc
2.1	1861	37.500	.60	1.50	4.00	15.00
	1867	54.212	.60	1.50	4.00	20.00

Mint mark: N

KM#	Date	Mintage	Fine	VF	XF	Unc
2.2	1861	23.055	.60	1.50	3.50	15.00
	1862	33.195	.60	1.50	3.50	15.00

Mint mark: T

KM#	Date	Mintage	Fine	VF	XF	Unc
2.3	1867	5.000	2.00	4.25	8.50	17.50

Mint mark: R

KM#	Date	Mintage	Fine	VF	XF	Unc
30	1895	.305	10.00	17.50	35.00	60.00
	1896	.282	25.00	50.00	100.00	150.00
	1897	4.415	.60	1.50	4.00	12.50
	1898	4.161	.60	1.50	4.00	12.50
	1900	2.735	.60	1.50	4.00	12.50

KM#	Date	Mintage	Fine	VF	XF	Unc
38	1903	5.000	.60	1.50	4.00	12.50
	1905	1.260	4.00	8.50	18.00	30.00
	1906	3.145	.60	1.50	3.50	7.50
	1907	.230	25.00	50.00	75.00	150.00
	1908	1.518	1.00	2.50	5.00	15.00

KM#	Date	Mintage	Fine	VF	XF	Unc
41	1908	.298	9.00	15.00	25.00	80.00
	1909	2.419	.60	1.50	3.00	15.00
	1910	.590	2.00	4.00	9.00	30.00
	1911	2.777	.60	1.50	3.00	15.00
	1912	.840	.60	2.00	5.00	16.00
	1914	1.648	.50	1.30	2.00	15.00
	1915	4.860	.50	1.30	2.50	15.00
	1916	1.540	.50	1.30	2.00	15.00
	1917	3.638	.50	1.30	2.00	15.00

5 CENTESIMI

COPPER
Mint mark: B

KM#	Date	Mintage	Fine	VF	XF	Unc
3.1	1861	3.809	15.00	30.00	50.00	125.00

Mint mark: M

KM#	Date	Mintage	Fine	VF	XF	Unc
3.2	1861	210.000	.60	1.50	6.00	40.00
	1867	24.000	.60	1.50	5.00	30.00

Mint mark: N

KM#	Date	Mintage	Fine	VF	XF	Unc
3.3	1861	103.707	.60	1.50	7.50	45.00
	1862	106.293	.60	1.50	7.50	45.00
	1867	46.000	.60	1.50	7.50	45.00

Mint mark: R

KM#	Date	Mintage	Fine	VF	XF	Unc
31	1895	.508	10.00	17.50	30.00	80.00
	1896	.380	10.00	20.00	35.00	100.00
	1900	2,000	250.00	350.00	500.00	1000.

NOTE: 2,000 of the 1900 dated coins were struck but most were remelted and not issued.

KM#	Date	Mintage	Fine	VF	XF	Unc
42	1908	.824	10.00	25.00	50.00	130.00
	1909	1.734	.75	1.75	3.50	15.00
	1912	.743	1.75	3.00	6.00	30.00
	1913 dot after D	1.964	4.00	10.00	15.00	50.00
	1913 w/o dot after D	Inc. Ab.	40.00	75.00	150.00	250.00
	1915	1.038	3.50	7.50	12.50	30.00
	1918	4.242	.75	1.75	3.50	15.00

KM#	Date	Mintage	Fine	VF	XF	Unc
59	1919	13.208	.75	2.00	3.00	10.00
	1920	33.372	.30	.75	2.00	5.00
	1921	80.111	.30	.75	2.00	5.00
	1922	42.914	.30	.75	2.00	5.00
	1923	29.614	.30	.75	2.00	5.00
	1924	20.352	.30	.75	2.00	5.00
	1925	40.460	.30	.75	2.00	5.00
	1926	21.158	.30	.75	2.00	5.00
	1927	15.800	.30	.75	2.00	5.00
	1928	16.090	.30	.75	2.00	5.00
	1929	29.000	.30	.75	2.00	5.00
	1930	22.694	.30	.75	2.00	5.00
	1931	20.000	.30	.75	2.00	5.00
	1932	11.456	.30	.75	2.00	5.00
	1933	20.720	.30	.75	2.00	5.00
	1934	16.000	.30	.75	2.00	5.00
	1935	11.000	.30	.75	2.00	5.00
	1936	9.462	.30	.75	2.00	5.00
	1937	.972	4.00	8.00	12.50	25.00

KM#	Date	Mintage	Fine	VF	XF	Unc
73	1936, yr. XIV	Inc. Ab.	2.00	4.00	8.00	15.00
	1937, yr. XV	7.207	.30	.75	1.00	3.00
	1938, yr. XVI	24.000	.20	.65	1.00	3.00
	1939, yr. XVII	22.000	.20	.65	1.00	3.00

ALUMINUM-BRONZE

KM#	Date	Mintage	Fine	VF	XF	Unc
73a	1939, yr. XVII	1.000	.30	.75	1.25	3.00
	1940, yr. XVIII	9.630	.30	.75	1.00	3.00
	1941, yr. XIX	16.340	.30	.75	1.00	3.00
	1942, yr. XX	25.200	.30	.75	1.25	3.00
	1943, yr. XXI	13.922	2.00	5.00	10.00	20.00

10 CENTESIMI

COPPER
Mint mark: M

KM#	Date	Mintage	Fine	VF	XF	Unc
11.1	1862	40.000	1.50	3.50	7.00	50.00
	1866	36.000	1.50	3.50	7.00	50.00

Mint mark: None

KM#	Date	Mintage	Fine	VF	XF	Unc
11.2	1862	—	1.50	3.50	7.00	50.00
	1863	80.000	1.50	3.50	7.00	50.00
	1866	—	15.00	25.00	35.00	50.00

Mint mark: H

KM#	Date	Mintage	Fine	VF	XF	Unc
11.3	1866	40.000	1.50	3.50	7.00	50.00
	1867	50.000	1.50	3.50	7.00	50.00

Mint mark: N

KM#	Date	Mintage	Fine	VF	XF	Unc
11.4	1866	67.650	1.50	3.50	7.00	50.00
	1867	31.360	1.50	3.50	7.00	50.00

Mint mark: OM

KM#	Date	Mintage	Fine	VF	XF	Unc
11.5	1866	20.000	1.50	3.50	7.00	50.00
	1866.	Inc. Ab.	1.50	3.50	7.00	50.00
	1867	—	1.50	3.50	7.00	50.00
	1867.	—	3.00	5.00	12.50	50.00

Mint mark: T

KM#	Date	Mintage	Fine	VF	XF	Unc
11.6	1866	16.350	1.50	3.50	7.00	50.00
	1867	18.640	1.50	3.50	7.00	50.00

Mint mark: B/I

KM#	Date	Mintage	Fine	VF	XF	Unc
27.1	1893	8.547	1.50	3.50	7.00	30.00
	1894	32.000	1.50	3.50	7.00	30.00

Mint mark: R

KM#	Date	Mintage	Fine	VF	XF	Unc
27.2	1893	28.000	1.50	3.50	8.00	50.00
	1894	5.910	5.00	10.00	25.00	50.00

Similar to 5 Centesimi, KM#42.

KM#	Date	Mintage	Fine	VF	XF	Unc
43	1908	—	1000.	1800.	2200.	3000.

50th Anniversary of Kingdom

KM#	Date	Mintage	Fine	VF	XF	Unc
51	1911	2.000	2.50	5.00	10.00	30.00

KM#	Date	Mintage	Fine	VF	XF	Unc
60	1919	.986	20.00	35.00	50.00	100.00
	1920	37.995	.50	1.25	4.00	10.00
	1921	66.510	.50	1.25	4.00	10.00
	1922	45.217	.50	1.25	4.00	10.00
	1923	31.529	.50	1.25	4.00	10.00
	1924	35.312	.50	1.25	4.00	10.00
	1925	22.370	.50	1.25	4.00	10.00
	1926	25.190	.50	1.25	4.00	10.00
	1927	22.673	.50	1.25	4.00	10.00
	1928	15.680	.50	2.00	7.50	20.00
	1929	15.593	.50	1.25	4.00	10.00
	1930	17.115	.50	1.25	4.00	10.00
	1931	10.750	.50	1.25	4.00	10.00
	1932	5.678	1.25	2.50	7.50	20.00
	1933	10.250	.50	1.25	4.00	10.00
	1934	18.300	.50	1.25	4.00	10.00
	1935	10.500	.50	1.25	4.00	10.00
	1936	8.770	.50	1.50	4.50	12.50
	1937	5.500	.50	1.50	4.50	12.50

KM#	Date	Mintage	Fine	VF	XF	Unc
74	1936, yr. XIV	Inc. Ab.	.75	1.50	3.00	12.50
	1937, yr. XV	7.212	.25	.75	1.50	4.00
	1938, yr. XVI	18.750	.25	.75	1.50	4.00
	1939, yr. XVII	24.750	.25	.75	1.50	4.00

ALUMINUM-BRONZE

KM#	Date	Mintage	Fine	VF	XF	Unc
74a	1939, yr. XVII	.750	.50	1.50	2.00	4.00
	1940, yr. XVIII	23.355	.20	.60	1.00	4.00
	1941, yr. XIX	27.050	.20	.60	1.00	4.00
	1942, yr. XX	18.100	.20	.60	1.00	4.00
	1943, yr. XXI	25.400	.25	.60	2.00	5.00

20 CENTESIMI

1.0000 g, .835 SILVER, .0268 oz ASW
Mint mark: T

KM#	Date	Mintage	Fine	VF	XF	Unc
12	1863 NB	461 pcs.	400.00	750.00	1500.	3000.

Mint mark: M

KM#	Date	Mintage	Fine	VF	XF	Unc
13.1	1863 BN	27.845	3.00	6.00	12.50	40.00

Mint mark: T

KM#	Date	Mintage	Fine	VF	XF	Unc
13.2	1863 BN	6.289	4.00	9.00	25.00	75.00
	1863 BN inverted BN	Inc. Ab.	10.00	25.00	60.00	175.00
	1867 BN	.866	20.00	50.00	100.00	300.00

COPPER-NICKEL
Mint mark: KB

KM#	Date	Mintage	Fine	VF	XF	Unc
28.1	1894	75.000	.40	1.00	3.00	8.00

Mint mark: R

KM#	Date	Mintage	Fine	VF	XF	Unc
28.2	1894	13.901	.60	1.50	3.00	12.00
	1895	11.099	.60	1.50	3.00	12.00

NICKEL

KM#	Date	Mintage	Fine	VF	XF	Unc
44	1908	14.315	.50	1.00	3.00	10.00
	1909	19.280	.50	1.00	3.00	10.00
	1910	21.887	.50	1.00	3.00	10.00
	1911	13.671	.50	1.00	3.00	10.00
	1912	21.040	.50	1.00	3.00	10.00
	1913	20.729	.50	1.00	3.00	10.00
	1914	14.308	.50	1.00	3.00	10.00
	1919	3.475	1.00	3.50	10.00	25.00
	1920	27.284	.50	1.00	3.00	10.00
	1921	50.372	.50	1.00	3.00	10.00
	1922	17.134	.50	1.00	3.00	10.00
	1926	500 pcs.	—	—	—	150.00
	1927	100 pcs.	—	—	—	200.00
	1928	50 pcs.	—	—	—	250.00
	1929	50 pcs.	—	—	—	250.00
	1930	50 pcs.	—	—	—	250.00
	1931	50 pcs.	—	—	—	250.00

KM#	Date	Mintage	Fine	VF	XF	Unc
44	1932	50 pcs.	—	—	—	250.00
	1933	50 pcs.	—	—	—	250.00
	1934	50 pcs.	—	—	—	250.00
	1935	50 pcs.	—	—	—	250.00

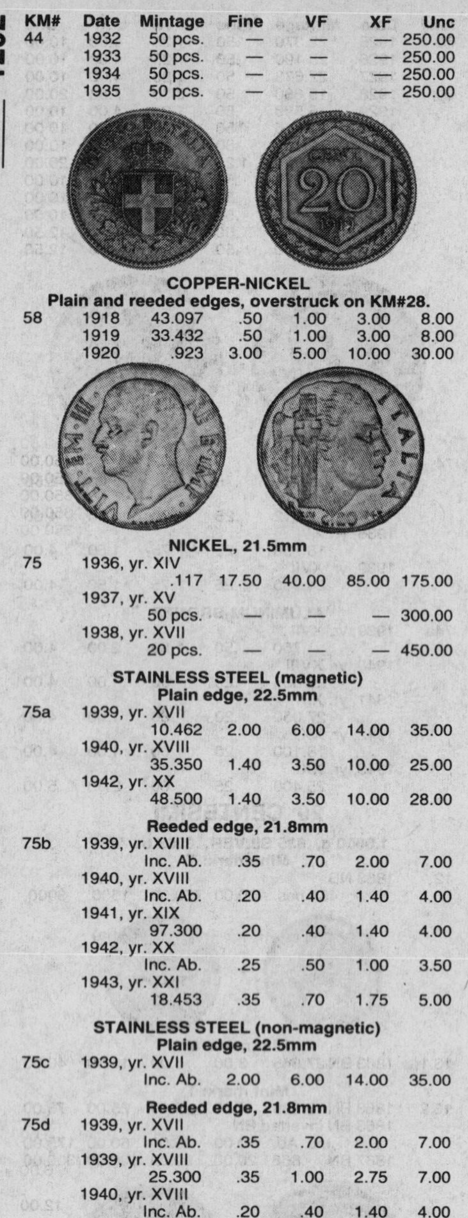

COPPER-NICKEL
Plain and reeded edges, overstruck on KM#28.

KM#	Date	Mintage	Fine	VF	XF	Unc
58	1918	43.097	.50	1.00	3.00	8.00
	1919	33.432	.50	1.00	3.00	8.00
	1920	.923	3.00	5.00	10.00	30.00

NICKEL, 21.5mm

KM#	Date	Mintage	Fine	VF	XF	Unc
75	1936, yr. XIV	.117	17.50	40.00	85.00	175.00
	1937, yr. XV	50 pcs.	—	—	—	300.00
	1938, yr. XVII	20 pcs.	—	—	—	450.00

STAINLESS STEEL (magnetic)
Plain edge, 22.5mm

KM#	Date	Mintage	Fine	VF	XF	Unc
75a	1939, yr. XVII	10.462	2.00	6.00	14.00	35.00
	1940, yr. XVIII	35.350	1.40	3.50	10.00	25.00
	1942, yr. XX	48.500	1.40	3.50	10.00	28.00

Reeded edge, 21.8mm

KM#	Date	Mintage	Fine	VF	XF	Unc
75b	1939, yr. XVIII	Inc. Ab.	.35	.70	2.00	7.00
	1940, yr. XVIII	Inc. Ab.	.20	.40	1.40	4.00
	1941, yr. XIX	97.300	.20	.40	1.40	4.00
	1942, yr. XX	Inc. Ab.	.25	.50	1.00	3.50
	1943, yr. XXI	18.453	.35	.70	1.75	5.00

STAINLESS STEEL (non-magnetic)
Plain edge, 22.5mm

KM#	Date	Mintage	Fine	VF	XF	Unc
75c	1939, yr. XVII	Inc. Ab.	2.00	6.00	14.00	35.00

Reeded edge, 21.8mm

KM#	Date	Mintage	Fine	VF	XF	Unc
75d	1939, yr. XVII	Inc. Ab.	.35	.70	2.00	7.00
	1939, yr. XVIII	25.300	.35	1.00	2.75	7.00
	1940, yr. XVIII	Inc. Ab.	.20	.40	1.40	4.00

25 CENTESIMI

NICKEL
Mint mark: R

KM#	Date	Mintage	Fine	VF	XF	Unc
36	1902	7.773	12.50	30.00	70.00	150.00
	1903	5.895	10.00	25.00	60.00	140.00

50 CENTESIMI

2.5000 g, .900 SILVER, .0723 oz ASW
Mint mark: FIRENZE

KM#	Date	Mintage	Fine	VF	XF	Unc
A4	1861 F	1.222	50.00	100.00	150.00	400.00

Mint mark: M

KM#	Date	Mintage	Fine	VF	XF	Unc
4.1	1861 BN	—	—	—	Rare	—

Mint mark: T

KM#	Date	Mintage	Fine	VF	XF	Unc
4.2	1861 B in shield	.045	—	—	Rare	—
	1862 BN	.185	35.00	75.00	150.00	400.00

Mint mark: N

KM#	Date	Mintage	Fine	VF	XF	Unc
4.3	1862	.630	20.00	45.00	100.00	250.00

2.5000 g, .835 SILVER, .0671 oz ASW
Mint mark: M

KM#	Date	Mintage	Fine	VF	XF	Unc
4a.1	1863 BN	4.706	4.00	7.00	12.00	30.00

Mint mark: T

KM#	Date	Mintage	Fine	VF	XF	Unc
4a.2	1863 BN	2.753	7.00	15.00	35.00	75.00

Mint mark: M

KM#	Date	Mintage	Fine	VF	XF	Unc
14.1	1863 BN	33.760	4.00	7.00	12.00	30.00
	1866 BN	19.199	12.50	20.00	30.00	45.00
	1867 BN	10.984	4.00	7.00	12.00	30.00

Mintmark: N

KM#	Date	Mintage	Fine	VF	XF	Unc
14.2	1863 BN	16.062	5.00	10.00	15.00	30.00
	1867 BN	7.838	5.00	10.00	15.00	30.00

Mint mark: T

KM#	Date	Mintage	Fine	VF	XF	Unc
14.3	1863 BN	6.301	5.00	10.00	15.00	30.00
	1867 BN	.396	35.00	85.00	175.00	400.00

Mint mark: R

KM#	Date	Mintage	Fine	VF	XF	Unc
26	1889	.635	25.00	40.00	75.00	200.00
	1892	.148	30.00	50.00	100.00	250.00

NICKEL
Plain edge

KM#	Date	Mintage	Fine	VF	XF	Unc
61.1	1919	3.700	2.50	5.00	20.00	50.00
	1920	29.450	.75	1.50	3.00	15.00
	1921	16.849	.75	1.50	3.00	15.00
	1924	.599	40.00	80.00	200.00	400.00
	1925	24.884	1.50	2.50	8.00	20.00
	1926	500 pcs.	—	—	—	175.00
	1927	100 pcs.	—	—	—	280.00
	1928	50 pcs.	—	—	—	350.00

Reeded edge

KM#	Date	Mintage	Fine	VF	XF	Unc
61.2	1919	Inc. Ab.	2.50	6.25	12.50	100.00
	1920	Inc. Ab.	2.50	6.25	12.50	100.00
	1921	Inc. Ab.	2.50	6.25	12.50	100.00
	1924	Inc. Ab.	25.00	50.00	75.00	250.00
	1925	Inc. Ab.	2.50	5.00	10.00	50.00
	1929	50 pcs.	—	—	—	300.00
	1930	50 pcs.	—	—	—	300.00
	1931	50 pcs.	—	—	—	300.00
	1932	50 pcs.	—	—	—	300.00
	1933	50 pcs.	—	—	—	300.00
	1934	50 pcs.	—	—	—	300.00
	1935	50 pcs.	—	—	—	300.00

KM#	Date	Mintage	Fine	VF	XF	Unc
76	1936, yr. XIV	.118	15.00	35.00	80.00	160.00
	1937, yr. XV	50 pcs.	—	—	—	300.00
	1938, yr. XVII	20 pcs.	—	—	—	450.00

STAINLESS STEEL (non-magnetic)

KM#	Date	Mintage	Fine	VF	XF	Unc
76a	1939, yr. XVII	9.373	.35	.75	2.00	7.00
	1939, yr. XVIII	10.005	.35	.75	2.00	7.00
	1940, yr. XVIII	19.005	.25	.60	1.50	4.50

STAINLESS STEEL (magnetic)

KM#	Date	Mintage	Fine	VF	XF	Unc
76b	1939, yr. XVII	Inc. Ab.	.35	.75	2.00	7.00
	1940, yr. XVIII	Inc. Ab.	.25	.60	1.50	4.50
	1941, yr. XIX	58.100	.25	.60	1.50	4.50
	1942, yr. XX	26.450	.25	.60	1.50	4.50
	1943, yr. XXI	.361	25.00	45.00	75.00	150.00

LIRA

5.0000 g, .900 SILVER, .1447 oz ASW
Mint mark: FIRENZE

KM#	Date	Mintage	Fine	VF	XF	Unc
A5	1861 F	.432	55.00	110.00	200.00	400.00

Mint mark: T

KM#	Date	Mintage	Fine	VF	XF	Unc
5.1	1861 B in shield	.019	—	—	Rare	—
	1862 BN	.105	50.00	100.00	200.00	400.00

Mint mark: N

KM#	Date	Mintage	Fine	VF	XF	Unc
5.2	1862	.497	30.00	65.00	150.00	300.00

5.0000 g, .835 SILVER, .1342 oz ASW
Mint mark: M

KM#	Date	Mintage	Fine	VF	XF	Unc
5a.1	1863 BN	24.054	2.00	5.00	10.00	40.00
	1867/3 BN	7.665	6.00	10.00	17.50	60.00
	1867 BN	I.A.	4.00	7.50	15.00	50.00

Mint mark: T

KM#	Date	Mintage	Fine	VF	XF	Unc
5a.2	1863 BN	2.270	4.00	7.50	15.00	50.00
	1867 BN	.335	25.00	50.00	150.00	300.00

Mint mark: M

KM#	Date	Mintage	Fine	VF	XF	Unc
15.1	1863 BN	29.837	2.00	5.00	12.50	50.00

Mint mark: T

KM#	Date	Mintage	Fine	VF	XF	Unc
15.2	1863 BN	3.839	60.00	125.00	200.00	375.00

Mint mark: R

KM#	Date	Mintage	Fine	VF	XF	Unc
24.1	1883	5,420	1000.	2000.	4800.	12,000.
	1884	1.995	4.00	10.00	25.00	100.00
	1886	6.095	2.50	6.00	20.00	90.00
	1892	.032	300.00	650.00	1500.	3250.
	1899	1.818	3.00	7.50	20.00	90.00
	1900	.318	5.00	12.50	35.00	150.00

Mint mark: M

KM#	Date	Mintage	Fine	VF	XF	Unc
24.2	1887	16.305	2.50	7.50	20.00	80.00

Mint mark: R

KM#	Date	Mintage	Fine	VF	XF	Unc
32	1901	2.590	5.00	12.50	25.00	100.00
	1902	4.084	3.50	7.50	20.00	90.00
	1905	.700	30.00	60.00	150.00	400.00
	1906	4.665	3.50	5.00	12.50	50.00
	1907	8.472	2.50	5.00	12.50	50.00

KM#	Date	Mintage	Fine	VF	XF	Unc
45	1908	2.212	20.00	40.00	80.00	200.00
	1909	3.475	3.50	7.50	20.00	100.00
	1910	5.525	2.50	5.00	12.50	60.00
	1912	5.865	2.50	4.00	9.00	35.00
	1913	16.177	2.00	3.50	6.00	25.00

KM#	Date	Mintage	Fine	VF	XF	Unc
57	1915	5.229	2.75	4.00	12.50	35.00
	1916	1.835	5.00	10.00	20.00	60.00
	1917	9.744	2.75	4.00	10.00	25.00

NICKEL

KM#	Date	Mintage	Fine	VF	XF	Unc
62	1922	82.267	.60	1.00	3.00	15.00
	1923	20.175	.60	1.00	3.00	15.00
	1924 closed 2					
		29.288	.60	1.00	3.00	15.00
	1926	500 pcs.	—	—	—	175.00
	1927	100 pcs.	—	—	—	280.00
	1928	19.996	1.00	2.00	10.00	30.00
	1929	50 pcs.	—	—	—	300.00
	1930	50 pcs.	—	—	—	300.00
	1931	50 pcs.	—	—	—	300.00
	1932	50 pcs.	—	—	—	300.00
	1933	50 pcs.	—	—	—	300.00
	1934	50 pcs.	—	—	—	300.00
	1935	50 pcs.	—	—	—	300.00

KM#	Date	Mintage	Fine	VF	XF	Unc
77	1936, yr. XIV					
		.119	15.00	35.00	80.00	165.00
	1937, yr. XV					
		50 pcs.	—	—	—	300.00
	1938, yr. XVII					
		20 pcs.	—	—	—	450.00

STAINLESS STEEL (non-magnetic)

KM#	Date	Mintage	Fine	VF	XF	Unc
77a	1939, yr. XVII					
		10.034	.40	1.50	4.00	14.00
	1939, yr. XVIII					
		15.977	.35	.75	1.50	6.00
	1940, yr. XVIII					
		25.997	.30	.60	1.25	5.00

STAINLESS STEEL (magnetic)

KM#	Date	Mintage	Fine	VF	XF	Unc
77b	1939, yr. XVII					
		Inc. Ab.	.40	1.50	4.00	14.00
	1939, yr. XVIII					
		Inc. Ab.	.35	.75	1.50	6.00
	1940, yr. XVIII					
		Inc. Ab.	.30	.60	1.25	5.00
	1941, yr. XIX					
		8.550	.50	1.75	5.00	16.00
	1942, yr. XX					
		5.700	.35	.75	1.50	6.00
	1943, yr. XXI					
		11.500	10.00	20.00	35.00	75.00

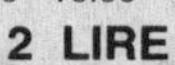

2 LIRE

10.0000 g, .900 SILVER, .2893 oz ASW

Mint mark: T

KM#	Date	Mintage	Fine	VF	XF	Unc
6.1	1861 B in shield					
		9,871	—	—	Rare	—

Mint mark: N

KM#	Date	Mintage	Fine	VF	XF	Unc
6.2	1862	062	150.00	300.00	600.00	1500.

10.0000 g, .835 SILVER, .2684 oz ASW

KM#	Date	Mintage	Fine	VF	XF	Unc
6a.1	1863 BN	10.090	6.50	17.50	40.00	150.00

Mint mark: T

KM#	Date	Mintage	Fine	VF	XF	Unc
6a.2	1863 BN	4.910	7.50	20.00	50.00	175.00

Mint mark: N

KM#	Date	Mintage	Fine	VF	XF	Unc
16.1	1863 BN	—	7.50	20.00	80.00	200.00

Mint mark: T

KM#	Date	Mintage	Fine	VF	XF	Unc
16.2	1863 BN	—	7.50	25.00	100.00	250.00

Mint mark: R

KM#	Date	Mintage	Fine	VF	XF	Unc
23	1881	4.141	5.00	10.00	40.00	150.00
	1882	2.859	5.00	10.00	40.00	150.00
	1883	3.500	5.00	10.00	40.00	150.00
	1884	4.500	5.00	10.00	40.00	150.00
	1885	.598	25.00	50.00	100.00	300.00
	1886	1.902	5.00	10.00	40.00	150.00
	1887	7.500	5.00	10.00	40.00	150.00
	1897	.848	7.50	12.50	40.00	150.00
	1898	1.320	25.00	50.00	100.00	400.00
	1899	.610	7.50	12.50	35.00	150.00

KM#	Date	Mintage	Fine	VF	XF	Unc
33	1901	.072	200.00	400.00	800.00	1500.
	1902	.549	40.00	80.00	150.00	400.00
	1903	.054	300.00	500.00	1000.	3000.
	1904	.157	125.00	250.00	450.00	700.00
	1905	1.643	10.00	20.00	50.00	200.00
	1906	.970	12.50	25.00	75.00	200.00
	1907	1.245	10.00	20.00	50.00	200.00

KM#	Date	Mintage	Fine	VF	XF	Unc
46	1908	2.283	6.00	15.00	50.00	150.00
	1910	.719	25.00	50.00	125.00	300.00
	1911	.535	30.00	60.00	150.00	400.00
	1912	2.166	6.00	15.00	50.00	150.00

50th Anniversary of Kingdom

KM#	Date	Mintage	Fine	VF	XF	Unc
52	1911	1.000	12.50	25.00	50.00	125.00

KM#	Date	Mintage	Fine	VF	XF	Unc
55	1914	10.390	4.00	6.00	11.00	30.00
	1915	7.948	4.00	6.00	11.00	30.00
	1916	10.923	4.00	6.00	11.00	30.00
	1917	6.123	6.00	12.50	25.00	60.00

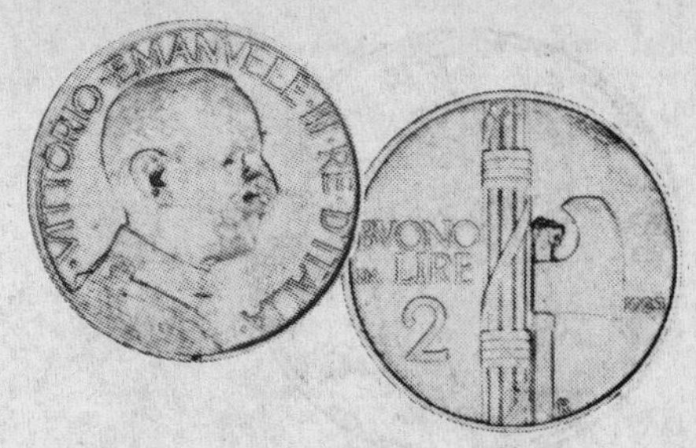

NICKEL

KM#	Date	Mintage	Fine	VF	XF	Unc
63	1923	32.260	1.00	2.00	5.00	20.00
	1924	45.051	1.00	2.00	5.00	20.00
	1925	14.628	1.00	2.00	5.00	30.00
	1926	5.101	5.00	10.00	50.00	150.00
	1927	1.632	25.00	50.00	100.00	300.00
	1928	50 pcs.	—	—	—	350.00
	1929	50 pcs.	—	—	—	350.00
	1930	50 pcs.	—	—	—	350.00
	1931	50 pcs.	—	—	—	350.00
	1932	50 pcs.	—	—	—	350.00
	1933	50 pcs.	—	—	—	350.00
	1934	50 pcs.	—	—	—	350.00
	1935	50 pcs.	—	—	—	350.00

KM#	Date	Mintage	Fine	VF	XF	Unc
78	1936, yr. XIV					
		.120	20.00	45.00	90.00	200.00
	1937, yr. XV					
		50 pcs.	—	—	—	350.00
	1938, yr. XVII					
		20 pcs.	—	—	—	500.00

STAINLESS STEEL (non-magnetic)

KM#	Date	Mintage	Fine	VF	XF	Unc
78a	1939, yr. XVII					
		2.900	.60	1.75	5.00	16.00
	1939, yr. XVIII					
		4.873	.40	.90	2.50	8.00
	1940, yr. XVIII					
		5.742	.40	.90	2.00	6.00

STAINLESS STEEL (magnetic)

KM#	Date	Mintage	Fine	VF	XF	Unc
78b	1939, yr. XVII					
		Inc. Ab.	.60	1.75	5.00	16.00
	1939, yr. XVIII					
		Inc. Ab.	.40	.90	2.50	8.00
	1940, yr. XVIII					
		Inc. Ab.	.40	.90	2.00	6.00
	1941, yr. XIX					
		1.865	.50	1.50	3.00	12.00
	1942, yr. XX					
		2.450	40.00	80.00	160.00	325.00
	1943, yr. XXI					
		.600	20.00	40.00	100.00	200.00

5 LIRE

25.0000 g, .900 SILVER, .7234 oz ASW

Mint mark: FIRENZE

Accession to Throne of Unified Italy

KM#	Date	Mintage	Fine	VF	XF	Unc
7	1861	.021	400.00	900.00	1800.	3500.

Mint mark: T

KM#	Date	Mintage	Fine	VF	XF	Unc
8.1	1861 B in shield					
		.160	175.00	375.00	650.00	1200.
	1862 BN	.051	50.00	100.00	200.00	550.00
	1865 BN	.491	15.00	30.00	70.00	200.00
	Mint mark: N					
8.2	1862 BN	.142	30.00	65.00	120.00	350.00
	1864 BN	.120	20.00	40.00	90.00	225.00
	1865 BN	.312	15.00	30.00	70.00	200.00
	1866 BN	.460	1000.	1500.	2000.	4000.
	Mint mark: M					
8.3	1869 BN	3.995	10.00	17.50	40.00	175.00
	1870 BN	5.969	10.00	17.50	40.00	150.00
	1871 BN	6.697	10.00	17.50	40.00	150.00
	1872 BN	7.093	10.00	17.50	40.00	150.00
	1873 BN	8.438	10.00	17.50	40.00	150.00
	1874 BN	12.000	10.00	17.50	40.00	150.00
	1875 BN	8.982	10.00	17.50	40.00	150.00
	Mint mark: R					
8.4	1870	—	50.00	100.00	200.00	300.00
	1871	.404	65.00	135.00	250.00	400.00
	1872	.029	300.00	500.00	1000.	2500.
	1873	.017	400.00	800.00	2000.	4000.
	1875	1.018	15.00	30.00	75.00	300.00
	1876	6.390	12.00	20.00	40.00	150.00
	1877	4.410	12.00	20.00	40.00	175.00
	1878	1.700	15.00	25.00	50.00	225.00

1.6129 g, .900 GOLD, .0466 oz AGW
Mint mark: T

KM#	Date	Mintage	Fine	VF	XF	Unc
17	1863 BN	.197	75.00	100.00	175.00	250.00
	1865 BN	.408	100.00	175.00	250.00	375.00
	1865 BN	—	Proof Reported, not confirmed			

25.0000 g, .900 SILVER, .7234 oz ASW
Mint mark: R

KM#	Date	Mintage	Fine	VF	XF	Unc
20	1878	.100	200.00	400.00	800.00	2000.
	1879	4.000	20.00	40.00	125.00	600.00

KM#	Date	Mintage	Fine	VF	XF	Unc
34	1901	114 pcs.	—	—	15,000.	20,000.

50th Anniversary of Kingdom

KM#	Date	Mintage	Fine	VF	XF	Unc
53	1911	.060	150.00	300.00	500.00	950.00

KM#	Date	Mintage	Fine	VF	XF	Unc
56	1914	.273	500.00	850.00	2500.	4000.

5.0000 g, .835 SILVER, .1342 oz ASW
Edge inscription: *FERT*.

KM#	Date	Mintage	Fine	VF	XF	Unc
67.1	1926	5.405	6.00	15.00	30.00	120.00
	1927	92.887	1.50	3.00	7.50	25.00
	1928	9.908	6.00	15.00	40.00	160.00
	1929	33.803	2.00	4.00	8.50	28.00
	1930	19.525	2.00	4.00	10.00	30.00
	1931	50 pcs.	—	—	—	350.00
67.1	1932	50 pcs.	—	—	—	350.00
	1933	50 pcs.	—	—	—	350.00
	1934	50 pcs.	—	—	—	350.00
	1935	50 pcs.	—	—	—	350.00
	Edge inscription: **FERT**					
67.2	1927	Inc. Ab.	2.00	5.00	10.00	35.00
	1928	Inc. Ab.	10.00	20.00	50.00	200.00
	1929	Inc. Ab.	3.00	6.00	12.00	40.00

KM#	Date	Mintage	Fine	VF	XF	Unc
79	1936, yr. XIV					
		1.016	10.00	20.00	40.00	100.00
	1937, yr. XV					
		.100	15.00	30.00	60.00	135.00
	1938, yr. XVIII					
		20 pcs.	—	—	—	500.00
	1939, yr. XVIII					
		20 pcs.	—	—	—	500.00
	1940, yr. XIX					
		20 pcs.	—	—	—	500.00
	1941, yr. XX					
		20 pcs.	—	—	—	500.00

10 LIRE

3.2258 g, .900 GOLD, 18mm, .0933 oz AGW
Mint mark: T

KM#	Date	Mintage	Fine	VF	XF	Unc
9.1	1861 B in shield					
		1,916	1500.	3000.	4500.	7500.

KM#	Date	Mintage	Fine	VF	XF	Unc
	18.5mm					
9.2	1863 BN	.543	75.00	100.00	150.00	225.00
	1863 BN	—	Proof Reported, not confirmed			
	1865 BN	.444	100.00	175.00	225.00	325.00
	19mm					
9.3	1863 BN	I.A.	70.00	95.00	125.00	175.00
	19.5mm					
9.4	1863 BN	I.A.	75.00	100.00	135.00	200.00

Mint mark: R

KM#	Date	Mintage	Fine	VF	XF	Unc
47	1910	5,202	—	—	Rare	—
	1912	6,796	700.00	1250.	2000.	3000.
	1926	40 pcs.	—	—	—	8800.
	1927	30 pcs.	—	—	—	6850.

10.0000 g, .835 SILVER, .2684 oz ASW
Edge inscription: *FERT*.

KM#	Date	Mintage	Fine	VF	XF	Unc
68.1	1926	1.748	65.00	135.00	275.00	600.00
	1927	44.801	7.00	15.00	40.00	80.00
	1928	6.652	25.00	65.00	150.00	300.00
	1929	6.800	35.00	75.00	175.00	350.00
	1930	3.668	60.00	125.00	250.00	500.00
	1931	50 pcs.	—	—	—	700.00
	1932	50 pcs.	—	—	—	700.00
	1933	50 pcs.	—	—	—	700.00
	1934	50 pcs.	—	—	—	700.00
	Edge inscription: **FERT**					
68.2	1927	Inc. Ab.	10.00	20.00	50.00	100.00
	1928	Inc. Ab.	75.00	150.00	300.00	600.00
	1929	Inc. Ab.	25.00	65.00	140.00	280.00

KM#	Date	Mintage	Fine	VF	XF	Unc
80	1936, yr. XIV	.619	15.00	30.00	60.00	135.00
	1937, yr. XV	50 pcs.	—	—	—	600.00
	1938, yr. XVII	20 pcs.	—	—	—	800.00
	1939, yr. XVIII	20 pcs.	—	—	—	800.00
	1940, yr. XIX	20 pcs.	—	—	—	800.00
	1941, yr. XX	20 pcs.	—	—	—	800.00

20 LIRE

6.4516 g, .900 GOLD, .1867 oz AGW
Mint mark: T

KM#	Date	Mintage	Fine	VF	XF	Unc
10.1	1861B in shield	3,267	125.00	200.00	300.00	500.00
	1861 T/F	I.A.	BV	120.00	130.00	150.00
	1862 BN	1.955	BV	100.00	110.00	125.00
	1863 BN	2.981	BV	100.00	110.00	125.00
	1864 BN	.609	BV	100.00	110.00	125.00
	1865 BN	3.109	BV	100.00	110.00	150.00
	1866 BN	.196	125.00	150.00	200.00	400.00
	1867 BN	.276	BV	100.00	110.00	150.00
	1868 BN	.340	BV	100.00	110.00	150.00
	1869 BN	.185	BV	100.00	110.00	150.00
	1870 BN	.055	125.00	200.00	350.00	800.00

Mint mark: R

KM#	Date	Mintage	Fine	VF	XF	Unc
10.2	1870	—	150.00	300.00	600.00	1450.
	1871	—	BV	125.00	200.00	400.00
	1873	2,174	400.00	800.00	1600.	3500.
	1874	.041	BV	100.00	110.00	155.00
	1875	.051	BV	100.00	110.00	155.00
	1876	.108	BV	100.00	110.00	125.00
	1877	.247	BV	100.00	110.00	125.00
	1878	.316	BV	100.00	110.00	125.00

Mint mark: M

KM#	Date	Mintage	Fine	VF	XF	Unc
10.3	1872 BN	—	100.00	150.00	250.00	500.00
	1873 BN	1.018	BV	100.00	110.00	145.00
	1874 BN	.255	BV	100.00	110.00	150.00

Mint mark: R

KM#	Date	Mintage	Fine	VF	XF	Unc
21	1879	.146	BV	100.00	110.00	125.00
	1880	.129	BV	100.00	110.00	125.00
	1881	.843	BV	100.00	110.00	125.00
	1882	6.970	BV	90.00	100.00	115.00
	1883	.182	BV	100.00	110.00	125.00
	1884	9,775	175.00	300.00	500.00	1200.
	1885	.165	BV	100.00	110.00	125.00
	1886	.059	BV	100.00	110.00	125.00
	1888	.111	BV	100.00	110.00	125.00
	1889	—	150.00	250.00	400.00	600.00
	1890	.068	BV	100.00	110.00	125.00
	1891	.032	BV	100.00	120.00	160.00
	1893	.041	BV	100.00	110.00	145.00
	1897	.038	BV	100.00	110.00	155.00

RED GOLD

KM#	Date	Mintage	Fine	VF	XF	Unc
21a	1882	Inc. Ab.	BV	110.00	125.00	175.00

6.4516 g, .900 GOLD, .1867 oz AGW

KM#	Date	Mintage	Fine	VF	XF	Unc
37.1	1902	181 pcs.	—	—	*Rare	—
	1903	1,800	450.00	800.00	1250.	1650.
	1905	8,715	250.00	400.00	650.00	900.00
	1908	—	—	—	Rare	—

***NOTE:** Stack's International sale 3-88 XF realized $13,200.

Obv: Small anchor at bottom indicates gold in coin is from Eritrea.

KM#	Date	Mintage	Fine	VF	XF	Unc
37.2	1902	115 pcs.	2500.	5500.	9500.*	14,500.

***NOTE:** Bowers and Merena Guia sale 3-88 Unc. realized $14,300.

Obv: Uniformed bust.

KM#	Date	Mintage	Fine	VF	XF	Unc
48	1910	*.033	—	—	—	30,000.
	1912	.059	275.00	400.00	650.00	850.00
	1926	40 pcs.	—	—	3000.	5500.
	1927	30 pcs.	—	—	—	7250.

***NOTE:** Six pieces currently known to exist.

1st Anniversary of Fascist Government

KM#	Date	Mintage	Fine	VF	XF	Unc
64	1923	.020	150.00	300.00	500.00	650.00

15.0000 g, .800 SILVER, .3858 oz ASW

KM#	Date	Mintage	Fine	VF	XF	Unc
69	1927, yr. V	100 pcs.	—	—	4000.	5500.
	1927, yr. VI	3.518	50.00	90.00	250.00	550.00
	1928, yr. VI	2.487	70.00	110.00	325.00	650.00
	1929, yr. VII	50 pcs.	—	—	—	1750.
	1930, yr. VIII	50 pcs.	—	—	—	1750.
	1931, yr. IX	50 pcs.	—	—	—	1750.
	1932, yr. X	50 pcs.	—	—	—	1750.
	1933, yr. XI	50 pcs.	—	—	—	1750.
	1934, yr. XII	50 pcs.	—	—	—	1750.

20.0000 g, .600 SILVER, .3858 oz ASW
10th Anniversary End of World War I

KM#	Date	Mintage	Fine	VF	XF	Unc
70	1928, yr. VI	—	75.00	160.00	300.00	700.00

NOTE: Similar 20 and 100 Lire pieces struck in gold are modern fantasies. Refer to *UNUSUAL WORLD COINS*, 3rd edition, Krause Publications, 1992.

15.0000 g, .800 SILVER, .3858 oz ASW

KM#	Date	Mintage	Fine	VF	XF	Unc
81	1936, yr. XIV	.010	250.00	500.00	1000.	2000.
	1937, yr. XV	50 pcs.	—	—	—	2500.
	1938, yr. XVII	20 pcs.	—	—	—	2750.
	1939, yr. XVIII	20 pcs.	—	—	—	2750.
	1940, yr. XIX	20 pcs.	—	—	—	3000.
	1941, yr. XX	20 pcs.	—	—	—	3000.

50 LIRE

16.1290 g, .900 GOLD, .4667 oz AGW
Mint mark: T

KM#	Date	Mintage	Fine	VF	XF	Unc
18	1864 BN	103 pcs.	10,000.	15,000.	27,500.	35,000.

Mint mark: R

KM#	Date	Mintage	Fine	VF	XF	Unc
25	1884	2,532	900.00	1500.	2000.	3000.
	1888	2,125	1000.	2000.	2750.	3750.
	1891	414 pcs.	1500.	2500.	4000.	7500.

KM#	Date	Mintage	Fine	VF	XF	Unc
49	1910	2,096	—	—	Rare	—
	1912	.011	450.00	750.00	1100.	1750.
	1926	40 pcs.	—	—	*Rare	—
	1927	30 pcs.	—	—	—	8750.

***NOTE:** Bowers and Merena Guia sale 3-88 Choice Unc. (cleaned) realized $8,250.

50th Anniversary of Kingdom

KM#	Date	Mintage	Fine	VF	XF	Unc
54	1911	.020	300.00	500.00	750.00	1250.

4.3995 g, .900 GOLD, .1273 oz AGW

KM#	Date	Mintage	Fine	VF	XF	Unc
71	1931, yr. IX	.032	100.00	135.00	175.00	275.00
	1931, yr. X	Inc. Ab.	200.00	300.00	400.00	600.00
	1932, yr. X	.012	200.00	300.00	400.00	600.00
	1933, yr. XI	6,463	300.00	400.00	600.00	800.00

KM#	Date	Mintage	Fine	VF	XF	Unc
82	1936, yr. XIV	790 pcs.	900.00	1500.	2750.	4000.

100 LIRE

32.2580 g, .900 GOLD, .9334 oz AGW
Mint mark: T

KM#	Date	Mintage	Fine	VF	XF	Unc
19.1	1864 BN	579 pcs.	2000.	4500.	8000.	12,000.

Mint mark: R

KM#	Date	Mintage	Fine	VF	XF	Unc
19.2	1872	661 pcs.	2000.	4500.	7500.	10,000.
	1878	294 pcs.	3500.	7000.	10,000.	17,500.

KM#	Date	Mintage	Fine	VF	XF	Unc
22	1880	145 pcs.	6000.	12,000.	16,000.	*25,000.
	1882	1,229	900.00	1500.	2500.	3750.
	1883	4,219	800.00	1250.	2250.	3500.
	1888	1,169	900.00	1500.	3000.	4500.
	1891	209 pcs.	2000.	4000.	7000.	10,000.

***NOTE:** Bowers and Merena Guia sale 3-88 Choice AU realized $24,200.

KM#	Date	Mintage	Fine	VF	XF	Unc
39	1903	916 pcs.	1500.	3000.	6000.	8000.
	1905	1,012	1250.	2500.	5000.	7000.

KM#	Date	Mintage	Fine	VF	XF	Unc
50	1910	2,013	—	—	Rare	—
	1912	4,946	—	1500.	2500.	3500.
	1926	40 pcs.	—	—	**Rare	—
	1927	30 pcs.	—	—	*Rare	—

***NOTE:** Stack's International sale 3-88 BU realized $18,700.
****NOTE:** Bowers and Merena Guia sale 3-88 Choice Unc. (cleaned) realized $12,650.

1st Anniversary of Fascist Government

KM#	Date	Mintage	Fine	VF	XF	Unc
65	1923 frosted finish	.020	750.00	1000.	1500.	2400.
	1923 bright finish	—	—	—	Rare	—

25th Year of Reign-10th Anniv. World War I Entry

KM#	Date	Mintage	Fine	VF	XF	Unc
66	1925	5,000	1000.	1500.	2500.	4000.
	1925	—	—		Matte Proof	4500.

8.7990 g, .900 GOLD, .2546 oz AGW

KM#	Date	Mintage	Fine	VF	XF	Unc
72	1931, yr. IX	.034	150.00	250.00	375.00	550.00
	1931, yr. X	Inc. Ab.	150.00	250.00	400.00	650.00
	1932, yr. X	9,081	150.00	250.00	400.00	650.00
	1933, yr. XI	6,464	175.00	275.00	450.00	750.00

KM#	Date	Mintage	Fine	VF	XF	Unc
83	1936, yr. XIV	812 pcs.	1000.	2000.	3000.	5000.

5.1900 g, .900 GOLD, .1502 oz AGW

KM#	Date	Mintage	Fine	VF	XF	Unc
84	1937, yr. XVI	249 pcs.	—	5000.	9000.	*14,500.
	1940, yr. XVIII	2 pcs.	—	—	Rare	—

***NOTE:** Bowers and Merena Guia sale 3-88 Unc realized $14,300.

REPUBLIC

LIRA

ALUMINUM
Mint mark: R

KM#	Date	Mintage	Fine	VF	XF	Unc
87	1946	.104	8.50	25.00	65.00	120.00
	1947	.012	50.00	120.00	220.00	400.00
	1948	9.000	.40	1.00	2.50	8.00
	1949	13.200	.40	1.00	2.50	8.00
	1950	1.942	1.00	2.00	6.00	12.50

KM#	Date	Mintage	Fine	VF	XF	Unc
91	1951	3.680	.20	.50	1.00	8.00
	1952	2.720	.20	.50	1.00	5.00
	1953	2.800	.20	.50	1.00	3.00
	1954	41.040	.10	.25	.50	1.85
	1955	32.640	.10	.25	.50	1.85
	1956	1.840	.20	.50	4.00	15.00
	1957	7.440	.10	.25	.50	2.00
	1958	5.280	.10	.25	.50	2.00
	1959	1.680	.10	.25	.50	2.00
	1968	.100	—	—	—	17.00
	1969	.310	—	—	—	5.00
	1970	1.011	—	—	—	2.50
	1980	1.500	—	—	—	1.50
	1981	.500	—	—	—	1.50
	1982	.085	—	—	—	2.50
	1983	.076	—	—	—	6.00
	1984	.077	—	—	—	4.00
	1985	.073	—	—	—	2.00
	1985	.020	—	—	Proof	3.00
	1986	—	—	—	—	2.00
	1986	—	—	—	Proof	3.00
	1987	.177	—	—	—	2.50
	1987	—	—	—	Proof	3.50
	1988	.077	—	—	—	2.00
	1989	—	—	—	—	2.00

2 LIRE

ALUMINUM
Mint mark: R

KM#	Date	Mintage	Fine	VF	XF	Unc
88	1946	.123	7.50	20.00	60.00	115.00
	1947	.012	50.00	120.00	225.00	425.00
	1948	7.200	.50	1.50	3.00	9.00
	1949	1.350	5.00	12.00	25.00	50.00
	1950	2.640	.60	1.75	4.00	12.00

KM#	Date	Mintage	Fine	VF	XF	Unc
94	1953	4.125	.25	.50	.75	4.00
	1954	22.500	.25	.50	.75	2.00
	1955	2.750	.25	.50	.75	3.50
	1956	1.500	1.00	3.00	5.00	15.00
	1957	6.313	.25	.50	.75	2.50
	1958	.125	20.00	60.00	140.00	200.00
	1959	2.000	.25	.50	.75	2.50
	1968	.100	—	—	—	15.00
	1969	.310	—	—	—	4.00
	1970	1.140	—	—	—	2.50
	1980	.500	—	—	—	1.00
	1981	.500	—	—	—	1.00
	1982	.085	—	—	—	2.50
	1983	.076	—	—	—	6.00
	1984	.077	—	—	—	4.00
	1985	.073	—	—	—	1.00
	1985	.020	—	—	Proof	2.50
	1986	—	—	—	—	1.00
	1986	—	—	—	Proof	2.50
	1987	.177	—	—	—	1.50
	1987	—	—	—	Proof	3.00
	1988	.077	—	—	—	1.00
	1989	—	—	—	—	1.00

5 LIRE

ALUMINUM
Mint mark: R

KM#	Date	Mintage	Fine	VF	XF	Unc
89	1946	.081	100.00	200.00	325.00	500.00
	1947	.017	125.00	225.00	400.00	600.00
	1948	25.125	.50	1.50	5.00	15.00
	1949	71.100	.30	.75	2.00	8.50
	1950	114.790	.30	.75	2.00	8.50

KM#	Date	Mintage	Fine	VF	XF	Unc
92	1951	40.260	.10	.25	.50	3.00
	1952	57.400	.10	.25	.50	4.00
	1953	196.200	.10	.25	.50	2.00
	1954	436.400	.10	.25	.50	1.50
	1955	159.000	.10	.25	.50	2.00
	1956	.400	15.00	50.00	250.00	800.00
	1966	1.200	.25	.50	1.00	1.50
	1967	10.600	.10	.25	.50	1.00
	1968	7.500	—	—	.10	.75
	1969	7.910	—	—	.10	.75
	1969 inverted I					
		.969	1.00	2.00	4.00	22.50
	1970	3.200	—	—	.10	.75
	1971	8.600	—	—	.10	.75
	1972	16.400	—	—	.10	.50
	1973	28.800	—	—	.10	.50
	1974	6.600	—	—	.10	.50
	1975	7.000	—	—	.10	.50
	1976	8.800	—	—	.10	.50
	1977	6.700	—	—	.10	.50
	1978	3.600	—	—	.10	.50
	1979	4.200	—	—	.10	.50
	1980	3.663	—	—	.10	.50
	1981	7.788	—	—	.10	.50
	1982	.855	—	—	.10	.50
	1983	14.020	—	—	.10	.50
	1984	.122	—	—	.10	.50
	1985	3.000	—	—	.10	.50
	1985	.020	—	—	Proof	1.50
	1986	5.000	—	—	.10	.50
	1986	—	—	—	Proof	1.50
	1987	7.000	—	—	.10	.50
	1987	—	—	—	Proof	1.50
	1988	5.000	—	—	.10	.50
	1989 coin rotation					
		—	—	—	.10	.50
	1989 medal rotation					
		—	—	—	—	10.00
	1990	—	—	—	.10	.50

10 LIRE

ALUMINUM
Mint mark: R

KM#	Date	Mintage	Fine	VF	XF	Unc
90	1946	.101	50.00	120.00	200.00	300.00
	1947	.012	200.00	600.00	1200.	1850.
	1948	14.400	1.00	4.00	20.00	60.00
	1949	49.500	.50	1.00	3.00	10.00
	1950	53.311	.50	1.00	3.00	10.00

KM#	Date	Mintage	Fine	VF	XF	Unc
93	1951	96.600	.10	.25	2.00	10.00
	1952	105.150	.10	.25	1.50	8.00
	1953	151.500	.10	.25	1.00	6.00
	1954	95.250	.50	1.00	5.00	40.00
	1955	274.950	.10	.15	1.00	3.00
	1956	76.650	.10	.25	1.25	6.00
93	1965	1.050	.25	.50	1.50	8.00
	1966	16.500	.10	.25	1.00	3.00
	1967	29.450	.10	.25	1.00	2.00
	1968	32.200	—	—	.10	.75
	1969	23.710	—	—	.10	.75
	1970	14.100	—	—	.10	.75
	1971	23.550	—	—	.10	.75
	1972	61.300	—	—	.10	.50
	1973	145.800	—	—	.10	.50
	1974	85.000	—	—	.10	.50
	1975	76.800	—	—	.10	.50
	1976	82.000	—	—	.10	.50
	1977	80.750	—	—	.10	.50
	1978	43.800	—	—	.10	.50
	1979	98.000	—	—	.10	.50
	1980	81.109	—	—	.10	.50
	1981	46.967	—	—	.10	.50
	1982	45.986	—	—	.10	.50
	1983	15.110	—	—	.10	.50
	1984	11.122	—	—	.10	.50
	1985	15.000	—	—	.10	.50
	1985	.020	—	—	Proof	2.50
	1986	16.000	—	—	.10	.50
	1986	—	—	—	Proof	2.50
	1987	13.000	—	—	.10	.50
	1987	—	—	—	Proof	2.50
	1988	13.000	—	—	.10	.50
	1989	—	—	—	.10	.50
	1990	—	—	—	.10	.50

20 LIRE

ALUMINUM-BRONZE
Mint mark: R

KM#	Date	Mintage	Fine	VF	XF	Unc
97.1	1957	*60.075	.20	.40	2.00	10.00
	1958	80.550	.20	.40	2.00	10.00
	1959	4.005	.50	1.25	5.00	50.00

***NOTE:** Two different types of sevens in date.

Plain edge

KM#	Date	Mintage	Fine	VF	XF	Unc
97.2	1968	.100	—	2.50	5.00	35.00
	1969	16.735	.10	.15	.25	1.00
	1970	31.500	.10	.15	.25	.65
	1971	12.375	.10	.15	.25	1.00
	1972	34.400	.10	.15	.25	.65
	1973	20.000	.10	.15	.25	.65
	1974	17.000	.10	.15	.20	.65
	1975	25.000	.10	.15	.20	.65
	1976	15.000	.10	.15	.20	.65
	1977	10.000	.10	.15	.20	.65
	1978	8.415	.10	.15	.20	.65
	1979	32.000	.10	.15	.20	.50
	1980	61.795	.10	.15	.20	.50
	1981	68.557	.10	.15	.20	.50
	1982	44.774	.10	.15	.20	.50
	1983	15.110	.10	.15	.20	.50
	1984	5.122	.10	.15	.20	.50
	1985	15.000	.10	.15	.20	.50
	1985	.020	—	—	Proof	3.00
	1986	13.000	.10	.15	.20	.50
	1986	—	—	—	Proof	3.00
	1987	8.234	.10	.15	.20	.50
	1987	—	—	—	Proof	3.00
	1988	13.000	.10	.15	.20	.50
	1989	—	.10	.15	.20	.50
	1990	—	.10	.15	.20	.50

50 LIRE

STAINLESS STEEL
Mint mark: R

KM#	Date	Mintage	Fine	VF	XF	Unc
95	1954	17.600	1.00	2.00	25.00	70.00
	1955	70.500	.50	1.00	15.00	50.00
	1956	69.400	.50	1.00	8.00	45.00
	1957	8.925	2.00	4.00	40.00	120.00
	1958	.825	4.00	10.00	80.00	220.00
	1959	8.800	.50	1.00	15.00	80.00
	1960	2.025	2.00	4.00	30.00	100.00
	1961	11.100	.50	1.00	5.00	40.00
	1962	17.700	.50	1.00	2.50	30.00
	1963	31.600	.20	.50	1.50	20.00
	1964	37.900	.20	.50	1.50	12.00
	1965	25.300	.20	.50	1.50	10.00
	1966	27.400	.20	.40	.80	5.00
	1967	28.000	.20	.40	.80	5.00
	1968	17.800	.20	.30	.50	1.50
	1969	23.010	.20	.30	.50	1.50
	1970	21.411	.10	.20	.50	1.50
	1971	33.410	.10	.20	.50	1.50
	1972	39.000	.10	.20	.50	1.50
	1973	48.700	.10	.20	.50	1.50
95	1974	64.100	.10	.20	.35	1.00
	1975	87.000	.10	.15	.25	1.00
	1976	180.600	.10	.15	.25	1.00
	1977	293.800	.10	.15	.25	1.00
	1978	416.808	.10	.15	.25	1.00
	1979	256.630	.10	.15	.25	1.00
	1980	—	.10	.15	.25	1.00
	1981	—	.10	.15	.25	1.00
	1982	—	.10	.15	.25	1.00
	1983	—	.10	.15	.25	1.00
	1984	—	.10	.15	.25	1.00
	1985	—	.10	.15	.25	1.00
	1985	.020	—	—	Proof	3.00
	1986	—	.10	.15	.25	1.00
	1986	—	—	—	Proof	3.00
	1987	14.682	.10	.15	.25	1.00
	1987	—	—	—	Proof	3.00
	1988	20.000	.10	.15	.25	1.00
	1989	—	.10	.15	.25	1.00

Reduced size

KM#	Date	Mintage	Fine	VF	XF	Unc
95a	1990	—	—	—	—	.35
	1991	—	—	—	—	.35
	1992	—	—	—	—	.35
	1993	—	—	—	—	.35

100 LIRE

STAINLESS STEEL
Mint mark: R

KM#	Date	Mintage	Fine	VF	XF	Unc
96	1955	8.600	1.00	4.00	30.00	200.00
	1956	99.800	.25	1.00	7.50	85.00
	1957	90.600	.25	1.00	15.00	120.00
	1958	25.640	.25	1.00	15.00	130.00
	1959	19.500	.25	1.00	15.00	120.00
	1960	20.700	.25	1.00	15.00	120.00
	1961	11.860	.25	1.00	18.00	150.00
	1962	21.700	.20	.50	5.00	60.00
	1963	33.100	.20	.50	2.00	25.00
	1964	31.300	.20	.50	1.00	15.00
	1965	37.000	.20	.50	1.00	15.00
	1966	52.500	.15	.25	.50	4.00
	1967	23.700	.15	.25	.50	4.00
	1968	34.200	.15	.25	.50	2.00
	1969	27.710	.15	.25	.50	2.00
	1970	25.011	.15	.25	.50	2.00
	1971	25.910	.15	.25	.50	2.00
	1972	31.170	.15	.25	.50	2.00
	1973	30.780	.15	.25	.50	3.00
	1974	83.880	.15	.25	.35	1.00
	1975	106.650	.15	.25	.35	1.00
	1976	160.020	.15	.25	.35	1.00
	1977	253.980	.15	.25	.35	1.00
	1978	343.626	.15	.25	.35	1.00
	1979	187.913	.15	.25	.35	1.00
	1980	—	.15	.25	.35	1.00
	1981	—	.15	.25	.35	1.00
	1982	—	.15	.25	.35	1.00
	1983	—	.15	.25	.35	1.00
	1984	—	.15	.25	.35	1.00
	1985	—	.15	.25	.35	1.00
	1985	.020	—	—	Proof	3.50
	1986	—	.15	.25	.35	1.00
	1986	—	—	—	Proof	3.50
	1987	25.000	.15	.25	.35	1.00
	1987	—	—	—	Proof	3.50
	1988	23.000	.15	.25	.35	1.00
	1989	—	.15	.25	.35	1.00

Reduced size

KM#	Date	Mintage	Fine	VF	XF	Unc
96a	1990	—	—	—	—	.50
	1991	—	—	—	—	.50
	1992	—	—	—	—	.50

100th Anniversary of Birth of Guglielmo Marconi

KM#	Date	Mintage	Fine	VF	XF	Unc
102	1974	50.000	.15	.25	.50	1.75

F.A.O. Issue

KM#	Date	Mintage	Fine	VF	XF	Unc
106	1979	78.340	.15	.25	.35	1.25

Centennial of Livorno Naval Acadamy

KM#	Date	Mintage	Fine	VF	XF	Unc
108	1981	40.000	.15	.25	.35	1.50

8.0000 g, .835 SILVER, .2148 oz ASW
900th Anniversary of University of Bologna

KM#	Date	Mintage	Fine	VF	XF	Unc
127	1988	.044	—	—	—	7.50
	1988	—	—	—	Proof	15.00

COPPER-NICKEL

KM#	Date	Mintage	Fine	VF	XF	Unc
159	1993	—	—	—	—	.75

200 LIRE

ALUMINUM-BRONZE
Mint mark: R

KM#	Date	Mintage	Fine	VF	XF	Unc
105	1977	15.900	.20	.25	.35	1.25
	1978	461.034	.20	.25	.35	1.25
	1979	212.745	.20	.25	.35	1.25
	1980	—	.20	.25	.35	1.25
	1981	—	.20	.25	.35	1.25
	1982	—	.20	.25	.35	1.25
	1983	—	.20	.25	.35	1.25
	1984	—	.20	.25	.35	1.25
	1985	—	.20	.25	.35	1.25
	1985	.020	—	—	Proof	4.00
	1986	—	.20	.25	.35	1.25
	1986	—	—	—	Proof	4.00
	1987	26.180	.20	.25	.35	1.25
	1987	—	—	—	Proof	4.00
	1988	37.000	.20	.25	.35	1.25
	1991	—	—	—	Proof	4.00

F.A.O. and International Women's Year

KM#	Date	Mintage	Fine	VF	XF	Unc
107	1980	50.000	.20	.25	.35	1.25

World Food Day

KM#	Date	Mintage	Fine	VF	XF	Unc
109	1981	50.000	.20	.25	.35	1.25

5.0000 g, .835 SILVER, .1342 oz ASW
900th Anniversary of University of Bologna
Obv: Similar to 100 Lire, KM#127.

KM#	Date	Mintage	Fine	VF	XF	Unc
128	1988	.044	—	—	—	10.00
	1988	—	—	—	Proof	25.00

BRONZITAL
Taranto Naval Yards

KM#	Date	Mintage	Fine	VF	XF	Unc
130	1989	—	—	—	—	1.25
	1989	—	—	—	Proof	4.00

5.0000 g, .835 SILVER, .1342 oz ASW
Soccer - Ball on World Globe

KM#	Date	Mintage	Fine	VF	XF	Unc
133	1989	—	—	—	—	15.00
	1989	—	—	—	Proof	30.00

Christopher Columbus - Coat of Arms & Dolphin
Obv: Similar to 500 Lire, KM#139.

KM#	Date	Mintage	Fine	VF	XF	Unc
138	1989	—	—	—	—	15.00
	1989	—	—	—	Proof	30.00

BRONZITAL
State Council Building

KM#	Date	Mintage	Fine	VF	XF	Unc
135	1990	—	—	—	—	1.25
	1990	—	—	—	Proof	4.00

9.0000 g, .835 SILVER, .2416 oz ASW
Italian Flora and Fauna

KM#	Date	Mintage	Fine	VF	XF	Unc
142	1991	—	—	—	—	15.00

ALUMINUM-BRONZE
Genoa Stamp Exposition

KM#	Date	Mintage	Fine	VF	XF	Unc
151	1992	100.000	—	—	—	1.25

70th Anniversary of Military Aviation

KM#	Date	Mintage	Fine	VF	XF	Unc
155	1993	—	—	—	—	1.35

500 LIRE

11.0000 g, .835 SILVER, .2953 oz ASW
Mint mark: R
(Dates appear on edge of coin in raised lettering.)

KM#	Date	Mintage	Fine	VF	XF	Unc
98	1958	24.240	—	BV	4.50	10.00
	1958	Inc. Ab.	—	—	Proof	30.00
	1959	19.360	—	BV	4.50	10.00
	1959	Inc. Ab.	—	—	Proof	30.00
	1960	24.080	—	BV	4.50	10.00
	1960	Inc. Ab.	—	—	Proof	30.00
	1961	6.560	—	BV	10.00	40.00
	1961	Inc. Ab.	—	—	Proof	75.00
	1964	4.880	—	BV	4.50	12.50
	1964	Inc. Ab.	—	—	Proof	30.00
	1965	3.120	—	BV	4.50	12.50
	1965	Inc. Ab.	—	—	Proof	30.00
	1966	13.120	—	BV	4.25	7.00
	1966	Inc. Ab.	—	—	Proof	25.00
	1967	2.480	—	BV	4.25	7.00
	1967	Inc. Ab.	—	—	Proof	25.00
	1968	.100	—	—	—	100.00
	1968	Inc. Ab.	—	—	Proof	120.00
	1969	.310	—	—	—	15.00
	1969	Inc. Ab.	—	—	Proof	30.00
	1970	1.140	—	—	—	10.00
	1970	Inc. Ab.	—	—	Proof	25.00
	1980	.500	—	—	—	10.00
	1980	Inc. Ab.	—	—	P/L	25.00
	1981	.500	—	—	—	15.00
	1981	Inc. Ab.	—	—	P/L	25.00
	1982	.115	—	—	—	15.00
	1982	Inc. Ab.	—	—	P/L	25.00
	1983	.076	—	—	—	80.00
	1983	Inc. Ab.	—	—	P/L	100.00
	1984	.077	—	—	—	40.00
	1984	Inc. Ab.	—	—	P/L	65.00
	1985	.073	—	—	—	30.00
	1985	.015	—	—	Proof	50.00
	1986	—	—	—	—	27.50
	1986	—	—	—	Proof	50.00
	1987	—	—	—	—	27.50
	1987	—	—	—	Proof	50.00
	1988	—	—	—	—	27.50
	1989	—	—	—	—	27.50

***NOTE:** Varieties exist in the 1966 issue.

Italian Unification Centennial

KM#	Date	Mintage	Fine	VF	XF	Unc
99	1961	27.120	—	BV	3.00	7.00
	1961	—	—	—	Proof	22.50

700th Anniversary of Birth of Dante Alighieri

KM#	Date	Mintage	Fine	VF	XF	Unc
100	1965	4.272	—	BV	3.50	8.00
	1965	—	—	—	Proof	15.00

100th Anniversary of Birth of Guglielmo Marconi

KM#	Date	Mintage	Fine	VF	XF	Unc
103	1974	.670	—	—	—	20.00
	1974	—	—	—	Proof	30.00

500th Anniversary of Birth of Michelangelo

KM#	Date	Mintage	Fine	VF	XF	Unc
104	1975	.286	—	—	—	30.00
	1975	—	—	—	Proof	45.00

2000th Anniversary of Virgil's Birth

KM#	Date	Mintage	Fine	VF	XF	Unc
110	1981(1982)	.341	—	—	—	18.00
	1981(1982)	—	—	—	Proof	28.00

ACMONITAL RING, BRONZITAL CENTER

KM#	Date	Mintage	Fine	VF	XF	Unc
111	1982	200.000	—	.40	.60	2.00
	1983	230.000	—	.40	.60	1.25
	1984	—	—	.40	.60	1.25
	1985	—	—	.40	.60	1.25
	1985	.020	—	—	Proof	18.00
	1986	—	—	.40	.60	1.25
	1986	—	—	—	Proof	15.00
	1987	200.000	—	.40	.60	1.25
	1987	—	—	—	Proof	20.00
	1988	142.000	—	.40	.60	1.25
	1988	—	—	—	Proof	25.00
	1989	—	—	.40	.60	1.25
	1989	—	—	—	Proof	20.00
	1990	—	—	.40	.60	1.25
	1990	—	—	—	Proof	20.00
	1991	—	—	.40	.60	1.25
	1991	—	—	—	Proof	20.00
	1992	—	—	.40	.60	1.25

11.0000 g, .835 SILVER, .2953 oz ASW
100th Anniversary - Death of Giuseppe Garibaldi

KM#	Date	Mintage	Fine	VF	XF	Unc
112	1982(1983)	.193	—	—	—	20.00
	1982(1983)	—	—	—	Proof	30.00

Galileo Galilei

KM#	Date	Mintage	Fine	VF	XF	Unc
113	1982(1983)	.198	—	—	—	20.00
	1982(1983)	—	—	—	Proof	30.00

Los Angeles Olympics

KM#	Date	Mintage	Fine	VF	XF	Unc
114	1984	.193	—	—	—	30.00
	1984	Inc. Ab.	—	—	Proof	40.00

First Italian President of Common Market

KM#	Date	Mintage	Fine	VF	XF	Unc
115	1985	.103	—	—	—	65.00
	1985	.029	—	—	Proof	85.00

Duino College

KM#	Date	Mintage	Fine	VF	XF	Unc
116	1985	.126	—	—	—	22.50
	1985	—	—	—	Proof	32.50

European Year of Music

KM#	Date	Mintage	Fine	VF	XF	Unc
117	1985	.096	—	—	—	20.00
	1985	—	—	—	Proof	30.00

Etruscan Culture

KM#	Date	Mintage	Fine	VF	XF	Unc
118	1985	.104	—	—	—	20.00
	1985	—	—	—	Proof	30.00

200th Anniversary - Birth of Alessandro Manzoni

KM#	Date	Mintage	Fine	VF	XF	Unc
123	1985	.091	—	—	—	35.00
	1985	.020	—	—	Proof	50.00

Soccer Championship - Mexico

KM#	Date	Mintage	Fine	VF	XF	Unc
119	1986	.091	—	—	—	30.00
	1986	.021	—	—	Proof	45.00

Year of Peace

KM#	Date	Mintage	Fine	VF	XF	Unc
120	1986	.090	—	—	—	25.00
	1986	.019	—	—	Proof	40.00

600th Anniversary - Birth of Donatello

KM#	Date	Mintage	Fine	VF	XF	Unc
124	1986	.073	—	—	—	35.00
	1986	.018	—	—	Proof	50.00

Year of the Family

KM#	Date	Mintage	Fine	VF	XF	Unc
121	1987	.085	—	—	—	35.00
	1987	.020	—	—	Proof	50.00

World Athletic Championships

KM#	Date	Mintage	Fine	VF	XF	Unc
122	1987	.080	—	—	—	30.00
	1987	.020	—	—	Proof	45.00

Giacomo Leopardi

KM#	Date	Mintage	Fine	VF	XF	Unc
132	1987	.058	—	—	—	50.00
	1987	.010	—	—	Proof	65.00

Summer Olympics - Seoul

KM#	Date	Mintage	Fine	VF	XF	Unc
125	1988	.070	—	—	—	35.00
	1988	.013	—	—	Proof	55.00

40th Anniversary of Constitution

KM#	Date	Mintage	Fine	VF	XF	Unc
126	1988	.067	—	—	—	30.00
	1988	.013	—	—	Proof	45.00

900th Anniversary - University of Bologna
Obv: Similar to 100 Lire, KM#127.

KM#	Date	Mintage	Fine	VF	XF	Unc
129	1988	.068	—	—	—	30.00
	1988	.013	—	—	Proof	45.00

100th Anniversary - Death of Giovanni Bosco

KM#	Date	Mintage	Fine	VF	XF	Unc
144	1988	.051	—	—	—	60.00
	1988	9,000	—	—	Proof	75.00

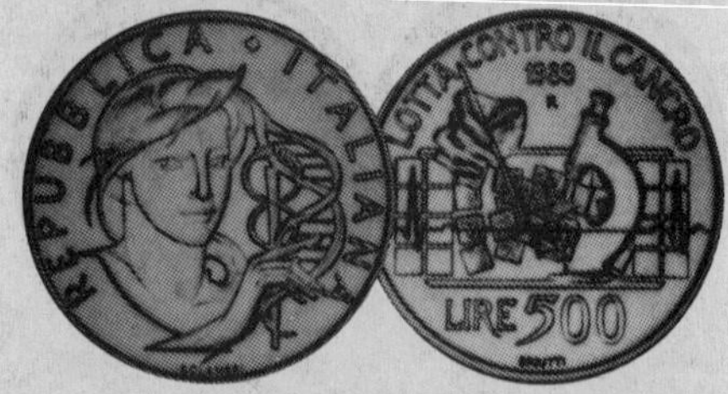

Fight Against Cancer

KM#	Date	Mintage	Fine	VF	XF	Unc
131	1989	.046	—	—	—	60.00

Soccer - Map of Italy on World Globe

KM#	Date	Mintage	Fine	VF	XF	Unc
134	1989	.086	—	—	—	35.00
	1989	.028	—	—	Proof	60.00

350th Anniversary - Death of Tommaso Campanella

KM#	Date	Mintage	Fine	VF	XF	Unc
145	1989	.051	—	—	—	40.00
	1989	.010	—	—	Proof	65.00

Christopher Columbus - Ships in Dock

KM#	Date	Mintage	Fine	VF	XF	Unc
139	1989	.075	—	—	—	35.00
	1989	.025	—	—	Proof	60.00

Soccer
Obv: Similar to KM#134. Rev: Dove w/ half globe - half soccer ball in background.

KM#	Date	Mintage	Fine	VF	XF	Unc
136	1990	.068	—	—	—	35.00
	1990	.025	—	—	Proof	60.00

Italian Presidency of the E.E.C. Council

KM#	Date	Mintage	Fine	VF	XF	Unc
137	1990	.054	—	—	—	35.00
	1990	.010	—	—	Proof	65.00

Columbus - Discovery of America

KM#	Date	Mintage	Fine	VF	XF	Unc
140	1990	.075	—	—	—	32.50
	1990	.025	—	—	Proof	60.00

500th Anniversary of Birth of Tizian

KM#	Date	Mintage	Fine	VF	XF	Unc
146	1990	—	—	—	—	35.00
	1990	—	—	—	Proof	60.00

15.0000 g, .835 SILVER, .4027 oz ASW
2100th Anniversary of Ponte Milvio

KM#	Date	Mintage	Fine	VF	XF	Unc
147	1991	.065	—	—	—	35.00
	1991	.015	—	—	Proof	60.00

Italian Flora and Fauna

KM#	Date	Mintage	Fine	VF	XF	Unc
143	1991	—	—	—	—	30.00

11.0000 g, .835 SILVER, .2953 oz ASW
Discovery of America - Old Map

KM#	Date	Mintage	Fine	VF	XF	Unc
148	1991	.075	—	—	—	32.50
	1991	.025	—	—	Proof	60.00

Lorenzo De'Medici

KM#	Date	Mintage	Fine	VF	XF	Unc
149	1992	—	—	—	—	32.50
	1992	—	—	—	Proof	60.00

Christopher Columbus

KM#	Date	Mintage	Fine	VF	XF	Unc
150	1992	—	—	—	—	32.50
	1992	—	—	—	Proof	60.00

15.0000 g, .835 SILVER, .4027 oz ASW
Rosini

KM#	Date	Mintage	Fine	VF	XF	Unc
152	1992	—	—	—	—	32.50

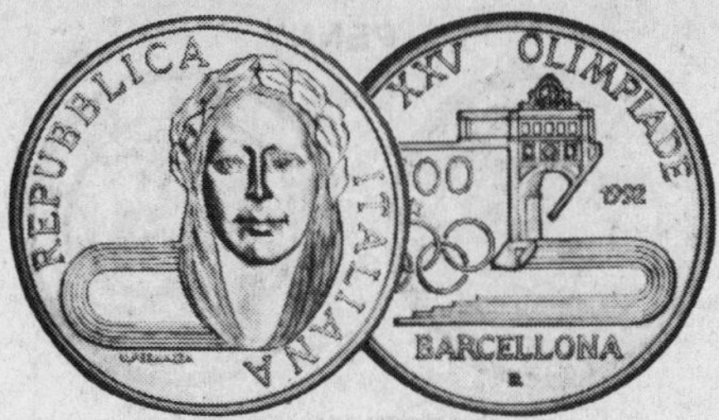

Olympics - Building and Track

KM#	Date	Mintage	Fine	VF	XF	Unc
153	1992	—	—	—	—	32.50

Flora and Fauna

KM#	Date	Mintage	Fine	VF	XF	Unc
154	1992	—	—	—	—	40.00

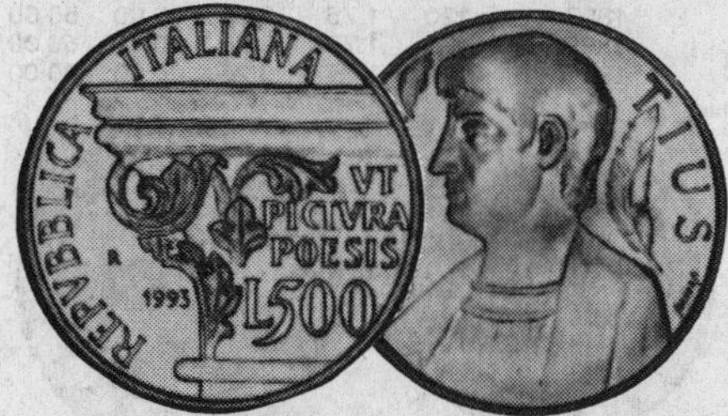

2000th Anniversary - Death of Horace, Poet

KM#	Date	Mintage	Fine	VF	XF	Unc
156	1993	—	—	—	—	25.00
	1993	—	—	—	Proof	45.00

Wildlife Protection-Storks and Swordfish

KM#	Date	Mintage	Fine	VF	XF	Unc
157	1993	—	—	—	—	27.50

University of Pisa

KM#	Date	Mintage	Fine	VF	XF	Unc
158	1993	—	—	—	—	25.00

ACMONITAL RING BRONZITAL CENTER
Centennial of Bank of Italy

KM#	Date	Mintage	Fine	VF	XF	Unc
160	1993	—	—	—	—	1.25

1000 LIRE

14.6000 g, .835 SILVER, .3920 oz ASW
Centennial of Rome as Capital

KM#	Date	Mintage	Fine	VF	XF	Unc
101	1970	3.011	—	—	—	15.00
	1970	—	—	—	Proof	25.00

MINT SETS (MS)

KM#	Date	Mintage	Identification	Issue Price	Mkt. Val.
MS1	1968(8)	100,000	KM91-96,97.2,98	6.50	160.00
MS2	1969(8)	310,000	KM91-96,97.2,98	6.50	15.00
MS3	1970(9)	1,011,000	KM91-96,97.2,98,101	—	20.00
MS4	1980(10)	257,000	KM91-96,97.2,98,105,107	—	18.00
MS5	1981(11)	163,000	KM91-96,97.2,98,105,	—	20.00
			108-109	—	20.00
MS6	1981(8)	—	KM92-93,95-96,97.2,105,	—	—
			108-109	—	—
MS7	1982(10)	120,000	KM91-96,97.2,98,105,111	—	18.00
MS9	1983(10)	77,000	KM91-96,97.2,98,105,111	—	145.00
MS11	1984(10)	77,000	KM91-96,97.2,98,105,111	—	60.00
MS13	1985(10)	17,000	KM91-96,97.2,105,111,123	—	40.00
MS14	1985(11)	75,000	KM91-96,97.2,98,105,111,	—	60.00
			123	—	60.00
MS17	1986(11)	73,000	KM91-96,97.2,98,105,111,	—	65.00
			124	—	65.00
MS18	1987(11)	58,000	KM91-96,97.2,98,105,111,	—	80.00
			132	—	80.00
MS19	1988(11)	51,000	KM91-96,97.2,98,105,111, 144	46.00	90.00
MS21	1988(3)	—	KM127-129	—	47.50
MS22	1989(11)	51,000	KM91-96,97.2,98,111,130, 145	—	75.00
MS23	1989(2)	—	KM133-134	—	50.00
MS24	1990(11)	—	KM91-94,95a-96a,97.2,98, 111,135,146	—	85.00
MS25	1991(11)	—	KM91-94,95a-96a,97.2,98, 105,111,147	50.00	70.00
MS26	1991(2)	—	KM142-143	—	45.00
MS27	1992(11)	—	KM91-94,95a-96a,97.2, 98,111,151,161	50.00	—
MS28	1993(11)	—	KM91-94,95a-96a,97.2 98,111,162,163	—	—

PROOF SETS (PS)

KM#	Date	Mintage	Identification	Issue Price	Mkt. Val.
PS1	1985(10)	5,000	KM91-96,97.2,105,111,123	—	75.00
PS2	1985(11)	15,000	KM91-96,97.2,98,105,111, 123	—	135.00
PS3	1986(10)	—	KM91-96,97.2,105,111,124	—	75.00
PS4	1986(11)	18,000	KM91-96,97.2,98,105,111, 124	—	135.00
PS5	1987(11)	10,000	KM91-96,97.2,98,105,111, 132	—	160.00
PS6	1988(11)	9,000	KM91-96,97.2,98,105,111, 144	100.00	165.00
PS7	1988(3)	—	KM127-129	—	90.00
PS8	1989(11)	10,000	KM91-96,97.2,98,111, 130,145	—	160.00
PS9	1990(11)	—	KM91-94,95a-96a,97.2,98, 111,135,146	—	155.00
PS10	1991(11)	—	KM91-94,95a-96a,97.2,98, 105,111,147	100.00	155.00
PS11	1992(11)	—	KM91-94,95a-96a,97.2, 98,111,151,161	90.00	—
PS12	1993(11)	—	KM91-94,95a-96a,97.2, 98,111,162,163	—	—

IVORY COAST

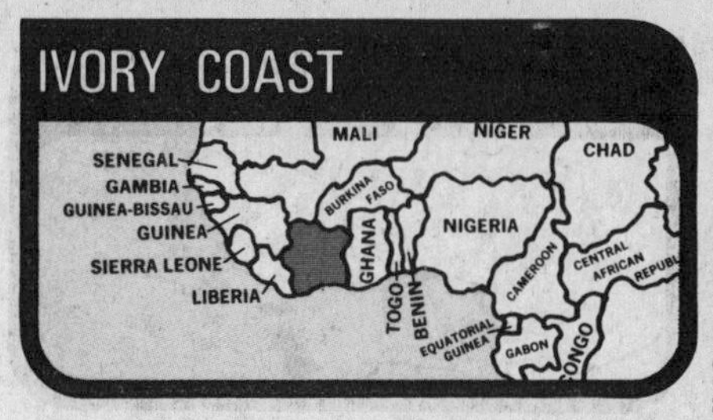

The Republic of the Ivory Coast, a former French Overseas territory located on the south side of the African bulge between Nigeria and Ghana, has an area of 124,504 sq. mi. (322,463 sq. km.) and a population of 11.8 million. Capital: Yamoussoukro. The predominantly agricultural economy is one of Africa's most prosperous. Coffee, tropical woods, cocoa, and bananas are exported.

The Ivory Coast was first visited by French and Portuguese navigators in the 15th century. French traders set up establishments in the 19th century, and gradually extended their influence along the coast and inland. The area was organized as a territory in 1893, and from 1904 to 1958 was a constituent unit of the Federation of French West Africa - as a Colony under the Third Republic and an Overseas Territory under the Fourth. In 1958 Ivory Coast became an autonomous republic within the French Community. Independence was attained on Aug. 7, 1960.

10 FRANCS

25.0000 g, .925 SILVER, .7434 oz ASW

KM#	Date	Mintage	VF	XF	Unc
1	1966	—	—	Proof	42.50

NOTE: Varieties exist in 2.9mm and 3.5mm planchets.

3.2000 g, .900 GOLD, .0926 oz AGW

KM#	Date	Mintage	VF	XF	Unc
2	1966	2,000	—	Proof	85.00

25 FRANCS

8.0000 g, .900 GOLD, .2315 oz AGW

KM#	Date	Mintage	VF	XF	Unc
3	1966	2,000	—	Proof	135.00

50 FRANCS

16.0000 g, .900 GOLD, .4630 oz AGW
Similar to 25 Francs, KM#3.

KM#	Date	Mintage	VF	XF	Unc
4	1966	2,000	—	Proof	265.00

100 FRANCS

32.0000 g, .900 GOLD, .9260 oz AGW

KM#	Date	Mintage	VF	XF	Unc
5	1966	2,000	—	Proof	525.00

PROOF SETS (PS)

KM#	Date	Mintage	Identification	Issue Price	Mkt. Val.
PS1	1966	2,000	KM2-5	—	1000.

Jamaica, a member of the British Commonwealth situated in the Caribbean Sea 90 miles south of Cuba, has an area of 4,244 sq. mi. (10,990 sq. km.) and a population of 2.1 million. Capital: Kingston. The economy is founded chiefly on mining, tourism and agriculture. Alumina, bauxite, sugar, rum and molasses are exported.

Jamaica was discovered by Columbus on May 3, 1494, and settled by Spain in 1509. The island was captured in 1655 by a British naval force under the command of Admiral William Penn, sent by Oliver Cromwell and ceded to Britain by the Treaty of Madrid, 1670. For more than 150 years, the Jamaican economy of sugar, slaves and piracy was one of the most prosperous in the new world. Dissension between the property-oriented island legislature and the home government prompted parliament to establish a crown colony government for Jamaica in 1866. From 1958 to 1961 Jamaica was a member of the West Indies Federation, withdrawing when Jamaican voters rejected the association. The colony attained independence on Aug. 6, 1962. Jamaica is a member of the Commonwealth of Nations. The Queen of England is Chief of State.

In 1758, the Jamaican Assembly authorized stamping a certain amount of Spanish milled coinage. Token coinage by merchants aided the island's monetary supply in the early 19th century. Sterling coinage was introduced in Jamaica in 1825, with the additional silver three halfpence under William IV and Victoria. Certain issues of three pence of William IV and Victoria were intended for colonial use, including Jamaica, as were the last dates of three pence for George VI.

There was an extensive token and work tally coinage for Jamaica in the late 19th and early 20th centuries.

A decimal standard currency system was adopted on Sept. 8, 1969.

RULERS

British, until 1962

MINT MARKS

H - Heaton
C - Ottawa
FM - Franklin Mint, U.S.A.**
(fm) - Franklin Mint, U.S.A.*
(RM) - Royal Mint

***NOTE:** During 1970 the Franklin Mint produced matte and proof coins (1 cent-1 dollar) using dies similar to/or Royal Mint without the FM mint mark.

****NOTE:** From 1975 the Franklin Mint has produced coinage in up to 3 different qualities. Qualities of issue are designated in ( ) after each date and are defined as follows:

(M) MATTE - Normal circulation strike or a dull finish produced by sandblasting special uncirculated (polish finish) or proof quality dies.

(U) SPECIAL UNCIRCULATED - Polished or proof-like in appearance without any frosted features.

(P) PROOF - The highest qualitty obtainable having mirror-like fields and frosted features.

MONETARY SYSTEM

4 Farthings = 1 Penny
12 Pence = 1 Shilling
8 Reales = 6 Shillings, 8 Pence
(Commencing 1969)
100 Cents = 1 Dollar

FARTHING

COPPER-NICKEL

KM#	Date	Mintage	Fine	VF	XF	Unc
15	1880	.192	1.50	2.50	12.00	32.50
	1880	—	—	—	Proof	225.00
	1882H	.384	1.00	1.75	10.00	27.50
	1882H	—	—	—	Proof	200.00
	1884	.096	2.00	4.00	20.00	50.00
	1884	—	—	—	Proof	250.00
	1885	.096	2.00	4.00	20.00	50.00
	1885	—	—	—	Proof	200.00
	1887	.192	1.50	2.50	12.00	32.50
	1887	—	—	—	Proof	200.00
	1888	.192	1.50	2.50	12.00	30.00
	1888	—	—	—	Proof	200.00
	1889	.192	1.50	2.50	12.50	32.50
	1890H	.096	2.00	4.00	20.00	50.00
	1891	.096	2.00	4.00	20.00	90.00
	1893	.096	2.00	4.00	20.00	70.00
15	1894	.144	1.75	3.25	15.00	40.00
	1894	—	—	—	Proof	200.00
	1895	.144	1.75	3.25	15.00	40.00
	1897	.144	1.75	3.25	15.00	40.00
	1899	.144	1.75	3.25	15.00	40.00
	1900	.144	1.75	3.25	15.00	40.00

Rev: Horizontal shading in arms.

KM#	Date	Mintage	Fine	VF	XF	Unc
18	1902	.144	1.75	3.25	15.00	40.00
	1903	.144	1.75	3.25	15.00	35.00

Rev: Vertical shading in arms.

KM#	Date	Mintage	Fine	VF	XF	Unc
21	1904	.192	1.00	2.50	12.00	32.50
	1904	—	—	—	Proof	200.00
	1905	.192	1.00	2.50	12.00	32.50
	1906	.528	1.00	2.00	8.00	25.00
	1907	.192	1.00	2.50	12.00	32.50
	1909	.144	2.00	4.00	15.00	40.00
	1910	.048	2.00	4.00	20.00	45.00

KM#	Date	Mintage	Fine	VF	XF	Unc
24	1914	.192	1.75	3.25	12.00	32.50
	1916H	.480	.75	1.50	4.00	20.00
	1916H	—	—	—	Proof	250.00
	1918C	.208	1.00	2.00	5.00	25.00
	1918C	—	—	—	Proof	200.00
	1919C	.401	.75	1.50	4.00	20.00
	1926	.240	.75	1.50	4.00	20.00
	1928	.480	.75	1.50	4.00	20.00
	1928	—	—	—	Proof	200.00
	1932	.480	.75	1.50	4.00	20.00
	1932	—	—	—	Proof	—
	1934	.480	.75	1.50	4.00	20.00
	1934	—	—	—	Proof	—

NICKEL-BRASS

KM#	Date	Mintage	Fine	VF	XF	Unc
27	1937	.480	.50	1.00	1.75	12.00
	1937	—	—	—	Proof	175.00

Obv: Larger head.

KM#	Date	Mintage	Fine	VF	XF	Unc
30	1938	.480	.20	.40	1.50	7.00
	1938	—	—	—	Proof	—
	1942	.480	.20	.40	1.50	7.00
	1945	.480	.20	.40	1.50	7.00
	1945	—	—	—	Proof	120.00
	1947	.192	.35	.70	2.00	12.00
	1947	—	—	—	Proof	120.00

Obv. leg: W/o AND EMPEROR OF INDIA.

KM#	Date	Mintage	Fine	VF	XF	Unc
33	1950	.288	.10	.25	.80	3.25
	1950	—	—	—	Proof	175.00
	1952	.288	.10	.25	.80	3.25
	1952	—	—	—	Proof	175.00

1/2 PENNY

COPPER-NICKEL

KM#	Date	Mintage	Fine	VF	XF	Unc
16	1869	.192	1.25	2.50	15.00	40.00
	1869	—	—	—	Proof	300.00
	1870	.240	1.25	2.50	15.00	45.00
	1870	—	—	—	Proof	500.00
	1871	.240	1.25	2.50	15.00	45.00
	1871	—	—	—	Proof	375.00
	1880	.192	1.25	2.50	15.00	45.00
	1880	—	—	—	Proof	475.00
	1882H	.096	2.00	5.00	20.00	80.00
	1882H	—	—	—	Proof	400.00
	1884	.096	2.00	5.00	20.00	55.00
	1884	—	—	—	Proof	400.00
	1885	.096	2.00	5.00	20.00	55.00
	1885	—	—	—	Proof	400.00
	1887	.072	4.00	8.00	40.00	85.00
	1888	.096	1.75	5.00	20.00	50.00
	1888	—	—	—	Proof	350.00
	1889	.096	2.00	5.00	25.00	60.00
	1890H	.120	1.75	3.25	20.00	50.00
	1891	.120	1.75	3.25	20.00	70.00
	1893	.144	1.75	3.25	20.00	50.00
	1894	.096	2.00	5.00	25.00	60.00
	1895	.096	2.00	5.00	25.00	60.00
	1897	.120	1.75	3.25	20.00	50.00
	1899	.120	1.75	3.25	20.00	50.00
	1900	.120	1.75	3.25	20.00	60.00

Rev: Horizontal shading in arms.

KM#	Date	Mintage	Fine	VF	XF	Unc
19	1902	.048	1.25	2.50	15.00	50.00
	1903	.048	1.25	2.50	15.00	50.00

Rev: Vertical shading in arms.

KM#	Date	Mintage	Fine	VF	XF	Unc
22	1904	.048	1.50	3.00	20.00	70.00
	1905	.048	1.50	3.00	20.00	60.00
	1906	.432	.35	.65	6.50	25.00
	1907	.504	.35	.65	6.50	25.00
	1909	.144	.45	.80	8.00	32.50
	1910	.144	.45	.80	8.00	32.50

KM#	Date	Mintage	Fine	VF	XF	Unc
25	1914	.096	1.25	2.50	15.00	60.00
	1916H	.192	.35	.65	4.00	20.00
	1918C	.251	.35	.65	4.00	20.00
	1918C	—	—	—	Proof	200.00
	1919C	.312	.35	.65	4.00	20.00
	1920	.480	.35	.65	4.00	20.00
	1926	.240	.35	.65	4.00	30.00
	1928	.120	.35	.65	4.00	20.00
	1928	—	—	—	Proof	200.00

NICKEL-BRASS

KM#	Date	Mintage	Fine	VF	XF	Unc
28	1937	.960	.50	1.00	2.50	12.00
	1937	—	—	—	Proof	175.00

Obv: Larger head.

KM#	Date	Mintage	Fine	VF	XF	Unc
31	1938	.960	.25	.50	2.50	12.00
	1938	—	—	—	Proof	175.00
	1940	.960	.25	.50	2.50	12.00
	1940	—	—	—	Proof	175.00
	1942	.960	.25	.50	2.50	12.00
	1945	.960	.25	.50	2.50	12.00
	1945	—	—	—	Proof	175.00
	1947	.960	.25	.50	2.50	12.00
	1947	—	—	—	Proof	200.00

Obv. leg: W/o AND EMPEROR OF INDIA.

KM#	Date	Mintage	Fine	VF	XF	Unc
34	1950	1.440	.10	.20	.30	3.25
	1950	—	—	—	Proof	175.00
	1952	1.200	.10	.20	.30	3.25
	1952	—	—	—	Proof	175.00

KM#	Date	Mintage	Fine	VF	XF	Unc
36	1955	1.440	.10	.15	.40	2.00
	1955	—	—	—	Proof	100.00
	1957	.600	.10	.20	.50	2.00
	1957	—	—	—	Proof	—
	1958	.960	.10	.20	.50	2.00
	1958	—	—	—	Proof	100.00
	1959	.960	.10	.20	.50	2.00
	1959	—	—	—	Proof	—
	1961	.480	.20	.40	1.00	4.00
	1961	—	—	—	Proof	—
	1962	.960	.10	.15	.30	1.75
	1962	—	—	—	Proof	100.00
	1963	.960	.10	.15	.30	1.75
	1963	—	—	—	Proof	100.00

Rev: New arms.

KM#	Date	Mintage	Fine	VF	XF	Unc
38	1964	1.440	.10	.15	.20	.80
	1965	1.200	.10	.15	.20	.80
	1966	1.680	.10	.15	.20	.80

COPPER-NICKEL-ZINC
Jamaican Coinage Centennial

KM#	Date	Mintage	Fine	VF	XF	Unc
41	1969	.030	.10	.15	.25	.75
	1969	5,000	—	—	Proof	2.50

PENNY

COPPER-NICKEL

KM#	Date	Mintage	Fine	VF	XF	Unc
17	1869	.144	2.00	6.50	25.00	60.00
	1869	—	—	—	Proof	225.00
	1870	.120	2.00	5.00	25.00	65.00
	1870	—	—	—	Proof	775.00
	1871	.120	2.00	5.00	25.00	65.00
	1871	—	—	—	Proof	600.00
	1880	.096	4.00	12.00	50.00	100.00
	1880	—	—	—	Proof	600.00
	1882H	.048	4.00	12.00	50.00	125.00
	1882H	—	—	—	Proof	500.00
	1882	Inc. Ab.	15.00	40.00	120.00	225.00
	1882	—	—	—	Proof	1000.
	1884	.048	4.00	12.00	50.00	100.00
	1884	—	—	—	Proof	500.00
	1885	.048	4.00	12.00	50.00	100.00
	1885	—	—	—	Proof	400.00
	1887	.024	3.00	14.00	60.00	160.00
	1888	.024	4.50	14.00	60.00	180.00
	1888	—	—	—	Proof	400.00
	1889	.024	4.50	14.00	60.00	160.00
	1890	.036	4.00	12.00	50.00	120.00
	1891	.036	4.00	12.00	50.00	120.00
	1893	.024	5.00	14.00	60.00	180.00
	1894	.036	4.00	12.00	50.00	120.00
	1895	.036	4.00	12.00	50.00	120.00
	1897	.024	4.50	14.00	60.00	180.00
	1899	.024	4.50	14.00	60.00	180.00
	1900	.024	4.50	14.00	60.00	160.00

Rev: Horizontal shading in arms.

KM#	Date	Mintage	Fine	VF	XF	Unc
20	1902	.060	2.25	4.75	25.00	60.00
	1903	.060	2.25	4.75	25.00	60.00

Rev: Vertical shading in arms.

KM#	Date	Mintage	Fine	VF	XF	Unc
23	1904	.024	2.25	6.50	27.50	80.00
	1904	—	—	—	Proof	250.00
	1905	.048	2.00	4.75	22.50	60.00
	1906	.156	1.25	2.50	12.00	40.00
	1907	.108	1.25	2.50	12.00	40.00
	1909	.144	1.25	2.50	12.00	40.00
	1910	.144	1.25	2.50	12.00	40.00

KM#	Date	Mintage	Fine	VF	XF	Unc
26	1914	.024	8.00	15.00	65.00	175.00
	1916H	.024	6.00	12.00	50.00	150.00
	1918C	.187	2.00	5.00	15.00	60.00
	1918C	—	—	—	Proof	200.00
	1919C	.251	1.25	4.75	12.00	50.00
	1920	.360	.75	2.50	9.50	32.50
	1926	.240	.75	2.50	9.50	30.00
	1928	.360	.75	2.50	9.50	30.00
	1928	—	—	—	Proof	200.00

NICKEL-BRASS

KM#	Date	Mintage	Fine	VF	XF	Unc
29	1937	1.200	1.00	1.75	3.25	12.00
	1937	—	—	—	Proof	200.00

Obv: Larger head.

KM#	Date	Mintage	Fine	VF	XF	Unc
32	1938	1.200	.35	.65	3.25	12.00
	1938	—	—	—	Proof	200.00
	1940	1.200	.35	.65	3.25	12.00
	1940	—	—	—	Proof	200.00
	1942	1.200	.35	.65	3.25	12.00
	1942	—	—	—	Proof	200.00
	1945	1.200	.35	.65	3.25	12.00
	1945	—	—	—	Proof	200.00
	1947	.480	.35	.65	3.25	12.00
	1947	—	—	—	Proof	200.00

Obv. leg: W/o AND EMPEROR OF INDIA.

KM#	Date	Mintage	Fine	VF	XF	Unc
35	1950	.600	.20	.35	1.50	8.00
	1950	—	—	—	Proof	200.00
	1952	.725	.20	.35	1.50	8.00
	1952	—	—	—	Proof	200.00

KM#	Date	Mintage	Fine	VF	XF	Unc
37	1953	1.200	.10	.20	.50	1.50
	1953	—	—	—	Proof	115.00
	1955	.960	.10	.25	1.00	4.00
	1955	—	—	—	Proof	115.00
	1957	.600	.10	.25	1.00	4.00
	1957	—	—	—	Proof	—
	1958	1.080	.10	.20	.30	3.00
	1958	—	—	—	Proof	100.00
	1959	1.368	.10	.20	.30	2.50
	1959	—	—	—	Proof	—
	1960	1.368	.10	.20	.30	2.50
	1960	—	—	—	Proof	—
	1961	1.368	.10	.20	.30	2.50
	1961	—	—	—	Proof	—
	1962	1.920	.10	.20	.30	2.50
	1962	—	—	—	Proof	100.00
	1963	.720	.25	.50	4.00	30.00
	1963	—	—	—	Proof	100.00

KM#	Date	Mintage	Fine	VF	XF	Unc
39	1964	.480	.10	.15	.25	.75
	1965	1.200	.10	.15	.20	.35
	1966	1.200	.10	.15	.20	.35
	1967	2.760	.10	.15	.20	.35

COPPER-NICKEL-ZINC
Jamaican Coinage Centennial

KM#	Date	Mintage	Fine	VF	XF	Unc
42	1969	.030	.10	.15	.30	.75
	1969	5,000	—	—	Proof	2.50

1-1/2 PENCE

.925 SILVER

From 1834 through 1870 colonial issue 1-1/2 pence were circulated in Ceylon and Jamaica. These are listed under Great Britain.

5 SHILLINGS

COPPER-NICKEL
VIII Commonwealth Games

KM#	Date	Mintage	Fine	VF	XF	Unc
40	1966	.190	—	1.25	1.50	2.00
	1966	.020	—	—	Proof	4.00

DECIMAL COINAGE

The Franklin Mint and Royal Mint have both been striking the 1 cent through 1 dollar coinage. The 1970 issues were all struck with dies similar to/or Royal Mint without the FM mint mark. The Royal Mint issues have the name JAMAICA extending beyond the native head dress feathers. Those struck after 1970 by the Franklin Mint have the name JAMAICA within the head dress feathers.

CENT

BRONZE
Ackee Fruit

KM#	Date	Mintage	VF	XF	Unc
45	1969	30.200	—	.10	.25
	1969	.019	—	Proof	.50
	1970(RM) small date	10.000	—	.10	.25
	1970FM(M) large date	5,000	—	.10	.25
	1970FM(P)	.012	—	Proof	.50
	1971(RM)	5.625	—	.10	.25

KM#	Date	Mintage	VF	XF	Unc
51	1971FM(M)	4,834	—	.10	.25
	1971FM(P)	.014	—	Proof	.50
	1972FM(M)	7,982	—	.10	.25
	1972FM(P)	.017	—	Proof	.50
	1973FM(M)	.029	—	.10	.25
	1973FM(P)	.028	—	Proof	.50
	1974FM(M)	.028	—	.10	.25
	1974FM(P)	.022	—	Proof	.50
	1975FM(M)	.036	—	.10	.25
	1975FM(U)	4,683	—	—	.25
	1975FM(P)	.016	—	Proof	.50

F.A.O. Issue

KM#	Date	Mintage	VF	XF	Unc
52	1971	.020	—	.10	.30
	1972	5.000	—	.10	.30
	1973	5.500	—	.10	.30
	1974	3.000	—	.10	.30

ALUMINUM
F.A.O. Issue

KM#	Date	Mintage	VF	XF	Unc
64	1975	15.000	—	.10	.20
	1976	16.000	—	.10	.20
	1977	—	—	.10	.20
	1978	8.400	—	.10	.20
	1980	10.000	—	.10	.20
	1981	8.000	—	.10	.20
	1982	10.000	—	.10	.20
	1983	1.342	—	—	.15
	1984	8.704	—	—	.15
	1985	5.112	—	—	.15
	1985	—	—	Proof	.50
	1986	17.534	—	—	.15
	1987	9.968	—	—	.15
	1987	—	—	Proof	.50
	1988	—	—	Proof	.50
	1989	—	—	Proof	.50
	1990	—	—	Proof	.50
	1991	—	—	—	.15
	1991	—	—	Proof	.50
	1992	—	—	Proof	.50
	1993	—	—	Proof	.50

KM#	Date	Mintage	VF	XF	Unc
68	1976FM(M)	.028	—	—	.15
	1976FM(U)	1,802	—	—	.25
	1976FM(P)	.024	—	Proof	.50
	1977FM(M)	.028	—	—	.15
	1977FM(U)	597 pcs.	—	—	1.50
	1977FM(P)	.010	—	Proof	.50
	1978FM(M)	.028	—	—	.15
	1978FM(U)	1,282	—	—	.40
	1978FM(P)	6,058	—	Proof	.60
	1979FM(M)	.028	—	—	.15
	1979FM(U)	2,608	—	—	.40
	1979FM(P)	4,049	—	Proof	.60
	1980FM(M)	.028	—	—	.15
	1980FM(U)	3,668	—	—	.35
	1980FM(P)	2,688	—	Proof	.75
	1981FM(U)	482 pcs.	—	—	1.50
	1981FM(P)	1,577	—	Proof	.75
	1982FM(U)	—	—	—	.35
	1982FM(P)	—	—	Proof	.75
	1984FM(U)	—	—	—	.35
	1984FM(P)	—	—	Proof	.75

Mule. 2 obverses of KM#64.

KM#	Date	Mintage	VF	XF	Unc
136	1982 FM	—	—	220.00	250.00

Mule. 2 reverses of KM#64.

KM#	Date	Mintage	VF	XF	Unc
137	1982FM	—	—	250.00	300.00

21st Anniversary of Independence

KM#	Date	Mintage	VF	XF	Unc
101	1983FM(U)	—	—	—	.35
	1983FM(P)	—	—	Proof	.75

5 CENTS

COPPER-NICKEL
Crocodile

KM#	Date	Mintage	VF	XF	Unc
46	1969	12.008	—	.10	.45
	1969	.030	—	Proof	.60
	1970FM(M)	5,000	—	.10	.35
	1970FM(P)	.012	—	Proof	.60
	1972	6.000	—	.10	.35
	1975	6.010	—	.10	.35
	1977	2.400	—	.10	.25
	1978	2.000	—	.10	.25
	1980	2.272	—	.10	.25
	1981	2.001	—	.10	.25
	1982	2.000	—	.10	.25
	1983	.992	—	.10	.25
	1984	3.508	—	.10	.25
	1985	4.760	—	.10	.25
	1985	—	—	Proof	.60
	1986	14.504	—	.10	.25
	1987	13.166	—	.10	.25
	1987	—	—	Proof	.60
	1988	9.780	—	.10	.25
	1988	—	—	Proof	.60
	1989	—	—	.10	.25
	1989	—	—	Proof	.60

NICKEL PLATED STEEL

KM#	Date	Mintage	VF	XF	Unc
46a	1990	—	—	.10	.25
	1990	—	—	Proof	.60
	1991	—	—	Proof	.60
	1992	—	—	.10	.25
	1992	—	—	Proof	.60
	1993	—	—	Proof	.60

COPPER-NICKEL

KM#	Date	Mintage	VF	XF	Unc
53	1971FM(M)	4,834	—	.10	.30
	1971FM(P)	.014	—	Proof	.50
	1972FM(M)	7,982	—	.10	.30
	1972FM(P)	.017	—	Proof	.50
	1973FM(M)	.017	—	.10	.30
	1973FM(P)	.028	—	Proof	.50
	1974FM(M)	.016	—	.10	.30
	1974FM(P)	.022	—	Proof	.50
	1975FM(M)	6,240	—	.10	.30
	1975FM(U)	4,683	—	—	.30
	1975FM(P)	.016	—	Proof	.50
	1976FM(M)	5,560	—	.10	.30
	1976FM(U)	1,802	—	—	.30
	1976FM(P)	.024	—	Proof	.50
	1977FM(M)	5,560	—	.10	.35
	1977FM(U)	597 pcs.	—	—	1.50
	1977FM(P)	.010	—	Proof	.50
	1978FM(M)	5,560	—	.10	.35
	1978FM(U)	1,282	—	—	.50
	1978FM(P)	6,058	—	Proof	.75
	1979FM(M)	5,560	—	.10	.35
	1979FM(U)	2,608	—	—	.50
	1979FM(P)	4,049	—	Proof	.75
	1980FM(M)	5,560	—	.10	.35
	1980FM(U)	3,668	—	—	.40
	1980FM(P)	2,688	—	Proof	1.00
	1981FM(U)	482 pcs.	—	—	1.50
	1981FM(P)	1,577	—	Proof	1.00
	1982FM(U)	—	—	—	.40
	1982FM(P)	—	—	Proof	1.00
	1984FM(U)	—	—	—	.40
	1984FM(P)	—	—	Proof	1.00

21st Anniversary of Independence

KM#	Date	Mintage	VF	XF	Unc
102	1983FM(U)	—	—	—	.40
	1983FM(P)	—	—	Proof	1.00

10 CENTS

COPPER-NICKEL
Lignum Vitae

KM#	Date	Mintage	VF	XF	Unc
47	1969	19.508	—	.10	.50
	1969	.030	—	Proof	.75
	1970FM(M)	5,000	—	.10	.50
	1970FM(P)	.012	—	Proof	.75
	1972	6.000	—	.10	.50
	1975	10.010	—	.10	.40
	1977	8.000	—	.10	.40
	1981	8.000	—	.10	.30
	1982	8.000	—	.10	.30
	1983	2.000	—	.10	.30
	1984	5.000	—	.10	.30
	1985	8.310	—	.10	.30
	1985	—	—	Proof	.75
	1986	21.677	—	.10	.30
	1987	29.089	—	.10	.30
	1987	—	—	Proof	.75
	1988	15.660	—	.10	.30
	1988	—	—	Proof	.75
	1989	—	—	.10	.30
	1989	—	—	Proof	.75

NICKEL PLATED STEEL

KM#	Date	Mintage	VF	XF	Unc
47a	1990	—	—	.10	.30
	1990	—	—	Proof	.75

COPPER-NICKEL

KM#	Date	Mintage	VF	XF	Unc
54	1971FM(M)	4,834	—	.10	.35
	1971FM(P)	.014	—	Proof	.75
	1972FM(M)	7,982	—	.10	.35
	1972FM(P)	.017	—	Proof	.75
	1973FM(M)	.015	—	.10	.35
	1973FM(P)	.028	—	Proof	.75
	1974FM(M)	.014	—	.10	.35
	1974FM(P)	.022	—	Proof	.75
	1975FM(M)	3,120	—	.10	.35
	1975FM(U)	4,683	—	—	.35
	1975FM(P)	.016	—	Proof	.75
	1976FM(M)	2,780	—	.10	.35
	1976FM(U)	1,802	—	—	.35
	1976FM(P)	.024	—	Proof	.75
	1977FM(M)	2,780	—	.10	.50
	1977FM(U)	597 pcs.	—	—	1.50
	1977FM(P)	.010	—	Proof	.75
	1978FM(M)	2,780	—	.10	.50
	1978FM(U)	4,062	—	—	.60
	1978FM(P)	6,058	—	Proof	1.00
	1979FM(M)	2,780	—	.10	.50
	1979FM(U)	2,608	—	—	.60
	1979FM(P)	4,049	—	Proof	1.00
	1980FM(M)	2,780	—	.10	.50
	1980FM(U)	3,668	—	—	.50
	1980FM(P)	2,688	—	Proof	1.50
	1981FM(U)	482 pcs.	—	—	1.50
	1981FM(P)	1,577	—	Proof	1.50
	1982FM(U)	—	—	—	.50
	1982FM(P)	—	—	Proof	1.50
	1984FM(U)	—	—	—	.50
	1984FM(P)	—	—	Proof	1.50

21st Anniversary of Independence

KM#	Date	Mintage	VF	XF	Unc
103	1983FM(U)	—	—	—	.50
	1983FM(P)	—	—	Proof	1.50

NICKEL PLATED STEEL
Paul Bogle

KM#	Date	Mintage	VF	XF	Unc
146	1991	—	—	—	.50
	1991	—	—	Proof	1.50
	1992	—	—	—	.50
	1992	—	—	Proof	1.50
	1993	—	—	—	.50
	1993	—	—	Proof	1.50

20 CENTS

COPPER-NICKEL
Mahoe Tree

KM#	Date	Mintage	VF	XF	Unc
48	1969	3.758	—	.20	.75
	1969	.030	—	Proof	1.00
	1970FM(M)	5,000	—	.20	.75
	1970FM(P)	.012	—	Proof	1.00
	1975	.010	—	.20	.85
	1982	1.000	—	.20	.65
	1984	2.000	—	.20	.65
	1986	2.530	—	.20	.65
	1987	5.545	—	.20	.65
	1987	—	—	Proof	1.00
	1988	5.016	—	.20	.65
	1988	—	—	Proof	1.00
	1989	—	—	.20	.65
	1989	—	—	Proof	1.00
	1990	—	—	Proof	1.00

KM#	Date	Mintage	VF	XF	Unc
55	1971FM(M)	4,834	—	.20	.50
	1971FM(P)	.014	—	Proof	1.00
	1972FM(M)	7,982	—	.20	.50
	1972FM(P)	.017	—	Proof	1.00
	1973FM(M)	.013	—	.20	.50
	1973FM(P)	.028	—	Proof	1.00
	1974FM(M)	.012	—	.20	.50
	1974FM(P)	.022	—	Proof	1.00
	1975FM(M)	1,560	—	.20	.50
	1975FM(U)	4,683	—	—	.50
	1975FM(P)	.016	—	Proof	1.00
	1976FM(M)	1,390	—	.20	.50
	1976FM(U)	1,802	—	—	.50
	1976FM(P)	.024	—	Proof	1.00

F.A.O. Issue

KM#	Date	Mintage	VF	XF	Unc
69	1976	3.000	—	.20	1.00
	1982	Inc. KM48	—	.20	1.00

KM#	Date	Mintage	VF	XF	Unc
73	1977FM(M)	1,390	—	.20	.75
	1977FM(U)	597 pcs.	—	—	2.00
	1977FM(P)	.010	—	Proof	1.00
	1978FM(M)	1,390	—	.20	.75
	1978FM(U)	1,282	—	—	.75
	1978FM(P)	6,058	—	Proof	1.50
	1979FM(M)	1,390	—	.20	.75
	1979FM(U)	2,608	—	—	.75
	1979FM(P)	4,049	—	Proof	1.50
	1980FM(M)	1,390	—	.20	.60
	1980FM(U)	3,668	—	—	.60
	1980FM(P)	2,688	—	Proof	2.00
	1981FM(U)	482 pcs.	—	—	2.00
	1981FM(P)	1,577	—	Proof	2.00
	1982FM(U)	—	—	—	.60
	1982FM(P)	—	—	Proof	2.00

KM#	Date	Mintage	VF	XF	Unc
73	1984FM(U)	—	—	—	.60
	1984FM(P)	—	—	Proof	2.00

World Food Day
Obv: JAMAICA more compact.

KM#	Date	Mintage	VF	XF	Unc
90	1981FM(M)	—	—	—	1.50

21st Anniversary of Independence

KM#	Date	Mintage	VF	XF	Unc
104	1983FM(U)	—	—	—	.60
	1983FM(P)	—	—	Proof	2.00

KM#	Date	Mintage	VF	XF	Unc
120	1981	—	—	—	.60
	1984	2.000	—	—	.60
	1985	2.988	—	—	.60
	1986	2.530	—	—	.60

25 CENTS

COPPER-NICKEL
Doctor Bird

KM#	Date	Mintage	VF	XF	Unc
49	1969	.758	—	.25	1.00
	1969	.030	—	Proof	1.50
	1970FM(M)	5,000	—	.25	1.00
	1970FM(P)	.012	—	Proof	1.50
	1973	.160	—	.25	1.00
	1975	3.110	—	.25	1.00
	1982	1.000	—	.25	1.00
	1984	2.002	—	.25	1.00
	1985	1.999	—	.25	1.00
	1985	—	—	Proof	1.50
	1986	2.635	—	.25	1.00
	1987	6.006	—	.25	1.00
	1987	—	—	Proof	1.50
	1988	3.034	—	.25	1.00
	1988	—	—	Proof	1.50
	1989	—	—	.25	1.00
	1989	—	—	Proof	1.50
	1990	—	—	Proof	1.50

KM#	Date	Mintage	VF	XF	Unc
56	1971FM(M)	4,834	—	.25	.75
	1971FM(P)	.014	—	Proof	1.25
	1972FM(M)	8,382	—	.25	.75
	1972FM(P)	.017	—	Proof	1.25
	1973FM(M)	.013	—	.25	.75
	1973FM(P)	.028	—	Proof	1.25

KM#	Date	Mintage	VF	XF	Unc
56	1974FM(M)	.012	—	.25	.75
	1974FM(P)	.022	—	Proof	1.25
	1975FM(M)	1,503	—	.25	.75
	1975FM(U)	4,683	—	—	.75
	1975FM(P)	.016	—	Proof	1.25
	1976FM(M)	1,112	—	.25	.75
	1976FM(U)	1,802	—	—	.75
	1976FM(P)	.024	—	Proof	1.25
	1977FM(M)	1,112	—	.25	1.25
	1977FM(U)	597 pcs.	—	—	3.00
	1977FM(P)	.010	—	Proof	1.25
	1978FM(M)	1,112	—	.25	1.25
	1978FM(U)	1,282	—	—	1.25
	1978FM(P)	6,058	—	Proof	2.00
	1979FM(M)	1,112	—	.25	1.25
	1979FM(U)	2,608	—	—	1.25
	1979FM(P)	4,049	—	Proof	2.00
	1980FM(M)	1,112	—	.25	1.00
	1980FM(U)	3,668	—	—	1.00
	1980FM(P)	2,688	—	Proof	3.00
	1981FM(U)	482 pcs.	—	—	3.00
	1981FM(P)	1,577	—	Proof	3.00
	1982FM(U)	—	—	—	1.00
	1982FM(P)	—	—	Proof	3.00
	1984FM(U)	—	—	—	1.00
	1984FM(P)	—	—	Proof	3.00

21st Anniversary of Independence

KM#	Date	Mintage	VF	XF	Unc
105	1983FM(U)	—	—	—	1.00
	1983FM(P)	—	—	Proof	3.00

25th Anniversary of Bank of Jamaica

KM#	Date	Mintage	VF	XF	Unc
154	1985	—	—	.75	3.50

NICKEL PLATED STEEL
Marcus Garvey

KM#	Date	Mintage	VF	XF	Unc
147	1991	—	—	—	1.00
	1991	—	—	Proof	3.00
	1992	—	—	—	1.00
	1992	—	—	Proof	3.00
	1993	—	—	Proof	3.00

50 CENTS

COPPER-NICKEL
Marcus Garvey

KM#	Date	Mintage	VF	XF	Unc
65	1975	12.010	.15	.50	1.50
	1984	2.000	.15	.50	1.50
	1985	2.119	.15	.50	1.50
	1985	—	—	Proof	3.00
	1986	3.404	.15	.50	1.50
	1987	5.545	.15	.50	1.50
	1988	10.505	.15	.50	1.50
	1988	—	—	Proof	3.00
	1989	—	.15	.50	1.50
	1989	—	—	Proof	3.00
	1990	—	—	Proof	3.00

KM#	Date	Mintage	VF	XF	Unc
70	1976FM(M)	1,112	—	.25	1.50
	1976FM(U)	1,802	—	—	1.50
	1976FM(P)	.024	—	Proof	1.50
	1977FM(M)	556 pcs.	—	.50	3.50
	1977FM(U)	597 pcs.	—	—	3.50
	1977FM(P)	.010	—	Proof	1.50
	1978FM(M)	556 pcs.	—	.50	3.50
	1978FM(U)	1,838	—	—	2.00
	1978FM(P)	6,058	—	Proof	2.50
	1979FM(M)	556 pcs.	—	.50	3.50
	1979FM(U)	1,282	—	—	2.50
	1979FM(P)	4,049	—	Proof	3.00
	1980FM(M)	556 pcs.	—	.50	3.50
	1980FM(U)	3,668	—	—	2.00
	1980FM(P)	2,688	—	Proof	3.00
	1981FM(U)	482 pcs.	—	—	3.50
	1981FM(P)	1,577	—	Proof	3.00
	1982FM(U)	—	—	—	2.00
	1982FM(P)	—	—	Proof	3.00
	1984FM(U)	—	—	—	2.00
	1984FM(P)	—	—	Proof	3.00

21st Anniversary of Independence

KM#	Date	Mintage	VF	XF	Unc
106	1983FM(U)	—	—	—	2.00
	1983FM(P)	—	—	Proof	4.00

100th Anniversary of Birth of Marcus Garvey
Obv: Similar to KM#70.
Rev: Similar to 10 Dollars, KM#128.

KM#	Date	Mintage	VF	XF	Unc
132	1987	500 pcs.	—	Proof	3.50

DOLLAR

COPPER-NICKEL
Sir Alexander Bustamante

KM#	Date	Mintage	VF	XF	Unc
50	1969	.047	—	1.00	2.00
	1969	.030	—	Proof	3.00
	1970FM(M)	5,000	—	.30	2.50
	1970FM(P)	.014	—	Proof	3.00

KM#	Date	Mintage	VF	XF	Unc
57	1971FM	5,024	—	.30	2.50
	1971FM(P)	.015	—	Proof	3.00
	1972F(M)	7,982	—	.30	2.00
	1972FM(P)	.017	—	Proof	3.00
	1973FM	.010	—	.30	2.00
	1973FM(P)	.028	—	Proof	3.00
	1974FM(M)	8,961	—	.30	2.00
	1974FM(P)	.022	—	Proof	3.00
	1975FM(M)	5,312	—	.30	2.50
	1975FM(U)	4,683	—	—	2.50
	1975FM(P)	.016	—	Proof	3.00
	1976FM(M)	284 pcs.	—	.50	17.50
	1976FM(U)	1,802	—	—	4.00
	1976FM(P)	.024	—	Proof	3.00
	1977FM(M)	287 pcs.	—	.50	17.50
	1977FM(U)	597 pcs.	—	—	8.00
	1977FM(P)	.010	—	Proof	3.00
	1978FM(U)	1,566	—	—	4.00
	1978FM(P)	6,058	—	Proof	4.00
	1979FM(M)	284 pcs.	—	.50	17.50
	1979FM(U)	2,608	—	—	4.00
	1979FM(P)	4,049	—	Proof	5.00

Reduced size, 34mm

KM#	Date	Mintage	VF	XF	Unc
84.1	1980FM(M)	284 pcs.	—	.50	15.00
	1980FM(U)	3,668	—	—	3.00
	1980FM(P)	2,688	—	Proof	10.00
	1981FM(U)	482 pcs.	—	—	8.00
	1981FM(P)	1,577	—	Proof	10.00
	1982FM(U)	—	—	—	4.00
	1982FM(P)	—	—	Proof	10.00

Reeded edge

KM#	Date	Mintage	VF	XF	Unc
84.2	1985	—	—	—	3.00
	1987	—	—	Proof	5.00
	1988	—	—	Proof	5.00
	1989	—	—	Proof	5.00

NICKEL-BRASS
Reeded edge w/inscription: Bank of Jamaica

KM#	Date	Mintage	VF	XF	Unc
84.2a	1990	—	—	Proof	5.00
	1991	—	—	Proof	5.00

NICKEL PLATED STEEL
Reeded edge w/o inscription

KM#	Date	Mintage	VF	XF	Unc
84.2b	1993	—	—	—	3.00

World Food Day

KM#	Date	Mintage	VF	XF	Unc
91	1981FM(U)	—	—	—	7.50

Soccer Games

KM#	Date	Mintage	VF	XF	Unc
96	1982	—	—	—	3.75

21st Anniversary of Independence

KM#	Date	Mintage	VF	XF	Unc
107	1983FM(U)	3,710	—	—	4.00
	1983FM(P)	609 pcs.	—	Proof	10.00

21st Anniversary of Independence

KM#	Date	Mintage	VF	XF	Unc
134	1983FM(P)	—	—	Proof	7.00

100th Anniversary of Birth of Bustamante

KM#	Date	Mintage	VF	XF	Unc
113	1984FM(U)	—	—	—	3.00
	1984FM(P)	268 pcs.	—	Proof	10.00

NICKEL-BRASS
Sir Alexander Bustamante

KM#	Date	Mintage	VF	XF	Unc
145	1990	—	—	—	2.25
	1991	—	—	—	2.25
	1992	—	—	Proof	10.00

BRASS PLATED STEEL

KM#	Date	Mintage	VF	XF	Unc
145a	1993	—	—	—	2.25
	1993	500 pcs.	—	Proof	10.00

5 DOLLARS

42.1500 g, .925 SILVER, 1.2536 oz ASW
Norman W.Manley
Obv: Similar to 1 Dollar, KM#50.

KM#	Date	Mintage	VF	XF	Unc
58	1971FM	4,072	—	—	12.50
	1971FM(P)	.013	—	Proof	10.00

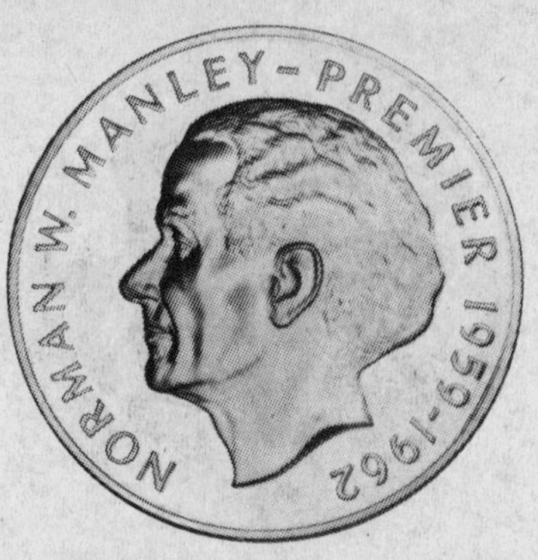

41.4800 g, .925 SILVER, 1.2336 oz ASW
Obv: Similar to 1 Dollar, KM#50.

KM#	Date	Mintage	VF	XF	Unc
59	1972FM	3,232	—	—	12.00
	1972FM(P)	.021	—	Proof	10.00
	1973FM	6,484	—	—	12.00
	1973FM(P)	.036	—	Proof	10.00

COPPER-NICKEL
Similar to KM#59, reduced size, 42mm.

KM#	Date	Mintage	VF	XF	Unc
62	1974FM(M)	8,661	—	—	4.00
	1975FM(M)	65 pcs.	—	—	—
	1975FM(U)	4,683	—	—	4.00
	1976FM(M)	56 pcs.	—	—	—
	1976FM(U)	1,802	—	—	6.00
	1977FM(M)	56 pcs.	—	—	—
	1977FM(U)	597 pcs.	—	—	10.00
	1978FM(U)	1,338	—	—	6.00
	1979FM(M)	56 pcs.	—	—	—
	1979FM(U)	2,608	—	—	6.00

37.6000 g, .500 SILVER, .6044 oz ASW

KM#	Date	Mintage	VF	XF	Unc
62a	1974FM(P)	.022	—	Proof	8.00
	1975FM(P)	.016	—	Proof	8.00
	1976FM(P)	.023	—	Proof	8.00
	1977FM(P)	.010	—	Proof	8.00
	1978FM(P)	6,058	—	Proof	12.00
	1979FM(P)	4,049	—	Proof	12.00

COPPER-NICKEL
Reduced size, 36mm

KM#	Date	Mintage	VF	XF	Unc
85.1	1980FM(M)	56 pcs.	—	—	—
	1980FM(U)	3,668	—	—	10.00
	1981FM(U)	482 pcs.	—	—	15.00
	1982FM(U)	—	—	—	6.00
	1984FM(U)	—	—	—	6.00

18.5600 g, .500 SILVER, .2983 oz ASW

KM#	Date	Mintage	VF	XF	Unc
85.1a	1980FM(P)	2,688	—	Proof	15.00
	1981FM(P)	1,577	—	Proof	15.00
	1982FM(P)	1,040	—	Proof	15.00
	1984FM(P)	268 pcs.	—	Proof	15.00
85.2	1985	—	—	—	15.00
	1987	—	—	Proof	15.00
	1988	—	—	Proof	15.00
	1989	—	—	Proof	15.00
	1990	500 pcs.	—	Proof	15.00
	1991	—	—	Proof	15.00
	1992	—	—	Proof	15.00
	1993	—	—	Proof	15.00

COPPER-NICKEL
21st Anniversary of Independence

KM#	Date	Mintage	VF	XF	Unc
108	1983FM(U)	—	—	—	6.00

18.5600 g, .500 SILVER, .2983 oz ASW

KM#	Date	Mintage	VF	XF	Unc
108a	1983FM(P)	—	—	Proof	15.00

NICKEL PLATED STEEL
Centennial of Birth of Norman Manley

KM#	Date	Mintage	VF	XF	Unc
157	1993	—	—	—	2.50

18.5000 g, .500 SILVER, .2984 oz ASW

KM#	Date	Mintage	VF	XF	Unc
157a	1993	*2,000	—	Proof	45.00

10 DOLLARS

49.2000 g, .925 SILVER, 1.4632 oz ASW
10th Anniversary of Independence

KM#	Date	Mintage	VF	XF	Unc
60	1972	.042	—	—	11.50
	1972	.033	—	Proof	12.50

COPPER-NICKEL
Sir Henry Morgan
Obv: Similar to 1 Dollar, KM#50.

KM#	Date	Mintage	VF	XF	Unc
63	1974FM(M)	.015	—	—	6.00

42.8000 g, .925 SILVER, 1.2728 oz ASW

KM#	Date	Mintage	VF	XF	Unc
63a	1974FM(P)	.042	—	Proof	12.00

COPPER-NICKEL
Christopher Columbus
Obv: Similar to 1 Dollar, KM#50.

KM#	Date	Mintage	VF	XF	Unc
66	1975FM(M)	30 pcs.	—	—	—
	1975FM(U)	5,758	—	—	9.00

42.8000 g, .925 SILVER, 1.2728 oz ASW

KM#	Date	Mintage	VF	XF	Unc
66a	1975FM(P)	.029	—	Proof	15.00

COPPER-NICKEL
Admiral Horatio Nelson
Obv: Similar to 1 Dollar, KM#50.

KM#	Date	Mintage	VF	XF	Unc
71	1976FM(M)	27 pcs.	—	—	—
	1976FM(U)	2,302	—	—	10.00

42.8000 g, .925 SILVER, 1.2728 oz ASW

KM#	Date	Mintage	VF	XF	Unc
71a	1976FM(P)	.031	—	Proof	18.00

COPPER-NICKEL
Admiral George Rodney
Obv: Similar to 1 Dollar, KM#50.

KM#	Date	Mintage	VF	XF	Unc
74	1977FM(M)	27 pcs.	—	—	—
	1977FM(U)	847 pcs.	—	—	22.50

42.8000 g, .925 SILVER, 1.2728 oz ASW

KM#	Date	Mintage	VF	XF	Unc
74a	1977FM(P)	.014	—	Proof	20.00

COPPER-NICKEL
Homerus Swallowtails
Obv: Similar to 1 Dollar, KM#50.

KM#	Date	Mintage	VF	XF	Unc
79	1979FM(M)	27 pcs.	—	—	—
	1979FM(U)	2,608	—	—	25.00

42.8000 g, .925 SILVER, 1.2728 oz ASW

KM#	Date	Mintage	VF	XF	Unc
79a	1979FM(P)	8,308	—	Proof	35.00

22.4500 g, .925 SILVER, .6677 oz ASW
International Year of the Child

KM#	Date	Mintage	VF	XF	Unc
80	1979	.020	—	Proof	12.50

30.2800 g, .500 SILVER, .4868 oz ASW.
10th Anniversary of Caribbean Development Bank

KM#	Date	Mintage	VF	XF	Unc
87	1980FM(P)	2,327	—	Proof	25.00

28.2800 g, .925 SILVER, .8410 oz ASW
Wedding of Prince Charles and Lady Diana

KM#	Date	Mintage	VF	XF	Unc
92	1981	.040	—	Proof	20.00

COPPER-NICKEL
American Crocodile

KM#	Date	Mintage	VF	XF	Unc
93	1981FM(U)	804 pcs.	—	—	35.00

22.4500 g, .925 SILVER, .6677 oz ASW

KM#	Date	Mintage	VF	XF	Unc
93a	1981FM(P)	3,216	—	Proof	37.50

COPPER-NICKEL
Jamaican Unity
Obv: Similar to 1 Dollar, KM#50.

KM#	Date	Mintage	VF	XF	Unc
75	1978FM(U)	1,559	—	—	12.50

42.8000 g, .925 SILVER, 1.2728 oz ASW

KM#	Date	Mintage	VF	XF	Unc
75a	1978FM(P)	.012	—	Proof	20.00

COPPER-NICKEL
Streamertail Hummingbirds

KM#	Date	Mintage	VF	XF	Unc
86	1980FM(M)	27 pcs.	—	—	—
	1980FM(U)	5,668	—	—	20.00

22.4500 g, .925 SILVER, .6677 oz ASW

KM#	Date	Mintage	VF	XF	Unc
86a	1980FM(P)	5,394	—	Proof	22.50

COPPER-NICKEL

Mongoose

KM#	Date	Mintage	VF	XF	Unc
97	1982FM(U)	—	—	—	20.00
	22.4500 g, .925 SILVER, .6677 oz ASW				
97a	1982FM(P)	1,852	—	Proof	35.00

Soccer Games

KM#	Date	Mintage	VF	XF	Unc
98	1982	9,775	—	Proof	27.50

COPPER-NICKEL
21st Anniversary of Independence

KM#	Date	Mintage	VF	XF	Unc
109	1983FM(U)	1,320	—	—	15.00
	22.4500 g, .925 SILVER, .6677 oz ASW				
109a	1983FM(P)	1,187	—	Proof	35.00

Royal Visit

KM#	Date	Mintage	VF	XF	Unc
111	1983	—	—	Proof	25.00

Summer Olympics - Sprinter

KM#	Date	Mintage	VF	XF	Unc
125	1984	—	—	Proof	37.50

COPPER-NICKEL
Blue Marlin
Obv: Similar to KM#86.

KM#	Date	Mintage	VF	XF	Unc
114	1984FM(U)	—	—	—	20.00
	22.4500 g, .925 SILVER, .6677 oz ASW				
114a	1984FM(P)	335 pcs.	—	Proof	50.00

Decade For Women

KM#	Date	Mintage	VF	XF	Unc
115	1984	1,100	—	Proof	30.00
	1985	610 pcs.	—	Proof	45.00

28.2800 g, .500 SILVER, .4546 oz ASW
XIII Commonwealth Games - Edinburgh

KM#	Date	Mintage	VF	XF	Unc
121	1986	.050	—	—	20.00
	28.2800 g, .925 SILVER, .8411 oz ASW				
121a	1986	.020	—	Proof	30.00

22.4500 g, .925 SILVER, .6677 oz ASW
Year of Youth

KM#	Date	Mintage	VF	XF	Unc
123	1985	1,000	—	Proof	37.50

25th Anniversary of Independence

KM#	Date	Mintage	VF	XF	Unc
133	1987	*500 pcs.	—	Proof	45.00

COPPER-NICKEL
Year of the Worker

KM#	Date	Mintage	VF	XF	Unc
138	1988	—	—	—	6.00
	22.4500 g, .925 SILVER, .6677 oz ASW				
138a	1988	*1,000	—	Proof	50.00

COPPER-NICKEL
Columbus Discovery of the New World

KM#	Date	Mintage	VF	XF	Unc
140	1989	—	—	—	6.00
	22.4500 g, .925 SILVER, .6677 oz ASW				
140a	1989	*5,500	—	Proof	50.00

COPPER-NICKEL
Arrival By Columbus In New World

KM#	Date	Mintage	VF	XF	Unc
144	1990	—	—	—	6.00
	22.4500 g, .925 SILVER, .6677 oz ASW				
144a	1990	*.011	—	Proof	50.00

100th Anniversary of Birth of Marcus Garvey.

KM#	Date	Mintage	VF	XF	Unc
128	1987	1,000	—	Proof	37.50

COPPER-NICKEL
Columbus Ship - Pinta

KM#	Date	Mintage	VF	XF	Unc
148	1991	—	—	—	6.00

22.4500 g, .925 SILVER, .6677 oz ASW

KM#	Date	Mintage	VF	XF	Unc
148a	1991	*5,500	—	Proof	50.00

500th Anniversary of Columbus Arrival

KM#	Date	Mintage	VF	XF	Unc
152	1992	5,500	—	Proof	50.00

40th Anniversary of Coronation of Queen Elizabeth II

KM#	Date	Mintage	VF	XF	Unc
155	1993	*5,500	—	Proof	50.00

20 DOLLARS

15.7484 g, .500 GOLD, .2531 oz AGW
10th Anniversary of Independence

KM#	Date	Mintage	VF	XF	Unc
61	1972	.030	—	—	120.00
	1972	.020	—	Proof	140.00

25 DOLLARS

136.0800 g, .925 SILVER, 4.0473 oz ASW
25th Anniversary of Coronation

KM#	Date	Mintage	VF	XF	Unc
76	1978	.011	—	—	47.50
	1978	.022	—	Proof	50.00

10th Anniversary of Investiture of Prince Charles

KM#	Date	Mintage	VF	XF	Unc
81	1979	.016	—	—	47.50
	1979	.025	—	Proof	50.00

136.0800 g, .500 SILVER, 2.1878 oz ASW
1980 Olympics

KM#	Date	Mintage	VF	XF	Unc
88	1980	—	—	—	75.00
	1980	6,969	—	Proof	90.00

136.0800 g, .925 SILVER, 4.0473 oz ASW
Wedding of Prince Charles and Lady Diana
Obv: Similar to 10 Dollars, KM#92.

KM#	Date	Mintage	VF	XF	Unc
94	1981	6,450	—	Proof	65.00

Soccer Games
Obv: Similar to 10 Dollars, KM#98.

KM#	Date	Mintage	VF	XF	Unc
99	1982	.030	—	Proof	70.00

Royal Visit

KM#	Date	Mintage	VF	XF	Unc
112	1983	—	—	Proof	70.00

Summer Olympics -Sprinter
Illustration reduced. Actual size: 63mm.

KM#	Date	Mintage	VF	XF	Unc
116	1984	3,300	—	Proof	95.00

23.4400 g, .925 SILVER, .6677 oz ASW
Decade For Women
Mule. Denomination error for 10 Dollars, KM#115.

KM#	Date	Mintage	VF	XF	Unc
126	1984	—	—	Proof	200.00

136.0800 g, .925 SILVER, 4.0473 oz ASW
Humpback Whale Protection
Obv: Similar to KM#112.

KM#	Date	Mintage	VF	XF	Unc
119	1985	2,600	—	Proof	100.00

World Championship Soccer - Mexico

KM#	Date	Mintage	VF	XF	Unc
127	1986	—	—	—	30.00

37.7800 g, .925 SILVER, 1.1236 oz ASW
25th Anniversary of Independence

KM#	Date	Mintage	VF	XF	Unc
130	1987	1,900	—	Proof	100.00

23.3300 g, .925 SILVER, .6939 oz ASW
Olympics - Relay Runners

KM#	Date	Mintage	VF	XF	Unc
141	1988	*.015	—	Proof	40.00

World Championship Soccer

KM#	Date	Mintage	VF	XF	Unc
142	1990	—	—	Proof	40.00

Columbus' Jamaican Landfall of 1494

KM#	Date	Mintage	VF	XF	Unc
150	1991	650 pcs.	—	—	155.00
	1991	*.025	—	Proof	60.00

Discovery of America - Landfall

KM#	Date	Mintage	VF	XF	Unc
151	1992	550 pcs.	—	—	155.00
	1992	*.025	—	Proof	60.00

100 DOLLARS

7.8300 g, .900 GOLD, .2265 oz AGW
Christopher Columbus

KM#	Date	Mintage	VF	XF	Unc
67	1975FM(M)	100 pcs.	—	—	175.00
	1975FM(U)	.010	—	—	110.00
	1975FM(P)	.021	—	Proof	140.00

Admiral Horatio Nelson

KM#	Date	Mintage	VF	XF	Unc
72	1976FM(M)	100 pcs.	—	—	180.00
	1976FM(P)	8,952	—	Proof	140.00

11.3400 g, .900 GOLD, .3281 oz AGW
25th Anniversary of Coronation

KM#	Date	Mintage	VF	XF	Unc
77	1978	—	—	—	150.00
	1978	5,835	—	Proof	165.00

10th Anniversary of Investiture of Prince Charles

KM#	Date	Mintage	VF	XF	Unc
82	1979	2,891	—	Proof	160.00

7.1300 g, .900 GOLD, .2063 oz AGW
21st Anniversary of Independence

KM#	Date	Mintage	VF	XF	Unc
110	1983FM(P)	638 pcs.	—	Proof	200.00

100th Anniversary of Birth of Bustamante

KM#	Date	Mintage	VF	XF	Unc
117	1984FM(P)	531 pcs.	—	Proof	150.00

136.0800 g, .925 SILVER, 4.0473 oz ASW
World Championship Soccer - Mexico
Illustration reduced. Actual size: 63mm.
Obv: Similar to KM#149.

KM#	Date	Mintage	VF	XF	Unc
122	1986	.020	—	Proof	110.00

11.3400 g, .900 GOLD, .3281 oz AGW
100th Anniversary of Birth of Marcus Garvey
Obv: Similar to KM#117.
Rev: Similar to 10 Dollars, KM#128.

KM#	Date	Mintage	VF	XF	Unc
129	1987	500 pcs.	—	Proof	300.00

136.0800 g, .925 SILVER, 4.0473 oz ASW
Streamertail Hummingbird
Illustration reduced. Actual size: 63mm.
Obv: Similar to 250 Dollars KM#124.

KM#	Date	Mintage	VF	XF	Unc
139	1987	—	—	Proof	125.00

Summer Olympics - Relay Race
Illustration reduced. Actual size: 63mm.
Obv: Similar to 10 Dollars, KM#111.

KM#	Date	Mintage	VF	XF	Unc
135	1988	.015	—	Proof	150.00

World Championship Soccer
Illustration reduced. Actual size: 63mm.
Obv: Similar to 25 Dollars, KM#142.

KM#	Date	Mintage	VF	XF	Unc
143	1990	—	—	Proof	150.00

137.8000 g, .925 SILVER, 4.0981 oz ASW
Olympics - Boxing
Illustration reduced. Actual size: 63mm.

KM#	Date	Mintage	VF	XF	Unc
149	1992	—	—	Proof	160.00

11.3400 g, .900 GOLD, .3281 oz ASW
Centennial of Birth of Norman Manley

KM#	Date	Mintage	VF	XF	Unc
158	1993	500 pcs.	—	Proof	475.00

250 DOLLARS

43.2200 g, .900 GOLD, 1.2507 oz AGW
25th Anniversary of Coronation

KM#	Date	Mintage	VF	XF	Unc
78	1978	3,005	—	Proof	550.00

10th Anniversary of Investiture of Prince Charles

KM#	Date	Mintage	VF	XF	Unc
83	1979	1,650	—	Proof	600.00

11.3400 g, .900 GOLD, .3281 oz AGW
1980 Olympics

KM#	Date	Mintage	VF	XF	Unc
89	1980	902 pcs.	—	Proof	320.00

Wedding of Prince Charles and Lady Diana
Obv: Similar to 10 Dollars, Y#60.

KM#	Date	Mintage	VF	XF	Unc
95	1981	1,491	—	Proof	250.00

Soccer Games

KM#	Date	Mintage	VF	XF	Unc
100	1982	694 pcs.	—	Proof	325.00

Decade For Women

KM#	Date	Mintage	VF	XF	Unc
118	1984	559 pcs.	—	Proof	300.00

11.3200 g, .900 GOLD, .3275 oz AGW
Royal Visit

KM#	Date	Mintage	VF	XF	Unc
124	1983	5,000	—	Proof	225.00

16.0000 g, .900 GOLD, .4630 oz AGW
25th Anniversary of Independence

KM#	Date	Mintage	VF	XF	Unc
131	1987	250 pcs.	—	Proof	400.00

500 DOLLARS

11.3400 g, .900 GOLD, .3281 oz AGW
Columbus Quincentennial - 500 on Ship Sail

KM#	Date	Mintage	VF	XF	Unc
153	1992	500 pcs.	—	Proof	480.00

.40th Anniversary of Coronation of Queen Elizabeth
Similar to 10 Dollars, KM#155.
Obv: Crowned portrait of the Queen. Rev: Arms.

KM#	Date	Mintage	VF	XF	Unc
155	1993	*500 pcs.	—	Proof	480.00

MINT SETS (MS)

KM#	Date	Mintage	Identification	Issue Price	Mkt. Val.
MS1	1969(2)	30,000	KM41-42	.90	2.00
MS2	1969(6)	30,000	KM45-50	—	6.50
MS3	1970(6)	5,000	KM45-50	16.00	6.50
MS4	1971(7)	4,072	KM51,53-58	19.50	20.00
MS5	1971(6)	4,834	KM51,53-57	—	8.00
MS6	1972(7)	2,982	KM51,53-57,59	19.75	20.00
MS7	1972(6)	4,000	KM51,53-57	10.00	8.00
MS8	1973(7)	6,404	KM51,53-57,59	19.75	20.00
MS9	1973(6)	3,000	KM51,53-57	9.95	8.00
MS10	1974(8)	8,361	KM51,53-57,59,63	25.00	18.00
MS11	1975(8)	4,683	KM51,53-57,62,66	27.50	20.00
MS12	1976(9)	1,802	KM53-57,62,68,70,71	27.50	25.00
MS13	1977(9)	597	KM53-54,56-57,62,68, 70,73,74	27.50	40.00
MS14	1978(9)	1,282	KM53-54,56-57,62,68, 70,73,75	27.50	35.00
MS15	1979(9)	2,608	KM53-54,56-57,62,68, 70,73,79	27.50	30.00
MS16	1980(9)	3,668	KM53-54,56,68,70,73, 84-86	30.00	25.00
MS17	1981(9)	482	KM53-54,56,68,70,73, 84-85,93	31.00	45.00
MS18	1982(9)	—	KM53-54,56,68,70,73, 84-85,97	31.00	35.00
MS19	1983(9)	1,210	KM101-109	37.00	35.00
MS20	1984(9)	—	KM53-54,56,68,70,73, 85,113-114	37.00	30.00

PROOF SETS (PS)

KM#	Date	Mintage	Identification	Issue Price	Mkt. Val.
PS1	1918C(3)	—	KM24-26	—	600.00
PS2	1928(3)	20	KM24-26	—	600.00
PS3	1937(3)	—	KM27-29	—	550.00
PS4	1969(6)	8,530	KM45-50	15.00	8.00
PS5	1969(2)	5,000	KM41-42	2.70	5.00
PS6	1970(6)	11,540	KM45-50	15.00	7.00
PS7	1971(7)	12,739	KM51,53-58	26.50	15.00
PS8	1971(6)	1,048	KM51,53-57	15.00	8.00
PS9	1972(7)	16,967	KM51,53-57,59	27.50	15.00
PS10	1973(7)	28,405	KM51,53-57,59	27.50	15.00
PS11	1974(8)	22,026	KM51,53-57,62a-63a	50.00	25.00
PS12	1975(8)	15,638	KM51,53-57,62a,66a	55.00	28.00
PS13	1976(9)	22,900	KM53-57,62a,68,70, 71a	55.00	30.00
PS14	1976(7)	1,503	KM53-57,68,70	22.50	12.50
PS15	1977(9)	10,054	KM53-54,56-57,62a, 68,70,73,74a	55.00	35.00
PS16	1978(9)	6,058	KM53-54,56-57,62a, 68,70,73,75a	59.00	40.00
PS17	1979(9)	4,049	KM53-54,56-57,62a, 68,70,73,79a	59.00	45.00
PS18	1980(9)	2,688	KM53-54,56,68,70, 73,84,85a,86a	90.00	50.00
PS19	1981(9)	1,577	KM53-54,56,68,70, 73,84,85a,93a	92.00	60.00
PS20	1982(9)	—	KM53-54,56,68,70, 73,84,85a,97a	92.00	70.00
PS21	1983(9)	1,210	KM101-107,108a-109a	—	72.50
PS22	1984(9)	—	KM53-54,56,68,70,73, 85a,113,114a	92.00	70.00
PS23	1985(9)	—	KM46-47,49,64-65,84, 85b,120,123	—	80.00
PS24	1987(9)	500	KM46-49,64,84a,85b, 132,133	90.00	80.00
PS25	1988(9)	500	KM46-49,64-65,84a, 85b,138a	115.00	80.00
PS26	1989(9)	*5,000	KM46-49,64-65,84a, 85b,140a	120.00	75.00
PS27	1990(9)	*500	KM46a-47a,48-49,64-65, 84a,85b,144	125.00	125.00
PS28	1991(7)	*500	KM46a,64,84a,85b, 146-148	—	75.00
PS29	1992(7)	*500	KM46a,64,85b,145 147,152	138.95	140.00
PS30	1993(7)	*500	KM46a,64,85b,145a, 146-147.155	—	140.00

JAPAN

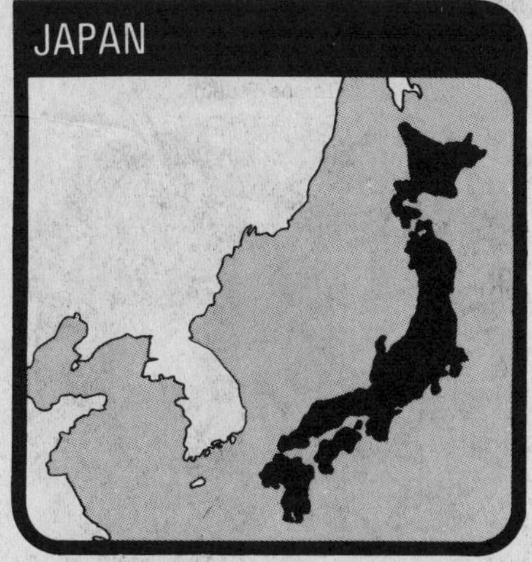

Japan, a constitutional monarchy situated off the east coast of Asia, has an area of 145,809 sq. mi. (377,835 sq. km.) and a population of 123.2 million. Capital: Tokyo. Japan, one of the major industrial nations of the world, exports machinery, motor vehicles, electronics and chemicals.

Japan, founded (so legend holds) in 660 B.C. by a direct descendant of the Sun Goddess, was first brought into contact with the west by a storm-blown Portuguese ship in 1542. European traders and missionaries proceeded to enlarge the contact until the Shogunate, sensing a military threat in the foreign presence, expelled all foreigners and restricted relations with the outside world in the 17th century. After Commodore Perry's U.S. flotilla visited in 1854, Japan rapidly industrialized, abolished the Shogunate and established a parliamentary form of government, and by the end of the 19th century achieved the status of a modern economic and military power. A series of wars with China and Russia, and participation with the Allies in World War I, enlarged Japan territorially but brought its interests into conflict with the Far Eastern interests of the United States, Britain and the Netherlands, causing it to align with the Axis Powers for the pursuit of World War II. After its defeat in World War II, Japan renounced military aggression as a political instrument, established democratic self-government, and quickly reasserted its position as an economic world power.

Japanese coinage of concern to this catalog includes those issued for the Ryukyu Islands (also called Liuchu), a chain of islands extending southwest from Japan toward Taiwan (Formosa), before the Japanese government converted the islands into a prefecture under the name Okinawa. Many of the provinces of Japan issued their own definitive coinage under the Shogunate.

RULERS

Shoguns

Iyenari, 1787-1837
Iyeoshi, 1837-1853
Iyesada, 1853-1858
Iyemochi, 1858-1866
Yoshinobu, 1866-1867

Emperors

Komei, 1847-1866
Mutsuhito (Meiji), 1867-1912

Years 1-45 明治 or 治明

Yoshihito (Taisho), 1912-1926

Years 1-15 大正 or 正大

Hirohito (Showa), 1926-1989

Years 1-64 昭和 or 和昭

Akihito (Heisei), 1989

Years 1 - 平成

NOTE: The personal name of the emperor is followed by the name that he chose for his regnal era.

MONETARY SYSTEM

Until 1870

Prior to the Meiji currency reform, there was no fixed exchange rate between the various silver, gold and copper "cash" coins (which previously included Chinese "cash") in circulation. Each coin exchanged on the basis of its own merits and the prevailing market conditions. The size and weight of the copper coins and the weight and fineness of the silver and gold coins varied widely. From time to time the government would declare an official exchange rate, but this was usually ignored. For gold and silver, nominal equivalents were:

16 Shu = 4 Bu = 1 Ryo

Commencing 1870

10 Rin = 1 Sen
100 Sen = 1 Yen

MONETARY UNITS

Momme 匁 Ryo 両

Bu 分 Shu 朱 Rin 厘

Sen 銭 Yen 円 or 圓 or 圓

MINT MARKS ON MON

A - 文 - Edo (Tokyo)
B - 佐佐佐 Sado
C - 十 - Jiuman Tsubo
D - 小 - Koume Mura
E - 一 - Ichi-no-se
F - 川 - Onagi-gawa
G - 元 - Osaka
H - 長 - Nagasaki
I - 足 - Ashio
J - 仙 - Sendai
K - 千 - Sendai
L - 久 - Kuji (Hitachi Ohta)
M - ト,ド - Mito
N - ノ - Aizu
O - イ - Ise
P - 盛 - Morioka
Q - 了 - Hiroshima
R - 山 Yamanouchi

NOTE: Dates shown in parentheses are the first year of minting. Most pieces were minted for several years afterwards, but the exact years minting took place are not known.

DATING

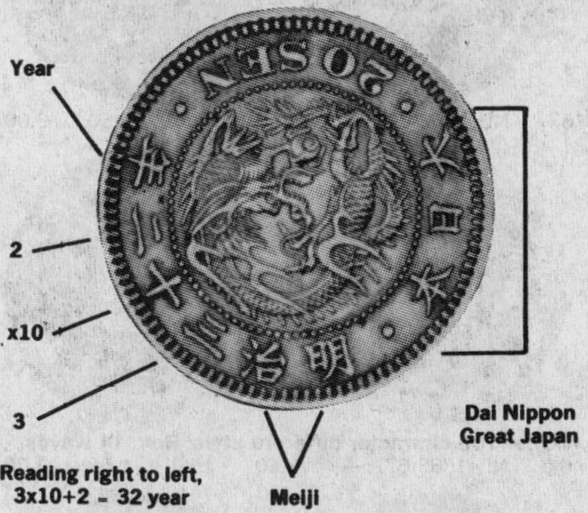

NOTE: In Showa yr. 23 (1948) inscriptions were reversed to read from left to right.

LEGENDS

Reading top-bottom, right-left.

Kanei Tsuho

Bunkyu-Eiho

EARLY COINAGE

Kanei Tsuho

MON

COPPER

C#	Date	Mint	VG	Fine	VF	XF
1.14	ND(1844) bosen					
		M	—	—	—	500.00

NOTE: C#1.5, 1.7 and 1.14 are known only as *bosen* seed or mother coins.

IRON
Rev: Plain.

C#	Date	Mint	VG	Fine	VF	XF
1.1a	ND(1739-1867)					
		—	2.00	5.00	7.50	15.00

Rev: Various mint marks.

C#	Date	Mint	VG	Fine	VF	XF
1.3a	ND(1862)	B	6.50	12.50	17.50	25.00
1.12	(1739;1838)					
		K	3.00	5.00	8.00	15.00

NOTE: Most copper 1 Mon pieces predate the coverage of this book. Those with mint marks B and K are *bosen* seed or mother coins.

4 MON

COPPER and BRASS
Rev: 11 waves.

C#	Date	Mint	VG	Fine	VF	XF
4.2	ND(1769-1860)					
		—	.30	.50	1.00	3.00

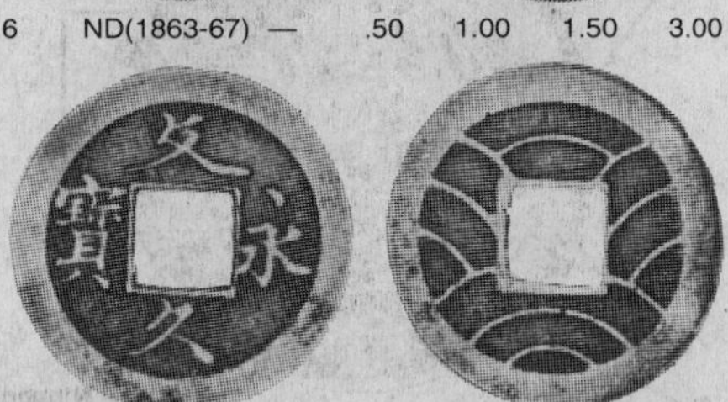

C#	Date	Mint	VG	Fine	VF	XF
6	ND(1863-67)	—	.50	1.00	1.50	3.00

Obv: Top character different style. Rev: 11 waves.

C#	Date	Mint	VG	Fine	VF	XF
6.a	ND(1863-67)	—	.50	1.00	1.50	3.00

Obv: As above but character at left abbreviated. Rev: 11 waves.

C#	Date	Mint	VG	Fine	VF	XF
6.b	ND(1863-67)	—	1.00	1.50	3.00	5.00

IRON
Rev: 11 waves; w/o mint mark.

C#	Date	Mint	VG	Fine	VF	XF
4.2a	ND(1866)	—	4.00	6.00	10.00	20.00

Rev: 11 waves and various mint marks.

C#	Date	Mint	VG	Fine	VF	XF
4.12	ND(1866)	K	3.00	6.00	12.00	20.00
4.14	(1866)	M	12.00	17.50	25.00	35.00
4.15	(1866)	N	5.00	10.00	17.50	25.00
4.16	(1866)	O	5.00	10.00	17.50	25.00
4.17	(1866)	P	5.00	10.00	17.50	25.00
4.18	(1866)	Q	250.00	300.00	400.00	500.00
4.19	(1866)	R	—	—	Rare	—

NOTE: Copper 4 Mon pieces similar to those listed only under iron issues are *bosen* seed or mother coins.

100 MON

(Tempo Tsuho)

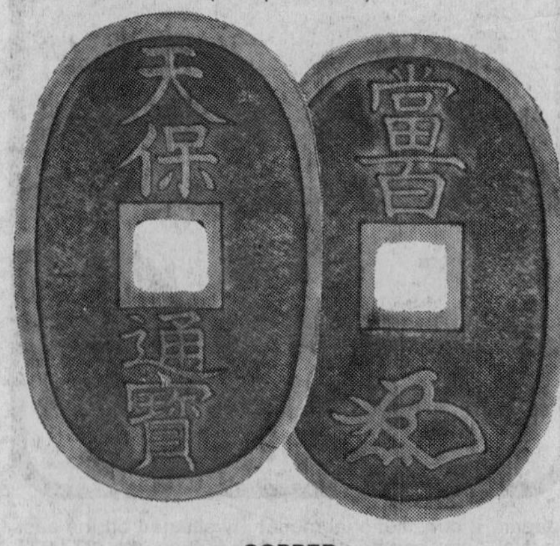

COPPER

C#	Date	Mint	VG	Fine	VF	XF
7	ND(1835-70)	—	2.50	5.00	7.00	10.00

MAMEITAGIN 'BEAN' SILVER

God of Plenty 'bean' Silver

KEY TO DATING MODERN MAMEITA GIN

'BUN'
GENBUN PERIOD
1736-1741
(Used 1736-1818)

'BUN'
BUNSEI PERIOD
1818-1830
(Used 1820-1837)

'HO'
TEMPO PERIOD
1830-1844
(Used 1837-1858)

'SEI'
ANSEI PERIOD
1854-1860
(Used 1859-1865)

One of the above characters is usually found on the obverse of C#8 or both sides of C#8a and C#8b. The same characters are found at both ends of chogin pieces C#9. Era designators were used continuously until the next one was introduced, regardless of intervening eras.

NOTE: Values are for pieces weighing 5-8 grams. Pieces over 10 grams may command up to twice the values shown; pieces under 5 grams somewhat less.

.460 SILVER
Obv: One or more large characters, w/o "God of Plenty". Era designator between characters.
Rev: Blank or w/chop marks.
Genbun

C#	Date	Mint	VG	Fine	VF	XF
8.1a	ND(1736-1818)					
		—	10.00	15.00	25.00	35.00

Obv: "God of Plenty" w/other large characters. Era designator between characters and on god's belly.

C#	Date	Mint	VG	Fine	VF	XF
8.1b	ND(1736-1818)					
		—	20.00	30.00	45.00	60.00

.360 SILVER
Obv: One or more large characters, w/o "God of Plenty". Era designator between characters.
Bunsei

C#	Date	Mint	VG	Fine	VF	XF
8.2a	ND(1820-37)	—	10.00	20.00	30.00	40.00

Obv: "God of Plenty" w/other large characters. Era designator between characters and on god's belly.

C#	Date	Mint	VG	Fine	VF	XF
8.2b	ND(1820-37)	—	20.00	40.00	60.00	80.00

.261 SILVER
Obv: One or more large characters, w/o "God of Plenty". Era designator between characters.
Tempo

C#	Date	Mint	VG	Fine	VF	XF
8.3a	ND(1837-58)	—	10.00	15.00	22.50	30.00

Obv: "God of Plenty" w/other large characters. Era designator between characters and on god's belly.

C#	Date	Mint	VG	Fine	VF	XF
8.3b	ND(1837-58)	—	12.50	25.00	40.[illegible]	55.00

.135 SILVER
Obv: One or more large characters, w/o "God of Plenty". Era designator between characters.
Ansei

C#	Date	Mint	VG	Fine	VF	XF
8.4a	ND(1859-65)	—	6.00	10.00	17.50	25.00

Obv: "God of Plenty" w/other large characters. Era designator between characters and on god's belly.

C#	Date	Mint	VG	Fine	VF	XF
8.4b	ND(1859-65)	—	100.00	150.00	225.00	300.00

.460 SILVER
Obv. and rev: "God of Plenty" design, era designator on belly.
Genbun

C#	Date	Mint	VG	Fine	VF	XF
8a.1	ND(1736-1818)					
		—	80.00	140.00	215.00	350.00

Obv: "God of Plenty" design.
Rev: Single *ho* or multiple era designator.
Genbun

C#	Date	Mint	VG	Fine	VF	XF
8b.1	ND(1736-1818)					
		—	800.00	1000.	1300.	1750.

.360 SILVER
Obv. and rev: "God of Plenty" design, era designator on belly.
Bunsei

C#	Date	Mint	VG	Fine	VF	XF
8a.2	ND(1820-37)	—	90.00	150.00	225.00	375.00

Obv: "God of Plenty" design.
Rev: Single *ho* or multiple era designator.
Bunsei

C#	Date	Mint	VG	Fine	VF	XF
8b.2	ND(1820-37)	—	1000.	1250.	1600.	2000.

.261 SILVER
Obv. and rev: "God of Plenty" design, era designator on belly.
Tempo

C#	Date	Mint	VG	Fine	VF	XF
8a.3a	ND(1837-58)	—	75.00	125.00	200.00	300.00

Obv: "God of Plenty", era designator on belly.
Rev: Character *ho* (treasure) on belly of "God of Plenty".

C#	Date	Mint	VG	Fine	VF	XF
8a.3b	ND(1837-58)	—	200.00	300.00	400.00	550.00

Obv: "God of Plenty" design.
Rev: Single or multiple era designator.
Tempo

C#	Date	Mint	VG	Fine	VF	XF
8b.3a	ND(1837-58)	—	1000.	1500.	2000.	2500.

Obv: "God of Plenty". Rev: Large single character *ho* (treasure).

C#	Date	Mint	VG	Fine	VF	XF
8b.3b.	ND(1837-58)	—	1000.	1500.	2000.	2500.

.135 SILVER
Obv. and rev: "God of Plenty" design.
Ansei

C#	Date	Mint	VG	Fine	VF	XF
8a.4	ND(1859-65)	—	70.00	110.00	175.00	250.00

Obv: "God of Plenty" design.
Rev: Single or multiple era designator.
Ansei

C#	Date	Mint	VG	Fine	VF	XF
8b.4a	ND(1859-65)	—	1250.	1750.	2250.	2750.

Obv: "God of Plenty". Rev: Large single character "*Ho*" (treasure).

C#	Date	Mint	VG	Fine	VF	XF
86.4b	ND(1859-65)	—	1000.	1500.	2000.	2500.

CHO GIN

All illustrations in this section are reduced 50%.

KEY TO DATING MODERN CHO GIN (SILVER)

GENBUN, 1736-1741　BUNSEI, 1818-1830

TEMPO, 1830-1844　ANSEI, 1854-1860

(Long Silver)

.460 SILVER
Obv: Era marks at each end. Miscellaneous marks elsewhere. Rev: Blank except for occasional chop marks.
Genbun

C#	Date	Mint	VG	Fine	VF	XF
9	ND(1736-1818)	—	125.00	225.00	375.00	600.00

.360 SILVER
Bunsei

C#	Date	Mint	VG	Fine	VF	XF
9a	ND(1820-37)	—	125.00	225.00	375.00	600.00

Illustrations Full Size

.261 SILVER
Tempo

C#	Date	Mint	VG	Fine	VF	XF
9b	ND(1837-58)	—	100.00	200.00	325.00	500.00

.135 SILVER
Ansei

C#	Date	Mint	VG	Fine	VF	XF
9c	ND(1859-65)	—	90.00	150.00	250.00	400.00

SHU

(Is Shu Gin)

.989 SILVER, 2.63 g
Bunsei

C#	Date	Mintage	VG	Fine	VF	XF
11	ND(1829-37)	139.915	45.00	70.00	90.00	125.00

KEY TO DATING LATER 1 SHU

常　KAEI PERIOD 1848-1854 (Used 1853-1865)

常　MEIJI PERIOD 1868-1912 (Used 1868-1869)

.968 SILVER, 1.89 g
Kaie

C#	Date	Mintage	VG	Fine	VF	XF
12	ND(1853-65)	159.245	4.50	6.00	12.00	17.50

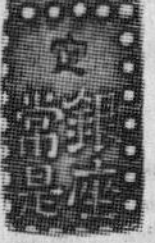

.880 SILVER, 1.88 g

Meiji
Rev: 3 top strokes are straight w/o curves or hooks.

C#	Date	Mintage	VG	Fine	VF	XF
12a	ND(1868-69)	18.742	10.00	15.00	22.50	30.00

NOTE: C#12 type 1 Shu are dated according to how the character illustrated is written on the reverse. Meiji 1 Shu are also known as Kaheishi 1 Shu.

2 SHU

(Nishu Gin)

.978 SILVER, 10.19 g
Meiwa-Ko-Nanryo

C#	Date	Mintage	VG	Fine	VF	XF
13	ND(1772-1824)	47.464	75.00	100.00	150.00	200.00

NOTE: Pieces struck on large planchets with full edge beads on obverse and reverse command a 50% premium.

.978 SILVER, 7.53 g
Bunsei-Shin-Nanryo

C#	Date	Mintage	VG	Fine	VF	XF
13a	ND(1824-30)	60.624	45.00	70.00	90.00	125.00

.845 SILVER, 13.62 g
Ansei

C#	Date	Mintage	VG	Fine	VF	XF
15	ND(1859)	.706	800.00	1250.	1800.	2500.

KEY TO DATING 1 BU

常是　TEMPO PERIOD 1830-1844 (Used 1837-1854)

ANSEI PERIOD 1854-1860 (Used 1859-1868)

MEIJI PERIOD 1868-1912 (Used 1868-1869)

NOTE: 1 Bu are dated according to how the two characters above are written on the reverse of the piece. There are other variations as well. Meiji Bu also are known as Kaheishi Bu.

BU

(Ichibu)

.991 SILVER, 8.66 g
Varieties of countermark
Tempo

C#	Date	Mintage	VG	Fine	VF	XF
16	ND(1837-54)	78.917	8.00	15.00	22.50	30.00

.873 SILVER, 8.63 g
Ansei

C#	Date	Mintage	VG	Fine	VF	XF
16a	ND(1859-68)	11.399	5.00	10.00	15.00	22.50

.807 SILVER, 8.66 g
Meiji

C#	Date	Mintage	VG	Fine	VF	XF
16b	ND(1868-69)	4.267	225.00	350.00	475.00	600.00

3 BU

(Sanbu)

(1859)

.903 SILVER
"Ansei Trade Dollar"
c/m: 4 characters on Mexico (Culiacan)
8 Reales, KM#377.3.

KM#	Date	Mintage	VG	Fine	VF	XF
101.1	ND(1846-58)	—	3000.	5000.	6500.	8000.

c/m: 4 characters on Mexico (Guanajuato)
8 Reales, KM#377.8.

KM#	Date	Mintage	VG	Fine	VF	XF
101.2	ND(1825-58)	—	3000.	5000.	6500.	8000.

c/m: 4 characters on Mexico City
8 Reales, KM#377.10.

KM#	Date	Mintage	VG	Fine	VF	XF
101.3	ND(1824-58)	—	3000.	5000.	6500.	8000.

c/m: 4 characters on Mexico (Zacatecas)
8 Reales, KM#377.13.

KM#	Date	Mintage	VG	Fine	VF	XF
101.4	ND(1825-58)	—	3000.	5000.	6500.	8000.

SHU

(Isshu)

.123 GOLD/.877 SILVER, 1.39 g
Bunsei

C#	Date	Mintage	VG	Fine	VF	XF
17	ND(1824-32)	46.723	200.00	300.00	400.00	550.00

2 SHU

(Nishu)

.298 GOLD/.702 SILVER, 1.62 g
Tempo

C#	Date	Mintage	VG	Fine	VF	XF
18	ND(1832-58)	103.070	15.00	22.50	30.00	37.50

.229 GOLD/.771 SILVER, 0.75 g
Manen

C#	Date	Mintage	VG	Fine	VF	XF
18a	ND(1860-69)	25.120	20.00	30.00	40.00	55.00

KEY TO DATING 1 AND 2 BU

GENBUN PERIOD 1 BU

文 1736-1741
(Used 1736-1818)

BUNSEI PERIOD 2 BU

文 1818-1830
TYPE A DATE MARK
(Used 1818-1828)

BUNSEI PERIOD 1 BU and 2 BU

文 1818-1830
TYPE B DATE MARK
(Used 1819-1829 on 1 Bu)
(Used 1828-1832 on 2 Bu)

TEMPO PERIOD

保 1830-1844
(Used 1837-1858)

ANSEI PERIOD

正 1854-1859
(Used 1859)

MANEN PERIOD
1859-1860
(Without era designator)

C#21b is dated according to its weight. C#21c and C#21d can be distinguished by the character to the left on the reverse.

KEY TO DATING C#21c and C#21d

MANEN PERIOD
1860-1861
(Used 1860)

MEIJI PERIOD
1868-1912
(Used 1868-1869)

BU

(Ichi Bu)

.653 GOLD/.347 SILVER, 3.25 g
Genbun
Rev: Written as flourish.
Dating mark in upper right corner.

C#	Date	Mintage	VG	Fine	VF	XF
19	ND(1736-1818)	—	75.00	100.00	150.00	225.00

.560 GOLD/.440 SILVER, 3.27 g
Bunsei
Rev: Type B mark.

C#	Date	Mintage	VG	Fine	VF	XF
20	ND(1819-29)	—	100.00	150.00	200.00	275.00

.568 GOLD/.432 SILVER, 2.80 g
Tempo

C#	Date	Mintage	VG	Fine	VF	XF
20a	ND(1837-58)	—	125.00	200.00	275.00	325.00

.570 GOLD/.430 SILVER, 2.24 g
Ansei

C#	Date	Mintage	VG	Fine	VF	XF
20b	ND(1859)	—	1500.	2500.	3500.	4750.

.574 GOLD/.426 SILVER, 0.82 g
Manen
Rev: W/o dating mark.

C#	Date	Mintage	VG	Fine	VF	XF
20c	ND(1860-67)	—	500.00	1000.	1500.	2000.

NOTE: Similar pieces without dating mark but weighing about 4 grams were made during the Kyoho era, 1716-34.

2 BU

(Ni Bu)

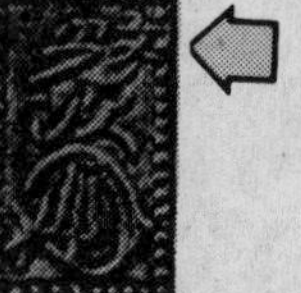

.563 GOLD/.437 SILVER, 6.52 g
Bunsei
Rev: Type A mark.

C#	Date	Mintage	VG	Fine	VF	XF
21	ND(1818-28)	5.972	300.00	450.00	650.00	850.00

.490 GOLD/.510 SILVER, 6.56 g
Bunsei
Rev: Type B mark.

C#	Date	Mintage	VG	Fine	VF	XF
21a	ND(1828-32)	4.066	250.00	400.00	550.00	700.00

.209 GOLD/.791 SILVER, 5.62 g
Ansei
Rev: W/o mark.

C#	Date	Mintage	VG	Fine	VF	XF
21b	ND(1856-60)	7.103	75.00	150.00	200.00	250.00

A.

B.

.229 GOLD/.771 SILVER, 3.00 g
Manen
Obv: Paulownia leaf type A. Rev: W/o mark.

C#	Date	Mintage	VG	Fine	VF	XF
21c.1	ND(1860-)	100.201	300.00	450.00	600.00	800.00

Manen
Obv: Paulownia leaf type B.

C#	Date	Mintage	VG	Fine	VF	XF
21c.2	ND(1860-)	I.A.	250.00	350.00	500.00	650.00

.223 GOLD/.777 SILVER, 3.00 g
Meiji

C#	Date	Mintage	VG	Fine	VF	XF
21d	ND(1868-69)	—	30.00	40.00	50.00	60.00

KOBAN

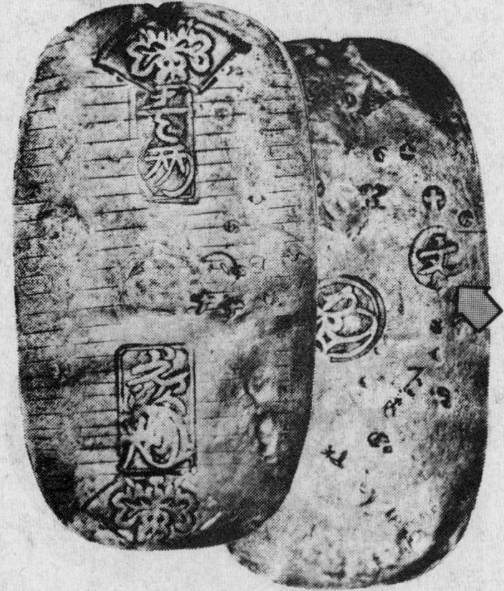

.653 GOLD/.347 SILVER, 13.13 g
Genbun

C#	Date	Mintage	VG	Fine	VF	XF
22	ND(1736-1818)	*17.436	1000.	1500.	2000.	2500.

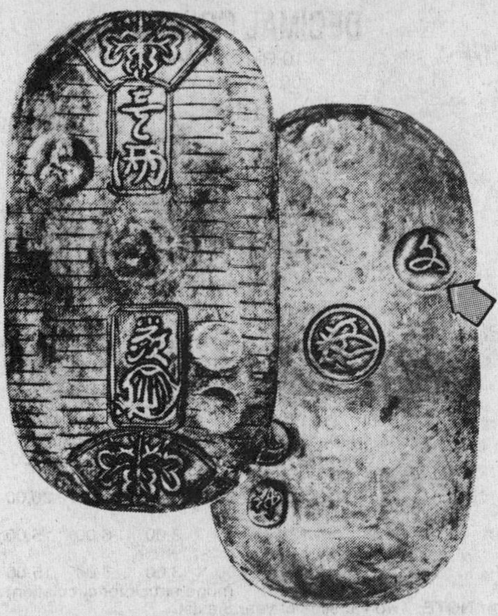

.559 GOLD/.441 SILVER, 13.13 g
Bunsei
Rev: Mark B.

C#	Date	Mintage	VG	Fine	VF	XF
22a	ND(1819-28)	*11.043	900.00	1400.	1800.	2250.

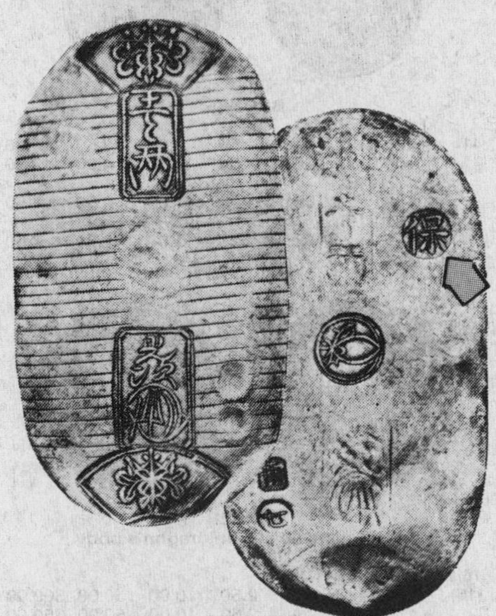

.568 GOLD/.432 SILVER, 11.25 g
Tempo

C#	Date	Mintage	VG	Fine	VF	XF
22b	ND(1837-1858)	*8.120	800.00	1200.	1500.	2000.

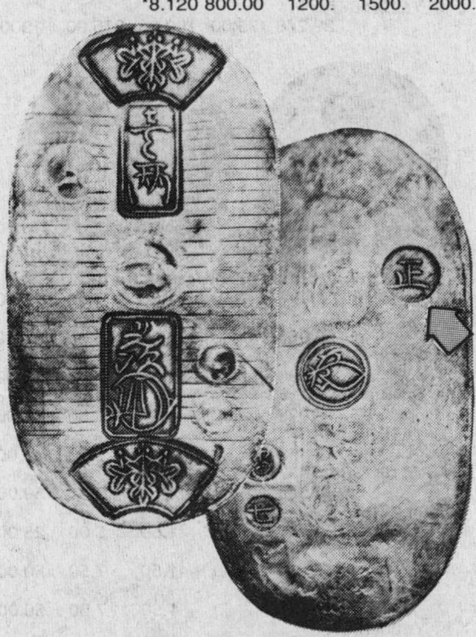

.570 GOLD/.430 SILVER, 8.97 g
Ansei

C#	Date	Mintage	VG	Fine	VF	XF
22c	ND(1859)	.351	3000.	4000.	6000.	8500.

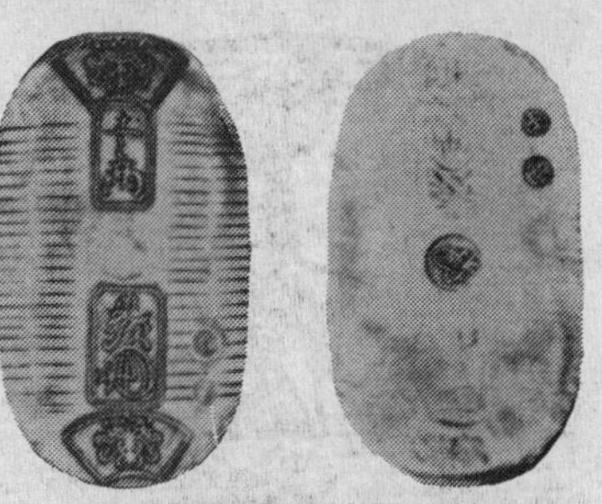

.574 GOLD/.426 SILVER, 3.30 g
Manen
Rev: W/o mark.

C#	Date	Mintage	VG	Fine	VF	XF
22d	(1860-67)	.625	550.00	850.00	1000.	1350.

***NOTE:** Koban mintage figures include Ichibu Kin.

GORYOBAN

(5 Ryo)

.842 GOLD/.158 SILVER, 33.75 g, 51x89mm
Tempo

C#	Date	Mintage	VG	Fine	VF	XF
23	ND(1837-43)	.034	5000.	8000.	12,000.	15,000.

OBAN

NOTE: Oban illustrations are reduced by 50%.

.676 GOLD/.324 SILVER, 165.38 g, 94x153mm
Kyoho

C#	Date	Mintage	VG	Fine	VF	XF
24.1	ND(1725-1837) original inking	8,515	—	—	65,000.	80,000.
	ND(1725-1837) re-inked during Tempo period	Inc. Ab.	—	—	50,000.	65,000.

.674 GOLD/.326 SILVER, 165.38 g, 95x157mm
Tempo

C#	Date	Mintage	VG	Fine	VF	XF
24.2	ND(1838-60)	1,887	—	—	60,000.	75,000.

.344 GOLD/.639 SILVER, 112.4 g, 81x137mm
Manen
Hand made horizontal crenulations.

C#	Date	Mintage	VG	Fine	VF	XF
24a.1	ND(1860-62)	.017	—	—	19,000.	27,500.

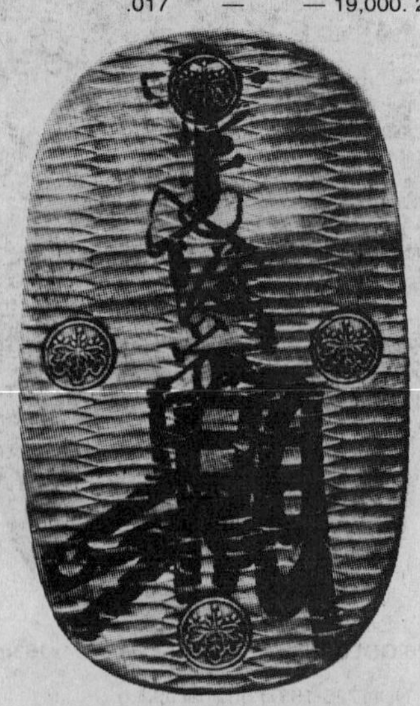

Machine made horizontal crenulations.

C#	Date	Mintage	VG	Fine	VF	XF
24a.2	ND(1860-62)	I.A.	—	—	17,500.	25,000.

DECIMAL COINAGE

10 Rin = 1 Sen
100 Sen = 1 Yen

RIN

COPPER

Y#	Date	Mintage	Fine	VF	XF	Unc
	Meiji					
15	Yr.6(1873)	6.979	4.50	10.00	20.00	40.00
	Yr.7(1874)	I.A.	2.00	4.00	8.00	30.00
	Yr.8(1875)	3.718	4.00	9.00	20.00	50.00
	Yr.9(1876)	.023	500.00	1200.	2250.	4000.
	Yr.10(1877)	I.A.	200.00	350.00	650.00	1000.
	Yr.13(1880)	810 pcs.	1000.	1500.	2750.	5000.
	Yr.15(1882)	3.632	2.00	5.00	8.00	20.00
	Yr.16(1883)	14.128	1.00	3.00	6.00	15.00
	Yr.17(1884)	16.009	1.00	3.00	6.00	15.00
	Yr.25(1892)	—	(none struck for circulation)			

NOTE: Two varieties of year 8 exist.

5 RIN

BRONZE

Y#	Date	Mintage	Fine	VF	XF	Unc
	Taisho					
41	Yr.5(1916)	8.000	.50	2.00	3.50	10.00
	Yr.6(1917)	5.287	.50	2.00	4.00	12.50
	Yr.7(1918)	11.661	.25	1.00	2.50	7.50
	Yr.8(1919)	17.130	.25	1.00	2.50	7.50

1/2 SEN

COPPER
Obv: Square scales on dragon's body.

Y#	Date	Mintage	Fine	VF	XF	Unc
	Meiji					
16.1 (16)	Yr.6(1873)	16.804	2.50	10.00	50.00	300.00
	Yr.7(1874)	I.A.	2.50	10.00	50.00	350.00
	Yr.8(1875)	17.037	.75	3.50	25.00	250.00
	Yr.9(1876)	24.292	.75	3.50	25.00	250.00
	Yr.10(1877)	29.278	75.00	150.00	275.00	1900.

Obv: V scales on dragon's body.

Y#	Date	Mintage	Fine	VF	XF	Unc
16.2 (16.1)	Yr.10(1877)	I.A.	.50	1.50	7.50	45.00
	Yr.12(1879)	29.963	7.50	30.00	50.00	800.00
	Yr.13(1880)	14.090	.50	1.50	7.50	50.00
	Yr.14(1881)	17.929	.50	1.50	7.50	50.00
	Yr.15(1882)	26.458	.50	1.50	7.50	50.00
	Yr.16(1883)	38.202	.50	1.50	7.50	50.00
	Yr.17(1884)	38.480	.50	1.50	5.00	25.00
	Yr.18(1885)	31.166	.50	1.50	7.50	50.00
	Yr.19(1886)	31.831	.50	1.50	7.50	50.00
	Yr.20(1887)	35.651	.50	1.50	7.50	50.00
	Yr.21(1888)	25.744	3.50	5.00	10.00	90.00
	Yr.25(1892)	—	(none struck for circulation)			

SEN

COPPER
Obv: Square scales on dragon's body.

Y#	Date	Mintage	Fine	VF	XF	Unc
	Meiji					
17.1	Yr.6(1873)	1.301	6.00	12.50	27.50	300.00
(17)	Yr.7(1874)	25.564	1.00	2.50	5.00	150.00
	Yr.8(1875)	32.832	.75	1.50	3.00	125.00
	Yr.9(1876)	38.048	.75	1.50	3.00	125.00
	Yr.10(1877)	98.041	.75	1.50	3.00	125.00

Obv: V scales on dragon's body.

Y#	Date	Mintage	Fine	VF	XF	Unc
17.2 (17.1)	Yr.13(1880)	33.947	.50	1.50	3.00	85.00
	Yr.14(1881)	16.123	1.50	2.50	6.50	125.00
	Yr.14(1881) large 4	Inc. Ab.	25.00	50.00	100.00	225.00
	Yr.15(1882)	19.150	.50	1.50	3.00	85.00
	Yr.16(1883)	47.613	.50	1.50	3.00	85.00
	Yr.17(1884)	53.702	.50	1.50	3.00	85.00
	Yr.18(1885)	46.846	.50	1.50	3.00	85.00
	Yr.19(1886)	26.886	.50	1.50	3.00	85.00
	Yr.20(1887)	22.249	.50	1.50	3.00	85.00
	Yr.21(1888)	25.864	.50	1.50	3.00	65.00
	Yr.25(1892)	—	(none struck for circulation)			

BRONZE

Y#	Date	Mintage	Fine	VF	XF	Unc
20	Yr.31(1898)	3.649	2.50	5.00	10.00	110.00
	Yr.32(1899)	9.764	2.00	4.50	8.00	55.00
	Yr.33(1900)	3.086	4.50	7.50	12.50	130.00
	Yr.34(1901)	5.555	2.00	4.50	8.00	55.00
	Yr.35(1902)	4.444	5.00	10.00	15.00	145.00
	Yr.39(1906)	—	(none struck for circulation)			
	Yr.42(1909)	—	(none struck for circulation)			

Y#	Date	Mintage	Fine	VF	XF	Unc
	Taisho					
35	Yr.2(1913)	15.000	2.00	3.00	5.00	30.00
	Yr.3(1914)	10.000	2.00	3.00	5.00	30.00
	Yr.4(1915)	13.000	2.00	3.00	5.00	30.00

Y#	Date	Mintage	Fine	VF	XF	Unc
42	Yr.5(1916)	19.193	.50	1.00	1.50	25.00
	Yr.6(1917)	27.183	.25	.50	1.00	20.00
	Yr.7(1918)	121.794	.25	.50	1.00	7.50
	Yr.8(1919)	209.959	.15	.25	.50	3.50
	Yr.9(1920)	118.829	.15	.25	.50	3.50
	Yr.10(1921)	252.440	.15	.25	.50	3.50
	Yr.11(1922)	253.210	.15	.25	.50	3.50
	Yr.12(1923)	155.500	.15	.25	.50	3.50
	Yr.13(1924)	106.250	.15	.25	.50	3.50

Y#	Date	Mintage	Fine	VF	XF	Unc
	Showa					
47	Yr.2(1927)	26.500	1.50	2.50	3.50	30.00
	Yr.4(1929)	3.000	3.50	7.50	15.00	35.00
	Yr.5(1930)	5.000	2.50	4.50	7.50	60.00
	Yr.6(1931)	25.001	.25	.50	1.50	10.00
	Yr.7(1932)	35.066	.25	.50	1.50	7.50
	Yr.8(1933)	38.936	.15	.25	.50	1.50
	Yr.9(1934)	100.004	.15	.25	.50	1.50
	Yr.10(1935)	200.009	.15	.25	.50	1.50
	Yr.11(1936)	109.170	.15	.25	.50	1.50
	Yr.12(1937)	133.196	.15	.25	.50	1.50
	Yr.13(1938)	87.649	.15	.25	.50	1.50

Y#	Date	Mintage	Fine	VF	XF	Unc
55	Yr.13(1938)	113.605	.15	.25	.50	1.50

四 四

TYPE A ALUMINUM TYPE B

Y#	Date	Mintage	Fine	VF	XF	Unc
56	Yr.13(1938)	45.502	—	.25	.50	8.50
	Yr.14(1939) Type A	444.602	—	.50	.75	12.00
	Yr.14(1939) Type B	Inc. Ab.	—	.25	.50	1.50
	Yr.15(1940)	602.110	—	.25	.50	1.50

0.6500 g

Y#	Date	Mintage	Fine	VF	XF	Unc
59	Yr.16(1941)	1016.620	—	—	.25	.50
	Yr.17(1942)	119.709	—	—	.25	.75
	Yr.18(1943)	1,163.949	—	—	.25	.50

Thinner, 0.5500 g

Y#	Date	Mintage	Fine	VF	XF	Unc
59a	Yr.18(1943)	627.191	—	—	.50	1.00

TIN-ZINC

Y#	Date	Mintage	Fine	VF	XF	Unc
62	Yr.19(1944)	1,641.661	—	—	.25	.50
	Yr.20(1945)	I.A.	—	—	.25	.75

REDDISH BROWN BAKED CLAY

KM#	Date	Mintage	Fine	VF	XF	Unc
110	ND(1945)	—	4.00	6.00	15.00	20.00

NOTE: Circulated for a few days before the end of WWII in Central Japan. Varieties of color exist.

2 SEN

BRONZE
Obv: Square scales on dragon's body.

Y#	Date	Mintage	Fine	VF	XF	Unc
	Meiji					
18.1	Yr.6(1873)	3.949	35.00	75.00	150.00	825.00
(18)	Yr.7(1874)	I.A.	2.50	5.00	10.00	375.00
	Yr.8(1875)	22.835	1.50	2.50	5.00	265.00
	Yr.9(1876)	25.817	1.50	2.50	5.00	265.00
	Yr.10(1877)	33.897	1.50	2.50	5.00	265.00

Obv: V scales on dragon's body.

Y#	Date	Mintage	Fine	VF	XF	Unc
18.2 (18.1)	Yr.10(1877)	43.290	1.50	2.50	5.00	115.00
	Yr.13(1880)	33.142	1.50	2.50	5.00	115.00
	Yr.14(1881)	38.475	1.50	2.50	5.00	115.00
	Yr.15(1882)	43.527	1.50	2.50	5.00	115.00
	Yr.16(1883)	19.476	1.50	2.50	5.00	115.00
	Yr.17(1884)	12.090	2.50	5.00	10.00	350.00
	Yr.25(1892)	—	(none struck for circulation)			

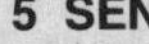

5 SEN

1.2500 g, .800 SILVER, .0321 oz ASW

Y#	Date	Mintage	Fine	VF	XF	Unc
	Meiji					
1	Yr.3(1870) shallow scales	1.501	150.00	250.00	350.00	550.00
	Yr.3(1870) deep scales	Inc. Ab.	200.00	300.00	450.00	875.00
	Yr.4(1871)	I.A.	250.00	350.00	500.00	900.00

Early variety. Rev: 66 rays, 79 beads.

Y#	Date	Mintage	Fine	VF	XF	Unc
6.1	Yr.4(1871)	1.665	30.00	75.00	150.00	250.00

Late variety. Rev: 53 rays, 65 beads.

Y#	Date	Mintage	Fine	VF	XF	Unc
6.2	Yr.4(1871)	I.A.	25.00	60.00	90.00	200.00

明	明	明
Type I Characters Not Connected	**Type II** Characters Connected	**Type III** Characters Not Connected, long vert. stroke

1.3400 g, .800 SILVER, .0344 oz ASW

Y#	Date	Mintage	Fine	VF	XF	Unc
22	Yr.6(1873) Type I	5.593	10.00	20.00	30.00	65.00
	Yr.6(1873) Type II	Inc. Ab.	50.00	75.00	125.00	250.00
	Yr.7(1874)	7.806	65.00	125.00	200.00	500.00
	Yr.8(1875)	6.396	10.00	20.00	30.00	50.00
	Yr.9(1876) Type I	5.546	10.00	20.00	30.00	65.00
	Yr.9(1876) Type II	Inc. Ab.	15.00	30.00	45.00	100.00
	Yr.10(1877)	22.024	10.00	20.00	30.00	50.00
	Yr.10(1880) Type III	Inc. Ab.	20.00	45.00	70.00	125.00
	Yr.13(1880)	79 pcs.	2500.	5000.	7500.	15,000.
	Yr.25(1892)	—	(none struck for circulation)			

NOTE: Varieties exist.

COPPER-NICKEL

Y#	Date	Mintage	Fine	VF	XF	Unc
19	Yr.22(1889)	28.841	1.25	2.50	5.00	55.00
	Yr.23(1890)	39.258	1.25	2.50	5.00	55.00
	Yr.24(1891)	15.924	1.50	3.00	7.50	100.00
	Yr.25(1892)	9.510	1.50	3.00	7.50	100.00
	Yr.26(1893)	8.531	1.50	3.00	7.50	100.00
	Yr.27(1894)	14.680	1.50	3.00	7.50	100.00
	Yr.28(1895)	1.030	50.00	100.00	200.00	1700.
	Yr.29(1896)	5.119	3.50	7.50	17.50	300.00
	Yr.30(1897)	7.857	1.50	3.00	7.50	100.00

NOTE: Varieties exist.

Y#	Date	Mintage	Fine	VF	XF	Unc
21	Yr.30(1897)	4.167	6.50	15.00	30.00	265.00
	Yr.31(1898)	18.197	4.00	8.00	15.00	115.00
	Yr.32(1899)	10.658	4.00	8.00	15.00	115.00
	Yr.33(1900)	2.426	7.50	15.00	25.00	235.00
	Yr.34(1901)	7.124	5.00	10.00	17.50	115.00
	Yr.35(1902)	2.448	10.00	25.00	35.00	285.00
	Yr.36(1903)	.372	150.00	250.00	400.00	2500.
	Yr.37(1904)	1.628	20.00	35.00	75.00	390.00
	Yr.38(1905)	6.000	5.00	10.00	17.50	115.00
	Yr.39(1906)	—	*(none struck for circulation)			

***NOTE:** Spink-Taisei Hong Kong sale 9-91 BU realized $10,000.

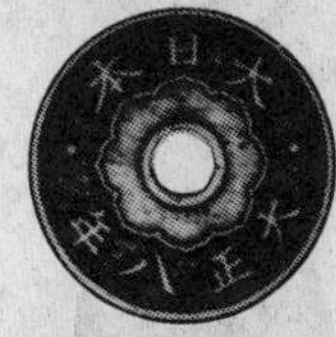

Y#	Date	Mintage	Fine	VF	XF	Unc
	Taisho					
43	Yr.6(1917)	6.781	7.50	15.00	25.00	50.00
	Yr.7(1918)	9.131	5.00	10.00	20.00	32.50
	Yr.8(1919)	44.980	3.00	6.00	10.00	15.00
	Yr.9(1920)	21.906	3.00	6.00	10.00	15.00

19.1mm

Y#	Date	Mintage	Fine	VF	XF	Unc
44	Yr.9(1920)	100.455	.35	.75	2.00	12.50
	Yr.10(1921)	133.020	.25	.50	1.50	4.00
	Yr.11(1922)	163.908	.25	.50	1.50	4.00
	Yr.12(1923)	80.000	.25	.50	1.50	4.00

Showa

Y#	Date	Mintage	Fine	VF	XF	Unc
48	Yr.7(1932)	8.000	.25	.50	1.75	5.00

NICKEL

Y#	Date	Mintage	Fine	VF	XF	Unc
53	Yr.8(1933)	16.150	.50	1.50	3.00	5.50
	Yr.9(1934)	33.851	.50	1.00	2.00	4.50
	Yr.10(1935)	13.680	1.00	2.00	3.50	7.50
	Yr.11(1936)	36.321	.50	1.00	2.00	4.50
	Yr.12(1937)	44.402	.50	1.00	2.00	4.50
	Yr.13(1938)	*10.000		4 known	Rare	—

***NOTE:** Almost entire mintage remelted.

ALUMINUM-BRONZE

Y#	Date	Mintage	Fine	VF	XF	Unc
57	Yr.13(1938)	40.001	.50	1.00	1.50	4.00
	Yr.14(1939)	97.903	.50	1.00	1.50	4.00
	Yr.15(1940)	34.501	.50	1.00	1.50	4.00

ALUMINUM

Variety 1 - 1.2000 g

Y#	Date	Mintage	Fine	VF	XF	Unc
60	Yr.15(1940)	167.638	—	—	.50	2.00
	Yr.16(1941)	242.361	—	—	.25	1.50

Variety 2 - 1.0000 g

Y#	Date	Mintage	Fine	VF	XF	Unc
60a	Yr.16(1941)	478.023	1.50	3.50	7.50	35.00
	Yr.17(1942)	I.A.	—	—	.25	1.00

Variety 3 - 0.8000 g

Y#	Date	Mintage	Fine	VF	XF	Unc
60b	Yr.18(1943)	276.493	—	—	.25	1.00

TIN-ZINC

Y#	Date	Mintage	Fine	VF	XF	Unc
63	Yr.19(1944)	70.003	—	.25	.50	1.50
65	Yr.20(1945)	180.008	—	—	.50	2.00
	Yr.21(1946)	I.A.	—	—	.50	2.00

REDDISH BROWN BAKED CLAY

KM#	Date	Mintage	Fine	VF	XF	Unc
111	Yr.20(1945)	—	50.00	75.00	100.00	175.00

NOTE: Not issued for circulation. Varieties of color exist.

10 SEN

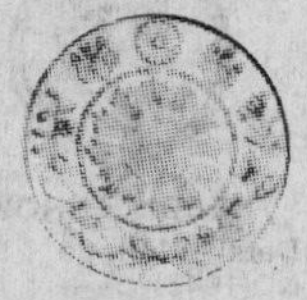

2.5000 g, .800 SILVER, .0643 oz ASW

Y#	Date	Mintage	Fine	VF	XF	Unc
	Meiji					
2	Yr.3(1870) shallow scales	6.102	12.50	25.00	35.00	130.00
	Yr.3(1870) deep scales	Inc. Ab.	20.00	35.00	55.00	175.00

2.6957 g, .800 SILVER, .0693 oz ASW

Y#	Date	Mintage	Fine	VF	XF	Unc
23	Yr.6(1873) Type I	5.109	5.00	10.00	15.00	40.00
	Yr.6(1873) Type II	Inc. Ab.	60.00	120.00	165.00	375.00

明 明

Type I Characters Not Connected — **Type II Characters Connected**

Y#	Date	Mintage	Fine	VF	XF	Unc
	Yr.7(1874)	10.221	160.00	275.00	425.00	950.00
	Yr.8(1875) Type II	8.977	15.00	30.00	50.00	135.00
	Yr.8(1875) Type I	Inc. Ab.	5.00	10.00	15.00	40.00
	Yr.9(1876)	11.890	5.00	10.00	15.00	40.00
	Yr.10(1877)	20.352	10.00	25.00	40.00	100.00
	Yr.13(1880)	77 pcs.	5000.	8000.	16,000.	27,500.
	Yr.18(1885)	9.763	3.00	7.50	12.00	30.00
	Yr.20(1887)	10.421	3.00	7.50	12.00	30.00
	Yr.21(1888)	8.177	3.00	7.50	15.00	35.00
	Yr.24(1891)	5.000	10.00	20.00	35.00	100.00
	Yr.25(1892)	5.000	10.00	20.00	35.00	100.00
	Yr.26(1893)	12.000	3.00	7.50	15.00	45.00
	Yr.27(1894)	11.000	3.00	7.50	18.00	100.00
	Yr.28(1895)	13.719	2.00	5.00	7.50	30.00
	Yr.29(1896)	15.080	2.00	5.00	7.50	30.00
	Yr.30(1897)	20.357	2.00	5.00	7.50	30.00
	Yr.31(1898)	13.643	3.00	7.50	10.00	35.00
	Yr.32(1899)	26.216	3.00	7.50	10.00	35.00
	Yr.33(1900)	8.183	6.00	12.50	20.00	100.00
	Yr.34(1901)	.797	125.00	175.00	250.00	750.00
	Yr.35(1902)	1.204	100.00	150.00	200.00	750.00
	Yr.37(1904)	11.106	2.50	5.00	7.50	30.00
	Yr.38(1905)	34.182	2.50	5.00	7.50	30.00
	Yr.39(1906)	4.710	2.50	5.00	7.50	30.00

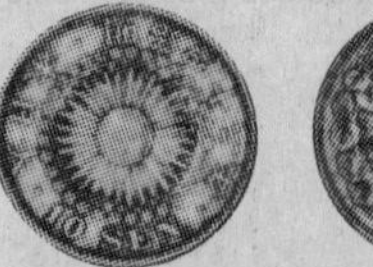

2.2500 g, .720 SILVER, .0521 oz ASW

Y#	Date	Mintage	Fine	VF	XF	Unc
29	Yr.40(1907)	12.000	2.50	5.00	7.50	50.00
	Yr.41(1908)					
29		12.273	2.50	5.00	7.50	50.00
	Yr.42(1909)	20.279	1.00	3.50	5.00	25.00
	Yr.43(1910)	20.339	1.00	3.50	5.00	25.00
	Yr.44(1911)	38.729	1.00	3.50	5.00	25.00
	Yr.45(1912)	10.755	1.00	3.50	5.00	25.00

Obv: Japanese character *first*.

Y#	Date	Mintage	Fine	VF	XF	Unc
	Taisho					
36.1	Yr.1(1912)	10.344	2.50	5.00	10.00	55.00

Y#	Date	Mintage	Fine	VF	XF	Unc
36.2	Yr.2(1913)	13.321	1.00	2.50	5.00	12.00
	Yr.3(1914)	10.325	1.00	2.50	5.00	12.00
	Yr.4(1915)	16.836	1.50	3.00	5.00	12.00
	Yr.5(1916)	10.324	1.00	2.50	4.00	12.00
	Yr.6(1917)	35.170	.75	2.00	3.00	10.00

COPPER-NICKEL

Y#	Date	Mintage	Fine	VF	XF	Unc
45	Yr.9(1920)	4.894	.35	.75	2.50	25.00
	Yr.10(1921)	61.870	.25	.50	1.50	5.00
	Yr.11(1922)	159.770	.25	.50	1.50	5.00
	Yr.12(1923)	190.010	.25	.50	1.50	4.50
	Yr.14(1925)	54.475	.25	.50	1.50	5.00
	Yr.15(1926)	58.675	.25	.50	1.50	5.00

Y#	Date	Mintage	Fine	VF	XF	Unc
	Showa					
49	Yr.2(1927)	36.050	.25	.50	1.50	5.00
	Yr.3(1928)	41.450	.25	.50	1.50	5.00
	Yr.4(1929)	10.000	.50	1.00	2.00	20.00
	Yr.6(1931)	1.850	.75	1.50	2.50	7.50
	Yr.7(1932)	23.151	.25	.50	1.50	5.00

NICKEL

Y#	Date	Mintage	Fine	VF	XF	Unc
54	Yr.8(1933)	14.570	.50	1.00	2.00	5.50
	Yr.9(1934)	37.351	.25	.75	1.50	4.75
	Yr.10(1935)	35.586	.30	1.00	1.75	5.25
	Yr.11(1936)	77.948	.25	.75	1.50	4.75
	Yr.12(1937)	40.001	.30	1.00	1.75	5.25

ALUMINUM-BRONZE

Y#	Date	Mintage	Fine	VF	XF	Unc
58	Yr.13(1938)	47.077	.35	.75	1.50	4.75
	Yr.14(1939)	121.796	.25	.50	1.00	4.50
	Yr.15(1940)	16.135	.50	1.00	2.00	10.00

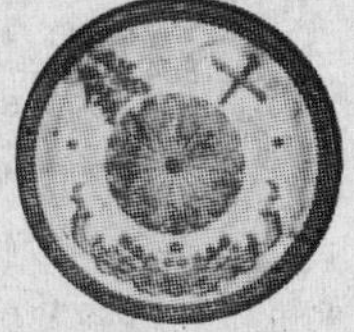

ALUMINUM, 1.5000 g

Y#	Date	Mintage	Fine	VF	XF	Unc
61	Yr.15(1940)	575.628	—	.20	.35	1.50
	Yr.16(1941)	I.A.	—	.20	.35	1.50

1.2000 g

Y#	Date	Mintage	Fine	VF	XF	Unc
61a	Yr.16(1941)	944.947	.10	.35	.50	2.00
	Yr.17(1942)	I.A.	—	.20	.35	1.50
	Yr.18(1943)	I.B.	.20	.50	2.00	5.00

1.0000 g

Y#	Date	Mintage	Fine	VF	XF	Unc
61b	Yr.18(1943)	756.037	—	.20	.35	1.50

TIN-ZINC

Y#	Date	Mintage	Fine	VF	XF	Unc
64	Yr.19(1944)	450.022	—	.20	.35	1.50

REDDISH BROWN BAKED CLAY

KM#	Date	Mintage	Fine	VF	XF	Unc
112	Yr.20(1945)	—	50.00	80.00	125.00	175.00

NOTE: Not issued for circulation. Varieties of color exist.

ALUMINUM

Y#	Date	Mintage	Fine	VF	XF	Unc
68	Yr.20(1945)	237.590	—	.20	.35	1.00
	Yr.21(1946)	I.A.	—	.20	.35	1.00

20 SEN

Yr.4 var.

5.0000 g, .800 SILVER, .1286 oz ASW

Meiji

Y#	Date	Mintage	Fine	VF	XF	Unc
3	Yr.3(1870) shallow scales	4.313	12.50	20.00	40.00	135.00
	Yr.3(1870) deep scales	Inc. Ab.	17.50	35.00	60.00	200.00
	Yr.4(1871)	I.A.	12.50	20.00	35.00	125.00
	Yr.4(1871) lower stroke incomplete	Inc. Ab.	75.00	100.00	150.00	300.00

明 **Type I Character Closed**

明 **Type II Character Open**

5.3800 g, .800 SILVER, .1383 oz ASW

Y#	Date	Mintage	Fine	VF	XF	Unc
24	Yr.6(1873) Type I	6.214	5.00	10.00	15.00	55.00
	Yr.6(1873) Type II	Inc. Ab.	65.00	125.00	250.00	650.00
	Yr.7(1874)	3.024	15.00	30.00	60.00	200.00

明 **Type I Characters Not Connected**

明 **Type II Characters Connected**

Y#	Date	Mintage	Fine	VF	XF	Unc
	Yr.8(1875) Type I	.612	100.00	150.00	275.00	750.00
	Yr.8(1875) Type II	Inc. Ab.	50.00	100.00	175.00	575.00
	Yr.9(1876) Type II	9.200	20.00	35.00	65.00	225.00
	Yr.9(1876) Type I	Inc. Ab.	5.00	10.00	15.00	65.00
	Yr.10(1877)	5.199	20.00	35.00	65.00	240.00
	Yr.13(1880)	96 pcs.	1750.	3250.	5500.	12,500.
	Yr.18(1885)	4.205	4.00	7.50	12.50	50.00
	Yr.20(1887)	4.794	4.00	7.50	12.50	50.00
	Yr.21(1888)	.703	60.00	125.00	200.00	1000.
	Yr.24(1891)	2.500	10.00	17.50	30.00	115.00
	Yr.25(1892)	3.054	7.50	15.00	25.00	100.00
	Yr.26(1893)	3.445	6.50	12.50	20.00	90.00
	Yr.27(1894)	4.500	5.50	10.00	15.00	140.00
	Yr.28(1895)	7.000	3.50	7.50	12.50	50.00
	Yr.29(1896)	2.599	7.50	15.00	25.00	100.00
	Yr.30(1897)	7.516	3.50	7.50	12.50	50.00
	Yr.31(1898)	17.984	3.50	7.50	12.50	50.00
	Yr.32(1899)	15.000	3.50	7.50	12.50	50.00
	Yr.33(1900)	.800	25.00	50.00	75.00	325.00
	Yr.34(1901)	.500	150.00	225.00	350.00	1900.
	Yr.37(1904)	5.250	3.50	7.50	12.50	50.00
	Yr.38(1905)	8.444	3.50	7.50	12.50	50.00

4.0500 g, .800 SILVER, .1042 oz ASW

Y#	Date	Mintage	Fine	VF	XF	Unc
30	Yr.39(1906)	6.555	3.50	7.50	18.00	200.00
	Yr.40(1907)	20.000	2.25	3.50	7.50	60.00
	Yr.41(1908)	15.000	2.25	3.50	7.50	60.00
	Yr.42(1909)	8.824	2.25	3.50	7.50	60.00
	Yr.43(1910)	21.175	2.25	3.50	7.50	60.00
	Yr.44(1911)	.500	60.00	120.00	250.00	1000.

50 SEN

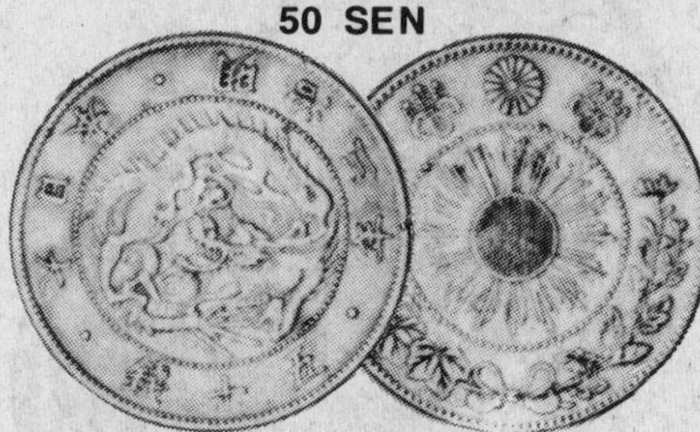

12.5000 g, .800 SILVER, .3215 oz ASW

Meiji

Y#	Date	Mintage	Fine	VF	XF	Unc
4	Yr.3(1870)	1.806	32.50	65.00	100.00	325.00
	Yr.4(1871)	I.A.	30.00	60.00	85.00	300.00

NOTE: Varieties exist.

Type II, large dragon

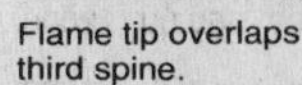

Flame tip overlaps third spine.

Type I, small dragon

Flame tip extends between third & fourth spine.

30.5mm

Type I: 19mm circle of dots around dragon.

Y#	Date	Mintage	Fine	VF	XF	Unc
4a.1 (4a)	Yr.4(1871)	2.648	50.00	100.00	150.00	300.00

Type II: 21mm circle of dots around dragon.

Y#	Date	Mintage	Fine	VF	XF	Unc
4a.2 (4a.1)	Yr.4(1871)	I.A.	400.00	800.00	1200.	3500.

13.5000 g, .800 SILVER, .3472 oz ASW

Y#	Date	Mintage	Fine	VF	XF	Unc
25	Yr.6(1873) Type I	3.447	25.00	35.00	65.00	250.00
	Yr.6(1873) Type II	Inc.Ab.	150.00	200.00	300.00	775.00
	Yr.7(1874)	.095	7500.	12,500.	20,000.	32,500.
	Yr.8(1875)	109 pcs.	8000.	11,000.	16,000.	27,500.
	Yr.9(1876)	1,251	2500.	4500.	6500.	14,000.
	Yr.10(1877)	.184	1250.	2000.	3750.	7000.
	Yr.13(1880)	179 pcs.	7500.	12,500.	20,000.	40,000.
	Yr.18(1885)	.409	125.00	175.00	275.00	900.00
	Yr.30(1897)	5.078	7.50	15.00	20.00	175.00
	Yr.31(1898)	22.797	6.50	12.50	17.50	120.00
	Yr.32(1899)	10.254	7.50	15.00	20.00	125.00
	Yr.33(1900)	3.280	10.00	18.00	30.00	220.00
	Yr.34(1901)	1.790	15.00	35.00	70.00	350.00
	Yr.35(1902)	1.023	50.00	85.00	150.00	625.00
	Yr.36(1903)	1.503	25.00	45.00	80.00	425.00
	Yr.37(1904)	5.373	7.50	12.50	18.00	125.00
	Yr.38(1905)	9.566	7.50	12.50	18.00	125.00

NOTE: Two varieties exist for year 6 in the character *Nen* (=year). The type II has a very long lower horizontal stroke.

10.1000 g, .800 SILVER, .2597 oz ASW

Y#	Date	Mintage	Fine	VF	XF	Unc
31	Yr.39(1906)	12.478	3.00	6.00	15.00	225.00
	Yr.40(1907)	24.062	3.00	6.00	12.50	60.00
	Yr.41(1908)	25.470	3.00	6.00	12.50	60.00
	Yr.42(1909)	21.998	3.00	6.00	12.50	60.00
	Yr.43(1910)	15.323	3.00	6.00	12.50	60.00
	Yr.44(1911)	9.900	3.00	6.00	12.50	60.00
	Yr.45(1912)	3.677	7.50	12.50	18.00	75.00

Obv: Japanese character *first*.

Taisho

Y#	Date	Mintage	Fine	VF	XF	Unc
37.1	Yr.1(1912)	1.928	12.50	20.00	35.00	150.00

Y#	Date	Mintage	Fine	VF	XF	Unc
37.2	Yr.2(1913)	5.910	3.00	7.50	17.50	60.00
	Yr.3(1914)	1.872	17.50	28.00	45.00	175.00
	Yr.4(1915)	2.011	15.00	25.00	40.00	160.00
	Yr.5(1916)	8.736	3.50	7.50	12.50	35.00
	Yr.6(1917)	9.963	3.50	7.50	12.50	35.00

4.9600 g, .720 SILVER, .1148 oz ASW

Y#	Date	Mintage	Fine	VF	XF	Unc
46	Yr.11(1922)	76.320	BV	1.50	5.00	20.00
	Yr.12(1923)	185.180	BV	1.50	3.00	15.00
	Yr.13(1924)	78.520	BV	1.50	3.00	15.00
	Yr.14(1925)	47.808	BV	1.50	3.00	17.50
	Yr.15(1926)	32.572	BV	1.50	3.00	17.50

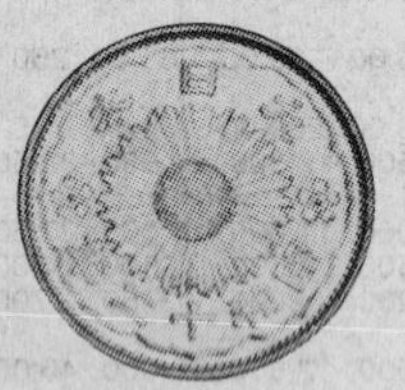

Y#	Date	Mintage	Fine	VF	XF	Unc
	Showa					
50	Yr.3(1928)	38.592	BV	1.00	2.50	10.00
	Yr.4(1929)	12.568	BV	1.50	5.00	25.00
	Yr.5(1930)	10.200	BV	2.00	5.50	15.00
	Yr.6(1931)	27.677	BV	1.00	2.50	10.00
	Yr.7(1932)	24.132	BV	1.00	2.50	10.00
	Yr.8(1933)	10.001	BV	2.00	7.00	20.00
	Yr.9(1934)	20.003	BV	1.50	2.50	10.00
	Yr.10(1935)	11.738	BV	1.50	2.50	10.00
	Yr.11(1936)	44.272	BV	1.50	2.50	7.50
	Yr.12(1937)	48.000	BV	1.50	2.50	7.50
	Yr.13(1938)	3.600	50.00	75.00	125.00	250.00

BRASS

Y#	Date	Mintage	Fine	VF	XF	Unc
67	Yr.21(1946)	268.187	.25	.50	1.00	2.50
	Yr.22(1947)	I.A.	—	650.00	1000.	1700.

NOTE: Coins dated Showa 22 (1947) were not released to circulation.

***NOTE:** Varieties exist.

Y#	Date	Mintage	Fine	VF	XF	Unc
69	Yr.22(1947)	849.234	.10	.20	.40	1.00
	Yr.23(1948)	I.A.	.10	.20	.40	1.00

YEN

Low Dot + High Dot
1.6700 g, .900 GOLD, 13.5mm, .0482 oz AGW

Y#	Date	Mintage	Fine	VF	XF	Unc
	Meiji					
9	Yr.4(1871) low dot	1.841	175.00	300.00	400.00	575.00
	Yr.4(1871) low dot	—		—	Proof	6500.
	Yr.4(1871) high dot	Inc. Ab.	250.00	375.00	500.00	750.00

Reduced size, 12mm

Y#	Date	Mintage	Fine	VF	XF	Unc
9a	Yr.7(1874)	.116	1500.	2500.	3250.	4500.
	Yr.9(1876)	138 pcs.	4500.	7500.	12,000.	16,000.
	Yr.10(1877)	7,246	6500.	12,500.	22,000.	32,000.
	Yr.13(1880)	112 pcs.	9500.	17,500.	26,000.	36,000.
	Yr.25(1892)	(none struck for circulation)				

圓 圓 圓

Type I Type II Type III
26.9568 g, .900 SILVER, .7800 oz ASW

Y#	Date	Mintage	Fine	VF	XF	Unc
	Meiji					
5.1 (5)	Yr.3(1870)Type 1	3.685	100.00	275.00	375.00	600.00
5.2 (5.1)	Yr.3(1870)Type 2	Inc.Ab.	125.00	300.00	400.00	650.00
5.3 (5.2)	Yr.3(1870)Type 3	Inc. Ab.	450.00	850.00	1500.	2250.

Type I, 38.6mm
Spiral on pearl held by dragon curls in counter clock wise direction from center.

Y#	Date	Mintage	Fine	VF	XF	Unc
A25.1 (A25)	Yr.7(1874)	.942	350.00	650.00	1250.	4500.

Spiral on pearl curls clockwise from center.

Y#	Date	Mintage	Fine	VF	XF	Unc
A25.2 (A25.1)	Yr.7(1874)	I.A.	300.00	600.00	1200.	2750.
	Yr.8(1875)	.139	2000.	3000.	5000.	12,500.
	Yr.11(1878)	.856	150.00	350.00	550.00	2000.
	Yr.12(1879)	1.913	750.00	1200.	1750.	4500.

Y#	Date	Mintage	Fine	VF	XF	Unc
(A25.1)	Yr.13(1880)	5.427	50.00	125.00	200.00	1000.
	Yr.14(1881)	2.927	75.00	150.00	225.00	1250.
	Yr.15(1882)	5.089	45.00	75.00	125.00	850.00
	Yr.16(1883)	3.636	45.00	75.00	150.00	900.00
	Yr.17(1884)	3.599	60.00	125.00	200.00	1100.
	Yr.18(1885)	4.296	45.00	75.00	125.00	850.00
	Yr.19(1886)	9.084	45.00	75.00	125.00	875.00
	Yr.20(1887)	8.275	85.00	150.00	325.00	1350.

NOTE: Two varieties of year 7 exist. Year 11 has varieties in the bottom leaf on reverse. Year 19 edge has 198 reeds.

Type II: Reduced size, 38.1mm.

Y#	Date	Mintage	Fine	VF	XF	Unc
A25.3 (A25.2)	Yr.19(1886)	I.A.	500.00	900.00	1750.	4000.
	Yr.20(1887)	I.A.	45.00	75.00	150.00	900.00
	Yr.21(1888)	9.477	25.00	50.00	75.00	400.00
	Yr.22(1889)	9.295	25.00	45.00	65.00	225.00
	Yr.23(1890)	7.292	25.00	45.00	65.00	220.00
	Yr.24(1891)	7.518	15.00	30.00	50.00	185.00
	Yr.25(1892) flame extends between fourth and fifth spine	11.187	100.00	200.00	400.00	1350.
	Yr.25(1892) flame overlaps third spine of dragon	I.A.	20.00	35.00	55.00	210.00
	Yr.26(1893)	10.403	20.00	35.00	55.00	260.00
	Yr.27(1894)	22.118	15.00	25.00	45.00	140.00
	Yr.28(1895)	21.098	15.00	25.00	45.00	140.00
	Yr.29(1896)	11.363	15.00	25.00	45.00	140.00
	Yr.30(1897)	2.448	15.00	30.00	50.00	155.00
	Yr.34(1901)	1.256	15.00	30.00	50.00	160.00
	Yr.35(1902)	.668	25.00	50.00	75.00	225.00
	Yr.36(1903)	5.131	15.00	27.50	42.50	140.00
	Yr.37(1904)	6.970	15.00	27.50	42.50	140.00
	Yr.38(1905)	5.031	15.00	27.50	42.50	140.00
	Yr.39(1906)	3.471	25.00	50.00	85.00	245.00
	Yr.41(1908)	.334	50.00	100.00	225.00	450.00
	Yr.45(1912)	5.000	12.50	25.00	42.50	120.00

NOTE: Year 19 has diameter of 38.3mm and edge has 217 reeds.

Y#	Date	Mintage	Fine	VF	XF	Unc
	Taisho					
38	Yr.3(1914)	11.500	12.50	22.50	35.00	120.00

'GIN' COUNTERMARKS

c/m: ***Gin*** **right on 1 Yen Meiji Year 3, (1870), Y#5.**

c/m: *Gin* left on 1 Yen, Meiji Years 7-30, (1874-1897), Y#A25.

In 1897 Japan demonetized the silver one Yen and Trade Dollar coins, and many were melted to provide bullion from which to produce subsidiary coins. However, some 20 million Trade Dollars and one Yen coins were countermarked with the character *Gin* (meaning silver) and shipped to Taiwan, Korea and Southern Manchuria for use in circulation there. The countermark was applied to indicate that the coin was to be treated simply as bullion and to prevent the coins from returning to Japan where they could be sold to the government for gold.

The actual countermarking was done by the Tokyo and Osaka Mints; the Osaka Mint putting its *Gin* on the left side, the Tokyo Mint putting its *Gin* on the right side. Only 2,100,000 coins were countermarked at the Tokyo Mint Mint as opposed to 18,350,000 countermarked at Osaka, making the Tokyo pieces scarcer than the Osaka pieces.

Formerly *Gin* marked coins were regarded as damaged and sold for about 80 per cent of the price of the same coin without countermark. Now, however, the *Gin* coins are being collected by date and placement of the mark, and some sell for more than a non-countermarked piece. Any additional chop marks are still considered defacement and reduce the value of a coin substantially.

Mint: Osaka
c/m: *Gin* left on 1 Yen, Y#5.

Y#	Date	Mintage	VG	Fine	VF	XF
28	Yr.3(1870)	—	125.00	250.00	350.00	600.00

Type I, 38.6mm
c/m: *Gin* left on 1 Yen, Y#A25.
Counterclockwise spiral on pearl.

Y#	Date	Mintage	VG	Fine	VF	XF
28a	Yr.7(1874)	—	250.00	400.00	800.00	1200.

Clockwise spiral on pearl.

Y#	Date	Mintage	VG	Fine	VF	XF
28a.1	Yr.7(1874)	—	200.00	350.00	700.00	1000.
	Yr.8(1875)	—	900.00	2000.	3200.	5200.
	Yr.11(1878)	—	100.00	200.00	400.00	720.00
	Yr.12(1879)	—	350.00	750.00	1200.	2000.
	Yr.13(1880)	—	30.00	60.00	120.00	200.00
	Yr.14(1881)	—	35.00	75.00	150.00	225.00
	Yr.15(1882)	—	15.00	35.00	75.00	135.00
	Yr.16(1883)	—	20.00	40.00	80.00	140.00
	Yr.17(1884)	—	35.00	75.00	150.00	225.00
	Yr.18(1885)	—	15.00	35.00	75.00	135.00
	Yr.19(1886)	—	20.00	40.00	80.00	140.00
	Yr.20(1887)	—	40.00	85.00	150.00	325.00

Type II, 38.1mm

Y#	Date	Mintage	VG	Fine	VF	XF
28a.2	Yr.19(1886)	—	300.00	500.00	800.00	1200.
	Yr.20(1887)	—	30.00	50.00	100.00	175.00
	Yr.21(1888)	—	12.00	25.00	45.00	75.00
	Yr.22(1889)	—	10.00	20.00	40.00	65.00
	Yr.23(1890)	—	10.00	20.00	40.00	65.00
	Yr.24(1891)	—	8.00	15.00	35.00	60.00
	Yr.25(1892) early variety					
		—	50.00	100.00	200.00	350.00
	Yr.25(1892) late variety					
		—	10.00	20.00	40.00	60.00
	Yr.26(1893)	—	10.00	20.00	40.00	60.00
	Yr.27(1894)	—	7.50	15.00	30.00	50.00
	Yr.28(1895)	—	7.50	15.00	30.00	50.00
	Yr.29(1896)	—	7.50	15.00	30.00	50.00
	Yr.30(1897)	—	10.00	20.00	40.00	60.00

Mint: Tokyo
c/m: *Gin* right on 1 Yen, Y#5.

Y#	Date	Mintage	VG	Fine	VF	XF
28.1	YR.3(1870)	—	125.00	250.00	350.00	650.00

Type I, 38.6mm
c/m: *Gin* right on 1 Yen, Y#A25.
Counterclockwise spiral on pearl.

Y#	Date	Mintage	VG	Fine	VF	XF
28a.3	Yr.7(1874)	—	250.00	400.00	800.00	1250.

Clockwise spiral on pearl.

Y#	Date	Mintage	VG	Fine	VF	XF
28a.4	Yr.7(1874)	—	200.00	350.00	750.00	1100.
	Yr.8(1875)	—	1000.	2200.	3250.	5400.
	Yr.11(1878)	—	100.00	200.00	350.00	750.00
	Yr.12(1879)	—	350.00	750.00	1250.	2000.
	Yr.13(1880)	—	30.00	60.00	125.00	200.00
	Yr.14(1881)	—	40.00	80.00	150.00	225.00
	Yr.15(1882)	—	20.00	40.00	75.00	145.00
	Yr.16(1883)	—	25.00	45.00	80.00	150.00
	Yr.17(1884)	—	35.00	75.00	150.00	225.00
	Yr.18(1885)	—	20.00	40.00	75.00	145.00
	Yr.19(1886)	—	25.00	45.00	80.00	150.00
	Yr.20(1887)	—	45.00	90.00	175.00	350.00

Type II, 38.1mm

Y#	Date	Mintage	VG	Fine	VF	XF
28a.5	Yr.19(1886)	—	350.00	550.00	850.00	1250.
	Yr.20(1887)	—	35.00	55.00	115.00	185.00
	Yr.21(1888)	—	15.00	30.00	50.00	85.00
	Yr.22(1889)	—	10.00	20.00	40.00	65.00
	Yr.23(1890)	—	10.00	20.00	40.00	65.00
	Yr.24(1891)	—	8.00	15.00	35.00	60.00
28a.5	Yr.25(1892) early variety					
		—	50.00	100.00	200.00	400.00
	Yr.25(1892) late variety					
		—	10.00	20.00	40.00	60.00
	Yr.26(1893)	—	10.00	20.00	40.00	60.00
	Yr.27(1894)	—	7.50	15.00	30.00	50.00
	Yr.28(1895)	—	7.50	15.00	30.00	50.00
	Yr.29(1896)	—	7.50	15.00	30.00	50.00
	Yr.30(1897)	—	10.00	20.00	40.00	60.00

REGULAR COINAGE

YEN

BRASS

Y#	Year	Date	Mintage	VF	XF	Unc
	Showa					
70	23	(1948)	451.209	.25	.50	2.00
	24	(1949)	Inc. Ab.	.15	.35	1.25
	25	(1950)	Inc. Ab.	.15	.35	1.25

ALUMINUM

Y#	Year	Date	Mintage	VF	XF	Unc
74	30	(1955)	381.700	—	—	.10
	31	(1956)	500.900	—	—	.10
	32	(1957)	492.000	—	—	.10
	33	(1958)	374.900	—	—	.10
	34	(1959)	208.600	—	—	.10
	35	(1960)	300.000	—	—	.10
	36	(1961)	432.400	—	—	.10
	37	(1962)	572.000	—	—	.10
	38	(1963)	788.700	—	—	.10
	39	(1964)	1665.100	—	—	.10
	40	(1965)	1743.256	—	—	.10
	41	(1966)	807.344	—	—	.10
	42	(1967)	220.600	—	—	.10
	44	(1969)	184.700	—	—	.10
	45	(1970)	556.400	—	—	.10
	46	(1971)	904.950	—	—	.10
	47	(1972)	1274.950	—	—	.10
	48	(1973)	1470.000	—	—	.10
	49	(1974)	1750.000	—	—	.10
	50	(1975)	1656.150	—	—	.10
	51	(1976)	928.800	—	—	.10
	52	(1977)	895.000	—	—	.10
	53	(1978)	864.000	—	—	.10
	54	(1979)	1015.000	—	—	.10
	55	(1980)	1145.000	—	—	.10
	56	(1981)	1206.000	—	—	.10
	57	(1982)	1017.000	—	—	.10
	58	(1983)	1086.000	—	—	.10
	59	(1984)	981.850	—	—	.10
	60	(1985)	837.150	—	—	.10
	61	(1986)	417.960	—	—	.10
	62	(1987)	955,520	—	—	.10
	62	(1987)	.230	—	Proof	1.50
	63	(1988)	1268.842	—	—	.10
	63	(1988)	.200	—	Proof	1.50
	64	(1989)	116.100	—	—	.50

Obv: Small tree.
Rev: Large 1 on wide ring in center, date below, w/Japanese *first* as third character.

Y#	Year	Date	Mintage	VF	XF	Unc
	Heisei					
95.1	1	(1989)	2366.770	—	—	.10
	1	(1989)	.200	—	Proof	1.50

Y#	Year	Date	Mintage	VF	XF	Unc
95.2	2	(1990)	2768.753	—	—	.10
	2	(1990)	.200	—	Proof	1.50
	3	(1991)	2300.900	—	—	.10
	3	(1991)	.220	—	Proof	1.50
	4	(1992)	1298.880	—	—	.10
	4	(1992)	.250	—	Proof	1.50
	5	(1993)	—	—	—	.10
	5	(1993)	—	—	Proof	1.50

2 YEN

3.3333 g, .900 GOLD, 17.48mm, .0964 oz AGW

Y#	Date	Mintage	Fine	VF	XF	Unc
	Meiji					
10	Yr.3(1870)	.883	850.00	950.00	1200.	1750.
	Yr.3(1870)	—	—	—	Proof	9500.

Reduced size 16.96mm, same weight

Y#	Date	Mintage	Fine	VF	XF	Unc
10a	Yr.7(1874)	—	Reported, not confirmed			
	Yr.9(1876)					
		178 pcs.	—	45,000.	60,000.	75,000.
	Yr.10(1877)					
		39 pcs.	—	45,000.	60,000.	75,000.
	Yr.13(1880)					
		87 pcs.	—	45,000.	60,000.	75,000.
	Yr.25(1892)	—	(none struck for circulation)			

5 YEN

8.3333 g, .900 GOLD, 23.8mm, .2411 oz AGW

Y#	Date	Mintage	Fine	VF	XF	Unc
	Meiji					
11	Yr.3(1870)	.273	1250.	1750.	2500.	3500.
	Yr.4(1871)	I.A.	1250.	1650.	2400.	3400.
	Yr.4(1871)	—	—	—	Proof	10,000.

Reduced size, 21.8mm, same weight

Y#	Date	Mintage	Fine	VF	XF	Unc
11a	Yr.5(1872)	1.057	750.00	1000.	1500.	2500.
	Yr.6(1873)	3.148	750.00	1000.	1500.	2500.
	Yr.7(1874)	.728	1500.	1800.	2500.	3500.
	Yr.8(1875)	.181	1750.	2000.	2500.	3500.
	Yr.9(1876)	.146	1850.	2100.	2850.	3750.
	Yr.10(1877)	.136	1900.	2200.	3000.	4200.
	Yr.11(1878)	.101	1900.	2200.	3000.	4200.
	Yr.13(1880)	.078	1900.	2200.	3000.	4200.
	Yr.14(1881)	.149	1900.	2200.	3000.	4200.
	Yr.15(1882)	.113	1900.	2200.	3000.	4200.
	Yr.16(1883)	.108	1900.	2200.	3000.	4200.
	Yr.17(1884)	.113	1900.	2200.	3000.	4200.
	Yr.18(1885)	.200	1900.	2200.	3000.	4200.
	Yr.19(1886)	.179	1900.	2200.	3000.	4200.
	Yr.20(1887)	.179	1900.	2200.	3000.	4200.
	Yr.21(1888)	.165	1900.	2200.	3000.	4200.
	Yr.22(1889)	.353	1900.	2200.	3000.	4200.
	Yr.23(1890)	.238	1900.	2200.	3000.	4200.
	Yr.24(1891)	.216	1900.	2200.	3000.	4200.
	Yr.25(1892)	.263	1900.	2200.	3000.	4200.
	Yr.26(1893)	.260	1900.	2200.	3000.	4200.
	Yr.27(1894)	.314	1900.	2200.	3000.	4200.
	Yr.28(1895)	.320	1900.	2200.	3000.	4200.
	Yr.29(1896)	.224	1900.	2200.	3000.	4200.
	Yr.30(1897)	.107	1900.	2200.	3000.	4200.

4.1666 g, .900 GOLD, .1205 oz AGW

Y#	Date	Mintage	Fine	VF	XF	Unc
32	Yr.30(1897)	.111	850.00	950.00	1200.	1800.
	Yr.31(1898)	.055	850.00	950.00	1200.	1800.
	Yr.36(1903)	.021	900.00	1000.	1300.	2100.

Y#	Date	Mintage	Fine	VF	XF	Unc
32	Yr.44(1911)	.059	900.00	1000.	1300.	2000.
	Yr.45(1912)	.059	850.00	1000.	1300.	2000.

Y#	Date	Mintage	Fine	VF	XF	Unc
	Taisho					
39	Yr.2(1913)	.040	950.00	1250.	1550.	2250.
	Yr.13(1924)	.076	850.00	1150.	1300.	1900.
	Showa					
51	Yr.5(1930)	.852	20,000.	35,000.	50,000.	65,000.

BRASS

Y#	Year	Date	Mintage	VF	XF	Unc
71	23	(1948)	74.520	.50	.75	12.50
	24	(1949)	179.692	.15	.40	8.00

Old script

Y#	Year	Date	Mintage	VF	XF	Unc
72	24	(1949)	111.896	.15	.25	9.00
	25	(1950)	181.824	.15	.25	6.50
	26	(1951)	197.980	.15	.25	6.50
	27	(1952)	55.000	.30	.60	15.00
	28	(1953)	45.000	.30	.60	6.50
	32	(1957)	10.000	4.00	8.00	15.00
	33	(1958)	50.000	.25	.50	3.50

New script

Y#	Year	Date	Mintage	VF	XF	Unc
72a	34	(1959)	33.000	.25	.50	3.00
	35	(1960)	34.800	.20	.40	3.00
	36	(1961)	61.000	.15	.35	2.50
	37	(1962)	126.700	.10	.30	1.50
	38	(1963)	171.800	.10	.30	1.50
	39	(1964)	379.700	.10	.30	1.50
	40	(1965)	384.200	.10	.30	1.50
	41	(1966)	163.100	.10	.30	1.50
	42	(1967)	26.000	.25	.50	1.50
	43	(1968)	114.000	—	.10	.15
	44	(1969)	240.000	—	.10	.15
	45	(1970)	340.000	—	.10	.15
	46	(1971)	362.050	—	.10	.15
	47	(1972)	562.950	—	.10	.15
	48	(1973)	745.000	—	.10	.15
	49	(1974)	950.000	—	.10	.15
	50	(1975)	970.000	—	.10	.15
	51	(1976)	200.000	—	.10	.15
	52	(1977)	340.000	—	.10	.15
	53	(1978)	318.000	—	.10	.15
	54	(1979)	317.000	—	.10	.15
	55	(1980)	385.000	—	.10	.15
	56	(1981)	95.000	—	.10	.15
	57	(1982)	455.000	—	.10	.15
	58	(1983)	410.000	—	.10	.15
	59	(1984)	202.850	—	.10	.15
	60	(1985)	153.150	—	.10	.15
	61	(1986)	113.960	—	.10	.15
	62	(1987)	631.545	—	.10	.15
	62	(1987)	.230	—	Proof	1.75
	63	(1988)	368.920	—	—	.15
	63	(1988)	.200	—	Proof	1.75
	64	(1989)	67.332	—	—	.65

Obv: Inscription and date separated by seed leaf. Japanese character *first* in date. Rev: Gear around hole, rice stalk above denomination.

Y#	Year	Date	Mintage	VF	XF	Unc
	Heisei					
96.1	1	(1989)	960.460	—	—	.35
	1	(1989)	.200	—	Proof	1.75

Y#	Year	Date	Mintage	VF	XF	Unc
96.2	2	(1990)	520.753	—	—	.35
	2	(1990)	.200	—	Proof	1.75
	3	(1991)	516.900	—	—	.35
	3	(1991)	.220	—	Proof	1.75
	4	(1992)	300.880	—	—	.35
	4	(1992)	.250	—	Proof	1.75
	5	(1993)	—	—	—	.35
	5	(1993)	—	—	Proof	1.75

10 YEN

16.6666 g, .900 GOLD, .4823 oz AGW

Y#	Date	Mintage	Fine	VF	XF	Unc
	Meiji					
12	Yr.4(1871)	1.867	3000.	3750.	4500.	6000.
	Yr.4(1871)	—	—	—	Proof	35,000.
	Modified design					
12a	Yr.9(1876)	1,925	15,000.	25,000.	54,000.	70,000.
	Yr.10(1877)	36 pcs.	20,000.	30,000.	70,000.	85,000.
	Yr.13(1880)	136 pcs.	20,000.	30,000.	70,000.	85,000.
	Yr.25(1892)	(none struck for circulation)				

8.3333 g, .900 GOLD, .2411 oz AGW

Y#	Date	Mintage	Fine	VF	XF	Unc
33	Yr.30(1897)	2.422	500.00	650.00	800.00	1200.
	Yr.31(1898)	3.176	500.00	650.00	800.00	1200.
	Yr.32(1899)	1.743	500.00	650.00	800.00	1200.
	Yr.33(1900)	1.114	500.00	650.00	800.00	1200.
	Yr.34(1901)	1.654	500.00	650.00	800.00	1200.
	Yr.35(1902)	3.023	500.00	650.00	800.00	1250.
	Yr.36(1903)	2.902	500.00	650.00	800.00	1250.
	Yr.37(1904)	.724	500.00	800.00	1250.	2100.
	Yr.40(1907)	.157	500.00	800.00	1250.	2100.
	Yr.41(1908)	1.160	500.00	650.00	800.00	1250.
	Yr.42(1909)	2.165	450.00	650.00	800.00	1200.
	Yr.43(1910)	8,982	5000.	8500.	13,500.	18,000.

BRONZE
Reeded edge

Y#	Year	Date	Mintage	VF	XF	Unc
	Showa					
73	26	(1951)	101.068	.15	.35	45.00
	27	(1952)	486.632	.15	.35	35.00
	28	(1953)	466.300	.15	.35	35.00
	29	(1954)	520.900	.15	.35	45.00
	30	(1955)	123.100	.15	.35	20.00
	32	(1957)	50.000	.25	.65	35.00
	33	(1958)	25.000	.40	1.00	45.00

Plain edge

Y#	Year	Date	Mintage	VF	XF	Unc
73a	34	(1959)	62.400	—	.15	9.00
	35	(1960)	225.900	—	.15	1.25
	36	(1961)	229.900	—	.15	1.25
	37	(1962)	284.200	—	.15	1.25
	38	(1963)	411.300	—	.15	.60
	39	(1964)	479.200	—	.15	.60
	40	(1965)	387.600	—	.15	.60
	41	(1966)	395.900	—	.15	.60
	42	(1967)	158.900	—	.15	.60
	43	(1968)	363.600	—	.15	.30
	44	(1969)	414.800	—	.15	.30
	45	(1970)	382.700	—	.15	.30
	46	(1971)	610.050	—	.15	.30
	47	(1972)	634.950	—	.15	.30
	48	(1973)	1345.000	—	.15	.20
	49	(1974)	1780.000	—	.15	.20
	50	(1975)	1280.260	—	.15	.20
	51	(1976)	1369.740	—	.15	.20
	52	(1977)	1467.000	—	.15	.20
	53	(1978)	1435.000	—	.15	.20
	54	(1979)	1207.000	—	.15	.20
	55	(1980)	1127.000	—	.15	.20
	56	(1981)	1369.000	—	.15	.20
	57	(1982)	890.000	—	.15	.20
	58	(1983)	870.000	—	.15	.20
	59	(1984)	533.850	—	.15	.20
	60	(1985)	335.150	—	.15	.20
	61	(1986)	68.960	—	.15	.50
	62	(1987)	165.545	—	.15	.20
	62	(1987)	.230	—	Proof	1.75
	63	(1988)	617.912	—	—	.20
	63	(1988)	.200	—	Proof	1.75
	64	(1989)	74.692	—	—	.75

Obv: Ancient phoenix temple Hoo-do surrounded by arabesque pattern.
Rev: Japanese character *first* in date.

Y#	Year	Date	Mintage	VF	XF	Unc
	Heisei					
97.1	1	(1989)	666.108	—	—	.45
	1	(1989)	.200	—	Proof	1.75

Y#	Year	Date	Mintage	VF	XF	Unc
97.2	2	(1990)	754.753	—	—	.45
	2	(1990)	.200	—	Proof	1.75
	3	(1991)	631.900	—	—	.45
	3	(1991)	.220	—	Proof	1.75
	4	(1992)	537.880	—	—	.45
	4	(1992)	.250	—	Proof	1.75
	5	(1993)	—	—	—	.45
	5	(1993)	—	—	Proof	1.75

20 YEN

33.3332 g, .900 GOLD, .9646 oz AGW

Y#	Date	Mintage	Fine	VF	XF	Unc
	Meiji					
13	Yr.3(1870)	.046	10,000.	16,500.	25,000.	37,500.
	Yr.3(1870)	—	—	—	Proof	57,500.
	Yr.9(1876)	954 pcs.	12,500.	21,500.	44,500.	65,000.
	Yr.10(1877)	29 pcs.	18,000.	38,000.	78,000.	110,000.
	Yr.13(1880)	103 pcs.	16,500.	35,000.	74,000.	100,000.
	Yr.25(1892)	—	(none struck for circulation)			

16.6666 g, .900 GOLD, .4823 oz AGW

Y#	Date	Mintage	Fine	VF	XF	Unc
34	Yr.30(1897)	1.861	600.00	1400.	2100.	2500.
	Yr.36(1903)	—	—	—	Rare	—
	Yr.37(1904)	2.759	600.00	1400.	2100.	2500.
	Yr.38(1905)	1.045	600.00	1400.	2100.	2500.
	Yr.39(1906)	1.331	700.00	1500.	2250.	2650.
	Yr.40(1907)	.817	700.00	1500.	2250.	2650.
	Yr.41(1908)	.458	1000.	1500.	2250.	3000.
	Yr.42(1909)	.557	1000.	1500.	2250.	3000.
	Yr.43(1910)	2.163	700.00	1400.	2100.	2500.
	Yr.44(1911)	1.470	600.00	1400.	2100.	2500.
	Yr.45(1912)	1.272	600.00	1400.	2100.	2500.

Obv: Japanese character *first* used in date.

Y#	Date	Mintage	Fine	VF	XF	Unc
	Taisho					
40.1	Yr.1(1912)	.177	750.00	1500.	2200.	2800.

Y#	Date	Mintage	Fine	VF	XF	Unc
40.2	Yr.2(1913)	.869	700.00	1400.	2100.	2400.
	Yr.3(1914)	1.042	700.00	1400.	2100.	2400.
	Yr.4(1915)	1.509	700.00	1400.	2100.	2400.
	Yr.5(1916)	2.376	700.00	1400.	2100.	2400.
	Yr.6(1917)	6.208	600.00	1500.	2000.	2400.
	Yr.7(1918)	3.118	700.00	1400.	2100.	2400.
	Yr.8(1919)	1.531	700.00	1400.	2100.	2400.
	Yr.9(1920)	.370	700.00	1400.	2100.	2550.

Y#	Date	Mintage	Fine	VF	XF	Unc
	Showa					
52	Yr.5(1930)	11.055	15,000.	25,000.	35,000.	45,000.
	Yr.6(1931)	7.526	17,500.	27,500.	37,500.	47,500.
	Yr.7(1932)	—	—	—	Rare	—

50 YEN

NICKEL

Y#	Year	Date	Mintage	VF	XF	Unc
	Showa					
75	30	(1955)	63.700	.50	1.00	17.50
	31	(1956)	91.300	.50	.75	17.50
	32	(1957)	39.000	.50	1.25	17.50
	33	(1958)	18.000	1.00	2.50	30.00

Y#	Year	Date	Mintage	VF	XF	Unc
76	34	(1959)	23.900	1.00	2.50	15.00
	35	(1960)	6.000	12.50	22.50	32.50
	36	(1961)	16.000	2.00	4.00	17.50
	37	(1962)	50.300	.50	1.00	5.00
	38	(1963)	55.000	.50	1.00	5.00
	39	(1964)	69.200	.50	1.00	4.00
	40	(1965)	189.300	.50	1.00	3.00
	41	(1966)	171.500	.50	1.00	2.50

COPPER-NICKEL

Y#	Year	Date	Mintage	VF	XF	Unc
81	42	(1967)	238.400	—	.50	.65
	43	(1968)	200.000	—	.50	.65
	44	(1969)	210.900	—	.50	.65
	45	(1970)	269.800	—	.50	.65
	46	(1971)	80.950	—	.50	.65
	47	(1972)	138.980	—	.50	.65
	48	(1973)	200.970	—	.50	.65
	49	(1974)	470.000	—	.50	.65
	50	(1975)	238.120	—	.50	.65
	51	(1976)	241.880	—	.50	.65
	52	(1977)	176.000	—	.50	.65
	53	(1978)	234.000	—	.50	.65
	54	(1979)	110.000	—	.50	.65
	55	(1980)	51.000	—	.50	.65
	56	(1981)	179.000	—	.50	.65
	57	(1982)	30.000	—	.50	.65
	58	(1983)	30.000	—	.50	.65
	59	(1984)	29.850	—	.50	.65
	60	(1985)	10.150	—	.50	.65
	61	(1986)	9.960	—	.50	.65
	62	(1987)	.545	—	—	70.00
	62	(1987)	.230	—	Proof	75.00
	63	(1988)	108.912	—	—	.65
	63	(1988)	.200	—	Proof	2.00

Obv: Japanese character *first* in date.

Y#	Year	Date	Mintage	VF	XF	Unc
	Heisei					
101.1	1	(1989)	244.800	—	—	.65
	1	(1989)	.200	—	Proof	2.00

Y#	Year	Date	Mintage	VF	XF	Unc
101.2	2	(1990)	274.753	—	—	.65
	2	(1990)	.200	—	Proof	2.00
	3	(1991)	208.900	—	—	.65
	3	(1991)	.220	—	Proof	2.00
	4	(1992)	48.880	—	—	.65
	4	(1992)	.250	—	Proof	2.00
101.2	5	(1993)	—	—	—	.65
	5	(1993)	—	—	Proof	2.00

100 YEN

4.8000 g, .600 SILVER .0926 oz ASW

Y#	Year	Date	Mintage	VF	XF	Unc
	Showa					
77	32	(1957)	30.000	1.00	2.00	9.00
	33	(1958)	70.000	1.00	2.00	6.00

Y#	Year	Date	Mintage	VF	XF	Unc
78	34	(1959)	110.000	1.00	2.00	9.00
	35	(1960)	50.000	1.00	2.00	9.00
	36	(1961)	15.000	1.00	2.00	9.00
	38	(1963)	45.000	1.00	2.00	6.00
	39	(1964)	10.000	1.25	3.50	6.00
	40	(1965)	62.500	1.00	2.00	3.75
	41	(1966)	97.500	1.00	2.00	3.75

1964 Olympic Games

Y#	Year	Date	Mintage	VF	XF	Unc
79	39	1964	80.000	1.00	2.00	3.50

COPPER-NICKEL

Y#	Year	Date	Mintage	VF	XF	Unc
82	42	(1967)	432.200	—	1.00	1.50
	43	(1968)	471.000	—	1.00	1.50
	44	(1969)	323.700	—	1.00	1.50
	45	(1970)	237.100	—	1.00	1.50
	46	(1971)	481.050	—	1.00	1.50
	47	(1972)	468.950	—	1.00	1.50
	48	(1973)	680.000	—	1.00	1.50
	49	(1974)	660.000	—	1.00	1.50
	50	(1975)	437.160	—	1.00	1.50
	51	(1976)	322.840	—	1.00	1.50
	52	(1977)	440.000	—	1.00	1.50
	53	(1978)	292.000	—	1.00	1.50
	54	(1979)	382.000	—	1.00	1.50
	55	(1980)	588.000	—	1.00	1.50
	56	(1981)	348.000	—	1.00	1.50
	57	(1982)	110.000	—	1.00	1.50
	58	(1983)	50.000	—	1.00	1.50
	59	(1984)	41.850	—	1.00	1.50
	60	(1985)	58.150	—	1.00	1.50
	61	(1986)	99.960	—	1.00	1.50
	62	(1987)	193.545	—	1.00	1.50
	62	(1987)	.230	—	Proof	5.00
	63	(1988)	362.912	—	1.00	1.50
	63	(1988)	.200	—	Proof	5.00

NOTE: Varieties exist for Yr.42.

Osaka Expo '70

Y#	Year	Date	Mintage	VF	XF	Unc
83	45	(1970)	40.000	1.25	2.25	5.00

Winter Olympic Games - Sapporo

Y#	Year	Date	Mintage	VF	XF	Unc
84	47	1972	30.000	3.00	5.00	7.50

Okinawa Expo '75

Y#	Year	Date	Mintage	VF	XF	Unc
85	50	(1975)	120.000	1.00	1.50	2.00

50th Anniversary of Reign

Y#	Year	Date	Mintage	VF	XF	Unc
86	51	(1976)	70.000	1.25	2.50	4.50

Rev: Japanese character *first* in date.

Heisei

Y#	Year	Date	Mintage	VF	XF	Unc
98.1	1	(1989)	368.800	—	—	1.50
	1	(1989)	.200	—	Proof	5.00

Y#	Year	Date	Mintage	VF	XF	Unc
98.2	2	(1990)	444.753	—	—	1.50
	2	(1990)	.200	—	Proof	5.00
	3	(1991)	374.900	—	—	1.50
	3	(1991)	.220	—	Proof	5.00
	4	(1992)	211.050	—	—	1.50
	4	(1992)	.250	—	Proof	5.00
	5	(1993)	—	—	—	1.50
	5	(1993)	—	—	Proof	5.00

500 YEN

COPPER-NICKEL

Showa

Y#	Year	Date	Mintage	VF	XF	Unc
87	57	(1982)	300.000	—	4.50	5.50
	58	(1983)	240.000	—	4.50	5.50
	59	(1984)	342.850	—	4.50	5.50
	60	(1985)	97.150	—	4.50	5.50
	61	(1986)	49.960	—	4.25	5.00
	62	(1987)	2.545	5.00	7.00	10.00
	62	(1987)	.230	—	Proof	25.00
	63	(1988)	148.018	—	—	5.00
	63	(1988)	.200	—	Proof	10.00
	64	(1989)	16.042	—	—	10.00

1985 Tsukuba Expo

Y#	Year	Date	Mintage	VF	XF	Unc
88	60	(1985)	70.000	—	4.50	6.00

100th Anniversary - Governmental Cabinet System

Y#	Year	Date	Mintage	VF	XF	Unc
89	60	(1985)	70.000	—	4.50	6.00

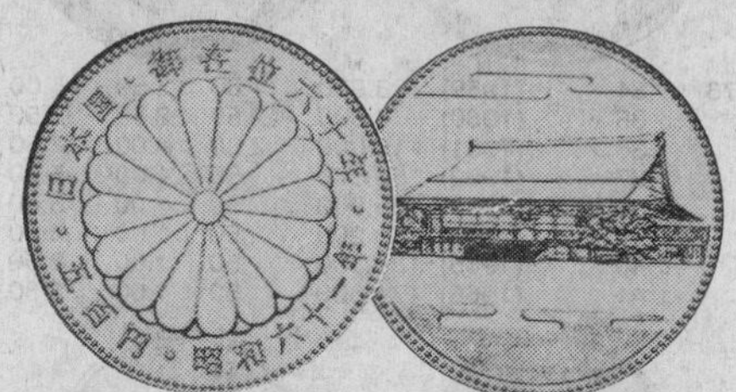

60 Years of Reign of Hirohito

Y#	Year	Date	Mintage	VF	XF	Unc
90	61	(1986)	50.000	—	4.50	6.00

Opening of Seikan Tunnel

Y#	Year	Date	Mintage	VF	XF	Unc
93	63	(1988)	20.000	—	—	8.00

Opening of Seto Bridge

Y#	Year	Date	Mintage	VF	XF	Unc
94	63	(1988)	20.000	—	—	8.00

Rev: Japanese character *first* in date.

Heisei

Y#	Year	Date	Mintage	VF	XF	Unc
99.1	1	(1989)	192.652	—	—	5.00
	1	(1989)	.200	—	Proof	10.00
99.2	2	(1990)	159.753	—	—	5.00
	2	(1990)	.200	—	Proof	10.00
	3	(1991)	169.900	—	—	5.00
	3	(1991)	.220	—	Proof	10.00
	4	(1992)	87.880	—	—	5.00
	4	(1992)	.250	—	Proof	10.00
	5	(1993)	—	—	—	5.00
	5	(1993)	—	—	Proof	10.00

Enthronement of Emperor Akihito

Y#	Year	Date	Mintage	VF	XF	Unc
102	2	(1990)	30.000	—	—	10.00

20th Anniversary - Reversion of Okinawa

Y#	Year	Date	Mintage	VF	XF	Unc
106	4	(1992)	19.053	—	—	12.00
	4	(1992)	.047	—	Proof	25.00

Royal Wedding of Crown Prince

Y#	Year	Date	Mintage	VF	XF	Unc
107	5	(1993)	30.000	—	—	10.00
	5	(1993)	.200	—	Proof	20.00

1000 YEN

20.0000 g, .925 SILVER, .5948 oz ASW
1964 Olympic Games

Showa

Y#	Year	Date	Mintage	VF	XF	Unc
80	39	1964	15.000	20.00	30.00	45.00

5000 YEN

15.0000 g, .925 SILVER, .4461 oz ASW
Osaka Exposition

Heisei

Y#	Year	Date	Mintage	VF	XF	Unc
100	2	1990	10.000	—	—	55.00

Centennial of Parliament

Y#	Year	Date	Mintage	VF	XF	Unc
103	2	(1990)	5.000	—	—	55.00

Centennial of Judicial System

Y#	Year	Date	Mintage	VF	XF	Unc
104	2	(1990)	5.000	—	—	55.00

15.000 g, 1.000 SILVER, .4823 oz ASW
Royal Wedding of Crown Prince

Y#	Year	Date	Mintage	VF	XF	Unc
108	5	(1993)	4.800	—	—	60.00
	5	(1993)	.200	—	Proof	100.00

10000 YEN

20.0000 g, .999 SILVER, .6430 oz ASW
60 Years of Reign of Hirohito

Y#	Year	Date	Mintage	VF	XF	Unc
91	61	(1986)	10.000	—	—	100.00

50,000 YEN

18.0000 g, 1.000 GOLD, .5788 oz AGW
Royal Wedding of Crown Prince

Y#	Year	Date	Mintage	VF	XF	Unc
109	5	(1993)	1.800	—	—	600.00
	5	(1993)	.100	—	Proof	850.00

100000 YEN

20.0000 g, .999 GOLD, .6430 oz AGW
60 Years of Reign of Hirohito

Y#	Year	Date	Mintage	VF	XF	Unc
92	61	(1986)	10.000	—	—	850.00
	62	(1987)	.876	—	—	850.00
	62	(1987)	.125	—	Proof	1000.

30.0000 g, .999 GOLD, .9646 oz AGW
Entbronement of Emperor Akihito

Y#	Year	Date	Mintage	VF	XF	Unc
	Heisei					
105	2	(1990)	1.900	—	—	850.00
	2	(1990)	.100	—	Proof	1200.

OCCUPATION COINAGE

The following issues were struck at the Osaka Mint for use in the Netherlands East Indies. The only inscription found on them is *Dai Nippon:* (Great Japan). The war situation had worsened to the point that shipping the coins became virtually impossible. Consequently, none of these coins were issued in the East Indies and almost the entire issue was lost or were remelted at the mint. Y#'s are for the Netherlands Indies and dates are from the Japanese Shinto dynastic calendar.

SEN

ALUMINUM

Y#	Date	Year	Mintage	VF	XF	Unc
22	2603	1943	233.190	75.00	100.00	150.00
	2604	1944	66.810	65.00	90.00	125.00

NOTE: 5 Sen listed as Pn48.

10 SEN

TIN ALLOY

Y#	Date	Year	Mintage	VF	XF	Unc
24	2603	1943	69.490	25.00	50.00	100.00
	2604	1944	110.510	20.00	40.00	75.00

TRADE COINAGE

TRADE DOLLAR

27.2200 g, .900 SILVER, .7876 oz ASW

Y#	Date	Mintage	Fine	VF	XF	Unc
	Meiji					
14	Yr.8(1875)	.097	300.00	650.00	1000.	2500.
	Yr.9(1876)	1.514	300.00	650.00	1000.	2500.
	Yr.10(1877)	1.125	300.00	650.00	1000.	2750.

'GIN' COUNTERMARKS

Mint: Osaka
c/m: *Gin* left on Trade Dollar, Y#14.

Y#	Date	Mintage	VG	Fine	VF	XF
28b.1	Yr.8(1875)	—	150.00	300.00	500.00	700.00
	Yr.9(1876)	—	150.00	300.00	500.00	700.00
	Yr.10(1877)	—	150.00	300.00	500.00	750.00

Mint: Tokyo
c/m: *Gin* right on Trade Dollar, Y#14.

Y#	Date	Mintage	VG	Fine	VF	XF
28b.2	Yr.8(1875)	—	175.00	350.00	550.00	750.00
	Yr.9(1876)	—	175.00	350.00	550.00	750.00
	Yr.10(1877)	—	175.00	350.00	550.00	800.00

MINT SETS (MS)

KM#	Date	Mintage	Identification	Issue Price	Mkt. Val.
MS1	1969(5)	6,162	Y72A,73A,74,81,82	1.25	650.00
MS2	1970(6)	26,000	Y72a,73A,74,81,82,83	2.00	50.00
MS3	1971(5)	14,653	Y72a,73a,74,81,82	1.60	115.00
MS4	1972(6)	30,000	Y72a,73a,74,81,82,84	2.90	50.00
MS5	1975(5)	720,000	Y72a,73a,74,81,82	2.30	5.00
MS6	1976(5)	580,000	Y72a,73a,74,81,82	2.80	5.00
MS7	1977(5)	520,000	Y72a,73a,74,81,82	3.00	7.50
MS8	1978(5)	488,000	Y72a,73a,74,81,82	3.50	7.50
MS9	1979(5)	400,000	Y72a,73a,74,81,82	3.80	9.00
MS10	1980(5)	520,000	Y72a,73a,74,81,82	3.20	8.00
MS11	1981(5)	568,000	Y72a,73a,74,81,82	4.00	7.50
MS12	1982(6)	632,000	Y72a,73a,74,81,82,87	6.80	9.00
MS13	1983(6)	502,000	Y72a,73a,74,81,82,87	6.80	25.00
MS14	1984(6)	520,000	Y72a,73a,74,81,82,87	7.40	25.00
MS15	1985(7)	720,000	Y72a-73a,74,81-82,87-88	8.50	20.00
MS16	1985(7)	102,000	Y72a-73a,74,81-82,87-88 Tsukuba Expo box	8.50	60.00
MS17	1985(7)	746,000	Y72a-73a,74,81-82,87,89	10.50	20.00
MS18	1986(7)	642,000	Y72a-73a,74,81-82,87,90	15.00	20.00
MS19	1986(6)	517,000	Y72a-73a,74,81-82,87	9.20	12.00
MS20	1987(6)	545,000	Y72a-73a,74,81-82,87	12.00	125.00
MS21	1987(6)	Inc. Ab.	Y72a-73a,74,81-82,87 cherry blossom box	12.00	135.00
MS22	1988(6)	605,021	Y72a-73a,74,81-82,87	12.40	15.00
MS23	1988(6)	41,979	Y72a-73a,74,81-82,87 cherry blossom box	12.40	20.00
MS24	1988(2)	400,000	Y93-94	15.20	20.00
MS25	1989(6)	647,000	Y95-99,101	12.80	30.00
MS26	1990(6)	600,000	Y95-99,101	—	30.00
MS27	1991(6)	600,000	Y95-99,101	13.00	14.00
MS28	1991(6)	10,000	Y95-99,101, Hiroshima cherry blossom box	13.60	60.00
MS29	1991(6)	50,000	Y95-99,101, Osaka cherry blossom box	13.60	24.00
MS30	1991(6)	40,000	Y95-99,101, 120th Anniversary box	13.60	20.00
MS31	1992(7)	650,000	Y95-99,101,106	18.40	25.00
MS32	1992(6)	20,000	Y95-99,101, Hiroshima cherry blossom box	13.60	30.00

KM#	Date	Mintage	Identification	Issue Price	Mkt. Val.
MS33	1992(6)	50,000	Y95-99,101, Osaka cherry blossom box	13.60	25.00
MS34	1992(6)	30,000	Y95-99,101, Toyama expo box	13.60	30.00
MS35	1993(7)	800,000	Y95-99,101,107	22.50	35.00
MS36	1993(6)	70,000	Y95-99,101, Osaka cherry blossom box	17.10	35.00
MS37	1993(6)	30,000	Y95-99,101, Hiroshima cherry blossom box	17.10	35.00
MS38	1993(6)	10,000	Y95-99,101, Tokyo coin expo box	17.10	45.00
MS39	1993(6)	30,000	Y95-99,101, Nagano Shinano expo box	17.10	30.00
MS40	1993(6)	100,000	Y95-99,101, Respect for the aged box	19.80	30.00
MS41	1993(3)	100,000	Y107-109	—	670.00
MS42	1993(2)	100,000	Y107-108	—	70.00

PROOF SETS (PS)

KM#	Date	Mintage	Identification	Issue Price	Mkt. Val.
PS1	1987(6)	230,000	Y72a-73a,74,81-82,87	37.40	150.00
PS2	1988(6)	200,000	Y72a-73a,74,81-82,87	46.50	75.00
PS3	1989(6)	200,000	Y95-99,101	47.90	75.00
PS4	1990(6)	200,000	Y95-99,101	47.90	75.00
PS5	1991(6)	220,000	Y95-99,101	58.75	75.00
PS6	1992(6)	250,000	Y95-99,101	55.65	80.00
PS7	1993(6)	—	Y95-99,101	—	80.00

PROVINCIAL COINAGE

AKITA

Capital city of Ugo Province (now Akita Prefecture) in northwest Honshu.

50 MON

LEAD or COPPER-PLATED LEAD

KM#	Date	Mintage	VG	Fine	VF	XF
2	ND(1862)	—	50.00	80.00	120.00	150.00

100 MON

COPPER

KM#	Date	Mintage	VG	Fine	VF	XF
4	ND(1862)	—	40.00	60.00	90.00	125.00

Obv: Short tail phoenix.

KM#	Date	Mintage	VG	Fine	VF	XF
6.1	ND(1862)	—	30.00	55.00	85.00	120.00

Obv: Long tail phoenix.

KM#	Date	Mintage	VG	Fine	VF	XF
6.2	ND(1862)	—	30.00	55.00	85.00	120.00

LEAD or COPPER-PLATED LEAD

KM#	Date	Mintage	VG	Fine	VF	XF
8	ND(1866)	—	50.00	80.00	120.00	150.00

BU

SILVER

KM#	Date	Mintage	VG	Fine	VF	XF
9	ND	—	1000.	1500.	2000.	2500.

4 MOMME 6 FUN

SILVER

KM#	Date	Mintage	VG	Fine	VF	XF
10	ND(1863)	—	125.00	250.00	350.00	450.00

9 MOMME 2 FUN

SILVER

KM#	Date	Mintage	VG	Fine	VF	XF
12	ND(1863)	—	400.00	600.00	750.00	900.00

HAKODATE

City on the southern end of Hokkaido. One of the ports opened by Perry's Treaty of 1854.

MON

IRON

Obv: 4 characters around round hole.
Rev: 1 character above hole.

KM#	Date	Mintage	VG	Fine	VF	XF
20	ND(1856)	—	3.00	6.00	12.00	25.00

COPPER

KM#	Date	Mintage	VG	Fine	VF	XF
20a	ND(1856)	—	—	—	100.00	175.00

NOTE: KM#20a is the *bosen* or mother coin used in

manufacturing KM#20.

HOSOKURA

A lead mining district in Rikuchu Province (now Iwate Prefecture) in northern Honshu.

100 MON

LEAD

KM#	Date	Mintage	VG	Fine	VF	XF
30	ND(1863)	—	150.00	250.00	400.00	500.00

KAGA

City and province (now Ishikawa Prefecture) on the Asian side of central Honshu.

NAN RYO

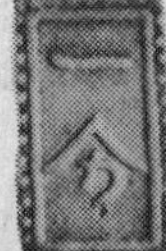

SILVER

KM#	Date	Mintage	VG	Fine	VF	XF
35	ND	—	1250.	1750.	2500.	3500.

MIMASAKA

Province in western Honshu, now part of Okayama Prefecture.

BU

SILVER

KM#	Date	Mintage	VG	Fine	VF	XF
46	ND	—	1200.	2000.	2750.	3500.

MORIOKA

Chief city of Rikuchu Province (now Iwate Prefecture) in northern Honshu.

100 MON

COPPER

KM#	Date	Mintage	VG	Fine	VF	XF
50	ND	—	800.00	1600.	2400.	3250.

8 MOMME

SILVER

KM#	Date	Mintage	VG	Fine	VF	XF
52	(1868)	—	1000.	1500.	2000.	2500.

SENDAI

Chief city of Rikuzen Province (now part of Miyagi Prefecture) in northern Honshu.

MON

IRON
Rev: Blank.

KM#	Date	Mintage	VG	Fine	VF	XF
60	ND(1784)	—	7.50	10.00	15.00	30.00

COPPER

KM#	Date	Mintage	VG	Fine	VF	XF
60a	ND(1784)	—	—	—	100.00	150.00

NOTE: KM#60a is the *bosen* or mother coin used in making the sand molds for casting KM#60.

TAJIMA

Province, now part of Hyogo Prefecture, on the Asian side of western Honshu.

NAN RYO

SILVER

KM#	Date	Mintage	VG	Fine	VF	XF
65	ND	—	1000.	1500.	2000.	2750.

TOSA

Province encompassing most of the southern coast of Shikoku, now Kochi Prefecture.

100 MON

COPPER

KM#	Date	Mintage	VG	Fine	VF	XF
70	ND(1865)	—	—	—	Rare	—

200 MON

COPPER

KM#	Date	Mintage	VG	Fine	VF	XF
72	ND(1865)	—	—	—	Rare	—

NOTE: A total of 8 types are reported for Tosa Province.

YONEZAWA

City in Uzen Province (now in Yamagata Prefecture) in north-central Honshu.

200 MON

LEAD

KM#	Date	Mintage	VG	Fine	VF	XF
80	ND(1866)	—	80.00	125.00	200.00	300.00

KM#	Date	Mintage	VG	Fine	VF	XF
82	ND(1866)	—	100.00	200.00	275.00	350.00

RYUKYU ISLANDS

OKINAWA
(Also called Liu-kiu and Loo-choo)

100 MON

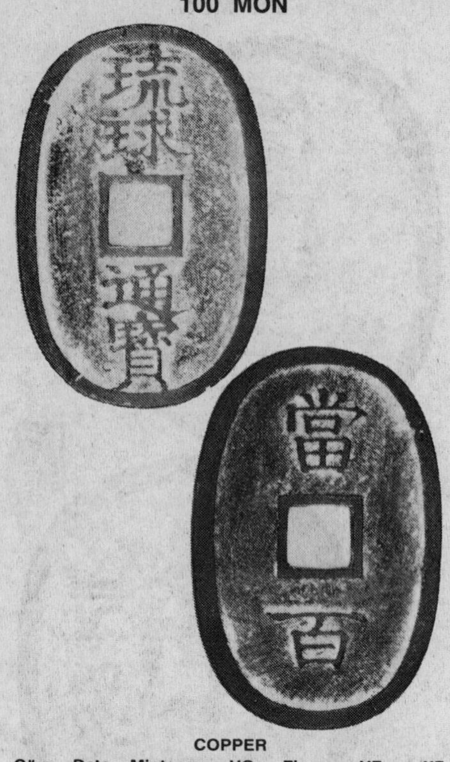

COPPER

C#	Date	Mintage	VG	Fine	VF	XF
100	ND(1862)	—	17.50	30.00	45.00	65.00

1/2 SHU

COPPER

C#	Date	Mintage	VG	Fine	VF	XF
115	ND(1862)	—	30.00	45.00	60.00	100.00

JERSEY

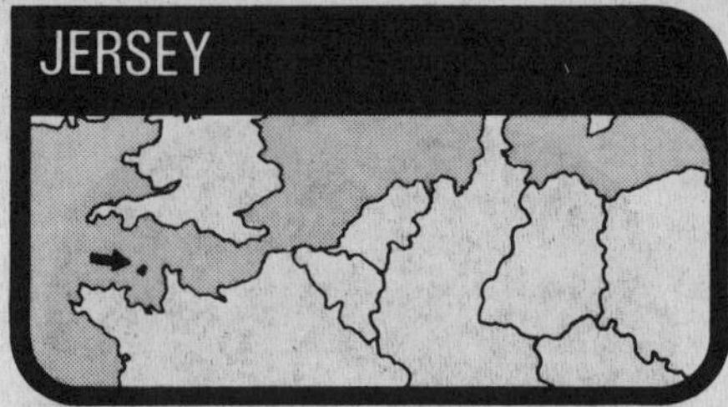

The Bailwick of Jersey, a British Crown dependency located in the English Channel 12 miles (19 km.) west of Normandy, France, has an area of 45 sq. mi. (117 sq. km.) and a population of 74,000. Capital: St. Helier. The economy is based on agriculture and cattle breeding - the importation of cattle is prohibited to protect the purity of the island's world-famous strain of milch cows.

Jersey was occupied by Neanderthal man 100,000 B.C., and by Iberians of 2000 B.C. who left their chamber tombs in the island's granite cliffs. Roman legions almost certainly visited the island although they left no evidence of settlement. The country folk of Jersey still speak an archaic form of Norman-French, lingering evidence of the Norman annexation of the island in 933 A.D. Jersey was annexed to England in 1206, 140 years after the Norman Conquest. The dependency is administered by its own laws and customs; laws enacted by the British Parliament do not apply to Jersey unless it is specifically mentioned. During World War II, German troops occupied the island from July 1, 1940 until May 9, 1945.

Coins of pre-Roman Gaul and of Rome have been found in abundance on Jersey.

RULERS

British

MINT MARKS

H - Heaton, Birmingham

MONETARY SYSTEM

Until 1877

13 Pence (Jersey) = 1 Shilling

Commencing 1877

12 Pence = 1 Shilling

5 Shillings = 1 Crown

20 Shillings = 1 Pound

1/52 SHILLING

COPPER

KM#	Date	Mintage	Fine	VF	XF	Unc
1	1841/0	.116	10.00	30.00	80.00	160.00
	1841	—	—	—	Proof	500.00
	1861	—	—	—	Proof	650.00

BRONZE

KM#	Date	Mintage	Fine	VF	XF	Unc
1a	1861	—	—	—	Proof	Rare

1/48 SHILLING

BRONZE

KM#	Date	Mintage	Fine	VF	XF	Unc
6	1877H	*.288	12.00	30.00	60.00	120.00
	1877H	—	—	—	Proof	200.00
	1877	—	—	—	Proof	225.00

***NOTE:** Issue withdrawn except for 38,400 pieces.

1/26 SHILLING

COPPER

KM#	Date	Mintage	Fine	VF	XF	Unc
2	1841	.233	2.50	12.00	40.00	100.00
	1841	—	—	—	Proof	650.00
	1844	.233	3.00	12.00	40.00	100.00
	1851	.160	3.00	12.00	40.00	100.00
	1858	.173	3.00	12.00	40.00	100.00
	1858	—	—	—	Proof	650.00
	1861	.173	3.00	12.00	40.00	100.00
	1861	—	—	—	Proof	650.00

BRONZE

KM#	Date	Mintage	Fine	VF	XF	Unc
4	1866	.173	1.00	6.00	30.00	50.00
	1866	—	—	—	Proof	225.00
	1870	.160	3.00	12.00	40.00	60.00
	1870	—	—	—	Proof	350.00
	1871	.160	2.00	10.00	35.00	55.00
	1871	—	—	—	Proof	350.00

1/24 SHILLING

BRONZE

KM#	Date	Mintage	Fine	VF	XF	Unc
7	1877H	.336	1.25	5.00	12.50	30.00
	1877H	—	—	—	Proof	200.00
	1877	—	—	—	Proof	250.00
	1888	.120	1.25	5.00	12.50	30.00
	1894	.120	1.25	5.00	12.50	30.00
	1894	—	—	—	Proof	400.00

KM#	Date	Mintage	Fine	VF	XF	Unc
9	1909	.120	1.00	3.00	12.00	25.00

KM#	Date	Mintage	Fine	VF	XF	Unc
11	1911	.072	1.00	3.00	12.00	25.00
	1913	.072	1.00	3.00	12.00	25.00
	1923	.072	1.00	3.00	12.00	25.00

KM#	Date	Mintage	Fine	VF	XF	Unc
13	1923	.072	.75	4.00	6.00	22.50
	1923	—	—	—	Proof	550.00
	1926	.120	.75	3.00	5.00	20.00
	1926	—	—	—	Proof	550.00

KM#	Date	Mintage	Fine	VF	XF	Unc
15	1931	.072	.50	1.00	3.50	15.00
	1931	—	—	—	Proof	165.00
	1933	.072	.50	1.00	3.50	15.00
	1933	—	—	—	Proof	165.00
	1935	.072	.50	1.00	3.50	15.00
	1935	—	—	—	Proof	165.00

KM#	Date	Mintage	Fine	VF	XF	Unc
17	1937	.072	.50	1.00	3.50	15.00
	1937	—	—	—	Proof	125.00
	1946	.072	.50	1.00	3.50	15.00
	1946	—	—	—	Proof	125.00
	1947	.072	.50	1.00	3.50	15.00
	1947	—	—	—	Proof	125.00

1/13 SHILLING

COPPER

KM#	Date	Mintage	Fine	VF	XF	Unc
3	1841	.116	1.00	13.50	50.00	175.00
	1841	—	—	—	Proof	800.00
	1844	.027	3.00	20.00	65.00	225.00
	1844	—	—	—	Proof	800.00
	1851	.160	1.50	13.50	50.00	160.00
	1851	—	—	—	Proof	800.00
	1858	.173	1.50	13.50	50.00	180.00
	1858	—	—	—	Proof	600.00
	1861	.173	1.50	13.50	50.00	160.00
	1861	—	—	—	Proof	600.00
	1865	—	—	—	Proof	350.00

BRONZE

KM#	Date	Mintage	Fine	VF	XF	Unc
5	1866	.173	1.00	6.50	35.00	100.00
	1866	—	—	—	Proof	225.00
	1866 w/o LCW on bust	—	—	—	Proof	250.00
	1870	.160	1.00	6.50	35.00	100.00
	1870	—	—	—	Proof	225.00
	1871	.160	1.00	6.50	35.00	100.00
	1871	—	—	—	Proof	325.00

1/12 SHILLING

BRONZE

KM#	Date	Mintage	Fine	VF	XF	Unc
8	1877H	.240	.50	3.00	15.00	50.00
	1877H	—	—	—	Proof	250.00
	1877	—	—	—	Proof	300.00
	1881	.075	1.00	7.00	27.50	65.00
	1888	.180	.50	3.00	15.00	50.00
	1894	.180	.50	3.00	15.00	50.00
	1894	—	—	—	Proof	400.00

KM#	Date	Mintage	Fine	VF	XF	Unc
10	1909	.180	.50	3.00	15.00	60.00

KM#	Date	Mintage	Fine	VF	XF	Unc
12	1911	.204	.25	1.50	7.00	35.00
	1913	.204	.25	1.50	7.00	35.00
	1923	.204	.25	1.50	7.00	35.00

KM#	Date	Mintage	Fine	VF	XF	Unc
14	1923	.301	.25	1.50	7.00	30.00
	1926	.083	.50	2.50	10.00	40.00

KM#	Date	Mintage	Fine	VF	XF	Unc
16	1931	.204	.25	1.00	3.50	12.00
	1931	—	—	—	Proof	125.00
	1933	.204	.25	1.00	3.50	12.00
	1933	—	—	—	Proof	125.00
	1935	.204	.25	1.00	3.50	12.00
	1935	—	—	—	Proof	125.00

KM#	Date	Mintage	Fine	VF	XF	Unc
18	1937	.204	.25	.50	3.00	10.00
	1937	—	—	—	Proof	125.00
	1946	.204	.25	.50	3.00	10.00
	1946	—	—	—	Proof	125.00
	1947	.444	.15	.25	1.50	7.50
	1947	—	—	—	Proof	125.00

Liberation Commemorative

KM#	Date	Mintage	Fine	VF	XF	Unc
19	1945	1.000	.15	.35	.75	5.00
	1945	—	—	—	Proof	100.00

NOTE: Struck between 1949-52.

KM#	Date	Mintage	Fine	VF	XF	Unc
20	1945	.720	.15	.25	.60	3.50
	1945	—	—	—	Proof	100.00

NOTE: Struck 1954.

KM#	Date	Mintage	Fine	VF	XF	Unc
21	1957	.720	.10	.15	.25	2.50
	1957	2,100	—	—	Proof	7.50
	1964	1.200	.10	.15	.25	1.00
	1964	.020	—	—	Proof	2.00

300th Anniversary of Accession of King Charles II

KM#	Date	Mintage	Fine	VF	XF	Unc
23	1960	1.200	.10	.15	.25	1.50
	1960	4,200	—	—	Proof	4.00

Mule. Obv: KM#20. Rev: KM#23.

KM#	Date	Mintage	Fine	VF	XF	Unc
24	1960	—	—	—	Proof	65.00

Norman Conquest

KM#	Date	Mintage	Fine	VF	XF	Unc
26	1966	1.200	.10	.15	.25	1.00
	1966	.030	—	—	Proof	2.00

1/4 SHILLING

(3 Pence)

NICKEL-BRASS

KM#	Date	Mintage	Fine	VF	XF	Unc
22	1957	2.000	.10	.15	.50	3.00
	1957	6,300	—	—	Proof	7.50
	1960	4,200	—	—	Proof	8.50

KM#	Date	Mintage	Fine	VF	XF	Unc
25	1964	1.200	.10	.15	.20	.75
	1964	.020	—	—	Proof	2.00

Norman Conquest

KM#	Date	Mintage	Fine	VF	XF	Unc
27	1966	1.200	.10	.15	.35	1.25
	1966	.030	—	—	Proof	2.00

5 SHILLINGS

COPPER-NICKEL
Norman Conquest
Obv: Similar to 1/4 Shilling, KM#12.

KM#	Date	Mintage	Fine	VF	XF	Unc
28	1966	.300	—	1.00	1.25	2.25
	1966	.030	—	—	Proof	5.00

DECIMAL COINAGE

100 New Pence = 1 Pound

Many of the following coins are also struck in silver, gold and platinum for collectors.

1/2 NEW PENNY

BRONZE

KM#	Date	Mintage	VF	XF	Unc
29	1971	3.000	—	.10	.20
	1980	.200	—	.10	.20
	1980	.010	—	Proof	1.35

1/2 PENNY

BRONZE

KM#	Date	Mintage	VF	XF	Unc
45	1981	.050	—	—	.10
	1981	.015	—	Proof	.90

NEW PENNY

BRONZE

KM#	Date	Mintage	VF	XF	Unc
30	1971	4.500	—	.10	.20
	1980	3.000	—	.10	.20
	1980	.010	—	Proof	1.80

PENNY

BRONZE

KM#	Date	Mintage	VF	XF	Unc
46	1981	.050	—	.10	.15
	1981	.015	—	Proof	1.10

Le Hocq Watch Tower, St. Clement

KM#	Date	Mintage	VF	XF	Unc
54	1983	.500	—	.10	.25
	1984	1.000	—	.10	.25
	1985	1.000	—	.10	.25
	1986	2.000	—	.10	.25
	1987	1.500	—	.10	.25
	1988	1.000	—	.10	.25
	1989	1.500	—	.10	.25
	1990	—	—	.10	.25
	1992	—	In sets only		.50

4.2000 g, .925 SILVER, .1249 oz ASW

KM#	Date	Mintage	VF	XF	Unc
54a	1983	5,000	—	Proof	5.00

2 NEW PENCE

BRONZE

KM#	Date	Mintage	VF	XF	Unc
31	1971	2.225	—	.10	.30
	1975	.750	—	.10	.40
	1980	2.000	—	.10	.30
	1980	.010	—	Proof	2.25

2 PENCE

BRONZE

KM#	Date	Mintage	VF	XF	Unc
47	1981	.050	—	.10	.20
	1981	.015	—	Proof	1.35

L'Hermitage, St. Helier

KM#	Date	Mintage	VF	XF	Unc
55	1983	.800	—	.10	.25
	1984	.750	—	.10	.25
	1985	.250	—	.10	.25
	1986	1.000	—	.10	.25
	1987	2.000	—	.10	.25
	1988	.750	—	.10	.25
	1989	1.000	—	.10	.25
	1990	2.600	—	.10	.25
	1992	—	In sets only		.50

8.4000 g, .925 SILVER, .2498 oz ASW

KM#	Date	Mintage	VF	XF	Unc
55a	1983	5,000	—	Proof	10.00

5 NEW PENCE

COPPER-NICKEL

KM#	Date	Mintage	VF	XF	Unc
32	1968	3.600	.10	.15	.50
	1980	.800	.10	.15	.50
	1980	.010	—	Proof	2.75

5 PENCE

COPPER-NICKEL

KM#	Date	Mintage	VF	XF	Unc
48	1981	.050	—	.10	.25
	1981	.015	—	Proof	1.80

Seymour Tower, Grouville, L'Avathison

KM#	Date	Mintage	VF	XF	Unc
56.1	1983	.400	—	.10	.25
	1984	.300	—	.10	.25
	1985	.600	—	.10	.25
	1986	.200	—	.10	.25
	1987	—	In sets only		.50
	1988	.400	—	.10	.25
	1989	—	—	.10	.25

6.6000 g, .925 SILVER, .1963 oz ASW

KM#	Date	Mintage	VF	XF	Unc
56.1a	1983	5,000	—	Proof	10.00

COPPER-NICKEL, Reduced size

KM#	Date	Mintage	VF	XF	Unc
56.2	1990	4.000	—	—	.35
	1991	2.000	—	—	.35
	1992	1.000	—	—	.50

10 NEW PENCE

COPPER-NICKEL

KM#	Date	Mintage	VF	XF	Unc
33	1968	1.500	.20	.35	1.00
	1975	1.022	.20	.30	.90
	1980	1.000	.20	.30	.75
	1980	.010	—	Proof	5.50

10 PENCE

COPPER-NICKEL

KM#	Date	Mintage	VF	XF	Unc
49	1981	.050	—	.20	.60
	1981	.015	—	Proof	2.25

La Houque Bie, Faldouet, St. Martin

KM#	Date	Mintage	VF	XF	Unc
57.1	1983	.030	—	.30	.50
	1984	.100	—	.30	.50
	1985	.100	—	.30	.50
	1986	.400	—	.30	.50
	1987	.800	—	.30	.50
	1988	.650	—	.30	.50
	1989	.700	—	.30	.50
	1990	.850	—	.30	.50
	1992	—	In sets only		1.00
	13.2000 g, .925 SILVER, .3926 oz ASW				
57.1a	1983	5,000	—	Proof	15.00
	COPPER-NICKEL, Reduced size				
57.2	1992	7.000	—	.30	.50

20 PENCE

COPPER-NICKEL
100th Anniversary of Lighthouse at Corbiere
Rev: Date below lighthouse.

KM#	Date	Mintage	VF	XF	Unc
53	1982	.200	—	.40	1.25
	5.8300 g, .925 SILVER, .1734 oz ASW				
53a	1982	1,500	—	Proof	15.00

COPPER-NICKEL
Obv: Date below bust.

KM#	Date	Mintage	VF	XF	Unc
66	1983	.400	—	.50	1.00
	1984	.250	—	.50	1.00
	1986	.100	—	.50	1.00
	1987	.100	—	.50	1.00
	1989	.100	—	.50	1.00
	1990	.150	—	.50	1.00
	1992	—	In sets only		2.00
	5.8300 g, .925 SILVER, .1734 oz ASW				
66a	1983	5,000	—	Proof	15.00

25 PENCE

COPPER-NICKEL
Queen's Silver Jubilee

KM#	Date	Mintage	VF	XF	Unc
44	1977	.262	.50	.75	2.50
	28.2800 g, .925 SILVER, .8411 oz ASW				
44a	1977	.025	—	Proof	30.00

50 NEW PENCE

COPPER-NICKEL

KM#	Date	Mintage	VF	XF	Unc
34	1969	.480	—	.90	1.50
	1980	.100	—	.90	1.50
	1980	.010	—	Proof	9.00

50 PENCE

5.4200 g, .925 SILVER, .1612 oz ASW
25th Wedding Anniversary

KM#	Date	Mintage	VF	XF	Unc
35	1972	.024	—	1.25	4.00
	1972	1,500	—	Proof	10.00

COPPER-NICKEL

KM#	Date	Mintage	VF	XF	Unc
50	1981	.050	—	1.00	1.50
	1981	.015	—	Proof	3.00

Grosnez Castle

KM#	Date	Mintage	VF	XF	Unc
58	1983	.050	—	1.00	1.50
	1984	.050	—	1.00	1.50
	1986	.030	—	1.00	1.50
	1987	.150	—	1.00	1.50
	1988	.130	—	1.00	1.50
	1989	.180	—	1.00	1.50
	1990	.370	—	1.00	1.50
	1992	—	In sets only		2.50
	15.5000 g, .925 SILVER, .4609 oz ASW				
58a	1983	5,000	—	Proof	10.00

COPPER-NICKEL
40th Anniversary of Liberation of 1945

KM#	Date	Mintage	VF	XF	Unc
63	1985	.065	—	1.00	1.50

POUND

10.8400 g, .925 SILVER, .3224 oz ASW
25th Wedding Anniversary

KM#	Date	Mintage	VF	XF	Unc
36	1972	.024	—	—	7.50
	1972	1,500	—	Proof	25.00

COPPER-NICKEL
Bicentennial Battle of Jersey

KM#	Date	Mintage	VF	XF	Unc
51	1981	.200	—	2.00	3.50
	1981	.015	—	Proof	10.00
	10.4500 g, .925 SILVER, .3108 oz ASW				
51a	1981	.010	—	Proof	22.50
	17.5500 g, .917 GOLD, .5174 oz AGW				
51b	1981	5,000	—	Proof	250.00

NICKEL-BRASS
Parish of St. Helier

KM#	Date	Mintage	VF	XF	Unc
59	1983	.100	—	2.00	3.50
	11.6800 g, .925 SILVER, .3474 oz ASW				
59a	1983	5,000	—	Proof	25.00
	19.6500 g, .917 GOLD, .5794 oz AGW				
59b	1983	*973 pcs.	—	Proof	350.00

NOTE: 497 pieces were remelted.

NICKEL-BRASS
Parish of St. Saviour

KM#	Date	Mintage	VF	XF	Unc
60	1984	.020	—	2.00	3.50
	11.6800 g, .925 SILVER, .3474 oz ASW				
60a	1984	2,500	—	Proof	35.00
	19.6500 g, .917 GOLD, .5794 oz AGW				
60b	1984	159 pcs.	—	Proof	400.00

NICKEL-BRASS
Parish of St. Brelade

KM#	Date	Mintage	VF	XF	Unc
61	1984	.020	—	2.00	3.50
	11.6800 g, .925 SILVER, .3474 oz ASW				
61a	1984	2,500	—	Proof	35.00
	19.6500 g, .917 GOLD, .5794 oz AGW				
61b	1984	133 pcs.	—	Proof	400.00

NICKEL-BRASS
Parish of St. Clement

KM#	Date	Mintage	VF	XF	Unc
62	1985	.025	—	2.00	3.50
	11.6800 g, .925 SILVER, .3474 oz ASW				
62a	1985	2,500	—	Proof	35.00
	19.6500 g, .917 GOLD, .5794 oz AGW				
62b	1985	124 pcs.	—	Proof	425.00

NICKEL-BRASS
Parish of St. Lawrence

KM#	Date	Mintage	VF	XF	Unc
65	1985	.010	—	2.00	3.50
	11.6800 g, .925 SILVER, .3474 oz ASW				
65a	1985	2,500	—	Proof	35.00
	19.6500 g, .917 GOLD, .5794 oz AGW				
65b	1985	108 pcs.	—	Proof	450.00

NICKEL-BRASS
Parish of St. Peter

KM#	Date	Mintage	VF	XF	Unc
68	1986	.010	—	2.00	3.50
	11.6800 g, .925 SILVER, .3474 oz ASW				
68a	1986	2,500	—	Proof	35.00
	19.6500 g, .917 GOLD, .5794 oz AGW				
68b	1986	146 pcs.	—	Proof	400.00

NICKEL-BRASS
Parish of Grouville

KM#	Date	Mintage	VF	XF	Unc
69	1986	.010	—	2.00	3.50
	11.6800 g, .925 SILVER, .3474 oz ASW				
69a	1986	2,500	—	Proof	35.00
	19.6500 g, .917 GOLD, .5794 oz AGW				
69b	1986	250 pcs.	—	Proof	400.00

NICKEL-BRASS
Parish of St. Martin
Obv: Similar to KM#69. Rev: Arms.

KM#	Date	Mintage	VF	XF	Unc
71	1987	.010	—	2.00	3.50
	11.6800 g, .925 SILVER, .3474 oz ASW				
71a	1987	2,500	—	Proof	35.00
	19.6500 g, .917 GOLD, .5794 oz AGW				
71b	1987	250 pcs.	—	Proof	400.00

NICKEL-BRASS
Parish of St. Ouen

KM#	Date	Mintage	VF	XF	Unc
72	1987	.010	—	2.00	3.50
	11.6800 g, .925 SILVER, .3474 oz ASW				
72a	1987	*2,500	—	Proof	35.00
	19.6500 g, .917 GOLD, .5794 oz AGW				
72b	1987	*250 pcs.	—	Proof	400.00

NICKEL-BRASS
Parish of Trinity

KM#	Date	Mintage	VF	XF	Unc
73	1988	.010	—	2.00	3.50
	11.6800 g, .925 SILVER, .3474 oz ASW				
73a	1988	*2,500	—	Proof	35.00
	19.6500 g, .917 GOLD, .5794 oz AGW				
73b	1988	*250 pcs.	—	Proof	400.00

NICKEL-BRASS
Parish of St. John

KM#	Date	Mintage	VF	XF	Unc
74	1988	.010	—	2.00	3.50
	11.6800 g, .925 SILVER, .3474 oz ASW				
74a	1988	*2,500	—	Proof	35.00
	19.6500 g, .917 GOLD, .5794 oz AGW				
74b	1988	*250 pcs.	—	Proof	400.00

NICKEL-BRASS
Parish of St. Mary's

KM#	Date	Mintage	VF	XF	Unc
75	1989	.025	—	2.00	3.50
	11.6800 g, .925 SILVER, .3474 oz ASW				
75a	1989	*2,500	—	Proof	35.00
	19.6500 g, .917 GOLD, .5794 oz AGW				
75b	1989	*250 pcs.	—	Proof	400.00

NICKEL-BRASS
Schooner "The Tickler"

KM#	Date	Mintage	VF	XF	Unc
84	1991	.015	—	—	3.50
	11.6800 g, .925 SILVER, .3474 oz ASW				
84a	1991	3,000	—	Proof	45.00
	19.6500 g, .917 GOLD, .5794 oz AGW				
84b	1991	*250 pcs.	—	Proof	550.00

NICKEL-BRASS
Sailing Ship - "Percy Douglas"

KM#	Date	Mintage	VF	XF	Unc
85	1991	.020	—	—	3.50
	11.6800 g, .925 SILVER, .3474 oz ASW				
85a	1991	3,000	—	Proof	45.00
	19.6500 g, .917 GOLD, .5794 oz AGW				
85b	1991	250 pcs.	—	Proof	550.00

NICKEL-BRASS
Sailing Ship - Hebe

KM#	Date	Mintage	VF	XF	Unc
86	1992	2,000	—	—	5.00
	11.6800 g, .925 SILVER, .3474 oz ASW				
86a	1992	*3,000	—	Proof	45.00
	19.6500 g, .917 GOLD, .5794 oz AGW				
86b	1992	*250 pcs.	—	Proof	550.00

NICKEL-BRASS
Ornamented Coat of Arms

KM#	Date	Mintage	VF	XF	Unc
87	1992	.020	—	—	3.50
	11.6800 g, .925 SILVER, .3474 oz ASW				
87a	1992	3,000	—	Proof	45.00
	19.6500 g, .917 GOLD, .5794 oz AGW				
87b	1992	250 pcs.	—	Proof	550.00

NICKEL-BRASS
Sailing Ship-Gemini

KM#	Date	Mintage	VF	XF	Unc
88	1993	—	—	—	3.50
	11.6800 g, .925 SILVER, .3474 oz ASW				
88a	1993	3,000	—	Proof	50.00
	19.6500 g, .917 GOLD, .5794 oz AGW				
88b	1993	250 pcs.	—	Proof	550.00

NICKEL-BRASS
Sailing Ship-Century

KM#	Date	Mintage	VF	XF	Unc
90	1993	—	—	—	3.50
	11.6800 g, .925 SILVER, .3474 oz ASW				
90a	1993	*3,000	—	Proof	50.00
	19.6500 g, .917 GOLD, .5794 oz AGW				
90b	1993	*250 pcs.	—	Proof	550.00

2 POUNDS

21.9000 g, .925 SILVER, .6513 oz ASW
25th Wedding Anniversary
Obv: Similar to 1 Pound, KM#36.

KM#	Date	Mintage	VF	XF	Unc
37	1972	.024	—	—	15.00
	1972	1,500	—	Proof	30.00

COPPER-NICKEL
Wedding of Prince Charles and Lady Diana

KM#	Date	Mintage	VF	XF	Unc
52	1981	.150	—	—	6.00
	28.2800 g, .925 SILVER, .8411 oz ASW				
52a	1981	.035	—	Proof	25.00
	15.9800 g, .917 GOLD, .4712 oz AGW				
52b	1981	1,500	—	Proof	250.00

COPPER-NICKEL
40th Anniversary of Liberation of 1945

KM#	Date	Mintage	VF	XF	Unc
64	1985	.020	—	—	6.00
	28.2800 g, .925 SILVER, .8411 oz ASW				
64a	1985	2,500	—	Proof	55.00
	47.5400 g, .917 GOLD, 1.4011 oz AGW				
64b	1985	40 pcs.	—	Proof	2000.

COPPER-NICKEL
XIII Commonwealth Games - Edinburgh
Obv: Similar to KM#70.

KM#	Date	Mintage	VF	XF	Unc
67.1	1986	5,000	—	—	6.00
	28.2800 g, .500 SILVER, .4546 oz ASW				
67.1a	1986	.020	—	—	25.00
	28.2800 g, .925 SILVER, .8411 oz ASW				
67.1b	1986	.020	—	Proof	50.00
	COPPER-NICKEL				
	Without edge inscription				
67.2	1986	—	—	—	7.50

World Wildlife Fund - Mauritius Pink Pigeon

KM#	Date	Mintage	VF	XF	Unc
70	1987	.023	—	—	7.00
	28.2800 g, .925 SILVER, .8411 oz ASW				
70a	1987	.025	—	Proof	50.00

COPPER-NICKEL
Royal Visit

KM#	Date	Mintage	VF	XF	Unc
76	1989	.010	—	—	6.00
	28.3000 g, .925 SILVER, .8411 oz ASW				
76a	1989	3,000	—	Proof	55.00

50th Anniversary of the Battle of Britain - Spitfire

KM#	Date	Mintage	VF	XF	Unc
77	1990	*.010	—	Proof	55.00

COPPER-NICKEL
90th Birthday of Queen Mother

KM#	Date	Mintage	VF	XF	Unc
83	1990	.010	—	—	8.00
	28.3500 g, .925 SILVER, .8432 oz ASW				
83a	1990	3,000	—	Proof	55.00
	15.9800 g, .917 GOLD, .4708 oz AGW				
83b	1990	90 pcs.	—	Proof	750.00

COPPER-NICKEL
40th Anniversary of Coronation of Queen Elizabeth II

KM#	Date	Mintage	VF	XF	Unc
89	ND(1993)	—	—	—	6.50
	28.2800 g, .925 SILVER, .8411 oz ASW				
89a	ND(1993)	*.010	—	Proof	55.00

2 POUNDS 50 PENCE

27.6000 g, .925 SILVER, .8208 oz ASW
25th Wedding Anniversary
Obv: Similar to 1 Pound, KM#36.

KM#	Date	Mintage	VF	XF	Unc
38	1972	.024	—	—	15.00
	1972	1,500	—	Proof	35.00

5 POUNDS

2.6200 g, .917 GOLD, .0772 oz AGW
25th Wedding Anniversary

KM#	Date	Mintage	VF	XF	Unc
39	1972	8,500	—	—	40.00
	1972	1,500	—	Proof	60.00

155.60000 g, .925 SILVER, 4.6215 oz ASW
50th Anniversary of the Battle of Britain - Spitfire
Illustration reduced. Actual size: 65mm
Obv: Similar to 2 Pounds, KM#77.

KM#	Date	Mintage	VF	XF	Unc
78	1990	*5,000	—	Proof	145.00

10 POUNDS

4.6400 g, .917 GOLD, .1368 oz AGW
25th Wedding Anniversary

KM#	Date	Mintage	VF	XF	Unc
40	1972	8,500	—	—	65.00
	1972	1,500	—	Proof	80.00

3.1300 g, .999 GOLD, .1005 oz AGW
50th Anniversary of the Battle of Britain
Obv: Similar to 50 Pounds, KM#81.

KM#	Date	Mintage	VF	XF	Unc
79	1990	*500 pcs.	—	Proof	120.00

20 POUNDS

9.2600 g, .917 GOLD, .2729 oz AGW
25th Wedding Anniversary

KM#	Date	Mintage	VF	XF	Unc
41	1972	8,500	—	—	125.00
	1972	1,500	—	Proof	160.00

25 POUNDS

11.9000 g, .917 GOLD, .3507 oz AGW
25th Wedding Anniversary

KM#	Date	Mintage	VF	XF	Unc
42	1972	8,500	—	—	150.00
	1972	1,500	—	Proof	200.00

7.8100 g, .999 GOLD, .2509 oz AGW
50th Anniversary of the Battle of Britain
Obv: Similar to 50 Pounds, KM#81.
Rev: Spitfire in flight over United Kingdom.

KM#	Date	Mintage	VF	XF	Unc
80	1990	*500 pcs.	—	Proof	250.00

50 POUNDS

22.6300 g, .917 GOLD, .6670 oz AGW
25th Wedding Anniversary

KM#	Date	Mintage	VF	XF	Unc
43	1972	8,500	—	—	325.00
	1972	1,500	—	Proof	375.00

15.6100 g, .999 GOLD, .5014 oz AGW
50th Anniversary of the Battle of Britain
Rev: Royal Air Force badge dividing dates.

KM#	Date	Mintage	VF	XF	Unc
81	1990	*500 pcs.	—	Proof	480.00

100 POUNDS

31.2100 g, .999 GOLD, 1.0025 oz AGW
50th Anniversary of the Battle of Britain
Rev: Spitfire in flight over United Kingdom.

KM#	Date	Mintage	VF	XF	Unc
82	1990	*500 pcs.	—	Proof	900.00

MINT SETS (MS)

KM#	Date	Mintage	Identification	Issue Price	Mkt. Val.
MS1	1972(9)	8,500	KM35-43	348.00	745.00
MS2	1972(4)	15,000	KM35-38	24.00	37.50
MS3	1983(7)	25,000	KM53-59	—	6.00
MS4	1987(7)	—	KM54-58,66,71	—	6.50
MS5	1992(7)	—	KM54-55,56.2,57.1, 58,66,86	22.50	22.50

PROOF SETS (PS)

KM#	Date	Mintage	Identification	Issue Price	Mkt. Val.
PS1	1957(4)	1,050	KM21,22 two each	—	30.00
PS2.1	1960(4)	2,100	KM22,23 two each	—	25.00
PS2.2	1960(4)	Inc. Ab.	KM22,24 two each	—	150.00
PS3	1964(4)	10,000	KM21,25 two each	—	8.00
PS4	1966(4)	15,000	KM26,27 two each	—	8.00
PS5	1966(2)	15,000	KM28 two pcs.	—	8.00
PS6	1972(9)	1,500	KM35-43	648.00	975.00
PS7	1980(6)	10,000	KM29-34	—	20.00
PS8	1981(7)	15,000	KM45-51	31.00	20.00
PS9	1983(7)	5,000	KM53a-59a	—	80.00
PS10	1990(4)	500	KM79-82	1595.	1750.

JORDAN

The Hashemite Kingdom of Jordan, a constitutional monarchy in southwest Asia, has an area of 37,738 sq. mi. (91,880 sq. km.) and a population of 3.5 million. Capital: Amman. Agriculture and tourism comprise Jordan's economic base. Chief exports are phosphates, tomatoes and oranges.

Jordan is the Edom and Moab of the time of Moses. It became part of the Roman province of Arabia in 106 A.D., was conquered by the Arabs in 633-36, and was part of the Ottoman Empire from the 16th century until World War I. At that time, the regions presently known as Jordan and Israel were mandated to Great Britain by the League of Nations as Transjordan and Palestine. In 1922 Transjordan was established as the semi-autonomous Emirate of Transjordan, ruled by the Hashemite Prince Abdullah but still nominally a part of the British mandate. The mandate over Transjordan was terminated in 1946, The country becoming the independent Hashemite Kingdom of Transjordan. The kingdom was renamed the Hashemite Kingdom of Jordan in 1950.

NOTE: Several 1964 and 1965 issues were limited to respective quantities of 3,000 and 5,000 examples struck to make up sets for sale to collectors.

TITLES

المملكة الاردنية الهاشمية

el-Mamlaka(t) el-Urduniya(t) el-Hashemiya(t)

RULERS

Abdullah Ibn al-Hussein, 1946-1951
Talal Ibn Abdullah, 1951-1952
Hussein Ibn Talal, 1952—

MONETARY SYSTEM

100 Fils = 1 Dirham
1000 Fils = 10 Dirhams = 1 Dinar
Commencing 1992
10 Piastres = 1 Dinar

FIL

BRONZE

KM#	Date	Year	Mintage	VF	XF	Unc
1	AH1368	1949	.350	1.00	1.50	3.00
	1368	1949	—	—	Proof	—

NOTE: *FIL* is an error for *FILS*, the correct Arabic singular.

FILS

BRONZE

KM#	Date	Year	Mintage	VF	XF	Unc
2	AH1368	1949	Inc. Ab.	.50	.90	2.00
	1368	1949	25 pcs.	—	Proof	60.00

KM#	Date	Year	Mintage	VF	XF	Unc
8	AH1374	1955	.200	.35	.50	1.00
	1374	1955	—	—	Proof	—
	1379	1960	.150	.40	.60	1.25
	1379	1960	—	—	Proof	—
	1382	1963	.200	.25	.50	1.00
	1382	1963	—	—	Proof	—
	1383	1964	3,000	1.50	3.00	5.00
	1385	1965	5,000	1.00	2.00	4.00
	1385	1965	.010	—	Proof	3.00

KM#	Date	Year	Mintage	VF	XF	Unc
		Hussein				
14	AH1387	1968	.060	.15	.25	.75

KM#	Date	Year	Mintage	VF	XF	Unc
35	AH1398	1978	—	.15	.25	.60
	1398	1978	.020	—	Proof	.75
	1401	1981	.100	.10	.20	.50
	1404	1984	.100	.10	.20	.50
	1406	1985	—	.10	.20	.50
	1406	1985	5,000	—	Proof	.75

5 FILS (1/2 QIRSH)

BRONZE

KM#	Date	Year	Mintage	VF	XF	Unc
3	AH1368	1949	3.300	.40	.75	1.50
	1368	1949	25 pcs.	—	Proof	80.00

KM#	Date	Year	Mintage	VF	XF	Unc
9	AH1374	1955	3.500	.35	.50	.75
	1374	1955	—	—	Proof	—
	1380	1960	.540	.50	.70	1.25
	1380	1960	—	—	Proof	—
	1382	1962	.250	.45	.70	1.25
	1382	1962	—	—	Proof	—
	1383	1964	3,000	—	4.50	7.50
	1384	1964	2.500	.30	.50	1.00
	1385	1965	5,000	1.25	2.50	4.00
	1385	1965	.010	—	Proof	5.00
	1387	1967	2.000	.10	.20	.40

KM#	Date	Year	Mintage	VF	XF	Unc
		Hussein				
15	AH1387	1968	.800	.10	.25	.50
	1390	1970	1.400	—	.20	.40
	1392	1972	.400	.10	.25	.65
	1394	1974	2.000	.10	.20	.40
	1395	1975	9.000	.10	.15	.30

KM#	Date	Year	Mintage	VF	XF	Unc
36	AH1398	1978	60.200	.10	.15	.30
	1398	1978	.020	—	Proof	1.25
	1406	1985	—	.10	.15	.30
	1406	1985	5,000	—	Proof	1.25

10 FILS (QIRSH, PIASTRE)

BRONZE

KM#	Date	Year	Mintage	VF	XF	Unc
4	AH1368	1949	2.700	.75	1.25	2.00
	1368	1949	25 pcs.	—	Proof	100.00

KM#	Date	Year	Mintage	VF	XF	Unc
10	AH1374	1955	1.500	.60	1.00	2.00
	1374	1955	—	—	Proof	—
	1380	1960	.060	1.25	2.00	3.50
	1380	1960	—	—	Proof	—
	1382	1962	2.300	.30	.50	1.00
	1382	1962	—	—	Proof	50.00
	1383	1964	1.253	.30	.50	1.00
	1385	1965	1.003	.20	.40	1.00
	1385	1965	.010	—	Proof	2.00
	1387	1967	1.000	.20	.35	1.00

KM#	Date	Year	Mintage	VF	XF	Unc
		Hussein				
16	AH1387	1968	.500	.20	.40	.75
	1390	1970	1.000	.20	.35	.60
	1392	1972	.600	.20	.40	.75
	1394	1974	1.000	.20	.40	.65
	1395	1975	5.000	.20	.35	.50

KM#	Date	Year	Mintage	VF	XF	Unc
37	AH1398	1978	30.000	.10	.15	.40
	1398	1978	.020	—	Proof	1.50
	1404	1984	10.000	.10	.15	.40
	1406	1985	—	.10	.15	.40
	1406	1985	5,000	—	Proof	1.50
	1409	1989	8,000	.10	.15	.40

20 FILS

COPPER-NICKEL

KM#	Date	Year	Mintage	VF	XF	Unc
5	AH1368	1949	1.570	.75	1.25	2.00
	1368	1949	25 pcs.	—	Proof	110.00

KM#	Date	Year	Mintage	VF	XF	Unc
13	AH1383	1964	3,000	1.50	3.00	5.00
	1385	1965	5,000	1.50	3.00	5.00
	1385	1965	.010	—	Proof	5.00

25 FILS (1/4 DIRHAM)

COPPER-NICKEL

KM#	Date	Year	Mintage	VF	XF	Unc
		Hussein				
17	AH1387	1968	.200	.15	.35	.75
	1390	1970	.240	.15	.35	.75
	1394	1974	.800	.15	.35	.75
	1395	1975	2.000	.15	.35	.75
	1397	1977	1.600	.15	.35	.75

KM#	Date	Year	Mintage	VF	XF	Unc
38	AH1398	1978	—	.20	.30	.75
	1398	1978	.020	—	Proof	2.00
	1401	1981	2.000	.20	.30	.75
	1404	1984	4.000	.20	.30	.75
	1406	1985	—	.20	.30	.75
	1406	1985	5,000	—	Proof	2.00
	1411	1991	5.000	.20	.30	.75

50 FILS (1/2 DIRHAM)

COPPER-NICKEL

KM#	Date	Year	Mintage	VF	XF	Unc
6	AH1368	1949	2.500	.75	2.00	3.50
	1368	1949	25 Pcs.	—	Proof	125.00

KM#	Date	Year	Mintage	VF	XF	Unc
11	AH1374	1955	2.500	.75	1.50	3.50
	1374	1955	—	—	Proof	—
	1382	1962	.750	.85	1.00	1.50
	1382	1962	—	—	Proof	—
	1383	1964	1.003	.50	.75	1.25
	1385	1965	1.505	.75	1.00	1.50
	1385	1965	.010	—	Proof	3.50

KM#	Date	Year	Mintage	VF	XF	Unc
		Hussein				
18	AH1387	1968	.400	.40	.75	1.75
	1390	1970	1.000	.40	.60	1.25
	1393	1973	—	.40	.60	1.25
	1394	1974	1.000	.40	.60	1.25
	1395	1975	2.000	.40	.60	1.25
	1397	1977	6.000	.40	.60	1.25

KM#	Date	Year	Mintage	VF	XF	Unc
39	AH1398	1978	6.168	.25	.50	1.25
	1398	1978	.020	—	Proof	2.50
	1400	1979	—	.25	.50	1.25
	1401	1981	5.000	.25	.50	1.25
	1404	1984	10.000	.25	.50	1.25
	1406	1985	—	.25	.50	1.25
	1406	1985	5,000	—	Proof	2.50
	1409	1989	6.000	.25	.50	1.25
	1411	1991	10.000	.25	.50	1.25

100 FILS (Dirham)

COPPER-NICKEL

KM#	Date	Year	Mintage	VF	XF	Unc
7	AH1368	1949	2.000	2.00	3.00	5.00
	1368	1949	25 pcs.	—	Proof	150.00

KM#	Date	Year	Mintage	VF	XF	Unc
12	AH1374	1955	.500	2.00	2.50	4.00
	1374	1955	—	—	Proof	—
	1382	1962	.600	1.00	1.50	3.00
	1382	1962	—	—	Proof	—
	1383	1964	3,000	1.50	3.00	5.00
	1385	1965	.405	1.00	1.25	2.50
	1385	1965	.010	—	Proof	4.00

Hussein

KM#	Date	Year	Mintage	VF	XF	Unc
19	AH1387	1968	.175	.75	1.50	2.50
	1395	1975	2.500	.40	1.00	2.00
	1397	1977	2.000	.40	1.00	2.00

KM#	Date	Year	Mintage	VF	XF	Unc
40	AH1398	1978	3.000	.40	1.00	2.00
	1398	1978	.020	—	Proof	3.00
	1400	1979	—	.40	1.00	2.00
	1401	1981	4.000	.40	1.00	2.00
	1404	1984	5.000	.40	1.00	1.50
	1406	1985	—	.40	1.00	1.50
	1406	1985	5,000	—	Proof	3.00
	1409	1989	4.000	.40	1.00	1.50
	1411	1991	6.000	.40	1.00	1.50

1/4 DINAR

COPPER-NICKEL
F.A.O. Issue

KM#	Date	Year	Mintage	VF	XF	Unc
20	AH1389	1969	.060	2.00	2.50	4.00

KM#	Date	Year	Mintage	VF	XF	Unc
28	AH1390	1970	.500	1.00	1.50	3.50
	1394	1974	.400	1.00	1.50	3.50
	1395	1975	.100	1.00	1.50	3.50
	1396	1976	—	1.00	1.50	3.50

19.0400 g, .925 SILVER, .5663 oz ASW
10th Anniversary of Central Bank of Jordan

KM#	Date	Year	Mintage	VF	XF	Unc
29	AH1394	1974	550 pcs.	—	Proof	60.00

.917 GOLD

KM#	Date	Year	Mintage	VF	XF	Unc
29a	AH1394	1974	100 pcs.	—	Proof	550.00

COPPER-NICKEL
25th Anniversary of Reign

KM#	Date	Year	Mintage	VF	XF	Unc
30	AH1397	1977	.200	1.00	2.00	4.00

KM#	Date	Year	Mintage	VF	XF	Unc
41	AH1398	1978	.200	1.00	2.00	3.50
	1398	1978	.020	—	Proof	4.00
	1401	1981	.800	.75	1.50	3.00
	1406	1985	—	.75	1.50	3.00
	1406	1985	5,000	—	Proof	4.00

1/2 DINAR

20.0000 g, .999 SILVER, .6424 oz ASW
Al Harraneh Palace

KM#	Date	Year	Mintage	VF	XF	Unc
21	AH1389	1969	6,100	—	Proof	20.00

COPPER-NICKEL
1400th Anniversary of Islam

KM#	Date	Year	Mintage	VF	XF	Unc
42	AH1400	1980	2.006	1.50	2.50	4.50

3/4 DINAR

30.0000 g, .999 SILVER, .9636 oz ASW
Shrine of the Nativity, Bethlehem
Obv: Similar to 1/2 Dinar, KM#21.

KM#	Date	Year	Mintage	VF	XF	Unc
22	AH1389	1969	5,800	—	Proof	40.00

DINAR

40.0000 g, .999 SILVER, 1.2848 oz ASW
Temple Hill, Jerusalem
Obv: Similar to 1/2 Dinar, KM#21.

KM#	Date	Year	Mintage	VF	XF	Unc
23	AH1389	1969	6,800	—	Proof	60.00

NICKEL-BRONZE
King's 50th Birthday

KM#	Date	Year	Mintage	VF	XF	Unc
47	AH1406	1985	—	—	—	7.50
	1406	1985	5,000	—	Proof	10.00

2 DINARS

5.5200 g, .900 GOLD, .1597 oz AGW
Forum In Jerash

KM#	Date	Year	Mintage	VF	XF	Unc
24	AH1389	1969	2,425	—	Proof	125.00

2-1/2 DINARS

28.2800 g, .925 SILVER, .8410 oz ASW
Conservation - Rhim Gazelle

KM#	Date	Year	Mintage	VF	XF	Unc
31	AH1397	1977	6,265	—	—	22.50
	AH1397	1977	5,011	—	Proof	30.00

3 DINARS

35.0000 g, .925 SILVER, 1.0409 oz ASW
Conservation - Palestine Sunbird
Obv: Similar to 2-1/2 Dinars, KM#31.

KM#	Date	Year	Mintage	VF	XF	Unc
32	AH1397	1977	6,263	—	—	25.00
	AH1397	1977	4,897	—	Proof	35.00

23.3300 g, .925 SILVER, .6938 oz ASW
International Year of the Child
Obv: Similar to 1/4 Dinar, KM#41.

KM#	Date	Year	Mintage	VF	XF	Unc
43	AH1401	1981	.021	—	Proof	15.00

5 DINARS

13.8200 g, .900 GOLD, .3999 oz AGW
Tomb in Petra

KM#	Date	Year	Mintage	VF	XF	Unc
25	AH1389	1969	1,950	—	Proof	300.00

10 DINARS

27.6400 g, .900 GOLD, .7998 oz AGW
Visit of Pope Paul VI

KM#	Date	Year	Mintage	VF	XF	Unc
26	AH1389	1969	1,870	—	Proof	500.00

30.0000 g, .925 SILVER, .8922 oz ASW
15th Century Hijrah Calendar
Obv: King Hussein. Rev: Mosques.

KM#	Date	Year	Mintage	VF	XF	Unc
44	AH1400	1980	.017	—	Proof	27.50

15.0000 g, .925 SILVER, .4610 oz ASW
King's 50th Birthday

KM#	Date	Year	Mintage	VF	XF	Unc
48	AH1406	1985	—	—	Proof	27.50

25 DINARS

69.1100 g, .900 GOLD, 1.9999 oz AGW
Dome of the Rock, Jerusalem

KM#	Date	Year	Mintage	VF	XF	Unc
27	AH1389	1969	1,000	—	Proof	1200.

15.0000 g, .917 GOLD, .4422 oz AGW
25th Anniversary of Reign

KM#	Date	Year	Mintage	VF	XF	Unc
33	AH1397					
		1977FM	4,724	—	Proof	225.00

40 DINARS

14.3100 g, .917 GOLD, .4216 oz AGW
15th Century Hijrah Calendar

KM#	Date	Year	Mintage	VF	XF	Unc
45	AH1400	1980	9,500	—	Proof	500.00

50 DINARS

15.9800 g, .917 GOLD, .4710 oz AGW
Five Year Plan

KM#	Date	Year	Mintage	VF	XF	Unc
50	AH1396	1976	250 pcs.	—	Proof	350.00

33.4370 g, .900 GOLD, .9676 oz AGW
Conservation - Houbara Bustard

KM#	Date	Year	Mintage	VF	XF	Unc
34	AH1397	1977	829 pcs.	—	—	450.00
	1397	1977	287 pcs.	—	Proof	750.00

17.0000 g, .917 GOLD, .5013 oz AGW
King's 50th Birthday
Similar to 10 Dinars, KM#48.

KM#	Date	Year	Mintage	VF	XF	Unc
49	AH1405	1985	2,000	—	Proof	325.00

60 DINARS

17.1700 g, .917 GOLD, .5062 oz AGW
International Year of the Child
Rev: Palace of Culture in Amman.

KM#	Date	Year	Mintage	VF	XF	Unc
46	AH1401	1981	.020	—	Proof	250.00

MONETARY REFORM

10 Piastres = 1 Dinar

2-1/2 PIASTRES

STAINLESS STEEL

KM#	Date	Year	Mintage	VF	XF	Unc
53	AH1413	1993	—	—	—	1.00

5 PIASTRES

NICKEL PLATED STEEL

KM#	Date	Year	Mintage	VF	XF	Unc
54	AH1413	1993	—	—	—	1.75

10 PIASTRES

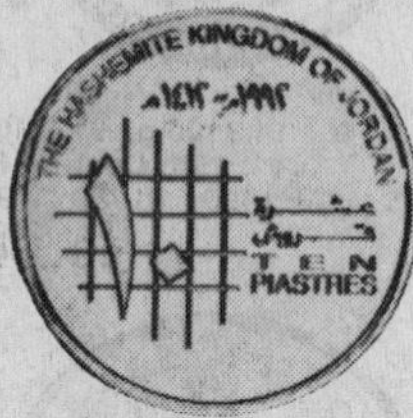

NICKEL PLATED STEEL

KM#	Date	Year	Mintage	VF	XF	Unc
55	AH1413	1993	—	—	—	2.25

DINAR

15.0000 g, .925 SILVER, .4461 oz ASW
40th Year of Reign

KM#	Date	Year	Mintage	VF	XF	Unc
51	AH1413	1993	—	—	Proof	20.00

8.5000 g, .917 GOLD, .2505 oz AGW
40th Year of Reign

KM#	Date	Year	Mintage	VF	XF	Unc
52	AH1413	1993	—	—	Proof	185.00

SPECIMEN SETS (SS)

KM#	Date	Mintage	Identification	Issue Price	Mkt. Val.
SS1	1964(6)	3,000	KM8-13	—	15.00
SS2	1965(6)	5,000	KM8-13	—	12.50
SS3	1968(6)	50	KM14-19	—	500.00

MINT SETS (MS)

KM#	Date	Mintage	Identification	Issue Price	Mkt. Val.
MS1	1985(8)	—	KM35-41,47	10.75	15.00
MS2	Mixed Date (6)	—	KM5(1949),8(1963),9(1962),10-11 (1964)12,(1962)	—	10.00

PROOF SETS (PS)

KM#	Date	Mintage	Identification	Issue Price	Mkt. Val.
PS1	1949(6)	25	KM2-7	—	625.00
PS2	1965(6)	10,000	KM8-12	14.40	17.50
PS3	1969(7)	—	KM21-27	396.00	2250.
PS4	1969(4)	—	KM24-27	—	2125.
PS5	1969(3)	5,800	KM21-23	36.00	135.00
PS6	1977(3)	1,000	KM31,32,34	780.00	825.00
PS7	1977(2)	9,000	KM31,32	60.00	65.00
PS8	1978(7)	20,000	KM35-41	27.00	15.00
PS9	1980(2)	—	KM44-45	365.00	525.00
PS10	1985(8)	5,000	KM35-41,47	31.00	25.00

Listings For

KATANGA: refer to Zaire

KEELING-COCOS ISLANDS: refer to Australia

KENYA

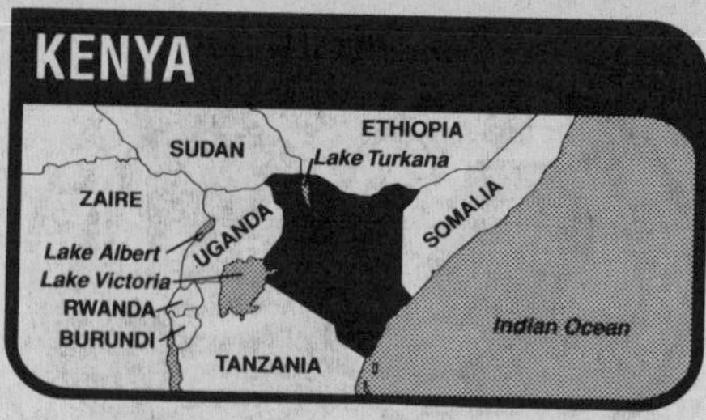

The Republic of Kenya, located on the east coast of Central Africa, has an area of 224,961 sq. mi (582,650 sq. km.) and a population of 20.1 million. Capital: Nairobi. The predominantly agricultural country exports coffee, tea and petroleum products.

The Arabs came to the coast of Kenya in the 8th century and established posts to conduct an ivory and slave trade. The Portuguese, the inveterate wanderers of the Age of Exploration, followed in the 16th century. After a lengthy and bitter struggle with the sultans of Zanzibar who controlled much of the southeastern coast of Africa, the Portuguese were driven away (late 17th century) and for many years Kenya was simply a port of call on the route to India. German and British interests in the 19th century produced agreements defining their respective spheres of influence. The British sphere was administraed by the Imperial East Africa Co. until 1895, when the British government purchased the company's rights in the East Africa Protectorate which, in 1920, was designated as Kenya Colony and protectorate - the latter being a 10-mile wide coastal strip together with Mombasa, Lamu and other small islands nominally retained by the Sultan of Zanzibar. Kenya achieved self-government in June of 1963 as a consequence of the 1952-60 Mau Mau terrorist campaign to secure land reforms and political rights for Africans. Independence was attained on Dec. 12, 1963. Kenya became a republic in 1964. It is a member of the Commonwealth of Nations. The president is Chief of State and Head of Government.

Mombasa was a thriving Arabic commercial center when first visited by Portuguese navigator Vasco da Gama in 1498. During the following two centuries Portugal made repeated efforts to capture the island stronghold but was unable to hold it against the assaults of the Muscat Arabs. In 1823 the ruling Mazuri family placed the city under British protection. Britain repudiated the protectorate and it was then seized by Seyyid Said of Oman, 1837, and annexed to Zanzibar. In 1887 the sultan of Zanzibar relinquished the port of Mombasa to British administration. It was occupied by the Imperial British East Africa Company and for the following two decades was the capital of British East Africa.

RULERS

British until 1964

MOMBASA

TITLES

ممباسه

Mombasa

MINT MARKS

H - Birmingham
C/M - Calcutta

MONETARY SYSTEM

4 Pice = 1 Anna
16 Anna = 1 Rupee

PICE

BRONZE, 24.9mm
Obv. and rev: Small letters.

KM#	Date	Mintage	Fine	VF	XF	Unc
1.1	AH1306/1888C/M	.630	.75	2.50	8.00	25.00
	1306/1888C/M	—	—	—	Proof	150.00

NOTE: Varieties in planchet thickness exist.

25.4mm
Obv: Small letters. Rev: Medium letters.

KM#	Date	Mintage	Fine	VF	XF	Unc
1.2	AH1306/1888C/M	Inc. Ab.	.50	2.00	7.00	20.00
	AH1306/1888C/M	—	—	—	Proof	200.00

Obv. and rev: Medium letters.

KM#	Date	Mintage	Fine	VF	XF	Unc
1.5	AH1306/1888C/M	Inc. Ab.	.50	2.00	7.00	20.00

Obv. and rev: Medium letters.

KM#	Date	Mintage	Fine	VF	XF	Unc
1.3	AH1306/1888H	2.352	.35	1.25	5.00	15.00
	AH1306/1888H	—	—	—	Proof	125.00

Obv. and rev: Large letters w/o serifs, dots between words.

KM#	Date	Mintage	Fine	VF	XF	Unc
1.4	AH1306/1888H	Inc. Ab.	.25	1.00	4.00	12.50
	1306/1888H	—	—	—	Proof	100.00

2 ANNAS

1.4600 g, .917 SILVER, .0430 oz ASW

KM#	Date	Mintage	Fine	VF	XF	Unc
2	1890H	.016	12.00	20.00	30.00	50.00
	1890H	—	—	—	Proof	90.00

1/4 RUPEE

(4 Annas)

2.9200 g, .917 SILVER, .0860 oz ASW

KM#	Date	Mintage	Fine	VF	XF	Unc
3	1890H	.012	15.00	25.00	35.00	75.00
	1890H	—	—	—	Proof	120.00

1/2 RUPEE

(8 Annas)

5.8300 g, .917 SILVER, .1719 oz ASW

KM#	Date	Mintage	Fine	VF	XF	Unc
4	1890H	.010	20.00	40.00	70.00	120.00
	1890H	—	—	—	Proof	140.00

RUPEE

11.6600 g, .917 SILVER, .3438 oz ASW

KM#	Date	Mintage	Fine	VF	XF	Unc
5	1888H	.094	10.00	25.00	50.00	125.00
	1888H	—	—	—	Proof	225.00

PROOF SETS (PS)

KM#	Date	Mintage	Identification	Issue Price	Mkt. Val.
PS1	1888H(2)	—	KM1,4,5	—	325.00
PS2	1890H(3)	—	KM2-4	—	350.00

KENYA

MONETARY SYSTEM

100 Cents = 1 Shilling

5 CENTS

NICKEL-BRASS
President Jomo Kenyatta

KM#	Date	Mintage	Fine	VF	XF	Unc
1	1966	28.000	—	.25	.50	1.00
	1966	27 pcs.	—	—	Proof	65.00
	1967	9.600	—	.25	.50	1.00
	1968	12.000	—	.25	.50	1.00

KM#	Date	Mintage	Fine	VF	XF	Unc
10	1969	.800	—	.50	1.25	3.50
	1969	15 pcs.	—	—	Proof	100.00
	1970	10.000	—	.15	.25	.50
	1971	29.680	—	.15	.25	.40
	1973	500 pcs.	—	—	Proof	15.00
	1974	5.599	—	.15	.25	.40
	1975	28.000	—	.15	.25	.40
	1978	23.168	—	.15	.25	.40

President Arap Moi

KM#	Date	Mintage	Fine	VF	XF	Unc
17	1980	—	—	.15	.25	.50
	1984	—	—	.15	.25	.75
	1987	—	—	.15	.25	.75
	1989	—	—	.15	.25	.50
	1990	—	—	.15	.25	.50
	1991	—	—	.15	.25	.50

10 CENTS

NICKEL-BRASS
President Jomo Kenyatta

KM#	Date	Mintage	Fine	VF	XF	Unc
2	1966	26.000	.20	.65	1.25	2.50
	1966	27 pcs.	—	—	Proof	65.00
	1967	7.300	.20	.65	1.25	2.50
	1968	12.000	.20	.65	1.25	2.50

KM#	Date	Mintage	Fine	VF	XF	Unc
11	1969	3.900	—	.15	.25	.65
	1969	15 pcs.	—	—	Proof	100.00
	1970	7.200	—	.15	.25	.65
	1971	32.400	—	.15	.25	.40
	1973	3.000	—	.15	.25	.75
	1973	500 pcs.	—	—	Proof	15.00
	1974	3.000	—	.15	.25	.75
	1975	3.000	—	.15	.25	.75
	1977	45.600	—	.15	.25	.75
	1978	22.600	—	.15	.25	.75

President Arap Moi

KM#	Date	Mintage	Fine	VF	XF	Unc
18	1980	—	—	.15	.25	1.00
	1984	—	—	.15	.25	1.25
	1986	—	—	.15	.25	1.25
	1987	—	—	.15	.25	1.25
	1989	—	—	.15	.25	1.00
	1990	—	—	.15	.25	1.00
	1991	—	—	.15	.25	1.00

25 CENTS

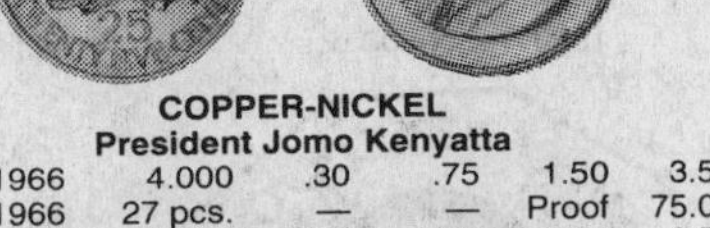

COPPER-NICKEL
President Jomo Kenyatta

KM#	Date	Mintage	Fine	VF	XF	Unc
3	1966	4.000	.30	.75	1.50	3.50
	1966	27 pcs.	—	—	Proof	75.00
	1967	4.000	.30	.75	1.50	3.50

KM#	Date	Mintage	Fine	VF	XF	Unc
12	1969	.200	.50	1.00	2.50	7.00
	1969	15 pcs.	—	—	Proof	110.00
	1973	500 pcs.	—	—	Proof	15.00

50 CENTS

COPPER-NICKEL
President Jomo Kenyatta

KM#	Date	Mintage	Fine	VF	XF	Unc
4	1966	4.000	.20	.40	1.00	3.00
	1966	27 pcs.	—	—	Proof	75.00
	1967	5.120	.20	.40	.85	2.50
	1968	6.000	.20	.40	.85	2.00

KM#	Date	Mintage	Fine	VF	XF	Unc
13	1969	.400	.50	1.00	2.00	4.00
	1969	15 pcs.	—	—	Proof	110.00
	1971	9.600	—	.20	.40	.75
	1973	3.360	.25	.50	1.00	2.00
	1973	500 pcs.	—	—	Proof	15.00
	1974	12.640	—	.20	.40	.75
	1975	8.000	—	.20	.40	.75
	1977	16.000	—	.20	.40	.75
	1978	20.480	—	.20	.40	.75

President Arap Moi

KM#	Date	Mintage	Fine	VF	XF	Unc
19	1980	—	—	.15	.35	1.00
	1989	—	—	.15	.35	1.00
	1990	—	—	.15	.35	1.00

SHILLING

COPPER-NICKEL
President Jomo Kenyatta

KM#	Date	Mintage	Fine	VF	XF	Unc
5	1966	20.000	.25	.50	1.00	3.00
	1966	27 pcs.	—	—	Proof	75.00
	1967	4.000	.25	.50	1.00	2.50
	1968	8.000	.20	.40	.80	2.00

KM#	Date	Mintage	Fine	VF	XF	Unc
14	1969	4.000	.15	.30	.75	1.75
	1969	15 pcs.	—	—	Proof	110.00
	1971	24.000	.10	.30	.65	1.50
	1973	2.480	.20	.40	.80	2.50
	1973	500 pcs.	—	—	Proof	20.00
	1974	13.520	.10	.30	.65	1.50
	1975	40.856	.10	.30	.65	1.50
	1978	20.000	.10	.30	.65	1.50

President Arap Moi

KM#	Date	Mintage	Fine	VF	XF	Unc
20	1980	—	.15	.30	.60	1.50
	1989	—	.15	.30	.60	1.50

2 SHILLINGS

COPPER-NICKEL
President Jomo Kenyatta

KM#	Date	Mintage	Fine	VF	XF	Unc
6	1966	3.000	1.00	2.00	3.50	7.50
	1966	27 pcs.	—	—	Proof	95.00
	1968	1.100	1.00	2.75	4.50	9.00

KM#	Date	Mintage	Fine	VF	XF	Unc
15	1969	.100	2.00	4.00	8.00	12.50
	1969	15 pcs.	—	—	Proof	120.00
	1971	1.920	.60	1.25	3.50	7.50
	1973	500 pcs.	—	—	Proof	25.00

5 SHILLINGS

BRASS
10th Anniversary of Independence

KM#	Date	Mintage	Fine	VF	XF	Unc
16	1973	.100	4.50	7.50	12.50	25.00
	1973	1,500	—	—	Proof	45.00

COPPER-NICKEL
President Arap Moi

23	1985	—	.50	1.00	2.00	4.00

100 SHILLINGS

7.6000 g, .917 GOLD, .2240 oz AGW
75th Anniversary - Birth of
President Jomo Kenyatta

KM#	Date	Mintage	VF	XF	Unc
7	1966	—	—	—	125.00
	1966	7,500	—	Proof	150.00

200 SHILLINGS

28.2800 g, .925 SILVER, .8410 oz ASW
Obv: President Moi. Rev: Coat of arms.

21	1979	9,500	—	Proof	45.00

250 SHILLINGS

19.0000 g, .917 GOLD, .5602 oz AGW
75th Anniversary - Birth of
President Jomo Kenyatta

8	1966	—	—	—	250.00
	1966	1,000	—	Proof	300.00

500 SHILLINGS

38.0000 g, .917 GOLD, 1.1204 oz AGW
75th Anniversary - Birth of
President Jomo Kenyatta

KM#	Date	Mintage	VF	XF	Unc
9	1966	—	—	—	550.00
	1966	500 pcs.	—	Proof	650.00

28.2800 g, .925 SILVER, .8410 oz ASW
10th Anniversary of Moi as President

24	1988	—	—	Proof	175.00

28.3300 g, .925 SILVER, .8425 oz ASW
25th Anniversary of Independence

25	1988	—	—	Proof	200.00

1000 SHILLINGS

28.0800 g, .925 SILVER, .8351 oz ASW
Silver Jubilee of Central Bank

KM#	Date	Mintage	VF	XF	Unc
26	1991	—	—	Proof	300.00

3000 SHILLINGS

40.0000 g, .917 GOLD, 1.1787 oz AGW
Obv: President Moi. Rev: Coat of arms.

22	1979	2,000	—	Proof	725.00

MINT SETS (MS)

KM#	Date	Mintage	Identification	Issue Price	Mkt. Val.
MS1	1966(3)	—	KM 7-9	—	925.00

PROOF SETS (PS)

PS1	1966(6)	27	KM 1-6	—	450.00
PS2	1966(3)	500	KM 7-9	152.60	1100.
PS3	1969(6)	15	KM 10-15	—	650.00
PS4	1973(7)	500	KM 10-16	—	150.00

Listings For

KIAO CHAU: refer to China

KIRIBATI

The Republic of Kiribati (formerly the Gilbert Islands), 30 coral atolls and islands spread over more than 1,000,000 sq. mi. (2,590,000 sq. km.) of the southwest Pacific Ocean, has an area of 332 sq. mi. (717 sq. km.) and a population of 64,200. Capital: Bairiki, on Tarawa. In addition to the Gilbert Islands proper, Kiribati includes Ocean Island, the Central and Southern Line Islands, and the Phoenix Islands, though possession of Canton and Enderbury of the Phoenix Islands is disputed with the United States. Most families engage in subsistence fishing. Copra and phosphates are exported, mostly to Australia and New Zealand.

The Gilbert Islands and the group formerly called the Ellice Islands (now Tuvalu) comprised a single British crown colony, the Gilbert and Ellice Islands.

The Islands were first sighted by Spanish mutineers in 1537. Succeeding visits were made by the English navigators John Byron (1764), James Cook (1777), and Thomas Gilbert and John Marshall (1788). An American, Edward Fanning, arrived in 1798. Britain declared a protectorate over the Gilbert and Ellice Islands, and in 1915 began the formation of a colony which was completed with the addition of the Phoenix Islands in 1937. The Central and Southern Line Islands were administratively attached to the Gilbert and Ellice Islands colony in 1972, and remained attached to the Gilberts when Tuvalu was created in 1975. The colony became self-governing in 1971. Kiribati attained independence on July 12, 1979.

RULERS

British until 1979

MONETARY SYSTEM

100 Cents = 1 Dollar

CENT

BRONZE
Frigate Bird

KM#	Date	Mintage	VF	XF	Unc
1	1979	.090	—	.10	.15
	1979	.010	—	Proof	.75
	1992	—	—	.10	.15

2 CENTS

BRONZE
B'abai Plant

KM#	Date	Mintage	VF	XF	Unc
2	1979	.025	—	.10	.20
	1979	.010	—	Proof	1.25
	1992	—	—	.10	.20

5 CENTS

COPPER-NICKEL
Tokai Lizard

KM#	Date	Mintage	VF	XF	Unc
3	1979	.020	.10	.15	.50
	1979	.010	—	Proof	2.00

10 CENTS

COPPER-NICKEL

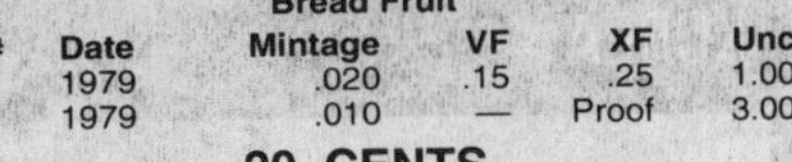

Bread Fruit

KM#	Date	Mintage	VF	XF	Unc
4	1979	.020	.15	.25	1.00
	1979	.010	—	Proof	3.00

20 CENTS

COPPER-NICKEL
Dolphins

KM#	Date	Mintage	VF	XF	Unc
5	1979	.020	.25	.50	1.50
	1979	.010	—	Proof	4.00

50 CENTS

COPPER-NICKEL
Panda Nut

KM#	Date	Mintage	VF	XF	Unc
6	1979	.020	.50	.75	2.00
	1979	.010	—	Proof	6.00

DOLLAR

COPPER-NICKEL
Outrigger Sailboat

KM#	Date	Mintage	VF	XF	Unc
7	1979	.020	.85	1.25	4.00
	1979	.010	—	Proof	8.00

2 DOLLARS

NICKEL-BRASS
10th Anniversary of Independence

KM#	Date	Mintage	VF	XF	Unc
14	1989	—	—	—	5.00

5 DOLLARS

28.1600 g, .500 SILVER, .4527 oz ASW
Independence

KM#	Date	Mintage	VF	XF	Unc
8	1979	1,545	—	—	20.00

28.1600 g, .925 SILVER, .8375 oz ASW

KM#	Date	Mintage	VF	XF	Unc
8a	1979	3,326	—	Proof	25.00

COPPER-NICKEL
2nd Anniversary of Independence and Wedding of Prince Charles and Lady Diana

KM#	Date	Mintage	VF	XF	Unc
10	1981	.050	—	—	6.00

28.6000 g, .925 SILVER, .8505 oz ASW

KM#	Date	Mintage	VF	XF	Unc
10a	1981	.025	—	Proof	25.00

COPPER-NICKEL
Royal Visit

KM#	Date	Mintage	VF	XF	Unc
12	1982	—	—	—	5.00

SILVER

KM#	Date	Mintage	VF	XF	Unc
12a	1982	—	—	Proof	60.00

10 DOLLARS

28.2800 g, .925 SILVER, .8411 oz ASW
5th Anniversary of Independence

KM#	Date	Mintage	VF	XF	Unc
13	1984	2,500	—	Proof	30.00

47.5200 g, .917 GOLD, 1.4012 oz AGW

KM#	Date	Mintage	VF	XF	Unc
13a	1984	50 pcs.	—	Proof	1850.

20 DOLLARS

31.4700 g, .925 SILVER, .9359 ASW
Soccer - World Cup '94

KM#	Date	Mintage	VF	XF	Unc
15	1993	*.010	—	Proof	45.00
		First Space Walk			
16	1993	*.015	—	Proof	40.00

150 DOLLARS

15.9800 g, .917 GOLD, .4711 oz AGW
Independence - Traditional Meeting House

KM#	Date	Mintage	VF	XF	Unc
9	1979	422 pcs.	—	—	250.00
	1979	386 pcs.	—	Proof	300.00
		2nd Anniversary of Independence and Wedding of Prince Charles and Lady Diana			
11	1981	750 pcs.	—	—	230.00
	1981	1,500	—	Proof	250.00

PROOF SETS (PS)

KM#	Date	Mintage	Identification	Issue Price	Mkt. Val.
PS1	1979(7)	10,000	KM1-7	34.00	25.00
PS2	1981(2)	—	KM10a,11	—	275.00

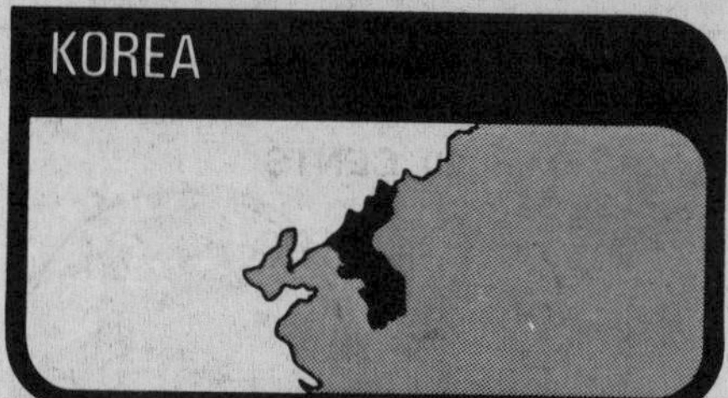

Korea, 'Land of the Morning Calm', occupies a mountainous peninsula in northeast Asia bounded by Manchuria, the Yellow Sea and the Sea of Japan.

According to legend, the first Korean dynasty, that of the House of Tangun, ruled from 2333 B.C. to 1122 B.C. It was followed by the dynasty of Kija, a Chinese scholar, which continued until 193 B.C. and brought a high civilization to Korea. The first recorded period in the history of Korea, the period of the Three Kingdoms, lasted from 57 B.C. to 935 A.D. and achieved the first political unification of the peninsula. The Kingdom of Koryo, from which Korea derived its name, was founded in 935 and continued until 1392, when it was superseded by the Yi Dynasty of King Yi. Sung Kye was to last until the Japanese annexation in 1910.

At the end of the 16th century Korea was invaded and occupied for 7 years by Japan, and from 1627 until the late 19th century it was a semi-independent tributary of China. Japan replaced China as the predominant foreign influence at the end of the Sino-Japanese War (1894-95), only to find her position threatened by Russian influence from 1896 to 1904. The Russian threat was eliminated by the Russo-Japanese War (1904-05) and in 1905 Japan established a direct protectorate over Korea. On Aug. 22, 1910, the last Korean ruler signed the treaty that annexed Korea to Japan as a government general in the Japanese Empire. Japanese suzerainty was maintained until the end of World War II.

From 1633 to 1891 the monetary system of Korea employed cast coins with a square center hole. Fifty-two agencies were authorized to procure these coins from a lesser number of coin foundries. They exist in thousands of varieties. Seed, or mother coins, were used to make the impressions in the molds in which the regular cash coins were cast. Czarist-Russian Korea experimented with Korean coins when Aliexiev of Russia, Korea's Financial Advisor, founded the First Asian Branch of the Russo-Korean Bank on March 1, 1898, and authorized the issuing of a set of new Korean coins with a crowned Russian-style quasi-eagle. British-Japanese opposition and the Russo-Japanese War operated to end the Russian coinage experiment in 1904.

RULERS

Yi Kwang (Sunjo Songhyo), 1801-1835
Yi Whan (Honjong Cholhyo), 1835-1850
Yi Chung (Choljong Yonghyo), 1850-1864
Yi Hyong (Kojong), 1864-1897
as Emperor Kwang Mu, 1897-1907
Japanese Puppet
Yung Hi (Sunjong), 1907-1910

MONETARY UNITS

文 Mun — 兩 Yang, Niang
分 Fun — 圜 Hwan, Warn
錢 Chon — 圓 Won, Whan, Hwan

IDENTIFICATION CHART

Kae Kuk (Founding of the Dynasty)

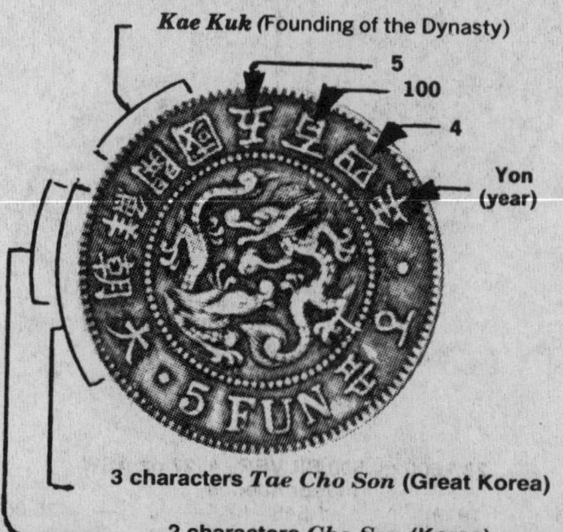

Obverse

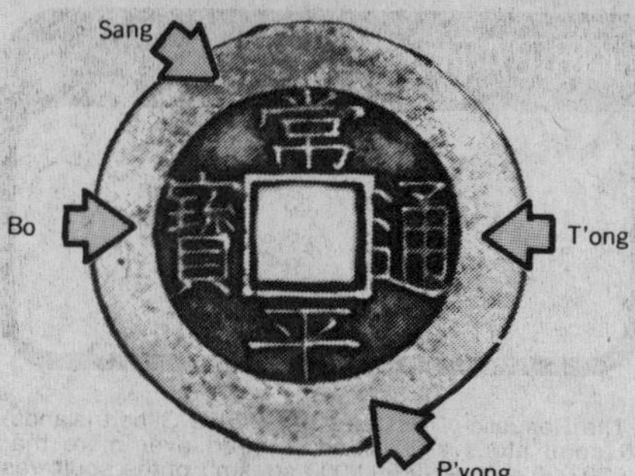

Sang P'yong T'ong Bo
"Always even currency"
Reverse

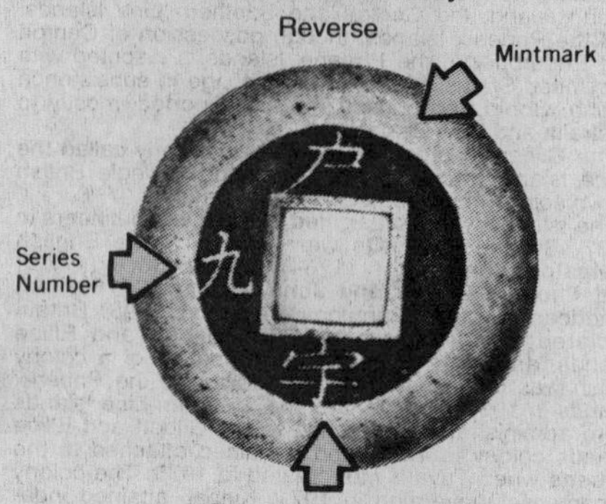

Furnace Designator

NOTE: The series number may be to the left, right or bottom of the center hole. The furnace designator may be either a numeral or a character from the THOUSAND CHARACTER CLASSIC.

SEED COINS

Seed coins are specially prepared examples, perfectly round, with sharp characters, used in the preparation of clay or sand molds.

Kyun 均
Government Tithe Office

Son 宣
Rice & Cloth Department

Chon 典
Central Government Mint

Mu 武
Palace Guard Office

Kum 禁
Court Guard Military Unit

Hun 訓 or 訓
Military Training Command

T'ong 統 or 統
T'ongyong Naval Office
Military Office in Seoul

Kyong 经
Government Office of Pukhan Mountain Fortress

Sim 沁
Kanghwa Township Military Office

Kae 

Kaesong Township Military Office

Song 松

Kaesong Township Military Office

I 利

Iwon Township Military Office

Ch'un 春 or 㫩

Ch'unch'on Township Military Office

Ch'on 川

Tanch'on Township Military Office

Ch'ang 

Ch'angdok Palace Mint
Ch'angwon Township Military Office

Ki 圻

Kwangju Township Military Office in Kyonggi Province

Kyong 

Kyonggi Provincial Office

Kyong Su 京水

Kyonggi Naval Station

P'yong 平

P'yongan Provincial Office

Ham 

Hamgyong Provincial Office

TREASURY DEPARTMENT

 or  **Ho (Ho Jo)**

MUN

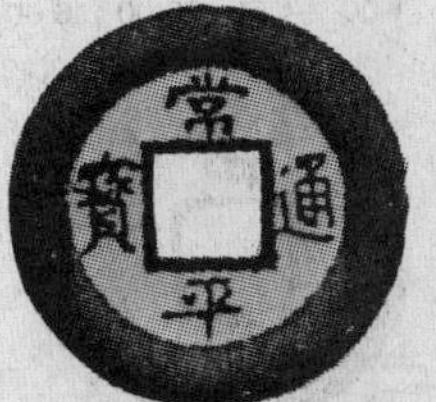

CAST COPPER or BRONZE, 26mm
Rev: *Ho* at top in different style, series number at bottom.

KM#	Date	Series	Good	VG	Fine	VF
9.1-9.10	ND(1806)	1-10	.75	1.00	1.50	2.50

Rev: *Ho* w/cross at top.

KM#	Date	Series	Good	VG	Fine	VF
9.15	ND(1806)	5	.75	1.00	1.50	2.50

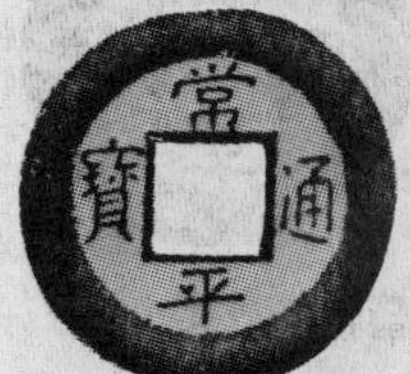

25mm
Rev: *Sip* (10) at bottom, additional series number at left.

KM#	Date	Series	Good	VG	Fine	VF
10.11-10.16	ND(1806)	11-16	.75	1.00	1.50	2.50

24mm
Rev: *I* (2) at bottom, series number at right.

KM#	Date	Series	Good	VG	Fine	VF
13.1-13.10	ND(1857)	1-10	2.00	3.50	5.00	10.00

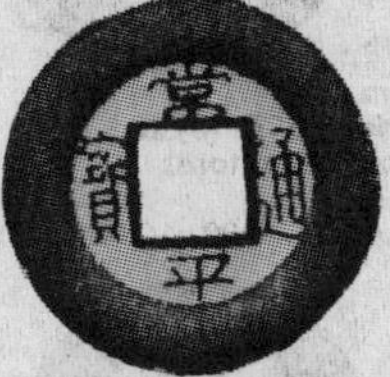

Rev: *I* (2) at bottom, series number at left.

KM#	Date	Series	Good	VG	Fine	VF
14.1-14.10	ND(1857)	1-10	3.00	4.50	7.50	15.00

25mm
Rev: *Sam* (3) at bottom, series number at right.

KM#	Date	Series	Good	VG	Fine	VF
15.1-15.10	ND(1832)	1-10	4.00	7.00	10.00	20.00

Rev: *Ho* w/o cross on top.

KM#	Date	Series	Good	VG	Fine	VF
15.11	ND(1832)	1	4.00	7.00	10.00	20.00

Rev: Dot in lower right field.

KM#	Date	Series	Good	VG	Fine	VF
15.14	ND(1832)	4	4.00	7.00	10.00	20.00

24mm
Rev: *Sam* (3) at bottom, series number at left.

KM#	Date	Series	Good	VG	Fine	VF
16.1-16.10	ND(1832)	1-10	4.00	7.00	10.00	20.00

***Ho* w/o cross on top.**

KM#	Date	Series	Good	VG	Fine	VF
16.14	ND(1832)	4	4.00	7.00	10.00	20.00

23mm
Rev: *Ho* in different style, *Sam* (3) at bottom, series number at left.

KM#	Date	Series	Good	VG	Fine	VF
17.1-17.10	ND(1857)	1-10	3.50	6.00	9.00	17.50

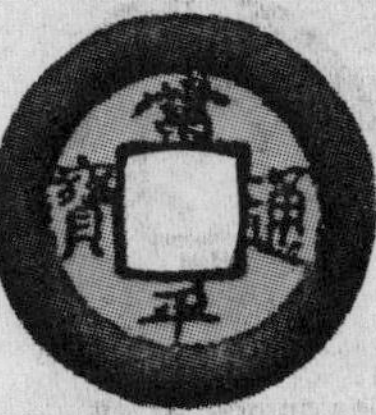

25mm
Rev: *O* (5) at bottom, series number at left.

KM#	Date	Series	Good	VG	Fine	VF
18.1	ND(1832)	1	1.25	2.25	3.50	5.00

Rev: Dot at right, series number at bottom.

KM#	Date	Series	Good	VG	Fine	VF
19.1-19.9	ND(1778-1806)	1-9	2.00	3.00	4.00	6.00

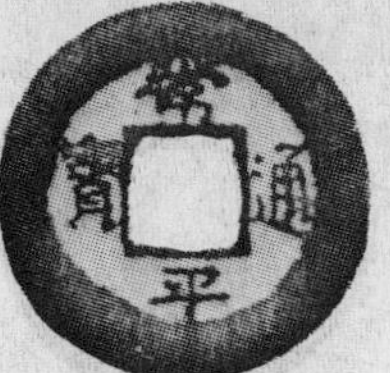

Rev: Dot at left, series number at bottom.

KM#	Date	Series	Good	VG	Fine	VF
20.1-20.6	ND(1778-1806)	1-6	4.00	7.00	10.00	20.00

24mm
Rev: Circle at right, series number at bottom.

KM#	Date	Series	Good	VG	Fine	VF
21.1-21.10	ND(1757-1806)	1-10	.75	1.00	1.50	2.50

23-25mm
Obv: 2 dot *Tong*, and *P'yong* w/hooks.

KM#	Date	Series	Good	VG	Fine	VF
21a.1-21a.10	ND(1757-1806)	1-10	.75	1.00	1.50	2.50

23mm
Rev: Circle at left, series number at bottom.

KM#	Date	Series	Good	VG	Fine	VF
22.1-22.10	ND(1757-1806)	1-10	.75	1.00	1.50	2.50

Obv: 2 dot *Tong* and *P'yong* w/hooks.

KM#	Date	Series	Good	VG	Fine	VF
22a.1-22a.10	ND(1757-1806)	1-10	.75	1.00	1.50	2.50

27mm
Rev: Circle at right, *Il* (1) at left, series number at bottom.

KM#	Date	Series	Good	VG	Fine	VF
23.1-23.4	ND(1814)	1-4	1.50	2.50	4.00	6.00

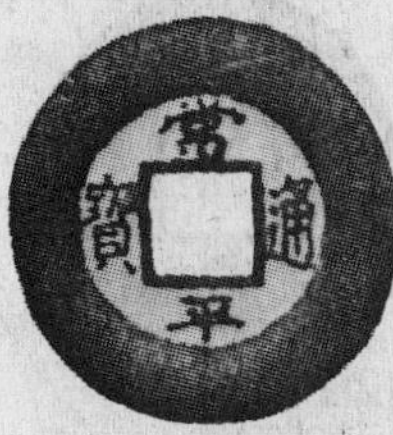

26mm
Rev: Circle at left, *Il* (1) at right, series number at bottom.

KM#	Date	Series	Good	VG	Fine	VF
24.1-24.10	ND(1840)	1-10	1.50	2.50	4.00	6.00

Rev: Circle at right, *I* (2) at left, series number at bottom.

KM#	Date	Series	Good	VG	Fine	VF
25.1-25.10	ND(1814)	1-10	1.50	2.50	4.00	6.00

25mm
Rev: Circle at left, *I* (2) at right, series number at bottom.

KM#	Date	Series	Good	VG	Fine	VF
26.1-26.10	ND(1814)	1-10	1.50	2.50	4.00	6.00

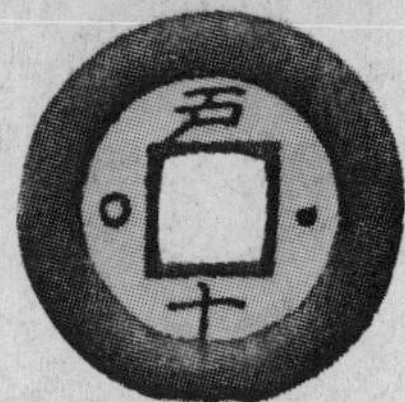

Rev: Dot at right, circle at left, series number at bottom.

KM#	Date	Series	Good	VG	Fine	VF
27.1-27.10	ND(1778-1806)	1-10	.75	1.00	1.50	2.50

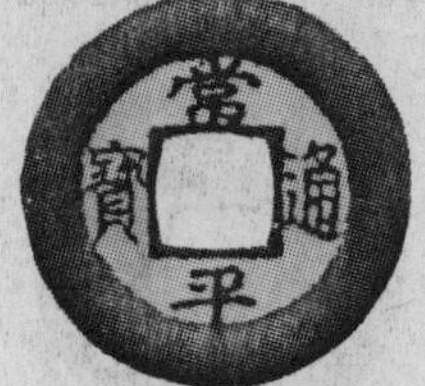

Rev: Circle at right, dot at left, series number at bottom.

KM#	Date	Series	Good	VG	Fine	VF
28.1-28.5	ND(1778-1806)	1-5	.75	1.00	1.50	2.50

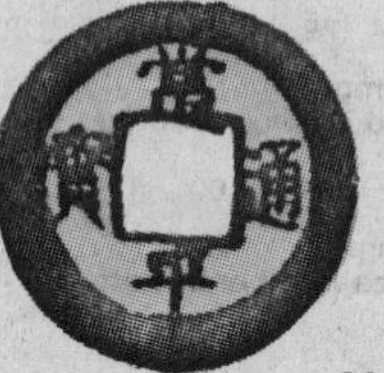

24mm
Rev: Crescent at right, series number at bottom.

KM#	Date	Series	Good	VG	Fine	VF
29.1-29.10	ND(1757-1806)	1-10	.75	1.00	1.50	2.50

23-24mm
Obv: W/o *P'yong*.

KM#	Date	Series	Good	VG	Fine	VF
29a.1-29a.10	ND(1757-1806)	1-10	.75	1.00	1.50	2.50

Rev: Star in crescent.

KM#	Date	Series	Good	VG	Fine	VF
29b.6	ND(1757-1806)	6	.75	1.00	1.50	2.50

Rev: Crescent at left, series number at bottom.

KM#	Date	Series	Good	VG	Fine	VF
30.1-30.10	ND(1757-1806)	1-10	.75	1.00	1.50	2.50

Obv: W/o *P'yong*, *tong* w/1 dot.

KM#	Date	Series	Good	VG	Fine	VF
30a.1-30a.10	ND(1757-1806)	1-10	.75	1.00	1.50	2.50

Obv: Star at lower left.

KM#	Date	Series	Good	VG	Fine	VF
30b.7	ND(1757-1806)	7	.75	1.00	1.50	2.50

25mm

KM#	Date	Series	Good	VG	Fine	VF
30c.1-30c.10	ND(1757-1806)	1-10	.75	1.00	1.50	2.50

Rev: Vertical line at right, crescent at left, number 9 at bottom.

KM#	Date	Series	Good	VG	Fine	VF
31.9	ND(1778-1806)	9	.75	1.00	1.50	2.50

25mm
Rev: Dot at right, crescent at left, series number at bottom.

KM#	Date	Series	Good	VG	Fine	VF
32.1-32.10	ND(1778-1806)	1-10	.75	1.00	1.50	2.50

Rev: Star in crescent.

KM#	Date	Series	Good	VG	Fine	VF
32.13		3	.75	1.00	1.50	2.50

26mm
Rev: Crescent at right, dot at left, series number at bottom.

KM#	Date	Series	Good	VG	Fine	VF
33.1-33.10	ND(1778-1806)	1-10	.75	1.00	1.50	2.50

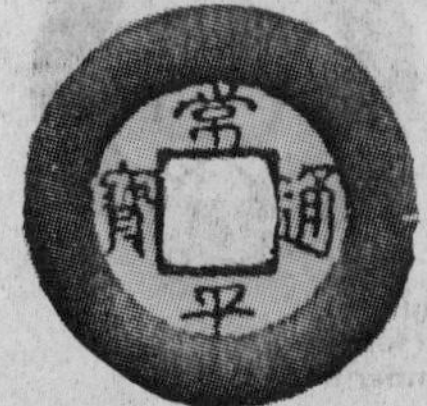

Rev: Crescent at right, *Il* (1) at left, series number at bottom.

KM#	Date	Series	Good	VG	Fine	VF
34.1-34.10	ND(1814)	1-10	1.50	2.50	4.00	6.00

Rev: *Il* (1) at right, crescent at left, series number at bottom.

KM#	Date	Series	Good	VG	Fine	VF
35.1-35.10	ND(1814)	1-10	1.50	2.50	4.00	6.00

25mm
Rev: Crescent at right, *Yuk* (6) at left, series number at bottom.

KM#	Date	Series	Good	VG	Fine	VF
36.1-36.6	ND(1857)	1-10	4.00	7.00	10.00	20.00

24mm
Small characters.
Rev: *Ch'on* at bottom, series number at right.

KM#	Date	Series	Good	VG	Fine	VF
37.1-37.11	ND(1832)	1-11	.75	1.00	1.50	2.50

23-26mm
Large characters.

KM#	Date	Series	Good	VG	Fine	VF
38.1-38.11	ND(1852)	1-11	.75	1.00	1.50	2.50

24mm
Small characters.
Rev: *Ch'on* at bottom, series number at left.

KM#	Date	Series	Good	VG	Fine	VF
39.1-39.10	ND(1832)	1-10	.75	1.00	1.50	2.50

25mm
Large characters.

KM#	Date	Series	Good	VG	Fine	VF
40.1-40.11	ND(1857)	1-11	.75	1.00	1.50	2.50

24mm
Rev: *Chi* at bottom, series number at left.

KM#	Date	Series	Good	VG	Fine	VF
41.1-41.10	ND(1852)	1-10	.75	1.00	1.50	2.50

Rev: *Hyon* at bottom, series number at right.

KM#	Date	Series	Good	VG	Fine	VF
42.1-42.10	ND(1852)	1-10	.75	1.00	1.50	2.50

Rev: Star at upper right.

KM#	Date	Series	Good	VG	Fine	VF
42.16	ND(1852)	6	.75	1.00	1.50	2.50

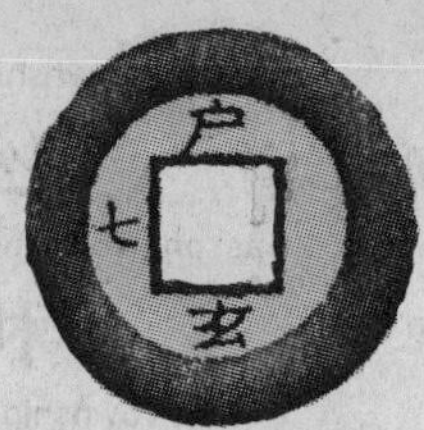

26mm
Obv. & rev: Small characters.
Rev: *Hyon* at bottom, series number at left.

KM#	Date	Series	Good	VG	Fine	VF
43.1-43.10	ND(1852)	1-10	.75	1.00	1.50	2.50

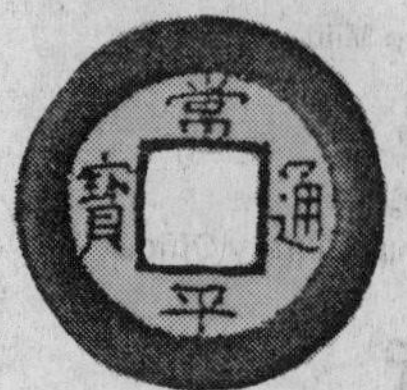

24mm
Obv. and rev: Large characters.
Rev: *Hyon* at bottom, series number at left.

KM#	Date	Series	Good	VG	Fine	VF
A43.1-A43.10	ND(1852)	1-10	.75	1.00	1.50	2.50

Rev: *Hwang* (yellow) at bottom, series number at right.

KM#	Date	Series	Good	VG	Fine	VF
44.1-44.10	ND(1832)	1-10	.75	1.00	1.50	2.50

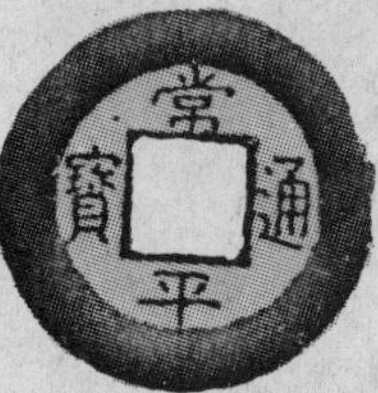

25mm
Rev: *U* at bottom.

KM#	Date	Series	Good	VG	Fine	VF
45	ND(1814)	—	1.50	2.50	4.00	6.00

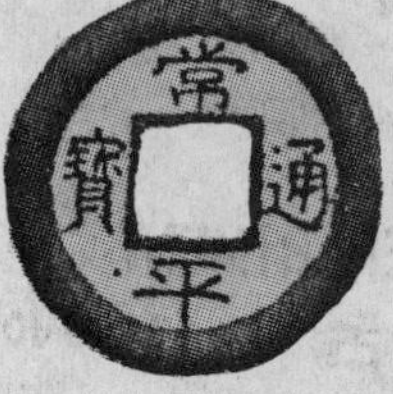

Rev: 19mm inner circle, *U* at bottom, series number at right.

KM#	Date	Series	Good	VG	Fine	VF
46.1-46.10	ND(1814)	1-10	1.00	1.50	3.00	6.00

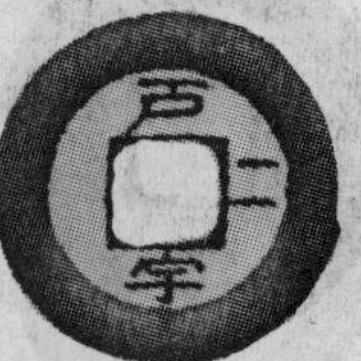

23mm
Rev: 16mm inner circle, *U* at bottom, series number at right.

KM#	Date	Series	Good	VG	Fine	VF
47.1-47.10	ND(1832)	1-10	.75	1.00	1.50	2.50

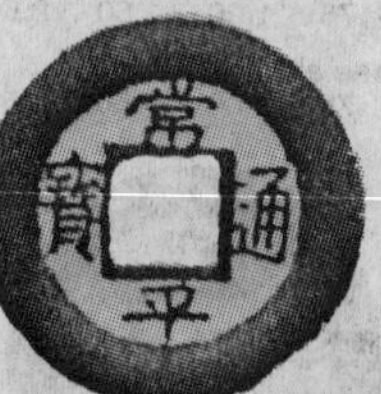

23-26mm
Rev: *U* at bottom, series number at left.

KM#	Date	Series	Good	VG	Fine	VF
48.1-48.10	ND(1814)	1-10	.75	1.00	1.50	2.50

25mm
Obv: Smaller *Po* at left.

KM#	Date	Series	Good	VG	Fine	VF
A48.1-A48.10	ND(1814)	1-10	.75	1.00	1.50	2.50

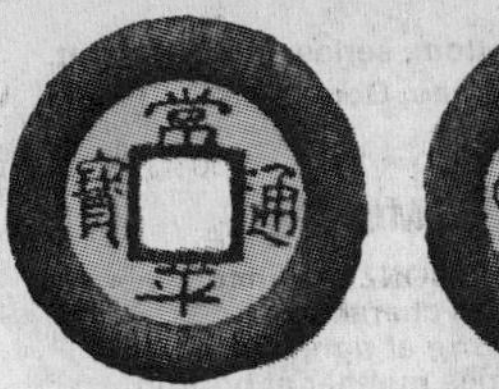
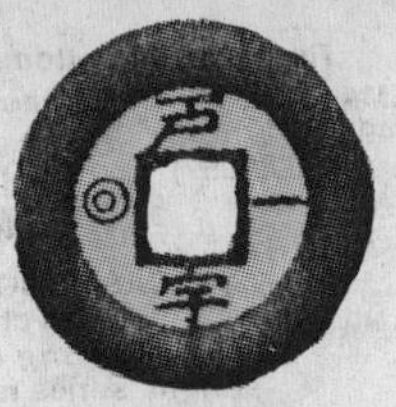

24mm
Rev: *U* at bottom, *Il* (1) at right, double circle at left.

KM#	Date	Series	Good	VG	Fine	VF
49	ND(1832)	—	1.50	2.50	4.00	6.00

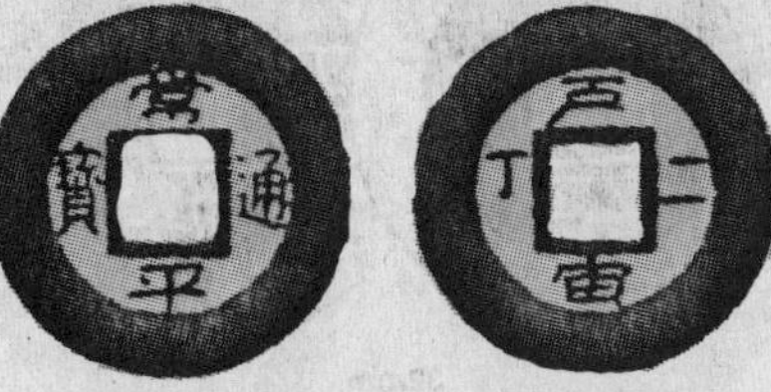

Rev: *Chu* at bottom, *Chong* at left, series number at right.

KM#	Date	Series	Good	VG	Fine	VF
50.1-50.10	ND(1832)	1-10	.75	1.00	1.50	2.50

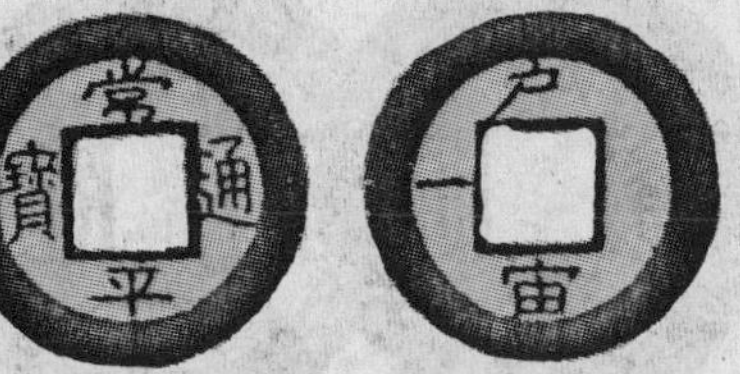

23-25mm
Rev: *Chu* at bottom, series number at left.

KM#	Date	Series	Good	VG	Fine	VF
51.1-51.10	ND(1852)	1-10	.75	1.00	1.50	2.50

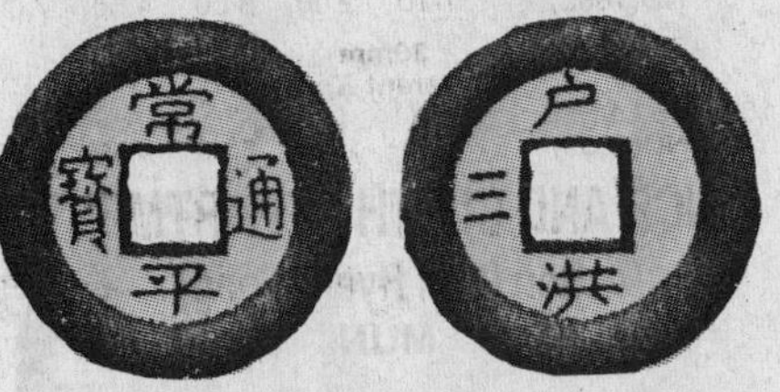

26mm
Rev: *Hong* at bottom, series number at left.

KM#	Date	Series	Good	VG	Fine	VF
52.1-52.10	ND(1852)	1-10	1.00	1.50	3.00	6.00

22-24mm

KM#	Date	Series	Good	VG	Fine	VF
53.1-53.10	ND(1852)	1-10	.75	1.00	1.50	2.50

Obv: *Tong* w/1 dot.

KM#	Date	Series	Good	VG	Fine	VF
53a.1-53a.10	ND(1852)	1-10	.75	1.00	1.50	2.50

23-25mm
Rev: *Il* (sun) at bottom, series number at left.

KM#	Date	Series	Good	VG	Fine	VF
54.1-54.10	ND(1852)	1-10	.75	1.00	1.50	2.50

Rev: *Wol* (moon) at bottom, series number at left.

KM#	Date	Series	Good	VG	Fine	VF
55.1-55.10	ND(1852)	1-10	.75	1.00	1.50	2.50

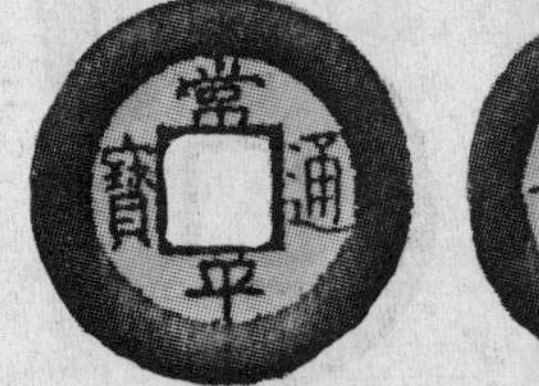

Rev: *Chin* at bottom, series number at left.

KM#	Date	Series	Good	VG	Fine	VF
56.1-56.10	ND(1852)	1-10	.75	1.00	1.50	2.50

24mm
Rev: *Yol* at bottom, series number at left.

KM#	Date	Series	Good	VG	Fine	VF
57.1-57.10	ND(1852)	1-10	.75	1.00	1.50	2.50

Rev: *Nae* at bottom, series number at left.

KM#	Date	Series	Good	VG	Fine	VF
58.1-58.10	ND(1852)	1-10	.75	1.00	1.50	2.50

Rev: *Wang* at bottom, series number at left.

KM#	Date	Series	Good	VG	Fine	VF
59.1-59.10	ND(1852)	1-10	.75	1.00	1.50	2.50

23mm
Rev: *Saeng* at bottom, series number at left.

KM#	Date	Series	Good	VG	Fine	VF
60.1-60.10	ND(1852)	1-10	.75	1.00	1.50	2.50

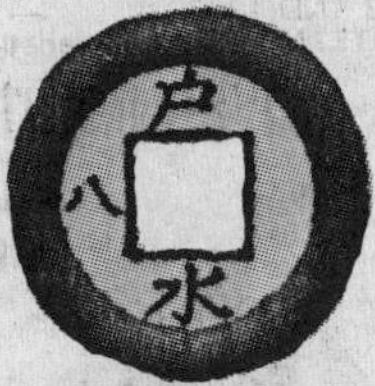

24mm
Rev: *Su* at bottom, series number at left.

KM#	Date	Series	Good	VG	Fine	VF
61.1-61.10	ND(1852)	1-10	.75	1.00	1.50	2.50

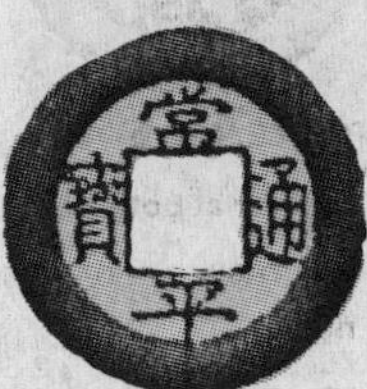

Rev: *Kwang* at bottom, series number at left.

KM#	Date	Series	Good	VG	Fine	VF
62.1-62.10	ND(1852)	1-10	.75	1.00	1.50	2.50

Rev: *Kwang* at bottom, dot at right, series number at left.

KM#	Date	Series	Good	VG	Fine	VF
63.6	ND(1852)	6	.75	1.00	1.50	2.50

25mm
Rev: *Kwang* at bottom, series number at right.

KM#	Date	Series	Good	VG	Fine	VF
64.2	ND(1852)	2	.75	1.00	1.50	2.50

23mm
Rev: *Mun* at bottom, series number at right.

KM#	Date	Series	Good	VG	Fine	VF
65.1-65.10	ND(1852)	1-10	.75	1.00	1.50	2.50

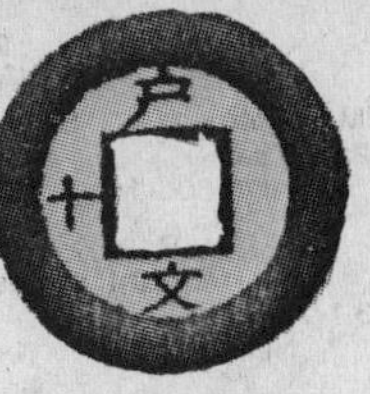

24mm
Rev: *Mun* at bottom, series number at left.

KM#	Date	Series	Good	VG	Fine	VF
66.1-66.10	ND(1832)	1-10	.75	1.00	1.50	2.50

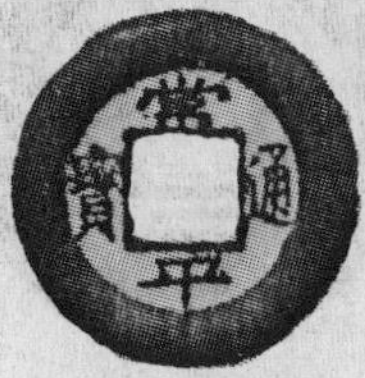

Rev: *Ho* in different style.

KM#	Date	Series	Good	VG	Fine	VF
67.1-67.10	ND(1832)	1-10	.75	1.00	1.50	2.50

25mm

KM#	Date	Series	Good	VG	Fine	VF
67.18	ND(1832)	8	.75	1.00	1.50	2.50

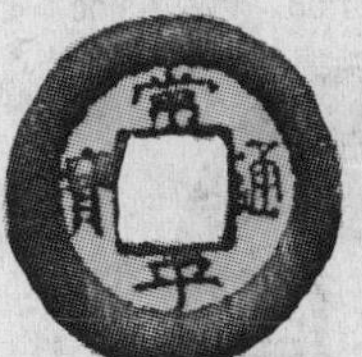

23mm
Rev: *Mun* at bottom, circle at left, series number at right.

KM#	Date	Series	Good	VG	Fine	VF
68.1-68.10	ND(1832)	1-10	.75	1.00	1.50	2.50

25mm
Rev: *Mun* at bottom, circle at right, series number at left.

KM#	Date	Series	Good	VG	Fine	VF
69.1-69.5	ND(1832)	1-5	1.25	2.50	4.00	6.00

24mm
Rev: *Ip* at bottom, series number at right.

KM#	Date	Series	Good	VG	Fine	VF
70.1-70.10	ND(1814)	1-10	.75	1.00	1.50	2.50

25mm
Rev: *Ho* w/o stem.

KM#	Date	Series	Good	VG	Fine	VF
70a.1-70a-10	ND(1814)	1-10	.75	1.00	1.50	2.50

23mm
Rev: *Ip* at bottom, series number at left.

KM#	Date	Series	Good	VG	Fine	VF
71.1-71.10	ND(1806-14)	1-10	.75	1.00	1.50	2.50

24mm
Obv: 1 dot *Tong*, and *P'yong* w/hooks.

KM#	Date	Series	Good	VG	Fine	VF
71a.1-71a.10	ND(1806-14)	1-10	.75	1.00	1.50	2.50

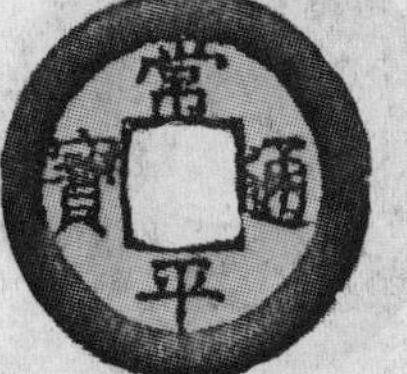

25mm
Rev: *Ip* at bottom, circle at left, series number at right.

KM#	Date	Series	Good	VG	Fine	VF
72.1-72.10	ND(1806-14)	1-10	.75	1.00	1.50	2.50

24mm
Wide rim.

KM#	Date	Series	Good	VG	Fine	VF
72a.1-72a.10	ND(1806-14)	1-10	.75	1.00	1.50	2.50

Rev: *Ip* at bottom, circle at right, series number at left.

KM#	Date	Series	Good	VG	Fine	VF
73.1-73.5	ND(1806-14)	1-5	4.00	7.00	10.00	20.00

5 MUN

CAST COPPER or BRONZE
30mm
Small characters, inner circle 21-22mm.
Rev: *Tang* at right, *O* (5) at left, series number at bottom.

KM#	Date	Series	Good	VG	Fine	VF
136.1-136.10	ND(1883)	1-10	1.00	1.75	3.00	4.50

31mm
Medium characters, inner circle 21-22mm.

KM#	Date	Series	Good	VG	Fine	VF
137.1-137.11	ND(1883)	1-11	1.00	1.75	3.00	4.50

30mm
Large characters, inner circle 21-22mm.

KM#	Date	Series	Good	VG	Fine	VF
138.1-138.11	ND(1883)	1-11	2.00	3.50	5.00	10.00

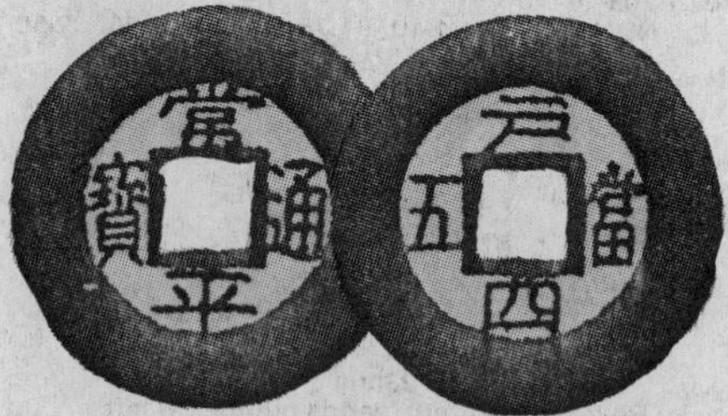

31mm
Inner circle 19mm

KM#	Date	Series	Good	VG	Fine	VF
139.1-139.10	ND(1883)	1-10	2.00	3.50	5.00	10.00

Rev: Small *Ho* at top, crescent under series number at bottom.

KM#	Date	Series	Good	VG	Fine	VF
140.1-140.10	ND(1883)	1-10	1.00	1.75	3.00	4.50

30mm
Rev: Wide *Ho* at top, crescent under series number at bottom.

KM#	Date	Series	Good	VG	Fine	VF
141.1-141.10	ND(1883)	1-10	1.50	2.50	4.50	8.50

Small characters, inner circle 19mm.
Rev: Crescent under series number at bottom.

KM#	Date	Series	Good	VG	Fine	VF
142.1-142.10	ND(1883)	1-10	2.00	3.50	5.00	10.00

100 MUN

CAST COPPER or BRONZE, 24.00 g, 39-40mm

KM#	Date	Series	Good	VG	Fine	VF
143	ND(1866)	—	3.00	5.00	7.00	10.00

NOTE: More than 40 varieties exist.

GOVERNMENT TITHE OFFICE

均 Kyun (Kyun Yok Ch'ong)

MUN

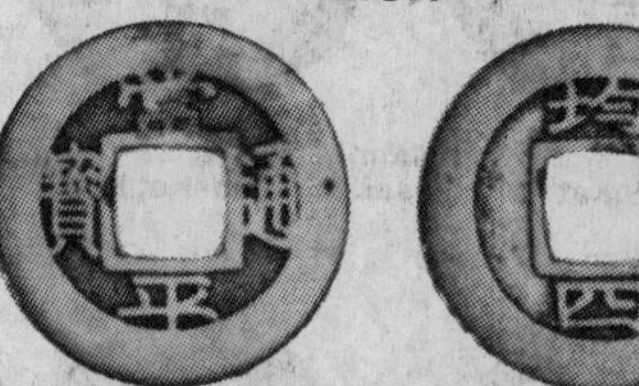

CAST COPPER or BRONZE, 4.00 g
24mm
Rev: *Kyun* at top, series number at bottom.

KM#	Date	Series	Good	VG	Fine	VF
147.1-147.10	ND(1807)	1-10	.75	1.00	1.50	2.50

Rev: Star at right.

KM#	Date	Series	Good	VG	Fine	VF
147.18	ND(1807)	8	.75	1.00	1.50	2.50
147.20	ND(1807)	10	.75	1.00	1.50	2.50

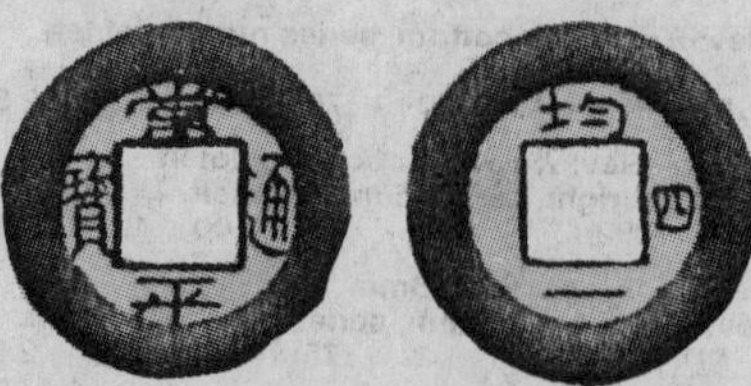

23mm
Rev: *Il* (1) at bottom, series number at right.

KM#	Date	Series	Good	VG	Fine	VF
148.1-148.10	ND(1857)	1-10	3.00	5.00	7.50	15.00

Rev: *Il* (1) at bottom, series number at left.

KM#	Date	Series	Good	VG	Fine	VF
149.1-149.10	ND(1857)	1-10	3.00	5.00	7.50	15.00

5 MUN

CAST BRONZE, 31mm
Small characters.
Rev: *Tang* at right, *O* (5) at right, series number at bottom.

KM#	Date	Series	Good	VG	Fine	VF
150.1-150.11	ND(1883)	1-11	1.00	1.50	2.50	4.00

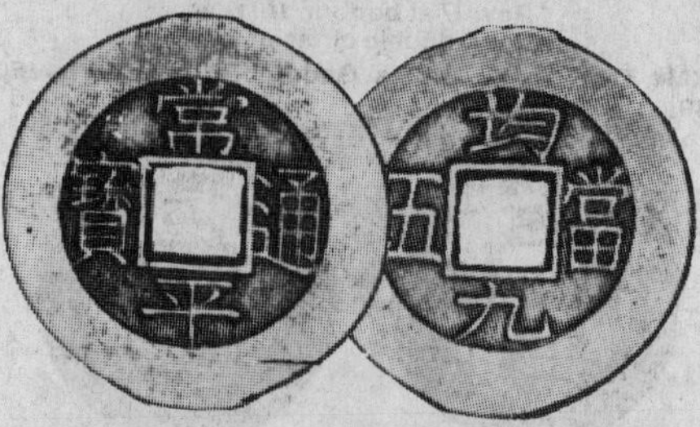

32mm
Medium characters.

KM#	Date	Series	Good	VG	Fine	VF
151.1-151.10	ND(1883)	1-10	1.50	2.50	4.00	6.00

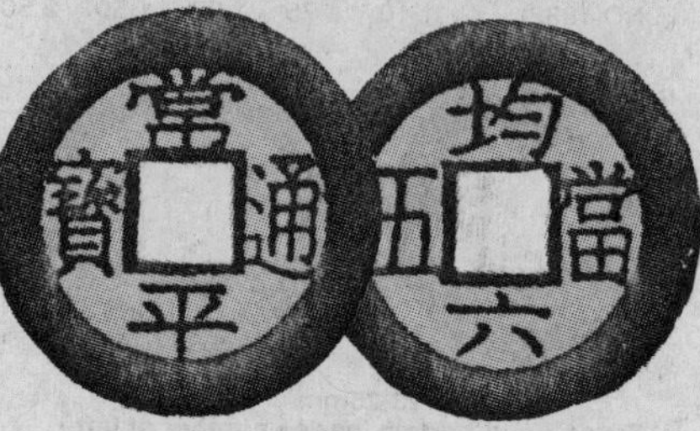

31mm
Large characters.

KM#	Date	Series	Good	VG	Fine	VF
152.1-152.10	ND(1883)	1-10	2.00	3.00	4.50	7.00

30mm
Different *Kyun*

KM#	Date	Series	Good	VG	Fine	VF
153.1-153.11	ND(1883)	1-11	2.00	3.00	4.50	7.00

RICE AND CLOTH DEPARTMENT

宣 Son (Son Hye Ch'ong) 惠

MUN

CAST COPPER or BRONZE, 4.00 g
25mm
Rev: Series number at bottom.

KM#	Date	Series	Good	VG	Fine	VF
174.1-174.6	ND(1814)	1-6	.75	1.00	1.75	3.00

Large characters.
Rev: *Hye* at top, series number at bottom.

KM#	Date	Series	Good	VG	Fine	VF
175.1-175.12	ND(1806)	1-12	.75	1.00	1.75	3.00

Small characters.

KM#	Date	Series	Good	VG	Fine	VF
176.1-176.12	ND(1806)	1-12	.75	1.00	1.75	3.00

26mm
Rev: *I* (2)at left, series number at bottom.

KM#	Date	Series	Good	VG	Fine	VF
177.1-177.7	ND(1836)	1-7	.75	1.00	1.75	3.00

CENTRAL GOVERNMENT MINT

典 **Chon (Chon Hwan' Guk)**

5 MUN

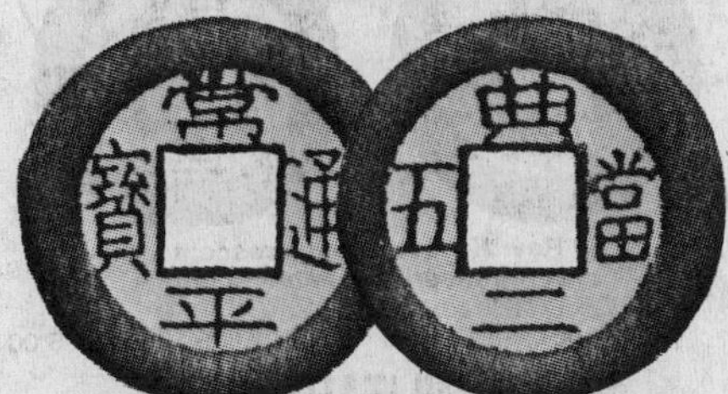

CAST BRONZE, 31mm
Large characters.
Rev: *Tang* at right, *O* (5) at left, series number at bottom.

KM#	Date	Series	Good	VG	Fine	VF
209.1-209.12	ND(1883)	1-12	1.00	1.75	3.00	5.00

32mm
Rev: Star below *Bo*.

KM#	Date	Series	Good	VG	Fine	VF
209.21	ND(1883)	1	1.00	1.75	3.00	5.00

32mm
Small characters.

KM#	Date	Series	Good	VG	Fine	VF
210.1-210.15	ND(1883)	1-15	1.00	1.75	3.00	5.00

Reduced size, 29mm

KM#	Date	Series	Good	VG	Fine	VF
211.1-211.12	ND(1883)	1-12	1.00	1.75	3.00	5.00

28mm
Rev: Dot below series number at bottom.

KM#	Date	Series	Good	VG	Fine	VF
212.1-212.3	ND(1883)	1-3	1.00	1.75	3.00	5.00

29mm
Obv: *P'yong* w/hooks.

KM#	Date	Series	Good	VG	Fine	VF
212.12	ND(1883)	2	1.00	1.75	3.00	5.00

PALACE GUARD OFFICE

武 **Mu (Mu Wi Yong)**

MUN

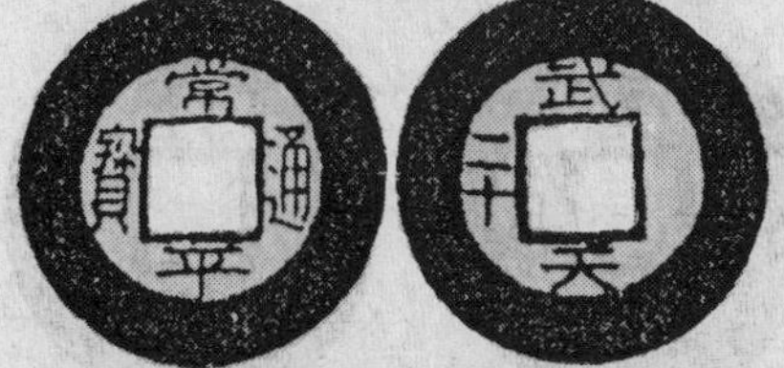

CAST BRONZE, 25-26mm, 4.00 g
Rev: *Ch'on* at bottom, series number at left.

KM#	Date	Series	Good	VG	Fine	VF
337.1-337.20	ND(1881)	1-20	1.00	1.75	3.00	5.00

Reduced size, 23-24mm

KM#	Date	Series	Good	VG	Fine	VF
338.1-338.20	ND(1881)	1-20	.75	1.00	1.50	2.50

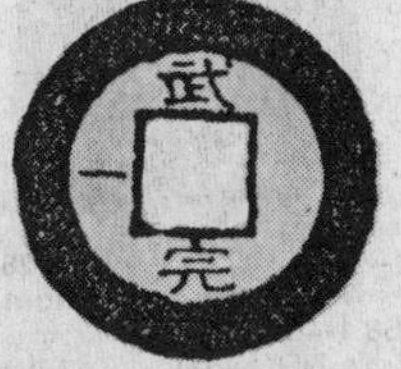

24mm
Rev: *Wan* at bottom, series number at left.

KM#	Date	Series	Good	VG	Fine	VF
339.1	ND(1881)	1	35.00	60.00	100.00	175.00

COURT GUARD

禁 **Kum (Kum Wi Yong)**

MUN

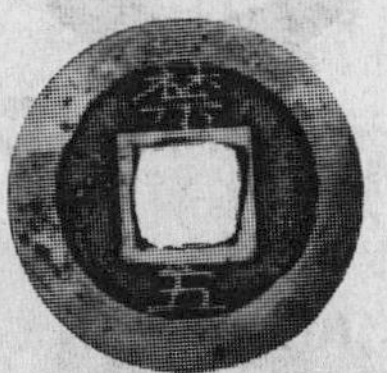

CAST BRONZE, 4.00 g, 23-25mm
Large characters.
Rev: *Kum* at top, series number at bottom.

KM#	Date	Series	Good	VG	Fine	VF
340.1-340.8	ND(1823)	1-8	.75	1.00	1.50	2.50

25mm
Small characters.

KM#	Date	Series	Good	VG	Fine	VF
341.1-341.8	ND(1823)	1-8	.75	1.00	1.50	2.50

Obv: Hooks in *P'yong*.

KM#	Date	Series	Good	VG	Fine	VF
341a.1-341a.8	ND(1823)	1-8	.75	1.00	1.50	2.50

23mm
Obv: *P'yong* w/o hooks.

KM#	Date	Series	Good	VG	Fine	VF
341b.1-341b.8	ND(1823)	1-8	.75	1.00	1.50	2.50

MILITARY TRAINING COMMAND

訓 or 訓 **Hun (Hul Ly On Do Gam)**

MUN

CAST BRONZE, 4.00 g, 25mm
Rev: *Hun* at top, series number at bottom.

KM#	Date	Series	Good	VG	Fine	VF
448.1-448.6	ND(1828)	1-6	.75	1.25	2.00	3.00

Rev: Star at upper left.

KM#	Date	Series	Good	VG	Fine	VF
448.14	ND(1828)	4	.75	1.25	2.00	3.00

25mm
Rev: *Ch'on* at bottom, series number at left.

KM#	Date	Series	Good	VG	Fine	VF
449.1-449.10	ND(1857)	1-10	.75	1.25	2.00	3.00

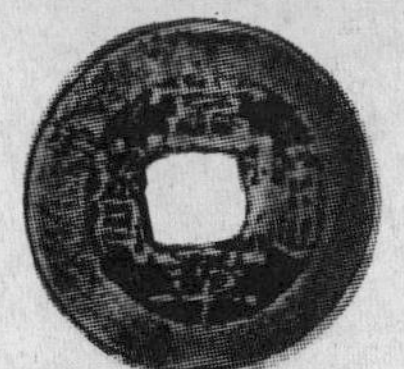

Rev: *Chong* at bottom, series number at left.

KM#	Date	Series	Good	VG	Fine	VF
450.1-450.10	ND(1857)	1-10	.75	1.25	2.00	3.00

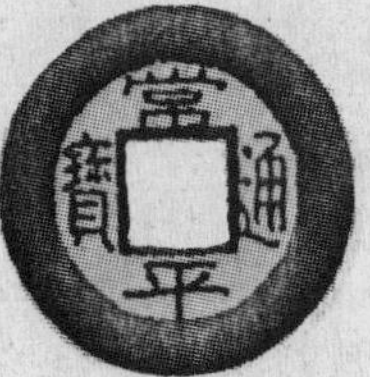
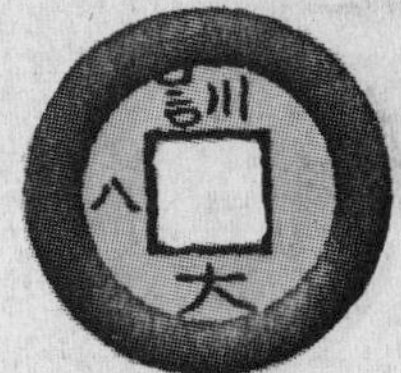

Rev: *Tae* at bottom, series number at left.

KM#	Date	Series	Good	VG	Fine	VF
451.1-451.10	ND(1857)	1-10	.75	1.25	2.00	3.00

Rev: *Kong* at bottom, series number at left.

KM#	Date	Series	Good	VG	Fine	VF
452.1-452.10	ND(1857)	1-10	.75	1.25	2.00	3.00

25mm
Rev: *Mun* at bottom, series number at right.

KM#	Date	Series	Good	VG	Fine	VF
453.1	ND(1857)	1	.75	1.25	2.00	3.00

24mm
Rev: *Mun* at bottom, series number at left.

KM#	Date	Series	Good	VG	Fine	VF
454.1-454.10	ND(1857)	1-10	.75	1.25	2.00	3.00

Rev: *Ch'on* (thousand) at bottom, series number at left.

KM#	Date	Series	Good	VG	Fine	VF
455.1-455.10	ND(1857)	1-10	.75	1.25	2.00	3.00

25mm
Rev: *Chung* at bottom, series number at right.

KM#	Date	Series	Good	VG	Fine	VF
456.1	ND(1857)	1	.75	1.25	2.00	3.00

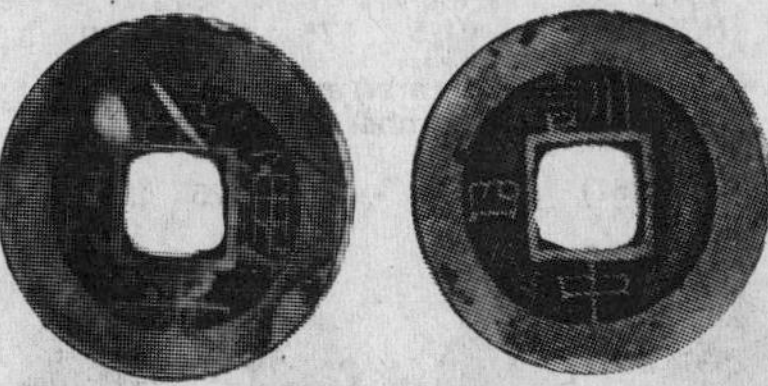

24mm
Rev: *Chung* at bottom, series number at left.

KM#	Date	Series	Good	VG	Fine	VF
457.1-457.10	ND(1857)	1-10	.75	1.25	2.00	3.00

Rev: Star at lower right.

KM#	Date	Series	Good	VG	Fine	VF
457.14	ND(1857)	4	.75	1.25	2.00	3.00

Rev: Star at right.

KM#	Date	Series	Good	VG	Fine	VF
457.16	ND(1857)	6	.75	1.25	2.00	3.00
457.17	ND(1857)	7	.75	1.25	2.00	3.00

25mm
Obv: Small characters.
Rev: *T'o* at bottom, series number at right.

KM#	Date	Series	Good	VG	Fine	VF
458.1-458.10	ND(1857)	1-10	.75	1.25	2.00	3.00

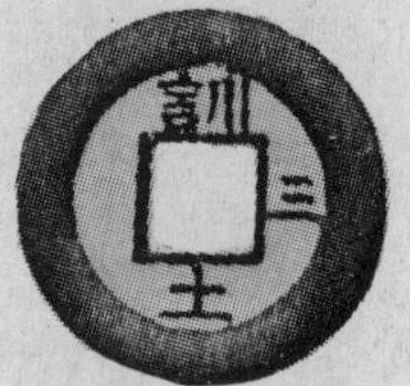

Obv: Large characters.

KM#	Date	Series	Good	VG	Fine	VF
459.1-459.10	ND(1857)	1-10	.75	1.25	2.00	3.00

Obv: Small characters.
Rev: *T'o* at bottom, series number at left.

KM#	Date	Series	Good	VG	Fine	VF
460.1-460.10	ND(1857)	1-10	.75	1.25	2.00	3.00

Obv: Large characters.

KM#	Date	Series	Good	VG	Fine	VF
461.1-461.10	ND(1857)	1-10	.75	1.25	2.00	3.00

Rev: *T'o* at bottom, series number at right, crescent at left.

KM#	Date	Series	Good	VG	Fine	VF
462.1-462.5	ND(1857)	1-5	.75	1.25	2.00	3.00

25mm
Obv: Small characters.
Rev: *T'o* at bottom, crescent at right, series number at left.

KM#	Date	Series	Good	VG	Fine	VF
463.1	ND(1857)	1	.75	1.25	2.00	3.00
463.2		2	.75	1.25	2.00	3.00
463.3		3	.75	1.25	2.00	3.00
463.4		4	2.00	3.00	4.00	6.50
463.5		5	2.00	3.00	4.00	6.50

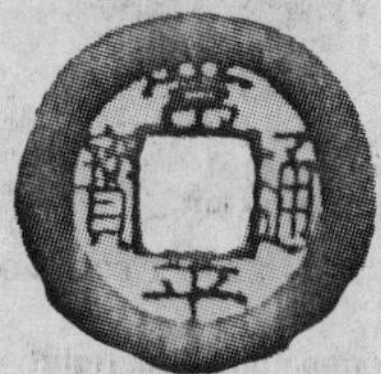 

24mm
Obv: Large characters.

KM#	Date	Series	Good	VG	Fine	VF
464.1-464.5	ND(1857)	1-5	.75	1.25	2.00	3.00

Rev: *Won* (first) at bottom, series number at right.

KM#	Date	Series	Good	VG	Fine	VF
465.1-465.10	ND(1857)	1-10	.75	1.25	2.00	3.00

25mm
Rev: *Won* at bottom, series number at left.

KM#	Date	Series	Good	VG	Fine	VF
466.1-466.10	ND(1857)	1-10	.75	1.25	2.00	3.00

Rev: *Won* at bottom, series number at right, crescent at left.

KM#	Date	Series	Good	VG	Fine	VF
467.1-467.5	ND(1857)	1-5	.75	1.25	2.00	3.00

26mm
Rev: *Saeng* at bottom, series number at right.

KM#	Date	Series	Good	VG	Fine	VF
468.1-468.10	ND(1857)	1-10	.75	1.25	2.00	3.00

25mm
Rev: *Saeng* at bottom, series number at left.

KM#	Date	Series	Good	VG	Fine	VF
469.1-469.10	ND(1857)	1-10	.75	1.25	2.00	3.00

24mm
Rev: *Saeng* at bottom, crescent at right, series number at left.

KM#	Date	Series	Good	VG	Fine	VF
470.1-470.5	ND(1857)	1-5	.75	1.25	2.00	3.00

25mm
Rev: *Chon* (perfect) at bottom, series number at right.

KM#	Date	Series	Good	VG	Fine	VF
471.1-471.10	ND(1857)	1-10	.75	1.25	2.00	3.00

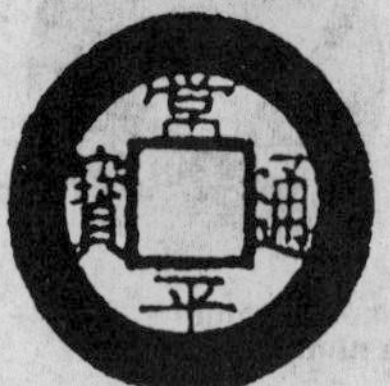 

24mm
Rev: *Chon* at bottom, series number at left.

KM#	Date	Series	Good	VG	Fine	VF
472.1-472.10	ND(1857)	1-10	.75	1.25	2.00	3.00

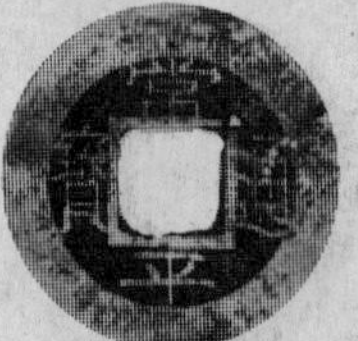 

23-25mm
Rev: *Chon* at bottom, crescent at right, series number at left.

KM#	Date	Series	Good	VG	Fine	VF
473.1-473.5	ND(1857)	1-5	.75	1.25	2.00	3.00

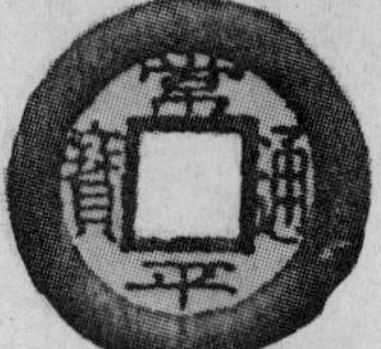 

24mm
Rev: *Kil* at bottom, series number at right.

KM#	Date	Series	Good	VG	Fine	VF
474.1-474.10	ND(1857)	1-10	6.00	10.00	15.00	25.00

Rev: *Kil* at bottom, series number at left.

KM#	Date	Series	Good	VG	Fine	VF
475.1-475.10	ND(1857)	1-10	6.00	10.00	15.00	25.00

Rev: *Kil* at bottom, crescent at right, series number at left.

KM#	Date	Series	Good	VG	Fine	VF
476.1-476.5	ND(1857)	1-5	6.00	10.00	15.00	25.00

SEOUL MILITARY OFFICE

統 T'ong (T'ong Wi Yong)

5 MON

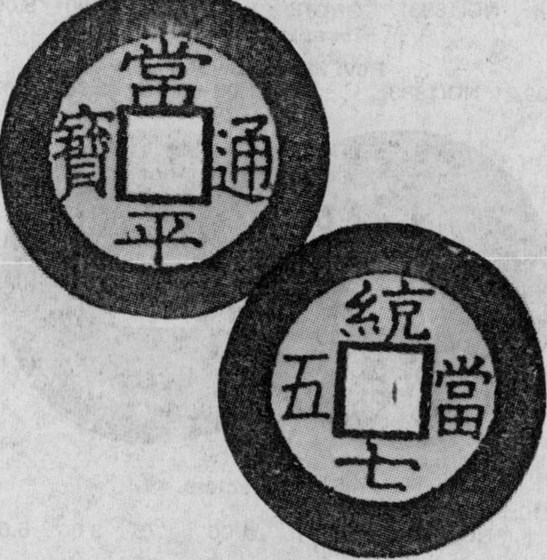

CAST BRONZE, 32mm
Inside diameter 20-22mm.
Rev: *Tang* at right, *O* (5) at left, series number at bottom.

KM#	Date	Series	Good	VG	Fine	VF
763.1-763.20	ND(1883)	1-20	1.00	1.50	2.25	3.50

Reduced size, 29mm, inside diameter 18-19mm.

KM#	Date	Series	Good	VG	Fine	VF
764.1-764.20	ND(1883)	1-20	1.00	1.50	2.25	3.50

GOVERNMENT OFFICE PUKHAN MOUNTAIN FORTRESS

经 Kyong (Kyong Ni Ch'ong)

MUN

CAST BRONZE, 4.00 g, 26mm

Rev: *Kyong* at top, series number at bottom.

KM#	Date	Series	Good	VG	Fine	VF
765.1-765.10	ND(1830)	1-10	1.00	1.50	2.25	3.50

Rev: *Sip* (10) at bottom and additional series number at left.

KM#	Date	Series	Good	VG	Fine	VF
766.1-766.6	ND(1830)	1-6	1.00	1.50	2.25	3.50

Rev: Star at left.

KM#	Date	Series	Good	VG	Fine	VF
766.11	ND(1830)	1	1.00	1.50	2.25	3.50

KANGWHA TOWNSHIP MILITARY OFFICE

沁 Sim (Kang Hwa Kwal Li Yong)

MUN

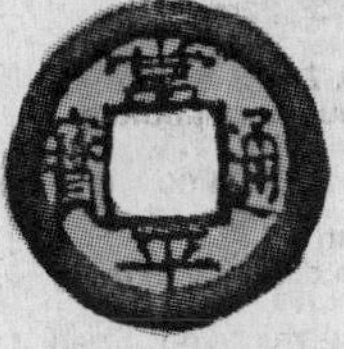

CAST BRONZE, 4.00 g, 22mm
Rev: *Sim* at top, *Won* (first) at bottom, dot at left.

KM#	Date	Series	Good	VG	Fine	VF
771	ND(1883)	—	1.75	2.50	3.50	5.00

25mm
Rev: *Won* (first) at bottom, series number at left.

KM#	Date	Series	Good	VG	Fine	VF
772.1-772.10	ND(1883)	1-10	6.00	10.00	16.50	25.00

22mm
Rev: *Won* (first) at bottom, series number at right, circle at left.

KM#	Date	Series	Good	VG	Fine	VF
773	ND(1883)	1	40.00	80.00	125.00	200.00

23mm
Wide rim.
Rev: *Won* (first) at bottom, series number at right, crescent at left.

KM#	Date	Series	Good	VG	Fine	VF
774.1-774.10	ND(1883)	1-10	6.00	10.00	16.50	25.00

21mm
Narrow rim.
Rev: *Won* (first) at bottom, series number at right, crescent at left.

KM#	Date	Series	Good	VG	Fine	VF
A774.1-A774.10	ND(1883)	1-10	6.00	10.00	16.50	25.00

5 MUN

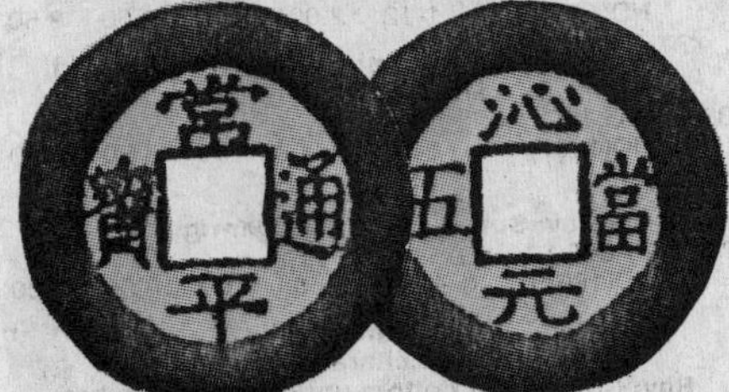

CAST BRONZE, 31mm
Rev: *Sim* at top, *Won* at bottom, *Tang* at right, *O* (5) at left.

KM#	Date	Series	Good	VG	Fine	VF
775	ND(1883)	—	3.50	6.50	10.00	15.00

30mm
Large characters.
Rev: Series number at bottom.

KM#	Date	Series	Good	VG	Fine	VF
776.1-776.11	ND(1883)	1-11	1.25	2.00	2.75	4.00

32mm
Small characters.

KM#	Date	Series	Good	VG	Fine	VF
777.1-777.10	ND(1883)	1-10	1.25	2.00	2.75	4.00

Rev: Crescent below series number.

KM#	Date	Series	Good	VG	Fine	VF
778.1-778.7	ND(1883)	1-7	8.00	12.00	20.00	30.00

Rev: Crescent at lower left.

KM#	Date	Series	Good	VG	Fine	VF
779.1-779.13	ND(1883)	1-13	3.00	5.00	8.00	12.00

KAESONG TOWNSHIP MILITARY OFFICE

開 Kae (Kae Song Kwal Li Yong)

MUN

CAST BRONZE, 4.00 g, 23.5mm
Large characters.
Rev: Series number at bottom.

KM#	Date	Series	Good	VG	Fine	VF
791.1-791.5	ND(1836)	1-5	.75	1.00	1.50	2.50

24.5mm
Rev: Circle at right, series number at bottom.

KM#	Date	Series	Good	VG	Fine	VF
793.1-793.10	ND(1816)	1-10	.75	1.00	1.50	2.50

Rev: Star at lower left.

KM#	Date	Series	Good	VG	Fine	VF
793.11	ND(1816)	1	.75	1.00	1.50	2.50

Rev: Star at upper left.

KM#	Date	Series	Good	VG	Fine	VF
793.17	ND(1816)	7	.75	1.00	1.50	2.50

24mm
Rev: Circle at left, series number at bottom.

KM#	Date	Series	Good	VG	Fine	VF
794.1-794.10	ND(1816)	1-10	.75	1.00	1.50	2.50

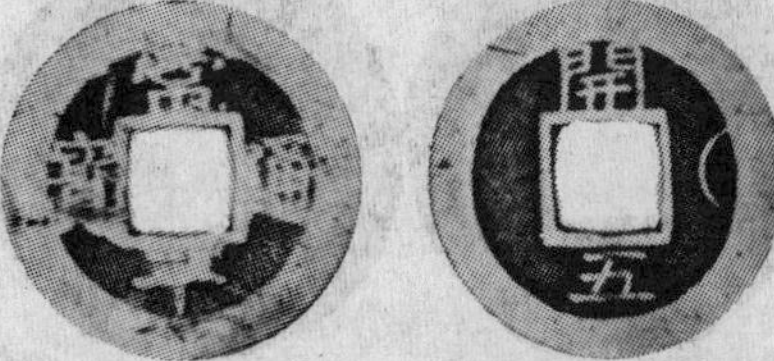

25mm
Rev: Crescent at right, series number at bottom.

KM#	Date	Series	Good	VG	Fine	VF
795.1-795.10	ND(1816)	1-10	.75	1.00	1.50	2.50

25.5mm
Small characters.
Rev: Crescent at right, series number at bottom.

KM#	Date	Series	Good	VG	Fine	VF
A795.1-A795.10	ND(1836)	1-10	2.50	6.00	10.00	15.00

Rev: Star at lower left.

KM#	Date	Series	Good	VG	Fine	VF
A795.13	ND(1836)	3	2.50	6.00	10.00	15.00

25mm
Rev: Crescent at left, series number at bottom.

KM#	Date	Series	Good	VG	Fine	VF
B795.1-B795.10	ND(1816)	1-10	.75	1.00	1.50	2.50

Small characters, wider rims.
Small crescent.

KM#	Date	Series	Good	VG	Fine	VF
C795.1-C795.10	ND(1836)	1-10	2.50	6.00	10.00	15.00

25mm
Rev: *Ch'on* at bottom, series number at right.

KM#	Date	Series	Good	VG	Fine	VF
796.1-796.10	ND(1836)	1-10	.75	1.00	1.50	2.50

Rev: *Ch'on* at bottom, *Sip* (10) at right, additional series number at left.

KM#	Date	Series	Good	VG	Fine	VF
797.1-797.5	ND(1836)	1-5	.75	1.00	1.50	2.50

Rev: *Ch'on* at bottom, series number at right, crescent at left.

KM#	Date	Series	Good	VG	Fine	VF
798.1-798.3	ND(1836)	1-3	.75	1.00	1.50	2.50

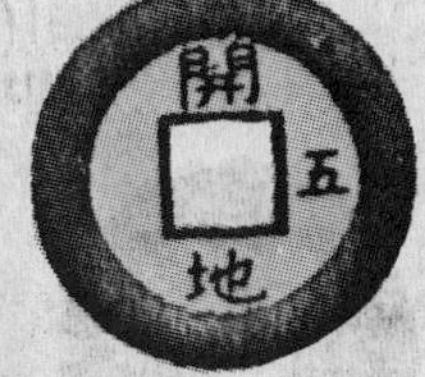

25.5mm
Rev: *Chi* at bottom, series number at right.

KM#	Date	Series	Good	VG	Fine	VF
799.1-799.10	ND(1836)	1-10	1.00	2.00	3.00	4.50

24.5mm
Rev: *Chi* at bottom, *Sip* (10) at right, additional series number at left.

KM#	Date	Series	Good	VG	Fine	VF
800.1-800.9	ND(1836)	1-9	1.00	2.00	3.00	4.50

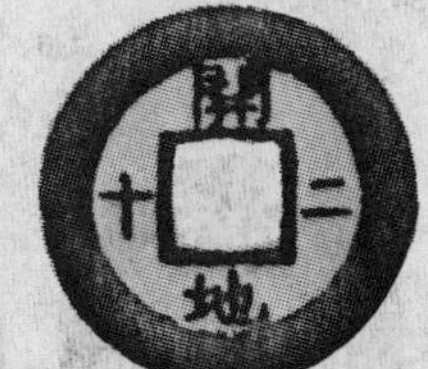

25mm
Rev: *Chi* at bottom, *I* (2) at right, *Sip* (10) at left.

KM#	Date	Series	Good	VG	Fine	VF
801.2	ND(1836)	2	1.00	2.00	3.00	4.50

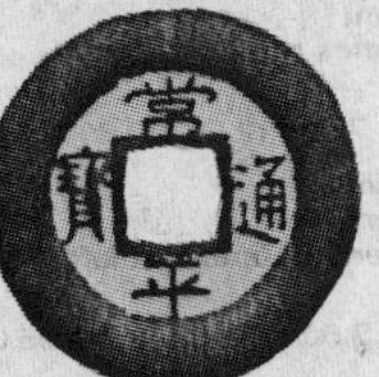

Rev: *Il* (sun) at bottom, series number at right.

KM#	Date	Series	Good	VG	Fine	VF
802.1-802.10	ND(1836)	1-10	1.00	2.00	3.00	4.50

22mm

KM#	Date	Series	Good	VG	Fine	VF
802.13	ND(1836)	3	1.00	2.00	3.00	4.50

24.5mm
Rev: *Il* (sun) at bottom, series number at left.

803.1-803.10 ND(1836)		1-10	1.00	2.00	3.00	4.50

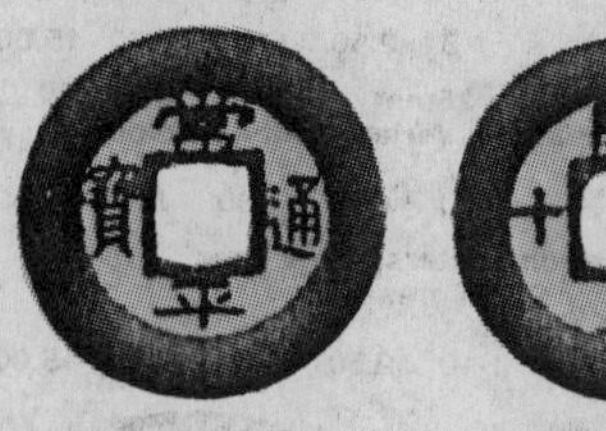

24mm
Rev: *T'o* at bottom, series number at left.

804.10 ND(1836)		10	—	—	Rare	—

松 Song (Song Do Kwal Li Yong)

NOTE: *Song Do* is another name for *Kae Song*.

MUN

CAST BRONZE, 4.00 g, 25mm
Rev: *Song* at top, series number at bottom.

805.1-805.10 ND(1882)		1-10	.75	1.00	1.50	2.50

IWON TOWNSHIP MILITARY OFFICE

利 I (I Won Kwal Li Yong)

MUN

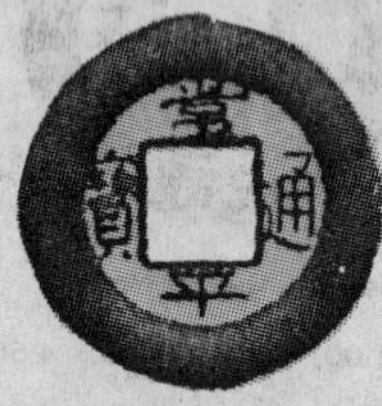

CAST BRONZE, 4.00 g, 24mm
Rev: *Chon* at bottom, series number at left.

834.1-834.6 ND(1882)		1-6	1.75	3.00	4.50	6.50

23mm
Rev: *Chi* at bottom, series number at right.

835.1-835.5 ND(1882)		1-5	7.50	12.50	20.00	35.00

24mm
Large characters.
Rev: *Chi* at bottom, series number at left.

836.1-836.5 ND(1882)		1-5	7.50	12.50	20.00	35.00

22mm
Small characters

837.1-837.5 ND(1882)		1-5	7.50	12.50	20.00	35.00

CH'UNCH'ON TOWNSHIP MILITARY OFFICE

Ch'un (Ch'un Ch'on Kwal Li Yong)

春 or 春 5 MUN

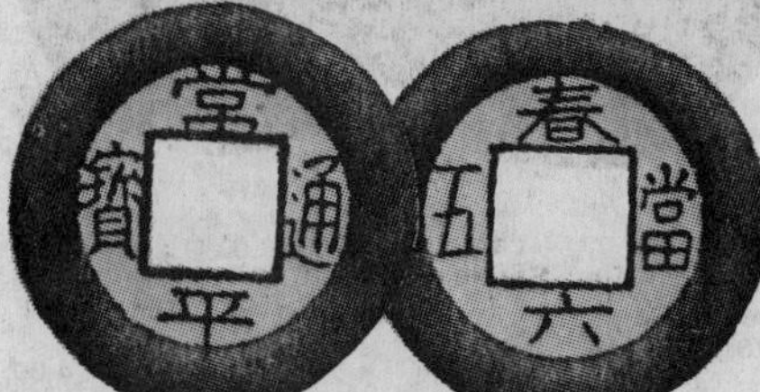

CAST BRONZE, 31mm
Large characters.
Rev: *Ch'un* at top, *Tang* at right, *O* (5) at left, series number at bottom.

KM#	Date	Series	Good	VG	Fine	VF
874.1-874.12	ND(1888)	1-12	1.00	1.75	2.75	4.00

30mm
Medium characters.

875.1-875.11	ND(1888)	1-11	1.00	1.75	2.75	4.00

Reduced size, 27mm

876.1-876.10	ND(1888)	1-10	1.00	1.75	2.75	4.00

28mm
Rev: *Ch'un* at top in different style.

877.1-877.20	ND(1888)	1-20	1.00	1.75	2.75	4.00

30mm

877a.1-877a.10	ND(1888)	1-10	1.00	1.75	2.75	4.00

29mm
Rev: Crescent at bottom under series number.

878.1-878.10	ND(1888)	1-10	2.00	3.00	4.00	6.00

28mm
Rev: Inverted crescent at bottom under series number.

879.1	ND(1888)	1	1.50	3.00	5.00	8.00
879.2-879.10		2-10	3.50	6.00	10.00	15.00
	ND(1888)	1-10	1.50	3.00	5.00	8.00

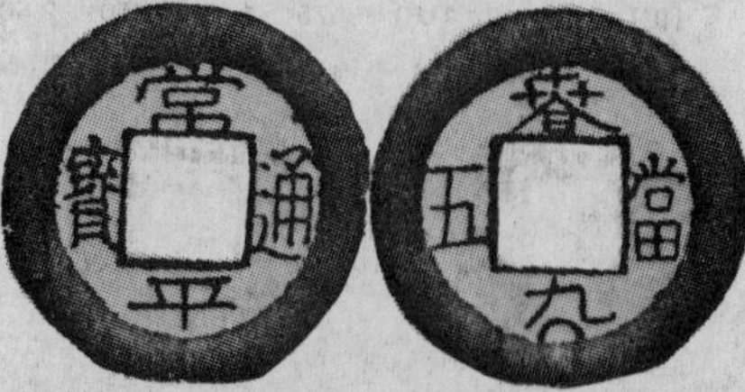

29-30mm
Rev: *Ch'un* at top in different style, crescent at bottom under series number.

KM#	Date	Series	Good	VG	Fine	VF
880.1-880.10	ND(1888)	1-10	2.00	3.00	4.00	6.00

27-28mm

A880.1-A880.20	ND(1888)	1-20	1.50	2.50	3.50	5.00

TANCH'ON TOWNSHIP MILITARY OFFICE

川 Chon (Tan Ch'on Kwal Li Yong)

5 MUN

CAST BRONZE, 32mm
Inside diameter 22mm.
Rev: *Ch'on* at top, *Tang* at right, *O* (5) at left, series number at bottom.

881.1-881.10	ND(1883)	1-10	2.25	4.00	6.00	8.50

28mm
Reduced size, inside diameter 20mm.

882.1-882.10	ND(1883)	1-10	2.75	5.00	7.50	11.00

CH'ANG DOK PALACE MINT

昌 Ch'ang (Ch'ang Dok Kung)

MUN

CAST BRONZE, 4.00 g, 23.5mm
Rev: *Ch'ang* at top, series number at bottom.

883.1	ND(1864-95)	1	3.50	6.00	10.00	16.00

NOTE Similar pieces without a series number are considered to be spurious.

CH'ANG WON TOWNSHIP MILITARY OFFICE

昌 Ch'ang (Ch'ang Won Kwal Li Yong)

5 MUN

CAST BRONZE, 31mm
Large characters.
Rev: *Ch'ang* at top, *Tang* at right, *O* (5) at left, series number at bottom.

884.1-884.12	ND(1887)	1-12	2.00	3.50	5.50	8.50

Reduced size, 29mm
Small characters.

885.1-885.12	ND(1887)	1-12	2.00	3.50	5.50	8.50

30mm
Rev: Sun or circle at upper right.

A885.1-A885.10	ND(1887)	1-10	2.50	4.00	6.00	10.00

31mm
Large characters.
Rev: Crescent at bottom under series number.

886.1-886.9	ND(1887)	1-9	2.00	3.50	5.50	8.50

Reduced size, 29mm
Small characters.

Rev: Crescent at bottom under series number.

KM#	Date	Series	Good	VG	Fine	VF
887.1-887.10	ND(1887)	1-10	2.00	3.50	5.50	8.50

30mm
Rev: Crescent at upper right.

KM#	Date	Series	Good	VG	Fine	VF
A887.1-A887.10	ND(1887)	1-10	2.50	4.00	6.00	10.00

KWANG JU TOWNSHIP MILITARY OFFICE

Kyonggi Province

圻 Ki (Kwang Ju Kwal Li Yong)

MUN

CAST BRONZE, 4.00 g, 25mm
Rev: *Ch'on* at bottom, series number at right.

KM#	Date	Series	Good	VG	Fine	VF
889.1-889.5	ND(1836)	1-5	1.00	1.50	2.50	4.00

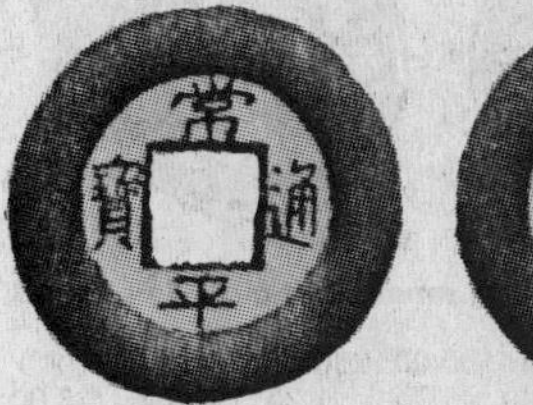

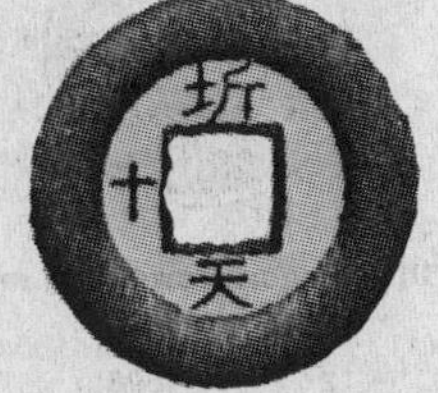

26mm
Large characters.
Rev: *Ch'on* at bottom, series number at left.

KM#	Date	Series	Good	VG	Fine	VF
890.1-890.10	ND(1836)	1-10	1.00	1.50	2.50	4.00

24mm
Small characters.

KM#	Date	Series	Good	VG	Fine	VF
A890.1-A890.10	ND(1836)	1-10	1.00	1.50	2.50	4.00

27mm
Rev: *Ch'on* at bottom, series number at right, circle at left.

KM#	Date	Series	Good	VG	Fine	VF
891.1-891.5	ND(1839)	1-5	3.50	6.00	10.00	18.00

Rev: Crescent at left, series number at right.

KM#	Date	Series	Good	VG	Fine	VF
892.1-892.10	ND(1836)	1-10	3.50	6.00	10.00	18.00

26.5mm
Rev: Crescent at right, series number at left.

KM#	Date	Series	Good	VG	Fine	VF
893.1-893.10	ND(1839)	1-10	3.50	6.00	9.00	16.00

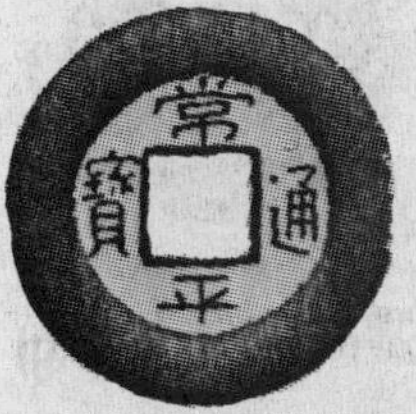

26mm
Rev: *I* (2) at bottom, series number at right.

KM#	Date	Series	Good	VG	Fine	VF
894.1-894.10	ND(1839)	1-10	5.00	8.50	13.50	20.00

Rev: *I* (2) at bottom, series number at left.

KM#	Date	Series	Good	VG	Fine	VF
895.1-895.10	ND(1839)	1-10	1.50	2.50	4.50	6.50

Rev: *I* (2) at bottom, crescent at right, series number at left.

KM#	Date	Series	Good	VG	Fine	VF
896.1-896.10	ND(1839)	1-10	5.00	8.00	12.50	20.00

KYONGGI PROVINCIAL OFFICE

京 Kyong (Kyong Gi Kam Yong)

5 MUN

CAST BRONZE, 29-30mm
Rev: *Kyong* at top, *Tang* at right, *O* (5) at left, series number at bottom.

KM#	Date	Series	Good	VG	Fine	VF
907	ND(1888)	1-27	1.00	1.50	2.50	4.00

P'YONGAN PROVINCIAL OFFICE

平 P'yong (P'yong An Kam Yong)

MUN

CAST BRONZE, 22mm, 4.00 g

KM#	Date	Series	Good	VG	Fine	VF
915.1	ND(1883)	1	.75	1.00	1.50	2.50
915.2		2	.75	1.00	1.50	2.50
915.3		3	.75	1.00	1.50	2.50
915.4		4	.75	1.00	1.50	2.50
915.5		5	.75	1.00	1.50	2.50
915.6		6	.75	1.00	1.50	2.50
915.7		7	.75	1.00	1.50	2.50
915.8		8	3.50	6.00	9.00	16.00
915.9		9	3.50	6.00	9.00	16.00
915.10		10	3.50	6.00	9.00	16.00
915.11		11	3.50	6.00	9.00	16.00

CAST BRONZE, 22mm, 4.00 g
Rev: Circle at left, series number at bottom.

KM#	Date	Series	Good	VG	Fine	VF
917.1-917.5	ND(1883)	1-5	.75	1.00	1.50	2.50

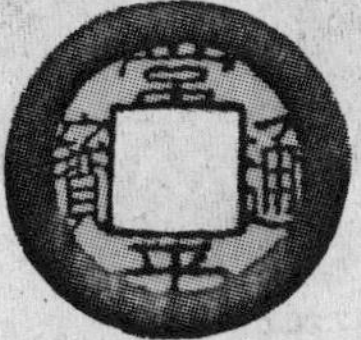

23mm
Rev: *Ch'on* at bottom, series number at left.

KM#	Date	Series	Good	VG	Fine	VF
918.1-918.11	ND(1891)	1-11	.75	1.00	1.50	2.50

21mm

KM#	Date	Series	Good	VG	Fine	VF
918.15	ND(1891)	5	.75	1.00	1.50	2.50

Rev: Star at upper left.

KM#	Date	Series	Good	VG	Fine	VF
918.17	ND(1891)	7	.75	1.00	1.50	2.50

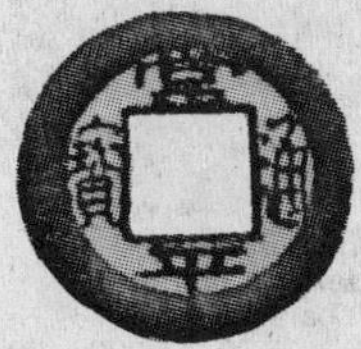

22mm
Rev: *Chi* at bottom, series number at left.

KM#	Date	Series	Good	VG	Fine	VF
919.1	ND(1891)	1	.75	1.00	1.50	2.50
919.4		4	.75	1.00	1.50	2.50

21mm
Rev: *Il* (sun) at bottom.

KM#	Date	Series	Good	VG	Fine	VF
920	ND(1891)	—	1.00	1.50	2.50	4.00

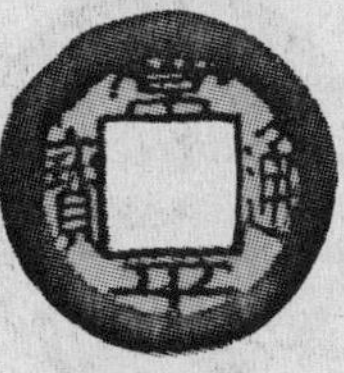

22mm
Rev: *Il* (sun) at bottom, series number at right.

KM#	Date	Series	Good	VG	Fine	VF
921.1-921.10	ND(1891)	1-10	.75	1.00	1.50	2.50

Rev: *Il* (sun) at bottom, series number at left.

KM#	Date	Series	Good	VG	Fine	VF
922.1-922.14	ND(1891)	1-14	.75	1.00	1.50	2.50

22.5mm
Rev: *Saeng* at bottom, series number at left.

KM#	Date	Series	Good	VG	Fine	VF
923.1-923.13	ND(1891)	1-13	.75	1.00	1.50	2.50

22mm
Rev: *Saeng* at bottom, series number at right, circle at left.

KM#	Date	Series	Good	VG	Fine	VF
924.1-924.10	ND(1891)	1-10	.75	1.00	1.50	2.50

5 MUN

CAST BRONZE, 31mm

KM#	Date	Series	Good	VG	Fine	VF
A970.1-A970.10	ND(1883)	1-10	1.00	2.00	3.00	5.00

HAMGYONG PROVINCIAL OFFICE

咸 Ham (Ham Gyong Kam Yong)

MUN

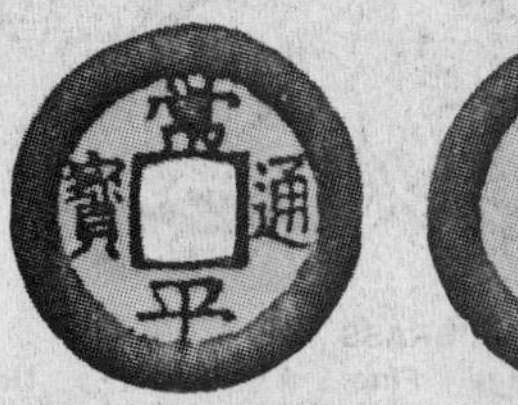

CAST BRONZE, 4.00 g, 24mm
Rev: *Ham* at top, series number at bottom.

KM#	Date	Series	Good	VG	Fine	VF
974.1-974.4	ND(1834)	1-4	1.00	1.75	2.50	4.00

TAE DONG TREASURY DEPARTMENT

CHON

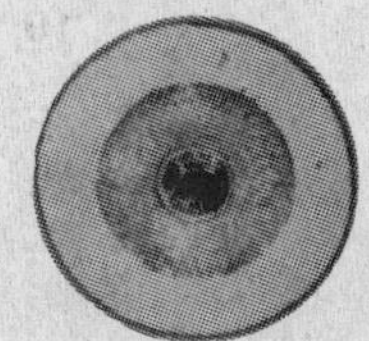

SILVER, 22mm
Rev: *Ho* in green, black or blue cloisonne enameled center circle.

KM#	Date	Mintage	VG	Fine	VF	XF
1081	ND(1882-83)	*	50.00	100.00	150.00	250.00

2 CHON

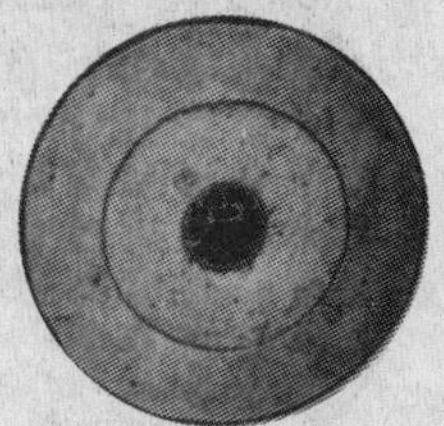

SILVER, 27mm
Rev: *Ho* in green, black or blue cloisonne enameled center circle.

KM#	Date	Mintage	VG	Fine	VF	XF
1082	ND(1882-83)	*	75.00	150.00	250.00	400.00

3 CHON

SILVER, 32.5mm
Rev: *Ho* in green, black or blue cloisonne enameled center circle.

KM#	Date	Mintage	VG	Fine	VF	XF
1083	ND(1882-83)	*	250.00	400.00	550.00	800.00

***NOTE:** Due to the added expense of adding the 'cloisonne' enamel during production the silver one, two & three Chon KM#1081-83 were discontinued in June, 1883. Examples with cloisonne missing are valued at about one half normal valuations. There are many types of trial sets of 1, 2 and 3 Chon in existence.

MILLED COINAGE

During the 1880's and 1890's, Korea experimented with several different types of machine-struck coins including a struck "Cash" coin with round center hole, KM#1100. Some pattern coins of this period exist, some of which may have actually entered circulation.

MONETARY SYSTEM
1888-1891
1000 Mun = 1 Warn

5 MUN

BRASS

KM#	Date	Mintage	Fine	VF	XF	Unc
1100	ND(1884)	—	150.00	300.00	450.00	600.00

COPPER, 3.25 g

KM#	Year	Date	Fine	VF	XF	Unc
1101	497	(1888)	60.00	120.00	200.00	400.00

10 MUN

COPPER, 6.50 g

KM#	Year	Date	Fine	VF	XF	Unc
1102	497	(1888)	125.00	265.00	400.00	700.00

WARN

26.9500 g, .900 SILVER, .7798 oz ASW

KM#	Year	Date	Fine	VF	XF	Unc
1103	497	(1888)	—	—	12,000.	20,000.

MONETARY REFORM

1892-1902
100 Fun = 1 Yang
5 Yang = 1 Whan

FUN

BRASS, 3.50 g
Obv: 3 characters, *Tae Cho-son* (Great Korea), to left of denomination.

KM#	Year	Date	Fine	VF	XF	Unc
1104	501	(1892)	10.00	35.00	75.00	250.00
	501	(1892)	—	—	Proof	1000.
	504	(1895)	10.00	35.00	75.00	250.00
	505	(1896)	17.50	65.00	125.00	300.00

Obv: 2 characters, *Cho-son* (Korea), to left of denomination.

KM#	Year	Date	Fine	VF	XF	Unc
1105	502	(1893)	15.00	50.00	100.00	250.00
	503	(1894)	—	Reported, not confirmed		
	504	(1895)	8.00	25.00	50.00	150.00
	505	(1896)	—	Reported, not confirmed		

5 FUN

COPPER, 17.20 g
Obv: 3 small characters, *Tae Cho-son*, leg. above dragon divided into two parts by a dot.

KM#	Year	Date	Fine	VF	XF	Unc
1106	501	(1892)	2.50	6.00	12.50	80.00
	501	(1892)	—	—	Proof	1200.
	505	(1896)	2.50	6.00	12.50	80.00

Obv: 2 characters, *Cho-son* (Korea), to left of denomination.

KM#	Year	Date	Fine	VF	XF	Unc
1107	502	(1893) small characters obv.	2.50	6.00	10.00	90.00
	502	(1893) large characters obv.	20.00	40.00	75.00	300.00
	503	(1894) large characters obv.	5.00	9.00	15.00	100.00
	504	(1895) large characters obv.	2.50	6.00	12.00	80.00
	505	(1896) small characters obv.	2.00	5.00	9.00	80.00

Obv: 3 large characters, *Tae Cho-son* (Great Korea) to left of denomination, w/o dot in leg. above dragon.

KM#	Year	Date	Fine	VF	XF	Unc
1108	504	(1895)	2.00	5.00	10.00	80.00
	505	(1896)	3.00	7.50	16.00	100.00

Kuang Mu

KM#	Year	Date	Fine	VF	XF	Unc
1116	2	(1898) small characters obv.	2.00	4.00	7.00	80.00
	2	(1898) medium characters obv.	15.00	35.00	70.00	250.00
	2	(1898) large characters obv.	50.00	100.00	200.00	400.00
	3	(1899)	150.00	225.00	500.00	1000.
	6	(1902)	3.50	6.50	12.00	90.00

1/4 YANG

COPPER-NICKEL
Obv: 3 characters, *Tae Cho-son* (Great Korea), to left of denomination.

KM#	Year	Date	Fine	VF	XF	Unc
1109	501	(1892)	10.00	25.00	50.00	150.00
	501	(1892)	—	—	Proof	2000.
	504	(1895)	10.00	25.00	50.00	150.00

Obv: 2 characters, *Cho-son* (Korea), to left of denomination.

KM#	Year	Date	Fine	VF	XF	Unc
1110	502	(1893)	5.00	12.00	25.00	100.00
	503	(1894)	20.00	50.00	150.00	200.00
	504	(1895)	150.00	300.00	500.00	1200.
	505	(1896)	5.00	12.00	25.00	100.00

Obv: Dragon crowded by small tight circle, 11.25mm, Kuang Mu

KM#	Year	Date	Fine	VF	XF	Unc
1117	1	(1897)	100.00	250.00	500.00	1000.
	2	(1898)	.75	1.25	2.00	8.00
	3	(1899) large characters obv.	100.00	250.00	500.00	1000.
	3	(1899) small characters obv.	100.00	250.00	500.00	1000.
	4	(1900)	125.00	300.00	550.00	1100.
	5	(1901)	100.00	250.00	500.00	1000.

NOTE: Many varieties of characters size and style exist for year 2 coins.

Obv: Larger circle around dragon.

KM#	Year	Date	Fine	VF	XF	Unc
1118	2	(1898)	7.50	12.50	25.00	100.00

NOTE: KM#1118 were counterfeits made on machinery supplied by the Japanese. These counterfeits were authorized for circulation by the Korean Government.

YANG

5.2000 g, .800 SILVER, .1338 oz ASW
Obv: 3 characters, *Tae Cho-son*.

KM#	Year	Date	Fine	VF	XF	Unc
1112	501	(1892)	65.00	100.00	150.00	400.00
	501	(1892)	—	—	Proof	5000.

Obv: 2 characters, *Cho-son*.

KM#	Year	Date	Fine	VF	XF	Unc
1113	502	(1893)	65.00	100.00	150.00	400.00

Obv: Wide spaced *Yang*.

Kuang Mu

KM#	Year	Date	Fine	VF	XF	Unc
1119	2	(1898)	80.00	150.00	250.00	450.00

Obv: Closely spaced *Yang*.

KM#	Year	Date	Fine	VF	XF	Unc
1120	2	(1898)	75.00	130.00	225.00	400.00

5 YANG

26.9500 g, .900 SILVER, .7798 oz ASW

KM#	Year	Mintage	Fine	VF	XF	Unc
1114	501(1892)	.020	700.00	1200.	1800.	2750.
	501(1892)	—	—	—	Proof	16,500.

WHAN

26.9500 g, .900 SILVER, .7798 oz ASW

KM#	Year	Mintage	Fine	VF	XF	Unc
1115	502(1893)	I.A.	2500.	5000.	10,000.	14,000.

MONETARY REFORM

RULERS

Kuang Mu, Years 5-11 (1901-1907AD)
Yung Hi, Years 1-4 (1907-1910AD)

MONETARY SYSTEM

100 Chon = 1 Won

RUSSIAN DOMINATION

1896-1904

CHON

BRONZE, 6.80 g

KM#	Year	Mintage	Fine	VF	XF	Unc
	Kuang Mu					
1121	6(1902)	3.001	1000.	2000.	3000.	5000.

5 CHON

COPPER-NICKEL, 4.30 g

KM#	Year	Mintage	Fine	VF	XF	Unc
	Kuang Mu					
1122	6(1902)	2.800	1150.	1650.	2500.	5000.

1/2 WON

13.5000 g, .800 SILVER, .3473 oz ASW

KM#	Year	Mintage	Fine	VF	XF	Unc
	Kuang Mu					
1123	5(1901)	1.831	2000.	5000.	7500.	12,000.

NOTE: Ponterio & Assoc. Witte Museum sale 8-89 choice BU realized $12,500.

JAPANESE PROTECTION

1905-1910

1/2 CHON

BRONZE, 3.56 g

KM#	Year	Mintage	Fine	VF	XF	Unc
	Kuang Mu					
1124	10(1906)	24.000	2.00	4.00	9.00	80.00
	11(1907)	*.800	—	—	Rare	—

2.10 g

KM#	Year	Mintage	Fine	VF	XF	Unc
	Yung Hi					
1136	1(1907)	*I.A.	60.00	150.00	325.00	650.00
	2(1908)	21.000	5.00	12.00	20.00	130.00
	3(1909)	8.200	6.00	13.00	22.50	140.00
	4(1910)	5.070	50.00	125.00	300.00	650.00

***NOTE:** Mintage for year 1 is included in the mintage for year 11 of KM#1124.

CHON

BRONZE, 7.13 g

KM#	Year	Mintage	Fine	VF	XF	Unc
	Kuang Mu					
1125	9(1905)	11.800	8.00	14.00	22.00	100.00
	10(1906)	I.A.	7.50	12.00	18.00	100.00

4.20 g

KM#	Year	Mintage	Fine	VF	XF	Unc
1132	11(1907)	11.200	3.50	7.00	12.00	80.00

KM#	Year	Mintage	Fine	VF	XF	Unc
	Yung Hi					
1137	1(1907)	I.A.	4.50	10.00	20.00	100.00
	2(1908)	6.800	3.00	6.00	10.00	80.00
	3(1909)	9.200	3.00	6.00	10.00	80.00
	4(1910)	3.500	3.50	8.00	17.00	90.00

5 CHON

COPPER-NICKEL, 4.50 g

KM#	Year	Mintage	Fine	VF	XF	Unc
	Kuang Mu					
1126	9(1905)	20.000	5.00	10.00	20.00	80.00
	11(1907)	160.0000	8.00	12.50	24.00	90.00

KM#	Year	Mintage	Fine	VF	XF	Unc
	Yung Hi					
1138	3(1909)	—	900.00	1400.	2400.	—

10 CHON

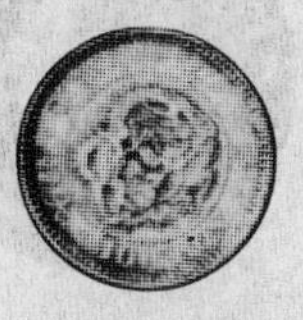

2.7000 g, .800 SILVER, .0695 oz ASW, 17.5mm, 1.5mm thick

KM#	Year	Mintage	Fine	VF	XF	Unc
	Kuang Mu					
1127	10(1906)	2.000	12.00	20.00	40.00	90.00

2.25 g, 1.0mm thick

KM#	Year	Mintage	Fine	VF	XF	Unc
1133	11(1907)	2.400	13.00	22.50	45.00	110.00

2.2500 g, .800 SILVER, .0578 oz ASW

KM#	Year	Mintage	Fine	VF	XF	Unc
	Yung Hi					
1139	2(1908)	6.300	10.00	14.00	25.00	60.00
	3(1909)	—	—	—	Rare	—
	4(1910)	9.500	7.00	12.00	22.00	50.00

20 CHON

5.3900 g, .800 SILVER, .1386 oz ASW, 22.5mm

KM#	Year	Mintage	Fine	VF	XF	Unc
	Kuang Mu					
1128	9(1905)	1.000	30.00	60.00	90.00	225.00
	10(1906)	2.500	25.00	45.00	70.00	150.00

4.0500 g, .800 SILVER, .1042 oz ASW

KM#	Year	Mintage	Fine	VF	XF	Unc
1134	11(1907)	1.500	15.00	25.00	40.00	110.00

4.5000 g, .800 SILVER, .1157 oz ASW

KM#	Year	Mintage	Fine	VF	XF	Unc
	Yung Hi					
1140	2(1908)	3.000	15.00	25.00	40.00	100.00
	3(1909)	2.000	15.00	25.00	40.00	100.00
	4(1910)	2.000	15.00	25.00	40.00	100.00

1/2 WON

13.4800 g, .800 SILVER, .3467 oz ASW

KM#	Year	Mintage	Fine	VF	XF	Unc
	Kuang Mu					
1129	9(1905)	.600	50.00	100.00	185.00	375.00
	10(1906)	1.200	50.00	100.00	175.00	350.00

10.1300 g, .800 SILVER, .2606 oz ASW

KM#	Year	Mintage	Fine	VF	XF	Unc
1135	11(1907)	1.000	50.00	100.00	175.00	350.00

KM#	Year	Mintage	Fine	VF	XF	Unc
	Yung Hi					
1141	2(1908)	1.400	65.00	110.00	200.00	400.00

5 WON

4.1666 g, .900 GOLD, .1206 oz AGW

KM#	Year	Mintage	Fine	VF	XF	Unc
	Yung Hi					
1142	2(1908)	.010	—	—	*Rare	—

***NOTE:** Swiss Bank sale No. 19 1-88 XF realized $113,100.

10 WON

8.3333 g, .900 GOLD, .2412 oz AGW

KM#	Year	Mintage	Fine	VF	XF	Unc
	Kuang Mu					
1130	10(1906)	5,012	—	20,000.	30,000.	42,500.

20 WON

16.6666 g, .900 GOLD, .4823 oz AGW

KM#	Year	Mintage	Fine	VF	XF	Unc
	Kuang Mu					
1131	10(1906)	2,506	—	20,000.	50,000.	80,000.
	Yung Hi					
1144	2(1908)	.040	—	20,000.	50,000.	80,000.
	3(1909)	.025	—	20,000.	50,000.	80,000.

PROOF SETS (PS)

KM#	Date	Mintage	Identification	Issue Price	Mkt. Val.
PS1	1892(5)	—	KM1104,1106,1109, 1112,1114	—	—

KOREA-NORTH

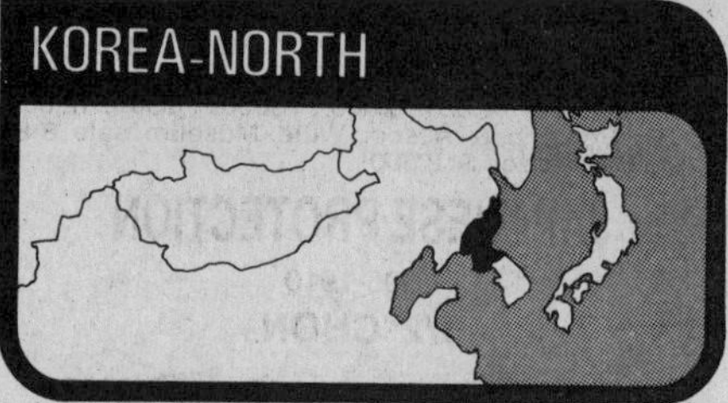

The Democratic Peoples Republic of Korea, situated in northeastern Asia on the northern half of the Korean peninsula between the Peoples Republic of China and the Republic of Korea, has an area of 46,540 sq. mi. (120,540 sq. km.) and a population of 20 million. Capital: Pyongyang. The economy is based on heavy industry and agriculture. Metals, minerals and farm produce are exported.

Japan replaced China as the predominant foreign influence in Korea in 1895 and annexed the peninsular country in 1910. Defeat in World War II brought an end to Japanese rule. U.S. troops entered Korea from the south and Soviet forces entered from the north. The Cairo conference (1943) had established that Korea should be 'free and independent'. The Potsdam conference (1945) set the 38th parallel as the line dividing the occupation forces of the United States and Russia. When Russia refused to permit a U.N. commission designated to supervise reunification elections to enter North Korea, an election was held in South Korea which established the Republic of Korea on Aug. 15, 1948. North Korea held an unsupervised election on Aug. 25, 1948, and on Sept. 9, 1948, proclaimed the establishment of the Democratic Peoples Republic of Korea.

NOTE: For earlier coinage see Korea.

MONETARY SYSTEM

100 Chon = 1 Won

CIRCULATION RESTRICTIONS

W/o star: KM#1-4 - General circulation
1 star: KM#5-8 - Issued to visitors from hard currency countries
2 stars: KM#9-12 - Issued to visitors from Communist countries

CHON

ALUMINUM

KM#	Date	Mintage	Fine	VF	XF	Unc
1	1959	—	.15	.25	.50	1.00
	1970	—	.20	.35	.75	1.50

Rev: Stars in field.

KM#	Date	Mintage	Fine	VF	XF	Unc
5	1959	—	—	—	.50	1.00

Rev: Star left of 1.

KM#	Date	Mintage	Fine	VF	XF	Unc
9	1959	—	—	—	.50	1.00

5 CHON

ALUMINUM

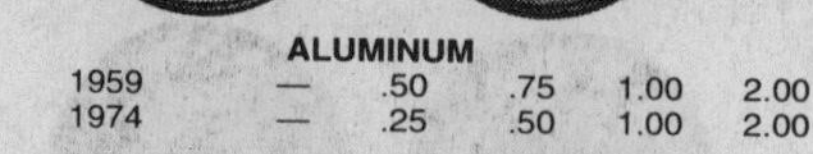

KM#	Date	Mintage	Fine	VF	XF	Unc
2	1959	—	.50	.75	1.00	2.00
	1974	—	.25	.50	1.00	2.00

Rev: Stars in field.

KM#	Date	Mintage	Fine	VF	XF	Unc
6	1974	—	—	—	1.00	2.00

Rev: Star left of 5.

KM#	Date	Mintage	Fine	VF	XF	Unc
10	1974	—	—	—	1.00	2.00

10 CHON

ALUMINUM

KM#	Date	Mintage	Fine	VF	XF	Unc
3	1959	—	.50	.75	1.00	2.00

Rev: Stars in field.

KM#	Date	Mintage	Fine	VF	XF	Unc
7	1959	—	—	—	1.00	2.00

Rev: Star left of 10.

KM#	Date	Mintage	Fine	VF	XF	Unc
11	1959	—	—	—	1.00	2.00

50 CHON

ALUMINUM

KM#	Date	Mintage	Fine	VF	XF	Unc
4	1978	—	.75	1.00	1.75	3.00

Rev: Stars in field.

KM#	Date	Mintage	Fine	VF	XF	Unc
8	1978	—	—	—	1.75	3.00

Rev: Star behind rider.

KM#	Date	Mintage	Fine	VF	XF	Unc
12	1978	—	—	—	1.75	3.00

WON

COPPER-NICKEL
Kim Il Sung's Birth Place

KM#	Date	Mintage	Fine	VF	XF	Unc
13	1987	—	—	—	Proof	4.00

Kim Il Sung's Arch of Triumph

KM#	Date	Mintage	Fine	VF	XF	Unc
14	1987	—	—	—	Proof	4.00

Kim Il Sung's Tower of Juche

KM#	Date	Mintage	Fine	VF	XF	Unc
15	1987	—	—	—	Proof	4.00

ALUMINUM

KM#	Date	Mintage	Fine	VF	XF	Unc
18	1987	—	—	—	—	3.50

5 WON

COPPER-NICKEL
Kim Il Sung's Arch of Triumph

KM#	Date	Mintage	Fine	VF	XF	Unc
22	1987	—	—	—	Proof	5.50

Kim Il Sung's Tower of Juche

KM#	Date	Mintage	Fine	VF	XF	Unc
23	1987	—	—	—	Proof	5.50

Kim Il Sung's Birth Place

KM#	Date	Mintage	Fine	VF	XF	Unc
25	1987	—	—	—	Proof	5.50

World Festival of Youth and Students

KM#	Date	Mintage	Fine	VF	XF	Unc
19	1989	—	—	—	—	6.00

20 WON

14.8000 g, .999 SILVER, .4758 oz ASW
World Festival of Youth and Students

KM#	Date	Mintage	Fine	VF	XF	Unc
20	1989	—	—	—	Proof	27.50

30 WON

17.0200 g, .999 SILVER, .5472 oz ASW
Friendship Art Festival

KM#	Date	Mintage	Fine	VF	XF	Unc
26	1989	—	—	—	Proof	30.00

50 WON

17.0000 g, .999 SILVER, .5466 oz ASW
80th Birthday of Kim Il Sung - Birthplace

KM#	Date	Mintage	Fine	VF	XF	Unc
52	1992	1,000	—	—	Proof	50.00

80th Birthday of Kim Il Sung - Portrait

KM#	Date	Mintage	Fine	VF	XF	Unc
54	1992	1,000	—	—	Proof	50.00

50th Birthday of Kim Jong Il

KM#	Date	Mintage	Fine	VF	XF	Unc
56	1992	1,000	—	—	Proof	50.00

200 WON

14.9700 g, .999 SILVER, .5000 oz ASW
Olympics - Equestrian
Obv: Silver content statement divided by emblem.

KM#	Date	Mintage	Fine	VF	XF	Unc
49	1991	—	—	—	Proof	55.00

Obv: Silver content statement below emblem.

KM#	Date	Mintage	Fine	VF	XF	Unc
50	1991	—	—	—	Proof	55.00

250 WON

7.7700 g, .999 GOLD, .2500 oz AGW
World Festival of Youth and Students

KM#	Date	Mintage	Fine	VF	XF	Unc
21	1989	—	—	—	Proof	275.00

500 WON

27.0000 g, .999 SILVER, .8681 oz ASW
World Championship Soccer - Mexico 86.

KM#	Date	Mintage	Fine	VF	XF	Unc
39	1987	—	—	—	Proof	50.00

Winter Olympics-Hockey

KM#	Date	Mintage	Fine	VF	XF	Unc
16	1988	.020	—	—	Proof	50.00

30th Anniversary of Gorch Fock

KM#	Date	Mintage	Fine	VF	XF	Unc
17	1988	—	—	—	Proof	50.00

World Championship Soccer

KM#	Date	Mintage	Fine	VF	XF	Unc
24	1988	—	—	—	Proof	40.00

F.A.O. - Food For All

KM#	Date	Mintage	Fine	VF	XF	Unc
36	1988	*2,000	—	—	Proof	50.00

Amerigo Vespucci

KM#	Date	Mintage	Fine	VF	XF	Unc
27	1989	—	—	—	Proof	45.00

31.8200 g, .999 SILVER, 1.0231 oz ASW
Fairy of Mt. Kungang

KM#	Date	Mintage	Fine	VF	XF	Unc
32	1989	—	—	—	Proof	45.00

27.0000 g, .999 SILVER, .8682 oz ASW
Calgary Winter Olympics - Figure Skater

KM#	Date	Mintage	Fine	VF	XF	Unc
33	1989	—	—	—	Proof	50.00

Barceloma Summer Olympics - Discus Thrower

KM#	Date	Mintage	Fine	VF	XF	Unc
34	1989	—	—	—	Proof	50.00

World Championship Soccer
Obv: Similar to KM#33.
Rev: Soccer player kicking ball.

KM#	Date	Mintage	Fine	VF	XF	Unc
37	1989	—	—	—	Proof	50.00

World Championship Soccer - Goalie

KM#	Date	Mintage	Fine	VF	XF	Unc
38	1989	—	—	—	Proof	50.00

Olympic Table Tennis

KM#	Date	Mintage	Fine	VF	XF	Unc
40	1990	—	—	—	Proof	45.00

Endangered Wildlife - Storks

KM#	Date	Mintage	Fine	VF	XF	Unc
41	1990	—	—	—	Proof	32.50

31.1000 g, .999 SILVER, 1.0000 oz ASW
World Championship Table Tennis - 2 Male Players

KM#	Date	Mintage	Fine	VF	XF	Unc
44	1991	—	—	—	Proof	35.00

World Championship Table Tennis - Male Player

KM#	Date	Mintage	Fine	VF	XF	Unc
45	1991	—	—	—	Proof	35.00

World Championship Table Tennis - Female Player

46	1991	—	—	—	Proof	35.00

World Championship Table Tennis - 3 Portraits

47	1991	—	—	—	Proof	35.00

27.0000 g, .999 SILVER, .8682 oz ASW
First Armoured Ship

48	1991	*.010	—	—	Proof	50.00

Environmental Protection - Flowers

KM#	Date	Mintage	Fine	VF	XF	Unc
59	1992	1,000	—	—	Proof	50.00

1994 Olympics - Speed Skating

60	1993	1,000	—	—	Proof	50.00

1994 Olympics - 2 Man Bobsled

61	1993	1,000	—	—	Proof	50.00

1500 WON

8.0000 g, .999 GOLD, .2572 oz AGW
Soccer

51	1991	—	—	—	Proof	250.00

2500 WON

15.5500 g, .999 GOLD, .5000 oz AGW
30th Anniversary of Gorch Fock
Obv: State emblem. Rev: Sailing ship.

35	1988	*500 pcs.	—	—	Proof	325.00

GOLD BULLION ISSUES

100 WON

3.1300 g, .999 GOLD, .1000 oz AGW
40th Anniversary of Peoples Republic

28	1988	—	—	—	Proof	75.00

250 WON

7.7800 g, .999 GOLD, .2500 oz AGW
40th Anniversary of Peoples Republic

29	1988	—	—	—	Proof	175.00

500 WON

15.5700 g, .999 GOLD, .5000 oz AGW
40th Anniversary of Peoples Republic

KM#	Date	Mintage	Fine	VF	XF	Unc
30	1988	—	—	—	Proof	300.00

1000 WON

31.1300 g, .999 GOLD, 1.0000 oz AGW
40th Anniversary of Peoples Republic

31	1988	—	—	—	Proof	575.00

1500 WON

15.5500 g, .999 GOLD, .5000 oz AGW
Inter-parliamentary Conference

42	1991	800 pcs.	—	—	Proof	400.00

Inter-parliamentary Conference

43	1991	800 pcs.	—	—	Proof	400.00

8.0000 g, .999 GOLD, .2572 oz AGW
Olympics - Gymnast

58	1990	*3,000	—	—	Proof	200.00

2000 WON

31.1000 g, .999 GOLD, 1.0000 oz AGW
80th Birthday of Kim Il Sung - Birthplace

53	1992	500 pcs.	—	—	Proof	700.00

80th Birthday of Kim Il Sung - Portrait

KM#	Date	Mintage	Fine	VF	XF	Unc
55	1992	500 pcs.	—	—	Proof	700.00

50th Birthday of Kim Jong Il

KM#	Date	Mintage	Fine	VF	XF	Unc
57	1992	500 pcs.	—	—	Proof	700.00

KOREA-SOUTH

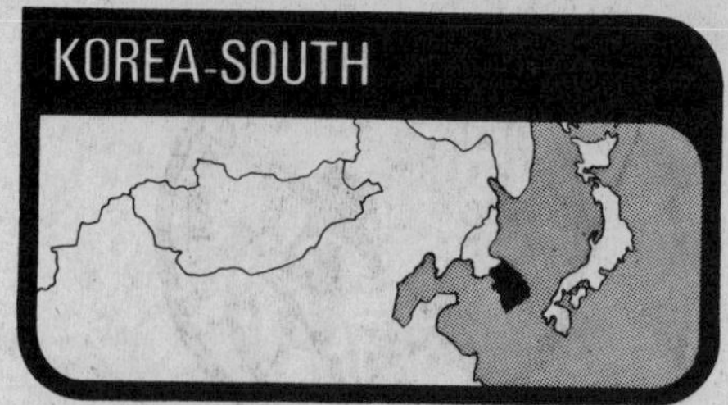

The Republic of Korea, situated in northeastern Asia on the southern half of the Korean peninsula between North Korea and the Korean Strait, has an area of 38,025 sq. mi. (98,480 sq. km.) and a population of 42.5 million. Capital: Seoul. The economy is based on agriculture and light and medium industry. Some of the world's largest oil tankers are built here. Automobiles, plywood, electronics, and textile products are exported.

Japan replaced China as the predominant foreign influence in Korea in 1895 and annexed the peninsular country in 1910. Defeat in World War II brought an end to Japanese rule. U.S. troops entered Korea from the south and Soviet forces entered from the north. The Cairo conference (1943) had established that Korea should be 'free and independent'. The Potsdam conference (1945) set the 38th parallel as the line dividing the occupation forces of the United States and Russia. When Russia refused to permit a U.N. commission designated to supervise reunification elections to enter North Korea, an election was held in South Korea on May 10, 1948. By its determination, the Republic of Korea was inaugurated on Aug. 15, 1948.

NOTE: For earlier coinage see Korea.

MINT MARKS

(a) - Paris, privy marks only

MONETARY SYSTEM

100 Chon = 1 Hwan

10 HWAN

BRONZE
Rose of Sharon

KM#	Date	Mintage	Fine	VF	XF	Unc
1	4292 (1959)	100.000	.20	.50	1.00	25.00
	4294 (1961)	100.000	.15	.25	.50	2.00

50 HWAN

NICKEL-BRASS
Iron Clad Turtle Boat

KM#	Date	Mintage	Fine	VF	XF	Unc
2	4292 (1959)	24.640	.20	.50	1.00	3.00
	4294 (1961)	20.000	.15	.30	.80	2.00

100 HWAN

COPPER-NICKEL
Syngman Rhee

KM#	Date	Mintage	Fine	VF	XF	Unc
3 (Y3)	4292 (1959)	49.640	.50	1.00	2.50	6.00

NOTE: Quantities of KM#1-3 dated 4292 in uncirculated condition were countermarked 'SAMPLE' in Korean for distribution to government and banking agencies. KM#3 was withdrawn from circulation June 10, 1962 and melted; KM#1 and KM#2 continued to circulate as 1 Won and 5 Won coins for 13 years respectively until demonitized and withdrawn from circulation March 22, 1975.

MONETARY REFORM

10 Hwan = 1 Won

Prior to the following issue, the Bank of Korea, on its authority, created a number of patterns in 1, 5 and 10 Won denominations, for example with the Kyongju Observatory design.

WON

BRASS
Rose of Sharon

KM#	Date	Mintage	Fine	VF	XF	Unc
4	1966	7.000	—	—	.10	4.00
	1967	48.500	—	—	.10	1.00

ALUMINUM

KM#	Date	Mintage	Fine	VF	XF	Unc
4a	1968	66.500	—	—	—	.10
	1969	85.000	—	—	—	.10
	1970	45.000	—	—	—	.10
	1974	12.000	—	—	.10	.15
	1975	10.000	—	—	.10	.15
	1976	20.000	—	—	—	.10
	1977	30.000	—	—	—	.10
	1978	30.000	—	—	—	.10
	1979	30.000	—	—	—	.10
	1980	20.000	—	—	—	.10
	1981	20.000	—	—	—	.10
	1982	30.000	—	—	—	.10
	1982	2,000	—	—	Proof	—

Rose of Sharon

KM#	Date	Mintage	Fine	VF	XF	Unc
31	1983	40.000	—	—	—	.10
	1984	20.000	—	—	—	.10
	1985	10.000	—	—	—	.10
	1987	10.000	—	—	—	.10
	1988	6.500	—	—	—	.10
	1989	10.000	—	—	—	.10
	1990	6.000	—	—	—	.10
	1991	5.000	—	—	—	.10

5 WON

BRONZE
Iron Clad Turtle Boat

KM#	Date	Mintage	Fine	VF	XF	Unc
5	1966	4.500	—	.15	.65	10.00
	1967	18.000	—	.10	.50	5.00
	1968	20.000	—	.10	.50	5.00
	1969	25.000	—	.10	.25	3.00
	1970	50.000	—	.10	.25	3.00

BRASS

KM#	Date	Mintage	Fine	VF	XF	Unc
5a	1970	Inc. Ab.	—	—	.10	2.25
	1971	64.038	—	—	—	.10
	1972	60.084	—	—	—	.10
	1977	1.000	—	—	.10	1.40
	1978	1.000	—	—	.10	1.30
	1979	1.000	—	—	.10	1.15
	1980	.100	—	.25	.50	3.00
	1981	.100	—	.25	.50	3.00
	1982	.100	—	.25	.50	3.00
	1982	2,000	—	—	Proof	—

KM#	Date	Mintage	Fine	VF	XF	Unc
32	1983	6.000	—	—	.10	.20
	1987	1.000	—	—	.10	.20
	1988	.500	—	—	.10	.20
	1989	.500	—	—	.10	.20
	1990	.600	—	—	.10	.20
	1991	.500	—	—	.10	.20

10 WON

BRONZE
Pagoda at Pul Guk Temple

KM#	Date	Mintage	Fine	VF	XF	Unc
6	1966	10.600	—	.15	.50	10.00
	1967	22.500	—	.15	.50	10.00

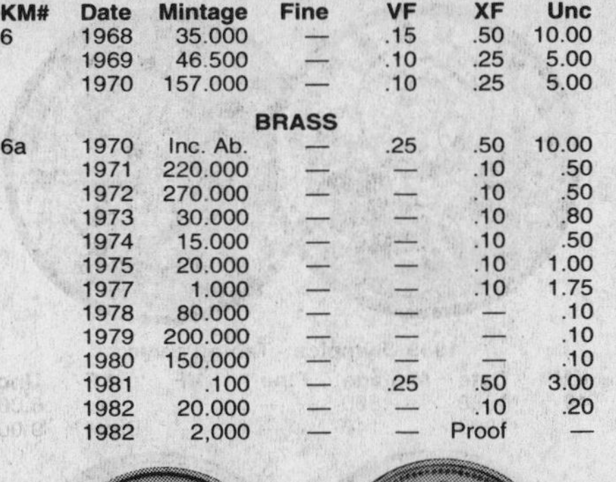

KM#	Date	Mintage	Fine	VF	XF	Unc
6	1968	35.000	—	.15	.50	10.00
	1969	46.500	—	.10	.25	5.00
	1970	157.000	—	.10	.25	5.00
			BRASS			
6a	1970	Inc. Ab.	—	.25	.50	10.00
	1971	220.000	—	—	.10	.50
	1972	270.000	—	—	.10	.50
	1973	30.000	—	—	.10	.80
	1974	15.000	—	—	.10	.50
	1975	20.000	—	—	.10	1.00
	1977	1.000	—	—	.10	1.75
	1978	80.000	—	—	—	.10
	1979	200.000	—	—	—	.10
	1980	150.000	—	—	—	.10
	1981	.100	—	.25	.50	3.00
	1982	20.000	—	—	.10	.20
	1982	2,000	—	—	Proof	—

KM#	Date	Mintage	Fine	VF	XF	Unc
33	1983	25.000	—	—	.10	.35
	1985	35.000	—	—	.10	.35
	1986	195.000	—	—	.10	.35
	1987	155.000	—	—	.10	.35
	1988	189.000	—	—	.10	.35
	1989	310.000	—	—	.10	.35
	1990	395.000	—	—	.10	.35
	1991	20.000	—	—	.10	.35
	1992	—	—	—	.10	.35

50 WON

2.8000 g, .999 SILVER, .0899 oz ASW
Kwan Soon Yu - Flag

KM#	Date	Year	Mintage	VF	XF	Unc
7	4303	1970	4,350	—	Proof	70.00
	4304	1971	—	—	Rare	—

COPPER-NICKEL
F.A.O. Issue

KM#	Date	Mintage	Fine	VF	XF	Unc
20	1972	6.000	—	.10	.30	2.50
	1973	40.000	—	.10	.20	1.00
	1974	25.000	—	.10	.20	1.00
	1977	1.000	—	.15	.25	2.00
	1978	1.500	—	.15	.25	1.40
	1979	20.000	—	—	.10	.25
	1980	10.000	—	—	.10	.25
	1981	25.000	—	—	.10	.20
	1982	40.000	—	—	.10	.20
	1982	2,000	—	—	Proof	—

F.A.O. Issue

KM#	Date	Mintage	Fine	VF	XF	Unc
34	1983	50.000	—	—	.10	.35
	1984	40.000	—	—	.10	.35
	1985	4.000	—	—	.10	.35
	1987	32.000	—	—	.10	.35
	1988	53.000	—	—	.10	.35
	1989	70.000	—	—	.10	.35
	1990	85.000	—	—	.10	.35
	1991	80.000	—	—	.10	.35
	1992	—	—	—	.10	.35

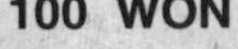

100 WON

5.6000 g, .999 SILVER, .1798 oz ASW

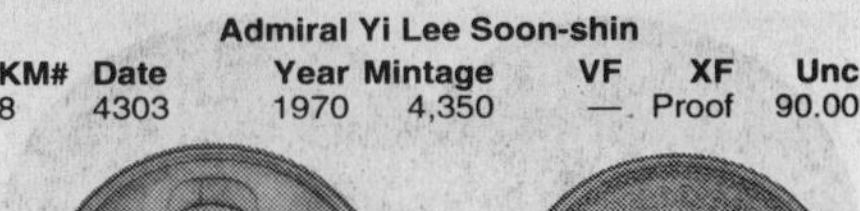

Admiral Yi Lee Soon-shin

KM#	Date	Year	Mintage	VF	XF	Unc
8	4303	1970	4,350	—	Proof	90.00

COPPER-NICKEL

KM#	Date	Mintage	Fine	VF	XF	Unc
9	1970	1.500	—	.50	.75	4.00
	1971	13.000	—	.15	.40	2.25
	1972	20.000	—	.15	.35	1.75
	1973*	80.000	—	.15	.30	1.00
	1974*	50.000	—	.15	.30	1.00
	1975	75.000	—	.15	.25	.60
	1977	30.000	—	.15	.25	.60
	1978	40.000	—	.15	.20	.35
	1979	130.000	—	.15	.20	.35
	1980	60.000	—	.15	.20	.35
	1981	.100	—	.25	.50	4.00
	1982	50.000	—	—	.15	.25
	1982	2,000	—	—	Proof	—

*NOTE: Die varieties exist.

30th Anniversary of Liberation

KM#	Date	Mintage	Fine	VF	XF	Unc
21	1975	4.998	—	.25	.50	1.25
	1975	2,000	—	—	Proof	125.00

1st Anniversary of the 5th Republic

KM#	Date	Mintage	Fine	VF	XF	Unc
24	1981	4.880	—	.25	.50	1.00
	1981 unfrosted					
		.018	—	—	Proof	30.00
	1981	2,000	—	—	Proof	175.00

Admiral Lee Soon-shin

KM#	Date	Mintage	Fine	VF	XF	Unc
35	1983	8.000	—	.15	.25	.50
	1984	40.000	—	.15	.25	.50
	1985	16.000	—	.15	.25	.50
	1986	131.000	—	.15	.25	.50
	1987	170.000	—	.15	.25	.50
	1988	298.000	—	.15	.25	.50
	1989	250.000	—	.15	.25	.50
	1990	185.000	—	.15	.25	.50
	1991	400.000	—	.15	.25	.50
	1992	—	—	.15	.25	.50

200 WON

11.2000 g, .999 SILVER, .3596 oz ASW
Celadon Vase

KM#	Date	Year	Mintage	VF	XF	Unc
10	4303	1970	4,200	—	Proof	115.00

250 WON

14.0000 g, .999 SILVER, .4497 oz ASW
Chung Hee Park

KM#	Date	Year	Mintage	VF	XF	Unc
11	4303	1970	4,100	—	Proof	135.00

500 WON

28.0000 g, .999 SILVER, .8994 oz ASW
Kyongju - Bodhisattva From the Cave Temple

KM#	Date	Year	Mintage	VF	XF	Unc
12	4303	1970	4,700	—	Proof	250.00

COPPER-NICKEL
42nd World Shooting Championships

KM#	Date	Mintage	Fine	VF	XF	Unc
22	1978	.980	—	.75	1.25	3.00
	1978 unfrosted					
		.018	—	—	Proof	60.00
	1978	2,000	—	—	Proof	225.00

Manchurian Crane

KM#	Date	Mintage	Fine	VF	XF	Unc
27	1982	15.000	—	—	.85	2.50
	1982	2,000	—	—	Proof	—
	1983	64.000	—	—	.85	2.50
	1984	70.000	—	—	.85	2.50
	1987	1.000	—	—	.85	2.50
	1988	27.000	—	—	.85	2.50
	1989	25.000	—	—	.85	2.50
	1990	60.000	—	—	.85	2.50
	1991	90.000	—	—	.85	2.50
	1992	—	—	—	.85	2.50
	1993	—	—	—	.85	2.50

1000 WON

56.0000 g, .999 SILVER, 1.7988 oz ASW
U.N. Forces in South Korea
Rev: Similar to 200 Won, KM#10.

KM#	Date	Year	Mintage	VF	XF	Unc
13	4303	1970	4,050	—	Proof	450.00

3.8700 g, .900 GOLD, .1119 oz AGW
Great South Gate in Seoul
Valcambi Mint

KM#	Date	Year	Mintage	VF	XF	Unc
14.1	4303	1970	1,500	—	Proof	400.00

Paris Mint

KM#	Date	Year	Mintage	VF	XF	Unc
14.2	4303	1970(a)	100 pcs.	—	Proof	1250.

NICKEL
1st Anniversary of the 5th Republic

KM#	Date	Mintage	Fine	VF	XF	Unc
25	1981	1.880	—	1.25	1.50	5.50
	1981 unfrosted					
		.018	—	—	Proof	40.00
	1981	2,000	—	—	Proof	225.00

COPPER-NICKEL
1988 Olympics - Dancers

KM#	Date	Mintage	Fine	VF	XF	Unc
28	1982	1.980	—	—	1.25	5.00
	1982 unfrosted					
		.010	—	—	Proof	25.00
	1982	.010	—	—	Proof	50.00

1988 Olympics - Drummer

KM#	Date	Mintage	Fine	VF	XF	Unc
36	1983	.330	—	—	1.25	5.00
	1983 unfrosted					
		.056	—	—	Proof	12.50
	1983	.101	—	—	Proof	22.50

200 Years of Catholic Church in Korea

KM#	Date	Mintage	Fine	VF	XF	Unc
39	1984	.572	—	—	1.25	5.00

10th Asian Games

KM#	Date	Mintage	Fine	VF	XF	Unc
41	1986	.930	—	—	1.25	5.50
	1986	.070	—	—	Proof	7.00

1988 Olympics - Basketball

KM#	Date	Mintage	Fine	VF	XF	Unc
46	1986	.560	—	—	—	6.00
	1986	.140	—	—	Proof	9.00

1988 Olympics - Tennis

KM#	Date	Mintage	Fine	VF	XF	Unc
47	1987	.560	—	—	—	6.00
	1987	.140	—	—	Proof	9.00

1988 Olympics - Handball

KM#	Date	Mintage	Fine	VF	XF	Unc
48	1987	.560	—	—	—	6.00
	1987	.140	—	—	Proof	9.00

1988 Olympics - Table Tennis

KM#	Date	Mintage	Fine	VF	XF	Unc
49	1988	.560	—	—	—	6.00
	1988	.140	—	—	Proof	9.00

Taejon International Exposition

KM#	Date	Mintage	Fine	VF	XF	Unc
78	1993	.590	—	—	—	5.00

2000 WON

NICKEL
1988 Olympics - Boxing

KM#	Date	Mintage	Fine	VF	XF	Unc
50	1986	.560	—	—	—	10.00
	1986	.140	—	—	Proof	15.00

1988 Olympics - Tae Kwon Do

KM#	Date	Mintage	Fine	VF	XF	Unc
51	1987	.560	—	—	—	10.00
	1987	.140	—	—	Proof	15.00

1988 Olympics - Wrestling

KM#	Date	Mintage	Fine	VF	XF	Unc
52	1987	.560	—	—	—	10.00
	1987	.140	—	—	Proof	15.00

1988 Olympics - Weight Lifting

KM#	Date	Mintage	Fine	VF	XF	Unc
53	1988	.560	—	—	—	10.00
	1988	.140	—	—	Proof	15.00

2500 WON

9.6800 g, .900 GOLD, .2801 oz AGW
Queen Mother Sunduk
Mint: Valcambi

KM#	Date	Year	Mintage	VF	XF	Unc
15.1	4303	1970	1,750	—	Proof	650.00
		Mint: Paris				
15.2	4303	1970(a)	100 pcs.	—	Proof	1500.

5000 WON

19.3600 g, .900 GOLD, .5602 oz AGW
Iron Clad Turtle Boat
Mint: Valcambi

KM#	Date	Year	Mintage	VF	XF	Unc
16.1	4303	1970	670 pcs.	—	Proof	1850.
		Mint: Paris				
16.2	4303	1970(a)	70 pcs.	—	Proof	2500.

23.0000 g, .900 SILVER, .6655 oz ASW
42nd World Shooting Championships

KM#	Date	Mintage	Fine	VF	XF	Unc
23	1978	.080	—	—	—	40.00
	1978 unfrosted					
		.020	—	—	Proof	110.00

16.8100 g, .925 SILVER, .5000 oz ASW
1988 Olympics - Tiger Mascot

KM#	Date	Mintage	Fine	VF	XF	Unc
54	1986	.092	—	—	—	15.00
	1986	.235	—	—	Proof	20.00

1988 Olympics - Rope Pulling

KM#	Date	Mintage	Fine	VF	XF	Unc
55	1986	.090	—	—	—	15.00
	1986	.217	—	—	Proof	20.00

1988 Olympic Stadium

KM#	Date	Mintage	Fine	VF	XF	Unc
60	1987	.073	—	—	—	15.00
	1987	.199	—	—	Proof	20.00

1988 Olympics - Chegi - Kicking

KM#	Date	Mintage	Fine	VF	XF	Unc
61	1987	.060	—	—	—	15.00
	1987	.180	—	—	Proof	20.00

1988 Olympics - Tae Kwon Do

KM#	Date	Mintage	Fine	VF	XF	Unc
66	1987	.058	—	—	—	15.00
	1987	.150	—	—	Proof	20.00

1988 Olympics - Girls on Swing

KM#	Date	Mintage	Fine	VF	XF	Unc
67	1987	.060	—	—	—	15.00
	1987	.147	—	—	Proof	20.00

1988 Olympics - Wrestling

KM#	Date	Mintage	Fine	VF	XF	Unc
70	1988	.059	—	—	—	15.00
	1988	.136	—	—	Proof	20.00

1988 Olympics - Boys Spinning Top

KM#	Date	Mintage	Fine	VF	XF	Unc
71	1988	.059	—	—	—	15.00
	1988	.134	—	—	Proof	20.00

Taejon International Exposition - Yarn Spinners

KM#	Date	Mintage	Fine	VF	XF	Unc
79	1993	.150	—	—	—	20.00

Taejon International Exposition - Folk Musicians

KM#	Date	Mintage	Fine	VF	XF	Unc
80	1993	.150	—	—	—	20.00

10000 WON

38.7200 g, .900 GOLD, 1.1205 oz AGW
President Chung Hee Park
Mint: Valcambi

KM#	Date	Year	Mintage	VF	XF	Unc
17.1	4303	1970	435 pcs.	—	Proof	5000.
		Mint: Paris				
17.2	4303	1970(a)	55 pcs.	—	Proof	6000.

15.0000 g, .900 SILVER, .4340 oz ASW
1988 Olympics - Great South Gate, Seoul

KM#	Date	Mintage	Fine	VF	XF	Unc
29	1982	.280	—	—	—	20.00
	1982 unfrosted					
		.010	—	—	Proof	45.00
	1982	.010	—	—	Proof	70.00

1988 Olympics - Pavilion of Kyongbok Palace

KM#	Date	Mintage	Fine	VF	XF	Unc
37	1983	.137	—	—	—	20.00
	1983 unfrosted					
		.056	—	—	Proof	30.00
	1983	.101	—	—	Proof	35.00

23.2600 g, .500 SILVER, .3739 oz ASW
200 Years of Catholic Church in Korea

KM#	Date	Mintage	Fine	VF	XF	Unc
40	1984	.152	—	—	—	25.00

23.0000 g, .900 SILVER, .6655 oz ASW
10th Asian Games - Badminton
Obv: Similar to 2000 Won, KM#50.

KM#	Date	Mintage	Fine	VF	XF	Unc
42	1986	.130	—	—	—	20.00
	1986	.070	—	—	Proof	30.00

10th Asian Games - Soccer
Obv: Similar to 2000 Won, KM#50.

KM#	Date	Mintage	Fine	VF	XF	Unc
43	1986	.130	—	—	—	20.00
	1986	.070	—	—	Proof	30.00

33.6200 g, .925 SILVER, 1.0000 oz ASW
1988 Olympics - Marathon

KM#	Date	Mintage	Fine	VF	XF	Unc
56	1986	.090	—	—	—	25.00
	1986	.229	—	—	Proof	30.00

1988 Olympics - Diving

KM#	Date	Mintage	Fine	VF	XF	Unc
57	1987	.090	—	—	—	25.00
	1987	.217	—	—	Proof	30.00

1988 Olympics - Archery

KM#	Date	Mintage	Fine	VF	XF	Unc
62	1987	.060	—	—	—	25.00
	1987	.182	—	—	Proof	30.00

1988 Olympics - Volleyball
Obv: Similar to KM#62.

KM#	Date	Mintage	Fine	VF	XF	Unc
63	1987	.072	—	—	—	25.00
	1987	.188	—	—	Proof	30.00

1988 Olympics - Gymnastics

KM#	Date	Mintage	Fine	VF	XF	Unc
74	1988	9,000	—	—	—	30.00
	1988	.097	—	—	Proof	40.00

1988 Olympics - Equestrian Events

KM#	Date	Mintage	Fine	VF	XF	Unc
75	1988	9,000	—	—	—	30.00
	1988	.097	—	—	Proof	40.00

1988 Olympics - Cycling

KM#	Date	Mintage	Fine	VF	XF	Unc
76	1988	8,700	—	—	—	30.00
	1988	.095	—	—	Proof	40.00

1988 Olympics - Soccer

KM#	Date	Mintage	Fine	VF	XF	Unc
77	1988	8,700	—	—	—	30.00
	1988	.083	—	—	Proof	40.00

Taejon International Exposition - Porcelain Celadon

KM#	Date	Mintage	Fine	VF	XF	Unc
81	1993	—	—	—	—	40.00

20000 WON

77.4000 g, .900 GOLD, 2.2398 oz AGW
Gold Crown - Silla Dynasty
Mint: Valcambi
Rev: Similar to 5000 Won, KM#16.1.

KM#	Date	Year	Mintage	VF	XF	Unc
18.1	4303	1970	382 pcs.	—	Proof	9000.
			Mint: Paris			
18.2	4303	1970(a)	52 pcs.	—	Proof	10,000.

23.0000 g, .900 SILVER, .6655 oz ASW
1st Anniversary of the 5th Republic

KM#	Date	Mintage	Fine	VF	XF	Unc
26	1981	.080	—	—	—	45.00
	1981 unfrosted					
		.018	—	—	Proof	55.00
	1981	2,000	—	—	Proof	350.00

1988 Olympics - Flame

KM#	Date	Mintage	Fine	VF	XF	Unc
30	1982	.180	—	—	—	35.00
	1982 unfrosted					
		.010	—	—	Proof	65.00
	1982	.010	—	—	Proof	90.00

1988 Olympics - Wrestlers

KM#	Date	Mintage	Fine	VF	XF	Unc
38	1983	.123	—	—	—	35.00
	1983 unfrosted					
		.056	—	—	Proof	40.00
	1983	.101	—	—	Proof	45.00

.900 SILVER
10th Asian Games - Runner
Obv: Similar to 1000 Won, KM#41.

KM#	Date	Mintage	Fine	VF	XF	Unc
44	1986	.130	—	—	—	40.00
	1986	.070	—	—	Proof	50.00

10th Asian Games - Pul Guk Temple - Kyong Ju
Obv: Similar to 1000 Won, KM#41.

KM#	Date	Mintage	Fine	VF	XF	Unc
45	1986	.130	—	—	—	40.00
	1986	.070	—	—	Proof	50.00

25000 WON

96.8000 g, .900 GOLD, 2.8012 oz AGW
King Sejong The Great
Mint: Valcambi
Illustration reduced. Actual size: 60mm
Rev: Similar to 5000 Won, KM#16.1.

KM#	Date	Year	Mintage	VF	XF	Unc
19.1	4303	1970	325 pcs.	—	Proof	15,000.
			Mint: Paris			
19.2	4303	1970(a)	25 pcs.	—	Proof	17,000.

16.8100 g, .925 GOLD, .5000 oz AGW
1988 Olympics - Folk Dancing

KM#	Date	Mintage	Fine	VF	XF	Unc
58	1986	.020	—	—	—	300.00
	1986	.111	—	—	Proof	300.00

1988 Olympics - Fan Dancing

KM#	Date	Mintage	Fine	VF	XF	Unc
64	1987	.020	—	—	—	300.00
	1987	.082	—	—	Proof	325.00

1988 Olympics - Kite Flying

KM#	Date	Mintage	Fine	VF	XF	Unc
68	1987	.020	—	—	—	300.00
	1987	.079	—	—	Proof	325.00
	1988	—	—	—	—	300.00
	1988	—	—	—	Proof	325.00

1988 Olympics - Korean Seesaw

KM#	Date	Mintage	Fine	VF	XF	Unc
72	1988	.019	—	—	—	300.00
	1988	.062	—	—	Proof	350.00

Taejon International Exposition - Celestial Globe

KM#	Date	Mintage	Fine	VF	XF	Unc
82	1993	.040	—	—	—	350.00

50000 WON

33.6200 g, .925 GOLD, 1.0000 oz AGW
1988 Olympics - History - Turtle Boat

KM#	Date	Mintage	Fine	VF	XF	Unc
59	1986	.030	—	—	Proof	650.00

1988 Olympics - Great South Gate
Obv: Similar to 10,000 Won, KM#62.

KM#	Date	Mintage	Fine	VF	XF	Unc
65	1987	.030	—	—	Proof	625.00

1988 Olympics - Horse and Rider
Obv: Similar to 10,000 Won, KM#62.

KM#	Date	Mintage	Fine	VF	XF	Unc
69	1987	.030	—	—	Proof	650.00

1988 Olympics - Pul Guk Temple
Obv: Similar to 10,000 Won, KM#62.

KM#	Date	Mintage	Fine	VF	XF	Unc
73	1988	.030	—	—	Proof	650.00

Taejon International Exposition - Tower of Great Light

KM#	Date	Mintage	Fine	VF	XF	Unc
83	1993	.010	—	—	—	750.00

MINT SETS (MS)

KM#	Date	Mintage	Identification	Issue Price	Mkt. Val.
MS1	Mixed dates(6)	*7,500	KM6a(1980)32,34-35 (1983),27,31(1984)	—	—
MS2	1986(5)	.130	KM41-45	113.00	145.00
MS3	1991(6)	—	KM27,31-35	—	12.00

***NOTE:** Issued as a presentation set for the World Bank Conference in Seoul, October 1985.

KM#	Date	Mintage	Identification	Issue Price	Mkt. Val.
MS4	1993(6)	10,000	KM78-83	1180.	1200.
MS5	1993(5)	30,000	KM78-82	443.00	450.00
MS6	1993(4)	50,000	KM78-81	97.00	100.00

PROOF SETS (PS)

KM#	Date	Mintage	Identification	Issue Price	Mkt. Val.
PS1	1970(12)	—	KM7-8,10-13,14.1-19.1	752.00	32,850.
PS2	1970(11)	—	KM7,8,10-13,14.2-18.2	—	22,350.
PS3	1970(6)	—	KM7-8,10-13	53.50	1100.
PS4	1970(6)	300	KM14.1-19.1	698.00	32,000.
PS5	1970(6)	25	KM14.2-19.2	—	38,250.
PS6	1982(6)	*2,000	KM4a-6a,9,20,27, (Presentation Set)	—	1000.
PS7	1986(5)	.070	KM41-45	170.00	170.00

***NOTE:** Original, intact sets are worth substantially more than their individual components.

KUWAIT

The State of Kuwait, a constitutional monarchy located on the Arabian Peninsula at the northwestern corner of the Persian Gulf, has an area of 6,880 sq. mi. (17,820 sq. km.) and a population of 1.7 million. Capital: Kuwait. Petroleum, the basis of the economy, provides 95 per cent of the exports.

The modern history of Kuwait began with the founding of the city of Kuwait, 1740, by tribesmen who wandered northward from the region of the Qatar Peninsula of eastern Arabia. Fearing that the Turks would take over the sheikhdom, Sheikh Mubarak entered into an agreement with Great Britain, 1899, placing Kuwait under the protection of Britain and empowering Britain to conduct its foreign affairs. Britain terminated the protectorate on June 19, 1961, giving Kuwait its independence (by a simple exchange of notes) but agreeing to furnish military aid on request.

Kuwait was invaded and occupied by an army from neighboring Iraq Aug. 2, 1990. Soon thereafter Iraq declared that the country would become a province of Iraq. An international coalition of military forces primarily based in Saudi Arabia led by the United States under terms set by the United Nations, attacked Iraqi military installations to liberate Kuwait. This occurred Jan. 16 1991 (Jan. 17 in Kuwait). Kuwait City was liberated Feb. 27, and a cease-fire was declared Feb. 28. New currency was introduced March 24, 1991.

TITLES

الكويت

al-Kuwait

RULERS

British, until 1961

LOCAL

Sabah Ibn Jabir al Sabah, 1756-1762

Abdallah Ibn Sabah al Sabah, 1762-1812

Jabir Ibn Abdallah al Sabah, 1812-1859

Sabah Ibn Jabir al Sabah, 1859-1866

Abdullah Ibn Sabah al Sabah, 1866-1892

Muhammad Ibn Sabah al Sabah, 1892-1896

Mubarak Ibn Sabah al Sabah, 1896-1915

Jabir Ibn Mubarak al Sabah, 1915-1917

Salim Ibn Mubarak al Sabah, 1917-1921

Ahmad Ibn Jabir al Sabah, 1921-1950

Abdullah Ibn Salim al Sabah, 1950-1965

Sabah Ibn Salim al Sabah, 1965-1977

Jabir Ibn Ahmad al Sabah, 1977—

MONETARY SYSTEM

1000 Fils = 1 Dinar

BAIZA

COPPER

KM#	Date	Year	Mintage	VF	XF	Unc
1	AH1304	(1887)	—	—	Rare	—

MODERN COINAGE

FILS

NICKEL-BRASS

KM#	Date	Year	Mintage	VF	XF	Unc
2	AH1380	1961	2.000	.50	1.00	1.50
	1380	1961	60 pcs.	—	Proof	30.00

KM#	Date	Year	Mintage	VF	XF	Unc
9	AH1382	1962	.500	.10	.15	.35
	1382	1962	60 pcs.	—	Proof	30.00
	1384	1964	.600	.25	.75	1.50
	1385	1966	.500	.25	.75	1.50
	1386	1967	1.875	.25	.75	1.50
	1389	1970	.375	.35	1.00	2.50
	1390	1971	.500	.25	.75	1.50
	1391	1971	.500	.25	.75	1.50
	1392	1972	.500	.25	.75	1.50
	1393	1973	.375	.35	1.00	2.50
	1395	1975	.500	.25	.75	1.50
	1396	1976	2.500	.15	.25	.50
	1397	1977	2.500	.15	.25	.50
	1399	1979	1.500	.15	.25	.50
	1400	1980	—	.15	.25	.50
	1408	1988	.500	.15	.25	.50

5 FILS

NICKEL-BRASS

KM#	Date	Year	Mintage	VF	XF	Unc
3	AH1380	1961	2.400	.60	1.25	2.00
	1380	1961	60 pcs.	—	Proof	35.00

KM#	Date	Year	Mintage	VF	XF	Unc
10	AH1382	1962	1.800	.10	.20	.45
	1382	1962	60 pcs.	—	Proof	35.00
	1384	1964	.600	.30	.75	2.00
	1386	1967	1.600	.20	.35	1.00
	1388	1968	.800	.30	.75	2.25
	1389	1969	—	.30	.75	2.25
	1389	1970	.600	.30	.75	2.25
	1390	1971	.600	.30	.75	2.25
	1391	1971	.600	.30	.75	2.25
	1392	1972	.800	.25	.65	1.75
	1393	1973	.800	.25	.65	1.75
	1394	1974	1.200	.10	.20	1.00
	1395	1975	5.020	.10	.20	.50
	1396	1976	.180	.35	1.00	3.00
	1397	1977	4.000	.10	.20	.40
	1399	1979	6.700	.10	.20	.40
	1400	1980	—	.10	.20	.40
	1401	1981	7.000	.10	.20	.40
	1403	1983	—	.10	.20	.40
	1405	1985	—	.10	.20	.40
	1407	1987	—	.10	.20	.40
	1408	1988	3.000	.10	.20	.40
	1410	1990	—	.10	.20	.40

10 FILS

NICKEL-BRASS

KM#	Date	Year	Mintage	VF	XF	Unc
4	AH1380	1961	2.600	.65	1.25	2.00
	1380	1961	60 pcs.	—	Proof	40.00

KM#	Date	Year	Mintage	VF	XF	Unc
11	AH1382	1962	1.360	.15	.25	.65
	1382	1962	60 pcs.	—	Proof	40.00
	1384	1964	.800	.35	.85	2.50
	1386	1967	1.360	.30	.75	1.75
	1388	1968	.672	.35	.85	2.50
	1389	1969	.480	.50	1.00	2.75
	1389	1970	.640	.35	.85	2.50
	1390	1971	.480	.50	1.00	2.75
	1391	1971	.800	.35	.85	2.50
	1392	1972	1.120	.15	.40	2.00
	1393	1973	1.440	.15	.40	2.00
	1394	1974	1.280	.15	.40	2.00
	1395	1975	5.280	.15	.25	.75
	1396	1976	2.400	.15	.25	.75
	1397	1977	—	.15	.25	.75
	1399	1979	6.160	.15	.25	.75
	1400	1980	—	.15	.25	.75
	1401	1981	8.320	.15	.25	.75
	1403	1983	—	.15	.25	.75
	1405	1985	—	.15	.25	.75
	1408	1988	5.000	.15	.25	.75

20 FILS

COPPER-NICKEL

KM#	Date	Year	Mintage	VF	XF	Unc
5	AH1380	1961	2.000	.75	1.50	2.50
	1380	1961	60 pcs.	—	Proof	45.00

KM#	Date	Year	Mintage	VF	XF	Unc
12	AH1382	1962	1.200	.25	.35	.75
	1382	1962	60 pcs.	—	Proof	45.00
	1384	1964	.480	.50	1.00	3.00
	1386	1967	1.280	.35	.85	2.00
	1388	1968	.672	.35	.85	2.50
	1389	1969	.800	.35	.85	2.50
	1389	1970	.480	.50	1.00	3.00
	1390	1971	.480	.50	1.00	3.00
	1391	1971	.960	.35	.85	2.00
	1392	1972	1.440	.20	.45	2.00
	1393	1973	1.280	.20	.45	2.00
	1394	1974	1.600	.20	.45	1.50
	1395	1975	2.400	.20	.30	1.25
	1396	1976	3.200	.20	.30	1.25
	1397	1977	3.400	.20	.30	1.25
	1399.	1979	5.520	.20	.30	1.25
	1400	1980	—	.20	.30	1.00
	1401	1981	8.960	.20	.30	1.00
	1403	1983	—	.20	.30	1.00
	1405	1985	—	.20	.30	1.00
	1408	1988	5.000	.20	.30	1.00

50 FILS

COPPER-NICKEL

KM#	Date	Year	Mintage	VF	XF	Unc
6	AH1380	1961	1.720	.85	1.75	2.75
	1380	1961	60 pcs.	—	Proof	60.00

KM#	Date	Year	Mintage	VF	XF	Unc
13	AH1382	1962	.900	.50	.75	1.25
	1382	1962	60 pcs.	—	Proof	60.00
	1384	1964	.300	.75	1.50	4.00
	1386	1967	.800	.40	.85	2.50
	1388	1968	.200	1.00	2.00	6.00
	1389	1969	.400	.50	1.00	3.00

KM#	Date	Year	Mintage	VF	XF	Unc
13	1389	1970	.500	.50	1.00	3.00
	1390	1971	.300	.75	1.50	4.00
	1391	1971	.500	.50	1.00	3.00
	1392	1972	.900	.50	.85	2.50
	1393	1973	.800	.50	.85	2.50
	1394	1974	1.000	.35	.50	2.00
	1395	1975	1.950	.35	.50	2.00
	1396	1976	2.250	.25	.35	2.00
	1397	1977	6.000	.25	.35	1.35
	1399	1979	6.050	.25	.35	1.35
	1400	1980	—	.25	.35	1.35
	1401	1981	3.000	.25	.35	1.35
	1403	1983	—	.25	.35	1.35
	1405	1985	—	.25	.35	1.35
	1407	1987	2.000	.25	.35	1.35
	1408	1988	3.000	.25	.35	1.35

100 FILS

COPPER-NICKEL

KM#	Date	Year	Mintage	VF	XF	Unc
7	AH1380	1961	1.260	1.00	2.00	3.50
	1380	1961	60 pcs.	—	Proof	90.00

KM#	Date	Year	Mintage	VF	XF	Unc
14	AH1382	1962	.640	.50	.65	1.50
	1382	1962	60 pcs.	—	Proof	90.00
	1384	1964	.160	1.75	3.00	6.00
	1386	1967	.640	1.00	1.50	3.00
	1388	1968	.160	1.75	3.00	6.00
	1389	1969	.320	1.00	2.00	4.00
	1391	1971	.240	1.25	2.00	4.00
	1392	1972	.400	1.00	1.50	3.00
	1393	1973	.480	1.00	1.50	3.00
	1394	1974	.480	1.00	1.50	3.00
	1395	1975	3.040	.50	.75	1.75
	1396	1976	—	.50	.75	1.75
	1397	1977	1.600	.50	.75	1.75
	1399	1979	3.040	.50	.75	1.75
	1400	1980	—	.50	.75	1.75
	1401	1981	2.960	.50	.75	1.75
	1403	1983	—	.50	.75	1.75
	1405	1985	—	.50	.75	1.75
	1407	1987	2.000	.50	.75	1.75
	1408	1988	2.000	.50	.75	1.75

2 DINARS

28.2800 g, .500 SILVER, .4546 oz ASW
15th Anniversary of Independence

KM#	Date	Year	Mintage	VF	XF	Unc
15		1976	—	.070	—	60.00

28.2800 g, .925 SILVER, .8411 oz ASW

KM#	Date	Year	Mintage	VF	XF	Unc
15a		1976	—	.053	Proof	100.00

5 DINARS

13.5720 g, .917 GOLD, .4001 oz AGW.

KM#	Date	Year	Mintage	VF	XF	Unc
8	AH1380	1961	*1,000	—	—	—

28.2800 g, .925 SILVER, .8411 oz ASW
15th Century of the Hijira

KM#	Date	Year	Mintage	VF	XF	Unc
16	AH1401	(1981)	.010	—	Proof	65.00

20th Anniversary of Independence
Rev: Similar to 100 Dinars, KM#19.

KM#	Date	Year	Mintage	VF	XF	Unc
18	(AH1401)	1981	.010	—	Proof	65.00

33.6250 g, .925 SILVER, 1.0000 oz ASW
25th Anniversary of Kuwait Currency
Obv: Arabic denomination, buildings, port scene and refinery.
Rev: English legend, falcon, dhow, building and map on globe.

KM#	Date	Year	Mintage	VF	XF	Unc
20	(AH1406)	1986	—	—	Proof	100.00

5th Islamic Summit Conference
Obv: Arabic, English and French legend, crescent and minaret. Rev: Dhow.

KM#	Date	Year	Mintage	VF	XF	Unc
22	AH1407	1987	—	—	Proof	100.00

50 DINARS

16.9660 g, .917 GOLD, .5000 oz AGW
25th Anniversary of Kuwait Independence
Obv: Arabic legend, arched design, falcon, tent, boat and pearl in a shell.
Rev: Radiant sun, mosque and assembly building, English and Arabic legend.

KM#	Date	Year	Mintage	VF	XF	Unc
21	AH1406	1986	—	—	Proof	275.00

5th Islamic Summit Conference
Obv: Arabic, English and French legend, crescent and minaret. Rev: Dhow.

KM#	Date	Year	Mintage	VF	XF	Unc
23	AH1407	1987	—	—	Proof	275.00

100 DINARS

15.9800 g, .917 GOLD, .4711 oz AGW
15th Century of the Hijira

KM#	Date	Year	Mintage	VF	XF	Unc
17	AH1401	(1981)	.010	—	Proof	400.00

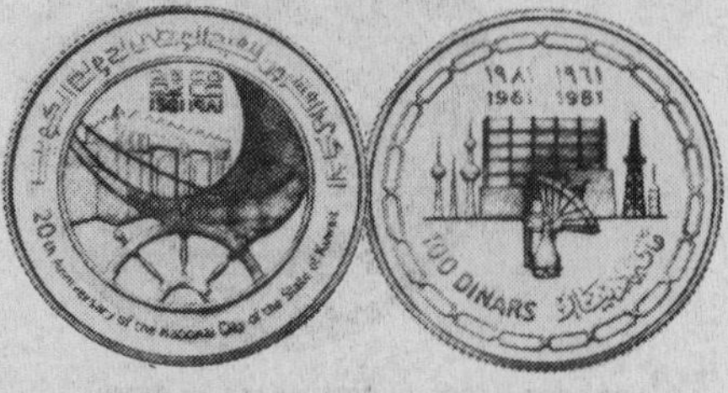

20th Anniversary of Independence

KM#	Date	Year	Mintage	VF	XF	Unc
19	(AH1401)	1981	.010	—	Proof	450.00

MINT SETS (MS)

KM#	Date	Mintage	Identification	Issue Price	Mkt. Val.
MS1	1393-94(6)	74	KM9-14	1.75	—
MS2	1396-97(6)	—	KM9-14	3.50	—

PROOF SETS (PS)

KM#	Date	Mintage	Identification	Issue Price	Mkt. Val.
PS1	1961(6)	60	KM2-7	—	300.00
PS2	1962(6)	60	KM9-14	—	300.00

LAOS

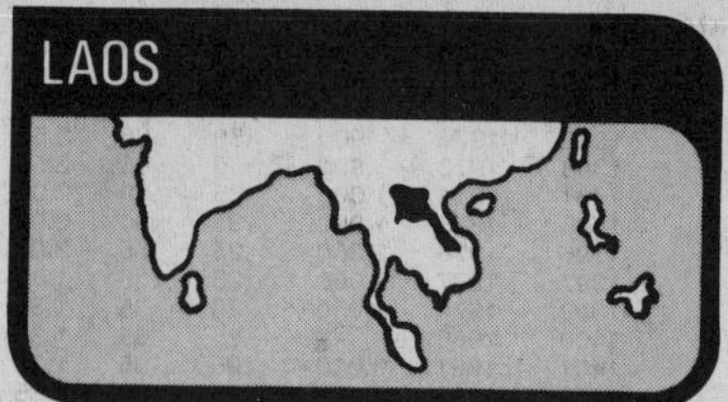

The Lao Peoples Democratic Republic, located on the Indo-Chinese Peninsula between the Socialist Republic of Vietnam and the Kingdom of Thailand, has an area of 91,429 sq. mi. (236,800 km.) and a population of 3.6 million. Capital Vientiane. Agriculture employs 95 per cent of the people. Tin, lumber and coffee are exported.

The first United Kingdom of Laos was established in the mid-14th century by King Fa Ngum who ruled an area including present Laos, northeastern Thailand, and the southern part of China's Yunnan province from his capital at Luang Prabang. Thailand and Vietnam obtained control over much of the present Lao territory in the 18th century and remained dominant until France established a protec- torate over the area in 1893 and incorporated it into the Union of Indo-China. The Independence of Laos was proclaimed in March of 1945, during the last days of the Japanese occupation of World War II. France reoccupied Laos in 1946, and established it as a constitutional monarchy within the French Union in 1949. In 1953 war erupted between the government and the Pathet Lao, a Communist movement supported by the Vietnamese Communist forces. Peace was declared in 1954 with Laos becoming fully independent in 1955 and the Pathet Lao being permitted to occupy two northern provinces. Civil war broke out again in 1960 with the United States supporting the government of the Kingdom of Laos and the North Vietnamese helping the Communist Pathet Lao, and continued, with intervals of truce and political compromise, until the formation of the Lao Peoples Democratic Republic on Dec. 2, 1975.

NOTE: For earlier coinage see French Indo-China.

RULERS

Sisavang Vong, 1949-1959
Savang Vatthana, 1959-1975

MONETARY SYSTEM

100 Cents = 1 Piastre
Commencing 1955
100 Att = 1 Kip

MINT MARKS

(a) - Paris, privy marks only
None - Berlin

NOTE: Private bullion issues previously listed here are now listed in *Unusual World Coins*, 3rd Edition, Krause Publications, Inc., 1992.

KINGDOM

10 CENTS

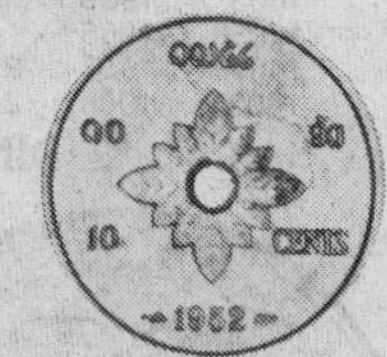

ALUMINUM

KM#	Date	Mintage	Fine	VF	XF	Unc
4	1952(a)	2.000	—	.15	.30	1.00

20 CENTS

ALUMINUM

KM#	Date	Mintage	Fine	VF	XF	Unc
5	1952(a)	3.000	—	.20	.40	1.00

50 CENTS

ALUMINUM

KM#	Date	Mintage	Fine	VF	XF	Unc
6	1952(a)	1.400	—	.35	.75	2.00

1000 KIP

10.0000 g, .925 SILVER, .2973 oz ASW
King Savang Vatthana Coronation

KM#	Date	Mintage	Fine	VF	XF	Unc
7	1971	—	—	—	—	20.00
	1971	*.020	—	—	Proof	30.00

2500 KIP

20.0000 g, .925 SILVER, .5947 oz ASW
King Savang Vatthana Coronation

KM#	Date	Mintage	Fine	VF	XF	Unc
8	1971	—	—	—	—	30.00
	1971	*.020	—	—	Proof	40.00

4000 KIP

4.0000 g, .900 GOLD, .1157 oz AGW
King Savang Vatthana Coronation

KM#	Date	Mintage	Fine	VF	XF	Unc
9	1971	*.010	—	—	Proof	70.00

5000 KIP

40.0000 g, .925 SILVER, 1.1895 oz ASW
King Savang Vatthana Coronation
Obv: Similar to 2500 Kip, KM#8.

KM#	Date	Mintage	Fine	VF	XF	Unc
10	1971	—	—	—	—	100.00
	1971	*.020	—	—	Proof	150.00

11.7000 g, .925 SILVER, .3479 oz ASW
Laotian Maiden

KM#	Date	Mintage	Fine	VF	XF	Unc
16	1975	400 pcs.	—	—	—	110.00
	1975	775 pcs.	—	—	Proof	135.00

Wat Phra Kio Museum, Vientiane

KM#	Date	Mintage	Fine	VF	XF	Unc
17	1975	400 pcs.	—	—	—	100.00
	1975	775 pcs.	—	—	Proof	125.00

8000 KIP

8.0000 g, .900 GOLD, .2315 oz AGW
King Savang Vatthana Coronation

KM#	Date	Mintage	Fine	VF	XF	Unc
11	1971	*.010	—	—	Proof	140.00

10000 KIP

80.0000 g, .925 SILVER, 2.3791 oz ASW
King Savang Vatthana Coronation
Obv: Similar to 2500 Kip, KM#8.

KM#	Date	Mintage	Fine	VF	XF	Unc
12	1971	—	—	—	—	150.00
	1971	*.020	—	—	Proof	250.00

23.5000 g, .925 SILVER, .6988 oz ASW
Wat Xieng - Thong Temple

KM#	Date	Mintage	Fine	VF	XF	Unc
18	1975	300 pcs.	—	—	—	175.00
	1975	650 pcs.	—	—	Proof	200.00

20000 KIP

20.0000 g, .900 GOLD, .5787 oz AGW
King Savang Vatthana Coronation

KM#	Date	Mintage	Fine	VF	XF	Unc
13	1971	*.010	—	—	Proof	325.00

40000 KIP

40.0000 g, .900 GOLD, 1.1575 oz AGW
King Savang Vatthana Coronation

KM#	Date	Mintage	Fine	VF	XF	Unc
14	1971	*.010	—	—	Proof	625.00

50000 KIP

3.6000 g, .900 GOLD, .1041 oz AGW
Obv: Bust of King Savang Vatthana.
Rev. That Luang Temple.

KM#	Date	Mintage	Fine	VF	XF	Unc
19	1975	100 pcs.	—	—	—	200.00
	1975	175 pcs.	—	—	Proof	275.00

Obv: Similar to 5000 Kip, KM#17.

KM#	Date	Mintage	Fine	VF	XF	Unc
20	1975	100 pcs.	—	—	—	175.00
	1975	175 pcs.	—	—	Proof	250.00

80000 KIP

80.0000 g, .900 GOLD, 2.3151 oz AGW
King Savang Vatthana Coronation
Obv: Similar to 20000 Kip, KM#13.

KM#	Date	Mintage	Fine	VF	XF	Unc
15	1971	—	—	—	Proof	1300.

100000 KIP

7.3200 g, .900 GOLD, .2118 oz AGW
Obv: Bust of King Savang Vatthana.
Rev: Statue of Buddha.

KM#	Date	Mintage	Fine	VF	XF	Unc
21	1975	100 pcs.	—	—	—	400.00
	1975	100 pcs.	—	—	Proof	500.00

MINT SETS (MS)

KM#	Date	Mintage	Identification	Issue Price	Mkt. Val.
MS1	1971(4)	—	KM7,8,10,12	—	300.00
MS1	1975(6)	100	KM16-21	—	1150.
MS2	1975(3)	300	KM16-18	—	375.00

PROOF SETS (PS)

KM#	Date	Mintage	Identification	Issue Price	Mkt. Val.
PS1	1971(5)	*10,000	KM9,11,13-15	467.00	2450.
PS2	1971(4)	*20,000	KM7,8,10,12	163.00	475.00
PS3	1975(6)	—	KM16-21	—	1375.
PS4	1975(3)	650	KM16-18	—	475.00
PS5	1975(3)	—	KM19-21	349.00	1000.

PEOPLES DEMOCRATIC REPUBLIC

MINT MARKS

None - Leningrad (50 Kip)

MONETARY SYSTEM

100 Att = 1 Kip

10 ATT

ALUMINUM

KM#	Date	Mintage	Fine	VF	XF	Unc
22	1980	—	—	.20	.40	.80

20 ATT

ALUMINUM

KM#	Date	Mintage	Fine	VF	XF	Unc
23	1980	—	—	.20	.40	.80

50 ATT

ALUMINUM

KM#	Date	Mintage	Fine	VF	XF	Unc
24	1980	—	—	.40	.80	1.20

KIP

COPPER-NICKEL
10th Anniversary of Peoples Democratic Republic

KM#	Date	Mintage	Fine	VF	XF	Unc
37	1985	—	—	.50	1.00	2.00

5 KIP

COPPER-NICKEL
10th Anniversary of Peoples Democratic Republic

KM#	Date	Mintage	Fine	VF	XF	Unc
38	1985	—	—	.75	1.50	3.00

10 KIP

COPPER-NICKEL
10th Anniversary of Peoples Democratic Republic

KM#	Date	Mintage	Fine	VF	XF	Unc
39	1985	—	—	1.25	2.50	5.00

World Soccer Championship-Italy 1990

KM#	Date	Mintage	Fine	VF	XF	Unc
30	1989	—	—	—	—	10.00

5 Mast Clipper

KM#	Date	Mintage	Fine	VF	XF	Unc
31	1988	.030	—	—	—	7.50

NICKEL BONDED STEEL

KM#	Date	Mintage	Fine	VF	XF	Unc
31a	1988	—	—	—	—	7.50

NICKEL PLATED STEEL
Olympics - Bicyclist

KM#	Date	Mintage	Fine	VF	XF	Unc
46	1991	—	—	—	—	12.50

20 KIP

COPPER-NICKEL
10th Anniversary of Peoples Democratic Republic

KM#	Date	Mintage	Fine	VF	XF	Unc
40	1985	—	—	1.50	2.50	5.00

50 KIP

COPPER-NICKEL
10th Anniversary of Peoples Democratic Republic

KM#	Date	Mintage	Fine	VF	XF	Unc
41	1985	—	—	2.00	3.00	6.50

38.2000 g, .900 SILVER, 1.1054 oz ASW
10th Anniversary of Peoples Republic
That Ing Hang

KM#	Date	Mintage	Fine	VF	XF	Unc
25	1985	2,000	—	—	Proof	40.00

10th Anniversary of Peoples Republic - That Luang

KM#	Date	Mintage	Fine	VF	XF	Unc
26	1985	2,000	—	—	Proof	40.00

10th Anniversary of Peoples Republic - Vat Phu

KM#	Date	Mintage	Fine	VF	XF	Unc
27	1985	2,000	—	—	Proof	40.00

10th Anniversary of Peoples Republic
Valley of Jars

KM#	Date	Mintage	Fine	VF	XF	Unc
28	1985	2,000	—	—	Proof	40.00

16.0000 g, .999 SILVER, .5145 oz ASW
5 Mast Clipper Ship "Prussia"

KM#	Date	Mintage	Fine	VF	XF	Unc
29	1988	2,000	—	—	Proof	45.00

12.0000 g, .999 SILVER, .3855 oz ASW
European Soccer Championship-Germany

KM#	Date	Mintage	Fine	VF	XF	Unc
32	1988	5,000	—	—	—	40.00

16.0000 g, .999 SILVER, .5145 oz ASW
World Soccer Championship-Mexico 86

KM#	Date	Mintage	Fine	VF	XF	Unc
33	ND(1988)	5,000	—	—	Proof	42.50

World Soccer Championship-Italy 1990

KM#	Date	Mintage	Fine	VF	XF	Unc
34	1989	5,000	—	—	Proof	42.50

Winter Olympics-Ice Dancing

KM#	Date	Mintage	Fine	VF	XF	Unc
35	1989	5,000	—	—	Proof	50.00

Summer Olympics-Water Polo

KM#	Date	Mintage	Fine	VF	XF	Unc
36	1989	5,000	—	—	Proof	50.00

12.0000 g, .999 SILVER, .3858 oz ASW
World Cup - Soccer

KM#	Date	Mintage	Fine	VF	XF	Unc
44	1991	—	—	—	—	35.00

20.0300 g, .999 SILVER, .6440 oz ASW
Wildlife - Tigers

KM#	Date	Mintage	Fine	VF	XF	Unc
45	1991	—	—	—	Proof	37.50

20.0000 g, .999 SILVER, .6430 oz ASW
Soccer - Goalie

KM#	Date	Mintage	Fine	VF	XF	Unc
47	1991	—	—	—	Proof	37.50

Protection of Nature - Elephant

KM#	Date	Mintage	Fine	VF	XF	Unc
48	1993	—	—	—	Proof	35.00

15.9400 g, .999 SILVER, .5120 oz ASW
Prehistoric Animals - Sauroctonus

KM#	Date	Mintage	Fine	VF	XF	Unc
49	1993	—	—	—	Proof	32.50

100 KIP

3.1500 g, .999 GOLD, .1012 oz AGW
Clipper Ship - Prussia
Obv: Emblem and legend above denomination.
Rev: 5 masted clipper ship.

KM#	Date	Mintage	Fine	VF	XF	Unc
42	1988	500 pcs.	—	—	—	150.00

That Louang Temple

KM#	Date	Mintage	Fine	VF	XF	Unc
43	1990	—	—	—	—	165.00

PROOF SETS (PS)

KM#	Date	Mintage	Identification	Issue Price	Mkt. Val.
PS1	1985(4)	2,000	KM25-28	—	160.00

Listings For

LAHEJ: refer to Yemen Republic

LATVIA

The Republic of Latvia, the central Baltic state in east Europe, has an area of 24,595 sq. mi. (43,601 sq. km.) and a population of *2.6 million. Capital: Riga. Livestock raising and manufacturing are the chief industries. Butter, bacon, fertilizers and telephone equipment are exported.

The Latvians, of Aryan descent, were nomadic tribesmen who settled along the Baltic prior to the 13th century. Lacking a central government, they were easily conquered by the German Teutonic Knights, Russia, Sweden and Poland. Following the third partition of Poland by Austria, Prussia and Russia in 1795, Latvia came under Russian domination and did not experience autonomy until the Russian Revolution of 1917 provided an opportunity for freedom. The Latvian Republic was established on Nov. 18, 1918. The republic was occupied by Soviet troops and annexed to the Soviet Union in 1940. Following the German occupation of 1941-44, it was retaken by Russia and reestablished as a member republic of the Soviet Union. Western countries, including the United States, did not recognize Latvia's incorporation into the Soviet Union.

The coinage, issued during Latvia's short tenure as a republic, is obsolete.

Latvia declared their independence from the USSR on August 22, 1991.

REPUBLIC COINAGE

MONETARY SYSTEM

100 Santimu = 1 Lats

SANTIMS

BRONZE

KM#	Date	Mintage	Fine	VF	XF	Unc
1	1922	5.000	.65	1.40	2.75	8.00
	1924	4.990	.65	1.40	2.75	8.00
	1926	5.000	.65	1.40	2.75	8.00
	1928 designers name below ribbon					
		5.000	.65	1.40	2.75	8.00
	1928 w/o designers name below ribbon					
		Inc. Ab.	2.00	5.00	10.00	32.50
	1932	5.000	.65	1.40	2.75	8.00
	1932	—	—	—	Proof	—
	1935	5.000	.65	1.40	2.75	8.00

KM#	Date	Mintage	Fine	VF	XF	Unc
10	1937	2.700	.65	1.40	2.75	8.00
	1938	1.900	.65	1.40	2.75	10.00
	1939	*3.400	.50	1.00	2.00	3.00

***NOTE:** Most were never placed into circulation.

2 SANTIMI

BRONZE

KM#	Date	Mintage	Fine	VF	XF	Unc
2	1922 designers name on obverse					
		10.000	1.00	2.00	4.00	9.00
	1922 w/o designers name					
		Inc. Ab.	5.00	10.00	17.50	35.00
	1926	5.000	.90	2.00	4.00	9.00
	1928	5.000	.90	2.00	4.00	9.00
	1932	5.000	.90	2.00	4.00	9.00
	1932	—	—	—	Proof	—

19mm

KM#	Date	Mintage	Fine	VF	XF	Unc
11.1	1937	.045	10.00	20.00	30.00	60.00

19.5mm

KM#	Date	Mintage	Fine	VF	XF	Unc
11.2	1939	*5.000	1.00	2.00	3.00	6.00

***NOTE:** Most were never placed into circulation.

5 SANTIMI

BRONZE

KM#	Date	Mintage	Fine	VF	XF	Unc
3	1922 designers name on obverse					
		15.000	.50	1.00	3.00	8.00
	1922 w/o designers name					
		Inc. Ab.	3.00	6.00	10.00	20.00

10 SANTIMU

NICKEL

KM#	Date	Mintage	Fine	VF	XF	Unc
4	1922	15.000	.50	1.00	3.00	6.00

20 SANTIMU

NICKEL

KM#	Date	Mintage	Fine	VF	XF	Unc
5	1922	15.000	.50	1.00	3.00	8.00

50 SANTIMU

NICKEL

KM#	Date	Mintage	Fine	VF	XF	Unc
6	1922	9.000	1.00	3.00	5.00	10.00

LATS

5.0000 g, .835 SILVER, .1342 oz ASW

KM#	Date	Mintage	Fine	VF	XF	Unc
7	1923	—	—	—	900.00	—
	1924	10.000	2.00	3.00	5.00	20.00

2 LATI

10.0000 g, .835 SILVER, .2684 oz ASW

KM#	Date	Mintage	Fine	VF	XF	Unc
8	1925	6.386	2.50	3.00	5.00	30.00
	1926	1.114	2.50	3.50	6.00	32.50

5 LATI

25.0000 g, .835 SILVER, .6712 oz ASW

KM#	Date	Mintage	Fine	VF	XF	Unc
9	1929	1.000	9.00	12.00	20.00	45.00
	1929	—	—	—	Proof	—
	1931	2.000	9.00	12.00	20.00	45.00
	1931	—	—	—	Proof	—
	1932	.600	9.00	12.00	20.00	45.00
	1932	—	—	—	Proof	—

MODERN COINAGE

SANTIMS

COPPER PLATED IRON

KM#	Date	Mintage	Fine	VF	XF	Unc
15	1992	—	—	—	—	.25

2 SANTIMI

BRONZE PLATED STEEL

KM#	Date	Mintage	Fine	VF	XF	Unc
21	1992	—	—	—	—	.50

5 SANTIMI

BRASS

KM#	Date	Mintage	Fine	VF	XF	Unc
16	1992	—	—	—	—	.75

10 SANTIMU

BRASS

KM#	Date	Mintage	Fine	VF	XF	Unc
17	1992	—	—	—	—	1.00

20 SANTIMU

BRASS

KM#	Date	Mintage	Fine	VF	XF	Unc
22	1992	—	—	—	—	1.25

50 SANTIMU

COPPER-NICKEL

KM#	Date	Mintage	Fine	VF	XF	Unc
13	1992	—	—	—	—	1.50

LATS

COPPER-NICKEL

KM#	Date	Mintage	Fine	VF	XF	Unc
12	1992	—	—	—	—	2.50

2 LATI

COPPER-NICKEL

KM#	Date	Mintage	Fine	VF	XF	Unc
14	1992	—	—	—	—	5.00

75th Anniversary of Declaration of Independence

KM#	Date	Mintage	Fine	VF	XF	Unc
18	1992	.050	—	—	Proof	8.00

10 LATU

25.1750 g, .925 SILVER, .7484 oz ASW
75th Anniversary of Declaration of Independence

KM#	Date	Mintage	Fine	VF	XF	Unc
19	1993	.030	—	—	Proof	25.00

100 LATU

13.3380 g, .833 GOLD, .2501 oz AGW
75th Anniversary of Declaration of Independence

KM#	Date	Mintage	Fine	VF	XF	Unc
20	1993	5,000	—	—	Proof	250.00

MINT SETS (MS)

KM#	Date	Mintage	Identification	Issue Price	Mkt. Val.
MS1	1992(8)	—	KM12-17,21-22	—	20.00

LEBANON

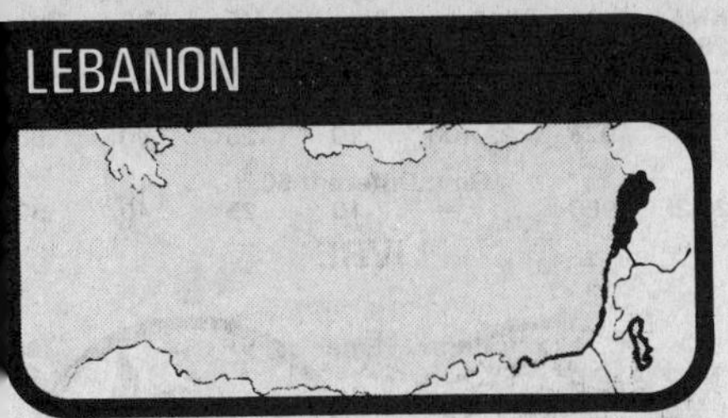

The Republic of Lebanon, situated on the eastern shore of the Mediterranean Sea between Syria and Israel, has an area of 4,015 sq. mi. (10,400 sq. km.) and a population of 3.5 million. Capital: Beirut. The economy is based on agriculture, trade and tourism. Fruit, other foodstuffs and textiles are exported.

Almost at the beginning of recorded history, Lebanon appeared as the well-wooded hinterland of the Phoenicians who exploited its famous forests of cedar. The mountains were a Christian refuge and a Crusader stronghold. Lebanon, the history of which is essentially the same as that of Syria, came under control of the Ottoman Turks early in the 16th century. Following the collapse of the Ottoman Empire after World War I, Lebanon, along with Syria, became a French mandate. The French drew a border around the predominantly Christian Lebanon Sanjak or administrative subdivision and on Sept. 1, 1920 proclaimed the area the State of Grand Lebanon (Etat du Grand Liban) a republic under French control. France announced the independence of Lebanon on Nov. 26, 1941, but the last British and French troops didn't leave until the end of August 1946.

TITLES

الجمهورية اللبنانية

al-Jomhuriya(t) al-Lubnaniya(t)

MINT MARKS

(a) - Paris, privy marks only
(u) - Utrecht, privy marks only

MONETARY SYSTEM

100 Piastres = 1 Livre (Pound)

FRENCH PROTECTORATE

1/2 PIASTRE

COPPER-NICKEL

KM#	Date	Mintage	Fine	VF	XF	Unc
9	1934(a)	.200	2.00	5.00	12.50	40.00
	1936(a)	1.200	1.25	3.00	7.50	25.00

ZINC

KM#	Date	Mintage	Fine	VF	XF	Unc
9a	1941(a)	1.000	.50	1.00	4.00	10.00

PIASTRE

COPPER-NICKEL

KM#	Date	Mintage	Fine	VF	XF	Unc
3	1925(a)	1.500	.50	2.00	7.50	25.00
	1931(a)	.300	1.00	4.00	12.50	45.00
	1933(a)	.500	1.00	4.00	10.00	45.00
	1936(a)	2.200	.50	1.00	6.50	20.00

ZINC

KM#	Date	Mintage	Fine	VF	XF	Unc
3a	1940(a)	2.000	.50	.75	4.00	10.00

2 PIASTRES

ALUMINUM-BRONZE

KM#	Date	Mintage	Fine	VF	XF	Unc
1	1924(a)	1.800	1.25	3.00	12.50	50.00

KM#	Date	Mintage	Fine	VF	XF	Unc
4	1925(a)	1.000	3.00	8.00	20.00	75.00

2-1/2 PIASTRES

ALUMINUM-BRONZE

KM#	Date	Mintage	Fine	VF	XF	Unc
10	1940(a)	1.000	1.00	2.00	3.50	12.00

5 PIASTRES

ALUMINUM-BRONZE

KM#	Date	Mintage	Fine	VF	XF	Unc
2	1924(a)	1.000	1.25	3.00	10.00	45.00

Rev: Both privy marks to left of '5'.

KM#	Date	Mintage	Fine	VF	XF	Unc
5.1	1925(a)	1.500	.75	1.50	8.00	30.00

Rev: Privy marks to left and right of 5 Piastres.

KM#	Date	Mintage	Fine	VF	XF	Unc
5.2	1925(a)	Inc. Ab.	1.00	2.00	7.50	30.00
	1931(a)	.400	1.50	4.00	12.50	40.00
	1933(a)	.500	1.50	4.00	12.50	40.00
	1936(a)	.900	1.00	2.00	7.50	25.00
	1940(a)	1.000	.75	1.50	5.00	15.00

10 PIASTRES

2.0000 g, .680 SILVER, .0437 oz ASW

KM#	Date	Mintage	Fine	VF	XF	Unc
6	1929	.880	3.00	7.00	25.00	70.00

25 PIASTRES

5.0000 g, .680 SILVER, .1093 oz ASW

KM#	Date	Mintage	Fine	VF	XF	Unc
7	1929	.600	3.00	7.00	25.00	75.00
	1933(a)	.200	4.50	15.00	40.00	125.00
	1936(a)	.400	3.50	10.00	27.50	85.00

50 PIASTRES

10.0000 g, .680 SILVER, .2186 oz ASW

KM#	Date	Mintage	Fine	VF	XF	Unc
8	1929	.500	5.00	10.00	40.00	125.00
	1933(a)	.100	7.00	20.00	65.00	185.00
	1936(a)	.100	7.00	17.50	50.00	150.00

WORLD WAR II COINAGE

1/2 PIASTRE

BRASS

KM#	Date	Mintage	Fine	VF	XF	Unc
11	ND	—	1.00	2.50	5.00	10.00

NOTE: Three varieties known. Usually crudely struck, off center, etc. Perfectly struck, centered unc. specimens command a considerable premium. Size of letters also vary.

PIASTRE

BRASS

KM#	Date	Mintage	Fine	VF	XF	Unc
12	ND	—	1.00	3.00	7.50	15.00

NOTE: Two varieties known. Usually crudely struck, off center, etc. Perfectly struck, centered unc. specimens command a considerable premium.

ALUMINUM

KM#	Date	Mintage	Fine	VF	XF	Unc
12a	ND	—	—	—	—	—

2-1/2 PIASTRES

ALUMINUM

KM#	Date	Mintage	Fine	VF	XF	Unc
13	ND	—	1.50	3.00	7.50	15.00

NOTE: Seven varieties known. Usually crudely struck, off center, etc. Perfectly struck, centered unc. specimens command a considerable premium.

ALUMINUM-BRONZE

KM#	Date	Mintage	Fine	VF	XF	Unc
13a	ND	—	—	650.00	850.00	—

5 PIASTRES

ALUMINUM

KM#	Date	Mintage	Fine	VF	XF	Unc
A14	ND	—	—	—	2000.	3000.

NOTE: Did not enter circulation in significant numbers.

REPUBLIC

PIASTRE

ALUMINUM-BRONZE

KM#	Date	Mintage	VF	XF	Unc	BU
19	1955(a)	4.000	—	.10	.15	.25

2-1/2 PIASTRES

ALUMINUM-BRONZE

KM#	Date	Mintage	Fine	VF	XF	Unc
20	1955(a)	5.000	—	.10	.15	.30

5 PIASTRES

ALUMINUM

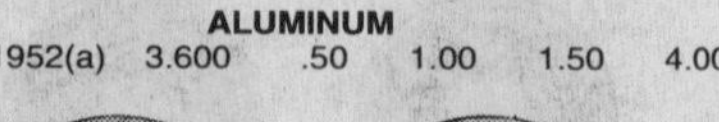

KM#	Date	Mintage	Fine	VF	XF	Unc
14	1952(a)	3.600	.50	1.00	1.50	4.00

KM#	Date	Mintage	Fine	VF	XF	Unc
18	1954	4.440	.10	.30	.50	1.25

ALUMINUM-BRONZE

KM#	Date	Mintage	Fine	VF	XF	Unc
21	1955(a)	3.000	.10	.20	.30	.50
	1961(a)	—	.10	.15	.20	.40

NICKEL-BRASS

KM#	Date	Mintage	Fine	VF	XF	Unc
25.1	1968	2.000	—	.10	.15	.20
	1969	4.000	—	.10	.15	.20
	1970	—	—	.10	.15	.25

KM#	Date	Mintage	Fine	VF	XF	Unc
25.2	1972(a)	12.000	—	—	.10	.15
	1975(a)	—	—	—	.10	.15
	1980	—	—	—	.10	.15

10 PIASTRES

ALUMINUM

KM#	Date	Mintage	Fine	VF	XF	Unc
15	1952(a)	3.600	.50	1.00	5.00	15.00

ALUMINUM-BRONZE

KM#	Date	Mintage	Fine	VF	XF	Unc
22	1955	2.175	.20	.40	.60	1.00

KM#	Date	Mintage	Fine	VF	XF	Unc
23	1955(a)	6.000	.10	.25	.50	.75

COPPER-NICKEL

KM#	Date	Mintage	Fine	VF	XF	Unc
24	1961	7.000	—	.10	.25	.50
	1961	—	—	—	Proof	—

NICKEL-BRASS

KM#	Date	Mintage	Fine	VF	XF	Unc
26	1968(a)	2.000	—	.10	.15	.25
	1969(a)	5.000	—	—	.10	.20
	1970(a)	8.000	—	—	.10	.20
	1972(a)	12.000	—	—	.10	.20
	1975(a)	—	—	—	.10	.20

25 PIASTRES

ALUMINUM-BRONZE

KM#	Date	Mintage	Fine	VF	XF	Unc
16.1	1952(u)	7.200	.10	.40	.60	1.00

Different inscription and larger date.

KM#	Date	Mintage	Fine	VF	XF	Unc
16.2	1961(u)	5.000	.10	.40	.50	.75

NICKEL-BRASS

KM#	Date	Mintage	Fine	VF	XF	Unc
27.1	1968	1.500	.10	.15	.25	.50
	1969	2.500	.10	.15	.20	.40
	1970	—	.10	.15	.20	.40
	1972	8.000	.10	.15	.20	.30
	1975	—	.10	.15	.20	.30

Rev: Different, wider, bold 25.

KM#	Date	Mintage	Fine	VF	XF	Unc
27.2	1980	—	.10	.15	.20	.30

50 PIASTRES

4.9710 g, .600 SILVER, .0959 oz ASW

KM#	Date	Mintage	Fine	VF	XF	Unc
17	1952(u)	7.200	BV	1.00	1.50	3.50

NICKEL

KM#	Date	Mintage	Fine	VF	XF	Unc
28.1	1968	2.000	.20	.40	.60	1.00
	1969	3.488	.10	.25	.40	.75
28.1	1970	2.000	.10	.25	.40	.50
	1971	2.000	.10	.25	.40	.50
	1975	—	.10	.25	.40	.50
	1978	22.400	.10	.25	.40	.50

Rev: Different 50.

KM#	Date	Mintage	Fine	VF	XF	Unc
28.2	1980	—	.10	.25	.40	.50

LIVRE

NICKEL
F.A.O. Issue

KM#	Date	Mintage	Fine	VF	XF	Unc
29	1968	.300	.25	.50	1.00	2.00

KM#	Date	Mintage	Fine	VF	XF	Unc
30	1975	—	.20	.40	.60	1.00
	1975	—	—	—	Proof	—
	1977	8.000	.20	.40	.60	1.00
	1980	12.000	.20	.40	.60	1.00
	1981	—	.20	.40	.60	1.00
	1986	—	.20	.40	.60	1.00

NOTE: Varieties exist.

COPPER-NICKEL
1980 Winter Olympics

KM#	Date	Mintage	Fine	VF	XF	Unc
32	1980	.040	—	—	Proof	10.00

5 LIVRES

NICKEL
F.A.O. Issue

KM#	Date	Mintage	Fine	VF	XF	Unc
31	1978	1.000	—	—	—	3.50

10 LIVRES

19.0000 g, .500 SILVER, .3054 oz ASW
1980 Winter Olympics

KM#	Date	Mintage	Fine	VF	XF	Unc
33	1980	.020	—	—	Proof	25.00

COPPER-NICKEL
World Food Day

KM#	Date	Mintage	Fine	VF	XF	Unc
35	1981	.015	—	—	—	6.00

400 LIVRES

8.0000 g, .900 GOLD, .2315 oz AGW
1980 Winter Olympics

KM#	Date	Mintage	Fine	VF	XF	Unc
34	1980	1,000	—	—	Proof	225.00

LESOTHO

The Kingdom of Lesotho, a constitutional monarchy located within the east-central part of the Republic of South Africa, has an area of 11,720 sq. mi. (30,350 sq. km.) and a population of 1.5 million. Capital: Maseru. The economy is based on subsistence agriculture and livestock raising. Wool, mohair, and cattle are exported.

Lesotho (formerly Basutoland) was sparsely populated until the end of the 16th century. Between the 16th and 19th centuries an influx of refugees from tribal wars led to the development of a distinct Basotho group. During the reign of tribal chief Moshesh I (1823-70), a series of wars with the Orange Free State resulted in the loss of large areas of territory to South Africa. Moshesh appealed to the British for help, and Basutoland was constituted a native state under British protection. In 1871 it was annexed to Cape Colony, but was restored to direct control by the Crown in 1884. From 1884 to 1959 legislative and executive authority was vested in a British High Commissioner. The constitution of 1959 recognized the expressed wish of the people for independence, which was attained on Oct. 4, 1966.

Lesotho is a member of the Commonwealth of Nations. The King of Lesotho is Chief of State.

RULERS

Moshoeshoe II, 1966

MONETARY SYSTEM

100 Licente/Lisente = 1 Maloti/Loti

SENTE

NICKEL-BRASS
Straw Hut

KM#	Date	Mintage	VF	XF	Unc
16	1979	4.500	—	.10	.35
	1979	.010	—	Proof	.50
	1980	—	—	.10	.35
	1980	.010	—	Proof	.50
	1981	2,500	—	Proof	.50
	1983	—	—	.10	.35
	1985	—	—	.10	.35
	1989	—	—	.10	.35

2 LISENTE

NICKEL-BRASS
Steer

KM#	Date	Mintage	VF	XF	Unc
17	1979	3.000	—	.10	.50
	1979	.010	—	Proof	1.00
	1980	—	—	.10	.50
	1980	.010	—	Proof	1.00
	1981	2,500	—	Proof	2.00
	1985	—	—	.10	.50
	1989	—	—	.10	.50

5 LICENTE/LISENTE

2.8900 g, .900 SILVER, .0836 oz ASW
Independence Attained

KM#	Date	Mintage	VF	XF	Unc
1	1966	5,000	—	Proof	6.00

NICKEL-BRASS
Aloe Plant

KM#	Date	Mintage	VF	XF	Unc
18	1979	2.700	—	.10	.50
18	1979	.010	—	Proof	1.25
	1980	—	—	.10	.50
	1980	.010	—	Proof	1.25
	1981	2,500	—	Proof	2.50
	1989	—	—	.10	.50

10 LICENTE/LISENTE

5.6800 g, .900 SILVER, .1643 oz ASW
Independence Attained

KM#	Date	Mintage	VF	XF	Unc
2	1966	5,000	—	Proof	6.00

COPPER-NICKEL
Angora Goat

KM#	Date	Mintage	VF	XF	Unc
19	1979	2.000	.10	.15	.75
	1979	.010	—	Proof	1.75
	1980	—	.10	.15	.75
	1980	.010	—	Proof	1.75
	1981	2,500	—	Proof	3.00
	1983	—	.10	.15	.75
	1989	—	.10	.15	.75

20 LICENTE

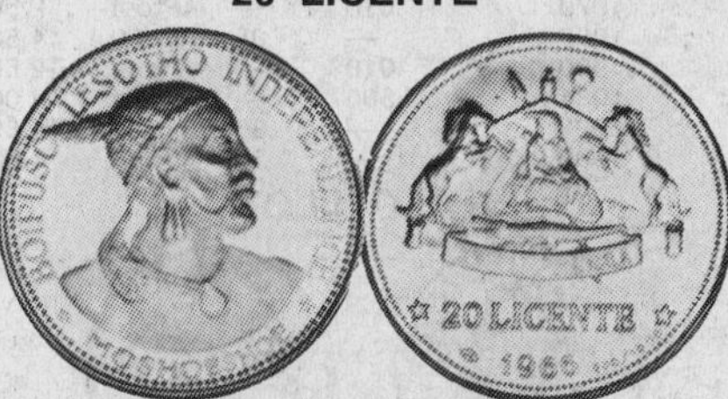

11.2800 g, .900 SILVER, .3263 oz ASW
Independence Attained

KM#	Date	Mintage	VF	XF	Unc
3	1966	5,000	—	Proof	10.00

25 LISENTE

COPPER-NICKEL
Woman in Native Costume Weaving Baskets

KM#	Date	Mintage	VF	XF	Unc
20	1979	1.200	.10	.20	1.25
	1979	.010	—	Proof	2.00
	1980	—	.10	.20	1.25
	1980	.010	—	Proof	2.00
	1981	2,500	—	Proof	3.50
	1989	—	.10	.20	1.25

50 LICENTE/LISENTE

28.1000 g, .900 SILVER, .8131 oz ASW
Independence Attained
Rev: Small 900/1000 at right of date.

KM#	Date	Mintage	VF	XF	Unc
4.1	1966	—	—	—	10.00
	1966	—	—	Proof	12.50

Rev: Large 900/1000 at right of date.

KM#	Date	Mintage	VF	XF	Unc
4.2	1966	—	—	—	10.00
	1966	5,000	—	Proof	12.50

Rev: Mint mark and fineness below date.

KM#	Date	Mintage	VF	XF	Unc
4.3	1966	—	—	—	10.00
	1966	—	—	Proof	12.50

COPPER-NICKEL
Horse and Rider

KM#	Date	Mintage	VF	XF	Unc
21	1979	.480	.35	.50	1.50
	1979	.010	—	Proof	2.50
	1980	—	.35	.50	1.50
	1980	.010	—	Proof	2.50
	1981	2,500	—	Proof	4.00
	1983	—	.35	.50	1.50
	1989	—	.35	.50	1.50

MALOTI/LOTI

3.9940 g, .917 GOLD, .1177 oz AGW
Independence Attained

KM#	Date	Mintage	VF	XF	Unc
5	1966	3,500	—	Proof	70.00

F.A.O. Issue

KM#	Date	Mintage	VF	XF	Unc
8	1969	3,000	—	Proof	65.00

COPPER-NICKEL

KM#	Date	Mintage	VF	XF	Unc
22	1979	1.275	.65	1.00	2.50
	1979	.010	—	Proof	4.00
	1980	—	.75	1.25	3.50
	1980	.010	—	Proof	4.00
	1981	2,500	—	Proof	6.00
	1989	—	.75	1.25	3.50

11.3100 g, .925 SILVER, .3363 oz ASW
Silver Jubilee of King Moshoeshoe II

KM#	Date	Mintage	VF	XF	Unc
46	1985	2,500	—	Proof	20.00

18.9800 g, .917 GOLD, .5626 oz AGW

KM#	Date	Mintage	VF	XF	Unc
46a	1985	500 pcs.	—	Proof	350.00

2 MALOTI

7.9880 g, .917 GOLD, .2355 oz. AGW
Independence Attained

KM#	Date	Mintage	VF	XF	Unc
6	1966	3,500	—	Proof	120.00

F.A.O. Issue

KM#	Date	Mintage	VF	XF	Unc
9	1969	3,000	—	Proof	120.00

4 MALOTI

15.9760 g, .917 GOLD, .4710 oz AGW
Independence Attained

KM#	Date	Mintage	VF	XF	Unc
7	1966	3,500	—	Proof	215.00

F.A.O. Issue

KM#	Date	Mintage	VF	XF	Unc
10	1969	3,000	—	Proof	250.00

10 MALOTI

39.9400 g, .917 GOLD, 1.1776 oz AGW
F.A.O. Issue

KM#	Date	Mintage	VF	XF	Unc
11	1969	3,000	—	Proof	650.00

25.0800 g, .925 SILVER, .7459 oz ASW
10th Anniversary of Independence

KM#	Date	Mintage	VF	XF	Unc
13	1976	2,300	—	—	20.00
	1976	2,100	—	Proof	30.00

28.2800 g, .925 SILVER, .8411 oz ASW
Monument of King Moshoeshoe I

KM#	Date	Mintage	VF	XF	Unc
23	1979	.010	—	—	15.00
	1979	5,000	—	Proof	20.00

12.0000 g, .500 SILVER, .1929 oz ASW

KM#	Date	Mintage	VF	XF	Unc
23a	1979	.010	—	—	10.00
	1979	5,000	—	Proof	15.00

28.2800 g, .925 SILVER, .8411 oz ASW
International Year of the Child
Similar to 15 Maloti, KM#25.

KM#	Date	Mintage	VF	XF	Unc
24	1979(1981)	—	—	—	15.00
	1979(1981)	.037	—	Proof	17.50

23.3300 g, .925 SILVER, .6938 oz ASW
World Soccer Championship

KM#	Date	Mintage	VF	XF	Unc
32	1982	3,582	—	Proof	40.00

World Soccer Championship

KM#	Date	Mintage	VF	XF	Unc
34	1982	3,000	—	Proof	40.00

31.1000 g, .500 SILVER, .5000 oz ASW
George Washington
Obv: Similar to KM#34.
Rev: Washington facing left.

KM#	Date	Mintage	VF	XF	Unc
40	1982	7,355	—	Proof	22.50

George Washington

Obv: Similar to KM#34.
Rev: Washington kneeling on one knee.

KM#	Date	Mintage	VF	XF	Unc
41	1982	4,200	—	Proof	25.00

George Washington - Crossing the Delaware

KM#	Date	Mintage	VF	XF	Unc
42	1982	.015	—	Proof	20.00

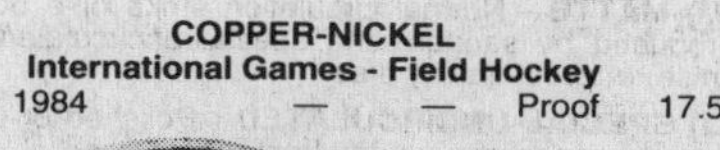

COPPER-NICKEL
International Games - Field Hockey

KM#	Date	Mintage	VF	XF	Unc
47	1984	—	—	Proof	17.50

23.3300 g, .925 SILVER, .6939 oz ASW
Decade For Women

KM#	Date	Mintage	VF	XF	Unc
49	1985	1,000	—	Proof	35.00

28.2800 g, .925 SILVER, .8411 oz ASW

Papal Visit

KM#	Date	Mintage	VF	XF	Unc
50	1988	*.015	—	Proof	45.00

15 MALOTI

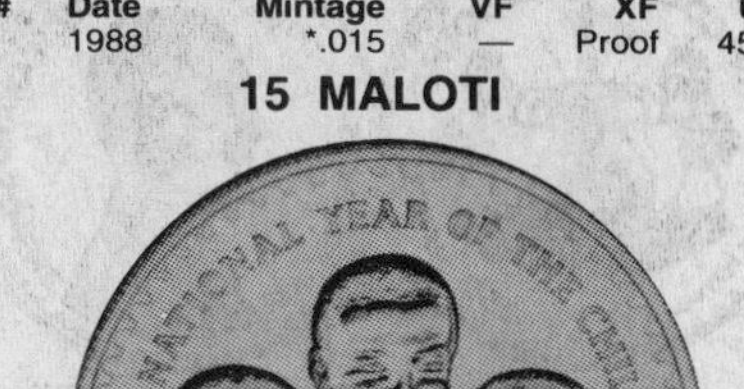

33.4000 g, .925 SILVER, .9933 oz ASW
International Year of the Child
Obv: Similar to 25 Maloti, KM#35.

KM#	Date	Mintage	VF	XF	Unc
25	1979	.018	—	—	17.50
	1979	7,500	—	Proof	22.50

.500 SILVER
15th Anniversary of Commonwealth Membership
Similar to 50 Maloti, KM#38.

KM#	Date	Mintage	VF	XF	Unc
37	1981	2,500	—	Proof	30.00

12.0000 g, .500 SILVER, .1929 oz ASW
15th Anniversary of Independence

KM#	Date	Mintage	VF	XF	Unc
53	1981	2,500	—	Proof	30.00

20 MALOTI

79.8810 g, .917 GOLD, 2.3553 oz AGW
F.A.O. Issue
Obv: Similar to 10 Maloti, KM#11.

KM#	Date	Mintage	VF	XF	Unc
12	1969	3,000	—	Proof	1250.

25 MALOTI

16.8200 g, .925 SILVER, .5003 oz ASW
Duke of Edinburgh Youth Awards

KM#	Date	Mintage	VF	XF	Unc
35	1981	5,000	—	Proof	35.00

28.2800 g, .925 SILVER, .8411 oz ASW
International Year of Disabled Persons

KM#	Date	Mintage	VF	XF	Unc
44	1983	—	—	—	25.00
	1983	—	—	Proof	35.00

30 MALOTI

.925 SILVER
Wedding of Prince Charles and Lady Diana

KM#	Date	Mintage	VF	XF	Unc
30	1981	.010	—	Proof	30.00

50 MALOTI

4.5000 g, .900 GOLD, .1302 oz AGW
10th Anniversary of Independence

KM#	Date	Mintage	VF	XF	Unc
14	1976	700 pcs.	—	—	120.00
	1976	1,910	—	Proof	110.00

33.6200 g, .925 SILVER, .9999 oz ASW
110th Anniversary of Death of King Moshoeshoe I

KM#	Date	Mintage	VF	XF	Unc
27	1980	2,500	—	—	30.00
	1980	1,400	—	Proof	45.00

15th Anniversary of Commonwealth Membership

KM#	Date	Mintage	VF	XF	Unc
38	1981	5,000	—	Proof	40.00

100 MALOTI

9.0000 g, .900 GOLD, .2604 oz AGW
10th Anniversary of Independence

KM#	Date	Mintage	VF	XF	Unc
15	1976	450 pcs.	—	—	175.00
	1976	1,410	—	Proof	160.00

200 MALOTI

15.9800 g, .900 GOLD, .4624 oz AGW
International Year of Disabled Persons

KM#	Date	Mintage	VF	XF	Unc
45	1983	500 pcs.	—	—	400.00
	1983	500 pcs.	—	Proof	450.00

250 MALOTI

33.9300 g, .917 GOLD, 1.0000 oz AGW
International Year of the Child
Similar to 15 Maloti, KM#25.

KM#	Date	Mintage	VF	XF	Unc
26	1979	2,500	—	—	475.00
	1979	2,000	—	Proof	525.00

31.1000 g, .917 GOLD, .9170 oz AGW
110th Anniversary of Death of King Moshoeshoe I
Obv: Similar to 50 Maloti, KM#27.

KM#	Date	Mintage	VF	XF	Unc
28	1980	1,500	—	—	450.00
	1980	3,000	—	Proof	475.00

15.9000 g, .917 GOLD, .4688 oz AGW
Wedding of Prince Charles and Lady Diana

KM#	Date	Mintage	VF	XF	Unc
31	1981	1,000	—	—	250.00
	1981	1,500	—	Proof	350.00

15.7500 g, .995 PLATINUM, .5039 oz APW

KM#	Date	Mintage	VF	XF	Unc
31a	1981	200 pcs.	—	Proof	550.00

7.1300 g, .900 GOLD, .2063 oz AGW
Soccer Games

KM#	Date	Mintage	VF	XF	Unc
33	1982	551 pcs.	—	Proof	250.00

16.9600 g, .917 GOLD, .5001 oz AGW
Duke of Edinburgh Youth Award

KM#	Date	Mintage	VF	XF	Unc
36	1981	1,500	—	Proof	275.00

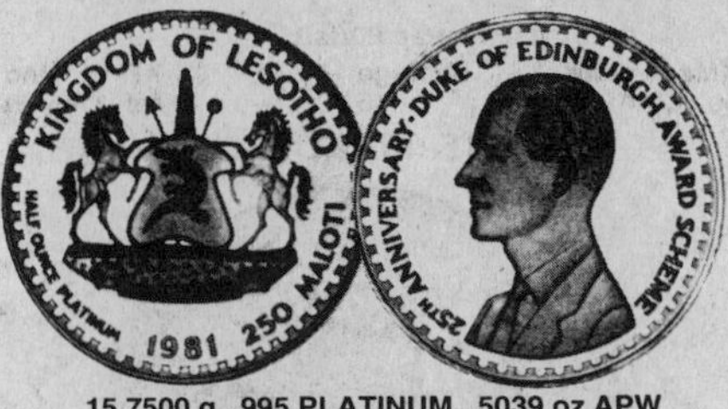

15.7500 g, .995 PLATINUM, .5039 oz APW

KM#	Date	Mintage	VF	XF	Unc
36a	1981	200 pcs.	—	Proof	550.00

15.9800 g, .917 GOLD, .4708 oz AGW
Papal Visit

KM#	Date	Mintage	VF	XF	Unc
51	1988	*750 pcs.	—	Proof	500.00

500 MALOTI

33.9300 g, .917 GOLD, 1.0000 oz AGW
110th Anniversary of Death of King Moshoeshoe I
Obv: Similar to 50 Maloti, KM#27.

KM#	Date	Mintage	VF	XF	Unc
29	1980	1,500	—	—	500.00
	1980	3,000	—	Proof	525.00

15th Anniversary of Commonwealth Membership

KM#	Date	Mintage	VF	XF	Unc
39	1981	500 pcs.	—	Proof	550.00

31.5000 g, .995 PLATINUM, 1.0078 oz APW

KM#	Date	Mintage	VF	XF	Unc
39a	1981	200 pcs.	—	Proof	825.00

MINT SETS (MS)

KM#	Date	Mintage	Identification	Issue Price	Mkt. Val.
MS1	1976(3)	450	KM13-15	194.00	315.00
MS2	1989(7)	—	KM16-22	—	10.00

PROOF SETS (PS)

KM#	Date	Mintage	Identification	Issue Price	Mkt. Val.
PS1	1966(7)	1,500	KM1-7	301.00	475.00
PS2	1966(5)	7	KM Pn5-9	—	—
PS3	1966(4)	2	KM Pn1-4	—	—
PS4	1966(4)	3,500	KM1-4	28.00	35.00
PS5	1966(3)	2,000	KM5-7	301.00	430.00
PS6	1969(5)	3,000	KM8-12	450.00	2450.
PS7	1976(3)	1,410	KM13-15	285.00	300.00
PS8	1976(2)	—	KM14-15	270.00	270.00
PS9	1976(2)	—	KM13-14	—	135.00
PS10	1979(7)	10,000	KM16-22	34.00	12.50
PS11	1980(8)	10,000	KM16-22,23a	51.00	25.00
PS12	1981(8)	2,500	KM16-22,30	55.00	45.00

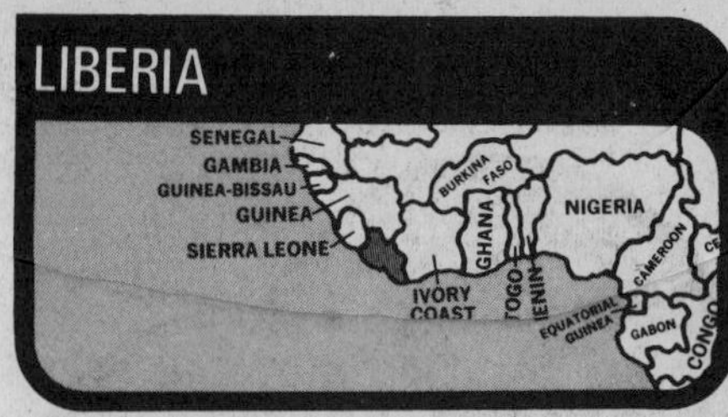

The Republic of Liberia, located on the southern side of the west African bulge between Sierra Leone and Ivory Coast, has an area of 43,000 sq. mi. (111,370 sq. km) and a population of 2.2 million. Capital: Monrovia. The major industries are agriculture, mining and lumbering. Iron ore, diamonds, rubber, coffee and coca are exported.

The Liberian coast was explored and charted by Portuguese navigator Pedro de Cintra in 1461. For the following three centuries Portuguese traders visited the area regularly to trade for gold, slaves and pepper. The modern country of Liberia, Africa's first republic, was settled in 1822 by the American Colonization Society as a homeland for American freed slaves, with the U.S. government furnishing funds and assisting in negotiations for procurement of land from the native chiefs. The various settlements united in 1839 to form the Commonwealth of Liberia, and in 1847 established the country as a republic with a constitution modeled after that of the United States.

U.S. money was declared legal tender in Liberia in 1943, replacing British West African currency.

Most of the Liberian pattern series, particularly of the 1888-90 period are acknowledged to have been 'unofficial' privately sponsored issues, but they are without exception avidly collected by most collectors of Liberian coins. The 'K' number designations on these pieces refer to a listing of Liberian patterns compiled and published by Ernst Kraus.

MINT MARKS

B - Bern, Switzerland
H - Heaton, Birmingham
(d) - Denver, U.S.
(l) - London
(s) - San Francisco, U.S.
FM - Franklin Mint, U.S.A.*

***NOTE:** During 1975-77 the Franklin Mint produced coinage in up to 3 different qualities. Qualities of issue are designated in ( ) after each date and are defined as follows:

(M) MATTE - Normal circulation strike or a dull finish produced by sandblasting special uncirculated (polish finish) or proof quality dies.

(U) SPECIAL UNCIRCULATED - Polished or prooflike in appearance without any frosted features.

(P) PROOF - The highest quality obtainable having mirror-like fields and frosted features.

MONETARY SYSTEM

100 Cents = 1 Dollar

1/2 CENT

BRASS

KM#	Date	Mintage	Fine	VF	XF	Unc
10	1937	1.000	.10	.25	.35	.5

COPPER-NICKEL

KM#	Date	Mintage	Fine	VF	XF	Unc
10a	1941	.025	.15	.35	.50	.7

CENT

COPPER
Rev: 2 stars.

KM#	Date	Mintage	Fine	VF	XF	Unc
1	1847	—	5.00	12.50	20.00	50.0
	1847	—	—	—	Proof	100.0

Rev: 4 stars.

KM#	Date	Mintage	Fine	VF	XF	Unc
3	1862	—	5.00	12.50	22.50	60.00
	1862/47	—	10.00	25.00	45.00	125.00
	1862	—	—	—	Proof	110.00

BRONZE

KM#	Date	Mintage	Fine	VF	XF	Unc
5	1896H	.358	2.00	5.00	12.50	30.00
	1896H	—	—	—	Proof	135.00
	1906H	.180	3.50	7.50	17.50	45.00
	1906H	—	—	—	Proof	135.00

BRASS

KM#	Date	Mintage	Fine	VF	XF	Unc
11	1937	1.000	.20	.50	1.50	6.00

COPPER-NICKEL

KM#	Date	Mintage	Fine	VF	XF	Unc
11a	1941	.250	.50	2.50	7.50	40.00

BRONZE

KM#	Date	Mintage	Fine	VF	XF	Unc
13	1960	.500	—	—	.10	.25
	1961	7.000	—	—	.10	.30
	1968(l)	3.000	—	—	.10	.15
	1968(s)	.014	—	—	Proof	.50
	1969	5,056	—	—	Proof	.50
	1970	3,464	—	—	Proof	1.00
	1971	3,032	—	—	Proof	1.00
	1972(d)	10.000	—	—	.10	.25
	1972(s)	4,866	—	—	Proof	.50
	1973	.011	—	—	Proof	.50
	1974	9,362	—	—	Proof	.50
	1975	5.000	—	—	.10	.15
	1975	4,056	—	—	Proof	.50
	1976	2,131	—	—	Proof	.50
	1977	2.500	—	—	.10	.35
	1977	920 pcs.	—	—	Proof	.50
	1978FM	7,311	—	—	Proof	.50
	1983FM	2.500	—	—	.10	.35
	1984	2.500	—	—	.10	.35

Edge inscription: O.A.U. July 1979.

KM#	Date	Mintage	Fine	VF	XF	Unc
13a	1979FM	1,857	—	—	Proof	1.00

2 CENTS

COPPER

Rev: 2 stars.

KM#	Date	Mintage	Fine	VF	XF	Unc
2	1847	—	5.00	10.00	20.00	50.00
	1847	—	—	—	Proof	120.00

Rev: 4 stars.

KM#	Date	Mintage	Fine	VF	XF	Unc
4	1862	—	5.00	10.00	25.00	75.00
	1862	—	—	—	Proof	175.00

BRONZE

KM#	Date	Mintage	Fine	VF	XF	Unc
6	1896H	.323	2.00	5.00	12.50	40.00
	1896H	—	—	—	Proof	160.00
	1906H	.108	4.00	8.00	20.00	60.00
	1906H	—	—	—	Proof	160.00

BRASS

KM#	Date	Mintage	Fine	VF	XF	Unc
12	1937	1.000	.10	.25	.75	5.00

COPPER-NICKEL

KM#	Date	Mintage	Fine	VF	XF	Unc
12a	1941	.810	.10	.25	.50	2.50
	1978FM	7,311	—	—	Proof	1.50

Edge inscription: O.A.U. July 1979.

KM#	Date	Mintage	Fine	VF	XF	Unc
12b	1979FM	1,857	—	—	Proof	2.00

5 CENTS

COPPER-NICKEL

KM#	Date	Mintage	Fine	VF	XF	Unc
14	1960	1.000	—	.10	.15	.50
	1961	3.200	—	.10	.15	.40
	1968	.015	—	—	Proof	.75
	1969	5,056	—	—	Proof	.75
	1970	3,464	—	—	Proof	1.25
	1971	3,032	—	—	Proof	1.25
	1972(d)	3.000	—	.10	.15	.25
	1972(s)	4,866	—	—	Proof	.75
	1973	.011	—	—	Proof	.75
	1974	9,362	—	—	Proof	.75
	1975	3.000	—	.10	.15	.25
	1975	4,056	—	—	Proof	.75
	1976	2,131	—	—	Proof	.75
	1977	—	—	.10	.15	.50
	1977	920 pcs.	—	—	Proof	.75
	1978FM	7,311	—	—	Proof	.75
	1983FM	1.000	—	.10	.15	.25
	1984	1.000	—	.10	.15	.25

Edge inscription: O.A.U. July 1979.

KM#	Date	Mintage	Fine	VF	XF	Unc
14a	1979FM	1,857	—	—	Proof	2.00

10 CENTS

2.3200 g, .925 SILVER, .0690 oz ASW

KM#	Date	Mintage	Fine	VF	XF	Unc
7	1896H	.020	4.00	10.00	22.50	100.00
	1896H	—	—	—	Proof	250.00
	1906H	.035	4.00	10.00	22.50	100.00
	1906H	—	—	—	Proof	250.00

2.0700 g, .900 SILVER, .0599 oz ASW

KM#	Date	Mintage	Fine	VF	XF	Unc
15	1960	1.000	BV	.75	1.25	3.00
	1961	1.200	BV	.75	1.25	3.00

COPPER-NICKEL, 2.10 g

KM#	Date	Mintage	Fine	VF	XF	Unc
15a.1	1966	2.000	—	.15	.25	.50

1.80 g

KM#	Date	Mintage	Fine	VF	XF	Unc
15a.2	1968	.014	—	—	Proof	1.25
	1969	5,056	—	—	Proof	1.25
	1970(d)	2.500	—	.15	.25	.50
	1970(s)	3,464	—	—	Proof	1.50
	1971	3,032	—	—	Proof	1.50
	1972	4,866	—	—	Proof	1.25
	1973	.011	—	—	Proof	1.00
	1974	9,362	—	—	Proof	1.00
	1975	4,500	—	.15	.20	.35
	1975	4,056	—	—	Proof	1.00
	1976	2,131	—	—	Proof	1.00
	1977	—	—	.15	.25	.75
	1977	920 pcs.	—	—	Proof	1.00
	1978FM	7,311	—	—	Proof	1.00
	1983FM	.500	—	.15	.25	.75
	1984FM	.500	—	.15	.25	.75
	1987	10.000	—	.15	.25	.75

Edge inscription: O.A.U. July 1979.

KM#	Date	Mintage	Fine	VF	XF	Unc
15b	1979FM	1,857	—	—	Proof	2.00

25 CENTS

5.8000 g, .925 SILVER, .1725 oz ASW

KM#	Date	Mintage	Fine	VF	XF	Unc
8	1896H	.015	4.00	10.00	30.00	110.00
	1896H	—	—	—	Proof	250.00
	1906H	.034	6.00	12.50	35.00	120.00
	1906H	—	—	—	Proof	250.00

5.1800 g, .900 SILVER, .1499 oz ASW

KM#	Date	Mintage	Fine	VF	XF	Unc
16	1960	.900	BV	1.50	2.00	4.50
	1961	1.200	BV	1.50	2.00	4.50

COPPER-NICKEL, 5.20 g

KM#	Date	Mintage	Fine	VF	XF	Unc
16a.1	1966	.800	—	.25	.65	1.25

4.80 g

KM#	Date	Mintage	Fine	VF	XF	Unc
16a.2	1968(d)	1.600	—	.25	.50	1.00
	1968(s)	.014	—	—	Proof	1.50
	1968	2.400				
		(restrike)	—	.25	.50	1.00
	1969	5,056	—	—	Proof	1.50
	1970	3,464	—	—	Proof	1.75
	1971	3,032	—	—	Proof	1.75
	1972	4,866	—	—	Proof	1.50
	1973	2.000	—	.25	.50	1.00
	1973	.011	—	—	Proof	1.25
	1974	9,362	—	—	Proof	1.25
	1975	1.600	—	.25	.50	1.00
	1975	4,056	—	—	Proof	1.25
	1976	.800	—	.25	.65	1.25
	1976	100 pcs.	—	—	Proof	25.00

F.A.O. Issue

KM#	Date	Mintage	Fine	VF	XF	Unc
30	1976	.800	—	.25	.75	1.75
	1976	2,131	—	—	Proof	3.50
	1977	920 pcs.	—	—	Proof	3.50
	1978FM	7,311	—	—	Proof	2.25

Edge inscription: O.A.U. July 1979.

KM#	Date	Mintage	Fine	VF	XF	Unc
30a	1979FM	1,857	—	—	Proof	3.50

50 CENTS

11.6000 g, .925 SILVER, .3450 oz ASW

KM#	Date	Mintage	Fine	VF	XF	Unc
9	1896H	5,000	7.50	15.00	45.00	250.00
	1896H	—	—	—	Proof	400.00
	1906H	.024	7.50	15.00	45.00	250.00
	1906H	—	—	—	Proof	400.00

10.3700 g, .900 SILVER, .3001 oz ASW

KM#	Date	Mintage	Fine	VF	XF	Unc
17	1960	1.100	BV	3.00	4.00	8.00
	1961	.800	BV	3.00	4.00	8.00

COPPER-NICKEL, 10.40 g

KM#	Date	Mintage	Fine	VF	XF	Unc
17a.1	1966	.200	—	.75	1.00	1.50

COPPER-NICKEL, 8.90 g

KM#	Date	Mintage	Fine	VF	XF	Unc
17a.2	1968(l)	1.000	—	.60	.80	1.50
	1968(s)	.014	—	—	Proof	1.50
	1969	5,056	—	—	Proof	1.50
	1970	3,464	—	—	Proof	2.50
	1971	3,032	—	—	Proof	2.50
	1972	4,866	—	—	Proof	1.50
	1973	1.000	—	.60	.75	1.25
	1973	.011	—	—	Proof	1.50
	1974	9,362	—	—	Proof	1.50
	1975	.800	—	.60	.75	1.25
	1975	4,056	—	—	Proof	1.50
	1976	1.000	—	.60	.75	1.25
	1976	100 pcs.	—	—	Proof	35.00

KM#	Date	Mintage	Fine	VF	XF	Unc
31	1976	—	—	.60	1.00	2.50
	1976	2,131	—	—	Proof	5.00
	1977	920 pcs.	—	—	Proof	5.00
	1978FM	7,311	—	—	Proof	3.50
	1987	1.800	—	.60	1.00	2.50

Edge inscription: O.A.U. July 1979.

KM#	Date	Mintage	Fine	VF	XF	Unc
31a	1979FM	1,857	—	—	Proof	5.00

DOLLAR

20.7400 g, .900 SILVER, .6001 oz ASW

KM#	Date	Mintage	Fine	VF	XF	Unc
18	1961	.200	BV	5.00	6.50	13.00
	1962	1.000	BV	5.00	6.50	12.00

COPPER-NICKEL, 20.70 g

KM#	Date	Mintage	Fine	VF	XF	Unc
18a.1	1966	1.000	—	1.00	1.50	2.25

COPPER-NICKEL, 18.00 g

KM#	Date	Mintage	Fine	VF	XF	Unc
18a.2	1968(l)	1.000	—	1.00	1.50	2.25
	1968(s)	.014	—	—	Proof	2.00
	1969	5,056	—	—	Proof	2.00
	1970(d)	2.000	—	1.00	1.50	3.00
	1970(s)	3,464	—	—	Proof	6.00
	1971	3,032	—	—	Proof	4.50
	1972	4,866	—	—	Proof	4.50
	1973	.011	—	—	Proof	3.00
	1974	9,362	—	—	Proof	3.00
	1975	.400	—	1.25	1.75	3.00
	1975	4,056	—	—	Proof	3.00
	1976	2,000	—	1.50	2.00	3.50
	1976	100 pcs.	—	—	Proof	50.00

KM#	Date	Mintage	Fine	VF	XF	Unc
32	1976	—	—	1.25	1.75	3.50
	1976	2,131	—	—	Proof	9.00
	1977	920 pcs.	—	—	Proof	11.50
	1978FM	7,311	—	—	Proof	12.50
	1987	1.500	—	1.25	1.75	3.50

Edge inscription: O.A.U. July 1979.

KM#	Date	Mintage	Fine	VF	XF	Unc
32a	1979FM	1,857	—	—	Proof	15.00

Preserve Planet Earth
Similar to 10 Dollars, KM#99.

KM#	Date	Mintage	Fine	VF	XF	Unc
98	1993	—	—	—	—	6.50

Nolan Ryan
Similar to 10 Dollars, KM#102.

KM#	Date	Mintage	Fine	VF	XF	Unc
101	1993	—	—	—	—	6.50

COPPER-NICKEL, 28.52 g
Preserve Planet Earth - Corythosaurus

KM#	Date	Mintage	Fine	VF	XF	Unc
109	1993	—	—	—	—	6.50

Preserve Planet Earth - Atchaeopteryx
Incorrect spelling.

KM#	Date	Mintage	Fine	VF	XF	Unc
112	1993	—	—	—	—	6.50

Preserve Planet Earth - Archaeopteryx
Correct spelling.

KM#	Date	Mintage	Fine	VF	XF	Unc
115	1994	—	—	—	—	7.00

2 DOLLARS

COPPER-NICKEL
FAO World Fisheries Conference

KM#	Date	Mintage	Fine	VF	XF	Unc
47	1983	.100	—	—	—	6.00

28.2800 g, .925 SILVER, .8411 oz ASW

KM#	Date	Mintage	Fine	VF	XF	Unc
47a	1983	.020	—	—	Proof	25.00

47.5400 g, GOLD

KM#	Date	Mintage	Fine	VF	XF	Unc
47b	1983	600 pcs.	—	—	Proof	1100.

2-1/2 DOLLARS

4.1796 g, .900 GOLD, .1209 oz AGW
Inauguration of President Tolbert

KM#	Date	Mintage	Fine	VF	XF	Unc
24	1972	—	—	—	Proof	80.00

5 DOLLARS

5.0000 g, .900 GOLD, .1447 oz AGW
25th Anniversary of Inter-Continental Hotels

KM#	Date	Mintage	Fine	VF	XF	Unc
62	1971	—	—	—	Proof	—

8.3592 g, .900 GOLD, .2419 oz AGW
Inauguration of President Tolbert

KM#	Date	Mintage	Fine	VF	XF	Unc
25	1972	—	—	—	Proof	160.00

34.1000 g, .900 SILVER, .9868 oz ASW

KM#	Date	Mintage	Fine	VF	XF	Unc
29	1973	500 pcs.	—	—	—	25.00
	1973	.028	—	—	Proof	12.00
	1974	.020	—	—	Proof	12.00
	1975	9,017	—	—	Proof	13.50
	1976	3,683	—	—	Proof	17.50
	1977	1,640	—	—	Proof	20.00
	1978FM	7,311	—	—	Proof	15.00

Edge inscription: O.A.U. July 1979.

KM#	Date	Mintage	Fine	VF	XF	Unc
29a	1979FM	1,857	—	—	Proof	25.00

COPPER-NICKEL
Military Memorial

KM#	Date	Mintage	Fine	VF	XF	Unc
44	1982	4.000	—	5.00	6.50	9.00
	1985	2.000	—	5.00	6.50	9.00

15.5500 g, .999 SILVER, .5000 oz ASW
Grand Prix - Gerhard Berger

KM#	Date	Mintage	Fine	VF	XF	Unc
73	1992	—	—	—	Proof	20.00

Grand Prix - Nigel Mansell
Similar to 10 Dollars, KM#75.

KM#	Date	Mintage	Fine	VF	XF	Unc
76	1992	*.050	—	—	Proof	20.00

Grand Prix - Aguri Suzuki
Similar to 10 Dollars, KM#84.

KM#	Date	Mintage	Fine	VF	XF	Unc
77	1992	*.050	—	—	Proof	20.00

Grand Prix - Ayrton Senna
Similar to 10 Dollars, KM#85.

KM#	Date	Mintage	Fine	VF	XF	Unc
78	1992	*.050	—	—	Proof	20.00

Grand Prix - Riccardo Patrese
Similar to 10 Dollars, KM#74.

KM#	Date	Mintage	Fine	VF	XF	Unc
79	1992	*.050	—	—	Proof	20.00

Grand Prix - Michael Schumacher
Similar to 10 Dollars, KM#86.

KM#	Date	Mintage	Fine	VF	XF	Unc
80	1992	*.050	—	—	Proof	20.00

Grand Prix - Alain Prost
Similar to 10 Dollars, KM#87.

KM#	Date	Mintage	Fine	VF	XF	Unc
81	1992	*.050	—	—	Proof	20.00

Grand Prix - Ukyo Katayama
Similar to 10 Dollars, KM#88.

KM#	Date	Mintage	Fine	VF	XF	Unc
82	1992	*.050	—	—	Proof	20.00

U.S. President Clinton
Similar to 10 Dollars, KM#68.

KM#	Date	Mintage	Fine	VF	XF	Unc
67	1993	*.050	—	—	Proof	20.00

Willy Brandt
Similar to 10 Dollars, KM#72.

KM#	Date	Mintage	Fine	VF	XF	Unc
97	1993	—	—	—	Proof	20.00

John F. Kennedy
Similar to 10 Dollars, KM#104.

KM#	Date	Mintage	Fine	VF	XF	Unc
103	1993	*.050	—	—	Proof	20.00

10 DOLLARS

11.7200 g, .900 GOLD, .3391 oz AGW
25th Anniversary of Inter-Continental Hotels

KM#	Date	Mintage	Fine	VF	XF	Unc
63	1971	—	—	—	Proof	—

16.7185 g, .900 GOLD, .4838 oz AGW
Inauguration of President Tolbert

KM#	Date	Mintage	Fine	VF	XF	Unc
26	1972	—	—	—	Proof	310.00

23.3300 g, .925 SILVER, .6939 oz ASW
Decade For Women
Rev: Coat of arms, denomination.

KM#	Date	Mintage	Fine	VF	XF	Unc
53	1985	—	—	—	Proof	25.00

31.1000 g, .999 SILVER, 1.0000 oz ASW
John F. Kennedy

KM#	Date	Mintage	Fine	VF	XF	Unc
54	1988	*.025	—	—	Proof	42.50

President Samuel Kanyon Doe
Similar to 250 Dollars, KM#56.

KM#	Date	Mintage	Fine	VF	XF	Unc
55	1988	*.025	—	—	Proof	42.50

U.S. President Bush
Similar to 250 Dollars, KM#58.

KM#	Date	Mintage	Fine	VF	XF	Unc
57	1989	*.025	—	—	Proof	42.50

Emperor Hirohito
Similar to 250 Dollars, KM#60.

KM#	Date	Mintage	Fine	VF	XF	Unc
59	1989	*.025	—	—	Proof	42.50

Willy Brandt

KM#	Date	Mintage	Fine	VF	XF	Unc
72	1992	—	—	—	Proof	40.00

Grand Prix - Riccardo Patrese

KM#	Date	Mintage	Fine	VF	XF	Unc
74	1992	*.025	—	—	Proof	40.00

Grand Prix - Nigel Mansell

KM#	Date	Mintage	Fine	VF	XF	Unc
75	1992	*.025	—	—	Proof	40.00

Grand Prix - Gerhard Berger

KM#	Date	Mintage	Fine	VF	XF	Unc
83	1992	*.025	—	—	Proof	40.00

Grand Prix - Aguri Suzuki

KM#	Date	Mintage	Fine	VF	XF	Unc
84	1992	*.025	—	—	Proof	40.00

Grand Prix - Ayrton Senna

KM#	Date	Mintage	Fine	VF	XF	Unc
85	1992	*.025	—	—	Proof	40.00

Grand Prix - Michael Schumacher

KM#	Date	Mintage	Fine	VF	XF	Unc
86	1992	*.025	—	—	Proof	40.00

Grand Prix - Alain Prost

KM#	Date	Mintage	Fine	VF	XF	Unc
87	1992	*.025	—	—	Proof	40.00

Grand Prix - Ykyo Katayama

KM#	Date	Mintage	Fine	VF	XF	Unc
88	1992	*.025	—	—	Proof	40.00

U.S. President Clinton

KM#	Date	Mintage	Fine	VF	XF	Unc
68	1993	*.025	—	—	Proof	37.50

Preserve Planet Earth - Protoceratops

KM#	Date	Mintage	Fine	VF	XF	Unc
99	1993	*.025	—	—	Proof	35.00

Nolan Ryan

KM#	Date	Mintage	Fine	VF	XF	Unc
102	1993	—	—	—	Proof	35.00

John F. Kennedy

KM#	Date	Mintage	Fine	VF	XF	Unc
104	1993	*.025	—	—	Proof	40.00

Preserve Planet Earth - Corythosaurus

KM#	Date	Mintage	Fine	VF	XF	Unc
110	1993	.025	—	—	Proof	35.00

Preserve Planet Earth - Atchaeopteryx
Incorrect spelling.

KM#	Date	Mintage	Fine	VF	XF	Unc
113	1993	*.025	—	—	Proof	35.00

Preserve Planet Earth - Archaeopteryx
Correct spelling.

KM#	Date	Mintage	Fine	VF	XF	Unc
116	1994	.025	—	—	Proof	35.00

12 DOLLARS

6.0000 g, .900 GOLD, .1736 oz AGW
President Tubman 70th Birthday

KM#	Date	Mintage	Fine	VF	XF	Unc
20	1965	400 pcs.	—	—	Proof	125.00

15 DOLLARS

1.0000 g, .9999 GOLD, .0321 oz AGW
Preserve Planet Earth - Compsognatbus

KM#	Date	Mintage	Fine	VF	XF	Unc
108	1993	—	—	—	Proof	32.50

20 DOLLARS

18.6500 g, .900 GOLD, .5397 oz AGW
William Vacanarat Shadrach Tubman

KM#	Date	Mintage	Fine	VF	XF	Unc
19	1964B	.010	—	—	—	275.00

.999 GOLD

KM#	Date	Mintage	Fine	VF	XF	Unc
19a	1964B-L	100 pcs.	—	—	Proof	350.00

NOTE: Of the total issue, 10,200 were struck of .900 fine gold and bear the "B" mint mark of the Bern Mint below the date, while 100 were struck (restrikes suspected) as proofs of .999 fine gold and are designated by the presence of a small "L" above date.

15.8100 g, .900 GOLD, .8768 oz AGW
25th Anniversary of Inter-Continental Hotels

KM#	Date	Mintage	Fine	VF	XF	Unc
64	1971	—	—	—	Proof	—

33.4370 g, .900 GOLD, .9675 oz AGW
Inauguration of President Tolbert

KM#	Date	Mintage	Fine	VF	XF	Unc
27	1972	—	—	—	Proof	450.00

28.2800 g, .925 SILVER, .8411 oz ASW
Year of the Scout
Obv: Coat of arms.

KM#	Date	Mintage	Fine	VF	XF	Unc
45	1983	.010	—	—	—	20.00
	1983	.010	—	—	Proof	30.00

International Year of Disabled Persons

KM#	Date	Mintage	Fine	VF	XF	Unc
48	1983	—	—	—	—	20.00
	1983	—	—	—	Proof	30.00

25 DOLLARS

23.3120 g, .900 GOLD, .6746 oz AGW
President Tubman 70th Birthday

KM#	Date	Mintage	Fine	VF	XF	Unc
21	1965B	3,000	—	—	—	350.00

.999 GOLD

KM#	Date	Mintage	Fine	VF	XF	Unc
21a	1965B-L	100 pcs.	—	—	Proof	400.00

President Tubman 75th Birthday

KM#	Date	Mintage	Fine	VF	XF	Unc
23	1970B	—	—	—	Proof	300.00

Sesquicentennial of Founding of Liberia

KM#	Date	Mintage	Fine	VF	XF	Unc
28	1972B	3,000	—	—	Proof	300.00

30 DOLLARS

15.0000 g, .900 GOLD, .4340 oz AGW
President Tubman 70th Birthday

KM#	Date	Mintage	Fine	VF	XF	Unc
22	1965	400 pcs.	—	—	Proof	225.00

50 DOLLARS

155.5150 g, .999 SILVER, 5.0000 oz ASW
U.S. President Clinton
Similar to 10 Dollars, KM#68.

KM#	Date	Mintage	Fine	VF	XF	Unc
69	1993	—	—	—	Proof	85.00

100 DOLLARS

6.0000 g, .900 GOLD, .1736 oz AGW
Inauguration of President Tolbert

KM#	Date	Mintage	Fine	VF	XF	Unc
33	1976	175 pcs.	—	—	Proof	175.00

10.9300 g, .900 GOLD, .3163 oz AGW
130th Anniversary of the Republic

KM#	Date	Mintage	Fine	VF	XF	Unc
36	1977FM(U)	787 pcs.	—	—	—	200.00
	1977FM(P)	4,250	—	—	Proof	150.00

Organization of African Unity Summit Conference

KM#	Date	Mintage	Fine	VF	XF	Unc
37	1979FM(P)	1,656	—	—	Proof	150.00

11.2000 g, .900 GOLD, .3241 oz AGW
Organization of African Unity

KM#	Date	Mintage	Fine	VF	XF	Unc
38	1979FM(P)	—	—		Proof	250.00

10.9300 g, .900 GOLD, .3163 oz AGW
5th Anniversary of Government

KM#	Date	Mintage	Fine	VF	XF	Unc
50	1985FM(P)	409 pcs.	—	—	Proof	450.00

7.1300 g, .900 GOLD, .2063 oz AGW
Decade For Women

KM#	Date	Mintage	Fine	VF	XF	Unc
61	1985	318 pcs.	—	—	Proof	220.00

311.0300 g, .999 SILVER, 10.0000 oz ASW
U.S. President Clinton

KM#	Date	Mintage	Fine	VF	XF	Unc
70	1993	—	—	—	Proof	165.00

6.2200 g, .999 GOLD, .2000 oz AGW
Preserve Planet Earth - Protoceratops

KM#	Date	Mintage	Fine	VF	XF	Unc
100	1993	*7,500	—	—	Proof	165.00

6.2200 g, .999 GOLD, .2000 oz AGW
Preserve Planet Earth - Corythosaurus

KM#	Date	Mintage	Fine	VF	XF	Unc
111	1993	7,500	—	—	Proof	165.00

Preserve Planet Earth - Atchaeopteryx
Incorrect spelling.

KM#	Date	Mintage	Fine	VF	XF	Unc
114	1993	*7,500	—	—	Proof	165.00

Correct spelling - Archaeopteryx.

KM#	Date	Mintage	Fine	VF	XF	Unc
117	1994	7,500	—	—	Proof	165.00

150 DOLLARS

500.0000 g, .999 SILVER, 16.0756 oz ASW
Illustration reduced. Actual size: 85mm.
Preserve Planet Earth - 2 Brachiosauros

KM#	Date	Mintage	Fine	VF	XF	Unc
106	1993	121 pcs.	—	—	Proof	325.00

200 DOLLARS

12.0000 g, .900 GOLD, .3472 oz AGW
Inauguration of President Tolbert

KM#	Date	Mintage	Fine	VF	XF	Unc
34	1976	100 pcs.	—	—	Proof	300.00

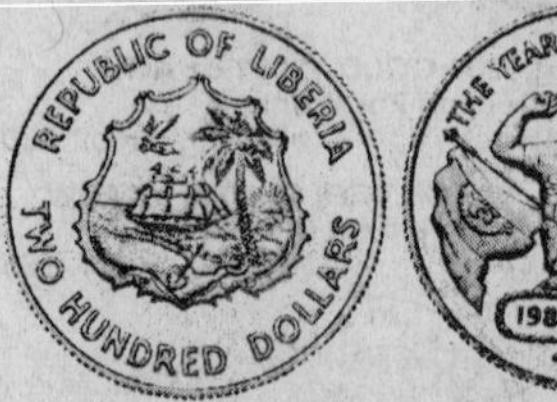

15.9800 g, .917 GOLD, .4712 oz AGW
Year of the Scout

KM#	Date	Mintage	Fine	VF	XF	Unc
46	1983	—	—	—	—	350.00
	1983	—	—	—	Proof	500.00

15.9800 g, .900 GOLD, .4624 oz AGW
International Year of Disabled Persons

KM#	Date	Mintage	Fine	VF	XF	Unc
49	1983	500 pcs.	—	—	—	325.00
	1983	500 pcs.	—	—	Proof	475.00

250 DOLLARS

15.5000 g, .999 GOLD, .5000 oz AGW
John F. Kennedy Memorial

KM#	Date	Mintage	Fine	VF	XF	Unc
52	1988	5,000	—	—	Proof	400.00

President Samuel Kanyon Doe

KM#	Date	Mintage	Fine	VF	XF	Unc
56	1988	*5,000	—	—	Proof	415.00

U.S. President Bush

KM#	Date	Mintage	Fine	VF	XF	Unc
58	1989	600 pcs.	—	—	Proof	415.00

Emperor Hirohito

KM#	Date	Mintage	Fine	VF	XF	Unc
60	1989	600 pcs.	—	—	Proof	415.00

Grand Prix - Nigel Mansell
Similar to 10 Dollars, KM#75.

KM#	Date	Mintage	Fine	VF	XF	Unc
89	1992	*5,000	—	—	Proof	375.00

Grand Prix - Gerhard Berger
Similar to 10 Dollars, KM#83.

KM#	Date	Mintage	Fine	VF	XF	Unc
90	1992	*5,000	—	—	Proof	375.00

Grand Prix - Aguri Suzuki
Similar to 10 Dollars, KM#84.

KM#	Date	Mintage	Fine	VF	XF	Unc
91	1992	*5,000	—	—	Proof	375.00

Grand Prix - Ayrton Senna
Similar to 10 Dollars, KM#85.

KM#	Date	Mintage	Fine	VF	XF	Unc
92	1992	*5,000	—	—	Proof	375.00

Grand Prix - Riccardo Patrese
Similar to 10 Dollars, KM#74.

KM#	Date	Mintage	Fine	VF	XF	Unc
93	1992	*5,000	—	—	Proof	375.00

Grand Prix - Michael Schumacher
Similar to 10 Dollars, KM#86.

KM#	Date	Mintage	Fine	VF	XF	Unc
94	1992	*5,000	—	—	Proof	375.00

Grand Prix - Alain Prost
Similar to 10 Dollars, KM#87.

KM#	Date	Mintage	Fine	VF	XF	Un
95	1992	*5,000	—	—	Proof	375.0

Grand Prix - Ukyo Katayama
Similar to 10 Dollars, KM#88.

KM#	Date	Mintage	Fine	VF	XF	Unc
96	1992	*5,000	—	—	Proof	375.0

U.S. President Clinton
Similar to 10 Dollars, KM#68.

KM#	Date	Mintage	Fine	VF	XF	Unc
71	1993	*5,000	—	—	Proof	375.0

John F. Kennedy
Similar to 10 Dollars, KM#104.

KM#	Date	Mintage	Fine	VF	XF	Unc
105	1993	*5,000	—	—	Proof	375.0

300 DOLLARS

1000.0000 g, .999 SILVER, 32.1512 oz ASW
Illustration reduced. Actual size: 100mm.
Preserve Planet Earth - Tyrannosaurus Rex
Attacking A Triceratops

KM#	Date	Mintage	Fine	VF	XF	Unc
107	1993	151 pcs.	—	—	Proof	500.0

400 DOLLARS

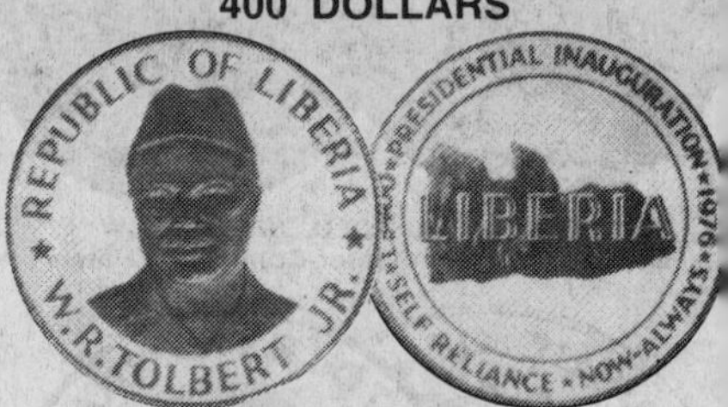

24.0000 g, .900 GOLD, .6945 oz AGW
Inauguration of President Tolbert

KM#	Date	Mintage	Fine	VF	XF	Unc
35	1976	25 pcs.	—	—	Proof	1250

PROOF SETS (PS)

KM#	Date	Mintage	Identification	Issue Price	Mkt. Va
PS1	1896H(5)	—	KM5-9	—	1125
PS2	1906H(5)	—	KM5-9	—	1125
PS3	1968(6)	14,396	KM13,14,15a-18a	15.25	7.5
PS4	1969(6)	5,056	KM13,14,15a-18a	15.25	7.5
PS5	1970(6)	3,464	KM13,14,15a-18a	15.25	12.5
PS6	1971(6)	3,032	KM13,14,15a-18a	15.25	10.0
PS7	1972(6)	4,866	KM13,14,15a-18a	15.50	9.0
PS8	1972(4)	—	KM24-27	—	100
PS9	1973(7)	10,542	KM13,14,15a-18a,29	27.00	18.0
PS10	1974(7)	9,362	KM13,14,15a-18a,29	27.00	18.0
PS11	1975(7)	4,056	KM13,14,15a-18a,29	31.50	20.0
PS12	1976(7)	2,131	KM13,14,15a,29-32	45.00	32.5
PS13	1977(7)	920	KM13,14,15a,29-32	45.00	37.5
PS14	1978(8)	7,311	KM12a,13,14,15a,29-32	47.00	35.0
PS15	1979(8)	1,857	KM12b,13a,14a,15b, 29a-32a marked O.A.U. JULY, 1979	45.00	50.0

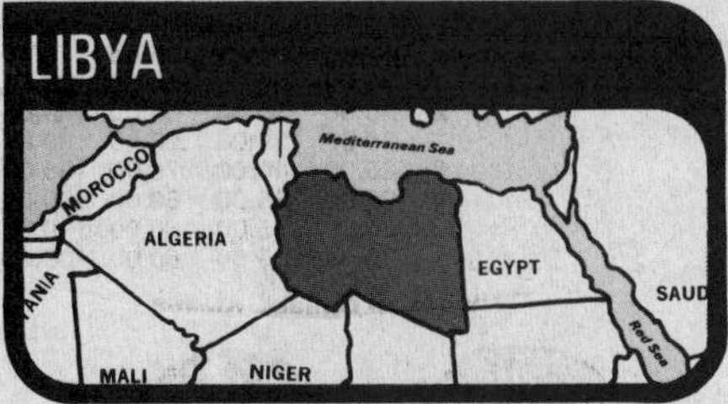

The Socialist Peoples Libyan Arab Jamahiriya, located on the north-central coast of Africa between Tunisia and Egypt, has an area of 679,362 sq. mi. (1,759,540 sq. km.) and a population of 3.9 million. Capital: Tripoli. Crude oil, which accounts for 90 per cent of the export earnings, is the mainstay of the economy.

Libya has been subjected to foreign rule throughout most of its history, various parts of it having been ruled by the Phoenicians, Carthaginians, Vandals, Byzantines, Greeks, Romans, Egyptians, and in the following centuries the Arabs' language, culture and religion were adopted by the indigenous population. Libya was conquered by the Ottoman Turks in 1553, and remained under Turkish domination, becoming a Turkish vilayet in 1835, until it was conquered by Italy and made into a colony in 1911. The name 'Libya', the ancient Greek name for North Africa exclusive of Egypt, was given to the colony by Italy in 1934. Libya came under Allied administration after the fall of Tripoli on Jan. 23, 1943, divided into zones of British and French control. On Dec. 24, 1951, in accordance with a United Nations resolution, Libya proclaimed its independence as a constitutional monarchy, thereby becoming the first country to achieve independence through the United Nations. The monarchy was overthrown by a coup d'etat on Sept. 1, 1969, and Libya was established as a republic.

TITLES

المملكة الليبية

al-Mamlaka(t) al-Libiya(t)

الجمهورية الليبية

al-Jomhuriya(t) al-Arabiya(t) al-Libiya(t)

TRIPOLI

Tripoli (formerly Ottoman Empire Area of antique Tripolitania, 700-146 B.C.), the capital city and chief port of the Libyan Arab Jamahiriya, is situated on the North African coast on a promontory stretching out into the Mediterranean Sea. It was probably founded by Phoenicians from Sicily, but was under Roman control from 146 B.C. until 450 A.D. Invasion by Vandals and conquest by the Byzantines preceded the Arab invasions of the 11th century which, by destroying the commercial centers of Sabratha and Leptis, greatly enhanced the importance of Tripoli, an importance maintained through periods of Norman and Spanish control. Tripoli fell to the Turks, who made it the capital of the vilayet of Tripoli in 1551 and remained in their hands until 1911, when it was occupied by the Italians who made it the capital of the Italian province of Tripolitania. British forces entered the city on Jan. 23, 1943, and administered it until establishment of the independent Kingdom of Libya on Dec. 24, 1951.

RULERS

Ottoman, until 1911

LOCAL PASHAS

Yusuf Pasha Qaramanli,
AH1210-1248/1796-1833AD (resigned)
Ali Pasha Qaramanli II,
AH1248-1250/1833-1835AD

MINTNAME

طرابلس غرب

Tarabalus Gharb = (Tripoli West)

The appellation *west* serving to distinguish it from Tripoli in Lebanon, which had been an Ottoman Mint in the 16th century. On some of the copper coins, *Gharb* is omitted; several types come both with and without *Gharb*. The mint closed between the 28th and 29th year of the reign of Mahmud II.

MONETARY SYSTEM

The monetary system of Tripoli was confused and is poorly understood. Theoretically, 40 Para were equal to one Piastre, but due to the debasement of the silver coinage, later issues are virtually pure copper, though the percentage of alloy varies radically even within a given year. The 10 Para and 20 Para pieces were a little heavier than the copper Paras, with which they could easily be confounded, except that the copper Paras were generally thicker, and bear simpler inscriptions. It is not known how many of the coppers were tariffed to the debased Piastre and its fractions. Some authorities consider the copper pieces to be Beshliks (5 Para coins).

The gold coinage came in two denominations, the Zeri Mahbub (2.4-2.5 g), and the Sultani Altin (3.3-3.4 g). The ratio of the billon Piastres to the gold coins fluctuated from day to day.

OTTOMAN COINAGE

MUSTAFA IV

AH1222-1223/1807-1808AD

30 PARA

SILVER, 35mm, 12.50 g

KM#	Date	Year	VG	Fine	VF	XF
70	AH1222	—	—	—	Rare	—

ZERI MAHBUB

GOLD, 21mm, 2.45 g
Similar to Zeri Mahbub, KM#56

KM#	Date	Year	VG	Fine	VF	XF
72	AH1222	—	—	—	Rare	—

SULTANI

GOLD, 25mm, 3.33 g

KM#	Date	Year	VG	Fine	VF	XF
73	AH1222	1	—	—	Rare	—

MAHMUD II

AH1223-1255/1808-1839AD

COPPER COINAGE

Under this rubric are included all pieces intended as paras. Many of the billon coins are so debased as to be nearly pure copper, but they can be distinguished from those coins intended as paras as they are much thinner, and bear different devices and inscriptions. Some pieces are also struck in brass.

In addition to pieces bearing no regnal year, the issuance of coppers seems to be restricted to two series, the first bearing years 12 & 13, the other years 20-27. The first group is related to an anomalous billon issue in the same years (Type D below), the second issue seems to be connected to the reduced weight series of years 21-25. The undated pieces were most probably struck during one of these two periods.

All of the following pieces appear to be of one denomination, probably a para, but vary in size from about 17-23mm.

PARA

COPPER

KM#	Date	Year	Good	VG	Fine	VF
75	AH1223	—	5.00	8.00	12.50	20.00
		12	6.00	10.00	18.50	35.00
		13	6.00	10.00	18.50	35.00
		20	6.00	10.00	17.50	30.00
	ND	—	4.00	7.00	10.00	18.00

Obv. leg: *Sultan/Mahmud Khan/ Azza Nasruhu.*

KM#	Date	Year	Good	VG	Fine	VF
77	AH1223	—	6.00	9.00	15.00	22.50
		20	6.00	10.00	16.50	25.00

Obv. leg: *Sultan/1223*. Rev. leg: *Mahmud/24.*

KM#	Date	Year	Good	VG	Fine	VF
79	AH1223	24	7.00	12.00	18.00	30.00

Obv: Toughra. Rev: Similar to KM#75, w/*Gharb.*

KM#	Date	Year	Good	VG	Fine	VF
81	AH1222(error)					
		—	8.00	12.50	20.00	45.00
	1223	—	6.00	10.00	18.00	30.00
	Rev: W/o *Gharb.*					
83	AH1223	—	2.50	5.00	10.00	20.00

Obv. Toughra and rev. leg. within square and 8 loops.

KM#	Date	Year	Good	VG	Fine	VF
85	AH1223	2	6.00	9.00	15.00	25.00
	Obv: Toughra. Rev: 6-line legend.					
87	AH1223	18	8.00	12.00	20.00	35.00

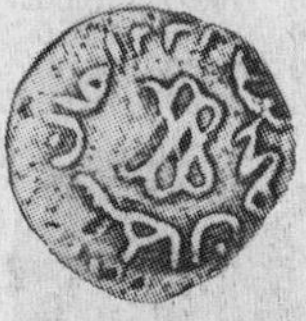

COPPER
Obv. leg: *Sultan Mahmud Khan 1223* w/year above arabesque.

KM#	Date	Year	Good	VG	Fine	VF
89	AH1223	25	3.00	6.00	10.00	20.00
		26	3.75	7.50	15.00	25.00
		62	(error) for year 26			
			3.75	7.50	15.00	35.00

NOTE: Several variations are found in the arrangement of the obverse legend. Year 29 is reported, but is likely a misreading of year 26.

Similar to KM#89 but year below arabesque.

KM#	Date	Year	Good	VG	Fine	VF
90	AH1223	25	3.75	7.50	15.00	25.00

Obv: W/o dot above B in DARB.

KM#	Date	Year	Good	VG	Fine	VF
91.1	ND	—	8.00	10.00	12.00	20.00

Obv. leg: *Duriba*. Rev. leg: *Fi Trablus.*

KM#	Date	Year	Good	VG	Fine	VF
91.2	ND	—	10.00	12.00	15.00	20.00

Obv. and rev. leg. within lozenge.

KM#	Date	Year	Good	VG	Fine	VF
93	AH1223	—	6.00	10.00	20.00	30.00

COPPER or BRASS
Obv. and rev. leg. arranged differently.

KM#	Date	Year	Good	VG	Fine	VF
95	AH1223	23	8.00	12.00	20.00	45.00

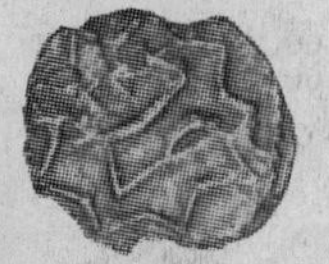

COPPER
Obv. and rev. leg. within 10-pointed stars.

KM#	Date	Year	Good	VG	Fine	VF
97	AH1223	23	6.00	9.00	15.00	25.00

Obv. leg: *Duriba/Fi/1223*. Rev: *Tarabalus/r.y.*

KM#	Date	Year	Good	VG	Fine	VF
99	AH1223	12	6.00	10.00	16.50	25.00
		13	6.00	10.00	16.50	25.00
		20	6.00	10.00	16.50	25.00
		21	6.00	10.00	16.50	25.00

Obv. leg: *Duriba/Fi/1223*. Rev: *Tarabalus/r.y.*

KM#	Date	Year	Good	VG	Fine	VF
101	AH1223	13	6.00	10.00	16.50	30.00
		21	6.00	10.00	16.50	30.00

3.79g, 20mm
Rev: *Tarabalus 22* in looped star of David.

KM#	Date	Year	Good	VG	Fine	VF
102	AH1123	22	10.00	15.00	20.00	35.00

Rev: 5 dots within wreath.

KM#	Date	Year	Good	VG	Fine	VF
103	AH1223	20	6.00	9.00	15.00	22.50

Rev: Arabesque within garland.

KM#	Date	Year	Good	VG	Fine	VF
105	AH1223	21	6.00	10.00	16.00	24.00

Obv: W/o *Gharb*. Rev: Rose within garland.

KM#	Date	Year	Good	VG	Fine	VF
107	AH1223	22	6.00	9.00	15.00	22.50

Rev: 5 stars.

KM#	Date	Year	Good	VG	Fine	VF
109	AH1223	25	6.00	10.00	16.50	25.00

Obv. leg: *Duriba/fi/Tarabalus/1223*.
Rev: *Gharb*.

KM#	Date	Year	Good	VG	Fine	VF
111	AH1223	21	5.00	8.00	12.00	20.00

Obv: Ornament. Rev: *Gharb*.

KM#	Date	Year	Good	VG	Fine	VF
112	AH1223	21	6.00	9.00	15.00	20.00

Obv. leg: *Duriba/Fi/Tarabalus/1223*.
Rev: Hexagram w/central dot.

KM#	Date	Year	Good	VG	Fine	VF
115	AH1223	—	5.00	8.00	15.00	22.50
		25	5.00	8.00	15.00	22.50
		27	5.00	8.00	15.00	22.50

Rev: Hexagram w/4-7 dots.

KM#	Date	Year	Good	VG	Fine	VF
117	AH1223	—	5.00	8.00	10.00	20.00

Obv: Similar to KM#111. Rev: Hexagram w/23.

KM#	Date	Year	Good	VG	Fine	VF
119	AH1223	23	6.00	10.00	18.00	24.00

BILLON COINAGE

The billon coinage of Mahmud II is extremely varied, with a plethora of types deriving largely from contemporary Turkish, Egyptian, and Tunisian prototypes. There is considerable controversy over the denominations of these coins, although they seem to be based on a Piastre (40 Paras, Kuruns) of about 16 grams from yrs. 1-13, of about 12 grams from yrs. 13-21, and of 10 grams from yrs. 21-25. A new style coinage was introduced in yr. 28, but it was apparently never issued in sizable quantities and confined to the one year.

There is considerable weight variation within each denomination, in some cases up to 20 percent higher or lower than the theoretical norm. There is not yet discernible correlation between type, denomination, year, and standard. Recent evidence indicates that the net silver content was frequently and repeatedly reduced, probably in rather small increments. Thus the existence of several types for a single denomination and regnal year may indicate a multiplicity of issues with a single year, but as the full series is still not known, the complete sequence for each denomination cannot yet be reconstructed Debasements were frequent: In the 4-year period covering years 21-24, ten changes in the values of coinage are recorded, but not all changes need have referred to the denominations and designs.

Except for a few isolated miscellaneous types, all of the billon coinage can be classed into five basic types:

TYPE A: Obv: Toughra, sometimes with adjacent symbol, (i.e. flower, tamgha with arrow heads, large tamgha, crescent, letter "nun", and figures "22" and "23"). Rev: Year/mintname/*1223*.

TYPE B: Obv: Toughra/mintname/*1223*. Rev: 4-line leg. giving Sultan's titles: *Sultan al-Bahrayn Wa Khaqan al-Bahrayn al Sultan Ibn al Sultan* (sometimes with stars).

TYPE C: Obv: Sultan's name/benediction/mintname/*1223*. (4-line leg.) Rev: Same as rev. of Type B.

TYPE D: Obv: Sultan's name (sometimes with *1223*). Rev: Year/mintname/*1223* (1223 omitted when on obv.)

TYPE E: Obv: 4-line leg: *Sultan al Barrayn wa Khaqan al Bahrayn al Sultan Mahmud Khan Azza Nasruhu* & year. Rev: Mintname/*1223* (this type copied from Tunis piastre & fractions).

In addition to the variations in type, there is considerable variation in the borders. No attempt has been made in these listings to distinguish the various types of borders, though it is quite possible that such distinctions may have been monetarily important.

STANDARD COINAGE

The following listings are arranged by standard, and then by denomination within each standard. The sizes of the coins can vary considerably within each issue. The weight can vary by up to 20 percent higher or lower than the amounts shown.

All of the coins were struck in low-grade billon, tending toward pure copper on some of the later issues. Most of the coins originally were lightly silver-washed, and specimens with the silver wash intact are now quite scarce.

FIRST STANDARD

Based on a Piastre (40 Para) of about 16.00 g.

5 PARA

BILLON, 22-23mm, Type B

KM#	Date	Year	Good	VG	Fine	VF
126	AH1223	1	20.00	35.00	60.00	100.00
		2	20.00	35.00	60.00	100.00
		7	20.00	35.00	60.00	100.00
		8	25.00	40.00	75.00	125.00
		9	20.00	35.00	60.00	100.00
		10	20.00	35.00	60.00	100.00
		11	20.00	35.00	60.00	100.00

10 PARA

SILVER, 1.35 g, 18mm
Rev: Ornament in circle for regnal year.

KM#	Date	Year	Good	VG	Fine	VF
127	AH1223	—	30.00	50.00	75.00	125.00

BILLON, 22-24mm, 2.46 g, Type A

KM#	Date	Year	Good	VG	Fine	VF
128	AH1223	—	15.00	25.00	75.00	125.00
		2	15.00	25.00	75.00	125.00

3.35 g

KM#	Date	Year	Good	VG	Fine	VF
130	AH1223	7	30.00	50.00	75.00	125.00

KM#	Date	Year	Good	VG	Fine	VF
131	AH1223	9	20.00	40.00	75.00	125.00

29-31mm, 3.89 g

KM#	Date	Year	Good	VG	Fine	VF
134	AH1223	9	20.00	35.00	60.00	100.00

24mm, 1.80 g

KM#	Date	Year	Good	VG	Fine	VF
135	AH1223	3	20.00	35.00	60.00	100.00

15 PARA

BILLON

KM#	Date	Year	Good	VG	Fine	VF
132	AH1223	7	15.00	25.00	50.00	80.00

20 PARA

BILLON, 31mm, 5.38-6.65 g, Type A

KM#	Date	Year	Good	VG	Fine	VF
136	AH1223	2	15.00	25.00	75.00	125.00
		7	15.00	25.00	75.00	125.00
137	AH1223	8	15.00	25.00	75.00	125.00

KM#	Date	Year	Good	VG	Fine	VF
138	AH1223	9	30.00	50.00	75.00	125.00

KM#	Date	Year	Good	VG	Fine	VF
139	AH1223	10	30.00	50.00	75.00	125.00
		11	30.00	50.00	75.00	125.00

40 PARA

BILLON, 37mm, 15.68 g, Type A

KM#	Date	Year	Good	VG	Fine	VF
140	AH1223	ND	45.00	75.00	125.00	200.00

12.025 g, Type B

KM#	Date	Year	Good	VG	Fine	VF
141	AH1223	1	50.00	100.00	175.00	300.00
		2	50.00	90.00	150.00	400.00
		3	50.00	75.00	125.00	300.00
		ornament	50.00	80.00	130.00	300.00

100 PARA

BILLON, 24.68 g, 43-44mm
Ornament w/dot on either side.

KM#	Date	Year	Good	VG	Fine	VF
142	AH1223	ND	100.00	175.00	275.00	400.00

Obv: Ornament right of toughra.

KM#	Date	Year	Good	VG	Fine	VF
143	AH1223	3	—	—	Rare	—
		4	—	—	Rare	—
		5	—	—	Rare	—

Obv: Flower right of toughra.

KM#	Date	Year	Good	VG	Fine	VF
144	AH1223	4	—	—	Rare	—
		5	—	—	Rare	—
		5	special form		Rare	—

SECOND STANDARD

Years 12-13
Based on a Piastre of about 14.00 g.

10 PARA

BILLON, 19mm, 2.90 g, Type D

KM#	Date	Year	Good	VG	Fine	VF
145	AH1223	12	15.00	25.00	75.00	125.00
		13	15.00	25.00	75.00	125.00

20 PARA

BILLON, 23mm, 4.41 g, Type D

KM#	Date	Year	Good	VG	Fine	VF
147	AH1223	12	12.50	25.00	60.00	100.00
		13	12.50	25.00	60.00	100.00

BILLON, 28mm, 6.35 g, Type B

KM#	Date	Year	Good	VG	Fine	VF
149	AH1223	13	35.00	60.00	100.00	150.00

40 PARA

BILLION, 35mm, Type B

KM#	Date	Year	Good	VG	Fine	VF
150	AH1223	13	45.00	75.00	115.00	160.00

THIRD STANDARD

Years 14-21
Based on a Piastre of about 12.00 g.

10 PARA

BILLON, 22-28mm, 3.09 g, Type A

KM#	Date	Year	Good	VG	Fine	VF
154	AH1223	19	30.00	50.00	70.00	100.00

Rev: Legend within square.

KM#	Date	Year	Good	VG	Fine	VF
155	AH1223	20	30.00	50.00	70.00	100.00

Type B, 22-25mm, 1.69-1.80 g

KM#	Date	Year	Good	VG	Fine	VF
156	AH1223	16	30.00	50.00	70.00	100.00
		17	30.00	50.00	70.00	100.00
		18	17.50	30.00	60.00	125.00

15 PARA

BILLON, 29mm, 3.70 g, Type E

KM#	Date	Year	Good	VG	Fine	VF
162	AH1223	17	20.00	40.00	75.00	125.00

20 PARA

BILLON, 23mm, 5.60 g, Type A

KM#	Date	Year	Good	VG	Fine	VF
164	AH1223	20	18.00	30.00	50.00	100.00

Type A, 5.59 g, 31mm

KM#	Date	Year	Good	VG	Fine	VF
166	AH1223	15	30.00	50.00	75.00	125.00
		20	30.00	50.00	75.00	125.00
		21	30.00	50.00	75.00	125.00

Type B

KM#	Date	Year	Good	VG	Fine	VF
168	AH1223	15	40.00	75.00	100.00	150.00

Type C, 6.43 g, 29mm

KM#	Date	Year	Good	VG	Fine	VF
170	AH1222	—	30.00	50.00	80.00	120.00
	1223	20	30.00	50.00	80.00	120.00

Type D, 5.10 g, 28mm

KM#	Date	Year	Good	VG	Fine	VF
172	AH1223	20	15.00	25.00	40.00	60.00

30 PARA

BILLON, 34mm, Type A

KM#	Date	Year	Good	VG	Fine	VF
174	AH1223	3	100.00	150.00	250.00	400.00

29mm, Type A

KM#	Date	Year	Good	VG	Fine	VF
176	AH1223	2	15.00	30.00	70.00	100.00

33-34mm, 7.73 g

KM#	Date	Year	Good	VG	Fine	VF
178	AH1223	17	35.00	55.00	80.00	125.00
		18	35.00	55.00	80.00	125.00
		Type E, 6.43 g				
179	AH1223	20	20.00	35.00	60.00	125.00

40 PARA

BILLON, 35mm, Type A, lozenge borders

KM#	Date	Year	Good	VG	Fine	VF
180	AH1223	21	40.00	60.00	100.00	160.00
		32mm, Type A, plain borders				
182	AH1223	20	35.00	55.00	90.00	150.00
		36-39mm, Type A, circular ornate borders				
184	AH1223	15	30.00	50.00	90.00	150.00
		19	30.00	50.00	90.00	150.00
		21	30.00	50.00	90.00	150.00

35-37mm, Type B

KM#	Date	Year	Good	VG	Fine	VF
186	AH1223	13	35.00	55.00	90.00	150.00
		14	35.00	55.00	90.00	150.00
		18	35.00	55.00	90.00	150.00
		20	35.00	55.00	90.00	150.00

Similar to KM#186 but letter *nun* beside toughra.

KM#	Date	Year	Good	VG	Fine	VF
187	AH1223	14	100.00	125.00	150.00	200.00

36mm, Type C

KM#	Date	Year	Good	VG	Fine	VF
188	AH1223	19	45.00	65.00	100.00	160.00
		20	45.00	65.00	100.00	160.00
		34mm, Type D				
190	AH1223	18	45.00	65.00	100.00	160.00
		33mm, 11.75 g, Type E				
192	AH1243	—	—	—	Rare	—

NOTE: KM#192 is dated to the actual year, as on similar coins of Tunis.

50 PARA

BILLON, 37mm, 15.44 g, Type A

KM#	Date	Year	Good	VG	Fine	VF
194	AH1243	—	—	—	Rare	—

NOTE: Refer to KM#182. The denomination of the above coin is very uncertain.

60 PARA

BILLON, 18.27 g, Type A

KM#	Date	Year	Good	VG	Fine	VF
196	AH1223	20	20.00	35.00	60.00	100.00

FOURTH STANDARD

Years 21-25

Based on a Piastre of approximately 10.00 g.

10 PARA

BILLON, 24mm, Type B

KM#	Date	Year	Good	VG	Fine	VF
201	AH1223	22	12.50	22.50	35.00	75.00
		24	18.00	30.00	45.00	75.00
		25	18.00	30.00	45.00	75.00

20 PARA

BILLON, 29-30mm, Type A

KM#	Date	Year	Good	VG	Fine	VF
203	AH1223	22	25.00	50.00	75.00	100.00
		23	20.00	35.00	50.00	70.00

Type B

KM#	Date	Year	Good	VG	Fine	VF
205	AH1223	22	18.00	30.00	45.00	65.00
		24	18.00	30.00	45.00	65.00
		25	18.00	30.00	45.00	65.00

30 PARA

BILLON, 35mm, Type A

KM#	Date	Year	Good	VG	Fine	VF
206	AH1223	24	60.00	90.00	150.00	200.00
		BILLON, 32mm, Type D				
207	AH1223	22	40.00	60.00	100.00	150.00

34mm

KM#	Date	Year	Good	VG	Fine	VF
209	AH1223	23	—	—	Rare	—

35mm

Similar to Type A, but w/large crescents at both sides similar to Turkey 10 Para, C#197 but w/o wreaths.

KM#	Date	Year	Good	VG	Fine	VF
211	AH1223	24	30.00	60.00	85.00	125.00

40 PARA

BILLON, Type A

KM#	Date	Year	Good	VG	Fine	VF
213	AH1223	21	40.00	60.00	100.00	150.00
		22	60.00	90.00	150.00	200.00
		24	25.00	40.00	60.00	85.00

Type B

KM#	Date	Year	Good	VG	Fine	VF
215	AH1223	21	65.00	100.00	150.00	225.00
		22	50.00	80.00	100.00	120.00
		24	50.00	80.00	100.00	120.00
		25	50.00	80.00	100.00	120.00

FIFTH STANDARD

Year 28 only

Uncertain metrology

MANGIR

COPPER, 0.914 g, 16mm
Obv: Toughra w/*Nuhas* (= copper) to right, year 28 to left.
Rev. leg: *Duriba/Fi/Tarabalus Gharb/1223.*

KM#	Date	Year	Good	VG	Fine	VF
217	AH1223	28	15.00	25.00	40.00	75.00

NOTE: Varieties exist.

5 PARA

BILLON, 1.855 g, 19mm
Type A, but obv. and rev. leg. within wreaths. W/*Fidda* (= Silver) to right of toughra, regnal year at left.

KM#	Date	Year	Good	VG	Fine	VF
216	AH1223	28	—	—	Rare	—

10 PARA

BILLON, 3.680 g, 21mm
Type A, but obv. and rev. leg. within wreaths. W/*Fidda* (= Silver) to right of toughra, regnal year at left.

KM#	Date	Year	Good	VG	Fine	VF
220	AH1223	28	—	—	Rare	—

20 PARA

BILLON, 7.05-7.73 g, 25-30mm
Type A, but obv. and rev. leg. within wreaths. W/*Fidda* (= Silver) to right of toughra, regnal year at left.

KM#	Date	Year	Good	VG	Fine	VF
218	AH1223	28	—	—	Rare	—

40 PARA

BILLON, 14.50-14.81 g, 36-38mm
Type A, but obv. and rev. leg. within wreaths. W/*Fidda* (= Silver) to right of toughra, regnal year at left.

KM#	Date	Year	Good	VG	Fine	VF
219	AH1223	28	—	—	Rare	—

ZERI MAHBUB

GOLD, 21-24mm, 2.30-2.50 g, Type B

KM#	Date	Year	VG	Fine	VF	XF
222	AH1223	12	100.00	175.00	250.00	350.00
		13	100.00	175.00	250.00	350.00
		14	100.00	175.00	250.00	350.00

Type E
Rev: Mintname above date.

KM#	Date	Year	VG	Fine	VF	XF
224	AH1223	18	100.00	175.00	250.00	350.00

KM#	Date	Year	VG	Fine	VF	XF
226	AH1223	20	100.00	175.00	250.00	350.00

SULTANI

GOLD, 33mm, 5.58 g
Obv: Toughra.

KM#	Date	Year	VG	Fine	VF	XF
227	AH1223	5	500.00	650.00	750.00	950.00

24-26mm, 3.20-3.40 g, Type C (variant)

KM#	Date	Year	VG	Fine	VF	XF
228	AH1223	6	100.00	175.00	250.00	350.00
		19	100.00	175.00	250.00	350.00
		ornament	100.00	175.00	250.00	350.00

Similar, but broader and thinner.

KM#	Date	Year	VG	Fine	VF	XF
230	AH1223	14	—	—	Rare	—

Rev: W/o lines dividing leg.

KM#	Date	Year	VG	Fine	VF	XF
232	AH1223	—	100.00	175.00	250.00	350.00

LIBYA

RULERS

Idris I, 1951-1969

MONETARY SYSTEM

10 Milliemes = 1 Piastre
100 Piastres = 1 Pound

MILLIEME

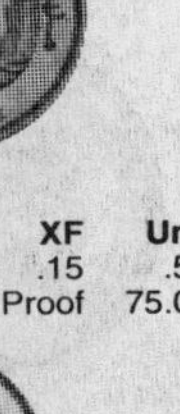

BRONZE

KM#	Date	Year	Mintage	VF	XF	Unc
1	—	1952	7.750	.10	.15	.50
	—	1952	32 pcs.	—	Proof	75.00

NICKEL-BRASS

KM#	Date	Year	Mintage	VF	XF	Unc
6	AH1385	1965	11.000	.10	.15	.25

2 MILLIEMES

BRONZE

KM#	Date	Year	Mintage	VF	XF	Unc
2	—	1952	6.650	.10	.25	.75
	—	1952	32 pcs.	—	Proof	75.00

5 MILLIEMES

BRONZE

KM#	Date	Year	Mintage	VF	XF	Unc
3	—	1952	7.680	.15	.35	1.00
	—	1952	32 pcs.	—	Proof	75.00

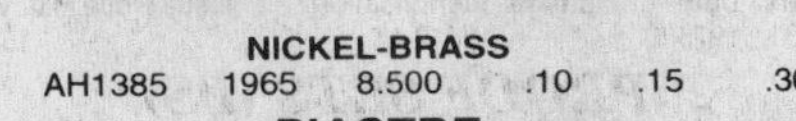

NICKEL-BRASS

KM#	Date	Year	Mintage	VF	XF	Unc
7	AH1385	1965	8.500	.10	.15	.30

PIASTRE

COPPER-NICKEL

KM#	Date	Year	Mintage	VF	XF	Unc
4	—	1952	10.200	.35	.60	1.25
	—	1952	32 pcs.	—	Proof	100.00

10 MILLIEMES

COPPER-NICKEL

KM#	Date	Year	Mintage	VF	XF	Unc
8	AH1385	1965	17.000	.10	.20	.40

2 PIASTRES

COPPER-NICKEL

KM#	Date	Year	Mintage	VF	XF	Unc
5	—	1952	6.075	.35	.75	1.50
	—	1952	32 pcs.	—	Proof	125.00

20 MILLIEMES

COPPER-NICKEL

KM#	Date	Year	Mintage	VF	XF	Unc
9	AH1385	1965	8.750	.15	.35	2.00

50 MILLIEMES

COPPER-NICKEL

KM#	Date	Year	Mintage	VF	XF	Unc
10	AH1385	1965	8.000	.25	.50	3.00

100 MILLIEMES

COPPER-NICKEL

KM#	Date	Year	Mintage	VF	XF	Unc
11	AH1385	1965	8.000	.50	1.00	3.50

SOCIALIST PEOPLES REPUBLIC

MONETARY SYSTEM

1000 Dirhams = 1 Dinar

DIRHAM

BRASS-CLAD STEEL

KM#	Date	Year	Mintage	VF	XF	Unc
12	AH1395	1975	20.000	.10	.25	1.00

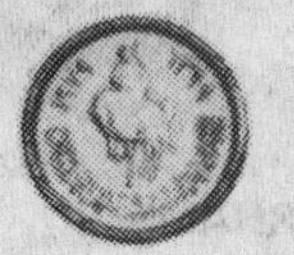
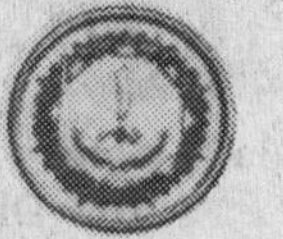

KM#	Date	Year	Mintage	VF	XF	Unc
18	AH1399	1979	1.000	.20	.50	1.50

5 DIRHAMS

BRASS-CLAD STEEL

KM#	Date	Year	Mintage	VF	XF	Unc
13	AH1395	1975	23.000	.10	.35	1.50

KM#	Date	Year	Mintage	VF	XF	Unc
19	AH1399	1979	2.000	.25	.65	2.00

10 DIRHAMS

COPPER-NICKEL-CLAD STEEL

KM#	Date	Year	Mintage	VF	XF	Unc
14	AH1395	1975	52.750	.10	.45	1.50

KM#	Date	Year	Mintage	VF	XF	Unc
20	AH1399	1979	4.000	.15	.65	2.50

20 DIRHAMS

COPPER-NICKEL-CLAD STEEL

KM#	Date	Year	Mintage	VF	XF	Unc
15	AH1395	1975	25.500	.25	.75	3.50

KM#	Date	Year	Mintage	VF	XF	Unc
21	AH1399	1979	6.000	.35	1.00	4.00

50 DIRHAMS

COPPER-NICKEL

KM#	Date	Year	Mintage	VF	XF	Unc
16	AH1395	1975	25.640	.40	1.25	4.50

KM#	Date	Year	Mintage	VF	XF	Unc
22	AH1399	1979	9.120	.50	1.50	5.00

100 DIRHAMS

COPPER-NICKEL

KM#	Date	Year	Mintage	VF	XF	Unc
17	AH1395	1975	15.433	.75	2.00	5.50

KM#	Date	Year	Mintage	VF	XF	Unc
23	AH1399	1979	15.000	.75	2.50	6.00

5 DINARS

28.2800 g, .925 SILVER, .8410 oz ASW
International Year of Disabled Persons

KM#	Date	Year	Mintage	VF	XF	Unc
24	—	1981	.020	—	—	25.00
	—	1981	.021	—	Proof	30.00

70 DINARS

15.9800 g, .917 GOLD, .4712 oz AGW
International Year of Disabled Persons

KM#	Date	Year	Mintage	VF	XF	Unc
25	—	1981	4,000	—	—	400.00
	—	1981	4,000	—	Proof	500.00

MINT SETS (MS)

KM#	Date	Mintage	Identification	Issue Price	Mkt. Val.
MS1	1975(6)	—	KM12-17	—	15.00

PROOF SETS (PS)

KM#	Date	Mintage	Identification	Issue Price	Mkt. Val.
PS1	1952(5)	32	KM1-5	—	450.00

LIECHTENSTEIN

The Principality of Liechtenstein, located in central Europe on the east bank of the Rhine between Austria and Switzerland, has an area of 61 sq. mi. (160 sq. km.) and a population of 27,200. Capital: Vaduz. The economy is based on agriculture and light manufacturing. Canned goods, textiles, ceramics and precision instruments are exported.

The lordships of Schellenburg and Vaduz were merged into the principality of Liechtenstein. It was a member of the Rhine Confederation from 1806 to 1815, and of the German Confederation from 1815 to 1866 when it became independent. Liechtenstein's long and close association with Austria was terminated by World War I. In 1921 it adopted the coinage of Switzerland, and two years later entered into a customs union with the Swiss, who also operated its postal and telegraph systems and represent it in international affairs. The tiny principality abolished its army in 1868 and has avoided involvement in all European wars since that time.

RULERS

Prince John II, 1858-1929
Prince Franz I, 1929-1938
Prince Franz Josef II, 1938-1990
Prince Hans Adam II, 1990-

MINT MARKS

A - Vienna
B - Bern
M - Munich (restrikes)

MONETARY SYSTEM

(1857-1868)

1-1/2 Florins = 1 Vereinsthaler

EIN (1) THALER

(Vereins)

18.5200 g, .900 SILVER, .5358 oz ASW

Y#	Date	Mintage	Fine	VF	XF	Unc
1	1862A	1,920	1250.	2000.	3500.	4250.
	1862A-M	—		(restrike)	Proof	25.00

29.5000 g, .900 GOLD, .8536 oz AGW

Y#	Date	Mintage	Fine	VF	XF	Unc
1a	1862A-M	.050		(restrike)	Proof	600.00

PLATINUM, 33.34 g

Y#	Date	Mintage	Fine	VF	XF	Unc
1b	1862A-M	—		(restrike)	Proof	1250.

MONETARY REFORM

100 Heller = 1 Krone

KRONE

5.0000 g, .835 SILVER, .1342 oz ASW

Y#	Date	Mintage	Fine	VF	XF	Unc
2	1900	.050	12.00	20.00	25.00	45.00
	1904	.075	12.00	20.00	25.00	45.00
	1910	.045	12.00	20.00	25.00	45.00
	1915	.075	12.00	20.00	25.00	45.00

2 KRONEN

10.0000 g, .835 SILVER, .2684 oz ASW

Y#	Date	Mintage	Fine	VF	XF	Unc
3	1912	.050	12.00	18.00	28.00	45.00
	1915	.038	15.00	20.00	35.00	60.00

5 KRONEN

24.0000 g, .900 SILVER, .6944 oz ASW

Y#	Date	Mintage	Fine	VF	XF	Unc
4	1900	5,000	250.00	400.00	600.00	750.00
	1904	.015	75.00	120.00	150.00	250.00
	1910	.010	75.00	150.00	200.00	275.00
	1915	.010	75.00	150.00	200.00	275.00

10 KRONEN

3.3875 g, .900 GOLD, .0980 oz AGW

Y#	Date	Mintage	Fine	VF	XF	Unc
5	1900	1,500	—	—	5000.	6000.

20 KRONEN

6.7750 g, .900 GOLD, .1960 oz AGW

Y#	Date	Mintage	Fine	VF	XF	Unc
6	1898	1,500	—	—	4250.	5000.

MONETARY REFORM

100 Rappen = 1 Frank

1/2 FRANK

2.5000 g, .835 SILVER, .0751 oz ASW

Y#	Date	Mintage	Fine	VF	XF	Unc
7	1924	*.030	65.00	125.00	160.00	215.00

***NOTE:** 15,745 pieces were remelted.

FRANK

5.0000 g, .835 SILVER, .1342 oz ASW

Y#	Date	Mintage	Fine	VF	XF	Unc
8	1924	*.060	30.00	60.00	100.00	150.00

***NOTE:** 45,355 pieces were remelted.

2 FRANKEN

10.0000 g, .835 SILVER, .2684 oz ASW

Y#	Date	Mintage	Fine	VF	XF	Unc
9	1924	*.050	40.00	90.00	150.00	175.00

***NOTE:** 41,707 pieces were remelted.

5 FRANKEN

25.0000 g, .900 SILVER, .7234 oz ASW

Y#	Date	Mintage	Fine	VF	XF	Unc
10	1924	*.015	250.00	350.00	450.00	700.00

***NOTE:** 11,260 pieces were remelted.

10 FRANKEN

3.2258 g, .900 GOLD, .0933 oz AGW

Y#	Date	Mintage	Fine	VF	XF	Unc
11	1930	2,500	—	650.00	850.00	1000.

Y#	Date	Mintage	Fine	VF	XF	Unc
13	1946B	.010	—	150.00	200.00	250.00

30.0000 g, .900 SILVER, .8682 oz ASW
50th Anniversary of Reign
Obv: Similar to 50 Franken, Y#21.

Y#	Date	Mintage	Fine	VF	XF	Unc
20	1988	.035	—	—	—	30.00

Succession of Hans-Adam II

Y#	Date	Mintage	Fine	VF	XF	Unc
22	1990	.035	—	—	—	25.00

20 FRANKEN

6.4516 g, .900 GOLD, .1867 oz AGW

Y#	Date	Mintage	Fine	VF	XF	Unc
12	1930	2,500	—	650.00	850.00	1500.

Y#	Date	Mintage	Fine	VF	XF	Unc
14	1946B	.010	—	175.00	275.00	350.00

25 FRANKEN

5.6450 g, .900 GOLD, .1633 oz AGW
Franz Josef II and Princess Gina

Y#	Date	Mintage	Fine	VF	XF	Unc
15	1956	.015	—	—	225.00	275.00

100th Anniversary of National Bank

Y#	Date	Mintage	Fine	VF	XF	Unc
18	1961	.020	—	—	—	250.00

50 FRANKEN

11.2900 g, .900 GOLD, .3267 oz AGW
Franz Josef II and Princess Gina

Y#	Date	Mintage	Fine	VF	XF	Unc
16	1956	.015	—	—	300.00	350.00

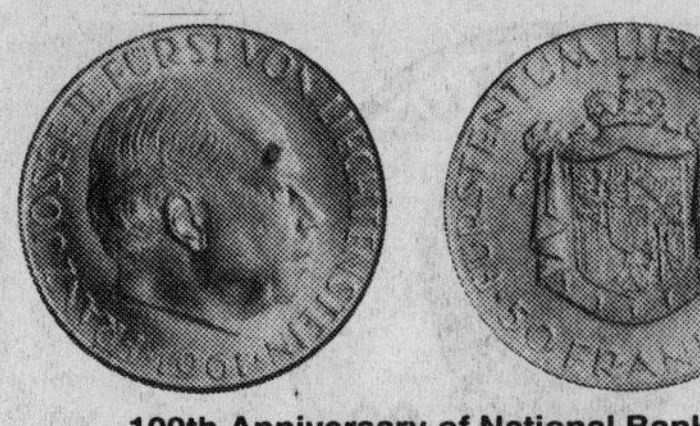

100th Anniversary of National Bank

Y#	Date	Mintage	Fine	VF	XF	Unc
19	1961	.020	—	—	—	325.00

10.0000 g, .900 GOLD, .2894 oz AGW
50th Anniversary of Reign

Y#	Date	Mintage	Fine	VF	XF	Unc
21	1988	.035	—	—	—	250.00

Succession of Hans-Adam II

Y#	Date	Mintage	Fine	VF	XF	Unc
23	1990	.025	—	—	—	175.00

100 FRANKEN

32.2580 g, .900 GOLD, .9335 oz AGW
Franz Josef II and Princess Gina

Y#	Date	Mintage	Fine	VF	XF	Unc
17	1952	4,000	—	—	3200.	3750.

LITHUANIA

The Republic of Lithuania, southernmost of the Baltic states in east Europe, has an area of 25,174 sq. mi. (65,201 sq. km.) and a population of *3.6 million. Capital: Vilnius. The economy is based on livestock raising and manufacturing. Hogs, cattle, hides and electric motors are exported.

Lithuania emerged as a grand duchy in the 14th century. In the 15th century it was a major power of central Europe, stretching from the Baltic to the Black Sea. It was joined with Poland in 1569. Following the third partition of Poland by Austria, Prussia and Russia, 1795, Lithuania came under Russian domination and did not regain its independence until shortly before the end of World War I when it declared itself a sovereign republic. The republic was occupied by Soviet troops and annexed to the U.S.S.R. in 1940. Following the German occupation of 1941-44, it was retaken by Russia and reestablished as a member republic of the Soviet Union. Western countries, including the United States, did not recognize Lithuania's incorporation into the Soviet Union.

Lithuania declared its independence March 11, 1990 and it was recognized by the United States on Sept. 2, 1991, followed by the Soviet government in Moscow on Sept. 6. They were seated in the UN General Assembly on Sept. 17, 1991.

MINT MARKS

LMK - Vilnius

REPUBLIC COINAGE

MONETARY SYSTEM

100 Centu = 1 Litas

CENTAS

ALUMINUM-BRONZE

KM#	Date	Mintage	Fine	VF	XF	Unc
71	1925	5.000	3.00	6.00	15.00	35.00

BRONZE

KM#	Date	Mintage	Fine	VF	XF	Unc
79	1936	9.995	2.00	4.00	9.00	20.00

2 CENTAI

BRONZE

KM#	Date	Mintage	Fine	VF	XF	Unc
80	1936	4.951	5.00	10.00	15.00	35.00

5 CENTAI

ALUMINUM-BRONZE

KM#	Date	Mintage	Fine	VF	XF	Unc
72	1925	12.000	2.00	4.00	10.00	22.50

BRONZE

KM#	Date	Mintage	Fine	VF	XF	Unc
81	1936	4.800	3.00	6.00	14.00	32.00

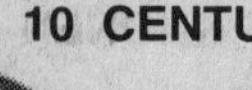

10 CENTU

ALUMINUM-BRONZE

KM#	Date	Mintage	Fine	VF	XF	Unc
73	1925	12.000	2.00	4.00	10.00	25.00

20 CENTU

ALUMINUM-BRONZE

KM#	Date	Mintage	Fine	VF	XF	Unc
74	1925	8.000	3.00	5.00	12.00	30.00

50 CENTU

ALUMINUM-BRONZE

KM#	Date	Mintage	Fine	VF	XF	Unc
75	1925	5.000	7.50	12.00	20.00	50.00

LITAS

2.7000 g, .500 SILVER, .0434 oz ASW

KM#	Date	Mintage	Fine	VF	XF	Unc
76	1925	5.985	2.00	4.00	10.00	30.00

2 LITU

5.4000 g, .500 SILVER, .0868 oz ASW

KM#	Date	Mintage	Fine	VF	XF	Unc
77	1925	3.000	6.00	9.00	12.00	25.00

5 LITAI

13.5000 g, .500 SILVER, .2170 oz ASW

KM#	Date	Mintage	Fine	VF	XF	Unc
78	1925	1.000	4.00	8.00	16.00	45.00
	1925	—	—	—	Proof	500.00

9.0000 g, .750 SILVER, .2170 oz ASW
Dr. Jonas Basanavicius
Obv: Designer's initials below bust, lettered edge.

KM#	Date	Mintage	Fine	VF	XF	Unc
82	1936	2.612	3.00	7.00	12.00	35.00

10 LITU

18.0000 g, .750 SILVER, .4340 oz ASW
Grand Duke Vytis Didysis
Lettered edge

KM#	Date	Mintage	Fine	VF	XF	Unc
83	1936	.720	7.00	12.50	20.00	50.00

20th Anniversary of Republic - President Smetona

84	1938	.170	15.00	25.00	30.00	70.00

MONETARY REFORM

100 Centas = 1 Litas

CENTAS

ALUMINUM

85	1991	—	—	—	—	.20

2 CENTAI

ALUMINUM

86	1991	—	—	—	—	.35

5 CENTAI

ALUMINUM

87	1991	—	—	—	—	.50

10 CENTU

BRONZE

88	1991	—	—	—	—	.60

20 CENTU

BRONZE

KM#	Date	Mintage	Fine	VF	XF	Unc
89	1991	—	—	—	—	.75

50 CENTU

BRONZE

90	1991	—	—	—	—	.85

LITAS

COPPER-NICKEL

91	1991	—	—	—	—	1.50

2 LITAI

COPPER-NICKEL

92	1991	—	—	—	—	1.75

5 LITAI

COPPER-NICKEL

93	1991	—	—	—	—	2.50

10 LITU

COPPER-NICKEL
Darius and Girenas

94	1993LMK	—	—	—	—	6.00

Papal Visit

95	1993LMK	—	—	—	—	6.00

MINT SETS (MS)

KM#	Date	Mintage	Identification	Issue Price	Mkt. Val.
MS1	1925(10)	—	KM71-75	—	800.00

LUXEMBOURG

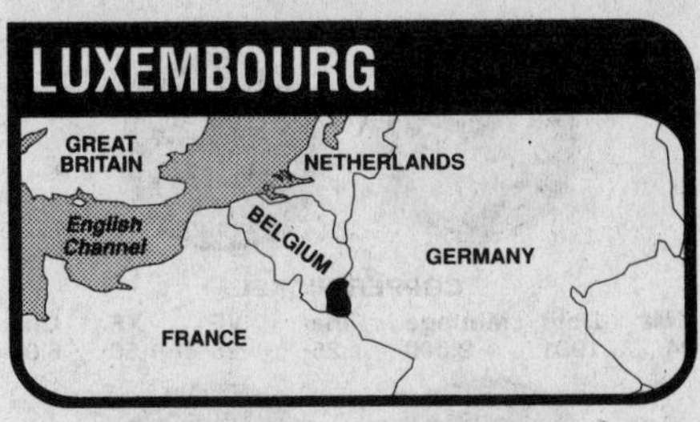

The Grand Duchy of Luxembourg is located in western Europe between Belgium, Germany and France, has an area of 998 sq. mi. (2,586 sq. km.) and a population of 377,100. Capital: Luxembourg. The economy is based on steel - Luxembourg's per capita production of 16 tons is the highest in the world.

Founded about 963, Luxembourg was a prominent country of the Holy Roman Empire; one of its sovereigns became Holy Roman Emperor as Henry VII, 1308. After being made a duchy by Emperor Charles IV, 1354, Luxembourg passed under the domination of Burgundy, Spain, Austria and France, 1443-1815, regaining autonomy under the Treaty of Vienna, 1815, as a grand duchy in union with the Netherlands, though ostensibly a member of the German Confederation. When Belgium seceded from the Kingdom of the Netherlands, 1830, Luxembourg was forced to cede its greater western section to Belgium. The tiny duchy left the German Confederation in 1867 when the Treaty of London recognized it as an independent state and guaranteed its perpetual neutrality. Luxembourg was occupied by Germany and liberated by American troops in both World Wars, and is the resting place of 5,000 American soldiers, including Gen. George S. Patton.

RULERS

William III (Netherlands), 1849-1890
Adolphe, 1890-1905
William IV, 1905-1912
Marie Adelaide, 1912-1919
Charlotte, 1919-1964
Jean, 1964

MINT MARKS

A - Paris
(b) - Brussels, privy marks only
(u) - Utrecht, privy marks only

PRIVY MARKS

Angels head, two headed eagle - Brussels
Anchor, hand - Paris, (1846-60)
Anchor, bee - Paris, (1860-79)
Sword, Caduceus - Utrecht (1846-74 although struck at Brussels until 1909)

MONETARY SYSTEM

100 Centimes = 1 Franc

2-1/2 CENTIMES

BRONZE

KM#	Date	Mintage	Fine	VF	XF	Unc
21	1854(u)	.640	1.00	3.00	7.50	25.00
	1870(u) dot above BARTH on rev.					
		.210	2.00	8.00	15.00	30.00
	1870(u) w/o dot above BARTH on rev.					
		Inc. Ab.	2.50	10.00	18.50	42.50
	1901(u)	.800	1.00	2.00	3.50	12.50
	1908(u)	.400	1.00	2.50	4.00	14.00

5 CENTIMES

BRONZE

KM#	Date	Mintage	Fine	VF	XF	Unc
22.1	1854(u)	.680	1.50	4.00	12.50	30.00
	1870(u)	.304	2.00	4.50	12.50	30.00
	Mint mark: A					
22.2	1855	.600	1.50	4.00	12.50	30.00
	1860	.200	7.50	15.00	25.00	60.00

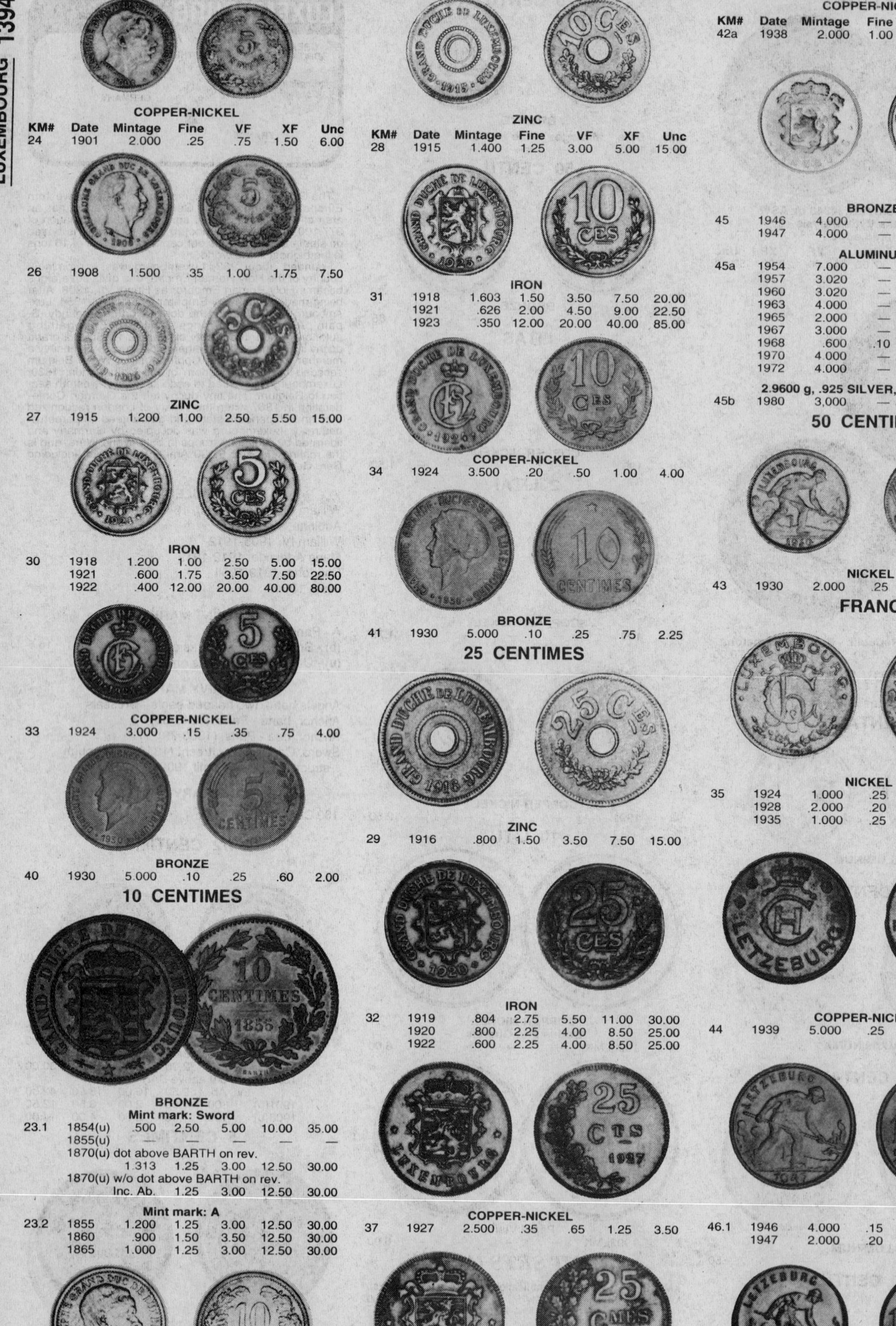

COPPER-NICKEL

KM#	Date	Mintage	Fine	VF	XF	Unc
24	1901	2.000	.25	.75	1.50	6.00
26	1908	1.500	.35	1.00	1.75	7.50

ZINC

KM#	Date	Mintage	Fine	VF	XF	Unc
27	1915	1.200	1.00	2.50	5.50	15.00

IRON

KM#	Date	Mintage	Fine	VF	XF	Unc
30	1918	1.200	1.00	2.50	5.00	15.00
	1921	.600	1.75	3.50	7.50	22.50
	1922	.400	12.00	20.00	40.00	80.00

COPPER-NICKEL

KM#	Date	Mintage	Fine	VF	XF	Unc
33	1924	3.000	.15	.35	.75	4.00

BRONZE

KM#	Date	Mintage	Fine	VF	XF	Unc
40	1930	5.000	.10	.25	.60	2.00

10 CENTIMES

BRONZE
Mint mark: Sword

KM#	Date	Mintage	Fine	VF	XF	Unc
23.1	1854(u)	.500	2.50	5.00	10.00	35.00
	1855(u)	—	—	—	—	—
	1870(u) dot above BARTH on rev.	1.313	1.25	3.00	12.50	30.00
	1870(u) w/o dot above BARTH on rev.	Inc. Ab.	1.25	3.00	12.50	30.00

Mint mark: A

KM#	Date	Mintage	Fine	VF	XF	Unc
23.2	1855	1.200	1.25	3.00	12.50	30.00
	1860	.900	1.50	3.50	12.50	30.00
	1865	1.000	1.25	3.00	12.50	30.00

COPPER-NICKEL

KM#	Date	Mintage	Fine	VF	XF	Unc
25	1901	4.000	.25	.75	1.50	7.50

ZINC

KM#	Date	Mintage	Fine	VF	XF	Unc
28	1915	1.400	1.25	3.00	5.00	15.00

IRON

KM#	Date	Mintage	Fine	VF	XF	Unc
31	1918	1.603	1.50	3.50	7.50	20.00
	1921	.626	2.00	4.50	9.00	22.50
	1923	.350	12.00	20.00	40.00	85.00

COPPER-NICKEL

KM#	Date	Mintage	Fine	VF	XF	Unc
34	1924	3.500	.20	.50	1.00	4.00

BRONZE

KM#	Date	Mintage	Fine	VF	XF	Unc
41	1930	5.000	.10	.25	.75	2.25

25 CENTIMES

ZINC

KM#	Date	Mintage	Fine	VF	XF	Unc
29	1916	.800	1.50	3.50	7.50	15.00

IRON

KM#	Date	Mintage	Fine	VF	XF	Unc
32	1919	.804	2.75	5.50	11.00	30.00
	1920	.800	2.25	4.00	8.50	25.00
	1922	.600	2.25	4.00	8.50	25.00

COPPER-NICKEL

KM#	Date	Mintage	Fine	VF	XF	Unc
37	1927	2.500	.35	.65	1.25	3.50

BRONZE

KM#	Date	Mintage	Fine	VF	XF	Unc
42	1930	1.000	.25	.75	1.50	5.00

COPPER-NICKEL

KM#	Date	Mintage	Fine	VF	XF	Unc
42a	1938	2.000	1.00	2.00	4.00	7.00

BRONZE

KM#	Date	Mintage	Fine	VF	XF	Unc
45	1946	4.000	—	.15	.25	.75
	1947	4.000	—	.15	.25	.75

ALUMINUM

KM#	Date	Mintage	Fine	VF	XF	Unc
45a	1954	7.000	—	—	—	.10
	1957	3.020	—	—	—	.10
	1960	3.020	—	—	—	.10
	1963	4.000	—	—	—	.10
	1965	2.000	—	—	—	.10
	1967	3.000	—	—	—	.10
	1968	.600	.10	.25	.50	1.00
	1970	4.000	—	—	—	.10
	1972	4.000	—	—	—	.10

2.9600 g, .925 SILVER, .0880 oz ASW

KM#	Date	Mintage	Fine	VF	XF	Unc
45b	1980	3,000	—	—	Proof	12.00

50 CENTIMES

NICKEL

KM#	Date	Mintage	Fine	VF	XF	Unc
43	1930	2.000	.25	.50	1.00	5.00

FRANC

NICKEL

KM#	Date	Mintage	Fine	VF	XF	Unc
35	1924	1.000	.25	.75	1.25	8.00
	1928	2.000	.20	.50	1.00	7.00
	1935	1.000	.25	.75	1.25	6.00

COPPER-NICKEL

KM#	Date	Mintage	Fine	VF	XF	Unc
44	1939	5.000	.25	.75	1.50	5.00
46.1	1946	4.000	.15	.35	.50	1.00
	1947	2.000	.20	.40	.75	1.00
46.2	1952	5.000	.10	.25	.50	1.00

KM#	Date	Mintage	Fine	VF	XF	Unc
46.3	1953	2.000	—	.10	.15	.40
	1955	1.000	—	.10	.15	.40
	1957	2.000	—	.10	.15	.40
	1960	2.000	—	.10	.15	.40
	1962	2.000	—	.10	.15	.40
	1964	2.000	—	.10	.15	.40

4.4500 g, .925 SILVER, .1323 oz ASW

KM#	Date	Mintage	Fine	VF	XF	Unc
46.3a	1980	3,000	—	—	Proof	20.00

COPPER-NICKEL

KM#	Date	Mintage	Fine	VF	XF	Unc
55	1965	3.000	—	—	.10	.20
	1966	1.000	—	—	.10	.20
	1968	3.000	—	—	.10	.20
	1970	3.000	—	—	.10	.20
	1972	3.000	—	—	.10	.20
	1973	3.000	—	—	.10	.20
	1976	3.000	—	—	.10	.20
	1977	1.000	—	—	.10	.20
	1978	3.000	—	—	.10	.20
	1979	2.775	—	—	.10	.20
	1980	4.000	—	—	.10	.20
	1981	5.000	—	—	.10	.20
	1982	3.000	—	—	.10	.20
	1983	3.000	—	—	.10	.20
	1984	3.000	—	—	.10	.20

4.4700 g, .925 SILVER, .1329 oz ASW

KM#	Date	Mintage	Fine	VF	XF	Unc
55a	1980	3,000	—	—	Proof	20.00

COPPER-NICKEL

KM#	Date	Mintage	Fine	VF	XF	Unc
59	1986	3.000	—	—	.10	.20
	1987	3.000	—	—	.10	.20

NICKEL-STEEL

KM#	Date	Mintage	Fine	VF	XF	Unc
63	1988	3.000	—	—	—	.40
	1989	3.000	—	—	—	.40
	1990	25.000	—	—	—	.40
	1991	—	—	—	—	.40
	1992	—	—	—	—	.40
	1993	—	—	—	—	.40

2 FRANCS

NICKEL

KM#	Date	Mintage	Fine	VF	XF	Unc
36	1924	1.000	1.00	2.25	4.00	15.00

5 FRANCS

8.0000 g, .750 SILVER, .1929 oz ASW

KM#	Date	Mintage	Fine	VF	XF	Unc
38	1929	2.000	BV	2.50	5.00	15.00

COPPER-NICKEL

KM#	Date	Mintage	Fine	VF	XF	Unc
50	1949	2.000	.30	.60	1.00	2.50

KM#	Date	Mintage	Fine	VF	XF	Unc
51	1962	2.000	.10	.25	.40	.75

6.7400 g, .925 SILVER, .2004 oz ASW

KM#	Date	Mintage	Fine	VF	XF	Unc
51a	1980	3,000	—	—	Proof	27.50

COPPER-NICKEL

KM#	Date	Mintage	Fine	VF	XF	Unc
56	1971	1.000	—	—	.15	.50
	1976	1.000	—	—	.15	.50
	1979	1.000	—	—	.15	.50
	1981	1.000	—	—	.15	.50

6.7800 g, .925 SILVER, .2016 oz ASW

KM#	Date	Mintage	Fine	VF	XF	Unc
56a	1980	3,000	—	—	Proof	27.50

BRASS

KM#	Date	Mintage	Fine	VF	XF	Unc
60.1	1986	9.000	—	—	.15	.40
	1987	7.000	—	—	.15	.40
	1988	2.000	—	—	.15	.40

Rev: Larger crown w/cross touching rim.

KM#	Date	Mintage	Fine	VF	XF	Unc
60.2	1988	Inc. Ab.	—	—	.15	.40

KM#	Date	Mintage	Fine	VF	XF	Unc
65	1989	2.000	—	—	—	.60
	1990	4.000	—	—	—	.60
	1991	—	—	—	—	.60
	1992	—	—	—	—	.60
	1993	—	—	—	—	.60

10 FRANCS

13.3900 g, .750 SILVER, .3228 oz ASW

KM#	Date	Mintage	Fine	VF	XF	Unc
39	1929	1.000	BV	4.50	9.00	25.00

NICKEL

KM#	Date	Mintage	Fine	VF	XF	Unc
57	1971	3.000	—	—	.30	.60
	1972	3.000	—	—	.30	.60
	1974	3.000	—	—	.30	.60
	1976	3.000	—	—	.30	.60
	1977	3.000	—	—	.30	.60
	1978	3.000	—	—	.30	.60
	1979	1.000	—	—	.30	.60
	1980	1.000	—	—	.30	.60

8.7900 g, .925 SILVER, .2614 oz ASW

KM#	Date	Mintage	Fine	VF	XF	Unc
57a	1980	3,000	—	—	Proof	30.00

20 FRANCS

8.5000 g, .835 SILVER, .2282 oz ASW
600th Anniversary John the Blind

KM#	Date	Mintage	Fine	VF	XF	Unc
47	1946	.100	—	—	8.00	16.50

BRONZE

KM#	Date	Mintage	Fine	VF	XF	Unc
58	1980	3.000	—	—	.60	1.00
	1981	3.000	—	—	.60	1.00
	1982	3.000	—	—	.60	1.00
	1983	2.000	—	—	.60	1.00

10.2100 g, .925 SILVER, .3036 oz ASW

KM#	Date	Mintage	Fine	VF	XF	Unc
58a	1980	3,000	—	—	Proof	35.00

6.2200 g, .999 GOLD, .200 oz AGW
150th Anniversary of the Grand Duchy

KM#	Date	Mintage	Fine	VF	XF	Unc
64	1989	.050	—	—	—	125.00

BRONZE

KM#	Date	Mintage	Fine	VF	XF	Unc
67	1990	1.100	—	—	—	2.00
	1991	—	—	—	—	2.00
	1992	—	—	—	—	2.00
	1993	—	—	—	—	2.00

50 FRANCS

12.5000 g, .835 SILVER, .3356 oz ASW
600th Anniversary John the Blind

KM#	Date	Mintage	Fine	VF	XF	Unc
48	1946	.100	—	—	12.50	18.00

NICKEL

KM#	Date	Mintage	Fine	VF	XF	Unc
62	1987	3.000	—	—	1.50	3.50
	1988	1.000	—	—	1.50	3.50

Similar to 5 Francs, KM#65.

KM#	Date	Mintage	Fine	VF	XF	Unc
66	1989	3.200	—	—	—	3.50
	1990	2.000	—	—	—	3.50
	1991	—	—	—	—	3.50
	1992	—	—	—	—	3.50
	1993	—	—	—	—	3.50

100 FRANCS

25.0000 g, .835 SILVER, .6711 oz ASW
600th Anniversary John the Blind

KM#	Date	Mintage	Fine	VF	XF	Unc
49	1946	.098	—	—	22.50	40.00
	1946 w/o designer's name	2,000 (restrike)	—	—	—	120.00

18.0000 g, .835 SILVER .4832 oz ASW

KM#	Date	Mintage	Fine	VF	XF	Unc
52	1963	.050	—	—	10.00	15.00

KM#	Date	Mintage	Fine	VF	XF	Unc
54	1964	.054	—	—	7.50	12.50

250 FRANCS

25.0000 g, .900 SILVER, .7234 oz ASW
Millennium of Luxembourg City

KM#	Date	Mintage	Fine	VF	XF	Unc
53.1	1963	.011	—	—	45.00	60.00

"Dark toned" by the mint

KM#	Date	Mintage	Fine	VF	XF	Unc
53.2	1963	8,500	—	—	50.00	70.00

MINT SETS (MS)

KM#	Date	Mintage	Identification	Issue Price	Mkt. Val.
MS1	1990	10,000	KM63,65.1,66-67	—	14.00
MS2	1991	10,000	KM63,65.1,66-67	—	14.00

PROOF SETS (PS)

KM#	Date	Mintage	Identification	Issue Price	Mkt. Val.
PS1	1980(7)	3,000	KM45b,46.3a,51a,55a-58a	—	175.00

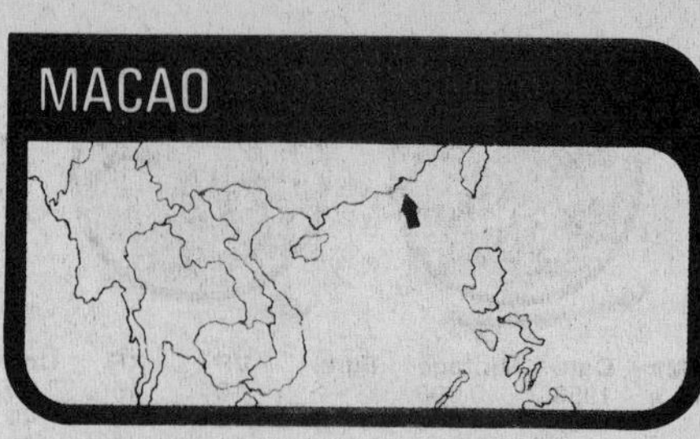

MACAO

The Province of Macao, a Portuguese overseas province located in the South China Sea 40 miles southwest of Hong Kong, consists of the peninsula of Macao and the islands of Taipa and Coloane. It has an area of 6.2 sq. mi. (16 sq. km.) and a population of 500,000. Capital: Macao. Macao's economy is based on light industry, commerce, tourism, fishing, and gold trading -Macao is one of the entirely free markets for gold in the world. Cement, textiles, fireworks, vegetable oils, and metal products are exported.

Established by the Portuguese in 1557, Macao is the oldest European settlement in the Far East. The Chinese, while agreeing to Portuguese settlement, did not recognize Portuguese sovereign rights and the Portuguese remained largely under control of the Chinese until 1849, when the Portuguese abolished the Chinese custom house and declared the independence of the port. The Manchu government formally recognized the Portuguese right to 'perpetual occupation' of Macao in 1887.

In 1987, Portugal and China agreed that Macao will become a Chinese Territory from 1999 on.

RULERS

Portuguese

MINT MARKS

(p) - Pobjoy Mint
(s) - Singapore Mint

Pobjoy Mint **Singapore Mint**

MONETARY SYSTEM

100 Avos = 1 Pataca

5 AVOS

BRONZE

KM#	Date	Mintage	VF	XF	Unc
1	1952	.500	1.00	2.00	5.00

NICKEL-BRASS

KM#	Date	Mintage	VF	XF	Unc
1a	1967	5.000	—	.10	.25

10 AVOS

BRONZE

KM#	Date	Mintage	VF	XF	Unc
2	1952	12.500	.30	.60	1.50

NICKEL-BRASS

KM#	Date	Mintage	VF	XF	Unc
2a	1967	5.525	.15	.25	.40
	1968	6.975	.15	.25	.40
	1975	20.000	.10	.20	.35
	1976	Inc. Ab.	.10	.20	.35

BRASS

KM#	Date	Mintage	VF	XF	Unc
20	1982	24.580	—	.10	.20
	1983	—	—	.10	.20
	1984	—	—	.10	.20
	1985	—	—	.10	.20
	1988	—	—	.10	.20

3.2000 g, .925 SILVER, .0952 oz ASW

KM#	Date	Mintage	VF	XF	Unc
20a	1982	2,000	—	Proof	7.50
	1983	2,500	—	Proof	5.00
	1984	2,500	—	Proof	5.00
	1985	2,500	—	Proof	5.00

4.0000 g, .917 GOLD, .1179 oz AGW

KM#	Date	Mintage	VF	XF	Unc
20b	1982	150 pcs.	—	Proof	100.00

4.5000 g, .950 PLATINUM, .1374 oz APW

KM#	Date	Mintage	VF	XF	Unc
20c	1982	375 pcs.	—	Proof	125.00

20 AVOS

BRASS

KM#	Date	Mintage	VF	XF	Unc
21	1982	9.960	—	.10	.25
	1983	—	—	.10	.25
	1984	—	—	.10	.25
	1985	—	—	.10	.25

4.6000 g, .925 SILVER, .1368 oz ASW

KM#	Date	Mintage	VF	XF	Unc
21a	1982	2,000	—	Proof	10.00
	1983	2,500	—	Proof	7.50
	1984	2,500	—	Proof	7.50
	1985	2,500	—	Proof	7.50

5.5000 g, .917 GOLD, .1621 oz AGW

KM#	Date	Mintage	VF	XF	Unc
21b	1982	150 pcs.	—	Proof	150.00

6.2000 g, .950 PLATINUM, .1893 oz APW

KM#	Date	Mintage	VF	XF	Unc
21c	1982	375 pcs.	—	Proof	175.00

50 AVOS

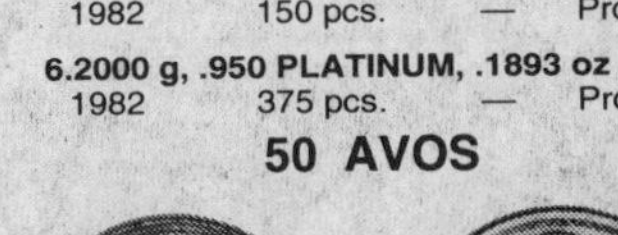

COPPER-NICKEL

KM#	Date	Mintage	VF	XF	Unc
3	1952	2.560	.50	1.00	3.00

KM#	Date	Mintage	VF	XF	Unc
7	1972	1.600	.25	.35	.75
	1973	4.840	.25	.35	.75

KM#	Date	Mintage	VF	XF	Unc
9	1978	3.000	.10	.30	.65

BRASS

KM#	Date	Mintage	VF	XF	Unc
22	1982	16.952	—	.10	.30
	1983	—	—	.10	.30
	1984	—	—	.10	.30
	1985	—	—	.10	.30

5.7000 g, .925 SILVER, .1695 oz ASW

KM#	Date	Mintage	VF	XF	Unc
22a	1982	2,000	—	Proof	12.50
	1983	2,500	—	Proof	10.00
	1984	2,500	—	Proof	10.00
	1985	2,500	—	Proof	10.00

7.4000 g, .917 GOLD, .2181 oz AGW

KM#	Date	Mintage	VF	XF	Unc
22b	1982	150 pcs.	—	Proof	175.00

8.4000 g, .950 PLATINUM, .2565 oz APW

KM#	Date	Mintage	VF	XF	Unc
22c	1982	375 pcs.	—	Proof	200.00

PATACA

3.0000 g, .720 SILVER, .0694 oz ASW

KM#	Date	Mintage	VF	XF	Unc
4	1952	4.500	1.00	2.00	4.00

NICKEL

KM#	Date	Mintage	VF	XF	Unc
6	1968	5.000	.35	.50	1.25
	1975	6.000	.20	.30	1.00

COPPER-NICKEL

KM#	Date	Mintage	VF	XF	Unc
6a	1980	—	.20	.30	1.00

Obv: High stars.

KM#	Date	Mintage	VF	XF	Unc
23.1	1982(s)	6.427	.20	.40	.80
	1983(s)	—	.20	.40	.80
	1984(s)	—	.20	.40	.80
	1985(s)	—	.20	.40	.80

9.0000 g, .925 SILVER, .2677 oz ASW

KM#	Date	Mintage	VF	XF	Unc
23.1a	1982(s)	2,000	—	Proof	15.00
	1983(s)	2,500	—	Proof	12.50
	1984(s)	2,500	—	Proof	12.50
	1985(s)	2,500	—	Proof	12.50

11.6000 g, .917 GOLD, .3420 oz AGW

KM#	Date	Mintage	VF	XF	Unc
23.1b	1982(s)	150 pcs.	—	Proof	250.00

13.2000 g, .950 PLATINUM, .4032 oz APW

KM#	Date	Mintage	VF	XF	Unc
23.1c	1982(s)	375 pcs.	—	Proof	325.00

COPPER-NICKEL
Obv: Low stars.

KM#	Date	Mintage	VF	XF	Unc
23.2	1982(p)	—	.20	.40	.80
	1983(p)	—	.20	.40	.80

5.7000 g, .925 SILVER, .1695 oz ASW

KM#	Date	Mintage	VF	XF	Unc
23.2a	1982(p)	—	—	Proof	15.00

COPPER-NICKEL

KM#	Date	Mintage	VF	XF	Unc
57	1992	—	—	—	1.25

5 PATACAS

15.0000 g, .720 SILVER, .3472 oz ASW

KM#	Date	Mintage	VF	XF	Unc
5	1952	.900	4.00	5.00	8.00

10.0000 g, .650 SILVER, .2089 oz ASW

KM#	Date	Mintage	VF	XF	Unc
5a	1971	.500	3.00	4.00	6.50

COPPER-NICKEL
Obv: High stars.

KM#	Date	Mintage	VF	XF	Unc
24.1	1982(s)	1.102	.75	1.25	2.50
	1983(s)	—	.75	1.25	2.50
	1984(s)	—	.75	1.25	2.50
	1985(s)	—	.75	1.25	2.50
	1988(s)	—	.75	1.25	2.50

10.7000 g, .925 SILVER, .3182 oz ASW

KM#	Date	Mintage	VF	XF	Unc
24.1a	1982(s)	2,000	—	Proof	30.00
	1983(s)	2,500	—	Proof	25.00
	1984(s)	2,500	—	Proof	25.00
	1985(s)	2,500	—	Proof	25.00

16.3000 g, .917 GOLD, .4808 oz AGW

KM#	Date	Mintage	VF	XF	Unc
24.1b	1982(s)	150 pcs.	—	Proof	350.00

18.4000 g, .950 PLATINUM, .5620 oz APW

KM#	Date	Mintage	VF	XF	Unc
24.1c	1982(s)	375 pcs.	—	Proof	425.00

COPPER-NICKEL
Obv: Low stars.

KM#	Date	Mintage	VF	XF	Unc
24.2	1982(p)	—	.75	1.25	2.50

10.7000 g, .925 SILVER, .3182 oz ASW

KM#	Date	Mintage	VF	XF	Unc
24.2a	1982(p)	—	—	Proof	30.00

COPPER-NICKEL

KM#	Date	Mintage	VF	XF	Unc
56	1992	—	—	—	3.50

20 PATACAS

18.0000 g, .650 SILVER, .3762 oz ASW
Opening of Macao-Taipa Bridge

KM#	Date	Mintage	VF	XF	Unc
8	1974	1.000	—	7.50	12.50

100 PATACAS

28.2800 g, .925 SILVER, .8411 oz ASW
25th Anniversary of Grand Prix

KM#	Date	Mintage	VF	XF	Unc
10	1978	610 pcs.	—	Proof	100.00

COPPER-NICKEL

KM#	Date	Mintage	VF	XF	Unc
10a	1978	—	—	—	325.00

28.2800 g, .925 SILVER, .8411 oz ASW
Rev: Racing car w/o advertising.

KM#	Date	Mintage	VF	XF	Unc
11	1978	5,500	—	Proof	35.00

Year of the Goat

KM#	Date	Mintage	VF	XF	Unc
14	1979(s)	5,500	—	Proof	35.00

Year of the Monkey

KM#	Date	Mintage	VF	XF	Unc
16	1980	—	—	—	35.00
	1980	2,000	—	Proof	50.00

Year of the Cockerel

KM#	Date	Mintage	VF	XF	Unc
18	1981(p)	1,000	—	—	35.00
	1981(p)	1,000	—	Proof	50.00

Year of the Dog

KM#	Date	Mintage	VF	XF	Unc
25	1982(p)	500 pcs.	—	—	40.00
	1982(p)	500 pcs.	—	Proof	65.00
	1982(s)	500 pcs.	—	—	40.00
	1982(s)	3,500	—	Proof	50.00

Year of the Pig

KM#	Date	Mintage	VF	XF	Unc
27	1983(s)	2,500	—	—	35.00
	1983(s)	2,500	—	Proof	45.00

Year of the Rat

KM#	Date	Mintage	VF	XF	Unc
29	1984(s)	2,000	—	—	35.00
	1984(s)	5,000	—	Proof	45.00

Year of the Ox

KM#	Date	Mintage	VF	XF	Unc
31	1985(s)	.010	—	—	35.00
	1985(s)	5,000	—	Proof	45.00

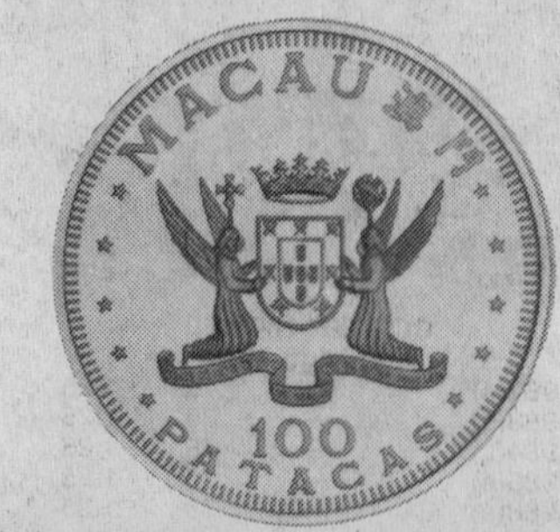

Visit of Portugal's President Eanes

KM#	Date	Mintage	VF	XF	Unc
33	1985(s)	3,000	—	—	30.00
	1985(s)	2,000	—	Proof	40.00

Year of the Tiger

KM#	Date	Mintage	VF	XF	Unc
34	1986(s)	2,000	—	—	50.00
	1986(s)	3,000	—	Proof	60.00

Year of the Rabbit

KM#	Date	Mintage	VF	XF	Unc
36	1987(s)	—	—	—	40.00
	1987(s)	5,000	—	Proof	45.00

Year of the Dragon
Similar to 1000 Patacas, KM#39.

KM#	Date	Mintage	VF	XF	Unc
38	1988	—	—	—	40.00
	1988	5,000	—	Proof	45.00

35th Anniversary of Grand Prix
Rev: Similar to 500 Patacas, KM#42.

KM#	Date	Mintage	VF	XF	Unc
40	1988	5,000	—	Proof	45.00

PLATINUM

KM#	Date	Mintage	VF	XF	Unc
40a	1988	10 pcs.	—	Proof	3350.

28.2800 g, .925 SILVER, .8411 oz ASW
Year of the Snake

Similar to 1000 Patacas, KM#45.

KM#	Date	Mintage	VF	XF	Unc
44	1989(s)	2,000	—	—	40.00
	1989(s)	3,000	—	Proof	55.00

Year of the Horse

KM#	Date	Mintage	VF	XF	Unc
46	1990(s)	1,000	—	—	40.00
	1990(s)	4,000	—	Proof	55.00

Year of the Goat
Similar to 1000 Patacas, KM#51.

KM#	Date	Mintage	VF	XF	Unc
48	1991(s)	1,000	—	—	150.00
	1991(s)	*4,000	—	Proof	50.00

Year of the Monkey

KM#	Date	Mintage	VF	XF	Unc
52	1992(s)	1,000	—	—	155.00
	1992(s)	*4,000	—	Proof	50.00

Year of the Rooster

KM#	Date	Mintage	VF	XF	Unc
58	1993	500 pcs.	—	—	160.00
	1993	*4,000	—	Proof	45.00

Macao Grand Prix

KM#	Date	Mintage	VF	XF	Unc
62	1993	5,000	—	Proof	50.00

250 PATACAS

3.9900 g, .917 GOLD, .1176 oz AGW
Year of the Goat
Similar to 1000 Patacas, KM#51.

KM#	Date	Mintage	VF	XF	Unc
49	1991	*2,500	—	Proof	100.00

Year of the Monkey
Obv: Similar to 1000 Patacas, KM#51. Rev: Monkey.

KM#	Date	Mintage	VF	XF	Unc
53	1992	*2,500	—	Proof	120.00

Year of the Rooster
Similar to 100 Patacas, KM#59.

KM#	Date	Mintage	VF	XF	Unc
59	1993	*2,500	—	Proof	120.00

500 PATACAS

7.9600 g, .917 GOLD, .2347 oz AGW
25th Anniversary of Grand Prix

KM#	Date	Mintage	VF	XF	Unc
12	1978	550 pcs.	—	Proof	325.00

Rev: Racing car w/o advertising.

KM#	Date	Mintage	VF	XF	Unc
13	1978	5,500	—	Proof	190.00

Year of the Goat

KM#	Date	Mintage	VF	XF	Unc
15	1979	5,500	—	Proof	175.00

155.5150 g, .999 SILVER, 5.0000 oz ASW
35th Anniversary of Grand Prix
Similar to KM#42.

KM#	Date	Mintage	VF	XF	Unc
41	1988	2,000	—	Proof	150.00

7.9881 g, .917 GOLD, .2354 oz AGW
35th Anniversary of Grand Prix

KM#	Date	Mintage	VF	XF	Unc
42	1988	4,500	—	Proof	225.00

Year of the Goat
Similar to 1000 Patacas, KM#51.

KM#	Date	Mintage	VF	XF	Unc
50	1991	*2,500	—	Proof	200.00

7.9900 g, .917 GOLD, .2352 oz AGW
Year of the Monkey
Obv: Similar to 1000 Patacas, KM#51. Rev: Monkey.

KM#	Date	Mintage	VF	XF	Unc
54	1992	*2,500	—	Proof	230.00

Year of the Rooster
Similar to 100 Patacas, KM#58.

KM#	Date	Mintage	VF	XF	Unc
60	1993	*2,500	—	Proof	230.00

155.6000 g, .999 SILVER, 5.0000 oz ASW
Macao Grand Prix

KM#	Date	Mintage	VF	XF	Unc
63	1993	2,000	—	Proof	150.00

7.9600 g, .917 GOLD, .2352 oz AGW

KM#	Date	Mintage	VF	XF	Unc
64	1993	4,500	—	Proof	250.00

1000 PATACAS

15.9760 g, .917 GOLD, .4711 oz AGW
Year of the Monkey

KM#	Date	Mintage	VF	XF	Unc
17	1980	5,500		Proof	400.00

Year of the Cockerel

KM#	Date	Mintage	VF	XF	Unc
19	1981	3,500	—	—	300.00
	1981	Inc. Ab.	—	Proof	325.00

Year of the Dog

KM#	Date	Mintage	VF	XF	Unc
26	1982	256 pcs.	—	—	350.00
	1982	255 pcs.	—	Proof	525.00

Year of the Pig

KM#	Date	Mintage	VF	XF	Unc
28	1983	400 pcs.	—	—	375.00
	1983	500 pcs.	—	Proof	475.00

Year of the Rat

KM#	Date	Mintage	VF	XF	Unc
30	1984	2,000	—	—	300.00
	1984	3,000	—	Proof	350.00

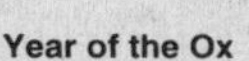

Year of the Ox

KM#	Date	Mintage	VF	XF	Unc
32	1985	.010	—	—	250.00
	1985	5,000	—	Proof	325.00

Year of the Tiger

35	1986	2,000	—	—	250.00
	1986	3,000	—	Proof	300.00

Year of the Rabbit

37	1987	—	—	—	250.00
	1987	5,000	—	Proof	300.00

Year of the Dragon

39	1988	5,000	—	Proof	300.00

Year of the Snake

45	1989	2,000	—	—	275.00
	1989	3,000	—	Proof	350.00

Year of the Horse

47	1990	2,000	—	—	275.00
	1990	3,000	—	Proof	350.00

Year of the Goat

51	1991	*500 pcs.	—	—	400.00
	1991	*4,500	—	Proof	475.00

Year of the Monkey

KM#	Date	Mintage	VF	XF	Unc
55	1992	*500 pcs.	—	—	400.00
	1992	*4,500	—	Proof	475.00

Year of the Rooster
Similar to 100 Patacas, KM#58.

61	1993	*500 pcs.	—	—	400.00
	1993	*4,500	—	Proof	475.00

10,000 PATACAS

155.5150 g, .999 GOLD, 5.0000 oz AGW
35th Anniversary of Grand Prix
Similar to 500 Patacas, KM#42.

43	1988	500 pcs.	—	Proof	3250.

Macao Grand Prix
Similar to 500 Patacas, KM#64.

65	1993	500 pcs.	—	Proof	3250.

PROOF SETS (PS)

KM#	Date	Mintage	Identification	Issue Price	Mkt. Val.
PS1	1982(5)	2,000	KM20a-24a	—	75.00
PS1b	1982(5)	150	KM20b-24b	—	1025.
PS1c	1982(5)	375	KM20c-24c	—	1250.
PS2	1983(5)	2,500	KM20a-24a	55.00	60.00
PS3	1984(5)	2,500	KM20a-24a	55.00	60.00
PS4	1985(5)	2,500	KM20a-24a	55.00	60.00
PS5	1987(2)	—	KM36-37	—	360.00
PS6	1988(2)	—	KM38-39	—	360.00
PS7	1991(3)	2,500	KM49-51	775.00	775.00
PS8	1992(3)	2,500	KM53-55	825.00	825.00
PS9	1993(3)	2,500	KM59-61	830.00	830.00

MACEDONIA

The Republic of Macedonia is land-locked, and is bordered in the north by Yugoslavia, to the east by Bulgaria, in the south by Greece and to the west by Albania and has an area of 9,923 sq. mi. (25,713 sq. km.) and a population at the 1991 census was 2,038,847, of which the predominating ethnic groups were Macedonians. The capital is Skopje.

The Slavs settled in Macedonia since the 6th century, who had been Christianized by Byzantium, were conquered by the non-Slav Bulgars in the 7th century and in the 9th century formed a Macedo-Bulgarian empire, the western part of which survived until Byzantine conquest in 1014. In the 14th century, it fell to Serbia, and in 1355 to the Ottomans. After the Balkan Wars of 1912-13 Turkey was ousted, and Serbia received the greater part of the territory, the balance going to Bulgaria and Greece. In 1918, Yugoslav Macedonia was incorporated into Serbia as 'South Serbia', becoming a republic in the S.F.R. of Yugoslavia. Claims to the historical Macedonian territory have long been a source of contention between Bulgaria and Greece.

On Nov. 20, 1991 parliament promulgated a new constitution, and declared its independence on Nov. 20, 1992, but failed to secure EC and US recognition owing to Greek objections to its use of the name "Macedonia".

On Dec. 11, 1992, the UN Security Council authorized the expedition of a small peacekeeping force to prevent hostilities spreading to Macedonia.

There is a 120-member single-chamber National Assembly.

50 DENI

BRASS
Seagull Flying Off Shore

KM#	Date	Mintage	Fine	VF	XF	Unc
1	1993	—	—	.10	.20	.50

DENAR

BRASS
Dog Standing Left

2	1993	—	—	.15	.30	.75

2 DENARI

BRASS
Fish Above Water

3	1993	—	—	.25	.50	1.25

5 DENARI

BRASS
Lynx

4	1993	—	—	.35	.75	1.75

MINT SETS (MS)

KM#	Date	Mintage	Identification	Mkt.Val.
MS1	1993(4)	—	KM1-4	5.50

MADAGASCAR

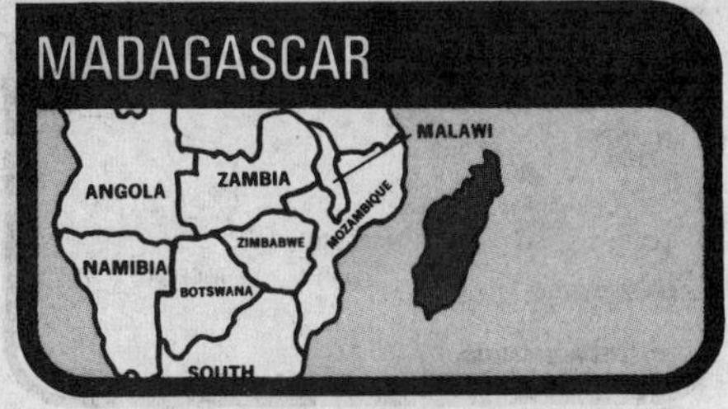

The Democratic Republic of Madagascar, an independent member of the French Community located in the Indian Ocean 250 miles (402 km.) off the southeast coast of Africa, has an area of 226,658 sq. mi. (587,040 sq. km.) and a population of 10 million. Capital: Antananarivo. The economy is primarily agricultural; large bauxite deposits are presently being developed. Coffee, vanilla, graphite, and rice are exported.

Successive waves of immigrants from south-east Asia, Africa, Arabia and India populated Madagascar beginning about 2,000 years ago. Diago Diaz, a Portuguese navigator, sighted the island of Madagascar on Aug. 10, 1500, when his ship became separated from an India-bound fleet. Attempts at settlement by the British during the reign of Charles I and by the French during the 17th and 18th centuries were of no avail, and the island became a refuge and supply base for Indian Ocean pirates. Despite considerable influence on the island, the British accepted the imposition of a French protectorate in 1886 in return for French recognition of Britain's sphere of influence in Zanzibar. Madagascar was made a French colony in 1896 after absolute control had been established by military force. Britain occupied the island after the fall of France, 1942, to prevent its seizure by the Japanese, returning it to the Free French in 1943. On Oct. 14, 1958, following a decade of intermittent but bitter warfare, Madagascar, as the Malagasy Republic, became an autonomous state within the French Community. On June 27, 1960, it became a sovereign, independent nation, though remaining nominally within the French Community. The Malagasy republic was renamed the Democratic Republic of Madagascar in 1975.

MONETARY SYSTEM

100 Centimes = 1 Franc

MINT MARKS

(a) - Paris, privy marks only
Pretoria

50 CENTIMES

BRONZE
Mint: Pretoria

KM#	Date	Mintage	Fine	VF	XF	Unc
1	1943	2.000	1.50	2.50	10.00	30.00

FRANC

BRONZE
Mint: Pretoria

KM#	Date	Mintage	Fine	VF	XF	Unc
2	1943	5.000	3.00	6.00	20.00	60.00

ALUMINUM

KM#	Date	Mintage	Fine	VF	XF	Unc
3	1948(a)	7.400	.15	.30	.50	2.00
	1958(a)	2.600	.15	.30	.50	2.25

2 FRANCS

ALUMINUM

KM#	Date	Mintage	Fine	VF	XF	Unc
4	1948(a)	10.000	.15	.35	.65	1.75

5 FRANCS

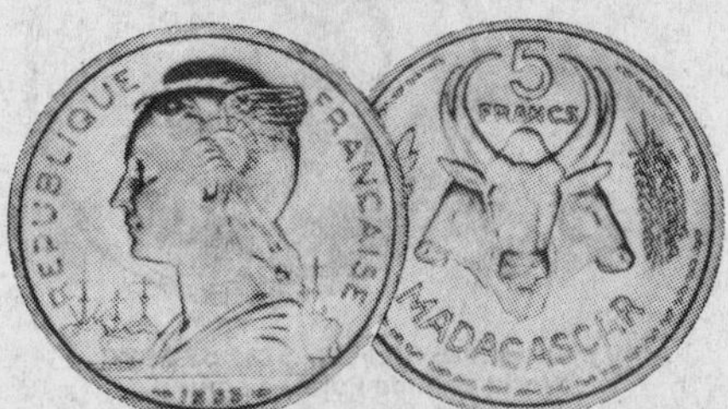

ALUMINUM

KM#	Date	Mintage	Fine	VF	XF	Unc
5	1953(a)	30.012	.25	.55	.85	2.00

10 FRANCS

ALUMINUM-BRONZE

KM#	Date	Mintage	Fine	VF	XF	Unc
6	1953(a)	25.000	.35	.65	1.25	3.00

20 FRANCS

ALUMINUM-BRONZE

KM#	Date	Mintage	Fine	VF	XF	Unc
7	1953(a)	15.000	.75	1.50	3.00	6.00

MALAGASY REPUBLIC

MINT MARKS

(a) - Paris, privy marks only

MONETARY SYSTEM

5 Francs = 1 Ariary

FRANC

STAINLESS STEEL

KM#	Date	Mintage	Fine	VF	XF	Unc
8	1965(a)	1.170	.10	.15	.30	1.00
	1966(a)	—	.10	.15	.30	1.00
	1970(a)	—	.10	.15	.30	1.00
	1974(a)	1.250	.10	.15	.30	1.00
	1975(a)	7.355	.10	.15	.30	1.00
	1976(a)	—	.10	.15	.30	1.00
	1977(a)	—	.10	.15	.30	1.00
	1979(a)	—	.10	.15	.30	1.00
	1980(a)	—	.15	.20	.40	1.20
	1981(a)	—	.15	.20	.40	1.20
	1982(a)	—	.15	.20	.40	1.20
	1983(a)	—	.15	.20	.40	1.20
	1986(a)	—	.15	.20	.40	1.20
	1987(a)	—	.15	.20	.40	1.20
	1988(a)	—	.15	.20	.40	1.20
	1989(a)	—	.15	.20	.40	1.20

2 FRANCS

STAINLESS STEEL

KM#	Date	Mintage	Fine	VF	XF	Unc
9	1965(a)	.760	.15	.25	.50	1.25
	1970(a)	—	.10	.20	.40	1.20
	1974(a)	1.250	.10	.20	.40	1.20
	1975(a)	8.250	.10	.20	.40	1.20
	1976(a)	—	.10	.20	.40	1.20
	1977(a)	—	.10	.20	.40	1.20
	1979(a)	—	.10	.20	.40	1.20
	1980(a)	—	.15	.25	.50	1.35
	1981(a)	—	.15	.25	.50	1.35
	1982(a)	—	.15	.25	.50	1.35
	1983(a)	—	.15	.25	.50	1.35
	1984(a)	—	.15	.25	.50	1.35
	1986(a)	—	.15	.25	.50	1.35
	1987(a)	—	.15	.25	.50	1.35
	1988(a)	—	.15	.25	.50	1.35
	1989(a)	—	.15	.25	.50	1.35

5 FRANCS - ARIARY

STAINLESS STEEL

KM#	Date	Mintage	Fine	VF	XF	Unc
10	1966(a)	—	.15	.25	.60	1.50
	1967(a)	—	.15	.25	.60	1.50
	1968(a)	7.500	.15	.25	.60	1.50
	1970(a)	—	.15	.25	.60	1.50
	1972(a)	19.100	.15	.25	.60	1.50
	1976(a)	—	.15	.25	.60	1.50
	1977(a)	—	.15	.25	.60	1.50
	1979(a)	—	.15	.25	.60	1.50
	1980(a)	—	.20	.30	.65	1.60
	1981(a)	—	.20	.30	.65	1.60
	1983(a)	—	.20	.30	.65	1.60
	1984(a)	—	.20	.30	.65	1.60
	1986(a)	—	.20	.30	.65	1.60
	1987(a)	—	.20	.30	.65	1.60
	1988(a)	—	.20	.30	.65	1.60
	1989(a)	—	.20	.30	.65	1.60

10 FRANCS - ROA (2) ARIARY

ALUMINUM-BRONZE
F.A.O. Issue

KM#	Date	Mintage	Fine	VF	XF	Unc
11	1970(a)	25.000	.20	.30	.70	1.75
	1971(a)	Inc. Ab.	.20	.30	.70	1.75
	1972(a)	Inc. Ab.	.20	.30	.70	1.75
	1973(a)	Inc. Ab.	.20	.30	.70	1.75
	1974(a)	—	.20	.30	.70	1.75
	1975(a)	—	.20	.30	.70	1.75
	1976(a)	9.500	.20	.30	.70	1.75
	1977(a)	—	.20	.30	.70	1.75
	1978(a)	—	.20	.30	.70	1.75
	1980(a)	—	.25	.35	.80	2.00
	1981(a)	—	.25	.35	.80	2.00
	1982(a)	—	.25	.35	.80	2.00
	1983(a)	—	.25	.35	.80	2.00
	1984(a)	—	.25	.35	.80	2.00
	1986(a)	—	.25	.35	.80	2.00
	1987(a)	3.200	.25	.35	.80	2.00
	1988(a)	—	.25	.35	.80	2.00
	1989(a)	—	.25	.35	.80	2.00

COPPER-PLATED STEEL

KM#	Date	Mintage	Fine	VF	XF	Unc
11a	1991	—	.25	.35	.80	2.00
	1992	—	.25	.35	.80	2.00

20 FRANCS - EFATRA (4) ARIARY

ALUMINUM-BRONZE
F.A.O. Issue

KM#	Date	Mintage	Fine	VF	XF	Unc
12	1970(a)	15.000	.25	.35	.75	2.25
	1971(a)	Inc. Ab.	.25	.35	.75	2.25
	1972(a)	Inc. Ab.	.30	.40	.80	2.50
	1973(a)	Inc. Ab.	.30	.40	.80	2.50
	1974(a)	—	.30	.40	.80	2.50
	1975(a)	—	.30	.40	.80	2.50
	1976(a)	2.700	.30	.40	.80	2.50
	1977(a)	—	.30	.40	.80	2.50
	1978(a)	—	.30	.40	.80	2.50
	1979(a)	—	.30	.40	.80	2.50

KM#	Date	Mintage	Fine	VF	XF	Unc
12	1981(a)	—	.35	.45	.85	2.75
	1982(a)	—	.35	.45	.85	2.75
	1983(a)	—	.35	.45	.85	2.75
	1984(a)	—	.35	.45	.85	2.75
	1986(a)	—	.35	.45	.85	2.75
	1987(a)	5.200	.35	.45	.85	2.75
	1988(a)	—	.35	.45	.85	2.75
	1989(a)	—	.35	.45	.85	2.75

FLEUR DE COIN SETS (SS)

KM#	Date	Mintage	Identification	Issue Price	Mkt. Val.
SS1	1970(5)	1,500	KM8-12	2.75	11.50

DEMOCRATIC REPUBLIC

5 ARIARY

COPPER PLATED STEEL
Rice Plant

KM#	Date	Mintage	Fine	VF	XF	Unc
17	1992	—	1.00	2.00	3.00	5.00

10 ARIARY

NICKEL
F.A.O. Issue

KM#	Date	Mintage	Fine	VF	XF	Unc
13	1978	8.001	1.50	2.50	4.50	10.00

9.0000 g, .925 SILVER, .2676 oz ASW

KM#	Date	Mintage	Fine	VF	XF	Unc
13a	1978	3,800	—	—	Proof	20.00

COPPER-NICKEL

KM#	Date	Mintage	Fine	VF	XF	Unc
13b	1983	—	1.00	2.00	4.00	9.00

10.0000 g, .917 GOLD, .2947 oz AGW
World Wildlife Fund - Ibis

KM#	Date	Mintage	Fine	VF	XF	Unc
16	1988	*5,000	—	—	Proof	225.50

STAINLESS STEEL
Cutting Peat

KM#	Date	Mintage	Fine	VF	XF	Unc
18	1992	—	1.00	2.00	4.00	8.00

20 ARIARY

NICKEL
F.A.O. Issue

KM#	Date	Mintage	Fine	VF	XF	Unc
14	1978	8.001	2.00	3.50	6.00	12.50

12.0000 g, .925 SILVER, .3569 oz ASW

KM#	Date	Mintage	Fine	VF	XF	Unc
14a	1978	3,800	—	—	Proof	25.00

COPPER-NICKEL

KM#	Date	Mintage	Fine	VF	XF	Unc
14b	1983	—	1.50	3.00	5.50	12.00

19.4400 g, .925 SILVER, .5782 oz ASW
World Wildlife Fund - Lemur

KM#	Date	Mintage	Fine	VF	XF	Unc
15	1988	*.025	—	—	Proof	50.00

STAINLESS STEEL
Tractor Pulling Plows

KM#	Date	Mintage	Fine	VF	XF	Unc
19	1992	—	1.50	2.50	4.50	10.00

50 ARIARY

STAINLESS STEEL

KM#	Date	Mintage	Fine	VF	XF	Unc
20	1992	—	2.50	4.00	8.00	15.00

PROOF SETS (PS)

KM#	Date	Mintage	Identification	Issue Price	Mkt. Val.
PS1	1978	3,800	KM13a,14a	38.00	45.00

MADEIRA ISLANDS

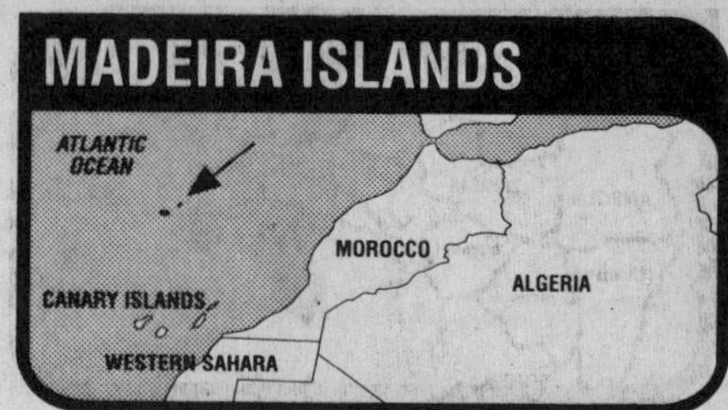

The Madeira Islands, which belong to Portugal, are located 360 miles (492 km.) off the northwest coast of Africa. They have an area of 307 sq. mi. (795 sq. km.) and a population of 270,976. The group consists of two inhabited islands named Madeira and Porto Santo and two groups of uninhabited rocks named Desertas and Selvagens. Capital: Funchal. The two staple products are wine and sugar. Bananas and pineapples are also produced for export.

Although the evidence is insufficient, it is thought that the Phoenicians visited Madeira at an early period. It is also probable that the entire archipelago was explored in early times by Genoese adventurers; an Italian map dated 1351 shows the Madeira Islands quite clearly. The Portuguese navigator Goncalvez Zarco first sighted Porto Santo in 1418, having been driven there by a storm while he was exploring the coast of West Africa. Madeira itself was discovered in 1420. The islands were uninhabited when visited by Zarco, but their colonization was immediately begun by Prince Henry the Navigator, aided by the knights of the Order of Christ. British troops occupied the islands in 1801, and again in 1807-14.

RULERS

Portuguese

V (5) REIS

COPPER

KM#	Date	Mintage	VG	Fine	VF	XF
1	1850	—	35.00	75.00	150.00	300.00

X (10) REIS

COPPER

KM#	Date	Mintage	VG	Fine	VF	XF
2	1842	—	7.50	15.00	30.00	60.00
	1850	—	—	—	Rare	—
	1852	—	7.50	15.00	30.00	60.00

XX (20) REIS

COPPER
Obv: Similar to 10 Reis, KM#2.

KM#	Date	Mintage	VG	Fine	VF	XF
3	1842	—	10.00	20.00	40.00	80.00
	1852	—	—	—	Rare	—

MODERN COINAGE

25 ESCUDOS

COPPER-NICKEL
Autonomy of Madeira - Zarco

KM#	Date	Mintage	Fine	VF	XF	Unc
4	1981	.750	—	—	—	3.50
	11.0000 g, .925 SILVER, .3272 oz ASW					
4a	1981	.020	—	—	Proof	12.00

100 ESCUDOS

COPPER-NICKEL
Autonomy of Madeira - Zarco

KM#	Date	Mintage	Fine	VF	XF	Unc
5	1981	.250	—	—	—	7.50
	16.5000 g, .925 SILVER, .4908 oz ASW					
5a	1981	.020	—	—	Proof	18.00

PROOF SETS (PS)

KM#	Date	Mintage	Identification	Issue Price	Mkt. Val.
PS1	1981(2)	20,000	KM4a-5a	42.00	30.00

MALAWI

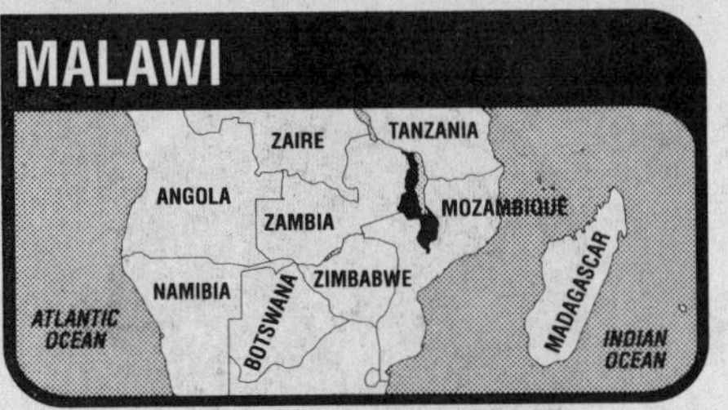

The Republic of Malawi (formerly Nyasaland), located in southeastern Africa to the west of Lake Malawi (Nyasa), has an area of 45,747 sq. mi. (118,480 sq. km.) and a population of 7 million. Capital: Lilongwe. The economy is predominantly agricultural. Tobacco, tea, peanuts and cotton are exported.

Although the Portuguese, heirs to the restless spirit of Prince Henry, were the first Europeans to reach the Malawi area, the first meaningful contact was made by missionary-explorer Dr. David Livingstone who arrived at Lake Malawi on Sept. 16, 1859, and remained to make extensive explorations in the 1860's. Subsequent clashes between settlements of Scottish missionaries and Arab slave traders, and the procurement of development rights by Cecil Rhodes, 1884, stimulated British interest and brought about the establishment of the Nyasaland protectorate in 1891. In 1953 Nyasaland reluctantly joined the Federation of Rhodesia and Nyasaland and, after prolonged protest, was granted self-government within the federation. Nyasaland became the independent nation of Malawi on July 6, 1964, and became a republic two years later. Malawi is a member of the Commonwealth of Nations. The president is the Chief of State and Head of Government.

NOTE: For earlier coinage see Rhodesia and Nyasaland.

MONETARY SYSTEM

12 Pence 1 Shilling
2 Shillings 1 Florin
5 Shillings 1 Crown
20 Shillings 1 Pound

PENNY

BRONZE

KM#	Date	Mintage	Fine	VF	XF	Unc
6	1967	6.000	.35	.65	1.25	2.50
	1968	3.600	2.50	5.00	10.00	20.00

6 PENCE

COPPER-NICKEL-ZINC
Rooster

KM#	Date	Mintage	Fine	VF	XF	Unc
1	1964	14.800	.25	.50	1.00	2.00
	1964	.010	—	—	Proof	1.25
	1967	6.000	.50	1.00	2.50	5.00

SHILLING

COPPER-NICKEL-ZINC
Cobs of Corn

KM#	Date	Mintage	Fine	VF	XF	Unc
2	1964	11.900	.35	.65	1.25	2.50
	1964	.010	—	—	Proof	1.25
	1968	3.000	.75	1.50	3.00	5.50

FLORIN

COPPER-NICKEL-ZINC
African Elephants

KM#	Date	Mintage	Fine	VF	XF	Unc
3	1964	6.500	.75	1.50	3.00	5.00
	1964	.010	—	—	Proof	2.50

1/2 CROWN

COPPER-NICKEL-ZINC
Dr. Hastings Kamuzu Banda

KM#	Date	Mintage	Fine	VF	XF	Unc
4	1964	6.400	1.00	2.00	4.00	6.00
	1964	.010	—	—	Proof	3.00

CROWN

NICKEL-BRASS
Day of the Republic-July 6, 1966

KM#	Date	Mintage	Fine	VF	XF	Unc
5	1966	.020	—	—	Proof	6.00

DECIMAL COINAGE

100 Tambala = 1 Kwacha

TAMBALA

BRONZE
Rooster

KM#	Date	Mintage	Fine	VF	XF	Unc
7.1	1971	15.000	.10	.15	.30	.60
	1971	4,000	—	—	Proof	1.00
	1973	5.000	.10	.15	.30	.60
	1974	12.500	.10	.15	.30	.60
	Obv: Accent mark above W in MALAWI.					
7.2	1975	—	.10	.15	.30	.60
	1976	10.000	.10	.15	.30	.60
	1977	10.000	.10	.15	.30	.60
	1979	15.000	.10	.15	.30	.60
	1982	15.000	.10	.15	.30	.60
	COPPER PLATED STEEL					
7a	1984	.201	.15	.20	.40	.80
	1985	—	.15	.20	.40	.80
	1985	.010	—	—	Proof	3.00
	1987	—	.15	.20	.40	.80
	1989	—	.15	.20	.40	.80
	1991	—	.15	.20	.40	.80

2 TAMBALA

BRONZE
Blue Crane

KM#	Date	Mintage	Fine	VF	XF	Unc
8.1	1971	10.000	.15	.30	.60	1.35
	1971	4,000	—	—	Proof	1.50
	1973	5.000	.15	.30	.60	1.35
	1974	5.000	.15	.30	.60	1.35

Obv: Accent mark above W in MALAWI.

KM#	Date	Mintage	Fine	VF	XF	Unc
8.2	1975	—	.15	.30	.60	1.35
	1976	5.000	.15	.30	.60	1.35
	1977	5.000	.15	.30	.60	1.35
	1979	7.637	.15	.30	.60	1.35
	1982	15.000	.15	.30	.60	1.35

COPPER PLATED STEEL

KM#	Date	Mintage	Fine	VF	XF	Unc
8a	1984	.150	.20	.40	.80	1.75
	1985	—	.20	.40	.80	1.75
	1985	.010	—	—	Proof	4.00
	1987	—	.20	.40	.80	1.75
	1989	—	.20	.40	.80	1.75
	1991	—	.20	.40	.80	1.75

5 TAMBALA

COPPER-NICKEL
Purple Heron

KM#	Date	Mintage	Fine	VF	XF	Unc
9.1	1971	7.000	.20	.40	.80	1.60
	1971	4,000	—	—	Proof	1.00

Obv: Accent mark above W in MALAWI.

KM#	Date	Mintage	Fine	VF	XF	Unc
9.2	1985	.010	—	—	Proof	5.00

NICKEL CLAD STEEL

KM#	Date	Mintage	Fine	VF	XF	Unc
9.2a	1989	—	.25	.50	1.00	2.00

10 TAMBALA

COPPER-NICKEL
Cobs of Corn

KM#	Date	Mintage	Fine	VF	XF	Unc
10.1	1971	4.000	.35	.65	1.25	2.50
	1971	4,000	—	—	Proof	2.00

Obv: Accent mark above W in MALAWI.

KM#	Date	Mintage	Fine	VF	XF	Unc
10.2	1985	.010	—	—	Proof	6.00

NICKEL CLAD STEEL

KM#	Date	Mintage	Fine	VF	XF	Unc
10.2a	1989	—	.40	.80	1.50	3.50

20 TAMBALA

COPPER-NICKEL
African Elephants

KM#	Date	Mintage	Fine	VF	XF	Unc
11.1	1971	3.000	.50	1.00	2.00	3.50
	1971	4,000	—	—	Proof	3.00

Obv: Accent mark above W in MALAWI.

KM#	Date	Mintage	Fine	VF	XF	Unc
11.2	1985	.010	—	—	Proof	7.00

NICKEL CLAD STEEL

KM#	Date	Mintage	Fine	VF	XF	Unc
11.2a	1989	—	.60	1.20	2.50	4.50

50 TAMBALA

COPPER-NICKEL
Dr. Hastings Kamuzu Banda

KM#	Date	Mintage	Fine	VF	XF	Unc
19	1986	—	2.00	4.00	7.00	12.00
	1989	—	2.00	4.00	7.00	12.00

KWACHA

COPPER-NICKEL
Decimalization of Coinage
Obv: Similar to 5 Kwacha, KM#15.

KM#	Date	Mintage	Fine	VF	XF	Unc
12	1971	.020	.75	1.50	3.00	6.00
	1971	4,000	—	—	Proof	5.50

BRASS
Rooster

KM#	Date	Mintage	Fine	VF	XF	Unc
20	1992	—	—	—	—	12.00
	1993	—	—	—	—	12.00

5 KWACHA

28.2800 g, .925 SILVER, .8410 oz ASW
Conservation - Crawshay's Zebras

KM#	Date	Mintage	Fine	VF	XF	Unc
15	1978	4,048	—	—	—	22.50
	1978	3,622	—	—	Proof	42.50

10 KWACHA

28.2800 g, .925 SILVER, .8411 oz ASW
10th Anniversary of Independence

KM#	Date	Mintage	Fine	VF	XF	Unc
13	1974	7,556	—	—	—	11.50
	1974	4,937	—	—	Proof	18.50

10th Anniversary of the Reserve Bank
Obv: Similar to KM#13.

KM#	Date	Mintage	Fine	VF	XF	Unc
14	1975	6,870	—	—	—	11.50
	1975	Inc. Ab.	—	—	Proof	18.50

.900 GOLD

KM#	Date	Mintage	Fine	VF	XF	Unc
14a	1975	—	—	—	—	1000.

35.0000 g, .925 SILVER, 1.0409 oz ASW
Conservation - Sable Antelope
Obv: Similar to 5 Kwacha, KM#15.

KM#	Date	Mintage	Fine	VF	XF	Unc
16	1978	4,009	—	—	—	25.00
	1978	3,416	—	—	Proof	45.00

28.2800 g, .925 SILVER, .8410 oz ASW
20th Anniversary of Reserve Bank

KM#	Date	Mintage	Fine	VF	XF	Unc
18	1985	4,000	—	—	Proof	25.00

47.5400 g, .917 GOLD, 1.4011 oz AGW

KM#	Date	Mintage	Fine	VF	XF	Unc
18a	1985	50 pcs.	—	—	Proof	1500.

28.2800 g, .925 SILVER, .8411 oz ASW
Save the Children Fund - Fishing

KM#	Date	Mintage	Fine	VF	XF	Unc
21	1992	*.020	—	—	Proof	40.00

20 KWACHA

10.0000 g, .917 GOLD, .2948 oz AGW
Save the Children Fund - Mother and Children

KM#	Date	Mintage	Fine	VF	XF	Unc
22	1992	*3,000	—	—	Proof	220.00

250 KWACHA

33.4370 g, .900 GOLD, .9676 oz AGW
Conservation - Nyala

KM#	Date	Mintage	Fine	VF	XF	Unc
17	1978	566 pcs.	—	—	—	600.00
	1978	208 pcs.	—	—	Proof	850.00

MINT SETS (MS)

KM#	Date	Mintage	Identification	Issue Price	Mkt. Val.
MS1	1971(6)	10,000	KM7-12	3.30	12.50
MS2	1978(2)	—	KM15,16	—	50.00

PROOF SETS (PS)

KM#	Date	Mintage	Identification	Issue Price	Mkt. Val.
PS1	1964(4)	10,000	KM1-4	10.00	8.00
PS2	1971(6)	4,000	KM7-12	8.70	12.50
PS3	1978(2)	—	KM15,16	—	90.00
PS4	1985(5)	10,000	KM7a-8a,9-11	30.00	25.00

Listings for

MALAYA: refer to Malaysia

MALAYA & BRITISH BORNEO: refer to Malaysia

MALAYSIA

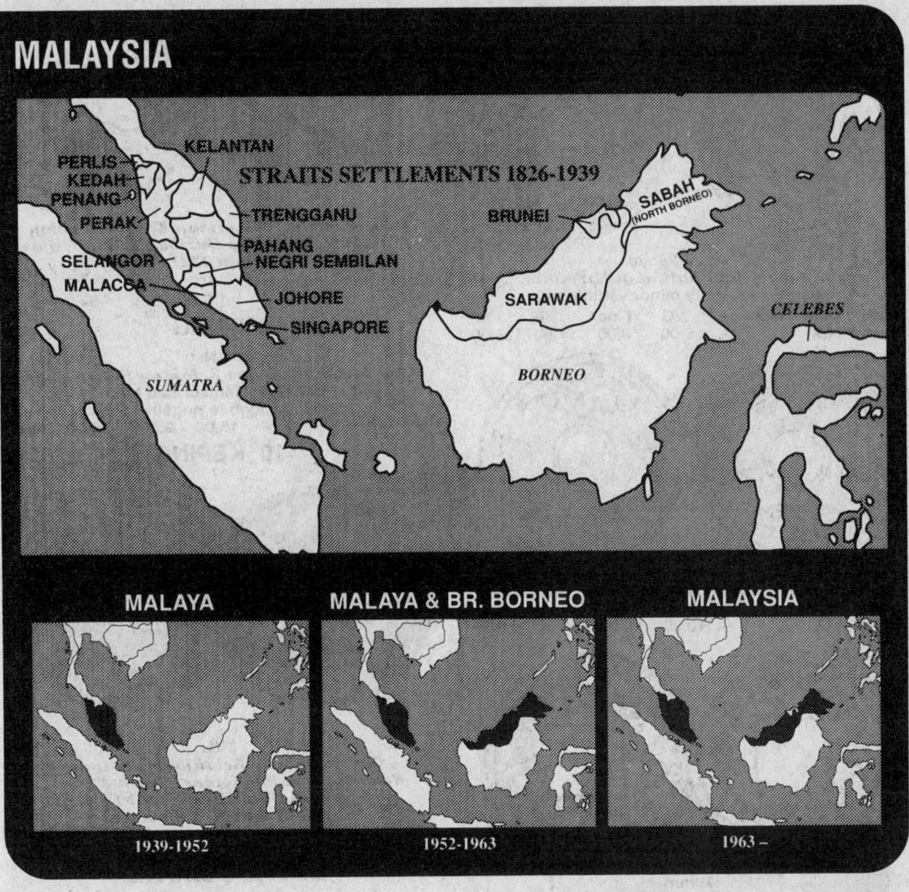

MONETARY SYSTEM

10 Pitis=1 Keping
900-4,000 Pitis=1 Ringgit (Dollar)
1280 Trah=1 Ringgit
100 Pice(cents)=1 Ringgit

DENOMINATIONS

The following Arabic legends appear for the denomination with an Arabic number above.

كفڠ (1) Keping — سكفڠ Sakeping — ساتكفڠ Satkeping

دوکفڠ (2) Dua Keping

NOTE: Many local merchant tokens, inscribed mainly in Chinese, exist for most of the Malay states. These have not been listed.

KEDAH

A state in northwestern Malaysia. Islam introduced in 15th century. Subject to Thailand from 1821-1909. Coins issued under Governor Tengku Anum.

TITLES

كداه

Kedah

SULTANS

Ahmad Taju'd-din Halim Shah, 1798-1843
Zainal Rashid al-Muazzam Shah, 1843-1854
Ahmad Taju'd-din Mukarram Shah, 1854-1879
Abdul-Hamim, 1882-1909

From 1821-1843, Kedah was actually under the control of the Siamese, and was ruled by Governor Tengku Anum.

TRA

TIN, 23mm
Obv: Arabic leg: *Tahun Alif 1224*. Rev: Arabic leg: *Balad Kedah Daru'l/Aman*. Irregular center hole.

KM#	Date	Mintage	Good	VG	Fine	VF
3	AH1224	—	20.00	35.00	50.00	75.00

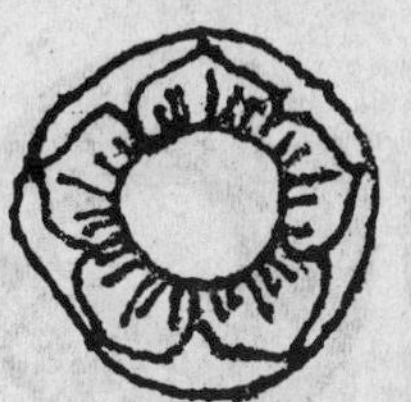

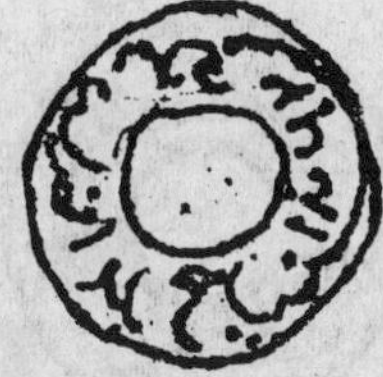

24mm
Obv: 5-petaled lotus blossom. Rev: Arabic leg: *Belanja Balad al-Perlis Kedah-Sanat 1262*. Irregular center hole.

KM#	Date	Mintage	Good	VG	Fine	VF
4	AH1262	—	20.00	35.00	50.00	75.00

18mm
Obv: Crude 12-pointed star. Rev: Arabic leg: *Belanja Balad Kedah Daru'l-Aman*. Irregular center hole.

KM#	Date	Mintage	Good	VG	Fine	VF
5	ND	—	20.00	30.00	45.00	65.00

KELANTAN

A state in northern Malaysia. Colonized by Javanese in 1300's. Subject to Thailand from 1780 to 1909.

TITLES

كلنتن

Kelantan

خليفة المؤمنين

Khalifat Al-Mu'minin

SULTANS

Muhammed I, 1800-1835
Muhammed II, 1835-1886
Ahmad, 1886-1889
Muhammed III, 1889-1891
Mansur, 1891-1899
Interregnum, 1899-1902
Muhammed IV, 1902-1919

PITIS

TIN, 24-29mm
Obv. Arabic leg: *Khalifat al-Mu'minin*. Rev: Same. Many minor variations.

KM#	Date	Mintage	VG	Fine	VF	XF
1	ND	—	5.00	8.00	14.00	25.00

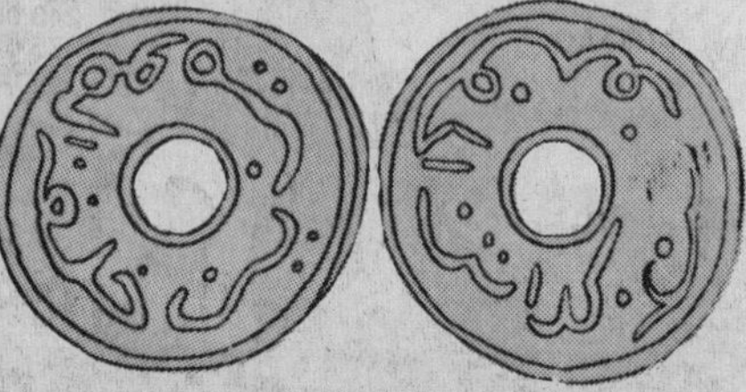

Obv: Similar to KM#1. Rev. Arabic leg: *Al-Julus Kelantan*.

KM#	Date	Mintage	VG	Fine	VF	XF
2	ND	—	10.00	15.00	30.00	50.00

28mm
Obv. Arabic leg: Similar to KM#1. Rev: *Sanat 1256*.

KM#	Date	Mintage	VG	Fine	VF	XF
4	AH1256	—	8.00	12.00	20.00	30.00

NOTE: This type has also been attributed to Legeh.

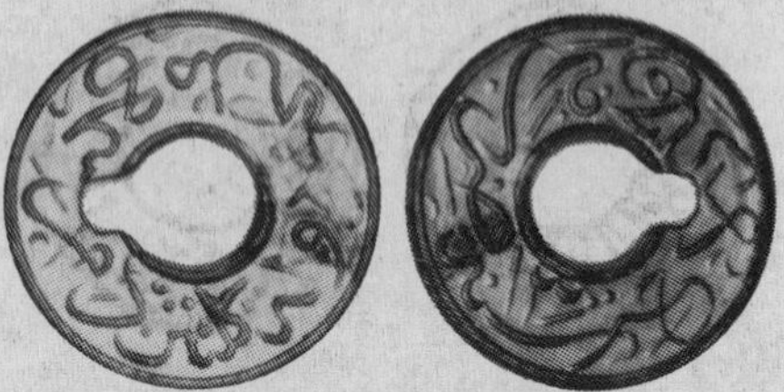

Obv. Arabic leg: *Dama Sama Mulka Daulat Kelantan*. Rev. Arabic leg: *Duriba Fi Jamadal Akhir 1300*.

KM#	Date	Mintage	VG	Fine	VF	XF
5	AH1300	—	8.00	12.00	20.00	30.00

Obv. Arabic leg: *Adim Mulkahu Belanjaan Kera Jaan Kelantan*. Rev. Arabic leg: *Sunia Fi Jumadal Ula Sanat 1314*.

KM#	Date	Mintage	VG	Fine	VF	XF
10	AH1314	—	5.00	8.00	16.00	30.00

NOTE: Legends are incuse.

Obv. Arabic leg: *Belanjaan Negri Kelantan Adama Mulkahu*. Rev. Arabic leg: *Sunia Fi Jumadal Ula Sanat 1321*.

KM#	Date	Mintage	VG	Fine	VF	XF
12	AH1321	—	8.00	12.00	20.00	30.00

Obv. Arabic leg: *Belanjaan Kerajaan Kelan Tan*. Rev. Arabic leg: *Duriba Fi Dhul Hijja Sanat 1321*.

KM#	Date	Mintage	VG	Fine	VF	XF
15	AH1321	—	1.50	2.50	3.50	7.00

KEPING

TIN
Obv. Arabic leg: *Negri Kelantan Satu Keping Sanat 1323*. Rev: Uninscribed but obv. leg. shows through in negative form.

KM#	Date	Mintage	VG	Fine	VF	XF
18	AH1323	—	15.00	25.00	35.00	50.00

10 KEPING

TIN
Obv. Arabic leg: *Belanjaan Kerajaan Kelantin Sepuloh Keping*. Rev. Arabic leg: *Sunia Fi Dhul Hijja Sanat 1321*. Border of diamonds around leg.

KM#	Date	Mintage	VG	Fine	VF	XF
20	AH1321	—	5.00	10.00	20.00	30.00

LOCAL COINAGE

KEMASIN

Town in Kelantan State

TITLES

كماسن

Kemasin

JOKOH

TIN, 29-30mm
Obv. Jawi leg: *Ini Pakai Di Kemasin Sanat 1300*. Rev: Chinese inscription & 5 c/m. Two vars.

KM#	Date	Mintage	VG	Fine	VF	XF
30	AH1300	—	20.00	40.00	60.00	100.00

PATANI, PATTANI

Refer to Thailand Local Issues.

MALACCA

A state of Malaysia on the west coast. It was settled from Sumatra in the 1300's. Occupied by the Portuguese in 1511. Captured by the Dutch in 1641. Held by the British from 1795 to 1802 and 1811 to 1818. Ceded to Britain in 1824.

The attribution of the following coins to Malacca is uncertain. All were struck in England, on behalf of merchants in Singapore. All have an Arabic legend *Tanah Melayu* (Land of the Malays) above a rooster.

KEPING

COPPER
Rev: Denomination at top written like a fraction.

KM#	Date	Mintage	Fine	VF	XF	Unc
8.1	AH1247	—	1.00	3.00	7.00	25.00
	BRASS					
8.1a	AH1247	—	—	—	—	—
	COPPER					
	Rev: Denomination written simply 1.					
8.2	AH1247	—	1.00	3.00	7.00	25.00
	AH1251	—	Reported, not confirmed			
	AH1147(error)		30.00	50.00	70.00	100.00
	AH1219(error)		2.50	6.00	15.00	30.00
	AH1241(error)		30.00	50.00	70.00	100.00
	AH1411(error)		2.50	6.00	15.00	40.00

2 KEPING

COPPER

KM#	Date	Mintage	Fine	VF	XF	Unc
14	AH1247	—	12.50	20.00	30.00	60.00

PAHANG

A state on the east coast of Malaysia. Subject to the Suvyaya kingdom in Sumatra in the 1200's. Shuttled from native kingdom to native kingdom after 1450. Became one of the Federated Malay States in 1895.

The following coins were minted by prominent Chinese in Pahang by permission of Sultan Ahmed. They were intended for general circulation within Pahang. Many other pieces issued by merchants and gambling houses exist, but will not be listed here.

TITLES

Pahang

GOVERNORS

Bendahara Sewa Raja Tun Ali, 1806-1857

Bendahara Sewa Raja Tun Mutahir, 1857-1863

SULTANS

Ahmed Al Muazzam, 1884-1914 ruled as Governor Bendahara Sewa Raja Ahmad from 1863 to 1884

Pahang Company

1/2 CENT

TIN
Obv: 4 Chinese characters *Ch'ien Sheng T'ung Pao*. Rev. value and Arabic leg: *Pahang Company* and 1/2 C.

KM#	Date	Mintage	Good	VG	Fine	VF
6	ND	—	15.00	20.00	40.00	60.00

Minted between 1884 and 1896.

CENT

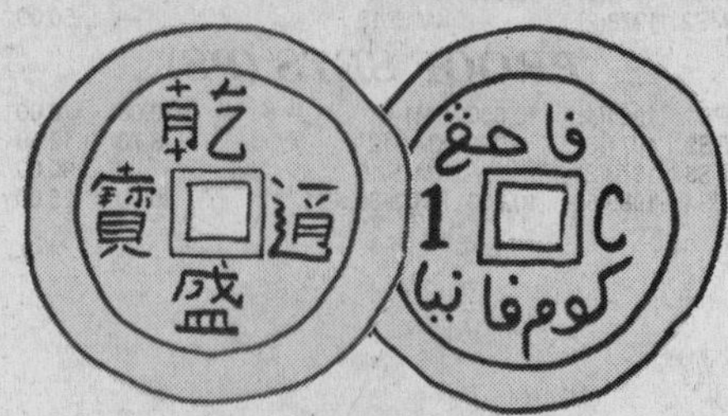

TIN
Rev: 1 C

KM#	Date	Mintage	Good	VG	Fine	VF
9	ND	—	15.00	20.00	40.00	60.00

Minted between 1884 and 1896.

Obv: Value and Chinese *Ch'ien Sheng T'ung Pao*. Rev: Date and Arabic leg.

KM#	Date	Mintage	Good	VG	Fine	VF
11	AH1301	—	10.00	15.00	30.00	50.00

PENANG

Pulu Penang-Prince of Wales Island

An island off the west coast of Malaysia. Ceded to the British in 1791 by the sultan of Kedah and was the first British settlement in Malaya. Also known as Pulu Penang and Prince of Wales Island - which title it retained until 1867.

The currency system depended on the Spanish dollar divided into 100 pice (or cents) until 1826 when 48 pice were deemed the equivalent of one Bengal rupee until 1830. The coins are considered in three groups:

(a) The Company bale mark series, consisting of copper 1/10, 1/2 and 1 pice of 1786/1787, and silver tenth, quarter and half dollars, dated 1788;

(b) Company coat of arms issues in copper between 1810 and 1828 in denominations of 1/2, 1 and double pice pieces; and

(c) Tin issues of local mintage pice pieces of 1800-1809, which are extremely rare.

TITLES

Pulu Penang ڤولو ڤنيڠ

MONETARY SYSTEM

100 Cents (Pice) = 1 Dollar

1/2 CENT

(1/2 Pice)

COPPER
Mint: Royal

KM#	Date	Mintage	Fine	VF	XF	Unc
11	1810	1.720	20.00	30.00	60.00	125.00
	1810	—	—	—	Proof	400.00

Mint: Madras

KM#	Date	Mintage	Fine	VF	XF	Unc
12	1825	.145	60.00	90.00	150.00	300.00
	1828	.414	50.00	80.00	140.00	300.00

NOTE: Wreath varies from 21 to 26 lily cups.

CENT

(Pice)

Tin, uniface, 40.35 g 元
Initial GL (Governor Leith) in ring.
c/m: Chinese character *Yuan*.

KM#	Date	Mintage	VG	Fine	VF	XF
8	ND(c.1800-03)	—	1250.	3000.	4500.	6000.

啓

TIN, uniface, 30.50 g
Initials GF (Governor Farguhar) in ring,
c/m: Chinese character *Ch'i*.

KM#	Date	Mintage	VG	Fine	VF	XF
9	ND(c.1805)	—	600.00	1150.	1850.	3000.

美

TIN, uniface, 30.00-32.00 g
Native initials A & C (Anderson & Clubley)
c/m: Chinese character *Mei*.

KM#	Date	Mintage	VG	Fine	VF	XF
10	1809	—	900.00	1500.	2500.	4000.

美

English initials A & C (Anderson & Clubley)

KM#	Date	Mintage	VG	Fine	VF	XF
11	1809	—	900.00	1500.	2500.	4000.

COPPER
Royal Mint
Rev: Leaves on wreath go clockwise.

KM#	Date	Mintage	Fine	VF	XF	Unc
13	1810 small date, small shield					
		1.827	17.50	35.00	70.00	100.00
	1810	—	—	—	Proof	350.00

Madras Mint

KM#	Date	Mintage	Fine	VF	XF	Unc
14	1825	.137	40.00	80.00	140.00	240.00
	1828	.236	35.00	75.00	130.00	240.00

NOTE: Wreaths vary from 21 to 27 lily cups.

2 CENTS

(2 Pice)

COPPER
Mint: Madras

KM#	Date	Mintage	Fine	VF	XF	Unc
15	1825	.130	40.00	80.00	140.00	240.00
	1825	—	—	—	Proof	375.00
	1828	.720	20.00	50.00	120.00	180.00

NOTE: Wreaths vary from 24 to 28 lily cups.

PERAK

A state on the west coast of Malaysia. Important tin deposits are in this state. Part of Malay kingdoms from early times. Perak was an independent state from 1824-1874. The only coin is one made in Birmingham, England and distributed by a Singapore importer.

TITLES

Negri Peraq نکري ڤيرق

SULTANS

Ahmadin, ?-1806
Abdul-Malik Mansur, 1806-1825
Abdullah Muazzam, 1825-1830
Shahabud-Din Riayat, 1831-1851
Abdullah Muhammad, 1851-1857
Jafar Muazzam, 1857-1865
Ali Al-Mukammal Inayat, 1865-1871
Ismail Muabidin, 1871-1874
Abdullah Muhammad, 1874-1877
Yusuf Sharifud-Din Mufzal, 1877-1887
Sir Idris Murshid Al-Azzam, 1887-1916
Abdul-Jalil, 1916-1918
Iskander, 1918-?

KEPING

COPPER
Obv. Arabic leg: *Negri Perak* (State of Perak). Rev. Arabic leg: *Satu Kepang 1251* (one Keping AH 1251).

KM#	Date	Mintage	VG	Fine	VF	XF
4	AH1251	—	2.50	5.00	15.00	35.00
	1251	—	—	—	Proof	120.00

PERLIS

See State of Kedah

SELANGOR

A state on the west coast of Malaysia. Played a part in the trading programs of both the Dutch and the British. Signed a treaty with Britain in 1818 and Britain took control of the state in 1874.

TITLES

Negeri Selangor نکري سلاغور

SULTANS

Ibrahim, 1777-1826
Muhammad, 1826-1857
Abdul-Samad, 1857-1898
Sulaiman, 1898-1938

PITIS

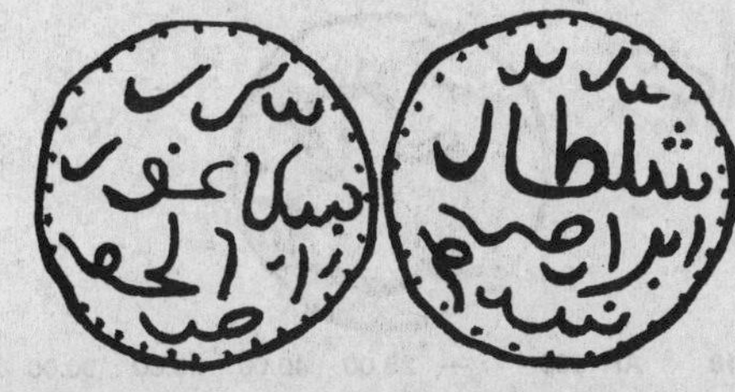

TIN
Obv. leg: Arabic
Negari Selangor Darul Ihsan.
Rev. leg: Arabic
Baginda Sultan Ibrahim Shah.

KM#	Date	Mintage	Fine	VF	XF	Unc
1	ND	—	—	—	—	—

KEPING

COPPER
Obv. Arabic leg: *Negri Selangor.*
Rev. Arabic leg: *Satu Keping 1251.*

3	AH1251	—	2.50	5.00	15.00	35.00

TRENGGANU

A state in eastern Malaysia on the shore of the south China Sea. Area of dispute between Malacca and Thailand with the latter emerging with possession. Trengganu became a British dependency in 1909.

TITLES

Khalifat al-Mu'minin خليفة المؤمنين

Trengganu ترغكانو

SULTANS

Zainal Abidin I,
Zainal Abidin II, 1793-1808
Ahmad I, 1808-1827
Abdul Rahman, 1827-1831
Daud, 1831
Mansur II, 1831-1836
Muhammed, 1836-1839
Baginda Omar, 1839-1876
Ahmad II, 1876-1881
Zainal Abidin III, 1881-1918
Muhammed, 1918-1920
Sulaiman, 1920-1942

PITIS

TIN

KM#	Date	Mintage	VG	Fine	VF	XF
9	AH1222	—	17.50	27.50	40.00	60.00

Legend points outward instead of inward.

10	AH1222	—	20.00	35.00	50.00	75.00

Khalifat al-Muminin 1251 Malik al-Adil.

11	AH1251	—	30.00	50.00	75.00	100.00

13	AH1265	—	25.00	40.00	65.00	90.00

Belanja Trengganu Sanat 1299.

KM#	Date	Mintage	VG	Fine	VF	XF
14	AH1299	—	25.00	40.00	65.00	90.00

KEPING

COPPER
Obv. Arabic leg: *Negri Trengganu* (State of Trengganu). Rev. Arabic leg: *Satu Keping 1251.*

12	AH1251	—	5.00	8.00	20.00	40.00
	AH1251	—	—	—	Proof	125.00

10 KEPING

TIN

15	AH1310	—	10.00	20.00	30.00	55.00

1/4 CENT

TIN
Similar to 1/2 Cent, KM#16.

17	AH1325	—	—	—	Rare	—

1/2 CENT

TIN

16	AH1322(recast)	—	—	—	15.00	

18	AH1325(recast)	—	—	—	15.00	

NOTE: Originals are rare.

CENT

TIN

19	AH1325	—	4.50	8.25	15.00	25.00

KM#	Date	Mintage	VG	Fine	VF	XF
20	AH1325	—	4.50	8.25	15.00	25.00

Although dated AH1325 (1907) this coin was actually struck in 1920 under Sultan Sulaiman. Authorized mintage was one million pieces. Beware of thin lead counterfeits.

STRAITS SETTLEMENTS

Straits Settlements, a former British crown colony situated on the Malay Peninsula of Asia, was formed in 1826 by combining the territories of Singapore, Penang and Malacca. The colony was administered by the East India Company until its abolition in 1853. Straits Settlements was a part of British India from 1858 to 1867 at which time it became a Crown Colony. This name was changed to Malaya in 1939.

RULERS

British

MINT MARKS

H - Heaton, Birmingham
W - Soho Mint
B - Bombay

MONETARY SYSTEM

100 Cents=1 Dollar

EAST INDIA COMPANY

1826-1858

1/4 CENT

COPPER
Rev. leg: EAST INDIA COMPANY

KM#	Date	Mintage	Fine	VF	XF	Unc
1	1845	34.327	3.00	10.00	22.00	65.00
	1845 WW on truncation					
		—	—	—	Proof	350.00

1/2 CENT

COPPER

2	1845	18.737	4.00	10.00	28.00	65.00
	1845	—	—	—	Proof	350.00
	1845 WW on truncation					
		Inc. Ab.	4.00	10.00	25.00	60.00
	1845 WW on truncation					
		—	—	—	Proof	400.00

CENT

COPPER

3	1845	18.526	5.00	15.00	35.00	80.00
	1845 WW on truncation					
		—	—	—	Proof	450.00

BRITISH INDIA GOVERNMENT

1858-1867

1/4 CENT

COPPER
Rev. leg: INDIA STRAITS

KM#	Date	Mintage	Fine	VF	XF	Unc
4	1862	3.368	50.00	125.00	250.00	475.00
	1862	—	—	—	Proof	925.00

1/2 CENT

COPPER

KM#	Date	Mintage	Fine	VF	XF	Unc
5	1862	4.590	25.00	50.00	150.00	300.00
	1862	—	—	—	Proof	700.00

CENT

COPPER

KM#	Date	Mintage	Fine	VF	XF	Unc
6	1862	9.321	6.00	15.00	35.00	120.00
	1862	—	—	—	Proof	450.00

COLONIAL ISSUES

1867-1939

1/4 CENT

COPPER
Rev. leg: STRAITS SETTLEMENTS, plain edge.

KM#	Date	Mintage	Fine	VF	XF	Unc
7	1872	—	—	—	Proof	375.00
	1872H	9.240	6.50	12.50	35.00	100.00
	1872H	—	—	—	Proof	300.00
	1873	—	120.00	160.00	300.00	700.00
	1873	—	—	—	Proof	800.00
	1875	—	—	—	Proof	600.00
	1875W	—	—	—	Proof	600.00
	1883	.200	300.00	600.00	1100.	2000.
	BRONZE					
7a	1884	8.000	2.50	8.50	30.00	70.00
	1884	—	—	—	Proof	250.00
	Reeded edge					
14	1889	2.000	2.50	7.50	30.00	70.00
	1889	—	—	—	Proof	250.00
	1890	—	—	—	Proof	600.00
	1891	—	—	—	Proof	400.00
	1898	1.600	2.00	5.00	22.00	55.00
	1898	—	—	—	Proof	250.00
	1899	2.400	2.00	4.00	20.00	50.00
	1901	2.000	2.00	4.00	20.00	50.00

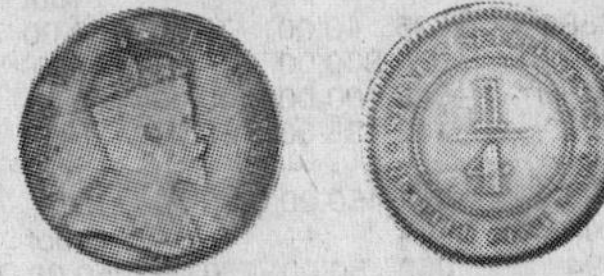

COPPER

KM#	Date	Mintage	Fine	VF	XF	Unc
17	1904 plain edge	—	—	—	Proof	500.00
	1904 milled edge	—	—	—	Proof	500.00
	1905	2.008	1.25	6.00	15.00	40.00
	1905	—	—	—	Proof	250.00
	1908	1.200	1.25	6.00	17.50	45.00

KM#	Date	Mintage	Fine	VF	XF	Unc
27	1916	4.000	1.00	2.00	4.50	12.00
	1916	—	—	—	Proof	220.00

1/2 CENT

COPPER
Plain edge

KM#	Date	Mintage	Fine	VF	XF	Unc
8	1872	—	—	—	Proof	350.00
	1872H	5.610	18.00	30.00	60.00	120.00
	1872H	—	—	—	Proof	350.00
	1873	—	35.00	65.00	140.00	400.00
	1874	—	—	—	Proof	400.00
	1875	—	—	—	Proof	400.00
	1875W	—	—	—	Proof	400.00
	1883	2.740	50.00	75.00	325.00	650.00
	BRONZE					
8a	1884	4.000	6.00	12.00	40.00	90.00
	1884	—	—	—	Proof	400.00

Reeded edge

KM#	Date	Mintage	Fine	VF	XF	Unc
15	1889	2.000	10.00	22.00	50.00	110.00
	1890	—	—	—	Proof	400.00
	1891	—	—	—	Proof	400.00

COPPER

KM#	Date	Mintage	Fine	VF	XF	Unc
18	1904	—	—	—	Proof	350.00
	1908	2.000	2.50	5.00	15.00	45.00

KM#	Date	Mintage	Fine	VF	XF	Unc
28	1916	3.000	1.00	2.50	7.50	15.00
	1916	—	—	—	Proof	300.00

BRONZE

KM#	Date	Mintage	Fine	VF	XF	Unc
37	1932	5.000	.75	1.00	3.00	10.00
	1932	—	—	—	Proof	240.00

CENT

COPPER
Plain edge

KM#	Date	Mintage	Fine	VF	XF	Unc
9	1872	—	—	—	Proof	350.00
	1872H	5.770	3.00	12.50	35.00	75.00
9	1872H	—	—	—	Proof	350.00
	1873	—	7.00	18.00	45.00	95.00
	1874	10.000	4.00	12.50	35.00	65.00
	1874H	10.000	4.00	12.50	35.00	65.00
	1874H	—	—	—	Proof	250.00
	1875	6.000	7.00	18.00	40.00	70.00
	1875	—	—	—	Proof	250.00
	1875W	—	7.00	18.00	40.00	70.00
	1875 W on truncation					
		—	—	—	Proof	250.00
	1876	—	6.50	15.00	35.00	70.00
	1877	—	6.50	15.00	35.00	70.00
	1878	—	60.00	175.00	400.00	900.00
	1883	8.640	6.50	15.00	40.00	90.00
	BRONZE					
9a	1884	6.000	1.00	5.00	15.00	50.00
	1884	—	—	—	Proof	250.00
	1885	7.412	10.00	25.00	60.00	150.00
	1886	1.512	20.00	40.00	100.00	200.00
	Reeded edge					
16	1887	8.988	1.25	5.00	17.50	60.00
	1888	10.000	1.25	5.00	17.50	60.00
	1889	6.010	1.25	5.00	17.50	60.00
	1890	11.006	1.25	5.00	17.50	60.00
	1890	—	—	—	Proof	250.00
	1891	6.004	1.00	5.00	17.50	60.00
	1894	9.034	1.00	5.00	17.50	60.00
	1895	4.446	1.00	5.00	17.50	60.00
	1897	18.040	1.00	5.00	17.50	60.00
	1898	2.086	4.00	12.00	30.00	70.00
	1898	—	—	—	Proof	220.00
	1900	2.914	1.00	4.00	15.00	50.00
	1901	15.230	1.00	4.00	12.50	40.00

COPPER

KM#	Date	Mintage	Fine	VF	XF	Unc
19	1903	7.053	1.50	4.50	13.50	37.50
	1903	—	—	—	Proof	200.00
	1904	6.467	1.50	4.50	13.50	37.50
	1904	—	—	—	Proof	200.00
	1906	7.504	3.50	8.00	22.50	60.00
	1907	5.015	1.00	4.00	15.00	40.00
	1908	Inc. Ab.	1.00	2.50	10.00	30.00
	1908	—	—	—	Proof	200.00

KM#	Date	Mintage	Fine	VF	XF	Unc
32	1919	20.165	.50	.75	6.00	20.00
	1919	—	—	—	Proof	175.00
	1920	55.000	.50	.75	3.00	12.50
	1920	—	—	—	Proof	150.00
	1926/0	5.000	2.00	5.00	10.00	25.00
	1926	Inc. Ab.	.50	.75	7.50	25.00

5 CENTS

1.3600 g, .800 SILVER, .0349 oz ASW

KM#	Date	Mintage	Fine	VF	XF	Unc
10	1871	.062	320.00	700.00	1200.	2000.
	1871	—	—	—	Proof	3000.
	1873	.060	550.00	1400.	1850.	2500.
	1874H	.060	50.00	100.00	185.00	350.00
	1876H	.040	500.00	1000.	1600.	2400.
	1877	.060	400.00	660.00	1100.	2000.
	1878	.260	15.00	35.00	90.00	200.00
	1878	—	—	—	Proof	350.00
	1879H	.100	120.00	200.00	400.00	600.00
	1880H	.090	140.00	300.00	550.00	800.00
	1881	.180	20.00	40.00	120.00	200.00
	1881	—	—	—	Proof	350.00
	1882H	.380	12.50	25.00	55.00	160.00
	1882H	—	—	—	Proof	350.00
	1883	.080	100.00	200.00	350.00	720.00
	1884	.440	5.00	12.00	35.00	90.00
	1884	—	—	—	Proof	350.00
	1885	.200	15.00	35.00	100.00	240.00
	1885	—	—	—	Proof	350.00
	1886	.340	7.50	12.50	28.00	80.00
	1887	.440	6.00	10.00	22.00	70.00
	1888	.590	5.00	10.00	20.00	65.00
	1889	1.000	2.00	4.00	15.00	50.00
	1889	—	—	—	Proof	350.00
	1890H	.440	6.00	17.50	48.00	80.00
	1890H	—	—	—	Proof	350.00

KM#	Date	Mintage	Fine	VF	XF	Unc
10	1891	.800	2.50	5.00	15.00	50.00
	1893	.440	3.50	6.00	20.00	60.00
	1894	.340	2.50	5.00	15.00	50.00
	1895	1.480	2.00	3.00	10.00	45.00
	1896	.960	2.00	3.00	10.00	45.00
	1897	.320	4.00	8.00	20.00	60.00
	1897H	.440	4.00	8.00	22.00	70.00
	1898	1.200	1.50	2.50	12.50	45.00
	1899	.078	3.00	6.00	20.00	60.00
	1900	2.720	1.50	2.50	12.50	40.00
	1900H	.400	5.00	10.00	22.00	60.00
	1901	3.000	1.50	2.50	12.50	45.00

KM#	Date	Mintage	Fine	VF	XF	Unc
20	1902	1.920	5.00	12.00	50.00	90.00
	1902	—	—	—	Proof	350.00
	1903	2.270	5.00	12.00	50.00	90.00
	1903	—	—	—	Proof	350.00

1.3600 g, .600 SILVER, .0262 oz ASW

KM#	Date	Mintage	Fine	VF	XF	Unc
20a	1910B	13.012	1.25	2.25	5.50	12.00
	1910B	—	—	—	Proof	350.00

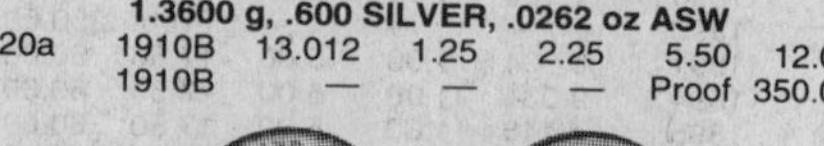

1.3600 g, .400 SILVER, .0174 oz ASW

KM#	Date	Mintage	Fine	VF	XF	Unc
31	1918	3.100	.50	1.25	5.00	12.00
	1919	6.900	.50	1.25	5.00	12.00
	1920	4.000	120.00	250.00	600.00	1200.

COPPER-NICKEL

KM#	Date	Mintage	Fine	VF	XF	Unc
34	1920	20.000	1.00	12.00	50.00	100.00
	1920	—	—	—	Proof	525.00

1.3600 g, .600 SILVER, .0262 oz ASW
Similar to KM#31, smaller bust, broader rim.

KM#	Date	Mintage	Fine	VF	XF	Unc
36	1926	10.000	.50	.75	4.00	12.00
	1926	—	—	—	Proof	240.00
	1935	3.000	.50	.75	4.00	9.00
	1935	—	—	—	Proof	240.00

10 CENTS

2.7100 g, .800 SILVER, .0697 oz ASW

KM#	Date	Mintage	Fine	VF	XF	Unc
11	1871	.248	15.00	25.00	65.00	150.00
	1871	—	—	—	Proof	250.00
	1872H	.230	15.00	25.00	62.50	130.00
	1872H	—	—	—	Proof	250.00
	1873	.210	25.00	45.00	110.00	180.00
	1874H	.180	12.50	20.00	45.00	90.00
	1876H	.120	30.00	65.00	130.00	250.00
	1877	.160	15.00	35.00	55.00	120.00
	1878	.470	5.00	10.00	25.00	60.00
	1878	—	—	—	Proof	250.00
	1879H	.250	12.50	20.00	45.00	90.00
	1879H	—	—	—	Proof	250.00
	1880H	.235	16.50	28.00	60.00	130.00
	1881	.460	4.00	8.00	25.00	60.00
	1881	—	—	—	Proof	250.00
	1882H	.430	4.00	8.00	25.00	60.00
	1882H	—	—	—	Proof	250.00
	1883	.160	25.00	50.00	100.00	200.00
	1883H	.610	120.00	220.00	400.00	800.00
	1883H	—	—	—	Proof	1100.
	1884 crosslet 4	1.240	3.00	5.00	12.00	50.00
	1884 plain 4	Inc. Ab.	3.00	5.00	12.00	50.00
	1884	—	—	—	Proof	250.00
	1885	.400	15.00	20.00	30.00	90.00
	1885	—	—	—	Proof	250.00
	1886	.790	3.00	5.00	12.00	45.00
	1886	—	—	—	Proof	250.00
	1887	.640	3.00	5.00	12.00	45.00
	1888	1.075	2.00	4.00	12.00	45.00
	1888	—	—	—	Proof	250.00

KM#	Date	Mintage	Fine	VF	XF	Unc
11	1889	1.500	2.00	3.00	7.50	40.00
	1889	—	—	—	Proof	250.00
	1890H	.730	3.50	6.00	15.00	50.00
	1890H	—	—	—	Proof	250.00
	1891	1.380	2.00	3.00	7.50	30.00
	1891	—	—	—	Proof	250.00
	1893	.980	2.00	3.00	7.50	30.00
	1893	—	—	—	Proof	250.00
	1894	1.640	2.00	3.00	7.50	30.00
	1895	2.324	2.00	3.00	7.50	25.00
	1896	2.256	2.00	3.00	7.50	25.00
	1897	.700	2.50	5.00	12.50	50.00
	1897H	.390	4.00	8.00	20.00	60.00
	1898	1.960	2.00	3.50	8.00	35.00
	1899	.286	2.00	3.50	8.00	35.00
	1900	2.960	2.00	3.50	8.00	35.00
	1900H	1.000	2.50	5.00	12.50	40.00
	1900H	—	—	—	Proof	250.00
	1901	2.700	2.00	3.00	7.00	25.00

KM#	Date	Mintage	Fine	VF	XF	Unc
21	1902	6.118	2.50	10.00	25.00	60.00
	1902	—	—	—	Proof	250.00
	1903	1.401	3.00	12.00	32.50	80.00
	1903	—	—	—	Proof	250.00

2.7100 g, .600 SILVER, .0522 oz ASW

KM#	Date	Mintage	Fine	VF	XF	Unc
21a	1909B	11.088	5.00	20.00	40.00	90.00
	1910B	1.657	1.00	2.00	3.00	10.00
	1910B	—	—	—	Proof	250.00

Obv: Dot below bust.

KM#	Date	Mintage	Fine	VF	XF	Unc
29	1916	.600	3.00	7.00	20.00	35.00
	1917	5.600	1.00	2.00	7.00	22.00

2.7100 g, .400 SILVER, .0348 oz ASW
Obv: Cross below bust.

KM#	Date	Mintage	Fine	VF	XF	Unc
29a	1918	7.500	1.00	2.50	8.00	22.00
	1919	11.500	1.00	2.50	8.00	22.00
	1920	4.000	5.00	15.00	40.00	115.00

2.7100 g, .600 SILVER, .0522 oz ASW
Obv: Plain field below bust.

KM#	Date	Mintage	Fine	VF	XF	Unc
29b	1926	20.000	1.00	1.50	5.00	15.00
	1926	—	—	—	Proof	225.00
	1927	23.000	.50	.75	1.00	3.25
	1927	—	—	—	Proof	225.00

20 CENTS

5.4300 g, .800 SILVER, .1396 oz ASW

KM#	Date	Mintage	Fine	VF	XF	Unc
12	1871	.016	380.00	750.00	1300.	1900.
	1871	—	—	—	Proof	2800.
	1872H	.040	120.00	250.00	400.00	700.00
	1873	.030	350.00	700.00	1200.	1850.
	1874H	.045	75.00	110.00	175.00	325.00
	1876H	.030	100.00	220.00	400.00	700.00
	1877	.055	65.00	100.00	185.00	375.00
	1878	.150	12.50	18.50	55.00	145.00
	1878	—	—	—	Proof	375.00
	1879H	.050	60.00	110.00	200.00	375.00
	1879H	—	—	—	Proof	450.00
	1880H	.085	30.00	50.00	100.00	220.00
	1880H	—	—	—	Proof	375.00
	1881/71	.100	25.00	40.00	100.00	250.00
	1881	Inc. Ab.	20.00	35.00	90.00	200.00
	1882H	.245	12.00	20.00	50.00	120.00
	1882H	—	—	—	Proof	375.00
	1883	.200	15.00	22.00	55.00	130.00
	1884	.220	5.00	10.00	27.50	65.00
	1884	—	—	—	Proof	375.00
	1885	.100	20.00	35.00	90.00	200.00
	1886	.245	5.00	7.50	20.00	50.00
	1886	—	. —	—	Proof	375.00
	1887	.220	5.00	7.50	15.00	45.00
	1888	.295	5.00	7.50	15.00	45.00
	1888	—	—	—	Proof	375.00
	1889	.420	3.00	5.00	15.00	40.00

KM#	Date	Mintage	Fine	VF	XF	Unc
12	1890H	.270	7.50	15.00	35.00	70.00
	1890H	—	—	—	Proof	300.00
	1891	.510	3.25	5.00	13.50	40.00
	1893	.310	3.25	5.00	13.50	40.00
	1894	.495	3.25	5.00	13.50	40.00
	1895	.580	3.25	5.00	13.50	40.00
	1896	.600	3.25	5.00	13.50	40.00
	1897	.150	8.00	15.00	30.00	80.00
	1897H	.185	8.00	15.00	30.00	80.00
	1898	.580	3.00	4.50	12.50	37.50
	1899	.204	3.00	4.50	12.50	37.50
	1900	.620	3.00	4.50	12.50	37.50
	1900H	.300	6.00	9.00	25.00	70.00
	1900H	—	—	—	Proof	375.00
	1901	.600	3.00	4.50	12.50	37.50

KM#	Date	Mintage	Fine	VF	XF	Unc
22	1902	1.105	6.00	15.00	50.00	120.00
	1902	—	—	—	Proof	300.00
	1903	1.150	6.00	15.00	50.00	120.00
	1903	—	—	—	Proof	300.00

5.4300 g, .600 SILVER, .1047 oz ASW

KM#	Date	Mintage	Fine	VF	XF	Unc
22a	1910B	3.276	2.00	3.50	10.00	25.00
	1910B	—	—	—	Proof	300.00

Obv: Dot below bust.

KM#	Date	Mintage	Fine	VF	XF	Unc
30	1916B	.545	4.00	10.00	30.00	70.00
	1916B	—	—	—	Proof	250.00
	1917B	.652	2.50	4.50	25.00	55.00

5.4300 g, .400 SILVER, .0698 oz ASW
Obv: Cross below bust.

KM#	Date	Mintage	Fine	VF	XF	Unc
30a	1919B	2.500	2.50	4.50	12.00	35.00
	1919B	—	—	—	Proof	250.00

5.4300 g, .600 SILVER, .1047 oz ASW
Obv: Plain field below bust.

KM#	Date	Mintage	Fine	VF	XF	Unc
30b	1926	2.500	1.50	3.00	12.00	35.00
	1926	—	—	—	Proof	250.00
	1927	3.000	1.50	2.50	6.00	12.00
	1927	—	—	—	Proof	250.00
	1935 round top 3	1.000	1.50	2.50	3.50	7.00
	1935 flat top 3	Inc. Ab.	1.50	2.50	3.50	7.00

50 CENTS

13.5769 g, .800 SILVER, .3492 oz ASW

KM#	Date	Mintage	Fine	VF	XF	Unc
13	1886	.060	50.00	120.00	270.00	850.00
	1886	—	—	—	Proof	2200.
	1887	.094	40.00	75.00	180.00	475.00
	1887	—	—	—	Proof	2200.
	1888	.096	40.00	75.00	180.00	475.00
	1889	.032	800.00	1350.	1750.	3300.
	1890H	.042	100.00	200.00	325.00	850.00
	1891	.112	35.00	50.00	125.00	300.00
	1891	—	—	—	Proof	2200.
	1893	.024	450.00	800.00	1350.	2200.
	1893	—	—	—	Proof	2750.
	1894	.052	50.00	150.00	250.00	500.00
	1895	.056	50.00	150.00	250.00	500.00
	1896	.120	25.00	50.00	120.00	280.00
	1897	.036	100.00	200.00	320.00	800.00
	1897H	.044	85.00	150.00	250.00	600.00
	1898	.160	25.00	50.00	120.00	280.00
	1899	.136	25.00	50.00	120.00	280.00
	1900	.088	35.00	70.00	150.00	320.00
	1900H	.040	100.00	175.00	350.00	775.00
	1901	.120	25.00	50.00	120.00	280.00

KM#	Date	Mintage	Fine	VF	XF	Unc
23	1902	.148	50.00	80.00	175.00	280.00
	1902	—	—	—	Proof	900.00
	1903	.193	50.00	80.00	175.00	280.00
	1903	—	—	—	Proof	900.00
	1904	—	—		Proof	1000.
	1905B raised	.498	35.00	65.00	135.00	260.00
	1905B raised	—	—	—	Proof	950.00
	1905B incuse	—	—	—	Proof	950.00

10.1000 g, .900 SILVER, .2922 oz ASW

KM#	Date	Mintage	Fine	VF	XF	Unc
24	1907	.464	5.50	10.00	22.00	60.00
	1907H	2.667	5.50	10.00	22.00	60.00
	1907H	—	—	—	Proof	200.00
	1908	2.869	7.00	12.50	27.50	80.00
	1908H	Inc. 1907H	7.00	10.00	22.00	60.00

8.4200 g, .500 SILVER, .1353 oz ASW

Obv: Cross below bust.

KM#	Date	Mintage	Fine	VF	XF	Unc
35.1	1920	3.900	1.50	2.50	4.00	8.00
	1920	—	—	—	Proof	250.00
	1921	2.579	2.00	3.00	5.00	10.00
	1921	—	—	—	Proof	250.00

Obv: Dot below bust.

KM#	Date	Mintage	Fine	VF	XF	Unc
35.2	1920	Inc. Ab.	120.00	185.00	300.00	550.00

DOLLAR

26.9500 g, .900 SILVER, .7799 oz ASW

KM#	Date	Mintage	Fine	VF	XF	Unc
25	1903	—	—	—	Proof	1000.
	1903B incuse	15.010	15.00	25.00	50.00	100.00
	1903B raised	Inc. Ab.	70.00	120.00	250.00	600.00
	1903B raised	—	—	—	Proof	1100.
	1904B	20.365	12.50	20.00	35.00	85.00
	1904B	—	—	—	Proof	1000.

20.2100 g, .900 SILVER, .5848 oz ASW
Reduced size, 34.5mm.

KM#	Date	Mintage	Fine	VF	XF	Unc
26	1907	6.842	7.50	10.00	20.00	65.00
	1907H	4.000	7.50	10.00	20.00	65.00
	1907H	—	—	—	Proof	550.00
	1908	4.152	7.50	10.00	20.00	65.00
	1908	—	—	—	Proof	550.00
	1909	1.014	10.00	15.00	25.00	85.00
	1909	—	—	—	Proof	550.00

16.8500 g, .500 SILVER, .2709 oz ASW

KM#	Date	Mintage	Fine	VF	XF	Unc
33	1919	6.000	15.00	30.00	90.00	140.00
	1919(restrike)		—	—	Proof	80.00
	1920	8.164	10.00	20.00	30.00	70.00
	1920(restrike)		—	—	Proof	80.00
	1925	—	450.00	850.00	1250.	—
	1925	—	—	—	Proof	3500.
	1925(restrike)		—	—	Proof	600.00
	1926	—	450.00	850.00	1250.	—
	1926	—	—	—	Proof	3500.
	1926(restrike)		—	—	Proof	600.00

SARAWAK

Sarawak is a former British colony located on the northwest coast of Borneo. The Japanese occupation during World War II so thoroughly devastated the economy that Rajah Sir Charles Vyner Brooke ceded it to Great Britain on July 1, 1946. In September, 1963 the colony joined the Federation of Malaysia.

RULERS

James Brooke, Rajah, 1841-1868
Charles J. Brooke, Rajah, 1868-1917
Charles V. Brooke, Rajah, 1917-1946

MINT MARKS

H - Heaton, Birmingham

MONETARY SYSTEM

100 Cents = 1 Dollar

1/4 CENT

COPPER

KM#	Date	Mintage	Fine	VF	XF	Unc
1	1863	—	40.00	80.00	150.00	300.00
	1863	—	—	—	Proof	550.00

BRONZED COPPER

KM#	Date	Mintage	Fine	VF	XF	Unc
1a	1863	—	—	—	Proof	725.00

COPPER

KM#	Date	Mintage	Fine	VF	XF	Unc
4	1870	.100	8.00	20.00	50.00	120.00
	1870	—	—	—	Proof	350.00
	1896H	.283	6.00	15.00	35.00	100.00
	1896H	—	—	—	Proof	350.00

1/2 CENT

COPPER

KM#	Date	Mintage	Fine	VF	XF	Unc
2	1863	—	12.50	35.00	85.00	200.00
	1863	—	—	—	Proof	550.00

BRONZED COPPER

KM#	Date	Mintage	Fine	VF	XF	Unc
2a	1863	—	—	—	Proof	700.00

COPPER

KM#	Date	Mintage	Fine	VF	XF	Unc
5	1870	.250	6.00	18.00	40.00	95.00
	1879	.640	6.00	18.00	40.00	95.00
	1879	—	—	—	Proof	350.00
	1896H	.327	4.00	12.00	30.00	85.00
	1896H	—	—	—	Proof	350.00

KM#	Date	Mintage	Fine	VF	XF	Unc
20	1933H	2.000	1.00	2.00	4.00	9.00
	1933H	—	—	—	Proof	240.00

CENT

COPPER

KM#	Date	Mintage	Fine	VF	XF	Unc
3	1863	—	7.00	18.00	40.00	120.00
	1863	—	—	—	Proof	400.00

BRONZED COPPER

KM#	Date	Mintage	Fine	VF	XF	Unc
3a	1863	—	—	—	Proof	600.00

COPPER

KM#	Date	Mintage	Fine	VF	XF	Unc
6	1870	—	2.50	6.00	15.00	40.00
	1870	—	—	—	Proof	200.00
	1870	—	—		Gilt Proof	200.00
	1879	.750	3.50	9.00	25.00	65.00
	1879	—	—	—	Proof	200.00
	1880	1.070	3.00	7.00	22.00	62.50
	1882	1.070	2.50	6.00	16.50	50.00
	1882	—	—	—	Proof	200.00
	1884	1.070	2.50	6.00	16.50	50.00
	1884	—	—	—	Proof	200.00
	1885	2.140	2.50	6.00	16.50	50.00
	1885	—	—	—	Proof	200.00
	1886	3.210	2.50	6.00	16.50	50.00
	1887	1.605	2.50	6.00	16.50	50.00
	1887	—	—	—	Proof	200.00
	1888	2.140	2.50	6.00	16.50	50.00
	1888	—	—	—	Proof	200.00
	1889	.535	2.50	6.00	16.50	50.00
	1889/8H	2.675	2.50	6.00	16.50	50.00
	1889H	Inc. Ab.	2.50	6.00	16.50	50.00
	1889H	—	—	—	Proof	200.00
	1890H	3.210	2.50	6.00	16.50	50.00
	1891	.535	5.00	10.00	25.00	55.00
	1891H	1.070	2.50	6.00	16.50	50.00

NOTE: Varieties exist.

KM#	Date	Mintage	Fine	VF	XF	Unc
7	1892H	2.178	2.50	6.00	16.50	50.00
	1892H	—	—	—	Proof	200.00
	1893H	1.634	2.50	6.00	16.50	50.00
	1894H	1.633	2.50	6.00	16.50	50.00
	1896H	2.178	2.50	6.00	16.50	50.00
	1896H	—	—	—	Proof	200.00
	1897H	1.089	2.50	6.00	16.50	50.00

COPPER-NICKEL

KM#	Date	Mintage	Fine	VF	XF	Unc
12	1920H	5.000	3.00	7.50	18.00	60.00

BRONZE

KM#	Date	Mintage	Fine	VF	XF	Unc
18	1927H	5.000	1.25	2.25	4.50	9.00
	1927H	—	—	—	Proof	210.00
	1929H	2.000	1.25	2.25	5.00	10.00
	1930H	3.000	1.25	2.25	5.00	10.00
	1930H	—	—	—	Proof	210.00
	1937H	3.000	1.25	2.25	4.50	9.00
	1941H*	3.000	250.00	350.00	525.00	900.00
	1942	—	—	Reported, not confirmed		

***NOTE:** Estimate 50 pcs. exist.

5 CENTS

1.3500 g, .800 SILVER, .0347 oz ASW

KM#	Date	Mintage	Fine	VF	XF	Unc
8	1900H	.200	20.00	40.00	65.00	120.00
	1900H	—	—	—	Proof	350.00
	1908H	.040	30.00	50.00	90.00	140.00
	1908H	—	—	—	Proof	350.00
	1911H	.040	30.00	50.00	90.00	140.00
	1913H	.100	25.00	50.00	80.00	120.00
	1913H	—	—	—	Proof	350.00
	1915H	.100	25.00	50.00	90.00	130.00
	1915H	—	—	—	Proof	350.00

1.3500 g, .400 SILVER, .0174 oz ASW

KM#	Date	Mintage	Fine	VF	XF	Unc
13	1920H	.100	40.00	60.00	100.00	180.00
	1920H	—	—	—	Proof	400.00

COPPER-NICKEL

KM#	Date	Mintage	Fine	VF	XF	Unc
14	1920H	.400	2.00	4.00	8.00	20.00
	1927H	.600	2.00	4.00	8.00	20.00
	1927H	—	—	—	Proof	275.00

10 CENTS

2.7100 g, .800 SILVER, .0697 oz ASW

KM#	Date	Mintage	Fine	VF	XF	Unc
9	1900H	.150	15.00	20.00	45.00	90.00
	1900H	—	—	—	Proof	350.00
	1906H	.050	20.00	30.00	55.00	100.00
	1906H	—	—	—	Proof	350.00
	1910H	.050	20.00	30.00	55.00	100.00
	1910H	—	—	—	Proof	350.00
	1911/10H	.100	20.00	30.00	60.00	120.00
	1911H	Inc. Ab.	15.00	20.00	40.00	90.00
	1913H	.100	15.00	20.00	40.00	90.00
	1913H	—	—	—	Proof	350.00
	1915H	.100	35.00	50.00	90.00	200.00
	1915H	—	—	—	Proof	350.00

KM#	Date	Mintage	Fine	VF	XF	Unc
15	1920H	.150	18.00	27.50	50.00	90.00
	1920H	—	—	—	Proof	350.00

COPPER-NICKEL

KM#	Date	Mintage	Fine	VF	XF	Unc
16	1920H	.800	2.00	4.00	8.00	17.50
	1927H	1.000	2.00	3.00	6.00	17.50
	1927H	—	—	—	Proof	300.00
	1934H	2.000	2.00	3.00	6.00	17.50
	1934H	—	—	—	Proof	300.00

20 CENTS

5.4300 g, .800 SILVER, .1396 oz ASW

KM#	Date	Mintage	Fine	VF	XF	Unc
10	1900H	.075	25.00	50.00	75.00	170.00
	1900H	—	—	—	Proof	550.00
	1906H	.025	30.00	62.50	110.00	220.00
	1906H	—	—	—	Proof	550.00
	1910H	.025	30.00	62.50	110.00	220.00
	1910H	—	—	—	Proof	550.00
	1911H	.015	30.00	62.50	110.00	220.00
	1913H	.025	30.00	62.50	110.00	220.00
	1913H	—	—	—	Proof	550.00
	1915H	.025	125.00	175.00	300.00	500.00
	1915H	—	—	—	Proof	725.00

5.4300 g, .400 SILVER, .0699 oz ASW

KM#	Date	Mintage	Fine	VF	XF	Unc
17	1920H	.025	65.00	120.00	220.00	400.00
	1920H	—	—	—	Proof	600.00
	1927H	.250	5.00	10.00	22.50	50.00
	1927H	—	—	—	Proof	400.00

50 CENTS

13.5700 g, .800 SILVER, .3490 oz ASW

KM#	Date	Mintage	Fine	VF	XF	Unc
11	1900H	.040	70.00	120.00	220.00	350.00
	1900H	—	—	—	Proof	1350.
	1906H	.010	225.00	325.00	500.00	950.00
	1906H	—	—	—	Proof	1350.

13.5700 g, .500 SILVER, .2181 oz ASW

KM#	Date	Mintage	Fine	VF	XF	Unc
19	1927H	.200	12.00	20.00	38.00	90.00
	1927H	—	—	—	Proof	400.00

BRITISH NORTH BORNEO

British North Borneo (now known as Sabah), a former British protectorate and crown colony, occupies the northern tip of the island of Borneo. The island of Labuan, which lies 6 miles off the northwest coast of the island of Borneo, was attached to Singapore settlement in 1907. It became an independent settlement of the Straits Colony in 1912 and was incorporated with British North Borneo in 1946.

RULERS

British

MINT MARKS

H - Heaton, Birmingham

MONETARY SYSTEM

100 Cents=1 Straits Dollar

1/2 CENT

BRONZE

KM#	Date	Mintage	Fine	VF	XF	Unc
1	1885H	.500	4.00	12.50	30.00	75.00
	1885H	—	—	—	Proof	160.00
	1886H	1.000	3.50	7.50	25.00	60.00
	1886H	—	—	—	Proof	160.00
	1887H	.500	3.50	7.50	25.00	60.00
	1891H	2.000	3.50	7.50	22.00	50.00
	1891H	—	—	—	Proof	160.00
	1907H	1.000	15.00	30.00	45.00	130.00

CENT

BRONZE

KM#	Date	Mintage	Fine	VF	XF	Unc
2	1882H	2.000	2.50	4.50	16.00	45.00
	1882H	—	—	—	Proof	125.00
	1884H	2.000	2.50	4.50	16.00	45.00
	1884H	—	—	—	Proof	125.00
	1885H	1.750	3.00	6.00	18.00	50.00
	1886H	5.000	2.50	4.50	16.00	45.00
	1886H	—	—	—	Proof	125.00
	1887H	6.000	2.50	4.50	16.00	45.00
	1887H	—	—	—	Proof	125.00
	1888H	6.000	2.50	4.50	16.00	45.00
	1888H	—	—	—	Proof	125.00
	1889H	9.000	2.50	4.50	16.00	45.00
	1890H	8.003	2.50	4.50	16.00	45.00
	1890H	—	—	—	Proof	125.00
	1891H	3.000	2.50	4.50	16.00	45.00
	1891H	—	—	—	Proof	125.00
	1894H	1.000	12.50	27.50	50.00	90.00
	1896H	1.000	12.50	27.50	50.00	90.00
	1907H	1.000	20.00	50.00	75.00	125.00
	1907H	—	—	—	Proof	400.00

COPPER-NICKEL

KM#	Date	Mintage	Fine	VF	XF	Unc
3	1904H	2.000	2.00	3.50	8.50	20.00
	1921H	1.000	2.00	3.50	12.50	22.50
	1935H	1.000	1.25	2.50	6.50	20.00
	1938H	1.000	1.25	2.50	6.50	20.00
	1941H	1.000	1.25	2.50	6.50	20.00

2-1/2 CENTS

COPPER-NICKEL

KM#	Date	Mintage	Fine	VF	XF	Unc
4	1903H	2.000	2.50	5.00	15.00	40.00
	1903H	—	—	—	Proof	300.00
	1920H	.280	5.00	15.00	30.00	65.00

5 CENTS

COPPER-NICKEL

KM#	Date	Mintage	Fine	VF	XF	Unc
5	1903H	1.000	2.50	5.00	15.00	35.00
	1920H	.100	5.00	10.00	30.00	55.00
	1921H	.500	2.50	5.00	15.00	35.00
	1927H	.150	3.00	5.00	15.00	35.00
	1928H	.150	2.00	4.00	12.00	30.00
	1938H	.500	1.50	3.00	7.50	15.00
	1940H	.500	1.50	3.00	7.50	15.00
	1941H	1.000	1.50	3.00	7.50	15.00

25 CENTS

2.8300 g, .500 SILVER, .0454 oz ASW

KM#	Date	Mintage	Fine	VF	XF	Unc
6	1929H	.400	10.00	15.00	25.00	45.00
	1929H	—	—	—	Proof	160.00

MALAYA

Malaya, a former member of the British Commonwealth located in the southern part of the Malay peninsula, consisted of 11 states: the unfederated Malay states of Johore, Kelantan, Kedah, Perlis and Trengganu; the federated Malay states of Negri-Sembilan, Pahang, Perak and Selangor; former members of the Straits Settlements Penang and Malacca. Malaya was occupied by the Japanese during the years 1942-1945. The only local opposition to the Japanese had come mainly from the Chinese Communists who then continued their guerilla operations after the Japanese had surrendered. They were finally defeated in 1956. Malaya was granted full independence on Aug. 31, 1957.

RULERS

British

MINT MARKS

I - Calcutta Mint(1941)
I - Bombay Mint(1945)
No Mint mark - Royal Mint

MONETARY SYSTEM

100 Cents = 1 Dollar

1/2 CENT

BRONZE

KM#	Date	Mintage	Fine	VF	XF	Unc
1	1940	6.000	.50	1.25	2.00	4.00
	1940	—	—	—	Proof	150.00

CENT

BRONZE

KM#	Date	Mintage	Fine	VF	XF	Unc
2	1939	20.000	.25	.40	.60	1.50
	1939	—	—	—	Proof	150.00
	1940	23.600	.25	.40	.60	1.50
	1940	—	—	—	Proof	—
	1941-I	33.620	.75	1.25	5.00	10.00

Reduced size.

KM#	Date	Mintage	Fine	VF	XF	Unc
6	1943	50.000	.10	.20	.35	.80
	1943	—	—	—	Proof	150.00
	1945	40.033	.10	.20	.35	.80
	1945	—	—	—	Proof	150.00

5 CENTS

1.3600 g, .750 SILVER, .0327 oz ASW

KM#	Date	Mintage	Fine	VF	XF	Unc
3	1939	2.000	.50	1.00	1.50	2.50
	1939	—	—	—	Proof	250.00
	1941	4.000	.40	.50	1.20	2.00
	1941	—	—	—	Proof	250.00
	1941-I	Inc. Ab.	.40	.50	1.20	2.00

1.3600 g, .500 SILVER, .0218 oz ASW

KM#	Date	Mintage	Fine	VF	XF	Unc
3a	1943	10.000	.30	.40	.65	1.50
	1943	—	—	—	Proof	250.00
	1945	8.800	.30	.40	.65	1.50
	1945	—	—	—	Proof	250.00
	1945-I	4.600	.50	.75	1.00	2.00

COPPER-NICKEL

KM#	Date	Mintage	Fine	VF	XF	Unc
7	1948	30.000	.10	.25	.75	2.00
	1948	—	—	—	Proof	220.00
	1950	40.000	.10	.25	.75	2.00
	1950	—	—	—	Proof	220.00

10 CENTS

2.7100 g, .750 SILVER, .0653 oz ASW

KM#	Date	Mintage	Fine	VF	XF	Unc
4	1939	10.000	.75	1.00	1.25	2.50
	1939	—	—	—	Proof	280.00
	1941	17.000	.75	1.00	1.25	2.50
	1941	—	—	—	Proof	280.00
	1941-I	—	—	—	Proof	Rare

2.7100 g, .500 SILVER, .0435 oz ASW

KM#	Date	Mintage	Fine	VF	XF	Unc
4a	1943	5.000	.75	1.00	1.50	2.50
	1943	—	—	—	Proof	280.00
	1945	3.152	.75	1.00	1.50	3.00
	1945-I	—	—	—	Proof	Rare

COPPER-NICKEL

KM#	Date	Mintage	Fine	VF	XF	Unc
8	1948	23.885	.15	.30	.75	2.25
	1948	—	—	—	Proof	280.00
	1949	26.115	.25	.50	1.20	3.00
	1949	—	—	—	Proof	280.00
	1950	65.000	.15	.30	.75	2.25
	1950	—	—	—	Proof	280.00

20 CENTS

5.4300 g, .750 SILVER, .1309 oz ASW

KM#	Date	Mintage	Fine	VF	XF	Unc
5	1939	8.000	1.25	1.75	2.25	4.50
	1939	—	—	—	Proof	280.00

5.4300 g, .500 SILVER, .0872 oz ASW

KM#	Date	Mintage	Fine	VF	XF	Unc
5a	1943	5.000	1.25	1.75	2.25	4.50
	1943	—	—	—	Proof	260.00
	1945	10.000	2.00	4.00	8.00	10.00
	1945-I	—	—	—	Proof	Rare

COPPER-NICKEL

KM#	Date	Mintage	Fine	VF	XF	Unc
9	1948	40.000	.30	.50	1.50	4.50
	1948	—	—	—	Proof	280.00
9	1950	20.000	.30	.50	1.50	4.50
	1950	—	—	—	Proof	280.00

MALAYA & BRITISH BORNEO

Malaya & British Borneo, a Currency Commission named the Board of Commissioners of Currency, Malaya and British Borneo, was initiated on Jan. 1, 1952, for the purpose of providing a common currency for use in Johore, Kelantan, Kedah, Perlis, Trengganu, Negri Sembilan, Pahang, Perak, Selangor, Penang, Malacca, Singapore, North Borneo, Sarawak and Brunei.

RULERS

British

MINT MARKS

KN - King's Norton, Birmingham
H - Heaton, Birmingham
No Mint mark - Royal Mint

MONETARY SYSTEM

100 Cents = 1 Dollar

CENT

BRONZE

KM#	Date	Mintage	VF	XF	Unc
5	1956	6.250	.10	.25	.50
	1956	—	—	Proof	125.00
	1957	12.500	.10	.25	.50
	1957	—	—	Proof	—
	1958	5.000	.10	.25	.50
	1958	—	—	Proof	125.00
	1961	10.000	.10	.20	.50
	1961	—	—	Proof	125.00

KM#	Date	Mintage	VF	XF	Unc
6	1962	45.000	—	.10	.35
	1962	*25 pcs.	—	Proof	125.00

5 CENTS

COPPER-NICKEL

KM#	Date	Mintage	VF	XF	Unc
	1953	20.000	.25	.50	1.50
	1953	—	—	Proof	200.00
	1957	10.000	.50	.75	2.00
	1957	—	—	Proof	—
	1957H	10.000	.50	.75	2.00
	1957KN	Inc. Ab.	1.25	1.75	3.00
	1958	10.000	.25	.50	1.50
	1958	—	—	Proof	200.00
	1958H	10.000	.50	.75	2.00
	1961	95.000	.15	.50	1.25
	1961	—	—	Proof	—
	1961H	5.000	2.00	4.00	9.00
	1961KN	Inc. Ab.	1.00	2.00	4.50

10 CENTS

COPPER-NICKEL

KM#	Date	Mintage	VF	XF	Unc
2	1953	20.000	.40	.80	2.00
	1953	—	—	Proof	200.00
	1956	10.000	.40	1.00	2.50
	1956	—	—	Proof	200.00
	1957H	10.000	.40	1.20	3.00
	1957H	—	—	Proof	200.00
	1957KN	10.000	.40	1.20	3.00
	1958	10.000	.40	.80	2.00
	1958	—	—	Proof	200.00
	1960	10.000	.40	.80	2.00
	1960	—	—	Proof	200.00
	1961	60.780	.20	.50	1.00
	1961	—	—	Proof	200.00
	1961H	69.220	.20	.50	1.00
	1961KN	Inc. Ab.	.50	.80	2.75

20 CENTS

COPPER-NICKEL

KM#	Date	Mintage	VF	XF	Unc
3	1954	10.000	.80	1.50	2.50
	1954	—	—	Proof	220.00
	1956	5.000	.75	1.25	2.00
	1956	—	—	Proof	220.00
	1957H	2.500	1.20	1.80	3.00
	1957KN	2.500	1.20	1.80	4.00
	1961	32.000	.50	.75	2.00
	1961	—	—	Proof	200.00
	1961H	23.000	.75	1.25	2.00

50 CENTS

COPPER-NICKEL, security edge

KM#	Date	Mintage	VF	XF	Unc
4.1	1954	8.000	1.00	2.00	4.50
	1954	—	—	Proof	280.00
	1955H	4.000	1.50	2.50	5.00
	1956	3.440	1.50	2.25	5.00
	1956	—	—	Proof	280.00
	1957H	2.000	1.50	2.50	5.00
	1957KN	2.000	2.00	2.75	6.00
	1958H	4.000	1.00	1.50	5.00
	1961	17.000	1.00	1.50	3.50
	1961	—	—	Proof	280.00
	1961H	4.000	1.50	2.50	5.00

Error, w/o security edge.

KM#	Date	Mintage	VF	XF	Unc
4.2	1954	Inc. Ab.	90.00	120.00	300.00
	1957KN	Inc. Ab.	90.00	120.00	300.00
	1958H	Inc. Ab.	90.00	120.00	300.00
	1961	Inc. Ab.	90.00	120.00	300.00
	1961H	Inc. Ab.	90.00	120.00	300.00

MALAYSIA

The independent limited constitutional monarchy of Malaysia, which occupies the southern part of the Malay Peninsula in southeast Asia and the northern part of the island of Borneo, has an area of 127,317 sq. mi. (329,750 sq. km.) and a population of 15.4 million. Capital: Kuala Lumpur. The economy is based on agriculture, mining and forestry. Rubber, tin, timber and palm oil are exported.

Malaysia came into being on Sept. 16, 1963, as a federation of Malaya (Johore, Kelantan, Kedah, Perlis, Trengganu, Negri-Sembilan, Pahang, Perak, Selangor, Penang, Malacca), Singapore, Sabah (British North Borneo) and Sarawak. Following two serious racial riots involving Malayans and Chinese, Singapore withdrew from the federation on Aug. 9, 1965, to become an independent republic within the British Commonwealth.

MINT MARKS

FM - Franklin Mint, U.S.A.*

***NOTE:** From 1975 the Franklin Mint has produced coinage in up to 3 different qualities. Qualities of issue are designated in ( ) after each date and are defined as follows:

(M) MATTE - Normal circulation strike or a dull finish produced by sandblasting special uncirculated (polish finish) or proof quality dies.

(U) SPECIAL UNCIRCULATED - Polished or proof-like in appearance without any frosted features.

(P) PROOF - The highest quality obtainable having mirror-like fields and frosted features.

MONETARY SYSTEM

100 Sen = 1 Ringgit (Dollar)

SEN

BRONZE
Parliament Building

KM#	Date	Mintage	VF	XF	Unc
1	1967	45.000	—	.10	.15
	1967	500 pcs.	—	Proof	5.00
	1968	10.500	—	.10	.15
	1970	2.535	.15	.50	1.50
	1971	30.012	—	.10	.15
	1973	39.264	—	.10	.15
	1980FM(P)	5,000	—	Proof	1.00
	1981FM(P)	6,628	—	Proof	1.00

COPPER-CLAD STEEL

KM#	Date	Mintage	VF	XF	Unc
1a	1973	Inc. Ab.	.15	.45	.65
	1976	24.694	—	.10	.15
	1977	24.437	—	.10	.15
	1978	30.861	—	.10	.15
	1979	15.714	—	.10	.15
	1980	16.151	—	.10	.15
	1981	24.633	—	.10	.15
	1982	37.295	—	.10	.15
	1983	12.140	—	.10	.15
	1984	26.260	—	.10	.15
	1985	52.402	—	.10	.15
	1986	48.920	—	.10	.15
	1987	37.409	—	.10	.15
	1988	56.749	—	.10	.15

BRONZE

KM#	Date	Mintage	VF	XF	Unc
1c	1976	100 pcs.	25.00	65.00	125.00

BRONZE CLAD STEEL
Drum

KM#	Date	Mintage	VF	XF	Unc
49	1989	—	—	—	.15
	1990	—	—	—	.15
	1991	—	—	—	.15
	1992	—	—	—	.15

5 SEN

COPPER-NICKEL

KM#	Date	Mintage	VF	XF	Unc
2	1967	75.464	—	.10	.20
	1967	500 pcs.	—	Proof	10.00
	1968	74.536	—	.10	.20
	1971	16.668	—	.30	.50
	1973	102.942	—	.10	.15
	1976	65.659	—	.10	.15
	1977	10.609	—	.30	.50
	1978	50.012	—	.10	.15
	1979	38.824	—	.10	.15
	1980	33.898	—	.10	.15
	1980FM(P)	6,628	—	Proof	2.00
	1981	51.490	—	.10	.15
	1981FM(P)	—	—	Proof	3.00
	1982	118.594	—	.10	.15
	1985	15.553	—	.10	.15
	1987	17.623	—	.10	.15
	1988	14.203	—	.10	.15

Top With String

KM#	Date	Mintage	VF	XF	Unc
50	1989	—	—	—	.15
	1990	—	—	—	.15
	1991	—	—	—	.15
	1992	—	—	—	.15

10 SEN

COPPER-NICKEL

KM#	Date	Mintage	VF	XF	Unc
3	1967	106.708	.10	.15	.30
	1967	500 pcs.	—	Proof	12.50
	1968	20.000	.10	.15	.30
	1971	.042	35.00	45.00	65.00
	1973	214.865	.10	.15	.30
	1976	148.809	.10	.15	.30
	1977	52.724	.10	.15	.30
	1978	21.154	.10	.15	.30
	1979	50.663	.10	.15	.30
	1980	51.802	.10	.15	.30
	1980FM(P)	6,628	—	Proof	3.00
	1981	236.639	.10	.15	.30
	1981FM(P)	—	—	Proof	5.00
	1982	145.639	—	.10	.25
	1983	30.840	—	.10	.25
	1988	—	—	.10	.25

Ceremonial Table

KM#	Date	Mintage	VF	XF	Unc
51	1989	—	—	—	.25
	1990	—	—	—	.25
	1991	—	—	—	.25
	1992	—	—	—	.25

20 SEN

COPPER-NICKEL

KM#	Date	Mintage	VF	XF	Unc
4	1967	19.560	.10	.30	.45
	1967	500 pcs.	—	Proof	17.50
	1968	35.440	.10	.30	.45
	1969	15.000	.15	.35	.50
	1970	1.054	.50	.75	1.00
	1971	9.968	.15	.35	.50
	1973	116.075	.10	.20	.35
	1976	61.534	.10	.20	.35
	1977	52.002	.10	.20	.35
	1978	6.847	.15	.30	.45
	1979	17.346	.10	.20	.35
	1980	32.842	.10	.20	.35
	1980FM(P)	6,628	—	Proof	4.00
	1981	144.128	.10	.20	.35
	1981FM(P)	—	—	Proof	6.00
	1982	97.905	—	.10	.25
	1983	—	—	.10	.25
	1987	34.330	—	.10	.25
	1988	72.110	—	.10	.25

Basket Containing Food and Utensils

KM#	Date	Mintage	VF	XF	Unc
52	1989	—	—	—	.35
	1990	—	—	—	.35
	1991	—	—	—	.35
	1992	—	—	—	.35

50 SEN

COPPER-NICKEL

KM#	Date	Mintage	VF	XF	Unc
5.1	1967	15.000	.25	.50	1.00
(5)	1967	500 pcs.	—	Proof	20.00
	1968	12.000	.25	.50	1.00
	1969	2.000	.50	.75	1.50

Error, w/o security edge.

KM#	Date	Mintage	VF	XF	Unc
5.2	1967	Inc. Ab.	75.00	140.00	240.00
(6)	1968	Inc. Ab.	75.00	140.00	240.00
	1969	Inc. Ab.	250.00	350.00	550.00

Lettered edge

KM#	Date	Mintage	VF	XF	Unc
5.3	1971	8.414	.30	.60	1.00
(8)	1973	48.250	.25	.50	.75
	1976	—	.25	.40	.60
	1977	17.721	.25	.40	.60
	1978	11.033	.25	.40	.60
	1979	5.361	.25	.40	.60
	1980	15.916	.25	.40	.60
	1980FM(P)	6,628	—	Proof	5.00
	1981	22.969	—	.25	.50
	1982	20.585	—	.25	.50
	1983	11.560	—	.25	.50
	1984	10.140	—	.25	.50
	1985	7.115	—	.25	.50
	1986	8.193	—	.25	.50
	1987	8.592	—	.25	.50
	1988	18.810	—	.25	.50

Plain edge

KM#	Date	Mintage	VF	XF	Unc
5.4	1981FM(P)	—	—	Proof	10.00

Ceremonial Kite

KM#	Date	Mintage	VF	XF	Unc
53	1989	—	—	—	.65
	1990	—	—	—	.65
	1991	—	—	—	.65
	1992	—	—	—	.65

RINGGIT

COPPER-NICKEL
10th Anniversary Bank Negara

KM#	Date	Mintage	VF	XF	Unc
7	1969	1.000	1.00	1.50	3.00

17.000 g, .925 SILVER, .5055 oz ASW

KM#	Date	Mintage	VF	XF	Unc
7a	1969	1,000	—	Proof	400.00

COPPER-NICKEL

KM#	Date	Mintage	VF	XF	Unc
9.1	1971	2.379	.50	.75	1.25
	1971	500 pcs.	—	Proof	800.00
	1980	.472	.60	.85	1.50
	1980FM(P)	6,628	—	Proof	10.00
	1981	.765	.60	.85	1.50
	1982	.202	.60	.85	1.50
	1984	.356	.60	.85	1.50
	1985	.302	.60	.85	1.50
	1986	1.500	.60	.85	1.50
	1987	.177	.60	.85	1.50

Plain edge

KM#	Date	Mintage	VF	XF	Unc
9.2	1981FM(P)	—	—	Proof	20.00

Kuala Lumpur Anniversary

KM#	Date	Mintage	VF	XF	Unc
12	1972	.500	.60	.85	2.50
	1972	500 pcs.	—	Proof	350.00

25th Anniversary Employee Provident Fund

KM#	Date	Mintage	VF	XF	Unc
13	1976FM(U)	.500	.60	.85	2.50
	1976FM(P)	7,810	—	Proof	18.00

3rd Malaysian 5 Year Plan

KM#	Date	Mintage	VF	XF	Unc
16	1976	1.000	.60	.75	2.00
	1976FM(P)	.017	—	Proof	12.00

9th South-East Asian Games

KM#	Date	Mintage	VF	XF	Unc
22	1977	1.000	.60	.75	2.00
	1977FM(P)	.011	—	Proof	17.50

20th Anniversary of Independence

KM#	Date	Mintage	VF	XF	Unc
25	1977	.500	.60	.75	2.00
	1977FM(P)	3,102	—	Proof	35.00

100th Anniversary of Natural Rubber Production

KM#	Date	Mintage	VF	XF	Unc
26	1977	.500	.60	.75	2.00

20th Anniversary of Bank Negara

KM#	Date	Mintage	VF	XF	Unc
27	1979	.300	.60	.75	2.00

17.0000 g, .925 SILVER, .5055 oz ASW

KM#	Date	Mintage	VF	XF	Unc
27a	1979	8,000	—	Proof	22.50
	1979FM(P)	6,628	—	Proof	30.00

COPPER-NICKEL
15th Century of Hegira

KM#	Date	Mintage	VF	XF	Unc
28	AH1401	.050	.60	.75	2.00

Tun Hussein Onn

KM#	Date	Mintage	VF	XF	Unc
29	1981	1.000	.50	.65	1.85
	1981	.010	—	Proof	15.00

25th Anniversary of Independence

KM#	Date	Mintage	VF	XF	Unc
32	1982	1.500	.50	.65	1.85
	1982	.015	—	Proof	12.00

5th Malaysian 5 Year Plan

KM#	Date	Mintage	VF	XF	Unc
36	1986	1.000	.50	.65	1.85
	1986	8,000	—	Proof	10.00

PATA Conference

KM#	Date	Mintage	VF	XF	Unc
39	1986	.500	.50	.65	1.85

16.8500 g, .500 SILVER, .2709 oz ASW

KM#	Date	Mintage	VF	XF	Unc
39a	1986	.011	—	Proof	10.00

COPPER-ZINC-TIN
30th Anniversary of Independence

KM#	Date	Mintage	VF	XF	Unc
43	1987	1.000	—	.60	1.75
	1987	2,000	—	Proof	10.00

ALUMINUM-BRONZE
Native Dagger and Scabbard

KM#	Date	Mintage	VF	XF	Unc
54	1989	—	—	—	1.75
	1990	—	—	—	1.75
	1991	—	—	—	1.75
	1992	—	—	—	1.75

5 RINGGIT

COPPER-NICKEL

KM#	Date	Mintage	VF	XF	Unc
10	1971	2.000	2.50	3.00	5.00
	1971	500 pcs.	—	Proof	850.00

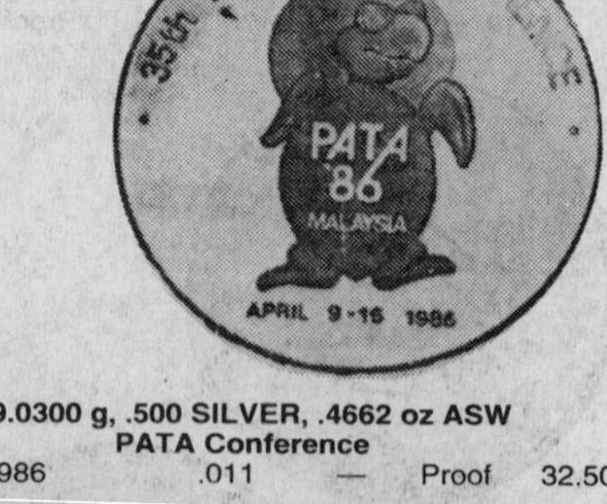

29.0300 g, .500 SILVER, .4662 oz ASW
PATA Conference

KM#	Date	Mintage	VF	XF	Unc
40	1986	.011	—	Proof	32.50

ALUMINUM-BRONZE
15th South East Asian Games

KM#	Date	Mintage	VF	XF	Unc
47	1989	.500	—	—	6.00
	1989	.050	—	Proof	12.50

Commonwealth Heads of State Meeting

KM#	Date	Mintage	VF	XF	Unc
55	1989	.150	—	—	6.00
	1989	8,000	—	Proof	12.50

100th Anniversary of Kuala Lumpur

KM#	Date	Mintage	VF	XF	Unc
59	1990	—	—	—	8.00

World Wildlife Fund - Stylized Bird

KM#	Date	Mintage	VF	XF	Unc
61	1992	—	—	—	5.00

10 RINGGIT

10.8200 g, .925 SILVER, .3218 oz ASW
3rd Malaysian 5 Year Plan

KM#	Date	Mintage	VF	XF	Unc
17	1976FM(U)	.200	—	—	8.00
	1976FM(P)	.010	—	Proof	15.00
	1980FM(P)	6,628	—	Proof	20.00

10.8200 g, .500 SILVER, .1740 oz ASW
30th Anniversary of Independence

KM#	Date	Mintage	VF	XF	Unc
44	1987	.050	—	—	6.00
	1987	.010	—	Proof	12.00

13.6000 g, .925 SILVER, .4045 oz ASW
Proclamation of Melaka as a Historical City

KM#	Date	Mintage	VF	XF	Unc
57	1989	.020	—	Proof	27.00

15 RINGGIT

28.2800 g, .925 SILVER, .8411 oz ASW
Conservation - Malaysian Gaur

KM#	Date	Mintage	VF	XF	Unc
19	1976	.040	—	—	20.00
	1976	8,113	—	Proof	30.00

16.7300 g, .800 SILVER, .5347 oz ASW
15th South East Asian Games

KM#	Date	Mintage	VF	XF	Unc
48	1989	.050	—	P/L	12.00
	1989	.020	—	Proof	25.00

20 RINGGIT

16.2300 g, .500 SILVER, .2609 oz ASW
Tun Hussein Onn

KM#	Date	Mintage	VF	XF	Unc
30	1981FM(U)	.100	—	—	12.50
	1981FM(P)	5,000	—	Proof	25.00

25 RINGGIT

35.0000 g, .925 SILVER, 1.0409 oz ASW
25th Anniversary Employee Provident Fund

KM#	Date	Mintage	VF	XF	Unc
14	1976FM(U)	.100	—	—	15.00
	1976FM(P)	7,796	—	Proof	55.00

Conservation - Rhinoceros Hornbill
Obv: Similar to 500 Ringgit, KM#21.

KM#	Date	Mintage	VF	XF	Unc
20	1976	.040	—	—	32.50
	1976	8,008	—	Proof	50.00

9th South-East Asian Games

KM#	Date	Mintage	VF	XF	Unc
23	1977FM(U)	.100	—	—	20.00
	1977FM(P)	5,877	—	Proof	65.00
	1980FM(P)	5,000	—	Proof	75.00

25th Anniversary of Independence
Obv: Similar to 1 Ringgit, KM#32.

KM#	Date	Mintage	VF	XF	Unc
33	1982	.154	—	—	15.00
	1982	7,000	—	Proof	30.00

35.0000 g, .500 SILVER, .5627 oz ASW
25th Anniversary of the National Bank

KM#	Date	Mintage	VF	XF	Unc
35	1984	.098	—	—	15.00
	1984	.010	—	Proof	35.00

5th Malaysian 5 Year Plan

KM#	Date	Mintage	VF	XF	Unc
37	1986	.080	—	—	15.00
	1986	5,000	—	Proof	30.00

23.3300 g, .925 SILVER, .6939 oz ASW
Women's Decade

KM#	Date	Mintage	VF	XF	Unc
41	ND(1985)	2,000	—	Proof	47.50

21.9000 g, .750 SILVER, .5281 oz ASW
Commonwealth Heads of State Meeting

KM#	Date	Mintage	VF	XF	Unc
56	1989	.030	—	—	15.00
	1989	8,000	—	Proof	30.00

100th Anniversary of Kuala Lumpur

KM#	Date	Mintage	VF	XF	Unc
60	1990	—	—	—	20.00

21.7700 g, .925 SILVER, .6474 oz ASW
World Wildlife Fund - Fish

KM#	Date	Mintage	VF	XF	Unc
62	1992	*.050	—	Proof	35.00

30 RINGGIT

22.0000 g, .850 SILVER, .6012 oz ASW
30th Anniversary of the National Bank

KM#	Date	Mintage	VF	XF	Unc
46	1989	.047	—	—	15.00
	1989	.010	—	Proof	30.00

100 RINGGIT

18.6600 g, .917 GOLD, .5502 oz AGW
Prime Minister Abdul Rahman Putra Al-haj

KM#	Date	Mintage	VF	XF	Unc
11	1971	.100	—	—	320.00
	1971	500 pcs.	—	Proof	900.00

200 RINGGIT

7.3000 g, .900 GOLD, .2112 oz AGW
3rd Malaysian 5 Year Plan

KM#	Date	Mintage	VF	XF	Unc
18	1976FM(U)	.051	—	—	100.00
	1976FM(P)	3,102	—	Proof	150.00

7.2200 g, .900 GOLD, .2089 oz AGW
9th South East Asian Games

KM#	Date	Mintage	VF	XF	Unc
24	1977FM(U)	.012	—	—	120.00
	1977FM(P)	975 pcs.	—	Proof	200.00

250 RINGGIT

10.1100 g, .900 GOLD, .2925 oz AGW
25th Anniversary Employee Provident Fund

KM#	Date	Mintage	VF	XF	Unc
15	1976FM(U)	.030	—	—	150.00
	1976FM(P)	7,706	—	Proof	200.00

8.1000 g, .900 GOLD, .2344 oz AGW
Women's Decade

KM#	Date	Mintage	VF	XF	Unc
42	1985	1,500	—	Proof	220.00

7.4300 g, .900 GOLD, .2150 oz AGW
30th Anniversary of Independence

KM#	Date	Mintage	VF	XF	Unc
45	1987	5,000	—	—	125.00
	1987	2,000	—	Proof	160.00

7.1300 g, .900 GOLD, .2063 oz AGW
15th South East Asian Games

KM#	Date	Mintage	VF	XF	Unc
58	1989	2,500	—	Proof	210.00

500 RINGGIT

33.4370 g, .900 GOLD, .9676 oz AGW
Conservation - Malayan Tapir

KM#	Date	Mintage	VF	XF	Unc
21	1976	2,894	—	—	550.00
	1976	508 pcs.	—	Proof	700.00

10.2600 g, .900 GOLD, .2969 oz AGW
Tun Hussein Onn

KM#	Date	Mintage	VF	XF	Unc
31	1981FM(U)	.020	—	—	250.00
	1981FM(P)	1,000	—	Proof	350.00

25th Anniversary of Independence
Similar to 1 Ringgit, KM#32.

KM#	Date	Mintage	VF	XF	Unc
34	1982	.020	—	—	250.00
	1982	1,000	—	Proof	350.00

5th Malaysian 5 Year Plan

KM#	Date	Mintage	VF	XF	Unc
38	1986	.010	—	—	250.00
	1986	1,000	—	Proof	350.00

MINT SETS (MS)

KM#	Date	Mintage	Identification	Issue Price	Mkt. Val.
MS1	1967(5)	10,000	KM1-5.1	—	10.00
MS2	1973(5)	2,000	KM1-4,5.3	—	2.50
MS3	1980(6)	2,000	KM1-4,5.3	—	3.50
MS4	1989(6)	2,000	KM49-54	—	4.00
MS5	1990(6)	2,000	KM49-54	—	4.00

PROOF SETS (PS)

KM#	Date	Mintage	Identification	Issue Price	Mkt. Val.
PS1	1967(5)	500	KM1-5.1	—	110.00
PS2	1976(3)	508	KM19-21	808.00	960.00
PS3	1976(2)	7,500	KM19-20	—	120.00
PS4	1976(3)	2,641	KM16-18	—	180.00
PS5	1976(3)	1,000	KM13-15	—	275.00
PS6	1977(3)	975	KM22-24	164.00	300.00
PS7	1980(9)	5,000	KM1,2-4,5.3,9.1,17, 23,27a	132.00	150.00
PS8	1981(6)	—	KM1-4,5.4,9.2	—	45.00
PS9	1981(3)	3,000	KM29-31	—	390.00
PS10	1982(3)	4,000	KM32-34	—	415.00
PS11	1986(3)	2,000	KM36-38	—	390.00
PS12	1986(2)	11,000	KM39a,40	—	42.50
PS13	1987(3)	1,000	KM43-45	—	185.00
PS14	1989(3)	2,500	KM47,48,58	—	250.00
PS15	1989(2)	20,000	KM47-48	—	37.50
PS16	1989(2)	15,000	KM55-56	—	42.50

MALDIVE ISLANDS

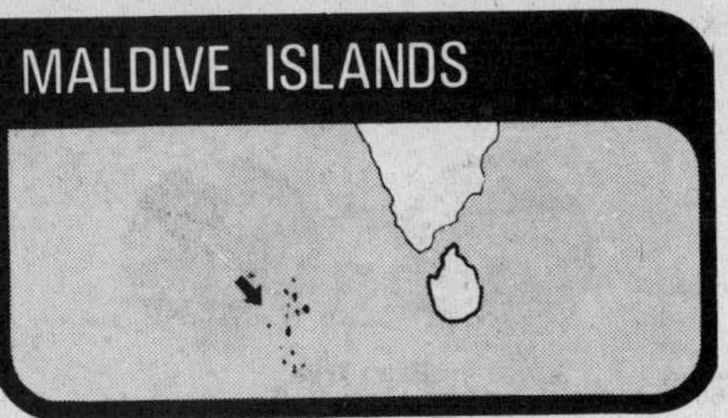

The Republic of Maldives, an archipelago of 2,000 coral islets in the northern Indian Ocean 417 miles (671 km.) west of Ceylon, has an area of 115 sq. mi. (298 sq. km.) and a population of 189,000. Capital: Malé. Fishing employs 95 percent of the male work force. Dried fish, copra and coir yarn are exported.

The Maldive Islands were visited by Arab traders and converted to Islam in 1153. After being harassed in the 16th and 17th centuries by Mopla pirates of the Malabar coast and Portuguese raiders, the Maldivians voluntarily placed themselves under the suzerainty of Ceylon. In 1887 the islands became an internally self-governing British protectorate and a nominal dependency of Ceylon. Traditionally a sultanate, the Maldives became a republic in 1953 but restored the sultanate in 1954. The Sultanate of the Maldive Islands attained complete internal and external autonomy on July 26, 1965, and on Nov. 11, 1968, again became a republic.

The coins of the Maldives, issued by request of the Sultan and without direct British sponsorship, are not definitively coins of the British Commonwealth.

RULERS

Muhammad Mu'in al-Din,
AH1213-1250/1798-1835AD
Muhammad Imad al-Din IV,
AH1250-1300/1835-1882AD
Ibrahim Nur al-Din,
AH1300-1318/1882-1900AD
Muhammad Imad al-Din V,
AH1318-1322/1900-1904AD
Muhammad Shams al-Din III,
AH1322-1353/1904-1935AD
Hasan Nur al-Din II,
AH1353-1364/1935-1945AD
Abdul-Majid Didi,
AH1364-1371/1945-1953AD
First Republic,
AH1371-1372/1953-1954AD
Muhammad Farid Didi,
AH1372-1388/1954-1968AD
Second Republic, AH1388 to date/1968AD to date

MINTNAME

Mahle (Male)

MONETARY SYSTEM

100 Lari = 1 Rupee (Rufiya)

NOTE: The metrology of the early coinage is problematical. There seem to have been three denominations: a double Larin of 8-10 g, a Larin of approximately 4.8 g, and a half Larin that varied from 1.1 to 2.4 g, known as the Bodu Larin, Larin and Kuda Larin, respectively. In some years probably when copper was cheap (AH1276 & 1294), the Kuda (1/2) Larin is found with weights as high as 3.7 g.

MUHAMMAD MU'IN AL-DIN ISKANDAR

AH1213-1250/1798-1835AD

KUDA (1/2) LARIN

COPPER/BRONZE/BRASS, 2.40 g

KM#	Date	Good	VG	Fine	VF
32	AH1216	3.00	5.00	7.50	10.00
	1219	3.00	5.00	7.50	10.00
	1220	3.00	5.00	7.50	10.00
	1221	3.00	5.00	7.50	10.00
	1230	5.00	7.50	12.00	18.00
	1238	3.50	6.00	9.00	12.50
	1239	4.00	6.50	10.00	15.00
	1248	3.00	5.00	7.50	9.00

NOTE: Varieties exist. Some specimens are struck on lightweight planchets, some being square in shape. The date on the reverse occurs in various places.

MUHAMMAD IMAD AL-DIN IV ISKANDAR

AH1250-1300/1835-1882AD

1/4 LARIN

BRONZE/BRASS, .090-1.20 g

KM#	Date	Good	VG	Fine	VF
34.1	AH1251	5.00	7.50	12.00	17.50
	1286	5.00	7.50	12.00	17.50
	1292	5.00	7.50	12.00	17.50
	1294	5.00	7.50	12.00	17.50
	1298	4.00	6.50	10.00	15.00

Obv. leg: Within border of small circles.
Rev: Date at top.

KM#	Date	Good	VG	Fine	VF
34.2	AH1286	—	—	Rare	—

NOTE: These lightweight coins are believed to have been intended as 1/4 larins since the dies with which they were struck are smaller than those for the kuda (1/2) larin, below. The issues dated AH1251 and 1298 are square or round.

KUDA (1/2) LARIN

BRONZE, 2.40 g

KM#	Date	Good	VG	Fine	VF
35.1	AH1252	4.00	6.50	10.00	15.00
	1257	2.50	3.50	6.00	9.00
	1258	2.50	3.50	6.00	9.00
	1276	2.50	3.50	6.00	9.00
	1280	2.50	3.50	6.00	9.00
	1286	2.50	3.00	5.00	8.00
	1287	4.00	6.50	10.00	15.00
	1292	2.50	3.50	6.00	9.00
	1294	3.00	5.00	7.50	10.00
	1295	—	—	—	—
	1298	.50	1.25	2.50	4.50

NOTE: Date on second and third lines on reverse.

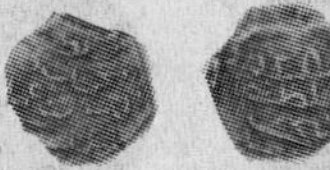

Rev: Date in top line.

KM#	Date	Good	VG	Fine	VF
35.2	AH1286	4.00	6.50	10.00	15.00

Obv: Leg. within border of small circles.
Rev: Leg. within quadrifoil.

KM#	Date	Good	VG	Fine	VF
35.3	AH1286	—	—	Rare	—

BODU (2) LARI

BRONZE, 8.60 g
Rev: Date in third line.

KM#	Date	Good	VG	Fine	VF
36.1	AH1294	5.00	8.50	12.50	17.50
	1298	5.00	8.50	12.50	17.50

Rev: Date in second line.

KM#	Date	Good	VG	Fine	VF
36.2	AH1298	7.50	12.50	20.00	30.00

IBRAHIM NUR AL-DIN ISKANDAR

AH1300-1318/1882-1900AD

1/4 LARIN/LARIN

BRONZE, 1.10 g

KM#	Date	Fine	VF	XF	Unc
37	AH1300	2.00	3.00	4.50	6.00

NOTE: Toward the end of this reign the standard was

reportedly revised by a factor of four, making this denomination officially one larin. The date occurs in different places on the reverse.

MUHAMMAD IMAD AL-DIN V ISKANDAR

AH1318-1322/1900-1904AD

LARIN

COPPER/BRASS, 0.80-1.10 g

KM#	Date	Fine	VF	XF	Unc
38	AH1318	1.00	1.50	2.00	4.00
	1319	3.00	4.50	6.00	8.00

2 LARIAT

COPPER/BRASS, 1.40-2.00 g

KM#	Date	Fine	VF	XF	Unc
39	AH1318	1.50	3.50	5.00	7.50
	1319	1.50	3.50	5.00	7.50

NOTE: Previously listed date AH1311 is merely poor die cutting of AH1319. Many die varieties exist.

4 LARIAT

COPPER/BRASS, 2.50-4.50 g
Plain or reeded edge.

KM#	Date	Fine	VF	XF	Unc
40.1	AH1320	1.50	2.50	4.50	8.00

NOTE: Many die varieties exist.

Rev: Arabic *Sanat* below date.

KM#	Date	Fine	VF	XF	Unc
40.2	AH1320	3.50	8.00	12.00	16.00

NOTE: Pattern or presentation pieces of Larin dated AH1318, 2 Lariat dated AH1319 and 4 Lariat dated AH1320 exist in silver or with silver plating.

MUHAMMAD SHAMS AL-DIN III ISKANDAR

AH1322-1353/1904-1935AD

LARIN

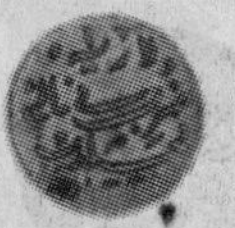

BRONZE, 0.90 g

KM#	Date	Fine	VF	XF	Unc
41	AH1331	1.00	1.25	1.50	2.50

Struck at Birmingham, England, Mint.

4 LARIAT

BRONZE, 3.30 g

KM#	Date	Fine	VF	XF	Unc
42	AH1331	1.00	1.50	2.50	5.00

Struck at Birmingham, England, Mint.

REPUBLIC

MONETARY SYSTEM
100 Laari = 1 Rupee

LAARI

BRONZE

KM#	Date	Year	Mintage	VF	XF	Unc
43	AH1379	1960	.300	.15	.25	.50
	1379	1960	1,270	—	Proof	2.25

ALUMINUM

KM#	Date	Year	Mintage	VF	XF	Unc
49	AH1389	1970	.500	.10	.20	.40
	1399	1979	—	.10	.20	.40
	1399	1979	.100	—	Proof	1.00

Palm Tree

KM#	Date	Year	Mintage	VF	XF	Unc
68	AH1404	1984	—	—	.10	.15
	1404	1984	—	—	Proof	2.00

2 LAARI

BRONZE

KM#	Date	Year	Mintage	VF	XF	Unc
44	AH1379	1960	.600	.20	.35	.75
	1379	1960	1,270	—	Proof	2.75

ALUMINUM

KM#	Date	Year	Mintage	VF	XF	Unc
50	AH1389	1970	.500	.15	.25	.50
	1399	1979	—	.15	.25	.50
	1399	1979	.100	—	Proof	1.00

5 LAARI

NICKEL-BRASS

KM#	Date	Year	Mintage	VF	XF	Unc
45	AH1379	1960	.300	.25	.40	.75
	1379	1960	1,270	—	Proof	3.50

ALUMINUM

KM#	Date	Year	Mintage	VF	XF	Unc
45a	AH1389	1970	.300	.20	.30	.40
	1399	1979	—	—	.10	.20
	1399	1979	—	—	Proof	2.00

Bonito Fish

KM#	Date	Year	Mintage	VF	XF	Unc
69	AH1404	1984	—	—	.10	.15
	1404	1984	—	—	Proof	2.00

10 LAARI

NICKEL-BRASS

KM#	Date	Year	Mintage	VF	XF	Unc
46	AH1379	1960	.600	.50	.75	1.50

ALUMINUM

KM#	Date	Year	Mintage	VF	XF	Unc
46a	AH1379	1960	1,270	1.00	1.50	2.00
	1399	1979	—	—	.10	.25
	1399	1979	—	—	Proof	2.00

Maldivian Sailing Ship - Dhivehi Odi

KM#	Date	Year	Mintage	VF	XF	Unc
70	AH1404	1984	—	—	.10	.20
	1404	1984	—	—	Proof	2.50

25 LAARI

NICKEL-BRASS

Security edge.

KM#	Date	Year	Mintage	VF	XF	Unc
47.1	AH1379	1960	.300	.60	1.00	1.50
	1379	1960	1,270	—	Proof	5.00

Reeded edge.

KM#	Date	Year	Mintage	VF	XF	Unc
47.2	AH1379	1960	—	2.00	3.50	6.00
	1399	1979	—	—	.10	.25
	1399	1979	.100	—	Proof	3.00

Mosque

KM#	Date	Year	Mintage	VF	XF	Unc
71	AH1404	1984	—	—	.15	.45
	1404	1984	—	—	Proof	3.50
	1411	1990	—	—	.15	.45

50 LAARI

NICKEL-BRASS
Security edge.

KM#	Date	Year	Mintage	VF	XF	Unc
48.1	AH1379	1960	.300	1.00	1.75	2.50
	1379	1960	1,270	—	Proof	7.00

Reeded edge.

KM#	Date	Year	Mintage	VF	XF	Unc
48.2	AH1379	1960	—	3.00	5.00	8.00
	1399	1979	—	.10	.20	.40
	1399	1979	.100	—	Proof	6.00

Turtle

KM#	Date	Year	Mintage	VF	XF	Unc
72	AH1404	1984	—	.15	.35	1.00
	1404	1984	—	—	Proof	5.00
	1411	1990	—	.15	.35	1.00

RUFIYAA

COPPER PLATED STEEL

KM#	Date	Year	Mintage	VF	XF	Unc
73	AH1402	1982	—	.20	.50	2.00

COPPER-NICKEL

KM#	Date	Year	Mintage	VF	XF	Unc
73a	AH1404	1984	—	.20	.50	2.00
	1404	1984	—	—	Proof	10.00

5 RUFIYAA

COPPER-NICKEL
F.A.O. Issue - Bonito Fish

KM#	Date	Year	Mintage	VF	XF	Unc
55	AH1397	1977	.015	—	2.00	3.50

F.A.O. Issue - Lobster

KM#	Date	Year	Mintage	VF	XF	Unc
57	AH1398	1978	7,000	—	3.00	5.00
			SILVER			
57a	AH1398	1978	1,887	—	Proof	30.00
			GOLD			
57b	AH1398	1978	—	—	Proof	650.00

10 RUFIYAA

COPPER-NICKEL
F.A.O. Issue

KM#	Date	Year	Mintage	VF	XF	Unc
59	AH1399	1979	—	—	3.50	9.00
			25.0000 g, .925 SILVER, .7435 oz ASW			
59a	AH1399	1979	3,000	—	Proof	22.00

COPPER-NICKEL
F.A.O. Issue

KM#	Date	Year	Mintage	VF	XF	Unc
62	AH1400	1980	—	—	3.00	8.00

20 RUFIYAA

28.2800 g, .500 SILVER, .4546 oz ASW
F.A.O. Issue Bonito and Bluefin Tuna

KM#	Date	Year	Mintage	VF	XF	Unc
56	AH1397	1977	.015	—	—	12.50

28.2800 g, .925 SILVER, .8410 oz ASW
International Year of the Child

KM#	Date	Year	Mintage	VF	XF	Unc
61	AH1399	1979	.012	—	Proof	20.00

COPPER-NICKEL
World Fisheries Conference

KM#	Date	Year	Mintage	VF	XF	Unc
65	AH1404	1984	.100	—	—	6.00
			28.2800 g, .925 SILVER, .8410 oz ASW			
65a	AH1404	1984	.020	—	Proof	30.00

19.4400 g, .925 SILVER, .5782 oz ASW
Decade for Women

KM#	Date	Year	Mintage	VF	XF	Unc
74	AH1405	1984	500 pcs.	—	Proof	40.00

25 RUFIYAA

28.0500 g, .500 SILVER, .4509 oz ASW
F.A.O. Issue - Sailing Ship

KM#	Date	Year	Mintage	VF	XF	Unc
58	AH1398	1978	7,140	—	—	30.00
	1398	1978	2,000	—	Proof	45.00
			GOLD			
58a	AH1398	1978	—	—	Proof	850.00

100 RUFIYAA

28.2800 g, .800 SILVER, .7274 oz ASW
F.A.O. Issue

KM#	Date	Year	Mintage	VF	XF	Unc
60	AH1399	1979	6,000	—	—	25.00
			28.2800 g, .925 SILVER, .8411 oz ASW			
60a	AH1399	1979	8,000	—	Proof	28.00

28.2800 g, .800 SILVER, .7274 oz ASW
F.A.O. Issue

KM#	Date	Year	Mintage	VF	XF	Unc
63	AH1400	1980	6,501	—	—	30.00
			28.2800 g, .925 SILVER, .8411 oz ASW			
63a	AH1400	1980	3,003	—	Proof	45.00

World Food Day
Obv: Similar to KM#60.

KM#	Date	Year	Mintage	VF	XF	Unc
64	AH1401	1981	.010	—	—	30.00
	1401	1981	5,000	—	Proof	40.00

International Year of Disabled Persons
Rev: Ancient Yin and Yang symbols.

KM#	Date	Year	Mintage	VF	XF	Unc
66	AH1404	1984	—	—	—	25.00
	1404	1984	—	—	Proof	35.00

15.9800 g, .917 GOLD, .4712 oz AGW

KM#	Date	Year	Mintage	VF	XF	Unc
67	AH1404	1984	500 pcs.	—	—	750.00
	1404	1984	500 pcs.	—	Proof	850.00

Commonwealth Finance Ministers Meeting

KM#	Date	Year	Mintage	VF	XF	Unc
75	AH1404	1984	100 pcs.	—	Proof	500.00

28.2800 g, .925 SILVER, .8411 oz ASW
Opening of Grand Mosque and Islamic Centre

KM#	Date	Year	Mintage	VF	XF	Unc
78	AH1404	1984	500 pcs.	—	Proof	70.00

Commonwealth Finance Ministers Meeting

KM#	Date	Year	Mintage	VF	XF	Unc
76	AH1405	1985	300 pcs.	—	Proof	75.00

250 RUFIYAA

31.4700 g, .925 SILVER, .9359 oz ASW
1992 Olympics - Swimming

KM#	Date	Year	Mintage	VF	XF	Unc
80	AH1410	1990	—	—	Proof	40.00

Maldivian Sailing Ship - Dhivehi Odi

KM#	Date	Year	Mintage	VF	XF	Unc
81	AH1410	1990	.015	—	Proof	40.00

World Cup Football Championship
Rev: Soccer ball trailing an inscribed ribbon.

KM#	Date	Year	Mintage	VF	XF	Unc
82	AH1410	1990	—	—	Proof	40.00

Soccer - World Cup '94

KM#	Date	Year	Mintage	VF	XF	Unc
83	AH1413	1993	—	—	Proof	45.00

Skylab Space Station

KM#	Date	Year	Mintage	VF	XF	Unc
84	AH1413	1993	—	—	Proof	45.00

MINT SETS (MS)

KM#	Date	Mintage	Identification	Issue Price	Mkt. Val.
MS1	1984(6)	—	KM68-73	8.75	6.50

PROOF SETS (PS)

KM#	Date	Mintage	Identification	Issue Price	Mkt. Val.
PS1	1960(6)	1,270	KM43-48	—	25.00
PS2	1979(6)	—	KM45a,46a,47-50	30.00	15.00
PS3	1979(2)	3,000	KM59a,60a	—	50.00
PS4	1984(6)	2,500	KM68-73	30.00	25.00

MALI

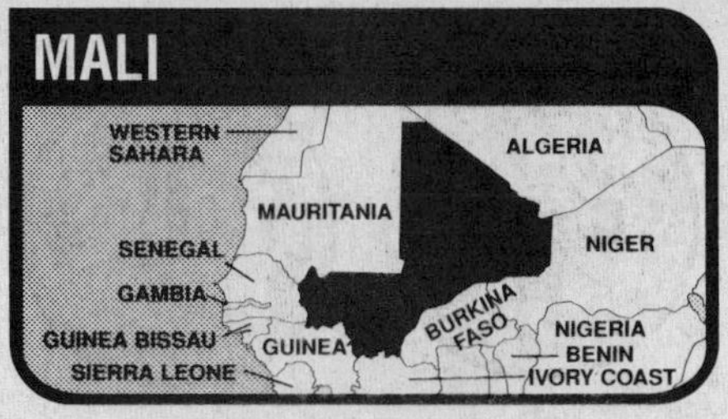

The Republic of Mali, a landlocked country in the interior of West Africa southwest of Algeria, has an area of 478,767 sq. mi. (1,240,000 sq. km.) and a population of 8.1 million. Capital: Bamako. Livestock, fish, cotton and peanuts are exported.

Malians are descendants of the ancient Malinke Kingdom of Mali that controlled the middle Niger from the 11th to the 17th centuries. The French penetrated the Sudan (now Mali) about 1880, and established their rule in 1898 after subduing fierce native resistance. In 1904 the area became the colony of Upper Senegal-Niger (changed to French Sudan in 1920), and became part of the French Union in 1946. In 1958 French Sudan became the Sudanese Republic with complete internal autonomy. Senegal joined with the Sudanese Republic in 1959 to form the Mali Federation which, in 1960, became a fully independent member of the French Community. Upon Senegal's subsequent withdrawal from the Federation, the Sudanese, on Sept. 22, 1960, proclaimed their nation the fully independent Republic of Mali and severed all ties with France.

MINT MARKS

(a) - Paris, privy marks only

5 FRANCS

ALUMINUM

KM#	Date	Mintage	Fine	VF	XF	Unc
2	1961	—	.15	.35	.70	1.50

10 FRANCS

25.0000 g, .900 SILVER, .7234 oz ASW
Independence Day

KM#	Date	Mintage	Fine	VF	XF	Unc
1	ND(1960)	.010	—	—	Proof	35.00

ALUMINUM

KM#	Date	Mintage	Fine	VF	XF	Unc
3	1961	—	.15	.35	.85	1.75

3.2000 g, .900 GOLD, .0926 oz AGW
President Modibo Keita
Similar to 25 Francs, KM#6.

KM#	Date	Mintage	Fine	VF	XF	Unc
5	1967	—	—	—	Proof	75.00

ALUMINUM

KM#	Date	Mintage	Fine	VF	XF	Unc
11	1976(a)	5.000	1.00	2.00	4.00	8.00

3.2000 g, .900 GOLD, .0926 oz AGW
Anniversary of Independence
Similar to 50 Francs, KM#15.

KM#	Date	Mintage	Fine	VF	XF	Unc
13	ND	—	—	—	—	—

25 FRANCS

ALUMINUM

KM#	Date	Mintage	Fine	VF	XF	Unc
4	1961	—	.25	.50	1.50	3.50

8.0000 g, .900 GOLD, .2315 oz AGW
President Modibo Keita

KM#	Date	Mintage	Fine	VF	XF	Unc
6	1967	—	—	—	Proof	135.00

ALUMINUM

KM#	Date	Mintage	Fine	VF	XF	Unc
12	1976(a)	5.000	1.25	2.50	5.00	10.00

.900 GOLD, .2315 oz AGW
Anniversary of Independence
Similar to 50 FRANCS, KM#15.

KM#	Date	Mintage	Fine	VF	XF	Unc
14	ND	—	— Reported, not confirmed			

50 FRANCS

16.0000 g, .900 GOLD, .4630 oz AGW
President Modibo Keita

KM#	Date	Mintage	Fine	VF	XF	Unc
7	1967	—	—	—	Proof	265.00

NICKEL-BRASS
F.A.O. Issue

KM#	Date	Mintage	Fine	VF	XF	Unc
9	1975(a)	10.000	.25	.50	1.00	2.00
	1977(a)	—	.25	.50	1.00	2.00

16.0000 g, .900 GOLD, .4630 oz AGW
Anniversary of Independence

KM#	Date	Mintage	Fine	VF	XF	Unc
15	ND	—	—	—	—	—

100 FRANCS

32.0000 g, .900 GOLD, .9260 oz AGW
President Modibo Keita

KM#	Date	Mintage	Fine	VF	XF	Unc
8	1967	—	—	—	Proof	525.00

NICKEL-BRASS
F.A.O. Issue

KM#	Date	Mintage	Fine	VF	XF	Unc
10	1975(a)	23.000	.50	1.00	2.00	4.00

32.0000 g, .900 GOLD, .9260 oz AGW
Anniversary of Indepdence Day
Similar to 50 Francs, KM#15.

KM#	Date	Mintage	Fine	VF	XF	Unc
16	ND	—	— Reported, not confirmed			

PROOF SETS (PS)

KM#	Date	Mintage	Identification	Issue Price	Mkt. Val.
PS1	1967(4)	—	KM5-8	—	1000.

MALTA

The Republic of Malta, an independent parliamentary democracy within the British Commonwealth, is situated in the Mediterranean Sea between Sicily and North Africa. With the islands of Gozo and Comino, Malta has an area of 122 sq. mi. (320 sq. km.) and a population of 386,000. Capital: Valletta. Malta has no proven mineral resources, an agriculture insufficient to its needs, and a small, but expanding, manufacturing facility. Clothing, textile yarns and fabrics, and knitted wear are exported.

For more than 3,500 years Malta was ruled, in succession by Phoenicians, Carthaginians, Romans, Arabs, Normans, the Knights of Malta, France and Britain. Napoleon seized Malta by treachery in 1798. The French were ousted by a Maltese insurrection assisted by Britain, and in 1814 Malta, of its own free will, became a part of the British Empire. Malta obtained full independence in Sept., 1964; electing to remain within the Commonwealth with the British monarch as the nominal head of state.

Malta became a republic on Dec. 13, 1974, but remained a member of the Commonwealth of Nations. The president is Chief of State. The prime minister is the Head of Government.

RULERS

British, until 1964

BRITISH COINAGE

MONETARY SYSTEM

4 Farthings = 1 Penny

1/3 FARTHING

COPPER

NOTE: From 1827 through 1913 homeland type 1/3 Farthing along with other coinage of Great Britain circulated in Malta. The 1/3 Farthing corresponded to the copper Grano or 1/12 penny. These are found listed under Great Britain.

DECIMAL COINAGE

10 Mils = 1 Cent

100 Cents = 1 Pound

MINT MARKS

FM - Franklin Mint, U.S.A.*

***NOTE:** From 1975 the Franklin Mint has produced coinage in up to 3 different qualities. Qualities of issue are designated in ( ) after each date and are defined as follows:

(M) MATTE - Normal circulation strike or a dull finish produced by sandblasting special uncirculated (polish finish) or proof quality dies.

(U) SPECIAL UNCIRCULATED - Polished or prooflike in appearance without any frosted features.

(P) PROOF - The highest quality obtainable having mirror-like fields and frosted features.

2 MILS

ALUMINUM
Maltese Cross

KM#	Date	Mintage	VF	XF	Unc
5	1972	.030	.10	.15	.30
	1972	.013	—	Proof	.50
	1976FM(M)	5,000	—	—	2.00
	1976FM(P)	.026	—	Proof	.50
	1977FM(U)	5,252	—	—	1.00
	1977FM(P)	6,884	—	Proof	1.00
	1978FM(U)	5,252	—	—	1.00
	1978FM(P)	3,244	—	Proof	1.00
	1979FM(U)	537 pcs.	—	—	3.00
	1979FM(P)	6,577	—	Proof	1.00
	1980FM(U)	385 pcs.	—	—	3.00
	1980FM(P)	3,451	—	Proof	1.00
	1981FM(U)	444 pcs.	—	—	3.00
	1981FM(P)	1,453	—	Proof	1.00

10th Anniversary of Decimalization

KM#	Date	Mintage	VF	XF	Unc
54	1982FM(U)	850 pcs.	—	—	3.00
	1982FM(P)	1,793	—	Proof	1.00

3 MILS

ALUMINUM
Bee and Honeycomb

KM#	Date	Mintage	VF	XF	Unc
6	1972	—	.10	.15	.40
	1972	8,000	—	Proof	.75
	1976FM(M)	5,000	—	—	2.50
	1976FM(P)	.026	—	Proof	.75
	1977FM(U)	5,252	—	—	1.50
	1977FM(P)	6,884	—	Proof	1.25
	1978FM(U)	5,252	—	—	2.50
	1978FM(P)	3,244	—	Proof	1.25
	1979FM(U)	537 pcs.	—	—	5.00
	1979FM(P)	6,577	—	Proof	1.25
	1980FM(U)	385 pcs.	—	—	5.00
	1980FM(P)	3,451	—	Proof	1.25
	1981FM(U)	449 pcs.	—	—	5.00
	1981FM(P)	1,453	—	Proof	1.25

10th Anniversary of Decimalization

KM#	Date	Mintage	VF	XF	Unc
55	1982FM(U)	850 pcs.	—	—	4.00
	1982FM(P)	1,793	—	Proof	1.25

5 MILS

ALUMINUM
Earthen Lampstand

KM#	Date	Mintage	VF	XF	Unc
7	1972	4.320	.10	.15	.40
	1972	.013	—	Proof	1.00
	1976FM(M)	5,000	—	—	3.00
	1976FM(P)	.026	—	Proof	1.00
	1977FM(U)	5,252	—	—	2.00
	1977FM(P)	6,884	—	Proof	1.50
	1978FM(U)	5,252	—	—	2.00
	1978FM(P)	3,244	—	Proof	1.50
	1979FM(U)	537 pcs.	—	—	7.00
	1979FM(P)	6,577	—	Proof	1.50
	1980FM(U)	385 pcs.	—	—	7.00
	1980FM(P)	3,451	—	Proof	1.50
	1981FM(U)	449 pcs.	—	—	7.00
	1981FM(P)	1,453	—	Proof	1.50

10th Anniversary of Decimalization

KM#	Date	Mintage	VF	XF	Unc
56	1982FM(U)	850 pcs.	—	—	5.00
	1982FM(P)	1,793	—	Proof	1.50

CENT

BRONZE
George Cross

KM#	Date	Mintage	VF	XF	Unc
8	1972	5.650	.10	.15	.40
	1972	.013	—	Proof	1.25
	1975	1.500	.10	.20	.50
	1976FM(M)	5,000	—	—	3.50
	1976FM(P)	.026	—	Proof	1.25
	1977	2.793	.10	.15	.40
	1977FM(U)	5,252	—	—	2.50
	1977FM(P)	6,884	—	Proof	1.75
	1978FM(U)	5,252	—	—	2.50
	1978FM(P)	3,244	—	Proof	1.75
	1979FM(U)	537 pcs.	—	—	9.00
	1979FM(P)	6,577	—	Proof	1.75
	1980FM(U)	385 pcs.	—	—	9.00
	1980FM(P)	3,451	—	Proof	1.75
	1981FM(U)	449 pcs.	—	—	9.00
	1981FM(P)	1,453	—	Proof	1.75
	1982	—	.10	.15	.25

10th Anniversary of Decimalization

KM#	Date	Mintage	VF	XF	Unc
57	1982FM(U)	850 pcs.	—	—	7.50
	1982FM(P)	1,793	—	Proof	1.75

COPPER-ZINC
Weasel
Obv: Similar to 1 Pound, KM#82.

KM#	Date	Mintage	VF	XF	Unc
78	1986	21.526	—	—	.10
	1986	.010	—	Proof	2.00

KM#	Date	Mintage	VF	XF	Unc
93	1991	—	—	—	.10

2 CENTS

COPPER-NICKEL
Penthesilea, Queen of the Amazons

KM#	Date	Mintage	VF	XF	Unc
9	1972	5.640	.10	.15	.40
	1972	.013	—	Proof	1.50
	1976	1.000	.15	.20	.60
	1976FM(M)	2,500	—	—	4.50
	1976FM(P)	.026	—	Proof	1.50
	1977	6.105	.10	.15	.40
	1977FM(U)	2,752	—	—	4.50
	1977FM(P)	6,884	—	Proof	2.50
	1978FM(U)	2,752	—	—	4.50
	1978FM(P)	3,244	—	Proof	2.50
	1979FM(U)	537 pcs.	—	—	12.00
	1979FM(P)	6,577	—	Proof	2.50
	1980FM(U)	385 pcs.	—	—	12.00
	1980FM(P)	3,451	—	Proof	2.50
	1981FM(U)	449 pcs.	—	—	12.00
	1981FM(P)	1,453	—	Proof	2.50
	1982	—	.10	.15	.30

10th Anniversary of Decimalization

KM#	Date	Mintage	VF	XF	Unc
58	1982FM(U)	850 pcs.	—	—	10.00
	1982FM(P)	1,793	—	Proof	2.50

Olive Branch
Obv: Similar to 1 Pound, KM#82.

KM#	Date	Mintage	VF	XF	Unc
79	1986	.280	—	—	.15
	1986	.010	—	Proof	3.00
94	1991	—	—	—	.15

5 CENTS

COPPER-NICKEL
Floral Alter in the Temple of Hagar Qim

KM#	Date	Mintage	VF	XF	Unc
10	1972	4.180	.20	.30	.50
	1972	.013	—	Proof	1.75
	1976	1.009	.20	.30	.60
	1976FM(M)	2,500	—	—	5.00
	1976FM(P)	.026	—	Proof	2.00
	1977	—	.20	.30	.50
	1977FM(U)	2,752	—	—	5.00
	1977FM(P)	6,884	—	Proof	3.00
	1978FM(U)	2,752	—	—	5.00
	1978FM(P)	3,244	—	Proof	3.00
	1979FM(U)	537 pcs.	—	—	15.00
	1979FM(P)	6,577	—	Proof	3.00
	1980FM(U)	385 pcs.	—	—	15.00
	1980FM(P)	3,451	—	Proof	3.00
	1981FM(U)	449 pcs.	—	—	15.00
	1981FM(P)	1,453	—	Proof	3.00

10th Anniversary of Decimalization

KM#	Date	Mintage	VF	XF	Unc
59	1982FM(U)	850 pcs.	—	—	12.50
	1982FM(P)	1,793	—	Proof	3.00

Fresh Water Crab

KM#	Date	Mintage	VF	XF	Unc
77	1986	.150	—	—	.25
	1986	.010	—	Proof	3.50
95	1991	—	—	—	.25

10 CENTS

COPPER-NICKEL
Barge of the Grand Master

KM#	Date	Mintage	VF	XF	Unc
11	1972	10.680	.40	.60	1.00
11	1972	.013	—	Proof	2.25
	1976FM(M)	1,000	—	—	6.00
	1976FM(P)	.026	—	Proof	2.50
	1977FM(U)	1,252	—	—	6.00
	1977FM(P)	6,884	—	Proof	3.50
	1978FM(U)	1,252	—	—	6.00
	1978FM(P)	3,244	—	Proof	3.50
	1979FM(U)	537 pcs.	—	—	17.50
	1979FM(P)	6,577	—	Proof	3.50
	1980FM(U)	385 pcs.	—	—	15.00
	1980FM(P)	3,451	—	Proof	3.50
	1981FM(U)	449 pcs.	—	—	15.00
	1981FM(P)	1,453	—	Proof	3.50

10th Anniversary of Decimalization

KM#	Date	Mintage	VF	XF	Unc
60	1982FM(U)	850 pcs.	—	—	13.00
	1982FM(P)	1,793	—	Proof	3.50
76	1986	4.188	—	.40	.60
	1986	.010	—	Proof	4.00

Obv: Similar to 5 Cents, KM#95.

KM#	Date	Mintage	VF	XF	Unc
96	1991	—	—	.40	.60

25 CENTS

BRASS
1st Anniversary of Republic of Malta

KM#	Date	Mintage	VF	XF	Unc
29	1975	4.750	1.00	1.50	2.50
	1975	—		Matte Proof	150.00

BRONZE

KM#	Date	Mintage	VF	XF	Unc
29a	1975	6,000	—	Proof	12.50

COPPER-NICKEL

KM#	Date	Mintage	VF	XF	Unc
29b	1976FM(M)	300 pcs.	—	—	40.00
	1976FM(P)	.026	—	Proof	3.00
	1977FM(U)	552 pcs.	—	—	20.00
	1977FM(P)	6,884	—	Proof	4.50
	1978FM(U)	552 pcs.	—	—	20.00
	1978FM(P)	3,244	—	Proof	4.50
	1979FM(U)	537 pcs.	—	—	20.00
	1979FM(P)	6,577	—	Proof	4.50
	1980FM(U)	385 pcs.	—	—	20.00
	1980FM(P)	3,451	—	Proof	4.50
	1981FM(U)	449 pcs.	—	—	20.00
	1981FM(P)	1,453	—	Proof	4.50

10th Anniversary of Decimalization

KM#	Date	Mintage	VF	XF	Unc
61	1982FM(U)	850 pcs.	—	—	15.00
	1982FM(P)	1,793	—	Proof	4.50

Ghirlanda Flower
Obv: Similar to 1 Pound, KM#82.

KM#	Date	Mintage	VF	XF	Unc
80	1986	3.090	—	—	1.00
	1986	.010	—	Proof	5.00

Obv: Similar to 5 Cents, KM#95.

KM#	Date	Mintage	VF	XF	Unc
97	1991	—	—	—	1.00

50 CENTS

COPPER-NICKEL
Great Siege Monument

KM#	Date	Mintage	VF	XF	Unc
12	1972	5.500	1.75	2.00	2.50
	1972	.013	—	Proof	3.50
	1976FM(M)	150 pcs.	—	—	90.00
	1976FM(P)	.026	—	Proof	5.00
	1977FM(U)	402 pcs.	—	—	25.00
	1977FM(P)	6,884	—	Proof	6.00
	1978FM(U)	402 pcs.	—	—	25.00
	1978FM(P)	3,244	—	Proof	6.00
	1979FM(U)	537 pcs.	—	—	25.00
	1979FM(P)	6,577	—	Proof	6.00
	1980FM(U)	385 pcs.	—	—	25.00
	1980FM(P)	3,451	—	Proof	6.00
	1981FM(U)	449 pcs.	—	—	25.00
	1981FM(P)	1,453	—	Proof	6.00

10th Anniversary of Decimalization

KM#	Date	Mintage	VF	XF	Unc
62	1982FM(U)	850 pcs.	—	—	20.00
	1982FM(P)	1,793	—	Proof	6.00

Tulliera Plant
Obv: Similar to 1 Pound, KM#82.

KM#	Date	Mintage	VF	XF	Unc
81	1986	2.086	—	—	4.00
	1986	.010	—	Proof	7.00

Obv: Similar to 5 Cents, KM#95.

KM#	Date	Mintage	VF	XF	Unc
98	1991	—	—	—	4.00

POUND

10.0000 g, .987 SILVER, .3173 oz ASW
Manwel Dimech

KM#	Date	Mintage	VF	XF	Unc
13	1972	.055	—	4.50	9.00

Sir Temi Zammit

KM#	Date	Mintage	VF	XF	Unc
19	1973	.030	—	4.50	9.00

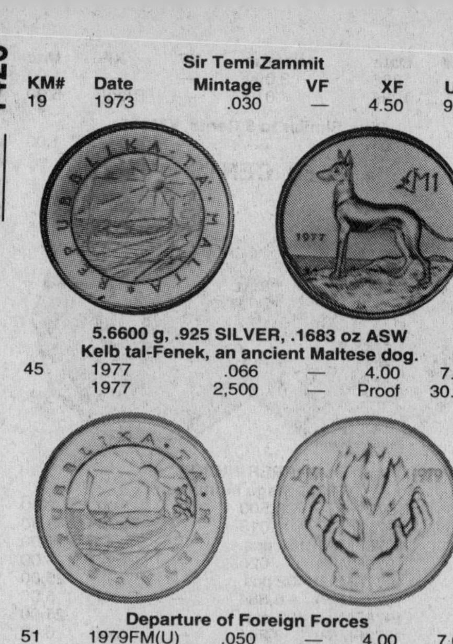

5.6600 g, .925 SILVER, .1683 oz ASW
Kelb tal-Fenek, an ancient Maltese dog.

KM#	Date	Mintage	VF	XF	Unc
45	1977	.066	—	4.00	7.00
	1977	2,500	—	Proof	30.00

Departure of Foreign Forces

KM#	Date	Mintage	VF	XF	Unc
51	1979FM(U)	.050	—	4.00	7.00
	1979FM(P)	7,871	—	Proof	20.00

COPPER-NICKEL
World Fisheries Conference

KM#	Date	Mintage	VF	XF	Unc
63	ND(1984)	.120	—	4.00	6.00

NICKEL
Merill Bird

KM#	Date	Mintage	VF	XF	Unc
82	1986	2.272	—	—	5.50
	1986	.010	—	Proof	8.00

Obv: Similar to 5 Cents, KM#95.

KM#	Date	Mintage	VF	XF	Unc
99	1991	—	—	—	5.50

2 POUNDS

20.0000 g, .987 SILVER, .6347 oz ASW
Fort St. Angelo

KM#	Date	Mintage	VF	XF	Unc
14	1972	.053	—	8.00	14.00

Tal-Imdina Gate
Obv: Similar to KM#14.

KM#	Date	Mintage	VF	XF	Unc
20	1973	.030	—	8.00	14.00

10.0000 g, .987 SILVER, .3173 oz ASW
Giovanni Francesco Abela

KM#	Date	Mintage	VF	XF	Unc
24	1974	.025	—	7.50	9.00

Obv: Similar to KM#24. Rev: Similar to KM#31.

KM#	Date	Mintage	VF	XF	Unc
30	1975	2,000	—	8.00	15.00

Alfonso Maria Galea

KM#	Date	Mintage	VF	XF	Unc
31	1975	.018	—	7.50	9.00

Guze Ellul Mercer

KM#	Date	Mintage	VF	XF	Unc
40	1976	.011	—	8.00	10.00

11.3100 g, .925 SILVER, .3363 oz ASW
Sir Luigi Preziosi

KM#	Date	Mintage	VF	XF	Unc
46	1977	.015	—	—	10.00
	1977	3,692	—	Proof	17.50

World Food Day

KM#	Date	Mintage	VF	XF	Unc
52	1981	1,500	—	—	16.50
	1981	.012	—	Proof	10.00

17.0000 g, .925 SILVER, .5056 oz ASW
25th Anniversary of Independence

KM#	Date	Mintage	VF	XF	Unc
88	1989	.075	—	—	12.50
	1989	7,500	—	Proof	35.00

4 POUNDS

20.0000 g, .987 SILVER, .6347 oz ASW
Cottonera Gate

KM#	Date	Mintage	VF	XF	Unc
25	1974	.024	—	14.50	18.50

Obv: Same as KM#25. Rev: Similar to KM#33.

KM#	Date	Mintage	VF	XF	Unc
32	1975	2,000	—	15.00	27.50

St. Agatha's Tower at Qammieh

KM#	Date	Mintage	VF	XF	Unc
33	1975	.018	—	14.50	18.50

Fort Manoel Gate

KM#	Date	Mintage	VF	XF	Unc
41	1976	.010	—	15.00	19.00

5 POUNDS

3.0000 g, .916 GOLD, .0883 oz AGW
Rev: Hand holding torch, map of Malta.

KM#	Date	Mintage	VF	XF	Unc
15	1972	.018	—	—	60.00

28.2800 g, .925 SILVER, .8411 oz ASW
Windmill of Xarolla

KM#	Date	Mintage	VF	XF	Unc
47	1977	.015	—	—	25.00
	1977	3,938	—	Proof	35.00

IYC - UNICEF

KM#	Date	Mintage	VF	XF	Unc
53	1981	.011	—	—	25.00

World Fisheries Conference

KM#	Date	Mintage	VF	XF	Unc
64	ND(1984)	.020	—	Proof	28.00

International Year of Disabled Persons

KM#	Date	Mintage	VF	XF	Unc
65	1983	—	—	—	25.00
	1983	—	—	Proof	40.00

20.0000 g, .925 SILVER, .5949 oz ASW
Maritime History - Strangier (1813)

KM#	Date	Mintage	VF	XF	Unc
67	1984	.015	—	P/L	20.00

Maritime History - Tigre (1839)

KM#	Date	Mintage	VF	XF	Unc
68	1984	.015	—	P/L	20.00

Maritime History - Wignacourt (1844)

KM#	Date	Mintage	VF	XF	Unc
69	1984	.015	—	P/L	20.00

Maritime History - Providenza (1848)

KM#	Date	Mintage	VF	XF	Unc
70	1984	.015	—	P/L	20.00

28.2800 g, .925 SILVER, .8411 oz ASW
Decade for Women

KM#	Date	Mintage	VF	XF	Unc
71	1984	.017	—	Proof	25.00

20.0000 g, .925 SILVER, .5949 oz ASW
Maritime History - Malta (1862)

KM#	Date	Mintage	VF	XF	Unc
72	1985	.015	—	P/L	20.00

Maritime History - Tagliaferro (1882)

KM#	Date	Mintage	VF	XF	Unc
73	1985	.015	—	P/L	20.00

Maritime History - L'Isle Adam (1883)

KM#	Date	Mintage	VF	XF	Unc
74	1985	.015	—	P/L	20.00

Maritime History - Maria Dacoutros (1902)

KM#	Date	Mintage	VF	XF	Unc
75	1985	.015	—	P/L	20.00

Maritime History - Valetta City (1917)

KM#	Date	Mintage	VF	XF	Unc
83	1986	.015	—	P/L	20.00

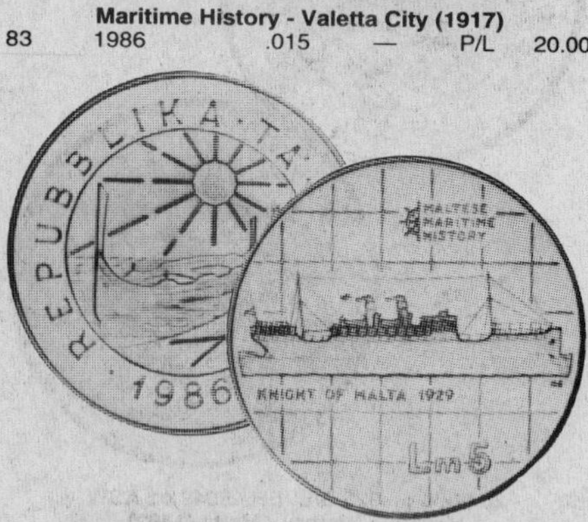

Maritime History - Knight of Malta (1929)

KM#	Date	Mintage	VF	XF	Unc
84	1986	.015	—	P/L	20.00

Maritime History - Saver (1943)

KM#	Date	Mintage	VF	XF	Unc
85	1986	.015	—	P/L	20.00

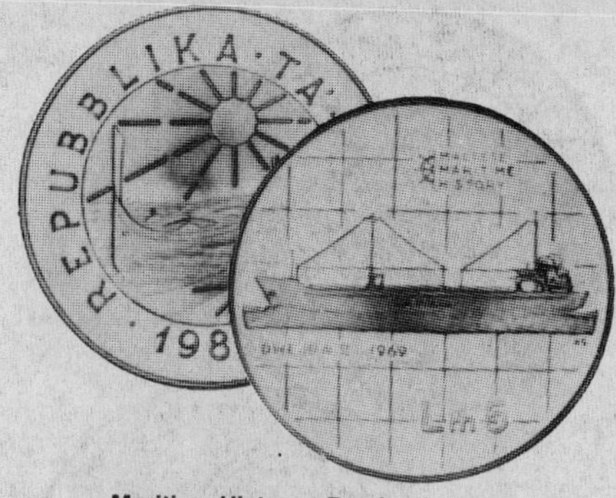

Maritime History - Dwejra II (1969)

KM#	Date	Mintage	VF	XF	Unc
86	1986	.015	—	P/L	20.00

28.2800 g, .925 SILVER, .8411 oz ASW
20th Anniversary of Central Bank of Malta

KM#	Date	Mintage	VF	XF	Unc
87	1988	*5,000	—	—	25.00
	1988	*2,000	—	Proof	45.00

28.6000 g, .925 SILVER, .8506 oz ASW
Papal Visit

KM#	Date	Mintage	VF	XF	Unc
90	1990	500 pcs.	—	—	32.50
	1990	4,000	—	Proof	55.00

28.2800 g, .925 SILVER, .8411 oz ASW
Entry of Malta to European Economic Community

KM#	Date	Mintage	VF	XF	Unc
91	1990	—	—	—	30.00
	1990	*4,000	—	Proof	50.00

Save The Children

KM#	Date	Mintage	VF	XF	Unc
92	1991	.020	—	Proof	40.00

50th Anniversary of George Cross Award

KM#	Date	Mintage	VF	XF	Unc
100	1992	*.010	—	Proof	47.50

25th Anniversary of Central Bank

KM#	Date	Mintage	VF	XF	Unc
102	1993	*1,500	—	—	32.50
	1993	*1,500	—	Proof	55.00

Quadricentennial of University of Malta

KM#	Date	Mintage	VF	XF	Unc
106	ND(1993)	*1,000	—	Proof	45.00

10 POUNDS

6.0000 g, .916 GOLD, .1767 oz AGW
Kenur, a Maltese stone charcoal stove.

16	1972	.016	—	—	100.00

3.0000 g, .916 GOLD, .0883 oz AGW
Watchtower

21	1973	9,078	—	—	60.00

Zerafa Flower

26	1974	9,124	—	—	60.00

Obv: Similar to KM#26. Rev: Similar to KM#35.

34	1975	2,000	—	—	75.00

Maltese Falcon

35	1975	6,448	—	—	90.00

Swallow-tail Butterfly

42	1976	4,448	—	—	100.00

20 POUNDS

12.0000 g, .916 GOLD, .3534 oz AGW
Merill Bird

17	1972	.016	—	—	225.00

6.0000 g, .916 GOLD, .1767 oz AGW
Dolphins Fountain at Floriana

22	1973	9,075	—	—	125.00

Gozo Boat

KM#	Date	Mintage	VF	XF	Unc
27	1974	8,700	—	—	125.00

Obv: Similar to KM#27. Rev: Similar to KM#37.

36	1975	2,000	—	—	150.00

Fresh Water Crab

37	1975	5,698	—	—	150.00

Storm Petrel Bird

43	1976	4,098	—	—	150.00

25 POUNDS

8.0000 g, .916 GOLD, .2356 oz AGW
First Gozo coin.

48	1977	4,000	—	—	125.00
	1977	3,249	—	Proof	150.00

7.9800 g, .916 GOLD, .2354 oz AGW
30th Anniversary of George Cross Award

101	1992	*500 pcs.	—	Proof	280.00

50 POUNDS

30.0000 g, .916 GOLD, .8836 oz AGW
Neptune

18	1972	.016	—	—	450.00

15.0000 g, .916 GOLD, .4418 oz AGW
Auberge de Castille at Valletta

23	1973	9,075	—	—	275.00

First Maltese Coin

KM#	Date	Mintage	VF	XF	Unc
28	1974	8,667	—	—	275.00

Ornamental stone balcony.

38	1975	2,000	—	—	300.00

39	1975	5,500	—	—	275.00

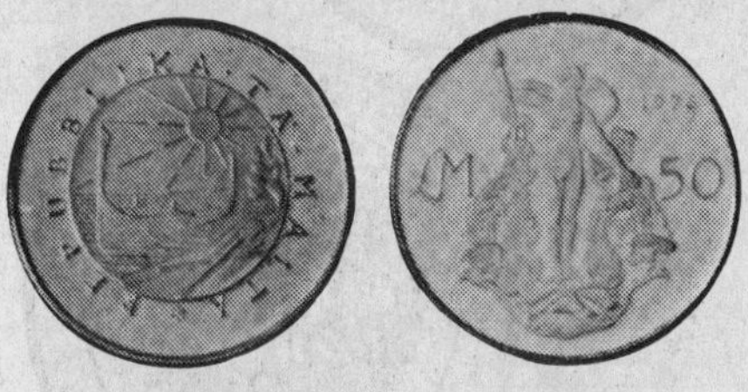

Ornamental Door Knocker

44	1976	3,748	—	—	275.00

Mnara

49	1977	4,000	—	—	275.00
	1977	846 pcs.	—	Proof	325.00

100 POUNDS

32.0000 g, .916 GOLD, .9425 oz AGW
Sculpture of Les Gavroches

50	1977	4,000	—	—	500.00
	1977	846 pcs.	—	Proof	650.00

15.9800 g, .917 GOLD, .4709 oz AGW
International Year of Disabled Persons

66	1983	700 pcs.	—	—	400.00
	1983	600 pcs.	—	Proof	500.00

17.0000 g, .917 GOLD, .5007 oz AGW
25th Anniversary of Independence

KM#	Date	Mintage	VF	XF	Unc
89	1989	5,000	—	—	355.00
	1989	2,500	—	Proof	400.00

EUROPEAN CURRENCY UNIT

POUND - 2 ECU

COPPER-NICKEL
Defense of Europe

KM#	Date	Mintage	VF	XF	Unc
103	1993	.025	—	—	10.00

5 POUNDS - 10 ECU

25.0000 g, .925 SILVER, .7435 oz ASW
Defense of Europe

KM#	Date	Mintage	VF	XF	Unc
104	1993	.035	—	Proof	40.00

25 POUNDS - 55 ECU

6.7200 g, .900 GOLD, .1945 oz AGW
Defense of Europe

KM#	Date	Mintage	VF	XF	Unc
105	1993	2,500	—	Proof	250.00

MINT SETS (MS)

KM#	Date	Mintage	Identification	Issue Price	Mkt. Val.
MS1	1972(8)	8,000	KM5-12	—	7.50
MS2	1972(4)	8,000	KM15-18	210.00	800.00
MS3	1972(2)	—	KM13,14	8.50	27.50
MS4	1973(3)	9,078	KM21-23	—	400.00
MS5	1973(2)	—	KM19,20	—	27.50
MS6	1974(3)	—	KM26-28	256.00	400.00
MS7	1974(2)	—	KM24,25	19.60	22.50
MS8	1975(5)	2,000	KM30,32,34,36,38	276.00	550.00
MS9	1975(3)	—	KM34,36,38	256.00	475.00
MS10	1975(2)	—	KM30,32	20.00	45.00
MS11	1975(3)	—	KM35,37,39	—	425.00
MS12	1976(3)	—	KM42-44	—	425.00
MS13	1976(2)	—	KM40-41	—	25.00
MS14	1977(9)	252	KM5-12,29b	—	65.00
MS15	1977(3)	4,000	KM48-50	610.00	900.00
MS16	1977(3)	15,000	KM45-47	34.50	36.50
MS17	1978(9)	252	KM5-12,29b	—	65.00
MS18	1979(9)	537	KM5-12,29b	—	110.00
MS19	1980(9)	385	KM5-12,29b	11.00	110.00
MS20	1981(9)	449	KM5-12,29b	13.25	110.00
MS21	1982(9)	850	KM54-62	13.25	120.00
MS22	1984(4)	15,000	KM67-70	72.00	75.00
MS23	1985(4)	15,000	KM72-75	72.00	75.00
MS24	1986(4)	15,000	KM83-86	72.00	75.00

PROOF SETS (PS)

KM#	Date	Mintage	Identification	Issue Price	Mkt. Val.
PS1	1972(8)	8,000	KM5-12 (plastic case)	—	12.50
PS2	1976(9)	26,248	KM5-12,29b	27.50	15.00
PS3	1977(9)	6,884	KM5-12,29b	31.50	22.50
PS4	1977(3)	750	KM48-50	909.00	1125.
PS5	1977(3)	2,500	KM45-47	72.00	80.00
PS6	1978(9)	3,244	KM5-12,29b	—	18.00
PS7	1979(10)	6,577	KM5-12,29b,51	41.50	30.00
PS8	1980(9)	3,451	KM5-12,29b	30.00	20.00
PS9	1981(9)	1,453	KM5-12,29b	25.30	25.00
PS10	1982(9)	1,793	KM54-62	32.00	25.00
PS11	1986(7)	10,000	KM76-82	29.75	30.00

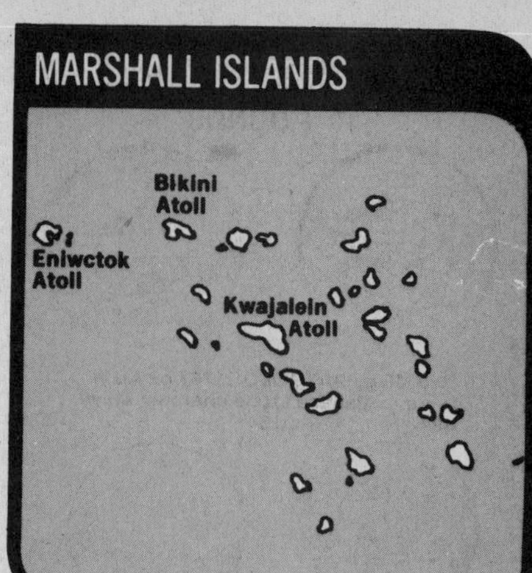

The Republic of the Marshall Islands, an archipelago which is one of the four island groups that make up what is commonly known as Micronesia, consists of 33 coral atolls comprised of over 1,150 islands or islets. It is located east of the Caroline Islands and west north-west of the Gilbert Islands half way between Hawaii and Australia. The Ratak chain to the east and the Ralik chain to the west comprise a total land area of 70 sq. mi. (181 sq. km.) with a population of 25,000 of which about 10 percent includes Americans who work at Kwajalein Missile Range. Majuro Atoll is the government and commercial center of the Republic.

Very little is known of the history of the islands before the 16th century. It is believed that many countries vessels visited the islands while searching for new trade routes to the East. In 1788, John Marshall, a British sea captain for whom the islands were named, explored them. The Marshalls have undergone successive domination by the Spanish, Germans, Japanese and Americans. It was the site of some of the fiercest fighting of the entire Pacific theater during World War II. At the conclusion of the war, the United States, under the direction of the United Nations administered the affairs of the Marshall Islands.

A constitutional government was formed on May 1, 1979 with Amata Kabua being elected as the head of the government. On October 1, 1986, the United States notified the United Nations that the Marshall Islands were to be recognized as a separate nation.

The monetary system is based on the U.S. dollar.

MINT MARKS

M - Medallic Art Co.
R - Roger Williams Mint, Conn.
S - Sunshine Mint

1/2 DOLLAR

15.5510 g, .999 SILVER, .5000 oz ASW
Independence and Bullion - Pandanus Fruit

KM#	Date	Mintage	VF	XF	Unc
1	1986	.010	—	Proof	12.50

DOLLAR

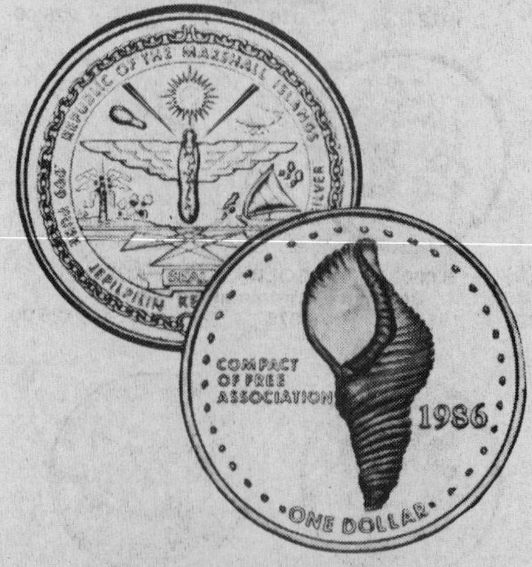

31.1030 g, .999 SILVER, 1.0000 oz ASW

Independence and Bullion - Triton Shell
Obv: Similar to 1/2 Dollar, KM#1.

KM#	Date	Mintage	VF	XF	Unc
2	1986	.010	—	Proof	27.50

5 DOLLARS

COPPER-NICKEL
U.S. Space Shuttle - Discovery

KM#	Date	Mintage	VF	XF	Unc
6	1988	.756	—	—	8.00
	1988M	.431	—	—	8.00

First Men on the Moon

KM#	Date	Mintage	VF	XF	Unc
13	1989	—	—	—	7.00

50th Anniversary of Battle of Britain

KM#	Date	Mintage	VF	XF	Unc
18	1990M	—	—	—	6.50

German Unification

KM#	Date	Mintage	VF	XF	Unc
33	1990M	—	—	—	7.00

Dwight David Eisenhower
Obv: Similar to KM#6.

KM#	Date	Mintage	VF	XF	Unc
38	1990M	—	—	—	6.50

Pearl Harbor

KM#	Date	Mintage	VF	XF	Unc
35	1991M	—	—	—	6.50

Space Shuttle Columbia

KM#	Date	Mintage	VF	XF	Unc
37	1991M	—	—	—	7.00

Desert Storm

KM#	Date	Mintage	VF	XF	Unc
40	1991R	—	—	—	6.50

P-40 Warhawk of Flying Tigers

KM#	Date	Mintage	VF	XF	Unc
49	1991M	—	—	—	6.50

Legends of Discovery - Tipnol

KM#	Date	Mintage	VF	XF	Unc
81	1992R	—	—	—	6.50

First Air Raid on Tokyo - Doolittle

KM#	Date	Mintage	VF	XF	Unc
84	1992R	—	—	—	6.50

Heroes of Corregidor

KM#	Date	Mintage	VF	XF	Unc
87	1992R	—	—	—	6.50

Battle of Midway

KM#	Date	Mintage	VF	XF	Unc
90	1992R	—	—	—	6.50

Humpback Whales

KM#	Date	Mintage	VF	XF	Unc
110	1993R	—	—	P/L	6.50

Heroes of the North Atlantic - Submarine

KM#	Date	Mintage	VF	XF	Unc
118	1993R	—	—	P/L	6.50

Heroes of Guadalcanal - Marine, Battleship & Airplanes

KM#	Date	Mintage	VF	XF	Unc
121	1993R	—	—	P/L	6.50

Elvis Presley

KM#	Date	Mintage	VF	XF	Unc
124	1993R	—	—	P/L	6.50

Common Dolphin

KM#	Date	Mintage	VF	XF	Unc
126	1993R	—	—	P/L	6.50

Christmas 1993

KM#	Date	Mintage	VF	XF	Unc
144	1993	—	—	—	6.50

Wright Brothers First Flight

KM#	Date	Mintage	VF	XF	Unc
148	1993	—	—	—	6.50

First Men on Moon

KM#	Date	Mintage	VF	XF	Unc
151	1994	—	—	—	6.50

10 DOLLARS

11.0000 g, .999 SILVER, .3533 oz ASW
Greg Louganis

KM#	Date	Mintage	VF	XF	Unc
147	1988	—	—	Proof	75.00

BRASS
Desert Storm

KM#	Date	Mintage	VF	XF	Unc
41	1991R	—	—	—	12.50

WWII American P-51 Mustang

KM#	Date	Mintage	VF	XF	Unc
59	1991S	*.050	—	—	12.50

WWII American B-29 Superfortress

KM#	Date	Mintage	VF	XF	Unc
60	1991S	*.050	—	—	12.50

WWII American B-25 Mitchell

KM#	Date	Mintage	VF	XF	Unc
61	1991S	*.050	—	—	12.50

WWII American PBY Catalina

KM#	Date	Mintage	VF	XF	Unc
62	1991S	*.050	—	—	12.50

WWII German BF 109 Messerschmitt

KM#	Date	Mintage	VF	XF	Unc
63	1991S	*.050	—	—	12.50

WWII British Spitfire

KM#	Date	Mintage	VF	XF	Unc
64	1991S	*.050	—	—	12.50

WWII Japanese A6M Reisen

KM#	Date	Mintage	VF	XF	Unc
5	1991S	*.050	—	—	12.50

WWII American F6F Hellcat

KM#	Date	Mintage	VF	XF	Unc
66	1991S	*.050	—	—	12.50

WWII Soviet Yak 9

KM#	Date	Mintage	VF	XF	Unc
67	1991S	*.050	—	—	12.50

WWII American B-17 Flying Fortress

KM#	Date	Mintage	VF	XF	Unc
68	1991S	*.050	—	—	12.50

WWII British Hawker Hurricane

KM#	Date	Mintage	VF	XF	Unc
69	1991S	*.050	—	—	12.50

The Heroes of Pearl Harbor
Obv: National seal.

KM#	Date	Mintage	VF	XF	Unc
73	1991	—	—	P/L	12.00

WWII British Mosquito

KM#	Date	Mintage	VF	XF	Unc
70	1991S	*.050	—	—	12.50

WWII British Lancaster

KM#	Date	Mintage	VF	XF	Unc
71	1991S	*.050	—	—	12.50

WWII American C-47 Skytrain

KM#	Date	Mintage	VF	XF	Unc
96	1991S	*.050	—	—	12.50

WWII American F4U Corsair

KM#	Date	Mintage	VF	XF	Unc
98	1991S	*.050	—	—	12.50

WWII American P-38 Lightning

KM#	Date	Mintage	VF	XF	Unc
101	1991	*.050	—	—	12.50

WWII Japanese G4M "Betty" Bomber

KM#	Date	Mintage	VF	XF	Unc
103	1991S	*.050	—	—	12.50

WWII Japanese KI-61 Hien "Tony"

KM#	Date	Mintage	VF	XF	Unc
107	1991S	*.050	—	—	12.50

WWII French D.520 Fighter

KM#	Date	Mintage	VF	XF	Unc
109	1991S	*.050	—	—	12.00

WWII German FW 190 Fighters

KM#	Date	Mintage	VF	XF	Unc
125	1991S	*.050	—	—	12.00

WWII American B-24 Liberator

KM#	Date	Mintage	VF	XF	Unc
131	1991S	*.050	—	—	12.00

WWII Italian S.M. 79 Sparviero

KM#	Date	Mintage	VF	XF	Unc
140	1991S	*.050	—	P/L	12.00

WWII German HE III Bombers

KM#	Date	Mintage	VF	XF	Unc
141	1991S	*.050	—	P/L	12.00

WWII Soviet IL-2 Shturmovik Ground Attack

KM#	Date	Mintage	VF	XF	Unc
142	1991S	*.050	—	—	12.50

WWII American P-51 Mustang

KM#	Date	Mintage	VF	XF	Unc
143	1991S	*.050	—	P/L	12.50

Legends of Discovery - Santa Maria

KM#	Date	Mintage	VF	XF	Unc
82	1992R	—	—	—	14.00

First Air Raid on Tokyo - Doolittle

KM#	Date	Mintage	VF	XF	Unc
85	1992R	—	—	—	12.50

Heroes of Corregidor

KM#	Date	Mintage	VF	XF	Unc
88	1992R	—	—	—	12.50

Battle of Midway

KM#	Date	Mintage	VF	XF	Unc
91	1992R	—	—	—	12.50

Heroes of the North Atlantic - Submarine

KM#	Date	Mintage	VF	XF	Unc
119	1993R	—	—	P/L	14.00

Heroes of Guadalcanal - Marine, Battleship & Airplanes

KM#	Date	Mintage	VF	XF	Unc
122	1993R	—	—	P/L	12.50

Common Dolphin

KM#	Date	Mintage	VF	XF	Unc
127	1993R	—	—	P/L	14.00

Elvis Presley

KM#	Date	Mintage	VF	XF	Unc
129	1993	—	—	P/L	12.50

Pacific Whales & Dolphins - Humpback Whales

KM#	Date	Mintage	VF	XF	Unc
132	1993	*.025	—	—	12.50

Pacific Whales & Dolphins - Risso's Dolphins

KM#	Date	Mintage	VF	XF	Unc
133	1993	*.025	—	—	12.50

Pacific Whales & Dolphins - Beluga Whales

KM#	Date	Mintage	VF	XF	Unc
134	1993	*.025	—	—	12.50

Pacific Whales & Dolphins - Hector's Dolphins

KM#	Date	Mintage	VF	XF	Unc
135	1993	*.025	—	—	12.50

Pacific Whales & Dolphins - Blue Whale

KM#	Date	Mintage	VF	XF	Unc
136	1993	*.025	—	—	12.50

Pacific Whales & Dolphins - Bottlenose Dolphin

KM#	Date	Mintage	VF	XF	Unc
137	1993	*.025	—	—	12.50

Pacific Whales & Dolphins - Killer Whale

KM#	Date	Mintage	VF	XF	Unc
138	1993	*.025	—	—	12.50

Pacific Whales & Dolphins - Baiji Dolphins

KM#	Date	Mintage	VF	XF	Unc
139	1993	*.025	—	—	12.50

Christmas 1993

KM#	Date	Mintage	VF	XF	Unc
145	1993	*.025	—	—	12.50

Wright Brothers First Flight

KM#	Date	Mintage	VF	XF	Unc
149	1993	—	—	—	12.50

First Men on the Moon

KM#	Date	Mintage	VF	XF	Unc
152	1994	—	—	—	12.50

20 DOLLARS

3.1100 g, .999 GOLD, .1000 oz AGW
Independence and Bullion - Sun

KM#	Date	Mintage	VF	XF	Unc
3	1986	*5,000	—	Proof	50.00

15.5517 g, .999 SILVER, .5000 oz ASW
First Men on Moon

KM#	Date	Mintage	VF	XF	Unc
153	1994	—	—	Proof	23.00

25 DOLLARS

33.9600 g, .925 SILVER, 1.0100 oz ASW
Greg Louganis-Back Dive

KM#	Date	Mintage	VF	XF	Unc
20	1988	*.280	—	—	60.00
	1988	*.350	—	Proof	100.00

Greg Louganis-Twister

KM#	Date	Mintage	VF	XF	Unc
21	1988	*.280	—	—	65.00
	1988	*.350	—	Proof	100.00

Greg Louganis-Jacknife

KM#	Date	Mintage	VF	XF	Unc
22	1988	*.280	—	—	65.00
	1988	*.350	—	Proof	100.00

50 DOLLARS

7.7750 g, .999 GOLD, .2500 oz AGW
Independence and Bullion - Coconut

KM#	Date	Mintage	VF	XF	Unc
4	1986	*5,000	—	Proof	125.00

31.1000 g, .999 SILVER, 1.0000 oz ASW
U.S. Space Shuttle - Discovery

KM#	Date	Mintage	VF	XF	Unc
12	1989	*.050	—	Proof	55.00
	1989S	Inc. Ab.	—	Proof	52.50

John Glenn in Space Orbit

KM#	Date	Mintage	VF	XF	Unc
7	1989	*.025	—	Proof	55.00
	1989S	Inc. Ab.	—	Proof	52.50

Neil Armstrong on the Moon
Obv: Similar to KM#12.

KM#	Date	Mintage	VF	XF	Unc
8	1989	*.025	—	Proof	55.00
	1989S	Inc. Ab.	—	Proof	52.50

American Space Station - Skylab
Obv: Similar to KM#12.

KM#	Date	Mintage	VF	XF	Unc
9	1989	*.025	—	Proof	37.50
	1989S	Inc. Ab.	—	Proof	32.50

Apollo - Sojus Joint Mission

KM#	Date	Mintage	VF	XF	Unc
10	1989	*.025	—	Proof	37.50
	1989S	Inc. Ab.	—	Proof	32.50

First Space Shuttle Flight

KM#	Date	Mintage	VF	XF	Unc
11	1989	*.025	—	Proof	37.50
	1989S	Inc. Ab.	—	Proof	32.50

First Man In Space - 1961

KM#	Date	Mintage	VF	XF	Unc
25	1989	*.025	—	Proof	40.00
	1989S	Inc. Ab.	—	Proof	37.50

First Probe of Venus - 1967

KM#	Date	Mintage	VF	XF	Unc
30	1989	*.025	—	Proof	40.00
	1989S	Inc. Ab.	—	Proof	37.50

First Men on the Moon

KM#	Date	Mintage	VF	XF	Unc
14	1989	*.050	—	Proof	37.50
	1989S	Inc. Ab.	—	Proof	32.50

First Woman In Space - 1963

KM#	Date	Mintage	VF	XF	Unc
26	1989	*.025	—	Proof	37.50
	1989S	Inc. Ab.	—	Proof	32.50

First Manned Orbit of the Moon - 1968

KM#	Date	Mintage	VF	XF	Unc
31	1989	*.025	—	Proof	37.50
	1989S	Inc. Ab.	—	Proof	32.50

First American Space Walk

KM#	Date	Mintage	VF	XF	Unc
15	1989	*.025	—	Proof	37.50
	1989S	Inc. Ab.	—	Proof	32.50

First Rendezvous In Space - 1965

KM#	Date	Mintage	VF	XF	Unc
27	1989	*.025	—	Proof	37.50
	1989S	Inc. Ab.	—	Proof	32.50

First Space Station Crew - 1971

KM#	Date	Mintage	VF	XF	Unc
32	1989	*.025	—	Proof	37.50
	1989S	Inc. Ab.	—	Proof	32.50

First Docking In Space

KM#	Date	Mintage	VF	XF	Unc
23	1989	*.025	—	Proof	37.50
	1989S	Inc. Ab.	—	Proof	32.50

First Space Walk - 1965

KM#	Date	Mintage	VF	XF	Unc
28	1989	*.025	—	Proof	37.50
	1989S	Inc. Ab.	—	Proof	32.50

First Manned Lunar Vehicle - 1971

KM#	Date	Mintage	VF	XF	Unc
50	1989	*.025	—	Proof	37.50
	1989S	Inc. Ab.	—	Proof	32.50

First Man-Made Satellite - 1957

KM#	Date	Mintage	VF	XF	Unc
24	1989	*.025	—	Proof	40.00
	1989S	Inc. Ab.	—	Proof	37.50

First Soft Landing on the Moon - 1966

KM#	Date	Mintage	VF	XF	Unc
29	1989	*.025	—	Proof	37.50
	1989S	Inc. Ab.	—	Proof	32.50

First American Satellite - 1958

KM#	Date	Mintage	VF	XF	Unc
51	1989	*.025	—	Proof	37.50
	1989S	Inc. Ab.	—	Proof	32.50

First Liquid Fuel Rocket Launch - 1926

KM#	Date	Mintage	VF	XF	Unc
52	1989	*.025	—	Proof	40.00
	1989S	Inc. Ab.	—	Proof	37.50

First Untethered Space Walk - 1984

KM#	Date	Mintage	VF	XF	Unc
53	1989	*.025	—	Proof	37.50
	1989S	Inc. Ab.	—	Proof	32.50

First Landing on Mars - 1976

KM#	Date	Mintage	VF	XF	Unc
54	1989	*.025	—	Proof	37.50
	1989S	Inc. Ab.	—	Proof	32.50

First Flyby of Saturn - 1979

KM#	Date	Mintage	VF	XF	Unc
55	1989	*.025	—	Proof	37.50
	1989S	Inc. Ab.	—	Proof	32.50

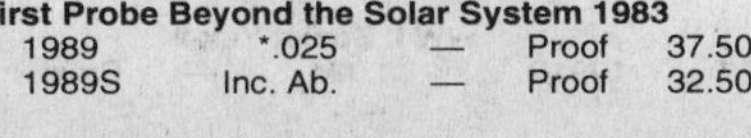

First Probe Beyond the Solar System 1983

KM#	Date	Mintage	VF	XF	Unc
56	1989	*.025	—	Proof	37.50
	1989S	Inc. Ab.	—	Proof	32.50

First Flyby of Jupiter - 1973

KM#	Date	Mintage	VF	XF	Unc
57	1989	*.025	—	Proof	37.50
	1989S	Inc. Ab.	—	Proof	32.50

50th Anniversary of Battle of Britain

KM#	Date	Mintage	VF	XF	Unc
19	1990M	*.050	—	Proof	60.00

German Unification

KM#	Date	Mintage	VF	XF	Unc
34	1990M	*.050	—	Proof	60.00

Dwight David Eisenhower

KM#	Date	Mintage	VF	XF	Unc
39	1990M	*.050	—	Proof	60.00

Pearl Harbor

KM#	Date	Mintage	VF	XF	Unc
36	1991M	*.050	—	Proof	60.00

Operation Desert Storm

KM#	Date	Mintage	VF	XF	Unc
42	1991R	—	—	Proof	60.00

WW II American P-51 Mustang

KM#	Date	Mintage	VF	XF	Unc
43	1991M	*.025	—	Proof	60.00

WW II American B-29 Superfortress

KM#	Date	Mintage	VF	XF	Unc
44	1991M	*.025	—	Proof	60.00

WW II German BF-109 Messerschmitt

KM#	Date	Mintage	VF	XF	Unc
45	1991M	*.025	—	Proof	60.00

WW II British Spitfire

KM#	Date	Mintage	VF	XF	Unc
46	1991M	*.025	—	Proof	60.00

WW II American PBY Catalina

KM#	Date	Mintage	VF	XF	Unc
47	1991M	*.025	—	Proof	60.00

WW II Japanese A6M Reisen

KM#	Date	Mintage	VF	XF	Unc
48	1991M	*.025	—	Proof	60.00

WW II P-40 Warhawk

KM#	Date	Mintage	VF	XF	Unc
58	1991M	*.025	—	Proof	60.00

Space Shuttle Columbia - 1981

KM#	Date	Mintage	VF	XF	Unc
72	1991M	*.025	—	Proof	60.00

WW II British Hurricane

KM#	Date	Mintage	VF	XF	Unc
74	1991S	*.024	—	Proof	60.00

WW II British Mosquito

KM#	Date	Mintage	VF	XF	Unc
75	1991S	*.024	—	Proof	60.00

WW II American B-24 Liberator

KM#	Date	Mintage	VF	XF	Unc
76	1991S	*.025	—	Proof	60.00

WW II American B-25 Mitchell

KM#	Date	Mintage	VF	XF	Unc
77	1991S	*.025	—	Proof	60.00

WW II American C-47 Skytrain

KM#	Date	Mintage	VF	XF	Unc
78	1991S	*.024	—	Proof	60.00

WW II American B-17 Flying Fortress

KM#	Date	Mintage	VF	XF	Unc
79	1991S	*.024	—	Proof	60.00

WW II American F4U Corsair

KM#	Date	Mintage	VF	XF	Unc
80	1991S	*.024	—	Proof	60.00

WW II American P-38 Lightning

KM#	Date	Mintage	VF	XF	Unc
93	1991S	*.025	—	Proof	60.00

WW II American F6F Hellcat

KM#	Date	Mintage	VF	XF	Unc
94	1991S	*.024	—	Proof	60.00

WW II Japanese G4M "Betty" Bomber

KM#	Date	Mintage	VF	XF	Unc
95	1991S	*.025	—	Proof	60.00

WW II Soviet Yak-9

KM#	Date	Mintage	VF	XF	Unc
97	1991S	*.024	—	Proof	60.00

WW II Japanese K1-61 Hien "Tony"

KM#	Date	Mintage	VF	XF	Unc
99	1991S	*.025	—	Proof	60.00

WW II French D-520 Fighter

100	1991S	*.025	—	Proof	60.00

WW II German FW 190 Fighters

102	1991S	*.024	—	Proof	60.00

WW II British Lancaster

104	1991S	*.025	—	Proof	60.00

WW II Italian S.M. 79 Sparviero Bombers

105	1991S	*.024	—	Proof	60.00

WW II German HE 111 Bombers

KM#	Date	Mintage	VF	XF	Unc
106	1991S	*.025	—	Proof	60.00

WW II Soviet IL-2 Shturmovik

108	1991S	*.024	—	Proof	60.00

Legends of Discovery - Greek Ship Argo

81	1992R	—	—	Proof	60.00

First Air Raid on Tokyo - Doolittle

86	1992R	—	—	Proof	65.00

Heroes of Corregidor

89	1992R	—	—	Proof	65.00

Battle of Midway

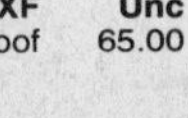

KM#	Date	Mintage	VF	XF	Unc
92	1992R	—	—	Proof	65.00

Pacific Whales & Dolphins - Humpback Whale

111	1993R	*.025	—	Proof	60.00

Pacific Whales & Dolphins - Risso's Dolphins

112	1993R	*.025	—	Proof	60.00

Pacific Whales & Dolphins - Beluga Whale

113	1993R	*.025	—	Proof	60.00

Pacific Whales & Dolphins - Hector's Dolphin

114	1993R	*.025	—	Proof	60.00

Pacific Whales & Dolphins - Blue Whales

115	1993R	*.025	—	Proof	60.00

Pacific Whales & Dolphins - Baiji Dolphins

116	1993R	*.025	—	Proof	60.00

Pacific Whales & Dolphins - Killer Whales

KM#	Date	Mintage	VF	XF	Unc
117	1993R	*.025	—	Proof	60.00

Heroes of the North Atlantic - Submarine

KM#	Date	Mintage	VF	XF	Unc
120	1993R	—	—	Proof	60.00

Heroes of Guadalcanal - Marine, Battleship & Airplanes

KM#	Date	Mintage	VF	XF	Unc
123	1993R	—	—	Proof	60.00

Common Dolphins

KM#	Date	Mintage	VF	XF	Unc
128	1993R	—	—	Proof	60.00

Elvis Presley

KM#	Date	Mintage	VF	XF	Unc
130	1993S	—	—	Proof	60.00

Christmas 1993

KM#	Date	Mintage	VF	XF	Unc
146	1993R	—	—	Proof	60.00

Wright Brothers First Flight

KM#	Date	Mintage	VF	XF	Unc
150	1993	—	—	Proof	60.00

First Men on Moon

KM#	Date	Mintage	VF	XF	Unc
154	1994	—	—	Proof	60.00

75 DOLLARS

155.6700 g, .999 SILVER, 5.0055 oz ASW
Illustration reduced. Actual size: 65mm
Greg Louganis - World's Greatest Diver

KM#	Date	Mintage	VF	XF	Unc
16	1988	*.175	—	Proof	225.00

100 DOLLARS

13.3300 g, .583 GOLD, .2499 oz AGW
Greg Louganis - World's Greatest Diver
Obv: National seal and legend. Rev: Diver.

KM#	Date	Mintage	VF	XF	Unc
17	1988	*.280	—	—	250.00
	1988	*.350	—	Proof	300.00

200 DOLLARS

31.1030 g, .999 GOLD, 1.0000 oz AGW
Independence and Bullion - Stick Chart

KM#	Date	Mintage	VF	XF	Unc
5	1986	*5,000	—	Proof	475.00

MINT SETS (MS)

KM#	Date	Mintage	Identification	Issue Price	Mkt. Val.
MS1	1988(3)	—	KM20-22	—	200.00
MS2	1988(4)	—	KM17,20-22	—	450.00
MS3	1992R	—	KM81-83	71.00	—
MS4	1992R	—	KM84-86	71.00	—
MS5	1992R	—	KM87-89	71.00	—
MS6	1992R	—	KM90-92	71.00	—
MS7	1992R	—	KM84,87,90	17.50	—
MS8	1992R	—	KM85,88,91	34.00	—
MS9	1992R	—	KM86,89,92	156.00	—

PROOF SETS (PS)

KM#	Date	Mintage	Identification	Issue Price	Mkt. Val.
PS1	1986(3)	5,000	KM3-5	1095.	650.00
PS2	1986(2)	.010	KM1-2	45.00	50.00
PS3	1988(3)	—	KM20-22	—	300.00
PS4	1988(4)	—	KM17,20-22	—	600.00
PS5	1991(3)	—	KM40-42	71.00	75.00
PS6	1993(3)	—	KM124,129-130	—	85.00

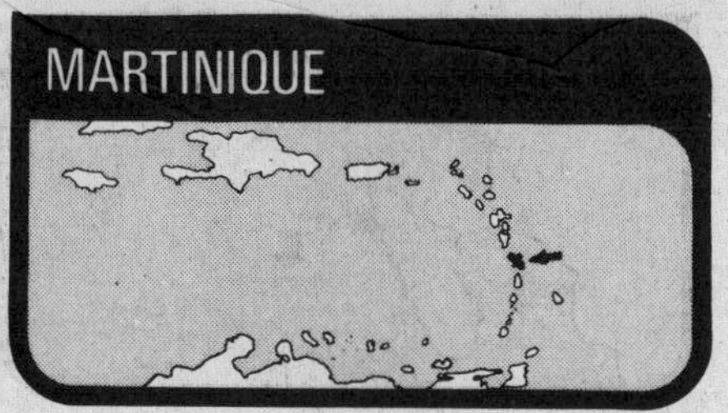

The French Overseas Department of Martinique, located in the Lesser Antilles of the West Indies between Dominica and Saint Lucia, has an area of 425 sq. mi. (1,100 sq. km.) and a population of 290,000. Capital: Fort-de-France. Agriculture and tourism are the major sources of income. Bananas, sugar, and rum are exported.

Christopher Columbus discovered Martinique, probably on June 15, 1502. France took possession on June 25, 1635, and has maintained possession since that time except for three short periods of British occupation during the Napoleonic Wars. A French department since 1946, Martinique voted a reaffirmation of that status in 1958, remaining within the new French Community. Martinique was the birthplace of Napoleon's Empress Josephine, and the site of the eruption of Mt. Pelee in 1902 that claimed 40,000 lives.

The official currency of Martinique is the French franc. The 1897-1922 coinage of the Colony of Martinique is now obsolete.

RULERS

British, 1793-1801
French, 1802-1809

MONETARY SYSTEM

15 Sols = 1 Escalin
20 Sols = 1 Livre
66 Livres = 4 Escudos = 6400 Reis

French Occupation

1802-1809

MONETARY SYSTEM

6400 Reis = 22 Livres

20 LIVRES

GOLD
c/m: 20 above eagle on false or lightweight Brazil 6400 Reis, KM#172.2.

KM#	Date	Mintage	VG	Fine	VF	XF
32	ND(1751-77)	—	950.00	1400.	1700.	2850.
	ND(1778-79)	—	700.00	1000.	1350.	2250.

c/m: 20 above eagle on false Brazil 6400 Reis, type of KM#199.

KM#	Date	Mintage	VG	Fine	VF	XF
31	ND(1777-86)	—	—	—	Rare	—

22 LIVRES

GOLD
c/m: 22 above eagle on Portuguese 4000 Reis, KM#184.

KM#	Date	Mintage	VG	Fine	VF	XF
38	ND(1707-22)	—	2500.	4000.	5500.	8500.

c/m: 22 above eagle on Brazil 6400 Reis, KM#151.

KM#	Date	Mintage	VG	Fine	VF	XF
39	ND(1735-50)	—	2000.	3500.	4500.	7500.

c/m: 22 above eagle on false Brazil 6400 Reis, type of KM#172.1.

KM#	Date	Mintage	VG	Fine	VF	XF
37	ND(1751-77)	—	1500.	2500.	3000.	5000.

c/m: 22 above eagle on Brazil 6400 Reis, KM#199.2.

KM#	Date	Mintage	VG	Fine	VF	XF
33	ND(1777-86)	—	1000.	1500.	1800.	3000.

c/m: 22 above eagle on Brazil 6400 Reis, KM#218.2.

KM#	Date	Mintage	VG	Fine	VF	XF
34	ND(1786-90)	—	1000.	1500.	1800.	3000.

c/m: 22 above eagle on Brazil 6400 Reis, KM#226.1.

KM#	Date	Mintage	VG	Fine	VF	XF
35	ND(1789-1805)	—	950.00	1400.	1700.	2850.

c/m: 22 above eagle on Portugal 4 Escudos, KM#240.

KM#	Date	Mintage	VG	Fine	VF	XF
36	ND(1750-76)	—	1250.	2000.	2450.	4000.

NOTE: There are many merchant c/m from Martinique during this period, but the above are probably the only official issues. There are also many counterfeits or fantasies attributed to the West Indies.

MONETARY REFORM

100 Centimes   1 Franc

50 CENTIMES

COPPER-NICKEL

KM#	Date	Mintage	VG	Fine	VF	XF
40	1897	.600	7.50	15.00	30.00	70.00
	1922	.500	5.00	10.00	25.00	55.00

FRANC

COPPER-NICKEL

KM#	Date	Mintage	VG	Fine	VF	XF
41	1897	.300	10.00	20.00	40.00	90.00
	1922	.350	7.50	15.00	35.00	70.00

MAURITANIA

The Islamic Republic of Mauritania, located in northwest Africa bounded by Spanish Sahara, Mali, Algeria, Senegal and the Atlantic Ocean, has an area of 397,955 sq. mi. (1,030,700 sq. km.) and a population of 1.9 million. Capital: Nouakchott. The economy centers about herding, agriculture, fishing and mining. Iron ore, copper concentrates and fish products are exported.

The indigenous Negroid inhabitants were driven out of Mauritania by Berber invaders of the Islamic faith in the 11th century. The Berbers in turn were conquered by Arab invaders, the Beni Hassan, in the 16th century. Arab traders carried on a gainful trade in gum arabic, gold and slaves with Portuguese, Dutch, English and French traders until late in the 19th century when France took control of the area and made it a part of French West Africa, in 1920. Mauritania became a part of the French Union in 1946 and was made an autonomous republic within the new French Community in 1958, when the Islamic Republic of Mauritania was proclaimed. The republic became independent on November 28, 1960, and withdrew from the French Community in 1966.

On June 28, 1973, in a move designed to emphasize its non-alignment with France, Mauritania converted its currency from the old French-supported C.F.A. franc unit to a new unit called the Ouguiya.

MONETARY SYSTEM

5 Khoum = 1 Ouguiya
100 Ouguiya = 500 CFA Francs

1/5 OUGUIYA

(Khoums)

ALUMINUM

KM#	Date	Year	Mintage	Fine	VF	XF	Unc
1	AH1393	1973	1.000	.75	1.50	2.50	4.00

OUGUIYA

COPPER-NICKEL-ALUMINUM
Rev: Arabic leg. in one line.

KM#	Date	Year	Mintage	Fine	VF	XF	Unc
2	AH1393	1973	—	3.00	6.00	12.00	20.00

Rev: Arabic leg. in two lines.

KM#	Date	Year	Mintage	Fine	VF	XF	Unc
6	AH1394	1974	—	2.50	5.50	10.00	18.50
	1401	1981	—	1.50	3.00	4.50	7.50
	1403	1983	—	1.00	2.00	3.50	6.50
	1406	1986	—	.75	1.50	2.50	4.50
	1407	1987	—	.50	1.00	2.00	4.00
	1410	1990	—	.50	1.00	2.00	4.00

5 OUGUIYA

COPPER-NICKEL-ALUMINUM

KM#	Date	Year	Mintage	Fine	VF	XF	Unc
3	AH1393	1973	—	2.50	5.50	10.00	15.00
	1394	1974	—	2.50	5.50	10.00	17.50
	1401	1981	—	2.00	4.00	6.00	12.50
	1404	1984	—	1.50	2.50	4.50	10.00
	1407	1987	—	.75	1.50	2.50	5.00
	1410	1990	—	.50	1.00	2.00	4.00

10 OUGUIYA

COPPER-NICKEL

KM#	Date	Year	Mintage	Fine	VF	XF	Unc
4	AH1393	1973	—	2.50	5.50	10.00	17.50
	1394	1974	—	2.50	5.50	10.00	17.50
	1401	1981	—	2.00	5.00	7.50	15.00
	1403	1983	—	1.25	2.50	4.50	9.00
	1407	1987	—	1.25	2.50	4.50	9.00
	1410	1990	—	.75	1.50	2.50	5.00
	1411	1991	—	.75	1.50	2.50	5.00

20 OUGUIYA

COPPER-NICKEL

KM#	Date	Year	Mintage	Fine	VF	XF	Unc
5	AH1393	1973	—	2.50	5.50	10.00	17.50
	1394	1974	—	2.50	5.50	10.00	17.50
	1403	1983	—	1.25	2.50	4.50	9.00
	1407	1987	—	1.25	2.50	4.50	9.00
	1410	1990	—	1.25	2.50	4.50	9.00

500 OUGUIYA

26.0800 g, .920 GOLD, .7714 oz AGW
15th Anniversary of Independence

KM#	Date	Mintage	Fine	VF	XF	Unc
7	1975(a)	1,800	—	—	—	450.00

MINT SETS (MS)

KM#	Date	Mintage	Identification	Issue Price	Mkt. Val.
MS1	1973(10)	—	KM1-5, two each	20.00	150.00

MAURITIUS

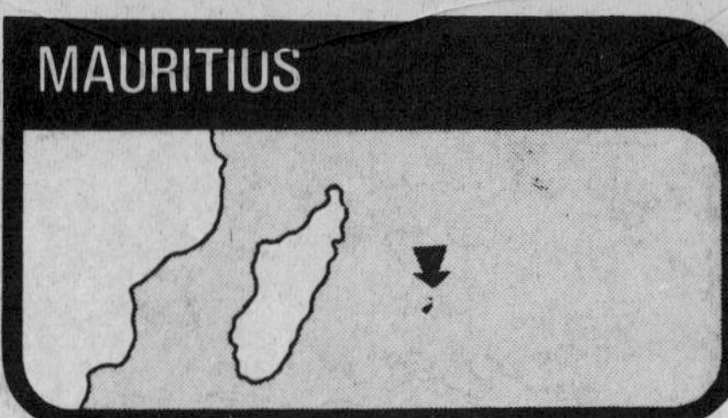

The island of Mauritius, a member nation of the Britis Commonwealth located in the Indian Ocean 500 mile (805 km.) east of Madagascar, has an area of 790 sq mi. (1,860 sq. km.) and a population of 1 million. Cap tal: Port Louis. Sugar provides 90 percent of the expo revenue.

Cartographic evidence indicates that Arabs and Malay arrived at Mauritius during the Middle Ages. Doming Fernandez, a Portuguese navigator, visited the island i the early 16th century, but Portugal made no attempt a settlement. The Dutch took possession, and named th island, in 1598. Their colony failed to prosper and wa abandoned in 1710. France claimed Mauritius in 171 and developed a strong and prosperous colony that er dured until the island was captured by the British, 181C during the Napoleonic Wars. British possession was con firmed by the Treaty of Paris, 1814. Mauritius becam independent on March 12, 1968. It is a member of th Commonwealth of Nations.

The first coins struck under British auspices for Mauritiu were undated (1822) and bore French legends.

RULERS

British, until 1968

MINT MARKS

H - Heaton, Birmingham
SA - Pretoria Mint

MONETARY SYSTEM

20 Sols (Sous) = 1 Livre
100 Cents = 1 Rupee

25 SOUS

.500 SILVER

KM#	Date	Mintage	VG	Fine	VF	X
1	ND(1822)	—	15.00	30.00	50.00	135.0
	ND(1822)	—	—	—	Proof	550.0

50 SOUS

.500 SILVER

KM#	Date	Mintage	VG	Fine	VF	X
2	ND(1822)	—	20.00	40.00	75.00	175.0
	ND(1822)	—	—	—	Proof	700.0

ANCHOR COINAGE

(1/16, 1/8, 1/4 & 1/2 Dollar)

NOTE: Coins dated 1820 were struck for Mauritius an colonies of the British West Indies. These circulated Mauritius until 1826 when they were shipped to th British West Indies where they will be found listed.

REGULAR COINAGE

100 Cents = 1 Rupee

CENT

BRONZE

KM#	Date	Mintage	Fine	VF	XF	Un
7	1877	—	—	—	Proof	175.0
	1877H	.700	2.00	4.00	22.50	65.0
	1877H	—	—	—	Proof	125.0
	1878	.250	3.00	13.00	50.00	135.0

KM#	Date	Mintage	Fine	VF	XF	Unc
7	1878	—	—	—	Proof	350.00
	1882H	.300	1.50	5.00	30.00	80.00
	1882H	—	—	—	Proof	150.00
	1883	.500	1.25	2.50	18.50	55.00
	1883	—	—	—	Proof	175.00
	1884	.500	1.25	2.50	18.50	55.00
	1884	—	—	—	Proof	175.00
	1888	.500	1.25	2.50	18.50	55.00
	1890H	.500	1.25	2.50	18.50	55.00
	1896	.500	1.25	2.50	18.50	55.00
	1897	1.000	1.00	2.00	12.00	40.00
	1897	—	—	—	Proof	175.00
12	1911	1.000	.75	1.50	12.00	40.00
	1912	.500	1.25	2.50	18.50	55.00
	1917	.500	.75	1.50	12.00	35.00
	1920	.500	1.50	3.00	22.50	60.00
	1921	.500	2.00	4.00	22.50	60.00
	1922	1.800	.50	1.00	8.00	25.00
	1923	.200	3.00	7.00	35.00	75.00
	1924	.200	3.00	7.00	35.00	75.00
21	1943SA	.520	.50	1.25	4.00	10.00
	1944SA	.500	.50	1.25	4.00	10.00
	1945SA	.500	.50	1.25	4.00	10.00
	1946SA	.500	.50	1.25	4.00	10.00
	1947SA	.500	.50	1.25	4.00	10.00
25	1949	.500	.75	1.25	2.50	7.50
	1949	—	—	—	Proof	100.00
	1952	.500	.75	1.25	2.50	7.50
	1952	—	—	—	Proof	100.00
31	1953	.500	.10	.25	.50	1.50
	1953	—	—	—	Proof	75.00
	1955	.501	.10	.25	.50	2.50
	1955	—	—	—	Proof	75.00
	1956	.500	.10	.20	.50	2.50
	1956	—	—	—	Proof	75.00
	1957	.501	.10	.20	.50	2.50
	1959	.501	.10	.20	.50	2.50
	1959	—	—	—	Proof	75.00
	1960	.500	.10	.20	.50	2.50
	1960	—	—	—	Proof	75.00
	1961	.500	.10	.20	.50	2.50
	1961	—	—	—	Proof	75.00
	1962	.500	.10	.20	.50	1.50
	1962	—	—	—	Proof	50.00
	1963	.500	.10	.20	.50	1.50
	1963	—	—	—	Proof	50.00
	1964	1.500	—	.10	.20	.50
	1964	—	—	—	Proof	50.00
	1965	1.500	—	.10	.20	.50
	1969	.500	—	.10	.15	.30
	1970	1.500	—	—	.10	.20
	1971	1.000	—	—	.10	.20
	1971	750 pcs.	—	—	Proof	20.00
	1975	.400	—	—	.10	.20
	1978	9,268	—	—	Proof	1.00

2 CENTS

BRONZE

KM#	Date	Mintage	Fine	VF	XF	Unc
8	1877	—	—	—	Proof	150.00
	1877H	.350	1.00	6.50	27.50	100.00
	1877H	—	—	—	Proof	300.00
	1878	.130	2.50	12.00	65.00	150.00
	1878	—	—	—	Proof	150.00
	1882H	.150	2.00	8.00	30.00	125.00
	1882H	—	—	—	Proof	275.00
	1883	.250	1.00	6.50	27.50	75.00
8	1884	.250	1.00	6.50	27.50	75.00
	1884	—	—	—	Proof	550.00
	1888	.250	.75	4.00	20.00	45.00
	1888	—	—	—	Proof	400.00
	1890H	.250	1.00	5.00	25.00	75.00
	1896	.188	1.00	5.00	25.00	85.00
	1897	1.000	.75	4.00	20.00	45.00
	1897	—	—	—	Proof	375.00
13	1911	.500	2.00	4.00	15.00	40.00
	1911	—	—	—	Proof	300.00
	1912	.250	3.00	5.00	30.00	70.00
	1917	.250	1.25	2.50	12.00	35.00
	1920	.250	1.50	3.00	20.00	45.00
	1921	.250	1.50	3.00	20.00	45.00
	1922	.900	.50	1.00	8.00	30.00
	1923	.400	1.25	2.50	18.50	45.00
	1924	.400	1.25	2.50	18.50	45.00
22	1943SA	.290	.75	2.00	4.00	10.00
	1944SA	.500	.75	2.00	4.00	10.00
	1945SA	.250	.75	2.00	4.00	10.00
	1946SA	.400	.75	2.00	4.00	10.00
	1947SA	.250	.75	2.00	4.00	10.00
26	1949	.250	.75	1.25	2.50	6.50
	1949	—	—	—	Proof	120.00
	1952	.250	.75	1.25	2.50	6.50
	1952	—	—	—	Proof	120.00
32	1953	.250	.10	.25	.50	2.50
	1953	—	—	—	Proof	100.00
	1954	—	—	—	Proof	300.00
	1955	.501	.10	.25	.50	2.50
	1955	—	—	—	Proof	100.00
	1956	.250	.10	.25	.50	3.50
	1956	—	—	—	Proof	100.00
	1957	.501	.10	.25	.50	3.50
	1959	.503	.10	.25	.50	3.50
	1959	—	—	—	Proof	100.00
	1960	.250	.10	.25	.50	3.50
	1960	—	—	—	Proof	100.00
	1961	.500	.10	.25	.50	3.50
	1961	—	—	—	Proof	100.00
	1962	.500	.10	.25	.50	1.50
	1962	—	—	—	Proof	75.00
	1963	.500	.10	.25	.50	1.50
	1963	—	—	—	Proof	75.00
	1964	1.00	—	.10	.25	.50
	1964	—	—	—	Proof	50.00
	1965	.750	.10	.20	.40	.60
	1966	.500	.10	.20	.40	.50
	1967	.250	.10	.20	.40	.50
	1969	.500	.10	.20	.40	.50
	1971	1.000	—	.10	.20	.40
	1971	750 pcs.	—	—	Proof	20.00
	1975	5.200	—	—	.10	.35
	1978	9,268	—	—	Proof	1.50

5 CENTS

BRONZE

KM#	Date	Mintage	Fine	VF	XF	Unc
9	1877	—	—	—	Proof	375.00
	1877H	3.00	3.00	10.00	55.00	175.00
	1877H	—	—	—	Proof	900.00
	1878	.050	6.00	20.00	90.00	300.00
	1878	—	—	—	Proof	200.00
	1882H	.060	5.00	15.00	80.00	250.00
	1882H	—	—	—	Proof	375.00
	1883	.100	3.00	12.00	65.00	125.00
	1884	.100	3.00	12.00	65.00	125.00
	1884	—	—	—	Proof	250.00
	1888	.100	1.50	7.50	40.00	80.00
	1890H	.100	2.50	12.00	70.00	180.00
	1897	.600	1.50	7.50	50.00	110.00
	1897	—	—	—	Proof	200.00
14	1917	.600	2.00	4.50	27.50	80.00
	1920	.200	2.00	4.50	32.50	100.00
	1921	.100	3.00	6.50	35.00	120.00
	1922	.360	2.00	4.50	32.50	100.00
	1923	.400	3.00	6.50	35.00	120.00
	1924	.400	2.00	4.50	32.50	100.00
20	1942SA	.940	1.50	2.50	6.50	15.00
	1944SA	1.000	1.25	1.75	4.00	10.00
	1945SA	.500	1.25	1.75	4.00	12.00
34	1956	.201	.25	.50	.75	5.00
	1956	—	—	—	Proof	100.00
	1957	.203	.25	.50	2.00	8.00
	1957	—	—	—	Proof	100.00
	1959	.801	.25	.50	1.00	4.00
	1959	—	—	—	Proof	75.00
	1960	.400	.25	.50	1.00	4.00
	1960	—	—	—	Proof	75.00
	1963	.200	.25	.50	1.00	2.00
	1963	—	—	—	Proof	70.00
	1964	.600	.25	.50	1.00	2.00
	1964	—	—	—	Proof	70.00
	1965	.200	.25	.50	.75	2.00
	1966	.200	.25	.50	.75	1.50
	1967	.200	.25	.50	.75	2.00
	1969	.500	.10	.15	.25	.50
	1970	.800	.10	.15	.25	.50
	1971	.500	.10	.15	.25	.50
	1971	750 pcs.	—	—	Proof	20.00
	1975	3.700	.10	.15	.25	.50
	1978	8.000	—	.10	.20	.50
	1978	9,268	—	—	Proof	2.00

10 CENTS

1.1660 g, .800 SILVER, .0300 oz ASW

KM#	Date	Mintage	Fine	VF	XF	Unc
10.1	1877	—	—	—	Proof	400.00
	1877H	.250	1.50	6.50	27.50	100.00
	1877H	—	—	—	Proof	300.00
	1878	.050	5.00	18.00	50.00	220.00
	1878	—	—	—	Proof	275.00
	1882H	.030	15.00	35.00	150.00	250.00
	1883	.100	3.00	10.00	40.00	200.00
	1883	—	—	—	Proof	275.00
	1886	.750	1.25	5.00	22.00	80.00
	1886	—	—	—	Proof	275.00
	1889H	.500	2.00	7.50	25.00	100.00
	1889	—	—	—	Proof	275.00
	1897	.500	2.00	7.50	25.00	80.00
	1897	—	—	—	Proof	400.00

Plain edge.

KM#	Date	Mintage	Fine	VF	XF	Unc
10.2	1877H	—	—	—	Proof	225.00

COPPER-NICKEL

KM#	Date	Mintage	Fine	VF	XF	Unc
24	1947	.500	.75	1.50	8.00	35.00
	1947	—	—	—	Proof	200.00
30	1952	.250	.50	.75	1.50	6.50
	1952	—	—	—	Proof	150.00
33	1954	.252	.20	.35	.75	2.50
	1954	—	—	—	Proof	150.00
	1957	.250	.20	.35	.75	2.50
	1959	.253	.20	.35	.75	2.50
	1959	—	—	—	Proof	175.00
	1960	.050	.20	.35	.75	2.00
	1960	—	—	—	Proof	175.00
	1963	.200	.15	.30	.60	1.50
	1963	—	—	—	Proof	175.00
	1964	.200	.15	.30	.60	1.00
	1965	.200	.15	.30	.60	1.00
	1966	.200	.10	.25	.50	.75
	1969	.200	.10	.25	.50	.75
	1970	.500	.10	.25	.50	.75
	1971	.300	.10	.25	.50	.75
	1971	750 pcs.	—	—	Proof	20.00
	1975	6.675	.10	.25	.50	.75
	1978	13.000	.10	.25	.50	.75
	1978	9,268	—	—	Proof	2.50

20 CENTS

2.3320 g, .800 SILVER, .0600 oz ASW

KM#	Date	Mintage	Fine	VF	XF	Unc
11.1	1877	—	—	—	Proof	750.00
	1877H	.375	5.00	20.00	75.00	300.00
	1877H	—	—	—	Proof	400.00
	1878	.050	10.00	30.00	150.00	400.00
	1878	—	—	—	Proof	300.00
	1882H	.015	15.00	50.00	225.00	475.00
	1883	.100	6.00	22.50	100.00	275.00
	1883	—	—	—	Proof	300.00
	1886	.750	4.00	16.00	40.00	150.00
	1886	—	—	—	Proof	300.00
	1889H	.250	5.00	20.00	60.00	225.00
	1899	.500	4.00	16.00	55.00	200.00
	1899	—	—	—	Proof	300.00

Plain edge.

KM#	Date	Mintage	Fine	VF	XF	Unc
11.2	1877H	—	—	—	Proof	750.00

1/4 RUPEE

2.9200 g, .916 SILVER, .0816 oz ASW

KM#	Date	Mintage	Fine	VF	XF	Unc
15	1934	.400	2.00	7.00	20.00	60.00
	1934	—	—	—	Proof	600.00
	1935	.400	2.00	7.00	20.00	60.00
	1935	—	—	—	Proof	750.00
	1936	.400	2.00	6.00	18.00	50.00
	1936	—	—	—	Proof	650.00
18	1938	2.000	3.00	10.00	30.00	80.00
	1938	—	—	—	Proof	375.00

2.9200 g, .500 SILVER, .0470 oz ASW

KM#	Date	Mintage	Fine	VF	XF	Unc
18a	1946	2.000	7.50	20.00	40.00	100.00
	1946	—	—	—	Proof	400.00

COPPER-NICKEL

KM#	Date	Mintage	Fine	VF	XF	Unc
27	1950	2.000	.50	1.00	2.00	9.50
	1950	—	—	—	Proof	175.00
	1951	1.000	.50	1.00	2.00	9.50
	1951	—	—	—	Proof	175.00
36	1960	1.000	.35	.75	1.00	2.00
	1960	—	—	—	Proof	100.00
	1964	.400	.25	.50	.75	1.50
	1964	—	—	—	Proof	100.00
	1965	.400	.25	.50	.75	1.25
	1970	.400	.20	.35	.60	1.00
	1971	.540	.25	.50	.75	1.25
	1971	750 pcs.	—	—	Proof	20.00
	1975	8.940	.15	.30	.50	.80
	1978	*8.800	.15	.30	.50	.80
	1978	9,268	—	—	Proof	3.50

***NOTE:** Variety exists with lower hole in 8 filled.

1/2 RUPEE

5.8300 g, .916 SILVER, .1717 oz ASW

KM#	Date	Mintage	Fine	VF	XF	Unc
16	1934	1.000	2.50	5.00	15.00	50.00
	1934	—	—	—	Proof	450.00

5.8300 g, .500 SILVER, .0937 oz ASW

KM#	Date	Mintage	Fine	VF	XF	Unc
23	1946	1.000	10.00	25.00	125.00	200.00
	1946	—	—	—	Proof	700.00

COPPER-NICKEL

KM#	Date	Mintage	Fine	VF	XF	Unc
28	1950	1.000	.50	1.00	1.75	9.00
	1950	—	—	—	Proof	175.00
	1951	.570	.75	1.25	2.00	9.50
	1951	—	—	—	Proof	225.00
37.1	1965	.200	.50	1.00	2.00	6.00
	1971	.400	.25	.50	.75	1.50
	1971	750 pcs.	—	—	Proof	25.00
	1975	4.160	.25	.50	.75	1.25
	1978	.400	.25	.50	.75	1.25
	1978	9,268	—	—	Proof	4.00

Error. W/o security edge.

KM#	Date	Mintage	Fine	VF	XF	Unc
37.2	1971	Inc. Ab.	—	—	—	—

RUPEE

11.6600 g, .916 SILVER, .3434 oz ASW

KM#	Date	Mintage	Fine	VF	XF	Unc
17	1934	1.500	4.00	8.00	20.00	50.00
	1934	—	—	—	Proof	600.00
19	1938	.200	8.00	15.00	45.00	150.00
	1938	—	—	—	Proof	500.00

COPPER-NICKEL

KM#	Date	Mintage	Fine	VF	XF	Unc
29.1	1950	1.500	.75	1.50	3.00	16.00
	1950	—	—	—	Proof	200.00
	1951	1.000	.50	1.25	2.00	12.00
	1951	—	—	—	Proof	300.00

Error. W/o security edge.

KM#	Date	Mintage	Fine	VF	XF	Unc
29.2	1951	Inc. Ab.	—	—	—	—
35.1	1956	1.000	.25	.75	1.50	7.50
	1956	—	—	—	Proof	200.00
	1964	.200	.50	1.00	3.00	5.00
	1971	.600	.25	.60	1.00	2.00
	1971	750 pcs.	—	—	Proof	50.00
	1975	4.525	.25	.60	1.00	2.00
	1978	2.000	.25	.60	1.00	2.00
	1978	9,268	—	—	Proof	5.00

Error. W/o security edge.

KM#	Date	Mintage	Fine	VF	XF	Unc
35.2	1971	Inc. Ab.	.25	.75	1.25	2.50

10 RUPEES

COPPER-NICKEL
Independence Commemorative

KM#	Date	Mintage	Fine	VF	XF	Unc
38	1971	.050	—	1.00	2.00	4.00
	20.0000 g, .925 SILVER, .5948 oz ASW					
38a	1971	750 pcs.	—	—	Proof	125.00

COPPER-NICKEL
Wedding of Prince Charles and Lady Diana

KM#	Date	Mintage	Fine	VF	XF	Unc
46	1981	—	—	1.00	2.00	4.00
	28.2800 g, .925 SILVER, .8411 oz ASW					
46a	1981	2,090	—	—	Proof	30.00

World Food Day
Obv: Similar to KM#46.

KM#	Date	Mintage	Fine	VF	XF	Unc
48	1981	.010	—	—	—	15.00
	1981	5,000	—	—	Proof	25.00

25 RUPEES

25.4000 g, .500 SILVER, .4083 oz ASW
Conservation - Blue Swallowtail

KM#	Date	Mintage	VF	XF	Unc
40	1975	—	—	—	20.00
	28.2800 g, .925 SILVER, .8411 oz ASW				
40a	1975(error)	12 pcs.	—	—	—
	1975	9,869	—	Proof	25.00

28.4000 g, .500 SILVER, .4565 oz ASW
Queen's Silver Jubilee

KM#	Date	Mintage	VF	XF	Unc
43	1977	—	—	—	10.00
	28.2800 g, .925 SILVER, .8411 oz ASW				
43a	1977	.047	—	Proof	12.50

10th Anniversary of Independence
Obv: Similar to 1000 Rupees, Y#39.

KM#	Date	Mintage	VF	XF	Unc
44	1978	.020	—	—	12.50
	1978	5,100	—	Proof	25.00

International Year of Disabled Persons

KM#	Date	Mintage	VF	XF	Unc
49	1982	.011	—	—	17.50
	1982	.010	—	Proof	22.50

50 RUPEES

32.1500 g, .500 SILVER, .5168 oz ASW
Conservation - Mauritius Kestrel

KM#	Date	Mintage	VF	XF	Unc
41	1975	—	—	—	22.50
	35.0000 g, .925 SILVER, 1.0409 oz ASW				
41a	1975	12 pcs.	—	—	—
	1975	9,513	—	Proof	30.00

200 RUPEES

15.5600 g, .917 GOLD, .4587 oz AGW
Independence Commemorative

KM#	Date	Mintage	VF	XF	Unc
39	1971	2,500	—	—	200.00
	1971	750 pcs.	—	Proof	350.00

1000 RUPEES

33.4370 g, .900 GOLD, .9676 oz AGW
Conservation - Mauritius Flycatcher

KM#	Date	Mintage	VF	XF	Unc
42	1975	1,966	—	—	450.00
	1975	716 pcs.	—	Proof	650.00

15.9800 g, .917 GOLD, .4711 oz AGW
10th Anniversary of Independence

KM#	Date	Mintage	VF	XF	Unc
45	1978	1,000	—	—	200.00
	1978	1,016	—	Proof	250.00

Wedding of Prince Charles and Lady Diana

KM#	Date	Mintage	VF	XF	Unc
47	1981	28 pcs.	—	—	600.00
	1981	22 pcs.	—	Proof	975.00

International Year of Disabled Persons

KM#	Date	Mintage	VF	XF	Unc
50	1982	45 pcs.	—	—	550.00
	1982	48 pcs.	—	Proof	950.00

MONETARY REFORM

CENT

COPPER PLATED STEEL

KM#	Date	Mintage	Fine	VF	XF	Unc
51	1987	*5,000	—	—	—	.15
	1987	*2,500	—	—	Proof	1.00

5 CENTS

COPPER PLATED STEEL

KM#	Date	Mintage	Fine	VF	XF	Unc
52	1987	*5,000	—	—	—	.30
	1987	*2,500	—	—	Proof	2.00
	1990	—	—	—	—	.30

20 CENTS

NICKEL PLATED STEEL

KM#	Date	Mintage	Fine	VF	XF	Unc
53	1987	*5,000	—	—	—	.50
	1987	*2,500	—	—	Proof	3.00
	1990	—	—	—	—	.50

1/2 RUPEE

NICKEL PLATED STEEL

KM#	Date	Mintage	Fine	VF	XF	Unc
54	1987	*5,000	—	—	—	.75
	1987	*2,500	—	—	Proof	5.00
	1990	—	—	—	—	.75

RUPEE

COPPER-NICKEL

KM#	Date	Mintage	Fine	VF	XF	Unc
55	1987	*5,000	—	—	—	1.50
	1987	*2,500	—	—	Proof	10.00
	1990	—	—	—	—	1.50

5 RUPEES

COPPER-NICKEL

KM#	Date	Mintage	Fine	VF	XF	Unc
56	1987	*5,000	—	—	—	3.00
	1987	*2,500	—	—	Proof	16.00
	1991	—	—	—	—	3.00

GOLD BULLION ISSUES

100 RUPEES

3.4120 g, .917 GOLD, .1000 oz AGW
Dodo Bird
Obv: Similar to 1,000 Rupees, KM#60.

KM#	Date	Mintage	VF	XF	Unc
57	1988	—	—	—	75.00

250 RUPEES

8.5130 g, .917 GOLD, .2500 oz AGW
Dodo Bird
Obv: Similar to 1,000 Rupees, KM#60.

KM#	Date	Mintage	VF	XF	Unc
58	1988	—	—	—	150.00

500 RUPEES

17.0250 g, .917 GOLD, .5000 oz AGW
Dodo Bird
Obv: Similar to 1,000 Rupees, KM#60.

KM#	Date	Mintage	VF	XF	Unc
59	1988	—	—	—	300.00

1000 RUPEES

34.0500 g, .917 GOLD, 1.0000 oz AGW
Dodo Bird

KM#	Date	Mintage	VF	XF	Unc
60	1988	—	—	—	600.00

MINT SETS (MS)

KM#	Date	Mintage	Identification	Issue Price	Mkt. Val.
MS1	1987(6)	*5,000	KM51-56	16.95	17.50
MS2	1988(4)	—	KM57-60	1250.	1125.

PROOF SETS (PS)

KM#	Date	Mintage	Identification	Issue Price	Mkt. Val.
PS1	1934(3)	20	KM15-17	—	2100.
PS2	1971(9)	750	KM31-37,38a,39	200.00	650.00
PS3	1975(2)	30,000	KM40a-41a	50.00	60.00
PS4	1978(7)	9,268	KM31-37	22.00	20.00
PS5	1981(2)	—	KM46a,47	—	1000.
PS6	1987(6)	*2,500	KM51-56	36.95	37.50

MAURITIUS & REUNION

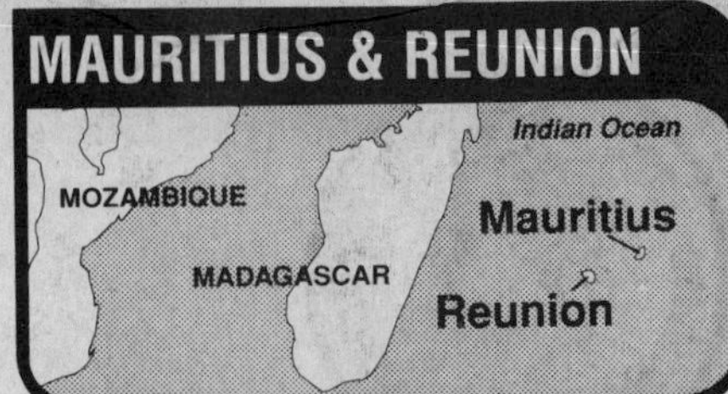

Mauritius and Reunion (Isles de France et de Bourbon), located in the Indian Ocean about 500 miles east of Madagascar, were at one time administered by France as a single colony. Ownership of Mauritius passed to Great Britain in 1810-14. Isle de Bourbon, renamed Reunion in 1793, remained a French possession and is now an overseas department.

RULERS

French until 1810

MONETARY SYSTEM

20 Sols (Sous) = 1 Livre

ISLE DE FRANCE ET BONAPARTE

Reunion had become the official name in 1792 but after the French Revolution and the beginning of the Napoleonic era (1801-1814) the name was changed to Isle de Bonaparte.

DIX (10) LIVRES

SILVER

KM#	Date	Mintage	VG	Fine	VF	XF
1	1810	—	200.00	325.00	500.00	900.00

NOTE: This coin was weakly struck on the obverse and reverse centers. Well struck examples command a premium.

MEXICO

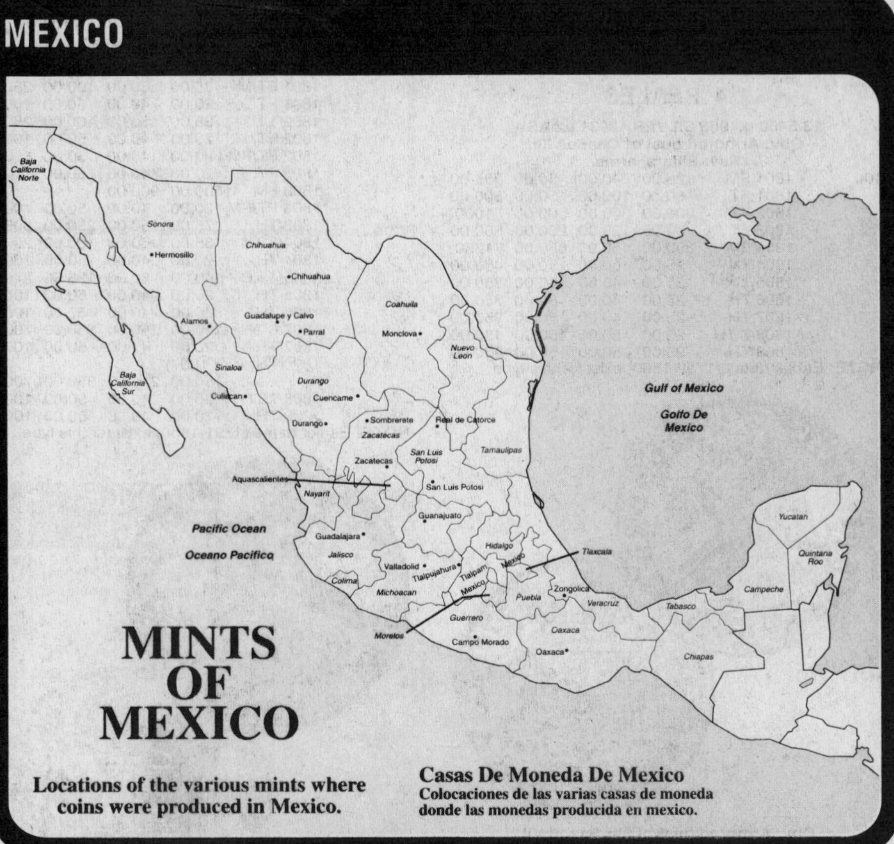

The United Mexican States, located immediately south of the United States has an area of 764,000 sq. mi. (1,972,550 sq. km.) and a population of 77.3 million. Capital: Mexico City. The economy is based on agriculture, manufacturing and mining. Oil, cotton, silver, coffee, and shrimp are exported.

Mexico was the site of highly advanced Indian civilizations. 1,500 years before conquistador Hernando Cortes conquered the wealthy Aztec empire of Montezuma, 1519-21, and founded a Spanish colony which lasted for nearly 300 years. During the Spanish period, Mexico, then called New Spain, stretched from Guatemala to the present states of Wyoming and California, its present northern boundary having been established by the secession of Texas (1836) and the 1846-48 war with the United States.

Independence from Spain was declared by Father Miguel Hidalgo on Sept. 16, 1810, (Mexican Independence Day) and was achieved by General Agustin de Iturbide in 1821. Iturbide became emperor in 1822 but was deposed when a republic was established a year later. For more than half a century following the birth of the republic, the political scene of Mexico was characterized by turmoil which saw two emperors (including the unfortunate Maximilian), several dictators and an average of one new government every nine months passing swiftly from obscurity to oblivion. The land, social, economic and labor reforms promulgated by the Reform Constitution of 1917 established the basis for sustained economic development and participative democracy that have made Mexico one of the most politically stable countries of modern Latin America.

COLONIAL MILLED COINAGE

RULERS

Charles IV, 1788-1808
Ferdinand VII, 1808-1821

MINT MARKS

Mo - Mexico City Mint

ASSAYERS INITIALS

Letter	Date	Name
F	1777-1803	Francisco Arance Cobos
M	1784-1801	Mariano Rodriguez
T	1801-1810	Tomas Butron Miranda
H	1803-1814	Henrique Buenaventura Azorin
J	1809-1833	Joaquin Davila Madrid
J	1812-1833	Jose Garcia Ansaldo

MONETARY SYSTEM

16 Pilones = 1 Real
8 Tlaco = 1 Real
16 Reales = 1 Escudo

1/8 (PILON)

(1/16 Real)

COPPER
Obv: Crowned F VII monogram.
Rev: Castles and lions in wreath.

KM#	Date	VG	Fine	VF	XF
59	1814	8.00	15.00	30.00	100.00
	1815	8.00	15.00	30.00	100.00

1/4 (TLACO)

(1/8 Real)

COPPER
Obv. leg: FERDIN. VII. . around crowned F.VII.

KM#	Date	VG	Fine	VF	XF
63	1814	10.00	20.00	40.00	125.00
	1815	10.00	20.00	40.00	125.00
	1816	10.00	20.00	40.00	125.00

2/4 (2 TLACO)

(1/4 Real)

COPPER
Obv. leg: FERDIN. VII. . around crowned F.VII.

KM#	Date	VG	Fine	VF	XF
64	1814	6.00	12.00	25.00	100.00
	1815/4	8.00	15.00	35.00	125.00
	1815	6.00	12.00	25.00	100.00
	1816	6.00	12.00	25.00	100.00
	1821	15.00	30.00	50.00	175.00

1/4 REAL

.8450 g, .903 SILVER, .0245 oz ASW
Obv: Castle. Rev: Lion.

KM#	Date	VG	Fine	VF	XF
62	1801	10.00	15.00	27.50	60.00
	1802	12.50	20.00	27.50	60.00
	1803	12.50	20.00	27.50	60.00
	1804	10.00	20.00	27.50	70.00
	1805/4	12.50	22.50	40.00	65.00
	1805	10.00	20.00	35.00	60.00
	1806	10.00	20.00	35.00	70.00
	1807/797	15.00	30.00	40.00	75.00
	1807	12.50	25.00	35.00	70.00
	1808	12.50	25.00	35.00	70.00
	1809/8	12.50	25.00	35.00	70.00
	1809	12.50	25.00	35.00	70.00
	1810	12.50	25.00	35.00	60.00
	1811	12.50	25.00	35.00	60.00
	1812	12.50	25.00	35.00	60.00
	1813	10.00	20.00	27.50	60.00
	1815	10.00	20.00	35.00	60.00
	1816	10.00	20.00	30.00	50.00

NOTE: Earlier dates (1796-1800) exist for this type.

1/2 REAL

1.6900 g, .903 SILVER, .0490 oz ASW
Obv: Armored bust of Charles IIII.
Rev: Pillars and arms.

KM#	Date	VG	Fine	VF	XF
72	1801 FM	6.50	10.00	20.00	75.00
	1801 FT	4.00	6.00	10.00	45.00
	1802 FT	4.00	6.00	10.00	45.00
	1803 FT	5.00	9.00	15.00	45.00
	1804 TH	4.00	6.00	10.00	45.00
	1805 TH	4.00	6.00	10.00	45.00
	1806 TH	4.00	6.00	10.00	45.00
	1807/6 TH	4.50	6.50	11.50	50.00
	1807 TH	4.00	6.00	10.00	45.00
	1808/7 TH	4.50	6.50	11.50	50.00
	1808 TH	4.00	6.00	10.00	45.00

NOTE: Earlier dates (1792-1800) exist for this type.

Obv: Armored bust of Ferdinand VII.

KM#	Date	VG	Fine	VF	XF
73	1808 TH	3.00	5.00	10.00	30.00
	1809 TH	3.00	5.00	10.00	30.00
	1810 TH	5.00	8.00	12.00	35.00
	1810 HJ	3.00	5.00	10.00	30.00
	1811 HJ	3.00	5.00	10.00	30.00
	1812 HJ	3.00	5.00	10.00	30.00
	1813 TH	3.50	6.00	10.00	30.00
	1813 JJ	10.00	20.00	40.00	100.00
	1813 HJ	7.50	15.00	30.00	90.00
	1814 JJ	5.00	8.00	12.00	35.00

Obv: Draped bust of Ferdinand VII.

KM#	Date	VG	Fine	VF	XF
74	1814 JJ	3.00	5.00	12.00	45.00
	1815 JJ	3.00	5.00	10.00	40.00
	1816 JJ	3.00	5.00	10.00	40.00
	1817/6 JJ	—	—	—	—
	1817 JJ	3.00	5.00	12.00	45.00
	1818/7 JJ	3.00	5.00	15.00	50.00
	1818 JJ	3.00	5.00	15.00	50.00
	1819 JJ	3.00	5.00	10.00	40.00
	1820 JJ	3.00	5.00	15.00	50.00
	1821 JJ	3.00	5.00	10.00	40.00

REAL

3.3800 g, .903 SILVER, .0981 oz ASW
Obv: Armored bust of Charles IIII.

KM#	Date	VG	Fine	VF	XF
81	1801 FM	8.00	15.00	25.00	80.00
	1801 FT	3.00	8.50	16.50	60.00
	1802 FM	3.00	8.50	16.50	60.00
	1802 FT	3.00	7.50	12.50	60.00
	1803 FT	3.00	8.50	16.50	60.00
	1804 TH	3.00	7.50	12.50	60.00
	1805 TH	3.00	8.50	16.50	60.00
	1806 TH	3.00	7.50	12.50	60.00
	1807/6 TH	3.50	8.50	13.50	65.00
	1807 TH	3.00	7.50	12.50	60.00
	1808/7 TH	3.50	8.50	13.50	65.00
	1808 TH	3.00	7.50	12.50	60.00

NOTE: Earlier dates (1792-1800) exist for this type.

Obv: Armored bust of Ferdinand VII.

KM#	Date	VG	Fine	VF	XF
82	1809 TH	4.00	7.50	15.00	100.00
	1810/09 TH	4.00	7.50	15.00	100.00
	1810 TH	4.00	7.50	15.00	100.00
	1810 HJ	6.00	10.00	20.00	125.00
	1811 HJ	4.00	7.50	15.00	100.00
	1811 TH	25.00	35.00	60.00	250.00
	1812 HJ	4.00	7.50	15.00	80.00
	1812 JJ	6.00	10.00	20.00	125.00
	1813 HJ	5.50	8.50	17.50	125.00
	1813 JJ	50.00	100.00	150.00	250.00
	1814 HJ	50.00	100.00	175.00	300.00
	1814 JJ	50.00	100.00	175.00	300.00

Obv: Draped bust of Ferdinand VII.

KM#	Date	VG	Fine	VF	XF
83	1814 JJ	25.00	50.00	100.00	350.00
	1815 JJ	5.50	8.50	17.50	125.00
	1815 HJ	15.00	30.00	60.00	150.00
	1816 JJ	4.00	7.50	12.50	75.00
	1817 JJ	4.00	7.50	12.50	75.00
	1818 JJ	30.00	60.00	125.00	500.00
	1819 JJ	5.50	8.50	17.50	75.00
	1820 JJ	5.00	8.50	17.50	75.00
	1821/0 JJ	7.50	12.50	27.50	110.00
	1821 JJ	5.00	8.50	12.50	50.00

2 REALES

6.7700 g, .903 SILVER, .1965 oz ASW
Obv: Armored bust of Carolus IIII.

KM#	Date	VG	Fine	VF	XF
91	1801 FT	5.00	10.00	15.00	100.00
	1801 FM	20.00	40.00	75.00	250.00
	1802 FT	5.00	10.00	15.00	100.00
	1803 FT	5.00	10.00	15.00	100.00
	1804 TH	5.00	10.00	15.00	100.00
	1805 TH	5.00	10.00	15.00	100.00
	1806/5 TH	5.50	11.50	16.50	110.00
	1806 TH	5.00	10.00	15.00	100.00
	1807/5 TH	5.50	11.50	16.50	110.00
	1807/6 TH	15.00	30.00	60.00	200.00
	1807 TH	5.00	10.00	15.00	100.00
	1808/7 TH	5.50	11.50	16.50	110.00
	1808 TH	5.00	10.00	15.00	100.00

NOTE: Earlier dates (1792-1800) exist for this type.

Obv: Armored bust of Ferdinand VII.

KM#	Date	VG	Fine	VF	XF
92	1809 TH	6.50	12.50	45.00	150.00
	1810 TH	6.50	12.50	45.00	150.00
	1810 HJ	6.50	12.50	45.00	150.00
	1811 HJ	6.50	12.50	45.00	150.00
	1811 HJ/TH	40.00	80.00	150.00	300.00
	1811 TH	100.00	200.00	300.00	750.00

Obv: Draped bust of Ferdinand VII.

KM#	Date	VG	Fine	VF	XF
93	1812 HJ	15.00	30.00	100.00	300.00
	1812 TH	60.00	125.00	250.00	500.00
	1812 JJ	10.00	20.00	60.00	200.00
	1813 HJ	40.00	100.00	200.00	500.00
	1813 JJ	20.00	60.00	125.00	350.00
	1813 TH	15.00	30.00	100.00	400.00
	1814/13 JJ	15.00	30.00	100.00	400.00
	1814 JJ	15.00	30.00	100.00	400.00
	1815 JJ	5.00	10.00	30.00	100.00
	1816 JJ	5.00	10.00	30.00	100.00
	1817 JJ	5.00	10.00	30.00	100.00
	1818 JJ	5.00	10.00	30.00	100.00

KM#	Date	VG	Fine	VF	XF
93	1819 JJ	5.00	10.00	30.00	100.00
	1820 JJ	125.00	—	—	—
	1821/0 JJ	5.00	10.00	30.00	110.00
	1821 JJ	5.00	10.00	30.00	100.00

4 REALES

13.5400 g, .903 SILVER, .3931 oz ASW
Obv: Armored bust of Charles IIII.
Rev: Pillars, arms.

KM#	Date	VG	Fine	VF	XF
100	1801 FM	25.00	40.00	80.00	350.00
	1801 FT	60.00	100.00	150.00	500.00
	1802 FT	200.00	300.00	500.00	1000.
	1803 FT	60.00	125.00	200.00	550.00
	1803 FM	350.00	450.00	650.00	1250.
	1804 TH	25.00	50.00	150.00	450.00
	1805 TH	25.00	40.00	80.00	350.00
	1806 TH	25.00	40.00	80.00	350.00
	1807 TH	25.00	40.00	80.00	350.00
	1808/7 TH	25.00	50.00	150.00	450.00
	1808 TH	25.00	50.00	150.00	450.00

NOTE: Earlier dates (1792-1800) exist for this type.

Obv: Armored bust of Ferdinand VII.

KM#	Date	VG	Fine	VF	XF
101	1809 HJ	75.00	125.00	175.00	450.00
	1810 TH	75.00	125.00	175.00	450.00
	1810 HJ	75.00	125.00	175.00	450.00
	1811 HJ	75.00	125.00	175.00	450.00
	1812 HJ	500.00	750.00	1000.	2000.

Obv: Draped bust of Ferdinand VII.

KM#	Date	VG	Fine	VF	XF
102	1816 JJ	150.00	200.00	350.00	600.00
	1817 JJ	250.00	400.00	500.00	1000.
	1818/7 JJ	250.00	400.00	500.00	1000.
	1818 JJ	250.00	400.00	500.00	1000.
	1819 JJ	175.00	250.00	350.00	700.00
	1820 JJ	175.00	250.00	350.00	700.00
	1821 JJ	75.00	125.00	200.00	425.00

8 REALES

Obv: Armored bust of Charles IIII.

KM#	Date	VG	Fine	VF	XF
109	1801/791 FM	35.00	60.00	100.00	250.00

KM#	Date	VG	Fine	VF	X
109	1801/0 FM	35.00	60.00	100.00	250.0
	1801/0 FT/FM	20.00	40.00	50.00	100.0
	1801 FM	20.00	40.00	100.00	250.0
	1801 FT/M	35.00	60.00	100.00	250.0
	1801 FT	20.00	40.00	50.00	100.0
	1802/1 FT	35.00	60.00	100.00	250.0
	1802 FT	20.00	40.00	50.00	100.0
	1802 FT/FM	20.00	40.00	50.00	100.0
	1803 FT	20.00	40.00	50.00	110.0
	1803 FM	600.00	900.00	—	—
	1803 FT/FM	20.00	40.00	50.00	100.0
	1803 TH	75.00	150.00	250.00	500.0
	1804/3 TH	35.00	60.00	100.00	250.0
	1804 TH	20.00	40.00	50.00	100.0
	1805/4 TH	40.00	80.00	125.00	275.0
	1805 TH	20.00	40.00	50.00	100.0
	1806 TH	20.00	40.00	50.00	100.0
	1807/6 TH	150.00	250.00	350.00	700.0
	1807 TH	20.00	40.00	50.00	100.0
	1870 TH(error 1807)	150.00	250.00	350.00	700.0
	1808/7 TH	20.00	40.00	50.00	100.0
	1808 TH	20.00	40.00	50.00	100.0

NOTE: Earlier dates (1791-1800) exist for this type.

Obv: Armored bust of Ferdinand VII.

KM#	Date	VG	Fine	VF	X
110	1808 TH	25.00	40.00	65.00	125.0
	1809/8 TH	25.00	40.00	65.00	125.0
	1809 HJ	25.00	40.00	65.00	125.0
	1809 HJ/TH	20.00	40.00	50.00	100.0
	1809 TH/JH	20.00	40.00	50.00	100.0
	1809 TH	20.00	40.00	50.00	100.0
	1810/09 HJ	25.00	40.00	65.00	125.0
	1810 HJ	25.00	40.00	65.00	125.0
	1810 HJ/TH	25.00	40.00	65.00	125.0
	1810 TH	75.00	150.00	300.00	600.0
	1811/0 HJ	20.00	40.00	50.00	100.0
	1811 HJ	20.00	40.00	50.00	100.0

Obv: Draped bust of Ferdinand VII.

KM#	Date	VG	Fine	VF	X
111	1811 HJ	20.00	40.00	60.00	125.0
	1812 HJ	50.00	75.00	125.00	250.0
	1812 JJ/HJ	20.00	40.00	50.00	90.0
	1812 JJ	20.00	40.00	50.00	90.0
	1813 HJ	50.00	75.00	125.00	250.0
	1813 JJ	20.00	40.00	50.00	90.0
	1814/3 HJ	1200.	2500.	5000.	—
	1814/3 JJ/HJ	20.00	40.00	50.00	90.0
	1814/3 JJ	20.00	40.00	50.00	90.0
	1814 JJ	20.00	40.00	50.00	90.0
	1814 HJ	500.00	800.00	1500.	3000

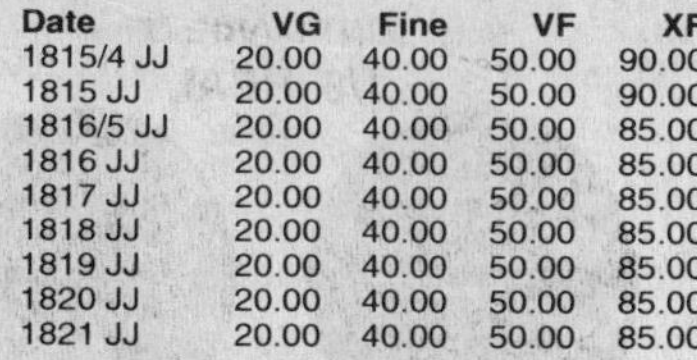

KM#	Date	VG	Fine	VF	XF
111	1815/4 JJ	20.00	40.00	50.00	90.00
	1815 JJ	20.00	40.00	50.00	90.00
	1816/5 JJ	20.00	40.00	50.00	85.00
	1816 JJ	20.00	40.00	50.00	85.00
	1817 JJ	20.00	40.00	50.00	85.00
	1818 JJ	20.00	40.00	50.00	85.00
	1819 JJ	20.00	40.00	50.00	85.00
	1820 JJ	20.00	40.00	50.00	85.00
	1821 JJ	20.00	40.00	50.00	85.00

1/2 ESCUDO

1.6900 g, .875 GOLD, .0475 oz AGW
Obv. leg: FERD.VII.D.G.HISP.ET IND.

KM#	Date	VG	Fine	VF	XF
112	1814 JJ	250.00	350.00	450.00	600.00
	1815/4 JJ	150.00	200.00	250.00	350.00
	1815 JJ	150.00	200.00	250.00	350.00
	1816 JJ	100.00	150.00	200.00	300.00
	1817 JJ	150.00	200.00	250.00	350.00
	1818 JJ	150.00	200.00	250.00	350.00
	1819 JJ	150.00	200.00	250.00	350.00
	1820 JJ	200.00	300.00	450.00	600.00

ESCUDO

3.3800 g, .875 GOLD, .0950 oz AGW
Obv: Armored bust of Charles IV.

KM#	Date	VG	Fine	VF	XF
120	1801 FT	125.00	200.00	250.00	350.00
	1801 FM	125.00	200.00	250.00	350.00
	1802 FT	125.00	200.00	250.00	350.00
	1803 FT	125.00	200.00	250.00	350.00
	1804/3 TH	125.00	200.00	250.00	350.00
	1804 TH	125.00	200.00	250.00	350.00
	1805 TH	125.00	200.00	250.00	350.00
	1806 TH	125.00	200.00	250.00	350.00
	1807 TH	125.00	200.00	250.00	350.00
	1808 TH	125.00	200.00	250.00	350.00

NOTE: Earlier dates (1792-1800) exist for this type.

Obv: Armored bust of Ferdinand VII.

KM#	Date	VG	Fine	VF	XF
121	1809 HJ	125.00	200.00	250.00	400.00
	1810 HJ	125.00	200.00	250.00	400.00
	1811 HJ	125.00	200.00	250.00	400.00
	1812 HJ	150.00	250.00	300.00	500.00

Obv: Undraped bust of Ferdinand VII.

KM#	Date	VG	Fine	VF	XF
122	1814 HJ	100.00	150.00	225.00	400.00
	1815 JJ	100.00	150.00	225.00	400.00
	1815 HJ	100.00	150.00	225.00	400.00
	1816 JJ	125.00	175.00	275.00	500.00
	1817 JJ	100.00	150.00	225.00	400.00
	1818 JJ	100.00	150.00	225.00	400.00
	1819 JJ	100.00	150.00	225.00	400.00
	1820 JJ	100.00	150.00	225.00	400.00

2 ESCUDOS

6.7700 g, .875 GOLD, .1904 oz AGW
Obv: Armored bust of Charles IV.

KM#	Date	VG	Fine	VF	XF
132	1801 FM	125.00	250.00	350.00	600.00
	1802 FT	125.00	250.00	350.00	600.00
	1803 FT	125.00	250.00	350.00	600.00
	1804 TH	125.00	250.00	350.00	600.00
	1805 TH	125.00	250.00	350.00	600.00
	1806 TH	125.00	250.00	350.00	600.00
	1807 TH	125.00	250.00	350.00	600.00
	1808 TH	125.00	250.00	350.00	600.00

NOTE: Earlier dates (1791-1800) exist for this type.

Obv: Undraped bust of Ferdinand VII.

KM#	Date	VG	Fine	VF	XF
134	1814 HJ	250.00	400.00	650.00	1200.
	1814 JJ	250.00	400.00	650.00	1200.
	1815 JJ	250.00	400.00	650.00	1200.
	1816 JJ	250.00	400.00	650.00	1200.
	1817 JJ	250.00	400.00	650.00	1200.
	1818 JJ	250.00	400.00	650.00	1200.
	1819 JJ	250.00	400.00	650.00	1200.
	1820 JJ	250.00	400.00	650.00	1200.

4 ESCUDOS

13.5400 g, .875 GOLD, .3809 oz AGW
Obv: Armored bust of Charles IIII.

KM#	Date	VG	Fine	VF	XF
144	1801 FM	300.00	500.00	750.00	1400.
	1801 FT	300.00	500.00	750.00	1400.
	1802 FT	300.00	500.00	750.00	1400.
	1803 FT	300.00	500.00	750.00	1400.
	1804/3 TH	300.00	500.00	750.00	1400.
	1804 TH	300.00	500.00	750.00	1400.
	1805 TH	300.00	500.00	750.00	1400.
	1806/5 TH	300.00	500.00	750.00	1400.
	1806 TH	300.00	500.00	750.00	1400.
	1807 TH	300.00	500.00	750.00	1400.
	1808/0 TH	300.00	500.00	750.00	1400.
	1808 TH	300.00	500.00	750.00	1400.

NOTE: Earlier dates (1792-1800) exist for this type.

Obv: Armored bust of Ferdinand VII.

KM#	Date	VG	Fine	VF	XF
145	1810 HJ	450.00	600.00	950.00	1600.
	1811 HJ	350.00	500.00	850.00	1400.
	1812 HJ	350.00	500.00	850.00	1400.

Obv: Undraped bust of Ferdinand VII.

KM#	Date	VG	Fine	VF	XF
146	1814 HJ	400.00	650.00	900.00	1600.
	1815 HJ	400.00	650.00	900.00	1600.
	1815 JJ	400.00	650.00	900.00	1600.
	1816 JJ	400.00	650.00	900.00	1600.
	1817 JJ	400.00	650.00	900.00	1600.
	1818 JJ	400.00	650.00	900.00	1600.
	1819 JJ	400.00	650.00	900.00	1600.
	1820 JJ	400.00	650.00	900.00	1600.

8 ESCUDOS

27.0700 g, .875 GOLD, .7616 oz AGW
Obv: Armored bust of Charles IIII.
Rev. leg: IN UTROQ. FELIX., arms, order chain.

KM#	Date	VG	Fine	VF	XF
159	1801/0 FT	400.00	500.00	700.00	1000.
	1801 FM	375.00	475.00	650.00	900.00
	1801 FT	375.00	475.00	650.00	900.00
	1802 FT	375.00	475.00	650.00	900.00
	1803 FT	375.00	475.00	650.00	900.00
	1804/3 TH	400.00	500.00	700.00	1000.
	1804 TH	375.00	475.00	650.00	900.00
	1805 TH	375.00	475.00	650.00	900.00
	1806 TH	375.00	475.00	650.00	900.00
	1807/6 TH	400.00	500.00	700.00	1000.
	1807 TH	450.00	550.00	750.00	1000.
	1808 TH	450.00	600.00	800.00	1100.

NOTE: Earlier dates (1791-1800) exist for this type.

Obv: Armored bust of Ferdinand VII.

KM#	Date	VG	Fine	VF	XF
160	1808 TH	400.00	500.00	750.00	1000.
	1809 HJ	400.00	500.00	750.00	1000.
	1810 HJ	375.00	475.00	650.00	875.00
	1811/0 HJ	400.00	500.00	750.00	1000.
	1811 HJ	400.00	500.00	750.00	1000.
	1811 JJ	375.00	475.00	650.00	875.00
	1812 JJ	375.00	475.00	650.00	875.00

Obv: Undraped bust of Ferdinand VII.

KM#	Date	VG	Fine	VF	XF
161	1814 JJ	375.00	475.00	650.00	850.00
	1815/4 JJ	400.00	500.00	700.00	1000.
	1815/4 HJ	400.00	500.00	700.00	1000.
	1815 JJ	375.00	475.00	650.00	850.00
	1815 HJ	375.00	475.00	650.00	850.00
	1816/5 JJ	400.00	500.00	700.00	1000.
	1816 JJ	375.00	475.00	650.00	850.00
	1817 JJ	375.00	475.00	650.00	850.00
	1818/7 JJ	375.00	475.00	650.00	850.00
	1818 JJ	375.00	475.00	650.00	850.00
	1819 JJ	375.00	475.00	650.00	850.00
	1820 JJ	375.00	475.00	650.00	850.00
	1821 JJ	400.00	500.00	700.00	1000.

PROCLAMATION MEDALLIC ISSUES (Q)

The 'Q' used in the following listings refer to STANDARD CATALOG OF MEXICAN COINS, PAPER MONEY, STOCKS, BONDS and MEDALS, Krause Publications, Inc., copyright 1981.

Chiapa

REAL

SILVER

Obv: Crowned arms between pillars, IR below, leg: FERNANDO VII REY DE ESPANA Y DE SUS INDIAS. Rev: Legend in 5 lines within wreath, PROCLA/MADO/ENCIUD/R.DECHIAPPA/1808.

KM#	Date	Fine	VF	XF	Unc
Q8	1808	22.50	35.00	50.00	—

2 REALES

SILVER

Obv. leg: FERNANDO VII REY DE ESPANA Y DE SUS INDIAS.

KM#	Date	Fine	VF	XF	Unc
Q10	1808	50.00	70.00	100.00	—

Queretaro

2 REALES

SILVER

Obv. leg: FERNANDO VII REY DE ESPANA.

KM#	Date	Fine	VF	XF	Unc
Q64	1808	35.00	50.00	75.00	—

4 REALES

SILVER

KM#	Date	Fine	VF	XF	Unc
Q-A66	1808	140.00	200.00	300.00	—

8 REALES

SILVER

KM#	Date	Fine	VF	XF	Unc
Q68	1808	300.00	425.00	600.00	—

WAR OF INDEPENDENCE

ROYALIST ISSUES

(1810-1821)

Provisional Mints

RULER

Ferdinand VII, 1808-1821

MINT MARKS

CA - Chihuahua
D - Durango
GA - Guadalajara
GO - Guanajuato
ZS - Zacatecas

MONETARY SYSTEM

16 Reales = 1 Escudo

CHIHUAHUA

The Chihuahua Mint was established by a decree of October 8, 1810 as a temporary mint. Their first coins were cast 8 reales using Mexico City coins as patterns and obliterating/changing the mint mark and moneyer initials. Two c/m were placed on the obverse - on the left, a T designating its having been received by the Royal Treasurer and on the right crowned pillars of Hercules with pomegranate beneath; the symbol of the comptroller.

In 1814 standard dies were available and from 1814 to 1822 standard 8 reales were struck. Only the one denomination was made at this mint.

MINT MARK: CA

8 REALES

CAST SILVER

Obv: Imaginary bust of Ferdinand VII; leg: FERDIN.VII.DEI.GRATIA. c/m: 'T' at left and pomegranate pillars at right.

KM#	Date	Good	VG	Fine	VF
123	1810 RP	—	—	Rare	—
	1811 RP	45.00	60.00	100.00	150.00
	1812 RP	30.00	40.00	60.00	90.00
	1813/2 RP	32.50	45.00	70.00	100.00
	1813 RP	30.00	40.00	60.00	90.00

27.0700 g, .903 SILVER, .7860 oz ASW
Obv: Draped bust of Ferdinand VII.
Rev: Similar to KM#123.

KM#	Date	VG	Fine	VF	XF
111.1	1813 RP	— Reported, not confirmed			
	1814 RP	— Reported, not confirmed			
	1815 RP	200.00	275.00	350.00	500.00
	1816 RP	80.00	125.00	150.00	275.00
	1817 RP	100.00	150.00	185.00	275.00
	1818 RP	100.00	150.00	185.00	275.00
	1819 RP	125.00	175.00	250.00	350.00
	1820 RP	200.00	275.00	350.00	500.00
	1821 RP	200.00	275.00	350.00	500.00
	1822 RP	400.00	600.00	800.00	1100.

NOTE: KM#111.1 is normally found counterstamped over earlier cast 8 Reales, KM#123.

DURANGO

The Durango mint was authorized as a temporary mint at the same time as the Chihuahua Mint, October 8, 1810. The mint opened sometime in 1811 and made coins of 6 denominations - 5 silver and 1 copper - during the period 1811 to 1822.

MINT MARK: D

1/8 REAL

COPPER

Obv: Crown above double F7 monogram. Rev: EN DURANGO, value, date.

KM#	Date	VG	Fine	VF	XF
60	1812	35.00	75.00	125.00	225.00
	1813	—	—	Rare	—
	1814	—	—	Rare	—

Rev: Spray added above date.

KM#	Date	VG	Fine	VF	XF
61	1814	15.00	25.00	50.00	85.00
	1815	15.00	25.00	50.00	85.00
	1816	15.00	25.00	50.00	85.00
	1817	15.00	25.00	50.00	80.00
	1818	15.00	25.00	50.00	80.00
	1818 OCTAVO DD REAL (error)	45.00	75.00	—	—

1/2 REAL

1.6900 g, .903 SILVER, .0491 oz ASW
Obv: Draped bust of Ferdinand VII.

KM#	Date	VG	Fine	VF	XF
74.1	1813 RM	250.00	350.00	600.00	1500.
	1814 MZ	250.00	350.00	600.00	1500.
	1816 MZ	250.00	350.00	600.00	1500.

REAL

3.3800 g, .903 SILVER, .0981 oz ASW
Obv: Draped bust of Ferdinand VII.

KM#	Date	VG	Fine	VF	XF
83.1	1813 RM	250.00	350.00	500.00	1250.
	1814 MZ	250.00	350.00	500.00	1250.
	1815 MZ	250.00	300.00	500.00	1250.

2 REALES

6.7700 g, .903 SILVER, .1966 oz ASW
Obv: Armored bust of Ferdinand VII.

KM#	Date	VG	Fine	VF	XF
92.2	1811 RM	200.00	300.00	400.00	1500.
	1812 RM	—	—	Rare	—

Obv: Draped bust of Ferdinand VII.

KM#	Date	VG	Fine	VF	XF
93.1	1812 MZ	200.00	300.00	400.00	1500.
	1812 RM	—	—	Rare	—
	1813 MZ	300.00	500.00	800.00	2500.
	1813 RM	300.00	500.00	800.00	2500.
	1814 MZ	300.00	500.00	800.00	2500.
	1815 MZ	300.00	500.00	800.00	2500.
	1816 MZ	300.00	500.00	800.00	2500.
	1817 MZ	300.00	500.00	800.00	2500.

4 REALES

13.5400 g, .903 SILVER, .3931 oz ASW
Obv: Draped bust of Ferdinand VII.

KM#	Date	VG	Fine	VF	XF
102.1	1814 MZ	500.00	1000.	1500.	4000.
	1816 MZ	400.00	800.00	1200.	3000.
	1817 MZ	400.00	800.00	1200.	3000.

8 REALES

27.0700 g, .903 SILVER, .7860 oz ASW
Obv: Armored bust of Ferdinand VII.

KM#	Date	VG	Fine	VF	XF
110.1	1811 RM	500.00	800.00	1200.	4000.
	1812 RM	300.00	500.00	800.00	3000.
	1813 MZ	300.00	500.00	800.00	3000.
	1814 MZ	300.00	500.00	800.00	3000.

Obv: Draped bust of Ferdinand VII.

KM#	Date	VG	Fine	VF	XF
111.2	1812 MZ	300.00	400.00	600.00	1500.
	1812 RM	125.00	175.00	275.00	800.00
	1813 RM	150.00	200.00	325.00	850.00
	1813 MZ	125.00	175.00	275.00	750.00
	1814 MZ	150.00	225.00	275.00	750.00
	1815 MZ	75.00	125.00	225.00	600.00
	1816 MZ	50.00	75.00	125.00	325.00
	1817 MZ	30.00	50.00	90.00	250.00
	1818 MZ	50.00	75.00	125.00	350.00
	1818 RM	50.00	75.00	125.00	325.00
	1818 CG/RM	100.00	125.00	150.00	350.00
	1818 CG	50.00	75.00	125.00	325.00
	1819 CG/RM	50.00	100.00	150.00	300.00
	1819 CG	30.00	60.00	100.00	250.00
	1820 CG	30.00	60.00	100.00	250.00
	1821 CG	30.00	40.00	50.00	150.00
	1822 CG	30.00	50.00	75.00	160.00

NOTE: Occasionally these are found struck over Guadalajara 8 reales and are very rare in general, specimens dated prior to 1816 are rather weakly struck.

GUADALAJARA

The Guadalajara Mint made its first coins in 1812 and the mint operated until April 30, 1815. It was to reopen in 1818 and continue operations until 1822. It was the only Royalist mint to strike gold coins, both 4 and 8 escudos. In addition to these it struck the standard 5 denominations in silver.

MINT MARK: GA

1/2 REAL

1.6900 g, .903 SILVER, .0491 oz ASW
Obv: Draped bust of Ferdinand VII.

KM#	Date	VG	Fine	VF	XF
74.2	1812 MR	—	—	Rare	—
	1814 MR	40.00	100.00	200.00	300.00
	1815 MR	200.00	350.00	500.00	1000.

REAL

3.3800 g, .903 SILVER, .0981 oz ASW
Obv: Draped bust of Ferdinand VII.

KM#	Date	VG	Fine	VF	XF
83.2	1814 MR	125.00	175.00	275.00	600.00
	1815 MR	—	—	Rare	—

2 REALES

6.7700 g, .903 SILVER, .1966 oz ASW
Obv: Draped bust of Ferdinand VII.

KM#	Date	VG	Fine	VF	XF
93.2	1812 MR	300.00	500.00	800.00	2500.
	1814 MR	75.00	125.00	200.00	600.00
	1815/4 MR	425.00	725.00	1100.	3600.
	1815 MR	400.00	700.00	1000.	3500.
	1821 FS	200.00	250.00	350.00	900.00

4 REALES

13.5400 g, .903 SILVER, .3931 oz ASW
Obv: Draped bust of Ferdinand VII.

KM#	Date	VG	Fine	VF	XF
102.2	1814 MR	40.00	65.00	150.00	250.00
	1815 MR	80.00	150.00	300.00	500.00

Obv: Large bust.

KM#	Date	VG	Fine	VF	XF
102.3	1814 MR	50.00	100.00	200.00	400.00

Obv: Large bust w/berries in laurel.

KM#	Date	VG	Fine	VF	XF
102.4	1814 MR	—	—	Rare	—

8 REALES

27.0700 g, .903 SILVER, .7860 oz ASW
Obv: Draped bust of Ferdinand VII.

KM#	Date	VG	Fine	VF	XF
111.3	1812 MR	1000.	1500.	3000.	4500.
	1813/2 MR	60.00	100.00	150.00	400.00
	1813 MR	60.00	100.00	150.00	400.00
	1814 MR	20.00	30.00	50.00	175.00
	1815 MR	150.00	200.00	250.00	750.00
	1818 FS	30.00	50.00	65.00	200.00
	1821/18 FS	30.00	50.00	75.00	200.00
	1821 FS	25.00	35.00	50.00	150.00
	1822/1 FS	30.00	50.00	75.00	200.00
	1822 FS	30.00	50.00	75.00	200.00

NOTE: Die varieties exist. Early dates are also encountered struck over other types.

4 ESCUDOS

13.5400 g, .875 GOLD, .3809 oz ASW
Obv: Uniformed bust of Ferdinand VII.

KM#	Date	VG	Fine	VF	XF
147	1812 MR	—	—	Rare	—

8 ESCUDOS

27.0700 g, .875 GOLD, .7616 oz AGW
Obv: Large uniformed bust of Ferdinand VII.

KM#	Date	VG	Fine	VF	XF
162	1812 MR	— Reported, not confirmed			
	1813 MR	4000.	7000.	10,000.	18,000.

Obv: Small uniformed bust of Ferdinand VII.

KM#	Date	VG	Fine	VF	XF
163	1813 MR	7000.	10,000.	15,000.	22,000.

Obv: Undraped bust of Ferdinand VII.

KM#	Date	VG	Fine	VF	XF
161.1	1821 FS	1500.	2500.	4500.	7500.

Obv: Draped bust of Ferdinand VII.

KM#	Date	VG	Fine	VF	XF
164	1821 FS	6000.	8500.	12,500.	20,000.

GUANAJUATO

Guanajuato Mint was authorized December 24, 1812 and started production shortly thereafter. For unknown reasons it closed on May 15, 1813. The mint was reopened in April of 1821 by the insurgent forces. They continued to make coins of the Spanish design to pay their army. After independence coins were made into the year 1822. Only the 2 and 8 reales coins were made.

MINT MARK: Go

2 REALES

6.7700 g, .903 SILVER, .1966 oz ASW
Obv: Draped bust of Ferdinand VII.

KM#	Date	VG	Fine	VF	XF
93.3	1821 JM	30.00	60.00	90.00	175.00
	1822 JM	25.00	45.00	65.00	125.00

8 REALES

27.0700 g, .903 SILVER, .7860 oz ASW
Obv: Draped bust of Ferdinand VII.

KM#	Date	VG	Fine	VF	XF
111.4	1812 JJ	750.00	1250.	1750.	2500.
	1813 JJ	125.00	175.00	275.00	600.00
	1821 JM	25.00	50.00	75.00	200.00
	1822/0 JM	40.00	100.00	150.00	300.00
	1822 JM	20.00	30.00	50.00	175.00

NUEVA VISCAYA

(Later became Durango State)

This 8 reales, intended for the province of Nueva Viscaya was minted in the newly opened Durango Mint during the months of February and March of 1811 before the regular coinage of Durango was started.

8 REALES

.903 SILVER
Obv, leg: MON.PROV. DE NUEV.VIZCAYA, arms of Durango. Rev: Royal arms.

KM#	Date	Good	VG	Fine	VF
181	1811 RM	1250.	2000.	2750.	4500.

NOTE: Several varieties exist.

OAXACA

The city of Oaxaca was in the midst of a coin shortage when it became apparent the city would be taken by insurgent forces. The Royalist forces under Lt. Gen. Saravia had some coins made. They were cast in a blacksmith shop and were made in 3 denominations - 1/2, 1 and 8 reales. They were made only briefly in 1812 before the city fell to the opposing forces.

1/2 REAL

.903 SILVER
Obv: Cross separating castle, lion, F,7O.
Rev. leg: OAXACA around shield.

KM#	Date	Good	VG	Fine	VF
166	1812	1000.	1500.	2500.	3500.

REAL

.903 SILVER

KM#	Date	Good	VG	Fine	VF
167	1812	300.00	600.00	1000.	2000.

8 REALES

.903 SILVER

KM#	Date	Good	VG	Fine	VF
168	1812 c/m:A	1200.	1800.	3000.	4500.
	1812 c/m:B	1200.	1800.	3000.	4500.
	1812 c/m:C	1200.	1800.	3000.	4500.
	1812 c/m:D	1200.	1800.	3000.	4500.
	1812 c/m:K	1200.	1800.	3000.	4500.
	1812 c/m:L	1200.	1800.	3000.	4500.
	1812 c/m:Mo	1200.	1800.	3000.	4500.
	1812 c/m:N	1200.	1800.	3000.	4500.
	1812 c/m:O	1200.	1800.	3000.	4500.
	1812 c/m:R	1200.	1800.	3000.	4500.
	1812 c/m:V	1200.	1800.	3000.	4500.
	1812 c/m:Z	1200.	1800.	3000.	4500.

NOTE: The above issue usually has a second c/m: O between crowned pillars.

REAL DEL CATORCE

(City in San Luis Potosi)

Real del Catorce is an important mining center in the state of San Luis Potosi. In 1811 an 8 reales coin was issued under very tedious conditions while the city was still in Royalist hands. Few survive.

8 REALES

.903 SILVER
Obv. leg: EL R.D. CATORC. POR FERNA. VII.
Rev. leg: MONEDA. PROVISIONAL.VALE.8R.

KM#	Date	VG	Fine	VF	XF
169	1811	2000.	4000.	7500.	15,000.

SAN FERNANDO DE BEXAR

Struck by Jose Antonio de la Garza, the 'jolas' are the only known coins issued under Spanish rule in the continental United States of America.

1/8 REAL

COPPER

KM#	Date	Mintage	Good	VG	Fine	VF
170	1818	8,000	500.00	750.00	1200.	1600.

KM#	Date	Mintage	Good	VG	Fine	VF
171	1818	Inc. Ab.	500.00	750.00	1200.	1600.

SAN LUIS POTOSI

Sierra De Pinos

Villa

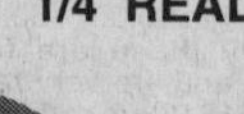

1/4 REAL

COPPER

KM#	Date	Good	VG	Fine	VF
A172	1814	85.00	125.00	185.00	250.00

SILVER

KM#	Date	Good	VG	Fine	VF
A172a	1814	—	—	Rare	—

SOMBRERETE

(Under Royalist Vargas)

The Sombrerete Mint opened on October 8, 1810 in an area that boasted some of the richest mines in Mexico. The mint operated until July 16, 1811 when it closed only to reopen in 1812 and finally to close for good at the end of 1812. The man in charge of the mines, Fernando Vargas, was also in charge of the coinage. All of the coins bear his name.

1/2 REAL

.903 SILVER
Obv. leg: FERDIN.VII.SOMBRERETE. . ., around crowned globes.
Rev. leg: VARGAS above lys in oval, sprays.

KM#	Date	VG	Fine	VF	XF
172	1811	35.00	60.00	100.00	175.00
	1812	50.00	90.00	150.00	225.00

REAL

.903 SILVER
Obv. leg: FERDIN.VII.SOMBRERETE. ., around crowned globes.
Rev. leg: VARGAS above lys in oval, sprays.

KM#	Date	VG	Fine	VF	XF
173	1811	40.00	60.00	100.00	160.00
	1812	30.00	40.00	80.00	125.00

2 REALES

.903 SILVER
Obv: R.CAXA.DE.SOMBRERETE, royal arms.
Rev. c/m: VARGAS, 1811, S between crowned pillars.

KM#	Date	VG	Fine	VF	XF
174	1811 SE	65.00	200.00	400.00	650.00

4 REALES

.903 SILVER
Obv. leg: R.CAXA.DE.SOMBRERETE, royal arms.
Rev. leg: Small VARGAS/1811.

KM#	Date	Good	VG	Fine	VF
175.1	1811	100.00	200.00	400.00	750.00

Rev: Large VARGAS/1812.

KM#	Date	Good	VG	Fine	VF
175.2	1812	50.00	150.00	250.00	400.00

8 REALES

.903 SILVER
Obv. leg: R.CAXA. DE SOMBRERETE.
Rev. c/m: VARGAS, date, S between crowned pillars.

KM#	Date	Good	VG	Fine	VF
176	1810	1000.	1500.	2500.	3500.
	1811	200.00	300.00	400.00	500.00

Obv. leg: R.CAXA. DE SOMBRETE, crowned arms.
Rev. leg: VARGAS/date/3

KM#	Date	Good	VG	Fine	VF
177	1811	100.00	150.00	200.00	300.00
	1812	100.00	150.00	200.00	300.00

VALLADOLID MICHOACAN

(Now Morelia)

Valladolid, capitol of Michoacan province, was a strategically important center for military thrusts into the adjoining provinces. The Royalists made every effort to retain the position. In 1813, with the advance of the insurgent forces, it became apparent that to maintain the position would be very difficult. During 1813 it was necessary to make coins in the city due to lack of traffic with other areas. These were made only briefly before the city fell and were also used by the insurgents with appropriate countermarks.

8 REALES

.903 SILVER
Obv: Royal arms in wreath, value at sides.
Rev: PROVISIONAL/DE VALLADOLID/1813.

KM#	Date	Good	VG	Fine	VF
178	1813	1000.	2000.	3000.	5000.

Obv: Bust, leg: FERDIN. VII.
Rev: Arms, pillars.

KM#	Date	Good	VG	Fine	VF
179	1813	1500.	2500.	3500.	5500.

ZACATECAS

The city of Zacatecas, in a rich mining area, has a long history of providing silver for the world. From the mid-1500's silver poured from its mines. On November 14, 1810 a mint began production for the Royalist cause. Zacatecas was the most prolific of the mints during the War of Independence. The 4 silver denominations were made here. The first type was a local type with the mountains of silver shown on the coins. These were made only in 1810 and 1811. Some of the 1811 were made by the insurgents after the town fell on April 15, 1811. The town was retaken by the Royalists on May 21, 1811. From then until 1822 the standard bust type of Ferdinand VII was made.

MINT MARKS: Z, ZS, Zs

1/2 REAL

.903 SILVER
Similar to KM#181 but w/local arms.
Flowers 1 and 4, castles 2 and 3.

KM#	Date	Good	VG	Fine	VF
180	1810	75.00	125.00	200.00	400.00
	1181 (error 1811)	30.00	50.00	75.00	150.00

Obv: Royal arms.
Rev. leg: MONEDA PROVISIONAL DE ZACATECAS., mountain.

KM#	Date	Good	VG	Fine	VF
181	1811	30.00	50.00	75.00	100.00

Obv: Provincial bust FERDIN. VII.
Rev. leg: MONEDA PROVISIONAL DE ZACATECAS.

KM#	Date	Good	VG	Fine	VF
182	1811	30.00	40.00	60.00	80.00
	1812	25.00	35.00	50.00	70.00

1.6900 g, .903 SILVER, .0491 oz ASW
Obv: Armored bust of Ferdinand VII.

KM#	Date	Good	VG	Fine	VF
73.1	1813 FP	30.00	60.00	100.00	175.00
	1813 AG	20.00	40.00	60.00	100.00
	1814 AG	15.00	30.00	60.00	100.00
	1815 AG	12.50	25.00	40.00	60.00
	1816 AG	10.00	15.00	25.00	50.00
	1817 AG	10.00	15.00	25.00	50.00
	1818 AG	10.00	15.00	25.00	50.00
	1819 AG	10.00	15.00	25.00	50.00

Obv: Draped bust Ferdinand VII.

KM#	Date	VG	Fine	VF	XF
74.3	1819 AG	8.00	12.00	25.00	50.00
	1820 AG	8.00	12.00	25.00	50.00
	1820 RG	5.00	10.00	20.00	45.00
	1821 AG	50.00	100.00	150.00	250.00
	1821 RG	5.00	10.00	20.00	45.00

REAL

.903 SILVER
Obv: Local arms w/flowers and castles.

KM#	Date	Good	VG	Fine	VF
183	1810	100.00	150.00	300.00	500.00
183	1181 (error 1811)	20.00	40.00	75.00	125.00

Obv: Royal arms.
Rev. leg: MONEDA PROVISIONAL DE ZACATECAS., mountain.

KM#	Date	Good	VG	Fine	VF
184	1811	15.00	30.00	50.00	100.00

Obv: Provincial bust, leg: FERDIN. VII.
Rev. leg: MONEDA PROVISIONAL DE ZACATECAS, arms, pillars.

KM#	Date	Good	VG	Fine	VF
185	1811	45.00	75.00	100.00	175.00
	1812	45.00	75.00	100.00	175.00

3.3800 g, .903 SILVER, .0981 oz ASW
Obv: Armored bust of Ferdinand VII.

KM#	Date	Good	VG	Fine	VF
82.1	1813 FP	50.00	100.00	150.00	250.00
	1814 FP	20.00	35.00	50.00	75.00
	1814 AG	20.00	35.00	50.00	75.00
	1815 AG	20.00	35.00	50.00	75.00
	1816 AG	10.00	20.00	30.00	60.00
	1817 AG	6.50	12.50	20.00	40.00
	1818 AG	6.50	12.50	20.00	40.00
	1819 AG	5.00	9.00	15.00	30.00
	1820 AG	4.00	7.50	12.50	25.00

Obv: Draped bust of Ferdinand VII.

KM#	Date	VG	Fine	VF	XF
83.3	1820 AG	5.00	10.00	17.50	40.00
	1820 RG	5.00	10.00	17.50	40.00
	1821 AG	15.00	30.00	45.00	75.00
	1821 AZ	10.00	20.00	30.00	60.00
	1821 RG	6.00	12.00	17.50	45.00
	1822 AZ	6.00	12.00	17.50	45.00
	1822 RG	15.00	30.00	45.00	75.00

2 REALES

.903 SILVER
Obv: Local arms w/flowers and castles.

KM#	Date	Good	VG	Fine	VF
186	1810	—	—	Rare	—
	1181 (error 1811)	25.00	40.00	60.00	100.00

Obv: Royal arms.
Rev. leg: MONEDA PROVISIONAL DE ZACATECAS., mountain above L.V.O.

KM#	Date	Good	VG	Fine	VF
187	1811	15.00	30.00	50.00	75.00

Obv: Armored bust, leg: FERDIN. VII.
Rev. leg: MONEDA PROVISIONAL DE ZACATECAS, crowned arms, pillars.

KM#	Date	Good	VG	Fine	VF
188	1811	40.00	75.00	150.00	225.00
	1812	30.00	60.00	125.00	200.00

6.7700 g, .903 SILVER, .1966 oz ASW
Obv: Large armored bust of Ferdinand VII.

KM#	Date	Good	VG	Fine	VF
92.1	1813 FP	37.50	50.00	75.00	125.00
	1814 FP	37.50	50.00	75.00	125.00
	1814 AG	37.50	50.00	75.00	125.00
	1815 AG	6.50	12.50	25.00	50.00
	1816 AG	6.50	12.50	25.00	50.00
	1817 AG	6.50	12.50	25.00	50.00
	1818 AG	6.50	12.50	25.00	50.00

Obv: Small armored bust of Ferdinand VII.

KM#	Date	Good	VG	Fine	VF
A92	1819 AG	25.00	50.00	100.00	200.00

Obv: Draped bust of Ferdinand VII.

KM#	Date	VG	Fine	VF	XF
93.4	1818 AG	6.50	12.50	20.00	40.00
	1819 AG	10.00	20.00	40.00	75.00
	1820 AG	10.00	20.00	40.00	75.00
	1820 RG	10.00	20.00	40.00	75.00
	1821 AG	10.00	20.00	40.00	75.00
	1821 AZ/RG	10.00	20.00	40.00	75.00
	1821 AZ	10.00	20.00	40.00	75.00
	1821 RG	10.00	20.00	40.00	75.00
	1822 AG	10.00	20.00	40.00	75.00
	1822 AZ	15.00	30.00	60.00	120.00
	1822 RG	10.00	20.00	40.00	75.00

8 REALES

.903 SILVER
Obv: Local arm w/flowers and castles.
Rev: Similar to KM#190.

KM#	Date	Good	VG	Fine	VF
189	1810	300.00	450.00	600.00	800.00
	1181 (error 1811)	100.00	150.00	225.00	300.00

NOTE: Also exists with incomplete date.

Obv. leg: FERDIN.VII.DEI. ., royal arms.
Rev. leg: MONEDA PROVISIONAL DE ZACATECAS, mountain above L.V.O.

KM#	Date	Good	VG	Fine	VF
190	1811	75.00	125.00	150.00	225.00

Obv: Armored bust of Ferdinand VII.
Rev. leg: MONEDA PROVISIONAL DE ZACATECAS, crowned arms, pillars.

KM#	Date	Good	VG	Fine	VF
191	1811	35.00	50.00	100.00	150.00
	1812	35.00	50.00	100.00	150.00

Obv: Draped bust of Ferdinand VII.
Rev. leg: MONEDA PROVISIONAL DE ZACATECAS, crowned arms, pillars.

KM#	Date	Good	VG	Fine	VF
192	1812	50.00	75.00	125.00	200.00

27.0700 g, .903 SILVER, .7860 oz ASW
Obv: Draped bust of Ferdinand VII.

KM#	Date	VG	Fine	VF	XF
111.5	1813 AG	125.00	200.00	250.00	350.00
	1813 FP	75.00	125.00	175.00	275.00
	1814 AG	100.00	150.00	200.00	300.00
	1814 AG D over horizontal D in IND				
		125.00	175.00	225.00	325.00
	1814 AG/FP	100.00	150.00	200.00	300.00
	1814 FP	150.00	250.00	350.00	450.00
	1815 AG	50.00	100.00	150.00	250.00
	1816 AG	35.00	50.00	65.00	125.00
	1817 AG	35.00	50.00	65.00	125.00
	1818 AG	30.00	40.00	50.00	100.00
	1819 AG	30.00	40.00	50.00	100.00
	1820 AG	30.00	40.00	50.00	100.00
	1820 RG	30.00	40.00	50.00	100.00
	1821/81 RG	75.00	150.00	225.00	300.00
	1821 RG	15.00	25.00	35.00	65.00
	1821 AZ	50.00	100.00	150.00	200.00
	1822 RG	40.00	60.00	100.00	175.00

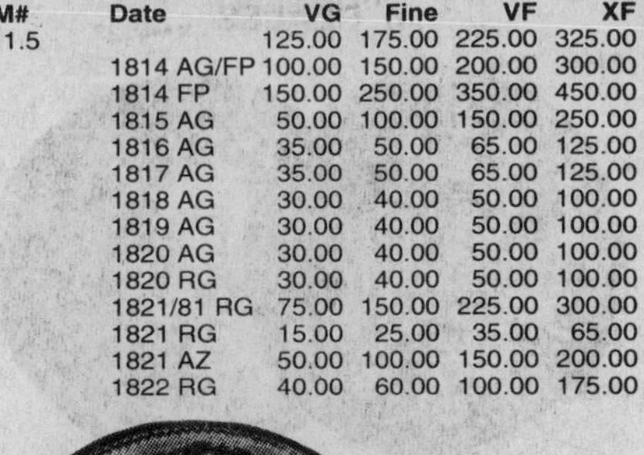

Rev: Crown with lower rear arc.

KM#	Date	VG	Fine	VF	XF
111.6	1821 RG	160.00	320.00	550.00	750.00

COUNTERMARKED COINAGE

Crown and Flag

(Refer to Multiple Countermarks)

LCM - La Comandancia Militar

NOTE: This countermark exists in 15 various sizes.

2 REALES

.903 SILVER
c/m: LCM on Mexico KM#92.

KM#	Date	Good	VG	Fine	VF
193.1	ND(1809) TH	100.00	150.00	200.00	275.00

c/m: LCM on Zacatecas KM#187.

KM#	Date	Good	VG	Fine	VF
193.2	ND(1811)	100.00	150.00	200.00	275.00

8 REALES

CAST SILVER
c/m: LCM on Chihuahua KM#123.

KM#	Date	Good	VG	Fine	VF
194.1	ND(1811) RP	100.00	200.00	300.00	450.00
	ND(1812) RP	100.00	200.00	300.00	450.00

.903 SILVER
c/m: LCM on Chihuahua KM#111.1 struck over KM#123.

KM#	Date	Good	VG	Fine	VF
194.2	ND(1815) RP	200.00	275.00	400.00	550.00
	ND(1817) RP	125.00	175.00	225.00	300.00
	ND(1820) RP	125.00	175.00	225.00	300.00
	ND(1821) RP	125.00	175.00	225.00	300.00

c/m: LCM on Durango KM#111.2.

KM#	Date	Good	VG	Fine	VF
194.3	ND(1812) RM	70.00	125.00	190.00	250.00
	ND(1821) CG	70.00	125.00	190.00	250.00

c/m: LCM on Guadalajara KM#111.3.

KM#	Date	Good	VG	Fine	VF
194.4	ND(1813) MR	150.00	225.00	300.00	475.00
	ND(1820) FS	—	—	Rare	—

c/m: LCM on Guanajuato KM#111.4.

KM#	Date	Good	VG	Fine	VF
194.5	ND(1813) JM	225.00	350.00	475.00	650.00

c/m: LCM on Nueva Vizcaya KM#165.

KM#	Date	Good	VG	Fine	VF
194.6	ND(1811) RM	—	—	Rare	—

c/m: LCM on Mexico KM#111.

KM#	Date	Good	VG	Fine	VF
194.7	ND(1811) HJ	125.00	225.00	350.00	600.00
	ND(1812) JJ	110.00	135.00	190.00	325.00
	ND(1817) JJ	50.00	65.00	85.00	125.00
	ND(1818) JJ	50.00	65.00	85.00	125.00
	ND(1820) JJ	—	—	—	—

c/m: LCM on Sombrerete KM#176.

KM#	Date	Good	VG	Fine	VF
194.8	ND(1811)	—	—	Rare	—
	ND(1812)	—	—	Rare	—

c/m: LCM on Zacatecas KM#190.

KM#	Date	Good	VG	Fine	VF
194.9	ND(1811)	225.00	350.00	450.00	—

c/m: LCM on Zacatecas KM#111.5.

KM#	Date	Good	VG	Fine	VF
194.10	ND(1813) FP	—	—	—	—
	ND(1814) AG	—	—	—	—
	ND(1822) RG	—	—	—	—

LCV - Las Cajas de Veracruz

(The Royal Treasury of the City of Veracruz)

L.C.V.

7 REALES

SILVER
c/m: LCV and 7 on underweight 8 Reales.

KM#	Date	Good	VG	Fine	VF
195	ND(-)	—	—	Rare	—

7-1/4 REALES

SILVER
c/m: LCV and 7-1/4 on underweight 8 Reales.

KM#	Date	Good	VG	Fine	VF
196	ND(-)	—	—	Rare	—

7-1/2 REALES

SILVER
c/m: LCV and 7-1/2 on underweight 8 Reales.

KM#	Date	Good	VG	Fine	VF
197	ND(-)	—	—	Rare	—

7-3/4 REALES

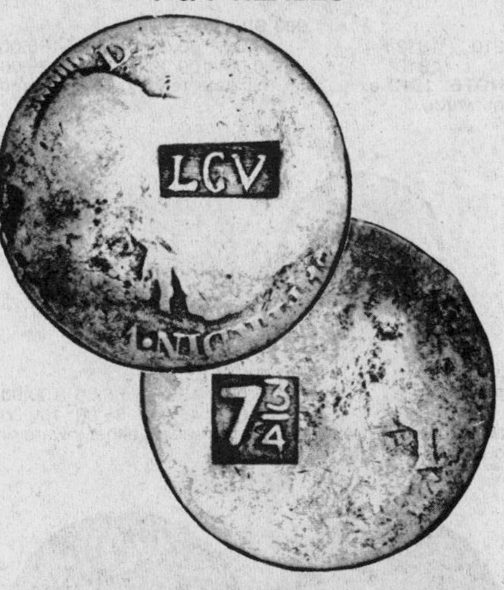

SILVER
c/m: LCV and 7-3/4 on underweight 8 Reales.

KM#	Date	Good	VG	Fine	VF
198	ND(-)	300.00	375.00	450.00	600.00

8 REALES

CAST SILVER
c/m: LCV on Chihuahua KM#123.

KM#	Date	Good	VG	Fine	VF
A198	ND(1811) RP	150.00	250.00	400.00	500.00

SILVER
c/m: LCV on Zacatecas KM#191.

KM#	Date	Good	VG	Fine	VF
199	ND(1811)	175.00	225.00	275.00	350.00
	ND(1812)	175.00	225.00	275.00	350.00

MS (Monogram) - Manuel Salcedo

8 REALES

SILVER
c/m: MS monogram on Mexico KM#110.

KM#	Date	Good	VG	Fine	VF
200	ND(1809) TH	150.00	250.00	400.00	500.00
	ND(1810) HJ	150.00	250.00	400.00	500.00
	ND(1811) HJ	150.00	250.00	400.00	500.00

MVA - Monclova

8 REALES

SILVER
c/m: MVA/1811 on Chihuahua KM#111.1; struck over cast Mexico KM#110.

KM#	Date	Good	VG	Fine	VF
201	ND(1809)	—	—	Rare	—
	ND(1816) RP	—	—	Rare	—
	ND(1821) RP	—	—	Rare	—

c/m: MVA/1812 on Chihuahua KM#111.1; struck over cast Mexico KM#109.

KM#	Date	Good	VG	Fine	VF
202.1	1812(1810)	125.00	175.00	250.00	350.00

c/m: MVA/1812 on cast Mexico KM#109.

KM#	Date	Good	VG	Fine	VF
202.2	1812(1798) FM	100.00	150.00	250.00	350.00
	1812(1802) FT	100.00	150.00	250.00	350.00

c/m: MVA/1812 on cast Mexico KM#110.

KM#	Date	Good	VG	Fine	VF
202.3	1812(1809) HJ	100.00	150.00	250.00	350.00
	1812(1809) TH	100.00	150.00	250.00	350.00
	1812(1810) HJ	100.00	150.00	250.00	350.00

c/m: MVA/1812 on Zacatecas KM#189.

KM#	Date	Good	VG	Fine	VF
202.5	1812(1813)	300.00	350.00	450.00	550.00

PDV - Provisional de Valladolid

VTIL - (Util = useful)

(Refer to Multiple countermarks)

INSURGENT COINAGE

Supreme National Congress Of America

1/2 REAL

COPPER
Obv. leg: FERDIN. VII DEI GRATIA, eagle on bridge.
Rev. leg: S.P.CONG.NAT.IND.
GUV.T., value, bow, quiver, etc.

KM#	Date	Good	VG	Fine	VF
203	1811	30.00	45.00	60.00	100.00

REAL

SILVER
Similar to 1/2 Real, KM#203.

KM#	Date	Good	VG	Fine	VF
204	1811	50.00	75.00	125.00	200.00

2 REALES

SILVER

KM#	Date	Good	VG	Fine	VF
205	1812	250.00	350.00	500.00	700.00

8 REALES

CAST SILVER

KM#	Date	Good	VG	Fine	VF
206	1811	150.00	250.00	350.00	500.00
	1812	150.00	250.00	350.00	500.00

STRUCK SILVER

KM#	Date	Good	VG	Fine	VF
207	1811	—	Rare	—	—
	1812	300.00	600.00	1000.	1500.

COPPER
Obv. leg: FERDIN.VII. . . ., eagle on bridge.
Rev. leg: PROVICIONAL POR LA SUPREMA JUNTA DE AMERICA, bow, sword and quiver.

KM#	Date	Good	VG	Fine	VF
208	1811	100.00	150.00	225.00	450.00
	1812	100.00	150.00	225.00	450.00

National Congress

1/2 REAL

COPPER
Obv. leg: VICE FERD. VII DEI GRATIA ET, eagle on bridge.
Rev. leg: S. P. CONG. NAT. IND.
GUV. T., value, bow, quiver, etc.

KM#	Date	Good	VG	Fine	VF
209	1811	50.00	100.00	150.00	200.00
	1812	30.00	60.00	100.00	150.00
	1813	30.00	60.00	100.00	150.00
	1814	50.00	100.00	150.00	200.00

.903 SILVER

KM#	Date	Good	VG	Fine	VF
210	1812	30.00	60.00	100.00	150.00
	1813	50.00	100.00	175.00	275.00

NOTE: 1812 exists with the date reading inwards and outwards.

REAL

.903 SILVER

KM#	Date	Good	VG	Fine	VF
211	1812	25.00	45.00	65.00	100.00
	1813	25.00	45.00	65.00	100.00

NOTE: 1812 exists with the date reading either inward or outward.

2 REALES

COPPER

KM#	Date	Good	VG	Fine	VF
212	1812	100.00	150.00	200.00	250.00
	1813	25.00	50.00	75.00	100.00
	1814	35.00	75.00	110.00	150.00

.903 SILVER

KM#	Date	Good	VG	Fine	VF
213	1813	125.00	250.00	300.00	400.00

NOTE: These dies were believed to be intended for the striking of 2 Escudos.

4 REALES

.903 SILVER
Mint: Mexico City

KM#	Date	Good	VG	Fine	VF
214	1813	500.00	1000.	2000.	3000.

8 REALES

.903 SILVER
Mint: Mexico City
Obv: Small crowned eagle.

KM#	Date	Good	VG	Fine	VF
215.1	1812	500.00	1000.	2000.	3500.

Obv: Large crowned eagle.

KM#	Date	Good	VG	Fine	VF
215.2	1813	500.00	1000.	2000.	3500.

American Congress

REAL

.903 SILVER
Obv: Eagle on cactus, leg: CONGRESO AMERICANO.
Rev: F.7 on spread mantle, leg: DEPOSIT D.L.AUCTORI J.

KM#	Date	Good	VG	Fine	VF
216	ND (1813)	35.00	65.00	100.00	150.00

Obv: Eagle on cactus, leg: CONGR.AMER.

Rev: F.7 on spread mantle,
leg: DEPOS.D.L.AUT.D.

KM#	Date	Good	VG	Fine	VF
217	ND(1813)	35.00	65.00	100.00	150.00

NUEVA GALICIA

(Later became Jalisco State)

Nueva Galicia was a province in early colonial times that was similar to modern Zacatecas, etc. The name was adopted again during the War of Independence. The only issue was an 1812 2 reales of rather enigmatic origin.

2 REALES

.903 SILVER
Obv. leg: PROVYCIONAL. . . . ., N.G. in center, date.

KM#	Date	Good	VG	Fine	VF
218	1813	1000.	3000.	6000.	10,000.

OAXACA

Oaxaca was the hub of insurgent activity in the south. The issues of Oaxaca represent various episodic strikings of coins, usually under dire circumstances, by various individuals. The copper coins were made because of urgency and were to be redeemed at its face value in gold or silver. The silver coins were made after the copper coins when silver was available to the insurgent forces. Coinage started in July, 1811 and ran until October 1814.

SUD

(Under General Morelos)

1/2 REAL

COPPER
Obv: Bow, SUD.
Rev: Morelos monogram Mo, date.

KM#	Date	Good	VG	Fine	VF
219	1811	7.50	12.50	20.00	30.00
	1812	7.50	12.50	20.00	30.00
	1813	6.00	10.00	17.50	25.00
	1814	10.00	17.50	25.00	35.00

NOTE: Uniface strikes exist of #219.

STRUCK SILVER

KM#	Date	Good	VG	Fine	VF
220.1	1811	—	—	—	—
	1812	—	—	—	—
	1813	—	—	—	—

CAST SILVER

KM#	Date	Good	VG	Fine	VF
220.2	1811	—	—	—	—
	1812	—	—	—	—
	1813	25.00	50.00	100.00	150.00

NOTE: Most silver specimens available on today's market are considered spurious.

SILVER
Obv. leg: PROVICIONAL DE OAXACA, bow, arrow.
Rev. leg: AMERICA MORELOS, lion.

KM#	Date	Good	VG	Fine	VF
221	1812	35.00	60.00	100.00	150.00
	1813	35.00	60.00	100.00	150.00

COPPER

KM#	Date	Good	VG	Fine	VF
221a	1812	27.50	42.50	70.00	100.00
	1813	20.00	35.00	60.00	85.00

Obv: Similar to KM#220.
Rev: Similar to KM#221 but w/1/2 at left of lion.

KM#	Date	Good	VG	Fine	VF
A222	1813	27.50	42.50	70.00	100.00

REAL

COPPER

KM#	Date	Good	VG	Fine	VF
222	1811	5.00	10.00	20.00	40.00
	1812	4.00	8.00	15.00	30.00
	1813	4.00	8.00	15.00	30.00

STRUCK SILVER

KM#	Date	Good	VG	Fine	VF
222a	1812	—	—	—	—
	1813	—	—	—	—

CAST SILVER

KM#	Date	Good	VG	Fine	VF
223	1812	—	—	—	—
	1813	40.00	75.00	125.00	175.00

NOTE: Most silver specimens available on today's market are considered spurious.

COPPER
Obv: Bow, arrow/SUD.
Rev. leg: AMERICA MORELOS, lion.

KM#	Date	Good	VG	Fine	VF
224	1813	27.50	42.50	75.00	110.00

SILVER

KM#	Date	Good	VG	Fine	VF
225	1813	—	—	Rare	—

2 REALES

COPPER

KM#	Date	Good	VG	Fine	VF
226.1	1811	12.50	25.00	50.00	100.00
	1812	2.50	3.75	5.00	10.00
	1813	2.50	3.75	5.00	10.00

Obv: 3 large stars added.

KM#	Date	Good	VG	Fine	VF
226.2	1814	10.00	20.00	40.00	60.00

Obv. leg: SUD-OXA, bow, arrow.
Rev: Morelos monogram, value, date.

KM#	Date	Good	VG	Fine	VF
227	1813	60.00	100.00	200.00	300.00
	1814	60.00	100.00	200.00	300.00

Obv. leg: SUD. OAXACA

KM#	Date	Good	VG	Fine	VF
228	1814	60.00	100.00	200.00	325.00

CAST SILVER

KM#	Date	Good	VG	Fine	VF
229	1812	60.00	100.00	150.00	225.00
	1812 filled D in SUD				
		60.00	100.00	150.00	225.00

NOTE: Most silver specimens available on today's market are considered spurious.

4 REALES

NOTE: All known examples are modern fabrications.

CAST SILVER

KM#	Date	Good	VG	Fine	VF
230	1811	—	—	—	—
	1812	—	—	—	—

Obv. leg: SUD-OXA, bow, arrow.
Rev: Morelos monogram.

KM#	Date	Good	VG	Fine	VF
231	1813	125.00	250.00	400.00	800.00

COPPER
Obv. leg: SUD-OXA, bow, arrow.
Rev: Morelos monogram.

KM#	Date	Good	VG	Fine	VF
232	1814	100.00	150.00	200.00	400.00

8 REALES

COPPER
Plain fields

KM#	Date	Good	VG	Fine	VF
233.1	1812	15.00	30.00	60.00	90.00

KM#	Date	Good	VG	Fine	VF
233.2	1812	6.00	8.00	12.00	15.00
	1813	6.00	8.00	12.00	15.00
	1814	10.00	12.00	15.00	20.00

Similar to KM#233.4 but lines below bow slant left.

KM#	Date	Good	VG	Fine	VF
233.3	1813	10.00	17.50	30.00	50.00

Obv: Lines below bow slant right.

KM#	Date	Good	VG	Fine	VF
233.4	1813	10.00	17.50	30.00	50.00

Ornate flowery fields

KM#	Date	Good	VG	Fine	VF
234	1811	75.00	125.00	150.00	225.00
	1812	4.00	5.00	7.50	15.00
	1813	4.00	5.00	7.50	15.00
	1814	10.00	15.00	25.00	50.00

CAST SILVER

KM#	Date	Good	VG	Fine	VF
235	1811	—	—	—	—
	1812	100.00	200.00	300.00	400.00
	1813	75.00	150.00	250.00	350.00
	1814	—	—	—	—

NOTE: Most silver specimens available on today's market are considered spurious.

.903 SILVER, struck
Obv: PROV. D. OAXACA, M monogram.
Rev: Lion shield w/or w/o bow above.

KM#	Date	Good	VG	Fine	VF
236	1812	—	—	Rare	—

Obv: W/o leg.

KM#	Date	Good	VG	Fine	VF
237	1813	—	—	Rare	—

Obv: Bow/M/SUD. .
Rev: PROV. DE, ..., arms.

KM#	Date	Good	VG	Fine	VF
238	1813	—	—	Rare	—

CAST SILVER
Similar to 4 Reales, KM#231.

KM#	Date	Good	VG	Fine	VF
239	1814	—	—	Rare	—

COPPER

KM#	Date	Good	VG	Fine	VF
240	1814	30.00	60.00	125.00	200.00

OAXACA spelled out

KM#	Date	Good	VG	Fine	VF
241	1814	—	—	Rare	—

Huautla

8 REALES

COPPER
Obv. leg: MONEDA PROVI.CIONAL PS.ES. around bow, arrow/SUD.
Rev. leg: FABRICADO EN HUAUTLA

KM#	Date	Good	VG	Fine	VF
242	1812	500.00	800.00	1200.	1750.

Tierra Caliente

(Hot Country)

Under General Morelos

1/2 REAL

COPPER
Obv: Bow, T.C., SUD.
Rev: Morelos monogram, value, date.

KM#	Date	Good	VG	Fine	VF
243	1813	40.00	70.00	125.00	200.00

REAL

COPPER
Similar to 1/2 Real, KM#243.

KM#	Date	Good	VG	Fine	VF
244	1813	15.00	30.00	50.00	80.00

2 REALES

COPPER
Similar to 1/2 Real, KM#243.

KM#	Date	Good	VG	Fine	VF
245	1813	10.00	25.00	35.00	50.00

KM#	Date	Good	VG	Fine	VF
246	1814	25.00	50.00	100.00	175.00

CAST SILVER

KM#	Date	Good	VG	Fine	VF
247	1814	—	—	Rare	—

8 REALES

COPPER

KM#	Date	Good	VG	Fine	VF
248	1813	10.00	20.00	40.00	75.00

CAST SILVER

KM#	Date	Good	VG	Fine	VF
249	1813	—	—	—	—

NOTE: Most specimens available on todays market are considered spurious.

PUEBLA

The coins of Puebla emanated from Zacatlan, the headquarters of the hit-and-run insurgent leader Osorno. The mint opened in April of 1812 and operated until the end of 1813. The coins were 2 reales in silver and 1 and 1/2 reales in copper.

Zacatlan

(Struck by General Osorno)

1/2 REAL

COPPER
Obv: Osorno monogram, ZACATLAN, date.
Rev: Crossed arrows, wreath, value.

KM#	Date	Good	VG	Fine	VF
250	1813	—	—	Rare	—

REAL

COPPER

KM#	Date	Good	VG	Fine	VF
251	1813	100.00	150.00	250.00	450.00

2 REALES

COPPER

KM#	Date	Good	VG	Fine	VF
252	1813	125.00	200.00	325.00	550.00

VERACRUZ

Veracruz was the province that housed the town of Zongolica. In this town 2 priests and a lawyer decided to raise an army to fight for independence. Because of their isolation from other insurgent forces they decided to make coins for their area. Records show that they planned to or did mint coins of 1/2, 1, 2, 4, and 8 reales denominations. Extant specimens are known for only the three higher values.

Zongolica

2 REALES

.903 SILVER
Obv. leg: VIVA FERNANDO VII Y AMERICA, bow and arrow.
Rev. leg: ZONGOLICA, value, crossed palm branch, sword, date.

KM#	Date	Good	VG	Fine	VF
253	1812	100.00	200.00	300.00	600.00

4 REALES

.903 SILVER
Similar to 2 Reales, KM#253.

KM#	Date	Good	VG	Fine	VF
254	1812	600.00	800.00	1200.	2000.

8 REALES

.903 SILVER

KM#	Date	Good	VG	Fine	VF
255	1812	1200.	1600.	3000.	6000.

COUNTERMARKED COINAGE

Congress Of Chilpanzingo

Type A: Hand holding bow and arrow between quiver w/arrows, sword and bow.

Type B: Crowned eagle on bridge.

1/2 REAL

SILVER
c/m: Type A on cast Mexico City KM#72.

KM#	Date	Good	VG	Fine	VF
256.1	ND(1812)	45.00	70.00	90.00	120.00

c/m: Type A on Zacatecas KM#181.

KM#	Date	Good	VG	Fine	VF
256.2	ND(1811)	55.00	75.00	100.00	125.00

REAL

SILVER
c/m: Type A on cast Mexico City KM#81.

KM#	Date	Good	VG	Fine	VF
A257	ND(1803)	20.00	30.00	50.00	80.00

2 REALES

SILVER
c/m: Type B on 1/4 cut of 8 Reales.

KM#	Date	Good	VG	Fine	VF
257.1	ND	—	—	Unique	—

c/m: Type B on Zacatecas KM#186.

KM#	Date	Good	VG	Fine	VF
257.2	ND(1811)	—	—	Unique	—

8 REALES

SILVER

KM#	Date	Good	VG	Fine	VF
	c/m: Type A on cast Mexico City KM#109.				
258.1	ND(1805) TH	45.00	65.00	85.00	125.00
	c/m: Type A on cast Mexico City KM#110.				
258.2	ND(1810) HJ	50.00	75.00	100.00	150.00
	c/m: Type A on cast Mexico City KM#111.				
258.3	ND(1811) HJ	45.00	65.00	85.00	125.00
	ND(1812) HJ	100.00	125.00	175.00	275.00
	c/m: Type B on Chihuahua KM#111.1.				
259.1	ND(1816) RP	200.00	250.00	300.00	350.00
	c/m: Type B on cast Mexico City KM#111.				
259.2	ND(1811) HJ	130.00	140.00	150.00	175.00

c/m: Type B on Valladolid KM#178.

KM#	Date	Good	VG	Fine	VF
259.3	ND(1813)	1000.	2000.	3000.	5000.

c/m: Type B on Zacatecas KM#190.

KM#	Date	Good	VG	Fine	VF
259.4	ND(1810)	400.00	500.00	600.00	750.00

Ensaie

8 REALES

SILVER
c/m: Eagle over ENSAIE on Mexico City KM#110.

KM#	Date	Good	VG	Fine	VF
260.1	ND(1811) HJ	150.00	200.00	275.00	350.00

c/m: Eagle over ENSAIE crude sling below on Zacatecas KM#189.

KM#	Date	Good	VG	Fine	VF
260.2	ND(1811)	200.00	400.00	600.00	800.00

c/m: Eagle over ENSAIE, crude sling below on Zacatecas KM#190.

KM#	Date	Good	VG	Fine	VF
260.3	ND(1810)	—	—	—	—
	ND(1811)	100.00	150.00	200.00	300.00

c/m: Eagle over ENSAIE, crude sling below on Zacatecas KM#191.

KM#	Date	Good	VG	Fine	VF
260.4	ND(1810)	500.00	700.00	900.00	1200.
	ND(1811)	275.00	325.00	400.00	500.00
	ND(1812)	225.00	275.00	300.00	400.00

Jose Maria Liceaga

J.M.L. with banner on cross, crossed olive branches. (J.M.L./V., D.s, S.M.,S.Y.S.L., Ve, A.P., s.r.a., Sea, P.G.,S.,S.M.,E.)

1/2 REAL

SILVER
c/m: JML/SM on cast Mexico City 1/2 Real.

KM#	Date	Good	VG	Fine	VF
A260	ND	100.00	150.00	200.00	275.00

2 REALES

SILVER
c/m: J.M.L./Ve on 1/4 cut of 8 Reales.

KM#	Date	Good	VG	Fine	VF
261.1	ND	175.00	225.00	300.00	—

c/m: J.M.L./V. on Zacatecas KM#186-187.

KM#	Date	Good	VG	Fine	VF
261.2	ND(1811)	200.00	225.00	250.00	300.00

c/m: J.M.L./DS on Zacatecas KM#186-187.

KM#	Date	Good	VG	Fine	VF
261.3	ND(1811)	200.00	235.00	275.00	325.00

c/m: J.M.L./S.M. on Zacatecas KM#186-187.

KM#	Date	Good	VG	Fine	VF
261.4	ND(1811)	200.00	235.00	275.00	325.00

c/m: J.M.L./S.Y. on Zacatecas KM#186-187.

KM#	Date	Good	VG	Fine	VF
261.5	ND(1811)	200.00	235.00	275.00	325.00

8 REALES

SILVER
c/m: J.M.L./D.S. on Zacatecas KM#189-190.

KM#	Date	Good	VG	Fine	VF
262.1	ND(1811)	250.00	325.00	425.00	550.00

c/m: J.M.L./E on Zacatecas KM#189-190.

KM#	Date	Good	VG	Fine	VF
262.2	ND(1811)	225.00	300.00	400.00	550.00

c/m: J.M.L./P.G. on Durango KM#111.2.

KM#	Date	Good	VG	Fine	VF
262.3	ND(1813) RM	200.00	275.00	375.00	525.00

c/m: J.M.L./S.F. on Zacatecas KM#189-190.

KM#	Date	Good	VG	Fine	VF
262.4	ND(1811)	200.00	275.00	375.00	525.00

c/m: J.M.L./S.M. on Zacatecas KM#189-190.

KM#	Date	Good	VG	Fine	VF
262.5	ND(1811)	200.00	275.00	375.00	525.00

c/m: J.M.L./V.E. on Zacatecas KM#189-190.

KM#	Date	Good	VG	Fine	VF
262.6	ND(1811)	200.00	275.00	375.00	525.00

Don Jose Maria De Linares

8 REALES

SILVER
c/m: LINA/RES* on Mexico City KM#110.

KM#	Date	Good	VG	Fine	VF
263.1	ND(1808) TH	300.00	350.00	425.00	525.00

c/m: LINA/RES * on Zacatecas KM#189-190.

KM#	Date	Good	VG	Fine	VF
263.2	ND(1811)	350.00	425.00	500.00	600.00

c/m: LINA/RES* on Zacatecas, KM#191-192.

KM#	Date	Good	VG	Fine	VF
263.3	ND(1812)	300.00	350.00	425.00	525.00

L.V.S. - Labor Vincit Semper

NOTE: Some authorities believe L.V.S. is for 'La Villa de Sombrerete'.

8 REALES

CAST SILVER
c/m: L.V.S. on Chihuahua KM#123.

KM#	Date	Good	VG	Fine	VF
264.1	ND(1811) RP	275.00	350.00	450.00	550.00
	ND(1812) RP	200.00	250.00	300.00	375.00

c/m: L.V.S. on Chihuahua KM#111.1 overstruck on KM#123.

KM#	Date	Good	VG	Fine	VF
264.2	ND(1816) RP	250.00	300.00	325.00	375.00
	ND(1817) RP	250.00	300.00	325.00	375.00
	ND(1818) RP	250.00	300.00	325.00	375.00
	ND(1819) RP	400.00	450.00	500.00	600.00
	ND(1820) RP	450.00	500.00	550.00	650.00

c/m: L.V.S. on Guadalajara KM#111.3.

KM#	Date	Good	VG	Fine	VF
264.3	ND(1817)	185.00	220.00	250.00	310.00

c/m: L.V.S. on Nueva Vizcaya KM#165.

KM#	Date	Good	VG	Fine	VF
264.4	ND(1811) RM	1150.	3150.	5250.	8250.

c/m: L.V.S. on Sombrerete KM#177.

KM#	Date	Good	VG	Fine	VF
264.5	ND(1811)	300.00	350.00	450.00	550.00
	ND(1812)	300.00	350.00	450.00	550.00

c/m: L.V.S. on Zacatecas KM#189-190.

KM#	Date	Good	VG	Fine	VF
264.6	ND(1811)	350.00	400.00	450.00	550.00

c/m: L.V.S. on Zacatecas KM#192.

KM#	Date	Good	VG	Fine	VF
264.7	ND(1813)	350.00	400.00	450.00	550.00

Morelos

Morelos monogram

Type A: Stars above and below monogram in circle.

Type B: Dots above and below monogram in oval.

Type C: Monogram in rectangle.

NOTE: Many specimens of Type C available in today's market are considered spurious.

2 REALES

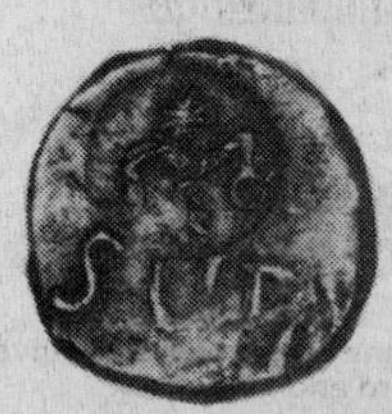

COPPER
c/m: Type A on Oaxaca Sud, KM#226.1.

KM#	Date	Good	VG	Fine	VF
A265	1812	—	—	—	—

8 REALES

SILVER
c/m: Type A on cast Mexico City KM#109.

KM#	Date	Good	VG	Fine	VF
265.1	ND(1797) FM	45.00	50.00	55.00	75.00
	ND(1798) FM	45.00	50.00	55.00	75.00
	ND(1800) FM	45.00	50.00	55.00	75.00
	ND(1807) TH	45.00	50.00	55.00	75.00

c/m: Type A on Mexico City KM#110.

KM#	Date	Good	VG	Fine	VF
265.2	ND(1809) TH	55.00	65.00	75.00	100.00
	ND(1811) HJ	55.00	65.00	75.00	100.00

c/m: Type A on Mexico City KM#111.

KM#	Date	Good	VG	Fine	VF
265.3	ND(1812) JJ	50.00	55.00	60.00	70.00

COPPER
c/m: Type A on Oaxaca Sud KM#233.

KM#	Date	Good	VG	Fine	VF
265.4	ND(1811)	12.50	17.50	25.00	35.00
	ND(1812)	12.50	17.50	25.00	35.00
	ND(1813)	12.50	17.50	25.00	35.00
	ND(1814)	12.50	17.50	25.00	35.00

CAST SILVER
c/m: Type A on Supreme National Congress KM#206.

KM#	Date	Good	VG	Fine	VF
265.5	ND(1811)	200.00	250.00	300.00	450.00

SILVER
c/m: Type A on Zacatecas KM#189-190.

KM#	Date	Good	VG	Fine	VF
265.6	ND(1811)	200.00	250.00	350.00	450.00

c/m: Type A on Zacatecas KM#191.

KM#	Date	Good	VG	Fine	VF
265.7	ND(1811)	200.00	250.00	350.00	450.00

c/m: Type B on Guatemala 8 Reales, C#67.

KM#	Date	Good	VG	Fine	VF
266.1	ND(1810) M	—	—	Rare	—

c/m: Type B on Mexico City KM#110.

KM#	Date	Good	VG	Fine	VF
266.2	ND(1809) TH	45.00	55.00	65.00	90.00

c/m: Type C on Zacatecas KM#189-190.

KM#	Date	Good	VG	Fine	VF
267	ND(1811)	300.00	350.00	400.00	500.00

Norte

Issued by the Supreme National Congress and the Army of the North.

c/m: Eagle on cactus; star to left; NORTE below.

1/2 REAL

SILVER
c/m: On Zacatecas KM#180.

KM#	Date	Good	VG	Fine	VF
268	ND(1811)	250.00	300.00	375.00	450.00

2 REALES

SILVER
c/m: On Zacatecas KM#187.

KM#	Date	Good	VG	Fine	VF
269	ND(1811)	225.00	275.00	325.00	400.00

c/m: On Zacatecas KM#188.

KM#	Date	Good	VG	Fine	VF
A269	ND(1812)	—	—	—	—

4 REALES

SILVER
c/m: On Sombrerete KM#175.

KM#	Date	Good	VG	Fine	VF
B269	ND(1812)	100.00	150.00	200.00	275.00

8 REALES

SILVER
c/m: On Chihuahua KM#111.1.

KM#	Date	Good	VG	Fine	VF
270.1	ND(1813) RP	250.00	350.00	450.00	550.00

c/m: On Guanajuato KM#111.4.

KM#	Date	Good	VG	Fine	VF
270.2	ND(1813) JM	400.00	550.00	700.00	800.00

c/m: On Zacatecas KM#189-190.

KM#	Date	Good	VG	Fine	VF
270.3	ND(1811)	300.00	400.00	500.00	650.00

c/m: On Zacatecas KM#191.

KM#	Date	Good	VG	Fine	VF
270.4	ND(1811)	200.00	300.00	400.00	550.00
	ND(1812)	200.00	300.00	400.00	550.00

Osorno

c/m: Osorno monogram.
(Jose Francisco Osorno)

1/2 REAL

SILVER
c/m: On Mexico City KM#72.

KM#	Date	Good	VG	Fine	VF
271.1	ND(1798) FM	65.00	100.00	150.00	200.00
	ND(1802) FT	65.00	100.00	150.00	200.00
	ND(1806)	65.00	100.00	150.00	200.00

c/m: On Mexico City KM#73.

KM#	Date	Good	VG	Fine	VF
271.2	ND(1809)	65.00	100.00	150.00	200.00

REAL

SILVER
c/m: On Mexico City KM#81.

KM#	Date	Good	VG	Fine	VF
272.1	ND(1803) FT	65.00	100.00	150.00	200.00
	ND(1803) FT	65.00	100.00	150.00	200.00

c/m: On Potosi Real.

KM#	Date	Good	VG	Fine	VF
272.2	ND	65.00	100.00	150.00	200.00

2 REALES

SILVER
c/m: On cast Mexico City KM#92.

KM#	Date	Good	VG	Fine	VF
A272.1	ND(1809) TH	75.00	125.00	175.00	250.00

c/m: On Zacatlan KM#252.

KM#	Date	Good	VG	Fine	VF
A272.2	ND(1813)	150.00	200.00	300.00	400.00

4 REALES

SILVER
c/m: On Mexico City KM#97.

KM#	Date	Good	VG	Fine	VF
273	ND(1782) FF	—	—	—	—

8 REALES

SILVER
c/m: On Lima 8 Reales, C#101.

KM#	Date	Good	VG	Fine	VF
274.1	ND(1811) JP	200.00	225.00	250.00	300.00

c/m: On Mexico City KM#110.

KM#	Date	Good	VG	Fine	VF
274.2	ND(1809) TH	125.00	150.00	225.00	300.00
	ND(1810) HJ	125.00	150.00	225.00	300.00
	ND(1811) HJ	125.00	150.00	225.00	300.00

S.J.N.G. - Suprema Junta National Gubernativa

(Refer to Multiple countermarks)

VILLA/GRAN

(Julian Villagran)

2 REALES

SILVER
c/m: On cast Mexico City KM#91.

KM#	Date	Good	VG	Fine	VF
298	ND(1799) FM	150.00	200.00	250.00	350.00
	ND(1802) FT	150.00	200.00	250.00	350.00

8 REALES

SILVER
c/m: VILLA/GRAN on cast Mexico City KM#109.

KM#	Date	Good	VG	Fine	VF
275	ND(1796) FM	200.00	250.00	300.00	350.00
	ND(1806) TH	200.00	250.00	300.00	350.00

UNCLASSIFIED COUNTERMARKS

General Vicente Guerrero

The countermark of an eagle facing left within a pearled oval has been attributed by some authors as that of General Vicente Guerrero, a leader of the insurgents in the south, 1816-1821.

1/2 REAL

SILVER
c/m: Eagle on Mexico City 1/2 Real.

KM#	Date	Good	VG	Fine	VF
276	ND	40.00	60.00	80.00	175.00

REAL

SILVER
c/m: Eagle on Mexico City KM#78.

KM#	Date	Good	VG	Fine	VF
277	ND(1772) FM	35.00	50.00	75.00	150.00

2 REALES

SILVER
c/m: Eagle on Mexico City KM#88.

KM#	Date	Good	VG	Fine	VF
278.1	ND(1784) FM	50.00	75.00	125.00	250.00

c/m: Eagle on Mexico City KM#91.

KM#	Date	Good	VG	Fine	VF
278.2	ND(1807) PJ	35.00	65.00	85.00	200.00

8 REALES

SILVER
c/m: Eagle on Zacatecas KM#191.

KM#	Date	Good	VG	Fine	VF
279	ND(1811)	100.00	150.00	200.00	350.00

ZMY

8 REALES

SILVER
c/m: ZMY on Zacatecas KM#191.

KM#	Date	Good	VG	Fine	VF
286	ND(1812)	100.00	150.00	210.00	275.00

MULTIPLE COUNTERMARKS

Many combinations of Royalist and Insurgent countermarks are found usually on the cast copies produced by the Chihuahua and Mexico City Mints and also the crude provisional mint issues of this period. Struck Mexico Mint coins were used for molds to cast necessity coinage and were countermarked to show issuing authority. Some were marked again by opposing forces or by friendly forces to allow circulation in their area of occupation. Some countermarks are only obtainable with companion markings.

Chilpanzingo Crown and Flag

8 REALES

SILVER
c/m: Chilpanzingo Type B and crown and flag on Zacatecas KM#189-190.

KM#	Date	Good	VG	Fine	VF
280	ND(1811)	—	—	—	—

Chilpanzingo/LVA

8 REALES

SILVER
c/m: Chilpanzingo Type A and LVA on Mexico City KM#109.

KM#	Date	Good	VG	Fine	VF
297	ND(1805) TH	—	—	—	—

Chilpanzingo/LVS

8 REALES

SILVER
c/m: Chilpanzingo Type A and script LVS on cast Mexico City KM#110.

KM#	Date	Good	VG	Fine	VF
281	ND(1809) HJ	50.00	75.00	150.00	250.00

Chilpanzingo/Morelos

8 REALES

SILVER
c/m: Chilpanzingo Type A and Morelos monogram Type A on cast Mexico City KM#109.

KM#	Date	Good	VG	Fine	VF
284	ND(1806) TH	35.00	45.00	55.00	150.00
	ND(1807) TH	—	—	—	—

c/m: Chilpanzingo Type A and Morelos monogram Type A on struck Mexico City KM#110.

KM#	Date	Good	VG	Fine	VF
285.1	ND(1809) TH	35.00	50.00	100.00	250.00

c/m: Chilpanzingo Type A and Morelos monogram Type A on cast Mexico City KM#110.

KM#	Date	Good	VG	Fine	VF
285.2	ND(1810) HJ	35.00	45.00	55.00	150.00
	ND(1811) HJ	—	—	—	—

c/m: Chilpanzingo Type A and Morelos monogram Type A on cast Mexico City KM#111.

KM#	Date	Good	VG	Fine	VF
285.3	ND(1811) HJ	—	—	—	—

Chilpanzingo/Morelos/LVS
8 REALES

SILVER
c/m: Chilpanzingo Type A, Morelos Type A and LVS monogram on cast Mexico City KM#110.

KM#	Date	Good	VG	Fine	VF
286	ND(1809) HJ	35.00	50.00	75.00	200.00

Chilpanzingo/P.D.V.
8 REALES

SILVER
c/m: Chilpanzingo Type B and P.D.V. (Provisional De Valladolid) on Valladolid KM#178.

KM#	Date	Good	VG	Fine	VF
287	ND(1813)	—	—	—	—

Chilpanzingo/S.J.N.G.
8 REALES

SILVER
c/m: Chilpanzingo Type B and S.J.N.G. (Suprema Junta Nacional Gubernativa) on Zacatecas KM#189-190.

KM#	Date	Good	VG	Fine	VF
288	ND(1811)	—	—	—	—

C.M.S./S.C.M.
2 REALES

SILVER
c/m: C.M.S. (Comandancia Militar Suriana) and eagle w/S.C.M. (Soberano Congreso Mexicano) on Mexico City 2 Reales.

KM#	Date	Good	VG	Fine	VF
289	ND	—	—	—	—

ENSAIE/J.M.L.
8 REALES

SILVER
c/m: ENSAIE and J.M.L. on Zacatecas, KM#190.

KM#	Date	Good	VG	Fine	VF
A290	ND(1811)	—	—	—	—

ENSAIE/VTIL
8 REALES

SILVER
c/m: ENSAIE and VTIL on Zacatecas KM#189-190.

KM#	Date	Good	VG	Fine	VF
290	ND(1811)	—	—	—	—

J.M.L./VTIL
2 REALES

SILVER
c/m: J.M.L./D.S. and VTIL on Zacatecas, KM#186.

KM#	Date	Good	VG	Fine	VF
A286	ND(1811)	75.00	125.00	175.00	250.00

c/m: J.M.L./V.E. and VTIL on Zacatecas KM#186.

KM#	Date	Good	VG	Fine	VF
B286	ND(1810)	75.00	125.00	175.00	250.00
	ND(1811)	75.00	125.00	175.00	250.00

8 REALES

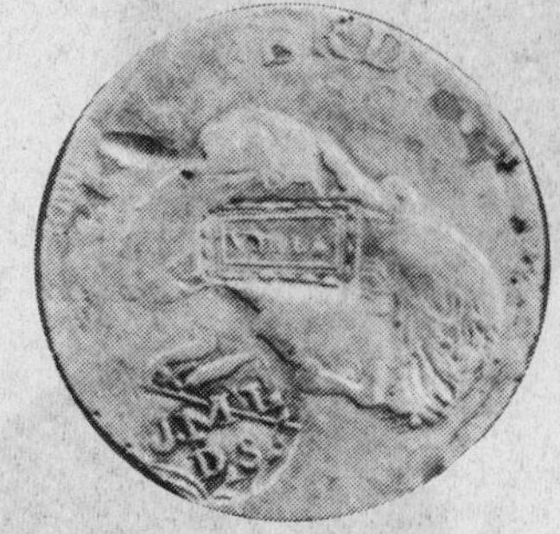

SILVER
c/m: J.M.L./D.S. and VTIL on Mexico City KM#110.

KM#	Date	Good	VG	Fine	VF
291	ND(1810) HJ	—	—	—	—

L.C.M./Morelos
8 REALES

SILVER
c/m: LCM and Morelos monogram Type A on cast Mexico City KM#109.

KM#	Date	Good	VG	Fine	VF
282	ND(1792) FM	—	—	—	—

Morelos/Morelos
8 REALES

SILVER
c/m: Morelos Type A and C on cast Mexico City KM#109.

KM#	Date	Good	VG	Fine	VF
283	ND(1806) TH	—	—	—	—

LCM/MVA-1812
8 REALES

SILVER
c/m: LCM and MVA/1812 on Chihuahua KM#123.

KM#	Date	Good	VG	Fine	VF
292	1812(1810) RP	—	—	—	—

c/m: LCM and MVA 1812 on Chihuahua KM#110.

KM#	Date	Good	VG	Fine	VF
A293	1812(1810) HJ	—	—	—	—

c/m: LCM and MVA/1812 on Chihuahua KM#111.1.

KM#	Date	Good	VG	Fine	VF
293	1812(1818)	200.00	300.00	450.00	700.00

L.V.A./Morelos

8 REALES

SILVER
c/m: Script LVA and Morelos monogram Type A on cast Mexico City KM#110.

KM#	Date	Good	VG	Fine	VF
294	ND(-) HJ	—	—	—	—

M.d.S./S.C.M.

2 REALES

SILVER
c/m: M.d.S. (Militar del Sur) and eagle w/S.C.M. (Soberano Congreso Mexicano) on Mexico City 2 Reales.

KM#	Date	Good	VG	Fine	VF
295	ND	—	—	—	—

OSORNO/VILLAGRAN

8 REALES

SILVER
c/m: Osorno monogram and VILLA/GRAN on cast Mexico City KM#110.

KM#	Date	Good	VG	Fine	VF
296	ND(1809) TH	—	—	—	—

S.J.N.G./VTIL

8 REALES

SILVER
c/m: S.J.N.G. and VTIL on Zacatecas KM#191.

KM#	Date	Good	VG	Fine	VF
297	ND	35.00	50.00	75.00	200.00

EMPIRE OF ITURBIDE

RULERS

Augustin I Iturbide, 1822-1823

MINT MARKS

Mo - Mexico City Mint

ASSAYERS INITIALS

JA - Jose Garcia Ansaldo, 1812-1833
JM - Joaquin Davila Madrid, 1809-1833

1/8 REAL

COPPER
Mint: Nueva Viscaya

KM#	Date	Mintage	Good	VG	Fine	VF
299	1821	—	25.00	50.00	85.00	150.00
	1822	—	7.50	12.50	25.00	45.00
	1823	—	7.50	12.50	25.00	45.00

1/4 REAL

COPPER
Mint: Nueva Viscaya

KM#	Date	Mintage	Good	VG	Fine	VF
300	1822	—	175.00	275.00	425.00	500.00

1/2 REAL

.903 SILVER
Mint mark: Mo

KM#	Date	Mintage	Fine	VF	XF	Unc
301	1822 JM	—	17.50	30.00	60.00	310.00
	1823 JM	—	12.50	25.00	50.00	285.00

REAL

.903 SILVER
Mint mark: Mo

KM#	Date	Mintage	Fine	VF	XF	Unc
302	1822 JM	—	50.00	110.00	225.00	750.00

2 REALES

.903 SILVER
Mint mark: Mo

KM#	Date	Mintage	Fine	VF	XF	Unc
303	1822 JM	—	25.00	55.00	225.00	800.00
	1823 JM	—	20.00	45.00	175.00	750.00

8 REALES

.903 SILVER
Mint mark: Mo

KM#	Date	Mintage	Fine	VF	XF	Unc
304	1822 JM	—	45.00	95.00	250.00	850.00

Obv: Bust similar to 8 Escudos, KM#313.
Rev: Similar to KM#304.

KM#	Date	Mintage	Fine	VF	XF	Unc
305	1822 JM	—	—	—	Rare	—

Type I. Obv: Leg. divided. Rev: 8 R.J.M. at upper left of eagle.

KM#	Date	Mintage	Fine	VF	XF	Unc
306.1	1822 JM	—	60.00	145.00	350.00	1250.

Rev: Cross on crown.

KM#	Date	Mintage	Fine	VF	XF	Unc
306.2	1822 JM	—	—	—	Rare	—

Type II. Obv: Similar to KM#306.
Rev: Similar to KM#310.

KM#	Date	Mintage	Fine	VF	XF	Unc
307	1822 JM	—	135.00	325.00	550.00	2150.

Type III. Obv: Continuous leg. w/long smooth

truncation. Rev: Similar to KM#306.

KM#	Date	Mintage	Fine	VF	XF	Unc
308	1822 JM	—	175.00	500.00	950.00	1400.

NOTE: Variety with long, straight truncation is valued at $5,000. in uncirculated condition.

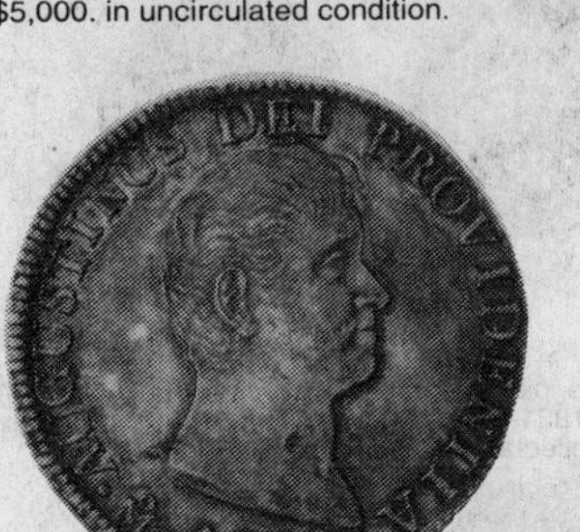

Type IV. Obv: Similar to KM#308.
Rev: Similar to KM#310.

KM#	Date	Mintage	Fine	VF	XF	Unc
309	1822 JM	—	50.00	125.00	225.00	800.00

Type V. Obv. continuous leg. w/short irregular truncation. Rev: 8 R.J.M. below eagle.

KM#	Date	Mintage	Fine	VF	XF	Unc
310	1822 JM	—	50.00	125.00	200.00	750.00
	1823 JM	—	50.00	125.00	200.00	750.00

Type VI. Obv: Bust w/long truncation.
Rev: Similar to KM#310.

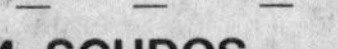

KM#	Date	Mintage	Fine	VF	XF	Unc
311	1822 JM	—	—	—	Rare	—

4 SCUDOS

.875 GOLD
Mint mark: Mo

KM#	Date	Mintage	Fine	VF	XF	Unc
312	1823 JM	—	1000.	1750.	2500.	4500.

8 SCUDOS

.875 GOLD
Mint mark: Mo
Obv. leg: AUGUSTINUS.

KM#	Date	Mintage	Fine	VF	XF	Unc
313.1	1822 JM	—	1200.	2000.	3500.	—

NOTE: Superior Casterline sale 5-89 choice AU realized $11,000.

Obv. leg: AUGSTINUS (error).

KM#	Date	Mintage	Fine	VF	XF	Unc
313.2	1822 JM	—	1250.	2250.	4000.	—

KM#	Date	Mintage	Fine	VF	XF	Unc
314	1823 JM	—	1000.	1800.	3000.	5000.

REPUBLIC

MINT MARKS

A, AS - Alamos
CE - Real de Catorce
CA,CH - Chihuahua
C, Cn, Gn(error) - Culiacan
D, Do - Durango
EoMo - Estado de Mexico
Ga - Guadalajara
GC - Guadalupe y Calvo
G, Go - Guanajuato
H, Ho - Hermosillo
M, Mo - Mexico City
O, OA - Oaxaca
SLP, PI, P, I/P - San Luis Potosi
Z, Zs - Zacatecas

ASSAYERS INITIALS

ALAMOS MINT

Initials	Years	Mintmaster
PG	1862-1868	Pascual Gaxiola
DL, L	1866-1879	Domingo Larraguibel
AM	1872-1874	Antonio Moreno
ML, L	1878-1895	Manuel Larraguibel

REAL DE CATORCE MINT

Initials	Years	Mintmaster
ML	1863	Mariano Leon

CHIHUAHUA MINT

Initials	Years	Mintmaster
MR	1831-1834	Mariano Cristobal Ramirez
AM	1833-1839	Jose Antonio Mucharraz
MJ	1832	Jose Mariano Jimenez
RG	1839-1856	Rodrigo Garcia
JC	1856-1865	Joaquin Campa
BA	1858	Bruno Arriada
FP	1866	Francisco Potts
JG	1866-1868	Jose Maria Gomez del Campo
MM, M	1868-1895	Manuel Merino
AV	1873-1880	Antonio Valero
EA	1877	Eduardo Avila
JM	1877	Jacobo Mucharraz
GR	1877	Guadalupe Rocha
MG	1880-1882	Manuel Gameros

CULIACAN MINT

Initials	Years	Mintmaster
CE	1846-1870	Clemente Espinosa de los Monteros
C	1870	???
PV	1860-1861	Pablo Viruega
MP, P	1871-1876	Manuel Onofre Parodi
GP	1876	Celso Gaxiola & Manuel Onofre Parodi
CG, G	1876-1878	Celso Gaxiola
JD, D	1878-1882	Juan Dominguez
AM, M	1882-1899	Antonio Moreno
F	1870	Fernando Ferrari
JQ, Q	1899-1903	Jesus S. Quiroz
FV, V	1903	Francisco Valdez
MH, H	1904	Merced Hernandez
RP, P	1904-1905	Ramon Ponce de Leon

DURANGO MINT

Initials	Years	Mintmaster
RL	1825-1832	???
RM	1830-1848	Ramon Mascarenas
OMC	1840	Octavio Martinez de Castro
CM	1848-1876	Clemente Moron
JMR	1849-1852,	Jose Maria Ramirez
CP, P	1853-1864, 1867-1873	Carlos Leon de la Pena
LT	1864-1865	???
JMP, P	1877	Carlos Miguel de la Palma
PE, E	1878	Pedro Espejo
TB, B	1878-1880	Trinidad Barrera
JP	1880-1894	J. Miguel Palma
MC, C	1882-1890	Manuel M. Canseco or Melchor Calderon
JB	1885	Jacobo Blanco
ND, D	1892-1895	Norberto Dominguez

ESTADO DE MEXICO MINT

Initials	Years	Mintmaster
L	1828-1830	Luis Valazquez de la Cadena
F	1828-1830	Francisco Parodi

GUADALAJARA MINT

Initials	Years	Mintmaster
FS	1818-1835	Francisco Suarez
JM	1830-1832	???
JG	1836-1839 1842-1867	Juan de Dios Guzman
MC	1839-1846	Manuel Cueras
JM	1867-1869	Jesus P. Manzano
IC, C	1869-1877	Ignacio Canizo y Soto
MC	1874-1875	Manuel Contreras
JA, A	1877-1881	Julio Arancivia
FS, S	1880-1882	Fernando Sayago
TB, B	1883-1884	Trinidad Barrera
AH, H	1884-1885	Antonio Hernandez y Prado
JS, S	1885-1895	Jose S. Schiafino

GUADALUPE Y CALVO MINT

Initials	Years	Mintmaster
MP	1844-1852	Manuel Onofre Parodi

GUANAJUATO MINT

Initials	Years	Mintmaster
JJ	1825-1826	Jose Mariano Jimenez
MJ, MR, JM, PG, PJ, PF		???
PM	1841-1848, 1853-1861	Patrick Murphy
YF	1862-1868	Yldefonso Flores
YE	1862-1863	Ynocencio Espinoza
FR	1870-1878	Faustino Ramirez
SB, RR	???	
RS	1891-1900	Rosendo Sandoval

HERMOSILLO MINT

Initials	Years	Mintmaster
PP	1835-1836	Pedro Peimbert
FM	1871-1876	Florencio Monteverde
MP	1866	Manuel Onofre Parodi
PR	1866-1875	Pablo Rubio
R	1874-1875	Pablo Rubio
GR	1877	Guadalupe Rocha
AF, F	1876-1877	Alejandro Fourcade
JA, A	1877-1883	Jesus Acosta
FM, M	1883-1886	Fernando Mendez
FG, G	1886-1895	Fausto Gaxiola

MEXICO CITY MINT

Because of the great number of assayers for this mint (Mexico City is a much larger mint than any of the others) there is much confusion as to which initial stands for which assayer at any one time. Therefore we feel that it would be of no value to list the assayers.

OAXACA MINT

Initials	Years	Mintmaster
AE	1859-1891	Agustin Endner
E	1889-1890	Agustin Endner
FR	1861-1864	Francisco de la Rosa
EN	1890	Eduardo Navarro Luna
N	1890	Eduardo Navarro Luna

POTOSI MINT

Initials	Years	Mintmaster
JS	1827-1842	Juan Sanabria
AM	1838,1843-1849	Jose Antonio Mucharraz
PS	1842-1843,1848-1849, 1857-1861,1867-1870	Pompaso Sanabria
S	1869-1870	Pomposo Sanabria
MC	1849-1859	Mariano Catano
RO	1859-1865	Romualdo Obregon
MH, H	1870-1885	Manuel Herrera Razo
O	1870-1873	Juan R. Ochoa
CA, G	1867-1870	Carlos Aguirre Gomez
BE, E	1879-1881	Blas Escontria
LC, C	1885-1886	Luis Cuevas
MR, R	1886-1893	Mariano Reyes

ZACATECAS MINT

Initials	Years	Mintmaster
A	1825-1829	Adalco
Z	1825-1826	Mariano Zaldivar
V	1824-1831	Jose Mariano Vela
O	1829-1867	Manuel Ochoa
M	1831-1867	Manuel Miner
VL	1860-1866	Vicente Larranaga
JS	1867-1868, 1876-1886	J.S. de Santa Ana
YH	1868-1874	Ygnacio Hierro
JA	1874-1876	Juan H. Acuna
FZ	1886-1905	Francisco de P. Zarate
FM	1904-1905	Francisco Mateos

Die Varieties

The basic designs were maintained throughout the Mexican Mints but many variances exist most notable in the eagle, cactus and sprays.

1835 Durango, 8 Escudos

A large winged eagle was portrayed on the earlier coinage of the new republic.

1849 Mexico City, 8 Escudos

The later eagle featured undersized wings.

1844 Durango, 8 Escudos

The early renditions of the hand held Liberty cap over open book were massive in the gold escudo series.

1864 Durango, 8 Escudos

A finer more petite style was adopted later on in the gold escudo series.

State and Federal Issues

1/16 REAL

(Medio Octavo)

COPPER
Mint: Jalisco
Obv. leg: DEPARTAMENTO DE JALISCO

KM#	Date	Mintage	Good	VG	Fine	VF
316	1860	—	3.00	5.00	10.00	50.00
	Obv. leg: ESTADO LIBRE DE JALISCO					
317	1861	—	3.00	5.00	10.00	50.00

Mint: Mexico City
Obv. leg: REPUBLICA MEXICANA

KM#	Date	Mintage	VG	Fine	VF	XF
315	1831	—	10.00	15.00	35.00	100.00
	1832/1	—	12.00	17.50	35.00	125.00
	1832	—	10.00	15.00	35.00	100.00
	1833	—	10.00	15.00	35.00	100.00
	BRASS					
315a	1832	—	15.00	22.50	60.00	150.00
	1833	—	12.00	17.50	50.00	100.00
	1835	—	400.00	800.00	1250.	2300.

1/8 REAL

(Octavo Real)

COPPER
Mint: Chihuahua
Obv. leg: ESTADO SOBERANO DE CHIHUAHUA

KM#	Date	Mintage	Good	VG	Fine	VF
318	1833	—	—	—	Rare	—
	1834	—	—	—	Rare	—
	1835/3	—	—	—	Rare	—

Obv. leg: ESTADO DE CHIHUAHUA

KM#	Date	Mintage	Good	VG	Fine	VF
319	1855	—	3.50	5.00	18.00	60.00

Mint: Durango
Rev. leg: LIBERTAD

KM#	Date	Mintage	Good	VG	Fine	VF
320	1824	—	5.00	10.00	35.00	100.00
	1828	—	150.00	250.00	400.00	900.00

NOTE: These pieces were frequently struck over 1/8 Real, dated 1821-23 of Nueva Vizcaya. All known examples are collectable contemporary counterfeits.

Rev. leg: OCTo.DE.R.DE DO., date.

KM#	Date	Mintage	Good	VG	Fine	VF
321	1828	—	6.00	15.00	35.00	100.00

Obv. leg: ESTADO DE DURANGO

KM#	Date	Mintage	Good	VG	Fine	VF
322	1833	—	—	—	Rare	—

Obv. leg: REPUBLICA MEXICANA

KM#	Date	Mintage	Good	VG	Fine	VF
323	1842/33	—	15.00	20.00	40.00	125.00
	1842	—	10.00	15.00	30.00	100.00

Obv. leg: REPUBLICA MEXICANA
Rev. leg: DEPARTAMENTO DE DURANGO

KM#	Date	Mintage	Good	VG	Fine	VF
324	1845	—	25.00	50.00	100.00	250.00
	1846	—	—	—	Rare	—
	1847	—	3.00	5.00	8.00	35.00

Obv. leg: REPUBLICA MEXICANA
Rev. leg: ESTADO DE DURANGO

KM#	Date	Mintage	Good	VG	Fine	VF
325	1851	—	3.00	5.00	8.00	30.00
	1852/1	—	3.00	5.00	8.00	30.00
	1852	—	3.00	5.00	8.00	30.00
	1854	—	6.00	10.00	17.50	65.00

Mint: Guanajuato
Obv. leg: ESTADO LIBRE DE GUANAJUATO

KM#	Date	Mintage	Good	VG	Fine	VF
326	1829	—	3.00	5.00	10.00	30.00
	1829 error w/GUANJUATO	—	3.00	5.00	10.00	30.00
	1830	—	8.00	12.00	20.00	75.00

BRASS

KM#	Date	Mintage	Good	VG	Fine	VF
327	1856	—	8.00	12.00	20.00	75.00

25mm

KM#	Date	Mintage	Good	VG	Fine	VF
328	1856	—	4.00	6.00	10.00	30.00
	1857	—	4.00	6.00	10.00	30.00

COPPER

KM#	Date	Mintage	Good	VG	Fine	VF
328a	1857	—	10.00	20.00	35.00	60.00

Mint: Jalisco
Obv. leg: ESTADO LIBRE DE JALISCO

KM#	Date	Mintage	Good	VG	Fine	VF
329	1828	—	3.00	5.00	8.00	25.00
	1831	—	100.00	200.00	300.00	400.00
	1832/28	—	3.00	5.00	8.00	25.00
	1832	—	3.00	5.00	8.00	25.00
	1833	—	3.00	5.00	8.00	25.00
	1834	—	50.00	100.00	175.00	300.00

KM#	Date	Mintage	Good	VG	Fine	VF
330	1856	—	4.00	7.00	10.00	25.00
	1857	—	4.00	7.00	10.00	25.00
	1858	—	4.00	7.00	10.00	25.00
	1861	—	100.00	200.00	300.00	400.00
	1862/1	—	4.00	7.00	10.00	25.00
	1862	—	4.00	7.00	10.00	25.00

Obv. leg: DEPARTAMENTO DE JALISCO

KM#	Date	Mintage	Good	VG	Fine	VF
331	1858	—	3.00	5.00	8.00	20.00
	1859	—	3.00	5.00	8.00	20.00
	1860/59	—	3.00	5.00	8.00	20.00
	1860	—	3.00	5.00	8.00	20.00
	1862	—	6.00	10.00	20.00	60.00

Mint: Mexico City
27mm
Obv. leg: REPUBLICA MEXICANA

KM#	Date	Mintage	VG	Fine	VF	XF
332	1829	—	450.00	900.00	1500.	2500.

21mm
Obv. leg: REPUBLICA MEXICANA

KM#	Date	Mintage	Good	VG	Fine	VF
333	1829	—	10.00	15.00	30.00	60.00
	1830	—	2.00	3.00	5.00	15.00
	1831	—	2.00	4.00	6.00	20.00
	1832	—	2.00	4.00	6.00	20.00
	1833/2	—	2.00	4.00	6.00	20.00
	1833	—	2.00	3.00	5.00	15.00
	1834	—	2.00	3.00	5.00	15.00
	1835/4	—	2.25	4.00	6.00	20.00
	1835	—	2.00	3.00	5.00	15.00

Obv. leg: LIBERTAD

KM#	Date	Mintage	Good	VG	Fine	VF
334	1841	—	7.00	15.00	30.00	75.00
	1842	—	3.00	5.00	10.00	30.00
	1850	—	15.00	20.00	30.00	80.00
	1861	—	8.00	12.00	25.00	70.00

Mint: Occidente
Obv. leg: ESTADO DE OCCIDENTE

KM#	Date	Mintage	Good	VG	Fine	VF
335	1828 reverse S					
		—	15.00	30.00	45.00	100.00
	1829	—	15.00	30.00	45.00	100.00

Mint: Potosi
Obv. leg: ESTADO LIBRE DE SAN LUIS POTOSI

KM#	Date	Mintage	Good	VG	Fine	VF
336	1829	—	6.00	9.00	15.00	50.00
	1830	—	8.00	12.00	20.00	60.00
	1831	—	5.00	8.00	12.00	40.00
	1859	—	5.00	8.00	12.00	40.00

Mint: Sonora
Obv. leg: ESTO LIBE Y SOBO DE SONORA, 28mm.

KM#	Date	Mintage	Good	VG	Fine	VF
337	1859	—	—	Rare	—	—

Mint: Zacatecas
Obv. leg: ESTo LIBe FEDo DE ZACATECAS

KM#	Date	Mintage	Good	VG	Fine	VF
338	1825	—	3.00	5.00	10.00	25.00
	1827	—	3.00	5.00	10.00	25.00
	1827 inverted A for V in OCTAVO					
		—	12.00	20.00	40.00	100.00
	1829	—	—	—	Rare	—
	1830	—	3.00	5.00	8.00	20.00
	1831	—	4.00	6.00	10.00	25.00
	1832	—	3.00	5.00	8.00	20.00
	1833	—	3.00	5.00	8.00	20.00
	1835	—	4.00	6.00	10.00	25.00
	1846	—	4.00	6.00	10.00	25.00
	1851	—	125.00	175.00	250.00	350.00
	1852	—	4.00	6.00	10.00	25.00
	1858	—	3.00	5.00	8.00	20.00
	1859	—	3.00	5.00	8.00	20.00
	1862	—	3.00	5.00	8.00	20.00
	1863 reversed 6 in date					
		—	3.00	5.00	8.00	20.00

Obv. leg: DEPARTAMENTO DE ZACATECAS

KM#	Date	Mintage	Good	VG	Fine	VF
339	1836	—	4.00	8.00	15.00	40.00
	1845	—	6.00	10.00	20.00	50.00
	1846	—	4.00	8.00	15.00	40.00

1/4 REAL

(Un Quarto/Una Quartilla)
(Copper/Brass Series)

COPPER
Mint: Chihuahua
Obv. leg: ESTADO SOBERANO DE CHIHUAHUA

KM#	Date	Mintage	Good	VG	Fine	VF
340	1833	—	8.00	12.00	35.00	75.00
	1834	—	5.00	8.00	12.00	50.00
	1835	—	5.00	8.00	12.00	50.00

Obv. leg: ESTADO LIBRE DE CHIHUAHUA

KM#	Date	Mintage	Good	VG	Fine	VF
341	1846	—	4.00	6.00	12.00	50.00

NOTE: Varieties with or without fraction bar.

Obv. leg: ESTADO DE CHIHUAHUA

KM#	Date	Mintage	Good	VG	Fine	VF
342	1855	—	3.00	5.00	10.00	50.00
	1856	—	3.00	5.00	10.00	50.00

Obv. leg: DEPARTAMENTO DE CHIHUAHUA

KM#	Date	Mintage	Good	VG	Fine	VF
343	1855	—	3.00	5.00	10.00	50.00
	1855 DE/reversed D and E					
		—	3.00	5.00	10.00	50.00

Obv. leg: E. CHIHA LIBERTAD

KM#	Date	Mintage	Good	VG	Fine	VF
344	1860	—	2.00	4.00	8.00	25.00
	1861	—	2.00	4.00	8.00	25.00
	1865/1	—	2.50	5.50	10.00	30.00
	1865	—	10.00	20.00	35.00	95.00
	1866/5	—	10.00	20.00	35.00	95.00
	1866	—	2.00	4.00	8.00	25.00

Mint: Durango
Obv. leg: REPUBLICA MEXICANA

KM#	Date	Mintage	Good	VG	Fine	VF
345	1845	—	—	—	Rare	—

Obv. leg: REPUBLICA MEXICANA
Rev: DURANGO, date, value.

KM#	Date	Mintage	Good	VG	Fine	VF
346	1858	—	—	—	Rare	—

Obv. leg: ESTADO DE DURANGO
Rev. leg: CONSTITUCION

KM#	Date	Mintage	Good	VG	Fine	VF
347	1858	—	3.00	6.00	12.00	50.00

NOTE: Variety exists in brass.

Obv. leg: DEPARTAMENTO DE DURANGO
Rev. leg: LIBERTAD EN EL ORDEN.

KM#	Date	Mintage	Good	VG	Fine	VF
348	1860	—	2.00	5.00	15.00	45.00
	1866	—	2.00	5.00	15.00	45.00

Obv. leg: ESTADO DE DURANGO
Rev. leg: INDEPENDENCIA Y LIBERTAD

KM#	Date	Mintage	Good	VG	Fine	VF
349	1866	—	3.00	5.00	12.00	45.00

Rev. leg: SUFRAGIO LIBRE

KM#	Date	Mintage	Good	VG	Fine	VF
350	1872	—	2.00	4.00	10.00	20.00

NOTE: Variety exists in brass.

Mint: Guanajuato
Obv. leg: ESTADO LIBRE DE GUANAJUATO

KM#	Date	Mintage	Good	VG	Fine	VF
351	1828	—	4.00	7.00	10.00	45.00
	1828 error w/GUANJUATO	—	4.00	7.00	10.00	45.00
	1829	—	4.00	7.00	10.00	45.00

Obv. leg: EST. LIB. DE GUANAXUATO
Rev. leg: OMNIA VINCIT LABOR

KM#	Date	Mintage	Good	VG	Fine	VF
352	1856	—	12.00	25.00	50.00	100.00
	1857	—	6.00	9.00	15.00	45.00
			BRASS			
352a	1856	—	4.00	7.00	10.00	30.00
	1857	—	4.00	7.00	10.00	30.00

COPPER
Mint: Jalisco
Obv. leg: ESTADO LIBRE DE JALISCO

KM#	Date	Mintage	Good	VG	Fine	VF
353	1828	—	4.00	6.00	12.00	35.00
	1829/8	—	3.00	5.00	8.00	35.00
	1829	—	3.00	5.00	8.00	35.00
	1830/20	—	3.00	5.00	8.00	30.00
	1830/29	—	3.00	5.00	8.00	30.00
	1830	—	3.00	5.00	8.00	30.00
	1831	—	—	—	Rare	—
	1832/20	—	3.00	5.00	8.00	30.00
	1832/28	—	3.00	5.00	8.00	30.00
	1832	—	3.00	5.00	8.00	30.00
	1833/2	—	3.00	5.00	8.00	30.00
	1834	—	3.00	5.00	8.00	30.00
	1835/3	—	3.00	5.00	8.00	30.00
	1835	—	3.00	5.00	8.00	30.00
	1836	—	—	—	Rare	—

Obv. leg: DEPARTAMENTO DE JALISCO

KM#	Date	Mintage	Good	VG	Fine	VF
354	1836	—	—	—	Rare	—

Obv. leg: ESTADO LIBRE DE JALISCO

KM#	Date	Mintage	Good	VG	Fine	VF
355	1858	—	3.00	5.00	8.00	20.00
	1861	—	3.00	5.00	10.00	25.00
	1862	—	3.00	5.00	8.00	20.00

Obv. leg: DEPARTAMENTO DE JALISCO

KM#	Date	Mintage	Good	VG	Fine	VF
356	1858	—	3.00	5.00	8.00	20.00
	1859/8	—	3.00	5.00	8.00	20.00
	1859	—	3.00	5.00	8.00	20.00
	1860	—	3.00	5.00	8.00	20.00

Mint: Mexico City

Obv. leg: REPUBLICA MEXICANA.

KM#	Date	Mintage	VG	Fine	VF	XF
357	1829	—	8.00	20.00	60.00	150.00

Reduced size.

KM#	Date	Mintage	VG	Fine	VF	XF
358	1829	—	12.00	25.00	50.00	150.00
	1830	—	2.00	3.00	4.00	10.00
	1831	—	2.00	3.00	4.00	10.00
	1832	—	5.50	10.00	20.00	35.00
	1833	—	2.00	3.00	4.00	10.00
	1834/3	—	2.00	3.00	4.00	10.00
	1834	—	2.00	3.00	4.00	10.00
	1835	—	2.00	3.00	4.00	10.00
	1836	—	2.00	3.00	4.00	10.00
	1837	—	5.00	10.00	20.00	40.00
			BRASS c/m: JM			
358a.1	1831	—	8.00	15.00	35.00	75.00
			W/o countermark			
358a.2	1831	—	—	—	—	—

COPPER
Mint: Potosi
Obv. leg: ESTADO LIBRE DE SAN LUIS POTOSI
Rev. leg: MEXICO LIBRE

KM#	Date	Mintage	Good	VG	Fine	VF
359	1828	—	3.00	4.00	6.00	15.00
	1829	—	3.00	4.00	6.00	15.00
	1830	—	3.00	4.00	6.00	15.00
	1832	—	3.00	4.00	6.00	15.00
	1859 large LIBRE	—	3.00	4.00	6.00	15.00
	1859 small LIBRE	—	3.00	4.00	6.00	15.00
	1860	—	3.00	4.00	6.00	15.00

Rev. leg: REPUBLICA MEXICANA

KM#	Date	Mintage	Good	VG	Fine	VF
360	1862	1,367	3.00	4.00	6.00	10.00
	1862 LIBR	Inc. Ab.	3.00	4.00	6.00	10.00

Milled edge
Obv. leg: ESTADO LIBRE Y SOBERANO DE S.L. POTOSI
Rev. leg: LIBERTAD Y REFORMA

KM#	Date	Mintage	Good	VG	Fine	VF
361	1867	3.177	3.00	4.00	7.00	20.00
	1867 AFG	I.A.	3.00	4.00	7.00	20.00
			Plain edge			
362	1867	Inc. Ab.	3.00	4.00	7.00	20.00
	1867 AFG	I.A.	3.00	4.00	7.00	20.00

Mint: Sinaloa
Obv. leg: ESTADO LIBRE Y SOBERANO DE SINALOA

KM#	Date	Mintage	Good	VG	Fine	VF
363	1847	—	3.00	5.00	8.00	20.00
	1848	—	3.00	5.00	8.00	20.00
	1859	—	2.00	3.00	4.00	9.00
	1861	—	2.00	3.00	4.00	9.00
	1862	—	2.00	3.00	4.00	9.00
	1863	—	2.50	3.50	5.00	10.00
	1864/3	—	2.50	3.50	5.00	10.00
	1864	—	2.00	3.00	4.00	9.00
	1865	—	2.00	3.00	4.00	9.00
	1866/5	7.401	2.50	3.50	5.00	10.00
	1866	Inc. Ab.	2.00	3.00	4.00	9.00

BRASS

KM#	Date	Mintage	Good	VG	Fine	VF
363a	1847	—	5.00	10.00	20.00	50.00

COPPER
Mint: Sonora
Obv. leg: EST.D.SONORA UNA CUART

KM#	Date	Mintage	Good	VG	Fine	VF
364	1831	—	—	—	Rare	—
	1832	—	3.00	5.00	9.00	50.00
	1833/2	—	2.50	4.00	7.00	40.00
	1833	—	2.50	4.00	7.00	40.00
	1834	—	2.50	4.00	7.00	40.00
	1835/3	—	2.50	4.00	7.00	40.00
	1835	—	2.50	4.00	7.00	40.00
	1836	—	2.50	4.00	7.00	40.00

Obv. leg: ESTO.LIBE.Y SOBO.DE SONORA

KM#	Date	Mintage	Good	VG	Fine	VF
365	1859	—	3.00	5.00	8.00	20.00
	1861/59	—	4.00	6.50	11.00	25.00
	1861	—	3.00	5.00	8.00	20.00
	1862	—	3.00	5.00	8.00	20.00
	1863/2	—	7.00	15.00	30.00	50.00

BRASS
Mint: Zacatecas
Obv. leg: ESTO LIBE FEDO DE ZACATECAS

KM#	Date	Mintage	Good	VG	Fine	VF
366	1824	—	—	—	Rare	—
	1825	—	3.00	5.00	8.00	20.00
	1826	—	100.00	150.00	200.00	300.00
	1827/17	—	3.00	5.00	8.00	20.00
	1829	—	3.00	5.00	8.00	20.00
	1830	—	3.00	5.00	8.00	20.00
	1831	—	50.00	100.00	125.00	250.00
	1832	—	3.00	5.00	8.00	20.00
	1833	—	3.00	5.00	8.00	20.00
	1834	—	—	—	Rare	—
	1835	—	3.00	5.00	8.00	20.00
	1846	—	3.00	5.00	8.00	20.00
	1847	—	3.00	5.00	8.00	20.00
	1852	—	3.00	5.00	8.00	20.00
	1853	—	3.00	5.00	8.00	20.00
	1855	—	5.00	10.00	20.00	65.00
	1858	—	3.00	5.00	8.00	20.00
	1859	—	3.00	5.00	8.00	20.00
	1860	—	100.00	150.00	200.00	300.00
	1862/57	—	3.50	5.00	8.00	20.00
	1862/59/7	—	10.00	20.00	40.00	80.00
	1862	—	3.00	5.00	8.00	20.00
366	1863/2	—	3.00	5.00	8.00	20.00
	1863	—	3.00	5.00	8.00	20.00
	1864/58	—	5.00	10.00	25.00	60.00

COPPER
Obv. leg: DEPARTAMENTO DE ZACATECAS

KM#	Date	Mintage	Good	VG	Fine	VF
367	1836	—	5.00	8.00	12.00	25.00
	1845	—	—	—	Rare	—
	1846	—	3.00	5.00	8.00	20.00

SILVER SERIES

0.8450 g, .903 SILVER, .0245 oz ASW
Mint mark: CA

KM#	Date	Mintage	VG	Fine	VF	XF
368	1843 RG	—	75.00	125.00	300.00	500.00

Mint mark: C

KM#	Date	Mintage	VG	Fine	VF	XF
368.1	1855 LR	—	50.00	100.00	200.00	400.00

Mint mark: Do

KM#	Date	Mintage	VG	Fine	VF	XF
368.2	1842 LR	—	12.00	20.00	40.00	125.00
	1843 LR	—	20.00	25.00	60.00	150.00

Mint mark: Ga

KM#	Date	Mintage	VG	Fine	VF	XF
368.3	1842 JG	—	2.50	5.50	8.00	20.00
	1843/2 JG	—	—	—	—	—
	1843 JG	—	6.00	9.00	12.50	30.00
	1843 MC	—	4.00	6.50	9.00	25.00
	1844 MC	—	4.00	6.50	9.00	25.00
	1844 LR	—	2.50	5.00	7.50	15.00
	1845 LR	—	2.50	4.50	7.50	15.00
	1846 LR	—	5.00	8.00	10.00	25.00
	1847 LR	—	4.00	6.50	9.00	25.00
	1848 LR	—	—	—	Rare	—
	1850 LR	—	—	—	Rare	—
	1851 LR	—	6.00	10.00	20.00	50.00
	1852 LR	—	50.00	100.00	135.00	200.00
	1854/3 LR	—	50.00	100.00	135.00	200.00
	1854 LR	—	5.00	10.00	12.50	30.00
	1855 LR	—	5.00	8.00	10.00	30.00
	1857 LR	—	6.50	10.00	15.00	27.50
	1862 LR	—	5.50	10.00	15.00	30.00

Mint mark: GC

KM#	Date	Mintage	VG	Fine	VF	XF
368.4	1844 LR	—	50.00	75.00	125.00	200.00

Mint mark: Go

KM#	Date	Mintage	VG	Fine	VF	XF
368.5	1842 PM	—	4.00	6.00	10.00	20.00
	1842 LR	—	2.00	4.00	8.00	15.00
	1843/2 LR	—	4.00	6.00	10.00	20.00
	1843 LR	—	2.00	4.00	8.00	15.00
	1844/3 LR	—	—	—	—	—
	1844 LR	—	2.00	4.00	8.00	15.00
	1845 LR	—	8.00	15.00	30.00	60.00
	1846/5 LR	—	—	—	—	—
	1846 LR	—	4.00	6.00	10.00	20.00
	1847 LR	—	2.00	4.00	8.00	15.00
	1848/7 LR	—	2.00	4.00	8.00	15.00
	1848 LR	—	2.00	4.00	8.00	15.00
	1849/7 LR	—	8.00	15.00	30.00	60.00
	1849 LR	—	2.00	4.00	8.00	15.00
	1850 LR	—	2.00	4.00	8.00	15.00
	1851 LR	—	2.00	4.00	8.00	15.00
	1852 LR	—	2.00	4.00	8.00	15.00
	1853 LR	—	2.00	4.00	8.00	15.00
	1855 LR	—	4.00	8.00	15.00	30.00
	1856/4 LR	—	—	—	—	—
	1856 LR	—	5.00	10.00	20.00	35.00
	1862/1 LR	—	3.00	5.00	10.00	20.00
	1862 LR	—	2.00	4.00	8.00	15.00
	1863 LR	—	2.00	4.00	8.00	15.00

Mint mark: Mo

KM#	Date	Mintage	VG	Fine	VF	XF
368.6	1842 LR	—	2.00	4.00	8.00	15.00
	1843 LR	—	2.00	4.00	8.00	15.00
	1844/3 LR	—	8.00	12.00	20.00	40.00
	1844 LR	—	4.00	6.00	10.00	20.00
	1845 LR	—	4.00	6.00	10.00	20.00
	1846 LR	—	2.00	4.00	8.00	15.00
	1850 LR	—	5.00	10.00	20.00	35.00
	1858 LR	—	4.00	8.00	15.00	30.00
	1859 LR	—	4.00	6.00	10.00	20.00
	1860 LR	—	4.00	6.00	10.00	20.00
	1861 LR	—	4.00	6.00	10.00	20.00
	1862 LR	—	4.00	6.00	10.00	20.00
	1863/53 LR	—	—	—	—	—
	1863 LR	—	4.00	6.00	10.00	20.00

Mint mark: S.L.Pi

KM#	Date	Mintage	VG	Fine	VF	XF
368.7	1842	—	2.00	4.00	8.00	15.00
	1843/2	—	4.00	6.00	10.00	20.00
	1843	—	2.00	4.00	8.00	15.00
	1844	—	2.00	4.00	8.00	15.00
	1845/3	—	4.00	6.00	10.00	25.00
368.7	1845/4	—	4.00	6.00	10.00	25.00
	1845	—	2.00	4.00	8.00	15.00
	1847/5	—	4.00	6.00	10.00	20.00
	1847	—	2.00	4.00	8.00	15.00
	1851/47	—	4.00	8.00	15.00	30.00
	1854	—	125.00	200.00	275.00	400.00
	1856	—	4.00	8.00	15.00	30.00
	1857	—	5.00	10.00	20.00	35.00
	1862/57	—	10.00	20.00	40.00	85.00

Mint mark: Zs

KM#	Date	Mintage	VG	Fine	VF	XF
368.8	1842/1 LR	—	4.00	8.00	15.00	30.00
	1842 LR	—	4.00	6.00	10.00	20.00

1/2 REAL

1.6900 g, .903 SILVER, .0490 oz ASW
Mint mark: Mo
Obv: Hooked neck eagle

KM#	Date	Mintage	Fine	VF	XF	Unc
369	1824 JM	—	40.00	60.00	125.00	500.00

Mint mark: A

KM#	Date	Mintage	VG	Fine	VF	XF
370	1862 PG	—	—	—	Rare	—

Mint mark: Ca
Obv: Facing eagle

KM#	Date	Mintage	VG	Fine	VF	XF
370.1	1844 RG	—	75.00	125.00	175.00	275.00
	1845 RG	—	75.00	125.00	150.00	250.00

Mint mark: C, Co

KM#	Date	Mintage	VG	Fine	VF	XF
370.2	1846 CE	—	30.00	50.00	75.00	150.00
	1848/7 CE	—	15.00	25.00	45.00	90.00
	1849/8 CE	—	15.00	25.00	45.00	90.00
	1849 CE	—	—	—	—	—
	1852 CE	—	12.50	20.00	40.00	80.00
	1853/1 CE	—	12.50	20.00	40.00	80.00
	1854 CE	—	20.00	35.00	50.00	100.00
	1856 CE	—	12.50	20.00	40.00	80.00
	1857/6 CE	—	20.00	35.00	50.00	100.00
	1857 CE	—	15.00	25.00	45.00	90.00
	1858 CE (error 1 for 1/2)	—	12.50	20.00	40.00	80.00
	1860/59 PV	—	20.00	35.00	50.00	100.00
	1860 PV	—	12.50	20.00	40.00	80.00
	1861 PV	—	12.50	20.00	40.00	80.00
	1863 CE (error 1 for 1/2)	—	15.00	25.00	45.00	90.00
	1867 CE	—	12.50	20.00	40.00	80.00
	1869 CE (error 1 for 1/2)	—	12.50	20.00	40.00	80.00

Mint mark: D, Do

KM#	Date	Mintage	VG	Fine	VF	XF
370.3	1832 RM	—	125.00	225.00	350.00	600.00
	1832 RM/L	—	—	—	—	—
	1833/2 RM/L	—	75.00	100.00	150.00	225.00
	1833/1 RM/L	—	12.50	20.00	40.00	80.00
	1833 RM	—	25.00	40.00	75.00	150.00
	1834/1 RM	—	25.00	40.00	75.00	150.00
	1834 RM	—	12.50	20.00	40.00	80.00
	1837/1 RM	—	12.50	20.00	40.00	80.00
	1837/4 RM	—	12.50	20.00	40.00	80.00
	1837/6 RM	—	12.50	20.00	40.00	80.00
	1841/33 RM	—	15.00	25.00	50.00	100.00
	1842/32 RM	—	12.50	20.00	40.00	80.00
	1842 RM	—	12.50	20.00	40.00	80.00
	1842 RM 8R (error)	—	12.50	20.00	40.00	80.00
	1842 RM 1/2/8R	—	12.50	20.00	40.00	80.00
	1843/33 RM	—	15.00	25.00	50.00	100.00
	1843 RM	—	—	—	—	—
	1845/31 RM	—	12.50	20.00	40.00	80.00
	1845/34 RM	—	12.50	20.00	40.00	80.00
	1845/35 RM	—	12.50	20.00	40.00	80.00
	1845 RM	—	15.00	25.00	50.00	100.00
	1846 RM	—	30.00	50.00	80.00	200.00
	1848/5 RM	—	35.00	55.00	110.00	250.00
	1848/36 RM	—	25.00	40.00	75.00	200.00
	1849 JMR	—	25.00	40.00	75.00	200.00
	1850 RM	—	—	—	Rare	—
	1850 JMR	—	25.00	40.00	75.00	200.00
	1851 JMR	—	20.00	35.00	50.00	100.00
	1852/1 JMR	—	65.00	125.00	250.00	600.00
	1852 JMR	—	30.00	50.00	80.00	200.00
	1853 CP	—	12.50	20.00	40.00	80.00
	1854 CP	—	25.00	40.00	75.00	200.00
	1855 CP	—	25.00	40.00	60.00	150.00
	1856/5 CP	—	20.00	35.00	50.00	100.00
	1857 CP	—	20.00	35.00	50.00	100.00
	1858/7 CP	—	20.00	35.00	50.00	100.00
	1859 CP	—	20.00	35.00	50.00	100.00
	1860/59 CP	—	40.00	65.00	135.00	300.00
	1861 CP	—	125.00	200.00	300.00	600.00
	1862 CP	—	25.00	40.00	60.00	125.00

KM#	Date	Mintage	Fine	VF	XF	Unc
370.3	1864 LT	—	50.00	100.00	200.00	450.00
	1869 CP	—	40.00	65.00	125.00	275.00

Mint mark: EoMo

KM#	Date	Mintage	Fine	VF	XF	Unc
370.4	1829 LF	—	175.00	300.00	450.00	1300.

Mint mark: Ga

KM#	Date	Mintage	Fine	VF	XF	Unc
370.5	1825 FS	—	25.00	40.00	75.00	150.00
	1826 FS	—	10.00	15.00	35.00	70.00
	1828/7 FS	—	12.50	20.00	40.00	80.00
	1829 FS	—	7.50	15.00	30.00	60.00
	1830/29 FS	—	40.00	60.00	100.00	200.00
	1831 LP	—	—	—	Rare	—
	1832 FS	—	10.00	20.00	35.00	70.00
	1834/3 FS	—	65.00	100.00	175.00	250.00
	1834 FS	—	10.00	20.00	35.00	70.00
	1835/4/3 FS/LP	—	15.00	25.00	40.00	80.00
	1837/6 JG	—	50.00	100.00	150.00	250.00
	1838/7 JG	—	15.00	25.00	40.00	80.00
	1839/8 JG/FS	—	35.00	75.00	150.00	250.00
	1839 MC	—	10.00	20.00	35.00	70.00
	1840/39 MC/JG	—	—	—	—	—
	1840 MC	—	15.00	25.00	40.00	80.00
	1841 MC	—	20.00	35.00	50.00	100.00
	1842/1 JG	—	15.00	25.00	40.00	80.00
	1842 JG	—	10.00	20.00	35.00	70.00
	1843/2 JG	—	15.00	30.00	50.00	100.00
	1843 JG	—	10.00	20.00	35.00	70.00
	1843 MC/JG	—	10.00	20.00	35.00	70.00
	1843 MC	—	10.00	20.00	35.00	70.00
	1844 MC	—	10.00	20.00	35.00	70.00
	1845 MC	—	10.00	20.00	35.00	70.00
	1845 JG	—	10.00	20.00	35.00	70.00
	1846 MC	—	10.00	20.00	35.00	70.00
	1846 JG	—	10.00	20.00	35.00	70.00
	1847 JG	—	10.00	20.00	35.00	70.00
	1848/7 JG	—	10.00	20.00	35.00	70.00
	1849 JG	—	10.00	20.00	35.00	70.00
	1850/49 JG	—	—	—	—	—
	1850 JG	—	10.00	20.00	35.00	70.00
	1851/0 JG	—	10.00	20.00	35.00	70.00
	1852 JG	—	10.00	20.00	35.00	70.00
	1853 JG	—	10.00	20.00	35.00	70.00
	1854 JG	—	10.00	20.00	35.00	70.00
	1855/4 JG	—	10.00	20.00	35.00	70.00
	1855 JG	—	10.00	20.00	35.00	70.00
	1856 JG	—	10.00	20.00	35.00	70.00
	1857 JG	—	10.00	20.00	35.00	70.00
	1858/7 JG	—	10.00	20.00	35.00	70.00
	1858 JG	—	10.00	20.00	35.00	70.00
	1859/7 JG	—	10.00	20.00	35.00	70.00
	1860/59 JG	—	10.00	20.00	35.00	70.00
	1861 JG	—	5.00	12.50	25.00	50.00
	1862/1 JG	—	15.00	25.00	40.00	80.00

Mint mark: GC

KM#	Date	Mintage	Fine	VF	XF	Unc
370.6	1844 MP	—	50.00	100.00	150.00	350.00
	1845 MP	—	25.00	50.00	100.00	200.00
	1846 MP	—	25.00	50.00	100.00	200.00
	1847 MP	—	25.00	50.00	100.00	300.00
	1848 MP	—	20.00	40.00	75.00	150.00
	1849 MP	—	25.00	50.00	100.00	200.00
	1850 MP	—	30.00	60.00	125.00	250.00
	1851 MP	—	25.00	50.00	100.00	200.00

Mint mark: Go

KM#	Date	Mintage	Fine	VF	XF	Unc
370.7	1826 MJ	—	125.00	250.00	400.00	1000.
	1827/6 MJ	—	7.50	15.00	30.00	75.00
	1828/7 MJ	—	7.50	15.00	30.00	75.00
	1828 MJ denomination 2/1	—	—	—	—	—
	1828 JG	—	—	—	—	—
	1828 MR	—	50.00	100.00	150.00	250.00
	1829/8 MJ	—	5.00	10.00	25.00	50.00
	1829 MJ	—	5.00	10.00	25.00	50.00
	1829 MJ reversed N in MEXICANA	—	5.00	10.00	25.00	50.00
	1830 MJ	—	5.00	10.00	25.00	50.00
	1831/29 MJ	—	15.00	30.00	60.00	150.00
	1831 MJ	—	10.00	20.00	40.00	80.00
	1832/1 MJ	—	7.50	15.00	30.00	75.00
	1832 MJ	—	7.50	15.00	30.00	75.00
	1833 MJ round top 3	—	10.00	20.00	40.00	80.00
	1833 MJ flat top 3	—	10.00	20.00	40.00	80.00
	1834 PJ	—	5.00	10.00	25.00	50.00
	1835 PJ	—	5.00	10.00	25.00	50.00
	1836/5 PJ	—	7.50	15.00	30.00	75.00
	1836 PJ	—	5.00	10.00	25.00	50.00
	1837 PJ	—	5.00	10.00	25.00	50.00
	1838/7 PJ	—	5.00	10.00	25.00	50.00
	1839 PJ	—	5.00	10.00	25.00	50.00
	1839 PJ (error: REPUBLIGA)	—	5.00	10.00	25.00	50.00
	1840/39 PJ	—	7.50	10.00	25.00	75.00
	1840 PJ straight J	—	5.00	10.00	25.00	50.00
	1840 PJ curved J	—	5.00	10.00	25.00	50.00
	1841/31 PJ	—	5.00	10.00	25.00	50.00
	1841 PJ	—	5.00	10.00	25.00	50.00
	1842/1 PJ	—	5.00	10.00	25.00	50.00
	1842/1 PM	—	5.00	10.00	25.00	50.00
	1842 PM/J	—	5.00	10.00	25.00	50.00
	1842 PJ	—	5.00	10.00	25.00	50.00
	1842 PM	—	5.00	10.00	25.00	50.00
	1843/33 PM 1/2 over 8					
370.7		—	5.00	10.00	25.00	50.00
	1843 PM convex wings	—	5.00	10.00	25.00	50.00
	1843 PM concave wings	—	5.00	10.00	25.00	50.00
	1844/3 PM	—	5.00	10.00	25.00	50.00
	1844 PM	—	10.00	20.00	40.00	90.00
	1845/4 PM	—	5.00	10.00	25.00	50.00
	1845 PM	—	5.00	10.00	25.00	50.00
	1846/4 PM	—	5.00	10.00	25.00	50.00
	1846/5 PM	—	5.00	10.00	25.00	50.00
	1846 PM	—	5.00	10.00	25.00	50.00
	1847/6 PM	—	7.50	15.00	30.00	60.00
	1847 PM	—	7.50	15.00	30.00	60.00
	1848/35 PM	—	5.00	10.00	25.00	50.00
	1848 PM	—	5.00	10.00	25.00	50.00
	1848 PF/M	—	5.00	10.00	25.00	50.00
	1849/39 PF	—	5.00	10.00	25.00	50.00
	1849 PF	—	5.00	10.00	25.00	50.00
	1849 PF (error: MEXCANA)	—	5.00	10.00	25.00	50.00
	1850 PF	—	5.00	10.00	25.00	50.00
	1851 PF	—	5.00	10.00	25.00	50.00
	1852/1 PF	—	5.00	10.00	25.00	50.00
	1852 PF	—	2.50	7.50	17.50	40.00
	1853 PF/R	—	5.00	10.00	25.00	50.00
	1853 PF	—	5.00	10.00	25.00	50.00
	1854 PF	—	5.00	10.00	25.00	50.00
	1855 PF	—	5.00	10.00	25.00	50.00
	1856/4 PF	—	5.00	10.00	25.00	50.00
	1856/5 PF	—	5.00	10.00	25.00	50.00
	1856 PF	—	5.00	10.00	25.00	50.00
	1857/6 PF	—	5.00	10.00	25.00	50.00
	1857 PF	—	5.00	10.00	25.00	50.00
	1858/7 PF	—	7.50	15.00	30.00	60.00
	1858 PF	—	5.00	10.00	25.00	50.00
	1859 PF	—	5.00	10.00	25.00	50.00
	1860 PF small 1/2	—	5.00	10.00	25.00	50.00
	1860 PF large 1/2	—	5.00	10.00	25.00	50.00
	1860/59 PF	—	5.00	10.00	25.00	50.00
	1861 PF small 1/2	—	5.00	10.00	25.00	50.00
	1861 PF large 1/2	—	5.00	10.00	25.00	50.00
	1862/1 YE	—	5.00	10.00	25.00	50.00
	1862 YE	—	2.50	7.50	17.50	40.00
	1862 YF	—	5.00	10.00	25.00	50.00
	1867 YF	—	2.50	7.50	17.50	40.00
	1868 YF	—	2.50	7.50	17.50	40.00

NOTE: Varieties exist.

Mint mark: Ho

KM#	Date	Mintage	Fine	VF	XF	Unc
370.8	1839 PP	—	—	—	Unique	—
	1862 FM	—	65.00	125.00	200.00	400.00
	1867 PR/FM 6/inverted 6, & 7/1	—	100.00	175.00	250.00	450.00

Mint mark: Mo

KM#	Date	Mintage	Fine	VF	XF	Unc
370.9	1825 JM	—	10.00	20.00	40.00	80.00
	1826/5 JM	—	10.00	20.00	40.00	80.00
	1826 JM	—	5.00	10.00	20.00	60.00
	1827/6 JM	—	5.00	10.00	20.00	60.00
	1827 JM	—	5.00	10.00	20.00	60.00
	1828/7 JM	—	7.50	15.00	25.00	75.00
	1828 JM	—	10.00	20.00	40.00	80.00
	1829 JM	—	7.50	15.00	25.00	75.00
	1830 JM	—	5.00	10.00	20.00	60.00
	1831 JM	—	5.00	10.00	20.00	60.00
	1832 JM	—	7.50	12.50	27.50	60.00
	1833 MJ	—	7.50	12.50	27.50	60.00
	1834 ML	—	5.00	10.00	20.00	60.00
	1835 ML	—	5.00	10.00	20.00	60.00
	1836/5 ML/MF	—	7.50	15.00	25.00	65.00
	1836 ML	—	7.50	15.00	25.00	65.00
	1838 ML	—	5.00	10.00	20.00	60.00
	1839/8 ML	—	5.00	10.00	25.00	65.00
	1839 ML	—	5.00	10.00	20.00	50.00
	1840 ML	—	5.00	10.00	20.00	50.00
	1841 ML	—	5.00	10.00	20.00	50.00
	1842 ML	—	5.00	10.00	20.00	50.00
	1842 MM	—	5.00	10.00	20.00	50.00
	1843 MM	—	10.00	20.00	40.00	80.00
	1844 MF	—	5.00	10.00	20.00	50.00
	1845/4 MF	—	5.00	10.00	25.00	60.00
	1845 MF	—	5.00	10.00	20.00	50.00
	1846 MF	—	5.00	10.00	20.00	50.00
	1847 RC	—	10.00	20.00	40.00	80.00
	1848/7 GC/RC	—	5.00	10.00	20.00	50.00
	1849 GC	—	5.00	10.00	20.00	50.00
	1850 GC	—	5.00	10.00	20.00	50.00
	1851 GC	—	5.00	10.00	20.00	50.00
	1852 GC	—	5.00	10.00	20.00	50.00
	1853 GC	—	5.00	10.00	20.00	50.00
	1854 GC	—	5.00	10.00	20.00	50.00
	1855 GC	—	5.00	10.00	20.00	50.00
	1855 GF/GC	—	7.50	12.50	25.00	65.00
	1856/5 GF	—	7.50	12.50	25.00	65.00
	1857 GF	—	5.00	10.00	20.00	50.00
	1858 FH	—	3.00	5.00	12.50	40.00
	1858/9 FH	—	5.00	10.00	20.00	50.00
	1859 FH	—	3.00	6.00	15.00	50.00
	1860 FH/GC	—	5.00	10.00	20.00	50.00
	1860/59 FH	—	7.50	12.50	25.00	65.00
	1860 FH	—	3.00	6.00	15.00	50.00
	1860 TH	—	5.00	10.00	20.00	50.00
	1861 CH	—	3.00	6.00	15.00	45.00
370.9	1862/52 CH	—	5.00	10.00	20.00	50.00
	1862 CH	—	3.00	6.00	15.00	45.00
	1863/55 TH/GC	—	5.00	10.00	20.00	50.00
	1863 CH/GC	—	5.00	10.00	20.00	50.00
	1863 CH	—	3.00	6.00	15.00	45.00

Mint mark: Pi

KM#	Date	Mintage	Fine	VF	XF	Unc
370.10	1831 JS	—	7.50	12.50	25.00	65.00
	1841/36 JS	—	20.00	40.00	75.00	125.00
	1842/1 PS	—	20.00	40.00	75.00	125.00
	1842/1 PS P/J	—	60.00	80.00	150.00	300.00
	1842 PS/JS	—	50.00	75.00	125.00	250.00
	1842 JS	—	20.00	40.00	75.00	125.00
	1843/2 PS	—	17.50	25.00	40.00	80.00
	1843 PS	—	15.00	25.00	35.00	70.00
	1843 AM	—	10.00	15.00	25.00	60.00
	1844 AM	—	10.00	15.00	30.00	65.00
	1845 AM	—	250.00	375.00	500.00	1500.
	1846/5 AM	—	40.00	75.00	125.00	200.00
	1847/6 AM	—	15.00	25.00	40.00	80.00
	1848 AM	—	15.00	25.00	40.00	80.00
	1849 MC/AM	—	15.00	25.00	40.00	80.00
	1849 MC	—	12.50	20.00	35.00	70.00
	1850/49 MC	—	—	—	—	—
	1850Pi MC	—	10.00	15.00	25.00	60.00
	1850P MC	—	—	—	—	—
	1851 MC	—	10.00	15.00	25.00	60.00
	1852 MC	—	10.00	20.00	30.00	65.00
	1853 MC	—	7.50	12.50	20.00	60.00
	1854 MC	—	7.50	12.50	20.00	60.00
	1855 MC	—	15.00	20.00	35.00	70.00
	1856 MC	—	15.00	25.00	50.00	100.00
	1857 MC	—	7.50	12.50	20.00	60.00
	1857 PS	—	10.00	15.00	30.00	65.00
	1858 MC	—	12.50	20.00	35.00	70.00
	1858 PS	—	12.50	20.00	35.00	70.00
	1859 MC	—	—	—	Rare	—
	1860/59 PS	—	12.50	20.00	35.00	70.00
	1861 RO	—	10.00	15.00	30.00	60.00
	1862/1 RO	—	15.00	25.00	50.00	125.00
	1862 RO	—	15.00	25.00	50.00	125.00
	1863/2 RO	—	15.00	25.00	45.00	100.00

Mint mark: Z, Zs

KM#	Date	Mintage	Fine	VF	XF	Unc
370.11	1826 AZ	—	5.00	10.00	20.00	60.00
	1826 AO	—	5.00	10.00	20.00	60.00
	1827 AO	—	5.00	10.00	20.00	60.00
	1828/7 AO	—	5.00	10.00	20.00	60.00
	1829 AO	—	5.00	10.00	20.00	60.00
	1830 OV	—	5.00	10.00	20.00	60.00
	1831 OV	—	25.00	50.00	75.00	150.00
	1831 OM	—	5.00	10.00	20.00	60.00
	1832 OM	—	5.00	10.00	20.00	60.00
	1833 OM	—	5.00	10.00	20.00	60.00
	1834 OM	—	5.00	10.00	20.00	60.00
	1835/4 OM	—	5.00	10.00	20.00	60.00
	1835 OM	—	5.00	10.00	20.00	60.00
	1836 OM	—	5.00	10.00	20.00	60.00
	1837 OM	—	10.00	20.00	40.00	80.00
	1838 OM	—	5.00	10.00	20.00	60.00
	1839 OM	—	7.50	15.00	30.00	65.00
	1840 OM	—	10.00	25.00	45.00	90.00
	1841 OM	—	10.00	25.00	45.00	90.00
	1842/1 OM	—	5.00	10.00	20.00	60.00
	1842 OM	—	5.00	10.00	20.00	60.00
	1843 OM	—	40.00	75.00	115.00	250.00
	1844 OM	—	5.00	10.00	20.00	60.00
	1845 OM	—	5.00	10.00	20.00	60.00
	1846 OM	—	7.50	15.00	30.00	65.00
	1847 OM	—	5.00	10.00	20.00	50.00
	1848 OM	—	5.00	10.00	20.00	50.00
	1849 OM	—	5.00	10.00	20.00	50.00
	1850 OM	—	5.00	10.00	20.00	50.00
	1851 OM	—	5.00	10.00	20.00	50.00
	1852 OM	—	5.00	10.00	20.00	50.00
	1853 OM	—	5.00	10.00	20.00	50.00
	1854/3 OM	—	5.00	10.00	20.00	50.00
	1854 OM	—	5.00	10.00	20.00	50.00
	1855/3 OM	—	7.50	15.00	30.00	65.00
	1855 OM	—	5.00	10.00	20.00	50.00
	1856 OM	—	5.00	10.00	20.00	50.00
	1857 MO	—	5.00	10.00	20.00	50.00
	1858 MO	—	5.00	10.00	20.00	50.00
	1859 MO	—	6.00	8.50	17.50	35.00
	1859 VL	—	6.00	8.50	17.50	40.00
	1860/50 VL inverted A for V	—	5.00	10.00	20.00	50.00
	1860/59 VL inverted A for V	—	5.00	10.00	20.00	50.00
	1860 MO	—	5.00	10.00	20.00	50.00
	1860 VL	—	5.00	10.00	20.00	50.00
	1861/0 VL inverted A for V	—	7.50	15.00	30.00	65.00
	1861 VL inverted A for V	—	5.00	10.00	20.00	50.00
	1862 VL inverted A for V	—	5.00	10.00	20.00	50.00
	1863/1 VL inverted A for V	—	7.50	15.00	30.00	65.00
	1863 VL inverted A for V	—	5.00	10.00	20.00	50.00
	1869 YH	—	5.00	10.00	20.00	50.00

REAL

3.3800 g, .903 SILVER, .0981 oz ASW

Mint mark: Do

KM#	Date	Mintage	Fine	VF	XF	Unc
371	1824 RL	—	2750.	3250.	4000.	5500.

Mint mark: Ca

KM#	Date	Mintage	Fine	VF	XF	Unc
372	1844 RG	—	500.00	1000.	1500.	2750.
	1845 RG	—	500.00	1000.	1500.	2750.
	1855 RG	—	100.00	150.00	225.00	450.00

Mint mark: C

KM#	Date	Mintage	Fine	VF	XF	Unc
372.1	1846 CE	—	12.50	25.00	40.00	110.00
	1848 CE	—	12.50	25.00	40.00	110.00
	1850 CE	—	12.50	25.00	40.00	110.00
	1851/0 CE	—	12.50	25.00	40.00	110.00
	1852/1 CE	—	7.50	15.00	30.00	100.00
	1853/2 CE	—	7.50	15.00	30.00	100.00
	1854 CE	—	7.50	15.00	30.00	100.00
	1856 CE	—	40.00	65.00	100.00	225.00
	1857/4 CE	—	10.00	20.00	35.00	100.00
	1857/6 CE	—	10.00	20.00	35.00	100.00
	1858 CE	—	5.00	7.50	15.00	100.00
	1859 CE	—	—	—	—	—
	1860 PV	—	5.00	7.50	15.00	100.00
	1861 PV	—	5.00	7.50	15.00	100.00
	1863 CE	3 known	—	—	1650.	2250.
	1869 CE	—	5.00	7.50	15.00	100.00

Mint mark: Do

KM#	Date	Mintage	Fine	VF	XF	Unc
372.2	1832/1 RM	—	5.00	10.00	20.00	90.00
	1832 RM/RL	—	10.00	15.00	30.00	100.00
	1832 RM	—	5.00	10.00	20.00	100.00
	1834/24 RM/RL	—	15.00	25.00	50.00	150.00
	1834/3 RM/RL	—	15.00	25.00	50.00	150.00
	1834 RM	—	10.00	20.00	40.00	110.00
	1836/4 RM	—	5.00	7.50	15.00	100.00
	1836 RM	—	5.00	7.50	15.00	100.00
	1837 RM	—	12.50	20.00	40.00	110.00
	1841 RM	—	7.50	15.00	30.00	100.00
	1842/32 RM	—	10.00	20.00	40.00	110.00
	1842 RM	—	7.50	15.00	30.00	100.00
	1843 RM	—	5.00	7.50	15.00	100.00
	1844/34 RM	—	15.00	25.00	45.00	125.00
	1845 RM	—	5.00	7.50	15.00	100.00
	1846 RM	—	7.50	15.00	30.00	100.00
	1847 RM	—	10.00	15.00	35.00	100.00
	1848/31 RM	—	10.00	15.00	35.00	100.00
	1848/33 RM	—	10.00	15.00	35.00	100.00
	1848/5 RM	—	10.00	15.00	35.00	100.00
	1848 RM	—	7.50	12.50	20.00	100.00
	1849/8 CM	—	10.00	15.00	30.00	100.00
	1850 JMR	—	15.00	25.00	45.00	125.00
	1851 JMR	—	15.00	25.00	45.00	120.00
	1852 JMR	—	15.00	25.00	45.00	120.00
	1853 CP	—	12.50	20.00	35.00	100.00
	1854/1 CP	—	10.00	15.00	25.00	100.00
	1854 CP	—	7.50	12.50	20.00	100.00
	1855 CP	—	10.00	15.00	25.00	100.00
	1856 CP	—	12.50	20.00	35.00	100.00
	1857 CP	—	12.50	20.00	35.00	100.00
	1858 CP	—	12.50	20.00	35.00	100.00
	1859 CP	—	7.50	12.50	20.00	100.00
	1860/59 CP	—	10.00	15.00	25.00	100.00
	1861 CP	—	15.00	25.00	40.00	110.00
	1862/1 CP	—	225.00	300.00	450.00	1250.
	1864 LT	—	15.00	25.00	40.00	110.00

Mint mark: EoMo

KM#	Date	Mintage	Fine	VF	XF	Unc
372.3	1828 LF	—	200.00	300.00	450.00	1500.

Mint mark: Ga

KM#	Date	Mintage	Fine	VF	XF	Unc
372.4	1826 FS	—	15.00	30.00	50.00	125.00
	1828/7 FS	—	15.00	30.00	50.00	125.00
	1829/8/7 FS	—	—	—	—	—
	1829 FS	—	15.00	30.00	50.00	125.00
	1830 FS	—	250.00	350.00	500.00	—
	1831 LP	—	15.00	30.00	50.00	125.00
	1831 LP/FS	—	300.00	450.00	600.00	—
	1832 FS	—	250.00	350.00	500.00	—
	1833/2 G FS	—	100.00	150.00	275.00	550.00
	1833 FS	—	75.00	125.00	225.00	500.00
	1834/3 FS	—	75.00	125.00	225.00	500.00
	1835 FS	—	—	—	—	—
	1837/6 JG/FS	—	12.50	20.00	35.00	100.00
	1838/7 JG/FS	—	12.50	20.00	35.00	100.00
	1839 JG	—	250.00	350.00	500.00	—
	1840 JG	—	12.50	20.00	35.00	100.00
372.4	1840 MC	—	7.50	12.50	25.00	70.00
	1841 MC	—	50.00	75.00	125.00	250.00
	1842/0 JG/MC	—	10.00	15.00	30.00	100.00
	1842 JG	—	7.50	12.50	20.00	100.00
	1843 JG	—	150.00	200.00	300.00	750.00
	1843 MC	—	5.00	7.50	15.00	100.00
	1844 MC	—	7.50	12.50	20.00	100.00
	1845 MC	—	10.00	15.00	25.00	100.00
	1845 JG	—	5.00	7.50	20.00	100.00
	1846 JG	—	12.50	20.00	35.00	100.00
	1847/6 JG	—	10.00	15.00	25.00	100.00
	1847 JG	—	10.00	15.00	25.00	100.00
	1848 JG	—	400.00	550.00	700.00	—
	1849 JG	—	7.50	12.50	20.00	100.00
	1850 JG	—	175.00	275.00	400.00	—
	1851 JG	—	10.00	15.00	25.00	100.00
	1852 JG	—	10.00	15.00	25.00	100.00
	1853/2 JG	—	10.00	15.00	25.00	100.00
	1854 JG	—	10.00	15.00	25.00	100.00
	1855 JG	—	15.00	25.00	40.00	100.00
	1856 JG	—	7.50	12.50	20.00	100.00
	1857/6 JG	—	12.50	20.00	35.00	100.00
	1858/7 JG	—	15.00	25.00	40.00	110.00
	1859/8 JG	—	25.00	50.00	75.00	150.00
	1860/59 JG	—	30.00	60.00	90.00	225.00
	1861/0 JG	—	20.00	30.00	50.00	125.00
	1861 JG	—	25.00	50.00	100.00	250.00
	1862 JG	—	7.50	12.50	20.00	100.00

Mint mark: GC

KM#	Date	Mintage	Fine	VF	XF	Unc
372.5	1844 MP	—	40.00	60.00	100.00	250.00
	1845 MP	—	40.00	60.00	100.00	250.00
	1846 MP	—	40.00	60.00	100.00	250.00
	1847 MP	—	40.00	60.00	100.00	250.00
	1848 MP	—	40.00	60.00	100.00	250.00
	1849/7 MP	—	40.00	60.00	100.00	250.00
	1849/8 MP	—	40.00	60.00	100.00	250.00
	1849 MP	—	40.00	60.00	100.00	250.00
	1850 MP	—	40.00	60.00	100.00	250.00
	1851 MP	—	40.00	60.00	100.00	250.00

Mint mark: Go

KM#	Date	Mintage	Fine	VF	XF	Unc
372.6	1826/5 JJ	—	5.00	7.50	15.00	85.00
	1826 MJ	—	4.00	6.00	15.00	85.00
	1827 MJ	—	4.00	6.00	15.00	65.00
	1827 JM	—	10.00	15.00	25.00	75.00
	1828/7 MR	—	4.00	6.00	15.00	85.00
	1828 MJ, straight J, small 8	—	4.00	6.00	15.00	85.00
	1828Go MJ, full J, large 8	—	4.00	6.00	15.00	85.00
	1828G MJ, full J, large 8	—	4.00	6.00	15.00	85.00
	1828 MR	—	4.00	6.00	15.00	85.00
	1829/8 MG small eagle	—	4.00	6.00	15.00	85.00
	1829 MJ small eagle	—	4.00	6.00	15.00	85.00
	1829 MJ large eagle	—	4.00	6.00	15.00	85.00
	1830 MJ small initials	—	4.00	6.00	15.00	85.00
	1830 MJ medium initials	—	4.00	6.00	15.00	85.00
	1830 MJ large initials	—	4.00	6.00	15.00	85.00
	1830 MJ reversed N in MEXICANA	—	4.00	6.00	15.00	85.00
	1831/0 MJ reversed N in MEXICANA	—	4.00	6.00	15.00	85.00
	1831 MJ	—	4.00	6.00	15.00	85.00
	1832/1 MJ	—	15.00	30.00	50.00	125.00
	1832 MJ	—	15.00	30.00	50.00	125.00
	1833 MJ top of 3 round	—	4.00	6.00	15.00	85.00
	1833 MJ top of 3 flat	—	4.00	6.00	15.00	85.00
	1834 PJ	—	4.00	6.00	15.00	85.00
	1835 PJ	—	7.50	12.50	20.00	85.00
	1836 PJ	—	4.00	6.00	15.00	85.00
	1837 PJ	—	15.00	30.00	50.00	125.00
	1838/7 PJ	—	10.00	20.00	35.00	85.00
	1839 PJ	—	4.00	6.00	15.00	85.00
	1840/39 PJ	—	4.00	6.00	15.00	85.00
	1840 PJ	—	4.00	6.00	15.00	85.00
	1841/31 PJ	—	10.00	20.00	35.00	85.00
	1841 PJ	—	4.00	6.00	15.00	85.00
	1842 PJ	—	4.00	6.00	15.00	85.00
	1842 PM	—	4.00	6.00	15.00	85.00
	1843 PM convex wings	—	4.00	6.00	15.00	85.00
	1843 PM concave wings	—	4.00	6.00	15.00	85.00
	1844 PM	—	4.00	6.00	15.00	85.00
	1845/4 PM	—	4.00	6.00	15.00	85.00
	1845 PM	—	4.00	6.00	15.00	85.00
	1846/5 PM	—	7.50	12.50	20.00	85.00
	1846 PM	—	4.00	6.00	15.00	85.00
	1847/6 PM	—	4.00	6.00	15.00	85.00
	1847 PM	—	4.00	6.00	15.00	85.00
	1848 PM	—	4.00	6.00	15.00	85.00
	1849 PF	—	10.00	20.00	35.00	85.00
	1850 PF	—	4.00	6.00	15.00	85.00
	1851 PF	—	10.00	20.00	35.00	100.00
	1853/2 PF	—	7.50	12.50	20.00	75.00
	1853 PF	—	4.00	6.00	15.00	75.00
	1854/3 PF	—	4.00	6.00	15.00	75.00
	1854 PF large eagle	—	4.00	6.00	15.00	75.00
372.6	1854 PF small eagle	—	4.00	6.00	15.00	75.00
	1855/3 PF	—	4.00	6.00	15.00	75.00
	1855/4 PF	—	4.00	6.00	15.00	75.00
	1855 PF	—	4.00	6.00	15.00	75.00
	1856/5 PF	—	4.00	6.00	15.00	75.00
	1856 PF	—	4.00	6.00	15.00	75.00
	1857/6 PF	—	4.00	6.00	15.00	75.00
	1857 PF	—	4.00	6.00	15.00	75.00
	1858 PF	—	4.00	6.00	15.00	75.00
	1859 PF	—	4.00	6.00	15.00	75.00
	1860/50 PF	—	4.00	6.00	15.00	75.00
	1860 PF	—	4.00	6.00	15.00	75.00
	1861 PF	—	4.00	6.00	15.00	75.00
	1862 YE	—	4.00	6.00	15.00	75.00
	1862/1 YF	—	7.50	12.50	20.00	75.00
	1862 YF	—	4.00	6.00	15.00	75.00
	1867 YF	—	4.00	6.00	15.00	75.00
	1868/7 YF	—	4.00	6.00	15.00	75.00

Mint mark: Ho

KM#	Date	Mintage	Fine	VF	XF	Unc
372.7	1867 small 7/1 PR	—	50.00	65.00	100.00	250.00
	1867 large 7/small 7 PR	—	50.00	65.00	100.00	250.00
	1868 PR	—	50.00	65.00	100.00	250.00

Mint mark: Mo

KM#	Date	Mintage	Fine	VF	XF	Unc
372.8	1825 JM	—	10.00	20.00	40.00	110.00
	1826 JM	—	7.50	15.00	30.00	100.00
	1827/6 JM	—	7.50	15.00	30.00	75.00
	1827 JM	—	5.00	10.00	20.00	70.00
	1828 JM	—	7.50	15.00	30.00	100.00
	1830/29 JM	—	5.00	10.00	20.00	100.00
	1830 JM	—	5.00	12.50	25.00	100.00
	1831 JM	—	100.00	200.00	300.00	750.00
	1832 JM	—	5.00	10.00	20.00	100.00
	1833/2 MJ	—	5.00	10.00	20.00	100.00
	1850 GC	—	5.00	10.00	20.00	100.00
	1852 GC	—	275.00	425.00	575.00	—
	1854 GC	—	10.00	20.00	40.00	100.00
	1855 GF	—	5.00	10.00	20.00	80.00
	1856 GF	—	5.00	10.00	20.00	80.00
	1857 GF	—	5.00	10.00	20.00	80.00
	1858 FH	—	5.00	10.00	20.00	80.00
	1859 FH	—	5.00	10.00	20.00	80.00
	1861 CH	—	5.00	10.00	20.00	80.00
	1862 CH	—	5.00	10.00	20.00	80.00
	1863/2 CH	—	7.50	12.50	25.00	80.00

Mint mark: Pi

KM#	Date	Mintage	Fine	VF	XF	Unc
372.9	1831 JS	—	5.00	10.00	20.00	125.00
	1837 JS	—	750.00	850.00	1000.	—
	1838/7 JS	—	250.00	300.00	375.00	—
	1838 JS	—	20.00	35.00	60.00	125.00
	1840/39 JS	—	7.50	15.00	30.00	125.00
	1840 JS	—	7.50	15.00	30.00	125.00
	1841 JS	—	7.50	15.00	30.00	125.00
	1842 JS	—	15.00	30.00	55.00	150.00
	1842 PS	—	5.00	10.00	20.00	125.00
	1843 PS	—	12.50	20.00	35.00	125.00
	1843 AM	—	40.00	60.00	80.00	150.00
	1844 AM	—	40.00	60.00	80.00	150.00
	1845 AM	—	7.50	15.00	30.00	125.00
	1846/5 AM	—	7.50	15.00	30.00	125.00
	1847/6 AM	—	7.50	15.00	30.00	125.00
	1847 AM	—	7.50	15.00	30.00	125.00
	1848/7 AM	—	7.50	15.00	30.00	125.00
	1849 PS	—	7.50	15.00	30.00	125.00
	1849/8 SP	—	60.00	100.00	150.00	—
	1849 SP	—	15.00	25.00	40.00	125.00
	1850 MC	—	5.00	10.00	20.00	125.00
	1851/0 MC	—	7.50	15.00	30.00	125.00
	1851 MC	—	7.50	15.00	30.00	125.00
	1852/1/0 MC	—	10.00	20.00	35.00	125.00
	1852 MC	—	7.50	15.00	30.00	125.00
	1853/1 MC	—	12.50	20.00	35.00	125.00
	1853 MC	—	10.00	20.00	35.00	125.00
	1854/3 MC	—	20.00	40.00	60.00	150.00
	1855/4 MC	—	20.00	40.00	60.00	150.00
	1855 MC	—	15.00	25.00	45.00	125.00
	1856 MC	—	15.00	25.00	45.00	125.00
	1857 PS	—	20.00	35.00	55.00	135.00
	1857 MC	—	20.00	40.00	60.00	150.00
	1858 MC	—	12.50	20.00	35.00	125.00
	1859 PS	—	10.00	15.00	30.00	125.00
	1860/59 PS	—	10.00	15.00	30.00	125.00
	1861 PS	—	7.50	12.50	20.00	125.00
	1861 RO	—	12.50	20.00	35.00	125.00
	1862/1 RO	—	12.50	20.00	35.00	90.00
	1862 RO	—	7.50	12.50	20.00	125.00

Mint mark: Zs

KM#	Date	Mintage	Fine	VF	XF	Unc
372.10	1826 AZ	—	5.00	12.50	35.00	120.00
	1826 AO	—	5.00	12.50	35.00	120.00
	1827 AO	—	5.00	12.50	35.00	120.00
	1828/7 AO	—	5.00	12.50	35.00	120.00
	1828 AO	—	5.00	12.50	35.00	120.00
	1828 AO inverted V for A	—	5.00	12.50	35.00	120.00
	1829 AO	—	5.00	12.50	35.00	120.00
	1830 ZsOV	—	5.00	12.50	35.00	120.00
	1830 ZOV	—	5.00	12.50	35.00	120.00
	1831 OV	—	5.00	12.50	35.00	120.00
	1831 OM	—	5.00	12.50	30.00	120.00
	1832 OM	—	5.00	12.50	30.00	120.00
	1833/2 OM	—	5.00	12.50	30.00	120.00
	1833 OM	—	5.00	12.50	30.00	120.00
	1834/3 OM	—	5.00	12.50	30.00	120.00
	1834 OM	—	5.00	12.50	30.00	120.00
	1835/4 OM	—	20.00	35.00	60.00	150.00

KM#	Date	Mintage	Fine	VF	XF	Unc
372.10	1835 OM	—	4.00	8.00	20.00	65.00
	1836/5 OM	—	4.00	8.00	20.00	85.00
	1836 OM	—	4.00	8.00	20.00	85.00
	1837 OM	—	4.00	8.00	20.00	85.00
	1838 OM	—	4.00	8.00	20.00	85.00
	1839 OM	—	4.00	8.00	20.00	85.00
	1840 OM	—	4.00	8.00	20.00	85.00
	1841 OM	—	20.00	40.00	60.00	150.00
	1842/1 OM	—	4.00	8.00	20.00	85.00
	1842 OM	—	4.00	8.00	20.00	85.00
	1843 OM	—	4.00	8.00	20.00	85.00
	1844 OM	—	4.00	8.00	20.00	85.00
	1845/4 OM	—	5.00	12.50	30.00	100.00
	1845 OM	—	4.00	8.00	20.00	85.00
	1846 OM old font and obv.					
		—	4.00	8.00	20.00	85.00
	1846 OM new font and obv.					
		—	4.00	8.00	20.00	85.00
	1847 OM	—	4.00	8.00	20.00	85.00
	1848 OM	—	4.00	8.00	20.00	85.00
	1849 OM	—	10.00	25.00	50.00	125.00
	1850 OM	—	4.00	6.00	15.00	85.00
	1851 OM	—	4.00	6.00	15.00	85.00
	1852 OM	—	4.00	6.00	15.00	85.00
	1853 OM	—	4.00	6.00	15.00	85.00
	1854/2 OM	—	4.00	6.00	15.00	85.00
	1854/3 OM	—	4.00	6.00	15.00	85.00
	1854 OM	—	4.00	6.00	15.00	85.00
	1855/4 OM	—	4.00	6.00	15.00	85.00
	1855 OM	—	4.00	6.00	15.00	85.00
	1855 MO	—	4.00	6.00	15.00	85.00
	1856 MO	—	4.00	6.00	15.00	85.00
	1856 MO/OM	—	4.00	6.00	15.00	85.00
	1857 MO	—	4.00	6.00	15.00	85.00
	1858 MO	—	4.00	6.00	15.00	85.00
	1859 MO	—	4.00	6.00	15.00	75.00
	1860 VL	—	4.00	6.00	15.00	75.00
	1861 VL	—	4.00	6.00	15.00	75.00
	1862 VL	—	5.00	12.50	30.00	100.00
	1868 JS	—	25.00	45.00	90.00	175.00
	1869 YH	—	4.00	8.00	20.00	75.00

2 REALES

6.7600 g, .903 SILVER, .1962 oz ASW

Mint mark: D, Do

Obv: Hooked-neck eagle.

KM#	Date	Mintage	Fine	VF	XF	Unc
373	1824 Do RL	—	50.00	125.00	300.00	850.00
	1824 D RL	—	100.00	200.00	500.00	1650.

Mint mark: Mo

KM#	Date	Mintage	Fine	VF	XF	Unc
373.1	1824 JM	—	20.00	50.00	100.00	350.00

Mint mark: A

Obv: Facing eagle, reeded edge.

KM#	Date	Mintage	Fine	VF	XF	Unc
374	1872 AM	.015	40.00	100.00	200.00	500.00

Mint mark: Ce

KM#	Date	Mintage	Fine	VF	XF	Unc
374.1	1863 ML	—	125.00	200.00	325.00	675.00

Mint mark: Ca

KM#	Date	Mintage	Fine	VF	XF	Unc
374.2	1832 MR	—	30.00	60.00	100.00	200.00
	1833 MR	—	30.00	60.00	125.00	500.00
	1834 MR	—	35.00	75.00	125.00	500.00
	1834 AM	—	35.00	75.00	125.00	500.00
	1835 AM	—	35.00	75.00	125.00	500.00
	1836 AM	—	20.00	40.00	80.00	200.00
	1844 RG	—	—	—	Unique	—
	1845 RG	—	20.00	40.00	80.00	200.00
	1855 RG	—	20.00	40.00	80.00	200.00

Mint mark: C

KM#	Date	Mintage	Fine	VF	XF	Unc
374.3	1846/1146 CE					
		—	25.00	50.00	100.00	225.00
	1847 CE	—	12.50	20.00	40.00	200.00
	1848 CE	—	12.50	20.00	40.00	200.00
	1850 CE	—	25.00	50.00	75.00	200.00
	1851 CE	—	12.50	20.00	40.00	200.00
	1852/1 CE	—	12.50	20.00	40.00	200.00
	1853/2 CE	—	12.50	20.00	40.00	200.00
	1854 CE	—	15.00	30.00	50.00	200.00
	1856 CE	—	20.00	35.00	70.00	200.00
	1857 CE	—	12.50	20.00	40.00	200.00
	1860 PV	—	12.50	20.00	40.00	200.00
	1861 PV	—	12.50	20.00	40.00	200.00
	1869 CE	—	12.50	20.00	40.00	200.00

Mint mark: Do

KM#	Date	Mintage	Fine	VF	XF	Unc
374.4	1826 RL	—	20.00	40.00	60.00	200.00
	1832 RM style of pre-1832					
374.4		—	20.00	40.00	60.00	200.00
	1832 RM style of post-1832					
		—	20.00	40.00	60.00	200.00
	1834/2 RM	—	20.00	40.00	60.00	200.00
	1834/3 RM	—	20.00	40.00	60.00	200.00
	1835/4 RM/RL					
		—	200.00	300.00	500.00	—
	1841/31 RM	—	50.00	75.00	125.00	250.00
	1841 RM	—	50.00	75.00	125.00	250.00
	1842/32 RM	—	12.50	20.00	40.00	200.00
	1843 RM/RL	—	12.50	20.00	40.00	200.00
	1844 RM	—	35.00	50.00	80.00	200.00
	1845/34 RM/RL					
		—	12.50	20.00	40.00	200.00
	1846/36 RM	—	100.00	150.00	200.00	350.00
	1848/36 RM	—	12.50	20.00	40.00	200.00
	1848/37 RM	—	12.50	20.00	40.00	200.00
	1848/7 RM	—	12.50	20.00	40.00	200.00
	1848 RM	—	12.50	20.00	40.00	200.00
	1849 CM/RM	—	12.50	20.00	40.00	200.00
	1849 CM	—	12.50	20.00	40.00	200.00
	1851 JMR/RL					
		—	12.50	20.00	40.00	200.00
	1852 JMR	—	12.50	20.00	40.00	200.00
	1854 CP/CR	—	30.00	50.00	80.00	200.00
	1855 CP	—	250.00	350.00	500.00	—
	1856 CP	—	100.00	150.00	250.00	500.00
	1858 CP	—	12.50	20.00	40.00	200.00
	1859/8 CP	—	12.50	20.00	40.00	200.00
	1861 CP	—	12.50	20.00	40.00	200.00

Mint mark: EoMo

KM#	Date	Mintage	Fine	VF	XF	Unc
374.5	1828 LF	—	325.00	525.00	900.00	2500.

Mint mark: Ga

KM#	Date	Mintage	Fine	VF	XF	Unc
374.6	1825 FS	—	20.00	40.00	80.00	200.00
	1826 FS	—	20.00	40.00	80.00	200.00
	1828/7 FS	—	100.00	150.00	225.00	400.00
	1829 FS	—	—	—	Rare	—
	1832/0 FS/LP					
		—	100.00	150.00	225.00	350.00
	1832 FS	—	12.50	20.00	40.00	200.00
	1833/2 FS/LP					
		—	12.50	20.00	40.00	200.00
	1834/27 FS	—	—	—	Rare	—
	1834 FS	—	12.50	20.00	40.00	200.00
	1835 FS	—	2100.	—	—	—
	1837 JG	—	12.50	20.00	40.00	200.00
	1838 JG	—	12.50	20.00	40.00	200.00
	1840/30 MC	—	12.50	20.00	40.00	200.00
	1841 MC	—	12.50	20.00	40.00	200.00
	1842/32 JG/MC					
		—	35.00	50.00	100.00	200.00
	1842 JG	—	20.00	40.00	80.00	200.00
	1843 JG	—	12.50	20.00	40.00	200.00
	1843 MC/JG	—	12.50	20.00	40.00	200.00
	1844 MC	—	12.50	20.00	40.00	200.00
	1845/3 MC/JG					
		—	12.50	20.00	40.00	200.00
	1845/4 MC/JG					
		—	12.50	20.00	40.00	200.00
	1845 JG	—	12.50	20.00	40.00	200.00
	1846 JG	—	12.50	20.00	40.00	200.00
	1847/6 JG	—	25.00	40.00	80.00	200.00
	1848/7 JG	—	12.50	20.00	40.00	200.00
	1849 JG	—	12.50	20.00	40.00	200.00
	1850/40 JG	—	12.50	20.00	40.00	200.00
	1851 JG	—	250.00	350.00	500.00	—
	1852 JG	—	12.50	20.00	40.00	200.00
	1853/1 JG	—	12.50	20.00	40.00	200.00
	1854/3 JG	—	250.00	350.00	500.00	—
	1855 JG	—	35.00	50.00	80.00	200.00
	1856 JG	—	12.50	20.00	40.00	200.00
	1857 JG	—	250.00	350.00	500.00	—
	1859/8 JG	—	12.50	20.00	40.00	200.00
	1859 JG	—	12.50	20.00	40.00	200.00
	1862/1 JG	—	12.50	20.00	40.00	200.00

Mint mark: GC

KM#	Date	Mintage	Fine	VF	XF	Unc
374.7	1844 MP	—	40.00	60.00	125.00	275.00
	1845 MP	—	40.00	60.00	125.00	275.00
	1846 MP	—	50.00	100.00	150.00	300.00
	1847 MP	—	35.00	50.00	100.00	250.00
	1848 MP	—	50.00	100.00	150.00	300.00
	1849 MP	—	50.00	100.00	150.00	300.00
	1850 MP	—	50.00	100.00	150.00	300.00
	1851/0 MP	—	50.00	100.00	150.00	300.00
	1851 MP	—	50.00	100.00	150.00	300.00

Mint mark: Go

KM#	Date	Mintage	Fine	VF	XF	Unc
374.8	1825 JJ	—	7.50	15.00	30.00	150.00
	1826/5 JJ	—	7.50	15.00	30.00	150.00
	1826 JJ	—	7.50	10.00	25.00	150.00
	1826 MJ	—	7.50	10.00	25.00	150.00
	1827/6 MJ	—	7.50	10.00	25.00	150.00
	1827 MJ	—	7.50	10.00	25.00	150.00
	1828/7 MR	—	7.50	15.00	30.00	150.00
	1828 MJ	—	7.50	10.00	20.00	150.00
	1828 JM	—	7.50	10.00	20.00	150.00
	1829 MJ	—	7.50	10.00	20.00	150.00
	1831 MJ	—	7.50	10.00	20.00	150.00
	1832 MJ	—	7.50	10.00	20.00	150.00
	1833 MJ	—	7.50	10.00	20.00	150.00
	1834 PJ	—	7.50	10.00	20.00	150.00
	1835/4 PJ	—	7.50	15.00	30.00	150.00
	1835 PJ	—	7.50	10.00	20.00	150.00
	1836 PJ	—	7.50	10.00	20.00	150.00
	1837/6 PJ	—	7.50	10.00	20.00	150.00
	1837 PJ	—	7.50	10.00	20.00	150.00
	1838/7 PJ	—	7.50	10.00	20.00	150.00
	1838 PJ	—	7.50	10.00	20.00	150.00
374.8	1839/8 PJ	—	7.50	15.00	30.00	150.00
	1839 PJ	—	7.50	10.00	20.00	150.00
	1840 PJ	—	7.50	10.00	20.00	150.00
	1841 PJ	—	7.50	10.00	20.00	150.00
	1842 PJ	—	7.50	10.00	20.00	150.00
	1842 PM/PJ	—	7.50	10.00	20.00	150.00
	1842 PM	—	7.50	10.00	20.00	150.00
	1843/2 PM concave wings, thin rays, sm. letters					
		—	7.50	10.00	20.00	150.00
	1843 PM convex wings, thick rays, lg. letters					
		—	7.50	10.00	20.00	150.00
	1844 PM	—	7.50	10.00	20.00	150.00
	1845/4 PM	—	7.50	10.00	20.00	150.00
	1845 PM	—	7.50	10.00	20.00	150.00
	1846/5 PM	—	10.00	15.00	35.00	150.00
	1846 PM	—	7.50	10.00	20.00	150.00
	1847 PM	—	7.50	10.00	20.00	150.00
	1848/7 PM	—	7.50	15.00	30.00	150.00
	1848 PM	—	7.50	15.00	30.00	150.00
	1848 PF	—	100.00	150.00	250.00	500.00
	1849/8 PF/PM					
		—	7.50	10.00	20.00	150.00
	1849 PF	—	7.50	10.00	20.00	150.00
	1850/40 PF	—	7.50	10.00	20.00	150.00
	1850 PF	—	7.50	10.00	20.00	150.00
	1851 PF	—	7.50	10.00	20.00	150.00
	1852/1 PF	—	7.50	10.00	20.00	150.00
	1852 PF	—	7.50	10.00	20.00	150.00
	1853 PF	—	7.50	10.00	20.00	150.00
	1854/3 PF	—	7.50	10.00	20.00	150.00
	1854 PF old font and obv.					
		—	7.50	10.00	20.00	150.00
	1854 PF new font and obv.					
		—	7.50	10.00	20.00	150.00
	1855 PF	—	7.50	10.00	20.00	150.00
	1855 PF star in G of mint mark					
		—	7.50	10.00	20.00	150.00
	1856/5 PF	—	10.00	15.00	35.00	150.00
	1856 PF	—	10.00	15.00	25.00	150.00
	1857/6 PF	—	7.50	10.00	20.00	150.00
	1857 PF	—	7.50	10.00	20.00	150.00
	1858/7 PF	—	7.50	10.00	20.00	150.00
	1858 PF	—	7.50	10.00	20.00	150.00
	1859/7 PF	—	7.50	10.00	20.00	150.00
	1859 PF	—	7.50	10.00	20.00	150.00
	1860/50 PF	—	7.50	10.00	20.00	150.00
	1860/59 PF	—	7.50	10.00	20.00	150.00
	1860 PF	—	7.50	10.00	20.00	150.00
	1861/51 PF	—	7.50	10.00	20.00	150.00
	1861/57 PF	—	7.50	10.00	20.00	150.00
	1861/0 PF	—	7.50	10.00	20.00	150.00
	1861 PF	—	7.50	10.00	20.00	150.00
	1862/1 YE	—	7.50	10.00	20.00	125.00
	1862 YE	—	7.50	10.00	20.00	125.00
	1862/57 YE	—	7.50	10.00	20.00	125.00
	1862 YE/PF	—	7.50	10.00	20.00	125.00
	1862 YF	—	7.50	10.00	20.00	125.00
	1863/52 YF	—	7.50	10.00	20.00	125.00
	1863 YF	—	7.50	10.00	20.00	125.00
	1867/57 YF	—	7.50	10.00	20.00	125.00
	1868/57 YF	—	10.00	15.00	25.00	125.00

NOTE: Varieties exist.

Mint mark: Ho

KM#	Date	Mintage	Fine	VF	XF	Unc
374.9	1861 FM	—	200.00	300.00	400.00	650.00
	1862/52 Ho FM/C. CE					
		—	250.00	350.00	500.00	—
	1867/1 PR/FM					
		—	75.00	150.00	250.00	500.00

Mint mark: Mo

KM#	Date	Mintage	Fine	VF	XF	Unc
374.10	1825 JM	—	10.00	15.00	30.00	175.00
	1826 JM	—	10.00	15.00	30.00	175.00
	1827 JM	—	10.00	15.00	30.00	175.00
	1828 JM	—	10.00	15.00	30.00	175.00
	1829/8 JM	—	10.00	15.00	30.00	175.00
	1829 JM	—	10.00	15.00	30.00	175.00
	1830 JM	—	40.00	60.00	125.00	250.00
	1831 JM	—	10.00	15.00	30.00	175.00
	1832 JM	—	100.00	200.00	400.00	—
	1833/2 MJ/JM					
		—	10.00	15.00	30.00	175.00
	1834 ML	—	50.00	100.00	200.00	400.00
	1836 ML	—	— Reported, not confirmed			
	1836 MF	—	10.00	15.00	30.00	175.00
	1837 ML	—	10.00	15.00	30.00	175.00
	1840 ML	—	150.00	225.00	350.00	—
	1841 ML	—	10.00	15.00	30.00	175.00
	1842 ML	—	—	—	Rare	—
	1847 RC	—	10.00	15.00	30.00	175.00
	1848 GC	—	10.00	15.00	30.00	175.00
	1849 GC	—	10.00	15.00	30.00	175.00
	1850 GC	—	10.00	15.00	30.00	175.00
	1851 GC	—	40.00	60.00	125.00	250.00
	1852 GC	—	10.00	15.00	30.00	175.00
	1853 GC	—	10.00	15.00	30.00	175.00
	1854/44 GC	—	10.00	15.00	30.00	175.00
	1855 GC	—	10.00	15.00	30.00	175.00
	1855 GF/GC	—	10.00	15.00	30.00	175.00
	1855 GF	—	10.00	15.00	30.00	175.00
	1856/5 GF/GC					
		—	10.00	15.00	30.00	175.00
	1857 GF	—	10.00	15.00	30.00	175.00
	1858 FH	—	7.50	12.50	25.00	150.00
	1858 FH/GF	—	7.50	12.50	25.00	150.00
	1859 FH	—	7.50	12.50	25.00	150.00
	1860 FH	—	7.50	12.50	25.00	150.00
	1860 TH	—	7.50	12.50	25.00	150.00
	1861 TH	—	— Reported, not confirmed			
	1861 CH	—	7.50	12.50	25.00	150.00
	1862 CH	—	7.50	12.50	25.00	150.00

KM#	Date	Mintage	Fine	VF	XF	Unc
374.10	1863 CH	—	7.50	12.50	25.00	150.00
	1863 TH	—	7.50	12.50	25.00	150.00
	1867 CH	—	7.50	12.50	25.00	150.00
	1868 CH	—	10.00	15.00	30.00	150.00
	1868 PH	—	7.50	12.50	25.00	150.00

NOTE: Varieties exist.

Mint mark: Pi

KM#	Date	Mintage	Fine	VF	XF	Unc
374.11	1829 JS	—	10.00	15.00	30.00	200.00
	1830/20 JS	—	20.00	30.00	60.00	200.00
	1837 JS	—	10.00	15.00	30.00	200.00
	1841 JS	—	10.00	15.00	30.00	200.00
	1842/1 JS	—	10.00	15.00	30.00	200.00
	1842 JS	—	10.00	15.00	30.00	200.00
	1842 PS	—	20.00	35.00	60.00	200.00
	1843 PS	—	12.50	20.00	40.00	200.00
	1843 AM	—	10.00	15.00	30.00	200.00
	1844 AM	—	10.00	15.00	30.00	200.00
	1845 AM	—	10.00	15.00	30.00	200.00
	1846 AM	—	10.00	15.00	30.00	200.00
	1849 MC	—	10.00	15.00	30.00	200.00
	1850 MC	—	10.00	15.00	30.00	200.00
	1856 MC	—	40.00	60.00	125.00	250.00
	1857 MC	—	—	—	—	—
	1858 MC	—	12.50	20.00	40.00	200.00
	1859 MC	—	50.00	70.00	100.00	200.00
	1861 PS	—	10.00	15.00	30.00	200.00
	1862 RO	—	12.50	20.00	40.00	200.00
	1863 RO	—	100.00	250.00	350.00	500.00
	1868 PS	—	10.00	15.00	30.00	200.00
	1869/8 PS	—	10.00	15.00	30.00	200.00
	1869 PS	—	10.00	15.00	30.00	200.00

Mint mark: Zs

KM#	Date	Mintage	Fine	VF	XF	Unc
374.12	1825 AZ	—	10.00	15.00	30.00	150.00
	1826 AV (A is inverted V)	—	7.50	10.00	25.00	150.00
	1826 AZ (A is inverted V)	—	7.50	10.00	25.00	150.00
	1826 AO	—	10.00	15.00	30.00	150.00
	1827 AO (A is inverted V)	—	6.00	8.00	12.00	150.00
	1828/7 AO	—	15.00	30.00	60.00	175.00
	1828 AO	—	7.50	10.00	25.00	100.00
	1828 AO (A is inverted V)	—	7.50	10.00	25.00	150.00
	1829 AO	—	7.50	10.00	25.00	150.00
	1829 OV	—	7.50	10.00	25.00	150.00
	1830 OV	—	7.50	10.00	25.00	150.00
	1831 OV	—	7.50	10.00	25.00	150.00
	1831 OM/OV	—	7.50	10.00	25.00	150.00
	1831 OM	—	7.50	10.00	25.00	150.00
	1832/1 OM	—	15.00	30.00	60.00	150.00
	1832 OM	—	7.50	10.00	25.00	150.00
	1833/27 OM	—	7.50	10.00	25.00	150.00
	1833/2 OM	—	7.50	10.00	25.00	150.00
	1833 OM	—	7.50	10.00	25.00	150.00
	1834 OM	—	40.00	60.00	125.00	200.00
	1835 OM	—	7.50	10.00	25.00	150.00
	1836 OM	—	7.50	10.00	25.00	150.00
	1837 OM	—	7.50	10.00	25.00	150.00
	1838 OM	—	15.00	30.00	60.00	150.00
	1839 OM	—	7.50	10.00	20.00	150.00
	1840 OM	—	7.50	10.00	20.00	150.00
	1841/0 OM	—	7.50	10.00	20.00	150.00
	1841 OM	—	7.50	10.00	20.00	150.00
	1842 OM	—	7.50	10.00	20.00	150.00
	1843 OM	—	7.50	10.00	20.00	150.00
	1844 OM	—	7.50	10.00	20.00	150.00
	1845 OM small letters and leaves	—	7.50	10.00	20.00	150.00
	1845 OM large letters and leaves	—	7.50	10.00	20.00	150.00
	1846 OM	—	7.50	10.00	20.00	150.00
	1847 OM	—	7.50	10.00	20.00	150.00
	1848 OM	—	7.50	10.00	20.00	150.00
	1849 OM	—	7.50	10.00	20.00	150.00
	1850 OM	—	7.50	10.00	20.00	150.00
	1851 OM	—	7.50	10.00	20.00	150.00
	1852 OM	—	7.50	10.00	20.00	150.00
	1853 OM	—	7.50	10.00	20.00	150.00
	1854/3 OM	—	7.50	10.00	20.00	150.00
	1854 OM	—	7.50	10.00	20.00	150.00
	1855/4 OM	—	7.50	10.00	20.00	150.00
	1855 OM	—	7.50	10.00	20.00	150.00
	1855 MO	—	7.50	10.00	20.00	150.00
	1856/5 MO	—	7.50	10.00	20.00	150.00
	1856 MO	—	7.50	10.00	20.00	150.00
	1857 MO	—	7.50	10.00	20.00	150.00
	1858 MO	—	7.50	10.00	20.00	150.00
	1859 MO	—	7.50	10.00	20.00	150.00
	1860/59 MO	—	7.50	10.00	20.00	150.00
	1860 MO	—	7.50	10.00	20.00	100.00
	1860 VL	—	7.50	10.00	20.00	150.00
	1861 VL	—	7.50	10.00	20.00	150.00
	1862 VL	—	7.50	10.00	20.00	100.00
	1863 MO	—	12.50	20.00	40.00	150.00
	1863 VL	—	7.50	10.00	20.00	150.00
	1864 MO	—	7.50	10.00	20.00	150.00
	1864 VL	—	7.50	10.00	20.00	150.00
	1865 MO	—	7.50	10.00	20.00	150.00
	1867 JS	—	7.50	10.00	20.00	150.00
	1868 JS	—	10.00	15.00	35.00	150.00
	1868 YH	—	7.50	10.00	20.00	150.00
	1869 YH	—	7.50	10.00	20.00	150.00
	1870 YH	—	7.50	10.00	20.00	150.00

NOTE: Varieties exist.

4 REALES

13.5400 g, .903 SILVER, .3925 oz ASW
Mint mark: Ce
Obv: Facing eagle.

KM#	Date	Mintage	Fine	VF	XF	Unc
375	1863 ML large C	—	200.00	500.00	850.00	4000.
	1863 ML small C	—	350.00	650.00	1250.	4750.

Mint mark: C

KM#	Date	Mintage	Fine	VF	XF	Unc
375.1	1846 CE	—	400.00	550.00	900.00	—
	1850 CE	—	75.00	125.00	250.00	600.00
	1852 CE	—	200.00	300.00	500.00	1250.
	1857 CE	—	—	—	Rare	—
	1858 CE	—	100.00	200.00	350.00	1000.
	1860 PV	—	25.00	50.00	125.00	600.00

Mint mark: Ga

KM#	Date	Mintage	Fine	VF	XF	Unc
375.2	1842/1 JG	—	—	Reported, not confirmed		
	1842 JG	—	—	Reported, not confirmed		
	1843 MC	—	20.00	40.00	80.00	400.00
	1844/3 MC	—	30.00	60.00	125.00	400.00
	1844 MC	—	20.00	40.00	80.00	400.00
	1845 MC	—	20.00	40.00	80.00	400.00
	1845 JG	—	20.00	40.00	80.00	400.00
	1846 JG	—	20.00	40.00	80.00	400.00
	1847 JG	—	40.00	80.00	150.00	400.00
	1848/7 JG	—	40.00	80.00	150.00	400.00
	1849 JG	—	40.00	80.00	150.00	400.00
	1850 JG	—	65.00	125.00	250.00	550.00
	1852 JG	—	—	—	Rare	—
	1854 JG	—	—	—	Rare	—
	1855 JG	—	100.00	200.00	400.00	1250.
	1856 JG	—	—	—	Rare	—
	1857/6 JG	—	65.00	125.00	250.00	550.00
	1858 JG	—	125.00	250.00	450.00	1250.
	1859/8 JG	—	125.00	250.00	450.00	1250.
	1860 JG	—	—	—	Rare	—
	1863/2 JG	—	150.00	300.00	1250.	6000.
	1863 JG	—	150.00	300.00	1250.	6000.

Mint mark: GC

KM#	Date	Mintage	Fine	VF	XF	Unc
375.3	1844 MP	—	1000.	2000.	3000.	—
	1845 MP	—	3000.	4000.	5000.	9000.
	1846 MP	—	1700.	2800.	—	—
	1847 MP	—	1500.	2500.	—	—
	1849 MP	—	2000.	3000.	—	—
	1850 MP	—	500.00	1000.	—	—

Mint mark: Go

KM#	Date	Mintage	Fine	VF	XF	Unc
375.4	1835 PJ	—	12.50	25.00	60.00	350.00
	1836/5 PJ	—	15.00	30.00	75.00	350.00
	1836 PJ	—	15.00	30.00	75.00	350.00
	1837 PJ	—	12.50	25.00	60.00	350.00
	1838/7 PJ	—	15.00	30.00	75.00	350.00
	1838 PJ	—	12.50	30.00	75.00	350.00
	1839 PJ	—	12.50	25.00	60.00	350.00
	1840/30 PJ	—	20.00	50.00	100.00	350.00
	1841/31 PJ	—	150.00	250.00	450.00	1250.
	1842 PJ	—	—	—	Rare	—
	1842 PM	—	15.00	30.00	75.00	350.00
	1843/2 PM eagle w/convex wings, thick rays	—	12.50	25.00	60.00	350.00
	1843 PM eagle w/concave wings, thin rays	—	12.50	25.00	60.00	350.00
	1844/3 PM	—	15.00	30.00	75.00	350.00
	1844 PM	—	20.00	50.00	100.00	350.00
	1845/4 PM	—	20.00	50.00	100.00	350.00
	1845 PM	—	20.00	50.00	100.00	350.00
	1846/5 PM	—	15.00	30.00	75.00	350.00
	1846 PM	—	15.00	30.00	75.00	350.00
	1847/6 PM	—	15.00	30.00	75.00	350.00
	1847 PM	—	15.00	30.00	75.00	350.00
	1848/7 PM	—	20.00	50.00	100.00	350.00
	1848 PM	—	20.00	50.00	100.00	350.00
	1849 PF	—	20.00	50.00	100.00	350.00
	1850 PF	—	12.50	25.00	60.00	350.00
	1851 PF	—	12.50	25.00	60.00	350.00
	1852 PF	—	15.00	30.00	75.00	350.00
	1853 PF	—	15.00	30.00	75.00	350.00
	1854 PF large eagle	—	15.00	30.00	75.00	350.00
	1854 PF small eagle	—	15.00	30.00	75.00	350.00
	1855/4 PF	—	15.00	30.00	75.00	350.00
	1855 PF	—	12.50	25.00	60.00	350.00
	1856 PF	—	12.50	25.00	60.00	350.00
	1857 PF	—	20.00	50.00	100.00	350.00
	1858 PF	—	20.00	50.00	100.00	350.00
	1859 PF	—	20.00	50.00	100.00	350.00
	1860/59 PF	—	15.00	30.00	75.00	350.00
	1860 PF	—	15.00	30.00	75.00	350.00
	1861/51 PF	—	15.00	30.00	75.00	350.00
	1861 PF	—	20.00	50.00	100.00	350.00
	1862/1 YE	—	15.00	30.00	75.00	350.00
	1862/1 YF	—	15.00	30.00	75.00	350.00
375.4	1862 YE/PF	—	15.00	30.00	75.00	350.00
	1862 YE	—	15.00	30.00	75.00	350.00
	1862 YF	—	15.00	30.00	75.00	350.00
	1863/53 YF	—	15.00	30.00	75.00	350.00
	1863 YF/PF	—	15.00	30.00	75.00	350.00
	1863 YF	—	15.00	30.00	75.00	350.00
	1867/57 YF/PF	—	15.00	30.00	75.00	350.00
	1868/58 YF/PF	—	15.00	30.00	75.00	350.00
	1870 FR	—	15.00	30.00	75.00	350.00

NOTE: Varieties exist. Some 1862 dates appear to be 1869 because of weak dies.

Mint mark: Ho

KM#	Date	Mintage	Fine	VF	XF	Unc
375.5	1861 FM	—	200.00	350.00	500.00	1850.
	1867/1 PR/FM	—	150.00	275.00	400.00	1750.

Mint mark: Mo

KM#	Date	Mintage	Fine	VF	XF	Unc
375.6	1827/6 JM	—	200.00	400.00	—	—
	1850 GC	—	—	—	Rare	—
	1852 GC	—	—	—	Rare	—
	1854 GC	—	—	—	Rare	—
	1855 GF/GC	—	50.00	100.00	200.00	500.00
	1855 GF	—	100.00	200.00	350.00	800.00
	1856 GF/GC	—	20.00	50.00	100.00	350.00
	1856 GF	—	—	—	Rare	—
	1859 FH	—	20.00	50.00	100.00	350.00
	1861 CH	—	15.00	30.00	75.00	300.00
	1862 CH	—	20.00	50.00	100.00	350.00
	1863/2 CH	—	20.00	50.00	100.00	350.00
	1863 CH	—	75.00	150.00	300.00	650.00
	1867 CH	—	20.00	50.00	100.00	350.00
	1868 CH/PH	—	30.00	75.00	150.00	400.00
	1868 CH	—	20.00	50.00	100.00	350.00
	1868 PH	—	30.00	75.00	150.00	400.00

Mint mark: O

KM#	Date	Mintage	Fine	VF	XF	Unc
375.7	1861 FR ornamental edge	—	225.00	450.00	700.00	2500.
	1861 FR herringbone edge	—	275.00	550.00	800.00	2500.
	1861 FR obliquely reeded edge	—	200.00	400.00	650.00	—

Mint mark: Pi

KM#	Date	Mintage	Fine	VF	XF	Unc
375.8	1837 JS	—	—	—	Rare	—
	1838 JS	—	150.00	250.00	400.00	800.00
	1842 PS	—	50.00	100.00	200.00	450.00
	1843/2 PS	—	50.00	100.00	200.00	450.00
	1843/2 PS 3 cut from 8 punch	—	50.00	100.00	200.00	450.00
	1843 AM	—	30.00	75.00	150.00	450.00
	1843 PS	—	50.00	100.00	200.00	450.00
	1844 AM	—	30.00	75.00	150.00	450.00
	1845/4 AM	—	20.00	50.00	100.00	450.00
	1845 AM	—	20.00	50.00	100.00	450.00
	1846 AM	—	20.00	50.00	100.00	450.00
	1847 AM	—	75.00	150.00	250.00	550.00
	1848 AM	—	—	—	Rare	—
	1849 MC/AM	—	20.00	50.00	100.00	450.00
	1849 MC	—	20.00	50.00	100.00	450.00
	1849 PS	—	20.00	50.00	100.00	450.00
	1850 MC	—	20.00	50.00	100.00	450.00
	1851 MC	—	20.00	50.00	100.00	450.00
	1852 MC	—	20.00	50.00	100.00	450.00
	1853 MC	—	20.00	50.00	100.00	450.00
	1854 MC	—	100.00	200.00	400.00	1100.
	1855 MC	—	200.00	350.00	500.00	1500.
	1856 MC	—	300.00	450.00	700.00	—
	1857 MC	—	—	—	Rare	—
	1857 PS	—	—	—	Rare	—
	1858 MC	—	100.00	200.00	400.00	1000.
	1859 MC	—	2000.	3000.	—	—
	1860 PS	—	300.00	450.00	700.00	—
	1861 PS	—	30.00	75.00	150.00	450.00
	1861 RO/PS	—	30.00	75.00	150.00	450.00
	1861 RO	—	50.00	100.00	200.00	450.00
	1862 RO	—	30.00	75.00	150.00	450.00
	1863 RO	—	30.00	75.00	150.00	450.00
	1864 RO	—	1600.	2600.	—	—
	1868 PS	—	30.00	75.00	150.00	450.00
	1869/8 PS	—	30.00	75.00	150.00	450.00
	1869 PS	—	30.00	75.00	150.00	450.00

Mint mark: Zs

KM#	Date	Mintage	Fine	VF	XF	Unc
375.9	1830 OM	—	20.00	50.00	100.00	350.00
	1831 OM	—	15.00	30.00	75.00	350.00
	1832/1 OM	—	20.00	50.00	100.00	350.00
	1832 OM	—	20.00	50.00	100.00	350.00
	1833/2 OM	—	20.00	50.00	100.00	350.00
	1833/27 OM	—	15.00	30.00	75.00	350.00
	1833 OM	—	15.00	30.00	75.00	350.00
	1834/3 OM	—	20.00	50.00	100.00	350.00
	1834 OM	—	15.00	30.00	75.00	350.00
	1835 OM	—	15.00	30.00	75.00	350.00
	1836 OM	—	15.00	30.00	75.00	350.00
	1837/5 OM	—	20.00	50.00	100.00	350.00
	1837/6 OM	—	20.00	50.00	100.00	350.00
	1837 OM	—	20.00	50.00	100.00	350.00
	1838/7 OM	—	15.00	30.00	75.00	350.00
	1839 OM	—	250.00	375.00	500.00	—
	1840 OM	—	—	—	Rare	—
	1841 OM	—	15.00	30.00	75.00	350.00
	1842 OM small letters	—	75.00	150.00	300.00	800.00
	1842 OM large letters	—	15.00	30.00	75.00	350.00
	1843 OM	—	15.00	30.00	75.00	350.00
	1844 OM	—	20.00	50.00	100.00	350.00
	1845 OM	—	20.00	50.00	100.00	350.00

KM#	Date	Mintage	Fine	VF	XF	Unc
375.9	1846/5 OM	—	25.00	60.00	125.00	350.00
	1846 OM	—	20.00	50.00	100.00	350.00
	1847 OM	—	15.00	30.00	75.00	350.00
	1848/6 OM	—	50.00	75.00	125.00	350.00
	1848 OM	—	20.00	50.00	100.00	350.00
	1849 OM	—	20.00	50.00	100.00	350.00
	1850 OM	—	20.00	50.00	100.00	350.00
	1851 OM	—	15.00	30.00	75.00	350.00
	1852 OM	—	15.00	30.00	75.00	350.00
	1853 OM	—	20.00	50.00	100.00	350.00
	1854/3 OM	—	30.00	75.00	150.00	350.00
	1855/4 OM	—	20.00	50.00	100.00	350.00
	1855 OM	—	15.00	30.00	75.00	350.00
	1856 OM	—	15.00	30.00	75.00	350.00
	1856 MO	—	20.00	50.00	100.00	350.00
	1857/5 MO	—	20.00	50.00	100.00	350.00
	1857 O/M	—	20.00	50.00	100.00	350.00
	1857 MO	—	15.00	30.00	75.00	350.00
	1858 MO	—	20.00	50.00	100.00	350.00
	1859 MO	—	15.00	30.00	75.00	350.00
	1860/59 MO	—	20.00	50.00	100.00	350.00
	1860 MO	—	15.00	30.00	75.00	350.00
	1860 VL	—	20.00	50.00	100.00	350.00
	1861/0 VL	—	20.00	50.00	100.00	350.00
	1861 VL	—	15.00	30.00	75.00	350.00
	1862/1 VL	—	20.00	50.00	100.00	350.00
	1862 VL	—	20.00	50.00	100.00	350.00
	1863 VL	—	20.00	50.00	100.00	350.00
	1863 MO	—	20.00	50.00	100.00	350.00
	1864 VL	—	15.00	30.00	75.00	350.00
	1868 JS	—	20.00	50.00	100.00	350.00
	1868 YH	—	15.00	30.00	75.00	350.00
	1869 YH	—	15.00	30.00	75.00	350.00
	1870 YH	—	15.00	30.00	75.00	350.00

8 REALES

27.0700 g, .903 SILVER, .7859 oz ASW

Mint mark: Do

Obv: Hooked-neck eagle.

KM#	Date	Mintage	Fine	VF	XF	Unc
376	1824 RL	—	200.00	350.00	1250.	2750.

NOTE: Varieties exist.

Mint mark: Go

KM#	Date	Mintage	Fine	VF	XF	Unc
376.1	1824 JM	—	200.00	325.00	1000.	3500.
	1825/4 JJ	—	550.00	800.00	1500.	6000.
	1825 JJ	—	500.00	750.00	1400.	5500.

Mint mark: Mo

KM#	Date	Mintage	Fine	VF	XF	Unc
376.2	1823 JM edge: circle and rectangle pattern					
		—	—	—	Rare	—
	1823 JM edge: laurel leaves					
		—	150.00	300.00	650.00	2500.
	1824 JM	—	125.00	250.00	450.00	2000.
	1824 JM (error) REPULICA					
		—	—	—	Rare	—

NOTE: These are rarely found with detail on the eagles breast and bring a premium if even slight feather detail is present there.

Mint mark: A, As

KM#	Date	Mintage	Fine	VF	XF	Unc
377	1864 PG	—	650.00	900.00	1200.	—
	1865/4 PG	—	—	—	Rare	—
	1865 PG	—	500.00	750.00	1000.	—
	1866/5 PG	—	—	—	Rare	—
	1866 PG	—	—	—	Rare	—
	1866 DL	—	—	—	Rare	—
	1867 DL	—	—	—	Rare	—
	1868 DL	—	50.00	90.00	150.00	300.00
	1869/8 DL	—	50.00	90.00	150.00	—
	1869 DL	—	50.00	80.00	120.00	300.00
	1870 DL	—	30.00	60.00	120.00	300.00
	1871 DL	—	20.00	35.00	75.00	200.00
	1872 AM/DL	—	25.00	50.00	100.00	300.00
	1872 AM	—	25.00	50.00	100.00	250.00
	1873 AM	.509	15.00	25.00	50.00	150.00
	1874 DL	—	15.00	25.00	50.00	150.00
	1875A DL 7/7	—	40.00	80.00	120.00	300.00
	1875A DL	—	15.00	25.00	50.00	150.00
	1875AsDL	—	30.00	60.00	110.00	250.00
	1876 DL	—	15.00	25.00	50.00	150.00
	1877 DL	.515	15.00	25.00	50.00	150.00
	1878 DL	.513	15.00	25.00	50.00	150.00
	1879 DL	—	20.00	35.00	75.00	175.00
	1879 ML	—	30.00	60.00	125.00	300.00
	1880 ML	—	12.00	15.00	30.00	140.00
	1881 ML	.966	12.00	15.00	30.00	140.00
	1882 ML	.480	12.00	15.00	30.00	140.00
	1883 ML	.464	12.00	15.00	30.00	140.00
	1884 ML	—	12.00	15.00	30.00	140.00
	1885 ML	.280	12.00	15.00	30.00	140.00
	1886 ML	.857	12.00	15.00	25.00	110.00
	1886/0 As/Cn ML/JD					
		I.A.	15.00	20.00	35.00	160.00
	1887 ML	.650	12.00	15.00	25.00	110.00
	1888/7 ML	.508	30.00	60.00	100.00	400.00
	1888 ML	I.A.	12.00	15.00	25.00	110.00
	1889 ML	.427	12.00	15.00	25.00	110.00
	1890 ML	.450	12.00	15.00	25.00	110.00
	1891 ML	.533	12.00	15.00	25.00	110.00
	1892 ML	.465	12.00	15.00	25.00	110.00
	1893 ML	.734	10.00	12.00	20.00	80.00
	1894 ML	.725	10.00	12.00	20.00	80.00
	1895 ML	.477	10.00	12.00	20.00	80.00

NOTE: Varieties exist.

Mint mark: Ce

KM#	Date	Mintage	Fine	VF	XF	Unc
377.1	1863 ML	—	375.00	625.00	1000.	2250.
	1863 CeML/PiMC					
		—	375.00	650.00	1100.	2750.

Mint mark: Ca

KM#	Date	Mintage	Fine	VF	XF	Unc
377.2	1831 MR	—	1000.	1750.	2250.	3250.
	1832 MR	—	125.00	200.00	300.00	600.00
	1833 MR	—	500.00	750.00	1250.	—
	1834 MR	—	—	—	Rare	—
	1834 AM	—	—	—	Rare	—
	1835 AM	—	150.00	250.00	400.00	800.00
	1836 AM	—	100.00	150.00	225.00	450.00
	1837 AM	—	—	—	Rare	—
	1838 AM	—	100.00	200.00	300.00	600.00
	1839 RG	—	1250.	2500.	—	—
	1840 RG 1 dot after date					
		—	400.00	600.00	800.00	1500.
	1840 RG 3 dots after date					
		—	400.00	600.00	800.00	1500.

KM#	Date	Mintage	Fine	VF	XF	Unc
377.2	1841 RG	—	50.00	100.00	150.00	300.00
	1842 RG	—	25.00	40.00	65.00	125.00
	1843 RG	—	40.00	80.00	125.00	250.00
	1844/1 RG	—	35.00	70.00	100.00	200.00
	1844 RG	—	25.00	40.00	65.00	125.00
	1845 RG	—	25.00	40.00	65.00	125.00
	1846 RG	—	30.00	60.00	100.00	250.00
	1847 RG	—	40.00	80.00	125.00	250.00
	1848 RG	—	30.00	60.00	100.00	200.00
	1849 RG	—	30.00	60.00	100.00	200.00
	1850/40 RG	—	40.00	80.00	125.00	250.00
	1850 RG	—	30.00	60.00	100.00	200.00
	1851/41 RG	—	100.00	200.00	300.00	500.00
	1851 RG	—	150.00	250.00	400.00	750.00
	1852/42 RG	—	150.00	250.00	400.00	750.00
	1852 RG	—	150.00	250.00	400.00	750.00
	1853/43 RG	—	150.00	250.00	400.00	750.00
	1853 RG	—	150.00	250.00	400.00	750.00
	1854/44 RG	—	100.00	200.00	300.00	500.00
	1854 RG	—	50.00	100.00	150.00	300.00
	1855/45 RG	—	100.00	200.00	350.00	650.00
	1855 RG	—	75.00	125.00	200.00	400.00
	1856/45 RG	—	200.00	400.00	600.00	1000.
	1856/5 JC	—	600.00	1000.	1250.	1750.
	1857 JC/RG	—	40.00	80.00	125.00	250.00
	1857 JC	—	50.00	100.00	150.00	250.00
	1858 JC	—	20.00	30.00	50.00	120.00
	1858 BA	—	—	—	Rare	—
	1859 JC	—	40.00	80.00	125.00	250.00
	1860 JC	—	20.00	40.00	90.00	175.00
	1861 JC	—	15.00	25.00	50.00	120.00
	1862 JC	—	15.00	25.00	50.00	120.00
	1863 JC	—	20.00	35.00	75.00	150.00
	1864 JC	—	20.00	35.00	75.00	150.00
	1865 JC	—	100.00	200.00	350.00	600.00
	1865 FP	—	—	—	Rare	—
	1866 JC	—	—	—	Rare	—
	1866 FP	—	—	—	Rare	—
	1866 JG	—	—	—	Rare	—
	1867 JG	—	100.00	200.00	350.00	600.00
	1868 JG	—	75.00	150.00	200.00	350.00
	1868 MM	—	50.00	100.00	150.00	300.00
	1869 MM	—	20.00	35.00	65.00	125.00
	1870 MM	—	20.00	35.00	65.00	125.00
	1871/0 MM	—	15.00	25.00	50.00	100.00
	1871 MM	—	15.00	25.00	50.00	100.00
	1871 MM first M/inverted M					
		—	20.00	35.00	65.00	125.00
	1873 MM	—	20.00	35.00	65.00	125.00
	1873 MM/T					
		—	15.00	25.00	50.00	100.00
	1874 MM	—	12.00	15.00	30.00	100.00
	1875 MM	—	12.00	15.00	30.00	100.00
	1876 MM	—	12.00	15.00	30.00	100.00
	1877 EA	.472	12.00	15.00	30.00	100.00
	1877 GR	I.A.	25.00	45.00	65.00	150.00
	1877 JM	I.A.	12.00	15.00	30.00	100.00
	1877 AV	I.A.	100.00	200.00	350.00	750.00
	1878 AV	.439	12.00	15.00	25.00	75.00
	1879 AV	—	12.00	15.00	25.00	75.00
	1880 AV	—	250.00	400.00	600.00	1200.
	1880 PM	—	500.00	750.00	1000.	1500.
	1880 MG normal initials					
		—	12.00	15.00	25.00	100.00
	1880 MG tall initials					
		—	12.00	15.00	25.00	100.00
	1880 MM	—	12.00	15.00	25.00	100.00
	1881 MG	1.085	10.00	12.00	20.00	60.00
	1882 MG	.779	10.00	12.00	20.00	60.00
	1882 MM	I.A.	10.00	12.00	20.00	60.00
	1882 MM M sideways					
		Inc. Ab.	20.00	40.00	90.00	150.00
	1883 sideways M MM					
		.818	—	—	—	—
	1883 MM	I.A.	10.00	12.00	20.00	60.00
	1884/3 MM	—	12.00	15.00	30.00	75.00
	1884 MM	—	10.00	12.00	20.00	60.00
	1885/4 MM					
		1.345	15.00	25.00	50.00	100.00
	1885/6 MM	I.A.	15.00	25.00	50.00	100.00
	1885 MM	I.A.	10.00	12.00	20.00	60.00
	1886 MM	2.483	10.00	12.00	20.00	60.00
	1887 MM	2.625	10.00	12.00	20.00	60.00
	1888/7 MM					
		2.434	15.00	25.00	50.00	100.00
	1888 MM	I.A.	10.00	12.00	20.00	60.00
	1889 MM	2.681	10.00	12.00	20.00	60.00
	1890 MM	2.137	10.00	12.00	20.00	60.00
	1891/0 MM					
		2.268	15.00	25.00	50.00	100.00
	1891 MM	I.A.	10.00	12.00	20.00	80.00
	1892 MM	2.527	10.00	12.00	20.00	60.00
	1893 MM	2.632	10.00	12.00	20.00	60.00
	1894 MM	2.642	10.00	12.00	20.00	60.00
	1895 MM	1.112	10.00	12.00	20.00	60.00

NOTE: Varieties exist.

Mint mark: C, Cn

KM#	Date	Mintage	Fine	VF	XF	Unc
377.3	1846 CE	—	150.00	300.00	800.00	1500.
	1847 CE	—	600.00	1000.	1500.	—
	1848 CE	—	150.00	300.00	600.00	1000.
	1849 CE	—	75.00	125.00	200.00	400.00
	1850 CE	—	75.00	125.00	200.00	400.00
	1851 CE	—	125.00	250.00	450.00	1000.
	1852/1 CE	—	100.00	150.00	250.00	500.00
	1852 CE	—	100.00	200.00	350.00	650.00
	1853/0 CE	—	200.00	350.00	700.00	1300.
	1853/2/0	—	200.00	400.00	750.00	1400.
	1853 CE thick rays					
		—	100.00	175.00	300.00	600.00

KM#	Date	Mintage	Fine	VF	XF	Unc
377.3	1853 CE (error:) MEXIGANA	—	200.00	350.00	650.00	—
	1854 CE	—	—	—	Rare	—
	1854 CE large eagle & hat	—	150.00	300.00	600.00	1000.
	1855/6 CE	—	40.00	60.00	100.00	200.00
	1855 CE	—	25.00	40.00	60.00	125.00
	1856 CE	—	50.00	100.00	175.00	350.00
	1857 CE	—	20.00	30.00	45.00	100.00
	1858 CE	—	30.00	40.00	60.00	125.00
	1859 CE	—	20.00	30.00	45.00	100.00
	1860/9 PV/CV	—	50.00	70.00	100.00	200.00
	1860/9 PV/E	—	50.00	70.00	100.00	200.00
	1860 CE	—	25.00	40.00	55.00	100.00
	1860 PV	—	40.00	60.00	80.00	150.00
	1861/0 CE	—	40.00	60.00	100.00	250.00
	1861 PV/CE	—	75.00	125.00	200.00	350.00
	1861 CE	—	20.00	35.00	50.00	150.00
	1862 CE	—	20.00	35.00	50.00	150.00
	1863/2 CE	—	30.00	50.00	75.00	200.00
	1863 CE	—	20.00	30.00	50.00	150.00
	1864 CE	—	30.00	60.00	100.00	300.00
	1865 CE	—	125.00	200.00	325.00	650.00
	1866 CE	—	—	—	Rare	—
	1867 CE	—	125.00	200.00	375.00	750.00
	1868/7 CE	—	30.00	40.00	75.00	150.00
	1868/8	—	50.00	100.00	150.00	300.00
	1868 CE	—	30.00	40.00	75.00	150.00
	1869 CE	—	30.00	40.00	75.00	175.00
	1870 CE	—	35.00	50.00	90.00	200.00
	1873 MP	—	50.00	100.00	150.00	300.00
	1874C MP	—	20.00	30.00	45.00	100.00
	1874CN MP	—	125.00	200.00	300.00	600.00
	1875 MP	—	12.00	15.00	20.00	75.00
	1876 GP	—	12.00	15.00	30.00	90.00
	1876 CG	—	12.00	15.00	20.00	75.00
	1877 CG	.339	12.00	15.00	20.00	75.00
	1877 Gn CG (error)	—	65.00	125.00	200.00	400.00
	1877 JA	I.A.	35.00	75.00	125.00	250.00
	1878/7 CG	.483	35.00	75.00	125.00	250.00
	1878 CG	I.A.	15.00	25.00	35.00	125.00
	1878 JD	I.A.	15.00	20.00	30.00	125.00
	1878 JD D/retrograde D	I.A.	20.00	30.00	40.00	150.00
	1879 JD	—	12.00	15.00	30.00	90.00
	1880/70 JD	—	15.00	20.00	30.00	90.00
	1880 JD	—	12.00	15.00	20.00	75.00
	1881/0 JD	1.032	15.00	20.00	30.00	90.00
	1881C JD	I.A.	12.00	15.00	20.00	75.00
	1881CnJD	I.A.	40.00	60.00	90.00	150.00
	1882 JD	.397	12.00	15.00	20.00	75.00
	1882 AM	I.A.	12.00	15.00	20.00	75.00
	1883 AM	.333	12.00	15.00	20.00	125.00
	1884 AM	—	12.00	15.00	20.00	75.00
	1885/6 AM	.227	20.00	30.00	45.00	100.00
	1885C AM	I.A.	75.00	125.00	250.00	500.00
	1885CnAM	I.A.	12.00	15.00	20.00	75.00
	1885GnAM (error)	Inc. Ab.	60.00	100.00	150.00	300.00
	1886 AM	.571	12.00	15.00	20.00	75.00
	1887 AM	.732	12.00	15.00	20.00	75.00
	1888 AM	.768	12.00	15.00	20.00	75.00
	1889 AM	1.075	12.00	15.00	20.00	75.00
	1890 AM	.874	10.00	12.00	18.00	60.00
	1891 AM	.777	10.00	12.00	18.00	60.00
	1892 AM	.681	10.00	12.00	18.00	60.00
	1893 AM	1.144	10.00	12.00	18.00	60.00
	1894 AM	2.118	10.00	12.00	18.00	60.00
	1895 AM	1.834	10.00	12.00	18.00	60.00
	1896 AM	2.134	10.00	12.00	18.00	60.00
	1897 AM	1.580	10.00	12.00	18.00	60.00

NOTE: Varieties exist.

Mint mark: Do

KM#	Date	Mintage	Fine	VF	XF	Unc
377.4	1825 RL	—	30.00	55.00	85.00	175.00
	1826 RL	—	40.00	100.00	250.00	500.00
	1827/6 RL	—	35.00	60.00	80.00	175.00
	1827 RL	—	30.00	50.00	75.00	150.00
	1828/7 RL	—	35.00	60.00	80.00	175.00
	1828 RL	—	25.00	50.00	75.00	150.00
	1829 RL	—	25.00	50.00	75.00	150.00
	1830 RM B on eagles claw	—	25.00	50.00	75.00	150.00
	1831 RM B on eagles claw	—	20.00	30.00	50.00	125.00
	1832 RM Mexican dies, B on eagles claw	—	25.00	50.00	100.00	200.00
	1832/1 RM/RL French dies	—	25.00	35.00	75.00	150.00
	1833/2 RM/RL	—	20.00	35.00	75.00	150.00
	1833 RM	—	15.00	30.00	50.00	125.00
	1834/3/2 RM/RL	—	20.00	35.00	75.00	150.00
	1834 RM	—	15.00	25.00	45.00	100.00
	1835/4 RM/RL	—	25.00	40.00	80.00	150.00
	1835 RM	—	20.00	35.00	55.00	125.00
	1836/1 RM	—	20.00	30.00	50.00	125.00
	1836/4 RM	—	20.00	30.00	50.00	125.00
	1836/5/4 RM/RL	—	75.00	150.00	250.00	500.00
	1836 RM	—	20.00	30.00	50.00	125.00
	1836 RM M on snake	—	20.00	30.00	50.00	125.00
	1837/1 RM	—	20.00	30.00	50.00	125.00
	1837 RM	—	20.00	30.00	50.00	125.00
	1838/1 RM	—	20.00	30.00	50.00	125.00
377.4	1838/7 RM	—	20.00	30.00	50.00	125.00
	1838 RM	—	20.00	30.00	50.00	125.00
	1839/1 RM/RL	—	20.00	30.00	50.00	125.00
	1839/1 RM	—	20.00	30.00	50.00	125.00
	1839 RM	—	20.00	30.00	50.00	125.00
	1840/38/31 RM	—	20.00	30.00	50.00	125.00
	1840/39 RM	—	20.00	30.00	50.00	125.00
	1840 RM	—	20.00	30.00	50.00	125.00
	1841/31 RM	—	25.00	50.00	75.00	175.00
	1842/31 RM B below cactus	—	125.00	250.00	400.00	750.00
	1842/31 RM	—	40.00	80.00	125.00	250.00
	1842/32 RM	—	40.00	80.00	125.00	250.00
	1842 RM eagle of 1832-41	—	20.00	30.00	50.00	125.00
	1842 RM pre 1832 eagle resumed	—	20.00	30.00	50.00	125.00
	1842 RM	—	40.00	80.00	125.00	250.00
	1843/33 RM	—	50.00	90.00	150.00	250.00
	1844/34 RM	—	100.00	200.00	300.00	500.00
	1844/35 RM	—	100.00	200.00	300.00	500.00
	1845/31 RM	—	35.00	75.00	125.00	250.00
	1845/34 RM	—	35.00	75.00	125.00	250.00
	1845/35 RM	—	35.00	75.00	125.00	250.00
	1845 RM	—	20.00	30.00	50.00	125.00
	1846/31 RM	—	20.00	30.00	50.00	125.00
	1846/36 RM	—	20.00	30.00	50.00	125.00
	1846 RM	—	20.00	30.00	50.00	125.00
	1847 RM	—	25.00	50.00	75.00	150.00
	1848/7 RM	—	125.00	250.00	400.00	750.00
	1848/7 CM/RM	—	100.00	200.00	350.00	700.00
	1848 CM/RM	—	100.00	200.00	350.00	700.00
	1848 RM	—	100.00	200.00	300.00	600.00
	1848 CM	—	50.00	100.00	200.00	400.00
	1849/39 CM	—	100.00	200.00	350.00	700.00
	1849 CM	—	100.00	200.00	350.00	700.00
	1849 JMR/CM oval 0	—	200.00	325.00	450.00	800.00
	1849 DoJMR oval O	—	200.00	400.00	600.00	1000.
	1849 DoJMR round O	—	200.00	400.00	600.00	1000.
	1850 JMR	—	100.00	150.00	250.00	500.00
	1851/0 JMR	—	100.00	150.00	250.00	500.00
	1851 JMR	—	100.00	150.00	250.00	500.00
	1852 CP/JMR	—	—	—	Rare	—
	1852 CP	—	—	—	Rare	—
	1852 JMR	—	175.00	250.00	375.00	550.00
	1853 CP/JMR	—	175.00	275.00	400.00	700.00
	1853 CP	—	200.00	350.00	600.00	1200.
	1854 CP	—	25.00	35.00	65.00	300.00
	1855 CP eagle type of 1854	—	50.00	100.00	175.00	350.00
	1855 CP eagle type of 1856	—	50.00	100.00	175.00	350.00
	1856 CP	—	50.00	100.00	175.00	350.00
	1857 CP	—	35.00	75.00	175.00	350.00
	1858/7 CP	—	25.00	35.00	70.00	150.00
	1858 CP	—	20.00	30.00	60.00	150.00
	1859 CP	—	20.00	30.00	60.00	150.00
	1860/59 CP	—	30.00	50.00	100.00	200.00
	1860 CP	—	20.00	30.00	60.00	150.00
	1861/0 CP	—	30.00	50.00	100.00	200.00
	1861 CP	—	20.00	30.00	50.00	125.00
	1862/1 CP	—	25.00	35.00	60.00	125.00
	1862 CP	—	20.00	30.00	55.00	100.00
	1863/2 CP	—	25.00	50.00	75.00	175.00
	1863/53 CP	—	30.00	60.00	90.00	200.00
	1863 CP	—	25.00	50.00	75.00	175.00
	1864 CP	—	100.00	150.00	250.00	500.00
	1864 LT	—	25.00	40.00	80.00	175.00
	1865 LT	—	—	—	Rare	—
	1866 CM	—	—	—	Rare	—
	1867 CM	—	—	—	Rare	—
	1867/6 CP	—	200.00	400.00	600.00	1200.
	1867 CP	—	175.00	300.00	500.00	1000.
	1867 CP/CM	—	175.00	300.00	500.00	1000.
	1867 CP/LT	—	175.00	300.00	500.00	1000.
	1868 CP	—	25.00	40.00	80.00	175.00
	1869 CP	—	20.00	30.00	50.00	125.00
	1870/69 CP	—	20.00	30.00	50.00	125.00
	1870/9 CP	—	20.00	30.00	50.00	125.00
	1870 CP	—	20.00	30.00	50.00	125.00
	1873 CP	—	125.00	225.00	325.00	600.00
	1873 CM	—	30.00	50.00	100.00	200.00
	1874/3 CM	—	12.00	15.00	20.00	100.00
	1874 CM	—	10.00	15.00	20.00	60.00
	1874 JH	—	—	—	Rare	—
	1875 CM	—	10.00	15.00	20.00	75.00
	1875 JH	—	100.00	175.00	275.00	500.00
	1876 CM	—	10.00	15.00	20.00	75.00
	1877 CM	.431	—	—	Rare	—
	1877 CP	I.A.	10.00	15.00	20.00	75.00
	1877 JMP	I.A.	—	—	Rare	—
	1878 PE	.409	15.00	25.00	40.00	90.00
	1878 TB	I.A.	10.00	15.00	20.00	75.00
	1879 TB	—	10.00	15.00	20.00	75.00
	1880/70 TB	—	150.00	250.00	375.00	650.00
	1880/70 TB/JP	—	150.00	250.00	375.00	650.00
	1880/70 JP	—	15.00	25.00	40.00	90.00
	1880 TB	—	150.00	250.00	375.00	650.00
	1880 JP	—	10.00	15.00	20.00	75.00
	1881 JP	.928	10.00	15.00	20.00	75.00
	1882 JP	.414	10.00	15.00	20.00	75.00
377.4	1882 MC/JP	Inc. Ab.	30.00	60.00	100.00	200.00
	1882 MC	I.A.	25.00	50.00	75.00	150.00
	1883/73 MC	.452	15.00	25.00	40.00	90.00
	1883 MC	I.A.	10.00	15.00	20.00	75.00
	1884/3 MC	—	20.00	30.00	60.00	110.00
	1884 MC	—	10.00	15.00	20.00	75.00
	1885 MC	.547	10.00	12.00	18.00	65.00
	1885 JB	I.A.	25.00	35.00	50.00	125.00
	1886/3 MC	.955	15.00	25.00	40.00	90.00
	1886 MC	I.A.	10.00	12.00	18.00	65.00
	1887 MC	1.004	10.00	12.00	18.00	65.00
	1888 MC	.996	10.00	12.00	18.00	65.00
	1889 MC	.874	10.00	12.00	18.00	65.00
	1890 MC	1.119	10.00	12.00	18.00	65.00
	1890 JP	I.A.	10.00	12.00	18.00	65.00
	1891 JP	1.487	10.00	12.00	18.00	65.00
	1892 JP	1.597	10.00	12.00	18.00	65.00
	1892 ND	I.A.	25.00	50.00	100.00	200.00
	1893 ND	1.617	10.00	12.00	18.00	65.00
	1894 ND	1.537	10.00	12.00	18.00	65.00
	1895/3 ND	.761	15.00	25.00	40.00	90.00
	1895 ND	I.A.	10.00	12.00	18.00	65.00

NOTE: Varieties exist.

Mint mark: EoMo

KM#	Date	Mintage	Fine	VF	XF	Unc
377.5	1828 LF/LP	—	500.00	1000.	2500.	—
	1828 LF	—	500.00	1000.	2500.	—
	1829 LF	—	400.00	800.00	1500.	—
	1830/20 LF	—	—	—	Rare	—
	1830 LF	—	1000.	2000.	3000.	—

Mint mark: Ga

KM#	Date	Mintage	Fine	VF	XF	Unc
377.6	1825 FS	—	150.00	275.00	425.00	850.00
	1826/5 FS	—	125.00	250.00	400.00	800.00
	1827/87 FS	—	125.00	250.00	400.00	800.00
	1827 FS	—	225.00	350.00	500.00	1000.
	1287 FS (error)		8500.	—	—	—
	1828 FS	—	200.00	375.00	550.00	1100.
	1829/8 FS	—	200.00	375.00	550.00	1100.
	1829 FS	—	175.00	325.00	475.00	950.00
	1830/29 FS	—	175.00	300.00	450.00	900.00
	1830 FS	—	100.00	175.00	300.00	600.00
	1830 LP/FS	—	—	—	Rare	—
	1831 LP	—	200.00	400.00	600.00	1200.
	1831 FS/LP	—	300.00	500.00	750.00	1500.
	1831 FS	—	—	—	—	—
	1832/1 FS	—	50.00	100.00	175.00	300.00
	1832/1 FS/LP	—	60.00	125.00	200.00	350.00
	1832 FS	—	25.00	50.00	100.00	200.00
	1833/2/1 FS/LP	—	45.00	75.00	125.00	250.00
	1833/2 FS	—	25.00	50.00	100.00	200.00
	1834/2 FS	—	60.00	125.00	200.00	350.00
	1834/3 FS	—	60.00	125.00	200.00	350.00
	1834/0 FS	—	60.00	125.00	200.00	350.00
	1834 FS	—	50.00	100.00	150.00	300.00
	1835 FS	—	25.00	50.00	100.00	200.00
	1836/1 JG/FS	—	40.00	80.00	125.00	250.00
	1836 FS	—	—	—	Rare	—
	1836 JG/FS	—	25.00	50.00	100.00	200.00
	1836 JG	—	25.00	50.00	100.00	200.00
	1837/6 JG/FS	—	50.00	100.00	175.00	300.00
	1837 JG	—	40.00	80.00	125.00	250.00
	1838/7 JG	—	100.00	175.00	300.00	550.00
	1838 JG	—	100.00	150.00	275.00	500.00
	1839 MC	—	100.00	200.00	300.00	550.00
	1839 MC/JG	—	100.00	200.00	300.00	550.00
	1839 JG	—	60.00	125.00	200.00	350.00
	1840/30 MC	—	50.00	75.00	150.00	275.00
	1840 MC	—	30.00	60.00	125.00	250.00
	1841 MC	—	30.00	60.00	125.00	250.00

KM#	Date	Mintage	Fine	VF	XF	Unc
377.6	1842/1 JG/MG	—	100.00	150.00	250.00	450.00
	1842/1 JG/MC	—	100.00	150.00	250.00	450.00
	1842 JG	—	25.00	50.00	100.00	200.00
	1842 JG/MG	—	25.00	50.00	100.00	200.00
	1843/2 MC/JG	—	25.00	50.00	100.00	200.00
	1843 MC/JG	—	25.00	50.00	100.00	200.00
	1843 JG	—	400.00	600.00	800.00	1500.
	1843 MC	—	50.00	100.00	150.00	300.00
	1844 MC	—	50.00	100.00	150.00	300.00
	1845 MC	—	75.00	150.00	250.00	450.00
	1845 JG	—	600.00	1000.	1500.	—
	1846 JG	—	40.00	80.00	150.00	300.00
	1847 JG	—	100.00	150.00	225.00	400.00
	1848/7 JG	—	55.00	85.00	125.00	250.00
	1848 JG	—	50.00	75.00	100.00	200.00
	1849 JG	—	90.00	125.00	175.00	300.00
	1850 JG	—	50.00	100.00	150.00	300.00
	1851 JG	—	125.00	200.00	350.00	650.00
	1852 JG	—	100.00	150.00	250.00	450.00
	1853/2 JG	—	125.00	175.00	250.00	475.00
	1853 JG	—	90.00	125.00	175.00	300.00
	1854/3 JG	—	65.00	90.00	125.00	250.00
	1854 JG	—	50.00	75.00	125.00	250.00
	1855/4 JG	—	50.00	100.00	150.00	275.00
	1855 JG	—	25.00	50.00	100.00	200.00
	1856/4 JG	—	60.00	125.00	175.00	300.00
	1856/5 56	—	60.00	125.00	175.00	300.00
	1856 JG	—	50.00	100.00	150.00	275.00
	1857 JG	—	50.00	100.00	225.00	400.00
	1858 JG	—	100.00	150.00	300.00	500.00
	1859/7 JG	—	25.00	50.00	100.00	175.00
	1859/8 JG	—	25.00	50.00	100.00	175.00
	1859 JG	—	20.00	40.00	80.00	125.00
	1860 JG w/o dot	—	400.00	800.00	1200.	2000.
	1860 JG dot in loop of eagles tail (base alloy)	—	—	—	Rare	—
	1861 JG	—	—	—	Rare	—
	1862 JG	—	—	—	Rare	—
	1863/52 JG	—	—	—	—	—
	1863/59 JG	—	45.00	50.00	85.00	135.00
	1863/2 JG	—	30.00	50.00	90.00	175.00
	1863/4 JG	—	40.00	60.00	125.00	200.00
	1863 JG	—	25.00	45.00	75.00	150.00
	1863 FV	—	—	—	Rare	—
	1867 JM	—	—	—	Rare	—
	1868/7 JM	—	50.00	75.00	125.00	200.00
	1868 JM	—	50.00	75.00	125.00	200.00
	1869 JM	—	50.00	75.00	125.00	200.00
	1869 IC	—	75.00	125.00	200.00	375.00
	1870/60 IC	—	60.00	90.00	150.00	275.00
	1870 IC	—	60.00	90.00	150.00	275.00
	1873 IC	—	15.00	25.00	50.00	125.00
	1874 IC	—	10.00	15.00	20.00	85.00
	1874 MC	—	25.00	50.00	100.00	200.00
	1875 IC	—	15.00	30.00	60.00	125.00
	1875 MC	—	10.00	15.00	20.00	85.00
	1876 IC	.559	15.00	30.00	50.00	100.00
	1876 MC	I.A.	125.00	175.00	250.00	375.00
	1877 IC	.928	10.00	15.00	20.00	85.00
	1877 JA	I.A.	10.00	15.00	20.00	85.00
	1878 JA	.764	10.00	15.00	20.00	85.00
	1879 JA	—	10.00	15.00	20.00	85.00
	1880/70 FS	—	15.00	25.00	50.00	125.00
	1880 JA	—	10.00	15.00	20.00	85.00
	1880 FS	—	10.00	15.00	20.00	85.00
	1881 FS	1.300	10.00	15.00	20.00	85.00
	1882/1 FS	.537	15.00	25.00	50.00	125.00
	1882 FS	I.A.	10.00	15.00	20.00	85.00
	1882 TB/FS	I.A.	75.00	150.00	250.00	450.00
	1882 TB	I.A.	50.00	100.00	175.00	300.00
	1883 TB	.561	15.00	25.00	40.00	125.00
	1884 TB	—	10.00	12.00	18.00	85.00
	1884 AH	—	10.00	12.00	18.00	85.00
	1885 AH	.443	10.00	12.00	18.00	85.00
	1885 JS	I.A.	30.00	60.00	100.00	200.00
	1886 JS	1.039	10.00	12.00	18.00	85.00
	1887 JS	.878	10.00	12.00	18.00	85.00
	1888 JS	1.159	10.00	12.00	18.00	85.00
	1889 JS	1.583	10.00	12.00	18.00	85.00
	1890 JS	1.658	10.00	12.00	18.00	85.00
	1891 JS	1.507	10.00	12.00	18.00	85.00
	1892/1 JS	1.627	15.00	25.00	50.00	125.00
	1892 JS	I.A.	10.00	12.00	18.00	75.00
	1893 JS	1.952	10.00	12.00	18.00	75.00
	1894 JS	2.046	10.00	12.00	18.00	75.00
	1895 JS	1.146	10.00	12.00	18.00	60.00

NOTE: Varieties exist. The 1830 LP/FS is currently only known with a Philippine countermark.

Mint mark: GC

KM#	Date	Mintage	Fine	VF	XF	Unc
377.7	1844 MP	—	350.00	500.00	1000.	2000.
	1844 MP (error) reversed S in Ds, Gs	—	400.00	600.00	1200.	2250.
	1845 MP eagle's tail square	—	125.00	225.00	300.00	600.00
	1845 MP eagle's tail round	—	225.00	450.00	650.00	1200.
	1846 MP eagle's tail square	—	100.00	150.00	350.00	750.00
	1846 MP eagle's tail round	—	100.00	150.00	350.00	750.00
	1847 MP	—	150.00	250.00	400.00	800.00
	1848 MP	—	175.00	300.00	500.00	900.00
	1849 MP	—	175.00	300.00	525.00	1000.
	1850 MP	—	175.00	300.00	575.00	1100.
	1851 MP	—	400.00	600.00	900.00	1600.
	1852 MP	—	500.00	800.00	1250.	2250.

Mint mark: Go

KM#	Date	Mintage	Fine	VF	XF	Unc
377.8	1825 JJ	—	40.00	70.00	150.00	300.00
	1826 JJ straight J's	—	40.00	80.00	175.00	350.00
	1826 JJ full J's	—	30.00	60.00	125.00	250.00
	1826 MJ	—	—	—	Rare	—
	1827 MJ	—	40.00	75.00	125.00	250.00
	1827 MJ/JJ	—	40.00	75.00	125.00	250.00
	1827 MR	—	100.00	200.00	350.00	600.00
	1828 MJ	—	30.00	60.00	125.00	250.00
	1828/7 MR	—	200.00	400.00	600.00	1200.
	1828 MR	—	200.00	400.00	600.00	1200.
	1829 MJ	—	20.00	35.00	55.00	150.00
	1830 MJ oblong beading and narrow J	—	20.00	30.00	55.00	150.00
	1830 MJ regular beading and wide J	—	20.00	30.00	55.00	150.00
	1831 MJ colon after date	—	12.00	20.00	30.00	100.00
	1831 MJ 2 stars after date	—	12.00	20.00	30.00	100.00
	1832 MJ	—	12.00	20.00	30.00	100.00
	1832 MJ 1 of date over inverted 1	—	20.00	35.00	65.00	125.00
	1833 MJ	—	12.00	20.00	30.00	100.00
	1833 JM	—	1000.	1500.	2000.	2500.
	1834 PJ	—	12.00	20.00	30.00	100.00
	1835 PJ star on cap	—	12.00	20.00	30.00	100.00
	1835 PJ dot on cap	—	12.00	20.00	30.00	100.00
	1836 PJ	—	12.00	20.00	30.00	100.00
	1837 PJ	—	12.00	20.00	30.00	100.00
	1838 PJ	—	12.00	20.00	30.00	100.00
	1839 PJ/JJ	—	12.00	20.00	30.00	100.00
	1839 PJ	—	12.00	20.00	30.00	100.00
	1840/30 PJ	—	20.00	30.00	50.00	150.00
	1840 PJ	—	12.00	20.00	30.00	125.00
	1841/31 PJ	—	12.00	20.00	30.00	100.00
	1841 PJ	—	12.00	20.00	30.00	100.00
	1842/31 PM/PJ	—	25.00	35.00	60.00	150.00
	1842 PJ	—	20.00	30.00	50.00	125.00
	1842 PM/PJ	—	12.00	20.00	30.00	100.00
	1842 PM	—	12.00	20.00	30.00	100.00
	1843 PM dot after date	—	12.00	20.00	30.00	100.00
	1843 PM triangle of dots after date	—	12.00	20.00	30.00	100.00
	1844 PM	—	12.00	20.00	30.00	100.00
	1845 PM	—	12.00	20.00	30.00	100.00
	1846/5 PM eagle type of 1845	—	20.00	30.00	50.00	150.00
	1846 PM early type of 1847	—	15.00	25.00	35.00	125.00
	1847 PM	—	12.00	20.00	30.00	75.00
	1848/7 PM	—	20.00	35.00	65.00	150.00
	1848 PM	—	20.00	35.00	65.00	150.00
	1848 PF	—	12.00	20.00	30.00	75.00
	1849 PF	—	12.00	20.00	30.00	75.00
	1850 PF	—	12.00	20.00	30.00	75.00
	1851/0 PF	—	20.00	30.00	50.00	100.00
	1851 PF	—	12.00	20.00	30.00	75.00
	1852/1 PF	—	20.00	30.00	50.00	100.00
	1852 PF	—	12.00	20.00	30.00	75.00
	1853/2 PF	—	20.00	30.00	50.00	100.00
	1853 PF	—	12.00	20.00	30.00	75.00
	1854 PF	—	12.00	20.00	30.00	75.00
	1855 PF large letters	—	12.00	20.00	30.00	75.00
	1855 PF small letters	—	12.00	20.00	30.00	75.00
	1856/5 PF	—	20.00	30.00	50.00	100.00
377.8	1856 PF	—	12.00	20.00	30.00	75.00
	1857/5 PF	—	20.00	30.00	50.00	100.00
	1857/6 PF	—	20.00	30.00	50.00	100.00
	1857 PF	—	12.00	20.00	30.00	75.00
	1858 PF	—	12.00	20.00	30.00	75.00
	1859/7 PF	—	20.00	30.00	50.00	100.00
	1859/8 PF	—	20.00	30.00	50.00	100.00
	1859 PF	—	12.00	20.00	30.00	75.00
	1860/50 PF	—	20.00	30.00	50.00	100.00
	1860/59 PF	—	12.00	18.00	25.00	85.00
	1860 PF	—	12.00	15.00	20.00	75.00
	1861/51 PF	—	15.00	20.00	30.00	100.00
	1861/0 PF	—	12.00	15.00	20.00	75.00
	1861 PF	—	12.00	15.00	20.00	75.00
	1862 YE/PF	—	12.00	15.00	20.00	75.00
	1862 YE	—	12.00	15.00	20.00	75.00
	1862 YF	—	12.00	15.00	20.00	75.00
	1862 YF/PF	—	12.00	15.00	20.00	75.00
	1863/53 YF	—	12.00	18.00	25.00	75.00
	1863/54 YF	—	15.00	20.00	30.00	100.00
	1863 YE	—	—	—	Rare	—
	1863 YF	—	12.00	15.00	20.00	75.00
	1867/57 YF	—	15.00	20.00	30.00	100.00
	1867 YF	—	12.00	15.00	20.00	75.00
	1868/58 YF	—	15.00	20.00	30.00	100.00
	1868 YF	—	12.00	15.00	20.00	75.00
	1870/60 FR	—	20.00	30.00	50.00	150.00
	1870 YF	—	—	—	Rare	—
	1870 FR/YF	—	12.00	18.00	25.00	85.00
	1870 FR	—	12.00	15.00	20.00	75.00
	1873 FR	—	12.00	15.00	20.00	75.00
	1874/3 FR	—	15.00	20.00	30.00	85.00
	1874 FR	—	15.00	25.00	35.00	100.00
	1875/6 FR	—	15.00	20.00	30.00	85.00
	1875 FR small circle w/dot on eagle	—	12.00	15.00	20.00	75.00
	1876/5 FR	—	15.00	20.00	30.00	85.00
	1876 FR	—	12.00	15.00	20.00	60.00
	1877 FR	2.477	12.00	15.00	20.00	60.00
	1878/7 FR	2.273	15.00	20.00	30.00	75.00
	1878/7 SM	—	15.00	20.00	30.00	75.00
	1878 FR	I.A.	12.00	15.00	20.00	65.00
	1878 SM,S/F	—	15.00	20.00	25.00	70.00
	1878 SM	—	12.00	15.00	20.00	65.00
	1879/7 SM	—	15.00	20.00	30.00	75.00
	1879/8 SM	—	15.00	20.00	30.00	75.00
	1879/8 SM/FR	—	15.00	20.00	30.00	75.00
	1879 SM	—	12.00	15.00	20.00	65.00
	1879 SM/FR	—	15.00	20.00	30.00	75.00
	1880/70 SB	—	15.00	20.00	30.00	75.00
	1880 SB/SM	—	12.00	15.00	20.00	65.00
	1881/71 SB	— 3.974	15.00	20.00	30.00	75.00
	1881/0 SB	I.A.	15.00	20.00	30.00	75.00
	1881 SB	I.A.	12.00	15.00	20.00	65.00
	1882 SB	2.015	12.00	15.00	20.00	75.00
	1883 SB	2.100	35.00	75.00	125.00	250.00
	1883 BR	I.A.	12.00	15.00	20.00	65.00
	1883 BR/SR	—	12.00	15.00	20.00	65.00
	1883 BR/SB	Inc. Ab.	12.00	15.00	20.00	65.00
	1884/73 BR	—	20.00	30.00	40.00	100.00
	1884/74 BR	—	20.00	30.00	40.00	100.00
	1884/3 BR	—	20.00	30.00	40.00	100.00
	1884 BR	—	12.00	15.00	20.00	65.00
	1884/74 RR	—	50.00	100.00	175.00	350.00
	1884 RR	—	50.00	100.00	175.00	350.00
	1885/75 RR	2.363	15.00	20.00	30.00	75.00
	1885 RR	I.A.	12.00	15.00	20.00	65.00
	1886/75 RR	4.127	15.00	20.00	25.00	70.00
	1886/76 RR	Inc. Ab.	12.00	15.00	20.00	65.00
	1886/5 RR/BR	Inc. Ab.	12.00	15.00	20.00	65.00
	1886 RR	I.A.	12.00	15.00	20.00	65.00
	1887 RR	4.205	10.00	15.00	20.00	65.00
	1888 RR	3.985	10.00	15.00	20.00	65.00
	1889 RR	3.646	10.00	15.00	20.00	65.00
	1890 RR	3.615	10.00	15.00	20.00	65.00
	1891 RS	3.197	10.00	15.00	20.00	65.00
	1891 RR	—	Contemporary counterfeit			
	1892 RS	3.672	10.00	15.00	20.00	65.00
	1893 RS	3.854	10.00	15.00	20.00	65.00
	1894 RS	4.127	10.00	15.00	20.00	65.00
	1895/1 RS	3.768	15.00	20.00	25.00	75.00
	1895/3 RS	I.A.	15.00	20.00	25.00	75.00
	1895 RS	I.A.	10.00	15.00	20.00	65.00
	1896/1 Go/As RS/ML	5.229	15.00	20.00	25.00	75.00
	1896/1 RS	I.A.	12.00	15.00	20.00	65.00
	1896 Go/Ga RS	Inc. Ab.	—	—	—	—
	1896 RS	I.A.	10.00	12.00	18.00	60.00
	1897 RS	4.344	10.00	12.00	18.00	60.00

NOTE: Varieties exist.

Mint mark: Ho

KM#	Date	Mintage	Fine	VF	XF	Unc
377.9	1835 PP	—	—	—	—	—
	1836 PP	—	—	—	Unique	—
	1839 PR	—	—	—	Unique	—
	1861 FM	—	—	—	Rare	—
	1862 FM	—	—	—	Rare	—
	1862 FM reeded edge	—	—	—	Rare	—
	1863 FM	—	150.00	300.00	800.00	—
	1864 FM	—	—	—	Rare	—
	1864 PR	—	—	—	Rare	—
	1865 FM	—	250.00	500.00	950.00	—
	1866 FM	—	—	—	Rare	—
	1866 MP	—	—	—	Rare	—
	1867 PR	—	100.00	175.00	275.00	500.00
	1868 PR	—	20.00	35.00	65.00	175.00
	1869 PR	—	40.00	60.00	125.00	250.00
	1870 PR	—	50.00	80.00	150.00	300.00
	1871/0 PR	—	50.00	75.00	125.00	250.00
	1871 PR	—	30.00	50.00	90.00	200.00
	1872/1 PR	—	35.00	60.00	90.00	200.00
	1872 PR	—	30.00	50.00	75.00	175.00
	1873 PR	.351	30.00	50.00	85.00	150.00
	1874 PR	—	15.00	20.00	40.00	125.00
	1875 PR	—	15.00	20.00	40.00	125.00
	1876 AF	—	15.00	20.00	40.00	125.00
	1877 AF	.410	20.00	30.00	50.00	150.00
	1877 GR	I.A.	100.00	150.00	225.00	400.00
	1877 JA	I.A.	25.00	50.00	85.00	175.00
	1878 JA	.451	15.00	20.00	40.00	100.00
	1879 JA	—	15.00	20.00	40.00	100.00
	1880 JA	—	15.00	20.00	40.00	100.00
	1881 JA	.586	15.00	20.00	40.00	100.00
	1882 HoJA O above H	.240	25.00	40.00	65.00	125.00
	1882 HoJA O after H	I.A.	25.00	40.00	65.00	125.00
	1883/2 JA	.204	225.00	375.00	550.00	1000.
	1883/2 FM/JA	I.A.	25.00	40.00	75.00	150.00
	1883 FM	I.A.	20.00	30.00	60.00	125.00
	1883 JA	I.A.	200.00	350.00	500.00	1000.
	1884/3 FM	—	20.00	25.00	50.00	125.00
	1884 FM	—	15.00	20.00	40.00	100.00
	1885 FM	.132	15.00	20.00	40.00	100.00
	1886 FM	.225	20.00	30.00	45.00	125.00
	1886 FG	I.A.	20.00	30.00	45.00	125.00
	1887 FG	.150	20.00	35.00	65.00	150.00
	1888 FG	.364	12.00	18.00	25.00	100.00
	1889 FG	.490	12.00	18.00	25.00	100.00
	1890 FG	.565	12.00	18.00	25.00	100.00
	1891 FG	.738	12.00	18.00	25.00	100.00
	1892 FG	.643	12.00	18.00	25.00	100.00
	1893 FG	.518	12.00	18.00	25.00	100.00
	1894 FG	.504	12.00	18.00	25.00	100.00
	1895 FG	.320	12.00	18.00	25.00	100.00

NOTE: Varieties exist.

Mint mark: Mo

KM#	Date	Mintage	Fine	VF	XF	Unc
377.10	1824 JM round tail	—	75.00	125.00	250.00	500.00
	1824 JM square tail	—	75.00	125.00	250.00	500.00
	1825 JM	—	25.00	35.00	50.00	150.00
	1826/5 JM	—	25.00	40.00	75.00	150.00
	1826 JM	—	20.00	30.00	50.00	125.00
	1827 JM medal alignment	—	25.00	35.00	50.00	125.00
	1827 JM coin alignment	—	25.00	35.00	50.00	125.00
	1828 JM	—	30.00	60.00	100.00	200.00
	1829 JM	—	20.00	30.00	50.00	125.00
	1830/20 JM	—	35.00	55.00	100.00	200.00
	1830 JM	—	30.00	50.00	90.00	175.00
	1831 JM	—	30.00	50.00	100.00	200.00

KM#	Date	Mintage	Fine	VF	XF	Unc
377.10	1832/1 JM	—	25.00	40.00	60.00	125.00
	1832 JM	—	20.00	30.00	40.00	100.00
	1833 MJ	—	25.00	40.00	80.00	175.00
	1833 ML	—	500.00	750.00	950.00	2000.
	1834/3 ML	—	25.00	35.00	50.00	125.00
	1834 ML	—	20.00	30.00	40.00	100.00
	1835 ML	—	20.00	30.00	40.00	125.00
	1836 ML	—	50.00	100.00	150.00	300.00
	1836 ML/MF	—	50.00	100.00	150.00	300.00
	1836 MF	—	30.00	50.00	80.00	175.00
	1836 MF/ML	—	35.00	60.00	90.00	200.00
	1837/6 ML	—	30.00	50.00	75.00	150.00
	1837/6 MM	—	30.00	50.00	75.00	150.00
	1837/6 MM/ML	—	30.00	50.00	75.00	150.00
	1837/6 MM/MF	—	30.00	50.00	75.00	150.00
	1837 ML	—	30.00	50.00	75.00	150.00
	1837 MM	—	75.00	125.00	175.00	325.00
	1838 MM	—	30.00	50.00	75.00	150.00
	1838 ML	—	20.00	35.00	60.00	125.00
	1838 ML/MM	—	20.00	35.00	60.00	125.00
	1839 ML	—	15.00	25.00	35.00	100.00
	1840 ML	—	15.00	25.00	35.00	100.00
	1841 ML	—	15.00	25.00	35.00	75.00
	1842 ML	—	15.00	25.00	35.00	75.00
	1842 MM	—	15.00	25.00	35.00	75.00
	1843 MM	—	15.00	25.00	35.00	75.00
	1844 MF/MM	—	—	—	—	—
	1844 MF	—	15.00	25.00	35.00	75.00
	1845/4 MF	—	15.00	25.00	35.00	75.00
	1845 MF	—	15.00	25.00	35.00	75.00
	1846/5 MF	—	15.00	25.00	35.00	100.00
	1846 MF	—	15.00	25.00	35.00	100.00
	1847/6 MF	—	—	—	Rare	—
	1847 MF	—	—	—	Rare	—
	1847 RC	—	20.00	30.00	40.00	100.00
	1847 RC/MF	—	15.00	25.00	35.00	75.00
	1848 GC	—	15.00	25.00	35.00	75.00
	1849/8 GC	—	20.00	35.00	50.00	100.00
	1849 GC	—	15.00	25.00	35.00	75.00
	1850/40 GC	—	25.00	50.00	100.00	200.00
	1850/49 GC	—	25.00	50.00	100.00	200.00
	1850 GC	—	20.00	40.00	75.00	150.00
	1851 GC	—	20.00	40.00	60.00	125.00
	1852 GC	—	15.00	30.00	45.00	100.00
	1853 GC	—	15.00	25.00	40.00	100.00
	1854 GC	—	15.00	25.00	40.00	100.00
	1855 GC	—	20.00	35.00	65.00	125.00
	1855 GF	—	12.00	15.00	20.00	75.00
	1855 GF/GC	—	12.00	15.00	20.00	75.00
	1856/4 GF	—	15.00	25.00	40.00	100.00
	1856/5 GF	—	15.00	25.00	40.00	100.00
	1856 GF	—	12.00	15.00	20.00	75.00
	1857 GF	—	10.00	15.00	20.00	75.00
	1858/7 FH/GF	—	10.00	15.00	20.00	75.00
	1858 FH	—	10.00	15.00	20.00	75.00
	1859 FH	—	10.00	15.00	20.00	75.00
	1860/59 FH	—	15.00	20.00	25.00	75.00
	1860 FH	—	10.00	15.00	20.00	65.00
	1860 TH	—	12.00	18.00	30.00	100.00
	1861 TH	—	10.00	15.00	20.00	75.00
	1861 CH	—	10.00	15.00	20.00	75.00
	1862 CH	—	10.00	15.00	20.00	75.00
	1863 CH	—	10.00	15.00	20.00	75.00
	1863 CH/TH	—	10.00	15.00	20.00	75.00
	1863 TH	—	10.00	15.00	20.00	75.00
	1867 CH	—	10.00	15.00	20.00	65.00
	1868 CH	—	10.00	15.00	20.00	65.00
	1868 CH/PH	—	10.00	15.00	20.00	65.00
	1868 PH	—	10.00	15.00	20.00	65.00
	1869 CH	—	10.00	15.00	20.00	65.00
	1873 MH	—	10.00	15.00	20.00	65.00
	1873 MH/HH	—	12.00	18.00	25.00	75.00
	1874/69 MH	—	15.00	25.00	45.00	100.00
	1874 MH	—	12.00	18.00	25.00	75.00
	1874 BH/MH	—	12.00	15.00	20.00	65.00
	1874 BH	—	10.00	15.00	20.00	65.00
	1875 BH	—	10.00	15.00	20.00	65.00
	1876/4 BH	—	12.00	18.00	25.00	75.00
	1876/5 BH	—	12.00	18.00	25.00	75.00
	1876 BH	—	10.00	15.00	20.00	65.00
	1877 MH	.898	10.00	15.00	20.00	65.00
	1877 MH/BH	Inc. Ab.	12.00	18.00	25.00	75.00
	1878 MH	2.154	10.00	15.00	20.00	65.00
	1879/8 MH	—	10.00	15.00	20.00	75.00
	1879 MH	—	10.00	15.00	20.00	65.00
	1880/79 MH	—	15.00	20.00	30.00	75.00
	1880 MH	—	10.00	15.00	20.00	75.00
	1881 MH	5.712	10.00	15.00	20.00	65.00
	1882/1 MH	2.746	12.00	15.00	20.00	75.00
	1882 MH	I.A.	10.00	15.00	20.00	65.00
	1883/2 MH	2.726	12.00	18.00	25.00	85.00
	1883 MH	I.A.	10.00	15.00	20.00	65.00
	1884/3 MH	—	15.00	20.00	30.00	75.00
	1884 MH	—	10.00	15.00	20.00	65.00
	1885 MH	3.649	10.00	15.00	20.00	65.00
	1886 MH	7.558	10.00	12.00	18.00	60.00
	1887 MH	7.681	10.00	12.00	18.00	60.00
	1888 MH	7.179	10.00	12.00	18.00	60.00
	1889 MH	7.332	10.00	15.00	20.00	65.00
	1890 MH	7.412	10.00	12.00	18.00	60.00
	1890 AM	I.A.	10.00	12.00	18.00	60.00
	1891 AM	8.076	10.00	12.00	18.00	60.00
	1892 AM	9.392	10.00	12.00	18.00	60.00
	1893 AM	10.773	10.00	12.00	18.00	55.00

KM#	Date	Mintage	Fine	VF	XF	Unc
377.10	1894 AM	12.394	10.00	12.00	18.00	45.00
	1895 AM	10.474	10.00	12.00	18.00	45.00
	1895 AB	I.A.	10.00	12.00	18.00	60.00
	1896 AB	9.327	10.00	12.00	18.00	60.00
	1896 AM	I.A.	10.00	12.00	18.00	60.00
	1897 AM	8.621	10.00	12.00	18.00	60.00

NOTE: Varieties exist. 1874 CP is a die struck counterfeit.

Mint mark: O, Oa

KM#	Date	Mintage	Fine	VF	XF	Unc
377.11	1858O AE	—	—	—	Rare	—
	1858OaAE	—	—	—	Rare	—
	1859 AE A in O of mm	—	250.00	550.00	1000.	—
	1860 AE A in O of mm	—	200.00	400.00	600.00	—
	1861 O FR	—	125.00	250.00	500.00	1000.
	1861OaFR	—	200.00	400.00	600.00	—
	1862O FR	—	40.00	80.00	200.00	375.00
	1862OaFR	—	65.00	125.00	250.00	450.00
	1863O FR	—	30.00	60.00	100.00	250.00
	1863O AE	—	30.00	60.00	100.00	250.00
	1863OaAE A in O of mm	—	100.00	150.00	250.00	450.00
	1863OaAE A above O in mm	—	—	—	Rare	—
	1864 FR	—	25.00	50.00	75.00	200.00
	1867 AE	—	40.00	80.00	150.00	400.00
	1868 AE	—	25.00	50.00	100.00	250.00
	1869 AE	—	30.00	60.00	100.00	250.00
	1873 AE	—	200.00	300.00	600.00	1250.
	1874 AE	.142	15.00	30.00	50.00	200.00
	1875/4 AE	.131	25.00	50.00	75.00	200.00
	1875 AE	I.A.	15.00	30.00	40.00	125.00
	1876 AE	.140	20.00	35.00	55.00	200.00
	1877 AE	.139	20.00	30.00	50.00	200.00
	1878 AE	.125	15.00	25.00	50.00	200.00
	1879 AE	.153	15.00	30.00	45.00	150.00
	1880 AE	.143	15.00	30.00	45.00	150.00
	1881 AE	.134	20.00	35.00	60.00	150.00
	1882 AE	.100	20.00	35.00	60.00	150.00
	1883 AE	.122	15.00	30.00	45.00	150.00
	1884 AE	.142	15.00	30.00	50.00	150.00
	1885 AE	.158	15.00	25.00	40.00	125.00
	1886 AE	.120	15.00	30.00	45.00	150.00
	1887/6 AE	.115	25.00	50.00	80.00	200.00
	1887 AE	I.A.	15.00	25.00	40.00	125.00
	1888 AE	.145	15.00	25.00	40.00	125.00
	1889 AE	.150	20.00	30.00	60.00	175.00
	1890 AE	.181	20.00	30.00	60.00	175.00
	1891 EN	.160	15.00	25.00	40.00	125.00
	1892 EN	.120	15.00	25.00	40.00	125.00
	1893 EN	.066	45.00	75.00	115.00	225.00

NOTE: Varieties exist.

Mint mark: Pi

KM#	Date	Mintage	Fine	VF	XF	Unc
377.12	1827 JS	—	—	—	Rare	—
	1828/7 JS	—	250.00	400.00	600.00	1200.
	1828 JS	—	200.00	350.00	500.00	1000.
	1829 JS	—	35.00	65.00	125.00	250.00
	1830 JS	—	30.00	50.00	100.00	200.00
	1831/0 JS	—	30.00	60.00	125.00	250.00
	1831 JS	—	25.00	35.00	65.00	200.00
	1832/22 JS	—	25.00	35.00	55.00	150.00
	1832 JS	—	25.00	35.00	55.00	150.00
	1833/2 JS	—	30.00	40.00	50.00	150.00
	1833 JS	—	20.00	30.00	40.00	125.00
	1834/3 JS	—	25.00	35.00	50.00	125.00
	1834 JS	—	15.00	25.00	40.00	125.00
	1835 JS denomination 8R	—	20.00	30.00	60.00	150.00
	1835 JS denomination 8Rs	—	15.00	25.00	40.00	125.00
	1836 JS	—	20.00	30.00	45.00	125.00
	1837 JS	—	30.00	50.00	80.00	175.00
	1838 JS	—	20.00	30.00	45.00	125.00
	1839 JS	—	20.00	40.00	60.00	125.00

KM#	Date	Mintage	Fine	VF	XF	Unc
377.12	1840 JS	—	20.00	30.00	50.00	125.00
	1841PiJS	—	25.00	40.00	80.00	175.00
	1841iPJS (error)	—	50.00	100.00	200.00	400.00
	1842/1 JS	—	40.00	60.00	90.00	175.00
	1842/1 PS/JS	—	35.00	55.00	85.00	175.00
	1842 JS eagle type of 1843	—	30.00	50.00	75.00	150.00
	1842 PS	—	30.00	50.00	75.00	150.00
	1842 PS/JS eagle type of 1841	—	30.00	50.00	75.00	150.00
	1843/2 PS round top 3	—	50.00	75.00	150.00	250.00
	1843 PS flat top 3	—	30.00	60.00	125.00	225.00
	1843 AM round top 3	—	20.00	30.00	50.00	125.00
	1843 AM flat top 3	—	20.00	30.00	50.00	125.00
	1844 AM	—	20.00	30.00	50.00	125.00
	1845/4 AM	—	25.00	50.00	100.00	225.00
	1845 AM	—	25.00	50.00	100.00	225.00
	1846/5 AM	—	25.00	35.00	50.00	125.00
	1846 AM	—	15.00	25.00	40.00	125.00
	1847 AM	—	30.00	50.00	80.00	150.00
	1848/7 AM	—	30.00	60.00	90.00	175.00
	1848 AM	—	30.00	50.00	80.00	150.00
	1849/8 PS/AM	—	—	—	Rare	—
	1849 PS/AM	—	—	—	Rare	—
	1849 MC/PS	—	60.00	125.00	250.00	500.00
	1849 AM	—	—	—	Rare	—
	1849 MC	—	60.00	125.00	250.00	500.00
	1850 MC	—	40.00	80.00	150.00	300.00
	1851 MC	—	125.00	200.00	300.00	600.00
	1852 MC	—	75.00	125.00	200.00	400.00
	1853 MC	—	125.00	175.00	300.00	600.00
	1854 MC	—	100.00	150.00	250.00	500.00
	1855 MC	—	100.00	150.00	250.00	500.00
	1856 MC	—	65.00	100.00	200.00	400.00
	1857 MC	—	—	—	Rare	—
	1857 PS/MC	—	150.00	225.00	375.00	700.00
	1857 PS	—	125.00	200.00	350.00	650.00
	1858 MC/PS	—	250.00	400.00	650.00	1200.
	1858 MC	—	250.00	400.00	650.00	1200.
	1858 PS	—	—	—	Rare	—
	1859/8 MC/PS	—	—	—	Rare	—
	1859 MC/PS	—	—	—	Rare	—
	1859 PS/PC	—	—	—	Rare	—
	1859 PS	—	—	—	Rare	—
	1860 FC	—	2000.	4000.	6500.	—
	1860 FE	—	—	—	Rare	—
	1860 MC	—	2000.	4000.	6500.	—
	1860 PS	—	400.00	600.00	900.00	1750.
	1861 PS	—	30.00	60.00	90.00	175.00
	1861 RO	—	25.00	35.00	55.00	125.00
	1862/1 RO	—	20.00	25.00	50.00	125.00
	1862 RO	—	15.00	20.00	40.00	100.00
	1862 RO oval O in RO	—	15.00	20.00	40.00	100.00
	1862 RO round O in RO, 6 is inverted 9	—	20.00	30.00	50.00	125.00
	1863/2 RO	—	25.00	35.00	65.00	150.00
	1863 RO	—	15.00	20.00	40.00	125.00
	1863 6/inverted 6	—	25.00	35.00	55.00	125.00
	1863 FC	—	—	—	Rare	—
	1864 RO	—	—	—	Rare	—
	1867 CA	—	—	—	Rare	—
	1867 LR	—	—	—	Rare	—
	1867 PS	—	30.00	60.00	125.00	275.00
	1868/7 PS	—	30.00	60.00	125.00	250.00
	1868 PS	—	20.00	30.00	50.00	125.00
	1869/8 PS	—	20.00	25.00	45.00	125.00
	1869 PS	—	15.00	20.00	40.00	125.00
	1870/69 PS	—	—	—	Rare	—
	1870 PS	—	—	—	Rare	—
	1873 MH	—	15.00	20.00	40.00	135.00
	1874/3 MH	—	15.00	20.00	30.00	125.00
	1874 MH	—	10.00	12.00	18.00	100.00
	1875 MH	—	10.00	12.00	18.00	100.00
	1876/5 MH	—	15.00	20.00	30.00	125.00
	1876 MH	—	10.00	12.00	18.00	100.00
	1877 MH	1.018	10.00	12.00	18.00	100.00
	1878 MH	1.046	12.00	15.00	25.00	125.00
	1879/8 MH	—	15.00	20.00	30.00	125.00
	1879 MH	—	10.00	12.00	18.00	100.00
	1879 BE	—	25.00	50.00	75.00	150.00
	1879 MR	—	30.00	50.00	100.00	200.00
	1880 MR	—	250.00	400.00	800.00	—
	1880 MH	—	10.00	12.00	18.00	100.00
	1881 MH	2.100	10.00	12.00	18.00	100.00
	1882/1 MH	1.602	15.00	20.00	30.00	125.00
	1882 MH	I.A.	10.00	12.00	18.00	100.00
	1883 MH	1.545	10.00	12.00	18.00	100.00
	1884/3 MH	—	15.00	20.00	30.00	125.00
	1884 MH/MM	—	12.00	15.00	20.00	85.00
	1884 MH	—	10.00	12.00	18.00	75.00
	1885/4 MH	1.736	15.00	20.00	30.00	125.00
	1885/8 MH	I.A.	15.00	20.00	30.00	125.00
	1885 MH	I.A.	10.00	12.00	18.00	75.00
	1885 LC	I.A.	12.00	18.00	25.00	100.00
	1886 LC	3.347	10.00	12.00	18.00	75.00
	1886 MR	I.A.	10.00	12.00	18.00	75.00
	1887 MR	2.922	10.00	12.00	18.00	75.00
	1888 MR	2.438	10.00	12.00	18.00	75.00
	1889 MR	2.103	10.00	12.00	18.00	75.00
	1890 MR	1.562	10.00	12.00	18.00	65.00
	1891 MR	1.184	10.00	12.00	18.00	65.00
	1892 MR	1.336	10.00	12.00	18.00	65.00
	1893 MR	.530	10.00	12.00	18.00	75.00

NOTE: Varieties exist.

Mint mark: Zs

KM#	Date	Mintage	Fine	VF	XF	Unc
377.13	1825 AZ	—	25.00	35.00	60.00	150.00
	1826/5 AZ	—	25.00	45.00	75.00	175.00
	1826 AZ	—	20.00	35.00	60.00	150.00
	1826 AV	—	225.00	450.00	700.00	1500.
	1826 AO	—	350.00	650.00	1000.	2000.
	1827 AO/AZ	—	35.00	50.00	125.00	250.00
	1827 AO	—	25.00	45.00	85.00	175.00
	1828 AO	—	15.00	20.00	40.00	125.00
	1829 AO	—	15.00	20.00	40.00	125.00
	1829 OV	—	50.00	90.00	150.00	300.00
	1830 OV	—	15.00	20.00	40.00	125.00
	1831 OV	—	25.00	50.00	90.00	175.00
	1831 OM	—	15.00	25.00	50.00	125.00
	1832/1 OM	—	20.00	25.00	40.00	125.00
	1832 OM	—	15.00	20.00	35.00	100.00
	1833/2 OM	—	20.00	30.00	40.00	125.00
	1833 OM/MM	—	15.00	25.00	35.00	100.00
	1833 OM	—	15.00	20.00	30.00	100.00
	1834 OM	—	15.00	20.00	30.00	100.00
	1835 OM	—	15.00	20.00	35.00	100.00
	1836/4 OM	—	20.00	30.00	45.00	125.00
	1836/5 OM	—	20.00	30.00	45.00	125.00
	1836 OM	—	15.00	20.00	30.00	100.00
	1837 OM	—	15.00	20.00	30.00	100.00
	1838/7 OM	—	20.00	30.00	40.00	125.00
	1838 OM	—	15.00	20.00	30.00	100.00
	1839 OM	—	15.00	20.00	30.00	100.00
	1840 OM	—	15.00	20.00	30.00	100.00
	1841 OM	—	15.00	20.00	30.00	100.00
	1842 OM eagle type of 1841	—	15.00	20.00	30.00	100.00
	1842 OM eagle type of 1843	—	15.00	20.00	30.00	100.00
	1843 OM	—	15.00	20.00	30.00	100.00
	1844 OM	—	15.00	20.00	30.00	100.00
	1845 OM	—	15.00	20.00	30.00	100.00
	1846 OM	—	15.00	20.00	30.00	100.00
	1847 OM	—	15.00	20.00	30.00	100.00
	1848/7 OM	—	20.00	30.00	40.00	125.00
	1848 OM	—	15.00	20.00	30.00	100.00
	1849 OM	—	15.00	20.00	30.00	100.00
	1850 OM	—	15.00	20.00	30.00	100.00
	1851 OM	—	15.00	20.00	30.00	100.00
	1852 OM	—	15.00	20.00	30.00	100.00
	1853 OM	—	30.00	45.00	65.00	200.00
	1854/3 OM	—	20.00	30.00	50.00	150.00
	1854 OM	—	15.00	25.00	40.00	125.00
	1855 OM	—	20.00	30.00	60.00	125.00
	1855 MO	—	30.00	60.00	90.00	175.00
	1856/5 MO	—	20.00	30.00	40.00	125.00
	1856 MO	—	15.00	20.00	30.00	100.00
	1857/5 MO	—	20.00	30.00	40.00	125.00
	1857 MO	—	15.00	20.00	30.00	100.00
	1858/7 MO	—	15.00	20.00	30.00	100.00
	1858 MO	—	15.00	20.00	30.00	100.00
	1859/8 MO	—	15.00	20.00	30.00	100.00
	1859 MO	—	15.00	20.00	30.00	100.00
	1859 VL/MO	—	25.00	50.00	75.00	150.00
	1859 VL	—	20.00	40.00	60.00	125.00
	1860/50 MO	—	10.00	12.00	18.00	75.00
	1860/59 MO	—	10.00	12.00	18.00	75.00
	1860 MO	—	10.00	12.00	18.00	75.00
	1860 VL/MO	—	10.00	12.00	18.00	75.00
	1860 VL	—	10.00	12.00	18.00	75.00
	1861/0 VL/MO	—	10.00	12.00	18.00	75.00
	1861/0 VL	—	10.00	12.00	18.00	75.00
	1861 VL	—	10.00	12.00	18.00	75.00
	1862/1 VL	—	15.00	20.00	30.00	100.00
	1862 VL	—	10.00	12.00	18.00	75.00
	1863 VL	—	10.00	12.00	18.00	75.00
	1863 MO	—	10.00	12.00	18.00	75.00
	1864/3 VL	—	15.00	20.00	30.00	100.00
	1864 VL	—	10.00	12.00	18.00	75.00
	1864 MO	—	15.00	20.00	30.00	100.00
	1865/4 MO	—	200.00	450.00	700.00	1500.
	1865 MO	—	175.00	400.00	600.00	1250.
	1866 VL	—	Contemporary counterfeit			
	1867 JS	—	—	—	Rare	—
	1868 JS	—	10.00	12.00	18.00	75.00
	1868 YH	—	10.00	12.00	18.00	75.00
	1869 YH	—	10.00	12.00	18.00	75.00
	1870 YH	—	—	—	Rare	—
	1873 YH	—	10.00	12.00	18.00	75.00
	1874 YH	—	10.00	12.00	18.00	75.00
	1874 JA/YA	—	10.00	12.00	18.00	75.00
	1874 JA	—	10.00	12.00	18.00	75.00
	1875 JA	—	10.00	12.00	18.00	75.00
	1876 JA	—	10.00	12.00	18.00	75.00
	1876 JS	—	10.00	12.00	18.00	75.00
	1877 JS	2.700	10.00	12.00	18.00	75.00
	1878 JS	2.310	10.00	12.00	18.00	75.00
	1879/8 JS	—	15.00	20.00	30.00	100.00
	1879 JS	—	10.00	12.00	18.00	75.00
	1880 JS	—	10.00	12.00	18.00	75.00
	1881 JS	5.592	10.00	12.00	18.00	75.00
	1882/1 JS	2.485	15.00	20.00	30.00	100.00
	1882 JS straight J	Inc. Ab.	10.00	12.00	18.00	60.00
	1882 JS full J	Inc. Ab.	10.00	12.00	18.00	60.00
	1883/2 JS	2.563	15.00	20.00	30.00	100.00
	1883 JS	I.A.	10.00	12.00	18.00	75.00
	1884 JS	—	10.00	12.00	18.00	75.00
	1885 JS	2.252	10.00	12.00	18.00	60.00
	1886/5 JS	5.303	15.00	20.00	30.00	100.00
	1886/8 JS	I.A.	15.00	20.00	30.00	100.00
	1886 JS	I.A.	10.00	12.00	18.00	60.00
	1886 FZ	I.A.	10.00	12.00	18.00	60.00
	1887ZsFZ	4.733	10.00	12.00	18.00	60.00
	1887Z FZ	I.A.	20.00	30.00	50.00	100.00
	1888/7 FZ	5.132	12.00	15.00	25.00	75.00
	1888 FZ	I.A.	10.00	12.00	18.00	60.00
	1889 FZ	4.344	10.00	12.00	18.00	60.00
	1890 FZ	3.887	10.00	12.00	18.00	60.00
	1891 FZ	4.114	10.00	12.00	18.00	60.00
	1892/1 FZ	4.238	12.00	15.00	25.00	75.00
	1892 FZ	I.A.	10.00	12.00	18.00	60.00
	1893 FZ	3.872	10.00	12.00	18.00	60.00
	1894 FZ	3.081	10.00	12.00	18.00	60.00
	1895 FZ	4.718	10.00	12.00	18.00	60.00
	1896 FZ	4.226	10.00	12.00	18.00	50.00
	1897 FZ	4.877	10.00	12.00	18.00	50.00

NOTE: Varieties exist.

1/2 ESCUDO

1.6900 g, .875 GOLD, .0475 oz AGW
Mint mark: C
Obv: Facing eagle.

KM#	Date	Mintage	VG	Fine	VF	XF
378	1848 CE	—	35.00	50.00	75.00	150.00
	1853 CE	—	35.00	50.00	75.00	150.00
	1854 CE	—	35.00	50.00	75.00	150.00
	1856 CE	—	50.00	100.00	150.00	250.00
	1857 CE	—	35.00	50.00	75.00	150.00
	1859 CE	—	35.00	50.00	75.00	150.00
	1860 CE	—	35.00	50.00	75.00	150.00
	1862 CE	—	35.00	50.00	75.00	125.00
	1863 CE	—	35.00	50.00	75.00	125.00
	1866 CE	—	35.00	50.00	75.00	125.00
	1867 CE	—	35.00	50.00	75.00	125.00
	1870 CE	—	—	—	—	—

Mint mark: Do

KM#	Date	Mintage	VG	Fine	VF	XF
378.1	1833 RM/RL	—	35.00	50.00	75.00	150.00
	1834/3 RM	—	35.00	50.00	75.00	150.00
	1835/3 RM	—	35.00	50.00	75.00	150.00
	1836/4 RM	—	35.00	50.00	75.00	150.00
	1837 RM	—	35.00	50.00	75.00	150.00
	1838 RM	—	40.00	60.00	100.00	175.00
	1843 RM	—	40.00	60.00	100.00	175.00
	1844/33 RM	—	40.00	60.00	100.00	175.00
	1844/33 RM/RL	—	40.00	60.00	100.00	175.00
	1846 RM	—	40.00	60.00	100.00	175.00
	1848 RM	—	40.00	60.00	100.00	175.00
	1850/33 JMR	—	40.00	60.00	100.00	175.00
	1851 JMR	—	40.00	60.00	100.00	200.00
	1852 JMR	—	40.00	60.00	100.00	175.00
	1853/33 CP	—	75.00	150.00	300.00	500.00
	1853 CP	—	35.00	50.00	75.00	150.00
	1854 CP	—	35.00	50.00	75.00	150.00
	1855 CP	—	35.00	50.00	75.00	150.00
	1859 CP	—	35.00	50.00	75.00	150.00
	1861 CP	—	35.00	50.00	75.00	150.00
	1864 LT	—	75.00	125.00	250.00	400.00

Mint mark: Ga

KM#	Date	Mintage	VG	Fine	VF	XF
378.2	1825 FS	—	40.00	60.00	100.00	175.00
	1829 FS	—	40.00	60.00	100.00	175.00
	1831 FS	—	40.00	60.00	100.00	175.00
	1834 FS	—	40.00	60.00	100.00	175.00
	1835 FS	—	40.00	60.00	100.00	175.00
	1837 JG	—	40.00	60.00	100.00	175.00
	1838 JG	—	40.00	60.00	100.00	175.00
	1839 JG	—	40.00	60.00	100.00	175.00
	1842 JG	—	40.00	60.00	100.00	175.00
	1847 JG	—	40.00	60.00	100.00	175.00
	1850 JG	—	35.00	50.00	75.00	150.00
	1852 JG	—	35.00	50.00	75.00	150.00

KM#	Date	Mintage	VG	Fine	VF	XF
378.2	1859 JG	—	40.00	60.00	100.00	175.00
	1861 JG	—	35.00	50.00	75.00	150.00

Mint mark: GC

KM#	Date	Mintage	VG	Fine	VF	XF
378.3	1846 MP	—	50.00	75.00	100.00	175.00
	1847 MP	—	50.00	75.00	100.00	175.00
	1848/7 MP	—	50.00	75.00	100.00	200.00
	1851 MP	—	50.00	75.00	100.00	175.00

Mint mark: Go

KM#	Date	Mintage	VG	Fine	VF	XF
378.4	1845 PM	—	30.00	40.00	65.00	125.00
	1849 PF	—	30.00	40.00	65.00	125.00
	1851/41 PF	—	30.00	40.00	65.00	125.00
	1851 PF	—	30.00	40.00	65.00	125.00
	1852 PF	—	30.00	40.00	65.00	125.00
	1853 PF	—	30.00	40.00	65.00	125.00
	1855 PF	—	30.00	50.00	80.00	150.00
	1857 PF	—	30.00	40.00	65.00	125.00
	1858/7 PF	—	30.00	40.00	65.00	125.00
	1859 PF	—	30.00	40.00	65.00	125.00
	1860 PF	—	30.00	40.00	65.00	125.00
	1861 PF	—	30.00	40.00	65.00	125.00
	1862/1 YE	—	30.00	40.00	65.00	125.00
	1863 YF	—	30.00	40.00	65.00	125.00

Mint mark: Mo

KM#	Date	Mintage	VG	Fine	VF	XF
378.5	1825/1 JM	—	50.00	75.00	125.00	200.00
	1825/4 JM	—	50.00	75.00	125.00	200.00
	1825 JM	—	30.00	40.00	80.00	150.00
	1827/6 JM	—	30.00	40.00	80.00	150.00
	1827 JM	—	30.00	40.00	80.00	150.00
	1829 JM	—	30.00	40.00	80.00	150.00
	1831/0 JM	—	30.00	40.00	80.00	150.00
	1831 JM	—	30.00	40.00	60.00	125.00
	1832 JM	—	30.00	40.00	60.00	125.00
	1833 MJ olive & oak branches reversed	—	30.00	50.00	90.00	175.00
	1834 ML	—	30.00	40.00	60.00	125.00
	1835 ML	—	30.00	40.00	80.00	150.00
	1838 ML	—	30.00	50.00	90.00	175.00
	1839 ML	—	30.00	50.00	90.00	175.00
	1840 ML	—	30.00	40.00	60.00	125.00
	1841 ML	—	30.00	40.00	60.00	125.00
	1842 ML	—	30.00	40.00	80.00	150.00
	1842 MM	—	30.00	40.00	80.00	150.00
	1843 MM	—	30.00	40.00	60.00	125.00
	1844 MF	—	30.00	40.00	60.00	125.00
	1845 MF	—	30.00	40.00	60.00	125.00
	1846/5 MF	—	30.00	40.00	60.00	125.00
	1846 MF	—	30.00	40.00	60.00	125.00
	1848 GC	—	30.00	40.00	60.00	125.00
	1850 GC	—	30.00	40.00	60.00	125.00
	1851 GC	—	30.00	40.00	60.00	125.00
	1852 GC	—	30.00	40.00	60.00	125.00
	1853 GC	—	30.00	40.00	60.00	125.00
	1854 GC	—	30.00	40.00	60.00	125.00
	1855 GF	—	30.00	40.00	60.00	125.00
	1856/4 GF	—	30.00	40.00	60.00	125.00
	1857 GF	—	30.00	40.00	60.00	125.00
	1858/7 FH/GF	—	35.00	50.00	75.00	150.00
	1858 FH	—	30.00	40.00	60.00	125.00
	1859 FH	—	30.00	40.00	60.00	125.00
	1860/59 FH	—	30.00	40.00	60.00	125.00
	1861 CH/FH	—	30.00	40.00	80.00	150.00
	1862 CH	—	30.00	40.00	60.00	125.00
	1863/57 CH/GF	—	30.00	40.00	60.00	125.00
	1868/58 PH	—	30.00	40.00	80.00	150.00
	1869/59 CH	—	30.00	40.00	80.00	150.00

Mint mark: Zs

KM#	Date	Mintage	VG	Fine	VF	XF
378.6	1860 VL	—	35.00	50.00	75.00	150.00
	1862/1 VL	—	35.00	50.00	75.00	150.00
	1862 VL	—	30.00	40.00	65.00	125.00

ESCUDO

3.3800 g, .875 GOLD, .0950 oz AGW
Mint mark: C
Obv: Facing eagle.

KM#	Date	Mintage	VG	Fine	VF	XF
379	1846 CE	—	75.00	100.00	200.00	350.00
	1847 CE	—	50.00	75.00	125.00	175.00
	1848 CE	—	50.00	75.00	125.00	175.00
	1849/8 CE	—	60.00	100.00	150.00	225.00
	1850 CE	—	50.00	75.00	125.00	175.00
	1851 CE	—	60.00	100.00	150.00	225.00
	1853/1 CE	—	60.00	100.00	150.00	225.00
	1854 CE	—	50.00	75.00	125.00	175.00
	1856/5/4 CE	—	60.00	100.00	150.00	225.00
	1856 CE	—	50.00	75.00	125.00	175.00
	1857/1 CE	—	60.00	100.00	150.00	225.00
	1857 CE	—	50.00	75.00	125.00	175.00
	1861 PV	—	50.00	75.00	125.00	175.00
	1862 CE	—	50.00	75.00	125.00	175.00
	1863 CE	—	50.00	75.00	125.00	175.00
	1866 CE	—	50.00	75.00	125.00	175.00
	1870 CE	—	50.00	75.00	125.00	175.00

Mint mark: Do

KM#	Date	Mintage	VG	Fine	VF	XF
379.1	1833/2 RM/RL	—	75.00	125.00	200.00	300.00
	1834 RM	—	60.00	100.00	150.00	200.00
	1835 RM	—	—	—	—	—
379.1	1836 RM/RL	—	60.00	100.00	150.00	200.00
	1838 RM	—	60.00	100.00	150.00	200.00
	1846/38 RM	—	75.00	125.00	200.00	300.00
	1850 JMR	—	75.00	125.00	175.00	225.00
	1851/31 JMR	—	75.00	125.00	200.00	300.00
	1851 JMR	—	75.00	125.00	175.00	225.00
	1853 CP	—	75.00	125.00	175.00	225.00
	1854/34 CP	—	75.00	125.00	175.00	225.00
	1854/44 CP/RP	—	75.00	125.00	175.00	225.00
	1855 CP	—	75.00	125.00	175.00	225.00
	1859 CP	—	75.00	125.00	175.00	225.00
	1861 CP	—	75.00	125.00	175.00	225.00
	1864 LT/CP	—	75.00	125.00	175.00	225.00

Mint mark: Ga

KM#	Date	Mintage	VG	Fine	VF	XF
379.2	1825 FS	—	60.00	90.00	125.00	200.00
	1826 FS	—	60.00	90.00	125.00	200.00
	1829 FS	—	—	—	—	—
	1831 FS	—	60.00	90.00	125.00	200.00
	1834 FS	—	60.00	90.00	125.00	200.00
	1835 JG	—	60.00	90.00	125.00	200.00
	1842 JG/MC	—	60.00	90.00	125.00	200.00
	1843 MC	—	60.00	90.00	125.00	200.00
	1847 JG	—	60.00	90.00	125.00	200.00
	1848/7 JG	—	60.00	90.00	125.00	200.00
	1849 JG	—	60.00	90.00	125.00	200.00
	1850/40 JG	—	60.00	125.00	225.00	325.00
	1850 JG	—	60.00	90.00	125.00	200.00
	1852/1 JG	—	60.00	90.00	125.00	200.00
	1856 JG	—	60.00	90.00	125.00	200.00
	1857 JG	—	60.00	90.00	125.00	200.00
	1859/7 JG	—	60.00	90.00	125.00	200.00
	1860/59 JG	—	60.00	90.00	125.00	200.00
	1860 JG	—	60.00	90.00	125.00	200.00

Mint mark: GC

KM#	Date	Mintage	VG	Fine	VF	XF
379.3	1844 MP	—	75.00	100.00	175.00	250.00
	1845 MP	—	75.00	100.00	175.00	250.00
	1846 MP	—	75.00	100.00	175.00	250.00
	1847 MP	—	75.00	100.00	175.00	250.00
	1848 MP	—	75.00	100.00	175.00	250.00
	1849 MP	—	75.00	100.00	175.00	250.00
	1850 MP	—	75.00	100.00	175.00	250.00
	1851 MP	—	75.00	100.00	175.00	250.00

Mint mark: Go

KM#	Date	Mintage	VG	Fine	VF	XF
379.4	1845 PM	—	60.00	75.00	125.00	200.00
	1849 PF	—	60.00	75.00	125.00	200.00
	1851 PF	—	60.00	75.00	125.00	200.00
	1853 PF	—	60.00	75.00	125.00	200.00
	1860 PF	—	75.00	125.00	200.00	300.00
	1862 YE	—	60.00	75.00	125.00	200.00

Mint mark: Mo

KM#	Date	Mintage	VG	Fine	VF	XF
379.5	1825 JM	—	50.00	70.00	100.00	150.00
	1827/6 JM	—	50.00	70.00	100.00	150.00
	1827 JM	—	50.00	70.00	100.00	150.00
	1830/29 JM	—	50.00	70.00	100.00	150.00
	1831 JM	—	50.00	70.00	100.00	150.00
	1832 JM	—	50.00	70.00	125.00	175.00
	1833 MJ	—	50.00	70.00	100.00	150.00
	1834 ML	—	50.00	70.00	125.00	175.00
	1841 ML	—	50.00	70.00	125.00	175.00
	1843 MM	—	50.00	70.00	100.00	150.00
	1845 MF	—	50.00	70.00	100.00	150.00
	1846/5 MF	—	50.00	70.00	100.00	150.00
	1848 GC	—	50.00	70.00	125.00	175.00
	1850 GC	—	50.00	70.00	125.00	175.00
	1856/4 GF	—	50.00	70.00	100.00	150.00
	1856/5 GF	—	50.00	70.00	100.00	150.00
	1856 GF	—	50.00	70.00	100.00	150.00
	1858 FH	—	50.00	70.00	125.00	175.00
	1859 FH	—	50.00	70.00	100.00	150.00
	1860 TH	—	50.00	70.00	125.00	175.00
	1861 CH	—	50.00	70.00	100.00	150.00
	1862 CH	—	50.00	70.00	125.00	175.00
	1863 TH	—	50.00	70.00	100.00	150.00
	1869 CH	—	50.00	70.00	100.00	150.00

Mint mark: Zs

KM#	Date	Mintage	VG	Fine	VF	XF
379.6	1853 OM	—	100.00	125.00	200.00	300.00
	1860/59 VL V is inverted A	—	75.00	100.00	200.00	350.00
	1860 VL	—	75.00	100.00	150.00	200.00
	1862 VL	—	75.00	100.00	150.00	200.00

2 ESCUDOS

6.7700 g, .875 GOLD, .1904 oz AGW
Mint mark: C
Obv: Facing eagle.

KM#	Date	Mintage	VG	Fine	VF	XF
380	1846 CE	—	100.00	150.00	225.00	325.00
	1847 CE	—	100.00	150.00	225.00	325.00
	1848 CE	—	100.00	150.00	225.00	325.00
	1852 CE	—	100.00	150.00	225.00	325.00
	1854 CE	—	100.00	175.00	250.00	375.00
	1856/4 CE	—	100.00	175.00	250.00	375.00
	1857 CE	—	100.00	150.00	225.00	325.00

Mint mark: Do

KM#	Date	Mintage	VG	Fine	VF	XF
380.1	1833 RM	—	300.00	450.00	700.00	1200.
	1837/4 RM	—	—	—	—	—
	1837 RM	—	—	—	—	—
	1844 RM	—	275.00	400.00	600.00	1000.

Mint mark: EoMo

KM#	Date	Mintage	VG	Fine	VF	XF
380.2	1828 LF	—	700.00	1000.	1750.	2500.

Mint mark: Ga

KM#	Date	Mintage	VG	Fine	VF	XF
380.3	1835 FS	—	100.00	150.00	225.00	325.00
	1836/5 JG	—	100.00	150.00	225.00	300.00
	1839/5 JG	—	—	—	—	—
	1839 JG	—	100.00	150.00	200.00	275.00
	1840 MC	—	100.00	150.00	200.00	275.00
	1841 MC	—	100.00	150.00	250.00	400.00
	1847/6 JG	—	100.00	150.00	225.00	300.00
	1848/7 JG	—	100.00	150.00	225.00	300.00
	1850/40 JG	—	100.00	150.00	200.00	250.00
	1851 JG	—	100.00	150.00	200.00	275.00
	1852 JG	—	100.00	150.00	225.00	325.00
	1853 JG	—	100.00	150.00	200.00	275.00
	1854/2 JG	—	—	—	—	—
	1858 JG	—	100.00	150.00	200.00	275.00
	1859/8 JG	—	100.00	150.00	225.00	300.00
	1859 JG	—	100.00	150.00	200.00	275.00
	1860/50 JG	—	100.00	150.00	225.00	300.00
	1860 JG	—	100.00	150.00	225.00	300.00
	1861/59 JG	—	100.00	150.00	200.00	275.00
	1861/0 JG	—	100.00	150.00	200.00	275.00
	1863/1 JG	—	100.00	150.00	200.00	275.00
	1870 IC	—	100.00	150.00	200.00	275.00

Mint mark: GC

KM#	Date	Mintage	VG	Fine	VF	XF
380.4	1844 MP	—	150.00	200.00	275.00	400.00
	1845 MP	—	750.00	1250.	2000.	3000.
	1846 MP	—	750.00	1250.	2000.	3000.
	1847 MP	—	125.00	175.00	350.00	500.00
	1848 MP	—	150.00	200.00	350.00	450.00
	1849 MP	—	150.00	200.00	300.00	400.00
	1850 MP	—	150.00	200.00	300.00	400.00

Mint mark: Go

KM#	Date	Mintage	VG	Fine	VF	XF
380.5	1845 PM	—	100.00	150.00	250.00	400.00
	1849 PF	—	100.00	150.00	250.00	400.00
	1853 PF	—	100.00	150.00	250.00	400.00
	1856 PF	—	100.00	150.00	250.00	400.00
	1859 PF	—	100.00	150.00	250.00	400.00
	1860/59 PF	—	100.00	150.00	250.00	400.00
	1860 PF	—	100.00	150.00	250.00	400.00
	1862 YE	—	100.00	150.00	250.00	400.00

Mint mark: Ho

KM#	Date	Mintage	VG	Fine	VF	XF
380.6	1861 FM	—	500.00	1000.	1500.	2000.

Mint mark: Mo

KM#	Date	Mintage	VG	Fine	VF	XF
380.7	1825 JM	—	100.00	150.00	200.00	275.00
	1827/6 JM	—	100.00	150.00	200.00	275.00
	1827 JM	—	100.00	150.00	200.00	275.00
	1830/29 JM	—	100.00	150.00	200.00	275.00
	1831 JM	—	100.00	150.00	200.00	275.00
	1833 ML	—	100.00	150.00	200.00	275.00
	1841 ML	—	100.00	150.00	200.00	275.00
	1844 MF	—	100.00	150.00	200.00	275.00
	1845 MF	—	100.00	150.00	200.00	275.00
	1846 MF	—	125.00	200.00	400.00	600.00
	1848 GC	—	100.00	150.00	200.00	275.00
	1850 GC	—	100.00	150.00	200.00	275.00
	1856/5 GF	—	100.00	150.00	200.00	275.00
	1856 GF	—	100.00	150.00	200.00	275.00
	1858 FH	—	100.00	150.00	200.00	275.00
	1859 FH	—	100.00	150.00	200.00	275.00
	1861 TH	—	100.00	150.00	200.00	275.00
	1861 CH	—	100.00	150.00	200.00	300.00
	1862 CH	—	100.00	150.00	200.00	300.00
	1863 TH	—	100.00	150.00	200.00	300.00
	1868 PH	—	100.00	150.00	200.00	300.00
	1869 CH	—	100.00	150.00	200.00	300.00

Mint mark: Zs

KM#	Date	Mintage	VG	Fine	VF	XF
380.8	1860 VL	—	150.00	300.00	600.00	1200.
	1862 VL	—	250.00	500.00	800.00	1200.
	1864 MO	—	150.00	300.00	600.00	1200.

4 ESCUDOS

13.5400 g, .875 GOLD, .3809 oz AGW
Mint mark: C
Facing eagle

KM#	Date	Mintage	VG	Fine	VF	XF
381	1846 CE	—	1200.	1700.	—	—
	1847 CE	—	400.00	650.00	850.00	1250.
	1848 CE	—	600.00	900.00	1250.	1750.

Mint mark: Do

KM#	Date	Mintage	VG	Fine	VF	XF
381.1	1832 RM/LR	—	—	—	Rare	—
	1832 RM	—	600.00	900.00	1250.	1750.
	1833 RM/RL	—	—	—	Rare	—
	1852 JMR	—	—	—	Rare	—

Mint mark: Ga

KM#	Date	Mintage	VG	Fine	VF	XF
381.2	1844 MC	—	500.00	750.00	1000.	1500.
	1844 JG	—	400.00	650.00	850.00	1250.

Mint mark: GC

KM#	Date	Mintage	VG	Fine	VF	XF
381.3	1844 MP	—	400.00	650.00	850.00	1250.
	1845 MP	—	350.00	500.00	700.00	1000.
	1846 MP	—	400.00	650.00	850.00	1250.
	1848 MP	—	400.00	650.00	850.00	1250.
	1850 MP	—	500.00	750.00	1000.	1500.

Mint mark: Go

KM#	Date	Mintage	VG	Fine	VF	XF
381.4	1829/8 MJ	—	250.00	400.00	550.00	750.00
	1829 JM	—	250.00	400.00	550.00	750.00
	1829 MJ	—	250.00	400.00	550.00	750.00
	1831 MJ	—	250.00	400.00	550.00	750.00
	1832 MJ	—	250.00	400.00	550.00	750.00
	1833 MJ	—	250.00	400.00	600.00	850.00
	1834 PJ	—	300.00	500.00	700.00	1000.
	1835 PJ	—	300.00	500.00	700.00	1000.
	1836 PJ	—	250.00	400.00	600.00	850.00
	1837 PJ	—	250.00	400.00	600.00	850.00
	1838 PJ	—	250.00	400.00	600.00	850.00
	1839 PJ	—	300.00	500.00	700.00	1000.
	1840 PJ	—	250.00	400.00	600.00	850.00
	1841 PJ	—	300.00	500.00	700.00	1000.
	1845 PM	—	250.00	400.00	600.00	850.00
	1847/5 YE	—	300.00	500.00	700.00	1000.
	1847 PM	—	300.00	500.00	700.00	1000.
	1849 PF	—	300.00	500.00	700.00	1000.
	1851 PF	—	300.00	500.00	700.00	1000.
	1852 PF	—	250.00	400.00	600.00	850.00
	1855 PF	—	250.00	400.00	600.00	850.00
	1857/5 PF	—	250.00	400.00	600.00	850.00
	1858/7 PF	—	250.00	400.00	600.00	850.00
	1858 PF	—	250.00	400.00	600.00	850.00
	1859/7 PF	—	300.00	500.00	700.00	1000.
	1860 PF	—	300.00	500.00	800.00	1200.
	1862 YE	—	250.00	400.00	600.00	850.00
	1863 YF	—	250.00	400.00	600.00	850.00

Mint mark: Ho

KM#	Date	Mintage	VG	Fine	VF	XF
381.5	1861 FM	—	1000.	1500.	2500.	4000.

Mint mark: Mo

KM#	Date	Mintage	VG	Fine	VF	XF
381.6	1825 JM	—	250.00	400.00	600.00	900.00
	1827/6 JM	—	250.00	400.00	550.00	850.00
	1829 JM	—	250.00	450.00	700.00	1000.
	1831 JM	—	250.00	450.00	700.00	1000.
	1832 JM	—	300.00	500.00	800.00	1200.
	1844 MF	—	250.00	450.00	700.00	1000.
	1850 GC	—	250.00	450.00	700.00	1000.
	1856 GF	—	250.00	400.00	550.00	850.00
	1857/6 GF	—	250.00	400.00	550.00	850.00
	1857 GF	—	250.00	400.00	550.00	850.00
	1858 FH	—	250.00	450.00	700.00	1000.
	1859/8 FH	—	250.00	450.00	700.00	1000.
	1861 CH	—	400.00	800.00	1200.	1600.
	1863 CH	—	250.00	450.00	700.00	1000.
	1868 PH	—	250.00	400.00	550.00	850.00
	1869 CH	—	250.00	400.00	500.00	800.00

Mint mark: O, Oa

KM#	Date	Mintage	VG	Fine	VF	XF
381.7	1861 FR	—	1500.	2500.	4000.	7000.

Mint mark: Zs

KM#	Date	Mintage	VG	Fine	VF	XF
381.8	1862 VL	—	750.00	1250.	2250.	3500.

8 ESCUDOS

27.0700 g, .875 GOLD, .7616 oz AGW
Mint mark: Mo
Obv: Hooked-neck eagle.

KM#	Date	Mintage	Fine	VF	XF	Unc
382.1	1823 JM snake's tail curved					
		—	3500.	6500.	10,000.	—

NOTE: Superior Casterline sale 5-89 choice AU realized $18,700.

KM#	Date	Mintage	Fine	VF	XF	Unc
382.2	1823 JM snake's tail looped					
		—	3500.	6500.	10,000.	—

Mint mark: A
Obv: Facing eagle.

KM#	Date	Mintage	Fine	VF	XF	Unc
383	1864 PG	—	650.00	1250.	2250.	—
	1866 DL	—	—	—	7500.	—
	1868/7 DL	—	1500.	2250.	3250.	—
	1869 DL	—	650.00	1250.	2250.	—
	1870 DL	—	1500.	2250.	3250.	—
	1872 AM	—	—	—	Rare	—

Mint mark: Ca

KM#	Date	Mintage	Fine	VF	XF	Unc
383.1	1841 RG	—	400.00	750.00	1250.	1750.
	1842 RG	—	375.00	500.00	1000.	1500.
	1843 RG	—	375.00	500.00	1000.	1500.
	1844 RG	—	350.00	500.00	1000.	1500.
	1845 RG	—	350.00	500.00	1000.	1500.
	1846 RG	—	500.00	1250.	1500.	2000.
	1847 RG	—	1000.	2500.	—	—
	1848 RG	—	350.00	500.00	1000.	1500.
	1849 RG	—	350.00	500.00	1000.	1500.
	1850/40 RG	—	350.00	500.00	1000.	1500.
	1851/41 RG	—	350.00	500.00	1000.	1500.
	1852/42 RG	—	350.00	500.00	1000.	1500.
	1853/43 RG	—	350.00	500.00	1000.	1500.
	1854/44 RG	—	350.00	500.00	1000.	1500.
	1855/43 RG	—	400.00	650.00	1250.	1750.
	1856/46 RG	—	350.00	500.00	750.00	1250.
	1857 JC/RG	—	350.00	500.00	750.00	1250.
	1858 JC	—	350.00	500.00	750.00	1250.
	1858 BA/RG	—	350.00	500.00	750.00	1250.
	1859 JC/RG	—	350.00	500.00	750.00	1250.
	1860 JC/RG	—	350.00	500.00	1000.	1500.
	1861 JC	—	375.00	500.00	750.00	1250.
	1862 JC	—	375.00	500.00	750.00	1250.
	1863 JC	—	500.00	1000.	1750.	2250.
	1864 JC	—	400.00	750.00	1250.	1750.
	1865 JC	—	750.00	1500.	2500.	3500.
	1866 JC	—	375.00	500.00	1000.	1500.
	1866 FP	—	600.00	1250.	2000.	2500.
	1866 JG	—	375.00	500.00	1000.	1500.
	1867 JG	—	375.00	500.00	750.00	1250.
	1868 JG concave wings					
		—	375.00	500.00	750.00	1250.
	1869 MM regular eagle					
		—	375.00	500.00	750.00	1250.
	1870/60 MM	—	375.00	500.00	750.00	1250.
	1871/61 MM	—	375.00	500.00	1000.	1500.

Mint mark: C

KM#	Date	Mintage	Fine	VF	XF	Unc
383.2	1846 CE	—	375.00	500.00	1000.	1750.
	1847 CE	—	375.00	500.00	800.00	1250.
	1848 CE	—	375.00	500.00	1000.	1750.
	1849 CE	—	375.00	450.00	700.00	1250.
	1850 CE	—	375.00	450.00	700.00	1250.
	1851 CE	—	375.00	500.00	800.00	1250.
	1852 CE	—	375.00	500.00	800.00	1250.
	1853/1 CE	—	375.00	450.00	700.00	1250.
	1854 CE	—	375.00	450.00	700.00	1250.
	1855/4 CE	—	375.00	500.00	1000.	1750.
	1855 CE	—	375.00	500.00	800.00	1250.
	1856 CE	—	375.00	450.00	700.00	1250.
	1857 CE	—	375.00	450.00	700.00	1250.
	1857 CE w/o periods after C's					
		—	—	—	—	—
	1858 CE	—	375.00	450.00	700.00	1250.
	1859 CE	—	375.00	450.00	700.00	1250.
	1860/58 CE	—	375.00	500.00	800.00	1250.
	1860 CE	—	375.00	500.00	800.00	1250.
	1860 PV	—	375.00	450.00	700.00	1250.
	1861 PV	—	375.00	500.00	800.00	1250.
	1861 CE	—	375.00	500.00	800.00	1250.
	1862 CE	—	375.00	500.00	800.00	1250.
	1863 CE	—	375.00	500.00	800.00	1250.
	1864 CE	—	375.00	450.00	700.00	1250.
	1865 CE	—	375.00	500.00	800.00	1250.
	1866/5 CE	—	375.00	450.00	700.00	1250.
	1866 CE	—	375.00	450.00	700.00	1250.
	1867 CB (error)					
		—	375.00	450.00	700.00	1250.
	1867 CE/CB	—	375.00	450.00	700.00	1250.
	1868 CB (error)					
		—	375.00	500.00	800.00	1250.
	1869 CE	—	375.00	500.00	800.00	1250.
	1870 CE	—	375.00	500.00	800.00	1250.

Mint mark: Do

KM#	Date	Mintage	Fine	VF	XF	Unc
383.3	1832 RM	—	850.00	1750.	2000.	3000.
	1833 RM/RL	—	375.00	500.00	800.00	1250.
	1834 RM	—	375.00	500.00	800.00	1250.
	1835 RM	—	375.00	500.00	800.00	1250.
	1836 RM/RL	—	375.00	500.00	800.00	1250.
	1836 RM M on snake					
		—	375.00	500.00	800.00	1250.
	1837 RM	—	375.00	500.00	800.00	1250.
	1838/6 RM	—	375.00	500.00	800.00	1250.
	1838 RM	—	375.00	500.00	800.00	1250.
	1839 RM	—	375.00	450.00	700.00	1250.
	1840/30 RM/RL					
		—	400.00	600.00	1000.	1750.
	1841/30 RM	—	550.00	750.00	1250.	2000.
	1841/31 RM	—	375.00	500.00	800.00	1250.
	1841/34 RM	—	375.00	500.00	800.00	1250.
	1841 RM/RL	—	375.00	500.00	800.00	1250.
	1842/32 RM	—	375.00	500.00	800.00	1250.
	1843/33 RM	—	550.00	750.00	1250.	2000.
	1843/1 RM	—	375.00	500.00	800.00	1250.
	1843 RM	—	375.00	500.00	800.00	1250.
	1844/34 RM/RL					
		—	500.00	1000.	1500.	2500.
	1844 RM	—	450.00	800.00	1250.	2000.
	1845/36 RM	—	400.00	600.00	1000.	1750.
	1845 RM	—	400.00	600.00	1000.	1750.
	1846 RM	—	375.00	500.00	800.00	1250.
	1847/37 RM	—	375.00	500.00	800.00	1250.
	1848/37 RM	—	—	—	—	—
	1848/38 CM	—	375.00	500.00	800.00	1250.
	1849/39 CM	—	375.00	500.00	800.00	1250.
	1849 JMR	—	400.00	750.00	1250.	2000.
	1850 JMR	—	400.00	750.00	1250.	2000.
	1851 JMR	—	400.00	750.00	1250.	2000.
	1852/1 JMR	—	450.00	800.00	1250.	2000.
	1852 CP	—	450.00	800.00	1250.	2000.
	1853 CP	—	450.00	800.00	1250.	2000.
	1854 CP	—	400.00	600.00	1000.	1750.
	1855/4 CP	—	375.00	500.00	800.00	1250.
	1855 CP	—	375.00	500.00	800.00	1250.
	1856 CP	—	400.00	600.00	1000.	1750.
	1857 CP French style eagle, 1832-57					
		—	375.00	500.00	800.00	1250.
	1857 CP Mexican style eagle					
		—	375.00	500.00	800.00	1250.
	1858 CP	—	375.00	500.00	800.00	1250.
	1859 CP	—	375.00	500.00	800.00	1250.
	1860/59 CP	—	450.00	700.00	1250.	2200.
	1861/0 CP	—	400.00	600.00	1000.	1750.
	1862/52 CP	—	375.00	500.00	800.00	1250.
	1862/1 CP	—	375.00	500.00	800.00	1250.
	1862 CP	—	375.00	500.00	800.00	1250.
	1863/53 CP	—	375.00	500.00	800.00	1250.
	1864 LT	—	375.00	500.00	800.00	1250.
	1865/4 LT	—	500.00	1000.	1650.	2750.

KM#	Date	Mintage	Fine	VF	XF	Unc
383.3	1866/4 CM	—	1250.	2000.	2500.	—
	1866 CM	—	400.00	600.00	1000.	1750.
	1867/56 CP	—	400.00	600.00	1000.	1750.
	1867/4 CP	—	375.00	500.00	800.00	1250.
	1868/4 CP/LT	—	—	—	—	—
	1869 CP	—	500.00	1250.	1750.	2750.
	1870 CP	—	400.00	600.00	1000.	1750.

Mint mark: EoMo

KM#	Date	Mintage	Fine	VF	XF	Unc
383.4	1828 LF	—	2500.	4500.	7500.	—
	1829 LF	—	2500.	4500.	7500.	—

Mint mark: Ga

KM#	Date	Mintage	Fine	VF	XF	Unc
383.5	1825 FS	—	500.00	1000.	1250.	1750.
	1826 FS	—	500.00	1000.	1250.	1750.
	1830 FS	—	500.00	1000.	1250.	1750.
	1836 FS	—	750.00	1500.	2000.	3000.
	1836 JG	—	1000.	2500.	3500.	—
	1837 JG	—	1000.	2500.	3500.	—
	1840 MC	—	750.00	1500.	2000.	3000.
	1841/31 MC	—	1000.	2500.	—	—
	1841 MC	—	850.00	1650.	2250.	—
	1842 JG	—	—	—	—	—
	1843 MC	—	—	—	—	—
	1845 MC	—	400.00	750.00	1000.	1500.
	1847 JG	—	2250.	—	—	—
	1849 JG	—	500.00	1000.	1250.	1750.
	1850 JG	—	400.00	750.00	1000.	1500.
	1851 JG	—	400.00	750.00	1000.	1500.
	1852/1 JG	—	500.00	1000.	1250.	1750.
	1855 JG	—	1000.	2500.	3500.	—
	1856 JG	—	400.00	750.00	1000.	1500.
	1857 JG	—	400.00	750.00	1000.	1500.
	1861/0 JG	—	500.00	1000.	1250.	1750.
	1861 JG	—	400.00	600.00	1000.	1750.
	1863/1 JG	—	500.00	1000.	1250.	1750.
	1866 JG	—	400.00	750.00	1000.	1500.

Mint mark: GC

KM#	Date	Mintage	Fine	VF	XF	Unc
383.6	1844 MP	—	550.00	750.00	1250.	2000.
	1845 MP eagle's tail square	—	550.00	750.00	1250.	2000.
	1845 MP eagle's tail round	—	550.00	750.00	1250.	2000.
	1846 MP eagle's tail square	—	450.00	650.00	1000.	1750.
	1846 MP eagle's tail round	—	450.00	650.00	1000.	1750.
	1847 MP	—	450.00	650.00	1000.	1750.
	1848 MP	—	550.00	750.00	1250.	2000.
	1849 MP	—	550.00	750.00	1250.	2000.
	1850 MP	—	450.00	650.00	1000.	1750.
	1851 MP	—	450.00	650.00	1000.	1750.
	1852 MP	—	550.00	750.00	1250.	2000.

Mint mark: Go

KM#	Date	Mintage	Fine	VF	XF	Unc
383.7	1828 MJ	—	700.00	1750.	2250.	3000.
	1829 MJ	—	600.00	1500.	2000.	2750.
	1830 MJ	—	375.00	500.00	750.00	1000.
	1831 MJ	—	600.00	1500.	2000.	2750.
	1832 MJ	—	500.00	1250.	1750.	2500.
	1833 MJ	—	375.00	500.00	750.00	1000.
	1834 PJ	—	375.00	500.00	750.00	1000.
	1835 PJ	—	375.00	500.00	750.00	1000.
	1836 PJ	—	400.00	650.00	900.00	1250.
	1837 PJ	—	400.00	650.00	900.00	1250.
	1838/7 PJ	—	375.00	500.00	750.00	1000.
	1838 PJ	—	375.00	500.00	800.00	1200.
	1839/8 PJ	—	375.00	500.00	750.00	1000.
	1839 PJ regular eagle	—	375.00	500.00	800.00	1200.
	1840 PJ concave wings	—	375.00	500.00	750.00	1000.
	1841 PJ	—	375.00	500.00	750.00	1000.
	1842 PJ	—	375.00	475.00	650.00	1000.
	1842 PM	—	375.00	500.00	750.00	1000.
	1843 PM small eagle	—	375.00	500.00	750.00	1000.
	1844/3 PM	—	400.00	650.00	900.00	1250.
	1844 PM	—	375.00	500.00	750.00	1000.
	1845 PM	—	375.00	500.00	750.00	1000.
	1846/5 PM	—	375.00	500.00	800.00	1200.
	1846 PM	—	375.00	500.00	750.00	1000.
	1847 PM	—	400.00	650.00	900.00	1250.
	1848/7 PM	—	375.00	500.00	750.00	1000.
	1848 PM	—	375.00	500.00	750.00	1000.
	1848 PF	—	375.00	500.00	750.00	1000.
	1849 PF	—	375.00	425.00	650.00	900.00
	1850 PF	—	375.00	425.00	650.00	900.00
	1851 PF	—	375.00	500.00	750.00	1000.
	1852 PF	—	375.00	500.00	750.00	1000.
	1853 PF	—	375.00	425.00	650.00	900.00
	1854 PF eagle of 1853	—	375.00	500.00	750.00	1000.
	1854 PF eagle of 1855	—	375.00	500.00	750.00	1000.
	1855/4 PF	—	400.00	650.00	900.00	1250.
	1855 PF	—	375.00	500.00	750.00	1000.
	1856 PF	—	375.00	500.00	750.00	1000.
	1857 PF	—	375.00	500.00	750.00	1000.
	1858 PF	—	375.00	500.00	750.00	1000.
	1859 PF	—	375.00	400.00	550.00	750.00
	1860/50 PF	—	375.00	425.00	650.00	900.00
	1860/59 PF	—	400.00	650.00	900.00	1250.
	1860 PF	—	375.00	500.00	750.00	1100.
	1861/0 PF	—	375.00	400.00	500.00	750.00
	1861 PF	—	375.00	400.00	500.00	750.00
	1862/1 YE	—	375.00	500.00	750.00	1000.
	1862 YE	—	375.00	500.00	750.00	1000.
	1862 YF	—	—	—	—	—
	1863/53 YF	—	375.00	500.00	750.00	1000.
	1863 PF	—	375.00	500.00	750.00	1000.
	1867/57 YF/PF	—	375.00	500.00	750.00	1000.
	1867 YF	—	375.00	500.00	750.00	1000.
	1868/58 YF	—	375.00	500.00	750.00	1000.
	1870 FR	—	375.00	425.00	650.00	900.00

Mint mark: Ho

KM#	Date	Mintage	Fine	VF	XF	Unc
383.8	1863 FM	—	400.00	650.00	1000.	2000.
	1864 FM	—	600.00	1250.	1750.	2750.
	1864 PR/FM	—	400.00	650.00	1000.	2000.
	1865 FM/PR	—	500.00	800.00	1250.	2500.
	1867/57 PR	—	400.00	650.00	1000.	2000.
	1868 PR	—	500.00	800.00	1250.	2500.
	1868 PR/FM	—	500.00	800.00	1250.	2500.
	1869 PR/FM	—	400.00	650.00	1000.	2000.
	1869 PR	—	400.00	650.00	1000.	2000.
	1870 PR	—	400.00	650.00	1000.	2000.
	1871/0 PR	—	500.00	800.00	1250.	2500.
	1871 PR	—	500.00	800.00	1250.	2500.
	1872/1 PR	—	600.00	1250.	1750.	2750.
	1873 PR	—	400.00	650.00	1000.	2000.

Large book.

Small book.

Mint mark: Mo

KM#	Date	Mintage	Fine	VF	XF	Unc
383.9	1824 JM lg. book reverse	—	500.00	1000.	1250.	2000.
	1825 JM sm. book reverse	—	375.00	450.00	600.00	1000.
	1826/5 JM	—	700.00	1750.	2250.	3000.
	1827 JM	—	375.00	600.00	725.00	1000.
	1828 JM	—	375.00	600.00	725.00	1000.
	1829 JM	—	375.00	600.00	725.00	1000.
	1830 JM	—	375.00	600.00	725.00	1000.
	1831 JM	—	375.00	600.00	725.00	1000.
	1832/1 JM	—	375.00	600.00	725.00	1000.
	1832 JM	—	375.00	600.00	725.00	1000.
	1833 MJ	—	400.00	750.00	1000.	1500.
	1833 ML	—	375.00	450.00	600.00	900.00
	1834 ML	—	375.00	450.00	600.00	900.00
	1835/4 ML	—	500.00	1000.	1250.	2000.
	1836 ML	—	375.00	450.00	600.00	900.00
	1836 MF	—	500.00	700.00	1200.	2000.
	1837/6 ML	—	375.00	450.00	600.00	900.00
	1838 ML	—	375.00	450.00	600.00	900.00
	1839 ML	—	375.00	450.00	600.00	900.00
	1840 ML	—	375.00	450.00	600.00	900.00
	1841 ML	—	375.00	450.00	600.00	900.00
	1842/1 ML	—	—	—	—	—
	1842 ML	—	375.00	450.00	600.00	900.00
	1842 MM	—	—	—	—	—
	1843 MM	—	375.00	450.00	600.00	900.00
	1844 MF	—	375.00	450.00	600.00	900.00
	1845 MF	—	375.00	450.00	600.00	900.00
	1846 MF	—	500.00	1000.	1250.	2000.
	1847 MF	—	950.00	2250.	—	—
	1847 RC	—	375.00	500.00	800.00	1250.
	1848 GC	—	375.00	450.00	600.00	900.00
	1849 GC	—	375.00	450.00	600.00	900.00
	1850 GC	—	375.00	450.00	600.00	900.00
	1851 GC	—	375.00	450.00	600.00	900.00
	1852 GC	—	375.00	450.00	600.00	900.00
	1853 GC	—	375.00	450.00	600.00	900.00
	1854/44 GC	—	375.00	450.00	600.00	900.00
	1854/3 GC	—	375.00	450.00	600.00	900.00
	1855 GF	—	375.00	450.00	600.00	900.00
	1856/5 GF	—	375.00	450.00	600.00	900.00
	1856 GF	—	375.00	450.00	600.00	900.00
	1857 GF	—	375.00	450.00	600.00	900.00
	1858 FH	—	375.00	450.00	600.00	900.00
	1859 FH	—	400.00	750.00	1000.	1500.
	1860 FH	—	375.00	450.00	600.00	900.00
	1860 TH	—	375.00	450.00	600.00	900.00
	1861/51 CH	—	375.00	450.00	600.00	900.00
	1862 CH	—	375.00	450.00	600.00	900.00
	1863/53 CH	—	375.00	450.00	600.00	900.00
	1863/53 TH	—	375.00	450.00	600.00	900.00
	1867 CH	—	375.00	450.00	600.00	900.00
	1868 CH	—	375.00	450.00	600.00	900.00
	1868 PH	—	375.00	450.00	600.00	900.00
	1869 CH	—	375.00	450.00	600.00	900.00

NOTE: Formerly reported 1825/3 JM is merely a reworked 5.

Mint mark: O

KM#	Date	Mintage	Fine	VF	XF	Unc
383.10	1858 AE	—	2000.	3000.	4000.	6000.
	1859 AE	—	1000.	2500.	3750.	5500.
	1860 AE	—	1000.	2500.	3750.	5500.
	1861 FR	—	450.00	900.00	1500.	2750.
	1862 FR	—	450.00	900.00	1500.	2750.
	1863 FR	—	450.00	900.00	1500.	2750.
	1864 FR	—	500.00	900.00	1500.	2750.
	1867 AE	—	450.00	900.00	1500.	2750.
	1868 AE	—	450.00	900.00	1500.	2750.
	1869 AE	—	450.00	900.00	1500.	2750.

Mint mark: Zs

KM#	Date	Mintage	Fine	VF	XF	Unc
383.11	1858 MO	—	400.00	750.00	1000.	2000.
	1859 MO	—	375.00	450.00	650.00	900.00
	1860/59 VL/MO	—	2000.	3000.	4000.	—
	1860/9 MO	—	400.00	750.00	1000.	2000.
	1860 MO	—	375.00	500.00	700.00	1000.
	1861/0 VL	—	375.00	500.00	700.00	1000.
	1861 VL	—	375.00	500.00	700.00	1000.
	1862 VL	—	375.00	500.00	700.00	1100.
	1863 VL	—	375.00	500.00	700.00	1000.
	1863 MO	—	375.00	500.00	700.00	1000.
	1864 MO	—	750.00	1000.	1500.	3000.
	1865 MO	—	375.00	500.00	700.00	1000.
	1865 MP	—	Contemporary counterfeit			
	1868 JS	—	400.00	600.00	800.00	1250.
	1868 YH	—	400.00	600.00	800.00	1250.
	1869 YH	—	400.00	600.00	800.00	1250.
	1870 YH	—	400.00	600.00	800.00	1250.
	1871 YH	—	400.00	600.00	800.00	1250.

EMPIRE OF MAXIMILIAN

RULER

Maximilian, Emperor, 1864-1867

MINT MARKS

Refer To Republic Coinage

MONETARY SYSTEM

100 Centavos = 1 Peso (8 Reales)

CENTAVO

COPPER
Mint mark: M

KM#	Date	Mintage	Fine	VF	XF	Unc
384	1864	—	35.00	60.00	150.00	900.00

5 CENTAVOS

1.3537 g, .903 SILVER, .0393 oz ASW
Mint mark: G

KM#	Date	Mintage	Fine	VF	XF	Unc
385	1864	.090	17.50	35.00	65.00	225.00
	1865	—	20.00	30.00	50.00	200.00
	1866	—	65.00	140.00	300.00	1800.

Mint mark: M

KM#	Date	Mintage	Fine	VF	XF	Unc
385.1	1864	—	12.50	20.00	40.00	200.00
	1866/4	—	25.00	40.00	75.00	365.00
	1866	—	20.00	35.00	65.00	350.00

Mint mark: P

KM#	Date	Mintage	Fine	VF	XF	Unc
385.2	1864	—	100.00	215.00	950.00	2000.

Mint mark: Z

KM#	Date	Mintage	Fine	VF	XF	Unc
385.3	1865	—	20.00	30.00	100.00	300.00

10 CENTAVOS

2.7073 g, .903 SILVER, .0786 oz ASW
Mint mark: G

KM#	Date	Mintage	Fine	VF	XF	Unc
386	1864	.045	17.50	35.00	65.00	225.00
	1865	—	25.00	40.00	80.00	275.00

Mint mark: M

KM#	Date	Mintage	Fine	VF	XF	Unc
386.1	1864	—	12.50	20.00	40.00	200.00
	1866/4	—	20.00	30.00	55.00	275.00
	1866/5	—	20.00	30.00	65.00	300.00
	1866	—	20.00	30.00	65.00	300.00

Mint mark: P

KM#	Date	Mintage	Fine	VF	XF	Unc
386.2	1864	—	60.00	110.00	200.00	550.00

Mint mark: Z

KM#	Date	Mintage	Fine	VF	XF	Unc
386.3	1865	—	25.00	50.00	120.00	450.00

50 CENTAVOS

13.5365 g, .903 SILVER, .3929 oz ASW
Mint mark: Mo

KM#	Date	Mintage	Fine	VF	XF	Unc
387	1866	.031	30.00	50.00	100.00	550.00

PESO

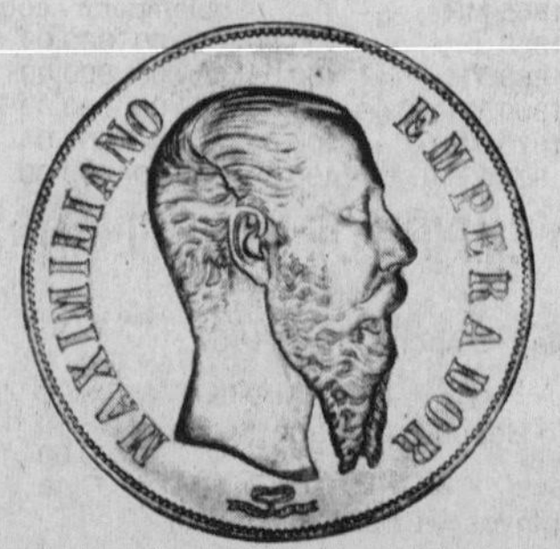

27.0700 g, .903 SILVER, .7857 oz ASW
Mint mark: Go

KM#	Date	Mintage	Fine	VF	XF	Unc
388	1866	—	300.00	425.00	650.00	2250.

Mint mark: Mo

KM#	Date	Mintage	Fine	VF	XF	Unc
388.1	1866	2.148	25.00	40.00	80.00	325.00
	1867	1.238	35.00	60.00	120.00	400.00

Mint mark: Pi

KM#	Date	Mintage	Fine	VF	XF	Unc
388.2	1866	—	40.00	80.00	150.00	600.00

20 PESOS

33.8400 g, .875 GOLD, .9520 oz AGW
Mint mark: Mo

KM#	Date	Mintage	Fine	VF	XF	Unc
389	1866	8,274	500.00	850.00	1150.	2250.

REPUBLIC
DECIMAL COINAGE

100 Centavos = 1 Peso

UN (1) CENTAVO

COPPER
Mint mark: Mo
Obv: Seated Liberty.

KM#	Date	Mintage	Fine	VF	XF	Unc
390	1863 round top 3, reeded edge	—	10.00	15.00	30.00	150.00
	1863 round top 3, plain edge	—	10.00	15.00	30.00	150.00
	1863 flat top 3	—	8.00	12.50	25.00	150.00

Mint mark: SLP

KM#	Date	Mintage	Fine	VF	XF	Unc
390.1	1863	1.025	10.00	25.00	50.00	300.00

Mint mark: As
Obv: Standing eagle.

KM#	Date	Mintage	Fine	VF	XF	Unc
391	1875	—	—	—	Rare	—
	1876	.050	100.00	200.00	300.00	650.00
	1880	—	25.00	50.00	100.00	400.00
	1881	—	30.00	60.00	125.00	250.00

Mint mark: Cn

KM#	Date	Mintage	Fine	VF	XF	Unc
391.1	1874	.266	12.50	17.50	35.00	150.00
	1875/4	.153	15.00	20.00	45.00	150.00
	1875	Inc. Ab.	10.00	15.00	25.00	150.00
391.1	1876	.154	5.00	8.00	15.00	150.00
	1877/6	.993	7.50	11.50	17.50	175.00
	1877	Inc. Ab.	6.00	9.00	15.00	150.00
	1880	.142	7.50	10.00	12.50	150.00
	1881	.167	7.50	10.00	25.00	175.00
	1897 large N in mm.	.300	2.50	5.00	12.00	50.00
	1897 small N in mm.	Inc. Ab.	2.50	5.00	9.00	45.00

Mint mark: Do

KM#	Date	Mintage	Fine	VF	XF	Unc
391.2	1879	.110	10.00	17.50	35.00	150.00
	1880	.069	40.00	90.00	175.00	500.00
	1891	—	8.00	11.00	30.00	150.00
	1891 Do/Mo	—	8.00	11.00	30.00	150.00

Mint mark: Ga

KM#	Date	Mintage	Fine	VF	XF	Unc
391.3	1872	.263	15.00	30.00	60.00	200.00
	1873	.333	6.00	9.00	25.00	150.00
	1874	.076	15.00	25.00	50.00	175.00
	1875	—	10.00	15.00	30.00	150.00
	1876	.303	3.00	6.00	17.50	150.00
	1877	.108	4.00	6.00	20.00	150.00
	1878	.543	4.00	6.00	15.00	150.00
	1881/71	.975	7.00	9.00	20.00	175.00
	1881	Inc. Ab.	7.00	9.00	20.00	175.00
	1889 Ga/Mo	—	3.50	5.00	25.00	125.00
	1890	—	4.00	7.50	20.00	100.00

Mint mark: Go

KM#	Date	Mintage	Fine	VF	XF	Unc
391.4	1874	—	20.00	40.00	80.00	250.00
	1875	.190	11.50	20.00	60.00	200.00
	1876	—	125.00	200.00	350.00	750.00
	1877	—	—	—	Rare	—
	1878	.576	8.00	11.00	30.00	175.00
	1880	.890	6.00	10.00	25.00	175.00

Mint mark: Ho

KM#	Date	Mintage	Fine	VF	XF	Unc
391.5	1875	3,500	450.00	—	—	—
	1876	8,508	50.00	100.00	225.00	500.00
	1880 short H, round O	.102	7.50	15.00	35.00	150.00
	1880 tall H, oval O	Inc. Ab.	7.50	15.00	35.00	150.00
	1881	.459	5.00	10.00	25.00	150.00

Mint mark: Mo

KM#	Date	Mintage	Fine	VF	XF	Unc
391.6	1869	1.874	7.50	25.00	60.00	200.00
	1870/69	1.200	10.00	25.00	60.00	225.00
	1870	Inc. Ab.	8.00	20.00	50.00	200.00
	1871	.918	8.00	15.00	40.00	200.00
	1872/1	1.625	6.50	10.00	30.00	200.00
	1872	Inc. Ab.	6.00	9.00	25.00	200.00
	1873	1.605	4.00	7.50	20.00	200.00
	1874/3	1.700	5.00	7.00	15.00	100.00
	1874	Inc. Ab.	3.00	5.50	15.00	100.00
	1874.	Inc. Ab.	5.00	10.00	25.00	200.00
	1875	1.495	6.00	8.00	30.00	100.00
	1876	1.600	3.00	5.50	12.50	100.00
	1877	1.270	3.00	5.50	13.50	100.00
	1878/5	1.900	7.50	11.00	22.50	125.00
	1878/6	Inc. Ab.	7.50	11.00	22.50	125.00
	1878/7	Inc. Ab.	7.50	11.00	20.00	125,00
	1878	Inc. Ab.	6.00	9.00	13.50	100.00
	1879/8	1.505	4.50	6.50	13.50	100.00
	1879	Inc. Ab.	3.00	5.50	11.50	75.00
	1880/70	1.130	5.50	7.50	15.00	100.00
	1880/72	I.A.	20.00	50.00	100.00	250.00
	1880/79	I.A.	15.00	35.00	75.00	175.00
	1880	Inc. Ab.	4.25	6.00	12.50	75.00
	1881	1.060	4.50	7.00	15.00	75.00
	1886	12.687	1.50	2.00	8.50	40.00
	1887	7.292	1.50	2.00	5.00	35.00
	1888/78	9.984	2.50	3.00	10.00	30.00
	1888/7	Inc. Ab.	2.50	3.00	10.00	30.00
	1888	Inc. Ab.	1.50	2.00	8.50	30.00
	1889	19.970	2.00	3.00	8.00	30.00
	1890/89	18.726	2.50	3.00	10.00	40.00
	1890/990	I.A.	2.50	3.00	10.00	40.00
	1890	Inc. Ab.	1.50	2.00	8.50	30.00
	1891	14.544	1.50	2.00	8.50	30.00
	1892	12.908	1.50	2.00	8.50	30.00
	1893/2	5.078	2.50	3.00	10.00	35.00
	1893	Inc. Ab.	1.50	2.00	8.50	30.00
	1894/3	1.896	3.00	6.00	15.00	50.00
	1894	Inc. Ab.	2.00	3.00	10.00	35.00
	1895/3	3.453	3.00	4.50	12.50	35.00
	1895/85	I.A.	3.00	6.00	15.00	50.00
	1895	Inc. Ab.	2.00	3.00	8.50	25.00
	1896	3.075	2.00	3.00	8.50	25.00
	1897	4.150	1.50	2.00	8.50	25.00

NOTE: Varieties exist.

Mint mark: Oa

KM#	Date	Mintage	Fine	VF	XF	Unc
391.7	1872	.016	300.00	500.00	1200.	—
	1873	.011	350.00	600.00	—	—
	1874	4,835	450.00	—	—	—
	1875	2,860	500.00	—	—	—

Mint mark: Pi

KM#	Date	Mintage	Fine	VF	XF	Unc
391.8	1871	—	—	—	Rare	—
	1877	.249	—	—	Rare	—
	1878	.751	12.50	25.00	50.00	200.00
	1891 Pi/Mo	—	10.00	17.50	35.00	150.00
	1891	—	8.00	15.00	30.00	150.00

Mint mark: Zs

KM#	Date	Mintage	Fine	VF	XF	Unc
391.9	1872	.055	22.50	30.00	100.00	300.00
	1873	1.460	4.00	8.00	25.00	150.00
	1874/3	.685	5.50	11.00	30.00	250.00
	1874	Inc. Ab.	4.00	8.00	25.00	200.00
	1875/4	.200	8.50	17.00	45.00	250.00

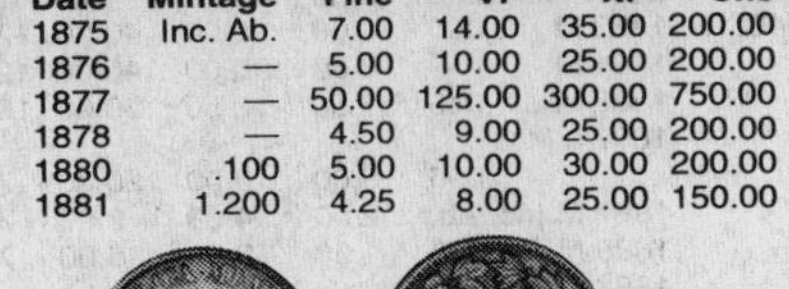

KM#	Date	Mintage	Fine	VF	XF	Unc
391.9	1875	Inc. Ab.	7.00	14.00	35.00	200.00
	1876	—	5.00	10.00	25.00	200.00
	1877	—	50.00	125.00	300.00	750.00
	1878	—	4.50	9.00	25.00	200.00
	1880	.100	5.00	10.00	30.00	200.00
	1881	1.200	4.25	8.00	25.00	150.00

COPPER-NICKEL
Mint: Mexico City

KM#	Date	Mintage	Fine	VF	XF	Unc
392	1882	99.955	7.50	12.50	17.50	35.00
	1883	Inc. Ab.	.50	.75	1.00	1.50

Obv: Restyled eagle.

KM#	Date	Mintage	Fine	VF	XF	Unc
393	1898	1.529	4.00	6.00	15.00	40.00

NOTE: Varieties exist.

Mint mark: C
Reduced size

KM#	Date	Mintage	Fine	VF	XF	Unc
394	1901	.220	15.00	22.50	35.00	65.00
	1902	.320	15.00	22.50	45.00	90.00
	1903	.536	7.50	12.50	20.00	45.00
	1904/3	.148	35.00	50.00	75.00	125.00
	1905	.110	100.00	150.00	300.00	550.00

NOTE: Varieties exist.

Mint mark: M,Mo

KM#	Date	Mintage	Fine	VF	XF	Unc
394.1	1899	.051	150.00	175.00	300.00	800.00
	1900 wide date	4.010	2.50	4.00	7.50	25.00
	1900 narrow date	Inc. Ab.	2.50	4.00	7.50	25.00
	1901	1.494	3.00	8.00	17.50	50.00
	1902/899	2.090	30.00	60.00	100.00	175.00
	1902	Inc. Ab.	2.25	4.00	10.00	35.00
	1903	8.400	1.50	2.25	4.00	20.00
	1904	10.250	1.50	2.00	4.00	20.00
	1905	3.643	2.25	4.00	10.00	40.00

NOTE: Varieties exist.

2 CENTAVOS

COPPER-NICKEL
Mint: Mexico City

KM#	Date	Mintage	Fine	VF	XF	Unc
395	1882	50.023	2.00	3.00	7.50	15.00
	1883/2	Inc. Ab.	2.00	3.00	7.50	15.00
	1883	Inc. Ab.	.50	.75	1.00	2.50

5 CENTAVOS

1.3530 g, .903 SILVER, .0392 oz ASW
Mint mark: Ca
Obv: Facing eagle. Rev: Denomination in wreath.

KM#	Date	Mintage	Fine	VF	XF	Unc
396	1868	—	40.00	65.00	125.00	400.00
	1869	*.030	25.00	40.00	100.00	350.00
	1870	.035	30.00	50.00	100.00	350.00

Mint mark: SLP

KM#	Date	Mintage	Fine	VF	XF	Unc
396.1	1863	—	75.00	125.00	350.00	1200.

Mint mark: Mo
Rev: Cap and rays.

KM#	Date	Mintage	Fine	VF	XF	Unc
397	1867/3	—	25.00	50.00	125.00	275.00
	1867	—	20.00	40.00	100.00	250.00
	1868/7	—	25.00	50.00	150.00	325.00
	1868	—	20.00	40.00	100.00	250.00

NOTE: Varieties exist.

Mint mark: P

KM#	Date	Mintage	Fine	VF	XF	Unc
397.1	1868/7	.034	25.00	50.00	125.00	300.00
	1868	Inc. Ab.	20.00	45.00	100.00	250.00
	1869	.014	200.00	300.00	600.00	—

Mint mark: As
Obv: Standing eagle.

KM#	Date	Mintage	Fine	VF	XF	Unc
398	1874 DL	—	10.00	20.00	40.00	150.00
	1875 DL	—	10.00	20.00	40.00	150.00
	1876 L	—	22.00	45.00	70.00	160.00
	1878 L mule, gold peso obverse	—	250.00	350.00	650.00	—
	1879 L mule, gold peso obverse	—	40.00	65.00	120.00	275.00
	1880 L mule, gold peso obverse	.012	55.00	85.00	165.00	325.00
	1886 L	.043	12.00	25.00	50.00	165.00
	1886 L mule, gold peso obverse	Inc. Ab.	55.00	85.00	165.00	300.00
	1887 L	.020	25.00	50.00	75.00	165.00
	1888 L	.032	12.00	25.00	50.00	125.00
	1889 L	.016	25.00	50.00	100.00	200.00
	1890 L	.030	25.00	50.00	85.00	175.00
	1891 L	8,000	65.00	125.00	200.00	400.00
	1892 L	.013	20.00	40.00	60.00	125.00
	1893 L	.024	10.00	20.00	45.00	90.00
	1895 L	.020	10.00	20.00	45.00	90.00

Mint mark: CH, Ca

KM#	Date	Mintage	Fine	VF	XF	Unc
398.1	1871 M	.014	20.00	40.00	100.00	250.00
	1873 M crude date	—	100.00	150.00	250.00	500.00
	1874 M crude date	—	25.00	50.00	75.00	150.00
	1886 M	.025	7.50	15.00	30.00	100.00
	1887 M	.037	7.50	15.00	30.00	100.00
	1887 Ca/MoM	Inc. Ab.	10.00	20.00	40.00	125.00
	1888 M	.145	1.50	3.00	6.00	25.00
	1889 M	.044	5.00	10.00	20.00	50.00
	1890 M	.102	1.50	3.00	6.00	25.00
	1891 M	.164	1.50	3.00	6.00	25.00
	1892 M	.085	1.50	3.00	6.00	25.00
	1892 M 9/inverted 9	Inc. Ab.	2.00	4.00	7.50	30.00
	1893 M	.133	1.50	3.00	6.00	25.00
	1894 M	.108	1.50	3.00	6.00	25.00
	1895 M	.074	2.00	4.00	7.50	30.00

Mint mark: Cn

KM#	Date	Mintage	Fine	VF	XF	Unc
398.2	1871 P	—	125.00	200.00	350.00	—
	1873 P	4,992	50.00	100.00	200.00	400.00
	1874 P	—	25.00	50.00	100.00	200.00
	1875 P	—	—	—	Rare	—
	1876 P	—	25.00	50.00	100.00	200.00
	1886 M	.010	25.00	50.00	100.00	200.00
	1887 M	.010	25.00	50.00	100.00	200.00
	1888 M	.119	1.50	3.00	6.00	30.00
	1889 M	.066	4.00	7.50	15.00	50.00
	1890 M	.180	1.50	3.00	6.00	25.00
	1890 D (error)	Inc. Ab.	125.00	175.00	250.00	—
	1891 M	.087	2.00	4.00	7.50	25.00
	1894 M	.024	4.00	7.50	15.00	40.00
	1896 M	.016	7.50	12.50	25.00	75.00
	1897 M	.223	1.50	2.50	5.00	20.00

Mint mark: Do

KM#	Date	Mintage	Fine	VF	XF	Unc
398.3	1874 M	—	100.00	150.00	225.00	500.00
	1877 P	4,795	75.00	125.00	225.00	450.00
	1878/7 E/P	4,300	200.00	300.00	450.00	—
	1879 B	—	125.00	200.00	350.00	—
	1880 B	—	—	—	Rare	—
	1881 P	3,020	300.00	500.00	800.00	—
	1887 C	.042	5.00	8.00	17.50	60.00
	1888/9 C	.091	6.00	10.00	20.00	70.00
	1888 C	Inc. Ab.	4.00	7.50	15.00	55.00
	1889 C	.049	3.50	6.00	12.50	50.00
	1890 C	.136	4.00	7.50	15.00	55.00
	1890 P	Inc. Ab.	5.00	8.00	17.50	60.00
	1891/0 P	.048	3.50	6.00	12.50	50.00
	1891 P	Inc. Ab.	3.00	5.00	10.00	45.00
	1894 D	.038	3.50	6.00	12.50	50.00

Mint mark: Ga

KM#	Date	Mintage	Fine	VF	XF	Unc
398.4	1877 A	—	15.00	30.00	60.00	150.00
	1881 S	.156	4.00	7.50	15.00	60.00
	1886 S	.087	2.00	4.00	7.50	25.00
	1888 S lg.G	.262	2.00	4.00	10.00	30.00
	1888 S sm.g	Inc. Ab.	2.00	4.00	10.00	30.00
	1889 S	.178	1.50	3.00	7.50	25.00
	1890 S	.068	4.00	7.50	12.50	35.00
	1891 S	.050	4.00	6.50	10.00	35.00
	1892 S	.078	2.00	4.00	7.50	25.00
	1893 S	.044	4.00	7.50	15.00	45.00

Mint mark: Go

KM#	Date	Mintage	Fine	VF	XF	Unc
398.5	1869 S	.080	15.00	30.00	75.00	175.00
	1871 S	.100	5.00	10.00	25.00	75.00
398.5	1872 S	.030	30.00	60.00	125.00	250.00
	1873 S	.040	30.00	60.00	125.00	250.00
	1874 S	—	7.00	12.00	25.00	75.00
	1875 S	—	8.00	15.00	30.00	75.00
	1876 S	—	8.00	15.00	30.00	75.00
	1877 S	—	7.00	12.00	20.00	75.00
	1878/7 S	.020	8.00	15.00	25.00	75.00
	1879 S	—	8.00	15.00	25.00	75.00
	1880 S	.055	15.00	30.00	60.00	200.00
	1881/0 S	.160	5.00	8.00	17.50	60.00
	1881 S	Inc. Ab.	4.00	6.00	12.00	45.00
	1886 R	.230	1.50	3.00	6.00	30.00
	1887 R	.230	1.50	2.50	5.00	30.00
	1888 R	.320	1.50	2.50	5.00	20.00
	1889 R	.060	4.00	6.00	12.00	45.00
	1890 R	.250	1.50	2.50	5.00	20.00
	1891/0 R	.168	1.80	3.00	6.00	30.00
	1891 R	Inc. Ab.	1.50	2.50	5.00	20.00
	1892 R	.138	1.50	3.00	6.00	25.00
	1893 R	.200	1.25	2.50	5.00	20.00
	1894 R	.200	1.25	2.50	5.00	20.00
	1896 R	.525	1.25	2.00	4.00	15.00
	1897 R	.596	1.50	2.00	4.00	15.00

Mint mark: Ho

KM#	Date	Mintage	Fine	VF	XF	Unc
398.6	1874/69 R	—	125.00	225.00	350.00	—
	1874 R	—	100.00	200.00	325.00	—
	1878/7 A	.022	—	—	Rare	—
	1878 A	Inc. Ab.	20.00	40.00	80.00	175.00
	1878 A mule, gold peso obverse	Inc. Ab.	40.00	80.00	150.00	300.00
	1880 A	.043	7.50	15.00	30.00	75.00
	1886 G	.044	5.00	10.00	20.00	75.00
	1887 G	.020	5.00	10.00	20.00	75.00
	1888 G	.012	7.50	15.00	30.00	85.00
	1889 G	.067	3.00	6.00	12.50	40.00
	1890 G	.050	3.00	6.00	12.50	40.00
	1891 G	.046	3.00	6.00	12.50	40.00
	1893 G	.084	2.50	5.00	10.00	30.00
	1894 G	.068	2.00	4.00	10.00	30.00

Mint mark: Mo

KM#	Date	Mintage	Fine	VF	XF	Unc
398.7	1869/8 C	.040	8.00	15.00	40.00	120.00
	1870 C	.140	4.00	7.00	20.00	60.00
	1871 C	.103	9.00	20.00	40.00	100.00
	1871 M	Inc. Ab.	7.50	12.50	25.00	60.00
	1872 M	.266	5.00	8.00	20.00	55.00
	1873 M	.020	40.00	60.00	100.00	225.00
	1874/69 M	—	7.50	15.00	30.00	75.00
	1874 M	—	4.00	7.00	17.50	50.00
	1874/3 B	—	5.00	8.00	22.50	55.00
	1874 B	—	5.00	8.00	22.50	55.00
	1875 B	—	4.00	7.00	15.00	50.00
	1875 B/M	—	6.00	9.00	17.50	60.00
	1876/5 B	—	4.00	7.00	15.00	50.00
	1876 B	—	4.00	7.00	12.50	50.00
	1877/6 M	.080	4.00	7.00	15.00	60.00
	1877 M	Inc. Ab.	4.00	7.00	12.50	60.00
	1878/7 M	.100	4.00	7.00	15.00	55.00
	1878 M	Inc. Ab.	2.50	5.00	12.50	45.00
	1879/8 M	—	8.00	12.50	22.50	55.00
	1879 M	—	4.50	7.00	15.00	50.00
	1879 M 9/inverted 9	—	10.00	15.00	25.00	75.00
	1880/76 M/B	—	5.00	7.50	15.00	50.00
	1880/76 M	—	5.00	7.50	15.00	50.00
	1880 M	—	4.00	6.00	12.00	40.00
	1881/0 M	.180	4.00	6.00	10.00	35.00
	1881 M	Inc. Ab.	3.00	4.50	9.00	35.00
	1886/0 M	.398	2.00	2.75	7.50	25.00
	1886/1 M	I.A.	2.00	2.75	7.50	25.00
	1886 M	Inc. Ab.	1.75	2.25	6.00	20.00
	1887 m	.720	1.75	2.00	5.00	20.00
	1887 M/m	I.A.	1.75	2.00	6.00	20.00
	1888/7 M	1.360	2.25	2.50	6.00	20.00
	1888 M	Inc. Ab.	1.75	2.00	5.00	20.00
	1889/8 M	1.242	2.25	2.50	6.00	20.00
	1889 M	Inc. Ab.	1.75	2.00	5.00	20.00
	1890/00 M	1.694	1.75	2.75	6.00	20.00
	1890 M	Inc. Ab.	1.50	2.00	5.00	20.00
	1891 M	1.030	1.75	2.00	5.00	20.00
	1892 M	1.400	1.75	2.00	5.00	20.00
	1892 M 9/inverted 9	Inc. Ab.	2.00	2.75	7.50	20.00
	1893 M	.220	1.75	2.00	5.00	15.00
	1894 M	.320	1.75	2.00	5.00	15.00
	1895 M	.078	3.00	5.00	8.00	25.00
	1896 B	.080	1.75	2.00	5.00	20.00
	1897 M	.160	1.75	2.00	5.00	15.00

NOTE: Varieties exist.

Mint mark: Oa

KM#	Date	Mintage	Fine	VF	XF	Unc
398.8	1890 E	.048	—	—	Rare	—
	1890 N	Inc. Ab.	65.00	125.00	200.00	350.00

Mint mark: Pi

KM#	Date	Mintage	Fine	VF	XF	Unc
398.9	1869 S	—	300.00	400.00	500.00	—
	1870 G/MoC	.020	—	—	Rare	—
	1870 O	Inc. Ab.	200.00	300.00	400.00	—
	1871 O	5,400	—	—	Rare	—
	1872 O	—	75.00	100.00	175.00	400.00
	1873	5,000	—	—	Rare	—
	1874 H	—	30.00	50.00	100.00	225.00
	1875 H	—	7.50	12.50	30.00	75.00
	1876 H	—	10.00	20.00	45.00	100.00
	1877 H	—	7.50	12.50	20.00	60.00
	1878/7 H	—	—	—	Rare	—
	1878 H	—	60.00	90.00	150.00	300.00

KM#	Date	Mintage	Fine	VF	XF	Unc
398.9	1880 H	6,200	—	—	Rare	—
	1881 H	4,500	—	—	Rare	—
	1886 R	.033	12.50	25.00	50.00	125.00
	1887/0 R	.169	4.00	7.50	15.00	45.00
	1887 R	Inc. Ab.	3.00	5.00	10.00	32.00
	1888 R	.210	2.00	4.00	9.00	30.00
	1889/7 R	.197	2.50	5.00	10.00	32.00
	1889 R	Inc. Ab.	2.00	4.00	9.00	30.00
	1890 R	.221	2.00	3.00	6.00	25.00
	1891/89 R/B	.176	2.00	4.00	8.00	25.00
	1891 R	Inc. Ab.	2.00	3.00	6.00	20.00
	1892/89 R	.182	2.00	4.00	8.00	25.00
	1892/0 R	I.A.	2.00	4.00	8.00	25.00
	1892 R	Inc. Ab.	2.00	3.00	6.00	20.00
	1893 R	.041	5.00	10.00	20.00	60.00

NOTE: Varieties exist.

Mint mark: Zs

KM#	Date	Mintage	Fine	VF	XF	Unc
398.10	1870 H	.040	12.50	25.00	50.00	125.00
	1871 H	.040	12.50	25.00	50.00	125.00
	1872 H	.040	12.50	25.00	50.00	125.00
	1873/2 H	.020	35.00	65.00	125.00	275.00
	1873 H	Inc. Ab.	25.00	50.00	100.00	250.00
	1874 H	—	7.50	12.50	25.00	75.00
	1874 A	—	40.00	75.00	150.00	300.00
	1875 A	—	7.50	12.50	25.00	75.00
	1876 A	—	50.00	75.00	100.00	200.00
	1876 S	—	12.50	25.00	50.00	125.00
	1877 S	—	3.00	6.00	12.00	40.00
	1878 S	.060	3.00	6.00	12.00	40.00
	1879/8 S	—	3.00	6.00	15.00	50.00
	1879 S	—	3.00	6.00	12.00	40.00
	1880/79 S	.130	6.00	10.00	20.00	60.00
	1880 S	Inc. Ab.	5.00	8.00	16.00	45.00
	1881 S	.210	2.50	5.00	10.00	35.00
	1886/4 S	.360	6.00	10.00	20.00	60.00
	1886 S	Inc. Ab.	2.00	3.00	6.00	20.00
	1886 Z	Inc. Ab.	5.00	10.00	25.00	65.00
	1887 Z	.400	2.00	3.00	6.00	25.00
	1888/7 Z	.500	2.00	3.00	6.00	25.00
	1888 Z	Inc. Ab.	2.00	3.00	6.00	25.00
	1889 Z	.520	2.00	3.00	6.00	25.00
	1889 Z 9/inverted 9	Inc. Ab.	2.00	3.00	6.00	25.00
	1889 ZsZ/MoM	Inc. Ab.	2.00	3.00	6.00	25.00
	1890 Z	.580	1.75	2.50	5.00	20.00
	1890 ZsZ/MoM	Inc. Ab.	2.00	3.00	6.00	25.00
	1891 Z	.420	1.75	2.50	5.00	20.00
	1892 Z	.346	1.75	2.50	5.00	20.00
	1893 Z	.258	1.75	2.50	5.00	20.00
	1894 Z	.228	1.75	2.50	5.00	20.00
	1894 ZoZ (error)	Inc. Ab.	2.00	4.00	8.00	30.00
	1895 Z	.260	1.75	2.50	5.00	20.00
	1896 Z	.200	1.75	2.50	5.00	20.00
	1896 6/inverted 6	Inc. Ab.	2.00	3.00	6.00	25.00
	1897/6 Z	.200	2.00	3.00	6.00	25.00
	1897 Z	Inc. Ab.	1.75	2.50	5.00	20.00

COPPER-NICKEL
Mint: Mexico City

KM#	Date	Mintage	Fine	VF	XF	Unc
399	1882	Inc. Ab.	.50	1.00	2.50	7.50
	1883	Inc. Ab.	25.00	50.00	80.00	250.00

.903 SILVER
Mint mark: Cn
Obv: Restyled eagle.

KM#	Date	Mintage	Fine	VF	XF	Unc
400	1898 M	.044	1.75	4.00	8.00	20.00
	1899 M	.111	5.50	8.50	20.00	50.00
	1899 Q	Inc. Ab.	1.75	2.25	4.50	12.50
	1900/800 Q	.239	3.50	5.00	12.50	30.00
	1900 Q round Q, single tail	Inc. Ab.	1.75	2.50	6.00	15.00
	1900 Q narrow C, oval Q	Inc. Ab.	1.75	2.50	6.00	15.00
	1900 Q wide C, oval Q	Inc. Ab.	1.75	2.50	6.00	15.00
	1901 Q	.148	1.75	2.25	4.50	12.50
	1902 Q narrow C, heavy serifs	.262	1.75	2.50	6.00	15.00
	1902 Q wide C, light serifs	Inc. Ab.	1.75	2.50	6.00	15.00
	1903/1 Q	.331	2.00	2.50	6.00	15.00
	1903 Q	Inc. Ab.	1.75	2.25	4.50	12.50
	1903/1898 V	Inc. Ab.	3.50	4.50	9.00	22.50
	1903 V	Inc. Ab.	1.75	2.25	4.50	12.50
	1904 H	.352	1.75	2.25	5.00	15.00

NOTE: Varieties exist.

Mint mark: Go

KM#	Date	Mintage	Fine	VF	XF	Unc
400.1	1898 R mule, gold peso obverse	.180	7.50	15.00	30.00	75.00
	1899 R	.260	1.75	2.25	4.50	12.50
	1900 R	.200	1.75	2.25	4.50	12.50

NOTE: Varieties exist.

Mint mark: Mo

KM#	Date	Mintage	Fine	VF	XF	Unc
400.2	1898 M	.080	2.00	4.00	7.00	25.00
	1899 M	.168	1.75	2.25	4.50	12.50
	1900/800 M	.300	4.50	6.50	10.00	30.00
	1900 M	Inc. Ab.	1.75	2.25	4.50	12.50
	1901 M	.100	1.75	2.25	4.50	12.50
	1902 M	.144	1.25	2.00	3.75	10.00
	1903 M	.500	1.25	2.00	3.75	10.00
	1904/804 M	1.090	1.75	2.50	6.00	15.00
	1904/94 M	I.A.	1.75	2.50	6.00	15.00
	1904 M	Inc. Ab.	1.25	2.00	6.00	12.50
	1905 M	.344	1.75	3.75	7.50	17.50

Mint mark: Zs

KM#	Date	Mintage	Fine	VF	XF	Unc
400.3	1898 Z	.100	1.75	2.25	4.50	12.50
	1899 Z	.050	2.00	3.00	7.00	20.00
	1900 Z	.055	1.75	2.50	5.00	15.00
	1901 Z	.040	1.75	2.50	5.00	15.00
	1902/1 Z	.034	2.00	4.50	9.00	22.50
	1902 Z	Inc. Ab.	1.75	3.75	7.50	17.50
	1903 Z	.217	1.25	2.00	5.00	12.50
	1904 Z	.191	1.75	2.50	5.00	12.50
	1904 M	Inc. Ab.	1.75	2.50	6.00	15.00
	1905 M	.046	2.00	4.50	9.00	22.50

10 CENTAVOS

2.7070 g, .903 SILVER, .0785 oz ASW
Mint mark: Ca
Obv: Eagle. Rev: Value within wreath.

KM#	Date	Mintage	Fine	VF	XF	Unc
401	1868/7	—	30.00	60.00	150.00	550.00
	1868	—	30.00	60.00	150.00	550.00
	1869	.015	25.00	50.00	125.00	600.00
	1870	.017	22.50	45.00	100.00	550.00

Mint mark: SLP

KM#	Date	Mintage	Fine	VF	XF	Unc
401.2	1863	—	75.00	150.00	275.00	900.00

Mint mark: Mo

KM#	Date	Mintage	Fine	VF	XF	Unc
402	1867/3	—	50.00	100.00	150.00	450.00
	1867	—	20.00	40.00	60.00	250.00
	1868/7	—	20.00	40.00	80.00	275.00
	1868	—	20.00	45.00	75.00	250.00

Mint mark: P

KM#	Date	Mintage	Fine	VF	XF	Unc
402.1	1868/7	.038	45.00	90.00	175.00	650.00
	1868	Inc. Ab.	20.00	40.00	100.00	550.00
	1869/7	4,900	55.00	125.00	250.00	800.00

Mint mark: As

KM#	Date	Mintage	Fine	VF	XF	Unc
403	1874 DL	—	20.00	40.00	80.00	175.00
	1875 L	—	5.00	10.00	25.00	90.00
	1876 L	—	10.00	18.00	40.00	110.00
	1878/7 L	—	10.00	18.00	45.00	120.00
	1878 L	—	5.00	10.00	30.00	100.00
	1879 L	—	10.00	18.00	40.00	110.00
	1880 L	.013	10.00	18.00	40.00	110.00
	1882 L	.022	10.00	18.00	40.00	110.00
	1883 L	8,520	25.00	50.00	100.00	225.00
	1884 L	—	7.50	12.50	35.00	100.00
	1885 L	.015	7.50	12.50	35.00	100.00
	1886 L	.045	7.50	12.50	35.00	100.00
	1887 L	.015	7.50	12.50	35.00	100.00
	1888 L	.038	7.50	12.50	35.00	100.00
	1889 L	.020	7.50	12.50	35.00	100.00
	1890 L	.040	7.50	12.50	35.00	100.00
	1891 L	.038	7.50	12.50	35.00	100.00
	1892 L	.057	5.00	10.00	25.00	90.00
	1893 L	.070	10.00	18.00	40.00	110.00

NOTE: Varieties exist.

Mint mark: CH,Ca

KM#	Date	Mintage	Fine	VF	XF	Unc
403.1	1871 M	8,150	15.00	30.00	60.00	150.00
	1873 M crude date	—	35.00	75.00	125.00	175.00
	1874 M	—	10.00	17.50	35.00	100.00
	1880/70 G	7,620	20.00	40.00	80.00	175.00
	1880 G/g	I.A.	15.00	25.00	50.00	125.00
	1881	340 pcs.	—	—	Rare	—

KM#	Date	Mintage	Fine	VF	XF	Unc
403.1	1883 M	9,000	10.00	20.00	40.00	125.00
	1884 M	—	10.00	20.00	40.00	125.00
	1886 M	.045	7.50	12.50	30.00	100.00
	1887/3 M/G	.096	5.00	10.00	20.00	75.00
	1887 M	Inc. Ab.	2.00	4.00	8.00	75.00
	1888 M	.299	1.50	2.50	5.00	75.00
	1888 Ca/Mo	Inc. Ab.	1.50	2.50	5.00	75.00
	1889/8 M	.115	2.00	4.00	8.00	75.00
	1889 M small 89 (5 Centavo font)	Inc. Ab.	2.00	4.00	8.00	75.00
	1890/80 M	.140	2.00	4.00	8.00	75.00
	1890/89 M	I.A.	2.00	4.00	8.00	75.00
	1890 M	Inc. Ab.	1.50	3.00	7.00	75.00
	1891 M	.163	1.50	3.00	7.00	75.00
	1892 M	.169	1.50	3.00	7.00	75.00
	1892 M 9/inverted 9	Inc. Ab.	2.00	4.00	8.00	75.00
	1893 M	.246	1.50	3.00	7.00	75.00
	1894 M	.163	1.50	3.00	7.00	75.00
	1895 M	.127	1.50	3.00	7.00	75.00

NOTE: Varieties exist.

Mint mark: Cn

KM#	Date	Mintage	Fine	VF	XF	Unc
403.2	1871 P	—	—	—	Rare	—
	1873 P	8,732	20.00	50.00	100.00	225.00
	1881 D	9,440	75.00	175.00	325.00	500.00
	1882 D	.012	75.00	125.00	200.00	400.00
	1885 M mule gold 2-1/2 Peso obv.	.018	25.00	50.00	100.00	200.00
	1886 M mule, gold 2-1/2 Peso obv.	.013	50.00	100.00	150.00	300.00
	1887 M	.011	20.00	40.00	75.00	175.00
	1888 M	.056	5.00	10.00	25.00	125.00
	1889 M	.042	5.00	10.00	20.00	75.00
	1890 M	.132	2.00	4.00	7.50	75.00
	1891 M	.084	5.00	10.00	20.00	75.00
	1892/1 M	.037	4.00	8.00	15.00	75.00
	1892 M	Inc. Ab.	2.50	5.00	10.00	75.00
	1894 M	.043	2.50	5.00	10.00	75.00
	1895 M	.023	2.50	5.00	10.00	60.00
	1896 M	.121	1.50	2.50	5.00	50.00

Mint mark: Do

KM#	Date	Mintage	Fine	VF	XF	Unc
403.3	1878 E	2,500	100.00	175.00	300.00	600.00
	1879 B	—	—	—	Rare	—
	1880/70 B	—	—	—	Rare	—
	1880/79 B	—	—	—	Rare	—
	1884 C	—	30.00	60.00	100.00	225.00
	1886 C	.013	75.00	150.00	300.00	500.00
	1887 C	.081	4.00	8.00	15.00	100.00
	1888 C	.031	6.00	12.00	30.00	100.00
	1889 C	.055	4.00	8.00	15.00	100.00
	1890 C	.050	4.00	8.00	15.00	100.00
	1891 P	.139	2.00	4.00	8.00	80.00
	1892 P	.212	2.00	4.00	8.00	80.00
	1892 D	Inc. Ab.	2.00	4.00	8.00	80.00
	1893 D	.258	2.00	4.00	8.00	80.00
	1893 D/C	I.A.	2.50	5.00	10.00	80.00
	1894 D	.184	1.50	3.00	6.00	80.00
	1894 D/C	I.A.	2.00	4.00	8.00	80.00
	1895 D	.142	1.50	3.00	6.00	80.00

Mint mark: Ga

KM#	Date	Mintage	Fine	VF	XF	Unc
403.4	1871 C	4,734	75.00	125.00	200.00	500.00
	1873/1 C	.025	10.00	15.00	35.00	150.00
	1873 C	Inc.Ab.	10.00	15.00	35.00	150.00
	1874 C	—	10.00	15.00	35.00	150.00
	1877 A	—	10.00	15.00	30.00	150.00
	1881 S	.115	5.00	10.00	25.00	150.00
	1883 B	.090	4.00	8.00	15.00	90.00
	1884 B	—	5.00	10.00	20.00	90.00
	1884 B/S	—	6.00	12.50	25.00	90.00
	1884 H	—	3.00	5.00	10.00	90.00
	1885 H	.093	3.00	5.00	10.00	90.00
	1886 S	.151	2.50	4.00	9.00	90.00
	1887 S	.162	1.50	3.00	6.00	90.00
	1888 S	.225	1.50	3.00	6.00	90.00
	1888 GaS/HoG	Inc. Ab.	1.50	3.00	6.00	90.00
	1889 S	.310	1.50	3.00	6.00	40.00
	1890 S	.303	1.50	3.00	6.00	40.00
	1891 S	.199	5.00	10.00	20.00	45.00
	1892 S	.329	1.50	3.00	6.00	40.00
	1893 S	.225	1.50	3.00	6.00	40.00
	1894 S	.243	3.00	6.00	12.00	40.00
	1895 S	.080	1.50	3.00	6.00	40.00

NOTE: Varieties exist.

Mint mark: Go

KM#	Date	Mintage	Fine	VF	XF	Unc
403.5	1869 S	7,000	20.00	40.00	80.00	200.00
	1871/0 S	.060	15.00	25.00	50.00	125.00
	1872 S	.060	15.00	25.00	50.00	125.00
	1873 S	.050	15.00	25.00	50.00	125.00
	1874 S	—	15.00	25.00	50.00	125.00
	1875 S	—	250.00	350.00	500.00	800.00
	1876 S	—	10.00	20.00	40.00	100.00
	1877 S	—	80.00	120.00	200.00	400.00
	1878/7 S	.010	10.00	20.00	45.00	110.00
	1878 S	Inc. Ab.	7.50	12.00	20.00	75.00
	1879 S	—	7.50	12.00	20.00	75.00
	1880 S	—	100.00	200.00	300.00	450.00
	1881/71 S	.100	3.00	5.00	10.00	75.00
	1881/0 S	I.A.	3.50	5.00	10.00	75.00
	1881 S	Inc. Ab.	3.00	5.00	10.00	75.00
	1882/1 S	.040	3.00	6.00	12.00	75.00
	1883 B	—	3.00	5.00	10.00	75.00
	1884 B	—	1.50	3.00	6.00	75.00
	1884 S	—	6.00	12.50	25.00	90.00
	1885 R	.100	1.50	3.00	6.00	75.00

KM#	Date	Mintage	Fine	VF	XF	Unc
403.5	1886 R	.095	3.00	5.00	10.00	75.00
	1887 R	.330	2.50	5.00	10.00	75.00
	1888 R	.270	1.50	3.00	6.00	75.00
	1889 R	.205	2.00	4.00	8.00	75.00
	1889 GoR/HoG	Inc. Ab.	3.00	5.00	10.00	75.00
	1890 R	.270	1.50	3.00	6.00	35.00
	1890 GoR/Cn M	Inc. Ab.	1.50	3.00	6.00	35.00
	1891 R	.523	1.50	3.00	6.00	35.00
	1891 GoR/HoG	Inc. Ab.	1.50	3.00	6.00	35.00
	1892 R	.440	1.50	3.00	6.00	35.00
	1893/1 R	.389	3.00	5.00	10.00	35.00
	1893 R	Inc. Ab.	1.50	3.00	6.00	35.00
	1894 R	.400	1.50	2.50	5.00	35.00
	1895 R	.355	1.50	2.50	5.00	35.00
	1896 R	.190	1.50	2.50	5.00	35.00
	1897 R	.205	1.50	2.50	5.00	35.00

NOTE: Varieties exist.

Mint mark: Ho

KM#	Date	Mintage	Fine	VF	XF	Unc
403.6	1874 R	—	30.00	60.00	100.00	200.00
	1876 F	3,140	200.00	300.00	450.00	750.00
	1878 A	—	5.00	10.00	15.00	85.00
	1879 A	—	25.00	50.00	90.00	175.00
	1880 A	—	3.00	6.00	12.50	85.00
	1881 A	.028	4.00	7.00	15.00	85.00
	1882/1 A	.025	5.00	10.00	20.00	85.00
	1882/1 a	I.A.	6.00	12.50	25.00	85.00
	1882 A	Inc. Ab.	4.00	7.00	15.00	85.00
	1883	7,000	65.00	100.00	200.00	400.00
	1884 A	—	35.00	75.00	150.00	300.00
	1884 M	—	7.50	15.00	30.00	85.00
	1885 M	.021	12.50	25.00	50.00	100.00
	1886 M	.010	—	—	Rare	—
	1886 G	Inc. Ab.	7.50	12.50	25.00	85.00
	1887 G	—	25.00	50.00	75.00	150.00
	1888 G	.025	6.00	12.50	25.00	85.00
	1889 G	.042	3.00	6.00	10.00	85.00
	1890 G	.048	3.00	6.00	10.00	85.00
	1891/80 G	.136	3.00	6.00	10.00	85.00
	1891/0 G	I.A.	3.00	6.00	10.00	85.00
	1891 G	Inc. Ab.	3.00	6.00	10.00	85.00
	1892 G	.067	3.00	6.00	10.00	85.00
	1893 G	.067	3.00	6.00	10.00	85.00

Mint mark: Mo

KM#	Date	Mintage	Fine	VF	XF	Unc
403.7	1869/8 C	.030	10.00	20.00	40.00	100.00
	1869 C	Inc. Ab.	8.00	17.50	35.00	90.00
	1870 C	.110	3.00	7.50	15.00	50.00
	1871 C	.084	50.00	75.00	125.00	250.00
	1871 M	Inc. Ab.	12.00	17.50	45.00	125.00
	1872/69 M	.198	10.00	20.00	35.00	100.00
	1872 M	Inc. Ab.	3.00	7.50	15.00	65.00
	1873 M	.040	10.00	15.00	30.00	75.00
	1874 M	—	5.00	10.00	20.00	65.00
	1874/64 B	—	5.00	10.00	20.00	65.00
	1874 B/M	—	20.00	40.00	60.00	125.00
	1874 B	—	5.00	10.00	15.00	65.00
	1875 B	—	20.00	40.00	60.00	125.00
	1876/5 B	—	3.00	5.00	9.00	65.00
	1876/5 B/M	—	3.00	5.00	9.00	65.00
	1877/6 M	—	3.00	5.00	9.00	65.00
	1877/6 M/B	—	3.00	5.00	9.00	65.00
	1877 M	—	3.00	5.00	9.00	65.00
	1878/7 M	.100	3.00	5.00	9.00	65.00
	1878 M	Inc. Ab.	3.00	5.00	9.00	65.00
	1879/69 M	—	3.00	5.00	9.00	65.00
	1879 M/C	—	3.00	5.00	9.00	65.00
	1880/79 M	—	3.00	5.00	9.00	65.00
	1881/0 M	.510	3.00	5.00	9.00	35.00
	1881 M	Inc. Ab.	3.00	5.00	9.00	35.00
	1882/1 M	.550	3.00	5.00	9.00	35.00
	1882 M	Inc. Ab.	3.00	5.00	9.00	35.00
	1883/2 M	.250	3.00	5.00	9.00	35.00
	1884 M	—	3.00	5.00	9.00	35.00
	1885 M	.470	3.00	5.00	9.00	35.00
	1886 M	.603	3.00	5.00	9.00	35.00
	1887 M	.580	3.00	5.00	9.00	35.00
	1888/7 MoM	.710	3.00	5.00	9.00	35.00
	1888 MoM	I.A.	3.00	5.00	9.00	35.00
	1888 MOM	I.A.	3.00	5.00	9.00	35.00
	1889/8 M	.622	3.00	5.00	9.00	35.00
	1889 M	Inc. Ab.	3.00	5.00	9.00	35.00
	1890/89 M	.815	3.00	5.00	9.00	35.00
	1890 M	Inc. Ab.	3.00	5.00	9.00	35.00
	1891 M	.859	1.50	2.50	7.00	25.00
	1892 M	1.030	1.50	2.50	7.00	25.00
	1893 M	.310	1.50	2.50	7.00	25.00
	1893 M/C	I.A.	1.50	2.50	7.00	25.00
	1894 M	.350	5.00	10.00	20.00	60.00
	1895 M	.320	1.50	2.50	7.00	25.00
	1896 B/G	.340	1.50	2.50	7.00	25.00
	1896 M	Inc. Ab.	35.00	70.00	100.00	150.00
	1897 M	.170	1.50	2.50	5.00	20.00

NOTE: Varieties exist.

Mint mark: Oa

KM#	Date	Mintage	Fine	VF	XF	Unc
403.8	1889 E	.021	200.00	400.00	600.00	—
	1890 E	.031	100.00	150.00	250.00	500.00
	1890 N	Inc. Ab.	—	—	Rare	—

Mint mark: Pi

KM#	Date	Mintage	Fine	VF	XF	Unc
403.9	1869/8 S	4,000	—	—	Rare	—
	1870/69 O	.018	—	—	Rare	—
	1870 G	Inc. Ab.	125.00	200.00	325.00	600.00
	1871 O	.021	50.00	100.00	150.00	300.00
	1872 O	.016	150.00	225.00	350.00	650.00
	1873 O	4,750	—	—	Rare	—

KM#	Date	Mintage	Fine	VF	XF	Unc
403.9	1874 H	—	25.00	50.00	100.00	200.00
	1875 H	—	75.00	125.00	200.00	400.00
	1876 H	—	75.00	125.00	200.00	400.00
	1877 H	—	75.00	125.00	200.00	400.00
	1878 H	—	250.00	500.00	750.00	—
	1879 H	—	—	—	—	—
	1880 H	—	150.00	250.00	350.00	—
	1881 H	7,600	250.00	350.00	500.00	—
	1882 H	4,000	—	—	Rare	—
	1883 H	—	125.00	200.00	300.00	500.00
	1884 H	—	25.00	50.00	100.00	200.00
	1885 H	.051	25.00	50.00	100.00	200.00
	1885 C	Inc. Ab.	—	—	Rare	—
	1886 C	.052	15.00	30.00	60.00	150.00
	1886 R	Inc. Ab.	5.00	10.00	20.00	65.00
	1887 R	.118	2.50	5.00	10.00	50.00
	1888 R	.136	2.50	5.00	10.00	50.00
	1889/7 R	.131	7.50	12.50	20.00	60.00
	1890 R	.204	1.50	3.00	7.50	40.00
	1891/89 R	.163	2.50	5.00	10.00	40.00
	1891 R	Inc. Ab.	1.50	3.50	6.00	30.00
	1892/0 R	.200	2.00	4.00	8.00	40.00
	1892 R	Inc. Ab.	1.50	2.50	5.00	40.00
	1893 R	.048	7.50	10.00	17.50	60.00

NOTE: Varieties exist.

Mint mark: Zs

KM#	Date	Mintage	Fine	VF	XF	Unc
403.10	1870 H	.020	100.00	150.00	200.00	400.00
	1871/0 H	.010	—	—	—	—
	1871 H	Inc. Ab.	—	—	—	—
	1872 H	.010	150.00	200.00	275.00	500.00
	1873 H	.010	250.00	350.00	600.00	—
	1874/3 H	—	50.00	75.00	150.00	300.00
	1874 A	—	200.00	300.00	500.00	—
	1875 A	—	5.00	10.00	25.00	100.00
	1876 A	—	5.00	10.00	25.00	100.00
	1876 S	—	100.00	200.00	300.00	500.00
	1877 S small S	—	7.50	12.50	25.00	100.00
	1877 S regular S	—	7.50	12.50	25.00	100.00
	1878/7 S	.030	5.00	10.00	20.00	80.00
	1878 S	Inc. Ab.	5.00	10.00	20.00	80.00
	1879 S	—	5.00	10.00	20.00	80.00
	1880 S	—	5.00	10.00	20.00	80.00
	1881/0 S	.120	3.00	6.00	12.50	50.00
	1881 S	Inc. Ab.	3.00	6.00	12.50	50.00
	1882/1 S	.064	12.50	25.00	50.00	125.00
	1882 S	Inc. Ab.	12.50	25.00	50.00	125.00
	1883/73 S	.102	2.00	4.00	8.00	50.00
	1883 S	Inc. Ab.	2.00	4.00	8.00	50.00
	1884/3 S	—	2.00	4.00	8.00	50.00
	1884 S	—	2.00	4.00	8.00	50.00
	1885 S	.297	1.50	2.50	5.00	50.00
	1885 S small S in mint mark	Inc. Ab.	2.50	4.00	8.00	50.00
	1885 Z w/o assayers initial (error)	Inc. Ab.	3.50	7.50	15.00	65.00
	1886 S	.274	1.50	2.50	5.00	30.00
	1886 Z	I.A.	12.50	25.00	50.00	125.00
	1887 ZsZ	.233	1.50	2.50	5.00	30.00
	1887 Z Z (error)	Inc. Ab.	3.50	7.50	15.00	50.00
	1888 ZsZ	.270	1.50	2.50	5.00	30.00
	1888 Z Z (error)	Inc. Ab.	3.50	7.50	15.00	40.00
	1889/7 Z/S	.240	4.00	8.00	12.50	40.00
	1889 Z/S	I.A.	1.50	4.00	8.00	30.00
	1889 Z	Inc. Ab.	1.50	2.50	5.00	30.00
	1890 ZsZ	.410	1.50	2.50	5.00	30.00
	1890 Z Z (error)	Inc. Ab.	3.75	7.50	15.00	40.00
	1891 Z	1.105	1.50	2.50	5.00	30.00
	1891 ZsZ double s	Inc. Ab.	2.00	4.00	7.00	30.00
	1892 Z	1.102	1.50	2.50	5.00	30.00
	1893 Z	1.011	1.50	2.50	5.00	25.00
	1894 Z	.892	1.50	2.50	5.00	30.00
	1895 Z	.920	1.50	2.50	5.00	30.00
	1896/5 ZsZ	.700	1.50	2.50	5.00	30.00
	1896 ZsZ	I.A.	1.50	2.50	5.00	30.00
	1896 Z Z (error)	Inc. Ab.	3.75	7.50	15.00	40.00
	1897/6 ZsZ	.900	2.00	5.00	10.00	30.00
	1897/6 Z Z (error)	Inc. Ab.	3.75	7.50	15.00	40.00
	1897 Z	Inc. Ab.	1.50	2.50	5.00	30.00

NOTE: Varieties exist.

Mint mark: Cn
Obv: Restyled eagle.

KM#	Date	Mintage	Fine	VF	XF	Unc
404	1898 M	9,870	50.00	100.00	150.00	300.00
	1899 Q round Q, single tail	.080	5.00	7.50	15.00	40.00
	1899 Q oval Q, double tail	Inc. Ab.	5.00	7.50	15.00	40.00
	1900 Q	.160	1.50	2.50	5.00	20.00
	1901 Q	.235	1.50	2.50	5.00	20.00
	1902 Q	.186	1.50	2.50	5.00	20.00
	1903 Q	.256	1.50	2.50	6.00	20.00
	1903 V	Inc. Ab.	1.50	2.50	5.00	15.00
	1904 H	.307	1.50	2.50	5.00	15.00

NOTE: Varieties exist.

Mint mark: Go

KM#	Date	Mintage	Fine	VF	XF	Unc
404.1	1898 R	.435	1.50	2.50	5.00	20.00
	1899 R	.270	1.50	2.50	5.00	25.00
	1900 R	.130	7.50	12.50	25.00	60.00

Mint mark: Mo

KM#	Date	Mintage	Fine	VF	XF	Unc
404.2	1898 M	.130	1.50	2.50	5.00	17.50
	1899 M	.190	1.50	2.50	5.00	17.50
	1900 M	.311	1.50	2.50	5.00	17.50
	1901 M	.080	2.50	3.50	7.00	20.00
	1902 M	.181	1.50	2.50	5.00	17.50
	1903 M	.581	1.50	2.50	5.00	17.50
	1904 M	1.266	1.25	2.00	4.50	15.00
	1904 MM (error)	Inc. Ab.	2.50	5.00	10.00	25.00
	1905 M	.266	2.00	3.75	7.50	20.00

Mint mark: Zs

KM#	Date	Mintage	Fine	VF	XF	Unc
404.3	1898 Z	.240	1.50	2.50	7.50	20.00
	1899 Z	.105	1.50	3.00	10.00	22.00
	1900 Z	.219	7.50	10.00	20.00	45.00
	1901 Z	.070	2.50	5.00	10.00	25.00
	1902 Z	.120	2.50	5.00	10.00	25.00
	1903 Z	.228	1.50	3.00	10.00	20.00
	1904 Z	.368	1.50	3.00	10.00	20.00
	1904 M	Inc. Ab.	1.50	3.00	10.00	25.00
	1905 M	.066	7.50	15.00	30.00	60.00

20 CENTAVOS

5.4150 g, .903 SILVER, .1572 oz ASW
Mint mark: Cn
Obv: Restyled eagle.

KM#	Date	Mintage	Fine	VF	XF	Unc
405	1898 M	.114	5.00	12.50	35.00	140.00
	1899 M	.044	12.00	20.00	45.00	225.00
	1899 Q	Inc. Ab.	20.00	35.00	100.00	250.00
	1900 Q	.068	6.50	12.50	35.00	140.00
	1901 Q	.185	5.00	10.00	30.00	120.00
	1902/802 Q	.098	6.00	10.00	30.00	120.00
	1902 Q	Inc. Ab.	4.00	9.00	30.00	120.00
	1903 Q	.093	4.00	9.00	30.00	120.00
	1904/3 H	.258	—	—	—	—
	1904 H	Inc. Ab.	5.00	10.00	30.00	120.00

Mint mark: Go

KM#	Date	Mintage	Fine	VF	XF	Unc
405.1	1898 R	.135	4.00	8.00	20.00	100.00
	1899 R	.215	4.00	8.00	20.00	100.00
	1900/800 R	.038	10.00	20.00	50.00	150.00

Mint mark: Mo

KM#	Date	Mintage	Fine	VF	XF	Unc
405.2	1898 M	.150	4.00	8.00	20.00	85.00
	1899 M	.425	4.00	8.00	20.00	85.00
	1900/800 M	.295	4.00	8.00	20.00	85.00
	1901 M	.110	4.00	8.00	20.00	85.00
	1902 M	.120	4.00	8.00	20.00	85.00
	1903 M	.213	4.00	8.00	20.00	85.00
	1904 M	.276	4.00	8.00	20.00	85.00
	1905 M	.117	6.50	20.00	50.00	150.00

NOTE: Varieties exist.

Mint mark: Zs

KM#	Date	Mintage	Fine	VF	XF	Unc
405.3	1898 Z	.195	5.00	10.00	20.00	100.00
	1899 Z	.210	5.00	10.00	20.00	100.00
	1900/800 Z	.097	5.00	10.00	20.00	100.00
	1901/0 Z	.130	25.00	50.00	100.00	250.00
	1901 Z	Inc. Ab.	5.00	10.00	20.00	100.00
	1902 Z	.105	5.00	10.00	20.00	100.00
	1903 Z	.143	5.00	10.00	20.00	100.00
	1904 Z	.246	5.00	10.00	20.00	100.00
	1904 M	Inc. Ab.	5.00	10.00	20.00	100.00
	1905 M	.059	10.00	20.00	50.00	150.00

25 CENTAVOS

6.7680 g, .903 SILVER, .1965 oz ASW
Mint mark: A,As

KM#	Date	Mintage	Fine	VF	XF	Unc
406	1874 L	—	20.00	40.00	90.00	200.00
	1875 L	—	15.00	30.00	70.00	200.00
	1876 L	—	30.00	50.00	100.00	200.00
	1877 L	.011	200.00	300.00	500.00	—
	1877.	Inc. Ab.	10.00	25.00	60.00	200.00
	1878 L	.025	10.00	25.00	60.00	200.00
	1879 L	—	10.00	25.00	60.00	200.00
	1880 L	—	10.00	25.00	60.00	200.00
	1880.L	—	10.00	25.00	60.00	200.00
	1881 L	8,800	500.00	700.00	—	—
	1882 L	7,777	15.00	35.00	80.00	200.00

KM#	Date	Mintage	Fine	VF	XF	Unc
406	1883 L	.028	10.00	25.00	60.00	200.00
	1884 L	—	10.00	25.00	60.00	200.00
	1885 L	—	20.00	40.00	90.00	200.00
	1886 L	.046	15.00	30.00	70.00	200.00
	1887 L	.012	12.50	27.50	65.00	200.00
	1888 L	.020	12.50	27.50	65.00	200.00
	1889 L	.014	12.50	27.50	65.00	200.00
	1890 L	.023	10.00	25.00	60.00	200.00

Mint mark: CA,CH,Ca

KM#	Date	Mintage	Fine	VF	XF	Unc
406.1	1871 M	.018	25.00	50.00	100.00	200.00
	1872 M very crude date					
		.024	50.00	100.00	150.00	300.00
	1883 M	.012	10.00	25.00	50.00	175.00
	1885/3 M	.035	10.00	25.00	50.00	175.00
	1885 M	Inc.Ab.	10.00	25.00	50.00	175.00
	1886 M	.022	10.00	25.00	50.00	175.00
	1887/6 M	.026	10.00	15.00	30.00	175.00
	1887 M	Inc. Ab.	10.00	15.00	30.00	175.00
	1888 M	.014	10.00	25.00	50.00	175.00
	1889 M	.050	10.00	15.00	30.00	175.00

Mint mark: Cn

KM#	Date	Mintage	Fine	VF	XF	Unc
406.2	1871 P	—	250.00	500.00	750.00	—
	1872 P	2,780	300.00	550.00	800.00	—
	1873 P	.020	100.00	150.00	250.00	500.00
	1874 P	—	20.00	50.00	125.00	250.00
	1875 P	—	250.00	500.00	750.00	—
	1876 P	—	—	—	Rare	—
	1878/7 D/S	—	100.00	150.00	250.00	500.00
	1878 D	—	100.00	150.00	250.00	500.00
	1879 D	—	15.00	35.00	70.00	175.00
	1880 D	—	250.00	500.00	750.00	—
	1881/0 D	.018	15.00	30.00	60.00	175.00
	1882 D	—	200.00	350.00	600.00	—
	1882 M	—	—	—	Rare	—
	1883 M	.015	50.00	100.00	150.00	300.00
	1884 M	—	20.00	40.00	80.00	175.00
	1885/4 M	.019	20.00	40.00	80.00	175.00
	1886 M	.022	12.50	20.00	50.00	175.00
	1887 M	.032	12.50	20.00	50.00	175.00
	1888 M	.086	7.50	15.00	30.00	175.00
	1889 M	.050	10.00	25.00	50.00	175.00
	1890 M	.091	7.50	17.50	40.00	175.00
	1892/0 M	.016	20.00	40.00	80.00	200.00
	1892 M	Inc. Ab.	20.00	40.00	80.00	200.00

Mint mark: Do

KM#	Date	Mintage	Fine	VF	XF	Unc
406.3	1873 P	892 pcs.	—	—	Rare	—
	1877 P	—	25.00	50.00	100.00	200.00
	1878/7 E	—	250.00	500.00	750.00	—
	1878 B	—	—	—	Rare	—
	1879 B	—	50.00	75.00	125.00	250.00
	1880 B	—	—	—	Rare	—
	1882 C	.017	25.00	50.00	100.00	225.00
	1884/3 C	—	25.00	50.00	100.00	200.00
	1885 C	.015	20.00	40.00	80.00	200.00
	1886 C	.033	15.00	30.00	60.00	200.00
	1887 C	.027	10.00	20.00	50.00	200.00
	1888 C	.025	10.00	20.00	50.00	200.00
	1889 C	.029	10.00	20.00	50.00	200.00
	1890 C	.068	7.50	15.00	40.00	200.00

Mint mark: Ga

KM#	Date	Mintage	Fine	VF	XF	Unc
406.4	1880 A	.038	25.00	50.00	100.00	200.00
	1881/0 S	.039	25.00	50.00	100.00	200.00
	1881 S	Inc. Ab.	25.00	50.00	100.00	200.00
	1882 S	.018	25.00	50.00	100.00	200.00
	1883/2 B/S	—	50.00	100.00	150.00	300.00
	1884 B	—	20.00	40.00	80.00	150.00
	1889 S	.030	20.00	40.00	80.00	150.00

Mint mark: Go

KM#	Date	Mintage	Fine	VF	XF	Unc
406.5	1870 S	.128	10.00	20.00	50.00	125.00
	1871 S	.172	10.00	20.00	50.00	125.00
	1872/1 S	.178	10.00	20.00	50.00	125.00
	1872 S	Inc. Ab.	10.00	20.00	50.00	125.00
	1873 S	.120	10.00	20.00	50.00	125.00
	1874 S	—	15.00	30.00	60.00	150.00
	1875/4 S	—	15.00	30.00	60.00	150.00
	1875 S	—	10.00	20.00	50.00	125.00
	1876 S	—	20.00	40.00	80.00	175.00
	1877 S	.124	10.00	20.00	50.00	125.00
	1878 S	.146	10.00	20.00	50.00	125.00
	1879 S	—	10.00	20.00	50.00	125.00
	1880 S	—	20.00	40.00	80.00	175.00
	1881 S	.408	7.50	17.50	45.00	125.00
	1882 S	.204	7.50	17.50	45.00	125.00
	1883 B	.168	7.50	17.50	45.00	125.00
	1884/69 B	—	7.50	17.50	45.00	125.00
	1884/3 B	—	7.50	17.50	45.00	125.00
	1884 B	—	7.50	17.50	45.00	125.00
	1885/65 R	.300	7.50	17.50	45.00	125.00
	1885/69 R	I.A.	7.50	17.50	45.00	125.00
	1885 R	Inc. Ab.	7.50	17.50	45.00	125.00
	1886/66 R	.322	7.50	17.50	45.00	125.00
	1886/69 R/S					
		Inc. Ab.	7.50	17.50	45.00	125.00
	1886/5/69R					
		Inc. Ab.	7.50	15.00	45.00	125.00
	1886 R	Inc. Ab.	7.50	15.00	45.00	125.00
	1887 R	.254	7.50	15.00	45.00	125.00
	1887 Go/Cn R/D					
		Inc. Ab.	7.50	15.00	45.00	125.00
	1888 R	.312	7.50	15.00	45.00	125.00
	1889/8 R	.304	7.50	15.00	45.00	125.00
	1889/8 Go/Cn R/D					
		Inc. Ab.	7.50	15.00	45.00	125.00
	1889 R	Inc. Ab.	7.50	15.00	45.00	125.00
	1890 R	.236	7.50	15.00	45.00	125.00

NOTE: Varieties exist.

Mint mark: Ho

KM#	Date	Mintage	Fine	VF	XF	Unc
406.6	1874 R	.023	10.00	20.00	40.00	125.00
	1874/64 R	I.A.	10.00	20.00	40.00	125.00
	1875 R	—	—	—	Rare	—
	1876/4 F/R					
		.034	10.00	20.00	50.00	150.00
	1876 F/R	I.A.	10.00	25.00	60.00	150.00
	1876 F	Inc. Ab.	10.00	25.00	55.00	135.00
	1877 F	—	10.00	20.00	50.00	125.00
	1878 A	.023	10.00	20.00	50.00	125.00
	1879 A	—	10.00	20.00	50.00	125.00
	1880 A	—	15.00	30.00	60.00	125.00
	1881 A	.019	15.00	30.00	60.00	125.00
	1882 A	8,120	20.00	40.00	80.00	150.00
	1883 M	2,000	100.00	200.00	300.00	600.00
	1884 M	—	12.50	25.00	50.00	150.00
	1885 M	—	10.00	20.00	50.00	125.00
	1886 G	6,400	30.00	60.00	125.00	250.00
	1887 G	.012	10.00	20.00	40.00	125.00
	1888 G	.020	10.00	20.00	40.00	125.00
	1889 G	.028	10.00	20.00	40.00	125.00
	1890/80 G	.018	25.00	50.00	100.00	125.00
	1890 G	Inc. Ab.	25.00	50.00	100.00	125.00

NOTE: Varieties exist.

Mint mark: Mo

KM#	Date	Mintage	Fine	VF	XF	Unc
406.7	1869 C	.076	10.00	25.00	50.00	125.00
	1870/9 C	.136	6.00	12.00	30.00	125.00
	1870 C	Inc. Ab.	6.00	12.00	30.00	125.00
	1871 M	.138	6.00	12.00	30.00	125.00
	1872 M	.220	6.00	12.00	30.00	125.00
	1873/1 M	.048	10.00	25.00	50.00	125.00
	1873 M	Inc. Ab.	10.00	25.00	50.00	125.00
	1874/69 B/M					
		—	10.00	25.00	50.00	125.00
	1874/3 M	—	10.00	25.00	50.00	125.00
	1874/3 B	—	10.00	25.00	50.00	125.00
	1874 M	—	6.00	12.00	30.00	125.00
	1874 B/M	—	10.00	25.00	50.00	125.00
	1875 B	—	6.00	12.00	30.00	125.00
	1876/5 B	—	7.50	15.00	40.00	125.00
	1876 B	—	6.00	12.00	30.00	125.00
	1877 M	.056	10.00	25.00	50.00	125.00
	1878/1 M	.120	10.00	25.00	50.00	125.00
	1878/7 M	I.A.	10.00	25.00	50.00	125.00
	1878 M	Inc. Ab.	6.00	12.00	30.00	125.00
	1879 M	—	10.00	20.00	40.00	125.00
	1880 M	—	7.50	15.00	35.00	125.00
	1881/0 M	.300	10.00	25.00	50.00	125.00
	1881 M	Inc. Ab.	10.00	25.00	50.00	125.00
	1882 M	.212	7.50	15.00	35.00	125.00
	1883 M	.108	7.50	15.00	35.00	125.00
	1884 M	—	10.00	20.00	40.00	125.00
	1885 M	.216	10.00	20.00	40.00	125.00
	1886/5 M	.436	7.50	15.00	35.00	125.00
	1886 M	Inc. Ab.	7.50	15.00	35.00	125.00
	1887 M	.376	7.50	15.00	35.00	125.00
	1888 M	.192	7.50	15.00	35.00	125.00
	1889 M	.132	7.50	15.00	35.00	125.00
	1890 M	.060	10.00	20.00	40.00	125.00

NOTE: Varieties exist.

Mint mark: Pi

KM#	Date	Mintage	Fine	VF	XF	Unc
406.8	1869 S	—	25.00	75.00	150.00	300.00
	1870 G	.050	10.00	30.00	75.00	150.00
	1870 O	Inc. Ab.	15.00	35.00	85.00	175.00
	1871 O	.030	10.00	30.00	75.00	150.00
	1872 O	.046	10.00	30.00	75.00	150.00
	1873 O	.013	15.00	40.00	90.00	175.00
	1874 H	—	15.00	40.00	90.00	200.00
	1875 H	—	10.00	20.00	60.00	150.00
	1876/5 H	—	15.00	30.00	80.00	175.00
	1876 H	—	10.00	25.00	65.00	150.00
	1877 H	.019	10.00	25.00	65.00	150.00
	1878 H	—	15.00	30.00	60.00	150.00
	1879/8 H	—	10.00	25.00	60.00	150.00
	1879 H	—	10.00	25.00	60.00	150.00
	1879 E	—	100.00	200.00	300.00	600.00
	1880 H	—	20.00	40.00	100.00	200.00
	1881 H	.050	20.00	40.00	80.00	175.00
	1881 E	Inc. Ab.	—	—	Rare	—
	1882 H	.020	10.00	20.00	60.00	150.00
	1883 H	.017	10.00	25.00	65.00	150.00
	1884 H	—	10.00	25.00	65.00	150.00
	1885 H	.043	10.00	20.00	60.00	150.00
	1886 C	.078	10.00	25.00	65.00	150.00
	1886 R	Inc. Ab.	7.50	20.00	50.00	150.00
	1886 R 6/inverted 6					
		Inc. Ab.	7.50	20.00	50.00	150.00
	1887 Pi/ZsR					
		.092	7.50	20.00	50.00	150.00
	1887 Pi/ZsB					
		Inc. Ab.	100.00	150.00	300.00	500.00
	1888 R	.106	7.50	20.00	50.00	150.00
	1888 Pi/ZsR					
		Inc. Ab.	10.00	20.00	50.00	150.00
	1888 R/B	I.A.	10.00	20.00	50.00	150.00
	1889 R	.115	7.50	15.00	40.00	150.00
	1889 Pi/ZsR					
		Inc. Ab.	10.00	20.00	50.00	150.00
	1889 R/B	I.A.	10.00	20.00	50.00	150.00
	1890 R	.064	10.00	20.00	50.00	150.00
	1890 Pi/ZsR/B					
		Inc. Ab.	7.50	15.00	40.00	150.00
	1890 R/B	I.A.	10.00	20.00	50.00	150.00

NOTE: Varieties exist.

Mint mark: Zs

KM#	Date	Mintage	Fine	VF	XF	Unc
406.9	1870 H	.152	6.00	15.00	50.00	125.00
	1871 H	.250	6.00	15.00	50.00	125.00
	1872 H	.260	6.00	15.00	50.00	125.00
406.9	1873 H	.132	6.00	15.00	50.00	125.00
	1874 H	—	10.00	20.00	60.00	125.00
	1874 A	—	10.00	20.00	60.00	125.00
	1875 A	—	7.00	20.00	60.00	125.00
	1876 A	—	6.00	15.00	50.00	125.00
	1876 S	—	6.00	15.00	50.00	125.00
	1877 S	.350	6.00	15.00	50.00	125.00
	1878 S	.252	6.00	15.00	50.00	125.00
	1879 S	—	6.00	15.00	50.00	125.00
	1880 S	—	6.00	15.00	50.00	125.00
	1881/0 S	.570	6.00	15.00	50.00	125.00
	1881 S	Inc. Ab.	6.00	15.00	50.00	125.00
	1882/1 S	.300	10.00	17.50	55.00	125.00
	1882 S	Inc. Ab.	6.00	15.00	50.00	125.00
	1883/2 S	.193	10.00	17.50	55.00	125.00
	1883 S	Inc. Ab.	6.00	15.00	50.00	125.00
	1884/3 S	—	10.00	17.50	55.00	125.00
	1884 S	—	6.00	15.00	50.00	125.00
	1885 S	.309	6.00	15.00	50.00	125.00
	1886/5 S	.613	6.00	15.00	50.00	125.00
	1886 S	Inc. Ab.	6.00	15.00	50.00	125.00
	1886 Z	Inc. Ab.	6.00	15.00	55.00	125.00
	1887 Z	.389	6.00	15.00	50.00	125.00
	1888 Z	.408	6.00	15.00	50.00	125.00
	1889 Z	.400	6.00	15.00	50.00	125.00
	1890 Z	.269	6.00	15.00	50.00	125.00

NOTE: Varieties exist.

50 CENTAVOS

13.5360 g, .903 SILVER, .3930 oz ASW

Mint mark: A,As

Rev: Balance scale.

KM#	Date	Mintage	Fine	VF	XF	Unc
407	1875 L	—	12.00	25.00	70.00	400.00
	1876/5 L	—	25.00	50.00	120.00	450.00
	1876 L	—	12.00	25.00	70.00	400.00
	1876.L	—	—	—	—	—
	1877 L	.026	15.00	30.00	85.00	450.00
	1878 L	—	12.00	25.00	70.00	400.00
	1879 L	—	25.00	50.00	120.00	450.00
	1880 L	.057	12.00	25.00	70.00	400.00
	1881 L	.018	15.00	30.00	80.00	450.00
	1884 L	6,286	65.00	120.00	250.00	650.00
	1885 As/HoL					
		.021	15.00	35.00	90.00	450.00
	1888 L	—	Contemporary counterfeits			

Mint mark: Ca, CHa

KM#	Date	Mintage	Fine	VF	XF	Unc
407.1	1883 M	.012	30.00	60.00	125.00	500.00
	1884 M	—	25.00	50.00	125.00	500.00
	1885 M	.013	15.00	35.00	90.00	400.00
	1886 M	.018	20.00	40.00	100.00	450.00
	1887 M	.026	25.00	65.00	150.00	500.00

Mint mark: Cn

KM#	Date	Mintage	Fine	VF	XF	Unc
407.2	1871 P	—	400.00	550.00	750.00	1500.
	1873 P	—	400.00	550.00	750.00	1500.
	1874 P	—	200.00	300.00	500.00	1000.
	1875/4 P	—	20.00	40.00	75.00	450.00
	1875 P	—	12.00	25.00	50.00	450.00
	1876 P	—	15.00	30.00	60.00	450.00
	1877/6 G	—	15.00	30.00	60.00	450.00
	1877 G	—	12.00	25.00	50.00	450.00
	1878 G	.018	20.00	40.00	75.00	450.00
	1878 D Cn/Mo					
		Inc. Ab.	30.00	60.00	100.00	450.00
	1878 D	Inc. Ab.	15.00	35.00	75.00	450.00
	1879 D	—	12.00	25.00	50.00	450.00
	1879 D/G	—	12.00	25.00	50.00	450.00
	1880 D	—	15.00	30.00	60.00	450.00
	1881/0 D	.188	15.00	30.00	60.00	450.00
	1881 D	Inc. Ab.	15.00	30.00	60.00	450.00
	1881 G	Inc. Ab.	125.00	175.00	275.00	550.00
	1882 D	—	175.00	225.00	325.00	1000.
	1882 G	—	100.00	250.00	300.00	1000.
	1883 D	.019	25.00	50.00	100.00	500.00
	1885/3 CN/Pi M/H					
		9,254	30.00	60.00	100.00	500.00
	1886 M/G	7,030	50.00	100.00	150.00	800.00
	1886 M	Inc. Ab.	40.00	80.00	150.00	800.00
	1887 M	.076	20.00	40.00	100.00	450.00
	1888 M	—	Contemporary counterfeits			
	1892 M	8,200	40.00	80.00	150.00	800.00

Mint mark: Do

KM#	Date	Mintage	Fine	VF	XF	Unc
407.3	1871 P	591 pcs.	—	—	Rare	—
	1873 P	4,010	150.00	250.00	500.00	1250.
	1873 M/P	I.A.	150.00	250.00	500.00	1250.
	1874 M	—	20.00	40.00	175.00	750.00
	1875 M	—	20.00	40.00	80.00	350.00
	1875 H	—	150.00	250.00	450.00	1000.
	1876/5 M	—	35.00	70.00	150.00	500.00
	1876 M	—	35.00	70.00	150.00	500.00
	1877 P	2,000	30.00	45.00	150.00	1250.
	1878 B	—	—	—	Rare	—
	1879 B	—	—	—	Rare	—
	1880 P	—	30.00	60.00	125.00	500.00
	1881 P	.010	40.00	80.00	150.00	550.00
	1882 C	8,957	30.00	75.00	200.00	800.00

KM#	Date	Mintage	Fine	VF	XF	Unc
407.3	1884/2 C	—	20.00	50.00	125.00	600.00
	1884 C	—	—	—	—	—
	1885 B	—	15.00	40.00	100.00	500.00
	1886 C	.016	15.00	40.00	100.00	500.00
	1887 Do/MoC	.028	15.00	40.00	100.00	500.00

Mint mark: Go

KM#	Date	Mintage	Fine	VF	XF	Unc
407.4	1869 S	—	15.00	35.00	75.00	550.00
	1870 S	.166	12.00	25.00	50.00	450.00
	1871 S	.148	12.00	25.00	50.00	450.00
	1872/1 S	.144	15.00	30.00	60.00	500.00
	1872 S	Inc. Ab.	12.00	25.00	50.00	450.00
	1873 S	.050	12.00	25.00	50.00	450.00
	1874 S	—	12.00	25.00	50.00	450.00
	1875 S	—	15.00	35.00	75.00	450.00
	1876/5 S	—	12.00	25.00	50.00	450.00
	1877 S	.076	12.00	25.00	60.00	450.00
	1878 S	.037	15.00	30.00	75.00	550.00
	1879 S	—	12.00	25.00	50.00	450.00
	1880 S	—	12.00	25.00	50.00	450.00
	1881/79 S	.032	15.00	30.00	60.00	500.00
	1881 S	Inc. Ab.	12.00	25.00	50.00	450.00
	1882 S	.018	12.00	25.00	50.00	450.00
	1883/2 B/S	—	15.00	30.00	60.00	500.00
	1883 B	—	12.00	25.00	50.00	450.00
	1883 S	—	—	—	Rare	—
	1884 B/S	—	15.00	30.00	75.00	500.00
	1885 R	.053	12.00	25.00	50.00	450.00
	1886/5 R/B	.059	15.00	30.00	60.00	500.00
	1886/5 R/S	Inc. Ab.	20.00	40.00	75.00	500.00
	1886 R	Inc. Ab.	20.00	40.00	75.00	450.00
	1887 R	.018	20.00	40.00	75.00	550.00
	1888 R	—	Contemporary counterfeits			

NOTE: Varieties exist.

Mint mark: Ho

KM#	Date	Mintage	Fine	VF	XF	Unc
407.5	1874 R	—	20.00	40.00	100.00	600.00
	1875/4 R	—	20.00	50.00	125.00	600.00
	1875 R	—	20.00	50.00	125.00	600.00
	1876/5 F/R	—	15.00	35.00	100.00	550.00
	1876 F	—	15.00	35.00	100.00	550.00
	1877 F	—	50.00	75.00	150.00	650.00
	1880/70 A	—	15.00	35.00	100.00	550.00
	1880 A	—	15.00	35.00	100.00	550.00
	1881 A	.013	15.00	35.00	100.00	550.00
	1882 A	—	75.00	150.00	250.00	750.00
	1888 G	—	Contemporary counterfeits			
	1894 G	.059	15.00	30.00	100.00	450.00
	1895 G	8,000	250.00	350.00	500.00	1250.

NOTE: Varieties exist.

Mint mark: Mo

KM#	Date	Mintage	Fine	VF	XF	Unc
407.6	1869 C	.046	15.00	35.00	95.00	600.00
	1870 C	.052	15.00	30.00	90.00	550.00
	1871 C	.014	40.00	75.00	150.00	650.00
	1871 M/C	I.A.	35.00	75.00	150.00	600.00
	1872/1 M	.060	35.00	75.00	150.00	550.00
	1872 M	Inc. Ab.	35.00	75.00	150.00	550.00
	1873 M	6,000	35.00	75.00	150.00	600.00
	1874/3 M	—	200.00	400.00	600.00	1250.
	1874/2 B	—	15.00	30.00	75.00	500.00
	1874/3 B/M	—	15.00	30.00	75.00	500.00
	1874 B	—	15.00	30.00	75.00	500.00
	1875 B	—	15.00	30.00	75.00	550.00
	1876/5 B	—	15.00	30.00	75.00	500.00
	1876 B	—	12.00	25.00	75.00	500.00
	1877/2 M	—	20.00	40.00	100.00	550.00
	1877 M	—	15.00	30.00	90.00	500.00
	1878/7 M	8,000	25.00	50.00	125.00	600.00
	1878 M	Inc. Ab.	15.00	35.00	100.00	550.00
	1879 M	—	25.00	50.00	125.00	550.00
	1880 M	—	100.00	150.00	250.00	750.00
	1881 M	.016	25.00	50.00	125.00	600.00
	1882/1 M	2,000	30.00	60.00	150.00	750.00
	1883/2 M	4,000	150.00	225.00	350.00	1000.
	1884 M	—	150.00	225.00	350.00	1000.
	1885 M	.012	30.00	60.00	150.00	600.00
	1886/5 M	.066	15.00	35.00	90.00	450.00
	1886 M	Inc. Ab.	12.00	25.00	75.00	400.00
	1887/6 M	.088	15.00	35.00	90.00	450.00
	1887 M	Inc. Ab.	15.00	35.00	75.00	450.00
	1888 M	—	Contemporary counterfeits			

Mint mark: Pi

KM#	Date	Mintage	Fine	VF	XF	Unc
407.7	1870/780 G	.050	25.00	45.00	110.00	500.00
	1870 G	Inc. Ab.	20.00	40.00	100.00	450.00
	1870 O	Inc. Ab.	20.00	40.00	100.00	450.00
	1871 O/G	.064	15.00	30.00	80.00	400.00
	1872 O	.052	15.00	30.00	80.00	400.00
	1872 O/G	I.A.	15.00	30.00	80.00	400.00
	1873 O	.032	20.00	40.00	100.00	450.00
	1873 H	Inc. Ab.	25.00	50.00	125.00	550.00
	1874 H/O	—	15.00	30.00	80.00	400.00
	1875 H	—	15.00	30.00	80.00	400.00
	1876 H	—	30.00	60.00	150.00	700.00
	1877 H	.034	20.00	40.00	100.00	450.00
	1878 H	9,700	20.00	40.00	100.00	450.00
	1879/7 H	—	15.00	35.00	90.00	450.00
	1879 H	—	15.00	35.00	90.00	400.00
	1880 H	—	20.00	40.00	100.00	450.00
	1881 H	.028	20.00	40.00	100.00	450.00
	1882 H	.022	15.00	30.00	80.00	400.00
	1883 H 8/8	.029	50.00	100.00	200.00	750.00
	1883 H	Inc. Ab.	15.00	30.00	80.00	400.00
407.7	1884 H	—	50.00	100.00	175.00	600.00
	1885/0 H	.045	20.00	40.00	100.00	450.00
	1885/4 H	I.A.	20.00	40.00	100.00	450.00
	1885 H	Inc. Ab.	25.00	50.00	125.00	450.00
	1885 C	Inc. Ab.	15.00	30.00	80.00	400.00
	1886/1 R	.092	50.00	100.00	175.00	600.00
	1886 C	Inc. Ab.	15.00	30.00	80.00	400.00
	1886 R	Inc. Ab.	15.00	30.00	80.00	400.00
	1887 R	.032	15.00	30.00	90.00	450.00
	1888 R	—	Contemporary counterfeits			

Mint mark: Zs

KM#	Date	Mintage	Fine	VF	XF	Unc
407.8	1870 H	.086	12.00	25.00	60.00	450.00
	1871 H	.146	12.00	25.00	50.00	400.00
	1872 H	.132	12.00	25.00	50.00	400.00
	1873 H	.056	12.00	25.00	50.00	400.00
	1874 H	—	12.00	25.00	50.00	400.00
	1874 A	—	—	—	Rare	—
	1875 A	—	12.00	25.00	50.00	400.00
	1876/5 A	—	15.00	30.00	60.00	450.00
	1876 A	—	12.00	25.00	50.00	400.00
	1876 S	—	100.00	200.00	350.00	750.00
	1877 S	.100	12.00	25.00	50.00	400.00
	1878/7 S	.254	15.00	30.00	60.00	450.00
	1878 S	Inc. Ab.	15.00	30.00	60.00	400.00
	1879 S	—	12.00	25.00	50.00	400.00
	1880 S	—	12.00	25.00	50.00	400.00
	1881 S	.201	12.00	25.00	50.00	400.00
	1882/1 S	2,000	50.00	100.00	250.00	650.00
	1882 S	Inc. Ab.	50.00	100.00	250.00	650.00
	1883 Zs/Za S	.031	30.00	60.00	100.00	450.00
	1883 S	Inc. Ab.	25.00	50.00	100.00	450.00
	1884/3 S	—	15.00	30.00	60.00	450.00
	1884 S	—	12.00	25.00	50.00	400.00
	1885/4 S	2,000	25.00	50.00	125.00	450.00
	1885 S	Inc. Ab.	25.00	50.00	125.00	450.00
	1886 Z	2,000	150.00	275.00	400.00	1000.
	1887 Z	.063	30.00	60.00	125.00	450.00

NOTE: Varieties exist.

PESO

27.0730 g, .903 SILVER, .7860 oz ASW
Mint mark: CH
Rev: Balance scale.

KM#	Date	Mintage	Fine	VF	XF	Unc
408	1872 P/M	.747	750.00	1500.	3500.	—
	1872 P	Inc. Ab.	350.00	700.00	1500.	—
	1872/1 M	I.A.	25.00	40.00	75.00	400.00
	1872 M	Inc. Ab.	17.50	25.00	50.00	250.00
	1873 M	.320	20.00	30.00	60.00	250.00
	1873 M/P	I.A.	25.00	40.00	75.00	350.00

Mint mark: Cn

KM#	Date	Mintage	Fine	VF	XF	Unc
408.1	1870 E	—	40.00	80.00	150.00	500.00
	1871/11 P	.478	25.00	45.00	90.00	350.00
	1871 P	Inc. Ab.	20.00	40.00	75.00	300.00
	1872 P	.209	20.00	40.00	75.00	300.00
	1873 P	.527	20.00	40.00	75.00	300.00

Mint mark: Do

KM#	Date	Mintage	Fine	VF	XF	Unc
408.2	1870 P	—	50.00	100.00	175.00	450.00
	1871 P	.427	25.00	50.00	75.00	300.00
	1872 P	.296	20.00	40.00	75.00	350.00
	1872 PT	I.A.	100.00	175.00	250.00	675.00
	1873 P	.203	25.00	45.00	85.00	350.00

Mint mark: Ga

KM#	Date	Mintage	Fine	VF	XF	Unc
408.3	1870 C	—	650.00	850.00	—	—
	1871 C	.829	25.00	65.00	135.00	600.00
	1872 C	.485	40.00	90.00	175.00	650.00
	1873/2 C	.277	40.00	90.00	175.00	700.00
	1873 C	Inc. Ab.	25.00	65.00	135.00	600.00

Mint mark: Go

KM#	Date	Mintage	Fine	VF	XF	Unc
408.4	1871/0 S	3.946	30.00	50.00	90.00	350.00
	1871/3 S	I.A.	20.00	35.00	70.00	250.00
	1871 S	Inc. Ab.	12.00	20.00	40.00	200.00
	1872 S	4.067	12.00	20.00	40.00	250.00
	1873/2 S	1.560	15.00	25.00	50.00	250.00
	1873 S	Inc. Ab.	12.00	20.00	45.00	200.00
	1873/Go/Mo/S/M	Inc. Ab.	12.00	20.00	45.00	250.00

Mint mark: Mo

KM#	Date	Mintage	Fine	VF	XF	Unc
408.5	1869 C	—	35.00	65.00	135.00	450.00
	1870/69 C	5.115	15.00	25.00	50.00	275.00
	1870 C	Inc. Ab.	12.00	20.00	40.00	250.00
	1870 M/C	I.A.	18.00	30.00	50.00	275.00
	1870 M	Inc. Ab.	18.00	30.00	50.00	275.00
	1871/0 M	6.974	15.00	25.00	50.00	275.00
	1871 M	Inc. Ab.	12.00	20.00	40.00	250.00
	1872/1 M/C	4.801	15.00	25.00	50.00	275.00
	1872 M	Inc. Ab.	12.00	20.00	40.00	250.00
	1873 M	1.765	12.00	20.00	40.00	250.00

NOTE: The 1869 C with large LEY on the scroll is a pattern.

Mint mark: Oa

KM#	Date	Mintage	Fine	VF	XF	Unc
408.6	1869 E	—	275.00	400.00	600.00	2000.
	1870 OAE small A	Inc. Ab.	15.00	30.00	75.00	400.00
	1870 OA E large A	Inc. Ab.	100.00	150.00	300.00	900.00
	1871/69 E	.140	30.00	50.00	125.00	550.00
	1871 OaE small A	Inc. Ab.	15.00	30.00	60.00	300.00
	1871 OA E large A	Inc. Ab.	15.00	30.00	75.00	400.00
	1872 OaE small A	.180	15.00	30.00	75.00	400.00
	1872 OA E large A	Inc. Ab.	50.00	100.00	200.00	450.00
	1873 E	.105	15.00	30.00	75.00	350.00

Mint mark: Pi

KM#	Date	Mintage	Fine	VF	XF	Unc
408.7	1870 S	1.967	200.00	350.00	500.00	1000.
	1870 S/A	I.A.	200.00	350.00	500.00	1000.
	1870 G	Inc. Ab.	25.00	50.00	125.00	450.00
	1870 H	Inc. Ab.	Contemporary counterfeit			
	1870 O/G	I.A.	25.00	35.00	125.00	450.00
	1870 O	Inc. Ab.	20.00	30.00	100.00	350.00
	1871/69 O	2.103	75.00	150.00	250.00	500.00
	1871 O/G	I.A.	15.00	30.00	60.00	300.00
	1872 O	1.873	15.00	30.00	60.00	300.00
	1873 O	.893	15.00	30.00	60.00	300.00
	1873 H	Inc. Ab.	15.00	30.00	60.00	300.00

NOTE: Varieties exist.

Mint mark: Zs

KM#	Date	Mintage	Fine	VF	XF	Unc
408.8	1870 H	4.519	12.00	30.00	40.00	200.00
	1871 H	4.459	12.00	20.00	40.00	200.00
	1872 H	4.039	12.00	20.00	40.00	200.00
	1873 H	1.782	12.00	20.00	40.00	200.00

NOTE: Varieties exist.

Mint mark: Cn
Liberty cap

KM#	Date	Mintage	Fine	VF	XF	Unc
409	1898 AM	1.720	10.00	15.00	30.00	65.00
	1898 Cn/MoAM	I.A.	15.00	30.00	90.00	150.00
	1899 AM	1.722	25.00	50.00	90.00	175.00
	1899 JQ	I.A.	10.00	15.00	50.00	125.00
	1900 JQ	1.804	10.00	15.00	30.00	80.00
	1901 JQ	1.473	10.00	15.00	30.00	80.00
	1902 JQ	1.194	10.00	15.00	45.00	125.00
	1903 JQ	1.514	10.00	15.00	30.00	80.00
	1903 FV	I.A.	25.00	50.00	100.00	225.00
	1904 MH	1.554	10.00	15.00	30.00	80.00
	1904 RP	I.A.	45.00	85.00	125.00	300.00
	1905 RP	.598	20.00	40.00	75.00	225.00

Mint mark: Go

KM#	Date	Mintage	Fine	VF	XF	Unc
409.1	1898 RS	4.256	10.00	15.00	35.00	75.00
	1898 Go/MoRS	Inc. Ab.	20.00	30.00	60.00	125.00
	1899 RS	3.207	10.00	15.00	30.00	75.00
	1900 RS	1.489	25.00	50.00	100.00	250.00

NOTE: Varieties exist.

Mint mark: Mo

KM#	Date	Mintage	Fine	VF	XF	Unc
409.2	1898 AM original strike - rev. w/139 Beads	10.156	7.50	10.00	17.50	60.00
	1898 AM restrike (1949) - rev. w/134 Beads	10.250	7.50	10.00	15.00	40.00
	1899 AM	7.930	10.00	12.50	20.00	70.00
	1900 AM	8.226	10.00	12.50	20.00	70.00
	1901 AM	14.505	7.50	10.00	20.00	70.00
	1902/1 AM	16.224	150.00	300.00	500.00	950.00
	1902 AM	I.A.	7.50	10.00	20.00	70.00
	1903 AM	22.396	7.50	10.00	20.00	70.00
	1903 MA (error)	Inc. Ab.	1500.	2500.	3500.	7500.
	1904 AM	14.935	7.50	10.00	20.00	70.00
	1905 AM	3.557	15.00	25.00	55.00	125.00

KM#	Date	Mintage	Fine	VF	XF	Unc
409.2	1908 AM	7.575	10.00	12.50	20.00	60.00
	1908 GV	I.A.	10.00	12.50	17.50	40.00
	1909 GV	2.924	10.00	12.50	17.50	45.00

NOTE: Varieties exist.

Mint mark: Zs

KM#	Date	Mintage	Fine	VF	XF	Unc
409.3	1898 FZ	5.714	10.00	12.50	20.00	60.00
	1899 FZ	5.618	10.00	12.50	20.00	65.00
	1900 FZ	5.357	10.00	12.50	20.00	65.00
	1901 AZ	5.706	4000.	6500.	10,000.	—
	1901 FZ	I.A.	10.00	12.50	20.00	60.00
	1902 FZ	7.134	10.00	12.50	20.00	60.00
	1903/2 FZ	3.080	12.50	15.00	50.00	125.00
	1903 FZ	I.A.	10.00	12.50	20.00	65.00
	1904 FZ	2.423	10.00	15.00	25.00	70.00
	1904 FM	I.A.	10.00	15.00	25.00	85.00
	1905 FM	.995	20.00	40.00	60.00	150.00

NOTE: Varieties exist.

1.6920 g, .875 GOLD, .0476 oz AGW

Mint mark: As

KM#	Date	Mintage	Fine	VF	XF	Unc
410	1888 L	—	—	—	Rare	—
	1888 AsL/MoM	—	—	—	Rare	—

Mint mark: Ca

KM#	Date	Mintage	Fine	VF	XF	Unc
410.1	1888 Ca/MoM	104 pcs.	—	—	Rare	—

Mint mark: Cn

KM#	Date	Mintage	Fine	VF	XF	Unc
410.2	1873 P	1,221	75.00	100.00	150.00	250.00
	1875 P	—	85.00	125.00	150.00	250.00
	1878 G	248 pcs.	100.00	175.00	225.00	450.00
	1879 D	—	100.00	150.00	175.00	275.00
	1881/0 D	338 pcs.	100.00	150.00	175.00	275.00
	1882 D	340 pcs.	100.00	150.00	175.00	275.00
	1883 D	—	100.00	150.00	175.00	275.00
	1884 M	—	100.00	150.00	175.00	275.00
	1886/4 M	277 pcs.	100.00	150.00	225.00	450.00
	1888/7 M	2,586	100.00	175.00	225.00	450.00
	1888 M	Inc. Ab.	65.00	100.00	150.00	250.00
	1889 M	—	—	—	Rare	—
	1891/89 M	969 pcs.	75.00	100.00	150.00	250.00
	1892 M	780 pcs.	75.00	100.00	150.00	250.00
	1893 M	498 pcs.	85.00	125.00	150.00	250.00
	1894 M	493 pcs.	80.00	125.00	150.00	250.00
	1895 M	1,143	65.00	100.00	150.00	250.00
	1896/5 M	1,028	65.00	100.00	150.00	250.00
	1897 M	785 pcs.	65.00	100.00	150.00	250.00
	1898 M	3,521	65.00	100.00	150.00	225.00
	1898 Cn/MoM	Inc. Ab.	65.00	100.00	150.00	250.00
	1899 Q	2,000	65.00	100.00	150.00	225.00
	1901/0 Q	2,350	65.00	100.00	150.00	225.00
	1902 Q	2,480	65.00	100.00	150.00	225.00
	1902 Cn/MoQ/C	Inc. Ab.	65.00	100.00	150.00	225.00
	1904 H	3,614	65.00	100.00	150.00	225.00
	1904 Cn/Mo/ H	Inc. Ab.	65.00	100.00	150.00	250.00
	1905 P	1,000	—	Reported, not confirmed		

Mint mark: Go

KM#	Date	Mintage	Fine	VF	XF	Unc
410.3	1870 S	—	100.00	125.00	150.00	250.00
	1871 S	500 pcs.	100.00	175.00	225.00	450.00
	1888 R	210 pcs.	125.00	200.00	250.00	500.00
	1890 R	1,916	75.00	100.00	150.00	250.00
	1892 R	533 pcs.	100.00	150.00	175.00	325.00
	1894 R	180 pcs.	150.00	200.00	250.00	500.00
	1895 R	676 pcs.	100.00	150.00	175.00	300.00
	1896/5 R	4,671	65.00	100.00	150.00	250.00
	1897/6 R	4,280	65.00	100.00	150.00	250.00
	1897 R	Inc. Ab.	65.00	100.00	150.00	250.00
	1898 R regular obv.	5,193	65.00	100.00	150.00	250.00
	1898 R mule, 5 Centavos obv., normal rev.	Inc. Ab.	75.00	100.00	150.00	250.00
	1899 R	2,748	65.00	100.00	150.00	250.00
	1900/800 R	864 pcs.	75.00	125.00	150.00	275.00

Mint mark: Ho

KM#	Date	Mintage	Fine	VF	XF	Unc
410.4	1875 R	310 pcs.	—	—	Rare	—
	1876 F	—	—	—	Rare	—
	1888 G/MoM	—	—	—	Rare	—

Mint mark: Mo

KM#	Date	Mintage	Fine	VF	XF	Unc
410.5	1870 C	2,540	40.00	60.00	80.00	175.00
	1871 M/C	1,000	50.00	100.00	150.00	225.00
	1872 M/C	3,000	40.00	60.00	80.00	175.00
	1873/1 M	2,900	40.00	60.00	80.00	175.00
	1873 M	Inc. Ab.	40.00	60.00	80.00	175.00
	1874 M	—	40.00	60.00	80.00	175.00
	1875 B/M	—	40.00	60.00	80.00	175.00
	1876/5 B/M	—	40.00	60.00	80.00	175.00
	1877 M	—	40.00	60.00	80.00	175.00
	1878 M	2,000	40.00	60.00	80.00	175.00
	1879 M	—	40.00	60.00	80.00	175.00
	1880/70 M	—	40.00	60.00	80.00	175.00
	1881/71 M	1,000	40.00	60.00	80.00	175.00
	1882/72 M	—	40.00	60.00	80.00	175.00
		—	40.00	60.00	80.00	175.00
	1883/72 M	1,000	40.00	60.00	80.00	175.00
	1884 M	—	40.00	60.00	80.00	175.00
	1885/71 M	—	40.00	60.00	80.00	175.00
	1885 M	—	40.00	60.00	80.00	175.00
	1886 M	1,700	40.00	60.00	80.00	175.00
	1887 M	2,200	40.00	60.00	80.00	175.00
	1888 M	1,000	40.00	60.00	80.00	175.00
	1889 M	500 pcs.	100.00	150.00	200.00	275.00
	1890 M	570 pcs.	100.00	150.00	200.00	275.00
	1891 M	746 pcs.	100.00	150.00	200.00	275.00
	1892/0 M	2,895	40.00	60.00	80.00	175.00
	1893 M	5,917	40.00	60.00	80.00	175.00
	1894 M	6,244	40.00	60.00	80.00	175.00
	1895 M	8,994	40.00	60.00	80.00	175.00
	1895 B	Inc. Ab.	40.00	60.00	80.00	175.00
	1896 B	7,166	40.00	60.00	80.00	175.00
	1896 M	Inc. Ab.	40.00	60.00	80.00	175.00
	1897 M	5,131	40.00	60.00	80.00	175.00
	1898/7 M	5,368	40.00	60.00	80.00	175.00
	1899 M	9,515	40.00	60.00	80.00	175.00
	1900/800 M	9,301	40.00	60.00	80.00	175.00
	1900/880 M	Inc. Ab.	40.00	60.00	80.00	175.00
	1900/890 M	Inc. Ab.	40.00	60.00	80.00	175.00
	1900 M	Inc. Ab.	40.00	60.00	80.00	175.00
	1901/801 M large date	8,293	40.00	60.00	80.00	175.00
	1901 M small date	Inc. Ab.	40.00	60.00	80.00	175.00
	1902 M large date	.011	40.00	60.00	80.00	175.00
	1902 M small date	Inc. Ab.	40.00	60.00	80.00	175.00
	1903 M large date	.010	40.00	60.00	80.00	175.00
	1903 M small date	Inc. Ab.	50.00	80.00	120.00	180.00
	1904 M	9,845	40.00	60.00	80.00	175.00
	1905 M	3,429	40.00	60.00	80.00	175.00

Mint mark: Zs

KM#	Date	Mintage	Fine	VF	XF	Unc
410.6	1872 H	2,024	125.00	150.00	175.00	250.00
	1875/3 A	—	125.00	150.00	200.00	300.00
	1878 S	—	125.00	150.00	175.00	250.00
	1888 Z	280 pcs.	175.00	225.00	300.00	650.00
	1889 Z	492 pcs.	150.00	175.00	225.00	425.00
	1890 Z	738 pcs.	150.00	175.00	225.00	425.00

2-1/2 PESOS

4.2300 g, .875 GOLD, .1190 oz AGW

Mint mark: As

KM#	Date	Mintage	Fine	VF	XF	Unc
411	1888 As/MoL	—	—	—	Rare	—

Mint mark: Cn

KM#	Date	Mintage	Fine	VF	XF	Unc
411.1	1893 M	141 pcs.	1500.	2000.	2500.	3500.

Mint mark: Do

KM#	Date	Mintage	Fine	VF	XF	Unc
411.2	1888 C	—	—	—	Rare	—

Mint mark: Go

KM#	Date	Mintage	Fine	VF	XF	Unc
411.3	1871 S	600 pcs.	1250.	2000.	2500.	3250.
	1888 Go/MoR	110 pcs.	1750.	2250.	2750.	3500.

Mint mark: Ho

KM#	Date	Mintage	Fine	VF	XF	Unc
411.4	1874 R	—	—	—	Rare	—
	1888 G	—	—	—	Rare	—

Mint mark: Mo

KM#	Date	Mintage	Fine	VF	XF	Unc
411.5	1870 C	820 pcs.	150.00	250.00	350.00	650.00
	1872 M/C	800 pcs.	150.00	250.00	350.00	650.00
	1873/2 M	—	200.00	350.00	750.00	1250.
	1874 M	—	200.00	350.00	750.00	1250.
	1874 B/M	—	200.00	350.00	750.00	1250.
	1875 B	—	200.00	350.00	750.00	1250.
	1876 B	—	250.00	500.00	1000.	1500.
	1877 M	—	200.00	350.00	750.00	1250.
	1878 M	400 pcs.	200.00	350.00	750.00	1250.
	1879 M	—	200.00	350.00	750.00	1250.
	1880/79 M	—	200.00	350.00	750.00	1250.
411.5	1881 M	400 pcs.	200.00	350.00	750.00	1250.
	1882 M	—	200.00	350.00	750.00	1250.
	1883/73 M	400 pcs.	200.00	350.00	750.00	1250.
	1884 M	—	250.00	500.00	1000.	1500.
	1885 M	—	200.00	350.00	750.00	1250.
	1886 M	400 pcs.	200.00	350.00	750.00	1250.
	1887 M	400 pcs.	200.00	350.00	750.00	1250.
	1888 M	540 pcs.	200.00	350.00	750.00	1250.
	1889 M	240 pcs.	150.00	300.00	525.00	850.00
	1890 M	420 pcs.	200.00	350.00	750.00	1250.
	1891 M	188 pcs.	200.00	350.00	750.00	1250.
	1892 M	240 pcs.	200.00	350.00	750.00	1250.

Mint mark: Zs

KM#	Date	Mintage	Fine	VF	XF	Unc
411.6	1872 H	1,300	200.00	350.00	500.00	1000.
	1873 H	—	175.00	325.00	450.00	700.00
	1875/3 A	—	200.00	350.00	750.00	1250.
	1877 S	—	200.00	350.00	750.00	1250.
	1878 S	300 pcs.	200.00	350.00	750.00	1250.
	1888 Zs/MoS	80 pcs.	300.00	500.00	1000.	1750.
	1889 Zs/MoZ	184 pcs.	250.00	450.00	950.00	1500.
	1890 Z	326 pcs.	200.00	350.00	750.00	1250.

CINCO (5) PESOS

8.4600 g, .875 GOLD, .2380 oz AGW

Mint mark: As

KM#	Date	Mintage	Fine	VF	XF	Unc
412	1875 L	—	—	—	—	—
	1878 L	383 pcs.	900.00	1700.	3000.	4500.

Mint mark: Ca

KM#	Date	Mintage	Fine	VF	XF	Unc
412.1	1888 M	120 pcs.	—	—	Rare	—

Mint mark: Cn

KM#	Date	Mintage	Fine	VF	XF	Unc
412.2	1873 P	—	300.00	600.00	1000.	1500.
	1874 P	—	—	—	—	—
	1875 P	—	300.00	500.00	700.00	1250.
	1876 P	—	300.00	500.00	700.00	1250.
	1877 G	—	300.00	500.00	700.00	1250.
	1882	174 pcs.	—	—	Rare	—
	1888 M	—	500.00	1000.	1350.	2000.
	1890 M	435 pcs.	250.00	500.00	750.00	1250.
	1891 M	1,390	250.00	400.00	500.00	1000.
	1894 M	484 pcs.	250.00	500.00	750.00	1600.
	1895 M	142 pcs.	500.00	750.00	1500.	2500.
	1900 Q	1,536	200.00	300.00	400.00	950.00
	1903 Q	1,000	200.00	300.00	400.00	800.00

Mintmark: Do

KM#	Date	Mintage	Fine	VF	XF	Unc
412.3	1873/2 P	—	700.00	1250.	1800.	3000.
	1877 P	—	700.00	1250.	1800.	3000.
	1878 E	—	700.00	1250.	1800.	3000.
	1879/7 B	—	700.00	1250.	1800.	3000.
	1879 B	—	700.00	1250.	1800.	3000.

Mint mark: Go

KM#	Date	Mintage	Fine	VF	XF	Unc
412.4	1871 S	1,600	400.00	800.00	1250.	2500.
	1887 R	140 pcs.	600.00	1200.	1500.	2750.
	1888 R	65 pcs.	—	—	Rare	—
	1893 R	16 pcs.	—	—	Rare	—

Mint mark: Ho

KM#	Date	Mintage	Fine	VF	XF	Unc
412.5	1874 R	—	1750.	2500.	3000.	4500.
	1877 R	990 pcs.	750.00	1250.	2000.	3000.
	1877 A	Inc. Ab.	650.00	1100.	1750.	2750.
	1888G	—	—	—	Rare	—

Mint mark: Mo

KM#	Date	Mintage	Fine	VF	XF	Unc
412.6	1870 C	550 pcs.	200.00	400.00	550.00	900.00
	1871/69 M	1,600	175.00	350.00	475.00	750.00
	1871 M	Inc. Ab.	175.00	350.00	475.00	750.00
	1872 M	1,600	175.00	350.00	475.00	750.00
	1873/2 M	—	200.00	400.00	550.00	850.00
	1874 M	—	200.00	400.00	550.00	850.00
	1875/3 B/M	—	200.00	400.00	550.00	950.00
	1875 B	—	200.00	400.00	550.00	950.00
	1876/5 B/M	—	200.00	400.00	550.00	1000.
	1877 M	—	250.00	450.00	750.00	1250.
	1878/7 M	400 pcs.	200.00	400.00	550.00	1250.
	1878 M	Inc. Ab.	200.00	400.00	550.00	1250.
	1879/8 M	—	200.00	400.00	550.00	1250.
	1880 M	—	200.00	400.00	550.00	1250.
	1881 M	—	200.00	400.00	550.00	1250.
	1882 M					

KM#	Date	Mintage	Fine	VF	XF	Unc
412.6		200 pcs.	250.00	450.00	750.00	1250.
	1883 M	200 pcs.	250.00	450.00	750.00	1250.
	1884 M	—	250.00	450.00	750.00	1250.
	1886 M	200 pcs.	250.00	450.00	750.00	1250.
	1887 M	200 pcs.	250.00	450.00	750.00	1250.
	1888 M	250 pcs.	200.00	400.00	550.00	1250.
	1889 M	190 pcs.	250.00	450.00	750.00	1250.
	1890 M	149 pcs.	250.00	450.00	750.00	1250.
	1891 M	156 pcs.	250.00	450.00	750.00	1250.
	1892 M	214 pcs.	250.00	450.00	750.00	1250.
	1893 M	1,058	200.00	400.00	500.00	800.00
	1897 M	370 pcs.	200.00	400.00	550.00	1000.
	1898 M	376 pcs.	200.00	400.00	550.00	1000.
	1900 M	1,014	175.00	350.00	450.00	750.00
	1901 M	1,071	175.00	350.00	450.00	750.00
	1902 M	1,478	175.00	350.00	450.00	750.00
	1903 M	1,162	175.00	350.00	450.00	750.00
	1904 M	1,415	175.00	350.00	450.00	750.00
	1905 M	563 pcs.	200.00	400.00	550.00	1500.

Mint mark: Zs

KM#	Date	Mintage	Fine	VF	XF	Unc
412.7	1874 A	—	200.00	400.00	500.00	750.00
	1875 A	—	200.00	400.00	500.00	1000.
	1877 S/A	—	200.00	400.00	550.00	1000.
	1878/7 S/A	—	200.00	400.00	550.00	1000.
	1883 S	—	175.00	375.00	500.00	750.00
	1888 Z	70 pcs.	1000.	1500.	2000.	3000.
	1889 Z	373 pcs.	200.00	300.00	500.00	850.00
	1892 Z	1,229	200.00	300.00	450.00	750.00

DIEZ (10) PESOS

16.9200 g, .875 GOLD, .4760 oz AGW
Mint mark: As
Rev: Balance scale.

KM#	Date	Mintage	Fine	VF	XF	Unc
413	1874 DL	—	—	—	Rare	—
	1875 L	642 pcs.	600.00	1250.	2500.	3500.
	1878 L	977 pcs.	500.00	1000.	2000.	3000.
	1879 L	1,078	500.00	1000.	2000.	3000.
	1880 L	2,629	500.00	1000.	2000.	3000.
	1881 L	2,574	500.00	1000.	2000.	3000.
	1882 L	3,403	500.00	1000.	2000.	3000.
	1883 L	3,597	500.00	1000.	2000.	3000.
	1884 L	—	—	—	Rare	—
	1885 L	4,562	500.00	1000.	2000.	3000.
	1886 L	4,643	500.00	1000.	2000.	3000.
	1887 L	3,667	500.00	1000.	2000.	3000.
	1888 L	4,521	500.00	1000.	2000.	3000.
	1889 L	5,615	500.00	1000.	2000.	3000.
	1890 L	4,920	500.00	1000.	2000.	3000.
	1891 L	568 pcs.	500.00	1000.	2000.	3000.
	1892 L	—	—	—	—	—
	1893 L	817 pcs.	500.00	1000.	2000.	3000.
	1894/3 L	1,658	—	—	—	—
	1894 L	Inc. Ab.	500.00	1000.	2000.	3000.
	1895 L	1,237	500.00	1000.	2000.	3000.

Mint mark: Ca

KM#	Date	Mintage	Fine	VF	XF	Unc
413.1	1888 M	175 pcs.	—	—	7500.	—

Mint mark: Cn

KM#	Date	Mintage	Fine	VF	XF	Unc
413.2	1881 D	—	400.00	600.00	1000.	1750.
	1882 D	874 pcs.	400.00	600.00	1000.	1750.
	1882 E	Inc. Ab.	400.00	600.00	1000.	1750.
	1883 D	221 pcs.	—	—	—	—
	1883 M	Inc. Ab.	400.00	600.00	1000.	1750.
	1884 D	—	400.00	600.00	1000.	1750.
	1884 M	—	400.00	600.00	1000.	1750.
	1885 M	1,235	400.00	600.00	1000.	1750.
	1886 M	981 pcs.	400.00	600.00	1000.	1750.
	1887 M	2,289	400.00	600.00	1000.	1750.
	1888 M	767 pcs.	400.00	600.00	1000.	1750.
	1889 M	859 pcs.	400.00	600.00	1000.	1750.
	1890 M	1,427	400.00	600.00	1000.	1750.
	1891 M	670 pcs.	400.00	600.00	1000.	1750.
	1892 M	379 pcs.	400.00	600.00	1000.	1750.
	1893 M	1,806	400.00	600.00	1000.	1750.
	1895 M	179 pcs.	500.00	1000.	1500.	2500.
	1903 Q	774 pcs.	400.00	600.00	1000.	1750.

Mint mark: Do

KM#	Date	Mintage	Fine	VF	XF	Unc
413.3	1872 P	1,755	350.00	550.00	850.00	1250.
	1873/2 P	1,091	350.00	550.00	900.00	1500.
	1873/2 M/P	Inc. Ab.	350.00	550.00	900.00	1500.
	1874 M	—	350.00	550.00	900.00	1500.
	1875 M	—	350.00	550.00	900.00	1500.
	1876 M	—	450.00	750.00	1250.	2000.
	1877 P	—	350.00	550.00	900.00	1500.
	1878 E	582 pcs.	350.00	550.00	900.00	1500.
	1879/8 B	—	350.00	550.00	900.00	1500.
	1879 B	—	350.00	550.00	900.00	1500.
	1880 P	2,030	350.00	550.00	900.00	1500.
	1881/79 P	2,617	350.00	550.00	900.00	1500.
	1882 P	1,528	—	—	Rare	—
	1882 C	Inc. Ab.	350.00	550.00	900.00	1500.
	1883 C	793 pcs.	450.00	750.00	1250.	2000.
	1884 C	108 pcs.	450.00	750.00	1250.	2000.

Mint mark: Ga

KM#	Date	Mintage	Fine	VF	XF	Unc
413.4	1870 C	490 pcs.	500.00	800.00	1000.	1500.
	1871 C	1,910	400.00	800.00	1500.	2250.
	1872 C	780 pcs.	500.00	1000.	2000.	2500.
	1873 C	422 pcs.	500.00	1000.	2000.	3000.
	1874/3 C	477 pcs.	500.00	1000.	2000.	3000.
	1875 C	710 pcs.	500.00	1000.	2000.	3000.
	1878 A	183 pcs.	600.00	1200.	2500.	3500.
	1879 A	200 pcs.	600.00	1200.	2500.	3500.
	1880 S	404 pcs.	500.00	1000.	2000.	3000.
	1881 S	239 pcs.	600.00	1200.	2500.	3500.
	1891 S	196 pcs.	600.00	1200.	2500.	3500.

Mint mark: Go

KM#	Date	Mintage	Fine	VF	XF	Unc
413.5	1872 S	1,400	800.00	1500.	2000.	3000.
	1887 R	80 pcs.	1250.	2000.	2500.	3500.
	1888 R	68 pcs.	1500.	2500.	3000.	4000.

Mint mark: Ho

KM#	Date	Mintage	Fine	VF	XF	Unc
413.6	1874 R	—	—	—	Rare	—
	1876 F	357 pcs.	—	—	Rare	—
	1878 A	814 pcs.	1750.	3000.	3500.	5500.
	1879 A	—	1000.	2000.	2500.	4000.
	1880 A	—	1000.	2000.	2500.	4000.
	1881 A	—	—	—	Rare	—

Mint mark: Mo

KM#	Date	Mintage	Fine	VF	XF	Unc
413.7	1870 C	480 pcs.	500.00	900.00	1200.	2000.
	1872/1 M/C	2,100	350.00	550.00	900.00	1400.
	1873 M	—	400.00	600.00	950.00	1500.
	1874/3 M	—	400.00	600.00	950.00	1500.
	1875 B/M	—	400.00	600.00	950.00	1500.
	1876 B	—	—	—	Rare	—
	1878 M	300 pcs.	400.00	600.00	950.00	1500.
	1879 M	—	—	—	—	—
	1881 M	100 pcs.	500.00	1000.	1600.	2500.
	1882 M	—	400.00	600.00	950.00	1500.
	1883 M	100 pcs.	600.00	1000.	1600.	2500.
	1884 M	—	600.00	1000.	1600.	2500.
	1885 M	—	400.00	600.00	950.00	1500.
	1886 M	100 pcs.	600.00	1000.	1600.	2500.
	1887 M	100 pcs.	600.00	1000.	1625.	2750.
	1888 M	144 pcs.	450.00	750.00	1200.	2000.
	1889 M	88 pcs.	600.00	1000.	1600.	2500.
	1890 M	137 pcs.	600.00	1000.	1600.	2500.
	1891 M	133 pcs.	600.00	1000.	1600.	2500.
	1892 M	45 pcs.	600.00	1000.	1600.	2500.
	1893 M	1,361	350.00	550.00	900.00	1400.
	1897 M	239 pcs.	400.00	600.00	950.00	1500.
	1898/7 M	244 pcs.	425.00	625.00	1000.	1750.
	1900 M	733 pcs.	400.00	600.00	950.00	1500.
	1901 M	562 pcs.	350.00	500.00	800.00	1400.
	1902 M	719 pcs.	350.00	500.00	800.00	1400.
	1903 M	713 pcs.	350.00	500.00	800.00	1400.
	1904 M	694 pcs.	350.00	500.00	800.00	1400.
	1905 M	401 pcs.	400.00	600.00	950.00	1500.

Mint mark: Oa

KM#	Date	Mintage	Fine	VF	XF	Unc
413.8	1870 E	4,614	400.00	600.00	900.00	1350.
	1871 E	2,705	400.00	600.00	900.00	1350.
	1872 E	5,897	400.00	600.00	900.00	1350.
	1873 E	3,537	400.00	600.00	950.00	1500.
	1874 E	2,205	400.00	600.00	1200.	1800.
	1875 E	312 pcs.	450.00	750.00	1400.	2250.
	1876 E	766 pcs.	450.00	750.00	1400.	2250.
	1877 E	463 pcs.	450.00	750.00	1400.	2250.
	1878 E	229 pcs.	450.00	750.00	1400.	2250.
	1879 E	210 pcs.	450.00	750.00	1400.	2250.
	1880 E	238 pcs.	450.00	750.00	1400.	2250.
	1881 E	961 pcs.	400.00	600.00	1200.	2000.
	1882 E	170 pcs.	600.00	1000.	1500.	2500.
	1883 E	111 pcs.	600.00	1000.	1500.	2500.
	1884 E	325 pcs.	450.00	750.00	1400.	2250.
	1885 E	370 pcs.	450.00	750.00	1400.	2250.
	1886 E	400 pcs.	450.00	750.00	1400.	2250.
	1887 E	—	700.00	1250.	2250.	4000.
	1888 E	—	—	—	—	—

Mint mark: Zs

KM#	Date	Mintage	Fine	VF	XF	Unc
413.9	1871 H	2,000	350.00	550.00	850.00	1200.
	1872 H	3,092	300.00	500.00	700.00	1000.
	1873 H	936 pcs.	400.00	600.00	950.00	1500.
	1874 H	—	400.00	600.00	950.00	1500.
	1875/3 A	—	400.00	600.00	1000.	1750.
	1876/5 S	—	400.00	600.00	1000.	1750.
	1877 S/H	506 pcs.	400.00	600.00	1000.	1750.
	1878 S	711 pcs.	400.00	600.00	1000.	1750.
	1879/8 S	—	450.00	750.00	1400.	2250.
	1879 S	—	450.00	750.00	1400.	2250.
	1880 S	2,089	350.00	550.00	950.00	1500.
	1881 S	736 pcs.	400.00	600.00	1000.	1750.
	1882 S	1,599	350.00	550.00	950.00	1500.
	1883/2 S	256 pcs.	400.00	600.00	1000.	1750.
	1884/3 S	—	350.00	550.00	950.00	1600.
	1884 S	—	350.00	550.00	950.00	1600.
	1885 S	1,588	350.00	550.00	950.00	1500.
	1886 S	5,364	350.00	550.00	950.00	1500.
	1887 Z	2,330	350.00	550.00	950.00	1500.
	1888 Z	4,810	350.00	550.00	950.00	1500.
	1889 Z	6,154	300.00	500.00	750.00	1350.
	1890 Z	1,321	350.00	550.00	950.00	1500.
	1891 Z	1,930	350.00	550.00	950.00	1500.
	1892 Z	1,882	350.00	550.00	950.00	1500.
	1893 Z	2,899	350.00	550.00	950.00	1500.
	1894 Z	2,501	350.00	550.00	950.00	1500.
	1895 Z	1,217	350.00	550.00	950.00	1500.

VEINTE (20) PESOS

33.8400 g, .875 GOLD, .9520 oz AGW
Mint mark: As
Rev: Balance scale.

KM#	Date	Mintage	Fine	VF	XF	Unc
414	1876 L	276 pcs.	—	—	Rare	—
	1877 L	166 pcs.	—	—	Rare	—
	1878 L	—	—	—	—	—
	1888 L	—	—	—	Rare	—

Mint mark: CH,Ca

KM#	Date	Mintage	Fine	VF	XF	Unc
414.1	1872 M	995 pcs.	500.00	650.00	950.00	2500.
	1873 M	950 pcs.	500.00	650.00	950.00	2500.
	1874 M	1,116	500.00	650.00	950.00	2500.
	1875 M	750 pcs.	500.00	650.00	950.00	2500.
	1876 M	600 pcs.	500.00	800.00	1250.	2750.
	1877	55 pcs.	—	—	Rare	—
	1882 M	1,758	500.00	650.00	950.00	2500.
	1883 M	161 pcs.	600.00	1000.	1500.	3000.
	1884 M	496 pcs.	500.00	650.00	950.00	2500.
	1885 M	122 pcs.	600.00	1000.	1500.	3000.
	1887 M	550 pcs.	500.00	650.00	950.00	2500.
	1888 M					

KM#	Date	Mintage	Fine	VF	XF	Unc
414.1		351 pcs.	500.00	650.00	950.00	2500.
	1889 M	464 pcs.	500.00	650.00	950.00	2500.
	1890 M	1,209	500.00	650.00	950.00	2500.
	1891 M	2,004	500.00	600.00	900.00	2250.
	1893 M	418 pcs.	500.00	650.00	950.00	2500.
	1895 M	133 pcs.	600.00	1000.	1500.	3000.

Mint mark: Cn

KM#	Date	Mintage	Fine	VF	XF	Unc
414.2	1870 E	3,749	500.00	650.00	950.00	2000.
	1871 P	3,046	500.00	650.00	950.00	2000.
	1872 P	972 pcs.	500.00	650.00	950.00	2000.
	1873 P	1,317	500.00	650.00	950.00	2000.
	1874 P	—	500.00	650.00	950.00	2000.
	1875 P	—	600.00	1200.	1800.	2500.
	1876 P	—	500.00	650.00	950.00	2000.
	1876 G	—	500.00	650.00	950.00	2000.
	1877 G	167 pcs.	600.00	1000.	1500.	3000.
	1878	842 pcs.	—	—	Rare	—
	1881/0 D	2,039	—	—	—	—
	1881 D	Inc. Ab.	500.00	650.00	950.00	2000.
	1882/1 D	736 pcs.	500.00	650.00	950.00	2000.
	1883 M	1,836	500.00	650.00	950.00	2000.
	1884 M	—	500.00	650.00	950.00	2000.
	1885 M	544 pcs.	500.00	650.00	950.00	2000.
	1886 M	882 pcs.	500.00	650.00	950.00	2000.
	1887 M	837 pcs.	500.00	650.00	950.00	2000.
	1888 M	473 pcs.	500.00	650.00	950.00	2000.
	1889 M	1,376	500.00	650.00	950.00	2000.
	1890 M	—	500.00	650.00	950.00	2000.
	1891 M	237 pcs.	500.00	900.00	1200.	2250.
	1892 M	526 pcs.	500.00	650.00	950.00	2000.
	1893 M	2,062	500.00	650.00	950.00	2000.
	1894 M	4,516	500.00	650.00	950.00	2000.
	1895 M	3,193	500.00	650.00	950.00	2000.
	1896 M	4,072	500.00	650.00	950.00	2000.
	1897/6 M	959 pcs.	500.00	650.00	950.00	2000.
	1897 M	Inc. Ab.	500.00	650.00	950.00	2000.
	1898 M	1,660	500.00	650.00	950.00	2000.
	1899 M	1,243	500.00	650.00	950.00	2000.
	1899 Q	Inc. Ab.	500.00	900.00	1200.	2250.
	1900 Q	1,558	500.00	650.00	950.00	2000.
	1901/0 Q	1,496	—	—	—	—
	1901 Q	Inc. Ab.	500.00	650.00	950.00	2000.
	1902 Q	1,059	500.00	650.00	950.00	2000.
	1903 Q	1,121	500.00	650.00	950.00	2000.
	1904 H	4,646	500.00	650.00	950.00	2000.
	1905 P	1,738	500.00	900.00	1200.	2250.

Mint mark: Do

KM#	Date	Mintage	Fine	VF	XF	Unc
414.3	1870 P	416 pcs.	1000.	1500.	2000.	2500.
	1871/0 P	1,073	1000.	1750.	2250.	2750.
	1871 P	Inc. Ab.	1000.	1500.	2000.	2500.
	1872/1 PT	—	1500.	3000.	4500.	7000.
	1876 M	—	1000.	1500.	2000.	2500.
	1877 P	94 pcs.	1500.	2250.	2750.	3250.
	1878	258 pcs.	—	—	Rare	—

Mint mark: Go

KM#	Date	Mintage	Fine	VF	XF	Unc
414.4	1870 S	3,250	500.00	650.00	900.00	1250.
	1871 S	.020	500.00	650.00	900.00	1250.
	1872 S	.018	500.00	650.00	900.00	1250.
	1873 S	7,000	500.00	650.00	900.00	1250.
	1874 S	—	500.00	650.00	900.00	1250.
	1875 S	—	500.00	650.00	900.00	1250.
	1876 S	—	500.00	650.00	900.00	1250.
	1876 M/S	—	—	—	—	—
	1877 M/S	.015	—	—	Rare	—
	1877 R	Inc. Ab.	500.00	650.00	900.00	1250.
	1877 S	Inc. Ab.	—	—	Rare	—
	1878/7 M/S	.013	650.00	1250.	2000.	2500.
	1878 M	Inc. Ab.	650.00	1250.	2000.	2500.
	1878 S	Inc. Ab.	500.00	650.00	900.00	1250.
	1879 S	8,202	500.00	800.00	1200.	2250.
	1880 S	7,375	500.00	650.00	900.00	1250.
	1881 S	4,909	500.00	650.00	900.00	1250.
	1882 S	4,020	500.00	650.00	900.00	1250.
	1883/2 B	3,705	550.00	750.00	1150.	2000.
	1883 B	Inc. Ab.	500.00	650.00	900.00	1250.
	1884 B	1,798	500.00	650.00	900.00	1250.
	1885 R	2,660	500.00	650.00	900.00	1250.
	1886 R	1,090	500.00	800.00	1200.	2000.
	1887 R	1,009	500.00	800.00	1200.	2000.
	1888 R	1,011	500.00	800.00	1200.	2000.
	1889 R	956 pcs.	500.00	800.00	1200.	2000.
	1890 R	879 pcs.	500.00	800.00	1200.	2000.
	1891 R	818 pcs.	500.00	800.00	1200.	2000.
	1892 R	730 pcs.	500.00	800.00	1200.	2000.
	1893 R	3,343	500.00	650.00	950.00	1600.
	1894/3 R	6,734	500.00	650.00	900.00	1250.
	1894 R	I.A.	500.00	650.00	900.00	1250.
	1895/3 R	7,118	500.00	650.00	900.00	1250.
	1895 R	I.A.	500.00	650.00	900.00	1250.
	1896 R	9,219	500.00	650.00	900.00	1250.
414.4	1897/6 R	6,781	500.00	650.00	900.00	1250.
	1897 R	I.A.	500.00	650.00	900.00	1250.
	1898 R	7,710	500.00	650.00	900.00	1250.
	1899 R	8,527	500.00	650.00	900.00	1250.
	1900 R	4,512	500.00	650.00	900.00	1250.

Mint mark: Ho

KM#	Date	Mintage	Fine	VF	XF	Unc
414.5	1874 R	—	—	—	Rare	—
	1875 R	—	—	—	Rare	—
	1876 F	—	—	—	Rare	—
	1888 G	—	—	—	Rare	—

Mint mark: Mo

KM#	Date	Mintage	Fine	VF	XF	Unc
414.6	1870 C	.014	500.00	600.00	800.00	1300.
	1871 M	.021	500.00	600.00	800.00	1300.
	1872/1 M	.011	500.00	600.00	800.00	1600.
	1872 M	I.A.	500.00	600.00	800.00	1300.
	1873 M	5,600	500.00	600.00	800.00	1300.
	1874/2 M	—	500.00	600.00	800.00	1350.
	1874/2 B	—	500.00	700.00	1000.	1600.
	1875 B	—	500.00	650.00	900.00	1500.
	1876 B	—	500.00	650.00	900.00	1500.
	1876 M	—	—	Reported, not confirmed		
	1877 M	2,000	500.00	700.00	1100.	2000.
	1878 M	7,000	500.00	650.00	900.00	1500.
	1879 M	—	500.00	650.00	900.00	1750.
	1880 M	—	500.00	650.00	900.00	1750.
	1881/0 M	.011	500.00	600.00	800.00	1350.
	1881 M	I.A.	500.00	600.00	800.00	1350.
	1882/1 M	5,800	500.00	600.00	800.00	1350.
	1882 M	I.A.	500.00	600.00	800.00	1350.
	1883/1 M	4,000	500.00	600.00	800.00	1350.
	1883 M	I.A.	500.00	600.00	800.00	1250.
	1884/3 M	—	500.00	650.00	900.00	1400.
	1884 M	—	500.00	650.00	900.00	1400.
	1885 M	6,000	500.00	650.00	900.00	1750.
	1886 M	.010	500.00	600.00	800.00	1500.
	1887 M	.012	500.00	600.00	800.00	1500.
	1888 M	7,300	500.00	600.00	800.00	1500.
	1889 M	6,477	500.00	600.00	900.00	1650.
	1890 M	7,852	500.00	600.00	800.00	1500.
	1891/0 M	8,725	500.00	600.00	800.00	1500.
	1891 M	I.A.	500.00	600.00	800.00	1500.
	1892 M	.011	500.00	600.00	800.00	1300.
	1893 M	.015	500.00	600.00	800.00	1300.
	1894 M	.014	500.00	600.00	800.00	1300.
	1895 M	.013	500.00	600.00	800.00	1300.
	1896 B	.014	500.00	600.00	800.00	1300.
	1897/6 M	.012	500.00	600.00	800.00	1300.
	1897 M	I.A.	500.00	600.00	800.00	1300.
	1898 M	.020	500.00	600.00	800.00	1300.
	1899 M	.023	500.00	600.00	800.00	1300.
	1900 M	.021	500.00	600.00	800.00	1300.
	1901 M	.029	500.00	600.00	800.00	1300.
	1902 M	.038	500.00	600.00	800.00	1300.
	1903/2 M	.031	500.00	600.00	800.00	1300.
	1903 M	I.A.	500.00	600.00	800.00	1300.
	1904 M	.052	500.00	600.00	800.00	1300.
	1905 M	9,757	500.00	600.00	800.00	1300.

Mint mark: Oa

KM#	Date	Mintage	Fine	VF	XF	Unc
414.7	1870 E	1,131	750.00	1500.	2500.	5000.
	1871 E	1,591	750.00	1500.	2500.	5000.
	1872 E	255 pcs.	1000.	1750.	3000.	7000.
	1888 E	170 pcs.	2000.	3000.	5000.	—

Mint mark: Zs

KM#	Date	Mintage	Fine	VF	XF	Unc
414.8	1871 H	1,000	3500.	6500.	7000.	9000.
	1875 A	—	4000.	6000.	7500.	9500.
	1878 S	441 pcs.	4000.	6000.	7500.	9500.
	1888 Z	50 pcs.	—	—	Rare	—
	1889 Z	640 pcs.	3500.	5500.	7000.	9000.

UNITED STATES

MINT MARK

o
M - Mexico City

CENTAVO

BRONZE, 20mm

KM#	Date	Mintage	Fine	VF	XF	Unc
415	1905	6.040	3.50	6.50	13.50	90.00
	1906 narrow date	*67.505	.50	1.00	1.75	14.00
	1906 wide date	Inc. Ab.	.80	1.50	2.75	17.00
	1910	8.700	2.00	3.00	7.50	80.00
	1911	16.450	.75	1.25	2.50	20.00
	1912	12.650	.90	1.50	3.50	32.00
	1913	12.850	.85	1.25	3.00	35.00
	1914	17.350	.75	1.00	2.50	12.50
	1915	2.277	11.50	25.50	72.50	300.00
	1916	.500	50.00	80.00	220.00	1150.
	1920	1.433	22.50	52.50	90.00	400.00
	1921	3.470	6.00	15.00	50.00	275.00
	1922	1.880	8.50	16.00	60.00	300.00
	1923	4.800	.75	1.00	2.00	13.50
	1924/3	2.000	57.50	125.00	250.00	475.00
415	1924	Inc. Ab.	4.50	7.50	22.50	275.00
	1925	1.550	5.00	10.00	22.50	225.00
	1926	5.000	1.00	2.00	4.00	26.00
	1927/6	6.000	25.00	42.50	60.00	140.00
	1927	Inc. Ab.	.65	2.75	4.50	32.50
	1928	5.000	.50	1.00	3.00	17.50
	1929	4.500	.75	1.00	2.00	18.50
	1930	7.000	.55	1.00	2.65	19.50
	1933	10.000	.25	.35	1.25	16.00
	1934	7.500	.40	1.00	3.50	35.00
	1935	12.400	.15	.25	.40	11.50
	1936	20.100	.15	.20	.30	9.00
	1937	20.000	.15	.25	.35	3.50
	1938	10.000	.10	.15	.30	2.50
	1939	30.000	.10	.15	.30	1.25
	1940	10.000	.20	.30	.60	6.50
	1941	15.800	.15	.25	.35	2.50
	1942	30.400	.15	.20	.30	1.25
	1943	4.310	.30	.50	.75	9.00
	1944	5.645	.15	.25	.50	7.50
	1945	26.375	.10	.15	.25	1.00
	1946	42.135	—	.10	.15	.45
	1947	13.445	—	.10	.15	1.00
	1948	20.040	—	.10	.15	1.00
	1949	6.235	.10	.20	.30	1.25

***NOTE:** 50,000,000 pcs. were struck at the Birmingham Mint.

NOTE: Varieties exist.

Zapata Issue
Reduced size, 16mm

KM#	Date	Mintage	Fine	VF	XF	Unc
416	1915	.179	10.00	25.00	42.00	75.00

BRASS, 16mm

KM#	Date	Mintage	VF	XF	Unc	BU
417	1950	12.815	.15	.30	1.65	2.00
	1951	25.740	.15	.25	.75	1.10
	1952	24.610	.10	.15	.40	.75
	1953	21.160	.10	.15	.40	.85
	1954	25.675	.10	.15	.75	1.10
	1955	9.820	.15	.25	.85	1.50
	1956	11.285	.15	.25	.70	1.15
	1957	9.805	.10	.15	.85	1.35
	1958	12.155	.10	.15	.40	.80
	1959	11.875	.10	.20	.70	1.25
	1960	10.360	—	.15	.35	.65
	1961	6.385	—	.15	.50	.85
	1962	4.850	—	.15	.50	.90
	1963	7.775	—	.15	.25	.45
	1964	4.280	—	.10	.15	.35
	1965	2.255	—	.10	.20	.40
	1966	1.760	.10	.15	.40	.70
	1967	1.290	.10	.15	.40	.70
	1968	1.000	.10	.25	.75	1.30
	1969	1.000	.10	.15	.70	1.25

Reduced size, 13mm.

KM#	Date	Mintage	VF	XF	Unc	BU
418	1970	1.000	.20	.35	1.25	1.70
	1972	1.000	.25	.40	1.50	1.90
	1973	1.000	1.50	3.00	7.50	12.00

2 CENTAVOS

BRONZE, 25mm

KM#	Date	Mintage	Fine	VF	XF	Unc
419	1905	.050	150.00	250.00	400.00	1000.
	1906/inverted 6	9.998	20.00	40.00	90.00	275.00
	1906 wide date	I.A.	5.00	11.50	22.50	77.50
	1906 narrow date	*I.A.	6.50	15.00	27.50	80.00
	1920	1.325	9.00	27.50	52.50	260.00
	1921	4.275	3.00	5.75	11.00	90.00
	1922	—	250.00	550.00	1500.	4000.
	1924	.750	10.00	22.50	50.00	400.00
	1925	3.650	2.50	4.00	9.75	40.00
	1926	4.750	1.25	2.75	5.75	35.00
	1927	7.250	.75	1.25	2.75	25.00
	1928	3.250	1.00	1.75	4.25	28.00
	1929	.250	70.00	175.00	435.00	875.00
	1935	1.250	5.00	10.00	25.00	195.00
	1939	5.000	.45	.85	1.50	20.00
	1941	3.550	.40	.50	1.50	20.00

*NOTE: 5,000,000 pcs. were struck at the Birmingham Mint.

Zapata Issue
Reduced size, 20mm

KM#	Date	Mintage	Fine	VF	XF	Unc
420	1915	.487	6.00	9.50	12.50	50.00

5 CENTAVOS

NICKEL

421	1905	1.420	6.00	10.00	25.00	275.00
	1906/5	10.615	12.00	20.00	50.00	325.00
	1906	*Inc. Ab.	.90	1.25	3.25	55.00
	1907	4.000	1.00	3.50	12.00	250.00
	1909	2.052	3.50	11.00	55.00	365.00
	1910	6.181	.90	1.75	6.00	65.00
	1911 narrow date					
		4.487	.75	1.50	5.00	75.00
	1911 wide date					
		Inc. Ab.	2.50	4.50	10.00	80.00
	1912 small mint mark					
		.420	85.00	100.00	200.00	700.00
	1912 large mint mark					
		Inc. Ab.	70.00	95.00	175.00	550.00
	1913	2.035	2.00	4.50	10.00	85.00
	1914	2.000	1.50	2.00	4.00	65.00

NOTE: 5,000,000 pcs. appear to have been struck at the Birmingham Mint in 1914 and all of 1909-1911. The Mexican Mint report does not mention receiving the 1914 dated coins.

NOTE: Varieties exist.

BRONZE

422	1914	2.500	10.00	24.00	45.00	225.00
	1915	11.424	1.50	5.00	16.00	150.00
	1916	2.860	16.00	35.00	180.00	675.00
	1917	.800	75.00	175.00	375.00	800.00
	1918	1.332	37.50	90.00	225.00	600.00
	1919	.400	140.00	225.00	375.00	900.00
	1920	5.920	3.50	9.00	45.00	200.00
	1921	2.080	11.00	25.00	75.00	300.00
	1924	.780	40.00	90.00	250.00	600.00
	1925	4.040	5.00	12.00	45.00	195.00
	1926	3.160	6.00	12.00	45.00	215.00
	1927	3.600	4.00	8.00	30.00	190.00
	1928 large date					
		1.740	9.00	18.00	67.50	225.00
	1928 small date					
		Inc. Ab.	25.00	45.00	90.00	375.00
	1929	2.400	6.00	10.00	35.00	165.00
	1930 large oval 0 in date					
		2.600	5.00	9.00	35.00	180.00
	1930 small square 0 in date					
		Inc. Ab.	55.00	95.00	225.00	550.00
	1931	—	500.00	700.00	1150.	3000.
	1933	8.000	1.25	2.00	3.00	25.00
	1934	10.000	1.25	1.75	2.50	22.50
	1935	21.980	.90	1.25	3.00	18.50

COPPER-NICKEL

KM#	Date	Mintage	VF	XF	Unc	BU
423	1936	46.700	.50	1.00	6.50	9.00
	1937	49.060	.40	1.00	5.75	8.00
	1938	3.340	5.50	11.50	62.00	—
	1940	22.800	.90	1.50	7.00	10.00
	1942	7.100	1.50	2.50	25.00	32.50

BRONZE
'Josefa' Ortiz de Dominguez

KM#	Date	Mintage	VF	XF	Unc	BU
424	1942	.900	27.50	75.00	350.00	450.00
	1943	54.660	.50	.75	3.00	3.75
	1944	53.463	.20	.25	.75	1.00
	1945	44.262	.25	.35	.90	1.65
	1946	49.054	.50	.90	2.00	2.75
	1951	50.758	.75	1.00	3.00	4.75
	1952	17.674	1.50	2.75	9.00	11.00
	1953	31.568	.50	1.00	2.75	4.00
	1954	58.680	.50	1.00	2.75	4.00
	1955	31.114	1.25	2.00	11.00	15.00

COPPER-NICKEL
'White Josefa'

425	1950	5.700	.80	1.50	6.00	8.00

NOTE: 5,600,000 pieces struck at Connecticut melted.

BRASS

426	1954 dot	—	11.00	30.00	230.00	250.00
	1954 w/o dot	—	9.00	21.00	125.00	175.00
	1955	12.136	.90	1.75	9.00	12.50
	1956	60.216	.20	.30	.90	1.50
	1957	55.288	.15	.20	.90	1.50
	1958	104.624	.15	.20	.50	1.00
	1959	106.000	.15	.20	.90	1.35
	1960	99.144	.10	.15	.40	.75
	1961	61.136	.10	.15	.40	.70
	1962	47.232	.10	.15	.30	.55
	1963	156.680	—	.10	.20	.35
	1964	71.168	—	.10	.20	.40
	1965	155.720	—	.10	.15	.35
	1966	124.944	—	.10	.30	.50
	1967	118.816	—	.10	.25	.40
	1968	189.588	—	.10	.25	.35
	1969	210.492	—	.10	.25	.35

COPPER-NICKEL

426a	1962	19 pcs.	300.00	—	—	—

BRASS
Reduced size, 18mm.

427	1970	163.368	—	.10	.30	.45
	1971	198.844	—	.10	.15	.30
	1972	225.000	—	.10	.15	.30
	1973 flat top 3					
		595.070	—	.10	.25	.40
	1973 round top 3					
		Inc. Ab.	—	.10	.15	.25
	1974	401.584	—	.10	.20	.30
	1975	342.308	—	.10	.25	.35
	1976	367.524	—	.10	.30	.50

NOTE: Due to some minor alloy variations this type is often encounntered with a bronze color toning.

10 CENTAVOS

2.5000 g, .800 SILVER, .0643 oz ASW

428	1905	3.920	6.25	8.00	35.00	47.50
	1906	8.410	6.00	7.25	25.00	32.50
	1907/6	5.950	50.00	125.00	250.00	350.00
	1907	Inc. Ab.	6.75	9.25	35.00	42.50
	1909	2.620	9.50	12.00	70.00	85.00
	1910/00	3.450	15.00	30.00	80.00	100.00
	1910	Inc. Ab.	9.50	12.50	20.00	25.00
	1911	2.550	7.50	10.00	42.50	50.00
	1912	1.350	9.75	14.00	110.00	140.00
	1913/2	1.990	10.00	20.00	40.00	65.00

KM#	Date	Mintage	VF	XF	Unc	BU
428	1913	Inc. Ab.	7.00	10.00	33.50	45.00
	1914	3.110	4.50	6.75	13.50	18.75

1.8125 g, .800 SILVER, .0466 oz ASW
Reduced size, 15mm.

429	1919	8.360	9.50	17.50	97.50	115.00

BRONZE

430	1919	1.232	25.00	60.00	410.00	495.00
	1920	6.612	15.00	45.00	400.00	475.00
	1921	2.255	35.00	75.00	800.00	1000.
	1935	5.970	17.00	30.00	90.00	140.00

1.6600 g, .720 SILVER, .0384 oz ASW

431	1925/15	5.350	20.00	50.00	100.00	120.00
	1925/3	Inc. Ab.	20.00	35.00	100.00	125.00
	1925	Inc. Ab.	2.50	4.75	30.00	40.00
	1926/16	2.650	30.00	60.00	150.00	170.00
	1926	Inc. Ab.	4.00	7.25	60.00	80.00
	1927	2.810	2.75	3.50	17.50	21.50
	1928	5.270	2.00	2.50	10.00	12.25
	1930	2.000	4.75	6.00	20.00	23.50
	1933	5.000	2.00	3.60	9.00	11.00
	1934	8.000	1.50	2.65	9.50	12.00
	1935	3.500	3.50	6.00	15.00	20.00

COPPER-NICKEL

432	1936	33.030	.40	.90	7.00	8.50
	1937	3.000	5.00	15.00	215.00	235.00
	1938	3.650	1.75	5.50	52.00	65.00
	1939	6.920	1.00	4.00	30.00	40.00
	1940	12.300	.50	1.25	5.00	6.50
	1942	14.380	.75	1.75	7.00	8.50
	1945	9.558	.40	.65	3.50	4.00
	1946	46.230	.30	.50	2.50	3.00

BRONZE
Benito Juarez

433	1955	1.818	1.00	3.50	22.50	28.00
	1956	5.255	.50	2.25	20.00	27.50
	1957	11.925	.20	.50	5.00	6.50
	1959	26.140	.20	.30	.50	.65
	1966	5.873	.15	.25	.45	.60
	1967	32.318	.15	.25	.35	.50

COPPER-NICKEL
Variety I
Rev: 5 full rows of kernels, sharp stem, wide date.

434.1	1974	6.000	—	.10	.35	.45
	1975	5.550	.10	.15	.45	.55
	1976	7.680	.10	.20	.30	.40
	1977	144.650	.50	2.00	2.50	3.50
	1978	271.870	—	2.00	2.50	3.50
	1979	375.660	—	.10	.30	.40
	1980/79	21.290	2.25	3.75	6.00	7.00
	1980	I.A.	1.25	2.00	4.50	5.00

Variety II
Rev: 5 full, plus 1 partial row at left, blunt stem, narrow date.

KM#	Date	Mintage	VF	XF	Unc	BU
434.2	1977	Inc. Ab.	—	.10	.20	.25
	1978	Inc. Ab.	—	.10	.20	.30
	1979	Inc. Ab.	.10	.50	1.00	2.00
	1980	Inc. Ab.	—	.10	.20	.30

20 CENTAVOS

5.0000 g, .800 SILVER, .1286 oz ASW

KM#	Date	Mintage	VF	XF	Unc	BU
435	1905	2.565	10.00	17.50	150.00	175.00
	1906	6.860	7.00	12.00	55.00	70.00
	1907 straight 7					—
		4.000	10.00	20.00	70.00	100.00
	1907 curved 7					—
		5.435	9.50	16.00	55.00	75.00
	1908	.350	85.00	160.00	1500.	—
	1910	1.135	11.00	18.00	80.00	90.00
	1911	1.150	17.50	37.50	125.00	150.00
	1912	.625	35.00	75.00	335.00	375.00
	1913	1.000	18.00	35.00	92.50	115.00
	1914	1.500	12.50	18.00	67.50	75.00

3.6250 g, .800 SILVER, .0932 oz ASW
Reduced size, 19mm.

KM#	Date	Mintage	VF	XF	Unc	BU
436	1919	4.155	30.00	60.00	210.00	250.00

BRONZE

KM#	Date	Mintage	VF	XF	Unc	BU
437	1920	4.835	37.50	95.00	400.00	475.00
	1935	20.000	6.50	9.00	65.00	100.00

3.3333 g, .720 SILVER, .0772 oz ASW

KM#	Date	Mintage	VF	XF	Unc	BU
438	1920	3.710	5.50	12.00	140.00	175.00
	1921	6.160	5.50	12.00	95.00	125.00
	1925	1.450	9.00	20.00	120.00	150.00
	1926/5	1.465	20.00	50.00	300.00	—
	1926	Inc. Ab.	5.50	12.00	90.00	130.00
	1927	1.405	4.50	7.50	80.00	115.00
	1928	3.630	3.00	5.50	15.00	18.00
	1930	1.000	3.50	7.00	25.00	27.50
	1933	2.500	2.75	3.25	10.00	12.00
	1934	2.500	2.50	3.25	12.00	14.00
	1935	2.460	2.75	3.25	10.00	12.00
	1937	10.000	2.50	3.00	4.50	5.50
	1939	8.800	2.00	2.50	4.00	4.50
	1940	3.000	2.00	2.50	4.00	4.50
	1941	5.740	2.00	2.50	3.00	3.75
	1942	12.460	2.00	2.25	3.00	3.75
	1943	3.955	1.50	2.00	3.50	4.25

BRONZE

KM#	Date	Mintage	VF	XF	Unc	BU
439	1943	46.350	.95	3.25	18.00	25.00
	1944	83.650	.50	.75	9.00	11.00
	1945	26.801	2.25	4.00	10.50	13.00
	1946	25.695	1.10	2.50	6.00	8.25
	1951	11.385	3.00	6.50	60.00	100.00
	1952	6.560	2.50	5.50	25.00	32.50
	1953	26.948	.35	.75	6.50	10.00
	1954	40.108	.35	.85	9.00	12.50
	1955	16.950	3.00	6.50	50.00	80.00

KM#	Date	Mintage	VF	XF	Unc	BU
440	1955					
		Inc. KM439	.75	1.75	15.00	20.00
	1956	22.431	.30	.35	3.00	4.00
	1957	13.455	.50	1.50	9.00	12.00
	1959	6.017	5.00	9.00	55.00	90.00
	1960	39.756	.15	.20	.90	1.25
	1963	14.869	.20	.30	.90	1.25
	1964	28.654	.15	.25	.75	1.10
	1965	74.162	.15	.25	.85	1.20
	1966	43.745	.15	.25	.90	1.30
	1967	46.487	.15	.25	1.10	1.50
	1968	15.477	.15	.30	1.10	1.65
	1969	63.647	.15	.25	1.00	1.50
	1970	76.287	.15	.20	.90	1.30
	1971	49.892	.30	.35	1.25	1.75

KM#	Date	Mintage	VF	XF	Unc	BU
441	1971					
		Inc. KM440	.15	.35	1.50	2.00
	1973	78.398	.15	.25	.95	1.50
	1974	34.200	.25	.35	1.25	1.75

COPPER-NICKEL
Francisco Madero

KM#	Date	Mintage	VF	XF	Unc	BU
442	1974	112.000	—	.10	.25	.30
	1975	611.000	.10	.15	.30	.35
	1976	394.000	.10	.15	.35	.45
	1977	394.350	.10	.15	.40	.45
	1978	527.950	.10	.15	.25	.30
	1979	524.615	—	.10	.25	.35
	1979 Doubled die obv. large/small letters					
		—	1.00	2.00	4.00	8.00
	1980	326.500	.10	.20	.40	.60
	1981 open 8					
		106.205	.25	.50	1.75	2.25
	1981 closed 8, high date					
		248.500	.25	.50	1.50	2.00
	1981 closed 8, low date					
		—	1.00	1.50	2.00	3.00
	1981/1982	—	30.00	60.00	125.00	150.00
	1982	286.855	.15	.40	.90	1.10
	1983 round top 3					
		100.930	.25	.40	1.75	2.25
	1983 flat top 3					
		Inc. Ab.	.25	.50	1.25	1.75
	1983	998 pcs.	—	—	Proof	18.00

NOTE: The 1981/1982 overdate is often mistaken as 1982/1981.

BRONZE
Olmec Culture

KM#	Date	Mintage	VF	XF	Unc	BU
491	1983	260.000	.10	.25	.90	1.10
	1983	53 pcs.	—	—	Proof	185.00
	1984	180.320	.20	.30	1.50	1.70

25 CENTAVOS

3.3330 g, .300 SILVER, .0321 oz ASW

KM#	Date	Mintage	VF	XF	Unc	BU
443	1950	77.060	.60	.75	1.75	2.25
	1951	41.172	.60	.75	1.60	2.00
	1952	29.264	.75	1.00	1.80	2.50
	1953	38.144	.60	.75	1.50	2.00

COPPER-NICKEL
Francisco Madero

KM#	Date	Mintage	VF	XF	Unc	BU
444	1964	20.686	—	.15	.25	.40
	1966 closed beak					
		.180	.50	1.00	2.50	3.00
	1966 open beak					
		Inc. Ab.	1.00	3.50	10.00	14.00

50 CENTAVOS

12.5000 g, .800 SILVER, .3215 oz ASW

KM#	Date	Mintage	VF	XF	Unc	BU
445	1905	2.446	17.50	25.00	150.00	175.00
	1906	16.966	6.00	10.00	30.00	40.00
	1907 straight 7					
		18.920	5.75	8.50	25.00	28.50
	1907 curved 7					
		14.841	5.00	7.50	23.00	25.00
	1908	.488	75.00	170.00	525.00	600.00
	1912	3.736	10.00	15.00	45.00	60.00
	1913/07	10.510	35.00	75.00	200.00	250.00
	1913/2	Inc. Ab.	15.00	25.00	55.00	70.00
	1913	Inc. Ab.	7.00	10.00	25.00	30.00
	1914	7.710	8.50	15.50	30.00	36.00
	1916	.480	60.00	90.00	225.00	275.00
	1917	37.112	5.00	7.00	18.00	20.00
	1918	1.320	85.00	135.00	250.00	300.00

9.0625 g, .800 SILVER, .2331 oz ASW
Reduced size, 27mm.

KM#	Date	Mintage	VF	XF	Unc	BU
446	1918/7	2.760	—	625.00	1250.	—
	1918	Inc. Ab.	20.00	60.00	325.00	400.00
	1919	29.670	10.00	20.00	100.00	115.00

8.3333 g, .720 SILVER, .1929 oz ASW

KM#	Date	Mintage	VF	XF	Unc	BU
447	1919	10.200	10.00	20.00	90.00	110.00
	1920	27.166	7.50	10.00	72.50	85.00
	1921	21.864	7.75	10.50	85.00	110.00
	1925	3.280	15.00	30.00	130.00	155.00
	1937	20.000	4.00	6.00	7.50	8.50
	1938	.100	50.00	100.00	300.00	350.00
	1939	10.440	4.00	8.00	12.00	15.00
	1942	.800	4.00	6.00	12.50	17.00
	1943	41.512	3.75	4.50	5.50	6.50
	1944	55.806	3.75	4.50	5.50	6.50
	1945	56.766	4.00	4.75	6.00	7.00

7.9730 g, .420 SILVER, .1076 oz ASW

KM#	Date	Mintage	VF	XF	Unc	BU
448	1935	70.800	2.50	3.25	5.25	6.00

6.6600 g, .300 SILVER, .0642 oz ASW
Cuauhtemoc

KM#	Date	Mintage	VF	XF	Unc	BU
449	1950	13.570	1.75	2.25	3.50	4.00
	1951	3.650	2.00	2.75	3.75	5.00

BRONZE

KM#	Date	Mintage	VF	XF	Unc	BU
450	1955	3.502	1.50	2.50	25.00	37.50
	1956	34.643	.85	1.25	3.25	4.50
	1957	9.675	.95	1.25	4.50	5.75
	1959	4.540	.40	.60	1.50	2.00

COPPER-NICKEL

KM#	Date	Mintage	VF	XF	Unc	BU
451	1964	43.806	—	.15	.30	.40
	1965	14.326	—	.10	.30	.45
	1966	1.726	.20	.40	1.30	1.75
	1967	55.144	.15	.20	.50	.60
	1968	80.438	—	.15	.50	.60
	1969	87.640	.15	.25	.75	1.00

Obv: Stylized eagle.

KM#	Date	Mintage	VF	XF	Unc	BU
452	1970	76.236	—	.20	1.00	1.30
	1971	125.288	—	.15	.90	1.30
	1972	16.000	1.00	2.00	3.50	4.75
	1975 Dots	177.958	.60	1.25	3.50	5.25
	1975 No dots	Inc. Ab.	.10	.15	.40	.60
	1976 Dots	37,480	.60	1.25	5.00	6.00
	1976 No dots	Inc. Ab.	.15	.20	.50	.65
	1977	12.410	6.00	10.00	32.50	42.50
	1978	85.400	.15	.25	.50	.65
	1979 round 2nd 9 in date	229.000	.15	.20	.50	.65
	1979 square 9's in date	Inc. Ab.	.15	.35	1.60	2.10
	1980 narrow date, square 9	89.978	.40	.75	2.00	2.50
	1980 wide date, round 9	178.188	.15	.25	1.00	1.15
	1981 rectangular 9, narrow date	142.212	.60	1.25	3.50	7.50
	1981 round 9, wide date	Inc. Ab.	.20	.50	1.25	1.75
	1982	45.474	.15	.40	1.50	2.00
	1983	90.318	.15	.50	2.00	2.50
	1983	998 pcs.	—	—	Proof	18.00

NOTE: Coins dated 1975 and 1976 exist with and without dots in centers of three circles on plumage on reverse. Edge varieties exist.

STAINLESS STEEL
Palenque Culture

KM#	Date	Mintage	VF	XF	Unc	BU
492	1983	99.540	—	.25	.75	1.00
	1983	53 pcs.	—	—	Proof	185.00

UN (1) PESO

27.0700 g, .903 SILVER, .7859 oz ASW
'Caballito'

KM#	Date	Mintage	VF	XF	Unc	BU
453	1910	3.814	35.00	50.00	170.00	200.00
	1911 long lower left ray on rev.	1.227	40.00	70.00	210.00	275.00
	1911 short lower left ray on rev.	Inc. Ab.	140.00	185.00	600.00	800.00
	1912	.322	100.00	225.00	325.00	400.00
	1913/2	2.880	40.00	70.00	275.00	350.00
	1913	Inc. Ab.	40.00	70.00	180.00	210.00
	1914	.120	525.00	950.00	2750.	—

18.1300 g, .800 SILVER, .4663 oz ASW

KM#	Date	Mintage	VF	XF	Unc	BU
454	1918	3.050	35.00	100.00	2500.	—
	1919	6.151	22.50	50.00	1200.	1800.

16.6600 g, .720 SILVER, .3856 oz ASW

KM#	Date	Mintage	VF	XF	Unc	BU
455	1920/10	8.830	40.00	80.00	300.00	—
	1920	Inc. Ab.	9.00	20.00	160.00	200.00
	1921	5.480	9.00	20.00	160.00	200.00
	1922	33.620	4.00	5.50	22.00	25.00
	1923	35.280	4.00	5.50	22.00	25.00
	1924	33.060	4.00	5.50	22.00	25.00
	1925	9.160	5.00	11.00	60.00	80.00
	1926	28.840	4.00	5.50	20.00	24.00
	1927	5.060	5.00	10.00	70.00	90.00
	1932	50.770	3.50	4.50	6.00	6.75
	1933/2	43.920	15.00	25.00	80.00	—
	1933	Inc. Ab.	3.50	4.50	6.00	6.75

KM#	Date	Mintage	VF	XF	Unc	BU
455	1934	22.070	4.00	5.00	10.00	12.50
	1935	8.050	4.50	6.25	12.00	13.50
	1938	30.000	3.50	4.00	7.00	8.25
	1940	20.000	3.25	3.75	5.50	6.25
	1943	47.662	3.50	3.75	5.00	5.50
	1944	39.522	3.50	3.75	5.00	5.50
	1945	37.300	3.50	3.75	5.00	5.50

14.0000 g, .500 SILVER, .2250 oz ASW
Jose Morelos y Pavon

KM#	Date	Mintage	VF	XF	Unc	BU
456	1947	61.460	2.50	3.00	5.00	5.50
	1948	22.915	3.00	4.50	6.00	7.00
	1949	*4.000	—	1000.	1850.	2750.
	1949		—	—	Proof	4000.

***NOTE:** Not released for circulation.

13.3300 g, .300 SILVER, .1285 oz ASW
Jose Morelos y Pavon

KM#	Date	Mintage	VF	XF	Unc	BU
457	1950	3.287	3.50	4.75	7.00	8.50

16.0000 g, .100 SILVER, .0514 oz ASW
100th Anniversary of Constitution

KM#	Date	Mintage	VF	XF	Unc	BU
458	1957	.500	4.50	6.00	14.00	16.50

Jose Morelos y Pavon

KM#	Date	Mintage	VF	XF	Unc	BU
459	1957	28.273	.75	1.00	2.50	3.00
	1958	41.899	.75	.95	1.85	2.60
	1959	27.369	1.60	2.00	5.50	7.00
	1960	26.259	.75	1.10	3.25	4.00
	1961	52.601	.60	.90	2.25	3.00
	1962	61.094	.60	.90	2.25	2.75
	1963	26.394	BV	.75	1.75	2.40
	1964	15.615	BV	.75	1.90	2.20
	1965	5.004	BV	.60	1.75	2.00
	1966	30.998	BV	.60	1.75	2.00
	1967	9.308	BV	.60	3.00	3.50

COPPER-NICKEL

Jose Morelos y Pavon

KM#	Date	Mintage	VF	XF	Unc	BU
460	1970 narrow date	102.715	.25	.35	.65	.85
	1970 wide date	Inc. Ab.	1.25	2.50	8.00	9.75
	1971	426.222	.20	.25	.50	.65
	1972	120.000	.20	.25	.40	.65
	1974	63.700	.20	.25	.65	.90

KM#	Date	Mintage	VF	XF	Unc	BU
	1975 tall narrow date	205.979	.25	.35	1.00	1.35

KM#	Date	Mintage	VF	XF	Unc	BU
	1975 short wide date	Inc. Ab.	.30	.40	.75	1.00
	1976	94.489	.15	.20	.50	.75
	1977 thick date	94.364	.20	.45	1.00	1.25
	1977 thin date	Inc. Ab.	1.00	2.75	10.00	15.00
	1978 closed 8	208.300	.20	.30	1.00	1.15
	1978 open 8	55.140	.75	1.50	11.00	15.00
	1979 thin date	117.884	.20	.30	.75	1.00
	1979 thick date	Inc. Ab.	.40	.50	1.30	1.90
	1980 closed 8	318.800	.25	.35	.80	1.00
	1980 open 8	23.865	.75	1.50	10.00	12.75
	1981 closed 8	413.349	.20	.30	.75	1.00
	1981 open 8	58.616	.50	1.25	7.00	8.50
	1982	235.000	.25	.50	2.25	2.50
	1983 wide date	100.000	.20	.30	3.00	3.50
	1983 narrow date	Inc. Ab.	.25	.45	1.20	1.50
	1983	1,051	—	—	Proof	18.00

STAINLESS STEEL
Jose Morelos y Pavon

KM#	Date	Mintage	VF	XF	Unc	BU
496	1984	722.802	—	.25	.80	1.00
	1985	985.000	—	.15	.50	.75
	1986	740.000	—	.15	.50	.75
	1987	250.000	—	.15	.50	.80
	1988	—	—	.25	.80	1.00

DOS (2) PESOS

1.6666 g, .900 GOLD, .0482 oz AGW

KM#	Date	Mintage	Fine	VF	XF	Unc
461	1919	1.670	—	BV	30.00	50.00
	1920	4.282	—	BV	30.00	50.00
	1944	.010	27.50	35.00	45.00	70.00
	1945	*.140	—	—		*BV + 20%*
	1946	.168	30.00	50.00	55.00	100.00
	1947	.025	27.50	40.00	45.00	65.00
	1948	.045	—	no specimens known		

***NOTE:** During 1951-1972 a total of 4,590,493 pieces were restruck, most likely dated 1945.

26.6667 g, .900 SILVER, .7717 oz ASW
Centennial of Independence

KM#	Date	Mintage	VF	XF	Unc	BU
462	1921	1.278	35.00	60.00	325.00	450.00

DOS Y MEDIO (2-1/2) PESOS

2.0833 g, .900 GOLD, .0602 oz AGW

KM#	Date	Mintage	Fine	VF	XF	Unc
463	1918	1.704	—	BV	35.00	60.00
	1919	.984	—	BV	35.00	70.00
	1920/10	.607	—	BV	65.00	120.00
	1920	Inc. Ab.	—	BV	35.00	60.00
	1944	.020	BV	35.00	40.00	70.00
	1945	*.180	—	—		*BV + 18%*
	1946	.163	BV	35.00	40.00	65.00
	1947	.024	200.00	250.00	300.00	550.00
	1948	.063	BV	35.00	40.00	65.00

***NOTE:** During 1951-1972 a total of 5,025,087 pieces were restruck, most likely dated 1945.

CINCO (5) PESOS

4.1666 g, .900 GOLD, .1205 oz AGW

KM#	Date	Mintage	Fine	VF	XF	Unc
464	1905	.018	100.00	150.00	200.00	600.00
	1906	4.638	—	BV	60.00	90.00
	1907	1.088	—	BV	60.00	90.00
	1910	.100	BV	65.00	75.00	140.00
	1918/7	.609	60.00	65.00	75.00	120.00
	1918	Inc. Ab.	—	BV	60.00	90.00
	1919	.506	—	BV	60.00	90.00
	1920	2.385	—	BV	60.00	80.00
	1955	*.048	—	—		*BV + 11%*

***NOTE:** During 1955-1972 a total of 1,767,645 pieces were restruck, most likely dated 1955.

30.0000 g, .900 SILVER, .8681 oz ASW
Cuauhtemoc

KM#	Date	Mintage	VF	XF	Unc	BU
465	1947	5.110	BV	6.50	9.00	10.00
	1948	26.740	BV	6.00	8.00	9.00

27.7800 g, .720 SILVER, .6431 oz ASW
Opening of Southern Railroad

KM#	Date	Mintage	VF	XF	Unc	BU
466	1950	.200	30.00	40.00	50.00	55.00

NOTE: It is recorded that 100,000 pieces were melted to be used for the 1968 Mexican Olympic 25 Pesos.

Miguel Hidalgo y Costilla

KM#	Date	Mintage	VF	XF	Unc	BU
467	1951	4.958	BV	5.50	8.00	9.50
	1952	9.595	BV	5.50	8.00	9.50
	1953	20.376	BV	5.25	7.50	9.50
	1954	.030	30.00	60.00	80.00	90.00

Bicentennial of Hidalgo Birth

KM#	Date	Mintage	VF	XF	Unc	BU
468	1953	1.000	BV	6.50	9.00	11.00

18.0500 g, .720 SILVER, .4178 oz ASW
Reduced size, 36mm.

KM#	Date	Mintage	VF	XF	Unc	BU
469	1955	4.271	4.00	5.00	6.00	7.00
	1956	4.596	4.00	5.00	6.00	7.00
	1957	3.464	4.00	5.00	6.00	7.00

100th Anniversary of Constitution

KM#	Date	Mintage	VF	XF	Unc	BU
470	1957	.200	5.50	9.00	13.50	15.50

Centennial of Carranza Birth

KM#	Date	Mintage	VF	XF	Unc	BU
471	1959	1.000	BV	5.00	9.00	10.00

Small date Large date

COPPER-NICKEL
Vicente Guerrero

KM#	Date	Mintage	VF	XF	Unc	BU
472	1971	28.457	.50	.75	2.50	3.25
	1972	75.000	.50	.75	2.00	2.25
	1973	19.405	1.20	1.50	6.00	7.50
	1974	34.500	.35	.80	1.75	2.25
	1976 small date					
		26.121	.75	1.25	3.50	4.25
	1976 large date					
		121.550	.10	.50	1.50	1.75
	1977	102.000	.50	.75	1.50	2.00
	1978	25.700	.50	1.50	5.50	6.75

Quetzalcoatl

KM#	Date	Mintage	VF	XF	Unc	BU
485	1980	266.900	.20	.50	1.75	2.25
	1981	30.500	.35	.50	2.00	3.25
	1982	20.000	.50	1.50	3.50	5.25
	1982	1,051	—	—	Proof	24.00
	1983	7 known	—	—	Proof	—
	1984	16.300	1.25	2.00	4.00	6.00
	1985	76.900	1.50	2.25	4.50	6.50

BRASS
Circulation Coinage

KM#	Date	Mintage	VF	XF	Unc	BU
502	1985	30.000	—	.10	.35	.50
	1987	81.900	6.00	7.50	12.50	15.00
	1988	76.600	—	.10	.25	.35

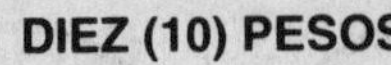

DIEZ (10) PESOS

8.3333 g, .900 GOLD, .2411 oz AGW
Miguel Hidalgo

KM#	Date	Mintage	Fine	VF	XF	Unc
473	1905	.039	120.00	135.00	150.00	225.00
	1906	2.949	—	BV	120.00	145.00
	1907	1.589	—	BV	120.00	145.00
	1908	.890	—	BV	120.00	145.00
	1910	.451	—	BV	120.00	145.00
	1916	.026	120.00	135.00	160.00	325.00
	1917	1.967	—	BV	120.00	145.00
	1919	.266	—	BV	120.00	145.00
	1920	.012	175.00	300.00	500.00	750.00
	1959	*.050	—	—		*BV + 7%*

***NOTE:** During 1961-1972 a total of 954,983 pieces were restruck, most likely dated 1959.

28.8800 g, .900 SILVER, .8357 oz ASW
Miguel Hidalgo

KM#	Date	Mintage	VF	XF	Unc	BU
474	1955	.585	BV	6.50	10.00	12.00
	1956	3.535	BV	5.50	8.50	11.00

100th Anniversary of Constitution

KM#	Date	Mintage	VF	XF	Unc	BU
475	1957	.100	12.00	25.00	42.00	47.50

150th Anniversary of War of Independence

KM#	Date	Mintage	VF	XF	Unc	BU
476	1960	1.000	BV	7.00	10.00	12.50

COPPER-NICKEL
Miguel Hidalgo
Thin flan, 1.6mm.

KM#	Date	Mintage	VF	XF	Unc	BU
477.1	1974	3.900	.50	1.75	3.25	4.00
	1974	—	—	—	Proof	600.00
	1975	1.000	1.00	3.50	10.00	17.50
	1976	74.500	.25	.75	1.75	2.25
	1977	79.620	.50	1.00	2.00	3.00

Thick flan, 2.3mm.

KM#	Date	Mintage	VF	XF	Unc	BU
477.2	1978	124.850	.50	1.00	2.50	2.75
	1979	57.200	.50	1.00	2.25	2.50
	1980	55.200	.50	1.00	2.75	3.50
	1981	222.768	.30	.60	2.00	2.25
	1982	151.770	.40	.75	2.50	3.25
	1982	1,051	—	—	Proof	24.00
	1983	3 known	—	—	Proof	—
	1985	58.000	1.25	1.75	6.00	7.50

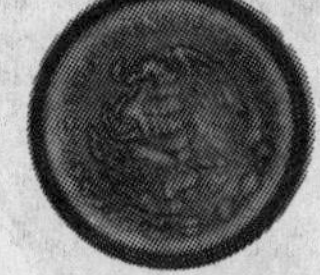

STAINLESS STEEL
Miguel Hidalgo

KM#	Date	Mintage	VF	XF	Unc	BU
512	1985	257.000	—	.15	.65	.85
	1986	392.000	—	.15	.65	1.50
	1987	305.000	—	.10	.50	.65
	1988	500.300	—	.10	.35	.40
	1989	—	—	.25	.75	1.25
	1990	—	—	.25	.75	1.25

NOTE: Date varieties exist.

VEINTE (20) PESOS

16.6666 g, .900 GOLD, .4823 oz AGW

KM#	Date	Mintage	Fine	VF	XF	Unc
478	1917	.852	—	BV	230.00	265.00
	1918	2.831	—	BV	230.00	275.00
	1919	1.094	—	BV	230.00	265.00
	1920/10	.462	—	BV	235.00	285.00
	1920	Inc. Ab.	—	BV	230.00	275.00
	1921/11	.922	—	BV	240.00	300.00
	1921	Inc. Ab.	—	BV	230.00	265.00
	1959	*.013	—	—		*BV + 4%*

***NOTE:** During 1960-1971 a total of 1,158,414 pieces were restruck, most likely dated 1959.

COPPER-NICKEL

KM#	Date	Mintage	VF	XF	Unc	BU
486	1980	84.900	.35	.70	2.75	3.50
	1981	250.573	.35	.70	2.50	3.25
	1982	236.892	.35	.70	2.75	3.50
	1982	1,051	—	—	Proof	25.00
	1983	3 known	—	—	Proof	—
	1984	55.000	1.00	1.50	6.00	7.50

BRASS
Guadalupe Victoria, First President

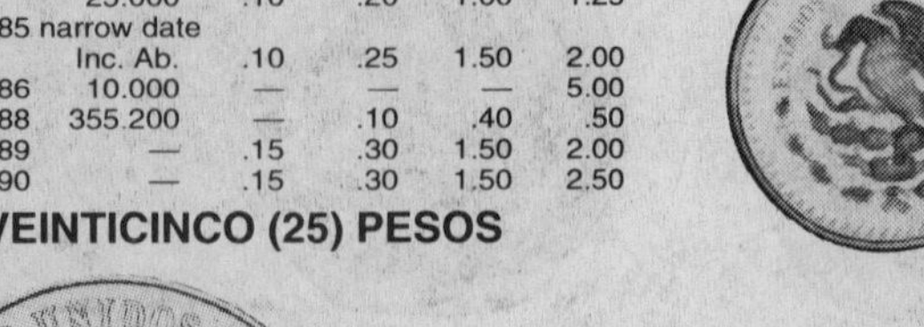

KM#	Date	Mintage	VF	XF	Unc	BU
508	1985 wide date					
		25.000	.10	.20	1.00	1.25
	1985 narrow date					
		Inc. Ab.	.10	.25	1.50	2.00
	1986	10.000	—	—	—	5.00
	1988	355.200	—	.10	.40	.50
	1989	—	.15	.30	1.50	2.00
	1990	—	.15	.30	1.50	2.50

VEINTICINCO (25) PESOS

22.5000 g, .720 SILVER, .5209 oz ASW
Summer Olympics - Mexico City
Type I, rings aligned.

KM#	Date	Mintage	VF	XF	Unc	BU
479.1	1968	27.182	BV	3.75	5.00	5.50

Type II, center ring low.

KM#	Date	Mintage	VF	XF	Unc	BU
479.2	1968	Inc. Ab.	BV	5.00	9.25	10.00

Normal tongue **Long curved tongue**
Type III, center rings low.
Snake with long curved tongue.

KM#	Date	Mintage	VF	XF	Unc	BU
479.3	1968	Inc. Ab.	BV	6.00	10.00	12.00

Benito Juarez

KM#	Date	Mintage	VF	XF	Unc	BU
480	1972	2.000	BV	4.00	6.00	7.50

7.7760 g, .720 SILVER, .1800 oz ASW, 24mm
1986 World Cup Soccer Games

KM#	Date	Mintage	VF	XF	Unc	BU
497	1985	.354	—	—	—	8.00

8.4060 g, .925 SILVER, .2450 oz ASW
Rev: W/o fineness statement.

KM#	Date	Mintage	VF	XF	Unc	BU
497a	1986	—	—	—	Proof	15.00

1986 World Cup Soccer Games

KM#	Date	Mintage	VF	XF	Unc	BU
503	1985	.277	—	—	Proof	15.00

1986 World Cup Soccer Games

KM#	Date	Mintage	VF	XF	Unc	BU
514	1985	.234	—	—	Proof	15.00

1986 World Cup Soccer Games

KM#	Date	Mintage	VF	XF	Unc	BU
519	1986	—	—	—	Proof	15.00

50 PESOS

41.6666 g, .900 GOLD, 1.2057 oz AGW
Centennial of Independence

KM#	Date	Mintage	Fine	VF	XF	Unc
481	1921	.180	—	—	BV	775.00
	1922	.463	—	—	BV	575.00
	1923	.432	—	—	BV	575.00
	1924	.439	—	—	BV	575.00
	1925	.716	—	—	BV	575.00
	1926	.600	—	—	BV	575.00
	1927	.606	—	—	BV	575.00
	1928	.538	—	—	BV	575.00
	1929	.458	—	—	BV	575.00
	1930	.372	—	—	BV	575.00
	1931	.137	—	—	BV	700.00
	1944	.593	—	—	BV	575.00
	1945	1.012	—	—	BV	575.00
	1946	1.588	—	—	BV	575.00
	1947	.309	—	—	*BV + 3%*	
	1947	—	—	—	—	Specimen 6500.

NOTE: During 1949-1972 a total of 3,975,654 pieces were restruck, most likely dated 1947.

COPPER-NICKEL
Coyolxauhqui

KM#	Date	Mintage	VF	XF	Unc	BU
490	1982	222.890	.65	.85	3.25	3.75
	1983	45.000	1.50	2.00	4.25	5.75
	1983	1,051	—	—	Proof	30.00
	1984	73.537	1.00	1.25	3.50	4.00
	1984	4 known	—	—	Proof	—

NOTE: Doubled die examples of 1982 and 1983 dates exist.

Benito Juarez

KM#	Date	Mintage	VF	XF	Unc	BU
495	1984	94.216	.25	1.00	1.50	2.25
	1985	296.000	.25	.75	1.50	2.25
	1986	50.000	5.00	7.00	10.00	12.00
	1987	210.000	—	—	1.00	1.25
	1988	80.200	5.00	7.00	9.00	11.50

STAINLESS STEEL

KM#	Date	Mintage	VF	XF	Unc	BU
495a	1988	353.300	—	.10	.50	.60
	1990	—	—	.25	1.00	2.00
	1992	—	—	.10	.50	.60

15.5520 g, .720 SILVER, .3601 oz ASW
1986 World Cup Soccer Games

KM#	Date	Mintage	VF	XF	Unc	BU
498	1985	.347	—	—	—	11.00

16.8310 g, .925 SILVER, .5000 oz ASW
Rev: W/o fineness statement.

KM#	Date	Mintage	VF	XF	Unc	BU
498a	1986	.010	—	—	Proof	22.50

1986 World Cup Soccer Games

KM#	Date	Mintage	VF	XF	Unc	BU
504	1985	.347	—	—	Proof	22.50

1986 World Cup Soccer Games

KM#	Date	Mintage	VF	XF	Unc	BU
515	1985	.234	—	—	Proof	22.50

1986 World Cup Soccer Games

KM#	Date	Mintage	VF	XF	Unc	BU
523	1986	.190	—	—	Proof	22.50

15.5500 g, .999 SILVER, .5000 oz ASW
50th Anniversary of Nationalization of Oil Industry

KM#	Date	Mintage	VF	XF	Unc	BU
532	1988	.030	—	—	12.00	15.00

CIEN (100) PESOS

Low 7's High 7's
27.7700 g, .720 SILVER, .6429 oz ASW
Jose Morelos y Pavon

KM#	Date	Mintage	VF	XF	Unc	BU
483	1977 low 7's, sloping shoulder					
		5.225	BV	5.00	7.00	10.00
	1977 high 7's, sloping shoulder					
		Inc. Ab.	BV	6.00	10.00	14.50

KM#	Date	Mintage	VF	XF	Unc	BU
484	1977 date in line, redesigned higher right shoulder					
		Inc. KM483	BV	4.00	5.25	5.75
	1978	9.879	BV	4.50	7.00	8.50
	1979	.784	BV	5.00	7.50	9.00
	1979	—	—	—	Proof	500.00

ALUMINUM-BRONZE
Venustiano Carranza

KM#	Date	Mintage	VF	XF	Unc	BU
493	1984	227.809	.20	.50	2.50	4.00
	1985	377.423	.15	.40	2.00	3.00
	1986	43.000	.75	1.25	4.00	6.00
	1987	165.000	—	.20	1.50	2.00
	1988	433.100	—	.20	.75	1.50
	1989	—	—	.20	1.00	1.75
	1990	—	—	.20	1.00	2.50
	1991	—	—	.20	1.00	2.50
	1992	—	—	.75	1.50	3.00

31.1030 g, .720 SILVER, .7201 oz ASW
1986 World Cup Soccer Games

KM#	Date	Mintage	VF	XF	Unc	BU
499	1985	.302	—	—	—	16.50

32.6250 g, .925 SILVER, 1.0000 oz ASW
Rev: W/o fineness statement.

KM#	Date	Mintage	VF	XF	Unc	BU
499a	1985	9,006	—	—	Proof	32.50

1986 World Cup Soccer Games
Rev: W/o fineness statement.

KM#	Date	Mintage	VF	XF	Unc	BU
505	1985	9,006	—	—	Proof	32.50

1986 World Cup Soccer Games
Rev: W/o fineness statement.

KM#	Date	Mintage	VF	XF	Unc	BU
521	1986	.208	—	—	Proof	32.50

1986 World Cup Soccer Games
Rev: W/o fineness statement.

KM#	Date	Mintage	VF	XF	Unc	BU
524	1986	.190	—	—	Proof	32.50

World Wildlife Fund - Monarch Butterflies

KM#	Date	Mintage	VF	XF	Unc	BU
537	1987	*.030	—	—	Proof	50.00

31.1030 g, .999 SILVER, 1.0000 oz ASW
50th Anniversary of Nationalization of Oil Industry

KM#	Date	Mintage	VF	XF	Unc	BU
533	1988	.010	—	—	22.00	30.00

33.6250 g, .925 SILVER, 1.0000 oz ASW
Save the Children

KM#	Date	Mintage	VF	XF	Unc	BU
539	1991	.030	—	—	Proof	45.00

27.0000 g, .925 SILVER, .8029 oz ASW

Ibero - American Series - Pillars

KM#	Date	Mintage	VF	XF	Unc	BU
540	1991	.050	—	—	Proof	42.50
	1992	.075	—	—	Proof	42.50

31.1030 g, .999 SILVER, 1.0000 oz ASW
Save the Whale

KM#	Date	Mintage	VF	XF	Unc	BU
566	1992	—	—	—	Proof	65.00

200 PESOS

COPPER-NICKEL
175th Anniversary of Independence

KM#	Date	Mintage	VF	XF	Unc	BU
509	1985	75.000	—	.25	3.00	4.00

75th Anniversary of 1910 Revolution

KM#	Date	Mintage	VF	XF	Unc	BU
510	1985	98.590	—	.25	3.25	4.75

1986 World Cup Soccer Games

KM#	Date	Mintage	VF	XF	Unc	BU
525	1986	50.000	—	.25	3.50	4.50

62.2060 g, .999 SILVER, 2.0000 oz ASW
1986 World Cup Soccer Games

KM#	Date	Mintage	VF	XF	Unc	BU
526	1986	.050	—	—	30.00	50.00

250 PESOS

8.6400 g, .900 GOLD, .2500 oz AGW
1986 World Cup Soccer Games

KM#	Date	Mintage	VF	XF	Unc	BU
500.1	1985	.100	—	—	—	110.00
	1986	—	—	—	—	110.00
	Rev: W/o fineness statement.					
500.2	1985	4,506	—	—	Proof	125.00
	1986	—	—	—	Proof	125.00

1986 World Cup Soccer Games

KM#	Date	Mintage	VF	XF	Unc	BU
506.1	1985	.088	—	—	—	115.00
	Rev: W/o fineness statement.					
506.2	1985	*.080	—	—	Proof	125.00

500 PESOS

17.2800 g, .900 GOLD, .5000 oz AGW
1986 World Cup Soccer Games
Obv: Eagle facing left w/snake in beak.

KM#	Date	Mintage	VF	XF	Unc	BU
501.1	1985	.102	—	—	—	210.00
	1986	—	—	—	—	210.00
	Rev: W/o fineness statement.					
501.2	1985	5,506	—	—	Proof	225.00
	1986	—	—	—	Proof	225.00

1986 World Cup Soccer Games

KM#	Date	Mintage	VF	XF	Unc	BU
507.1	1985	—	—	—	—	215.00
	Rev: W/o fineness statement.					
507.2	1985	—	—	—	Proof	225.00

33.4500 g, .925 SILVER, 1.0000 oz ASW
75th Anniversary of 1910 Revolution

KM#	Date	Mintage	VF	XF	Unc	BU
511	1985	.040	—	—	Proof	40.00

COPPER-NICKEL
Francisco Madero

KM#	Date	Mintage	VF	XF	Unc	BU
529	1986	20.000	—	.75	1.75	2.50
	1987	180.000	—	.75	1.75	2.50
	1988	230.000	—	.50	1.50	2.00
	1989	—	—	.50	1.50	2.00
	1990	—	—	.50	1.50	2.00

17.2800 g, .900 GOLD, .5000 oz AGW
50th Anniversary of Nationalization of Oil Industry
Similar to 5000 Pesos, KM#531.

KM#	Date	Mintage	VF	XF	Unc	BU
534	1988	—	—	—	—	225.00

1000 PESOS

17.2800 g, .900 GOLD, .5000 oz AGW
175th Anniversary of Independence

KM#	Date	Mintage	VF	XF	Unc	BU
513	1985	—	—	—	Proof	275.00

31.1030 g, .999 GOLD, 1.0000 oz AGW
1986 World Cup Soccer Games

KM#	Date	Mintage	VF	XF	Unc	BU
527	1986	—	—	—	—	675.00

34.5590 g, .900 GOLD, 1.0000 oz AGW
50th Anniversary of Nationalization of Oil Industry
Similar to 5000 Pesos, KM#531.

KM#	Date	Mintage	VF	XF	Unc	BU
535	1988	—	—	—	Proof	550.00

ALUMINUM-BRONZE
Juana de Asbaje

KM#	Date	Mintage	VF	XF	Unc	BU
536	1988	229.300	—	1.00	2.00	2.75
	1989	—	—	.75	1.75	2.50
	1990	—	—	1.00	2.00	2.75
	1992	—	—	.75	1.75	2.50

2000 PESOS

62.2000 g, .999 GOLD, 2.0000 oz AGW
1986 World Cup Soccer Games

KM#	Date	Mintage	VF	XF	Unc	BU
528	1986	—	—	—	—	1250.

5000 PESOS

COPPER-NICKEL
50th Anniversary of Nationalization of Oil Industry

KM#	Date	Mintage	VF	XF	Unc	BU
531	1988	50.000	—	2.75	4.75	6.00

MONETARY REFORM

1 New Peso = 1000 Old Pesos

5 CENTAVOS

STAINLESS STEEL

KM#	Date	Mintage	VF	XF	Unc
546	1992	—	—	—	.15

10 CENTAVOS

STAINLESS STEEL

KM#	Date	Mintage	VF	XF	Unc
547	1992	—	—	—	.20
	1993	—	—	—	.20

20 CENTAVOS

ALUMINUM-BRONZE

KM#	Date	Mintage	VF	XF	Unc
548	1992	—	—	—	.30
	1993	—	—	—	.30

50 CENTAVOS

ALUMINUM-BRONZE

KM#	Date	Mintage	VF	XF	Unc
549	1992	—	—	—	.60

NEW PESO

STAINLESS STEEL RING,
ALUMINUM-BRONZE CENTER

KM#	Date	Mintage	VF	XF	Unc
550	1992	—	—	—	1.10
	1994	—	—	—	1.10

2 NEW PESOS

STAINLESS STEEL RING,
ALUMINUM-BRONZE CENTER

KM#	Date	Mintage	VF	XF	Unc
551	1992	—	—	—	2.25
	1993	—	—	—	2.25

5 NEW PESOS

STAINLESS STEEL RING,
ALUMINUM-BRONZE CENTER

KM#	Date	Mintage	VF	XF	Unc
552	1992	—	—	—	4.25
	1993	—	—	—	4.25

10 NEW PESOS

ALUMINUM-BRONZE RING, .925 SILVER CENTER

KM#	Date	Mintage	VF	XF	Unc
553	1992	—	—	—	6.50
	1993	—	—	—	6.50

20 NEW PESOS

ALUMINUM-BRONZE RING, .925 SILVER CENTER

KM#	Date	Mintage	VF	XF	Unc
561	1993	—	—	—	9.50

SILVER BULLION ISSUES

NEW PESO

7.7580 g, .999 SILVER, .2498 oz ASW
Bajorrelieve Del El Tajin

KM#	Date	Mintage	VF	XF	Unc
567	1993	—	—	—	3.50

2 NEW PESOS

15.5516 g, .999 SILVER, .4995 oz ASW
Bajorrelieve Del El Tajin

KM#	Date	Mintage	VF	XF	Unc
568	1993	—	—	—	5.50

5 NEW PESOS

31.1035 g, .999 SILVER, .9991 oz ASW
Bajorrelieve Del El Tajin

KM#	Date	Mintage	VF	XF	Unc
569	1993	—	—	—	8.50

10 NEW PESOS

155.5175 g, .999 SILVER, 4.9956 oz ASW
Illustration reduced. Actual size: 64.9mm.
Piramide Del El Tajin

KM#	Date	Mintage	VF	XF	Unc
570	1993	—	—	—	45.00

25 PESOS

7.7758 g, .999 SILVER, .2500 oz ASW
Eagle Warrior

KM#	Date	Mintage	VF	XF	Unc
554	1992	—	—	—	3.50
	1992	.010	—	Proof	25.00

50 PESOS

15.5517 g, .999 SILVER, .5000 oz ASW
Eagle Warrior

KM#	Date	Mintage	VF	XF	Unc
555	1992	—	—	—	5.50
	1992	.010	—	Proof	30.00

100 PESOS

31.1035 g, .999 SILVER, 1.0000 oz ASW
Eagle Warrior

KM#	Date	Mintage	VF	XF	Unc
556	1992	—	—	—	10.00
	1992	.030	—	Proof	37.50

Xochipilli - The God of Joy, Music and Dance

KM#	Date	Mintage	VF	XF	Unc
562	1992	.030	—	Proof	37.50

Brasero Efigie - The God of Rain

KM#	Date	Mintage	VF	XF	Unc
563	1992	.030	—	Proof	37.50

Huehueteotl - The God of Fire

KM#	Date	Mintage	VF	XF	Unc
564	1992	.030	—	Proof	37.50

10000 PESOS

155.5175 g, .999 SILVER, 5.0000 oz ASW
Illustration reduced. Actual size: 65mm.
Native Warriors Taking Female Captive

KM#	Date	Mintage	VF	XF	Unc
557	1992	—	—	—	45.00
	1992	.010	—	Proof	95.00

1/20 ONZA TROY de PLATA

(1/20 Troy Ounce of Silver)

1.5551 g, .999 SILVER, .0500 oz ASW

KM#	Date	Mintage	VF	XF	Unc	BU
542	1991	.054	—	—	—	3.00
	1992	—	—	—	—	2.00
	1993	—	—	—	—	1.75

1/10 ONZA TROY de PLATA

(1/10 Troy Ounce of Silver)

3.1103 g, .999 SILVER, .1000 oz ASW

KM#	Date	Mintage	VF	XF	Unc	BU
543	1991	.050	—	—	—	3.00
	1992	—	—	—	—	2.25
	1993	—	—	—	—	2.00

1/4 ONZA TROY de PLATA

(1/4 Troy Ounce of Silver)

7.7758 g, .999 SILVER, .2500 oz ASW

KM#	Date	Mintage	VF	XF	Unc	BU
544	1991	.050	—	—	—	4.00
	1992	—	—	—	—	3.25
	1993	—	—	—	—	3.00

1/2 ONZA TROY de PLATA

(1/2 Troy Ounce of Silver)

15.5517 g, .999 SILVER, .5000 oz ASW

KM#	Date	Mintage	VF	XF	Unc	BU
545	1991	.051	—	—	—	6.00
	1992	—	—	—	—	5.00
	1993	—	—	—	—	5.00

ONZA TROY de PLATA

(Troy Ounce of Silver)

33.6250 g, .925 SILVER, 1.0000 oz ASW
Obv: Mint mark above coin press.

KM#	Date	Mintage	VF	XF	Unc	BU
M49a	1949	1.000	12.50	17.50	25.00	30.00

Type 1. Obv: Wide spacing between DE MONEDA
Rev: Mint mark below balance scale.

KM#	Date	Mintage	VF	XF	Unc	BU
M49b.1	1978	.280	BV	8.00	16.00	20.00

Type 2. Obv: Close spacing between DE MONEDA

KM#	Date	Mintage	VF	XF	Unc	BU
M49b.2	1978	Inc. Ab.	—	BV	13.00	18.00

Type 3. Rev: Left scale pan points to U in UNA.

KM#	Date	Mintage	VF	XF	Unc	BU
M49b.3	1979	4.508	—	BV	15.50	17.50

Type 4. Rev: Left scale pan points between U and N of UNA.

KM#	Date	Mintage	VF	XF	Unc	BU
M49b.4	1979	Inc. Ab.	—	BV	13.00	15.00

Type 5.

KM#	Date	Mintage	VF	XF	Unc	BU
M49b.5	1980	6.104	—	BV	12.00	13.50
	1980/70	I.A.	—	BV	15.50	17.50

LIBERTAD

(Onza Troy de Plata)

31.1000 g, .999 SILVER, 1.0000 oz ASW
Libertad

KM#	Date	Mintage	VF	XF	Unc	BU
494.1	1982	1.050	—	BV	7.00	9.00
	1983	1.268	—	BV	7.00	10.00
	1983	998 pcs.	—	—	Proof	275.00
	1984	1.014	—	BV	7.00	10.00
	1985	2.017	—	BV	7.00	9.50
	1986	1.699	—	BV	10.00	12.50
	1986	.030	—	—	Proof	22.00
	1987	.500	—	BV	20.00	30.00
	1987	.012	—	—	Proof	40.00
	1988	1.501	—	BV	16.00	27.50
	1988	*8,000	Proof Reported, not confirmed			
	1989	1.397	—	BV	10.00	12.50
	1989	3,500	—	—	Proof	45.00

Reeded edge.

KM#	Date	Mintage	VF	XF	Unc	BU
494.2	1988	*2,000	—	—	Proof	100.00
	1990	1.200	—	BV	8.00	10.00
	1990	—	—	—	Proof	20.00
	1991	1.651	—	BV	8.00	10.00
	1991	—	—	—	Proof	25.00

Obv: Eight dots below eagles left talons.
Rev: Revised design and lettering.

KM#	Date	Mintage	VF	XF	Unc	BU
494.3	1991	Inc. Ab.	—	BV	10.00	15.00
	1992	—	—	BV	7.00	9.50
	1992	—	—	—	Proof	25.00

Obv: Seven dots below eagles left talons, dull claws on right talon, thick letters.

KM#	Date	Mintage	VF	XF	Unc	BU
494.4	1993	—	—	BV	7.00	9.00

GOLD BULLION ISSUES

250 PESOS

7.7758 g, .999 GOLD, .2500 oz AGW
Native Culture - Sculpture of Jaguar Head

KM#	Date	Mintage	VF	XF	Unc
558	1992	—	—	—	100.00
	1992	.010	—	Proof	250.00

500 PESOS

15.5517 g, .999 GOLD, .5000 oz AGW
Native Culture - Sculpture of Jaguar Head

KM#	Date	Mintage	VF	XF	Unc
559	1992	—	—	—	200.00
	1992	.010	—	Proof	400.00

1000 PESOS

31.1035 g, .999 GOLD, 1.0000 oz AGW
Native Culture - Sculpture of Jaguar Head

KM#	Date	Mintage	VF	XF	Unc
560	1992	—	—	—	400.00
	1992	.010	—	Proof	600.00

1/20 ONZA ORO PURO

(1/20 Ounce of Pure Gold)

1.7500 g, .900 GOLD, .0500 oz AGW
Obv: Winged Victory. Rev: Calendar stone.

KM#	Date	Mintage	VF	XF	Unc	BU
530	1987	—	—	—		*BV + 30%*
	1988	—	—	—		*BV + 30%*
	1991	.010	—	—		*BV + 30%*
	1992	—	—	—		*BV + 30%*

1/10 ONZA ORO PURO

(1/10 Ounce of Pure Gold)

3.5000 g, .900 GOLD, .1000 oz AGW

KM#	Date	Mintage	VF	XF	Unc	BU
541	1991	.010	—	—		*BV + 20%*
	1992	—	—	—		*BV + 20%*

1/4 ONZA ORO PURO

(1/4 Ounce of Pure Gold)

8.6396 g, .900 GOLD, .2500 oz AGW

KM#	Date	Mintage	VF	XF	Unc	BU
487	1981	.313	—	—		*BV + 11%*
	1991	.010	—	—		*BV + 11%*
	1992	—	—	—		*BV + 11%*

1/2 ONZA ORO PURO

(1/2 Ounce of Pure Gold)

17.2792 g, .900 GOLD, .5000 oz AGW

KM#	Date	Mintage	VF	XF	Unc	BU
488	1981	.193	—	—		*BV + 8%*
	1989	3,500	—	—	Proof	400.00
	1991	.010	—	—		*BV + 8%*
	1992	—	—	—		*BV + 8%*

ONZA ORO PURO

(1 Ounce of Pure Gold)

34.5585 g, .900 GOLD, 1.0000 oz AGW

KM#	Date	Mintage	VF	XF	Unc	BU
489	1981	.596	—	—		*BV + 3%*
	1985	—	—	—		*BV + 3%*
	1988	—	—	—		*BV + 3%*
	1991	.010	—	—		*BV + 3%*
	1992	—	—	—		*BV + 3%*

(50 PESOS)

41.6666 g, .900 GOLD, 1.2057 oz AGW

KM#	Date	Mintage	VF	XF	Unc	BU
482	1943	.089	—	—	BV	525.00

PLATINUM BULLION ISSUES

1/4 ONZA

(1/4 ounce)

7.7775 g, .999 PLATINUM, .2500 oz APW

KM#	Date	Mintage	VF	XF	Unc
538	1989	3,500	—	—	Proof 200.00

MINT SETS (MS)

KM#	Date	Mintage	Identification	Issue Price	Mkt. Val.
MS1	1977(16)	500	—	—	600.00
MSa2	1977(9)	—	434.1,434.2,442,452, 460 thick date, 460 thin date,472,477.1,484,Type 2 for 3 ring binder	—	125.00
MS2	1978(9)	500	KM434.1,434.2,442,452, 460 open 8, 460 closed 8, 472,477,484,Type 1 flat pack	—	200.00
MS3	1978(9)	—	KM434.1,434.2,442,452, 460 open 8, 460 closed 8, 472,477.2,484,Type 2 for 3 ring binder	—	100.00
MS4	1979(8)	—	KM434.2,442,452 square 9, 452 round 9, 460(2), 472, 477.2,484, Type 1 flat pack	11.00	12.00
MS5	1979(8)	—	KM434.1,434.2,442,452 square 9, 452 round 9, 460,477,484, Type 2 for 3 ring binder	11.00	11.00
MS6	1980(9)	—	KM434.2, 442, 452 square 9, 452 round 9, 460 open 8, 460 closed 8, 477.2, 485-486	4.20	15.00
MS7	1981(9)	—	KM442 open 8, 442 closed 8, 452 rectangular 9, 452 round 9, 460 open 8, 460 closed 8, 477.2, 485,486	—	18.50
MS8	1982(7)	—	KM442,452,460,477,485, 486,490	—	16.50
MS9	1983(11)	—	KM442(2), 452(2), 460(2), 490(1), 491(2), 492(2)	—	15.00
MS10	1983(9)	—	KM442(2),452(2),460(2), 490(1),491(2),492(2) for 3 ring binder	—	13.50
MS11	1984(8)	—	KM485-486,490-491,493, 495(2),496	—	20.00
MS12	1985(12)	—	KM477.2,485,493(2), 495(2),496,502,508,509, 510,512	—	17.50
MS13	1986(7)	—	KM493,495,496,508,512, 525,529	—	17.50
MS14	1985/1986(7)	—	KM493,495-496,502,508 509,512	—	—
MS15	1987(9)	—	KM493,495(2),496,502(2), 512, 529(2)	—	40.00
MS16	1988(8)	—	KM493,495a,502,508,512, 529,531,536	—	25.00

NOTE: The 1978 and 1979 sets were issued in 2 varieties of plastic holders, one of which has holes for insertion in an official 3 ring binder which was sold for $3.30.

NOTE: In 1989 The Banco de Mexico began preparing mint sets by year with coins dated from 1971 thru 1988, MSa2 is such a set.

PROOF SETS (PS)

KM#	Date	Mintage	Identification	Issue Price	Mkt. Val.
PS1	1982/1983(8)	998	KM442,452,460,485, 477.2,486,490,494	495.00	425.00
PS2	1982/1983(8)	*2	KM460,477.2,485,486, 490,491,492,PnB169 (in white box with Mo. in gold)	—	—
PS3	1982/1983(7)	*23	KM460,477.2,485,486, 490,491,492(in white box with Mo in gold)	—	560.00
PS4	1982/1983(7)	*17	KM460,477.2,485,486, 490,491,492 (in white box)	—	560.00
PS5	1982/1983(7)	*8	KM460,477.2,485,486, 490,491,492 (in white box)	—	560.00
PS6	1983(7)	3	KM460,477.2,485,486, 490,491,492	—	—
PS7	1985/1986(12)	—	KM497a-499a,503-505, 514-515,519,521, 523-524	—	250.00
PS8	1985(4)	—	KM500.2-501.2,506.2, 507.2	—	700.00
PS9	1985(3)	—	KM499a,514,515 (in blue box)	—	70.00
PS10	1985(3)	—	KM503-505 (in blue box)	—	70.00
PS11	1985(2)	—	KM511,513	—	325.00
PS12	1989(3)	3,500	KM488,494,538, Rainbow	730.00	650.00

***NOTE:** KM#PS2, PS3, PS4 and PS5 are commonly referred to as pattern proof sets.

LOCAL COINAGE

This representation of local coinage is not to be considered as complete. Correspondence is welcomed by our editorial staff on any new varieties.

Ahualulco

OCTAVO - 1/8 REAL

COPPER, uniface
AHUALULCO and 1813 around 1/8 in circle.

KM#	Date	Good	VG	Fine	VF
L1	1813	17.50	25.00	35.00	50.00
	Script AHO, 1/8 below.				
L2	ND	12.50	17.50	25.00	35.00

Ameca

OCTAVO - 1/8 REAL

COPPER, uniface
Church flanked by trees.

KM#	Date	Good	VG	Fine	VF
L6	1824	12.50	17.50	25.00	35.00

TLACO DE AMECA around QTG monogram in circle.

KM#	Date	Good	VG	Fine	VF
L7	ND	12.50	17.50	25.00	35.00
	AME/CA 1811 in circle.				
L8	1811	17.50	25.00	35.00	50.00
	Octagonal planchet.				
L9	1811	17.50	25.00	35.00	50.00
	F 1/8 Z within wavy circle.				
L10	ND	17.50	25.00	35.00	50.00

T.Z. AMECA 1833 around value.

KM#	Date	Good	VG	Fine	VF
L11	1833	12.50	17.50	25.00	35.00

V.F AMECA 1858 below value.

KM#	Date	Good	VG	Fine	VF
L12	1858	12.50	17.50	25.00	35.00

Amescua

OCTAVO - 1/8 REAL

COPPER, uniface
Mexican Eagle

KM#	Date	Good	VG	Fine	VF
L15	1828	12.50	17.50	25.00	35.00

Date below eagle.

KM#	Date	Good	VG	Fine	VF
L16	1838	13.50	20.00	28.50	40.00

Atencinco

OCTAVO - 1/8 REAL

COPPER, uniface
ATENCINCO in outer border, 8 leaved rosette above branch in center.

KM#	Date	Good	VG	Fine	VF
L19	ND	15.00	20.00	28.00	40.00

Atotonilco

OCTAVO - 1/8 REAL

COPPER, uniface
ATOTONILCO ANO DE 1808 in outer border, L.S.S./JUSU/ESES in circle.

KM#	Date	Good	VG	Fine	VF
L22	1808	27.50	37.50	52.50	75.00

Obv. leg: ATOTONILCO ANO DE in outer border, 1821 in center. Rev. leg: E T P D Z around outer border.

KM#	Date	Good	VG	Fine	VF
L23	1821	17.50	25.00	35.00	50.00

Obv. leg: VILL ATOTONILCO in outer border, 1826 in center. Rev. leg: 1/8 in center, stars in outer border.

KM#	Date	Good	VG	Fine	VF
L24	1826	17.50	25.00	35.00	50.00

Campeche

CENTAVO

BRASS

KM#	Date	Good	VG	Fine	VF
L27	1861	8.50	12.50	20.00	28.00

Catorce

1/4 REAL

COPPER
Obv. leg: FONDOS PUBLICO around border, 1/4 below flower and raised rectangle. Rev. leg: DE CATORCE 1822 around border, eagle on cactus.

KM#	Date	Good	VG	Fine	VF
L30	1822	13.50	22.50	30.00	40.00

Celaya

OCTAVO - 1/8 REAL

COPPER
Obv. leg: EN/CELAYA/DE/1803. Rev. leg: LUIS/VASQUE/S, branches below, flower above.

KM#	Date	Good	VG	Fine	VF
L33	1803	27.50	37.50	52.50	75.00

COPPER, uniface
VINDERI/QUE/CELALLA/1808

KM#	Date	Good	VG	Fine	VF
L34	1808	27.50	37.50	52.50	75.00

VISCARA/CELAYA/1814 w/ornament above.

KM#	Date	Good	VG	Fine	VF
L35	1814	17.50	25.00	35.00	50.00

Chilchota

OCTAVO - 1/8 REAL

COPPER
Obv: Head to right, leg: CHILCHOTA UN OCTAVO, date below. Rev: Wreath in center, leg: RESPONSAVIDAD DE MURGVIA.

KM#	Date	Good	VG	Fine	VF
L38	1858	17.50	25.00	35.00	50.00

Colima

OCTAVO - 1/8 REAL

COPPER
Obv. leg: VILLA DE COLIMA around border as continuous leg. Rev: Blank.

KM#	Date	Good	VG	Fine	VF
L41	1813	12.50	17.50	25.00	37.50

Obv. leg: VILLA DE COLIMA and date in 3 lines. Rev: Blank.

KM#	Date	Good	VG	Fine	VF
L42	1814	12.50	17.50	25.00	37.50

Obv. leg: QUART COLIMA 1816 in 3 lines in wreath. Rev: Colima monogram in wreath.

KM#	Date	Good	VG	Fine	VF
L43	1816	12.50	17.50	25.00	37.50

KM#	Date	Good	VG	Fine	VF
L44	1819	15.00	22.50	30.00	45.00

Obv. leg: QUARTo DE COLIMA around border; date in center circle. Rev: Colima monogram in wreath.

KM#	Date	Good	VG	Fine	VF
L45	1824	15.00	22.50	30.00	45.00

Obv. leg: OCTO DE COLIMA around border, date in center circle. Rev. leg: OCTAVO within wreath, pellet in center.

KM#	Date	Good	VG	Fine	VF
L46	1824	15.00	22.50	30.00	45.00

Obv. leg: OCTO DE COLA in 3 lines.

KM#	Date	Good	VG	Fine	VF
L47	1824	15.00	22.50	30.00	45.00
	1828	15.00	22.50	30.00	45.00

Obv. leg: OCTO DE COLIMA in 3 lines. Rev. leg: ANO DE 1830 in 3 lines.

KM#	Date	Good	VG	Fine	VF
L48	1830	15.00	22.50	30.00	45.00

Cotija

OCTAVO - 1/8 REAL

COPPER
Obv: Seated Liberty w/staff and liberty cap, leg: DE.D.JOSE NUNES. Rev: Value and date in wreath, leg: COMMERCIO. D. COTIJA.

KM#	Date	Good	VG	Fine	VF
L51	ND	13.50	20.00	28.50	40.00

Cuido

OCTAVO - 1/8 REAL

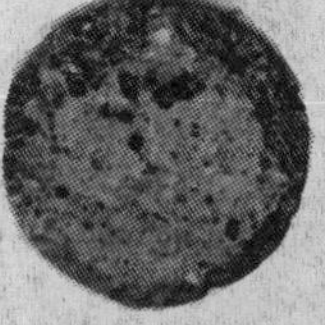

COPPER, uniface
"CUIDO" above "1/8" in spray.

KM#	Date	Good	VG	Fine	VF
L52	ND	13.50	20.00	28.50	40.00

Guadalajara

OCTAVO - 1/8 REAL

COPPER, uniface
Eagle w/wings spread, leg: GUADALAXARA.

KM#	Date	Good	VG	Fine	VF
L57	ND	27.50	37.50	52.50	75.00

Lagos

1/4 REAL

BRONZE
Obv: 2 globes w/crown above, wreath and 1/4 below. Rev: Coat of arms of Lagos.

KM#	Date	Good	VG	Fine	VF
L59	ND	100.00	150.00	200.00	250.00

SILVER

KM#	Date	Good	VG	Fine	VF
L59a	ND	150.00	200.00	300.00	500.00

Merida

1/2 GRANO

LEAD
Obv. leg: PART/DE LA SO/CIED in center.

MERIDADE YUCATAN around border, 1859 below. Rev. leg: 1/2/GRANO/DE PESO/FUERTE.

KM#	Date	Good	VG	Fine	VF
L60	1859	15.00	18.50	25.00	35.00

Pazcuaro

OCTAVO - 1/8 REAL

COPPER
Obv: Town at base of mountains, lake in foreground, value 1/8 above. Rev: Woman walking right, carrying bag, fish net and fish.

L63	ND	12.50	17.50	25.00	35.00

NOTE: Also in brass and cast in bronze.

Obv: 1/8 PAZCUARO. Rev: Crude portrait?.

L64	ND	12.50	17.50	25.00	35.00

Progreso

OCTAVO - 1/8 REAL

COPPER
Obv: Radiant star above open book.
Rev: Value 1/8 in double wreath.

L66	1858	17.50	25.00	35.00	50.00

CENTAVO

LEAD
Obv. leg: MUNICIPALIDAD DE PROGRESSO UN CENT, 1873 in center.
Rev: Flank in oval band.

L67	1873	13.50	20.00	27.50	40.00

Quitupan

OCTAVO - 1/8 REAL

COPPER
Obv: Bow and 2 arrows in center, leg: QUITUPAN. .1854. Rev: 1/8 in center, leg: IGNACIO BUENROSTO, monogram c/m.

L69	1854	17.50	25.00	35.00	50.00

Tacambaro

OCTAVO - 1/8 REAL

COPPER
Obv: Winged caduceus in sprays.
Rev: Value 1/8 in sprays.

L72	ND	13.50	20.00	28.50	40.00

Taretan

OCTAVO - 1/8 REAL

COPPER
Obv: Head of man right. Rev: Tree.

KM#	Date	Good	VG	Fine	VF
L75	1858	16.00	28.00	42.50	60.00

Tlazasalca

OCTAVO - 1/8 REAL

COPPER
Obv: 2 mountains, date below.
Rev: Value 1/8 in wreath.

L78	1853	17.50	25.00	35.00	50.00

Xalostotitlan

OCTAVO - 1/8 REAL

COPPER
Obv: Crown in center, leg: AYVNTAMIENTO ILVSTRE.
Rev: 4 in center, leg: DE XALOSTOTITLAN. 1820.

L54	1820	23.50	37.50	52.50	75.00

Zamora

OCTAVO - 1/8 REAL

COPPER

L80	1842	8.50	12.50	22.50	37.50
	1848	8.50	12.50	22.50	37.50
	1854	8.50	12.50	22.50	37.50
	1858	8.50	12.50	22.50	37.50

COPPER or BRONZE
Obv: Eagle on cactus above sprays.
Rev: Liberty cap, bow and arrows above sprays.
W/or w/o various c/m.

L81	1852	8.50	12.50	22.50	37.50
	1853	8.50	12.50	22.50	37.50
	1856	8.50	12.50	22.50	37.50
	1857	8.50	12.50	22.50	37.50
	1858	8.50	12.50	22.50	37.50

NOTE: These pieces are also found with various countermarks. "Za" in a dentilated circle is the most common. "1/8" in a circular c/m is also encountered.

Zapotlan

OCTAVO - 1/8 REAL

COPPER, uniface
ZAPO/TLAN/1813

KM#	Date	Good	VG	Fine	VF
L84	1813	18.50	30.00	42.50	60.00

REVOLUTION 1910-1917

The Mexican independence movement, which is of interest and concern to collectors because of the war-fareinduced activity of local and state mints, began with the Sept. 16, 1810 march on the capital led by Father Miguel Hidalgo, a well-intentioned man of imagination and courage who proved to be an inept organizer and leader. Hidalgo was captured and executed within 10 months. His revolution, led by such as Morelos, Guerrero and Iturbide, continued and culminated in Mexican independence in 1821. Turbulent years followed. From 1821 to 1877 there were two emperors, several dictators and enough presidents to provide a change of government on the average of once every nine months. Porfirio Diaz, who had the longest tenure of any dictator in Latin American history, seized power in 1877 and did not relinquish it until 1911.

The final phase of Mexico's lengthy revolutionary period began in 1910 and lasted through the adoption of a liberal constitution and the election of a new congress in 1917. The 1910-1917 revolution was agrarian in character and intended to destroy the regime of Diaz and make Mexico economically and diplomatically independent. The republic experienced a state of upheaval that saw most of the leading figures of the revolution (Villa, Carranza, Obregon, Zapata, Calles) fighting each other at one time or another. Carranza eventually emerged as the most powerful figure of the early revolution. As de facto president in 1916, he convened a constitutional convention which produced a constitution in which the aims of the revolution were formulized. Obregon, perhaps the ablest general and wiliest politician of the lot, became Mexico's elected president in 1920, bringing the most disastrous but significant decade in Mexico's history to an end.

AGUASCALIENTES

Aguascalientes is a state in central Mexico. Its coin issues, struck by authority of Pancho Villa, represent his deepest penetration into the Mexican heartland. Lack of silver made it necessary to make all denominations in copper.

CENTAVO

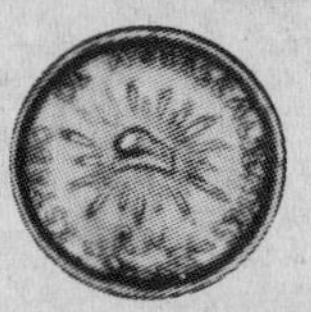

COPPER

KM#	Date	VG	Fine	VF	XF
601	1915 lg. date reeded edge	25.00	40.00	60.00	90.00
	1915 lg. date plain edge	250.00	350.00	450.00	—
	1915 sm. date reeded edge	20.00	30.00	50.00	75.00
	1915 sm. date plain edge	30.00	50.00	75.00	115.00

SILVER

KM#	Date	Mintage	VG	Fine	VF
601a	1915 lg. date	50 pcs.	—	275.00	450.00
	1915 small date	Inc. Ab.	—	275.00	450.00

2 CENTAVOS

COPPER

KM#	Date	VG	Fine	VF	XF
602.1	1915 round front 2	40.00	100.00	200.00	350.00

KM#	Date	VG	Fine	VF	XF
602.2	1915 square front 2, reeded edge	35.00	60.00	85.00	200.00
	1915 square front 2, plain edge	40.00	70.00	100.00	225.00

SILVER

KM#	Date	Mintage	VG	Fine	VF
602a	1915	50 pcs.	—	600.00	1000.

5 CENTAVOS

COPPER

KM#	Date	VG	Fine	VF	XF
603	1915	10.00	15.00	25.00	35.00

Obv: Vertically shaded 5.

KM#	Date	VG	Fine	VF	XF
604.1	1915 reeded edge	10.00	15.00	25.00	35.00
	1915 plain edge	100.00	150.00	225.00	325.00

Obv: Horizontally shaded 5.

KM#	Date	VG	Fine	VF	XF
604.2	1915 reeded edge	15.00	20.00	35.00	50.00
	1915 plain edge	20.00	30.00	50.00	75.00

SILVER

KM#	Date	Mintage	VG	Fine	VF
604a	1915	50 pcs.	—	1000.	1500.

20 CENTAVOS

COPPER
Rev: With flat bottomed 2.

KM#	Date	VG	Fine	VF	XF
605	1915	4.50	6.00	9.00	22.00

SILVER

KM#	Date	Mintage	VG	Fine	VF
605a	1915	50 pcs.	—	1200.	2000.

COPPER
Rev: With wavy bottomed 2.

KM#	Date	VG	Fine	VF	XF
606	1915	4.50	6.00	9.00	20.00

Obv: Pointed winged Eagle.

KM#	Date	VG	Fine	VF	XF
600	1915	15.00	20.00	35.00	60.00

SILVER

KM#	Date	VG	Fine	VF	XF
600a	1915	800.00	1200.	1600.	—

NOTE: Varieties exist with both plain and milled edges and many variations in the shading of the numerals.

CHIHUAHUA

Chihuahua is a northern state of Mexico bordering the U.S. It was the arena that introduced Pancho Villa to the world. Villa, an outlaw, was given a title when asked by Madero to participate in maintaining order during Madero's presidency. After Madero's death in February 1913 Villa became a persuasive leader. Chihuahua was where he made his first coins - the Parral series. The "Army of the North" pesos also came from this state. This coin helped Villa recruit soldiers because of his ability to pay in silver while others were paying in worthless paper.

HIDALGO DEL PARRAL

"FUERZAS CONSTITUCIONALISTAS"

2 CENTAVOS

COPPER

KM#	Date	VG	Fine	VF	XF
607	1913	2.50	4.00	8.00	15.00

BRASS

KM#	Date	VG	Fine	VF	XF
607a	1913	60.00	80.00	100.00	200.00

50 CENTAVOS

SILVER
Reeded edge

KM#	Date	VG	Fine	VF	XF
608	1913	9.00	15.00	20.00	35.00

Plain edge

KM#	Date	VG	Fine	VF	XF
609	1913	40.00	60.00	80.00	125.00

PESO

SILVER
Rev: 1 through PESO and ball BOLITA.

KM#	Date	VG	Fine	VF	XF
610	1913	900.00	1200.	1800.	2000.

Obv: Similar to KM#610.
Rev: 1 above PESO.

KM#	Date	VG	Fine	VF	XF
611	1913	35.00	50.00	75.00	150.00

CONSTITUTIONALIST ARMY

"EJERCITO CONSTITUCIONALISTA"

5 CENTAVOS

COPPER
Rev: Small rosettes at date.

KM#	Date	VG	Fine	VF	XF
612	1914	20.00	30.00	50.00	80.00

Rev: Large ornamental spear heads at date.

KM#	Date	VG	Fine	VF	XF
613	1914	1.00	2.50	3.50	4.50
	1915	1.00	2.50	3.50	4.50

NOTE: Numerous varieties exist.

CAST COPPER

KM#	Date	VG	Fine	VF	XF
613b	1914	75.00	100.00	200.00	250.00

BRASS

KM#	Date	VG	Fine	VF	XF
613a	1914	—	—	—	—
	1915	—	—	—	—

NOTE: Numerous varieties exist.

COPPER
Rev: Double lined V.

KM#	Date	VG	Fine	VF	XF
614	1915 MS	150.00	250.00	325.00	500.00
	1915 SS	—	—	Unique	—

Rev: Solid V.

KM#	Date	VG	Fine	VF	XF
614a	1915	—	—	Rare	—

Mule. Obv: KM#614. Rev: Rev. of KM#612.

KM#	Date	VG	Fine	VF	XF
614b	1915	—	350.00	—	—

Mule. Obv: KM#614. Rev: Obv. of KM#612.

KM#	Date	VG	Fine	VF	XF
614c	1915	—	—	Rare	—

10 CENTAVOS

COPPER

KM#	Date	VG	Fine	VF	XF
615	1915	1.25	2.50	3.50	5.00

BRASS

KM#	Date	VG	Fine	VF	XF
615a	1915	—	—	—	—

NOTE: Many varieties exist.

ARMY OF THE NORTH

"EJERCITO DEL NORTE"

PESO

SILVER

KM#	Date	VG	Fine	VF	XF
619	1915	15.00	25.00	35.00	65.00

COPPER

KM#	Date	VG	Fine	VF	XF
619a	1915	450.00	750.00	1000.	1500.

DURANGO

A state in north central Mexico. Another area of operation for Pancho Villa. The "Muera Huerta" peso originates in this state. The coins were made in Cuencame under the orders of Generals Cemceros and Contreras.

CUENCAME

"MUERA HUERTA"
(Death to Huerta)

PESO

SILVER
Rev: 1914 below UN PESO with 3 stars at each side.

KM#	Date	VG	Fine	VF	XF
620	1914	800.00	1000.	1400.	2500.

Obv. and rev: Continuous border.

KM#	Date	VG	Fine	VF	XF
621	1914	60.00	90.00	120.00	225.00

COPPER

KM#	Date	VG	Fine	VF	XF
621a	1914	175.00	375.00	500.00	900.00

NOTE: Varieties exist.

SILVER
Obv: Dot and dash border.

KM#	Date	VG	Fine	VF	XF
622	1914	60.00	100.00	150.00	250.00

20 PESOS

NOTE: The so called 20 Pesos gold Muera Huerta pieces are modern fantasies. Refer to *Unusual World Coins*, 3rd edition, 1989, Krause Publications, Inc.

ESTADO DE DURANGO

CENTAVO

COPPER

KM#	Date	VG	Fine	VF	XF
625	1914	2.00	3.00	5.00	7.50

BRASS

KM#	Date	VG	Fine	VF	XF
625a	1914	9.00	15.00	20.00	30.00

LEAD

KM#	Date	VG	Fine	VF	XF
625b	1914	20.00	40.00	65.00	90.00

COPPER
Obv. and rev: 2 obverses of KM#625.

KM#	Date	VG	Fine	VF	XF
625c	1914	25.00	50.00	100.00	150.00

CAST LEAD
Rev: Retrograde N.

KM#	Date	VG	Fine	VF	XF
624	1914	45.00	75.00	100.00	200.00

COPPER

KM#	Date	VG	Fine	VF	XF
626	1914	15.00	30.00	45.00	60.00

BRASS

KM#	Date	VG	Fine	VF	XF
626a	1914	35.00	50.00	75.00	150.00

LEAD

KM#	Date	VG	Fine	VF	XF
626b	1914	20.00	35.00	50.00	75.00

KM#	Date	VG	Fine	VF	XF
		COPPER			
627	1914	6.00	10.00	15.00	25.00
		LEAD			
627a	1914	20.00	35.00	50.00	65.00

KM#	Date	VG	Fine	VF	XF
		ALUMINUM			
628	1914	.65	1.00	2.00	3.00

5 CENTAVOS

COPPER
Obv. leg: ESTADO DE DURANGO.

KM#	Date	VG	Fine	VF	XF
629	1914	1.25	2.00	4.00	7.50

Obv. leg: E. DE DURANGO. Rev: Thin 5.

KM#	Date	VG	Fine	VF	XF
630	1914	125.00	275.00	375.00	500.00

Rev: Thick 5.

KM#	Date	VG	Fine	VF	XF
631	1914	1.25	2.00	4.00	7.50
		BRASS			
631a	1914	30.00	40.00	50.00	85.00
		LEAD			
631b	1914	45.00	70.00	100.00	180.00

KM#	Date	VG	Fine	VF	XF
		COPPER			
632	1914	3.00	5.00	9.00	15.00
		LEAD			
632a	1914	50.00	75.00	100.00	150.00

Obv: 3 stars below 1914. Rev: 5 CVS.

KM#	Date	VG	Fine	VF	XF
633	1914	—	400.00	800.00	—

KM#	Date	VG	Fine	VF	XF
		BRASS			
634	1914	.50	1.00	1.50	2.00
		COPPER			
634a	1914	75.00	100.00	150.00	225.00

NOTE: There are numerous varieties of these general types of the Durango 1 and 5 Centavo pieces.

GUERRERO

Guerrero is a state on the southwestern coast of Mexico. It was one of the areas of operation of Zapata and his forces in the south of Mexico. Seven different mints were operated by the Zapata forces in this state. The date ranges were from 1914 to 1917 and denominations from 2 centavos to 2 pesos. Some were cast but most were struck and the rarest coin of the group is the Suriana 1915 2 pesos.

2 CENTAVOS

COPPER

KM#	Date	VG	Fine	VF	XF
638 (666)	1915	75.00	125.00	175.00	250.00

3 CENTAVOS

COPPER

KM#	Date	VG	Fine	VF	XF
635	1915	500.00	1000.	1500.	2000.

5 CENTAVOS

COPPER

KM#	Date	VG	Fine	VF	XF
636	1915GRO	600.00	1000.	1300.	1750.

10 CENTAVOS

COPPER

KM#	Date	VG	Fine	VF	XF
637	1915GRO	—	—	Rare	—

20 CENTAVOS

Previously listed #638 dated 1915GRO existing in copper and in silver has been determined to be spurious.

25 CENTAVOS

SILVER

KM#	Date	VG	Fine	VF	XF
639	1915	300.00	400.00	525.00	650.00

50 CENTAVOS

SILVER

KM#	Date	VG	Fine	VF	XF
640	1915	900.00	1500.	2100.	3000

UN (1) PESO

0.30 g, 1.000 FINE GOLD/SILVER
Obv: Star before UN PESO.

KM#	Date	VG	Fine	VF	XF
641	1914	15.00	25.00	35.00	65.0

NOTE: Many die varieties exist.

Obv: Star before and after UN PESO.

KM#	Date	VG	Fine	VF	XF
642	1914	50.00	75.00	100.00	150.0
	1915	600.00	1000.	1500.	2000

DOS (2) PESOS

0.595 g, 1.000 FINE GOLD/SILVER

KM#	Date	VG	Fine	VF	XF
643	1914GRO	12.50	22.50	35.00	60.0

NOTE: Many varieties exist.

KM#	Date	VG	Fine	VF	XF
644	1915GRO	65.00	85.00	160.00	250.00

COPPER

KM#	Date	VG	Fine	VF	XF
644a	1915GRO	400.00	600.00	800.00	1000.

ATLIXTAC

10 CENTAVOS

COPPER

KM#	Date	VG	Fine	VF	XF
645	1915	3.00	4.00	6.50	9.00

Obv: Stars in leg.

KM#	Date	VG	Fine	VF	XF
646	1915	3.00	4.00	6.50	9.00

CACAHUATEPEC

5 CENTAVOS

COPPER

KM#	Date	VG	Fine	VF	XF
648	1917	12.00	25.00	40.00	75.00

20 CENTAVOS

SILVER

KM#	Date	VG	Fine	VF	XF
649	1917	75.00	125.00	200.00	250.00

50 CENTAVOS

SILVER

KM#	Date	VG	Fine	VF	XF
650	1917	50.00	75.00	100.00	150.00

UN (1) PESO

SILVER

KM#	Date	VG	Fine	VF	XF
651	1917 L.V.Go	1250.	2250.	3500.	4250.

CACALOTEPEC

20 CENTAVOS

SILVER

KM#	Date	VG	Fine	VF	XF
652	1917	800.00	1400.	1800.	2250.

CAMPO MORADO

C.M., C.M.GRO, CoMoGro, CAMPO Mo

5 CENTAVOS

COPPER

KM#	Date	VG	Fine	VF	XF
653	1915C.M.	9.00	15.00	22.50	35.00

10 CENTAVOS

COPPER

KM#	Date	VG	Fine	VF	XF
654	1915C.M.GRO	6.00	10.00	17.50	27.50

20 CENTAVOS

COPPER

KM#	Date	VG	Fine	VF	XF
655	1915C.M.GRO	15.00	25.00	35.00	50.00

50 CENTAVOS

COPPER

Obv: UN PESO effaced below eagle.

KM#	Date	VG	Fine	VF	XF
656	1915C.M.GRO	12.00	20.00	30.00	60.00

Regular obverse

KM#	Date	VG	Fine	VF	XF
657	1915C.M.GRO	6.00	10.00	13.50	20.00

BASE SILVER

KM#	Date	VG	Fine	VF	XF
657a	1915C.M.GRO	165.00	275.00	400.00	575.00

UN (1) PESO

0.300 g, 1.000 FINE GOLD/SILVER

Obv: Date below eagle.

KM#	Date	VG	Fine	VF	XF
658	1914Co Mo Gro	450.00	650.00	850.00	1100.

BRASS

KM#	Date	VG	Fine	VF	XF
658a	1914Co Mo Gro	—	—	Unique	2500.

0.300 g, 1.000 FINE GOLD/SILVER

Rev: Date below Liberty cap.

KM#	Date	VG	Fine	VF	XF
659	1914 CAMPO Mo	15.00	30.00	45.00	60.00

DOS (2) PESOS

0.595 g, 1.000 FINE GOLD/SILVER

KM#	Date	VG	Fine	VF	XF
660	1915 Co. Mo.	15.00	25.00	35.00	55.00

Rev: Star before and after Co. Mo.

KM#	Date	VG	Fine	VF	XF
661	1915 Co.Mo.	1200.	2000.	3000.	4500.

KM#	Date	VG	Fine	VF	XF
662	1915 C.M.GRO	20.00	30.00	50.00	65.00

COPPER

KM#	Date	VG	Fine	VF	XF
662a	1915 C.M.GRO	—	—	—	900.00

CHILPANCINGO

10 CENTAVOS

SILVER (cast)

KM#	Date	VG	Fine	VF	XF
663	1914	700.00	1000.	1500.	2000.

NOTE: Counterfeits exist.

20 CENTAVOS

SILVER (cast)

KM#	Date	VG	Fine	VF	XF
664	1914	700.00	1000.	1500.	2000.

NOTE: Counterfeits exist.

SURIANA

DOS (2) PESOS

0.595 g, 1.000 FINE GOLD/SILVER

KM#	Date	VG	Fine	VF	XF
665	1915	—	23,000.	—	

NOTE: Superior Munoz Sale Part 1, 6-78 (The Bothamely Specimen).

TAXCO

2 CENTAVOS

COPPER

Obv. leg: EDO.DE.GRO above eagle.

KM#	Date	VG	Fine	VF	XF
667	1915 O/T	25.00	40.00	60.00	90.00

5 CENTAVOS

COPPER

KM#	Date	VG	Fine	VF	XF
668	1915	9.00	15.00	20.00	25.00

10 CENTAVOS

COPPER

KM#	Date	VG	Fine	VF	XF
669	1915	9.00	15.00	20.00	30.00

50 CENTAVOS

COPPER

Obv. leg: Large letters.

KM#	Date	VG	Fine	VF	XF
670	1915	15.00	25.00	50.00	65.00

SILVER

KM#	Date	VG	Fine	VF	XF
671	1915	20.00	30.00	40.00	70.00

UN (1) PESO

0.300 g, 1.000 FINE GOLD/SILVER

Obv: Star before UN PESO. Rev: Star before G.

KM#	Date	VG	Fine	VF	XF
672	1915	12.00	20.00	25.00	35.00

Obv: Star before UN PESO. Rev: W/o star before G.

KM#	Date	VG	Fine	VF	XF
673	1915	250.00	300.00	400.00	500.00

Obv: W/o star before UN PESO.

KM#	Date	VG	Fine	VF	XF
674	1915	75.00	150.00	275.00	400.00

JALISCO

Jalisco is a state on the west coast of Mexico. The few coins made for this state show that the "Army of the North" did not restrict their operations to the northern border states. The coins were made in Guadalajara under the watchful eye of General Dieguez, commander of this segment of Villa's forces.

GUADALAJARA

CENTAVO

COPPER

KM#	Date	VG	Fine	VF	XF
675	1915	9.50	15.00	20.00	25.00

2 CENTAVOS

COPPER

KM#	Date	VG	Fine	VF	XF
676	1915	9.50	15.00	17.50	22.50

5 CENTAVOS

COPPER

KM#	Date	VG	Fine	VF	XF
677	1915	6.50	12.00	15.00	20.00

BRASS

KM#	Date	VG	Fine	VF	XF
677a	1915	—	—	Rare	—

10 CENTAVOS

COPPER

KM#	Date	VG	Fine	VF	XF
678	1915	—	—	1800.	2400.

PESO

COPPER

KM#	Date	VG	Fine	VF	XF
A678	1915	—	—	—	8000.

MEXICO, ESTADO DE

Estado de Mexico is a state in central Mexico that surrounds the Federal District on 3 sides. The issues by the Zapata forces in this state have two distinctions - the Amecameca pieces are the crudest and the Toluca cardboard piece is the most unusual. General Tenorio authorized the crude incuse Amecameca pieces.

AMECAMECA

5 CENTAVOS

BRASS

KM#	Date	VG	Fine	VF	XF
679	ND	—	—	Unique	—

Hand stamped

KM#	Date	VG	Fine	VF	XF
680	ND	75.00	100.00	150.00	200.00

10 CENTAVOS

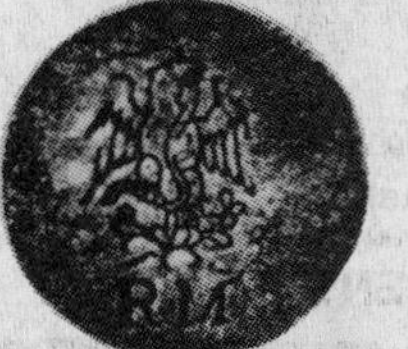

BRASS, hand stamped

KM#	Date	VG	Fine	VF	XF
681	ND	60.00	90.00	125.00	160.00

NOTE: Varieties exist.

20 CENTAVOS

BRASS, hand stamped

KM#	Date	VG	Fine	VF	XF
682	ND	15.00	22.50	35.00	60.00

NOTE: Varieties exist.

COPPER, hand stamped
Obv: Eagle over A.D.J.

KM#	Date	VG	Fine	VF	XF
683	ND	7.50	12.50	20.00	35.00

BRASS

KM#	Date	VG	Fine	VF	XF
683a	ND	—	—	125.00	175.00

25 CENTAVOS

BRASS

KM#	Date	VG	Fine	VF	XF
684	ND	—	—	Unique	—

COPPER, hand stamped
Obv: Eagle over sprays.

KM#	Date	VG	Fine	VF	XF
685	ND	15.00	25.00	40.00	80.00

BRASS, hand stamped

KM#	Date	VG	Fine	VF	XF
685a	ND	—	—	50.00	100.00

50 CENTAVOS

COPPER, hand stamped
Obv: Eagle over sprays.

KM#	Date	VG	Fine	VF	XF
686	ND	5.00	8.00	12.00	20.00

BRASS, hand stamped

KM#	Date	VG	Fine	VF	XF
686a	ND	75.00	100.00	150.00	200.00

COPPER
Contemporary counterfeit, hand engraved.

KM#	Date	VG	Fine	VF	XF
687	ND	12.00	20.00	32.50	50.00

NOTE: KM#687 - ¢ clears top of 5 while KM#686a has the stem of ¢ above the 5.

MEXICO, DISTRITO FEDERAL

See also general listings for 1 Centavo, KM#416 and 2 Centavos, KM#417 dated 1915 struck by Revolutionary forces under E. Zapata.

TENANCINGO, TOWN

2 CENTAVOS

COPPER
Rev: W/o TM below denomination.

KM#	Date	VG	Fine	VF	XF
688.1	1915	—	—	350.00	—

Rev: W/TM below denomination.

KM#	Date	VG	Fine	VF	XF
688.2	1915	—	200.00	300.00	—

5 CENTAVOS

COPPER
Rev: Lined C.

KM#	Date	VG	Fine	VF	XF
689.1	1915	5.00	10.00	15.00	25.00

Rev: Solid C.

KM#	Date	VG	Fine	VF	XF
689.2	1915	50.00	100.00	200.00	300.00

10 CENTAVOS

COPPER
Rev: W/o dot in C.

KM#	Date	VG	Fine	VF	XF
690.1	1916	10.00	15.00	20.00	30.00

Rev: Dot in C.

KM#	Date	VG	Fine	VF	XF
690.2	1916	50.00	100.00	200.00	300.00

20 CENTAVOS

COPPER

KM#	Date	VG	Fine	VF	XF
691	1915	25.00	40.00	55.00	75.00

TOLUCA, CITY

5 CENTAVOS

GREY CARDBOARD
Obv: W/o dot after TOLUCA.

KM#	Date	VG	Fine	VF	XF
692.1	1915	15.00	25.00	35.00	45.00

Obv: Dot after TOLUCA.

KM#	Date	VG	Fine	VF	XF
692.2	1915	15.00	25.00	35.00	45.00

20 CENTAVOS

COPPER
20 within C in circular countermark on 1 Centavo, KM#415.

KM#	Date	VG	Fine	VF	XF
693	ND	20.00	30.00	45.00	60.00

NOTE: Varieties exist.

40 CENTAVOS

COPPER
40 within C in circular countermark on 2 Centavos, KM#419.

KM#	Date	VG	Fine	VF	XF
694	ND	25.00	40.00	55.00	70.00

NOTE: Varieties exist.

MORELOS

Morelos is a state in south central Mexico, adjoining the federal district on the south. It was the headquarters of Emiliano Zapata. His personal quarters were at Tlatizapan in Morelos. The Morelos coins from 2 centavos to 1 peso were all copper except one type of 1 peso in silver. The 2 operating Zapatista mints in Morelos were Atlihuayan and Tlaltizapan.

2 CENTAVOS

COPPER
E.L.DE MORELOS

KM#	Date	VG	Fine	VF	XF
695	1915	1000.	1400.	1800.	2250.

5 CENTAVOS

COPPER
E. DE MOR. 1915.

KM#	Date	VG	Fine	VF	XF
696	1915	300.00	500.00	1000.	3500.

10 CENTAVOS

COPPER

KM#	Date	VG	Fine	VF	XF
697	1915	12.00	20.00	27.50	35.00

Date effaced from die

KM#	Date	VG	Fine	VF	XF
698	ND	12.00	20.00	32.50	50.00

KM#	Date	VG	Fine	VF	XF
699	1915	1000.	1500.	2000.	2500.

KM#	Date	VG	Fine	VF	XF
700	1916	5.00	10.00	15.00	20.00

20 CENTAVOS

COPPER

KM#	Date	VG	Fine	VF	XF
701	1915	9.00	15.00	21.50	30.00

50 CENTAVOS

COPPER
Obv: MOR beneath eagle. Rev: 50C monogram.

KM#	Date	VG	Fine	VF	XF
702	1915	300.00	500.00	900.00	1300.

Obv: Sprays beneath eagle.

KM#	Date	VG	Fine	VF	XF
703	1915	12.50	17.50	27.50	32.50

NOTE: The above exists with a silver and also a brass wash.

Rev: REFORMA LIBERTAD JUSTICIA Y LEY.

KM#	Date	VG	Fine	VF	XF
706	1915	350.00	500.00	800.00	1000.

Obv: MORELOS below eagle.

KM#	Date	VG	Fine	VF	XF
704	1916	12.50	17.50	27.50	32.50

UN (1) PESO

SILVER

KM#	Date	VG	Fine	VF	XF
708	1916	450.00	750.00	1000.	1500.

COPPER

KM#	Date	VG	Fine	VF	XF
708a	1916	450.00	750.00	1000.	1500.

OAXACA

Oaxaca is one of the southern states in Mexico. The coins issued in this state represent the most prolific series of the Revolution. Most of the coins bear the portrait of Benito Juarez and were issued by a provisional government in the state. The exceptions are the rectangular 1 and 3 centavos pieces that begin the series.

UN (1) CENTAVO

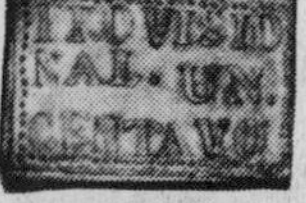

COPPER

KM#	Date	VG	Fine	VF	XF
709	1915	60.00	90.00	125.00	150.00

KM#	Date	VG	Fine	VF	XF
710	1915	12.00	17.50	25.00	40.00

BRASS

KM#	Date	VG	Fine	VF	XF
710a	1915	50.00	100.00	175.00	225.00

TRES (3) CENTAVOS

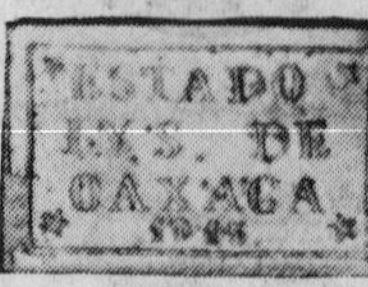

COPPER
Rev. leg: PROVISIO. . . . .

KM#	Date	VG	Fine	VF	XF
711	1915	60.00	100.00	125.00	150.00

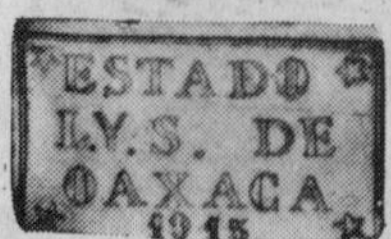
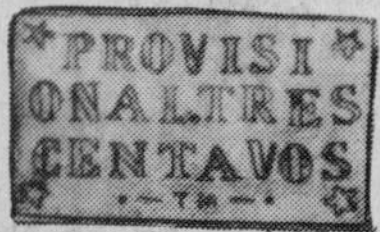

Rev. leg: PROVISI. . . . .

KM#	Date	VG	Fine	VF	XF
712	1915	600.00	1000.	1500.	2000.

Rev: W/o TM below denomination.

KM#	Date	VG	Fine	VF	XF
713.1	1915	3.00	5.00	10.00	15.00

Rev: W/TM below denomination.

KM#	Date	VG	Fine	VF	XF
713.2	1915	100.00	150.00	250.00	350.00

KM#	Date	VG	Fine	VF	XF
714	1915	6.00	9.00	14.00	20.00

5 CENTAVOS

COPPER

JAN.15 1915, incuse lettering

KM#	Date	VG	Fine	VF	XF
715	1915	—	—	Rare	—

Obv: Facing bust of Juarez.

KM#	Date	VG	Fine	VF	XF
716	1915	—	—	—	3000.

Obv: 2nd bust, low relief w/long pointed truncation.

KM#	Date	VG	Fine	VF	XF
717	1915	1.50	3.00	4.50	7.00

Obv: 5th bust, heavy w/short unfinished lapels.

KM#	Date	VG	Fine	VF	XF
718	1915	1.50	2.50	4.00	6.00

Obv: 6th bust, curved bottom.

KM#	Date	VG	Fine	VF	XF
719	1915	1.50	2.50	4.00	6.00

Obv: 7th bust, short truncation w/closed lapels.

KM#	Date	VG	Fine	VF	XF
720	1915	1.50	3.00	4.50	7.00

Obv: 8th bust, short curved truncation.

KM#	Date	VG	Fine	VF	XF
721	1915	1.50	2.50	4.00	6.00

10 CENTAVOS

COPPER

Obv: 2nd bust, low relief w/long-pointed truncation.

KM#	Date	VG	Fine	VF	XF
722	1915	1.50	2.50	4.00	6.00

Obv. and rev. leg: Retrograde.

KM#	Date	VG	Fine	VF	XF
723	1915	—	—	Rare	—

Obv: 4th bust, bold, unfinished truncation using 1 Peso obv. die of KM#740.

KM#	Date	VG	Fine	VF	XF
724	1915	3.00	5.00	7.00	9.00

Obv: 5th bust, heavy w/short unfinished lapels centered high.

KM#	Date	VG	Fine	VF	XF
725	1915	1.50	2.50	4.00	6.00

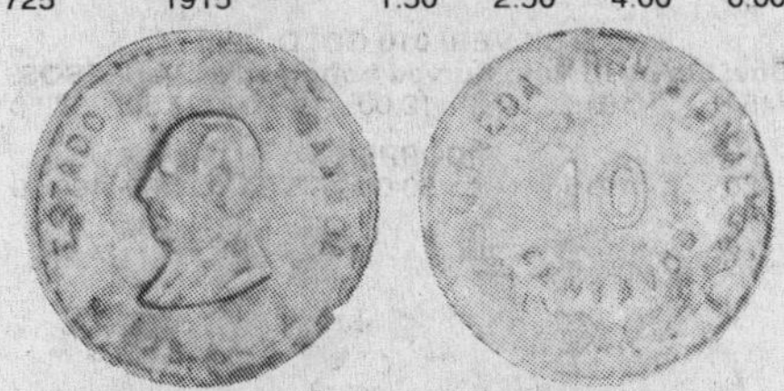

Obv: 6th bust, curved bottom.

KM#	Date	VG	Fine	VF	XF
726	1915	1.50	2.50	4.00	6.00

Obv: 7th bust, short truncation w/closed lapels.

KM#	Date	VG	Fine	VF	XF
727.1	1915	1.50	2.50	4.00	6.00

Rev: T below bow, M below 1st leaf.

KM#	Date	VG	Fine	VF	XF
727.2	1915	—	—	Rare	—

Obv: c/s: GV on 7th bust, short truncation w/closed lapels. Rev: Similar to KM#727.1.

KM#	Date	VG	Fine	VF	XF
727.3	1915	100.00	200.00	250.00	350.00

NOTE: Letters GV correspond to General Garcia Vigil.

20 CENTAVOS

SILVER

Obv: 2nd bust, low relief w/long-pointed truncation.

KM#	Date	VG	Fine	VF	XF
728	1915	500.00	750.00	1200.	1500.

COPPER

Obv: 4th bust, bold unfinished truncation using 1 Peso obv. die

KM#	Date	VG	Fine	VF	XF
729.1	1915	1.50	3.00	4.50	7.00

c/s: Liberty cap.

KM#	Date	VG	Fine	VF	XF
729.2	1915	100.00	150.00	200.00	275.00

Obv: 5th bust, heavy, w/short unfinished lapels using 20 Pesos obv. die.

KM#	Date	VG	Fine	VF	XF
730	1915	5.00	7.00	10.00	15.00

Obv: 6th bust, curved bottom.

KM#	Date	VG	Fine	VF	XF
731.1	1915	1.50	2.50	4.00	6.00

Similar to KM#731.1 but w/4th bust.

KM#	Date	VG	Fine	VF	XF
731.2	1915	—	—	Unique	—

Obv: 6th bust.

KM#	Date	VG	Fine	VF	XF
732	1915	1.50	2.50	4.00	6.00

Obv: 7th bust, short truncation w/closed lapels.

KM#	Date	VG	Fine	VF	XF
733	1915	1.50	3.00	4.50	7.00

50 CENTAVOS

SILVER
Obv: 5th bust, heavy w/short unfinished lapels, centered high.

KM#	Date	VG	Fine	VF	XF
734	1915	10.00	20.00	40.00	85.00

Obv: 6th bust, curved bottom.

KM#	Date	VG	Fine	VF	XF
735	1915	6.00	9.00	14.00	22.50

Obv: 7th bust, short truncation w/closed lapels.

KM#	Date	VG	Fine	VF	XF
736	1915	6.00	9.00	15.00	25.00

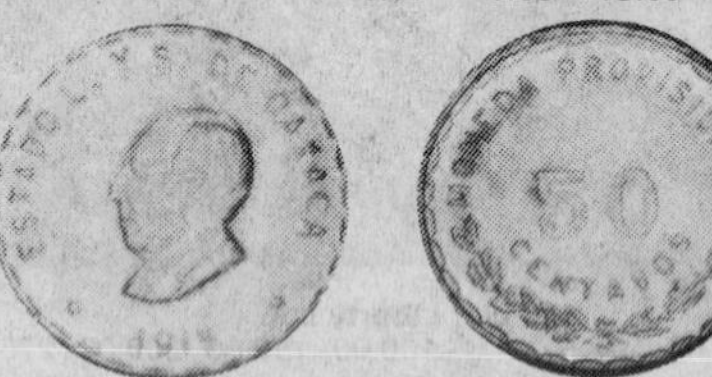

Obv: 8th bust, short truncation w/pronounced curve.

KM#	Date	VG	Fine	VF	XF
737	1915	6.50	10.00	16.00	30.00

BILLON
Obv: 9th bust, high nearly straight truncation.

KM#	Date	VG	Fine	VF	XF
739	1915	—	—	—	2000.

COPPER

KM#	Date	VG	Fine	VF	XF
739a	1915	—	—	—	—

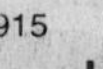
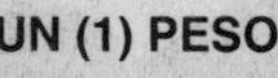

UN (1) PESO

SILVER
Obv: 4th bust, w/heavy unfinished truncation.

KM#	Date	VG	Fine	VF	XF
740.1	1915	3.00	5.00	8.50	14.00

Rev: TM below bow on wreath.

KM#	Date	VG	Fine	VF	XF
740.2	1915	150.00	200.00	250.00	350.00

Obv: 5th bust, heavy, w/short unfinished lapels, centered high.

KM#	Date	VG	Fine	VF	XF
741	1915	6.00	9.00	14.00	22.50

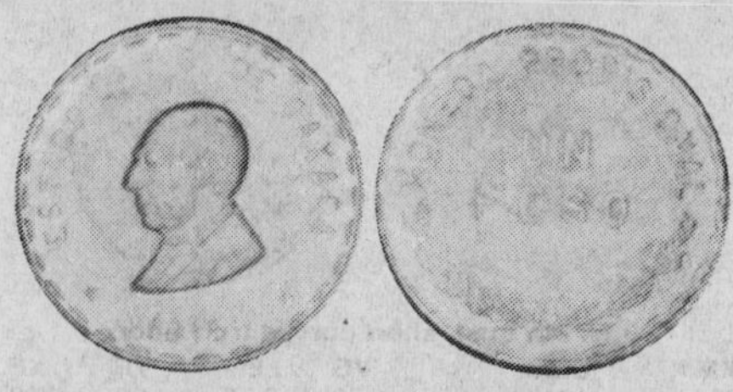

Obv: 6th bust, curved bottom line.

KM#	Date	VG	Fine	VF	XF
742	1915	6.00	9.00	14.00	22.50

Obv: 7th bust, short truncation w/closed lapels.

KM#	Date	VG	Fine	VF	XF
743	1915	4.00	6.00	10.00	16.00

Rev: TM below bow on wreath.

KM#	Date	VG	Fine	VF	XF
743a	1915	35.00	75.00	150.00	200.00

DOS (2) PESOS

SILVER
Obv: 4th bust, using 1 Peso obv. die.

KM#	Date	VG	Fine	VF	XF
744	1915	12.00	20.00	25.00	35.00

.902 SILVER/.010 GOLD, 22mm
Obv: 5th bust. Rev: Curved bottomed 2 over PESOS.

KM#	Date	VG	Fine	VF	XF
745	1915	12.00	20.00	27.50	37.50

COPPER

KM#	Date	VG	Fine	VF	XF
745a	1915	50.00	75.00	110.00	160.00

SILVER
Obv: 6th bust. Rev: 2 PESOS.

KM#	Date	VG	Fine	VF	XF
746	1915	10.00	15.00	27.50	45.00

KM#	Date	VG	Fine	VF	XF
A747	1915	—	—	185.00	275.00

NOTE: Obverse die is free hand engraved.

Obv: 6th bust. Rev: DOS PESOS.

KM#	Date	VG	Fine	VF	XF
747.1	1915	10.00	15.00	25.00	40.00

Obv: 6th bust. Rev: DOS PESOS.

KM#	Date	VG	Fine	VF	XF
747.2	1915.	10.00	15.00	25.00	40.00

Obv: 6th bust, periods after L and S.
Rev: DOS PESOS.

KM#	Date	VG	Fine	VF	XF
747.3	1915.	10.00	15.00	25.00	40.00

.902 SILVER
Obv: 7th bust, short truncation w/closed lapels, 22mm.

KM#	Date	VG	Fine	VF	XF
748	1915	12.00	20.00	40.00	60.00

SILVER
Obv: 10th, small nude bust.

KM#	Date	VG	Fine	VF	XF
749	1915	—	—	Unique	2300.

5 PESOS

.175 GOLD
Obv: 3rd bust, heavy, w/short unfinished lapels.

KM#	Date	VG	Fine	VF	XF
750	1915	150.00	200.00	275.00	375.00

.902 SILVER
Obv: 7th bust, short truncation w/closed lapels.

KM#	Date	VG	Fine	VF	XF
751	1915	30.00	50.00	75.00	115.00

COPPER

KM#	Date	VG	Fine	VF	XF
751a	1915	65.00	100.00	200.00	300.00

10 PESOS

.150 GOLD
Obv: 4th bust.

KM#	Date	VG	Fine	VF	XF
A752	1915	—	—	Rare	—

.175 GOLD

Obv: 5th bust.

KM#	Date	VG	Fine	VF	XF
752	1915	200.00	275.00	375.00	500.00

COPPER

752a	1915	300.00	500.00	1000.	2000.

20 PESOS

.150 GOLD
Obv: 4th bust.

A753	1915	—	—	Unique	—

.175 GOLD
Obv: 5th bust, heavy, w/short unfinished lapels, centered high.

753	1915	400.00	600.00	800.00	1000.

Obv: 7th bust, short truncation w/closed lapels.

754	1915	200.00	300.00	400.00	625.00

60 PESOS

.859 GOLD, reeded edge

KM#	Date	Fine	VF	XF	Unc
755	1916	—	—	Rare	—

NOTE: Bowers and Merena Guia sale 3-88 Unc. realized $13,200.

GOLD

755a	1916 (restrike)	—	—	2250.	3500.

SILVER, reeded edge

755b	1916 (restrike)	—	—	—	25.00

COPPER, plain edge

755c	1916 (restrike)	—	—	—	15.00

PUEBLA

A state of central Mexico. Puebla was a state that occasionally saw Zapata forces active within its boundaries. Also active, and an issuer of coins, was the Madero brigade who issued coins with their name 2 years after Madero's death. The state issue of 2, 5, 10 and 20 centavos saw limited circulation and recent hoards have been found of some values.

CHICONCUAUTLA

MADERO BRIGADE

10 CENTAVOS

COPPER

KM#	Date	VG	Fine	VF	XF
756	1915	7.50	12.50	17.50	25.00

20 CENTAVOS

COPPER
Rev: TRANSITORIO between rosettes.

757	1915	2.50	4.00	6.00	9.00

Rev: TRANSITORIO w/o rosettes.

758	1915	7.00	12.00	17.00	25.00

TETELA DEL ORO Y OCAMPO

2 CENTAVOS

COPPER, 17mm

759	1915	12.50	20.00	28.00	50.00
	1915(restrikes)	2.00	3.00	5.00	7.50

Rev. leg. ends: E.DE PU.

760	1915	15.00	25.00	35.00	75.00

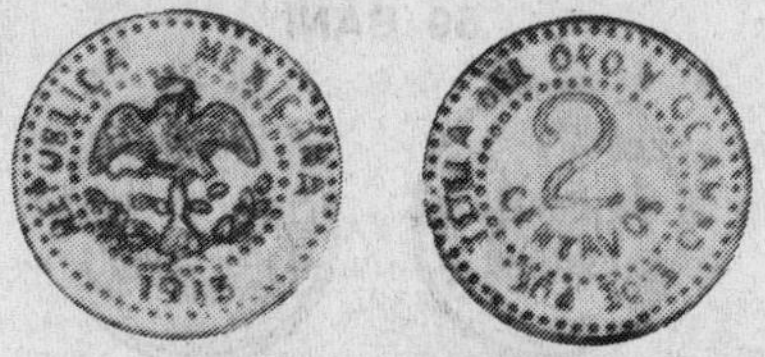

Rev. leg. ends: E.DE PUE.

761	1915	9.00	15.00	22.50	35.00

5 CENTAVOS

COPPER

762	1915	50.00	100.00	150.00	250.00

20 CENTAVOS

COPPER

KM#	Date	VG	Fine	VF	XF
764	1915	50.00	100.00	150.00	225.00

SINALOA

A state along the west coast of Mexico. The cast pieces of this state have been attributed to two people - Generals Rafael Buelna and Juan Carrasco. The cap and rays 8 reales is usually attributed to General Buelna and the rest of the series to Carrasco. Because of their crude nature it is questionable whether separate series or mints can be determined.

BUELNA/CARRASCO ISSUES

NOTE: These are all crude sand cast coins using regular coins to prepare the mold. Prices below give a range for how much of the original coin from which the mold was prepared is visible.

20 CENTAVOS

SILVER (cast)
Sand molded using regular 20 Centavos.

KM#	Date	Good	VG	Fine	VF
765	ND(1898-1905)	200.00	300.00	—	—

50 CENTAVOS

SILVER (cast)
Sand molded using regular 50 Centavos, KM#445.

766	ND(1905-18)	200.00	300.00	—	—

Obv: W/additional c/m: G.C.

767	ND(1905-18)	200.00	350.00	500.00	600.00

PESO

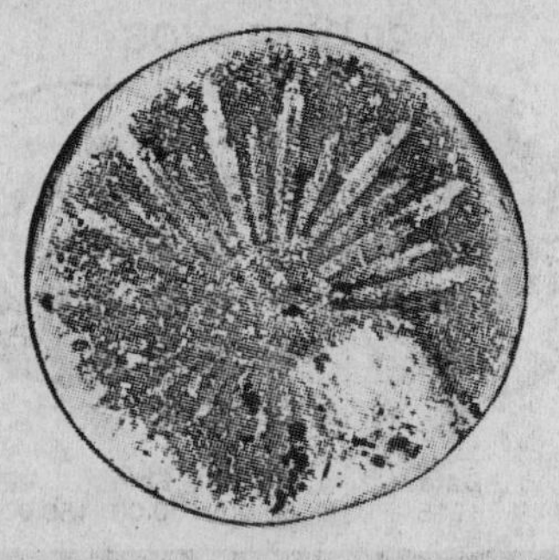

SILVER (cast)
Sand molded using regular 8 Reales, KM#377.

KM#	Date	Good	VG	Fine	VF
768.1	ND(1824-97)	17.50	35.00	45.00	65.00
	Obv: W/additional c/m: G.C.				
768.2	ND(1824-97)	25.00	45.00	100.00	150.00

Sand molded using regular Peso, KM#409.

KM#	Date	Good	VG	Fine	VF
769	ND(1898-1909)	17.50	35.00	45.00	65.00

Rev: W/additional c/m: G.C.

KM#	Date	Good	VG	Fine	VF
770	ND(1898-1909)	30.00	60.00	140.00	200.00

MOLDOVA

The Republic of Moldova (formerly the Moldavian S.S.R.) is bordered in the east and south by the Ukraine and on the west by Romania. It has an area of 13,000 sq. mi. (33,700 sq. km.) and a population of 4.4 million. Fish, agricultural products including canned goods, steel, concrete and dairy products are leading industries.

The Moldavian A.S.S.R. was created on Oct. 12, 1924, as part of the Ukrainian S.S.R., a Soviet protest against the recovery of Bessarabia by Romania. In 1940 Romania yielded to a Soviet ultimatum and ceded Bessarabia to the U.S.S.R. and the Soviet government formed a Moldavian S.S.R. comprised of the major part of Bessarabia. In June 1941, the Romanians allied with Germany reincorporated the whole of Bessarabia into Romania. Soviet armies reconquered it late in 1944 restoring the Moldavian S.S.R. A new constitution was adopted in April 1978. A declaration of republican sovereignty was adopted in June 1990 and the area was renamed Moldova, an independent republic, declared in Aug. 1991. In Dec. 1991 Moldova became a member of the Commonwealth of Independent States. Separatists and governement forces clashed in 1992. A joint declaration by Russian and Moldavian presidents on July 3, 1992 envisaged a demarcation line held by neutral forces and withdrawl of the Russian army from Transdniestria, which had developed into a self-styled republic.

RULERS

Romanian, until 1940

MONETARY SYSTEM

100 Bani = 1 Leu

BAN

ALUMINUM

KM#	Date	Mintage	VF	XF	Unc
1	1993	—	—	—	.50

5 BANI

ALUMINUM

KM#	Date	Mintage	VF	XF	Unc
2	1993	—	—	—	.75

25 BANI

ALUMINUM

KM#	Date	Mintage	VF	XF	Unc
3	1993	—	—	—	1.00

50 BANI

ALUMINUM

KM#	Date	Mintage	VF	XF	Unc
4	1993	—	—	—	1.25

LEU

NICKEL CLAD STEEL

KM#	Date	Mintage	VF	XF	Unc
5	1992	—	—	—	2.50

5 LEI

NICKEL CLAD STEEL

KM#	Date	Mintage	VF	XF	Unc
6	1993	—	—	—	5.50

Listings For

MOMBASA: refer to Kenya

MONACO

The Principality of Monaco, located on the Mediterranean coast nine miles from Nice, has an area of 0.58 sq. mi. (1.9 sq. km.) and a population of 26,000. Capital: MonacoVille. The economy is based on tourism and the manufacture of cosmetics, gourmet foods and highly specialized electronics. Monaco also derives its revenue from a tobacco monopoly and the sale of postage stamps for philatelic purpose. Gambling in Monte Carlo accounts for only a small fraction of the country's revenue.

Monaco derives its name from 'Monoikos', the Greek surname for Hercules, the mythological strong man who, according to legend, formed the Monacan headland during one of his twelve labors. Monaco has been ruled by the Grimaldi dynasty since 1297 - Prince Rainier III, the present and 31st monarch of Monaco, is still of that line - except for a period during the French Revolution until Napoleon's downfall when the Principality was annexed to France. Since 1865, Monaco has maintained a customs union with France which guarantees its privileged position as long as the royal line remains intact. Under the new constitution proclaimed on December 17, 1962, the Prince shares his power with an 18-member unicameral National Council.

RULERS

Honore IV, 1795-1819
Honore V, 1819-1841
Florestan I, 1841-1856
Charles III, 1856-1889
Albert I, 1889-1922
Louis II, 1922-1949
Rainier III, 1949

MINT MARKS

M - Monaco
A - Paris

PRIVY MARKS

(a) - Paris (privy marks only)
C and clasped hands - Francois Cabinas, mint director, 1837-1838
(p) - Thunderbolt - Poissy

MONETARY SYSTEM

10 Centimes = 1 Decime
10 Decimes = 1 Franc

CINQ (5) CENTIMES

CAST BRASS
Mint mark: M
Obv: Large head, BORREL F. below.

KM#	Date	Mintage	VG	Fine	VF	XF
95.1	1837 C	—	5.00	12.00	25.00	60.00
	COPPER, struck					
95.1a	1837 C	—	3.50	7.00	15.00	50.00

CAST BRASS
Obv: Small head, BORREL F. below.

KM#	Date	Mintage	VG	Fine	VF	XF
95.2	1837 C	—	4.00	10.00	20.00	50.00
	1838 C	—	— Reported, not confirmed			
	COPPER, struck					
95.2a	1837 C	—	3.50	7.00	15.00	45.00
	1838 C	—	12.00	25.00	50.00	125.00

UN (1) DECIME

COPPER, struck
Mint mark: M
Obv: BORREL F. below head.
Rev: Knot of wreath tied.

KM#	Date	Mintage	VG	Fine	VF	XF
97.1	1838 C	—	10.00	15.00	50.00	110.00
	BRASS, cast					
97.1a	1838 C	—	7.50	12.00	60.00	115.00

COPPER, struck
Obv: Smaller head, BORREL F. below.
Rev: Knot of wreath untied.

KM#	Date	Mintage	VG	Fine	VF	XF
97.2	1838 C	—	25.00	55.00	150.00	350.00
	BRASS, struck					
97.2a	1838 C	—	50.00	150.00	250.00	400.00

50 CENTIMES

ALUMINUM-BRONZE

KM#	Date	Mintage	Fine	VF	XF	Unc
110	1924(p)	.150	7.00	12.00	20.00	50.00
113	1926(p)	.100	8.00	15.00	30.00	60.00

FRANC

ALUMINUM-BRONZE

KM#	Date	Mintage	Fine	VF	XF	Unc
111	1924(p)	.150	6.00	12.00	20.00	45.00

KM#	Date	Mintage	Fine	VF	XF	Unc
114	1926(p)	.100	7.00	15.00	25.00	50.00

ALUMINUM

KM#	Date	Mintage	Fine	VF	XF	Unc
120	ND(1943a)	2.500	.50	1.00	2.00	5.00
	ALUMINUM-BRONZE					
120a	ND(1945a)	1.509	.50	1.00	2.00	5.00

2 FRANCS

ALUMINUM-BRONZE

KM#	Date	Mintage	Fine	VF	XF	Unc
112	1924(p)	.075	12.50	20.00	40.00	100.00

KM#	Date	Mintage	Fine	VF	XF	Unc
115	1926(p)	.075	12.50	20.00	40.00	90.00

ALUMINUM

KM#	Date	Mintage	Fine	VF	XF	Unc
121	ND(1943a)	1.250	.75	1.50	5.00	15.00
	ALUMINUM-BRONZE					
121a	ND(1945a)	1.080	.50	1.00	2.50	6.50

5 FRANCS

25.0000 g, .900 SILVER, .7234 oz ASW
Mint mark: M

KM#	Date	Mintage	Fine	VF	XF	Unc
96	1837	—	350.00	750.00	1250.	3500.

ALUMINUM

KM#	Date	Mintage	Fine	VF	XF	Unc
122	1945(a)	1.000	1.50	3.00	8.00	18.00

10 FRANCS

COPPER-NICKEL

KM#	Date	Mintage	Fine	VF	XF	Unc
123	1946(a)	1.000	1.50	3.00	7.00	15.00

ALUMINUM-BRONZE

KM#	Date	Mintage	Fine	VF	XF	Unc
130	1950(a)	.500	.50	1.00	2.00	5.00
	1951(a)	.500	.50	1.00	2.00	5.00

VINGT (20) FRANCS

6.4516 g, .900 GOLD, .1867 oz AGW

KM#	Date	Mintage	Fine	VF	XF	Unc
98	1878A	.025	120.00	200.00	300.00	600.00
	1879A	.050	80.00	150.00	200.00	500.00

COPPER-NICKEL

KM#	Date	Mintage	Fine	VF	XF	Unc
124	1947(a)	1.000	2.00	4.00	8.00	18.00

ALUMINUM-BRONZE

KM#	Date	Mintage	Fine	VF	XF	Unc
131	1950(a)	.500	.75	1.50	3.00	8.00
	1951(a)	.500	.75	1.50	3.00	8.00

CINQUANTE (50) FRANCS

ALUMINUM-BRONZE

KM#	Date	Mintage	Fine	VF	XF	Unc
132	1950(a)	.500	1.50	3.00	8.00	18.00

CENT (100) FRANCS

32.2580 g, .900 GOLD, .9335 oz AGW

KM#	Date	Mintage	Fine	VF	XF	Unc
99	1882A	5,000	400.00	600.00	800.00	1200.
	1884A	.015	BV	500.00	650.00	850.00
	1886A	.015	BV	500.00	650.00	850.00

KM#	Date	Mintage	Fine	VF	XF	Unc
105	1891A	.020	BV	500.00	600.00	750.00
	1895A	.020	BV	500.00	600.00	750.00
	1896A	.020	BV	500.00	600.00	750.00
	1901A	.015	BV	500.00	600.00	750.00
	1904A	.010	BV	500.00	600.00	750.00

COPPER-NICKEL

KM#	Date	Mintage	Fine	VF	XF	Unc
133	1950(a)	.500	2.00	4.00	8.00	18.00

KM#	Date	Mintage	Fine	VF	XF	Unc
134	1956(a)	.500	1.50	3.00	6.50	15.00

MONETARY REFORM

100 Old Francs = 1 New Franc

CENTIME

STAINLESS STEEL

KM#	Date	Mintage	Fine	VF	XF	Unc
155	1976(a)	.025	—	.10	.25	3.50
	1977(a)	.025	—	.10	.25	3.50
	1978(a)	.075	—	.10	.25	3.50
	1979(a)	.075	—	.10	.25	3.50
	1982(a)	.010	—	.10	.25	3.50

5 CENTIMES

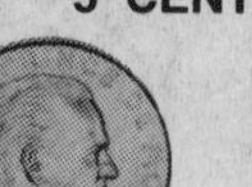

COPPER-ALUMINUM-NICKEL

KM#	Date	Mintage	Fine	VF	XF	Unc
156	1976(a)	.025	—	.15	.30	4.00
156	1977(a)	.025	—	.15	.30	4.00
	1978(a)	.075	—	.15	.30	4.00
	1979(a)	.075	—	.15	.30	4.00
	1982(a)	.010	—	.15	.30	4.00

10 CENTIMES

ALUMINUM-BRONZE

KM#	Date	Mintage	Fine	VF	XF	Unc
142	1962(a)	.750	—	.10	.20	1.00
	1974(a)	.179	—	.10	.20	1.75
	1975(a)	.172	—	.10	.20	1.75
	1976(a)	.178	—	.10	.20	1.75
	1977(a)	.172	—	.10	.20	1.75
	1978(a)	.112	—	.10	.20	2.00
	1979(a)	.112	—	.10	.20	2.00
	1982(a)	.100	—	.10	.20	2.00

20 CENTIMES

ALUMINUM-BRONZE

KM#	Date	Mintage	Fine	VF	XF	Unc
143	1962(a)	.750	—	.15	.25	1.25
	1974(a)	.104	—	.15	.25	2.25
	1975(a)	.097	—	.15	.25	2.25
	1976(a)	.103	—	.15	.25	2.25
	1977(a)	.097	—	.15	.25	2.25
	1978(a)	.081	—	.15	.25	2.25
	1979(a)	.081	—	.15	.25	2.25
	1982(a)	.100	—	.15	.25	2.25

50 CENTIMES

ALUMINUM-BRONZE

KM#	Date	Mintage	Fine	VF	XF	Unc
144	1962(a)	.375	—	1.00	2.00	5.00

1/2 FRANC

NICKEL

KM#	Date	Mintage	Fine	VF	XF	Unc
145	1965(a)	.375	.25	.50	1.00	2.00
	1968(a)	.250	.25	.50	1.00	2.00
	1974(a)	.069	.25	.50	1.00	2.75
	1975(a)	.070	.25	.50	1.00	2.75
	1976(a)	.068	.25	.50	1.00	2.75
	1977(a)	.062	.25	.50	1.00	2.75
	1978(a)	.414	.25	.50	1.00	2.25
	1979(a)	.414	.25	.50	1.00	2.25
	1982(a)	.457	.25	.50	1.00	2.25
	1989(a)	—	.25	.50	1.00	2.25

FRANC

NICKEL

KM#	Date	Mintage	Fine	VF	XF	Unc
140	1960(a)	.500	.30	.65	1.25	2.75
	1966(a)	.175	.35	.75	1.50	3.00
	1968(a)	.250	.35	.75	1.50	3.00
	1974(a)	.194	.35	.75	1.50	3.00
	1975(a)	.195	.35	.75	1.50	3.00
	1976(a)	.193	.35	.75	1.50	3.00
	1977(a)	.188	.35	.75	1.50	3.00
	1978(a)	.783	.35	.75	1.50	3.00
	1979(a)	.783	.35	.75	1.50	3.00
	1982(a)	.525	.35	.75	1.50	3.00
	1986(a)	—	.30	.60	1.25	2.75
	1989(a)	—	.30	.60	1.25	2.50

2 FRANCS

NICKEL

KM#	Date	Mintage	Fine	VF	XF	Unc
157	1979(a)	.162	.55	.75	1.50	3.50
	1981(a)	.275	.55	.75	1.50	3.50
	1982(a)	.446	.55	.75	1.50	3.50

5 FRANCS

12.0000 g, .835 SILVER, .3221 oz ASW

KM#	Date	Mintage	Fine	VF	XF	Unc
141	1960(a)	.125	—	—	7.50	11.00
	1966(a)	.125	—	—	7.50	11.00

NICKEL-CLAD COPPER-NICKEL

KM#	Date	Mintage	Fine	VF	XF	Unc
150	1971(a)	.250	—	1.50	2.50	4.50
	1974(a)	.152	—	1.50	2.50	4.50
	1975(a)	8,000	—	2.00	5.00	10.00
	1976(a)	8,000	—	2.00	5.00	10.00
	1977(a)	.042	—	2.00	5.00	10.00
	1978(a)	.022	—	2.00	5.00	10.00
	1979(a)	.022	—	2.00	5.00	10.00
	1982(a)	.152	—	2.00	5.00	10.00
	1989(a)	—	—	2.00	5.00	10.00

10 FRANCS

25.0000 g, .900 SILVER, .7234 oz ASW
10th Wedding Anniversary of Prince and Princess

KM#	Date	Mintage	Fine	VF	XF	Unc
146	1966(a)	.038	—	—	—	25.00

COPPER-NICKEL-ALUMINUM

25th Anniversary of Reign

KM#	Date	Mintage	Fine	VF	XF	Unc
151	1974(a)	.025	—	2.50	3.50	7.50

KM#	Date	Mintage	Fine	VF	XF	Unc
154	1975(a)	.025	—	2.25	3.25	7.50
	1976(a)	.016	—	2.50	3.50	8.50
	1977(a)	.050	—	2.25	2.75	5.00
	1978(a)	.228	—	2.25	2.75	5.00
	1979(a)	.228	—	2.25	2.75	5.00
	1981(a)	.235	—	2.25	2.75	5.00
	1982(a)	.230	—	2.25	2.75	5.00

Princess Grace

KM#	Date	Mintage	Fine	VF	XF	Unc
160	1982(a)	.030	—	—	—	12.50

NICKEL-ALUMINUM-BRONZE
Prince Pierre Foundation

KM#	Date	Mintage	Fine	VF	XF	Unc
162	1989(a)	—	—	—	—	6.50

ALUMINUM-BRONZE RING, STEEL CENTER

KM#	Date	Mintage	Fine	VF	XF	Unc
163	1989(a)	—	—	—	—	6.00
	1991(a)	—	—	—	—	6.00

20 FRANCS

COPPER-ALUMINUM-NICKEL center within NICKEL ring within COPPER-ALUMINUM-NICKEL ring
Prince's Palace

KM#	Date	Mintage	Fine	VF	XF	Unc
165	1992(a)	—	—	—	—	10.00

50 FRANCS

30.0000 g, .900 SILVER, .8681 oz ASW
25th Anniversary of Reign
Commemorative edge inscription.

KM#	Date	Mintage	Fine	VF	XF	Unc
152.1	1974(a)	.025	—	—	—	45.00
	Plain edge					
152.2	1975(a)	7,500	—	—	—	60.00
	1976(a)	6,000	—	—	—	65.00

100 FRANCS

15.0000 g, .900 SILVER, .4340 oz ASW
Heir Apparent Prince Albert

KM#	Date	Mintage	Fine	VF	XF	Unc
161	1982(a)	.030	—	—	—	85.00

40th Anniversary of Reign

KM#	Date	Mintage	Fine	VF	XF	Unc
164	1989(a)	.045	—	—	—	85.00

SPECIMEN SETS (SS)

Fleur de Coin

KM#	Date	Mintage	Identification	Issue Price	Mkt. Val.
SS1	1974(7)	*7,000	KM140,142-143,145, 150-151,152.1	45.00	115.00

***NOTE:** 3,000 of the above sets were not released.

KM#	Date	Mintage	Identification	Issue Price	Mkt. Val.
SS2	1975(7)	7,500	KM140,142-143,145, 150,152.2,154	—	100.00
SS3	1976(9)	6,000	KM140,142-143,145, 150,152.2,154-156	—	110.00
SS6	1982(11)	10,000	KM140,142-143,145, 150,154-157,160-161	—	135.00

MONGOLIA

The State of Mongolia, (formerly the Mongolian Peoples Republic) a landlocked country in central Asia between Russia and the People's Republic of China, has an area of 604,250 sq. mi. (1,565,000 sq. km.) and a population of 2.26 million. Capital: Ulan Bator. Animal herds and flocks are the chief economic asset. Wool, cattle, butter, meat and hides are exported.

Mongolia (often referred to as Outer Mongolia), one of the world's oldest countries, attained its greatest power in the 13th century when Genghis Khan and his successors conquered all of China and extended their influence westward as far as Hungary and Poland. The empire dissolved in later centuries and in 1691 was brought under suzerainty of the Manchus, who had conquered China in 1644. After the Chinese republican movement led by Sun Yat-sen overthrew the Manchus and set up the Chinese Republic in 1911, Mongolia, with the support of Russia, proclaimed their independence from China and, on March 13, 1921 a Provisional Peoples Government was established and later, on Nov. 26, 1924 the government proclaimed the Mongolian Peoples Republic.

Although nominally a dependency of China, Outer Mongolia voted at a plebiscite Oct. 20, 1945 to sever all ties with China and become an independent nation. Opposition to the communist party developed in late 1989 and after demonstrations and hunger strikes, the Politburo resigned on March 12, 1990 and the new State of Mongolia was organized.

On Feb. 12, 1992 it became the first to discard communism as the national political system by adopting a new constitution.

For earlier issues see Russia - Tannu Tuva.

MONETARY SYSTEM

100 Mongo = 1 Tugrik

PEOPLES REPUBLIC

MONGO

COPPER

KM#	Year	Date	Fine	VF	XF	Unc
1	15	(1925)	5.00	7.00	10.00	17.50

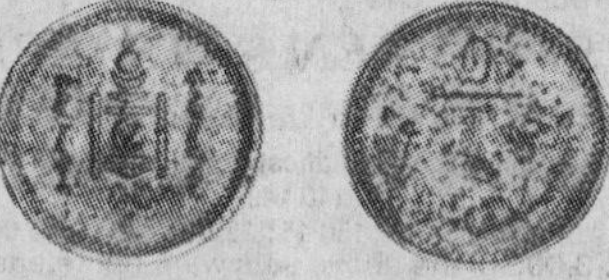

ALUMINUM-BRONZE

KM#	Year	Date	Fine	VF	XF	Unc
9	27	(1937)	2.50	3.50	6.00	12.00

KM#	Year	Date	Fine	VF	XF	Unc
15	35	(1945)	2.00	3.00	5.00	10.00

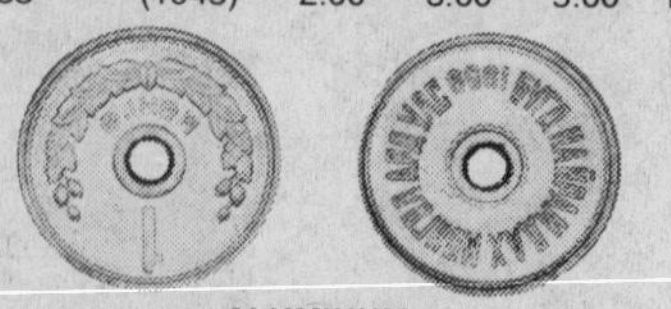

ALUMINUM

KM#	Date	Mintage	Fine	VF	XF	Unc
21	1959	9.000	.25	.75	1.25	2.00

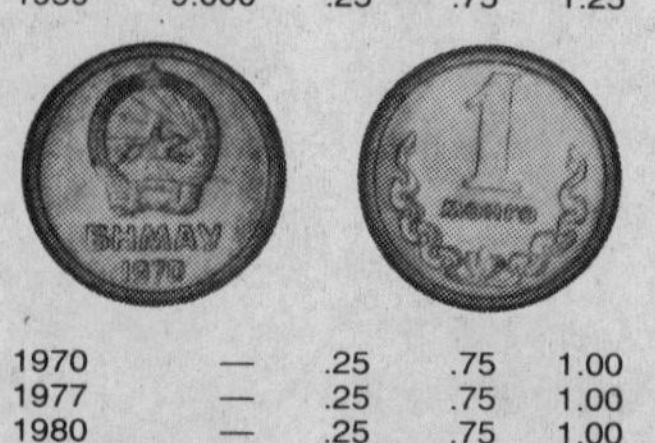

KM#	Date	Mintage	Fine	VF	XF	Unc
27	1970	—	.25	.75	1.00	1.50
	1977	—	.25	.75	1.00	1.50
	1980	—	.25	.75	1.00	1.50
	1981	—	.25	.75	1.00	1.50

2 MONGO

COPPER

KM#	Year	Date	Fine	VF	XF	Unc
2	15	(1925)	5.00	8.00	10.00	18.00

ALUMINUM-BRONZE

KM#	Year	Date	Fine	VF	XF	Unc
10	27	(1937)	2.50	3.50	5.00	10.00

KM#	Year	Date	Fine	VF	XF	Unc
16	35	(1945)	1.00	2.00	3.50	6.00

ALUMINUM

KM#	Date	Mintage	Fine	VF	XF	Unc
22	1959	4.000	.25	1.00	2.00	3.00

KM#	Date	Mintage	Fine	VF	XF	Unc
28	1970	—	.25	1.00	2.00	3.00
	1977	—	.25	1.00	2.00	3.00
	1980	—	.25	1.00	2.00	3.00
	1981	—	.25	1.00	2.00	3.00

5 MONGO

COPPER

KM#	Year	Date	Fine	VF	XF	Unc
3	15	(1925)	6.00	12.50	17.50	30.00

ALUMINUM-BRONZE

KM#	Year	Date	Fine	VF	XF	Unc
11	27	(1937)	2.75	3.50	5.00	10.00

KM#	Year	Date	Fine	VF	XF	Unc
17	35	(1945)	2.25	3.50	4.50	7.50

ALUMINUM

KM#	Date	Mintage	Fine	VF	XF	Unc
23	1959	2.400	.25	1.00	2.00	3.00

KM#	Date	Mintage	Fine	VF	XF	Unc
29	1970	—	.25	1.00	2.00	3.00
	1977	—	.25	1.00	2.00	3.00
	1980	—	.25	1.00	2.00	3.00
	1981	—	.25	1.00	2.00	3.00

10 MONGO

1.7996 g, .500 SILVER, .0289 oz ASW

KM#	Year	Date	Fine	VF	XF	Unc
4	Yr.15(1925)		1.500	3.00	5.00	8.00	15.00

COPPER-NICKEL

KM#	Year	Date	Fine	VF	XF	Unc
12	27	(1937)	2.00	3.50	6.00	12.00

KM#	Year	Date	Fine	VF	XF	Unc
18	35	(1945)	2.00	3.50	5.00	9.00

ALUMINUM

KM#	Date	Mintage	Fine	VF	XF	Unc
24	1959	3.000	.75	1.50	3.00	5.00

COPPER-NICKEL

KM#	Date	Mintage	Fine	VF	XF	Unc
30	1970	—	.75	1.50	2.50	4.00
	1977	—	.75	1.50	2.50	4.00
	1980	—	.75	1.50	2.50	4.00
	1981	—	.75	1.50	2.50	4.00

15 MONGO

2.6994 g, .500 SILVER, .0433 oz ASW

KM#	Date	Mintage	Fine	VF	XF	Unc
5	Yr.15(1925)	.417	3.50	6.00	10.00	17.50

COPPER-NICKEL

KM#	Year	Date	Fine	VF	XF	Unc
13	27	(1937)	2.00	3.00	5.00	10.00

KM#	Year	Date	Fine	VF	XF	Unc
19	35	(1945)	2.25	2.75	4.00	7.00

ALUMINUM

KM#	Date	Mintage	Fine	VF	XF	Unc
25	1959	4.600	.25	1.00	2.00	3.50

COPPER-NICKEL

KM#	Date	Mintage	Fine	VF	XF	Unc
31	1970	—	.25	1.00	2.00	3.00
	1977	—	.25	1.00	2.00	3.00
	1980	—	.25	1.00	2.00	3.00
	1981	—	.25	1.00	2.00	3.00

20 MONGO

3.5992 g, .500 SILVER, .0578 oz ASW

KM#	Date	Mintage	Fine	VF	XF	Unc
6	Yr.15(1925)	1.625	5.00	8.00	12.00	20.00

COPPER-NICKEL

KM#	Year	Date	Fine	VF	XF	Unc
14	27	(1937)	3.00	5.00	8.00	16.00

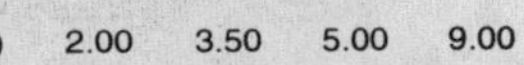

KM#	Year	Date	Fine	VF	XF	Unc
20	35	(1945)	2.00	3.50	5.00	9.00

ALUMINUM

KM#	Date	Mintage	Fine	VF	XF	Unc
26	1959	3.600	.75	1.50	2.50	3.50

COPPER-NICKEL

KM#	Date	Mintage	Fine	VF	XF	Unc
32	1970	—	.50	1.00	2.00	3.00
	1977	—	.50	1.00	2.00	3.00
	1980	—	.50	1.00	2.00	3.00
	1981	—	.50	1.00	2.00	3.00

50 MONGO

9.9979 g, .900 SILVER, .2893 oz ASW

KM#	Date	Mintage	Fine	VF	XF	Unc
7	Yr.15(1925)	.920	8.50	12.50	20.00	35.00

COPPER-NICKEL

KM#	Date	Mintage	Fine	VF	XF	Unc
33	1970	—	.50	1.50	2.50	5.00
	1977	—	.50	1.50	2.50	5.00
	1980	—	.50	1.50	2.50	5.00
	1981	—	.50	1.50	2.50	5.00

TUGRIK

19.9957 g, .900 SILVER, .5786 oz ASW

KM#	Date	Mintage	Fine	VF	XF	Unc
8	Yr.15(1925)	.400	15.00	18.00	25.00	45.00

ALUMINUM-BRONZE
50th Anniversary of the Revolution
Date on edge.

KM#	Date	Mintage	Fine	VF	XF	Unc
34	1971	—	5.00	7.00	9.00	12.00
	COPPER-NICKEL					
34a	1971	—	6.00	8.00	12.00	18.00
	18.4000 g, SILVER					
34b	1971	—	—	—	Proof	50.00
	30.3000 g, GOLD					
34c	1971	5-10 pcs.	—	—	Proof	2500.

ALUMINUM-BRONZE
60th Anniversary of the Revolution

KM#	Date	Mintage	Fine	VF	XF	Unc
41	1981	—	—	—	4.50	8.00

Soviet - Mongolian Space Flight

KM#	Date	Mintage	Fine	VF	XF	Unc
42	1981	—	—	—	3.50	6.50

60th Anniversary of the State Bank

KM#	Date	Mintage	Fine	VF	XF	Unc
43	1984	—	—	—	3.50	6.00

NOTE: Edge varieties exist.

60th Anniversary of the Peoples Republic

KM#	Date	Mintage	Fine	VF	XF	Unc
44	1984	—	—	—	3.50	6.00

Year of Peace

KM#	Date	Mintage	Fine	VF	XF	Unc
48	1986	—	—	—	3.50	6.00

65th Anniversary of the Revolution

KM#	Date	Mintage	Fine	VF	XF	Unc
49	1986	—	—	—	3.50	6.00

170th Anniversary of Birth of Karl Marx

KM#	Date	Mintage	Fine	VF	XF	Unc
52	1988	—	—	—	—	8.00

10 TUGRIK

COPPER-NICKEL
50th Anniversary of State Bank

KM#	Date	Mintage	VF	XF	Unc
35	1974	—	—	—	7.50

25 TUGRIK

28.2800 g, .925 SILVER, .8411 oz ASW
Conservation - Argali Sheep

KM#	Date	Mintage	VF	XF	Unc
36	1976	5,348	—	—	22.50
	1976	6,096	—	Proof	30.00

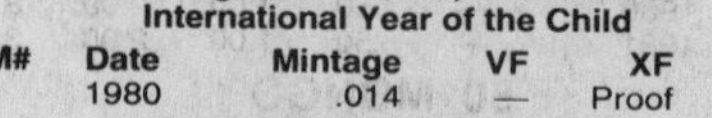

19.4400 g, .925 SILVER, .5781 oz ASW
International Year of the Child

KM#	Date	Mintage	VF	XF	Unc
39	1980	.014	—	Proof	20.00

Decade For Women

KM#	Date	Mintage	VF	XF	Unc
47	1984	1,249	—	Proof	35.00

28.2800 g, .925 SILVER, .8411 oz ASW
World Wildlife Fund - Panther

KM#	Date	Mintage	VF	XF	Unc
50	1987	850 pcs.		Matte Unc.	140.00
	1987	.025	—	Proof	50.00

Save the Children Fund

KM#	Date	Mintage	VF	XF	Unc
54	1989	.020	—	Proof	40.00

50 TUGRIK

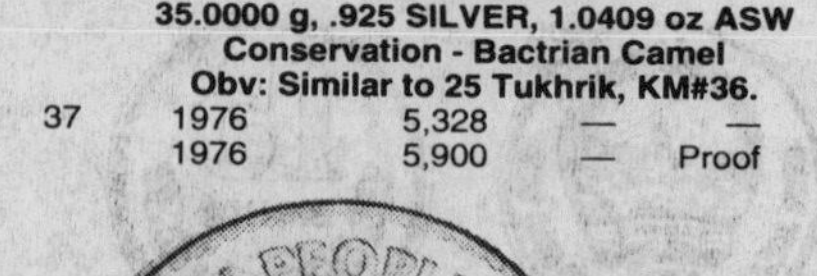

35.0000 g, .925 SILVER, 1.0409 oz ASW
Conservation - Bactrian Camel
Obv: Similar to 25 Tukhrik, KM#36.

KM#	Date	Mintage	VF	XF	Unc
37	1976	5,328	—	—	30.00
	1976	5,900	—	Proof	40.00

31.1000 g, .999 SILVER, 1.0000 oz ASW
Discovery of America - Columbus

KM#	Date	Mintage	VF	XF	Unc
57.1	1992	.020	—	Proof	50.00

Mule. Obv: KM#61. Rev: KM#57.

KM#	Date	Mintage	VF	XF	Unc
57.2	1992	—	—	Proof	60.00

100 TUGRIK

28.0000 g, .900 SILVER, .8102 oz ASW
Dinosaurs-Nemectosaurus

KM#	Date	Mintage	VF	XF	Unc
53	1989	1,000	—	—	75.00

Secret History of the Mongols
Obv: State emblem above denomination within English leg.
Rev: Portrait of Genghis Khan in light clothing.

KM#	Date	Mintage	VF	XF	Unc
55	1990	*4,000	—	—	50.00

1.5600 g, .999 GOLD, .0500 oz AGW
Discovery of America - Columbus
Similar to 50 Tugrik, KM#57.

KM#	Date	Mintage	VF	XF	Unc
58	1992	*.010	—	Proof	70.00

200 TUGRIK

3.1100 g, .999 GOLD, .1000 oz AGW
Discovery of America - Columbus
Similar to 50 Tugrik, KM#57.

KM#	Date	Mintage	VF	XF	Unc
59	1992	*.010	—	Proof	90.00

250 TUGRIK

7.1300 g, .900 GOLD, .2062 oz AGW
Decade for Women

KM#	Date	Mintage	VF	XF	Unc
45	1984	510 pcs.	—	Proof	225.00

300 TUGRIK

7.7700 g, .999 GOLD, .2500 oz AGW
Japanese Royal Wedding
Similar to 500 Tugrik, KM#73.

KM#	Date	Mintage	VF	XF	Unc
72	1993	*500 pcs.	—	Proof	250.00

750 TUGRIK

33.4370 g, .900 GOLD, .9676 oz AGW
Conservation - Przewalski Horses

KM#	Date	Mintage	VF	XF	Unc
38	1976	929 pcs.	—	—	600.00
	1976	374 pcs.	—	Proof	850.00

18.7900 g, .900 GOLD, .5437 oz AGW
International Year of the Child

KM#	Date	Mintage	VF	XF	Unc
40	1980	.032	—	Proof	250.00

1000 TUGRIK

20.7000 g, .900 GOLD, .5990 oz AGW
Secret History of the Mongols
Obv: State emblem above denomination within English leg.
Rev: Portrait of Genghis Khan in heavy clothing.

KM#	Date	Mintage	VF	XF	Unc
56	1990	*1,000	—	—	425.00

31.1000 g, .999 GOLD, 1.0000 oz AGW
Discovery of America - Columbus

KM#	Date	Mintage	VF	XF	Unc
60	1992	2,000	—	Proof	690.00

STATE OF MONGOLIA

50 TUGRIK

31.1000 g, .999 SILVER, 1.0000 oz ASW
Year of the Rooster

KM#	Date	Mintage	VF	XF	Unc
61	1993	.020	—	Proof	50.00

Japanese Royal Wedding

KM#	Date	Mintage	VF	XF	Unc
69	1993	1,962	—	Proof	60.00

Year of the Dog

KM#	Date	Mintage	VF	XF	Unc
75	1994	4,000	—	Proof	50.00

100 TUGRIK

1.5600 g, .999 GOLD, .0500 oz AGW
Year of the Rooster
Similar to 50 Tugrik, KM#61.

KM#	Date	Mintage	VF	XF	Unc
62	1992	.030	—	Proof	65.00

Japanese Royal Wedding
Similar to 50 Tugrik, KM#69.

KM#	Date	Mintage	VF	XF	Unc
70	1993	*3,000	—	Proof	75.00

200 TUGRIK

3.1100 g, .999 GOLD, .1000 oz AGW
Year of the Rooster
Similar to 50 Tugrik, KM#61.

KM#	Date	Mintage	VF	XF	Unc
63	1993	500 pcs.	—	Proof	100.00

Japanese Royal Wedding
Similar to 50 Tugrik, KM#69.

KM#	Date	Mintage	VF	XF	Unc
71	1993	100 pcs.	—	Proof	100.00

Year of the Dog

KM#	Date	Mintage	VF	XF	Unc
76	1994	500 pcs.	—	Proof	100.00

250 TUGRIK

155.5000 g, .999 SILVER, 5.0000 oz ASW
Year of the Rooster
Similar to 50 Tugrik, KM#61.

KM#	Date	Mintage	VF	XF	Unc
64	1992	300 pcs.	—	Proof	300.00

Illustration reduced. Actual size: 65mm.
Year of the Dog

KM#	Date	Mintage	VF	XF	Unc
77	1994	200 pcs.	—	Proof	300.00

31.4700 g, .925 SILVER, .9359 oz ASW
Wildlife - Wolves

KM#	Date	Mintage	VF	XF	Unc
80	1993	*.015	—	Proof	40.00

500 TUGRIK

15.5500 g, .999 GOLD, .5000 oz AGW
Japanese Royal Wedding
Similar to 500 Tugrik, KM#73.

KM#	Date	Mintage	VF	XF	Unc
73	1993	160 pcs.	—	Proof	450.00

600 TUGRIK

373.2000 g, .999 SILVER, 12.0000 oz ASW
Year of the Rooster
Similar to 50 Tugrik, KM#61.

KM#	Date	Mintage	VF	XF	Unc
65	1992	200 pcs.	—	Proof	500.00

1000 TUGRIK

31.1000 g, .999 GOLD, 1.0000 oz AGW
Year of the Rooster
Similar to 50 Tugrik, KM#61.

KM#	Date	Mintage	VF	XF	Unc
66	1992	1,000	—	Proof	700.00

Japanese Royal Wedding

KM#	Date	Mintage	VF	XF	Unc
74	1993	145 pcs.	—	Proof	800.00

31.1035 g, .999 GOLD, 1.0000 oz AGW
Year of the Dog

78	1994	300 pcs.	—	Proof	700.00

5000 TUGRIK

155.5000 g, .999 GOLD, 5.0000 oz AGW
Year of the Rooster
country name at right. Rev: Rooster.

67	1992	500 pcs.	—	Proof	2750.

Year of the Dog

79	1994	25 pcs.	—	Proof	2750.

12000 TUGRIK

373.2000 g, .999 GOLD, 12.0000 oz AGW
Year of the Rooster
Similar to 50 Tugrik, KM#61.

68	1992	25 pcs.	—	Proof	—

BULLION ISSUES

4000 TUGRIK

15.5940 g, .9999 GOLD, .5000 oz AGW
Chinggis Khan

81	1992	*9,000	—	Proof	650.00

8000 TUGRIK

31.1620 g, .9999 GOLD, 1.0000 oz AGW
Chinggis Khan

82	1992	*3,000	—	Proof	1200.

250,000 TUGRIK

1000.1000 g, .9999 GOLD, 32.1575 oz AGW
Illustration reduced. Actual size: 85mm.
Chinggis Khan

KM#	Date	Mintage	VF	XF	Unc
83	1992	*300 pcs.	—	Proof	30,600.

Listings For

MONTENEGRO: refer to Yugoslavia

MONTSERRAT

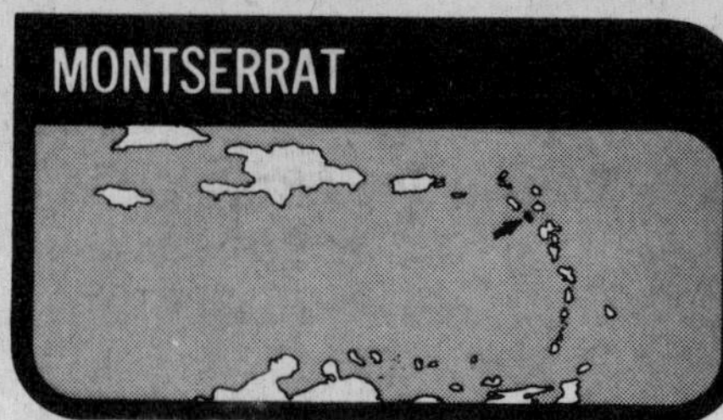

Montserrat, a British crown colony located in the Lesser Antilles of the West Indies 27 miles (43 km.) southwest of Antigua, has an area of 38 sq. mi. (100 sq. km.) and a population of 18,500. Capital: Plymouth. The island - actually a range of volcanic peaks rising from the Caribbean - exports cotton, limes and vegetables.

Columbus discovered Montserrat in 1493 and named it after Monserrado, a mountain in Spain. It was colonized by the English in 1632 and, except for brief periods of French occupancy in 1667 and 1782-83, has remained a British possession from that time. Currency of the British Caribbean Territories (Eastern Group) was used until later when the East Caribbean States coinage was introduced. Until becoming a separate colony in 1956, Montserrat was a presidency of the Leeward Islands.

The early 19th century countermarks of a crowned 3, 4, 7, 9 or 18 over M as documented by Major Pridmore have been more correctly listed under St. Bartholomew.

RULERS

British

MONETARY SYSTEM

100 Cents = 1 Dollar

4 DOLLARS

COPPER-NICKEL
F.A.O. Issue

KM#	Date	Mintage	Fine	VF	XF	Unc
30	1970	.013	—	—	6.00	8.00
	1970	2,000	—	—	Proof	20.00

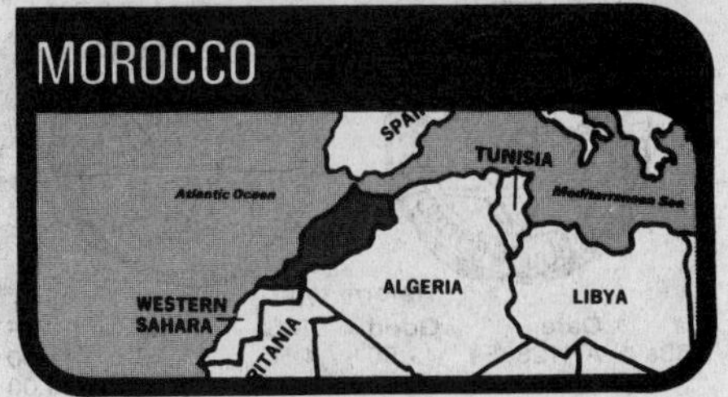

The Kingdom of Morocco, situated on the northwest corner of Africa, has an area of 275,117 sq. mi. (446,550 sq. km.) and a population of 22.5 million. Capital: Rabat. The economy is essentially agricultural. Phosphates, fresh and preserved vegetables, canned fish, and raw materials are exported.

Morocco's strategic position at the gateway to western Europe has been the principal determinant of its violent, frequently unfortunate history. Time and again the fertile plain between the rugged Atlas Mountains and the sea has echoed the battle's trumpet as Phoenicians, Romans, Vandals, Visigoths, Byzantine Greeks and Islamic Arabs successively conquered and occupied the land. Modern Morocco is a remnant of an early empire formed by the Arabs at the close of the 7th century which encompassed all of northwest Africa and most of the Iberian Peninsula. During the 17th and 18th centuries, while under the control of native dynasties, it was the headquarters of the famous Sale pirates. Morocco's strategic position involved it in the competition of 19th century European powers for political influence in Africa, and resulted in the division of Morocco into French and Spanish spheres of interest which were established as protectorates in 1912. Morocco became independent on March 2, 1956, after France agreed to end its protectorate. Spain signed similar agreements on April 7 of the same year.

TITLES

المعربية

Al-Maghribiya(t)

المملكة المغربية

Al-Mamlaka(t) al-Maghribiya(t)

المحمدية الشريفة

Al-Mohammediya(t) esh-Sherifiya(t)

RULERS

Filali Sharifs

Suleiman II
AH1206-1238/1792-1822AD
'Abd al-Rahman II
AH1238-1276/1822-1859AD
Mohammed IV
AH1276-1290/1859-1873AD
Al-Hasan I (Moulai Hasan)
AH1290-1311/1873-1894AD
'Abd al-Aziz
AH1311-1326/1894-1908AD
Al-Hafiz
AH1326-1330/1908-1912AD

French Protectorate
AH1330/1912AD

Yusuf
AH1330-1346/1912-1927AD
Mohammed V
AH1346-1375/1927-1955AD

Kingdom

Mohammed V
AH1376-1381/1956-1962AD
Al-Hasan II
AH1381/1962AD

EARLY COINAGE

Prior to the introduction of modern machine-struck coinage in Morocco in AH1299 (= 1882AD), a variety of primitive cast bronze coins and crudely hammered silver and gold were in circulation, together with considerable quantities of foreign coins.

The cast bronze were produced in several denominations, multiples of the basic unit. the Falus. The size of the coins is variable, and the distinction of the various denominations is not always clear, particularly on the issues of Sulaiman. The early types are varied, but beginning about AH1218, the reverse bears the seal of Solomon, and the obverse contains the date and/or mint. Error strikes with the seal of Solomon on both sides exist. The date is inscribed in European numerals, the mint, when present, is written out in Arabic script. Many of the issues are quite barbarous, with illegible dates and mints, and occasionally light in weight. These barbarous issues may have been contemporary counterfeits, and are of little numismatic value. The bronze pieces were cast in trees, and occasionally, entire or partial 'trees' are found on the market.

The silver and gold coins usually have the mintname on one side and the date on the other. The silver unit was the dirham of about 2.7 grams (but only about 2.0 grams from circa AH 1266-78), and the gold unit was the benduqi of about 3.25 grams. There were no fixed rates of exchange between coins of different metals.

Prices are for specimens with clearly legible dates and mintnames (if any). Illegible, barbarous, and defectively produced pieces are worth much less.

MINTS

(a) - Paris privy marks only

Bi - Angland (Birmingham) بانكلند

Ln = bi-Angland (London) بانكلند

Lr = al-'Araish (Larache) العرايش

Lr = al-'Araisah (Larache) العرايشة

As = Asfi (Safi) اسفي

Pa = bi-Bariz (Paris) بباريز

Be = Berlin برلين

EM = Essaouir (Mogador) السويرة

Fs = Fes (Fas, Fez) فاس

FH = Fes Hazrat فاس حضرة

KH = al-Kitaoua Hazrat الكتوة حضرة

Ma = Madrid مدريد

MH = Marakesh Hazrat مراكش حضرة

Mr = Marrakesh (Marakesh) مراكش

Mk = Miknas (Meknes) مكناس

Miknasah مكناسة

MB = Moulay-Ibrahim مولاي ابراهيم

Py - Poissy Inscribed "Paris" but with thunderbolt privy mark.

Rb = Rabat رباط

RF = Rabat al-Fath رباط الفتح

Si = Sijilmasah سجلماسة

Sus سوس

Sr = al-Suwair الصوير

Sh = al-Suwairah الصويرة

Tg = Tanjah (Tangier) طنجة

Te = Tetuan تطوان

(NM) = No mint name on coin.

NOTE: Some of the above forms of the mintnames are shown as they appear on the coins, not in regular Arabic script.

The following coins are divided by reign. However, all of the coins are anonymous, and the distinction by reign is purely artificial. There is much variation within each type, and several of the subtypes overlap more than one reign. The coinage of Sulaiman II and Abd al-Rahman II are listed only by type (dates through AH1276 inclusive); those of Muhammad IV (beginning AH1277 inclusive) and those of Al Hasan I (Moulai Hasan) are broken down by mint and date. The date listings for these two rulers, however, are believed to be very incomplete.

Suleiman II

AH1206-1238/1792-1822AD

FALUS

BRONZE

C#	Date	Good	VG	Fine	VF
95	AH1209-38	1.50	2.50	6.00	15.00

2 FALUS

BRONZE

C#	Date	Good	VG	Fine	VF
96	AH1209-38	2.00	3.00	6.00	15.00

4 FALUS

BRONZE

C#	Date	Good	VG	Fine	VF
98	AH1212-17	6.00	10.00	15.00	25.00

1/2 DIRHAM

SILVER, 15-18mm, 1.22 g

C#	Date	Good	VG	Fine	VF
105	AH1211-16	5.00	8.50	15.00	25.00

DIRHAM

SILVER, 17-20mm, 2.44-2.70 g

C#	Date	Good	VG	Fine	VF
108	AH1211-37	4.00	7.00	14.00	20.00

1/2 BENDUQI

GOLD, 1.76 g
Mintname: Hadrat Fes

C#	Date	VG	Fine	VF	XF
114	AH1232	90.00	150.00	250.00	375.00
	1236	90.00	150.00	250.00	375.00

BENDUQI

GOLD, 3.52 g
Mintname: Hadrat Fes

C#	Date	VG	Fine	VF	XF
115	AH1216	70.00	100.00	150.00	225.00
	1217	70.00	100.00	150.00	225.00
	1218	70.00	100.00	150.00	225.00
	1219	70.00	100.00	150.00	225.00
	1220	70.00	100.00	150.00	225.00
	1224	70.00	100.00	150.00	225.00

C#	Date	VG	Fine	VF	XF
115	1234	70.00	100.00	150.00	225.00
	1235	70.00	100.00	150.00	225.00
	1238	70.00	100.00	150.00	225.00

NOTE: Earlier dates (AH1209-14) exist for this type.

'Abd al-Rahman

AH1238-1276/1822-1859AD

1/2 FALUS

(Zelagh)

BRONZE, 13-14mm
Rev: Flower design.

C#	Date	Good	VG	Fine	VF
120	ND	2.00	3.50	6.00	10.00

Rev: Date.

C#	Date	Good	VG	Fine	VF
121	AH1245	5.00	10.00	20.00	40.00
	1263	5.00	10.00	20.00	40.00
	1268	5.00	10.00	20.00	40.00
	1270	5.00	10.00	20.00	40.00

FALUS

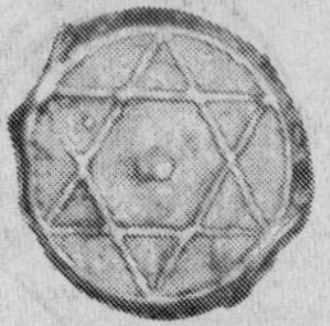

BRONZE, 17-20mm

C#	Date	Good	VG	Fine	VF
122	AH1240-76	1.00	3.00	5.00	8.00

NOTE: Many varieties exist.

2 FALUS

BRONZE, 22mm

C#	Date	Good	VG	Fine	VF
126	AH1240-76	1.00	2.00	4.00	6.00

NOTE: Many varieties exist.

3 FALUS

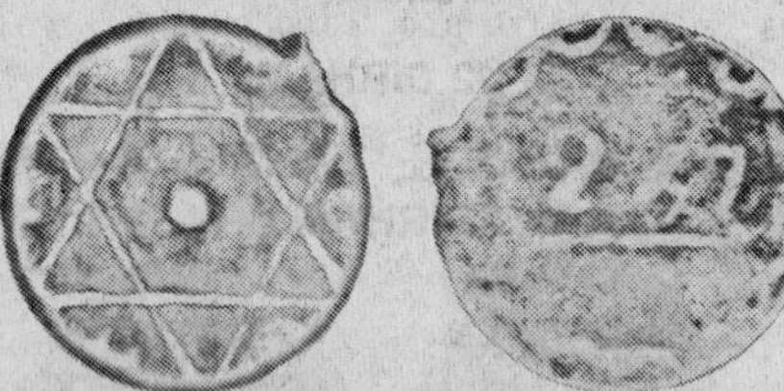

BRONZE, 25-28mm

C#	Date	Good	VG	Fine	VF
128	AH1264-69	2.50	4.50	7.50	12.50

NOTE: Many varieties exist.

1/2 DIRHAM

SILVER, 15-18mm, 1.30-1.40 g

C#	Date	Good	VG	Fine	VF
135	AH1241-64	3.50	6.00	10.00	20.00

DIRHAM

SILVER, 17-20mm, 2.70 g

C#	Date	Good	VG	Fine	VF
140	AH1240-52	4.00	7.00	11.00	22.50

Reduced standard, 2.00 g.

C#	Date	Good	VG	Fine	VF
140a	AH1266-76	3.25	6.00	10.00	20.00

1/2 BENDUQI

GOLD, 1.76 g

Mintname: Hadrat Fes

C#	Date	VG	Fine	VF	XF
145	AH1240	75.00	125.00	175.00	250.00
	1247	75.00	125.00	175.00	250.00
	1248	75.00	125.00	175.00	250.00
	1252	75.00	125.00	175.00	250.00

BENDUQI

GOLD, 3.52 g
Mintname: Hadrat Fes

C#	Date	VG	Fine	VF	XF
150.1	AH1241	75.00	125.00	175.00	250.00
	1242	60.00	90.00	135.00	185.00
	1243	60.00	90.00	135.00	185.00
	1244	60.00	90.00	135.00	185.00
	1245	60.00	90.00	135.00	185.00
	1246	60.00	90.00	135.00	185.00
	1247	60.00	90.00	135.00	185.00
	1248	60.00	90.00	135.00	185.00
	1249	60.00	90.00	135.00	185.00
	1250	60.00	90.00	135.00	185.00
	1251	60.00	90.00	135.00	185.00
	1252	60.00	90.00	135.00	185.00
	1253	60.00	90.00	135.00	185.00
	1254	60.00	90.00	135.00	185.00
	1255	60.00	90.00	135.00	185.00
	1256	60.00	90.00	135.00	185.00
	1257	60.00	90.00	135.00	185.00
	1258	60.00	90.00	135.00	185.00
	1259	60.00	90.00	135.00	185.00
	1266	60.00	90.00	135.00	185.00
	1267	60.00	90.00	135.00	185.00
	1269	60.00	90.00	135.00	185.00
	1270	60.00	90.00	135.00	185.00
	1271	60.00	90.00	135.00	185.00
	1272	60.00	90.00	135.00	185.00
	1273	60.00	90.00	135.00	185.00
	1274	60.00	90.00	135.00	185.00
	1275	60.00	90.00	135.00	185.00

Mintname: Meknes

C#	Date	VG	Fine	VF	XF
150.2	AH1247	—	—	—	—

Mohammed IV

AH1276-1290/1859-1873AD

FALUS

BRONZE, 17mm
Early types.

C#	Date	Good	VG	Fine	VF
160	AH1277(NM)	1.00	2.00	4.00	10.00
	1277Fs	1.00	2.00	4.00	10.00
	1278(NM)	1.00	2.00	4.00	10.00
	1278Te	2.00	3.00	6.00	15.00
	1278Fs	1.00	2.00	4.00	10.00
	1279Te	2.00	3.00	6.00	15.00
	1280	1.00	2.00	4.00	10.00
	1281Te	2.00	3.00	6.00	15.00
	1281(NM)	1.00	2.00	4.00	10.00

NOTE: Varieties exist.

Reform type
Similar to 2 Falus, C#163a.

C#	Date	Good	VG	Fine	VF
160a	AH1283Fs	2.00	3.00	10.00	20.00
	1283Mr	2.00	3.00	10.00	20.00
	1284Fs	2.00	3.00	10.00	20.00
	1285Fs	2.00	3.00	10.00	20.00
	1286Fs	2.00	3.00	10.00	20.00
	1287Fs	2.00	3.00	10.00	20.00
	1288Fs	2.00	3.00	10.00	20.00
	1289Fs	2.00	3.00	10.00	20.00

NOTE: Varieties exist.

2 FALUS

BRONZE, 21-24mm
Early types.

C#	Date	Good	VG	Fine	VF
163	AH1277Te	1.25	2.50	6.00	15.00
	1277Fs	1.00	2.00	·4.00	10.00
	1277Mr	1.00	2.00	4.00	10.00
	1277(NM)	1.00	2.00	4.00	10.00
	1278Fs	1.00	2.00	4.00	10.00
	1278Te	1.25	2.50	6.00	15.00
	1278(NM)	1.00	2.00	4.00	10.00
	1279Fs	1.00	2.00	4.00	10.00
	1279(NM)	1.00	2.00	4.00	10.00
	1280(NM)	1.00	2.00	4.00	10.00
	1281Fs	1.00	2.00	4.00	10.00
	1281Te	1.25	2.50	6.00	15.00
	1281(NM)	1.00	2.00	4.00	10.00

NOTE: 1281 Fz found also with retrograde '2' in date. Varieties exist.

Reform type

C#	Date	Good	VG	Fine	VF
163a	AH1283Fs	2.50	4.50	6.50	11.00
	1283Mr	2.00	3.00	5.00	10.00
	1284Fs	2.00	3.00	5.00	10.00
	1285Fs	2.00	3.00	5.00	10.00
	1285Mr	2.00	3.00	5.00	10.00
	1286Fs	2.00	3.00	5.00	10.00
	1287Fs	2.00	3.00	5.00	10.00
	1288Fs	2.00	3.00	5.00	10.00
	1288Mr	2.00	3.00	5.00	10.00
	1289Fs	2.00	3.00	5.00	10.00
	1290Fs	2.00	3.00	5.00	10.00

NOTE: Varieties exist.

3 FALUS

BRONZE, 26-29mm
Reform types.

C#	Date	Good	VG	Fine	VF
166	AH1278Mr	2.00	3.00	5.00	8.00
	1280Fs	2.00	3.00	5.00	8.00
	1283Fs	1.75	3.25	5.00	8.00
	1283Mr	2.00	3.50	5.50	9.00
	1284Fs	1.50	3.00	4.50	7.50
	1284Mr	1.25	2.25	3.50	6.00
	1285Fs	1.25	2.25	3.50	6.50
	1285Mr	1.25	2.25	3.50	6.50
	1286/5Mr	1.75	3.25	5.00	8.00
	1286Fs	2.25	4.00	6.00	10.00
	1286Mr	1.00	1.75	2.75	4.50
	1287Fs	2.00	3.00	5.00	9.00
	1287Mr	2.00	3.00	5.00	9.00
	1288/7Fs	2.25	4.00	6.00	10.00
	1288Fs	.75	1.50	2.50	4.00
	1288Mr	1.00	1.75	3.00	5.00
	1289/79Mr	1.20	2.00	3.50	6.00
	1289/8Mr	1.20	2.00	3.50	6.00
	1289Fs	1.00	1.75	3.00	5.00
	1289Mr	1.50	2.75	4.00	6.50
	1290Fs	1.00	1.75	3.00	5.00

NOTE: Some AH1280 Fs are a poorly engraved 1284 Fs. Varieties exist.

1/4 DIRHAM

(Mazuna)

SILVER, 0.65 g, 13mm

C#	Date	Good	VG	Fine	VF
170	AH1284Fs	4.00	6.50	10.00	17.50
	1284Mr	4.00	6.50	10.00	17.50
	1286Fs	4.00	6.50	10.00	17.50
	1288Fs	4.00	6.50	10.00	17.50

1/2 DIRHAM

SILVER, 15-18mm, 1.30-1.40 g

C#	Date	Good	VG	Fine	VF
175	AH1283Fs	3.00	5.50	8.50	15.00
	1284Fs	3.00	5.50	8.50	15.00
	1284Mr	4.00	7.00	11.00	20.00
	1284Rb	4.25	8.00	12.50	25.00
	1286Fs	3.00	5.50	8.50	15.00
	1288Fs	3.00	5.50	8.50	15.00

DIRHAM

SILVER, 17-20mm
Light standard, 2.00 g.

C#	Date	Good	VG	Fine	VF
176	AH1277Fs	4.50	8.00	12.50	20.00
	1278Fs	4.50	8.00	12.50	20.00

Heavy standard, 2.70 g.

C#	Date	Good	VG	Fine	VF
176a	AH1283Fs	4.00	7.00	12.00	18.00
	1284Fs	3.25	6.00	12.00	18.00
	1284Mr	3.75	7.00	12.00	20.00

C#	Date	Good	VG	Fine	VF
176a	1284Rb	3.75	7.00	12.00	20.00
	1285Fs	4.00	7.00	12.00	20.00
	1286Fs	3.25	6.00	11.00	18.00
	1288Rb	4.00	7.00	12.00	20.00

Al-Hasan I

(Moulai Hasan)

AH1290-1311/1873-1894AD

2 FALUS

BRONZE

182	AH1295 uncertain mint	—	—	—	—

NOTE: All known specimens appear to be counterfeits or misread dates having inverted 6.

4 FALUS

BRONZE

183	AH1291Mr	—	—	—	—
	1291Fs	5.00	8.00	12.50	22.50
	1295Mr	3.50	6.50	10.00	16.50
	1295Fs	3.50	6.50	10.00	16.50

DIRHAM

SILVER

187	AH1291Fs	15.00	20.00	40.00	65.00
	1299Fs	15.00	20.00	40.00	65.00

MONETARY REFORM

MONETARY SYSTEM

Until 1921

50 Mazunas = 1 Dirham
10 Dirhams = 1 Rial

NOTES

Various copper and silver coins dated AH1297-1311 are believed to be patterns. Copper coins similar to Y#14-17, but without denomination on reverse, are patterns.

On the silver coins the denominations are written in words and each series has its own characteristic names:

Y#4-8 (1299-1314) Denomination in Shar'i Dirhams.

Y#9-13 (1313-1319) Denomination in 'Preferred' Dirhams.

Y#18-22 (1320-1323) Denomination in fractions of a Rial, but on the 3 larger sizes, the equivalent is given in "Urti parts", 1 Rial 20 = Urti parts.

Y#23-25 (1329) Denomination in Dirhams and in fraction of a Rial.

Y#30-33 (1331-1336) Denomination in Yusuti or "Treasury" Dirhams.

On most of the larger denominations, the denomination is given in the form of a rhymed couplet.

1/2 MAZUNA

BRONZE

Y#	Date	Mintage	Fine	VF	XF	Unc
C1	AH1310Fs	—	200.00	350.00	600.00	1000.

NOTE: Some authorities consider Y#C1 to be a Mazuna.

MAZUNA

BRONZE

B1	AH1310Fs	—	150.00	300.00	550.00	900.00

NOTE: Some authorities consider Y#B1 to be a 2 Mazuna.

2-1/2 MAZUNAS

BRONZE

1	AH1310Fs	—	125.00	250.00	500.00	800.00

NOTE: Some authorities consider Y#1 to be a 3 Mazuna.

5 MAZUNAS

BRONZE

Y#	Date	Mintage	Fine	VF	XF	Unc
2	AH1310Fs	—	60.00	100.00	200.00	500.00

10 MAZUNAS

BRONZE

3	AH1310Fs	—	65.00	125.00	250.00	600.00

1/2 DIRHAM

(1/20 Rial)

1.4558 g, .835 SILVER, .0391 oz ASW

4	AH1299Pa	2.200	1.50	3.00	6.00	18.00
	1299Pa	—	—	—	Proof	200.00
	1309Pa	1.700	2.25	5.00	12.00	25.00
	1310Pa	1.700	2.00	4.00	9.00	20.00
	1311Pa	1.700	2.00	4.00	9.00	20.00
	1312Pa	1.700	2.00	4.00	9.00	20.00
	1313Pa	1.700	2.00	4.00	9.00	20.00
	1314Pa	1.700	5.00	12.50	25.00	45.00

DIRHAM

(1/10 Rial)

2.9116 g, .835 SILVER, .0782 oz ASW

5	AH1299Pa	6.800	2.00	4.00	8.00	20.00
	1309Pa	1.700	2.75	8.00	20.00	35.00
	1310Pa	1.800	2.75	7.00	15.00	30.00
	1311Pa	.800	2.75	7.50	17.00	35.00
	1312Pa	.800	2.75	7.50	17.00	35.00
	1313Pa	.800	3.00	8.00	22.50	35.00
	1314Pa					
		Inc. Y10	10.00	22.00	38.00	80.00

2-1/2 DIRHAMS

(1/4 Rial)

7.2790 g, .835 SILVER, .1954 oz ASW

6	AH1299Pa	2.100	3.00	10.00	20.00	30.00
	1299Pa	—	—	—	Proof	250.00
	1309Pa	.700	4.00	12.00	30.00	60.00
	1310Pa	.400	4.00	12.00	30.00	60.00
	1311Pa	.800	4.00	12.00	30.00	60.00
	1312Pa	.300	4.00	12.00	32.00	65.00
	1313Pa	.300	4.00	12.00	32.00	65.00
	1314Pa	—	20.00	45.00	80.00	145.00

5 DIRHAMS

(1/2 Rial)

14.5580 g, .835 SILVER, .3908 oz ASW

Y#	Date	Mintage	Fine	VF	XF	Unc
7	AH1299Pa	1.400	8.00	15.00	30.00	65.00
	1299Pa	—	—	—	Proof	400.00
	1309Pa	.280	8.00	20.00	35.00	100.00
	1310Pa	.170	8.00	20.00	35.00	90.00
	1311Pa	.170	8.00	20.00	35.00	90.00
	1312Pa	.170	8.00	20.00	35.00	90.00
	1313Pa	.170	15.00	30.00	55.00	150.00
	1314Pa					
		Inc. Y12	100.00	175.00	300.00	750.00

10 DIRHAMS

(Rial)

29.1160 g, .900 SILVER, .8425 oz ASW

8	AH1299Pa	.870	15.00	30.00	50.00	140.00

'Abd al-Aziz

AH1311-1326/1894-1908AD

MAZUNA

BRONZE

14	AH1320Be	5 pcs.	—	—	Proof	750.00
	1320Bi	3.000	2.00	5.00	9.00	20.00
	1320Fs	—	20.00	35.00	50.00	120.00
	1321Bi	.900	2.50	6.00	12.00	35.00

NOTE: 5 million examples of 1320 Pa were struck and melted, but at least one specimen is known to exist.

2 MAZUNAS

BRONZE

15.1	AH1320Be	5 pcs.	—	—	Proof	750.00
	1320Bi	1.500	2.00	5.00	10.00	25.00
	1320Bi	—	—	—	Proof	250.00
	1320Fs	—	2.00	5.00	10.00	25.00
	1320Pa	—	—	—	Proof	—
	1321Bi	.450	2.00	5.00	10.00	25.00
	1321Pa	6.500	2.00	5.00	10.00	25.00
	1322Fs	—	2.00	5.00	10.00	25.00
	1323Fs	—	2.00	5.00	10.00	25.00

NOTE: Varieties exist.

Rev: Rim design reversed.

Y#	Date	Mintage	Fine	VF	XF	Unc
15.2	AH1320Fs	—	10.00	25.00	35.00	60.00

5 MAZUNAS

BRONZE

Y#	Date	Mintage	Fine	VF	XF	Unc
16	AH1320Be	*5 pcs.	—	—	Proof	600.00
	1320Bi	2.400	1.00	3.00	7.00	25.00
	1320Bi	—	—	—	Proof	325.00
	1320Fs	—	10.00	25.00	50.00	100.00
	1320Pa	—	—	—	—	—
	1321Bi	.720	2.00	4.00	8.00	32.00
	1321Fs	—	Reported, not confirmed			
	1321Pa	7.950	5.00	10.00	20.00	37.50
	1322Fs	—	25.00	60.00	100.00	150.00

***NOTE:** An additional 799,764 pieces are reported struck, but very few are known.

NOTE: Varieties exist.

10 MAZUNAS

BRONZE

Y#	Date	Mintage	Fine	VF	XF	Unc
17	AH1320Be	2.400	1.25	2.50	6.00	25.00
	1320Bi	1.200	1.50	4.00	6.50	25.00
	1320Fs	—	8.00	20.00	50.00	110.00
	1321Be	2.600	1.25	3.00	6.00	25.00
	1321Bi	.360	1.00	2.00	3.25	25.00
	1321Fs	—	8.00	20.00	45.00	100.00
	1323Fs lg.10	—	35.00	60.00	75.00	150.00
	1323Fs sm.10	—	35.00	60.00	75.00	150.00

1/2 DIRHAM

1.4558 g, .835 SILVER, .0391 oz ASW
Rev: Arrow heads point outward.

Y#	Date	Mintage	Fine	VF	XF	Unc
9.1	AH1313Be	.560	15.00	17.50	22.50	40.00

Rev: Arrow heads point inward.

Y#	Date	Mintage	Fine	VF	XF	Unc
9.2	AH1314Pa	2.200	7.50	12.50	17.50	35.00
	1315Pa	1.190	2.50	4.00	7.50	20.00
	1316Pa	2.280	2.50	5.00	10.00	25.00
	1317Pa	1.700	2.00	4.00	7.50	25.00
	1318Pa	1.715	4.00	8.00	12.00	25.00
	1319Pa	—	2.50	5.00	10.00	28.00

1.2500 g, .835 SILVER, .0336 oz ASW

Y#	Date	Mintage	Fine	VF	XF	Unc
18	AH1320Ln	3.920	1.25	4.00	10.00	25.00
	1320Pa	2.400	1.50	4.00	10.00	25.00
	1321Ln	2.105	Inc. 1320Ln			
			3.00	5.00	10.00	25.00

DIRHAM

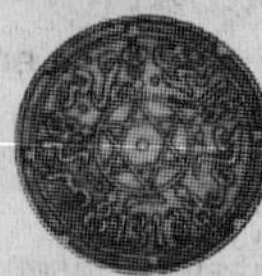

2.9116 g, .835 SILVER, .0782 oz AGW
Rev: Arrow heads point outward.

Y#	Date	Mintage	Fine	VF	XF	Unc
10.1	AH1313Be	.430	6.00	12.50	22.00	45.00

Rev: Arrow heads point inward.

Y#	Date	Mintage	Fine	VF	XF	Unc
10.2	AH1314Pa	1.400	3.00	7.00	15.00	32.00
	1315Pa	.860	3.00	7.00	15.00	32.00
	1316Pa	.860	3.00	7.00	15.00	32.00
	1317Pa	.860	3.00	7.00	15.00	32.00
	1318Pa	.858	3.00	7.00	15.00	32.00

2.5000 g, .835 SILVER, .0671 oz ASW

Y#	Date	Mintage	Fine	VF	XF	Unc
19	AH1320Ln	2.940	3.00	8.00	15.00	40.00
	1321Ln	.770	3.00	8.00	15.00	40.00

2-1/2 DIRHAMS

7.2790 g, .835 SILVER, .1954 oz ASW
Rev: Arrow heads point outward.

Y#	Date	Mintage	Fine	VF	XF	Unc
11.1	AH1313Be	.220	7.50	15.00	25.00	80.00
	1315Be	.640	5.00	10.00	15.00	55.00
	1318Be	.146	10.00	40.00	75.00	140.00

Rev: Arrow heads point inward.

Y#	Date	Mintage	Fine	VF	XF	Unc
11.2	AH1314Pa	1.036	5.00	8.00	10.00	22.00
	1315Pa	.340	5.00	10.00	15.00	55.00
	1316Pa	.400	5.00	15.00	50.00	80.00
	1317Pa	.340	5.00	15.00	50.00	80.00
	1318Pa	.340	10.00	35.00	60.00	115.00

6.2500 g, .835 SILVER, .1678 oz ASW

Y#	Date	Mintage	Fine	VF	XF	Unc
20	AH1320Be	.380	4.00	12.50	20.00	50.00
	1320Ln	3.056	4.00	10.00	12.50	40.00
	1320Pa	.640	4.00	11.00	17.50	45.00
	1321Be	4.450	4.00	7.00	10.00	32.50
	1321Ln	1.889	4.00	7.00	10.00	32.50
	1321Ln	—	—	—	Proof	375.00
	1321Pa	—	40.00	60.00	125.00	275.00

5 DIRHAMS

14.5580 g, .835 SILVER, .3908 oz ASW
Rev: Arrow heads point outward.

Y#	Date	Mintage	Fine	VF	XF	Unc
12.1	AH1313Be	.110	15.00	30.00	60.00	125.00
	1315Be	.360	10.00	16.00	35.00	85.00
	1318Be	.073	20.00	50.00	75.00	130.00

Rev: Arrow heads point inward.

Y#	Date	Mintage	Fine	VF	XF	Unc
12.2	AH1314Pa	.517	10.00	20.00	60.00	120.00
	1315Pa	.160	10.00	16.00	35.00	80.00
	1316Pa	.220	10.00	20.00	35.00	100.00
	1317Pa	.170	10.00	20.00	35.00	100.00
	1318Pa	.177	12.50	25.00	50.00	120.00

12.5000 g, .835 SILVER, .3356 oz ASW

Y#	Date	Mintage	Fine	VF	XF	Unc
21	AH1320Be	2.510	7.00	15.00	30.00	75.00
	1320Ln	.900	7.00	15.00	30.00	75.00
	1321Be	—	—	—	Rare	—
	1321Ln	1.041	7.00	15.00	30.00	75.00
21	1321Ln	—	—	—	Proof	450.00
	1321Pa	1.800	7.00	17.50	35.00	85.00
	1322Pa	.540	7.00	20.00	40.00	100.00
	1323Pa	1.090	7.00	20.00	40.00	100.00

10 DIRHAMS

29.1160 g, .900 SILVER, .8425 oz ASW

Y#	Date	Mintage	Fine	VF	XF	Unc
13	AH1313Be	.050	75.00	150.00	200.00	325.00
	1313Be	—	—	—	Proof	800.00

25.0000 g, .900 SILVER, .7234 oz ASW

Y#	Date	Mintage	Fine	VF	XF	Unc
22	AH1320Ln	.330	17.50	25.00	40.00	120.00
	1320Ln	—	—	—	Proof	Rare
	1321Pa	.300	20.00	27.50	40.00	120.00

Al-Hafiz

AH1326-1330/1908-1912AD

2-1/2 DIRHAMS

6.2500 g, .835 SILVER, .1678 oz ASW

Y#	Date	Mintage	Fine	VF	XF	Unc
23	AH1329Pa	3.130	4.00	8.50	18.00	40.00

5 DIRHAMS

12.5000 g, .835 SILVER, .3356 oz ASW

Y#	Date	Mintage	Fine	VF	XF	Unc
24	AH1329Pa	4.660	7.00	10.00	25.00	90.00

10 DIRHAMS

25.0000 g, .900 SILVER, .7234 oz ASW

Y#	Date	Mintage	Fine	VF	XF	Unc
25	AH1329Pa	7.040	10.00	20.00	40.00	100.00

Yusuf

AH1330-1346/1912-1927AD

MAZUNA

BRONZE

Y#	Date	Mintage	Fine	VF	XF	Unc
26	AH1330Pa	1.850	2.00	5.00	15.00	30.00

2 MAZUNAS

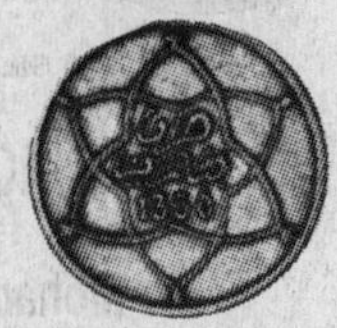

BRONZE

Y#	Date	Mintage	Fine	VF	XF	Unc
27	AH1330Pa	2.790	2.00	4.00	12.00	30.00

NOTE: Coins reportedly dated 1331 Pa probably bore date 1330.

5 MAZUNAS

BRONZE

Y#	Date	Mintage	Fine	VF	XF	Unc
28.1	AH1330Pa	3.180	2.00	5.00	11.00	25.00
	1340Pa	—	2.00	4.00	10.00	22.50

Rev: Privy marks.

Y#	Date	Mintage	Fine	VF	XF	Unc
28.2	1340Pa	2.000	1.00	2.00	5.00	25.00
	1340Py	2.010	2.00	5.00	8.00	27.50

10 MAZUNAS

BRONZE

Y#	Date	Mintage	Fine	VF	XF	Unc
29.1	AH1330Pa	1.500	.75	2.50	10.00	30.00
	1340Pa	1.000	.75	1.50	7.50	25.00

Rev: Privy marks.

Y#	Date	Mintage	Fine	VF	XF	Unc
29.2	AH1340Py	1.000	1.00	3.00	12.00	30.00

DIRHAM

2.5000 g, .835 SILVER, .0671 oz ASW

Y#	Date	Mintage	Fine	VF	XF	Unc
30	AH1331Pa	.500	30.00	45.00	75.00	200.00
	1331Pa	—	—	—	Proof	800.00

2-1/2 DIRHAMS

6.2500 g, .835 SILVER, .1678 oz ASW

Y#	Date	Mintage	Fine	VF	XF	Unc
31	AH1331Pa	2.500	30.00	45.00	90.00	225.00

5 DIRHAMS

.835 SILVER

Y#	Date	Mintage	Fine	VF	XF	Unc
32	AH1331Pa	1.500	7.00	16.00	25.00	60.00
	1336Pa	11.500	6.00	11.00	20.00	50.00

10 DIRHAMS

25.0000 g, .900 SILVER, .7234 oz ASW

Y#	Date	Mintage	Fine	VF	XF	Unc
33	AH1331Pa	7.000	9.00	20.00	35.00	70.00
	1336Pa	2.600	9.00	17.50	25.00	55.00

FRENCH PROTECTORATE

MONETARY SYSTEM

100 Centimes = 1 Franc

100 Francs = 1 Dirham

NOTE: Y46-51 were struck for more than 20 years without change of date, until a new currency was introduced in 1974. Final mintage statistics are not yet available.

25 CENTIMES

COPPER-NICKEL

Obv. and rev: W/o privy marks.

Y#	Date	Mintage	Fine	VF	XF	Unc
34.1	ND (1921)Pa	13.000	1.00	3.00	8.00	40.00

Rev: Thunderbolt above CENTIMES.

Y#	Date	Mintage	Fine	VF	XF	Unc
34.2	ND (1924)Py	6.020	1.00	3.00	8.00	40.00

Rev: Thunderbolt and torch at left and right of CENTIMES.

Y#	Date	Mintage	Fine	VF	XF	Unc
34.3	ND(1924)Py	Inc. Ab.	1.00	3.00	8.00	40.00

50 CENTIMES

NICKEL

Obv. and rev: W/o privy marks.

Y#	Date	Mintage	Fine	VF	XF	Unc
35.1	ND(1921)Pa	11.000	.50	1.00	6.50	45.00

Rev: Thunderbolt at bottom.

Y#	Date	Mintage	Fine	VF	XF	Unc
35.2	ND(1924)Py	3.000	1.00	2.00	8.00	45.00

FRANC

NICKEL

Obv. and rev: W/o privy marks.

Y#	Date	Mintage	Fine	VF	XF	Unc
36.1	ND(1921)Pa	13.510	.50	1.00	6.50	37.50

Rev: Thunderbolt below 1.

Y#	Date	Mintage	Fine	VF	XF	Unc
36.2	ND(1924)Py	3.000	1.25	2.50	10.00	55.00

Mohammed V

AH1346-1375/1927-1955AD

50 CENTIMES

ALUMINUM-BRONZE

Y#	Date	Year	Mintage	VF	XF	Unc
40	AH1364(a)	1945	—	.20	1.50	2.50

FRANC

ALUMINUM-BRONZE

Y#	Date	Year Mintage	VF	XF	Unc
41	AH1364(a)1945	12.000	.25	1.00	2.50

ALUMINUM

46	AH1370(a)1951	—	.10	.25	1.00

2 FRANCS

ALUMINUM-BRONZE

42	AH1364(a)1945	12.000	.50	2.50	6.00

ALUMINUM

47	AH1370(a)1951	—	.10	.50	2.00

5 FRANCS

5.0000 g, .680 SILVER, .1093 oz ASW

37	AH1347(a)	—	4.000	2.50	7.00	32.00
	1352(a)	—	5.000	1.50	4.00	18.00

ALUMINUM-BRONZE

Y#	Date	Mintage	Fine	VF	XF	Unc
43	AH1365(a)	20.000	.15	.35	.60	1.50

ALUMINUM

48	AH1370(a)	—	.10	.15	.30	1.00

10 FRANCS

10.0000 g, .680 SILVER, .2186 oz ASW

Y#	Date	Mintage	Fine	VF	XF	Unc
38	AH1347(a)	1.600	4.00	10.00	22.00	80.00
	1352(a)	2.900	2.25	3.00	8.00	27.50

COPPER-NICKEL

44	AH1366(a)	20.000	.35	.75	1.00	1.50

ALUMINUM-BRONZE

49	AH1371(a)	—	.10	.35	.75	1.50

20 FRANCS

20.0000 g, .680 SILVER, .4372 oz ASW

39	AH1347(a)	—	5.00	12.00	32.50	80.00
	1352(a)	2.000	5.00	8.00	25.00	50.00

COPPER-NICKEL

45	AH1366(a)	6.000	.25	.50	1.00	2.00
	1366	—	—	—	Proof	50.00

ALUMINUM-BRONZE

50	AH1371(a)	—	.10	.25	.75	1.50

50 FRANCS

ALUMINUM-BRONZE

Y#	Date	Mintage	Fine	VF	XF	Unc
51	AH1371(a)	—	.25	.50	.65	1.00

100 FRANCS

2.5000 g, .720 SILVER, .0579 oz ASW

Y#	Date	Year Mintage	VF	XF	Unc
A54	AH1370(a)1951	10.000	—	—	200.00

NOTE: Most were remelted.

52	AH1372(a)1953	5.000	2.50	3.50	5.00

200 FRANCS

8.0000 g, .720 SILVER, .1851 oz ASW

53	AH1372(a)1953	9.200	2.00	4.00	8.00

KINGDOM

1956

Mohammed V

AH1376-1381/1956-1962AD

500 FRANCS

22.5000 g, .900 SILVER, .6511 oz ASW

54	AH1376(a)1956	2.000	8.00	10.00	15.00

MONETARY REFORM

100 Francs = 1 Dirham

DIRHAM

6.0000 g, .600 SILVER, .1157 oz ASW

Y#	Date	Year	Mintage	VF	XF	Unc
55	AH1380(a)	1960	30.600	1.00	2.50	5.00

Al-Hasan II

AH1381/1962AD

DIRHAM

NICKEL

Y#	Date	Year	Mintage	VF	XF	Unc
56	AH1384(a)	1965	35.000	.50	.75	1.00
	1388(a)	1968	—	.50	.75	1.00
	1389(a)	1969	—	.50	.75	1.00

5 DIRHAM

11.7500 g, .720 SILVER, .2720 oz ASW

Y#	Date	Year	Mintage	VF	XF	Unc
57	AH1384(a)	1965	1,800	5.00	7.00	12.50
	1384(a)	1965	200 pcs.	—	Proof	50.00

MONETARY REFORM

1974

100 Santimat = 1 Dirham

SANTIM

ALUMINUM

Y#	Date	Year	Mintage	VF	XF	Unc
58	AH1394	1974	14.200	—	.50	1.25
	1394	1974	.020	—	Proof	1.00
	1395	1975	1.700	—	.10	1.00
	1395	1975	.014	—	Proof	2.50

.917 GOLD

Y#	Date	Year	Mintage	VF	XF	Unc
58a	AH1394	1974	30 pcs.	—	Proof	450.00

5 SANTIMAT

BRASS
F.A.O. Issue

Y#	Date	Year	Mintage	VF	XF	Unc
59	AH1394	1974	71.800	—	.15	.30
	1394	1974	.020	—	Proof	1.00
	1395	1975	11.000	—	.10	.25
	1398	1978	12.600	—	.10	.25

.917 GOLD

Y#	Date	Year	Mintage	VF	XF	Unc
59a	AH1394	1974	30 pcs.	—	Proof	450.00

BRASS
F.A.O. Issue

Y#	Date	Year	Mintage	VF	XF	Unc
83	AH1407	1987	—	—	—	.25

10 SANTIMAT

BRASS
F.A.O. Issue

Y#	Date	Year	Mintage	VF	XF	Unc
60	AH1394	1974	93.800	—	.15	.30
	1394	1974	.020	—	Proof	1.50
	1395	1975	10.900	—	.10	.20
	1398	1978	1.000	—	.10	.30

.917 GOLD

Y#	Date	Year	Mintage	VF	XF	Unc
60a	AH1394	1974	30 pcs.	—	Proof	550.00

BRASS
F.A.O. Issue

Y#	Date	Year	Mintage	VF	XF	Unc
84	AH1407	1987	—	—	—	.25

20 SANTIMAT

BRASS

Y#	Date	Year	Mintage	VF	XF	Unc
61	AH1394	1974	25.000	.30	.40	.50
	1394	1974	—	—	Proof	2.00
	1395	1975	10.700	.10	.15	.35
	1397	1977	22.800	.10	.15	.35
	1398	1978	2.200	.10	.15	.35

.917 GOLD

Y#	Date	Year	Mintage	VF	XF	Unc
61a	AH1394	1974	30 pcs.	—	Proof	650.00

BRASS
F.A.O. Issue
Obv: Arms. Rev: Ornamental design, value and date.

Y#	Date	Year	Mintage	VF	XF	Unc
85	AH1407	1987	—	—	—	.35

50 SANTIMAT

COPPER-NICKEL

Y#	Date	Year	Mintage	VF	XF	Unc
62	AH1394	1974	48.900	.20	.40	.60
	1394	1974	.020	—	Proof	2.50
	1398	1978	1.100	.25	.50	.75

.917 GOLD

Y#	Date	Year	Mintage	VF	XF	Unc
62a	AH1394	1974	30 pcs.	—	Proof	650.00

1/2 DIRHAM

COPPER-NICKEL
Obv: Portrait of King.
Rev: Arms above denomination.

Y#	Date	Year	Mintage	VF	XF	Unc
87	AH1407	1987	—	—	—	1.00

DIRHAM

COPPER-NICKEL

Y#	Date	Year	Mintage	VF	XF	Unc
63	AH1394	1974	21.900	.30	.50	.75
	1394	1974	.020	—	Proof	4.00
	1398	1978	18.100	.15	.35	.75

.917 GOLD

Y#	Date	Year	Mintage	VF	XF	Unc
63a	AH1394	1974	30 pcs.	—	Proof	800.00

COPPER-NICKEL
Obv: Portrait of King.
Rev: Arms above denomination.

Y#	Date	Year	Mintage	VF	XF	Unc
88	AH1407	1987	—	—	—	2.00

5 DIRHAMS

COPPER-NICKEL
World Food Conference

Y#	Date	Year	Mintage	VF	XF	Unc
64	AH1395	1975	.500	—	1.00	3.50
	1395	1975	500 pcs.	—	Proof	8.00

12.0000 g, .925 SILVER, .3569 oz ASW

Y#	Date	Year	Mintage	VF	XF	Unc
64a	AH1395	1975	200 pcs.	—	Proof	75.00

23.6500 g, .900 GOLD, .6844 oz AGW

Y#	Date	Year	Mintage	VF	XF	Unc
64b	AH1395	1975	20 pcs.	—	Proof	1000.

COPPER-NICKEL

Y#	Date	Year	Mintage	VF	XF	Unc
72 (A63)	AH1400	1980	10.000	1.00	4.00	6.00

STAINLESS STEEL RING,
ALUMINUM-BRONZE CENTER

Y#	Date	Year	Mintage	VF	XF	Unc
82	AH1407	1987	—	1.00	2.50	4.00

50 DIRHAMS

35.0000 g, .925 SILVER, 1.0409 oz ASW
20th Anniversary of Independence

Y#	Date	Year	Mintage	VF	XF	Unc
65	AH1395	1975	6,000	—	—	25.00
	1395	1975	4,400	—	Proof	45.00

60.1400 g, .900 GOLD, 1.7404 oz AGW

Y#	Date	Year	Mintage	VF	XF	Unc
65a	AH1395	1975	40 pcs.	—	Proof	1500.

35.0000 g, .925 SILVER, 1.0409 oz ASW
International Women's Year
Obv: Similar to Y#65.

Y#	Date	Year	Mintage	VF	XF	Unc
67	AH1395	1975	6,000	—	—	30.00
	1395	1975	4,400	—	Proof	50.00

60.1400 g, .900 GOLD, 1.7404 oz AGW

67a	AH1395	1975	20 pcs.	—	Proof	1850.

35.0000 g, .925 SILVER, 1.0409 oz ASW
50th Birthday King Hassan

Y#	Date	Year	Mintage	VF	XF	Unc
76	AH1399	1979	5,000	—	—	30.00
	1399	1979	500 pcs.	—	Proof	50.00

60.1400 g, .900 GOLD, 1.7404 oz AGW

76a	AH1399	1979	70 pcs.	—	Proof	1400.

Anniversary Green March

Y#	Date	Year	Mintage	VF	XF	Unc
79	AH1406	1986	—	—	—	25.00

Visit of the Pope

80	AH1406	1986	2,000	—	Proof	45.00

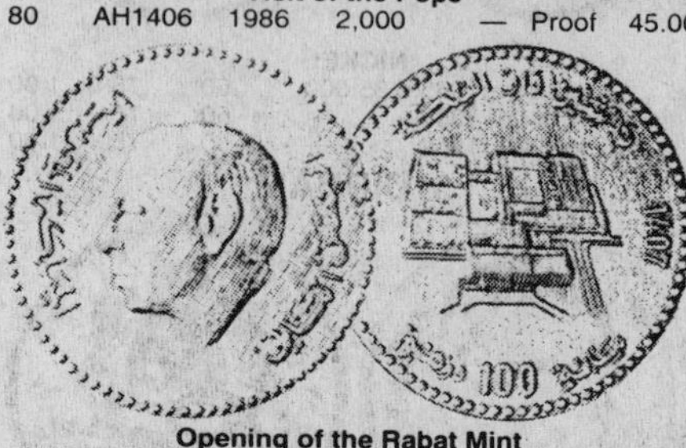

Opening of the Rabat Mint

86	AH1407	1987	—	—	—	25.00
	1407	1987	—	—	Proof	50.00

35.0000 g, .925 SILVER, 1.0409 oz ASW
Anniversary Green March
Obv: Similar to Y#65.

68	AH1396	1976	.011	—	—	20.00
	1396	1976	4,400	—	Proof	35.00
	1397	1977	3,500	—	—	35.00
	1397	1977	200 pcs.	—	Proof	55.00
	1398	1978	5,000	—	—	30.00
	1398	1978	300 pcs.	—	Proof	50.00
	1399	1979	3,000	—	—	35.00
	1399	1979	300 pcs.	—	Proof	50.00
	1400	1980	1,000	—	—	40.00
	1400	1980	200 pcs.	—	Proof	55.00

60.1400 g, .900 GOLD, 1.7404 oz AGW

68a	AH1396	1976	20 pcs.	—	Proof	1800.
	1397	1977	20 pcs.	—	Proof	1800.
	1398	1978	70 pcs.	—	Proof	1200.
	1399	1979	70 pcs.	—	Proof	1200.
	1400	1980	30 pcs.	—	Proof	1500.

35.0000 g, .925 SILVER, 1.0409 oz ASW
International Year of the Child
Obv: Similar to Y#65.

70	AH1399	1979	5,000	—	—	30.00
	1399	1979	500 pcs.	—	Proof	50.00

60.1400 g, .900 GOLD, 1.7404 oz AGW

70a	AH1399	1979	70 pcs.	—	Proof	1200.

100 DIRHAMS

25.0000 g, .925 SILVER, .7436 oz ASW
9th Mediterranean Games

75	AH1403	1983	5,000	—	—	25.00
	1403	1983	500 pcs.	—	Proof	60.00

15.0000 g, .925 SILVER, .4461 oz ASW
Olympic Games - Rings

77	AH1405	1985	2,300	—	—	25.00
	1405	1985	300 pcs.	—	Proof	70.00

25th Year of Reign of King Hassan

78	AH1406	1985	1,200	—	—	25.00
	1406	1985	200 pcs.	—	Proof	75.00

150 DIRHAMS

35.0000 g, .925 SILVER, 1.0409 oz ASW
15th Hejira Calendar Century
Obv: Similar to Y#73.

74	AH1401	1980	3,000	—	—	30.00
	1401	1980	300 pcs.	—	Proof	50.00

60.1400 g, .900 GOLD, 1.7404 oz AGW

74a	AH1401	1980	30 pcs.	—	Proof	1800.

35.0000 g, .925 SILVER, 1.0409 oz ASW
20th Anniversary King Hassan's Coronation

Y#	Date	Year	Mintage	VF	XF	Unc
73	AH1401	1981	3,000	—	—	30.00
	1401	1981	300 pcs.	—	Proof	50.00

60.1400 g, .900 GOLD, 1.7404 oz AGW

Y#	Date	Year	Mintage	VF	XF	Unc
73a	AH1401	1981	30 pcs.	—	Proof	1800.

200 DIRHAMS

15.0000 g, .925 SILVER, .4461 oz ASW
Moroccan - American Friendship Treaty

Y#	Date	Year	Mintage	VF	XF	Unc
81	AH1408	1987	*5,000	—	Proof	40.00

First Francophonie Games

Y#	Date	Year	Mintage	VF	XF	Unc
91	AH1409	1989	5,000	—	—	20.00
	1409	1989	500 pcs.	—	Proof	50.00

250 DIRHAMS

6.4500 g, .900 GOLD, .1867 oz AGW
Birthday of King Hassan

Y#	Date	Year	Mintage	VF	XF	Unc
66	AH1395	1975	5,000	—	—	100.00
	1395	1975	1,270	—	Proof	150.00
	1396	1976	3,200	—	—	100.00
	1396	1976	450 pcs.	—	Proof	175.00
	1397	1977	3,000	—	—	100.00
	1397	1977	800 pcs.	—	Proof	130.00
	1398	1978	2,000	—	—	100.00
	1398	1978	150 pcs.	—	Proof	200.00
	1399	1979	508 pcs.	—	—	150.00
	1399	1979	398 pcs.	—	Proof	175.00

500 DIRHAMS

12.9000 g, .900 GOLD, .3733 oz AGW
Birthday of King Hassan

Y#	Date	Year	Mintage	VF	XF	Unc
71	AH1399	1979	3,000	—	—	200.00
	1399	1979	300 pcs.	—	Proof	300.00
	1400	1980	100 pcs.	—	—	400.00
	1400	1980	100 pcs.	—	Proof	500.00
	1401	1981	100 pcs.	—	—	400.00
	1401	1981	100 pcs.	—	Proof	500.00
	1402	1982	100 pcs.	—	—	400.00
	1402	1982	100 pcs.	—	Proof	500.00
	1403	1983	2,500	—	—	200.00
	1403	1983	Inc. Ab.	—	Proof	200.00
	1404	1984	100 pcs.	—	—	400.00
	1404	1984	100 pcs.	—	Proof	500.00
	1405	1985	275 pcs.	—	—	250.00
	1405	1985	125 pcs.	—	Proof	475.00

MINT SETS (MS)

(Fleur de Coin)

KM#	Date	Mintage	Identification	Issue Price	Mkt. Val.
MS1	1951-65(8)	—	Y46-51,56,57	—	17.50

PROOF SETS (PS)

KM#	Date	Mintage	Identification	Issue Price	Mkt. Val.
PS1	1974-75(7)	.020	Y58-64	20.00	20.00
PS2	1974(6)	30	Y58a-63a	—	3200.

MOZAMBIQUE

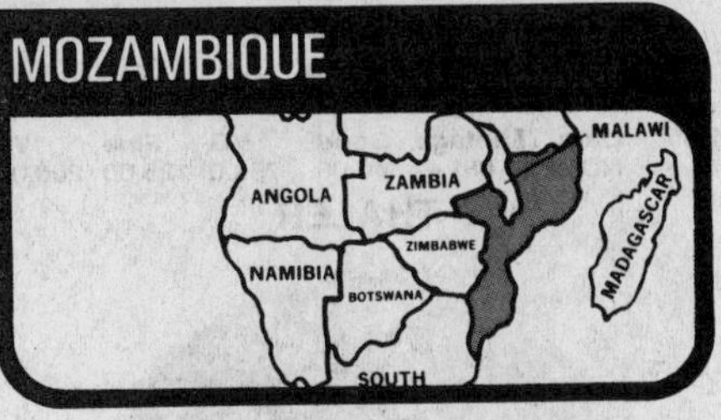

The Republic of Mozambique, a former overseas province of Portugal stretching for 1,430 miles (2,301 km.) along the southeast coast of Africa, has an area of 302,330 sq. mi. (801,590 sq. km.) and a population of 14.1 million, 99 percent of whom are native Africans of the Bantu tribes. Capital: Maputo. Agriculture is the chief industry. Cashew nuts, cotton, sugar, copra and tea are exported.

Vasco de Gama explored all the coast of Mozambique in 1498 and found Arab trading posts already established along the coast. Portuguese settlement dates from the establishment of the trading post of Mozambique in 1505. Within five years Portugal absorbed all the former Arab sultanates along the east African coast. The area was organized as a colony in 1907 and became an overseas province in 1952. In Sept. of 1974, after more than a decade of guerrilla warfare with the forces of the Mozambique Liberation Front, Portugal agreed to the independence of Mozambique, effective June 25, 1975. The Socialist party, led by President Joaquim Chissano was in power until the 2nd of November, 1990 when they became a republic.

RULERS

Portuguese, until 1975

MONETARY SYSTEM

2880 Reis = 6 Cruzados = 1 Onca

COLONIAL COINAGE

REIS

COPPER

KM#	Date	Mintage	Fine	VF	XF	Unc
24	1853	.100	10.00	20.00	40.00	70.00

II (2) REIS

COPPER

KM#	Date	Mintage	Fine	VF	XF	Unc
25	1853	.100	10.00	20.00	35.00	60.00

NOTE: The V Reis, X Reis and XX Reis pieces dated 1853 were issued for circulation in Mozambique. These are also attributed to Portugal and will be found under their appropriate listings.

20 REIS

COPPER

KM#	Date	Mintage	VG	Fine	VF	XF
18	1820	—	7.00	15.00	30.00	60.00

NOTE: For coins with c/m '10' refer to Brazil listings. Some 20 Reis coins previously listed here are now listed in St. Thomas and Prince Islands.

Similar to 40 Reis, KM#22.

KM#	Date	Mintage	VG	Fine	VF	XF
21	1840	.040	7.00	15.00	30.00	60.00

40 REIS

COPPER

KM#	Date	Mintage	VG	Fine	VF	XF
19	1820	—	6.00	12.00	25.00	55.00

NOTE: For coins with c/m '20' refer to Brazil listings. Some 40 Reis coins previously listed here are now listed in St. Thomas and Prince Islands.

KM#	Date	Mintage	VG	Fine	VF	XF
22	1840	.020	10.00	20.00	35.00	75.00

80 REIS

COPPER

KM#	Date	Mintage	VG	Fine	VF	XF
20	1820	—	10.00	20.00	35.00	75.00

NOTE: Other 80 Reis coins previously listed here are now listed in St. Thomas and Prince Islands.

Similar to 40 Reis, KM#22.

KM#	Date	Mintage	VG	Fine	VF	XF
23	1840	.010	12.00	25.00	40.00	85.00

ONCA

SILVER
Obv: Small date, lettering.

KM#	Date	Mintage	VG	Fine	VF	XF
26.1	1843	—	50.00	150.00	300.00	—

Obv: Large date, lettering.

KM#	Date	Mintage	VG	Fine	VF	XF
26.2	1845	—	70.00	165.00	350.00	—
	1847	—	50.00	150.00	300.00	—

NOTE: Varieties of reverse exist.

1-1/4 MATICAES

7.20 g, GOLD, Rectangular, 11x17mm

KM#	Date	Mintage	VG	Fine	VF	XF
31	ND(1835)	—	550.00	1300.	3000.	—

c/m: Rosette on KM#31.

KM#	Date	Mintage	VG	Fine	VF	XF
32	ND(1851)	—	300.00	700.00	1500.	—

2-1/2 MATICAES

14.50 g, GOLD

KM#	Date	Mintage	VG	Fine	VF	XF
33	ND(1835)	—	700.00	1000.	2000.	—

c/m: Rosette on KM#33.

KM#	Date	Mintage	VG	Fine	VF	XF
34	ND(1851)	—	250.00	450.00	750.00	—

COUNTERMARKED COINAGE

Decree of January 5, 1889

This decree ordained that all foreign silver coinage circulating in Mozambique was to be countermarked with a crowned PM within a circle. These coins were eventually to be replaced or exchanged by current Portuguese coinage upon their entry into the public treasury. The following list is a basic guide. Caution should be exercised as counterfeits exist. Grades noted are for the basic coin as the countermark is normally found in better condition than the coin bearing it.

6 PENCE

.925 SILVER

c/m: Crowned PM on Great Britain 6 Pence, KM#751.

KM#	Date	Mintage	Good	VG	Fine	VF
35	ND(1870)	—	25.00	40.00	65.00	100.00

SHILLING

.925 SILVER

c/m: Crowned PM on Great Britain 1 Shilling, KM#734.

KM#	Date	Mintage	Good	VG	Fine	VF
36	ND(1860)	—	25.00	40.00	65.00	100.0C

1/2 RUPEE

.917 SILVER

KM#	Date	Mintage	Good	VG	Fine	VF
c/m: Crowned PM on India 1/2 Rupee, KM#455.						
A37	ND(1840)	—	12.50	20.00	32.50	50.00
c/m: Crowned PM on India 1/2 Rupee, KM#456.						
37	ND(1840)	—	12.50	20.00	32.50	50.00
c/m: Crowned PM on India 1/2 Rupee, KM#472.						
A38	ND(1862-76)	—	10.00	15.00	25.00	40.00
c/m: Crowned PM on India 1/2 Rupee, KM#491.						
38	ND(1877-88)	—	10.00	15.00	25.00	40.00

RUPEE

.917 SILVER

KM#	Date	Mintage	Good	VG	Fine	VF
c/m: Crowned PM on India Rupee, KM#450.						
39	ND(1835)	—	35.00	60.00	100.00	150.00
c/m: Crowned PM on India Rupee, KM#457.						
A40	ND(1840)	—	20.00	30.00	50.00	80.00
c/m: Crowned PM on India Rupee, KM#458.						
40	ND(1840)	—	20.00	30.00	50.00	80.00
c/m: Crowned PM on India Rupee, KM#473.						
A41	ND(1862-76)	—	10.00	15.00	25.00	40.00

KM#	Date	Mintage	Good	VG	Fine	VF
c/m: Crowned PM on India Rupee, KM#492.						
41	ND(1877-88)	—	10.00	15.00	25.00	40.00
c/m: Crowned PM on India-Portuguese Rupia, KM#12.						
42	ND(1881-82)	—	20.00	30.00	50.00	80.00
c/m: Crowned PM on Mombasa Rupee, KM#5.						
43	ND(1888)	—	25.00	37.50	62.50	100.00

8 REALES

SILVER

c/m: Crowned PM on Mexico 8 Reales, KM#377.

KM#	Date	Mintage	Good	VG	Fine	VF
44	ND(1825-88)	—	40.00	75.00	125.00	200.00

THALER

SILVER

KM#	Date	Mintage	Good	VG	Fine	VF
c/m: Crowned PM on Austria Maria Theresa Thaler, KM#T1.						
45	ND(1780)	—	25.00	40.00	65.00	100.00
c/m: Crowned PM on Austria-Graz Thaler, KM#464.						
AA46	ND(1806-10)	—	30.00	50.00	80.00	140.00
c/m: Crowned PM on Austria Thaler, KM#473.						
A46	ND(1811-15)	—	30.00	50.00	80.00	140.00

KM#	Date	Mintage	Good	VG	Fine	VF
c/m: Crowned PM on Austria Thaler, KM#493.						
46	ND(1817-24)	—	30.00	50.00	80.00	140.00
c/m: Crowned PM on Austria Thaler, KM#494.						
47	ND(1824-30)	—	30.00	50.00	80.00	140.00

Decree of January 19, 1889

1889-1895

During the reign of D. Carlos I, a substitution of an indented PM (Provincia de Mocambique) which replaced the crowned PM of D. Luis I, was countermarked on all foreign silver coinage circulating in Mozambique. These coins were to be replaced or exchanged by Portuguese coinage on their entry into the public treasury.

1/4 RUPEE

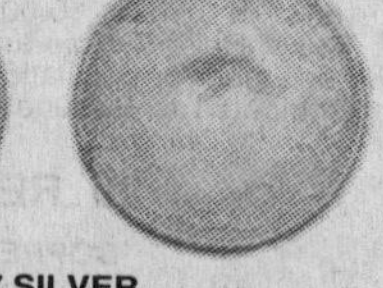

.917 SILVER

KM#	Date	Mintage	Good	VG	Fine	VF
c/m: PM on India 1/4 Rupee, KM#470.						
A48	ND(1862-76)	—	15.00	22.50	37.50	60.00
c/m: PM on India 1/4 Rupee, KM#490.						
48	ND(1877-88)	—	15.00	22.50	37.50	60.00

1/2 RUPEE

.917 SILVER

c/m: PM on India 1/2 Rupee, KM#455.

KM#	Date	Mintage	Good	VG	Fine	VF
A49	ND(1840)	—	12.50	20.00	32.50	50.00

KM#	Date	Mintage	Good	VG	Fine	VF
c/m: PM on India 1/2 Rupee, KM#456.						
49	ND(1840)	—	12.50	20.00	32.50	50.00
c/m: PM on India 1/2 Rupee, KM#472.						
50	ND(1862-76)	—	10.00	15.00	25.00	40.00
c/m: PM on German East Africa 1/2 Rupie, KM#4.						
51	ND(1891)	—	40.00	75.00	125.00	200.00

RUPEE

.917 SILVER

KM#	Date	Mintage	Good	VG	Fine	VF
c/m: PM on India Rupee, KM#450.						
52	ND(1835)	—	35.00	60.00	100.00	150.00
c/m: PM on India Rupee, KM#457.						
A53	ND(1840)	—	20.00	30.00	50.00	80.00
c/m: PM on India Rupee, KM#458.						
53	ND(1840)	—	20.00	30.00	50.00	80.00

c/m: PM on India Rupee, KM#473.

KM#	Date	Mintage	Good	VG	Fine	VF
A54	ND(1862-76)	—	20.00	30.00	50.00	80.00

KM#	Date	Mintage	Good	VG	Fine	VF
c/m: PM on India Rupee, KM#492.						
54	ND(1877-88)	—	20.00	30.00	50.00	80.00
c/m: PM on India-Portuguese Rupia, KM#12.						
55	ND(1881)	—	20.00	30.00	50.00	80.00
c/m: PM on Mombasa Rupee, KM#5.						
56	ND(1888)	—	25.00	37.50	62.50	100.00

c/m: PM on German East Africa Rupie, KM#2.

KM#	Date	Mintage	Good	VG	Fine	VF
57	ND(1890-94)	—	40.00	75.00	125.00	200.00

THALER

SILVER

KM#	Date	Mintage	Good	VG	Fine	VF
c/m: PM on Austria Maria Theresa Thaler, KM#T1.						
58	ND(1780)	—	25.00	40.00	65.00	100.00
c/m: PM on Austria Thaler, KM#473.						
59	ND(1817-24)	—	30.00	50.00	80.00	140.00

c/m: PM on Austria Thaler, KM#494.

KM#	Date	Mintage	Good	VG	Fine	VF
60	ND(1824-30)	—	30.00	50.00	80.00	140.00

DECIMAL COINAGE

100 Centavos = 1 Escudo

10 CENTAVOS

BRONZE

KM#	Date	Mintage	Fine	VF	XF	Unc
63	1936	2.000	.75	1.75	6.00	18.00

KM#	Date	Mintage	Fine	VF	XF	Unc
72	1942	2.000	.50	1.25	2.50	10.00

KM#	Date	Mintage	Fine	VF	XF	Unc
83	1960	3.750	—	.15	.25	1.00
	1961	10.300	—	—	.15	.75

20 CENTAVOS

BRONZE

KM#	Date	Mintage	Fine	VF	XF	Unc
64	1936	2.500	.85	2.00	8.00	30.00

KM#	Date	Mintage	Fine	VF	XF	Unc
71	1941	2.000	.85	2.00	7.00	22.50

KM#	Date	Mintage	Fine	VF	XF	Unc
75	1949	8.000	.25	.75	2.00	5.00
	1950	12.500	.25	.75	1.25	3.00

KM#	Date	Mintage	Fine	VF	XF	Unc
85	1961	12.500	—	.10	.15	1.00

Reduced size, 16mm

KM#	Date	Mintage	Fine	VF	XF	Unc
88	1973	1.798	6.00	12.00	20.00	40.00
	1974	13.044	6.00	12.00	20.00	40.00

50 CENTAVOS

COPPER-NICKEL

KM#	Date	Mintage	Fine	VF	XF	Unc
65	1936	2.500	1.00	3.00	10.00	35.00

BRONZE

KM#	Date	Mintage	Fine	VF	XF	Unc
73	1945	2.500	.50	1.50	7.00	20.00

NICKEL-BRONZE

KM#	Date	Mintage	Fine	VF	XF	Unc
76	1950	20.000	.30	1.00	2.50	7.50
	1951	16.000	.30	1.00	2.50	7.50

BRONZE

KM#	Date	Mintage	Fine	VF	XF	Unc
81	1953	5.010	.25	.50	1.50	6.00
	1957	24.990	—	.15	.25	3.00

KM#	Date	Mintage	Fine	VF	XF	Unc
89	1973	6.841	—	.15	.25	2.00
	1974	23.810	—	.15	.25	2.00

ESCUDO

COPPER-NICKEL

KM#	Date	Mintage	Fine	VF	XF	Unc
66	1936	2.000	2.00	5.00	10.00	60.00

BRONZE

KM#	Date	Mintage	Fine	VF	XF	Unc
74	1945	2.000	1.00	3.00	8.00	25.00

NICKEL-BRONZE

KM#	Date	Mintage	Fine	VF	XF	Unc
77	1950	10.000	.60	1.25	2.25	10.00
	1951	10.000	.50	1.00	2.00	7.00

BRONZE

KM#	Date	Mintage	Fine	VF	XF	Unc
82	1953	2.013	.30	.75	1.25	6.00
	1957	2.987	.20	.50	1.00	6.00
	1962	.600	.30	.75	1.25	4.50
	1963	3.258	—	.15	.50	4.00
	1965	5.000	—	.10	.35	2.00
	1968	4.500	—	.10	.35	2.00
	1969	1.642	—	.15	.50	2.50
	1973	.501	.20	.50	.75	4.50
	1974	25.281	—	.10	.30	1.50

2-1/2 ESCUDOS

3.5000 g, .650 SILVER, .0731 oz ASW

KM#	Date	Mintage	Fine	VF	XF	Unc
61	1935	1.200	5.00	10.00	25.00	70.00

KM#	Date	Mintage	Fine	VF	XF	Unc
68	1938	1.000	3.00	6.00	10.00	28.00
	1942	1.200	2.00	4.00	6.00	18.00
	1950	4.000	1.25	2.50	4.00	10.00
	1951	4.000	1.50	3.00	5.00	12.50

COPPER-NICKEL

KM#	Date	Mintage	Fine	VF	XF	Unc
78	1952	4.000	.30	.75	1.50	7.50
	1953	4.000	.30	.75	1.50	4.50
	1954	4.000	.15	.35	.65	1.50
	1955	4.000	.30	.75	1.50	5.00
	1965	8.000	.10	.25	.50	1.25
	1973	1.767	.20	.50	.75	2.25

5 ESCUDOS

7.0000 g, .650 SILVER, .1463 oz ASW

KM#	Date	Mintage	Fine	VF	XF	Unc
62	1935	1.000	2.00	5.00	18.00	45.00

KM#	Date	Mintage	Fine	VF	XF	Unc
69	1938	.800	3.00	6.00	20.00	50.00
	1949	8.000	1.50	3.50	9.00	20.00

4.0000 g, .650 SILVER, .0835 oz ASW

KM#	Date	Mintage	Fine	VF	XF	Unc
84	1960	8.000	.50	1.00	1.50	4.50

COPPER-NICKEL

KM#	Date	Mintage	Fine	VF	XF	Unc
86	1971	8.000	.20	.50	1.00	2.25
	1973	3.352	.20	.50	1.75	3.50

10 ESCUDOS

12.5000 g, .835 SILVER, .3356 oz ASW

KM#	Date	Mintage	Fine	VF	XF	Unc
67	1936	.497	7.00	15.00	27.50	65.00

KM#	Date	Mintage	Fine	VF	XF	Unc
70	1938	.530	6.00	12.00	22.00	50.00

5.0000 g, .720 SILVER, .1157 oz ASW

KM#	Date	Mintage	Fine	VF	XF	Unc
79	1952	1.503	2.00	4.00	8.00	20.00
	1954	1.335	2.00	4.00	8.00	20.00
	1955	1.162	2.00	4.00	8.00	20.00
	1960	2.000	.75	1.50	2.50	5.50

5.0000 g, .680 SILVER, .1093 oz ASW

KM#	Date	Mintage	Fine	VF	XF	Unc
79a	1966	.500	1.00	2.00	5.00	10.00

COPPER-NICKEL

KM#	Date	Mintage	Fine	VF	XF	Unc
79b	1968	5.000	.30	.60	1.75	4.50
	1970	4.000	.30	.60	1.50	3.50
	1974	3.366	.30	.60	1.75	5.00

20 ESCUDOS

10.0000 g, .720 SILVER, .2315 oz ASW

KM#	Date	Mintage	Fine	VF	XF	Unc
80	1952	1.004	1.50	3.00	5.00	8.00
	1955	.996	1.75	3.50	5.50	9.00
	1960	2.000	1.25	2.50	4.50	7.00

10.0000 g, .680 SILVER, .2186 oz ASW

KM#	Date	Mintage	Fine	VF	XF	Unc
80a	1966	.250	—	3.50	6.50	10.00

NICKEL

KM#	Date	Mintage	Fine	VF	XF	Unc
87	1971	2.000	.35	.75	1.75	3.50
	1972	1.158	.35	.75	2.00	4.00

PEOPLES REPUBLIC

100 Centimos = 1 Metica

CENTIMO

ALUMINUM

KM#	Date	Mintage	Fine	VF	XF	Unc
90	1975	15.050	—	—	125.00	185.00

2 CENTIMOS

COPPER-ZINC

KM#	Date	Mintage	Fine	VF	XF	Unc
91	1975	8.242	—	—	80.00	120.00

5 CENTIMOS

COPPER-ZINC

KM#	Date	Mintage	Fine	VF	XF	Unc
92	1975	14.898	—	—	80.00	120.00

10 CENTIMOS

COPPER-ZINC

KM#	Date	Mintage	Fine	VF	XF	Unc
93	1975	18.000	—	—	80.00	120.00

20 CENTIMOS

COPPER-NICKEL

KM#	Date	Mintage	Fine	VF	XF	Unc
94	1975	8.050	—	—	150.00	225.00

50 CENTIMOS

COPPER-NICKEL

KM#	Date	Mintage	Fine	VF	XF	Unc
95	1975	3.050	—	—	175.00	250.00

METICA

COPPER-NICKEL

KM#	Date	Mintage	Fine	VF	XF	Unc
96	1975	2.550	—	—	50.00	80.00

2-1/2 METICAS

COPPER-NICKEL

KM#	Date	Mintage	Fine	VF	XF	Unc
97	1975	1.500	—	—	125.00	200.00

MONETARY REFORM

100 Centavos = 1 Metical

50 CENTAVOS

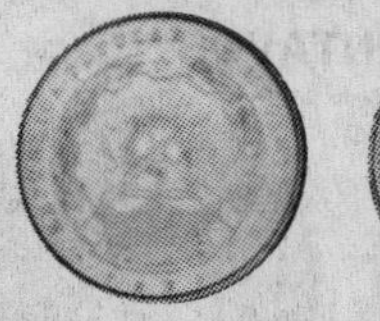

ALUMINUM
Musical Instrument

KM#	Date	Mintage	Fine	VF	XF	Unc
98	1980	5.160	.15	.30	.60	1.00
	1982	—	.15	.30	.60	1.00

METICAL

BRASS
Female Student

KM#	Date	Mintage	Fine	VF	XF	Unc
99	1980	.032	.30	.60	1.25	2.00
	1982	—	.30	.60	1.25	2.00

ALUMINUM

KM#	Date	Mintage	Fine	VF	XF	Unc
99a	1986	—	.25	.50	1.00	1.50

2-1/2 METICAIS

ALUMINUM, 1.80-2.00 g
Ship and Crane in Harbor

KM#	Date	Mintage	Fine	VF	XF	Unc
100	1980	1.088	.25	.50	1.00	1.75
	1982	—	.25	.50	1.00	1.75
	1986	—	.25	.50	1.00	1.75

NOTE: Edge varieties exist.

5 METICAIS

ALUMINUM
Tractor

KM#	Date	Mintage	Fine	VF	XF	Unc
101	1980	7.736	.35	.75	1.25	2.00
	1982	—	.35	.75	1.25	2.00
	1986	—	.35	.75	1.25	2.00

10 METICAIS

COPPER-NICKEL
Industrial Skyline

KM#	Date	Mintage	Fine	VF	XF	Unc
102	1980	.152	.50	1.00	1.75	3.25
	1981	—	.50	1.00	1.75	3.25

ALUMINUM

KM#	Date	Mintage	Fine	VF	XF	Unc
102a	1986	—	.35	.75	1.25	2.25

20 METICAIS

COPPER-NICKEL
Panzer Tank

KM#	Date	Mintage	Fine	VF	XF	Unc
103	1980	.078	.75	1.50	2.50	5.00

ALUMINUM

KM#	Date	Mintage	Fine	VF	XF	Unc
103a	1986	—	.60	1.20	2.00	3.50

50 METICAIS

COPPER-NICKEL
World Fisheries Conference

KM#	Date	Mintage	Fine	VF	XF	Unc
106	1983	.130	2.50	5.00	7.00	10.00

22.0000 g, .925 SILVER, .6543 oz ASW

KM#	Date	Mintage	Fine	VF	XF	Unc
106a	1983	.021	—	—	Proof	35.00

22.0000 g, .900 GOLD, .6366 oz AGW

KM#	Date	Mintage	Fine	VF	XF	Unc
106b	1983	135 pcs.	—	—	Proof	1200.

ALUMINUM
Woman and Soldier With Provisions

KM#	Date	Mintage	Fine	VF	XF	Unc
112	1986	—	.75	1.50	2.50	6.00

250 METICAIS

28.2800 g, .925 SILVER, .8411 oz ASW
10th Anniversary of Independence

KM#	Date	Mintage	Fine	VF	XF	Unc
107	1985	2,000	—	—	Proof	45.00

COPPER-NICKEL

KM#	Date	Mintage	Fine	VF	XF	Unc
107a	1985	—	—	—	—	10.00

500 METICAIS

19.4000 g, .800 SILVER, .4990 oz ASW
5th Anniversary of Independence

KM#	Date	Mintage	Fine	VF	XF	Unc
104	1980	5,000	—	—	Proof	35.00

16.0000 g, .999 SILVER, .5145 oz ASW
Defense of Nature - Lions

KM#	Date	Mintage	Fine	VF	XF	Unc
110	1989	2,000	—	—	Proof	50.00

Defense of Nature - Moorish Idol Fish

KM#	Date	Mintage	Fine	VF	XF	Unc
111	1989	2,000	—	—	Proof	50.00

Defense of Nature - Giraffes

KM#	Date	Mintage	Fine	VF	XF	Unc
113	1990	2,000	—	—	Proof	50.00

1000 METICAIS

COPPER-NICKEL
Visit of Pope John Paul II

KM#	Date	Mintage	Fine	VF	XF	Unc
109	1988	*.080	—	—	—	6.00

28.2800 g, .925 SILVER, .8411 oz ASW

KM#	Date	Mintage	Fine	VF	XF	Unc
109a	1988	*3,500	—	—	Proof	42.50

2000 METICAIS

17.5000 g, .917 GOLD, .5158 oz AGW
10th Anniversary of Independence

KM#	Date	Mintage	Fine	VF	XF	Unc
108	1985	100 pcs.	—	—	Proof	750.00

5000 METICAIS

17.2790 g, .900 GOLD, .5000 oz AGW
5th Anniversary of Independence
Obv: State emblem above denomination.
Rev: Figure at left, corn plants in background, tractor above.

KM#	Date	Mintage	Fine	VF	XF	Unc
105	1980	2,000	—	—	Proof	350.00

MINT SETS (MS)

KM#	Date	Mintage	Identification	Issue Price	Mkt. Val.
MS1	1980(6)	—	KM98-103	—	15.00

SPECIMEN SETS (SS)

KM#	Date	Mintage	Identification	Issue Price	Mkt. Val.
SS1	1975(8)	—	KM90-97	—	2400.

Listings For

MUKALLA: refer to Yemen Democratic Republic
MUSCAT & OMAN: refer to Oman

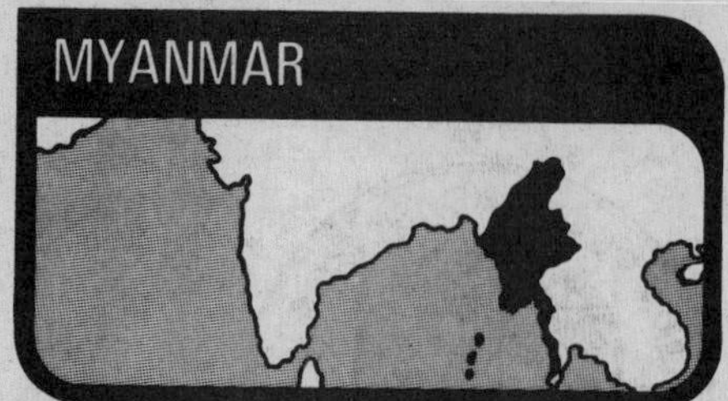

The Union of Myanmar, a country of Southeast Asia fronting on the Bay of Bengal and the Andaman Sea, has an area of 261,218 sq. mi. (678,500 sq. km.) and a population of 38.8 million. Capital: Yangon (Rangoon). Myanmar is an agricultural country heavily dependent on its leading product (rice) which occupies two-thirds of the cultivated area and accounts for 40 per cent of the value of exports. Mineral resources are extensive, but production is low. Petroleum, lead, tin, silver, zinc, nickel cobalt, and precious stones are exported.

The first European to reach Burma, about 1435, was Nicolo Di Conti, a merchant of Venice. During the beginning of the reign of Bodawpaya (1781-1819AD) the kingdom comprised most of the same area as it does today including Arakan which was taken over in 1784-85. The British East India Company, while unsuccessful in its 1612 effort to establish posts along the Bay of Bengal, was enabled by the Anglo-Burmese Wars of 1824-86 to expand to the whole of Burma and to secure its annexation to British India. In 1937, Burma was separated from India, becoming a separate British colony with limited self-government. Burma became an independent nation outside the British Commonwealth on Jan. 4, 1948, the constitution of 1948 providing for a parliamentary democracy and the nationalization of certain industries. However, political and economic problems persisted, and on March 2, 1962, Gen. Ne Win took over the government, suspended the constitution, installed himself as chief of state, and pursued a socialistic program with nationalization of nearly all industry and trade. On Jan. 4, 1974, a new constitution adopted by referendum established Burma as a 'socialist republic' under one-party rule. The country name was changed to Myanmar in 1989.

The coins issued by kings Mindon and Thibaw between 1852 and 1885 circulated in Upper Burma. Indian coins were current in Lower Burma, which was annexed in 1852. Burmese coins are frequently known by the equivalent Indian denominations, although their values are inscribed in Burmese units. Upper Burma was annexed in 1885 and the Burmese coinage remained in circulation until 1889, when Indian coins became current throughout Burma. Coins were again issued in the old Burmese denominations after independence in 1948, but these were replaced by decimal issues in 1952. The Chula-Sakarat (CS) dating is sometimes referred to as BE-Burmese Era and began in 638AD.

RULERS

Bodawpaya, CS1143-1181/ 1782-1819AD

Bagyidaw, CS1181-1198/ 1819-1837AD

Tharawaddy, CS1198-1207/ 1837-46AD

Pagan, CS1207-1214/1846-53AD

Mindon, CS1214-1240/1853-78AD

Thibaw, CS1240-1248/1880-85AD

British, 1886-1948

MONETARY SYSTEM

(Until 1952)

4 Pyas = 1 Pe
2 Pe = 1 Mu
2 Mu = 1 Mat
5 Mat = 1 Kyat

NOTE: Originally 10 light Mu = 1 Kyat but later on 8 heavy Mu = 1 Kyat.

Indian Equivalents

1 Silver Kyat = 1 Rupee = 16 Annas
1 Gold Kyat = 1 Mohur = 16 Rupees

1/8 PYA

LEAD

KM#	Date	Year	Good	VG	Fine	VF
22.1	BE1230	(1868)	—	—	Rare	—

Obv: Legend closer together.

KM#	Date	Year	Good	VG	Fine	VF
22.2	BE1231	(1869)	30.00	50.00	75.00	125.00

1/4 PYA

LEAD, 21-22mm

Obv: Hare crouching left. Rev: Leg. in wreath.

KM#	Date	Year	Good	VG	Fine	VF
23	CS1231	(1869)	25.00	40.00	60.00	100.00

1/4 PE

(Pice)

COPPER

KM#	Date	Year	Good	VG	Fine	VF
17	CS1227	(1865)	2.50	4.50	7.50	13.50

Rev: W/o stars above and below leg.

KM#	Date	Year	Good	VG	Fine	VF
18	CS1227	(1865)	2.50	4.50	7.50	15.00
	IRON					
18a	CS1227	(1865)	22.50	35.00	55.00	85.00

COPPER

Rev: Flower petals at top of wreath upright.

KM#	Date	Year	Good	VG	Fine	VF
25.1	CS1240	(1878)	2.50	4.50	10.00	25.00

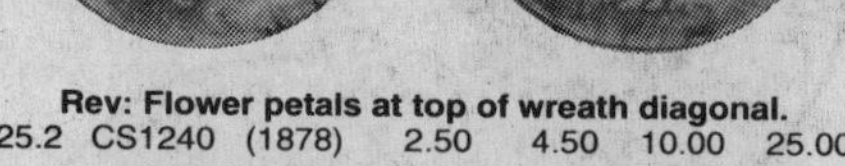

Rev: Flower petals at top of wreath diagonal.

KM#	Date	Year	Good	VG	Fine	VF
25.2	CS1240	(1878)	2.50	4.50	10.00	25.00
	BRASS					
25a	CS1240	(1878)	7.50	12.50	22.50	35.00

TIN

KM#	Date	Year	Good	VG	Fine	VF
25b	CS1240	(1878)	—	—	—	—

2 PYAS

COPPER

KM#	Date	Year	Good	VG	Fine	VF
24	CS1231	(1869)	17.50	30.00	50.00	75.00

PE

0.7300 g, .917 SILVER, .0215 oz ASW

KM#	Date	Year	Fine	VF	XF	Unc
6.1	CS1214	(1852)	12.50	27.50	60.00	100.00
	Accent mark omitted from value.					
6.2	CS1214	(1852)	12.50	27.50	60.00	100.00
	Figure J omitted from date.					
6.3	CS1214	(1852)	12.50	27.50	60.00	100.00
	2 dots omitted from value.					
6.4	CS1214	(1852)	12.50	27.50	60.00	100.00
	Accent marks and 2 dots omitted.					
6.5	CS1214	(1852)	12.50	27.50	60.00	100.00

MU

1.4600 g, .917 SILVER, .0430 oz ASW

KM#	Date	Year	Fine	VF	XF	Unc
7.1	CS1214	(1852)	5.00	10.00	17.50	90.00

Rev: Dot above top left character in denomination.

KM#	Date	Year	Fine	VF	XF	Unc
7.2	CS1214	(1852)	—	—	Proof	450.00

MAT

2.9200 g, .917 SILVER, .0860 oz ASW

KM#	Date	Year	Fine	VF	XF	Unc
8.1	CS1214	(1852)	7.50	12.50	50.00	100.00
	1214	(1852)	—	—	Proof	—
	Tail omitted from last digit of date.					
8.2	CS1214	(1852)	7.50	12.50	50.00	100.00

5 MU

(1/2 Rupee)

5.8300 g, .917 SILVER, .1718 oz ASW

KM#	Date	Year	Fine	VF	XF	Unc
9	CS1214	(1852)	12.50	22.50	70.00	150.00
	CS1214	(1852)	—	—	Proof	—

KYAT

(Rupee)

11.6600 g, .917 SILVER, .3436 oz ASW

KM#	Date	Year	Fine	VF	XF	Unc
10	CS1214	(1852)	7.50	12.50	35.00	150.00
	CS1214	(1852)	—	—	Proof	—

SILVER, 16.23 g

Obv: Peacock w/spread tail, flanked by two groups of 5 rosettes.

KM#	Date	Year	Good	VG	Fine	VF
11	CS1214	(1852)	150.00	350.00	500.00	850.00

Obv: Peacock in full display w/circular feather ends.

KM#	Date	Year	Good	VG	Fine	VF
12	CS1214	(1852)	250.00	500.00	1000.	1500.

SILVER, 39mm, 16.45 g
Obv: Shwepyizoe bird. Rev: Leg. above date.

KM#	Date	Year	Good	VG	Fine	VF
15	BE2396	(1853)	—	—	—	—

SILVER, 32mm, 15.75 g
Obv: Peacock w/folded tail flanked by floral garlands.

KM#	Date	Year	Good	VG	Fine	VF
16	CS1222	(1860)	—	—	—	—

PE

.900 GOLD
Obv: Facing peacock. Rev: Value in wreath.

KM#	Date	Year	Good	VG	Fine	VF
13	CS1214	(1852)	35.00	60.00	85.00	135.00

GOLD, 0.67 g

KM#	Date	Year	Good	VG	Fine	VF
19	CS1228	(1866)	35.00	60.00	95.00	175.00

MU

.900 GOLD
Obv: Facing peacock. Rev: Value in wreath.

KM#	Date	Year	Good	VG	Fine	VF
14	CS1214	(1852)	60.00	100.00	150.00	200.00

2 MU 1 PE

GOLD, 2.75 g

KM#	Date	Year	VG	Fine	VF	XF
20	CS1228	(1866)	125.00	175.00	250.00	450.00

5 MU
(1/2 Mohur)

GOLD, 5.85 g

KM#	Date	Year	Good	VG	Fine	VF
26	CS1240	(1878)	—	—	Rare	—

KYAT
(Mohur)

GOLD, 11.94 g

KM#	Date	Year	Good	VG	Fine	VF
21	CS1228	(1866)	—	—	Rare	—

REPUBLIC

2 PYAS

COPPER-NICKEL

KM#	Date	Mintage	Fine	VF	XF	Unc
27	1949	7.000	.25	.50	1.00	3.00
	1949	100 pcs.	—	—	Proof	100.00

PE

COPPER-NICKEL

KM#	Date	Mintage	Fine	VF	XF	Unc
28	1949	8.000	.35	.75	1.50	4.00
	1949	100 pcs.	—	—	Proof	100.00
	1950	9.500	.35	.75	1.50	4.00
	1950	—	—	—	Proof	—
	1951	6.500	.50	1.00	2.00	5.00
	1951	—	—	—	Proof	—

2 PE

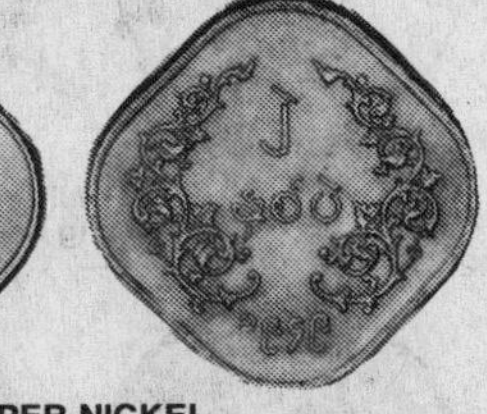

COPPER-NICKEL

KM#	Date	Mintage	Fine	VF	XF	Unc
29	1949	7.100	.50	1.00	2.00	5.00
	1949	100 pcs.	—	—	Proof	100.00
	1950	8.500	.50	1.00	2.00	5.00
	1950	—	—	—	Proof	—
	1951	7.480	.50	1.00	2.00	5.00
	1951	—	—	—	Proof	—

4 PE

NICKEL

KM#	Date	Mintage	Fine	VF	XF	Unc
30	1949	6.500	1.25	2.50	5.00	15.00
	1949	100 pcs.	—	—	Proof	100.00
	1950	6.120	1.00	2.00	4.00	12.00

8 PE

NICKEL

KM#	Date	Mintage	Fine	VF	XF	Unc
31	1949	3.270	1.50	3.00	6.00	25.00
	1949	100 pcs.	—	—	Proof	100.00
	1950	3.900	1.25	2.50	5.00	20.00
	1950	—	—	—	Proof	—

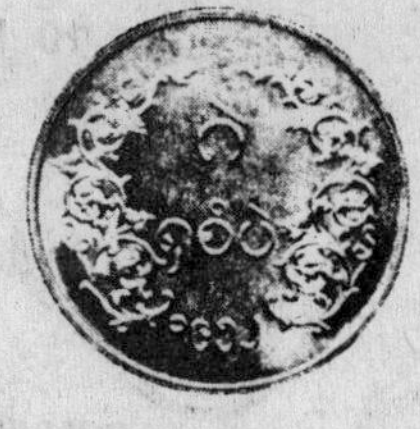

COPPER-NICKEL

KM#	Date	Year	Mintage	Fine	VF	XF	Unc
31a	CS1314	1952	1.642	50.00	100.00	150.00	200.00
	1314	1952	—	—	—	Proof	400.00

DECIMAL COINAGE

100 Pyas = 1 Kyat

PYA

BRONZE

KM#	Date	Year	Mintage	Fine	VF	XF	Unc
32	CS1314	1952	.500	.10	.15	.20	.35
	1314	1952	100 pcs.	—	—	Proof	60.00
	1315	1953	14.000	.10	.15	.20	.35
	1315	1953	—	—	—	Proof	—
	1317	1955	30.000	.10	.15	.20	.35
	1317	1955	—	—	—	Proof	—
	1318	1956	100 pcs.	—	—	Proof	60.00
	1324	1962	100 pcs.	—	—	Proof	60.00
	1327	1965	15.000	.10	.15	.20	.35
	1327	1965	—	—	—	Proof	—

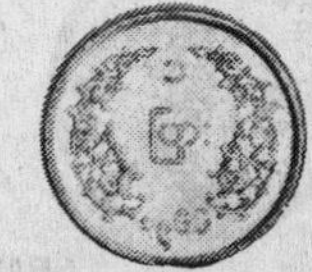

ALUMINUM
Aung San

KM#	Date	Year	Mintage	Fine	VF	XF	Unc
38	CS1328	1966	8.000	.10	.15	.25	.50

5 PYAS

COPPER-NICKEL

KM#	Date	Year	Mintage	Fine	VF	XF	Unc
33	CS1314	1952	20.000	.10	.15	.35	.75
	1314	1952	100 pcs.	—	—	Proof	65.00
	1315	1953	59.700	.10	.15	.35	.75
	1315	1953	—	—	—	Proof	—
	1317	1955	40.272	.10	.15	.35	.75
	1317	1955	—	—	—	Proof	—
	1318	1956	20.000	.10	.15	.35	.75
	1318	1956	100 pcs.	—	—	Proof	65.00
	1323	1961	12.000	.10	.15	.35	.75
	1323	1961	—	—	—	Proof	—
	1324	1962	10.000	.10	.15	.35	.75
	1324	1962	100 pcs.	—	—	Proof	65.00
	1325	1963	40.400	.10	.15	.25	.60
	1325	1963	—	—	—	Proof	—
	1327	1965	43.600	.10	.15	.20	.40
	1327	1965	—	—	—	Proof	—
	1328	1966	20.000	.10	.15	.20	.40
	1328	1966	—	—	—	Proof	—

ALUMINUM
Aung San

KM#	Date	Year	Mintage	Fine	VF	XF	Unc
39	CS1328	1966	—	.10	.20	.35	.60

ALUMINUM-BRONZE
F.A.O. Issue - Rice Plant

KM#	Date	Year	Mintage	Fine	VF	XF	Unc
51		1987	—	.10	.20	.40	.70

10 PYAS

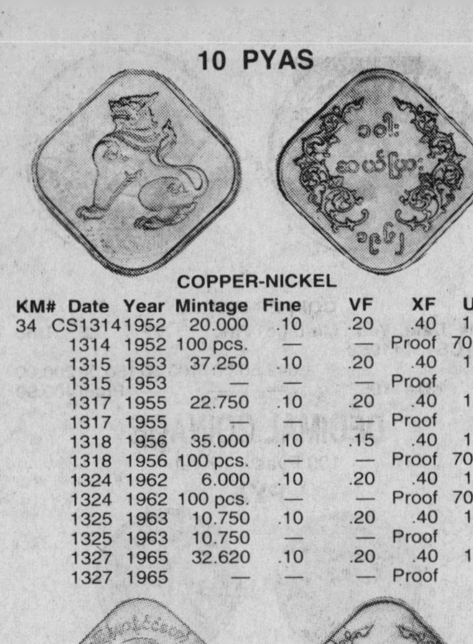

COPPER-NICKEL

KM#	Date	Year	Mintage	Fine	VF	XF	Unc
34	CS1314	1952	20.000	.10	.20	.40	1.00
	1314	1952	100 pcs.	—	—	Proof	70.00
	1315	1953	37.250	.10	.20	.40	1.00
	1315	1953	—	—	—	Proof	—
	1317	1955	22.750	.10	.20	.40	1.00
	1317	1955	—	—	—	Proof	—
	1318	1956	35.000	.10	.15	.40	1.00
	1318	1956	100 pcs.	—	—	Proof	70.00
	1324	1962	6.000	.10	.20	.40	1.00
	1324	1962	100 pcs.	—	—	Proof	70.00
	1325	1963	10.750	.10	.20	.40	1.00
	1325	1963	10.750	—	—	Proof	—
	1327	1965	32.620	.10	.20	.40	1.00
	1327	1965	—	—	—	Proof	—

ALUMINUM
Aung San

KM#	Date	Year	Mintage	Fine	VF	XF	Unc
40	CS1328	1966	—	.15	.30	.60	1.00

BRASS
F.A.O. Issue - Rice Plant

KM#	Year	Mintage	Fine	VF	XF	Unc
49	1983	—	.10	.20	.40	.80

25 PYAS

COPPER-NICKEL

KM#	Date	Year	Mintage	Fine	VF	XF	Unc
35	CS1314	1952	13.540	.10	.20	.50	1.25
	1314	1952	100 pcs.	—	—	Proof	75.00
	1316	1954	18.000	.10	.20	.50	1.25
	1316	1954	—	—	—	Proof	—
	1317	1955	—	—	—	Proof	75.00
	1318	1956	14.000	.10	.20	.50	1.25
	1318	1956	100 pcs.	—	—	Proof	75.00
	1321	1959	6.000	.10	.20	.50	1.25
	1321	1959	—	—	—	Proof	—
	1323	1961	4.000	.10	.20	.50	1.25
	1323	1961	—	—	—	Proof	—
	1324	1962	3.200	.10	.20	.50	1.25
	1324	1962	100 pcs.	—	—	Proof	75.00
	1325	1963	16.000	.10	.15	.30	.75
	1325	1963	—	—	—	Proof	—
	1327	1965	26.000	.10	.15	.30	.75
	1327	1965	—	—	—	Proof	—

ALUMINUM
Aung San

KM#	Date	Year	Mintage	Fine	VF	XF	Unc
41	CS1328	1966	—	.15	.30	.60	1.00

BRONZE
F.A.O. Issue - Rice Plant

KM#	Date	Year	Mintage	Fine	VF	XF	Unc
48		1980	—	.15	.30	.60	1.00

F.A.O. Issue - Rice Plant

KM#	Year	Mintage	Fine	VF	XF	Unc
50	1986	—	.10	.20	.35	.60

COPPER PLATED STEEL

KM#	Year	Mintage	Fine	VF	XF	Unc
50a	1991	—	.15	.50	.60	1.00

50 PYAS

COPPER-NICKEL

KM#	Date	Year	Mintage	Fine	VF	XF	Unc
36	CS1314	1952	2.500	.20	.50	.75	1.75
	1314	1952	100 pcs.	—	—	Proof	80.00
	1316	1954	12.000	.20	.50	.75	1.75
	1316	1954	—	—	—	Proof	—
	1318	1956	8.000	.20	.50	.75	1.75
	1318	1956	100 pcs.	—	—	Proof	80.00
	1323	1961	2.000	.15	.40	.75	1.75
	1323	1961	—	—	—	Proof	—
	1324	1962	.600	.25	.75	1.25	2.25
	1324	1962	100 pcs.	—	—	Proof	80.00
	1325	1963	4.800	.15	.25	.65	1.25
	1325	1963	—	—	—	Proof	—
	1327	1965	2.800	.15	.40	.75	1.75
	1327	1965	—	—	—	Proof	—
	1328	1966	3.400	.10	.30	.75	1.75
	1328	1966	—	—	—	Proof	—

ALUMINUM
Aung San

KM#	Date	Year	Mintage	Fine	VF	XF	Unc
42	CS1328	1966	—	.15	.40	1.00	2.00

BRASS
F.A.O. Issue - Rice Plant

KM#	Date	Mintage	Fine	VF	XF	Unc
46	1975	—	.15	.25	.65	1.25
	1976	—	.15	.25	.65	1.25

KYAT

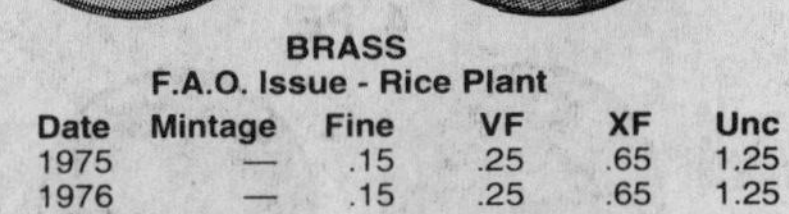

COPPER-NICKEL

KM#	Date	Year	Mintage	Fine	VF	XF	Unc
37	CS1314	1952	2.500	.35	.75	1.50	3.00
	1314	1952	100 pcs.	—	—	Proof	85.00
	1315	1953	7.500	.25	.50	1.00	2.00
	1315	1953	—	—	—	Proof	—
	1318	1956	3.500	.35	.75	1.50	3.00
	1318	1956	100 pcs.	—	—	Proof	85.00
	1324	1962	100 pcs.	—	—	Proof	85.00
	1327	1965	1.000	.35	.75	1.50	3.00
	1327	1965	—	—	—	Proof	—

F.A.O. Issue - Rice Plant

KM#	Date	Mintage	Fine	VF	XF	Unc
47	1975	20.000	.25	.50	1.00	2.00

UNION OF BURMA

Patriotic Liberation Army

MU

2.0000 g, 1.000 GOLD, .0643 oz AGW
Obv: UNION OF BURMA GOVERNMENT 1970-1971 around peacock. Rev. leg: U NU in star SHWE MUZI below.

KM#	Date	Mintage	VF	XF	Unc
43	1970-71	—	—	—	100.00

2 MU

4.0000 g, 1.000 GOLD, .1286 oz AGW

KM#	Date	Mintage	VF	XF	Unc
44	1970-71	—	—	—	200.00

4 MU

8.0000 g, 1.000 GOLD, .2572 oz AGW

KM#	Date	Mintage	VF	XF	Unc
45	1970-71	—	—	—	400.00

PROOF SETS (PS)

KM#	Date	Mintage	Identification	Issue Price	Mkt. Val.
PS1	1949(5)	100	KM27-31	—	500.00
PS2	1952(6)	100	KM32-37	—	435.00
PS3	1956(6)	100	KM32-37	—	435.00
PS4	1962(6)	100	KM32-37	—	435.00

NAMIBIA

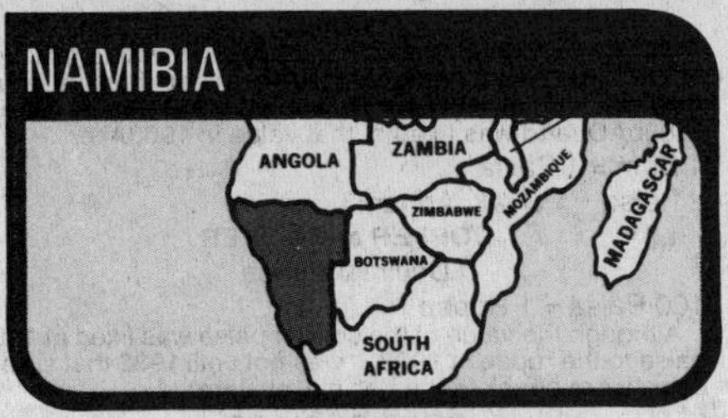

The Republic of Namibia, (formerly the international territory of Namibia), which was once the German colonial territory of German South West Africa, and later South West Africa, is situated on the Atlantic coast of southern Africa, bounded on the north by Angola, on the east by Botswana, and on the south by South Africa. It has an area of 318,261 sq. mi. (824,290 sq. km.) and a population of *1.4 million. Capital: Windhoek. Diamonds, copper, lead, zinc, and cattle are exported.

South Africa undertook the administration of South West Africa under the terms of a League of Nations mandate on Dec. 17, 1920. When the League of Nations was dissolved in 1946, its supervisory authority for South West Africa was inherited by the United Nations. In 1946 the UN denied South Africa's request to annex South West Africa. South Africa Africa responded by refusing to place the territory under a UN trusteeship. In 1950 the International Court of Justice ruled that South Africa could not unilaterally modify the international status of South West Africa. A 1966 UN resolution declaring the mandate terminated was rejected by South Africa, and the status of the area remains in dispute. In June 1968 the UN General Assembly voted to rename the territory Namibia. In 1971 the International Court of Justice ruled that South Africa's presence in Namibia was illegal. In Dec. 1973 the UN appointed a UN Commissioner and a multi-racial Advisory Council was appointed. An interim government was formed in 1977 and independence was to be declared by Dec. 31, 1978. This resolution was rejected by major UN powers. In April 1978 South Africa accepted a plan for UN-supervised elections which led to a political abstention by the South West Africa People's Organization (SWAPO) party leading to dissolvement of the Minister's Council and National Assembly in Jan. 1983. A Multi-Party Conference (MPC) was formed in May 1984 which held talks with SWAPO. The MPC petitioned South Africa for self-government and on June 17, 1985 the Transitional Government of National Unity was installed. Negotiations were held in 1988 between Angola, Cuba, and South Africa reaching a peaceful settlement on Aug. 5, 1988. By April 1989 Cuban troops were to withdraw from Angola and South African troops from Namibia. The Transitional Government resigned on Feb. 28, 1988 for the upcoming elections of the constituent assembly in Nov. 1989. Independence was finally achieved on March 21, 1990.

MONETARY SYSTEM

1 Namibia Dollar = 1 South African Rand

5 CENTS

NICKEL PLATED STEEL

KM#	Date	Mintage	VF	XF	Unc
1	1993	—	—	.15	.25

10 CENTS

NICKEL PLATED STEEL

KM#	Date	Mintage	VF	XF	Unc
2	1993	—	—	.25	.50

50 CENTS

NICKEL PLATED STEEL

KM#	Date	Mintage	VF	XF	Unc
3	1993	—	—	.50	1.00

DOLLAR

BRASS

KM#	Date	Mintage	VF	XF	Unc
4	1993	—	—	1.00	2.00

5 DOLLARS

BRASS

KM#	Date	Mintage	VF	XF	Unc
5	1993	—	—	3.00	6.00

NAURU ISLAND

Pacific Ocean

NAURU

SOLOMON ISLANDS

Nauru, formerly Pleasant Island, is an island republic in the western Pacific Ocean west of the Gilbert Islands. It has an area of 8-1/2 sq. mi. and a population of 7,254. It is known for its phosphate deposits.

The island was discovered in 1798. It was annexed by Germany in 1888 and made a part of the Marshall Island protectorate. In 1914 the island was occupied by Australia and placed under mandate in 1919. During World War II it was seized by the Japanese in August, 1942. It became a joint Australian, British and New Zealand trust territory in 1947 and remained as such until it became an independent republic in 1968.

RULERS

British, until 1968

MONETARY SYSTEM

100 Cents = 1 Dollar

10 DOLLARS

38.7000 g, .925 SILVER, 1.1508 oz ASW
Silver Jubilee of Independence

KM#	Date	Mintage	VF	XF	Unc
1	1993	1,000	—	Proof	55.00
	31.4700 g, .925 SILVER, .9359 oz ASW **Noah's Ark**				
2	1993	*.015	—	Proof	45.00

Listings For

NEJD: refer to Saudi Arabia

NEPAL

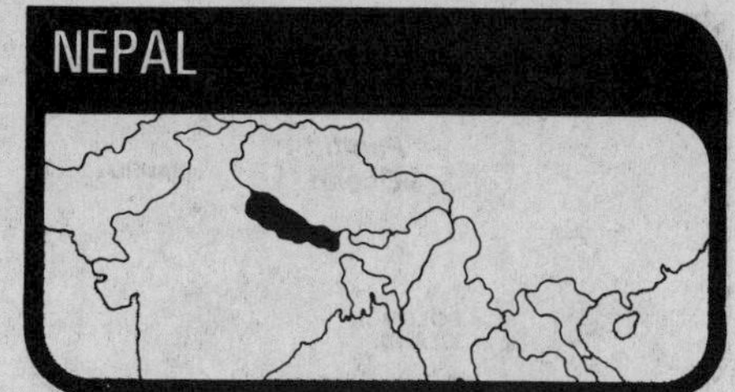

The Kingdom of Nepal, the world's only surviving Hindu kingdom, is a landlocked country occupying the southern slopes of the Himalayas. It has an area of 56,136 sq. mi. (140,800 sq. km.) and a population of 18 million. Capital: Kathmandu. Nepal has deposits of coal, copper, iron and cobalt, but they are largely unexploited. Agriculture is the principal economic activity. Rice, timber and jute are exported, with tourism the other major foreign exchange earner.

Apart from a brief Muslim invasion in the 14th century, Nepal was able to avoid the mainstream of Northern Indian politics, because of its impregnable position in the mountains. It is therefore a unique survivor of the medieval Hindu and Buddhist culture of Northern India, which was largely destroyed by the successive waves of Muslim invasions.

Prior to the late 18th century, Nepal, as we know it today, was divided among a number of small states. Unless otherwise stated, the term "Nepal" applies to the small fertile valley, about 4,500 ft. above sea level, in which the three main cities of Kathmandu, Patan and Bhatgaon are situated.

During the reign of King Yaksha Malla (1428-1482AD), the Nepalese kingdom, with capital at Bhatgaon, was extended northwards into Tibet, and also controlled a considerable area to the south of the hills. After Yaksha Malla's death, the Kingdom was divided among his sons, so four kingdoms were established with capitals at Bhatgaon, Patan, Kathmandu and Banepa, all situated within the small valley, less than 20 miles square. Banepa was quickly absorbed within the territory of Bhatgaon, but the other 3 kingdoms remained until 1769. The internecine strife between the 3 kings effectively stopped Nepal from becoming a major military force during this period, although with its fertile land and strategic position, it was by far the wealthiest and most powerful of the Himalayan states.

Apart from agriculture, Nepal owed its prosperity to its position on one of the easiest trade routes between the great monasteries of central Tibet, and India. Nepal made full use of this, and a trading community was set up in Lhasa during the 16th century, and Nepalese coins became the accepted currency medium in Tibet.

The seeds of discord between Nepal and Tibet were sown during the first half of the 18th century, when the Nepalese debased the coinage, and the fate of the Malla kings of Nepal was sealed when Prithvi Narayan Shah, King of the small state of Gorkha, to the west of Kathmandu, was able to gain control of the transhimalayan trade routes during the years after 1750.

Prithvi Narayan spent several years consolidating his position in hill areas before he finally succeeded in conquering the Kathmandu Valley in 1768, where he established the Shah dynasty, and moved his capital to Kathmandu.

After Prithvi Narayan's death a period of political instability ensued which lasted until the 1840's when the Rana family reduced the monarch to a figurehead and established the post of hereditary Prime Minister. A popular revolution in 1950 toppled the Rana family and reconstituted power in the throne. In 1959 King Mahendra declared Nepal a constitutional monarchy, and in 1962 a new constitution set up a system of panchayat (village council) democracy.

DATING

Nepal Samvat Era (NS)

All coins of the Malla kings of Nepal are dated in the Nepal Samvat era (NS). Year 1 NS began in 881, so to arrive at the AD date add 880 to the NS date. This era was exclusive to Nepal, except for one gold coin of Prana Narayan of Cooch Behar.

Saka Era (SE)

Up until 1888AD all coins of the Gorkha Dynasty were dated in the Saka era (SE). To convert from Saka to AD take Saka date + 78 = AD date. Coins dated with this era have SE before the date in the following listing.

Vikrama Samvat Era (VS)

From 1888AD most copper coins were dated in the Vikram Samvat (VS) era. To convert take VS date - 57 = AD date. Coins with this era have VS before the year in the listing. With the exception of a few gold coins struck in 1890 & 1892, silver and gold coins only changed to the VS era in 1911AD, but now this era is used for all coins struck in Nepal.

RULERS

SHAH DYNASTY

Rana Bahadur

रण वहादु

SE1699-1720/1777-1799AD

Queens of Rana Bahadur

Girvan Yuddha Vikrama

गीर्वाण युद्ध विक्रम सा

SE1720-1738/1799-1816AD

Queens of Girvan Yuddha Vikrama:
Siddhi Lakshmi

सिद्धि लक्ष्मी

Goraksha Rajya Lakshmi

गोरक्ष राज्य लक्ष्मी

Rajendra Vikrama

राजेन्द्र विक्रम

SE1738-1769/1816-1847AD

Queens of Rajendra Vikrama:
Samrajya Lakshmi

साम्राज्य लक्ष्मी

Rajya Lakshmi

राज्य लक्ष्मी

Surendra Vikrama

सुरेन्द्र बिक्रम सा

SE1769-1803/1847-1881AD

Queens of Surendra Vikrama:
Trailokya Raja Lakshmi

त्रैलोक्य राज्य लक्ष्मी

Sura Raja Lakshmi

सुर राज लक्ष्मी

Deva Raja Lakshmi

देवराज लक्ष्मी

Punyakumari Raja Lakshmi

पुण्यकुमारी राज्य लक्ष्मी

Prithvi Vira Vikrama

पृथ्वी वीर विक्रम

SE1803-1833/1881-1911AD
VS1938-1968/

Queens of Prithvi Vira Vikrama:
Lakshmi Divyeswari

लक्ष्मी दिव्येश्वरी

Tribhuvana Vira Vikrama

त्रिभुवनवीर विक्रम

VS1968-2007, 2007-2011/
1911-1950, 1951-1955AD

Jnanendra Vira Vikrama

ज्ञानेन्द्रवीर विक्रम

VS2007/1950-1951AD

Mahendra Vira Vikrama

महेन्द्रवीर विक्रम

VS2012-2028/1955-1972AD

Queens of Mahendra Vira Vikrama:
Ratna Rajya Lakshmi

रत्न राज लक्ष्मी

Birendra Bir Bikram

वीरेन्द्र वीर विक्रम

VS2028/1972-AD

Queen of Birendra
Aishvarya Rajya Lakshmi

ऐश्वर्य राज्य लक्ष्मी देवी

VS2028-/1972-AD

MONETARY SYSTEM

COPPER

Initially the copper paisa was not fixed in value relative to the silver coins, and generally fluctuated in value from 1/32 mohar in 1865AD to around 1/50 mohar after c1880AD, and was fixed at that value in 1903AD.

4 Dam = 1 Paisa
2 Paisa = 1 Dyak, Adhani

COPPER and SILVER

Decimal Series

100 Paisa = 1 Rupee

Although the value of the copper paisa was fixed at 100 paisa to the rupee in 1903, it was not until 1932 that silver coins were struck in the decimal system.

GOLD COINAGE

Nepalese gold coinage until recently did not carry any denominations and was traded for silver, etc. at the local bullion exchange rate. The three basic weight standards used in the following listing are distinguished for convenience, although all were known as Asarphi (gold coin) locally as follows:

GOLD MOHAR

5.60 g Multiples and Fractions

TOLA

12.48 g Multiples and Fractions

GOLD RUPEE or ASARPHI

11.66 g Multiples and Fractions
(Reduced to 10.00 g in 1966)

NOTE: In some instances the gold and silver issues were struck from the same dies.

NUMERALS

Nepal has used more variations of numerals on their coins than any other nation. The commonest are illustrated in the numeral chart in the introduction. The chart below illustrates some variations encompassing the last four centuries.

1	2	3	4	5	6	7	8	9	0
१	२	३	४	५	६	७	८	९	०
१	२		४	५	६	७	८	९	
१			४	५	६	७	८	९	
				५	६	७	८	९	
				५	६		८	९	
				५	६			९	
								९	

NUMERICS

Half	आधा
One	एक
Two	दुइ
Four	चार
Five	पाँच
Ten	दस
Twenty	विस
Twenty-five	पचीस
Fifty	पचास
Hundred	सय

DENOMINATIONS

Paisa	पैसा
Dam	दाम
Mohar	मोहर
Rupee	रुपैयाँ
Ashrapi	अश्रफी
Asarphi	असर्फी

DIE VARIETIES

Although the same dies were usually used both for silver and gold minor denominations, the gold Mohar is easily recognized being less ornate. The following illustrations are of a silver Mohar, KM#602 and a gold Mohar KM#615 issued by Surendra Vikrama Saha Deva in the period SE1769-1803/ 1847-1881AD. Note the similar reverse legend. The obverse usually will start with the character for the word Shri either in single or multiples, the latter as Shri Shri Shri or Shri 3.

OBVERSE

SILVER SE1791 | GOLD SE1793

LEGEND

श्री श्रीश्री सुरेन्द्र बिक्रम साहदेव

Shri Shri Shri Surendra Vikrama Saha Deva (date).

REVERSE

SILVER | GOLD

LEGEND (in center)

श्री ३ भवानी

Shri 3 Bhavani (around outer circle)

श्री श्री श्री गोरषनाथ

Shri Shri Shri Gorakhanatha

SHAH DYNASTY

RANA BAHADUR

SE1699-1720/1777-1799AD

Silver Coinage

1/4 MOHAR

In the name of Queen Raja Rajesvari

SILVER, 1.40 g

KM#	Date	Year	VG	Fine	VF	XF
496	SE1723	(1801)	7.00	10.00	15.00	22.50
	1724	(1802)	7.00	10.00	15.00	22.50

NOTE: Earlier dates (1789-1800) exist for this type.

In the name of Queen Amara Rajesvari

KM#	Date	Year	VG	Fine	VF	XF
497	SE1725	(1802)	50.00	75.00	85.00	100.00

In the name of Queen Suvarna Prabha

KM#	Date	Year	VG	Fine	VF	XF
498	SE1723	(1801)	5.50	9.00	13.50	20.00

In the name of Queen Mahamahesvari

KM#	Date	Year	VG	Fine	VF	XF
499	SE1725	(1803)	65.00	75.00	85.00	100.00

In the name of Queen Lalita Tripura Sundari

KM#	Date	Year	VG	Fine	VF	XF
500	SE1728	(1806)	10.00	13.50	18.50	25.00
	1729	(1807)	10.00	13.50	18.50	25.00
	1738	(1816)	7.00	10.00	15.00	22.50
	1741	(1819)	5.00	8.50	12.50	18.50
	1744	(1822)	10.00	13.50	18.50	25.00

In the name of Queen Lalita Tripura Sundari

3/8 MOHAR

SILVER

KM#	Date	Year	VG	Fine	VF	XF
A501	SE1726	(1804)	250.00	320.00	400.00	500.00

Gold Coinage

1/4 MOHAR

In the name of Queen Raja Rajesvari

GOLD, 1.40 g

KM#	Date	Year	Good	VG	Fine	VF
509	SE1723	(1801)	40.00	50.00	70.00	90.00
	1724	(1802)	40.00	50.00	70.00	90.00

NOTE: Earlier date (1794) exists for this type.

In the name of Queen Amara Rajesvari

KM#	Date	Year	Good	VG	Fine	VF
510	SE1724	(1802)	85.00	100.00	125.00	150.00

In the name of Queen Suvarna Prabha

KM#	Date	Year	Good	VG	Fine	VF
511.1	SE1723	(1801)	40.00	50.00	70.00	90.00

In the name of Queen Mahamahesvari

KM#	Date	Year	Good	VG	Fine	VF
511.2	SE1725	(1803)	150.00	250.00	350.00	500.00

In the name of Queen Lalita Tripura Sundari

KM#	Date	Year	VG	Fine	VF	XF
512	SE1728	(1806)	40.00	50.00	65.00	85.00
	1729	(1807)	40.00	50.00	65.00	85.00
	1741	(1819)	40.00	50.00	65.00	85.00

GIRVAN YUDDHA VIKRAMA

SE1720-1738/1799-1816AD

Copper Coinage

DAM

COPPER, 1.00 g

KM#	Date	Year	VG	Fine	VF	XF
517	VS1861	(1804)	.75	1.25	2.25	3.50

2 DAM

COPPER, 2.00 g

KM#	Date	Year	VG	Fine	VF	XF
A517	VS1861	(1804)	1.50	2.00	4.00	8.00

PAISA

COPPER, 7.60 g

KM#	Date	Year	VG	Fine	VF	XF
C517	VS1859	(1801)	—	7.00	15.00	20.00

2 PAISA

(Dhyak)

COPPER, 20.00 g

KM#	Date	Year	VG	Fine	VF	XF
B517	ND	—	3.00	5.00	10.00	15.00

4 PAISA

(Ganda)

COPPER, 40.00 g

KM#	Date	Year	VG	Fine	VF	XF
D517	ND	—	4.00	6.00	10.00	15.00

Silver Coinage

DAM

Actual Size | 2 x Actual Size

SILVER, uniface, 0.04 g

KM#	Date	Year	VG	Fine	VF	XF
518	ND	(1799-1816)	4.00	8.00	11.50	16.00

1/32 MOHAR

SILVER, uniface, 0.18 g

KM#	Date	Year	VG	Fine	VF	XF
519	ND	(1799-1816)	8.00	13.50	18.50	25.00

1/16 MOHAR

SILVER, 0.35 g

KM#	Date	Year	VG	Fine	VF	XF
520	ND	(1799-1816)	7.50	11.50	16.50	22.50

NOTE: Varieties exist.

1/8 MOHAR

SILVER, 0.70 g

Obv: Shri above sword.

KM#	Date	Year	VG	Fine	VF	XF
521	ND	(1799-1816)	6.00	10.00	13.50	18.50

Obv: Umbrella above sword.

KM#	Date	Year	VG	Fine	VF	XF
522	ND	(1799-1816)	6.00	10.00	13.50	18.50

Obv: Wreath above sword.

KM#	Date	Year	VG	Fine	VF	XF
523	ND	(1799-1816)	6.00	10.00	13.50	18.50

In the name of Queen Siddhi Lakshmi

1/4 MOHAR

SILVER,1.40 g

KM#	Date	Year	VG	Fine	VF	XF
524	SE1730	(1808)	10.00	13.50	18.50	25.00
	1733	(1811)	10.00	13.50	18.50	25.00
	1735	(1813)	10.00	13.50	18.50	25.00

In the name of Queen Goraksha Rajya Lakshmi

KM#	Date	Year	VG	Fine	VF	XF
525	SE1738	(1816)	65.00	75.00	85.00	100.00

1/2 MOHAR

SILVER, 2.77 g

KM#	Date	Year	VG	Fine	VF	XF
526	1728	(1806)	7.50	12.50	20.00	30.00
	1729	(1807)	7.50	12.50	20.00	30.00
	1730	(1808)	5.00	8.50	15.00	22.50
	1733	(1811)	7.50	12.50	20.00	30.00

NOTE: Earlier date (1799) exists for this type.

3/4 MOHAR

SILVER, 4.20 g

KM#	Date	Year	VG	Fine	VF	XF
527	SE1727	(1805)	100.00	200.00	250.00	300.00

MOHAR

SILVER, 5.60 g
Obv: 3 *Shri's* above square.

KM#	Date	Year	VG	Fine	VF	XF
529	SE1723	(1801)	4.50	6.50	9.00	11.50
	1724	(1802)	4.50	6.50	9.00	11.50
	1725	(1803)	4.50	6.50	9.00	11.50
	1728	(1806)	4.50	6.50	9.00	11.50
	1729	(1807)	4.50	6.50	9.00	11.50
	1730	(1808)	4.50	6.50	9.00	11.50
	1731	(1809)	4.50	6.50	9.00	11.50
	1732	(1810)	4.50	6.50	9.00	11.50
	1733	(1811)	4.50	6.50	9.00	11.50
	1734	(1812)	4.50	6.50	9.00	11.50
	1735	(1813)	4.50	6.50	9.00	11.50
	1736	(1814)	4.50	6.50	9.00	11.50
	1737	(1815)	4.50	6.50	9.00	11.50
	1738	(1816)	4.50	6.50	9.00	11.50

NOTE: Earlier dates (1799-1800) exist for this type.

Mule. Obv: KM#547. Rev: KM#529.

KM#	Date	Year	VG	Fine	VF	XF
530	SE1728	(1806)	50.00	80.00	100.00	125.00
	1729	(1807)	50.00	80.00	100.00	125.00

1-1/2 MOHARS

SILVER, 8.40 g

KM#	Date	Year	VG	Fine	VF	XF
531	SE1725	(1803)	25.00	35.00	50.00	75.00
	1726	(1804)	25.00	35.00	50.00	75.00

KM#	Date	Year	VG	Fine	VF	XF
532	SE1727	(1805)	75.00	125.00	175.00	250.00

3 MOHARS

SILVER, 16.80 g
Obv: Flourishes outside central legend.

KM#	Date	Year	VG	Fine	VF	XF
A533	SE1725	(1803)	—	150.00	200.00	250.00

Obv: W/o flourishes outside central legend.

KM#	Date	Year	VG	Fine	VF	XF
533	SE1725	(1803)	—	150.00	200.00	250.00

Similar to 1-1/2 Mohars, KM#532.

KM#	Date	Year	VG	Fine	VF	XF
534	SE1726	(1804)	—	200.00	300.00	400.00

Gold Coinage

DAM

GOLD, uniface, 0.044 g

KM#	Date	VG	Fine	VF	XF
535	ND (1799-1816)	10.00	14.00	20.00	30.00

1/32 MOHAR

GOLD, uniface, 0.175 g

KM#	Date	VG	Fine	VF	XF
536	ND (1799-1816)	14.00	20.00	25.00	40.00

1/16 MOHAR

GOLD, 0.35 g

KM#	Date	VG	Fine	VF	XF
537	ND (1799-1816)	14.00	20.00	25.00	40.00

NOTE: Three varieties exist.

1/8 MOHAR

GOLD, 0.70 g
Obv: *Shri* above sword.

KM#	Date	VG	Fine	VF	XF
538	ND (1799-1816)	22.50	27.50	40.00	60.00

Obv: Umbrella above sword.

KM#	Date	VG	Fine	VF	XF
539	ND (1799-1816)	22.50	27.50	40.00	60.00

In the name of Queen Siddhi Lakshmi

1/4 MOHAR

GOLD, 1.40 g

KM#	Date	Year	VG	Fine	VF	XF
540.1	SE1730	(1808)	40.00	50.00	65.00	85.00

KM#	Date	Year	VG	Fine	VF	XF
540.3	SE1732	(1810)	40.00	50.00	65.00	85.00
	1733	(1811)	40.00	50.00	65.00	85.00

KM#	Date	Year	VG	Fine	VF	XF
540.4	SE1736	(1814)	40.00	50.00	65.00	85.00

In the name of Queen Goraksha Rajyalakshmi

KM#	Date	Year	VG	Fine	VF	XF
540.2	SE1738	(1816)	120.00	150.00	170.00	200.00

1/2 MOHAR

GOLD, 2.80 g

KM#	Date	Year	VG	Fine	VF	XF
541	SE1728	(1806)	70.00	80.00	100.00	125.00
	1729	(1807)	70.00	80.00	100.00	125.00
	1730	(1808)	70.00	80.00	100.00	125.00

NOTE: Earlier date (1799) exists for this type.

KM#	Date	Year	VG	Fine	VF	XF
542	SE1732	(1810)	150.00	200.00	250.00	300.00
	1733	(1811)	150.00	200.00	250.00	300.00
543	SE1736	(1814)	150.00	200.00	250.00	300.00

MOHAR

GOLD, 5.60 g
Similar to KM#529.

KM#	Date	Year	VG	Fine	VF	XF
544	SE1723	(1801)	125.00	150.00	175.00	200.00
	1724	(1802)	125.00	150.00	175.00	200.00
	1728	(1806)	125.00	150.00	175.00	200.00

NOTE: Earlier date (1799) exists for this type.

Obv: Square in center.

KM#	Date	Year	VG	Fine	VF	XF
546	SE1733	(1811)	150.00	175.00	225.00	250.00

1-1/2 MOHARS

GOLD, 8.40 g

KM#	Date	Year	VG	Fine	VF	XF
547	SE1726	(1804)	185.00	225.00	275.00	350.00
	1728	(1806)	185.00	225.00	275.00	350.00
	1729	(1807)	185.00	225.00	275.00	350.00

Rev: Hexagon.

KM#	Date	Year	VG	Fine	VF	XF
548	SE1736	(1814)	185.00	225.00	275.00	350.00

2 MOHARS

GOLD, 11.20 g
Obv: Square in center.

KM#	Date	Year	VG	Fine	VF	XF
550	SE1733	(1811)	250.00	275.00	325.00	375.00

PRESENTATION ISSUES

In the name of Queen Goraksha Rajya Lakshmi

RUPEE

GOLD, 11.66 g

KM#	Date	Year	VG	Fine	VF	XF
551	SE1735	(1813)	400.00	500.00	550.00	600.00

RAJENDRA VIKRAMA

SE1738-1769/1816-1847AD

Silver Coinage

DAM

Actual Size 2 x Actual Size

SILVER, uniface, 0.04 g

KM#	Date	Year	VG	Fine	VF	XF
553	ND	(1816-47)	4.00	6.00	8.00	12.50

1/32 MOHAR

SILVER, uniface, 0.18 g

KM#	Date	Year	VG	Fine	VF	XF
554	ND	(1816-47)	5.50	9.00	12.50	17.50

1/16 MOHAR

SILVER, 0.35 g

KM#	Date	Year	VG	Fine	VF	XF
555	ND	(1816-47)	5.00	8.50	12.00	17.00

1/8 MOHAR

SILVER, 0.70 g
Obv: *Shri* above sword.

KM#	Date	Year	VG	Fine	VF	XF
556	ND	(1816-47)	3.00	5.00	8.50	15.00

Obv: Umbrella above sword.

KM#	Date	Year	VG	Fine	VF	XF
557	ND	(1816-47)	3.00	5.00	8.50	15.00

In the name of Queen Samrajya Lakshmi

1/4 MOHAR

SILVER, 1.40 g

KM#	Date	Year	VG	Fine	VF	XF
558	SE1745	(1823)	8.50	12.50	18.50	25.00
	1746	(1824)	5.00	8.50	12.50	18.50
	1753	(1831)	5.00	8.50	12.50	18.50
	1755	(1833)	5.00	8.50	12.50	18.50

KM#	Date	Year	VG	Fine	VF	XF
559	SE1746	(1824)	5.00	8.50	12.50	18.50
	1759	(1837)	5.00	8.50	12.50	18.50

Obv: Wreath above vase.

KM#	Date	Year	VG	Fine	VF	XF
560	SE1746	(1824)	5.00	8.50	12.50	18.50
	1753	(1831)	5.00	8.50	12.50	18.50
	1759	(1837)	5.00	8.50	12.50	18.50

In the name of Queen Rajya Lakshmi

KM#	Date	Year	VG	Fine	VF	XF
561.1	SE1764	(1842)	8.50	12.50	18.50	25.00
	1766	(1844)	8.50	12.50	18.50	25.00
	1767	(1845)	8.50	12.50	18.50	25.00

Struck w/gold dies. Rev: Circle.

KM#	Date	Year	VG	Fine	VF	XF
561.2	SE1764	(1842)	30.00	40.00	55.00	75.00

1/2 MOHAR

SILVER, 2.80 g
Mule. Obv: KM#563. Rev: KM#526.

KM#	Date	Year	VG	Fine	VF	XF
562	SE1730	(1808)	15.00	25.00	40.00	60.00

KM#	Date	Year	VG	Fine	VF	XF
563	SE1738	(1816)	3.50	6.50	10.00	15.00
	1744	(1822)	7.50	12.50	20.00	30.00
	1746	(1824)	4.50	7.50	12.50	17.50

KM#	Date	Year	VG	Fine	VF	XF
564	SE1746	(1824)	3.50	6.50	10.00	15.00
	1753	(1831)	3.50	6.50	10.00	15.00
	1755	(1833)	3.50	6.50	10.00	15.00
	1757	(1835)	3.50	6.50	10.00	15.00
	1759	(1837)	3.50	6.50	10.00	15.00
	1762	(1840)	3.50	7.50	12.50	16.50
	1764	(1842)	3.50	7.50	12.00	16.50
	1765	(1843)	3.50	7.50	12.00	16.50
	1766	(1844)	3.50	7.50	12.00	16.50

MOHAR

SILVER, 5.60 g
Rev: Moon and sun.

KM#	Date	Year	VG	Fine	VF	XF
565.1	SE1738	(1816)	50.00	90.00	120.00	150.00

KM#	Date	Year	VG	Fine	VF	XF
565.2	SE1738	(1816)	4.50	6.50	9.00	11.50
	1739	(1817)	4.50	6.50	9.00	11.50
	1740	(1818)	4.50	6.50	9.00	11.50
	1741	(1819)	4.50	6.50	9.00	11.50
	1742	(1820)	4.50	6.50	9.00	11.50
	1743	(1821)	4.50	6.50	9.00	11.50
	1744	(1822)	4.50	6.50	9.00	11.50
	1745	(1823)	4.50	6.50	9.00	11.50
	1746	(1824)	4.50	6.50	9.00	11.50
	1747	(1825)	4.50	6.50	9.00	11.50
	1748	(1826)	4.50	6.50	9.00	11.50
	1749	(1827)	4.50	6.50	9.00	11.50
	1750	(1828)	4.50	6.50	9.00	11.50
	1751	(1829)	4.50	6.50	9.00	11.50
	1752	(1830)	4.50	6.50	9.00	11.50
	1753	(1831)	4.50	6.50	9.00	11.50
	1754	(1832)	4.50	6.50	9.00	11.50
	1755	(1833)	4.50	6.50	9.00	11.50
	1756	(1834)	4.50	6.50	9.00	11.50
	1757	(1835)	4.50	6.50	9.00	11.50
	1758	(1836)	4.50	6.50	9.00	11.50
	1759	(1837)	4.50	6.50	9.00	11.50
	1760	(1838)	4.50	6.50	9.00	11.50
	1761	(1839)	7.00	10.00	13.50	17.50
	1762	(1840)	7.00	10.00	13.50	17.50
	1764	(1842)	4.50	6.50	9.00	11.50
	1765	(1843)	7.00	10.00	13.50	17.50
	1766	(1844)	4.50	6.50	9.00	11.50
	1767	(1845)	4.50	6.50	9.00	11.50
	1768	(1846)	4.50	7.50	12.50	16.50
	1769	(1847)	7.00	10.00	13.50	17.50

Obv: *Sri 3* at top.

KM#	Date	Year	VG	Fine	VF	XF
566	SE1740	(1818)	7.00	10.00	13.50	17.50

Obv: Ornamentation reversed.

KM#	Date	Year	VG	Fine	VF	XF
567	SE1762	(1840)	7.00	10.00	13.50	17.50

2 MOHARS

SILVER, 11.20 g

KM#	Date	Year	VG	Fine	VF	XF
568	SE1738	(1816)	25.00	35.00	50.00	75.00
	1740	(1818)	25.00	35.00	50.00	75.00
	1742	(1820)	25.00	35.00	50.00	75.00
	1743	(1821)	25.00	35.00	50.00	75.00
	1744	(1822)	25.00	35.00	50.00	75.00
	1753	(1831)	25.00	35.00	50.00	75.00
	1757	(1835)	25.00	35.00	50.00	75.00
	1764	(1842)	25.00	35.00	50.00	75.00

Gold Coinage

DAM

GOLD, uniface, 0.04 g

KM#	Date	Year	VG	Fine	VF	XF
569	ND	(1816-47)	10.00	14.00	20.00	30.00

1/32 MOHAR

GOLD, uniface, 0.18 g

KM#	Date	Year	VG	Fine	VF	XF
570	ND	(1816-47)	14.00	20.00	25.00	40.00

1/16 MOHAR

GOLD, 0.35 g

KM#	Date	Year	VG	Fine	VF	XF
571	ND	(1816-47)	14.00	20.00	25.00	40.00

1/8 MOHAR

GOLD, 0.70 g

KM#	Date	Year	VG	Fine	VF	XF
572	ND	(1816-47)	22.50	27.50	35.00	50.00

In the name of Queen Samrajya Lakshmi

1/4 MOHAR

GOLD, 1.40 g

KM#	Date	Year	VG	Fine	VF	XF
573.1	SE1746	(1824)	40.00	50.00	65.00	85.00
	1757	(1835)	40.00	50.00	65.00	85.00
	1758	(1836)	40.00	50.00	65.00	85.00
	1759	(1837)	40.00	50.00	65.00	85.00

NOTE: Varieties exist.

KM#	Date	Year	VG	Fine	VF	XF
573.2	SE1757	(1835)	40.00	50.00	65.00	85.00

In the name of Queen Rajya Lakshmi

KM#	Date	Year	VG	Fine	VF	XF
574	SE1764	(1842)	40.00	50.00	65.00	85.00

1/2 MOHAR

GOLD, 2.80 g

KM#	Date	Year	VG	Fine	VF	XF
575	SE1741	(1819)	150.00	200.00	250.00	300.00

KM#	Date	Year	VG	Fine	VF	XF
576	SE1744	(1822)	65.00	75.00	85.00	100.00
	1746	(1824)	65.00	75.00	85.00	100.00
	1753	(1831)	65.00	75.00	85.00	100.00

KM#	Date	Year	VG	Fine	VF	XF
577	SE1757	(1835)	65.00	75.00	85.00	100.00

KM#	Date	Year	VG	Fine	VF	XF
578	SE1757	(1835)	65.00	75.00	85.00	100.00
	1758	(1836)	65.00	75.00	85.00	100.00
	1762	(1840)	65.00	75.00	85.00	100.00
	1764	(1842)	65.00	75.00	85.00	100.00
	1766	(1844)	65.00	75.00	85.00	100.00

MOHAR

GOLD, 24mm, 5.60 g
Obv: Square in center.

KM#	Date	Year	VG	Fine	VF	XF
579	SE1738	(1816)	125.00	150.00	175.00	200.00

27mm
Obv: Circle in center.

KM#	Date	Year	VG	Fine	VF	XF
580	SE1741	(1819)	125.00	150.00	175.00	200.00
	1758	(1836)	125.00	150.00	175.00	200.00
	1760	(1838)	125.00	150.00	175.00	200.00
	1764	(1842)	125.00	150.00	175.00	200.00
	1766	(1844)	125.00	150.00	175.00	200.00
	1768	(1846)	125.00	150.00	175.00	200.00

27mm
Obv: Square in center.

KM#	Date	Year	VG	Fine	VF	XF
581	SE1746	(1824)	135.00	160.00	200.00	250.00
	1757	(1835)	135.00	160.00	200.00	250.00

2 MOHARS

GOLD, 11.20 g

KM#	Date	Year	VG	Fine	VF	XF
582	SE1738	(1816)	250.00	275.00	325.00	375.00
582	1741	(1819)	250.00	275.00	325.00	375.00
	1768	(1846)	250.00	275.00	325.00	375.00

Obv: Square in center.

KM#	Date	Year	VG	Fine	VF	XF
583	SE1746	(1824)	250.00	275.00	325.00	375.00
	1757	(1835)	— Reported, not confirmed			

PRESENTATION ISSUES

In the name of Rajendra Vikrama

RUPEE

GOLD, 11.66 g

KM#	Date	Year	VG	Fine	VF	XF
584	SE1759	(1837)	400.00	500.00	550.00	600.00

2 RUPEES

GOLD, 23.32 g

KM#	Date	Year	VG	Fine	VF	XF
585	SE1762	(1840)	750.00	1000.	1250.	1500.

SURENDRA VIKRAMA

SE1769-1803/1847-1881AD

Copper Coinage

DAM

COPPER

KM#	Date	Year	Good	VG	Fine	VF
586	SE(17)88	(1866)	2.00	3.50	5.00	7.50
	(17)90	(1868)	.75	1.25	2.25	3.50
	(17)91	(1869)	.75	1.25	2.25	3.50
	(17)92	(1870)	.75	1.25	2.25	3.50
	(17)93	(1871)	.75	1.25	2.25	3.50
	(17)94	(1872)	.75	1.25	2.25	3.50
	(17)96	(1874)	.75	1.25	2.25	3.50
	(17)97	(1875)	.75	1.25	2.25	3.50
	(17)98	(1876)	.75	1.25	2.25	3.50
	(17)99	(1877)	.75	1.25	2.25	3.50
	(18)02	(1880)	— Reported, not confirmed			

Machine struck

KM#	Date	Year	Good	VG	Fine	VF
586.1	SE(17)90	(1868)	30.00	45.00	85.00	175.00

1/2 PAISA

COPPER

KM#	Date	Year	Good	VG	Fine	VF
587	SE1802	(1880)	20.00	30.00	35.00	50.00

PAISA

 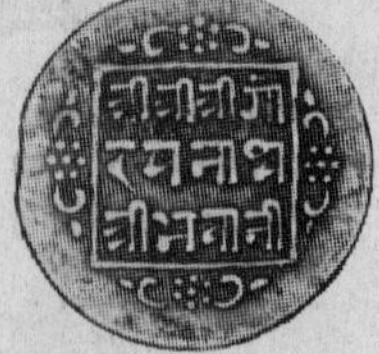

COPPER
Rev. leg: 12 characters.

KM#	Date	Year	Good	VG	Fine	VF
588	SE1787	(1865)	1.75	3.00	5.00	8.00

Obv. and rev: Border of dots.

KM#	Date	Year	Good	VG	Fine	VF
589	SE1787	(1865)	3.00	5.00	7.50	10.00

Rev. leg: 9 characters.

KM#	Date	Year	Good	VG	Fine	VF
590	SE1787	(1865)	1.50	2.00	3.50	5.00
	1788	(1866)	1.50	2.00	3.50	5.00
	1789	(1867)	1.50	2.00	3.50	5.00
	1790	(1868)	1.50	2.00	3.50	5.00
	1791	(1869)	1.50	2.00	3.50	5.00
	1792	(1870)	1.50	2.00	3.50	5.00
	1793	(1871)	1.50	2.00	3.50	5.00
	1794	(1872)	1.50	2.00	3.50	5.00
	1796	(1874)	1.50	2.00	3.50	5.00
	1797	(1875)	1.50	2.00	3.50	5.00
	1798	(1876)	1.50	2.00	3.50	5.00
	1799	(1877)	1.50	2.00	3.50	5.00
	1802	(1880)	15.00	20.00	25.00	35.00

2 PAISA

(Dak)

COPPER
Rev. leg: 12 characters.

KM#	Date	Year	Good	VG	Fine	VF
591	SE1787	(1865)	30.00	40.00	50.00	75.00

Rev. leg: 9 characters.

KM#	Date	Year	Good	VG	Fine	VF
592	SE1788	(1866)	2.00	3.50	5.00	10.00
	1790	(1868)	1.50	2.50	3.50	6.00
	1791	(1869)	1.50	2.50	3.50	6.00
	1796	(1874)	1.75	3.00	4.00	8.00
	1798	(1876)	1.75	3.00	4.00	8.00
	1802	(1880)	30.00	40.00	50.00	75.00

NOTE: Varieties exist.

Silver Coinage

DAM

SILVER, uniface, 0.04 g

KM#	Date	Year	VG	Fine	VF	XF
593	ND	(1847-81)	5.00	7.50	10.00	15.00

1/32 MOHAR

SILVER, uniface, 0.18 g

KM#	Date	Year	VG	Fine	VF	XF
594	ND	(1847-81)	6.00	10.00	13.50	18.50

1/16 MOHAR

SILVER, 0.35 g

KM#	Date	Year	VG	Fine	VF	XF
595	ND	(1847-81)	6.00	10.00	13.50	18.50

1/8 MOHAR

SILVER, 0.70 g

KM#	Date	Year	VG	Fine	VF	XF
596	ND	(1847-81)	5.00	8.50	12.50	17.50

In the name of Queen Trailokya Raja Lakshmi

1/4 MOHAR

SILVER, 1.40 g

KM#	Date	Year	VG	Fine	VF	XF
597	SE1769	(1847)	15.00	20.00	30.00	40.00
	1770	(1848)	15.00	20.00	30.00	40.00
	1772	(1850)	15.00	20.00	30.00	40.00

In the name of Queen Sura Raja Lakshmi

KM#	Date	Year	VG	Fine	VF	XF
598.1	SE1769	(1847)	15.00	25.00	35.00	45.00
	1770	(1848)	15.00	25.00	35.00	45.00
	1772	(1850)	15.00	25.00	35.00	45.00
	1775	(1853)	15.00	25.00	35.00	45.00
	1776	(1854)	15.00	25.00	35.00	45.00
	1782	(1860)	15.00	25.00	35.00	45.00
	1787	(1865)	15.00	25.00	35.00	45.00
	1788	(1866)	15.00	25.00	35.00	45.00

Struck with gold dies

KM#	Date	Year	VG	Fine	VF	XF
598.2	SE1777	(1855)	40.00	50.00	75.00	100.00

In the name of Queen Deva Raja Lakshmi

KM#	Date	Year	VG	Fine	VF	XF
599	SE1769	(1847)	9.00	13.50	20.00	30.00
	1770	(1848)	9.00	13.50	20.00	30.00
	1772	(1850)	9.00	13.50	20.00	30.00
	1773	(1851)	9.00	13.50	20.00	30.00
	1775	(1853)	9.00	13.50	20.00	30.00
	1776	(1854)	9.00	13.50	20.00	30.00

In the name of Queen Punyakumari Raja Lakshmi

KM#	Date	Year	VG	Fine	VF	XF
600	SE1802	(1880)	40.00	50.00	75.00	100.00

1/2 MOHAR

SILVER, 2.80 g

KM#	Date	Year	VG	Fine	VF	XF
601	SE1769	(1847)	5.00	8.50	13.50	20.00
	1770	(1848)	5.00	8.50	13.50	20.00
	1771	(1849)	5.00	8.50	13.50	20.00
	1772	(1850)	5.00	8.50	13.50	20.00
	1773	(1851)	15.00	20.00	25.00	30.00
	1775	(1853)	15.00	20.00	25.00	30.00
	1776	(1854)	15.00	20.00	25.00	30.00
	1787	(1865)	15.00	20.00	25.00	30.00
	1802	(1880)	15.00	20.00	25.00	30.00

MOHAR

SILVER, 5.60 g

KM#	Date	Year	VG	Fine	VF	XF
602	SE1769	(1847)	4.50	6.50	9.00	11.50
	1770	(1848)	4.50	6.50	9.00	11.50
	1771	(1849)	4.50	6.50	9.00	11.50
	1772	(1850)	4.50	6.50	9.00	11.50
	1773	(1851)	4.50	6.50	9.00	11.50
	1774	(1852)	7.00	10.00	13.50	17.50
	1775	(1853)	4.50	6.50	9.00	11.50
	1776	(1854)	4.50	6.50	9.00	11.50
	1777	(1855)	4.50	6.50	9.00	11.50
	1778	(1856)	4.50	6.50	9.00	11.50
	1779	(1857)	4.50	6.50	9.00	11.50
	1780	(1858)	4.50	6.50	9.00	11.50
	1781	(1859)	4.50	6.50	9.00	11.50
	1782	(1860)	4.50	7.50	12.50	16.50
	1785	(1863)	7.00	10.00	13.50	17.50
	1786	(1864)	4.50	6.50	9.00	11.50
	1787	(1865)	4.50	6.50	9.00	11.50
	1788	(1866)	4.50	6.50	9.00	11.50
	1789	(1867)	4.50	6.50	9.00	11.50
	1790	(1868)	4.50	6.50	9.00	11.50
	1791	(1869)	4.50	6.50	9.00	11.50
	1792	(1870)	4.50	6.50	9.00	11.50
	1793	(1871)	4.50	6.50	9.00	11.50
	1794	(1872)	4.50	6.50	9.00	11.50
	1796	(1874)	4.50	6.50	9.00	11.50
	1797	(1875)	4.50	6.50	9.00	11.50
	1800	(1878)	4.50	6.50	9.00	11.50
	1801	(1879)	4.50	6.50	9.00	11.50
	1802	(1880)	4.50	6.50	9.00	11.50
	1803	(1881)	4.50	6.50	9.00	11.50

Machine struck, plain edge

KM#	Date	Year	VG	Fine	VF	XF
602.1	SE1786	(1864)	12.50	15.00	20.00	27.50
	1787	(1865)	7.50	10.00	15.00	22.50
	1788	(1866)	12.50	15.00	20.00	27.50
	1789	(1867)	12.50	15.00	20.00	27.50

Struck using gold dies.

KM#	Date	Year	VG	Fine	VF	XF
602.2	SE1801	(1879)	12.50	15.00	20.00	27.50

2 MOHARS

SILVER, 11.20 g

KM#	Date	Year	VG	Fine	VF	XF
603	SE1769	(1847)	22.50	30.00	40.00	55.00
	1770	(1848)	22.50	30.00	40.00	55.00
	1771	(1849)	22.50	30.00	40.00	55.00
	1772	(1850)	22.50	30.00	40.00	55.00
	1777	(1855)	22.50	30.00	40.00	55.00
	1782	(1860)	22.50	30.00	40.00	55.00
	1796	(1874)	22.50	30.00	40.00	55.00
	1797	(1875)	22.50	30.00	40.00	55.00
	1801	(1879)	17.50	20.00	25.00	40.00
	1802	(1880)	22.50	30.00	40.00	55.00

Machine struck, milled edge

KM#	Date	Year	VG	Fine	VF	XF
603.1	SE1786	(1864)	—	—	Rare	—

26-28mm
Struck w/regular gold dies

KM#	Date	Year	VG	Fine	VF	XF
603.2	SE1801	(1879)	11.50	20.00	28.50	50.00
	1802	(1880)	22.50	30.00	40.00	55.00

Gold Coinage

DAM

Actual Size 2 x Actual Size

GOLD, uniface, 0.04 g
Legend in 2 lines.

KM#	Date	Year	VG	Fine	VF	XF
604	ND	(1847-81)	7.50	10.00	12.50	15.00

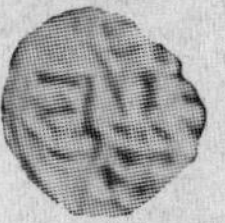

Actual Size 2 X Actual Size

Legend in 3 lines.

KM#	Date	Year	VG	Fine	VF	XF
A604	ND	(1847-81)	15.00	20.00	25.00	30.00

1/32 MOHAR

GOLD, uniface, 0.18 g

KM#	Date	Year	VG	Fine	VF	XF
605	ND	(1847-81)	14.00	20.00	25.00	32.50

1/16 MOHAR

GOLD, 0.35 g

KM#	Date	Year	VG	Fine	VF	XF
606	ND	(1847-81)	14.00	20.00	25.00	32.50

1/8 MOHAR

GOLD, 0.70 g

KM#	Date	Year	VG	Fine	VF	XF
607	ND	(1847-81)	22.50	27.50	35.00	45.00

In the name of Queen Trailokya Raja Lakshmi

1/4 MOHAR

GOLD, 1.40 g

KM#	Date	Year	VG	Fine	VF	XF
A608	SE1769	(1847)	40.00	50.00	65.00	85.00
	1770	(1848)	40.00	50.00	65.00	85.00

In the name of Queen Sura Raja Lakshmi

KM#	Date	Year	VG	Fine	VF	XF
608	SE1769	(1847)	40.00	50.00	65.00	85.00
	1787	(1865)	40.00	50.00	65.00	85.00
	1790	(1868)	40.00	50.00	65.00	85.00

In the name of Queen Deva Raja Lakshmi

KM#	Date	Year	VG	Fine	VF	XF
609	SE1770	(1848)	40.00	50.00	65.00	85.00

In the name of Queen Punyakumari Raja Lakshmi

KM#	Date	Year	VG	Fine	VF	XF
610	SE1802	(1880)	55.00	75.00	100.00	135.00

1/2 MOHAR

GOLD, 2.80 g

KM#	Date	Year	VG	Fine	VF	XF
611	SE1769	(1847)	65.00	75.00	85.00	100.00
	1770	(1848)	65.00	75.00	85.00	100.00
	1802	(1880)	65.00	75.00	85.00	100.00

Rev: W/o horizontal lines.

KM#	Date	Year	VG	Fine	VF	XF
612	SE1790	(1868)	65.00	75.00	85.00	100.00

In the name of Queen Deva Raja Lakshmi

MOHAR

GOLD, 5.60 g

KM#	Date	Year	VG	Fine	VF	XF
613	SE1769	(1847)	115.00	125.00	145.00	175.00
	1791	(1869)	115.00	125.00	145.00	175.00
	1794	(1872)	115.00	125.00	145.00	175.00
	1802	(1880)	115.00	125.00	145.00	175.00

1/2 TOLA

GOLD, 21.5mm, 6.24 g

KM#	Date	Year	VG	Fine	VF	XF
614.1	SE1773	(1851)	125.00	135.00	160.00	200.00

Larger size, 26.5mm

KM#	Date	Year	VG	Fine	VF	XF
614.2	SE1786	(1864)	125.00	135.00	160.00	200.00
	1787	(1865)	125.00	135.00	160.00	200.00

TOLA

GOLD, 12.48 g

KM#	Date	Year	VG	Fine	VF	XF
615	SE1769	(1847)	265.00	285.00	310.00	350.00
	1773	(1851)	265.00	285.00	310.00	350.00
	1774	(1852)	265.00	285.00	310.00	350.00
	1778	(1856)	265.00	285.00	310.00	350.00
	1780	(1858)	265.00	285.00	310.00	350.00
	1786	(1864)	265.00	285.00	310.00	350.00
	1787	(1865)	265.00	285.00	310.00	350.00
	1791	(1869)	265.00	285.00	310.00	350.00
	1793	(1871)	265.00	285.00	310.00	350.00
	1794	(1872)	265.00	285.00	310.00	350.00
	1802	(1880)	265.00	285.00	310.00	350.00

2 RUPEES

GOLD
Similar to 1 Tola, KM#615.

KM#	Date	Year	VG	Fine	VF	XF
616	SE1794	(1872)	450.00	525.00	650.00	800.00

PRESENTATION ISSUES

In the name of Queen Trailokyaraja Lakshmi

RUPEE

GOLD, 11.66 g

KM#	Date	Year	VG	Fine	VF	XF
617.1	SE1769	(1847)	400.00	500.00	550.00	600.00

KM#	Date	Year	VG	Fine	VF	XF
617.2	SE1771	(1849)	285.00	350.00	425.00	500.00

2 RUPEES

SILVER

618 SE1769 (1847) — Reported, not confirmed

GOLD, 23.32 g

KM#	Date	Year	VG	Fine	VF	XF
619	SE1769	(1847)	750.00	1000.	1250.	1500.
	1771	(1849)	750.00	1000.	1250.	1500.

PRITHVI VIRA VIKRAMA

SE1803-1833/VS1938-1968
1881-1911AD

Copper Coinage

DAM

COPPER

KM#	Date	Year	Fine	VF	XF	Unc
620.1	SE(18)18	(1896)	7.50	12.00	15.00	20.00
	(18)19	(1897)	7.50	12.00	15.00	20.00

KM#	Date	Year	Fine	VF	XF	Unc
620.2	VS(19)64	(1907)	7.50	12.00	15.00	20.00

KM#	Date	Year	Fine	VF	XF	Unc
621	VS(19)68	(1911)	4.50	7.50	10.00	17.50

1/2 PAISA

COPPER

KM#	Date	Year	Fine	VF	XF	Unc
622	VS(19)64	(1907)	4.50	7.50	10.00	17.50
	(19)68	(1911)	4.50	7.50	10.00	17.50

PAISA

COPPER
Obv: Trident. Rev. leg: 4 lines.

KM#	Date	Year	Good	VG	Fine	VF
623	SE1810	(1888)	30.00	50.00	75.00	100.00

Obv: Crossed khukris, circular leg. border of flowers.

KM#	Date	Year	Good	VG	Fine	VF
624	VS1945	(1888)	30.00	50.00	75.00	100.00

Obv: 2 footprints above khukris.

KM#	Date	Year	Good	VG	Fine	VF
625	VS1945	(1888)	3.00	5.00	8.50	13.50
	1948	(1891)	9.00	15.00	22.50	35.00

Obv. and rev: Border of XXX's.

KM#	Date	Year	Good	VG	Fine	VF
626	VS1948	(1891)	1.00	1.50	3.00	5.00
	1949	(1892)	2.00	3.00	5.00	8.00

Obv. and rev: Border of crescents.

KM#	Date	Year	Good	VG	Fine	VF
627	VS1949	(1892)	1.00	1.50	3.00	5.00
	1950	(1893)	1.00	1.50	3.00	5.00
	1951	(1894)	1.25	1.75	3.50	6.00

Obv. and rev: Leg. within wreaths.

KM#	Date	Year	Good	VG	Fine	VF
628	VS1949	(1892)	1.00	1.50	3.00	5.00
	1950	(1893)	1.00	1.50	3.00	5.00
	1951	(1894)	1.00	1.50	3.00	5.00
	1952	(1895)	1.00	1.50	3.00	5.00
	1953	(1896)	1.00	1.50	3.00	5.00
	1954	(1897)	1.00	1.50	3.00	5.00
	1955	(1898)	1.00	1.50	3.00	5.00
	1956	(1899)	1.00	1.50	3.00	5.00
	1957	(1900)	1.00	1.50	3.00	5.00
	1959	(1902)	1.00	1.50	3.00	5.00
	1960	(1903)	1.00	1.50	3.00	5.00
	1961	(1904)	1.00	1.50	3.00	5.00
	1962	(1905)	1.00	1.50	3.00	5.00
	1963	(1906)	1.00	1.50	3.00	5.00
	1964	(1907)	1.00	1.50	3.00	5.00

NOTE: Varieties in wreaths exist.

Obv. and rev: Leg. within squares.

KM#	Date	Year	Good	VG	Fine	VF
629	VS1959	(1902)	1.00	1.50	2.50	4.00
	1962	(1905)	1.00	1.50	2.50	4.00
	1963	(1906)	1.00	1.50	2.50	4.00
	1964	(1907)	1.00	1.50	2.50	4.00
	1965	(1908)	1.00	1.50	2.50	4.00
	1966	(1909)	1.00	1.50	2.50	4.00
	1967	(1910)	1.00	1.50	2.50	4.00
	1968	(1911)	1.00	1.50	2.50	4.00

Obv: Leg. within square. Rev: Leg. within circle.

KM#	Date	Year	Good	VG	Fine	VF
630	VS1959	(1902)	7.50	12.50	20.00	33.50

KM#	Date	Year	Fine	VF	XF	Unc
631	VS1964	(1907)	5.50	9.00	15.00	22.50
	1968	(1911)	8.50	13.50	20.00	30.00

2 PAISA

(Dak)

COPPER
Obv. and rev: Circular legends.

KM#	Date	Year	Good	VG	Fine	VF
632	VS1948	(1891)	2.00	3.00	5.00	8.00
	1949	(1892)	2.50	3.50	5.00	8.00
	1950	(1893)	2.50	3.50	5.00	8.00

Obv: Leg. within square. Rev: Leg. within circle.

KM#	Date	Year	Good	VG	Fine	VF
633	VS1959	(1902)	12.50	17.50	25.00	50.00

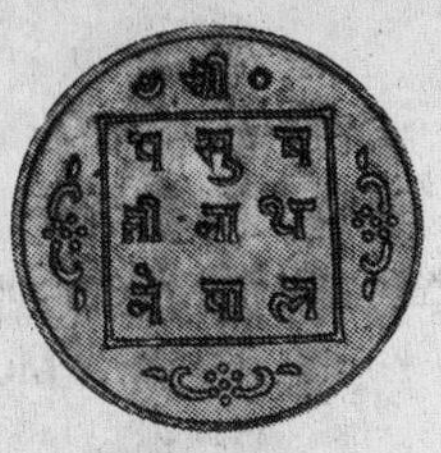

KM#	Date	Year	Fine	VF	XF	Unc
634	VS1964	(1907)	8.50	13.50	20.00	30.00
	1968	(1911)	9.00	15.00	22.50	35.00

Silver Coinage

DAM

SILVER, uniface, 0.04 g
5 characters around sword

KM#	Date	Fine	VF	XF	Unc
635	ND (1881-1911)	8.00	10.00	15.00	25.00

4 characters around sword

KM#	Date	Fine	VF	XF	Unc
636	ND (1881-1911)	15.00	25.00	30.00	40.00

1/32 MOHAR

SILVER, uniface, 0.18 g
Sun and moon

KM#	Date	Year	VG	Fine	VF	XF
637	ND	(1881-1911)	5.00	8.50	12.50	16.50

W/o sun and moon

KM#	Date	Year	VG	Fine	VF	XF
638	ND	(1881-1911)	5.00	8.50	12.50	16.50

1/16 MOHAR

SILVER, 0.35 g

KM#	Date	Year	Fine	VF	XF	Unc
639	ND	(1881-1911)	6.00	10.00	13.50	20.00

NOTE: Varieties exist.

1/8 MOHAR

SILVER, 0.70 g

KM#	Date	Fine	VF	XF	Unc
640	ND (1881-1911)	7.50	12.50	18.50	27.50

NOTE: Varieties exist.

1/4 MOHAR

SILVER, 1.40 g
Rev: 2 moons.

KM#	Date	Year	VG	Fine	VF	XF
641	SE1804	(1882)	15.00	17.50	25.00	35.00
	1806	(1884)	20.00	25.00	35.00	45.00
	1808	(1886)	15.00	17.50	25.00	35.00
	1811	(1889)	20.00	25.00	35.00	45.00

Rev: Moon and spiral sun.

KM#	Date	Year	VG	Fine	VF	XF
642	SE1816	(1894)	1.75	3.00	5.00	7.00
	1817	(1895)	1.75	3.00	5.00	7.00

Rev: Moon and dot for sun.

KM#	Date	Year	VG	Fine	VF	XF
643	SE1827	(1905)	1.75	3.00	5.00	7.00

Machine struck

KM#	Date	Year	VG	Fine	VF	XF
644	SE1833	(1911)	1.75	3.00	5.00	7.00
	1833	(1911)	—	—	Proof	25.00

1/2 MOHAR

SILVER, 2.77 g

KM#	Date	Year	VG	Fine	VF	XF
645	SE1803	(1881)	15.00	20.00	25.00	30.00
	1804	(1882)	15.00	20.00	25.00	30.00

Obv: Leg. modified.

KM#	Date	Year	VG	Fine	VF	XF
646	SE1805	(1883)	15.00	20.00	25.00	30.00

Machine struck, plain edge.

KM#	Date	Year	Fine	VF	XF	Unc
647	SE1816	(1894)	3.00	5.00	7.00	10.00
	1817	(1895)	3.00	5.00	7.00	10.00 •
	1824	(1902)	20.00	25.00	30.00	35.00

NOTE: Varieties exist.

KM#	Date	Year	Fine	VF	XF	Unc
648	SE1826	(1904)	3.00	5.00	7.00	10.00
	1827	(1905)	3.00	5.00	7.00	10.00
	1829	(1907)	3.50	5.50	8.50	11.50

Machine struck, milled edge.

KM#	Date	Year	Fine	VF	XF	Unc
649	SE1832	(1910)	20.00	25.00	30.00	35.00
	1833	(1911)	2.25	3.50	5.00	7.00
	1833	(1911)	—	—	Proof	35.00

MOHAR

SILVER, 5.60 g
Handstruck

KM#	Date	Year	VG	Fine	VF	XF
650	SE1803	(1881)	4.50	6.50	9.00	11.50
	1804	(1882)	4.50	6.50	9.00	11.50

Machine struck, plain edge

KM#	Date	Year	Fine	VF	XF	Unc
651.1	SE1803	(1881)	15.00	25.00	35.00	50.00
	1804	(1882)	4.50	6.50	8.00	10.00
	1805	(1883)	4.50	6.50	8.00	10.00
	1806	(1884)	4.50	6.50	8.00	10.00
	1807	(1885)	4.50	6.50	8.00	10.00
	1808	(1886)	4.50	6.50	8.00	10.00
	1809	(1887)	4.50	6.50	8.00	10.00
	1810	(1888)	4.50	6.50	8.00	10.00
	1811	(1889)	15.00	25.00	35.00	50.00
	1816	(1894)	4.50	6.50	8.00	10.00
	1817	(1895)	4.50	6.50	8.00	10.00
	1818	(1896)	4.50	6.50	8.00	10.00
	1819	(1897)	4.50	6.50	8.00	10.00
	1820	(1898)	4.50	6.50	8.00	10.00
	1821	(1899)	4.50	6.50	8.00	10.00
	1822	(1900)	4.50	6.50	8.00	10.00
	1823	(1901)	4.50	6.50	8.00	10.00
	1824	(1902)	4.50	6.50	8.00	10.00
	1825	(1903)	4.50	6.50	8.00	10.00
	1826	(1904)	4.50	6.50	8.00	10.00
	1827	(1905)	4.50	6.50	8.00	10.00

Machine struck, milled edge

KM#	Date	Year	Fine	VF	XF	Unc
651.2	SE1826	(1904)	4.50	6.50	8.00	10.00
	1827	(1905)	4.50	6.50	8.00	10.00
	1828	(1906)	4.50	6.50	8.00	10.00
	1829	(1907)	4.50	6.50	8.00	10.00
	1830	(1908)	4.50	6.50	8.00	10.00
	1831	(1909)	4.50	6.50	8.00	10.00
	1832	(1910)	4.50	6.50	8.00	10.00
	1833	(1911)	—	25.00	35.00	50.00

NOTE: The date 1833 was only issued in presentation sets.

Rev: Gold die, in error.

KM#	Date	Year	Fine	VF	XF	Unc
652	SE1825	(1903)	10.00	15.00	25.00	32.50

2 MOHARS

SILVER, 27mm, 11.20 g
Hand struck using gold dies.

KM#	Date	Year	Fine	VF	XF	Unc
A653	SE1803	(1881)	40.00	60.00	80.00	100.00

Machine struck, plain edge.

KM#	Date	Year	Fine	VF	XF	Unc
653	SE1804	(1882)	40.00	60.00	80.00	100.00
	1811	(1889)	40.00	60.00	80.00	100.00
	1817	(1895)	8.00	12.50	17.50	25.00

Machine struck using gold dies, plain edge, 29mm.

KM#	Date	Year	Fine	VF	XF	Unc
654	SE1821	(1899)	10.00	15.00	25.00	45.00

Machine struck, milled edge, 27mm

KM#	Date	Year	Fine	VF	XF	Unc
655	SE1829	(1907)	15.00	27.50	40.00	60.00
	1831	(1909)	6.00	9.00	12.50	20.00

Machine struck, 29mm

KM#	Date	Year	Fine	VF	XF	Unc
656	SE1832	(1910)	7.00	9.00	11.50	18.50
	1833	(1911)	6.00	8.00	10.00	16.50

4 MOHARS

SILVER, 22.40 g
Plain edge

KM#	Date	Year	Fine	VF	XF	Unc
657	SE1817	(1895)	60.00	100.00	140.00	200.00

Milled edge

KM#	Date	Year	Fine	VF	XF	Unc
658	SE1833	(1911)	60.00	100.00	140.00	200.00

Gold Coinage

DAM

GOLD, uniface, 0.04 g
5 characters around sword.
Similar to 1/64 Mohar, KM#664.

KM#	Date	Year	Fine	VF	XF	Unc
659	ND	(1881-1911)	10.00	14.00	20.00	27.50

4 characters around sword.
Similar to 1/64 Mohar, KM#663.

KM#	Date	Year	Fine	VF	XF	Unc
660	ND	(1881-1911)	10.00	14.00	20.00	27.50

Actual Size 2 x Actual Size
Circle around characters.

KM#	Date	Year	Fine	VF	XF	Unc
661	ND	(1881-1911)	10.00	14.00	20.00	27.50

Actual Size 2 x Actual Size
2 characters below sword.

KM#	Date	Year	Fine	VF	XF	Unc
662	ND	(1881-1911)	10.00	14.00	20.00	27.50

1/64 MOHAR

Actual Size 2 x Actual Size
GOLD, uniface, 0.09 g
Obv: 4 characters around sword.

KM#	Date	Year	Fine	VF	XF	Unc
663	ND	(1881-1911)	12.50	17.50	22.50	30.00

Actual Size 2 x Actual Size
Obv: 5 characters around sword.

KM#	Date	Year	Fine	VF	XF	Unc
664	ND	(1881-1911)	12.50	17.50	22.50	30.00

1/32 MOHAR

GOLD, uniface, 0.18 g
5 characters around sword.

KM#	Date	Year	Fine	VF	XF	Unc
665	ND	(1881-1911)	20.00	40.00	75.00	100.00

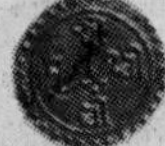

4 characters around sword.

KM#	Date	Year	Fine	VF	XF	Unc
666	ND	(1881-1911)	15.00	30.00	75.00	100.00

1/16 MOHAR

GOLD, 0.35 g

KM#	Date	Year	Fine	VF	XF	Unc
667	ND	(1881-1911)	15.00	40.00	75.00	100.00

KM#	Date	Year	Fine	VF	XF	Unc
668	SE(18)33	(1911)	15.00	30.00	75.00	100.00

1/8 MOHAR

GOLD, 0.70 g
Obv: 6 characters.

KM#	Date	Year	Fine	VF	XF	Unc
669.1	ND	(1881-1911)	22.50	40.00	75.00	100.00

Obv: 5 characters.

KM#	Date	Year	Fine	VF	XF	Unc
669.2	ND	(1881-1911)	22.50	40.00	75.00	100.00

NOTE: Varieties exist.

KM#	Date	Year	Fine	VF	XF	Unc
670	SE(18)33	(1911)	22.50	40.00	75.00	100.00

1/4 MOHAR

GOLD, 1.40 g

KM#	Date	Year	Fine	VF	XF	Unc
671.1	SE1808	(1886)	45.00	60.00	80.00	100.00
	1811	(1889)	45.00	60.00	80.00	100.00
	1817	(1895)	40.00	50.00	60.00	75.00
	1823	(1901)	45.00	60.00	80.00	100.00
	1829	(1907)	40.00	50.00	60.00	75.00

KM#	Date	Year	Fine	VF	XF	Unc
671.2	SE1833	(1911)	40.00	50.00	60.00	75.00

1/2 MOHAR

GOLD, 2.80 g

KM#	Date	Year	Fine	VF	XF	Unc
672.1	SE1805	(1883)	65.00	75.00	85.00	100.00

KM#	Date	Year	Fine	VF	XF	Unc
672.2	SE1817	(1895)	65.00	75.00	85.00	100.00

KM#	Date	Year	Fine	VF	XF	Unc
672.3	SE1823	(1901)	70.00	80.00	100.00	125.00

KM#	Date	Year	Fine	VF	XF	Unc
672.4	SE1829	(1907)	65.00	75.00	85.00	100.00

KM#	Date	Year	Fine	VF	XF	Unc
672.5	SE1833	(1911)	65.00	75.00	85.00	100.00

MOHAR

GOLD, 5.60 g

KM#	Date	Year	Fine	VF	XF	Unc
673.1	SE1804	(1882)	115.00	125.00	145.00	175.00
	1805	(1883)	115.00	125.00	145.00	175.00
	1809	(1887)	115.00	125.00	145.00	175.00
	1817	(1895)	115.00	125.00	145.00	175.00
	1820	(1898)	115.00	125.00	140.00	165.00
	1823	(1901)	115.00	125.00	140.00	165.00
	1825	(1903)	115.00	125.00	140.00	165.00
	1826	(1904)	115.00	125.00	140.00	165.00
	1827	(1905)	115.00	125.00	140.00	165.00

Milled edge

KM#	Date	Year	Fine	VF	XF	Unc
673.2	SE1828	(1906)	115.00	125.00	140.00	165.00
	1829	(1907)	115.00	125.00	140.00	165.00
	1831	(1909)	115.00	125.00	140.00	165.00
	1833	(1911)	115.00	125.00	140.00	165.00
673.3	VS1949	(1892)	115.00	125.00	145.00	175.00

TOLA

GOLD, 12.48 g
Oblique edge milling.

KM#	Date	Year	Fine	VF	XF	Unc
674.1	SE1803	(1881)	250.00	275.00	300.00	335.00
	1805	(1883)	250.00	275.00	300.00	335.00
	1810	(1888)	250.00	275.00	300.00	335.00
	1811	(1889)	250.00	275.00	300.00	335.00

Vertical edge milling.

KM#	Date	Year	Fine	VF	XF	Unc
674.2	SE1803	(1881)	250.00	275.00	300.00	335.00
	1804	(1882)	250.00	275.00	300.00	335.00

Plain edge.

KM#	Date	Year	Fine	VF	XF	Unc
674.3	SE1807	(1885)	250.00	275.00	300.00	325.00
	1817	(1895)	250.00	275.00	300.00	325.00
	1820	(1898)	250.00	275.00	300.00	325.00
	1823	(1901)	250.00	275.00	300.00	325.00
	1824	(1902)	250.00	275.00	300.00	325.00
	1825	(1903)	250.00	275.00	300.00	325.00
	1826	(1904)	250.00	275.00	300.00	325.00

Vertical edge milling.

KM#	Date	Year	Fine	VF	XF	Unc
675.1	SE1828	(1906)	250.00	275.00	300.00	325.00
	1829	(1907)	250.00	275.00	300.00	325.00
	1831	(1909)	250.00	275.00	300.00	325.00
	1832	(1910)	250.00	275.00	300.00	325.00
	1833	(1911)	250.00	275.00	300.00	325.00

Plain edge.

KM#	Date	Year	Fine	VF	XF	Unc
675.2	VS1947	(1890)	250.00	275.00	300.00	325.00

Oblique edge milling.

KM#	Date	Year	Fine	VF	XF	Unc
675.3	VS1949	(1892)	250.00	275.00	300.00	325.00

DUITOLA ASARPHI

GOLD, 23.32 g

KM#	Date	Year	Fine	VF	XF	Unc
676	SE1811	(1889)	600.00	700.00	800.00	1000.

Rev: Die of 4 Mohars, KM#657.

KM#	Date	Year	Fine	VF	XF	Unc
677	SE1817	(1895)	600.00	700.00	800.00	1000.

Plain edge.

KM#	Date	Year	Fine	VF	XF	Unc
678	SE1817	(1895)	600.00	700.00	800.00	1000.
	1825	(1902)	600.00	700.00	800.00	1000.

Milled edge, 27mm.

KM#	Date	Year	Fine	VF	XF	Unc
679	SE1829	(1907)	600.00	650.00	750.00	800.00

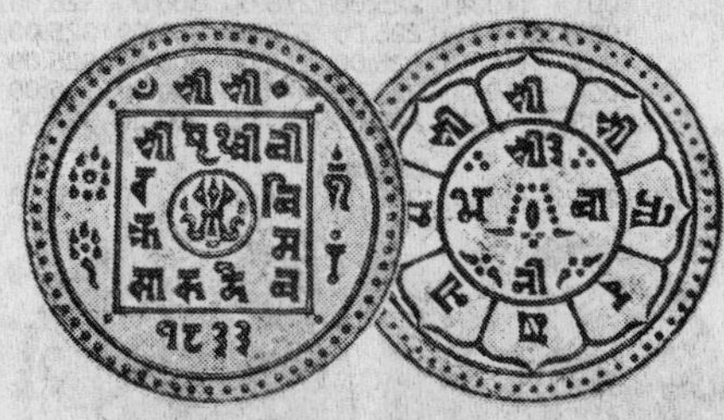

Milled edge, 29mm.

KM#	Date	Year	Fine	VF	XF	Unc
680	SE1833	(1911)	600.00	650.00	750.00	800.00

QUEEN LAKSHMI DIVYESWARI

(Regent for Tribhuvana Vira Vikrama)

Silver Coinage

1/2 MOHAR

SILVER, 2.77 g

KM#	Date	Year	Fine	VF	XF	Unc
681	VS1971	(1914)	4.00	6.00	9.00	11.50

MOHAR

SILVER, 5.60 g

KM#	Date	Year	Fine	VF	XF	Unc
682	VS1971	(1914)	4.50	6.50	9.00	11.50

Gold Coinage

MOHAR

GOLD, 5.60 g

KM#	Date	Year	Fine	VF	XF	Unc
683	VS1971	(1914)	100.00	125.00	145.00	175.00

TRIBHUVANA VIRA VIKRAMA

VS1968-2007/1911-1950AD

Copper Coinage

1/2 PAISA

COPPER

KM#	Date	Year	Fine	VF	XF	Unc
684	VS1978	(1921)	—	—	50.00	75.00
	1985	(1928)	—	—	50.00	75.00

NOTE: Struck only for presentation sets.

PAISA

COPPER
Machine struck

KM#	Date	Year	Good	VG	Fine	VF
685.1	VS1968	(1911)	10.00	20.00	50.00	75.00

Hand struck

KM#	Date	Year	Good	VG	Fine	VF
685.2	VS1969	(1912)	1.00	1.50	2.25	3.50
	1970	(1913)	1.00	1.50	2.25	3.50
	1971	(1914)	1.00	1.50	2.25	3.50
	1972	(1915)	1.00	1.50	2.25	3.50
	1973	(1916)	1.00	1.50	2.25	3.50
	1974	(1917)	1.00	1.50	2.25	3.50
	1975	(1918)	1.00	1.50	2.25	3.50
	1976	(1919)	1.00	1.50	2.25	3.50
	1977	(1920)	1.00	1.50	2.25	3.50

13.5 mm

KM#	Date	Year	Fine	VF	XF	Unc
686.1	VS1975	(1918)	—	—	37.50	50.00

11.5 mm

KM#	Date	Year	Good	VG	Fine	VF
686.2	VS1975	(1918)	—	—	60.00	90.00

NOTE: The above issues are believed to be patterns.

Machine struck, 3.75 g

KM#	Date	Year	Fine	VF	XF	Unc
687.1	VS1975	(1918)	1.25	1.75	3.00	6.00
(687.2)	1976	(1919)	1.25	1.75	3.00	6.00
	1977	(1920)	1.25	1.75	3.00	6.00
	1977 inverted date	(1920)	3.00	4.50	7.50	15.00

NOTE: Varieties of the Khukris exist.

Crude, hand struck

KM#	Date	Year	Good	VG	Fine	VF
687.2	VS1978	(1921)	2.00	3.00	4.50	7.50
(687.1)	1979	(1922)	2.00	3.00	4.50	7.50
	1980	(1923)	4.00	5.00	7.50	12.50
	1981	(1924)	4.00	5.00	7.50	12.50
	1982	(1925)	4.00	5.00	7.50	12.50
	1983	(1926)	4.00	5.00	7.50	12.50

NOTE: Varieties of the Khukris exist.

Machine struck, reduced weight, 2.80 g

KM#	Date	Year	Fine	VF	XF	Unc
688	VS1978	(1921)	1.25	1.75	3.00	6.00
	1979	(1922)	1.25	1.75	3.00	6.00
	1980	(1923)	1.50	3.00	5.00	10.00
	1981	(1924)	1.50	3.00	5.00	10.00
	1982	(1925)	1.25	1.75	3.00	6.00
	1984	(1927)	1.25	1.75	3.00	6.00
	1985	(1928)	1.25	1.75	3.00	6.00
	1986	(1929)	1.25	1.75	3.00	6.00
	1987	(1930)	1.25	1.75	3.00	6.00

2 PAISA

COPPER
Machine struck, 7.50 g

KM#	Date	Year	VG	Fine	VF	XF
689.1	VS1976	(1919)	1.00	2.00	3.00	5.00
(689.2)	1977	(1920)	1.00	2.00	3.00	5.00
	1977 inverted date	(1920)	3.50	5.00	8.50	13.50

NOTE: Varieties of the Khukris exist.

Crude struck

KM#	Date	Year	Good	VG	Fine	VF
689.2	VS1978	(1921)	1.00	2.00	3.50	6.00
(689.1)	1979	(1922)	1.00	2.00	3.50	6.00
	1980	(1923)	1.00	2.00	3.50	6.00
	1981	(1924)	1.00	2.00	3.50	6.00
	1982	(1925)	1.00	2.00	3.50	6.00
	1983	(1926)	1.00	2.00	3.50	6.00
	1984	(1927)	1.00	2.00	3.50	6.00
	1985	(1928)	1.00	2.00	3.50	6.00
	1986	(1929)	1.50	2.50	4.00	7.00
	1987	(1930)	1.50	2.50	4.00	7.00
	1988	(1931)	2.00	3.00	5.00	8.50

NOTE: Varieties of the Khukris exist.

Machine struck, reduced weight, 5.00 g

KM#	Date	Year	VG	Fine	VF	XF
689.3	VS1978	(1921)	1.00	2.00	3.00	4.50
	1979	(1922)	1.00	2.00	3.00	4.50
	1980	(1923)	1.00	2.00	3.00	4.50
	1981	(1924)	1.00	2.00	3.00	4.50
	1982	(1925)	1.00	2.00	3.00	4.50
	1983	(1926)	1.00	2.00	3.00	4.50
	1984	(1927)	1.00	2.00	3.00	4.50
	1991	(1934)	1.50	2.50	4.00	6.00

5 PAISA

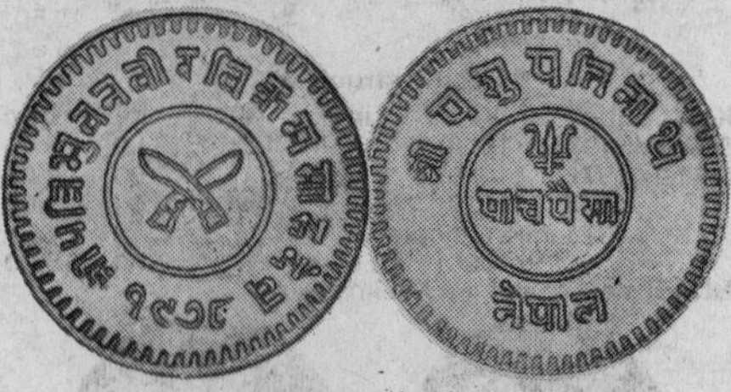

COPPER
Machine struck, 18.00 g

KM#	Date	Year	Fine	VF	XF	Unc
690.1	VS1976	(1919)	6.00	10.00	14.00	20.00
(690.2)	1977	(1920)	1.25	2.25	3.50	6.00
	1977 inverted date					
		(1920)	3.00	5.00	8.50	12.50

NOTE: Varieties of the Khukris exist.

***NOTE:** Previously listed date VS1975 (1918) is considered a pattern.

Crude struck

KM#	Date	Year	Fine	VF	XF	Unc
690.2	VS1978	(1921)	1.75	3.00	5.00	7.50
(690.1)	1979	(1922)	1.75	3.00	5.00	7.50
	1980	(1923)	1.75	3.00	5.00	7.50
	1981	(1924)	1.75	3.00	5.00	7.50
	1982	(1925)	1.75	3.00	5.00	7.50
	1983	(1926)	1.75	3.00	5.00	7.50
	1984	(1927)	1.75	3.00	5.00	7.50
	1985	(1928)	1.75	3.00	5.00	7.50
	1986	(1929)	1.75	3.00	5.00	7.50
	1987	(1930)	1.75	3.00	5.00	7.50
	1988	(1931)	6.00	10.00	14.00	20.00

NOTE: Varieties of the Khukris exist.

Machine struck, reduced weight, 14.00 g

KM#	Date	Year	Fine	VF	XF	Unc
690.3	VS1978	(1921)	1.25	2.25	3.50	5.00
	1979	(1922)	1.25	2.25	3.50	5.00
	1980	(1923)	1.25	2.25	3.50	5.00
	1981	(1924)	1.25	2.25	3.50	5.00
	1982	(1925)	1.25	2.25	3.50	5.00
	1983	(1926)	1.25	2.25	3.50	5.00
	1984	(1927)	1.25	2.25	3.50	5.00
	1991	(1934)	15.00	20.00	25.00	30.00

NOTE: Varieties exist with both open and closed handles on Khukris.

Silver Coinage

DAM

SILVER, uniface, 0.04 g

KM#	Date	Year	Fine	VF	XF	Unc
691	ND	(1911-1950)	15.00	25.00	30.00	50.00

1/4 MOHAR

SILVER, 1.40 g

KM#	Date	Year	VG	Fine	VF	XF
692	VS1969	(1912)	1.75	3.00	5.00	7.00
	1970	(1913)	1.75	3.00	5.00	7.00

1/2 MOHAR

SILVER, 2.80 g

KM#	Date	Year	Fine	VF	XF	Unc
693	VS1968	(1911)	2.25	3.50	5.00	7.00
	1970	(1913)	2.25	3.50	5.00	7.00

MOHAR

SILVER, 5.60 g

KM#	Date	Year	Fine	VF	XF	Unc
694	VS1968	(1911)	4.50	6.50	8.00	10.00
	1969	(1912)	4.50	6.50	8.00	10.00
	1971	(1914)	4.50	6.50	8.00	10.00

2 MOHARS

SILVER, 11.20 g

KM#	Date	Year	Fine	VF	XF	Unc
695	VS1968	(1911)	BV	7.50	10.00	16.50
	1969	(1912)	BV	7.50	10.00	16.50
	1970	(1913)	BV	7.50	10.00	16.50
	1971	(1914)	BV	7.50	10.00	16.50
	1972	(1915)	BV	7.50	10.00	16.50
	1973	(1916)	BV	7.50	10.00	16.50
	1974	(1917)	BV	7.50	10.00	16.50
	1975	(1918)	BV	7.50	10.00	16.50
	1976	(1919)	BV	7.50	10.00	16.50
	1977	(1920)	BV	7.50	10.00	16.50
	1978	(1921)	BV	7.50	10.00	16.50
	1979	(1922)	BV	7.50	10.00	16.50
	1980	(1923)	BV	7.50	10.00	16.50
	1982	(1925)	BV	7.50	10.00	16.50
	1983	(1926)	BV	7.50	10.00	16.50
	1984	(1927)	BV	7.50	10.00	16.50
	1985	(1928)	BV	7.50	10.00	16.50
	1986	(1929)	BV	7.50	10.00	16.50
	1987	(1930)	BV	7.50	10.00	16.50
	1988	(1931)	BV	7.50	10.00	16.50
	1989	(1932)	BV	7.50	10.00	16.50

4 MOHARS

SILVER, 22.40 g

KM#	Date	Year	Fine	VF	XF	Unc
696	VS1971	(1914)	40.00	75.00	125.00	175.00

Gold Coinage

DAM

GOLD, uniface, 0.04 g

KM#	Date	Year	Fine	VF	XF	Unc
697	ND	(1911-50)	25.00	40.00	75.00	100.00

1/32 MOHAR

GOLD, uniface, 0.18 g

KM#	Date	Year	Fine	VF	XF	Unc
698	ND	(1911-50)	35.00	60.00	90.00	125.00

1/16 MOHAR

GOLD, 0.35 g

KM#	Date	Year	Fine	VF	XF	Unc
699	VS(19)77	(1920)	50.00	90.00	120.00	150.00

1/8 MOHAR

GOLD, 0.70 g

KM#	Date	Year	Fine	VF	XF	Unc
700	VS(19)76	(1919)	75.00	120.00	150.00	200.00

1/2 MOHAR

GOLD, 2.80 g

KM#	Date	Year	
701	VS1969	(1912)	— Reported, not confirmed
717	VS1995	(1938)	— Reported, not confirmed

MOHAR

GOLD, 5.60 g

KM#	Date	Year	Fine	VF	XF	Unc
702	VS1969	(1912)	100.00	125.00	140.00	175.00
	1975	(1918)	100.00	125.00	140.00	175.00
	1978	(1921)	100.00	125.00	140.00	175.00
	1979	(1922)	100.00	125.00	140.00	175.00
	1981	(1924)	100.00	125.00	140.00	175.00
	1983	(1926)	100.00	125.00	140.00	175.00
	1985	(1928)	100.00	125.00	140.00	175.00
	1986	(1929)	100.00	125.00	140.00	175.00
	1987	(1930)	100.00	125.00	140.00	175.00
	1989	(1932)	100.00	125.00	140.00	175.00
	1990	(1933)	100.00	125.00	140.00	175.00
	1991	(1934)	100.00	125.00	140.00	175.00
	1998	(1941)	100.00	125.00	140.00	175.00
	1999	(1942)	100.00	125.00	140.00	175.00
	2000	(1943)	100.00	125.00	140.00	175.00
	2003	(1946)	100.00	125.00	140.00	175.00
	2005	(1948)	100.00	125.00	140.00	175.00

KM#	Date	Mintage	Fine	VF	XF	Unc
722	VS1993(1936)					
		.376	— Reported, not confirmed			
	1994(1937)					
		.283	— Reported, not confirmed			

(TOLA) ASHRAPHI

GOLD, 12.48 g, 26.5 g

KM#	Date	Year	Fine	VF	XF	Unc
703.1	VS1969	(1912)	225.00	275.00	300.00	325.00
	1974	(1917)	225.00	275.00	300.00	325.00
	1975	(1918)	225.00	275.00	300.00	325.00
	1976	(1919)	225.00	275.00	300.00	325.00
	1977	(1920)	225.00	275.00	300.00	325.00
	1978	(1921)	225.00	275.00	300.00	325.00
	1979	(1922)	225.00	275.00	300.00	325.00
	1980	(1923)	225.00	275.00	300.00	325.00
	1981	(1924)	225.00	275.00	300.00	325.00
	1982	(1925)	225.00	275.00	300.00	325.00
	1983	(1926)	225.00	275.00	300.00	325.00
	1984	(1927)	225.00	275.00	300.00	325.00
	1985	(1928)	225.00	275.00	300.00	325.00
	1986	(1929)	225.00	275.00	300.00	325.00
	1987	(1930)	225.00	275.00	300.00	325.00
	1988	(1931)	225.00	275.00	300.00	325.00
	1989	(1932)	225.00	275.00	300.00	325.00
	1990	(1933)	225.00	275.00	300.00	325.00
	1991	(1934)	225.00	275.00	300.00	325.00
	1998	(1941)	225.00	275.00	300.00	325.00
	1999	(1942)	225.00	275.00	300.00	325.00
	2000	(1943)	225.00	275.00	300.00	325.00
	2003	(1946)	225.00	275.00	300.00	325.00

29.5mm

KM#	Date	Year	Fine	VF	XF	Unc
703.2	VS2005	(1948)	225.00	275.00	300.00	325.00

Obv: Trident in center.

KM#	Date	Year	Fine	VF	XF	Unc
727	VS1992	(1935)	235.00	250.00	285.00	325.00

DUITOLA ASARPHI

GOLD

Similar to 1 Tola, KM#703.

KM#	Date	Year	Fine	VF	XF	Unc
728	VS2005	(1948)	450.00	500.00	550.00	650.00

DECIMAL COINAGE

100 Paisa = 1 Rupee

1/4 PAISA

COPPER

KM#	Date	Year				
704	VS2000	(1943)	15.00	25.00	30.00	40.00
	2004	(1947)	15.00	25.00	30.00	40.00

1/2 PAISA

COPPER

KM#	Date	Year	Mintage	VF	XF	Unc
705	VS2004	(1947)	—	25.00	30.00	40.00

PAISA

COPPER

KM#	Date	Mintage	Fine	VF	XF	Unc
706	VS1990(1933)	—	.75	1.50	3.00	5.00
	1991(1934)	—	.75	1.50	3.00	5.00
	1992(1935)	—	.75	1.50	3.00	5.00
	1993(1936)	—	.75	1.50	3.00	5.00
	1994(1937)	.456	.75	1.50	3.00	5.00
	1995(1938)	—	.75	1.50	3.00	5.00
	1996(1939)	—	.75	1.50	3.00	5.00
	1997(1940)		.75	1.50	3.00	5.00

KM#	Date	Year	Fine	VF	XF	Unc
707	VS2005	(1948)	.75	1.25	1.75	2.50

BRASS

KM#	Date	Year	Fine	VF	XF	Unc
707a	VS2001	(1944)	.30	.50	.75	1.00
	2003	(1946)	.30	.50	.75	1.00
	2004	(1947)	3.00	5.00	7.00	10.00
	2005	(1948)	.30	.50	.75	1.00
	2006	(1949)	.60	1.00	1.25	1.75

2 PAISA

COPPER

KM#	Date	Year	VG	Fine	VF	XF
708	VS1992	(1935)	3.00	5.00	8.50	13.50

KM#	Date	Mintage	Fine	VF	XF	Unc
709.1	VS1992(1935)	—	2.00	4.00	6.50	10.00
	1993(1936)	.473	1.00	2.00	3.00	5.00
	1994(1937)	1.133	1.00	2.00	3.00	5.00
	1995(1938)	—	1.00	2.00	3.00	5.00
	1996(1939)	—	1.00	2.00	3.00	5.00
	1997(1940)	—	2.00	4.00	6.50	10.00

KM#	Date	Year	Fine	VF	XF	Unc
709.2	VS1992	(1935)	.60	1.00	1.75	3.00
	1994	(1937)	.50	.75	1.50	2.50
	1995	(1938)	2.00	3.50	5.00	7.50
	1996	(1939)	.30	.50	1.00	1.50
	1997	(1940)	.50	.75	1.50	2.50
	1998	(1941)	.50	.75	1.50	2.50
	1999	(1942)	.50	.75	1.50	2.50

KM#	Date	Year	Fine	VF	XF	Unc
710	VS1999	(1942)	.30	.50	1.00	2.00
	2000	(1943)	.30	.50	1.00	2.00
	2003	(1945)	.30	.50	1.00	2.00
	2005	(1948)	3.00	5.00	7.00	10.00

BRASS

KM#	Date	Year	Fine	VF	XF	Unc
710a	VS1999	(1942)	.30	.50	1.00	2.00
	2000	(1943)	.30	.50	1.00	2.00
	2001	(1944)	.30	.50	1.00	2.00
	2005	(1948)	1.75	3.00	5.00	7.50
	2008	(1951)	.30	.50	1.00	2.00
	2009	(1952)	.30	.50	1.00	2.00
	2010	(1953)	.30	.50	1.00	2.00

5 PAISA

COPPER

KM#	Date	Mintage	Fine	VF	XF	Unc
711	VS1992(1935)	—	1.50	3.00	4.50	6.50
	1993(1936)	.878	1.50	3.00	4.50	6.50
	1994(1937)	.403	1.50	3.00	4.50	6.50
	1995(1938)	—	1.00	2.00	3.00	5.00
	1996(1939)	—	1.50	3.00	4.50	6.50
	1997(1940)	—	1.50	3.00	4.50	6.50
	1998(1941)	—	— Reported, not confirmed			

COPPER-NICKEL-ZINC

KM#	Date	Year	Fine	VF	XF	Unc
712	VS2000	(1943)	.65	1.00	1.50	2.50
	2009	(1952)	1.75	3.00	5.00	8.50
	2010	(1953)	1.25	2.00	3.00	5.00

COPPER-NICKEL

KM#	Date	Year	Fine	VF	XF	Unc
712a	VS2010	(1953) (restrike)	.65	1.00	1.50	2.50

1/16 RUPEE

SILVER

KM#	Date	Year	Fine	VF	XF	Unc
713	VS(19)96	(1939)	12.50	20.00	32.50	50.00

20 PAISA

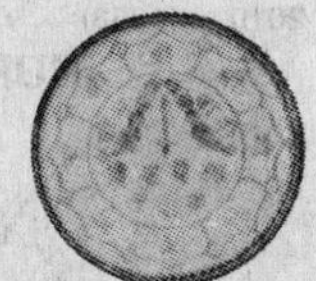

2.2161 g, .333 SILVER, .0237 oz ASW

KM#	Date	Year	Fine	VF	XF	Unc
714	VS1989	(1932)	2.25	4.00	5.00	6.50
	1991	(1934)	1.75	3.50	4.50	6.00
	1992	(1935)	1.75	3.50	4.50	6.00
	1993	(1936)	1.75	3.50	4.50	6.00
	1994	(1937)	3.75	6.50	10.00	15.00
	1995	(1938)	1.75	3.50	4.50	6.00
	1996	(1939)	1.75	3.50	4.50	6.00
	1997	(1940)	1.75	3.50	4.50	6.00
	1998	(1941)	1.75	3.50	4.50	6.00
	1999	(1942)	1.75	3.50	4.50	6.00
	2000	(1943)	1.75	3.50	4.50	6.00
	2001	(1944)	1.75	3.50	4.50	6.00
	2003	(1945)	1.75	3.50	4.50	6.00
	2004	(1947)	1.75	3.50	4.50	6.00
715	VS1989	(1932)	2.25	4.00	6.00	8.50

***NOTE:** The date VS1989 is given in different style characters. Refer to 50 Paisa KM#719 and 1 Rupee, KM#724 for style.

KM#	Date	Year	Fine	VF	XF	Unc
716	VS2006	(1949)	.75	1.00	1.25	1.75
	2007	(1950)	— Reported, not confirmed			
	2009	(1952)	.75	1.00	1.50	2.50
	2010	(1953)	.75	1.00	1.50	2.50

50 PAISA

5.5403 g, .800 SILVER, .1425 oz ASW

KM#	Date	Year	Fine	VF	XF	Unc
718	VS1989	(1932)	5.50	6.50	8.00	10.00
	1991	(1934)	2.50	4.50	7.00	10.00
	1992	(1935)	2.50	4.50	7.00	10.00
	1993	(1936)	2.50	4.50	7.00	10.00
	1994	(1937)	2.50	4.50	7.00	10.00
	1995	(1938)	2.50	4.50	7.00	10.00
	1996	(1939)	2.50	4.50	7.00	10.00
	1997	(1940)	2.50	4.50	7.00	10.00
	1998	(1941)	2.50	4.50	7.00	10.00
	1999	(1942)	2.50	4.50	7.00	10.00
	2000	(1943)	2.50	4.50	7.00	10.00
	2001	(1944)	2.50	4.50	7.00	10.00
	2003	(1946)	2.50	4.50	7.00	10.00
	2004	(1947)	2.50	4.50	7.00	10.00
	2005	(1948)	2.50	4.50	7.00	10.00

KM#	Date	Year	Fine	VF	XF	Unc
719	VS1989	(1932)	2.50	4.50	7.00	9.00

NOTE: The date is given in different characters.

5.5403 g, .333 SILVER, .0593 oz ASW
Obv: 4 dots around trident.

KM#	Date	Year	Fine	VF	XF	Unc
720	VS2005	(1948)	45.00	65.00	90.00	125.00

Obv: W/o dots around trident.

KM#	Date	Year	Fine	VF	XF	Unc
721	VS2006	(1949)	1.50	2.00	2.75	4.50
	2007	(1950)	1.50	2.00	2.75	4.50
	2009/7	(1952/0)	1.50	2.25	3.00	5.00
	2009	(1952)	1.50	2.00	2.75	4.50
	2010	(1953)	1.50	2.00	2.75	4.50

RUPEE

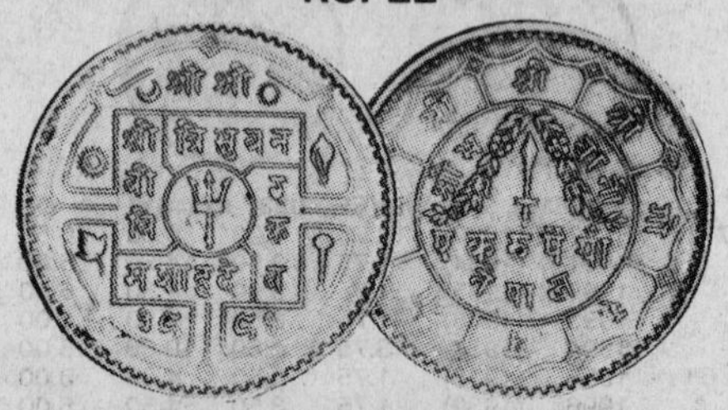

11.0806 g, .800 SILVER, .2850 oz ASW

KM#	Date	Mintage	Fine	VF	XF	Unc
723	VS1989(1932)	—	2.50	5.00	8.00	20.00
	1991(1934)	—	2.50	5.00	8.00	16.50
	1992(1935)	—	2.50	5.00	8.00	16.50
	1993(1936)	1.717	2.50	5.00	8.00	16.50
	1994(1937)	2.097	2.50	5.00	8.00	16.50
	1995(1938)	—	2.50	5.00	8.00	16.50
	1996(1939)	—	2.50	5.00	8.00	16.50
	1997(1940)	—	2.50	5.00	8.00	16.50
	1998(1941)	—	2.50	5.00	8.00	16.50
	1999(1942)	—	2.50	5.00	8.00	16.50
	2000(1943)	—	2.50	5.00	8.00	16.50
	2001(1944)	—	2.50	5.00	8.00	16.50
	2003(1946)	—	2.50	5.00	8.00	16.50
	2005(1948)	—	2.50	5.00	8.00	16.50

KM#	Date	Year	Fine	VF	XF	Unc
724	VS1989	(1932)	7.50	10.00	12.50	15.00

NOTE: The date is given in different characters.

11.0806 g, .333 SILVER, .1186 oz ASW
Obv: 4 dots around trident.

KM#	Date	Year	Fine	VF	XF	Unc
725	VS2005	(1948)	5.00	7.50	10.00	13.50

Obv: W/o dots around trident.

KM#	Date	Year	Fine	VF	XF	Unc
726	VS2006	(1949)	2.50	3.50	5.00	7.50
	2007	(1950)	2.50	3.50	5.00	7.50
	2008	(1951)	2.50	3.50	5.00	7.50
	2009	(1951)	2.50	3.50	5.00	7.50
	2010	(1952)	2.50	3.50	5.00	7.50

JNANENDRA VIRA VIKRAMA

VS2007/1950-1951AD

50 PAISA

5.5403 g, .333 SILVER, .0593 oz ASW

KM#	Date	Year	Mintage	VF	XF	Unc
729	VS2007	(1950)	26 pcs.	175.00	275.00	350.00

RUPEE

11.0806 g, .333 SILVER, .1186 oz ASW

KM#	Date	Year	Fine	VF	XF	Unc
730	VS2007	(1950)	4.50	6.50	9.00	12.50

MOHAR

GOLD

KM#	Date	Year	Fine	VF	XF	Unc
731	VS2007	(1950)	—	—	Rare	—

TOLA

GOLD

KM#	Date	Year	Fine	VF	XF	Unc
732	VS2007	(1950)	—	—	Rare	—

TRIVHUVANA VIRA VIKRAMA

VS2007-2011/1951-1955AD

50 PAISA

COPPER-NICKEL

KM#	Date	Year	Fine	VF	XF	Unc
740	VS2010	(1953)	.50	1.00	2.00	3.00
	2011	(1954)	.35	.75	1.50	2.00

RUPEE

COPPER-NICKEL
Equal denticles at rim.

KM#	Date	Year	Fine	VF	XF	Unc
742	VS2010	(1953)	.75	1.25	2.00	3.50
	2011	(1954)	.75	1.25	2.00	3.50

Unequal denticles at rim.

KM#	Date	Year	Fine	VF	XF	Unc
743	VS2011	(1954)	.75	1.25	2.00	3.50

ANONYMOUS COINAGE

PAISA

BRASS, 18mm

KM#	Date	Year	Fine	VF	XF	Unc
733	VS2010	(1953)	8.00	15.00	20.00	25.00
	2011	(1954)	17.50	25.00	35.00	40.00
	2012	(1955) (restrike)	—	1.00	1.50	2.00

17.5mm

KM#	Date	Year	Fine	VF	XF	Unc
734	VS2012	(1955)	1.25	2.00	2.50	3.50

2 PAISA

BRASS

KM#	Date	Year	Fine	VF	XF	Unc
735	VS2010	(1953)	12.50	20.00	37.50	60.00
	2011	(1954)	30.00	40.00	50.00	75.00
	2011	(1954)	(restrike)		1.50	2.50

KM#	Date	Year	Fine	VF	XF	Unc
749	VS2012	(1955)	.30	.50	.75	1.50
	2013	(1956)	.30	.50	.75	1.50
	2014	(1957)	.30	.50	.75	1.50

4 PAISA

BRASS

KM#	Date	Year	Fine	VF	XF	Unc
754	VS2012	(1955)	1.00	1.75	3.00	5.00

5 PAISA

BRONZE, 3.89 g

KM#	Date	Year	Fine	VF	XF	Unc
736	VS2010	(1953)	2.75	4.50	7.00	10.00
	2011	(1954)	.65	1.00	2.75	5.00
	2012	(1955)	.30	.50	.75	1.00
	2013	(1956)	.30	.50	.75	1.00
	2014	(1957)	.30	.50	.75	1.00

COPPER-NICKEL, 4.04 g (OMS?)

KM#	Date	Year	Fine	VF	XF	Unc
736a	VS2014	(1957)	— Reported, not confirmed			

10 PAISA

BRONZE

KM#	Date	Year	Fine	VF	XF	Unc
737	VS2010	(1953)	2.75	4.50	7.00	10.00
	2011	(1954)	.15	.25	.50	1.00
	2011	(1954)		(restrike)	.15	.25
	2012	(1955)	.15	.25	.50	1.00

20 PAISA

COPPER-NICKEL

KM#	Date	Year	Fine	VF	XF	Unc
738	VS2010	(1953)	12.50	20.00	30.00	40.00
	2010	(1953)		(restrike)	2.50	3.00
	2011	(1954)	32.50	40.00	50.00	60.00

25 PAISA

COPPER-NICKEL

KM#	Date	Year	Fine	VF	XF	Unc
739	VS2010	(1953)	2.00	3.50	4.50	6.00
	2011	(1954)	2.00	3.50	4.50	6.00
	2012	(1955)	1.25	2.00	2.50	3.50
	2014	(1957)	1.25	2.00	2.50	3.50

1/2 ASARPHI

GOLD, 5.80 g
Portrait type.

KM#	Date	Year	Mintage	VF	XF	Unc
741	VS2010	(1953)	—	120.00	140.00	160.00

NOTE: KM#741 is believed to be a restrike.

ASARPHI

GOLD, 11.66 g

KM#	Date	Year	Mintage	VF	XF	Unc
744	VS2010	(1953)	—	175.00	200.00	250.00

MAHENDRA VIRA VIKRAMA

VS2012-2028/1955-1972AD

PAISA

BRASS
Mahendra Coronation

KM#	Date	Year	Fine	VF	XF	Unc
745	VS2013	(1956)	.30	.50	.75	1.00

Rev: Numerals w/shading.

KM#	Date	Year	Fine	VF	XF	Unc
746	VS2014	(1957)	.10	.15	.25	.40
	2015	(1958)	.10	.15	.25	.40
	2018	(1961)	.10	.15	.25	.40
	2019	(1962)	.10	.15	.25	.40
	2020	(1963)	.10	.15	.25	.40

Rev: Numerals w/o shading.

KM#	Date	Year	Fine	VF	XF	Unc
747	VS2021	(1964)	.10	.15	.20	.30
	2022	(1965)	.10	.15	.25	.40

ALUMINUM
National Flower

KM#	Date	Year	Mintage	VF	XF	Unc
748	VS2023	(1966)	—	.10	.15	.25
	2025	(1968)	—	.10	.15	.25
	2026	(1969)	—	.10	.15	.25
	2027	(1970)	2,187	—	Proof	1.25
	2028	(1971)	—	.10	.15	.25
	2028	(1971)	2,380	—	Proof	1.25

2 PAISA

BRASS
Mahendra Coronation
Narrow rim

KM#	Date	Year	Fine	VF	XF	Unc
750.1	VS2013	(1956)	.30	.50	.75	1.00

Wide rim

KM#	Date	Year	Fine	VF	XF	Unc
750.2	VS2013	(1956)	.30	.50	.75	1.00

Rev: Numerals w/shading.

KM#	Date	Year	Fine	VF	XF	Unc
751	VS2014	(1957)	.10	.15	.25	.40
	2015	(1958)	.10	.15	.25	.40
	2016	(1959)	.10	.15	.25	.40
	2018	(1961)	.10	.15	.25	.40
	2019	(1962)	.10	.15	.25	.40
	2020	(1963)	.10	.15	.25	.40

Rev: Numerals w/o shading.

KM#	Date	Year	Fine	VF	XF	Unc
752	VS2021	(1964)	.10	.15	.20	.35
	2022	(1965)	.10	.15	.25	.50
	2023	(1966)	.10	.15	.25	.50

ALUMINUM
Himalayan Monal

KM#	Date	Year	Mintage	VF	XF	Unc
753	VS2023	(1966)	—	.10	.15	.25
	2024	(1967)	—	.10	.15	.25
	2025	(1968)	—	.10	.15	.25
	2026	(1969)	—	.10	.15	.25
	2027	(1970)	—	.10	.15	.25
	2027	(1970)	2,187	—	Proof	1.50
	2028	(1971)	—	.10	.15	.25
	2028	(1971)	2,380	—	Proof	1.50

5 PAISA

BRONZE
Mahendra Coronation
Wide rim w/accent mark.

KM#	Date	Year	Fine	VF	XF	Unc
756.1	VS2013	(1956)	10.00	20.00	30.00	40.00

W/o accent mark.

KM#	Date	Year	Fine	VF	XF	Unc
756.3	VS2013	(1956)	1.00	2.00	3.00	5.00

Narrow rim

KM#	Date	Year	Fine	VF	XF	Unc
756.2	VS2013	(1956)	(restrike)			
			.35	.60	1.00	1.50

Rev: Numerals w/shading.

KM#	Date	Year	Fine	VF	XF	Unc
757	VS2014	(1957)	.10	.20	.30	.75
	2015	(1958)	.10	.20	.30	.75
	2016	(1959)	.10	.30	.50	1.00
	2017	(1960)	.10	.20	.30	.75
	2018	(1961)	.10	.20	.30	.75
	2019	(1962)	.10	.20	.30	.75
	2020	(1963)	.10	.20	.30	.75

ALUMINUM-BRONZE
Rev: Numerals w/o shading.

KM#	Date	Year	Fine	VF	XF	Unc
758	VS2021	(1964)	.50	1.00	1.50	2.50

BRONZE

KM#	Date	Year	Fine	VF	XF	Unc
758a	VS2021	(1964)	.10	.15	.25	.50
	2022	(1965)	.10	.15	.30	.60
	2023	(1966)	.10	.15	.30	.60

ALUMINUM

KM#	Date	Year	Mintage	VF	XF	Unc
759	VS2023	(1966)	—	.15	.25	.50
	2024	(1967)	—	.10	.20	.35
	2025	(1968)	—	.10	.20	.35
	2026	(1969)	—	.10	.20	.25
	2027	(1970)	—	.10	.20	.35
	2027	(1970)	2,187	—	Proof	1.75
	2028	(1971)	—	.10	.20	.35
	2028	(1971)	2,038	—	Proof	1.75

10 PAISA

BRONZE
Mahendra Coronation

KM#	Date	Year	Fine	VF	XF	Unc
761	VS2013	(1956)	.25	.50	.75	1.50

Rev: Numerals w/shading.

KM#	Date	Year	Fine	VF	XF	Unc
762	VS2014	(1957)	2.75	4.50	7.00	10.00
	2015	(1958)	.15	.25	.50	.75
	2016	(1959)	3.00	5.00	7.00	10.00
	2018	(1961)	.15	.25	.50	.75
	2019	(1962)	.15	.25	.50	.75
	2020	(1963)	.15	.25	.50	.75

ALUMINUM-BRONZE
Rev: Numerals w/o shading.

KM#	Date	Year	Fine	VF	XF	Unc
763	VS2021	(1964)	.75	1.25	2.00	3.00

BRONZE, 25mm
Modified design

KM#	Date	Year	Fine	VF	XF	Unc
764	VS2021	(1964)	.10	.15	.25	.50
	2022	(1965)	.10	.15	.25	.50
	2023	(1966)	.10	.15	.25	.50

BRASS

KM#	Date	Year	Mintage	VF	XF	Unc
765	VS2023	(1966)	—	.15	.25	.50
	2024	(1967)	—	.15	.25	.50
	2025	(1968)	—	15.00	17.50	20.00
	2026	(1969)	—	.10	.20	.35
	2027	(1970)	—	.10	.20	.35
	2027	(1970)	2,187	—	Proof	2.00
	2028	(1971)	—	.10	.20	.35
	2028	(1971)	2,380	—	Proof	2.00

F.A.O. Issue

KM#	Date	Year	Mintage	VF	XF	Unc
766	VS2028	(1971)	1.500	.10	.15	.20

25 PAISA

COPPER-NICKEL
Mahendra Coronation

KM#	Date	Year	Fine	VF	XF	Unc
770	VS2013	(1956)	.30	.50	.70	1.00

Obv: 4 characters in line above trident.
Rev: Small character at bottom (outer circle).

KM#	Date	Year	Fine	VF	XF	Unc
771	VS2015	(1958)	1.50	2.50	4.00	6.00
	2018	(1961)	.25	.40	.60	.80
	2020	(1963)	.25	.40	.60	.80
	2022	(1965)	2.00	3.50	6.00	9.00

2.9900 g, .950 SILVER, .0913 oz ASW

KM#	Date	Year	Fine	VF	XF	Unc
771a	VS2017/615	(1960)	—	—	—	100.00

COPPER-NICKEL
Rev: Large different character at bottom.

KM#	Date	Year	Fine	VF	XF	Unc
772	VS2021	(1964)	.30	.50	.70	1.00
	2022	(1965)	.30	.50	.70	1.00
	2023	(1966)	.30	.50	.70	1.00

Obv: 5 characters in line above trident.

KM#	Date	Year	Mintage	VF	XF	Unc
773	VS2024	(1967)	—	.35	.50	.75
	2025	(1968)	—	15.00	20.00	25.00
	2026	(1969)	—	.35	.50	.75
	2027	(1970)	—	.35	.50	.75
	2027	(1970)	2,187	—	Proof	2.50
	2028	(1971)	—	.35	.50	.75
	2028	(1971)	2,380	—	Proof	2.50

50 PAISA

COPPER-NICKEL
Mahendra Coronation

KM#	Date	Year	Fine	VF	XF	Unc
776	VS2013	(1956)	.35	.75	1.00	1.50

Rev: Small character at bottom (outer circle).

KM#	Date	Year	Fine	VF	XF	Unc
777	VS2011	(1954)	.50	1.00	1.50	3.00
	2012	(1955)	.25	.50	.75	1.00
	2013	(1956)	.25	.50	1.00	2.00
	2014	(1957)	.25	.50	1.00	2.00
	2015	(1958)	.25	.50	1.00	2.00
	2016	(1959)	.25	.50	1.00	2.00
	2017	(1960)	.25	.30	.75	1.25
	2018	(1961)	.25	.50	1.00	2.00
	2020	(1963)	.25	.30	.75	1.50

Rev: Large different character at bottom.

KM#	Date	Year	Fine	VF	XF	Unc
778	VS2021	(1964)	.25	.35	.50	.75
	2022	(1965)	.25	.50	.75	1.50
	2023	(1966)	.25	.50	.75	1.00

Reduced size, 23.5mm
Obv: 4 characters in line above trident.

KM#	Date	Year	Fine	VF	XF	Unc
779	VS2023	(1966)	.25	.50	.75	1.50

Obv: 5 characters in line above trident.

KM#	Date	Year	Mintage	VF	XF	Unc
780	VS2025	(1968)	—	.30	.50	1.00
	2026	(1969)	—	.30	.50	.85
	2027	(1970)	2,187	—	Proof	3.00
	2028	(1971)	2,380	—	Proof	3.00

RUPEE

COPPER-NICKEL, 29.6mm

KM#	Date	Year	Fine	VF	XF	Unc
784	VS2011	(1954)	1.25	2.25	3.50	5.00
	2012	(1955)	1.00	1.75	2.50	4.00

Reduced size, 28.8mm.
Rev: Small character at bottom (outer circle).

KM#	Date	Year	Fine	VF	XF	Unc
785	VS2012	(1955)	.50	.85	1.25	1.75
	2013	(1956)	.50	.85	1.25	1.75
	2014	(1957)	.50	.85	1.25	1.75
	2015	(1958)	.50	.85	1.25	1.75
	2016	(1959)	.50	.85	1.25	1.75
	2018	(1961)	.50	.85	1.25	1.75
	2020	(1963)	.50	.85	1.25	1.75

Rev: Large character at bottom.

KM#	Date	Year	Fine	VF	XF	Unc
786	VS2021	(1964)	.50	.75	1.00	1.50
	2022	(1965)	.50	1.00	1.50	2.50
	2023	(1966)	4.50	7.50	10.00	15.00

Reduced size, 27mm.
Obv: 4 characters in line above trident.

KM#	Date	Year	Fine	VF	XF	Unc
787	VS2023	(1966)	.75	1.00	1.35	2.00

Obv: 5 characters in line above trident.

KM#	Date	Year	Mintage	VF	XF	Unc
788	VS2025	(1968)	—	1.00	1.50	2.00
	2026	(1969)	—	1.00	1.40	2.00
	2027	(1970)	2,187	—	Proof	4.50
	2028	(1971)	2,380	—	Proof	4.50

COPPER-NICKEL
Mahendra Coronation

KM#	Date	Year	Fine	VF	XF	Unc
790	VS2013	(1956)	—	1.25	1.75	2.50

10 RUPEES

15.6000 g, .600 SILVER, .3009 oz ASW
F.A.O. Issue

KM#	Date	Year	Mintage	VF	XF	Unc
794	VS2025	(1968)	1.000	3.00	4.00	8.00

1/6 ASARPHI

GOLD, 1.90 g
Mahendra Coronation

KM#	Date	Year	Fine	VF	XF	Unc
767	VS2013	(1956)	—	50.00	60.00	100.00

1/5 ASARPHI

GOLD, 2.33 g

KM#	Date	Year	Fine	VF	XF	Unc
768	VS2010	(1953)	—	50.00	60.00	100.00
	2012	(1955)	—	Reported, not confirmed		

1/4 ASARPHI

GOLD, 2.90 g

KM#	Date	Year	Fine	VF	XF	Unc
774	VS2010	(1953)	60.00	70.00	80.00	100.00
	2012	(1955)	—	Reported, not confirmed		

NOTE: Coins dated VS2010 are believed to be restrikes.

Reduced weight, 2.50 g.

KM#	Date	Year	Fine	VF	XF	Unc
775	VS2026	(1969)	—	—	75.00	100.00

1/2 ASARPHI

GOLD, 5.80 g
Mahendra Coronation

KM#	Date	Year	Fine	VF	XF	Unc
781	VS2013	(1956)	—	120.00	135.00	160.00

KM#	Date	Year	Fine	VF	XF	Unc
782	VS2012	(1955)	—	120.00	135.00	160.00
	2019	(1962)	—	120.00	135.00	160.00

5.00 g
Virendra Marriage

KM#	Date	Year	Fine	VF	XF	Unc
783	VS2026	(1969)	—	—	150.00	175.00

ASARPHI

GOLD

KM#	Date	Year	Mintage	VF	XF	Unc
789	VS2012	(1955)	—	225.00	250.00	300.00
	2019	(1962)	—	225.00	250.00	300.00

Mahendra Coronation

KM#	Date	Year	Mintage	VF	XF	Unc
791	VS2013	(1956)	—	225.00	250.00	300.00

10.00 g

KM#	Date	Year	Mintage	VF	XF	Unc
792	VS2026	(1969)	—	225.00	250.00	300.00

2 ASARPHI

GOLD

KM#	Date	Year	Fine	VF	XF	Unc
793	VS2012	(1955)	—	500.00	550.00	625.00

In the name of Queen Ratna Rajya Lakshmi

50 PAISA

COPPER-NICKEL

KM#	Date	Year	Mintage	VF	XF	Unc
795	VS2012	(1955)	3,000	100.00	125.00	150.00

RUPEE

COPPER-NICKEL

KM#	Date	Year	Mintage	VF	XF	Unc
797	VS2012	(1955)	2,000	100.00	150.00	175.00

1/2 ASARPHI

GOLD

KM#	Date	Year	Mintage	VF	XF	Unc
796	VS2012	(1955)	Reported, not confirmed			

ASARPHI

GOLD, 11.66 g

KM#	Date	Year	Mintage	VF	XF	Unc
798	VS2012	(1955)	Reported, not confirmed			

VIRENDRA VIR VIKRAMA

VS2028-/1972-AD

PAISA

ALUMINUM
National Flower

KM#	Date	Year	Mintage	VF	XF	Unc
799	VS2028	(1972)	.010	.20	.30	.40
	2029	(1972)	3.036	.10	.15	.25
	2029	(1972)	3,943	—	Proof	.60
	2030	(1973)	1.279	.10	.15	.25
	2030	(1973)	8,891	—	Proof	.40
	2031	(1974)	.430	.10	.15	.25
	2031	(1974)	.011	—	Proof	.40
	2032	(1975)	.324	.10	.15	.25
	2033	(1976)	.217	—	.10	.25
	2034	(1977)	1.040	.10	.15	.25
	2035	(1978)	.394	.10	.15	.25
	2036	(1979)	—	.10	.15	.25

Virendra Coronation

KM#	Date	Year	Mintage	VF	XF	Unc
800	VS2031	(1974)	.075	.10	.15	.25

COPPER-NICKEL

KM#	Date	Year	Mintage	VF	XF	Unc
800a	VS2031	(1974)	1,000	—	Proof	2.50

ALUMINUM

KM#	Date	Year	Mintage	VF	XF	Unc
1012	VS2039	(1982)	—	4.00	6.00	8.00
	2040	(1983)	.042	Reported, not confirmed		

2 PAISA

ALUMINUM
Himalayan Monal

KM#	Date	Year	Mintage	VF	XF	Unc
801	VS2028	(1972)	8,319	.20	.30	.50
	2029	(1972)	5.206	.10	.15	.25
	2029	(1972)	3,943	—	Proof	.70
	2030	(1973)	2.563	.10	.15	.25
	2030	(1973)	8,891	—	Proof	.50
	2031	(1974)	.011	—	Proof	.50
	2033	(1976)	.072	.10	.15	.30
	2035	(1978)	.026	.10	.15	.30

5 PAISA

ALUMINUM

KM#	Date	Year	Mintage	VF	XF	Unc
802	VS2028	(1972)	3.700	.10	.20	.35
	2029	(1972)	23.578	.10	.20	.35
	2029	(1972)	3,943	—	Proof	.85
	2030	(1973)	12.320	.10	.20	.35
	2030	(1973)	8,891	—	Proof	.60
	2031	(1974)	15.730	.10	.20	.35
	2031	(1974)	.011	—	Proof	.60
	2032	(1975)	19.747	.10	.20	.35
	2033	(1976)	29.619	.10	.20	.30
	2034	(1977)	27.222	.10	.20	.30
	2035	(1978)	27.613	.10	.20	.30
	2036	(1979)	—	.10	.20	.30
	2037	(1980)	13.235	.10	.20	.30
	2038	(1981)	15.137	.10	.20	.30
	2039	(1982)	8.971	.10	.20	.30

F.A.O. Issue

KM#	Date	Year	Mintage	VF	XF	Unc
803	VS2031	(1974)	4.584	—	.10	.15

Virendra Coronation

KM#	Date	Year	Mintage	VF	XF	Unc
804	VS2031	(1974)	2.869	.10	.25	.50

COPPER-NICKEL

KM#	Date	Year	Mintage	VF	XF	Unc
804a	VS2031	(1974)	1,000	—	Proof	3.00

ALUMINUM

KM#	Date	Year	Mintage	VF	XF	Unc
1013	VS2039	(1982)	8.971	7.00	10.00	15.00
	2040	(1983)	6.430	—	.10	.25
	2041	(1984)	9.634	—	.10	.25
	2042	(1985)	.058	—	.10	.25
	2043	(1986)	2.937	—	.10	.25
	2044	(1987)	3.126	—	.10	.25
	2045	(1988)	1.030	—	.10	.25
	2046	(1989)	—	—	.10	.25
	2047	(1990)	—	—	.10	.25

10 PAISA

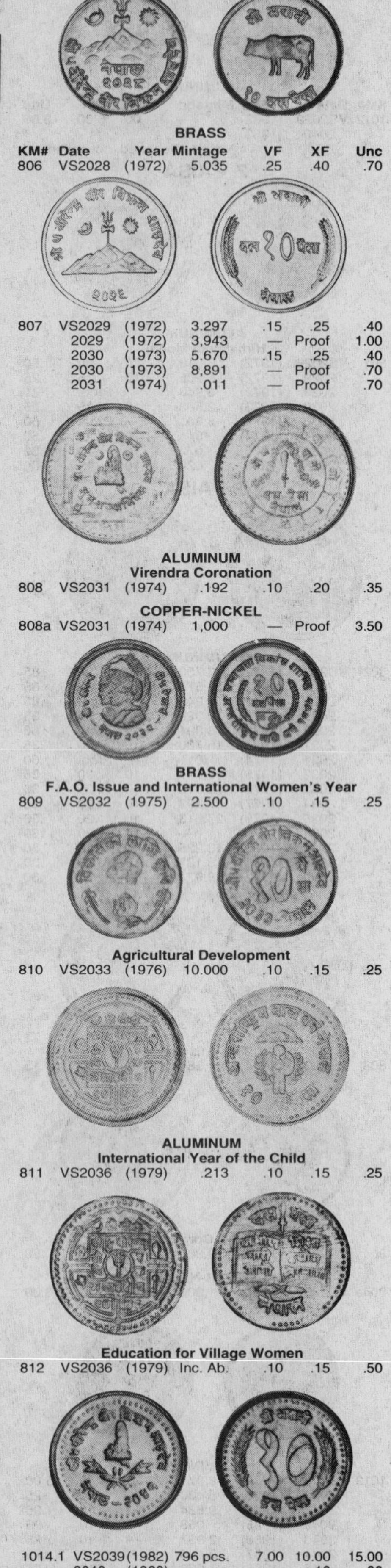

BRASS

KM#	Date	Year	Mintage	VF	XF	Unc
806	VS2028	(1972)	5.035	.25	.40	.70

KM#	Date	Year	Mintage	VF	XF	Unc
807	VS2029	(1972)	3.297	.15	.25	.40
	2029	(1972)	3,943	—	Proof	1.00
	2030	(1973)	5.670	.15	.25	.40
	2030	(1973)	8,891	—	Proof	.70
	2031	(1974)	.011	—	Proof	.70

ALUMINUM
Virendra Coronation

KM#	Date	Year	Mintage	VF	XF	Unc
808	VS2031	(1974)	.192	.10	.20	.35

COPPER-NICKEL

KM#	Date	Year	Mintage	VF	XF	Unc
808a	VS2031	(1974)	1,000	—	Proof	3.50

BRASS
F.A.O. Issue and International Women's Year

KM#	Date	Year	Mintage	VF	XF	Unc
809	VS2032	(1975)	2.500	.10	.15	.25

Agricultural Development

KM#	Date	Year	Mintage	VF	XF	Unc
810	VS2033	(1976)	10.000	.10	.15	.25

ALUMINUM
International Year of the Child

KM#	Date	Year	Mintage	VF	XF	Unc
811	VS2036	(1979)	.213	.10	.15	.25

Education for Village Women

KM#	Date	Year	Mintage	VF	XF	Unc
812	VS2036	(1979)	Inc. Ab.	.10	.15	.50

KM#	Date	Year	Mintage	VF	XF	Unc
1014.1	VS2039	(1982)	796 pcs.	7.00	10.00	15.00
	2040	(1983)	—	—	.10	.30
	2041	(1984)	7.834	—	.10	.30
	2042	(1985)	.099	—	.10	.30

Rev: Smaller corn ears.

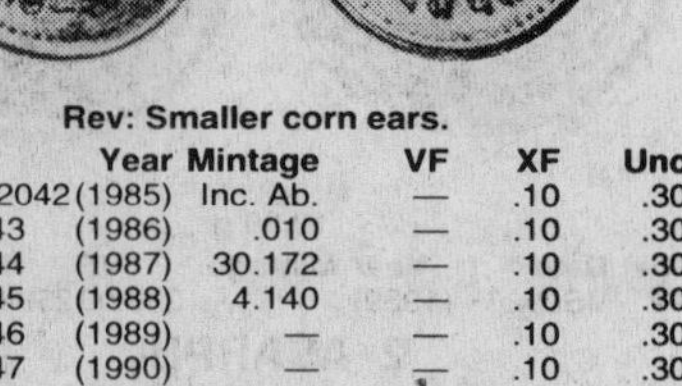

KM#	Date	Year	Mintage	VF	XF	Unc
1014.2	VS2042	(1985)	Inc. Ab.	—	.10	.30
	2043	(1986)	.010	—	.10	.30
	2044	(1987)	30.172	—	.10	.30
	2045	(1988)	4.140	—	.10	.30
	2046	(1989)	—	—	.10	.30
	2047	(1990)	—	—	.10	.30
	2048	(1991)	—	—	.10	.30

20 PAISA

BRASS
F.A.O. Issue

KM#	Date	Year	Mintage	VF	XF	Unc
813	VS2035	(1978)	.234	.35	.75	1.00

International Year of the Child

KM#	Date	Year	Mintage	VF	XF	Unc
814	VS2036	(1979)	.030	.35	.75	1.00

25 PAISA

COPPER-NICKEL

KM#	Date	Year	Mintage	VF	XF	Unc
815	VS2028	(1972)	5,691	.40	.60	.80
	2029	(1972)	3,943	—	Proof	1.25
	2030	(1973)	8.676	.30	.40	.50
	2030	(1973)	8,891	—	Proof	.80
	2031	(1974)	1.172	.35	.50	.75
	2031	(1974)	.011	—	Proof	.80
	2032	(1975)	4.584	.30	.40	.50
	2033	(1976)	1.837	.30	.40	.50
	2034	(1977)	3.808	.30	.40	.50
	2035	(1978)	5.964	.30	.40	.50
	2036	(1979)	—	.30	.40	.50
	2037	(1980)	2.047	.30	.40	.50
	2038	(1981)	1.580	.30	.40	.50
	2039	(1982)	7.185	.30	.40	.50

Virendra Coronation

KM#	Date	Year	Mintage	VF	XF	Unc
816.1	VS2031	(1974)	.431	.35	.50	.75

Reeded edge.

KM#	Date	Year	Mintage	VF	XF	Unc
816.2	VS2031	(1974)	1,000	—	Proof	4.00

BRASS
World Food Day

KM#	Date	Year	Mintage	VF	XF	Unc
817	VS2038	(1981)	2.000	—	.10	.30

International Year of Disabled Persons

KM#	Date	Year	Mintage	VF	XF	Unc
818	VS2038	(1981)	Inc. Ab.	.10	.25	.50

ALUMINUM

KM#	Date	Year	Mintage	VF	XF	Unc
1015	VS2039	(1982)				
			Inc. KM815	4.00	6.00	8.00
	2040	(1983)	7.603	.10	.25	.50
	2041	(1984)	15.534	.10	.25	.50
	2042	(1985)	12.586	.10	.25	.50
	2043	(1986)	.054	.10	.25	.50
	2044	(1987)	13.633	.10	.25	.50
	2045	(1988)	13.046	.10	.25	.50
	2046	(1989)	—	.10	.25	.50
	2047	(1990)	—	.10	.25	.50
	2048	(1991)	—	.10	.25	.50
	2050	(1993)	—	.10	.25	.50

50 PAISA

COPPER-NICKEL

KM#	Date	Year	Mintage	VF	XF	Unc
821	VS2028	(1972)	5,343	.35	.50	1.00
	2029	(1972)	.347	.35	.50	.90
	2029	(1972)	3,943	—	Proof	1.50
	2030	(1973)	.998	.35	.50	.90
	2030	(1973)	8,891	—	Proof	1.00
	2031	(1974)	.016	.35	.50	1.00
	2031	(1974)	.011	—	Proof	1.00
	2032	(1975)	.227	.35	.50	.90
	2033	(1976)	3.446	.35	.50	.75
	2034	(1977)	6.016	.35	.50	.75
	2035	(1978)	2.355	.35	.50	.75
	2036	(1979)	—	.35	.50	.75
	2037	(1980)	4.861	.35	.50	.75
	2038	(1981)	.929	.35	.50	.75
	2039	(1982)	2.954	.35	.50	.75

STAINLESS STEEL
Obv: Smaller trident in center.

KM#	Date	Year	Mintage	VF	XF	Unc
821a	VS2045	(1988)	—	.20	.30	.50

COPPER-NICKEL, 1mm thick
Virendra Coronation

KM#	Date	Year	Mintage	VF	XF	Unc
822.1	VS2031	(1974)	.136	.50	.75	1.25

Reeded edge, 1.5mm thick.

KM#	Date	Year	Mintage	VF	XF	Unc
822.2	VS2031	(1974)	1,000	—	Proof	5.00

World Food Day

KM#	Date	Year	Mintage	VF	XF	Unc
823	VS2038	(1981)	2.000	.10	.30	.60

International Year of Disabled Persons

KM#	Date	Year	Mintage	VF	XF	Unc
824	VS2038	(1981)	Inc. Ab.	.50	.75	1.25

Family Planning

KM#	Date	Year	Mintage	VF	XF	Unc
1016	VS2041	(1984)	—	.10	.25	.50

19mm

KM#	Date	Year	Mintage	VF	XF	Unc
1018	VS2039	(1982)	Inc. Ab.	.10	.25	.50
	2040	(1983)	.072	.10	.25	.50
	2041	(1984)	5.917	.10	.25	.50

STAINLESS STEEL, 23.5mm

KM#	Date	Year	Mintage	VF	XF	Unc
1018a	VS2044	(1987)	6.341	.10	.25	.50
	2045	(1988)	7.350	.10	.25	.50
	2046	(1989)	—	.10	.25	.50
	2047	(1990)	—	.10	.25	.50

RUPEE

COPPER-NICKEL

KM#	Date	Year	Mintage	VF	XF	Unc
828	VS2028	(1972)	5,030	.50	1.00	2.00
	2029	(1972)	.022	.50	1.00	1.50
	2029	(1972)	3,943	—	Proof	2.50
	2030	(1973)	5,667	.50	1.00	2.00
	2030	(1973)	8,891	—	Proof	2.00
	2031	(1974)	.011	—	Proof	1.50
	2033	(1976)	.058	.50	1.00	1.50
	2034*	(1977)	30.000	.25	.50	1.00
	2035	(1978)	—	.25	.50	1.00
	2036	(1979)	—	.25	.50	1.00
	2036*	(1980)	30.000	.25	.50	1.00

***NOTE:** These 2 dates were struck at the Canberra Mint.

STAINLESS STEEL
Obv: Smaller trident in center.

KM#	Date	Year	Mintage	VF	XF	Unc
828a	VS2045	(1988)	—	.25	.50	1.00

COPPER-NICKEL, 2mm thick
Virendra Coronation

KM#	Date	Year	Mintage	VF	XF	Unc
829.1	VS2031	(1974)	—	.75	1.25	1.75

Reeded edge, 2.5mm thick.

KM#	Date	Year	Mintage	VF	XF	Unc
829.2	VS2031	(1974)	1,000	—	Proof	6.00

F.A.O. Issue and International Women's Year

KM#	Date	Year	Mintage	VF	XF	Unc
831	VS2032	(1975)	1.500	.25	.50	1.25

Family Planning

KM#	Date	Year	Mintage	VF	XF	Unc
1019	VS2041	(1984)	.021	—	—	.75

STAINLESS STEEL

KM#	Date	Year	Mintage	VF	XF	Unc
1061	VS2048	(1991)	—	—	Proof	2.00
	2049	(1992)	—	.25	.50	1.00

2 RUPEES

COPPER-NICKEL
World Food Day

KM#	Date	Year	Mintage	VF	XF	Unc
832	VS2038	(1981)	1.000	.50	.75	1.50

F.A.O. Issue

KM#	Date	Year	Mintage	VF	XF	Unc
1025	VS2039	(1982)	.366	.50	.75	1.50

Family Planning

KM#	Date	Year	Mintage	VF	XF	Unc
1020	VS2041	(1984)	.011	.50	.75	1.50

5 RUPEES

COPPER-NICKEL
Rural Women's Advancement

KM#	Date	Year	Mintage	VF	XF	Unc
833	VS2037	(1980)	.050	.75	1.25	2.50

National Bank Silver Jubilee

KM#	Date	Year	Mintage	VF	XF	Unc
834	VS2038	(1981)	.064	.75	1.25	2.75

Circulation Coinage

KM#	Date	Year	Mintage	VF	XF	Unc
1009	VS2039	(1982)	Inc. Ab.	.50	1.00	2.00
	2040	(1983)	.478	.30	.50	1.00

Family Planning

KM#	Date	Year	Mintage	VF	XF	Unc
1017	VS2041	(1984)	.458	.50	1.00	2.00

Year of Youth

KM#	Date	Year	Mintage	VF	XF	Unc
1023	VS2042	(1985)	1.124	—	—	2.50

Social Services

KM#	Date	Year	Mintage	VF	XF	Unc
1047	VS2042	(1985)	Inc. Ab.	—	—	3.50

World Food Day

KM#	Date	Year	Mintage	VF	XF	Unc
1028	VS2043	(1986)	.099	—	—	2.50

15th World Buddhist Conference

KM#	Date	Year	Mintage	VF	XF	Unc
1042	VS2043	(1986)	.135	—	—	3.50

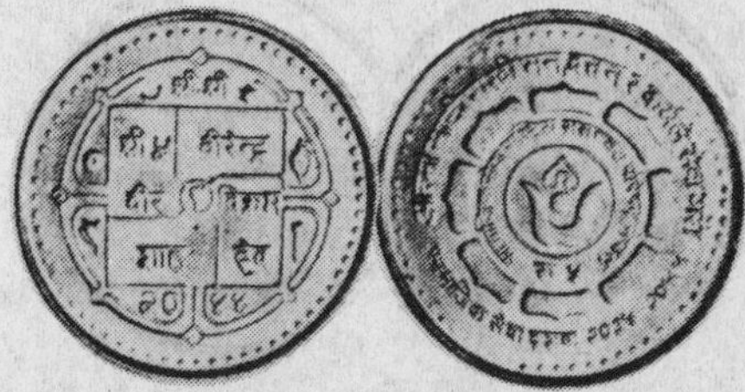

10th Year of National Social Security Administration

KM#	Date	Year	Mintage	VF	XF	Unc
1030	VS2044	(1987)	.104	—	—	2.50

3rd SAARC Summit

KM#	Date	Year	Mintage	VF	XF	Unc
1043	VS2044	1987	2,000	—	—	4.50

COPPER-NICKEL
World Food Day

KM#	Date	Year	Mintage	VF	XF	Unc
1053	VS2047	(1990)	—	—	—	4.00

New Constitution

KM#	Date	Year	Mintage	VF	XF	Unc
1063	VS2047	(1990)	—	—	—	3.25

Parliament Session

KM#	Date	Year	Mintage	VF	XF	Unc
1062	VS2048	(1991)	—	—	—	3.00

10 RUPEES

COPPER-NICKEL
30th Anniversary of Ascent of Mt. Everest
Obv: Similar to 5 Rupees, KM#833.

KM#	Date	Year	Mintage	VF	XF	Unc
1004	VS2040	1983	2,000	—	—	12.50

20 RUPEES

14.8500 g, .500 SILVER, .2387 oz ASW
F.A.O. Issue and International Women's Year

KM#	Date	Year	Mintage	VF	XF	Unc
836	VS2032	(1975)	.050	—	3.50	7.00

International Year of the Child

KM#	Date	Year	Mintage	VF	XF	Unc
837	VS2036	(1979)	—	—	2.50	5.00

15.0000 g, .925 SILVER, .4461 oz ASW

KM#	Date	Year	Mintage	VF	XF	Unc
837a	VS2036	(1979)	1,000	—	Proof	27.50

25 RUPEES

25.6000 g, .500 SILVER, .4115 oz ASW
Virendra Coronation

KM#	Date	Year	Mintage	VF	XF	Unc
838	VS2031	(1974)	.075	—	4.00	8.00

28.2800 g, .925 SILVER, .8411 oz ASW

KM#	Date	Year	Mintage	VF	XF	Unc
838a	VS2031	(1974)	1,000	—	Proof	35.00

NOTE: Struck in 1979.

25.6000 g, .500 SILVER, .4115 oz ASW
Conservation - Monal Pheasant

KM#	Date	Year	Mintage	VF	XF	Unc
839	VS2031 (1974-75)		.011	—	—	14.00

28.2800 g, .925 SILVER, .8411 oz ASW

KM#	Date	Year	Mintage	VF	XF	Unc
839a	VS2031 (1974-75)		.011	—	Proof	18.00

12.0000 g, .250 SILVER, .0965 oz ASW

KM#	Date	Year	Mintage	VF	XF	Unc
1051	VS2041	(1984)	—	—	—	5.00

8.0000 g, .250 SILVER, .0643 oz ASW
F.A.O. Issue

KM#	Date	Year	Mintage	VF	XF	Unc
835	VS2031	(1974)	.039	—	4.00	6.00

25th Anniversary of Panchayat

KM#	Date	Year	Mintage	VF	XF	Unc
1048	VS2042	(1985)	9.962	—	—	5.00

50 RUPEES

31.8000 g, .500 SILVER, .5112 oz ASW
Conservation - Red Panda
Obv: Similar to 25 Rupees, KM#839.

KM#	Date	Year	Mintage	VF	XF	Unc
841	VS2031	(1974-75)	.011	—	—	18.00

35.0000 g, .925 SILVER, 1.0409 oz ASW

KM#	Date	Year	Mintage	VF	XF	Unc
841a	VS2031	(1974-75)	.010	—	Proof	22.00

25.0000 g, .500 SILVER, .4018 oz ASW
Education for Village Women

KM#	Date	Year	Mintage	VF	XF	Unc
842	VS2036	(1979)	.015	—	—	12.50

25.0000 g, .925 SILVER, .7436 oz ASW

KM#	Date	Year	Mintage	VF	XF	Unc
842a	VS2036	(1979)	1,000	—	Proof	32.50

14.9000 g, .500 SILVER, .2395 oz ASW
International Year of Disabled Persons

KM#	Date	Year	Mintage	VF	XF	Unc
843	VS2038	1981	.016	—	—	10.00

15.0000 g, .400 SILVER, .1929 oz ASW
International Year of the Child
Similar to 100 Rupees, KM#851.

A851 VS2038 (1981) Reported, not confirmed

15.0000 g, .500 SILVER, .2406 oz ASW
50th Anniversary of Kathmandu Mint

KM#	Date	Year	Mintage	VF	XF	Unc
1046	VS2039	(1982)	8,765	—	—	15.00

100 RUPEES

25.4900 g, .500 SILVER, .4050 oz ASW
World Food Day

KM#	Date	Year	Mintage	VF	XF	Unc
850	VS2038	(1981)	.021	—	—	10.00
	2038	(1981)	.010	—	Proof	15.00

19.4400 g, .500 SILVER, .3125 oz ASW
International Year of the Child

KM#	Date	Year	Mintage	VF	XF	Unc
851	VS2038	(1981)	9,270	—	Proof	25.00

31.1000 g, .925 SILVER, .9250 oz ASW
30th Anniversary of Ascent of Mt. Everest
Obv: Similar to 5 Rupees, KM#833.

KM#	Date	Year	Mintage	VF	XF	Unc
1005	VS2040	(1983)	1,500	—	Proof	60.00

15.0000 g, .500 SILVER. .2411 oz ASW
Year of Youth

KM#	Date	Year	Mintage	VF	XF	Unc
1024	VS2042	1985	8,199	—	—	12.00

200 RUPEES

15.0000 g, .600 SILVER, .2894 oz ASW
10th Year of National Social Security Administration

KM#	Date	Year	Mintage	VF	XF	Unc
1031	VS2044	(1987)	4.145	—	—	25.00

250 RUPEES

28.2800 g, .925 SILVER, .8411 oz ASW
10th Anniversary of Reign

KM#	Date	Year	Mintage	VF	XF	Unc
1007	VS2038	(1982)	.010	—	Proof	30.00

Year of the Scout

KM#	Date	Year	Mintage	VF	XF	Unc
1010	VS2039	(1982)	.010	—	—	27.50
	2039	(1982)	Inc. Ab.	—	Proof	35.00

19.4400 g, .925 SILVER, .5782 oz ASW
Wildlife Preservation - Deer

KM#	Date	Year	Mintage	VF	XF	Unc
1026	VS2043	(1986)	.020	—	Proof	30.00

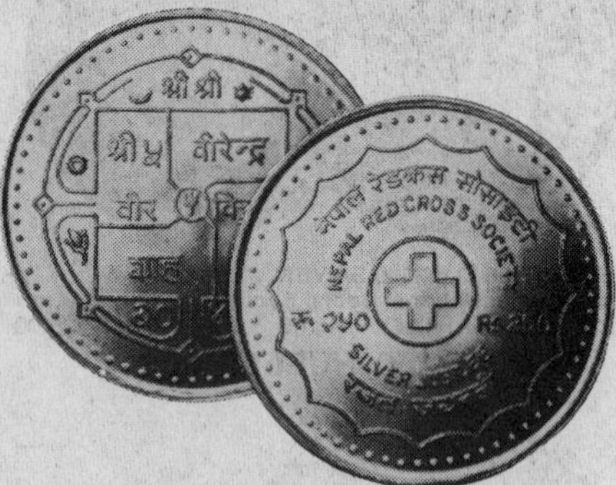

Silver Jubilee of Nepal Red Cross Society

KM#	Date	Year	Mintage	VF	XF	Unc
1049	VS2045	(1988)	6,360	—	—	25.00

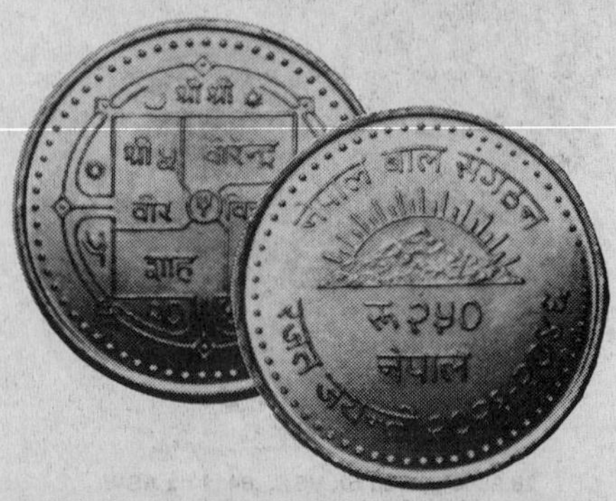

25th Anniversary of Nepalese Power Company

KM#	Date	Year	Mintage	VF	XF	Unc
1052	VS2046	(1989)	—	—	—	25.00

Save The Children

KM#	Date	Year	Mintage	VF	XF	Unc
1055	VS2047	1990	.020	—	Proof	25.00

300 RUPEES

25.2900 g, .500 SILVER, .4066 oz ASW
First Scout Jamboree in Nepal

KM#	Date	Year	Mintage	VF	XF	Unc
1029	VS2043	1987	6,967	—	—	30.00

25.0000 g, .925 SILVER, .7436 oz ASW
3rd SAARC Summit

KM#	Date	Year	Mintage	VF	XF	Unc
1044	VS2044	1987	5,000	—	—	35.00

18.0500 g, .925 SILVER, .5368 oz ASW
Rastriya Banijya Bank

KM#	Date	Year	Mintage	VF	XF	Unc
1057	VS2047	(1990)	—	—	—	25.00

18.3150 g, .925 SILVER, .5447 oz ASW
New Constitution

KM#	Date	Year	Mintage	VF	XF	Unc
1064	VS2047	1990	—	—	—	30.00

Parliament Session

KM#	Date	Year	Mintage	VF	XF	Unc
1065	VS2048	1991	—	—	—	30.00

350 RUPEES

23.3000 g, .500 SILVER, .3746 oz ASW
Crown Prince, Sacred Thread Ceremony

KM#	Date	Year	Mintage	VF	XF	Unc
1032	VS2044	(1987)	5,217	—	—	30.00

500 RUPEES

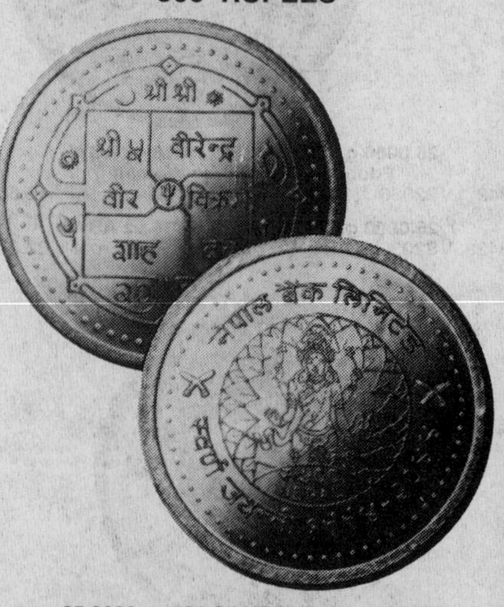

35.0000 g, .500 SILVER, .5627 oz ASW
50th Anniversary of National Bank

KM#	Date	Year	Mintage	VF	XF	Unc
1035	VS2044	(1987)	.019	—	—	45.00

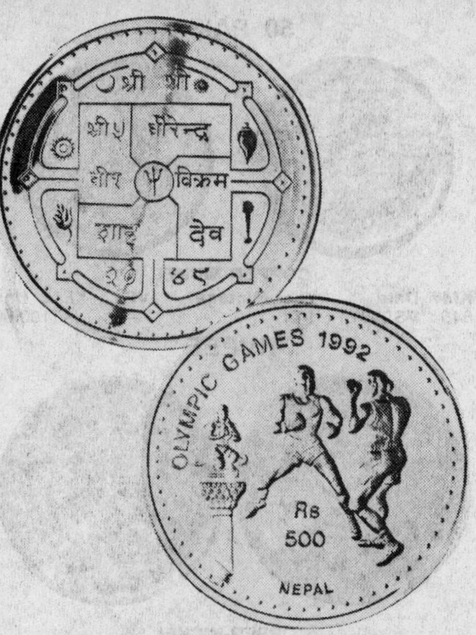

31.4700 g, .925 SILVER, .9359 oz ASW
Olympics - Boxers

KM#	Date	Year	Mintage	VF	XF	Unc
1058	VS2049	(1992)	—	—	—	60.00

31.7500 g, .925 SILVER, .9443 oz ASW
Olympics - Cross Country Skiing

KM#	Date	Year	Mintage	VF	XF	Unc
1066	VS2050	(1993)	—	—	Proof	60.00

600 RUPEES

31.1030 g, .999 SILVER, 1.0000 oz ASW
60th Birthday - Queen Mother

KM#	Date	Year	Mintage	VF	XF	Unc
041	VS2045	(1988)	5,000	—	Proof	50.00

1000 RUPEES

33.4370 g, .900 GOLD, .9676 oz AGW
Conservation - Great Indian Rhinoceros

KM#	Date	Year	Mintage	VF	XF	Unc
844	VS2031	(1974)	2,176	—	—	500.00
	2031	(1974)	671 pcs.	—	Proof	650.00

NOTE: Very small quantity restruck in 1979.

Rural Women's Advancement

KM#	Date	Year	Mintage	VF	XF	Unc
1000	VS2037	(1980)	500 pcs.	—	Proof	150.00

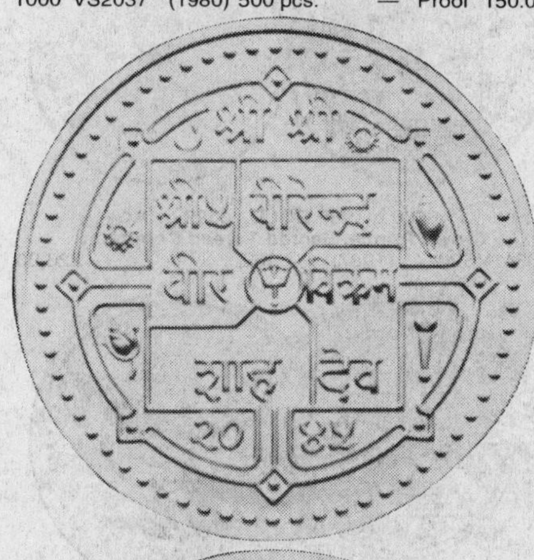

155.5150 g, .999 SILVER, 5.0000 oz ASW
Snow Leopard
Illustration reduced. Actual size: 65mm

KM#	Date	Year	Mintage	VF	XF	Unc
1036	VS2045	(1988)	*5,000		Proof	175.00

1/10 ASARPHI

3.1100 g, .999 GOLD, .1000 oz AGW
Snow Leopard
Similar to 1 Asarphi, KM#1040.

KM#	Date	Year	Mintage	VF	XF	Unc
1037	VS2045	(1988)	*.010	—	—	45.00
	2045	(1988)	2,000	—	Proof	60.00

1/4 ASARPHI

2.5000 g, .999 GOLD, .0804 oz AGW

Virendra Coronation

KM#	Date	Year	Mintage	VF	XF	Unc
816a	VS2031	(1974)	500 pcs.	—	—	100.00

KM#	Date	Year	Mintage	VF	XF	Unc
819	VS2028	(1971)	4 pcs.	—	—	—
	2030	(1973)	—	—	—	90.00
	2031	(1974)	—	—	—	90.00
	2036	(1979)	—	—	—	90.00
	2037	(1980)	48 pcs.	—	—	90.00

2.5000 g, .900 GOLD, .0724 oz AGW

KM#	Date	Year	Mintage	VF	XF	Unc
1050	VS2039	(1982)	11 pcs.	—	—	—

7.7700 g, .999 GOLD, .2500 oz AGW
Snow Leopard
Similar to 1 Asarphi, KM#1040.

KM#	Date	Year	Mintage	VF	XF	Unc
1038	VS2045	1988	*8,000	—	—	120.00
	2045	1988	*2,000	—	Proof	145.00

2.5000 g, .999 GOLD, .0804 oz AGW
Similar to 1 Asarphi, KM#1054.

KM#	Date	Year	Mintage	VF	XF	Unc
1059	VS2047	(1990)	—	—	—	90.00

1/2 ASARPHI

5.0000 g, .999 GOLD, .1607 oz AGW
Virendra Coronation

KM#	Date	Year	Mintage	VF	XF	Unc
822a	VS2031	(1974)	500 pcs.	—	—	150.00

KM#	Date	Year	Mintage	VF	XF	Unc
825	VS2028	(1971)	4 pcs.	—	—	—
	2030	(1973)	—	—	—	150.00
	2031	(1974)	—	—	—	150.00
	2036	(1979)	36 pcs.	—	—	150.00
	2037	(1980)	45 pcs.	—	—	150.00

NOTE: Reports indicate a mintage of 44 pcs. struck in .960 Gold in 1980.

5.0000 g, .900 GOLD, .1447 oz AGW

KM#	Date	Year	Mintage	VF	XF	Unc
1021	VS2039	(1982)	23 pcs.	—	—	—

5.8300 g, .960 GOLD, .1800 oz AGW
Crown Prince, Sacred Thread Ceremony

KM#	Date	Year	Mintage	VF	XF	Unc
1033	VS2044	(1987)	2,774	—	—	110.00

15.5500 g, .999 GOLD, .5000 oz AGW
Snow Leopard
Similar to 1 Asarphi, KM#1040.

KM#	Date	Year	Mintage	VF	XF	Unc
1039	VS2045	1988	*8,000	—	—	220.00
	2045	1988	*2,000	—	Proof	245.00

5.0000 g, .999 GOLD, .1600 oz AGW
Similar to 1 Asarphi, KM#1054.

KM#	Date	Year	Mintage	VF	XF	Unc
1060	VS2047	(1990)	—	—	—	150.00

ASARPHI

10.0000 g, .999 GOLD, .3215 oz AGW

KM#	Date	Year	Mintage	VF	XF	Unc
827	VS2028	(1971)	*4 pcs.	—	—	—
	2030	(1973)	50 pcs.	—	—	325.00
	2031	(1974)	—	—	—	300.00
	2033	(1976)	—	—	—	300.00
	2036	(1979)	52 pcs.	—	—	300.00
	2037	(1980)	30 pcs.	—	—	300.00

NOTE: Reports indicate a mintage of 44 pcs. struck in .960 Gold in 1980.

Virendra Coronation

829a VS2031 (1974)*500 pcs. — Proof 300.00

10.0000 g, .500 WHITE GOLD, .1608 oz AGW

829b VS2031 (1974)*250 pcs. — Proof 350.00
(845)

NOTE: Struck by Singapore Mint, sometimes referred to as 1000 Rupees.

11.6600 g, .900 GOLD, .3374 oz AGW
International Year of the Child

852 VS2038 (1981) 4,055 — Proof 220.00

10.0000 g, .500 GOLD, .1608 oz AGW
30th Anniversary of Ascent of Mt. Everest
Obv: Similar to 5 Rupees, KM#833.

1006 VS2040 (1983) 350 pcs. — Proof 260.00

15.9800 g, .900 GOLD, .4624 oz AGW
10th Anniversary of Reign

KM#	Date	Year	Mintage	VF	XF	Unc
1008	VS2038	(1981)	27 pcs.	—	—	450.00
	2038	(1981)	5,092	—	Proof	250.00

15.9800 g, .917 GOLD, .4712 oz AGW
Year of the Scout

1011 VS2039 (1982) 2,000 — — 400.00

10.0000 g, .900 GOLD, .2894 oz AGW

KM#	Date	Year	Mintage	VF	XF	Unc
1022	VS2039	(1982)	25 pcs.	—	—	—

11.6600 g, .900 GOLD, .3374 oz AGW
Wildlife Protection - Ganges River Dolphins

1027 VS2043 (1986) 5,000 — Proof 250.00

11.6600 g, .960 GOLD, .3599 oz AGW
Crown Prince, Sacred Thread Ceremony

1034 VS2044 (1987) 1,962 — — 220.00

31.1000 g, .9999 GOLD, 1.0000 oz AGW
Snow Leopard

KM#	Date	Year	Mintage	VF	XF	Unc
1040	VS2045	1988	*.010	—	—	450.00
	2045	1988	2,000	—	Proof	560.00

15.0000 g, .900 GOLD, .4340 oz AGW
3rd SAARC Summit
Similar to 300 Rupees, KM#1044.
Obv: Divided square in wheel design.
Rev: Stylized 7 pigeons within bull's horn logo.

1045 VS2044 1987 1,000 — — 350.00

10.0000 g, .999 GOLD, .3215 oz AGW
The New Constitution

1054 VS2047 1990 — — — 250.00

11.6600 g, .900 GOLD, .3374 oz AGW
Save The Children

1056 VS2047 1990 3,000 — Proof 250.00

In the name of Queen Aishvarya Rajya Lakshmi

50 PAISA

COPPER-NICKEL

KM#	Date	Year	Mintage	VF	XF	Unc
846	VS2031	(1974)	—	—	—	100.0

RUPEE

COPPER-NICKEL

848 VS2031 (1974) — — — 150.0

1/2 ASARPHI

GOLD

847 VS2031 (1974) Reported, not confirme

ASARPHI

GOLD

849 VS2031 (1974) Reported, not confirme

NOTE: The above coins were struck and sent to th Royal Palace. Few have emerged.

MINT SETS (MS)

KM#	Date	Mintage	Identification	Issue Price	Mkt. Val
MS1	1932(3)	—	—	—	—
MS2	1949(3)	—	KM716,718,723 restrikes	—	8.0
MS3	1953(8)	—	KM733,735-740,742	—	160.0
MS-A4	Mixed date (3)	—	KM709.2(1996),711(1995), 737(2011)	—	7.0
MS4	1955(3)	—	KM712(2000),733,749 (2012)	.85	5.0
MS5	1956(7)	—	KM745,750,756.2,761, 770,776,790	—	50.0
MS6	1956(7)	—	KM745,750,756.3,761, 770,776,790 restrikes	—	13.5
MS7	1957(4)	—	KM740(2011)742,738 (2010),769(2014)	2.05	12.0
MS8	1957(6)	—	KM709.1(1996),755 (2014),760(2011) 2 pcs. each	.85	7.0
MS9	1964(7)	—	KM747,752,758,763, 772,778,785	—	10.0
MS10	1964(7)	—	KM747,752,758a,764, 772,778,785	—	5.0
MS11	1965(7)	—	KM747,752(2022),758, 763,772,778,786 (2021)	2.75	10.0
MS12	1966(7)	—	KM748,753,759,765, 772,779,787	—	7.0
MS13	1967(7)	—	KM748,753,759,765, 772,779,787	—	5.0
MS14	1972(7)	—	KM799,801,802,806, 815,821,828	—	5.0
MS15	1974(7)	—	KM800,804,808,816, 822,829,838	—	12.5
MS16	1974(2)	—	KM839,841	32.50	35.0
MS17	1975(5)	—	KM808,816,822,829, 838	—	13.0
MS18	1975(3)	—	KM809,831,836	—	9.0

PROOF SETS (PS)

KM#	Date	Mintage	Identification	Issue Price	Mkt. Val
PS1	1911	—	Copper, Silver	—	—
PS2	1911	—	Gold	—	—
PS3	1970(7)	2,187	KM748,753,759,765, 773,780,788	10.00	15.0
PS4	1971(7)	2,380	KM748,753,759,765, 773,780,788	10.00	15.0
PS5	1972(7)	3,943	KM799,801,802,807, 815,821,828	10.00	8.5
PS6	1973(7)	8,891	KM799,801,802,807, 815,821,828	10.00	6.0
PS7	1974(7)	10,543	KM799,801,802,807, 815,821,828	10.00	5.5
PS8	1974(2)	30,000	KM839a,841a	50.00	50.0
PS9	(1979)(7)*	1,000	KM800a,804a,808a, 816,822,829,838a (dated 1974)	62.00	62.0

***NOTE:** Coins dated 2031 (1974) but this set was issued in 1979 ostensibly to celebrate the 5th Anniversary of the Coronation.

KM#	Date	Mintage	Identification	Issue Price	Mkt. Val
PS10	1988(4)	2,000	KM1037-1040	—	1000

NETHERLANDS

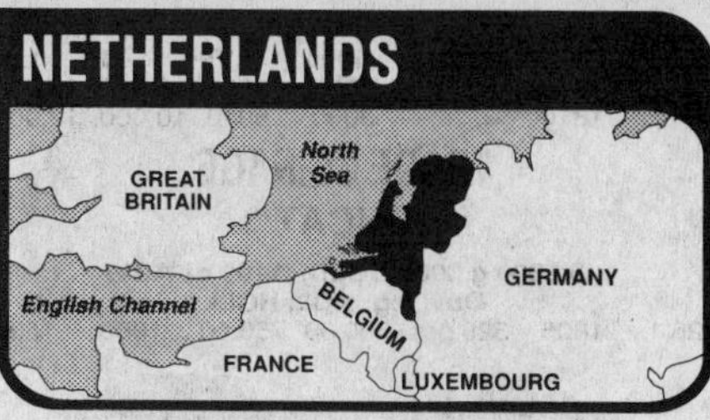

The Kingdom of the Netherlands, a country of western Europe fronting on the North Sea and bordered by Belgium and Germany, has an area of 15,770 sq. mi. (41,500 sq. km.) and a population of 15.3 million. Capital: Amsterdam, but the seat of government is at The Hague. The economy is based on dairy farming and a variety of industrial activities. Chemicals, yarns and fabrics, and meat products are exported.

After being a part of Charlemagne's empire in the 8th and 9th centuries, the Netherlands came under control of Burgundy and the Austrian Hapsburgs, and finally was subjected to Spanish dominion in the 16th century. Led by William of Orange, the Dutch revolted against Spain in 1568. The seven northern provinces formed the Union of Utrecht and declared their independence in 1581, becoming the Republic of the United Netherlands. In the following century, the 'Golden Age' of Dutch history, the Netherlands became a great sea and colonial power, a patron of the arts and a refuge for the persecuted. The United Dutch Republic ended in 1795 when the French formed the Batavian Republic. Napoleon made his brother Louis, the King of Holland in 1806, however he abdicated in 1810 when Napoleon annexed Holland. The French were expelled in 1813, and all the provinces of Holland and Belgium were merged into the Kingdom of the United Netherlands under William I, in 1814. The Belgians withdrew in 1830 to form their own kingdom, the last substantial change in the configuration of European Netherlands.

WORLD WAR II COINAGE

Coinage of the Netherlands Homeland Types - KM#152, 153, 163, 164, 161.1 and 161.2 - were minted by U.S. mints in the name of the government in exile and its remaining Curacao and Surinam Colonies during the years 1941-45. The Curacao and Surinam strikings, distinguished by the presence of a palm tree in combination with a mint mark (P-Philadelphia; D-Denver; S-San Francisco) flanking the date, are incorporated under those titles in this volume. Pieces of this period struck in the name of the homeland bear an acorn and mint mark and are incorporated in the following tabulation.

NOTE: Excepting the World War II issues struck at U.S. mints, all of the modern coins were struck at the Utrecht Mint and bear the caduceus mint mark of that facility. They also bear the mintmasters marks.

RULERS

BATAVIAN REPUBLIC

French domination, 1795-1806

KINGDOM OF HOLLAND

French Protectorate

Louis Napoleon, 1806-1810

FRENCH ANNEXATION

Napoleon I, 1810-1814

KINGDOM OF THE NETHERLANDS

William I, 1815-1840
William II, 1840-1849
William III, 1849-1890
Wilhelmina I, 1890-1948
Juliana, 1948-1980
Beatrix, 1980

MINT MARKS

B - Brussels (Belgium), 1821-1830
D - Denver, 1943-1945
P - Philadelphia, 1941-1945
S - San Francisco, 1944-1945

MINT PRIVY MARKS

Date	Privy Mark
Harderwijk (Gelderland)	
1782-1806	Ear of corn
Dordrecht (Holland)	
1600-1806	Rosette
1795-1806	None
Enkhuizen (West Friesland)	
1796-1803	Star
Hoorn (West Friesland)	
1803-1809	Star
Kampen (Overyssel)	
1763-1764,1795-1807	
Utrecht (Utrecht)	
1738-1805	Shield
Utrecht	
1806-present	Caduceus

MINTMASTERS PRIVY MARKS

Date	Privy Mark
Brussels Mint	
1821-1830	Palm branch
U. S. Mints	
1941-1945	Palm tree
Utrecht Mint	
1806-1810	Bee
1810-1813	Mast
1815-1816	Cloverleaf
1817	Child in swaddling clothes
1818-1840	Torch
1839-1846	Fleur de lis
1846-1874	Sword
1874	Sword in scabbard
1875-1887	Broadaxe
1887	Broadaxe and star
1888-1909	Halberd
1909	Halberd and star
1909-1933	Seahorse
1933-1942	Grapes
1943-1945	No privy mark
1945-1969	Fish
1969-1979	Cock
1980	Cock and star (temporal)
1980-1988	Anvil with hammer
1989	Bow and arrow

NOTE: A star adjoining the privy mark indicates that the piece was struck at the beginning of the term of office of a successor. (The star was used only if the successor had not chosen his own mark yet.)

MONETARY SYSTEM

8 Duits = 1 Stuiver (Stiver)
6 Stuivers = 1 Schelling
20 Stuivers = 1 Gulden (Guilder or Florin)
50 Stuivers = 1 Rijksdaalder (Silver Ducat)
60 Stuivers = 1 Ducaton (Silver Rider)
14 Gulden = 1 Golden Rider

Commencing 1815

100 Cents = 1 Gulden
2-1/2 Gulden = 1 Rijksdaalder

BATAVIAN REPUBLIC

Prior to 1806, the Netherlands was a confederation of seven provinces, each producing coins similar in design but differing in the coat of arms or inscription. Generally the coins of each province contained an abbreviation of the name of the province somewhere in the inscription. Under the Batavian Republic, the following abbreviations were used.

PROVINCE ABBREVIATIONS

G, GEL - Gelderland
HOL, HOLL - Holland
TRANSI - Overijsel
TRA, TRAI, TRAIECTUM - Utrecht
WESTF, WESTRI - Westfriesland
ZEL, ZEELANDIA - Zeeland

3 GULDEN

.915 SILVER
Obv. leg: HOL, HOLL

KM#	Date	Mintage	Fine	VF	XF	Unc
9.2	1801	—	90.00	160.00	240.00	350.00

NOTE: Earlier dates (1795-1800) exist for this type.

RIJKSDAALDER

.868 SILVER
Obv. leg: G, GEL

KM#	Date	Mintage	Fine	VF	XF	Unc
10.1	1801	—	300.00	450.00	600.00	850.00
	1802	Inc. Ab.	300.00	450.00	600.00	850.00

NOTE: Earlier dates (1795-1800) exist for this type.

Obv. leg: HOL, HOLL

KM#	Date	Mintage	Fine	VF	XF	Unc
10.2	1801/0	—	200.00	300.00	400.00	650.00
	1801	Inc. Ab.	175.00	250.00	350.00	500.00
	1802	Inc. Ab.	175.00	250.00	350.00	500.00
	1806	Inc. Ab.	950.00	1400.	2000.	2500.

NOTE: Earlier dates (1796-1800) exist for this type.

Obv. leg: TRAIECTUM, TRA, TRAI

KM#	Date	Mintage	Fine	VF	XF	Unc
10.4	1801	—	65.00	100.00	150.00	200.00
	1801 small 8-0	Inc. Ab.	65.00	100.00	150.00	200.00
	1802	Inc. Ab.	65.00	100.00	150.00	200.00
	1803 long sword	Inc. Ab.	65.00	100.00	150.00	200.00
	1803 short sword	Inc. Ab.	65.00	100.00	150.00	200.00
	1804	Inc. Ab.	65.00	100.00	150.00	200.00
	1805/797	I.A.	65.00	100.00	150.00	200.00
	1805	Inc. Ab.	65.00	100.00	150.00	200.00

NOTE: Earlier dates (1795-1800) exist for this type.

TRADE COINAGE

DUCAT

3.5000 g, .986 GOLD, .1109 oz AGW
Obv. leg: G, GEL

KM#	Date	Mintage	Fine	VF	XF	Unc
11.1	1801	—	150.00	250.00	350.00	500.00
	1802	Inc. Ab.	150.00	250.00	350.00	500.00
	1803	—	650.00	1300.	2000.	2500.

NOTE: Earlier dates (1795-1800) exist for this type.

Obv. leg: HOL, HOLL

KM#	Date	Mintage	Fine	VF	XF	Unc
11.2	1801 w/o star	—	90.00	150.00	200.00	200.00
	1801 star	—	220.00	475.00	700.00	1000.
	1802 w/o star	—	90.00	155.00	200.00	300.00
	1802 star	—	200.00	375.00	500.00	700.00
	1803 w/o star	—	100.00	220.00	275.00	500.00
	1804 w/o star	—	100.00	220.00	275.00	500.00
	1805 w/o star	—	200.00	375.00	600.00	850.00

NOTE: Coins with the star were struck at the Enkhuizen Mint with a total mintage of 630,455. Coins without the star were struck at the Dordrecht Mint with a total mintage of 2,861,825.
NOTE: Earlier dates (1795-1800) exist for this type.

Obv. leg: TRAIECTUM, TRA, TRAI

KM#	Date	Mintage	Fine	VF	XF	Unc
11.3	1801	.960	70.00	130.00	200.00	300.00
	1802	1.705	70.00	130.00	200.00	300.00
	1803	2.089	70.00	130.00	200.00	275.00
	1804/3	.870	80.00	170.00	250.00	325.00
	1804	Inc. Ab.	80.00	170.00	250.00	325.00
	1805	1.300	70.00	130.00	200.00	275.00

NOTE: Earlier dates (1795-1800) exist for this type.

2 DUCAT

7.0000 g, .986 GOLD, .2219 oz AGW
Obv. leg: HOL, HOLL
Similar to 1 Ducat KM#11.2

KM#	Date	Mintage	Fine	VF	XF	Unc
12.1	1802	—	700.00	1300.	2000.	2500.

NOTE: Earlier date (1795) exists for this type.

Obv. leg: TRAIECTUM, TRA, TRAI
Similar to 1 Ducat, KM#11.3.

KM#	Date	Mintage	Fine	VF	XF	Unc
12.2	1801	.215	350.00	700.00	1000.	1250.
	1802	.115	500.00	1000.	1500.	2000.
	1803	.365	350.00	700.00	1000.	1250.
	1804	.250	350.00	700.00	1000.	1250.
	1805	.301	350.00	700.00	1000.	1250.

NOTE: Earlier dates (1795-1800)) exist for this type.

KINGDOM OF HOLLAND

10 STUIVERS

SILVER
Mint: Utrecht

KM#	Date	Mintage	Fine	VF	XF	Unc
30	1808	—	—	—	Rare	—
	1809	—	300.00	700.00	1200.	1500.

FLORIN

SILVER
Mint: Utrecht

KM#	Date	Mintage	Fine	VF	XF	Unc
29	1807	—	550.00	1200.	1750.	2500.

GULDEN

SILVER
Mint: Utrecht

KM#	Date	Mintage	Fine	VF	XF	Unc
31	1808	—	300.00	700.00	1200.	1500.
	1809	—	300.00	700.00	1200.	1500.
	1810	—	300.00	700.00	1200.	1500.

RIJKSDAALDER

.868 SILVER
Mint: Utrecht
Obv. leg: . . . . .TRAI.

KM#	Date	Mintage	Fine	VF	XF	Unc
25	1806	.580	125.00	220.00	300.00	350.00
	1807	.151	150.00	250.00	325.00	400.00
	1808	.343	125.00	220.00	300.00	350.00

SILVER

KM#	Date	Mintage	Fine	VF	XF	Unc
36	1809	—	900.00	1600.	2100.	3000.

KM#	Date	Mintage	Fine	VF	XF	Unc
37	1809	—	1200.	1900.	3000.	3500.

50 STUIVERS

SILVER
Mint: Utrecht

KM#	Date	Mintage	Fine	VF	XF	Unc
28	1807	300 pcs.	900.00	1650.	2250.	2800.
	1808	2.466	100.00	175.00	250.00	325.00

2-1/2 GULDEN

SILVER
Mint: Utrecht

KM#	Date	Mintage	Fine	VF	XF	Unc
32	1808	—	1000.	2000.	2500.	3000.

10 GULDEN

6.8250 g, .917 GOLD, .2012 oz AGW
Mint: Utrecht

KM#	Date	Mintage	Fine	VF	XF	Unc
33	1808	—	1500.	3000.	4500.	6000.
	1810	—	1500.	3000.	4500.	6000.

20 GULDEN

13.6500 g, .917 GOLD, .4024 oz AGW

Mint: Utrecht

KM#	Date	Mintage	Fine	VF	XF	Unc
34	1808	—	3000.	6000.	10,000.	12,000
	1810	—	3000.	6000.	10,000.	12,000

TRADE COINAGE

DUCAT

3.5000 g, .986 GOLD, .1109 oz AGW
Obv. leg: HOL, HOLL

KM#	Date	Mintage	Fine	VF	XF	Unc
26.1	1806	526 pcs.	500.00	750.00	1000.	1500

Obv. leg: TRAIECTUM, TRA, TRAI
Mint: Utrecht

KM#	Date	Mintage	Fine	VF	XF	Unc
26.2	1806 sm.dt.	.794	110.00	190.00	260.00	350.0
	1807 small date, straight 7	.622	110.00	190.00	260.00	350.0
	1808/7	.037	175.00	300.00	350.00	450.0
	1808	Inc. Ab.	140.00	250.00	325.00	375.0

Mint: St. Petersburg

KM#	Date	Mintage	Fine	VF	XF	Unc
26.3	1806 lg.dt.	1.300	110.00	190.00	260.00	350.0
	1807 large date, curved 7	1.940	110.00	190.00	260.00	350.0

KM#	Date	Mintage	Fine	VF	XF	Unc
35	1808	.283	200.00	375.00	525.00	700.0
	1809	Inc. Ab.	200.00	375.00	525.00	700.0

KM#	Date	Mintage	Fine	VF	XF	Unc
38	1809	2.371	200.00	375.00	525.00	700.0
	1810	Inc. Ab.	200.00	375.00	525.00	700.0

2 DUCAT

7.0000 g, .986 GOLD, .2218 oz AGW
Mint: Utrecht
Obv. leg: TRAIECTUM, TRA, TRAI

KM#	Date	Mintage	Fine	VF	XF	Unc
27	1806	.199	500.00	800.00	1200.	1500
	1807	.156	500.00	800.00	1200.	1500
	1808	—	500.00	800.00	1200.	1500

FRENCH ANNEXATION

From 1810 to 1814, the Netherlands were a part o France. During this period, homeland type coins were no minted. Regular French coins were struck at the Utrech Mint at this time, and are identified by the fish and mas privy marks. These coins are listed under France.

KINGDOM OF THE NETHERLANDS

1/2 CENT

COPPER

KM#	Date	Mintage	Fine	VF	XF	Unc
51	1818	—	650.00	1500.	2000.	3500
	1819	.144	150.00	450.00	800.00	2450
	1821	3.500	35.00	75.00	125.00	200.0
	1821B	.271	85.00	150.00	300.00	550.0
	1821B	—	—	—	Proof	900.0
	1822	9.888	17.50	35.00	75.00	100.0
	1822B	3.969	35.00	75.00	125.00	200.0
	1823	10.000	15.00	35.00	75.00	100.0
	1823B	13.228	15.00	35.00	75.00	100.0
	1824	2.402	35.00	85.00	150.00	225.0
	1824B	3.430	35.00	85.00	150.00	225.0
	1826	—	200.00	300.00	500.00	800.0
	1826B	2.076	35.00	85.00	150.00	225.0
	1827	4.574	15.00	35.00	75.00	100.0
	1827B	3.337	15.00	35.00	75.00	100.0
	1828	1.358	50.00	100.00	200.00	300.0
	1828B	4.034	15.00	35.00	75.00	100.0
	1829	3.347	15.00	35.00	75.00	100.0
	1831	3.850	15.00	35.00	75.00	100.0

KM#	Date	Mintage	Fine	VF	XF	Unc
51	1832	10.328	15.00	35.00	75.00	100.00
	1833	.150	150.00	300.00	500.00	1100.
	1837	2.602	15.00	30.00	70.00	100.00
68	1841	2.600	20.00	45.00	90.00	120.00
	1843	3.120	20.00	45.00	90.00	120.00
	1846	.600	25.00	60.00	110.00	160.00
	1847	2.000	25.00	50.00	100.00	130.00

KM#	Date	Mintage	Fine	VF	XF	Unc
90	1850	2.000	10.00	25.00	50.00	75.00
	1851	2.051	10.00	25.00	50.00	75.00
	1852	2.028	40.00	80.00	120.00	240.00
	1853	2.000	10.00	25.00	50.00	75.00
	1854	3.000	10.00	22.00	35.00	60.00
	1855	.999	80.00	200.00	350.00	800.00
	1857	4.155	10.00	22.00	30.00	55.00
	1859	4.052	10.00	22.00	30.00	55.00
	1861	1.446	20.00	40.00	70.00	90.00
	1862	2.026	8.00	20.00	30.00	55.00
	1863	2.428	8.00	20.00	30.00	55.00
	1864	2.016	8.00	20.00	30.00	55.00
	1865	2.006	8.00	20.00	30.00	55.00
	1867	2.008	8.00	20.00	30.00	55.00
	1869	2.014	8.00	20.00	30.00	55.00
	1870	2.004	8.00	20.00	30.00	55.00
	1872	2.026	8.00	20.00	30.00	55.00
	1873	2.026	8.00	20.00	30.00	55.00
	1875	2.026	8.00	20.00	30.00	55.00
	1876	2.020	8.00	20.00	30.00	55.00
	1877	1.400	15.00	35.00	50.00	75.00

BRONZE

Obv: 17 small shields in field, leg: KONINGRIJK. . .

KM#	Date	Mintage	Fine	VF	XF	Unc
109	1878	4.000	5.00	10.00	20.00	35.00
	1883	.800	50.00	100.00	160.00	200.00
	1884	17.200	2.50	5.00	15.00	25.00
	1885	7.800	3.00	7.50	18.00	30.00
	1886	2.200	25.00	60.00	110.00	140.00
	1891	5.000	5.00	10.00	20.00	35.00
	1894	5.000	5.00	10.00	20.00	35.00
	1898	2.000	20.00	50.00	100.00	140.00
	1900	3.000	14.00	25.00	50.00	70.00
	1901	6.000	3.00	7.00	12.50	25.00

Obv: 15 large shields in field around larger lion, smaller date and leg. Rev: CENT in larger letters.

KM#	Date	Mintage	Fine	VF	XF	Unc
133	1903	10.000	2.00	5.00	10.00	20.00
	1906	10.000	2.00	5.00	10.00	20.00

KM#	Date	Mintage	Fine	VF	XF	Unc
138	1909	5.000	2.00	4.00	7.00	11.00
	1911	5.000	2.00	4.00	7.00	11.00
	1912	5.000	2.00	4.00	7.00	11.00
	1914	5.000	2.00	4.00	7.00	11.00
	1915	2.500	8.00	17.50	30.00	40.00
	1916	4.000	3.00	6.00	11.00	15.00
	1917	5.000	2.00	4.00	7.00	11.00
	1921	1.500	9.00	22.50	35.00	50.00
	1922/1	—	40.00	80.00	150.00	250.00
	1922	2.500	7.00	15.00	25.00	35.00
	1928	4.000	2.00	4.00	7.00	11.00
	1930	6.000	2.00	4.00	7.00	11.00
	1934	5.000	1.50	3.50	6.00	7.50
	1936	5.000	1.50	3.50	6.00	7.50
	1937	1.600	2.00	5.00	8.00	12.00
	1938	8.400	1.25	3.00	5.00	7.50
	1940	6.000	1.25	3.00	5.00	7.50

CENT

COPPER

KM#	Date	Mintage	Fine	VF	XF	Unc
47	1817	—	600.00	2000.	3500.	5000.
	1818	—	600.00	2000.	3500.	5000.
	1819	.165	220.00	600.00	1250.	2000.
	1821	10.325	15.00	30.00	60.00	100.00
	1821B	.113	220.00	600.00	1150.	1750.
	1822	18.462	15.00	30.00	60.00	100.00
	1822B	6.718	17.50	45.00	100.00	150.00
	1823	22.300	15.00	30.00	60.00	100.00
	1823B	11.272	17.50	45.00	100.00	150.00
	1824	5.450	40.00	90.00	175.00	250.00

KM#	Date	Mintage	Fine	VF	XF	Unc
47	1824B	.144	175.00	450.00	1000.	1750.
	1826	4.600	17.50	45.00	100.00	150.00
	1826B	7.824	17.50	45.00	100.00	150.00
	1827	27.450	15.00	30.00	60.00	100.00
	1827B	20.966	15.00	30.00	60.00	100.00
	1828	8.261	15.00	30.00	60.00	100.00
	1828B	7.608	17.50	45.00	100.00	150.00
	1830	1.750	40.00	90.00	125.00	175.00
	1831	4.161	17.50	45.00	100.00	150.00
	1837	5.203	12.50	30.00	55.00	100.00

BRONZE

KM#	Date	Mintage	Fine	VF	XF	Unc
100	1860	2.032	10.00	25.00	45.00	75.00
	1861	2.050	10.00	25.00	45.00	75.00
	1862	2.026	10.00	25.00	45.00	75.00
	1863	10.246	4.00	9.00	16.00	25.00
	1864	2.026	10.00	25.00	45.00	75.00
	1870	4.010	7.00	15.00	30.00	45.00
	1873	3.026	9.00	17.50	35.00	55.00
	1875	3.015	9.00	17.50	35.00	55.00
	1876	13.047	4.00	9.00	16.00	25.00
	1877	11.026	4.00	9.00	16.00	25.00

Obv: 15 small shields in field, leg: KONINGRIJK

KM#	Date	Mintage	Fine	VF	XF	Unc
107	1877	6.100	6.00	13.00	30.00	45.00
	1878	53.900	1.50	4.00	9.00	15.00
	1880	20.000	2.50	6.00	16.50	30.00
	1881	10.000	2.50	6.00	16.50	30.00
	1882/1	—	7.00	15.00	40.00	70.00
	1882	5.000	5.00	10.00	25.00	35.00
	1883	15.000	2.50	6.00	16.50	30.00
	1884	10.000	2.50	6.00	16.50	30.00
	1892	5.000	6.00	15.00	30.00	55.00
	1896	3.000	10.00	30.00	60.00	80.00
	1897	2.500	10.00	30.00	60.00	80.00
	1898	5.000	6.00	15.00	25.00	50.00
	1899	5.100	6.00	15.00	25.00	50.00
	1900 large date	12.400	4.00	10.00	20.00	40.00
	1900 small date	Inc. Ab.	4.00	10.00	20.00	40.00
	1900	—	—	—	Proof	185.00

Obv: 15 large shields in field, leg: KONINKRIJK

KM#	Date	Mintage	Fine	VF	XF	Unc
130	1901	10.000	3.00	7.00	20.00	35.00

Obv: 10 large shields in field, leg: KONINGRIJK.

KM#	Date	Mintage	Fine	VF	XF	Unc
131	1901	10.000	3.00	7.00	20.00	35.00

Obv: 15 medium shields in field, leg: KONINGRIJK.

KM#	Date	Mintage	Fine	VF	XF	Unc
132	1902	10.000	2.00	5.00	10.00	25.00
	1904	15.000	2.00	5.00	10.00	25.00
	1905	10.000	2.00	5.00	10.00	25.00
	1906	9.000	2.00	5.00	10.00	25.00
	1907	6.000	15.00	35.00	65.00	90.00

SILVER
Plain edge.

KM#	Date	Mintage	Fine	VF	XF	Unc
132a	1906	—	—	—	Proof	875.00

KM#	Date	Mintage	Fine	VF	XF	Unc
152	1913	5.000	6.00	15.00	30.00	45.00
	1914	9.000	2.00	5.00	10.00	20.00
	1915	10.800	2.00	5.00	10.00	20.00
	1916	21.700	1.00	3.00	6.00	12.00
	1916	—	—	—	Proof	110.00
	1917	20.000	1.00	3.00	6.00	12.00
	1918	10.000	2.00	5.00	10.00	15.00
	1919	6.000	3.00	6.00	15.00	20.00
	1920	11.400	1.00	3.00	6.00	12.00
	1921	12.600	1.00	3.00	6.00	12.00
	1922	20.000	1.00	3.00	6.00	12.00
	1924	1.400	25.00	50.00	100.00	120.00
	1925	18.600	1.00	3.00	6.00	12.00
	1926	10.000	1.00	3.00	6.00	12.00
	1927	10.000	1.00	3.00	6.00	12.00
	1928	10.000	1.00	3.00	6.00	12.00
	1929	20.000	1.00	3.00	6.00	12.00
	1930	10.000	1.00	3.00	6.00	12.00
	1931	3.400	8.00	20.00	35.00	50.00
	1937	10.000	1.00	3.00	5.00	7.50
	1938	16.600	1.00	2.50	3.50	7.00
	1939	22.000	1.00	2.50	3.50	7.00
	1940	24.600	1.00	2.50	3.50	7.00
	1941	66.600	.50	1.00	2.00	3.00

NOTE: For similar coins dated 1942P see Netherlands Antilles (Curacao); 1943P, 1957-1960 see Surinam.

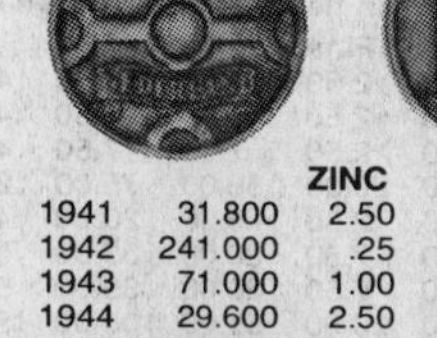

ZINC

KM#	Date	Mintage	Fine	VF	XF	Unc
170	1941	31.800	2.50	6.00	15.00	22.00
	1942	241.000	.25	.75	2.00	4.50
	1943	71.000	1.00	3.00	5.00	10.00
	1944	29.600	2.50	6.00	15.00	22.00

BRONZE

KM#	Date	Mintage	VF	XF	Unc	BU
175	1948	130.400	.25	.50	1.50	10.00
	1948	—	—	—	Proof	40.00

KM#	Date	Mintage	VF	XF	Unc	BU
180	1950	91.000	.10	.25	.75	5.00
	1950	—	—	—	Proof	45.00
	1951	45.800	.10	.25	.75	5.00
	1951	—	—	—	Proof	45.00
	1952	68.000	.10	.25	.75	5.00
	1952	—	—	—	Proof	45.00
	1953	54.000	.10	.25	.75	5.00
	1953	—	—	—	Proof	45.00
	1954	54.000	.10	.25	.75	5.00
	1954	—	—	—	Proof	45.00
	1955	52.000	.10	.25	.75	5.00
	1955	—	—	—	Proof	45.00
	1956	34.800	.10	.25	.75	5.00
	1956	—	—	—	Proof	45.00
	1957	48.000	.10	.25	.75	5.00
	1957	—	—	—	Proof	45.00
	1958	34.000	.10	.25	.75	5.00
	1958	—	—	—	Proof	40.00
	1959	36.000	.10	.25	.75	5.00
	1959	—	—	—	Proof	35.00
	1960	40.000	.10	.25	.75	5.00
	1960	—	—	—	Proof	35.00
	1961	52.000	—	.10	.35	3.00
	1961	—	—	—	Proof	35.00
	1962	57.000	—	.10	.35	3.00
	1962	—	—	—	Proof	35.00
	1963	70.000	—	.10	.35	3.00
	1963	—	—	—	Proof	35.00
	1964	73.000	—	.10	.35	3.00
	1964	—	—	—	Proof	35.00
	1965	91.000	—	.10	.35	2.00
	1965	—	—	—	Proof	35.00
	1966 large date	104.000	—	.10	.25	2.00
	1966 large date	—	—	—	Proof	35.00
	1966 small date	Inc. Ab.	—	.10	.25	2.00
	1966 small date	—	—	—	Proof	20.00
	1967	140.000	—	.10	.25	2.00
	1967	—	—	—	Proof	25.00
	1968	28.000	—	.10	.25	2.00
	1968	—	—	—	Proof	20.00
	1969 fish privy mark	50.000	—	.10	.25	2.00
	1969 fish privy mark	—	—	—	Proof	20.00
	1969 cock privy mark	50.000	—	.10	.25	2.00
	1969 cock privy mark	—	—	—	Proof	20.00
	1970	100.000	—	.10	.15	1.50
	1970	—	—	—	Proof	20.00

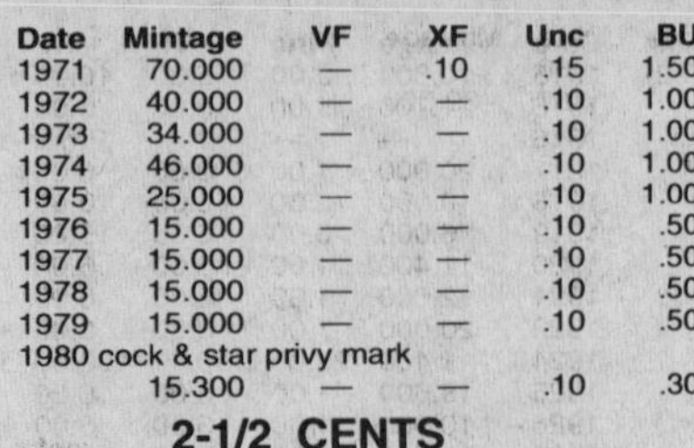

KM#	Date	Mintage	VF	XF	Unc	BU
180	1971	70.000	—	.10	.15	1.50
	1972	40.000	—	—	.10	1.00
	1973	34.000	—	—	.10	1.00
	1974	46.000	—	—	.10	1.00
	1975	25.000	—	—	.10	1.00
	1976	15.000	—	—	.10	.50
	1977	15.000	—	—	.10	.50
	1978	15.000	—	—	.10	.50
	1979	15.000	—	—	.10	.50
	1980 cock & star privy mark	15.300	—	—	.10	.30

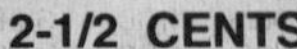

2-1/2 CENTS

BRONZE

Obv: 17 small shields in field, leg: KONINGRIJK.

KM#	Date	Mintage	Fine	VF	XF	Unc
108	1877	4.000	2.50	7.50	17.50	40.00
	1880	4.000	2.50	7.50	17.50	40.00
	1881	4.000	2.50	7.50	17.50	40.00
	1883	.400	20.00	50.00	75.00	125.00
	1884	3.600	3.50	9.00	20.00	45.00
	1886	2.000	7.50	20.00	35.00	55.00
	1890	2.000	7.50	20.00	35.00	55.00
	1894	1.000	20.00	55.00	100.00	150.00
	1898	1.600	15.00	35.00	65.00	100.00

Obv: 15 large shields in field.

KM#	Date	Mintage	Fine	VF	XF	Unc
134	1903	4.000	2.50	5.00	15.00	30.00
	1904	4.000	2.50	5.00	15.00	30.00
	1905	4.000	2.50	5.00	15.00	30.00
	1906	8.000	2.50	5.00	15.00	30.00

KM#	Date	Mintage	Fine	VF	XF	Unc
150	1912	2.000	7.50	20.00	35.00	45.00
	1913	4.000	3.50	7.50	15.00	25.00
	1914	2.000	7.50	20.00	35.00	45.00
	1915	3.000	6.50	14.00	25.00	35.00
	1916	8.000	3.00	5.00	12.50	20.00
	1918	4.000	3.50	7.50	15.00	25.00
	1919	2.000	7.50	15.00	30.00	40.00
	1929	8.000	2.00	4.00	8.00	12.50
	1941	19.800	1.00	2.00	3.00	5.00

ZINC

KM#	Date	Mintage	Fine	VF	XF	Unc
171	1941	27.600	2.50	7.50	10.00	25.00
	1942	*.200	650.00	2250.	4250.	9000.

***NOTE:** Almost entire issue melted, about 30 pcs. known.

5 CENTS

.8200 g, .569 SILVER, .0150 oz ASW

KM#	Date	Mintage	Fine	VF	XF	Unc
52	1818	2,500	450.00	800.00	1500.	1750.
	1818	—	—	—	Proof	3000.
	1819	3,000	300.00	600.00	1000.	1250.
	1819	—	—	—	Proof	2650.
	1822	.047	220.00	440.00	650.00	800.00
	1825B	.900	35.00	60.00	120.00	150.00
	1826B	1.021	35.00	60.00	120.00	150.00
	1827	.534	25.00	50.00	75.00	100.00
	1827B	.284	40.00	80.00	130.00	175.00
	1828B	.397	35.00	70.00	120.00	150.00

.6850 g, .640 SILVER, .0141 oz ASW

KM#	Date	Mintage	Fine	VF	XF	Unc
74	1848	100 pcs.	600.00	1300.	2000.	3000.
	1848	—	—	—	Proof	2500.

KM#	Date	Mintage	Fine	VF	XF	Unc
91	1850	3.037	3.00	7.00	15.00	25.00
	1853	.011	200.00	450.00	600.00	1000.
	1853	—	—	—	Proof	1400.
	1855	.515	5.00	12.00	20.00	35.00
	1859	.400	5.00	12.00	20.00	35.00
	1862. dot after date	.400	5.00	12.00	20.00	35.00
	1862 w/o dot after date	Inc. Ab.	5.00	12.00	20.00	35.00
	1863	.640	5.00	12.00	20.00	35.00
	1868	.200	30.00	55.00	125.00	175.00
	1869	.500	5.00	12.00	20.00	35.00
	1876	.200	7.00	20.00	35.00	50.00
	1879	.200	7.00	20.00	35.00	50.00
	1879	—	—	—	Proof	160.00
	1887	.100	25.00	45.00	75.00	90.00

NOTE: Varieties exist for 1850 dated coins.

COPPER-NICKEL

KM#	Date	Mintage	Fine	VF	XF	Unc
137	1907	6.000	4.00	12.00	22.50	35.00
	1908	5.430	5.00	15.00	27.50	45.00
	1909	2.570	30.00	70.00	110.00	135.00

KM#	Date	Mintage	Fine	VF	XF	Unc
153	1913	6.000	1.50	2.50	10.00	25.00
	1914	7.400	1.50	2.50	10.00	25.00
	1923	10.000	1.50	2.50	10.00	25.00
	1929	8.000	1.50	2.50	12.50	25.00
	1932	2.000	10.00	25.00	40.00	60.00
	1933	1.400	40.00	70.00	110.00	135.00
	1934	2.600	7.50	17.50	27.50	45.00
	1936	2.600	7.50	17.50	27.50	45.00
	1938	4.200	3.00	7.00	15.00	25.00
	1939	4.600	3.00	7.00	15.00	25.00
	1940	7.200	2.50	5.00	12.50	25.00

NOTE: For a similar coin dated 1943, see Netherlands Antilles (Curacao).

ZINC

KM#	Date	Mintage	Fine	VF	XF	Unc
172	1941	32.200	2.00	4.00	10.00	20.00
	1942	11.800	4.00	8.00	15.00	30.00
	1943	7.000	10.00	22.50	40.00	70.00

BRONZE

KM#	Date	Mintage	VF	XF	Unc	BU
176	1948	23.600	.50	.75	2.00	15.00
	1948	—	—	—	Proof	80.00

KM#	Date	Mintage	VF	XF	Unc	BU
181	1950	20.000	.10	.25	.75	5.00
	1950	—	—	—	Proof	50.00
	1951	16.200	.10	.25	.75	5.00
	1951	—	—	—	Proof	50.00
	1952	14.400	.10	.25	.75	5.00
	1952	—	—	—	Proof	50.00
	1953	12.000	.10	.25	.75	5.00
	1953	—	—	—	Proof	50.00
	1954	14.000	.10	.25	.75	5.00
	1954	—	—	—	Proof	50.00
	1955	11.400	.10	.25	.75	5.00
	1955	—	—	—	Proof	50.00
	1956	7.400	.15	.35	1.00	6.00
	1956	—	—	—	Proof	50.00
	1957	16.000	.10	.25	.75	5.00
	1957	—	—	—	Proof	50.00
	1958	9.000	.10	.25	.75	6.00
	1958	—	—	—	Proof	50.00
	1960	11.000	.10	.25	.75	5.00
	1960	—	—	—	Proof	40.00
	1961	12.000	.10	.25	.50	3.00
	1961	—	—	—	Proof	40.00
	1962	15.000	.10	.25	.50	3.00
	1962	—	—	—	Proof	40.00
	1963	18.000	.10	.25	.50	3.00
	1963	—	—	—	Proof	40.00
	1964	21.000	.10	.25	.50	3.00
	1964	—	—	—	Proof	40.00
	1965	28.000	.10	.25	.50	3.00
	1965	—	—	—	Proof	40.00
	1966	22.000	.10	.25	.50	3.00
	1966	—	—	—	Proof	40.00
	1967 leaves far from rim	32.000	—	.10	.25	3.00
	1967 leaves far from rim	—	—	—	Proof	50.00
	1967 leaves touching rim	Inc. Ab.	.15	.50	1.00	4.00
	1967 leaves touching rim	—	—	—	Proof	40.00
	1969 fish privy mark	5.000	.15	.50	1.00	3.50
	1969 fish privy mark	—	—	—	Proof	40.00
	1969 cock privy mark	11.000	—	.10	.25	2.00
	1969 cock privy mark	—	—	—	Proof	40.00
	1970	22.000	—	.10	.25	1.00
	1970	—	—	—	Proof	25.00
	1970 date close to rim	Inc. Ab.	—	.10	.25	1.00
	1970 date close to rim	—	—	—	Proof	20.00
	1971	25.000	—	.10	.25	1.00
	1972	25.000	—	.10	.25	1.00
	1973	22.000	—	.10	.25	1.00
	1974	20.000	—	—	.10	.50
	1975	46.000	—	—	.10	.50
	1976	50.000	—	—	.10	.50
	1977	50.000	—	—	.10	.50
	1978	60.000	—	—	.10	.50
	1979	80.000	—	—	.10	.50
	1980 cock & star privy mark	252.500	—	—	.10	.30

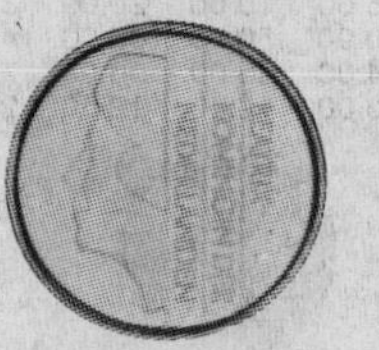

KM#	Date	Mintage	VF	XF	Unc	BU
202	1982	47.100	—	—	.10	.20
	1982	.010	—	—	Proof	10.00
	1983	60.200	—	—	.10	.20
	1983	.015	—	—	Proof	7.50
	1984	70.700	—	—	.10	.20
	1984	.020	—	—	Proof	4.00
	1985	36.100	—	—	.10	.20
	1985	.017	—	—	Proof	4.00
	1986	7.700	—	—	.10	.20
	1986	.020	—	—	Proof	4.00
	1987	33.300	—	—	—	.10
	1987	.018	—	—	Proof	4.00
	1988	22.600	—	—	—	.10
	1988	.020	—	—	Proof	4.00
	1989	27.100	—	—	—	.10
	1989	.015	—	—	Proof	4.00
	1990	39.300	—	—	—	.10
	1990	.015	—	—	Proof	4.00
	1991	73.000	—	—	—	.10
	1991	.014	—	—	Proof	4.00
	1992	52.600	—	—	—	.10
	1993	*50.100	—	—	—	.10
	1994	*55.100	—	—	—	.10

NICKEL

KM#	Date	Mintage	VF	XF	Unc	BU
202a	1987	—	—	—	—	—
	1991	—	—	—	—	—

10 CENTS

1.6900 g, .569 SILVER, .0309 oz ASW

KM#	Date	Mintage	Fine	VF	XF	Unc
53	1818	60 pcs.	1250.	2500.	4000.	11,000.
	1818	—	—	—	Proof	9000.
	1819	.025	275.00	600.00	1000.	1500.
	1822	.113	200.00	400.00	700.00	1000
	1823B	.178	110.00	220.00	375.00	850.00
	1825	.972	30.00	45.00	90.00	140.00
	1825B	1.727	30.00	45.00	90.00	140.00
	1826	2.138	25.00	40.00	85.00	130.00

KM#	Date	Mintage	Fine	VF	XF	Unc
53	1826B	1.430	30.00	50.00	100.00	180.00
	1827	5.895	17.50	32.50	70.00	110.00
	1827B	1.711	25.00	40.00	85.00	110.00
	1828	2.036	25.00	40.00	85.00	130.00
	1828B	1.168	30.00	45.00	90.00	145.00

1.4000 g, .640 SILVER, .0288 oz ASW

KM#	Date	Mintage	Fine	VF	XF	Unc
75	1848	6.859	20.00	55.00	120.00	160.00
	1848	—	—	—	Proof	375.00
	1849. dot after date					
		4.051	15.00	45.00	90.00	110.00
	1849 w/o dot after date					
		Inc. Ab.	35.00	90.00	175.00	425.00

KM#	Date	Mintage	Fine	VF	XF	Unc
80	1849	6.204	20.00	55.00	90.00	140.00
	1850	7.270	20.00	55.00	90.00	165.00
	1853	1.104	45.00	90.00	130.00	200.00
	1855	.745	50.00	100.00	150.00	220.00
	1855 low 5					
		Inc. Ab.	50.00	100.00	150.00	220.00
	1856	1.000	20.00	55.00	90.00	150.00
	1859	1.000	20.00	55.00	90.00	150.00
	1862	.800	45.00	100.00	160.00	220.00
	1863	1.240	20.00	55.00	80.00	125.00
	1868	.200	100.00	300.00	500.00	800.00
	1869	1.000	20.00	55.00	80.00	125.00
	1871	1.000	20.00	55.00	80.00	125.00
	1873	1.000	20.00	55.00	80.00	125.00
	1874 sword privy mark					
		.800	90.00	250.00	400.00	850.00
	1874 sword in scabbard privy mark					
		2.000	40.00	100.00	150.00	200.00
	1876	1.000	12.50	35.00	70.00	100.00
	1877	1.000	12.50	35.00	70.00	100.00
	1878	1.000	12.50	35.00	70.00	100.00
	1879	1.000	12.50	35.00	70.00	100.00
	1880	1.000	12.50	35.00	70.00	100.00
	1881	2.000	12.50	35.00	70.00	100.00
	1882	2.000	12.50	35.00	70.00	100.00
	1884	1.000	12.50	35.00	70.00	100.00
	1885	2.000	12.50	35.00	70.00	100.00
	1887	1.600	12.50	35.00	70.00	100.00
	1889	2.800	10.00	30.00	60.00	80.00
	1890	2.600	10.00	30.00	60.00	80.00

KM#	Date	Mintage	Fine	VF	XF	Unc
16	1892 thin head					
		2.000	12.00	35.00	70.00	90.00
	1893	2.000	12.00	35.00	70.00	90.00
	1894	1.500	12.00	35.00	70.00	90.00
	1895	1.000	17.50	55.00	90.00	135.00
	1896	2.000	12.00	35.00	70.00	90.00
	1897	7.850	6.00	20.00	40.00	60.00

Obv: Small head, divided legend.

KM#	Date	Mintage	Fine	VF	XF	Unc
19	1898	2.000	22.50	60.00	120.00	180.00
	1901	2.000	20.00	55.00	100.00	160.00

Obv: Large head.

KM#	Date	Mintage	Fine	VF	XF	Unc
35	1903	6.000	8.00	25.00	45.00	70.00

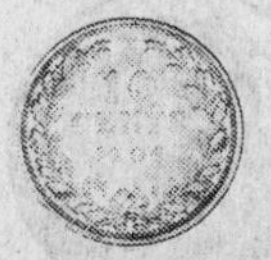

Obv: Small head, continuous legend.

KM#	Date	Mintage	Fine	VF	XF	Unc
36	1904	3.000	10.00	32.50	65.00	80.00
	1905	2.000	15.00	40.00	80.00	110.00
	1906	4.000	9.00	25.00	45.00	65.00

KM#	Date	Mintage	Fine	VF	XF	Unc
145	1910	2.250	25.00	60.00	100.00	150.00
	1911	4.000	9.00	25.00	55.00	70.00
	1912	4.000	9.00	25.00	55.00	70.00
	1913	5.000	9.00	25.00	55.00	70.00
	1914	9.000	3.00	10.00	20.00	35.00
	1915	5.000	3.00	10.00	20.00	35.00
	1916	5.000	3.00	10.00	20.00	35.00
	1917	10.000	2.00	7.50	15.00	30.00
	1918	20.000	1.50	5.00	12.50	25.00
	1919	10.000	2.00	7.50	15.00	30.00
	1921	5.000	3.00	10.00	20.00	35.00
	1925	5.000	3.00	10.00	20.00	35.00

KM#	Date	Mintage	Fine	VF	XF	Unc
163	1926	2.700	7.00	18.00	30.00	55.00
	1927	2.300	7.00	18.00	30.00	65.00
	1928	10.000	.75	3.00	7.50	15.00
	1930	5.000	1.50	4.50	10.00	17.50
	1934	2.000	7.00	18.00	30.00	55.00
	1935	8.000	1.00	3.00	7.50	15.00
	1936	15.000	.50	1.00	2.00	5.00
	1937	18.600	.50	1.00	2.00	5.00
	1938	21.400	.50	1.00	2.00	5.00
	1939	20.000	.50	1.00	2.00	5.00
	1941	43.000	.50	.75	1.50	4.00
	1943P acorn privy mark					
		Inc. Be.	1.00	2.00	3.00	20.00
	1944P	120.000	.50	.75	1.00	2.50
	1944D	25.400	1150.	2250.	3000.	5000.
	1944S	64.040	1.00	2.00	3.00	22.50
	1945P	90.560	175.00	350.00	500.00	700.00

NOTE: For similar coins dated 1941P-1943P with palm tree privy mark, see Netherlands Antilles (Curacao) and Surinam.

ZINC

KM#	Date	Mintage	Fine	VF	XF	Unc
173	1941	29.800	1.00	2.00	7.50	20.00
	1942	95.600	.25	.50	2.50	15.00
	1943	29.000	1.00	2.00	7.50	20.00

NICKEL

KM#	Date	Mintage	VF	XF	Unc	BU
177	1948	69.200	.25	.50	1.00	7.00
	1948	—	—	—	Proof	90.00

KM#	Date	Mintage	VF	XF	Unc	BU
182	1950	56.600	.10	.25	.50	4.50
	1950	—	—	—	Proof	60.00
	1951	54.200	.10	.25	.50	4.50
	1951	—	—	—	Proof	60.00
	1954	8.200	.10	.35	.75	6.50
	1954	—	—	—	Proof	60.00
	1955	18.200	.10	.25	.50	4.50
	1955	—	—	—	Proof	60.00
	1956	12.000	.10	.25	.50	4.50
	1956	—	—	—	Proof	60.00
	1957	18.600	.10	.25	.50	4.50
	1957	—	—	—	Proof	60.00
	1958	34.000	.10	.25	.50	4.50
	1958	—	—	—	Proof	60.00
	1959	44.000	.10	.25	.50	4.50
	1959	—	—	—	Proof	50.00
	1960	12.000	.10	.25	.50	4.50
	1960	—	—	—	Proof	50.00
	1961	25.000	—	.10	.25	4.50
	1961	—	—	—	Proof	50.00
	1962	30.000	—	.10	.25	4.50
	1962	—	—	—	Proof	50.00
	1963	35.000	—	.10	.25	4.50
	1963	—	—	—	Proof	60.00
	1964	41.000	—	.10	.25	4.50
	1964	—	—	—	Proof	60.00
	1965	59.000	—	.10	.25	4.50
	1965	—	—	—	Proof	60.00
	1966	44.000	—	—	.10	2.00

KM#	Date	Mintage	VF	XF	Unc	BU
182	1966	—	—	—	Proof	50.00
	1967	39.000	—	—	.10	2.00
	1967	—	—	—	Proof	50.00
	1968	42.000	—	—	.10	2.00
	1968	—	—	—	Proof	40.00
	1969 fish privy mark					
		29.100	—	—	.10	2.00
	1969 fish privy mark					
		—	—	—	Proof	40.00
	1969 cock privy mark					
		24.000	—	—	.10	2.00
	1969 cock privy mark					
		—	—	—	Proof	40.00
	1970	50.000	—	—	.10	1.50
	1970	—	—	—	Proof	40.00
	1971	55.000	—	—	.10	1.50
	1972	60.000	—	—	.10	1.50
	1973	90.000	—	—	.10	1.25
	1974	75.000	—	—	.10	1.00
	1975	110.000	—	—	.10	1.00
	1976	85.000	—	—	.10	1.00
	1977	100.000	—	—	.10	1.00
	1978	110.000	—	—	.10	1.00
	1979	120.000	—	—	.10	1.00
	1980 cock & star privy mark					
		195.300	—	—	.10	.50

KM#	Date	Mintage	VF	XF	Unc	BU
203	1982	10.300	—	—	.10	.25
	1982	.010	—	—	Proof	10.00
	1983	38.200	—	—	—	.25
	1983	.015	—	—	Proof	8.00
	1984	42.200	—	—	.10	.25
	1984	.020	—	—	Proof	4.00
	1985	29.100	—	—	.10	.25
	1985	.017	—	—	Proof	4.00
	1986	23.100	—	—	.10	.25
	1986	.020	—	—	Proof	4.00
	1987	21.700	—	—	.10	.25
	1987	.018	—	—	Proof	4.00
	1988	2.200	—	.10	.20	.50
	1988	.020	—	—	Proof	4.00
	1989	5.300	—	—	—	.25
	1989	.015	—	—	Proof	4.00
	1990	13.300	—	—	—	.25
	1990	.015	—	—	Proof	4.00
	1991	41.000	—	—	—	.25
	1991	.014	—	—	Proof	4.00
	1992	41.200	—	—	—	.25
	1993	*40.000	—	—	—	.25
	1994	*40.000	—	—	—	.25

25 CENTS

4.2300 g, .569 SILVER, .0773 oz ASW

KM#	Date	Mintage	Fine	VF	XF	Unc
48	1817	—	525.00	1500.	3000.	4500.
	1817	—	—	—	Proof	8750.
	1818	—	525.00	1500.	3000.	4500.
	1819	.013	300.00	600.00	1000.	1750.
	1819	—	—	—	Proof	3000.
	1822	.116	220.00	400.00	750.00	1000.
	1823B	1.334	35.00	70.00	100.00	130.00
	1824B	6.033	25.00	45.00	70.00	100.00
	1825	10.311	25.00	45.00	70.00	100.00
	1825B	2.608	35.00	70.00	100.00	130.00
	1826	12.282	25.00	45.00	70.00	100.00
	1826B	7.299	25.00	45.00	70.00	100.00
	1827B	1.822	35.00	70.00	100.00	130.00
	1828B	.334	150.00	300.00	650.00	900.00
	1829	.106	150.00	350.00	750.00	1000.
	1829B	1.256	45.00	90.00	150.00	200.00
	1830	1.534	45.00	90.00	150.00	200.00
	1830B	.902	50.00	90.00	150.00	200.00

3.5750 g, .640 SILVER, .0736 oz ASW

KM#	Date	Mintage	Fine	VF	XF	Unc
76	1848. dot after date					
		10.730	20.00	50.00	100.00	150.00
	1848.	—	—	—	Proof	300.00
	1848 w/o dot after date					
		Inc. Ab.	25.00	90.00	150.00	175.00
	1849/89	8.059	150.00	330.00	500.00	625.00
	1849	Inc. Ab.	15.00	40.00	85.00	115.00

KM#	Date	Mintage	Fine	VF	XF	Unc
81	1849	Inc.KM76	140.00	300.00	500.00	750.00
	1850	2.207	110.00	270.00	400.00	600.00
	1853	7,974	250.00	500.00	1000.	1500.
	1853	—	—	—	Proof	3000.
	1887	.100	140.00	300.00	500.00	750.00
	1889	.200	125.00	270.00	350.00	550.00
	1890. dot after date	.600	80.00	175.00	275.00	450.00
	1890 w/o dot after date	Inc. Ab.	110.00	250.00	400.00	475.00

KM#	Date	Mintage	Fine	VF	XF	Unc
115	1891	2 pcs.	—	—	—	—
	1892	.800	17.50	50.00	90.00	130.00
	1893	.800	17.50	50.00	90.00	130.00
	1894	1.000	15.00	50.00	90.00	130.00
	1895	1.200	15.00	50.00	90.00	130.00
	1895 slanted mint mark	Inc. Ab.	75.00	150.00	350.00	450.00
	1896	.600	35.00	110.00	180.00	250.00
	1897	3.100	10.00	40.00	70.00	100.00

Obv: Bust w/small truncation.

KM#	Date	Mintage	Fine	VF	XF	Unc
120.1	1898	.400	80.00	200.00	350.00	575.00
	1901	1.600	12.50	45.00	90.00	120.00

Obv: Bust w/wider truncation.

KM#	Date	Mintage	Fine	VF	XF	Unc
120.2	1901	Inc. Ab.	50.00	150.00	275.00	400.00
	1902	1.200	15.00	45.00	80.00	110.00
	1903	1.200	15.00	45.00	80.00	110.00
	1904	1.600	15.00	45.00	80.00	110.00
	1905	1.200	15.00	45.00	80.00	110.00
	1906	2.000	12.00	40.00	65.00	90.00

KM#	Date	Mintage	Fine	VF	XF	Unc
146	1910	.880	30.00	90.00	160.00	225.00
	1910	—	—	—	Proof	300.00
	1911	1.600	15.00	45.00	75.00	120.00
	1912	1.600	15.00	45.00	75.00	120.00
	1913	1.200	20.00	60.00	100.00	150.00
	1914	5.600	5.00	25.00	50.00	80.00
	1915	2.000	6.00	25.00	50.00	100.00
	1916	2.000	6.00	25.00	50.00	100.00
	1917	4.000	5.00	22.50	45.00	85.00
	1918	6.000	4.00	17.50	35.00	60.00
	1919	4.000	5.00	22.50	45.00	85.00
	1925	2.000	5.00	25.00	50.00	85.00

KM#	Date	Mintage	Fine	VF	XF	Unc
164	1926	2.000	12.50	35.00	50.00	100.00
	1928	8.000	1.50	3.00	7.50	20.00
	1939	4.000	1.50	4.00	6.00	10.00
	1940	9.000	1.00	2.00	4.00	7.50
	1941	40.000	.75	1.00	2.00	4.00
	1943P acorn privy mark	Inc. Be.	1.00	2.00	4.00	15.00
	1944P acorn privy mark	40.000	.75	1.00	2.00	4.00
	1945P acorn privy mark	92.000	80.00	180.00	350.00	450.00

NOTE: For similar coins dated 1941P and 1943P with palm tree privy mark, see Netherlands Antilles (Curacao).

ZINC

KM#	Date	Mintage	Fine	VF	XF	Unc
174	1941	34.600	.50	1.50	8.00	30.00
	1942	27.800	.50	1.50	8.00	30.00
	1943	13.600	3.00	10.00	20.00	60.00

NICKEL

KM#	Date	Mintage	VF	XF	Unc	BU
178	1948	27.400	.25	.50	1.50	10.00
	1948	—	—	—	Proof	90.00

KM#	Date	Mintage	VF	XF	Unc	BU
183	1950	43.000	.20	.30	.60	5.00
	1950	—	—	—	Proof	65.00
	1951	33.200	.20	.30	.60	5.00
	1951	—	—	—	Proof	65.00
	1954	6.400	.50	1.50	2.50	8.00
	1954	—	—	—	Proof	65.00
	1955	10.000	.20	.30	.60	5.00
	1955	—	—	—	Proof	65.00
	1956	8.000	.20	.30	.60	4.00
	1956	—	—	—	Proof	65.00
	1957	8.000	.20	.30	.60	4.00
	1957	—	—	—	Proof	65.00
	1958	15.000	.20	.30	.60	4.00
	1958	—	—	—	Proof	65.00
	1960	9.000	.20	.30	.60	4.00
	1960	—	—	—	Proof	60.00
	1961	6.000	.40	1.25	2.00	7.50
	1961	—	—	—	Proof	50.00
	1962	12.000	.20	.30	.60	3.50
	1962	—	—	—	Proof	50.00
	1963	18.000	.20	.30	.60	3.50
	1963	—	—	—	Proof	50.00
	1964	25.000	.20	.30	.60	3.50
	1964	—	—	—	Proof	50.00
	1965	18.000	.20	.30	.60	3.50
	1965	—	—	—	Proof	50.00
	1966	25.000	—	.20	.30	1.50
	1966	—	—	—	Proof	50.00
	1967	18.000	—	.20	.30	1.50
	1967	—	—	—	Proof	60.00
	1968	26.000	—	.20	.30	1.50
	1968	—	—	—	Proof	60.00
	1969 fish privy mark	14.000	—	.20	.30	1.50
	1969 fish privy mark	—	—	—	Proof	60.00
	1969 cock privy mark	21.000	—	.20	.30	1.50
	1969 cock privy mark	—	—	—	Proof	60.00
	1970	39.000	—	.20	.30	1.50
	1970	—	—	—	Proof	60.00
	1971	40.000	—	.20	.30	1.50
	1972	50.000	—	.20	.30	1.50
	1973	45.000	—	.20	.30	1.50
	1974	10.000	—	.20	.30	1.50
	1975	25.000	—	.20	.30	1.00
	1976	64.000	—	.20	.30	1.00
	1977	55.000	—	.20	.30	1.00
	1978	35.000	—	.20	.30	1.00
	1979	45.000	—	.20	.30	1.00
	1980 cock & star privy mark	159.300	—	—	.20	.75

ALUMINUM

KM#	Date	Mintage	VF	XF	Unc	BU
183a	1980	15 pcs.	—	—	—	400.00

NICKEL

KM#	Date	Mintage	VF	XF	Unc	BU
204	1982	18.300	—	—	.20	.25
	1982	.010	—	—	Proof	15.00
	1983	18.200	—	—	.20	.25
	1983	.015	—	—	Proof	12.00
204	1984	19.200	—	—	.20	.25
	1984	.020	—	—	Proof	6.00
	1985	29.100	—	—	.20	.25
	1985	.017	—	—	Proof	6.00
	1986	20.300	—	—	.20	.25
	1986	.020	—	—	Proof	6.00
	1987	30.100	—	—	.20	.25
	1987	.018	—	—	Proof	6.00
	1988	17.400	—	—	.20	.25
	1988	.020	—	—	Proof	6.00
	1989	30.500	—	—	—	.25
	1989	.015	—	—	Proof	6.00
	1990	23.100	—	—	—	.25
	1990	.015	—	—	Proof	6.00
	1991	25.000	—	—	—	.25
	1991	.014	—	—	Proof	6.00
	1992	41.500	—	—	—	.25
	1993	*35.000	—	—	—	.25
	1994	*35.000	—	—	—	.25

1/2 GULDEN

(50 Cents)

5.3800 g, .893 SILVER, .1544 oz ASW

KM#	Date	Mintage	Fine	VF	XF	Unc
54	1818	.051	130.00	250.00	650.00	900.00
	1819	.043	130.00	250.00	650.00	900.00
	1819	—	—	—	Proof	1250.
	1822 engraver's name below bust	.119	130.00	250.00	450.00	700.00
	1822 w/o engraver's name	Inc. Ab.	250.00	475.00	700.00	1000.
	1829B	.180	130.00	250.00	450.00	700.00
	1830B	.100	130.00	250.00	450.00	700.00

5.0000 g, .945 SILVER, .1519 oz ASW

Reeded edge.

KM#	Date	Mintage	Fine	VF	XF	Unc
73.1	1846	—	600.00	1500.	3000.	4000.
	1846	—	—	—	Proof	3000.
	1847	1.111	35.00	100.00	250.00	400.00
	1847	—	—	—	Proof	700.00
	1848	4.050	15.00	60.00	150.00	250.00

Lettered edge.

KM#	Date	Mintage	Fine	VF	XF	Unc
73.2	1846	—	—	—	Proof	3500.

KM#	Date	Mintage	Fine	VF	XF	Unc
92	1850	—	750.00	1750.	3000.	4000.
	1850	—	—	—	Proof	3800.
	1853/43	1,711	400.00	1000.	2000.	3000.
	1857	3.606	15.00	40.00	75.00	150.00
	1858	7.604	12.50	35.00	60.00	115.00
	1859	3.001	15.00	40.00	75.00	150.00
	1860	6.603	12.50	35.00	60.00	125.00
	1861	6.001	12.50	35.00	60.00	125.00
	1862	4.002	12.50	35.00	60.00	125.00
	1863	5.152	12.50	35.00	60.00	125.00
	1864	4.001	12.50	35.00	60.00	125.00
	1866	1.402	25.00	70.00	150.00	250.00
	1868 open 8	4.004	12.50	35.00	60.00	125.00
	1868 closed 8	Inc. Ab.	12.50	35.00	60.00	120.00

KM#	Date	Mintage	Fine	VF	XF	Unc
121.1	1898	2.000	25.00	60.00	150.00	200.00
	1898	—	—	—	Proof	600.00

Rev: W/o 50 C. below shield.

KM#	Date	Mintage	Fine	VF	XF	Unc
121.2	1904	1.000	35.00	85.00	150.00	250.00
	1905	4.000	10.00	25.00	50.00	100.00
	1906	1.000	35.00	85.00	150.00	250.00
	1907	3.300	10.00	25.00	50.00	100.00
	1907	—	—	—	Proof	300.00
	1908	4.000	10.00	25.00	50.00	100.00
	1909	3.000	10.00	25.00	50.00	100.00

KM#	Date	Mintage	Fine	VF	XF	Unc
147	1910	4.000	10.00	30.00	80.00	150.00
	1912	4.000	10.00	30.00	80.00	150.00
	1913	8.000	8.00	17.50	40.00	100.00
	1919	8.000	8.00	17.50	40.00	100.00

5.0000 g, .720 SILVER, .1157 oz ASW

KM#	Date	Mintage	Fine	VF	XF	Unc
160	1921	5.000	1.50	3.00	6.00	22.50
	1921	—	—	—	Proof	200.00
	1922	11.240	1.25	2.50	5.00	15.00
	1928	5.000	1.50	3.00	6.00	22.50
	1929	9.500	1.25	2.50	5.00	12.50
	1930	18.500	1.25	2.50	4.00	10.00

GULDEN

(100 Cents)

10.7600 g, .893 SILVER, .3089 oz ASW

KM#	Date	Mintage	Fine	VF	XF	Unc
55	1818	.043	400.00	750.00	1500.	2000.
	1818	—	—	—	Proof	2250.
	1819	.252	160.00	400.00	600.00	1000.
	1820	.543	85.00	175.00	275.00	500.00
	1821	1.239	85.00	175.00	275.00	500.00
	1822	.080	300.00	700.00	1500.	2000.
	1823	.732	85.00	175.00	275.00	500.00
	1823	—	—	—	Proof	900.00
	1823B	.025	650.00	1500.	2000.	2500.
	1824	1.096	85.00	175.00	275.00	500.00
	1824 dash between crown & shield					
		Inc. Ab.	85.00	160.00	225.00	325.00
	1828	.062	300.00	600.00	1250.	1700.
	1829B	.383	200.00	400.00	750.00	1200.
	1831/21	.120	200.00	400.00	750.00	1200.
	1831	Inc. Ab.	200.00	400.00	750.00	1200.
	1832/21	1.362	80.00	160.00	275.00	500.00
	1832/23	I.A.	80.00	160.00	275.00	500.00
	1832/24	I.A.	80.00	160.00	275.00	500.00
	1832/24 dash between crown & shield					
		Inc. Ab.	80.00	160.00	275.00	500.00
	1832/28	I.A.	80.00	160.00	275.00	500.00
	1832	Inc. Ab.	80.00	160.00	275.00	500.00
	1837	.383	80.00	160.00	275.00	500.00

10.0000 g, .945 SILVER, .3038 oz ASW

KM#	Date	Mintage	Fine	VF	XF	Unc
5	1840	.099	60.00	130.00	250.00	500.00
	1840	—	—	—	Proof	2000.

KM#	Date	Mintage	Fine	VF	XF	Unc
66	1840	2 pcs.	—	—	Rare	—
	1842	.661	80.00	225.00	500.00	750.00
	1842	—	—	—	Proof	900.00
	1842 shorter bust					
		Inc. Ab.	175.00	375.00	700.00	1150.
	1842	—	—	—	Proof	1250.
	1843	1.720	60.00	135.00	200.00	400.00
	1844	1.575	60.00	135.00	200.00	400.00
	1845	3.803	20.00	50.00	90.00	150.00
	1845 dash between crown & shield					
		.221	60.00	115.00	200.00	400.00
	1846 fleur de lis privy mark					
		.901	30.00	80.00	130.00	200.00
	1846 sword privy mark					
		3.772	20.00	45.00	100.00	150.00
	1847	8.280	15.00	35.00	65.00	125.00
	1848	13.615	15.00	35.00	65.00	125.00
	1849	.650	55.00	140.00	200.00	400.00

KM#	Date	Mintage	Fine	VF	XF	Unc
93	1850	10 pcs.	—	—	Rare	—
	1850	—	—	—	Proof	4000.
	1850 reeded edge					
		—	—	—	Rare	—
	1851	2.125	22.50	60.00	120.00	175.00
	1853/0	.652	275.00	350.00	625.00	850.00
	1853/1	Inc. Ab.	275.00	350.00	625.00	850.00
	1853	Inc. Ab.	150.00	250.00	400.00	650.00
	1854	4.511	17.50	35.00	55.00	110.00
	1855	5.133	17.50	35.00	55.00	110.00
	1856	4.955	17.50	35.00	55.00	110.00
	1857	2.125	22.50	40.00	80.00	130.00
	1858	4.199	17.50	35.00	70.00	120.00
	1859	2.717	17.50	35.00	70.00	130.00
	1860	4.036	17.50	30.00	65.00	120.00
	1861	5.079	15.00	30.00	65.00	120.00
	1863	7.986	15.00	30.00	65.00	120.00
	1864	3.600	15.00	30.00	65.00	120.00
	1865	6.402	15.00	30.00	65.00	120.00
	1866	1.002	27.50	65.00	125.00	200.00
	1867	*4 pcs.	—	—	Proof	10,000.

KM#	Date	Mintage	Fine	VF	XF	Unc
117	1892	3.500	10.00	30.00	80.00	150.00
	1896	.100	100.00	260.00	700.00	1000.
	1896	—	—	—	Proof	1500.
	1897	2.500	15.00	35.00	100.00	175.00

KM#	Date	Mintage	Fine	VF	XF	Unc
122.1	1898	2.000	35.00	70.00	150.00	325.00
	1901	2.000	30.00	65.00	135.00	300.00
	1901	—	—	—	Proof	400.00

Rev: W/o 100 C. below shield.

KM#	Date	Mintage	Fine	VF	XF	Unc
122.2	1904	2.000	17.50	35.00	70.00	135.00
	1905	1.000	35.00	65.00	140.00	250.00
	1906	.500	200.00	350.00	550.00	700.00
	1906	—	—	—	Proof	1000.
	1907	5.100	12.00	30.00	65.00	110.00
	1908	4.700	12.00	30.00	65.00	110.00
	1909	2.000	20.00	45.00	80.00	140.00

KM#	Date	Mintage	Fine	VF	XF	Unc
148	1910	1.000	45.00	100.00	275.00	400.00
	1910	—	—	—	Proof	600.00
	1911	2.000	50.00	100.00	200.00	350.00
	1912	3.000	12.50	25.00	55.00	110.00
	1913	8.000	10.00	25.00	55.00	110.00
	1914	15.785	10.00	20.00	50.00	110.00
	1915	14.215	10.00	20.00	50.00	110.00
	1916	5.000	25.00	50.00	90.00	175.00
	1917	2.300	30.00	50.00	90.00	175.00

10.0000 g, .720 SILVER, .2315 oz ASW
Obv. leg. ends below truncation.

KM#	Date	Mintage	Fine	VF	XF	Unc
161.1	1922	9.550	4.00	9.00	20.00	40.00
	1922	—	—	—	Proof	350.00
	1923	8.050	4.00	9.00	20.00	40.00
	1924	8.000	4.00	12.50	35.00	55.00
	1928	6.150	4.00	7.50	18.00	30.00
	1929	32.350	BV	5.00	7.50	15.00
	1930	13.500	BV	5.00	7.50	17.50
	1931	38.100	BV	5.00	7.50	15.00
	1938	5.000	6.00	12.50	20.00	40.00
	1939	14.200	BV	5.00	7.50	15.00
	1940	21.300	BV	5.00	7.50	15.00
	1940	—	—	—	Proof	175.00
	1944P acorn privy mark					
		I.A.	70.00	150.00	225.00	350.00

Obv. leg. ends at right of truncation.

KM#	Date	Mintage	Fine	VF	XF	Unc
161.2	1944P acorn privy mark					
		105.125	20.00	30.00	60.00	75.00
	1945P acorn privy mark					
		25.375	250.00	450.00	600.00	1200.

NOTE: For similar coins dated 1943D with palm tree privy mark, see Netherlands East Indies.

6.5000 g, .720 SILVER, .1504 oz ASW

KM#	Date	Mintage	VF	XF	Unc	BU
184	1954	6.600	—	BV	4.00	8.00
	1954	—	—	—	Proof	75.00

KM#	Date	Mintage	VF	XF	Unc	BU
184	1955	37.500	—	BV	2.50	6.00
	1955	—	—	—	Proof	75.00
	1956	38.900	—	BV	2.50	6.00
	1956	—	—	—	Proof	75.00
	1957	27.000	—	BV	2.50	6.00
	1957	—	—	—	Proof	75.00
	1958	30.000	—	BV	2.50	8.00
	1958	—	—	—	Proof	75.00
	1963	5.000	—	BV	4.00	12.50
	1963	—	—	—	Proof	90.00
	1964	9.000	—	BV	2.50	5.00
	1964	—	—	—	Proof	90.00
	1965	21.000	—	BV	2.00	4.00
	1965	—	—	—	Proof	90.00
	1966	5.000	—	BV	3.00	8.00
	1966	—	—	—	Proof	90.00
	1967	7.000	—	BV	4.00	10.00
	1967	—	—	—	Proof	120.00
		NICKEL				
184a	1967	31.000	—	—	.75	2.50
	1967	—	—	—	Proof	55.00
	1968	61.000	—	—	.75	2.50
	1969 fish	27.500	—	—	.75	2.50
	1969 fish	—	—	—	Proof	50.00
	1969 cock					
		15.500	—	—	.75	2.50
	1969 cock	—	—	—	Proof	50.00
	1970	18.000	—	—	.75	2.50
	1970	—	—	—	Proof	50.00
	1971	50.000	—	—	.65	1.75
	1972	60.000	—	—	.65	1.75
	1973	27.000	—	—	.65	1.75
	1975	9.000	—	—	.65	1.75
	1976	32.000	—	—	.65	1.75
	1977	38.000	—	—	.65	1.75
	1978	30.000	—	—	.65	1.50
	1979	25.000	—	—	.65	1.50
	1980 cock & star privy mark					
		118.300	—	—	.65	1.25

Investiture of New Queen

KM#	Date	Mintage	VF	XF	Unc	BU
200	1980	30.500	—	—	.65	1.25
		SILVER				
200a	1980	157 pcs.	—	—	Rare	—
		GOLD				
200b	1980	7 pcs.	—	—	Rare	—

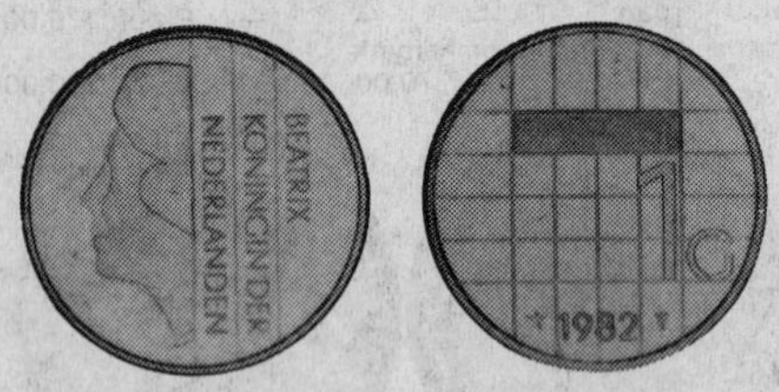

NICKEL

KM#	Date	Mintage	VF	XF	Unc	BU
205	1982	31.300	—	—	—	1.00
	1982	.010	—	—	Proof	20.00
	1983	5.200	—	—	—	1.00
	1983	.015	—	—	Proof	15.00
	1984	4.200	—	—	—	1.00
	1984	.020	—	—	Proof	7.50
	1985	3.100	—	—	—	1.00
	1985	.017	—	—	Proof	7.50
	1986	12.100	—	—	—	1.00
	1986	.018	—	—	Proof	7.50
	1987	20.100	—	—	—	1.00
	1987	.020	—	—	Proof	7.50
	1988	13.600	—	—	—	1.00
	1988	.020	—	—	Proof	7.50
	1989	1.100	—	—	—	2.00
	1989	.015	—	—	Proof	7.50
	1990	1.100	—	—	—	1.00
	1990	.015	—	—	Proof	7.50
	1991	.400	—	—	—	2.00
	1991	.014	—	—	Proof	7.50
	1992	10.000	—	—	—	1.00
	1993	*10.100	—	—	—	1.00
	1994	*14.100	—	—	—	1.00

RIJKSDAALDER

Mint: Utrecht

28.0780 g, .868 SILVER, .7836 ASW

KM#	Date	Mintage	Fine	VF	XF	Unc
46	1815	12 pcs.	—	—	Proof	8000.
	1816	.174	550.00	900.00	1200.	2000.
	1816	—	—	—	Proof	2000.

2-1/2 GULDEN

25.0000 g, .945 SILVER, .7596 oz ASW

KM#	Date	Mintage	Fine	VF	XF	Unc
67	1840	.044	125.00	250.00	500.00	1000.
	1840	—	—	—	Proof	1600.

KM#	Date	Mintage	Fine	VF	XF	Unc
69	1841	.054	200.00	500.00	1100.	2000.
	1841	—	—	—	Proof	2200.
	1842	1.010	50.00	100.00	225.00	500.00
	1843	.643	60.00	125.00	250.00	600.00
	1843	—	—	—	Proof	900.00
	1844	.279	100.00	200.00	350.00	700.00
	1845	3.270	25.00	50.00	150.00	300.00
	1845 dash between crown & shield					
		.504	40.00	75.00	150.00	350.00
	1845 dot on band of privy mark					
		.154	40.00	75.00	150.00	350.00
	1846 Fleur de lis privy mark					
		3.630	20.00	50.00	150.00	300.00
	1846	—	—	—	Proof	850.00
69	1846 sword privy mark					
		—	20.00	50.00	150.00	250.00
	1847	9.465	15.00	30.00	90.00	200.00
	1848	8.333	15.00	30.00	90.00	200.00
	1849	2.049	25.00	70.00	160.00	300.00

KM#	Date	Mintage	Fine	VF	XF	Unc
82	1849	.439	60.00	175.00	300.00	500.00
	1849	—	—	—	Proof	950.00
	1850	5.008	18.00	35.00	90.00	200.00
	1851	3.647	18.00	35.00	90.00	200.00
	1852	4.547	18.00	35.00	90.00	200.00
	1853/2	.234	100.00	300.00	425.00	650.00
	1853	Inc. Ab.	75.00	200.00	350.00	525.00
	1854/2	4.335	60.00	150.00	300.00	500.00
	1854	Inc. Ab.	18.00	35.00	90.00	200.00
	1855	2.082	18.00	35.00	90.00	200.00
	1856	.909	45.00	110.00	200.00	350.00
	1857	3.353	18.00	35.00	90.00	200.00
	1858	8.357	18.00	35.00	90.00	150.00
	1859	4.307	18.00	35.00	100.00	175.00
	1860	.847	50.00	100.00	200.00	350.00
	1861	.876	40.00	100.00	200.00	350.00
	1862	3.304	20.00	35.00	100.00	175.00
	1863	.051	300.00	600.00	1200.	1800
	1864	2.034	18.00	30.00	60.00	150.00
	1865	2.288	18.00	30.00	60.00	150.00
	1866	3.563	18.00	30.00	60.00	150.00
	1867	4.949	15.00	25.00	60.00	125.00
	1868	4.040	15.00	25.00	60.00	125.00
	1869	5.046	15.00	25.00	60.00	125.00
	1870	6.640	12.00	22.50	45.00	100.00
	1871	6.875	12.00	22.50	45.00	100.00
	1872	13.416	12.00	22.50	45.00	100.00
	1873	5.515	12.00	22.50	45.00	100.00
	1874 sword privy mark					
		3.040	12.00	22.50	45.00	100.00
	1874 sword in scabbard privy mark					
		9.756	12.00	22.50	45.00	100.00

KM#	Date	Mintage	Fine	VF	XF	Unc
123	1898	.100	175.00	275.00	550.00	950.00
	1898	—	—	—	Proof	3000

25.0000 g, .720 SILVER, .5787 oz ASW

KM#	Date	Mintage	Fine	VF	XF	Unc
165	1929	4.400	7.00	12.00	20.00	65.00

KM#	Date	Mintage	Fine	VF	XF	Unc
165	1930	11.600	5.00	9.00	14.00	30.00
	1931	4.400	5.00	9.00	14.00	30.00
	1932	6.320	5.00	10.00	16.00	35.00
	1932 deep hair lines					
		Inc. Ab.	100.00	175.00	250.00	400.00
	1933	3.560	9.00	15.00	25.00	55.00
	1937	4.000	7.00	10.00	17.50	35.00
	1938	2.000	9.00	15.00	25.00	55.00
	1938 deep hair lines					
		Inc. Ab.	45.00	90.00	150.00	275.00
	1939	3.760	7.00	11.00	17.50	35.00
	1940	4.640	20.00	30.00	50.00	90.00

NOTE: For similar coins dated 1943D with palm tree privy mark, see Netherlands East Indies.

15.0000 g, .720 SILVER, .3472 oz ASW

KM#	Date	Mintage	VF	XF	Unc	BU
185	1959	7.200	—	BV	5.00	12.50
	1959	—	—	—	Proof	175.00
	1960	12.800	—	BV	5.00	12.50
	1960	—	—	—	Proof	175.00
	1961	10.000	—	BV	5.00	12.50
	1961	—	—	—	Proof	175.00
	1962	5.000	—	BV	6.25	15.00
	1962	—	—	—	Proof	175.00
	1963	4.000	BV	6.25	12.50	25.00
	1963	—	—	—	Proof	175.00
	1964	2.800	BV	7.50	12.50	25.00
	1964	—	—	—	Proof	175.00
	1966	5.000	—	BV	6.25	15.00
	1966	—	—	—	Proof	175.00

NICKEL

KM#	Date	Mintage	VF	XF	Unc	BU
191	1969 fish privy mark					
		1.200	1.50	3.50	5.00	7.50
	1969 fish privy mark					
		—	—	—	Proof	70.00
	1969 cock privy mark					
		15.600	—	—	1.50	3.00
	1969 cock privy mark					
		—	—	—	Proof	70.00
	1970	22.000	—	—	1.50	3.00
	1970	—	—	—	Proof	70.00
	1971	8.000	—	—	1.50	3.00
	1972	20.000	—	—	1.50	3.00
	1978	5.000	—	—	1.50	3.00
	1980 cock & star privy mark					
		37.300	—	—	1.50	2.00

400th Anniversary of the Union of Utrecht

KM#	Date	Mintage	VF	XF	Unc	BU
197	1979	25.000	—	—	1.50	2.00

Investiture of New Queen

KM#	Date	Mintage	VF	XF	Unc	BU
201	1980	30.500	—	—	—	2.00

SILVER

KM#	Date	Mintage	VF	XF	Unc	BU
201a	1980	157 pcs.	—	—	Rare	—

GOLD

KM#	Date	Mintage	VF	XF	Unc	BU
201b	1980	7 pcs.	—	—	Rare	—

NICKEL

KM#	Date	Mintage	VF	XF	Unc	BU
206	1982	14.300	—	—	—	2.00
	1982	.010	—	—	Proof	35.00
	1983	3.800	—	—	—	2.00
	1983	.015	—	—	Proof	27.50
	1984	5.200	—	—	—	2.00
	1984	.020	—	—	Proof	16.00
	1985	3.100	—	—	—	2.00
	1985	.017	—	—	Proof	16.00
	1986	5.800	—	—	—	2.00
	1986	.020	—	—	Proof	16.00
	1987	2.500	—	—	—	2.00
	1987	.018	—	—	Proof	16.00
	1988	6.200	—	—	—	2.00
	1988	.020	—	—	Proof	16.00
	1989	4.100	—	—	—	2.00
	1989	.015	—	—	Proof	16.00
	1990	1.100	—	—	—	2.00
	1990	.015	—	—	Proof	16.00
	1991	.400	—	—	—	3.00
	1991	.014	—	—	Proof	16.00
	1992	.400	—	—	—	3.00
	1993	*.515	—	—	—	2.50
	1994	*1.100	—	—	—	2.00

3 GULDEN

39.2900 g, .893 SILVER, .9270 oz ASW

KM#	Date	Mintage	Fine	VF	XF	Unc
49	1817	12 pcs.	—	—	Rare	—
	1817	—	—	—	Proof	12,000.
	1818	.116	300.00	450.00	800.00	1200.
	1819/8	.151	750.00	1000.	1400.	2000.
	1819	Inc. Ab.	270.00	450.00	800.00	1200.
	1820	.713	270.00	450.00	800.00	1200.
	1821	.277	270.00	450.00	800.00	1200.
	1821 w/o engraver's name					
		Inc. Ab.	500.00	750.00	1000.	1500.
	1821 medal rotation					
		—	750.00	1000.	1400.	2000.
	1822	.296	500.00	750.00	1000.	1700.
	1822 w/o engraver's name					
		Inc. Ab.	500.00	750.00	1000.	1700.
	1823	.255	500.00	750.00	850.00	1200.
	1823B	.014	1500.	3000.	7000.	10,000.
	1824	.644	300.00	450.00	800.00	1200.
	1824 dash between crown & shield					
		Inc. Ab.	300.00	450.00	800.00	1200.
	1830/20	.246	300.00	450.00	800.00	1200.
	1830/24	I.A.	300.00	450.00	800.00	1200.
	1830/24 dash between crown & shield					
		Inc. Ab.	325.00	500.00	900.00	1500.
	1830	Inc. Ab.	300.00	450.00	800.00	1200.
	1831/24	.117	300.00	450.00	800.00	1200.
	1831/24 dash between crown & shield					
		Inc. Ab.	300.00	450.00	800.00	1200.
	1831	Inc. Ab.	300.00	450.00	800.00	1200.
	1832/21	.371	300.00	450.00	800.00	1200.

KM#	Date	Mintage	Fine	VF	XF	Unc
49	1832/22	I.A.	300.00	450.00	800.00	1200.
	1832/23	I.A.	300.00	450.00	800.00	1200.
	1832/24	I.A.	300.00	450.00	800.00	1200.
	1832/24 dash between crown & shield					
		Inc. Ab.	300.00	450.00	800.00	1200.
	1832	Inc. Ab.	300.00	450.00	800.00	1200.

5 GULDEN

3.3645 g, .900 GOLD, .0973 oz AGW

KM#	Date	Mintage	Fine	VF	XF	Unc
60	1826B	.843	80.00	200.00	300.00	550.00
	1827	.518	175.00	275.00	375.00	850.00
	1827B	1.629	80.00	200.00	300.00	500.00

KM#	Date	Mintage	Fine	VF	XF	Unc
72	1843	1,595	300.00	900.00	1500.	2000.

Obv: Bust right.
Rev: Crowned arms within branches.

KM#	Date	Mintage	Fine	VF	XF	Unc
77	1848	50 pcs.	700.00	1750.	2500.	3250.
	1848	—	—	—	Proof	3250.

KM#	Date	Mintage	Fine	VF	XF	Unc
94	1850	—	600.00	1500.	2000.	2500.
	1850	—	—	—	Proof	2250.
	1851	.010	300.00	1000.	1500.	2000.

KM#	Date	Mintage	Fine	VF	XF	Unc
151	1912	1.000	50.00	75.00	125.00	175.00
	1912	120 pcs.	—		Matte Proof	700.00

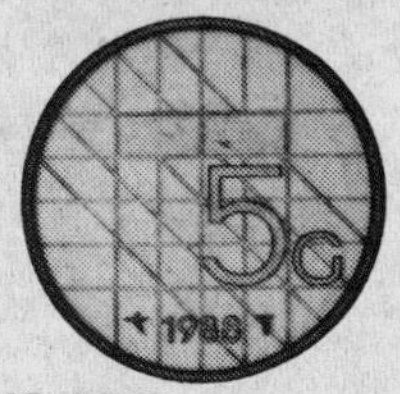

BRONZE CLAD NICKEL

KM#	Date	Mintage	VF	XF	Unc	BU
210	1987	2 pcs.	—	—	—	—
	1988	73.700	—	—	—	3.50
	1988	.020	—	—	Proof	5.00
	1989	69.000	—	—	—	3.50
	1989	.015	—	—	Proof	5.00
	1990	48.000	—	—	—	3.50
	1990	.015	—	—	Proof	5.00
	1991	17.000	—	—	—	3.50
	1991	.014	—	—	Proof	5.00
	1992	.400	—	—	—	4.50
	1993	*.400	—	—	—	4.50
	1994	*.400	—	—	—	4.50

10 GULDEN

6.7290 g, .900 GOLD, .1947 oz AGW

KM#	Date	Mintage	Fine	VF	XF	Unc
56	1818	—	1000.	1500.	2000.	4000.
	1819	.107	650.00	1000.	1350.	2250.
	1820	.033	650.00	1000.	1350.	2250.
	1822	.048	650.00	1000.	1500.	3000.
	1823	.266	150.00	275.00	350.00	800.00
	1824	.336	150.00	275.00	350.00	800.00
	1824B	3.735	150.00	275.00	350.00	800.00
	1825	.228	150.00	275.00	350.00	800.00
	1825B	3.821	150.00	275.00	350.00	800.00
	1826	—	1000.	1500.	2000.	4000.
	1826B	.079	600.00	850.00	1200.	2000.
	1827	.134	450.00	575.00	900.00	1500.

KM#	Date	Mintage	Fine	VF	XF	Unc
56	1827B	—	600.00	850.00	1200.	2000.
	1828	.015	900.00	1400.	1800.	3500.
	1828B	.562	150.00	275.00	350.00	800.00
	1829	9,484	650.00	1000.	1350.	2250.
	1829B	.084	650.00	1000.	1350.	2250.
	1830/20	—	—	—	—	800.00
	1830/28	.568	1000.	1200.	1500.	3000.
	1830	Inc.Ab.	150.00	275.00	350.00	800.00
	1831/0	.099	600.00	850.00	1200.	2000.
	1831	Inc. Ab.	150.00	275.00	350.00	800.00
	1832/1	1.372	600.00	850.00	1200.	2000.
	1832	Inc. Ab.	150.00	275.00	350.00	800.00
	1833	.721	150.00	275.00	350.00	800.00
	1837	.458	150.00	275.00	350.00	800.00
	1839	.326	150.00	275.00	350.00	800.00
	1840	2.760	150.00	275.00	350.00	600.00

KM#	Date	Mintage	Fine	VF	XF	Unc
71	1842	860 pcs.	1100.	2000.	3000.	4000.

KM#	Date	Mintage	Fine	VF	XF	Unc
78	1848	*50 pcs.	1500.	2500.	3750.	5000.
	1848	—	—	—	Proof	6000.

KM#	Date	Mintage	Fine	VF	XF	Unc
95	1850	—	900.00	1800.	2500.	3250.
	1850	—	—	—	Proof	4000.
	1851	.010	500.00	1000.	1750.	2500.

KM#	Date	Mintage	Fine	VF	XF	Unc
105	1875	4.110	—	BV	100.00	115.00

KM#	Date	Mintage	Fine	VF	XF	Unc
106	1876	1.581	—	BV	100.00	120.00
	1877	1.108	—	BV	100.00	120.00
	1879/7	.581	125.00	175.00	250.00	350.00
	1879	Inc. Ab.	—	BV	100.00	120.00
	1880	.050	BV	110.00	145.00	175.00
	1885	.067	BV	110.00	145.00	175.00
	1886	.054	100.00	125.00	165.00	200.00
	1887	.041	100.00	125.00	165.00	200.00
	1888	.036	125.00	250.00	350.00	450.00
	1889	.205	—	BV	100.00	120.00

KM#	Date	Mintage	Fine	VF	XF	Unc
118	1892	61 pcs.	1500.	3000.	5000.	6000.
	1892	—	—	—	Proof	9000.
	1895/1	149 pcs.	1400.	2500.	4000.	5500.
	1895/1	—	—	—	Proof	5500.
	1895	Inc. Ab.	900.00	2000.	3500.	5000.
	1897	.454	—	BV	100.00	150.00

KM#	Date	Mintage	Fine	VF	XF	Unc
124	1898	.099	125.00	175.00	225.00	350.00

KM#	Date	Mintage	Fine	VF	XF	Unc
149	1911	.775	—	BV	100.00	120.00
	1911	8 pcs.	—	—	Proof	1750.
	1912	3.000	—	BV	100.00	120.00
	1913	1.133	—	BV	100.00	120.00
	1917	4.000	—	BV	100.00	120.00

KM#	Date	Mintage	Fine	VF	XF	Unc
162	1925	2.000	—	BV	100.00	120.00
	1925	12 pcs.	—	—	Proof	1500.
	1926	2.500	—	BV	100.00	120.00
	1926	—	—	—	Proof	1300.
	1927	1.000	—	BV	100.00	120.00
	1932	4.324	—	BV	100.00	120.00
	1933	2.462	—	BV	100.00	120.00

25.0000 g, .720 SILVER, .5787 oz ASW
25th Anniversary of Liberation

KM#	Date	Mintage	VF	XF	Unc	BU
195	1970	6.000	—	—	8.00	10.00
	1970	.020	—	—	P/L	27.50
	1970	40 pcs.	—	—	Proof	300.00

25th Anniversary of Reign

KM#	Date	Mintage	VF	XF	Unc	BU
196	1973	4.500	—	—	8.00	10.00
	1973	.106	—	—	Proof	22.50

20 GULDEN

13.4580 g, .900 GOLD, .3894 oz AGW
Obv: Bust right.
Rev: Crowned arms within branches.

KM#	Date	Mintage	Fine	VF	XF	Unc
79	1848	*50 pcs.	1250.	3000.	4500.	6000

KM#	Date	Mintage	Fine	VF	XF	Unc
96	1850	—	1250.	2500.	3500.	4500
	1850	—	—	—	Proof	4500
	1851	2,500	600.00	1500.	2500.	3000
	1853	136 pcs.	1000.	2250.	3000.	4000

50 GULDEN

25.0000 g, .925 SILVER, .7435 oz ASW
Dutch-American Friendship

KM#	Date	Mintage	VF	XF	Unc	BU
207	1982	.190	—	—	—	50.00
	1982	.050	—	—	Proof	75.00
		GOLD				
207a	1982	2 pcs.	—	—	—	2000

25.0000 g, .925 SILVER, .7435 oz ASW
400th Anniversary of Death of William of Orange

KM#	Date	Mintage	VF	XF	Unc	BU
208	1984	.950	—	—	—	30.00
	1984	.106	—	—	P/L	35.00
	1984	.056	—	—	Proof	55.00

Golden Wedding Anniversary
Queen Mother and Prince Bernhard

KM#	Date	Mintage	VF	XF	Unc	BU
209	1987	1.050	—	—	—	30.00
	1987	.081	—	—	P/L	40.00
	1987	.053	—	—	Proof	60.00

300th Anniversary of William and Mary

KM#	Date	Mintage	VF	XF	Unc	BU
212	1988	.750	—	—	—	30.00
	1988	.053	—	—	P/L	35.00
	1988	.036	—	—	Proof	50.00

GOLD

KM#	Date	Mintage	VF	XF	Unc	BU
212a	1988	4 pcs.	—	—	Rare	—

25.0000 g, .925 SILVER, .7435 oz ASW
100 Years of Queens

KM#	Date	Mintage	VF	XF	Unc	BU
214	1990	.750	—	—	—	30.00
	1990	.051	—	—	P/L	35.00
	1990	.035	—	—	Proof	50.00

Silver Wedding Anniversary

KM#	Date	Mintage	VF	XF	Unc	BU
215	1991	.600	—	—	—	30.00
	1991	.047	—	—	P/L	35.00
	1991	.035	—	—	Proof	50.00

TRADE COINAGE

DUCAT

3.5000 g, .983 GOLD, .1106 oz AGW
Mint: Utrecht

KM#	Date	Mintage	Fine	VF	XF	Unc
45	1814	2.930	120.00	225.00	275.00	400.00
	1815	.673	120.00	225.00	275.00	400.00
	1815 cloverleaf					
		.614	120.00	225.00	275.00	400.00
	1816	.221	130.00	250.00	325.00	500.00

KM#	Date	Mintage	Fine	VF	XF	Unc
50.1	1817	.495	220.00	400.00	600.00	750.00
	1818	1.552	80.00	130.00	200.00	300.00
	1819	.111	100.00	200.00	275.00	400.00
	1820	.010	200.00	350.00	500.00	700.00
	1821	.015	200.00	350.00	500.00	700.00
	1822	.012	200.00	350.00	500.00	700.00
	1824B	8,000	350.00	700.00	1200.	1500.
	1825	.119	100.00	200.00	275.00	400.00
	1825B	.056	200.00	350.00	500.00	700.00
	1827	.138	130.00	250.00	325.00	450.00
	1827B	.027	220.00	400.00	500.00	700.00
	1828/7	.622	120.00	225.00	275.00	400.00
50.1	1828	Inc. Ab.	120.00	225.00	275.00	400.00
	1828B	.534	100.00	200.00	275.00	400.00
	1829/8B	.247	200.00	350.00	500.00	700.00
	1829B	Inc. Ab.	200.00	350.00	500.00	700.00
	1829	1.153	80.00	130.00	180.00	250.00
	1830B	.011	300.00	425.00	650.00	850.00
	1831	.411	80.00	130.00	180.00	250.00
	1833	.247	100.00	200.00	275.00	400.00
	1836/5	.236	150.00	325.00	650.00	850.00
	1836	Inc. Ab.	110.00	225.00	325.00	500.00
	1839	.151	80.00	170.00	250.00	350.00
	1840 Fleur de lis privy mark					
		.103	110.00	225.00	300.00	450.00

Mint: St. Petersburg

KM#	Date	Mintage	Fine	VF	XF	Unc
50.2	1818	1.350	80.00	130.00	175.00	250.00
	1827	.350	130.00	250.00	325.00	450.00
	1828	1.300	120.00	225.00	275.00	375.00
	1829	.150	80.00	130.00	175.00	200.00
	1830	2.000	80.00	130.00	175.00	200.00
	1831	1.000	80.00	130.00	175.00	200.00
	1832	1.000	100.00	200.00	275.00	350.00
	1833	.350	100.00	200.00	275.00	350.00
	1834	.150	200.00	350.00	500.00	700.00
	1835	.650	110.00	225.00	325.00	425.00
	1836	.300	110.00	225.00	325.00	450.00
	1837	1.400	80.00	170.00	250.00	350.00
	1838	1.200	80.00	170.00	250.00	350.00
	1839	1.350	80.00	170.00	250.00	350.00
	1840 torch privy mark					
		—	80.00	175.00	250.00	350.00
70.1	1841 torch privy mark					
		3.904	80.00	150.00	200.00	300.00

Mint: Utrecht

KM#	Date	Mintage	Fine	VF	XF	Unc
70.2	1841 Fleur de lis privy mark					
		.096	100.00	200.00	300.00	450.00

KM#	Date	Mintage	Fine	VF	XF	Unc
83.1	1849	.014	70.00	140.00	200.00	300.00
	1872	.030	200.00	500.00	800.00	1400.
	1873	.040	200.00	500.00	800.00	1400.
	1874	.044	200.00	500.00	800.00	1400.
	1876	.044	200.00	500.00	800.00	1400.
	1877	.015	200.00	500.00	800.00	1400.
	1878	.087	200.00	500.00	800.00	1400.
	1879	.020	200.00	500.00	800.00	1400.
	1880	.025	200.00	500.00	800.00	1400.
	1885	.081	125.00	350.00	600.00	1000.
	1894	.030	110.00	225.00	300.00	450.00
	1895/55	.058	125.00	250.00	350.00	800.00
	1895/59	I.A.	110.00	225.00	300.00	450.00
	1895	Inc. Ab.	90.00	175.00	270.00	350.00
	1899	.061	90.00	175.00	270.00	350.00
	1901	.029	110.00	220.00	275.00	500.00
	1903	.091	90.00	180.00	270.00	350.00
	1905	.088	90.00	180.00	270.00	350.00
	1906	.029	110.00	220.00	275.00	450.00
	1908	.091	90.00	180.00	270.00	350.00
	1909 halberd w/star privy mark					
		.106	80.00	150.00	250.00	350.00
	1909 sea horse privy mark					
		.030	130.00	250.00	300.00	450.00
	1910	.421	80.00	150.00	225.00	350.00
	1910	—	—	—	Proof	700.00
	1912	.148	80.00	150.00	225.00	350.00
	1913	.205	80.00	150.00	225.00	350.00
	1914	.247	80.00	150.00	225.00	350.00
	1916	.117	80.00	150.00	225.00	350.00
	1916	—	—	—	Proof	450.00
	1917	.217	BV	65.00	80.00	120.00
	1920	.293	BV	65.00	80.00	120.00
	1921	.409	BV	60.00	70.00	100.00
	1922	.050	80.00	150.00	225.00	400.00
	1923	.107	BV	75.00	150.00	250.00
	1924	.084	BV	75.00	150.00	250.00
	1925	.573	BV	60.00	70.00	100.00
	1925	Inc. Ab.	—	—	Proof	250.00
	1926	.191	BV	60.00	80.00	120.00
	1927	.654	—	BV	50.00	65.00
	1928	.572	—	BV	50.00	65.00
	1932	.088	100.00	250.00	350.00	450.00
	1937	.117	BV	80.00	100.00	140.00

Mint: St. Petersburg

KM#	Date	Mintage	Fine	VF	XF	Unc
83.2	1849	4.750	70.00	140.00	200.00	300.00

Similar to KM#190.2 but knight w/right leg bent.

KM#	Date	Mintage	Fine	VF	XF	Unc
190.1	1960	3,605	—	—	P/L	475.00
	1972	.029	—	—	P/L	75.00
	1974	.087	—	—	P/L	70.00
	1974 medal struck					
		2,000	—	—	P/L	350.00

KM#	Date	Mintage	Fine	VF	XF	Unc
190.1	1975	.205	—	—	P/L	65.00
	1976	*.038	—	—	P/L	180.00
	1978	.029	—	—	P/L	90.00
	1985	.104	—	—	P/L	80.00

*NOTE: Of the original 37,844 pieces struck, 32,000 were melted.

Obv: Knight w/left leg bent, larger letters in legend.

KM#	Date	Mintage	Fine	VF	XF	Unc
190.2	1986	.095	—	—	P/L	80.00
	1989	.024	—	—	Proof	90.00
	1990	.018	—	—	Proof	90.00
	1991	.012	—	—	Proof	85.00
	1992	.014	—	—	Proof	85.00
	1993	—	—	—	Proof	95.00

2 DUCAT

6.9880 g, .983 GOLD, .2209 oz AGW
Mint: Utrecht

KM#	Date	Mintage	Fine	VF	XF	Unc
97	1854	—	—	—	10,000.	12,000.
	1854	—	—	—	Proof	9000.
	1867	—	—	—	—	20,000.

KM#	Date	Mintage	Fine	VF	XF	Unc
211	1988	.024	—	—	P/L	140.00
	1989	.018	—	—	Proof	150.00
	1991	.010	—	—	Proof	150.00
	1992	.012	—	—	Proof	150.00

SILVER BULLION ISSUES

SILVER DUCAT

28.2500 g, .875 SILVER, .7948 oz ASW

KM#	Date	Mintage	Fine	VF	XF	Unc
213	1989	.036	—	—	Proof	50.00
	1992	.017	—	—	Proof	60.00
	1993	—	—	—	Proof	60.00

SELECT SETS (SS)

Fleur de Coin

KM#	Date	Mintage	Identification	Issue Price	Mkt. Val.
SS1	1971(6)	1,000	KM180-183,184a,191	—	70.00
SS1a	1972(1)	2,000	KM191	—	8.00
SS2	1972(5)	2,000	KM180-183,184a	—	45.00
SS3	1973(5)	10,000	KM180-183,184a	—	35.00
SS4	1974(3)	10,000	KM180-182	—	15.00
SS5	1975(6)	12,000	*KM180-183,184a	—	30.00
SS6	1976(5)	15,000	KM180-183,184a	—	55.00
SS7	1977(5)	17,000	KM180-183,184a	—	50.00
SS8	1978(6)	21,500	KM180-183,184a,191	6.50	30.00
SS9	1979(6)	50,000	KM180-183,184a,197	6.50	12.50
SS10	1980(6)	249,732	KM180-183,184a,191	—	6.00
SS11	1980(2)	504,000	KM200-201	—	6.00
SS12	1980(2)	157 pcs.	KM200-201, Silver	—	1000.
SS13	1980(2)	7 pcs.	KM200b-201b, Gold	—	—
SS14	1982(5)	242,701	KM202-206	12.00	7.50
SS15	1983(5)	156,165	KM202-206	—	8.50
SS16	1984(5)	131,748	KM202-206	12.00	10.00
SS17	1985(5)	113,079	KM202-206	—	12.50
SS18	1986(5)	112,190	KM202-206	—	15.00
SS19	1987(5)	120,800	KM202-206, Utrecht medal	—	22.00
SS20	1988(6)	132,800	KM202-206,210, Groningen medal	16.00	22.00
SS21	1989(6)	103,600	KM202-206,210, Flevoland medal	13.50	17.50
SS22	1990(6)	102,700	KM202-206,210, N-Brabant medal	16.50	16.50
SS23	1991(6)	100,000	KM202-206,210, Drenthe medal	14.50	14.50
SS24	1992(6)	94,000	KM202-206,210, Zeeland medal	14.50	14.50
SS25	1992(6)	3,000	KM202-206,210, numismatic year medal	—	20.00
SS26	1993(6)	—	KM202-206,210, Limburg medal	14.50	14.50
SS27	1993(6)	2,500	KM202-206,210, V.O.C. medal	20.00	20.00

*NOTE: Set also includes 1974 25 cents.

PROOF SETS (PS)

KM#	Date	Mintage	Identification	Issue Price	Mkt. Val.
PS1	1948(4)	50	KM175-178 w/PROEF	—	800.00
PS2	1948(4)	—	KM175-178	—	300.00
PS3	1949(4)	—	KM180-183 head left	—	Rare
PS4	1950(4)	—	KM180-183 w/PROEF	—	700.00
PS5	1950(4)	—	KM180-183	—	325.00
PS6	1951(4)	—	KM180-183	—	275.00
PS7	1952(2)	—	KM180-181	—	275.00
PS8	1953(2)	—	KM180-181	—	275.00
PS9	1954(5)	—	KM180-184	—	275.00
PS10	1955(5)	—	KM180-184	—	250.00
PS11	1956(5)	—	KM180-184	—	250.00
PS12	1957(5)	—	KM180-184	—	250.00
PS13	1958(5)	—	KM180-184	—	250.00
PS14	1959(3)	—	KM180,182,185	—	450.00
PS15	1960(5)	—	KM180-183,185	—	450.00
PS16	1961(5)	—	KM180-183,185	—	450.00
PS17	1962(5)	40	KM180-183,185	—	450.00
PS18	1963(6)	40	KM180-185	—	475.00
PS19	1964(6)	40	KM180-185	—	475.00
PS20	1965(5)	—	KM180-184	—	250.00
PS21	1966(6)	—	KM180-185	—	450.00
PS22	1967(5)	—	KM180-183,184a	—	200.00
PS23	1968(3)	—	KM180,182-183	—	175.00
PS24	1969(6) Cock	—	KM180-183,184a,191	—	250.00
PS25	1969(6) Fish	—	KM180-183,184a,191	—	250.00
PS26	1970(6)	—	KM180-183,184a,191	—	250.00

NOTE: From 1970 until 1982 no proof sets were struck for collectors. Approximately 60 V.I.P. sets per year had been struck and presented to various officials, etc.

KM#	Date	Mintage	Identification	Issue Price	Mkt. Val.
PS27	1982(5)	10,000	KM202-206	35.00	145.00
PS28	1983(5)	15,000	KM202-206	35.00	60.00
PS29	1984(5)	20,406	KM202-206	35.00	40.00
PS30	1985(5)	17,100	KM202-206	35.00	50.00
PS31	1986(5)	19,500	KM202-206	35.00	40.00
PS32	1987(5)	18,100	KM202-206, Utrecht medal	35.00	40.00
PS33	1988(6)	19,550	KM202-206,210, Groningen medal	53.50	55.00
PS34	1989(6)	15,300	KM202-206,210, Flevoland medal	50.00	55.00
PS35	1989(3)	6,400	KM190.2,211,213	260.00	260.00
PS36	1990(6)	15,100	KM202-206,210, N. Brabant medal	—	55.00
PS37	1991(6)	14,240	KM202-206,210, Drenthe medal	—	55.00
PS38	1992(6)	12,600	KM202-206,210, Zeeland medal	53.50	55.00
PS40	1993(6)	—	KM202-206,210, Limburg medal	—	55.00

NETHERLANDS ANTILLES

The Netherlands Antilles, comprises two groups of islands in the West Indies: Bonaire and Curacao and their dependencies near the Venezuelan coast and St. Eustatius, Saba, and the southern part of St. Martin (St. Maarten) southeast of Puerto Rico. The island group has an area of 371 sq. mi. (960 sq. km.) and a population of 225,000. Capital: Willemstad. Chief industries are the refining of crude oil and tourism. Petroleum products and phosphates are exported.

On Dec. 15, 1954, the Netherlands Antilles were given complete domestic autonomy and granted equality within the Kingdom with Surinam and the Netherlands. On Jan. I, 1986, Aruba achieved "status aparte" as the third state under the Dutch crown which is a step towards total independence.

ST. EUSTATIUS

St. Eustatius (Sint Eustatius, Statia), a Netherlands West Indian island located in the Leeward Islands of the Lesser Antilles nine miles northwest of St. Kitts, has an area of 12 sq. mi. (21 sq. km.) and a population of about 2,000. It is part of the Netherlands Antilles. The island's capital is Oranjestad. The chief industries are farming, fishing, and tourism.

Between 1630 and 1640 the Dutch seized Curacao, Saba, St. Martin and St. Eustatius, all valuable as piloting and smuggling depots. The territorial acquisitions were confirmed to the Dutch by the Treaty of Munster in 1648. Under the guidance of merchants from Flushing, St. Eustatius became a prosperous entrepot of neutral trade. On Feb. 3, 1781, British Admiral George Rodney, acting under orders, captured the island and confiscated much valuable booty. Before passing permanently into Dutch hands, St. Eustatius was attacked or captured several times by the French and English, and was in English hands during the Napoleonic Wars from 1810 to 1814.

RULERS

Dutch

MONETARY SYSTEM

6 Stuivers = 1 Reaal

COUNTERMARKED COINAGE

SE incuse countermark on French Guiana 2 Sous coins was official.

These were followed by raised SE countermarks (on a variety of worn billon & silver coins) generally thought to be forgeries.

From 1809 all coins had to be revalidated with a P countermark, which stood for Pierre dit Flamand, the artisan who designed the mark. Both raised and incuse SE varieties as well as unmarked coins were revalidated.

STUIVER

COPPER
c/m: Raised SE.

KM#	Date	Mintage	Good	VG	Fine	VF
1.2	ND(1797-1809)		40.00	65.00	90.00	175.00

BILLON

KM#	Date	Mintage	Good	VG	Fine	VF
1.2a	ND(1797-1809)		40.00	65.00	90.00	175.00

SILVER

KM#	Date	Mintage	Good	VG	Fine	VF
1.2b	ND(1797-1809)		100.00	150.00	200.00	250.00

BRITISH OCCUPATION

STUIVER

VARIOUS METALS
c/m: P revalidation on older SE.

KM#	Date	Mintage	Good	VG	Fine	VF
4	ND(1809-12)		30.00	50.00	80.00	150.00

2 REALES

SILVER
c/m: P in circle of dots.

KM#	Date	Mintage	Good	VG	Fine	VF
7.1	ND(1810-12)		50.00	70.00	110.00	190.00

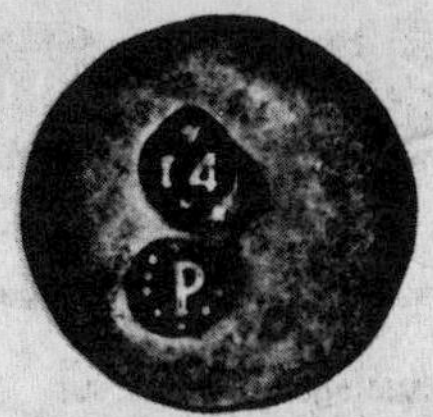

c/m: P in circle of dots on St. Bartholomew 14 Stuivers, KM#11.

M#	Date	Mintage	Good	VG	Fine	VF
.2	ND(1810-12)		—	—	Rare	—

ST. MARTIN

St. Martin (Sint Maarten), the only island in the Antilles wned by two European powers (France and the letherlands), is located in the Leeward Islands of the esser Antilles five miles south of the British island of Anuilla. The French northern section of the island (St. lartin) is a dependency of the French Department of uadeloupe. It has an area of 20 sq. mi. (51 sq. km.) nd a population of about 4,500. Capital: Le Marigot. The utch southern section of the island (Sint Maarten) has n area of 17 sq. mi. (34 sq. km.) and a population of bout 8,000. Capital: Philipsburg. The chief industries re farming, fishing, and tourism. Salt, horses, and mules re exported.

Although nominally a Spanish possession at the time, St. artin was occupied by French freebooters in 1638, but hen Spain relinquished claim to the island in 1648 it as peaceably divided between France and Holland in ecognition of the merchant communities already established on the island by nationals of both powers. St. Mar- n has remained under dual French-Dutch ownership to e present time, except for a period during the Napoonic Wars when the British seized and occupied it.

The northern section of the island uses the coins and urrency of France.

MONETARY SYSTEM

Stuivers = 1 Reaal
0 Stuivers = 1 Gulden
2 (later 15) Reaals = 1 Peso

COUNTERMARKED COINAGE

2 STUIVERS

BILLON
c/m: StM in beaded circle plus incuse M on French Guiana 2 Sous.

ND(1820) — 70.00 110.00 140.00 175.00

/m: Incuse Fleur-de-Lys on French Guiana 2 Sous.

ND(1805) — 100.00 150.00 200.00 250.00

SILVER
c/m: Raised Fleur-de-Lis

ND(1805) — 30.00 50.00 75.00 100.00

/m: Incuse Fleur-de-Lys plus S t M in beaded circle.

ND(1805) — 50.00 80.00 130.00 200.00

18 STUIVERS

SILVER
/m: ST. MARTIN and arrows on 1/5 cut of Spanish or Spanish Colonial 8 Reales.

2 ND(1809) — 75.00 150.00 275.00 450.00

CURACAO

The island of Curacao, the largest of the Netherlands ntilles, which is an autonomous part of the Kingdom of ne Netherlands located in the Caribbean Sea 40 miles ff the coast of Venezuela, has an area of 173 sq. mi. 472 sq. km.) and a population of 127,900. Capital: Villemstad. The chief industries are banking and ourism. Salt, phosphates and cattle are exported.

Curacao was discovered by Spanish navigator Alonso le Ojeda in 1499 and was settled by Spain in 1527. The Dutch West India Company took the island from Spain in 634 and administered it until 1787, when it was surrendered to the United Netherlands. The Dutch held it thereafter except for two periods during the Napoleonic Wars, 1800-1803 and 1807-16, when it was occupied by the British. During World War II, Curacao refined 60 percent of the oil used by the Allies; the refineries were protected by U.S. troops after Germany invaded the Netherlands in 1940.

During the second occupation of the Napoleonic period, the British created an emergency coinage for Curacao by cutting the Spanish dollar into 5 equal segments and countermarking each piece with a rosette indent.

BATAVIAN REPUBLIC

MONETARY SYSTEM

1 Cent (U.S.) = 2-1/2 Stuivers
6 Stuivers = 1 Reaal
8 Realen = 1 Peso, 1793-1801
12 Realen = 1 Peso, 1801-18
6 Pesos = 1 Johannes (unmarked), 1799-1815
8 Pesos = 1 Johannes (c/m), 1799-1815
7-1/2 Pesos = 1 Johannes (c/m), 1815-27

9 STUIVERS

SILVER
c/m: 9 in oval indent on Spanish Colonial 1 Real.

KM#	Date	Mintage	Good	VG	Fine	VF
4	ND 1801	—	150.00	200.00	250.00	325.00

NOTE: The above coins along with similar coins bearing the numbers 3, 5, 14-18 are of questionable origin. Thus, they are not listed in Craig. Pridmore states these as unattributable.

3 REAAL

SILVER
c/m: 5-petalled rosace in circle on 1/4 cut of Spanish or Spanish Colonial 8 Reales

KM#	Date	Mintage	VG	Fine	VF	XF
7	ND(c.1810)	.030	600.00	1200.	1800.	2200.

BRITISH OCCUPATION

1807-1816

3 REAAL

SILVER
Reconstructed 5 segments
c/m: 5-petalled rosace in circle on 1/5 cut of Spanish or Spanish Colonial 8 reales

13 ND(1815) .040 65.00 125.00 250.00 400.00

3-1/2 REAAL

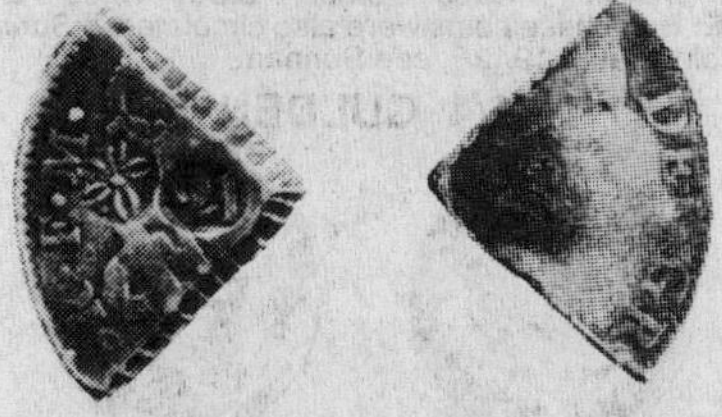

SILVER
c/m: Additional 21 in oval indent on KM#13.

16 ND(1814) — 1500. 2500. 3850. 5500.

6 PESOS

GOLD
Obv. c/m: GI, L, MH and B at edges, GH in center on false Brazil 6400 Reis type of KM#172.2
Rev. c/m: W.

KM#	Date	Mintage	VG	Fine	VF	XF
19	ND(1815)	—	—	—	Unique	—

Obv. c/m: GI, L, MH and B at edges, GH in center on Brazil 6400 Reis, KM#199.1.
Rev. c/m: W.

KM#	Date	Mintage	VG	Fine	VF	XF
20	ND(1815)	—	—	—	Unique	—

NETHERLANDS RESTORED

1816

MONETARY REFORM

15 Realen = 1 Peso, 1818-22
7 Stuivers = 1 Reaal, 1822-27
10 Stuivers = 1 Franc, 1822-27
5 Francs = 1 Dollar
20 Stuivers = 1 Gulden, 1827-99
2/5 Peso = 1 Gulden, 1827-96
5/7 Peso = 1 Gulden, 1896-97
1 Peso = 1 Gulden, 1897-99

STUIVER

.300 SILVER

KM#	Date	Mintage	Fine	VF	XF	Unc
24	1822	.529	50.00	80.00	135.00	225.00

NOTE: Struck also in 1840-41, circulating at that time as a 2 Cent piece.

1/4 REAAL

SILVER

KM#	Date	Mintage	Fine	VF	XF	Unc
25	1821	Unique?	—	—	—	—

REAAL

SILVER

KM#	Date	Mintage	Fine	VF	XF	Unc
		Rev: 4 acorns.				
26.1	1821	.121	90.00	150.00	250.00	500.00
		Rev: 7 acorns.				
26.2	1821	Inc. Ab.	90.00	150.00	250.00	500.00
		Rev: 8 acorns.				
26.3	1821	Inc. Ab.	90.00	150.00	250.00	500.00
		Rev: 9 acorns.				
26.4	1821	Inc. Ab.	90.00	150.00	250.00	500.00
		Rev: 12 acorns.				
26.5	1821	Inc. Ab.	90.00	150.00	250.00	500.00

1/4 GUILDER

SILVER
Reconstructed 4 segments
c/m: C in oval indent on 1/4 cut of Netherlands 1 Gulden.

KM#	Date	Mintage	VG	Fine	VF	XF
27	ND(1838)	.024	70.00	130.00	200.00	325.00

3 REAAL

SILVER
Reconstructed 5 segments
c/m: 3 in circle on 1/5 cut of Spanish or Spanish Colonial 8 Reales.

KM#	Date	Mintage	VG	Fine	VF	XF
28	ND(1818)	.078	55.00	90.00	150.00	250.00

c/m: 3 in dentilated circle on 1/5 cut of Spanish or Spanish Colonial 8 Reales.

KM#	Date	Mintage	VG	Fine	VF	XF
29	ND(1819-25)	—	80.00	130.00	210.00	360.00

5 REAAL

SILVER
c/m: 5 in circle on 1/3 cut of Spanish or Spanish Colonial 8 Reales.

KM#	Date	Mintage	VG	Fine	VF	XF
30	ND(1818)	3,000	2500.	5000.	8500.	14,500.

MODERN COINAGE

MONETARY SYSTEM
100 Cents = 1 Gulden

CENT

BRONZE

KM#	Date	Mintage	Fine	VF	XF	Unc
39	1942P	2.500	4.25	7.50	12.50	20.00

NOTE: This coin was also circulated in Surinam. For similar coins dated 1943P & 1957-1960, see Surinam.

KM#	Date	Mintage	Fine	VF	XF	Unc
41	1944D	3.000	.75	1.75	3.00	7.00
	1947(u)	1.500	1.00	2.00	6.00	12.00
	1947(u)	80 pcs.	—	—	Proof	20.00

2-1/2 CENTS

BRONZE

KM#	Date	Mintage	Fine	VF	XF	Unc
42	1944D	1.000	.65	1.00	2.00	4.00
	1947(u)	.500	.65	1.25	3.00	7.00
	1947(u)	80 pcs.	—	—	Proof	20.00
	1948(u)	1.000	.50	.75	1.50	3.00
	1948(u)	75 pcs.	—	—	Proof	20.00

5 CENTS

COPPER-NICKEL

KM#	Date	Mintage	Fine	VF	XF	Unc
40	1943	8.595	1.75	3.50	6.50	10.00

NOTE: The above piece does not bear either a palm tree privy mark or a mint mark, but it was struck expressly for use in Curacao and Surinam. This homeland type of KM#153 was last issued in the Netherlands in 1940.

KM#	Date	Mintage	Fine	VF	XF	Unc
47	1948	1.000	1.00	2.00	4.00	8.00
	1948	75 pcs.	—	—	Proof	40.00

1/10 GULDEN

1.4000 g, .640 SILVER, .0288 oz ASW

KM#	Date	Mintage	Fine	VF	XF	Unc
36	1901(u)	.300	12.50	25.00	50.00	100.00
	1901(u)	40 pcs.	—	—	Proof	150.00

KM#	Date	Mintage	Fine	VF	XF	Unc
43	1944D	1.500	1.00	2.00	3.50	6.00
	1947(u)	1.000	1.00	2.00	3.00	5.00
	1947(u)	80 pcs.	—	—	Proof	60.00

KM#	Date	Mintage	Fine	VF	XF	Unc
48	1948(u)	1.000	1.50	2.50	4.00	9.00
	1948(u)	75 pcs.	—	—	Proof	60.00

10 CENTS

1.4000 g, .640 SILVER, .0288 oz ASW

KM#	Date	Mintage	Fine	VF	XF	Unc
37	1941P	.800	5.00	10.00	15.00	30.00
	1943P	4.500	3.00	6.00	10.00	20.00

NOTE: Both these coins were also circulated in Surinam. For coins dated 1942P, see Surinam.

1/4 GULDEN

3.5800 g, .640 SILVER, .0736 oz ASW

KM#	Date	Mintage	Fine	VF	XF	Unc
35	1900(u)	.480	7.50	25.00	65.00	125.00
	1900(u)	40 pcs.	—	—	Proof	200.00

KM#	Date	Mintage	Fine	VF	XF	Un
44	1944D	1.500	1.00	2.00	4.50	7.5
	1947(u)	1.000	1.00	2.00	4.50	7.5
	1947(u)	80 pcs.	—	—	Proof	80.0

25 CENTS

3.5800 g, .640 SILVER, .0736 oz ASW

KM#	Date	Mintage	Fine	VF	XF	Unc
38	1941P	1.100	2.50	5.00	8.00	15.0
	1943/1P	2.500	2.00	4.00	8.50	17.5
	1943P	Inc.Ab.	1.50	3.00	6.00	12.5

NOTE: Both these coins were also circulated in Surinan For similar coins dated 1943, 1944 & 1945-P with aco mint mark see Netherlands.

GULDEN

10.0000 g, .720 SILVER, .2315 oz ASW

KM#	Date	Mintage	Fine	VF	XF	Unc
45	1944D	.500	3.50	6.50	12.50	26.0

2-1/2 GULDEN

25.0000 g, .720 SILVER, .5787 oz ASW

KM#	Date	Mintage	Fine	VF	XF	Unc
46	1944D	.200	3.00	4.50	6.50	12.0

PROOF SETS (PS)

KM#	Date	Mintage	Identification	Issue Price	Mkt. Va
PS1	1901(2)	40	KM36(1901), KM35(1900)	—	400.0
PS2	1947(4)	80	KM41-44	—	180.0
PS3	1948(3)	75	KM42,47-48	—	120.0

NETHERLANDS ANTILLES

RULERS

Juliana, 1948-1980
Beatrix, 1980

MINT MARKS

Utrecht - privy marks only
Y - York Mint
FM - Franklin Mint, U.S.A.

NOTE: From 1975 the Franklin Mint has produce coinage in up to 3 different qualities. Qualities of issu are designated in ( ) after each date and are defined a follows:

(M) MATTE - Normal circulation strike or a dull finis produced by sandblasting special uncirculated (polis finish) or proof quality dies.

(U) SPECIAL UNCIRCULATED - Polished or proof-lik in appearance without any frosted features.

(P) PROOF - The highest quality obtainable having mirror-like fields and frosted features.

MONETARY SYSTEM

100 Cents = 1 Gulden

CENT

BRONZE

KM#	Date	Mintage	Fine	VF	XF	Unc
1	1952	1.000	2.00	4.00	8.00	15.00
	1952	100 pcs.	—	—	Proof	45.00
	1954	1.000	1.00	2.00	4.50	10.00
	1954	200 pcs.	—	—	Proof	20.00
	1957	1.000	1.00	2.00	4.50	10.00
	1957	250 pcs.	—	—	Proof	20.00
	1959	1.000	.75	1.75	3.25	7.50
	1959	250 pcs.	—	—	Proof	20.00
	1960	300 pcs.	—	—	Proof	20.00
	1961	1.000	.25	1.00	2.00	4.00
	1961	—	—	—	Proof	20.00
	1963	1.000	.25	1.00	2.00	4.00
	1963	—	—	—	Proof	20.00
	1964	—	—	—	Proof	25.00
	1965	1.200	.30	1.25	2.50	5.00
	1965	—	—	—	Proof	20.00
	1967	.850	.75	1.75	3.00	6.00
	1967	—	—	—	Proof	20.00
	1968 fish	.900	.50	1.00	2.00	4.00
	1968 star & fish					
		.700	1.25	2.50	5.00	7.50
	1970	.200	1.25	2.50	5.00	7.50
	1970	—	—	—	Proof	20.00

KM#	Date	Mintage	Fine	VF	XF	Unc
8	1969	200 pcs.	—	—	Proof	25.00
	1970	1.200	.10	.25	.50	1.00
	1970	—	—	—	Proof	17.50
	1971	3.000	.10	.20	.35	.75
	1971	—	—	—	Proof	17.50
	1972	1.000	.10	.20	.35	.75
	1973	3.000	.10	.15	.30	.50
	1973	—	—	—	Proof	17.50
	1974	3.000	.10	.15	.30	.50
	1974	—	—	—	Proof	17.50
	1975	2.000	.10	.15	.30	.50
	1975	—	—	—	Proof	17.50
	1976	3.000	—	.10	.15	.25
	1977	4.000	—	.10	.15	.25
	1978	2.000	—	.10	.15	.25
			ALUMINUM			
8a	1979	7.500	—	.10	.15	.25
	1979	—	—	—	Proof	7.50
	1980	2.500	—	.10	.15	.25
	1981	2.400	—	.10	.15	.25
	1982	2.400	—	.10	.15	.25
	1983	2.900	—	.10	.15	.25
	1984	3.600	—	.10	.15	.25
	1985	3.000	—	.10	.15	.25

KM#	Date	Mintage	Fine	VF	XF	Unc
32	1989	1.350	—	—	—	.20
	1990	2.700	—	—	—	.20
	1991	4.000	—	—	—	.20
	1992	.050	—	—	—	.25

2-1/2 CENTS

BRONZE

KM#	Date	Mintage	Fine	VF	XF	Unc
5	1956	.400	.75	2.00	4.00	8.00
	1956	500 pcs.	—	—	Proof	26.00
	1959	1.000	.25	1.25	2.50	5.00
	1959	250 pcs.	—	—	Proof	30.00
	1965 fish	.500	.75	1.50	2.75	4.00
	1965	—	—	—	Proof	25.00
	1965 fish & star					
		.150	.75	1.75	3.50	7.50

KM#	Date	Mintage	Fine	VF	XF	Unc
9	1969	200 pcs.	—	—	Proof	30.00
	1970	.500	.15	.35	1.00	2.00
	1970	—	—	—	Proof	20.00
	1971	3.000	.10	.20	.30	.50
	1971	—	—	—	Proof	20.00
	1973	1.000	.10	.20	.30	.50
	1973	—	—	—	Proof	20.00
	1974	1.000	.10	.20	.30	.50
	1974	—	—	—	Proof	20.00
	1975	1.000	.10	.20	.30	.50
	1976	1.000	.10	.20	.30	.50
	1977	1.000	.10	.20	.30	.50
	1978	1.500	.10	.20	.30	.50
			ALUMINUM			
9a	1979	2.000	—	.10	.15	.25
	1979	—	—	—	Proof	10.00
	1980	2.000	—	.10	.15	.25
	1981	1.000	—	.10	.15	.25
	1982	1.000	—	.10	.15	.25
	1983	1.000	—	.10	.15	.25
	1984	1.000	—	.10	.15	.25
	1985	—	—	.10	.15	.25

5 CENTS

COPPER-NICKEL

KM#	Date	Mintage	Fine	VF	XF	Unc
6	1957	.500	.75	1.50	3.00	6.00
	1957	250 pcs.	—	—	Proof	40.00
	1962	.250	2.00	4.00	8.00	15.00
	1962	200 pcs.	—	—	Proof	30.00
	1963	.400	.75	1.25	2.50	4.00
	1963	—	—	—	Proof	30.00
	1965	.500	.75	1.25	2.50	4.00
	1965	—	—	—	Proof	30.00
	1967	.600	.75	1.25	2.50	4.00
	1967	—	—	—	Proof	30.00
	1970	.450	.75	1.25	2.50	4.00
	1970	—	—	—	Proof	30.00

Obv: Straight legend and inscription.

KM#	Date	Mintage	Fine	VF	XF	Unc
A13	1969	200 pcs.	—	—	Proof	120.00

KM#	Date	Mintage	Fine	VF	XF	Unc
13	1971	2.000	.10	.25	.50	.75
	1971	—	—	—	Proof	22.50
	1974	.500	.50	1.25	2.50	5.00
	1974	—	—	—	Proof	22.50
	1975	2.000	.10	.25	.50	.75
	1975	—	—	—	Proof	22.50
	1976	1.500	.10	.25	.50	.75
	1977	1.000	.10	.25	.50	.75
	1978	1.500	.10	.25	.50	.75
	1979	1.500	.10	.25	.50	.75
	1979	—	—	—	Proof	12.50
	1980	1.500	—	.10	.25	.50
	1981	1.000	—	.10	.25	.50
	1982	1.000	—	.10	.25	.50
	1983	1.000	—	.10	.25	.50
	1984	1.500	—	.10	.25	.50
	1985	1.500	—	.10	.25	.50

ALUMINUM

KM#	Date	Mintage	Fine	VF	XF	Unc
33	1989	.900	—	—	—	.35
	1990	1.800	—	—	—	.35
	1991	2.500	—	—	—	.35
	1992	.600	—	—	—	.35

1/10 GULDEN

1.4000 g, .640 SILVER, .0288 oz ASW

KM#	Date	Mintage	Fine	VF	XF	Unc
3	1954	.200	5.00	10.00	15.00	25.00
	1954	200 pcs.	—	—	Proof	40.00
	1956	.250	.50	2.50	4.25	7.00
	1956	500 pcs.	—	—	Proof	30.00
	1957	.250	.50	2.00	4.50	8.00
	1957	250 pcs.	—	—	Proof	40.00
	1959	.250	.50	2.00	4.50	8.00
	1959	250 pcs.	—	—	Proof	40.00
	1960	.400	.50	1.50	3.00	5.00
	1960	300 pcs.	—	—	Proof	30.00
	1962	.400	.50	1.50	3.00	5.00
	1962	200 pcs.	—	—	Proof	35.00
	1963	.900	.50	1.25	2.50	4.00
	1963	—	—	—	Proof	35.00
	1966 fish	1.000	.50	1.25	2.50	4.00
	1966 fish & star					
		.200	1.25	2.00	3.50	6.00
	1970	.300	.75	1.25	2.50	4.00
	1970	—	—	—	Proof	35.00

10 CENTS

NICKEL

KM#	Date	Mintage	Fine	VF	XF	Unc
10	1969	200 pcs.	—	—	Proof	40.00
	1970	1.000	.25	.45	.75	1.25
	1970	—	—	—	Proof	25.00
	1971	3.000	.10	.20	.35	.75
	1971	—	—	—	Proof	25.00
	1974	1.000	.25	.45	.75	1.25
	1974	—	—	—	Proof	25.00
	1975	1.500	.10	.30	.50	1.00
	1975	—	—	—	Proof	25.00
	1976	2.000	.10	.20	.35	.75
	1977	1.000	.10	.20	.35	.75
	1978	1.500	.10	.15	.25	.50
	1979	1.500	.10	.15	.25	.50
	1979	—	—	—	Proof	12.50
	1980	1.500	—	.15	.25	.50
	1981	1.000	—	.20	.35	.75
	1982	1.000	—	.20	.35	.75
	1983	1.000	—	.20	.35	.75
	1984	1.000	—	.20	.35	.75
	1985	1.000	—	.20	.35	.75

NICKEL BONDED STEEL

KM#	Date	Mintage	Fine	VF	XF	Unc
34	1989	.900	—	—	—	.75
	1990	1.800	—	—	—	.75
	1991	2.500	—	—	—	.75
	1992	.900	—	—	—	.75

1/4 GULDEN

3.5800 g, .640 SILVER, .0736 oz ASW

KM#	Date	Mintage	Fine	VF	XF	Unc
4	1954	.200	3.00	5.00	10.00	17.50
	1954	200 pcs.	—	—	Proof	45.00
	1956	.200	3.00	5.00	10.00	17.50
	1956	500 pcs.	—	—	Proof	40.00
	1957	.200	3.00	5.00	10.00	17.50
	1957	250 pcs.	—	—	Proof	45.00
	1960	.240	2.00	3.50	6.00	10.00
	1960	300 pcs.	—	—	Proof	40.00
	1962	.240	1.25	2.50	4.50	9.00
	1962	200 pcs.	—	—	Proof	40.00
	1963	.300	1.25	2.00	3.50	6.00
	1963	—	—	—	Proof	40.00
	1965	.500	1.25	2.50	4.50	9.00
	1965	—	—	—	Proof	40.00
	1967 fish	.310	1.25	2.50	4.50	9.00
	1967 fish	—	—	—	Proof	40.00
	1967 fish & star					
		.200	1.25	3.00	5.25	10.00
	1970	.150	1.25	3.00	5.25	10.00
	1970	—	—	—	Proof	35.00

25 CENTS

NICKEL

KM#	Date	Mintage	Fine	VF	XF	Unc
11	1969	200 pcs.	—	—	Proof	45.00
	1970	.750	.25	.75	1.50	3.25
	1970	—	—	—	Proof	30.00
	1971	3.000	.25	.35	.60	1.00
	1971	—	—	—	Proof	30.00
	1975	1.000	.25	.35	.60	1.00
	1975	—	—	—	Proof	30.00
	1976	1.000	.25	.35	.60	1.00
	1977	1.000	.25	.35	.60	1.00
	1978	1.000	.25	.35	.50	.80
	1979	1.000	.25	.35	.50	.80
	1979	—	—	—	Proof	17.50
	1980	1.000	.25	.50	.50	.80
	1981	1.000	.20	.30	.40	.60
	1982	1.000	.20	.30	.40	.60
	1983	1.000	.20	.30	.40	.60
	1984	1.000	.20	.30	.40	.60
	1985	.750	.20	.30	.40	.60

NICKEL BONDED STEEL

KM#	Date	Mintage	Fine	VF	XF	Unc
35	1989	.900	—	—	—	.75
	1990	1.800	—	—	—	.75
	1991	2.000	—	—	—	.75
	1992	.900	—	—	—	.75

50 CENTS

AUREATE STEEL

KM#	Date	Mintage	Fine	VF	XF	Unc
36	1989	.300	—	—	—	1.00
	1990	.600	—	—	—	1.00
	1991	.500	—	—	—	1.00
	1992	.050	—	—	—	1.50

GULDEN

10.0000 g, .720 SILVER, .2315 oz ASW

KM#	Date	Mintage	Fine	VF	XF	Unc
2	1952	1.000	1.75	3.50	7.50	12.50
	1952	100 pcs.	—	—	Proof	175.00
	1963	.100	2.00	4.00	8.00	16.00
	1963	—	—	—	Proof	100.00
	1964 fish	.300	1.75	3.00	5.00	8.50
	1964 fish & star	.200	3.00	5.00	10.00	17.50
	1964	—	—	—	Proof	100.00
	1970	.050	2.50	4.50	10.00	17.50
	1970	—	—	—	Proof	100.00

NICKEL

KM#	Date	Mintage	Fine	VF	XF	Unc
12	1969	200 pcs.	—	—	Proof	170.00
	1970	.500	.75	1.50	2.50	5.00
	1970	—	—	—	Proof	50.00
	1971	3.000	—	1.00	2.00	4.00
	1971	—	—	—	Proof	50.00
	1978	.500	—	.75	1.25	2.50
	1979	.500	—	.75	1.25	2.50
	1979	—	—	—	Proof	25.00
	1980 cock & star	.500	—	—	.75	1.75

KM#	Date	Mintage	Fine	VF	XF	Unc
24	1980 anvil	.200	—	—	.75	1.75
	1981	.200	—	—	.75	1.75
	1982	.500	—	—	.75	1.75
	1983	.500	—	—	.75	1.75
	1984	.500	—	—	.75	1.75
	1985	.400	—	—	.75	1.75

AUREATE STEEL

KM#	Date	Mintage	Fine	VF	XF	Unc
37	1989	.700	—	—	—	1.50
	1990	1.400	—	—	—	1.50
	1991	2.000	—	—	—	1.50
	1992	1.200	—	—	—	1.50

2-1/2 GULDEN

25.0000 g, .720 SILVER, .5787 oz ASW

KM#	Date	Mintage	Fine	VF	XF	Unc
7	1964	.200	3.00	5.00	7.00	12.00
	1964	—	—	—	Proof	200.00

NICKEL

KM#	Date	Mintage	Fine	VF	XF	Unc
19	1978	.100	1.50	2.00	3.00	6.00
	1979	.200	—	1.50	2.00	3.50
	1979	—	—	—	Proof	35.00
	1980 cock & star	.200	—	1.50	2.00	3.50

KM#	Date	Mintage	Fine	VF	XF	Unc
25	1980 anvil	.100	—	1.50	2.50	4.00
	1981	.100	—	1.50	2.50	4.00
	1982	.100	—	1.50	2.50	4.0
	1984	.013	—	1.75	3.50	5.0
	1985	.013	—	1.75	3.50	5.0

AUREATE STEEL

KM#	Date	Mintage	Fine	VF	XF	Unc
38	1989	.020	—	—	—	4.0
	1990	.050	—	—	—	3.5
	1991	.050	—	—	—	3.5
	1992	.025	—	—	—	4.0

5 GULDEN

3.3600 g, .900 GOLD, .0972 oz AGW
Obv: Bust of Queen Beatrix left.

KM#	Date	Mintage	Fine	VF	XF	Unc
26	1980(1982)	.016	—	—	Proof	60.0

10 GULDEN

25.0000 g, .720 SILVER, .5787 oz ASW
150th Anniversary of Bank

KM#	Date	Mintage	Fine	VF	XF	Unc
20	1978	.035	—	—	—	12.5
	1978	.015	—	—	Proof	20.0

6.7200 g, .900 GOLD, .1945 oz AGW
Obv: Bust of Queen Beatrix left.

KM#	Date	Mintage	Fine	VF	XF	Unc
27	1980(1982)	6,000	—	—	Proof	125.0

25 GULDEN

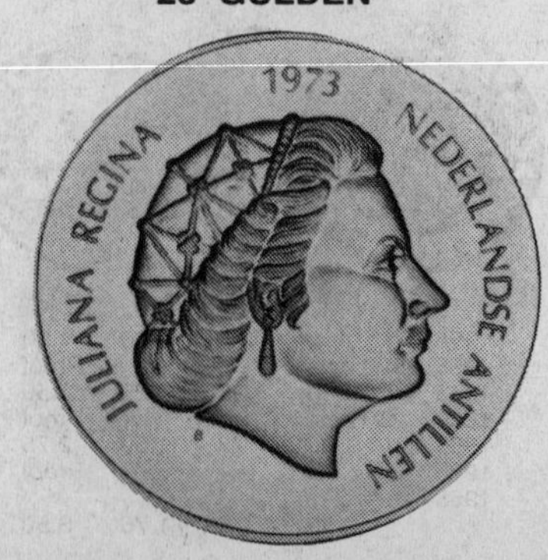

41.7000 g, .925 SILVER, 1.2401 oz ASW
25th Anniversary of Reign

KM#	Date	Mintage	Fine	VF	XF	Unc
14	1973	.040	—	—	—	15.00
	1973	.020	—	—	Proof	20.00

U.S. Bicentennial

KM#	Date	Mintage	Fine	VF	XF	Unc
15	1976FM(M)					
		200 pcs.	—	—	—	175.00
	1976FM(U)					
		9,425	—	—	—	35.00
	1976FM(P)	.013	—	—	Proof	40.00

Peter Stuyvesant

KM#	Date	Mintage	Fine	VF	XF	Unc
17	1977FM(U)					
		2,000	—	—	—	200.00

27.2200 g, .925 SILVER, .8095 oz ASW
International Year of the Child

KM#	Date	Mintage	Fine	VF	XF	Unc
22	1979	1,000	—	—	—	125.00
	1979	4,000	—	—	P/L	45.00
	1979	.017	—	—	Proof	18.50

25.0000 g, .925 SILVER, .7435 oz ASW
Pope John Paul II

KM#	Date	Mintage	Fine	VF	XF	Unc
39	1990	.010	—	—	—	20.00
	1990	.010	—	—	Proof	40.00

50 GULDEN

3.3600 g, .900 GOLD, .0972 oz AGW
75th Anniversary of the Royal Covenant

KM#	Date	Mintage	Fine	VF	XF	Unc
23	1979	.011	—	—	—	45.00
	1979	.064	—	—	Proof	50.00

24.0000 g, .500 SILVER, .3859 oz ASW

KM#	Date	Mintage	Fine	VF	XF	Unc
28	1980	8,600	—	—	—	35.00
	1980	.016	—	—	Proof	30.00

25.0000 g, .925 SILVER, .7435 oz ASW
Dutch-American Friendship

KM#	Date	Mintage	Fine	VF	XF	Unc
30	1982	.040	—	—	Proof	32.50

Mikve Israel Emanuel Synagogue

KM#	Date	Mintage	Fine	VF	XF	Unc
31	1982	.010	—	—	Proof	60.00

100 GULDEN

6.7200 g, .900 GOLD, .1944 oz AGW
150th Anniversary of Bank

KM#	Date	Mintage	Fine	VF	XF	Unc
21	1978	.027	—	—	—	90.00
	1978	.024	—	—	Proof	100.00

200 GULDEN

7.9500 g, .900 GOLD, .2300 oz AGW
U.S. Bicentennial

KM#	Date	Mintage	Fine	VF	XF	Unc
16	1976FM(M)					
		100 pcs.	—	—	—	300.00
	1976FM(U)					
		5,726	—	—	—	165.00
	1976FM(P)	.015	—	—	Proof	175.00

Peter Stuyvesant

KM#	Date	Mintage	Fine	VF	XF	Unc
18	1977FM(M)					
		2,000	—	—	—	200.00
	1977FM(U)					
		654 pcs.	—	—	—	300.00
	1977FM(P)					
		6,878	—	—	Proof	200.00

300 GULDEN

5.0400 g, .900 GOLD, .1458 oz AGW
Abdication of Queen Juliana

KM#	Date	Mintage	Fine	VF	XF	Unc
29.1	1980FM(U)	.012	—	—	—	75.00
	1980FM(P)	.037	—	—	Proof	90.00
	Rev: W/o mint mark.					
29.2	1980	Inc. Ab.	—	—	Proof	250.00

MINT SETS (MS)

KM#	Date	Mintage	Identification	Issue Price	Mkt. Val.
MS1	1971(7)	—	KM8-13 + Curacao KM46	—	22.00
MS2	1979(7)	11,500	KM8a,9a,10-13,19	—	17.50
MS3	1980(7)	18,500	KM8a,9a,10-13,19	—	15.00
MS4	1980(2)	23,000	KM24-25	—	7.50
MS5	1981(7)	23,500	KM8a,9a,10-12,24,25	—	10.00
MS6	1982(7)	10,000	KM8a,9a,10-12,24,25	—	12.00
MS7	1983(6)	25,000	KM8a,9a,10-12.24 + medallion	14.00	11.50
MS8	1984(7)	26,000	KM8a,9a,10-12,24,25	14.50	10.00
MS9	1985(7)	24,000	KM8a,9a,10-12,24,25	—	10.00
MS10	1989(7)	15,000	KM32-38	—	12.50
MS11	1990(7)	10,000	KM32-38	13.00	12.50
MS12	1991(7)	12,100	KM32-38	13.50	12.50
MS13	1992(7)	—	KM32-38	—	12.50

PROOF SETS (PS)

KM#	Date	Mintage	Identification	Issue Price	Mkt. Val.
PS1	1952(2)	100	KM1,2	—	220.00
PS2	1954(3)	200	KM1,3-4	—	100.00
PS3	1956(3)	500	KM3-5	—	100.00
PS4	1957(4)	250	KM1,3-4,6	—	145.00
PS5	1959(3)	250	KM1,3,5	—	90.00
PS6	1960(3)	300	KM1,3-4	—	90.00
PS7	1962(3)	200	KM3-4,6	—	100.00
PS8	1963(5)	—	KM1-4,6	—	225.00
PS9	1964(3)	—	KM1,2,7	—	325.00
PS10	1965(4)	—	KM1,4-6	—	105.00
PS11	1967(3)	—	KM1,4,6	—	80.00
PS12	1969(6)	200	KM8-12,A13	—	425.00
PS13	1970(10)	—	KM1-4,6,8-12	—	350.00
PS14	1971(6)	—	KM8-13	—	165.00
PS15	1973(3)	—	KM8,9,14	—	87.50
PS16	1974(4)	—	KM8-10,13	—	85.00
PS17	1975(4)	—	KM8,10-11,13	—	240.00
PS18	1976(2)	.013	KM15,16	187.50	325.00
PS19	1979(7)	—	KM8a,9a,10-13,19	—	120.00

Listings For

NETHERLANDS EAST INDIES: refer to Indonesia

NEW BRUNSWICK: refer to Canada

NEW CALEDONIA

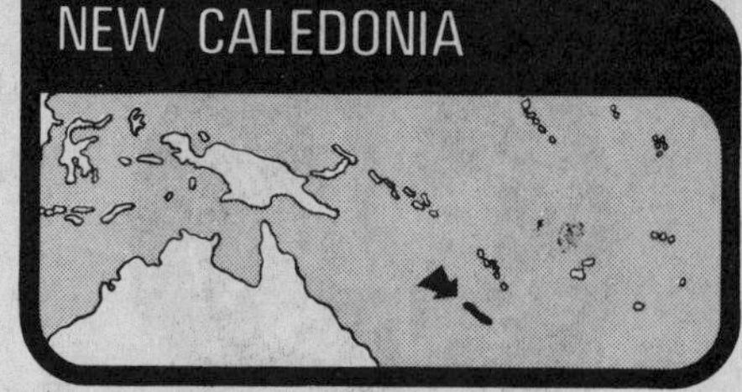

The French Overseas Territory of New Caledonia, a group of about 25 islands in the South Pacific, is situated about 750 miles (1,207 km.) east of Australia. The territory, which includes the dependencies of Ile des Pins, Loyalty Islands, Ile Huon, Isles Belep, Isles Chesterfield, and Ile Walpole, has a total land area of 7,358 sq. mi. (19,060 sq. km.) and a population of *156,000. Capital: Noumea. The islands are rich in minerals; New Caledonia has the world's largest known deposit of nickel. Nickel, nickel castings, coffee and copra are exported.

The first European to sight New Caledonia was the British navigator Capt. James Cook in 1774. The French took possession in 1853, and established a penal colony on the island in 1854. The European population of the colony remained disproportionately convict until 1894. New Caledonia became an overseas territory within the French Community in 1946, and in 1958 and 1972 chose to remain affiliated with France.

MINT MARKS

(a) - Paris, privy marks only

MONETARY SYSTEM

100 Centimes = 1 Franc

50 CENTIMES

ALUMINUM

KM#	Date	Mintage	VF	XF	Unc
1	1949(a)	1.000	.50	1.00	3.50

FRANC

ALUMINUM

KM#	Date	Mintage	VF	XF	Unc
2	1949(a)	4.000	.25	.75	2.50

KM#	Date	Mintage	VF	XF	Unc
8	1971(a)	1.000	.25	.75	2.00

Obv. leg: I.E.O.M. added.

KM#	Date	Mintage	VF	XF	Unc
10	1972(a)	.600	.25	.75	2.50
	1973(a)	1.000	.15	.25	.75
	1977(a)	1.500	.15	.25	.75
	1979(a)	—	.10	.20	.50
	1981(a)	1.000	.10	.20	.50
	1982(a)	1.000	.10	.20	.50
	1983(a)	—	.10	.20	.50
	1984(a)	—	.10	.20	.50
	1985(a)	—	.10	.20	.50
	1988(a)	—	.10	.20	.50
	1989(a)	—	.10	.20	.50
	1990(a)	—	.10	.20	.50

2 FRANCS

ALUMINUM

KM#	Date	Mintage	VF	XF	Unc
3	1949(a)	3.000	.50	1.50	4.50
9	1971(a)	1.000	.25	1.00	2.00
	Obv. leg: I.E.O.M. added.				
14	1973(a)	.400	.20	.75	2.50
	1977(a)	1.500	.20	.50	1.00
	1979(a)	—	.20	.40	.65
	1982(a)	1.000	.20	.35	.65
	1983(a)	—	.20	.35	.65
	1987(a)	—	.20	.35	.65
	1989(a)	—	.20	.35	.65
	1990(a)	—	.20	.35	.65

5 FRANCS

ALUMINUM

KM#	Date	Mintage	VF	XF	Unc
4	1952(a)	4.000	.50	1.00	3.50
	Obv. leg: I.E.O.M. added.				
16	1983(a)	—	.50	1.00	2.50
	1986(a)	1.000	.50	1.00	2.50
	1989(a)	—	.50	1.00	2.50
	1990(a)	—	.50	1.00	2.50
	1991(a)	—	.50	1.00	2.50

10 FRANCS

NICKEL

KM#	Date	Mintage	VF	XF	Unc
5	1967(a)	.400	1.00	2.00	4.50
	1970(a)	1.000	.50	.75	2.50

Obv. leg: I.E.O.M. added.

KM#	Date	Mintage	VF	XF	Unc
11	1972(a)	.600	.50	.75	2.00
	1973(a)	.400	.50	.75	2.00
	1977(a)	1.000	.50	.75	1.00

KM#	Date	Mintage	VF	XF	Unc
11	1979(a)	—	.35	.50	1.00
	1983(a)	—	.35	.50	1.00
	1986(a)	—	.35	.50	1.00
	1989(a)	—	.35	.50	1.00
	1990(a)	—	.35	.50	1.00

20 FRANCS

NICKEL

KM#	Date	Mintage	VF	XF	Unc
6	1967(a)	.300	1.25	2.50	5.00
	1970(a)	1.200	.60	1.00	2.00

Obv. leg: I.E.O.M. added.

KM#	Date	Mintage	VF	XF	Unc
12	1972(a)	.700	.75	1.00	2.00
	1977(a)	.350	.75	1.00	3.00
	1979(a)	—	.50	.85	1.50
	1983(a)	—	.50	.85	1.50
	1986(a)	—	.50	.85	1.50
	1990(a)	—	.50	.85	1.50

50 FRANCS

NICKEL

KM#	Date	Mintage	VF	XF	Unc
7	1967(a)	.700	1.50	3.00	7.00

Obv. leg: I.E.O.M. added.

KM#	Date	Mintage	VF	XF	Unc
13	1972(a)	.300	1.50	2.00	5.00
	1979(a)	—	1.50	2.00	5.00
	1983(a)	—	1.50	2.00	5.00
	1987(a)	—	1.50	2.00	5.00
	1991(a)	—	1.50	2.00	5.00

100 FRANCS

NICKEL-BRONZE

KM#	Date	Mintage	VF	XF	Unc
15	1976(a)	2.000	1.50	2.50	6.00
	1979(a)	—	1.50	2.50	6.00
	1984(a)	—	1.50	2.50	6.00
	1987(a)	—	1.50	2.50	6.00
	1988(a)	—	1.50	2.50	6.00
	1991(a)	—	1.50	2.50	6.00

FLEUR DE COIN SETS (SS)

KM#	Date	Mintage	Identification	Issue Price	Mkt. Val.
SS1	1967(3)	2,200	KM5-7	10.00	17.50

NOTE: This set issued with New Hebrides and French Polynesia 1967 set.

Listings For

NEWFOUNDLAND: refer to Canada

NEW GUINEA: refer to Papua New Guinea

NEW HEBRIDES: refer to Vanuatu

NEW ZEALAND

New Zealand, a parliamentary state located in the Southwestern Pacific 1,250 miles (2,011 km.) east of Australia, has an area of 103,883 sq. mi. (268,680 sq. km.) and a population of *3.4 million. Capital: Wellington. Wool, meat, dairy products and some manufactured items are exported.

The first European to sight New Zealand was the Dutch navigator Abel Tasman in 1642. The islands were explored by British navigator Capt. James Cook who surveyed it in 1769 and annexed the land to Great Britain. The British government disavowed the annexation and for the next 70 years the only white settlers to arrive were adventurers attracted by the prospects of lumbering, sealing and whaling. Great Britain annexed the land in 1840 by treaty with the native chiefs and made it a dependency of New South Wales. The colony was granted self-government in 1852, a ministerial form of government in 1856, and full dominion status on Sept. 26, 1907. Full internal and external autonomy, which New Zealand had in effect possessed for many years, was formally extended in 1947. New Zealand is a member of the Commonwealth of Nations. The Queen of England is Chiefof State.

Prior to 1933 English coins were the official legal tender but Australian coins were accepted in small transactions. Currency fluctuations caused a distintive New Zealand coinage to be introduced in 1933. The 1935 Waitangi crown and proof set were originally intended to mark the introduction but delays caused their date to be changed to 1935. The 1940 halfcrown marked the centennial of British rule, the 1949 and 1953 crowns commemorated Royal visits and the 1953 proof set marked the coronation of Queen Elizabeth.

Decimal Currency was introduced in 1967 with special sets commemorating the last issued of pound sterling and the first of the decimal issues. Since then dollars and sets of coins have been issued nearly every year.

RULERS

British

MONETARY SYSTEM

12 Pence = 1 Shilling
2 Shillings = 1 Florin
2 Shillings & 6 Pence = Half Crown
5 Shillings = 1 Crown
20 Shillings = 1 Pound
2 Dollars = 1 Pound

1/2 PENNY

BRONZE
Hei Tiki

KM#	Date	Mintage	Fine	VF	XF	Unc
12	1940	3.432	.35	.65	1.75	8.00
	1940	—	—	—	Proof	200.00
	1941	.960	.25	.65	2.00	10.00
	1941	—	—	—	Proof	250.00
	1942	1.960	.35	.75	3.50	17.50
	1944	2.035	.25	.50	2.00	9.00
	1945	1.516	.25	.35	1.00	5.00
	1945	—	—	—	Proof	200.00
	1946	3.120	.25	.50	1.00	5.00
	1946	—	—	—	Proof	200.00
	1947	2.726	.25	.50	1.00	5.00
	1947	—	—	—	Proof	175.00

KM#	Date	Mintage	Fine	VF	XF	Unc
20	1949	1.766	.10	.25	1.00	6.00
	1949	—	—	—	Proof	175.00
	1950	1.426	.10	.25	1.25	7.00
	1950	—	—	—	Proof	200.00
	1951	2.342	.10	.25	1.00	7.00
	1951	—	—	—	Proof	175.00
	1952	2.400	.10	.20	.50	2.50
	1952	—	—	—	Proof	175.00

Obv: W/o shoulder strap.

KM#	Date	Mintage	Fine	VF	XF	Unc
23.1	1953	.720	.10	.25	1.00	4.00
	1953	7,000	—	—	Proof	8.00
	1953	—	—	Matte	Proof	125.00
	1954	.240	.75	1.25	3.50	20.00
	1954	—	—	—	Proof	150.00
	1955	.240	.50	1.25	3.50	20.00
	1955	—	—	—	Proof	150.00

Obv: W/shoulder strap.

KM#	Date	Mintage	Fine	VF	XF	Unc
23.2	1956	1.200	.10	.35	1.00	6.00
	1956	—	—	—	Proof	150.00
	1957	1.440	.10	.35	.75	5.00
	1957	—	—	—	Proof	150.00
	1958	1.920	.10	.30	.50	2.00
	1958	—	—	—	Proof	150.00
	1959	1.920	.10	.20	.50	2.00
	1959	—	—	—	Proof	150.00
	1960	2.400	.10	.15	.40	1.50
	1960	—	—	—	Proof	150.00
	1961	2.880	.10	.15	.40	1.50
	1961	—	—	—	Proof	150.00
	1962	2.880	.10	.15	.40	1.25
	1962	—	—	—	Proof	150.00
	1963	1.680	.10	.15	.30	1.00
	1963	—	—	—	Proof	150.00
	1964	2.885	.10	.15	.20	.50
	1964	—	—	—	Proof	150.00
	1965	5.177	.10	.15	.20	.50
	1965	.025	—	—	Proof	1.50

PENNY

BRONZE
Tui Bird

KM#	Date	Mintage	Fine	VF	XF	Unc
13	1940	5.424	.35	1.00	2.00	12.00
	1940	—	—	—	Proof	250.00
	1941	1.200	.25	1.00	5.00	22.00
	1942	3.120	.25	1.00	6.00	45.00
	1942	—	—	—	Proof	300.00
	1943	8.400	.25	.50	3.00	8.00
	1943	—	—	—	Proof	250.00
	1944	3.696	.25	.50	2.50	8.00
	1944	—	—	—	Proof	250.00
	1945	4.764	.25	.50	2.50	8.00
	1945	—	—	—	Proof	250.00
	1946	6.720	.25	.50	2.50	8.00
	1946	—	—	—	Proof	250.00
	1947	5.880	.25	.50	2.50	8.00
	1947	—	—	—	Proof	250.00

BRONZE, burnished

KM#	Date	Mintage	Fine	VF	XF	Unc
13a	1945	—	—	—	40.00	120.00

NOTE: Struck in error by the Royal Mint on Great Britain blanks.

BRONZE

KM#	Date	Mintage	Fine	VF	XF	Unc
21	1949	2.016	.20	.60	2.50	10.00
	1949	—	—	—	Proof	250.00
	1950	5.784	.15	.50	1.75	7.00
	1950	—	—	—	Proof	200.00
	1951	6.888	.15	.50	1.75	7.00
	1951	—	—	—	Proof	200.00
	1952	10.800	.15	.50	1.00	5.00
	1952	—	—	—	Proof	175.00

Obv: W/o shoulder strap.

KM#	Date	Mintage	Fine	VF	XF	Unc
24.1	1953	2.400	.10	.25	1.50	5.00
	1953	7,000	—	—	Proof	15.00
	1953	—	—	Matte	Proof	125.00
	1954	1.080	.25	1.00	5.00	18.00
	1954	—	—	—	Proof	200.00
	1955	3.720	.10	.25	1.50	6.50
	1955	—	—	—	Proof	175.00
	1956	Inc. Be.	8.00	15.00	70.00	200.00

Obv: W/shoulder strap.

KM#	Date	Mintage	Fine	VF	XF	Unc
24.2	1956	3.600	.10	.20	1.00	4.50
	1956	—	—	—	Proof	175.00
	1957	2.400	.10	.20	.75	3.50
	1957	—	—	—	Proof	175.00
	1958	10.800	.10	.20	.50	2.00
	1958	—	—	—	Proof	175.00
	1959	8.400	.10	.20	.50	2.00
	1959	—	—	—	Proof	175.00
	1960	7.200	.10	.20	.50	1.75
	1960	—	—	—	Proof	150.00
	1961	7.200	.10	.20	.50	1.25
	1961	—	—	—	Proof	150.00
	1962	6.000	—	.10	.45	1.25
	1962	—	—	—	Proof	150.00
	1963	2.400	—	.10	.20	.75
	1963	—	—	—	Proof	150.00
	1964	18.000	—	.10	.15	.50
	1964	—	—	—	Proof	150.00
	1965	.175	—	.10	.35	1.50
	1965	.025	—	—	Proof	3.50

3 PENCE

1.4100 g, .500 SILVER, .0226 oz ASW
Crossed Patu

KM#	Date	Mintage	Fine	VF	XF	Unc
1	1933	6.000	.35	.75	3.50	18.00
	1933	*20 pcs.	—	—	Proof	500.00
	1934	6.000	.35	.75	3.50	18.00
	1934	—	—	—	Proof	1650.
	1935	.040	35.00	85.00	165.00	450.00
	1935	364 pcs.	—	—	Proof	600.00
	1936	2.760	.35	.75	3.50	18.00
	1936	—	—	—	Proof	500.00

KM#	Date	Mintage	Fine	VF	XF	Unc
7	1937	2.880	.35	.75	2.75	16.00
	1937	—	—	—	Proof	450.00
	1939	3.000	.35	.75	2.75	16.00
	1939	—	—	—	Proof	450.00
	1940	2.000	.35	1.25	4.50	20.00
	1940	—	—	—	Proof	450.00
	1941	1.760	.50	1.50	6.50	35.00
	1941	—	—	—	Proof	400.00
	1942	3.120	.30	.75	1.50	10.00
	1942 w/1 dot	Inc. Ab.	1.00	4.00	50.00	225.00
	1943	4.400	.30	.60	1.25	6.50
	1944	2.840	.30	.60	1.25	6.50
	1944	—	—	—	Proof	400.00
	1945	2.520	.30	.60	1.00	4.00
	1945	—	—	—	Proof	400.00
	1946	6.080	.30	.60	1.00	4.00
	1946	—	—	—	Proof	400.00

COPPER-NICKEL

KM#	Date	Mintage	Fine	VF	XF	Unc
7a	1947	6.400	.15	.35	3.00	12.00
	1947	*20 pcs.	—	—	Proof	350.00

KM#	Date	Mintage	Fine	VF	XF	Unc
15	1948	4.000	.15	.35	2.00	10.00
	1948	—	—	—	Proof	200.00
	1950	.800	.25	1.00	5.00	30.00
	1950	—	—	—	Proof	250.00
	1951	3.600	.15	.35	1.25	8.00
	1951	—	—	—	Proof	200.00
	1952	8.000	.15	.35	1.25	7.00
	1952	—	—	—	Proof	200.00

Obv: W/o shoulder strap.

KM#	Date	Mintage	Fine	VF	XF	Unc
25.1	1953	4.000	.15	.35	.75	2.50
	1953	7,000	—	—	Proof	15.00
	1953	—	—	Matte	Proof	150.00
	1954	4.000	.15	.35	.75	3.00
	1954	—	—	—	Proof	200.00
	1955	4.000	.15	.35	.75	3.00
	1955	—	—	—	Proof	200.00
	1956	Inc. Be.	1.25	2.00	12.00	90.00
	1956	—	—	—	Proof	300.00

Obv: W/shoulder strap.

KM#	Date	Mintage	Fine	VF	XF	Unc
25.2	1956	4.800	.10	.20	.50	2.25
	1956	—	—	—	Proof	200.00
	1957	8.000	.10	.20	.30	2.00
	1957	—	—	—	Proof	200.00
	1958	4.800	.10	.20	.30	2.00
	1958	—	—	—	Proof	200.00
	1959	4.000	.10	.20	.30	2.00
	1959	—	—	—	Proof	200.00
	1960	4.000	.10	.20	.30	1.50
	1960	—	—	—	Proof	200.00
	1961	4.800	.10	.15	.30	1.00
	1961	—	—	—	Proof	200.00
	1962	6.000	.10	.15	.30	.75
	1962	—	—	—	Proof	200.00
	1963	4.000	.10	.15	.25	.50
	1963	—	—	—	Proof	200.00
	1964	6.400	.10	.15	.25	.50
	1964	—	—	—	Proof	200.00
	1965	4.175	—	.10	.15	.50
	1965	.027	—	—	Proof	1.00

6 PENCE

2.8300 g, .500 SILVER, .0454 oz ASW
Huia Bird

KM#	Date	Mintage	Fine	VF	XF	Unc
2	1933	3.000	.60	1.25	4.50	25.00
	1933	*20 pcs.	—	—	Proof	500.00
	1934	3.600	.60	1.25	4.50	25.00
	1934	—	—	—	Proof	1650
	1935	.560	2.00	6.00	25.00	175.00
	1935	364 pcs.	—	—	Proof	300.00
	1936	1.480	.75	2.25	6.50	35.00
	1936	—	—	—	Proof	—

KM#	Date	Mintage	Fine	VF	XF	Unc
8	1937	1.280	.50	1.50	4.50	30.00
	1937	—	—	—	Proof	400.00
	1939	.700	.50	1.50	4.50	30.00
	1939	—	—	—	Proof	400.00
	1940	.800	.50	2.25	6.50	35.00
	1940	—	—	—	Proof	400.00
	1941	.440	2.00	4.00	45.00	300.00
	1941	—	—	—	Proof	600.00
	1942	.360	2.00	4.00	20.00	175.00
	1943	1.800	.50	1.00	3.00	12.50
	1944	1.160	.50	1.00	3.50	17.50
	1944	—	—	—	Proof	350.00
	1945	.940	.50	1.00	3.50	16.50
	1945	—	—	—	Proof	350.00
	1946	2.120	.50	1.00	2.00	10.00
	1946	—	—	—	Proof	350.00

COPPER-NICKEL

KM#	Date	Mintage	Fine	VF	XF	Unc
8a	1947	3.200	.50	1.00	4.50	30.00
	1947	*20 pcs.	—	—	Proof	350.00

KM#	Date	Mintage	Fine	VF	XF	Unc
16	1948	2.000	.30	.60	1.50	12.00
	1948	—	—	—	Proof	300.00
	1950	.800	.40	1.25	8.00	80.00
	1950	—	—	—	Proof	300.00
	1951	1.800	.30	.50	.75	3.50
	1951	—	—	—	Proof	300.00
	1952	3.200	.30	.50	2.00	7.50
	1952	—	—	—	Proof	250.00

Obv: W/o shoulder strap.

KM#	Date	Mintage	Fine	VF	XF	Unc
26.1	1953	1.200	.15	.30	.75	4.00
	1953	7,000	—	—	Proof	12.50
	1953	—	—	Matte	Proof	150.00
	1954	1.200	.15	.30	1.50	7.00
	1954	—	—	—	Proof	200.00
	1955	1.600	.15	.30	1.50	9.00
	1957	Inc. Be.	1.00	2.00	16.00	100.00
	1957	—	—	—	Proof	500.00

Obv: W/shoulder strap.

KM#	Date	Mintage	Fine	VF	XF	Unc
26.2	1955	—	—	—	Proof	2800.
	1956	2.000	.20	.50	1.25	3.00
	1956	—	—	—	Proof	200.00
	1957	2.400	.20	.50	.75	2.00
	1957	—	—	—	Proof	200.00
	1958	3.000	.15	.50	.75	2.00
	1958	—	—	—	Proof	200.00
	1959	2.000	.15	.50	.75	2.00
	1959	—	—	—	Proof	200.00
	1960	1.600	.15	.25	.40	1.25
	1960	—	—	—	Proof	200.00
	1961	.800	.10	.15	.25	1.00
	1961	—	—	—	Proof	200.00
	1962	1.200	.10	.15	.25	1.00
	1962	—	—	—	Proof	200.00
	1963	.800	.10	.15	.25	1.00
	1963	—	—	—	Proof	200.00
	1964	7.800	—	.10	.15	.75
	1964	—	—	—	Proof	200.00
	1965	8.575	—	—	.10	.75
	1965	.025	—	—	Proof	1.00

SHILLING

5.6500 g, .500 SILVER, .0908 oz ASW
Maori

KM#	Date	Mintage	Fine	VF	XF	Unc
3	1933	3.000	2.00	3.50	12.50	85.00
	1933	*20 pcs.	—	—	Proof	650.00
	1934	3.600	2.00	4.00	8.00	65.00
	1934	—	—	—	Proof	2100.
	1935	.560	3.00	5.00	16.00	125.00
	1935	364 pcs.	—	—	Proof	300.00

KM#	Date	Mintage	Fine	VF	XF	Unc
9	1937	.890	1.50	3.50	7.50	65.00
	1937	—	—	—	Proof	600.00
	1940	.500	1.50	3.50	5.00	80.00
	1940	—	—	—	Proof	600.00
	1941	.360	2.00	5.00	20.00	175.00
	1941	—	—	—	Proof	600.00
	1942	.240	2.00	4.00	16.00	125.00
	1943	.900	1.00	2.00	5.00	35.00
	1944	.480	1.00	2.00	5.00	45.00
	1944	—	—	—	Proof	600.00
	1945	1.030	1.00	2.00	4.00	20.00
	1945	—	—	—	Proof	600.00
	1946	1.060	1.00	2.00	4.00	20.00
	1946	—	—	—	Proof	600.00

COPPER-NICKEL

KM#	Date	Mintage	Fine	VF	XF	Unc
9a	1947	2.800	.75	2.00	16.00	75.00
	1947	—	—	—	Proof	400.00

KM#	Date	Mintage	Fine	VF	XF	Unc
17	1948	1.000	.60	1.25	12.00	50.00
	1948	—	—	—	Proof	400.00
	1950	.600	.60	1.25	12.00	50.00
	1950	—	—	—	Proof	400.00
	1951	1.200	.60	1.25	12.00	45.00
	1951	—	—	—	Proof	400.00
	1952	.600	.60	1.25	12.00	40.00
	1952	—	—	—	Proof	400.00

Obv: W/o shoulder strap.

KM#	Date	Mintage	Fine	VF	XF	Unc
27.1	1953	.200	.60	1.00	2.00	8.00
	1953	7,000	—	—	Proof	15.00
	1953	—	—		Matte Proof	150.00
	1955	.200	.60	1.25	5.00	50.00
	1955	—	—	—	Proof	400.00

Obv: W/shoulder strap.

KM#	Date	Mintage	Fine	VF	XF	Unc
27.2	1956	.800	.60	1.00	1.50	5.00
	1956	—	—	—	Proof	400.00
	1957	.800	.60	1.00	1.50	5.00
	1957	—	—	—	Proof	400.00
	1958	1.000	.30	.60	1.00	4.00
	1958	—	—	—	Proof	400.00
	1959	.600	.30	.60	1.00	4.00
	1959	—	—	—	Proof	400.00
	1960	.600	.30	.60	1.00	4.00
	1960	—	—	—	Proof	400.00
	1961	.400	.15	.30	.60	2.00
	1961	—	—	—	Proof	400.00
	1962	1.000	.15	.30	.50	1.25
	1962	—	—	—	Proof	400.00
	1963	.600	.15	.30	.50	1.00
	1963	—	—	—	Proof	400.00
	1964	3.400	.10	.15	.30	.75
	1964	—	—	—	Proof	400.00
	1965	4.475	.10	.15	.30	.75
	1965	.025	—	—	Proof	1.50

FLORIN

11.3100 g, .500 SILVER, .1818 oz ASW
Kiwi

KM#	Date	Mintage	Fine	VF	XF	Unc
4	1933	2.100	1.50	4.00	16.00	75.00
	1933	*20 pcs.	—	—	Proof	700.00
	1934	2.850	1.50	4.00	16.00	70.00
	1934	—	—	—	Proof	2250.
	1935	.755	2.00	7.00	40.00	125.00
	1935	364 pcs.	—	—	Proof	350.00
	1936	.150	6.00	20.00	90.00	600.00
	1936	—	—	—	Proof	1500.

KM#	Date	Mintage	Fine	VF	XF	Unc
10.1	1937	1.190	1.50	2.50	10.00	50.00
	1937	—	—	—	Proof	700.00
	1940	.500	3.00	12.00	90.00	550.00
	1940	—	—	—	Proof	900.00
	1941	.820	1.50	3.00	7.00	45.00
	1941	—	—	—	Proof	700.00
	1942	.150	1.50	4.00	20.00	75.00
	1943	1.400	1.50	2.50	7.00	40.00
	1944	.140	1.75	6.00	30.00	125.00
	1944	—	—	—	Proof	900.00
	1945	.515	1.50	2.00	6.00	35.00
	1945	—	—	—	Proof	700.00
	1946	1.200	1.50	2.50	12.00	70.00
	1946	—	—	—	Proof	700.00

Rev: Flat back on kiwi.

KM#	Date	Mintage	Fine	VF	XF	Unc
10.2	1946	Inc. Ab.	2.00	8.00	70.00	265.00

COPPER-NICKEL

KM#	Date	Mintage	Fine	VF	XF	Unc
10.2a	1947	2.500	.75	2.00	25.00	100.00
	1947	—	—	—	Proof	500.00

KM#	Date	Mintage	Fine	VF	XF	Unc
18	1948	1.750	.75	1.50	20.00	65.00
	1948	—	—	—	Proof	450.00
	1949	3.500	.75	1.25	16.00	60.00
	1949	—	—	—	Proof	450.00
	1950	3.500	.65	1.25	2.00	16.50
	1950	—	—	—	Proof	450.00
	1951	1.000	.65	1.25	2.00	16.50
	1951	—	—	—	Proof	450.00

Obv: W/o shoulder strap.

KM#	Date	Mintage	Fine	VF	XF	Unc
28.1	1953	.250	.50	.75	1.50	5.00
	1953	7,000	—	—	Proof	20.00
	1953	—	—		Matte Proof	200.00

Obv: W/shoulder strap.

KM#	Date	Mintage	Fine	VF	XF	Unc
28.2	1961	1.500	.15	.25	.50	2.00
	1961	—	—	—	Proof	400.00
	1962	1.500	.15	.25	.50	2.00
	1962	—	—	—	Proof	400.00
	1963	.100	.15	.60	1.00	3.00
	1963	—	—	—	Proof	400.00
	1964	7.000	.15	.20	.35	1.00
	1964	—	—	—	Proof	400.00
	1965	9.425	.15	.20	.35	1.00
	1965	.025	—	—	Proof	2.00

1/2 CROWN

14.1400 g, .500 SILVER, .2273 oz ASW

KM#	Date	Mintage	Fine	VF	XF	Unc
5	1933	2.000	3.00	12.00	25.00	125.00
	1933	*20 pcs.	—	—	Proof	750.00
	1934	2.720	3.00	12.00	16.00	120.00
	1934	—	—	—	Proof	2400.
	1935	.612	3.00	22.50	40.00	225.00
	1935	364 pcs.	—	—	Proof	650.00

KM#	Date	Mintage	Fine	VF	XF	Unc
11	1937	.672	3.00	9.50	12.00	85.00
	1937	—	—	—	Proof	750.00
	1941	.776	3.00	9.00	8.00	75.00
	1941	—	—	—	Proof	750.00
	1942	.240	3.00	9.50	16.00	100.00
	1943	1.120	1.50	4.00	10.00	60.00
	1944	.180	2.50	6.00	35.00	200.00
	1944	—	—	—	Proof	750.00
	1945	.420	1.50	3.00	10.00	80.00
	1945	—	—	—	Proof	750.00
	1946	.960	1.50	2.50	7.00	70.00
	1946	—	—	—	Proof	750.00

New Zealand Centennial - Maori Wahine

KM#	Date	Mintage	Fine	VF	XF	Unc
14	1940	.101	3.50	7.50	10.00	27.50
	1940	—	—	—	Proof	5500.

COPPER-NICKEL

KM#	Date	Mintage	Fine	VF	XF	Unc
11a	1947	1.600	.60	2.50	12.00	100.00
	1947	*20 pcs.	—	—	Proof	600.00

KM#	Date	Mintage	Fine	VF	XF	Unc
19	1948	1.400	.60	2.00	12.00	90.00
	1948	—	—	—	Proof	550.00
	1949	2.800	.60	2.00	9.00	75.00
	1949	—	—	—	Proof	550.00
	1950	3.600	.60	1.50	2.50	12.00
	1950	—	—	—	Proof	550.00
	1951	1.200	.60	1.00	2.00	9.00
	1951	—	—	—	Proof	550.00

Obv: W/o shoulder strap.

KM#	Date	Mintage	Fine	VF	XF	Unc
29.1	1953	.120	.75	1.25	2.00	6.50
	1953	7,000	—	—	Proof	25.00
	1953	—	—	—	Matte Proof	250.00

Obv: W/shoulder strap.

KM#	Date	Mintage	Fine	VF	XF	Unc
29.2	1961	.080	.60	.80	1.50	4.00
	1961	—	—	—	Proof	500.00
	1962	.600	.50	.70	1.00	3.00
	1962	—	—	—	Proof	500.00
	1963	.400	.50	.70	1.00	2.00
	1963	—	—	—	Proof	500.00
	1965	.175	.50	.70	1.00	2.50
	1965	.025	—	—	Proof	3.00

CROWN

28.2800 g, .500 SILVER, .4546 oz ASW
Treaty of Waitangi in 1840
Woka Nene and Governor Hobson

KM#	Date	Mintage	Fine	VF	XF	Unc
6	1935	764 pcs.	1150.	1350.	1750.	2250.
	1935	364 pcs.	—	—	Proof	2900.

Proposed Royal Visit
Silver Fern Leaf

KM#	Date	Mintage	Fine	VF	XF	Unc
22	1949	.200	3.00	4.00	6.00	12.00
	1949	*3 pcs.	—	—	Proof	4000.

COPPER-NICKEL
Queen Elizabeth II Coronation

KM#	Date	Mintage	Fine	VF	XF	Unc
30	1953	.250	—	1.50	2.50	5.50
	1953	7,000	—	—	Proof	30.00
	1953	4-10 pcs.	—	—	Matte Proof	350.00

DECIMAL COINAGE

MINTS

(c) Royal Australian Mint, Canberra
(l) Royal Mint, Llantrisant
(o) Royal Canadian Mint, Ottawa

MONETARY SYSTEM

100 Cents = 1 Dollar

CENT

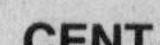

BRONZE
Silver Fern Leaf

KM#	Date	Mintage	VF	XF	Unc
31	1967	120.250	—	.15	.25
	1967	.050	—	Proof	1.50
	1968	.035	—	.15	1.25
	1968	.040	—	Proof	2.00
	1969	.050	—	.15	1.25
	1969	.050	—	Proof	2.00
	1970	10.090	—	.15	.75
	1970	.020	—	Proof	1.25
	1971(c) serifs on date numerals				
		10.000	—	.10	2.50
	1971(l) w/o serifs				
		.015	—	.10	4.00
	1971(l)	5,000	—	Proof	15.00
	1972	10.055	—	.10	2.75
	1972	8,045	—	Proof	6.00
	1973	15.055	—	.10	2.75
	1973	8,000	—	Proof	6.00
	1974	35.035	—	.10	1.00
31	1974	8,000	—	Proof	5.00
	1975	60.015	—	.10	.75
	1975	.010	—	Proof	5.00
	1976	20.016	—	.10	.75
	1976	.011	—	Proof	5.00
	1977	.020	—	.20	6.50
	1977	.012	—	Proof	5.50
	1978(o)	15.023	—	.10	.50
	1978(o)	.015	—	Proof	4.00
	1979(o)	35.025	—	.10	.50
	1979(o)	.016	—	Proof	4.00
	1980(l) round 0 in date				
		.027	—	.10	1.00
	1980(l)	.017	—	Proof	4.00
	1980(o) oval 0 in date				
		40.000	—	.10	.50
	1981(o) serif on 1				
		10.000	—	.10	.50
	1981(l) flat 1	.025	—	.10	1.00
	1981(l) flat 1	.018	—	Proof	4.00
	1982(o) shaped 2				
		10.000	—	.10	.25
	1982(l) straight 2				
		.025	—	.10	1.00
	1982(l) straight 2				
		.018	—	Proof	3.00
	1983(o) blunt 3				
		40.000	—	.10	.25
	1983(l) stylized 3				
		.025	—	.10	1.00
	1983(l) stylized 3				
		.018	—	Proof	3.00
	1984(o)	30.000	—	.10	.25
	1984(l)	.025	—	—	.50
	1984(l)	.015	—	Proof	1.75
	1985(o)	40.000	—	—	.25
	1985(c)	.020	—	—	.50
	1985(c)	.012	—	Proof	1.25

Obv: Similar to 1 Dollar, KM#57.

KM#	Date	Mintage	VF	XF	Unc
58	1986(o)	25.000	—	—	.15
	1986(l)	.018	—	—	.30
	1986(l)	.010	—	Proof	1.25
	1987(o)	27.500	—	—	.15
	1987(l)	.018	—	—	.30
	1987(l)	.010	—	Proof	1.25
	1988(l)	.015	—	—	8.00
	1988(l)	9,000	—	Proof	1.25

NOTE: The 1988 one cent was only struck for sets, no circulated strikes are available.

2 CENTS

BRONZE
Kowhai Leaves

KM#	Date	Mintage	VF	XF	Unc
32	1967	75.250	—	.15	.25
	1967	.050	—	Proof	1.00
	1968	.035		.15	1.50
	1968	.040	—	Proof	1.50
	1969	20.560	—	.15	1.00
	1969	.050	—	Proof	1.50
	1970	.030	—	.15	1.75
	1970	.020	—	Proof	1.50
	1971(c) serifs on date numerals				
		15.050	—	.10	4.25
	1971(l) w/o serifs				
		.015	—	.10	3.25
	1971(l)	5,000	—	Proof	17.00
	1972	17.525	—	.10	4.50
	1972	8,045	—	Proof	6.50
	1973	38.565	—	.10	3.00
	1973	8,000	—	Proof	6.25
	1974	50.015	—	.10	1.00
	1974	8,000	—	Proof	4.00
	1975	20.015	—	.10	.75
	1975	.010	—	Proof	4.00
	1976	15.016	—	.10	.75
	1976	.011	—	Proof	4.00
	1977	20.000	—	.10	.75
	1977	.012	—	Proof	4.00
	1978	.023	—	.10	4.75
	1978	.015	—	Proof	4.00
	1979	.025	—	.10	4.75
	1979	.016	—	Proof	4.00
	1980(l) round 0 in date				
		.027	—	.10	1.25
	1980(l)	.017	—	Proof	3.50
	1980(o) oval 0 in date				
		10.000	—	.10	1.25
	1981(o) serif on 1				
		25.000	—	.10	1.25
	1981(l) flat 1	.025	—	.10	1.25
	1981(l) flat 1	.018	—	Proof	3.50
	1982(o) shaped 2				
		50.000	—	.10	1.25
	1982(l) straight 2				
		.025	—	.10	1.35
	1982(l) straight 2				
		.018	—	Proof	3.50
	1983(o) blunt 3				
		15.000	—	.10	1.25

KM#	Date	Mintage	VF	XF	Unc
32	1983(l) stylized 3	.025	—	.10	1.00
	1983(l) stylized 3	.018	—	Proof	3.50
	1984(o)	10.000	—	.10	.50
	1984(l)	.025	—	.10	1.25
	1984(l)	.015	—	Proof	2.00
	1985(o)	22.500	—	.10	.25
	1985(c)	.020	—	—	1.35
	1985(c)	.012	—	Proof	1.50

Mule. Obv: Bahamas 5 Cent, KM#3. Rev: KM#32.

KM#	Date	Mintage	VF	XF	Unc
33	ND(1967)	*.050	15.00	20.00	35.00

Obv: Similar to 1 Dollar, KM#57.

KM#	Date	Mintage	VF	XF	Unc
59	1986(l)	.018	—	—	6.50
	1986(l)	.010	—	Proof	1.50
	1987(o)	36.250	—	—	.50
	1987(l)	.018	—	—	1.50
	1987(l)	.010	—	Proof	1.50
	1988(l)	.015	—	—	6.50
	1988(l)	9,000	—	Proof	1.50

5 CENTS

COPPER-NICKEL
Tuatara

KM#	Date	Mintage	VF	XF	Unc
34	1967	26.250	—	.15	.50
	1967 w/o sea line	Inc. Ab.	1.00	2.50	25.00
	1967	.050	—	Proof	1.25
	1968	.035	—	.15	1.50
	1968	.040	—	Proof	2.00
	1969	10.310	—	.15	.50
	1969	.050	—	Proof	1.60
	1970	11.182	—	.15	.70
	1970	.020	—	Proof	2.00
	1971(c) serifs on date numerals	11.520	—	.10	4.50
	1971(l) w/o serifs	.015	—	.10	3.50
	1971(l)	5,000	—	Proof	20.00
	1972	20.015	—	.10	1.75
	1972	8,045	—	Proof	7.00
	1973	4.039	—	.10	2.00
	1973	8,000	—	Proof	6.50
	1974	18.015	—	.10	2.25
	1974	8,000	—	Proof	5.00
	1975	32.015	—	.10	1.25
	1975	.010	—	Proof	5.50
	1976	.016	—	.10	8.00
	1976	.011	—	Proof	5.00
	1977	.020	—	.10	5.50
	1977	.012	—	Proof	5.00
	1978	20.023	—	.10	.50
	1978	.015	—	Proof	5.00
	1979	.025	—	.10	3.75
	1979	.016	—	Proof	5.00
	1980(l) round 0 in date	.027	—	.10	1.00
	1980(l)	.017	—	Proof	5.00
	1980(o) oval 0 in date	12.000	—	.10	1.00
	1981(o) serif on 1	20.000	—	.10	1.00
	1981(l) flat 1	.025	—	.10	1.00
	1981(l) flat 1	.018	—	Proof	4.00
	1982(o) shaped 2	50.000	—	.10	1.00
	1982(l) straight 2	.025	—	.10	1.00
	1982(l) straight 2	.018	—	Proof	4.00
	1983(l)	.025	—	.10	2.10
	1983(l)	.018	—	Proof	4.00
	1984(l)	.025	—	.10	2.10
	1984(l)	.015	—	Proof	4.00
	1985(o)	14.000	—	.10	.50
	1985(c)	.020	—	.10	1.50
	1985(c)	.012	—	Proof	4.00

Mule. Obv: KM#34. Rev: Canada 10 Cent, KM#77.

KM#	Date	Mintage	VF	XF	Unc
64	1981(o) serif on 1	—	—	—	—

KM#	Date	Mintage	VF	XF	Unc
60	1986(o)	18.000	—	.10	.50
	1986(l)	.018	—	—	1.00
	1986(l)	.010	—	Proof	4.00
	1987(o)	60.000	—	.10	.50
	1987(l)	.018	—	—	1.00
	1987(l)	.010	—	Proof	4.00
	1988(o)	16.000	—	.10	.50
	1988(l)	.015	—	—	1.00
	1988(l)	9,000	—	Proof	4.00
	1989	36.000	—	—	.25
	1989	—	—	Proof	4.00
	1990	—	—	—	1.00
	1990	.010	—	Proof	4.00
	1991	—	—	—	2.00
	1991	9,000	—	Proof	4.00
	1992	—	—	—	3.50
	1992	9,000	—	Proof	4.00
	1993	—	—	—	.75
	1993	—	—	Proof	4.00

1990 Anniversary Celebrations

KM#	Date	Mintage	VF	XF	Unc
72	1990	.010	—	—	1.00

3.2700 g, .925 SILVER, .0973 oz ASW

KM#	Date	Mintage	VF	XF	Unc
72a	1990	.010	—	Proof	12.00

10 CENTS

COPPER-NICKEL
Maori Mask

KM#	Date	Mintage	VF	XF	Unc
35	1967	17.250	—	.15	.45
	1967	.050	—	Proof	1.50
	1968	.035	—	.15	1.00
	1968	.040	—	Proof	2.50
	1969	3.050	—	.15	1.00
	1969	.050	—	Proof	2.00

KM#	Date	Mintage	VF	XF	Unc
41	1970	2.076	—	.15	1.00
	1970	.020	—	Proof	2.00
	1971(c) serifs on date numerals	2.800	1.00	3.50	35.00
	1971(l) w/o serifs	.015	—	.15	3.50
	1971(l)	5,000	—	Proof	30.00
	1972	2.039	—	.15	3.25
	1972	8,000	—	Proof	10.00
	1973	3.525	—	.10	1.75
	1973	8,000	—	Proof	7.50
	1974	4.619	—	.10	1.75
	1974	8,000	—	Proof	7.50
	1975	7.015	—	.10	1.75
	1975	.010	—	Proof	6.00
	1976	5.016	—	.10	1.75
	1976	.011	—	Proof	6.00
	1977	5.000	—	.10	1.25
	1977	.012	—	Proof	6.00
	1978	16.023	—	.10	1.25
	1978	.015	—	Proof	5.00
	1979	6.000	—	.10	1.00
	1979	.016	—	Proof	5.00
	1980(l) round 0 in date	.027	—	.10	1.00
	1980(l)	.017	—	Proof	5.00
	1980(o) oval 0 in date	28.000	—	.10	1.00
	1981(o)	5.000	—	.10	1.50
	1981(l)	.025	—	.10	1.00
	1981(l)	.018	—	Proof	5.00
	1982(o)	18.000	—	.10	1.00
	1982(l)	.025	—	.10	1.00
	1982(l)	.018	—	Proof	5.00

KM#	Date	Mintage	VF	XF	Unc
41	1983(l)	.025	—	.10	2.00
	1983(l)	.018	—	Proof	4.50
	1984(l)	.025	—	.10	2.00
	1984(l)	.015	—	Proof	4.50
	1985(o)	8.000	—	.10	1.00
	1985(c)	.020	—	—	1.00
	1985(c)	.012	—	Proof	4.50

KM#	Date	Mintage	VF	XF	Unc
61	1986(l)	.018	—	.10	4.50
	1986(l)	.010	—	Proof	4.50
	1987(o)	21.000	—	.10	.50
	1987(l)	.018	—	.10	1.00
	1987(l)	.010	—	Proof	4.50
	1988(o)	24.000	—	.10	.50
	1988(l)	.015	—	.10	1.50
	1988(l)	9,000	—	Proof	4.50
	1989	9.000	—	—	.50
	1989	—	—	Proof	4.50
	1990	—	—	—	1.50
	1990	.010	—	Proof	4.50
	1991	—	—	—	2.00
	1991	9,000	—	Proof	4.50
	1992	—	—	—	2.00
	1992	9,000	—	Proof	4.50
	1993	—	—	—	1.00
	1993	—	—	Proof	4.50

1990 Anniversary Celebrations

KM#	Date	Mintage	VF	XF	Unc
73	1990	.010	—	—	2.00

6.5300 g, .925 SILVER, .1942 oz ASW

KM#	Date	Mintage	VF	XF	Unc
73a	1990	.010	—	Proof	12.00

20 CENTS

COPPER-NICKEL
Kiwi

KM#	Date	Mintage	VF	XF	Unc
36	1967	13.250	—	.20	.75
	1967	.050	—	Proof	1.75
	1968	.035	—	.20	1.00
	1968	.040	—	Proof	3.00
	1969	2.500	—	.20	1.00
	1969	.050	—	Proof	2.50
	1970	.030	—	.20	1.25
	1970	.020	—	Proof	3.00
	1971(c) serifs on date numerals	1.600	1.00	4.50	35.00
	1971(l) w/o serifs	.015	—	.20	2.50
	1971(l)	5,000	—	Proof	50.00
	1972	1.531	—	.15	2.50
	1972	8,000	—	Proof	15.00
	1973	3.043	—	.15	2.50
	1973	8,000	—	Proof	8.00
	1974	4.527	—	.15	4.50
	1974	8,000	—	Proof	9.00
	1975	5.015	—	.15	1.75
	1975	.012	—	Proof	7.50
	1976	7.516	—	.15	1.50
	1976	.011	—	Proof	7.00
	1977	7.500	—	.15	1.50
	1977	.012	—	Proof	7.50
	1978	2.523	—	.15	1.25
	1978	.015	—	Proof	6.00
	1979	8.000	—	.15	1.25
	1979	.016	—	Proof	6.00
	1980(l) round 0 in date	.027	—	.15	1.50
	1980(l)	.017	—	Proof	6.00
	1980(o) oval 0 in date	9.000	—	.15	1.00
	1981(o) serif on 1	7.500	—	.15	1.00
	1981(l) flat 1	.025	—	.15	1.00
	1981(l) flat 1	.018	—	Proof	5.00
	1982(o) shaped 2	17.500	—	.15	1.00

KM#	Date	Mintage	VF	XF	Unc
36	1982(l) straight 2				
		.025	—	.15	1.00
	1982(l) straight 2				
		.018	—	Proof	5.00
	1983(o) blunt 3				
		2.500	—	.15	1.80
	1983(l) stylized 3				
		.025	—	.15	1.80
	1983(l) stylized 3				
		.018	—	Proof	5.00
	1984(o)	1.500	—	.15	1.50
	1984(l)	.025	—	.15	1.50
	1984(l)	.018	—	Proof	5.00
	1985(o)	6.000	—	.15	1.50
	1985(c)	.020	—	.15	1.50
	1985(c)	.012	—	Proof	5.00

Obv: Similar to 1 Dollar, KM#57.

KM#	Date	Mintage	VF	XF	Unc
62	1986(o)	12.500	—	.15	1.00
	1986(l)	.018	—	.25	1.00
	1986(l)	.010	—	Proof	5.00
	1987(o)	14.000	—	.15	1.00
	1987(l)	.018	—	.25	1.00
	1987(l)	.010	—	Proof	5.00
	1988(o)	12.500	—	.15	.50
	1988(l)	.015	—	.25	1.25
	1988(l)	9,000	—	Proof	5.00
	1989	5.000	—	—	1.00
	1989	—	—	Proof	5.00

1990 Anniversary Celebrations

KM#	Date	Mintage	VF	XF	Unc
74	1990	.010	—	—	2.50

13.0700 g, .925 SILVER, .3887 oz ASW

KM#	Date	Mintage	VF	XF	Unc
74a	1990	.010	—	Proof	12.00

COPPER-NICKEL

KM#	Date	Mintage	VF	XF	Unc
81	1990	5.000	—	—	.25
	1990	—	—	Proof	5.00
	1991	—	—	—	2.00
	1991	9,000	—	Proof	5.00
	1992	—	—	—	3.50
	1992	9,000	—	Proof	5.00
	1993	—	—	—	2.00
	1993	—	—	Proof	5.00

50 CENTS

COPPER-NICKEL
H.M.S. Endeavour

KM#	Date	Mintage	VF	XF	Unc
37	1967	10.250	—	.45	.75
	1967 dot above 1				
		Inc. Ab.	1.50	3.00	28.00
	1967	.050	—	Proof	2.00
	1968	.035	—	.45	2.00
	1968	.040	—	Proof	3.50
	1970	.030	—	.45	2.00
	1970	.050	—	Proof	3.50
	1971(c) serifs on date numerals				
		1.123	1.00	5.00	35.00
	1971(l) w/o serifs				
		.015	—	.35	4.50
	1971(l)	5,000	—	Proof	50.00
	1972	1.423	—	.35	4.50
	1972	8,045	—	Proof	20.00
	1973	2.523	—	.35	4.00
	1973	8,000	—	Proof	12.50
	1974	1.215	—	.35	3.50
	1974	8,000	—	Proof	12.50
	1975	3.815	—	.35	3.00
	1975	.010	—	Proof	9.00

KM#	Date	Mintage	VF	XF	Unc
37	1976	2.016	—	.35	1.50
	1976	.011	—	Proof	9.00
	1977	2.000	—	.35	1.50
	1977	.012	—	Proof	9.00
	1978	2.023	—	.35	1.50
	1978	.015	—	Proof	7.00
	1979	2.400	—	.35	2.00
	1979	.016	—	Proof	7.00
	1980(l) round 0 in date				
		.027	—	.35	1.50
	1980(l)	.017	—	Proof	7.00
	1980(o) oval in date				
		8.000	—	.35	1.50
	1981(o) serif on 1				
		4.000	—	.35	1.50
	1981(l) flat 1	.025	—	.35	1.50
	1981(l) flat 1	.018	—	Proof	7.00
	1982(o) shaped 2				
		6.000	—	.35	1.50
	1982(l) straight 2				
		.025	—	.35	2.00
	1982(l) straight 2				
		.018	—	Proof	7.00
	1983(l)	.025	—	.35	2.00
	1983(o)	—	—	.35	2.50
	1983(l)	.018	—	Proof	7.00
	1984(o)	2.000	—	.35	2.50
	1984(l)	.025	—	.35	2.00
	1984(l)	.015	—	Proof	6.00
	1985(o)	2.000	—	.35	2.50
	1985(c)	.020	—	.35	2.00
	1985(c)	.012	—	Proof	6.00

200th Anniversary Captain Cook's Voyage
Similar to KM#37.
Edge inscribed COOK BI-CENTENARY 1769-1969

KM#	Date	Mintage	VF	XF	Unc
39	1969	.050	—	.75	2.50
	1969	.050	—	Proof	4.00

KM#	Date	Mintage	VF	XF	Unc
63	1986(o)	5.200	—	.35	1.00
	1986(l)	.018	—	.50	1.50
	1986(l)	.010	—	Proof	6.00
	1987(o)	3.600	—	.35	1.00
	1987(l)	.018	—	.50	1.50
	1987(l)	.010	—	Proof	6.00
	1988(o)	8.800	—	.35	1.00
	1988(l)	.015	—	.50	.75
	1988(l)	9,000	—	Proof	6.00
	1989	—	—	—	1.50
	1989	—	—	Proof	6.00
	1990	—	—	—	1.50
	1990	.010	—	Proof	6.00
	1991	—	—	—	1.50
	1991	9,000	—	Proof	6.00
	1992	—	—	—	1.50
	1992	9,000	—	Proof	6.00
	1993	—	—	—	1.50
	1993	—	—	Proof	6.00

1990 Anniversary Celebrations

KM#	Date	Mintage	VF	XF	Unc
75	1990	.010	—	—	3.50

15.7400 g, .925 SILVER, .4682 oz ASW

KM#	Date	Mintage	VF	XF	Unc
75a	1990	.010	—	Proof	25.00

DOLLAR

COPPER-NICKEL
Decimalization Commemorative, lettered edge

KM#	Date	Mintage	VF	XF	Unc
38.1	1967	.450	—	.75	1.50
	1967	.050	—	Proof	3.00

Regular Issue, reeded edge

KM#	Date	Mintage	VF	XF	Unc
38.2	1971	.045	—	2.50	8.00
	1971	5,000	—	Proof	55.00
	1972	.042	—	2.00	6.00
	1972	8,045	—	Proof	20.00
	1972 RAM case				
		3,000	—	Proof	55.00
	1973	.037	—	2.00	6.00
	1973	.016	—	Proof	7.00
	1975	.030	—	2.00	6.00
	1975	.020	—	Proof	7.00
	1976	.036	—	2.25	6.50
	1976	.022	—	Proof	7.00

200th Anniversary Captain Cook's Voyage

KM#	Date	Mintage	VF	XF	Unc
40	1969	.400	—	1.00	2.00
	1969	.050	—	Proof	4.00

Royal Visit - Mount Cook

KM#	Date	Mintage	VF	XF	Unc
42	1970	.285	—	1.00	2.00
	1970	.020	—	Proof	5.00

Cook Islands

KM#	Date	Mintage	VF	XF	Unc
43	1970	.025	—	8.00	12.00
	1970	5,030	—	Proof	45.00

Commonwealth Games

KM#	Date	Mintage	VF	XF	Unc
44	1974	.515	—	1.00	1.75
	27.2160 g, .925 SILVER, .8095 oz ASW				
44a	1974	.018	—	Proof	22.50

COPPER-NICKEL
New Zealand Day - Kotuku

KM#	Date	Mintage	VF	XF	Unc
45	1974	.050	—	4.00	10.00
	1974	5,000	—	Proof	80.00

Waitangi Day - Treaty House

KM#	Date	Mintage	VF	XF	Unc
46	1977	.090	—	2.50	5.00
	27.2160 g, .925 SILVER, .8095 oz ASW				
46a	1977	.027	—	Proof	17.50

COPPER-NICKEL
25th Anniversary of Coronation - Parliament

KM#	Date	Mintage	VF	XF	Unc
47	1978	.123	—	1.00	2.25
	27.2160 g, .925 SILVER, .8095 oz ASW				
47a	1978	.033	—	Proof	12.00

COPPER-NICKEL

KM#	Date	Mintage	VF	XF	Unc
48	1979	.110	—	1.00	2.50
	27.2160 g, .925 SILVER, .8095 oz ASW				
48a	1979	.035	—	Proof	10.00

COPPER-NICKEL
Fantail

KM#	Date	Mintage	VF	XF	Unc
49	1980	.112	—	1.00	2.50
	27.2160 g, .925 SILVER, .8095 oz ASW				
49a	1980	.037	—	Proof	15.00

COPPER-NICKEL
Royal Visit
English Oak and N.Z. Kauri

KM#	Date	Mintage	VF	XF	Unc
50	1981	.100	—	1.00	2.50
	27.2160 g, .925 SILVER, .8095 oz ASW				
50a	1981	.038	—	Proof	12.00

COPPER-NICKEL
Takahe

KM#	Date	Mintage	VF	XF	Unc
51	1982	.065	—	1.25	3.00

27.2160 g, .925 SILVER, .8095 oz ASW

KM#	Date	Mintage	VF	XF	Unc
51a	1982	.035	—	Proof	15.00

COPPER-NICKEL
Royal Visit

KM#	Date	Mintage	VF	XF	Unc
52	1983	.040	—	2.00	4.00
	27.2160 g, .925 SILVER, .8095 oz ASW				
52a	1983	.017	—	Proof	18.00

COPPER-NICKEL
50 Years of New Zealand Coinage

KM#	Date	Mintage	VF	XF	Unc
53	1983	.065	—	1.00	2.50
	27.2160 g, .925 SILVER, .8095 oz ASW				
53a	1983	.035	—	Proof	13.50

COPPER-NICKEL
Chatham Island Black Robin

KM#	Date	Mintage	VF	XF	Unc
54	1984	.065	—	2.00	6.00
	27.2160 g, .925 SILVER, .8095 oz ASW				
54a	1984	.030	—	Proof	15.00

COPPER-NICKEL
Black Stilt
Obv: Similar to KM#38.1.

KM#	Date	Mintage	VF	XF	Unc
55	1985	.060	—	1.00	2.50
	27.2160 g, .925 SILVER, .8095 oz ASW				
55a	1985	.025	—	Proof	16.00

COPPER-NICKEL
Royal Visit

KM#	Date	Mintage	VF	XF	Unc
56	1986	.040	—	1.25	3.00

27.2160 g, .925 SILVER, .8095 oz ASW

KM#	Date	Mintage	VF	XF	Unc
56a	1986	.013	—	Proof	22.50

COPPER-NICKEL
Kakapo

KM#	Date	Mintage	VF	XF	Unc
57	1986	.053	—	1.00	2.50

27.2160 g, .925 SILVER, .8095 oz ASW

KM#	Date	Mintage	VF	XF	Unc
57a	1986	.021	—	Proof	16.00

COPPER-NICKEL
National Parks Centennial

KM#	Date	Mintage	VF	XF	Unc
65	1987	.053	—	1.25	3.00

27.2160 g, .925 SILVER, .8095 oz ASW

KM#	Date	Mintage	VF	XF	Unc
65a	1987	.021	—	Proof	15.00

COPPER-NICKEL
Yellow-eyed Penguin

KM#	Date	Mintage	VF	XF	Unc
66	1988	*.045	—	1.50	5.00

27.2160 g, .925 SILVER, .8095 oz ASW

KM#	Date	Mintage	VF	XF	Unc
66a	1988	*.019	—	Proof	35.00

COPPER-NICKEL
XIV Commonwealth Games-Runner
Obv: Similar to KM#66.

KM#	Date	Mintage	VF	XF	Unc
67	1989	—	—	1.25	3.50

27.2160 g, .925 SILVER, .8095 oz ASW

KM#	Date	Mintage	VF	XF	Unc
67a	1989	.080	—	Proof	17.50

COPPER-NICKEL
XIV Commonwealth Games-Gymnast
Obv: Similar to KM#66.

KM#	Date	Mintage	VF	XF	Unc
68	1989	—	—	1.25	3.50

27.2160 g, .925 SILVER, .8095 oz ASW

KM#	Date	Mintage	VF	XF	Unc
68a	1989	—	—	Proof	17.50

COPPER-NICKEL
XIV Commonwealth Games-Swimmer
Obv: Similar to KM#66.

KM#	Date	Mintage	VF	XF	Unc
69	1989	—	—	1.25	3.50

27.2160 g, .925 SILVER, .8095 oz ASW

KM#	Date	Mintage	VF	XF	Unc
69a	1989	—	—	Proof	17.50

COPPER-NICKEL
XIV Commonwealth Games-Weightlifter
Obv: Similar to KM#66.

KM#	Date	Mintage	VF	XF	Unc
70	1989	—	—	1.25	3.50

27.2160 g, .925 SILVER, .8095 oz ASW

KM#	Date	Mintage	VF	XF	Unc
70a	1989	—	—	Proof	17.50

COPPER-NICKEL
1990 Anniversary Celebrations - Treaty of Waitangi

KM#	Date	Mintage	VF	XF	Unc
76	1990	.040	—	1.25	3.00

27.2160 g, .925 SILVER, .8095 oz ASW

KM#	Date	Mintage	VF	XF	Unc
76a	1990	.014	—	Proof	30.00

ALUMINUM-BRONZE
Kiwi Bird

KM#	Date	Mintage	VF	XF	Unc
78	1990	40.000	—	—	2.00
	1991	10.000	—	—	2.00
	1991	.020	—	Proof	5.00
	1992	.015	—	—	2.00
	1992	9,000	—	Proof	5.00
	1993	—	—	—	2.00
	1993	—	—	Proof	5.00

8.0000 g, .925 SILVER, .2380 oz ASW

KM#	Date	Mintage	VF	XF	Unc
78a	1990	.010	—	Proof	10.00

2 DOLLARS

ALUMINUM-BRONZE
White Heron

KM#	Date	Mintage	VF	XF	Unc
79	1990	28.000	—	—	2.50
	1991	10.000	—	—	3.50
	1991	.020	—	Proof	7.00
	1992	.015	—	—	3.00
	1992	9,000	—	Proof	8.00

10.0000 g, .925 SILVER, .2974 oz ASW

KM#	Date	Mintage	VF	XF	Unc
79a	1990	.010	—	Proof	15.00

COPPER-ALUMINUM-NICKEL
Kingfisher

KM#	Date	Mintage	VF	XF	Unc
87	1993	—	—	—	2.50

10.0000 g, .925 SILVER, .2974 oz ASW

KM#	Date	Mintage	VF	XF	Unc
87a	1993	—	—	Proof	15.00

5 DOLLARS

ALUMINUM-BRONZE
ANZAC Memorial

KM#	Date	Mintage	VF	XF	Unc
71	1990	—	—	—	4.00
	1990	.060	—	Proof	20.00

COPPER-NICKEL
Rugby World Cup

KM#	Date	Mintage	VF	XF	Unc
80	1991	—	—	—	7.50
	27.6000 g, .925 SILVER, .8208 oz ASW				
80a	1991	.015	—	Proof	35.00

COPPER-NICKEL
25th Anniversary of Decimal Currency

KM#	Date	Mintage	VF	XF	Unc
82	1992	.019	—	—	10.00
	27.2200 g, .925 SILVER, .8096 oz ASW				
82a	1992	8,000	—	Proof	32.50
	COPPER-NICKEL				
	Mythological Maori Hero - Kupe				
83	1992	.040	—	—	6.00
	Abel Tasman				
84	1992	.040	—	—	6.00
	Captain James Cook				
85	1992	.040	—	—	6.00
	Christopher Columbus				
86	1992	.040	—	—	6.00

40th Anniversary of Coronation

KM#	Date	Mintage	VF	XF	Unc
88	1993	—	—	—	9.00
	27.2200 g, .925 SILVER, .8095 oz ASW				
88a	1993	*.015	—	Proof	35.00
	47.5250 g, .917 GOLD, 1.4010 oz AGW				
88b	1993	*500 pcs.	—	Proof	850.00
	31.4700 g, .955 SILVER, .9662 oz ASW				
	Hooker Sea Lion				
89	1993	.020	—	Proof	35.00

150 DOLLARS

16.9500 g, .917 GOLD, .4996 oz AGW
Kiwi

KM#	Date	Mintage	VF	XF	Unc
77	1990	3,200	—	Proof	350.00

SELECT SETS (SS)

KM#	Date	Mintage	Identification	Issue Price	Mkt. Val.
SS1	1965(7)	75,000	KM23.2-29.2	2.50	10.00

MINT SETS (MS)

KM#	Date	Mintage	Identification	Issue Price	Mkt. Val.
MS1	1965(7)	100,000	KM23.2-29.2	2.00	4.50
MS2	1967(7)	250,000	KM31-32,34-37,38.1	4.50	3.00
MS4	1968(6)	35,000	KM31-32,34-37	2.15	3.50
MS5	1969(7)	50,000	KM31-32,34-36,39-40	3.25	5.50
MS7	1970(7)	30,000	KM31-32,34,36-37,41-42	3.50	5.50
MS10	1971(7)	15,000	KM31-32,34,36-37,38.2,41	3.50	15.00
MS12	1972(7)	15,000	KM31-32,34,36-37,38.2,41	3.50	8.00
MS14	1973(7)	15,000	KM31-32,34,36-37,38.2,41	3.50	10.00
MS17	1974(7)	15,000	KM31-32,34,36-37,41,44	4.35	12.00
MS20	1975(7)	15,000	KM31-32,34,36-37,38.2,41	4.50	6.00
MS22	1976(7)	16,000	KM31-32,34,36-37,38.2,41	4.75	10.00
MS23	1977(7)	20,000	KM31-32,34,36-37,41,46	4.75	8.00
MS24	1978(7)	23,000	KM31-32,34,36-37,41,47	5.25	7.00
MS25	1979(7)	25,000	KM31-32,34,36-37,41,48	5.50	8.00
MS26	1980(7)	27,000	KM31-32,34,36-37,41,49	5.75	10.00
MS27	1981(7)	25,000	KM31-32,34,36-37,41,50	5.75	6.00
MS28	1982(7)	25,000	KM31-32,34,36-37,41,51	6.00	8.00
MS29	1983(7)	25,000	KM31-32,34,36-37,41,53	6.25	10.00
MS30	1984(7)	25,000	KM31-32,34,36-37,41,54	4.75	11.00
MS31	1985(7)	20,000	KM31-32,34,36-37,41,55	4.00	12.00
MS32	1986(7)	18,000	KM57-63	5.00	10.00
MS33	1987(7)	18,000	KM58-65	7.50	11.00
MS34	1988(7)	15,000	KM58-63,66	8.00	20.00
MS35	1989(5)	14,600	KM60-63,67	11.00	14.00
MS36	1990(6)	18,000	KM60-61,63,78-79,81	13.00	12.00
MS37	1990(5)	10,000	KM72-76	11.00	30.00
MS38	1991(7)	—	KM60-61,63,78-81	16.00	15.50
MS39	1992(7)	15,000	KM60-61,63,78-79,81-82	15.00	15.50
MS40	1992(4)	40,000	KM83-86	—	20.00

PROOF SETS (PS)

KM#	Date	Mintage	Identification	Issue Price	Mkt. Val.
PS1	1933(5)	*20 pcs.	KM1-5	—	3000.
PS2	1934(5)	—	KM1-5	—	10,000.
PS3	1935(6)	364 pcs.	KM1-6	—	4000.
PS4	1937(5)	*20 pcs.	KM7-11	—	3000.
PS5	1947(5)	—	KM7a-11a	—	2500.
PS6	1953(8)	7,000	KM23-30	—	80.00
PS7	1953(8)	—	KM23-30, Matte Proof	—	1500.
PS8	1954(4)	—	KM23-26	—	1000.
PS9	1964(6)	—	KM23-28	—	1500.
PS10	1965(7)	25,000	KM23.2-29.2 flat pack	—	10.00
PS11	1965(7)	400	KM23.2-29.2 red plush case	—	120.00
PS12	1967(7)	50,000	KM31-32,34-38 flat pack	10.00	4.00
PS13	1967(7)	400	KM31-32,34-38 blue plush case	—	120.00
PS14	1968(6)	40,000	KM31-32,34-37	7.00	4.50
PS15	1969(7)	50,000	KM31-32,34-36,39-40	7.00	6.00
PS16	1970(7)	20,000	KM31-32,34,36-37, 41-42	7.00	8.50
PS17	1971(7)	5,000	KM31-32,34,36-37, 38.2,41	15.00	100.00
PS18	1972(7)	8,045	KM31-32,34,36-37, 38.2,41	16.00	20.00
PS19	1973(7)	8,000	KM31-32,34,36-37, 38.2,41	16.00	16.50
PS20	1974(7)	8,000	KM31-32,34,36-37, 41,44a	14.00	27.50
PS21	1975(7)	10,000	KM31-32,34,36-37, 38.2,41	18.50	10.00
PS22	1976(7)	11,000	KM31-32,34,36-37, 38.2,41	19.00	10.00
PS23	1977(7)	12,000	KM31-32,34,36-37, 41,46a	19.50	16.50
PS24	1978(7)	15,000	KM31-32,34,36-37, 41,47a	23.50	16.50
PS25	1979(7)	16,000	KM31-32,34,36-37, 41,48a	25.50	14.50
PS26	1980(7)	17,000	KM31-32,34,36-37, 41,49a	42.00	20.00
PS27	1981(7)	18,000	KM31-32,34,36-37, 41,50a	37.00	14.00
PS28	1982(7)	18,000	KM31-32,34,36-37, 41,51a	33.00	16.50
PS29	1983(7)	18,000	KM31-32,34,36-37, 41,53a	40.00	16.50
PS30	1984(7)	15,000	KM31-32,34,36-37, 41,54a	28.00	16.50
PS31	1985(7)	11,500	KM31-32,34,36-37, 41,55a	27.00	20.00
PS32	1986(7)	10,000	KM57a,58-63	30.00	22.50
PS33	1987(7)	10,000	KM58-63,65a	38.00	20.00
PS34	1988(7)	9,000	KM58-63,66a	43.00	45.00
PS35	1989(5)	10,000	KM60-63,67a	44.50	35.00
PS36	1989(4)	8,600	KM67a-70a	132.00	65.00
PS37	1990(6)	10,000	KM60-61,63,78a-79a,81	52.00	40.00
PS38	1990(5)	10,000	KM72a-76a	110.00	95.00
PS39	1991(7)	—	KM60-61,63,78-79, 80a,81	61.00	47.50
PS40	1992(7)	9,000	KM60-61,63,78-79, 81,82a	58.00	50.00
PS41	1993(6)	—	KM60-61,63,78,81,87a	75.00	70.00

The Republic of Nicaragua, situated in Central America between Honduras and Costa Rica, has an area of 50,193 sq. mi. (129,494 sq. km.) and a population of *3.7 million. Capital: Managua. Agriculture, mining (gold and silver) and hardwood logging are the principal industries. Cotton, meat, coffee and sugar are exported.

Columbus sighted the coast of Nicaragua on Sept. 12, 1502 during the course of his last voyage of discovery. It was first visited in 1522 by conquistadores from Panama, under the command of Gil Gonzalez. The first settlements were established in 1524 at Granada and Leon by Francisco Hernandez de Cordoba. Nicaragua was incorporated, for administrative purpose, in the Captaincy General of Guatemala, which included every Central American state but Panama. Nicaragua's first governor was Pedro Arias Davila, appointed on June 1, 1827. The Captaincy General declared its independence from Spain on Sept. 15, 1821. The next year Nicaragua united with the Mexican Empire of Augustin de Iturbide, then in 1823 with the Central American Republic. When the federation was dissolved, Nicaragua declared itself an independent republic on April 30, 1838.

Dissension between the Liberals and Conservatives kept Nicaragua in turmoil, which made it possible for William Walker to make himself President in 1855. The two major political parties finally united to drive him out and in 1857 he was expelled. Comparative peace followed, but by 1912, Nicaragua had requested the U.S. Marines to restore order which began U.S. involvement until the Good Neighbor Policy was adopted in 1933. Anastasio Somoza Garcia assumed the Presidency in 1936. Elections were held beginning in 1963 to choose their officials.

MINT MARKS

H - Heaton, Birmingham
HF - Huguenin Freres, Le Locle
Mo - Mexico City
- Philadelphia, Pa.
- Sherritt
- Waterbury, Ct.

MONETARY SYSTEM

100 Centavos = 1 Peso

CENTAVO

COPPER-NICKEL

KM#	Date	Mintage	Fine	VF	XF	Unc
1	1878	.500	3.00	6.00	20.00	80.00
	1878	—	—	—	Proof	400.00

5 CENTAVOS

1.2500 g, .800 SILVER, .0322 oz ASW

KM#	Date	Mintage	Fine	VF	XF	Unc
2	1880H	.256	2.50	5.00	15.00	125.00
	1880H	—	—	—	Proof	250.00

KM#	Date	Mintage	Fine	VF	XF	Unc
5	1887H	1.000	2.00	4.00	10.00	50.00
	1887H	—	—	—	Proof	300.00

COPPER-NICKEL

KM#	Date	Mintage	Fine	VF	XF	Unc
8	1898	2.000	.75	2.00	8.00	35.00

KM#	Date	Mintage	Fine	VF	XF	Unc
9	1899	2.000	.50	1.50	7.00	25.00

10 CENTAVOS

2.5000 g, .800 SILVER, .0643 oz ASW

KM#	Date	Mintage	Fine	VF	XF	Unc
3	1880H	.552	4.00	8.00	25.00	75.00
	1880H	—	—	—	Proof	225.00

KM#	Date	Mintage	Fine	VF	XF	Unc
6	1887H	1.500	1.00	2.50	10.00	60.00
	1887H	—	—	—	Proof	350.00

20 CENTAVOS

5.0000 g, .800 SILVER, .1286 oz ASW

KM#	Date	Mintage	Fine	VF	XF	Unc
4	1880H	.288	3.00	7.50	35.00	125.00
	1880H	—	—	—	Proof	350.00

KM#	Date	Mintage	Fine	VF	XF	Unc
7	1887H	1.000	2.00	5.00	20.00	50.00
	1887H	—	—	—	Proof	500.00

MONETARY REFORM

100 Centavos = 1 Cordoba
12-1/2 Pesos = 1 Cordoba

1/2 CENTAVO

BRONZE

KM#	Date	Mintage	Fine	VF	XF	Unc
10	1912H	.900	1.00	2.50	10.00	30.00
	1912H	—	—	—	Proof	275.00
	1915H	.320	1.50	4.00	18.00	60.00
	1916H	.720	1.50	4.00	12.00	55.00
	1917	.720	1.50	4.00	12.00	45.00
	1922	.400	2.00	5.00	20.00	75.00
	1924	.400	1.00	3.00	12.00	50.00
	1934	.500	1.00	3.00	10.00	35.00
	1936	.600	.50	.75	5.00	20.00
	1937	1.000	.40	.60	4.00	15.00

CENTAVO

BRONZE

KM#	Date	Mintage	Fine	VF	XF	Unc
11	1912H	.450	1.00	3.00	10.00	35.00
	1912H	—	—	—	Proof	275.00
	1914H	.300	3.00	6.00	18.00	50.00
	1915H	.500	2.00	5.00	15.00	55.00
	1916H	.450	2.00	5.00	15.00	50.00
	1917	.450	2.00	5.00	15.00	50.00
	1919	.750	1.00	4.00	12.50	40.00

KM#	Date	Mintage	Fine	VF	XF	Unc
11	1920	.700	1.00	4.00	12.50	40.00
	1922	.500	1.00	4.00	12.50	45.00
	1924	.300	1.00	5.00	15.00	50.00
	1927	.250	1.50	7.50	18.00	65.00
	1928	.500	1.00	4.00	12.00	35.00
	1929	.500	1.00	4.00	12.00	30.00
	1930	.250	1.50	7.50	18.00	60.00
	1934	.500	1.00	3.00	6.00	20.00
	1935	.500	.50	2.00	4.00	15.00
	1936	.500	.50	2.00	4.00	15.00
	1937	1.000	.10	.50	3.00	12.50
	1938	2.000	.10	.50	3.00	10.00
	1940	2.000	.10	.50	3.00	10.00

BRASS

KM#	Date	Mintage	Fine	VF	XF	Unc
20	1943	1.000	.50	1.50	4.50	18.00

5 CENTAVOS

COPPER-NICKEL

KM#	Date	Mintage	Fine	VF	XF	Unc
12	1912H	.460	1.00	3.00	12.50	50.00
	1912H	—	—	—	Proof	300.00
	1914H	.300	1.00	4.00	18.00	60.00
	1915H	.160	2.00	5.00	25.00	100.00
	1919	.100	1.00	4.00	20.00	80.00
	1920	.150	1.00	3.00	15.00	70.00
	1927	.100	2.00	5.00	25.00	80.00
	1928	.100	1.00	3.00	18.00	50.00
	1929	.100	1.00	3.00	15.00	45.00
	1930	.100	1.00	3.00	15.00	40.00
	1934	.200	1.00	3.00	12.50	35.00
	1935	.200	1.00	3.00	12.50	35.00
	1936	.300	.50	1.00	5.00	18.00
	1937	.300	.50	1.00	5.00	18.00
	1938	.800	.50	1.00	5.00	15.00
	1940	.800	.50	1.00	5.00	12.50

BRASS
Plain edge

KM#	Date	Mintage	Fine	VF	XF	Unc
21	1943	2.000	.50	2.50	10.00	35.00

COPPER-NICKEL
B.N.N. on edge

KM#	Date	Mintage	Fine	VF	XF	Unc
24.1	1946	4.000	.10	.25	2.50	10.00
	1946	—	—	—	Proof	200.00
	1950	—	.10	.25	2.50	10.00
	1952	4.000	.10	.25	3.50	15.00
	1952	—	—	—	Proof	250.00
	1954	4.000	.10	.15	.25	5.00
	1954	—	—	—	Proof	250.00
	1956	5.000	.10	.15	.50	5.00
	1956	—	—	—	Proof	250.00

B.C.N. on edge

KM#	Date	Mintage	Fine	VF	XF	Unc
24.2	1962	3.000	—	.10	.15	.75
	1962	—	—	—	Proof	150.00
	1964	4.000	—	.10	.15	.75
	1965	10.000	—	.10	.15	.75

Reeded edge

KM#	Date	Mintage	Fine	VF	XF	Unc
24.3	1972	.020	—	—	Proof	2.50

NICKEL CLAD STEEL

KM#	Date	Mintage	Fine	VF	XF	Unc
24.3a	1972	10.000	—	—	.10	.25

ALUMINUM
F.A.O. Issue

KM#	Date	Mintage	Fine	VF	XF	Unc
27	1974	2.000	—	—	.40	1.00

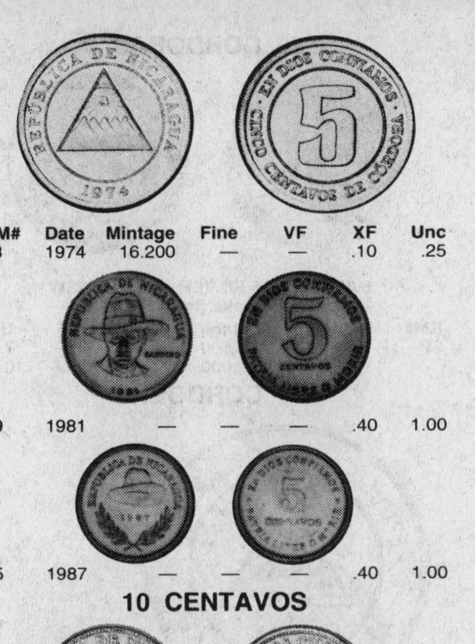

KM#	Date	Mintage	Fine	VF	XF	Unc
28	1974	16.200	—	—	.10	.25
49	1981	—	—	—	.40	1.00
55	1987	—	—	—	.40	1.00

10 CENTAVOS

2.5000 g, .800 SILVER, .0643 oz ASW

KM#	Date	Mintage	Fine	VF	XF	Unc
13	1912H	.230	1.50	3.50	15.00	60.00
	1912H	—	—	—	Proof	250.00
	1914H	.220	2.50	7.50	25.00	80.00
	1927	.500	1.00	2.00	7.50	50.00
	1928	1.000	.50	1.50	6.00	35.00
	1930	.150	1.50	3.00	15.00	60.00
	1935	.250	1.00	2.00	5.00	35.00
	1936	.250	1.00	2.00	5.00	25.00

NOTE: All dates of KM#13 are struck with medal rotation except 1935 which appears only in coin rotation.

COPPER-NICKEL
B.N.N. on edge

KM#	Date	Mintage	Fine	VF	XF	Unc
17.1	1939	2.500	.50	1.00	4.00	25.00
	1939	—	—	—	Proof	150.00
	1946	2.000	.25	.50	2.00	15.00
	1946	—	—	—	Proof	200.00
	1950	2.000	.25	.50	3.00	15.00
	1950	—	—	—	Proof	200.00
	1952	1.500	.25	.50	3.00	15.00
	1952	—	—	—	Proof	200.00
	1954	3.000	.10	.25	1.50	5.00
	1954	—	—	—	Proof	200.00
	1956	5.000	.10	.20	1.00	2.00
	1956	—	—	—	Proof	200.00

B.C.N. on edge

KM#	Date	Mintage	Fine	VF	XF	Unc
17.2	1962	4.000	—	.10	.15	1.25
	1962	—	—	—	Proof	225.00
	1964	4.000	—	.10	.15	1.50
	1965	12.000	—	.10	.15	.75

Reeded edge

KM#	Date	Mintage	Fine	VF	XF	Unc
17.3	1972	.020	—	—	Proof	2.50

NICKEL CLAD STEEL

KM#	Date	Mintage	Fine	VF	XF	Unc
17.3a	1972	10.000	—	.10	.15	.30

BRASS
Reeded edge

KM#	Date	Mintage	Fine	VF	XF	Unc
22	1943	2.000	.50	1.00	5.00	35.00

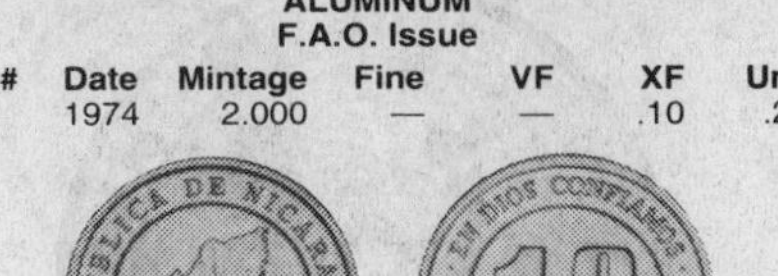

ALUMINUM
F.A.O. Issue

KM#	Date	Mintage	Fine	VF	XF	Unc
29	1974	2.000	—	—	.10	.25

KM#	Date	Mintage	Fine	VF	XF	Unc
30	1974	20.000	—	—	.10	.20

COPPER-NICKEL

KM#	Date	Mintage	Fine	VF	XF	Unc
31	1975	2.000	—	—	—	—
	1978	—	—	—	.40	1.25

ALUMINUM

KM#	Date	Mintage	Fine	VF	XF	Unc
50	1981	—	—	—	.15	.50

KM#	Date	Mintage	Fine	VF	XF	Unc
56	1987	—	—	—	.15	.50

25 CENTAVOS

6.2500 g, .800 SILVER, .1607 oz ASW

KM#	Date	Mintage	Fine	VF	XF	Unc
14	1912H	.320	2.00	5.00	30.00	70.00
	1912H	—	—	—	Proof	350.00
	1914H	.100	4.00	6.00	35.00	100.00
	1928	.200	2.00	5.00	20.00	45.00
	1929	.020	7.00	15.00	50.00	110.00
	1930	.020	7.00	15.00	50.00	100.00
	1936	.100	2.00	3.00	15.00	35.00

COPPER-NICKEL
B.N.N. on edge

KM#	Date	Mintage	Fine	VF	XF	Unc
18.1	1939	1.000	.50	1.50	6.50	30.00
	1939	—	—	—	Proof	250.00
	1946	1.000	.25	.50	1.50	12.50
	1946	—	—	—	Proof	280.00
	1950	1.000	.25	.50	1.50	10.00
	1950	—	—	—	Proof	300.00
	1952	1.000	.25	.50	1.50	7.00
	1952	—	—	—	Proof	280.00
	1954	2.000	.10	.20	.50	6.00
	1954	—	—	—	Proof	280.00
	1956	3.000	.10	.20	.50	2.50
	1956	—	—	—	Proof	280.00

B.C.N. on edge

KM#	Date	Mintage	Fine	VF	XF	Unc
18.2	1964	3.000	.10	.20	.40	2.00
	1965	4.400	.10	.20	.30	.75

Reeded edge

KM#	Date	Mintage	Fine	VF	XF	Unc
18.3	1972	4.000	—	.10	.15	.35
	1972	.020	—	—	Proof	2.50
	1974	6.000	—	.10	.15	.35

BRASS
Reeded edge

KM#	Date	Mintage	Fine	VF	XF	Unc
23	1943	1.000	.50	1.50	8.50	35.00

NICKEL CLAD STEEL
Mint: Sherritt

KM#	Date	Mintage	Fine	VF	XF	Unc
51	1981	—	—	—	.25	.75
	1985	—	—	—	—	—

ALUMINUM

KM#	Date	Mintage	Fine	VF	XF	Unc
57	1987	—	—	—	.25	1.00

50 CENTAVOS

12.5000 g, .800 SILVER, .3215 oz ASW

KM#	Date	Mintage	Fine	VF	XF	Unc
15	1912H	.260	5.00	12.50	35.00	125.00
	1912H	—	—	—	Proof	500.00
	1929	.020	7.00	15.00	50.00	200.00

COPPER-NICKEL
B.N.N. on edge

KM#	Date	Mintage	Fine	VF	XF	Unc
19.1	1939	1.000	.50	2.00	7.50	40.00
	1939	—	—	—	Proof	250.00
	1946	.500	.50	1.00	5.00	30.00
	1946	—	—	—	Proof	300.00
	1950	.500	.50	1.50	7.50	35.00
	1950	—	—	—	Proof	300.00
	1952	1.000	.25	1.00	5.00	20.00
	1952	—	—	—	Proof	300.00
	1954	2.000	.15	.50	2.00	5.00
	1954	—	—	—	Proof	300.00
	1956	2.000	.15	.25	1.00	4.00
	1956	—	—	—	Proof	300.00

B.C.N. on edge

KM#	Date	Mintage	Fine	VF	XF	Unc
19.2	1965	.600	.50	1.25	3.50	8.00
	1965	—	—	—	Proof	150.00

Reeded edge

KM#	Date	Mintage	Fine	VF	XF	Unc
19.3	1972	—	—	—	—	—
	1972	.020	—	—	Proof	2.50
	1974	2.000	.10	.25	.50	2.00

KM#	Date	Mintage	Fine	VF	XF	Unc
42	1980 Mo	5.000	.10	.25	.50	1.75
	1981 Mo	—	.10	.25	.50	1.75

NICKEL CLAD STEEL

KM#	Date	Mintage	Fine	VF	XF	Unc
42a	1983	—	—	—	.40	1.00
	1985	—	—	—	—	—

ALUMINUM-BRONZE

KM#	Date	Mintage	Fine	VF	XF	Unc
58	1987	—	—	—	.40	1.00

UN (1) CORDOBA

25.0000 g, .900 SILVER, .7234 oz ASW

KM#	Date	Mintage	Fine	VF	XF	Unc
16	1912H	.035	20.00	35.00	100.00	1350.
	1912H	—	—	—	Proof	1500.

COPPER-NICKEL
Reeded edge

KM#	Date	Mintage	Fine	VF	XF	Unc
26	1972	20.000	.10	.20	.50	2.00
	1972	—	—	—	Proof	5.00

KM#	Date	Mintage	Fine	VF	XF	Unc
43	1980 Mo	10.000	.10	.20	.50	2.00
	1981 Mo	—	.10	.20	.50	2.00
	1983	—	.10	.20	.50	2.00

NICKEL CLAD STEEL

KM#	Date	Mintage	Fine	VF	XF	Unc
43a	1984	—	—	.10	.50	2.00
	1985	—	—	.10	.50	2.00

ALUMINUM-BRONZE

KM#	Date	Mintage	Fine	VF	XF	Unc
59	1987	—	—	—	.50	2.00

27.0000 g, .925 SILVER, .8029 oz ASW
Ibero - American Series - 2 Figures

KM#	Date	Mintage	Fine	VF	XF	Unc
77	1991	.050	—	—	Proof	47.50

5 CORDOBAS

COPPER-NICKEL

KM#	Date	Mintage	Fine	VF	XF	Unc
44	1980	10.000	.15	.25	1.00	2.50

NICKEL CLAD STEEL

KM#	Date	Mintage	Fine	VF	XF	Unc
44a	1984	—	—	.25	1.00	3.00

ALUMINUM-BRONZE

KM#	Date	Mintage	Fine	VF	XF	Unc
60	1987	—	—	—	1.00	2.50

10 CORDOBAS

25.7000 g, .999 SILVER, .8263 oz ASW
Soccer

KM#	Date	Mintage	VF	XF	Unc
76	1991	—	—	Proof	50.00

19.9500 g, .999 SILVER, .6408 oz ASW
Spanish Royal Visit

KM#	Date	Mintage	VF	XF	Unc
78	1991	—	—	Proof	50.00

20 CORDOBAS

5.0300 g, .925 SILVER, .1496 oz ASW
Earthquake Relief Issue

KM#	Date	Mintage	VF	XF	Unc
32	1975	2,500	—	—	7.50
	1975	2,000	—	Proof	10.00

50 CORDOBAS

35.6000 g, .900 GOLD, 1.0300 oz AGW
100th Anniversary of Birth of Ruben Dario

KM#	Date	Mintage	VF	XF	Unc
25	1967HF	*.017	—	P/L	500.00

***NOTE:** Originally 500 pcs. were issued in blue boxes with certificates. An additional 16,000 pieces were struck later on. Boxed originals command a premium.

12.5700 g, .925 SILVER, .3738 oz ASW
U.S. Bicentennial

KM#	Date	Mintage	VF	XF	Unc
33	1975	2,000	—	—	10.00
	1975	2,000	—	Proof	15.00

Earthquake Relief Issue

KM#	Date	Mintage	VF	XF	Unc
34	1975	2,500	—	—	9.00
	1975	2,000	—	Proof	12.50

16.6000 g, .825 SILVER, .4403 oz ASW
Winter Olympics - Skier

KM#	Date	Mintage	VF	XF	Unc
61	1988	.010	—	Proof	50.00

Summer Olympics - Sailboat

KM#	Date	Mintage	VF	XF	Unc
62	1988	.010	—	Proof	50.00

100 CORDOBAS

25.1400 g, .925 SILVER, .6668 oz ASW
U.S. Bicentennial

KM#	Date	Mintage	VF	XF	Unc
35	1975	2,000	—	—	25.00
	1975	2,000	—	Proof	35.00

Earthquake Relief Issue

KM#	Date	Mintage	VF	XF	Unc
36	1975	2,700	—	—	20.00
	1975	2,000	—	Proof	32.50

200 CORDOBAS

2.1000 g, .900 GOLD, .0608 oz AGW
Pieta

KM#	Date	Mintage	VF	XF	Unc
37	1975	1,200	—	—	60.00
	1975	1,650	—	Proof	75.00

250 CORDOBAS

171.0700 g, .999 SILVER, 5.4946 oz ASW
Spanish Royal Visit
Obv: Similar to KM#78.

KM#	Date	Mintage	VF	XF	Unc
79	1992	—	—	Proof	160.00

500 CORDOBAS

5.4000 g, .900 GOLD, .1563 oz AGW
Colonial Church

KM#	Date	Mintage	VF	XF	Unc
38	1975	320 pcs.	—	—	250.00
	1975	100 pcs.	—	Proof	400.00

Earthquake Relief Issue

KM#	Date	Mintage	VF	XF	Unc
39	1975	1,000	—	—	150.00
	1975	1,650	—	Proof	225.00

14.0000 g, .925 SILVER, .4164 oz ASW
A.C. Sandino

KM#	Date	Mintage	VF	XF	Unc
45	1980 Mo	.021	—	Proof	25.00

Dobas Carlos Fonseca

KM#	Date	Mintage	VF	XF	Unc
46	1980 Mo	.021	—	Proof	25.00

Rigoberto Lopez Perez

KM#	Date	Mintage	VF	XF	Unc
47	1980 Mo	.021	—	Proof	25.00

14.0000 g, .999 SILVER, .4502 oz ASW
Birthplace of Augusto Cesar Sandino

KM#	Date	Mintage	VF	XF	Unc
69	1984	—	—	Proof	40.00

Generals Sandino, Estrada and Umanzor

KM#	Date	Mintage	VF	XF	Unc
70	1984	—	—	Proof	40.00

50th Anniversary of the Murder of
General Augusto Cesar Sandino

KM#	Date	Mintage	VF	XF	Unc
73	1984	—	—	Proof	40.00

ALUMINUM

KM#	Date	Mintage	VF	XF	Unc
63	1987	—	—	2.00	6.00

1000 CORDOBAS

9.5000 g, .900 GOLD, .2749 oz AGW
U.S. Bicentennial

KM#	Date	Mintage	VF	XF	Unc
40	1975	3,380	—	—	200.00
	1975	2,270	—	Proof	225.00

20.0000 g, .900 GOLD, .5788 oz AGW
1st Anniversary of Revolution

KM#	Date	Mintage	VF	XF	Unc
48	1980 Mo	6,000	—	Proof	450.00

20.0000 g, .917 GOLD, .5896 oz AGW
50th Anniversary of the Murder of
General Augusto Cesar Sandino

KM#	Date	Mintage	VF	XF	Unc
52	1984	1,000	—	Proof	500.00

Rev: Birthplace of Augusto Cesar Sandino.

KM#	Date	Mintage	VF	XF	Unc
53	1984	1,000	—	Proof	500.00

Rev: Generals Sandino, Estrada and Umanzor.

KM#	Date	Mintage	VF	XF	Unc
54	1984	1,000	—	Proof	500.00

2000 CORDOBAS

19.2000 g, .900 GOLD, .5556 oz AGW
U.S. Bicentennial

KM#	Date	Mintage	VF	XF	Unc
41	1975	320 pcs.	—	—	400.00
	1975	100 pcs.	—	Proof	700.00

16.6000 g, .825 SILVER, .4404 oz ASW
Soccer - 1 Player

KM#	Date	Mintage	VF	XF	Unc
65	1988	—	—	Proof	60.00

10000 CORDOBAS

20.0000 g, .999 SILVER, .6431 oz ASW
Discovery of Nicaragua by Columbus

KM#	Date	Mintage	VF	XF	Unc
64	1989	*.010	—	Proof	50.00

26.4000 g, .999 SILVER, .8480 oz ASW
Soccer - 2 Players

KM#	Date	Mintage	VF	XF	Unc
66	1990	.010	—	Proof	50.00

26.0000 g, .999 SILVER, .8352 oz ASW
Discovery of America - Sailing Ship

KM#	Date	Mintage	VF	XF	Unc
67	1990	—	—	Proof	45.00

1992 Summer Olympics - Bicyclist

KM#	Date	Mintage	VF	XF	Unc
68	1990	—	—	Proof	40.00

Wildlife - Tiger

KM#	Date	Mintage	VF	XF	Unc
71	1990	—	—	Proof	50.00

20.4000 g, .999 SILVER, .6553 oz ASW
1992 Summer Olympics - Equestrian

KM#	Date	Mintage	VF	XF	Unc
72.1	1990	.010	—	Proof	50.00

20.0000 g, .999 SILVER, .6431 oz ASW
Rev: "999" added at 4 o'clock.

KM#	Date	Mintage	VF	XF	Unc
72.2	1990	Inc. Ab.	—	Proof	40.00

25.9000 g, .999 SILVER, .8320 oz ASW
1992 Summer Olympics - Tennis

KM#	Date	Mintage	VF	XF	Unc
74	1990	.010	—	Proof	40.00

20.0000 g, .999 SILVER, .6431 oz ASW
1992 Winter Olympics - Figure Skater

KM#	Date	Mintage	VF	XF	Unc
75	1990	—	—	Proof	40.00

MINT SETS (MS)

KM#	Date	Mintage	Identification	Issue Price	Mkt. Val.
MS1	1975(5)	—	KM37-41	—	925.00
MS2	1975(5)	2,250	KM32-36	—	72.50

PROOF SETS (PS)

KM#	Date	Mintage	Identification	Issue Price	Mkt. Val.
PS1	1912(7)	10	KM10-16	—	3250.
PS2	1912(3)	2	Pn10,Pn12,Pn14	—	—
PS3	1912(7)	1	Pn11,Pn13,Pn15-19	—	—
PS4	1972(5)	20,000	KM17.3-19.3,24.3,26	8.00	15.00
PS5	1975(7)	—	KM32,33,35,37,38,40,41	—	1165.
PS6	1975(5)	2,000	KM32-36	—	110.00
PS7	1975(3)	—	KM32,33,35	115.00	60.00
PS8	1975(3)	—	KM34,36,39	—	170.00
PS9	1975(2)	—	KM37,39	—	300.00

NIGER

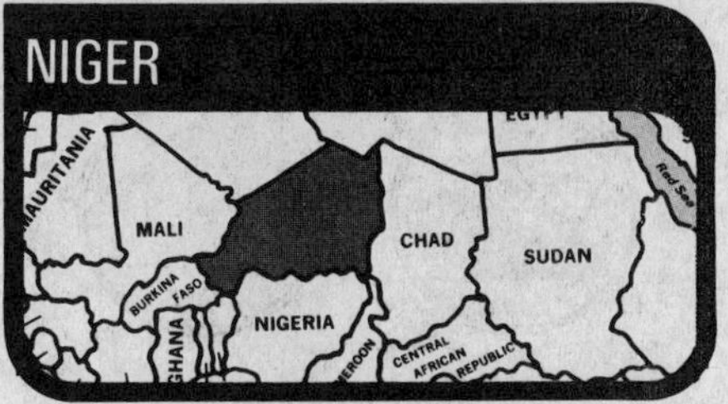

The Republic of Niger, located in West Africa's Sahara region 1,000 miles (1,609 km.) from the Mediterranean shore, has an area of 489,191 sq. mi. (1,267,000 sq. km.) and a population of *7.4 million. Capital: Niamey. The economy is based on subsistence agriculture and livestock raising. Peanuts, peanut oil, and livestock are exported.

Although four-fifths of Niger is arid desert, it was, some 6,000 years ago inhabited and an important economic crossroads. Its modern history began in the 19th century with the beginning of contacts with British and German explorers searching for the mouth of the Niger River. Niger was incorporated into French West Africa in 1896, but it was 1922 before all native resistance was quelled and Niger became a French colony. In 1958 the voters approved the new French Constitution and elected to become an autonomous republic within the French Community. On Aug. 3, 1960, Niger withdrew from the Community and proclaimed its independence.

10 FRANCS

4.2000 g, .900 GOLD, .1215 oz AGW
Independence Commemorative

KM#	Date	Mintage	VF	XF	Unc
1	1960	1,000	—	Proof	60.00

3.2000 g, .900 GOLD, .0926 oz AGW

KM#	Date	Mintage	VF	XF	Unc
7	1968	1,000	—	Proof	100.00

24.5400 g, .900 SILVER, .7100 oz ASW
Sharp details, raised rim.

KM#	Date	Mintage	VF	XF	Unc
8.1	1968	1,000	—	Proof	60.00

20.2000 g, .900 SILVER, .5845 oz ASW
Dull details, machined down rim.

KM#	Date	Mintage	VF	XF	Unc
8.2	1968	(restrike)	—	—	—

NOTE: Exists with and without accent marks above first E in REPUBLIQUE.

25 FRANCS

8.0000 g, .900 GOLD, .2315 oz AGW
Independence Commemorative

KM#	Date	Mintage	VF	XF	Unc
2	1960	1,000	—	Proof	125.00

KM#	Date	Mintage	VF	XF	Unc
9	1968	1,000	—	Proof	175.00

50 FRANCS

16.0000 g, .900 GOLD, .4630 oz AGW
Independence Commemorative

KM#	Date	Mintage	VF	XF	Unc
3	1960	1,000	—	Proof	250.00

KM#	Date	Mintage	VF	XF	Unc
10	1968	1,000	—	Proof	450.00

100 FRANCS

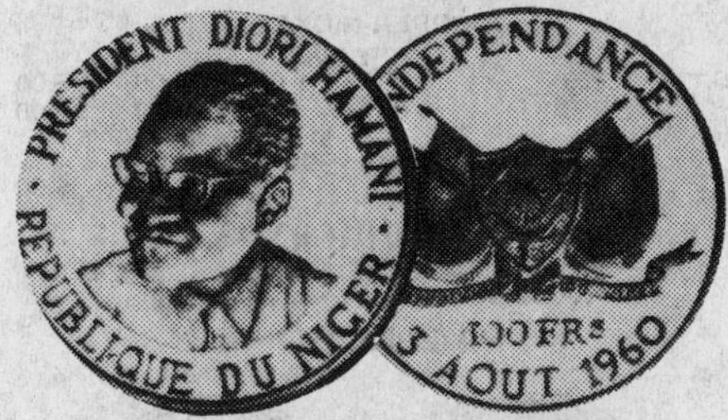

32.0000 g, .900 GOLD, .9260 oz AGW
Independence Commemorative

KM#	Date	Mintage	VF	XF	Unc
4	1960	1,000	—	Proof	525.00

KM#	Date	Mintage	VF	XF	Unc
11	1968	1,000	—	Proof	600.00

500 FRANCS

10.0000 g, .900 SILVER, .2893 oz ASW
Independence Commemorative

KM#	Date	Mintage	VF	XF	Unc
5	1960	—	—	Proof	30.00

1000 FRANCS

20.0000 g, .900 SILVER, .5787 oz ASW
Independence Commemorative

KM#	Date	Mintage	VF	XF	Unc
6	1960	—	—	Proof	45.00

PROOF SETS (PS)

KM#	Date	Mintage	Identification	Issue Price	Mkt. Val.
PS1	1960(4)	1,000	KM1-4	—	960.00
PS2	1968(4)	—	KM7,9-11	—	1325.

NIGERIA

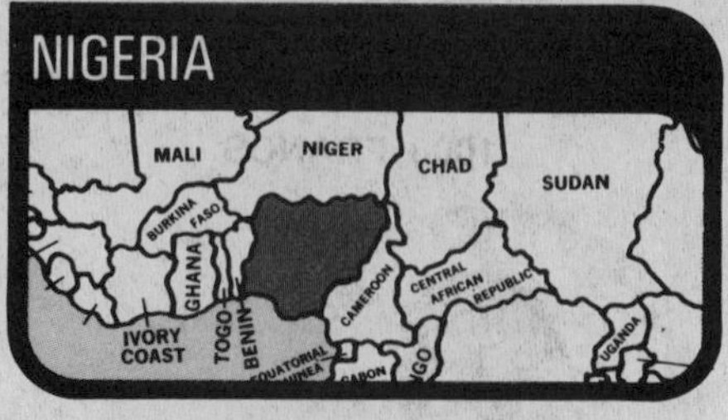

The Federal Republic of Nigeria, situated on the Atlantic coast of Africa between Benin and Cameroon, has an area of 356,669 sq. mi. (923,770 sq. km.) and a population of *115.2 million. Capital: Lagos. The economy is based on petroleum and agriculture. Crude oil, cocoa, tobacco and tin are exported.

Following the Napoleonic Wars, the British expanded their trade with the interior of Nigeria. British claims to a sphere of influence in that area were recognized by the Berlin Conference of 1885, and in the following year the Royal Niger Company was chartered. Direct British control of the territory was initiated in 1900, and in 1914 the amalgamation of Northern and Southern Nigeria into the Colony and Protectorate of Nigeria was effected. In 1960, following a number of territorial and constitutional changes, Nigeria was granted independence within the British Commonwealth as a federation of the Northern, Western and Eastern regions. Nigeria altered its political relationship with Great Britain on Oct. 1, 1963, by proclaiming itself a republic. It did, however, elect to remain a member of the Commonwealth of Nations. The Supreme Commander of Armed Forces is the Head of the Federal Military Government.

On May 30, 1967, the Eastern Region of the republic - an area occupied principally by the proud and resourceful Ibo tribe - seceded from Nigeria and proclaimed itself the independent Republic of Biafra with Odumegwu Ojukwu as Chief of State. Civil war erupted and raged for 31 months. Casualties, including civilian, were about two million, the majority succumbing to malnutrition and disease. Biafra surrendered to the federal government on January 15, 1970.

For earlier coinage refer to British West Africa.

RULERS

Elizabeth II, 1952-1963

MONETARY SYSTEM

12 Pence = 1 Shilling
20 Shillings = 1 Pound

1/2 PENNY

BRONZE

KM#	Date	Mintage	VF	XF	Unc
1	1959	52.800	.10	.20	.50
	1959	6,031	—	Proof	2.00

PENNY

BRONZE

KM#	Date	Mintage	VF	XF	Unc
2	1959	93.368	.10	.20	.75
	1959	6,031	—	Proof	2.50

3 PENCE

NICKEL-BRASS

KM#	Date	Mintage	VF	XF	Unc
3	1959	52.000	.15	.30	1.00
	1959	6,031	—	Proof	3.50

6 PENCE

COPPER-NICKEL

KM#	Date	Mintage	VF	XF	Unc
4	1959	35.000	.25	.50	1.50
	1959	6,031	—	Proof	5.00

SHILLING

COPPER-NICKEL

KM#	Date	Mintage	VF	XF	Unc
5	1959	18.000	.50	1.00	2.50
	1959	6,031	—	Proof	6.50
	1961	48.584	.50	1.00	2.50
	1961	—	—	Proof	—
	1962	39.416	.50	1.00	2.50

2 SHILLINGS

COPPER-NICKEL
Security edge

KM#	Date	Mintage	VF	XF	Unc
6.1	1959	15.000	1.00	2.00	5.00
	1959	6,031	—	Proof	9.00

Reeded edge

KM#	Date	Mintage	VF	XF	Unc
6.2	1959	Inc. Ab.	1.00	2.00	5.00

REPUBLIC

100 Kobo = 1 Naira (10 Shillings)

1/2 KOBO

BRONZE

KM#	Date	Mintage	VF	XF	Unc
7	1973	166.618	.45	1.00	2.50
	1973	.010	—	Proof	2.50

KOBO

BRONZE

KM#	Date	Mintage	VF	XF	Unc
8	1973	586.944	.25	.50	1.50
	1973	.010	—	Proof	3.00
	1974	14.500	.25	.50	1.50
	1987	—	.25	.50	1.50
	1988	—	.25	.50	1.50

COPPER PLATED STEEL

KM#	Date	Mintage	VF	XF	Unc
8a	1991	—	—	—	.50

5 KOBO

COPPER-NICKEL

KM#	Date	Mintage	VF	XF	Unc
9	1973	96.920	.35	.75	1.75
	1973	.010	—	Proof	4.00
	1974	—	.35	.75	1.75
	1976	9.800	.35	.75	1.75
	1987	—	.35	.75	1.75
	1988	—	.35	.75	1.75
	1989	—	.35	.75	1.75

10 KOBO

COPPER-NICKEL

KM#	Date	Mintage	VF	XF	Unc
10	1973	340.870	.50	1.00	2.00
	1973	.010	—	Proof	5.50
	1974	—	.50	1.00	2.00
	1976	7.000	.50	1.00	2.00
	1987	—	.50	1.00	2.00
	1988	—	.50	1.00	2.00
	1989	—	.50	1.00	2.00
	1990	—	.50	1.00	2.00

COPPER PLATED STEEL

KM#	Date	Mintage	VF	XF	Unc
12	1991	—	—	—	.75

25 KOBO

COPPER-NICKEL

KM#	Date	Mintage	VF	XF	Unc
11	1973	4.616	1.00	2.50	5.00
	1973	.010	—	Proof	7.50
	1975	—	1.00	2.50	5.00

COPPER PLATED STEEL

KM#	Date	Mintage	VF	XF	Unc
11a	1991	—	—	—	1.00

50 KOBO

NICKEL PLATED STEEL

KM#	Date	Mintage	VF	XF	Unc
13	1991	—	—	—	2.00

NAIRA

NICKEL PLATED STEEL

KM#	Date	Mintage	VF	XF	Unc
14	1991	—	—	—	4.50

PROOF SETS (PS)

KM#	Date	Mintage	Identification	Issue Price	Mkt. Val.
PS1	1959(6)	1,031	KM1-6, red case, originals	—	30.00
PS2	1959(6)	5,000	KM1-6, blue case, restrikes	—	15.00
PS3	1973(5)	10,200	KM7-11	14.70	22.50

BIAFRA

MONETARY SYSTEM

12 Pence = 1 Shilling

3 PENCE

ALUMINUM

KM#	Date	Mintage	VF	XF	Unc
1	1969	—	20.00	35.00	55.00

SHILLING

ALUMINUM

KM#	Date	Mintage	VF	XF	Unc
2	1969	—	12.50	17.50	25.00

Obv. value: ONE SHILLING

KM#	Date	Mintage	VF	XF	Unc
3	1969	—	—	175.00	275.00

2-1/2 SHILLINGS

ALUMINUM

KM#	Date	Mintage	VF	XF	Unc
4	1969	—	15.00	20.00	35.00

CROWN

SILVER

Independence and Liberty

KM#	Date	Mintage	VF	XF	Unc
5	1969	—	—	Rare	—

POUND

19.7600 g, .750 SILVER, .4765 oz ASW

KM#	Date	Mintage	VF	XF	Unc
6	1969	—	—	60.00	85.00

3.9940 g, .917 GOLD, .1177 oz AGW

2nd Anniversary of Independence

Obv: Similar to 25 Pounds, KM#11.

KM#	Date	Mintage	VF	XF	Unc
7	1969	3,000	—	Proof	70.00

2 POUNDS

7.9881 g, .917 GOLD, .2354 oz AGW

2nd Anniversary of Independence

Obv: Similar to 25 Pounds, KM#11.

KM#	Date	Mintage	VF	XF	Unc
8	1969	3,000	—	Proof	140.00

5 POUNDS

15.9761 g, .917 GOLD, .4710 oz AGW

2nd Anniversary of Independence

Obv: Similar to 25 Pounds, KM#11.

KM#	Date	Mintage	VF	XF	Unc
9	1969	3,000	—	Proof	270.00

10 POUNDS

39.9403 g, .917 GOLD, 1.1776 oz AGW

2nd Anniversary of Independence

Obv: Similar to 25 Pounds, KM#11.

KM#	Date	Mintage	VF	XF	Unc
10	1969	3,000	—	Proof	650.00

25 POUNDS

79.8805 g, .917 GOLD, 2.3553 oz AGW

2nd Anniversary of Independence

KM#	Date	Mintage	VF	XF	Unc
11	1969	3,000	—	Proof	1320.

PROOF SETS (PS)

KM#	Date	Mintage	Identification	Issue Price	Mkt. Val.
PS1	1969(5)	3,000	KM7-11	464.00	2450.

Listings For

NIGERIA - BRITISH WEST AFRICA: refer to British West Africa

NIUE

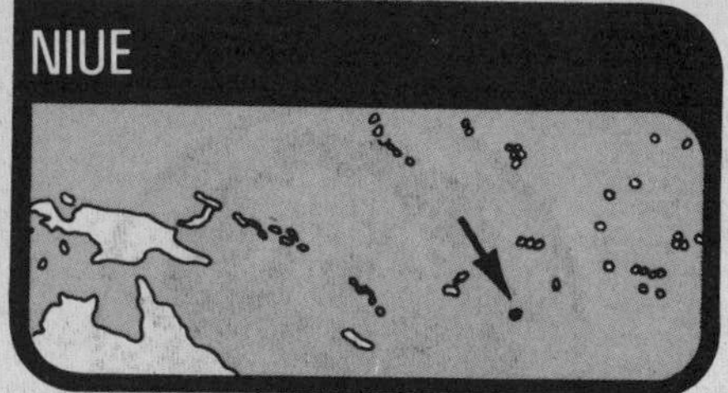

Niue, or Savage Island, a dependent state of New Zealand is located in the Pacific Ocean east of Tonga and south-east of Samoa. The size is 100 sq. mi. (260 sq. km.) with a population of *2,000. Chief village and port is Alofi. Bananas and copra are exported.

Discovered by Captain Cook in 1774, it was originally part of the Cook Islands administration but has been separate since 1922.

5 DOLLARS

COPPER-NICKEL
Olympic Tennis - Boris Becker

KM#	Date	Mintage	VF	XF	Unc
1	1987	.080	—	—	5.50

Olympic Tennis - Steffi Graf

KM#	Date	Mintage	VF	XF	Unc
5	1987	.050	—	—	5.50

Tennis - Steffi Graf

KM#	Date	Mintage	VF	XF	Unc
11	1988	—	—	—	6.00

Soccer - Franz Beckenbauer

KM#	Date	Mintage	VF	XF	Unc
12	1988	—	—	—	5.00

Tennis Navratilova, Graf and Evert

KM#	Date	Mintage	VF	XF	Unc
15	1988	—	—	—	5.50

John F. Kennedy

KM#	Date	Mintage	VF	XF	Unc
17	1988	.080	—	—	6.50

General Douglas MacArthur

KM#	Date	Mintage	VF	XF	Unc
22	1989	—	—	—	6.00

Davis Cup Tennis

KM#	Date	Mintage	VF	XF	Unc
24	1989	*.050	—	—	6.50

General Dwight D. Eisenhower

KM#	Date	Mintage	VF	XF	Unc
29	1990	—	—	—	6.00

General George S. Patton

KM#	Date	Mintage	VF	XF	Unc
31	1990	—	—	—	6.00

Admiral William Halsey
Rev: Portrait above ships.

KM#	Date	Mintage	VF	XF	Unc
33	1990	—	—	—	6.00

Franklin D. Roosevelt
Rev: Portrait.

KM#	Date	Mintage	VF	XF	Unc
35	1990	—	—	—	6.00

Winston Churchill
Rev: Portrait.

KM#	Date	Mintage	VF	XF	Unc
37	1990	—	—	—	6.00

10.0000 g, .500 SILVER, .1608 oz ASW
The Bounty

KM#	Date	Mintage	VF	XF	Unc
55	1992	*.150	—	—	12.50

9.9300 g, .500 SILVER, .1596 oz ASW
World Cup Soccer - Player & Statue of Liberty

KM#	Date	Mintage	VF	XF	Unc
58	1991	—	—	—	18.00

10.0000 g, .500 SILVER, .1608 oz ASW
Endangered Wildlife - Jaguar

KM#	Date	Mintage	VF	XF	Unc
60	1992	*.025	—	Proof	15.00

Olympics 1996 - Sprinter

KM#	Date	Mintage	VF	XF	Unc
61	1992	—	—	Proof	18.00

Protect Our World - Oak Tree

KM#	Date	Mintage	VF	XF	Unc
62	1993	—	—	Proof	15.00

10 DOLLARS

10.0000 g, .925 SILVER, .2974 oz ASW
Summer Olympics - Runners

KM#	Date	Mintage	VF	XF	Unc
46	1991	—	—	—	20.00

Summer Olympics - Discus Thrower

KM#	Date	Mintage	VF	XF	Unc
56	1991	—	—	Proof	20.00

31.5300 g, .999 SILVER, 1.0128 oz ASW
World Cup Soccer - Hand Shake

KM#	Date	Mintage	VF	XF	Unc
59	1991	—	—	Proof	40.00

20 DOLLARS

31.4700 g, .925 SILVER, .9359 oz ASW
40th Anniversary of Coronation

KM#	Date	Mintage	VF	XF	Unc
57	1993	*.010	—	Proof	55.00

Protect Our World - Hand Holding Seedling

KM#	Date	Mintage	VF	XF	Unc
63	1993	*.010	—	Proof	40.00

Kennedy and Statue of Liberty

KM#	Date	Mintage	VF	XF	Unc
64	1993	—	—	Proof	40.00

50 DOLLARS

27.1000 g, .625 SILVER, .5446 oz ASW
Olympic Tennis - Boris Becker

KM#	Date	Mintage	VF	XF	Unc
2	1987	.020	—	Proof	42.50

Olympic Tennis - Steffi Graf
Similar to 5 Dollars, KM#5.

KM#	Date	Mintage	VF	XF	Unc
6	1987	.020	—	Proof	42.50

Tennis - Steffi Graf
Similar to 5 Dollars, KM#11.

KM#	Date	Mintage	VF	XF	Unc
13	1988	*.020	—	Proof	42.50

Soccer - Franz Beckenbauer
Similar to 5 Dollars, KM#12.

KM#	Date	Mintage	VF	XF	Unc
14	1988	*.020	—	Proof	42.50

Tennis - Navratilova, Graf and Evert
Similar to 5 Dollars, KM#15.

KM#	Date	Mintage	VF	XF	Unc
16	1988	*.020	—	Proof	42.50

28.2800 g, .925 SILVER, .8411 oz ASW
John F. Kennedy
Similar to 5 Dollars, KM#17.

KM#	Date	Mintage	VF	XF	Unc
18	1988	.020	—	Proof	42.50

31.1030 g, .999 SILVER, 1.0000 oz ASW
General Douglas MacArthur
Obv: Similar to KM#2.

KM#	Date	Mintage	VF	XF	Unc
23	1989	*.050	—	Proof	35.00

28.2800 g, .925 SILVER, .8411 oz ASW
Davis Cup Tennis

KM#	Date	Mintage	VF	XF	Unc
25	1989	*.020	—	Proof	38.50

1992 Olympics - Rowing

KM#	Date	Mintage	VF	XF	Unc
27	1989	—	—	Proof	50.00

31.1030 g, .999 SILVER, 1.0000 oz ASW
General Dwight D. Eisenhower

KM#	Date	Mintage	VF	XF	Unc
30	1990	*.050	—	Proof	55.00

General George S. Patton

KM#	Date	Mintage	VF	XF	Unc
32	1990	*.050	—	Proof	55.00

Admiral William Halsey

KM#	Date	Mintage	VF	XF	Unc
34	1990	*.050	—	Proof	55.00

Franklin D. Roosevelt

KM#	Date	Mintage	VF	XF	Unc
36	1990	*.050	—	Proof	55.00

Winston Churchill

KM#	Date	Mintage	VF	XF	Unc
38	1990	*.050	—	Proof	55.00

28.2800 g, .925 SILVER, .8411 oz ASW
Soccer - 2 Players
Obv: Similar to 200 Dollars, KM#42.

KM#	Date	Mintage	VF	XF	Unc
43	1988	—	—	Proof	50.00

Tennis - Steffi Graf

KM#	Date	Mintage	VF	XF	Unc
44	1989	—	—	Proof	35.00

38.2000 g, .925 SILVER, 1.1361 oz ASW
Soccer - Player Kicking Ball

KM#	Date	Mintage	VF	XF	Unc
47	1990	—	—	Proof	60.00

155.5175 g, .999 SILVER, 5.0000 oz ASW
Kennedy and Apollo Rocket

KM#	Date	Mintage	VF	XF	Unc
65	1993	—	—	Proof	200.00

7.7760 g, .583 GOLD, .1458 oz AGW
John F. Kennedy

KM#	Date	Mintage	VF	XF	Unc
66	1993	—	—	Proof	110.00

100 DOLLARS

155.5175 g, .999 SILVER, 5.0000 oz ASW
Illustration reduced. Actual size: 65mm
Olympic Tennis - Boris Becker

KM#	Date	Mintage	VF	XF	Unc
3	1987	*5,000	—	Proof	125.00

Illustration reduced. Actual size: 65mm

Olympic Tennis - Steffi Graf

KM#	Date	Mintage	VF	XF	Unc
7	1987	*5,000	—	Proof	125.00

John F. Kennedy
Similar to 5 Dollars, KM#17.

KM#	Date	Mintage	VF	XF	Unc
19	1988	3,000	—	Proof	125.00

Soccer - Franz Beckenbauer
Similar to 5 Dollars, KM#12.

KM#	Date	Mintage	VF	XF	Unc
21	1988	—	—	Proof	125.00

Illustration reduced. Actual size: 65mm
Olympic Tennis - Steffi Graf

KM#	Date	Mintage	VF	XF	Unc
28	1989	—	—	Proof	125.00

Navratilova, Graf and Evert
Similar to 250 Dollars, KM#41.

KM#	Date	Mintage	VF	XF	Unc
40	1988	*3,000	—	Proof	125.00

200 DOLLARS

311.0350 g, .999 SILVER, 10.0000 oz ASW
Olympic Tennis - Boris Becker
Similar to 50 Dollars, KM#2.

KM#	Date	Mintage	VF	XF	Unc
4	1987	*3,000	—	Proof	165.00

Olympic Tennis - Steffi Graf
Similar to 50 Dollars, KM#5.

KM#	Date	Mintage	VF	XF	Unc
8	1987	*3,000	—	Proof	165.00

6.9117 g, .900 GOLD, .2000 oz AGW
General Douglas MacArthur

KM#	Date	Mintage	VF	XF	Unc
42	1989	*2,500	—	Proof	220.00

General Dwight D. Eisenhower

KM#	Date	Mintage	VF	XF	Unc
45	1990	2,500	—	Proof	220.00

General George S. Patton

KM#	Date	Mintage	VF	XF	Unc
50	1989	—	—	Proof	220.00

Admiral William Halsey

KM#	Date	Mintage	VF	XF	Unc
51	1990	—	—	Proof	220.00

President Franklin Delano Roosevelt

KM#	Date	Mintage	VF	XF	Unc
52	1990	—	—	Proof	220.00

Sir Winston Churchill

KM#	Date	Mintage	VF	XF	Unc
53	1990	—	—	Proof	220.00

250 DOLLARS

8.4830 g, .917 GOLD, .2500 oz AGW
Olympic Tennis - Boris Becker

KM#	Date	Mintage	VF	XF	Unc
9	1987	1,000	—	Proof	425.00

Olympic Tennis - Steffi Graf

KM#	Date	Mintage	VF	XF	Unc
10	1987	1,000	—	Proof	400.00

10.0000 g, .917 GOLD, .2948 oz AGW
John F. Kennedy

KM#	Date	Mintage	VF	XF	Unc
20	1988	5,000	—	Proof	175.00

Soccer - Beckenbauer

KM#	Date	Mintage	VF	XF	Unc
39	1988	*5,000	—	Proof	175.00

Navratilova, Graf and Evert

KM#	Date	Mintage	VF	XF	Unc
41	1988	*5,000	—	Proof	200.00

Olympic Tennis - Steffi Graf
Rev: Steffi holding cup and racket.

KM#	Date	Mintage	VF	XF	Unc
48	1988	—	—	Proof	250.00

Davis Cup Tennis

KM#	Date	Mintage	VF	XF	Unc
26	1989	500 pcs.	—	Proof	225.00

Olympic Tennis - Steffi Graf
Rev: Steffi concentrating on service.

KM#	Date	Mintage	VF	XF	Unc
49	1989	3,000	—	Proof	225.00

Soccer - Italian

KM#	Date	Mintage	VF	XF	Unc
54	1990	*2,500	—	Proof	225.00

Listings For

NORTH KOREA: refer to Korea
NORTH VIETNAM: refer to Vietnam

NORWAY

The Kingdom of Norway, a constitutional monarchy located in northwestern Europe, has an area of 150,000 sq. mi. (324,220 sq. km.), including the island territories of Spitzbergen (Svalbard) and Jan Mayen, and a population of *4.2 million. Capital: Oslo. The diversified economic base of Norway includes shipping, fishing, forestry, agriculture, and manufacturing. Nonferrous metals, paper and paperboard, paper pulp, iron, steel and oil are exported.

A united Norwegian kingdom was established in the 9th century, the era of the indomitable Norse Vikings who ranged far and wide, visiting the coasts of northwestern Europe, the Mediterranean, Greenland and North America. In the 13th century the Norse kingdom was united briefly with Sweden, then passed through inheritance in 1380 to the rule of Denmark which was maintained until 1814. In 1814 Norway fell again under the rule of Sweden. The union lasted until 1905 when the Norwegian Parliament arranged a peaceful separation and invited a Danish prince (King Haakon VII) to ascend the throne of an independent Kingdom of Norway. His son Olav V became King in 1957. Just prior to his death on Jan. 17, 1991, King Olav committed 10,000 troops to the Persian Gulf.

RULERS

Danish, until 1814
Swedish, until 1905
Haakon VII, 1905-1957
Olav V, 1957-1991
Harald V, 1991

MINT MARKS

(h) Crossed hammers - Kongsberg

MINTMASTERS INITIALS

Letter	Date	Name
AB,B	1961-1980	Arne Jon Bakken
AB*	1980	Ole R. Kolberg
B	1861	Brynjulf Bergslien
CHL,star(s)	1836-1888	Caspar Herman Langberg
I,IT	1880-1926	Ivar Trondsen, engraver
IGM	1797-1806	Johan Georg Madelung
IGP	1807-1824	Johan Georg Prahm
JMK	1825-1836	Johan Michael Kruse
K	1981	Ole R. Kolberg
M	1815-1830	Gregorius Middelthun
OH	1959	Oivind Hansen, engraver

MONETARY SYSTEM

1794-1873
120 Skilling = 1 Speciedaler

1/2 SKILLING

COPPER

KM#	Date	Mintage	VG	Fine	VF	XF
305.1	1839	.613	2.50	5.00	15.00	40.00
	1840	2.558	2.00	4.00	7.50	25.00
	1841	1.683	2.00	4.00	7.50	25.00

Rev: Star below hammers.

KM#	Date	Mintage	VG	Fine	VF	XF
305.2	1841	Inc. Ab.	1.00	2.50	6.00	20.00

KM#	Date	Mintage	Fine	VF	XF	Unc
324	1863	.480	5.00	12.50	35.00	85.00

KM#	Date	Mintage	Fine	VF	XF	Unc
329	1867	3.600	1.00	2.00	7.00	20.00

SKILLING

COPPER, 25mm
Obv: Crowned FR monogram.
Rev: 5-petalled rosettes, by 1 and below date.

KM#	Date	Mintage	VG	Fine	VF	XF
274.1	1809	.346	7.50	12.50	20.00	50.00

Rev: 8-petalled rosettes, by 1 and below date.

KM#	Date	Mintage	VG	Fine	VF	XF
274.2	1809	Inc. Ab.	7.50	12.50	20.00	50.00

Rev: Ovals by 1 and below date.

KM#	Date	Mintage	VG	Fine	VF	XF
274.3	1809	Inc. Ab.	7.50	12.50	20.00	50.00

KM#	Date	Mintage	VG	Fine	VF	XF
281	1812	5.453	1.00	2.50	5.00	10.00
	*1812 w/o crossed hammers below date					
		Inc. Ab.	20.00	45.00	75.00	120.00

*Beware of removed mint mark or altered coin.

KM#	Date	Mintage	VG	Fine	VF	XF
284	1816	1.659	4.00	10.00	25.00	75.00

KM#	Date	Mintage	VG	Fine	VF	XF
286	1819	3.817	4.00	10.00	25.00	55.00
	1820	Inc. Ab.	3.00	7.00	17.50	55.00
	1824	6,000	30.00	50.00	110.00	250.00
	1825	—	250.00	500.00	750.00	1500.
	1827	.034	30.00	50.00	100.00	225.00
	1828	.038	500.00	1000.	—	—
	1831/28	1.440	35.00	60.00	135.00	255.00
	1831	Inc. Ab.	35.00	60.00	135.00	255.00
	1832	Inc. Ab.	22.50	40.00	85.00	175.00
	1833	.126	22.50	40.00	85.00	175.00
	1834	—	1250.	—	—	—

KM#	Date	Mintage	Fine	VF	XF	Unc
335	1870	1.200	2.00	7.00	15.00	60.00

2 SKILLING

1.5000 g, .250 SILVER, .0120 oz ASW

KM#	Date	Mintage	VG	Fine	VF	XF
270	1801 IGM	1.109	20.00	5.00	9.00	20.00
	1802 IGM	2.854	20.00	5.00	9.00	20.00
	1803 IGM	2.410	20.00	5.00	9.00	20.00
	1804 IGM	3.634	4.00	10.00	18.00	35.00
	1805 IGM	2.412	3.00	8.00	15.00	30.00
	1807 IGP	3.507	2.00	5.00	9.00	18.00

NOTE: Earlier date (1800) exists for this type.

COPPER
Rev: 8-petalled rosettes by 2 and below date.

KM#	Date	Mintage	VG	Fine	VF	XF
280.1	1810	3.449	2.00	4.00	8.00	20.00

Rev: Cross.

KM#	Date	Mintage	VG	Fine	VF	XF
280.2	1810	Inc. Ab.	2.00	4.00	8.00	20.00
	1811	1.190	2.50	6.00	12.00	25.00

Rev: 5 petalled rosettes by 2 and below date.

280.3	1811	—	2.50	6.00	12.00	25.00

295	1822	.963	7.00	20.00	45.00	110.00
	1824	.549	7.00	20.00	45.00	110.00
	1825	.510	12.00	30.00	75.00	175.00
	1827	.288	12.00	30.00	65.00	150.00
	1828	.453	10.00	25.00	60.00	140.00
	1831/28	.723	7.00	17.50	40.00	100.00
	1831	Inc. Ab.	7.00	17.50	40.00	100.00
	1832	Inc. Ab.	7.00	17.50	40.00	100.00
	1833	.060	8.00	20.00	45.00	110.00
	1834	.880	40.00	80.00	140.00	300.00

1.5000 g, .250 SILVER, .0120 oz ASW, 17mm

297	1825	.240	7.00	15.00	30.00	60.00

310	1842	1.500	2.00	4.00	10.00	20.00
	1843	Inc. Ab.	3.00	7.50	15.00	30.00

Rev: Rosettes,

KM#	Date	Mintage	Fine	VF	XF	Unc
336.1	1870	.900	3.00	5.00	10.00	25.00
	1871	.900	3.00	5.00	10.00	25.00

Rev: Stars.

336.2	1871	1.140	3.00	5.00	10.00	25.00

3 SKILLING

2.2500 g, .250 SILVER, .0181 oz ASW
Rev: Rosettes.

330.1	1868	.499	5.00	8.00	16.00	40.00
	1869	.103	10.00	16.00	32.50	85.00

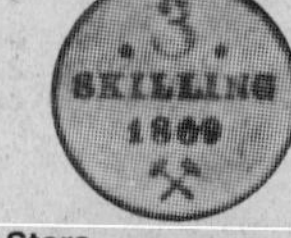

Rev: Stars.

330.2	1869	.600	5.00	8.00	16.00	45.00

Rev: Rosettes.

338.1	1872	.504	5.00	8.00	16.00	45.00

Rev: Stars.

338.2	1872	.576	5.00	8.00	16.00	45.00
	1873	.600	5.00	8.00	16.00	45.00

4 SKILLING

COPPER
Rev: Rosettes by 4 and below date.

KM#	Date	Mintage	VG	Fine	VF	XF
275.1	1809	.251	12.50	30.00	70.00	150.00

Rev: Stars by 4 and below date.

275.2	1809	Inc. Ab.	17.50	40.00	85.00	190.00
	1810					
	2 pcs. known		—	—	Rare	—

2.0500 g, .250 SILVER, .0165 oz ASW

276.1	1809 IGP rev. leg: SKILLE:	2.228	3.00	6.00	14.00	32.50
276.2	1809 IGP rev. leg: SKILLE =	Inc. Ab.	3.00	6.00	14.00	32.50

3.0000 g, .250 SILVER, .0241 oz ASW

298	1825 JMK	.333	6.00	12.50	25.00	50.00

311	1842	.750	3.00	7.00	20.00	50.00

KM#	Date	Mintage	Fine	VF	XF	Unc
337	1871	.559	7.00	12.50	25.00	50.00

6 SKILLING

COPPER
Obv: Crowned shield. Rev: Value.

KM#	Date	Mintage	VG	Fine	VF	XF
282	1813	.109	3.00	6.00	15.00	32.50

8 SKILLING

2.7300 g, .375 SILVER, .0329 oz ASW

KM#	Date	Mintage	VG	Fine	VF	XF
277	1809 IGP	1.350	5.00	10.00	20.00	45.00

3.3700 g, .500 SILVER, .0542 oz ASW

285	1817 IGP	.241	10.00	20.00	50.00	135.00

KM#	Date	Mintage	VG	Fine	VF	XF
287	1819 IGP	.101	15.00	30.00	75.00	150.00

1.9300 g, .875 SILVER, .0543 oz ASW

299	1825	.016	15.00	25.00	50.00	110.00
	1827/5	.014	15.00	25.00	50.00	110.00

12 SKILLING

COPPER
Obv: Crowned shield. Rev: Value.

KM#	Date	Mintage	VG	Fine	VF	XF
283	1813	.739	3.00	6.00	12.50	30.00

2.8900 g, .875 SILVER, .0813 oz ASW
Plain border

314.1	1845	.631	6.00	10.00	22.50	50.00
	1846	.250	6.50	10.00	25.00	55.00
	1847	.256	6.50	10.00	25.00	55.00
	1848	.316	6.50	10.00	25.00	55.00

Beaded border

314.2	1850 leg: V KONGE	.287	6.50	10.00	25.00	55.00
	1850 leg: V.KONGE	Inc. Ab.	7.00	13.00	25.00	60.00
	1852	.313	5.00	10.00	22.50	50.00
	1853	.360	5.00	10.00	22.50	50.00
	1854	.301	5.00	10.00	22.50	50.00
	1855	.450	5.00	10.00	22.50	50.00
	1856/5	.812	4.50	9.00	20.00	40.00
	1856	Inc. Ab.	4.00	7.00	18.00	35.00

Obv: Small head.

KM#	Date	Mintage	Fine	VF	XF	Unc
320	1861	2,500	450.00	800.00	1400.	2500.
	1862	2.500	450.00	800.00	1400.	2500.

Obv: Large head.

326	1865	.152	50.00	100.00	200.00	400.00

339	1873	.490	30.00	45.00	75.00	200.00

24 SKILLING

7.3100 g, .687 SILVER, .1615 oz ASW

KM#	Date	Mintage	VG	Fine	VF	XF
288	1819 IGP	.050	20.00	40.00	80.00	150.00

5.7300 g, .875 SILVER, .1612 oz ASW

KM#	Date	Mintage	VG	Fine	VF	XF
296	1823 IGP	.125	37.50	75.00	130.00	275.00
	1824 JMK	7,800	40.00	80.00	175.00	325.00

KM#	Date	Mintage	VG	Fine	VF	XF
300	1825	4,600	45.00	90.00	200.00	340.00
	1827/5	.027	30.00	65.00	135.00	250.00
	1827	Inc. Ab.	30.00	65.00	135.00	250.00
	1830	5,800	55.00	110.00	225.00	425.00
	1831/0	2,400	—	—	Rare	—
	1833	—	110.00	225.00	400.00	650.00
	1834	—	110.00	225.00	400.00	650.00
	1835	2,500	90.00	175.00	325.00	575.00
	1836	2,500	90.00	175.00	350.00	600.00

5.7800 g, .875 SILVER, .1626 oz ASW
Plain border

KM#	Date	Mintage	VG	Fine	VF	XF
315.1	1845	.357	8.00	17.50	40.00	75.00
	1846	.383	9.00	20.00	45.00	85.00
	1847	.217	9.00	20.00	45.00	85.00
	1848	.150	11.00	25.00	50.00	95.00

Beaded border

KM#	Date	Mintage	VG	Fine	VF	XF
315.2	1850	.102	11.00	25.00	50.00	100.00
	1852	.254	9.00	20.00	45.00	85.00
	1853	.327	9.00	20.00	45.00	85.00
	1854	.212	11.00	25.00	50.00	100.00
	1855	.204	8.00	17.50	40.00	80.00

Obv: Small head.

KM#	Date	Mintage	Fine	VF	XF	Unc
321	1861	13 pcs.	—	—	*Rare	—
	1862	1,200	500.00	900.00	1600.	2500.

***NOTE:** Heritage Long Beach sale 10-88 P/L BU realized $11,275.

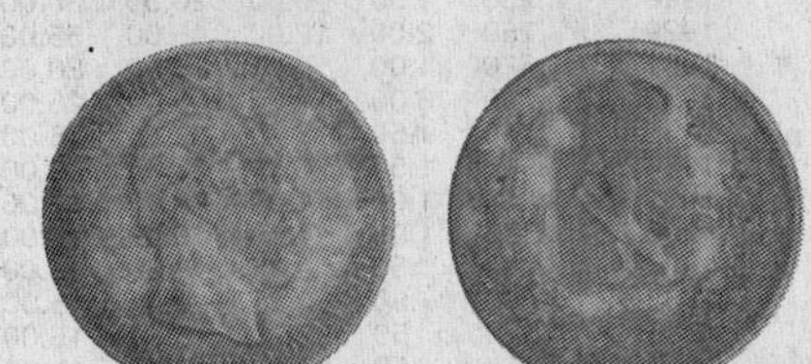

Obv: Large head.

KM#	Date	Mintage	Fine	VF	XF	Unc
327	1865	.079	75.00	125.00	275.00	500.00

1/15 SPECIE DALER

3.3700 g, .500 SILVER, .0542 oz ASW
Obv: Value, crowned oval arms. Rev: Value, date.

KM#	Date	Mintage	VG	Fine	VF	XF
271	1801 IGM	.382	5.00	10.00	15.00	50.00
	1802 IGM	.149	5.00	10.00	15.00	50.00

NOTE: Earlier dates (1795-1800) exist for this type.

1/5 SPECIE DALER

7.3100 g, .687 SILVER, .1615 oz ASW

KM#	Date	Mintage	VG	Fine	VF	XF
272	1801 IGM	.163	15.00	30.00	60.00	110.00
	1803 IGM	.092	15.00	30.00	60.00	110.00

NOTE: Earlier dates (1796-1800) exist for this type.

1/3 SPECIE DALER

9.6300 g, .875 SILVER, .2709 oz ASW
Similar to KM#273.

KM#	Date	Mintage	VG	Fine	VF	XF
266	1801 IGM	.108	25.00	55.00	110.00	225.00
	1802 IGM	.065	30.00	60.00	120.00	250.00
	1803 IGM	.024	35.00	65.00	125.00	260.00

NOTE: Earlier dates (1795-1800) exist for this type.

Obv: Bust right w/o bow, P.G. below portrait.

KM#	Date	Mintage	VG	Fine	VF	XF
273	1803 IGM	I.A.	125.00	250.00	500.00	1250.

1/2 SPECIE DALER

14.4500 g, .875 SILVER, .4065 oz ASW

KM#	Date	Mintage	VG	Fine	VF	XF
289	1819	.302	60.00	120.00	250.00	475.00
	1821	.069	40.00	70.00	120.00	230.00
	1823/1	6,100	90.00	180.00	325.00	650.00
	1824/1	.033	40.00	80.00	150.00	275.00
	1824	Inc. Ab.	40.00	80.00	150.00	275.00

KM#	Date	Mintage	VG	Fine	VF	XF
302	1827 SKI:	.070	40.00	75.00	135.00	290.00
	1827. SKI.	I.A.	40.00	75.00	135.00	290.00
	1829	5,100	150.00	300.00	500.00	850.00
	1830	8,000	90.00	180.00	300.00	550.00
	1831	9,000	90.00	180.00	300.00	550.00
	1832	4,700	90.00	180.00	300.00	550.00
	1833	1,500	90.00	180.00	300.00	550.00
	1834/29	.018	50.00	90.00	175.00	325.00
	1834	Inc. Ab.	50.00	90.00	175.00	325.00
	1835	9,000	50.00	90.00	175.00	325.00
	1835 star below mint mark					
		Inc. Ab.	—	—	Rare	—
	1836	4,000	60.00	120.00	225.00	350.00

KM#	Date	Mintage	VG	Fine	VF	XF
312	1844	.231	35.00	65.00	120.00	230.00

KM#	Date	Mintage	VG	Fine	VF	XF
316	1846	.146	35.00	65.00	120.00	230.00
	1847	.047	35.00	65.00	120.00	230.00
	1848	.015	40.00	70.00	140.00	275.00
	1849	.142	30.00	65.00	120.00	230.00
	1850	Inc. Ab.	30.00	65.00	120.00	230.00
	1855	.010	100.00	200.00	375.00	625.00

KM#	Date	Mintage	Fine	VF	XF	Unc
322	1861	500 pcs.	—	—	Rare	—
	1861 B below bust					
		13 pcs.	—	—	*Rare	—
	1862	.064	135.00	225.00	385.00	900.00

***NOTE:** Heritage Long Beach sale 10-88 P/L BU realized $14,575.

Obv: Larger head.

KM#	Date	Mintage	Fine	VF	XF	Unc
328	1865	700 pcs.	—	—	*Rare	—

***NOTE:** Oslo Mynthandel sale 10-89 VF realized $12,750.

KM#	Date	Mintage	Fine	VF	XF	Unc
340	1873	4,200	4500.	6000.	8500.	12,000.

SPECIE DALER

28.8900 g, .875 SILVER, .8127 oz ASW

KM#	Date	Mintage	VG	Fine	VF	XF
290	1819 IGP	.024	125.00	300.00	500.00	800.00
	1821 IGP	.101	75.00	120.00	250.00	500.00
	1823 IGP	.016	200.00	450.00	850.00	1500.
	1824/1 JMK					
		.121	60.00	125.00	275.00	525.00
	1824 JMK	I.A.	60.00	125.00	275.00	525.00

KM#	Date	Mintage	VG	Fine	VF	XF
301	1826	.025	70.00	140.00	275.00	500.00
	1826 initial M					
		Inc. Ab.	750.00	1500.	3000.	4500.
	1827/6	.132	60.00	120.00	230.00	425.00
	1827	Inc. Ab.	60.00	120.00	230.00	425.00
	1829/7	.016	75.00	170.00	350.00	600.00

KM#	Date	Mintage	VG	Fine	VF	XF
301	1829	Inc. Ab.	75.00	170.00	350.00	600.00
	1830	.026	60.00	120.00	275.00	500.00
	1831	.031	80.00	175.00	400.00	650.00
	1832	.024	80.00	175.00	400.00	650.00
	1833	2,732	500.00	1000.	2000.	3000.
	1834	.103	60.00	120.00	230.00	425.00
	1835	.040	60.00	120.00	230.00	425.00
	1835 star below mint mark					
		Inc. Ab.	200.00	500.00	900.00	1500.
	1836	.052	65.00	150.00	275.00	500.00

KM#	Date	Mintage	VG	Fine	VF	XF
313	1844	.302	60.00	120.00	230.00	435.00

KM#	Date	Mintage	VG	Fine	VF	XF
317	1846	.067	50.00	100.00	200.00	350.00
	1847	.140	50.00	100.00	200.00	350.00
	1848	.081	50.00	100.00	200.00	350.00
	1849	.114	50.00	100.00	200.00	350.00
	1850	.124	50.00	100.00	200.00	350.00
	1855	.148	50.00	100.00	200.00	350.00
	1856	.114	55.00	110.00	220.00	350.00
	1857	.160	55.00	110.00	220.00	350.00

Rev: Similar to KM#313.

KM#	Date	Mintage	Fine	VF	XF	Unc
323	1861	.044	225.00	450.00	800.00	1750.
	1861 B below bust					
		13 pcs.	—	—	Rare	—
	1862	.062	225.00	450.00	800.00	1750.

Rev: Similar to KM#313.

KM#	Date	Mintage	Fine	VF	XF	Unc
325	1864	.130	175.00	325.00	500.00	1000.
	1865	.086	175.00	325.00	500.00	1000.
	1867	.030	400.00	750.00	1250.	2750.
	1868	.114	200.00	400.00	750.00	1750.
	1869	.057	200.00	350.00	600.00	1250.

DECIMAL COINAGE

100 Ore = 1 Krone (30 Skilling)

ORE

BRONZE

KM#	Date	Mintage	VF	XF	Unc	BU
352	1876	8.000	8.00	15.00	60.00	80.00
	1877	2.166	25.00	45.00	115.00	150.00
	1878	1.834	37.50	60.00	160.00	200.00
	1884	3.378	8.00	15.00	60.00	80.00
	1885	.622	110.00	150.00	250.00	300.00
	1889	3.000	7.00	15.00	30.00	45.00
	1891	3.000	8.00	17.50	35.00	50.00
	1893	3.000	8.00	17.50	35.00	50.00
	1897	3.000	8.00	17.50	35.00	50.00
	1899	4.500	4.00	10.00	25.00	30.00
	1902	4.500	4.00	10.00	25.00	30.00

NOTE: Varieties exist.

KM#	Date	Mintage	VF	XF	Unc	BU
361	1906	3.000	4.00	9.00	17.50	20.00
	1907	2.550	4.00	10.00	22.50	25.00

KM#	Date	Mintage	VF	XF	Unc	BU
367	1908	1.450	15.00	25.00	75.00	90.00
	1910	2.480	2.50	7.00	25.00	27.50
	1911	3.270	2.50	7.00	30.00	32.50
	1912	2.850	7.00	15.00	85.00	100.00
	1913	2.840	2.50	6.00	20.00	22.00
	1914	5.020	2.50	5.00	20.00	22.00
	1915	1.540	15.00	25.00	110.00	125.00
	1921	3.805	35.00	50.00	125.00	175.00
	1922	Inc. Ab.	2.00	12.00	35.00	50.00
	1923	.770	12.00	25.00	65.00	90.00
	1925	3.000	1.50	10.00	35.00	45.00
	1926	2.200	1.50	10.00	35.00	45.00
	1927	.800	7.00	17.50	60.00	80.00
	1928	3.000	.75	4.00	18.00	20.00
	1929	4.990	.75	4.00	15.00	16.50
	1930 lg.dt.					
		2.010	1.00	5.00	20.00	22.00
	1930 sm.dt.					
		I.A.	1.00	5.00	20.00	22.00
	1931	2.000	1.00	5.00	20.00	22.00
	1932	2.500	1.00	5.00	20.00	22.00
	1933	2.000	1.00	5.00	15.00	16.50
	1934	2.000	1.00	5.00	15.00	16.50
	1935	5.495	.75	2.00	9.00	10.00
	1936	6.855	.75	2.00	9.00	10.00
	1937	6.020	.50	1.25	5.00	6.00
	1938	4.920	.50	1.25	5.00	6.00
	1939	2.500	.50	1.25	7.00	8.00
	1940	5.010	.50	1.25	5.00	6.00
	1941	12.260	.25	1.25	5.00	6.00
	1946	2.200	.25	1.25	7.00	8.50
	1947	4.870	.25	.75	4.00	5.00
	1948	9.405	.25	.75	3.50	4.00
	1949	2.785	.25	.75	5.00	6.00
	1950	5.730	.25	.75	3.50	4.00
	1951	16.670	.25	.75	3.50	4.00
	1952	Inc. Ab.	.25	.75	2.50	3.00

IRON

KM#	Date	Mintage	VF	XF	Unc	BU
367a	1918	6.000	8.00	15.00	30.00	45.00
	1919	12.930	3.50	10.00	20.00	22.50
	1920	4.445	10.00	20.00	40.00	60.00
	1921	2.270	35.00	55.00	125.00	140.00

World War II German Occupation

KM#	Date	Mintage	VF	XF	Unc	BU
387	1941	13.410	.50	1.50	9.00	10.00
	1942	37.710	.50	1.50	3.50	4.50
	1943	33.030	.50	1.50	3.50	4.50
	1944	8.820	.75	2.00	7.00	8.00
	1945	1.740	8.00	12.50	25.00	28.00

BRONZE

KM#	Date	Mintage	VF	XF	Unc	BU
398	1952					
		Inc. KM367	.10	.80	3.00	5.00
	1953	7.440	.10	.80	3.00	3.50
	1954	7.650	.10	.80	3.00	3.50
	1955	8.635	.10	.80	3.00	3.50
	1956	11.705	.10	.80	3.00	3.50
	1957	15.750	.10	.60	2.00	2.50

KM#	Date	Mintage	VF	XF	Unc	BU
403	1958	2.820	.50	2.00	5.00	7.00
	1959	9.120	.20	.75	4.00	6.00
	1960	7.890	.10	.25	2.00	2.50
	1961	5.671	.10	.25	2.00	2.50
	1962	12.180	.10	.20	1.00	1.25
	1963	8.010	.10	.25	2.00	2.50
	1964	11.020	—	.10	.60	.75
	1965	8.081	—	.10	1.25	1.50
	1966	12.431	—	.10	.80	1.00
	1967	13.026	—	.10	.60	.75
	1968	.126	1.00	2.00	5.00	7.00
	1969	6.291	—	.10	.35	.50
	1970	6.608	—	.10	.35	.50
	1971	18.966	—	.10	.25	.40
	1972	21.103	—	.10	.25	.40

2 ORE

BRONZE

KM#	Date	Mintage	VF	XF	Unc	BU
353	1876	1.774	7.00	16.00	65.00	80.00
	1877	1.976	6.00	14.00	45.00	55.00
	1884	1.000	9.00	20.00	60.00	75.00
	1889	1.000	6.00	12.50	35.00	45.00
	1891	1.000	5.00	10.00	45.00	55.00
	1893	1.000	5.00	10.00	45.00	55.00
	1897	1.000	5.00	10.00	45.00	55.00
	1899	1.000	5.00	10.00	45.00	55.00
	1902	1.005	4.00	8.00	30.00	40.00

KM#	Date	Mintage	VF	XF	Unc	BU
362	1906	.500	7.00	25.00	100.00	150.00
	1907	.980	4.00	10.00	45.00	75.00

KM#	Date	Mintage	VF	XF	Unc	BU
371	1909	.520	10.00	30.00	125.00	165.00
	1910	.500	10.00	30.00	200.00	250.00
	1911	.195	10.00	30.00	125.00	175.00
	1912	.805	10.00	30.00	125.00	175.00
	1913	2.010	2.00	6.00	40.00	50.00
	1914	2.990	2.00	6.00	40.00	50.00
	1915	Inc. Ab.	8.00	20.00	125.00	150.00
	1921	2.028	1.00	10.00	40.00	50.00
	1922	2.288	1.00	10.00	40.00	50.00
	1923	.745	2.00	10.00	75.00	90.00
	1928	2.250	1.00	5.00	20.00	30.00
	1929	.750	2.00	12.00	45.00	55.00
	1931	1.570	1.00	5.00	20.00	30.00
	1932	.630	6.00	15.00	100.00	125.00
	1933	.750	1.50	6.00	35.00	45.00
	1934	.500	1.50	6.00	35.00	45.00
	1935	2.223	1.00	4.00	20.00	22.00
	1936	4.533	1.00	4.00	20.00	22.00
	1937	3.790	.50	2.25	10.00	15.00
	1938	3.765	.50	2.25	10.00	15.00
	1939	4.420	.50	2.25	10.00	15.00
	1940	2.655	.50	2.25	10.00	15.00
	1946	1.575	.50	3.00	10.00	15.00
	1947	4.679	.25	1.00	5.00	10.00
	1948	1.003	3.00	4.00	12.00	16.00
	1949	1.455	.25	1.00	5.00	7.00
	1950	5.790	.25	1.00	4.00	6.00
	1951	10.540	.25	1.00	4.00	6.00
	1952	Inc. Ab.	.25	1.00	4.00	6.00

IRON

KM#	Date	Mintage	VF	XF	Unc	BU
371a	1917	.720	115.00	175.00	350.00	425.00
	1918	1.280	50.00	80.00	150.00	200.00
	1919	3.365	15.00	35.00	70.00	100.00
	1920	2.635	15.00	45.00	85.00	150.00

World War II German Occupation

KM#	Date	Mintage	VF	XF	Unc	BU
394	1943	6.575	.75	1.50	5.50	7.00
	1944	9.805	.75	1.50	5.50	7.00
	1945	2.520	3.00	5.00	12.50	15.00

BRONZE

KM#	Date	Mintage	VF	XF	Unc	BU
399	1952	Inc. Ab.	.10	.80	5.00	6.50
	1953	6.705	.10	.80	4.00	5.50
	1954	2.805	.10	.80	4.00	5.50
	1955	3.600	.10	.80	4.00	5.50
	1956	6.780	.10	.80	4.00	5.50
	1957	6.090	.10	.80	4.00	5.50

Rev: Small lettering.

KM#	Date	Mintage	VF	XF	Unc	BU
404	1958	2.700	.50	1.50	5.00	6.50

Rev: Large lettering.

KM#	Date	Mintage	VF	XF	Unc	BU
410	1959	4.125	.20	1.00	4.00	5.50
	1960	3.735	.10	.75	4.00	5.50
	1961	4.477	.10	.30	1.50	2.00
	1962	6.205	.10	.30	1.50	2.00
	1963	4.840	.10	.30	1.50	2.00
	1964	7.250	.10	.15	1.00	1.25
	1965	6.241	.10	.25	1.75	2.50
	1966	10.485	—	.10	1.50	2.00
	1967	11.993	—	.10	1.00	1.25
	1968	3,467				
		In mint sets only			650.00	800.00
	1969	.316	1.00	1.50	3.00	4.50
	1970	6.794	—	.10	.50	.80
	1971	15.462	—	.10	.40	.60
	1972	15.898	—	.10	.30	.50

5 ORE

BRONZE

KM#	Date	Mintage	VF	XF	Unc	BU
349	1875	.354	35.00	100.00	350.00	450.00
	1876	1.647	8.00	35.00	100.00	150.00
	1878	.500	20.00	50.00	225.00	275.00
	1896	1.000	6.00	30.00	100.00	125.00
	1899	.700	6.00	30.00	100.00	125.00
	1902	.705	6.00	30.00	100.00	125.00

KM#	Date	Mintage	VF	XF	Unc	BU
364	1907	.200	9.00	35.00	150.00	185.00

KM#	Date	Mintage	VF	XF	Unc	BU
368	1908	.600	35.00	60.00	200.00	250.00
	1911	.480	7.50	40.00	125.00	175.00
	1912	.520	10.00	50.00	300.00	375.00
	1913	1.000	2.50	17.50	85.00	110.00
	1914	1.000	2.50	17.50	85.00	110.00
	1915	Inc. Ab.	20.00	65.00	250.00	350.00
	1916	.300	12.50	30.00	150.00	200.00
	1921	.683	6.00	40.00	150.00	200.00
	1922	2.296	5.00	25.00	90.00	110.00
	1923	.456	7.50	40.00	150.00	200.00
	1928	.848	3.00	15.00	65.00	85.00
	1929	.452	9.00	30.00	150.00	200.00
	1930	1.292	2.50	17.50	65.00	85.00
	1931	.808	2.50	17.50	65.00	85.00
	1932	.500	10.00	30.00	90.00	110.00
	1933	.300	10.00	40.00	175.00	250.00
	1935	.496	5.00	15.00	60.00	80.00
	1936	.760	2.50	12.50	35.00	50.00
	1937	1.552	1.50	10.00	30.00	35.00
	1938	1.332	1.50	10.00	30.00	35.00
	1939	1.370	1.50	8.00	25.00	35.00
	1940	2.554	1.00	6.00	20.00	25.00
	1941	3.576	1.00	5.00	15.00	18.00
	1951	8.128	.50	2.00	10.00	12.00
	1952	Inc. Ab.	3.50	8.00	30.00	50.00

IRON

KM#	Date	Mintage	VF	XF	Unc	BU
368a	1917	1.700	40.00	60.00	100.00	125.00
	1918/7	.432	185.00	325.00	600.00	800.00
	1918	Inc. Ab.	175.00	300.00	575.00	800.00
	1919	3.464	30.00	50.00	100.00	150.00
	1920	1.629	60.00	90.00	200.00	250.00

World War II German Occupation

KM#	Date	Mintage	VF	XF	Unc	BU
388	1941	6.608	1.50	4.50	22.00	28.00
	1942	10.312	1.50	4.00	11.00	15.00
	1943	6.184	2.00	6.00	17.50	25.00
	1944	4.256	5.00	10.00	22.00	28.00
	1945	.408	150.00	225.00	350.00	450.00

BRONZE

KM#	Date	Mintage	VF	XF	Unc	BU
400	1952	Inc. KM368	1.00	2.00	12.50	30.00
	1953	6.216	1.00	2.00	8.00	12.50
	1954	4.536	1.00	2.00	8.00	12.50
	1955	6.570	1.00	2.00	8.00	12.50
	1956	2.959	1.00	2.00	10.00	15.00
	1957	5.624	1.00	2.00	7.00	10.00

KM#	Date	Mintage	VF	XF	Unc	BU
405	1958	2.205	2.00	5.00	20.00	30.00
	1959	3.208	.50	2.00	7.00	10.00
	1960	5.519	.20	1.00	6.00	9.00
	1961	4.554	.20	1.00	5.00	8.00
	1962	7.764	.15	.75	3.50	5.00
	1963	3.204	.15	.75	3.50	5.00
	1964	6.108	.10	.50	1.75	2.50
	1965	6.841	.10	.50	1.75	2.50
	1966	8.415	.10	.50	1.75	2.50
	1967	9.071	.10	.50	1.75	2.50
	1968	4.286	.10	.80	2.50	3.50
	1969	4.328	.10	.30	1.00	1.50
	1970	7.351	.10	.30	.75	1.25
	1971	13.450	.10	.30	1.00	1.50

KM#	Date	Mintage	VF	XF	Unc	BU
405	1972	19.002	—	.10	.40	.75
	1973	9.584	—	.10	.40	.75

KM#	Date	Mintage	VF	XF	Unc	BU
415	1973	52.886	—	.10	.25	.35
	1974	37.150	—	.10	.25	.35
	1975	32.479	—	.10	.25	.35
	1976	24.233	—	.10	.15	.25
	1977	29.646	—	.10	.15	.25
	1978	13.838	—	.10	.15	.25
	1979	25.255	—	.10	.15	.25
	1980	12.315	—	.10	.15	.25
	1980 w/o star	27.515	—	.10	.15	.25
	1981	24.529	—	.10	.15	.25
	1982	16.849	—	.10	.15	.25

10 ORE

(3 Skilling)

1.5000 g, .400 SILVER, .0192 oz ASW

KM#	Date	Mintage	VF	XF	Unc	BU
345	1874	2.000	20.00	40.00	125.00	200.00
	1875	.996	40.00	75.00	200.00	250.00

KM#	Date	Mintage	VF	XF	Unc	BU
350	1875	1.008	65.00	125.00	300.00	400.00
	1876	1.992	20.00	40.00	85.00	100.00
	1877	.588	90.00	140.00	300.00	400.00
	1878	.612	50.00	90.00	250.00	300.00
	1880	.600	40.00	60.00	120.00	150.00
	1882	.760	30.00	45.00	75.00	90.00
	1883	1.250	20.00	40.00	60.00	70.00
	1888	.500	35.00	55.00	100.00	125.00
	1889	.750	17.50	32.50	55.00	70.00
	1890	1.000	15.00	32.50	50.00	60.00
	1892	2.000	12.50	27.50	45.00	60.00
	1894	1.500	12.50	27.50	45.00	60.00
	1897	1.500	7.50	22.50	40.00	50.00
	1898	2.000	7.50	22.50	40.00	50.00
	1899	2.500	7.50	22.50	40.00	50.00
	1901	2.021	7.50	22.50	40.00	50.00
	1903	1.501	7.50	22.50	40.00	50.00

KM#	Date	Mintage	VF	XF	Unc	BU
372	1909	2.000	7.50	17.50	40.00	60.00
	1911	1.650	8.50	17.50	45.00	75.00
	1912	2.350	7.50	17.50	40.00	50.00
	1913	2.000	6.00	12.50	30.00	40.00
	1914	1.180	11.00	20.00	40.00	50.00
	1915	2.820	3.00	6.00	14.00	16.00
	1916	1.500	9.00	18.00	40.00	50.00
	1917	5.950	2.00	4.00	6.50	8.00
	1918/7	1.650	—	—	—	—
	1918	Inc. Ab.	2.50	7.50	14.00	16.00
	1919	7.800	2.00	4.00	6.50	8.00

COPPER-NICKEL

KM#	Date	Mintage	VF	XF	Unc	BU
378	1920	2.535	15.00	20.00	35.00	50.00
	1921	6.465	10.00	12.50	25.00	35.00
	1922	3.965	10.00	12.50	25.00	35.00
	1923	7.135	15.00	20.00	35.00	50.00

KM#	Date	Mintage	VF	XF	Unc	BU
383	1924	12.079	.75	7.50	30.00	40.00
	1925	7.051	.75	7.50	35.00	45.00
	1926	11.764	.75	7.50	30.00	40.00
	1927	.527	12.50	80.00	300.00	450.00
	1937	5.000	.75	4.00	12.50	22.00
	1938	3.413	.75	4.00	12.00	16.50
	1939	1.538	2.50	8.00	20.00	25.00
	1940	4.800	.75	1.50	8.00	10.00
	1941	10.150	.75	1.50	6.50	8.00
	1945	1.719	.25	1.50	12.00	16.50
	1946	3.723	.25	1.50	5.00	7.00
	1947	7.257	.25	1.50	4.00	5.00
	1948	3.105	.25	2.00	4.00	5.50
	1949	11.546	.25	1.50	4.00	5.50
	1951	5.150	.25	1.50	4.00	5.50

NICKEL-BRASS
World War II Government in exile.

KM#	Date	Mintage	VF	XF	Unc	BU
391	1942	*6.000	—	100.00	150.00	200.00

NOTE: All melted down except for 9,667.

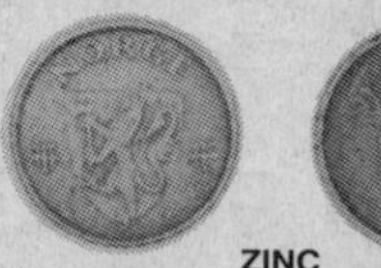
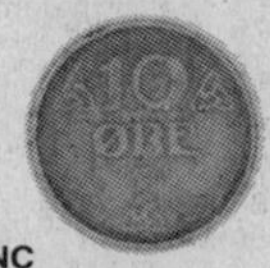

ZINC
World War II Nazi Occupation

KM#	Date	Mintage	VF	XF	Unc	BU
389	1941	15.310	2.00	5.00	15.00	25.00
	1942	50.388	1.00	3.00	6.00	10.00
	1943	13.378	2.00	4.50	12.00	20.00
	1944	3.549	12.50	25.00	75.00	125.00
	1945	5.646	8.00	15.00	30.00	50.00

COPPER-NICKEL

KM#	Date	Mintage	VF	XF	Unc	BU
396	1951	17.400	.30	2.00	15.00	20.00
	1952	Inc. Ab.	.20	1.25	5.00	10.00
	1953	7.700	.20	1.25	5.00	10.00
	1954	10.105	.20	1.25	6.00	12.00
	1955	9.830	.20	1.25	12.50	16.00
	1956	10.066	.20	1.25	5.00	10.00
	1957	22.900	.20	1.25	5.00	10.00

Rev: Small lettering.

KM#	Date	Mintage	VF	XF	Unc	BU
406	1958	1.425	1.50	2.50	6.50	12.50

Rev: Large lettering.

KM#	Date	Mintage	VF	XF	Unc	BU
411	1959	2.500	.75	2.50	7.50	10.00
	1960	12.490	.10	.50	3.00	5.00
	1961	10.386	.10	.50	3.00	5.00
	1962	16.210	.10	.50	2.00	3.00
	1963	17.560	.10	.50	2.00	3.00
	1964	9.781	.10	.25	.75	1.25
	1965	10.561	.10	.50	3.00	4.50
	1966	16.610	.10	.50	1.75	2.25
	1967	18.243	.10	.30	1.75	2.25
	1968	24.698	.10	.30	1.75	2.25
	1969	27.157	.10	.20	1.25	2.00
	1970	.639	1.00	2.00	3.50	5.00
	1971	8.904	.10	.15	.75	1.25
	1972	24.834	—	.10	.35	.75
	1973	22.301	—	.10	.35	.75

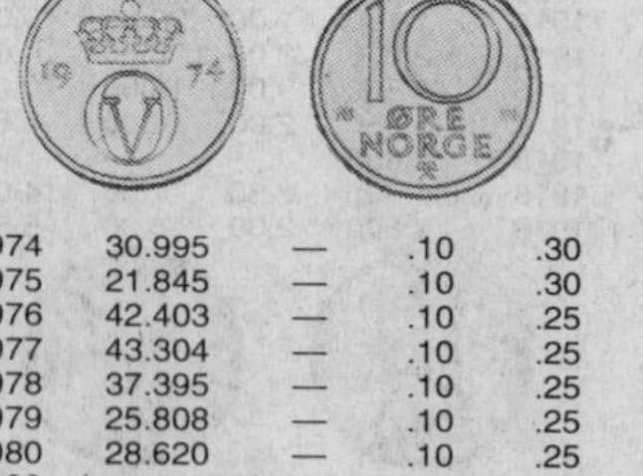

KM#	Date	Mintage	VF	XF	Unc	BU
416	1974	30.995	—	.10	.30	.50
	1975	21.845	—	.10	.30	.50
	1976	42.403	—	.10	.25	.35
	1977	43.304	—	.10	.25	.35
	1978	37.395	—	.10	.25	.35
	1979	25.808	—	.10	.25	.35
	1980	28.620	—	.10	.25	.35
	1980 w/o star	14.050	—	.10	.25	.35
	1981	43.083	—	.10	.25	.35
	1982	40.974	—	.10	.25	.35
	1983	45.637	—	.10	.25	.35
	1984	100.066	—	.10	.20	.30
	1985	103.108	—	.10	.20	.30
	1986	146.392	—	.10	.20	.30
	1987	166.040	—	.10	.20	.30
	1988	94.677	—	.10	.20	.30
	1989	97.274	—	.10	.20	.30
	1990	150.290	—	.10	.20	.30
	1991	—	—	.10	.20	.30
	1992	—	—	.10	.20	.30

25 ORE

2.4000 g, .600 SILVER, .0463 oz ASW

KM#	Date	Mintage	VF	XF	Unc	BU
354	1876	3.200	15.00	40.00	100.00	125.00

KM#	Date	Mintage	VF	XF	Unc	BU
360	1896	.400	30.00	80.00	200.00	250.00
	1898	.400	30.00	80.00	200.00	250.00
	1899	.600	16.00	40.00	85.00	100.00
	1900	.400	30.00	70.00	185.00	200.00
	1901	.607	16.00	40.00	85.00	100.00
	1902	.612	16.00	40.00	85.00	100.00
	1904	.600	16.00	40.00	85.00	100.00

KM#	Date	Mintage	VF	XF	Unc	BU
373	1909	.600	20.00	40.00	80.00	95.00
	1911	.400	30.00	55.00	110.00	125.00
	1912	.200	75.00	130.00	250.00	325.00
	1913	.400	25.00	50.00	110.00	125.00
	1914	.400	25.00	55.00	115.00	135.00
	1915	1.032	10.00	20.00	40.00	50.00
	1916	.368	30.00	55.00	125.00	150.00
	1917	.400	30.00	50.00	120.00	150.00
	1918/6	.800	17.50	32.50	40.00	50.00
	1918	Inc. Ab.	10.00	20.00	35.00	45.00
	1919	1.600	8.00	15.00	25.00	35.00

COPPER-NICKEL

KM#	Date	Mintage	VF	XF	Unc	BU
381	1921	4.800	10.00	15.00	25.00	32.50
	1922	14.200	10.00	15.00	25.00	32.50
	1923	5.200	20.00	27.50	45.00	55.00

KM#	Date	Mintage	VF	XF	Unc	BU
382	1921	Inc. KM381	5.00	25.00	200.00	300.00
	1922	Inc. KM381	4.00	18.00	140.00	200.00
	1923	Inc. KM381	3.00	15.00	100.00	150.00

KM#	Date	Mintage	VF	XF	Unc	BU
384	1924	4.000	2.00	6.00	40.00	50.00
	1927	6.200	1.50	6.00	40.00	50.00
	1929	.800	5.00	17.50	85.00	110.00
	1939	1.220	.75	3.00	20.00	30.00
	1940	1.160	.75	3.00	20.00	30.00
	1946	1.850	.50	1.50	5.00	8.00
	1947	2.592	.50	1.50	3.50	5.50
	1949	2.602	.50	1.50	3.50	5.50
	1950	2.800	.50	1.50	3.50	5.50

NICKEL-BRASS
World War II Government in exile.

KM#	Date	Mintage	VF	XF	Unc	BU
392	1942	*2.400	—	100.00	150.00	200.00

***NOTE:** All melted down except for 10,300 pieces.

ZINC
World War II German Occupation

KM#	Date	Mintage	VF	XF	Unc	BU
395	1943	14.105	1.50	3.50	15.00	25.00
	1944	3.031	7.50	17.50	35.00	50.00
	1945	3.010	10.00	20.00	45.00	60.00

COPPER-NICKEL

KM#	Date	Mintage	VF	XF	Unc	BU
401	1952	4.060	.25	1.00	5.00	15.00
	1953	3.320	.25	1.00	7.50	20.00
401	1954	3.140	.25	1.00	5.00	15.00
	1955	2.000	.25	1.00	15.00	40.00
	1956	3.980	.25	1.00	5.00	15.00
	1957	7.660	.25	1.00	5.00	15.00

KM#	Date	Mintage	VF	XF	Unc	BU
407	1958	1.316	1.00	2.50	12.00	20.00
	1959	1.184	1.00	2.50	12.00	20.00
	1960	3.964	.10	1.00	4.50	6.50
	1961	4.656	.10	.90	3.50	5.50
	1962	6.304	.10	.90	3.50	5.50
	1963	3.640	.10	.90	3.50	5.50
	1964	4.953	.10	.40	1.25	2.00
	1965	2.798	.10	.60	2.50	4.00
	1966	6.075	.10	.60	1.50	2.50
	1967	6.641	.10	.60	1.50	2.50
	1968	4.963	.10	.40	1.25	2.00
	1969	12.427	.10	.15	.75	1.50
	1970	1.545	.10	.60	3.00	5.00
	1971	5.247	—	.10	.50	1.00
	1972	7.929	—	.10	.50	1.00
	1973	8.516	—	.10	.50	1.00

KM#	Date	Mintage	VF	XF	Unc	BU
417	1974	8.048	—	.10	.30	.50
	1975	15.595	—	.10	.30	.50
	1976	24.721	—	.10	.20	.40
	1977	20.150	—	.10	.20	.40
	1978	11.259	—	.10	.20	.40
	1979	16.666	—	.10	.20	.40
	1980	6.289	—	.10	.20	.40
	1980 w/o star	8.176	—	.10	.20	.40
	1981	17.971	—	.10	.20	.40
	1982	16.863	—	.10	.20	.40

50 ORE

(15 Skilling)

5.0000 g, .600 SILVER, .0964 oz ASW

KM#	Date	Mintage	VF	XF	Unc	BU
346	1874	.160	90.00	190.00	450.00	500.00
	1875	.640	100.00	225.00	500.00	600.00

Rev: W/o 15 SK.

KM#	Date	Mintage	VF	XF	Unc	BU
356	1877	.800	35.00	125.00	350.00	400.00
	1880	.120	125.00	225.00	550.00	650.00
	1885	.100	140.00	250.00	600.00	700.00
	1887	.200	55.00	100.00	225.00	250.00
	1888	.100	80.00	175.00	350.00	450.00
	1889	.200	35.00	75.00	160.00	200.00
	1891	.400	25.00	50.00	120.00	150.00
	1893	.600	20.00	45.00	120.00	150.00
	1895	.200	25.00	55.00	130.00	155.00
	1896	.500	25.00	60.00	140.00	160.00
	1897	.200	40.00	75.00	200.00	250.00
	1898	.300	25.00	60.00	140.00	150.00
	1899	.200	30.00	65.00	175.00	250.00
	1900	.300	20.00	50.00	130.00	155.00
	1901	.404	20.00	50.00	130.00	155.00
	1902	.301	20.00	50.00	130.00	155.00
	1904	.101	100.00	200.00	350.00	500.00

KM#	Date	Mintage	VF	XF	Unc	BU
374	1909	.200	35.00	65.00	115.00	135.00
	1911	.200	40.00	75.00	125.00	160.00
	1912	.200	60.00	100.00	180.00	220.00
	1913	.200	40.00	75.00	160.00	200.00
	1914	.800	9.00	17.50	40.00	60.00
	1915	.300	25.00	50.00	100.00	125.00

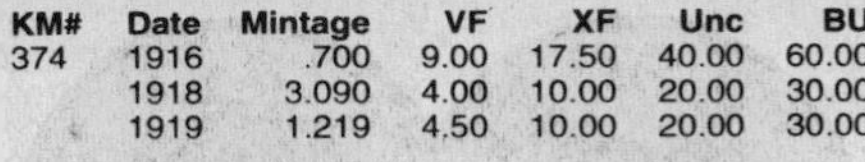

KM#	Date	Mintage	VF	XF	Unc	BU
374	1916	.700	9.00	17.50	40.00	60.00
	1918	3.090	4.00	10.00	20.00	30.00
	1919	1.219	4.50	10.00	20.00	30.00

COPPER-NICKEL

KM#	Date	Mintage	VF	XF	Unc	BU
379	1920	1.236	35.00	50.00	80.00	100.00
	1921	7.345	12.50	20.00	35.00	45.00
	1922	3.000	12.50	20.00	35.00	45.00
	1923	4.540	65.00	85.00	135.00	160.00

KM#	Date	Mintage	VF	XF	Unc	BU
380	1920	Inc. KM379	50.00	150.00	650.00	700.00
	1921	Inc. KM379	8.00	50.00	350.00	400.00
	1922	Inc. KM379	6.00	40.00	200.00	250.00
	1923	Inc. KM379	6.00	35.00	150.00	200.00

KM#	Date	Mintage	VF	XF	Unc	BU
386	1926	2.000	1.50	12.50	40.00	60.00
	1927	2.502	1.50	10.00	40.00	60.00
	1928/7	1.458	2.50	12.00	40.00	60.00
	1928	Inc. Ab.	1.50	12.50	40.00	60.00
	1929	.600	5.00	30.00	250.00	400.00
	1939	.900	.60	4.00	30.00	50.00
	1940	2.193	.50	3.00	14.00	16.50
	1941	2.373	.50	3.00	10.00	15.00
	1945	1.354	.50	2.00	17.50	22.50
	1946	1.533	.50	3.00	10.00	15.00
	1947	2.465	.50	3.00	9.00	12.50
	1948	5.911	.40	1.50	7.50	12.00
	1949	1.030	1.00	4.00	14.00	16.50

NICKEL-BRASS
World War II Government in Exile

KM#	Date	Mintage	VF	XF	Unc	BU
393	1942	*1.600	—	110.00	150.00	170.00

***NOTE:** All melted down except for 9,238.

ZINC
World War II Nazi Occupation

KM#	Date	Mintage	VF	XF	Unc	BU
390	1941	7.761	3.00	7.50	35.00	75.00
	1942	7.606	2.50	6.00	20.00	30.00
	1943	3.349	20.00	50.00	100.00	135.00
	1944	1.542	15.00	30.00	60.00	85.00
	1945	.226	250.00	400.00	550.00	650.00

COPPER-NICKEL

KM#	Date	Mintage	VF	XF	Unc	BU
402	1953	2.370	.60	1.50	12.00	17.50
	1954	.230	9.00	50.00	200.00	400.00
	1955	1.930	.40	2.00	25.00	32.50
	1956	1.630	.40	2.00	25.00	32.50
	1957	1.800	.40	2.00	12.50	18.00

KM#	Date	Mintage	VF	XF	Unc	BU
408	1958	1.560	.75	2.50	20.00	35.00
	1959	.340	2.00	10.00	45.00	60.00
	1960	1.584	.10	1.50	6.50	10.00
	1961	2.425	.10	.75	4.00	6.50
	1962	3.064	.10	.75	4.00	6.50
	1963	2.168	.10	.75	4.00	6.50
	1964	2.692	.10	.50	3.00	5.00
	1965	1.248	.75	2.50	15.00	20.00
	1966	4.262	.10	.25	1.50	3.00
	1967	4.001	.10	.25	1.50	3.00
	1968	5.431	.10	.25	1.50	3.00
	1969	7.591	.10	.25	.75	1.50
	1970	.481	.75	2.00	5.00	7.00
	1971	2.489	.10	.15	.50	1.25
	1972	4.453	.10	.15	.50	1.00
	1973	3.317	.10	.15	.50	1.00

KM#	Date	Mintage	VF	XF	Unc	BU
418	1974	8.494	.10	.15	.40	.60
	1975	10.123	.10	.15	.40	.60
	1976	15.177	.10	.15	.30	.50
	1977	19.412	.10	.15	.25	.40
	1978	15.305	.10	.15	.25	.40
	1979	10.152	.10	.15	.25	.40
	1980	7.082	.10	.15	.25	.40
	1980 w/o star	7.066	.10	.15	.25	.40
	1981	3.402	.10	.15	.25	.40
	1982	11.157	.10	.15	.25	.40
	1983	15.762	.10	.15	.25	.40
	1984	8.615	.10	.15	.25	.40
	1985	4.444	.10	.15	.25	.40
	1986	4.178	.10	.15	.25	.40
	1987	5.167	.10	.15	.25	.40
	1988	9.610	.10	.15	.25	.40
	1989	5.785	.10	.15	.25	.40
	1990	1.729	.10	.15	.25	.40
	1991	2.924	.10	.15	.25	.40
	1992	—	.10	.15	.25	.40
	1992	—	—	—	Proof	—
	1993	—	.10	.15	.25	.40

KRONE

(30 Skilling)

7.5000 g, .800 SILVER, .1929 oz ASW

KM#	Date	Mintage	VF	XF	Unc	BU
351	1875	.600	170.00	325.00	750.00	1000.

Rev: W/o 30 SK.

KM#	Date	Mintage	VF	XF	Unc	BU
357	1877	1.000	50.00	150.00	380.00	425.00
	1878	.060	750.00	1600.	3800.	4250.
	1879	.140	125.00	350.00	700.00	800.00
	1881	.080	125.00	400.00	800.00	1000.
	1882	.120	100.00	350.00	700.00	800.00
	1885	.100	75.00	240.00	485.00	525.00
	1887	.100	75.00	225.00	475.00	500.00
	1888	.075	150.00	400.00	850.00	1000.
	1889	.200	45.00	100.00	265.00	350.00
	1890	.200	45.00	100.00	265.00	350.00
	1892	.150	50.00	110.00	265.00	350.00
	1893	.100	50.00	110.00	265.00	350.00
	1894	.100	50.00	125.00	350.00	450.00
	1895/4	.100	55.00	125.00	275.00	325.00
	1895	Inc. Ab.	60.00	135.00	300.00	350.00
	1897	.250	40.00	80.00	190.00	250.00
	1898	.150	50.00	125.00	300.00	400.00
	1900	.250	40.00	80.00	165.00	200.00
	1901	.152	40.00	80.00	200.00	250.00
	1904	.100	90.00	175.00	400.00	450.00

KM#	Date	Mintage	VF	XF	Unc	BU
369	1908 crossed hammers on shield	.180	50.00	85.00	155.00	175.00
	1908 crossed hammers w/o shield	.170	40.00	70.00	130.00	150.00
	1910	.100	100.00	200.00	400.00	450.00
	1912	.200	60.00	100.00	225.00	250.00
	1913	.230	40.00	85.00	200.00	225.00
	1914	.602	20.00	40.00	70.00	90.00
	1915	.498	22.50	45.00	75.00	100.00
	1916	.400	25.00	50.00	150.00	200.00
	1917	.600	17.50	25.00	60.00	75.00

COPPER-NICKEL

KM#	Date	Mintage	VF	XF	Unc	BU
385	1925	8.686	3.00	15.00	85.00	120.00
	1926	1.984	4.00	20.00	135.00	160.00
	1927	1.000	5.00	30.00	275.00	350.00
	1936	.700	5.50	35.00	275.00	350.00
	1937	1.000	4.00	25.00	150.00	200.00
	1938	.926	2.50	15.00	85.00	120.00
	1939	2.253	1.50	7.50	45.00	60.00
	1940	3.890	1.00	5.00	30.00	40.00
	1946	5.499	.50	2.50	14.00	16.00
	1947	.802	2.00	10.00	45.00	60.00
	1949	7.846	.50	2.50	10.00	12.00
	1950	9.942	.50	2.50	10.00	12.00
	1951	4.761	.50	2.50	10.00	12.00

KM#	Date	Mintage	VF	XF	Unc	BU
397	1951	3.819	.50	2.00	15.00	25.00
	1953	1.465	.50	2.00	25.00	50.00
	1954	3.045	.50	2.00	25.00	50.00
	1955	1.970	.50	2.00	25.00	50.00
	1956	4.300	.50	2.00	20.00	45.00
	1957	7.630	.50	2.00	18.00	25.00

KM#	Date	Mintage	VF	XF	Unc	BU
409	1958	.540	7.00	30.00	150.00	250.00
	1959	4.450	.20	2.00	20.00	30.00
	1960	1.790	.20	2.00	15.00	20.00
	1961	3.934	.20	.75	10.00	12.00
	1962	6.015	.20	.75	10.00	12.00
	1963	4.677	.20	.75	10.00	12.00
	1964	3.469	.20	.50	4.00	6.00
	1965	3.222	.20	.75	20.00	30.00
	1966	3.084	.20	.40	4.00	6.00
	1967	6.680	.20	.40	5.00	10.00
	1968	6.149	.20	.50	6.00	10.00
	1969	5.186	.20	.35	2.00	3.00
	1970	8.637	.20	.40	8.00	10.00
	1971	10.258	.20	.35	1.50	2.00
	1972	13.179	.20	.35	1.00	1.50
	1973	9.140	.20	.35	1.00	1.50

KM#	Date	Mintage	VF	XF	Unc	BU
419	1974	16.537	.20	.35	.75	1.00
	1975	26.044	.20	.35	.75	1.00
	1976	35.927	.20	.35	.45	.75

KM#	Date	Mintage	VF	XF	Unc	BU
419	1977	26.264	.20	.35	.45	.75
	1978	23.360	.20	.35	.45	.75
	1979	15.897	.20	.35	.45	.75
	1980	5.918	.20	.35	1.75	2.25
	1981	16.308	.20	.35	.45	.75
	1982	29.187	.20	.35	.45	.75
	1983	34.293	.20	.35	.45	.75
	1984	3.677	.20	.35	.75	1.25
	1985	10.985	.20	.35	.45	.75
	1986	5.612	.20	.35	.45	.75
	1987	11.015	.20	.35	.45	.75
	1988	14.880	.20	.35	.45	.75
	1989	5.605	.20	.35	.45	.75
	1990	8.804	.20	.35	.45	.75
	1990	.015	—	—	Proof	125.00
	1991	15.080	.20	.35	.45	.75

KM#	Date	Mintage	VF	XF	Unc	BU
436	1992	—	.20	.35	.45	.75
	1992	—	—	—	Proof	—

2 KRONER

15.0000 g, .800 SILVER, .3858 oz ASW

KM#	Date	Mintage	VF	XF	Unc	BU
359	1878	.300	75.00	220.00	575.00	700.00
	1885	.025	375.00	900.00	2000.	2500.
	1887*	.025	375.00	900.00	2000.	2500.
	1888	.025	400.00	1000.	2200.	3000.
	1890	.100	55.00	150.00	400.00	475.00
	1892	.050	100.00	275.00	750.00	900.00
	1893	.075	80.00	200.00	550.00	700.00
	1894	.075	80.00	200.00	550.00	700.00
	1897	.050	100.00	250.00	750.00	900.00
	1898	.050	100.00	250.00	750.00	900.00
	1900	.125	50.00	120.00	250.00	325.00
	1902	.153	50.00	120.00	250.00	325.00
	1904	.076	75.00	150.00	275.00	350.00

NOTE: Restrikes are made by the Royal Mint, Norway in gold, silver and bronze.

Norway Independence
Obv: Large shield.

KM#	Date	Mintage	VF	XF	Unc	BU
363	1906	.100	15.00	25.00	35.00	50.00

Obv: Smaller shield.

KM#	Date	Mintage	VF	XF	Unc	BU
365	1907	.055	30.00	50.00	80.00	100.00

Border Watch

KM#	Date	Mintage	VF	XF	Unc	BU
366	1907	.028	125.00	225.00	375.00	500.00

KM#	Date	Mintage	VF	XF	Unc	BU
370	1908	.200	30.00	60.00	115.00	135.00
	1910	.150	50.00	100.00	225.00	300.00
	1912	.150	45.00	100.00	225.00	300.00
	1913	.270	25.00	50.00	100.00	125.00
	1914	.255	30.00	60.00	110.00	130.00
	1915	.225	30.00	60.00	110.00	130.00
	1916	.250	50.00	90.00	150.00	200.00
	1917	.378	17.50	30.00	70.00	100.00

Constitution Centennial

KM#	Date	Mintage	VF	XF	Unc	BU
377	1914	.226	10.00	17.50	37.50	75.00

5 KRONER

COPPER-NICKEL

KM#	Date	Mintage	VF	XF	Unc	BU
412	1963	7.074	1.00	3.00	10.00	12.50
	1964	7.346	1.00	2.00	6.00	8.00
	1965	2.233	1.00	2.50	45.00	50.00
	1966	2.502	1.00	2.50	20.00	25.00
	1967	.583	1.75	5.00	20.00	35.00
	1968	1.813	1.00	2.00	7.50	10.00
	1969	2.404	1.00	2.00	6.00	8.00
	1970	.202	2.50	5.00	12.50	15.00
	1971	.178	2.50	6.00	15.00	17.50
	1972	2.281	—	1.00	2.25	2.75
	1973	2.778	—	1.00	2.25	2.75

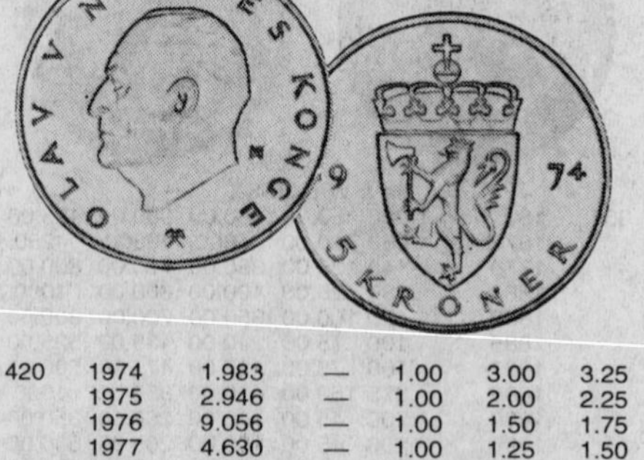

KM#	Date	Mintage	VF	XF	Unc	BU
420	1974	1.983	—	1.00	3.00	3.25
	1975	2.946	—	1.00	2.00	2.25
	1976	9.056	—	1.00	1.50	1.75
	1977	4.630	—	1.00	1.25	1.50
	1978	5.853	—	1.00	1.25	1.50
	1979	6.818	—	1.00	1.25	1.50
	1980	1.578	—	1.00	2.00	2.25
	1981	1.105	—	1.00	1.50	1.75
	1982	3.920	—	1.00	1.25	1.50
	1983	2.932	—	1.00	1.25	1.50
	1984	1.233	—	1.00	1.50	1.75
	1985	1.441	—	1.00	1.25	1.50
	1987	.900	—	1.00	2.00	2.25
	1988	.865	—	1.00	2.00	2.25

100th Anniversary of Krone System

KM#	Date	Mintage	VF	XF	Unc	BU
421	1975	1.192	1.00	1.50	2.50	2.75

150th Anniversary Emmigration to America

KM#	Date	Mintage	VF	XF	Unc	BU
422	1975	1.223	1.00	1.50	2.50	2.75

350th Anniversary of Norwegian Army

KM#	Date	Mintage	VF	XF	Unc	BU
423	1978	2.990	1.00	1.50	2.00	2.25

300th Anniversary of the Mint

KM#	Date	Mintage	VF	XF	Unc	BU
428	1986	2.345	1.00	1.50	2.00	2.25
	1986	5,000	—	—	P/L	25.00

175th Anniversary of the National Bank

KM#	Date	Mintage	VF	XF	Unc	BU
430	1991	.544	—	—	6.00	7.00

Harald V

KM#	Date	Mintage	VF	XF	Unc	BU
437	1992	*.500	—	—	1.25	1.50
	1992	—	—	—	Proof	—

***NOTE:** 100,000 of the 1992 dated coins are in mint sets.

10 KRONER

(2-1/2 Speciedaler)

4.4803 g, .900 GOLD, .1296 oz AGW

KM#	Date	Mintage	Fine	VF	XF	Unc
347	1874	.024	200.00	450.00	700.00	1000.

KM#	Date	Mintage	Fine	VF	XF	Unc
358	1877	.020	250.00	450.00	650.00	900.00
	1902	.025	175.00	350.00	500.00	750.00

KM#	Date	Mintage	Fine	VF	XF	Unc
375	1910	.053	90.00	150.00	300.00	450.00

20.0000 g, .900 SILVER, .5787 oz ASW
Constitution Sesquicentennial

KM#	Date	Mintage	VF	XF	Unc	BU
413	1964	1.408	—	6.00	7.00	8.00

NOTE: Edge lettering varieties exist.

COPPER-ZINC-NICKEL

KM#	Date	Mintage	VF	XF	Unc	BU
427	1983	20.193	—	1.75	3.00	5.00
	1984	26.169	—	1.75	2.50	3.00
	1985	22.458	—	1.75	2.50	3.00
	1986	29.060	—	1.75	2.50	3.00
	1987	8.809	—	1.75	2.50	3.00
	1988	2.630	—	1.75	2.50	3.00
	1989	3.259	—	1.75	2.50	3.00
	1990	3.004	—	1.75	2.50	3.00
	1991	—	—	1.75	2.50	3.00

20 KRONER

(5 Speciedaler)

8.9606 g, .900 GOLD, .2593 oz AGW

KM#	Date	Mintage	Fine	VF	XF	Unc
348	1874	.198	150.00	250.00	450.00	650.00
	1875	.105	150.00	250.00	450.00	650.00

KM#	Date	Mintage	Fine	VF	XF	Unc
355	1876	.109	150.00	200.00	400.00	550.00
	1877	.038	150.00	250.00	450.00	725.00
	1878	.139	150.00	200.00	400.00	550.00
	1879	.046	150.00	200.00	400.00	550.00
	1883	.036	3000.	6000.	9000.	12,500.
	1886	.101	150.00	200.00	400.00	550.00
	1902	.050	150.00	200.00	400.00	550.00

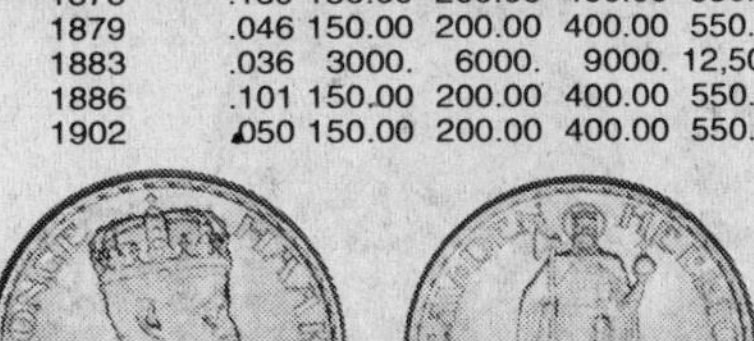

KM#	Date	Mintage	Fine	VF	XF	Unc
376	1910	.250	165.00	225.00	350.00	500.00

25 KRONER

29.0000 g, .875 SILVER, .8159 oz ASW
25th Anniversary of Liberation

KM#	Date	Mintage	VF	XF	Unc	BU
414	1970	1.204	—	—	—	9.00

50 KRONER

27.0000 g, .925 SILVER, .8030 oz ASW
75th Birthday of King Olav V

KM#	Date	Mintage	VF	XF	Unc	BU
424	1978	.800	—	—	12.00	15.00

16.8100 g, .925 SILVER, .5000 oz ASW
1994 Olympics - Skiers

KM#	Date	Mintage	VF	XF	Unc	BU
431	1991	*.218	—	—	Proof	28.00

1994 Olympics - Child Skiing

KM#	Date	Mintage	VF	XF	Unc	BU
432	1991	*.218	—	—	Proof	28.00

1994 Olympics - Grandfather and Child

KM#	Date	Mintage	VF	XF	Unc	BU
438	1992	*.156	—	—	Proof	30.00

1994 Olympics - 2 Children on Sled

KM#	Date	Mintage	VF	XF	Unc	BU
439	1992	*.156	—	—	Proof	30.00

1994 Olympics - Cross Country Skiers

KM#	Date	Mintage	VF	XF	Unc	BU
447	1993	*.156	—	—	Proof	30.00

1994 Olympics - Children Ice Skating

KM#	Date	Mintage	VF	XF	Unc	BU
448	1993	*.156	—	—	Proof	30.00

100 KRONER

24.7300 g, .925 SILVER, .7355 oz ASW
25th Anniversary of King Olaf's Reign

KM#	Date	Mintage	VF	XF	Unc	BU
426	1982	.800	—	—	20.00	22.50

33.6200 g, .925 SILVER, 1.0000 oz ASW
1994 Olympics - Cross Country Skier
Obv: Similar to 50 Kroner, KM#431.

433	1991	*.218	—	—	Proof	55.00

1994 Olympics - 2 Speed Skaters

434	1991	*.218	—	—	Proof	55.00

1994 Olympics - Ski Jumper

440	1992	*.156	—	—	Proof	60.00

1994 Olympics - Hockey Players

KM#	Date	Mintage	VF	XF	Unc	BU
441	1992	*.156	—	—	Proof	60.00

World Cycling Championships - 1 Cyclist

443	1993	.040	—	—	Proof	60.00

World Cycling Championships - 7 Cyclists

444	1993	.040	—	—	Proof	60.00

1994 Olympics - Figure Skater

449	1993	*.218	—	—	Proof	50.00

1994 Olympics - Alpine Skier

KM#	Date	Mintage	VF	XF	Unc	BU
450	1993	*.218	—	—	Proof	50.00

175 KRONER

26.5000 g, .925 SILVER, .7882 oz ASW
175th Anniversary of Constitution

429	1989	.085	—	—	90.00	100.00
	1989	.015	—	—	P/L	350.00

200 KRONER

26.8000 g, .625 SILVER, .5385 oz ASW
35th Anniversary of Liberation

425	1980	.298	—	—	37.50	42.50

1500 KRONER

17.0000 g, .917 GOLD, .5000 oz AGW
1994 Olympics - Ancient Norwegian Skier
Obv: Portrait of Olav V right.

KM#	Date	Mintage	Fine	VF	XF	Unc
435	1991	*.045	—	—	Proof	400.00

1994 Olympics - Birkebeiners

KM#	Date	Mintage	Fine	VF	XF	Unc
442	1992	*.030	—	—	Proof	425.00

World Cycling Championships - 2 Antique Cyclists

KM#	Date	Mintage	Fine	VF	XF	Unc
445	1993	.020	—	—	Proof	450.00

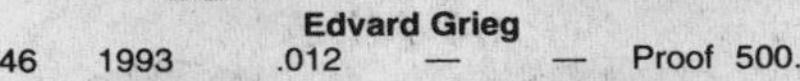

Edvard Grieg

KM#	Date	Mintage	Fine	VF	XF	Unc
446	1993	.012	—	—	Proof	500.00

1994 Olympics - Telemark Skier

KM#	Date	Mintage	Fine	VF	XF	Unc
451	1993	*.030	—	—	Proof	425.00

MINT SETS (MS)

KM#	Date	Mintage	Identification	Issue Price	Mkt. Val.
MS1	1960(7)	200	KM403,405,407-411	—	—
MS2	1961(7)	475	KM403,405,407-411	—	—
MS3	1962(7)	570	KM403,405,407-411	—	—
MS4	1963(8)	370	KM403,405,407-412	—	—
MS6	1964(8)	1,260	KM403,405,407-412	—	—
MS7	1965(8)	1,800	KM403,405,407-412, plastic	—	150.00
MS8	1966(8)	1,400	KM403,405,407-412, plastic	—	100.00
MS9	1967(8)	2,490	KM403,405,407-412, soft plastic	—	100.00
MS11	1968(8)	1,167	KM403,405,407-412, soft plastic	—	850.00
MS12	1968(8)	2,300	KM403,405,407-412, sandhill	—	875.00
MS13	1969(8)	3,140	KM403,405,407-412, soft plastic	—	20.00
MS14	1969(8)	7,450	KM403,405,407-412, sandhill	—	40.00
MS15	1970(8)	2,005	KM403,405,407-412, soft plastic	—	50.00
MS16	1970(8)	7,311	KM403,405,407-412, sandhill	—	70.00
MS17	1971(8)	2,010	KM403,405,407-412, soft plastic	—	50.00
MS18	1971(8)	4,055	KM403,405,407-412, sandhill	—	75.00
MS19	1972(8)	6,549	KM403,405,407-412, soft plastic	—	15.00
MS20	1972(8)	6,435	KM403,405,407-412, sandhill	—	35.00
MS21	1973(7)	7,085	KM405,407-409,411 412,415,soft plastic	—	12.00
MS22	1973(7)	13,090	KM405,407-409,411 412,415,sandhill	—	25.00
MS23	1974(6)	10,275	KM415-420,soft plastic	—	8.00
MS24	1974(6)	29,695	KM415-420,sandhill	—	12.00
MS25	1975(8)	30,207	KM415-422,sandhill	5.00	27.50
MS26	1975(7)	5,287	KM415-421,soft plastic	5.00	20.00
MS27	1976(6)	5,000	KM415-420,soft plastic	3.00	7.00
MS28	1976(6)	25,000	KM415-420,sandhill	3.00	10.00
MS29	1977(6)	5,000	KM415-420,soft plastic	3.40	12.00
MS30	1977(6)	25,000	KM415-420,sandhill	3.40	25.00
MS31	1978(6)	5,000	KM415-420,soft plastic	3.40	14.00
MS32	1978(6)	30,000	KM415-420,sandhill	3.40	25.00
MS33	1979(6)	8,000	KM415-420,soft plastic	3.40	6.00
MS34	1979(6)	50,000	KM415-420,sandhill	3.40	9.00
MS35	1980(6)	10,000	KM415-420,soft plastic	3.40	7.00
MS36	1980(6)	70,000	KM415-420,sandhill	3.40	15.00
MS37	1981(6)	100,000	KM415-420,hard plastic	4.25	8.00
MS38	1982(6)	102,650	KM415-420	4.50	10.00
MS39	1983(4)	102,300	KM416,418-420	5.00	8.00
MS40	1984(5)	101,000	KM416,418-420,427	5.00	8.00
MS41	1985(5)	110,000	KM416,418-420,427	5.00	8.00
MS42	1986(5)	100,000	KM416,418-419,427-428	7.00	12.00
MS43	1987(5)	85,000	KM416,418-420,427	7.00	12.00
MS44	1988(5)	102,000	KM416,418-420,427	7.00	10.00
MS45	1989(4)	101,000	KM416,418-419,427	8.00	12.00
MS46	1990(4)	103,000	KM416,418-419,427	8.00	12.00
MS47	1991/1992(5)	100,000	KM416,418,427,436-437	—	8.50

PROOF SETS (PS)

KM#	Date	Mintage	Identification	Issue Price	Mkt. Val.
PS1	1992(3)	—	KM418,436-437	—	—
PS2	1993(3)	—	KM443-445	—	570.00

Listings For

NOVA SCOTIA: refer to Canada

OMAN

The Sultanate of Oman (formerly Muscat and Oman), an independent monarchy located in the southeastern part of the Arabian Peninsula, has an area of 82,030 sq. mi. (212,460 sq. km.) and a population of *1.3 million. Capital: Muscat. The economy is based on agriculture, herding and petroleum. Petroleum products, dates, fish and hides are exported.

The first European contact with Muscat and Oman was made by the Portuguese who captured Muscat, the capital and chief port, in 1508. They occupied the city, utilizing it as a naval base and factory and holding it against land and sea attacks by Arabs and Persians until finally ejected by local Arabs in 1650. It was next occupied by the Persians who maintained control until 1741, when it was taken by Ahmed ibn Sa'id of the present ruling family. Muscat and Oman was the most powerful state in Arabia during the first half of the 19th century, until weakened by the persistent attack of interior nomadic tribes, British influence, initiated by the signing of a treaty of friendship with the Sultanate in 1798, remains a dominant fact of the civil and military phases of the government, although Britain recognizes the Sultanate as a sovereign state and there is no colonial relationship between them.

Sultan Said bin Taimur was overthrown by his son, Qabus bin Said, on July 23, 1970. The new sultan changed the nation's name to Sultanate of Oman.

TITLES

Muscat مسقط

Oman عمان

MUSCAT & OMAN

RULERS

Feisal bin Turee,
AH1285-1332/1888-1913AD
Taimur bin Feisal
AH1332-1351/1913-1932AD
Sa'id bin Taimur,
AH1351-1390/1932-1970AD
Qabus bin Sa'id, AH1390-/1970-AD

MONETARY SYSTEM

Until 1970

4 Baisa = 1 Anna
64 Baisa = 1 Rupee
200 Baisa = 1 Riyal

Commencing 1970

1000 Baisa = 1 Riyal

COLONIAL COINAGE

1/12 ANNA

COPPER

KM#	Date	Mintage	VG	Fine	VF	XF
1	AH1311	—	25.00	35.00	60.00	125.00

1/4 ANNA

COPPER

KM#	Date	Mintage	Good	VG	Fine	VF
2	AH1311	—	6.00	10.00	18.00	40.00

COPPER or BRASS
Birmingham Mint
Symetrical five.

KM#	Date	Mintage	Good	VG	Fine	VF
3.1	AH1315	19.110	.20	.50	1.00	2.00
	Nonsymetrical five.					
3.2	AH1315	I.A.	1.00	2.00	3.00	5.00

NOTE: A much cruder issue with many die varieties known. Perhaps struck at Bombay, India.

LOCAL COINAGE

1/4 ANNA

COPPER

KM#	Date	Mintage	Good	VG	Fine	VF
4.1	AH1312	—	2.00	3.25	5.00	8.50

Obv. and rev: W/o inner circle.

KM#	Date	Mintage	Good	VG	Fine	VF
4.2	AH1312	—	2.00	3.25	5.00	8.50

Rev: KM#2.

KM#	Date	Mintage	Good	VG	Fine	VF
5	AH1312//1311	—	2.50	4.25	6.00	10.00

KM#	Date	Mintage	Good	VG	Fine	VF
6	AH1311	—	—	—	—	—
	1312	—	—	—	—	—
	1313	—	2.50	4.25	6.00	10.00

Mule. Obv: KM#6. Rev: KM#2.

KM#	Date	Mintage	Good	VG	Fine	VF
7	AH1313//1311	—	—	—	—	—

KM#	Date	Mintage	Good	VG	Fine	VF
8.1	AH1312	—	2.50	4.25	6.00	10.00

Obv. and rev: Dentilated borders.

KM#	Date	Mintage	Good	VG	Fine	VF
8.2	AH1312	—	2.50	4.25	6.00	10.00

KM#	Date	Mintage	Good	VG	Fine	VF
9.1	AH1313	—	2.50	4.25	6.00	10.00

Obv: Legend begins at top w/o star or dot.
Rev: 4-line inscription within denticled border.

KM#	Date	Mintage	Good	VG	Fine	VF
9.2	AH1313	—	—	—	—	—

KM#	Date	Mintage	Good	VG	Fine	VF
10.1	AH1314	—	3.00	5.00	7.00	12.50

Obv: Large date, value on 1 line.

KM#	Date	Mintage	Good	VG	Fine	VF
10.2	AH1314	—	3.00	5.00	7.00	12.50

KM#	Date	Mintage	Good	VG	Fine	VF
11	AH1314	—	3.00	5.00	7.00	12.50
12.1	AH1315	—	2.00	3.25	5.00	8.50

Rev: Legend style varies.

KM#	Date	Mintage	Good	VG	Fine	VF
12.2	AH1315	—	2.00	3.25	5.00	8.50

KM#	Date	Mintage	Good	VG	Fine	VF
13	AH5131 (error) date retrograde	—	4.00	6.50	10.00	17.50

Rev: W/o star.

KM#	Date	Mintage	Good	VG	Fine	VF
14	AH1316	—	2.50	4.00	6.00	10.00
	Rev: Star between wreath points.					
15	AH1316	—	12.50	20.00	30.00	50.00
16	AH1318	—	Reported, not confirmed			
	Mule. Obv: KM#6. Rev: KM#14.					
17	AH1315	—	—	—	—	—

NOTE: There are numerous varieties of each year of the native issues, varying in both obverse and reverse legends, in the presence or absence of wreath borders, etc.

COUNTERMARKED COINAGE

1/4 ANNA

COPPER
c/m: *ST* in Arabic on 1/4 Anna, KM#3.

KM#	Date	Mintage	Good	VG	Fine	VF
19.1	ND(AH1311-18)	—	15.00	25.00	40.00	60.00

NOTE: ST for Sultan Taimur.

c/m: *SS* or *S* in Arabic on 1/4 Anna, KM#3.

KM#	Date	Mintage	Good	VG	Fine	VF
19.2	ND(AH1311-18)	—	30.00	50.00	80.00	120.00

NOTE: c/m always appears on obv. of KM#3. SS or S for Sultan Said.

MONETARY REFORM

2 BAISA

COPPER-NICKEL

KM#	Date	Mintage	Fine	VF	XF	Unc
25	AH1365	—	.50	.75	1.00	2.00
	1365	—	—	—	Proof	4.00

NOTE: Coins of AH1365 have the monetary unit spelled Baiza; on all other coins it is spelled Baisa.

NOTE: Most of the proof issues of the AH1359 and 1365 dated coins of Muscat & Oman now on the market are probably later restrikes produced by the Bombay Mint.

BRONZE

KM#	Date	Mintage	Fine	VF	XF	Unc
36	AH1390	4.000	.10	.15	.25	.40
	1390	—	—	—	Proof	1.50

3 BAISA

BRONZE

KM#	Date	Mintage	Fine	VF	XF	Unc
30	AH1378	8.000	.50	.75	1.25	2.00
	1378	—	—	—	Proof	—

NOTE: Struck for use in Dhofar province.

KM#	Date	Mintage	Fine	VF	XF	Unc
32	AH1380	10.000	.35	.50	.60	1.00
	1380	Inc. Ab.	—	—	Proof	—

5 BAISA

COPPER-NICKEL

KM#	Date	Mintage	Fine	VF	XF	Unc
26	AH1365	—	1.00	1.25	1.50	2.00
	1365	—	—	—	Proof	5.00
33	AH1381	5.000	.40	.60	1.00	1.50
	1381	Inc. Ab.	—	—	Proof	—

BRONZE

KM#	Date	Mintage	Fine	VF	XF	Unc
37	AH1390	3.400	—	.10	.15	.25
	1390	—	—	—	Proof	2.00

10 BAISA

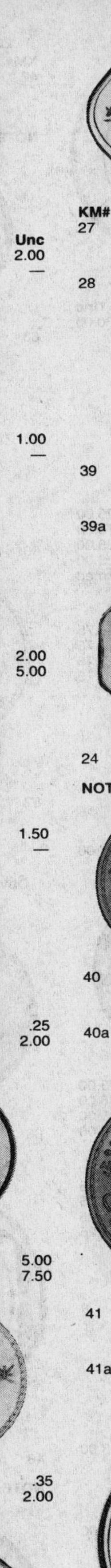

COPPER-NICKEL

KM#	Date	Mintage	Fine	VF	XF	Unc
22	AH1359	—	2.50	3.25	4.00	5.00
	1359	—	—	—	Proof	7.50

Struck for use in Dhofar province.

BRONZE

KM#	Date	Mintage	Fine	VF	XF	Unc
38	AH1390	4.500	.10	.15	.20	.35
	1390	—	—	—	Proof	2.00

20 BAISA

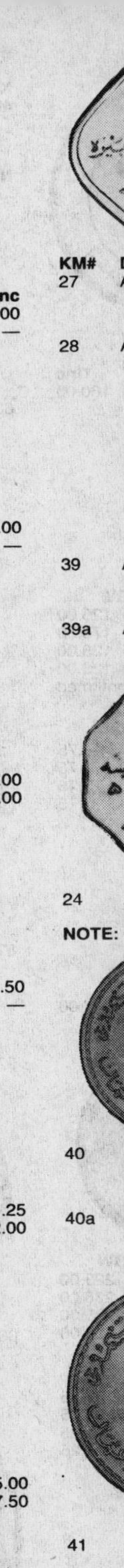

COPPER-NICKEL

KM#	Date	Mintage	Fine	VF	XF	Unc
23	AH1359	—	3.00	5.00	7.50	10.50
	1359	—	—	—	Proof	13.50

NOTE: Struck for use in Dhofar province.

KM#	Date	Mintage	Fine	VF	XF	Unc
27	AH1365	—	1.00	2.00	2.75	4.00
	1365	—	—	—	Proof	6.50

Mule. Obv: KM#23. Rev: KM#27.

KM#	Date	Mintage	Fine	VF	XF	Unc
28	AH1359/1365 (restrike)				—	17.50

25 BAISA

COPPER-NICKEL

KM#	Date	Mintage	Fine	VF	XF	Unc
39	AH1390	2.000	.10	.15	.30	.50
	1390	—	—	—	Proof	2.50

6.0100 g, .916 GOLD, .1771 oz AGW

KM#	Date	Mintage	Fine	VF	XF	Unc
39a	AH1390					
		350 pcs.	—	—	Proof	125.00

50 BAISA

COPPER-NICKEL

KM#	Date	Mintage	Fine	VF	XF	Unc
24	AH1359	—	.20	6.50	8.50	12.50
	1359	—	—	—	Proof	16.50

NOTE: Struck for use in Dhofar province.

KM#	Date	Mintage	Fine	VF	XF	Unc
40	AH1390	1.600	.15	.30	.50	.75
	1390	—	—	—	Proof	3.50

12.8100 g, .916 GOLD, .3775 oz AGW

KM#	Date	Mintage	Fine	VF	XF	Unc
40a	AH1390					
		350 pcs.	—	—	Proof	225.00

100 BAISA

COPPER-NICKEL

KM#	Date	Mintage	Fine	VF	XF	Unc
41	AH1390	1.000	.30	.45	.60	1.00
	1390	—	—	—	Proof	5.00

22.6300 g, .916 GOLD, .6670 oz AGW

KM#	Date	Mintage	Fine	VF	XF	Unc
41a	AH1390					
		350 pcs.	—	—	Proof	375.00

1/2 DHOFARI RIYAL

14.0300 g. .833 SILVER, .3758 oz ASW

KM#	Date	Mintage	Fine	VF	XF	Unc
29	AH1367	.200	12.00	14.00	18.00	25.00
	1367	—	—	—	Proof	40.00

NOTE: Struck for use in Dhofar province.

24.0300 g, .917 GOLD, .6780 oz AGW

KM#	Date	Mintage	Fine	VF	XF	Unc
29a	AH1367	2 pcs.	—	—	Proof	2000.

1/2 SAIDI RIYAL

.500 SILVER

KM#	Date	Mintage	Fine	VF	XF	Unc
34	AH1380	.696	3.00	3.50	4.75	7.50
	1380	—	—	—	Proof	75.00
	1381	—	3.00	3.50	4.75	7.50

25.6000 g, .916 GOLD, 33mm, .7540 oz AGW

KM#	Date	Mintage	Fine	VF	XF	Unc
34a	AH1381					
		150 pcs.	—	—	Proof	550.00
	1382					
		100 pcs.	—	—	Proof	550.00
	1390					
		350 pcs.	—	—	Proof	400.00
	1391					
		224 pcs.	—	—	—	—

SAIDI RIYAL

28.0700 g, .833 SILVER, .7518 oz ASW

KM#	Date	Mintage	Fine	VF	XF	Unc
31	AH1378	1.000	—	12.00	15.00	20.00
	1378					
		100 pcs.	—	—	Proof	650.00

28.0700 g, .500 SILVER, .4512 oz ASW

KM#	Date	Mintage	Fine	VF	XF	Unc
31a	AH1378	.400	—	10.00	12.50	15.00

46.6500 g, .916 GOLD, 33.7mm, 1.3740 oz AGW

KM#	Date	Mintage	Fine	VF	XF	Unc
31b	AH1378					
		100 pcs.	—	—	Proof	1000.
	1390					
		350 pcs.	—	—	Proof	725.00
	1391					
		224 pcs.	—	—	—	—

15 SAIDI RIYALS

7.9900 g, .916 GOLD, .2353 oz AGW

KM#	Date	Mintage	Fine	VF	XF	Unc
35	AH1381	2,000	—	—	—	150.00
	1381	460 pcs.	—	—	Proof	250.00

NOTE: An additional 460 pieces reported struck in 1971 and 1972, bearing the date AH1391.

MINT SETS (MS)

KM#	Date	Mintage	Identification	Issue Price	Mkt. Val.
MS1	AH1390(6)	5,500	KM36-41	—	3.50

PROOF SETS (PS)

KM#	Date	Mintage	Identification	Issue Price	Mkt. Val.
PS1	AH1359,65,67 (6)	—	KM22-26,29	—	75.00
PS2	AH1359,65,67 (6)	—	KM22,24-27,29	—	70.00
PS3	AH1390(6)	2,102	KM36-41	11.00	16.50
PS4	AH1390(3)	350	KM39a-41a	—	725.00

NOTE: Sets of 5 coins comprising KM22,24,25,26 and 27 or 28 have been marketed in recent years. They are Bombay mint restrikes.

SULTANATE OF OMAN

5 BAIZA

BRONZE

KM#	Date	Year	Mintage	VF	XF	Unc
50	AH1395	(1975)	4.000	.10	.15	.30
	1400	(1980)	5.000	.10	.15	.30
	1406	(1986)	—	.10	.15	.30
	1410	(1990)	—	.10	.15	.30

Sultan Qaboos Sports Complex
Obv: National emblem.

KM#	Date	Year	Mintage	VF	XF	Unc
76	AH1410	1990	2,000	—	Proof	5.00

10 BAIZA

BRONZE
F.A.O. Issue

KM#	Date	Year	Mintage	VF	XF	Unc
51	AH1395	(1975)	1.500	.10	.15	.30

KM#	Date	Year	Mintage	VF	XF	Unc
52	AH1395	(1975)	4.000	.10	.15	.30
	1400	(1980)	5.250	.10	.15	.30
	1406	(1986)	1.000	.10	.15	.30
	1410	(1990)	—	.10	.15	.30

Central Bank of Oman
Obv: National emblem.

KM#	Date	Year	Mintage	VF	XF	Unc
77	AH1410	1990	2,000	—	Proof	5.00

15 BAIZA

20.0000 g, .925 SILVER, .5949 oz ASW
15th Anniversary of Reign of Sultan

KM#	Date	Year	Mintage	VF	XF	Unc
75	AH1406	(1985)	2,000	—	Proof	160.00

25 BAIZA

5.9600 g, .917 GOLD, 18mm, .1757 oz AGW

KM#	Date	Year	Mintage	VF	XF	Unc
45	AH1392	—	250 pcs.	—	—	125.00
	1392	—	50 pcs.	—	Proof	175.00
	1394	(1974)	250 pcs.	—	Proof	125.00
	1395	(1975)	250 pcs.	—	Proof	125.00
	1397	(1977)	1,000	Reported, not confirmed		

NOTE: Struck for presentation purposes.

COPPER-NICKEL

KM#	Date	Year	Mintage	VF	XF	Unc
45a	AH1395	(1975)	3.500	.15	.25	.75
	1400	(1980)	3.330	.15	.25	.75
	1406	(1986)	2.000	.15	.25	.75
	1410	(1990)	—	.15	.25	.75

Royal Hospital
Obv: National emblem.

KM#	Date	Year	Mintage	VF	XF	Unc
78	AH1410	1990	2,000	—	Proof	7.00

50 BAIZA

12.8900 g, .917 GOLD, 24mm, .3801 oz AGW

KM#	Date	Year	Mintage	VF	XF	Unc
46	AH1392	—	250 pcs.	—	—	225.00
	1392	—	50 pcs.	—	Proof	275.00
	1394	(1974)	250 pcs.	—	Proof	225.00
	1395	(1975)	250 pcs.	—	Proof	225.00

NOTE: Struck for presentation purposes.

COPPER-NICKEL

KM#	Date	Year	Mintage	VF	XF	Unc
46a	AH1395	(1975)	2.000	.20	.40	1.25
	1400	(1980)	4.510	.20	.40	1.25
	1406	(1986)	2.000	.20	.40	1.25
	1410	(1990)	—	.20	.40	1.25

Irrigation Canal
Obv: National emblem.

KM#	Date	Year	Mintage	VF	XF	Unc
79	AH1410	1990	2,000	—	Proof	8.00

75 BAIZA

12.0000 g, .917 GOLD, .3537 oz AGW
Tenth National Day of Oman

KM#	Date	Year	Mintage	VF	XF	Unc
69	AH1404	(1984)	500 pcs.	—	Proof	275.00

100 BAIZA

22.7400 g, .917 GOLD, 28.5mm, .6705 oz AGW

KM#	Date	Year	Mintage	VF	XF	Unc
47	AH1392	—	250 pcs.	—	—	350.00
	1392	—	50 pcs.	—	Proof	425.00
	1394	(1974)	250 pcs.	—	Proof	350.00
	1395	(1975)	250 pcs.	—	Proof	350.00

NOTE: Struck for presentation purposes.

COPPER-NICKEL

KM#	Date	Year	Mintage	VF	XF	Unc
68	AH1404	(1984)	4.000	.35	.50	1.50

Sultan Qaboos University
Obv: National emblem.

KM#	Date	Year	Mintage	VF	XF	Unc
80	AH1410	1990	2,000	—	Proof	10.00

ALUMINUM-BRONZE CENTER, COPPER-NICKEL RING
100 Years of Coinage

KM#	Date	Year	Mintage	VF	XF	Unc
82	AH1411	1991	—	—	—	4.50

1/4 OMANI RIAL

12.8900 g, .917 GOLD, .3799 oz AGW
Fort al Hazam
Obv: Similar to 1/2 Omani Rial, KM#58. Rev: Fort.

KM#	Date	Year	Mintage	VF	XF	Unc
57	AH1397	(1977)	1,000	—	Proof	200.00

ALUMINUM-BRONZE

KM#	Date	Year	Mintage	VF	XF	Unc
66	AH1400	1980	2.000	.75	1.00	2.00

1/2 OMANI RIAL

25.6000 g, .917 GOLD, .7548 oz AGW

KM#	Date	Year	Mintage	VF	XF	Unc
48	AH1394	(1974)	250 pcs.	—	—	650.00
	1397	(1977)	1,000	—	—	600.00

NOTE: Struck for presentation purposes.

19.6700 g, .917 GOLD, .5797 oz AGW
Fort Marbat

KM#	Date	Year	Mintage	VF	XF	Unc
58	AH1397	(1977)	1,000	—	Proof	300.00

COPPER-NICKEL
F.A.O. Issue

KM#	Date	Year	Mintage	VF	XF	Unc
64	AH1398	1978	.015	2.75	3.50	5.00

ALUMINUM-BRONZE

KM#	Date	Year	Mintage	VF	XF	Unc
67	AH1400	1980	—	2.75	3.50	5.00

10.0000 g, .917 GOLD, .2947 oz AGW
Youth Year

KM#	Date	Year	Mintage	VF	XF	Unc
70	AH1404	(1984)	400 pcs.	—	Proof	225.00

OMANI RIAL

46.6500 g, .917 GOLD, 1.3755 oz AGW

KM#	Date	Year	Mintage	VF	XF	Unc
44	AH1391	(1971)	224 pcs.	—	Proof	725.00
	1392	(1972)	—	—	Proof	725.00
	1394	(1974)	250 pcs.	—	Proof	725.00

NOTE: Struck for presentation purposes.

25.6000 g, .917 GOLD, .7545 oz AGW
Fort Buraimi
Obv: Similar to 1/2 Omani Rial, Y#22. Rev: Fort.

KM#	Date	Year	Mintage	VF	XF	Unc
59	AH1397	(1977)	1,000	—	Proof	400.00

15.0000 g, .500 SILVER, .2412 oz ASW
F.A.O. Issue

KM#	Date	Year	Mintage	VF	XF	Unc
65	AH1398	1978	.015	—	7.50	10.00

20.0000 g, .917 GOLD, .5894 oz AGW
Youth Year

KM#	Date	Year	Mintage	VF	XF	Unc
71	AH1404	(1984)	300 pcs.	—	Proof	350.00

2 RIALS

20.0000 g, .925 SILVER, .5948 oz ASW
Sultan Said

KM#	Date	Year	Mintage	VF	XF	Unc
81	AH1411	1990	2,000	—	Proof	50.00

2-1/2 OMANI RIALS

25.3100 g, .925 SILVER, .7528 oz ASW
Conservation - Caracal

KM#	Date	Year	Mintage	VF	XF	Unc
60	AH1397	(1977)	4,407	—	—	32.50

28.2800 g, .925 SILVER, .8411 oz ASW

KM#	Date	Year	Mintage	VF	XF	Unc
60a	AH1397	(1977)	4,539	—	Proof	40.00

World Wildlife Fund - Eagles

KM#	Date	Year	Mintage	VF	XF	Unc
73	AH1407	1987	.025	—	Proof	30.00

Save the Children

KM#	Date	Year	Mintage	VF	XF	Unc
83	AH1411	1991	—	—	Proof	35.00

5 OMANI RIALS

31.6500 g, .925 SILVER, .9414 oz ASW
Conservation - Arabian Whit Oryx

KM#	Date	Year	Mintage	VF	XF	Unc
61	AH1397	(1977)	4,401	—	—	35.00

35.0000 g, .925 SILVER, 1.0409 oz ASW

KM#	Date	Year	Mintage	VF	XF	Unc
61a	AH1397	(1977)	4,359	—	Proof	45.00

45.6500 g, .917 GOLD, 1.3454 oz AGW
Sultan Qabus bin Said

KM#	Date	Year	Mintage	VF	XF	Unc
62	AH1397	(1977)	1,000	—	Proof	850.00

15 OMANI RIALS

7.9900 g, .917 GOLD, .2355 oz AGW, 22mm

KM#	Date	Year	Mintage	VF	XF	Unc
49	AH1394	(1974)	300 pcs.	—	—	200.00

NOTE: Struck for presentation purposes.

25 OMANI RIALS

10.0000 g, .917 GOLD, .2947 oz AGW
World Wildlife Fund - Masked Booby

KM#	Date	Year	Mintage	VF	XF	Unc
74	AH1407	1987	5,000	—	Proof	175.00

75 OMANI RIALS

33.4370 g, .900 GOLD, .9676 oz AGW
Conservation - Arabian Tahr

KM#	Date	Year	Mintage	VF	XF	Unc
63	AH1397	(1977)	825 pcs.	—	—	500.00
	1397	(1977)	325 pcs.	—	Proof	750.00

World Wildlife

KM#	Date	Year	Mintage	VF	XF	Unc
72	AH1404	(1984)	200 pcs.	—	Proof	1000.

PROOF SETS (PS)

KM#	Date	Mintage	Identification	Issue Price	Mkt. Val.
PS1	AH1394(3)	250	KM45-47	—	700.00
PS2	AH1395(3)	250	KM45-47	—	700.00
PS3	AH1397(3)	—	KM60a,61a,63	780.00	850.00
PS4	AH1397(2)	—	KM60a,61a	60.00	85.00
PS5	AH1410(6)	2,000	KM76-81	84.50	85.00

PAKISTAN

The Islamic Republic of Pakistan, located on the Indian sub-continent between India and Afghanistan, has an area of 310,404 sq. mi. (803,940 sq. km.) and a population of *110.4 million. Capital: Islamabad. Pakistan is mainly an agricultural land. Yarn, cotton, rice, and leather are exported.

Afghan and Turkish intrusions into northern India between the 11th and 18th centuries resulted in large numbers of Indians being converted to Islam. The idea of a separate Moslem state independent of Hindu India developed in the 1930's and was agreed to by Britain in 1946. The Islamic majority areas of India, consisting of the separate geographic entities known as East and West Pakistan, achieved self-government as Pakistan, with dominion status in the British Commonwealth, when the British withdrew from India on Aug. 14, 1947. Pakistan became a republic in 1956. When a basic constitutional crisis initiated by the election of Dec. 1, 1970 - the first direct general election in Pakistani history - could not be resolved by the leaders of East and West Pakistan, the East Pakistanis seceded from the Islamic Republic of Pakistan (March 26, 1971) and formed the independent People's Republic of Bangladesh. After many years of vacillation between civilian and military regimes, the people of Pakistan held a free national election in November, 1988 and installed a democratic government under a parliamentary system.

TITLE

باكستان

Pakistan

MONETARY SYSTEM

3 Pies = 1 Pice
4 Pice = 1 Anna
16 Annas = 1 Rupee

PIE

BRONZE

KM#	Date	Mintage	Fine	VF	XF	Unc
11	1951	2.950	.10	.20	.30	.50
	1951	—	—	—	Proof	1.25
	1953	.110	.10	.40	.60	1.00
	1953	—	—	—	Proof	1.00
	1955	.211	.10	.40	.60	1.00
	1956	3.390	.10	.15	.25	.35
	1957	—	.10	.15	.25	.35

PICE

BRONZE

KM#	Date	Mintage	Fine	VF	XF	Unc
1	1948	101.070	.10	.15	.20	.40
	1948	—	—	—	Proof	1.50
	1949	25.740	.10	.15	.20	.35
	1951	14.050	.10	.15	.20	.40
	1952	41.680	.10	.15	.20	.35

NOTE: Varieties exist.

NICKEL-BRASS

KM#	Date	Mintage	Fine	VF	XF	Unc
12	1953	47.540	.10	.15	.20	.35
	1953	—	—	—	Proof	1.25
	1955	31.280	.10	.15	.20	.35
	1956	9.710	.15	.20	.25	.50
	1957	57.790	.10	.15	.20	.35
	1958	52.470	.10	.15	.20	.35
	1959	41.620	.10	.15	.20	.35

1/2 ANNA

COPPER-NICKEL

KM#	Date	Mintage	Fine	VF	XF	Unc
2	1948	73.920	.10	.15	.20	.25
	1948	—	—	—	Proof	1.50
	1949 dot after date	16.940	.20	.25	.35	.50
	1951	75.360	.10	.15	.20	.25

NICKEL-BRASS

KM#	Date	Mintage	Fine	VF	XF	Unc
13	1953	8.350	.10	.20	.25	.35
	1953	—	—	—	Proof	1.25
	1955	17.310	.10	.15	.20	.30
	1958	38.250	.10	.15	.20	.25

ANNA

COPPER-NICKEL

KM#	Date	Mintage	Fine	VF	XF	Unc
3	1948	73.460	.10	.20	.30	.50
	1948	—	—	—	Proof	1.50
	1949	11.140	.10	.20	.25	.50
	1949 dot after date	Inc. KM8	.15	.25	.30	.50
	1951	40.800	.10	.20	.25	.40
	1952	15.430	.10	.20	.25	.35

KM#	Date	Mintage	Fine	VF	XF	Unc
8	1950	94.830	3.00	4.50	6.50	10.00
	1950	—	—	—	Proof	15.00

KM#	Date	Mintage	Fine	VF	XF	Unc
14	1953	9.350	.10	.15	.20	.30
	1953	—	—	—	Proof	1.50
	1954	35.360	.10	.15	.20	.25
	1955	6.230	.10	.15	.20	.30
	1956	4.580	.10	.15	.20	.35
	1957	12.500	.10	.15	.20	.25
	1958	44.320	.10	.15	.20	.25

2 ANNAS

COPPER-NICKEL

KM#	Date	Mintage	Fine	VF	XF	Unc
4	1948	55.930	.15	.25	.35	.60
	1948	—	—	—	Proof	1.50
	1949	19.720	.15	.25	.35	.60
	1949 dot after date	Inc. KM9	.20	.30	.40	.75
	1951	33.130	.15	.25	.35	.60

KM#	Date	Mintage	Fine	VF	XF	Unc
9	1950	21.190	3.50	5.00	7.50	12.50
	1950	—	—	—	Proof	20.00

KM#	Date	Mintage	Fine	VF	XF	Unc
15	1953	7.910	.10	.15	.20	.50
	1953	—	—	—	Proof	1.50
	1954	5.740	.10	.15	.20	.50
	1955	6.230	.10	.15	.20	.50
	1956	1.370	.10	.20	.35	.75
	1957	2.570	.10	.15	.30	.60
	1958	6.200	.10	.15	.20	.50
	1959	8.010	.10	.15	.20	.50

1/4 RUPEE

NICKEL

KM#	Date	Mintage	Fine	VF	XF	Unc
5	1948	52.680	.20	.30	.40	.65
	1948	—	—	—	Proof	2.25
	1949	46.000	.20	.30	.35	.40
	1951	19.120	.20	.30	.35	.40

KM#	Date	Mintage	Fine	VF	XF	Unc
10	1950	19.400	5.00	7.50	12.00	20.00
	1950	—	—	—	Proof	25.00

1/2 RUPEE

NICKEL

KM#	Date	Mintage	Fine	VF	XF	Unc
6	1948	33.260	.40	.60	.75	1.00
	1948	—	—	—	Proof	2.00
	1949	20.300	.40	.60	.75	1.00
	1951	11.430	.40	.65	.90	1.25

RUPEE

NICKEL

KM#	Date	Mintage	Fine	VF	XF	Unc
7	1948	46.200	.75	1.25	2.00	3.50
	1948	—	—	—	Proof	4.00
	1949	37.100	.75	1.25	2.00	3.50

NOTE: Varieties exist.

DECIMAL COINAGE

100 Paisa (Pice) = 1 Rupee

PICE

BRONZE

KM#	Date	Mintage	Fine	VF	XF	Unc
6	1961	74.910	.10	.20	.25	.35

PAISA

BRONZE

KM#	Date	Mintage	Fine	VF	XF	Unc
7	1961	134.650	—	.10	.15	.20
	1961	—	—	—	Proof	1.50
	1962	149.380	—	.10	.15	.20
	1963	127.810	—	.10	.15	.20

KM#	Date	Mintage	Fine	VF	XF	Unc
24	1964	39.890	.10	.25	.50	1.00
	1964	—	—	—	Proof	1.50
	1965	69.660	.10	.25	.50	1.00

NICKEL-BRASS

KM#	Date	Mintage	Fine	VF	XF	Unc
24a	1965	32.950	—	.10	.15	.20
	1966	179.370	—	.10	.15	.20

ALUMINUM

KM#	Date	Mintage	Fine	VF	XF	Unc
29	1967	170.070	—	—	.10	.15
	1968	—	—	—	.10	.15
	1969	—	—	—	.10	.15
	1970	204.606	—	—	.10	.15
	1971	191.880	—	—	.10	.15
	1972	108.510	—	—	.10	.15
	1973	Inc. Ab.	—	—	.10	.15

F.A.O. Issue - Cotton

KM#	Date	Mintage	Fine	VF	XF	Unc
33	1974	14.230	—	—	—	.10
	1975	43.000	—	—	—	.10
	1976	49.180	—	—	—	.10
	1977	62.750	—	—	—	.10
	1978	20.380	—	—	—	.10
	1979	5.630	—	—	—	.10

2 PAISA

BRONZE

KM#	Date	Mintage	Fine	VF	XF	Unc
25	1964	67.660	.10	.15	.20	.25
	1964	—	—	.15	Proof	1.50
	1965	27.880	.10	.15	.20	.25
	1966	50.590	.10	.15	.20	.25

ALUMINUM

KM#	Date	Mintage	Fine	VF	XF	Unc
28	1966	11.940	.10	.15	.20	.25
	1967	73.970	—	.10	.15	.20
	1968	—	—	.10	.15	.20

KM#	Date	Mintage	Fine	VF	XF	Unc
25a	1968	—	—	—	.10	.15
	1969	—	—	—	.10	.15
	1970	24.401	—	—	.10	.15
	1971	10.140	—	—	.10	.20
	1972	4.040	—	.10	.15	.25
	1974	3.600	—	.10	.15	.25

F.A.O. Issue - Rice Plant

KM#	Date	Mintage	Fine	VF	XF	Unc
34	1974	3.600	—	—	.10	.15
	1975	4.020	—	—	.10	.15
	1976	5.750	—	—	.10	.15

5 PICE

NICKEL-BRASS

KM#	Date	Mintage	Fine	VF	XF	Unc
18	1961	40.050	—	.10	.15	.25
	1961	—	—	—	Proof	1.50

5 PAISA

NICKEL-BRASS

KM#	Date	Mintage	Fine	VF	XF	Unc
19	1961	40.790	—	—	.10	.20
	1961	—	—	—	Proof	1.50
	1962	48.200	—	—	.10	.20
	1963	45.020	—	—	.10	.20

KM#	Date	Mintage	Fine	VF	XF	Unc
26	1964	82.730	—	—	.10	.20
	1965	72.570	—	—	.10	.20
	1966	32.900	—	—	.10	.20
	1967	24.470	—	—	.10	.20
	1968	—	—	.10	.15	.35
	1969	5.690	—	.10	.15	.35
	1970	24.655	—	—	.10	.30
	1971	23.860	—	—	.10	.30
	1972	40.345	—	—	.10	.30
	1973	Inc. Ab.	—	—	.10	.30
	1974	7.695	—	—	.15	.30

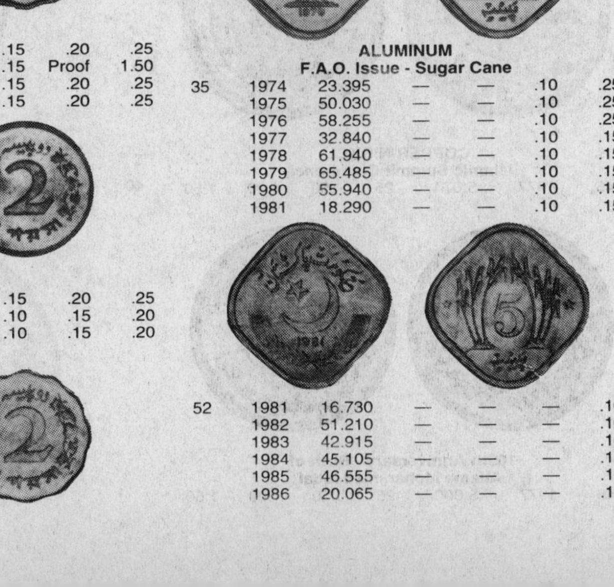

ALUMINUM
F.A.O. Issue - Sugar Cane

KM#	Date	Mintage	Fine	VF	XF	Unc
35	1974	23.395	—	—	.10	.25
	1975	50.030	—	—	.10	.25
	1976	58.255	—	—	.10	.25
	1977	32.840	—	—	.10	.15
	1978	61.940	—	—	.10	.15
	1979	65.485	—	—	.10	.15
	1980	55.940	—	—	.10	.15
	1981	18.290	—	—	.10	.15

KM#	Date	Mintage	Fine	VF	XF	Unc
52	1981	16.730	—	—	—	.10
	1982	51.210	—	—	—	.10
	1983	42.915	—	—	—	.10
	1984	45.105	—	—	—	.10
	1985	46.555	—	—	—	.10
	1986	20.065	—	—	—	.10
	1987	37.710	—	—	—	.10
	1988	40.150	—	—	—	.10

10 PICE

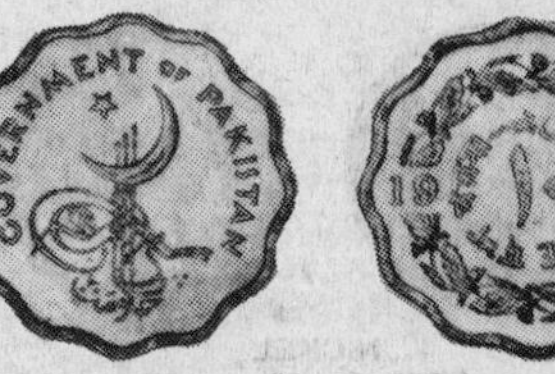

COPPER-NICKEL

KM#	Date	Mintage	Fine	VF	XF	Unc
20	1961	22.230	.10	.15	.25	.50

10 PAISA

COPPER-NICKEL

KM#	Date	Mintage	Fine	VF	XF	Unc
21	1961	31.090	—	.10	.15	.35
	1961	—	—	—	Proof	2.00
	1962	29.440	—	.10	.15	.35
	1963	19.760	—	.10	.15	.35

KM#	Date	Mintage	Fine	VF	XF	Unc
27	1964	52.580	—	—	.10	.25
	1965	51.540	—	—	.10	.25
	1966	—	—	—	.10	.25
	1967	16.430	—	—	.10	.25
	1968	—	—	—	.10	.25

Reduced size

KM#	Date	Mintage	Fine	VF	XF	Unc
31	1969	—	—	—	.10	.25
	1970	30.250	—	—	.10	.25
	1971	26.270	—	—	.10	.25
	1972	24.845	—	—	.10	.25
	1973	Inc. Ab.	—	—	.10	.25
	1974	4.780	—	—	.10	.25

ALUMINUM
F.A.O. Issue - Grain Spears

KM#	Date	Mintage	Fine	VF	XF	Unc
36	1974	18.640	—	—	—	.10
	1975	28.875	—	—	.10	.25
	1976	43.755	—	—	.10	.25
	1977	29.045	—	—	.10	.20
	1978	55.185	—	—	.10	.20
	1979	56.100	—	—	.10	.20
	1980	40.985	—	—	.10	.20
	1981	15.500	—	—	.10	.20

KM#	Date	Mintage	Fine	VF	XF	Unc
53	1981	7.995	—	—	.10	.15
	1982	39.770	—	—	.10	.15
	1983	44.705	—	—	.10	.15
	1984	35.255	—	—	.10	.15
	1985	41.545	—	—	.10	.15
	1986	43.280	—	—	.10	.15
	1987	39.090	—	—	.10	.15
	1988	42.510	—	—	.10	.15

KM#	Date	Mintage	Fine	VF	XF	Unc
53	1989	—	—	—	.10	.15
	1990	—	—	—	.10	.15

25 PAISA

NICKEL

KM#	Date	Mintage	Fine	VF	XF	Unc
22	1963	16.900	.10	.15	.20	.30
	1964	7.990	.10	.15	.25	.40
	1965	9.290	.10	.15	.25	.40
	1966	6.650	.10	.15	.25	.40
	1967	3.740	.10	.15	.25	.40

COPPER-NICKEL

KM#	Date	Mintage	Fine	VF	XF	Unc
30	1967	(?)5.500	.10	.15	.20	.30
	1968	(?)5.500	.10	.15	.20	.30
	1969	—	.10	.15	.20	.30
	1970	30.392	—	.10	.15	.25
	1971	12.664	—	.10	.15	.25
	1972	10.824	—	.10	.15	.25
	1973	—	—	.10	.15	.25
	1974	9.756	—	.10	.15	.25

KM#	Date	Mintage	Fine	VF	XF	Unc
37	1975	14.264	—	.10	.15	.25
	1976	20.440	—	.10	.15	.25
	1977	22.092	—	.10	.15	.25
	1978	33.544	—	.10	.15	.25
	1979	29.648	—	.10	.15	.25
	1980	49.556	—	.10	.15	.25
	1981	33.952	—	.10	.15	.25

KM#	Date	Mintage	Fine	VF	XF	Unc
58	1981	5.648	—	.10	.15	.25
	1982	28.940	—	.10	.15	.25
	1983	40.844	—	.10	.15	.25
	1984	50.988	—	.10	.15	.25
	1985	53.748	—	.10	.15	.25
	1986	75.764	—	.10	.15	.25
	1987	53.560	—	.10	.15	.25
	1988	58.900	—	.10	.15	.25
	1989	—	—	.10	.15	.25
	1992	—	—	.10	.15	.25

50 PAISA

NICKEL

KM#	Date	Mintage	Fine	VF	XF	Unc
23	1963	8.110	.10	.20	.30	.50
	1964	4.580	.15	.25	.40	.70
	1965	8.980	.10	.20	.30	.50
	1966	2.860	.15	.25	.50	1.00
	1967	—	Reported, not confirmed			
	1968	—	.10	.20	.30	.50
	1969	—	.10	.20	.30	.50

COPPER-NICKEL

KM#	Date	Mintage	Fine	VF	XF	Unc
32	1969	—	.10	.20	.30	.70
	1970	—	.10	.15	.25	.50
	1971	4.670	.10	.15	.25	.50
32	1972	4.900	.10	.15	.25	.50
	1974	1.128	.15	.20	.30	.70

KM#	Date	Mintage	Fine	VF	XF	Unc
38	1975	9.180	.10	.15	.25	.50
	1976	—	.10	.15	.25	.50
	1977	5.548	.10	.15	.25	.50
	1978	18.252	.10	.15	.25	.50
	1979	14.596	.10	.15	.25	.50
	1980	22.332	.10	.15	.25	.50
	1981	13.552	.10	.15	.25	.50

100th Anniversary - Birth of Mohammad Ali Jinnah

KM#	Date	Mintage	Fine	VF	XF	Unc
39	1976	5.600	.10	.15	.25	.60

1400th Hegira Anniversary

KM#	Date	Year	Mintage	VF	XF	Unc
51	AH1401	(1981)	—	.10	.25	.85

KM#	Date	Mintage	Fine	VF	XF	Unc
54	1981	4.612	—	.10	.15	.50
	1982	15.844	—	.10	.15	.50
	1983	9.608	—	.10	.15	.50
	1984	17.520	—	.10	.15	.50
	1985	20.144	—	.10	.15	.50
	1986	14.116	—	.10	.15	.50
	1987	23.044	—	.10	.15	.50
	1988	37.140	—	.10	.15	.50
	1990	—	—	.10	.15	.50
	1991	—	—	.10	.15	.50

RUPEE

COPPER-NICKEL
Islamic Summit Conference

KM#	Date	Mintage	Fine	VF	XF	Unc
45	1977	5.074	.25	.50	1.00	1.50

100th Anniversary - Birth of
Allama Mohammad Iqbal

KM#	Date	Mintage	Fine	VF	XF	Unc
46	1977	5.000	.25	.50	1.00	1.50

1400th Hegira Anniversary

KM#	Date	Year	Mintage	VF	XF	Unc
55	AH1401	(1981)	.045	—	—	2.[illegible]

World Food Day

KM#	Date	Mintage	Fine	VF	XF	Unc
56	1981	.045	—	—	—	2.[illegible]

26.5mm

KM#	Date	Mintage	Fine	VF	XF	Unc
57.1	1979	—	—	.10	.25	1.0
	1980	14.522	—	.10	.25	1.0
	1981	12.038	—	.10	.25	1.0

25mm

KM#	Date	Mintage	Fine	VF	XF	Unc
57.2	1981	4.084	—	.10	.25	1.0
	1982	27.878	—	.10	.25	1.0
	1983	18.746	—	.10	.25	1.[illegible]
	1984	14.562	—	.10	.25	1.[illegible]
	1985	4.934	—	.10	.25	1.0
	1986	11.840	—	.10	.25	1.0
	1987	50.416	—	.10	.25	1.0
	1988	10.644	—	.10	.25	1.0

100 RUPEES

28.2800 g, .925 SILVER, .8411 oz ASW
Conservation - Tropogan Pheasant

KM#	Date	Mintage	Fine	VF	XF	Unc
40	1976	5,120	—	—	—	25.0
	1976	5,837	—	—	Proof	30.0

20.4400 g, .925 SILVER, .6079 oz ASW
100th Anniversary of Birth of Mohammad Ali Jinnah

KM#	Date	Mintage	Fine	VF	XF	Unc
41	1976	1,300	—	—	—	25.00
	1976	2,800	—	—	Proof	25.00

Islamic Summit Conference

KM#	Date	Mintage	Fine	VF	XF	Unc
47	1977	1,500	—	—	—	22.50
	1977	2,500	—	—	Proof	22.50

100th Anniversary - Birth of Allama Mohammad Iqbal

KM#	Date	Mintage	Fine	VF	XF	Unc
48	1977	3,000	—	—	—	30.00
	1977	300 pcs.	—	—	Proof	50.00

150 RUPEES

35.0000 g, .925 SILVER, 1.0409 oz ASW
Conservation - Gavial Crocodile
Obv: Similar to 100 Rupees, KM#40.

KM#	Date	Mintage	Fine	VF	XF	Unc
42	1976	5,119	—	—	—	32.50
	1976	5,637	—	—	Proof	35.00

500 RUPEES

4.5000 g, .917 GOLD, .1325 oz AGW

100th Anniversary - Birth of Mohammad Ali Jinnah

KM#	Date	Mintage	Fine	VF	XF	Unc
43	1976	500 pcs.	—	—	—	100.00
	1976	500 pcs.	—	—	Proof	165.00

3.6400 g, .917 GOLD, .1073 oz AGW
100th Anniversary - Birth of Allama Mohammad Iqbal

KM#	Date	Mintage	Fine	VF	XF	Unc
49	1977	500 pcs.	—	—	—	100.00
	1977	200 pcs.	—	—	Proof	200.00

1000 RUPEES

9.0000 g, .917 GOLD, .2650 oz AGW
Islamic Summit Conference

KM#	Date	Mintage	Fine	VF	XF	Unc
50	1977	400 pcs.	—	—	—	175.00
	1977	400 pcs.	—	—	Proof	300.00

3000 RUPEES

33.4370 g, .900 GOLD, .9676 oz AGW
Conservation - Astor Markhor

KM#	Date	Mintage	Fine	VF	XF	Unc
44	1976	902 pcs.	—	—	—	500.00
	1976	273 pcs.	—	—	Proof	750.00

MIXED DATE MINT SETS (MS)

KM#	Date	Mintage	Identification	Issue Price	Mkt. Val.
MS1	1948/51/53(8)	—	KM5-7,11-15	4.00	5.00
MS2	1948/61(6)	—	KM5-7,17,19,21	2.00	4.00
MS3	1948/64(7)	—	KM7,22-27	2.00	4.00
MS4	1948/74(7)	—	KM7,30,32-36	2.00	4.00
MS5	1948/75(7)	—	KM7,33-38	—	4.50
MS6	1951/53(5)	—	KM11-15	—	4.00

NOTE: Restrikes have been issued for most of these sets.

MINT SETS (MS)

KM#	Date	Mintage	Identification	Issue Price	Mkt. Val.
MS1	1948(7)	—	KM1-7	—	8.00
MS4	1961(3)	—	KM17,19,21	—	3.50
MS7	1976(2)	—	KM41,43	63.00	125.00
MS8	1976(2)	—	KM40,42	—	60.00
MS9	1977(2)	—	KM47,50	—	200.00

PROOF SETS (PS)

KM#	Date	Mintage	Identification	Issue Price	Mkt. Val.
PS1	1948(7)	5,000	KM1-7	4.00	14.50
PS2	1950(3)	—	KM8-10	—	60.00
PS3	1953(5)	—	KM11-15	2.00	6.50
PS4	1961(3)	—	KM17,19,21	1.00	5.00
PS5	1976(2)	—	KM41,43	90.50	190.00
PS6	1976(2)	—	KM40,42	—	70.00
PS7	1977(2)	—	KM47,50	—	325.00

PALAU ISLANDS

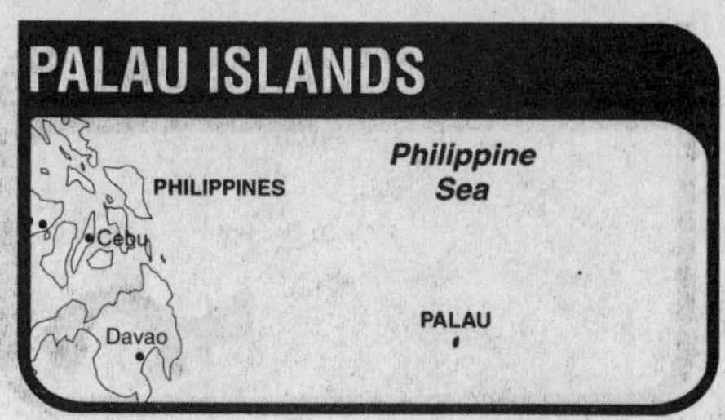

Palau, a group of about 100 islands and islets, is generally considered a part of the Caroline Islands. It is located about 1,000 miles southeast of Manila and about the same distance southwest of Saipan and has an area of 179 sq. mi. and a population of 12,116. Capital: Koror.

The islands were administered as part of the Caroline Islands under the Spanish regime until they were sold to Germany in 1899. Seized by Japan in 1914, it was mandated to them in 1919 and Koror was made the administrative headquarters of all the Japanese mandated islands in 1921. During World War II the islands were taken by the Allies, in 1944, with the heaviest fighting taking place on Peleliu. They became part of the U.S. Trust Territory of the Pacific Islands in 1947. In 1980 they became internally self-governing and independent. Control over foreign policy, except defense, was approved in 1986.

DOLLAR

COPPER-NICKEL
Rev: W/Plastic Applique
Oceanic Environment Conservation

KM#	Date	Mintage	VF	XF	Unc
1	1992	*.050	—	Proof	27.50

5 DOLLARS

25.0000 g, .900 SILVER, .7234 oz ASW
Rev: W/Plastic Applique
Oceanic Environment Conservation

KM#	Date	Mintage	VF	XF	Unc
2	1992	*6,000	—	Proof	65.00

Listings For

PALESTINE: refer to Israel

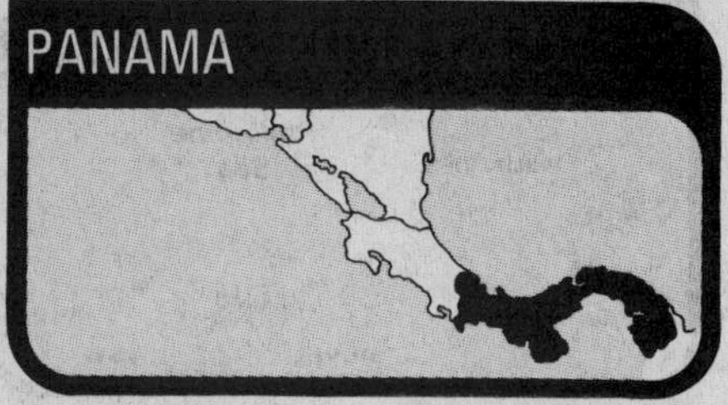

The Republic of Panama, a Central American country situated between Costa Rica and Colombia, has an area of 29,762 sq. mi. (78,200 sq. km.) and a population of *2.4 million. Capital: Panama City. The Panama Canal is the country's biggest asset; servicing world related transit trade and international commerce. Bananas, refined petroleum, sugar and shrimp are exported.

Panama was visited by Christopher Columbus in 1502 during his fourth voyage to America, and explored by Vasco Nunez de Balboa in 1513. Panama City, founded in 1519, was a primary transshipment center for treasure and supplies to and from Spain's American colonies. Panama declared its independence in 1821 and joined the Confederation of Greater Colombia. In 1903, after Colombia rejected a treaty enabling the United States to build a canal across the Isthmus, Panama with the support of the United States proclaimed its independence from Colombia and became a sovereign republic.

The 1904 2-1/2 centesimos known as the 'Panama Pill' or 'Panama Pearl' is one of the world's smaller silver coins and a favorite with collectors.

MINT MARKS

FM - Franklin Mint, U.S.A.*

CHI in circle - Valcambi Mint, Balerna, Switzerland

***NOTE:** From 1975 the Franklin Mint has produced coinage in up to 3 different qualities. Qualities of issue are designated in ( ) after each date and are defined as follows:

(M) MATTE - Normal circulation strike or a dull finish produced by sandblasting special uncirculated (polish finish) or proof quality dies.

(U) SPECIAL UNCIRCULATED - Polished or proof-like in appearance without any frosted features.

(P) PROOF - The highest quality obtainable having mirror-like fields and frosted features.

MONETARY SYSTEM

100 Centesimos = 1 Balboa

1/2 CENTESIMO

COPPER-NICKEL

KM#	Date	Mintage	Fine	VF	XF	Unc
6	1907	1.000	.50	1.00	2.00	5.00
	1907	—	—	—	Proof	—

NOTE: Previously listed re-engraved overdates were struck from very common doubled dies. The plain date in unc. is scarcer.

CENTESIMO

BRONZE
Urraca

KM#	Date	Mintage	Fine	VF	XF	Unc
14	1935	.200	2.00	5.00	12.00	65.00
	1937	.200	1.00	2.50	7.00	50.00

50th Anniversary of the Republic

KM#	Date	Mintage	Fine	VF	XF	Unc
17	1953	1.500	.10	.15	.35	3.00
	1953	4 pcs.	—	—	Proof	700.00

KM#	Date	Mintage	VF	XF	Unc
22	1961	2.500	.15	.25	2.00
	1962	2.000	.15	.25	1.00
22	1962	*50 pcs.	—	Proof	200.00
	1966	3.000	.10	.15	.75
	1966	.013	—	Proof	1.00
	1967	7.600	.10	.15	.75
	1967	.020	—	Proof	1.00
	1968	25.000	.10	.15	.75
	1968	.023	—	Proof	1.00
	1969	.014	—	Proof	1.00
	1970	9,528	—	Proof	1.00
	1971	.011	—	Proof	1.00
	1972	.013	—	Proof	1.00
	1973	.017	—	Proof	1.00
	1974	*10.000	.10	.15	.25
	1974	*.018	—	Proof	1.00
	1975	10.000	.10	.15	.25
	1977	10.000	.10	.15	.25
	1978	10.000	.10	.15	.25
	1979	10.000	.10	.15	.25
	1980	20.500	.10	.15	.25
	1981	20.000	.10	.15	.25
	1983FM(P)	—	—	Proof	1.50
	1983	5.000	.10	.15	.25
	1984FM(P)	—	—	Proof	1.50
	1985FM(P)	**	—	Proof	1.50
	1986	20.000	.10	.15	.25
	1987	20.000	—	—	.10
	1991	30.000	—	—	.10

NOTE: Varieties exist.
***NOTE:** 1974 circulation coins were struck at West Point and New York, the proof coins at San Francisco.
****NOTE:** Unauthorized striking.

COPPER COATED ZINC

KM#	Date	Mintage	VF	XF	Unc
22a	1980	—	.10	.15	.25
	1981	—	.10	.15	.25
	1982	—	.10	.15	.25
	1983	45.000	.10	.15	.25

KM#	Date	Mintage	VF	XF	Unc
33.1	1975(RCM)	.500	.10	.20	.50
	1975FM(M)	.125	.10	.25	1.00
	1975FM(U)	1,410	—	—	3.00
	1975FM(P)	.041	—	Proof	.50
	1976(RCM)	.050	.10	.20	1.00
	1976FM(M)	.063	.10	.20	1.00
	1976FM(P)	.012	—	Proof	.50
	1977FM(U)	.063	.10	.20	1.00
	1977FM(P)	9,548	—	Proof	.50
	1979FM(U)	.020	.10	.20	1.00
	1979FM(P)	5,949	—	Proof	.50
	1980FM(U)	.040	.10	.20	1.00
	1981FM(P)	1,973	—	Proof	1.00
	1982FM(U)	5,000	.50	1.00	3.00
	1982FM(P)	1,480	—	Proof	1.00

Edge lettering: 1830 BOLIVAR 1980

KM#	Date	Mintage	VF	XF	Unc
33.2	1980FM(P)	2,629	—	Proof	1.00

75th Anniversary of Independence

KM#	Date	Mintage	VF	XF	Unc
45	1978FM(U)	.050	.10	.20	1.00
	1978FM(P)	.011	—	Proof	1.25

COPPER PLATED ZINC

KM#	Date	Mintage	VF	XF	Unc
124	1991	15.000	.10	.15	.25

1-1/4 CENTESIMOS

BRONZE

KM#	Date	Mintage	Fine	VF	XF	Unc
15	1940	1.600	.50	1.00	3.50	12.00

2-1/2 CENTESIMOS

1.2500 g, .900 SILVER, .0362 oz ASW

KM#	Date	Mintage	Fine	VF	XF	Unc
1	1904	.400	4.00	6.00	12.50	22.50
	1904	*12 pcs.	—	—	Proof	R,NC

NOTE: The above piece is popularly referred to as th Panama Pill.

COPPER-NICKEL
Rev. leg: DOS Y MEDIOS

KM#	Date	Mintage	Fine	VF	XF	Un
7.1	1907	.800	1.00	3.00	12.50	60.0
	1907	*5 pcs.	—	—	Proof	R,N

Rev. leg: DOS Y MEDIO

KM#	Date	Mintage	Fine	VF	XF	Un
7.2	1916	.800	1.00	3.50	20.00	100.0
	1918*	7 known	—	—	—	250

***NOTE:** Unauthorized issue, 1 million pieces melte June 1918.

KM#	Date	Mintage	Fine	VF	XF	Un
8	1929	1.000	1.00	3.00	18.00	100.0
	1929	—	—	—	Proof	–

KM#	Date	Mintage	Fine	VF	XF	Un
16	1940	1.200	.50	1.00	3.50	12.5

COPPER-NICKEL CLAD COPPER
F.A.O. Issue

KM#	Date	Mintage	VF	XF	Un
32	1973	2.000	—	.10	.2
	1975	1.000	—	.10	.5

Victoriano Lorenzo

KM#	Date	Mintage	VF	XF	Un
34.1	1975(RCM)	.040	.35	.60	1.0
	1975FM(M)	.050	.35	.60	1.0
	1975FM(U)	1,410	1.00	1.75	2.5
	1975FM(P)	.041	—	Proof	1.0
	1976(RCM)	.020	.35	.60	1.0
	1976FM(M)	.025	.35	.60	1.0
	1976FM(P)	.024	—	Proof	1.0
	1977FM(U)	.025	.35	.60	1.0
	1977FM(P)	9,548	—	Proof	1.0
	1979FM(U)	.012	.35	.60	1.0
	1979FM(P)	5,949	—	Proof	1.0
	1980FM(U)	.040	.35	.60	1.0
	1981FM(P)	1,973	—	Proof	2.0
	1982FM(U)	2,000	.75	1.50	2.2
	1982FM(P)	1,480	—	Proof	2.5

Edge lettering: 1830 BOLIVAR 1980

KM#	Date	Mintage	VF	XF	Un
34.2	1980FM(P)	2,629	—	Proof	1.0

75th Anniversary of Independence

KM#	Date	Mintage	VF	XF	Un
46	1978FM(U)	.040	.25	.50	1.0
	1978FM(P)	.011	—	Proof	1.0

KM#	Date	Mintage	VF	XF	Un
85	1983FM(P)	—	—	Proof	2.5
	1984FM(P)	—	—	Proof	2.5
	1985FM(P)	*	—	Proof	2.5

***NOTE:** Unauthorized striking.

5 CENTESIMOS

2.5000 g, .900 SILVER, .0723 oz ASW

KM#	Date	Mintage	Fine	VF	XF	Unc
2	1904	1.500	2.50	5.00	12.50	50.00
	1904	12 pcs.	—	—	Proof	1000.
	1916	.100	35.00	60.00	125.00	275.00

COPPER-NICKEL

KM#	Date	Mintage	Fine	VF	XF	Unc
9	1929	.500	2.00	4.00	12.00	75.00
	1932	.332	2.00	4.00	12.50	80.00

KM#	Date	Mintage	VF	XF	Unc
23.1	1961	1.000	.50	1.25	2.50

KM#	Date	Mintage	VF	XF	Unc
23.2	1962	2.600	.10	.20	1.00
	1962	*25 pcs.	—	Proof	350.00
	1966	4.900	.10	.20	.50
	1966	.013	—	Proof	1.00
	1967	2.600	.10	.20	.50
	1967	.020	—	Proof	1.00
	1968	6.000	.10	.20	.50
	1968	.023	—	Proof	1.00
	1969	.014	—	Proof	1.00
	1970	5.000	.10	.20	.50
	1970	9,528	—	Proof	1.00
	1971	.011	—	Proof	1.00
	1972	.013	—	Proof	1.00
	1973	5.000	.10	.20	.50
	1973	.017	—	Proof	1.00
	1974	.019	—	Proof	1.00
	1975	5.000	.10	.15	.40
	1982	8.000	.10	.15	.40
	1983	7.500	.10	.15	.40
	1993	—	—	Proof	1.50

NOTE: The 1962 & 1966 Royal Mint strikes are normally sharper in detail. The stars on the reverse above the eagle are flat while previous dates are raised.

NOTE: Varieties exist.

Carlos J. Finlay

KM#	Date	Mintage	VF	XF	Unc
35.1	1975(RCM)	.080	.25	.50	1.00
	1975FM(M)	.015	.25	.50	1.00
	1975FM(U)	1,410	—	—	2.50
	1975FM(P)	.041	—	Proof	1.00
	1976(RCM)	.020	.25	.50	1.00
	1976FM(M)	.013	.25	.50	1.00
	1976FM(P)	.012	—	Proof	1.00
	1977FM(U)	.013	.25	.50	1.00
	1977FM(P)	9,548	—	Proof	1.00
	1979FM(U)	.012	.25	.50	1.00
	1979FM(P)	5,949	—	Proof	1.00
	1980FM(U)	.043	.25	.50	1.00
	1981FM(P)	1,973	—	Proof	1.50
	1982FM(U)	3,000	.75	1.25	2.00
	1982FM(P)	1,480	—	Proof	1.50

Edge lettering: 1830 BOLIVAR 1980

KM#	Date	Mintage	VF	XF	Unc
35.2	1980FM(P)	2,629	—	Proof	1.50

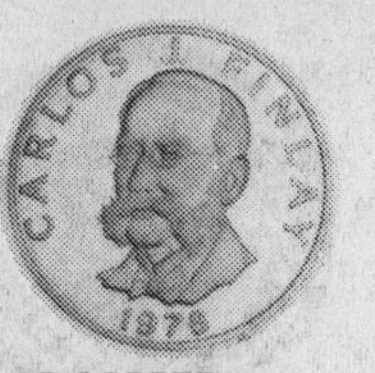

COPPER-NICKEL CLAD COPPER
75th Anniversary of Independence

KM#	Date	Mintage	VF	XF	Unc
47	1978FM(U)	.030	—	—	1.00
	1978FM(P)	.011	—	Proof	1.00

KM#	Date	Mintage	VF	XF	Unc
86	1983FM(P)	—	—	Proof	2.50
	1984FM(P)	—	—	Proof	2.50
	1985FM(P)	*	—	Proof	3.50

***NOTE:** Unauthorized striking.

10 CENTESIMOS

5.0000 g, .900 SILVER, .1447 oz ASW

KM#	Date	Mintage	Fine	VF	XF	Unc
3	1904	1.100	3.50	7.50	25.00	100.00
	1904	12 pcs.	—	—	Proof	1000.

1/10 BALBOA

2.5000 g, .900 SILVER, .0723 oz ASW
High relief.

KM#	Date	Mintage	Fine	VF	XF	Unc
10.1	1930	.500	1.75	3.00	9.50	35.00
	1930	20 pcs.	—		Matte Proof	1500.
	1931	.200	2.50	5.00	15.00	100.00
	1932	.150	3.00	6.00	15.00	120.00
	1933	.100	5.00	10.00	25.00	150.00
	1934	.075	7.50	15.00	40.00	200.00
	1947	1.000	.75	1.50	3.00	12.00

Low relief.

KM#	Date	Mintage	Fine	VF	XF	Unc
10.2	1962	5.000	—	BV	1.00	1.50
	1962	*25 pcs.	—	—	Proof	500.00

COPPER-NICKEL CLAD COPPER

KM#	Date	Mintage	VF	XF	Unc
10a	1966TI	6.955	.25	.35	1.00
	1966TII	1.000	.50	2.00	5.00
	1966	.013	—	Proof	1.00
	1967	.020	—	Proof	1.00
	1968	5.000	.20	.30	1.00
	1968	.023	—	Proof	1.00
	1969	.014	—	Proof	1.00
	1970	7.500	.15	.25	.50
	1970	9,528	—	Proof	1.00
	1971	.011	—	Proof	1.00
	1972	.013	—	Proof	1.00
	1973	10.000	.15	.20	.50
	1973	.017	—	Proof	1.00
	1974	.018	—	Proof	1.00
	1975	.500	.25	.50	1.00
	1980	5.000	.15	.25	.75
	1982	7.740	.10	.20	.50
	1983	7.750	.10	.20	.50
	1986	1.000	.10	.20	1.50
	1993	—	—	Proof	1.50

NOTE: The 1966 exists in two varieties, Type I is similar to the 1962 strike on a thick flan (London) with diamonds on both sides of DE and Type II is similar to the 1947 strikes on a thin flan (U.S.) with elongated diamonds on both sides of DE.

2.5000 g, .900 SILVER, .0723 oz ASW
50th Anniversary of the Republic

KM#	Date	Mintage	Fine	VF	XF	Unc
18	1953	3.300	BV	.75	1.50	2.50

KM#	Date	Mintage	Fine	VF	XF	Unc
24	1961	2.500	BV	.75	1.50	2.00

COPPER-NICKEL CLAD COPPER

KM#	Date	Mintage	VF	XF	Unc
87	1983FM(P)	—	—	Proof	3.00
	1984FM(P)	—	—	Proof	3.00
	1985FM(P)	*	—	Proof	5.00

***NOTE:** Unauthorized striking.

10 CENTESIMOS

COPPER-NICKEL CLAD COPPER
Manuel E. Amador

KM#	Date	Mintage	VF	XF	Unc
36.1	1975(RCM)	.050	.20	.50	1.00
	1975FM(M)	.013	.20	.50	1.00
	1975FM(U)	1,410	—	—	2.50
	1975FM(P)	.041	—	Proof	1.00
	1976(RCM)	.020	.20	1.00	1.50
	1976FM(M)	6,250	.50	1.25	2.00
	1976FM(P)	.012	—	Proof	1.00
	1977FM(U)	6,250	.50	1.25	2.00
	1977FM(P)	9,548	—	Proof	1.00
	1979FM(U)	.010	.20	.50	1.00
	1979FM(P)	5,949	—	Proof	1.00
	1980FM(U)	.040	.20	.50	1.00
	1981FM(P)	1,973	—	Proof	1.50
	1982FM(U)	2,500	.75	1.50	2.50
	1982FM(P)	1,480	—	Proof	1.50

Edge lettering: 1830 BOLIVAR 1980

KM#	Date	Mintage	VF	XF	Unc
36.2	1980FM(P)	2,629	—	Proof	2.50

75th Anniversary of Independence

KM#	Date	Mintage	VF	XF	Unc
48	1978FM(U)	.020	.20	.50	1.00
	1978FM(P)	.011	—	Proof	1.25

25 CENTESIMOS

12.5000 g, .900 SILVER, .3617 oz ASW

KM#	Date	Mintage	Fine	VF	XF	Unc
4	1904	1.600	5.00	10.00	30.00	120.00
	1904	12 pcs.	—	—	Proof	1000.

1/4 BALBOA

6.2500 g, .900 SILVER, .1809 oz ASW
High relief.

KM#	Date	Mintage	Fine	VF	XF	Unc
11.1	1930	.400	2.50	4.00	15.00	65.00
	1930	20 pcs.	—	Matte Proof		2000.
	1931	.048	15.00	30.00	200.00	1750.
	1932	.126	2.50	5.00	40.00	350.00
	1933	.120	2.50	5.00	20.00	175.00
	1934	.090	2.50	5.00	20.00	125.00
	1947	.700	1.50	3.00	6.00	25.00

Low relief.

KM#	Date	Mintage	Fine	VF	XF	Unc
11.2	1962	4.000	BV	1.00	2.00	3.00
	1962	25 pcs.	—	—	Proof	500.00

COPPER-NICKEL CLAD COPPER

KM#	Date	Mintage	VF	XF	Unc
11a	1966	7.400	.35	.50	1.00
	1966	.013	—	Proof	2.00
	1967	.020	—	Proof	1.50
	1968	1.200	.35	.60	1.25
	1968	.023	—	Proof	1.50
	1969	.014	—	Proof	1.50
	1970	2.000	.35	.50	1.00
	1970	9,528	—	Proof	2.00
	1971	.011	—	Proof	1.50
	1972	.013	—	Proof	1.50
	1973	.800	.40	1.00	1.50
	1973	.017	—	Proof	1.50
	1974	.018	—	Proof	1.50
	1975	1.500	.35	.50	.75
	1979	2.000	.25	.35	.50
	1980	2.000	.25	.35	.50
	1982	3.000	.25	.35	.50
	1983	6.000	.25	.35	.50
	1986 (RCM)	3.000	.25	.35	1.50
	1993	—	—	Proof	2.00

6.2500 g, .900 SILVER, .1809 oz ASW
50th Anniversary of the Republic

KM#	Date	Mintage	Fine	VF	XF	Unc
19	1953	1.200	BV	1.50	3.00	15.00

KM#	Date	Mintage	Fine	VF	XF	Unc
25	1961	2.000	BV	1.25	2.00	4.00

COPPER-NICKEL CLAD COPPER

KM#	Date	Mintage	VF	XF	Unc
88	1983FM(P)	—	—	Proof	4.00
	1984FM(P)	—	—	Proof	4.00
	1985FM(P)	*	—	Proof	7.50

*NOTE: Unauthorized striking.

25 CENTESIMOS

COPPER-NICKEL CLAD COPPER
Justo Arosemena

KM#	Date	Mintage	VF	XF	Unc
37.1	1975(RCM)	.040	.25	.50	1.00
	1975FM(M)	5,000	1.00	1.75	3.00
	1975FM(U)	1,410	—	—	4.00
	1975FM(P)	.041	—	Proof	1.00
	1976(RCM)	.012	.35	.50	1.00
	1976FM(M)	2,500	.75	1.50	2.50
	1976FM(P)	.012	—	Proof	1.00
	1977FM(U)	2,500	.75	1.50	2.50
	1977FM(P)	9,548	—	Proof	1.00
	1979FM(U)	4,000	.50	1.00	1.50
	1979FM(P)	5,949	—	Proof	1.00
	1980FM(U)	4,000	.50	1.00	1.50
	1981FM(P)	1,973	—	Proof	2.00
	1982FM(U)	2,000	.75	1.50	2.00
	1982FM(P)	1,480	—	Proof	2.00

Edge lettering: 1830 BOLIVAR 1980

KM#	Date	Mintage	VF	XF	Unc
37.2	1980FM(P)	2,629	—	Proof	2.00

75th Anniversary of Independence

KM#	Date	Mintage	VF	XF	Unc
49	1978FM(U)	8,000	.35	.50	1.00
	1978FM(P)	.011	—	Proof	1.50

50 CENTESIMOS

25.0000 g, .900 SILVER, .7235 oz ASW

KM#	Date	Mintage	Fine	VF	XF	Unc
5	1904	1.800*	12.00	20.00	50.00	250.00
	1904	12 pcs.	—	—	Proof	1500.
	1905	1.000*	20.00	40.00	100.00	400.00

*NOTE: 1,000,000 melted in 1931 to issue 1 Balboa coin at San Francisco Mint.

1/2 BALBOA

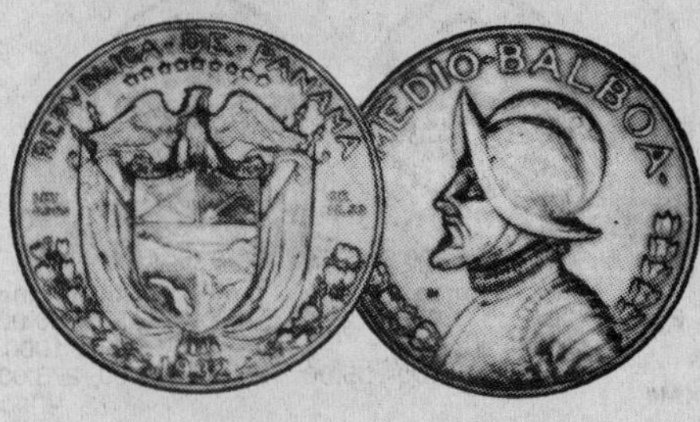

12.5000 g, .900 SILVER, .3617 oz ASW
High relief.

KM#	Date	Mintage	Fine	VF	XF	Unc
12.1	1930	.300	3.50	8.00	25.00	95.00
	1930	20 pcs.	—	Matte Proof		2500.
	1932	.063	5.00	12.00	175.00	1000.
	1933	.120	4.00	6.00	45.00	300.00
	1934	.090	4.00	6.00	50.00	350.00
	1947	.450	BV	3.50	10.00	35.00

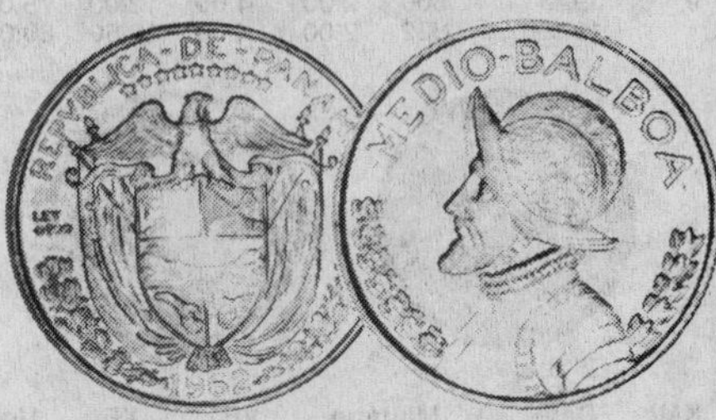

Low relief.

KM#	Date	Mintage	Fine	VF	XF	Unc
12.2	1962	.700	BV	2.50	3.50	6.50
	1962	25 pcs.	—	—	Proof	750.00

12.5000 g, .400 CLAD SILVER, .1608 oz ASW
Obv: Normal helmet.

KM#	Date	Mintage	VF	XF	Unc
12a.1	1966	1.000	1.50	2.00	5.00
	1966	.013	—	Proof	3.00
	1967	.300	1.50	2.00	5.00
	1967	.020	—	Proof	3.00
	1968	1.000	1.50	2.00	5.00
	1968	.023	—	Proof	3.00
	1969	.014	—	Proof	3.00
	1970	.610	1.50	2.00	5.00
	1970	9,528	—	Proof	4.00
	1971	.011	—	Proof	3.00
	1972	.013	—	Proof	3.00
	1993	—	—	Proof	4.00

Error: Type II helmet rim incomplete

KM#	Date	Mintage	VF	XF	Unc
12a.2	1966	Inc. Ab.	5.00	3.50	17.50

COPPER-NICKEL CLAD COPPER

KM#	Date	Mintage	VF	XF	Unc
12b	1973	1.000	1.00	1.25	1.50
	1973	.017	—	Proof	2.00
	1974	.018	—	Proof	2.00
	1975	1.200	.75	1.25	1.50
	1979	1.000	—	.75	1.00
	1980	.400	—	.75	1.00
	1982	.400	—	.75	1.00
	1983	1.850	—	.75	1.00
	1986	.200	.75	1.50	5.00

12.5000 g, .900 SILVER, .3617 oz ASW
50th Anniversary of the Republic

KM#	Date	Mintage	Fine	VF	XF	Unc
20	1953	.600	—	BV	3.00	6.00

KM#	Date	Mintage	Fine	VF	XF	Unc
26	1961	.350	—	BV	4.00	7.00

COPPER-NICKEL CLAD COPPER

KM#	Date	Mintage	VF	XF	Unc
89	1983FM(P)	—	—	Proof	6.00
	1984FM(P)	—	—	Proof	6.00
	1985FM(P)	*	—	Proof	12.50

***NOTE:** Unauthorized striking.

50 CENTESIMOS

COPPER-NICKEL CLAD COPPER
Fernando de Lesseps

KM#	Date	Mintage	VF	XF	Unc
38.1	1975(RCM)	.020	1.00	1.50	2.00
	1975FM(M)	2,000	1.50	3.00	5.00
	1975FM(U)	1,410	—	—	6.50
	1975FM(P)	.041	—	Proof	2.00
	1976(RCM)	.012	1.00	1.50	2.00
	1976FM(M)	1,250	1.00	2.00	3.00
	1976FM(P)	.012	—	Proof	2.00
	1977FM(U)	1,250	1.00	2.00	3.00
	1977FM(P)	9,548	—	Proof	2.00
	1979FM(U)	2,000	1.00	2.00	3.00
	1979FM(P)	5,949	—	Proof	2.00
	1980FM(U)	2,000	1.00	2.00	3.00
	1981FM(P)	1,973	—	Proof	3.00
	1982FM(U)	1,000	1.00	2.00	3.00
	1982FM(P)	1,480	—	Proof	3.00

Edge lettering: 1830 BOLIVAR 1980

KM#	Date	Mintage	VF	XF	Unc
38.2	1980FM(P)	2,629	—	Proof	3.00
	1980FM(P) (error) w/o edge lettering				
		Inc. Ab.	—	Proof	65.00

75th Anniversary of Independence

KM#	Date	Mintage	VF	XF	Unc
50	1978FM(U)	8,000	1.00	2.00	4.00
	1978FM(P)	.011	—	Proof	5.00

BALBOA

26.7300 g, .900 SILVER, .7735 oz ASW
Vasco Nunez de Balboa

KM#	Date	Mintage	Fine	VF	XF	Unc
13	1931	.200	6.00	8.00	17.50	80.00
	1931	20 pcs.	—	Matte Proof		3000.
	1934	.225	6.00	7.50	15.00	80.00
	1947	.500	BV	4.00	5.00	12.50

50th Anniversary of the Republic
Obv: Similar to KM#13.

KM#	Date	Mintage	Fine	VF	XF	Unc
21	1953	.050	5.00	8.00	10.00	25.00

KM#	Date	Mintage	VF	XF	Unc
27	1966	.300	—	—	10.00
	1966	.013	—	Proof	15.00
	1967	.020	—	Proof	12.00
	1968	.023	—	Proof	12.00
	1969	.014	—	Proof	12.00
	1970	.013	—	Proof	15.00
	1971	.018	—	Proof	12.00
	1972	.023	—	Proof	12.00
	1973	.030	—	Proof	12.00
	1974	.030	—	Proof	12.00

NOTE: More than 200,000 of 1966 dates were melted down in 1971 for silver for the 20 Balboas.

COPPER-NICKEL CLAD COPPER

KM#	Date	Mintage	VF	XF	Unc
39.1	1975FM(M)	4,035	—	—	15.00
	1975FM(U)	1,410	—	—	25.00
	1976FM(M)	625 pcs.	—	—	40.00
	1977FM(U)	625 pcs.	—	—	40.00
	1979FM(U)	1,000	—	—	30.00
	1980FM(U)	1,000	—	—	25.00
	1982FM(U)	500 pcs.	—	—	40.00

26.7300 g, .925 SILVER, .7950 oz ASW

KM#	Date	Mintage	VF	XF	Unc
39.1a	1975FM(P)	.045	—	Proof	12.00
	1976FM(P)	.014	—	Proof	12.00
	1977FM(P)	.011	—	Proof	12.00
	1979FM(P)	7,160	—	Proof	12.00

20.7400 g, .500 SILVER, .3334 oz ASW

KM#	Date	Mintage	VF	XF	Unc
39.1b	1981FM(P)	2,633	—	Proof	18.00
	1982FM(P)	1,837	—	Proof	18.00

COPPER-NICKEL CLAD COPPER
Obv: Erroronеous silver content (LEY .925) below arms.

KM#	Date	Mintage	VF	XF	Unc
39.2	1975	.010	—	—	7.00
	1976	.012	—	—	7.00

20.7400 g, .500 SILVER, .3334 oz ASW
Edge lettering: 1830 BOLIVAR 1980

KM#	Date	Mintage	VF	XF	Unc
39.3	1980FM(P)	2,629	—	Proof	18.00

COPPER-NICKEL CLAD COPPER
Obv: Erroneous silver content (LEY .500) below arms.

KM#	Date	Mintage	VF	XF	Unc
39.4	1982FM(U)	11 pcs.	—	—	750.00

75th Anniversary of Independence

KM#	Date	Mintage	VF	XF	Unc
51	1978FM(U)	4,000	—	—	10.00

.925 SILVER

KM#	Date	Mintage	VF	XF	Unc
51a	1978FM(P)	.013	—	Proof	16.00

COPPER-NICKEL

Death of General Omar Torrijos

KM#	Date	Mintage	VF	XF	Unc
76	1982	.200	—	1.50	3.50
	1982 frosted obverse and reverse				
		200 pcs.	—	Proof	150.00
	1982 frosted obverse				
		50 pcs.	—	Proof	200.00
	1983	.200	—	1.50	3.50
	1984	.200	—	1.50	3.50

***NOTE:** 50 pieces with frosted obverse only and 200 pieces with frosted obverse and reverse.

KM#	Date	Mintage	VF	XF	Unc
90	1983FM(M)	—	—	—	5.00

20.7400 g, .500 SILVER, .3334 oz ASW

KM#	Date	Mintage	VF	XF	Unc
90a	1983FM(P)	1,602	—	Proof	22.50
	1984FM(P)	1,044	—	Proof	22.50
	1985FM(P)	954 pcs.	—	Proof	40.00

5 BALBOAS

35.7000 g, .925 SILVER, 1.0617 oz ASW
11th Central American and Caribbean Games

KM#	Date	Mintage	VF	XF	Unc
28	1970FM	1.647	—	—	7.00
	1970FM(M)	.603	—	—	7.00
	1970FM(P)	.059	—	Proof	10.00

35.0000 g, .900 SILVER, 1.0128 oz ASW
F.A.O. Issue
Obv: Similar to Y#28.

KM#	Date	Mintage	VF	XF	Unc
30	1972	.070	—	—	10.00
	1972	.010	—	Proof	20.00

COPPER-NICKEL CLAD COPPER
Belisario Porras
Obv: Similar to KM#28.

KM#	Date	Mintage	VF	XF	Unc
40.1	1975FM(M)	5,125	—	—	10.00
	1975FM(U)	1,410	—	—	20.00
	1976FM(M)	125 pcs.	—	—	75.00
	1977FM(U)	125 pcs.	—	—	75.00
	1979FM(U)	1,000	—	—	15.00
	1980FM(U)	1,000	—	—	15.00
	1982FM(U)	1,200	—	—	15.00

35.1200 g, .925 SILVER, 1.0446 oz ASW

KM#	Date	Mintage	VF	XF	Unc
40.1a	1975FM(P)	.041	—	Proof	15.00
	1976FM(P)	.012	—	Proof	15.00
	1977FM(P)	9,548	—	Proof	15.00
	1979FM(P)	5,949	—	Proof	15.00

23.3300 g, .500 SILVER, .3751 oz ASW

KM#	Date	Mintage	VF	XF	Unc
40.1b	1981FM(P)	1,973	—	Proof	30.00
	1982FM(P)	1,480	—	Proof	30.00

COPPER-NICKEL CLAD COPPER
Obv: Erroneous silver content
(LEY .925) below arms.

KM#	Date	Mintage	VF	XF	Unc
40.2	1975	4,000	—	—	8.50
	1976	5,000	—	—	8.50

23.3300 g, .500 SILVER, .3751 oz ASW
Edge lettering: 1830 BOLIVAR 1980

KM#	Date	Mintage	VF	XF	Unc
40.3	1980FM(P)	2,629	—	Proof	20.00

Obv: Erroneous silver content
(LEY .925) below arms.

KM#	Date	Mintage	VF	XF	Unc
40.4	1982FM(P)	—	—	Proof	75.00

COPPER-NICKEL CLAD COPPER
Obv: Erroneous silver content
(LEY .500) below arms.

KM#	Date	Mintage	VF	XF	Unc
40.5	1982FM(U)	200 pcs.	—	—	50.00

75th Anniversary of Independence

KM#	Date	Mintage	VF	XF	Unc
52	1978FM(U)	2,000	—	—	15.00

35.1200 g, .925 SILVER, 1.0446 oz ASW

KM#	Date	Mintage	VF	XF	Unc
52a	1978FM(P)	.011	—	Proof	25.00

Panama Canal Treaty Implementation

KM#	Date	Mintage	VF	XF	Unc
58	1979FM(P)	6,854	—	Proof	20.00

24.1100 g, .500 SILVER, .3875 oz ASW
Champions of Boxing

KM#	Date	Mintage	VF	XF	Unc
63	1980	1,261	—	Proof	40.00

24.1600 g, .925 SILVER, .7186 oz ASW
Champions of Soccer

KM#	Date	Mintage	VF	XF	Unc
77	1982	9,446	—	Proof	35.0

23.3300 g, .500 SILVER, .3751 oz ASW

KM#	Date	Mintage	VF	XF	Unc
91	1983FM(P)	1,776	—	Proof	30.0
	1984FM(P)	889 pcs.	—	Proof	30.0

Discovery of the Pacific Ocean

KM#	Date	Mintage	VF	XF	Unc
04	1985FM(P)	765 pcs.	—	Proof	100.00

10 BALBOAS

42.4800 g, .925 SILVER, 1.2635 oz ASW
Panama Canal Treaty Ratification

KM#	Date	Mintage	VF	XF	Unc
3	1978FM(P)	.012	—	Proof	22.50

NICKEL

KM#	Date	Mintage	VF	XF	Unc
3a	1978	.300	—	12.00	20.00

42.4800 g, .925 SILVER, 1.2635 oz ASW
Panama Canal Treaty Implementation

KM#	Date	Mintage	VF	XF	Unc
9	1979FM(P)	7,229	—	Proof	30.00

26.5000 g, .500 SILVER, .4260 oz ASW
Balseria Game

KM#	Date	Mintage	VF	XF	Unc
4	1980	1,267	—	Proof	40.00

Champions of Soccer

KM#	Date	Mintage	VF	XF	Unc
78	1982	9,076	—	Proof	30.00

International Year of the Child

KM#	Date	Mintage	VF	XF	Unc
79	1982	8,460	—	Proof	30.00

20 BALBOAS

129.5900 g, .925 SILVER, 3.8544 oz ASW
Illustration reduced. Actual size: 61mm.
150th Anniversary of
Central American Independence.
Obv: Similar to 5 Balboas, KM#28.

KM#	Date	Mintage	VF	XF	Unc
29	1971FM(M)	.069	—	—	32.50
	1971FM(P)	.040	—	Proof	40.00

Illustration reduced. Actual size: 61mm.
Regular Issue, Simon Bolivar
Obv: Similar to 5 Balboas, KM#28.

KM#	Date	Mintage	VF	XF	Unc
31	1972FM(M)	.037	—	—	35.00
	1972FM(P)	.048	—	Proof	40.00
	1973FM(M)	.094	—	—	30.00
	1973FM(P)	.074	—	Proof	40.00
	1974FM(M)	.099	—	—	30.00
	1974FM(P)	.161	—	Proof	40.00
	1975FM(M)	2,500	—	—	55.00
	1975FM(U)	—	—	—	120.00
	1975FM(P)	.062	—	Proof	40.00
	1976FM(M)	2,500	—	—	60.00
	1976FM(P)	.022	—	Proof	45.00

Illustration reduced. Actual size: 61mm.
Vasco Nunez de Balboa
Obv: Similar to 5 Balboas, KM#28.

KM#	Date	Mintage	VF	XF	Unc
44	1977FM(U)	2,879	—	—	65.00
	1977FM(P)	.024	—	Proof	55.00
	1979FM(U)	2,500	—	—	65.00
	1979FM(P)	.013	—	Proof	60.00

75th Anniversary of Independence
Rev: Similar to KM#44.

KM#	Date	Mintage	VF	XF	Unc
54	1978FM(U)	2,500	—	—	70.00
	1978FM(P)	.023	—	Proof	50.00

119.8800 g, .500 SILVER, 1.9273 oz ASW
Simon Bolivar Death Sesquicentenarium
Obv: Similar to 5 Balboas, KM#28.

KM#	Date	Mintage	VF	XF	Unc
65	1980FM(U)	1,000	—	—	120.00
	1980FM(P)	3,714	—	Proof	80.00

118.5700 g, .500 SILVER, 1.9060 oz ASW
Simon Bolivar, El Libertador

KM#	Date	Mintage	VF	XF	Unc
71	1981FM(U)	500 pcs.	—	—	135.00
	1981FM(P)	3,528	—	Proof	85.00

2.1400 g, .500 GOLD, .0344 oz AGW
Figure of Eight Butterfly

KM#	Date	Mintage	VF	XF	Unc
72	1981FM(U)	205 pcs.	—	—	125.00
	1981FM(P)	4,445	—	Proof	45.00

119.8800 g, .500 SILVER, 1.9273 oz ASW
Balboa, Discoveror of the Pacific

KM#	Date	Mintage	VF	XF	Unc
80	1982FM(P)	2,352	—	Proof	120.00

2.1400 g, .500 GOLD, .0344 oz AGW
Hummingbird

KM#	Date	Mintage	VF	XF	Unc
81	1982FM(U)	140 pcs.	—	—	125.00
	1982FM(P)	3,445	—	Proof	50.00

Banded Butterfly Fish

KM#	Date	Mintage	VF	XF	Unc
92	1983FM(U)	—	—	—	125.00
	1983FM(P)	1,671	—	Proof	55.00

118.5700 g, .500 SILVER, 1.9060 oz ASW
200th Anniversary of Birth of Bolivar
Obv: Similar to 5 Balboas, KM#77.

KM#	Date	Mintage	VF	XF	Unc
93	1983FM(U)	500 pcs.	—	—	80.00
	1983FM(P)	3,186	—	Proof	50.00

2.1400 g, .500 GOLD, .0344 oz AGW
Puma

KM#	Date	Mintage	VF	XF	Unc
97	1984FM(U)	100 pcs.	—	—	175.00
	1984FM(P)	357 pcs.	—	Proof	80.00

119.8800 g, .500 SILVER, 1.9273 oz ASW
Balboa and Indian Guide

KM#	Date	Mintage	VF	XF	Unc
98	1984FM(P)	1,760	—	Proof	150.00

2.1400 g, .500 GOLD, .0344 oz AGW
Harpy Eagle

KM#	Date	Mintage	VF	XF	Unc
102	1985FM(P)	817 pcs.	—	Proof	80.00

119.8800 g, .500 SILVER, 1.9273 oz ASW
Discovery of the Pacific Ocean

KM#	Date	Mintage	VF	XF	Unc
105	1985FM(P)	1,402	—	Proof	145.00

50 BALBOAS

5.3700 g, .500 GOLD, .0861 oz AGW
Christmas 1981

KM#	Date	Mintage	VF	XF	Unc
73	1981FM(U)	154 pcs.	—	—	150.00
	1981FM(P)	1,940	—	Proof	75.00

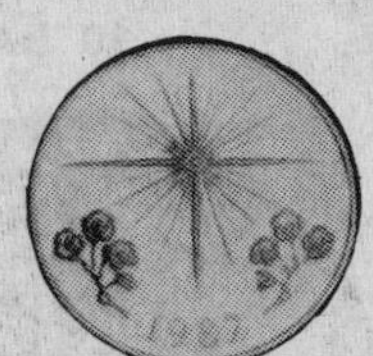

Christmas 1982

KM#	Date	Mintage	VF	XF	Unc
82	1982FM(U)	60 pcs.	—	—	200.00
	1982FM(P)	1,361	—	Proof	80.00

Christmas 1983

KM#	Date	Mintage	VF	XF	Unc
94	1983FM(U)	—	—	—	150.00
	1983FM(P)	1,283	—	Proof	85.00

Peace of Christmas

KM#	Date	Mintage	VF	XF	Unc
99	1984FM(P)	—	—	Proof	200.00

75 BALBOAS

10.6000 g, .500 GOLD, .1704 oz AGW
75th Anniversary of Independence

KM#	Date	Mintage	VF	XF	Unc
55	1978FM(U)	410 pcs.	—	—	110.0
	1978FM(P)	9,161	—	Proof	90.0

100 BALBOAS

8.1600 g, .900 GOLD, .2361 oz AGW
500th Anniversary of Birth of Balboa

KM#	Date	Mintage	VF	XF	Unc
41	1975FM(U)	.044	—	—	100.0
	1975FM(P)	.075	—	Proof	100.0
	1976FM(M)	50 pcs.	—	—	350.0
	1976FM(U)	3,013	—	—	110.0
	1976FM(P)	.011	—	Proof	100.0
	1977FM(M)	50 pcs.	—	—	350.0
	1977FM(U)	324 pcs.	—	—	145.0
	1977FM(P)	5,092	—	Proof	125.0

Peace and Progress

KM#	Date	Mintage	VF	XF	Unc
6	1978FM(M)	50 pcs.	—	—	350.00
	1978FM(U)	300 pcs.	—	—	200.00
	1978FM(P)	6,086	—	Proof	130.00

Pre-Columbian Art - Golden Turtle

KM#	Date	Mintage	VF	XF	Unc
0	1979FM(M)	50 pcs.	—	—	350.00
	1979FM(U)	240 pcs.	—	—	200.00
	1979FM(P)	4,829	—	Proof	125.00

Pre-Columbian Art - Golden Condor

KM#	Date	Mintage	VF	XF	Unc
6	1980FM(U)	209 pcs.	—	—	225.00
	1980FM(P)	2,411	—	Proof	175.00

7.1300 g, .500 GOLD, .1146 oz AGW
Panama Canal Centennial

KM#	Date	Mintage	VF	XF	Unc
7	1980FM(U)	77 pcs.	—	—	250.00
	1980FM(P)	2,468	—	Proof	100.00

Pre-Columbian Art - Cocle Indian Ceremonial Mask

KM#	Date	Mintage	VF	XF	Unc
4	1981FM(U)	174 pcs.	—	—	185.00
	1981FM(P)	1,841	—	Proof	110.00

Pre-Columbian Art - Indian Design

KM#	Date	Mintage	VF	XF	Unc
3	1982FM(U)	26 pcs.	—	—	350.00
	1982FM(P)	578 pcs.	—	Proof	175.00

Pre-Columbian Art - Cocle Indian Birds

KM#	Date	Mintage	VF	XF	Unc
5	1983FM(U)	—	—	—	220.00
	1983FM(P)	1,308	—	Proof	110.00

Pre-Columbian Art - Indian Art

KM#	Date	Mintage	VF	XF	Unc
100	1984FM(U)	—	—	—	275.00
	1984FM(P)	—	—	Proof	175.00

150 BALBOAS

9.3000 g, .999 PLATINUM, .2987 oz APW
150th Anniversary Pan-American Congress

KM#	Date	Mintage	VF	XF	Unc
43	1976FM(M)	30 pcs.	—	—	750.00
	1976FM(U)	510 pcs.	—	—	200.00
	1976FM(P)	.013	—	Proof	175.00

7.6700 g, .500 GOLD, .1233 oz AGW
Simon Bolivar Death Sesquicentenarium

KM#	Date	Mintage	VF	XF	Unc
68	1980FM(U)	169 pcs.	—	—	200.00
	1980FM(P)	1,837	—	Proof	125.00

200 BALBOAS

9.5000 g, .980 PLATINUM, .2994 oz APW
Panama Canal Treaty Implementation

KM#	Date	Mintage	VF	XF	Unc
61	1979FM(P)	2,178	—	Proof	200.00

9.3300 g, .980 PLATINUM, .2940 oz APW
Champions of Boxing

KM#	Date	Mintage	VF	XF	Unc
69	1980	219 pcs.	—	Proof	400.00

500 BALBOAS

41.7000 g, .900 GOLD, 1.2067 oz AGW
500th Anniversary of Birth of Balboa

KM#	Date	Mintage	VF	XF	Unc
42	1975FM(M)	10 pcs.	—	—	1500.
	1975FM(U)	1,496	—	—	525.00
	1975FM(P)	9,824	—	Proof	500.00
	1976FM(M)	10 pcs.	—	—	1500.
	1976FM(U)	160 pcs.	—	—	625.00
	1976FM(P)	2,669	—	Proof	550.00
	1977FM(M)	10 pcs.	—	—	1500.
	1977FM(U)	59 pcs.	—	—	725.00
	1977FM(P)	1,980	—	Proof	550.00

30th Anniversary of Organization of American States
Obv: Similar to KM#42.

KM#	Date	Mintage	VF	XF	Unc
57	1978FM(M)	10 pcs.	—	—	1500.
	1978FM(U)	106 pcs.	—	—	600.00
	1978FM(P)	2,009	—	Proof	550.00

Golden Jaguar
Obv: Similar to KM#42.

KM#	Date	Mintage	VF	XF	Unc
62	1979FM(U)	130 pcs.	—	—	750.00
	1979FM(P)	1,657	—	Proof	600.00

37.1800 g, .500 GOLD, .5977 oz AGW
White Herons
Obv: Similar to KM#42.

KM#	Date	Mintage	VF	XF	Unc
70	1980FM(U)	54 pcs.	—	—	775.00
	1980FM(P)	612 pcs.	—	Proof	625.00

Sailfish
Obv: Similar to KM#42.

KM#	Date	Mintage	VF	XF	Unc
75	1981FM(U)	41 pcs.	—	—	850.00
	1981FM(P)	487 pcs.	—	Proof	650.00

Death of General Omar Torrijos
Obv: Similar to KM#42.

KM#	Date	Mintage	VF	XF	Unc
84	1982FM(U)	97 pcs.	—	—	700.00
	1982FM(P)	398 pcs.	—	Proof	525.00

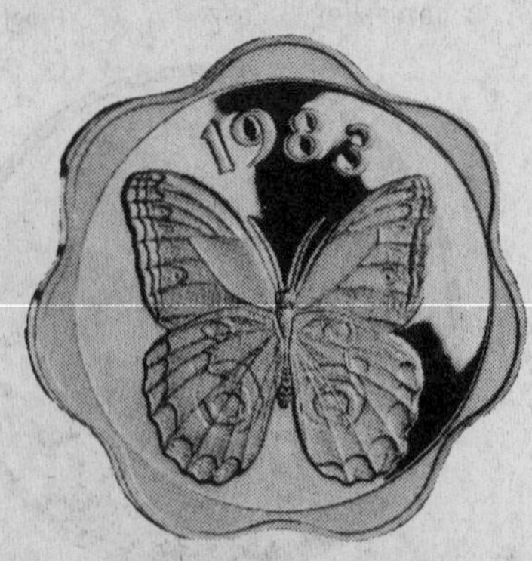

Owl Butterfly

KM#	Date	Mintage	VF	XF	Unc
96	1983FM(U)	100 pcs.	—	—	800.00
	1983FM(P)	469 pcs.	—	Proof	900.00

37.1200 g, .500 GOLD, .5968 oz AGW
Golden Eagle

KM#	Date	Mintage	VF	XF	Unc
101	1984FM(U)	10 pcs.	—	—	2000.
	1984FM(P)	156 pcs.	—	Proof	800.00

37.1800 g, .500 GOLD, .5977 oz AGW
National Eagle

KM#	Date	Mintage	VF	XF	Unc
103	1985FM(P)	184 pcs.	—	Proof	1450.

MINT SETS (MS)

KM#	Date	Mintage	Identification	Issue Price	Mkt. Val.
MS1	1975(8)	1,410	KM33.1-40.1	25.00	65.00

PROOF SETS (PS)

KM#	Date	Mintage	Identification	Issue Price	Mkt. Val.
PS1	1904(5)	*12	KM1-5	—	5000.
PS2	1930(3)	20	KM10-12	—	Rare
PS3	1962(5)	25	KM10-12,22,23.2	—	2300.
PS4	1966(6)	12,701	KM10a-11a,12a.1,22, 23.2,27	15.25	25.00
PS5	1967(6)	19,983	KM10a-11a,12a.1,22, 23.2,27	15.25	17.50
PS6	1968(6)	23,210	KM10a-11a,12a.1,22, 23.2,27	15.25	17.50
PS7	1969(6)	14,000	KM10a-11a,12a.1,22, 23.2,27	15.25	17.50
PS8	1970(6)	9,528	KM10a-11a,12a.1,22, 23.2,27	15.25	20.00
PS9	1971(6)	10,696	KM10a-11a,12a.1,22, 23.2,27	15.25	15.00
PS10	1972(6)	13,322	KM10a-11a,12a.1,22, 23.2,27	15.25	15.00
PS11	1973(6)	16,946	KM10a-11a,12b,22, 23.2,27	17.50	16.50
PS12	1974(6)	17,521	KM10a-11a,12b,22, 23.2,27	17.50	16.5
PS13	1975(9)	37,041	KM31,33.1-38.1,39.1a-40.1a	130.00	80.0
PS14	1975(8)	4,057	KM31,34.1-38.1,39.1a-40.1a	50.00	30.0
PS15	1976(9)	10,610	KM31,33.1-38.1,39.1a-40.1a	102.00	80.0
PS16	1976(8)	1,792	KM33.1-38.1,39.1a-40.1a	50.00	30.0
PS17	1976(2)	11,479	KM31,34.1	51.00	40.0
PS18	1977(9)	8,093	KM33.1-38.1,39.1a-40.1a,44	100.00	90.0
PS19	1977(8)	1,455	KM33.1-38.1,39.1a-40.1a	50.00	30.0
PS20	1978(9)	9,667	KM45-50,51a,52a,54	110.00	100.0
PS21	1978(8)	1,122	KM45-50,51a,52a,54	—	40.0
PS22	1979(9)	4,974	KM33.1-38.1,39.1a-40.1a,44	132.00	100.0
PS23	1979(8)	975	KM33.1-38.1,39.1a-		
PS23			40.1a	60.00	35.0
PS24	1979(2)	1,775	KM58-59	125.00	55.0
PS25	1980(9)	1,686	KM33.2-38.2,39.3-40.3,65	287.00	150.0
PS26	1980(8)	943	KM33.2-38.2,39.3-40.3,	87.00	40.0
PS27	1981(9)	1,279	KM33.1-38.1,39.1b-40.1b,71	212.00	150.0
PS28	1981(8)	694	KM33.1-38.1,39.1b-40.1b	87.00	35.0
PS29	1982(9)	746	KM33.1-38.1,39.1b-40.1b,80	212.00	200.0
PS30	1982(9)	Error set	KM33-38,39.1b,40.4, 80	212.00	250.0
PS31	1982(8)	734	KM33-38,39.1b-40.1b	87.00	35.0
PS32	1982(8)	Error set	KM33-38,39.1b,40.4	—	120.0
PS33	1983(9)	—	KM22,85-89,90a,91,93	87.00	155.0
PS34	1983(8)	—	KM22,85-89,90a,91	—	70.0
PS35	1984(9)	—	KM22,85-89,90a,91,98	—	200.0
PS36	1984(8)	—	KM22,85-89,90a,91	72.00	70.0
PS37	1985(8)	765	KM22,85-89,90a,104	72.00	175.0
PS38	1988(5)	5,000	KM106a-109a,110	295.00	175.0
PS39	1993(4)	—	KM10a-11a,12a.1,23.2	—	12.5

PALO SECO

Palo Seco Leper Colony was established in Balboa Canal Zone in 1907. It is known today as Palo Sec Hospital. The original issue of tokens totaled $1,800.0 of which $1,492.75 was destroyed on November 28 1955. The issue was backed by United States Currenc and was replaced by United States circulation coinage.

Leprosarium Token Coinage (Tn)

CENT

COPPER

KM#	Date	Mintage	VG	Fine	VF
Tn1	ND(1919)	—	25.00	45.00	85.0

5 CENTS

BRASS

KM#	Date	Mintage	VG	Fine	VF
Tn2	ND(1919)	—	30.00	50.00	100.0

10 CENTS

ALUMINUM

KM#	Date	Mintage	VG	Fine	VF
Tn3	ND(1919)	—	60.00	85.00	165.0

25 CENTS

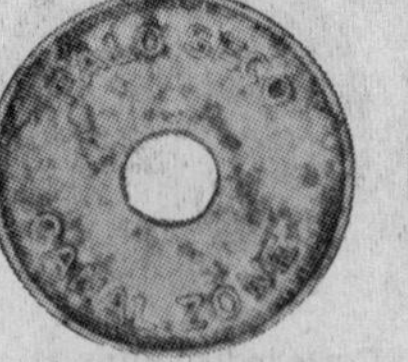

ALUMINUM

KM#	Date	Mintage	VG	Fine	VF
Tn4	ND(1919)	—	70.00	120.00	200.00

50 CENTS

ALUMINUM

KM#	Date	Mintage	VG	Fine	VF
Tn5	ND(1919)	—	90.00	140.00	250.00

DOLLAR

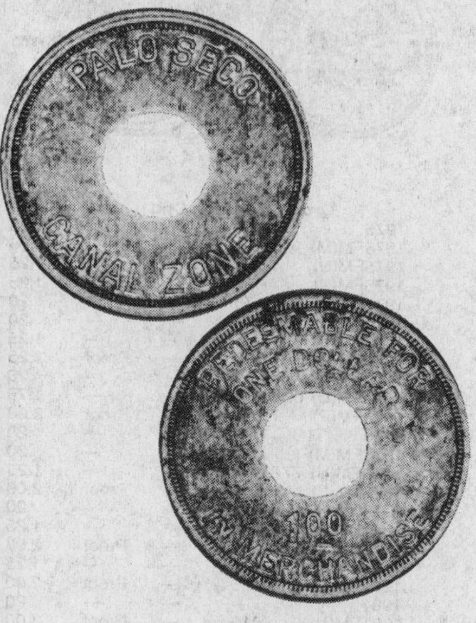

ALUMINUM

KM#	Date	Mintage	VG	Fine	VF
Tn6	ND(1919)	—	135.00	225.00	325.00

PAPUA NEW GUINEA

Papua New Guinea, an independent member of the British Commonwealth, occupies the eastern half of the island of New Guinea. It lies north of Australia near the equator and borders on West Irian. The country, which includes nearby Bismark archipelago, Buka and Bougainville, has an area of 178,260 sq. mi. (461,690 sq. km.) and a population of *3.7 million who are divided into more than 1,000 seperate tribes speaking more than 700 mutually unintelligible languages. Capital: Port Moresby. The economy is agricultural, and exports copra, rubber, cocoa, coffee, tea, gold and copper.

In 1884 Germany annexed the area known as German New Guinea (also Neu Guinea or Kaiser Wilhelmsland) comprising the northern section of eastern New Guinea, and granted its administration and development to the Neu-Guinea Compagnie. Administration reverted to Germany in 1889 following the failure of the company to exercise adequate administration. While a German protectorate, German New Guinea had an area of 92,159 sq. mi. (238,692 sq. km.) and a population of about 250,000. Capital: Herbertshohe, 1 of 4 capitals of German New Guinea. The seat of government was transferred to Rabaul in 1910. Copra was the chief crop. Australian troops occupied German New Guinea in Aug. 1914, shortly after Great Britain declared war on Germany. It was mandated to Australia by the Leage of Nations in 1920, known as the Territory of New Guinea. The territory was invaded and most of it was occupied by Japan in 1942. Following the Japanese surrender, it came under U.N. trusteeship, Dec. 13, 1946, with Australia as the administering power.

The Papua and New Guinea act, 1949, provided for the government of Papua and New Guinea as one administrative unit. On Dec. 1, 1973, Papua New Guinea became selfgoverning with Australia retaining responsibility for defense and foreign affairs. Full independence was achieved on Sept. 16, 1975. Papua New Guinea is a member of the Commonwealth of Nations. The Queen of England is Chief of State.

GERMAN NEW GUINEA

RULERS

German, 1884-1914

MINT MARKS

A - Berlin

MONETARY SYSTEM

100 Pfennig = 1 Mark

PFENNIG

COPPER

KM#	Date	Mintage	Fine	VF	XF	Unc
1	1894A	.033	20.00	40.00	90.00	150.00
	1894A	—	—	—	Proof	400.00

2 PFENNIG

COPPER

KM#	Date	Mintage	Fine	VF	XF	Unc
2	1894A	.017	35.00	65.00	120.00	200.00
	1894A	—	—	—	Proof	550.00

10 PFENNIG

COPPER

KM#	Date	Mintage	Fine	VF	XF	Unc
3	1894A	.024	30.00	60.00	140.00	300.00
	1894A	—	—	—	Proof	1250.

1/2 MARK

2.7780 g, .900 SILVER, .0804 oz ASW

KM#	Date	Mintage	Fine	VF	XF	Unc
4	1894A	.016	50.00	100.00	200.00	350.00
	1894A	—	—	—	Proof	550.00

MARK

5.5560 g, .900 SILVER, .1608 oz ASW

KM#	Date	Mintage	Fine	VF	XF	Unc
5	1894A	.033	50.00	100.00	200.00	400.00
	1894A	—	—	—	Proof	700.00

2 MARK

11.1110 g, .900 SILVER, .3215 oz ASW

KM#	Date	Mintage	Fine	VF	XF	Unc
6	1894A	.013	125.00	225.00	450.00	850.00
	1894A	—	—	—	Proof	1200.

5 MARK

27.7780 g, .900 SILVER, .8039 oz ASW

KM#	Date	Mintage	Fine	VF	XF	Unc
7	1894A	.019	—	800.00	1200.	2000.
	1894A	—	—	—	Proof	3500.

10 MARK

3.9820 g, .900 GOLD, .1152 oz AGW

KM#	Date	Mintage	Fine	VF	XF	Unc
8	1895A	2,000	—	4000.	8250.	10,000.
	1895A	—	—	—	Proof	12,500.

20 MARK

7.9650 g, .900 GOLD, .2305 oz AGW

KM#	Date	Mintage	Fine	VF	XF	Unc
9	1895A	1,500	—	4000.	8500.	11,500.
	1895A	—	—	—	Proof	15,000.

PROOF SETS (PS)

KM#	Date	Mintage	Identification	Issue Price	Mkt. Val.
PS1	1894(7)	—	KM1-7	—	8150.

NEW GUINEA

New Guinea, the world's largest island after Greenland, was discovered by Spanish navigator Jorge de Menezes, who landed on the northwest shore in 1527. European interests, attracted by exaggerated estimates of the resources of the area, resulted in the island being claimed in part by Spain, the Netherlands, Great Britain and Germany.

RULERS

British 1910-1952

MONETARY SYSTEM

12 Pence = 1 Shilling
20 Shillings = 1 Pound

1/2 PENNY

COPPER-NICKEL

KM#	Date	Mintage	Fine	VF	XF	Unc
1	1929	.025	—	—	350.00	500.00
	1929	—	—	—	Proof	750.00

NOTE: Entire mintage returned to Melbourne Mint which later sold 400 pcs. in sets with KM#2. Balance of mintage was destroyed.

NICKEL

KM#	Date	Mintage	Fine	VF	XF	Unc
1a	1929	20 pcs.	—	—	Proof	750.00

PENNY

COPPER-NICKEL

KM#	Date	Mintage	Fine	VF	XF	Unc
2	1929	.063	—	—	350.00	500.00
	1929	—	—	—	Proof	750.00

NOTE: Entire mintage returned to Melbourne Mint which later sold 400 pcs. in sets with KM#1. Balance of mintage was destroyed.

NICKEL

KM#	Date	Mintage	Fine	VF	XF	Unc
2a	1929	20 pcs.	—	—	Proof	750.00

BRONZE

KM#	Date	Mintage	Fine	VF	XF	Unc
6	1936	.360	1.25	1.75	3.50	7.00
	1936	—	—	—	Proof	300.00

KM#	Date	Mintage	Fine	VF	XF	Unc
7	1938	.360	3.00	6.00	10.00	18.00
	1944	.240	1.50	2.75	5.00	9.00

3 PENCE

COPPER-NICKEL

KM#	Date	Mintage	Fine	VF	XF	Unc
3	1935	1.200	3.00	6.00	10.00	35.00
	1935	—	—	—	Proof	250.00

KM#	Date	Mintage	Fine	VF	XF	Unc
10	1944	.500	2.00	4.00	8.50	27.50

6 PENCE

COPPER-NICKEL

KM#	Date	Mintage	Fine	VF	XF	Unc
4	1935	2.000	3.50	7.50	10.00	35.00
	1935	—	—	—	Proof	250.00

KM#	Date	Mintage	Fine	VF	XF	Unc
9	1943	.130	6.00	9.00	15.00	45.00

SHILLING

5.3800 g, .925 SILVER, .1600 oz ASW

KM#	Date	Mintage	Fine	VF	XF	Unc
5	1935	2.100	1.00	2.00	3.50	6.00
	1936	1.360	1.00	2.00	3.50	6.00

KM#	Date	Mintage	Fine	VF	XF	Unc
8	1938	3.400	1.00	2.00	3.50	6.00
	1945	2.000	1.00	2.00	3.50	6.00

PROOF SETS (PS)

KM#	Date	Mintage	Identification	Issue Price	Mkt. Val.
PS1	1929(2)	—	KM1,2	—	1500.
PS2	1929(2)	20	KM1a,2a	—	1500.

PAPUA NEW GUINEA

MINT MARKS

FM - Franklin Mint, U.S.A.*

***NOTE:** From 1975 the Franklin Mint has produced coinage in up to 3 different qualities. Qualities of issue are designated in ( ) after each date and are defined as follows:

(M) MATTE - Normal circulation strike or a dull finish produced by sandblasting special uncirculated (polish finish) or proof quality dies.

(U) SPECIAL UNCIRCULATED - Polished or proof-like in appearance without any frosted features.

(P) PROOF - The highest quality obtainable having mirror-like fields and frosted features.

MONETARY SYSTEM

100 Toea = 1 Kina

TOEA

BRONZE
Paradise Bird - Wing Butterfly

KM#	Date	Mintage	VF	XF	Unc
1	1975	14.400	—	.15	.25
	1975FM(M)	.083	—	—	.30
	1975FM(U)	4,134	—	—	1.00
	1975FM(P)	.067	—	Proof	1.00
	1976	25.175	—	—	.15
	1976FM(M)	.084	—	—	.15
	1976FM(U)	976 pcs.	—	—	1.00
	1976FM(P)	.016	—	Proof	1.00
	1977FM(M)	.084	—	—	.15
	1977FM(U)	603 pcs.	—	—	1.50
	1977FM(P)	7,721	—	Proof	1.50
	1978	—	—	—	.20
	1978FM(M)	.083	—	—	.15
	1978FM(U)	777 pcs.	—	—	1.00
	1978FM(P)	5,540	—	Proof	1.50
	1979FM(M)	.084	—	—	.15
	1979FM(U)	1,366	—	—	1.00
1	1979FM(P)	2,728	—	Proof	1.50
	1980FM(U)	1,160	—	—	1.00
	1980FM(P)	2,125	—	Proof	1.50
	1981	—	—	—	1.00
	1981FM(M)	—	—	—	.15
	1981FM(P)	.010	—	Proof	2.00
	1982FM(M)	—	—	—	1.00
	1982FM(P)	—	—	Proof	2.00
	1983	—	—	—	.15
	1983FM(U)	360 pcs.	—	—	.15
	1983FM(P)	—	—	Proof	2.00
	1984	—	—	—	.15
	1984FM(P)	—	—	Proof	2.00
	1987	—	—	—	.15
	1990	—	—	—	.15

2 TOEA

BRONZE
Ornate Butterfly Cod

KM#	Date	Mintage	VF	XF	Unc
2	1975	11.400	—	.10	.25
	1975FM(M)	.042	—	—	.30
	1975FM(U)	4,134	—	—	1.25
	1975FM(P)	.067	—	Proof	1.25
	1976	15.175	—	.10	.20
	1976FM(M)	.042	—	—	.20
	1976FM(U)	976 pcs.	—	—	1.25
	1976FM(P)	.016	—	Proof	1.25
	1977FM(M)	.042	—	—	.20
	1977FM(U)	603 pcs.	—	—	1.75
	1977FM(P)	7,721	—	Proof	2.00
	1978	—	—	—	.20
	1978FM(M)	.042	—	—	.20
	1978FM(U)	777 pcs.	—	—	1.25
	1978FM(P)	5,540	—	Proof	2.00
	1979FM(M)	.042	—	—	.20
	1979FM(U)	1,366	—	—	1.25
	1979FM(P)	2,728	—	Proof	2.00
	1980FM(U)	1,160	—	—	1.25
	1980FM(P)	2,125	—	Proof	2.00
	1981	—	—	—	.20
	1981FM(P)	.010	—	Proof	3.00
	1982FM(M)	—	—	—	1.25
	1982FM(P)	—	—	Proof	3.00
	1983	—	—	—	.20
	1983FM(U)	360 pcs.	—	—	2.00
	1983FM(P)	—	—	Proof	3.00
	1984	—	—	—	.20
	1984	—	—	Proof	3.00
	1987	—	—	—	.20
	1990	—	—	—	.20

5 TOEA

COPPER-NICKEL
Plateless Turtle

KM#	Date	Mintage	VF	XF	Unc
3	1975	11.000	.15	.25	.45
	1975FM(M)	.017	—	—	.55
	1975FM(U)	4,134	—	—	1.50
	1975FM(P)	.067	—	Proof	1.50
	1976	24.000	.15	.25	.45
	1976FM(M)	.017	—	—	.50
	1976FM(U)	976 pcs.	—	—	1.50
	1976FM(P)	.016	—	Proof	1.50
	1977FM(M)	.017	—	—	.55
	1977FM(U)	603 pcs.	—	—	2.00
	1977FM(P)	7,721	—	Proof	2.50
	1978	2,000	—	—	3.00
	1978FM(M)	.017	—	—	.55
	1978FM(U)	777 pcs.	—	—	1.50
	1978FM(P)	5,540	—	Proof	2.50
	1979	—	—	—	.40
	1979FM(M)	.017	—	—	.55
	1979FM(U)	1,366	—	—	1.50
	1979FM(P)	2,728	—	Proof	2.50
	1980FM(U)	1,160	—	—	1.50
	1980FM(P)	2,125	—	Proof	2.50
	1981FM(P)	.010	—	Proof	4.00
	1982	—	—	—	.40
	1982FM(M)	—	—	—	1.50
	1982FM(P)	—	—	Proof	4.00
	1983FM(U)	360 pcs.	—	—	2.50
	1983FM(P)	—	—	Proof	4.00
	1984	—	—	—	.40
	1984FM(P)	—	—	Proof	4.00
	1987	—	—	—	.40
	1990	—	—	—	.40

10 TOEA

COPPER-NICKEL
Cuscus

KM#	Date	Mintage	VF	XF	Unc
4	1975	8.600	.20	.35	.65
	1975FM(M)	8,300	—	—	1.00
	1975FM(U)	4,134	—	—	1.75
	1975FM(P)	.067	—	Proof	2.00
	1976	—	.20	.35	.65
	1976FM(M)	8,300	—	—	1.00
	1976FM(U)	976 pcs.	—	—	1.75
	1976FM(P)	.016	—	Proof	2.00
	1977FM(M)	8,300	—	—	1.00
	1977FM(U)	603 pcs.	—	—	2.25
	1977FM(P)	7,721	—	Proof	3.00
	1978FM(M)	8,300	—	—	1.00
	1978FM(U)	777 pcs.	—	—	1.75
	1978FM(P)	5,540	—	Proof	3.00
	1979FM(M)	8,300	—	—	1.00
	1979FM(U)	1,366	—	—	1.75
	1979FM(P)	2,728	—	Proof	3.00
	1980FM(U)	1,160	—	—	1.75
	1980FM(P)	2,125	—	Proof	3.00
	1981FM(P)	.010	—	Proof	5.00
	1982FM(M)	—	—	—	1.75
	1982FM(P)	—	—	Proof	5.00
	1983FM(U)	360 pcs.	—	—	2.75
	1983FM(P)	—	—	Proof	5.00
	1984FM(P)	—	—	Proof	5.00

20 TOEA

COPPER-NICKEL
Cassowary

KM#	Date	Mintage	VF	XF	Unc
5	1975	15.500	.30	.65	1.25
	1975FM(M)	4,150	—	—	2.35
	1975FM(U)	4,134	—	—	2.35
	1975FM(P)	.067	—	Proof	3.00
	1976FM(M)	4,150	—	—	2.25
	1976FM(U)	976 pcs.	—	—	2.25
	1976FM(P)	.016	—	Proof	3.00
	1977FM(M)	4,150	—	—	2.25
	1977FM(U)	603 pcs.	—	—	2.75
	1977FM(P)	7,721	—	Proof	4.00
	1978	2.500	.45	1.00	1.50
	1978FM(M)	4,150	—	—	2.25
	1978FM(U)	777 pcs.	—	—	2.25
	1978FM(P)	5,540	—	Proof	4.00
	1979FM(M)	4,150	—	—	2.25
	1979FM(U)	1,366	—	—	2.25
	1979FM(P)	2,728	—	Proof	4.00
	1980FM(U)	1,160	—	—	2.25
	1980FM(P)	2,125	—	Proof	4.00
	1981	—	.25	.50	1.00
	1981FM(P)	.010	—	Proof	6.00
	1982FM(M)	—	—	—	2.25
	1982FM(P)	—	—	Proof	6.00
	1983FM(U)	360 pcs.	—	—	3.25
	1983FM(P)	—	—	Proof	6.00
	1984	—	.25	.50	1.00
	1984FM(P)	—	—	Proof	6.00
	1987	—	.25	.50	1.00
	1990	—	.25	.50	1.00

50 TOEA

COPPER-NICKEL
South Pacific Festival of Arts

KM#	Date	Mintage	VF	XF	Unc
5	1980	—	.75	1.25	2.50
	1980FM(U)	1,160	—	—	15.00
	1980FM(P)	2,125	—	Proof	10.00

9th South Pacific Games

KM#	Date	Mintage	VF	XF	Unc
31	1991	.025	—	—	15.00

KINA

COPPER-NICKEL
Sea and River Crocodiles

KM#	Date	Mintage	VF	XF	Unc
6	1975	2.000	1.35	2.00	3.00
	1975FM(M)	829 pcs.	—	—	10.00
	1975FM(U)	4,134	—	—	3.25
	1975FM(P)	.067	—	Proof	3.25
	1976FM(M)	829 pcs.	—	—	10.00
	1976FM(U)	976 pcs.	—	—	3.00
	1976FM(P)	.016	—	Proof	4.00
	1977FM(M)	829 pcs.	—	—	10.00
	1977FM(U)	603 pcs.	—	—	15.00
	1977FM(P)	7,721	—	Proof	5.00
	1978FM(M)	829 pcs.	—	—	10.00
	1978FM(U)	777 pcs.	—	—	3.00
	1978FM(P)	5,540	—	Proof	5.00
	1979FM(M)	829 pcs.	—	—	10.00
	1979FM(U)	1,366	—	—	3.00
	1979FM(P)	2,728	—	Proof	6.50
	1980FM(U)	1,160	—	—	3.00
	1980FM(P)	2,125	—	Proof	6.50
	1981FM(P)	.010	—	Proof	3.00
	1982FM(M)	—	—	—	3.00
	1982FM(P)	—	—	Proof	8.00
	1983FM(U)	360 pcs.	—	—	16.50
	1983FM(P)	—	—	Proof	8.00
	1984FM(P)	—	—	Proof	8.00

5 KINA

COPPER-NICKEL
New Guinea Eagle

KM#	Date	Mintage	VF	XF	Unc
7	1975FM(M)	166 pcs.	—	—	40.00
	1975FM(U)	4,134	—	—	7.50
	1976FM(M)	166 pcs.	—	—	40.00
	1976FM(U)	976 pcs.	—	—	12.50
	1977FM(M)	166 pcs.	—	—	40.00
	1977FM(U)	603 pcs.	—	—	25.00
	1978FM(M)	166 pcs.	—	—	40.00
	1978FM(U)	777 pcs.	—	—	12.50
	1979FM(M)	166 pcs.	—	—	40.00
	1979FM(U)	1,366	—	—	10.00
	1980FM(U)	1,160	—	—	10.00

27.6000 g, .500 SILVER, .4436 oz ASW

KM#	Date	Mintage	VF	XF	Unc
7a	1975FM(P)	.067	—	Proof	6.50
7a	1976FM(P)	.016	—	Proof	7.50
	1977FM(P)	7,721	—	Proof	10.00
	1978FM(P)	5,540	—	Proof	10.00
	1979FM(P)	2,728	—	Proof	12.50
	1980FM(P)	2,125	—	Proof	12.50

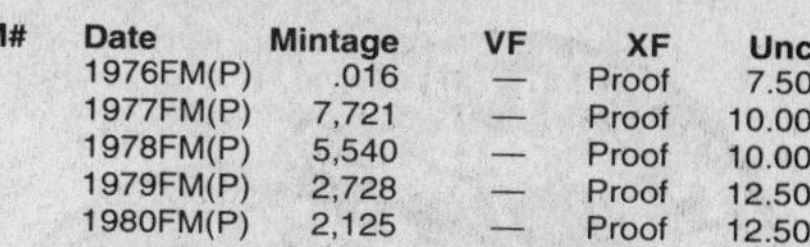

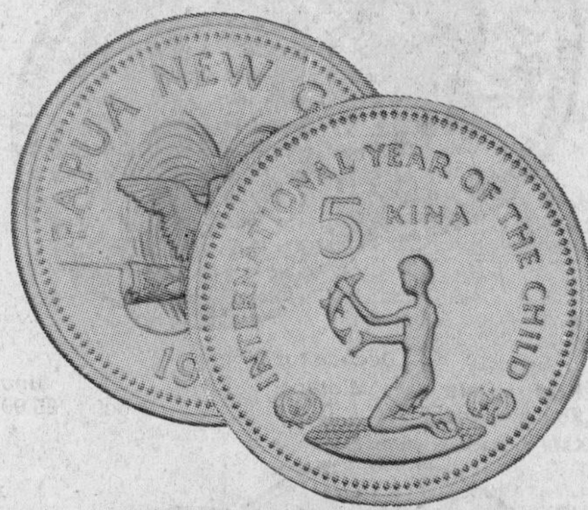

28.2800 g, .500 SILVER, .4656 oz ASW
International Year of the Child

KM#	Date	Mintage	VF	XF	Unc
18	1981	8,775	—	—	20.00

COPPER-NICKEL
Defense of the Kokoda Trail
Obv: Similar to 20 Toea, KM#5.

KM#	Date	Mintage	VF	XF	Unc
20	1982FM(M)	—	—	—	10.00

28.2800 g, .925 SILVER, .8411 oz ASW

KM#	Date	Mintage	VF	XF	Unc
20a	1982FM(P)	1,795	—	Proof	40.00

COPPER-NICKEL
10th Anniversary of Bank of Papua New Guinea
Obv: Similar to 20 Toea, KM#5.

KM#	Date	Mintage	VF	XF	Unc
23	1983FM(U)	360 pcs.	—	—	10.00

28.2800 g, .925 SILVER, .8411 oz ASW

KM#	Date	Mintage	VF	XF	Unc
23a	1983FM(P)	673 pcs.	—	Proof	40.00

New Parliament Building

KM#	Date	Mintage	VF	XF	Unc
25a	1984FM(P)	—	—	Proof	40.00

Decade for Women

KM#	Date	Mintage	VF	XF	Unc
28	1984FM(P)	1,050	—	Proof	25.00

23.3300 g, .925 SILVER, .6938 oz ASW
Butterfly

34	1992	500 pcs.	—	—	145.00

10 KINA

COPPER-NICKEL
Bird of Paradise

8	1975FM(M)	82 pcs.	—	—	75.00
	1975FM(U)	4,134	—	—	12.50
	1976FM(M)	82 pcs.	—	—	75.00
	1976FM(U)	976 pcs.	—	—	15.00
	1978FM(M)	168 pcs.	—	—	60.00
	1978FM(U)	777 pcs.	—	—	17.50
	1979FM(M)	82 pcs.	—	—	75.00
	1979FM(U)	1,366	—	—	15.00
	1980FM(U)	776 pcs.	—	—	15.00
	1983FM(U)	360 pcs.	—	—	17.50

41.6000 g, .925 SILVER, 1.2371 oz ASW

8a	1975FM(P)	.079	—	Proof	10.00
	1976FM(P)	.021	—	Proof	12.50
	1978FM(P)	7,352	—	Proof	15.00
	1979FM(P)	4,147	—	Proof	22.50
	1980FM(P)	2,752	—	Proof	27.50
	1983FM(P)	1,025	—	Proof	30.00

COPPER-NICKEL
Silver Jubilee of Queen Elizabeth II

KM#	Date	Mintage	VF	XF	Unc
11	1977FM(M)	82 pcs.	—	—	80.00
	1977FM(U)	603 pcs.	—	—	30.00

40.5000 g, .925 SILVER, 1.2046 oz ASW

11a	1977FM(P)	.014	—	Proof	15.00

COPPER-NICKEL
Royal Visit
Obv: Similar to 5 Kina, KM#7.

21	1982FM(M)	—	—	—	20.00

40.5000 g, .925 SILVER, 1.2046 oz ASW

21a	1982FM(P)	1,185	—	Proof	60.00

35.6000 g, .925 SILVER, 1.0587 oz ASW
Papal Visit
Obv: Similar to 5 Kina, KM#7.

26a	1984FM(P)	597 pcs.	—	Proof	55.00

42.1200 g, .925 SILVER, 1.2528 oz ASW
9th South Pacific Games

30a	1991	3,000	—	Proof	40.00

1.5710 g, .999 GOLD, .0504 oz AGW
Butterfly

33	1992	—	—	P/L	—

1.5710 g, .995 PLATINUM, .0502 oz APW

KM#	Date	Mintage	VF	XF	Unc
33a	1992	—	—	P/L	—

100 KINA

9.5700 g, .900 GOLD, .2769 oz AGW
Independence Commemorative

9	1975FM(M)	100 pcs.	—	—	300.00
	1975FM(U)	8,081	—	—	115.00
	1975FM(P)	.018	—	Proof	120.00

1st Anniversary of Independence

10	1976FM(M)	100 pcs.	—	—	300.00
	1976FM(U)	250 pcs.	—	—	150.00
	1976FM(P)	8,020	—	Proof	125.00

Papuan Hornbill

12	1977FM(M)	100 pcs.	—	—	300.00
	1977FM(U)	362 pcs.	—	—	150.00
	1977FM(P)	3,460	—	Proof	150.00

Bird Wing Butterfly

13	1978FM(U)	400 pcs.	—	—	250.00
	1978FM(P)	4,751	—	Proof	450.00

4 Faces of the Nation

14	1979FM(M)	102 pcs.	—	—	300.00
	1979FM(U)	286 pcs.	—	—	150.00
	1979FM(P)	3,492	—	Proof	175.00

7.8300 g, .500 GOLD, .1258 oz AGW
South Pacific Festival of Arts

16	1980	7,500	—	Proof	125.00

9.5700 g, .900 GOLD, .2769 oz AGW
5th Anniversary of Independence

M#	Date	Mintage	VF	XF	Unc
7	1980FM(M)	30 pcs.	—	—	400.00
	1980FM(P)	1,118	—	Proof	200.00

Prime Minister, Sir Julius Chan

9	1981FM(P)	685 pcs.	—	Proof	225.00

Royal Visit

2	1982FM(P)	484 pcs.	—	Proof	275.00

10th Anniversary of Bank of Papua New Guinea

	1983FM(P)	378 pcs.	—	Proof	335.00

100th Anniversary of Founding of British and German Protectorates

	1984FM(P)	274 pcs.	—	Proof	350.00

Butterfly - Ornithoptera Alexandrae

	1990	500 pcs.	—	—	250.00
	1990	*5,000	—	Proof	325.00
	1992	*5,000	—	Proof	350.00

9.5700 g, .995 PLATINUM, .3061 oz APW

a	1992	500 pcs.	—	—	360.00
	1992	*5,000	—	Proof	365.00

MINT SETS (MS)

KM#	Date	Mintage	Identification	Issue Price	Mkt. Val.
S1	1975FM(8)	4,134	KM1-8	30.00	25.00
S2	1976FM(8)	976	KM1-8	30.00	37.50
S3	1977FM(8)	603	KM1-7,11	30.00	60.00
S4	1978FM(8)	777	—	30.00	40.00
S5	1979FM(8)	1,366	KM1-8	31.00	35.00
S6	1980FM(9)	—	KM1-8,15	35.00	35.00
MS7	1982FM(8)	—	KM1-6,20,21	36.00	35.00
MS8	1983FM(8)	360	KM1-6,8,23	36.00	35.00

PROOF SETS (PS)

KM#	Date	Mintage	Identification	Issue Price	Mkt. Val.
PS1	1975FM(8)	42,340	KM1-6,7a,8a	60.00	30.00
PS2	1976FM(8)	16,323	KM1-6,7a,8a	60.00	30.00
PS3	1977FM(8)	7,721	KM1-6,7a,11a	60.00	42.00
PS4	1978FM(8)	5,540	KM1-6,7a,8a	70.00	45.00
PS5	1979FM(8)	2,728	KM1-6,7a,8a	72.00	50.00
PS6	1980FM(9)	—	KM1-6,7a,8a,15	130.00	65.00
PS7	1981FM(6)	10,000	KM1-6	29.00	12.50
PS8	1982FM(8)	—	KM1-6,20a,21a	92.00	100.00
PS9	1983FM(8)	—	KM1-6,8a,23a	132.00	120.00
PS10	1984FM(8)	—	KM1-6,25a-26a	133.00	120.00

PARAGUAY

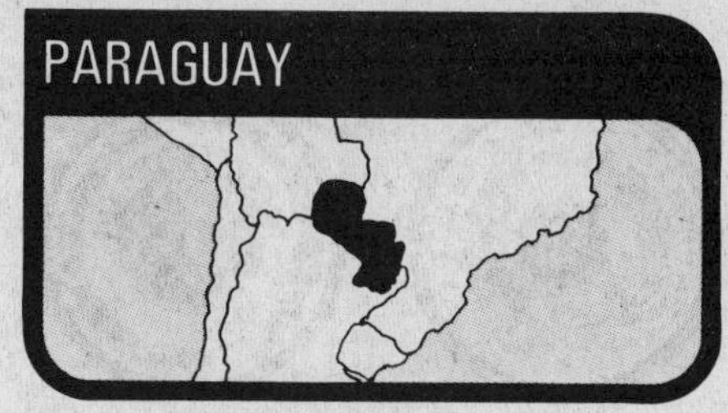

The Republic of Paraguay, a landlocked country in the heart of South America surrounded by Argentina, Bolivia and Brazil, has an area of 157,048 sq. mi. (406,750 sq. km.) and a population of *4.5 million, 95 percent of whom are of mixed Spanish and Indian descent. Capital: Asuncion. The country is predominantly agrarian, with no important mineral deposits or oil reserves. Meat, timber, hides, oilseeds, tobacco and cotton account for 70 percent of Paraguay's export revenue.

Paraguay was first visited by Alejo Garcia, a shipwrecked Spaniard, in 1524. The interior was explored by Sebastian Cabot in 1527 and 1528, when he sailed up the Parana and Paraguay rivers. Asuncion, which would become the center of a Spanish colonial province embracing much of southern South America, was established by the Spanish explorer Juan de Salazar on Aug. 15, 1537. For a century and a half the history of Paraguay was largely the history of the agricultural colonies established by the Jesuits in the south and east to Christianize the Indians. In 1811, following the outbreak of the South American wars of independence, Paraguayan patriots overthrew the local Spanish authorities and proclaimed their country's independence.

During the Triple Alliance War (1864-1870) in which Paraguay faced Argentina, Brazil and Uruguay, Asuncion's ladies gathered in an Assembly on Feb. 24, 1867 and decided to give up their jewelry in order to help the national defense. The President of the Republic, Francisco Solano Lopez accepted the offering and ordered one twentieth of it be used to mint the first Paraguayan gold coins according to the Decree of the 11th of Sept., 1867.

Two dies were made, one by Bouvet, and another by an American, Leonard Charles, while only the die made by Bouvet was eventually used.

MINT MARKS

HF - LeLocle

CONTRACTORS

(Chas. J.) SHAW - for Ralph Heaton, Birmingham Mint

MONETARY SYSTEM

100 Centesimos = 1 Peso

1/12 REAL

COPPER

KM#	Date	Mintage	Fine	VF	XF	Unc
1.1*	1845 Birmingham	2.880	5.00	15.00	50.00	100.00

Crude issue struck at Asuncion Mint.

KM#	Date	Mintage	Fine	VF	XF	Unc
1.2*	1845	.288	5.00	25.00	75.00	150.00

***NOTE:** Struck with medal die alignment. Coin strike varieties exist. After 1847 they were revalued at 1/24th Real.

4 PESOS FUERTES

6.5700 g, .900 GOLD, .1901 oz AGW
First Paraguayan Gold Coin

A2	1867	—	5500.	7500.	10,000.	—

DECIMAL COINAGE

100 Centavos (Centesimos)
= 1 Peso

CENTESIMO

COPPER
Rev: SHAW to right of date.

KM#	Date	Mintage	Fine	VF	XF	Unc
2	1870	—	2.00	5.00	20.00	40.00

2 CENTESIMOS

COPPER
Rev: SHAW to right of date.

KM#	Date	Mintage	Fine	VF	XF	Unc
3	1870	—	2.50	7.50	25.00	50.00

4 CENTESIMOS

COPPER
Rev: SHAW to right of date.

KM#	Date	Mintage	Fine	VF	XF	Unc
4.1	1870	—	3.00	10.00	30.00	75.00

Crude issue struck at Asuncion.
Obv: W/o ribbon bow on sprays.
Rev: W/o SHAW to right of date.

KM#	Date	Mintage	VG	Fine	VF	XF
4.2	1870	—	50.00	100.00	200.00	500.00
	Rev: SAEZ to right of date.					
4.3	1870	—	50.00	75.00	150.00	300.00

NOTE: Varieties exist.

5 CENTAVOS

COPPER-NICKEL

KM#	Date	Mintage	Fine	VF	XF	Unc
6	1900	.400	1.00	2.00	10.00	25.00
	1903	.600	1.00	2.00	6.50	15.00

KM#	Date	Mintage	Fine	VF	XF	Unc
9	1908	.400	1.50	5.00	30.00	75.00

10 CENTAVOS

COPPER-NICKEL

KM#	Date	Mintage	Fine	VF	XF	Unc
7	1900	.800	1.00	2.50	10.00	22.50
	1903	1.200	1.00	2.00	6.50	15.00

KM#	Date	Mintage	Fine	VF	XF	Unc
10	1908	.800	2.50	5.00	25.00	70.00

20 CENTAVOS

COPPER-NICKEL

KM#	Date	Mintage	Fine	VF	XF	Unc
8	1900	.500	1.00	3.00	10.00	30.00
	1903	.750	1.00	2.00	7.50	17.50

KM#	Date	Mintage	Fine	VF	XF	Unc
11	1908	1.000	2.50	5.00	25.00	70.00

50 CENTAVOS

COPPER-NICKEL

KM#	Date	Mintage	Fine	VF	XF	Unc
12	1925	4.000	.50	1.50	5.00	10.00

ALUMINUM

KM#	Date	Mintage	Fine	VF	XF	Unc
15	1938	.400	.50	1.00	3.50	7.50

PESO

25.0000 g, .900 SILVER, .7233 oz ASW

KM#	Date	Mintage	Fine	VF	XF	Unc
5	1889	.600*	50.00	90.00	135.00	350.0

***NOTE:** Unknown quantity melted.

COPPER-NICKEL

KM#	Date	Mintage	Fine	VF	XF	Unc
13	1925	3.500	.50	1.00	5.00	8.0

ALUMINUM

KM#	Date	Mintage	Fine	VF	XF	Unc
16	1938	—	.50	1.50	3.00	6.5

2 PESOS

COPPER-NICKEL

KM#	Date	Mintage	Fine	VF	XF	Unc
14	1925	2.500	.50	1.00	6.00	9.0

ALUMINUM

KM#	Date	Mintage	Fine	VF	XF	Unc
17	1938	—	.50	1.50	3.00	6.5

5 PESOS

COPPER-NICKEL

KM#	Date	Mintage	Fine	VF	XF	Unc
18	1939	4.000	1.00	2.50	7.50	15.0

10 PESOS

COPPER-NICKEL

KM#	Date	Mintage	Fine	VF	XF	Unc
19	1939	4.000	1.00	2.00	7.00	14.0

MONETARY REFORM

100 Centimos = 1 Guarani

CENTIMO

ALUMINUM-BRONZE
Flower

KM#	Date	Mintage	Fine	VF	XF	Unc
20	1944	3.500	.10	.50	1.00	2.00
	1948HF	2.000	.10	.50	1.00	2.00
	1950HF	1.096	.10	.25	1.00	2.00

5 CENTIMOS

ALUMINUM-BRONZE
Passion Flower

KM#	Date	Mintage	Fine	VF	XF	Unc
21	1944	2.195	.10	.50	1.00	2.50
	1947HF	13.111	.10	.20	.50	1.00

10 CENTIMOS

ALUMINUM-BRONZE
Orchid

KM#	Date	Mintage	Fine	VF	XF	Unc
22	1944	.975	.25	.75	2.50	5.00
	1947	6.656	.10	.25	.50	1.00
	1947HF	—	.10	.25	.50	1.00

KM#	Date	Mintage	Fine	VF	XF	Unc
25	1953	5.000	.10	.15	.30	.60

NOTE: Medal rotation dies.

15 CENTIMOS

ALUMINUM-BRONZE

KM#	Date	Mintage	Fine	VF	XF	Unc
26	1953	5.000	.10	.15	.30	.60

NOTE: Medal rotation dies.

25 CENTIMOS

ALUMINUM-BRONZE
Orchid

KM#	Date	Mintage	Fine	VF	XF	Unc
23	1944	.700	.25	1.00	3.00	10.00
	1948HF	.600	.25	.75	2.50	7.00
	1951HF	1.000	.25	.75	1.25	3.00

KM#	Date	Mintage	Fine	VF	XF	Unc
27	1953	2.000	.10	.15	.30	.75

NOTE: Medal rotation dies.

50 CENTIMOS

ALUMINUM-BRONZE

KM#	Date	Mintage	Fine	VF	XF	Unc
24	1944	2.485	.25	1.00	2.00	5.00
	1951	2.893	.25	.75	1.50	2.50

KM#	Date	Mintage	Fine	VF	XF	Unc
28	1953	2.000	.10	.15	.30	.75

NOTE: Medal rotation dies.

GUARANI

STAINLESS STEEL

KM#	Date	Mintage	Fine	VF	XF	Unc
151	1975	10.000	—	—	.15	.50
	1975	1,000	—	—	Proof	6.00
	1976	12.000	—	—	.10	.40
	1976	1,000	—	—	Proof	8.00

F.A.O. Issue

KM#	Date	Mintage	Fine	VF	XF	Unc
165	1978	15.000	—	—	.15	.50
	1980	13.000	—	—	.15	.50
	1980	1,000	—	—	Proof	5.00
	1984	15.000	—	—	.10	.30
	1986	15.000	—	—	.10	.30
	1988	15.000	—	—	.10	.30

NOTE: Varieties exist.

5 GUARANIES

STAINLESS STEEL

KM#	Date	Mintage	Fine	VF	XF	Unc
152	1975	7.500	—	—	.15	.50
	1975	1,000	—	—	Proof	6.00

F.A.O. Issue

KM#	Date	Mintage	Fine	VF	XF	Unc
166	1978	10.000	—	—	.15	.60
	1980	12.000	—	—	.15	.60
	1980	1,000	—	—	Proof	5.00
	1984	15.000	—	—	.10	.40
	1986	15.000	—	—	.10	.40
	1988	—	—	—	.10	.40

NOTE: Varieties exist.

NICKEL-BRONZE

KM#	Date	Mintage	Fine	VF	XF	Unc
166a	1992	15.000	—	—	.15	.50

10 GUARANIES

STAINLESS STEEL

KM#	Date	Mintage	Fine	VF	XF	Unc
153	1975	10.000	—	.10	.20	.75
	1975	1,000	—	—	Proof	8.00
	1976	10.000	—	.10	.20	.75
	1976	1,000	—	—	Proof	10.00

F.A.O. Issue

KM#	Date	Mintage	Fine	VF	XF	Unc
167	1978	15.000	—	.10	.20	.75
	1980	15.000	—	.10	.20	.75
	1980	1,000	—	—	Proof	7.00
	1984	20.000	—	.10	.15	.50
	1986	35.000	—	.10	.15	.50
	1988	40.000	—	.10	.15	.50

NOTE: Varieties exist.

NICKEL-BRONZE
F.A.O. Issue - Cow

KM#	Date	Mintage	Fine	VF	XF	Unc
178	1990	40.000	—	—	—	.50

50 GUARANIES

STAINLESS STEEL

KM#	Date	Mintage	Fine	VF	XF	Unc
154	1975	9.500	.20	.40	.60	1.25
	1975	1,000	—	—	Proof	10.00

General Estigarribia

KM#	Date	Mintage	Fine	VF	XF	Unc
169	1980	10.700	.20	.40	.60	1.25
	1980	1,000	—	—	Proof	9.00
	1986	15.000	.20	.40	.60	1.25
	1988	25.000	.20	.30	.50	1.00

NOTE: Varieties exist.

COPPER-ZINC-NICKEL
Acaray River Dam

KM#	Date	Mintage	Fine	VF	XF	Unc
179	1992	35.000	—	—	—	1.75

100 GUARANIES

COPPER-ZINC-NICKEL

KM#	Date	Mintage	Fine	VF	XF	Unc
177	1990	35.000	—	—	—	2.25

BRASS PLATED STEEL

KM#	Date	Mintage	Fine	VF	XF	Unc
177a	1993	35.000	—	—	—	2.00

25.0000 g, .999 SILVER, .8030 oz ASW
General A. Stroessner
Obv: Arms.

KM#	Date	Mintage	VF	XF	Unc
31	1972	*.010	—	Proof	50.00

Munich Olympics - Runner

KM#	Date	Mintage	VF	XF	Unc
32	1972	*.010	—	Proof	90.00

Munich Olympics - Broad Jumper
Obv: Arms. Rev: Broad Jumper.

KM#	Date	Mintage	VF	XF	Unc
33	1972	*.010	—	Proof	90.00

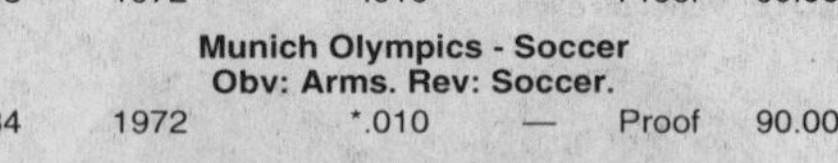

Munich Olympics - Soccer
Obv: Arms. Rev: Soccer.

KM#	Date	Mintage	VF	XF	Unc
34	1972	*.010	—	Proof	90.00

Munich Olympics - Hurdler
Obv: Arms.

KM#	Date	Mintage	VF	XF	Unc
35	1972	*.010	—	Proof	90.00

Munich Olympics
Obv: Arms. Rev: High jumper.

KM#	Date	Mintage	VF	XF	Unc
36	1972	*.010	—	Proof	90.00

Munich Olympics - Boxer
Obv: Arms.

KM#	Date	Mintage	VF	XF	Unc
37	1972	*.010	—	Proof	90.00
	1973	—	—	Proof	90.00

Mariscal Jose F. Estigarriba
Obv: Arms.

KM#	Date	Mintage	VF	XF	Unc
59	1973	*.010	—	Proof	50.00

Mariscal Francisco Solano Lopez
Obv: Arms.

KM#	Date	Mintage	VF	XF	Unc
60	1973	*.010	—	Proof	50.00

General Jose E. Diaz
Obv: Arms.

KM#	Date	Mintage	VF	XF	Unc
61	1973	*.010	—	Proof	50.00

General Bernardino Caballero
Obv: Arms.

KM#	Date	Mintage	VF	XF	Unc
62	1973	*.010	—	Proof	50.00

Teotihucana Culture
Obv: Arms.

KM#	Date	Mintage	VF	XF	Unc
63	1973	*.010	—	Proof	60.00

Huasteca Culture
Obv: Arms.

KM#	Date	Mintage	VF	XF	Unc
64	1973	*.010	—	Proof	60.00

Mixteca Culture
Obv: Arms.

KM#	Date	Mintage	VF	XF	Unc
65	1973	*.010	—	Proof	60.00

Veracruz Ceramica
Obv: Arms.

KM#	Date	Mintage	VF	XF	Unc
66	1973	*.010	—	Proof	60.00

Veracruz Culture
Obv: Arms.

KM#	Date	Mintage	VF	XF	Unc
67	1973	*.010	—	Proof	60.00

Albrecht Durer
Obv: Arms.

M#	Date	Mintage	VF	XF	Unc
8	1973	*.010	—	Proof	65.00

Johann Wolfgang Goethe
Obv: Arms.

9	1973	*.010	—	Proof	65.00

Abraham Lincoln
Obv: Arms.

07	1974	*.010	—	Proof	65.00

Ludwig van Beethoven
Obv: Arms.

08	1974	*.010	—	Proof	75.00

Otto von Bismarck
Obv: Arms.

09	1974	*.010	—	Proof	75.00

Albert Einstein
Obv: Arms.

110	1974	*.010	—	Proof	75.00

Giuseppe Garibaldi
Obv: Arms.

KM#	Date	Mintage	VF	XF	Unc
111	1974	*.010	—	Proof	50.00

Alessandro Manzoni
Obv: Arms.

112	1974	*.010	—	Proof	50.00

William Tell
Obv: Arms.

113	1974	*.010	—	Proof	50.00

John F. Kennedy
Obv: Arms.

114	1974	*.010	—	Proof	50.00

Konrad Adenauer
Obv: Arms.

115	1974	*.010	—	Proof	50.00

Winston Churchill
Obv: Arms.

KM#	Date	Mintage	VF	XF	Unc
116	1974	*.010	—	Proof	50.00

Pope John XXIII
Obv: Arms.

117	1974	*.010	—	Proof	65.00

Pope Paul VI
Obv: Arms.

118	1974	*.010	—	Proof	50.00

Parliament of Paraguay
Obv: Arms.

155	1975	*.010	—	Proof	50.00

Apollo 11
Obv: Arms.

156	1975	*.010	—	Proof	65.00

Apollo 15
Obv: Arms.

KM#	Date	Mintage	VF	XF	Unc
157	1975	*.010	—	Proof	65.00

Friendship Bridge
Obv: Arms.

KM#	Date	Mintage	VF	XF	Unc
158	1975	*.010	—	Proof	50.00

Holy Trinity Church
Obv: Arms.

KM#	Date	Mintage	VF	XF	Unc
159	1975	*.010	—	Proof	50.00

Ruins of Humaita
Obv: Arms.

KM#	Date	Mintage	VF	XF	Unc
160	1975	*.010	—	Proof	50.00

300 GUARANIES

26.6000 g, .720 SILVER, .6157 oz ASW
4th Term of President Stroessner

KM#	Date	Mintage	Fine	VF	XF	Unc
29	1968	.250	—	—	6.00	9.00

1500 GUARANIES

10.7000 g, .900 GOLD, .3096 oz AGW
General A. Stroessner

KM#	Date	Mintage	VF	XF	Unc
38	1972	*1,500	—	Proof	300.00

Munich Olympics - Runner
Obv: Arms. Rev: Runner.

KM#	Date	Mintage	VF	XF	Unc
39	1972	*1,500	—	Proof	800.00

Munich Olympics - Broad Jumper
Obv: Arms. Rev: Broad Jumper.

KM#	Date	Mintage	VF	XF	Unc
40	1972	*1,500	—	Proof	800.00

Munich Olympics - Soccer
Obv: Arms. Rev: Soccer.

KM#	Date	Mintage	VF	XF	Unc
41	1972	*1,500	—	Proof	800.00

Munich Olympics - Hurdler
Obv: Arms.

KM#	Date	Mintage	VF	XF	Unc
42	1972	*1,500	—	Proof	800.00

Munich Olympics - High Jumper
Obv: Arms. Rev: High Jumper.

KM#	Date	Mintage	VF	XF	Unc
43	1972	*1,500	—	Proof	800.00

Munich Olympics - Boxer
Obv: Arms. Rev: Boxer.

KM#	Date	Mintage	VF	XF	Unc
44	1972	*1,500	—	Proof	800.00
	1973	—	—	Proof	800.00

Estigarribia
Obv: Arms.

KM#	Date	Mintage	VF	XF	Unc
70	1973	*1,500	—	Proof	450.00

Mariscal Francisco Solano Lopez
Obv: Arms.

KM#	Date	Mintage	VF	XF	Unc
71	1973	*1,500	—	Proof	450.00

General Jose E. Diaz
Obv: Arms.

KM#	Date	Mintage	VF	XF	Unc
72	1973	*1,500	—	Proof	450.00

General Bernardino Caballero
Obv: Arms.

KM#	Date	Mintage	VF	XF	Unc
73	1973	*1,500	—	Proof	450.00

Teotihucana Culture
Obv: Arms. Rev: Sculpture.

KM#	Date	Mintage	VF	XF	Unc
74	1973	*1,500	—	Proof	450.00

Huasteca Culture
Obv: Arms. Rev: Sculpture.

KM#	Date	Mintage	VF	XF	Unc
75	1973	*1,500	—	Proof	450.00

Mixteca Culture
Obv: Arms. Rev: Pitcher in shape of animal.

KM#	Date	Mintage	VF	XF	Unc
76	1973	*1,500	—	Proof	450.00

Veracruz Ceramica
Obv: Arms. Rev: Vase.

KM#	Date	Mintage	VF	XF	Unc
77	1973	*1,500	—	Proof	450.00

Veracruz Culture
Obv: Arms. Rev: Sculpted head.

KM#	Date	Mintage	VF	XF	Unc
78	1973	*1,500	—	Proof	450.00

Albrecht Durer
Obv: Arms.

KM#	Date	Mintage	VF	XF	Unc
79	1973	*1,500	—	Proof	450.00

Johann Wolfgang Goethe
Obv: Arms.

KM#	Date	Mintage	VF	XF	Unc
80	1973	*1,500	—	Proof	450.00

Abraham Lincoln
Obv: Arms.

KM#	Date	Mintage	VF	XF	Unc
119	1974	*1,500	—	Proof	450.00

Ludwig van Beethoven
Obv: Arms.

KM#	Date	Mintage	VF	XF	Unc
120	1974	*1,500	—	Proof	850.00

Otto von Bismarck

KM#	Date	Mintage	VF	XF	Unc
121	1974	*1,500	—	Proof	450.00

Albert Einstein

KM#	Date	Mintage	VF	XF	Unc
122	1974	*1,500	—	Proof	450.00

Giuseppe Garibaldi
Obv: Arms.

KM#	Date	Mintage	VF	XF	Unc
123	1974	*1,500	—	Proof	450.00

Alessandro Manzoni

Obv: Arms.

M#	Date	Mintage	VF	XF	Unc
24	1974	*1,500	—	Proof	450.00

William Tell
Obv: Arms.

M#	Date	Mintage	VF	XF	Unc
25	1974	*1,500	—	Proof	450.00

John F. Kennedy

M#	Date	Mintage	VF	XF	Unc
26	1974	*1,500	—	Proof	450.00

Konrad Adenauer

M#	Date	Mintage	VF	XF	Unc
27	1974	*1,500	—	Proof	450.00

Winston Churchill

M#	Date	Mintage	VF	XF	Unc
28	1974	*1,500	—	Proof	450.00

Pope John XXIII

M#	Date	Mintage	VF	XF	Unc
29	1974	*1,500	—	Proof	450.00

Pope Paul VI

M#	Date	Mintage	VF	XF	Unc
130	1974	*1,500	—	Proof	450.00

Parliament of Paraguay
Obv: Arms.

M#	Date	Mintage	VF	XF	Unc
179	1975	*1,500	—	Proof	450.00

Apollo 11
Obv: Arms.

M#	Date	Mintage	VF	XF	Unc
180	1975	*1,500	—	Proof	550.00

Apollo 15
Obv: Arms.

M#	Date	Mintage	VF	XF	Unc
181	1975	*1,500	—	Proof	550.00

Friendship Bridge
Obv: Arms.

KM#	Date	Mintage	VF	XF	Unc
182	1975	*1,500	—	Proof	450.00

Holy Trinity Church
Obv: Arms.

KM#	Date	Mintage	VF	XF	Unc
183	1975	*1,500	—	Proof	450.00

Ruins of Humaita
Obv: Arms.

KM#	Date	Mintage	VF	XF	Unc
184	1975	*1,500	—	Proof	450.00

3000 GUARANIES

21.3000 g, .900 GOLD, .6164 oz AGW
General A. Stroessner

KM#	Date	Mintage	VF	XF	Unc
45	1972	*1,500	—	Proof	450.00

Munich Olympics - Runner

KM#	Date	Mintage	VF	XF	Unc
46	1972	*1,500	—	Proof	1600.

Munich Olympics - Broad Jumper

KM#	Date	Mintage	VF	XF	Unc
47	1972	*1,500	—	Proof	1600.

Munich Olympics - Soccer

KM#	Date	Mintage	VF	XF	Unc
48	1972	*1,500	—	Proof	1600.

Munich Olympics - Hurdler

KM#	Date	Mintage	VF	XF	Unc
49	1972	*1,500	—	Proof	1600.

Munich Olympics - High Jumper

KM#	Date	Mintage	VF	XF	Unc
50	1972	*1,500	—	Proof	1600.

Munich Olympics - Boxer

KM#	Date	Mintage	VF	XF	Unc
51	1972	*1,500	—	Proof	1600.
	1973	—	—	Proof	1600.

Estigarribia

KM#	Date	Mintage	VF	XF	Unc
81	1973	*1,500	—	Proof	750.00

Mariscal Francisco Solano Lopez

KM#	Date	Mintage	VF	XF	Unc
82	1973	*1,500	—	Proof	750.00

General Jose E. Diaz

KM#	Date	Mintage	VF	XF	Unc
83	1973	*1,500	—	Proof	750.00

General Bernardino Caballero

KM#	Date	Mintage	VF	XF	Unc
84	1973	*1,500	—	Proof	750.00

Teotihucana Culture

KM#	Date	Mintage	VF	XF	Unc
85	1973	*1,500	—	Proof	750.00

Huasteca Culture

KM#	Date	Mintage	VF	XF	Unc
86	1973	*1,500	—	Proof	750.00

Mixteca Culture
Rev: Pitcher in shape of animal.

KM#	Date	Mintage	VF	XF	Unc
87	1973	*1,500	—	Proof	750.00

Veracruz Ceramica
Rev: Vase.

KM#	Date	Mintage	VF	XF	Unc
88	1973	*1,500	—	Proof	750.00

Veracruz Culture
Rev: Sculpted head.

KM#	Date	Mintage	VF	XF	Unc
89	1973	*1,500	—	Proof	750.00

Albrecht Durer

KM#	Date	Mintage	VF	XF	Unc
90	1973	*1,500	—	Proof	750.00

Johann Wolfgang Goethe

KM#	Date	Mintage	VF	XF	Unc
91	1973	*1,500	—	Proof	750.00

Abraham Lincoln

KM#	Date	Mintage	VF	XF	Unc
131	1974	*1,500	—	Proof	750.00

Ludwig van Beethoven

KM#	Date	Mintage	VF	XF	Unc
132	1974	*1,500	—	Proof	1500.

Otto von Bismarck

KM#	Date	Mintage	VF	XF	Unc
133	1974	*1,500	—	Proof	750.00

Albert Einstein

KM#	Date	Mintage	VF	XF	Unc
134	1974	*1,500	—	Proof	750.00

Giuseppe Garibaldi

KM#	Date	Mintage	VF	XF	Unc
135	1974	*1,500	—	Proof	750.00

Alessandro Manzoni

KM#	Date	Mintage	VF	XF	Unc
136	1974	*1,500	—	Proof	750.00

William Tell

KM#	Date	Mintage	VF	XF	Unc
137	1974	*1,500	—	Proof	750.00

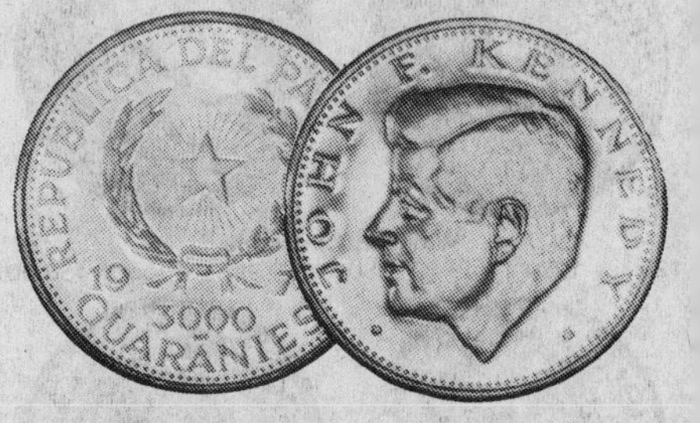

John F. Kennedy

KM#	Date	Mintage	VF	XF	Unc
138	1974	*1,500	—	Proof	750.00

Konrad Adenauer

KM#	Date	Mintage	VF	XF	Unc
139	1974	*1,500	—	Proof	750.00

Winston Churchill

KM#	Date	Mintage	VF	XF	Unc
140	1974	*1,500	—	Proof	750.00

Pope John XXIII

KM#	Date	Mintage	VF	XF	Unc
141	1974	*1,500	—	Proof	750.00

Pope Paul VI

M#	Date	Mintage	VF	XF	Unc
2	1974	*1,500	—	Proof	750.00

Iglesia De Santisima Trinidad

M#	Date	Mintage	VF	XF	Unc
61	1975	—	—	Proof	700.00

Parliament of Paraguay

M#	Date	Mintage	VF	XF	Unc
62	1975	—	—	Proof	700.00

Friendship Bridge

M#	Date	Mintage	VF	XF	Unc
63	1975	—	—	Proof	700.00

Humaita Ruins

M#	Date	Mintage	VF	XF	Unc
64	1975	—	—	Proof	700.00

Apollo 11

M#	Date	Mintage	VF	XF	Unc
75	1975	—	—	Proof	1100.

Apollo 15

KM#	Date	Mintage	VF	XF	Unc
176	1975	—	—	Proof	1100.

4500 GUARANIES

31.9000 g, .900 GOLD, .9231 oz AGW
General A. Stroessner
Obv: Arms.

KM#	Date	Mintage	VF	XF	Unc
52	1972	*1,500	—	Proof	750.00

KM#	Date	Mintage	VF	XF	Unc
	Munich Olympics - Runner **Obv: Arms.**				
53 (M23)	1972	*1,500	—	Proof	2750.
	Munich Olympics Broad Jumper **Obv: Arms. Rev: Broad jumper.**				
54	1972	*1,500	—	Proof	2750.
	Munich Olympics - Soccer **Obv: Arms. Rev: Soccer.**				
55	1972	*1,500	—	Proof	2750.
	Munich Olympics - Hurdler **Obv: Arms. Rev: Hurdler.**				
56	1972	*1,500	—	Proof	2750.
	Munich Olympics - High Jumper **Obv: Arms. Rev: High Jumper.**				
57	1972	*1,500	—	Proof	2750.
	Munich Olympics - Boxer **Obv: Arms. Rev: Boxer.**				
58	1972	*1,500	—	Proof	2750.
	1973	—	—	Proof	2750.
	Mariscal Jose F. Estigarribia **Obv: Arms.**				
92	1973	*1,500	—	Proof	1150.
	Mariscal Francisco Solano Lopez **Obv: Arms.**				
93	1973	*1,500	—	Proof	1150.
	General Jose E. Diaz **Obv: Arms.**				
94	1973	*1,500	—	Proof	1150.
	General Bernardino Caballero **Obv: Arms.**				
95	1973	*1,500	—	Proof	1150.
	Teotihucana Culture **Obv: Arms. Rev: Sculpture.**				
96	1973	*1,500	—	Proof	1150.
	Huasteca Culture **Obv: Arms. Rev: Sculpture.**				
97	1973	*1,500	—	Proof	1150.
	Mixteca Culture **Obv: Arms. Rev: Pitcher in shape of animal.**				
98	1973	*1,500	—	Proof	1150.
	Veracruz Ceramica **Obv: Arms. Rev: Vase.**				
99	1973	*1,500	—	Proof	1150.
	Veracruz Culture **Obv: Arms. Rev: Sculpted head.**				
100	1973	*1,500	—	Proof	1150.
	Albrecht Durer **Obv: Arms.**				
101	1973	*1,500	—	Proof	1150.
	Johann Wolfgang Goethe **Obv: Arms.**				
102	1973	*1,500	—	Proof	1150.
	Ludwig van Beethoven **Obv: Arms.**				
103	1974	*1,500	—	Proof	2150.
	Otto von Bismarck **Obv: Arms.**				
104	1974	*1,500	—	Proof	1150.
	Giuseppe Garibaldi **Obv: Arms.**				
105	1974	*1,500	—	Proof	1150.

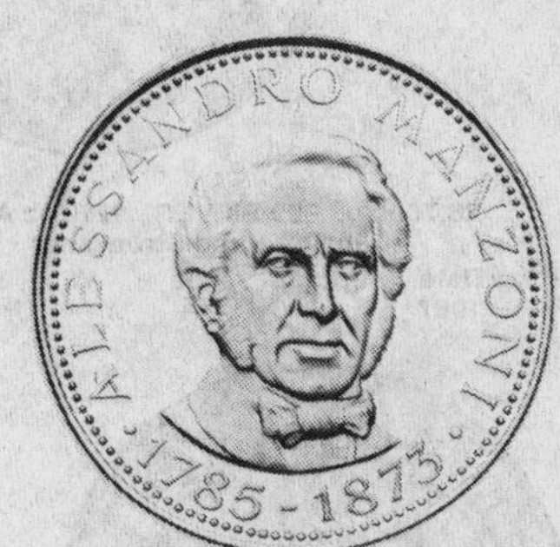

KM#	Date	Mintage	VF	XF	Unc
	Alessandro Manzoni				
106	1974	*1,500	—	Proof	1150.
	Abraham Lincoln **Obv: Arms.**				
143	1974	*1,500	—	Proof	1150.
	Albert Einstein **Obv: Arms.**				
144	1974	*1,500	—	Proof	1150.
	William Tell **Obv: Arms.**				
145	1974	*1,500	—	Proof	1150.
	John F. Kennedy **Obv: Arms.**				
146	1974	*1,500	—	Proof	1150.
	Konrad Adenauer **Obv: Arms.**				
147	1974	*1,500	—	Proof	1150.
	Winston Churchill **Obv: Arms.**				
148	1974	*1,500	—	Proof	1150.
	Pope John XXIII **Obv: Arms.**				
149	1974	*1,500	—	Proof	1150.
	Pope Paul VI **Obv: Arms.**				
150	1974	*1,500	—	Proof	1150.
	Parliament of Paraguay **Obv: Arms.**				
185	1975	*1,500	—	Proof	1150.
	Apollo 11 **Obv: Arms.**				
186	1975	*1,500	—	Proof	1250.
	Apollo 15 **Obv: Arms.**				
187	1975	*1,500	—	Proof	1250.
	Friendship Bridge **Obv: Arms.**				
188	1975	*1,500	—	Proof	1150.
	Holy Trinity Church **Obv: Arms.**				
189	1975	*1,500	—	Proof	1150.
	Ruins of Humaita **Obv: Arms.**				
190	1975	*1,500	—	Proof	1150.

NOTE: Mintage limits were never met for most Paraguayan gold coins. All may be considered very scarce.

10,000 GUARANIES

46.0100 g, .900 GOLD, 1.3315 oz AGW
4th Term of President Stroessner
Similar to 300 Guaranies KM#29.

KM#	Date	Mintage	Fine	VF	XF	Unc
30	1968	*50 pcs.	—	—	Proof	4500.

***NOTE:** KM#30 struck for presentation.

28.7000 g, .999 SILVER, .9219 oz ASW
Caballero and Stroessner

KM#	Date	Mintage	Fine	VF	XF	Unc
171	1987	1,000	—	—	Proof	42.50

8th Term of President A. Stroessner

KM#	Date	Mintage	Fine	VF	XF	Unc
173	1988	1,000	—	—	Proof	42.50

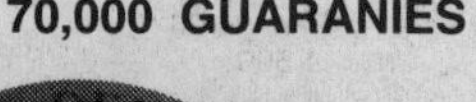

70,000 GUARANIES

46.0000 g, .900 GOLD, 1.3310 oz AGW
6th Term of President A. Stroessner

KM#	Date	Mintage	Fine	VF	XF	Unc
168	1978	300 pcs.	—	—	Proof	850.00

100,000 GUARANIES

46.0000 g, .900 GOLD, 1.3310 oz AGW
7th Term of President A. Stroessner

KM#	Date	Mintage	Fine	VF	XF	Unc
170	1983	300 pcs.	—	—	Proof	950.00

250,000 GUARANIES

46.0000 g, .917 GOLD, 1.3561 oz AGW
Caballero - Stroessner

KM#	Date	Mintage	Fine	VF	XF	Unc
172	1987	*500 pcs.	—	—	Proof	800.00

***NOTE:** 250 pieces remelted.

300,000 GUARANIES

46.0000 g, .917 GOLD, 1.3561 oz AGW
8th Term of President A. Stroessner

KM#	Date	Mintage	Fine	VF	XF	Unc
174	1988	*500 pcs.	—	—	Proof	800.00

***NOTE:** 250 pieces remelted.

PROOF SETS (PS)

KM#	Date	Mintage	Identification	Issue Price	Mkt. Val.
PS1	1972(24)	—	KM31-36,38-43,45-50,52-57	—	—
PS2	1973(48)	—	KM37,44,51,58-102	—	—
PS3	1974(48)	—	KM103-150	—	—
PS4	1975(24)	—	KM155-164,175-176,179-190	—	—
PS5	1975(4)	1,000	KM151-154	—	25.00
PS6	1976(2)	1,000	KM151,153	—	20.00
PS7	1980(4)	1,000	KM165-167,169	—	25.00

Listings For

PERSIA: refer to Iran

PERU

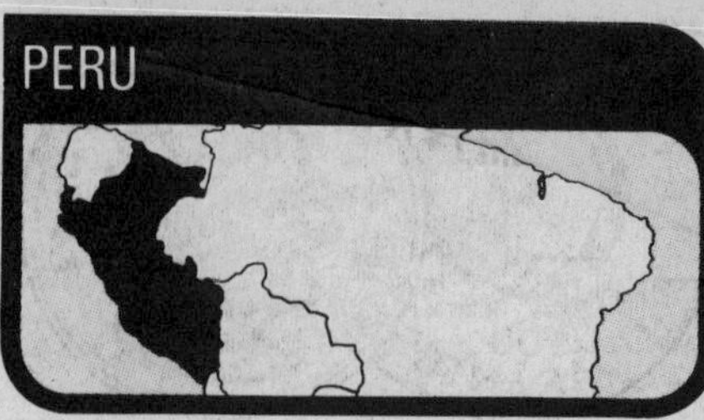

The Republic of Peru, located on the Pacific coast of South America, has an area of 496,225 sq. mi. (1,285,220 sq. km.) and a population of *21.4 million. Capital: Lima. The diversified economy includes mining, fishing and agriculture. Fish meal, copper, sugar, zinc and iron ore are exported.

Once part of the great Inca Empire that reached from northern Ecuador to central Chile, Peru was conquered in 1531-33 by Francisco Pizarro. Desirable as the richest of the Spanish viceroyalties, it was torn by warfare between avaricious Spaniards until the arrival in 1569 of Francisco de Toledo, who initiated 2-1/2 centuries of efficient colonial rule which made Lima the most aristocratic colonial capital and the stronghold of Spain's American possessions. Jose de San Martin of Argentina proclaimed Peru's independence on July 28, 1821; Simon Bolivar of Venezuela secured it in December, 1824 when he defeated the last Spanish army in South America. After several futile attempts to re-establish its South American empire, Spain recognized Peru's independence in 1879.

Andres de Santa Cruz, whose mother was a high-ranking Inca, was the best of Bolivia's early presidents, and temporarily united Peru and Bolivia 1836-39, thus realizing his dream of a Peruvian/Bolivian confederation. This prompted the separate coinages of North and South Peru. Peruvian resistance and Chilean intervention finally broke up the confederation, sending Santa Cruz into exile. A succession of military strongman presidents ruled Peru until Marshall Castilla revitalized Peruvian politics in the mid-19th century and repulsed Spain's attempt to reclaim its one-time colony. Subsequent loss of southern territory to Chile in the War of the Pacific, 1879-81, and gradually increasing rejection of foreign economic domination, combined with recent serious inflation, affected the country numismatically.

RULERS

Spanish, until 1822

MINT MARKS

AREQUIPA, AREQ = Arequipa
AYACUCHO = Ayacucho
(B) = Brussels
CUZCO (monogram), Cuzco, Co.
Cuzco
L, LIMAE (monogram), Lima
(monogram), LIMA = Lima
(L) = London
PASCO (monogram), Pasco, Paz, Po
= Pasco
P,(P) = Philadelphia
S = San Francisco
(W) = Waterbury, CT, USA

NOTE: The LIMAE monogram appears in three forms. The early LM monogram form looks like a dotted L with M. The later LIMAE monogram has all the letters of LIMAE more readily distinguishable. The third form appears as an M monogram during early Republican issues.

MINT ASSAYERS INITIALS

The letter(s) following the dates of Peruvian coins are the assayer's initials appearing on the coins. They generally appear at the 11 o'clock position on the Colonial coinage and at the 5 o'clock position along the rim on the obverse or reverse on the Republican coinage.

MONETARY SYSTEM

16 Reales = 2 Pesos = 1 Escudo

DATING

Peruvian 5, 10 and 20 centavos, issued from 1918-1944, bear the dates written in Spanish. The following table translates those written dates into numerals:

1918 - UN MIL NOVECIENTOS DIECIOCHO
1919 - UN MIL NOVECIENTOS DIECINUEVE
1920 - UN MIL NOVECIENTOS VEINTE
1921 - UN MIL NOVECIENTOS VEINTIUNO
1923 - UN MIL NOVECIENTOS VEINTITRES
1926 - UN MIL NOVECIENTOS VEINTISEIS
1934 - UN MIL NOVECIENTOS TREINTICUATRO
1935 - UN MIL NOVECIENTOS TREINTICINCO
1937 - UN MIL NOVECIENTOS TREINTISIETE
1939 - UN MIL NOVECIENTOS TREINTINUEVE
1940 - UN MIL NOVECIENTOS CUARENTA
1941 - UN MIL NOVECIENTOS CUARENTIUNO

U. S. Mints

1942 - MIL NOVECIENTOS CUARENTA Y DOS

Lima Mint

1942 - UN MIL NOVECIENTOS CUARENTIDOS

U. S. Mints

1943 - MIL NOVECIENTOS CUARENTA Y TRES

944 - MIL NOVECIENTOS CUARENTA Y CUATRO

Lima Mint

944 - MIL NOVECIENTOS CUARENTICUATRO

MILLED COINAGE

1/4 REAL

.8500 g, .903 SILVER, .0247 oz ASW
Mint mark: L
Obv: Castle, L at left, 1/4 at right.

KM#	Date	Mintage	VG	Fine	VF	XF
02.2	1801	—	7.50	12.50	20.00	40.00
	1802	—	10.00	15.00	30.00	60.00
	1803	—	10.00	15.00	30.00	60.00
	1804	—	10.00	15.00	30.00	60.00
	1805	—	10.00	15.00	30.00	60.00
	1806	—	7.50	12.50	20.00	40.00
	1807	—	7.50	12.50	20.00	40.00
	1808	—	7.50	12.50	20.00	40.00

NOTE: Earlier dates (1796-1800) exist for this type.

KM#	Date	Mintage	VG	Fine	VF	XF
108	1809	—	25.00	45.00	65.00	80.00
	1810	—	6.00	10.00	20.00	35.00
	1811	—	8.00	13.50	30.00	45.00
	1812	—	8.00	13.50	30.00	45.00
	1813	—	6.00	10.00	20.00	35.00
	1814	—	6.00	10.00	20.00	35.00
	1815	—	9.00	15.00	30.00	45.00
	1816	—	6.00	10.00	22.50	35.00
	1817	—	6.00	10.00	22.50	35.00
	1818	—	6.00	10.00	22.50	35.00
	1819	—	6.00	10.00	22.50	35.00
	1820	—	6.00	10.00	22.50	35.00
	1821	—	6.00	10.00	22.50	35.00
	1823	—	30.00	45.00	70.00	100.00
	1825	—	45.00	75.00	100.00	150.00

NOTE: Most 1809 dates found are actually dated 1802, where the base of the 2 is weakly struck.

1/2 REAL

1.6500 g, .903 SILVER, .0479 oz ASW
Mint mark: LIMAE (monogram)
Obv. leg: CAROLUS IIII, bust. Rev: Arms, pillars.

KM#	Date	Mintage	VG	Fine	VF	XF
93	1801 IJ	—	3.00	6.00	10.00	22.50
	1802 IJ	—	3.00	6.00	10.00	22.50
	1803 IJ	—	4.50	9.00	15.00	30.00
	1803 JP	—	3.00	6.00	9.00	20.00
	1804 JP	—	3.00	6.00	9.00	20.00
	1805 JP	—	3.00	6.00	10.00	22.50
	1805 IJ	—	10.00	18.50	35.00	50.00
	1806 JP	—	3.00	6.00	10.00	22.50
	1807 JP	—	3.00	6.00	9.00	20.00
	1808 JP	—	3.00	6.00	10.00	20.00

NOTE: Earlier dates (1791-1800) exist for this type.

Obv. leg: FERDND. VII. . ., Lima bust.
Rev: Arms, pillars.

KM#	Date	Mintage	VG	Fine	VF	XF
103.1	1808 JP	—	40.00	65.00	100.00	150.00

Obv. leg: FERDIN. VII.

KM#	Date	Mintage	VG	Fine	VF	XF
103.2	1809 JP	—	13.50	22.50	37.50	85.00
	1810 JP	—	7.50	12.50	22.50	65.00
	1811 JP	—	7.50	12.50	22.50	65.00

Obv: Standard bust.

KM#	Date	Mintage	VG	Fine	VF	XF
113	1811 JP	—	6.00	10.00	20.00	45.00
	1812 JP	—	2.75	5.00	10.00	20.00
	1813 JP	—	2.75	5.00	10.00	20.00
	1814 JP	—	3.50	7.00	13.50	30.00
	1815 JP	—	2.75	5.00	10.00	20.00
	1816 JP	—	2.75	5.00	10.00	20.00
	1817 JP	—	2.75	5.00	10.00	20.00
	1818 JP	—	2.75	5.00	10.00	20.00
	1819 JP	—	2.75	5.00	10.00	20.00
	1820 JP	—	2.75	5.00	10.00	20.00
	1821 JP	—	2.75	5.00	10.00	20.00

REAL

3.2500 g, .903 SILVER, .0944 oz ASW
Obv. leg: CAROLUS IIII. . ., bust of Charles IV.
Rev: Similar to KM#109.

KM#	Date	Mintage	VG	Fine	VF	XF
94	1801 IJ	—	6.00	10.00	20.00	40.00
	1802 IJ	—	15.00	25.00	40.00	65.00
	1803 IJ	—	12.00	20.00	40.00	100.00
	1803 JP	—	9.00	15.00	35.00	100.00
	1804 IJ	—	12.00	20.00	50.00	100.00
	1804 JP	—	12.00	20.00	50.00	100.00
	1805 JP	—	9.00	15.00	35.00	100.00
	1806 JP	—	6.00	10.00	20.00	50.00
	1807 JP	—	6.00	10.00	20.00	40.00
	1808 JP	—	25.00	40.00	100.00	140.00

NOTE: Earlier dates (1791-1800) exist for this type.

Obv. leg: FERDIN VII. . ., Lima bust.

KM#	Date	Mintage	VG	Fine	VF	XF
109	1808 JP	—	—	—	Rare	—
	1809 JP	—		Reported, not confirmed		

KM#	Date	Mintage	VG	Fine	VF	XF
109	1810 JP	—	15.00	25.00	45.00	250.00
	1811 JP	—	15.00	25.00	45.00	250.00

Obv. leg: FERDIN. VII. . ., standard bust.

KM#	Date	Mintage	VG	Fine	VF	XF
114.1	1811 JP	—	25.00	40.00	70.00	125.00
	1812 JP	—	5.00	9.00	15.00	30.00
	1813 JP	—	5.00	9.00	15.00	35.00
	1814 JP	—	3.50	7.00	12.50	30.00
	1815 JP	—	7.00	12.00	16.00	35.00
	1816 JP	—	4.00	7.00	12.50	30.00
	1817 JP	—	4.00	7.00	12.50	30.00
	1818 JP	—	4.00	7.00	12.50	30.00
	1819 JP	—	4.00	7.00	12.50	30.00
	1820 JP	—	4.00	7.00	12.50	30.00
	1821 JP	—	4.00	7.00	12.50	30.00
	1823 JP	—	15.00	25.00	60.00	110.00

Mint mark: CUZCO (monogram)

KM#	Date	Mintage	VG	Fine	VF	XF
114.2	1824/3 T	—	40.00	70.00	150.00	275.00
	1824 T	—	50.00	100.00	175.00	350.00

2 REALES

6.5000 g, .903 SILVER, .1887 oz ASW
Mint mark: LIMAE (monogram)
Obv. leg: CAROLUS IIII, bust of Charles IV.
Rev: Similar to KM#104.2.

KM#	Date	Mintage	VG	Fine	VF	XF
95	1801 IJ	—	6.00	10.00	15.00	30.00
	1802 IJ	—	6.00	10.00	15.00	25.00
	1803 IJ	—	12.00	20.00	35.00	70.00
	1803 JP	—	6.00	10.00	15.00	30.00
	1804 IJ	—	9.00	15.00	25.00	50.00
	1804 JP	—	6.00	10.00	15.00	25.00
	1805 JP	—	5.00	9.00	12.50	22.50
	1806 JP	—	6.00	10.00	15.00	25.00
	1807 JP	—	6.00	10.00	15.00	30.00
	1808 JP	—	6.00	10.00	15.00	30.00

NOTE: Earlier dates (1791-1800) exist for this type.

Obv. leg: FERDND. VII. . ., Lima bust.
Rev: Arms, pillars.

KM#	Date	Mintage	VG	Fine	VF	XF
104.1	1808 JP	—	35.00	60.00	150.00	250.00
	1809 JP	—	—	—	Rare	—

Obv. leg: FERDIN. VII. . ., Lima bust.

KM#	Date	Mintage	VG	Fine	VF	XF
104.2	1808 JP	—	90.00	150.00	250.00	400.00
	1809 JP	—	—	—	Rare	—
	1810 JP	—	6.00	10.00	15.00	30.00
	1811 JP	—	15.00	25.00	45.00	75.00

Obv. leg: FERDIN. VII. . ., standard bust.

KM#	Date	Mintage	VG	Fine	VF	XF
115.1	1811 JP	—	12.00	20.00	35.00	85.00
	1812 JP	—	4.75	8.50	12.50	17.50
	1813 JP	—	4.75	8.50	12.50	17.50
	1814 JP	—	6.00	10.00	14.00	25.00
	1815 JP	—	6.00	10.00	15.00	25.00
	1816 JP	—	4.75	8.50	12.50	17.50
	1817 JP	—	4.75	8.50	12.50	17.50
	1818 JP	—	4.75	8.50	12.50	17.50
	1819 JP	—	4.75	8.50	12.50	17.50
	1820 JP	—	4.75	8.50	12.50	17.50
	1821 JP	—	4.75	8.50	12.50	17.50
	1823 JP	—	6.00	10.00	15.00	25.00

Mint mark: CUZCO (monogram)

KM#	Date	Mintage	VG	Fine	VF	XF
115.2	1824 T	—	125.00	200.00	300.00	500.00

Mint mark: LIMAE (monogram)

KM#	Date	Mintage	VG	Fine	VF	XF
115.3	1826 IR	—	75.00	125.00	250.00	375.00

NOTE: KM#115.3 was struck in Callao by Royalists prior to final capitulation on January 22, 1826.

4 REALES

13.0000 g, .903 SILVER, .3774 oz ASW
Mint: Lima
Obv. leg: CAROLUS IIII. . .

KM#	Date	Mintage	VG	Fine	VF	XF
96	1801 IJ	—	25.00	45.00	90.00	150.00
	1802 IJ	—	30.00	50.00	100.00	175.00
	1803 IJ	—	75.00	125.00	200.00	350.00
	1803 JP	—	45.00	75.00	125.00	250.00
	1804 JP	—	25.00	45.00	100.00	175.00
	1805 JP	—	25.00	40.00	100.00	175.00
	1806 JP	—	25.00	40.00	100.00	175.00
	1807 JP	—	25.00	45.00	100.00	175.00
	1808 JP	—	45.00	75.00	125.00	250.00

NOTE: Earlier dates (1791-1800) exist for this type.

Obv. leg: FERDND. VII. . ., Lima bust.
Rev: Arms, pillars.

KM#	Date	Mintage	VG	Fine	VF	XF
105.1	1808 JP	—	75.00	125.00	250.00	475.00

Obv. leg: FERDIN. VII. . ., Lima bust.

KM#	Date	Mintage	VG	Fine	VF	XF
105.2	1810 JP	—	65.00	125.00	250.00	500.00
	1811 JP	—	65.00	125.00	250.00	500.00

Obv. leg: FERDIN. VII. . ., standard bust.

KM#	Date	Mintage	VG	Fine	VF	XF
116	1811 JP	—	—	—	Rare	—
	1812 JP	—	25.00	40.00	100.00	150.00
	1813 JP	—	75.00	125.00	200.00	350.00
	1814 JP	—	75.00	125.00	200.00	350.00
	1815 JP	—	60.00	100.00	175.00	250.00
	1816 JP	—	20.00	30.00	100.00	150.00
	1817 JP	—	20.00	30.00	100.00	150.00
	1818 JP	—	20.00	30.00	100.00	150.00
	1819 JP	—	20.00	30.00	100.00	150.00
	1820 JP	—	20.00	30.00	75.00	100.00
	1821 JP	—	20.00	30.00	75.00	150.00

8 REALES

25.0000 g, .903 SILVER, .7259 oz ASW
Mint mark: LIMAE (monogram)
Rev: Similar to KM#117.2.

KM#	Date	Mintage	VG	Fine	VF	XF
97	1801 IJ	4.223	25.00	32.50	50.00	85.00
	1802 IJ	3.875	25.00	32.50	50.00	85.00
	1803 IJ	—	35.00	60.00	100.00	125.00
	1803 JP	—	25.00	32.50	50.00	85.00
	1804 JP	3.979	25.00	32.50	50.00	85.00
	1805 JP	4.030	25.00	32.50	50.00	85.00
	1806 JP	4.199	25.00	32.50	50.00	85.00
	1807 JP	3.562	25.00	32.50	50.00	85.00
	1808 JP	4.017	25.00	32.50	50.00	85.00

NOTE: Earlier dates (1791-1800) exist for this type.

Obv. leg: FERDND. VII. . ., imaginary bust.
Rev: Arms, pillars.

KM#	Date	Mintage	VG	Fine	VF	XF
106.1	1808 JP	I.A.	150.00	250.00	425.00	800.00
	1809 JP	4.197	100.00	200.00	280.00	450.00

Obv. leg: FERDIN. VII. . . ., imaginary bust.

KM#	Date	Mintage	VG	Fine	VF	XF
106.2	1809 JP	I.A.	30.00	60.00	100.00	225.00
	1810 JP	4.380	30.00	60.00	100.00	225.00
	1811 JP	4.412	30.00	50.00	75.00	150.00

Obv. leg: FERDIN. VII. . ., standard bust.

KM#	Date	Mintage	VG	Fine	VF	XF
117.1	1811 JP	I.A.	50.00	90.00	140.00	225.00
	1812 JP	3.800	25.00	32.50	45.00	75.00
	1813 JP	4.033	25.00	32.50	45.00	75.00
	1814 JP	3.599	25.00	32.50	45.00	75.00
	1815 JP	3.642	25.00	32.50	45.00	75.00
	1816 JP	—	25.00	32.50	45.00	75.00
	1817 JP wide date					
		—	25.00	32.50	45.00	75.00
	1817 JP narrow date					
		—	25.00	32.50	45.00	75.00
	1818 JP	—	25.00	32.50	45.00	75.00
	1819 JP	3.139	25.00	32.50	45.00	75.00
	1820 JP	—	25.00	32.50	45.00	75.00
	1821 JP	—	25.00	32.50	45.00	75.00
	1822 JP	—	Reported, not confirmed			
	1823 JP	—	100.00	175.00	250.00	400.00
	1824 JP	—	Reported, not confirmed			
	1824 JM	—	100.00	150.00	300.00	500.00

Mint mark: CUZCO (monogram)

KM#	Date	Mintage	VG	Fine	VF	XF
117.2	1824 T	—	60.00	100.00	175.00	350.00
	1824 G	—	90.00	150.00	250.00	550.00
	1824 G/T	—	—	—	Rare	—

1/2 ESCUDO

1.6875 g, .875 GOLD, .0475 oz AGW
Mint mark: LIMAE (monogram)

KM#	Date	Mintage	VG	Fine	VF	XF
125	1814 JP	—	225.00	450.00	800.00	1400.
	1815 JP	—	225.00	450.00	800.00	1400.
	1816 JP	—	225.00	450.00	800.00	1400.
	1817 JP	—	225.00	450.00	800.00	1400.
	1818 JP	—	225.00	450.00	800.00	1400.
	1819 JP	—	225.00	450.00	800.00	1400.
	1820 JP	—	225.00	450.00	800.00	1400.
	1821 JP	—	225.00	450.00	800.00	1400.

ESCUDO

3.3750 g, .875 GOLD, .0949 oz AGW
Mint mark: LIMAE (monogram)
Obv. leg: CAROL. IIII. . ., bust of Charles IV.
Rev: Similar to KM#126.

KM#	Date	Mintage	VG	Fine	VF	XF
80	1801 IJ	—	100.00	150.00	250.00	350.00
	1802 IJ	—	100.00	150.00	250.00	350.00
	1803 IJ	—	100.00	150.00	250.00	350.00
	1803 JP	—	100.00	150.00	250.00	350.00
	1804 JP	—	100.00	150.00	250.00	350.00
	1805 JP	—	100.00	150.00	250.00	350.00
	1806 JP	—	100.00	150.00	250.00	350.00
	1807 JP	—	100.00	150.00	250.00	350.00
	1808 JP	—	100.00	150.00	250.00	350.00

NOTE: Earlier dates (1789-1800) exist for this type.

Obv. leg: FERDIN. VII. . ., uniformed Lima bust.

KM#	Date	Mintage	VG	Fine	VF	XF
110	1809 JP	—	Reported, not confirmed			
	1810 JP	—	200.00	400.00	650.00	950.00
	1811 JP	—	300.00	600.00	1000.	1500.
	1812 JP	—	350.00	700.00	1150.	1650.

Obv. leg: FERDIN. VII. . ., standard bust.

KM#	Date	Mintage	VG	Fine	VF	XF
119	1812 JP	—	150.00	300.00	500.00	700.00
	1813 JP	—	125.00	250.00	400.00	600.00
	1814 JP	—	150.00	300.00	500.00	700.00

Obv. leg: FERDIN. VII. . ., laureate undraped bust.

KM#	Date	Mintage	VG	Fine	VF	XF
126	1814 JP	—	150.00	225.00	350.00	450.00
	1815 JP	—	100.00	150.00	250.00	350.00
	1816 JP	—	100.00	150.00	250.00	350.00
	1817 JP	—	100.00	150.00	250.00	350.00
	1818 JP	—	100.00	150.00	250.00	350.00
	1819 JP	—	150.00	225.00	350.00	450.00
	1820 JP	—	100.00	150.00	250.00	350.00
	1821 JP	—	125.00	200.00	300.00	400.00

2 ESCUDOS

6.7500 g, .875 GOLD, .1899 oz AGW
Obv. leg: CAROL IIII, bust of Charles IV.

KM#	Date	Mintage	VG	Fine	VF	XF
100	1804 JP	—	125.00	225.00	400.00	600.00
	1805 JP	—	175.00	275.00	500.00	800.00
	1806 JP	—	175.00	275.00	500.00	800.00
	1808 PJ	—	225.00	325.00	600.00	900.00

NOTE: Earlier dates (1792-1800) exist for this type.

Obv. leg: FERDIN. VII. . ., uniformed Lima bust.
Rev: Crowned arms, order chain.

KM#	Date	Mintage	VG	Fine	VF	XF
111	1809 JP	—	300.00	550.00	1000.	1500.
	1810 JP	—	300.00	550.00	1000.	1500.
	1811 JP	—	300.00	550.00	1000.	1500.

Obv. leg: FERDIN. VII. . ., standard bust.

KM#	Date	Mintage	VG	Fine	VF	XF
120	1812 JP	—	225.00	450.00	700.00	1100.
	1813 JP	—	225.00	450.00	700.00	1100.

Obv. leg: FERDIN. VII. . ., laureate undraped bust

KM#	Date	Mintage	VG	Fine	VF	XF
127	1814 JP	—	200.00	350.00	550.00	900.00
	1815 JP	—	200.00	350.00	550.00	900.00
	1816 JP	—	200.00	350.00	550.00	900.00
	1817 JP	—	200.00	350.00	550.00	900.00
	1818 JP	—	200.00	350.00	550.00	900.00
	1819 JP	—	200.00	350.00	550.00	900.00
	1820 JP	—	200.00	350.00	550.00	900.00
	1821 JP	—	200.00	350.00	550.00	900.00

4 ESCUDOS

13.5000 g, .875 GOLD, .3798 oz AGW
Mint mark: LIMAE (monogram)
Obv. leg: CAROL. IV. . . . .

KM#	Date	Mintage	VG	Fine	VF	XF
98	1801 IJ	—	500.00	750.00	1300.	2000.
	1804 JP	—	500.00	750.00	1300.	2000.
	1805 JP	—	500.00	750.00	1300.	2000.
	1806 JP	—	500.00	750.00	1300.	2000.
	1807 JP	—	500.00	750.00	1300.	2000.

NOTE: Earlier dates (1791-1800) exist for this type.

Obv. leg: FERDIN. VII. . ., uniformed Lima bust.

KM#	Date	Mintage	VG	Fine	VF	XF
112	1809 JP	—	1250.	1750.	2500.	4000.
	1810 JP	—	1000.	1500.	2250.	3500.

Obv: Large laureate draped bust of Ferdinand VII.

KM#	Date	Mintage	VG	Fine	VF	XF
121	1812 JP	—	1250.	1750.	2250.	3500.

Obv: Small laureate draped bust of Ferdinand VII.

KM#	Date	Mintage	VG	Fine	VF	XF
122	1812 JP	—	800.00	1250.	1750.	2500.
	1813 JP	—	800.00	1250.	1750.	2500.

Obv: Laureate, undraped bust of Ferdinand VII.

M#	Date	Mintage	VG	Fine	VF	XF
28	1814 JP	—	600.00	1000.	1500.	2250.
	1815 JP	—	500.00	750.00	1250.	2000.
	1816 JP	—	600.00	1000.	1500.	2250.
	1817 JP	—	1200.	1750.	2250.	3500.
	1818 JP	—	600.00	1000.	1500.	2250.
	1819 JP	—	800.00	1200.	1750.	2500.
	1820 JP	—	800.00	1200.	1750.	2500.
	1821 JP	—	800.00	1200.	1750.	2500.

8 ESCUDOS

27.0000 g, .875 GOLD, .7596 oz AGW
Mint mark: LIMAE (monogram)
Obv. leg: CAROL. IIII, bust of Charles IV.

	Date	Mintage	VG	Fine	VF	XF
01	1801 IJ	—	400.00	500.00	800.00	1100.
	1802 IJ	—	400.00	500.00	800.00	1100.
	1803 IJ	—	400.00	500.00	800.00	1100.
	1803 JP	—	400.00	500.00	900.00	1300.
	1804 IJ	—	600.00	900.00	1800.	3000.
	1804 JP	—	400.00	500.00	900.00	1300.
	1805 JP	—	400.00	500.00	800.00	1100.
	1806 JP	—	400.00	500.00	800.00	1100.
	1807 JP	—	400.00	500.00	800.00	1100.
	1808 JP	—	400.00	500.00	800.00	1100.

NOTE: Earlier dates (1792-1800) exist for this type.

Obv. leg: FERDIN. VII. . ., uniformed Lima bust.
Rev: Crowned arms, order chain.

	Date	Mintage	VG	Fine	VF	XF
107	1808 JP	—	900.00	1800.	3000.	4500.
	1809 JP	—	600.00	1000.	1750.	2500.
	1810 JP	—	600.00	1000.	1750.	2500.
	1811 JP	—	600.00	1000.	1750.	2500.
	1812 JP	—	800.00	1250.	2500.	3500.

Obv: Large laureate draped bust of Ferdinand VII.

KM#	Date	Mintage	VG	Fine	VF	XF
118	1811 JP	—	900.00	1750.	3000.	5000.
	1812 JP	—	600.00	1000.	1750.	2500.

Obv: Small laureate draped bust of Ferdinand VII.

KM#	Date	Mintage	VG	Fine	VF	XF
124	1812 JP	—	750.00	1250.	2000.	2500.
	1813 JP	—	750.00	1250.	2000.	2500.

KM#	Date	Mintage	VG	Fine	VF	XF
129.1	1814 JP	—	400.00	500.00	800.00	1100.
	1815 JP	—	400.00	500.00	800.00	1100.
	1816 JP	—	400.00	500.00	900.00	1300.
	1817 JP	—	400.00	500.00	800.00	1100.
	1818 JP	—	400.00	500.00	800.00	1100.
	1819 JP	—	400.00	500.00	800.00	1100.
	1820 JP	—	400.00	500.00	800.00	1100.
	1821 JP	—	400.00	500.00	900.00	1300.

Mint mark: Co
Obv: Similar to KM#129.1.

KM#	Date	Mintage	VG	Fine	VF	XF
129.2	1824 G	—	800.00	1250.	2500.	4000.

PROVISIONAL COINAGE

(Republican)

1/4 REAL

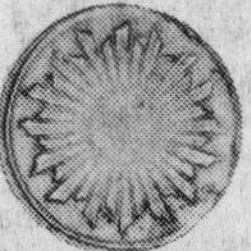

COPPER

KM#	Date	Mintage	VG	Fine	VF	XF
135	1822	—	6.00	13.50	28.00	50.00

OCTAVO DE (1/8) PESO

(1 Real)

COPPER
Mint mark: LIMA (monogram)

KM#	Date	Mintage	VG	Fine	VF	XF
137	1823	—	4.25	10.00	18.00	37.50
	1823 V	—	15.00	35.00	50.00	110.00

QUARTO DE (1/4) PESO

(2 Reales)

COPPER
Mint mark: LIMA (monogram)

KM#	Date	Mintage	VG	Fine	VF	XF
138	1823	—	3.25	6.75	12.50	27.50
	1823 V	—	10.00	15.00	27.50	55.00

NOTE: Restrikes of KM#137 and 138 were issued in 1921 using the original dies.

8 REALES

25.0000 g, .903 SILVER, .7259 oz ASW
Mint mark: LIMA (monogram)
Peru Libre Type

KM#	Date	Mintage	VG	Fine	VF	XF
136	1822 JP	—	50.00	75.00	135.00	300.00
	1823 JP	—	50.00	75.00	135.00	250.00

COUNTERMARKED COINAGE

(Royalist)

8 REALES

SILVER
c/m: Crown above 1824 on KM#136.

KM#	Date	Year	VG	Fine	VF	XF
130	1824	1822 JP	70.00	100.00	160.00	320.00
	1824	1823 JP	50.00	80.00	125.00	250.00

NOTE: The crown/1824 countermark appears to have been applied without any discretion to obverse or reverse. Although being very collectable neither variety carries a premium over the other.

REPUBLIC

1/4 REAL

.8400 g, .903 SILVER, .0243 oz ASW
Mint: Lima

KM#	Date	Mintage	VG	Fine	VF	XF
143.1	1826	—	3.50	6.50	14.00	27.50
	1827	—	2.50	4.75	10.00	17.50
	1828	—	3.50	6.50	14.00	27.50
	1829/8	—	4.75	8.50	17.50	37.50
	1830/28	—	3.00	6.00	14.00	27.50
	1831/0	—	2.50	4.75	10.00	17.50
	1831	—	3.50	6.00	13.00	25.00
	1832	—	5.25	11.00	22.50	45.00
	1833	—	3.00	5.75	12.00	25.00
	1834/3	—	5.00	7.50	15.00	30.00
	1834	—	3.50	6.00	13.00	27.50
	1835	—	6.50	13.50	26.00	55.00
	1836/5	—	10.00	15.00	30.00	50.00
	1836	—	5.00	10.00	22.50	45.00
	1837	—	5.00	10.00	22.50	45.00
	1839/8	—	5.00	10.00	22.50	45.00
	1839	—	4.25	8.50	17.00	35.00
	1840	—	4.25	8.50	17.00	35.00
	1841/0	—	3.50	6.00	13.00	25.00
	1841	—	4.00	8.00	16.00	35.00
	1842/32	—	4.00	8.00	16.00	35.00
	1842	—	2.50	4.75	10.00	17.50
	1843/33	—	4.00	8.00	16.00	35.00
	1843	—	2.50	4.75	10.00	17.50
	1845	—	3.00	5.75	12.00	22.50
	1846	—	2.50	4.75	10.00	17.50
	1846/3	—	2.50	5.00	12.00	20.00
	1847/6	—	5.00	12.50	25.00	50.00
	1847	—	3.50	7.00	16.00	30.00
	1848/38	—	4.25	8.50	20.00	40.00
	1848	—	4.25	8.50	20.00	40.00
	1849/38	—	4.25	8.50	20.00	40.00
	1849/8	—	4.25	8.50	20.00	40.00
	1849	—	3.50	7.00	16.00	30.00
	1850	—	2.50	5.00	12.00	20.00
	1851/21	—	2.00	4.00	10.00	18.00
	1851/31	—	2.00	4.00	10.00	18.00
	1853/1	—	2.50	5.00	12.00	20.00
	1855/35	—	1.50	3.00	5.00	15.00
	1855/3	—	1.50	3.00	5.00	15.00
	1855	—	1.50	3.00	5.00	15.00
	1856/45	—	2.50	5.00	12.00	20.00
	1856	—	1.50	3.00	5.00	15.00

Mint: Arequipa

KM#	Date	Mintage	VG	Fine	VF	XF
143.2	1839	—	100.00	175.00	350.00	500.00

1/2 REAL

1.6900 g, .903 SILVER, .0490 oz ASW
Mint mark: LIMAE (monogram)
Obv. leg: REPUB.PERUANA.

KM#	Date	Mintage	VG	Fine	VF	XF
144.1	1826 JM	—	3.50	7.50	15.00	25.00
	1827 JM	—	5.50	12.50	25.00	40.00
	1828 JM	—	3.50	7.50	15.00	25.00
	1829/8 JM	—	7.00	15.00	35.00	60.00
	1830 JM	—	7.00	15.00	35.00	60.00
	1831 MM	—	4.00	7.50	17.50	30.00
	1832 MM	—	4.00	7.50	17.50	30.00
	1833/2	—	4.00	7.50	17.50	30.00
	1833 MM	—	2.50	6.00	12.50	20.00
	1834 MM	—	2.50	6.00	12.50	20.00
	1835/3 MM	—	4.50	9.00	18.50	32.00
	1835 MM	—	4.50	9.00	18.50	32.00
	1835 MT/M	—	7.00	15.00	35.00	60.00

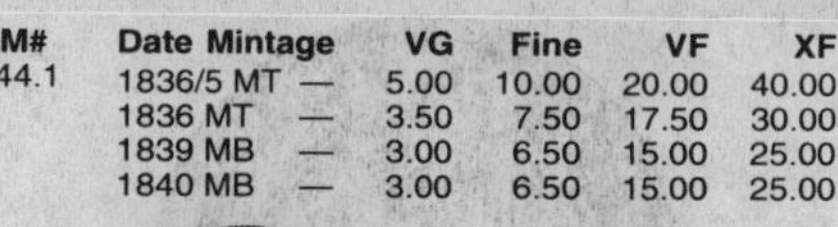

KM#	Date	Mintage	VG	Fine	VF	XF
144.1	1836/5 MT	—	5.00	10.00	20.00	40.00
	1836 MT	—	3.50	7.50	17.50	30.00
	1839 MB	—	3.00	6.50	15.00	25.00
	1840 MB	—	3.00	6.50	15.00	25.00

Mint mark: CUZCO (monogram)

KM#	Date	Mintage	VG	Fine	VF	XF
144.2	1827 GM	—	12.50	25.00	50.00	95.00
	1828 G	—	12.50	25.00	50.00	95.00
	1829/8 G	—	10.00	20.00	40.00	80.00
	1829 G	—	12.50	25.00	50.00	95.00
	1830/28 G	—	10.00	20.00	40.00	80.00
	1830 G	—	7.50	15.00	25.00	50.00
	1831 G	—	5.00	10.00	20.00	45.00
	1835 B	—	5.00	10.00	20.00	45.00

Mint mark: CUZCO

KM#	Date	Mintage	VG	Fine	VF	XF
144.3	1833 B	—	3.00	6.00	11.00	30.00
	1834 B	—	3.50	6.50	12.00	35.00

1.6500 g, .667 SILVER, .0354 oz ASW
Mint mark: AREQ
Obv. leg: REPUB. PERUANA

KM#	Date	Mintage	VG	Fine	VF	XF
144.4	1836 M	—	5.00	12.00	25.00	50.00

1.6500 g, .903 SILVER, .0479 oz ASW
Mint mark: LIMA (monogram)

KM#	Date	Mintage	VG	Fine	VF	XF
144.5	1840 MMB	—	10.00	20.00	35.00	65.00
	1841/0 MMB	—	15.00	30.00	50.00	85.00

Obv. leg: REP. PERUANA 10D. 20G

KM#	Date	Mintage	VG	Fine	VF	XF
144.7	1840 MB	—	5.50	12.00	25.00	55.00
	1841 MB	—	5.50	12.00	25.00	45.00
	1842 MB	—	5.50	12.00	25.00	45.00
	1843 MB	—	4.00	8.00	16.00	32.00
	1845 MB	—	3.00	6.00	12.00	25.00
	1846 MB	—	3.00	7.00	14.00	28.00
	1847 MB	—	9.00	15.00	28.00	65.00
	1849 MB	—	6.00	12.00	25.00	55.00
	1850 MB	—	3.00	6.00	12.00	25.00
	1851 MB	—	4.00	7.50	15.00	30.00
	1852 MB	—	5.00	10.00	20.00	45.00
	1853/1 MB	—	15.00	20.00	30.00	75.00
	1853/2 MB	—	Reported, not confirmed			
	1853 MB	—	15.00	20.00	30.00	75.00
	1854 MB	—	4.00	7.50	15.00	30.00
	1855 MB	—	3.00	5.50	10.00	17.50
	1856 MB	—	3.00	5.50	10.00	17.50

NOTE: Varieties exist.

REAL

3.3800 g, .903 SILVER, .0981 oz ASW
Mint mark: LIMAE (monogram)
Obv. leg: REPUB. PERUANA

KM#	Date	Mintage	VG	Fine	VF	XF
145.1	1826 JM	—	12.00	25.00	45.00	90.00
	1827 JM	—	4.50	9.00	16.00	30.00
	1828 JM	—	4.50	9.00	16.00	30.00
	1829 JM	—	Reported, not confirmed			
	1830 JM	—	8.50	17.50	35.00	60.00
	1831 JM	—	10.00	20.00	42.50	80.00
	1831 MM	—	—	—	—	—
	1832 MM	—	7.50	15.00	27.50	50.00
	1833/2 MM	—	10.00	20.00	40.00	75.00
	1834 MM	—	5.50	10.00	18.00	35.00
	1835/3	—	Reported, not confirmed			
	1836 MT	—	10.00	20.00	40.00	75.00
	1839 MB	—	7.50	15.00	27.50	50.00
	1840 MB	—	4.50	9.00	16.00	30.00

Mint mark: CUZco (monogram)
Obv. leg: REPUB. PERUANA

KM#	Date	Mintage	VG	Fine	VF	XF
145.2	1827 GM	—	15.00	35.00	60.00	100.00
	1828 G	—	15.00	35.00	60.00	100.00
	1829/8 G	—	20.00	40.00	75.00	125.00
	1829 G	—	20.00	40.00	75.00	125.00
	1830 G	—	20.00	40.00	75.00	125.00
	1831/21 G	—	20.00	40.00	75.00	125.00
	1831/0 G	—	20.00	40.00	75.00	125.00
	1831 G	—	20.00	40.00	75.00	125.00

Mint mark: CUZCO

KM#	Date	Mintage	VG	Fine	VF	XF
145.3	1834 B	—	45.00	80.00	150.00	225.00

Obv. leg: REP. PERUANA 10D 20G
Mint mark: LIMAE: (monogram)

KM#	Date	Mintage	VG	Fine	VF	XF
145.4	1841 MB	—	—	—	—	—
	1842 MB	—	10.00	20.00	40.00	75.00
	1843 MB	—	10.00	20.00	40.00	75.00
	1846 MB	—	10.00	20.00	40.00	75.00
	1847/6 MB	—	12.00	25.00	47.50	90.00
	1849 MB	—	5.50	10.00	18.00	35.00
	1850 MB	—	3.50	7.00	12.50	20.00
	1851 MB	—	4.00	8.00	14.00	25.00
	1855 MB	—	4.50	9.00	16.00	30.00
	1856/5 MB	—	3.50	7.00	12.50	20.00

2 REALES

6.7700 g, .903 SILVER, .1965 oz ASW
Mint mark: LIMAE (monogram)
Obv. leg: REPUB. PERUANA

KM#	Date	Mintage	VG	Fine	VF	XF
141.1	1825 JM	—	12.00	25.00	40.00	80.00
	1826 JM	—	4.00	7.00	15.00	30.00
	1827 JM	—	5.00	10.00	18.00	40.00
	1828/27 JM	—	—	—	—	—
	1828 JM	—	3.00	6.50	12.50	25.00
	1828 JM inverted reverse	—	6.00	12.00	25.00	50.00
	1829 JM	—	16.00	35.00	65.00	125.00
	1830/29 JM	—	9.00	17.50	35.00	75.00
	1830 JM	—	9.00	17.50	35.00	75.00
	1831 MM	—	9.00	17.50	35.00	75.00
	1832/1 MM	—	9.00	17.50	35.00	75.00
	1832 MM	—	5.00	10.00	18.00	40.00
	1833 MM	—	8.00	15.00	25.00	50.00
	1834/3 MM	—	10.00	20.00	40.00	80.00
	1834 MM	—	8.00	15.00	25.00	50.00
	1835 MM	—	150.00	300.00	—	—
	1836 MT	—	150.00	350.00	—	—
	1839 MB	—	8.00	15.00	25.00	50.00
	1840 MB	—	4.00	8.00	15.00	35.00

Mint mark: CUZco (monogram)
Obv. leg: REPUB. PERUANA

KM#	Date	Mintage	VG	Fine	VF	XF
141.2	1827 GM	—	35.00	65.00	100.00	165.00
	1828 G	—	25.00	55.00	80.00	145.00
	1829 G	—	25.00	55.00	80.00	145.00
	1830 G	—	30.00	60.00	85.00	150.00
	1831 G	—	35.00	65.00	100.00	165.00

6.7700 g, .667 SILVER, .1452 oz ASW

KM#	Date	Mintage	VG	Fine	VF	XF
141.2a	1835 B	—	6.50	12.50	18.50	40.00

Mint mark: LIMAE (monogram)
Obv. leg: REP. PERUANA 10D 20G

KM#	Date	Mintage	VG	Fine	VF	XF
141.3	1840 MB	—	12.00	25.00	40.00	80.00
	1841/0 MB	—	10.00	22.00	35.00	65.00
	1841 MB	—	4.50	10.00	20.00	45.00
	1842 MB	—	4.50	10.00	20.00	45.00
	1843 MB	—	8.00	15.00	25.00	60.00
	1845 MB	—	10.00	20.00	40.00	80.00
	1846 MB	—	15.00	30.00	50.00	100.00
	1848/6 MB	—	5.00	12.00	22.00	50.00
	1848 MB	—	5.00	12.00	22.00	50.00
	1849 MB	—	4.00	8.00	15.00	30.00
	1850 MB	—	4.00	8.00	15.00	30.00
	1851 MB	—	4.50	10.00	20.00	45.00
	1854 MB	—	8.00	15.00	25.00	60.00
	1855 MB	—	10.00	20.00	40.00	80.00
	1856 MB	—	8.00	15.00	25.00	60.00

NOTE: Varieties exist.

Mint: Pasco
Obv. leg: REPUB. PERUANA

KM#	Date	Mintage	VG	Fine	VF	XF
141.4	1843 M	—	400.00	750.00	—	—

4 REALES

13.0000 g, .667 SILVER, .2788 oz ASW
Mint mark: CUZco (monogram)

M#	Date	Mintage	VG	Fine	VF	XF
51.1	1835 B	—	3.00	7.00	16.50	55.00
	1836 B	—	2.00	3.75	9.00	42.50

OTE: Many die varieties.

Mint mark: AREQ
Obv. leg: REPUB PERUANA

51.2	1836 M	—	25.00	45.00	100.00	200.00
	1839 MV	—	25.00	45.00	100.00	200.00
	1840 MV	—	25.00	45.00	100.00	200.00

13.5400 g, .903 SILVER, .3931 oz ASW
Mint mark: LIMA (monogram)
Obv. leg: REP. PERUANA

51.3	1842 MB	—	20.00	35.00	70.00	150.00
	1843/2 MB	—	10.00	17.50	35.00	85.00
	1843 MB	—	10.00	17.50	35.00	85.00
	1845 MB	—	15.00	25.00	50.00	125.00
	1846 MB	—	20.00	35.00	70.00	150.00
	1848 MB	—	7.00	15.00	30.00	50.00
	1849 MB	—	15.00	25.00	50.00	125.00
	1850 MB	—	9.00	20.00	35.00	75.00
	1851 MB	—	8.00	17.50	32.50	70.00
	1854 MB	—	5.00	9.00	15.00	40.00
	1855/4 MB	—	5.00	9.00	15.00	40.00
	1855 MB	—	10.00	15.00	30.00	65.00
	1856 MB	—	40.00	75.00	125.00	250.00

Mint mark: PAZCO (monogram)
Obv. leg: REPUB. PERUANA, 10Ds20Gs.

151.4	1843 M	—	20.00	45.00	120.00	250.00

Mint mark: PASCO
Obv. leg: REPUB. PERUANA 10Ds20Gs.

151.5	1844 M	—	8.50	17.50	47.50	125.00

Obv. leg: REPUBLICA PERUANA, w/o fineness.

KM#	Date	Mintage	VG	Fine	VF	XF
151.6	1844 M	—	10.00	22.50	65.00	165.00
	1845 M	4 known	140.00	180.00	—	—

Mint mark: PASCO (monogram)
Obv. leg: REP. PERUANA 10Ds20Gs.

151.7	1844 M	—	Reported, not confirmed			
	1855 N.S.	—	—	—	Rare	—

Mint mark: PASCO
Obv. leg: REPUB. PERUANA. 10Ds20Gs.

151.8	1855	—	25.00	55.00	120.00	275.00

Obv. leg: REP. PERUANA 10D 20G

151.9	1855 M	—	8.50	17.50	40.00	100.00

NOTE: Most coins of this variety have small engravers initial B in wreath above arms. At least one example is known with JB in relief.

Obv. leg: REP. PERUANA.

151.10	1856 Z in 0	—	75.00	175.00	300.00	—
	1857 Z in 0	—	20.00	40.00	75.00	150.00
	1857 AF	—	85.00	190.00	325.00	—
	1857	—	150.00	350.00	750.00	—

8 REALES

27.0700 g, .903 SILVER, .7859 oz ASW
Mint mark: LIMA (monogram)
Obv. leg: REPUB. PERUANA
Rev: Small figure of Liberty.

142.1	1825 JM	—	20.00	35.00	55.00	130.00
	1826 JM	—	12.50	17.50	35.00	100.00
	1827 JM	—	12.50	17.50	35.00	100.00
	1828 JM	—	60.00	85.00	150.00	350.00

Mint mark: CUZco (monogram)

KM#	Date	Mintage	VG	Fine	VF	XF
142.2	1826 GM	—	35.00	55.00	100.00	225.00
	1826 G	—	15.00	30.00	60.00	120.00
	1827 GM	—	15.00	30.00	60.00	120.00
	1827 G	—	35.00	55.00	100.00	225.00
	1828/7 G	—	15.00	30.00	60.00	120.00
	1828 G	—	15.00	30.00	60.00	120.00
	1829 G	—	35.00	55.00	100.00	225.00
	1829 G REPMB (error)	—	—	—	Rare	—

Mint mark: LIMAE (monogram)
Rev: Large figure of Liberty.

142.3	1828 JM	—	10.00	15.00	25.00	65.00
	1829 JM	—	11.00	17.00	30.00	75.00
	1830 JM	—	11.00	17.00	30.00	75.00
	1831 JM	—	35.00	60.00	115.00	250.00
	1831 MM	—	11.00	17.00	30.00	75.00
	1832 MM	—	10.00	15.00	25.00	60.00
	1833 MM	—	10.00	15.00	25.00	60.00
	1833 MM POR AL UNION (error)	—	—	—	Rare	—
	1834 MM	—	10.00	15.00	25.00	60.00
	1835 MM	—	11.00	17.00	30.00	75.00
	1835 MM POR AL UNION (error)	—	—	—	Rare	—
	1835 MT	—	11.00	17.00	30.00	75.00
	1836 MT	—	10.00	15.00	25.00	60.00
	1836 TM	—	30.00	50.00	100.00	250.00
	1838 MB	—	20.00	30.00	55.00	125.00
	1839 MB	—	12.00	20.00	40.00	90.00
	1840 MB	—	10.00	15.00	25.00	60.00

Mint mark: CUZCO

142.4	1830 G	—	12.00	20.00	35.00	80.00
	1831 G	—	12.00	20.00	35.00	80.00
	1832 B	—	12.50	22.50	40.00	90.00
	1833 B	—	15.00	25.00	45.00	100.00
	1833 BoAr	—	15.00	25.00	45.00	100.00
	1834 BoAr	—	15.00	25.00	45.00	100.00

Mint mark: CUZco (monogram)

KM#	Date	Mintage	VG	Fine	VF	XF
142.5	1835 B	—	30.00	50.00	100.00	200.00

Mint mark: AREQ

KM#	Date	Mintage	VG	Fine	VF	XF
142.7	1839 MV	—	800.00	1500.	3500.	7000.
	1840 MV	—	600.00	1200.	3000.	6000.

Mint mark: LIMAE (monogram)
Obv. leg: REP. PERUANA 10DS 20GS
Rev: Similar to KM#142.3.

KM#	Date	Mintage	VG	Fine	VF	XF
142.8	1840 MB	—	30.00	55.00	100.00	200.00
	1841/0 MB	—	25.00	50.00	85.00	100.00
	1841 MB	—	12.00	22.00	32.00	75.00

Mint mark: CUZco (monogram)
Obv. leg: 10Ds20Gs.

KM#	Date	Mintage	VG	Fine	VF	XF
142.9	1840 A	—	15.00	30.00	60.00	125.00

Mint mark: LIMAE (monogram)

Obv. leg: REPUB. PERUANA 10Ds 20Gs.

KM#	Date	Mintage	VG	Fine	VF	XF
142.10	1841 MB	—	1500.	3500.	6750.	—
	1842 MB	—	12.00	20.00	60.00	175.00
	1843 MB	—	10.00	17.50	50.00	140.00
	1843 MB POR AL UNION (error)	—	120.00	150.00	175.00	350.00
	1843 MB inverted V in LA	—	125.00	150.00	175.00	350.00
	1844 MB	—	20.00	35.00	85.00	250.00
	1845 MB	—	10.00	17.50	50.00	140.00
	1846 MB	—	10.00	25.00	75.00	200.00
	1847/6 MB	—	25.00	50.00	100.00	325.00
	1847 MB	—	25.00	50.00	100.00	325.00
	1848/7 MB	—	10.00	25.00	75.00	200.00
	1848 MB	—	10.00	25.00	75.00	200.00
	1849/8/7 MB	—	50.00	125.00	300.00	600.00
	1849 MB	—	50.00	125.00	300.00	600.00
	1850/49 MB	—	50.00	100.00	200.00	300.00
	1850 MB ornamented edge	—	10.00	25.00	75.00	200.00
	1850 MB roped edge	—	30.00	60.00	150.00	450.00
	1851 MB	—	15.00	35.00	95.00	250.00
	1852 MB	—	20.00	45.00	120.00	300.00

23.9734 g, .903 SILVER, .6960 oz ASW
Reeded edge.

KM#	Date	Mintage	VG	Fine	VF	XF
142.10a	1855 MB	—	8.00	17.50	40.00	75.00

27.0700 g, .903 SILVER, .7859 oz ASW
Mint mark: AREQ
Obv. leg: REPUB. PERUANA. . . . . 10Ds20Gs.

KM#	Date	Mintage	VG	Fine	VF	XF
142.11	1841 M	—	2500.	4500.	7500.	12,000.

Mint: Pasco
Obv. leg: REPUB. PERUANA

KM#	Date	Mintage	VG	Fine	VF	XF
142.6	1836 MO	—	—	—	Rare	—

NOTE: Swiss Bank Corp. sale 20 9-88 holed fine realized $10,500.

Mint mark: LIMAE (monogram)
Obv. leg: Small REPUBLICA PERUANA, small date.
Rev: Small letters in legend.

KM#	Date	Mintage	VG	Fine	VF	XF
142.12	1853 MB	—	40.00	90.00	200.00	500.00

Mint: Pasco
Obv. leg: REPUB PERUANA. 10Ds20Gs.

KM#	Date	Mintage	VG	Fine	VF	XF
142.13	1857 Z in 0	—	—	—	10,000.	20,000.
	1857 Z in 0 PRO LA UNION (error)	—	—	—	*Rare	—

***NOTE:** Superior December Sale 12-90 VF realized $20,900.

1/2 ESCUDO

1.6875 g, .875 GOLD, .0475 oz AGW
Mint mark: LIMAE (monogram)

KM#	Date	Mintage	VG	Fine	VF	XF
146.1	1826 JM	—	45.00	90.00	150.00	200.00
	1827 JM	—	60.00	125.00	225.00	300.00
	1828 JM	—	35.00	70.00	115.00	150.00
	1829 JM	—	30.00	50.00	80.00	100.00
	1833 MM	—	35.00	70.00	115.00	150.00
	1836 TM	—	35.00	70.00	115.00	150.00
	1836 MM	—	—	—	—	—
	1839 MB	—	60.00	125.00	225.00	300.00
	1840 MB	—	30.00	50.00	80.00	100.00
	1841 MB	—	35.00	70.00	115.00	150.00
	1842 MB	—	60.00	125.00	225.00	300.00
	1850 MB	—	35.00	70.00	115.00	150.00
	1851 MB	—	75.00	150.00	300.00	425.00
	1856 MB	—	45.00	90.00	150.00	200.00

NOTE: For coins of this type dated 1838 M, see North Peru.

Mint mark: CUZCO

KM#	Date	Mintage	VG	Fine	VF	XF
146.2	1826 GM	—	35.00	60.00	95.00	125.00

ESCUDO

3.3750 g, .875 GOLD, .0949 oz AGW
Mint mark: LIMAE (monogram)
Obv. leg: REPUBLICA PERUANA

KM#	Date	Mintage	VG	Fine	VF	XF
147.1	1826 JM	—	70.00	120.00	200.00	300.00
	1827 JM	—	95.00	165.00	265.00	350.00
	1828/7 JM	—	70.00	120.00	200.00	300.00
	1828 JM	—	70.00	120.00	200.00	300.00
	1829 JM	—	55.00	85.00	135.00	200.00
	1833 MM	—	Reported, not confirmed			

Mint mark: CUZCO

KM#	Date	Mintage	VG	Fine	VF	XF
147.2	1826 GM	—	100.00	160.00	240.00	400.00
	1830 G	—	100.00	160.00	240.00	400.00

Mint mark: CUZco (monogram)

KM#	Date	Mintage	VG	Fine	VF	XF
147.3	1840 A	—	55.00	85.00	135.00	200.00
	1845 A	—	55.00	70.00	95.00	150.00
	1846 A	—	55.00	85.00	135.00	200.00

Mint mark: LIMAE (monogram)
Obv. leg: REPUB. PERUANA

KM#	Date	Mintage	VG	Fine	VF	XF
147.4	1855 MB	—	70.00	120.00	200.00	300.00

2 ESCUDOS

6.7500 g, .875 GOLD, .1899 oz AGW
Mint mark: LIMAE (monogram)
Obv. leg: REPUBLICA PERUANA

KM#	Date	Mintage	VG	Fine	VF	XF
149.1	1828 JM	—	150.00	200.00	275.00	500.00
	1829 JM	—	100.00	130.00	175.00	250.00

Obv. leg: REPUB. PERUANA

KM#	Date	Mintage	VG	Fine	VF	XF
149.2	1850 MB	—	125.00	175.00	250.00	400.00
	1851 MB	—	110.00	150.00	200.00	300.00
	1853 MB	—	95.00	115.00	140.00	200.00
	1854 MB	—	125.00	175.00	250.00	400.00
	1855 MB	—	125.00	175.00	250.00	400.00

4 ESCUDOS

13.5000 g, .875 GOLD, .3798 oz AGW
Mint mark: LIMA

KM#	Date	Mintage	VG	Fine	VF	XF
150.1	1828 JM	—	—	—	Rare	—

Mint mark: LIMAE (monogram)

KM#	Date	Mintage	VG	Fine	VF	XF
150.2	1850 MB	—	225.00	350.00	500.00	750.00
	1853 MB	—	300.00	475.00	650.00	1000.

Obv. leg: Small lettering.
Rev: Flat base below Liberty.

KM#	Date	Mintage	VG	Fine	VF	XF
150.3	1854 MB	—	200.00	300.00	450.00	650.00

Obv. leg: REPUB. PERUANA

KM#	Date	Mintage	VG	Fine	VF	XF
150.4	1855 MB	—	185.00	210.00	300.00	450.00

8 ESCUDOS

27.0000 g, .875 GOLD, .7596 oz AGW
Mint mark: LIMAE (monogram)
Obv. leg: REPUBLICA PERUANA

KM#	Date	Mintage	VG	Fine	VF	XF
148.1	1826 JM	—	350.00	375.00	500.00	800.00
	1827 JM	—	350.00	400.00	550.00	1000.
	1828 JM	—	350.00	500.00	800.00	1500.
	1829/8 JM	—	350.00	400.00	550.00	1000.
	1829 JM	—	350.00	400.00	550.00	1000.
	1833 MM	—	350.00	375.00	500.00	800.00
	1840 MB	—	350.00	500.00	800.00	1500.

Mint mark: CUZCO

KM#	Date	Mintage	VG	Fine	VF	XF
148.2	1826 GM	—	350.00	550.00	750.00	1400.
	1827 G	—	350.00	550.00	750.00	1400.
	1828/7 G	—	350.00	450.00	600.00	1100.
	1828 G	—	350.00	450.00	600.00	1100.
	1829 G	—	350.00	550.00	750.00	1400.
	1830 G	—	350.00	450.00	600.00	1100.
	1831 G	—	350.00	375.00	550.00	900.00
	1832 VOARSH	—	350.00	400.00	600.00	1000.
	1833 BoAr	—	350.00	375.00	550.00	900.00
	1834 BoAr	—	350.00	400.00	600.00	1000.

Mint mark: CUZco (monogram)

KM#	Date	Mintage	VG	Fine	VF	XF
148.3	1835 B	—	350.00	450.00	650.00	1200.
	1836 B	—	350.00	500.00	800.00	1500.
	1839 A	—	350.00	500.00	800.00	1500.
	1840 A	—	350.00	400.00	600.00	1000.
	1843 A	—	350.00	450.00	650.00	1200.
	1844 A	—	350.00	500.00	800.00	1500.
	1845 A	—	350.00	375.00	550.00	900.00

Mint mark: LIMA (monogram)
Obv. and rev: Large letters in legends.

KM#	Date	Mintage	VG	Fine	VF	XF
148.6	1850 MB	—	350.00	375.00	500.00	900.00

Obv. and rev: Small letters in legends.

KM#	Date	Mintage	VG	Fine	VF	XF
148.4	1853 MB	—	400.00	600.00	900.00	1500.
	1854 MB	—	350.00	375.00	450.00	750.00
	1855 MB	—	350.00	375.00	500.00	850.00

Obv. leg: REPUB. PERUANA

KM#	Date	Mintage	VG	Fine	VF	XF
148.5	1855 MB	—	350.00	375.00	450.00	750.00

NORTH PERU

STATE COINAGE

Estado Nor-Peruano

1/2 REAL

1.6900 g, .903 SILVER, .0490 oz ASW
Mint: Lima

KM#	Date	Mintage	VG	Fine	VF	XF
154	1836 TM	—	13.50	32.50	85.00	225.00
	1837 TM	—	7.00	15.00	30.00	75.00
	1837 M	—	10.00	25.00	60.00	100.00
	1838 M	—	10.00	25.00	60.00	100.00
	1838 MB	—	10.00	25.00	60.00	100.00
	1838 MT	—	Reported, not confirmed			

REAL

3.3800 g, .903 SILVER, .0981 oz ASW

KM#	Date	Mintage	VG	Fine	VF	XF
158	1838 MB	—	80.00	175.00	300.00	450.00

2 REALES

6.7700 g, .903 SILVER, .1965 oz ASW

KM#	Date	Mintage	VG	Fine	VF	XF
157	1837 JM	—	—	—	Rare	—
	1838 MB	—	—	—	Rare	—

8 REALES

27.0700 g, .903 SILVER, .7859 oz ASW

KM#	Date	Mintage	VG	Fine	VF	XF
155	1836 TM	—	12.00	20.00	35.00	125.00
	1837 TM	—	10.00	17.50	30.00	95.00
	1837 M	—	12.00	20.00	35.00	100.00
	1838 M	—	12.00	20.00	35.00	100.00
	1838 MB	—	10.00	17.50	30.00	90.00
	1839 MB	—	12.00	20.00	35.00	100.00

1/2 ESCUDO

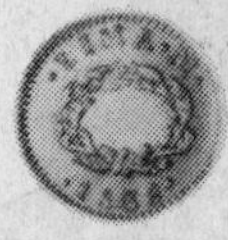

1.6875 g, .875 GOLD, .0475 oz AGW

KM#	Date	Mintage	VG	Fine	VF	XF
159	1838 M	—	100.00	200.00	350.00	500.00

NOTE: This coin is identical to the Republic type, KM#146.1 and can only be identified by the date.

ESCUDO

3.3750 g, .875 GOLD, .0949 oz AGW

KM#	Date	Mintage	VG	Fine	VF	XF
160	1838 M	—	500.00	1000.	1500.	2000.

2 ESCUDOS

6.7500 g, .875 GOLD, .1899 oz AGW

KM#	Date	Mintage	VG	Fine	VF	XF
161	1838 M	—	1500.	2000.	2500.	3000.

4 ESCUDOS

13.5000 g, .875 GOLD, .3798 oz AGW

KM#	Date	Mintage	VG	Fine	VF	XF
162	1838 M	—	2000.	3000.	5000.	10,000.

8 ESCUDOS

27.0000 g, .875 GOLD, .7596 oz AGW

KM#	Date	Mintage	VG	Fine	VF	XF
156	1836 TM	—	—	—	Rare	—
	1838 M	—	1500.	2500.	3500.	6000.

REPUBLIC COINAGE

Rep. Nor-Peruano

1/2 REAL

1.6900 g, .903 SILVER, .0490 oz ASW

KM#	Date	Mintage	VG	Fine	VF	XF
163	1839 MB	—	42.50	100.00	175.00	300.00

8 REALES

27.0700 g, .903 SILVER, .7859 oz ASW

KM#	Date	Mintage	VG	Fine	VF	XF
164	1839 MB	—	350.00	650.00	1150.	2000.

SOUTH PERU

STATE COINAGE

Estado Sud Peruano

1/2 REAL

1.6900 g, .667 SILVER, .0362 oz ASW
Mint: Cuzco

KM#	Date	Mintage	VG	Fine	VF	XF
166	1837 B	—	8.50	20.00	45.00	145.00

8 ESCUDOS

27.0000 g, .875 GOLD, .7596 oz AGW

KM#	Date	Mintage	VG	Fine	VF	XF
167	1837 BA	—	400.00	600.00	900.00	1650.

REPUBLIC COINAGE

Repub. Sud Peruano

1/2 REAL

1.6500 g, .667 SILVER, .0354 oz ASW
Mint mark: AREQ(uipa)

KM#	Date	Mintage	VG	Fine	VF	XF
168	1837	—	7.50	18.50	37.50	115.00
	1838/7	—	—	—	—	—

2 REALES

6.5000 g, .667 SILVER, .1391 oz ASW
Mint: Cuzco

KM#	Date	Mintage	VG	Fine	VF	XF
169.1	1837 BA	—	3.75	10.00	23.50	67.50

Mint mark: AREQ(uipa)

KM#	Date	Mintage	VG	Fine	VF	XF
169.2	1838	—	5.50	15.00	35.00	90.00

4 REALES

13.5400 g, .667 SILVER, .2899 oz ASW
Mint mark: AREQ (uipa).

KM#	Date	Mintage	VG	Fine	VF	XF
172	1838 MV	—	8.50	20.00	47.50	110.00

8 REALES

27.0700 g, .903 SILVER, .7859 oz ASW
Mint mark: CUZCO
Rev. leg: FEDERACION

KM#	Date	Mintage	VG	Fine	VF	XF
170.1	1837 BA incuse edge lettering					
		—	20.00	45.00	80.00	175.00
	1837 BA raised edge lettering					
		5 known	200.00	350.00	500.00	—

Rev. leg: Small letters, CONFEDERACION • B • A •.

KM#	Date	Mintage	VG	Fine	VF	XF
170.2	1837 BA	—	25.00	55.00	120.00	300.00

Rev. leg: Large letters, CONFEDERACION • B • A •.

KM#	Date	Mintage	VG	Fine	VF	XF
170.4	1837 MS	—	45.00	70.00	140.00	350.00
	1838 BA	—	20.00	45.00	75.00	125.00
	1838 MS	—	20.00	45.00	75.00	125.00
	1839 MS	—	50.00	100.00	225.00	375.00

Mint mark: AREQ(uipa)

KM#	Date	Mintage	VG	Fine	VF	XF
170.3	1838 MV	—	600.00	1200.	2500.	5500.
	1839 MV	—	1650.	3250.	5250.	—

1/2 ESCUDO

1.6875 g, .875 GOLD, .0475 oz AGW
Mint mark: CUZCO (monogram)

KM#	Date	Mintage	VG	Fine	VF	XF
173	1838 MS	—	75.00	140.00	220.00	450.00

ESCUDO

3.3750 g, .875 GOLD, .0949 oz AGW

KM#	Date	Mintage	VG	Fine	VF	XF
174	1838 MS	—	90.00	160.00	280.00	525.00

8 ESCUDOS

27.0000 g, .875 GOLD, .7596 oz AGW

KM#	Date	Mintage	VG	Fine	VF	XF
171	1837 BA	—	400.00	600.00	900.00	1900.
	1838 MS	—	400.00	550.00	800.00	1750.

TRANSITIONAL COINAGE

Issued during the changeover to the decimal system.

MEDIO (1/2) REAL

1.2500 g, .900 SILVER, .0361 oz ASW
Mint: Lima

KM#	Date	Mintage	Fine	VF	XF	Unc
177	1858 MB	—	4.75	11.00	27.50	60.00

KM#	Date	Mintage	Fine	VF	XF	Unc
180	1859 YB	—	4.50	9.50	22.50	50.00
	1860/59 YB	—	4.50	9.50	22.50	50.00
	1860 YB	—	3.25	8.00	16.50	38.50
	1861 YB	—	4.50	9.50	22.50	50.00

NOTE: Die varieties exist.

REAL

2.5000 g, .900 SILVER, .0723 oz ASW

KM#	Date	Mintage	Fine	VF	XF	Unc
181	1859 YB	—	5.00	12.00	25.00	55.00
	1860 YB	—	3.00	6.50	12.50	30.00
	1861 YB	—	5.50	14.00	30.00	65.00

NOTE: Die varieties exist.

25 CENTAVOS

6.2500 g, .900 SILVER, .1808 oz ASW

KM#	Date	Mintage	Fine	VF	XF	Unc
182	1859/8 YB	—	22.50	52.50	100.00	235.00
	1859 YB	—	40.00	75.00	150.00	335.00

NOTE: Die varieties exist.

50 CENTIMOS

12.1000 g, .900 SILVER, .3501 oz ASW

KM#	Date	Mintage	Fine	VF	XF	Unc
178	1858 MB	—	13.50	25.00	55.00	115.00
	1858 MB	—	—	—	Proof	—

50 CENTAVOS

12.1000 g, .900 SILVER, .3501 oz ASW
Rev: Liberty w/short hair.

KM#	Date	Mintage	Fine	VF	XF	Unc
179.1	1858 MB	—	16.00	32.50	65.00	240.00
	1858 YB	—	13.50	27.50	55.00	150.00
	1859 YB	—	15.00	40.00	85.00	200.00

Rev: Liberty w/long hair.

KM#	Date	Mintage	Fine	VF	XF	Unc
179.2	1858 YB	—	12.00	22.50	45.00	140.00
	1859/8 YB/Y	—	12.00	22.50	45.00	140.00
	1859 YB/Y	—	9.00	20.00	40.00	125.00

NOTE: Die varieties exist.

4 ESCUDOS

13.5000 g, .875 GOLD, .3798 oz AGW

KM#	Date	Mintage	Fine	VF	XF	Unc
184	1863 YB	—	—	—	Rare	—

8 ESCUDOS

27.0000 g, .875 GOLD, .7596 oz AGW

KM#	Date	Mintage	Fine	VF	XF	Unc
183	1862 YB	—	400.00	500.00	700.00	1250.
	1863/2 YB	—	350.00	450.00	550.00	900.00
	1863 YB	—	350.00	450.00	550.00	900.00

DECIMAL COINAGE

100 Centavos (10 Dineros) = 1 Sol
10 Soles = 1 Libra

CENTAVO

COPPER-NICKEL

KM#	Date	Mintage	Fine	VF	XF	Unc
187.1	1863	1.000	1.00	2.50	6.00	22.50
	1863	—	—	—	Proof	—
	1864	Inc. Ab.	1.25	3.50	7.50	25.00

NOTE: Wreath varieties exist.

BRONZE

KM#	Date	Mintage	Fine	VF	XF	Unc
187.1a	1875	—	1.50	3.50	6.00	20.00
	1876	—	1.00	3.00	5.00	15.00
	1877	—	2.00	5.00	10.00	30.00
	1878	—	10.00	15.00	25.00	65.00

NOTE: Date varieties exist.

Sharper diework

KM#	Date	Mintage	Fine	VF	XF	Unc
187.2	1919 (P)	4.000	.50	1.00	2.50	8.50

Thick planchet
Small date and legend.

KM#	Date	Mintage	Fine	VF	XF	Unc
208.1	1901	.600	1.00	2.50	4.00	14.00
	1904	1.000	4.50	8.00	14.00	45.00

Large date and legend.

KM#	Date	Mintage	Fine	VF	XF	Unc
208.2	1933	.275	1.50	3.00	5.50	16.00
	1934	1.185	.75	1.50	2.50	7.50
	1935	1.105	.75	1.50	2.50	7.50
	1936	.565	1.50	3.00	5.50	16.00
	1937/6	.735	1.00	2.00	4.00	12.00
	1937	Inc. Ab.	.75	1.50	2.50	7.50
	1938	.340	.75	1.50	2.50	7.50
	1939	1.225	1.50	3.00	5.50	15.00
	1940	1.250	1.50	3.00	5.50	15.00
	1941	2.593	.40	.75	1.50	6.00

NOTE: Varieties exist.

Thin planchet

KM#	Date	Mintage	Fine	VF	XF	Unc
208a	1941	Inc.KM208	.40	.75	1.50	6.00
	1942	2.865	.50	1.00	1.75	7.50
	1943	—	Reported, not confirmed			
	1944	—	4.00	9.00	16.00	40.00

KM#	Date	Mintage	Fine	VF	XF	Unc
211	1909	.252	7.50	15.00	20.00	50.00
	1909/999 R	I.A.	7.50	15.00	20.00	50.00

KM#	Date	Mintage	Fine	VF	XF	Unc
211	1909 R	Inc. Ab.	7.50	15.00	20.00	50.00
	1915	.250	3.00	6.00	10.00	25.00
	1916	.360	1.00	2.00	4.50	14.00
	1916 R	Inc. Ab.	1.00	2.00	4.50	14.00
	1917	.830	1.00	2.00	4.00	14.00
	1917 R	Inc. Ab.	1.00	2.00	4.00	14.00
	1918	1.060	1.00	2.00	4.00	12.00
	1918 R	Inc. Ab.	1.00	2.00	4.00	12.00
	1920 R	.360	1.00	2.50	4.50	15.00
	1933 R	Inc. KM208	1.00	2.50	4.50	15.00
	1934	Inc.KM208	4.50	8.00	14.00	45.00
	1935 R	Inc. KM208	4.00	7.00	12.00	40.00
	1936 R	Inc. KM208	1.50	3.50	6.00	15.00
	1937	—	—	—	—	—
	1937 R	Inc. KM208	1.50	3.50	6.00	15.00
	1939 R	Inc. KM208	4.50	8.00	14.00	45.00

NOTE: Engravers initial R appeared below ribbon on most or all new dies, but often became weak or filled. Most coins show at least a faint trace of R. Date varieties also exist.

Thin planchet.

KM#	Date	Mintage	Fine	VF	XF	Unc
211a	1941	Inc.KM208	1.00	2.00	3.50	12.50
	1942	Inc. KM208a	.50	1.00	1.75	7.50
	1943	—	2.50	5.00	12.50	30.00
	1944	2.490	.15	.40	.75	2.50
	1945	2.157	.15	.40	.75	2.50
	1946	3.198	.15	.40	.75	2.00
	1947	2.976	.15	.40	.75	2.50
	1948	3.195	.15	.40	.75	2.00
	1949	1.104	.25	.65	1.25	3.50

NOTE: Many varieties exist.

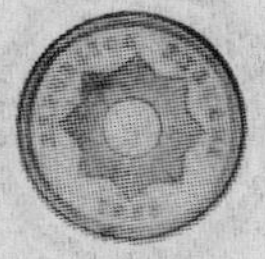

ZINC

KM#	Date	Mintage	Fine	VF	XF	Unc
227	1950	3.196	.35	.75	1.25	4.00
	1951	3.289	.25	.40	.65	2.00
	1952	3.050	.25	.40	.65	2.00
	1953	3.260	.35	.60	1.00	3.00
	1954	3.215	.75	1.50	2.50	8.00
	1955	3.400	.25	.40	.65	2.00
	1956	2.500	.25	.40	.65	2.00
	1957	4.400	.40	.85	1.50	5.00
	1958	2.600	.35	.60	1.00	3.00
	1959	3.200	.25	.40	.65	2.00
	1960/50	3.060	.35	.60	1.00	3.00
	1960	Inc. Ab.	.75	1.50	3.00	6.00
	1961/51	2.600	.35	.60	1.00	3.00
	1962/52	2.600	.25	.40	.65	2.00
	1963/53	2.400	.25	.40	.65	2.00
	1963	Inc. Ab.	.25	.40	.65	2.00
	1965	.360	.75	1.50	2.50	8.00

NOTE: Varieties exist. Copper plated examples of type dated 1951 are known.

2 CENTAVOS

COPPER-NICKEL

KM#	Date	Mintage	Fine	VF	XF	Unc
188.1	1863	1.000	1.50	4.00	12.50	27.50
	1863	—	—	—	Proof	—
	1864	Inc. Ab.	1.50	4.00	12.50	27.50

COPPER or BRONZE

KM#	Date	Mintage	Fine	VF	XF	Unc
188.1a	1876	—	1.00	3.00	6.00	17.50
	1877	—	1.00	4.00	8.50	25.00
	1878	—	1.00	3.00	7.00	20.00
	1879	*	1.00	3.00	7.00	20.00
	1879 B	—	—	—	—	—

***NOTE:** Coin and medal rotations exist.

Modified dies.

KM#	Date	Mintage	Fine	VF	XF	Unc
188.2	1895 (W)	—	.75	1.75	4.00	9.50

Sharper diework

KM#	Date	Mintage	Fine	VF	XF	Unc
188.3	1919 (P)	3.000	.35	.75	2.00	6.50

Thick planchet

KM#	Date	Mintage	Fine	VF	XF	Unc
212.1	1917 C	.073	4.00	6.50	10.00	25.00
	1918/17	.580	3.50	6.00	9.00	22.50
	1918/17 C	I.A.	3.50	6.00	9.00	22.50
	1918	Inc. Ab.	3.50	6.00	12.00	30.00
	1918 C	Inc. Ab.	3.50	6.00	12.00	30.00
	1920/7 C	.328	—	—	—	—
	1920	Inc. Ab.	1.00	1.75	3.00	10.00
	1920 C	Inc. Ab.	1.00	1.75	3.00	10.00
	1933	.285	1.00	1.75	3.00	10.00
	1933 C	Inc. Ab.	1.00	1.75	3.00	10.00
	1934	.973	.75	1.50	2.50	9.00
	1934 C	Inc. Ab.	.75	1.50	2.50	9.00
	1935	.950	.75	1.50	2.50	9.00
	1935 C	Inc. Ab.	.75	1.50	2.50	9.00
	1936	.763	.75	1.50	2.50	9.00
	1936/5 C	I.A.	1.50	2.50	5.00	15.00
	1936 C	Inc. Ab.	.75	1.25	2.25	7.50
	1937	.963	.75	1.50	2.50	9.00
	1937 C	Inc. Ab.	.75	1.50	2.50	9.00
	1938 C	.428	1.00	1.75	3.00	10.00
	1939/8 C	—	Reported, not confirmed			
	1939/8	—	1.50	2.50	5.00	15.00
	1939 C inverted A for V in CENTAVOS	.783	.75	1.50	2.50	9.00
	1940	—	—	—	—	—
	1940 C	.565	1.00	1.75	3.00	10.00
	1941/0	I.A.	—	—	—	—
	1941/0 C	I.A.	—	—	—	—
	1941/22	I.A.	—	—	—	—
	1941	Inc. Ab.	—	—	—	—
	1941 C	Inc. Ab.	2.00	5.00	10.00	15.00

NOTE: Engravers initial C appeared below ribbon on most or all new dies, but often became weak or filled. Most coins show at least a faint trace of C. Other varieties also exist.

Thin planchet

KM#	Date	Mintage	Fine	VF	XF	Unc
212.2	1941/32	.870	—	—	—	—
	1941/33 C	I.A.	1.00	2.00	3.50	10.00
	1941/33	I.A.	—	—	—	—
	1941/38	I.A.	—	—	—	—
	1941/38 C	I.A.	1.00	2.00	3.50	10.00
	1941/39 C	I.A.	1.00	2.00	3.50	10.00
	1941/0	I.A.	1.00	2.00	3.50	10.00
	1941	Inc. Ab.	.35	.75	1.25	4.00
	1942/22	4.418	—	—	—	—
	1942/32	4.418	—	—	—	—
	1942	Inc. Ab.	.25	.50	1.00	3.00
	1943/2	1.829	.50	1.00	2.00	7.00
	1943	Inc. Ab.	.50	1.00	2.00	7.00
	1944	2.068	.75	1.50	3.00	9.00
	1945	2.288	.75	1.50	3.00	9.00
	1946	2.121	.25	.50	.75	2.50
	1947	1.280	.25	.50	.75	2.50
	1948	1.518	.25	.50	.75	3.00
	1949/8	.938	.25	.60	3.50	5.00
	1949	Inc. Ab.	—	—	—	—

NOTE: Varieties exist.

ZINC

KM#	Date	Mintage	Fine	VF	XF	Unc
228	1950	1.702	.35	.75	1.25	4.00
	1951	3.289	.35	.75	1.25	4.00
	1952	1.155	.35	.75	1.25	4.00
	1953	1.150	.40	.85	1.50	5.00
	1954	—	2.50	5.00	9.00	30.00
	1955	1.185	.35	.75	1.25	4.00
	1956	.400	.50	1.00	2.00	6.00
	1957	.520	1.50	3.00	6.00	20.00
	1958	.200	1.25	2.50	4.50	15.00

NOTE: Copper plated examples of type dated 1951 exist.

1/2 DINERO

1.2500 g, .900 SILVER, .0362 oz ASW
Mint: Lima
Obv: Small wreath.
Rev: Denomination in curved line.

KM#	Date	Mintage	Fine	VF	XF	Unc
189	1863 YB	—	1.00	2.00	5.00	15.00
	1864 YB	—	1.50	3.00	7.50	25.00

NOTE: Engraver's initials RB appear left of shield on reverse. Roman numeral I in 1/2 on 1863 dated coins.

Mint: Cuzco

KM#	Date	Mintage	VG	Fine	VF	XF
189a	1885 JM	—	75.00	150.00	300.00	600.00

NOTE: S in wreath on obverse and engravers initials left of shield, Roman numeral I in 1/2 on reverse.

Mint: Lima
Obv: Large wreath.
Rev: Denomination in straight line.

KM#	Date	Mintage	Fine	VF	XF	Unc
206	1890 TF	.870	1.50	3.00	6.00	15.00
	1891 TF	.160	2.00	3.50	8.00	20.00
	1892 TF	.228	1.00	2.00	4.50	12.00
	1893 TF	—	25.00	50.00	95.00	165.00
	1895 TF	.422	1.00	2.00	5.00	14.00
	1896 TF	.456	2.00	4.00	9.00	22.50
	1896 F.	Inc. Ab.	1.00	2.00	4.50	12.00
	1896.F.	Inc. Ab.	1.00	2.00	4.50	12.00
	1896,F.(error) PBRUANA	Inc. Ab.	—	—	—	—
	1897 JF	.320	.75	1.25	2.50	7.00
	1897 VN	I.A.	3.50	7.00	16.00	37.50
	1898/7 VN	.600	1.00	2.00	5.00	14.00
	1898 VN	I.A.	.75	1.50	3.50	10.00
	1898 JF	I.A.	.60	1.25	2.50	7.00
	1899/8 JF	.500	1.00	1.75	4.00	11.00
	1899 JF	I.A.	.60	1.25	2.50	7.00
	1900/890 JF	.400	.60	1.25	2.50	7.00
	1901/801 JF	.500	.60	1.25	2.50	7.00
	1901/801/701 JF	Inc. Ab.	.60	1.25	2.50	7.00
	1901/891/791	Inc. Ab.	.60	1.25	2.00	6.00
	1901/891 JF	Inc. Ab.	.60	1.25	2.00	6.00
	1901 JF	I.A.	.75	1.50	3.50	9.00
	1902/802 JF	.616	.60	1.25	2.00	6.00
	1902/892 JF	Inc. Ab.	.60	1.25	2.00	6.00
	1902/92	I.A.	.60	1.25	2.00	6.00
	1902 JF	I.A.	.75	1.50	3.50	9.00
	1903/803 JF	1.798	.50	1.00	1.75	4.50
	1903/893 JF	Inc. Ab.	.50	1.00	1.75	4.50
	1903/897 JF	Inc. Ab.	1.00	1.75	4.00	11.00
	1903 JF	I.A.	.75	1.50	3.00	7.50
	1904/804 JF	.723	.60	1.25	2.00	6.00
	1904/804 JF (error FFLIZ)	Inc. Ab.	2.00	4.50	8.00	12.50
	1904/893 JF	Inc. Ab.	.60	1.25	2.00	6.00
	1904/894 JF	Inc. Ab.	.60	1.25	2.00	6.00
	1904/894 JF (error FFLIZ)	Inc. Ab.	2.00	4.50	8.00	12.50
	1904 JF	I.A.	.75	1.50	3.00	7.50
	1904 JF (error FFLIZ)	Inc. Ab.	2.00	4.50	8.00	12.50
	1905/805 JF	1.400	.75	1.50	3.50	9.00
	1905/893 JF	Inc. Ab.	1.00	2.00	4.50	12.00
	1905/894	Inc. Ab.	1.00	2.00	4.50	12.00
	1905/895 JF	Inc. Ab.	.50	1.25	2.00	6.00
	1905/3 JF	I.A.	1.00	2.00	4.50	12.00
	1905 JF	I.A.	.75	1.50	3.00	7.50
	1906/806 JF	.900	.75	1.50	3.50	9.00
	1906/886 JF	Inc. Ab.	.75	1.50	3.50	9.00
	1906/895 JF	Inc. Ab.	.75	1.50	3.50	9.00
	1906/896 JF	Inc. Ab.	.50	1.25	2.00	6.00
	1906 JF	I.A.	.75	1.50	3.00	9.00
	1907 FG	.600	.60	1.25	2.00	6.00
	1908/7 FG	.200	1.50	3.00	6.00	15.00
	1908 FG	I.A.	.75	1.50	3.50	9.00
	1909/7 FG	—	3.00	6.00	12.50	27.50
	1909 FG	—	.75	1.50	3.50	9.00
	1910 FG	.640	.50	1.00	1.75	4.50
	1911 FG	.460	.50	1.25	2.00	6.00
	1912 FG	.120	.60	1.25	2.50	7.00
	1913 FG	.480	.50	1.00	1.75	4.50
	1914/04 FG	—	1.00	2.50	5.50	15.00
	1914/03 FG	—	1.00	2.50	5.50	15.00
	1914/3 FG	—	.75	1.50	3.50	9.00
	1914 FG	—	.50	1.00	1.75	4.50
	1916/3 FG	.860	.50	1.00	1.75	4.50

KM#	Date	Mintage	Fine	VF	XF	Unc
206	1916/3 FG (error) FERUANA	—	1.00	2.00	4.50	12.50
	1916 FG	I.A.	.35	.75	1.25	3.00
	1916/5 FG (error) PERUANA	Inc. Ab.	1.00	2.00	4.50	12.50
	1916/5 FG (error) FERUANA	Inc. Ab.	1.00	2.00	4.50	12.50
	1916 FG (error) FERUANA	Inc. Ab.	1.00	2.00	4.50	12.50
	1916	—	—	—	Matte	—
	1917 FG	.140	.50	1.00	1.75	4.50

NOTE: Most coins 1900-06 show faint to strong traces of 9/8 or 90/89 in date. Non-overdates without such traces are scarce. Most coins of 1907-17 have engravers initial R at left of shield tip on reverse. Many other varieties exist.

5 CENTAVOS

COPPER-NICKEL
Mint: Philadelphia
Obv. date: UN MIL NOVECIENTOS DIECIOCHO.

KM#	Date	Mintage	Fine	VF	XF	Unc
213.1	1918	4.000	.50	1.25	2.50	10.00
	1919	10.000	.40	1.00	2.00	7.00
	1923	2.000	1.00	2.00	3.50	12.50
	1926	4.000	1.50	3.00	6.00	20.00

Mint: London

KM#	Date	Mintage	Fine	VF	XF	Unc
213.2	1934	4.000	.75	2.00	3.00	8.50
	1934	—	—	—	Proof	—
	1935	4.000	.50	1.25	2.00	6.00
	1935	—	—	—	Proof	—
	1937	2.000	.75	2.00	3.00	8.50
	1937	—	—	—	Proof	—
	1939	2.000	.50	1.25	2.00	6.00
	1939	—	—	—	Proof	—
	1940	2.000	.50	1.25	2.00	6.00
	1940	—	—	—	Proof	—
	1941	2.000	.50	1.25	2.00	6.00
	1941	—	—	—	Proof	—

BRASS
Mint: Philadelphia
Obv. date: MIL NOVECIENTOS CUARENTA Y DOS.

KM#	Date	Mintage	Fine	VF	XF	Unc
213.2a.1	1942	4.000	1.00	3.00	5.00	12.00
	1943	4.000	1.00	3.00	5.00	12.00
	1944	4.000	1.00	2.75	4.50	10.00

Mint mark: S

KM#	Date	Mintage	Fine	VF	XF	Unc
213.2a.2	1942	4.000	1.00	3.00	5.00	12.00
	1943	4.000	2.50	4.50	8.00	20.00

Mint: Lima
Obv. date: MIL NOVECIENTOS CUARENTICUATRO.

KM#	Date	Mintage	Fine	VF	XF	Unc
213.2a.3	1944	1.106	1.50	3.50	6.00	15.00

Thick planchet, short legend.

KM#	Date	Mintage	Fine	VF	XF	Unc
223.1	1945	2.768	.35	.75	1.50	4.00
	1946/5	4.270	1.00	2.50	5.00	14.00
	1946	Inc. Ab.	.25	.50	1.00	3.50

Long legend.

KM#	Date	Mintage	Fine	VF	XF	Unc
223.3	1947	7.683	.25	.50	1.00	3.00
	1948	6.711	.25	.50	1.00	3.00
	1949/8	5.550	1.00	2.00	4.00	10.00
	1949	Inc. Ab.	1.00	2.00	4.00	10.00
	1950	7.933	.25	.50	1.00	3.00
	195.1	8.064	.25	.50	1.00	3.00

Thin planchet

KM#	Date	Mintage	Fine	VF	XF	Unc
223.2	1951	Inc. Ab.	.10	.25	.50	2.50
	1952	7.840	.10	.25	.50	2.50
	1953	6.976	.10	.25	.50	2.50
	1953 AFP	—	—	—	—	—
	1954	6.244	.10	.20	.40	1.00
	1955	8.064	.10	.20	.40	2.00
	1956	16.200	—	.10	.35	1.50
	1957 small date	16.000	—	.10	.25	.75
	1957 lg.dt.	I.A.	—	.10	.25	.75
	1958	4.600	—	.10	.25	1.00
	1959	8.300	—	.10	.25	1.00
	1960/50	9.900	—	—	Rare	—
	1960	Inc. Ab.	—	.10	.25	.75
	1961	10.200	—	.10	.20	.75
	1962	11.064	—	.10	.20	.75
	1963	12.012	—	.10	.20	.75
	1964/3	12.304	—	.10	.35	1.50
	1964	Inc. Ab.	—	—	.10	.75
	1965 small date	12.500	—	—	.10	.50
223.2	1965 lg. dt.	I.A.	—	—	.10	.50
	1965	—	—	—	Proof	20.00

NOTE: Varieties exist.

President Castilla

KM#	Date	Mintage	Fine	VF	XF	Unc
232	1954	2.080	1.25	2.50	5.00	10.00

400th Anniversary of Lima Mint

KM#	Date	Mintage	Fine	VF	XF	Unc
290	1965	.712	—	—	.10	.25
	1965	—	—	—	Proof	100.00

Obv: Large arms.
Reeded edge

KM#	Date	Mintage	Fine	VF	XF	Unc
244.1	1966*	14.620	—	—	.10	.20
	1966	1,000	—	—	Proof	2.50

***NOTE:** PAREJA in field at lower left of arms.

SILVER PLATED BRASS

KM#	Date	Mintage	Fine	VF	XF	Unc
244.1a	1967	—	—	—	—	—

BRASS
Plain edge

KM#	Date	Mintage	Fine	VF	XF	Unc
244.2	1967	14.088	—	—	.10	.20
	1968	17.880	—	—	.10	.20
	1969	17.880	—	—	—	.10
	1970	—	—	—	—	.10
	1971	24.320	—	—	—	.10
	1972	24.342	—	—	—	.10
	1973	25.074	—	—	—	.10

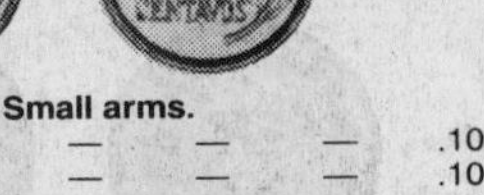

Obv: Small arms.

KM#	Date	Mintage	Fine	VF	XF	Unc
244.3	1973	Inc. Ab.	—	—	—	.10
	1974	—	—	—	—	.10
	1975	—	—	—	—	.10

DINERO

2.5000 g, .900 SILVER, .0723 oz ASW
Mint: Lima
Obv: Small wreath.
Rev: Denomination in curved line.

KM#	Date	Mintage	Fine	VF	XF	Unc
190	1863 YB	—	1.25	2.25	4.50	17.50
	1864/3 YB	—	1.25	2.25	4.00	15.00
	1864 YB	—	1.50	2.50	5.00	22.00
	1865/3 YB	—	3.50	7.50	15.00	45.00
	1865 YB	—	2.00	5.00	10.00	45.00
	1866/5 YB	—	1.25	2.25	4.00	15.00
	1866 YB	—	1.00	1.75	3.50	12.50
	1870/60 YJ	—	3.00	6.00	15.00	45.00
	1870/60 YJ/YB	—	—	—	—	—
	1870/69 YJ/YB	—	1.25	2.25	4.00	15.00
	1870 YJ	—	1.25	2.25	4.50	17.50
	1870 YJ/B	—	1.25	2.25	4.00	15.00
	1872/62 YJ/B	—	65.00	125.00	200.00	325.00
	1872 YJ	—	35.00	75.00	125.00	200.00
	1874 YJ	—	1.25	2.25	4.50	17.50
	1875 YJ	—	1.00	1.75	3.50	12.50
	1877 YJ.	—	2.00	5.00	10.00	35.00
	1877 Y.J.	—	3.00	5.00	15.00	50.00

NOTE: Engravers initials R.B. at left of shield on reverse of 1863-77. Varieties exist.

Mint: Cuzco

KM#	Date	Mintage	VG	Fine	VF	XF
190a	1886 JM	—	20.00	40.00	80.00	150.00

NOTE: Engravers initials FB left of shield on reverse.

Mint: Lima
Obv: Large wreath.
Rev: Denomination in straight line.

KM#	Date	Mintage	Fine	VF	XF	Unc
204.1	1888 TF	.010	50.00	90.00	150.00	250.00
	1890 TF	.400	1.25	2.25	5.00	20.00
	1891 TF	.060	3.00	7.50	15.00	38.00
	1892 TF	.069	3.00	7.50	15.00	38.00

Rev: Denomination in curved line.

KM#	Date	Mintage	Fine	VF	XF	Unc
204.2	1893 TF	.023	4.00	8.00	17.50	60.00
	1894/3 TF	—	15.00	30.00	60.00	100.00
	1895/3 TF	.090	5.00	15.00	25.00	45.00
	1895 TF	I.A.	4.00	8.00	17.50	70.00
	1896/5 TF	.534	2.50	6.00	12.50	25.00
	1896 TF	I.A.	3.00	6.00	12.00	30.00
	1896/5 F	I.A.	1.00	1.75	3.50	10.00
	1896 F	Inc. Ab.	3.00	6.00	12.00	28.00
	1897 JF	.511	1.00	1.75	3.50	10.00
	1897 VN	I.A.	1.00	1.75	3.50	10.00
	1898/7 JF	.200	3.00	6.00	12.00	28.00
	1898 JF	I.A.	1.25	2.25	4.00	12.50
	1900/90 JF	.550	1.00	2.00	3.25	10.00
	1900/98 JF	I.A.	1.25	2.25	4.00	12.50
	1900/890 JF	I.A.	1.00	2.00	3.50	10.00
	1900/898 JF	I.A.	1.00	2.00	3.50	10.00
	1900/897 JF	I.A.	1.00	2.00	3.50	10.00
	1900/89 JF	I.A.	1.00	2.00	3.50	10.00
	1900 JF	I.A.	1.25	2.25	4.00	12.50
	1902/1 JF	.375	1.00	2.00	3.50	10.00
	1902/891 JF	I.A.	1.00	2.00	3.50	10.00
	1902/892 JF	I.A.	1.00	2.00	3.50	10.00
	1902/897 JF	I.A.	1.00	2.00	3.50	10.00
	1902 JF	I.A.	1.00	2.00	3.50	10.00
	1903/803 JF	.887	1.00	2.00	3.50	10.00
	1903/892 JF	I.A.	.75	2.00	3.50	8.00
	1903/92 JF	I.A.	.75	2.00	3.50	8.00
	1903 JF	I.A.	.75	1.75	2.50	6.00
	1904 JF	.380	1.00	2.00	4.00	12.50
	1905/3 JF	.700	1.00	2.50	4.00	10.00
	1905 JF	I.A.	.75	2.00	3.50	8.00
	1906 JF	.826	.75	2.00	3.50	8.00
	1907 JF	.500	—	—	Rare	—
	1907 FG/JF	Inc. Ab.	1.25	2.50	4.50	10.00
	1907 FG	I.A.	1.00	1.75	3.00	8.00
	1908 FG/JF	.200	1.00	2.25	4.00	10.00
	1908 FG/GF	I.A.	1.00	2.25	4.00	10.00
	1908 FG	I.A.	1.00	1.75	3.00	8.00
	1909 FG	—	2.00	4.00	8.00	15.00
	1909 FG/FO	—	2.00	4.00	8.00	15.00
	1909 FG/FF	—	2.00	4.00	8.00	15.00
	1910 FG	.210	.60	1.25	2.50	8.00
	1910 FG/JF	I.A.	1.00	2.25	4.00	12.50
	1910 FG/JG	I.A.	1.00	2.25	4.00	12.50
	1911 FG	.200	.75	1.50	3.00	8.00
	1911 FG/JF	I.A.	1.00	2.25	4.00	12.50
	1911 FG/JG	I.A.	1.00	2.25	4.00	12.50
	1912 FG	.400	.60	1.25	2.50	8.00
	1912/02 FG/JF	I.A.	1.00	2.25	4.00	12.50
	1912 FG/JF	I.A.	1.00	2.25	4.00	12.50
	1912 FG/JG	I.A.	1.00	2.25	4.00	12.50
	1913/1 FG/JF	I.A.	1.00	2.25	4.00	12.50
	1913/2 FG	.360	1.00	2.25	4.00	12.50
	1913/7 FG/G	I.A.	1.00	2.25	4.00	12.50
	1913 FG	I.A.	.60	1.25	2.50	8.00
	1913 FG/G	I.A.	.60	1.25	2.50	8.00
	1913 FG/JB	I.A.	.60	1.25	2.50	8.00
	1916 FG large date	.430	1.25	2.50	4.50	10.00
	1916 FG small date	I.A.	.60	1.25	2.00	6.00
	1916 FG/JG	I.A.	2.00	5.00	7.50	15.00

NOTE: Varieties exist.

10 CENTAVOS

COPPER-NICKEL
Mint: Philadelphia
Obv. date: UN MIL NOVECIENTOS DIECIOCHO.

KM#	Date	Mintage	Fine	VF	XF	Unc
214.1	1918	3.000	.40	1.00	2.00	7.00
	1919	2.500	.40	1.00	2.00	7.00
	1920	3.080	.35	.75	1.50	6.00
	1921	6.920	.35	.75	1.50	6.00
	1926	3.000	2.50	5.00	8.50	22.50

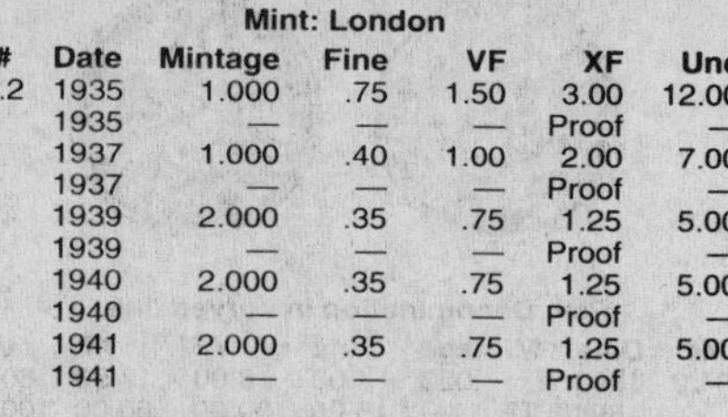

Mint: London

KM#	Date	Mintage	Fine	VF	XF	Unc
214.2	1935	1.000	.75	1.50	3.00	12.00
	1935	—	—	—	Proof	—
	1937	1.000	.40	1.00	2.00	7.00
	1937	—	—	—	Proof	—
	1939	2.000	.35	.75	1.25	5.00
	1939	—	—	—	Proof	—
	1940	2.000	.35	.75	1.25	5.00
	1940	—	—	—	Proof	—
	1941	2.000	.35	.75	1.25	5.00
	1941	—	—	—	Proof	—

BRASS
Mint: Philadelphia
Date is spelled out w/a "Y".

KM#	Date	Mintage	Fine	VF	XF	Unc
214a.1	1942	2.000	1.50	3.00	6.00	16.00
	1943	2.000	1.50	3.00	6.00	16.00
	1944	2.000	1.50	3.50	7.00	20.00

Mint mark: S

KM#	Date	Mintage	Fine	VF	XF	Unc
214a.2	1942	2.000	6.00	12.00	20.00	45.00
	1943	2.000	1.50	3.00	6.00	16.00

Mint: Lima
Date is spelled out with an I.

KM#	Date	Mintage	Fine	VF	XF	Unc
214a.3	1942	—	5.00	9.00	15.00	35.00
	1944	—	3.50	7.00	12.00	30.00

Thick planchet
Obv: Short legend.

KM#	Date	Mintage	Fine	VF	XF	Unc
224.1	1945	2.810	.25	.50	1.50	4.00
	1946/5	4.863	.50	1.00	2.50	8.00
	1946	Inc. Ab.	.35	.75	2.00	7.00

Thin planchet, 1.3mm
Obv: Long legend.

KM#	Date	Mintage	Fine	VF	XF	Unc
224.2	1951	Inc. Ab.	.10	.20	.40	2.00
	1951 AFP	—	—	—	—	—
	1952	6.694	.10	.20	.40	3.00
	1952 AFP	—	—	—	—	—
	1953	5.668	.10	.20	.40	2.00
	1953 AFP	—	—	—	—	—
	1954	7.786	—	.10	.35	1.50
	1954 AFP	—	—	—	—	—
	1955	6.690	—	.10	.35	1.50
	1955 AFP	—	—	—	—	—
	1956/5	8.410	.10	.35	.75	3.50
	1956	Inc. Ab.	—	.10	.25	.75
	1956 AFP	—	—	—	—	—
	1957	8.420	—	.10	.25	.75
	1957 AFP	—	—	—	—	—
	1958	10.380	—	.10	.25	1.00
	1958 AFP	—	—	—	—	—
	1959	8.300	—	.10	.25	.75
	1959 AFP	—	—	—	—	—
	1960	12.600	—	.10	.25	.50
	1961	12.700	—	.10	.15	.60
	1962	14.598	—	.10	.15	.50
	1963	16.100	—	.10	.15	.50
	1964	16.504	—	.10	.15	.60
	1965	17.808	—	.10	.15	.50
	1965	—	—	—	Proof	25.00

NOTE: Date varieties exist.

Thick planchet.
Obv: Long legend.

KM#	Date	Mintage	Fine	VF	XF	Unc
226.1	1947	6.806	.25	.50	1.00	3.00
	1948	5.771	.25	.50	1.25	4.00
	1949/8	4.730	.50	1.00	1.50	7.50

Obv: Different legend.

KM#	Date	Mintage	Fine	VF	XF	Unc
226.2	1949	Inc. Ab.	.25	.50	1.25	4.00
	1950	5.298	.25	.50	1.00	3.00
	1951	7.324	6.00	10.00	15.00	35.00
	1951/0 AFP	—	—	—	—	—
	1951 AFP	—	—	—	—	—

President Castilla

KM#	Date	Mintage	Fine	VF	XF	Unc
233	1954	1.818	1.50	3.00	6.00	12.50

400th Anniversary of Lima Mint

KM#	Date	Mintage	Fine	VF	XF	Unc
237	1965	.572	—	—	.10	.35
	1965	—	—	—	Proof	150.00

Obv: Large arms.
Reeded edge

KM#	Date	Mintage	Fine	VF	XF	Unc
245.1	1966*	14.930	—	—	.10	.25
	1966	1,000	—	—	Proof	2.50

NOTE: Date varieties exist.
***NOTE:** PAREJA in field at lower left of arms.

SILVER PLATED BRASS

KM#	Date	Mintage	Fine	VF	XF	Unc
245.1a	1967	—	—	—	—	—

BRASS
Plain edge

KM#	Date	Mintage	Fine	VF	XF	Unc
245.2	1967	19.330	—	—	.10	.25
	1968	24.390	—	—	.10	.25
	1969	24.390	—	—	.10	.25
	1970	29.110	—	—	.10	.20
	1971	30.590	—	—	.10	.20
	1972	34.442	—	—	.10	.20
	1973	33.864	—	—	.10	.20

NOTE: Date varieties exist.

Obv: Small arms.

KM#	Date	Mintage	Fine	VF	XF	Unc
245.3	1973	Inc. Ab.	—	—	.10	.15
	1974	—	—	—	.10	.15
	1975	10.430	—	—	.10	.15

KM#	Date	Mintage	Fine	VF	XF	Unc
263	1975	—	—	—	.10	.15

1/5 SOL

5.0000 g, .900 SILVER, .1447 oz ASW
Mint: Lima
Obv: Small wreath.
Rev: Denomination in curved line.

KM#	Date	Mintage	Fine	VF	XF	Unc
191	1863 YB	—	1.75	4.00	8.00	45.00
	1864/3 YB	—	2.00	5.00	10.00	55.00
	1864/3 YB-DD	—	—	25.00	55.00	225.00
	1864 YB	—	1.50	3.50	7.00	35.00
	1864 YB-DD	—	—	25.00	55.00	225.00
	1865/4 YB	—	2.00	5.00	10.00	55.00
	1865 YB	—	1.50	3.50	7.00	45.00
	1866/5 YB	—	2.00	4.50	8.50	40.00
	1866 YB	—	1.50	3.00	6.00	30.00
	1867 YB	—	1.50	3.50	7.00	35.00
	1869 YB	—	8.00	15.00	25.00	85.00
	1874 YJ	—	1.75	4.00	7.50	40.00
	1874 YJ/YB	—	—	—	—	—
	1875 YB	—	—	—	—	—
	1875/65 YJ	—	2.50	5.00	10.00	55.00
	1875 YJ	—	1.75	4.00	7.50	40.00

NOTE: Engraver's initials RB appear left of shield on reverse. Varieties exist.

Mint: Arequipa

KM#	Date	Mintage	Fine	VF	XF	Unc
191a	1885 A.C.	—	275.00	425.00	850.00	1750.

Mint: Lima
Obv: Large wreath.
Rev: Denomination in straight line,
Libertad in relief.

KM#	Date	Mintage	Fine	VF	XF	Unc
205.1	1888 TF	.550	1.75	3.50	6.00	17.50
	1889 TF	—	—	—	Rare	—
	1890/88 TF	.085	4.50	9.00	18.00	45.00
	1890 TF	I.A.	3.50	7.00	15.00	40.00
	1891 TF	.064	5.00	10.00	20.00	60.00
	1892 TF	.128	1.75	3.50	7.00	20.00

Rev: Libertad incuse.

KM#	Date	Mintage	Fine	VF	XF	Unc
205.2	1893 TF-JR	.049	5.00	10.00	20.00	60.00
	1895 TF-JR	I.A.	7.00	15.00	30.00	75.00
	1896 TF-JR	.586	1.50	3.00	5.50	14.00
	1896 F-JR	I.A.	1.75	3.50	7.00	20.00
	1897 JF	.745	1.50	3.00	5.50	14.00
	1897 JF-JR	I.A.	1.50	3.00	5.50	14.00
	1897 VN	I.A.	1.75	3.50	6.00	15.00
	1898 JF	.350	1.50	3.00	5.50	14.00
	1899/88 JF	.700	1.50	3.00	5.50	12.50
	1899/8	I.A.	1.50	3.00	5.50	12.50
	1899 JF	I.A.	1.50	3.00	5.50	12.00
	1899 JF-JR	I.A.	—	—	—	—
	1900/800 JF	.750	2.00	4.00	8.00	17.50
	1900/800 JF-JR		2.00	4.00	8.00	17.50
		I.A.	1.75	3.50	6.00	15.00
	1900/890 JF	I.A.	1.75	3.50	6.00	15.00
	1900 JF	I.A.	1.50	3.00	5.50	12.00
	1901 JF	.638	1.50	3.00	5.50	12.00
	1903/1 JF	.702	2.00	4.00	7.00	17.50
	1903/13 JF	I.A.	1.75	3.50	6.00	15.00
	1903 JF	I.A.	1.50	3.00	5.50	12.00
	1906 JF	.660	1.50	3.00	5.50	12.00
	1907 JF	1.370	1.25	2.00	4.00	6.00
	1907 FG	I.A.	1.50	3.00	5.50	12.00
	1908/7 FG	.560	1.75	3.50	6.00	15.00
	1908 FG	I.A.	1.50	3.00	5.50	12.00
	1909 FG	.042	2.00	4.00	9.00	27.50
	1910/00 FG	.165	3.00	7.00	12.00	25.00
	1910 FG	I.A.	3.00	7.00	12.00	25.00
	1911 FG	.250	1.50	3.00	5.50	9.00
	1911 FG-R	I.A.	1.50	3.00	5.50	9.00
	1912 FG	.300	1.25	2.00	4.00	6.00
	1912 FG-R	I.A.	1.50	3.00	5.50	9.00
	1913 FG	.223	1.75	3.50	6.00	15.00
	1913 FG-R	I.A.	1.75	3.50	6.00	15.00
	1914 FG	.010	5.00	10.00	20.00	40.00
	1915 FG	—	25.00	35.00	60.00	100.00
	1916 FG	.425	2.00	5.00	10.00	25.00
	1916 FG-R	I.A.	1.50	3.00	5.00	9.00
	1917 FG-R	.020	8.00	15.00	30.00	60.00

NOTE: Some coins 1893-1900 have engravers initials JR left of shield tip on reverse and some 1911-17 have R in same location. Die varieties exist.

20 CENTAVOS

COPPER-NICKEL
Mint: Philadelphia
Obv. date: UN MIL NOVECIENTOS DIECIOCHO.

KM#	Date	Mintage	Fine	VF	XF	Unc
215.1	1918	2.500	.40	1.00	2.50	8.00
	1919	1.250	.50	1.25	3.00	10.00
	1920	1.464	.50	1.25	3.00	10.00
	1921	8.536	.35	.85	2.00	7.00
	1926	2.500	.75	2.50	6.00	20.00

Mint: London

KM#	Date	Mintage	Fine	VF	XF	Unc
215.2	1940	1.000	.25	.75	1.75	5.50

KM#	Date	Mintage	Fine	VF	XF	Unc
	1940	—	—	—	Proof	125.00
	1941	1.000	.35	1.00	2.50	7.50
	1941	—	—	—	Proof	125.00

BRASS
Mint: Philadelphia
Obv. date: MIL NOVECIENTOS CUARENTA Y TRES.

KM#	Date	Mintage	Fine	VF	XF	Unc
215a.1	1942	.500	3.00	6.00	12.50	50.00
	1943	.500	3.00	6.00	12.50	50.00
	1944	.500	4.00	7.50	15.00	55.00

Mint mark: S

KM#	Date	Mintage	Fine	VF	XF	Unc
215a.2	1942	.500	6.00	12.00	25.00	90.00
	1943	.500	3.00	6.00	12.50	60.00

Mint: Lima
Thick planchet
Obv: Large head, divided leg.

KM#	Date	Mintage	Fine	VF	XF	Unc
221.1	1942	.300	1.00	2.50	5.00	12.50
	1943	1.900	.75	1.50	2.50	7.50
	1944	2.963	.60	1.25	2.00	6.00

Obv: Large head w/AFP on truncation, continuous leg.

KM#	Date	Mintage	Fine	VF	XF	Unc
221.2	1946	3.410	.25	.50	.85	3.00
	1947	4.307	.25	.50	.85	3.00
	1948	3.578	.25	.50	.85	3.00
	1949/8	2.709	.75	1.50	2.50	6.50

Obv: Different legend.

KM#	Date	Mintage	Fine	VF	XF	Unc
221.4	1949	Inc. Ab.	.50	1.00	1.75	4.50
	1950	2.427	1.00	1.75	3.00	8.00
	1951	2.941	3.00	7.50	12.50	30.00

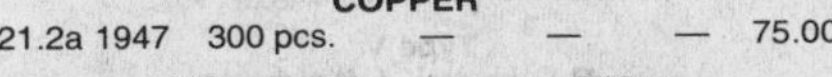

COPPER

KM#	Date	Mintage	Fine	VF	XF	Unc
221.2a	1947	300 pcs.	—	—	—	75.00

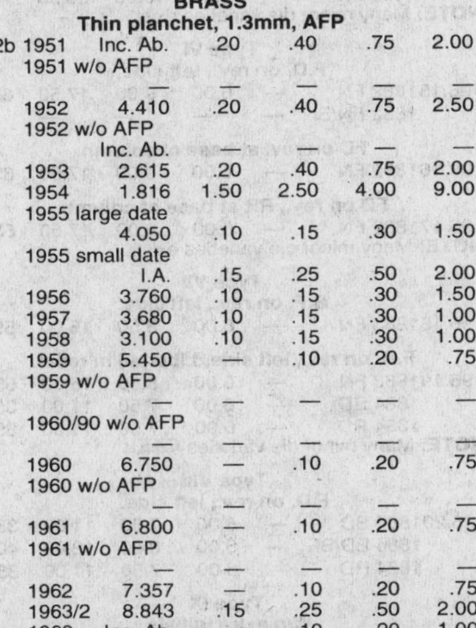

BRASS
Thin planchet, 1.3mm, AFP

KM#	Date	Mintage	Fine	VF	XF	Unc
221.2b	1951	Inc. Ab.	.20	.40	.75	2.00
	1951 w/o AFP	—	—	—	—	—
	1952	4.410	.20	.40	.75	2.50
	1952 w/o AFP	Inc. Ab.	—	—	—	—
	1953	2.615	.20	.40	.75	2.00
	1954	1.816	1.50	2.50	4.00	9.00
	1955 large date	4.050	.10	.15	.30	1.50
	1955 small date	I.A.	.15	.25	.50	2.00
	1956	3.760	.10	.15	.30	1.50
	1957	3.680	.10	.15	.30	1.00
	1958	3.100	.10	.15	.30	1.00
	1959	5.450	—	.10	.20	.75
	1959 w/o AFP	—	—	—	—	—
	1960/90 w/o AFP	—	—	—	—	—
	1960	6.750	—	.10	.20	.75
	1960 w/o AFP	—	—	—	—	—
	1961	6.800	—	.10	.20	.75
	1961 w/o AFP	—	—	—	—	—
	1962	7.357	—	.10	.20	.75
	1963/2	8.843	.15	.25	.50	2.00
	1963	Inc. Ab.	—	.10	.20	1.00
	1964	9.550	—	.10	.20	.75
221.2b	1965	—	—	.10	.20	.75
	1965 w/o AFP	—	—	—	—	—
	1965	—	—	—	Proof	30.00

NOTE: Date varieties exist.

Obv: Small head, continuous leg.

KM#	Date	Mintage	Fine	VF	XF	Unc
221.3	1945	3.043	.25	.50	.75	1.50
	1945 w/o AFP	—	—	—	—	—
	1946/5	Inc. Ab.	.25	.65	1.00	2.00
	1946	Inc. Ab.	.25	.50	.75	1.50
	1946 AFP	I.A.	—	—	—	—

President Castilla

KM#	Date	Mintage	Fine	VF	XF	Unc
234	1954	.799	2.25	4.50	10.00	16.50

KM#	Date	Mintage	Fine	VF	XF	Unc
264	1975	—	—	—	.10	.20

25 CENTAVOS

BRASS
400th Anniversary of Lima Mint

KM#	Date	Mintage	Fine	VF	XF	Unc
238	1965	1.113	—	.10	.15	.35
	1965	—	—	—	Proof	200.00

Reeded edge. Obv: Large arms.

KM#	Date	Mintage	Fine	VF	XF	Unc
246.1	1966*	9.300	—	.10	.15	.25
	1966	1,000	—	—	Proof	2.50

***NOTE:** PAREJA in field at lower left of arms.

SILVER PLATED BRASS

KM#	Date	Mintage	Fine	VF	XF	Unc
246.1a	1967	—	—	—	—	—

BRASS
Plain edge.

KM#	Date	Mintage	Fine	VF	XF	Unc
246.2	1967	8.150	—	.10	.15	.25
	1968	7.440	—	.10	.15	.25
	1968 AP	I.A.	—	.10	.15	.25
	1969 AP on rev.	7.440	—	.10	.15	.25
	1969 w/o AP	Inc. Ab.	—	—	—	—
	1970	6.341	—	.10	.15	.25
	1971	3.196	—	.10	.15	.25
	1972	5.523	—	.10	.15	.25
	1973	7.492	.10	.15	.20	.50

Obv: Small arms.

KM#	Date	Mintage	Fine	VF	XF	Unc
259	1973	Inc. Ab.	—	.10	.15	.25
	1974	—	—	.10	.15	.25
	1975	—	—	.10	.15	.25

1/2 SOL

12.5000 g, .900 SILVER, .3617 oz ASW
Mint: Lima
Obv: Small wreath.
Rev: Denomination in curved line.

KM#	Date	Mintage	Fine	VF	XF	Unc
195	1864 YB	—	5.00	10.00	20.00	60.00
	1864 YB-D*	—	100.00	150.00	250.00	400.00
	1865 YB	—	4.00	8.50	15.00	55.00

NOTE: Engraver's initials RB appear left of shield on reverse. Date varieties exist.
***NOTE:** See 1 Sol, KM#196.2.

Obv: Large wreath.
Rev: Denomination in straight line.

KM#	Date	Mintage	Fine	VF	XF	Unc
203	1907 FG-JR	1.000	BV	4.00	6.50	14.00
	1908/7 FG-JR	.030	8.00	15.00	35.00	100.00
	1908 FG-JR	I.A.	12.00	25.00	45.00	125.00
	1914 FG-JR	.173	BV	4.50	9.00	20.00
	1915 FG-JR	.570	BV	3.50	5.50	12.00
	1916 FG	.384	BV	3.50	5.50	12.00
	1916 FG-JR	—	BV	3.50	5.50	12.00
	1917 FG-JR	.178	BV	4.00	7.50	20.00

NOTE: Most coins 1907-17 have engravers initials JR left of shield tip on reverse. Date varieties exist.

12.5000 g, .500 SILVER, .2009 oz ASW

KM#	Date	Mintage	Fine	VF	XF	Unc
216	1922 LIBERTAD incuse, J.R. on rev.	.465	2.50	4.50	10.00	30.00
	1922 LIBERTAD in relief	Inc. Ab.	2.50	4.50	10.00	30.00
	1923 LIBER/TAD GM round top 3	2.520	BV	2.50	6.00	20.00
	1923 flat top 3	Inc. Ab.	BV	2.50	5.50	17.50
	1924 GM	.238	3.00	6.00	12.00	40.00
	1926 GM	.694	BV	3.50	7.00	20.00
	1927 GM	2.640	BV	2.50	5.50	15.00
	1928/7 GM	3.028	—	—	—	—
	1928 GM	I.A.	BV	2.50	5.50	15.00
	1929 GM	3.068	BV	2.50	5.50	15.00
	1935 AP	2.653	BV	2.50	5.00	14.00
	1935	—	—	—	—	—

NOTE: Engravers initials appear on stems of obverse wreath. Date varieties exist.

BRASS
Mint: London
Obv: 3 palm leaves point to llama on shield.

KM#	Date	Mintage	Fine	VF	XF	Unc
220.1	1935	10.000	.50	1.25	2.25	7.00
	1941	4.000	.50	1.25	2.25	7.00

Mint: Philadelphia

KM#	Date	Mintage	Fine	VF	XF	Unc
220.2	1942	4.000	1.50	3.00	5.00	15.00
	1943	4.000	3.00	6.50	12.50	35.00
	1944	Inc. Ab.	1.50	3.00	5.00	15.00

Mint mark: S

KM#	Date	Mintage	Fine	VF	XF	Unc
220.3	1942	1.668	1.50	3.00	5.00	15.00
	1943	6.332	1.50	3.00	5.00	15.00

NOTE: The coins struck in Philadelphia and San Francisco have a serif on the "4" of the date; the Lima and London coins do not.

Mint: Lima
Obv: 1 palm leaf points to llama on shield.

KM#	Date	Mintage	Fine	VF	XF	Unc
220.4	1941	2.000	3.00	6.50	12.50	35.00

Obv: 1 palm leaf points to llama on shield.

KM#	Date	Mintage	Fine	VF	XF	Unc
220.4	1941	2.000	3.00	6.50	12.50	35.00
	1942	Inc. Ab.	1.50	3.00	5.00	15.00
	1942 AP	—	—	—	—	—
	1943	2.000	.50	1.00	2.00	8.00
	1944/2	4.000	—	—	—	—
	1944	Inc. Ab.	.40	.85	1.75	7.00
	1944 AP	I.A.	—	—	—	—
	1945	4.000	.75	1.50	3.00	10.00

NOTE: Dates 1941-44 have thick flat-top 4 w/o serifs. 1945 has narrow 4 like KM#220.5.

Obv: 3 palm leaves point to llama on shield.

KM#	Date	Mintage	Fine	VF	XF	Unc
220.5	1942 long-top 2	Inc. Ab.	1.50	3.00	5.00	15.00
	1944	Inc. Ab.	.75	1.50	3.00	10.00
	1944 AP	I.A.	.50	1.00	2.00	7.00
	1945	Inc. Ab.	.75	1.50	3.00	10.00
	1945 AP	I.A.	.75	1.50	3.00	10.00
	1946/5 AP	3.744	2.00	3.50	6.50	17.50
	1946 AP	I.A.	.40	.75	1.25	4.00
	1947 AP	6.066	.40	.75	1.25	5.00
	1947	Inc. Ab.	.40	.75	1.25	5.00
	1948	3.324	.40	.75	1.25	4.00
	1949/8	.420	1.00	2.00	4.00	12.00
	1949	Inc. Ab.	1.50	3.00	6.00	18.00
	1950	.091	1.25	2.25	4.50	15.00
	1951/8	.930	.50	1.00	2.00	7.00
	1951	Inc. Ab.	.50	1.00	2.00	7.00
	1952	.935	.75	1.50	3.00	10.00
	1953	.817	.50	1.00	2.00	7.00
	1954	.637	.75	1.50	3.00	10.00
	1955	1.383	.15	.35	.75	4.00
	1956	2.309	.10	.25	.40	1.50
	1957	2.700	.10	.25	.50	2.00
	1958	2.691	.10	.25	.40	1.50
	1959	3.609	.10	.25	.40	1.50
	1960	5.600	.10	.20	.35	.75
	1961	4.400	.10	.20	.35	.75
	1962	3.540	.10	.20	.35	1.00
	1963	4.345	.10	.20	.35	.75
	1964	5.315	.10	.20	.35	1.50
	1965	7.090	.10	.20	.35	1.75
	1965	—	—	—	Proof	50.00

NOTE: 1942, 1944 AP and all 1945-49 have narrow 4 w/o serif on crossbar. 1944 w/o AP has flat-top 4 like KM#220.4. Engravers initials AP appear on wreath stems of some 1944-45, all 1946 and some 1947 coins. Varieties exist.

400th Anniversary of Lima Mint

KM#	Date	Mintage	Fine	VF	XF	Unc
239	1965	10.971	—	.10	.15	.35
	1965	—	—	—	Proof	400.00

Obv: Large arms. Rev: Vicuna.

KM#	Date	Mintage	Fine	VF	XF	Unc
247	1966	13.720	—	.10	.20	.40
	1966	—	—	—	Proof	4.00
	1967	15.500	—	.10	.20	.35
	1968	13.890	—	.10	.20	.40
	1969	13.890	—	.10	.20	.40
	1970	11.901	—	.10	.20	.40
	1971	7.524	—	.15	.20	.40
	1972	19.441	—	.10	.20	.40
	1973	14.951	—	.10	.20	.40

SILVER PLATED BRASS

KM#	Date	Mintage	Fine	VF	XF	Unc
247a	1967	—	—	—	—	—

Obv: Small arms.

KM#	Date	Mintage	Fine	VF	XF	Unc
260	1973	Inc. Ab.	—	.10	.20	.40
	1974/1	—	—	.10	.20	.40
	1974	14.518	—	.10	.20	.40
	1975	14.039	—	.10	.20	.40
265	1975	62.682	—	.10	.20	.30
	1976	369.828	—	.10	.20	.30
	1977	18.943	—	.10	.20	.30

9.3500 g, .900 GOLD, .2706 oz AGW
150th Anniversary Battle of Ayacucho

KM#	Date	Mintage	Fine	VF	XF	Unc
268	1976	.010	—	—	—	150.00

SOL

25.0000 g, .900 SILVER, .7234 oz ASW
Mint: Lima
Type I
Obv: Small wreath above shield has ribbon ties.
Rev: Shield below liberty's hand is tilted.
Santiago issues have LIMA on the coin.

KM#	Date	Mintage	Fine	VF	XF	Unc
196.1	1864/54 YB	—	6.00	8.50	15.00	55.00
	1864/54 Y.B	—	6.00	8.50	15.00	55.00
	1864/54 Y.B Roman I in date	—	6.00	8.50	15.00	55.00
	1864/54 Y.B w/Y.B inverted	—	6.00	8.50	15.00	55.00
	1864/54 Y.B R-B on stems/ribbon by date	—	9.00	16.00	30.00	90.00
	1865/55 YB	—	6.00	9.00	17.50	65.00
	1865/55 Y.B	—	6.00	9.00	14.00	65.00
	1865/55 Y.B/B.B	—	6.00	9.00	17.50	65.00
	1866/56 YB	—	6.00	8.00	12.00	40.00
	1866/55 Y.B	—	6.00	9.00	17.50	65.00
	1866/56 Y.B	—	6.00	8.00	12.00	40.00
	1867/57 Y.B	—	6.00	8.00	12.00	40.00
	1868/58 Y.B	—	6.00	8.00	12.00	40.00
	1868/58 Y.B BP on rev., left side	—	6.00	9.00	17.50	65.00

NOTE: Many minor die varieties, all coins are overdates.

Obv: DERTEANO on bottom row of coins falling from cornucopia.

KM#	Date	Mintage	Fine	VF	XF	Unc
196.2	1864/54 Y.B Arabic date	—	60.00	150.00	400.00	1500.
	1864/54 Y.B Roman I in date	—	100.00	175.00	500.00	1700.
	1864 Y.B Arabic date	—	—	—	Rare	—

NOTE: There are numerous minor die varieties such as D's in the denticles around the border on the obv.

Type II

KM#	Date	Mintage	Fine	VF	XF	Unc
196.3	1868 YB Roman I	—	6.00	9.00	17.50	65.00
	1868 YB Arabic 1/Roman I	—	10.00	20.00	35.00	100.00
	1868 YB Arabic 1	—	10.00	20.00	35.00	100.00
	1868 YB Arabic 1 BP on rev., left side	—	6.00	8.00	12.00	40.00
	1868 YB Arabic 1 Llama has 5 legs	—	6.00	9.00	17.50	70.00
	1869 YB Arabic 1	—	6.00	7.50	11.00	30.00
	1869 YB Arabic 1 BP on rev., left side	—	6.00	7.50	12.00	40.00
	1869 YB Roman I	—	6.00	8.00	12.00	40.00
	1870 YB	—	Reported, not confirmed			
	1870 YJ	—	6.00	7.50	12.00	40.00
	1870 YJ dot below 7 in date	—	6.00	7.50	12.00	40.00
	1871 YJ	—	6.00	7.50	11.00	30.00
	1871 YJ dot above 1 in date	—	6.00	7.50	11.00	30.00
	1871 YJ dot below 1 in date	—	6.00	7.50	11.00	30.00
	1871 YJ dot below 7 in date	—	6.00	7.50	11.00	30.00
	1872 YJ	—	6.00	7.50	11.00	30.00
	1872 YJ dot below 7 in date	—	7.00	10.00	15.00	35.00
	1873 YJ	—	10.00	20.00	40.00	135.00
	1874 YJ	—	6.00	7.50	11.00	30.00
	1875 YJ	—	6.00	7.50	11.00	35.00
	1876 YJ	—	Reported, not confirmed			

NOTE: Many minor die varieties exist.

Mint: Santiago

KM#	Date	Mintage	Fine	VF	XF	Unc
196.4	1873 LD Arabic 1	.445	7.50	15.00	25.00	75.00
	1873 LD/backwards D, Arabic 1	—	12.00	20.00	35.00	100.00
	1873 LD Arabic 1/Roman I	—	12.00	20.00	35.00	100.00
	1873 LD Roman I	—	9.00	17.50	30.00	90.00

NOTE: Many minor die varieties exist.

Type III
Letters R.B. on stems flanking date.

KM#	Date	Mintage	Fine	VF	XF	Unc
196.5	1879 YJ	—	6.00	8.50	15.00	55.00
	1880/70 YJ	—	17.50	37.50	75.00	250.00
	1880/8 YJ	—	12.00	25.00	50.00	200.00
	1880 YJ	—	12.00	25.00	50.00	150.00

Letters R.B. on ribbon of wreath, 3 berries in bunch.

KM#	Date	Mintage	Fine	VF	XF	Unc
196.6	1880 YJ	—	20.00	45.00	85.00	350.00

W/o extra letters on stem, 3 berries

KM#	Date	Mintage	Fine	VF	XF	Unc
196.29	1880 YJ	—	12.00	25.00	50.00	150.00

2 berries in bunch.

KM#	Date	Mintage	Fine	VF	XF	Unc
196.7	1880 YJ	—	15.00	35.00	75.00	200.00

W/o extra letters, 2 berries in bunch.

KM#	Date	Mintage	Fine	VF	XF	Unc
196.8	1880 YJ	—	12.00	25.00	50.00	200.00

NOTE: Many minor die varieties exist.

Type IV

KM#	Date	Mintage	Fine	VF	XF	Unc
196.9	1881 BF	—	6.00	12.00	20.00	60.00

Rev: Letters R.L. on base of column.

KM#	Date	Mintage	Fine	VF	XF	Unc
196.10	1881 BF	—	6.00	12.00	20.00	60.00

NOTE: Many minor die varieties exist.

Type V
B.F. on rev., left side.

KM#	Date	Mintage	Fine	VF	XF	Unc
196.11	1881 BF	—	6.00	9.00	17.50	65.00

R.B. on rev., left side.

KM#	Date	Mintage	Fine	VF	XF	Unc
196.12	1881 BF	—	6.00	9.00	17.50	65.00
	1882 BF	—	6.00	8.50	15.00	55.00

F.D. on rev., left side.

KM#	Date	Mintage	Fine	VF	XF	Unc
196.13	1882 BF	—	6.00	8.50	15.00	55.00

FD on rev. at base of column.

KM#	Date	Mintage	Fine	VF	XF	Unc
196.14	1882 BF	—	6.00	9.00	17.50	65.00
	1882 FN	—	6.00	10.00	20.00	70.00

NOTE: Many minor die varieties exist.

Type VI
F.D. on rev., left side.

KM#	Date	Mintage	Fine	VF	XF	Unc
196.15	1882 FN	—	6.00	9.00	17.50	65.00
	1882 FN/BN	—	—	—	—	—

FD on rev. at base of column.

KM#	Date	Mintage	Fine	VF	XF	Unc
196.16	1882 FN	—	6.00	9.00	17.50	65.00

FD on rev., RB at base of column.

KM#	Date	Mintage	Fine	VF	XF	Unc
196.17	1882 FN	—	6.00	9.00	17.50	65.00

NOTE: Many minor die varieties exist.

Type VII
B.F. on rev., left side.

KM#	Date	Mintage	Fine	VF	XF	Unc
196.18	1883 FN	—	6.00	8.50	15.00	55.00

F.D. on rev., left side, Libertad in relief.

KM#	Date	Mintage	Fine	VF	XF	Unc
196.19	1883 FN	—	6.00	8.50	15.00	55.00
	1884 BD	—	6.00	7.50	11.00	35.00
	1884 RD	—	6.00	7.50	11.00	35.00

NOTE: Many minor die varieties exist.

Type VIII
F.D. on rev., left side.

KM#	Date	Mintage	Fine	VF	XF	Unc
196.20	1884 BD	—	6.00	7.50	11.00	35.00
	1884 BD/BF	—	6.00	8.00	12.00	40.00
	1884 RD	—	6.00	7.50	11.00	35.00

Type IX
W/o extra initials.

KM#	Date	Mintage	Fine	VF	XF	Unc
196.21	1884 RD	—	7.00	9.00	15.00	50.00

Type X
Rev: Libertad incuse.

KM#	Date	Mintage	Fine	VF	XF	Unc
196.22	1885 RD	—	6.00	7.50	15.00	30.00
	1885 RD/BD	—	6.00	7.50	15.00	30.00
	1885 RD/BF	—	6.00	7.50	15.00	30.00
	1885 TD	—	6.00	7.50	15.00	30.00
	1885 TD/BD	—	6.00	7.50	15.00	30.00
	1885 TD/BF	—	6.00	7.50	15.00	30.00
	1885 TD/TF	—	6.00	7.50	15.00	30.00
	1886/5 TF	—	17.50	37.50	75.00	300.00
	1886/5 TF/BR	—	17.50	37.50	100.00	200.00
	1886 TF	—	6.00	8.50	15.00	55.00
	1887/6 TF	—	6.00	7.50	11.00	30.00
	1887/6 TF/BF	—	6.00	7.50	11.00	30.00
	1887 TF	—	6.00	7.00	10.00	27.50
	1887 TF/BF	—	6.00	7.00	10.00	27.50

NOTE: Many minor die varieties exist.

Rev: R on base of column.

KM#	Date	Mintage	Fine	VF	XF	Unc
196.23	1885 RD	—	6.00	8.50	15.00	50.00

Type XI
Rev: Shield below Liberty's hand is tilted. UN SOL is in a straight line, Libertad in relief.

KM#	Date	Mintage	Fine	VF	XF	Unc
196.24	1888 TF	3.147	6.00	7.00	11.00	30.00
	1888 TF/BF	I.A.	6.00	7.00	11.00	30.00
	1889 TF	2.842	6.00	7.00	10.00	27.50
	1889 TF/BF	I.A.	6.00	7.00	10.00	27.50
	1890/80 TF/BF	2.304	6.00	9.00	15.00	55.00
	1890 TF/BF	Inc. Ab.	6.00	7.00	10.00	27.50
	1890 TF	I.A.	6.00	7.00	10.00	27.50
	1891/81 TF	2.981	6.00	8.00	12.00	32.50
	1891/81 TF/BF	Inc. Ab.	6.00	8.00	12.00	32.50
	1891 TF/BF	Inc. Ab.	6.00	7.00	10.00	27.50
	1891 TF	I.A.	6.00	7.00	10.00	27.50
	1892 TF	2.270	6.00	7.00	10.00	27.50
	1892 TF/BF	Inc. Ab.	6.00	7.00	10.00	27.50

NOTE: Date varieties exist.

Rev. leg: Inverted V for A in LA.

KM#	Date	Mintage	Fine	VF	XF	Unc
196.25	1889 TF/BF	I.A.	15.00	30.00	60.00	100.00

NOTE: Many minor die varieties exist, especially for the 1888 issues.

Type XII
Legends have smaller lettering, 37mm. Rev: Libertad incuse.

KM#	Date	Mintage	Fine	VF	XF	Unc
196.26	1393/893 TF (error date)	—	30.00	45.00	90.00	200.00
	1893 TF	—	6.00	7.00	10.00	27.50
	1894 TF	4.358	6.00	7.00	10.00	27.50
	1895 TF	4.111	6.00	7.00	10.00	27.50
	1896 TF	2.511	6.00	8.00	12.00	40.00
	1896 F	I.A.	6.00	7.00	10.00	27.50
	1897 JF	.234	7.00	12.00	20.00	90.00
	1914 FG	.620	6.00	7.00	8.00	22.50
	1915/4 FG	1.736	6.00	8.00	11.00	40.00
	1915 FG	Inc. Ab.	6.00	7.00	8.00	20.00

NOTE: Varieties exist.

Rev: LIBERTAD incuse, 36.5mm.

KM#	Date	Mintage	Fine	VF	XF	Unc
196.27	1916 FG	1.927	6.00	7.00	8.00	20.00

Type XIII
Rev: LIBERTAD in relief.

KM#	Date	Mintage	Fine	VF	XF	Unc
196.28	1916 FG	I.A.	6.00	7.00	8.00	20.00

25.0000 g, .500 SILVER, .4019 oz ASW
Obv: Fineness omitted. Rev: LIBERTAD in relief.

KM#	Date	Mintage	Fine	VF	XF	Unc
217.1	1922	—	—	—	Rare	—
	1923	3,600	25.00	50.00	100.00	300.00

Rev: LIBERTAD incuse.

KM#	Date	Mintage	Fine	VF	XF	Unc
217.2	1923	1,400	40.00	85.00	200.00	500.00

Mint: Philadelphia

Small letters

KM#	Date	Mintage	Fine	VF	XF	Unc
218.1	1923	*2.369	BV	4.00	8.00	15.00
	1924/824	*3.113	5.00	10.00	20.00	40.00
	1924/3	*I.A.	5.00	10.00	20.00	40.00
	1924	Inc. Ab.	BV	4.00	8.00	15.00
	1925	*1.291	BV	4.00	8.00	17.50
	1926	*2.157	BV	4.00	8.00	15.00

***NOTE:** The Philadelphia and Lima strikings may be distinguished by the fact that the letters in the legends are smaller on those pieces produced at Philadelphia. All bear the name of the Lima Mint.

Mint: Lima
Large letters
Obv: Engraver's initials GM on stems flanking date.

KM#	Date	Mintage	Fine	VF	XF	Unc
218.2	1924	.096	5.00	10.00	20.00	65.00
	1925	1.005	BV	4.00	8.00	15.00
	1930	.076	BV	4.00	8.00	15.00
	1931	.024	BV	4.00	9.00	18.00
	1933	5,000	6.00	12.00	20.00	40.00
	1934/3	2.855	BV	4.00	9.00	18.00
	1934	Inc. Ab.	BV	3.00	6.00	12.00
	1935	.695	BV	4.00	8.00	17.50

BRASS

KM#	Date	Mintage	Fine	VF	XF	Unc
222	1943	10.000	.35	1.25	3.00	8.00
	1944	Inc. Ab.	.35	1.25	3.00	7.00
	1945	—	.50	1.50	3.50	9.00
	1946	1.752	.50	1.50	3.00	8.00
	1947	3.302	.35	1.00	2.00	6.00
	1948	1.992	.35	1.00	2.00	6.00
	1949/8	.751	2.00	4.00	7.00	20.00
	1949	Inc. Ab.	3.50	7.50	12.00	25.00
	1950	1.249	7.00	10.00	15.00	25.00
	1951/0	2.094	.25	.50	1.50	6.00
	1951	Inc. Ab.	.25	.50	1.50	6.00
	1952	2.037	.25	.50	1.50	6.00
	1953	1.243	3.00	6.00	10.00	25.00
	1954	1.220	.35	.75	1.75	6.00
	1955	1.323	.35	.75	1.75	6.00
	1956	3.450	.15	.35	.75	3.00
	1957	3.086	.15	.35	1.00	5.00
	1958	3.390	.15	.35	.75	3.00
	1959	4.975	.15	.35	1.00	5.00
	1960	5.800	.15	.35	.75	1.50
	1961	5.200	.15	.35	.75	2.00
	1962	5.102	.15	.35	.75	1.50
	1963	5.499	.15	.35	.75	2.00
	1964	5.888	.15	.35	.75	2.00
	1965	5.504	.15	.35	.75	2.00
	1965	—	—	—	Proof	75.00

NOTE: Date varieties exist.

400th Anniversary of Lima Mint

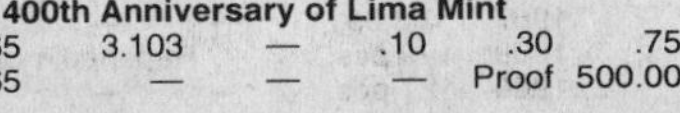

KM#	Date	Mintage	Fine	VF	XF	Unc
240	1965	3.103	—	.10	.30	.75
	1965	—	—	—	Proof	500.00

KM#	Date	Mintage	Fine	VF	XF	Unc
248	1966	16.410	—	.10	.25	.50
	1966	1,000	—	—	Proof	5.00
	1967	13.920	—	.10	.25	.50
	1968	12.260	—	.10	.25	.50
	1969	12.260	—	.10	.25	.50
	1970	12.336	—	.10	.25	.50
	1971	11.927	—	.10	.25	.50
	1972	3.945	—	.10	.25	.50
	1973	12.856	—	.10	.25	.50
	1974	14.966	—	.10	.25	.50
	1975	—	—	.10	.25	.50

SILVER PLATED BRASS

KM#	Date	Mintage	Fine	VF	XF	Unc
248a	1967	—	—	—	—	—

BRASS, 21mm

KM#	Date	Mintage	Fine	VF	XF	Unc
266.1	1975	354.485	—	—	.10	.25
	1976	114.660	—	—	.10	.25

17mm
Mint mark: LIMA (monogram)

KM#	Date	Mintage	Fine	VF	XF	Unc
266.2	1978	9.000	—	—	.10	.20
	1979	4.842	—	—	.10	.20
	1980	28.826	—	—	.10	.20
	1981	51.630	—	—	.10	.20
	1982	4.155	—	—	.10	.20

23.4000 g, .900 GOLD, .6772 oz AGW
150th Anniversary Battle of Ayacucho

KM#	Date	Mintage	Fine	VF	XF	Unc
269	1976	.010	—	—	—	450.00

5 SOLES

8.0645 g, .900 GOLD, .2334 oz AGW
Mint mark: LIMA

KM#	Date	Mintage	Fine	VF	XF	Unc
192	1863 YB	—	125.00	150.00	225.00	375.00

2.3404 g, .900 GOLD, .0677 oz AGW
Mint: Lima

KM#	Date	Mintage	Fine	VF	XF	Unc
235	1956	4,510	—	—	—	50.00
	1957	2,146	—	—	—	50.00
	1958	3,325	Reported, not confirmed			
	1959	1,536	—	—	—	50.00
	1960	8,133	—	—	—	50.00
	1961	1,154	—	—	—	50.00
	1962	1,550	—	—	—	50.00
	1963	3,945	—	—	—	50.00
	1964	2,063	—	—	—	50.00
	1965	.014	—	—	—	50.00
	1966	4,738	—	—	—	50.00
	1967	3,651	—	—	—	50.00
	1968	129 pcs.	Reported, not confirmed			
	1969	127 pcs.	—	—	—	175.00

COPPER-NICKEL
Mint: Paris

KM#	Date	Mintage	Fine	VF	XF	Unc
252	1969	10.000	.20	.40	.60	1.50

150th Anniversary of Independence
Mint mark: LIMA (monogram)

KM#	Date	Mintage	Fine	VF	XF	Unc
254	1971	3.480	.20	.40	.80	2.00

Regular Issue

KM#	Date	Mintage	Fine	VF	XF	Unc
257	1972	2.068	—	.10	.35	1.00
	1973	.475	—	.10	.35	1.00
	1974	—	—	.10	.35	1.50
	1975	—	—	.10	.35	1.50

KM#	Date	Mintage	Fine	VF	XF	Unc
267	1975	—	—	.10	.35	1.00
	1976	17.016	—	.10	.35	1.00
	1977	94.272	—	.10	.35	1.00

BRASS

KM#	Date	Mintage	Fine	VF	XF	Unc
271	1978	38.016	—	.10	.20	.50
	1979	64.524	—	.10	.20	.50
	1980	76.964	—	.10	.20	.50
	1981	31.632	—	.10	.20	.50
	1982	23.262	—	.10	.20	.50
	1983	650 pcs.	20.00	30.00	40.00	60.00

10 SOLES

16.1290 g, .900 GOLD, .4667 oz AGW
Mint mark: LIMA

KM#	Date	Mintage	Fine	VF	XF	Unc
193	1863 YB	—	225.00	250.00	300.00	500.00

4.6807 g, .900 GOLD, .1354 oz AGW
Mint: Lima

KM#	Date	Mintage	Fine	VF	XF	Unc
236	1956	5,410	—	—	BV	75.00
	1957	1,300	—	—	BV	75.00
	1958	3,325	Reported, not confirmed			
	1959	1,103	—	—	BV	75.00
236	1960	7,178	—	—	BV	75.00
	1961	1,634	—	—	BV	75.00
	1962	1,676	—	—	BV	75.00
	1963	3,372	—	—	BV	75.00
	1964	1,554	—	—	BV	75.00
	1965	.014	—	—	BV	75.00
	1966	2,601	—	—	BV	75.00
	1967	3,002	—	—	BV	75.00
	1968	100 pcs.	—	BV	100.00	200.00
	1969	100 pcs.	—	BV	100.00	200.00

COPPER-NICKEL
Mint: Paris

KM#	Date	Mintage	Fine	VF	XF	Unc
253	1969	15.000	.25	.50	.75	1.75

150th Anniversary of Independence
Mint mark: LIMA (monogram)

KM#	Date	Mintage	Fine	VF	XF	Unc
255	1971	2.460	.25	.50	1.00	2.50

KM#	Date	Mintage	Fine	VF	XF	Unc
258	1972	2.235	—	.10	.40	1.25
	1973	1.765	—	.10	.40	1.25
	1974	—	—	.10	.40	1.25
	1975	—	—	.10	.40	1.25

BRASS
Obv: Large arms, small letters.
Inner circle 19.1mm.

KM#	Date	Mintage	Fine	VF	XF	Unc
272.1	1978	46.970	—	.10	.40	.75

Obv: Small arms, large letters.
Inner circle 17.2mm.

KM#	Date	Mintage	Fine	VF	XF	Unc
272.2	1978	—	—	.10	.40	.75
	1979	82.220	—	.10	.40	.75
	1980	99.595	—	.10	.40	.75
	1981	25.660	—	.10	.40	.75
	1982	61.035	—	.10	.40	.75
	1983	15.820	—	.10	.40	.75

150th Anniversary of Birth of Admiral Grau

KM#	Date	Mintage	Fine	VF	XF	Unc
287	1984	30.000	—	—	.10	.25

20 SOLES

32.2581 g, .900 GOLD, .9334 oz AGW
Mint mark: LIMA

KM#	Date	Mintage	Fine	VF	XF	Unc
194	1863 YB	—	450.00	475.00	500.00	650.00

9.3614 g, .900 GOLD, .2709 oz AGW
Mint: Lima

KM#	Date	Mintage	Fine	VF	XF	Unc
229	1950	1,800	—	—	BV	150.00
	1951	9,264	—	—	BV	150.00
	1952	424 pcs.	—	—	BV	200.00
	1953	1,435	—	—	BV	150.00
	1954	1,732	—	—	BV	150.00
	1955	1,971	—	—	BV	150.00
	1956	1,201	—	—	BV	150.00
	1957	.011	—	—	BV	150.00
	1958	.011	—	—	BV	150.00
	1959	.012	—	—	BV	150.00
	1960	7,753	—	—	BV	150.00
	1961	1,825	—	—	BV	150.00
	1962	2,282	—	—	BV	150.00
	1963	3,892	—	—	BV	150.00
	1964	1,302	—	—	BV	150.00
	1965	.012	—	—	BV	150.00
	1966	4,001	—	—	BV	150.00
	1967	5,003	—	—	BV	150.00
	1968	640 pcs.	—	—	BV	200.00
	1969	640 pcs.	—	—	BV	200.00

8.0000 g, .900 SILVER, .2315 oz ASW
400th Anniversary of Lima Mint

KM#	Date	Mintage	Fine	VF	XF	Unc
241	1965	.150	—	—	—	5.00

7.9700 g, .900 SILVER, .2306 oz ASW
100th Anniversary of Peru-Spain Naval Battle

KM#	Date	Mintage	Fine	VF	XF	Unc
249	1966	4,001	—	—	—	20.00

50 SOLES

33.4363 g, .900 GOLD, .9675 oz AGW

KM#	Date	Mintage	Fine	VF	XF	Unc
219	1930	5,584	475.00	625.00	950.00	1600.
	1931	5,538	475.00	625.00	950.00	1500.
	1967	.010	—	—	—	500.00
	1968	300 pcs.	—	—	—	750.00
	1969	403 pcs.	—	—	—	750.00

23.4056 g, .900 GOLD, .6772 oz AGW
Mint: Lima

KM#	Date	Mintage	Fine	VF	XF	Unc
230	1950	1,927	—	—	BV	350.00
	1951	5,292	—	—	BV	350.00
	1952	1,201	—	—	BV	350.00
	1953	1,464	—	—	BV	350.00
	1954	1,839	—	—	BV	350.00
	1955	1,898	—	—	BV	350.00
	1956	.011	—	—	BV	350.00
	1957	.011	—	—	BV	350.00
	1958	.011	—	—	BV	350.00
	1959	5,734	—	—	BV	350.00
	1960	2,139	—	—	BV	350.00
	1961	1,110	—	—	BV	350.00
	1962	3,319	—	—	BV	350.00
	1963	3,089	—	—	BV	350.00
	1964/3	2,425	—	—	BV	350.00
	1964	Inc. Ab.	—	—	BV	350.00
	1965	.023	—	—	BV	350.00
	1966	3,409	—	—	BV	350.00
	1967	5,805	—	—	BV	350.00
	1968	443 pcs.	—	—	BV	450.00
	1969	443 pcs.	—	—	BV	450.00
	1970	553 pcs.	—	—	BV	450.00

400th Anniversary of Lima Mint

KM#	Date	Mintage	Fine	VF	XF	Unc
242	1965	.017	—	—	—	350.00

100th Anniversary of Peru-Spain Naval Battle

KM#	Date	Mintage	Fine	VF	XF	Unc
250	1966	6,409	—	—	—	550.00

21.4500 g, .800 SILVER, .5517 oz ASW
150th Anniversary of Independence
Mint mark: LIMA (monogram)

KM#	Date	Mintage	Fine	VF	XF	Unc
256	1971	.100	—	—	—	8.00

ALUMINUM-BRONZE

KM#	Date	Mintage	Fine	VF	XF	Unc
273	1979	1.323	—	.10	.20	.35
	1980	42.573	—	.10	.20	.35
	1981	19.923	—	.10	.20	.35
	1982 LIMA	18.471	—	.10	.20	.35
	1982 w/o mm	Inc. Ab.	—	.10	.20	.35
	1983	8.175	—	.10	.20	.35

BRASS
150th Anniversary of Birth of Admiral Grau

KM#	Date	Mintage	Fine	VF	XF	Unc
297	1984	11.475	—	—	—	.10
	1985	8.525	—	—	—	.10

100 SOLES

46.8071 g, .900 GOLD, 1.3544 oz AGW
Mint: Lima

KM#	Date	Mintage	Fine	VF	XF	Unc
231	1950	1,176	—	—	BV	700.00
	1951	8,241	—	—	BV	650.00
	1952	126 pcs.	—	—	2000.	3000.
	1953	498 pcs.	—	—	BV	750.00
	1954	1,808	—	—	BV	650.00
	1955	901 pcs.	—	—	BV	750.00
	1956	1,159	—	—	BV	650.00
	1957	550 pcs.	—	—	BV	750.00
	1958	101 pcs.	—	—	3000.	4000.
	1959	4,710	—	—	BV	650.00
	1960	2,207	—	—	BV	650.00
	1961	6,982	—	—	BV	650.00
	1962	9,678	—	—	BV	650.00
	1963	7,342	—	—	BV	650.00
	1964	.011	—	—	BV	650.00
	1965	.023	—	—	BV	650.00
	1966	3,409	—	—	BV	650.00
	1967	6,431	—	—	BV	650.00
	1968	540 pcs.	—	—	BV	750.00
	1969	540 pcs.	—	—	BV	750.00
	1970	425 pcs.	—	—	BV	750.00

400th Anniversary of Lima Mint

KM#	Date	Mintage	Fine	VF	XF	Unc
243	1965	.027	—	—	—	650.00

100th Anniversary of Peru-Spain Naval Battle

KM#	Date	Mintage	Fine	VF	XF	Unc
251	1966	6,253	—	—	—	825.00

22.4500 g, .800 SILVER, .5774 oz ASW
Centennial Peru-Japan Trade Relations
Mint mark: LIMA (monogram)

KM#	Date	Mintage	Fine	VF	XF	Unc
261	1973	.375	—	—	—	17.50

COPPER-NICKEL

KM#	Date	Mintage	Fine	VF	XF	Unc
283	1980	100.000	—	.10	.35	.70
	1982	—	—	.10	.35	.70

BRASS

150th Anniversary of Birth of Admiral Grau
Mint mark: LIMA (monogram)

KM#	Date	Mintage	Fine	VF	XF	Unc
288	1984	20.000	—	.10	.20	.50

200 SOLES

22.0000 g, .800 SILVER, .5659 oz ASW
Aviation Heroes-Chavez and Quinones

KM#	Date	Mintage	Fine	VF	XF	Unc
262	1974	.025	—	—	—	15.00
	1975	.090	—	—	—	10.00
	1976	.025	—	—	—	15.00
	1977	3,000	—	—	—	20.00
	1978	3,000	—	—	—	20.00

400 SOLES

28.1000 g, .900 SILVER, .8131 oz ASW
150th Anniversary Battle of Ayacucho
Mint mark: LIMA (monogram)
Obv: Similar to 200 Soles, Y#77.

KM#	Date	Mintage	Fine	VF	XF	Unc
270	1976	.350	—	—	—	10.00

500 SOLES

BRASS
150th Anniversary of Birth of Admiral Grau
Mint mark: LIMA (monogram)

KM#	Date	Mintage	Fine	VF	XF	Unc
289	1984	16.962	—	.10	.20	.75

Admiral Grau
Rev: Portrait w/o date below.

KM#	Date	Mintage	Fine	VF	XF	Unc
310	1985	13.038	—	.10	.20	.75

1000 SOLES

15.5500 g, .500 SILVER, .2500 oz ASW
National Congress
Mint mark: LIMA (monogram)

KM#	Date	Mintage	Fine	VF	XF	Unc
275	1979	.200	—	—	—	5.00

5000 SOLES

33.6300 g, .925 SILVER, 1.0000 oz ASW
100th Anniversary of Battle of Iquique
Mint mark: LIMA (monogram)

KM#	Date	Mintage	Fine	VF	XF	Unc
276	1979	.100	—	—	—	22.50

23.3700 g, .925 SILVER, .6951 oz ASW
Champions of Soccer

KM#	Date	Mintage	Fine	VF	XF	Unc
284	1982	8,250	—	—	Proof	35.00

Champions of Soccer

KM#	Date	Mintage	Fine	VF	XF	Unc
285	1982	8,300	—	—	Proof	35.00

10000 SOLES

16.8000 g, .925 SILVER, .4997 oz ASW
Battle of La Brena and General Caceres
Mint mark: LIMA (monogram)

KM#	Date	Mintage	Fine	VF	XF	Unc
286	1982	.100	—	—	—	5.50

50000 SOLES

16.9700 gm., .917 GOLD, .5004 oz AGW
Alfonso Urgarte
Mint mark: LIMA (monogram)

KM#	Date	Mintage	Fine	VF	XF	Unc
277	1979	.010	—	—	—	300.00

Elias Aguirre

KM#	Date	Mintage	Fine	VF	XF	Unc
278	1979	.010	—	—	—	300.00

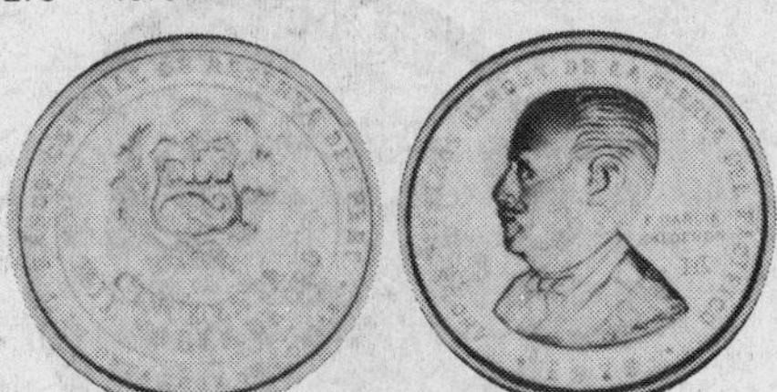

F. Garcia Calderon

KM#	Date	Mintage	Fine	VF	XF	Unc
279	1979	.010	—	—	—	300.00

100000 SOLES

33.9000 g, .917 GOLD, .9995 oz AGW
Francisco Bolognese
Mint mark: LIMA (monogram)

KM#	Date	Mintage	Fine	VF	XF	Unc
280	1979	.010	—	—	—	550.00

Andres A. Caceres

KM#	Date	Mintage	Fine	VF	XF	Unc
281	1979	.010	—	—	—	550.00

Miguel Grau

KM#	Date	Mintage	Fine	VF	XF	Unc
282	1979	.010	—	—	—	550.00

PROVISIONAL COINAGE

5 CENTAVOS

COPPER-NICKEL

KM#	Date	Mintage	Fine	VF	XF	Unc
197	1879	12.000	1.00	1.75	3.50	6.00
	1880	2.000	1.50	3.00	6.00	10.00

10 CENTAVOS

COPPER-NICKEL

KM#	Date	Mintage	Fine	VF	XF	Unc
198	1879	3.005	1.00	2.00	6.00	10.00
	1880	4.000	1.00	1.50	2.50	5.00

20 CENTAVOS

COPPER-NICKEL

KM#	Date	Mintage	Fine	VF	XF	Unc
199	1879	.498	4.00	8.00	20.00	75.00

PESETA COINAGE

1/2 REAL

1.2500 g, .900 SILVER, .0362 oz ASW
Mint: Ayacucho

KM#	Date	Mintage	Fine	VF	XF	Unc
202	1882 LM	—	250.00	500.00	800.00	1750.

NOTE: Most specimens have been holed or soldered (and sometimes repaired) and are worth much less than market valuations shown.

PESETA

5.0000 g, .900 SILVER, .1447 oz ASW
Mint: LIMA
Obv: B below wreath.

KM#	Date	Mintage	Fine	VF	XF	Unc
200.1	1880 BF	—	2.50	4.50	10.00	45.00

Obv: W/dot after B below wreath.

KM#	Date	Mintage	Fine	VF	XF	Unc
200.2	1880 BF	—	2.50	4.50	10.00	45.00

5 PESETAS

25.0000 g, .900 SILVER, .7234 oz ASW
Mint: Lima
Obv: B below wreath.

KM#	Date	Mintage	Fine	VF	XF	Unc
201.1	1880 BF	—	15.00	22.50	50.00	200.00

Obv: W/dot after B below wreath.

KM#	Date	Mintage	Fine	VF	XF	Unc
201.2	1880 BF	—	12.00	20.00	45.00	180.00

Mint: Ayacucho
Rev: Similar to KM#201.1.

KM#	Date	Mintage	Fine	VF	XF	Unc
201.3	1881 B	—	80.00	200.00	400.00	900.00
	1882 LM	—	50.00	100.00	200.00	500.00

MONETARY REFORM

1986 - 1990
1000 Soles de Oro = 1 Inti

CENTIMO

BRASS
Mint mark: LIMA (monogram)

KM#	Date	Mintage	Fine	VF	XF	Unc
291	1985	4.180	—	—	—	.20
	1986	.020	—	—	—	.20
	1987	—	—	—	—	.20
	1988	—	—	—	—	.20

5 CENTIMOS

BRASS
Mint mark: LIMA (monogram)

KM#	Date	Mintage	Fine	VF	XF	Unc
292	1985	20.000	—	—	—	.30
	1986	—	—	—	—	.30
	1987	—	—	—	—	.30
	1988	—	—	—	—	.30

10 CENTIMOS

BRASS
Mint mark: LIMA (monogram)

KM#	Date	Mintage	Fine	VF	XF	Unc
293	1985	143.900	—	—	—	.50
	1986	48.730	—	—	—	.50
	1987	42.370	—	—	—	.50
	1988	—	—	—	—	.50

20 CENTIMOS

BRASS
Mint mark: LIMA (monogram)

KM#	Date	Mintage	Fine	VF	XF	Unc
294	1985	4.739	—	—	—	.75
	1986	96.699	—	—	—	.75
	1987	59.668	—	—	—	.75
	1988	—	—	—	—	.75

50 CENTIMOS

BRASS
Mint mark: LIMA (monogram)

KM#	Date	Mintage	Fine	VF	XF	Unc
295	1985	43.320	—	—	—	1.00
	1986	72.802	—	—	—	1.00
	1987	63.878	—	—	—	1.00
	1988	80.000	—	—	—	1.00

1/2 INTI

16.8000 g, .925 SILVER, .4997 oz ASW
Mint mark: LIMA (monogram)
Pachacutec

KM#	Date	Mintage	Fine	VF	XF	Unc
301	1989	—	—	—	—	17.50

INTI

COPPER-NICKEL
Mint mark: LIMA (monogram)

KM#	Date	Mintage	Fine	VF	XF	Unc
296	1985	15.760	—	—	—	1.50
	1986	87.240	—	—	—	1.50
	1987	120.000	—	—	—	1.50
	1988	17.304	—	—	—	1.50

5 INTIS

COPPER-NICKEL
Mint mark: LIMA (monogram)
Admiral Grau

KM#	Date	Mintage	Fine	VF	XF	Unc
300	1985	3,972	—	—	—	—
	1986	.028	—	—	—	2.00
	1987	20.106	—	—	—	2.00
	1988	34.084	—	—	—	2.00

100 INTIS

11.1100 g, .925 SILVER, .3271 oz ASW
Mint mark: LIMA (monogram)
150th Anniversary of Birth of Marshal Caceres

KM#	Date	Mintage	Fine	VF	XF	Unc
298	1986	.010	—	—	—	10.00

200 INTIS

22.0400 g, .925 SILVER, .6543 oz ASW
Mint mark: LIMA (monogram)
150th Anniversary of Birth of Marshal Caceres

KM#	Date	Mintage	Fine	VF	XF	Unc
299	1986	—	—	—	—	20.00

MONETARY REFORM

1991 -

1/M Intis = 1 Nuevo Sol
100 (New) Centimos = 1 Nuevo Sol

CENTIMO

BRASS
Mint mark: LIMA (monogram)

KM#	Date	Mintage	Fine	VF	XF	Unc
303	1991	—	—	—	—	.25
	1993	—	—	—	—	.25

5 CENTIMOS

BRASS
Mint mark: LIMA (monogram)

KM#	Date	Mintage	Fine	VF	XF	Unc
304	1991	—	—	—	—	.35
	1992	—	—	—	—	.35
	1993	—	—	—	—	.35

10 CENTIMOS

BRASS
Mint mark: LIMA (monogram)

KM#	Date	Mintage	Fine	VF	XF	Unc
305	1991	—	—	—	—	.60
	1992	—	—	—	—	.60
	1993	—	—	—	—	.60

20 CENTIMOS

BRASS
Mint mark: LIMA (monogram)

KM#	Date	Mintage	Fine	VF	XF	Unc
306	1991	—	—	—	—	.80
	1993	—	—	—	—	.80

50 CENTIMOS

COPPER-NICKEL

KM#	Date	Mintage	Fine	VF	XF	Unc
307	1991	—	—	—	—	1.50
	1994	—	—	—	—	1.50

NUEVO SOL

27.0000 g, .925 SILVER, .8029 oz ASW
Ibero - American Series

KM#	Date	Mintage	Fine	VF	XF	Unc
302	1991	.060	—	—	Proof	42.50

COPPER-NICKEL

KM#	Date	Mintage	Fine	VF	XF	Unc
308.1	1991	—	—	—	—	5.00
	1992	—	—	—	—	5.00
	1994	—	—	—	—	5.00

Rev: W/F. DIAZ below wreath.

KM#	Date	Mintage	Fine	VF	XF	Unc
308.2	1991	—	—	—	Rare	—

20 NUEVO SOLES

33.6250 g, .925 SILVER, 1.0000 oz ASW
Rio De Janeiro Protocol

KM#	Date	Mintage	Fine	VF	XF	Unc
309	1992	.050	—	—	—	25.00

TRADE COINAGE

1/5 LIBRA (POUND)

1.5976 g, .917 GOLD, .0471 oz AGW
Mint: Lima

KM#	Date	Mintage	Fine	VF	XF	Unc
210	1905 ROZF	.045	—	BV	25.00	35.00
	1905 GOZF	I.A.	—	BV	25.00	35.00
	1906 GOZF	.106	—	BV	25.00	35.00
	1907 GOZF	.031	—	BV	25.00	35.00
	1907 GOZG	—	—	BV	25.00	35.00
	1910 GOZG	—	—	BV	25.00	35.00
	1911 GOZF	.062	—	BV	25.00	35.00
	1911 GOZG	—	—	BV	25.00	35.00
	1912 GOZG	—	—	BV	25.00	35.00
	1912 POZG	—	—	BV	25.00	35.00
	1913 POZG	.060	—	BV	25.00	35.00
	1914 POZG	.025	—	BV	25.00	35.00
	1914 PBLG	I.A.	—	BV	25.00	35.00
	1915	.010	—	BV	25.00	35.00
	1916	.013	Reported, not confirmed			
	1917	3,896	—	BV	25.00	35.00
	1918	.016	—	BV	25.00	35.00
	1919	.010	—	BV	25.00	35.00
	1920	.072	—	BV	25.00	35.00
	1922	8,110	—	BV	25.00	35.00
	1923	.027	—	BV	25.00	35.00
	1924	—	—	BV	25.00	35.00
	1925	.020	—	BV	25.00	35.00
	1926	.011	—	BV	25.00	35.00
	1927	.014	—	BV	25.00	35.00
	1928	9,322	—	BV	25.00	35.00
	1929	8,971	—	BV	25.00	35.00
	1930	9,991	—	BV	35.00	50.00
	1931	8,722	Reported, not confirmed			
	1932	8,430	Reported, not confirmed			

KM#	Date	Mintage	Fine	VF	XF	Unc
210	1946	.010	Reported, not confirmed			
	1947	.010	Reported, not confirmed			
	1948	.015	Reported, not confirmed			
	1949	.011	Reported, not confirmed			
	1951 BBR	4,637	Reported, not confirmed			
	1952 BBR	6,337	Reported, not confirmed			
	1953 BBR	9,821	—	—	—	40.00
	1954	9,473	Reported, not confirmed			
	1955 ZBR	.010	—	—	—	40.00
	1956 ZBR	8,116	—	—	—	32.50
	1957 ZBR	6,345	Reported, not confirmed			
	1958 ZBR	5,098	—	—	—	32.50
	1959 ZBR	6,308	—	—	—	32.50
	1960 ZBR	6,083	—	—	—	32.50
	1961 ZBR	.012	—	—	—	32.50
	1962 ZBR	5,431	—	—	—	32.50
	1963 ZBR	.011	—	—	—	32.50
	1964 ZBR	.025	—	—	—	32.50
	1965 ZBR	.019	—	—	—	32.50
	1966 ZBR	.060	—	—	—	32.50
	1967 BBR	9,914	—	—	—	32.50
	1968 BBR	4,781	—	—	—	32.50
	1968 BBB	I.A.	—	—	—	32.50
	1969 BBB	.015	—	—	—	32.50

1/2 LIBRA (POUND)

3.9940 g, .917 GOLD, .1177 oz AGW

KM#	Date	Mintage	Fine	VF	XF	Unc
209	1902 ROZF	7,800	—	BV	50.00	65.00
	1903 ROZF	7,245	—	BV	50.00	65.00
	1904 ROZF	8,360	—	BV	50.00	65.00
	1905 ROZF	8,010	—	BV	50.00	65.00
	1905 GOZF	I.A.	—	BV	50.00	65.00
	1906 GOZF	9,176	—	BV	50.00	65.00
	1907 GOZF	.010	—	BV	50.00	65.00
	1907 GOZG	—	—	BV	50.00	65.00
	1908 GOZG	8,180	—	BV	50.00	65.00
	1909 GOZG	6,799	Reported, not confirmed			
	1910 GOZG	4,221	Reported, not confirmed			
	1911 GOZG	.014	Reported, not confirmed			
	1912 GOZG	.016	Reported, not confirmed			
	1913 POZG	.020	—	BV	50.00	65.00
	1914 PBLG	—	Reported, not confirmed			
	1916	1,900	Reported, not confirmed			
	1917	8,133	Reported, not confirmed			
	1918	8,800	Reported, not confirmed			
	1919	8,765	Reported, not confirmed			
	1930	1,889	Reported, not confirmed			
	1946	7,750	Reported, not confirmed			
	1947	3,146	Reported, not confirmed			
	1948	.012	Reported, not confirmed			
	1949	.020	Reported, not confirmed			
	1950	5,890	Reported, not confirmed			
	1951	.018	Reported, not confirmed			
	1952 BBR	8,345	Reported, not confirmed			
	1953 BBR	9,210	—	—	—	65.00
	1954 ZBR	9,220	Reported, not confirmed			
	1955 ZBR	.014	—	—	—	65.00
	1956 ZBR	7,385	Reported, not confirmed			
	1957 ZBR	8,472	Reported, not confirmed			
	1958 ZBR	.011	Reported, not confirmed			
	1959 ZBR	5,236	Reported, not confirmed			
	1960 ZBR	.016	Reported, not confirmed			
	1961 ZBR	752 pcs.	—	—	BV	100.00
	1962 ZBR	4,286	—	—	BV	60.00
	1963 ZBR	908 pcs.	—	—	BV	100.00
	1964 ZBR	.010	—	—	BV	60.00
	1965 ZBR	5,490	—	—	BV	60.00
	1966 ZBR	.044	—	—	BV	60.00

KM#	Date	Mintage	Fine	VF	XF	Unc
209	1967 ZBR	—	—	—	BV	60.00
	1968 BBB	.014	—	—	BV	60.00
	1968 PBB	I.A.	—	—	BV	60.00
	1969 BBB	4,400	—	—	BV	60.00

LIBRA (POUND)

7.9881 g, .917 GOLD, .2354 oz AGW

KM#	Date	Mintage	Fine	VF	XF	Unc
207	1898 ROZF	—	—	BV	100.00	125.00
	1899 ROZF	—	—	BV	100.00	125.00
	1900 ROZF	.064	—	BV	100.00	125.00
	1901 ROZF	.081	—	BV	100.00	125.00
	1902 ROZF	.089	—	BV	100.00	125.00
	1903 ROZF	.100	—	BV	100.00	125.00
	1904 ROZF	.033	—	BV	100.00	125.00
	1905 ROZF	.141	—	BV	100.00	125.00
	1905 GOZF	—	—	BV	100.00	125.00
	1906 GOZF	.201	—	BV	100.00	125.00
	1907 GOZF	.123	—	BV	100.00	125.00
	1907 GOZG	I.A.	—	BV	100.00	125.00
	1908 GOZG	.036	—	BV	100.00	125.00
	1909 GOZG	.052	—	BV	100.00	125.00
	1910 GOZG	.047	—	BV	100.00	125.00
	1911 GOZG	.042	—	BV	100.00	125.00
	1912 GOZG	.054	—	BV	100.00	125.00
	1912 POZG	I.A.	—	BV	100.00	125.00
	1913 POZG	—	—	BV	100.00	125.00
	1914 POZG	—	—	BV	100.00	125.00
	1914 PBLG	.119	—	BV	100.00	125.00
	1915 PVG	.091	—	BV	100.00	125.00
	1915 PMQG	I.A.	—	BV	100.00	125.00
	1915	Inc. Ab.	—	BV	100.00	125.00
	1916	.582	—	BV	100.00	125.00
	1917	1.928	—	BV	100.00	125.00
	1918	.600	—	BV	100.00	125.00
	1919	Inc. Ab.	—	BV	100.00	125.00
	1920	.152	—	BV	100.00	125.00
	1921	Inc. Ab.	—	BV	100.00	125.00
	1922	.013	—	BV	100.00	125.00
	1923	.015	—	BV	100.00	125.00
	1924	8,113	—	BV	100.00	125.00
	1925	9,068	—	BV	100.00	125.00
	1926	4,596	—	BV	100.00	125.00
	1927	8,360	—	BV	100.00	125.00
	1928	2,184	—	BV	100.00	125.00
	1929	3,119	—	BV	100.00	125.00
	1930	1,050	—	BV	100.00	125.00
	1959 ZBR	605 pcs.	—	—	BV	225.00
	1961 ZBR	402 pcs.	—	—	BV	210.00
	1962 ZBR	6,203	—	—	BV	150.00
	1963 ZBR	302 pcs.	—	—	BV	250.00
	1964 ZBR	.013	—	—	BV	125.00
	1965 ZBR	9,917	—	—	BV	125.00
	1966 ZBR	.039	—	—	BV	125.00
	1967 BBR	2,002	—	—	BV	160.00
	1968 BBR	7,307	—	—	BV	175.00
	1969 BBR	7,307	—	—	BV	175.00

SPECIMEN 'FDC' SETS (SS)

(Flor De Cuno)

KM#	Date	Mintage	Identification	Issue Price	Mkt. Val.
SS1	1967(5)	—	KM244.1a-247.1a,248a	—	—

PROOF SETS (PS)

KM#	Date	Mintage	Identification	Issue Price	Mkt. Val.
PS1	1886(7)	6 known	KM-PnA25,25,A26-E26	—	4500.
PS2	1965(5)	*10	KM237-240,290	—	1500.
PS3	1965(5)	—	KM220.5,221.2b,222, 223.2-224.2	—	200.00
PS4	1966(5)	*1,000	KM244.1-247.1,248	—	16.50

The Republic of the Philippines, an archipelago in the western Pacific 500 miles (805 km.) from the southeast coast of Asia, has an area of 115,830 sq. mi. (300,000 sq. km.) and a population of *64.9 million. Capital: Manila. The economy of the 7,000-island group is based on agriculture, forestry and fishing. Timber, coconut products, sugar and hemp are exported.

Migration to the Philippines began about 30,000 years ago when land bridges connected the islands with Borneo and Sumatra. Ferdinand Magellan claimed the islands for Spain in 1521. The first permanent settlement was established by Miguel de Legazpi at Cebu in April of 1565; Manila was established in 1572. A British expedition captured Manila and occupied the Spanish colony in Oct. of 1762, but it was returned to Spain by the treaty of Paris, 1763. Spain held the Philippines amid a growing movement of Filipino nationalism until 1898 when they were ceded to the United States at the end of the Spanish-American War. The Philippines became a self-governing commonwealth of the United States in 1935, and attained independence as the Republic of the Philippines on July 4, 1946.

RULERS

Spanish until 1898

MINT MARKS

(b) Brussels, privy marks only
BSP - Bangko Sentral Pilipinas
D - Denver, 1944-1945
(Lt) - Llantrisant
M, MA - Manila
S - San Francisco, 1903-1947
SGV - Madrid
(Sh) - Sherritt
(US) - United States
FM - Franklin Mint, U.S.A.*
(VDM) - Vereinigte Deutsche Metall Werks; Altona, W. Germany
Star - Manila (Spanish)

***NOTE:** From 1975 through 1977 the Franklin Mint has produced coinage in up to 3 different qualities. Beginning in 1978 only (U) and (P) were struck. Qualities of issue are designated in ( ) after each date and are defined as follows:

(M) MATTE - Normal circulation strike or a dull finish produced by sandblasting special uncirculated (polish finish) or proof quality dies.

(U) SPECIAL UNCIRCULATED - Polished or proof-like in appearance without any frosted features.

(P) PROOF - The highest quality obtainable having mirror-like fields and frosted features.

MONETARY SYSTEM

8 Octavos = 4 Quartos = 1 Real
8 Reales = 1 Peso

COLONIAL COINAGE

OCTAVO

COPPER
Mint mark: M

KM#	Date	Mintage	Good	VG	Fine	VF
5	1805F	—	15.00	30.00	50.00	80.00
	1806F	—	15.00	30.00	50.00	80.00

NOTE: Earlier date (1798) exists for this type.

KM#	Date	Mintage	Fine	VF	XF	Unc
8	1820F	—	10.00	20.00	40.00	100.00
	1829F	—	60.00	80.00	150.00	500.00
	1830F	—	12.00	30.00	50.00	250.00

QUARTO

COPPER
Mint mark: M

Similar to KM#7.

KM#	Date	Mintage	Good	VG	Fine	VF
6	1805F	—	8.00	12.50	25.00	40.00
	1806F	—	8.00	12.50	25.00	40.00
	1807F	—	8.00	12.50	25.00	40.00

NOTE: Earlier dates (1798-1800) exist for this type.

KM#	Date	Mintage	VG	Fine	VF	XF
7	1817F	—	40.00	60.00	125.00	200.00
	1819 (retrograde) P181	—	100.00	160.00	325.00	500.00
	1820F	—	10.00	20.00	40.00	60.00
	1821F	—	10.00	20.00	40.00	60.00
	1822F	—	—	—	Rare	—
	1822 (error) 2281 w/retrograde 2's	—	30.00	50.00	80.00	150.00
	1823F	—	15.00	25.00	45.00	100.00
	1824F	—	—	—	Rare	—
	1826F	—	10.00	20.00	40.00	60.00
	1827F	—	—	—	Rare	—
	1828F	—	10.00	20.00	45.00	80.00
	1829F	—	10.00	20.00	40.00	65.00
	1830F	—	10.00	20.00	40.00	65.00
	1831F	—	40.00	60.00	80.00	150.00
	1833F	—	40.00	60.00	80.00	150.00

NOTE: Varieties exist.

KM#	Date	Mintage	Good	VG	Fine	VF
9	1822F	—	25.00	40.00	60.00	150.00
	1823F	—	15.00	25.00	45.00	90.00
	1824F	—	30.00	50.00	80.00	200.00

Mint mark: MA

KM#	Date	Mintage	Good	VG	Fine	VF
10	1834F	—	12.00	20.00	40.00	60.00

KM#	Date	Mintage	Good	VG	Fine	VF
13	1835F	—	30.00	50.00	80.00	150.00

2 QUARTOS

COPPER
Mint mark: MA

KM#	Date	Mintage	Good	VG	Fine	VF
11	1834F	—	60.00	120.00	200.00	350.00

KM#	Date	Mintage	Good	VG	Fine	VF
14	1835F	—	50.00	80.00	150.00	250.00

4 QUARTOS

COPPER
Mint mark: MA

KM#	Date	Mintage	Good	VG	Fine	VF
12	1834F	—	100.00	150.00	225.00	500.00

KM#	Date	Mintage	Good	VG	Fine	VF
15	1835F	—	80.00	120.00	180.00	350.00

COUNTERSTAMPED COINAGE

(8 REALES)

MANILA/1828

Type I

Obv. c/s: MANILA/1828 within serrated circle.
Rev. leg: HABILITADO POR EL REY N.S.D. FERN. VII. around crowned Spanish royal arms.

This counterstamp was inaugurated on October 13, 1828 by the Captain-General of the Philippines. The outer serrated border was intended to obliterate the legends on the foreign dollars being overstruck. This failed to work satisfactorily and this method was soon discontinued.

SILVER

KM#	Date	Year	Good	VG	Fine	VF
	c/s: Type I on Bolivia 8 Soles, KM#97.					
16	1828	(1827 JM)	125.00	200.00	300.00	500.00
	c/s: Type I on Bolivia 8 Reales, KM#84.					
17	1828	(1808-25)	125.00	200.00	225.00	300.00
	c/s: Type I on Mexico 8 Reales, KM#376.					
18	1828	(1823-5)	125.00	200.00	250.00	400.00
	c/s: Type I on Mexico City 8 Reales, KM#309.					
19	1828	(1822 JM)	—	—	Rare	—
	c/s: Type I on Mexico City 8 Reales, KM#310.					
20	1828	(1822-23 JM)	225.00	400.00	600.00	800.00
	c/s: Type I on Mexico 8 Reales, KM#376.					
38	1828	(1823-24)	100.00	175.00	200.00	300.00
	c/s: Type I on Mexico 8 Reales, KM#377.					
21	1828	(1824-8)	100.00	175.00	200.00	300.00
	c/s: Type I on Peru (Lima) 8 Reales, KM#117.1.					
22	1828	(1810-24)	100.00	160.00	200.00	300.00
	c/s: Type I on Peru (Lima) 8 Reales, KM#136.					
23	1828	(1822-3)	100.00	160.00	200.00	300.00
	c/s: Type I on Peru (Lima) 8 Reales, KM#142.1.					
24	1828	(1825-8)	80.00	150.00	200.00	350.00

c/s: Type I on Peru (Lima) 8 Reales, KM#142.3.

KM#	Date	Year	Good	VG	Fine	VF
5	1828	(1828)	65.00	125.00	175.00	300.00

c/s: Type I on Peru (Cuzco) 8 Reales, KM#142.2.

6	1828	(1826-28)	80.00	150.00	200.00	300.00

NOTE: Other coin types may exist with this particular counterstamp.

MANILA/1828

Type II

Obv. c/s: MANILA/1828. Rev: Crowned Spanish royal arms without legends and serrated circles.

SILVER

c/s: Type II on Bolivia 8 Reales, KM#84.

27	1828	(1808-25)	90.00	160.00	200.00	300.00

c/s: Type II on Mexico 8 Reales, KM#376.

28	1828	(1823-25)	100.00	175.00	200.00	300.00

c/s: Type II on Mexico 8 Reales, KM#377.

29	1828	(1824-28)	90.00	160.00	200.00	300.00

c/s: Type II on Peru (Lima) 8 Reales, KM#117.1.

30	1828	(1810-24)	70.00	130.00	200.00	300.00

c/s: Type II on Peru (Lima) 8 Reales, KM#136.

31	1828	(1822-23)	70.00	130.00	200.00	300.00

c/s: Type II on Peru (Lima) 8 Reales, KM#142.1.

32	1828	(1825-28)	80.00	150.00	200.00	325.00

c/s: Type II on Peru (Lima) 8 Reales, KM#142.3.

33	1828	(1828)	60.00	90.00	130.00	200.00

NOTE: Other coin types may exist with this particular counterstamp.

(8 ESCUDOS)

MANILA/1829

Type III

c/s: MANILA/1829.

Rev: Crowned Spanish royal arms.

GOLD

c/s: Type III on Mexico City 8 Escudos, KM#383.

34	1829	(1825JM)	—	—	—	—

NOTE: The above is in the collection of Fabrica Nacional de Moneda y Timbre de Madrid (Spain).

(8 REALES)

MANILA/1830

Type IV

c/s: MANILA/1830 within serrated circle .

Rev. leg. HABILITADO POR EL REY N.S.D.FERN.VII. around crowned Spanish royal arms.

SILVER

Type IV on Bolivia 8 Soles, KM#97.

KM#	Date	Year	Good	VG	Fine	VF
35	1830	(1827-30)	1500.	1800.	2200.	3000.

NOTE: Rare double stamped obverse coin illustrated, Bank Leu Bostonian sale 10-90 VF realized $16,380.

c/s: Type IV on Mexico 8 Reales, KM#376.

36	1830	(1823-25)	1500.	1800.	2200.	3000.

c/s: Type IV on Mexico 8 Reales, KM#377.

37	1830	(1824-30)	1500.	1800.	2200.	3000.

NOTE: Other coin types may exist with this particular counterstamp.

COUNTERMARKED COINAGE

(8 REALES)

FERDINAND VII

SILVER

Oval Type V   Round Type V

Actual size 9-10mm

These countermarks were introduced by decree of October 27, 1832 due to the problems encountered with the larger countermarks of 1828-1830. Pierced or holed coins were declared not valid but later were countermarked directly over the hole with Type V or Type VI countermarks and circulated freely. The latter types exist countermarked on both sides directly over the hole and are very scarce. These countermarks were retired in 1834 after the death of Ferdinand VII and replaced with a new die of Isabel II, Type VI. Coins with either Type V countermark dated after 1834 can be considered counterfeit.

(REAL)

SILVER

c/m: F.7.o on Mexico 1 Real.

40	ND	—	—	—	Rare	—

(2 REALES)

SILVER

c/m: F.7.o on Mexico 2 Reales, KM#372.

41	ND	(1825-34)	75.00	100.00	200.00	300.00

c/m: F.7.o on Peru 2 Reales, KM#141.

42	ND	(1825-34)	75.00	100.00	200.00	300.00

(4 REALES)

SILVER

c/m: F.7.o on Mexico 4 Reales.

43	ND	—	200.00	300.00	400.00	700.00

(8 REALES)

SILVER

c/m: F.7.o on Argentina 8 Reales, KM#5.

44.1	ND	(1813)	50.00	80.00	150.00	250.00

c/m: F.7.o on Argentina 8 Reales, KM#14.

44.2	ND	(1815)	50.00	80.00	150.00	250.00

c/m: F.7.o on Argentina 8 Soles, KM#15.

45	ND	(1815)	50.00	80.00	150.00	250.00

c/m: F.7.o on Argentina 8 Reales, KM#20.

46	ND	(1826-34)	60.00	100.00	175.00	275.00

c/m: F.7.o on Bolivia 8 Reales, KM#55.

KM#	Date	Year	Good	VG	Fine	VF
47	ND	(1773-89)	75.00	110.00	200.00	300.00

c/m: F.7.o on Bolivia 8 Reales, KM#64.

48	ND	(1789-91)	60.00	100.00	190.00	275.00

c/m: F.7.o on Bolivia 8 Reales, KM#73.

49	ND	(1791-1808)	60.00	100.00	160.00	250.00

c/m: F.7.o on Bolivia 8 Reales, KM#84.

50	ND	(1808-25)	60.00	100.00	160.00	250.00

c/m: F.7.o on Bolivia 8 Soles, KM#97.

51	ND	(1827-34)	25.00	35.00	50.00	80.00

c/m: F.7.o on Brazil 960 Reis, KM#307.

52	ND	(1809-18)	125.00	175.00	300.00	500.00

c/m: F.7.o on Brazil 960 Reis, KM#326.

53	ND	(1818-22)	125.00	175.00	400.00	600.00

c/m: F.7.o on Brazil 960 Reis, KM#368.

54	ND	(1823-7)	125.00	175.00	300.00	500.00

c/m: F.7.o on Central American Republic (Guatemala) 8 Reales, KM#4.

55	ND	(1824-34)	75.00	120.00	180.00	250.00

c/m: F.7.o on Chile 1 Peso, KM#82.

56	ND	(1817-34)	50.00	75.00	100.00	150.00

c/m: F.7.O on Columbia, Cundinamarca Province 8 Reales, KM#6.

KM#	Date	Year	Good	VG	Fine	VF
57	ND	(1820-21)	50.00	75.00	100.00	150.00

c/m: F.7.o on France 5 Francs, C#189.

KM#	Date	Year	Good	VG	Fine	VF
A58	1826D	—	350.00	500.00	800.00	1200.

c/m. in oval: F.7.o on Kingdom of Italy 5 Lire, C#10.1.

KM#	Date	Year	Good	VG	Fine	VF
58	1809	—	—	—	Rare	—

c/m: F.7.o on Mexico City 8 Reales, KM#105.

KM#	Date	Year	Good	VG	Fine	VF
59	ND	(1760-71)	—	—	Rare	—

c/m: F.7.o on Mexico City 8 Reales, KM#106.

KM#	Date	Year	Good	VG	Fine	VF
60	ND	(1772-89)	80.00	100.00	175.00	225.00

c/m: F.7.o on Mexico City 8 Reales, KM#107.

KM#	Date	Year	Good	VG	Fine	VF
61	ND	(1789-90FM)	60.00	100.00	175.00	225.00

c/m: F.7.o on Mexico City 8 Reales, KM#108.

KM#	Date	Year	Good	VG	Fine	VF
62	ND	(1790FM)	60.00	100.00	175.00	225.00

c/m: F.7.o on Mexico City 8 Reales, KM#109.

KM#	Date	Year	Good	VG	Fine	VF
63	ND	(1791-1808)	50.00	90.00	150.00	215.00

c/m: F.7.o on Mexico City 8 Reales, KM#110.

KM#	Date	Year	Good	VG	Fine	VF
64	ND	(1808-11)	60.00	100.00	175.00	220.00

c/m: F.7.o on Mexico City 8 Reales, KM#111.

KM#	Date	Year	Good	VG	Fine	VF
65	ND	(1811-21)	60.00	110.00	150.00	220.00

c/m: F.7.o on Mexico City 8 Reales, KM#304.

KM#	Date	Year	Good	VG	Fine	VF
66	ND	(1822JM)	50.00	100.00	150.00	250.00

c/m: F.7.o on Mexico City 8 Reales, KM#305.

KM#	Date	Year	Good	VG	Fine	VF
67	ND	(1822JM)	50.00	100.00	150.00	250.00

c/m: F.7.o on Mexico City 8 Reales, KM#306.

KM#	Date	Year	Good	VG	Fine	VF
68	ND	(1822JM)	50.00	100.00	150.00	250.00

c/m: F.7.o on Mexico City 8 Reales, KM#307.

KM#	Date	Year	Good	VG	Fine	VF
69	ND	(1822JM)	75.00	150.00	250.00	450.00

c/m: F.7.o on Mexico City 8 Reales, KM#308.

KM#	Date	Year	Good	VG	Fine	VF
70	ND	(1822JM)	70.00	140.00	200.00	350.00

c/m: F.7.o on Mexico City 8 Reales, KM#309.

KM#	Date	Year	Good	VG	Fine	VF
71	ND	(1822JM)	—	—	Rare	—

c/m: F.7.o on Mexico City 8 Reales, KM#310.

KM#	Date	Year	Good	VG	Fine	VF
72	ND	(1822-3JM)	50.00	100.00	150.00	250.00

c/m: F.7.o on Mexico (Guanajuato) 8 Reales, KM#376.1.

KM#	Date	Year	Good	VG	Fine	VF
73	ND	(1823-5)	45.00	80.00	125.00	200.00

c/m: F.7.o on Mexico 8 Reales, KM#377.

KM#	Date	Year	Good	VG	Fine	VF
74	ND	(1824-34)	30.00	50.00	60.00	80.00

c/m: F.7.o on Peru (Lima) 8 Reales, KM#78.

KM#	Date	Year	Good	VG	Fine	VF
75	ND	(1772-89)	60.00	100.00	150.00	250.00

c/m: F.7.o on Peru (Lima) 8 Reales, KM#87.

KM#	Date	Year	Good	VG	Fine	VF
76	ND	(1789-91)	60.00	100.00	150.00	250.00

c/m: F.7.o on Peru (Lima) 8 Reales, KM#97.

KM#	Date	Year	Good	VG	Fine	VF
77	ND	(1791-1808)	60.00	80.00	125.00	200.00

c/m: F.7.o on Peru (Lima) 8 Reales, KM#106.

KM#	Date	Year	Good	VG	Fine	VF
78	ND	(1808-11)	60.00	85.00	130.00	200.00

c/m: F.7.o on Peru (Lima) 8 Reales, KM#117.1.

KM#	Date	Year	Good	VG	Fine	VF
79	ND	(1810-24)	60.00	80.00	125.00	175.00

c/m: F.7.o on Peru (Lima) 8 Reales, KM#136.

KM#	Date	Year	Good	VG	Fine	VF
80	ND	(1822-3)	35.00	60.00	90.00	125.00

c/m: F.7.o on Peru (Lima) 8 Reales, KM#130.

KM#	Date	Year	Good	VG	Fine	VF
81	ND	(1824)	60.00	90.00	150.00	200.00

c/m. in oval: F.7.o on Peru (Lima) 8 Reales, KM#142.1.

KM#	Date	Year	Good	VG	Fine	VF
82	ND	(1825-8)	—	—	Rare	—

c/m: F.7.o on Peru (Lima) 8 Reales, KM#142.3.

KM#	Date	Year	Good	VG	Fine	VF
83	ND	(1828-34)	30.00	45.00	60.00	75.00

c/m: F.7.O on Peru (Cuzco) 8 Reales, KM#142.4.

KM#	Date	Year	Good	VG	Fine	VF
84	ND	(1830-34)	75.00	100.00	175.00	300.00

8 ESCUDOS

GOLD
c/m: F.7.o on Chile 8 Escudos, KM#84.

KM#	Date	Year	Good	VG	Fine	VF
85	ND	1822FD	3000.	3500.	4000.	5000.
		1825I	—	—	Unique	—
		1826I	—	—	Unique	—

c/m: F.7.o on Colombia 8 Escudos, KM#82.2.

KM#	Date	Year	Good	VG	Fine	VF
A86	ND	1825	—	—	Rare	*—

***NOTE:** Superior Ebsen sale 6-87 VF realized $13,750.

c/m: F.7.o on Mexico - Estado 8 Escudos, KM#383.4.

KM#	Date	Year	Good	VG	Fine	VF
86	ND	1829LF	—	—	Unique	—

NOTE: Other coin types may exist with this particular countermark.

ISABEL II

SILVER
Type VI

This countermark was introduced after the death of Ferdinand VII on December 20, 1834. It exists with several varieties of crowns. Countermarking of foreign coins was halted in Manila by the edict of March 31, 1837 after Spain had recognized the independence of Mexico, Peru, Colombia, Bolivia, Chile and other former colonies in Central and South America. Coins with the Type VI countermarked after 1837 can be considered counterfeit.

(REAL)

SILVER
c/m: Y • II • on Mexico - Zacatecas Real, KM#372.10.

KM#	Date	Year	Good	VG	Fine	VF
87	ND	(1826-37)	75.00	125.00	175.00	300.00

(2 REALES)

SILVER
c/m: Y • II • on Mexico - Zacatecas 2 Reales, KM#374.12.

KM#	Date	Year	Good	VG	Fine	VF
88	ND	(1825-37)	60.00	100.00	150.00	250.00

c/m: Y • II • on Peru (Lima) 2 Reales, KM#104.2.

KM#	Date	Year	Good	VG	Fine	VF
A90	ND	(1808-1811)	90.00	160.00	250.00	400.00

c/m: Y • II • on Peru (Lima) 2 Reales, KM#141.

KM#	Date	Year	Good	VG	Fine	VF
90	ND	(1825-37)	60.00	100.00	150.00	200.00

(GULDEN)

.920 SILVER
c/m: Y • II • on Netherlands-Holland 1 Gulden, Cr#C13.

KM#	Date	Year	Good	VG	Fine	VF
89	ND	(1793)	120.00	150.00	200.00	300.00

(4 REALES)

SILVER
c/m: Y • II • on Bolivia 4 Reales, KM#54.

KM#	Date	Year	Good	VG	Fine	VF
91	ND	(1788)	250.00	400.00	600.00	900.00

c/m: Y • II • on Mexico - Zacatecas 4 Reales, KM#375.9.

KM#	Date	Year	Good	VG	Fine	VF
92	ND	(1832)	200.00	300.00	450.00	750.00

(8 REALES)

SILVER

c/m: Y • II • on Argentina 8 Reales, KM#5.

KM#	Date	Year	Good	VG	Fine	VF
93.1	ND	(1813)	60.00	100.00	150.00	200.00

c/m: Y • II • on Argentina 8 Reales, KM#14.

KM#	Date	Year	Good	VG	Fine	VF
93.2	ND	(1815)	60.00	100.00	150.00	200.00

c/m: Y • II • on Argentina 8 Soles, KM#15.

KM#	Date	Year	Good	VG	Fine	VF
94	ND	(1815)	60.00	100.00	150.00	350.00

c/m: Y • II • on Argentina 8 Reales, KM#20.

KM#	Date	Year	Good	VG	Fine	VF
95	ND	(1826-37)	60.00	100.00	150.00	250.00

c/m: Y • II • on Bolivia 8 Reales, KM#55.

KM#	Date	Year	Good	VG	Fine	VF
96	ND	(1773-89)	65.00	110.00	160.00	250.00

c/m: Y • II • on Bolivia 8 Reales, KM#64.

KM#	Date	Year	Good	VG	Fine	VF
97	ND	(1789-91)	65.00	110.00	160.00	250.00

c/m: Y • II • on Bolivia 8 Reales, KM#73.

KM#	Date	Year	Good	VG	Fine	VF
98	ND	(1791-1808)	65.00	100.00	150.00	200.00

c/m: Y • II • on Bolivia 8 Reales, KM#84.

KM#	Date	Year	Good	VG	Fine	VF
99	ND	(1808-25)	60.00	90.00	140.00	190.00

c/m: Y • II • on Bolivia 8 Sueldos, KM#97.

KM#	Date	Year	Good	VG	Fine	VF
100	ND	(1827-37)	25.00	35.00	45.00	80.00

c/m: Y • II • on Brazil 960 Reis, KM#307.

KM#	Date	Year	Good	VG	Fine	VF
101	ND	(1809-18)	125.00	175.00	250.00	375.00

c/m: Y • II • on Brazil 960 Reis, KM#326.

KM#	Date	Year	Good	VG	Fine	VF
102	ND	(1818-22)	125.00	175.00	250.00	375.00

c/m: Y • II • on Brazil 960 Reis, KM#368.

KM#	Date	Year	Good	VG	Fine	VF
103	ND	(1823-30)	125.00	175.00	250.00	375.00

c/m: Y • II • on Brazil 960 Reis, KM#385.

KM#	Date	Year	Good	VG	Fine	VF
104	ND	(1832-4)	—	—	Rare	—

c/m: Y • II • on Brazil 1200 Reis, KM#454.

KM#	Date	Year	Good	VG	Fine	VF
105	ND	(1834-7)	150.00	300.00	400.00	600.00

c/m: Y • II • on Central American Republic - Guatemala 8 Reales, KM#4.

KM#	Date	Year	Good	VG	Fine	VF
106.1	ND	(1824-37)	100.00	200.00	300.00	500.00

c/m: Y • II • on obv. and rev. of Central American Republic - Guatemala 8 Reales, KM#4.

KM#	Date	Year	Good	VG	Fine	VF
106.2	ND	(1824 NG)	100.00	200.00	300.00	500.00

c/m: Y • II • on Central American Republic - Costa Rica 8 Reales, KM#22.

KM#	Date	Year	Good	VG	Fine	VF
107	ND	(1831)	150.00	300.00	400.00	600.00

c/m: Y • II • on Chile 1 Peso, KM#82.

KM#	Date	Year	Good	VG	Fine	VF
108	ND	(1817-34)	50.00	75.00	100.00	125.00

c/m: Y • II • on Colombia 8 Reales, KM#89.

KM#	Date	Year	Good	VG	Fine	VF
109	ND	(1834-6)	40.00	60.00	80.00	120.00

c/m: Y • II • on Mexico City 8 Reales, KM#104.

KM#	Date	Year	Good	VG	Fine	VF
110	ND	(1747-60)	—	—	Rare	—

c/m: Y • II • on Mexico City 8 Reales, KM#105.

KM#	Date	Year	Good	VG	Fine	VF
111	ND	(1760-71)	—	—	Rare	—

c/m: Y • II • on Mexico City 8 Reales, KM#106.

KM#	Date	Year	Good	VG	Fine	VF
112	ND	(1772-89)	60.00	120.00	160.00	250.00

c/m: Y • II • on Mexico City 8 Reales, KM#107.

KM#	Date	Year	Good	VG	Fine	VF
113	ND	(1789-90FM)	60.00	120.00	150.00	200.00

c/m: Y / II • on Mexico City 8 Reales, KM#108.

KM#	Date	Year	Good	VG	Fine	VF
114	ND	(1790FM)	60.00	120.00	170.00	250.00

c/m: Y / II • on Mexico City 8 Reales, KM#109.

KM#	Date	Year	Good	VG	Fine	VF
115	ND	(1791-1808)	50.00	100.00	150.00	200.00

c/m: Y • II • on Mexico City 8 Reales, KM#110.

KM#	Date	Year	Good	VG	Fine	VF
116	ND	(1808-11)	50.00	100.00	150.00	200.00

c/m: Y • 11 • on Mexico - Chihuahua 8 Reales, KM#111.1.

KM#	Date	Year	Good	VG	Fine	VF
117.1	ND	(1815-22)	100.00	150.00	220.00	300.00

c/m: Y • II • on Mexico - Durango 8 Reales, KM#111.2.

KM#	Date	Year	Good	VG	Fine	VF
117.2	ND	(1811-21)	50.00	100.00	150.00	200.00

c/m: Y • II • on Mexico City 8 Reales, KM#111.

KM#	Date	Year	Good	VG	Fine	VF
119	ND	(1811-21)	50.00	100.00	150.00	200.00

c/m: Y • II • on Mexico - Zacatecas 8 Reales, KM#111.5.

KM#	Date	Year	Good	VG	Fine	VF
118	ND	(1813-22)	50.00	100.00	150.00	200.00

c/m: Y • II • on Mexico - Zacatecas 8 Reales, KM#189.

KM#	Date	Year	Good	VG	Fine	VF
120	ND	(1811)	100.00	150.00	220.00	300.00

c/m: Y • II • on Mexico City 8 Reales, KM#304.

KM#	Date	Year	Good	VG	Fine	VF
121	ND	(1822JM)	50.00	85.00	135.00	175.00

c/m: Y • II • on Mexico City 8 Reales, KM#305.

KM#	Date	Year	Good	VG	Fine	VF
122	ND	(1822JM)	50.00	100.00	140.00	200.00

c/m: Y • II • on Mexico City 8 Reales, KM#306.

KM#	Date	Year	Good	VG	Fine	VF
123	ND	(1822JM)	50.00	100.00	140.00	200.00

c/m: Y • II • on Mexico City 8 Reales, KM#307.

KM#	Date	Year	Good	VG	Fine	VF
124	ND	(1822JM)	50.00	100.00	140.00	180.00

c/m: Y • II • on Mexico City 8 Reales, KM#308.

KM#	Date	Year	Good	VG	Fine	VF
125	ND	(1822JM)	50.00	100.00	140.00	180.00

c/m: Y • II • on Mexico City 8 Reales, KM#309.

KM#	Date	Year	Good	VG	Fine	VF
126	ND	(1822JM)	—	—	Rare	—

c/m: Y • II • on Mexico City 8 Reales, KM#310.

KM#	Date	Year	Good	VG	Fine	VF
127	ND	(1822-3JM)	40.00	80.00	125.00	180.00

c/m: Y • II • on Mexico 8 Reales, KM#376.

KM#	Date	Year	Good	VG	Fine	VF
128	ND	(1823-4)	50.00	100.00	140.00	200.00

c/m: Y • II • on Mexico 8 Reales, KM#377.

KM#	Date	Year	Good	VG	Fine	VF
129	ND	(1824-37)	30.00	45.00	60.00	90.00

c/m: Y • II • on Peru (Lima) 8 Reales, KM#64.

KM#	Date	Year	Good	VG	Fine	VF
130	ND	(1760-72)	50.00	100.00	150.00	200.00

c/m: Y • II • on Peru (Lima) 8 Reales, KM#78.

KM#	Date	Year	Good	VG	Fine	VF
131	ND	(1772-89)	50.00	100.00	150.00	200.00

c/m: Y • II • on Peru (Lima) 8 Reales, KM#87.

KM#	Date	Year	Good	VG	Fine	VF
132	ND	(1789-91)	60.00	110.00	175.00	200.00

c/m: Y • II • on Peru (Lima) 8 Reales, KM#97.

KM#	Date	Year	Good	VG	Fine	VF
133	ND	(1791-1808)	50.00	100.00	150.00	200.00

c/m: Y • II • on Peru (Lima) 8 Reales, KM#106.

KM#	Date	Year	Good	VG	Fine	VF
134	ND	(1808-11)	50.00	100.00	150.00	200.00

c/m: Y • II • on Peru (Lima) 8 Reales, KM#117.1

KM#	Date	Year	Good	VG	Fine	VF
135	ND	(1810-24)	45.00	65.00	85.00	125.00

c/m: Y • II • on Peru (Lima) 8 Reales, KM#136.

KM#	Date	Year	Good	VG	Fine	VF
136	ND	(1822-3)	35.00	50.00	75.00	100.00

c/m: Y • II • on Peru (Lima) 8 Reales, KM#130.

KM#	Date	Year	Good	VG	Fine	VF
137	ND	(1824)	125.00	175.00	250.00	350.00

c/m: Y • II • on Peru (Lima) 8 Reales, KM#142.1.

KM#	Date	Year	Good	VG	Fine	VF
138.1	ND	(1825-8)	25.00	35.00	45.00	60.00

c/m: Y • II • on Peru (Lima) 8 Reales, KM#142.3.

KM#	Date	Year	Good	VG	Fine	VF
138.2	ND	(1828-37)	25.00	35.00	45.00	60.00

c/m: Y • II • on Peru (Cuzco)
8 Reales, KM#142.4.

KM#	Date	Year	Good	VG	Fine	VF
138.4	ND	(1830-34)	45.00	75.00	120.00	180.00

c/m: Y • II • on Philippines, KM#80.

KM#	Date	Year	Good	VG	Fine	VF
139	ND	(1822-3)	90.00	135.00	225.00	300.00

NOTE: Coins bearing both Type V or Type VI countermarks with other countermarks are very scarce. Certain holed or pierced coins are sometimes found with an additional set of countermarks usually struck on both sides over the hole to approve it for normal circulation. These are very scarce.

ESCUDO

GOLD
c/m: Y • II • on Colombia 1 Escudo, KM#81.2.

KM#	Date	Year	Good	VG	Fine	VF
140	ND	(1827FM)	—	—	Unique	—

8 ESCUDO

GOLD
c/m: Y • II • on Colombia
8 Escudos, KM#82.1.

KM#	Date	Year	Good	VG	Fine	VF
141.1	ND	(1826JF)	3000.	3500.	4000.	6500.
	ND	(1831RS)	4000.	5000.	6000.	10,000.
	ND	(1832RS)	—	—	—	*12,800.
	ND	(1835RS)	—	—	—	*16,500.

c/m: Y • II • on Colombia
8 Escudos, KM#82.2.

KM#	Date	Year	Good	VG	Fine	VF
141.2	ND	(1833UR)	3000.	3500.	4000.	6500.

c/m: Y • II • on Mexico City Iturbide
8 Scudos, KM#313.1.

KM#	Date	Year	Good	VG	Fine	VF
141.3	ND	(1822)	—	—	—	*16,500.

c/m: Y • II • on Mexico City
8 Escudos, KM#383.9.

KM#	Date	Year	Good	VG	Fine	VF
141.4	ND	(1834ML)	—	—	—	**13,200.

c/m: Y • II • on Argentina-Provincias Del Rio
De La Plata 8 Escudos, KM#21.

KM#	Date	Year	Good	VG	Fine	VF
141.5	ND	(1828P)	3000.	3500.	4000.	6500.

***NOTE:** Glendining's John J. Ford Jr. sale 10-89.
****NOTE:** Sotheby's Geneva gold coins of the Hispanic world sale 5-90.
NOTE: The above countermarks have been reported on other coins, (i.e. U.S. 1/2 Dollar, Dollar, and Spanish 20 Reales).

DECIMAL COINAGE

1861-1897
100 Centavos = 1 Peso

CENTAVO

COPPER, 25mm.
Obv: Boy head of Alfonso XIII of Spain .
Rev: Crowned arms between branches.

KM#	Date	Mintage	Fine	VF	XF	Unc
152	1894	—	1600.	2000.	2500.	3000.

2 CENTAVOS

COPPER, 30mm.
Obv: Boy head of Alfonso XIII of Spain.
Rev: Crowned arms between branches.

KM#	Date	Mintage	Fine	VF	XF	Unc
153	1894	—	2000.	2400.	2750.	3500.

10 CENTIMOS

2.5960 g, .900 SILVER, .0751 oz ASW

KM#	Date	Mintage	Fine	VF	XF	Unc
145	1864	4,586	75.00	150.00	400.00	1600.
	1865	.082	20.00	50.00	125.00	1000.
	1866	.039	30.00	60.00	150.00	1200.
	1867/6	.124	20.00	50.00	125.00	1000.
	1867	Inc. Ab.	20.00	40.00	100.00	950.00
	1868	*.139	6.00	12.00	25.00	125.00

NOTE: An additional 450,000 pieces were struck between 1870-74, all dated 1868.

2.5960 g, .835 SILVER, .0697 oz ASW

KM#	Date	Mintage	Fine	VF	XF	Unc
148	1880	.015	150.00	250.00	600.00	2500.
	1881/0	.624	25.00	45.00	125.00	400.00
	1881	Inc. Ab.	10.00	25.00	80.00	350.00
	1882/1	.525	20.00	40.00	125.00	400.00
	1882	Inc. Ab.	10.00	25.00	85.00	400.00
	1883/1	.983	15.00	30.00	85.00	350.00
	1883/2	Inc. Ab.	15.00	30.00	85.00	350.00
	1883	Inc. Ab.	10.00	20.00	80.00	300.00
	1884	.010	150.00	200.00	500.00	2000.
	1885/3	—	4.50	8.00	18.00	65.00
	1885	Inc. Ab.	3.00	6.00	12.00	45.00

***NOTE:** An additional 5,432,614 pieces were struck between 1886-1898, all dated 1885.

20 CENTIMOS

5.1920 g, .900 SILVER, .1502 oz ASW

KM#	Date	Mintage	Fine	VF	XF	Unc
146	1864	.067	40.00	60.00	120.00	1600.
	1865	.239	10.00	25.00	65.00	1000.
	1866/5	.134	15.00	35.00	90.00	1200.
	1866	Inc. Ab.	20.00	40.00	100.00	1250.
	1867	.138	15.00	30.00	80.00	1200.
	1868	*.418	5.00	8.00	15.00	150.00

***NOTE:** An additional 708,400 pieces were struck between 1869-1874, all dated 1868.

5.1920 g, .835 SILVER, .1394 oz ASW

KM#	Date	Mintage	Fine	VF	XF	Unc
149	1880	.070	30.00	60.00	120.00	1250.
	1881/0	1.029	10.00	20.00	40.00	300.00
	1881	Inc. Ab.	10.00	18.00	50.00	300.00
	1882/1	.968	12.00	24.00	55.00	500.00
	1882	Inc. Ab.	12.00	24.00	55.00	500.00
	1883/2	1.972	12.00	20.00	40.00	350.00
	1883/horizontal 8	Inc. Ab.	12.00	20.00	40.00	300.00
	1883	Inc. Ab.	10.00	16.00	30.00	300.00
	1884	.859	20.00	30.00	75.00	500.00
	1885	*1.344	5.00	8.00	12.50	70.00

***NOTE:** An additional 4,092,205 pieces were struck between 1886-1898, all dated 1885.

50 CENTIMOS

12.9800 g, .900 SILVER, .3756 oz ASW

KM#	Date	Mintage	Fine	VF	XF	Unc
147	1865	.081	30.00	60.00	150.00	1500.
	1866	7,442	300.00	450.00	700.00	5000.
	1867	6,870	250.00	400.00	600.00	4000.
	1868/58	*.423	10.00	18.00	50.00	200.00
	1868/7	Inc. Ab.	10.00	18.00	50.00	200.00
	1868	Inc. Ab.	7.50	15.00	45.00	200.00

***NOTE:** An additional 200,800 pieces were struck between 1869-1874, all dated 1868.

12.9800 g, .835 SILVER, .3485 oz ASW

KM#	Date	Mintage	Fine	VF	XF	Unc
150	1880	.127	100.00	125.00	275.00	2200.
	1881	2.480	10.00	20.00	40.00	500.00

KM#	Date	Mintage	Fine	VF	XF	Unc
150	1882/0	1.890	12.50	30.00	60.00	650.00
	1882/1	Inc. Ab.	12.50	30.00	60.00	650.00
	1882	Inc. Ab.	10.00	20.00	40.00	650.00
	1883	2.221	10.00	20.00	40.00	500.00
	1884	.023	80.00	125.00	250.00	2000.
	1885/3	*22.700	5.00	10.00	24.00	85.00
	1885	I.A.	3.50	7.50	18.00	65.00

***NOTE:** An additional 22,649,115 pieces were struck between 1886-1898, all dated 1885.

PESO

1.6915 g, .875 GOLD, .0476 oz AGW

KM#	Date	Mintage	Fine	VF	XF	Unc
142	1861/0	.237	45.00	65.00	90.00	225.00
	1861	Inc. Ab.	45.00	65.00	90.00	225.00
	1862/1	.143	45.00	65.00	90.00	225.00
	1862	Inc. Ab.	45.00	65.00	90.00	225.00
	1863/2	.236	45.00	65.00	90.00	225.00
	1863	Inc. Ab.	45.00	65.00	90.00	225.00
	1864/0	.274	45.00	65.00	90.00	225.00
	1864	Inc. Ab.	50.00	75.00	100.00	250.00
	1865/0	.189	55.00	90.00	125.00	250.00
	1865	Inc. Ab.	45.00	65.00	90.00	225.00
	1866/5	.077	160.00	200.00	300.00	1250.
	1866	Inc. Ab.	160.00	200.00	300.00	1250.
	1867	.012	450.00	800.00	1250.	3000.
	1868/6	*.028	45.00	70.00	100.00	200.00
	1868/7	Inc. Ab.	45.00	70.00	100.00	200.00
	1868	Inc. Ab.	40.00	50.00	70.00	135.00

***NOTE:** An additional 372,724 pieces were struck between 1869-1874, all dated 1868.

25.0000 g, .900 SILVER, .7234 oz ASW

KM#	Date	Mintage	Fine	VF	XF	Unc
154	1897 SGV	6.000	25.00	35.00	75.00	300.00

2 PESOS

3.3830 g, .875 GOLD, .0952 oz AGW

KM#	Date	Mintage	Fine	VF	XF	Unc
143	1861/0	.265	60.00	90.00	110.00	325.00
	1861	Inc. Ab.	60.00	90.00	110.00	325.00
	1862/1	.237	60.00	90.00	110.00	325.00
	1862	Inc. Ab.	60.00	90.00	110.00	325.00
	1863/2	.176	60.00	90.00	110.00	325.00
	1863	Inc. Ab.	60.00	90.00	110.00	325.00
	1864/0	.181	60.00	90.00	110.00	325.00
	1864/3	Inc. Ab.	60.00	90.00	110.00	325.00
	1864	Inc. Ab.	70.00	100.00	140.00	350.00
	1865	.034	150.00	225.00	350.00	750.00
	1866/5	.016	600.00	800.00	1250.	2500.
	1866	Inc. Ab.	600.00	800.00	1250.	2500.
	1868/6	*.048	55.00	70.00	90.00	200.00
	1868	Inc. Ab.	60.00	75.00	100.00	225.00

NOTE: An additional 304,691 pieces were struck between 1869-1873, all dated 1868.

4 PESOS

6.7661 g, .875 GOLD, .1903 oz AGW

KM#	Date	Mintage	Fine	VF	XF	Unc
144	1861	.183	120.00	150.00	190.00	375.00
	1862/1	.507	120.00	150.00	170.00	325.00
	1862	Inc. Ab.	120.00	150.00	170.00	325.00
	1863	.475	120.00	150.00	170.00	325.00
	1864	.461	120.00	150.00	175.00	350.00
	1865	.241	120.00	200.00	275.00	600.00
	1866/65	.044	500.00	750.00	1500.	3000.
	1866	Inc. Ab.	500.00	750.00	1500.	3000.
	1867	1,530	—	—	Rare	—
	1868	*.036	100.00	120.00	150.00	300.00

***NOTE:** 1,521,505 were struck between 1869-1873, all dated 1868.

KM#	Date	Mintage	Fine	VF	XF	Unc
151	1880	—	—	—	Rare	—
	1881	—	2500.	3500.	6000.	8000.
	1882	—	500.00	750.00	1250.	2000.
	1883	—	—	Reported, not confirmed		
	1884	—	—	Reported, not confirmed		
	1885	—	2500.	3500.	6000.	8000.

REVOLUTIONARY COINAGE

Island of Panay

CENTAVO

COPPER
Obv: Helmeted head right, leg.
Rev: Sun in triangle, leg.

KM#	Date	Mintage	VG	Fine	VF	XF
156	1899	—	—	—	2000.	2400.
		c/m: M behind head.				
157	1899	—	—	—	2000.	2400.

Town of Malolos

2 CENTAVOS

COPPER
Obv: Large date.

KM#	Date	Mintage	VG	Fine	VF	XF
158.1	1899	—	—	—	2000.	2400.
		Obv: Small date.				
158.2	1899	—	—	—	2000.	2400.

KM#	Date	Mintage	VG	Fine	VF	XF
159	1899	—	—	—	2000.	2400.

UNITED STATES ADMINISTRATION

1903-1935
100 Centavos = 1 Peso

1/2 CENTAVO

BRONZE

KM#	Date	Mintage	Fine	VF	XF	Unc
162	1903	12.084	.50	1.00	2.00	10.00
	1903	2,558	—	—	Proof	40.00
	1904	5.654	.50	1.00	2.50	15.00
	1904	1,355	—	—	Proof	50.00
	1905	471 pcs.	—	—	Proof	100.00
	1906	500 pcs.	—	—	Proof	80.00
	1908	500 pcs.	—	—	Proof	80.00

CENTAVO

BRONZE

KM#	Date	Mintage	Fine	VF	XF	Unc
163	1903	10.790	.50	1.00	2.00	15.00
	1903	2,558	—	—	Proof	40.00
	1904	17.040	.50	1.00	2.00	15.00
	1904	1,355	—	—	Proof	50.00
	1905	10.000	.50	1.00	2.00	22.50
	1905	471 pcs.	—	—	Proof	90.00
	1906	500 pcs.	—	—	Proof	50.00
	1908	500 pcs.	—	—	Proof	50.00
	1908S	2.187	1.00	2.00	6.00	30.00
	1909S	1.738	2.50	6.00	12.00	75.00
	1910S	2.700	1.00	2.00	6.00	30.00
	1911S	4.803	.50	2.00	6.00	25.00
	1912S	3.000	1.00	2.00	6.00	30.00
	1913S	5.000	.75	2.00	6.00	25.00
	1914S	5.000	.50	2.00	5.00	25.00
	1915S	2.500	10.00	20.00	50.00	200.00
	1916S	4.330	5.00	10.00	25.00	100.00
	1917/6S	7.070	2.50	5.00	10.00	70.00
	1917S	Inc. Ab.	.75	2.00	5.00	30.00
	1918S	11.660	.75	2.00	3.00	20.00
	1918S large S	Inc. Ab.	15.00	30.00	70.00	250.00
	1919S	4.540	.75	2.00	5.00	25.00
	1920S	2.500	4.00	8.00	16.00	90.00
	1920	3.552	1.00	2.00	3.00	25.00
	1921	7.283	.50	1.00	3.00	25.00
	1922	3.519	.50	1.00	3.00	25.00
	1925M	9.332	.25	1.00	3.00	25.00
	1926M	9.000	.25	1.00	3.00	25.00
	1927M	9.270	.25	1.00	3.00	25.00
	1928M	9.150	.25	1.00	3.00	25.00
	1929M	5.657	.75	1.50	3.00	22.00
	1930M	5.577	.75	1.50	3.00	22.00
	1931M	5.659	.75	1.50	3.00	22.00
	1932M	4.000	.75	2.00	3.00	25.00
	1933M	8.393	.50	.75	3.00	20.00
	1934M	3.179	1.00	2.00	3.00	25.00
	1936M	17.455	.50	1.00	3.00	12.00

5 CENTAVOS

COPPER-NICKEL

KM#	Date	Mintage	Fine	VF	XF	Unc
164	1903	8.910	.50	1.00	2.50	15.00
	1903	2,558	—	—	Proof	60.00
	1904	1.075	.60	1.50	3.50	25.00
	1904	1,355	—	—	Proof	65.00
	1905	471 pcs.	—	—	Proof	125.00
	1906	500 pcs.	—	—	Proof	100.00
	1908	500 pcs.	—	—	Proof	100.00
	1916S	.300	10.00	20.00	50.00	275.00
	1917S	2.300	1.00	2.00	5.00	50.00
	1918S	2.780	1.00	2.00	5.00	50.00
	1919S	1.220	1.00	3.00	6.00	60.00
	1920	1.421	2.00	4.00	8.00	90.00
	1921	2.132	2.00	4.00	8.00	80.00
	1925M	1.000	2.00	4.00	8.00	80.00
	1926M	1.200	2.00	4.50	10.00	65.00
	1927M	1.000	2.00	4.00	8.00	70.00
	1928M	1.000	2.00	4.50	10.00	85.00

Mule. Obv: KM#164. Rev: 20 Centavos, KM#170.

KM#	Date	Mintage	Fine	VF	XF	Unc
173	1918S	—	100.00	200.00	450.00	1750.

KM#	Date	Mintage	Fine	VF	XF	Unc
175	1930M	2.905	1.00	2.00	3.00	40.00
	1931M	3.477	1.00	2.00	3.00	40.00
	1932M	3.956	1.00	2.00	3.00	40.00
	1934M	2.154	1.00	3.00	5.00	45.00
	1935M	2.754	1.00	2.00	4.00	40.00

10 CENTAVOS

2.6924 g, .900 SILVER, .0779 oz ASW

KM#	Date	Mintage	Fine	VF	XF	Unc
165	1903	5.103	1.50	2.00	3.00	25.00
	1903	2,558	—	—	Proof	75.00
	1903S	1.200	6.00	10.00	25.00	175.00
	1904	.011	7.50	12.50	25.00	100.00
	1904	1,355	—	—	Proof	90.00
	1904S	5.040	1.50	2.00	3.00	40.00
	1905	471 pcs.	—	—	Proof	135.00
	1906	500 pcs.	—	—	Proof	125.00

2.0000 g, .750 SILVER, .0482 oz ASW

KM#	Date	Mintage	Fine	VF	XF	Unc
169	1907	1.501	1.50	3.00	5.00	45.00
	1907S	4.930	1.00	2.50	3.50	40.00
	1908	500 pcs.	—	—	Proof	150.00
	1908S	3.364	1.00	1.75	3.50	40.00
	1909S	.312	8.00	20.00	40.00	220.00
	1910S	5-10 pcs.	Unknown in any collection			
	1911S	1.101	1.50	3.50	8.00	45.00
	1912S	1.010	1.50	4.00	8.00	50.00
	1913S	1.361	1.50	4.50	8.50	50.00
	1914S	1.180	2.50	5.00	12.50	150.00
	1915S	.450	7.00	15.00	30.00	200.00
	1917S	5.991	.75	1.75	2.50	20.00
	1918S	8.420	.75	1.75	2.50	20.00
	1919S	1.630	1.00	1.75	3.50	30.00
	1920	.520	4.00	5.00	10.00	65.00
	1921	3.863	.75	1.50	2.50	22.50
	1929M	1.000	.75	1.50	2.50	25.00
	1935M	1.280	.75	1.25	2.50	22.50

20 CENTAVOS

5.3849 g, .900 SILVER, .1558 oz ASW

KM#	Date	Mintage	Fine	VF	XF	Unc
166	1903	5.353	2.00	3.00	4.00	30.00
	1903	2,558	—	—	Proof	75.00
	1903S	.150	10.00	20.00	50.00	180.00
	1904	.011	12.00	25.00	40.00	120.00
	1904	1,355	—	—	Proof	90.00
	1904S	2.060	2.00	3.00	4.00	35.00
	1905	471 pcs.	—	—	Proof	200.00
	1905S	.420	6.00	8.00	17.50	80.00
	1906	500 pcs.	—	—	Proof	180.00

4.0000 g, .750 SILVER, .0965 oz ASW

KM#	Date	Mintage	Fine	VF	XF	Unc
170	1907	1.251	2.00	4.00	6.00	50.00
	1907S	3.165	2.00	3.00	5.00	35.00
	1908	500 pcs.	—	—	Proof	150.00
	1908S	1.535	2.00	3.00	5.00	35.00
	1909S	.450	3.00	8.00	20.00	185.00
	1910S	.500	3.00	8.00	20.00	200.00
	1911S	.505	3.00	8.00	20.00	150.00
	1912S	.750	2.00	5.00	10.00	100.00
	1913S/S	.949	7.00	15.00	25.00	150.00
	1913S	Inc. Ab.	2.00	5.00	8.00	75.00
	1914S	.795	1.50	3.00	8.00	75.00
	1915S	.655	1.50	3.00	15.00	120.00
	1916S	1.435	1.00	3.00	10.00	90.00
	1917S	3.151	.80	2.00	4.00	25.00
	1918S	5.560	.80	2.00	4.00	25.00
	1919S	.850	.80	2.00	6.00	40.00
	1920	1.046	1.00	3.00	10.00	90.00
	1921	1.843	.80	2.00	3.00	25.00
	1929M	1.970	.80	2.00	3.00	25.00

Mule. Obv: KM#170. Rev: 5 Centavos, KM#164.

KM#	Date	Mintage	Fine	VF	XF	Unc
174	1928/7M	.100	4.00	10.00	50.00	300.00

50 CENTAVOS

13.4784 g, .900 SILVER, .3900 oz ASW

KM#	Date	Mintage	Fine	VF	XF	Unc
167	1903	3.102	3.00	6.00	12.50	75.00
	1903	2,558	—	—	Proof	125.00
	1903S	—	2000.	3500.	5000.	—
	1904	.011	15.00	25.00	35.00	125.00
	1904	1,355	—	—	Proof	165.00
	1904S	2.160	3.00	6.50	12.50	125.00
	1905	471 pcs.	—	—	Proof	325.00
	1905S	.852	3.00	8.00	20.00	165.00
	1906	500 pcs.	—	—	Proof	275.00

10.0000 g, .750 SILVER, .2411 oz ASW

KM#	Date	Mintage	Fine	VF	XF	Unc
171	1907	1.201	2.00	5.00	10.00	75.00
	1907S	2.112	2.00	4.00	8.00	65.00
	1908	500 pcs.	—	—	Proof	275.00
	1908S	1.601	2.00	4.00	8.00	65.00
	1909S	.528	3.00	6.00	10.00	135.00
	1917S	.674	3.00	6.00	10.00	125.00
	1918S	2.202	2.00	4.00	6.00	60.00
	1919S	1.200	2.00	4.50	6.50	75.00
	1920	.420	2.00	4.00	6.00	50.00
	1921	2.317	2.00	4.00	6.00	25.00

PESO

26.9568 g, .900 SILVER, .7800 oz ASW

KM#	Date	Mintage	Fine	VF	XF	Unc
168	1903	2.791	6.00	12.00	30.00	165.00
	1903	2,558	—	—	Proof	250.00
	1903S	11.361	6.00	10.00	25.00	120.00
	1904	.011	35.00	65.00	125.00	275.00
	1904	1,355	—	—	Proof	260.00
	1904S	6.600	6.00	12.00	25.00	125.00
	1905	471 pcs.	—	—	Proof	850.00
	1905S	6.056	10.00	12.00	30.00	150.00
	1906	500 pcs.	—	—	Proof	500.00
	1906S	.201	400.00	700.00	1500.	5000.

20.0000 g, .800 SILVER, .5144 oz ASW

KM#	Date	Mintage	Fine	VF	XF	Unc
172	1907					
		2 pcs. known	—	—	Proof	Rare
	1907S	10.276	BV	5.00	10.00	80.00
	1908	500 pcs.	—	—	Proof	500.00
	1908S	20.955	BV	5.00	10.00	75.00
	1909S	7.578	BV	5.00	10.00	80.00
	1910S	3.154	BV	6.00	12.50	100.00
	1911S	.463	10.00	16.00	60.00	550.00
	1912S	.680	10.00	16.00	60.00	600.00

COMMONWEALTH

CENTAVO

BRONZE

KM#	Date	Mintage	Fine	VF	XF	Unc
179	1937M	15.790	.25	1.00	1.75	12.00
	1938M	10.000	.25	.75	1.50	10.00
	1939M	6.500	.25	1.00	2.00	15.00
	1940M	4.000	.25	.75	1.25	8.00
	1941M	5.000	.50	1.00	2.00	15.00
	1944S	58.000	.10	.15	.20	.50

5 CENTAVOS

COPPER-NICKEL

KM#	Date	Mintage	Fine	VF	XF	Unc
180	1937M	2.494	.75	1.50	3.00	17.50
	1938M	4.000	.50	1.25	2.00	10.00
	1941M	2.750	.75	1.50	2.50	15.00

COPPER-NICKEL-ZINC

KM#	Date	Mintage	Fine	VF	XF	Unc
180a	1944	21.198	.10	.15	.50	2.00
	1944S	14.040	.10	.15	.25	.75
	1945S	72.796	.10	.15	.20	.50

10 CENTAVOS

2.0000 g, .750 SILVER, .0482 oz ASW

KM#	Date	Mintage	Fine	VF	XF	Unc
181	1937M	3.500	.50	1.00	2.50	15.00
	1938M	3.750	.50	.75	1.75	10.00
	1938M M inverted W					
		—	—	—	—	—
	1941M	2.500	.50	1.00	2.00	12.00
	1944D	31.592	—	BV	.75	1.50
	1945D	137.208	—	BV	.50	1.00

20 CENTAVOS

4.0000 g, .750 SILVER, .0965 oz ASW

KM#	Date	Mintage	Fine	VF	XF	Unc
182	1937M	2.665	BV	1.00	2.25	12.00
	1938M	3.000	BV	1.00	2.00	8.00
	1941M	1.500	BV	1.00	2.00	8.00
	1944D	28.596	—	BV	1.00	2.50
	1944D/S	—	—	—	—	75.00
	1945D	82.804	—	BV	.75	1.50

50 CENTAVOS

10.0000 g, .750 SILVER, .2411 oz ASW
Establishment of the Commonwealth

KM#	Date	Mintage	Fine	VF	XF	Unc
176	1936	.020	15.00	25.00	35.00	65.00

KM#	Date	Mintage	Fine	VF	XF	Unc
183	1944S	19.187	—	BV	2.50	4.50
	1945S	18.120	—	BV	2.50	4.50

PESO

20.0000 g, .900 SILVER, .5787 oz ASW
Establishment of the Commonwealth
Presidents Roosevelt And Quezon

KM#	Date	Mintage	Fine	VF	XF	Unc
177	1936	.010	40.00	50.00	65.00	125.00

Establishment of the Commonwealth
Governor General Murphy And President Quezon
Rev: Similar to KM#177.

KM#	Date	Mintage	Fine	VF	XF	Unc
178	1936	.010	40.00	50.00	65.00	125.00

REPUBLIC

CENTAVO

BRONZE

KM#	Date	Mintage	Fine	VF	XF	Unc
186	1958	20.000	—	—	.10	.25
	1960	40.000	—	—	.10	.15
	1962	30.000	—	—	.10	.15
	1963	130.000	—	—	.10	.15

5 CENTAVOS

BRASS

KM#	Date	Mintage	Fine	VF	XF	Unc
187	1958	10.000	—	—	.10	.20
187	1959	10.000	—	—	.10	.20
	1960	40.000	—	—	.10	.15
	1962	40.000	—	—	.10	.20
	1963	50.000	—	—	.10	.15
	1964	100.000	—	—	—	.10
	1966	10.000	—	—	.10	.20

10 CENTAVOS

NICKEL-BRASS

KM#	Date	Mintage	Fine	VF	XF	Unc
188	1958	10.000	—	.10	.15	.25
	1960	70.000	—	.10	.15	.20
	1962	50.000	—	.10	.15	.20
	1963	50.000	—	.10	.15	.20
	1964	100.000	—	—	.10	.20
	1966	110.000	—	—	.10	.20

25 CENTAVOS

NICKEL-BRASS
Obv: 8 smoke rings from volcano.

KM#	Date	Mintage	Fine	VF	XF	Unc
189.1	1958	10.000	.10	.20	.25	.50
	1960	10.000	.10	.20	.30	.50
	1962	40.000	—	.10	.25	.50
	1964	49.800	—	.10	.20	.35
	1966	50.000	—	.10	.20	.40

Obv: 6 smoke rings from volcano.

KM#	Date	Mintage	Fine	VF	XF	Unc
189.2	1966	40.000	—	.10	.20	.40

50 CENTAVOS

10.0000 g, .750 SILVER, .2411 oz ASW
General Douglas Mac Arthur

KM#	Date	Mintage	Fine	VF	XF	Unc
184	1947S	.200	—	BV	2.50	4.00

NICKEL-BRASS

KM#	Date	Mintage	Fine	VF	XF	Unc
190	1958	5.000	.20	.30	.45	1.00
	1964	25.000	.10	.20	.30	.60

1/2 PESO

12.5000 g, .900 SILVER, .3617 oz ASW
100th Anniversary - Birth of Dr. Jose Rizal

KM#	Date	Mintage	Fine	VF	XF	Unc
191	1961	.100	—	—	3.00	5.00

PESO

20.0000 g, .900 SILVER, .5787 oz ASW
General Douglas Mac Arthur

KM#	Date	Mintage	Fine	VF	XF	Unc
185	1947S	.100	—	BV	7.00	12.50

26.6000 g, .900 SILVER, .7697 oz ASW
100th Anniversary - Birth of Dr. Jose Rizal

KM#	Date	Mintage	Fine	VF	XF	Unc
192	1961	.100	—	—	5.00	8.00

100th Anniversary - Birth of Andres Bonifacio

KM#	Date	Mintage	Fine	VF	XF	Unc
193	1963	.100	—	—	5.00	8.00

100th Anniversary - Birth of Apolinario Mabini

KM#	Date	Mintage	Fine	VF	XF	Unc
194	1964	.100	—	—	5.00	8.00

25th Anniversary of Bataan Day

KM#	Date	Mintage	Fine	VF	XF	Unc
195	1967	.100	—	—	5.00	8.00

NOTE: KM#195 is a proof-like issue.

MONETARY REFORM

100 Sentimos = 1 Piso

SENTIMO

ALUMINUM
Lapu-Lapu

KM#	Date	Mintage	VF	XF	Unc
196	1967	10.000	—	—	.10
	1968	27.940	—	—	.10
	1969	12.060	—	—	.10
	1970	130.000	—	—	.10
	1974	165.000	—	—	.10
	1974	.010	—	Proof	5.00

KM#	Date	Mintage	VF	XF	Unc
205	1975FM(M)	.108	—	—	.10
	1975FM(U)	5,875	—	—	2.00
	1975FM(P)	.037	—	Proof	1.50
	1975 Lt	10.000	—	—	.10
	1975(US)	60.190	—	—	.10
	1976FM(M)	.010	—	—	.10
	1976FM(U)	1,826	—	1.00	2.50
	1976FM(P)	9,901	—	Proof	2.00
	1976(US)	60.000	—	—	.10
	1977	4.808	—	—	.10
	1977FM(M)	.010	—	—	1.00
	1977FM(U)	354 pcs.	—	—	4.00
	1977FM(P)	4,822	—	Proof	2.00
	1978	24.813	—	—	.10
	1978FM(U)	.010	—	—	1.00
	1978FM(P)	4,792	—	Proof	2.00

Rev: Redesigned seal.

KM#	Date	Mintage	VF	XF	Unc
224	1979BSP	—	—	—	.10
	1979FM(U)	.010	—	—	1.00
	1979FM(P)	3,645	—	Proof	2.00
	1980BSP	12.601	—	—	.10
	1980FM(U)	.010	—	—	1.00
	1980FM(P)	3,133	—	Proof	2.00
	1981BSP	33.391	—	—	.10
	1981FM(U)	—	—	—	1.00
	1981FM(P)	1,795	—	Proof	2.00
	1982BSP	51.730	—	—	.10
	1982FM(P)	—	—	Proof	2.00

King Lapu-Lapu - Sea Shell

KM#	Date	Mintage	VF	XF	Unc
238	1983	62.090	—	—	.10
	1983	—	—	Proof	2.00
	1984	.320	—	—	.10
	1985	.016	—	—	.10
	1986	.080	—	—	.10
	1987	13.570	—	—	.10
	1988	26.861	—	—	.10
	1989	—	—	—	.10
	1990	—	—	—	.10

5 SENTIMOS

BRASS
Melchora Aquino

KM#	Date	Mintage	VF	XF	Unc
197	1967	40.000	—	—	.10
	1968	50.000	—	—	.10
	1970	5.000	—	.10	.20
	1972	71.744	—	—	.10
	1974	90.025	—	—	.10
	1974	.010	—	Proof	5.00

KM#	Date	Mintage	VF	XF	Unc
206	1975FM(M)	.104	—	—	.10
	1975FM(U)	5,875	—	—	2.50
	1975FM(P)	.037	—	Proof	2.00
	1975(US)	98.928	—	—	.10
	1975 Lt	10.000	—	—	.10
	1976FM(M)	.010	—	—	1.50
	1976FM(U)	1,826	—	—	5.00
	1976FM(P)	9,901	—	Proof	2.50
	1976(US)	98.000	—	—	.10
	1977	19.367	—	—	.10
	1977FM(M)	.010	—	—	1.50
	1977FM(U)	354 pcs.	—	—	4.00
	1977FM(P)	4,822	—	Proof	2.50
	1978	61.838	—	—	.10
	1978FM(U)	.010	—	—	1.50
	1978FM(P)	4,792	—	Proof	2.50

Rev: Redesigned seal.

KM#	Date	Mintage	VF	XF	Unc
225	1979BSP	12.805	—	—	.10
	1979FM(U)	.010	—	—	1.00
	1979FM(P)	3,645	—	Proof	2.50
	1980BSP	111.339	—	—	.10
	1980FM(U)	.010	—	—	1.00
	1980FM(P)	3,133	—	Proof	2.50
	1981BSP	—	—	—	.10
	1981FM(U)	—	—	—	1.00
	1981FM(P)	1,795	—	Proof	3.00
	1982BSP	—	—	—	.10
	1982FM(P)	—	—	Proof	3.00

ALUMINUM
Waling-Waling Orchid

KM#	Date	Mintage	VF	XF	Unc
239	1983	100.016	—	—	.10
	1983	—	—	Proof	2.00
	1984	141.744	—	—	.10
	1985	50.416	—	—	.10
	1986	11.664	—	—	.10
	1987	79.008	—	—	.10
	1988	90.487	—	—	.10
	1989	—	—	—	.10
	1990	—	—	—	.10
	1991	—	—	—	.10

10 SENTIMOS

COPPER-NICKEL
Francisco Baltasar

KM#	Date	Mintage	VF	XF	Unc
198	1967	50.000	—	—	.10
	1968	60.000	—	—	.10
	1969	40.000	—	—	.10
	1970	50.000	—	—	.10
	1971	80.000	—	—	.10
	1972	121.390	—	—	.10
	1974	60.208	—	—	.10
	1974	.010	—	Proof	7.50

KM#	Date	Mintage	VF	XF	Unc
207	1975FM(M)	.104	—	—	.10
	1975FM(U)	5,875	—	—	2.50
	1975FM(P)	.037	—	Proof	2.00
	1975(VDM)	10.000	—	—	.10
	1975(US)	50.000	—	—	.10
	1976FM(M)	.010	—	—	.15
	1976FM(U)	1,826	—	—	6.00
	1976FM(P)	9,901	—	Proof	3.00
	1976(US)	50.000	—	—	.10
	1977	29.314	—	—	.10
	1977FM(M)	.010	—	—	1.50
	1977FM(U)	354 pcs.	—	—	6.50
	1977FM(P)	4,822	—	Proof	3.00
	1978	60.042	—	—	.10
	1978FM(U)	.010	—	—	2.00
	1978FM(P)	4,792	—	Proof	3.00

Rev: Redesigned seal.

KM#	Date	Mintage	VF	XF	Unc
226	1979BSP	6.446	—	—	.10
	1979FM(U)	.010	—	—	1.00
	1979FM(P)	3,645	—	Proof	3.00
	1980BSP	—	—	—	.10
	1980FM(U)	.010	—	—	1.00
	1980FM(P)	3,133	—	Proof	3.25
	1981BSP	—	—	—	.10
	1981FM(U)	—	—	—	1.00
	1981FM(P)	1,795	—	Proof	3.50
	1982BSP	—	—	—	.10
	1982FM(P)	—	—	Proof	3.50

NOTE: Varieties with thick and thin legends exist for coins with BSP mint mark.

ALUMINUM
World Conference on Fisheries - F.A.O.
Rev: Fish's name in error: PANDAKA PYGMEA

KM#	Date	Mintage	VF	XF	Unc
240.1	1983	95.640	—	—	.10
	1983	—	—	Proof	3.00
	1987	Inc. Be.	—	—	.10

Rev: Fish's name: PANDAKA PYGMAEA

KM#	Date	Mintage	VF	XF	Unc
240.2	1983	—	—	—	.10
	1984	235.900	—	—	.10
	1985	90.169	—	—	.10
	1986	4.270	—	—	.10
	1987	99.520	—	—	.10
	1988	117.166	—	—	.10
	1989	—	—	—	.10
	1990	—	—	—	.10
	1991	—	—	—	.10
	1992	—	—	—	.10

25 SENTIMOS

COPPER-NICKEL
Juan Luna

KM#	Date	Mintage	VF	XF	Unc
199	1967	40.000	—	.10	.25
	1968	10.000	—	.10	.25
	1969	10.000	—	.10	.25
	1970	40.000	—	.10	.25
	1971	60.000	—	.10	.25
	1972	90.000	—	.10	.25
	1974	10.000	—	.10	.25
	1974	.010	—	Proof	15.00

KM#	Date	Mintage	VF	XF	Unc
208	1975FM(M)	.104	—	—	.40
	1975FM(U)	5,875	—	—	3.50
	1975FM(P)	.037	—	Proof	3.00
	1975(US)	10.000	—	.10	.25
	1975(VDM)	10.000	—	.10	.25
	1976FM(M)	.010	—	.10	.25
	1976FM(U)	1,826	—	—	8.00
	1976FM(P)	9,901	—	Proof	3.50
	1976(US)	10.000	—	.10	.25
	1977	24.654	—	.10	.25
	1977FM(M)	.010	—	—	1.50
	1977FM(U)	354 pcs.	—	—	8.00
	1977FM(P)	4,822	—	Proof	4.50
	1978	40.466	—	.10	.25
	1978FM(U)	.010	—	—	2.50
	1978FM(P)	4,792	—	Proof	4.00

Rev: Redesigned seal.

KM#	Date	Mintage	VF	XF	Unc
227	1979BSP	20.725	—	.10	.25
	1979FM(U)	.010	—	—	1.50
	1979FM(P)	3,645	—	Proof	4.50
	1980BSP	—	—	.10	.25
	1980FM(U)	.010	—	—	1.50
	1980FM(P)	3,133	—	Proof	4.50
	1981BSP	—	—	.10	.25
	1981FM(U)	—	—	—	1.50
	1981FM(P)	1,795	—	Proof	5.00
	1982BSP	—	—	.10	.25
	1982FM(P)	—	—	Proof	5.00

BRASS
Butterfly

KM#	Date	Mintage	VF	XF	Unc
241.1	1983	92.944	—	.10	.25
	1983	—	—	Proof	3.00
	1984	254.324	—	.10	.25
	1985	84.922	—	.10	.25
	1986	65.284	—	.10	.25
	1987	1.680	—	.10	.25
	1988	51.062	—	—	.25
	1989	—	—	—	.25
	1990	—	—	—	.25

Reduced size.

KM#	Date	Mintage	VF	XF	Unc
241.2	1991	—	—	—	.25
	1992	—	—	—	.25
	1994	—	—	—	.25

50 SENTIMOS

COPPER-NICKEL-ZINC
Marcelo H. del Pilar

KM#	Date	Mintage	VF	XF	Unc
200	1967	20.000	.10	.20	.50
	1971	10.000	.10	.20	.60
	1972 serif on 2				
		30.000	.10	.20	.50
	1972 plain 2	20.517	.10	.20	.50
	1974	5.004	.10	.20	.60
	1974	.010	—	Proof	25.00
	1975	5.714	.10	.20	.60

COPPER-NICKEL
Monkey-eating Eagle
Eagle's name - PITHECOPHAGA

KM#	Date	Mintage	VF	XF	Unc
242.1	1983	27.644	—	.10	.25
	1983	—	—	Proof	5.00
	1984	121.408	—	.10	.25
	1985	107.048	—	.10	.25
	1986	120.000	—	.10	.25
	1987	1.078	—	.10	.25
	1988	24.008	—	.10	.25
	1989	—	—	.10	.25
	1990	—	—	.10	.25

Error. Eagle's name - PITHECOBHAGA

KM#	Date	Mintage	VF	XF	Unc
242.2	1983	Inc. Ab.	—	.10	.25

BRASS
Reduced size.

KM#	Date	Mintage	VF	XF	Unc
242.3	1991	—	—	.10	.25
	1992	—	—	.10	.25

PISO

26.4500 g, .900 SILVER, .7653 oz ASW
Centennial Birth of Aguinaldo

KM#	Date	Mintage	VF	XF	Unc
201	1969	.100	—	5.00	8.00

NOTE: These coins are 'proof-like' issues.

NICKEL
Pope Paul VI Visit

KM#	Date	Mintage	VF	XF	Unc
202	1970	.070	—	1.00	2.00

26.4500 g, .900 SILVER, .7653 oz ASW

KM#	Date	Mintage	VF	XF	Unc
202a	1970	.030	—	7.00	12.50

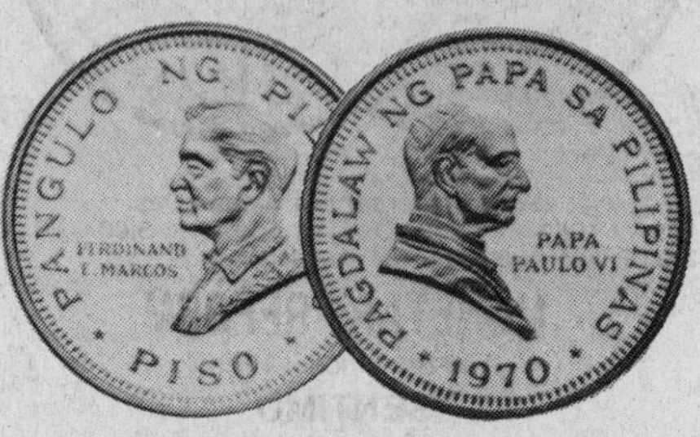

19.3000 g, .917 GOLD, .5691 oz AGW

KM#	Date	Mintage	VF	XF	Unc
202b	1970	1,000	—	—	400.00

COPPER-NICKEL
Jose Rizal

KM#	Date	Mintage	VF	XF	Unc
203	1972	121.821	.15	.25	.75
	1974	45.631	.15	.25	.75
	1974	.010	—	Proof	37.50

KM#	Date	Mintage	VF	XF	Unc
209.1	1975FM(M)	.104	—	—	1.00
	1975FM(U)	5,877	—	—	3.50
	1975FM(P)	.037	—	Proof	3.00
	1975(VDM)	10.000	.15	.25	.75
	1975(US)	30.000	.15	.25	.75
	1976FM(M)	.010	—	—	1.00
	1976FM(U)	1,826	—	—	10.00
	1976FM(P)	9,901	—	Proof	5.00
	1976(US)	30.000	.15	.25	.75
	1977	14.771	.15	.25	.75
	1977FM(M)	.012	—	—	4.00
	1977FM(U)	354 pcs.	—	—	10.00
	1977FM(P)	4,822	—	Proof	5.50
	1978	19.408	.15	.25	.75
	1978FM(U)	.010	—	—	4.00
	1978FM(P)	4,792	—	Proof	5.50

Rev. leg: ISANG BANSA ISANG DIWA below shield.

KM#	Date	Mintage	VF	XF	Unc
209.2	1979BSP	.321	.15	.25	1.00
	1979FM(U)	.010	—	—	2.50
	1979FM(P)	3,645	—	Proof	6.00
	1980BSP	19.693	.15	.25	.75
	1980FM(U)	.010	—	—	2.50
	1980FM(P)	3,133	—	Proof	12.50
	1981BSP	7.944	.15	.25	.75
	1981FM(U)	—	—	—	3.00
	1981FM(P)	1,795	—	Proof	6.00
	1982FM(P)	—	—	Proof	6.00
	1982BSP large date				
		52.110	.15	.25	.75
	1982BSP small date				
		Inc. Ab.	.15	.25	.75

Tamaraw Bull

KM#	Date	Mintage	VF	XF	Unc
243.1	1983	55.869	.10	.20	.50
	1983	—	—	Proof	7.00
	1984	4.997	.10	.20	.50
	1985	182.592	.10	.20	.50
	1986	19.072	.10	.20	.50
	1987	1.391	.10	.20	.50
	1988	54.636	—	—	.50
	1989	—	—	—	.50
	1990	—	—	—	.50

STAINLESS STEEL
Reduced size.

KM#	Date	Mintage	VF	XF	Unc
243.2	1992	—	—	—	.50

COPPER-NICKEL
Philippine Cultures Decade

KM#	Date	Mintage	VF	XF	Unc
251	1989	—	—	—	1.00

Waterfall, Ship and Flower

KM#	Date	Mintage	VF	XF	Unc
257	1991	—	—	—	1.00

2 PISO

COPPER-NICKEL
Andres Bonifacio

KM#	Date	Mintage	VF	XF	Unc
244	1983	15.640	.15	.30	1.00
	1983	—	—	Proof	10.00
	1984	121.111	.15	.30	1.00
	1985	115.211	.15	.30	1.00
	1986	25.260	.15	.30	1.00
	1987	2.196	.15	.30	1.00
	1988	16.094	—	—	1.00
	1989	—	—	—	1.00
	1990	—	—	—	1.00

Elpidio Quirino

KM#	Date	Mintage	VF	XF	Unc
253	ND(1991)	10.000	—	—	1.50

Jose Laurel

KM#	Date	Mintage	VF	XF	Unc
256	ND(1992)	—	—	—	1.50

STAINLESS STEEL
Andres Bonifacio

KM#	Date	Mintage	VF	XF	Unc
258	1991	—	—	—	1.00

5 PISO

NICKEL
Ferdinand E. Marcos

KM#	Date	Mintage	VF	XF	Unc
210.1	1975FM(M)	3,850	—	—	15.00
	1975FM(U)	7,875	—	—	10.00
210.1	1975FM(P)	.039	—	Proof	7.50
	1975(Sh)	20.000	.50	.75	1.50
	1976FM(M)	.010	—	—	5.00
	1976FM(U)	1,826	—	—	17.50
	1976FM(P)	9,901	—	Proof	7.50
	1977FM(M)	.010	—	—	5.00
	1977FM(U)	354 pcs.	—	—	15.00
	1977FM(P)	4,822	—	Proof	7.50
	1978FM(U)	.010	—	—	5.00
	1978FM(P)	4,792	—	Proof	7.50
	1982	—	.50	.75	1.50

Obv. leg: ISANG BANSA ISANG DIWA below shield.

KM#	Date	Mintage	VF	XF	Unc
210.2	1979FM(U)	.010	—	—	3.00
	1979FM(P)	3,645	—	Proof	8.00
	1980FM(U)	.010	—	—	3.00
	1980FM(P)	3,133	—	Proof	8.00
	1981FM(U)	.011	—	—	3.00
	1981FM(P)	1,795	—	Proof	10.00
	1982FM(P)	—	—	Proof	10.00

NICKEL-BRASS
Emilio Aquinaldo - Pterocarpus Indicus Flower

KM#	Date	Mintage	VF	XF	Unc
259	1991	—	—	—	3.50

10 PISO

NICKEL
People Power Revolution

KM#	Date	Mintage	VF	XF	Unc
250	1988	—	—	—	8.00

25 PISO

26.4000 g, .900 SILVER, .7639 oz ASW
25th Anniversary of Bank

KM#	Date	Mintage	VF	XF	Unc
204	1974	.090	—	—	10.00
	1974	.010	—	Proof	17.50

25.0000 g, .500 SILVER, .4018 oz ASW
Emilio Aguinaldo

KM#	Date	Mintage	VF	XF	Unc
211	1975FM(M)	.010	—	—	10.00
	1975FM(U)	5,875	—	—	15.00
	1975FM(P)	.037	—	Proof	15.00

F.A.O. Issue

KM#	Date	Mintage	VF	XF	Unc
214	1976FM(M)	.022	—	—	12.00
	1976FM(U)	1,826	—	—	40.00
	1976FM(P)	9,901	—	Proof	20.00

Banoiue Rice Terraces

KM#	Date	Mintage	VF	XF	Unc
217	1977FM(M)	.010	—	—	15.00
	1977FM(U)	354 pcs.	—	—	50.00
	1977FM(P)	4,822	—	Proof	30.00

100th Anniversary of Birth of Quezon

KM#	Date	Mintage	VF	XF	Unc
221	1978FM(U)	.010	—	—	14.00
	1978FM(P)	9,930	—	Proof	16.00

UN Conference on Trade and Development

KM#	Date	Mintage	VF	XF	Unc
228	1979FM(U)	.010	—	—	15.00
	1979FM(P)	7,093	—	Proof	20.00

100th Anniversary - Birth of Gen. Douglas MacArthur

KM#	Date	Mintage	VF	XF	Unc
230	1980FM(U)	9,800	—	—	17.50
	1980FM(P)	6,318	—	Proof	37.50

World Food Day

KM#	Date	Mintage	VF	XF	Unc
232	1981FM(U)	.010	—	—	15.00
	1981FM(P)	3,033	—	Proof	22.50

Presidents Marcos and Reagan

KM#	Date	Mintage	VF	XF	Unc
235	1982	8,000	—	—	50.00
	1982	250 pcs.	—	Proof	525.00

18.4100 g, .925 SILVER, .5475 oz ASW
President Aquino Visit in Washington

KM#	Date	Mintage	VF	XF	Unc
246	1986	*1,000	—	Proof	200.00

50 PISO

27.4000 g, .925 SILVER, .8148 oz ASW
3rd Anniversary of the New Society

KM#	Date	Mintage	VF	XF	Unc
212	1975FM(M)	.010	—	—	14.00
	1975FM(U)	7,875	—	—	17.50
	1975FM(P)	.054	—	Proof	12.50

I.M.F. Meeting

KM#	Date	Mintage	VF	XF	Unc
215	1976	5,477	—	Proof	17.50
	1976FM(M)	.010	—	—	14.00
	1976FM(U)	1,826	—	—	60.00
	1976FM(P)	.015	—	Proof	14.00

Inauguration of New Mint Facilities

KM#	Date	Mintage	VF	XF	Unc
218	1977FM(M)	.010	—	—	16.50
	1977FM(U)	354 pcs.	—	—	80.00
	1977FM(P)	6,704	—	Proof	22.50

100th Anniversary of Birth of Quezon

KM#	Date	Mintage	VF	XF	Unc
222	1978FM(U)	.010	—	—	15.00
	1978FM(P)	9,969	—	Proof	20.00

International Year of the Child

KM#	Date	Mintage	VF	XF	Unc
229	1979FM(U)	.010	—	—	14.00
	1979FM(P)	.027	—	Proof	12.50

Pope John Paul II Visit

KM#	Date	Mintage	VF	XF	Unc
233	1981FM(U)	.010	—	—	30.00
	1981FM(P)	3,353	—	Proof	60.00

40th Anniversary of Bataan-Corregidor

KM#	Date	Mintage	VF	XF	Unc
236	1982FM(U)	.013	—	—	15.00
	1982FM(P)	4,626	—	Proof	40.00

100 PISO

25.0000 g, .500 SILVER, .4019 oz ASW
75th Anniversary of Philippine National University

KM#	Date	Mintage	VF	XF	Unc
245	1983	.015	—	—	15.00
	1983	2,000	—	Proof	35.00

150 PISO

16.8200 g, .925 SILVER, .5002 oz ASW
Southeast Asian Games - Logo

KM#	Date	Mintage	VF	XF	Unc
254	1991	5,000	—	Proof	30.00

200 PISO

25.0000 g, .925 SILVER, .7436 oz ASW
World Wildlife Fund - Mindoro Buffalo

KM#	Date	Mintage	VF	XF	Unc
248	1987	.025	—	Proof	25.00

Save the Children Fund

KM#	Date	Mintage	VF	XF	Unc
252	1990	*.020	—	Proof	45.00

500 PISO

28.0000 g, .925 SILVER, .8328 oz ASW
People Power Revolution

KM#	Date	Mintage	VF	XF	Unc
249	1988	*7,500	—	Proof	50.00

1000 PISO

9.9500 g, .900 GOLD, .2879 oz AGW
3rd Anniversary of the New Society

KM#	Date	Mintage	VF	XF	Unc
213	1975	.023	—	—	135.00
	1975	.013	—	Proof	150.00

1500 PISO

20.5500 g, .900 GOLD, .5947 oz AGW

I.M.F. Meeting

KM#	Date	Mintage	VF	XF	Unc
216	1976	5,500	—	—	275.00
	1976	6,500	—	Proof	300.00

5th Anniversary of the New Society

219	1977	4,000	—	—	275.00
	1977	6,000	—	Proof	300.00

Inauguration of New Mint Facilities

223	1978	3,000	—	—	300.00
	1978	3,000	—	Proof	325.00

9.9500 g, .900 GOLD, .2879 oz AGW
Pope John Paul II Visit

234	1981	1,000	—	Proof	350.00

9.7800 g, .900 GOLD, .2830 oz AGW
40th Anniversary of Bataan-Corregidor

237	1982FM(U)	1,000	—	—	300.00
	1982FM(P)	445 pcs.	—	Proof	550.00

2500 PISO

14.5700 g, .500 GOLD, .2342 oz AGW
100th Anniversary - Birth of
Gen. Douglas MacArthur

231	1980FM(P)	3,073	—	Proof	350.00

15.0000 g, .500 GOLD, .2414 oz AGW
President Aquino Visit in Washington

KM#	Date	Mintage	VF	XF	Unc
247	1986	250 pcs.	—	Proof	600.00

5000 PISO

68.7400 g, .900 GOLD, 1.9893 oz AGW
5th Anniversary of the New Society

220	1977FM(U)	100 pcs.	—	—	1400.
	1977FM(P)	3,832	—	Proof	1200.

10000 PESOS

33.5500 g, .925 GOLD, 1.0000 oz AGW
People Power

255	1992	1,600	—	Proof	850.00

MINT SETS (MS)

KM#	Date	Mintage	Identification	Issue Price	Mkt. Val.
MS1	1936(3)	—	KM176-178	—	325.00
MS2	1947(2)	—	KM184-185	—	20.00
MS3	1958(5)	—	KM186-190	—	2.50
MS4	1970(2)	—	KM202,202a	—	15.00
MS5	1975(8)	*5,877	KM205-208,209.1, 210-212	33.50	35.00
MS6	1975(8)	3,850	KM205-208,209.1, 210-212	—	55.00
MS7	1976(8)	1,826*	KM205-210,214-215	—	150.00
MS8	1976(8)	10,000	KM205-210,214-215	—	35.00
MS9	1977(8)	354*	KM205-210,217-218	—	175.00
MS10	1977(8)	10,000	KM205-210,217-218	—	35.00
MS11	1978(8)	10,000	KM205-210,221-222	—	35.00
MS12	1979(8)	10,000	KM209.2-210.2,224-229	—	35.00
MS13	1980(7)	9,800	KM209.2-210.2,224-227, 230	—	25.00
MS14	1981(8)	10,000	KM209.2-210.2,224-227, 232-233	—	50.00
MSA15	1983(8)	—	KM238-239,240.2,241, 242.1,243-245BRM	—	17.50
MS15	1983(7)	—	KM238-239,240.1,241, 242.1,243-244	—	6.00
MS16	1989(7)	—	KM238-239,240.2,241, 242.1,243-244	—	6.00
MS17	1990(7)	—	KM238-239,240.2,241, 242.1,243-244	—	6.00

***NOTE:** Enclosed in Franklin Mint folder.

PROOF SETS (PS)

KM#	Date	Mintage	Identification	Issue Price	Mkt. Val.
PS1	1903(7)	2,558	KM162-168	—	600.00
PS1i	1903(7)	Inc. Ab.	KM162-168 (impaired)	—	350.00
PS2	1904(7)	1,355	KM162-168	—	800.00
PS2i	1904(7)	Inc. Ab.	KM162-168 (impaired)	—	450.00
PS3	1905(7)	471	KM162-168	—	1250.
PS3i	1905(7)	Inc. Ab.	KM162-168 (impaired)	—	550.00
PS4	1906(7)	500	KM162-168	—	1100.
PS4i	1906(7)	Inc. Ab.	KM162-168 (impaired)	—	500.00
PS5	1908(7)	500	KM162-164,169-172	—	1000.
PS5i	1908(7)	Inc. Ab.	KM162-164,169-172 (impaired)	—	500.00
PS6	1958(5)	—	KM186-190	—	—
PS7	1974(6)	*10,000	KM196-200,203	—	95.00
PS8	1975(8)	36,516	KM205-208,209.1-210.1, 211-212	67.00	50.00
PS9	1975(6)	—	KM205-208,209.1-210.1	—	—
PS10	1976(8)	9,901	KM205-208,209.1-210.1, 214-215	67.00	60.00
PS11	1977(8)	4,822	KM205-208,209.1-210.1, 217-218	70.00	80.00
PS12	1978(8)	4,792	KM205-208,209.1-210.1, 220-221	70.00	75.00
PS13	1978(2)	3,911	KM221-222	46.00	50.00
PS14	1979(8)	3,645	KM209.2-210.2,224-229	68.00	60.00
PS15	1979(2)	2,448	KM228-229	47.50	35.00
PS16	1980(7)	3,133	KM209.2-210.2,224-227, 230	65.00	50.00
PS17	1981(8)	1,795	KM209.2-210.2,224-227, 232-233	—	115.00
PS18	1982(7)	—	KM209.2-210.2,224-227, 236	52.00	70.00
PS19	1983(8)	—	KM238-239,240.1,241, 242.1,243-245	50.00	70.00
PS20	1986(2)	—	KM246-247	—	950.00

***NOTE:** Not released to the general public.

CULION ISLAND

LEPROSARIUM COINAGE

Culion Leper Colony

The Culion Leper Colony was established around 1903 on the island of Culion about 150 miles southeast of Manila by the Commission of Public Health. The first issue of coins valid only in the colony was produced by a private firm, Frank & Company. Later issues were struck at the Manila Mint.

MINT MARKS

PM = Philippine Mint at Manila

MONETARY SYSTEM

100 Centavos = 1 Peso

1/2 CENTAVO

ALUMINUM

KM#	Date	Mintage	Fine	VF	XF	Unc
1	1913	.017	.50	1.00	2.00	5.00

NOTE: Some authorities doubt that this coin circulated.

CENTAVO

ALUMINUM

KM#	Date	Mintage	Good	VG	Fine	VF
2	1913	.033	25.00	45.00	80.00	150.00

COPPER-NICKEL
Similar to KM#4 but 1st die; better strike.

3	1927PM	.030	5.00	10.00	15.00	40.00

2nd die, poor strike.

4	1927PM	Inc. Ab.	6.00	12.00	20.00	45.00

Obv: Bust of Rizal in circle.
Rev: PHILIPPINE HEALTH SERVICE/

LEPER COIN ONE CENTAVO.

KM#	Date	Mintage	Good	VG	Fine	VF
5	1930	—	Reported, not confirmed			

5 CENTAVOS

ALUMINUM

6	1913	6,600	30.00	60.00	150.00	250.00

COPPER-NICKEL

7	1927	.016	2.50	5.00	8.00	15.00

10 CENTAVOS

ALUMINUM

Similar to 1/2 Centavo, KM#1.

8	1913	6,600	4.00	6.50	10.00	35.00

Similar to 1 Peso, KM#14.

9	1920	.020	2.50	5.00	7.50	20.00

COPPER-NICKEL

KM#	Date	Mintage	VG	Fine	VF	XF
10	1930	.017	1.00	2.00	3.50	10.00

NOTE: One pattern exists in copper, but it has not been authenticated.

20 CENTAVOS

ALUMINUM

Similar to 1/2 Centavo, KM#1.

KM#	Date	Mintage	Good	VG	Fine	VF
11	1913	.010	5.00	10.00	18.00	50.00

12	1920	.010	2.50	5.00	10.00	20.00

COPPER-NICKEL

KM#	Date	Mintage	VG	Fine	VF	XF
13	1922PM	.010	5.00	10.00	17.50	30.00

PESO

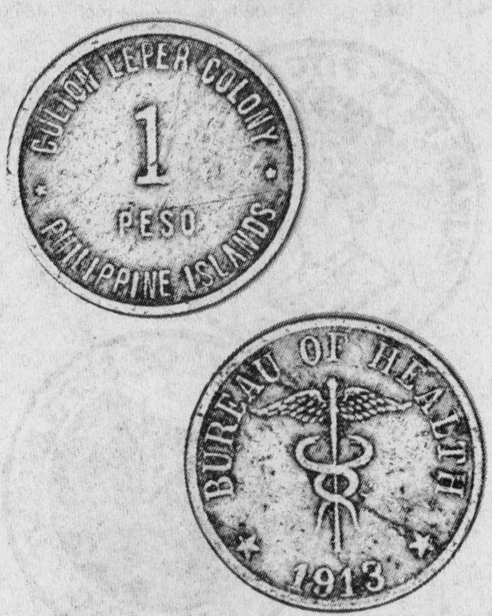

ALUMINUM

KM#	Date	Mintage	VG	Fine	VF	XF
14	1913	8,600	1.50	3.50	7.50	25.00

NOTE: This coin exists with thick and thin planchets.

15	1920	4,000	3.00	8.00	15.00	35.00

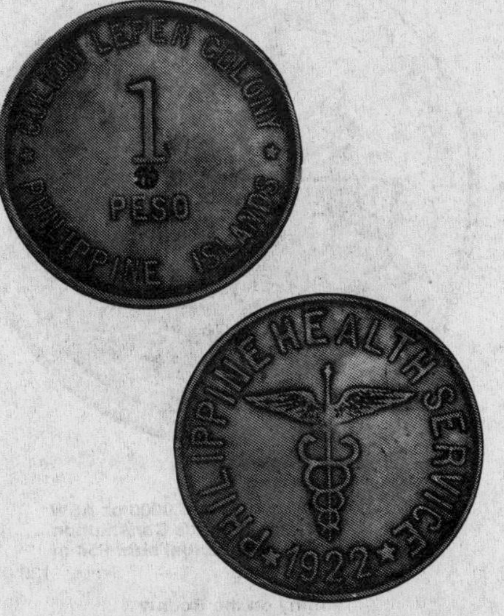

COPPER-NICKEL

16	1922PM	8,280	3.00	7.00	12.00	20.00

Similar to KM#16, but caduceus has curved wings.

17	1922PM	Inc. Ab.	20.00	35.00	50.00	100.00

KM#	Date	Mintage	VG	Fine	VF	XF
18	1925	.020	1.00	2.50	5.00	10.00

PITCAIRN ISLANDS

A small volcanic island, along with the uninhabited islands of Oeno, Henderson, and Ducie, constitute the British Colony of Pitcairn Islands. The main island has an area of about 2 sq. mi. (47 sq. km.) and a population of *68. It is located 1350 miles southeast of Tahiti. The islanders subsist on fishing, garden produce and crops. The sale of postage stamps and carved curios to passing ships brings cash income.

Discovered in 1767 by a British naval officer, Pitcairn was not occupied until 1790 when Fletcher Christian and nine mutineers from the British ship, HMS Bounty, along with some Tahitian men and women went ashore, and survived in obscurity until discovered by American whalers in 1808.

Adamstown is the chief settlement, located on the north coast, one of the few places that island-made longboats can land. The primary religion is Seventh-day Adventist and a public school provides basic education. In 1898 the settlement was placed under the jurisdiction of the Commissioner for the Western Pacific. Since 1952, the colony has been governed through locally elected officers and an island council.

New Zealand currency has been used since July 10, 1967.

DOLLAR

COPPER-NICKEL
Drafting of Pitcairn Islands Constitution

KM#	Date	Mintage	VF	XF	Unc
3	1988	—	—	—	6.50
	28.2800 g, .925 SILVER, .8411 oz ASW				
3a	1988	—	—	Proof	45.00

COPPER-NICKEL
Mutiny on the Bounty

KM#	Date	Mintage	VF	XF	Unc
4	1989	*.050	—	—	6.50
	28.2800 g, .925 SILVER, .8411 oz ASW				
4a	1989	*.020	—	Proof	45.00

COPPER-NICKEL
Burning of the HMAV Bounty

KM#	Date	Mintage	VF	XF	Unc
7	1990	—	—	—	6.50
	28.2800 g, .925 SILVER, .8411 oz ASW				
7a	1990	.010	—	Proof	45.00

50 DOLLARS

155.6000 g, .999 SILVER, 5.0000 oz ASW
Drafting of Pitcairn Islands Constitution
Illustration reduced. Actual size: 65mm

KM#	Date	Mintage	VF	XF	Unc
1	1988	*.010	—	Proof	130.00
	Mutiny on the Bounty **Similar to 250 Dollars, KM#2.**				
5	1989	*.010	—	Proof	130.00
	Burning of the HMAV Bounty **Similar to 250 Dollars, KM#9.**				
8	1990	*2,500	—	Proof	145.00

250 DOLLARS

15.9800 g, .917 GOLD, .4708 oz AGW
Drafting of Pitcairn Islands Constitution

KM#	Date	Mintage	VF	XF	Unc
2	1988	*2,500	—	Proof	350.00

Mutiny on the Bounty

KM#	Date	Mintage	VF	XF	Unc
6	1989	*2,500	—	Proof	350.00

Burning of the HMAV Bounty

KM#	Date	Mintage	VF	XF	Unc
9	1990	*500 pcs.	—	Proof	450.00

POLAND

The Republic of Poland, located in central Europe, has an area of 120,725 sq. mi. (312,680 sq. km.) and a population of *38.2 million. Capital: Warsaw. The economy is essentially agricultural, but industrial activity provides the products for foreign trade. Machinery, coal, coke, iron, steel and transport equipment are exported.

Poland, which began as a Slavic duchy in the 10th century and reached its peak of power between the 14th and 16th centuries, has had a turbulent history of invasion, occupation or partition by Mongols, Turkey, Hungary, Sweden, Austria, Prussia and Russia.

The first partition took place in 1772. Prussia took Polish Pomerania. Russia took part of the eastern provinces. Austria took Galicia, in which lay the fortress city of Kracow (Crakow). The second partition occurred in 1793 when Russia took another slice of the eastern provinces and Prussia took what remained of western Poland. The third partition, 1795, literally removed Poland from the map. Russia took what was left of the eastern provinces. Prussia seized most of central Poland, including Warsaw. Austria took what was left of the south. Napoleon restored to Poland much of the territory lost to Prussia and Austria, but after his defeat another partition returned the Duchy of Warsaw to Prussia, made Kracow into a tiny republic, and declared what remained to be the Kingdom of Poland under the czar and in permanent union with Russia.

Poland re-emerged as an independent state recognized by the Treaty of Versailles on June 28, 1919, and maintained its independence until 1939 when it was invaded by, and partitioned between, Germany and Russia. Poland's present boundaries were determined by the U.S.-BritishRussian agreement of Aug. 16, 1945. The Polish CommunistSocialist faction won a decisive victory at the polls in 1947 and established a 'Peoples Republic' of the Soviet type in 1952. On December 29, 1989 Poland was proclaimed the Republic of Poland.

RULERS

Friedrich August I, King of Saxony,
As Grand Duke, 1807-1814
Alexander I, Czar of Russia,
As King, 1815-1825
Nicholas (Mikolay) I, Czar of Russia,
As King, 1825-1855

MINT MARKS

MV,MW, MW-monogram - Warsaw Mint, 1965
FF - Stuttgart Germany 1916-1917
(w) - Warsaw 1925-39
Other letters appearing with date denote the Mint Master at the time the coin was struck.

MINTMASTERS INITIALS

WARSAW MINT

Letter	Date	Name
IB	1811-27	Jakub Benik
IP	1834-35	Jerzy (George) Pusch
IPH	1765-92	Johannes Philippus Holzhaeusser
JS	1810-11	John Stockmann
KG	1829-34	Carl Gronau

MONETARY SYSTEM

Until 1815

1 Solidus = 1 Schilling
3 Solidi = 2 Poltura = 1 Grosz
3 Poltura = 1-1/2 Grosze = 1 Polturak
6 Groszy = 1 Szostak
18 Groszy = 1 Tympf
30 Groszy = 4 Silbergroschen = 1 Zloty
1 Talar = 1 Zloty
6 Zlotych = 1 Reichsthaler
8 Zlotych = 1 Speciesthaler
5 Speciesthaler = 1 August D'or
3 Ducats = 1 Stanislaus D'or

GRAND DUCHY OF WARSAW

GROSZ

COPPER

C#	Date	Mintage	VG	Fine	VF	XF
81	1810 IS	.742	1.75	3.00	6.00	12.50
	1811 IS	4.358	1.75	2.50	5.00	10.00
	1811 IB	Inc. Ab.	1.75	2.50	5.00	10.00
	1812 IB	6.377	1.75	2.50	5.00	10.00
	1814 IB	3.072	1.75	2.50	5.00	10.00

3 GROSZE

COPPER

C#	Date	Mintage	VG	Fine	VF	XF
82	1810 IS	1.008	2.00	4.50	9.00	18.00
	1811 IS	5.479	2.00	3.00	7.50	15.00
	1811 IB	Inc. Ab.	2.00	3.00	7.50	15.00
	1812 IB	6.816	2.00	3.00	7.50	15.00
	1813 IB	1.139	2.00	4.50	9.00	18.00
	1814 IB	3.427	2.00	3.00	7.50	15.00

5 GROSZY

2.2000 g, .210 SILVER, .0148 oz ASW

C#	Date	Mintage	VG	Fine	VF	XF
83	1811 IS	11.595	4.00	7.00	15.00	25.00
	1811 IB	Inc. Ab.	4.00	7.00	15.00	25.00
	1812 IB	3.405	4.00	7.00	15.00	25.00

10 GROSZY

2.9900 g, .245 SILVER, .0235 oz ASW

C#	Date	Mintage	VG	Fine	VF	XF
84	1810 IS	—	6.00	15.00	30.00	60.00
	1812 IB	.951	5.00	10.00	16.50	35.00
	1813 IB	3.549	5.00	10.00	15.00	30.00

1/6 TALARA

4.9800 g, .535 SILVER, .0856 oz ASW

C#	Date	Mintage	VG	Fine	VF	XF
85	1811 IS	.113	9.00	15.00	45.00	90.00
	1812 IB	.223	9.00	15.00	45.00	90.00
	1813 IB	.106	15.00	25.00	50.00	160.00
	1814 IB	1.492	9.00	15.00	40.00	80.00

1/3 TALARA

8.6600 g, .625 SILVER, .1740 oz ASW

C#	Date	Mintage	VG	Fine	VF	XF
86	1810 IS	.123	10.00	15.00	45.00	90.00
	1811 IS	.993	10.00	15.00	30.00	75.00
	1812 IB	2.804	10.00	15.00	30.00	75.00
	1813 IB	1.916	10.00	15.00	30.00	75.00
	1814 IB	4.611	10.00	15.00	30.00	75.00

TALAR

22.9200 g, .720 SILVER, .5305 oz ASW

C#	Date	Mintage	VG	Fine	VF	XF
87	1811 IB	4,488	50.00	150.00	300.00	650.00
	1812 IB	.036	50.00	100.00	200.00	400.00
	1814 IB	.014	50.00	100.00	250.00	550.00

TRADE COINAGE

DUCAT

3.5000 g, .986 GOLD, .1109 oz AGW

C#	Date	Mintage	VG	Fine	VF	XF
88	1811 IB	8,546	250.00	400.00	600.00	950.00
	1813 IB	3,000	450.00	800.00	1400.	2000.

CONGRESS KINGDOM OF POLAND

MONETARY SYSTEM

30 Groszy = 15 Russian Kopeks = 1 Zloty
10 Zlotych = 1-1/2 Rubles

GROSZ

COPPER

C#	Date	Mintage	VG	Fine	VF	XF
93	1816 IB	1.873	1.00	2.00	4.00	8.00
	1817 IB	3.092	1.00	2.00	4.00	8.00
	1818 IB	4.035	1.00	2.00	4.00	8.00
	1818	Inc. Ab.	6.00	12.50	20.00	45.00
	1819 IB	Inc. Be.	1.00	2.50	5.00	10.00
	1820 IB	.372	1.00	2.50	5.00	8.00
	1821 IB	.571	1.00	2.50	5.00	8.00
	1822 IB	Inc.C#94	6.00	10.00	17.50	35.00

NOTE: Varieties of eagles exist.

(Mining)

Rev. leg: Z MIEDZI KRALOWEY.

C#	Date	Mintage	VG	Fine	VF	XF
94	1822 IB	2.721	1.75	2.50	5.00	10.00
	1823 IB	5.046	1.75	2.50	5.00	10.00
	1824 IB	5.413	1.75	2.50	5.00	10.00
	1825 IB	2.108	1.75	2.50	5.00	10.00
	1826 IB	—	—	—	—	—

C#	Date	Mintage	VG	Fine	VF	XF
105	1828 FH	1.190	1.00	2.00	4.00	8.00
	1829 FH	.931	1.00	2.00	4.00	8.00
	1830 FH	1.569	1.00	2.00	4.00	8.00
	1830 KG	I.A.	1.00	2.00	4.00	8.00
	1831 KG	1.777	1.00	2.00	4.00	8.00
	1832 KG	1.559	1.00	2.00	4.00	8.00
	1833 KG	.375	1.00	2.00	4.00	8.00
	1834 KG	.427	1.00	2.00	4.00	8.00
	1834 IP	I.A.	1.00	2.00	4.00	8.00
	1835 IP	.542	1.00	2.00	4.00	8.00

C#	Date	Mintage	VG	Fine	VF	XF
106	1835MW	I.A.	2.00	4.00	8.00	15.00
	1836MW	.839	2.00	4.00	8.00	15.00
	1837MW	1.016	1.00	2.00	4.00	8.00
	1837WM	I.A.	—	—	Rare	—
	1838MW	.488	1.00	2.00	4.00	8.00
	1839MW	.670	1.00	2.00	4.00	8.00
	1840MW	.243	1.00	2.00	4.00	8.00

NOTE: Varieties exist.

Rev: W/o wreath, pearl rim.

C#	Date	Mintage	VG	Fine	VF	XF
106a	1840MW	I.A.	7.50	12.50	17.50	30.00

Rev: JEDEN or IEDEN above value.

C#	Date	Mintage	VG	Fine	VF	XF
107	1840MW	Inc. C106	—	—	Rare	—
	1841MW	.372	—	—	Rare	—

3 GROSZE

COPPER

Plain edge, struck w/o collar

C#	Date	Mintage	VG	Fine	VF	XF
95.1	1817 IB	.843	2.00	4.00	8.00	16.00
	1818 IB	.157	4.00	8.00	17.50	25.00

NOTE: Varieties of eagles exist.

Reeded edge, struck in collar

C#	Date	Mintage	VG	Fine	VF	XF
95.2	1818 IB	—	—	—	Rare	—
	1819 IB	.187	2.00	4.00	8.00	16.00
	1820 IB	.089	2.00	5.00	10.00	20.00

(Mining)

Rev. leg: Z MIEDZI KRAIOWEY.

C#	Date	Mintage	VG	Fine	VF	XF
108	1826 IB	.570	7.00	10.00	15.00	25.00
	1827 IB	Inc. Ab.	7.00	10.00	15.00	25.00

Rev. leg: 3/GROSZE/POLSKI.

C#	Date	Mintage	VG	Fine	VF	XF
109	1827 FH	.495	2.50	5.00	10.00	20.00
	1828 FH	1.159	2.00	4.00	8.00	16.00
	1829 FH	1.057	2.00	4.00	8.00	16.00
	1829	—	7.00	10.00	15.00	25.00
	1830 FH	.891	2.00	4.00	8.00	16.00
	1830 KG	I.A.	12.50	20.00	35.00	75.00
	1831 FH	1.773	—	—	Rare	—
	1831 KG	1.343	2.00	4.00	8.00	16.00
	1832 FH	.030	—	—	Rare	—
	1832 KG	I.A.	2.00	4.00	8.00	16.00
	1833 KG	.515	2.00	4.00	8.00	16.00
	1834 KG	.346	2.50	5.00	10.00	20.00
	1834 IP	I.A.	2.50	5.00	10.00	20.00
	1835 IP	.185	4.00	8.00	16.00	30.00

Rev: Wreath surrounds value.

C#	Date	Mintage	VG	Fine	VF	XF
110.1	1835MW	I.A.	2.00	4.00	8.00	16.00
	1836MW	.244	2.00	4.00	8.00	16.00
	1837MW	.398	2.00	4.00	8.00	16.00
	1838MW	.288	2.00	4.00	8.00	16.00
	1839MW	.333	2.00	4.00	8.00	16.00

NOTE: Varieties exist.

Obv: Eagle's heads larger, shield smaller.

C#	Date	Mintage	VG	Fine	VF	XF
110.2	1839MW	I.A.	2.00	4.00	8.00	16.00
	1840MW	.118	2.00	4.00	8.00	16.00
	1840WW	I.A.	7.00	10.00	15.00	25.00
	1841MW	.242	4.00	7.50	15.00	25.00

5 GROSZY

1.4500 g, .192 SILVER, .0090 oz ASW

Obv: Eagle's wings smaller. Rev. value: 5 GROSZY.

Smooth edge

C#	Date	Mintage	VG	Fine	VF	XF
96.1	1816 IB	2.700	6.00	8.50	12.00	22.50

Reeded edge

C#	Date	Mintage	VG	Fine	VF	XF
96.2	1817 IB	Inc. Ab.		—	Rare	—

Obv: Redesigned shield.

C#	Date	Mintage	VG	Fine	VF	XF
96.3	1818 IB	3.056	2.50	5.00	12.00	22.50
	1819 IB	5.532	2.50	5.00	12.00	22.50
	1820 IB	3.481	2.50	5.00	12.00	22.50
	1821 IB	1.651	2.50	5.00	12.00	22.50
	1822 IB	1.282	2.50	5.00	12.00	22.50
	1823 IB	2.098	2.50	5.00	12.00	22.50
	1824 IB	.235	5.00	7.50	17.50	35.00
	1825 IB	.350	2.50	6.00	15.00	30.00
111	1826 IB	2.079	2.50	5.00	12.00	22.50
	1827 IB	1.904	2.50	5.00	12.00	22.50
	1827 FH	I.A.	2.50	5.00	15.00	25.00
	1828 FH	.403	2.50	5.00	15.00	25.00
	1829 FH	.714	2.50	5.00	15.00	25.00
	1829 KG	I.A.	—	—	Rare	—
	1830 FH	.571	2.50	5.00	15.00	25.00
	1831 KG	I.A.	3.00	8.00	17.50	30.00
	1832 KG	.154	10.00	15.00	30.00	60.00

C#	Date	Mintage	VG	Fine	VF	XF
111a	1836MW	.159	2.50	5.00	15.00	25.00
	1838MW	.173	2.50	5.00	15.00	25.00
	1839MW	.380	2.50	5.00	15.00	25.00
	1840MW	.127	2.50	5.00	17.50	20.00

Obv: Similar to 25 Zlotych, C#118.

C#	Date	Mintage	VG	Fine	VF	XF
112	1841	—	—	—	Proof	Rare

10 GROSZY

2.9000 g, .192 SILVER, .0180 oz ASW

Obv: Eagle.

C#	Date	Mintage	VG	Fine	VF	XF
97	1816 IB	.750	5.00	10.00	15.00	25.00
	1820 IB	.793	8.00	12.00	17.50	35.00
	1821 IB	.707	5.00	10.00	15.00	25.00
	1822 IB	1.238	5.00	10.00	15.00	25.00
	1823 IB	.262	10.00	15.00	20.00	40.00
	1825 IB	.750	7.50	10.00	15.00	30.00
113	1826 IB	.750	4.00	7.50	12.50	25.00
	1827 IB	.737	4.00	7.50	12.50	25.00
	1827 FH	I.A.	8.00	12.50	20.00	40.00
	1828 FH	.529	4.00	7.50	12.50	25.00
	1830 FH	.145	6.00	10.00	15.00	30.00
	1830 KG	I.A.	4.00	7.50	12.50	25.00
	1831 KG	16.604	6.00	10.00	15.00	30.00
	1832 KG	—	—	—	Rare	—
	1833 KG	—	—	—	Rare	—

C#	Date	Mintage	VG	Fine	VF	XF
113a	1835MW	.869	4.00	7.50	12.50	25.00
	1836MW	1.736	4.00	7.50	12.50	25.00
	1837MW	.767	4.00	7.50	12.50	25.00
	1838MW	1.735	4.00	7.50	12.50	25.00
	1839MW	.060	4.00	7.50	12.50	25.00
	1840MW	63.349	3.00	6.00	10.00	15.00
	1840WW	I.A.	6.00	12.00	15.00	30.00

ZLOTY

4.5500 g, .593 SILVER, .0872 oz ASW

Obv: Large head. Rev: Eagle, lettered edge.

C#	Date	Mintage	VG	Fine	VF	XF
98	1818 IB	2.253	6.00	10.00	20.00	40.00
	1818 IB struck in collar	—	—	—	Rare	—
	1819 IB	1.208	6.00	10.00	20.00	40.00
	1819 IB struck in collar	—	—	—	Rare	—

Obv: Smaller head.

C#	Date	Mintage	VG	Fine	VF	XF
98a	1818 IB	Inc. Ab.	—	—	Rare	—
	1822 IB	.287	6.00	10.00	20.00	40.00
	1823 IB	.052	6.00	10.00	20.00	40.00
	1824 IB	.119	6.00	10.00	20.00	40.00
	1825 IB	.084	6.00	10.00	20.00	40.00

Obv: Large head.

C#	Date	Mintage	VG	Fine	VF	XF
114.1	1827 IB	.106	6.00	10.00	20.00	35.00
	1828 FH	.092	6.00	10.00	20.00	35.00
	1829 FH	.124	6.00	10.00	20.00	35.00
	1830 FH	.614	6.00	10.00	20.00	35.00
	1831 KG	—	6.00	10.00	20.00	35.00
	1832 KG	1.112	6.00	10.00	20.00	35.00

NOTE: Varieties exist.

Obv: Small head.

C#	Date	Mintage	VG	Fine	VF	XF
114.2	1832 KG	I.A.	6.00	10.00	20.00	35.00
	1833 KG	.041	6.50	11.00	25.00	40.00
	1834 IP	.201	6.00	10.00	20.00	35.00

ZLOTY-15 KOPEKS

3.0700 g, .868 SILVER, .0857 oz ASW

C#	Date	Mintage	VG	Fine	VF	XF
129	1832 НГ	.049	6.50	10.00	15.00	30.00
	1833 НГ	.655	6.50	10.00	15.00	30.00
	1834 НГ	.030	7.50	12.50	20.00	40.00
	1834MW	.042	15.00	30.00	60.00	100.00
	1835 НГ	.150	6.50	10.00	15.00	30.00
	1835MW	2.192	5.00	7.50	10.00	25.00
	1836 НГ	1.450	6.50	10.00	15.00	30.00
	1836MW	3.331	5.00	7.50	10.00	25.00
	1837 НГ	.080	6.50	10.00	15.00	30.00
	1837MW	3.028	5.00	7.50	10.00	25.00
	1838 НГ	1.410	10.00	20.00	40.00	80.00
	1838MW	3.617	5.00	7.50	10.00	25.00
	1839 НГ	1.510	6.50	10.00	15.00	30.00
	1839 НГ	I.A.	—	—	Proof	Rare
	1839MW	3.586	5.00	7.50	10.00	25.00
	1840 НГ	1.060	6.50	10.00	15.00	30.00
	1840MW	.487	6.50	10.00	15.00	30.00
	1841 НГ	1.060	—	—	Proof	Rare
	1841MW	1.320	10.00	17.50	30.00	60.00

NOTE: Varieties exist.

40 GROSZY-20 KOPEKS

4.1000 g, .868 SILVER, .1144 oz ASW

C#	Date	Mintage	VG	Fine	VF	XF
130	1842MW	.051	10.00	15.00	20.00	35.00
	1843MW	.037	10.00	15.00	20.00	35.00
	1844MW	—	10.00	15.00	20.00	35.00
	1845MW	.062	10.00	15.00	20.00	35.00
	1846MW	—	—	—	Rare	—
	1848MW	.027	10.00	15.00	20.00	35.00
	1850MW	.038	10.00	15.00	20.00	35.00

50 GROSZY-25 KOPEKS

5.1800 g, .868 SILVER, .1445 oz ASW

C#	Date	Mintage	VG	Fine	VF	XF
131	1842MW	.057	10.00	15.00	25.00	50.00
	1843MW	.028	10.00	15.00	25.00	40.00
	1844MW	—	10.00	20.00	45.00	90.00
	1845MW	.052	10.00	15.00	25.00	40.00
	1846MW	.561	10.00	15.00	25.00	40.00
	1847MW	.485	10.00	15.00	25.00	40.00
	1848MW	.168	10.00	15.00	25.00	40.00
	1850MW	1.489	10.00	15.00	25.00	40.00

2 ZLOTE

9.0900 g, .593 SILVER, .1733 oz ASW
Lettered edge.

C#	Date	Mintage	VG	Fine	VF	XF
99	1816 IB	1.393	10.00	15.00	25.00	50.00
	1817 IB	1.084	10.00	15.00	25.00	50.00
	1818 IB	1.321	10.00	15.00	25.00	50.00
	1819 IB	1.241	10.00	15.00	25.00	50.00
	1820 IB	1.970	10.00	20.00	40.00	80.00

Obv: Medium head. Reeded edge, struck in collar.

C#	Date	Mintage	VG	Fine	VF	XF
99a	1819 IB	—	—	—	Rare	—
	1820 IB	Inc. Ab.	10.00	15.00	25.00	60.00
	1821 IB	.997	10.00	15.00	25.00	50.00
	1822 IB	.093	10.00	15.00	25.00	60.00
	1823 IB	.446	10.00	15.00	25.00	50.00
	1824 IB	.348	10.00	15.00	25.00	50.00
	1825 IB	.229	10.00	15.00	25.00	50.00

Obv: Laureated head

C#	Date	Mintage	VG	Fine	VF	XF
115	1826 IB	.065	10.00	15.00	30.00	60.00
	1828 FH	.119	10.00	15.00	25.00	50.00
	1830 FH	.306	10.00	15.00	25.00	50.00

2 ZLOTE-30 KOPEKS

6.2100 g, .868 SILVER, .1733 oz ASW

C#	Date	Mintage	VG	Fine	VF	XF
132	1834MW	.024	12.00	20.00	35.00	65.00
	1835MW	2.229	7.50	10.00	20.00	40.00
	1836MW	2.589	7.50	10.00	20.00	40.00
	1837MW	1,544	10.00	15.00	25.00	50.00
	1838MW	1,978	10.00	15.00	25.00	50.00
	1839MW	2,037	10.00	15.00	25.00	50.00
	1840MW	.306	10.00	15.00	25.00	50.00
	1841MW	1,261	10.00	15.00	25.00	50.00

5 ZLOTYCH

15.5900 g, .868 SILVER, .4351 oz ASW

C#	Date	Mintage	VG	Fine	VF	XF
100	1816 IB	.971	30.00	60.00	120.00	250.00
	1817 IB	2.585	25.00	45.00	80.00	200.00
	1818 IB	.201	30.00	60.00	130.00	275.00

NOTE: Large and small crown varieties exist.

C#	Date	Mintage	VG	Fine	VF	XF
116	1829 FH	1.234	15.00	25.00	45.00	80.00
	1830 FH	.287	22.50	32.50	55.00	100.00
	1830 KG	I.A.	22.50	32.50	55.00	100.00
	1831 KG	.023	22.50	32.50	55.00	100.00
116	1832 KG	.639	15.00	25.00	45.00	80.00
	1833 KG	.445	15.00	25.00	45.00	80.00
	1834 KG	.414	22.50	32.50	60.00	120.00
	1834 IP	—	22.50	32.50	55.00	100.00

NOTE: Large and small bust varieties exist.

Obv. leg. w/retrograde 'S'

C#	Date	Mintage	VG	Fine	VF	XF
116a	1833 KG	Inc. Ab.	22.50	32.50	55.00	100.00

5 ZLOTYCH-3/4 RUBLE

15.5400 g, .868 SILVER, .4337 oz ASW

C#	Date	Mintage	VG	Fine	VF	XF
133	1833 НГ	.258	12.00	20.00	30.00	50.00
	1834 НГ	.206	12.00	20.00	30.00	50.00
	1834MW	.086	12.00	20.00	30.00	50.00
	1835 НГ	.107	12.00	20.00	30.00	50.00
	1835MW	.540	10.00	15.00	20.00	40.00
	1836 НГ	.078	12.00	20.00	30.00	50.00
	1836MW	1.196	10.00	15.00	20.00	40.00
	1837 НГ	.262	12.00	20.00	30.00	50.00
	1837MW	1.000	10.00	15.00	20.00	40.00
	1838 НГ	.012	50.00	85.00	135.00	225.00
	1838MW	1.996	10.00	15.00	20.00	40.00
	1839 НГ	—	—	—	Rare	—
	1839 НГ	—	—	—	Proof	Rare
	1839MW	2.689	10.00	15.00	20.00	40.00
	1840 НГ	2,001	—	—	Rare	—
	1840MW	2.482	10.00	15.00	20.00	40.00
	1841 НГ	—	—	—	Rare	—
	1841MW	1.274	10.00	15.00	20.00	40.00

10 ZLOTYCH

31.1000 g, .868 SILVER, .8679 oz ASW

C#	Date	Mintage	VG	Fine	VF	XF
101.1	1820 IB	534 pcs.	—	—	Rare	—
	1821 IB	1,195	150.00	250.00	400.00	550.00
	1822 IB	233 pcs.	—	—	Rare	—

C#	Date	Mintage	VG	Fine	VF	XF
101.2	1823 IB	1,124	150.00	250.00	400.00	550.00
	1824 IB	513 pcs.	—	—	Rare	—
	1825 IB	—	—	—	Rare	—

Obv: Laureate head.

C#	Date	Mintage	VG	Fine	VF	XF
117	1827 IB	123 pcs.	—	—	Rare	—
	1827 FH	I.A.	—	—	Rare	—

10 ZLOTYCH-1-1/2 RUBLES

31.1000 g, .868 SILVER, .8679 oz ASW

C#	Date	Mintage	VG	Fine	VF	XF
134	1833 НГ	.127	20.00	30.00	60.00	100.00
	1834 НГ	.064	25.00	40.00	80.00	150.00
	1835 НГ	.262	20.00	35.00	60.00	100.00
	1835MW	3,081	40.00	80.00	120.00	200.00
	1836 НГ	.134	20.00	35.00	60.00	100.00
	1836MW	.220	20.00	35.00	60.00	100.00
	1837 НГ	.036	40.00	80.00	120.00	200.00
	1837MW	.194	20.00	35.00	60.00	100.00
	1838 НГ	13 pcs.	—	—	Rare	—
	1838MW	.010	100.00	200.00	325.00	475.00
	1839 НГ	7,006	125.00	275.00	450.00	750.00
	1839 НГ	I.A.	—	—	Proof	Rare
	1839MW	2,295	40.00	80.00	150.00	350.00
	1840 НГ	2,001	—	—	Rare	—
	1840MW	2,747	40.00	80.00	150.00	350.00
	1841 НГ	—	—	—	Rare	—
	1841MW	.037	40.00	80.00	120.00	200.00

20 ZLOTYCH-3 RUBLES

3.8900 g, .917 GOLD, .1147 oz AGW

C#	Date	Mintage	Fine	VF	XF	Unc
136.1	1834MW	243 pcs.	250.00	500.00	1000.	2000.
	1835MW	350 pcs.	250.00	500.00	1000.	2000.
	1836MW	307 pcs.	250.00	500.00	1000.	2000.
	1837MW	423 pcs.	250.00	500.00	1000.	2000.
	1838MW	66 pcs.	500.00	900.00	1500.	3000.
	1839MW	57 pcs.	500.00	900.00	1500.	3000.
	1840MW	—	800.00	1500.	2000.	3500.

Mintmark: St. Petersburg СПБ

C#	Date	Mintage	Fine	VF	XF	Unc
136.2	1834 ПД	.077	150.00	225.00	300.00	425.00
	1835 ПД	.052	150.00	225.00	300.00	425.00
	1836 ПД	.010	175.00	275.00	350.00	450.00
	1837 ПД	.030	150.00	225.00	300.00	425.00
	1838 ПД	.017	175.00	275.00	350.00	450.00
	1839 ПД	.011	175.00	300.00	375.00	475.00

C#	Date	Mintage	Fine	VF	XF	Unc
136.3	1840 ПД	5.473	225.00	375.00	450.00	525.00
	1841 ПД		Unique	—	Proof	—

***NOTE:** Superior Pipito sale 12-87 Proof realized $12,100.

25 ZLOTYCH

4.8900 g, .917 GOLD, .1442 oz AGW

C#	Date	Mintage	Fine	VF	XF	Unc
102	1817 IB	.096	175.00	350.00	475.00	700.00
	1818 IB	.055	150.00	250.00	375.00	550.00
	1819 IB	1,124	150.00	250.00	375.00	550.00

Struck in collar

C#	Date	Mintage	Fine	VF	XF	Unc
102a	1818 IB	.086	—	—	Rare	—
	1822 IB	479 pcs.	300.00	550.00	1000.	1500.
	1823 IB	612 pcs.	500.00	900.00	1500.	2000.
	1824 IB	636 pcs.	400.00	600.00	1200.	1800.
	1825 IB	134 pcs.	400.00	600.00	1200.	1800.
	1828 IB	385 pcs.	400.00	600.00	1200.	1800.

C#	Date	Mintage	Fine	VF	XF	Unc
118	1828 FH	241 pcs.	500.00	900.00	1500.	2000.
	1829 FH	66 pcs.	600.00	1000.	1600.	2200.
	1830 FH	618 pcs.	500.00	900.00	1500.	2000.
	1832 KG	152 pcs.	500.00	900.00	1500.	2000.
	1833 KG	424 pcs.	500.00	900.00	1500.	2000.

50 ZLOTYCH

9.7800 g, .917 GOLD, .2884 oz AGW

C#	Date	Mintage	Fine	VF	XF	Unc
103	1817 IB	.017	250.00	400.00	600.00	1000.
	1818 IB	.050	250.00	500.00	700.00	1150.
	1819 IB	.020	250.00	500.00	750.00	1250.

9.7367 g, .917 GOLD, .2871 oz AGW

C#	Date	Mintage	Fine	VF	XF	Unc
103.1	1817 IB	—	—	—	Proof	—

9.7800 g, .917 GOLD, .2884 oz AGW
Obv: Small head.

C#	Date	Mintage	Fine	VF	XF	Unc
103a	1819 IB	Inc. Ab.	250.00	400.00	600.00	1000.
	1820 IB	7,098	250.00	400.00	650.00	1000.
	1821 IB	2,638	250.00	500.00	750.00	1250.
	1822 IB	1,610	250.00	500.00	750.00	1250.
	1823 IB	181 pcs.	450.00	800.00	1500.	2500.
	1827 IB	70 pcs.	650.00	1150.	1650.	2650.

C#	Date	Mintage	Fine	VF	XF	Unc
119	1827 FH	62 pcs.	700.00	1200.	1700.	2800.
	1829 FH	238 pcs.	500.00	1100.	1500.	2500.

9.7367 g, .917 GOLD, .2871 oz AGW

C#	Date	Mintage	Fine	VF	XF	Unc
119.1	1829 FH	237 pcs.	—	—	Proof	—

REVOLUTIONARY COINAGE

1830-1831

3 GROSZE

COPPER

C#	Date	Mintage	VG	Fine	VF	XF
120	1831 KG	1.112	3.50	7.50	18.00	40.00

NOTE: Varieties in eagle exist.

10 GROSZY

2.8000 g, .192 SILVER, .0173 oz ASW

C#	Date	Mintage	VG	Fine	VF	XF
121	1831 KG	6.038	5.00	10.00	20.00	50.00

NOTE: Varieties in eagle exist.

2 ZLOTE

8.9800 g, .593 SILVER, .1712 oz ASW

C#	Date	Mintage	VG	Fine	VF	XF
123	1831 KG	.171	15.00	25.00	45.00	70.00

NOTE: Varieties exist.

5 ZLOTYCH

15.4900 g, .868 SILVER, .4323 oz ASW

C#	Date	Mintage	VG	Fine	VF	XF
124	1831 KG	.023	25.00	45.00	85.00	140.00

NOTE: Varieties in fraction numerator fineness exist.

TRADE COINAGE

DUCAT

3.5000 g, .986 GOLD, .1109 oz AGW
Obv: Eagle in legend at 1 o'clock.

C#	Date	Mintage	Fine	VF	XF	Unc
125	1831	.162	125.00	200.00	300.00	500.00

WWI OCCUPATION COINAGE

Germany released a 1, 2 and 3 Kopek coinage series in 1916 which circulated during their occupation of Poland. They will be found listed as Germany KM#21, 22 and 23.

GERMAN-AUSTRIAN REGENCY

100 Fenigow = 1 Marka

FENIG

IRON

Y#	Date	Mintage	Fine	VF	XF	Unc
4	1918 FF	51.484	1.00	2.00	3.50	7.00
	1918 FF	—	—	—	Proof	200.00

5 FENIGOW

IRON

Y#	Date	Mintage	Fine	VF	XF	Unc
5	1917 FF	18.700	.50	1.00	1.50	4.00
	1917 FF	—	—	—	Proof	100.00
	1918 FF	22.690	.50	1.00	1.50	4.00
	1918 FF	—	—	—	Proof	200.00

Mule. Obv: German KM#15. Rev: Poland Y#5.

Y#	Date	Mintage	Fine	VF	XF	Unc
5.1	1917 FF	—	50.00	100.00	150.00	200.00

10 FENIGOW

IRON

Y#	Date	Mintage	Fine	VF	XF	Unc
6	1917 FF obv. leg. touches edge	33.000	7.50	15.00	20.00	25.00
	1917 FF	—	—	—	Proof	100.00
	1917 FF obv. leg. away from edge	Inc. Ab.	.50	1.00	2.00	6.50
	1918 FF obv. leg. touches edge	14.990	.50	1.00	2.50	7.50
	1918 FF obv. leg. away from edge	Inc. Ab.	.50	1.00	2.50	7.50
	1918 FF obv. leg. away from edge	—	—	—	Proof	200.00

ZINC

Y#	Date	Mintage	Fine	VF	XF	Unc
6a	1917 FF	—	25.00	45.00	85.00	150.00

Mule. Obv: Y#6.
Rev: German 10 Pfennig, KM#20.

Y#	Date	Mintage	Fine	VF	XF	Unc
6.1	1917 FF	—	50.00	100.00	150.00	200.00

20 FENIGOW

IRON

Y#	Date	Mintage	Fine	VF	XF	Unc
7	1917 FF	1.900	2.00	4.00	6.00	10.00
	1918 FF	19.260	1.00	2.00	3.00	7.00

ZINC

Y#	Date	Mintage	Fine	VF	XF	Unc
7a	1917FF	—	35.00	60.00	100.00	200.00

REPUBLIC COINAGE

100 Groszy = 1 Zloty

GROSZ

BRASS

Y#	Date	Mintage	Fine	VF	XF	Unc
8	1923	—	18.00	25.00	45.00	100.00

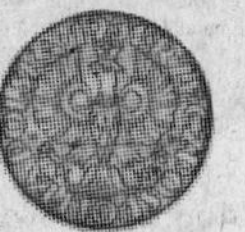

BRONZE

Y#	Date	Mintage	Fine	VF	XF	Unc
8a	1923	30.000	.25	.50	.75	5.00
	1925(w)	40.000	.25	.50	.75	5.00
	1927(w)	17.000	.25	.50	.75	5.00
	1928(w)	13.600	.25	.50	.75	5.00
	1930(w)	22.500	.25	.50	.75	5.00
	1931(w)	9.000	.50	1.00	7.00	17.50
	1932(w)	12.000	.50	1.00	5.00	10.00
	1933(w)	7.000	.50	1.00	5.00	10.00
	1934(w)	5.900	1.25	3.50	6.00	20.00
	1935(w)	7.300	.75	1.50	3.50	8.00
	1936(w)	12.600	.25	.50	2.00	5.00
	1937(w)	17.370	.25	.50	.75	2.00
	1938(w)	20.530	.25	.50	.75	2.00
	1939(w)	12.000	.25	.50	.75	2.00

2 GROSZE

BRASS

Y#	Date	Mintage	Fine	VF	XF	Unc
9	1923	20.500	.30	.75	2.50	6.00

BRONZE

Y#	Date	Mintage	Fine	VF	XF	Unc
9a	1925(w)	39.000	.20	.40	.75	5.00
	1927(w)	15.300	.50	2.00	4.50	10.00
	1928(w)	13.400	.50	2.00	4.50	10.00
	1930(w)	20.000	.20	.40	.75	5.00
	1931(w)	9.500	1.75	2.50	4.50	10.00
	1932(w)	6.500	2.00	4.00	8.00	16.00
	1933(w)	7.000	2.00	4.00	8.00	16.00
	1934(w)	9.350	1.75	3.00	7.50	15.00
	1935(w)	5.800	.20	.40	.75	5.00
	1936(w)	5.800	.20	.40	.60	2.50
	1937(w)	17.360	.20	.40	.60	2.50
	1938(w)	20.530	.20	.40	.60	2.50
	1939(w)	12.000	.20	.40	.60	2.50

5 GROSZY

BRASS

Y#	Date	Mintage	Fine	VF	XF	Unc
10	1923	32.000	.50	1.00	2.00	5.00

BRONZE

Y#	Date	Mintage	Fine	VF	XF	Unc
10a	1923	350 pcs.	—	—	Proof	150.00
	1925(w)	45.500	.20	.40	4.00	8.00
	1928(w)	8.900	.20	.40	5.00	10.00
	1930(w)	14.200	.20	.40	5.00	10.00
	1931(w)	1.500	.50	1.00	10.00	25.00
	1934(w)	.420	5.00	7.50	20.00	50.00
	1935(w)	4.660	.20	.40	.60	5.00
	1936(w)	4.660	.20	.40	.60	2.25
	1937(w)	9.050	.20	.40	.60	2.25
	1938(w)	17.300	.20	.40	.60	2.25
	1939(w)	10.000	.20	.40	.60	2.25

10 GROSZY

NICKEL

Y#	Date	Mintage	Fine	VF	XF	Unc
11	1923	100.000	.20	.45	.80	1.25

20 GROSZY

NICKEL

Y#	Date	Mintage	Fine	VF	XF	Unc
12	1923	150.000	.35	.75	1.25	2.00
	1923	10 pcs.	—	—	Proof	300.00

50 GROSZY

NICKEL

Y#	Date	Mintage	Fine	VF	XF	Unc
13	1923	100.000	.40	.80	1.50	3.50
	1923	10 pcs.	—	—	Proof	350.00

ZLOTY

5.0000 g, .750 SILVER, .1206 oz ASW

Y#	Date	Mintage	Fine	VF	XF	Unc
15	1924 (Paris) torches at sides of date					
		16.000	1.50	5.00	15.00	40.00
	1925 (London) dot after date					
		24.000	1.50	4.00	10.00	32.50
	1924 (Birmingham)					
		8 pcs.	—	—	Proof	600.00

NICKEL

Y#	Date	Mintage	Fine	VF	XF	Unc
14	1929(w)	32.000	.50	1.00	1.75	5.00

2 ZLOTE

10.0000 g, .750 SILVER, .2411 oz ASW

Y#	Date	Mintage	Fine	VF	XF	Unc
16	1924 (Paris) torches at sides of date					
		8.200	4.00	9.00	15.00	50.00
	1924H (Birmingham)					
		1.200	17.50	35.00	100.00	250.00
	1924 (Birmingham)					
		60 pcs.	—	—	Proof	600.00
	1924 (Philadelphia) w/o torches					
		.800	10.00	20.00	40.00	120.00
	1925 (London) dot after date					
		11.000	4.00	9.00	15.00	45.00
	1925 (Philadelphia)					
		5.200	6.50	15.00	30.00	65.00

4.4000 g, .750 SILVER, .1061 oz ASW

Y#	Date	Mintage	Fine	VF	XF	Unc
20	1932(w)	15.700	1.50	2.00	4.00	10.00
	1933(w)	9.250	1.50	2.00	4.00	10.00
	1934(w)	.250	3.00	5.00	8.00	15.00

Y#	Date	Mintage	Fine	VF	XF	Unc
27	1934(w)	10.425	2.00	5.00	10.00	30.00
	1936(w)	.075	20.00	35.00	65.00	180.00

15th Anniversary of Gdynia Seaport

Y#	Date	Mintage	Fine	VF	XF	Unc
30	1936(w)	3.918	3.00	5.00	8.00	20.00

5 ZLOTYCH

25.0000 g, .900 SILVER, .7234 oz ASW
Adoption of the Constitution

Y#	Date	Mintage	Fine	VF	XF	Unc
17.1	1925(w)	100 pcs.	150.00	300.00	700.00	1500.

GOLD
Adoption of the Constitution
Obv: Monogram by date. Rev: 100 pearls in circle.

Y#	Date	Mintage	Fine	VF	XF	Unc
17.1a	1925(w)	2 pcs.	—	—	Rare	—

25.0000 g, .900 SILVER, .7234 oz ASW
Obv: W/o monogram by date.

Y#	Date	Mintage	Fine	VF	XF	Unc
17.2	1925(w)	1,000	—	—	450.00	950.00
			BRONZE			
17.2a	1925(w)	100 pcs.	—	—	200.00	300.00
			BRASS			
17.2b	1925(w)	60 pcs.	—	—	225.00	350.00
			GOLD			
17.2c	1925(w)	1 pc.	—	—	Rare	—

25.0000 g, .900 SILVER, .7234 oz ASW
Obv: Monogram by date.
Rev: 81 pearls in circle.

Y#	Date	Mintage	Fine	VF	XF	Unc
17.3	1925(w)	1,000	—	—	450.00	950.00

Obv: W/o monogram by date, w/o mint mark.

Y#	Date	Mintage	Fine	VF	XF	Unc
17.4	1925(w)	1,000	—	—	450.00	950.00
			TOMBAK			
17.4a	1925(w)	100 pcs.	—	—	200.00	300.00

18.0000 g, .750 SILVER, .4340 oz ASW

Y#	Date	Mintage	Fine	VF	XF	Unc
18	1928(w) conjoined arrow and 'K' mint mark	7.500	15.00	30.00	55.00	160.00
	1928 error 'SUPRMA' edge inscription	Inc. Ab.	40.00	75.00	100.00	225.00
	1928 w/o mint mark	*10.000	12.50	22.50	45.00	140.00
	1930(w)	5.900	20.00	40.00	75.00	200.00
	1931(w)	2.200	40.00	90.00	175.00	350.00
	1932(w)	3.100	90.00	175.00	250.00	—

***NOTE:** 4,300,000 struck in London and 5,700,000 in Belgium.

Centennial of 1830 Revolution

Y#	Date	Mintage	Fine	VF	XF	Unc
19.1	1930(w)	1.000	12.00	25.00	50.00	150.00
			High relief.			
19.2	1930(w)	200 pcs.	70.00	100.00	175.00	350.00

11.0000 g, .750 SILVER, .2652 oz ASW

Y#	Date	Mintage	Fine	VF	XF	Unc
21	1932 (Warsaw)	1.000	15.00	30.00	80.00	175.00
	1932 (London) w/o mint mark	3.000	4.00	5.00	7.50	25.00
	1933(w)	11.000	3.50	4.50	7.50	22.50
	1933(w)	100 pcs.	—	—	Proof	—
	1934(w)	.250	5.00	7.50	10.00	35.00

Rifle Corps Aug. 6, 1914

Y#	Date	Mintage	Fine	VF	XF	Unc
25	1934(w)	.300	4.00	6.00	12.50	30.00

Jozef Piesudski

Y#	Date	Mintage	Fine	VF	XF	Unc
28	1934(w)	6.510	2.50	4.00	7.00	20.00
	1935(w)	1.800	3.00	4.50	8.00	20.00
	1936(w)	1.000	3.00	4.50	8.00	20.00
	1938(w)	.289	5.00	7.50	15.00	30.00

15th Anniversary of Gdynia Seaport

Y#	Date	Mintage	Fine	VF	XF	Unc
31	1936(w)	1.000	6.00	8.00	14.00	25.00

10 ZLOTYCH

3.2258 g, .900 GOLD, .0933 oz AGW
Boleslaus I

Y#	Date	Mintage	VF	XF	Unc
32	1925(w)	.050	55.00	75.00	100.00

22.0000 g, .750 SILVER, .5305 oz ASW

Y#	Date	Mintage	Fine	VF	XF	Unc
22	1932 (Warsaw)	3.100	5.00	8.00	12.50	25.00
	1932 (London) w/o mint mark	6.000	5.00	8.00	12.50	25.00
	1932(w)	100 pcs.	—	—	Proof	—
	1933(w)	2.800	5.00	8.00	12.50	25.00
	1933(w)	100 pcs.	—	—	Proof	—

Jan III Sobieski's Victory Over the Turks

Y#	Date	Mintage	Fine	VF	XF	Unc
23	1933(w)	.300	10.00	20.00	35.00	65.00
	1933(w)	100 pcs.	—	—	Proof	—

70th Anniversary of 1863 Insurrection

Y#	Date	Mintage	Fine	VF	XF	Unc
24	1933(w)	.300	10.00	20.00	45.00	90.00
	1933(w)	100 pcs.	—	—	Proof	—

Rifle Corps Aug. 6, 1914

Y#	Date	Mintage	Fine	VF	XF	Unc
26	1934(w)	.300	7.50	12.50	35.00	70.00

Jozef Piesudski

Y#	Date	Mintage	Fine	VF	XF	Unc
29	1934(w)	.200	10.00	20.00	40.00	85.00
	1935(w)	1.670	6.00	9.00	15.00	30.00
	1936(w)	2.130	6.00	9.00	15.00	30.00
	1937(w)	.908	6.00	10.00	18.00	40.00
	1938(w)	.234	10.00	15.00	30.00	70.00
	1939(w)	—	10.00	15.00	30.00	65.00

20 ZLOTYCH

6.4516 g, .900 GOLD, .1867 oz AGW
Boleslaus I

Y#	Date	Mintage	VF	XF	Unc
33	1925(w)	.027	100.00	110.00	150.00

WWII GERMAN OCCUPATION

GROSZ

ZINC

Y#	Date	Mintage	Fine	VF	XF	Unc
34	1939(w)	33.909	.50	1.25	2.50	5.00

5 GROSZY

ZINC

Y#	Date	Mintage	Fine	VF	XF	Unc
35	1939(w)	15.324	1.75	3.50	4.00	6.50

10 GROSZY

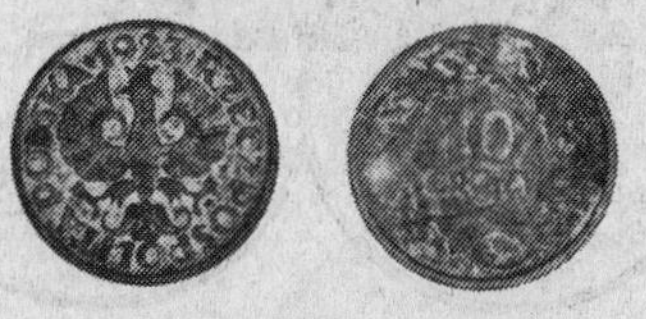

ZINC

Y#	Date	Mintage	Fine	VF	XF	Unc
36	1923(w)	42.175	.10	.20	.30	1.50

NOTE: Actually struck in 1941-44.

20 GROSZY

ZINC

Y#	Date	Mintage	Fine	VF	XF	Unc
37	1923(w)	40.025	.15	.25	.50	1.50

NOTE: Actually struck in 1941-44.

50 GROSZY

NICKEL PLATED IRON

Y#	Date	Mintage	Fine	VF	XF	Unc
38	1938(w)	32.000	1.00	2.00	4.00	7.50

IRON

Y#	Date	Mintage	Fine	VF	XF	Unc
38a	1938	—	1.25	2.50	5.00	8.50

POST WAR COINAGE

GROSZ

ALUMINUM

Y#	Date	Mintage	Fine	VF	XF	Unc
39	1949	400.116	.10	.20	.50	1.00

2 GROSZE

ALUMINUM

Y#	Date	Mintage	Fine	VF	XF	Unc
40	1949	300.106	.10	.25	.75	2.00

5 GROSZY

BRONZE

Y#	Date	Mintage	Fine	VF	XF	Unc
41	1949	300.000	.10	.25	.50	1.50

ALUMINUM

Y#	Date	Mintage	Fine	VF	XF	Unc
41a	1949	200.000	.10	.25	1.00	3.00

10 GROSZY

COPPER-NICKEL

Y#	Date	Mintage	Fine	VF	XF	Unc
42	1949	200.000	.20	.40	.60	1.75

ALUMINUM

Y#	Date	Mintage	Fine	VF	XF	Unc
42a	1949	31.047	.10	.25	1.00	3.00

20 GROSZY

COPPER-NICKEL

Y#	Date	Mintage	Fine	VF	XF	Unc
43	1949	133.383	.30	.60	.75	2.00

ALUMINUM

Y#	Date	Mintage	Fine	VF	XF	Unc
43a	1949	197.472	.10	.25	1.00	4.00

50 GROSZY

COPPER-NICKEL

Y#	Date	Mintage	Fine	VF	XF	Unc
44	1949	109.000	.50	.75	1.00	2.50

ALUMINUM

Y#	Date	Mintage	Fine	VF	XF	Unc
44a	1949	59.393	.10	.25	1.50	5.00

ZLOTY

COPPER-NICKEL

Y#	Date	Mintage	Fine	VF	XF	Unc
45	1949	87.053	1.00	1.50	2.25	4.00

ALUMINUM

Y#	Date	Mintage	Fine	VF	XF	Unc
45a	1949	43.000	.10	.25	2.50	7.50

PEOPLES REPUBLIC

5 GROSZY

ALUMINUM

Y#	Date	Mintage	VF	XF	Unc
A46	1958	53.521	—	.10	.20
	1959	28.564	—	.10	.15
	1960	12.246	—	.50	1.00
	1961	29.502	—	.10	.20
	1962	90.257	—	.10	.15
	1963	20.878	—	.10	.15
	1965MW	5.050	—	1.00	2.00
	1967MW	10.056	—	.50	1.00
	1968MW	10.196	—	.50	1.00
	1970MW	20.095	—	.10	.20
	1971MW	20.000	—	.10	.20
	1972MW	10.000	—	.10	.20

10 GROSZY

ALUMINUM

Y#	Date	Mintage	VF	XF	Unc
AA47	1961	73.400	—	.50	1.00
	1962	25.362	—	2.00	4.00
	1963	40.434	—	.50	1.50
	1965MW	50.521	—	1.00	2.00
	1966MW	70.749	—	.50	1.50
	1967MW	62.059	—	.50	1.50
AA47	1968MW	62.204	—	.50	1.50
	1969MW	71.566	—	.50	1.00
	1970MW	38.844	—	.10	.50
	1971MW	50.000	—	.10	.50
	1972MW	60.000	—	.10	.50
	1973MW	80.000	—	.10	.25
	1974	50.000	—	—	—
	1975MW	50.000	—	.10	.15
	1976MW	100.000	—	—	.10
	1977MW	100.000	—	—	.10
	1978MW	71.204	—	—	.10
	1979MW	73.191	—	—	.10
	1980MW	60.623	—	—	.10
	1981MW	70.000	—	—	.10
	1983MW	9.600	—	—	.10
	1985MW	9.957	—	—	.10

NOTE: Varieties in date size exist.

20 GROSZY

ALUMINUM

Y#	Date	Mintage	VF	XF	Unc
A47	1957	3.940	—	3.50	15.00
	1961	53.108	—	.75	2.00
	1962	19.140	—	1.00	4.00
	1963	41.217	—	.50	2.00
	1965MW	32.022	—	.50	2.00
	1966MW	23.860	—	.50	2.00
	1967MW	29.099	—	.50	2.00
	1968MW	29.191	—	.50	2.00
	1969MW	40.227	—	.50	1.50
	1970MW	20.028	—	.10	1.00
	1971MW	20.000	—	.10	1.00
	1972MW	60.000	—	.10	1.00
	1973	50.000	—	.10	.50
	1973MW	65.000	—	.10	.50
	1975MW	50.000	—	.10	.50
	1976MW large date	100.000	—	.10	.50
	1976MW small date	Inc. Ab.	—	.10	.50
	1977MW	80.730	—	.10	.20
	1978MW	50.730	—	.10	.20
	1979MW	45.252	—	.10	.20
	1980MW	30.020	—	.10	.20
	1981MW	60.082	—	.10	.20
	1983MW	10.041	—	.10	.20
	1985	16.227	—	.10	.20
	1985MW	—	—	.10	.20

NOTE: Date varieties exist.

50 GROSZY

ALUMINUM

Y#	Date	Mintage	VF	XF	Unc
48.1	1957	91.316	.10	1.00	2.50
	1965MW	22.090	.10	.50	1.00
	1967MW	2.027	.15	1.50	5.00
	1968MW	2.065	.15	1.50	5.00
	1970MW	3.273	.15	.30	1.50
	1971MW	7.000	.10	.25	1.00
	1972MW	10.000	.10	.25	.50
	1973MW	39,000	.10	.20	.50
	1974MW	33.000	.10	.20	.50
	1975	25.000	.10	.20	.50
	1976	25.000	.10	.20	.40
	1977MW	50.000	.10	.20	.40
	1978	18.600	.10	.20	.40
	1978MW	50.020	.10	.20	.40
	1982MW	16.067	.10	.20	.40
	1983MW	39.667	.10	.20	.40
	1984MW	44.217	.10	.20	.40
	1985MW	49.052	.10	.20	.40

Obv: Redesigned eagle.

Y#	Date	Mintage	VF	XF	Unc
48.2	1986MW	45.796	.10	.20	.40
	1986MW	5,000	—	Proof	3.50
	1987MW	21.257	.10	.20	.40
	1987MW	5,000	—	Proof	3.50
	1988MW	—	.10	.20	.40

ZLOTY

ALUMINUM

Y#	Date	Mintage	VF	XF	Unc
49.1	1957	58.631	.10	1.50	3.00
	1965MW	15.015	.10	1.00	2.00
	1966MW	18.185	.15	1.00	2.00
	1967MW	1.002	.25	1.50	6.00
	1968MW	1.176	.25	1.50	6.00
	1969MW	3.024	.20	1.00	2.00
	1970MW	6.016	.15	.50	1.50
	1971MW	6.000	.15	.50	1.00
	1972MW	7.000	.15	.50	1.00
	1973MW	15.000	.10	.50	1.00
	1974MW	42.000	.10	.15	.50
	1975	22.000	.10	.15	.50
	1975MW	33.000	.10	.15	.50
	1976	22.000	.10	.50	1.00
	1977MW	65.000	.10	.50	1.00
	1978	16.400	.10	.50	1.50
	1978MW	80.000	.10	.50	1.00
	1980MW	100.002	.10	.15	.50
	1981MW	4.082	.10	.15	1.00
	1982MW	59.643	.10	.15	.30
	1983MW	49.636	.10	.15	.25
	1984MW	61.036	.10	.15	.25
	1985MW	167.939	.10	.15	.25

Obv: Redesigned eagle.

Y#	Date	Mintage	VF	XF	Unc
49.2	1986MW	130.697	.10	.15	.25
	1986MW	5,000	—	Proof	3.50
	1987MW	100.081	.10	.15	.25
	1987MW	5,000	—	Proof	3.50
	1988MW	96.400	.10	.15	.25
	1988MW	5,000	—	Proof	3.50

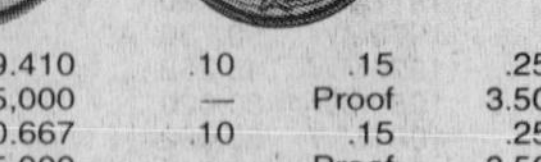

Y#	Date	Mintage	VF	XF	Unc
49.3	1989MW	49.410	.10	.15	.25
	1989MW	5,000	—	Proof	3.50
	1990MW	30.667	.10	.15	.25
	1990MW	5,000	—	Proof	3.50

2 ZLOTE

ALUMINUM

Y#	Date	Mintage	VF	XF	Unc
46	1958	83.640	.20	1.50	3.50
	1959	7.170	.50	4.00	10.00
	1960	36.131	.20	.50	2.00
	1970MW	2.014	.30	1.00	3.00
	1971MW	3.000	.20	1.00	3.00
	1972MW	3.000	.20	1.00	3.00
	1973MW	10.000	.15	.50	1.50
	1974MW	46.000	.15	.30	1.00

BRASS

Y#	Date	Mintage	VF	XF	Unc
80.1	1975	25.000	.15	.25	.50
	1976	60.000	.15	.25	.50
	1977	50.000	.15	.25	.50
	1978	2.600	.15	.25	1.75
	1978MW	2.382	.15	.25	1.75
	1979MW	85.752	.15	.25	.50
	1980MW	66.610	.15	.25	.50
	1981MW	40.306	.15	.25	.50
	1982MW	45.318	.15	.25	.50
	1983MW	35.244	.15	.25	.50
	1984MW	59.999	.15	.25	.50
	1985MW	100.300	.15	.25	.50

Obv: Redesigned eagle.

Y#	Date	Mintage	VF	XF	Unc
80.2	1986MW	60.718	.15	.25	.50
	1986MW	5,000	—	Proof	3.50
	1987MW	44.673	.15	.25	.50
	1987MW	5,000	—	Proof	3.50
	1988MW	94.651	.15	.25	.50
	1988MW	5,000	—	Proof	3.50

ALUMINUM, 17.9mm

Y#	Date	Mintage	VF	XF	Unc
80.3	1989MW	91.494	.10	.20	.40
	1989MW	5,000	—	Proof	3.50
	1990MW	40.723	.10	.20	.40
	1990MW	5,000	—	Proof	3.50

5 ZLOTYCH

ALUMINUM

Y#	Date	Mintage	VF	XF	Unc
47	1958	1.328	7.50	12.50	20.00
	1959	56.811	.25	1.50	3.00
	1960	16.301	.25	1.50	4.00
	1971MW	1.000	.50	3.00	10.00
	1973MW	5.000	.20	1.00	3.00
	1974MW	46.000	.20	.50	1.00

BRASS

Y#	Date	Mintage	VF	XF	Unc
81.1	1975	25.000	.20	.40	.80
	1976	60.000	.20	.40	.80
	1977	50.000	.20	.40	.80
	1979MW	5.098	.20	.40	1.50
	1980MW	10.100	.20	.40	.80
	1981MW	4.008	.20	.40	2.00
	1982MW	25.379	.20	.40	.80
	1983MW	30.531	.20	.40	.80
	1984MW	85.598	.20	.40	.80
	1985MW	20.501	.20	.40	.80

24mm
Obv: Redesigned eagle.

Y#	Date	Mintage	VF	XF	Unc
81.2	1986MW	57.108	.20	.40	.80
	1986MW	5,000	—	Proof	3.50
	1987MW	58.843	.20	.40	.80
	1987MW	5,000	—	Proof	3.50
	1988MW	18.668	.20	.40	.80
	1988MW	5,000	—	Proof	3.50

ALUMINUM, 20mm

Y#	Date	Mintage	VF	XF	Unc
81.3	1989MW	30.253	.15	.30	.60
	1989MW	5,000	—	Proof	3.50
	1990MW	38.248	.15	.30	.60
	1990MW	5,000	—	Proof	3.50

10 ZLOTYCH

COPPER-NICKEL, 31mm
Tadeusz Kosciuszko

Y#	Date	Mintage	VF	XF	Unc
50	1959	13.107	.50	1.75	2.5
	1960	27.551	.50	1.00	2.0
	1966MW	4.157	1.00	8.00	20.0

Reduced size, 28mm.

Y#	Date	Mintage	VF	XF	Unc
50a	1969MW	5.428	.50	1.50	5.0
	1970MW	13.783	.50	1.00	1.7
	1971MW	12.000	.50	1.00	1.7
	1972MW	10.000	.50	1.00	1.7
	1973MW	3.900	.50	2.00	8.0

Mikolaj Kopernik

Y#	Date	Mintage	VF	XF	Unc
51	1959	12.559	.75	1.25	2.5
	1965MW	3.000	1.00	5.00	15.0

Reduced size

Y#	Date	Mintage	VF	XF	Unc
51a	1967MW	2.128	.75	2.00	6.0
	1968MW	9.389	.75	1.25	2.0
	1969MW	8.612	.75	1.25	2.0

600th Anniversary of Jagiello University
Legends raised

Y#	Date	Mintage	VF	XF	Unc
52	1964	2.610	.50	1.25	2.5

Legends incuse

Y#	Date	Mintage	VF	XF	Unc
52a	1964	2.612	.50	1.25	2.5

700th Anniversary of Warsaw

Y#	Date	Mintage	VF	XF	Unc
54	1965MW	3.492	.50	1.25	2.50

700th Anniversary of Warsaw

Y#	Date	Mintage	VF	XF	Unc
55	1965MW	2.000	.50	1.25	2.50

200th Anniversary of Warsaw Mint

Y#	Date	Mintage	VF	XF	Unc
56	1966MW	.102	2.00	6.00	20.00

20th Anniversary - Death of General Swierczewski

Y#	Date	Mintage	VF	XF	Unc
58	1967MW	2.000	.50	1.00	2.00

Marie Curie Centennial of Birth

Y#	Date	Mintage	VF	XF	Unc
59	1967MW	2.000	.50	1.00	2.00

25th Anniversary Peoples Army

Y#	Date	Mintage	VF	XF	Unc
60	1968MW	2.000	.50	1.00	2.00

25th Anniversary Peoples Republic

Y#	Date	Mintage	VF	XF	Unc
61	1969MW	2.000	.50	1.00	2.00

25th Anniversary Provincial Annexations

Y#	Date	Mintage	VF	XF	Unc
62	1970MW	2.000	.50	1.00	2.00

F.A.O. Issue

Y#	Date	Mintage	VF	XF	Unc
63	1971MW	2.000	.50	1.00	2.00

Battle of Upper Silesia 50th Anniversary

Y#	Date	Mintage	VF	XF	Unc
64	1971MW	2.000	.50	1.00	2.00

50th Anniversary Gdynia Seaport

Y#	Date	Mintage	VF	XF	Unc
65	1972MW	2.000	.50	1.00	2.00

Boleslaw Prus

Y#	Date	Mintage	VF	XF	Unc
73	1975MW	35.000	.25	.65	1.00
	1976MW	20.000	.25	.65	1.00
	1977MW	25.000	.25	.65	1.00
	1978MW	4.007	.25	.65	2.00
	1981MW	2.655	.25	1.00	3.50
	1982MW	16.341	.25	.65	1.00
	1983MW	14.248	.25	.65	1.00
	1984MW	19.064	.25	.65	1.00

Adam Mickiewicz

Y#	Date	Mintage	VF	XF	Unc
74	1975MW	35.000	.25	.65	1.00
	1976MW	20.000	.25	.65	1.00

25mm

Y#	Date	Mintage	VF	XF	Unc
152.1	1984MW	15.756	.20	.50	1.00
	1985MW	5.282	.20	.50	1.00
	1986MW	31.043	.20	.50	1.00
	1986MW	5,000	—	Proof	4.00
	1987MW	69.636	.20	.50	1.00
	1987MW	5,000	—	Proof	4.00
	1988MW	102.493	.20	.50	1.00
	1988MW	5,000	—	Proof	4.00

BRASS, 21.8mm

Y#	Date	Mintage	VF	XF	Unc
152.2	1989MW	80.800	.20	.40	.80
	1989MW	5,000	—	Proof	4.00
	1990MW	106.892	.20	.40	.80
	1990MW	5,000	—	Proof	4.00

20 ZLOTYCH

COPPER-NICKEL

Y#	Date	Mintage	VF	XF	Unc
67	1973	25.000	.25	1.00	2.50
	1974	12.000	.25	.75	1.50
	1976	20.000	.25	.75	1.50

Marceli Nowotko

Y#	Date	Mintage	VF	XF	Unc
69	1974MW	10.000	.25	1.00	2.50
	1975	10.000	.25	1.00	2.00
	1976	20.000	.25	.75	1.50
	1976MW	30.000	.25	.75	1.50
	1977MW	16.000	.25	1.00	2.00
	1983MW	.152	.25	5.00	12.50

25th Anniversary of the Comcon

Y#	Date	Mintage	VF	XF	Unc
70	1974MW	2.000	.75	1.50	2.50

International Women's Year

Y#	Date	Mintage	VF	XF	Unc
75	1975MW	2.000	.75	1.50	2.50

Maria Konopnicka

Y#	Date	Mintage	VF	XF	Unc
95	1978MW	2.010	.75	1.50	2.50

First Polish Cosmonaut

Y#	Date	Mintage	VF	XF	Unc
97	1978MW	2.009	.75	1.50	2.50

International Year of the Child

Y#	Date	Mintage	VF	XF	Unc
99	1979MW	2.007	1.00	1.75	3.50

1980 Olympics - Runner

Y#	Date	Mintage	VF	XF	Unc
108	1980MW	2.012	1.00	1.75	5.00
	1980MW	100 pcs.	—	Proof	—

50th Anniversary of Ship "Dar Pomorza"

Y#	Date	Mintage	VF	XF	Unc
112	1980MW	2.007	1.00	1.75	3.50

Circulation Coinage

Y#	Date	Mintage	VF	XF	Unc
153.1	1984MW	12.703	.25	.60	1.25
	1985MW	15.514	.25	.60	1.25
	1986MW	37.959	.25	.60	1.25
	1986MW	5,000	—	Proof	4.00
	1987MW	22.213	.25	.60	1.25
	1987MW	5,000	—	Proof	4.00
	1988MW	14.994	.25	.60	1.25
	1988MW	5,000	—	Proof	4.00

Reduced size, 23.9mm

Y#	Date	Mintage	VF	XF	Unc
153.2	1989MW	95.974	.25	.50	1.00
	1989MW	5,000	—	Proof	4.00
	1990MW	104.712	.25	.50	1.00
	1990MW	5,000	—	Proof	4.00

50 ZLOTYCH

12.6400 g, .750 SILVER, .3048 .OZ ASW
Fryderyk Chopin

Y#	Date	Mintage	VF	XF	Unc
66	1972MW	.050	—	Proof	15.00
	1974MW	.010	—	Proof	22.50

COPPER-NICKEL
Duke Mieszko I

Y#	Date	Mintage	VF	XF	Unc
100	1979MW	2.640	1.00	2.00	5.00

King Boleslaw I Chrobry

Y#	Date	Mintage	VF	XF	Unc
114	1980MW	2.564	1.00	2.00	5.00

Duke Kazimierz I Odnowiciel

Y#	Date	Mintage	VF	XF	Unc
117	1980MW	2.504	1.00	2.00	5.00

General Broni Wladyslaw Sikorski

Y#	Date	Mintage	VF	XF	Unc
122	1981MW	2.505	1.00	2.00	5.00

King Boleslaw II Smialy

Y#	Date	Mintage	VF	XF	Unc
124	1981MW	2.538	1.00	2.00	4.00

World Food Day

Y#	Date	Mintage	VF	XF	Ur
127	1981MW	2.524	1.00	2.00	4.(

King Wladyslaw I Herman

Y#	Date	Mintage	VF	XF	Unc
128	1981MW	2.500	1.00	2.00	4.(

King Boleslaw III Krzywousty

Y#	Date	Mintage	VF	XF	Unc
133	1982MW	2.616	1.00	2.00	4.(

150th Anniversary of Great Theater

Y#	Date	Mintage	VF	XF	Unc
142	1983MW	.615	1.00	4.00	8.(

King Jan III Sobieski

Y#	Date	Mintage	VF	XF	Unc
145	1983MW	2.576	1.00	2.00	4.(

Ignacy Lukasiewicz

Y#	Date	Mintage	VF	XF	Unc
146	1983MW	.612	1.00	4.00	8.(

#	Date	Mintage	VF	XF	Unc
16	1990MW	28.707	—	—	2.00
	1990MW	5,000	—	Proof	10.00

100 ZLOTYCH

20.0000 g, .900 SILVER, .5787 oz ASW
Polish Millenium

7	1966MW	.198	—	6.50	12.50

16.5000 g, .625 SILVER, .3316 oz ASW
500th Anniversary - Birth of Nikolaus Kopernikus

8	1973MW	.051	—	Proof	15.00
	1974MW	.050	—	Proof	10.00

40th Anniversary - Death of
Maria Sklodowska Curie

1	1974MW	.050	—	Proof	10.00

Royal Castle in Warsaw

6	1975MW	.050	—	Proof	12.00

Ignacy Jan Paderewski

7	1975MW	.060	—	Proof	6.50

Helena Modrzejewska

Y#	Date	Mintage	VF	XF	Unc
78	1975MW	.060	—	Proof	6.50

Tadeusz Kosciuszko

82	1976MW	.100	—	Proof	7.00

Kazimierz Pulaski

84	1976MW	.100	—	Proof	7.00

Environment Protection - Bison

87	1977MW	.030	—	Proof	25.00

Henryk Sienkiewicz

88	1977MW	.020	—	Proof	10.00

Wladyslaw Reymont

89	1977MW	.020	—	Proof	10.00

Wawel Castle in Krakow

Y#	Date	Mintage	VF	XF	Unc
91	1977MW	.030	—	Proof	12.50

Adam Mickiewicz

92	1978MW	.030	—	Proof	12.50

Environment Protection - Moose

93	1978MW	.030	—	Proof	25.00

100th Anniversary - Birth of Janusz Korczak

94	1978MW	.030	—	Proof	10.00

Environment Protection - Beaver

96	1978MW	.030	—	Proof	25.00

Henryk Wieniawski

98	1979MW	.030	—	Proof	12.00

Ludwik Zamenhof

Y#	Date	Mintage	VF	XF	Unc
103	1979MW	.030	—	Proof	12.00

Environment Protection - Lynx

Y#	Date	Mintage	VF	XF	Unc
104	1979MW	.020	—	Proof	25.00

Environment Protection - Chamois

Y#	Date	Mintage	VF	XF	Unc
105	1979MW	.020	—	Proof	22.50

450th Anniversary - Birth of Jan Kochanowski

Y#	Date	Mintage	VF	XF	Unc
120	1980MW	.010	—	Proof	17.50

1980 Olympics - Runner
Rev: Olympic rings and runner.

Y#	Date	Mintage	VF	XF	Unc
109	1980MW	.010	—	Proof	35.00

Environment Protection - Cappercaillie

Y#	Date	Mintage	VF	XF	Unc
121	1980MW	.018	—	Proof	17.50

General Broni Wladyslaw Sikowski

Y#	Date	Mintage	VF	XF	Unc
123	1981MW	.012	—	Proof	15.00

Environment Protection - Horse

Y#	Date	Mintage	VF	XF	Unc
126	1981MW	.012	—	Proof	20.00

14.1700 g, .750 SILVER, .3417 oz ASW
Visit of Pope John Paul II

Y#	Date	Mintage	VF	XF	Unc
136	1982	8,700	—	—	40.00
	1982	3,750	—	Proof	80.00
	1985	1 pc.	—	—	—
	1985	5 pcs.	—	Proof	—
	1986	80 pcs.	—	—	—
	1986	128 pcs.	—	Proof	—

16.5000 g, .625 SILVER, .3316 oz ASW
Environment Protection - Stork

Y#	Date	Mintage	VF	XF	Unc
141	1982MW	.012	—	Proof	25.00

Wildlife Protection - Bear

Y#	Date	Mintage	VF	XF	Unc
147	1983MW	8,000	—	Proof	30.00

COPPER-NICKEL
Wincenty Witos

Y#	Date	Mintage	VF	XF	Unc
148	1984MW	1.530	—	—	4.00

40th Anniversary of Peoples Republic

Y#	Date	Mintage	VF	XF	Un
151	1984MW	2.595	—	—	4.0

King Przemyslaw II

Y#	Date	Mintage	VF	XF	Unc
155	1985MW	2.924	—	—	4.0

NICKEL PLATED STEEL
Polish Women's Memorial Hospital Center

Y#	Date	Mintage	VF	XF	Unc
157	1985MW	1.927	—	—	4.0

COPPER-NICKEL
King Wladyslaw I Lokietek

Y#	Date	Mintage	VF	XF	Unc
160	1986MW	2.540	—	—	4.0
	1986MW	5,000	—	Proof	12.0

King Kazimierz III

Y#	Date	Mintage	VF	XF	Unc
167	1987MW	2.479	—	—	5.0
	1987MW	5,000	—	Proof	12.0

70th Anniversary of Wielkopolskiego Insurrection

Y#	Date	Mintage	VF	XF	Unc
182	1988MW	2.513	—	—	3.5
	1988MW	5,000	—	Proof	12.0

Queen Jadwiga 1384-1399

Y#	Date	Mintage	VF	XF	Unc
183	1988MW	2.469	—	—	3.50
	1988MW	5,000	—	Proof	12.00

Y#	Date	Mintage	VF	XF	Unc
214	1990MW	37.341	—	—	2.50
	1990MW	5,000	—	Proof	12.00

200 ZLOTYCH

14.4700 g, .625 SILVER, .2907 oz ASW
30th Anniversary Polish Peoples Republic

Y#	Date	Mintage	VF	XF	Unc
72	1974MW	13.062	—	—	3.00
	1974MW	6,000	—	Proof	25.00

14.4700 g, .750 SILVER, .3490 oz ASW
30th Anniversary Victory Over Fascism

Y#	Date	Mintage	VF	XF	Unc
79	1975MW	1.826	—	—	5.00
	1975MW	2,600	—	Proof	25.00

14.4700 g, .625 SILVER, .2907 oz ASW
XXI Olympics - Rings and Torch

Y#	Date	Mintage	VF	XF	Unc
86	1976MW	2.072	—	—	5.00
	1976MW	.011	—	Proof	25.00

Duke Mieszko I

Y#	Date	Mintage	VF	XF	Unc
101	1979MW	.012	—	Proof	25.00

17.6000 g, .750 SILVER, .4244 oz ASW
Winter Olympics - Ski jumper
Rev: Torch below skier.

Y#	Date	Mintage	VF	XF	Unc
110	1980MW	.032	—	Proof	45.00

Rev: W/o torch.

Y#	Date	Mintage	VF	XF	Unc
110a	1980MW	.028	—	Proof	20.00

King Boleslaw I Chrobry

Y#	Date	Mintage	VF	XF	Unc
115	1980MW	.012	—	Proof	25.00

Duke Kazimierz I

Y#	Date	Mintage	VF	XF	Unc
118	1980MW	.012	—	Proof	15.00

King Bolaslaw II Smialy

Y#	Date	Mintage	VF	XF	Unc
125	1981MW	.012	—	Proof	20.00

King Wladyslaw I Herman

Y#	Date	Mintage	VF	XF	Unc
129	1981MW	.012	—	Proof	20.00

World Soccer Championship Games in Spain

Y#	Date	Mintage	VF	XF	Unc
130	1982MW	.021	—	Proof	16.50

King Boleslaw III Krzywousty

Y#	Date	Mintage	VF	XF	Unc
132	1982MW	.012	—	Proof	20.00

28.1300 g, .750 SILVER, .6784 oz ASW
Visit of Pope John Paul II
Obv: Similar to Y#132.

Y#	Date	Mintage	VF	XF	Unc
137	1982	3,000	—	—	60.00
	1982	3,650	—	Proof	80.00
	1985	1 pc.	—	—	—
	1985	5 pcs.	—	Proof	—
	1986	32 pcs.	—	—	—
	1986	75 pcs.	—	Proof	—

17.6000 g, .750 SILVER, .4244 oz ASW
King Jan III Sobieski

Y#	Date	Mintage	VF	XF	Unc
143	1983MW	.011	—	Proof	25.00

Winter Olympics - Ice Skater

Y#	Date	Mintage	VF	XF	Unc
149	1984MW	.015	—	Proof	25.00

Summer Olympics - Hurdler

Y#	Date	Mintage	VF	XF	Unc
150	1984MW	.016	—	Proof	25.00

500 ZLOTYCH

30.0000 g, .900 GOLD, .8681 oz AGW
Tadeusz Kosciuszko

83	1976MW	2,318	—	—	500.00

Kazimierz Pulaski

85	1976MW	2,315	—	—	500.00

16.5000 g, .625 SILVER, .3283 oz ASW
Environment Protection - Swan

154	1984MW	.010	—	Proof	30.00

16.5000 g, .750 SILVER, .3979 oz ASW
King Przemyslaw II

156	1985MW	8,000	—	Proof	22.50

40th Anniversary of United Nations

158	1985MW	.010	—	Proof	20.00

Environmental Protection - Squirrel

Y#	Date	Mintage	VF	XF	Unc
159	1985MW	8,000	—	Proof	20.00

King Wladyslaw I Lokietek

161	1986MW	8,000	—	Proof	17.50

Environment Protection - Owl

162	1986MW	.012	—	Proof	25.00

Soccer - Ball in Net

225	1986MW	.016	—	Proof	30.00

Olympics - Equestrian

165	1987MW	.015	—	Proof	40.00

European Championship Soccer Games

166	1987MW	.012	—	Proof	40.00

Winter Olympics - Ice Hockey Goalie

Y#	Date	Mintage	VF	XF	Unc
172	1987MW	.015	—	Proof	40.00

King Kazimierz III

173	1987MW	8,000	—	Proof	25.00

Queen Jadwiga 1384-1399

181	1988MW	8,000	—	Proof	25.00

Colosseum in Rome - Soccer 1990

184	1988MW	7,000	—	Proof	22.50

COPPER-NICKEL
50th Anniversary of Beginning of WWII

185	1989MW	10.135	—	—	3.00
	1989MW	5,000	—	Proof	10.00

King Wladyslaw II 1386-1434

194	1989MW	2.544	—	—	3.00
	1989MW	5,000	—	Proof	10.00

1000 ZLOTYCH

3.4000 g, .900 GOLD, .0984 oz AGW
Visit of Pope John Paul II

Y#	Date	Mintage	VF	XF	Unc
138	1982	900 pcs.	—	—	125.00
	1982	1,700	—	Proof	150.00
	1985	*1 pc.	—	—	600.00
	1985	*2 pcs.	—	Proof	800.00
	1986	*83 pcs.	—	—	250.00
	1986	*53 pcs.	—	Proof	300.00

14.5000 g, .750 SILVER, .3497 oz ASW
Visit of Pope John Paul II

Y#	Date	Mintage	VF	XF	Unc
144	1982MW	.803	—	—	12.50
	1983MW	1.530	—	—	10.00
	1983MW	.010	—	Proof	25.00

3.1100 g, .999 GOLD, .1000 oz AGW
Papal Visit in America

Y#	Date	Mintage	VF	XF	Unc
168	1987MW	201 pcs.	—	Proof	250.00

10th Anniversary of Pope John Paul II

Y#	Date	Mintage	VF	XF	Unc
174	1988MW	1,000	—	Proof	125.00

Pope John Paul II
Obv: Similar to Y#174.
Rev: Similar to 20,000 Zlotych, Y#190.

Y#	Date	Mintage	VF	XF	Unc
186	1989MW	*1,000		In sets only	125.00

2000 ZLOTYCH

8.0000 g, .900 GOLD, .2315 oz AGW
Fryderyk Chopin

Y#	Date	Mintage	VF	XF	Unc
90	1977MW	4,000	—	Proof	125.00

Duke Mieszko I

Y#	Date	Mintage	VF	XF	Unc
102	1979MW	3,000	—	Proof	125.00

Mikolaj Kopernik

Y#	Date	Mintage	VF	XF	Unc
106	1979MW	5,000	—	Proof	125.00

Maria Sklodowska Curie

Y#	Date	Mintage	VF	XF	Unc
107	1979MW	5,000	—	Proof	125.00

Winter Olympics - Ski Jumper
Obv: Similar to Y#107.

Y#	Date	Mintage	VF	XF	Unc
111	1980MW	5,250	—	Proof	125.00

King Boleslaw I Chrobry

Y#	Date	Mintage	VF	XF	Unc
116	1980MW	2,500	—	Proof	150.00

Kazimierz I

Y#	Date	Mintage	VF	XF	Unc
119	1980MW	2,500	—	Proof	150.00

Boleslaw II

Y#	Date	Mintage	VF	XF	Unc
135 (126)	1981MW	3,000	—	Proof	150.00

Wladyslaw I Herman
Similar to 200 Zlotych, Y#129.

Y#	Date	Mintage	VF	XF	Unc
131	1981MW	3,113	—	Proof	150.00

6.8000 g, .900 GOLD, .1968 oz AGW
Visit of Pope John Paul II

Y#	Date	Mintage	VF	XF	Unc
139	1982	500 pcs.	—	—	250.00
	1982	1,250	—	Proof	300.00
	1985	*1 pc.	—	—	800.00
	1985	*2 pcs.	—	Proof	1000.
	1986	*54 pcs.	—	—	400.00
	1986	*79 pcs.	—	Proof	450.00

Boleslaw III

Y#	Date	Mintage	VF	XF	Unc
234	1982	—	—	—	—

7.7700 g, .999 GOLD, .2500 oz AGW
Papal Visit in America

Y#	Date	Mintage	VF	XF	Unc
169	1987MW	201 pcs.	—	Proof	350.00

10th Anniversary of Pope John Paul II

Y#	Date	Mintage	VF	XF	Unc
175	1988	1,000	—	Proof	200.00

Pope John Paul II
Obv: Similar to Y#175.
Rev: Similar to 20,000 Zlotych, Y#190.

Y#	Date	Mintage	VF	XF	Unc
187	1989MW	*1,000		In sets only	200.00

5000 ZLOTYCH

15.5500 g, .999 GOLD, .5000 oz AGW
Papal Visit in America

Y#	Date	Mintage	VF	XF	Unc
170	1987MW	201 pcs.	—	Proof	550.00

10th Anniversary of Pope John Paul II

Y#	Date	Mintage	VF	XF	Unc
176	1988MW	1,000	—	Proof	300.00

Pope John Paul II
Obv: Similar to Y#176.
Rev: Similar to 20,000 Zlotych, Y#190.

Y#	Date	Mintage	VF	XF	Unc
188	1989MW	*1.000		In sets only	300.00

17.2700 g, .750 SILVER, .4165 oz ASW
Torun - Kopernicus

Y#	Date	Mintage	VF	XF	Unc
191	1989MW	.020	—	Proof	32.50

Torunia Town Hall

Y#	Date	Mintage	VF	XF	Unc
192	1989MW	.020	—	Proof	32.50

Henryk Sucharski

Y#	Date	Mintage	VF	XF	Unc
193	1989MW	.025	—	Proof	30.00

King Wladyslaw II - Bust

Y#	Date	Mintage	VF	XF	Unc
197	1989MW	8,000	—	Proof	35.00

King Wladyslaw II - Half Length

Y#	Date	Mintage	VF	XF	Unc
198	1989MW	2,500	—	Proof	45.00

10,000 ZLOTYCH

34.5000 g, .900 GOLD, .9984 oz AGW
Visit of Pope John Paul II

Y#	Date	Mintage	VF	XF	Unc
140	1982	200 pcs.	—	—	1250.
	1982	700 pcs.	—	Proof	1500.
	1985	*1 pc.	—	Proof	—
	1986	*6 pcs.	—	—	1750.
	1986	*13 pcs.	—	Proof	1850.

19.0600 g, .750 SILVER, .4582 oz ASW
Papal Visit

Y#	Date	Mintage	VF	XF	Unc
164	1987MW	.908	—	—	25.00
	1987MW	.015	—	Proof	40.00

31.1030 g, .999 GOLD, 1.0000 oz AGW
Papal Visit in America

Y#	Date	Mintage	VF	XF	Unc
171	1987MW	201 pcs.	—	Proof	1150.

10th Anniversary of Pope John Paul II

Y#	Date	Mintage	VF	XF	Unc
177	1988MW	1,000	—	—	550.00
	1988MW	1,000	—	Proof	600.00

31.1030 g, .999 SILVER, 1.0000 oz ASW

Y#	Date	Mintage	VF	XF	Unc
177a	1988MW	5,000	—	—	40.00
	1988MW	—	—	Proof	50.00

Pope John Paul - Christmas

Y#	Date	Mintage	VF	XF	Unc
179	1988MW	5,000	—	Proof	30.00

31.1030 g, .999 GOLD, 1.0000 oz AGW
Pope John Paul II

Y#	Date	Mintage	VF	XF	Unc
189	1989MW	*2,000	—	Proof	575.00

31.1000 g, .999 SILVER, 1.0000 oz ASW

Y#	Date	Mintage	VF	XF	Unc
189a	1989MW	—	—	—	40.00
	1989MW	5,000	—	Proof	50.00

COPPER-NICKEL
10th Anniversary of Solidarity

Y#	Date	Mintage	VF	XF	Unc
195	1990MW	15.164	—	—	7.00
	1990MW	5,000	—	Proof	15.00

NICKEL PLATED STEEL
200th Anniversary of Polish Constitution

Y#	Date	Mintage	VF	XF	Unc
217	1991MW	2.605	—	—	6.00

COPPER-NICKEL
Wladyslaw III

Y#	Date	Mintage	VF	XF	Unc
246	1992 MW	—	—	—	4.50

20,000 ZLOTYCH

19.0000 g, .750 SILVER, .4558 oz ASW
Soccer - Ball, Map and Globe

Y#	Date	Mintage	VF	XF	Unc
223	1989	.025	—	Proof	50.00

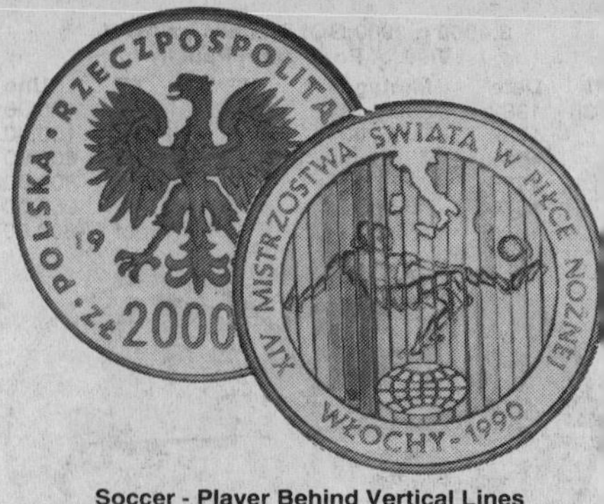

Soccer - Player Behind Vertical Lines

Y#	Date	Mintage	VF	XF	Un
224	1989	.025	—	Proof	50.0

COPPER-NICKEL CENTER, BRASS RING
225th Anniversary of Warsaw Mint

Y#	Date	Mintage	VF	XF	Un
215	1991MW	.100	—	—	15.0

3.1100 g, .999 GOLD, .1000 oz AGW
Solidarity
Obv: Similar to 10,000 Zlotych, Y#171.
Rev: Solidarity monument w/city view background

Y#	Date	Mintage	VF	XF	Un
219	1990	1,004	—	Proof	125.0

COPPER-NICKEL
Barn Swallows

Y#	Date	Mintage	VF	XF	Un
243	1993 MW	—	—	—	5.5

Lancut Castle

Y#	Date	Mintage	VF	XF	Un
244	1993 MW	—	—	—	5.5

Kazimierz IV

Y#	Date	Mintage	VF	XF	Un
256	1993	1.500	—	—	6.0

Olympics - Slalom Skier

Y#	Date	Mintage	VF	XF	Un
261	1993	.988	—	—	10.0

50,000 ZLOTYCH

19.3000 g, .750 SILVER, .4654 oz ASW
70 Years of Polish Independence

#	Date	Mintage	VF	XF	Unc
80	1988	1.000	—	—	20.00
	1988	.020	—	Proof	45.00

13.1000 g, .999 GOLD, .4212 oz AGW
Solidarity
Rev: Solidarity monument w/city view background.

20	1990	1,001	—	Proof	275.00

COPPER-NICKEL
200th Anniversary of Order Virtuti Militari

29	1992	.100	—	Proof	15.00

100,000 ZLOTYCH

31.1000 g, .999 SILVER, 1.0000 oz ASW
10th Anniversary of Solidarity

96	1990	.500	—	—	20.00

31.1000 g, .999 GOLD, 1.0000 oz AGW

96a	1990	1,001	—	Proof	650.00

Fryderyk Chopin

Y#	Date	Mintage	VF	XF	Unc
199	1990	.010	—	Proof	22.00

Tadeusz Kosciuszko

200	1990	.010	—	Proof	22.00

Marszalek Pilsudski

201	1990	.010	—	Proof	22.00

15.5500 g, .999 GOLD, .5000 oz AGW
Solidarity
Rev: Solidarity monument w/city view background.

221	1990	*1,000	—	Proof	300.00

NOTE: Y#202, 203 and 204 are 200,000 Zlotych coins struck in silver. Y#205, 206 and 207 are 200,000 Zlotych coins struck in gold.

16.5000 g, .750 SILVER, .3979 oz ASW
Major Henrik Dobrzanski - Hubal - Equestrians

235	1990	.012	—	Proof	37.50

Defense of Narvik - Polish Troops

236	1991	.012	—	Proof	37.50

Unification of Upper Silesia and Poland

Y#	Date	Mintage	VF	XF	Unc
227	1992	.012	—	Proof	37.50

200,000 ZLOTYCH

373.2420 g, .999 GOLD, 12.0000 oz AGW
Papal Visit in America
Illustration reduced. Actual size: 70mm

163	1987	101 pcs.	—	Proof	6500.

10th Anniversary of Pope John Paul II
Illustration reduced. Actual size: 70mm

178	1988MW	300 pcs.	—	Proof	5500.

Pope John Paul II
Illustration reduced. Actual size: 70mm.
Obv: Similar to 10,000 Zlotych, Y#179.

Y#	Date	Mintage	VF	XF	Unc
190	1989MW	*200 pcs.	—	Proof	6000.

155.5000 g, .999 SILVER, 5.0000 oz ASW
Fryderyk Chopin
Similar to 100,000 Zlotych, Y#199.

202	1990	.010	—	Proof	100.00

31.1000 g, .999 GOLD, 1.0000 oz AGW

205	1990	.010	—	Proof	500.00

155.5000 g, .999 SILVER, 5.0000 oz ASW
Tadeusz Kosciuszko
Similar to 100,000 Zlotych, Y#200.

203	1990	.010	—	Proof	100.00

31.1000 g, .999 GOLD, 1.0000 oz AGW

206	1990	.010	—	Proof	500.00

155.5000 g, .999 SILVER, 5.0000 oz ASW
Marszalck Pilsudski
Similar to 100,000 Zlotych, Y#201.

204	1990	.010	—	Proof	100.00

31.1000 g, .999 GOLD, 1.0000 oz AGW

207	1990	.010	—	Proof	500.00

31.1000 g, .999 GOLD, 1.0000 oz AGW
Solidarity
Rev: Solidarity monument w/city view background.

222	1990	*1,000	—	Proof	600.00

19.0600 g, .999 SILVER, .6122 oz ASW
Gen. Dyw. Stefan Rowecki "Grot"

240	1990	—	—	Proof	30.00

19.2650 g, .999 SILVER, .6188 oz ASW
Gen. Komorowski

250	1990	—	—	Proof	30.00

38.9000 g, .999 SILVER, 1.2496 oz ASW
200th Anniversary of Polish Constitution

Y#	Date	Mintage	VF	XF	Unc
218	1991	.100	—	—	30.00

31.1000 g, .925 SILVER, .9250 oz ASW
Albertville Olympics - Slalom Skier

226	1991	.020	—	Proof	37.50

Barcelona Olympics - Weightlifter

228	1991	.020	—	Proof	37.50

31.1600 g, .925 SILVER, .9267 oz ASW
Barcelona Olympics - 2 Sailboats

Y#	Date	Mintage	VF	XF	Unc
241	1991	—	—	Proof	37.50

19.3300 g, .750 SILVER, .4661 oz ASW
70th Anniversary of Posnan Fair

242	1991	—	—	Proof	30.00

Gen. Okulicki

251	1991	—	—	Proof	30.00

Gen. Tokarzewski - Karaszewicz

252	1991	—	—	Proof	30.00

31.1000 g, .999 SILVER, 1.0000 oz ASW
Discovery of America - Portrait and Ship

#	Date	Mintage	VF	XF	Unc
30	1992	.020	—	Proof	45.00

Seville Expo '92

#	Date	Mintage	VF	XF	Unc
31	1992	.045	—	Proof	35.00

16.5000 g, .750 SILVER, .3979 oz ASW
Polish Protection of WWII Sea Convoys

#	Date	Mintage	VF	XF	Unc
32	1992	.015	—	Proof	30.00

Stanislaw Staszic

#	Date	Mintage	VF	XF	Unc
33	1992	.020	—	Proof	30.00

Wladyslaw III - Chest Length Bust

Y#	Date	Mintage	VF	XF	Unc
253	1992	—	—	Proof	30.00

Wladyslaw III - Shoulder Length Bust

Y#	Date	Mintage	VF	XF	Unc
254	1992	—	—	Proof	30.00

16.5000 g, .750 SILVER, .3979 oz ASW
750th Anniversary of City of Stettin

Y#	Date	Mintage	VF	XF	Unc
255	1993	—	—	Proof	30.00

Kazimierz IV

Y#	Date	Mintage	VF	XF	Unc
257	1993	.015	—	Proof	30.00

Kazimierz IV - Enthroned

Y#	Date	Mintage	VF	XF	Unc
258	1993	5,000	—	Proof	35.00

Polish Partisans Sabotaging Railways - WWII

Y#	Date	Mintage	VF	XF	Unc
259	1993	.010	—	Proof	35.00

31.1600 g, .925 SILVER, .9267 oz ASW
50th Anniversary of Warsaw Ghetto Uprising

Y#	Date	Mintage	VF	XF	Unc
245	1993	—	—	Proof	40.00

1994 Olympics - Lillehammer

Y#	Date	Mintage	VF	XF	Unc
247	1993	—	—	Proof	45.00

31.1450 g, .999 SILVER, 1.0004 oz ASW
Barn Swallows

Y#	Date	Mintage	VF	XF	Unc
248	1993	—	—	Proof	45.00

Lancut Castle

Y#	Date	Mintage	VF	XF	Unc
249	1993	—	—	Proof	45.00

31.1000 g, .999 SILVER, .9990 oz ASW
Aerial View of Zamosc

Y#	Date	Mintage	VF	XF	Unc
260	1993	.020	—	Proof	40.00

500,000 ZLOTYCH

62.2000 g, .999 GOLD, 2.0000 oz AGW
Fryderyk Chopin
Similar to 100,000 Zlotych, Y#199.

Y#	Date	Mintage	VF	XF	Unc
208	1990	2,000	—	Proof	1000.

Tadeusz Kosciuszko
Similar to 100,000 Zlotych, Y#200.

Y#	Date	Mintage	VF	XF	Unc
209	1990	2,000	—	Proof	1000.

Marszalek Pilsudski
Similar to 100,000 Zlotych, Y#201.

Y#	Date	Mintage	VF	XF	Unc
210	1990	2,000	—	Proof	1000.

1,000,000 ZLOTYCH

373.2000 g, .999 GOLD, 12.0000 oz AGW
Fryderyk Chopin
Similar to 100,000 Zlotych, Y#199.

Y#	Date	Mintage	VF	XF	Unc
211	1990	250 pcs.	—	Proof	6,500.

Tadeusz Kosciuszko
Similar to 100,000 Zlotych, Y#200.

Y#	Date	Mintage	VF	XF	Unc
212	1990	250 pcs.	—	Proof	6,500.

Marszalek Pilsudski
Similar to 100,000 Zlotych, Y#201.

Y#	Date	Mintage	VF	XF	Unc
213	1990	250 pcs.	—	Proof	6,500.

SPECIMEN SETS (SS)

KM#	Date	Mintage	Identification	Issue Price	Mkt. Val.
SS1	1831(5)	—	C120,121,123-125, including 1 Zloty banknote	—	1500.

PROOF SETS (PS)

KM#	Date	Mintage	Identification	Issue Price	Mkt. Val.
PS1	1986(6)	5,000	Y48.2,49.2,80.2,81.2, 152.1,153.1	—	85.00
PS2	1987(7)	500	Y48.2,49.2,80.2,81.2, 152.1,153.1,167	—	85.00
PS3	1987(5)	6	Y140,163,168-170	—	—
PS4	1987(4)	300	Y140,168-170	—	—
PS5	1987(4)	201	Y168-171	—	—
PS6	1988(7)	5,000	Y49.2,80.2,81.2,152.1, 153.1,182,183, mint medal	—	85.00
PS7	1988(4)	1,000	Y174-177	—	1125.
PS8	1989(7)	5,000	Y49.3,80.3,81.3,152.2, 153.2,185,194	—	85.00
PS9	1989(4)	1,000	Y186-189	1595.	1100.
PS10	1990(4)	1,000	Y219-222	1495.	1300.

DANZIG

A seaport on the northern coast of Poland giving access to the Baltic Sea. An important port from early times. Has at different times belonged to the Teutonic Knights, Pomerania, Russia, and Prussia. Danzig was a free city from 1919 to 1939 during which most of its modern coinage was made.

RULERS

Friedrich Wilhelm III (of Prussia), 1797-1840
Marshal Lefebvre (as Duke), 1807-1814

MINT MARKS

A - Berlin

MINTMASTERS INITIALS

Letter	Date	Name
M	1808-12	Johann Ludwig Meyer

MONETARY SYSTEM

3 Schilling = 1 Groschen

SCHILLING

COPPER

KM#	Date	Mintage	VG	Fine	VF	XF
135	1801A	—	6.00	12.00	25.00	40.00

KM#	Date	Mintage	VG	Fine	VF	XF
136	1808 M	—	6.00	12.00	25.00	40.00
	1812 M	—	6.00	12.00	25.00	40.00

EIN (1) GROSCHEN

COPPER

KM#	Date	Mintage	VG	Fine	VF	XF
137	1809 M	—	7.50	15.00	25.00	50.00
	1812 M	—	7.50	15.00	25.00	50.00

FREE CITY

MONETARY SYSTEM

Until 1923
100 Pfennig = 1 Mark
Commencing 1923
100 Pfennig, Pfennige = 1 Gulden

PFENNIG

BRONZE

KM#	Date	Mintage	Fine	VF	XF	Unc
140	1923	4.000	1.00	3.00	5.00	10.00
	1923	—	—	—	Proof	50.00
	1926	1.500	1.50	4.00	8.00	16.00
	1929	1.000	2.50	7.50	12.00	20.00
	1930	2.000	1.25	3.50	6.50	12.00
	1937	3.000	1.25	3.50	6.50	12.00

2 PFENNIG

BRONZE

KM#	Date	Mintage	Fine	VF	XF	Unc
141	1923	1.000	1.75	4.50	7.50	15.00
	1923	—	—	—	Proof	65.00
	1926	1.750	1.75	4.50	7.50	15.00
	1937	.500	2.75	6.50	11.00	18.50

5 PFENNIG

COPPER-NICKEL

KM#	Date	Mintage	Fine	VF	XF	Unc
142	1923	3.000	1.25	2.75	6.00	12.00
	1923	—	—	—	Proof	100.00
	1928	1.000	3.50	8.25	14.00	27.50
	1928	—	—	—	Proof	175.00

ALUMINUM-BRONZE

KM#	Date	Mintage	Fine	VF	XF	Unc
151	1932	4.000	1.25	2.25	6.00	16.00

10 PFENNIG

COPPER-NICKEL

KM#	Date	Mintage	Fine	VF	XF	Unc
143	1923	5.000	2.00	3.00	8.00	18.00
	1923	—	—	—	Proof	115.00

ALUMINUM-BRONZE

KM#	Date	Mintage	Fine	VF	XF	Unc
152	1932	5.000	1.50	2.50	7.00	17.00

1/2 GULDEN

2.5000 g, .750 SILVER, .0603 oz ASW

KM#	Date	Mintage	Fine	VF	XF	Unc
144	1923	1.000	7.50	20.00	40.00	65.00
	1923	—	—	—	Proof	150.00
	1927	.400	17.50	35.00	70.00	125.00
	1927	—	—	—	Proof	250.00

NICKEL

KM#	Date	Mintage	Fine	VF	XF	Unc
153	1932	1.400	8.00	25.00	37.50	60.00

GULDEN

5.0000 g, .750 SILVER, .1206 oz ASW

M#	Date	Mintage	Fine	VF	XF	Unc
45	1923	2.500	11.00	22.50	40.00	65.00
	1923	—	—	—	Proof	200.00

NICKEL

54	1932	2.500	8.00	25.00	35.00	55.00

2 GULDEN

10.0000 g, .750 SILVER, .2411 oz ASW

46	1923	1.250	25.00	55.00	100.00	175.00
	1923	—	—	—	Proof	250.00

10.0000 g, .500 SILVER, .1608 oz ASW

55	1932	1.250	—	150.00	200.00	300.00

5 GULDEN

25.0000 g, .750 SILVER, .6028 oz ASW

47	1923	.700	65.00	135.00	210.00	325.00
	1923	—	—	—	Proof	550.00
	1927	.160	150.00	250.00	375.00	600.00
	1927	—	—	—	Proof	1000.

14.8200 g, .500 SILVER, .2382 oz ASW

KM#	Date	Mintage	Fine	VF	XF	Unc
156	1932	.430	125.00	225.00	350.00	950.00

157	1932	.430	150.00	350.00	850.00	1500.

NICKEL

158	1935	.800	100.00	160.00	235.00	450.00

10 GULDEN

NICKEL

159	1935	.380	300.00	500.00	700.00	1350.

25 GULDEN

7.9881 g, .917 GOLD, .2354 oz AGW

148	1923	800 pcs.	—	1500.	1800.	2500.
	1923	200 pcs.	—	—	Proof	3250.

NOTE: This issue was presented to members of the Senate.

150	1930	*4,000	—	—	6500.	9000.

NOTE: Not released for circulation; a few were given in V.I.P. presentation cases on September 1, 1939.

PROOF SETS (PS)

KM#	Date	Mintage	Identification	Issue Price	Mkt. Val.
PS1	1923(8)	—	KM140-147	—	1300.

EAST PRUSSIA

An area on the southeastern coast of the Baltic Sea. Part of the area is in present day Poland and part in the U.S.S.R. A possession of Prussia from 1525 until 1945. Coinage for the area made by the Prussian kings except for brief occupation by Russia from 1756-1762 when Russia produced special coin types for the area.

RULERS

Friedrich Wilhelm III (of Prussia)
1797-1840

MINT MARKS

A - Berlin
E - Konigsberg
G - Glatz, Silesia

NOTE: For gold listings refer to Konigsberg Mint under Brandenburg and Prussia (German States).

PRUSSIAN COINAGE

SCHILLING

COPPER

C#	Date	Mintage	VG	Fine	VF	XF
53	1804A	—	1.50	3.25	6.00	11.00
	1805A	—	1.50	3.25	6.00	11.00
	1806A	—	1.50	3.25	6.00	11.00

54	1810A	—	1.50	3.25	6.00	11.00

1/2 GROSCHEN

COPPER

56	1811A	—	3.00	7.00	15.00	25.00

GROSCHEN

COPPER

58	1810	—	1.75	4.50	8.00	14.00
	1811A	—	1.75	4.50	8.00	14.00

3 GROSCHEN

BILLON

60	1801A	—	3.50	9.00	15.00	25.00
	1802A	—	3.50	9.00	15.00	25.00
	1803A	—	3.50	9.00	15.00	25.00
	1805A	—	3.50	9.00	15.00	25.00
	1806A	—	3.50	9.00	15.00	25.00
	1807A	—	3.50	9.00	15.00	25.00

NOTE: Earlier date (1800) exists for this type.

60a	1807G	—	3.50	9.00	15.00	25.00
	1808G	—	3.50	9.00	15.00	25.00

KRAKOW

A city in southern Poland, the third largest in the country. Formed an independent republic in 1815 that lasted until 1846 at which time the city reverted to Austria. Coins made for the republic in 1835.

MONETARY SYSTEM

30 Groszy = 1 Zloty

5 GROSZY

BILLON

11	1835	—	10.00	20.00	30.00	50.00

10 GROSZY

SILVER

12	1835	—	10.00	20.00	30.00	50.00

ZLOTY

SILVER

C#	Date	Mintage	VG	Fine	VF	XF
13	1835	—	15.00	22.50	35.00	55.00

POSEN

A province of Prussia from 1793-1918. Became part of the Grand Duchy of Warsaw. Returned to Prussia after the Congress of Vienna (1815). A special coin issue was made as a provincial issue for the Grand Duchy of Posen by Prussia immediately after repossession.

RULERS

Friedrich Wilhelm III (of Prussia)
1797-1840

MINT MARKS

A - Berlin
B - Breslau

GROSCHEN

COPPER

KM#	Date	Mintage	VG	Fine	VF	XF
30	1816A	—	5.00	10.00	15.00	25.00
	1816B	—	5.00	10.00	15.00	25.00
	1817A	—	5.00	10.00	15.00	25.00

3 GROSCHEN

COPPER

KM#	Date	Mintage	VG	Fine	VF	XF
31	1816A	—	—	—	Rare	—
	1816B	—	5.00	15.00	20.00	30.00
	1817A	—	5.00	15.00	20.00	40.00

ZAMOSC

A Fortress commune in south-eastern Poland twice besieged by Russians.

MONETARY SYSTEM

30 Groszy = 1 Zloty

SIEGE COINAGE

Issued by the Saxon-Polish garrison under General Hauke.

MINT MARK

(b) - flaming bomb

6 GROSZY

COPPER

KM#	Date	Mintage	VG	Fine	VF	XF
1	1813	1,330	150.00	275.00	500.00	800.00

Rev: W/o outer leg.

KM#	Date	Mintage	VG	Fine	VF	XF
2	1813	Inc. Ab.	200.00	350.00	600.00	1000.

Rev: W/o palm fronds.

KM#	Date	Mintage	VG	Fine	VF	XF
3	1813	Inc. Ab.	—	—	Rare	—

2 ZLOTY

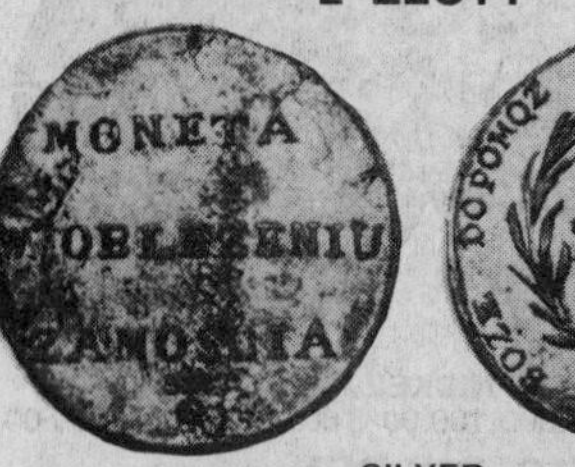

SILVER

KM#	Date	Mintage	VG	Fine	VF	XF
5	1813(b)	7,830	100.00	175.00	225.00	375.00

Obv: W/o mint mark.

KM#	Date	Mintage	VG	Fine	VF	XF
6	1813	Inc. Ab.	135.00	235.00	300.00	500.00

Obv: Legend in 4 lines.

KM#	Date	Mintage	VG	Fine	VF	XF
7	1813	Inc. Ab.	150.00	250.00	300.00	500.00

NOTE: Varieties exist.

PORTUGAL

The Portuguese Republic, located in the western part the Iberian Peninsula in southwestern Europe, has a area of 35,553 sq. mi. (92,080 sq. km.) and a popul tion of *10.5 million. Capital: Lisbon. Portugal's econom is based on agriculture, tourism, minerals, fisheries ar a rapidly expanding industrial sector. Textiles account f 33" of the exports and Portuguese wine has becom world famous. Portugal has become Europe's numb one producer of copper and the world's largest produc of cork.

After centuries of domination by Romans, Visigoths ar Moors, Portugal emerged in the 12th century as an ind pendent kingdom financially and philosophical prepared for the great period of exploration that wou follow. Attuned to the inspiration of Prince Henry th Navigator (1394-1460), Portugal's daring explorers the 15th and 16th centuries roamed the world's ocear from Brazil to Japan in an unprecendented burst energy and endeavor that culminated in 1494 with Po tugal laying claim to half the transoceanic world. Unfo tunately for the fortunes of the tiny kingdom, th Portuguese population was too small to colonize this va territory. Less than a century after Portugal laid claim half the world, English, French and Dutch trading con panies had seized the lion's share of the world colonies and commerce, and Portugal's place as a imperial power was lost forever. The monarchy was ove thrown in 1910 and a republic established.

On April 25, 1974, the government of Portugal wa seized by a military junta which reached agreement providing for independence for the Portuguese oversea provinces of Portuguese Guinea (Guinea-Bissau Mozambique, Cape Verde Islands, Angola, and S Thomas and Prince Islands (Sao Tome and Principe).

On January 1, 1986, Portugal became the elevent member of the European Economic Community and i the first half of 1992 held its first EEC Presidency.

RULERS

Joao, As Prince Regent, 1799-1816
Joao, As King (Joao VI), 1816-1826
Pedro IV, 1826-1828
Miguel, 1828-1834
Maria II, 1834-1853
Pedro V, 1853-1861
Luiz I, 1861-1889
Carlos I, 1889-1908
Manuel II, 1908-1910
Republic, 1910 to date

MINT MARKS

A - Paris (1891-1892, Copper only)
L - Lisbon
P - Porto
No Mint mark - Lisbon

MONETARY SYSTEM

1826-1836

7500 Reis = 1 Peca

Beginning in 1836 all coins were expressed in terms Reis and arranged in a decimal sequence, (until 1910).

Commencing 1836

20 Reis = 1 Vintem
100 Reis = 1 Tostao
480 Reis = 24 Vintens = 1 Cruzado
1600 Reis = 1 Escudo
6400 Reis = 4 Escudos = 1 Peca

Commencing 1910

100 Centavos = 1 Escudo

NOTE: The primary denomination was the Peca weighing 14.34 g, tariffed at 6400 Reis until 1825, and a 7500 Reis after 1826. The weight was not changed.

III (3) REIS

COPPER

Obv: JOANNES. . . ., around shield. Rev: Leg. aroun wreath, date and denomination within.

KM#	Date	Mintage	VG	Fine	VF	X
334	1804	.123	4.25	8.50	17.50	45.0

Obv: Crowned arms.
Rev: Value and date in branches.

KM#	Date	Mintage	VG	Fine	VF	X
354	1818	—	15.00	35.00	70.00	135.0

V (5) REIS

COPPER

Obv. leg: JOANNES. . ., arms.
Rev. leg. ends: PRINCEPS.

KM#	Date	Mintage	VG	Fine	VF	X
325	1801	—	20.00	40.00	85.00	175.0

NOTE: Earlier date (1800) exists for this type.

Rev. leg. ends: REGENS.

KM#	Date	Mintage	VG	Fine	VF	X
335	1804	—	Reported, not confirme			

KM#	Date	Mintage	VG	Fine	VF	XF
346	1812	.399	1.00	2.00	6.00	12.50
	1813	.539	2.00	3.00	7.00	15.00
	1814	.448	2.25	4.50	10.00	25.00

Mule. Obv: KM#305. Rev: KM#346.

KM#	Date	Mintage	VG	Fine	VF	XF
347	1812	—	5.25	11.25	22.50	45.00

Obv: Arms, JOANNES VI.
Rev: PORTUGALIAE. . . REX, value in wreath.

KM#	Date	Mintage	VG	Fine	VF	XF
355	1818	—	50.00	110.00	225.00	450.00
	1819	.011	4.00	8.00	17.50	35.00
	1820	—	3.50	7.00	15.00	30.00
	1823	.032	4.00	8.00	17.50	35.00
	1824	.098	1.50	3.00	6.00	12.50

Obv. leg: MICHAEL I DEI GRATIA, crowned arms.
Rev: Leg. around wreath, value within, date below.

KM#	Date	Mintage	VG	Fine	VF	XF
389	1829	.401	1.25	2.50	5.00	12.50

NOTE: For similar coins dated 1830 but w/titles of MariaII see Azores.

Titles of Maria II
Obv: Square shield.

KM#	Date	Mintage	VG	Fine	VF	XF
398	1833	—	65.00	125.00	250.00	400.00

(Struck at Porto.)

KM#	Date	Mintage	VG	Fine	VF	XF
408	1836	5,593	15.00	25.00	40.00	80.00

X (10) REIS

COPPER
Obv. leg: JOANNES. . ., arms.
Rev. leg. ends: PRINCEPS.

KM#	Date	Mintage	VG	Fine	VF	XF
327	1801	—	—	—	Rare	—

NOTE: Earlier date (1800) exists for this type.

Rev. leg. ends: REGENS.

KM#	Date	Mintage	VG	Fine	VF	XF
333	1803	—	20.00	37.50	75.00	150.00

KM#	Date	Mintage	VG	Fine	VF	XF
348	1812	.332	1.25	2.50	8.00	20.00
	1813	.276	1.25	2.50	8.00	20.00

Obv. leg: JOANNES VI. . ., arms.
Rev. leg: PORTUGALIAE. . . REX, value in wreath.

KM#	Date	Mintage	VG	Fine	VF	XF
356	1818	—	20.00	40.00	80.00	150.00
	1819	.806	1.50	3.00	6.00	12.50
	1820	6,773	10.00	22.50	45.00	90.00
	1822	.021	10.00	20.00	40.00	80.00
	1823	.044	2.00	4.25	9.00	20.00
	1824	.064	2.00	3.50	7.00	15.00
	1825	—	Reported, not confirmed			

KM#	Date	Mintage	VG	Fine	VF	XF
390	1829	.056	2.00	3.50	6.00	15.00
(C89)	1831	.345	1.00	4.25	10.00	25.00
	1833	.070	5.50	11.50	22.50	45.00

NOTE: For similar coins dated 1830 but with titles of Maria II see Azores.

Similar to 5 Reis, KM#408.

KM#	Date	Mintage	VG	Fine	VF	XF
399	1833	—	50.00	100.00	175.00	300.00

(Struck at Porto.)

Obv: Large crowned shield.

KM#	Date	Mintage	VG	Fine	VF	XF
406	1835	.287	2.50	6.00	12.00	25.00
	1836	.227	1.50	3.50	7.50	15.00
	1837	.360	6.00	10.00	17.50	35.00

Obv: Small crowned shield.

KM#	Date	Mintage	VG	Fine	VF	XF
409	1837	Inc. Ab.	2.00	4.25	8.50	17.50
	1838	.645	1.50	3.00	6.50	12.50
	1839	.469	1.50	3.00	6.50	12.50

20 REIS

(Vintem)

SILVER
Obv: Globe. Rev: Cross w/rosettes in angles.

KM#	Date	VG	Fine	VF	XF
330	ND(1799-1816)	2.25	4.25	8.50	17.50

BRONZE
Titles of Maria II

KM#	Date	Mintage	VG	Fine	VF	XF
400	1833	—	10.00	20.00	35.00	75.00

(Struck at Porto.)

40 REIS

(Pataco)

BRONZE
Plain edge

KM#	Date	Mintage	VG	Fine	VF	XF
345.1	1811	.163	6.25	12.50	20.00	50.00
	1812	1.384	3.25	6.25	12.50	30.00
	1813	1.762	2.50	5.00	10.00	25.00
	1814	.542	2.50	5.00	10.00	25.00
	1815	.118	10.00	20.00	35.00	75.00
	1817	—	Reported, not confirmed			

Milled edge

KM#	Date	Mintage	VG	Fine	VF	XF
345.2	1814	Inc. Ab.	8.50	17.50	35.00	90.00
365	1819	.422	3.00	6.00	12.50	35.00

KM#	Date	Mintage	VG	Fine	VF	XF
370	1820	1.579	2.00	3.50	6.25	25.00
	1821	1.575	2.00	3.50	6.25	25.00
	1822	2.370	2.00	3.50	6.25	25.00
	1823	2.621	2.00	3.50	6.25	25.00
	1824	3.051	2.00	3.50	6.25	25.00
	1825	1.124	2.50	4.00	7.50	30.00

Similar to KM#345.1.

KM#	Date	Mintage	VG	Fine	VF	XF
371	1821	—	25.00	60.00	115.00	225.00
	1823	—	20.00	50.00	90.00	175.00

Rev: Similar to KM#345.1.

KM#	Date	Mintage	VG	Fine	VF	XF
373	1826	1.253	3.25	6.25	12.50	40.00
	1827	1.447	2.50	5.00	10.00	30.00
	1828	1.378	2.50	5.00	10.00	30.00

Obv: Large high crown.

KM#	Date	Mintage	VG	Fine	VF	XF
380	1828	1.378	4.00	8.00	15.00	40.00
	1829	1.678	3.00	5.00	10.00	35.00

Obv: Small lower crown.

KM#	Date	Mintage	VG	Fine	VF	XF
391	1829	Inc. KM380	2.25	4.25	7.50	20.00
	1830	1.783	2.25	4.25	7.50	20.00
	1831	1.391	2.25	4.25	7.50	20.00
	1832	1.780	2.25	4.25	7.50	20.00
	1833	1.631	2.25	4.25	7.50	20.00
	1834	—	Reported, not confirmed			

Titles of Maria II
Similar to 20 Reis, KM#400, shield flared outward at upper corners, value in wreath.

KM#	Date	Mintage	VG	Fine	VF	XF
401	1833	—	6.25	12.50	20.00	45.00

(Struck at Porto.)

Shield w/right-angle upper corners.

KM#	Date	Mintage	VG	Fine	VF	XF
402	1833	—	2.00	3.75	7.50	22.50
	1834	—	2.00	3.75	7.50	22.50
	1847	—	3.50	7.50	17.50	45.00

The 1833-34 coins were struck at Lisbon, the 1847 at Porto. Varieties of the 1833 and 1834 coins have a vertical axis instead of horizontal. Values are 1833 $27.50 in XF, 1834 $35.00 in XF.

50 REIS

(1/2 Tostao)

SILVER
Obv. leg: JOANNES. . . . ET ALG. . . .
Rev. leg: IN HOC . . . . ., cross.

KM#	Date	Mintage	VG	Fine	VF	XF
310	ND(1799-1816)	—	7.50	20.00	45.00	120.00

SILVER
Obv. leg. ends: P. REGENS.

KM#	Date	Mintage	VG	Fine	VF	XF
311	ND(1799-1816)	—	7.50	20.00	45.00	120.00

KM#	Date	Mintage	VG	Fine	VF	XF
350	ND(1799-1816)	.010	5.50	12.50	30.00	75.00

Obv. leg: MICHAEL I. . . . REX, crowned value.
Rev. leg: IN HOC. . ., cross.

KM#	Date	Mintage	VG	Fine	VF	XF
381	ND(1828-34)	—	10.00	20.00	40.00	100.00

60 REIS

(3 Vintens)

Obv. leg: JOANNES. . . . ET ALG., arms.
Rev. leg: IN HOC. . . , cross.

KM#	Date	Mintage	VG	Fine	VF	XF
312	ND(1799-1816)	—	3.00	5.00	12.00	30.00

SILVER, 1.83 g
Obv. leg. ends: P. REGENS.

KM#	Date	Mintage	VG	Fine	VF	XF
313	ND(1799-1816)	—	2.50	4.50	10.00	25.00

Obv: Crowned arms above globe.

KM#	Date	Mintage	VG	Fine	VF	XF
351	ND(1799-1816)	—	3.50	6.50	15.00	40.00

Obv. leg: PETRUS IV. . . . REX, arms.

KM#	Date	Mintage	VG	Fine	VF	XF
374	ND(1816-26)	.036	85.00	175.00	385.00	850.00

Obv. leg: MICHAEL I. . ., crowned arms.

KM#	Date	Mintage	VG	Fine	VF	XF
382	ND(1828-34)	—	3.50	6.50	15.00	40.00

LXXX (80) REIS

Tostao

NOTE: Worth 100 Reis, though marked LXXX = 80 Reis.

SILVER
Mint: Lisbon
Obv. leg: JOANNES . . . ET. ALG.
Rev. leg: IN HOC. . ., cross.

KM#	Date	Mintage	VG	Fine	VF	XF
314	ND(1799-1816)	—	5.00	10.00	25.00	60.00

Obv. leg. ends: P. REGENS

KM#	Date	Mintage	VG	Fine	VF	XF
315	ND(1799-1816)	—	4.50	8.00	20.00	50.00

KM#	Date	Mintage	VG	Fine	VF	XF
352	ND(1799-1816)	—	5.00	10.00	22.50	55.00

Obv. leg: PETRUS IV . . . . REX, crowned value.

KM#	Date	Mintage	VG	Fine	VF	XF
375	ND(1816-26)	9,986	250.00	550.00	1150.	2800.

Obv. leg: MICHAEL I . . ., crowned value, large high crown.

KM#	Date	Mintage	VG	Fine	VF	XF
383	ND(1828-34)	—	15.00	25.00	50.00	100.00

Obv: Small lower crown.

KM#	Date	Mintage	VG	Fine	VF	XF
384	ND(1828-34)	—	350.00	650.00	1000.	1500.

120 REIS

(6 Vintens)

SILVER
Mint: Lisbon
Obv. leg: JOANNES. . . . . ET ALG, arms.
Rev. leg: IN HOC. . . . ., cross.

KM#	Date	Mintage	VG	Fine	VF	XF
316	ND(1799-1816)	—	6.00	12.00	30.00	75.00

Obv. leg. ends: P. REGENS.

KM#	Date	Mintage	VG	Fine	VF	XF
317	ND(1799-1816)	—	4.50	8.00	20.00	50.00

KM#	Date	Mintage	VG	Fine	VF	XF
353	ND(1799-1816)	—	6.50	12.00	30.00	75.00

Obv. leg: PETRUS IV . . . . REX, crowned arms.

KM#	Date	Mintage	VG	Fine	VF	XF
376	ND(1816-26)	.018	175.00	350.00	750.00	1900.

Obv. leg: MICHAEL I . . . ., crowned arms.

KM#	Date	Mintage	VG	Fine	VF	XF
385	ND(1828-34)	—	5.00	10.00	20.00	50.00

200 REIS

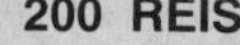

SILVER
Mint: Porto
Obv. leg: JOANNES . . . . P. REGENS., arms.

KM#	Date	Mintage	VG	Fine	VF	XF
340	1806	—	60.00	100.00	170.00	325.00
	1807	—	—	—	Rare	—
	1808	—	20.00	35.00	60.00	125.00
	1809	.022	35.00	60.00	100.00	200.00
	1816	—	50.00	90.00	150.00	300.00

KM#	Date	Mintage	VG	Fine	VF	XF
357	1818	.021	30.00	60.00	120.00	225.00
	1819	.024	30.00	65.00	135.00	250.00
	1820	2,818	30.00	60.00	125.00	225.00
	1821	2,293	80.00	175.00	350.00	650.00
	1822	6,483	40.00	85.00	175.00	325.00

Obv. leg: MICHAEL I . . ., crowned arms.

KM#	Date	Mintage	VG	Fine	VF	XF
392	1829	3,584	17.50	30.00	50.00	100.00
	1830	6,594	22.50	40.00	65.00	125.00

400 REIS

SILVER
Obv. leg. ends: ET. ALG.
Rev: Similar to KM#331.

KM#	Date	Mintage	VG	Fine	VF	XF
318	1801	.196	50.00	90.00	150.00	300.00
	1802	—	—	—	Rare	—

NOTE: Earlier dates (1799-1800) exist for this type.

Obv. leg. ends: P.REGENS

KM#	Date	Mintage	VG	Fine	VF	XF
331	1802	—	25.00	40.00	65.00	125.00
	1805	—	15.00	25.00	40.00	80.00
	1807	—	9.00	15.00	25.00	50.00
	1808	—	9.00	15.00	25.00	50.00
	1809	—	9.00	15.00	25.00	50.00
	1810	—	9.00	15.00	25.00	50.00
	1811	—	9.00	17.50	30.00	60.00
	1812	—	9.00	15.00	25.00	50.00
	1813	—	9.00	15.00	25.00	50.00
	1814	—	8.00	12.50	20.00	50.00
	1815	—	8.00	12.50	20.00	50.00
	1816	—	8.00	12.50	20.00	50.00
	1816 VINECS (error for VINCES)	—	50.00	100.00	175.00	350.00

1.0720 g, .917 GOLD, .0316 oz AGW
Obv. leg: JOANNES P.R. in crowned wreath.

KM#	Date	Mintage	VG	Fine	VF	XF
341	1807	8,857	65.00	125.00	225.00	350.00

SILVER

KM#	Date	Mintage	VG	Fine	VF	XF
358	1818	2.337	9.00	15.00	30.00	55.00
	1819	1.432	9.00	15.00	30.00	55.00
	1820	1.845	9.00	15.00	30.00	55.00
	1821	1.937	9.00	15.00	30.00	55.00

KM#	Date	Mintage	VG	Fine	VF	XF
358	1822	.568	10.00	20.00	40.00	80.00
	1823	.667	15.00	30.00	60.00	125.00
	1825	.028	32.50	55.00	90.00	175.00

1.0720 g, .917 GOLD, .0316 oz AGW
Obv. leg: JOAN VI in crowned wreath.

KM#	Date	Mintage	VG	Fine	VF	XF
359	1818	4,401	85.00	150.00	200.00	325.00
	1819	1,387	100.00	175.00	250.00	400.00
	1820	200 pcs.	250.00	350.00	550.00	825.00
	1821	266 pcs.	200.00	300.00	450.00	675.00

SILVER
Obv. leg: PETRUS IV . . . . REX., arms.

KM#	Date	Mintage	VG	Fine	VF	XF
377	1826	.259	32.50	55.00	90.00	175.00
	1827	—	None known to have survived			

.906 SILVER
Similar to KM#331.

KM#	Date	Mintage	VG	Fine	VF	XF
386	1828	.135	50.00	90.00	150.00	300.00
	1829	.022	250.00	500.00	1000.	2000.
	1830	.029	40.00	65.00	115.00	225.00
	1831	.065	35.00	60.00	100.00	200.00
	1832	.108	35.00	60.00	100.00	200.00
	1833	.708	35.00	60.00	100.00	200.00
	1834	.705	—	—	Rare	—

Obv. leg: *MARIA II. . . . REGINA*, arms.

KM#	Date	Mintage	VG	Fine	VF	XF
403.1	1833	—	500.00	1000.	1750.	3000.

(Struck in Porto.)

Obv. leg: Stars removed (Lisbon issues).

KM#	Date	Mintage	VG	Fine	VF	XF
403.2	1833	.798	10.00	17.50	30.00	75.00
	1834	1.864	9.00	15.00	25.00	50.00
	1835	3.433	9.00	15.00	25.00	45.00
	1836	.829	9.00	15.00	25.00	55.00
	1837	.194	100.00	200.00	350.00	650.00

1000 REIS

(Quartinho)

(1200 Reis)

2.6800 g, .917 GOLD, .0790 oz AGW

KM#	Date	Mintage	VG	Fine	VF	XF
360	1818	3,144	125.00	250.00	375.00	600.00
	1819	1,247	150.00	300.00	475.00	700.00
	1820	270 pcs.	250.00	425.00	600.00	1000.
	1821	275 pcs.	250.00	425.00	600.00	1000.

1/2 ESCUDO

(800 Reis)

1.7920 g, .917 GOLD, .0528 oz AGW
Obv. leg: JOANNES D.G. PORT. ET ALG. P. REGENS.

KM#	Date	Mintage	VG	Fine	VF	XF
337	1805	3,278	75.00	150.00	275.00	450.00
	1806	—	100.00	200.00	375.00	600.00
	1807	5,253	75.00	150.00	275.00	450.00

Obv. leg: JOANNES VI D.G. PORT. . .

KM#	Date	Mintage	VG	Fine	VF	XF
361	1818	270 pcs.	200.00	350.00	500.00	1000
	1819	5,536	100.00	250.00	400.00	600.00
	1820	82 pcs.	—	—	Rare	—
	1821	286 pcs.	200.00	350.00	500.00	1000

ESCUDO

(1600 Reis)

3.5850 g, .917 GOLD, .1057 oz AGW
Obv. leg: JOANNES D.G. PORT ET ALG. P. REGENS.

M#	Date	Mintage	VG	Fine	VF	XF
38	1805	—	—	—	Rare	—
	1807	800 pcs.	200.00	450.00	750.00	1200.

Obv. leg: JOANNES VI D.G. PORT . . . . REX, bust.

62	1818	1,804	200.00	350.00	550.00	850.00
	1819	1,523	200.00	350.00	550.00	850.00
	1821	270 pcs.	300.00	500.00	700.00	1000.

1/2 PECA

(3200 Reis)
Revalued to 3750 Reis in 1826.

7.1500 g, .917 GOLD, .2107 oz AGW
Obv. leg: JOANNES D.G. PORT ET ALG. P. REGENS, bust.

39	1805	74 pcs.	—	—	Rare	—

42	1807	483 pcs.	250.00	400.00	600.00	1000.

63	1818	100 pcs.	300.00	500.00	750.00	1200.
	1819	1,700	200.00	350.00	500.00	1000.
	1820	242 pcs.	—	—	Rare	—
	1821	196 pcs.	—	—	Rare	—
	1822	.014	150.00	250.00	375.00	600.00
	1823	—	—	—	Rare	—

79	1827	1,713	300.00	500.00	750.00	1200.

87	1828	242 pcs.	450.00	750.00	1250.	2000.

KM#	Date	Mintage	VG	Fine	VF	XF
396	1830	525 pcs.	500.00	800.00	1250.	2500.
	1831	225 pcs.	600.00	900.00	1500.	3000.

PECA

(6400 Reis)
Revalued to 7500 Reis in 1826.

14.3420 g, .917 GOLD, .4228 oz AGW

332	1802	.030	500.00	1000.	1500.	2250.

336	1804	476 pcs.	500.00	1000.	2000.	4000.
	1805	.027	225.00	375.00	550.00	900.00
	1806	.041	225.00	350.00	500.00	750.00
	1807	.036	250.00	425.00	750.00	1100.
	1808	.027	250.00	425.00	750.00	1100.
	1809	.013	250.00	425.00	750.00	1100.
	1812	.025	250.00	425.00	750.00	1100.
	1813	5,590	275.00	500.00	900.00	1400.
	1814	21 pcs.	—	—	Rare	—
	1815	305 pcs.	500.00	1000.	2000.	4000.
	1816	—	—	—	Rare	—
	1817	620 pcs.		Reported, not confirmed		

NOTE: Similar pieces with "R" after date were struck in Rio de Janeiro and are found listed under Brazil.

364	1818	291 pcs.	400.00	800.00	1250.	2000.
	1819	1,727	250.00	500.00	750.00	1400.
	1820	1,687	225.00	450.00	650.00	1200.
	1821	391 pcs.	400.00	800.00	1250.	2000.
	1822	.030	225.00	300.00	425.00	600.00
	1823	.027	225.00	300.00	425.00	600.00
	1824	1,553	300.00	400.00	500.00	600.00

NOTE: Similar pieces with "R" after date were struck in Rio de Janeiro and are listed under Brazil.

378	1826	10,883	350.00	650.00	1100.	1800.
	1828	1,255	500.00	1000.	1500.	2500.

NOTE: Similar pieces dated 1826 with square shield on reverse are patterns.

KM#	Date	Mintage	VG	Fine	VF	XF
388	1828	Inc. KM378	500.00	1000.	1500.	2750.

Modified design

397	1830	2,274	300.00	600.00	900.00	1500.
	1831	1,618	400.00	800.00	1250.	2000.

Obv: Bare head of queen.

404	1833	1,265	600.00	1250.	2500.	5000.

405	1833	—	500.00	1000.	1500.	2750.
	1834	.032	250.00	450.00	700.00	1000.

Obv. leg. continuous.

407	1835	2,989	350.00	600.00	850.00	1400.

COUNTERMARKED COINAGE

40 REIS

COPPER
c/m: GCP in a circle on 40 Reis, KM#402.

C#	Date	Mintage	Good	VG	Fine	VF
415.1	1833	—	5.00	15.00	25.00	50.00

C#	Date	Mintage	Good	VG	Fine	VF
415.1	1847	.218	3.00	7.00	15.00	35.00

c/m: Dot added below GCP on 40 Reis, KM#402.

C#	Date	Mintage	Good	VG	Fine	VF
415.2	1847	Inc. Ab.	4.00	10.00	20.00	40.00

(870 REIS)

In 1834, the Portuguese government ordered that the countermarking of all Spanish and Spanish colonial 8 Reales in circulation with the crowned arms of Portugal, to indicate a revaluation to 870 Reis.

SILVER

c/m: On Bolivia (Potosi) 8 Reales, KM#55.

KM#	Date	Year	Good	VG	Fine	VF
440.1	ND	(1773-89)	50.00	100.00	150.00	200.00

c/m: On Bolivia (Potosi) 8 Reales, KM#74.

KM#	Date	Year	Good	VG	Fine	VF
440.2	ND	(1789-91)	60.00	125.00	175.00	250.00

c/m: On Bolivia (Potosi) 8 Reales, KM#73.

KM#	Date	Year	Good	VG	Fine	VF
440.3	ND	(1791-1808)	40.00	75.00	110.00	150.00

c/m: On Bolivia (Potosi) 8 Reales, KM#84.

KM#	Date	Year	Good	VG	Fine	VF
404.4	ND	(1808-25)	35.00	70.00	100.00	135.00

c/m: On Brazil 960 Reis, KM#326.

KM#	Date	Year	Good	VG	Fine	VF
440.5	ND	(1818-22)	65.00	125.00	200.00	250.00

c/m: On Chile (Santiago) 8 Reales, KM#51.

KM#	Date	Year	Good	VG	Fine	VF
440.6	ND	(1791-1808)	125.00	225.00	350.00	500.00

c/m: On Guatemala 8 Reales, KM#69.

KM#	Date	Year	Good	VG	Fine	VF
440.7	ND	(1808-22)	125.00	200.00	250.00	400.00

c/m: On Mexico 8 Reales, KM#103.

KM#	Date	Year	Good	VG	Fine	VF
440.8	ND	(1732-47)	100.00	175.00	225.00	300.00

c/m: On Mexico 8 Reales, KM#104.

KM#	Date	Year	Good	VG	Fine	VF
440.9	ND	(1747-60)	80.00	135.00	200.00	300.00

c/m: On Mexico 8 Reales, KM#105.

KM#	Date	Year	Good	VG	Fine	VF
440.10	ND	(1760-72)	100.00	150.00	200.00	350.00

c/m: On Mexico 8 Reales, KM#106.

KM#	Date	Year	Good	VG	Fine	VF
440.11	ND	(1772-89)	25.00	50.00	75.00	100.00

c/m: On Mexico 8 Reales, KM#107.

KM#	Date	Year	Good	VG	Fine	VF
440.12	ND	(1789-90)	35.00	65.00	85.00	125.00

c/m: On Mexico 8 Reales, KM#109.

KM#	Date	Year	Good	VG	Fine	VF
440.13	ND	(1791-1808)	25.00	50.00	75.00	100.00

c/m: On Mexico 8 Reales, KM#110.

KM#	Date	Year	Good	VG	Fine	VF
440.14	ND	(1808-11)	25.00	50.00	75.00	100.00

c/m: On Mexico 8 Reales, KM#111.

KM#	Date	Year	Good	VG	Fine	VF
440.15	ND	(1811-21)	25.00	50.00	75.00	100.00

c/m: On Mexico (Durango) 8 Reales, KM#111.2.

KM#	Date	Year	Good	VG	Fine	VF
440.16	ND	(1812-22)	125.00	225.00	350.00	500.00

c/m: On Mexico (Guadalajara) 8 Reales, KM#111.3.

KM#	Date	Year	Good	VG	Fine	VF
440.17	ND	(1812-22)	60.00	125.00	150.00	250.00

c/m: On Mexico (Guanajuato) 8 Reales, KM#111.4.

KM#	Date	Year	Good	VG	Fine	VF
440.18	ND	(1812-22)	60.00	125.00	150.00	250.00

c/m: On Mexico (Zacatecas) 8 Reales, KM#111.5.

KM#	Date	Year	Good	VG	Fine	VF
440.19	ND	(1813-22)	35.00	75.00	100.00	150.00

c/m: On Peru (Lima) 8 Reales, KM#87.

KM#	Date	Year	Good	VG	Fine	VF
440.20	ND	(1789-91)	40.00	75.00	100.00	150.00

c/m: On Peru (Lima) 8 Reales, KM#97.

KM#	Date	Year	Good	VG	Fine	VF
440.21	ND	(1791-1808)	35.00	65.00	95.00	125.00

c/m: On Peru (Lima) 8 Reales, KM#106.

KM#	Date	Year	Good	VG	Fine	VF
440.22	ND	(1808-11)	35.00	65.00	95.00	125.00

c/m: On Peru (Lima) 8 Reales, KM#117.

KM#	Date	Year	Good	VG	Fine	VF
440.33	ND	(1810-24)	30.00	60.00	90.00	125.00

c/m: On Spain (Cadiz) 8 Reales, C#136.

KM#	Date	Year	Good	VG	Fine	VF
440.34	ND	(1810-15)	60.00	100.00	150.00	250.00

c/m: On Spain (Madrid) 8 Reales, C#71.

KM#	Date	Year	Good	VG	Fine	VF
440.35	ND	(1789-1808)	65.00	125.00	175.00	275.00

c/m: On Spain (Madrid) 20 Reales, C#92.

KM#	Date	Year	Good	VG	Fine	VF
440.36	ND	(1808-13)	65.00	125.00	175.00	275.00

c/m: On Spain (Madrid) 8 Reales, C#136.

KM#	Date	Year	Good	VG	Fine	VF
440.37	ND	(1812-33)	35.00	65.00	95.00	125.00

c/m: On Spain (Seville) 8 Reales, C#40.

KM#	Date	Year	Good	VG	Fine	VF
440.38	ND	(1772-88)	125.00	250.00	350.00	500.00

c/m: On Spain (Seville) 8 Reales, C#71.

KM#	Date	Year	Good	VG	Fine	VF
440.39	ND	(1788-1808)	85.00	150.00	225.00	300.00

c/m: On Spain (Seville) 8 Reales, C#136.

KM#	Date	Year	Good	VG	Fine	VF
440.40	ND	(1809-30)	45.00	75.00	110.00	150.00

c/m: On Spain (Valencia) 8 Reales, C#136a.

KM#	Date	Year	Good	VG	Fine	VF
440.41	ND	(1809-11)	125.00	175.00	250.00	500.00

(30,000 REIS)

In 1847, the crowned arms countermark was applied to the Dobrao of John V. Value was raised 50%.

GOLD

c/m: Crowned arms on Brazil 20,000 Reis, KM#117.

KM#	Date	Year	VG	Fine	VF	XF
499 (467)	ND(1847)	1724-27	1500.	2500.	4000.	5500

DECIMAL COINAGE

New denominations, all expressed in terms of Reis, were introduced by Maria II in 1836, to bring Portugal's currency into decimal form. Some of the coins retained old names, as follows:

1000 Reis Silver - Coroa
100 Reis Silver - Tostao

The diameter of the new copper coins, first minted by Maria II in 1837, was smaller than the earlier coinage, but the weight was unaltered. However, in 1882, Luis I reduced the size and weight of the copper currency.

The 1 Reis and 2 Reis pieces dated 1853 were issued for circulation on Mozambique and will be found in those listings.

3 REIS

COPPER

KM#	Date	Mintage	Fine	VF	XF	Unc
517	1868	.100	2.00	4.00	7.00	12.50

KM#	Date	Mintage	Fine	VF	XF	Unc
517	1874	.280	2.00	4.00	7.00	12.50
	1875	1.200	2.00	4.00	8.00	15.00

5 REIS

COPPER

KM#	Date	Mintage	VG	Fine	VF	XF
480	1840	.174	2.00	4.00	8.00	22.00
	1843	3,621	5.00	8.00	15.00	40.00
	1848	.147	2.00	4.00	8.00	28.00
	1850	.180	2.00	4.00	8.00	28.00
	1852	.292	2.00	4.00	8.00	28.00
	1853	*.097	3.00	6.00	10.00	25.00

***NOTE:** Struck for circulation primarily in Mozambique.

KM#	Date	Mintage	Fine	VF	XF	Unc
513	1867	.737	1.50	3.00	7.00	12.50
	1868	.740	1.50	3.00	7.00	12.50
	1871	.240	10.00	20.00	40.00	70.00
	1872	.700	1.50	3.00	7.00	12.50
	1873	.600	8.00	15.00	27.50	50.00
	1874	1.080	1.00	2.00	5.00	11.50
	1875	2.200	1.00	2.00	5.00	11.50
	1876	.320	8.00	15.00	35.00	60.00
	1877	.620	8.00	15.00	30.00	50.00
	1878	Inc. Ab.	2.00	4.00	10.00	15.00
	1879	.332	2.00	4.00	10.00	15.00
	1882	—	Reported, not confirmed			

BRONZE

KM#	Date	Mintage	Fine	VF	XF	Unc
525	1882	5.200	.50	1.00	2.50	7.00
	1883	4.700	.50	1.00	2.50	7.50
	1884	1.730	.75	1.50	3.25	10.00
	1885	3.200	.50	1.25	2.75	8.00
	1886	4.170	1.00	2.25	5.00	12.00

KM#	Date	Mintage	Fine	VF	XF	Unc
530	1890	.430	.75	1.50	2.00	4.00
	1891	Inc. Ab.	.50	1.00	2.00	4.00
	1892/1	1.510	.50	1.50	3.00	9.00
	1892	Inc. Ab.	.25	.75	1.50	4.00
	1893	3.280	.25	.75	1.50	4.50
	1896	.567	.25	.75	1.50	4.50
	1897	1.120	1.00	3.00	5.00	10.00
	1898	.700	.25	.75	1.50	4.50
	1899	1.220	.25	.75	1.50	4.00
	1900	1.110	1.00	3.00	5.00	10.00
	1901	1.070	1.00	3.00	5.00	10.00
	1904	.720	.50	1.00	2.50	6.00
	1905	1.340	.25	.75	1.50	4.00
	1906/0	1,260	.30	1.00	2.50	6.00
	1906/9	Inc. Ab.	.30	1.00	2.50	6.00
	1906	Inc. Ab.	.25	.75	1.50	4.00

KM#	Date	Mintage	Fine	VF	XF	Unc
555	1910	1.000	.25	.75	1.25	3.50

10 REIS

COPPER

Obv: Plain shield, struck in collared dies.

KM#	Date	Mintage	VG	Fine	VF	XF
470	1837	—	2.00	5.00	10.00	25.00
470	1838	—	2.00	5.00	10.00	25.00
	1839	—	2.00	5.00	10.00	25.00

Obv: Ornate shield.

KM#	Date	Mintage	VG	Fine	VF	XF
481	1840	.392	2.00	3.00	6.50	15.00
	1841	.476	2.00	3.00	6.50	15.00
	1842	1.131	2.00	3.00	6.50	15.00
	1843	.837	2.00	3.00	6.50	15.00
	1844	.620	2.00	3.00	6.50	15.00
	1845	.545	2.00	3.00	6.50	15.00
	1846	1.166	2.00	3.00	6.50	15.00
	1847	.057	5.00	10.00	20.00	45.00
	1850	.443	2.00	3.00	6.50	15.00
	1851	1.236	2.00	3.00	6.50	15.00
	1852	.558	2.00	3.00	6.50	15.00
	1853	*.046	2.00	3.00	6.50	15.00

***NOTE:** Struck for circulation primarily in Mozambique.

KM#	Date	Mintage	Fine	VF	XF	Unc
514	1867	.300	1.00	2.50	5.00	12.00
	1868	.450	2.50	5.00	10.00	20.00
	1870	Inc. Ab.	15.00	25.00	50.00	100.00
	1871	.360	2.50	5.00	10.00	20.00
	1873	2.000	.75	1.50	3.50	10.00
	1874	.220	5.00	10.00	20.00	40.00
	1878	—	Reported, not confirmed			

BRONZE

KM#	Date	Mintage	Fine	VF	XF	Unc
526	1882	14.795	1.00	2.00	4.50	10.00
	1883	Inc. Ab.	1.00	2.00	4.50	10.00
	1884	10.190	1.00	2.00	4.50	10.00
	1885	8.100	1.00	2.00	4.50	10.00
	1886	3.915	1.25	2.50	7.50	15.00

KM#	Date	Mintage	Fine	VF	XF	Unc
532	1891	3.445	1.00	2.00	5.00	12.50
	1891A	.895	2.50	6.00	15.00	35.00
	1892	9.298	1.00	2.00	5.00	12.50
	1892A	5.769	1.00	2.00	5.00	12.50

20 REIS

COPPER

KM#	Date	Mintage	VG	Fine	VF	XF
482	1847	2.484	3.00	6.00	12.00	25.00
	1848	.801	3.00	6.00	12.00	25.00
	1849	2.269	3.00	6.00	12.00	25.00
	1850	1.803	3.00	6.00	12.00	25.00
	1851	.842	3.00	6.00	12.00	25.00
	1852	1.215	3.00	6.00	12.00	25.00
	1853	*.946	3.00	6.00	12.00	25.00

***NOTE:** Struck for circulation primarily in Mozambique.

KM#	Date	Mintage	Fine	VF	XF	Unc
515	1867	.745	1.25	2.50	5.00	10.00
	1870	—	15.00	30.00	50.00	100.00
	1871	.360	3.00	6.00	10.00	20.00
	1872	.050	Reported, not confirmed			
	1873	2.500	1.00	2.00	3.00	8.00
	1874	1.575	1.00	2.00	4.00	10.00

BRONZE

KM#	Date	Mintage	Fine	VF	XF	Unc
527	1882	17.235	1.00	2.00	5.00	18.00
	1883	Inc. Ab.	1.00	2.00	5.00	18.00
	1884	17.200	1.00	2.00	5.00	18.00
	1885	18.493	1.00	2.00	5.00	18.00
	1886	4.573	1.00	2.00	6.00	20.00

KM#	Date	Mintage	Fine	VF	XF	Unc
533	1891	3.282	1.00	2.00	4.00	16.00
	1891A	6.016	1.00	2.00	5.00	18.00
	1892/1	15.411	1.25	2.50	5.00	18.00
	1892	Inc. Ab.	1.00	2.00	4.00	16.00
	1892A	.658	1.50	4.00	10.00	30.00

50 REIS

1.2500 g, .917 SILVER, .0368 oz ASW

KM#	Date	Mintage	VG	Fine	VF	XF
493	1855	.048	4.00	10.00	15.00	30.00

KM#	Date	Mintage	VG	Fine	VF	XF
493	1861	.800	1.00	2.00	5.00	10.00
506	1862	.017	2.00	6.00	10.00	20.00
	1863	.215	1.00	3.00	6.00	12.00
	1864	.050	4.00	7.00	12.00	30.00
	1868	—	Reported, not confirmed			
	1874	.060	2.00	6.00	10.00	20.00
	1875	Inc. Ab.	10.00	20.00	30.00	65.00
	1876	.100	1.00	3.00	5.00	10.00
	1877	.100	1.00	3.00	5.00	10.00
	1879	.080	1.00	3.00	5.00	10.00
	1880	.320	1.00	3.00	5.00	10.00
	1886	.060	3.00	7.00	16.00	50.00
	1887	.040	10.00	25.00	60.00	175.00
	1888	Inc. Be.	—	—	Rare	—
	1889	1.000	1.00	1.50	2.50	6.50
536	1893	.620	2.00	4.00	7.00	12.50

COPPER-NICKEL

KM#	Date	Mintage	Fine	VF	XF	Unc
545	1900	8.000	.50	1.00	2.00	6.00

100 REIS

2.9600 g, .917 SILVER, .0873 oz ASW
Obv: Young head
Reeded edge

KM#	Date	Mintage	VG	Fine	VF	XF
473	1838	2,505	20.00	40.00	80.00	180.00
	1842	—	Reported, not confirmed			
	1843	—	5.00	9.00	17.50	45.00
	1848	—	Reported, not confirmed			

Obv: Mature head.

KM#	Date	Mintage	VG	Fine	VF	XF
485	1851	9,205	3.50	7.50	15.00	35.00

Obv: Older head.

KM#	Date	Mintage	VG	Fine	VF	XF
488	1853	.066	3.50	7.50	12.50	30.00

2.5000 g, .917 SILVER, .0737 oz ASW

KM#	Date	Mintage	VG	Fine	VF	XF
490	1854	.535	2.50	5.50	12.50	25.00

Obv: Young head.

KM#	Date	Mintage	VG	Fine	VF	XF
497	1857	.043	20.00	40.00	80.00	160.00
	1858	—	20.00	40.00	80.00	160.00
	1859	.455	2.00	4.00	10.00	25.00
	1860	—	Reported, not confirmed			
	1861	.762	2.00	4.00	10.00	25.00
510	1864	.198	3.00	6.00	12.00	30.00
	1865	.100	3.00	6.00	12.00	30.00
	1866	.010	25.00	40.00	90.00	180.00
	1869	.010	25.00	40.00	75.00	160.00
	1871	.060	4.50	9.00	18.00	40.00
	1872	.060	4.00	8.00	16.00	35.00
	1873	—	Reported, not confirmed			
	1874	.170	2.50	5.00	10.00	25.00
	1875	.130	2.25	4.50	9.00	22.50
	1876	.220	1.50	3.00	6.00	12.00
	1877	.120	2.00	4.00	10.00	22.50
	1878	.030	5.00	10.00	20.00	40.00
	1879	.560	1.50	2.00	5.00	10.00
	1880	.440	1.50	2.00	5.00	10.00
	1881	Inc. Ab.	17.50	37.50	75.00	150.00
	1886	.750	1.50	2.00	5.00	10.00
	1888	.500	1.50	2.00	5.00	10.00
	1889	1.500	1.00	1.50	3.50	7.50
531	1890	.700	1.25	2.50	6.00	12.00
	1891	.270	2.00	5.00	10.00	20.00
	1893	1.050	1.00	2.00	5.00	10.00
	1894	Inc. Ab.	15.00	30.00	60.00	120.00
	1895	—	Reported, not confirmed			
	1898	.655	1.50	3.00	7.00	15.00

COPPER-NICKEL

KM#	Date	Mintage	Fine	VF	XF	Unc
546	1900	16.000	.25	.75	2.00	6.00

2.5000 g, .835 SILVER, .0671 oz ASW

KM#	Date	Mintage	Fine	VF	XF	Unc
548	1909	6.363	1.00	2.00	4.00	8.00
	1910	Inc. Ab.	1.00	2.00	3.00	5.00

200 REIS

5.9200 g, .917 SILVER, 1746 oz ASW
Obv: Young head.
Reeded edge

KM#	Date	Mintage	VG	Fine	VF	XF
474	1838	2,177	10.00	20.00	50.00	120.00
	1841	868 pcs.	20.00	40.00	80.00	170.00
	1842	—	Reported, not confirmed			
	1843	1,181	7.50	12.50	25.00	65.00
	1846	—	Reported, not confirmed			
	1848	—	Reported, not confirmed			

5.0000 g, .917 SILVER, .1474 oz ASW

KM#	Date	Mintage	VG	Fine	VF	XF
491	1854	.292	2.50	5.00	10.00	30.00
	1855	.793	2.50	5.00	10.00	30.00
499	1858	—	2.50	5.00	10.00	30.00
	1859	.117	Reported, not confirmed			
	1860	—	2.50	5.00	10.00	30.00
	1861	.202	20.00	40.00	80.00	160.00
507	1862	.696	3.00	6.00	10.00	30.00
	1863	.421	3.00	7.50	15.00	35.00
	1865	.050	6.50	12.50	25.00	60.00

Second bust
Similar to 100 Reis, KM#510.

KM#	Date	Mintage	VG	Fine	VF	XF
512	1866	.010	35.00	70.00	150.00	300.00
	1867	.010	25.00	55.00	110.00	225.00
	1868	5,000	25.00	50.00	100.00	225.00
	1871	.075	8.50	17.50	35.00	75.00
	1872	.070	10.00	20.00	40.00	80.00
	1875	.070	5.00	10.00	20.00	45.00
	1876	.080	30.00	60.00	120.00	250.00
	1877	.030	8.50	17.50	35.00	75.00
	1878	.020	20.00	45.00	90.00	180.00
	1879	5,050	37.50	75.00	150.00	350.00
	1880	.150	2.50	5.00	10.00	22.50
	1886	.340	2.00	4.00	9.00	20.00
	1887	3.600	1.75	3.00	7.00	15.00
	1888	.700	2.00	4.00	9.00	20.00
534	1891	2.365	1.50	2.50	5.00	12.00
	1892	.788	1.50	2.50	6.00	15.00
	1893/2	1.205	3.00	6.00	12.00	30.00
	1893	Inc. Ab.	2.50	5.00	10.00	25.00
	1901	.205	15.00	30.00	60.00	150.00
	1903	.200	4.00	7.50	15.00	35.00

400th Anniversary Discovery of India

KM#	Date	Mintage	VG	Fine	VF	XF
537	1898	.250	2.00	4.00	6.00	12.50
	1898	—	—	P/L	Unc	25.00

5.0000 g, .835 SILVER, .1342 oz ASW

KM#	Date	Mintage	VG	Fine	VF	XF
549	1909	7.656	1.50	3.00	5.00	10.00

500 REIS

14.8000 g, .917 SILVER, .4364 oz ASW

KM#	Date	Mintage	VG	Fine	VF	XF
471	1837	1,266	75.00	150.00	300.00	600.00
	1838	2,645	65.00	125.00	250.00	500.00
	1839	2,084	65.00	125.00	250.00	500.00
	1841	.022	6.00	12.00	25.00	50.00
	1842	.135	7.00	7.50	18.00	40.00
	1843	.105	7.50	15.00	30.00	65.00
	1844	4,265	10.00	20.00	40.00	80.00
	1845	—	12.50	25.00	50.00	100.00
	1846	.074	5.00	10.00	22.00	45.00
	1847	.775	4.00	7.50	15.00	30.00
	1848	.024	7.50	15.00	30.00	60.00
	1849	.059	6.00	12.00	25.00	50.00
	1850	.041	7.50	15.00	30.00	60.00
	1851	.155	4.00	7.50	15.00	35.00
	1853	.022	25.00	50.00	100.00	200.00

12.5000 g, .917 SILVER, .3684 oz ASW
Obv. leg: PETRUS.V. . ., young head.

KM#	Date	Mintage	VG	Fine	VF	XF
492	1854	.592	6.00	12.00	25.00	60.00
494	1855	1.210	4.00	8.00	20.00	45.00
	1856	1.478	4.00	8.00	20.00	40.00

KM#	Date	Mintage	VG	Fine	VF	XF
98	1857	1.949	6.00	10.00	22.50	50.00
	1858	3.091	4.00	8.00	20.00	45.00
	1859	2.660	4.00	8.00	20.00	45.00

KM#	Date	Mintage	VG	Fine	VF	XF
09	1863	.148	4.00	6.50	15.00	45.00
	1864	.341	3.50	5.50	10.00	30.00
	1865	.406	3.50	5.50	10.00	30.00
	1866	.378	3.50	5.50	10.00	22.50
	1867	.458	3.50	5.50	10.00	22.50
	1868	.388	3.50	5.50	10.00	22.50
	1870	798 pcs.	3.50	5.00	8.00	20.00
	1871	.228	3.50	5.00	8.00	20.00
	1872	.576	25.00	45.00	100.00	250.00
	1875	.140	17.50	30.00	60.00	140.00
	1876	.280	12.50	22.50	40.00	100.00
	1877	.050	10.00	15.00	25.00	60.00
	1879	.788	3.50	5.00	8.00	18.00
	1886	.300	3.50	5.00	8.00	18.00
	1887	.432	3.50	5.00	8.00	18.00
	1888	2.740	3.50	5.00	8.00	16.00
	1889	.960	3.50	5.00	8.00	16.00

KM#	Date	Mintage	VG	Fine	VF	XF
535	1891	12.476	3.50	4.50	7.50	15.00
	1892/1	4.716	5.00	8.00	12.00	25.00
	1892	Inc. Ab.	3.50	4.50	7.50	15.00
	1893	2.494	4.00	6.00	10.00	20.00
	1894	.254	50.00	100.00	150.00	350.00
	1895	.216	10.00	20.00	45.00	90.00
	1896	5.120	3.50	4.50	7.50	15.00
	1898	1.320	3.50	4.50	8.00	16.00
	1899	3.100	3.50	4.50	7.50	15.00
	1900	.200	25.00	50.00	100.00	200.00
	1901	1.050	5.00	10.00	20.00	40.00
	1903	.680	4.00	6.00	10.00	20.00
	1904	—		Reported, not confirmed		
	1906	.240	5.00	10.00	20.00	40.00
	1907	.384	4.00	6.00	10.00	20.00
	1908	1.840	4.00	6.00	10.00	20.00

400th Anniversary Discovery of India

KM#	Date	Mintage	VG	Fine	VF	XF
538	1898	.300	5.00	7.50	10.00	20.00
	1898	—	—	P/L	Unc	35.00

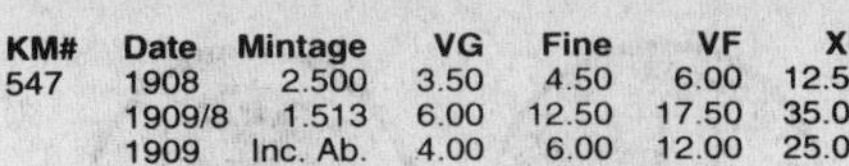

KM#	Date	Mintage	VG	Fine	VF	XF
547	1908	2.500	3.50	4.50	6.00	12.50
	1909/8	1.513	6.00	12.50	17.50	35.00
	1909	Inc. Ab.	4.00	6.00	12.00	25.00

Peninsular War Centennial

KM#	Date	Mintage	VG	Fine	VF	XF
556	1910	.200	10.00	15.00	25.00	50.00

Marquis De Pombal

KM#	Date	Mintage	VG	Fine	VF	XF
557	1910	.400	6.50	11.50	17.50	35.00
	1910	—	—	—	Proof	600.00

1000 REIS

29.6000 g, .917 SILVER, .8727 oz ASW

KM#	Date	Mintage	VG	Fine	VF	XF
472	1837	2,295	80.00	100.00	200.00	450.00
	1838	3,959	35.00	60.00	100.00	300.00
	1842	1,515	—	—	Rare	—
	1843	—	—	Reported, not confirmed		
	1844	—	20.00	40.00	75.00	150.00
	1845	10,724	20.00	40.00	75.00	150.00

1.7900 g, .917 GOLD, .0528 oz AGW

KM#	Date	Mintage	VG	Fine	VF	XF
486	1851	.012	40.00	50.00	65.00	125.00

1.7735 g, .917 GOLD, .0523 oz AGW

KM#	Date	Mintage	VG	Fine	VF	XF
495	1855	.068	35.00	40.00	55.00	100.00

25.0000 g, .917 SILVER, .7368 oz ASW
400th Anniversary Discovery of India

KM#	Date	Mintage	VG	Fine	VF	XF
539	1898	.300	10.00	12.00	15.00	35.00
	1898	—	—	P/L	Unc	75.00

KM#	Date	Mintage	VG	Fine	VF	XF
540	1899	1.500	10.00	12.00	15.00	30.00
	1900	3 known	—	—	Proof	7500.

Peninsular War Centennial

KM#	Date	Mintage	VG	Fine	VF	XF
558	1910	.200	15.00	25.00	40.00	90.00
	1910	—	—	—	Proof	900.00

2000 REIS

3.5470 g, .917 GOLD, .1045 oz AGW
Obv: Boy head.

KM#	Date	Mintage	Fine	VF	XF	Unc
496	1856	.038	65.00	100.00	200.00	300.00
	1857	.044	60.00	90.00	150.00	250.00

Obv: Young head.

KM#	Date	Mintage	Fine	VF	XF	Unc
500	1858	.013	60.00	90.00	150.00	275.00

KM#	Date	Mintage	Fine	VF	XF	Unc
500	1859	.016	60.00	90.00	150.00	275.00
	1860	.053	60.00	90.00	150.00	250.00

Rev: Arms in spray.

KM#	Date	Mintage	Fine	VF	XF	Unc
511	1864	.101	60.00	100.00	150.00	250.00
	1865	.095	60.00	100.00	150.00	250.00
	1866	.086	60.00	100.00	150.00	250.00

Rev: Mantled arms.

KM#	Date	Mintage	Fine	VF	XF	Unc
518	1868	.024	65.00	125.00	200.00	300.00
	1869	.011	65.00	125.00	200.00	300.00
	1870	500 pcs.	300.00	600.00	1000.	1500.
	1871	500 pcs.	200.00	400.00	700.00	1000.
	1872	1,000	125.00	200.00	375.00	550.00
	1874	5,000	75.00	150.00	250.00	350.00
	1875	2,000	100.00	175.00	275.00	350.00
	1876	5,000	75.00	150.00	250.00	350.00
	1877	2,250	100.00	175.00	275.00	400.00
	1878	.022	65.00	125.00	200.00	300.00
	1881	1,000	150.00	200.00	400.00	600.00
	1888	500 pcs.	200.00	400.00	750.00	1200.

2500 REIS

4.7800 g, .917 GOLD, .1410 oz AGW
Obv: Young head.

KM#	Date	Mintage	Fine	VF	XF	Unc
475	1838	1,114	300.00	500.00	800.00	1200.

4.4800 g, .917 GOLD, .1321 oz AGW

KM#	Date	Mintage	Fine	VF	XF	Unc
487	1851	.058	100.00	175.00	275.00	400.00

KM#	Date	Mintage	Fine	VF	XF	Unc
489	1853	1,010	250.00	450.00	650.00	1000.

5000 REIS

9.5600 g, .917 GOLD, .2819 oz AGW
Obv: Young head.

KM#	Date	Mintage	Fine	VF	XF	Unc
476.1	1838	2,410	200.00	250.00	500.00	800.00
	1845	401 pcs.	500.00	1000.	2000.	3000.

8.9600 g, .917 GOLD, .2642 oz AGW

KM#	Date	Mintage	Fine	VF	XF	Unc
476.2	1851	.057	175.00	225.00	325.00	500.00

8.8675 g, .917 GOLD, .2613 oz AGW
Obv: Young head.

KM#	Date	Mintage	Fine	VF	XF	Unc
505	1860	.052	150.00	175.00	200.00	350.00
	1861	.081	150.00	175.00	200.00	350.00

KM#	Date	Mintage	Fine	VF	XF	Unc
508	1862	.166	150.00	175.00	200.00	350.00
	1863	.038	150.00	175.00	200.00	350.00

Rev: Mantled arms.

KM#	Date	Mintage	Fine	VF	XF	Unc
516	1867	.045	150.00	175.00	200.00	350.00
	1868	.064	150.00	175.00	200.00	350.00
	1869	.077	150.00	175.00	200.00	350.00
	1870	.061	150.00	175.00	200.00	350.00
	1871	.047	150.00	175.00	200.00	350.00
	1872	.028	150.00	175.00	200.00	350.00
	1874	6,800	150.00	175.00	200.00	350.00
	1875	.010	150.00	175.00	200.00	350.00
	1876	.015	150.00	175.00	200.00	350.00
	1877	9,400	175.00	200.00	350.00	600.00
	1878	8,400	150.00	175.00	200.00	350.00
	1880	7,000	350.00	500.00	800.00	1200.
	1883	.023	150.00	175.00	200.00	350.00
	1886	.027	150.00	175.00	200.00	350.00
	1887	.044	150.00	175.00	200.00	350.00
	1888	4,800	150.00	175.00	200.00	350.00
	1889	9,000	150.00	175.00	200.00	350.00

10,000 REIS

17.7350 g, .917 GOLD, .5227 oz AGW

KM#	Date	Mintage	Fine	VF	XF	Unc
520	1878	.023	275.00	300.00	400.00	700.00
	1879	.036	275.00	300.00	400.00	700.00
	1880	.030	275.00	300.00	400.00	700.00
	1881	.019	275.00	300.00	425.00	750.00
	1882	.015	275.00	350.00	425.00	750.00
	1883	8,500	275.00	300.00	425.00	750.00
	1884	.013	275.00	300.00	425.00	750.00
	1885	.021	275.00	300.00	425.00	950.00
	1886	1,800	300.00	400.00	600.00	1000.
	1888	7,000	350.00	500.00	700.00	1250.
	1889	4,400	350.00	500.00	700.00	1250.

REPUBLIC

100 Centavos = 1 Escudo

CENTAVO

BRONZE

KM#	Date	Mintage	Fine	VF	XF	Unc
565	1917	2.250	.15	.30	.50	2.50
	1918	22.996	.15	.30	.50	2.50
	1920	12.535	.20	.35	.75	4.00
	1921	4.492	.75	1.50	2.00	10.00
	1922	Inc. Ab.	—	—	Rare	—

2 CENTAVOS

IRON

KM#	Date	Mintage	Fine	VF	XF	Unc
567	1918	.170	12.50	25.00	45.00	100.00

BRONZE

KM#	Date	Mintage	Fine	VF	XF	Unc
568	1918	4.295	.10	.25	.50	3.00
	1920	10.109	.10	.25	.50	3.00
	1921	.679	2.00	3.00	5.00	15.00

4 CENTAVOS

COPPER NICKEL

KM#	Date	Mintage	Fine	VF	XF	Unc
566	1917	4.961	.15	.25	.75	4.50
	1919	10.067	.15	.25	.75	4.50

5 CENTAVOS

BRONZE

KM#	Date	Mintage	Fine	VF	XF	Unc
569	1920	.114	2.50	5.00	7.50	15.00
	1921	5.916	.20	.90	2.50	4.00
	1922	Inc. Ab.	20.00	35.00	50.00	85.00

KM#	Date	Mintage	Fine	VF	XF	Unc
572	1924	6.480	.10	.25	.75	3.00
	1925	7.260	.25	.75	1.75	5.00
	1927	26.320	.10	.20	.50	2.00

10 CENTAVOS

2.5000 g, .835 SILVER, .0671 oz ASW

KM#	Date	Mintage	Fine	VF	XF	Unc
563	1915	3.418	1.00	1.50	2.50	7.50

COPPER-NICKEL

KM#	Date	Mintage	Fine	VF	XF	Unc
570	1920	1.120	.15	.30	.85	5.00
	1921	1.285	.15	.30	.85	5.00

BRONZE

KM#	Date	Mintage	Fine	VF	XF	Unc
573	1924	1.210	1.00	2.00	3.50	12.50
	1925	9.090	.15	.30	.85	5.00
	1926	26.250	.15	.25	.50	4.00
	1930	1.730	5.00	10.00	20.00	50.00
	1938	2.000	2.50	4.00	10.00	30.00
	1940	3.384	.75	1.50	2.25	6.00

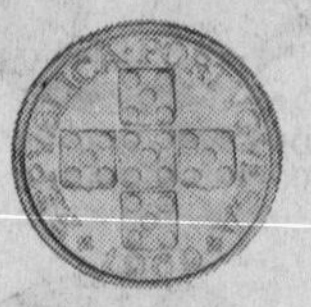

KM#	Date	Mintage	Fine	VF	XF	Unc
583	1942	1.035	.15	.30	.50	10.00
	1943	18.765	.10	.15	.25	8.00
	1944	5.090	.15	.30	.50	8.00
	1945	6.090	.15	.30	.50	10.00
	1946	7.740	.15	.30	.50	10.00
	1947	9.283	.15	.30	.50	5.50
	1948	5.900	.15	.30	.50	5.50
	1949	15.240	.10	.15	.25	3.00
	1950	8.860	.10	.20	.50	6.50
	1951	5.040	.10	.20	.50	6.50
	1952	4.960	.10	.20	.50	10.00
	1953	7.548	.10	.20	.50	6.00

KM#	Date	Mintage	Fine	VF	XF	Unc
583	1954	2.452	.10	.15	.25	6.00
	1955	10.000	—	.10	.15	3.00
	1956	3.336	—	.10	.15	3.00
	1957	6.654	—	.10	.15	2.00
	1958	7.320	—	.10	.15	2.00
	1959	7.140	—	.10	.15	2.00
	1960	15.055	—	.10	.15	1.25
	1961	5.020	—	.10	.15	.70
	1962	14.980	—	.10	.15	.45
	1963	5.393	—	.10	.15	.80
	1964	10.257	—	.10	.15	.45
	1965	15.550	—	.10	.15	.70
	1966	10.200	—	.10	.15	.45
	1967	18.592	—	.10	.15	.45
	1968	22.515	—	.10	.15	.45
	1969	3.871	—	.10	.15	.60

ALUMINUM

KM#	Date	Mintage	VF	XF	Unc
594	1969	—	40.00	60.00	100.00
	1970	—	—	Rare	—
	1971	25.673	—	—	.10
	1972	10.558	—	—	.10
	1973	3.149	—	—	.10
	1974	17.043	—	—	.10
	1975	22.410	—	—	.10
	1976	19.907	—	—	.10
	1977	8.431	—	—	.10
	1978	2.205	—	—	.10
	1979	9.083	—	—	.10

20 CENTAVOS

5.0000 g, .835 SILVER, .1342 oz ASW

KM#	Date	Mintage	Fine	VF	XF	Unc
562	1913	.540	3.00	7.50	15.00	30.00
	1916	.706	2.25	4.50	10.00	22.50

COPPER-NICKEL

KM#	Date	Mintage	Fine	VF	XF	Unc
571	1920	1.568	.25	.50	1.25	7.00
	1921	3.030	.25	.50	1.25	7.00
	1922	.580	75.00	125.00	225.00	375.00

BRONZE

KM#	Date	Mintage	Fine	VF	XF	Unc
574	1924	6.220	.25	.75	2.25	9.00
	1925	10.580	.25	.75	2.25	9.00

KM#	Date	Mintage	Fine	VF	XF	Unc
584	1942	10.170	.10	.20	.50	18.00
	1943	Inc. Ab.	.10	.20	.50	18.00
	1944	7.290	.10	.20	.50	15.00
	1945	7.552	.10	.20	.50	15.00
	1948	2.750	.15	.30	1.00	15.00
	1949	12.250	.10	.15	.30	10.00
	1951	3.185	.15	.30	1.00	15.00
	1952	1.815	.50	1.00	4.00	15.00
	1953	9.426	—	.10	.30	6.00
	1955	5.574	—	.10	.30	4.00
	1956	5.000	—	.10	.30	4.00
	1957	1.450	—	.10	.30	6.00
	1958	7.470	—	.10	.30	3.00
	1959	4.780	—	.10	.30	2.00
	1960	4.790	—	.10	.30	2.00
584	1961	5.180	—	.10	.30	1.50
	1962	2.500	—	.10	.50	4.00
	1963	7.990	—	.10	.30	1.25
	1964	7.010	—	.10	.15	.70
	1965	7.365	—	.10	.15	.80
	1966	8.075	—	.10	.15	.50
	1967	9.220	—	.10	.15	.50
	1968	10.372	—	.10	.15	.50
	1969	8.657	—	.10	.15	.60

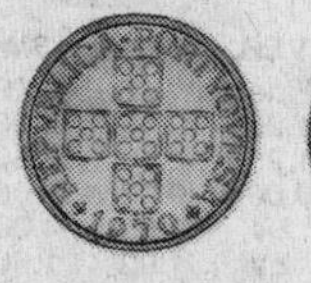

KM#	Date	Mintage	VF	XF	Unc
595	1969	10.891	—	.10	.15
	1970	16.120	—	.10	.15
	1971	1.933	—	.10	.40
	1972	16.354	—	.10	.15
	1973	4.900	—	.10	.15
	1974	26.975	—	.10	.15

50 CENTAVOS

12.5000 g, .835 SILVER, .3356 oz ASW

KM#	Date	Mintage	Fine	VF	XF	Unc
561	1912	1.695	3.25	5.00	10.00	22.50
	1913	4.443	3.25	5.00	7.50	22.50
	1914	4.992	3.25	5.00	7.50	15.00
	1916	5.080	3.25	5.00	7.50	15.00

ALUMINUM-BRONZE

KM#	Date	Mintage	Fine	VF	XF	Unc
575	1924	.810	10.00	17.50	25.00	45.00
	1925	—	150.00	300.00	500.00	800.00
	1926	4.340	.15	.50	2.00	8.00

COPPER-NICKEL

KM#	Date	Mintage	Fine	VF	XF	Unc
577	1927	2.330	.25	.50	2.50	15.00
	1928	6.823	.25	.50	2.50	15.00
	1929	9.779	.25	.50	2.50	15.00
	1930	1.116	.25	.50	3.00	22.50
	1931	7.127	.25	.50	2.50	15.00
	1935*	.902	1.00	2.00	10.00	45.00
	1938	.923	.50	1.00	8.00	40.00
	1940	2.000	—	.10	.50	17.50
	1944	2.974	—	.10	.25	15.00
	1945	5.700	—	.10	.25	20.00
	1946	4.334	—	.10	.35	20.00
	1947	6.998	—	.10	.35	12.00
	1951	4.610	—	.10	.25	8.00
	1952	2.421	.10	.25	.50	17.50
	1953	2.369	.10	.25	.50	10.00
	1955	3.057	—	.10	.25	6.00
	1956	3.003	—	.10	.25	6.00
	1957	3.940	—	.10	.25	4.00
	1958	2.687	—	.10	.25	2.50
	1959	4.027	—	.10	.25	2.50
	1960	2.592	—	.10	.20	2.00
	1961	3.324	—	.10	.15	.75
	1962	6.678	—	.10	.15	.75
	1963	2.346	—	.10	.20	1.00
	1964	7.654	—	—	.10	.50
	1965	3.366	—	—	.10	.50
	1966	6.085	—	—	.10	.50
	1967	19.391	—	—	.10	.35
	1968	11.448	—	—	.10	.35

***NOTE:** For exclusive use in Azores.

BRONZE

KM#	Date	Mintage	VF	XF	Unc
596	1969	3.481	—	.10	.15
	1970	17.280	—	.10	.15
	1971	9.139	—	.10	.15
	1972	24.729	—	.10	.15
	1973	35.588	—	.10	.15
	1974	28.719	—	.10	.15
	1975	17.793	—	.10	.15
	1976	23.734	—	.10	.15
	1977	16.340	—	.10	.15
	1978	48.348	—	.10	.15
	1979	61.652	—	.10	.15

ESCUDO

25.0000 g, .835 SILVER, .6711 oz ASW
October 5, 1910, Birth of the Republic

KM#	Date	Mintage	Fine	VF	XF	Unc
560	1910	*1.000	12.00	16.00	22.50	60.00

***NOTE:** Struck in 1914.

KM#	Date	Mintage	Fine	VF	XF	Unc
564	1915	1.818	8.00	10.00	14.00	40.00
	1916	1.405	8.00	10.00	14.00	40.00

ALUMINUM-BRONZE

KM#	Date	Mintage	Fine	VF	XF	Unc
576	1924	2.709	.50	1.50	4.00	8.00
	1926	2.346	10.00	20.00	30.00	65.00

COPPER-NICKEL

KM#	Date	Mintage	Fine	VF	XF	Unc
578	1927	1.917	.50	1.00	4.00	15.00
	1928	7.462	.50	1.00	4.00	15.00
	1929	1.617	.50	1.00	4.00	15.00
	1930	1.911	1.50	3.00	15.00	60.00
	1931	2.039	1.50	3.00	15.00	60.00
	1935*	—	15.00	25.00	50.00	150.00
	1939	.304	2.50	5.00	20.00	75.00
	1940	1.259	.50	1.00	3.00	18.00
	1944	.993	2.50	5.00	10.00	75.00
	1945	Inc. Ab.	.25	.50	2.00	12.00
	1946	2.507	.25	.50	2.00	12.00
	1951	2.500	.25	.50	1.50	6.00
	1952	2.500	.50	1.00	3.50	12.50
	1957	1.656	.10	.25	1.00	4.00
	1958	1.447	.10	.25	1.00	4.00
	1959	1.908	.10	.25	.75	3.00
	1961	2.505	.10	.25	.50	2.00
	1962	2.757	.10	.25	.50	2.00
	1964	1.611	.10	.25	.50	2.00
	1965	1.683	.10	.25	.50	2.00
	1966	2.607	.10	.20	.40	1.00
	1968	4.099	.10	.20	.40	1.00

***NOTE:** For exclusive use in Azores.

BRONZE

KM#	Date	Mintage	VF	XF	Unc
597	1969	3.020	.10	.15	.25
	1970	6.009	.10	.15	.20
	1971	7.860	.10	.15	.20
	1972	3.815	.10	.15	.30
	1973	20.467	.10	.15	.20
	1974	11.444	.10	.15	.20
	1975	8.473	.10	.15	.30
	1976	7.353	.10	.15	.20
	1977	6.218	.10	.15	.20
	1978	7.061	.10	.15	.20
	1979	14.241	.10	.15	.20
	1980	16.780	.10	.15	.20

NICKEL-BRASS

KM#	Date	Mintage	VF	XF	Unc
614	1981	30.165	—	.10	.20
(611)	1982	53.018	—	.10	.20
	1983	53.165	—	.10	.20
	1984	59.463	—	.10	.20
	1985	46.832	—	.10	.20
	1986	8.030	—	.10	.20

World Roller Hockey Championship Games

KM#	Date	Mintage	VF	XF	Unc
612	ND(1983)	1.990	—	.10	.20

KM#	Date	Mintage	VF	XF	Unc
631	1986	14.882	—	.10	.20
	1987	21.922	—	.10	.20
	1988	17.168	—	.10	.20
	1989	17.194	—	.10	.20
	1990	19.008	—	.10	.20
	1991	21.500	—	—	.20
	1992	22.000	—	—	.20
	1993	10.505	—	—	.20
	1994	—	—	—	.20

2-1/2 ESCUDOS

3.5000 g, .650 SILVER, .0731 oz ASW

KM#	Date	Mintage	Fine	VF	XF	Unc
580	1932	2.592	1.25	2.50	5.00	14.00
	1933	2.457	1.25	2.50	6.50	17.50
	1937	1.000	30.00	50.00	120.00	220.00
	1940	2.763	BV	2.00	4.00	7.50
	1942	3.847	BV	1.00	1.50	5.00
	1943	8.302	BV	1.00	1.50	4.00
	1944	9.134	BV	1.00	1.50	4.00
	1945	6.316	BV	1.00	1.50	5.00
	1946	3.208	BV	1.00	1.50	5.00
	1947	2.610	BV	1.00	1.50	5.00
	1948	1.814	1.25	2.50	5.00	10.00
	1951	4.000	BV	1.00	1.50	3.00

COPPER-NICKEL

KM#	Date	Mintage	VF	XF	Unc
590	1963	12.711	.10	.20	.50
	1964	17.948	.10	.20	.50
	1965	19.512	.10	.20	.50
	1966	3.828	.30	.50	2.50
	1967	5.545	.10	.20	.50
	1968	6.087	.10	.20	.50
	1969	9.969	.10	.20	.50
	1970	2.400	.10	.20	1.50
	1971	6.791	.10	.20	.35
	1972	6.713	.10	.20	1.50
	1973	9.104	.10	.20	.35
	1974	22.743	.10	.20	.35
	1975	16.624	.10	.20	.35
	1976	21.516	.10	.20	.40
	1977	45.726	.10	.20	.40
	1978	27.375	.10	.20	.40
	1979	44.804	.10	.20	.40
	1980	22.319	.10	.20	.40
	1981	25.420	.10	.20	.40
	1982	45.910	.10	.20	.40
	1983	62.946	.10	.20	.40
	1984	58.210	.10	.20	.40
	1985	60.142	.10	.20	.40

100th Anniversary of Death of Alexandre Herculano

KM#	Date	Mintage	VF	XF	Unc
605	1977	5.990	.10	.15	.50
	1977	.013	—	Proof	2.00

World Roller Hockey Championship Games

KM#	Date	Mintage	VF	XF	Unc
613	ND(1983)	1.990	—	.10	.50

F.A.O. Issue

KM#	Date	Mintage	VF	XF	Unc
617	1983	.995	—	.10	.50

5 ESCUDOS

7.0000 g, .650 SILVER, .1463 oz ASW

KM#	Date	Mintage	Fine	VF	XF	Unc
581	1932	.800	3.00	6.00	12.50	35.00
	1933	6.717	BV	1.50	3.00	12.50
	1934	1.012	BV	2.50	5.00	18.00
	1937	1.500	4.00	10.00	40.00	60.00
	1940	1.500	BV	2.50	5.00	15.00
	1942	2.051	BV	2.00	3.00	10.00
	1943	1.354	BV	2.50	4.00	10.00
	1946	.404	2.50	3.50	5.00	12.50
	1947	2.420	BV	2.00	2.50	6.00
	1948	2.018	BV	2.00	2.50	6.00
	1951	.966	BV	2.00	2.50	6.00

500th Anniversary - Death of Prince Henry the Navigator

KM#	Date	Mintage	Fine	VF	XF	Unc
587	1960	.800	—	2.00	3.00	7.00
	1960	—	—	—	Matte	20.00

COPPER-NICKEL

KM#	Date	Mintage	VF	XF	Unc
591	1963	2.200	.10	.25	2.50
	1964	4.268	.10	.25	.60
	1965	7.294	.10	.25	.50
	1966	8.120	.10	.25	.50
	1967	8.128	.10	.25	.50
	1968	5.023	.10	.25	.50
	1969	3.571	.10	.25	.60
	1970	1.200	.10	.25	2.00
	1971	2.721	.10	.25	.60
	1972	1.880	.10	.25	2.00
	1973	2.836	.10	.25	.60
	1974	3.984	.10	.25	.60
	1975	7.496	.10	.25	.60
	1976	11.379	.10	.25	.60
	1977	29.058	.10	.25	.60
	1978	.672	.30	.50	3.00
	1979	19.546	.10	.25	.60
	1980	46.244	.10	.25	.60
	1981	15.267	.10	.25	.60
	1982	31.318	.10	.25	.60
	1983	51.056	.10	.25	.60
	1984	46.794	.10	.25	.60
	1985	45.441	.10	.25	.60
	1986	18.753	.10	.25	.60

100th Anniversary - Death of Alexandre Herculano

KM#	Date	Mintage	VF	XF	Unc
606	1977	9.176	.25	.50	1.00
	1977	.010	—	Proof	5.00

World Roller Hockey Championship Games

KM#	Date	Mintage	VF	XF	Unc
615	ND(1983)	1.990	.25	.50	1.00

F.A.O. Issue

KM#	Date	Mintage	VF	XF	Unc
618	1983	.995	.25	.50	1.00

NICKEL-BRASS

KM#	Date	Mintage	VF	XF	Unc
632	1986	21.426	.10	.25	.50
	1987	40.548	.10	.25	.50
	1988	19.382	.10	.25	.50
	1989	27.641	.10	.25	.50
	1990	77.977	.10	.25	.50
	1991	32.000	—	—	.50
	1992	16.000	—	—	.50
	1993	8.300	—	—	.50
	1994	—	—	—	.50

10 ESCUDOS

12.5000 g, .835 SILVER, .3356 oz ASW
Battle of Ourique

KM#	Date	Mintage	Fine	VF	XF	Unc
579	1928	.200	6.00	12.00	18.00	45.00

KM#	Date	Mintage	Fine	VF	XF	Unc
582	1932	3.220	3.00	6.00	9.00	30.00
	1933	1.780	6.00	12.50	22.50	50.00
	1934	.400	5.00	7.50	20.00	60.00
	1937	.500	10.00	20.00	40.00	150.00
	1940	1.200	3.00	6.00	18.00	50.00
	1942	.186	40.00	90.00	180.00	350.00
	1948	.507	5.00	8.00	20.00	40.00

12.5000 g, .680 SILVER, .2732 oz ASW

KM#	Date	Mintage	Fine	VF	XF	Unc
586	1954	5.764	BV	2.50	4.00	6.00
	1955	4.056	BV	2.50	4.00	6.00

500th Anniversary - Death of
Prince Henry the Navigator

KM#	Date	Mintage	Fine	VF	XF	Unc
588	1960	.200	—	4.00	8.00	15.00
	1960	—	—	—	Matte	30.00

COPPER-NICKEL-CLAD-NICKEL

KM#	Date	Mintage	VF	XF	Unc
600	1971	3.876	.20	.40	2.00
	1972	2.694	.20	.40	2.00
	1973	5.418	.20	.40	2.00
	1974	4.043	.20	.40	2.00

NICKEL-BRASS

KM#	Date	Mintage	VF	XF	Unc
633	1986	12.818	.20	.40	1.00
	1987	32.815	.20	.40	1.00
	1988	32.579	.20	.40	1.00
	1989	12.788	.20	.40	1.00
	1990	26.500	.20	.40	1.00
	1991	9.500	—	—	1.00
	1992	5.600	—	—	1.00
	1993	.020	In mint sets only		10.00
	1994	.020	In mint sets only		10.00

Rural World

KM#	Date	Mintage	VF	XF	Unc
638	1987	2.000	.40	.60	1.50

20 ESCUDOS

21.0000 g, .800 SILVER, .5401 oz ASW
25th Anniversary of Financial Reform

KM#	Date	Mintage	VF	XF	Unc
585	1953	1.000	5.00	7.50	10.00
	1953	—	—	Matte	—

NOTE: A small quantity of KM#585, 587, 588, 589 & 592 were later given a matte finish by the Lisbon Mint on private contract.

500th Anniversary - Death of
Prince Henry the Navigator

KM#	Date	Mintage	VF	XF	Unc
589	1960	.200	10.00	20.00	30.00
	1960	—	—	Matte	60.00

10.0000 g, .650 SILVER, .2090 oz ASW
Opening of Salazar Bridge

KM#	Date	Mintage	VF	XF	Unc
592	1966	2.000	2.00	3.00	4.50
	1966	200 pcs.	—	Matte	35.00

COPPER-NICKEL

KM#	Date	Mintage	VF	XF	Unc
634	1986	45.361	.15	.25	1.00
	1987	68.216	.15	.25	1.00
	1988	57.482	.15	.25	1.00
	1989	25.060	.15	.25	1.00
	1990	.050	In mint sets only		10.00
	1991	.050	In mint sets only		10.00
	1992	.020	In mint sets only		10.00
	1993	.020	In mint sets only		10.00
	1994	.020	In mint sets only		10.00

25 ESCUDOS

COPPER-NICKEL

KM#	Date	Mintage	VF	XF	Unc
607	1977	7.657	.40	.80	1.50
	1978	12.277	.40	.80	1.50

100th Anniversary - Death of Alexandre Herculano

KM#	Date	Mintage	VF	XF	Unc
608	1977	5.990	.50	.90	1.75
	1977	.013	—	Proof	7.00

International Year of the Child

KM#	Date	Mintage	VF	XF	Unc
609	1979	.990	.50	.90	1.75
	1979	.010	—	P/L	7.00

Increased size, 28.5mm.

KM#	Date	Mintage	VF	XF	Unc
610	1980	.750	.40	.80	1.50
	1981	19.924	.40	.80	1.50
	1982	12.158	.40	.80	1.50
	1983	5.622	.40	.80	1.50
	1984	3.453	.40	.80	1.50
	1985	25.027	.40	.80	1.50
	1986	—	.40	.80	1.50

World Roller Hockey Championship Games

KM#	Date	Mintage	VF	XF	Unc
616	ND(1983)	1.990	.50	1.00	2.00

F.A.O. Issue

KM#	Date	Mintage	VF	XF	Unc
619	1983	.995	.50	1.00	2.00

10th Anniversary of Revolution
Obv: Waves breaking over arms. Rev: Stylized 25.

KM#	Date	Mintage	VF	XF	Unc
623	1984	1.980	.40	.75	1.50

International Year of Disabled Persons

KM#	Date	Mintage	VF	XF	Unc
624	ND(1984)	1.990	.40	.75	1.50

600th Anniversary - Battle of Aljubarrota

KM#	Date	Mintage	VF	XF	Unc
627	1985	.500	.50	1.00	2.00

10.8300 g, .925 SILVER, .3270 oz ASW

KM#	Date	Mintage	VF	XF	Unc
627a	1985	.020	—	—	15.00
	1985	5,000	—	Proof	30.00

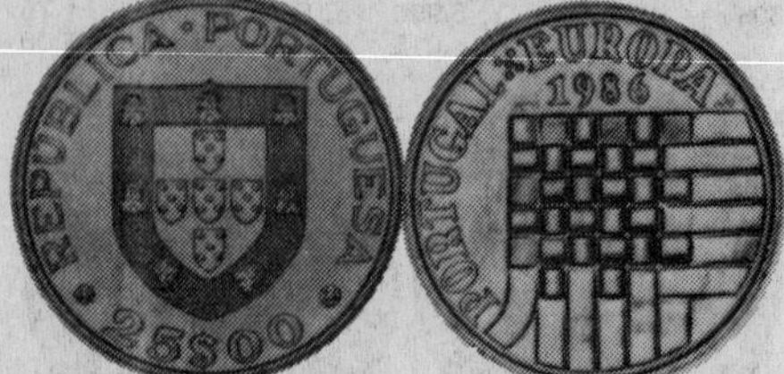

COPPER-NICKEL
Admission to European Common Market

KM#	Date	Mintage	VF	XF	Unc
635	1986	4.990	.40	.75	1.50

11.0000 g, .925 SILVER, .3272 oz ASW

KM#	Date	Mintage	VF	XF	Unc
635a	1986	5,000	—	Proof	60.00

50 ESCUDOS

18.0000 g, .650 SILVER, .3761 oz ASW
500th Anniversary - Birth of Pedro Alvares Cabral

KM#	Date	Mintage	VF	XF	Unc
593	1968	1.000	—	—	6.00
	1968	400 pcs.	—	Matte	30.00

NOTE: A small quantity of KM593, 598, 599, 601 & 602 were later given a matte finish by the Lisbon Mint on private contract.

500th Anniversary - Birth of Vasco Da Gama

KM#	Date	Mintage	VF	XF	Unc
598	1969	1.000	—	—	6.00
	1969	400 pcs.	—	Matte	30.00

Centennial - Birth of Marshal Carmona

KM#	Date	Mintage	VF	XF	Unc
599	1969	.500	—	—	6.00
	1969	400 pcs.	—	Matte	30.00

125th Anniversary - Bank of Portugal

KM#	Date	Mintage	VF	XF	Unc
601	1971	.500	—	—	7.50
	1971	—	—	Matte	30.00

400th Anniversary of Heroic Epic 'Os Lusiadas'

KM#	Date	Mintage	VF	XF	Unc
602	1972	1.000	—	—	7.50
	1972	—	—	Matte	30.00

COPPER-NICKEL

KM#	Date	Mintage	VF	XF	Unc
636	1986	51.110	—	—	3.00
	1987	28.248	—	—	3.00
	1988	41.905	—	—	3.00
	1989	18.327	—	—	3.00
	1990	.050	In mint sets only		15.00
	1991	2.000	—	—	3.00
	1992	.020	In mint sets only		15.00
	1993	.020	In mint sets only		15.00
	1994	.020	In mint sets only		15.00

100 ESCUDOS

18.0000 g, .650 SILVER, .3762 oz ASW
1974 Revolution

KM#	Date	Mintage	VF	XF	Unc
603	1974(76)	.950	—	—	5.00
	1974(76)	.010	—	Proof	15.00

COPPER-NICKEL
International Year of Disabled Persons

KM#	Date	Mintage	VF	XF	Unc
625	ND(1984)	.990	.75	1.00	3.00

50th Anniversary - Death of Fernando Pessoa - Poet

KM#	Date	Mintage	VF	XF	Unc
628	1985	.480	.75	1.00	4.00
	16.5000 g, .925 SILVER, .4907 oz ASW				
628a	1985	5,000	—	Proof	90.00

COPPER-NICKEL
800th Anniversary - Death of King Alfonso Henriques

KM#	Date	Mintage	VF	XF	Unc
629	1985	.500	.75	1.00	3.00
	16.5000 g, .925 SILVER, .4907 oz ASW				
629a	1985	.020	—	—	25.00
	1985	5,000	—	Proof	75.00

COPPER-NICKEL
600th Anniversary - Battle of Aljubarrota

KM#	Date	Mintage	VF	XF	Unc
630	1985	.500	.75	1.00	3.00
	16.5000 g, .925 SILVER, .4907 oz ASW				
630a	1985	.020	—	—	25.00
	1985	5,000	—	Proof	70.00

COPPER-NICKEL
World Cup Soccer - Mexico

KM#	Date	Mintage	VF	XF	Unc
637	1986	.500	.75	1.00	3.50
	16.5000 g, .925 SILVER, .4907 oz ASW				
637a	1986	.050	—	—	22.50
	1986	.020	—	Proof	50.00

COPPER-NICKEL
Golden Age of Portuguese Discoveries - Gil Eanes

KM#	Date	Mintage	VF	XF	Unc
639	1987	1.000	.75	1.00	3.00
	16.5000 g, .925 SILVER, .4907 oz ASW				
639a	1987	.050	—	—	22.50
	1987	.022	—	Proof	45.00
	24.0000 g, .917 GOLD, .7075 oz AGW				
639b	1987	5,772	—	—	550.00

COPPER-NICKEL
Golden Age of Portuguese Discoveries - Nuno Tristao

KM#	Date	Mintage	VF	XF	Unc
640	1987	1.000	.75	1.00	3.00
	16.5000 g, .925 SILVER, .4907 oz ASW				
640a	1987	.050	—	—	22.50
	1987	.020	—	Proof	45.00
	24.0000 g, .917 GOLD, .7075 oz AGW				
640b	1987	5,497	—	—	550.00
	31.1190 g, .999 PALLADIUM, 1.0000 oz APW				
640c	1987	323 pcs.	—	—	450.00
	1987	2,000	—	Proof	650.00

COPPER-NICKEL
Golden Age of Portuguese Discoveries - Diogo Cao

KM#	Date	Mintage	VF	XF	Unc
641	1987	1.000	.75	1.00	3.00
	16.5000 g, .925 SILVER, .4907 oz ASW				
641a	1987	.050	—	—	22.50
	1987	.020	—	Proof	45.00

24.0000 g, .917 GOLD, .7075 oz AGW

KM#	Date	Mintage	VF	XF	Unc
641b	1987	5,256	—	—	550.00
	1987	5,387	—	Proof	900.00

COPPER-NICKEL
Amadeo De Souza Cardoso

KM#	Date	Mintage	VF	XF	Unc
644	1987	.800	.75	1.00	3.50
	21.0000 g, .925 SILVER, .6246 oz ASW				
644a	1987	.030	—	—	20.00
	1987	.015	—	Proof	40.00

COPPER-NICKEL
Golden Age of Portuguese Discoveries - Bartolomeu Dias

KM#	Date	Mintage	VF	XF	Unc
642	1988	1.000	.75	1.00	3.00
	16.5000 g, .925 SILVER, .4907 oz ASW				
642a	1988	.050	—	—	22.50
	1988	.020	—	Proof	45.00
	24.0000 g, .917 GOLD, .7077 oz AGW				
642b	1988	5,503	—	—	450.00
	31.1190 g, .999 PLATINUM, 1.0000 oz APW				
642c	1988	907 pcs.	—	—	750.00
	1988	2,000	—	Proof	1450.

ALUMINUM-BRONZE CENTER, COPPER-NICKEL RING
Pedro Nunes

KM#	Date	Mintage	VF	XF	Unc
	Edge: 5 reeded and 5 plain sections.				
645.1	1989	20.000	—	1.00	2.25
	1990	52.000	—	1.00	2.25
	1991	45.500	—	1.00	2.25
	1992	14.500	—	1.00	2.25
	1993	.020	In mint sets only		20.00
	Edge: 6 reeded and 6 plain sections.				
645.2	1991	—	—	1.00	2.25

COPPER-NICKEL
Discovery of the Canary Islands

KM#	Date	Mintage	VF	XF	Unc
646	1989	2.000	—	—	3.00
	21.0000 g, .925 SILVER, .6246 ASW				
646a	1989	.050	—	—	20.00
	1989	.023	—	Proof	35.00
	24.0000 g, .917 GOLD, .7077 oz AGW				
646b	1989	2,981	—	Proof	625.00

COPPER-NICKEL
Discovery of Madeira

KM#	Date	Mintage	VF	XF	Unc
647	1989	2.000	—	—	3.00
21.0000 g, .925 SILVER, .6246 oz ASW					
647a	1989	.050	—	—	20.00
	1989	.020	—	Proof	35.00
24.0000 g, .917 GOLD, .7077 oz AGW					
647b	1989	2,996	—	Proof	625.00
31.1190 g, .999 PALLADIUM, 1.0000 oz APW					
647c	1989	2,500	—	Proof	600.00

COPPER-NICKEL
Discovery of the Azores

KM#	Date	Mintage	VF	XF	Unc
648	1989	2.000	—	—	3.00
21.0000 g, .925 SILVER, .6246 oz ASW					
648a	1989	.050	—	—	20.00
	1989	.020	—	Proof	35.00
24.0000 g, .917 GOLD, .7077 oz AGW					
648b	1989	5,495	—	Proof	580.00

COPPER-NICKEL
Celestial Navigation

KM#	Date	Mintage	VF	XF	Unc
649	1990	2.000	—	—	3.50
21.0000 g, .925 SILVER, .6246 oz ASW					
649a	1990	.050	—	—	20.00
	1990	.020	—	Proof	35.00
24.0000 g, .917 GOLD, .7077 oz AGW					
649b	1990	2,958	—	Proof	625.00
31.1190 g, .999 PLATINUM, 1.0000 oz APW					
649c	1990	2,500	—	Proof	1500.

COPPER-NICKEL
350th Anniversary - Restoration of Portuguese Independence

KM#	Date	Mintage	VF	XF	Unc
651	1990	1.000	—	—	3.00
18.5000 g, .925 SILVER, .5502 oz ASW					
651a	1990	.025	—	—	15.00
	1990	.010	—	Proof	35.00

COPPER-NICKEL
Camilo Castelo Branco

KM#	Date	Mintage	VF	XF	Unc
656	1990	1.000	—	—	3.00
18.5000 g, .925 SILVER, .5502 oz ASW					
656a	1990	.025	—	—	15.00
	1990	.010	—	Proof	35.00

COPPER-NICKEL
Antero De Quental

KM#	Date	Mintage	VF	XF	Unc
664	1991	—	—	—	3.00
26.5000 g, .925 SILVER, .7881 oz ASW					
664a	1991	.020	—	—	15.00
	1991	.030	—	Proof	35.00

200 ESCUDOS

COPPER-NICKEL CENTER, ALUMINUM-BRONZE RING
Garcia De Orta

KM#	Date	Mintage	VF	XF	Unc
655	1991	33.000	—	—	4.75
	1992	11.000	—	—	4.75
	1993	.020	In mint sets only		30.00

COPPER-NICKEL
Columbus and Portugal

KM#	Date	Mintage	VF	XF	Unc
658	1991	1.500	—	—	4.50
26.5000 g, .925 SILVER, .7880 oz ASW					
658a	1991	.010	—	—	20.00
	1991	.015	—	Proof	35.00
27.2000 g, .917 GOLD, .8000 oz AGW					
658b	1991	3,500	—	Proof	550.00
31.1190 g, .999 PLATINUM, 1.0000 oz APW					
658c	1991	2,500	—	Proof	650.00
31.1190 g, .999 PALLADIUM, 1.0000 oz APW					
658d	1991	2,500	—	Proof	320.00

COPPER-NICKEL
Westward Navigation - Stylized Ship

KM#	Date	Mintage	VF	XF	Unc
659	1991	1.500	—	—	4.50
26.5000 g, .925 SILVER, .7880 oz ASW					
659a	1991	.010	—	—	20.00
	1991	.015	—	Proof	35.00
27.2000 g, .917 GOLD, .8000 oz AGW					
659b	1991	3,500	—	Proof	550.00
31.1190 g, .999 PLATINUM, 1.0000 oz APW					
659c	1991	2,500	—	Proof	650.00
31.1190 g, .999 PALLADIUM, 1.0000 oz APW					
659d	1991	2,500	—	Proof	350.00

COPPER-NICKEL
New World - America - Columbus and Ships

KM#	Date	Mintage	VF	XF	Unc
660	1992	1.300	—	—	4.50
26.5000 g, .925 SILVER, .7880 oz ASW					
660a	1992	.010	—	—	20.00
	1992	.015	—	Proof	35.00
27.2000 g, .917 GOLD, .8000 oz AGW					
660b	1992	6,000	—	Proof	550.00
31.1190 g, .999 PLATINUM, 1.0000 oz APW					
660c	1992	2,500	—	Proof	650.00
31.1190 g, .999 PALLADIUM, 1.0000 oz APW					
660d	1992	2,500	—	Proof	350.00

COPPER-NICKEL
Joao Rodrigues Cabrilho - Map

KM#	Date	Mintage	VF	XF	Unc
661	1992	1.300	—	—	4.50
	26.5000 g, .925 SILVER, .7880 oz ASW				
661a	1992	.010	—	—	20.00
	1992	.015	—	Proof	35.00
	27.2000 g, .917 GOLD, .8000 oz AGW				
661b	1992	3,500	—	Proof	550.00
	31.1190 g, .999 PLATINUM, 1.0000 oz APW				
661c	1992	2,500	—	Proof	1500.
	31.1190 g, .999 PALLADIUM, 1.0000 oz APW				
661d	1992	2,500	—	Proof	350.00

COPPER-NICKEL
Olympics - Stylized Runner

KM#	Date	Mintage	VF	XF	Unc
662	1992	1.000	—	—	4.50
	26.5000 g, .925 SILVER, .7881 oz ASW				
662a	1992	.010	—	—	20.00
	1992	.017	—	Proof	40.00

COPPER-NICKEL
Portugal's Presidency of the European Community

KM#	Date	Mintage	VF	XF	Unc
663	1992	1.000	—	—	4.50
	26.5000 g, .925 SILVER, .7881 oz ASW				
663a	1992	.010	—	—	20.00
	1992	.010	—	Proof	40.00

COPPER-NICKEL
Tanegashima - Site 1st Portuguese Landing in Japan

KM#	Date	Mintage	VF	XF	Unc
665	1993	1.000	—	—	5.00
	26.5000 g, .925 SILVER, .7881 oz ASW				
665a	1993	.030	—	—	25.00
	1993	.022	—	Proof	45.00
	27.2000 g, .917 GOLD, .8020 oz AGW				
665b	1993	7,000	—	Proof	630.00

COPPER-NICKEL
Espingarda

KM#	Date	Mintage	VF	XF	Unc
666	1993	1.000	—	—	5.00
	26.5000 g, .925 SILVER, .7881 oz ASW				
666a	1993	.030	—	—	25.00
	1993	.020	—	Proof	45.00
	27.2000 g, .917 GOLD, .8020 oz AGW				
666b	1993	7,000	—	Proof	630.00
	31.1190 g, .999 PALLADIUM, 1.0000 oz APW				
666c	1993	2,000	—	Proof	350.00

COPPER-NICKEL
Enviados Daimios Kiushu

KM#	Date	Mintage	VF	XF	Unc
667	1993	1.000	—	—	5.00
	26.5000 g, .925 SILVER, .7881 oz ASW				
667a	1993	.030	—	—	25.00
	1993	.020	—	Proof	45.00
	27.2000 g, .917 GOLD, .8020 oz AGW				
667b	1993	7,000	—	Proof	630.00

COPPER-NICKEL
Arte Namban

KM#	Date	Mintage	VF	XF	Unc
668	1993	1.000	—	—	5.00
	26.5000 g, .925 SILVER, .7881 oz ASW				
668	1993	.030	—	—	25.00
	1993	.022	—	Proof	45.00
	27.2000 g, .917 GOLD, .8020 oz AGW				
668b	1993	7,000	—	Proof	630.00
	31.1190 g, .999 PLATINUM, 1.000 oz APW				
668c	1993	2,000	—	Proof	700.00

250 ESCUDOS

25.0000 g, .680 SILVER, .5466 oz ASW
1974 Revolution

KM#	Date	Mintage	VF	XF	Unc
604	1974(76)	.950	—	—	8.00
(Y80)	1974(76)	.010	—	Proof	20.00

COPPER-NICKEL
World Fisheries Conference

KM#	Date	Mintage	VF	XF	Unc
626	1984	.024	2.00	2.50	6.00

23.0000 g, .925 SILVER, .6841 oz ASW

KM#	Date	Mintage	VF	XF	Unc
626a	1984	8,000	—	Proof	65.00

COPPER-NICKEL
Seoul Olympics - Runners

KM#	Date	Mintage	VF	XF	Unc
643	1988	.850	2.00	2.50	5.00

28.0000 g, .925 SILVER, .8327 oz ASW

KM#	Date	Mintage	VF	XF	Unc
643a	1988	.070	—	—	30.00
	1988	.030	—	Proof	50.00

COPPER-NICKEL
850th Anniversary of Founding of Portugal

KM#	Date	Mintage	VF	XF	Unc
650	1989	.750	—	—	6.00

28.0000 g, .925 SILVER, .8327 oz ASW

KM#	Date	Mintage	VF	XF	Unc
650a	1989	.015	—	—	25.00
	1989	.030	—	Proof	40.00

500 ESCUDOS

7.0000 g, .835 SILVER, .1879 oz ASW
XVII European Art Exhibition

KM#	Date	Mintage	VF	XF	Unc
620	1983	.200	—	—	10.00
	1983	8,500	—	Proof	30.00

750 ESCUDOS

12.5000 g, .835 SILVER, .3356 oz ASW
XVII European Art Exhibition

KM#	Date	Mintage	VF	XF	Unc
621	1983	.200	—	—	10.00
	1983	8,500	—	Proof	30.00

1000 ESCUDOS

21.0000 g, .835 SILVER, .5638 oz ASW
XVII European Art Exhibition

KM#	Date	Mintage	VF	XF	Unc
622	1983	.200	—	—	17.50
	1983	8,500	—	Proof	35.00

17.0000 g, .925 SILVER, .5056 oz ASW
400th Anniversary of Death of Louis de Camoes

KM#	Date	Mintage	VF	XF	Unc
611	1980(1983)	.150	—	—	20.00
	1980(1983)	.010	—	Proof	50.00

27.0000 g, .500 SILVER, .4340 oz ASW
Ibero - American Series

KM#	Date	Mintage	VF	XF	Unc
657	1992	.326	—	—	17.50

27.0000 g, .925 SILVER, .8029 oz ASW

KM#	Date	Mintage	VF	XF	Unc
657a	1992	.030	—	Proof	45.00

MINT SETS (MS)

KM#	Date	Mintage	Identification	Issue Price	Mkt. Val.
MS1	1960(3)	—	KM587-589	—	50.00
MS2	1983(4)	10,000	KM612-613,615-616	3.00	7.00
MS3	1983(3)	50,000	KM620-622	30.00	50.00
MS4	1983(3)	5,000	KM617-619	4.00	8.00
MS5	1984(2)	10,000	KM624-625	3.00	5.00
MS6	1985(2)	20,000	KM627a,630a	20.00	40.00
MS7	1986(5)	50,000	KM631-634,636	6.00	6.00
MS8	1987/8(4)	40,000	KM639a-642a	78.00	90.00
MS9	1987/8(4)	5,000	KM639b-642b	2080.	2200.
MS10	1987(6)	50,000	KM631-634,636,638	10.00	10.00
MS11	1988(5)	30,000	KM631-634,636	10.00	10.00
MS12	1989(6)	*50,000	KM631-634,636,645	12.00	12.00
MS13	1990(6)	*50,000	KM631-634,636,645	15.00	30.00
MS14	1989/90(4)	30,000	KM646a-649a	79.50	80.00
MS15	1991(7)	—	KM631-634,636,645,655	17.50	17.50
MS16	1992(7)	—	KM631-634,636,645,655	—	20.00
MS17	1993(4)	30,000	KM665a-668a	79.50	100.00

PROOF SETS (PS)

KM#	Date	Mintage	Identification	Issue Price	Mkt. Val.
PS1	1960(3)	—	KM587-589, matte finish	—	—
PS2	1974(2)	10,000	KM603-604	6.00	35.00
PS3	1977(3)	10,000	KM605-606,608	2.50	15.00
PS4	1983(3)	8,500	KM620-622	60.00	90.00
PS5	1985(2)	5,000	KM627a,630a	40.00	100.00
PS6	1985(2)	5,000	KM628-628a	35.00	100.00
PS7	1987(4)	20,000	KM639a-642a	128.00	180.00
PS8	1987/88(4)	2,000	KM639a,640c,641b,642c Prestige	2200.	2850.
PS9	1989/90(4)	20,000	KM646a-649a	137.50	145.00
PS10	1989/90(4)	5,000	KM646b-649b	2425.	2450.
PS11	1989/90(4)	2,500	KM646a,647c,648b,649c Prestige	2650.	2700.
PS12	1991/92(4)	15,000	KM658a-661a	150.00	180.00
PS13	1991/92(4)	3,500	KM658b-661b	2350.	2350.
PS14	1991/92(4)	2,500	KM658c-661c Prestige	2400.	2600.
PS15	1993(4)	22,000	KM665a-668a	150.00	175.00
PS16	1993(4)	5,000	KM665b-668b	1980.	2000.
PS17	1993(4)	2,000	KM665a,666c,667b,668c Prestige	2300.	2300.

Listings For

PORTUGUESE GUINEA: refer to Guinea-Bissau

PORTUGUESE INDIA: refer to Indian Enclaves

PRINCE EDWARD ISLAND: refer to Canada

PUERTO RICO

The Commonwealth of Puerto Rico, the easternmost island of the Greater Antilles in the West Indies, has an area of 3,435 sq. mi. (9,104 sq. km.) and a population of 3.3 million. Capital: San Juan. The commonwealth has its own constitution and elects its own governor. Its people are citizens of the United States, liable to the draft - but not to federal taxation. The chief industries of Puerto Rico are manufacturing, agriculture, and tourism. Manufactured goods, cement, dairy and livestock products, sugar, rum and coffee are exported, mainly to the United States.

Puerto Rico ('Rich Port') was discovered by Columbus who landed on the island and took possession for Spain on Oct. 19, 1493 - the only time Columbus set foot on the soil of what is now a possession of the United States. The first settlement, Caparra, was established by Ponce de Leon in 1508. The early years of the colony were not promising. Considerable gold was found, but the supply was soon exhausted. Efforts to enslave the Indians caused violent reprisals. Hurricanes destroyed crops and homes. French, Dutch, and English freebooters burned the towns. Puerto Rico remained a Spanish possession until 1898, when it was ceded to the United States following the SpanishAmerican War. Puerto Ricans were granted a measure of self-government and U.S. citizenship in 1917. Effective July 25, 1952, a Congressional resolution elevated Puerto Rico to the status of a free commonwealth associated with the United States.

RULERS

Spanish until 1898

ASSAYERS INITIALS

G - Antonio Garcia Gonzalez
P - Felix Miguel Peiro Rodrigo

MONETARY SYSTEM

100 Centavos = 1 Peso

COUNTERMARKED COINAGE

In 1884 a large number of holed coins were countermarked at Puerto Rico's seven customs houses to legitimatize them with a device very similar to a fleur-de-lys. These coins were redeemed in 1894.

5 CENTIMOS

BRONZE

c/m: Lys on Spanish 5 Centimos, Y#69.

KM#	Date	Year	Good	VG	Fine	VF
1	ND	(1877-79)	75.00	125.00	175.00	275.00

10 CENTIMOS

BRONZE

c/m: Lys on Spanish 5 Centimos, Y#69.

KM#	Date	Year	Good	VG	Fine	VF
2	ND	(1877-79)	75.00	125.00	175.00	275.00

1/5 DOLLAR

SILVER

c/m: Lys on U.S. 20 Cent piece, Y#28.

KM#	Date	Year	Good	VG	Fine	VF
3	ND	(1875-78)	250.00	350.00	500.00	800.00

1/4 DOLLAR

SILVER

c/m: Lys on U.S. Bust Quarter, C#29.

KM#	Date	Year	Good	VG	Fine	VF
4	ND	(1815-28)	125.00	175.00	275.00	425.00

c/m: Lys on U.S. Seated Liberty Quarter, Y#30.

KM#	Date	Year	Good	VG	Fine	VF
5	ND	(1853)	100.00	150.00	250.00	350.00

c/m: Lys on U.S. Seated Liberty Quarter, Y#29.

KM#	Date	Year	Good	VG	Fine	VF
6	ND	(1838-65)	100.00	150.00	225.00	325.00

c/m: Lys on U.S. Seated Liberty Quarter, Y#31.

KM#	Date	Year	Good	VG	Fine	VF
7	ND	(1866-91)	100.00	150.00	225.00	325.00

c/m: Lys on Spanish or Spanish Colonial 2 Reales.

KM#	Date	Year	Good	VG	Fine	VF
8	ND	(1759-71)	100.00	150.00	225.00	325.00

1/2 DOLLAR

SILVER

c/m: Lys on U.S. Half Dollar, C#32.

KM#	Date	Year	Good	VG	Fine	VF
9	ND	(1807-36)	250.00	350.00	450.00	750.00

c/m: Lys on U.S. Half Dollar, Y#37.

KM#	Date	Year	Good	VG	Fine	VF
10	ND	(1839-66)	125.00	175.00	250.00	400.00

c/m: Lys on U.S. Half Dollar, Y#39.

KM#	Date	Year	Good	VG	Fine	VF
11	ND	(1866-91)	125.00	175.00	250.00	400.00

c/m: Lys on Spanish or Spanish Colonial 4 Reales.

KM#	Date	Year	Good	VG	Fine	VF
12	ND	(1791-1808)	200.00	300.00	350.00	500.00

DOLLAR

SILVER

c/m: Lys on U.S. bust type Dollar, C#34a.

KM#	Date	Year	Good	VG	Fine	VF
13	ND	(1798-1803)	450.00	525.00	650.00	1000.

c/m: Lys on U.S. Trade Dollar, Y#44.

KM#	Date	Year	Good	VG	Fine	VF
14	ND	(1873-78)	200.00	300.00	400.00	600.00

c/m: Lys on Spanish or Spanish Colonial 8 Reales.

KM#	Date	Year	Good	VG	Fine	VF
15	ND	(1772-89)	200.00	300.00	400.00	600.00

REGULAR COINAGE

5 CENTAVOS

1.2500 g, .900 SILVER, .0361 oz ASW

KM#	Date	Mintage	Fine	VF	XF	Unc
20	1896 PGV	.600	15.00	25.00	45.00	175.00

10 CENTAVOS

2.5000 g, .900 SILVER, .0723 oz ASW

KM#	Date	Mintage	Fine	VF	XF	Unc
21	1896 PGV	.700	20.00	35.00	60.00	250.00

20 CENTAVOS

5.0000 g, .900 SILVER, .1446 oz ASW

KM#	Date	Mintage	Fine	VF	XF	Unc
22	1895 PGV	3.350	35.00	60.00	90.00	300.00

40 CENTAVOS

10.0000 g, .900 SILVER, .2893 oz ASW

KM#	Date	Mintage	Fine	VF	XF	Unc
23	1896 PGV	.725	125.00	250.00	500.00	2750.

PESO

25.0000 g, .900 SILVER, .7234 oz ASW

KM#	Date	Mintage	Fine	VF	XF	Unc
24	1895 PGV	8.500	125.00	250.00	450.00	1100.

VIEQUES ISLAND

(Crab Island)

Vieques (Crab) Island, located to the east of Puerto Rico is the largest of the Commonwealth's offshore islands. Two-thirds of the island are leased to the U.S. navy. The neighboring island to the north, Culebra, was leased to the navy until 1974, when the naval station was closed and bombardment exercises ceased. Puerto Rico's offshore island to the west, Mona, situated between the main island and the Dominican Republic, has been unpopulated since the late 16th century, and is of no numismatic significance.

COUNTERMARKED COINAGE

Type I

c/m: 12 Rayed Sunburst

COPPER

c/m: On U.S. Nova Constellatio Cent

KM#	Date	Good	VG	Fine	VF
1	ND(1783-5)	50.00	75.00	125.00	200.00

SILVER

KM#	Date	Good	VG	Fine	VF
	c/m: On Danish West Indies 2 Skilling, KM#13.				
2	ND(1837)	40.00	55.00	85.00	125.00
	c/m: On Danish West Indies 2 Skilling, KM#19.				
3	ND(1848)	40.00	55.00	85.00	125.00
	c/m: On Danish West Indies 10 Skilling, KM#16.				
4	ND(1845)	45.00	65.00	100.00	140.00
	c/m: On Danish West Indies 20 Skilling, KM#17.				
5	ND(1840)	50.00	75.00	125.00	200.00

c/m: On Danish 18th century silver coin.

KM#	Date	Good	VG	Fine	VF
6	ND	50.00	85.00	110.00	175.00

c/m: On Spanish 2 Reales, C#134.

KM#	Date	Good	VG	Fine	VF
7	ND(1825)	85.00	125.00	150.00	225.00

Type II

c/m: V in 12 Rayed Sunburst

c/m: On 1/2 cut of Spanish Colonial 2 Reales

KM#	Date	Good	VG	Fine	VF
8	ND	100.00	135.00	175.00	250.00

QATAR

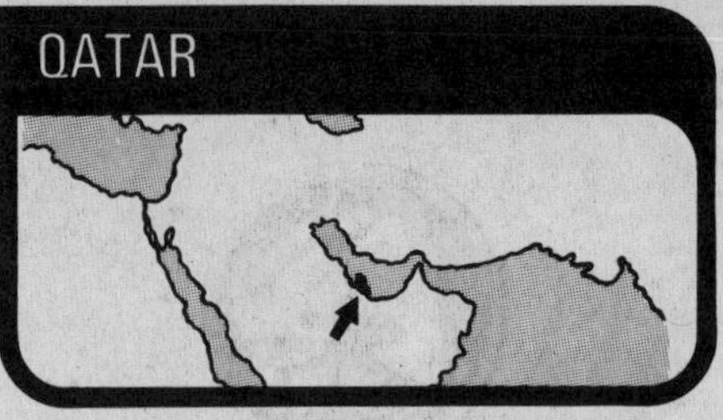

The State of Qatar, an emirate in the Persian Gulf between Bahrain and Trucial Oman, has an area of 4,247 sq. mi. (11,000 sq. km.) and a population of *469,000. Capital: Doha. Oil is the chief industry and export.

Qatar was under Turkish control from 1872 until the beginning of World War I when the Ottoman Turks evacuated the Qatar Peninsula. In 1916 Sheikh Abdullah placed Qatar under the protection of Great Britain and gave Britain responsibility for its defense and foreign relations. Qatar joined with Dubai in a Monetary Union and issued coins and paper money in 1966 and 1969. When Britain announced in 1968 that it would end treaty relationships with the Persian Gulf sheikhdoms in 1971, this union was dissolved, Qatar joined Bahrain and the seven trucial sheikhdoms (the latter now called the United Arab Emirates) in an effort to form a union of Arab Emirates. However the nine sheikhdoms were unable to agree on terms of union, and Qatar declared its independence as the State of Qatar on Sept. 3, 1971.

TITLES

Daulat Qatar

RULERS

Khalifa, 1972

MONETARY SYSTEM

100 Dirhem = 1 Riyal

DIRHEM

BRONZE

KM#	Date	Year	Mintage	VF	XF	Unc
2	AH1393	1973	.500	.10	.20	.50

5 DIRHEMS

BRONZE

KM#	Date	Year	Mintage	VF	XF	Unc
3	AH1393	1973	1.000	.10	.20	.60
	1398	1978	1.000	.10	.20	.60

10 DIRHEMS

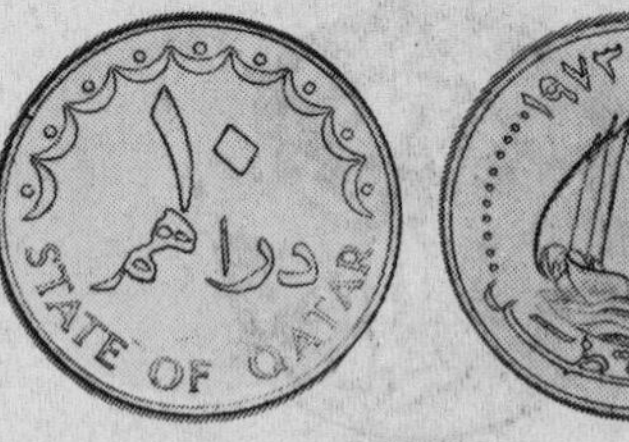

BRONZE

KM#	Date	Year	Mintage	VF	XF	Unc
1	AH1392	1972	1.500	.20	.35	.80
	1393	1973	1.500	.20	.35	.80

25 DIRHEMS

COPPER-NICKEL

KM#	Date	Year	Mintage	VF	XF	Unc
4	AH1393	1973	1.500	.25	.45	1.00
	1396	1976	2.000	.25	.45	1.00
	1398	1978	—	.25	.45	1.00
	1401	1981	—	.25	.45	1.00
	1407	1987	—	.25	.45	1.00
	1410	1990	—	.25	.45	1.00

50 DIRHEMS

COPPER-NICKEL

KM#	Date	Year	Mintage	VF	XF	Unc
5	AH1393	1973	1.500	.40	.80	1.50
	1398	1978	2.000	.40	.80	1.50
	1401	1981	—	.40	.80	1.50
	1407	1987	—	.40	.80	1.50
	1410	1990	—	.40	.80	1.50

QATAR & DUBAI

The State of Qatar, which occupies the Qatar Peninsula jutting into the Persian Gulf from eastern Saudi Arabia, has an area of 4,247 sq. mi. (11,000 sq. km.) and a population of *469,000. Capital: Doha. The traditional occupations of pearling, fishing, and herding have been replaced in economics by petroleum-related industries. Crude oil, petroleum products, and tomatoes are exported.

Dubai is one of the seven sheikhdoms comprising the United Arab Emirates (formerly Trucial States) located along the southern shore of the Persian Gulf. It has a population of about 60,000. Capital (of the United Arab Emirates): Abu Dhabi.

Qatar, which initiated protective treaty relations with Great Britain in 1820, achieved independence on Sept. 3, 1971, upon withdrawal of the British military presence from the Persian Gulf, and replaced its special treaty arrangement with Britain with a treaty of general friendship. Dubai attained independence on Dec. 1, 1971, upon termination of Britain's protective treaty with the trucial Sheikhdoms, and on Dec. 2, 1971, entered into the union of the United Arab Emirates.

Despite the fact that the Emirate of Qatar and the Sheikhdom of Dubai were merged under a monetary union, the two territories were governed independently from each other. Qatar now uses its own currency while Dubai uses the United Arab Emirates currency and coins.

TITLES

قطرودبي

Qatar Wa Dubai

RULERS

Ahmad II, 1960-1972

MONETARY SYSTEM

100 Dirhem = 1 Riyal

DIRHEM

BRONZE

KM#	Date	Year	Mintage	VF	XF	Unc
1	AH1386	1966	1.000	.10	.20	.50

5 DIRHEMS

BRONZE

KM#	Date	Year	Mintage	VF	XF	Unc
2	AH1386	1966	2.000	.10	.20	.60
	1389	1969	2.000	.10	.20	.60

10 DIRHEMS

BRONZE

KM#	Date	Year	Mintage	VF	XF	Unc
3	AH1386	1966	2.000	.20	.35	.80

25 DIRHEMS

COPPER-NICKEL

KM#	Date	Year	Mintage	VF	XF	Unc
4	AH1386	1966	2.000	.25	.45	1.00
	1389	1969	2.000	.25	.45	1.00

50 DIRHEMS

COPPER-NICKEL

KM#	Date	Year	Mintage	VF	XF	Unc
5	AH1386	1966	2.000	.40	.80	1.50

Listings For

QUAITI: refer to Yemen Republic

RAS AL KHAIMA: refer to United Arab Emirates

REUNION

The Department of Reunion, an overseas department of France located in the Indian Ocean 400 miles (640 km.) east of Madagascar, has an area of 969 sq. mi. (2,510 sq. km.) and a population of *566,000. Capital: Saint-Denis. The island's volcanic soil is extremely fertile. Sugar, vanilla, coffee and rum are exported.

Although first visited by Portuguese navigators in the 16th century, Reunion was uninhabited when claimed for France by Capt. Goubert in 1638. It was first colonized as Isle de Bourbon by the French in 1662 as a layover station for ships rounding the Cape of Good Hope to India. It was renamed Reunion in 1793. The island remained in French possession except for the period of 1810-15, when it was occupied by the British. Reunion became an overseas department of France in 1946, and in 1958 voted to continue that status within the new French Union.

During the first half of the 19th century, Reunion was officially known as Isle de Bonaparte (1801-14) and Isle de Bourbon (1814-48). Reunion coinage of those periods is so designated.

ISLE DE BOURBON

The Restoration of the House of Bourbon in France caused the name of the Reunion Island to be changed to Isle de Bourbon from 1814-1848.

RULERS

Louis XVIII, 1814-1828

MONETARY SYSTEM

100 Centimes = 1 Franc

10 CENTIMES

BILLON

KM#	Date	Mintage	VG	Fine	VF	XF
1	1816A	.150	12.50	35.00	75.00	200.00

REUNION

MINT MARKS

(a) - Paris, privy marks only

MONETARY SYSTEM

100 Centimes = 1 Franc

50 CENTIMES

COPPER-NICKEL

KM#	Date	Mintage	Fine	VF	XF	Unc
4	1896	1.000	15.00	35.00	90.00	275.00

FRANC

COPPER-NICKEL

KM#	Date	Mintage	Fine	VF	XF	Unc
5	1896	.500	35.00	60.00	150.00	350.00

KM#	Date	Mintage	VF	XF	Unc
	ALUMINUM				
6.1	1948(a)	3.000	.25	.50	1.75
	1964(a)	1.000	.25	.50	2.00
	1968(a)	.450	.50	1.00	3.50
	1969(a)	.500	.50	.75	2.50
	1971(a)	.800	.50	.75	2.00
	1973(a)	.500	.50	.75	2.50
	Thinner Planchet				
6.2	1969(a)	Inc. Ab.	.65	1.25	4.00

Mule. Obv: French Colonial. Rev: KM#6.1.

KM#	Date	Mintage	VF	XF	Unc
7	1948(a)	Inc. Ab.	—	—	—

2 FRANCS

ALUMINUM

KM#	Date	Mintage	VF	XF	Unc
8	1948(a)	2.000	.25	.75	2.50
	1968(a)	.100	2.50	4.50	8.00
	1969(a)	.150	1.50	2.50	5.00
	1970(a)	.300	.75	1.50	3.00
	1971(a)	.300	.75	1.50	3.00
	1973(a)	.500	.75	1.50	3.00

5 FRANCS

ALUMINUM

KM#	Date	Mintage	VF	XF	Unc
9	1955(a)	3.000	.50	.75	2.00
	1969(a)	.100	2.50	5.00	8.00
	1970(a)	.200	1.50	3.00	6.00
	1971(a)	.100	1.50	3.00	6.00
	1972(a)	.300	.75	1.50	2.50
	1973(a)	.250	.75	1.50	2.50

10 FRANCS

KM#	Date	Mintage	VF	XF	Unc
	ALUMINUM-BRONZE				
10	1955(a)	1.500	.45	.65	2.00
	1962(a)	.700	1.50	3.00	6.00
	1964(a)	1.000	.45	.65	2.00
	ALUMINUM NICKEL BRONZE				
10a	1969(a)	.300	1.00	2.00	5.00
	1970(a)	.300	1.00	2.00	4.00
	1971(a)	.200	1.50	3.50	7.00
	1972(a)	.400	1.00	2.00	5.00
	1973(a)	.700	.75	1.50	2.50

20 FRANCS

KM#	Date	Mintage	VF	XF	Unc
	ALUMINUM-BRONZE				
11	1955(a)	1.250	.65	1.00	3.00
	1960(a)	.100	2.75	5.50	9.00
	1961(a)	.300	2.25	4.50	7.00
	1962(a)	.190	2.75	5.00	8.00
	1964(a)	.750	.75	1.50	2.50
	ALUMINUM NICKEL BRONZE				
11a	1969(a)	.200	2.75	5.00	8.00
	1970(a)	.200	2.75	5.00	8.00
	1971(a)	.200	2.75	5.00	8.00
	1972(a)	.300	2.00	3.00	3.00
	1973(a)	.550	.75	1.50	2.50

50 FRANCS

NICKEL

KM#	Date	Mintage	VF	XF	Unc
12	1962(a)	1.000	1.25	2.25	4.00
	1964(a)	.500	2.00	3.00	5.00
	1969(a)	.100	2.75	5.00	8.00
	1970(a)	.100	2.75	5.00	8.00
	1973(a)	.350	2.00	3.00	3.50

100 FRANCS

NICKEL

KM#	Date	Mintage	VF	XF	Unc
13	1964(a)	2.000	1.00	1.50	2.50
	1969(a)	.200	2.25	4.00	6.00
	1970(a)	.150	2.25	4.50	8.00
	1971(a)	.100	2.75	6.00	12.50
	1972(a)	.400	2.00	3.00	4.00
	1973(a)	.200	2.25	4.00	6.00

FLEUR DE COIN SETS (SS)

KM#	Date	Mintage	Identification	Issue Price	Mkt. Val.
SS1	1964(5)	—	KM6.1,10-13	—	10.00

NOTE: This set issued with Comoros set.

Listings For

RHODESIA: refer to Zimbabwe

RHODESIA & NYASALAND: refer to Zimbabwe

RIAU ARCHIPELAGO: refer to Indonesia

ROMANIA

CZECHOSLOVAKIA
UKRAINE
MOLDOVA
AUSTRIA
HUNGARY
CROATIA
BOSNIA
SERBIA
BULGARIA
Black Sea

The Republic of Romania, a Balkan country in southeast Europe, has an area of 91,699 sq. mi. (237,500 sq. km.) and a population of *23.2 million. Capital: Bucharest. The economy is predominantly agricultural; heavy industry and oil have become increasingly important since 1959. Machinery, foodstuffs, raw minerals and petroleum products are exported.

The area of Romania, generally referred to as Dacia by the ancient Romans, was subjected to wave after wave of barbarian conquest and foreign domination before its independence (of Turkey) was declared in 1877. In 1881 it became a monarchy under Carol I, changing to a constitutional monarchy with a bicameral legislature in 1888. The government was reorganized along Fascist lines in 1940, and in the following year Romania joined Germany's attack on the Soviet Union for recovering the region of Bessarabia annexed by Stalin in 1940. The country was subsequently occupied by the Russian Army which actively supported the program and goals of the Romanian Communists. On Nov. 19, 1946, a Communistdominated government was installed and prompted the abdication of King Michael. Romania became a 'People's Republic' on Dec. 30, 1947. which was later proclaimed a Socialist Republic in 1965.

On Dec. 22, 1989 the Communist Socialist Republic government under the dictatorship of Nicolas Ceausescu was overthrown by organized freedom fighters in Bucharest. Ceausescu and his wife were later executed by a firing squad. The new government has established the Republic of Romania.

RULERS

Carol I (as Prince), 1866-81 (as King), 1881-1914
Ferdinand I, 1914-1927
Mihai I, 1927-1930
Carol II, 1930-1940
Mihai I, 1940-1947

MINT MARKS

(a) - Paris, privy marks only
(b) - Brussels, privy marks only
B - Bucharest (1870-1900)
B - Hamburg
C - Bucharest (1935)
FM - Franklin Mint
H - Heaton
HF - Huguenin, Le Locle
J - Hamburg
KN - Kings Norton
(p) - Thunderbolt - Poissy
V - Vienna
W - Watt (James Watt & Co.)
Huguenin - Le Locle

MONETARY SYSTEM

100 Bani = 1 Leu

BANU

COPPER

KM#	Date	Mintage	Fine	VF	XF	Unc
1	1867H	2.500	4.00	8.00	25.00	60.00
	1867H	Inc. Ab.	—	—	Proof	75.00
	1867WATT & CO.	2.500	6.00	12.00	25.00	70.00
	1867WATT & CO.	—	—	—	Proof	90.00

BAN

KM#	Date	Mintage	Fine	VF	XF	Unc
	GILT BRONZE **Similar to 2 Bani, KM#18.**					
A18	1883	500 pcs.	—	—	—	1200.
	BRONZE					
A18a	1888	500 pcs.	—	—	—	900.00

NOTE: Presentation issues for Queen Elizabeth of Romania.

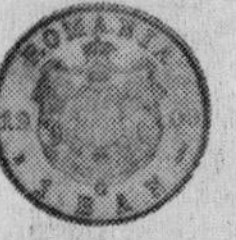

COPPER

KM#	Date	Mintage	Fine	VF	XF	Unc
26	1900B	20.007	1.50	2.25	5.50	16.00
	1900B	—	—	—	Proof	50.00

NOTE: Varieties exist.

2 BANI

COPPER

KM#	Date	Mintage	Fine	VF	XF	Unc
2	1867HEATON	5.000	2.50	6.00	12.00	30.00
	1867HEATON	Inc. Ab.	—	—	Proof	60.00
	1867WATT & CO.	5.000	3.00	7.50	14.00	35.00
	1867WATT & CO.	—	—	—	Proof	85.00

19.5mm
Obv leg: CAROL I DOMNUL (Prince)

KM#	Date	Mintage	Fine	VF	XF	Unc
11.1	1879B	.500	5.00	10.00	25.00	50.00

20mm

KM#	Date	Mintage	Fine	VF	XF	Unc
11.2	1879B	Inc. Ab.	4.00	8.00	18.00	35.00
	1880B	10.500	3.00	6.00	12.00	25.00
	1881B	1.250	15.00	20.00	35.00	120.00

Obv. leg: CAROL I REGE (King)

KM#	Date	Mintage	Fine	VF	XF	Unc
18	1882B	5.000	4.00	8.00	18.00	45.00

Rev: ROMANIA added above shield.

KM#	Date	Mintage	Fine	VF	XF	Unc
27	1900B	20.000	1.00	2.00	5.00	12.00

NOTE: Varieties exist.

5 BANI

COPPER

KM#	Date	Mintage	Fine	VF	XF	Unc
3	1867HEATON	12.500	2.50	5.00	10.00	25.00
	1867HEATON	—	—	—	Proof	80.00
	1867WATT & CO.	12.500	3.00	6.00	12.00	40.00
	1867WATT & CO.	—	—	—	Proof	100.00

Obv. leg: CAROL I REGE (King)

KM#	Date	Mintage	Fine	VF	XF	Unc
19	1882B	5.000	1.00	2.50	12.00	30.00
	1883B	3.000	1.00	2.00	10.00	28.00
	1884B	8.400	1.00	2.00	8.00	25.00
	1885B	3.600	2.00	4.00	15.00	40.00

COPPER-NICKEL

KM#	Date	Mintage	Fine	VF	XF	Unc
28	1900	20.000	1.00	2.50	7.00	15.00

KM#	Date	Mintage	Fine	VF	XF	Unc
31	1905	2.000	.50	1.00	3.00	9.00
	1905	—	—	—	Proof	25.00
	1906	48.000	.25	.50	2.00	8.00
	1906J	24.000	.25	.50	1.50	5.00

10 BANI

COPPER

KM#	Date	Mintage	Fine	VF	XF	Unc
4	1867HEATON	12.500	2.00	7.00	15.00	30.00
	1867HEATON	Inc. Ab.	—	—	Proof	75.00
	1867WATT & CO.	12.500	2.00	7.00	18.00	35.00
	1867WATT & CO.	—	—	—	Proof	95.00

COPPER-NICKEL

KM#	Date	Mintage	Fine	VF	XF	Unc
29	1900	15.000	.75	2.00	5.00	15.00
	1900	—	—	—	Proof	60.00

KM#	Date	Mintage	Fine	VF	XF	Unc
32	1905	10.820	.50	1.00	3.50	10.00
	1906	24.180	.25	.75	2.50	9.00
	1906J	17.000	.25	.75	1.50	6.00

20 BANI

COPPER-NICKEL

KM#	Date	Mintage	Fine	VF	XF	Unc
30	1900	2.500	3.00	9.00	25.00	70.00

KM#	Date	Mintage	Fine	VF	XF	Unc
33	1905	2.500	.50	2.50	9.00	30.00
	1906	3.000	.50	2.00	8.00	25.00
	1906J	2.500	.50	2.00	5.00	18.00

25 BANI

ALUMINUM

KM#	Date	Mintage	Fine	VF	XF	Unc
44	1921HF	20.000	.50	1.00	2.50	7.50

NOTE: Sizes of center hole vary from 3.8-4.3mm.

50 BANI

2.5000 g, .835 SILVER, .0671 oz ASW

KM#	Date	Mintage	Fine	VF	XF	Unc
9	1873(b)	4.800	2.50	8.00	20.00	45.00
	1876(b)	2.117	3.00	12.00	30.00	70.00

KM#	Date	Mintage	Fine	VF	XF	Unc
13	1881V	1.000	5.00	15.00	35.00	120.00

Rev: Large letters.

KM#	Date	Mintage	Fine	VF	XF	Unc
21.1	1884B	1.000	3.00	7.50	25.00	65.00

Obv: Different head.

KM#	Date	Mintage	Fine	VF	XF	Unc
21.2	1885B	.200	6.00	18.00	40.00	150.00

Rev: Small letters.

KM#	Date	Mintage	Fine	VF	XF	Unc
23	1894	.600	4.00	8.00	18.00	45.00
	1900	3.838	2.50	6.00	12.00	30.00
	1901	.194	6.00	15.00	35.00	95.00

KM#	Date	Mintage	Fine	VF	XF	Unc
41	1910	3.600	1.50	3.00	8.00	14.00
	1910	—	—	—	Proof	150.00
	1911	3.000	2.00	4.00	10.00	16.00
	1912	1.800	1.50	3.00	8.00	14.00
	1914	1.600	1.25	2.00	4.00	10.00
	1914	—	—	—	Proof	90.00

NOTE: Edge varieties exist.

ALUMINUM

KM#	Date	Mintage	Fine	VF	XF	Unc
45	1921HF	30.000	.50	1.00	3.50	9.00

NOTE: Sizes of center hole vary from 3.8-4.2mm.

LEU

5.0000 g, .835 SILVER, .1342 oz ASW

KM#	Date	Mintage	Fine	VF	XF	Unc
6	1870C	.400	20.00	45.00	120.00	350.00
	1870C medal rotation	Inc. Ab.	—	—	—	—

KM#	Date	Mintage	Fine	VF	XF	Unc
6	1870B	Inc. Ab.	100.00	225.00	375.00	800.00
	1870 B medal rotation	Inc. Ab.	—	—	—	—

KM#	Date	Mintage	Fine	VF	XF	Unc
10	1873(b)	4.443	4.00	8.00	17.50	60.00
	1874(b)	4.511	5.00	12.00	25.00	85.00
	1876(b)	.225	35.00	75.00	150.00	350.00

NOTE: Varieties exist.

Obv. leg: CAROL I DOMNUL (Prince).

KM#	Date	Mintage	Fine	VF	XF	Unc
14	1881V	1.800	8.00	16.00	45.00	125.00
	1881V	—	—	—	Proof	—

Obv. leg: CAROL I REGE (King).

KM#	Date	Mintage	Fine	VF	XF	Unc
22	1884B	1.000	6.00	15.00	35.00	85.00
	1885B	.400	9.00	27.50	55.00	140.00
	1885B	—	—	—	Proof	—

KM#	Date	Mintage	Fine	VF	XF	Unc
24	1894	1.500	4.00	7.50	16.00	55.00
	1894	—	—	—	Proof	—
	1900	.799	5.00	10.00	22.00	65.00
	1901	.370	6.00	15.00	35.00	90.00
	1901	—	—	—	Proof	—

Carol I 40th Anniversary of Reign

KM#	Date	Mintage	Fine	VF	XF	Unc
34	1906	2.500	4.00	8.00	15.00	35.00
	1906	—	—	—	Proof	85.00

KM#	Date	Mintage	Fine	VF	XF	Unc
42	1910	4.600	3.00	6.00	8.00	16.00
	1910	—	—	—	Proof	180.00
	1911	2.573	4.00	8.00	12.00	25.00
	1912	3.540	3.00	5.00	7.00	14.00
	1914	4.283	2.00	3.00	6.00	12.00
	1914	—	—	—	Proof	—

NOTE: Edge varieties exist.

COPPER-NICKEL

KM#	Date	Mintage	Fine	VF	XF	Unc
46	1924(b)	100.000	.50	1.50	3.50	8.50
	1924(p)	100.006	.50	1.50	3.50	8.50

NICKEL-BRASS

KM#	Date	Mintage	Fine	VF	XF	Unc
56	1938B	27.900	.10	.50	1.00	2.50
	1939B	72.200	.10	.50	1.50	3.00
	1940B	Inc. Ab.	.10	.50	1.00	2.50
	1941B	Inc. Ab.	.10	.50	1.50	3.50

2 LEI

10.0000 g, .835 SILVER, .2684 oz ASW

KM#	Date	Mintage	Fine	VF	XF	Unc
8	1872(b)	.262	6.00	15.00	55.00	175.00
	1872	—	—	—	Proof	500.00
	1873(b)	1.745	4.00	10.00	30.00	80.00
	1875(b)	3.092	4.00	9.00	25.00	70.00
	1876(b)	.653	6.00	15.00	50.00	150.00

KM#	Date	Mintage	Fine	VF	XF	Unc
15	1881V	1.150	12.00	30.00	75.00	200.00

KM#	Date	Mintage	Fine	VF	XF	Unc
25	1894	.600	8.00	16.00	45.00	150.00
	1894	—	—	—	Proof	—
	1900	.087	12.00	30.00	85.00	220.00
	1901	.012	350.00	500.00	750.00	1500.

KM#	Date	Mintage	Fine	VF	XF	Unc
43	1910	1.800	4.00	8.00	15.00	30.00
	1910	—	—	—	Proof	200.00
	1911	1.000	6.00	12.00	25.00	35.00
	1912	1.500	4.00	7.00	12.00	20.00
	1914	2.452	3.00	5.00	8.00	15.00
	1914	—	—	—	Proof	—

NOTE: Edge varieties exist.

COPPER-NICKEL

KM#	Date	Mintage	Fine	VF	XF	Unc
47	1924(b)	50.000	.60	1.75	4.00	9.50
	1924(p)	50.008	.60	1.75	4.00	9.50

ZINC

KM#	Date	Mintage	Fine	VF	XF	Unc
58	1941	101.778	.35	.75	1.75	5.00

5 LEI

25.0000 g, .900 SILVER, .7234 oz ASW

KM#	Date	Mintage	Fine	VF	XF	Unc
12	1880B name near rim	1.800	17.50	35.00	80.00	180.00
	1880B name near truncation	Inc. Ab.	20.00	40.00	90.00	200.00
	1881B	2.200	15.00	30.00	55.00	160.00

KM#	Date	Mintage	Fine	VF	XF	Unc
16	1881B	.570	25.00	60.00	140.00	275.00

Lettered Edge

KM#	Date	Mintage	Fine	VF	XF	Unc
17.1	1881B	1.230	15.00	35.00	85.00	250.00
	1882B	1.100	15.00	40.00	90.00	275.00
	1883B	*2.300	15.00	30.00	50.00	150.00
	1884B	.300	25.00	75.00	140.00	375.00
	1885B	.040	90.00	175.00	400.00	800.00

***NOTE:** Varieties in crown on mantle exist.

Reeded Edge

KM#	Date	Mintage	Fine	VF	XF	Unc
17.2	1901B	.082	40.00	85.00	160.00	275.00
	1901B	—	—	—	Proof	—

Carol I 40th Anniversary of Reign

KM#	Date	Mintage	Fine	VF	XF	Unc
35	1906	.200	40.00	65.00	160.00	320.00
	1906	—	—	—	Proof	950.00

NICKEL-BRASS
King Mihai I

KM#	Date	Mintage	Fine	VF	XF	Unc
48	1930H	15.000	1.00	2.50	6.00	17.50
	1930KN	15.000	1.00	3.50	8.00	20.00
	1930(a)	30.000	.50	2.50	5.00	12.00

ZINC

KM#	Date	Mintage	Fine	VF	XF	Unc
61	1942	140.000	.50	1.00	2.00	4.00

10 LEI

NICKEL-BRASS
King Carol II

KM#	Date	Mintage	Fine	VF	XF	Unc
49	1930	15.000	1.00	3.00	7.50	22.00
	1930	—	—	—	Proof	—
	1930(a)	30.000	1.00	3.00	7.00	20.00
	1930H	7.500	2.50	4.50	10.00	27.50
	1930KN	7.500	3.00	7.00	15.00	35.00

12-1/2 LEI

4.0323 g, .900 GOLD, .1167 oz AGW
Carol I 40th Anniversary of Reign

KM#	Date	Mintage	Fine	VF	XF	Unc
36	1906	.032	75.00	95.00	125.00	275.00

20 LEI

6.4516 g, .900 GOLD, .1867 oz AGW
Obv. leg: CAROL I DOMNULU (Prince), light beard.
Reeded edge.

KM#	Date	Mintage	Fine	VF	XF	Unc
5	1868(b)	200 pcs.	—	4000.	5000.	7500.

Obv. leg: CAROL I DOMNUL (Prince), heavy beard.

KM#	Date	Mintage	Fine	VF	XF	Unc
7	1870C	5,000	500.00	750.00	1250.	2400.

Obv. leg: CAROL I REGE (King).

KM#	Date	Mintage	Fine	VF	XF	Unc
20	1883B	.150	95.00	125.00	150.00	220.00
	1884	.035	200.00	300.00	550.00	900.00
	1890B	.196	100.00	150.00	175.00	240.00

Carol I 40th Anniversary of Reign

KM#	Date	Mintage	Fine	VF	XF	Unc
37	1906(b)	.015	125.00	150.00	200.00	350.00

NICKEL-BRASS
King Mihai I

KM#	Date	Mintage	Fine	VF	XF	Unc
50	1930 London	40.000	2.00	6.50	17.50	35.00
	1930	—	—	—	Proof	—
	1930H	5.000	3.00	8.00	25.00	50.00
	1930KN	5.000	3.00	10.00	30.00	60.00

KM#	Date	Mintage	Fine	VF	XF	Unc
51	1930	6.750	1.50	4.00	12.00	22.00
	1930	—	—	—	Proof	—
	1930(a)	17.500	1.50	3.00	10.00	20.00
	1930H	7.750	2.00	6.00	16.00	37.50
	1930KN	7.750	2.50	9.00	25.00	55.00

ZINC

KM#	Date	Mintage	Fine	VF	XF	Unc
62	1942	44.000	.75	1.50	3.00	6.00
	1943	25.783	1.00	2.25	4.00	8.00
	1944	5.034	1.50	3.00	4.50	10.00

25 LEI

8.0645 g, .900 GOLD, .2333 oz AGW

Carol I 40th Anniversary of Reign

KM#	Date	Mintage	Fine	VF	XF	Unc
38	1906(b)	.024	150.00	200.00	250.00	450.00

50 LEI

16.1290 g, .900 GOLD, .4667 oz AGW
Carol I 40th Anniversary of Reign

KM#	Date	Mintage	Fine	VF	XF	Unc
39	1906(b)	.028	250.00	300.00	450.00	800.00

NICKEL

KM#	Date	Mintage	Fine	VF	XF	Unc
55	1937	*12.000	1.25	2.50	4.50	7.50
	1938	*8.000	3.75	7.50	15.00	27.50

***NOTE:** 16.731 melted.

100 LEI

32.2580 g, .900 GOLD, .9335 oz AGW
Carol I 40th Anniversary of Reign

KM#	Date	Mintage	Fine	VF	XF	Unc
40	1906(b)	3,000	600.00	800.00	1200.	2250.

12.0000 g, .500 SILVER, .1929 oz ASW

KM#	Date	Mintage	Fine	VF	XF	Unc
52	1932(a)	2.000	9.00	18.00	40.00	120.00
	1932	16.400	5.00	10.00	20.00	50.00
	1932	—	—	—	Proof	250.00

NICKEL

KM#	Date	Mintage	Fine	VF	XF	Unc
54	1936	20.230	1.00	2.00	4.00	9.00
	1938	*3.250	7.50	12.00	25.00	65.00

*NOTE: 17.030 melted.

NICKEL-CLAD STEEL

KM#	Date	Mintage	Fine	VF	XF	Unc
64	1943	40.590	.50	1.00	1.50	5.00
	1944	21.289	.50	1.50	2.50	7.00

200 LEI

6.0000 g, .835 SILVER, .1611 oz ASW

63	1942	30.025	1.50	3.00	5.00	10.00

BRASS

66	1945	1.399	1.50	3.00	5.00	12.00

NOTE: Many of these coins were privately silver plated.

250 LEI

13.5000 g, .750 SILVER, .3255 oz ASW

53	1935	4.500	10.00	20.00	40.00	130.00

12.0000 g, .835 SILVER, .3222 oz ASW

57	1939	10.000	5.00	7.50	15.00	30.00
	1940	8.000	10.00	25.00	60.00	140.00

Rev: Date divided by portcullis.
Lettered edge: TOTUL PENTRU TARA.

59.1	1940	—	—	—	Rare	—

Rev: Date not divided.
Lettered edge: TOTUL PENTRU TARA

59.2	1941	2.250	8.00	15.00	35.00	60.00

Lettered edge: NIHIL SINE DEO

59.3	1941(p)	13.750	6.00	9.00	12.00	20.00

500 LEI

25.0000 g, .835 SILVER, .6711 oz ASW

KM#	Date	Mintage	Fine	VF	XF	Unc
60	1941	.775	8.00	12.00	17.00	25.00

12.0000 g, .700 SILVER, .2701 oz ASW

65	1944	9.731	2.50	3.50	5.00	8.00

BRASS

67	1945	3.422	2.00	3.00	4.50	8.00

NOTE: Many of these coins were privately silver plated.

ALUMINUM

68	1946	5.823	1.00	2.50	5.00	10.00

NOTE: W/o designers name result of filled die.

2000 LEI

BRASS

69	1946	24.619	1.00	2.50	4.00	7.00

NOTE: Many of these coins were privately silver plated.

10000 LEI

BRASS

KM#	Date	Mintage	Fine	VF	XF	Unc
76	1947	11.850	2.00	4.00	6.00	13.00

NOTE: Many of these coins were privately silver plated.

25000 LEI

12.5000 g, .700 SILVER, .2814 oz ASW

70	1946	2.372	2.00	4.00	6.00	12.00

100000 LEI

25.0000 g, .700 SILVER, .5626 oz ASW

71	1946	2.002	6.00	8.00	12.50	22.00

MONETARY REFORM

1000 Bani = 1 Leu

50 BANI

BRASS

72	1947	13.266	1.00	2.00	3.00	9.00

LEU

BRASS

73	1947	88.341	.75	2.00	3.00	7.50

2 LEI

BRONZE

KM#	Date	Mintage	Fine	VF	XF	Unc
74	1947	40.000	1.00	2.50	4.50	10.00

5 LEI

ALUMINUM

KM#	Date	Mintage	Fine	VF	XF	Unc
75	1947	56.026	1.00	2.00	5.00	13.50

PEOPLES REPUBLIC

1947-1965

LEU

COPPER-NICKEL-ZINC

KM#	Date	Mintage	Fine	VF	XF	Unc
78	1949	—	.75	1.50	3.00	6.00
	1950	—	.75	1.50	3.25	6.50
	1951	—	1.00	2.50	7.00	18.50

ALUMINUM

KM#	Date	Mintage	Fine	VF	XF	Unc
78a	1951	—	1.00	2.00	3.00	4.50
	1952	—	5.00	15.00	30.00	60.00

2 LEI

ALUMINUM-BRONZE

KM#	Date	Mintage	Fine	VF	XF	Unc
79	1950	—	1.00	2.50	5.00	10.00
	1951	—	2.00	6.00	15.00	30.00

ALUMINUM

KM#	Date	Mintage	Fine	VF	XF	Unc
79a	1951	—	1.25	2.50	3.50	7.50
	1952	—	6.00	15.00	32.00	70.00

5 LEI

ALUMINUM

KM#	Date	Mintage	Fine	VF	XF	Unc
77	1948	—	1.00	1.50	3.00	7.00
	1949	—	1.00	1.50	2.50	5.00
	1950	—	1.00	1.50	2.50	5.00
	1951	—	1.00	2.50	5.00	15.00

20 LEI

ALUMINUM

KM#	Date	Mintage	Fine	VF	XF	Unc
80	1951	—	7.50	15.00	25.00	65.00

MONETARY REFORM

100 Bani = 1 Leu

BAN

ALUMINUM-BRONZE
Obv: W/o star at top of arms.

KM#	Date	Mintage	Fine	VF	XF	Unc
81.1	1952	—	.10	.20	.30	1.00

Obv: Star at top of arms.

KM#	Date	Mintage	Fine	VF	XF	Unc
81.2	1953	—	1.00	2.00	6.00	15.00
	1954	—	2.50	6.00	15.00	32.50

3 BANI

ALUMINUM-BRONZE
Obv: W/o star at top of arms.

KM#	Date	Mintage	Fine	VF	XF	Unc
82.1	1952	—	1.00	2.00	4.50	12.50

Obv: Star at top of arms.

KM#	Date	Mintage	Fine	VF	XF	Unc
82.2	1953	—	.50	1.00	2.00	4.50
	1954	—	2.00	5.00	12.00	28.00

5 BANI

ALUMINUM-BRONZE
Obv: W/o star at top of arms.

KM#	Date	Mintage	Fine	VF	XF	Unc
83.1	1952	—	.50	1.00	2.50	6.00

Obv: Star at top of arms.

KM#	Date	Mintage	Fine	VF	XF	Unc
83.2	1953	—	.25	.50	2.00	4.00
	1954	—	.25	.50	2.00	4.00
	1955	—	.25	.50	2.00	4.00
	1956	—	.20	.45	1.00	2.50
	1957	—	.30	.60	2.50	5.00

NICKEL-CLAD STEEL
Obv: RPR on ribbon in arms.

KM#	Date	Mintage	Fine	VF	XF	Unc
89	1963	—	.20	.50	1.00	2.00

10 BANI

COPPER-NICKEL
Obv: W/o star at top of arms.

KM#	Date	Mintage	Fine	VF	XF	Unc
84.1	1952	—	1.50	3.50	9.00	22.00

Obv: Star at top of arms, leg: ROMANA.

KM#	Date	Mintage	Fine	VF	XF	Unc
84.2	1954	—	.20	1.00	2.50	6.50

Obv. leg: ROMINA

KM#	Date	Mintage	Fine	VF	XF	Unc
84.3	1955	—	.10	.20	.50	1.25
	1956	—	.10	.20	.50	1.25

15 BANI

NICKEL-CLAD STEEL

KM#	Date	Mintage	Fine	VF	XF	Unc
87	1960	—	.10	.20	.40	.80

25 BANI

COPPER-NICKEL
Obv: W/o star at top of arms.

KM#	Date	Mintage	Fine	VF	XF	Unc
85.1	1952	—	.60	1.50	4.00	12.00

Obv: Star at top of arms, leg: ROMANA.

KM#	Date	Mintage	Fine	VF	XF	Unc
85.2	1953	—	.20	.75	2.00	4.00
	1954	—	.20	.60	1.50	3.00

Obv. leg: ROMINA.

KM#	Date	Mintage	Fine	VF	XF	Unc
85.3	1955	—	.15	.35	.80	2.50

NICKEL-CLAD STEEL

KM#	Date	Mintage	Fine	VF	XF	Unc
88	1960	—	.15	.25	.35	.75

50 BANI

COPPER-NICKEL

KM#	Date	Mintage	Fine	VF	XF	Unc
86	1955	—	1.00	2.00	4.00	7.50
	1956	—	1.50	3.00	5.50	12.00

LEU

NICKEL-CLAD STEEL

KM#	Date	Mintage	Fine	VF	XF	Unc
90	1963	—	.25	.50	.75	1.50

3 LEI

NICKEL-CLAD STEEL

KM#	Date	Mintage	Fine	VF	XF	Unc
91	1963	—	.25	.50	1.00	2.50

SOCIALIST REPUBLIC

1965-1989

5 BANI

NICKEL-CLAD STEEL
Obv: ROMANIA on ribbon in arms.

KM#	Date	Mintage	Fine	VF	XF	Unc
92	1966	—	.10	.20	.30	.70

ALUMINUM

KM#	Date	Mintage	Fine	VF	XF	Unc
92a	1975	—	—	—	.10	.20

15 BANI

NICKEL-CLAD STEEL

KM#	Date	Mintage	Fine	VF	XF	Unc
93	1966	—	—	.10	.20	.75

ALUMINUM

KM#	Date	Mintage	Fine	VF	XF	Unc
93a	1975	—	—	—	.10	.25

25 BANI

NICKEL-CLAD STEEL

KM#	Date	Mintage	Fine	VF	XF	Unc
94	1966	—	—	.15	.30	.65

ALUMINUM

KM#	Date	Mintage	Fine	VF	XF	Unc
94a	1982	—	—	.10	.25	.60

LEU

NICKEL-CLAD STEEL

KM#	Date	Mintage	Fine	VF	XF	Unc
95	1966	—	.10	.25	.50	1.00

3 LEI

NICKEL-CLAD STEEL

KM#	Date	Mintage	Fine	VF	XF	Unc
96	1966	—	.25	.50	1.00	3.00

5 LEI

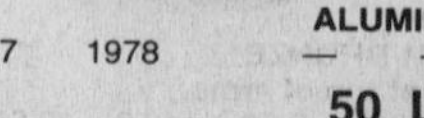

ALUMINUM

KM#	Date	Mintage	Fine	VF	XF	Unc
97	1978	—	—	.50	1.00	2.50

50 LEI

13.8800 g, .925 SILVER, .4128 oz ASW
2050th Anniversary of First Independent State
Obv: Similar to 100 Lei, KM#98.

KM#	Date	Mintage	Fine	VF	XF	Unc
100	1983FM	7,000	—	—	Proof	65.00
	1983FM	*1,000	—	—	Proof	200.00

*NOTE: Serially numbered on the edges.

100 LEI

27.7500 g, .925 SILVER, .8253 oz ASW
2050th Anniversary of First Independent State

KM#	Date	Mintage	Fine	VF	XF	Unc
98	1982FM	7,500	—	—	Proof	80.00
	1983FM	7,000	—	—	Proof	85.00
	1983FM	*1,000	—	—	Proof	300.00

*NOTE: Serially numbered on the edges.

500 LEI

.900 GOLD

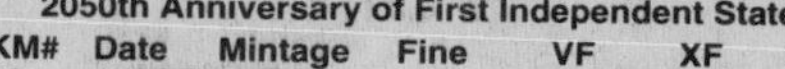

2050th Anniversary of First Independent State

KM#	Date	Mintage	Fine	VF	XF	Unc
99	1982FM	7,500	—	—	Proof	400.00
	1983FM	7,000	—	—	Proof	400.00
	1983FM	*1,000	—	—	Proof	450.00

*NOTE: Serially numbered on the edges.

1000 LEI

14.4000 g, .900 GOLD, .4167 oz AGW
2050th Anniversary of First Independent State
Obv: Similar to 500 Lei, KM#99.

KM#	Date	Mintage	Fine	VF	XF	Unc
101	1983FM	7,000	—	—	Proof	525.00
	1983FM	*1,000	—	—	Proof	900.00

*NOTE: Serially numbered on the edges.

REPUBLIC

1989-

LEU

BRONZE CLAD STEEL

KM#	Date	Mintage	Fine	VF	XF	Unc
113	1992 CD	—	—	—	—	.75

KM#	Date	Mintage	Fine	VF	XF	Unc
115	1993	—	—	—	—	.75

5 LEI

ALUMINUM
Mihai Vitcazul
Similar to 100 Lei, KM#111.

KM#	Date	Mintage	Fine	VF	XF	Unc
112	1991	3 known	—	—	—	—

NOTE: Mintage unissued and remelted.

NICKEL PLATED STEEL

KM#	Date	Mintage	Fine	VF	XF	Unc
114	1992 CD VG	—	—	—	—	1.00
	1993	—	—	—	—	1.00

10 LEI

NICKEL CLAD STEEL
Anniversary of Revolution

KM#	Date	Mintage	Fine	VF	XF	Unc
108	1990	30.000	—	.50	1.00	2.00
	1991	31.303	—	.25	.50	1.25
	1992	—	—	.25	.50	1.25

KM#	Date	Mintage	Fine	VF	XF	Unc
116	1993	—	—	—	—	1.50

20 LEI

BRASS CLAD STEEL
King Stefan Cel Mare

KM#	Date	Mintage	Fine	VF	XF	Unc
109	1991	43.200	—	—	—	3.50
	1992	—	—	—	—	3.50
	1993	—	—	—	—	3.50

50 LEI

BRASS CLAD STEEL
Alexandru Joan Cuza

KM#	Date	Mintage	Fine	VF	XF	Unc
110	1991	29.600	—	—	—	4.00
	1992	—	—	—	—	4.00
	1993	—	—	—	—	4.00

100 LEI

NICKEL PLATED STEEL
Mihai Viteazul

KM#	Date	Mintage	Fine	VF	XF	Unc
111	1991	12.600	—	—	—	9.00
	1992	—	—	—	—	9.00
	1993	—	—	—	—	9.00

NOTE: Edge varieties exist.

PROOF SETS (PS)

KM#	Date	Mintage	Identification	Issue Price	Mkt. Val.
PS1	1982(2)	7,000	KM98-99	429.00	480.00
PS2	1983(4)	1,000	KM98-99,101,110 edge numbering	850.00	1850.

Listings For

RUANDA & URUNDI: refer to Rwanda-Burundi and Zaire

RUSSIA

Russia, formerly the central power of the Union of Soviet Socialist Republics and now of the Commonwealth of Independent States occupies the northern part of Asia and the eastern part of Europe, in 1991 had an area of 8,649,538 sq. mi. (22,402,200 sq. km.) and a population of *288.7 million. Capital: Moscow. Exports include iron and steel, crude oil, timber, and nonferrous metals.

The first Russian dynasty was founded in Novgorod by the Viking Rurik in 862 A.D. Under Yaroslav the Wise (1019-54) the subsequent Kievan state became one of the great commercial and cultural centers of Europe before falling to the Mongols of the Batu Khan, 13th century, who were suzerains of Russia until late in the 15th century when Ivan III threw off the Mongol yoke. The Russian Empire was enlarged, solidified and Westernized during the reigns of Ivan the Terrible, Peter the Great and Catherine the Great, and by 1881 extended to the Pacific and into Central Asia. Contemporary Russian history began in March of 1917 when Tsar Nicholas II abdicated under pressure and was replaced by a provisional government composed of both radical and conservative elements. This government rapidly lost ground to the Bolshevik wing of the Socialist Democratic Labor Party which attained power following the Bolshevik Revolution which began on Nov. 7, 1917. After the Russian Civil War, the regional governments, national states and armies became federal republics of the Russian Socialist Federal Soviet Republic. These autonomous republics united to form the Union of Soviet Socialist Republics that was established as a federation under the premiership of Lenin on Dec. 30, 1922.

In the fall of 1991, events moved swiftly in the Soviet Union. Estonia, Latvia and Lithuania won their independence and were recognized by Moscow, Sept. 6. The Commonwealth of Independent States was formed Dec. 8, 1991 in Mensk by Belarus, Russia and Ukraine. It was expanded at a summit Dec. 21, 1991 to include 11 of the 12 remaining republics (excluding Georgia) of the old USSR.

EMPIRE

RULERS

Alexander I, 1801-1825
Nicholas I, 1825-1855
Alexander II, 1855-1881
Alexander III, 1881-1894
Nicholas II, 1894-1917

MINT MARKS

ЕМ - Ekaterinburg, 1762-1876
ИМ - Izhora, 1811-1821
КМ - Kolpino (Izhora), 1810
КМ - Kolyvan, 1767-1830 (later Souzan)
Л - Leningrad, 1991
М - Moscow, 1990
СПБ - St. Petersburg, 1724-1915
СПМ St. Petersburg (Izhora), 1840-1843
СМ - Souzan (Kolyvan), 1831-1847
ВМ - Warsaw, 1850-1864
MW - Warsaw, 1842-1854
Star (on rim) - Paris, 1896-1899
2 Stars (on rim) - Brussels, 1897-1899

(l) - LM monogram in oval - Leningrad

(m) - MM monogram in oval - Moscow

MINTMASTERS INITIALS

EKATERINBURG MINT

Initials	Years	Mintmaster
НМ	1810-21	Nicholai Mundt
ИФ	1811	Ivan Felkner
ФГ	1811-23	Franz German
ПГ	1823-25	Peter Gramatchikov
ИШ	1825	Ivan Shevkunov
ИК	1825-30	Ivan Kolobov
ФХ	1830-37	Fedor Khvochinski
КТ	1837	Konstantin Tomson
НА	1837-39	Nicholai Alexeev

IZHORA (KOLPINO) MINT

Initials	Years	Mintmaster
МК	1810-11	Mikhail Kleiner
ПС	1811-14	Paul Stupitzyn
ЯБ	1820-21	Yakov Vilson

KOLYVAN and SOUZAN MINTS

Initials	Years	Mintmaster
ПБ	1810-11	Peter Berezowski
АМ	1812-17	Alexei Maleev
ДБ	1817-18	Dmitri Bikhto
АД	1818-21	Alexander Deichmann
АМ	1821-30	Andrei Mevius

LENINGRAD MINT

Initials	Years	Mintmaster
АГ	1921-1922	A.F. Hartman
ПЛ	1922-1927	P.V. Latishev

LONDON MINT

Initials	Years	Mintmaster
Т.Р.	1924	Thomas Ross
ФР	1924	Thomas Ross

ST. PETERSBURG MINT

Initials	Years	Mintmaster
ФЦ	1797-1801	Fedor Tsetreus
АИ	1801-03	Alexie Ivanov
ФГ	1803-17	Fedor Gelman
ХЛ	1804-05	Khristopher Leo
МК	1808-09	Mikhail Kleiner
МФ	1812-22	Mikhail Fedorov
ПС	1811-25	Paul Stupitzyn
ПД	1820-38	Paul Danilov
НГ	1825-42	Nikolai Grachev

Initials	Years	Mintmaster
АЧ	1839-43	Alexei Chadov
КБ	1844-46	Constantine Butenev
АГ	1846-57	Alexander Gertov
ПА	1847-52	Paul Alexiev
НІ	1848-77	Nicholai Iossa
ФБ	1856-61	Fedor Blum
ПФ	1858-62	Paul Follendorf
МИ	1861-63	Mikhail Ivanov
АБ	1863	Alexander Belozerov
АС	1864-65	Aggei Svechin
НФ	1864-82	Nikolai Follendorf
СШ	1865-66	Sergei Shostak
ДС	1882-83	Dmitri Sabaneev
АГ	1883-99	Appolon Grasgov
ЭБ	1899-1913	Elikum Babayntz
ФЗ	1899-1901	Felix Zaleman
АР	1901-05	Alexander Redko
ВС	1913-17	Victor Smirnov

NOTE: St. Petersburg Mint became Petrograd in 1914 and Leningrad in 1924. It was renamed St. Petersburg in 1991.

MONETARY SYSTEM

1/4 Kopek = Polushka ПОЛУШКА
1/2 Kopek = Denga, Denezhka
ДЕНГА, ДЕНЕЖКА
Kopek КОПѢЙКА
(2, 3 & 4) Kopeks КОПѢЙКИ
(5 and up) Kopeks КОПѢЕКЪ
(1924 - 5 and up) Kopeks КОПЕЕК
3 Kopeks = Altyn, Altynnik
АЛТЫНЪ, АЛТЫННИКЪ
10 Kopeks = Grivna, Grivennik
ГРИВНА, ГРИВЕННИКЪ
25 Kopeks = Polupoltina, Polupoltinnik
ПОЛУПОЛТИНА
ПОЛУПОЛТИННИКЪ
50 Kopeks = Poltina, Poltinnik
ПОЛТИНА, ПОЛТИННИКЪ
100 Kopeks = Rouble, Ruble РУБЛЪ
10 Roubles = Imperial ИМПЕРIАЛЪ
10 Roubles = Chervonetz ЧЕРВОНЕЦ

NOTE: Mintage figures for years after 1885 are for fiscal years and may or may not reflect actual rarity, the commemorative and 1917 silver figures being exceptions.

NOTE: For silver coins with Zlotych and Kopek or Ruble denominations see Poland.

NOTE: For gold coins with Zlotych and Ruble denominations see Poland.

NOTE: Gold coins of 1 ducat or chervonetz denomination with both multiples and fractions are known before Peter I. Most Russian authorities agree that these pieces were not meant to be coins but were only made as awards for the military. The higher the rank of the individual the larger the gold piece. Thus the range was from a gold denga for a common soldier to a "Portugal" or 10 ducat size for a high ranking officer.

POLUSHKA

(1/4 Kopek)

COPPER, 3.00 g
Mint mark: ЕМ

C#	Date	Mintage	VG	Fine	VF	XF
92.2	1801	—	—	—	Rare	—

NOTE: Earlier dates (1797-1800) exist for this type.

C#	Date	Mintage	VG	Fine	VF	XF
111.1	1803	.012	15.00	30.00	60.00	120.00
	1804	20 pcs.	—	—	Rare	—
	1805	.025	15.00	30.00	60.00	120.00
	1808	—	25.00	50.00	100.00	200.00
	1810	—	25.00	50.00	100.00	200.00

Mint mark: КМ

C#	Date	Mintage	VG	Fine	VF	XF
111.2	1803	—	20.00	40.00	80.00	160.00
	1804	—	20.00	40.00	80.00	160.00
	1805	—	20.00	40.00	80.00	160.00
	1807	—	20.00	40.00	80.00	160.00

Mint mark: ЕМ

C#	Date	Mintage	VG	Fine	VF	XF
142.1	1840	10.793	2.00	4.00	8.00	20.00
	1841	3.230	2.00	4.00	8.00	20.00
	1842	1.600	2.00	4.00	8.00	20.00
	1843	1.664	2.00	4.00	8.00	20.00

Mint mark: СПМ

C#	Date	Mintage	VG	Fine	VF	XF
142.2	1840	6.400	4.00	7.50	15.00	30.00
	1841	6.400	3.00	6.00	12.00	24.00
	1842	12.800	3.00	6.00	12.00	24.00

Mint mark: СМ

C#	Date	Mintage	VG	Fine	VF	XF
142.3	1839	.450	12.50	25.00	50.00	100.00
	1840	2.573	4.00	7.50	15.00	30.00
	1841	3.571	4.00	7.50	15.00	30.00
	1842	3.960	4.00	7.50	15.00	30.00
	1843	2.006	4.00	7.50	15.00	30.00
	1844	3.400	4.00	7.50	15.00	30.00
	1845	3.000	4.00	7.50	15.00	30.00
	1846	3.000	4.00	7.50	15.00	30.00

Mint mark: ЕМ

C#	Date	Mintage	VG	Fine	VF	XF
147.1	1850	5.184	1.50	3.00	5.00	10.00
	1851	7.776	1.50	3.00	5.00	10.00
	1852	1.178	1.50	3.00	5.00	10.00
	1853	5.382	1.50	3.00	5.00	10.00
	1854	4.538	1.50	3.00	5.00	10.00
	1855	6.442	3.00	6.00	13.00	25.00

Mint mark: ВМ

C#	Date	Mintage	VG	Fine	VF	XF
147.3	1850	—	7.00	12.00	25.00	50.00
	1851	.080	7.00	12.00	25.00	50.00
	1852	.080	7.00	12.00	25.00	50.00
	1853	.040	7.00	12.00	25.00	50.00

Mint mark: ЕМ
Plain border

Y#	Date	Mintage	Fine	VF	XF	Unc
1.1	1855	6.422	2.00	4.00	8.00	20.00
	1856	6.000	2.00	4.00	8.00	20.00
	1857	6.000	2.00	4.00	8.00	20.00
	1858	6.970	2.00	4.00	8.00	20.00
	1859	3.834	2.00	4.00	8.00	20.00

Mint mark: ВМ

Y#	Date	Mintage	Fine	VF	XF	Unc
1.2	1855	.040	7.00	15.00	30.00	60.00
	1860	—	7.00	15.00	30.00	60.00

Mint mark: ЕМ
Toothed border

Y#	Date	Mintage	Fine	VF	XF	Unc
1.3	1858	—	—	—	Rare	—
	1859	—	2.00	4.00	8.00	20.00
	1860	—	60.00	120.00	200.00	300.00
	1861	.192	3.00	6.00	12.00	25.00
	1862	.992	2.00	4.00	8.00	20.00
	1863	.300	4.00	8.00	15.00	30.00
	1864	.403	4.00	8.00	15.00	30.00
	1865	.122	2.00	4.00	8.00	20.00
	1866	.326	2.00	4.00	8.00	20.00
	1867	.832	10.00	20.00	40.00	80.00

Mint mark: ВМ

Y#	Date	Mintage	Fine	VF	XF	Unc
1.4	1860	—	—	—	Rare	—
	1861	3.160	3.00	6.00	15.00	35.00

Mint mark: ЕМ

Y#	Date	Mintage	Fine	VF	XF	Unc
7.1	1867	Inc.Y1.3	10.00	17.00	35.00	70.00
	1868	.700	2.00	5.00	10.00	20.00
	1869	.615	2.00	5.00	10.00	20.00
	1870	.435	2.00	5.00	10.00	20.00
	1871	.155	2.00	5.00	10.00	20.00
	1872	.540	2.00	5.00	10.00	20.00
	1873	.823	2.00	5.00	10.00	20.00
	1874	.340	2.00	5.00	10.00	20.00
	1875	.300	1.25	2.50	5.00	10.00
	1876	—	40.00	80.00	150.00	300.00

Mint mark: СПБ

Y#	Date	Mintage	Fine	VF	XF	Unc
7.2	1867	24 pcs.	—	—	Rare	—
	1868	.060	3.00	6.00	12.00	25.00
	1869	.092	3.00	6.00	12.00	25.00
	1870	.020	3.50	7.50	15.00	30.00
	1871	—	—	—	Rare	—
	1876	.800	1.25	2.50	5.00	15.00
	1877	.720	1.25	2.50	5.00	15.00
	1878	1.100	1.25	2.50	5.00	15.00
	1879	.280	1.50	3.00	6.00	15.00
	1880	.180	3.00	5.00	9.00	20.00
	1881	.060	3.00	5.00	9.00	20.00

Y#	Date	Mintage	Fine	VF	XF	Unc
29	1881	.200	2.50	5.00	10.00	20.00
	1882	.060	2.50	5.00	10.00	20.00
	1883	.240	1.50	3.00	6.00	12.00
	1884	.140	2.50	4.00	8.00	20.00
	1885	.480	1.50	3.00	6.00	12.00
	1886	1.060	1.25	2.50	5.00	10.00
	1887	1.000	1.25	2.50	5.00	10.00
	1888	.200	1.50	3.00	6.00	12.00
	1889	.181	2.50	4.00	8.00	20.00
	1890	Inc. Ab.	1.50	3.00	6.00	12.00
	1891	.400	1.50	3.00	6.00	12.00
	1892	.918	1.25	2.50	5.00	12.00
	1893	.740	1.25	2.50	5.00	12.00

Y#	Date	Mintage	Fine	VF	XF	Unc
47.1	1894	—	6.00	12.00	25.00	40.00
	1895	.060	2.50	5.00	10.00	20.00
	1896	5.960	.50	1.00	2.00	7.00
	1897	3.040	.50	1.00	2.00	7.00
	1898	8.000	.50	1.00	2.00	7.00
	1899	8.000	.50	1.00	2.00	7.00
	1900	4.000	.50	1.00	2.00	7.00
	1909	2.000	1.00	2.00	4.00	12.00
	1910	8.000	4.00	8.00	15.00	30.00
	Common date	—	—	—	Proof	35.00

Mint: Petrograd - w/o mint mark

Y#	Date	Mintage	Fine	VF	XF	Unc
47.2	1915	.500	2.00	5.00	10.00	20.00
	1916	1.200	40.00	80.00	150.00	300.00

DENGA

(1/2 Kopek)

COPPER, 6.50 g
Mint mark: ЕМ
Obv: Monogram. Rev: Value, date.

C#	Date	Mintage	VG	Fine	VF	XF
93.2	1801	.026	7.50	15.00	30.00	60.00

NOTE: Earlier dates (1797-1800) exist for this type.

C#	Date	Mintage	VG	Fine	VF	XF
112.1	1804	20 pcs.	—	—	Rare	—
	1805	.040	50.00	100.00	175.00	225.00
	1808	—	—	—	Rare	—
	1810	—	—	—	Rare	—

Mint mark: КМ

C#	Date	Mintage	VG	Fine	VF	XF
112.2	1804	—	40.00	80.00	150.00	300.00
	1805	—	40.00	80.00	150.00	300.00
	1807	—	40.00	80.00	150.00	300.00

Obv: Type 2 eagle

C#	Date	Mintage	VG	Fine	VF	XF
116.2	1811 ПБ	—	5.00	10.00	20.00	40.00

Mint mark: ЕМ
Obv: Type 3 eagle

C#	Date	Mintage	VG	Fine	VF	XF
116.3	1811 НМ plain edge					
		.135	3.75	7.50	15.00	30.00
	1811 НМ reeded edge					
		Inc. Ab.	3.75	7.50	15.00	30.00
	1813 НМ	.024	4.00	8.00	15.00	30.00
	1815 НМ	.059	4.00	8.00	15.00	30.00
	1818 НМ					
		23.410	2.00	4.00	8.00	15.00
	1819 НМ	1.360	2.00	4.00	8.00	15.00
	1822 ФГ	—	25.00	50.00	100.00	200.00
	1825 ИК	.555	3.00	6.00	12.00	25.00

Mint mark: ИМ

C#	Date	Mintage	VG	Fine	VF	XF
116.4	1810 ФГ	.026	25.00	50.00	100.00	200.00
	1810 МК	I.A.	3.50	7.00	15.00	30.00
	1811 МК	.160	2.50	5.00	10.00	20.00
	1812 ПС	.510	2.50	5.00	10.00	20.00
	1813 ПС	1.220	2.50	5.00	10.00	20.00
	1814 ПС	2.250	2.50	5.00	10.00	20.00
	1814 СП	I.A.	2.50	5.00	10.00	20.00

Mint mark: КМ

C#	Date	Mintage	VG	Fine	VF	XF
116.5	1812 АМ	—	4.00	8.00	15.00	30.00
	1813 АМ	—	4.00	8.00	15.00	30.00
	1814 АМ	—	4.00	8.00	15.00	30.00
	1815 АМ	—	4.00	8.00	15.00	30.00
	1816 АМ	—	4.00	8.00	15.00	30.00
	1817 АМ	—	4.00	8.00	15.00	30.00

Mint mark: СПБ

C#	Date	Mintage	VG	Fine	VF	XF
16.6	1810 ФГ	—	6.00	12.00	25.00	50.00
	1811 МК	.075	3.00	6.00	12.00	25.00
	1812 ПС	—	25.00	50.00	100.00	200.00

Mint mark: ЕМ

C#	Date	Mintage	VG	Fine	VF	XF
135.1	1827 ИК	2.165	3.00	6.00	12.00	25.00
	1828 ИК	—	3.00	6.00	12.00	25.00

Mint mark: СПБ

C#	Date	Mintage	VG	Fine	VF	XF
135.2	1828	—	25.00	50.00	100.00	200.00

COPPER, 4.00 g
Mint mark: ЕМ

C#	Date	Mintage	VG	Fine	VF	XF
143.1	1840	10.999	2.00	4.00	8.00	15.00
	1841	3.384	2.00	4.00	8.00	15.00
	1842	3.600	2.00	4.00	8.00	15.00
	1843	2.580	2.00	4.00	8.00	15.00

Mint mark: СПБ

C#	Date	Mintage	VG	Fine	VF	XF
143.2	1840	—	6.00	12.00	25.00	50.00

Mint mark: СПМ

C#	Date	Mintage	VG	Fine	VF	XF
143.3	1840	6.400	2.00	4.00	8.00	15.00
	1841	6.400	2.00	4.00	8.00	15.00
	1842	12.800	2.00	4.00	8.00	15.00

Mint mark: СМ

C#	Date	Mintage	VG	Fine	VF	XF
143.4	1839	.454	4.00	8.00	15.00	30.00
	1840	2.560	2.00	4.00	8.00	15.00
	1841	3.542	2.00	4.00	8.00	15.00
	1842	3.960	2.00	4.00	8.00	15.00
	1843	2.006	2.00	4.00	8.00	15.00
	1844	3.400	2.00	4.00	8.00	15.00
	1845	3.000	2.00	4.00	8.00	15.00
	1846	3.000	2.00	4.00	8.00	15.00
	1847	2.532	2.00	4.00	8.00	15.00

Mint mark: МШ

C#	Date	Mintage	VG	Fine	VF	XF
143.5	1848	.087	30.00	60.00	120.00	225.00

Mint mark: ЕМ

C#	Date	Mintage	VG	Fine	VF	XF
148.1	1850	3.562	1.00	2.00	4.00	8.00
	1851	6.426	1.00	2.00	4.00	8.00
	1852	14.672	1.00	2.00	4.00	8.00
	1853	12.243	1.00	2.00	4.00	8.00
	1854	13.754	1.00	2.00	4.00	8.00
	1855	20.510	1.50	3.00	6.00	12.00

Mint mark: ВМ

C#	Date	Mintage	VG	Fine	VF	XF
148.3	1850	1.840	2.00	4.00	8.00	15.00
	1851	1.200	2.00	4.00	8.00	15.00
	1852	1.231	2.00	4.00	8.00	15.00
	1853	.804	2.00	4.00	8.00	15.00
	1854	.352	2.00	4.00	8.00	15.00
	1855	6.380	4.00	8.00	15.00	30.00

Mint mark: ЕМ
Plain border

Y#	Date	Mintage	Fine	VF	XF	Unc
2.1	1855	Inc.C148.1	2.00	4.00	8.00	20.00
	1856	6.000	2.00	4.00	8.00	20.00
	1857	6.000	2.00	4.00	8.00	20.00
	1858	11.147	2.00	4.00	8.00	20.00
	1859	5.871	2.00	4.00	8.00	20.00

Mint mark: ВМ

Y#	Date	Mintage	Fine	VF	XF	Unc
2.2	1855	6.380	5.00	10.00	20.00	40.00
	1856	4.278	5.00	10.00	20.00	40.00
	1857	1.909	5.00	10.00	20.00	40.00
	1858	.311	5.00	10.00	20.00	40.00
	1859	3.719	5.00	10.00	20.00	40.00
	1860	1.861	4.00	8.00	16.00	35.00

Mint mark: ЕМ
Toothed border

Y#	Date	Mintage	Fine	VF	XF	Unc
2.3	1859	—	2.00	4.00	8.00	20.00
	1860	2.838	2.00	5.00	10.00	20.00
	1861	2.277	2.00	5.00	10.00	20.00
	1862	3.072	2.00	5.00	10.00	20.00
	1863	1.011	2.00	5.00	10.00	20.00
	1864	1.116	3.00	6.00	12.00	30.00
	1865	.560	50.00	100.00	200.00	300.00
	1866	.333	4.00	8.00	15.00	40.00
	1867	.390	8.00	15.00	30.00	70.00

Mint mark: ВМ

Y#	Date	Mintage	Fine	VF	XF	Unc
2.4	1861	2.819	4.00	8.00	15.00	30.00
	1862	1.036	4.00	8.00	15.00	30.00
	1863	2.400	6.00	12.50	25.00	50.00

Mint mark: ЕМ

Y#	Date	Mintage	Fine	VF	XF	Unc
8.1	1867	Inc.Y2.3	7.00	15.00	30.00	60.00
	1868	1.190	1.50	3.00	6.00	12.00
	1869	.593	1.50	3.00	6.00	12.00
	1870	.510	2.00	4.00	8.00	15.00
	1871	.223	1.50	3.00	6.00	12.00
	1872	.365	1.50	3.00	6.00	12.00
	1873	.963	1.50	3.00	6.00	12.00
	1874	.300	1.50	3.00	6.00	12.00
	1875	.321	3.00	6.00	12.00	25.00
	1876	Inc. Ab.	50.00	100.00	200.00	325.00

Mint mark: СПБ

Y#	Date	Mintage	Fine	VF	XF	Unc
8.2	1867	—	5.00	10.00	20.00	40.00
	1868	.060	3.00	6.00	12.00	25.00
	1869	.145	2.00	4.50	9.00	17.50
	1870	.025	5.00	10.00	20.00	40.00
	1871	—	—	—	Rare	—
	1876	.770	1.00	2.25	4.50	9.00
	1877	1.290	1.00	2.25	4.50	9.00
	1878	1.120	1.00	2.25	4.50	9.00
	1879	.740	1.00	2.25	4.50	9.00
	1880	1.260	1.00	2.25	4.50	9.00
	1881	.420	1.00	2.25	4.50	9.00

Y#	Date	Mintage	Fine	VF	XF	Unc
30	1881	.440	1.00	2.25	4.50	15.00
	1882	.350	1.00	2.25	4.50	9.00
	1883	.540	1.00	2.25	4.50	9.00
	1884	.550	1.00	2.25	4.50	9.00
	1885	.680	1.00	2.25	4.50	9.00
	1886	.560	1.00	2.25	4.50	9.00
	1887	.600	1.00	2.25	4.50	9.00
	1888	.610	1.00	2.25	4.50	9.00
	1889	4.650	1.00	2.00	4.00	7.50
	1890	2.040	1.00	2.00	4.00	7.50
	1892	2.271	1.00	2.00	4.00	7.50
	1893	3.900	1.00	2.00	4.00	7.50
	1894	—	1.00	2.00	4.00	7.50

Y#	Date	Mintage	Fine	VF	XF	Unc
48.1	1894	—	5.00	10.00	20.00	40.00
	1895	2.992	1.00	2.00	4.00	8.00
	1896	1.340	1.00	2.00	4.00	8.00
	1897	60.000	.25	.50	1.00	5.00
	1898	76.000	.25	.50	1.00	5.00
	1899	76.000	.25	.50	1.00	5.00
	1900	36.000	.25	.50	1.00	5.00
	1908	8.000	.25	.50	1.00	5.00
	1909	49.500	.25	.50	1.00	4.00
	1910	24.000	.25	.50	1.00	5.00
	1911	35.800	.25	.50	1.00	5.00
	1912	28.000	.25	.50	1.00	5.00
	1913	50.000	.25	.50	1.00	5.00
	1914	14.000	.25	.50	1.00	5.00
	Common date	—	—	—	Proof	35.00

Mint: Petrograd - w/o mint mark

Y#	Date	Mintage	Fine	VF	XF	Unc
48.2	1915	12.000	.25	.50	1.00	5.00
	1916	9.400	.25	.50	1.00	5.00

KOPEK

COPPER, 4.00 g
Mint mark: ЕМ
Obv: Monogram. Rev: Value, date.

C#	Date	Mintage	VG	Fine	VF	XF
94.2	1801	1.708	3.00	6.00	12.00	25.00

NOTE: Earlier dates (1797-1800) exist for this type.

C#	Date	Mintage	VG	Fine	VF	XF
113.1	1804	200 pcs.	50.00	100.00	200.00	300.00
	1805	.114	20.00	40.00	80.00	150.00

Mint mark: КМ

C#	Date	Mintage	VG	Fine	VF	XF
113.2	1804	—	20.00	40.00	80.00	160.00
	1805	—	25.00	50.00	100.00	200.00
	1807	—	25.00	50.00	100.00	200.00

Obv: Type 2 eagle.

C#	Date	Mintage	VG	Fine	VF	XF
117.2	1811 ПБ	—	—	—	Rare	—

Mint mark: ЕМ
Obv: Type 3 eagle.

C#	Date	Mintage	VG	Fine	VF	XF
117.3	1811 НМ	1.926	1.50	3.00	6.00	12.00
	1811 НМ reeded edge	—	—	—	Rare	—
	1813 НМ	.030	25.00	50.00	100.00	200.00
	1815 НМ	.031	25.00	50.00	100.00	200.00
	1818 НМ	55.750	1.50	3.00	6.00	12.00
	1819 НМ	35.030	1.50	3.00	6.00	12.00
	1821 НМ	10.160	1.50	3.00	6.00	12.00
	1822 ФГ	10.265	1.50	3.00	6.00	12.00
	1823 ФГ	10.350	1.50	3.00	6.00	12.00
	1824 ПГ	—	1.50	3.00	6.00	12.00
	1825 ИК	—	1.50	3.00	6.00	12.00

NOTE: Varieties exist.

Mint mark: ИМ

C#	Date	Mintage	VG	Fine	VF	XF
117.4	1811 МК	.490	1.50	3.00	6.00	12.00
	1812 ПС	1.040	1.50	3.00	6.00	12.00
	1813 ПС	1.980	1.50	3.00	6.00	12.00
	1814 ПС	3.740	1.50	3.00	6.00	12.00
	1820 ЯБ	—	1.50	3.00	6.00	12.00
	1821 ЯБ	—	1.50	3.00	6.00	12.00

Mint mark: КМ

C#	Date	Mintage	VG	Fine	VF	XF
117.5	1810	—	25.00	50.00	100.00	200.00
	1811 ПБ	—	1.50	3.00	6.00	10.00
	1812 АМ	—	2.50	5.00	10.00	20.00
	1813 АМ	—	2.50	5.00	10.00	20.00
	1814 АМ	—	2.50	5.00	10.00	20.00
	1815 АМ	—	2.50	5.00	10.00	20.00
	1816 АМ	—	2.50	5.00	10.00	20.00
	1817 АМ	—	2.50	5.00	10.00	20.00
	1818 АД	—	2.50	5.00	10.00	20.00
	1818 ДБ	—	2.50	5.00	10.00	20.00
	1819 АД	—	2.50	5.00	10.00	20.00
	1820 АД	—	2.50	5.00	10.00	20.00
	1821 АМ	—	2.50	5.00	10.00	20.00
	1822 АМ	—	2.50	5.00	10.00	20.00
	1823 АМ	—	2.50	5.00	10.00	20.00
	1824 АМ	—	2.50	5.00	10.00	20.00
	1825 АМ	—	2.50	5.00	10.00	20.00

Mint mark: СПБ

C#	Date	Mintage	VG	Fine	VF	XF
117.6	1810 ФГ	.093	25.00	50.00	100.00	200.00
	1810 МК	I.A.	2.00	4.00	8.00	15.00
	1811 МК	.260	1.50	3.00	6.00	10.00

Mint mark: ЕМ

C#	Date	Mintage	VG	Fine	VF	XF
136.1	1827 ИК	2.646	1.50	3.00	6.00	12.00
	1828 ИК	43.015	1.50	3.00	6.00	12.00
	1829 ИК	48.215	1.50	3.00	6.00	12.00
	1830 ИК	2.100	1.50	3.00	6.00	12.00

Mint mark: КМ

C#	Date	Mintage	VG	Fine	VF	XF
136.2	1826 АМ	6.250	2.50	5.00	10.00	20.00
	1827 АМ	6.250	2.50	5.00	10.00	20.00
	1828 АМ	5.000	2.50	5.00	10.00	20.00
	1829 АМ	5.000	2.50	5.00	10.00	20.00
	1830 АМ	5.000	2.50	5.00	10.00	20.00

Mint mark: СПБ

C#	Date	Mintage	VG	Fine	VF	XF
136.3	1828	—	25.00	50.00	100.00	225.00

Mint mark: ЕМ

C#	Date	Mintage	VG	Fine	VF	XF
138.1	1830 ФХ	—	25.00	50.00	100.00	200.00
	1831 ФХ	13.050	1.50	3.00	6.00	12.00
	1832 ФХ	3.400	1.50	3.00	6.00	12.00
	1833 ФХ	2.883	1.50	3.00	6.00	12.00
	1834 ФХ	5.020	1.50	3.00	6.00	12.00
	1835 ФХ	6.570	1.50	3.00	6.00	12.00
	1836 ФХ	2.100	1.50	3.00	6.00	12.00
	1837 КТ	4.890	1.50	3.00	6.00	12.00
	1837 НА	I.A.	1.50	3.00	6.00	12.00
	1838 НА	1.043	25.00	50.00	100.00	200.00

Mint mark: СПБ

C#	Date	Mintage	VG	Fine	VF	XF
138.2	1830	29 pcs.	—	—	Rare	—

Mint mark: СМ

C#	Date	Mintage	VG	Fine	VF	XF
138.3	1831	2.000	2.50	5.00	10.00	20.00
	1832	2.000	2.50	5.00	10.00	20.00
	1833	.045	2.50	5.00	10.00	20.00
	1834	2.000	2.50	5.00	10.00	20.00
	1835	2.000	2.50	5.00	10.00	20.00
	1836	.100	2.50	5.00	10.00	20.00
	1837	1.000	2.50	5.00	10.00	20.00
	1838	1.800	2.50	5.00	10.00	20.00
	1839	.020	20.00	40.00	80.00	120.00

Mint mark: ЕМ

C#	Date	Mintage	VG	Fine	VF	XF
144.1	1840	20.778	1.00	2.00	4.00	8.00
	1841	19.341	1.00	2.00	4.00	8.00
	1842	13.851	1.00	2.00	4.00	8.00
	1843	12.520	1.00	2.00	4.00	8.00
	1844	—	1.00	2.00	4.00	8.00

Mint mark: СПБ

C#	Date	Mintage	VG	Fine	VF	XF
144.2	1840	11.200	5.00	10.00	20.00	40.00

Mint mark: СПМ

C#	Date	Mintage	VG	Fine	VF	XF
144.3	1840	Inc. Ab.	1.00	2.00	4.00	8.00
	1841	11.200	1.00	2.00	4.00	8.00
	1842	11.200	1.00	2.00	4.00	8.00
	1843	11.200	1.00	2.00	4.00	8.00

Mint mark: СМ

C#	Date	Mintage	VG	Fine	VF	XF
144.4	1839	.795	2.00	4.00	8.00	15.00
	1840	4.500	1.50	3.00	6.00	12.00
	1841	6.120	1.50	3.00	6.00	12.00
	1842	7.002	1.50	3.00	6.00	12.00
	1843	3.498	1.50	3.00	6.00	12.00
	1844	5.250	1.50	3.00	6.00	12.00
	1845	5.250	1.50	3.00	6.00	12.00
	1846	5.250	1.50	3.00	6.00	12.00
	1847	2.368	3.00	6.00	12.00	25.00

Mint mark: ЕМ

C#	Date	Mintage	VG	Fine	VF	XF
149.1	1850	1.843	.50	1.00	3.00	7.00
	1851	4.790	.50	1.00	3.00	7.00
	1852	14.006	.50	1.00	3.00	7.00
	1853	21.328	.50	1.00	3.00	7.00
	1854	22.397	.50	1.00	3.00	7.00
	1855	24.594	1.00	2.00	4.00	10.00

Mint mark: ВМ

C#	Date	Mintage	VG	Fine	VF	XF
149.3	1850	—	2.00	4.00	8.00	15.00
	1851	.797	2.00	4.00	8.00	15.00
	1852	.311	2.00	4.00	8.00	15.00
	1853	.391	2.00	4.00	8.00	15.00
	1855	Inc.C149.1	2.00	4.00	8.00	15.00

Mint mark: ЕМ

Obv: Crowned small A. Plain border.

Y#	Date	Mintage	Fine	VF	XF	Unc
3.1	1855	Inc.C149.1	1.00	2.00	6.00	15.00
	1856	10.641	1.00	2.00	6.00	15.00
	1857	5.659	1.00	2.00	6.00	15.00
	1858	13.731	1.00	2.00	6.00	15.00
	1859	11.059	1.00	2.00	6.00	15.00

Mint mark: ВМ

Obv: Crowned tall A. Rev: Large date.

Y#	Date	Mintage	Fine	VF	XF	Unc
3.2	1855	Inc.C149.3	2.00	4.00	12.00	25.00
	1856	3.337	2.00	4.00	12.00	25.00
	1858	1.528	2.00	4.00	12.00	25.00
	1859	3.109	2.00	4.00	12.00	25.00
	1860	3.766	2.00	4.00	12.00	25.00

Mint mark: ЕМ

Obv: Crowned small A. Toothed border.

Y#	Date	Mintage	Fine	VF	XF	Unc
3.3	1859	—	1.00	2.00	4.00	10.00
	1860	8.306	1.00	2.00	4.00	10.00
	1861	10.130	1.00	2.00	4.00	10.00
	1862	10.165	1.00	2.00	4.00	10.00
	1863	6.544	1.00	2.00	4.00	10.00
	1864	4.400	1.00	2.00	4.00	10.00
	1865	14.230	1.00	2.00	4.00	10.00
	1866	12.304	1.00	2.00	4.00	10.00
	1867	5.851	5.00	10.00	20.00	40.00

Mint mark: ВМ

Obv: Crowned tall A

Y#	Date	Mintage	Fine	VF	XF	Unc
3.4	1861	1.800	2.50	5.00	10.00	20.00
	1862	2.100	2.50	5.00	10.00	20.00
	1863	2.854	2.50	5.00	10.00	20.00
	1864	1.046	2.50	5.00	10.00	20.00

Mint mark: ЕМ

Y#	Date	Mintage	Fine	VF	XF	Unc
9.1	1867	Inc.Y3.3	3.00	6.00	12.00	25.00
	1868	6.305	.50	1.00	3.00	10.00
	1869	10.230	.50	1.00	3.00	10.00
	1870	9.875	.50	1.00	3.00	10.00
	1871	2.880	.50	1.00	3.00	10.00
	1872	5.713	.50	1.00	3.00	10.00
	1873	5.213	.50	1.00	3.00	10.00
	1874	5.013	.50	1.00	3.00	10.00
	1875	6.438	.50	1.00	3.00	10.00
	1876	1.755	4.00	8.00	15.00	30.00

Mint mark: СПБ

Y#	Date	Mintage	Fine	VF	XF	Unc
9.2	1867	—	2.00	4.00	8.00	20.00
	1868	.750	1.00	2.00	4.00	10.00
	1869	.739	1.00	2.00	4.00	10.00
	1870	1.143	1.00	2.00	4.00	10.00
	1871	—	—	—	Rare	—
	1876	2.930	.50	1.00	2.00	6.00
	1877	7.065	.50	1.00	2.00	6.00
	1878	8.241	.50	1.00	2.00	6.00
	1879	9.045	.50	1.00	2.00	6.00
	1880	7.730	.50	1.00	2.00	6.00
	1881	8.415	.50	1.00	2.00	6.00
	1882	5.685	.50	1.00	2.00	6.00
	1883	7.830	.50	1.00	2.00	6.00
	1884	2.500	.50	1.00	2.00	6.00
	1885	3.400	.50	1.00	2.00	6.00
	1886	3.210	.50	1.00	2.00	6.00
	1887	6.000	.25	.50	1.00	5.00
	1888	6.000	.25	.50	1.00	5.00
	1889	9.000	.25	.50	1.00	5.00
	1890	6.905	.25	.50	1.00	5.00
	1891	10.875	.25	.50	1.00	5.00
	1892	5.640	.25	.50	1.00	5.00
	1893	13.395	.25	.50	1.00	5.00
	1894	15.490	.25	.50	1.00	5.00
	1895	18.200	.25	.50	1.00	4.50
	1896	22.960	.25	.50	1.00	4.50
	1897	30.000	.25	.50	1.00	4.50
	1898	50.000	.25	.50	1.00	4.50
	1899	50.000	.25	.50	1.00	4.50
	1900	30.000	.25	.50	1.00	4.50
	1901	30.000	.25	.50	1.00	4.50
	1902	20.000	2.50	5.00	10.00	20.00
	1903	74.400	.25	.50	1.00	4.50
	1904	30.600	.25	.50	1.00	4.50
	1905	23.000	.25	.50	1.00	4.50
	1906	20.000	.25	.50	1.00	4.50
	1907	20.000	.25	.50	1.00	4.50
	1908	40.000	.25	.50	1.00	4.50
	1909	27.500	.25	.50	1.00	4.50
	1910	36.500	.25	.50	1.00	4.50
	1911	38.150	.25	.50	1.00	4.50
	1912	31.850	.25	.50	1.00	4.50
	1913	61.500	.25	.50	1.00	4.50
	1914	32.500	.25	.50	1.00	4.50
	Common date	—	—	—	Proof	35.00

Mint: Petrograd - w/o mint mark

Y#	Date	Mintage	Fine	VF	XF	Unc
9.3	1915	58.000	.25	.50	1.00	4.50
	1916	46.500	.25	.50	1.00	4.50
	1917	—	—	—	Unique	—

2 KOPEKS

COPPER

Mint mark: ЕМ

C#	Date	Mintage	VG	Fine	VF	XF
95.3	1801	27.380	4.00	8.00	15.00	30.00

NOTE: Earlier dates (1797-1800) exist for this type.

Mint mark: КМ

NOTE: Later date (1801) exists for this type.

C#	Date	Mintage	VG	Fine	VF	XF
95.4	1801	—	7.50	15.00	30.00	60.00

NOTE: Earlier dates (1797-1800) exist for this type.

Mint mark: ЕМ

C#	Date	Mintage	VG	Fine	VF	XF
114.1	1802	45.798	10.00	20.00	40.00	100.00
	1803	.298	25.00	50.00	100.00	200.00
	1804	—	—	—	Rare	—

Mint mark: КМ

C#	Date	Mintage	VG	Fine	VF	XF
114.2	1804	—	25.00	50.00	100.00	200.00
	1805	—	25.00	50.00	100.00	200.00
	1807	—	25.00	50.00	100.00	200.00

Mint mark: ЕМ
Obv: Type 1 eagle.

C#	Date	Mintage	VG	Fine	VF	XF
118.1	1810 НМ	79.364	1.50	2.50	5.00	10.00

NOTE: Exists with large and small date.

Mint mark: КМ
Obv: Type 2 eagle.

C#	Date	Mintage	VG	Fine	VF	XF
118.2	1810	—	4.00	8.00	15.00	30.00
	1810 ПБ	—	4.00	8.00	15.00	30.00
	1811 ПБ	—	4.00	8.00	15.00	30.00
	1812	—	4.00	8.00	15.00	30.00

Mint mark: ЕМ
Obv: Type 3 eagle.

C#	Date	Mintage	VG	Fine	VF	XF
118.3	1810 НМ	129.000	1.50	2.50	5.00	10.00
	1811 НМ plain edge	Inc. Ab.	1.50	2.50	5.00	10.00
	1811 НМ reeded edge	Inc. Ab.	1.50	2.50	5.00	10.00
	1812 НМ	132.085	1.50	2.50	5.00	10.00
	1812 НМ inverted 2	Inc. Ab.	1.50	2.50	5.00	10.00
	1813 НМ	64.980	1.50	2.50	5.00	10.00
	1814 НМ	110.000	1.50	2.50	5.00	10.00
	1815 НМ	44.970	1.50	2.50	5.00	10.00
	1816 НМ	64.150	1.50	2.50	5.00	10.00
	1817 НМ	75.000	1.50	2.50	5.00	10.00
	1818 НМ	60.625	1.50	2.50	5.00	10.00
	1818 ФГ	I.A.	1.50	2.50	5.00	10.00
	1819 НМ	100.468	1.50	2.50	5.00	10.00
	1820 НМ	75.180	1.50	2.50	5.00	10.00
	1821 НМ	55.170	1.50	2.50	5.00	10.00
	1821 ФГ	I.A.	1.50	2.50	5.00	10.00

C#	Date	Mintage	VG	Fine	VF	XF
118.3	1822 ФГ	44.867	1.50	2.50	5.00	10.00
	1823 ФГ	44.935	1.50	2.50	5.00	10.00
	1823 ПГ	I.A.	—	—	Rare	—
	1824 ПГ	36.600	1.50	2.50	5.00	10.00
	1825 ПГ	73.856	1.50	2.50	5.00	10.00
	1825 ИШ	I.A.	1.50	2.50	5.00	10.00
	1825 ИК	I.A.	1.50	2.50	5.00	10.00
137.1	1826 ИК	50.450	2.50	5.00	10.00	20.00
	1827 ИК	34.065	2.50	5.00	10.00	20.00
	1828 ИК	14.475	2.50	5.00	10.00	20.00
	1829 ИК	13.790	2.50	5.00	10.00	20.00
	1830 ИК	15.450	2.50	5.00	10.00	20.00

NOTE: Varieties exist.

Mint mark: ИМ

C#	Date	Mintage	VG	Fine	VF	XF
118.4	1810 МК	—	1.50	2.50	5.00	10.00
	1811 ПС	I.A.	1.50	2.50	5.00	10.00
	1811 МК	—	1.50	2.50	5.00	10.00
	1812 ПС	—	1.50	2.50	5.00	10.00
	1813 ПС	—	1.50	2.50	5.00	10.00
	1814 ПС	—	1.50	2.50	5.00	10.00
	1814	—	1.50	2.50	5.00	10.00

Mint mark: КМ

C#	Date	Mintage	VG	Fine	VF	XF
118.5	1812 АМ	—	1.50	2.50	5.00	10.00
	1813 АМ	—	1.50	2.50	5.00	10.00
	1814 АМ	—	1.50	2.50	5.00	10.00
	1815 АМ	—	1.50	2.50	5.00	10.00
	1816 АМ	—	1.50	2.50	5.00	10.00
	1817 АМ	—	1.50	2.50	5.00	10.00
	1817 АБ	—	1.50	2.50	5.00	10.00
	1818 ДБ	—	1.50	2.50	5.00	10.00
	1819 АД	—	1.50	2.50	5.00	10.00
	1820 АД	—	1.50	2.50	5.00	10.00
	1821 АД	—	1.50	2.50	5.00	10.00
	1821 АМ	—	1.50	2.50	5.00	10.00
	1822 АМ	—	1.50	2.50	5.00	10.00
	1823 АМ	—	1.50	2.50	5.00	10.00
	1824 АМ	—	1.50	2.50	5.00	10.00
	1825 АМ	—	1.50	2.50	5.00	10.00
137.2	1826 АМ	9.375	2.50	5.00	10.00	20.00
	1827 АМ	I.A.	2.50	5.00	10.00	20.00
	1828 АМ	15.000	2.50	5.00	10.00	20.00
	1829 АМ	15.000	2.50	5.00	10.00	20.00
	1830 АМ	15.000	2.50	5.00	10.00	20.00

Mint mark: СПБ

C#	Date	Mintage	VG	Fine	VF	XF
118.6	1810 ФГ	—	1.50	2.50	5.00	10.00
	1810 МК	—	1.50	2.50	5.00	10.00
	1810 ПС	—	1.50	2.50	5.00	10.00
	1811 МК	—	1.50	2.50	5.00	10.00
	1811 ПС	—	1.50	2.50	5.00	10.00
	1812 ПС	—	1.50	2.50	5.00	10.00
	1813 ПС	—	1.50	2.50	5.00	10.00
	1814 ПС	—	3.00	6.00	12.00	25.00
	1818	—	20.00	40.00	80.00	150.00
137.3	1828	—	25.00	50.00	100.00	200.00

Mint: Kolpino

C#	Date	Mintage	VG	Fine	VF	XF
118.7	1810 МК	—	20.00	40.00	80.00	150.00

Mint mark: ЕМ

C#	Date	Mintage	VG	Fine	VF	XF
139.1	1830 ФХ	—	20.00	40.00	80.00	150.00
	1831 ФХ	—	20.00	40.00	80.00	150.00
	1833 ФХ	.261	3.00	6.00	12.00	25.00
	1837 НА	16.845	3.00	6.00	12.00	25.00
	1838 НА	6.623	3.00	6.00	12.00	25.00
	1839 НА	8.250	3.00	6.00	12.00	25.00

Mint mark: СПБ

C#	Date	Mintage	VG	Fine	VF	XF
139.2	1830	29 pcs.	—	—	Rare	—

Mint mark: СМ

C#	Date	Mintage	VG	Fine	VF	XF
139.3	1831	1.500	2.50	4.50	8.00	15.00
	1832	1.500	2.50	4.50	8.00	15.00
	1833	.539	2.50	4.50	8.00	15.00
	1834	1.500	2.50	4.50	8.00	15.00
	1835	1.500	2.50	4.50	8.00	15.00
	1836	1.350	2.50	4.50	8.00	15.00
	1837	1.000	2.50	4.50	8.00	15.00
	1838	10.500	2.50	4.50	8.00	15.00
	1839	7.073	2.50	4.50	8.00	15.00

Mint mark: ЕМ

C#	Date	Mintage	VG	Fine	VF	XF
145.1	1840	20.778	2.00	4.00	7.00	12.00
	1841	14.999	2.00	4.00	7.00	12.00
	1842	12.446	2.00	4.00	7.00	12.00
	1843	11.020	2.00	4.00	7.00	12.00
	1844	5.500	2.00	4.00	7.00	12.00

Mint mark: СПБ

C#	Date	Mintage	VG	Fine	VF	XF
145.2	1840	—	6.00	12.00	25.00	50.00
	1841	—	25.00	50.00	100.00	200.00

Mint mark: СПМ

C#	Date	Mintage	VG	Fine	VF	XF
145.3	1840	4.800	1.50	2.50	5.00	10.00
	1841	Inc. Ab.	1.50	2.50	5.00	10.00
	1842	4.800	1.50	2.50	5.00	10.00
	1843	4.800	1.50	2.50	5.00	10.00

Mint mark: СМ

C#	Date	Mintage	VG	Fine	VF	XF
145.4	1839	.341	1.50	2.50	5.00	10.00
	1840	1.929	1.50	2.50	5.00	10.00
	1841	2.636	1.50	2.50	5.00	10.00
	1842	3.000	1.50	2.50	5.00	10.00
	1843	1.500	1.50	2.50	5.00	10.00
	1844	2.250	1.50	2.50	5.00	10.00
	1845	2.250	1.50	2.50	5.00	10.00
	1846	2.250	1.50	2.50	5.00	10.00
	1847	2.209	1.50	2.50	5.00	10.00

Mint mark: МШ

C#	Date	Mintage	VG	Fine	VF	XF
145.5	1848	.031	20.00	40.00	80.00	150.00

Mint mark: ЕМ

C#	Date	Mintage	VG	Fine	VF	XF
150.1	1850	2.206	1.50	3.00	6.00	12.00
	1851	8.356	1.50	3.00	6.00	12.00
	1852	6.874	1.50	3.00	6.00	12.00
	1853	7.561	1.50	3.00	6.00	12.00
	1854	4.541	1.50	3.00	6.00	12.00
(Y4.1)	1855	8.587	.50	1.00	2.00	5.00
	1856	9.167	.50	1.00	2.00	5.00
	1857	3.359	.50	1.00	2.00	5.00
	1858	10.028	.50	1.00	2.00	5.00
	1859	14.772	.50	1.00	2.00	5.00

Mint mark: ВМ

C#	Date	Mintage	VG	Fine	VF	XF
150.3	1850	—	10.00	20.00	40.00	80.00
	1851	.298	5.00	10.00	20.00	40.00
	1852	.202	5.00	10.00	20.00	40.00
	1853	2,642	—	—	Rare	—
	1854	.148	5.00	10.00	20.00	40.00
(Y4.2)	1855	1.347	1.00	2.00	6.00	12.00
	1856	1.190	1.00	2.00	6.00	12.00
	1858	.750	1.00	2.00	6.00	12.00
	1859	1.595	1.00	2.00	6.00	12.00
	1860	1.605	—	—	Rare	—

Mint mark: ЕМ
Obv: Ribbons added to crown.

Y#	Date	Mintage	Fine	VF	XF	Unc
4a.1	1859	14.772	1.00	2.00	5.00	15.00
	1860	19.239	1.00	2.00	5.00	15.00
	1861	18.547	1.00	2.00	5.00	15.00
	1862	16.889	1.00	2.00	5.00	15.00
	1863	21.703	1.00	2.00	5.00	15.00

Y#	Date	Mintage	Fine	VF	XF	Unc
4a.1	1864	14.175	1.00	2.00	5.00	15.00
	1865	26.921	1.00	2.00	5.00	15.00
	1866	21.890	1.00	2.00	5.00	15.00
	1867	8.970	1.00	2.00	5.00	15.00
		Mint mark: BM				
4a.2	1860	1.605	3.00	6.00	12.00	25.00
	1861	.586	3.00	6.00	12.00	25.00
	1862	.966	3.00	6.00	12.00	25.00
	1863	1.739	3.00	6.00	12.00	25.00

Y#	Date	Mintage	Fine	VF	XF	Unc
		Mint mark: EM				
10.1	1867	.150	5.00	10.00	20.00	40.00
	1868	18.200	.50	1.00	2.00	10.00
	1869	22.174	.50	1.00	2.00	10.00
	1870	21.884	.50	1.00	2.00	10.00
	1871	7.058	.50	1.00	2.00	10.00
	1872	12.734	.50	1.00	2.00	10.00
	1873	7.364	.50	1.00	2.00	10.00
	1874	8.551	.50	1.00	2.00	10.00
	1875	10.451	.50	1.00	2.00	10.00
	1876	2.905	.50	1.00	2.00	10.00
		Mint mark: СПБ				
10.2	1867	—	3.00	6.00	12.00	25.00
	1868	.659	1.50	3.00	6.00	15.00
	1869	.643	1.50	3.00	6.00	15.00
	1870	.231	2.00	4.00	8.00	20.00
	1871	—	—	—	Rare	—
	1876	3.240	.50	1.00	2.00	8.00
	1877	5.010	.50	1.00	2.00	8.00
	1878	8.093	.50	1.00	2.00	8.00
	1879	7.380	.50	1.00	2.00	8.00
	1880	6.525	.50	1.00	2.00	8.00
	1881	7.299	.50	1.00	2.00	8.00
	1882	4.478	.50	1.00	2.00	8.00
	1883	6.230	.50	1.00	2.00	8.00
	1884	2.625	.50	1.00	2.00	8.00
	1885	3.070	.50	1.00	2.00	8.00
	1886	3.123	.50	1.00	2.00	8.00
	1887	1.725	.50	1.00	2.00	8.00
	1888	1.823	.50	1.00	2.00	8.00
	1889	2.815	.50	1.00	2.00	8.00
	1890	2.538	.50	1.00	2.00	8.00
	1891	2.788	.50	1.00	2.00	8.00
	1892	.918	2.00	4.00	8.00	20.00
	1893	10.295	.50	1.00	2.00	5.00
	1894	8.600	.50	1.00	2.00	5.00
	1895	9.122	.50	1.00	2.00	5.00
	1896	14.675	.50	1.00	2.00	5.00
	1897	9.500	.50	1.00	2.00	5.00
	1898	17.500	.50	1.00	2.00	5.00
	1899	17.500	.50	1.00	2.00	5.00
	1900	20.500	.50	1.00	2.00	5.00
	1901	20.000	.50	1.00	2.00	5.00
	1902	10.000	.50	1.00	2.00	5.00
	1903	29.200	.50	1.00	2.00	5.00
	1904	13.300	.50	1.00	2.00	5.00
	1905	15.000	.50	1.00	2.00	5.00
	1906	6.250	.50	1.00	2.00	5.00
	1907	7.500	.50	1.00	2.00	5.00
	1908	19.000	.50	1.00	2.00	5.00
	1909	16.250	.50	1.00	2.00	5.00
	1910	12.000	.50	1.00	2.00	5.00
	1911	17.200	.50	1.00	2.00	5.00
	1912	17.050	.50	1.00	2.00	5.00
	1913	26.000	.50	1.00	2.00	5.00
	1914	20.000	.50	1.00	2.00	5.00
	Common date	—	—	—	Proof	35.00
		Mint: Petrograd - w/o mint mark				
10.3	1915	33.750	.50	1.00	2.00	5.00
	1916	31.500	.50	1.00	2.00	5.00

3 KOPEKS

COPPER

C#	Date	Mintage	VG	Fine	VF	XF
		Mint mark: EM				
146.1	1840	5.230	3.00	6.00	12.00	25.00
	1841	13.417	3.00	6.00	12.00	25.00
	1842	13.700	3.00	6.00	12.00	25.00
	1843	14.578	3.00	6.00	12.00	25.00
	1844	4.840	3.00	6.00	12.00	25.00
		Mint mark: СПБ				
146.2	1840	—	20.00	40.00	80.00	150.00
		Mint mark: СПМ				
146.3	1840	2.133	5.00	10.00	20.00	40.00
	1841	2.133	5.00	10.00	20.00	40.00
	1842	2.133	5.00	10.00	20.00	40.00
	1843	2.133	5.00	10.00	20.00	40.00
		Mint mark: CM				
146.4	1839	.142	10.00	20.00	50.00	100.00
	1840	.827	4.00	7.50	15.00	30.00
	1841	1.171	4.00	7.50	15.00	30.00
	1842	1.360	4.00	7.50	15.00	30.00
	1843	.669	4.00	7.50	15.00	30.00
	1844	1.000	4.00	7.50	15.00	30.00
	1845	1.000	4.00	7.50	15.00	30.00
	1846	1.000	4.00	7.50	15.00	30.00
	1847	1.000	4.00	7.50	15.00	30.00
		Mint mark: МШ				
146.5	1848	.017	50.00	90.00	175.00	325.00

C#	Date	Mintage	VG	Fine	VF	XF
		Mint mark: EM				
		Obv: First variety - 6 coats of arms.				
151.1	1850	.184	2.00	4.00	7.50	15.00
	1851	3.448	2.00	4.00	7.50	15.00
	1852	5.444	2.00	4.00	7.50	15.00
	1853	3.719	2.00	4.00	7.50	15.00
	1854	1.351	2.00	4.00	7.50	15.00
(Y5.1)	1855	2.835	1.00	2.00	4.00	8.00
	1856	6.700	1.00	2.00	4.00	8.00
	1857	4.726	1.00	2.00	4.00	8.00
	1858	10.662	1.00	2.00	4.00	8.00
	1859	15.821	1.00	2.00	4.00	8.00
	Common date		—	—	Proof	200.00
		Mint mark: BM				
151.3	1850	.050	4.00	7.50	15.00	30.00
	1851	.100	4.00	7.50	15.00	30.00
	1852	.100	4.00	7.50	15.00	30.00
	1853	.089	4.00	7.50	15.00	30.00
	1854	.161	4.00	7.50	15.00	30.00
(Y5.2)	1856	.417	2.50	5.00	10.00	20.00
	1857	.021	7.50	12.50	25.00	50.00
	1858	.712	2.50	5.00	10.00	20.00
	1859	.400	5.00	7.50	15.00	30.00

Y#	Date	Mintage	Fine	VF	XF	Unc
		Mint mark: EM				
		Obv: Second variety - 8 coats of arms.				
5a.1	1859	—	2.00	4.00	8.00	25.00
	1860	14.010	2.00	4.00	8.00	25.00
	1861	7.738	2.00	4.00	8.00	25.00
	1862	10.377	2.00	4.00	8.00	25.00
	1863	3.939	2.00	4.00	8.00	25.00
	1864	6.121	4.00	8.00	15.00	30.00
	1865	5.740	40.00	80.00	150.00	250.00
	1866	6.611	2.00	4.00	8.00	25.00
	1867	1.786	4.00	8.00	15.00	30.00
		Mint mark: BM				
5a.2	1860	.283	7.50	15.00	30.00	75.00
	1861	.284	6.00	12.50	25.00	60.00
	1862	.200	6.00	12.50	25.00	60.00
	1863	.401	9.00	17.50	35.00	80.00

Y#	Date	Mintage	Fine	VF	XF	Unc
		Mint mark: EM				
11.1	1867	.160	2.00	4.00	8.00	20.00
	1868	6.059	1.00	2.00	4.00	15.00
	1869	5.526	1.00	2.00	4.00	15.00
	1870	5.018	1.00	2.00	4.00	15.00
	1871	1.585	1.00	2.00	4.00	15.00
	1872	3.018	1.00	2.00	4.00	15.00
	1873	4.704	1.00	2.00	4.00	15.00
	1874	4.419	1.00	2.00	4.00	15.00
	1875	3.595	1.00	2.00	4.00	15.00
	1876	.890	1.00	2.00	4.00	15.00
		Mint mark: СПБ				
11.2	1867	54 pcs.	4.00	7.50	15.00	30.00
	1868	.910	2.00	4.00	8.00	20.00
	1869	.723	2.00	4.00	8.00	20.00
	1870	.080	6.00	12.00	25.00	50.00
	1871	—	40.00	80.00	150.00	250.00
	1876	4.863	.75	1.50	3.00	12.00
	1877	5.902	.75	1.50	3.00	12.00
	1878	6.355	.75	1.50	3.00	12.00
	1879	7.355	.75	1.50	3.00	12.00
	1880	6.773	.75	1.50	3.00	12.00
	1881	6.141	.75	1.50	3.00	12.00
	1882	4.280	.75	1.50	3.00	12.00
	1883	1.061	.75	1.50	3.00	12.00
	1884	2.975	.75	1.50	3.00	12.00
	1891	1.983	2.00	3.00	6.00	20.00
	1892	.648	2.00	3.00	6.00	20.00
	1893	6.365	.50	1.00	2.00	8.00
	1894	4.803	.50	1.00	2.00	8.00
	1895	5.417	.50	1.00	2.00	8.00
	1896	7.923	.50	1.00	2.00	8.00
	1897	6.667	.50	1.00	2.00	8.00
	1898	11.667	.50	1.00	2.00	8.00
	1899	11.667	.50	1.00	2.00	8.00
	1900	16.667	.50	1.00	2.00	8.00
	1901	10.000	.50	1.00	2.00	8.00
	1902	3.333	.50	1.00	2.00	8.00
	1903	11.400	.50	1.00	2.00	8.00
	1904	6.934	.50	1.00	2.00	8.00
	1905	3.333	.50	1.00	2.00	8.00
	1906	5.667	.50	1.00	2.00	8.00
	1907	2.500	.50	1.00	2.00	8.00
	1908	12.667	.50	1.00	2.00	8.00
	1909	6.733	.50	1.00	2.00	8.00
	1910	6.667	.50	1.00	2.00	8.00
	1911	9.467	.50	1.00	2.00	8.00
	1912	8.533	.50	1.00	2.00	8.00
	1913	15.333	.50	1.00	2.00	8.00
	1914	8.167	.50	1.00	2.00	8.00
	Common date	—	—	—	Proof	35.00
		Mint: Petrograd - w/o mint mark				
11.3	1915	19.833	.50	1.00	2.00	15.00
	1916	25.667	.50	1.00	2.00	15.00

5 KOPEKS

1.0400 g, .868 SILVER, .0290 oz ASW

C#	Date	Mintage	VG	Fine	VF	XF
		Mint mark: CM				
96.1a	1801 АИ	.010	17.50	35.00	70.00	120.00
	1801 ФЧ	I.A.	—	—	Rare	—

NOTE: Earlier dates (1798-1800) exist for this type.

COPPER
Mint mark: ЕМ

C#	Date	Mintage	VG	Fine	VF	XF
115.1	1802	12.592	10.00	20.00	40.00	80.00
	1803	31.820	9.00	17.50	32.50	65.00
	1804	26.268	9.00	17.50	32.50	65.00
	1805	16.519	10.00	20.00	40.00	80.00
	1806	38.416	7.50	15.00	30.00	65.00
	1807	10.667	10.00	20.00	40.00	80.00
	1808	10.001	10.00	20.00	40.00	80.00
	1809	10.140	10.00	20.00	40.00	80.00
	1810	15.802	10.00	20.00	40.00	80.00

NOTE: Varieties exist.

Mint mark: КМ

C#	Date	Mintage	VG	Fine	VF	XF
115.2	1802	4.000	12.50	25.00	50.00	100.00
	1803	3.600	12.50	25.00	50.00	100.00
	1804	4.000	12.50	25.00	50.00	100.00
	1805	5.000	12.50	25.00	50.00	100.00
	1806	5.000	15.00	30.00	60.00	120.00
	1807	5.000	15.00	30.00	60.00	120.00
	1808	5.000	15.00	30.00	60.00	120.00
	1809	5.000	15.00	30.00	60.00	120.00
	1810	—	15.00	30.00	60.00	120.00

NOTE: Varieties exist.

1.0366 g, .868 SILVER, .0289 oz ASW
Mint mark: СПБ

C#	Date	Mintage	VG	Fine	VF	XF
126	1810 ФГ	—	50.00	100.00	200.00	300.00
	1811 ФГ	.080	10.00	20.00	40.00	80.00
	1811	Inc. Ab.	—	—	Rare	—
	1812 МФ	—	—	—	Rare	—
	1813 ПС	.620	3.00	6.00	12.00	25.00
	1814 ПС	1.300	3.00	6.00	12.00	25.00
	1814 МФ	I.A.	3.00	6.00	12.00	25.00
	1815 МФ	3.000	3.00	6.00	12.00	25.00
	1815	Inc. Ab.	—	—	Rare	—
	1816 МФ	1.040	3.00	6.00	12.00	25.00
	1816 ПС	I.A.	3.00	6.00	12.00	25.00
	1817 ПС	.120	3.00	6.00	12.00	25.00
	1818 ПС	.340	3.00	6.00	12.00	25.00
	1819 ПС	.920	3.00	6.00	12.00	25.00
	1820 ПС	.460	3.00	6.00	12.00	25.00
	1820 ПД	I.A.	3.00	6.00	12.00	25.00
	1821 ПД	2.000	3.00	6.00	12.00	25.00
	1822 ПД	1.060	3.00	6.00	12.00	25.00
	1823 ПД	2.300	3.00	6.00	12.00	25.00
	1824 ПД	1.740	3.00	6.00	12.00	25.00
	1825 ПД	1.160	3.00	6.00	12.00	25.00
	1825 НГ	I.A.	—	—	Rare	—
152.3	1826 НГ	1.340	3.00	6.00	12.00	25.00

C#	Date	Mintage	VG	Fine	VF	XF
156	1826 НГ	Inc. C152.3	3.00	6.00	12.00	25.00
	1827 НГ	1.769	3.00	6.00	12.00	25.00
	1828 НГ	.060	5.00	10.00	20.00	40.00
	1829 НГ	.080	5.00	10.00	20.00	40.00
	1830 НГ	1.500	3.00	6.00	12.00	25.00
	1831 НГ	.520	3.00	6.00	12.00	25.00

COPPER
Mint mark: ЕМ

C#	Date	Mintage	VG	Fine	VF	XF
140.1	1830 ФХ	—	25.00	50.00	100.00	200.00
	1831 ФХ	41.120	3.50	6.50	12.50	25.00
	1831	—	4.00	8.00	15.00	30.00
	1832 ФХ	30.080	3.50	6.50	12.50	25.00
	1833 ФХ	14.332	3.50	6.50	12.50	25.00
	1834 ФХ	41.785	3.50	6.50	12.50	25.00
	1835 ФХ	41.763	3.50	6.50	12.50	25.00
	1836 ФХ	31.332	3.50	6.50	12.50	25.00
	1837 ФХ	19.745	4.00	8.00	15.00	30.00
	1837 КТ	I.A.	3.50	6.50	12.50	25.00
	1837 НА	I.A.	3.50	6.50	12.50	25.00
	1838 НА	24.430	3.50	6.50	12.50	25.00
	1839 НА	1.400	4.00	8.00	15.00	30.00

Mint mark: СПБ

C#	Date	Mintage	VG	Fine	VF	XF
140.2	1830	25 pcs.	—	—	Rare	—

Mint mark: СМ

C#	Date	Mintage	VG	Fine	VF	XF
140.3	1831	5.900	4.00	7.50	15.00	30.00
	1832	5.900	4.00	7.50	15.00	30.00
	1833	6.295	4.00	7.50	15.00	30.00
	1834	5.900	4.00	7.50	15.00	30.00
	1835	5.000	4.00	7.50	15.00	30.00
	1836	5.240	4.00	7.50	15.00	30.00
	1837	5.200	4.00	7.50	15.00	30.00
	1838	1.420	4.00	7.50	15.00	30.00
	1839	1.400	7.50	15.00	30.00	60.00

1.0366 g, .868 SILVER, .0289 oz ASW
Mint mark: СПБ

C#	Date	Mintage	VG	Fine	VF	XF
163	1832 НГ	.224	1.00	2.00	4.00	12.00
	1833 НГ	1.026	1.00	2.00	4.00	12.00
	1834 НГ	.780	1.00	2.00	4.00	12.00
	1835 НГ	1.010	1.00	2.00	4.00	12.00
	1836 НГ	.900	1.00	2.00	4.00	12.00
	1837 НГ	1.140	1.00	2.00	4.00	12.00
	1838 НГ	2.400	1.00	2.00	4.00	12.00
	1839 НГ	1,002	20.00	40.00	80.00	150.00
	1839 НГ	I.A.	—	—	Proof	Rare
	1840 НГ	.420	1.50	3.00	6.00	15.00
	1841 НГ	.100	1.50	3.00	6.00	15.00
	1842 АЧ	.100	1.50	3.00	6.00	15.00
	1843 АЧ	.400	1.50	3.00	6.00	15.00
	1844 КБ	.401	1.50	3.00	6.00	15.00
	1845 КБ	1.740	1.00	2.00	4.00	10.00
	1846 ПА	.280	1.00	2.00	4.00	10.00
	1847 ПА	1.010	1.00	2.00	4.00	10.00
	1848 НI	1.000	1.00	2.00	4.00	10.00
	1849 ПА	1.020	1.00	2.00	4.00	10.00
	1850 ПА	1.300	1.00	2.00	4.00	10.00
	1851 ПА	1.000	1.00	2.00	4.00	10.00
	1852 ПА	.900	1.00	2.00	4.00	10.00
	1852 НI	I.A.	—	—	Rare	—
	1853 НI	.900	1.00	2.00	7.50	20.00
	1854 НI	.500	1.00	2.00	7.50	20.00
(Y13)	1855 НI	.640	1.00	2.00	4.00	10.00
	1856 ФБ	.680	1.00	2.00	4.00	10.00
	1857 ФБ	.080	2.00	4.00	8.00	15.00
	1858 ФБ	.040	2.50	5.00	10.00	20.00

COPPER
Mint mark: ЕМ
Obv: 6 coats of arms.

C#	Date	Mintage	Fine	VF	XF	Unc
152.1	1850	.373	4.00	7.50	15.00	40.00
	1851	2.241	4.00	7.50	15.00	40.00
	1852	3.961	4.00	7.50	15.00	40.00
	1853	1.474	30.00	60.00	120.00	200.00
	1854	.356	4.00	7.50	15.00	40.00
(Y6.1)	1855	.740	3.00	6.00	12.00	25.00
	1856	5.146	2.00	4.00	8.00	20.00
	1857	8.675	2.00	4.00	8.00	20.00
	1858	19.561	2.00	4.00	8.00	20.00
	1859	19.441	2.00	4.00	8.00	20.00

Mint mark: ВМ

C#	Date	Mintage	Fine	VF	XF	Unc
152.4	1850	—	15.00	25.00	50.00	120.00
	1851	.024	15.00	25.00	50.00	120.00
	1852	.016	15.00	25.00	50.00	120.00
	1853	.040	15.00	25.00	50.00	120.00
(Y6.2)	1856	.040	15.00	25.00	50.00	120.00

Mint mark: ЕМ
Obv: 8 coats of arms.

Y#	Date	Mintage	Fine	VF	XF	Unc
6a	1858	—	—	—	Rare	—
	1859	Inc. Ab.	2.00	4.00	8.00	20.00
	1860	25.260	2.00	4.00	8.00	20.00
	1861	28.022	2.00	4.00	8.00	20.00
	1862	22.055	2.00	4.00	8.00	20.00
	1863	22.511	2.00	4.00	8.00	20.00
	1864	26.042	2.00	4.00	8.00	20.00
	1865	38.943	2.00	4.00	8.00	20.00
	1866	24.767	2.00	4.00	8.00	20.00
	1867	11.697	4.00	8.00	16.00	40.00

1.0366 g, .750 SILVER, .0250 oz ASW
Mint mark: СПБ
Obv: Ribbons added to crown.

Y#	Date	Mintage	Fine	VF	XF	Unc
19.1	1859	.120	—	—	Rare	—
	1859 ФБ	I.A.	4.00	8.00	16.00	40.00
	1860 ФБ	.020	4.00	8.00	16.00	40.00

Obv: Redesigned eagle, engrailed edge.

Y#	Date	Mintage	Fine	VF	XF	Unc
19.2	1860 ФБ	.180	2.00	4.00	10.00	25.00
	1861 ФБ	.360	2.00	4.00	10.00	25.00
	1861 МИ	I.A.	4.00	8.00	16.00	40.00
	1861	—	—	—	Rare	—
	1862 МИ	.400	2.00	4.00	10.00	25.00
	1863 АБ	.200	2.00	4.00	10.00	25.00
	1864 НФ	.240	2.00	4.00	10.00	25.00
	1865 НФ	.240	2.00	4.00	10.00	25.00
	1866 НФ	.190	2.00	4.00	10.00	25.00
	1866 НI	I.A.	10.00	20.00	45.00	100.00

.8998 g, .500 SILVER, .0144 oz ASW
Reeded edge

Y#	Date	Mintage	Fine	VF	XF	Unc
19a.1	1867 НI	.180	1.75	3.50	7.50	25.00
	1868 НI	.240	1.75	3.50	7.50	25.00
	1869 НI	.170	1.75	3.50	7.50	25.00
	1870 НI	.220	1.75	3.50	7.50	25.00
	1871 НI	.200	1.75	3.50	7.50	25.00
	1872 НI	.180	1.75	3.50	7.50	25.00
	1873 НI	.160	1.75	3.50	7.50	25.00
	1874 НI	.200	1.75	3.50	7.50	25.00
	1875 НI	.200	1.75	3.50	7.50	25.00
	1876 НI	.240	1.75	3.50	7.50	25.00
	1877 НI	.200	1.75	3.50	7.50	25.00
	1877 НФ	I.A.	5.00	10.00	20.00	50.00
	1878 НФ	.220	1.75	3.50	7.50	25.00
	1878 НI	I.A.	7.50	15.00	30.00	75.00
	1879 НФ	.140	1.75	3.50	7.50	25.00
	1880 НФ	.240	1.75	3.50	7.50	25.00
	1881 НФ	.200	1.75	3.50	7.50	25.00
	1882 НФ	1.760	1.00	2.00	4.00	10.00
	1883 ДС	1.000	1.00	2.00	4.00	10.00
	1883 АГ	I.A.	1.00	2.00	4.00	10.00
	1884 АГ	3.460	1.00	2.00	4.00	10.00
	1885 АГ	1.700	1.00	2.00	4.00	10.00
	1886 АГ	2.000	1.00	2.00	4.00	10.00
	1887 АГ	3.000	1.00	2.00	4.00	10.00
	1888 АГ	4.000	1.00	2.00	4.00	10.00
	1889 АГ	3.500	1.00	2.00	4.00	10.00
	1890 АГ	8,000	1.00	2.00	4.00	10.00
	1891 АГ	2.000	1.00	2.00	4.00	10.00
	1892 АГ	8.000	1.00	2.00	4.00	10.00
	1893 АГ	2.000	1.00	2.00	4.00	10.00
	1897 АГ	2.029	1.00	2.00	4.00	10.00
	1898 АГ	3.980	1.00	2.00	4.00	10.00
	1899 АГ	4.605	1.00	2.00	4.00	10.00
	1899 ЗБ	I.A.	1.00	2.00	4.00	10.00
	1900 ФЗ	5.205	1.00	2.00	4.00	10.00
	1901 ФЗ	5.790	1.00	2.00	4.00	10.00
	1901 АР	I.A.	1.00	2.00	4.00	10.00
	1902 АР	6.000	1.00	2.00	4.00	10.00
	1903 АР	9.000	1.00	2.00	4.00	10.00
	1904 АР	10 pcs.	—	—	Rare	—
	1905 АР	10.000	1.00	2.00	4.00	10.00
	1906 ЭБ	4.000	1.00	2.00	4.00	10.00
	1908 ЭБ	.400	1.00	2.00	4.00	10.00
	1909 ЭБ	3.100	1.00	2.00	4.00	10.00

Y#	Date	Mintage	Fine	VF	XF	Unc
19a.1	1910 ЭБ	2.500	1.00	2.00	4.00	10.00
	1911 ЭБ	2.700	1.00	2.00	4.00	10.00
	1912 ЭБ	3.000	1.00	2.00	4.00	10.00
	1913 ЭБ	1.300	2.00	4.00	8.00	25.00
	1913 ВС	I.A.	1.00	2.00	4.00	10.00
	1914 ВС	I.A.	1.00	2.00	4.00	10.00

Mint: Petrograd - w/o mint mark

Y#	Date	Mintage	Fine	VF	XF	Unc
19a.2	1915 ВС	3.000	1.00	2.00	4.00	10.00

COPPER
Mint mark: ЕМ

Y#	Date	Mintage	Fine	VF	XF	Unc
12.1	1867	1.459	3.00	6.00	12.00	25.00
	1868	23.019	1.00	3.00	6.00	20.00
	1869	20.277	1.00	3.00	6.00	20.00
	1870	21.158	1.00	3.00	6.00	20.00
	1871	6.304	1.00	3.00	6.00	20.00
	1872	11.890	1.00	3.00	6.00	20.00
	1873	13.052	1.00	3.00	6.00	20.00
	1874	12.879	1.00	3.00	6.00	20.00
	1875	19.624	1.00	3.00	6.00	20.00
	1876	5.329	1.00	3.00	6.00	20.00

Mint mark: СПБ

Y#	Date	Mintage	Fine	VF	XF	Unc
12.2	1867	44 pcs.	4.00	7.50	15.00	40.00
	1868	.821	2.00	4.00	8.00	30.00
	1869	.942	2.00	4.00	8.00	30.00
	1870	.028	5.00	10.00	20.00	40.00
	1871	—	50.00	100.00	175.00	300.00
	1876	4.655	1.00	3.00	6.00	20.00
	1877	7.184	1.00	3.00	6.00	20.00
	1878	12.542	1.00	3.00	6.00	20.00
	1879	14.652	1.00	3.00	6.00	20.00
	1880	6.773	1.00	3.00	6.00	20.00
	1881	13.824	1.00	3.00	6.00	20.00
	1911	3.800	6.00	12.50	25.00	50.00
	1912	2.700	10.00	17.50	35.00	70.00

Mint: Petrograd - w/o mint mark

Y#	Date	Mintage	Fine	VF	XF	Unc
12.3	1916	8.000	40.00	80.00	150.00	250.00
	1917	—		—	Rare	—

10 KOPEKS

(Grivennik)

2.0700 g, .868 SILVER, .0578 oz ASW

C#	Date	Mintage	VG	Fine	VF	XF
97.1a	1801 АИ	.010	25.00	50.00	100.00	200.00
	1801 ФЦ	I.A.	25.00	50.00	100.00	200.00

NOTE: Earlier dates (1798-1799) exist for this type.

2.0732 g, .868 SILVER, .0578 oz ASW
Mint mark: СПБ

C#	Date	Mintage	VG	Fine	VF	XF
119	1802 АИ	.190	25.00	50.00	100.00	200.00
	1803 АИ	.040	35.00	70.00	130.00	250.00
	1804 ФГ	.380	25.00	50.00	100.00	200.00
	1805 ФГ	.112	25.00	50.00	100.00	200.00

C#	Date	Mintage	VG	Fine	VF	XF
119a	1808 ФГ	—	35.00	70.00	130.00	250.00
	1809 МК	.035	25.00	50.00	100.00	200.00
	1810 ФГ	.077	25.00	50.00	100.00	200.00

C#	Date	Mintage	VG	Fine	VF	XF
127	1810 ФГ	—	5.00	10.00	20.00	40.00
	1811 ФГ	.930	2.50	5.00	10.00	20.00
	1812 МФ	—	—	—	Rare	—
	1813 ПС	1.010	2.50	5.00	10.00	20.00
	1814 ПС	2.120	2.50	5.00	10.00	20.00
	1814 СП	I.A.	—	—	Rare	—
	1814 МФ	I.A.	2.50	5.00	10.00	20.00
	1815 МФ	2.000	2.50	5.00	10.00	20.00
	1816 МФ	.250	2.50	5.00	10.00	20.00
	1816 ПС	I.A.	2.50	5.00	10.00	20.00
	1817 ПС	.160	2.50	5.00	10.00	20.00
	1818 ПС	.630	2.50	5.00	10.00	20.00
	1819 ПС	1.520	2.50	5.00	10.00	20.00
	1820 ПС	.520	2.50	5.00	10.00	20.00
	1820 ПД	I.A.	2.50	5.00	10.00	20.00
	1821 ПД	2.250	2.50	5.00	10.00	20.00
	1822 ПД	2.070	2.50	5.00	10.00	20.00
	1823 ПД	3.850	2.50	5.00	10.00	20.00
	1824 ПД	1.330	2.50	5.00	10.00	20.00
	1825 ПД	1.350	2.50	5.00	10.00	20.00
	1825 НГ	I.A.	5.00	10.00	20.00	40.00
152.7	1826 НГ	2.050	2.50	5.00	10.00	20.00

C#	Date	Mintage	VG	Fine	VF	XF
157	1826 НГ	Inc. C152.7	2.50	5.00	10.00	20.00
	1827 НГ	1.290	2.50	5.00	10.00	20.00
	1828 НГ	.370	2.50	5.00	10.00	20.00
	1829 НГ	.040	3.00	10.00	20.00	40.00
	1830 НГ	.500	2.50	5.00	10.00	20.00
	1831 НГ	.450	2.50	5.00	10.00	20.00

COPPER
Mint mark: ЕМ

C#	Date	Mintage	VG	Fine	VF	XF
141.1	1830 ФХ	—	20.00	40.00	80.00	150.00
	1831 ФХ	2.640	7.50	15.00	30.00	60.00
	1832 ФХ	7.620	7.50	15.00	30.00	60.00
	1833 ФХ	6.968	7.50	15.00	30.00	60.00
	1834 ФХ	9.134	7.50	15.00	30.00	60.00
	1835 ФХ	5.175	7.50	15.00	30.00	60.00
	1836 ФХ	7.240	7.50	15.00	30.00	60.00
	1837 ФХ	9.728	7.50	15.00	30.00	60.00
	1837 КТIФХ	—	15.00	30.00	60.00	120.00
	1837 КТ	I.A.	7.50	15.00	30.00	60.00
	1837 НА	I.A.	7.50	15.00	30.00	60.00
	1838 НА	5.468	7.50	15.00	30.00	60.00
	1839 НА	.350	8.50	17.50	35.00	70.00

Mint mark: СПБ

C#	Date	Mintage	VG	Fine	VF	XF
141.2	1830	25 pcs.	—	—	Rare	—

Mint mark: СМ

C#	Date	Mintage	VG	Fine	VF	XF
141.3	1831	.510	25.00	50.00	100.00	200.00
	1832	.510	25.00	50.00	100.00	200.00
	1833	.700	8.50	17.50	35.00	70.00
	1834	.510	8.50	17.50	35.00	70.00
	1835	.500	8.50	17.50	35.00	70.00
	1836	.600	8.50	17.50	35.00	70.00
	1837	.500	8.50	17.50	35.00	70.00
	1838	.350	8.50	17.50	35.00	70.00
	1839	.350	10.00	20.00	40.00	80.00

2.0700 g, .868 SILVER, .0577 oz ASW
Mint mark: СПБ

C#	Date	Mintage	VG	Fine	VF	XF
164.1	1832 НГ	.104	4.00	8.00	15.00	30.00
	1833 НГ	.880	2.00	4.00	8.00	15.00
	1834 НГ	.400	2.00	4.00	8.00	15.00
	1835 НГ	.940	2.00	4.00	8.00	15.00
	1836 НГ	.490	2.00	4.00	8.00	15.00
	1837 НГ	2.360	2.00	4.00	8.00	15.00
	1838 НГ	.500	2.00	4.00	8.00	15.00
	1839 НГ	2.411	2.00	4.00	8.00	15.00
	1839 НГ	I.A.	—	—	Proof	Rare
	1840 НГ	.190	2.00	4.00	8.00	15.00
	1841 НГ	.500	2.00	4.00	8.00	15.00
	1842 НГ	—	—	—	Rare	—
	1842 АЧ	.300	2.00	4.00	8.00	15.00
	1843 АЧ	.180	2.00	4.00	8.00	15.00
	1844 КБ	.461	2.00	4.00	8.00	15.00
	1845 КБ	2.435	2.00	4.00	8.00	15.00
	1846 ПА	.810	2.00	4.00	8.00	15.00
	1847 ПА	3.180	2.00	4.00	8.00	15.00
	1848 НІ	1.860	2.00	4.00	8.00	15.00
	1849 ПА	3.110	2.00	4.00	8.00	15.00
	1850 ПА	2.450	2.00	4.00	8.00	15.00
	1851 ПА	1.500	2.00	4.00	8.00	15.00
	1852 ПА	1.350	2.00	4.00	8.00	15.00
	1852 НІ	I.A.	2.00	4.00	8.00	15.00
	1853 НІ	1.350	2.00	4.00	8.00	15.00
	1854 НІ	1.000	2.00	4.00	8.00	15.00
(Y14.1)	1855 НІ	3.201	2.00	4.00	8.00	15.00
	1856 ФБ	1.940	2.00	4.00	8.00	15.00
	1857 ФБ	3.110	2.00	4.00	8.00	15.00
	1858 ФБ	2.600	2.00	4.00	8.00	15.00

Mint mark: МШ

C#	Date	Mintage	VG	Fine	VF	XF
164.2	1854	—	—	—	Rare	—
(Y14.2)	1855	.103	25.00	50.00	100.00	200.00

2.0732 g, .750 SILVER, .0499 oz ASW
Mint mark: СПБ
Type 1, reticulated edge.

Y#	Date	Mintage	Fine	VF	XF	Unc
20.1	1859 ФБ	3.920	1.00	2.00	4.00	15.00
	1860 ФБ	.580	1.00	2.00	4.00	15.00

Type 2, eagle redesigned.

Y#	Date	Mintage	Fine	VF	XF	Unc
20.2	1860 ФБ	2.810	1.00	2.00	4.00	15.00
	1861 ФБ	5.660	1.00	2.00	4.00	15.00
	1861 МИ	I.A.	1.00	2.00	4.00	15.00
	1861	19.300	1.00	2.00	4.00	15.00
	1862 МИ	5.800	1.00	2.00	4.00	15.00
	1863 АБ	5.750	1.00	2.00	4.00	15.00
	1864 НФ	3.740	1.00	2.00	4.00	15.00
	1865 НФ	3.886	1.00	2.00	4.00	15.00
	1866 НФ	2.533	1.00	2.00	4.00	15.00
	1866 НІ	I.A.	1.00	2.00	4.00	15.00

1.7996 g, .500 SILVER, .0289 oz ASW
Mint mark: СПБ
Reeded edge

Y#	Date	Mintage	Fine	VF	XF	Unc
20a.2	1867 НІ	6.445	.50	1.00	3.00	10.00
	1868 НІ	4.740	.50	1.00	3.00	10.00
	1869 НІ	3.710	.50	1.00	3.00	10.00
	1870 НІ	3.310	.50	1.00	3.00	10.00
	1871 НІ	4.195	.50	1.00	3.00	10.00
	1872 НІ	2.130	.50	1.00	3.00	10.00
	1873 НІ	2.620	.50	1.00	3.00	10.00
	1874 НІ	2.520	.50	1.00	3.00	10.00
	1875 НІ	3.590	.50	1.00	3.00	10.00
	1876 НІ	4.900	.50	1.00	3.00	10.00
	1877 НІ	2.090	.50	1.00	3.00	10.00
	1877 НФ	I.A.	.50	1.00	3.00	12.00
	1878 НФ	6.920	.50	1.00	3.00	10.00
	1878 НІ	I.A.	5.00	10.00	20.00	50.00
	1879 НФ	6.890	.50	1.00	3.00	10.00
	1880 НФ	6.740	.50	1.00	3.00	10.00
	1881 НФ	2.950	.50	1.00	3.00	10.00
	1882 НФ	.920	.50	1.00	3.00	10.00
	1883 ДС	1.520	.50	1.00	3.00	10.00
	1883 АГ	I.A.	.50	1.00	3.00	10.00
	1884 АГ	1.710	.50	1.00	3.00	10.00
	1885 АГ	1.300	.50	1.00	3.00	10.00
	1886 АГ	2.000	.50	1.00	3.00	10.00
	1887 АГ	4.000	.50	1.00	3.00	10.00
	1888 АГ	2.000	.50	1.00	3.00	10.00
	1889 АГ	5.000	.50	1.00	3.00	10.00
	1890 АГ	3.750	.50	1.00	3.00	10.00
	1891 АГ	3.240	.50	1.00	3.00	10.00
	1893 АГ	4.250	.50	1.00	3.00	10.00
	1894 АГ	4.000	.50	1.00	3.00	10.00
	1895 АГ	1.000	.50	1.00	3.00	10.00
	1896 АГ	2.010	.50	1.00	3.00	10.00
	1897 АГ	3.150	.50	1.00	3.00	10.00
	1898 АГ	6.610	.50	1.00	2.00	5.00
	1899 АГ	14.000	.50	1.00	2.00	5.00
	1899 ЗБ	I.A.	.50	1.00	2.00	5.00
	1900 ФЗ	2.603	.50	1.00	2.00	5.00
	1901 ФЗ	15.000	.50	1.00	2.00	5.00
	1901 АР	I.A.	.50	1.00	2.00	5.00
	1902 АР	17.000	.50	1.00	2.00	5.00
	1903 АР	28.500	.50	1.00	2.00	5.00
	1904 АР	20.000	.50	1.00	2.00	5.00
	1905 АР	25.000	.50	1.00	2.00	5.00
	1906 ЭБ	17.500	.50	1.00	2.00	5.00
	1907 ЭБ	20.000	.50	1.00	2.00	5.00
	1908 ЭБ	8.210	.50	1.00	2.00	5.00
	1909 ЭБ	25.290	.50	1.00	2.00	5.00
	1910 ЭБ	20.000	.50	1.00	2.00	5.00
	1911 ЭБ	19.180	.50	1.00	2.00	5.00
	1912 ЭБ	20.000	.50	1.00	2.00	5.00
	1913 ЭБ	7.250	.50	1.00	2.00	5.00
	1913 ВС	I.A.	.50	1.00	2.00	5.00
	1914 ВС	51.250	.50	1.00	2.00	5.00
	Common date	—	—	—	Proof	100.00

Mint: Petrograd - w/o mint mark

Y#	Date	Mintage	Fine	VF	XF	Unc
20a.3	1915 ВС	82.500	.50	.75	1.00	3.00
	1916 ВС	121.500	.50	.75	1.00	3.00
	1917 ВС	17.600	—	25.00	35.00	75.00

Mint: Osaka, Japan-w/o mint mark

Y#	Date	Mintage	Fine	VF	XF	Unc
20a.1	1916	70.001	1.00	2.00	4.00	10.00

15 KOPEKS

For similar coins not listed here refer to Poland.

3.1097 g, .750 SILVER, .0750 oz ASW
Mint mark: СПБ
Reticulated edge

Y#	Date	Mintage	Fine	VF	XF	Unc
21	1860 ФБ	4.480	1.25	1.50	3.00	12.50
	1861 ФБ	10.120	1.25	1.50	3.00	12.50
	1861 МИ	I.A.	1.25	1.50	3.00	12.50
	1861	13.300	1.25	1.50	3.00	12.50
	1862 МИ	10.000	1.25	1.50	3.00	12.50
	1863 АБ	9.960	1.25	1.50	3.00	12.50
	1864 НФ	10.715	1.25	1.50	3.00	12.50
	1865 НФ	10.703	1.25	1.50	3.00	12.50
	1866 НФ	6.329	1.25	1.50	3.00	12.50
	1866 НІ	I.A.	1.25	1.50	3.00	12.50

2.6994 g, .500 SILVER, .0434 oz ASW

Y#	Date	Mintage	Fine	VF	XF	Unc
21a.2	1867 НІ	8.720	.75	1.00	3.00	10.00
	1868 НІ	7.460	.75	1.00	3.00	10.00
	1869 НІ	8.120	.75	1.00	3.00	10.00
	1870 НІ	9.380	.75	1.00	3.00	10.00
	1871 НІ	9.460	.75	1.00	3.00	10.00
	1872 НІ	5.880	.75	1.00	3.00	10.00
	1873 НІ	7.960	.75	1.00	3.00	10.00
	1874 НІ	6.960	.75	1.00	3.00	10.00
	1875 НІ	7.480	.75	1.00	3.00	10.00
	1876 НІ	9.760	.75	1.00	3.00	10.00
	1877 НІ	4.360	.75	1.00	3.00	10.00
	1877 НФ	I.A.	2.00	5.00	12.50	25.00
	1878 НФ	1.116	.75	1.00	3.00	10.00
	1879 НФ	12.504	.75	1.00	3.00	10.00
	1880 НФ	11.655	.75	1.00	3.00	10.00
	1881 НФ	4.900	.75	1.00	3.00	10.00
	1882 НФ	1.470	.75	1.00	3.00	10.00
	1882 ДС	Inc. Ab.	10.00	20.00	30.00	60.00
	1883 ДС	4.020	.75	1.00	3.00	10.00
	1883 АГ	I.A.	.75	1.00	3.00	10.00
	1884 АГ	2.720	.75	1.00	3.00	10.00
	1885 АГ	1.420	.75	1.00	3.00	10.00
	1886 АГ	1.840	.75	1.00	3.00	10.00
	1887 АГ	3.000	.75	1.00	3.00	10.00
	1888 АГ	—	5.00	10.00	20.00	40.00
	1889 АГ	2.835	.75	1.00	2.00	6.00
	1890 АГ	3.500	.75	1.00	2.00	6.00
	1891 АГ	4.710	.75	1.00	2.00	6.00
	1893 АГ	6.500	.75	1.00	2.00	6.00
	1896 АГ	3.160	.75	1.00	2.00	6.00
	1897 АГ	I.A.	.75	1.00	2.00	6.00
	1898 АГ	3.000	.75	1.00	2.00	6.00
	1899 АГ	12.665	.75	1.00	2.00	6.00
	1899 ЗБ	I.A.	.75	1.00	2.00	6.00
	1900 ФЗ	12.665	.75	1.00	2.00	5.00
	1901 ФЗ	6.670	.75	1.00	2.00	5.00
	1901 АР	I.A.	.75	1.00	2.00	5.00
	1902 АР	28.667	.75	1.00	2.00	5.00
	1903 АР	16.667	.75	1.00	2.00	5.00
	1904 АР	15.600	.75	1.00	2.00	5.00
	1905 АР	24.000	.75	1.00	2.00	5.00
	1906 ЭБ	23.333	.75	1.00	2.00	5.00
	1907 ЭБ	30.000	.75	1.00	2.00	5.00
	1908 ЭБ	29.000	.75	1.00	2.00	5.00
	1909 ЭБ	21.667	.75	1.00	2.00	5.00
	1911 ЭБ	3.313	.75	1.00	2.00	5.00
	1912 ЭБ	13.333	.75	1.00	2.00	5.00
	1912 ВС	Inc. Ab.	2.00	5.00	12.50	25.00
	1913 ЭБ	5.300	5.00	10.00	20.00	40.00
	1913 ВС	I.A.	.75	1.00	2.00	5.00
	1914 ВС	43.367	.75	1.00	2.00	5.00

Mint: Petrograd - w/o mint mark

Y#	Date	Mintage	Fine	VF	XF	Unc
21a.3	1915 ВС	59.333	.75	1.50	2.00	4.00
	1916 ВС	96.773	.75	1.50	2.00	4.00
	1917 ВС	14.320	—	25.00	35.00	75.00

Mint: Osaka, Japan-w/o mint mark
Reeded edge

Y#	Date	Mintage	Fine	VF	XF	Unc
21a.1	1916	96.666	BV	1.00	2.00	5.00

20 KOPEKS

4.1463 g, .868 SILVER, .1157 oz ASW
Mint mark: СПБ

C#	Date	Mintage	VG	Fine	VF	XF
128	1810 ФГ	.250	5.00	10.00	20.00	30.00
128	1811 ФГ	1.969	2.50	5.00	10.00	20.00
	1813 ПС	1.900	2.50	5.00	10.00	20.00
	1814 ПС	1.850	2.50	5.00	10.00	20.00
	1814 МФ	I.A.	2.50	5.00	10.00	20.00
	1815 МФ	1.025	2.50	5.00	10.00	20.00
	1816 МФ	.115	6.00	12.50	25.00	50.00
	1816 ПС	I.A.	2.50	5.00	10.00	20.00
	1817 ПС	1.545	2.50	5.00	10.00	20.00
	1818 ПС	2.000	2.50	5.00	10.00	20.00
	1819 ПС	1.705	2.50	5.00	10.00	20.00
	1820 ПС	1.895	2.50	5.00	10.00	20.00
	1820 ПД	I.A.	2.50	5.00	10.00	20.00
	1821 ПД	3.025	2.50	5.00	10.00	20.00
	1822 ПД	2.100	2.50	5.00	10.00	20.00
	1823 ПД	7.075	2.50	5.00	10.00	20.00
	1823	—	—	—	Rare	—
	1824 ПД	1.750	2.50	5.00	10.00	20.00
	1825 ПД	1.375	2.50	5.00	10.00	20.00
	1825 НГ	I.A.	6.00	12.50	25.00	50.00

Similar to C#128.

C#	Date	Mintage	VG	Fine	VF	XF
153	1826 НГ	2.815	2.50	5.00	10.00	20.00

Obv: Eagle w/wings pointed down.

C#	Date	Mintage	VG	Fine	VF	XF
158	1826 НГ	Inc. C153	4.50	9.00	17.50	35.00
	1827 НГ	.465	4.50	9.00	17.50	35.00
	1828 НГ	.050	7.50	15.00	30.00	60.00
	1829 НГ	.250	4.50	9.00	17.50	35.00
	1830 НГ	1.175	4.50	9.00	17.50	35.00
	1831 НГ	.385	4.50	9.00	17.50	35.00

Obv: Variety I eagle.

C#	Date	Mintage	VG	Fine	VF	XF
165	1832 НГ	.097	3.00	6.00	10.00	25.00
	1833 НГ	.435	2.50	5.00	10.00	20.00
	1834 НГ	.320	2.50	5.00	10.00	20.00
	1835 НГ	.500	2.50	5.00	10.00	20.00
	1836 НГ	1.280	2.50	5.00	10.00	20.00
	1837 НГ	1.300	2.50	5.00	10.00	20.00
	1838 НГ	1.635	2.50	5.00	10.00	20.00
	1839 НГ	4.030	2.50	5.00	10.00	20.00
	1839 НГ	I.A.	—	—	Proof	Rare
	1840 НГ	2.075	2.50	5.00	10.00	20.00
	1841 НГ	.025	6.00	12.00	20.00	40.00
	1842 АЧ	—	20.00	40.00	80.00	150.00
	1843 АЧ	—	20.00	40.00	80.00	150.00
	1844 КБ	—	20.00	40.00	80.00	150.00
	1845 КБ	.105	2.50	5.00	10.00	20.00
	1846 ПА	.630	2.50	5.00	10.00	20.00
	1847 ПА	3.923	2.50	5.00	10.00	20.00
	1848 НІ	2.636	2.50	5.00	10.00	20.00
	1849 ПА	3.250	2.50	5.00	10.00	20.00
	1850 ПА	3.075	2.50	5.00	10.00	20.00
	1851 ПА	2.000	2.50	5.00	10.00	20.00
	1852 НІ	1.800	—	—	Rare	—
	1852 ПА	I.A.	2.50	5.00	10.00	20.00
	1853 НІ	1.800	2.50	5.00	10.00	20.00
	1854 НІ	.990	2.50	5.00	10.00	20.00
(Y15)	1855 НІ	3.090	2.50	5.00	10.00	20.00
	1856 ФБ	3.240	2.50	5.00	10.00	20.00
	1857 ФБ	4.275	2.50	5.00	10.00	20.00
	1857 MW	—	6.00	12.50	25.00	50.00
	1858 ФБ	4.150	2.50	5.00	10.00	20.00

4.1463 g, .750 SILVER, .0999 oz ASW
Reticulated edge

Y#	Date	Mintage	Fine	VF	XF	Unc
22.1	1859 ФБ	3.960	1.50	3.00	5.00	15.00
	1860 ФБ	1.070	1.50	3.00	5.00	15.00

Obv: Eagle redesigned.

Y#	Date	Mintage	Fine	VF	XF	Unc
22.2	1860 ФБ	14.440	1.50	3.00	5.00	15.00
22.2	1861 ФБ	19.500	1.50	3.00	5.00	15.00
	1861 МИ	I.A.	1.50	3.00	5.00	15.00
	1861	19.000	1.50	3.00	5.00	15.00
	1862 МИ	19.500	1.50	3.00	5.00	15.00
	1863 АБ	19.230	1.50	3.00	5.00	15.00
	1864 НФ	20.060	1.50	3.00	5.00	15.00
	1865 НФ	20.048	1.50	3.00	5.00	15.00
	1866 НФ	10.067	1.50	3.00	5.00	15.00
	1866 НІ	Inc. Ab.	1.50	3.00	5.00	15.00

NOTE: Varieties of eagle exist for 1860 dated coins.

3.5992 g, .500 SILVER, .0579 oz ASW
Reeded edge

Y#	Date	Mintage	Fine	VF	XF	Unc
22a.1	1867 НІ	15.355	1.00	2.00	3.00	12.00
	1868 НІ	11.975	1.00	2.00	3.00	12.00
	1869 НІ	17.017	1.00	2.00	3.00	12.00
	1870 НІ	16.255	1.00	2.00	3.00	12.00
	1871 НІ	18.860	1.00	2.00	3.00	12.00
	1872 НІ	11.980	1.00	2.00	3.00	12.00
	1873 НІ	15.185	1.00	2.00	3.00	12.00
	1874 НІ	14.850	1.00	2.00	3.00	12.00
	1875 НІ	15.545	1.00	2.00	3.00	12.00
	1876 НІ	16.255	1.00	2.00	3.00	12.00
	1877 НІ	6.950	1.00	2.00	3.00	12.00
	1877 НФ	I.A.	1.00	2.00	3.00	12.00
	1878 НФ	25.335	1.00	2.00	3.00	12.00
	1878 НІ	I.A.	5.00	10.00	20.00	50.00
	1879 НФ	23.070	1.00	2.00	3.00	12.00
	1880 НФ	22.605	1.00	2.00	3.00	12.00
	1881 НФ	9.350	1.00	2.00	3.00	12.00
	1882 НФ	3.535	1.00	2.00	3.00	12.00
	1883 ДС	4.270	1.00	2.00	3.00	12.00
	1883 АГ	I.A.	1.00	2.00	3.00	12.00
	1884 АГ	2.595	1.00	2.00	3.00	12.00
	1885 АГ	1.610	1.00	2.00	3.00	12.00
	1886 АГ	2.625	1.00	2.00	3.00	12.00
	1887 АГ	2.500	1.00	2.00	3.00	12.00
	1888 АГ	3.035	1.00	2.00	3.00	12.00
	1889 АГ	1.964	1.00	2.00	3.00	12.00
	1890 АГ	3.500	1.00	2.00	3.00	12.00
	1891 АГ	6.105	1.00	2.00	3.00	12.00
	1893 АГ	7.500	1.00	2.00	3.00	12.00
	1901 ФЗ	7.750	BV	1.00	2.00	5.00
	1901 АР	I.A.	10.00	20.00	40.00	80.00
	1902 АР	10.000	BV	1.00	2.00	5.00
	1903 АР	I.A.	BV	1.00	2.00	5.00
	1904 АР	13.000	BV	1.00	2.00	5.00
	1905 АР	11.000	BV	1.00	2.00	5.00
	1906 ЭБ	15.000	BV	1.00	2.00	5.00
	1907 ЭБ	20.000	BV	1.00	2.00	5.00
	1908 ЭБ	5.000	BV	1.00	2.00	5.00
	1909 ЭБ	18.875	BV	1.00	2.00	5.00
	1910 ЭБ	11.000	BV	1.00	2.00	5.00
	1911 ЭБ	7.100	BV	1.00	2.00	5.00
	1912 ЭБ	15.000	BV	1.00	2.00	5.00
	1912 ВС	I.A.	5.00	10.00	20.00	40.00
	1913 ЭБ	4.250	BV	1.00	2.00	5.00
	1913 ВС	I.A.	BV	1.00	2.00	5.00
	1914 ВС	52.750	BV	1.00	2.00	5.00

NOTE: Edge varieties exist for 1906 dated coins.

Mint: Petrograd - w/o mint mark

Y#	Date	Mintage	Fine	VF	XF	Unc
22a.2	1915 ВС	105.500	BV	1.00	2.00	4.00
	1916 ВС	131.670	BV	1.00	2.00	4.00
	1917 ВС	3.500	—	35.00	55.00	100.00
	Common date	—	—	—	Proof	125.00

POLUPOLTINNIK

5.1800 g, .868 SILVER, .1446 oz ASW

C#	Date	Mintage	VG	Fine	VF	XF
98.1a	1801 АИ	.068	25.00	50.00	100.00	225.00
	1801 ОЦ	I.A.	—	—	Rare	—

NOTE: Earlier dates (1798-1799) exist for this type.

4.1400 g, .868 SILVER, .1155 oz ASW
Mint mark: СПБ

C#	Date	Mintage	VG	Fine	VF	XF
121	1802 АИ	.324	50.00	100.00	175.00	250.00
	1803 АИ	.152	60.00	110.00	200.00	275.00
	1803 ФГ	I.A.	60.00	120.00	200.00	350.00
	1804 ФГ	.168	50.00	100.00	175.00	250.00
	1805 ФГ	.137	60.00	110.00	200.00	275.00

C#	Date	Mintage	VG	Fine	VF	XF
121a	1808 ФГ	—	—	—	Rare	—
	1809 МК	.040	60.00	120.00	200.00	275.00
	1809 ФГ	I.A.	—	—	Rare	—
	1810 ФГ	.066	60.00	120.00	200.00	275.00

25 KOPEKS

5.1830 g, .868 SILVER, .1446 oz ASW
Mint mark: СПБ

C#	Date	Mintage	VG	Fine	VF	XF
159	1827 НГ	1.860	5.00	10.00	25.00	50.00
	1828 НГ	.320	6.00	12.50	35.00	65.00
	1829 НГ	1.200	5.00	10.00	20.00	50.00
	1830 НГ	1.160	5.00	10.00	20.00	50.00
	1831 НГ	.484	5.00	10.00	20.00	50.00

NOTE: Edge varieties exist for 1828 dated coins.

For similar coins not listed here refer to Poland.

Obv: Variety I eagle.

C#	Date	Mintage	VG	Fine	VF	XF
166.1	1832 НГ	.308	3.50	8.00	15.00	30.00
	1833 НГ	.260	3.50	8.00	15.00	30.00
	1834 НГ	.260	3.50	8.00	15.00	30.00
	1835 НГ	.356	3.50	8.00	15.00	30.00
	1836 НГ	1.072	3.50	8.00	15.00	30.00
	1837 НГ	1.144	3.50	8.00	15.00	30.00
	1838 НГ	2.672	3.50	8.00	15.00	30.00
	1839 НГ	2.738	3.50	8.00	15.00	30.00
	1839 НГ	I.A.	—	—	Proof	Rare
	1840 НГ	.604	3.50	8.00	15.00	30.00
	1841 НГ	.020	20.00	40.00	80.00	150.00
	1842 АЧ	—	20.00	40.00	80.00	150.00
	1843 АЧ	—	20.00	40.00	80.00	150.00
	1844 КБ	.021	3.50	8.00	15.00	30.00
	1845 КБ	.569	3.50	8.00	15.00	30.00
	1846 ПА	.576	3.50	8.00	15.00	30.00
	1847 ПА	4.824	2.50	6.00	12.50	25.00
	1848 НI	2.636	2.50	6.00	12.50	25.00
	1849 ПА	3.440	2.50	6.00	12.50	25.00
	1850 ПА	3.740	2.50	6.00	12.50	25.00
	1851 ПА	2.400	2.50	6.00	12.50	25.00
	1852 ПА	2.160	2.50	6.00	12.50	25.00
	1852 НI	I.A.	10.00	20.00	40.00	80.00
	1853 НI	2.160	2.50	6.00	12.50	25.00
	1853	—	10.00	20.00	40.00	80.00
	1854 НI	1.148	2.50	6.00	12.50	25.00
(Y16.1)	1855 НI	10.396	2.50	5.00	7.50	12.50
	1856 ФБ	4.444	2.50	5.00	10.00	20.00
	1857 ФБ	5.420	2.50	5.00	10.00	20.00
	1858 ФБ	5.528	2.50	5.00	10.00	20.00
	1858	Inc. Ab.	5.00	10.00	20.00	40.00
	Common date		—	—	Proof	200.00

NOTE: Varieties of eagle and crown exist.

Mint mark: MW

C#	Date	Mintage	VG	Fine	VF	XF
166.2	1854	.033	10.00	20.00	40.00	80.00
(Y16.2)	1857	—	10.00	20.00	40.00	80.00

Mint mark: СПБ
Obv: Eagle redesigned.

Y#	Date	Mintage	Fine	VF	XF	Unc
23	1859 ФБ	4.400	5.00	10.00	20.00	60.00
	1860 ФБ	1.052	7.50	15.00	30.00	80.00
	1861 ФБ	.116	12.50	25.00	50.00	125.00
	1861 МИ	Inc. Ab.	12.50	25.00	50.00	125.00
	1862 МИ	.036	15.00	37.50	75.00	150.00
	1863 АБ	.036	15.00	37.50	75.00	150.00
	1864 НФ	.068	15.00	37.50	75.00	150.00
23	1865 НФ	.016	15.00	37.50	75.00	150.00
	1866 НФ	.036	15.00	37.50	75.00	150.00
	1866 НI	I.A.	15.00	37.50	75.00	150.00
	1867 НI	.048	15.00	37.50	75.00	150.00
	1868 НI	.040	15.00	37.50	75.00	150.00
	1869 НI	.020	15.00	37.50	75.00	150.00
	1870 НI	.044	15.00	37.50	75.00	150.00
	1871 НI	.024	15.00	37.50	75.00	150.00
	1872 НI	.044	15.00	37.50	75.00	150.00
	1873 НI	.036	15.00	37.50	75.00	150.00
	1874 НI	.032	15.00	37.50	75.00	150.00
	1875 НI	.024	15.00	37.50	75.00	150.00
	1876 НI	.040	15.00	37.50	75.00	150.00
	1877 НI	1.776	7.50	15.00	30.00	80.00
	1877	Inc. Ab.	15.00	37.50	75.00	150.00
	1877 НФ	I.A.	7.50	15.00	30.00	80.00
	1878 НФ	1.768	5.00	10.00	20.00	40.00
	1879 НФ	.032	15.00	37.50	75.00	150.00
	1880 НФ	.078	12.50	25.00	50.00	125.00
	1881 НФ	2,001	25.00	50.00	75.00	150.00
	1882 НФ	2,007	25.00	50.00	75.00	150.00
	1883 ДС	2,008	25.00	50.00	75.00	150.00
	1883 АГ	Inc. Ab.	25.00	50.00	75.00	200.00
	1884 АГ	2,004	25.00	50.00	75.00	175.00
	1885 АГ	1,011	25.00	50.00	75.00	200.00

4.9990 g, .900 SILVER, .1446 oz ASW
Mint: St. Petersburg-w/o mint mark

Y#	Date	Mintage	Fine	VF	XF	Unc
44	1886 АГ	4,058	25.00	50.00	90.00	175.00
	1887 АГ	.028	20.00	40.00	80.00	150.00
	1888 АГ	4,007	25.00	50.00	90.00	175.00
	1889 АГ	1,002	50.00	75.00	125.00	250.00
	1890 АГ	2,006	25.00	50.00	90.00	175.00
	1891 АГ	.024	25.00	50.00	90.00	175.00
	1892 АГ	4,006	25.00	50.00	90.00	175.00
	1893 АГ	8,008	25.00	50.00	90.00	175.00
	1894 АГ	—	15.00	30.00	60.00	100.00
	Common date	—	—	—	Proof	450.00

Y#	Date	Mintage	Fine	VF	XF	Unc
57	1895	1.000	8.00	15.00	40.00	80.00
	1896	27.212	5.00	10.00	20.00	35.00
	1898	1 pc.	—	—	Proof	7500.
	1900	.560	15.00	30.00	60.00	125.00
	1901	*150 pcs.	75.00	125.00	250.00	400.00

30 KOPEKS

Refer to Poland

POLTINA

(1/2 Rouble)

14.6200 g, .868 SILVER, .4080 oz ASW
Mint mark: СМ
Obv: Monograms in cruciform.
Rev: Legend in square.

C#	Date	Mintage	VG	Fine	VF	XF
99.1a	1801 ОМ	.172	40.00	75.00	150.00	275.00
	1801 ФЦ	I.A.	40.00	75.00	150.00	275.00

NOTE: Earlier dates (1797-1800) exist for this type.

10.3600 g, .868 SILVER, .2892 oz ASW
Mint mark: СПБ

C#	Date	Mintage	VG	Fine	VF	XF
123	1802 АИ	.104	25.00	50.00	100.00	250.00
	1803 АИ	.242	25.00	50.00	100.00	250.00
	1804 ФГ	.230	25.00	50.00	100.00	250.00
	1805 ФГ	.315	25.00	50.00	100.00	250.00

C#	Date	Mintage	VG	Fine	VF	XF
123a	1809 МК	.011	—	—	Rare	—
	1810 ФГ	.079	50.00	75.00	150.00	300.00

C#	Date	Mintage	VG	Fine	VF	XF
129	1810 ФГ Inc. C123a		6.00	12.00	30.00	70.00
	1811 ФГ	.090	6.00	12.00	30.00	70.00
	1812 МФ	.045	6.00	12.00	30.00	70.00
	1813 ПС	.580	6.00	12.00	30.00	70.00
	1814 ПС	.662	6.00	12.00	30.00	70.00
	1814 МФ	I.A.	6.00	12.00	30.00	70.00
	1815 МФ	1.700	6.00	12.00	30.00	70.00
	1816 МФ	.270	6.00	12.00	30.00	70.00
	1816 ПС	I.A.	6.00	12.00	30.00	70.00
	1817 ПС	2.820	6.00	12.00	30.00	70.00
	1818 ПС	4.250	6.00	12.00	30.00	70.00
	1819 ПС	2.430	6.00	12.00	30.00	70.00
	1819	Inc. Ab.	—	—	Rare	—
	1820 ПС	1.356	—	—	Rare	—
	1820 ПД	I.A.	6.00	12.00	30.00	70.00
	1821 ПД	.480	6.00	12.00	30.00	70.00
	1822 ПД	.090	6.00	12.00	30.00	70.00
	1823 ПД	.200	6.00	12.00	30.00	70.00
	1824 ПД	.320	6.00	12.00	30.00	70.00
	1825 ПД	.152	6.00	12.00	30.00	70.00
	1826 НГ	.201	6.00	12.00	30.00	70.00

C#	Date	Mintage	VG	Fine	VF	XF
160	1826 НГ Inc. C129		15.00	30.00	70.00	165.00
	1826 ПД	—	—	—	Rare	—
	1827 НГ	.164	15.00	30.00	70.00	165.00
	1828 НГ	.274	15.00	30.00	70.00	165.00
	1829 НГ	.880	15.00	30.00	70.00	165.00
	1830 НГ	.290	15.00	30.00	70.00	165.00
	1831 НГ	.140	15.00	30.00	70.00	165.00

Variety I eagle

C#	Date	Mintage	VG	Fine	VF	XF
167.1	1832 НГ	.050	10.00	20.00	40.00	100.00
	1833 НГ	.082	10.00	20.00	40.00	100.00
	1834 НГ	.046	10.00	20.00	40.00	100.00
	1835 НГ	.020	10.00	20.00	40.00	100.00
	1836 НГ	.140	7.50	15.00	30.00	60.00
	1837 НГ	.104	7.50	15.00	30.00	60.00
	1838 НГ	.004	—	—	Rare	—
	1839 НГ	1.830	5.00	10.00	25.00	45.00
	1840 НГ	.960	5.00	10.00	25.00	45.00
	1841 НГ	.010	15.00	30.00	60.00	125.00
	1842 НГ	—	—	—	Rare	—
	1842 АЧ	.214	5.00	10.00	25.00	40.00
	1843 АЧ	—	10.00	20.00	40.00	100.00
	1844 КБ	.348	5.00	10.00	25.00	45.00
	1845 КБ	2.009	5.00	10.00	25.00	45.00
	1846 ПА	.460	5.00	10.00	25.00	45.00
	1847 ПА	.615	5.00	10.00	25.00	45.00
	1848 НI	1.560	5.00	10.00	25.00	45.00
	1849 ПА	.450	5.00	10.00	25.00	45.00
	1850 ПА	.530	5.00	10.00	25.00	45.00
	1851 ПА	.800	5.00	10.00	25.00	45.00
	1852 ПА	.720	5.00	10.00	25.00	45.00

C#	Date	Mintage	VG	Fine	VF	XF
167.1	1852 НI	I.A.	7.50	15.00	35.00	60.00
	1853 НI	.720	5.00	10.00	25.00	45.00
	1854 НI	.440	5.00	10.00	25.00	45.00
(Y17)	1855 НI	.714	5.00	15.00	25.00	45.00
	1856 ФБ	.450	5.00	15.00	25.00	45.00
	1857 ФБ	1.650	5.00	15.00	25.00	45.00
	1858 ФБ	1.112	5.00	15.00	25.00	50.00
	Common date		—	—	Proof	300.00

NOTE: Varieties of eagle and wreath exist.

Mint mark: МШ

C#	Date	Mintage	VG	Fine	VF	XF
167.2	1842	.076	7.50	15.00	30.00	60.00
	1843	.023	10.00	20.00	40.00	80.00
	1844	.116	7.50	15.00	30.00	60.00
	1845	.138	7.50	15.00	30.00	60.00
	1846	.308	7.50	15.00	30.00	60.00
	1847	.783	7.50	15.00	30.00	60.00
	1854	.269	7.50	15.00	30.00	60.00

NOTE: Varieties of eagle exist.

Mint mark: СПБ
Variety II eagle

Y#	Date	Mintage	Fine	VF	XF	Unc
24	1859 ФБ	1.392	10.00	20.00	40.00	100.00
	1860 ФБ	.192	20.00	40.00	85.00	175.00
	1861 ФБ	.064	25.00	50.00	100.00	200.00
	1861 МИ	I.A.	40.00	80.00	150.00	300.00
	1862 МИ	.024	30.00	60.00	125.00	250.00
	1863 АБ	.022	30.00	60.00	125.00	250.00
	1864 НФ	.034	30.00	60.00	125.00	250.00
	1865 НФ	.024	30.00	60.00	125.00	250.00
	1866 НФ	.022	30.00	60.00	125.00	250.00
	1866 НI	I.A.	30.00	60.00	125.00	250.00
	1867 НI	.026	30.00	60.00	125.00	250.00
	1868 НI	.030	30.00	60.00	125.00	250.00
	1869 НI	.020	30.00	60.00	125.00	250.00
	1870 НI	6,000	40.00	80.00	150.00	300.00
	1871 НI	.020	30.00	60.00	125.00	250.00
	1872 НI	.022	30.00	60.00	125.00	250.00
	1873 НI	.036	30.00	60.00	125.00	250.00
	1874 НI	.016	30.00	60.00	125.00	250.00
	1875 НI	.014	30.00	60.00	125.00	250.00
	1876 НI	.024	30.00	60.00	125.00	250.00
	1876	Inc. Ab.	40.00	80.00	150.00	300.00
	1877 НI	1.034	10.00	20.00	40.00	100.00
	1877 НФ	I.A.	15.00	30.00	60.00	125.00
	1878 НФ	.778	10.00	20.00	40.00	100.00
	1879 НФ	.014	30.00	60.00	125.00	250.00
	1880 НФ	.042	25.00	50.00	100.00	200.00
	1881 НФ	1,011	40.00	80.00	150.00	300.00
	1882 НФ	1,007	40.00	80.00	150.00	300.00
	1883 ДС	1,008	40.00	80.00	150.00	300.00
	1883 АГ	I.A.	50.00	100.00	200.00	400.00
	1884 АГ	1,004	40.00	80.00	150.00	300.00
	1885 АГ	511 pcs.	50.00	100.00	200.00	400.00

NOTE: Edge varieties exist.

50 KOPEKS

9.9980 g, .900 SILVER, .2893 oz ASW
Mint: St. Petersburg-w/o mint mark

Y#	Date	Mintage	Fine	VF	XF	Unc
45	1886 АГ	2,058	15.00	30.00	80.00	250.00
	1887 АГ	.026	20.00	40.00	80.00	250.00
	1888 АГ	2,007	15.00	30.00	80.00	250.00
	1889 АГ	1,002	20.00	40.00	80.00	250.00
	1890 АГ	2,006	15.00	30.00	80.00	250.00
	1891 АГ	.024	20.00	40.00	80.00	250.00
	1892 АГ	2,006	15.00	30.00	80.00	250.00
	1893 АГ	4,008	15.00	30.00	80.00	250.00
	1894 АГ	—	15.00	25.00	75.00	200.00
	Common date	—	—	—	Proof	750.00

Mint mark: Star on rim

Y#	Date	Mintage	Fine	VF	XF	Unc
58.1	1896	.245	10.00	20.00	40.00	80.00
58.1	1897	46.755	7.50	12.50	25.00	60.00
	1899	10.000	7.50	12.50	25.00	60.00

Mint: St. Petersburg-w/o mint mark

Y#	Date	Mintage	Fine	VF	XF	Unc
58.2	1895 АГ	5.400	5.00	10.00	25.00	65.00
	1896 АГ	17.402	5.00	8.00	15.00	55.00
	1898 АГ	—	—	—	Proof	1250.
	1899 ЗБ	15.442	5.00	10.00	25.00	65.00
	1899 ФЗ	I.A.	5.00	10.00	25.00	65.00
	1899 АГ	I.A.	5.00	10.00	25.00	65.00
	1900 ФЗ	3.360	5.00	10.00	25.00	65.00
	1901 АР	.412	5.00	12.50	35.00	80.00
	1901 ФЗ	I.A.	5.00	12.50	35.00	80.00
	1902 АР	.036	10.00	20.00	40.00	100.00
	1903 АР	19 pcs.	200.00	300.00	550.00	1150.
	1904 АР	4,010	100.00	200.00	400.00	700.00
	1906 ЭБ	.010	25.00	50.00	100.00	200.00
	1907 ЭБ	.200	10.00	20.00	40.00	100.00
	1908 ЭБ	.040	10.00	20.00	40.00	100.00
	1909 ЭБ	.050	10.00	20.00	40.00	100.00
	1910 ЭБ	.150	10.00	20.00	40.00	100.00
	1911 ЭБ	.800	10.00	20.00	40.00	80.00
	1912 ЭБ	7.085	5.00	8.00	15.00	45.00
	1913 ЭБ	6.420	7.50	15.00	35.00	70.00
	1913 ВС	I.A.	5.00	10.00	20.00	45.00
	1914 ВС	1.200	5.00	10.00	20.00	45.00
	Common date	—	—	—	Proof	400.00

75 KOPEKS

Refer to Poland

ROUBLE

20.7300 g, .868 SILVER, .5785 oz ASW
Reduced size, 38mm.

C#	Date	Mintage	VG	Fine	VF	XF
101a	1801 АИ	3.143	20.00	40.00	90.00	150.00
	1801 ФЦ	I.A.	20.00	40.00	90.00	150.00
	1801 ОМ	I.A.	—	—	Rare	—

NOTE: Earlier dates (1798-1800) exist for this type.

Mint mark: СПБ
Alexander I

C#	Date	Mintage	VG	Fine	VF	XF
125	1802 АИ	5.360	20.00	40.00	80.00	150.00
	1803 АИ	2.429	20.00	40.00	80.00	150.00
	1803 ФГ	I.A.	25.00	50.00	100.00	200.00
	1804 ФГ	4.355	20.00	40.00	80.00	150.00
	1805 ФГ	2.020	20.00	40.00	80.00	150.00

C#	Date	Mintage	VG	Fine	VF	XF
125a	1807 ФГ	.533	25.00	50.00	90.00	150.00
	1808 ФГ	1.701	25.00	50.00	90.00	150.00
	1808 МК	I.A.	25.00	50.00	90.00	150.00
	1809 МК	2.177	25.00	50.00	90.00	150.00
	1809 ФГ	I.A.	25.00	50.00	90.00	150.00
	1810 ФГ	1.682	25.00	50.00	100.00	200.00

C#	Date	Mintage	VG	Fine	VF	XF
130	1810 ФГ					
		Inc. C125a	250.00	400.00	650.00	1100.
	1811 ФГ	2.675	10.00	20.00	35.00	75.00
	1812 МФ	4.076	10.00	20.00	35.00	75.00
	1813 ПС	5.210	10.00	20.00	35.00	75.00
	1814 МФ	3.600	10.00	20.00	35.00	75.00
	1814 ПС	I.A.	10.00	20.00	35.00	75.00
	1814	Inc. Ab.	15.00	30.00	50.00	90.00
	1815 МФ	4.750	10.00	20.00	35.00	75.00
	1816 МФ	1.782	10.00	20.00	35.00	75.00
	1816 ПС	I.A.	10.00	20.00	35.00	75.00
	1817 ПС	11.775	10.00	20.00	35.00	75.00
	1818 ПС	16.275	10.00	20.00	35.00	75.00
	1818 СП	I.A.	10.00	20.00	35.00	75.00
	1818	Inc. Ab.	15.00	30.00	50.00	90.00
	1819 ПС	6.355	10.00	20.00	35.00	75.00
	1820 ПС	1.962	10.00	20.00	35.00	75.00
	1820 ПД	I.A.	10.00	20.00	35.00	75.00
	1821 ПД	.840	10.00	20.00	35.00	75.00
	1822 ПД	3.120	10.00	20.00	35.00	75.00
	1823 ПД	2.955	10.00	20.00	35.00	75.00
	1824 ПД	2.035	10.00	20.00	35.00	75.00
	1825 ПД	1.461	10.00	20.00	35.00	75.00
	1825 НГ	I.A.	10.00	20.00	40.00	100.00
(155)	1826 НГ	.730	15.00	35.00	75.00	125.00

C#	Date	Mintage	Fine	VF	XF	Unc
161	1826 НГ					
		Inc.C155	35.00	75.00	125.00	275.00
	1827 НГ	.584	27.50	50.00	100.00	250.00
	1828 НГ	2.530	25.00	45.00	90.00	250.00
	1829 НГ	5.510	25.00	45.00	90.00	250.00
	1830 НГ	6.010	25.00	45.00	90.00	250.00
	1831 НГ	3.670	25.00	45.00	90.00	250.00

NOTE: Edge varieties exist.

C#	Date	Mintage	Fine	VF	XF	Unc
168.1	1832 НГ	1.941	18.00	25.00	60.00	150.00
	1833 НГ	1.711	18.00	25.00	60.00	150.00
	1834 НГ	2.270	18.00	25.00	60.00	150.00
	1835 НГ	.244	25.00	40.00	75.00	175.00
	1836 НГ	1.102	18.00	25.00	60.00	150.00
	1837 НГ	1.478	18.00	25.00	60.00	150.00
	1838 НГ	.232	25.00	40.00	75.00	175.00
	1839 НГ	.036	—	—	*Rare	—
	1839 НГ	I.A.	—	—	Proof	Rare
	1840 НГ	2.627	18.00	25.00	60.00	150.00
	1841 НГ	6.155	18.00	25.00	60.00	150.00
	1842 АЧ	4.965	18.00	25.00	60.00	150.00
	1843 АЧ	5.320	18.00	25.00	60.00	150.00
	1844 КБ	2.933	18.00	25.00	60.00	150.00
	1845 КБ	.683	18.00	25.00	60.00	150.00
	1846 ПА	3.523	18.00	25.00	60.00	150.00
	1847 ПА	.563	20.00	30.00	70.00	165.00
	1848 НI	1.542	18.00	25.00	60.00	150.00

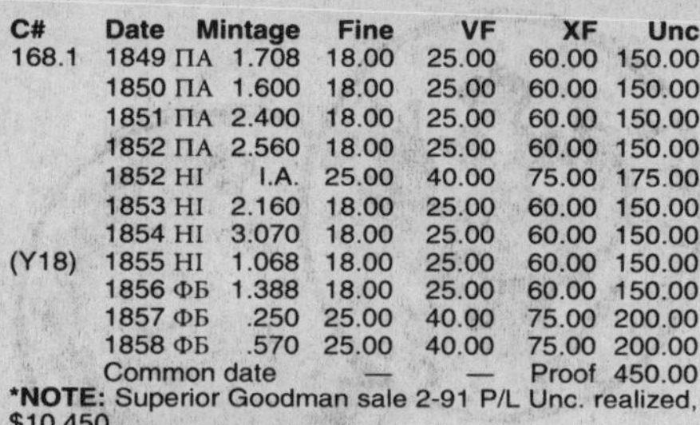

C#	Date	Mintage	Fine	VF	XF	Unc
168.1	1849 ПА	1.708	18.00	25.00	60.00	150.00
	1850 ПА	1.600	18.00	25.00	60.00	150.00
	1851 ПА	2.400	18.00	25.00	60.00	150.00
	1852 ПА	2.560	18.00	25.00	60.00	150.00
	1852 НІ	I.A.	25.00	40.00	75.00	175.00
	1853 НІ	2.160	18.00	25.00	60.00	150.00
	1854 НІ	3.070	18.00	25.00	60.00	150.00
(Y18)	1855 НІ	1.068	18.00	25.00	60.00	150.00
	1856 ФБ	1.388	18.00	25.00	60.00	150.00
	1857 ФБ	.250	25.00	40.00	75.00	200.00
	1858 ФБ	.570	25.00	40.00	75.00	200.00
	Common date		—	—	Proof	450.00

***NOTE:** Superior Goodman sale 2-91 P/L Unc. realized, $10,450.

Mint mark: MW

C#	Date	Mintage	Fine	VF	XF	Unc
168.2	1842	.257	22.50	35.00	75.00	135.00
	1843	.267	22.50	35.00	75.00	135.00
	1844	2.364	22.50	35.00	75.00	135.00
	1845	.345	25.00	45.00	95.00	150.00
	1846	.511	22.50	35.00	75.00	135.00
	1847	.987	22.50	35.00	75.00	135.00

Mint mark: СПБ
Alexander I Monument

C#	Date	Mintage	Fine	VF	XF	Unc
169	1834	.015	75.00	150.00	325.00	500.00
	1834	—	—	—	Proof	Rare

Battle of Borodino Memorial

C#	Date	Mintage	Fine	VF	XF	Unc
170	1839 НГ	.160	65.00	125.00	250.00	485.00

NOTE: The 1841 Marriage "Rouble" is a medal.

Mint: St. Petersburg-w/o mint mark
Nicholas I Memorial

Y#	Date	Mintage	Fine	VF	XF	Unc
28	1859	.050	60.00	110.00	190.00	325.00

Mint mark: СПБ

Y#	Date	Mintage	Fine	VF	XF	Unc
25	1859 ФБ	.014	75.00	150.00	300.00	500.00
	1860 ФБ	.018	50.00	100.00	150.00	350.00
	1861 ФБ	.076	50.00	100.00	150.00	350.00
	1861 МИ	I.A.	50.00	100.00	150.00	350.00
	1862 МИ	.022	50.00	100.00	150.00	350.00
	1863 АБ	.005	75.00	150.00	300.00	500.00
	1864 НФ	.114	25.00	50.00	100.00	225.00
	1865 НФ	.115	25.00	50.00	100.00	225.00
	1866 НІ	.110	25.00	50.00	100.00	225.00
	1866 НФ	I.A.	25.00	50.00	100.00	225.00
	1867 НІ	.425	17.50	25.00	50.00	135.00
	1868 НІ	.775	17.50	25.00	50.00	135.00
	1869 НІ	.285	17.50	25.00	50.00	135.00
	1870 НІ	.386	17.50	25.00	50.00	135.00
	1871 НІ	.884	17.50	25.00	50.00	135.00
	1872 НІ	.978	17.50	25.00	50.00	135.00
	1873 НІ	.673	17.50	25.00	50.00	135.00
	1874 НІ	.648	17.50	25.00	50.00	135.00
	1875 НІ	.687	17.50	25.00	50.00	135.00
	1876 НІ	.778	17.50	25.00	50.00	135.00
	1877 НІ	6.923	15.00	20.00	35.00	100.00
	1877 НФ	I.A.	15.00	20.00	35.00	100.00
	1878 НФ	8.087	15.00	20.00	35.00	100.00
	1879 НФ	.611	17.50	25.00	50.00	135.00
	1880 НФ	.521	17.50	25.00	50.00	135.00
	1881 НФ	.699	17.50	25.00	50.00	135.00
	1882 НФ	.434	17.50	25.00	50.00	135.00
	1883 ДС	.425	17.50	25.00	50.00	135.00
	1883 АГ	I.A.	50.00	100.00	150.00	400.00
	1884 АГ	.355	17.50	25.00	50.00	135.00
	1885 АГ	.500	17.50	25.00	50.00	135.00

Mint: St. Petersburg-w/o mint mark
Alexander III Coronation

Y#	Date	Mintage	Fine	VF	XF	Unc
43	1883	.279	35.00	50.00	90.00	240.00

19.9960 g, .900 SILVER, .5786 oz ASW
Mintmasters initials and stars found on edge.

Y#	Date	Mintage	Fine	VF	XF	Unc
46	1886 АГ	.488	20.00	40.00	75.00	225.00
	1887 АГ	.491	20.00	40.00	75.00	225.00
	1888 АГ	.498	20.00	40.00	75.00	225.00
	1889 АГ	1,002	125.00	250.00	500.00	1000.
	1890 АГ	.090	25.00	50.00	100.00	275.00
	1891 АГ	1.117	20.00	40.00	80.00	250.00
	1892 АГ	2.131	20.00	40.00	70.00	200.00
	1893 АГ	1.485	20.00	40.00	70.00	200.00
	1894 АГ	3,007	50.00	100.00	250.00	500.00
	Common date	—	—	—	Proof	1200.

Mint mark: 2 stars on rim

Y#	Date	Mintage	Fine	VF	XF	Unc
59.1	1897	26.000	10.00	17.50	30.00	85.00
	1898	14.000	10.00	17.50	30.00	85.00
	1899	10.000	10.00	17.50	30.00	85.00

Mint mark: Star on rim

Y#	Date	Mintage	Fine	VF	XF	Unc
59.2	1896	12.000	10.00	17.50	30.00	85.00
	1898	5.000	10.00	17.50	30.00	85.00

Mint: St. Petersburg-w/o mint mark

Y#	Date	Mintage	Fine	VF	XF	Unc
59.3	1895 АГ	1.240	12.00	20.00	35.00	100.00
	1896 АГ	12.540	10.00	17.50	30.00	85.00
	1897 АГ	18.515	10.00	17.50	30.00	85.00
	1898 АГ	18.725	10.00	17.50	30.00	85.00
	1899 ЗБ	6.503	10.00	17.50	30.00	85.00
	1899 ФЗ	I.A.	10.00	17.50	30.00	85.00
	1900 ФЗ	3.484	10.00	17.50	35.00	100.00
	1901 ФЗ	2.608	10.00	17.50	35.00	90.00
	1901 АР	I.A.	12.00	20.00	40.00	100.00
	1902 АН	.140	20.00	30.00	50.00	150.00
	1903 АР	.056	40.00	80.00	180.00	400.00
	1904 АР	.012	40.00	80.00	180.00	400.00
	1905 АР	.021	40.00	80.00	180.00	400.00
	1906 ЭБ	.046	40.00	80.00	180.00	400.00
	1907 ЭБ	.400	20.00	30.00	50.00	150.00
	1908 ЭБ	.130	20.00	30.00	50.00	150.00
	1909 ЭБ	.051	40.00	80.00	180.00	400.00
	1910 ЭБ	.075	25.00	40.00	80.00	200.00
	1911 ЭБ	.129	25.00	40.00	80.00	200.00
	1912 ЭБ	2.111	15.00	25.00	50.00	125.00
	1913 ЭБ	.022	50.00	100.00	200.00	450.00
	1913 ВС	I.A.	50.00	100.00	200.00	450.00
	1914 ВС	.536	25.00	35.00	90.00	250.00
	1915 ВС	*5,000	30.00	60.00	125.00	250.00
	Common date	—	—	—	Proof	900.00

NOTE: Varieties exist with plain edge. These are mint errors and rare.

Nicholas II Coronation

Y#	Date	Mintage	Fine	VF	XF	Unc
60	1896 АГ	.191	25.00	40.00	70.00	150.00
	1896 АГ	—	—	—	Proof	500.00

Alexander II Memorial

Y#	Date	Mintage	Fine	VF	XF	Unc
61	1898 АГ	*5,000	125.00	225.00	350.00	850.00
	1898 АГ	—	—	—	Proof	1200.

Napoleon Defeat Centennial

Y#	Date	Mintage	Fine	VF	XF	Unc
68	1912 ЭБ	.027	60.00	110.00	160.00	300.00
	1912 ЭБ	—	—	—	Proof	800.00

Alexander III Memorial

Y#	Date	Mintage	Fine	VF	XF	Unc
69	1912 ЭБ	900 pcs.	200.00	400.00	750.00	1250.
	1912 ЭБ	—	—	—	Proof	1600.

Mint: St. Petersburg-w/o mint mark
300th Anniversary Romanov Dynasty

Y#	Date	Mintage	Fine	VF	XF	Unc
70	1913 ВС	1.472	12.50	20.00	35.00	90.00

200th Anniversary Battle of Gangut

Y#	Date	Mintage	Fine	VF	XF	Unc
71	1914 ВС	*.030	400.00	600.00	1200.	2500.

***NOTE:** Only 317 pieces were issued.

1-1/2 ROUBLES/10 ZLOTYCH

For similar coins not listed here refer to Poland.

31.1000 g, .868 SILVER, .8679 oz ASW
Mint: St. Petersburg-w/o mint mark

C#	Date	Mintage	Fine	VF	XF	Unc
A172	1835	36 pcs.	—	—	5000.	10,000.

Obv: Designer's initials ПУ on truncation.

C#	Date	Mintage	Fine	VF	XF	Unc
172.1	1836	50 pcs.	—	—	5000.	7700.

Rev: Die break at rim lower right.

C#	Date	Mintage	Fine	VF	XF	Unc
172.2	1836	(restrike)	—	—	2500.	4000.

Obv: Designer's name below bust.

C#	Date	Mintage	Fine	VF	XF	Unc
172.3	1836	Inc. Ab.	—	—	5000.	7500.

Obv: W/o designer's name or initials.

C#	Date	Mintage	Fine	VF	XF	Unc
172.4	1836	Inc. Ab.	—	—	5500.	8500.

NOTE: The above coins were struck as presentation pieces.

Mint mark: СПБ
Battle of Borodino Memorial
Obv: Long rays.

C#	Date	Mintage	Fine	VF	XF	Unc
173.1	1839	6,000	400.00	800.00	1100.	1750.

Obv: Short rays.

C#	Date	Mintage	Fine	VF	XF	Unc
173.2	1839	Inc. Ab.	500.00	900.00	1450.	2250.

3 ROUBLES

10.3500 g, PLATINUM, .3327 oz APW
Mint mark: СПБ

C#	Date	Mintage	Fine	VF	XF	Unc
177	1828	.020	250.00	425.00	650.00	1000.
	1829	.043	225.00	350.00	525.00	750.00
	1830	.106	225.00	350.00	525.00	750.00
	1831	.087	225.00	350.00	525.00	750.00
	1832	.066	225.00	350.00	525.00	750.00
	1833	.085	250.00	400.00	600.00	850.00
	1834	.091	225.00	300.00	500.00	750.00
	1835	.139	250.00	400.00	600.00	800.00
	1836	.044	275.00	350.00	550.00	750.00
	1837	.046	275.00	350.00	550.00	750.00
	1838	.049	275.00	350.00	550.00	750.00
	1839	6 pcs.	—	—	Proof	3500.
	1840	3 pcs.	—	—	Proof	3000.
	1841	.017	250.00	400.00	600.00	850.00
	1842	.146	225.00	350.00	500.00	650.00
	1843	.172	225.00	350.00	550.00	750.00
	1844	.215	225.00	375.00	600.00	850.00
	1845	.050	250.00	425.00	650.00	900.00
	Common date	—	—	—	Proof	1450.

NOTE: The low mintage figures incorporated in the following listings of Russian platinum issues are not necessarily reflective of relative scarcity as many of the issues were restruck at later dates, using original dies in unrecorded quantities.

For similar coins not listed here refer to Poland.

3.9260 g, .917 GOLD, .1157 oz AGW

Y#	Date	Mintage	Fine	VF	XF	Unc
26	1869 НІ	.143	175.00	225.00	300.00	400.00
	1870 НІ	.200	175.00	225.00	300.00	400.00
	1871 НІ	.200	175.00	225.00	300.00	400.00
	1872 НІ	.100	175.00	225.00	300.00	400.00
	1873 НІ	.077	175.00	225.00	300.00	400.00
	1874 НІ	.270	175.00	225.00	300.00	400.00
	1875 НІ	.100	175.00	225.00	300.00	400.00

Y#	Date	Mintage	Fine	VF	XF	Unc
26	1876 HI	.063	175.00	225.00	300.00	400.00
	1877 HI	.050	175.00	225.00	300.00	400.00
	1877 НФ	I.A.	175.00	225.00	300.00	400.00
	1878 НФ	.194	175.00	225.00	300.00	400.00
	1879 НФ	5 pcs.	—	—	—	1900.
	1880 НФ	.100	175.00	225.00	300.00	400.00
	1881 НФ	.048	175.00	225.00	300.00	400.00
	1882 НФ	6 pcs.	—	2200.	3500.	5000.
	1883 ДС	9,007	175.00	225.00	350.00	500.00
	1883 АГ	I.A.	—	—	Rare	—
	1884 АГ	.047	175.00	225.00	350.00	500.00
	1885 АГ	.029	175.00	250.00	375.00	550.00
	Common date	—	—	—	Proof	1200.

5 ROUBLES

6.0800 g, .986 GOLD, .1928 oz AGW
Mint mark: СМ
Obv: Monograms in cruciform. Rev: Leg. in square.

C#	Date	Mintage	Fine	VF	XF	Unc
104.1	1801 АИ	.180	250.00	400.00	800.00	1200.

NOTE: Earlier dates (1798-1800) exist for this type.

Mint mark: СПБ

C#	Date	Mintage	Fine	VF	XF	Unc
131	1802	15 pcs.	—	—	Rare	—
	1803 ХЛ	6 pcs.	—	—	Rare	—
	1804 ХЛ	.037	250.00	400.00	800.00	1200.
	1805 ХЛ	8,109	250.00	400.00	800.00	1200.
	1806 ХЛ	2 pcs.	—	—	Rare	—

6.5440 g, .917 GOLD, .1929 oz AGW

C#	Date	Mintage	Fine	VF	XF	Unc
132	1817 ФГ	.710	130.00	180.00	300.00	500.00
	1818 МФ	1.520	130.00	200.00	325.00	550.00
	1819 МФ	.963	130.00	180.00	300.00	500.00
	1822 МФ	—	130.00	180.00	300.00	500.00
	1823 ПС	.440	130.00	180.00	300.00	500.00
	1824 ПС	.276	130.00	180.00	300.00	500.00
	1825 ПС	.101	400.00	700.00	1200.	2000.
	1825 ПС	—	—	—	Proof	3000.
	1825 ПД	I.A.	300.00	500.00	800.00	1400.

C#	Date	Mintage	Fine	VF	XF	Unc
174	1826 ПД	.212	130.00	180.00	300.00	500.00
	1827 ПД	—	300.00	500.00	900.00	1500.
	1828 ПД	.604	130.00	180.00	300.00	500.00
	1829 ПД	.733	130.00	180.00	300.00	500.00
	1830 ПД	.490	130.00	180.00	300.00	500.00
	1831 ПД	.846	150.00	300.00	400.00	650.00

Discovery of Gold at Kolyvan Mines

C#	Date	Mintage	Fine	VF	XF	Unc
176	1832 ПД	1,000	600.00	1200.	2200.	3500.
	1832	—	—	—	Proof	4500.

C#	Date	Mintage	Fine	VF	XF	Unc
175.1	1832 ПД	.481	100.00	120.00	140.00	175.00
	1833 ПД	.829	100.00	120.00	140.00	175.00
	1834 ПД	1.346	100.00	120.00	140.00	175.00
	1835 ПД	1.440	100.00	120.00	140.00	175.00
	1835	Inc. Ab.	—	—	Rare	—
	1836 ПД	.953	100.00	120.00	140.00	175.00
	1837 ПД	.048	150.00	200.00	250.00	400.00
	1838 ПД	.302	100.00	120.00	140.00	175.00

C#	Date	Mintage	Fine	VF	XF	Unc
175.1	1839 АЧ	1.609	100.00	120.00	140.00	175.00
	1840 АЧ	1.277	100.00	120.00	140.00	175.00
	1841 АЧ	1.668	100.00	120.00	140.00	175.00
	1842 АЧ	2.180	100.00	120.00	140.00	175.00
	1843 АЧ	1.852	100.00	120.00	140.00	175.00
	1844 КБ	2.365	100.00	120.00	140.00	175.00
	1845 КБ	2.842	100.00	120.00	140.00	175.00
	1846 АГ	3.442	100.00	120.00	140.00	175.00
	Common date	—	—	—	Proof	2000.

Mint mark: МШ

C#	Date	Mintage	Fine	VF	XF	Unc
175.2	1842	695 pcs.	700.00	1000.	1500.	2500.
	1846	62 pcs.	1000.	1500.	2000.	3000.
	1848	485 pcs.	700.00	1000.	1500.	2500.
	1849	133 pcs.	700.00	1000.	1500.	2500.
	Common date	—	—	—	Proof	3000.

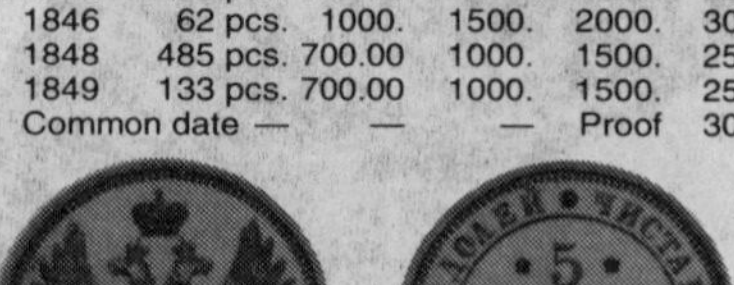

Mint mark: СПБ
Different eagle

C#	Date	Mintage	Fine	VF	XF	Unc
175.3	1846 АГ	Inc. C175.1	100.00	120.00	140.00	170.00
	1847 АГ	3.900	100.00	150.00	200.00	275.00
	1848 АГ	2.900	100.00	120.00	140.00	170.00
	1849 АГ	3.100	100.00	120.00	140.00	170.00
	1850 АГ	3.900	100.00	120.00	140.00	170.00
	1851 АГ	3.400	100.00	120.00	140.00	170.00
	1852 АГ	3.900	100.00	120.00	140.00	170.00
	1853 АГ	3.900	100.00	120.00	140.00	170.00
	1854 АГ	3.900	100.00	120.00	140.00	170.00

Y#	Date	Mintage	Fine	VF	XF	Unc
A26	1855 АГ	3.400	100.00	120.00	135.00	165.00
	1856 АГ	3.800	100.00	120.00	135.00	165.00
	1857 АГ	4.500	100.00	120.00	135.00	165.00
	1858 АГ	3.500	100.00	120.00	135.00	165.00
	1858 ПФ	—	100.00	120.00	135.00	165.00
	Common date	—	—	—	Proof	2000.

Y#	Date	Mintage	Fine	VF	XF	Unc
B26	1859 ПФ	3.900	100.00	120.00	135.00	160.00
	1860 ПФ	3.600	100.00	120.00	135.00	160.00
	1861 ПФ	3.500	100.00	120.00	135.00	160.00
	1862 ПФ	6.354	100.00	120.00	135.00	160.00
	1863 МИ	7.200	100.00	120.00	135.00	160.00
	1864 АС	3.900	100.00	120.00	135.00	160.00
	1865 АС	3.902	100.00	120.00	135.00	160.00
	1865 СШ	I.A.	100.00	120.00	135.00	160.00
	1866 СШ	3.900	100.00	120.00	135.00	160.00
	1866 HI	I.A.	100.00	120.00	135.00	160.00
	1867 HI	3.494	100.00	120.00	135.00	160.00
	1868 HI	3.400	100.00	120.00	135.00	160.00
	1869 HI	3.900	100.00	120.00	135.00	160.00
	1870 HI	5.000	100.00	120.00	135.00	160.00
	1871 HI	.800	100.00	120.00	135.00	160.00
	1872 HI	2.400	100.00	120.00	135.00	160.00
	1873 HI	3.000	100.00	120.00	135.00	160.00
	1874 HI	4.800	100.00	120.00	135.00	160.00
	1875 HI	4.000	100.00	120.00	135.00	160.00
	1876 HI	6.000	100.00	120.00	135.00	150.00
	1877 HI	6.600	100.00	120.00	135.00	150.00
	1877 НФ	I.A.	100.00	120.00	135.00	150.00
	1878 НФ	6.800	100.00	120.00	135.00	150.00
	1879 НФ	7.225	100.00	120.00	135.00	150.00
	1880 НФ	6.200	100.00	120.00	135.00	150.00
	1881 НФ	5.500	100.00	120.00	135.00	150.00
	1882 НФ	4.547	100.00	120.00	135.00	150.00
	1883 ДС	5.632	100.00	120.00	135.00	150.00
	1883 АГ	I.A.	100.00	120.00	135.00	150.00
	1884 АГ	4.801	100.00	120.00	135.00	150.00
	1885 АГ	5.433	100.00	120.00	135.00	150.00
	Common date	—	—	—	Proof	1750.

6.4516 g, .900 GOLD, .1867 oz AGW

Mint: St. Petersburg-w/o mint mark

Y#	Date	Mintage	Fine	VF	XF	Unc
42	1886 АГ	.351	BV	110.00	125.00	160.00
	1887 АГ	3.261	BV	110.00	125.00	150.00
	1888 АГ	5.257	BV	110.00	125.00	150.00
	1889 АГ	4.200	BV	110.00	125.00	150.00
	1890 АГ	5.600	BV	110.00	125.00	150.00
	1891 АГ	.541	BV	110.00	125.00	150.00
	1892 АГ	.128	BV	110.00	125.00	160.00
	1893 АГ	.598	BV	110.00	125.00	150.00
	1894 АГ	.598	BV	110.00	125.00	150.00
	Common date	—	—	—	Proof	1350.

NOTE: Edge varieties exist.

Y#	Date	Mintage	Fine	VF	XF	Unc
A61	1895 АГ	36 pcs.	—	2250.	4500.	6000.
	1896 АГ	33 pcs.	—	2250.	4500.	6000.

4.3013 g, .900 GOLD, .1244 oz AGW

Y#	Date	Mintage	Fine	VF	XF	Unc
62	1897 АГ	5.372	—	BV	60.00	75.00
	1898 АГ	52.378	—	BV	60.00	70.00
	1899 ЗБ	20.400	—	BV	60.00	75.00
	1899 ФЗ	I.A.	—	BV	60.00	75.00
	1900 ФЗ	.031	—	BV	80.00	110.00
	1901 ФЗ	7.500	—	BV	65.00	80.00
	1901 АР	I.A.	—	BV	65.00	80.00
	1902 АР	6.240	—	BV	65.00	80.00
	1903 АР	5.148	—	BV	65.00	80.00
	1904 АР	2.016	—	BV	70.00	100.00
	1906 ЭБ	10 pcs.	—	—	2000.	2500.
	1907 ЭБ	109 pcs.	—	—	900.00	1250.
	1909 ЭБ	—	BV	60.00	75.00	90.00
	1910 ЭБ	.200	BV	60.00	75.00	100.00
	1911 ЭБ	.100	BV	60.00	75.00	100.00
	Common date	—	—	—	Proof	850.00

6 ROUBLES

20.7100 g, PLATINUM, .6655 oz APW
Mint mark: СПБ

C#	Date	Mintage	Fine	VF	XF	Unc
178	1829	828 pcs.	1000.	2000.	2750.	3500.
	1830	8,610	1000.	1750.	2500.	3250.
	1831	2,784	1000.	1750.	2500.	3250.
	1832	1,502	1000.	2000.	2750.	3500.
	1833	302 pcs.	1000.	2000.	2750.	3500.
	1834	11 pcs.	1250.	2500.	3200.	5000.
	1835	107 pcs.	1000.	2000.	2500.	3250.
	1836	11 pcs.	—	—	Proof	6000.
	1837	253 pcs.	1000.	2000.	2750.	3500.
	1838	12 pcs.	—	—	Rare	—
	1839	2 pcs.	—	—	Rare	—
	1840	1 pc.	—	—	Rare	—
	1841	170 pcs.	1000.	2000.	2750.	3500.
	1842	121 pcs.	1000.	2000.	2750.	3500.
	1843	127 pcs.	1000.	2000.	2750.	3500.
	1844	4 pcs.	—	—	Rare	—
	1845	2 pcs.	—	—	Rare	—
	Common date	—	—	—	Proof	5000.

7 ROUBLES 50 KOPEKS

6.4516 g, .900 GOLD, .1867 oz AGW
Mint: St. Petersburg-w/o mint mark

Y#	Date	Mintage	Fine	VF	XF	Unc
63	1897 АГ	16.829	BV	100.00	125.00	200.00

10 ROUBLES

12.1700 g, .986 GOLD, .3858 oz AGW
Mint mark: СПБ

C#	Date	Mintage	Fine	VF	XF	Unc
133	1802	.074	2500.	3000.	3500.	4500.
	1802 АИ	I.A.	2500.	3000.	3500.	4500.
	1804 ХЛ	.072	2500.	3000.	3500.	4500.
	1805 ХЛ	.055	1500.	2000.	2150.	4250.
	1806 ХЛ	126 pcs.	—	—	Rare	—

12.9039 g, .900 GOLD, .3734 oz AGW
Mint: St. Petersburg-w/o mint mark

Y#	Date	Mintage	Fine	VF	XF	Unc
A42	1886 АГ	.057	200.00	300.00	500.00	750.00
	1887 АГ	.475	200.00	250.00	350.00	600.00
	1888 АГ	.023	200.00	300.00	500.00	750.00
	1889 АГ	.343	200.00	250.00	350.00	600.00
	1890 АГ	.015	200.00	300.00	500.00	750.00
	1891 АГ	3,010	250.00	400.00	650.00	900.00
	1892 АГ	8,006	250.00	400.00	650.00	900.00
	1893 АГ	1,008	250.00	400.00	650.00	900.00
	1894 АГ	1,007	250.00	400.00	650.00	900.00
	Common date	—	—	—	Proof	2800.

Rev. leg: ИМПЕРІАЛЪ (IMPERIAL).

Y#	Date	Mintage	Fine	VF	XF	Unc
A63	1895 АГ	125 pcs.	—	3000.	3500.	4000.
	1896 АГ	125 pcs.	—	3000.	3500.	4000.
	1897 АГ	125 pcs.	—	3000.	3500.	4000.

8.6026 g, .900 GOLD, .2489 oz AGW

Y#	Date	Mintage	Fine	VF	XF	Unc
64	1898 АГ	.200	—	BV	120.00	170.00
	1899 АГ	27.600	—	BV	110.00	130.00
	1899 ФЗ	I.A.	—	BV	110.00	130.00
	1899 ЗБ	I.A.	—	BV	120.00	160.00
	1900 ФЗ	6.021	—	BV	120.00	160.00
	1901 ФЗ	2.377	—	BV	120.00	160.00
	1901 АР	I.A.	—	BV	120.00	160.00
	1902 АР	2.019	—	BV	120.00	160.00
	1903 АР	2.817	—	BV	120.00	160.00
	1904 АР	1.025	—	BV	120.00	160.00
	1906 ЭБ	10 pcs.	—	—	Proof	3200.
	1909 ЭБ	.050	BV	110.00	125.00	200.00
	1910 ЭБ	.100	BV	110.00	125.00	200.00
	1911 ЭБ	.050	BV	110.00	125.00	200.00
	Common date	—	—	—	Proof	1800.

12 ROUBLES

41.4100 g, PLATINUM, 1.3311 oz APW
Mint mark: СПБ

C#	Date	Mintage	Fine	VF	XF	Unc
179	1830	119 pcs.	2000.	3250.	4500.	9000.
	1831	1,463	1650.	2750.	4000.	6500.
	1832	1,102	1650.	2750.	4000.	6500.
	1833	255 pcs.	2000.	3250.	4500.	9000.
	1834	11 pcs.	—	—	Proof	8000.
	1835	127 pcs.	2000.	3250.	4500.	9000.
	1836	11 pcs.	—	—	Proof	8000.
	1837	53 pcs.	2000.	3500.	5500.	10,000.
	1838	12 pcs.	—	—	Rare	—
	1839	2 pcs.	—	—	Rare	—
	1840	1 pc.	—	—	Rare	—
	1841	75 pcs.	2000.	3500.	5500.	10,000.
	1842	115 pcs.	2000.	3300.	5500.	10,000.
	1843	122 pcs.	2000.	3500.	5500.	10,000.
	1844	4 pcs.	—	—	Proof	7000.
	1845	2 pcs.	—	—	Rare	—
	Common date	—	—	—	Proof	6500.

NOTE: Varieties exist.

15 ROUBLES

12.9039 g, .900 GOLD, .3734 oz AGW
Mint: St. Petersburg-w/o mint mark

Y#	Date	Mintage	Fine	VF	XF	Unc
65	1897 АГ	11.900	BV	170.00	190.00	225.00

25 ROUBLES

32.7200 g, .917 GOLD, .9640 oz AGW
Mint mark: СПБ

C#	Date	Mintage	Fine	VF	XF	Unc
27	1876	100 pcs.	—	—	Proof	17,600.

NOTE: Realized in Stack's International sale 3-88.

32.2500 g, .900 GOLD, .9332 oz AGW
Mint: St. Petersburg-w/o mint mark
Rev. leg: 2-1/2 ИМПЕРІАЛА (IMPERIALS).

Y#	Date	Mintage	Fine	VF	XF	Unc
A65	1896	300 pcs.	—	4000.	5000.	7000.
	1908	150 pcs.	—	5500.	7500.	9500.
	1908	25 pcs.	—	—	Proof	13,000.

37 ROUBLES 50 KOPEKS

32.2500 g, .900 GOLD, .9335 oz AGW
Mint: St. Petersburg-w/o mint mark
Rev. leg: 100 ФРАНКОВЪ (Francs).

Y#	Date	Mintage	Fine	VF	XF	Unc
B65	1902	225 pcs.	—	4000.	5000.	9000.
	1902	—	—	—	Proof	15,400.

NOTE: Realized in Stack's International sale 3-88.

COPPER-NICKEL
Rev: Letter "P" after "1902 G".
Plain edge

Y#	Date	Mintage	Fine	VF	XF	Unc
B65a	1902 G P (restrike)	—	—	—	—	

PCOCP (R.S.F.S.R.)

РСФСР (Россиискои Социалистическои ФедератиЯ вноИ Советскои РеспуБлики) R.S.F.S.R. (Russian Soviet Federated Socialist Republic)

MONETARY SYSTEM
100 Kopeks = 1 Rouble

10 KOPEKS

1.8000 g, .500 SILVER, .0289 oz ASW

Y#	Date	Mintage	Fine	VF	XF	Unc
80	1921	.950	5.00	10.00	25.00	50.00
	1921	—	—	—	Proof	250.00
	1922	18.640	1.00	2.00	4.00	10.00
	1922	—	—	—	Proof	115.00
	1923	33.424	1.00	2.00	4.00	8.00
	1923	—	—	—	Proof	60.00

15 KOPEKS

2.7000 g, .500 SILVER, .0434 oz ASW

Y#	Date	Mintage	Fine	VF	XF	Unc
81	1921	.933	6.00	12.00	30.00	60.00
	1921	—	—	—	Proof	275.00
	1922	13.633	2.00	3.00	6.00	15.00
	1922	—	—	—	Proof	140.00
	1923	28.504	1.50	2.50	4.50	9.00
	1923	—	—	—	Proof	80.00

20 KOPEKS

3.6000 g, .500 SILVER, .0578 oz ASW

Y#	Date	Mintage	Fine	VF	XF	Unc
82	1921	.825	6.00	12.00	30.00	60.00
	1921	—	—	—	Proof	300.00
	1922	14.220	2.00	4.00	8.00	18.00
	1922	—	—	—	Proof	165.00
	1923	27.580	2.00	3.50	7.00	12.00
	1923	—	—	—	Proof	100.00

NOTE: Varieties exist.

50 KOPEKS

9.9980 g, .900 SILVER, .2893 oz ASW
Mintmasters initials on edge.

Y#	Date	Mintage	Fine	VF	XF	Unc
83	1921 АГ	1.400	5.00	7.00	10.00	25.00
	1921 АГ	—	—	—	Proof	325.00
	1922 АГ	8.224	10.00	15.00	25.00	60.00
	1922 АГ	—	—	—	Proof	350.00
	1922 ПЛ	I.A.	5.00	7.00	10.00	25.00
	1922 ПЛ	—	—	—	Proof	250.00

ROUBLE

19.9960 g, .900 SILVER, .5786 oz ASW
Mintmasters initials on edge.

Y#	Date	Mintage	Fine	VF	XF	Unc
84	1921 АГ	1.000	6.00	12.00	20.00	65.00
	1921 АГ	—	—	—	Proof	425.00
	1922 АГ	2.050	10.00	20.00	40.00	100.00
	1922 АГ	—	—	—	Proof	600.00
	1922 ПЛ	I.A.	10.00	20.00	40.00	100.00
	1922 ПЛ	—	—	—	Proof	450.00

CCCP (U.S.S.R.)

CCCP (Союз Советских Социалистических Республик) U.S.S.R. (Union of Soviet Socialist Republics).

MONETARY SYSTEM
100 Kopecks = 1 Rouble

1/2 KOPEK

COPPER

Y#	Date	Mintage	Fine	VF	XF	Unc
75	1925	45.380	3.50	7.50	14.50	30.00
	1927	—	3.50	7.50	14.50	30.00
	1927	—	—	—	Proof	100.00
	1928	—	4.50	8.00	16.50	35.00

KOPEK

BRONZE

Y#	Date	Mintage	Fine	VF	XF	Unc
76	1924 reeded edge					
		34.705	2.00	4.00	8.00	20.00
	1924 reeded edge					
		—	—	—	Proof	125.00
	1924 plain edge					
		Inc. Ab.	30.00	60.00	120.00	250.00
	1925	141.806	45.00	90.00	160.00	275.00

ALUMINUM-BRONZE

Y#	Date	Mintage	Fine	VF	XF	Unc
91	1926	87.915	.50	1.00	1.50	5.50
	1926	—	—	—	Proof	60.00
	1927	—	.50	1.00	1.50	5.00
	1928	—	.50	1.00	1.50	5.00
	1929	95.950	.50	1.00	1.50	5.00
	1930	85.351	.50	1.00	1.50	5.00
	1931	106.100	.50	1.00	1.50	5.00
	1932	56.900	.50	1.00	1.50	5.00
	1933	111.257	.50	1.00	1.50	5.00
	1934	100.245	.50	1.00	1.50	5.00
	1935	66.405	.50	1.00	2.00	6.00

NOTE: Varieties exist.

Y#	Date	Mintage	Fine	VF	XF	Unc
98	1935	Inc.Y91	.50	1.00	2.50	9.00
	1936	132.204	.50	1.00	2.00	7.50

Y#	Date	Mintage	Fine	VF	XF	Unc
105	1937	—	.25	.50	.75	1.50
	1938	—	.25	.50	.75	1.50
	1939	—	.25	.50	.75	1.50
	1940	—	.25	.50	.75	1.50
	1941	—	.50	1.00	2.00	6.00
	1945	—	.50	1.00	2.00	6.00
	1946	—	.50	1.00	2.00	6.00

NOTE: Varieties exist.

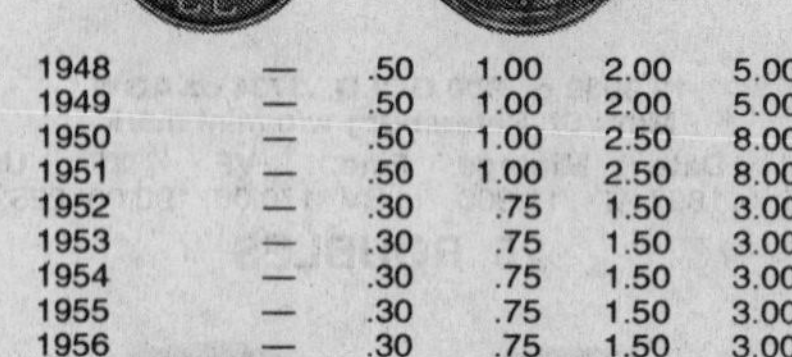

Y#	Date	Mintage	Fine	VF	XF	Unc
112	1948	—	.50	1.00	2.00	5.00
	1949	—	.50	1.00	2.00	5.00
	1950	—	.50	1.00	2.50	8.00
	1951	—	.50	1.00	2.50	8.00
	1952	—	.30	.75	1.50	3.00
	1953	—	.30	.75	1.50	3.00
	1954	—	.30	.75	1.50	3.00
	1955	—	.30	.75	1.50	3.00
	1956	—	.30	.75	1.50	3.00

NOTE: Varieties exist.

Y#	Date	Mintage	Fine	VF	XF	Unc
119	1957	—	1.00	2.00	4.00	12.00

BRASS

Y#	Date	Mintage	Fine	VF	XF	Unc
126	1961	—	.10	.15	.25	1.00
	1962	—	.10	.15	.25	.50
	1963	—	.10	.15	.25	.50
	1964	—	.20	.30	.50	2.00
	1965	—	.10	.15	.25	.50
	1966	—	.10	.15	.25	.50
	1967	—	.10	.15	.25	.50
	1968	—	.10	.15	.25	.50
	1969	—	.10	.15	.25	.50
	1970	—	.10	.15	.25	.50
	1971	—	.10	.15	.25	.50
	1972	—	.10	.15	.25	.50
	1973	—	.10	.15	.25	.50
	1974	—	.10	.15	.25	.50
	1975	—	.10	.15	.25	.50
	1976	—	.10	.15	.25	.50
	1977	—	.10	.15	.25	.50
	1978	—	.10	.15	.25	.50
	1979	—	.10	.15	.25	.50
	1980	—	.10	.15	.25	.50
	1981	—	.10	.15	.25	.50
	1982	—	.10	.15	.25	.50
	1983	—	.10	.15	.25	.50
	1984	—	.10	.15	.25	.50
	1985	—	.10	.15	.25	.50
	1986	—	.10	.15	.25	.50
	1987	—	.10	.15	.25	.50
	1988	—	.10	.15	.25	.50
	1989	—	.10	.15	.20	.35
	1990	—	.10	.15	.20	.35
	1991(m)	—	.10	.15	.20	.35
	1991(l)	—	.10	.15	.20	.35

NOTE: Varieties exist.

2 KOPEKS

BRONZE

Y#	Date	Mintage	Fine	VF	XF	Unc
77	1924 reeded edge					
		119.996	3.50	7.50	15.00	35.00
	1924 plain edge		30.00	60.00	120.00	250.00
	1925	Inc. Ab.	—	—	Rare	—

NOTE: Varieties exist.

ALUMINUM-BRONZE

Y#	Date	Mintage	Fine	VF	XF	Unc
92	1926	105.053	.25	.50	1.00	3.00
	1926	—	—	—	Proof	65.00
	1927	—	—	—	Rare	—
	1928	—	.25	.50	1.00	3.00
	1929	80.000	.25	.50	1.00	4.00
	1930	134.186	.25	.50	1.00	3.00
	1931	99.523	.25	.50	1.00	3.00
	1932	39.573	.35	.65	1.25	3.50
	1933	54.874	.50	1.00	2.00	6.00
	1934	61.574	.35	.65	1.25	3.50
	1935	81.121	.35	.65	1.50	4.00

NOTE: Varieties exist.

Y#	Date	Mintage	Fine	VF	XF	Unc
99	1935	—	.50	1.00	2.50	9.00
	1936	94.354	.25	.50	2.00	7.00

NOTE: Varieties exist.

Y#	Date	Mintage	Fine	VF	XF	Unc
106	1937	—	.25	.50	1.00	2.50
	1938	—	.25	.50	1.00	2.50
	1939	—	.25	.50	1.00	2.50
	1940	—	.25	.50	1.00	2.50
	1941	—	.25	.50	1.00	2.50
	1945	—	.50	1.00	2.00	5.00
	1946	—	.25	.50	1.00	4.00
	1948	—	40.00	70.00	130.00	225.00

Y#	Date	Mintage	Fine	VF	XF	Unc
113	1948	—	.25	.50	1.00	2.50
	1949	—	.25	.50	1.00	2.50
	1950	—	.25	.50	1.00	2.50
	1951	—	.50	1.00	2.00	6.00
	1952	—	.25	.50	1.00	3.00
	1953	—	.20	.50	1.00	2.00
	1954	—	.20	.50	1.00	2.00
	1955	—	.20	.50	1.00	2.00
	1956	—	.20	.50	1.00	2.00

NOTE: Varieties exist.

Y#	Date	Mintage	Fine	VF	XF	Unc
120	1957	—	.50	1.00	2.50	9.00

BRASS

Y#	Date	Mintage	Fine	VF	XF	Unc
127	1961	—	.10	.15	.25	.50
	1962	—	.10	.15	.25	.50
	1963	—	.10	.15	.25	.50
	1964	—	.15	.25	.50	1.00
	1965	—	.10	.15	.25	.50

Y#	Date	Mintage	Fine	VF	XF	Unc
7	1966	—	.10	.15	.25	.50
	1967	—	.10	.15	.25	.50
	1968	—	.10	.15	.25	.50
	1969	—	.10	.15	.25	.50
	1970	—	.10	.15	.25	.50
	1971	—	.10	.15	.25	.50
	1972	—	.10	.15	.25	.50
	1973	—	.10	.15	.25	.50
	1974	—	.10	.15	.25	.50
	1975	—	.10	.15	.25	.50
	1976	—	.10	.15	.25	.50
	1977	—	.10	.15	.25	.50
	1978	—	.10	.15	.25	.50
	1979	—	.10	.15	.25	.50
	1980	—	.10	.15	.25	.50
	1981	—	.10	.15	.25	.50
	1982	—	.10	.15	.25	.50
	1983	—	.10	.15	.25	.50
	1984	—	.10	.15	.25	.50
	1985	—	.10	.15	.25	.50
	1986	—	.10	.15	.25	.50
	1987	—	.10	.15	.25	.50
	1988	—	.10	.15	.25	.50
	1989	—	.10	.15	.20	.35
	1990	—	.10	.15	.20	.35
	1991(m)	—	.10	.15	.20	.35
	1991(l)	—	.10	.15	.20	.35

OTE: Varieties exist.

3 KOPEKS

BRONZE

Y#	Date	Mintage	Fine	VF	XF	Unc
8	1924 reeded edge					
		101.283	50.00	100.00	175.00	275.00
	1924 plain edge					
		Inc. Ab.	3.50	7.50	15.00	35.00

OTE: Varieties exist.

ALUMINUM-BRONZE

Y#	Date	Mintage	Fine	VF	XF	Unc
3	1926	19.940	1.25	2.00	4.00	7.00
	1926	—	—	—	Proof	75.00
	1926 obv. of Y#100		—	—	Rare	—
	1927	—	5.00	10.00	20.00	40.00
	1928	—	1.00	2.00	4.00	7.00
	1929	50.150	1.00	2.00	4.00	8.00
	1930	74.159	.25	.50	1.00	4.00
	1931	121.168	.25	.50	1.00	4.00
	1931 w/o CCCP obv.		—	—	Rare	—
	1932	37.718	.25	.50	1.00	4.00
	1933	44.764	.25	.50	2.00	6.00
	1934	44.529	.25	.50	2.00	6.00
	1935	58.303	.25	.50	2.50	7.00

IOTE: Varieties exist.

Y#	Date	Mintage	Fine	VF	XF	Unc
00	1935	—	.50	2.00	5.00	14.00
	1936	62.757	.25	1.00	4.00	10.00

IOTE: Varieties exist.

Y#	Date	Mintage	Fine	VF	XF	Unc
07	1937	—	.25	.50	1.00	4.00
	1938	—	.25	.50	1.00	4.00
	1939	—	.25	.50	1.00	4.00
	1940	—	.25	.50	1.00	3.00
	1941	—	.25	.50	1.00	4.00
	1943	—	.25	.50	1.00	5.00
	1945	—	.50	1.00	3.00	9.00
	1946	—	.25	.50	1.00	5.00
	1948	—	40.00	70.00	130.00	225.00

IOTE: Varieties exist.

Y#	Date	Mintage	Fine	VF	XF	Unc
114	1948	—	.25	.50	1.00	5.00
	1949	—	.25	.50	1.00	4.00
	1950	—	.25	.50	1.00	4.00
	1951	—	.50	1.00	2.00	7.00
	1952	—	.25	.50	1.00	4.00
	1953	—	.25	.50	1.00	3.00
	1954	—	.25	.50	1.00	3.00
	1955	—	.25	.50	1.00	3.00
	1956	—	.25	.50	1.00	3.00
	1957	—	2.50	5.00	10.00	30.00

NOTE: Varieties exist.

Y#	Date	Mintage	Fine	VF	XF	Unc
121	1957	—	.50	1.00	2.50	9.00

BRASS

Y#	Date	Mintage	Fine	VF	XF	Unc
128	1961	—	.10	.15	.25	.60
	1962	—	.10	.15	.25	.60
	1965	—	.10	.15	.25	.60
	1966	—	.10	.15	.25	.60
	1967	—	.10	.15	.25	.60
	1968	—	.10	.15	.25	.60
	1969	—	.10	.15	.25	.60
	1970	—	.10	.15	.25	.60
	1971	—	.10	.15	.25	.60
	1972	—	.10	.15	.25	.60
	1973	—	.10	.15	.25	.60
	1974	—	.10	.15	.25	.60
	1975	—	.10	.15	.25	.60
	1976	—	.10	.15	.25	.60
	1977	—	.10	.15	.25	.60
	1978	—	.10	.15	.25	.60
	1979	—	.10	.15	.25	.60
	1980	—	.10	.15	.25	.60
	1981	—	.10	.15	.25	.60
	1982	—	.10	.15	.25	.60
	1983	—	.10	.15	.25	.60
	1984	—	.10	.15	.25	.60
	1985	—	.10	.15	.25	.60
	1986	—	.10	.15	.25	.60
	1987	—	.10	.15	.25	.60
	1988	—	.10	.15	.25	.60
	1989	—	.10	.15	.20	.40
	1990	—	.10	.15	.20	.40
	1991(m)	—	.10	.15	.20	.40
	1991(l)	—	.10	.15	.20	.40

NOTE: Varieties exist.

5 KOPEKS

BRONZE

Y#	Date	Mintage	Fine	VF	XF	Unc
79	1924 reeded edge					
		88.510	50.00	100.00	175.00	275.00
	1924 plain edge					
		Inc. Ab.	5.00	10.00	20.00	50.00

NOTE: Varieties exist.

ALUMINUM-BRONZE

Y#	Date	Mintage	Fine	VF	XF	Unc
94	1926	14.697	1.00	2.00	6.00	10.00
	1926	—	—	—	Proof	85.00
	1927	—	2.00	4.00	12.00	30.00
	1928	—	.50	1.00	2.00	6.00
	1929	20.220	.50	1.00	2.00	6.00
	1930	44.490	.50	1.00	1.50	5.00
	1931	89.540	.50	1.00	1.50	5.00
	1932	65.100	.50	1.00	1.50	5.00
	1933	18.135	3.00	6.00	15.00	50.00
	1934	5.354	2.00	4.00	12.00	30.00
	1935	11.735	3.00	6.00	15.00	50.00

NOTE: Varieties exist.

Y#	Date	Mintage	Fine	VF	XF	Unc
101	1935	—	2.00	4.00	9.00	26.00
	1936	5.242	2.00	4.00	9.00	28.00

NOTE: Varieties exist.

Y#	Date	Mintage	Fine	VF	XF	Unc
108	1937	—	2.00	4.00	9.00	28.00
	1938	—	.25	.50	1.00	4.00
	1939	—	.25	.50	1.00	4.00
	1940	—	.25	.50	1.00	3.00
	1941	—	.25	.50	1.00	4.00
	1943	—	.25	.50	1.00	4.00
	1945	—	1.00	2.00	5.00	12.00
	1946	—	.25	.50	1.00	6.00

NOTE: Varieties exist.

Y#	Date	Mintage	Fine	VF	XF	Unc
115	1948	—	.25	.50	1.50	5.00
	1949	—	.25	.50	1.00	4.00
	1950	—	.25	.50	1.00	4.00
	1951	—	.50	1.00	2.00	5.00
	1952	—	.25	.50	1.00	4.00
	1953	—	.25	.50	1.00	4.00
	1954	—	.25	.50	1.00	4.00
	1955	—	.25	.50	1.00	4.00
	1956	—	.25	.50	1.00	4.00

NOTE: Varieties exist.

Y#	Date	Mintage	Fine	VF	XF	Unc
122	1957	—	1.00	2.00	3.00	9.00

NOTE: Varieties exist.

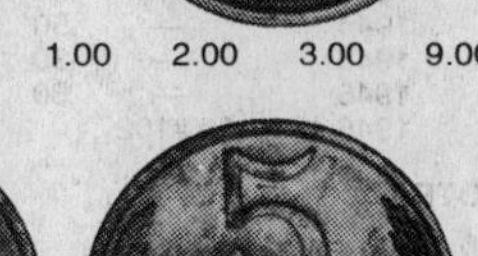

Y#	Date	Mintage	Fine	VF	XF	Unc
129	1961	—	.10	.15	.30	.75
	1962	—	.10	.15	.30	.75
	1965	—	.25	.50	1.00	3.00
	1966	—	.20	.30	.75	2.00
	1967	—	.15	.25	.50	1.50
	1968	—	.15	.25	.50	1.50
	1969	—	.20	.30	.75	2.00
	1970	—	.50	1.00	2.00	5.00
	1971	—	.15	.25	.50	1.50
	1972	—	.15	.25	.50	1.50
	1973	—	.10	.15	.30	.75
	1974	—	.10	.15	.30	.75
	1975	—	.10	.15	.30	.75

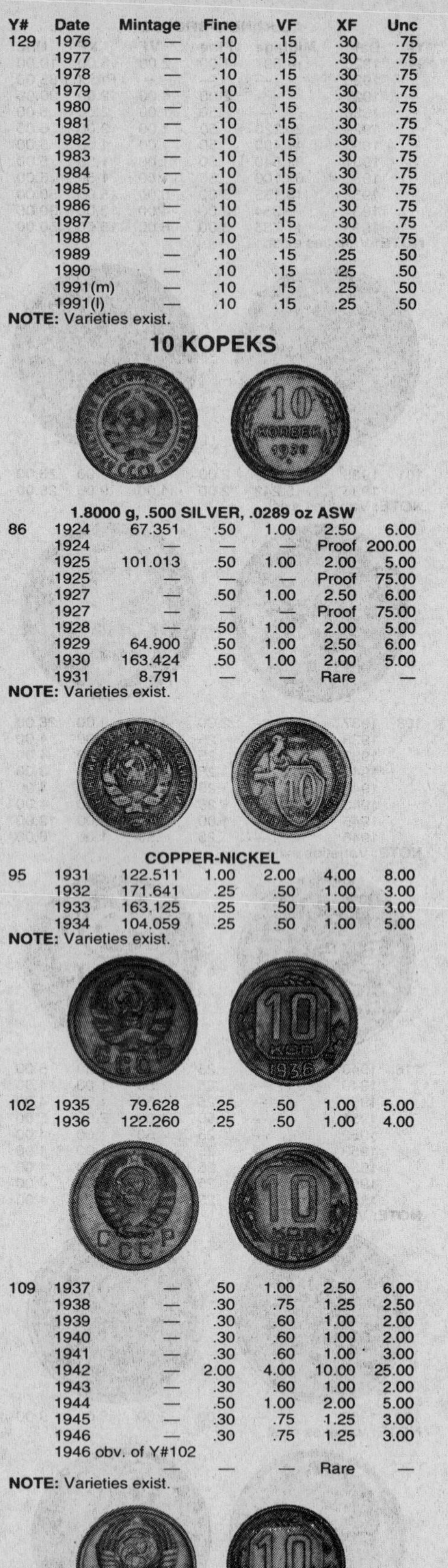

Y#	Date	Mintage	Fine	VF	XF	Unc
129	1976	—	.10	.15	.30	.75
	1977	—	.10	.15	.30	.75
	1978	—	.10	.15	.30	.75
	1979	—	.10	.15	.30	.75
	1980	—	.10	.15	.30	.75
	1981	—	.10	.15	.30	.75
	1982	—	.10	.15	.30	.75
	1983	—	.10	.15	.30	.75
	1984	—	.10	.15	.30	.75
	1985	—	.10	.15	.30	.75
	1986	—	.10	.15	.30	.75
	1987	—	.10	.15	.30	.75
	1988	—	.10	.15	.30	.75
	1989	—	.10	.15	.25	.50
	1990	—	.10	.15	.25	.50
	1991(m)	—	.10	.15	.25	.50
	1991(l)	—	.10	.15	.25	.50

NOTE: Varieties exist.

10 KOPEKS

1.8000 g, .500 SILVER, .0289 oz ASW

Y#	Date	Mintage	Fine	VF	XF	Unc
86	1924	67.351	.50	1.00	2.50	6.00
	1924	—	—	—	Proof	200.00
	1925	101.013	.50	1.00	2.00	5.00
	1925	—	—	—	Proof	75.00
	1927	—	.50	1.00	2.50	6.00
	1927	—	—	—	Proof	75.00
	1928	—	.50	1.00	2.00	5.00
	1929	64.900	.50	1.00	2.50	6.00
	1930	163.424	.50	1.00	2.00	5.00
	1931	8.791	—	—	Rare	—

NOTE: Varieties exist.

COPPER-NICKEL

Y#	Date	Mintage	Fine	VF	XF	Unc
95	1931	122.511	1.00	2.00	4.00	8.00
	1932	171.641	.25	.50	1.00	3.00
	1933	163.125	.25	.50	1.00	3.00
	1934	104.059	.25	.50	1.00	5.00

NOTE: Varieties exist.

Y#	Date	Mintage	Fine	VF	XF	Unc
102	1935	79.628	.25	.50	1.00	5.00
	1936	122.260	.25	.50	1.00	4.00

Y#	Date	Mintage	Fine	VF	XF	Unc
109	1937	—	.50	1.00	2.50	6.00
	1938	—	.30	.75	1.25	2.50
	1939	—	.30	.60	1.00	2.00
	1940	—	.30	.60	1.00	2.00
	1941	—	.30	.60	1.00	3.00
	1942	—	2.00	4.00	10.00	25.00
	1943	—	.30	.60	1.00	2.00
	1944	—	.50	1.00	2.00	5.00
	1945	—	.30	.75	1.25	3.00
	1946	—	.30	.75	1.25	3.00
	1946 obv. of Y#102	—	—	—	Rare	—

NOTE: Varieties exist.

Obv: 8 and 7 ribbons on wreath.

Y#	Date	Mintage	Fine	VF	XF	Unc
116	1948	—	.25	.50	2.00	5.00
	1949	—	.25	.50	1.00	3.00
	1950	—	.25	.50	1.00	2.00
	1951	—	.25	.50	1.00	5.00
	1952	—	.25	.50	1.00	4.00
	1953	—	.25	.50	1.00	2.00
	1954	—	.25	.50	1.00	2.00
	1955	—	.25	.50	1.00	2.00
	1956	—	.25	.50	1.00	2.00
	1956 rev. of Y#123	—	50.00	75.00	150.00	250.00

NOTE: Varieties exist.

Obv: 7 and 7 ribbons on wreath.

Y#	Date	Mintage	Fine	VF	XF	Unc
123	1957 rev. of Y#116	—	50.00	75.00	150.00	250.00
	1957	—	.25	.50	2.00	6.00

COPPER-NICKEL-ZINC

Y#	Date	Mintage	Fine	VF	XF	Unc
130.1	1961	—	.10	.20	.35	.75
	1962	—	.10	.20	.35	.75
	1965	—	.10	.20	.35	.75
	1966	—	.10	.20	.35	.75
	1967	—	.10	.20	.35	.75
	1968	—	.10	.20	.35	.75
	1969	—	.10	.20	.35	.75
	1970	—	.10	.20	.35	.75
	1971	—	.10	.20	.35	.75
	1972	—	.10	.20	.35	.75
	1973	—	.10	.20	.35	.75
	1974	—	.10	.20	.35	.75
	1975	—	.10	.20	.35	.75
	1976	—	.10	.20	.35	.75
	1977	—	.10	.20	.35	.75
	1978	—	.10	.20	.35	.75
	1979	—	.10	.20	.35	.75
	1980	—	.10	.20	.35	.75
	1981	—	.10	.20	.35	.75
	1982	—	.10	.20	.35	.75
	1983	—	.10	.20	.35	.75
	1984	—	.10	.20	.35	.75
	1985	—	.10	.20	.35	.75
	1986	—	.10	.20	.35	.75
	1987	—	.10	.20	.35	.75
	1988	—	.10	.20	.35	.75
	1989	—	.10	.20	.30	.50
	1990	—	.10	.20	.30	.50
	1991(l)	—	.10	.20	.30	.50
	1991(m)	—	.10	.20	.30	.50

Mint mark: M

Y#	Date	Mintage	Fine	VF	XF	Unc
130.2	1990	—	.10	.20	.30	.50

50th Anniversary of Revolution

Y#	Date	Mintage	Fine	VF	XF	Unc
136	1967	49.789	—	.20	.30	1.00
	1967	.211	—	—	BU	—

15 KOPEKS

2.7000 g, .500 SILVER, .0434 oz ASW

Y#	Date	Mintage	Fine	VF	XF	Unc
87	1924	72.426	.75	1.00	2.00	6.00
	1924	—	—	—	Proof	200.00
	1925	112.709	1.00	1.00	2.00	4.00
	1925	—	—	—	Proof	75.00
	1927	—	1.00	1.00	2.00	4.00
	1927	—	—	—	Proof	75.00
	1928	—	1.00	1.00	2.00	4.00
	1929	46.400	1.00	1.00	2.00	4.50
	1930	79.868	1.00	1.00	2.00	4.00
	1931	5.099	—	—	Rare	—

NOTE: Varieties exist.

COPPER-NICKEL

Y#	Date	Mintage	Fine	VF	XF	Unc
96	1931	75.859	.50	1.00	1.75	4.00
	1932	136.046	.50	1.00	1.75	3.50
	1933	127.591	.50	1.00	1.75	3.50
	1934	58.367	.50	1.00	2.50	5.00

NOTE: Varieties exist.

Y#	Date	Mintage	Fine	VF	XF	Unc
103	1935	51.308	.50	1.00	1.75	4.00
	1936	52.183	.35	.75	1.50	3.00

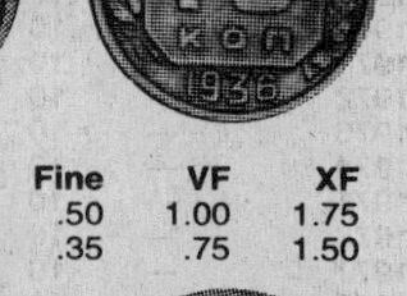

Y#	Date	Mintage	Fine	VF	XF	Unc
110	1937	—	.35	.75	1.50	3.00
	1938	—	.30	.50	1.00	2.00
	1939	—	.30	.50	1.00	2.00
	1940	—	.30	.50	1.00	2.00
	1941	—	.30	.50	1.00	2.00
	1942	—	2.00	4.00	10.00	25.00
	1943	—	.35	.75	1.25	2.50
	1944	—	1.00	2.00	5.00	10.00
	1945	—	.50	1.25	2.50	5.00
	1946	—	.35	.75	2.00	4.00

NOTE: Varieties exist.

Y#	Date	Mintage	Fine	VF	XF	Unc
117	1948	—	.35	.75	2.00	4.00
	1949	—	.35	.75	1.50	3.50
	1950	—	.30	.50	1.00	2.00
	1951	—	.50	1.00	2.50	8.00
	1952	—	.30	.50	1.00	2.00
	1953	—	.30	.50	1.00	2.00
	1954	—	.30	.50	1.00	2.00
	1955	—	.30	.50	1.00	2.00
	1956	—	.30	.50	1.00	2.00

NOTE: Varieties exist.

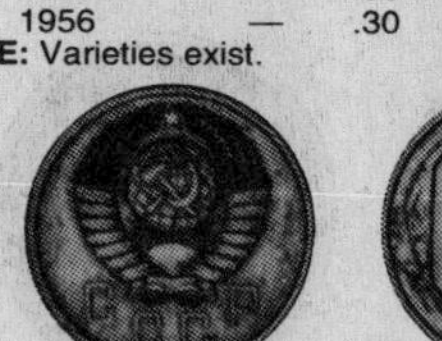

Y#	Date	Mintage	Fine	VF	XF	Unc
124	1957	—	.30	.50	1.00	5.00

COPPER-NICKEL-ZINC

Y#	Date	Mintage	Fine	VF	XF	Unc
131	1961	—	.10	.20	.40	.75
	1962	—	.10	.20	.40	1.00
	1965	—	.10	.20	.40	.75
	1966	—	.10	.20	.40	.75
	1967	—	.10	.20	.40	.75
	1968	—	.10	.20	.40	.75
	1969	—	.10	.20	.40	.75
	1970	—	.10	.20	.40	.75
	1971	—	.10	.20	.40	.75
	1972	—	.10	.20	.40	.75
	1973	—	.10	.20	.40	.75
	1974	—	.10	.20	.40	.75
	1975	—	.10	.20	.40	.75
	1976	—	.10	.20	.40	.75
	1977	—	.10	.20	.40	.75
	1978	—	.10	.20	.40	.75
	1979	—	.10	.20	.40	.75
	1980	—	.10	.20	.40	.75
	1981	—	.10	.20	.40	.75
	1982	—	.10	.20	.40	.75
	1983	—	.10	.20	.40	.75
	1984	—	.10	.20	.40	.75
	1985	—	.10	.20	.40	.75
	1986	—	.10	.20	.40	.75
	1987	—	.10	.20	.40	.75
	1988	—	.10	.20	.40	.75
	1989	—	.10	.20	.30	.50
	1990	—	.10	.20	.30	.50
	1991(l)	—	.10	.20	.30	.50
	1991(m)	—	.10	.20	.30	.50

50th Anniversary of Revolution

#	Date	Mintage	Fine	VF	XF	Unc
37	1967	49.789	.15	.30	.50	1.50
	1967	.211	—	—	BU	—

20 KOPEKS

3.6000 g, .500 SILVER, .0578 oz ASW

8	1924	93.810	1.00	1.75	3.00	7.00
	1924	—	—	—	Proof	225.00
	1925	135.188	1.00	1.75	3.00	6.00
	1925	—	—	—	Proof	75.00
	1927	—	1.00	1.75	3.00	8.00
	1928	—	1.00	1.75	3.00	6.00
	1929	67.250	1.00	1.75	3.00	6.00
	1930	125.658	1.00	1.75	3.00	6.00
	1931	9.530	—	—	Rare	—

COPPER-NICKEL

7	1931	82.200	.50	1.00	2.00	4.00
	1932	175.350	.50	1.00	2.00	4.00
	1933	143.927	.50	1.00	2.00	4.00
	1934	70.425	—	—	Rare	—

OTE: Varieties exist.

04	1935	125.165	.50	1.00	2.00	4.50
	1936	52.968	.50	1.00	2.00	5.00

OTE: Varieties exist.

11	1937	—	.40	.60	1.00	2.00
	1938	—	.40	.60	1.00	2.00
	1939	—	.40	.60	1.00	2.00
	1940	—	.40	.60	1.00	2.00
	1941	—	.40	.60	1.00	2.00
	1942	—	.50	.75	1.50	3.00
	1943	—	.40	.60	1.00	2.00
	1944	—	.60	1.25	2.50	5.00
	1945	—	.40	.60	1.50	3.00
	1946	—	.45	.75	2.00	4.00

OTE: Varieties exist.

18	1948	—	.45	.75	1.50	4.00
	1949	—	.45	.75	1.50	4.00
	1950	—	1.00	2.00	5.00	10.00
	1951	—	.50	1.00	2.50	7.00
	1952	—	.40	.60	1.00	2.00
	1953	—	.40	.60	1.00	2.00
	1954	—	.40	.60	1.00	2.00
	1955	—	.40	.60	1.00	2.00
	1956	—	.40	.60	1.00	2.00

OTE: Varieties exist.

25	1957	—	.40	.60	1.00	4.00

COPPER-NICKEL-ZINC

Y#	Date	Mintage	Fine	VF	XF	Unc
132.1	1961	—	.15	.30	.50	1.00
	1962	—	.15	.35	.75	1.50
	1965	—	.15	.30	.50	1.00
	1966	—	.15	.30	.50	1.00
	1967	—	.15	.30	.50	1.00
	1968	—	.15	.30	.50	1.00
	1969	—	.15	.30	.50	1.00
	1970	—	.15	.30	.50	1.00
	1971	—	.15	.30	.50	1.00
	1972	—	.15	.30	.50	1.00
	1973	—	.15	.30	.50	1.00
	1974	—	.15	.30	.50	1.00
	1975	—	.15	.30	.50	1.00
	1976	—	.15	.30	.50	1.00
	1977	—	.15	.30	.50	1.00
	1978	—	.15	.30	.50	1.00
	1979	—	.15	.30	.50	1.00
	1980	—	.15	.30	.50	1.00
	1981	—	.15	.30	.50	1.00
	1982	—	.15	.30	.50	1.00
	1983	—	.15	.30	.50	1.00
	1984	—	.15	.30	.50	1.00
	1985	—	.15	.30	.50	1.00
	1986	—	.15	.30	.50	1.00
	1987	—	.15	.30	.50	1.00
	1988	—	.15	.30	.50	1.00
	1989	—	.10	.20	.30	.75
	1990	—	.10	.20	.30	.75
	1991(l)	—	.10	.20	.30	.75
	1991(m)	—	.10	.20	.30	.75

NOTE: Varieties exist.

Mint mark: Л

132.2	1991	—	.10	.20	.30	.50

50th Anniversary of Revolution

138	1967	49.789	.40	.60	.75	2.00
	1967	.211	—	—	Proof	—

50 KOPEKS

9.9980 g, .900 SILVER, .2893 oz ASW
Edge: Weight shown in old Russian units.

89.1	1924 ПЛ	26.559	5.00	7.00	10.00	22.50
	1924 ПЛ	—	—	—	Proof	250.00
	1924 ТР	40.000	5.00	7.00	10.00	22.50

Edge: Weight shown in grams only.

89.2	1925 ПЛ	43.558	5.00	7.00	10.00	22.50
	1925 ПЛ	—	—	—	Proof	125.00
	1926 ПЛ	24.374	5.00	7.00	10.00	22.50
	1926 ПЛ	—	—	—	Proof	125.00
	1927 ПЛ	—	5.00	7.00	12.00	32.50
	1927 ПЛ	—	—	—	Proof	165.00

NOTE: Varieties exist.

COPPER-NICKEL-ZINC

Plain edge

Y#	Date	Mintage	Fine	VF	XF	Unc
133.1	1961	—	1.00	2.00	5.00	12.00

NOTE: Varieties exist.

Lettered edge

133.2	1964	—	.20	.40	.75	1.50
	1965	—	.20	.40	.75	1.50
	1966	—	.20	.40	.75	1.50
	1967	—	.20	.40	.75	1.50
	1968	—	.20	.40	.75	1.50
	1969	—	.20	.40	.75	1.50
	1970	—	.20	.40	.75	1.50
	1971	—	.20	.40	.75	1.50
	1972	—	.20	.40	.75	1.50
	1973	—	.20	.40	.75	1.50
	1974	—	.20	.40	.75	1.50
	1974	—	—	—	Proof	—
	1975	—	.20	.40	.75	1.50
	1976	—	.20	.40	.75	1.50
	1977	—	.20	.40	.75	1.50
	1978	—	.20	.40	.75	1.50
	1979	—	.20	.40	.75	1.50
	1980	—	.20	.40	.75	1.50
	1981	—	.20	.40	.75	1.50
	1982	—	.20	.40	.75	1.50
	1983	—	.20	.40	.75	1.50
	1984	—	.20	.40	.75	1.50
	1985	—	.20	.40	.75	1.50
	1986	—	.20	.40	.75	1.50
	1987	—	.20	.40	.75	1.50
	1988	—	.20	.40	.75	1.50
	1989	—	.15	.25	.50	1.00
	1990	—	.15	.25	.50	1.00
	1991 M	—	.15	.25	.50	1.00
	1991 L	—	.15	.25	.50	1.00

50th Anniversary of Revolution

139	ND(1967)	49.789	—	1.00	1.50	2.50
	ND(1967)	.211	—	—	BU	—

ROUBLE

19.9960 g, .900 SILVER, .5786 oz ASW
Edge: 18 grams (42.21d).

90.1	1924 ПЛ	12.998	7.50	12.50	25.00	75.00
	1924 ПЛ	—	—	—	Proof	750.00

NOTE: Varieties exist.

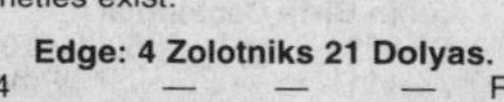

Edge: 4 Zolotniks 21 Dolyas.

90.2	1924	—	—	—	Rare	—

COPPER-NICKEL-ZINC
Plain edge

Y#	Date	Mintage	Fine	VF	XF	Unc
134.1	1961	—	2.00	3.50	6.00	15.00
	Lettered edge					
134.2	1964	—	.40	.75	1.50	2.50
	1965	—	.40	.75	1.50	2.50
	1966	—	.40	.75	1.50	2.50
	1967	—	.40	.75	1.50	2.50
	1968	—	.40	.75	1.50	2.50
	1969	—	.40	.75	1.50	2.50
	1970	—	.40	.75	1.50	2.50
	1971	—	.40	.75	1.50	2.50
	1972	—	.40	.75	1.50	2.50
	1973	—	.40	.75	1.50	2.50
	1974	—	.40	.75	1.50	2.50
	1975	—	.40	.75	1.50	2.50
	1976	—	.40	.75	1.50	2.50
	1977	—	.40	.75	1.50	2.50
	1978	—	.40	.75	1.50	2.50
	1979	—	.40	.75	1.50	2.50
	1980	—	.40	.75	1.50	2.50
	1981	—	.40	.75	1.50	2.50
	1982	—	.40	.75	1.50	2.50
	1983	—	.40	.75	1.50	2.50
	1984	—	.40	.75	1.50	2.50
	1985	—	.40	.75	1.50	2.50
	1986	—	.40	.75	1.50	2.50
	1987	—	.40	.75	1.50	2.50
	1988	—	.40	.75	1.50	2.50
	1989	—	.25	.50	1.00	2.50
	1990	—	.25	.50	1.00	2.50
	1991(m)	—	.25	.50	1.00	2.50
	1991(l)	—	.25	.50	1.00	2.50

20th Anniversary of World War II Victory

Y#	Date	Mintage	Fine	VF	XF	Unc
135.1	1965	59.989	—	.50	1.00	2.00
	1965	.011	—	—	Proof	6.00
	Edge inscription: 1988.N.					
135.2	1965	.055		(restrike)	Proof	3.00

50th Anniversary of Bolshevik Revolution

Y#	Date	Mintage	Fine	VF	XF	Unc
140.1	1967	52.289	—	.50	1.00	2.00
	1967	.211	—	—	BU	5.00
	Edge inscription: 1988.N.					
140.2	1967	.055		(restrike)	Proof	4.00

Lenin Birth Centennial

Y#	Date	Mintage	Fine	VF	XF	Unc
141	1970	99.889	—	.50	1.00	2.00
	1970	.111	—	—	Proof	5.00

30th Anniversary of World War II Victory
Date on edge

Y#	Date	Mintage	Fine	VF	XF	Unc
142.1	1975	14.989	—	.50	1.00	2.00
	1975	1.011	—	—	Proof	4.00

NOTE: Varieties exist.

Y#	Date	Mintage	Fine	VF	XF	Unc
	Edge inscription: 1988.N.					
142.2	1975	.055		(restrike)	Proof	3.00

60th Anniversary of Bolshevik Revolution

Y#	Date	Mintage	Fine	VF	XF	Unc
143.1	1977	4.987	—	.50	1.00	2.00
	1977	.013	—	—	Proof	7.00
	Edge inscription: 1988.N.					
143.2	1977	.055		(restrike)	Proof	3.00

1980 Olympics - Emblem

Y#	Date	Mintage	Fine	VF	XF	Unc
144	1977	8.665	—	.50	1.00	2.00
	1977	.335	—	—	Proof	4.00

1980 Olympics Moscow Kremlin

Y#	Date	Mintage	Fine	VF	XF	Unc
153.1	1978	6.491	—	.50	1.00	2.00
	1978	.510	—	—	Proof	4.00
	Rev: Clock on tower shows Roman 6 instead of 4.					
153.2	1978	Inc. Ab.	—	10.00	20.00	30.00

1980 Olympics Moscow University

Y#	Date	Mintage	Fine	VF	XF	Unc
164	1979	4.666	—	.50	1.00	2.00
	1979	.335	—	—	Proof	4.00

NOTE: Varieties in window arrangements exist.

1980 Olympics Monument, Sputnik and Sojuz

Y#	Date	Mintage	Fine	VF	XF	Unc
165	1979	4.666	—	.50	1.00	2.00
	1979	.335	—	—	Proof	4.00

COPPER-NICKEL
1980 Olympics Dolgorukij Monument

Y#	Date	Mintage	Fine	VF	XF	Unc
177	1980	4.491	—	.50	1.00	2.00
	1980	.510	—	—	Proof	4.00

1980 Olympics

Y#	Date	Mintage	Fine	VF	XF	Unc
178	1980	4.491	—	.50	1.00	2.00
	1980	.510	—	—	Proof	4.00

20th Anniversary of Manned Space Flights-Yuri Gagarin

Y#	Date	Mintage	Fine	VF	XF	Unc
188.1	1981	3.962	—	.50	1.00	2.00
	1981	.038	—	—	Proof	4.00
	Edge inscription: 1988.N.					
188.2	1981	.055		(restrike)	Proof	3.00

Russian-Bulgarian Friendship

Y#	Date	Mintage	Fine	VF	XF	Unc
189.1	1981	1.984	—	.50	1.00	2.00
	1981	.016	—	—	Proof	6.00
	Edge inscription: 1988.N.					
189.2	1981	.055		(restrike)	Proof	3.00

60th Anniversary of the Soviet Union

Y#	Date	Mintage	Fine	VF	XF	Unc
90.1	ND(1982)	1.921	—	.50	1.50	3.00
	ND(1982)	.079	—	—	Proof	6.00

Edge inscription: 1988.N.

Y#	Date	Mintage	Fine	VF	XF	Unc
90.2	ND(1982)	.055	(restrike)		Proof	4.00

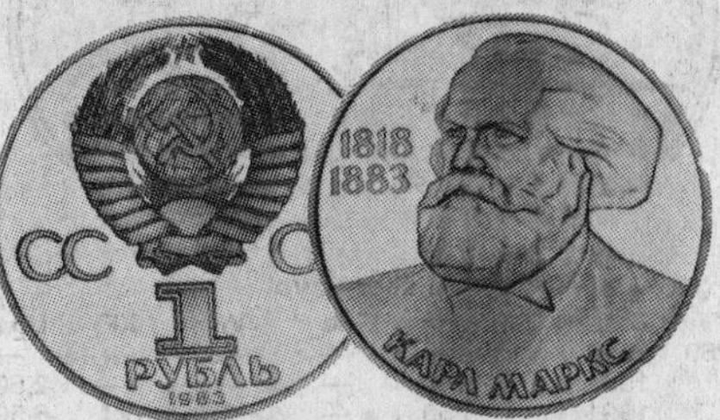

Centennial of Death of Karl Marx

Y#	Date	Mintage	Fine	VF	XF	Unc
91.1	1983	1.921	—	.50	1.50	3.00
	1983	.079	—	—	Proof	6.00

Edge inscription: 1988.N.

Y#	Date	Mintage	Fine	VF	XF	Unc
91.2	1983	.055	(restrike)		Proof	4.00

20th Anniversary of First Woman in Space - Valentina Tereshkova

Y#	Date	Mintage	Fine	VF	XF	Unc
192.1	1983	1.945	—	.50	1.00	2.00
	1983	.055	—	—	Proof	4.00

Edge inscription: 1988.N.

Y#	Date	Mintage	Fine	VF	XF	Unc
192.2	1983	.055	(restrike)		Proof	3.00

Ivan Fedorov - First Russian Printer

Y#	Date	Mintage	Fine	VF	XF	Unc
193.1	1983	1.965	—	.50	1.00	2.00
	1983	.035	—	—	Proof	4.00

Edge inscription: 1988.N.

Y#	Date	Mintage	Fine	VF	XF	Unc
193.2	1983	.055	(restrike)		Proof	3.00

150th Anniversary - Birth of Dimitri Ivanovich Mendeleyev

Y#	Date	Mintage	Fine	VF	XF	Unc
194.1	1984	1.965	—	.50	1.00	2.00
	1984	.035	—	—	Proof	4.00

Edge inscription: 1988.N.

Y#	Date	Mintage	Fine	VF	XF	Unc
194.2	1984	.055	(restrike)		Proof	3.00

125th Anniversary - Birth of Alexander Popov

Y#	Date	Mintage	Fine	VF	XF	Unc
195.1	1984	1.965	—	.50	1.00	2.00
	1984	.035	—	—	Proof	4.00

Edge inscription: 1988.N.

Y#	Date	Mintage	Fine	VF	XF	Unc
195.2	1984	.055	(restrike)		Proof	3.00

185th Anniversary of Birth of Alexander Sergeevich Pushkin

Y#	Date	Mintage	Fine	VF	XF	Unc
196.1	1984	1.965	—	.50	1.00	2.00
	1984	.035	—	—	Proof	4.00

Edge inscription: 1988.N.

Y#	Date	Mintage	Fine	VF	XF	Unc
196.2	1984	.055	(restrike)		Proof	3.00
	1985 (error)	—	—	—	—	—

115th Anniv. - Birth of Vladimir Lenin

Y#	Date	Mintage	Fine	VF	XF	Unc
197.1	1985	1.960	—	.50	1.50	3.00
	1985	.040	—	—	Proof	6.00

Edge inscription: 1988.N.

Y#	Date	Mintage	Fine	VF	XF	Unc
197.2	1985	.055	(restrike)		Proof	4.00
	1988 (error)	—	—	—	—	—

40th Anniversary of World War II Victory

Y#	Date	Mintage	Fine	VF	XF	Unc
198.1	1985	5.960	—	.50	1.00	2.00
	1985	.040	—	—	Proof	4.00

Edge inscription: 1988.N.

Y#	Date	Mintage	Fine	VF	XF	Unc
198.2	1985	.055	(restrike)		Proof	3.00

12th World Youth Festival in Moscow

Y#	Date	Mintage	Fine	VF	XF	Unc
199.1	1985	5.960	—	.50	1.00	2.00
	1985	.040	—	—	Proof	4.00

Edge inscription: 1988.N.

Y#	Date	Mintage	Fine	VF	XF	Unc
199.2	1985	.055	(restrike)		Proof	3.00

165th Anniversary - Birth of Friedrich Engels

Y#	Date	Mintage	Fine	VF	XF	Unc
200.1	1985	1.960	—	.50	1.50	3.00
	1985	.040	—	—	Proof	6.00

Edge inscription: 1988.N.

Y#	Date	Mintage	Fine	VF	XF	Unc
200.2	1983 (error)	—	—	—	—	—
	1985	.055	(restrike)		Proof	4.00

International Year of Peace

Y#	Date	Mintage	Fine	VF	XF	Unc
201.1	1986	3.955	—	.50	1.00	2.00
	1986	.045	—	—	Proof	4.00

Edge inscription: 1988.N.

Y#	Date	Mintage	Fine	VF	XF	Unc
201.2	1986	.055	(restrike)		Proof	3.00

Rouble written РУБЛЬ

Y#	Date	Mintage	Fine	VF	XF	Unc
201.3	1986	—	—	—	—	—

275th Anniversary - Birth of Mikhail Lomonosov

Y#	Date	Mintage	Fine	VF	XF	Unc
202.1	1986	1.965	—	.50	1.00	2.00
	1986	.035	—	—	Proof	4.00

Edge inscription: 1988.N.

Y#	Date	Mintage	Fine	VF	XF	Unc
202.2	1984 (mule)	—	—	—	—	—
	1986	.055	(restrike)		Proof	3.00

175th Anniversary - Battle of Borodino - Soldiers

Y#	Date	Mintage	Fine	VF	XF	Unc
203	1987	3.780	—	.50	1.00	2.00
	1987	.220	—	—	Proof	4.00

NOTE: Varieties exist w/wheat in coat of arms.

175th Anniversary - Battle of Borodino - Kutzov Monument

Y#	Date	Mintage	Fine	VF	XF	Unc
204	1987	3.780	—	.50	1.00	2.00
	1987	.220	—	—	Proof	5.00

NOTE: Varieties exist w/wheat in coat of arms.

130th Anniversary - Birth of Constantin Tsiolkovsy

Y#	Date	Mintage	Fine	VF	XF	Unc
205	1987	3.830	—	.50	1.00	2.00
	1987	.170	—	—	Proof	6.00

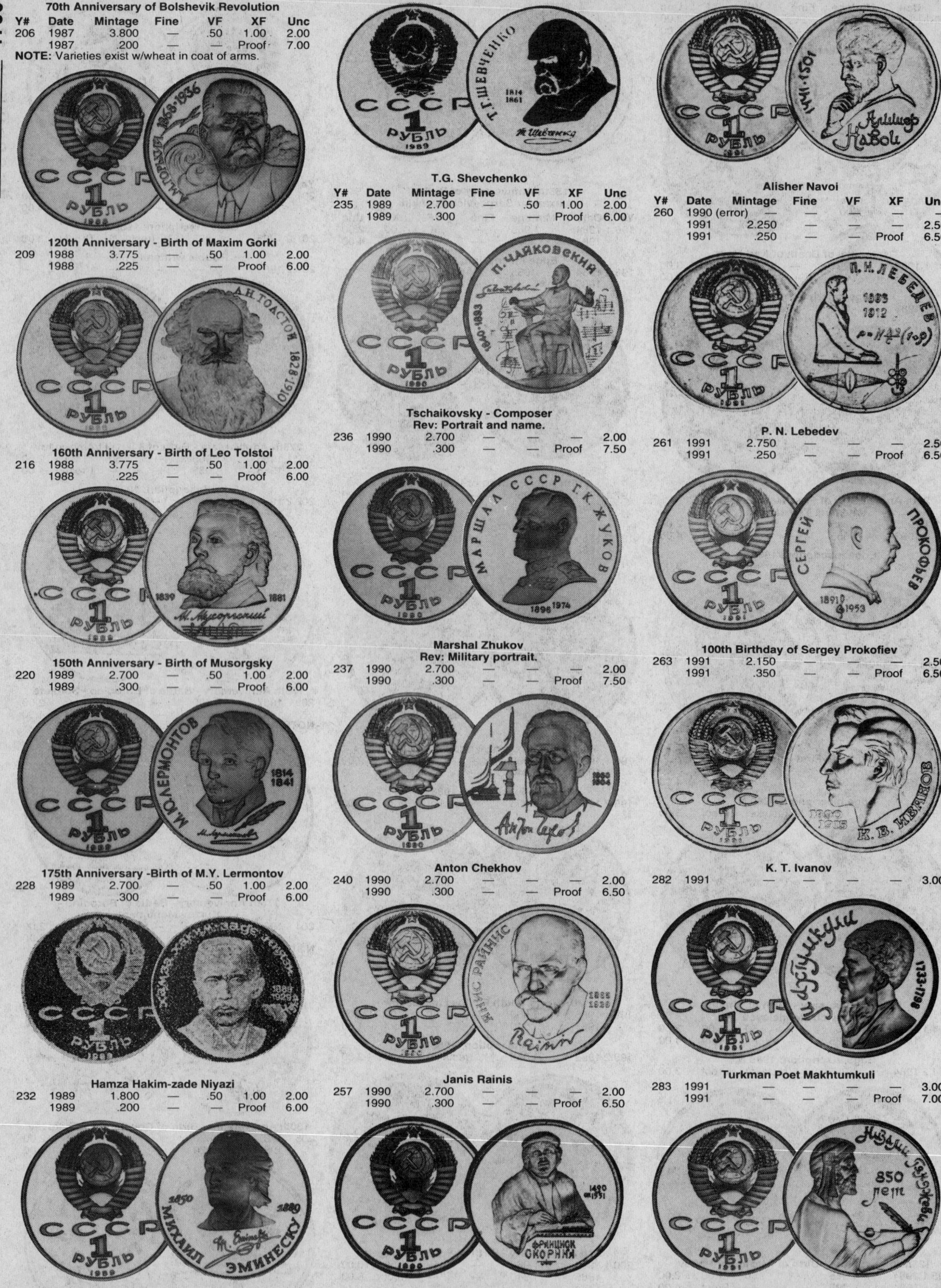

70th Anniversary of Bolshevik Revolution

Y#	Date	Mintage	Fine	VF	XF	Unc
206	1987	3.800	—	.50	1.00	2.00
	1987	.200	—	—	Proof	7.00

NOTE: Varieties exist w/wheat in coat of arms.

120th Anniversary - Birth of Maxim Gorki

Y#	Date	Mintage	Fine	VF	XF	Unc
209	1988	3.775	—	.50	1.00	2.00
	1988	.225	—	—	Proof	6.00

160th Anniversary - Birth of Leo Tolstoi

Y#	Date	Mintage	Fine	VF	XF	Unc
216	1988	3.775	—	.50	1.00	2.00
	1988	.225	—	—	Proof	6.00

150th Anniversary - Birth of Musorgsky

Y#	Date	Mintage	Fine	VF	XF	Unc
220	1989	2.700	—	.50	1.00	2.00
	1989	.300	—	—	Proof	6.00

175th Anniversary -Birth of M.Y. Lermontov

Y#	Date	Mintage	Fine	VF	XF	Unc
228	1989	2.700	—	.50	1.00	2.00
	1989	.300	—	—	Proof	6.00

Hamza Hakim-zade Niyazi

Y#	Date	Mintage	Fine	VF	XF	Unc
232	1989	1.800	—	.50	1.00	2.00
	1989	.200	—	—	Proof	6.00

100th Anniversary - Death of Mihai Eminescu

Y#	Date	Mintage	Fine	VF	XF	Unc
233	1989	1.800	—	.50	1.00	2.00
	1989	.200	—	—	Proof	6.00

T.G. Shevchenko

Y#	Date	Mintage	Fine	VF	XF	Unc
235	1989	2.700	—	.50	1.00	2.00
	1989	.300	—	—	Proof	6.00

Tschaikovsky - Composer
Rev: Portrait and name.

Y#	Date	Mintage	Fine	VF	XF	Unc
236	1990	2.700	—	—	—	2.00
	1990	.300	—	—	Proof	7.50

Marshal Zhukov
Rev: Military portrait.

Y#	Date	Mintage	Fine	VF	XF	Unc
237	1990	2.700	—	—	—	2.00
	1990	.300	—	—	Proof	7.50

Anton Chekhov

Y#	Date	Mintage	Fine	VF	XF	Unc
240	1990	2.700	—	—	—	2.00
	1990	.300	—	—	Proof	6.50

Janis Rainis

Y#	Date	Mintage	Fine	VF	XF	Unc
257	1990	2.700	—	—	—	2.00
	1990	.300	—	—	Proof	6.50

Francisk Scorina

Y#	Date	Mintage	Fine	VF	XF	Unc
258	1990	2.700	—	—	—	2.00
	1990	.300	—	—	Proof	6.50

Alisher Navoi

Y#	Date	Mintage	Fine	VF	XF	Unc
260	1990 (error)	—	—	—	—	—
	1991	2.250	—	—	—	2.50
	1991	.250	—	—	Proof	6.50

P. N. Lebedev

Y#	Date	Mintage	Fine	VF	XF	Unc
261	1991	2.750	—	—	—	2.50
	1991	.250	—	—	Proof	6.50

100th Birthday of Sergey Prokofiev

Y#	Date	Mintage	Fine	VF	XF	Unc
263	1991	2.150	—	—	—	2.50
	1991	.350	—	—	Proof	6.50

K. T. Ivanov

Y#	Date	Mintage	Fine	VF	XF	Unc
282	1991	—	—	—	—	3.00

Turkman Poet Makhtumkuli

Y#	Date	Mintage	Fine	VF	XF	Unc
283	1991	—	—	—	—	3.00
	1991	—	—	—	Proof	7.00

Nizami Gyanzhevi - Poet

Y#	Date	Mintage	Fine	VF	XF	Unc
284	1991	2.200	—	—	—	3.00
	1991	.300	—	—	Proof	7.00

Olympics - Wrestlers

Y#	Date	Mintage	Fine	VF	XF	Unc
289	1991	.500	—	—	Proof	8.50

Olympics - Javelin Thrower

Y#	Date	Mintage	Fine	VF	XF	Unc
290	1991	.500	—	—	Proof	8.50

Olympics - Cyclist and Charioteer

Y#	Date	Mintage	Fine	VF	XF	Unc
291	1991	.500	—	—	Proof	8.50

Olympics - Weight Lifters

Y#	Date	Mintage	Fine	VF	XF	Unc
299	1991	.500	—	—	Proof	8.50

Olympics - Broad Jumpers

Y#	Date	Mintage	Fine	VF	XF	Unc
300	1991	.500	—	—	Proof	8.50

Olympics - Runners

Y#	Date	Mintage	Fine	VF	XF	Unc
302	1991	.500	—	—	Proof	8.50

Government Bank Issues

Mint mark: Leningrad monogram

Y#	Date	Mintage	Fine	VF	XF	Unc
293	1991	—	—	—	—	.75

3 ROUBLES

COPPER-NICKEL
70th Anniversary of Bolshevik Revolution

Y#	Date	Mintage	Fine	VF	XF	Unc
207	1987	2.300	—	—	—	4.00
	1987	.200	—	—	Proof	6.00

34.5580 g, .900 SILVER, 1.0000 oz ASW
1000th Anniversary of Russian Architecture
Cathedral of St. Sophia in Kiev

Y#	Date	Mintage	Fine	VF	XF	Unc
210	1988	*.035	—	—	Proof	70.00

1000th Anniversary of Minting in Russia
Coin Design of St. Vladimir, 977-1015

Y#	Date	Mintage	Fine	VF	XF	Unc
211	1988	*.035	—	—	Proof	70.00

33.3000 g, .900 SILVER, 1.0000 oz ASW
500th Anniversary United Russia - Kremlin
Obv: State emblem and denomination.

Y#	Date	Mintage	Fine	VF	XF	Unc
222	1989	*.040	—	—	Proof	40.00

500th Anniversary of the First All Russian Coinage

Y#	Date	Mintage	Fine	VF	XF	Unc
223	1989	*.040	—	—	Proof	40.00

COPPER-NICKEL
Armenian Earthquake Relief

Y#	Date	Mintage	Fine	VF	XF	Unc
234	1989	2.700	—	—	—	4.00
	1989	.300	—	—	Proof	7.00

31.1000 g, .900 SILVER, .9000 oz ASW
Capt. Cook on Unalaska Island

Y#	Date	Mintage	Fine	VF	XF	Unc
242	1990	*.025	—	—	Proof	70.00

34.5600 g, .900 SILVER, 1.0000 oz ASW
World Summit for Children

Y#	Date	Mintage	Fine	VF	XF	Unc
247	1990	.020	—	—	Proof	45.00

31.1000 g, .900 SILVER, .9000 oz ASW
Peter the Great's Fleet

Y#	Date	Mintage	Fine	VF	XF	Unc
248	1990	.040	—	—	Proof	60.00

St. Peter and Paul Fortress in Leningrad

Y#	Date	Mintage	Fine	VF	XF	Unc
249	1990	.040	—	—	Proof	60.00

5 ROUBLES

Yuri Gagarin Monument

Y#	Date	Mintage	Fine	VF	XF	Unc
262	1991	.035	—	—	Proof	75.00

Fort Ross in California

Y#	Date	Mintage	Fine	VF	XF	Unc
264	1991	*.025	—	—	Proof	100.00

34.5590 g, .900 SILVER, 1.0000 oz ASW
Bolshoi Theater

Y#	Date	Mintage	Fine	VF	XF	Unc
274	1991	.040	—	—	Proof	55.00

Moscow's Arch of Triumph

Y#	Date	Mintage	Fine	VF	XF	Unc
275	1991	.040	—	—	Proof	55.00

COPPER-NICKEL
50th Anniversary of Defense of Moscow

Y#	Date	Mintage	Fine	VF	XF	Unc
301	1991	—	—	—	—	4.50
	1991	—	—	—	Proof	12.00

16.6700 g, .900 SILVER, .4824 oz ASW
Mint: Leningrad
1980 Olympics
Rev: Scenes of Kiev.

Y#	Date	Mintage	Fine	VF	XF	Unc
145	1977	.250	—	—	—	5.00
	1977	.121	—	—	Proof	7.00

Mints: Leningrad and Moscow
1980 Olympics
Rev: Scenes of Leningrad.

Y#	Date	Mintage	Fine	VF	XF	Unc
146	1977	.250	—	—	—	5.00
	1977	.121	—	—	Proof	7.00

Mint: Leningrad
1980 Olympics
Rev: Scenes of Minsk.

Y#	Date	Mintage	Fine	VF	XF	Unc
147	1977	.250	—	—	—	5.00
	1977	.121	—	—	Proof	7.00

Mints: Leningrad and Moscow
1980 Olympics
Rev: Scenes of Tallinn.

Y#	Date	Mintage	Fine	VF	XF	Unc
148	1977	.252	—	—	—	5.00
	1977	.122	—	—	Proof	7.00

Mint: Leningrad
1980 Olympics - Racing

Y#	Date	Mintage	Fine	VF	XF	Unc
154	1978	.227	—	—	—	5.00
	1978	.118	—	—	Proof	7.00

1980 Olympics - Swimming

Y#	Date	Mintage	Fine	VF	XF	Unc
155	1978	.227	—	—	—	5.00
	1978	.118	—	—	Proof	7.00

Mints: Leningrad and Moscow
1980 Olympics - High Jumping

Y#	Date	Mintage	Fine	VF	XF	Unc
156	1978	.221	—	—	—	5.00
	1978	.119	—	—	Proof	7.00

1980 Olympics - Equestrian Show Jumping

Y#	Date	Mintage	Fine	VF	XF	Unc
157	1978	.221	—	—	—	5.00
	1978	.119	—	—	Proof	7.00

1980 Olympics - Weightlifting

Y#	Date	Mintage	Fine	VF	XF	Unc
166	1979	.207	—	—	—	5.00
	1979	.108	—	—	Proof	7.00

1980 Olympics - Hammer Throw

Y#	Date	Mintage	Fine	VF	XF	Unc
167	1979	.207	—	—	—	5.00
	1979	.108	—	—	Proof	7.00

1980 Olympics - Archery

Y#	Date	Mintage	Fine	VF	XF	Unc
179	1980	.126	—	—	—	5.00
	1980	.095	—	—	Proof	7.00

1980 Olympics - Gymnastics

Y#	Date	Mintage	Fine	VF	XF	Unc
80	1980	.126	—	—	—	5.00
	1980	.095	—	—	Proof	7.00

Mint: Leningrad
1980 Olympics - Equestrian - Isindi

Y#	Date	Mintage	Fine	VF	XF	Unc
81	1980	.126	—	—	—	5.00
	1980	.096	—	—	Proof	7.00

1980 Olympics - Gorodki - Stick Throwing

Y#	Date	Mintage	Fine	VF	XF	Unc
82	1980	.126	—	—	—	5.00
	1980	.096	—	—	Proof	7.00

COPPER-NICKEL
70th Anniversary of Bolshevik Revolution

Y#	Date	Mintage	Fine	VF	XF	Unc
208	1987	1.300	—	—	—	10.00
	1987	.200	—	—	Proof	20.00

Leningrad Peter the Great

Y#	Date	Mintage	Fine	VF	XF	Unc
217	1988	1.675	—	—	—	6.00
	1988	.325	—	—	Proof	10.00

Novgorod Monument to the Russian Millenium

Y#	Date	Mintage	Fine	VF	XF	Unc
218	1988	1.675	—	—	—	6.00
	1988	.325	—	—	Proof	10.00

St. Sophia Cathedral in Kiev

Y#	Date	Mintage	Fine	VF	XF	Unc
219	1988	1.675	—	—	—	6.00
	1988	.325	—	—	Proof	10.00

Pokrowsky Cathedral in Moscow

Y#	Date	Mintage	Fine	VF	XF	Unc
221	1989	1.700	—	—	—	6.00
	1989	.300	—	—	Proof	10.00

Samarkand

Y#	Date	Mintage	Fine	VF	XF	Unc
229	1989	1.700	—	—	—	6.00
	1989	.300	—	—	Proof	10.00

Cathedral of the Annunciation in Moscow

Y#	Date	Mintage	Fine	VF	XF	Unc
230	1989	1.700	—	—	—	6.00
	1989	.300	—	—	Proof	10.00

St. Petersburg Palace

Y#	Date	Mintage	Fine	VF	XF	Unc
241	1990	2.700	—	—	—	6.00
	1990	.300	—	—	Proof	10.00

Uspenski Cathedral

Y#	Date	Mintage	Fine	VF	XF	Unc
246	1990	2.700	—	—	—	6.00
	1990	.300	—	—	Proof	10.00

Matenadarin Depository of Ancient Armenian Manuscripts

Y#	Date	Mintage	Fine	VF	XF	Unc
259	1990	2.700	—	—	—	6.00
	1990	.300	—	—	Proof	10.00

Cathedral of the Archangel Michael in Moscow

Y#	Date	Mintage	Fine	VF	XF	Unc
271	1991	—	—	—	—	6.50
	1991	—	—	—	Proof	12.50

State Bank Building in Moscow

Y#	Date	Mintage	Fine	VF	XF	Unc
272	1991	—	—	—	—	6.50
	1991	—	—	—	Proof	12.50

David Sasunsky Monument

Y#	Date	Mintage	Fine	VF	XF	Unc
273	1991	—	—	—	—	6.50
	1991	—	—	—	Proof	12.50

Government Bank Issues

BRASS CENTER, COPPER-NICKEL RING
Wildlife - Owl

Y#	Date	Mintage	Fine	VF	XF	Unc
280	1991	.500	—	—	—	3.50
	1991	.050	—	—	BU	9.00

Wildlife - Mountain Goat

Y#	Date	Mintage	Fine	VF	XF	Unc
281	1991	.500	—	—	—	3.50
	1991	.050	—	—	BU	9.00

COPPER-NICKEL

Y#	Date	Mintage	Fine	VF	XF	Unc
294	1991(l)	—	—	—	—	2.50

10 ROUBLES

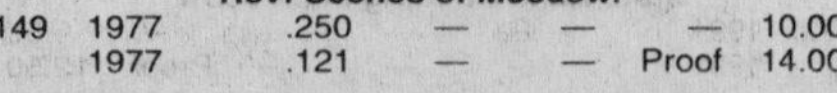

33.3000 g, .900 SILVER, .9636 oz ASW
Mints: Leningrad and Moscow
1980 Olympics
Rev: Scenes of Moscow.

Y#	Date	Mintage	Fine	VF	XF	Unc
149	1977	.250	—	—	—	10.00
	1977	.121	—	—	Proof	14.00

Mint: Leningrad
1980 Olympics
Obv: Similar to Y#149.
Rev: Map of USSR.

Y#	Date	Mintage	Fine	VF	XF	Unc
150	1977	.250	—	—	—	10.00
	1977	.121	—	—	Proof	14.00

1980 Olympics - Cycling
Obv: Similar to Y#149.

Y#	Date	Mintage	Fine	VF	XF	Unc
158.1	1978	.227	—	—	—	10.00
	1978	.118	—	—	Proof	14.00

Rev: W/o mint mark.

Y#	Date	Mintage	Fine	VF	XF	Unc
158.2	1978	*100 pcs.	—	—	—	110.00

Mints: Leningrad and Moscow
1980 Olympics - Canoeing
Obv: Similar to Y#149.

Y#	Date	Mintage	Fine	VF	XF	Unc
159	1978	.226	—	—	—	10.00
	1978	.118	—	—	Proof	14.00

1980 Olympics - Equestrian Sport
Obv: Similar to Y#149.

Y#	Date	Mintage	Fine	VF	XF	Unc
160	1978	.226	—	—	—	10.00
	1978	.118	—	—	Proof	14.00

1980 Olympics - Pole Vaulting
Obv: Similar to Y#149.

Y#	Date	Mintage	Fine	VF	XF	Unc
161	1978	.221	—	—	—	10.00
	1978	.119	—	—	Proof	14.00

1980 Olympics - Basketball
Obv: Similar to Y#149.

Y#	Date	Mintage	Fine	VF	XF	Unc
168	1979	.221	—	—	—	10.00
	1979	.119	—	—	Proof	14.00

1980 Olympics - Volleyball
Obv: Similar to Y#149.

Y#	Date	Mintage	Fine	VF	XF	Unc
169	1979	.221	—	—	—	10.00
	1979	.119	—	—	Proof	14.00

Mint: Leningrad
1980 Olympics - Boxing
Obv: Similar to Y#149.

Y#	Date	Mintage	Fine	VF	XF	Unc
170	1979	.207	—	—	—	12.00
	1979	.108	—	—	Proof	15.00

Mints: Leningrad and Moscow
1980 Olympics - Judo
Obv: Similar to Y#149.

Y#	Date	Mintage	Fine	VF	XF	Unc
171	1979	.207	—	—	—	12.00
	1979	.108	—	—	Proof	15.00

Mint: Leningrad
1980 Olympics - Lifting of the Weight
Obv: Similar to Y#149.

Y#	Date	Mintage	Fine	VF	XF	Unc
172	1979	.207	—	—	—	12.00
	1979	.108	—	—	Proof	15.00

Mints: Leningrad and Moscow
1980 Olympics - Wrestling
Obv: Similar to Y#149.

Y#	Date	Mintage	Fine	VF	XF	Unc
183	1980	.126	—	—	—	12.00
	1980	.095	—	—	Proof	15.00

Mint: Leningrad
1980 Olympics - Tug of War
Obv: Similar to Y#149.

Y#	Date	Mintage	Fine	VF	XF	Unc
184	1980	.126	—	—	—	12.00
	1980	.095	—	—	Proof	15.00

1980 Olympics - Reindeer Racing
Obv: Similar to Y#149.

Y#	Date	Mintage	Fine	VF	XF	Unc
185	1980	.126	—	—	—	12.00
	1980	.095	—	—	Proof	15.00

Government Bank Issues

ALUMINUM-BRONZE CENTER,
COPPER-NICKEL RING
Mint mark: Leningrad monogram

Y#	Date	Mintage	Fine	VF	XF	Unc
295	1991	—	—	—	—	5.00
	1992	—	—	—	—	5.00

25 ROUBLES

31.1000 g, .999 PALLADIUM, 1.0000 oz APW
Monument to Vladimir, Grand Duke of Kiev and
Millenium of Christianity in Russia
Obv: Similar to 10 Roubles, Y#149.

Y#	Date	Mintage	Fine	VF	XF	Unc
212	1988	7,000	—	—	—	280.00

500th Anniversary of Russian State - Ivan III

Y#	Date	Mintage	Fine	VF	XF	Unc
224	1989	*.012	—	—	Proof	250.00

250th Anniversary - Discovery of Russian
America - Ship - St. Peter

Y#	Date	Mintage	Fine	VF	XF	Unc
243	1990	6,500	—	—	Proof	300.00

250th Anniversary - Discovery of Russian
America - Ship - St. Paul

Y#	Date	Mintage	Fine	VF	XF	Unc
244	1990	6,500	—	—	Proof	300.00

500th Anniversary of Russian State -
Peter the Great

Y#	Date	Mintage	Fine	VF	XF	Unc
250	1990	.012	—	—	Proof	225.00

Three Saints Harbor - Russian Settlement in America
Obv: State emblem. Rev: Sailboat in harbor.

Y#	Date	Mintage	Fine	VF	XF	Unc
265	1991	*6,500	—	—	Proof	300.00

Novo Archangelsk 1799
Obv: State emblem. Rev: 3 masted ship at
coastal outpost.

Y#	Date	Mintage	Fine	VF	XF	Unc
266	1991	*6,500	—	—	Proof	300.00

500th Anniversary of Russian State -
Abolition of Serfdom in Russia
Obv: State emblem.

Y#	Date	Mintage	Fine	VF	XF	Unc
276	1991	*.012	—	—	Proof	250.00

50 ROUBLES

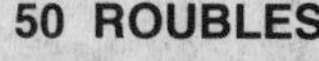

8.6397 g, .900 GOLD, .2500 oz AGW
1000th Anniversary of Russian Architecture -
Cathedral of St. Sophia in Novgorod
Obv: Similar to 100 Roubles, Y#A163.

Y#	Date	Mintage	Fine	VF	XF	Unc
213	1988	.025	—	—	—	125.00

500th Anniversary of Russian State -
Cathedral of the Ascension
Obv: State emblem and denomination.

Y#	Date	Mintage	Fine	VF	XF	Unc
225	1989	*.025	—	—	Proof	165.00

500th Anniversary of Russian State -
Moscow Church of the Archangel

Y#	Date	Mintage	Fine	VF	XF	Unc
251	1990	.025	—	—	Proof	150.00

8.6440 g, .900 GOLD, .2500 oz AGW
500th Anniversary of Russian State -
St. Isaac Cathedral in St. Petersburg

Y#	Date	Mintage	Fine	VF	XF	Unc
277	1991	.025	—	—	Proof	165.00

100 ROUBLES

17.2800 g, .900 GOLD, .5000 oz AGW
Mints: Leningrad and Moscow
1980 Olympics - Symbols

Y#	Date	Mintage	Fine	VF	XF	Unc
A163	1977	.044	—	—	—	200.00
	1977	.038	—	—	Proof	250.00

1980 Olympics - Lenin Stadium

Y#	Date	Mintage	Fine	VF	XF	Unc
151	1978	.062	—	—	—	200.00
	1978	.045	—	—	Proof	250.00

1980 Olympics - Waterside Grandstand

Y#	Date	Mintage	Fine	VF	XF	Unc
162	1978	.057	—	—	—	200.00
	1978	.030	—	—	Matte	—
	1978	.043	—	—	Proof	250.00

1980 Olympics - Velodrome Building

Y#	Date	Mintage	Fine	VF	XF	Unc
173	1979	.055	—	—	—	200.00
	1979	.042	—	—	Proof	250.00

Mint: Moscow
1980 Olympics - Druzhba Sports Hall

Y#	Date	Mintage	Fine	VF	XF	Unc
174	1979	.054	—	—	—	200.00
	1979	.038	—	—	Proof	250.00

1980 Olympics - Torch

Y#	Date	Mintage	Fine	VF	XF	Unc
186	1980	.025	—	—	—	200.00
	1980	.028	—	—	Proof	250.00

17.2794 g, .900 GOLD, .5000 oz AGW
1000th Anniversary of Minting in Russia -
Coin Design of St. Vladimir, 977-1015
Obv: Similar to Y#186.

Y#	Date	Mintage	Fine	VF	XF	Unc
214	1988	.014	—	—	—	285.00

500th Anniversary of Russian State -
Seal of Ivan III.
Obv: State emblem and denomination.

Y#	Date	Mintage	Fine	VF	XF	Unc
226	1989	*.014	—	—	Proof	300.00

15.5500 g, .900 GOLD, .4500 oz AGW
500th Anniversary of Russian State -
Peter the Great

Y#	Date	Mintage	Fine	VF	XF	Unc
252	1990	.014	—	—	Proof	285.00

17.5000 g, .900 GOLD, .5000 oz AGW
500th Anniversary of Russian State -
Tolstoi Monument

Y#	Date	Mintage	Fine	VF	XF	Unc
278	1991	.014	—	—	Proof	300.00

150 ROUBLES

15.5400 g, .999 PLATINUM, .4991 oz APW
Mint: Leningrad
1980 Olympics - Symbols

Y#	Date	Mintage	Fine	VF	XF	Unc
152	1977	9,910	—	—		*BV + 10%*
	1977	.024	—	—	Proof	350.00

1980 Olympics - Throwing Discus

Y#	Date	Mintage	Fine	VF	XF	Unc
163	1978	.013	—	—		*BV + 10%*
	1978	.020	—	—	Proof	350.00

1980 Olympics - Greek Wrestlers

Y#	Date	Mintage	Fine	VF	XF	Unc
175	1979	.014	—	—		*BV + 10%*
	1979	.019	—	—	—	350.00

1980 Olympics - Roman Chariot Race

Y#	Date	Mintage	Fine	VF	XF	Unc
176	1979	9,728	—	—		*BV + 10%*
	1979	.017	—	—	Proof	350.00

1980 Olympics - Ancient Greek Runners

Y#	Date	Mintage	Fine	VF	XF	Unc
187	1980	7,820	—	—		*BV + 10%*
	1980	.013	—	—	Proof	350.00

15.5500 g, .999 PLATINUM, .5000 oz APW
1000th Anniversary of Russian Literature -
Grand Duke Igor Writing Poetry
Obv: Similar to Y#187.

Y#	Date	Mintage	Fine	VF	XF	Unc
215	1988	.016	—	—	—	350.00

500th Anniversary of Russian State -
Ugra River Encounter
Obv: State emblem and denomination.

Y#	Date	Mintage	Fine	VF	XF	Unc
227	1989	*.016	—	—	Proof	350.00

250th Anniversary - Discovery of Russian America -
Ship - St. Gavriil
Obv: Similar to Y#187.
Rev: 1 masted ship sailing right.

Y#	Date	Mintage	Fine	VF	XF	Unc
245	1990	6,500	—	—	Proof	475.00

500th Anniversary of Russian State -
Battle of Poltava River

Y#	Date	Mintage	Fine	VF	XF	Unc
253	1990	.016	—	—	Proof	350.00

250th Anniversary - Discovery of Russian America -
Bishop Viniaminov

Y#	Date	Mintage	Fine	VF	XF	Unc
267	1991	*6,500	—	—	Proof	475.00

17.5000 g, .999 PLATINUM, .5000 oz APW
250th Anniversary of Russian State - War of Liberation Against Napoleon

#	Date	Mintage	Fine	VF	XF	Unc
79	1991	.016	—	—	Proof	375.00

RUSSIA

(Commonwealth of Independent States)

10 KOPEKS

COPPER CLAD STEEL
Kremlin Tower and Dome

#	Date	Mintage	Fine	VF	XF	Unc
96	1991 M	—	.10	.15	.25	.35

50 KOPEKS

COPPER-NICKEL
Mint mark: Л

#	Date	Mintage	Fine	VF	XF	Unc
92	1991	—	.15	.25	.35	.50

ROUBLE

COPPER-NICKEL
Rebirth of Russian Sovereignty and Democracy

#	Date	Mintage	Fine	VF	XF	Unc
03	1992	.669	—	—	—	2.50
	1992	1.301	—	—	P/L	6.50

Jacob Kolas

#	Date	Mintage	Fine	VF	XF	Unc
05	1992	—	—	—	—	2.50
	1992	—	—	—	Proof	6.50

Admiral Nakhimov

#	Date	Mintage	Fine	VF	XF	Unc
06	1992	—	—	—	—	2.50
	1992	—	—	—	Proof	6.50

BRASS CLAD STEEL
Double Headed White Russian Eagle

#	Date	Mintage	Fine	VF	XF	Unc
11	1992	—	—	—	—	1.00

COPPER-NICKEL
Yanka Kupala

Y#	Date	Mintage	Fine	VF	XF	Unc
320	1992	1.000	—	—	—	2.50
	1992	.200	—	—	P/L	3.50
	1992	.350	—	—	Proof	6.50

N.I. Lobachevsky

Y#	Date	Mintage	Fine	VF	XF	Unc
321	1992	1.000	—	—	—	2.50

Vladimir Ivanovich Vernadsky

Y#	Date	Mintage	Fine	VF	XF	Unc
319.1	1993	.450	—	—	—	2.50
	1993	.015	—	—	P/L	3.50
	1993	.035	—	—	Proof	6.50

Obv: W/o mint mark below eagle's claw.

Y#	Date	Mintage	Fine	VF	XF	Unc
319.2	1993	—	—	—	—	2.50

Gavrila Romanovich Derzhavin

Y#	Date	Mintage	Fine	VF	XF	Unc
325	1993	—	—	—	—	2.50

K.A. Temryazyev

Y#	Date	Mintage	Fine	VF	XF	Unc
326	1993	—	—	—	—	2.50

Y#	Date	Mintage	Fine	VF	XF	Unc
327	1993	—	—	—	—	2.50

15.5500 g, .900 SILVER, .4500 oz ASW
Red Book Wildlife Series - Tiger

Y#	Date	Mintage	Fine	VF	XF	Unc
335	1993	—	—	—	Proof	12.50

Red Book Wildlife Series - Horned Owl

Y#	Date	Mintage	Fine	VF	XF	Unc
336	1993	—	—	—	Proof	12.50

Red Book Wildlife Series - Mountain Goat

Y#	Date	Mintage	Fine	VF	XF	Unc
337	1993	—	—	—	Proof	12.50

3 ROUBLES

COPPER-NICKEL
International Space Year

Y#	Date	Mintage	Fine	VF	XF	Unc
297	1992	—	—	—	—	4.50
	1992	—	—	—	Proof	10.00

Battle of Chudskoye Lake

Y#	Date	Mintage	Fine	VF	XF	Unc
298	1992	.600	—	—	—	4.50
	1992	.400	—	—	Proof	10.00

WWII Allied Supply Convoys to Murmansk

Y#	Date	Mintage	Fine	VF	XF	Unc
304	1992	.700	—	—		4.50
	1992	.300	—	—	Proof	10.00

1st Anniversary - Defeat of Communist Attempted Coup

Y#	Date	Mintage	Fine	VF	XF	Unc
317	1992	—	—	—	—	4.50
	1992	—	—	—	Proof	10.00

Battle of Stalingrad

Y#	Date	Mintage	Fine	VF	XF	Unc
318	1993	—	—	—	Proof	10.00

50th Anniversary - Battle of Kursk

Y#	Date	Mintage	Fine	VF	XF	Unc
328	1993	—	—	—	—	5.00

5 ROUBLES

BRASS CLAD STEEL
Double Headed White Russian Eagle

Y#	Date	Mintage	Fine	VF	XF	Unc
312	1992	—	—	—	—	1.50

Kazakhstan

Y#	Date	Mintage	Fine	VF	XF	Unc
322	1992	—	—	—	Proof	10.00

Troitsk - Sergievsk Monastery

Y#	Date	Mintage	Fine	VF	XF	Unc
324	1993	—	—	—	—	6.00
	1993	—	—	—	Proof	10.00

COPPER-NICKEL
2500 Years of Turkmenistan

Y#	Date	Mintage	Fine	VF	XF	Unc
339	1993	—	—	—	Proof	6.50

10 ROUBLES

ALUMINUM-BRONZE CENTER,
COPPER-NICKEL RING
Wildlife - Red Breasted Kazarka

Y#	Date	Mintage	Fine	VF	XF	Unc
307	1992	—	—	—	—	6.00

Wildlife - Tiger

Y#	Date	Mintage	Fine	VF	XF	Unc
308	1992	—	—	—	—	6.00

Wildlife - Cobra

Y#	Date	Mintage	Fine	VF	XF	Unc
309	1992	—	—	—	—	6.00

COPPER-NICKEL
Double Headed White Russian Eagle

Y#	Date	Mintage	Fine	VF	XF	Unc
313	1992	—	—	—	—	1.50

20 ROUBLES

COPPER-NICKEL
Double Headed White Russian Eagle

Y#	Date	Mintage	Fine	VF	XF	Unc
314	1992	—	—	—	—	2.00

50 ROUBLES

ALUMINUM-BRONZE CENTER,
COPPER-NICKEL RING
Double Headed White Russian Eagle

Y#	Date	Mintage	Fine	VF	XF	Unc
315	1992	—	—	—	—	2.50

ALUMINUM - BRONZE

Y#	Date	Mintage	Fine	VF	XF	Unc
329	1993	—	—	—	—	2.50

ALUMINUM-BRONZE CENTER,
COPPER-NICKEL RING
Wildlife - Bear

Y#	Date	Mintage	Fine	VF	XF	Unc
330	1993	—	—	—	—	6.00

Wildlife - Gecko

Y#	Date	Mintage	Fine	VF	XF	Unc
331	1993	—	—	—	—	6.00

Wildlife - Grouse

Y#	Date	Mintage	Fine	VF	XF	Unc
332	1993	—	—	—	—	6.00

Wildlife - Egret

Y#	Date	Mintage	Fine	VF	XF	Unc
333	1993	—	—	—	—	6.00

Wildlife - Porpoise

Y#	Date	Mintage	Fine	VF	XF	Unc
334	1993	—	—	—	—	6.00

100 ROUBLES

COPPER-NICKEL CENTER, ALUMINUM-BRONZE RING
Double Headed White Russian Eagle

Y#	Date	Mintage	Fine	VF	XF	Unc
316	1992	—	—	—	—	3.00

COPPER-NICKEL-ZINC

Y#	Date	Mintage	Fine	VF	XF	Unc
338	1993	—	—	—	—	4.00

SILVER BULLION ISSUES

3 ROUBLES

34.7500 g, .900 SILVER, 1.0056 oz ASW
Mint: Moscow
Bolshoy Ballet

Y#	Date	Mintage	Fine	VF	XF	Unc
323	1993	.125	—	—	—	10.00
	1993	.040	—	—	Proof	20.00

GOLD BULLION ISSUES

10 ROUBLES

2.6600 g, .585 GOLD, .0500 oz AGW
Bolshoy Ballet
Obv: Similar to 50 Roubles, Y#287.

Y#	Date	Mintage	Fine	VF	XF	Unc
285	1991	6,000	—	—	—	50.00

25 ROUBLES

5.3200 g, .585 GOLD, .1000 oz AGW
Bolshoy Ballet
Obv: Similar to 50 Roubles, Y#287.

Y#	Date	Mintage	Fine	VF	XF	Unc
286	1991	5,000	—	—	—	100.00

3.1100 g, .999 GOLD, 1.000 oz AGW

Y#	Date	Mintage	Fine	VF	XF	Unc
286a	1991	1,500	—	—	Proof	250.00

50 ROUBLES

13.3000 g, .585 GOLD, .2500 oz AGW
Bolshoy Ballet

Y#	Date	Mintage	Fine	VF	XF	Unc
287	1991	2,400	—	—	—	250.00

7.7800 g, .999 GOLD, .2500 oz AGW

Y#	Date	Mintage	Fine	VF	XF	Unc
287a	1991	1,500	—	—	Proof	450.00

100 ROUBLES

26.5900 g, .585 GOLD, .5000 oz AGW
Bolshoy Ballet

Y#	Date	Mintage	Fine	VF	XF	Unc
288	1991	1,200	—	—	—	500.00

15.5500 g, .999 GOLD, .5000 oz AGW

Y#	Date	Mintage	Fine	VF	XF	Unc
288a	1991	1,500	—	—	Proof	750.00

PALLADIUM BULLION ISSUES

5 ROUBLES

7.7758 g, .999 PALLADIUM, .2500 oz APW
Ballerina - Hugging Herself

Y#	Date	Mintage	Fine	VF	XF	Unc
268	1991	9,000	—	—	—	60.00

10 ROUBLES

15.5500 g, .999 PALLADIUM, .5000 oz APW
Ballerina - Hugging Herself
Obv: Similar to Y#269.

Y#	Date	Mintage	Fine	VF	XF	Unc
238	1990	*.015	—	—	—	130.00

Ballerina - Arms and Left Leg Behind Her

Y#	Date	Mintage	Fine	VF	XF	Unc
269	1991	.010	—	—	—	110.00

25 ROUBLES

31.1035 g, .999 PALLADIUM, 1.0000 oz APW
Ballerina - Hugging Herself

Y#	Date	Mintage	Fine	VF	XF	Unc
231	1989	.027	—	—	—	160.00
	1989	3,000	—	—	Proof	500.00

Ballerina - Arms and Left Leg Behind Her
Similar to Y#231.

Y#	Date	Mintage	Fine	VF	XF	Unc
239	1990	.027	—	—	—	160.00
	1990	3,000	—	—	Proof	450.00

Ballerina - Right Arm Extends Upward

Y#	Date	Mintage	Fine	VF	XF	Unc
270	1991	.010	—	—	—	145.00
	1991	3,000	—	—	Proof	425.00

TRADE COINAGE

CHERVONETZ

(10 Roubles)

8.6026 g, .900 GOLD, .2489 oz AGW
Obv: РСФСР below arms.
Mintmasters initials on edge

Y#	Date	Mintage	Fine	VF	XF	Unc
85	1923 ПЛ	2.751	130.00	160.00	200.00	250.00
	1923 ПЛ	—	—	—	Proof	1350.
	1975	.250	—	—		*BV + 10%*
	1976 ЛМД	1.000	—	—		*BV + 10%*
	1977 ММД	1.000	—	—		*BV + 10%*
	1977 ЛМД	1.000	—	—		*BV + 10%*
	1978 ММД	.350	—	—		*BV + 10%*
	1979 ММД	1.000	—	—		*BV + 10%*
	1980 ММД	.900	—	—		*BV + 10%*
	1980 ММД	.100	—	—	Proof	150.00
	1981	1.000	—	—		*BV + 10%*
	1982	.065	—	—		*BV + 10%*
	Obv: CCCP below arms.					
A86	1925	.600	—	—	Unique	—

MINT SETS (MS)

KM#	Date	Mintage	Identification	Issue Price	Mkt. Val.
MS1	1957(4)	—	Y122-125	2.25	35.00
MS2	1961(9)	—	Y126-132,133.1,134.1	4.50	32.00
MS3	1962(7)	—	Y126-132	2.25	4.50
MS4	1964(4)	—	Y126,127,133.2,134.2	2.55	4.00
MS5	1965(9)	—	Y126-132,133.2,134.2	4.50	10.00
MS6	1966(9)	—	Y126-132,133.2,134.2	4.50	10.00
MS7	1967(9)	—	Y126-132,133.2,134.2	4.50	10.00
MS8	1967(5)	211,250	Y136-140	6.00	10.00
MS9	1968(9)	—	Y126-132,133a,134a and mint token.	6.00	10.00
MS10	1969(9)	—	Y126-132,133.2,134.2	7.00	10.00
MS11	1970(9)	—	Y126-132,133.2,134.2	11.00	10.00
MS12	1971(9)	—	Y126-132,133.2,134.2	6.00	10.00
MS13	1972(9)	10,000	Y126-132,133.2,134.2	7.00	10.00
MS14	1973(9)	8,000	Y126-132,133.2,134.2	11.00	10.00
MS15	1974(9)	27,500	Y126-132,133.2,134.2, square mint token.	11.00	10.00
MS16	1975(9)	27,000	Y126-132,133.2,134.2	11.00	10.00
MS17	1976(9)	55,000	Y126-132,133.2,134.2	11.00	10.00
MS18	1977(9)	58,750	Y126-132,133.2,134.2	11.00	10.00
MS19	1978(9)	62,500	Y126-132,133.2,134.2	11.00	10.00
MS20	1979(9)	75,000	Y126-132,133a,134a	19.00	10.00
MS21	1980(9)	—	Y126-132,133a,134a	19.00	10.00
MS22	1981(9)	—	Y126-132,133a,134a	—	10.00
MS23	1982(9)	—	Y126-132,133a,134a	—	10.00
MS24	1983(9)	—	Y126-132,133a,134a	—	10.00
MS25	1984(9)	—	Y126-132,133a,134a	—	10.00
MS26	1985(9)	—	Y126-132,133a,134a	—	10.00
MS27	Mixed date (9)	—	Y135,140-143,188-190	—	30.00
MS28	Mixed date (8)	—	Y135,140-143,188-189	—	25.00
MS29	1987(9)	—	Y126-131,132.1,133.2-134.2	—	10.00
MS30	1988(9)	—	Y126-133,134.2	—	10.00
MS31	1989(9)	—	Y126-133,134.2	—	10.00
MS32	1990(9)	—	Y126-133,134.2	—	12.00
MS33	1991(3)	—	Y268-270	245.00	275.00
MS34	1992(6)	—	Y311-316	15.00	15.00

PROOF SETS (PS)

KM#	Date	Mintage	Identification	Issue Price	Mkt. Val.
PS1	Mixed date (5)	—	Y152,163,175-176,187	—	1500.
PS2	1987(3)	—	Y206-208	—	37.50
PS3	1991(3)	1,500	Y286a-288a	—	1450.

RUSSIAN CAUCASIA

Russian Caucasia, a natural area in Russia located between the Black and Caspian Seas, was a region of mystery and myth to the Ancient Greeks. It was there that Prometheus was bound for the eagle's torment and the Argonauts sought the Golden Fleece. For more than a thousand years Caucasia was the refuge for wave after wave of migrating peoples. Greeks, Romans, Persians, Turks, Huns, Mongols and finally the Russians invaded the treeless steppes and wooded highlands of this rangeflanked granite bridge between Europe and Asia. Russian aggression, heroically resisted by the independent mountain races, began early in the 18th century and continued until the last opposition was stifled. The several states of Caucasia made a futile attempt to establish an independent federated republic during the Russian February Revolution of 1917, but were quickly reconquered after the triumph of Bolshevism over the Kerensky administration.

The following areas of Russian Caucasia were coin-issuing entities of interest to numismatics.

ARMAVIR

Armavir is a town located in Southern Russia north of the Caucasus.

LOCAL CURRENCY UNDER THE WHITE RUSSIANS

ROUBLE

COPPER
Reeded edge, thin planchet, monogram below tail.

KM#	Date	Mintage	VG	Fine	VF	XF
1	1918	—	75.00	150.00	250.00	400.00

3 ROUBLES

COPPER
Monogram below tail, reeded edge.

KM#	Date	Mintage	VG	Fine	VF	XF
2.1	1918	—	40.00	80.00	150.00	250.00
	Monogram below claw.					
2.2	1918	—	50.00	100.00	175.00	275.00

5 ROUBLES

COPPER

KM#	Date	Mintage	VG	Fine	VF	XF
3	1918	—	150.00	225.00	400.00	550.00

AZERBAIJAN

For previously listed coins refer to Azerbaijan Republic.

DAGHESTAN

Dagestan

Daghestan is a mountainous republic bounded on the north by Chechno-Ingush, on the south by Azerbaijan, on the east by the Caspian Sea, and on the west by Georgia. It was annexed from Persia in 1723. The republic was created in 1921 from the former province of Daghestan.

RULERS

Emir Uzun-Hayir (Uzun-Kheir)
AH1338-1339/1919-1920AD

MINTNAME

Daghistan داغستان

2-1/2 TOMAN

A 2-1/2 Toman coin was reportedly struck, but no specimens are known.

5 TOMAN

BRASS

KM#	Date	Mintage	Fine	VF	XF
2	AH1338	—	—	—	—

10 TOMAN

BRASS

KM#	Date	Mintage	Fine	VF	XF
3	AH1338	—	—	—	—
	COPPER **Struck over Russia 2 Kopek, Y#10.**				
4	AH1338	—	—	—	—

GEORGIA

The Georgia Republic, a former kingdom bounded on the north by Russia, on the south by Armenia and Turkey, on the east by Azerbaijan, and on the west by the Black Sea. After centuries of rule by Turkey or Persia Georgia became a vassal of Russia in 1783. It came under direct rule in September, 1801. Russia recognized Georgia's independence in 1920, invaded the country in 1921, and made it a constituent republic of the U.S.S.R in 1936.

Independence was declared March 31, 1991. Civil war was eased when the President fled the capital on Jan. 6 1992 and a Military Council took over functions of the government. All Soviet troops have been ordered out of the country and Soviet owned businesses have been seized. They have applied for admission into the UN and have asked to join the Commonwealth of Independent States but have been refused by both. Capital: Tbilisi.

RULERS

David, Regent
AH1215-1216/1801AD

MONETARY SYSTEM

5 Dinar = 1 Puli (Kazbegi)
4 Puli = 1 Bisti
2-1/2 Bisti = 1 Shahi
4 Shahi = 1 Abazi (Abbasi)
5 Abazi = 1 Rouble

Mintname

Tiflis تفليس

RUSSIAN ISSUES

Struck under the authority of Alexander I (1801-25) and Nicholas I (1825-55) of Russia at the Tiflis (Tbilisi) Mint.

MINTMASTERS INITIALS

Letter	Date	Name
AT	1810-1831	A. Trifonov
BK	1831-1834	Vasilij Klejmenov

MONETARY SYSTEM

5 Dinars = 1 Puli
2 Puli = 1 Kopek
4 Puli = 1 Bisti
50 Bisti = 1 Abaze

DATING

The dates are shown in a quantitive manner ex. 1000 plus 800 plus 10 plus 9 = 1819.

NOTE: The fine style 1 and 2 Abaze coins of 1828 are patterns, struck at St. Petersburg.

PULI

COPPER

KM#	Date	Mintage	VG	Fine	VF	XF
70	1804	4,000	—	—	Rare	—
	1805	Inc. Ab.	50.00	100.00	175.00	275.00
	1806	.015	50.00	100.00	175.00	275.00

2 PULI

COPPER

KM#	Date	Mintage	VG	Fine	VF	XF
71	1804	3,000	—	—	Rare	—
	1805	Inc. Ab.	60.00	120.00	200.00	325.00
	1806	.034	30.00	60.00	100.00	150.00
	1808	.012	30.00	60.00	100.00	150.00
	1810	.050	30.00	60.00	100.00	150.00

BISTI

COPPER

KM#	Date	Mintage	VG	Fine	VF	XF
72	1804	1,000	—	—	Rare	—
	1805	Inc. Ab.	65.00	125.00	175.00	275.00
	1806	.025	20.00	40.00	80.00	150.00
	1808	.020	20.00	40.00	80.00	150.00
	1810	.315	20.00	40.00	80.00	150.00

1/2 ABAZI

.917 SILVER

KM#	Date	Mintage	VG	Fine	VF	XF
73	1804 ПЗ	5,000	—	—	Rare	—
	1805 ПЗ	I.A.	25.00	50.00	100.00	200.00
	1810 AT	398 pcs.	—	—	Rare	—
	1813 AT	2,000	—	—	Rare	—
	1820 AT	4,000	30.00	60.00	110.00	225.00
	1821 AT	I.A.	25.00	50.00	100.00	200.00
	1822 AK	1,000	25.00	50.00	100.00	200.00
	1823 AK	4,000	25.00	50.00	100.00	200.00
	1824 AK	4,000	25.00	50.00	100.00	200.00
	1826 AT	5,000	25.00	50.00	100.00	200.00
	1827 AT	7,000	25.00	50.00	100.00	200.00
	1828 AT	.016	15.00	30.00	60.00	100.00
	1831 AT	—	25.00	50.00	100.00	225.00
	1832 BK	—	25.00	50.00	100.00	200.00
	1833 BK	—	25.00	50.00	95.00	200.00

ABAZI

SILVER, 19mm

KM#	Date	Mintage	VG	Fine	VF	XF
	1804 ПЗ	—	—	—	Rare	—
	1805 ПЗ	.019	15.00	30.00	45.00	65.00
	1806 ПЗ	.023	15.00	30.00	50.00	80.00
	1806 AK	I.A.	15.00	30.00	45.00	65.00
	1807 AK	9,000	15.00	30.00	45.00	65.00
	1808 AK	.014	15.00	30.00	45.00	65.00
	1809 AK	.017	15.00	30.00	45.00	65.00
	1810 AT	4,000	25.00	50.00	75.00	110.00
	1811 AT	1,000	—	—	Rare	—
	1812 AT	9,000	15.00	30.00	50.00	80.00
	1813 AT	7,000	15.00	30.00	50.00	80.00
	1814 AT	3,000	15.00	30.00	45.00	65.00
	1815 AT	3,000	20.00	40.00	60.00	90.00
	1816 AT	.012	15.00	30.00	45.00	65.00
	1818 AT	8,000	15.00	30.00	45.00	65.00
	1819 AT	.010	15.00	30.00	45.00	65.00

KM#	Date	Mintage	VG	Fine	VF	XF
74	1820 AT	.012	15.00	30.00	45.00	65.00
	1821 AT	.014	15.00	30.00	45.00	65.00
	1822 AT	5,000	20.00	40.00	60.00	90.00
	1822 AK	I.A.	15.00	30.00	45.00	65.00
	1823 AK	5,000	15.00	30.00	45.00	65.00
	1824 AK	5,000	15.00	30.00	45.00	65.00
	1826 AT	5,000	15.00	30.00	45.00	65.00
	1828 AT	—	—	—	Rare	—
	1830 AT	—	15.00	30.00	45.00	65.00
	1831 AT	—	15.00	30.00	45.00	65.00

2 ABAZI

.917 SILVER, 23mm

KM#	Date	Mintage	VG	Fine	VF	XF
75	1804 ПЗ	.033	—	—	Rare	—
	1805 ПЗ	I.A.	15.00	30.00	50.00	80.00
	1806 AK	.042	15.00	30.00	50.00	80.00
	1807 AK	.071	15.00	30.00	50.00	80.00
	1807 AT	I.A.	30.00	60.00	90.00	150.00
	1808 AK	.065	15.00	30.00	50.00	80.00
	1809 AK	.086	15.00	30.00	50.00	80.00
	1810 AK	.020	17.50	35.00	55.00	85.00
	1811 AT	.005	20.00	40.00	60.00	90.00
	1812 AT	.059	15.00	30.00	50.00	80.00
	1813 AT	.048	15.00	30.00	50.00	80.00
	1814 AT	.020	15.00	30.00	50.00	80.00
	1815 AT	.021	15.00	30.00	50.00	80.00
	1816 AT	.079	15.00	30.00	50.00	80.00
	1818 AT	.085	15.00	30.00	50.00	80.00
	1819 AT	.105	15.00	30.00	50.00	80.00
	1820 AT	.112	15.00	30.00	50.00	80.00
	1821 AT	.075	15.00	30.00	50.00	80.00
	1822 AT	.024	22.50	45.00	65.00	100.00
	1822 AK	I.A.	15.00	30.00	50.00	80.00
	1823 AK	.039	15.00	30.00	50.00	80.00
	1824 AK	.032	15.00	30.00	50.00	80.00
	1826 AT	.075	15.00	30.00	50.00	80.00
	1827 AT	.172	15.00	30.00	50.00	80.00
	1828 AT	.126	15.00	30.00	50.00	80.00
	1829 AT	.213	12.50	25.00	40.00	60.00
	1830 AT	.273	12.50	25.00	40.00	60.00
	1831 AT	.338	12.50	25.00	40.00	60.00
	1831 BK	I.A.	12.50	25.00	40.00	60.00
	1832 BK	.210	12.50	25.00	40.00	60.00
	1833 BK	.114	15.00	30.00	50.00	80.00

KARABAGH

Karabagh, a former Khanate in Azerbaijan was under the control of the Ottomans until 996AD when Persia regained control. The principal mint was located in Panahabad, now the town of Shusha. They broke away from Persia in the second half of the 1700's and were abandoned to the in 1822.

The Nagorno-Karabakh was established as an autonomous region with Azerbaijan in 1923. They elected for independence in 1991.

RULERS

Ibrahim Khalil Khan,
AH1177-1221/1763-1806AD
Mahdi Quli Khan Muzatfar,
AH1221-1235/1806-1822AD

MINTNAME

بناه باد

Panahabad (Shusha)

MONETARY SYSTEM

Derived from the Safavid Persian System

1 Bisti=20 Dinars
1 Abbasi=200 Dinars

All coins are anonymous except KM#5, which is in the name of Fath'ali Shah of Iran.

The silver abbasi of Karabagh circulated widely in Iran, where it came to be known as a "Panabadi", a term later used for the half Kran in Iran.

IBRAHIM KHALIL KHAN

AH1177-1221/1763-1806AD

ABBASI

SILVER

In the name of Fath'ali Shah

KM#	Date	Good	VG	Fine	VF
5	AH1216	10.00	20.00	35.00	65.00

MAHDI QULI KHAN MUZATFAR

AH1221-1235/1806-1822AD

ABBASI

SILVER

Obv: Russian crown and branches. Rev: Mintname.

KM#	Date	Good	VG	Fine	VF
6	AH1222	10.00	20.00	37.50	70.00

Obv: Kalimah. Rev: Mintname and date.

KM#	Date	Good	VG	Fine	VF
7	AH1221	8.00	15.00	30.00	55.00

Obv: Date and unread inscription. Rev: Mintname. (Date sometimes also on reverse.)

KM#	Date	Good	VG	Fine	VF
8	AH1228	5.00	10.00	25.00	45.00
	1229	5.00	10.00	25.00	45.00
	1230	5.00	10.00	25.00	45.00
	1231	5.00	10.00	25.00	45.00
	1232	5.00	10.00	25.00	45.00
	1233	5.00	10.00	25.00	45.00
	1234	5.00	10.00	25.00	45.00
	1235	5.00	10.00	25.00	45.00
	1236	5.00	10.00	25.00	45.00
	1237	5.00	10.00	25.00	45.00

NOTE: The above listing of types is incomplete. In addition, more dates of the listed type likely exist.

SCHAMAKHI

Schamakhi, later the capital of Shirwan, is a former khanate located in Azerbaijan. It was taken by the Ottomans in 1578. Restored to Persian rule in 1607, it remained so throughout much of its later history until liberated by the Russians who annexed the khanate in 1820.

RULERS

Persian until annexed to Russia in 1813

MINTNAME

Shamakha شماخه

Shamakhi شماخ

MONETARY SYSTEM

20 Dinars = 1 Bisti
10 Bisti = 1 Abbasi

ABBASI

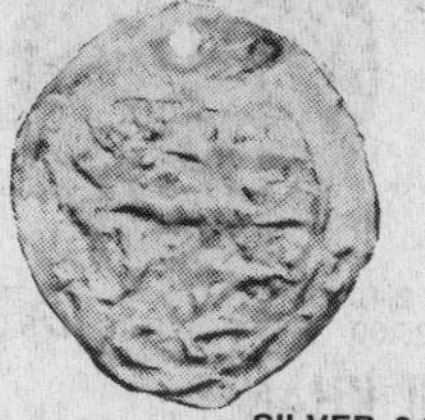

SILVER, 2.00-2.30 g

KM#	Date	Good	VG	Fine	VF
20	AH1223	16.50	32.50	70.00	100.00
	1227	15.00	30.00	65.00	90.00
	1228	15.00	30.00	65.00	90.00
	1229	15.00	30.00	65.00	90.00
	1230	15.00	30.00	65.00	90.00
	1231	15.00	30.00	65.00	90.00
	1232	15.00	30.00	65.00	90.00
	1233	15.00	30.00	65.00	90.00
	1234	15.00	30.00	65.00	90.00
	1235	15.00	30.00	65.00	90.00

SHEKI

Sheki, a former khanate in Russian Caucasia, was once part of Shirwan (under Ottoman rule). It was occupied and then annexed by Russia in 1820. Sheki is now part of Azerbaijan.

RULERS

Ja'far Quli Khan,
AH1221-1230/1806-1815AD
Ismail Khan,
AH1230-1234/1815-1819AD
Annexed to Russia in 1819

MONETARY SYSTEM

200 Dinars = 1 Abbasi
20 Dinars = 1 Bisti

MINTNAME

نخوي

Nukha

JA'FAR QULI KHAN

AH1221-1230/1806-1815AD

BISTI

COPPER
Obv: Crowned date, 6-pointed star below.
Rev: Leg. w/mint name below.

KM#	Date	Good	VG	Fine	VF
10	AH1221	25.00	45.00	80.00	150.00
	1222	25.00	45.00	80.00	150.00

Obv: Rosette and sprig below date.

KM#	Date	Good	VG	Fine	VF
11	1223	25.00	45.00	80.00	150.00
	1226	25.00	45.00	80.00	150.00

KM#	Date	Good	VG	Fine	VF
12	AH1228	25.00	45.00	80.00	150.00
	1233	25.00	45.00	80.00	150.00

ABBASI

SILVER, 2.10-2.30 g

KM#	Date	Good	VG	Fine	VF
5	AH1218	25.00	55.00	110.00	175.00

ISMAIL KHAN

AH1230-1234/1815-1819AD

1/2 ABBASI

SILVER, 1.10-1.20 g

KM#	Date	Good	VG	Fine	VF
15	AH1231	25.00	55.00	110.00	175.00
	1232	25.00	55.00	110.00	175.00

ABBASI

SILVER, 2.10-2.30 g

KM#	Date	Good	VG	Fine	VF
16	AH1232	25.00	55.00	110.00	175.00

TANNU TUVA

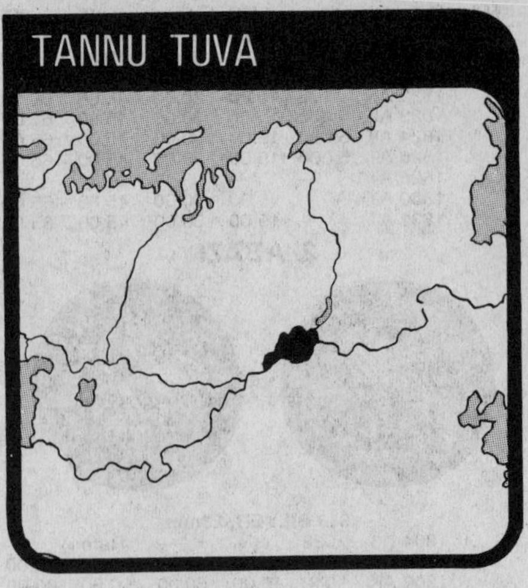

The Tannu-Tuva Peoples Republic (Tuva), an autonomous part of Russia located in central Asia on the northwest border of Outer Mongolia, has an area of 64,000 sq. mi. (165,760 sq. km.) and a population of about 175,000. Capital: Kyzyl. The economy is based on herding, forestry and mining.

As Urianghi, Tuva was part of Outer Mongolia of the Chinese Empire when tsarist Russia, after fomenting a separatist movement, extended its protection to the mountainous country in 1914. Tuva declared its independence as the Tannu-Tuva Peoples Republic in 1921 under the auspices of the Tuva Peoples Revolutionary Party. In 1926, following Russia's successful mediation of the resultant Tuvinian-Mongolian territorial dispute, TannuTuva and Outer Mongolia formally recognized each other's independence. The Tannu-Tuva Peoples Republic became an autonomous region of the U.S.S.R. on Oct. 13, 1944.

MONETARY SYSTEM

100 Kopejek (Kopeks) = 1 Aksha

KOPEJEK

ALUMINUM-BRONZE

KM#	Date	Mintage	VG	Fine	VF	XF
1	1934	—	17.50	25.00	35.00	60.00

2 KOPEJEK

ALUMINUM-BRONZE

KM#	Date	Mintage	VG	Fine	VF	XF
2	1933	—	—	—	—	—
	1934	—	20.00	27.50	45.00	70.00

3 KOPEJEK

ALUMINUM-BRONZE

KM#	Date	Mintage	VG	Fine	VF	XF
3	1933	—	—	—	—	—
	1934	—	17.50	25.00	35.00	60.00

5 KOPEJEK

ALUMINUM-BRONZE

KM#	Date	Mintage	VG	Fine	VF	XF
4	1934	—	20.00	27.50	45.00	70.00

10 KOPEJEK

COPPER-NICKEL

KM#	Date	Mintage	VG	Fine	VF	XF
5	1934	—	20.00	27.50	45.00	70.00

15 KOPEJEK

COPPER-NICKEL

KM#	Date	Mintage	VG	Fine	VF	XF
6	1934	—	20.00	27.50	45.00	70.00

20 KOPEJEK

COPPER-NICKEL

KM#	Date	Mintage	VG	Fine	VF	XF
7	1934	—	20.00	27.50	45.00	70.00

RUSSIAN TURKESTAN

Turkestan is the name conventionally used to designate ne extensive area of desert plains and low plateaus in Central Asia lying between Siberia on the north, Chinese Sinkiang and Afghanistan on the south, the Caspian Sea on the west, and Mongolia and the Gobi desert on the east. The region was occupied by Turkic nomads as early as the 6th century. They were organized as tribal tates for a time and, except for a few oasis cities, were elatively undisturbed by successive invasions by Mongols. Gradually, separate independent Islamic emirates developed around the cities of Bukhara, Khiva and Khokand. The eastern part of Turkestan, (Chinese Sinkiang) fell to the Chinese Communists in Oct. of 1949. The domination of Russia over most of the Turkic peoples of Asia began late in the 15th century when Ivan I brought the Mongol occupation of Russia to an end. By 900 the whole of Central Asia to the borders of China, Afghanistan and Persia had come under Russian uzerainty. Western Turkestam was established as an autonomous Soviet Socialist Republic in 1920. J. V. Stalin, then People's Commissar of Nationalities, objected to the formation of a single Turkish nation within he U.S.S.R. and effected the partition of the republic into he Soviet Socialist Republics of Uzbekistan, Turkmenistan, Kazakhstan, Kirghizstan and Tajikistan.

NOTE: The numerals '0' and '5' have variant forms in Russian Turkestan:

0 ○ instead of •

5 ل or ل instead of ۵ ٥

Note that the circle is used for 'zero', not for 'five' in Turkestan.

EMIRATE OF BUKHARA

Bukhara, a city and former emirate in southern Russian Turkestan, formed part (Sogdiana) of the Seleucid mpire after the conquest of Alexander the Great and emained an important regional center, sometimes city tate, until the 19th century. It became virtually a Russian assal in 1868 as a consequence of the Czarist invasion f 1866, following which it gradually became a part of Russian Turkestan and then part of Uzbekistan S.S.R., ow Uzbekistan.

RULERS

Haidar Tora,
AH1215-1242/1800-1826AD
Nasr Allah,
AH1242-1277/1826-1860AD
Muzaffar al-Din,
AH1277-1284/1860-1867AD
Russian Vassal,
AH1284-1336/1868-1917AD
Independent, AH1336-1338/1917-1920AD

MINTNAME

بخارا

Bukhara

HAIDAR TORA

(Amir Said Mir Haidar)
AH1215-1242/1800-1826AD

FALUS

COPPER
Obv. and rev: Legends.

C#	Date	Good	VG	Fine	VF
8	AH1232	3.00	5.00	10.00	20.00

Obv. and rev: Legend within Greek border.

C#	Date	Good	VG	Fine	VF
51	AH1221	3.50	6.50	12.50	25.00
	1228	3.50	6.50	12.50	25.00
	1229	3.50	6.50	12.50	25.00
	1241	3.50	6.50	12.50	25.00
	1242	3.50	6.50	12.50	25.00

Rev: Fish.

C#	Date	Good	VG	Fine	VF
52	AH1241	—	7.50	15.00	30.00

2 FALUS

SILVER

C#	Date	VG	Fine	VF	XF
54	AH1227	8.00	15.00	25.00	50.00
	1228	8.00	15.00	25.00	50.00

TENGA

SILVER, 2.50-3.00 g

C#	Date	VG	Fine	VF	XF
55	AH1216	8.00	15.00	25.00	45.00
	1217	8.00	15.00	25.00	45.00
	1223//1217	9.00	16.50	27.50	50.00
	1226	8.00	15.00	25.00	45.00
	1228//1215	9.00	16.50	27.50	50.00
	1230//1231	9.00	16.50	27.50	50.00
	1231//1216	9.00	16.50	27.50	50.00
	1232//1231	9.00	16.50	27.50	50.00
	1233//1218	9.00	16.50	27.50	50.00
	1234	8.00	15.00	25.00	45.00
	1235	8.00	15.00	25.00	45.00
	1236	8.00	15.00	25.00	45.00

In his own name

TILLA

GOLD
Obv: Teardrop. Rev: Circle.

C#	Date	VG	Fine	VF	XF
61	AH1217//1216	95.00	120.00	175.00	225.00
	1218	85.00	110.00	160.00	200.00
	1219	85.00	110.00	160.00	200.00
	1220//1216	95.00	120.00	175.00	225.00

NOTE: Earlier dates (AH1215) exist for this type.

Rev: Octagon.

C#	Date	VG	Fine	VF	XF
62	AH1221	100.00	150.00	225.00	300.00
	1222	100.00	150.00	225.00	300.00
	1225	100.00	150.00	225.00	300.00
	1226	100.00	150.00	225.00	300.00
	1227	100.00	150.00	225.00	300.00
	1229	100.00	150.00	225.00	300.00

Obv: Teardrop. Rev: Circle.

C#	Date	VG	Fine	VF	XF
63	AH1225	75.00	100.00	150.00	175.00

In the name of Ma'sum Ibn Danyal

Obv: Teardrop border

C#	Date	VG	Fine	VF	XF
65	AH1229	85.00	110.00	160.00	200.00
	1230/1229	95.00	120.00	175.00	225.00
	1230	85.00	110.00	160.00	200.00
	1231	85.00	110.00	160.00	200.00
	1233//1033(sic)	95.00	120.00	175.00	225.00
	1233//1232	95.00	120.00	175.00	225.00
	1234	85.00	110.00	160.00	200.00

C#	Date	VG	Fine	VF	XF
65a	AH1233	75.00	100.00	150.00	185.00
	1234	75.00	100.00	150.00	185.00
	1235	75.00	100.00	150.00	185.00

C#	Date	VG	Fine	VF	XF
66	AH1236//1235	75.00	100.00	150.00	185.00
	1236	75.00	100.00	150.00	185.00
	1239//1240	85.00	110.00	175.00	225.00
	1241	75.00	100.00	150.00	185.00

HUSSAIN SAYYID

AH1242/1826AD

TENGA

SILVER

C#	Date	VG	Fine	VF	XF
70	AH1241//1242	20.00	50.00	75.00	100.00

NASRULLAH

AH1242-1277/1826-1860AD

FALUS

BRASS

C#	Date	VG	Fine	VF	XF
71	AH1244	10.00	20.00	35.00	70.00

In the name of Haidar Tora

TENGA

SILVER

C#	Date	VG	Fine	VF	XF
72	AH1244	50.00	70.00	100.00	135.00

ANONYMOUS COINAGE

FALUS

COPPER or BRASS

C#	Date	Good	VG	Fine	VF
90	AH1277	5.00	8.50	15.00	22.50
	1281	5.00	8.50	15.00	22.50
	1284	5.00	8.50	15.00	22.50
	1285	5.00	8.50	15.00	22.50

BRONZE or BRASS

Y#	Date	VG	Fine	VF	XF
(Y1)	AH1322	8.50	16.50	25.00	45.00
	1324	8.50	16.50	25.00	45.00

In the name of Ma'sum Ibn Danyal

TENGA

SILVER, 3.20 g

C#	Date	VG	Fine	VF	XF
75	AH1242	8.50	15.00	30.00	45.00
	1244	8.50	15.00	30.00	45.00
	1245	8.50	15.00	30.00	45.00
	1247	8.50	15.00	30.00	45.00
	1248	8.50	15.00	30.00	45.00
	1249	8.50	15.00	30.00	45.00
	1255	8.50	15.00	30.00	45.00
	1257	8.50	15.00	30.00	45.00
	1258	8.50	15.00	30.00	45.00

C#	Date	VG	Fine	VF	XF
75	1261	10.00	20.00	40.00	75.00
	1263	8.50	15.00	30.00	45.00
	1265	8.50	15.00	30.00	45.00
	1267	8.50	15.00	30.00	45.00
	1269	8.50	15.00	30.00	45.00
	1271	8.50	15.00	30.00	45.00
	1273	8.50	15.00	30.00	45.00
	1275	8.50	15.00	30.00	45.00
	1276	8.50	15.00	30.00	45.00
	1277	8.50	15.00	30.00	45.00

C#	Date	VG	Fine	VF	XF
(C91)	AH1278	7.00	13.50	25.00	40.00
	1279	7.00	13.50	25.00	40.00
	1281	7.00	13.50	25.00	40.00
	1282	7.00	13.50	25.00	40.00
	1283	7.00	13.50	25.00	40.00
	1284	7.00	13.50	25.00	40.00
	1285	7.00	13.50	25.00	40.00
	1293//1283	20.00	30.00	45.00	60.00
	1293//1284	20.00	30.00	45.00	60.00
	1293	7.00	13.50	25.00	40.00
	1294//1293	20.00	30.00	45.00	60.00
	1294//1296	20.00	30.00	45.00	60.00
	1294	7.00	13.50	25.00	40.00
	1295	20.00	30.00	45.00	60.00
	1296	7.00	13.50	25.00	40.00
	1297//1298	20.00	30.00	45.00	60.00
	1297	7.00	13.50	25.00	40.00
	1298	7.00	13.50	25.00	40.00
	1299//1298	20.00	30.00	45.00	60.00
	1299	7.00	13.50	25.00	40.00
	1300	7.00	13.50	25.00	40.00
	1301//1299	20.00	30.00	45.00	60.00
	1301	7.00	13.50	25.00	40.00
	1303	7.00	13.50	25.00	40.00

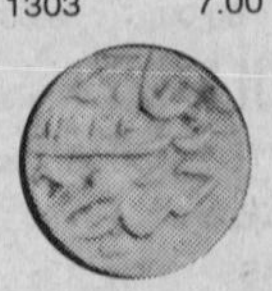

Thin and thick flan

Y#	Date	VG	Fine	VF	XF
(Y2)	1304	6.50	12.50	20.00	30.00
	1305//1304	10.00	16.50	27.50	40.00
	1305	6.50	12.50	20.00	30.00
	1306//1305	10.00	16.50	27.50	40.00
	1306//1307	10.00	16.50	27.50	40.00
	1306//1308	10.00	16.50	27.50	40.00
	1306	6.50	12.50	20.00	30.00
	1307	6.50	12.50	20.00	30.00
	1308//1309	10.00	16.50	27.50	40.00
	1308	6.50	12.50	20.00	30.00
	1309//1310	10.00	16.50	27.50	40.00
	1309	6.50	12.50	20.00	30.00
	1310//1315	10.00	16.50	27.50	40.00
	1310	6.50	12.50	20.00	30.00
	1311	6.50	12.50	20.00	30.00
	1315	6.50	12.50	20.00	30.00
	1316	6.50	12.50	20.00	30.00
	1319	6.50	12.50	20.00	30.00
	1320	6.50	12.50	20.00	30.00
	1322	6.50	12.50	20.00	30.00
	1323//1322	10.00	16.50	27.50	40.00
	1323	6.50	12.50	20.00	30.00

TILLA

GOLD

C#	Date	VG	Fine	VF	XF
85	AH1243//1242	85.00	110.00	165.00	200.00
	1243	75.00	100.00	150.00	185.00
	1244//1245	85.00	110.00	165.00	200.00

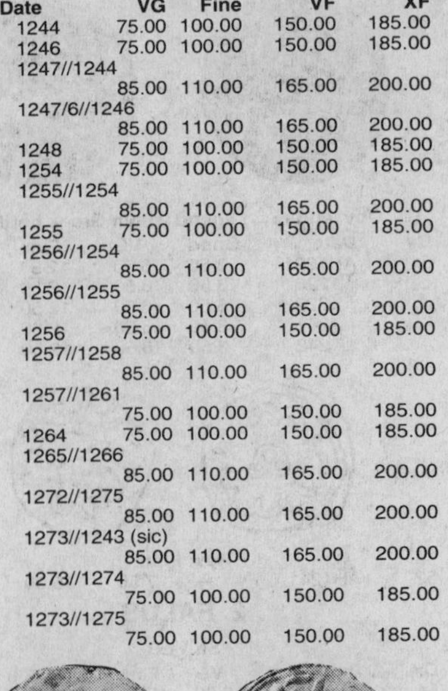

C#	Date	VG	Fine	VF	XF
85	1244	75.00	100.00	150.00	185.00
	1246	75.00	100.00	150.00	185.00
	1247//1244	85.00	110.00	165.00	200.00
	1247/6//1246	85.00	110.00	165.00	200.00
	1248	75.00	100.00	150.00	185.00
	1254	75.00	100.00	150.00	185.00
	1255//1254	85.00	110.00	165.00	200.00
	1255	75.00	100.00	150.00	185.00
	1256//1254	85.00	110.00	165.00	200.00
	1256//1255	85.00	110.00	165.00	200.00
	1256	75.00	100.00	150.00	185.00
	1257//1258	85.00	110.00	165.00	200.00
	1257//1261	75.00	100.00	150.00	185.00
	1264	75.00	100.00	150.00	185.00
	1265//1266	85.00	110.00	165.00	200.00
	1272//1275	85.00	110.00	165.00	200.00
	1273//1243 (sic)	85.00	110.00	165.00	200.00
	1273//1274	75.00	100.00	150.00	185.00
	1273//1275	75.00	100.00	150.00	185.00

C#	Date	VG	Fine	VF	XF
(C95)	AH1278	70.00	90.00	115.00	150.00
	1279	70.00	90.00	115.00	150.00
	1283	70.00	90.00	115.00	150.00
	1284	70.00	90.00	115.00	150.00
	1285	70.00	90.00	115.00	150.00
	1289	70.00	90.00	115.00	150.00
	1291	60.00	85.00	115.00	150.00
	1294	60.00	85.00	115.00	150.00
	1296//1300	75.00	100.00	125.00	175.00
	1296	60.00	85.00	115.00	150.00
	1297	60.00	85.00	115.00	150.00
	1299	60.00	85.00	115.00	150.00

NOTE: The date combination of obv: AH1279 and rev: AH1285 is reported for the above coin.

Y#	Date	VG	Fine	VF	XF
(Y3)	AH1303	75.00	100.00	125.00	165.00
	1306	75.00	100.00	125.00	165.00
	1309	75.00	100.00	125.00	165.00
	1315	75.00	100.00	125.00	165.00
	1316	75.00	100.00	125.00	165.00
	1319	75.00	100.00	125.00	165.00
	1325	75.00	100.00	125.00	165.00
	1327	75.00	100.00	125.00	165.00
	1328	75.00	100.00	125.00	165.00
	1329	75.00	100.00	125.00	165.00

ALIM IBN SAYYID MIR AMIN

AH1329-1338/1911-1920AD
Independent after AH1336/1917AD

FALUS

COPPER
Dates on obverse and reverse.

#	Date	VG	Fine	VF	XF
A4	AH132x-1332	—	—	—	—

Rev: "2" or "4" in circle.

#	Date	VG	Fine	VF	XF
4	AH1332	5.00	8.50	15.00	22.50
	1334	7.50	12.00	18.00	25.00

Date range 1331-36 reported, but unconfirmed.

Rev: "32" or "302" in a circle

Y#	Date	VG	Fine	VF	XF
4.1	AH1321	5.00	8.50	15.00	30.00
	1322	5.00	8.50	15.00	30.00
	1323	5.00	8.50	15.00	30.00
	1324	5.00	8.50	15.00	30.00
	1326	5.00	8.50	15.00	30.00
	1329	5.00	8.50	15.00	30.00
	1330	5.00	8.50	15.00	30.00
	1331	5.00	8.50	15.00	30.00
	1332	5.00	8.50	15.00	30.00
	1333	5.00	8.50	15.00	30.00
	1335	5.00	8.50	15.00	30.00
	(13)36	15.00	25.00	40.00	60.00

4 FALUS

COPPER

Y#	Date	VG	Fine	VF	XF
5	AH1334	8.00	12.50	20.00	35.00
	1335	8.00	12.50	20.00	35.00

8 FALUS

COPPER

Y#	Date	VG	Fine	VF	XF
A5	AH1335	8.00	12.50	20.00	35.00

1/2 TENGA

BRONZE

Y#	Date	VG	Fine	VF	XF
A6	AH1336	—	—	—	—

NOTE: Varieties w/star under mint exist.

TENGA

BRONZE, 15mm

Y#	Date	VG	Fine	VF	XF
6	AH1336	15.00	25.00	37.50	65.0

17-18mm

Y#	Date	VG	Fine	VF	XF
6a	AH1336	15.00	25.00	35.00	60.0
	1337	15.00	25.00	35.00	60.0

2 TENGA

BRONZE or BRASS
Obv. and rev: Greek border.

Y#	Date	VG	Fine	VF	XF
7	AH1336	15.00	25.00	35.00	55.0
	1337	15.00	25.00	35.00	55.0

Obv. and rev: Dotted inner circle.

Y#	Date	VG	Fine	VF	XF
7.1	AH1336	20.00	30.00	50.00	75.
	1337	20.00	30.00	50.00	75.

3 TENGA

BRONZE or BRASS

Y#	Date	VG	Fine	VF	XF
8	AH1336	15.00	25.00	35.00	50.00
	1337	15.00	25.00	35.00	50.00

4 TENGA

BRONZE or BRASS

Y#	Date	VG	Fine	VF	XF
9	AH1336	25.00	45.00	65.00	90.00

5 TENGA

BRONZE or BRASS

Y#	Date	VG	Fine	VF	XF
10	AH1336	22.50	35.00	50.00	75.00
	1337	22.50	35.00	50.00	75.00

10 TENGA

BRONZE or BRASS

Y#	Date	VG	Fine	VF	XF
11	AH1337	10.00	17.50	30.00	50.00
	1338//1337	10.00	17.50	30.00	50.00

20 TENGA

BRONZE or BRASS

Y#	Date	VG	Fine	VF	XF
12	AH1336	22.50	35.00	50.00	75.00
	1337	22.50	35.00	50.00	75.00

KHANATE OF KHIVA

Khiva, a present town once a great kingdom under the names of Chorasmia, Khwarezm and Urgenj, is located in Russian Turkestan east of the Caspian Sea and south of the Aral Sea. Russia established relations with Khiva in the 17th century, occupied it in 1873, and annexed it in 1875. In AH1338/1920AD it became Khwarezm Soviet People's Republic and later became part of the Uzbekistan S.S.R., now Uzbekistan.

RULERS

Muhammad Rahim
AH1221-1241/1805-1825AD
Allah Quli
AH1241-1258/1825-1842AD
Rahim Quli
AH1258-1261/1842-1845AD
Muhammad Amin
AH1261-1271/1845-1855AD
Abd Allah
AH1271-1272/1855-1856AD
Qutlugh Muhammad
AH1272/1856AD
Sayyid Muhammad Khan
AH1272-1282/1856-1865AD
Sayyid Muhammad Rahim
AH1282-1289/1865-1872AD
Sayid Muhammad Rahim, Russian Vassal
AH1290-1313/1873-1896AD
Sayyid Abdullah Khan and Junaid Khan
AH1337-1338/1918-1920AD

MINTNAME

Khwarezm خوارزم

MUHAMMAD RAHIM

AH122x-1241/1825AD

TENGA

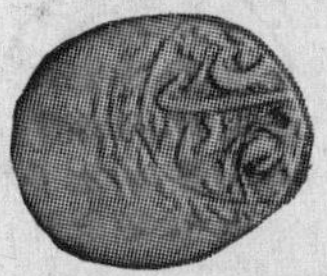

SILVER, 3.00 g

C#	Date	VG	Fine	VF	XF
40	AH1232	15.00	30.00	50.00	85.00
	1235	15.00	30.00	50.00	85.00

ALLAH QULI

AH1241-1258/1825-1842AD

TENGA

SILVER, 3.00 g

C#	Date	VG	Fine	VF	XF
50	AH1247	15.00	30.00	50.00	85.00
	1248	15.00	30.00	50.00	85.00
	1258	15.00	30.00	50.00	85.00

NOTE: Varieties exist.

MUHAMMAD AMIN

AH1261-1271/1845-1855AD

TENGA

SILVER, 3.00 g

C#	Date	VG	Fine	VF	XF
60	AH1262	12.50	25.00	40.00	75.00
	1263	12.50	25.00	40.00	75.00
	1264	12.50	25.00	40.00	75.00
	1265	12.50	25.00	40.00	75.00
	1266	12.50	25.00	40.00	75.00
	1267	12.50	25.00	40.00	75.00
	1268	12.50	25.00	40.00	75.00
	1269	12.50	25.00	40.00	75.00

1/2 TILLA

GOLD

C#	Date	VG	Fine	VF	XF
65	AH1261	200.00	350.00	500.00	750.00
	1265	200.00	350.00	500.00	750.00

Rev. leg. in octagonal frame.

C#	Date	VG	Fine	VF	XF
65a	AH1270	200.00	350.00	500.00	750.00
	1271	200.00	350.00	500.00	750.00

QUTLUGH MUHAMMAD

AH1271-1272/1855-1856AD

1/2 TILLA

GOLD

Y#	Date	VG	Fine	VF	XF
A1	AH1271	250.00	450.00	750.00	1100.
	1272	250.00	450.00	750.00	1100.

SAYYID MUHAMMAD KHAN

AH1272-1282/1856-1865AD

FALUS

COPPER

Y#	Date	VG	Fine	VF	XF
1	AH1272	20.00	35.00	50.00	75.00
	1274	20.00	35.00	50.00	75.00
	1275	20.00	35.00	50.00	75.00
	1277	20.00	35.00	50.00	75.00
	1278	20.00	35.00	50.00	75.00
	1279	20.00	35.00	50.00	75.00
	1280	20.00	35.00	50.00	75.00

TENGA

SILVER, 3.00 g
Obv: Date in center. Rev: Ornamented.

Y#	Date	VG	Fine	VF	XF
2	AH1273	10.00	25.00	45.00	75.00
	1274	10.00	25.00	45.00	75.00
	1275	10.00	25.00	45.00	75.00
	1276	10.00	25.00	45.00	75.00
	1277	10.00	25.00	45.00	75.00
	1278	10.00	25.00	45.00	75.00
	1279	10.00	25.00	45.00	75.00
	1280	10.00	25.00	45.00	75.00
	1281	10.00	25.00	45.00	75.00

TILLA

GOLD

Y#	Date	VG	Fine	VF	XF
A3	AH1276	275.00	450.00	700.00	1000.
	1277	275.00	450.00	700.00	1000.

SAYYID MUHAMMAD RAHIM

AH1282-1289/1865-1872AD

FALUS

COPPER

Y#	Date	VG	Fine	VF	XF
3	AH1286	12.50	25.00	50.00	75.00
	1290	12.50	25.00	50.00	75.00
	1308	12.50	25.00	50.00	75.00
	1310	12.50	25.00	50.00	75.00
	1311	12.50	25.00	50.00	75.00

TENGA

SILVER

Y#	Date	VG	Fine	VF	XF
6	AH1282	8.00	20.00	30.00	45.00
	1283	8.00	20.00	30.00	45.00

Y#	Date	VG	Fine	VF	XF
6	1284//1283				
		10.00	26.50	40.00	60.00
	1284	8.00	20.00	30.00	45.00
	1285	8.00	20.00	30.00	45.00
	1288	8.00	20.00	30.00	45.00
	1287	10.00	21.50	42.50	70.00
	1294	10.00	21.50	42.50	70.00
	1294//1295				
		10.00	21.50	42.50	70.00
	1298	10.00	21.50	42.50	70.00
	1301	10.00	21.50	42.50	70.00
	1303	10.00	21.50	42.50	70.00
	1305	10.00	21.50	42.50	70.00
	1306	10.00	21.50	42.50	70.00
	1307	10.00	21.50	42.50	70.00
	1308	10.00	21.50	42.50	70.00
	1311	10.00	21.50	42.50	70.00
	1312	10.00	21.50	42.50	70.00

SAYYID ABDULLAH KHAN and JUNAID KHAN

AH1337-1338/1918-1920AD

TENGA

SILVER

Y#	Date	VG	Fine	VF	XF
8	AH1337	100.00	175.00	250.00	—

2-1/2 TENGA

COPPER or BRASS
Obv: Sun rising.

Y#	Date	VG	Fine	VF	XF
9.1	AH1337	27.50	37.50	50.00	90.00

Obv: Full sun in sky.

Y#	Date	VG	Fine	VF	XF
9.2	AH1337	27.50	37.50	50.00	90.00

NOTE: Many die varieties exist.

5 TENGA

COPPER or BRASS
Obv: Full sun in sky.
Rev: Leg. in small circle, date above.

Y#	Date	VG	Fine	VF	XF
10.1	AH1337	37.50	52.50	70.00	110.00

Rev: Leg. in small circle, date below.

Y#	Date	VG	Fine	VF	XF
10.2	AH1337	37.50	52.50	70.00	110.00

NOTE: Many die varieties exist.

KHOQAND

Khoqand, a town and former khanate in eastern Turkestan, was a powerful state in the 18th century. Russian superiority in the area was recognized following the holy war of 1875 and was annexed in 1875. It regained its independence briefly during 1918-1920 and became a Soviet Peoples Republic briefly between 1920-1924, and finally was absorbed into Uzbekistan S.S.R.

RULERS

Muhammad Ali Khan
AH1238-1256/1822-1840AD
Sher Ali
AH1258-1261/1842-1845AD
Muhammad Khudayar Khan
AH1261-1275/1845-1858AD
Muhammad Fuland, Rebel
AH1275-1290/1858-1873AD
Malla Khan
AH1275-1275/1858-1862AD
Shah Murad
AH1278-1279/1862AD
Muhammad Khudayar Khan
AH1279-1280/1862-1863AD
Sayyid Sultan
AH1280-1282/1863-1864AD
Muhammad Khudayer Khan
AH1282-1292/1865-1875AD
Independent until AH1283/1866AD
Russian Vassal AH1283-1293/
1866-1876AD
Nasir al-Din
AH1292-1293/1875-1876AD
Annexed To Russia, 1875-1876AD

MINTNAMES

Until AH1257, the coinage of Khoqand was struck at two mints.

Fe - Fergana(t) فرغانة

Kd - Khoqand خوقند

MUHAMMAD ALI KAHN

AH1238-1256/1822-1840AD

PUL

COPPER

C#	Date	VG	Fine	VF	XF
60	AH1249 (Kd)	6.00	12.50	20.00	35.00

C#	Date	VG	Fine	VF	XF
63	AH1252(Fa)	15.00	35.00	50.00	70.00

TENGA

SILVER

C#	Date	VG	Fine	VF	XF
65	AH1241	10.00	22.50	37.50	55.00
	1243	10.00	22.50	37.50	55.00
	1244	10.00	22.50	37.50	55.00

C#	Date	VG	Fine	VF	XF
A66	ND(Kd)	—	—	—	—

Obv: Teardrop. Rev: Hexagon.

C#	Date	VG	Fine	VF	XF
66	AH1245	15.00	25.00	40.00	65.00

TILLA

GOLD

C#	Date	VG	Fine	VF	XF
67	AH1247(Fa)	—	—	—	—

C#	Date	VG	Fine	VF	XF
68	AH1252	75.00	100.00	150.00	250.00
	1254	75.00	100.00	150.00	250.00
	1255	75.00	100.00	150.00	250.00
	1256	75.00	100.00	150.00	250.00
	1257	75.00	100.00	150.00	250.00

SHER ALI

AH1258-1261/1842-1845AD

FALUS

COPPER

C#	Date	VG	Fine	VF	XF
—	AH1259	—	—	—	—

TILLA

GOLD

C#	Date	VG	Fine	VF	XF
78	AH1259/1258				
		100.00	125.00	150.00	225.00
	1259	80.00	100.00	135.00	175.00
	1260	80.00	100.00	135.00	175.00

MUHAMMAD KHUDAYAR KHAN

2nd Reign
AH1261-1275/1845-1858AD

PUL

COPPER

C#	Date	VG	Fine	VF	XF
87	AH 1265	8.00	14.00	23.50	35.0
	1269	8.00	14.00	23.50	35.0

TENGA

SILVER

C#	Date	VG	Fine	VF	XF
95	AH1266//1268				
		31.50	50.00	75.00	100.0
	1266	25.00	40.00	60.00	80.0
	1269	25.00	40.00	60.00	80.0
	1270	25.00	40.00	60.00	80.0
	1271	25.00	40.00	60.00	80.0
	1272	25.00	40.00	60.00	80.0
	1273	25.00	40.00	60.00	80.0
	1274	25.00	40.00	60.00	80.0
	1275	25.00	40.00	60.00	80.0

TILLA

GOLD

C#	Date	VG	Fine	VF	XF
100	AH1260	75.00	100.00	150.00	250.0
	1261//1264				
		95.00	125.00	190.00	325.0
	1261	75.00	100.00	150.00	250.0
	1262//1261				
		95.00	125.00	190.00	325.0
	1263	75.00	100.00	150.00	250.0
	1264	75.00	100.00	150.00	250.0
	1265	75.00	100.00	150.00	250.0
	1266	75.00	100.00	150.00	250.0
	1270	75.00	100.00	150.00	250.0
	1272	75.00	100.00	150.00	250.0
	1273	75.00	100.00	150.00	250.0
	1274	75.00	100.00	150.00	250.0
	1275	75.00	100.00	150.00	250.0

Obv: New title.

C#	Date	VG	Fine	VF	XF
100.5	AH1261//1262				
		125.00	275.00	400.00	550.0
	1265	125.00	275.00	400.00	550.0

MUHAMMAD FULAD

Rebel
AH1275-1290/1858-1873AD

TENGA

SILVER

C#	Date	VG	Fine	VF	XF
105	AH1292	15.00	25.00	40.00	60.0
	1293	15.00	25.00	40.00	60.0

TILLA

GOLD

C#	Date	VG	Fine	VF	XF
110	AH1275-90	70.00	85.00	100.00	125.00

MALLA KHAN

AH1275-1278/1858-1862AD

PUL

COPPER

C#	Date	VG	Fine	VF	XF
112	AH1277	10.00	20.00	32.50	60.00

TENGA

SILVER

C#	Date	VG	Fine	VF	XF
115	AH1275	27.50	55.00	70.00	85.00
	1276	27.50	55.00	70.00	85.00
	1277	27.50	55.00	70.00	85.00

TILLA

GOLD

C#	Date	VG	Fine	VF	XF
118	AH1275	125.00	175.00	225.00	300.00
	1276	125.00	175.00	225.00	300.00
	1277	125.00	175.00	225.00	300.00
	1278	125.00	175.00	225.00	300.00

SHAH MURAD

AH1278-1279/1862AD

TILLA

GOLD

C#	Date	VG	Fine	VF	XF
128	AH1278	100.00	125.00	150.00	175.00

MUHAMMAD KHUDAYAR KHAN

3rd Reign

AH1279-1280/1862-1863AD

TENGA

SILVER

Obv. & rev: Teardrop borders.

C#	Date	VG	Fine	VF	XF
130	AH1279	30.00	60.00	100.00	150.00

TILLA

GOLD

C#	Date	VG	Fine	VF	XF
135	AH-	Reported, not confirmed			

SAYYID SULTAN

AH1280-1282/1863-1865AD

TENGA

SILVER

C#	Date	VG	Fine	VF	XF
140	AH1280	42.50	75.00	125.00	175.00
	1281	42.50	75.00	125.00	175.00
	1285	42.50	75.00	125.00	175.00

TILLA

GOLD

C#	Date	VG	Fine	VF	XF
145	AH1280	100.00	115.00	140.00	165.00
	1281	100.00	115.00	140.00	165.00

MUHAMMAD KHUDAYAR KHAN

4th Reign

AH1282-1292/1865-1875AD

PUL

COPPER

C#	Date	VG	Fine	VF	XF
148	AH1287	6.00	13.50	26.50	37.50

TENGA

SILVER

C#	Date	VG	Fine	VF	XF
151	AH1282	25.00	40.00	60.00	80.00
	1283	25.00	40.00	60.00	80.00
	1284	25.00	40.00	60.00	80.00
	1285	25.00	40.00	60.00	80.00
	1286	25.00	40.00	60.00	80.00
	1287	25.00	40.00	60.00	80.00
	1289	25.00	40.00	60.00	80.00
	1291	25.00	40.00	60.00	80.00
	1292	25.00	40.00	60.00	80.00

In the name of Malla Khan

C#	Date	VG	Fine	VF	XF
152	AH1289	30.00	50.00	80.00	100.00

TILLA

GOLD

C#	Date	VG	Fine	VF	XF
155	AH1282	70.00	80.00	100.00	140.00
	1283	70.00	80.00	100.00	140.00
	1285	70.00	80.00	100.00	140.00
	1288	70.00	80.00	100.00	140.00

NASIR AL DIN

AH1292-1293/1875-1875AD

TILLA

GOLD

C#	Date	VG	Fine	VF	XF
165	AH1292	Reported, not confirmed			

KHWAREZM PEOPLES REPUBLIC

AH1338-1343/1920-1924AD

20 ROUBLES

BRONZE or BRASS

Y#	Date	VG	Fine	VF	XF
1	AH1338	22.50	30.00	40.00	65.00
	1339	20.00	30.00	40.00	65.00
	1340	20.00	30.00	40.00	65.00

25 ROUBLES

BRONZE or BRASS

Rev: 8 pointed star.

Y#	Date	VG	Fine	VF	XF
2	AH1339	17.50	30.00	40.00	65.00

Rev: 12 pointed star.

Y#	Date	VG	Fine	VF	XF
2.1	AH1339	17.50	30.00	40.00	65.00

100 ROUBLES

BRONZE or BRASS

Y#	Date	VG	Fine	VF	XF
3	AH1339	17.50	25.00	32.50	55.00

500 ROUBLES

BRONZE or BRASS

Y#	Date	VG	Fine	VF	XF
4	AH1339	50.00	75.00	200.00	275.00

Y#	Date	VG	Fine	VF	XF
4a	AH1339	20.00	30.00	40.00	65.00
	1340	20.00	30.00	40.00	65.00

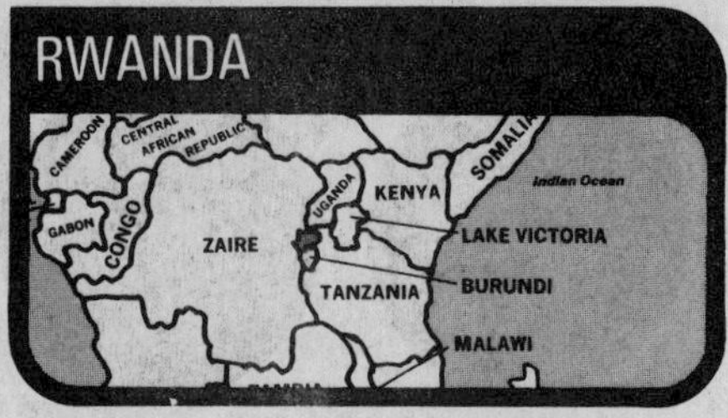

The Republic of Rwanda, located in central Africa between the Republic of the Congo and Tanzania, has an area of 10,169 sq. mi. (26,340 sq. km.) and a population of 7.3 million. Capital: Kigali. The economy is based on agriculture and mining. Coffee and tin are exported.

German Lieutenant Count von Goetzen was the first European to visit Rwanda, 1894. Four years later the court of the Mwami (the Tutsi king of Rwanda) willingly permitted the kingdom to become a protectorate of Germany. In 1916, during the African campaigns of World War I, Belgian troops from Congo occupied Rwanda. After the war it, together with Burundi, became a Belgian League of Nations mandate under the name of the Territory of Ruanda-Urundi. Following World War II, Ruanda-Urundi became a Belgian administered U.N. trust territory. The Tutsi monarchy was deposed by the U.N. supervised election of 1961, after which Belgium granted Rwanda internal autonomy. On July 1, 1962, the U.N. terminated the Belgian trusteeship and granted full independence to both Rwanda and Burundi.

For earlier coinage see Belgian Congo, and Rwanda and Burundi.

MINT MARKS

(a) - Paris, privy marks only
(b) - Brussels, privy marks only

MONETARY SYSTEM

100 Centimes = 1 Franc

1/2 FRANC

ALUMINUM

KM#	Date	Mintage	VF	XF	Unc
9	1970	5.000	.50	1.00	2.00

FRANC

COPPER-NICKEL

KM#	Date	Mintage	VF	XF	Unc
5	1964(b)	3.000	5.00	10.00	20.00
	1965(b)	4.500	.50	1.00	2.00

ALUMINUM

KM#	Date	Mintage	VF	XF	Unc
8	1969	5.000	.50	1.50	3.00

KM#	Date	Mintage	VF	XF	Unc
12	1974	13.000	.15	.25	.65
	1977(a)	15.000	.15	.25	.65
	1985	—	.10	.15	.65

2 FRANCS

ALUMINUM
F.A.O. Issue

KM#	Date	Mintage	VF	XF	Unc
10	1970	5.000	.10	.20	.50

5 FRANCS

BRONZE

KM#	Date	Mintage	VF	XF	Unc
6	1964(b)	4.000	.25	.50	1.75
	1965(b)	3.000	5.00	10.00	20.00

KM#	Date	Mintage	VF	XF	Unc
13	1974	.7.000	1.00	3.00	6.00
	1977(a)	7.002	1.00	2.00	4.00
	1987	—	.15	.25	.75

10 FRANCS

3.7500 g, .900 GOLD, .1085 oz AGW

KM#	Date	Mintage	VF	XF	Unc
1	1965	10,000	—	—	60.00
	1965	—	—	Proof	65.00

COPPER-NICKEL

KM#	Date	Mintage	VF	XF	Unc
7	1964(b)	6.000	1.00	2.00	5.00

KM#	Date	Mintage	VF	XF	Unc
14.1	1974	6.000	3.00	5.00	9.00

Reduced size.

KM#	Date	Mintage	VF	XF	Unc
14.2	1985	—	.25	.50	1.25

20 FRANCS

BRASS

KM#	Date	Mintage	VF	XF	Unc
15	1977(a)	22.000	1.00	2.00	4.00

25 FRANCS

7.5000 g, .900 GOLD, .2170 oz AGW
Similar to 10 Francs, KM#1.

KM#	Date	Mintage	VF	XF	Unc
2	1965	4,000	—	Proof	100.00

50 FRANCS

15.0000 g, .900 GOLD, .4340 oz AGW
Similar to 10 Francs, KM#1.

KM#	Date	Mintage	VF	XF	Unc
3	1965	3,000	—	Proof	175.00

BRASS

KM#	Date	Mintage	VF	XF	Unc
16	1977(a)	9.000	2.50	3.50	7.00

100 FRANCS

30.0000 g, .900 GOLD, .8681 oz AGW

KM#	Date	Mintage	VF	XF	Unc
4	1965	3,000	—	Proof	360.00

31.2300 g, .999 SILVER, 1.0041 oz ASW
Nelson Mandela

KM#	Date	Mintage	VF	XF	Unc
18	1990	—	—	—	30.00
	1990	*.050	—	Proof	40.00

200 FRANCS

18.0000 g, .800 SILVER, .4630 oz ASW
10th Anniversary of Independence and F.A.O. Issue

KM#	Date	Mintage	VF	XF	Unc
11	1972	.030	—	6.50	12.00

1000 FRANCS

31.6400 g, .999 SILVER, 1.0173 oz ASW
25th Anniversary of National Bank

KM#	Date	Mintage	VF	XF	Unc
7	1989	—	—	—	50.00

2000 FRANCS

7.8000 g, .999 GOLD, .2500 oz AGW
Nelson Mandela
Similar to 5000 Francs, KM#20.

KM#	Date	Mintage	VF	XF	Unc
19	1990	*.050	—		Proof 200.00

5000 FRANCS

15.5300 g, .999 GOLD, .5000 oz AGW
Nelson Mandela

KM#	Date	Mintage	VF	XF	Unc
20	1990	3,000	—		Proof 400.00

PROOF SETS (PS)

KM#	Date	Mintage	Identification	Issue Price	Mkt. Val.
PS1	1961(4)	3,000	KM#1-4	—	700.00

RWANDA-BURUNDI

Rwanda-Burundi, a Belgian League of Nations mandate and United Nations trust territory comprising the provinces of Rwanda and Burundi of the former colony of German East Africa, was located in central Africa between the present Republic of the Congo, Uganda and mainland Tanzania. The mandate-trust territory had an area of 20,916 sq. mi. (54,272 sq. km.) and a population of 4.3 million.

For specific statistics and history of Rwanda and of Burundi see individual entries.

When Rwanda and Burundi were formed into a mandate for administration by Belgium, their names were changed to Ruanda and Urundi and they were organized as an integral part of the Belgian Congo. During the mandate-trust territory period, they utilized the coinage of the Belgian Congo, which from 1954 through 1960 carried the appropriate dual identification. After the Belgian Congo acquired independence as the Republic of the Congo, the provinces of Ruanda and Urundi reverted to their former names of Rwanda and Burundi and utilized a common currency issued by a Central Bank (B.E.R.B.) established for that purpose until the time when, as independent republics, each issued its own national coinage.

For earlier coinage see Belgian Congo.

FRANC

BRASS

KM#	Date	Mintage	VF	XF	Unc
1	1960	2.000	2.50	5.00	10.00
	1961	16.000	.35	.75	1.50
	1964	3.000	2.50	5.00	10.00

NOTE: For later coinage see individual listings under Rwanda and Burundi.

COPPER-NICKEL
Mule. Obv: Rwanda-Burundi, KM#1.
Rev: Belgium, 1 Franc KM#142 or KM#143.

KM#	Date	Mintage	VF	XF	Unc
2	1961	50 pcs.	—	—	—

Listings For

SAARLAND: refer to Germany/West

ST. BARTHOLOMEW

St. Bartholomew (St. Barthelemy, St. Barts), a French island possession located in the Leeward Islands of the West Indies about 15 miles northwest of Guadeloupe, of which it is a dependency, has an area of 10 sq. mi. (26 sq. km.) and a population of about 3,000. Capital: BasseTerre, on the island of that name. The treeless island produces sugar, bananas, and rum.

St. Bartholomew was occupied by France in 1648 and sold to Sweden in 1784. In 1877 it was reacquired, by purchase, by France.

The coins issued under Sweden for St. Bartholomew - crown-countermarked U.S. coins, Cayenne sous, Swedish and Polish billon -have been extensively counterfeited.

RULERS

French, until 1784, 1877—
Swedish, 1784-1877

MONETARY SYSTEM

1797-1821

6 Stivers = 1 Bit
12 Bits = 8 Spanish Reales

1821-1846
(actually used to 1864)

6 Stivers = 1 Bit (Courant)
18-3/4 Bits (Courant) = 8 Reales

1864-1878

100 Cents = 1 Dollar

COUNTERMARKED COINAGE

Proclamation of December 30, 1808

3 STIVERS

SILVER
c/m: Crowned 3/M on Spanish Colonial 1/2 Real.

KM#	Date	Mintage	Good	VG	Fine	VF
4	ND(1808)	—	125.00	225.00	450.00	800.00

4 STIVERS

SILVER
c/m: Crowned 4/M on Spanish Colonial 1/2 Real.

KM#	Date	Mintage	Good	VG	Fine	VF
5	ND(1808)	—	125.00	225.00	450.00	800.00

7 STIVERS

SILVER
c/m: Crowned 7/M on Spanish Colonial 1 Real.

KM#	Date	Mintage	Good	VG	Fine	VF
7	ND(1808)	—	125.00	225.00	450.00	800.00

9 STIVERS

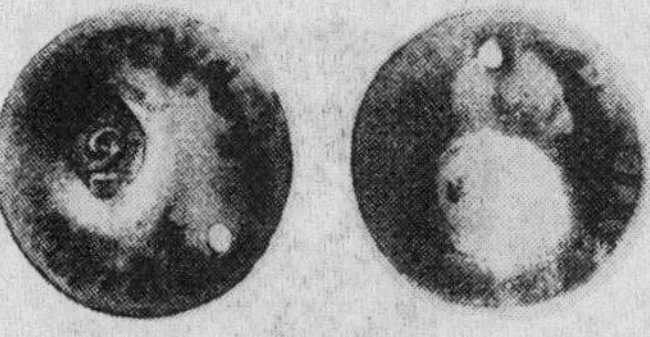

SILVER
c/m: Crowned 9/M on Spanish Colonial 1 Real.

KM#	Date	Mintage	Good	VG	Fine	VF
8	ND(1808)	—	150.00	250.00	550.00	1000.

c/m: Crowned 9/M on Spanish 1 Real.

KM#	Date	Mintage	Good	VG	Fine	VF
9	ND(1808)	—	150.00	250.00	500.00	900.00

14 STIVERS

SILVER

c/m: Crowned 14/M on Spanish Colonial 2 Reales.

KM#	Date	Mintage	Good	VG	Fine	VF
11	ND(1808)	—	200.00	300.00	600.00	1200.

NOTE: For St. Bartholomew countermarked 14 Stivers with additional countermark P in circle of dots see Saint Eustatius in Netherlands Antilles.

18 STIVERS

SILVER

c/m: Crowned 18/M on Spanish Colonial 2 Reales.

KM#	Date	Mintage	Good	VG	Fine	VF
13	ND(1808)	—	200.00	300.00	600.00	1200.

NOTE: Many contemporary counterfeits of the 1808 countermarks exist.

Proclamation of July 9, 1834

STIVER

SILVER

c/m: Type I crown on Curacao Stiver, KM#24.

KM#	Date	Mintage	Good	VG	Fine	VF
3	ND(1834)	—	75.00	150.00	300.00	500.00

2 SOU

BILLON

c/m: Type II crown on Cayenne 2 Sou, KM#1.

KM#	Date	Mintage	Good	VG	Fine	VF
2.1	ND(1834-64)	—	65.00	115.00	160.00	225.00

c/m: Type III crown on Cayenne 2 Sou, KM#1.

KM#	Date	Mintage	Good	VG	Fine	VF
2.2	ND(1834-64)	—	65.00	115.00	160.00	225.00

c/m: Type IV crown on Cayenne 2 Sou, KM#1.

KM#	Date	Mintage	Good	VG	Fine	VF
2.3	ND(1834-64)	—	75.00	125.00	175.00	250.00

c/m: Type V crown on Cayenne 2 Sou, KM#1.

KM#	Date	Mintage	Good	VG	Fine	VF
2.4	ND(1834-64)	—	75.00	125.00	175.00	250.00

c/m: Type VI crown on Cayenne 2 Sou, KM#1.

KM#	Date	Mintage	Good	VG	Fine	VF
2.5	ND(1834-64)	—	85.00	135.00	190.00	275.00

c/m: Type VII crown on Cayenne 2 Sou, KM#1.

KM#	Date	Mintage	Good	VG	Fine	VF
2.6	ND(1834-64)	—	85.00	135.00	190.00	275.00

NOTE: The crown countermark of 1834 was extensively counterfeited and imitated for over a century and a half from the period of issue. Spanish and Spanish colonial hosts are almost assuredly counterfeit.

Listings For

St. Eustatius: refer to Netherlands Antilles.

ST. HELENA & ASCENSION

St. Helena, a British colony located about 1,150 mile (1,850 km.) from the west coast of Africa, has an are of 47 sq. mi. (410 sq. km.) and a population of *7,00 Capital: Jamestown. Flax, lace, and rope are produce for export Ascension and Tristan da Cunha ar dependencies of St. Helena.

The island was discovered and named by the Port guese navigator Joao de Nova Castella in 1502. Th Portuguese imported livestock, fruit trees, and veg tables but established no permanent settlement. Th Dutch occupied the island temporarily, 1645-51. The o ginal European settlement was founded by represe tatives of the British East India Company sent to anne the island after the departure of the Dutch. The Dutc returned and captured St. Helena from the British c New Year's Day, 1673, but were in turn ejected by British force under Sir Richard Munden. Thereafter S Helena was the undisputed possession of Great Britai The island served as the place of exile for Napoleo several Zulu chiefs, and an ex-sultan of Zanzibar.

RULERS

British

MINT MARKS

PM - Pobjoy Mint

MONETARY SYSTEM

12 Pence = 1 Shilling

BRITISH EAST INDIA COMPANY

(1651-1834)

HALF PENNY

COPPER

KM#	Date	Mintage	Fine	VF	XF	Un
4	1821	—	7.00	15.00	45.00	100.0
	1821	—	—	—	Proof	150.0
			BRONZE			
4a	1821	—	—	—	Proof	150.0
			GILT BRONZE			
4b	1821	—	—	—	Proof	Rar

ST. HELENA

MONETARY SYSTEM

100 Pence = 1 Pound

25 PENCE (CROWN)

COPPER-NICKEL
St. Helena Tercentenary

KM#	Date	Mintage	Fine	VF	XF	Unc
5	1973	.100	—	—	—	3.00
	28.2800 g, .925 SILVER, .8411 oz ASW					
5a	1973	.010	—	—	Proof	20.00

COPPER-NICKEL
Queen's Silver Jubilee

KM#	Date	Mintage	Fine	VF	XF	Unc
6	1977	.050	—	—	—	3.00
	28.2800 g, .925 SILVER, .8411 oz ASW					
6a	1977	.025	—	—	Proof	16.50

COPPER-NICKEL
25th Anniversary of Coronation

KM#	Date	Mintage	Fine	VF	XF	Unc
7	1978PM	—	—	—	—	3.00
	28.2800 g, .925 SILVER, .8411 oz ASW					
7a	1978PM	.070	—	—	—	15.00
	1978PM	.025	—	—	Proof	22.00

COPPER-NICKEL
80th Birthday of Queen Mother

KM#	Date	Mintage	Fine	VF	XF	Unc
8	1980	.100	—	—	—	3.00
	28.2800 g, .925 SILVER, .8411 oz ASW					
8a	1980	.025	—	—	—	15.00

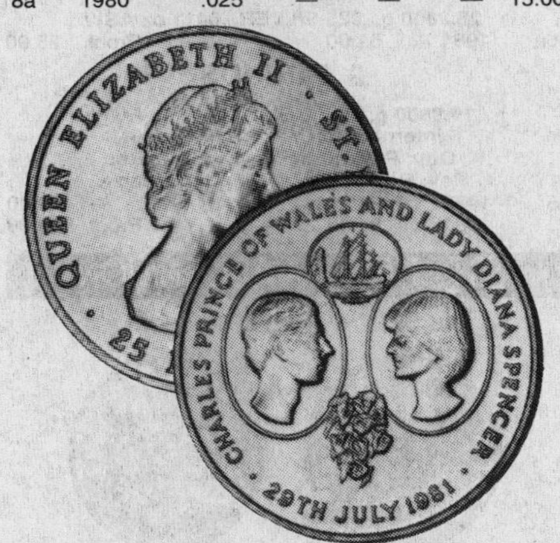

COPPER-NICKEL
Wedding of Prince Charles and Lady Diana

KM#	Date	Mintage	Fine	VF	XF	Unc
9	1981	.050	—	—	—	3.00
	28.2800 g, .925 SILVER, .8411 oz ASW					
9a	1981	.030	—	—	Proof	25.00

International Year of the Scout
Obv: Portrait of Queen.

KM#	Date	Mintage	Fine	VF	XF	Unc
10	1983	.010	—	—	—	17.50
	1983	.010	—	—	Proof	25.00

50 PENCE

COPPER-NICKEL
150th Anniversary of Colony of St. Helena

KM#	Date	Mintage	Fine	VF	XF	Unc
12	1984	.010	—	—	—	3.00
	28.2800 g, .925 SILVER, .8411 oz ASW					
12a	1984	5,000	—	—	Proof	30.00

47.5400 g, .917 GOLD, 1.4017 oz AGW

KM#	Date	Mintage	Fine	VF	XF	Unc
12b	1984	150 pcs.	—	—	Proof	850.00

COPPER-NICKEL
Royal Visit of Prince Andrew

KM#	Date	Mintage	Fine	VF	XF	Unc
13	1984	.125	—	—	—	3.00
	28.2800 g, .925 SILVER, .8411 oz ASW					
13a	1984	5,000	—	—	Proof	30.00

2 POUNDS

15.9800 g, .917 GOLD, .4712 oz AGW
International Year of the Scout

KM#	Date	Mintage	Fine	VF	XF	Unc
11	1983	2,000	—	—	—	450.00
	1983	2,000	—	—	Proof	500.00

ASCENSION ISLAND

An island of volcanic origin, Ascension Island lies in the south Atlantic 700 miles (1,100 km.) northwest of St. Helena. It has an area of 34 sq. mi. (88 sq. km.) on an island 9 miles (14 km.) long and 6 miles (10 km.) wide. Approximate population: 1,146. Although having little vegetation and scant rainfall, the island has a very healthy climate. The island is the nesting place for large numbers of sea turtles and sooty terns. Phosphates and guano are the chief natural sources of income.

The island was discovered on Ascension Day, 1501, by Joao da Nova, a Portuguese navigator. It lay unoccupied until 1815 when occupied by the British. It was under Admiralty rule until 1922 when it was annexed as a dependency of St. Helena. During World War II an airfield was built that has been used as a fueling stop for transatlantic flights to Southern Europe, North Africa and the Near East.

RULERS

British

MINT MARKS

PM - Pobjoy Mint

25 PENCE (CROWN)

COPPER-NICKEL
25th Anniversary of Coronation

KM#	Date	Mintage	Fine	VF	XF	Unc
1	1978PM	—	—	—	—	3.50
	28.2800 g, .925 SILVER, .8411 oz ASW					
1a	1978PM	.070	—	—	—	15.00
	1978PM	.025	—	—	Proof	25.00

Mule. Obv: Isle of Man crown.
Rev: Ascension KM#1.

KM#	Date	Mintage	Fine	VF	XF	Unc
2	1978PM (error)	367 pcs.	—	—	200.00	250.00

COPPER-NICKEL
Wedding of Prince Charles and Lady Diana

KM#	Date	Mintage	Fine	VF	XF	Unc
3	1981PM	.050	—	—	—	4.00

28.2800 g, .925 SILVER, .8411 oz ASW

KM#	Date	Mintage	Fine	VF	XF	Unc
3a	1981	500 pcs.	—	—	Proof	50.00

International Year of the Scout

KM#	Date	Mintage	Fine	VF	XF	Unc
4	1983	.010	—	—	—	25.00
	1983	.010	—	—	Proof	35.00

50 PENCE

COPPER-NICKEL
Royal Visit of Prince Andrew

KM#	Date	Mintage	Fine	VF	XF	Unc
6	1984	.125	—	—	—	4.00

28.2800 g, .925 SILVER, .8411 oz ASW

KM#	Date	Mintage	Fine	VF	XF	Unc
6a	1984	5,000	—	—	Proof	25.00

2 POUNDS

15.9800 g, .917 GOLD, .4712 oz AGW
International Year of the Scout
Obv: Portrait of Queen Elizabeth.
Rev: Boy Scout viewing landscape.

KM#	Date	Mintage	Fine	VF	XF	Unc
5	1983	2,000	—	—	—	450.00
	1983	2,000	—	—	Proof	500.00

ST. HELENA-ASCENSION

PENNY

BRONZE

KM#	Date	Mintage	Fine	VF	XF	Unc
1	1984	—	—	—	—	.15
	1984	*.010	—	—	Proof	1.25

Obv: Similar to 2 Pence, KM#12.

KM#	Date	Mintage	Fine	VF	XF	Unc
13	1991	—	—	—	—	.15

2 PENCE

BRONZE

KM#	Date	Mintage	Fine	VF	XF	Unc
2	1984	—	—	—	.10	.25
	1984	*.010	—	—	Proof	1.50

KM#	Date	Mintage	Fine	VF	XF	Unc
12	1991	—	—	—	.10	.25

5 PENCE

COPPER-NICKEL

KM#	Date	Mintage	Fine	VF	XF	Unc
3	1984	—	—	—	.10	.35
	1984	—	—	—	Proof	1.75

Obv: Similar to 2 Pence, KM#12.

KM#	Date	Mintage	Fine	VF	XF	Unc
14	1991	—	—	—	.10	.35

10 PENCE

COPPER-NICKEL

KM#	Date	Mintage	Fine	VF	XF	Unc
4	1984	—	—	—	.20	.50
	1984	—	—	—	Proof	2.00

Obv: Similar to 2 Pence, KM#12.

KM#	Date	Mintage	Fine	VF	XF	Unc
15	1991	—	—	—	.20	.50

50 PENCE

COPPER-NICKEL

KM#	Date	Mintage	Fine	VF	XF	Unc
5	1984	—	—	—	1.00	1.50
	1984	—	—	—	Proof	2.50

Wedding of Prince Andrew and Sarah Ferguson

KM#	Date	Mintage	Fine	VF	XF	Unc
7	1986	.013	—	—	—	4.00

28.2800 g, .925 SILVER, .8411 oz ASW

KM#	Date	Mintage	Fine	VF	XF	Unc
7a	1986	2,500	—	—	Proof	25.00

47.5400 g, .917 GOLD, 1.4017 oz AGW

KM#	Date	Mintage	Fine	VF	XF	Unc
7b	1986	50 pcs.	—	—	Proof	1200.

COPPER-NICKEL

165th Anniversary of Napoleon's Death

KM#	Date	Mintage	Fine	VF	XF	Unc
	1986	.050	—	—	—	5.00

Obv: Similar to 2 Pence, KM#12.

KM#	Date	Mintage	Fine	VF	XF	Unc
6	1991	—	—	—	—	5.00

POUND

NICKEL-BRASS
Sooty Tern

KM#	Date	Mintage	Fine	VF	XF	Unc
	1984	—	—	—	1.75	3.25
	1984	—	—	—	Proof	3.50

9.5000 g, .925 SILVER, .2826 oz ASW

KM#	Date	Mintage	Fine	VF	XF	Unc
a	1984	.010	—	—	Proof	20.00

NICKEL-BRASS
Obv: Similar to 2 Pence, KM#12.

KM#	Date	Mintage	Fine	VF	XF	Unc
7	1991	—	—	—	1.75	3.25

2 POUNDS

COPPER-NICKEL
Queen Mother

KM#	Date	Mintage	Fine	VF	XF	Unc
11	1990	—	—	—	—	12.00

28.2800 g, .925 SILVER, .8411 oz ASW

KM#	Date	Mintage	Fine	VF	XF	Unc
11a	1990	*.050	—	—	Proof	50.00

40th Anniversary of Coronation of Elizabeth II

KM#	Date	Mintage	Fine	VF	XF	Unc
18	ND(1993)	*.010	—	—	Proof	55.00

25 POUNDS

155.0000 g, .999 SILVER, 4.9839 oz ASW
165th Anniversary of Napoleon's Death
Illustration reduced. Actual size: 65mm
Obv: Similar to 50 Pence, KM#7.

KM#	Date	Mintage	Fine	VF	XF	Unc
9	1986	.015	—	—	Proof	100.00

50 POUNDS

32.2600 g, .999 PLATINUM, 1.0051 oz APW
165th Anniversary of Napoleon's Death

KM#	Date	Mintage	Fine	VF	XF	Unc
10	1986	5,000	—	—	Proof	550.00

MINT SETS (MS)

KM#	Date	Mintage	Identification	Issue Price	Mkt. Val.
MS1	1984	—	KM1-6	—	5.50

PROOF SETS (PS)

KM#	Date	Mintage	Identification	Issue Price	Mkt. Val.
PS1	1984	—	KM1-6	—	25.00

ST. KITTS & NEVIS

St. Kitts (St. Christopher), a West Indian island located in the Leeward Islands southeast of Puerto Rico, is the principal component of a British associated state composed of the islands of St. Kitts, Nevis, and Anguilla. The associated state has an area of 104 sq. mi. (360 sq. km.) and a population of *40,000. Capital: Basseterre, on St. Kitts. The islands export sugar, molasses, rum, cotton, and coconuts.

St. Kitts was discovered by Columbus in 1493 and was settled by Thomas Warner, an Englishman, in 1623. The island was ceded to the British by the Treaty of Utrecht, 1713. France protested British occupancy, and on three occasions between 1616 and 1782 seized the island and held it for short periods. St. Kitts used the coins and currency of the British Caribbean Territories (Eastern Group).

In early 1967 St. Kitts was united politically with Nevis and Anguilla to form a self-governing British associated state. In June 1967 Anguilla declared its independence of the federated state, and in Feb. 1969 unilaterally severed all ties with Britain and established the Republic of Anguilla. Britain refused to accept the unilateral movement and installed a commissioner to govern Anguilla, which remains a nominal part of the associated state. The political status of the three islands will be decided in the near future by a referendum.

From approximately 1750-1830, billon 2 sous of the French colony of Cayenne were countermarked 'SK' and used on St. Kitts. They were valued at 1-1/3 Pence.

RULERS

British

MONETARY SYSTEM

19th Century

108 Pence = 9 Shillings =
12 Bits = 1 Dollar

20th Century

100 Cents = 1 Dollar

NOTE: The grades shown describe the condition of the raised countermarks, not the host coin itself, which is typically well worn.

SAINT KITTS

COUNTERMARKED COINAGE

1-1/2 PENCE

Black Dog

BILLON
c/m: S on French Colonies 24 Deniers, C#6.

KM#	Date	Year	Good	VG	Fine	VF
1	ND	(1801)	50.00	75.00	100.00	125.00

2-1/4 PENCE

BILLON
c/m: S.K. on French Guyana 2 Sous, C#1.

KM#	Date	Year	Good	VG	Fine	VF
2	ND (1809-1812)		50.00	75.00	100.00	125.00

1/8 DOLLAR

SILVER
c/m: S on cut 1/8 section of Spanish 8 Reales.

KM#	Date	Year	Good	VG	Fine	VF
3	ND	(1801)	200.00	500.00	800.00	1000.

1/4 DOLLAR

SILVER
c/m: S on cut 1/4 section of Spanish 8 Reales.

KM#	Date	Year	Good	VG	Fine	VF
4	ND	(1801)	200.00	500.00	800.00	1000.

1/2 DOLLAR

SILVER
c/m: S on cut 1/2 section of Spanish 8 Reales.

KM#	Date	Year	Good	VG	Fine	VF
5	ND	(1801)	200.00	500.00	800.00	1000.

NEVIS

Nevis, a component of one of the West Indies Associated States, is located in the Leeward Islands and has an area of 50 sq. mi. (105 sq. km.) and a population of about 12,000. Charleston is the chief town and port. Sea-island cotton is the chief crop, and some sugar is produced.

Nevis was discovered by Columbus in 1493. It was first colonized by the English in 1628. Admiral De Grasse captured the island for France in 1782, but it was restored to Britain the following year. Alexander Hamilton, first Secretary of the Treasury, was born on Nevis in 1757.

RULERS

British

MONETARY SYSTEM

72 Black Dogs = 1 Dollar

COUNTERMARKED COINAGE

BLACK DOG

BILLON
c/m: NEVIS on French Guiana 2 Sous.

KM#	Date	Mintage	Good	VG	Fine	VF
1	ND(1801)	—	60.00	80.00	120.00	150.00

4 BLACK DOGS

SILVER
c/m: NEVIS above incuse 4.

KM#	Date	Mintage	Good	VG	Fine	VF
2	ND	—	200.00	500.00	850.00	1650.

6 BLACK DOGS

SILVER
c/m: NEVIS above incuse 6.

KM#	Date	Mintage	Good	VG	Fine	VF
3	ND	—	225.00	550.00	900.00	1750.

7 BLACK DOGS

SILVER
c/m: NEVIS above incuse 7.

KM#	Date	Mintage	Good	VG	Fine	VF
4	ND	—	200.00	500.00	850.00	1650.

9 BLACK DOGS

SILVER
c/m: NEVIS above incuse 9 on Spanish Colonial 1 Real.

KM#	Date	Mintage	Good	VG	Fine	VF
5.1	ND	—	200.00	450.00	800.00	1600.

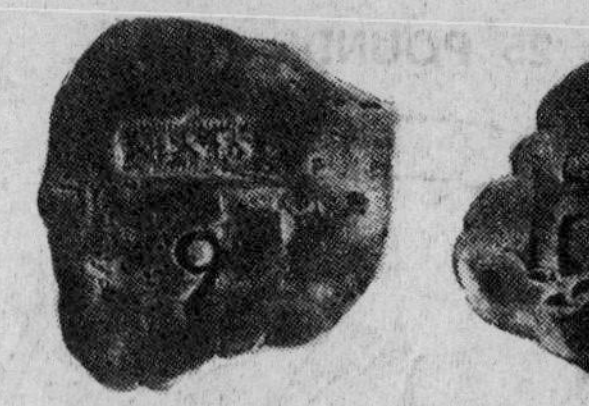

c/m: NEVIS above incuse 9 on Potosi 1 Real.

KM#	Date	Mintage	Good	VG	Fine	VF
5.2	ND(1684)	—	450.00	900.00	1500.	—

ST. KITTS & NEVIS (St. Christopher & Nevis)

4 DOLLARS

COPPER-NICKEL
F.A.O. Issue

KM#	Date	Mintage	Fine	VF	XF	Unc
1	1970	.013	—	—	3.00	9.00
	1970	2,000	—	—	Proof	20.00

10 DOLLARS

COPPER-NICKEL
Royal Visit

KM#	Date	Mintage	Fine	VF	XF	Unc
3	1985	.100	—	—	—	7.50

28.2800 g, .925 SILVER, .8411 oz ASW

KM#	Date	Mintage	Fine	VF	XF	Unc
3a	1985	5,000	—	—	Proof	35.00

47.5400 g, .917 GOLD, 1.4013 oz AGW

KM#	Date	Mintage	Fine	VF	XF	Unc
3b	1985	250 pcs.	—	—	Proof	1200.

20 DOLLARS

COPPER-NICKEL
200th Anniversary of Battle of the Saints

KM#	Date	Mintage	VF	XF	Un
4 (1)	1982	—	—	—	11.5

28.2800 g, .925 SILVER, .8411 oz ASW

KM#	Date	Mintage	VF	XF	Un
4a (1a)	1982	2,500		Proof	40.0

COPPER-NICKEL
Attainment of Independence

KM#	Date	Mintage	Fine	VF	XF	Unc
2	1983	—	—	—	—	15.0

28.2800 g, .925 SILVER, .8411 oz ASW

KM#	Date	Mintage	Fine	VF	XF	Unc
2a	1983	5,000	—	—	Proof	35.0

100 DOLLARS

7.9900 g, .917 GOLD, .2356 oz AGW
200th Anniversary of Siege of Brimstone Hill

KM#	Date	Mintage	VF	XF	Unc
5 (2)	1982	250 pcs.	—	—	250.0
	1982	15 pcs.	—	Proof	650.0

129.5900 g, .925 SILVER, 3.8543 oz ASW
Illustration reduced. Actual size: 63mm
Tropical Birds - Hummingbird
Obv: Coat of arms.

KM#	Date	Mintage	VF	XF	Unc
6 (3)	1988	*.010	—	Proof	120.00

ST. LUCIA

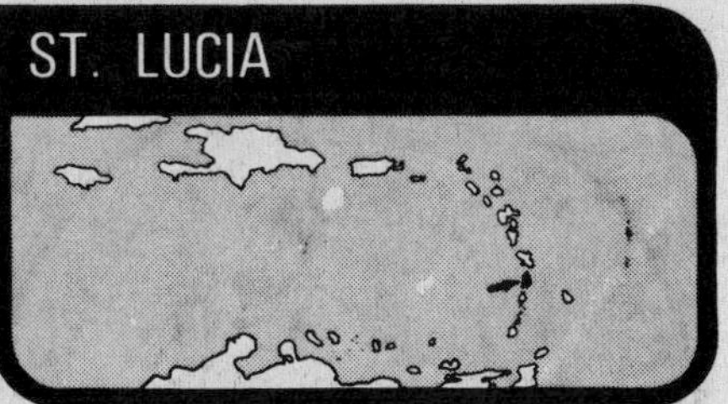

Saint Lucia, an independent island nation located in the Windward Islands of the West Indies between St. Vincent and Martinique, has an area of 238 sq. mi. (620 sq. km.) and a population of *150,000. Capital: Castries. The economy is agricultural. Bananas, copra, cocoa, sugar and logwood are exported.

Saint Lucia was discovered by Columbus in 1502. The first attempts at settlement undertaken by the British in 1605 and 1638 were frustrated by sickness and the determined hostility of the fierce Carib inhabitants. The French settled it in 1650 and made a treaty with the natives. Until 1814, when the island became a definite British possession, it was the scene of a continuous conflict between the British and French which saw the island change hands on at least 14 occasions. In 1967, under the West Indies Act, Saint Lucia was established as a British associated state, self-governing in internal affairs. Complete independence was attained on February 22, 1979. Saint Lucia is a member of the Commonwealth of Nations. The Queen of England is Chief ofState.

Prior to 1950, the island used sterling, which was superseded by the currency of the British Caribbean Territories (Eastern Group) and the East CaribbeanStates.

RULERS

British

MONETARY SYSTEM

12 Deniers = 1 Sou
15 Sous = 1 Escalin
20 Sous = 1 Livre
6 Black Dogs = 4 Stampees
= 1 Bit = 9 Pence

COUNTERMARKED COLONIAL COINAGE

1811

3 STAMPEES

SILVER
c/m: Circle w/crenalated edges on 1/4 cut of Spanish or Spanish Colonial 2 Reales.

KM#	Date	Mintage	Good	VG	Fine	VF
5	ND(1811)	—	—	—	—	—

ESCALIN

SILVER, 2.00 G
c/m: Circle on 1/3 cut of Spanish or Spanish Colonial 2 Reales.

KM#	Date	Mintage	Good	VG	Fine	VF
6	ND(1811)	—	150.00	250.00	375.00	550.00

1-1/2 ESCALINS

SILVER
c/m: Two circles on 1/4 cut of Spanish or Spanish Colonial 4 Reales.

KM#	Date	Mintage	Good	VG	Fine	VF
7	ND(1811)	—	250.00	400.00	600.00	850.00

2 ESCALINS

SILVER, 4.00 g
c/m: Three circles on 1/3 cut of Spanish or Spanish Colonial 4 Reales.

KM#	Date	Mintage	Good	VG	Fine	VF
8	ND(1811)	—	300.00	500.00	700.00	950.00

1813

2 LIVRES, 5 SOUS

SILVER, 5.30 g
c/m: S:Lucie on 1/3 outer cut of Spanish or Spanish Colonial 8 Reales.

KM#	Date	Mintage	Good	VG	Fine	VF
9	ND(1813)	—	40.00	80.00	150.00	275.00

6 LIVRES, 15 SOUS

SILVER, 15.00 g
c/m: S:Lucie on 1/3 center cut of Spanish or Spanish Colonial 8 Reales.

KM#	Date	Mintage	Good	VG	Fine	VF
10	ND(1813)	—	75.00	150.00	300.00	550.00

NOTE: There are no known genuine examples existing today of any other similar varieties cut from Spanish or Spanish Colonial 2 and 4 Reales with this countermark.

MODERN COINAGE

MONETARY SYSTEM

100 Cents = 1 Dollar

4 DOLLARS

COPPER-NICKEL
F.A.O. Issue

KM#	Date	Mintage	VF	XF	Unc
11	1970	.013	—	3.00	9.00
	1970	2,000	—	Proof	20.00

5 DOLLARS

COPPER-NICKEL
Papal Visit
Obv: Similar to 10 Dollars, KM#12.

KM#	Date	Mintage	VF	XF	Unc
14	1986	—	—	—	7.00

28.2800 g, .925 SILVER, .8411 oz ASW

KM#	Date	Mintage	VF	XF	Unc
14a	1986	2,120	—	Proof	40.00

10 DOLLARS

COPPER-NICKEL
200th Anniversary of Battle of the Saints

KM#	Date	Mintage	VF	XF	Unc
12	1982	—	—	—	11.50
	28.2800 g, .925 SILVER, .8411 oz ASW				
12a	1982	2,500	—	Proof	35.00

COPPER-NICKEL
Royal Visit

KM#	Date	Mintage	VF	XF	Unc
13	1985	.100	—	—	7.50
	28.2800 g, .925 SILVER, .8411 oz ASW				
13a	1985	5,000	—	Proof	35.00
	47.5400 g, .917 GOLD, 1.4013 oz AGW				
13b	1985	250 pcs.	—	Proof	1100.

28.2800 g, .925 SILVER, .8411 oz ASW
Commonwealth Finance Ministers Meeting

KM#	Date	Mintage	VF	XF	Unc
16	1986	1,000	—	Proof	30.00

100 DOLLARS

129.5900 g, .925 SILVER, 3.8543 oz ASW
Illustration reduced. Actual size: 63mm
Tropical Birds - Two Parrots

KM#	Date	Mintage	VF	XF	Unc
17	1988	*.010	—	Proof	120.00

500 DOLLARS

15.9800 g, .917 GOLD, .4709 oz AGW
Papal Visit

KM#	Date	Mintage	VF	XF	Unc
15	1986	100 pcs.	—	Proof	850.00

ST. PIERRE & MIQUELON

The Territorial Collectivity of St. Pierre and Miquelon, French overseas territory located 10 miles (16 km.) o the south coast of Newfoundland, has an area of 93 sc mi. (242 sq. km.) and a population of *6,000. Capita St. Pierre. The economy of the barren archipelago i based on cod fishing and fur farming. Fish and fish pro ducts, and mink and silver fox pelts are exported.

The islands, occupied by the French in 1604, were cap tured by the British in 1702 and held until 1763 when the were returned to the possession of France and employe as a fishing station. They passed between France an England on six more occasions between 1778 and 181 when they were awarded permanently to France by th Treaty of Paris. The rugged, soil-poor granite islands which will support only evergreen shrubs, are all tha remain to France of her extensive colonies in Nort America. In 1958 St. Pierre and Miquelon voted in favo of the new constitution of the Fifth Republic of France thereby choosing to remain within the new French Com munity.

RULERS

French

MINT MARKS

(a) - Paris, privy marks only

MONETARY SYSTEM

100 Centimes = 1 Franc

FRANC

ALUMINUM

KM#	Date	Mintage	Fine	VF	XF	Unc
1	1948(a)	.600	.50	.75	1.25	3.50

2 FRANCS

ALUMINUM

KM#	Date	Mintage	Fine	VF	XF	Unc
2	1948(a)	.300	.75	1.00	2.00	5.00

ST. THOMAS & PRINCE

The Democratic Republic of Sao Tome and Principe (formerly the Portuguese overseas province of St. Thomas and Prince Islands) is located in the Gulf of Guinea 150 miles (241 km.) off the west African coast. It has an area of 372 sq. mi. (960 sq. km.) and a population of *121,000. Capital: Sao Tome. The economy of the islands is based on cocoa, copra and coffee.

St. Thomas and St. Prince were uninhabited when discovered by Portuguese navigators Joao de Santarem and Pedro de Escobar in 1470. After the failure of their initial settlement, 1485, the Portuguese successfully colonized St. Thomas with a colony of prisoners and exiled Jews, 1493. An initial prosperity based on the sugar trade gave way to a time of misfortune, 1567-1709, that saw the colony attacked and occupied or plundered by the French and Dutch, ravaged by the slave revolt of 1595; and finally rendered destitute by the transfer of the world sugar trade to Brazil. In the late 1800s, the colony turned from the production of sugar to cocoa, the basis of its present economy

The islands were designated a Portuguese overseas province in 1951. On April 25, 1974, the government of Portugal was seized by a military junta which reached agreements providing for independence for the Portuguese overseas provinces of Portuguese Guinea (Guinea-Bissau), Mozambique, Cape Verde Islands, Angola, and St. Thomas and Prince Islands. The Democratic Republic of Sao Tome and Principe was declared on July 12, 1975.

RULERS

Portuguese, until 1975

MINT MARKS

R = Rio

20 REIS

COPPER

KM#	Date	Mintage	VG	Fine	VF	XF
A1	1813R	.010	10.00	15.00	25.00	50.00
	1815R	—	10.00	15.00	25.00	50.00

KM#	Date	Mintage	VG	Fine	VF	XF
D1	1819 Rio	—	2.00	4.50	10.00	25.00
	1820	—	2.00	4.50	10.00	25.00
	1825	.028	3.00	5.00	11.50	30.00

NOTE: Previously listed in Mozambique.

40 REIS

COPPER

KM#	Date	Mintage	VG	Fine	VF	XF
B1	1813 Rio	.015	12.00	20.00	30.00	65.00
	1815 Rio	—	20.00	30.00	45.00	75.00
E1	1819 Rio	—	3.75	7.50	15.00	30.00
	1820 Bahia	—	3.50	7.50	15.00	30.00
	1821 Lisbon	—	2.00	4.50	9.00	20.00
	1822	—	20.00	30.00	45.00	75.00
	1825	.024	4.00	6.00	11.50	22.50

NOTE: The difference between the Bahia and Lisbon coins is slight. The crown on the Bahia issue being rounder, approximately 2mm between the crown and rim.

NOTE: Previously listed in Mozambique.

80 REIS

COPPER

KM#	Date	Mintage	VG	Fine	VF	XF
C1	1813R	.015	10.00	15.00	22.50	50.00
F1	1819 Rio	—	7.50	12.50	20.00	45.00
	1820	—	5.00	8.00	12.50	30.00
	1825	.014	5.00	8.00	12.50	30.00

NOTE: Previously listed in Mozambique.

MONETARY REFORM

MONETARY SYSTEM

100 Centavos = 1 Escudo

10 CENTAVOS

NICKEL-BRONZE

KM#	Date	Mintage	Fine	VF	XF	Unc
2	1929	.500	1.00	2.00	5.00	15.00

BRONZE

KM#	Date	Mintage	Fine	VF	XF	Unc
15	1962	.500	.10	.20	.50	2.00

ALUMINUM

KM#	Date	Mintage	Fine	VF	XF	Unc
15a	1971	1.000	—	.10	.25	.75

20 CENTAVOS

NICKEL-BRONZE

KM#	Date	Mintage	Fine	VF	XF	Unc
3	1929	.250	1.25	2.50	6.00	16.00

BRONZE
18mm

KM#	Date	Mintage	Fine	VF	XF	Unc
16.1	1962	.250	.10	.25	.50	3.00

16mm

KM#	Date	Mintage	Fine	VF	XF	Unc
16.2	1971	.750	—	.10	.25	1.25

50 CENTAVOS

NICKEL-BRONZE

KM#	Date	Mintage	Fine	VF	XF	Unc
1	1928	—	10.00	20.00	75.00	450.00
	1929	.400	2.50	5.00	25.00	250.00

KM#	Date	Mintage	Fine	VF	XF	Unc
8	1948	.080	1.00	2.00	10.00	45.00

COPPER-NICKEL

KM#	Date	Mintage	Fine	VF	XF	Unc
10	1951	.048	1.00	2.00	10.00	45.00

BRONZE
20mm

KM#	Date	Mintage	Fine	VF	XF	Unc
17.1	1962	.480	.15	.30	.60	2.25

22mm

KM#	Date	Mintage	Fine	VF	XF	Unc
17.2	1971	.600	.10	.20	.50	1.00

ESCUDO

COPPER-NICKEL

KM#	Date	Mintage	Fine	VF	XF	Unc
4	1939	.100	4.00	8.00	35.00	175.00

NICKEL-BRONZE

KM#	Date	Mintage	Fine	VF	XF	Unc
9	1948	.060	2.00	4.00	10.00	50.00

COPPER-NICKEL

KM#	Date	Mintage	Fine	VF	XF	Unc
11	1951	.018	3.00	7.00	20.00	70.00

BRONZE

KM#	Date	Mintage	Fine	VF	XF	Unc
18	1962	.160	.20	.50	1.50	5.00
	1971	.350	.10	.25	.50	1.50

2-1/2 ESCUDOS

3.5000 g, .650 SILVER, .0732 oz ASW

KM#	Date	Mintage	Fine	VF	XF	Unc
5	1939	.080	4.50	9.00	25.00	150.00
	1948	.120	2.50	5.00	12.50	75.00

KM#	Date	Mintage	Fine	VF	XF	Unc
12	1951	.064	2.50	5.00	8.00	30.00

COPPER-NICKEL

KM#	Date	Mintage	Fine	VF	XF	Unc
19	1962	.140	.20	.50	1.50	4.00
	1971	.250	.10	.25	.50	1.50

5 ESCUDOS

7.0000 g, .650 SILVER, .1462 oz ASW

KM#	Date	Mintage	Fine	VF	XF	Unc
6	1939	.060	6.00	12.00	30.00	175.00
	1948	.100	4.50	8.50	17.50	85.00

25mm

KM#	Date	Mintage	Fine	VF	XF	Unc
13	1951	.072	2.50	5.00	15.00	37.50

4.0000 g, .600 SILVER, .0771 oz ASW
22mm

KM#	Date	Mintage	Fine	VF	XF	Unc
20	1962	.088	.65	1.25	2.50	6.50

COPPER-NICKEL

KM#	Date	Mintage	Fine	VF	XF	Unc
22	1971	.100	.35	.75	1.50	3.50

10 ESCUDOS

12.5000 g, .835 SILVER, .3356 oz ASW

KM#	Date	Mintage	Fine	VF	XF	Unc
7	1939	.040	7.00	15.00	35.00	250.00

12.5000 g, .720 SILVER, .2894 oz ASW

KM#	Date	Mintage	Fine	VF	XF	Unc
14	1951	.040	2.50	5.00	15.00	32.50

COPPER-NICKEL

KM#	Date	Mintage	Fine	VF	XF	Unc
23	1971	.100	.50	1.00	2.00	6.50

20 ESCUDOS

NICKEL

KM#	Date	Mintage	Fine	VF	XF	Unc
24	1971	.075	.70	1.50	3.00	7.00

50 ESCUDOS

18.0000 g, .650 SILVER, .3762 oz ASW
500th Anniversary of Discovery

KM#	Date	Mintage	Fine	VF	XF	Unc
21	1970	.150	—	—	—	6.00
	1970	*200 pcs.	—	—	Matte	—

NOTE: The "Matte" or "Matte-proof" versions were produced at the Lisbon Mint on private contract.

REPUBLIC

MONETARY SYSTEM

100 Centimos = 1 Dobra

50 CENTIMOS

BRASS
F.A.O. Issue

KM#	Date	Mintage	VF	XF	Unc
25	1977	2.000	.10	.15	.35
	1977	2,500	—	Proof	3.00

DOBRA

BRASS
F.A.O. Issue

KM#	Date	Mintage	VF	XF	Unc
26	1977	1.500	.10	.15	.50
	1977	2,500	—	Proof	3.00

2 DOBRAS

COPPER-NICKEL
F.A.O. Issue

KM#	Date	Mintage	VF	XF	Unc
27	1977	1.000	.20	.30	.85
	1977	2,500	—	Proof	3.50

5 DOBRAS

COPPER-NICKEL
F.A.O. Issue

KM#	Date	Mintage	VF	XF	Unc
28	1977	.750	.30	.50	1.25
	1977	2,500	—	Proof	5.00

10 DOBRAS

COPPER-NICKEL
F.A.O. Issue

KM#	Date	Mintage	VF	XF	Unc
29	1977	.300	.60	1.00	2.75
	1977	2,500	—	Proof	5.00

20 DOBRAS

COPPER-NICKEL
F.A.O. Issue

KM#	Date	Mintage	VF	XF	Unc
30	1977	.500	1.00	1.50	3.25
	1977	2,500	—	Proof	7.50

50 DOBRAS

COPPER-NICKEL
F.A.O. Issue

KM#	Date	Mintage	VF	XF	Unc
52	1990	—	—	—	3.00

100 DOBRAS

COPPER-NICKEL
World Fisheries Conference

KM#	Date	Mintage	VF	XF	Unc
41	ND(1984)	1.000	—	—	7.00

28.2800 g, .925 SILVER, .8411 oz ASW

KM#	Date	Mintage	VF	XF	Unc
41a	ND(1984)	.020	—	Proof	27.50

47.5400 g, .917 GOLD, 1.4017 oz AGW

KM#	Date	Mintage	VF	XF	Unc
41b	ND(1984)	100 pcs.	—	Proof	1450.

COPPER-NICKEL
10th Anniversary of Independence

KM#	Date	Mintage	VF	XF	Unc
42	ND(1985)	—	—	—	6.00

28.2800 g, .925 SILVER, .8411 oz ASW

KM#	Date	Mintage	VF	XF	Unc
42a	ND(1985)	1,000	—	Proof	35.00

47.5400 g, .917 GOLD, 1.4017 oz AGW

KM#	Date	Mintage	VF	XF	Unc
42b	ND(1985)	50 pcs.	—	Proof	1500.

250 DOBRAS

17.4000 g, .925 SILVER, .5175 oz ASW
Independence - World Population

KM#	Date	Mintage	VF	XF	Unc
31	1977	450 pcs.	—	—	45.00
	1977	750 pcs.	—	Proof	42.50

Independence - World Friendship

KM#	Date	Mintage	VF	XF	Unc
32	1977	450 pcs.	—	—	45.00
	1977	800 pcs.	—	Proof	42.50

Independence - Folklore

KM#	Date	Mintage	VF	XF	Unc
33	1977	300 pcs.	—	—	45.00
	1977	600 pcs.	—	Proof	42.50

Independence - World Unity

KM#	Date	Mintage	VF	XF	Unc
34	1977	400 pcs.	—	—	45.00
	1977	700 pcs.	—	Proof	42.50

Independence - Mother and Child

KM#	Date	Mintage	VF	XF	Unc
35	1977	350 pcs.	—	—	45.00
	1977	700 pcs.	—	Proof	42.50

500 DOBRAS

COPPER-NICKEL
Elvis Presley

KM#	Date	Mintage	VF	XF	Unc
70	1993	—	—	—	12.50

1000 DOBRAS

23.3300 g, .925 SILVER, .6938 oz ASW
Soccer - 2 Players

KM#	Date	Mintage	VF	XF	Unc
44	1990	.015	—	Proof	50.00

Soccer - 2 Players Running

KM#	Date	Mintage	VF	XF	Unc
45	1990	.015	—	Proof	50.00

20.0000 g, .999 SILVER, .6431 oz ASW
National Independence

KM#	Date	Mintage	VF	XF	Unc
49	1990	—	—	Proof	50.00

25.9600 g, .999 SILVER, .8347 oz ASW
Soccer - 2 Players and Ball

KM#	Date	Mintage	VF	XF	Unc
48	1990	—	—	Proof	50.00

Vasco Da Gama

KM#	Date	Mintage	VF	XF	Unc
50	1990	—	—	Proof	50.00

Olympics and Discovery of America

KM#	Date	Mintage	VF	XF	Unc
53	1990	—	—	Proof	50.00

Soccer - 1 Player
Obv: Similar to KM#45. Rev: 1 soccer player.

KM#	Date	Mintage	VF	XF	Unc
47	1991	—	—	Proof	50.00

COPPER-NICKEL
Atlanta Olympics - Wrestlers

KM#	Date	Mintage	VF	XF	Unc
54	ND	—	—	Proof	30.00

Atlanta Olympics - Soccer Players

KM#	Date	Mintage	VF	XF	Unc
55	ND	—	—	Proof	30.00

Atlanta Olympics - Boxer

KM#	Date	Mintage	VF	XF	Unc
56	ND	—	—	Proof	30.00

Atlanta Olympics - Bicyclist

KM#	Date	Mintage	VF	XF	Unc
57	ND	—	—	Proof	30.00

Atlanta Olympics - Karate Competitors

KM#	Date	Mintage	VF	XF	Unc
58	ND	—	—	Proof	30.00

Atlanta Olympics - Runner

KM#	Date	Mintage	VF	XF	Unc
59	ND	—	—	Proof	30.00

Atlanta Olympics - Field Hockey Players

KM#	Date	Mintage	VF	XF	Unc
60	ND	—	—	Proof	30.00

Atlanta Olympics - 4 Track and Field Events

KM#	Date	Mintage	VF	XF	Unc
61	ND	—	—	Proof	30.00

Atlanta Olympics - Surfer

KM#	Date	Mintage	VF	XF	Unc
62	ND	—	—	Proof	30.00

Atlanta Olympics - Swimmers

KM#	Date	Mintage	VF	XF	Unc
63	ND	—	—	Proof	30.00

Atlanta Olympics - 3 Gymnastic Events

KM#	Date	Mintage	VF	XF	Unc
64	ND	—	—	Proof	30.00

Atlanta Olympics - Tennis Players

KM#	Date	Mintage	VF	XF	Unc
65	ND	—	—	Proof	30.00

25.0000 g, .925 SILVER, .7242 oz ASW
Elvis Presley

KM#	Date	Mintage	VF	XF	Unc
71	1993	—	—	Proof	50.00

2500 DOBRAS

6.4800 g, .900 GOLD, .1875 oz AGW
Independence - World Friendship

KM#	Date	Mintage	VF	XF	Unc
36	1977	100 pcs.	—	—	300.00
	1977	170 pcs.	—	Proof	275.00

Independence - World Population

KM#	Date	Mintage	VF	XF	Unc
37	1977	100 pcs.	—	—	300.00
	1977	170 pcs.	—	Proof	275.00

Independence - Folklore

KM#	Date	Mintage	VF	XF	Unc
38	1977	100 pcs.	—	—	300.00
	1977	170 pcs.	—	Proof	275.00

Independence - World Unity

KM#	Date	Mintage	VF	XF	Unc
39	1977	100 pcs.	—	—	300.00
	1977	170 pcs.	—	Proof	275.00

Independence - Mother and Child

KM#	Date	Mintage	VF	XF	Unc
40	1977	100 pcs.	—	—	300.00
	1977	170 pcs.	—	Proof	275.00

3500 DOBRAS

136.0800 g, .925 SILVER, 4.3755 oz ASW
Illustration reduced. Actual size: 63mm.
Wildlife Protection - Sea Turtle

KM#	Date	Mintage	VF	XF	Unc
46	1990	750 pcs.	—	Proof	175.00

10,000 DOBRAS

7.7750 g, .900 GOLD, .2250 oz AGW
Sea Turtle

KM#	Date	Mintage	VF	XF	Unc
51	1992	500 pcs.	—	Proof	300.00

25,000 DOBRAS

15.5500 g, .999 GOLD, .5000 oz AGW
Elvis Presley
Obv: National emblem. Rev: Portrait w/microphone.

KM#	Date	Mintage	VF	XF	Unc
72	1993	—	—	Proof	300.00

EUROPEAN CURRENCY UNION

500 DOBRAS - 1 ECU

COPPER-NICKEL
15th Anniversary of Association With
European Common Market

KM#	Date	Mintage	VF	XF	Unc
67	1993	.020	—	—	12.00

2500 DOBRAS - 5 ECU

25.0000 g, .925 SILVER, .7434 oz ASW
15th Anniversary of Association With
European Common Market

KM#	Date	Mintage	VF	XF	Unc
68	1993	.012	—	Proof	47.50

25000 DOBRAS - 50 ECU

6.7200 g, .900 GOLD, .1944 oz AGW
15th Anniversary of Association With
European Common Market
Similar to 2500 Dobras, 5 Ecu, KM#68.
Obv: National emblem. Rev: Old harbor scene.

KM#	Date	Mintage	VF	XF	Unc
69	1993	1,000	—	Proof	225.00

MINT SETS (MS)

KM#	Date	Mintage	Identification	Issue Price	Mkt. Val.
MS1	1977(5)	—	KM31-35	71.00	225.00
MS2	1977(5)	100	KM36-40	655.00	1500.

PROOF SETS (PS)

KM#	Date	Mintage	Identification	Issue Price	Mkt. Val.
PS1	1977(5)	—	KM31-35	93.50	215.00
PS2	1977(5)	170	KM36-40	805.00	1375.

St. Vincent and the Grenadines, consisting of the island of St. Vincent and the northern Grenadines (a string of islets stretching southward from St. Vincent), is located in the Windward Islands of the West Indies, West of Barbados and south of St. Lucia. The tiny nation has an area of 150 sq. mi. (340 sq. km.) and a population of *105,000. Capital: Kingstown. Arrowroot, cotton, sugar, molasses, rum and cocoa are exported. Tourism is a principal industry.

St. Vincent was discovered by Columbus on Jan. 22, 1498, but was left undisturbed for more than a century. The British began colonization early in the 18th century against bitter and prolonged Carib resistance. The island was taken by the French in 1779, but was restored to the British in 1783, at the end of the American Revolution. St. Vincent and the northern Grenadines became a British associated state in Oct. 1969. Independence under the name of St. Vincent and the Grenadines was attained at midnight of Oct. 26, 1979. The new nation chose to become a member of the Commonwealth of Nations with the Queen of England as Chief of State.

A local coinage was introduced in 1797, with the gold withdrawn in 1818 and the silver in 1823. This was replaced by sterling. From the mid-1950's, St. Vincent used the currency of the British Caribbean Territories (Eastern Group), then that of the East Caribbean States.

RULERS

British

MONETARY SYSTEM

1797-1811

8 Shillings, 3 Pence = 11 Bits = 1 Dollar

Commencing 1811

9 Shillings = 12 Bits = 1 Dollar

Commencing 1979

100 Cents = 1 Dollar

COUNTERMARKED COINAGE

BLACK DOG

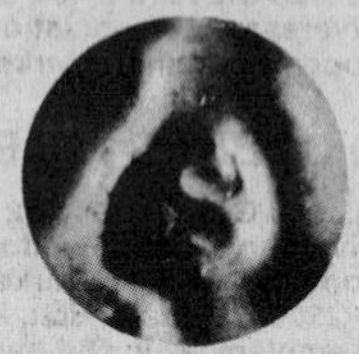

BILLON

c/m: Retrograde S within octagonal indent.

KM#	Date	Year	Good	VG	Fine	VF
7	ND	(1814)	25.00	50.00	75.00	100.00

STAMPEE

BILLON

c/m: Retrograde S within octagonal indent on French Colonial coin bearing a crowned C c/m.

KM#	Date	Year	Good	VG	Fine	VF
8	ND	(1814)	25.00	50.00	75.00	100.00

VI BITS

SILVER

c/m: S/VI on 23mm center disk cut from Spanish or Spanish Colonial 8 Reales.

KM#	Date	Year	Good	VG	Fine	VF
10	ND	(1811-14)	550.00	800.00	1100.	1550.

IX BITS

SILVER

c/m: S/IX on Spanish or Spanish American 4 Reales.

KM#	Date	Year	Good	VG	Fine	VF
11	ND	(1811-14)	2500.	3500.	4750.	6000.

XII BITS

SILVER

c/m: S/XII on holed Mexico 8 Reales, KM#109.

KM#	Date	Year	Good	VG	Fine	VF
12.2	ND	(1802 FT)	2750.	3750.	5000.	6500.

c/m: S/XII on holed Mexico 8 Reales, KM#110.

KM#	Date	Year	Good	VG	Fine	VF
12.3	ND	(1809 TH)	2750.	3750.	5000.	6500.

1798-1818

The countermarking of various gold coins in circulation on Saint Vincent was authorized by an Act of August 1, 1798. Standard weight for a gold "Joe" was set at 11.66 g with a denomination of 66 Shillings. Full weight gold was marked 3 times with the letter S. Underweight gold could be brought up to proper weight by plugging and marking the plug with a letter S, under the guidance of at least 1 Council member and 2 Assemblymen. Ongoing concerns and practical implementation made this act subject to review and in all likelihood alterations were made resulting in the various plugged and full weight examples listed below. All countermarked "Joes" were recalled in 1818.

66 SHILLINGS

GOLD, 11.50-11.66 g

c/m: S (3 times) on Brazil 6400 Reis, KM#149.

KM#	Date	Year	Good	VG	Fine	VF
17	ND	(17x8)	1500.	2250.	3500.	5000.

c/m: S (3 times) on Brazil 6400 Reis, KM#199.2.

KM#	Date	Year	Good	VG	Fine	VF
18	ND	(1786)	1500.	2250.	3500.	5000.

c/m: S (3 times) on plugged Brazil 6400 Reis, KM#199.2.

KM#	Date	Year	Good	VG	Fine	VF
19	ND	(1779)	1500.	2500.	4000.	6000.

Obv. c/m: S (3 times). Rev. c/m: IS on the plug of a false Brazil 6400 Reis, KM#172.2.

KM#	Date	Year	Good	VG	Fine	VF
5.1	ND	(1773)	—	—	Rare	—

Obv. c/m: S (3 times). Rev. c/m: IS on the plug of a false Brazil 6400 Reis, KM#199.2.

KM#	Date	Year	Good	VG	Fine	VF
5.2	ND	(178x)	—	—	Rare	—

Obv. c/m: S (3 times) and GH on the plug of a false Brazil 6400 Reis, KM#172.2.

KM#	Date	Year	Good	VG	Fine	VF
6	ND	(1767)	—	—	Rare	—

6 POUNDS 12 SHILLINGS

GOLD, 23.40 g

c/m: S (3 times) on Brazil 12,800 Reis, KM#150.

KM#	Date	Year	VG	Fine	VF	XF
16	ND	(1732)	—	—	*Rare	—

***NOTE:** Glendining's Ford sale 9-89 VF realized $12,800.

MODERN COINAGE

4 DOLLARS

COPPER-NICKEL

F.A.O. Issue

KM#	Date	Mintage	VF	XF	Unc
13	1970	.013	—	3.00	9.00
	1970	2,000	—	Proof	20.00

10 DOLLARS

COPPER-NICKEL
Royal Visit

KM#	Date	Mintage	VF	XF	Unc
14	1985	.100	—	—	7.50
	28.2800 g, .925 SILVER, .8411 oz ASW				
14a	1985	5,000	—	Proof	30.00
	47.5400 g, .917 GOLD, 1.4013 oz AGW				
14b	1985	250 pcs.	—	Proof	900.00

100 DOLLARS

129.5900 g, .925 SILVER, 3.8543 oz ASW
Illustration reduced. Actual size: 63mm
Tropical Birds - Pelican
Obv: Coat of arms.

KM#	Date	Mintage	VF	XF	Unc
15	1988	*.010	—	Proof	120.00

Listings For

SAMOA: refer to Western Samoa

SAN MARINO

The Republic of San Marino, the oldest and smallest republic in the world is located in north central Italy entirely surrounded by the Province of Emilia-Romagna. It has an area of 24 sq. mi. (60 sq. km.) and a population of *23,000. Capital: San Marino. The principal economic activities are farming, livestock raising, cheesemaking, tourism and light manufacturing. Building stone, lime, wheat, hides and baked goods are exported. The government derives most of its revenue from the sale of postage stamps for philatelic purposes.

According to tradition, San Marino was founded about 350AD by a Christian stonecutter as a refuge against religious persecution. While gradually acquiring the institutions of an independent state, it avoided the factional fights of the Middle Ages and, except for a brief period in fief to Cesare Borgia, retained its freedom despite attacks on its sovereignty by the Papacy, the Lords of Rimini, Napoleon and Mussolini. In 1862 San Marino established a customs union with, and put itself under the protection of, Italy. A Communist-Socialist coalition controlled the Government for 12 years after World War II. The Christian Democratic Party has been the core of government since 1957. In 1978 a Communist-Socialist coalition again came into power and remained in control until 1991.

San Marino has its own coinage, but Italian and Vatican City coins and currency are also in circulation.

MINT MARKS

M - Milan
R - Rome

MONETARY SYSTEM

100 Centesimi = 1 Lira

5 CENTESIMI

COPPER

KM#	Date	Mintage	Fine	VF	XF	Unc
1	1864M	.280	4.00	7.00	20.00	100.00
	1869M	.600	3.00	6.00	12.00	30.00
	1894R	.600	3.00	5.00	10.00	25.00

BRONZE

KM#	Date	Mintage	Fine	VF	XF	Unc
12	1935R	.400	1.25	2.00	3.00	5.50
	1936R	.400	1.25	2.00	3.00	5.50
	1937R	.400	1.25	2.00	3.00	5.50
	1938R	.200	1.50	2.25	3.50	6.50

10 CENTESIMI

COPPER

KM#	Date	Mintage	Fine	VF	XF	Unc
2	1875(m)	.150	4.00	8.00	25.00	60.00
	1893R	.150	4.00	7.50	22.00	45.00
	1894R	.150	4.00	7.50	22.00	45.00

BRONZE

KM#	Date	Mintage	Fine	VF	XF	Unc
13	1935R	.300	1.50	2.25	3.50	7.00
	1936R	.300	1.50	2.25	3.50	7.00
	1937R	.300	1.50	2.25	3.50	7.00
	1938R	.400	1.50	2.25	3.50	7.00

50 CENTESIMI

2.5000 g, .835 SILVER, .0671 oz ASW

KM#	Date	Mintage	Fine	VF	XF	Unc
3	1898R	.040	10.00	17.50	25.00	45.00

LIRA

5.0000 g, .835 SILVER, .1342 oz ASW

KM#	Date	Mintage	Fine	VF	XF	Unc
4	1898R	.020	17.50	27.50	37.50	75.00
	1906R	.030	15.00	22.50	35.00	65.00

ALUMINUM

KM#	Date	Mintage	VF	XF	Unc
14	1972	.291	—	.10	.20

KM#	Date	Mintage	VF	XF	Unc
22	1973	.291	—	.10	.20
30	1974	.276	—	.10	.20

KM#	Date	Mintage	VF	XF	Unc
40	1975	.291	—	.10	.20

KM#	Date	Mintage	VF	XF	Unc
51	1976	.195	—	.10	.20

F.A.O. Issue

KM#	Date	Mintage	VF	XF	Unc
63	1977	1.180	—	.10	.20

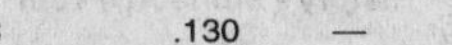

KM#	Date	Mintage	VF	XF	Unc
76	1978	.130	—	.15	.30

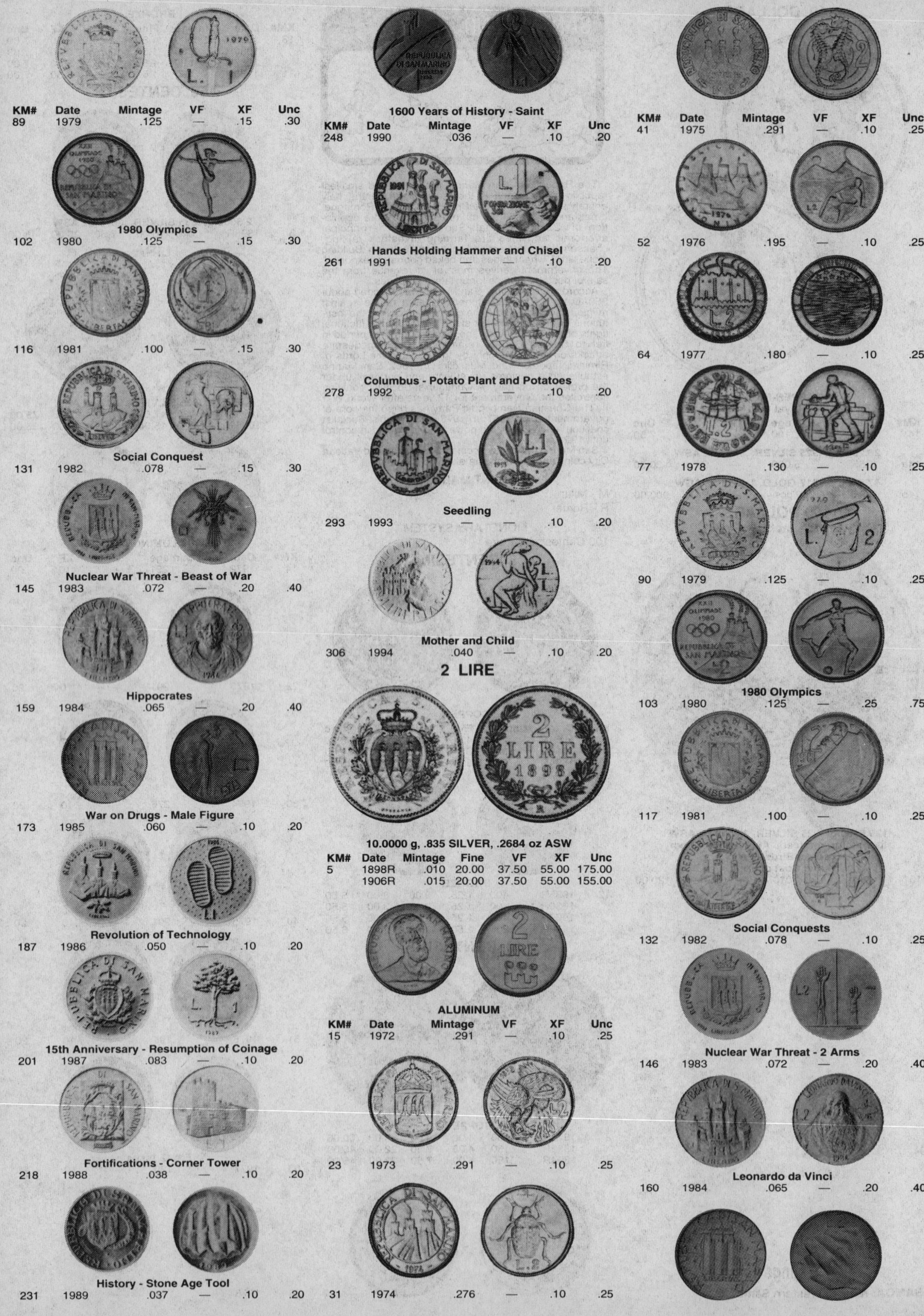

KM#	Date	Mintage	VF	XF	Unc
89	1979	.125	—	.15	.30

1980 Olympics

KM#	Date	Mintage	VF	XF	Unc
102	1980	.125	—	.15	.30
116	1981	.100	—	.15	.30

Social Conquest

KM#	Date	Mintage	VF	XF	Unc
131	1982	.078	—	.15	.30

Nuclear War Threat - Beast of War

KM#	Date	Mintage	VF	XF	Unc
145	1983	.072	—	.20	.40

Hippocrates

KM#	Date	Mintage	VF	XF	Unc
159	1984	.065	—	.20	.40

War on Drugs - Male Figure

KM#	Date	Mintage	VF	XF	Unc
173	1985	.060	—	.10	.20

Revolution of Technology

KM#	Date	Mintage	VF	XF	Unc
187	1986	.050	—	.10	.20

15th Anniversary - Resumption of Coinage

KM#	Date	Mintage	VF	XF	Unc
201	1987	.083	—	.10	.20

Fortifications - Corner Tower

KM#	Date	Mintage	VF	XF	Unc
218	1988	.038	—	.10	.20

History - Stone Age Tool

KM#	Date	Mintage	VF	XF	Unc
231	1989	.037	—	.10	.20

1600 Years of History - Saint

KM#	Date	Mintage	VF	XF	Unc
248	1990	.036	—	.10	.20

Hands Holding Hammer and Chisel

KM#	Date	Mintage	VF	XF	Unc
261	1991	—	—	.10	.20

Columbus - Potato Plant and Potatoes

KM#	Date	Mintage	VF	XF	Unc
278	1992	—	—	.10	.20

Seedling

KM#	Date	Mintage	VF	XF	Unc
293	1993	—	—	.10	.20

Mother and Child

KM#	Date	Mintage	VF	XF	Unc
306	1994	.040	—	.10	.20

2 LIRE

10.0000 g, .835 SILVER, .2684 oz ASW

KM#	Date	Mintage	Fine	VF	XF	Unc
5	1898R	.010	20.00	37.50	55.00	175.00
	1906R	.015	20.00	37.50	55.00	155.00

ALUMINUM

KM#	Date	Mintage	VF	XF	Unc
15	1972	.291	—	.10	.25
23	1973	.291	—	.10	.25
31	1974	.276	—	.10	.25
41	1975	.291	—	.10	.25
52	1976	.195	—	.10	.25
64	1977	.180	—	.10	.25
77	1978	.130	—	.10	.25
90	1979	.125	—	.10	.25

1980 Olympics

KM#	Date	Mintage	VF	XF	Unc
103	1980	.125	—	.25	.75
117	1981	.100	—	.10	.25

Social Conquests

KM#	Date	Mintage	VF	XF	Unc
132	1982	.078	—	.10	.25

Nuclear War Threat - 2 Arms

KM#	Date	Mintage	VF	XF	Unc
146	1983	.072	—	.20	.40

Leonardo da Vinci

KM#	Date	Mintage	VF	XF	Unc
160	1984	.065	—	.20	.40

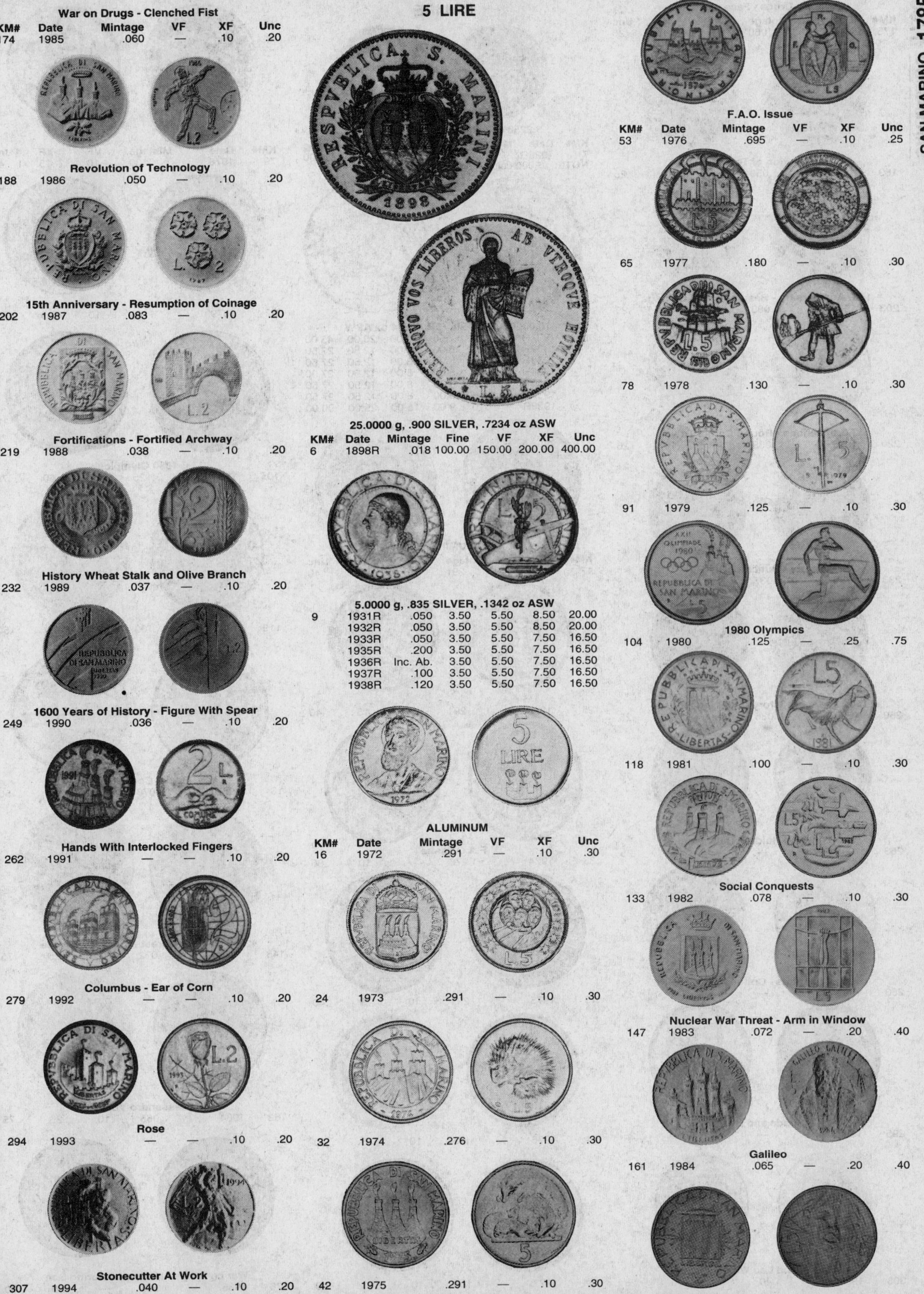

KM#	Date	Mintage	VF	XF	Unc
	War on Drugs - Clenched Fist				
174	1985	.060	—	.10	.20
	Revolution of Technology				
188	1986	.050	—	.10	.20
	15th Anniversary - Resumption of Coinage				
202	1987	.083	—	.10	.20
	Fortifications - Fortified Archway				
219	1988	.038	—	.10	.20
	History Wheat Stalk and Olive Branch				
232	1989	.037	—	.10	.20
	1600 Years of History - Figure With Spear				
249	1990	.036	—	.10	.20
	Hands With Interlocked Fingers				
262	1991	—	—	.10	.20
	Columbus - Ear of Corn				
279	1992	—	—	.10	.20
	Rose				
294	1993	—	—	.10	.20
	Stonecutter At Work				
307	1994	.040	—	.10	.20

5 LIRE

25.0000 g, .900 SILVER, .7234 oz ASW

KM#	Date	Mintage	Fine	VF	XF	Unc
6	1898R	.018	100.00	150.00	200.00	400.00

5.0000 g, .835 SILVER, .1342 oz ASW

KM#	Date	Mintage	Fine	VF	XF	Unc
9	1931R	.050	3.50	5.50	8.50	20.00
	1932R	.050	3.50	5.50	8.50	20.00
	1933R	.050	3.50	5.50	7.50	16.50
	1935R	.200	3.50	5.50	7.50	16.50
	1936R	Inc. Ab.	3.50	5.50	7.50	16.50
	1937R	.100	3.50	5.50	7.50	16.50
	1938R	.120	3.50	5.50	7.50	16.50

ALUMINUM

KM#	Date	Mintage	VF	XF	Unc
16	1972	.291	—	.10	.30
24	1973	.291	—	.10	.30
32	1974	.276	—	.10	.30
42	1975	.291	—	.10	.30
	F.A.O. Issue				
53	1976	.695	—	.10	.25
65	1977	.180	—	.10	.30
78	1978	.130	—	.10	.30
91	1979	.125	—	.10	.30
	1980 Olympics				
104	1980	.125	—	.25	.75
118	1981	.100	—	.10	.30
	Social Conquests				
133	1982	.078	—	.10	.30
	Nuclear War Threat - Arm in Window				
147	1983	.072	—	.20	.40
	Galileo				
161	1984	.065	—	.20	.40

KM#	Date	Mintage	VF	XF	Unc
	War on Drugs - Face of Addict				
175	1985	.060	—	.10	.25
	Revolution of Technology				
189	1986	.050	—	.10	.25
	15th Anniversary - Resumption of Coinage				
203	1987	.083	—	.10	.25
	Fortifications - Round Corner Tower				
220	1988	.038	—	.10	.25
	History - Bunch of Grapes				
233	1989	.037	—	.10	.25
	1600 Years of History - 2 Facing Figures				
250	1990	.036	—	.10	.25
	Hand Holding Quill				
263	1991	—	—	.10	.25
	Columbus - Cotton Plants				
280	1992	—	—	.10	.25
	Spade and Hoe				
295	1993	—	—	.10	.25
	Marino and Leo With Tools				
308	1994	.040	—	.10	.25

10 LIRE

3.2258 g, .900 GOLD, .0933 oz AGW

KM#	Date	Mintage	Fine	VF	XF	Unc
7	1925R	.020	200.00	300.00	400.00	750.00

NOTE: 16,000 coins remelted at the mint.

10.0000 g, .835 SILVER, .2684 oz ASW

KM#	Date	Mintage	Fine	VF	XF	Unc
10	1931R	.025	7.50	10.00	20.00	45.00
	1932R	.025	6.00	8.00	12.50	27.50
	1933R	.025	6.00	8.00	12.50	27.50
	1935R	.030	6.00	8.00	12.50	27.50
	1936R	Inc. Ab.	6.00	8.00	12.50	27.50
	1937R	.015	6.00	8.00	12.50	27.50
	1938R	.010	9.00	15.00	25.00	90.00

ALUMINUM

KM#	Date	Mintage	VF	XF	Unc
17	1972	.291	.10	.15	.40
25	1973	.291	.10	.15	.40
	F.A.O. Issue				
33	1974	1.276	—	.10	.30
43	1975	.291	.10	.15	.40
54	1976	.195	.10	.15	.40
66	1977	.180	.10	.15	.40

KM#	Date	Mintage	VF	XF	Un
79	1978	.130	.10	.15	.4
92	1979	.125	.10	.15	.4
	1980 Olympics				
105	1980	.125	.25	.50	.7
119	1981	.100	.10	.20	.5
	Social Conquests				
134	1982	.078	.10	.20	.50
	Nuclear War Threat - 2 Arms in Frame				
148	1983	.072	.10	.25	.75
	Alessandro Volta				
162	1984	.065	.10	.25	.75
	War on Drugs - Mother Lecturing Son				
176	1985	.060	—	.10	.30

Revolution of Technology

KM#	Date	Mintage	VF	XF	Unc
190	1986	.050	—	.10	.30

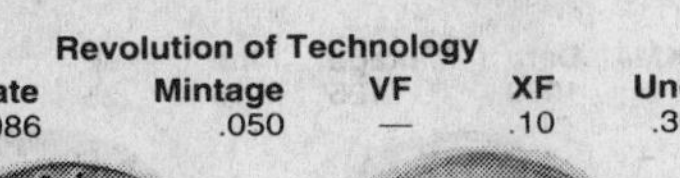

15th Anniversary - Resumption of Coinage

KM#	Date	Mintage	VF	XF	Unc
204	1987	.083	—	.10	.30

Fortifications - Sloping Fortress Wall

KM#	Date	Mintage	VF	XF	Unc
221	1988	.038	—	.10	.30

History - Ancient Pottery

KM#	Date	Mintage	VF	XF	Unc
234	1989	.037	—	.10	.30

1600 Years of History - Soldier

KM#	Date	Mintage	VF	XF	Unc
251	1990	.036	—	.10	.30

Hand Holding Castle Tower

KM#	Date	Mintage	VF	XF	Unc
264	1991	—	—	.10	.30

Columbus - Dolphin and Ship

KM#	Date	Mintage	VF	XF	Unc
281	1992	—	—	.10	.30

Corinthian Column

KM#	Date	Mintage	VF	XF	Unc
296	1993	—	—	.10	.30

Marino and Leo Working

KM#	Date	Mintage	VF	XF	Unc
309	1994	.040	—	.10	.30

20 LIRE

6.4516 g, .900 GOLD, .1867 oz AGW

KM#	Date	Mintage	Fine	VF	XF	Unc
8	1925R	9,334	300.00	600.00	1000.	2200.

NOTE: 7,334 coins were remelted at the mint.

15.0000 g, .800 SILVER, .3858 oz ASW

KM#	Date	Mintage	Fine	VF	XF	Unc
11	1931R	.010	20.00	40.00	80.00	175.00
	1932R	.010	35.00	70.00	120.00	250.00
	1933R	.010	25.00	45.00	90.00	180.00
	1935R	.010	30.00	50.00	100.00	200.00
	1936R	Inc. Ab.	30.00	50.00	100.00	200.00

20.0000 g, .800 SILVER, .5145 oz ASW

KM#	Date	Mintage	Fine	VF	XF	Unc
11a	1935R					
		1 pc. known	550.00	900.00	1800.	3000.
	1937R	5,100	100.00	175.00	350.00	600.00
	1938R	2,500	150.00	250.00	700.00	1200.

ALUMINUM-BRONZE

KM#	Date	Mintage	VF	XF	Unc
18	1972	.291	.10	.25	.50

KM#	Date	Mintage	VF	XF	Unc
26	1973	.291	.10	.25	.50
34	1974	.276	.10	.25	.50

F.A.O. Issue

KM#	Date	Mintage	VF	XF	Unc
44	1975	.291	.10	.25	.50

KM#	Date	Mintage	VF	XF	Unc
55	1976	.195	.10	.25	.50
67	1977	.180	.10	.25	.50

KM#	Date	Mintage	VF	XF	Unc
80	1978	.130	.10	.25	.50
93	1979	.125	.10	.30	.50

1980 Olympics

KM#	Date	Mintage	VF	XF	Unc
106	1980	.125	.25	.50	1.00

KM#	Date	Mintage	VF	XF	Unc
120	1981	.100	.10	.30	.60

Social Conquests

KM#	Date	Mintage	VF	XF	Unc
135	1982	.078	.10	.25	.50

Nuclear War Threat - Torch Above Man

KM#	Date	Mintage	VF	XF	Unc
149	1983	.072	.10	.30	.75

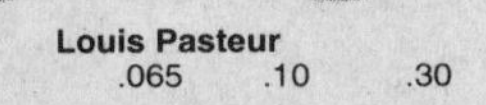

Louis Pasteur

KM#	Date	Mintage	VF	XF	Unc
163	1984	.065	.10	.30	.75

War on Drugs - Open Hand

KM#	Date	Mintage	VF	XF	Unc
177	1985	.060	—	.10	.50

Revolution of Technology

KM#	Date	Mintage	VF	XF	Unc
191	1986	.050	—	.10	.50

15th Anniversary - Resumption of Coinage

KM#	Date	Mintage	VF	XF	Unc
205	1987	.083	—	.10	.50

Fortifications - Small Fortified Gate

KM#	Date	Mintage	VF	XF	Unc
222	1988	.038	—	.10	.50

History - Sword and Flag

KM#	Date	Mintage	VF	XF	Unc
235	1989	.037	—	.10	.50

1600 Years of History - Figure Straddling Denomination

KM#	Date	Mintage	VF	XF	Unc
252	1990	.096	—	.10	.50

Gloved Hand Rejecting Cardinal Ring

KM#	Date	Mintage	VF	XF	Unc
265	1991	—	—	.10	.50

Columbus Landing on Hispaniola

KM#	Date	Mintage	VF	XF	Unc
282	1992	—	—	.10	.50

Scroll and Arch

KM#	Date	Mintage	VF	XF	Unc
297	1993	—	—	.10	.50

Workers Pulling Stone

KM#	Date	Mintage	VF	XF	Unc
310	1994	.040	—	.10	.50

50 LIRE

STEEL

KM#	Date	Mintage	Fine	VF	XF	Unc
19	1972	.291	.15	.25	.50	1.00
27	1973	.291	.15	.25	.50	1.00
35	1974	.276	.15	.25	.50	1.00
45	1975	.831	.15	.25	.50	1.00
56	1976	.195	.15	.25	.50	1.00
68	1977	.180	.15	.25	.50	1.00
81	1978	.130	.15	.25	.50	1.00

KM#	Date	Mintage	Fine	VF	XF	Unc
94	1979	.125	.15	.25	.50	1.00

1980 Olympics - Downhill Skier

KM#	Date	Mintage	Fine	VF	XF	Unc
107	1980	.125	.25	.50	1.00	2.00
121	1981	.100	.15	.25	.50	1.00

Social Conquests

KM#	Date	Mintage	Fine	VF	XF	Unc
136	1982	.078	.15	.25	.50	1.00

Nuclear War Threat - Beast Above Woman

KM#	Date	Mintage	Fine	VF	XF	Unc
150	1983	.072	.20	.40	.80	1.50

Pierre and Marie Curie

KM#	Date	Mintage	Fine	VF	XF	Unc
164	1984	.065	.20	.40	.80	1.50

War on Drugs - Stylized Figures

KM#	Date	Mintage	Fine	VF	XF	Unc
178	1985	.110	—	.10	.15	.75

Revolution of Technology

KM#	Date	Mintage	Fine	VF	XF	Unc
192	1986	.050	—	.10	.15	.75

15th Anniversary - Resumption of Coinage

KM#	Date	Mintage	Fine	VF	XF	Unc
206	1987	.093	—	.10	.15	.75

Fortifications - Ramp Leading to Gate House

KM#	Date	Mintage	Fine	VF	XF	Unc
223	1988	.038	—	.10	.15	.75

History - Cross Bow

KM#	Date	Mintage	Fine	VF	XF	Unc
236	1989	.087	—	.10	.15	.75

1600 Years of History - Bird

KM#	Date	Mintage	Fine	VF	XF	Unc
253	1990	.052	—	.10	.15	.75

Hand Holding Cannon Barrels and Wheat Stalks

KM#	Date	Mintage	Fine	VF	XF	Unc
266	1991	—	—	.10	.15	.75

Columbus - Seagulls Flying Over Radiant Seascape

KM#	Date	Mintage	Fine	VF	XF	Unc
283	1992	—	—	.10	.15	.75

Wheat Growing Through Barbed Wire

KM#	Date	Mintage	Fine	VF	XF	Unc
298	1993	—	—	.10	.15	.75

STAINLESS STEEL
Two Stonecutters

KM#	Date	Mintage	Fine	VF	XF	Unc
311	1994	.040	—	.10	.15	.75

100 LIRE

STEEL

KM#	Date	Mintage	Fine	VF	XF	Unc
20	1972	.291	.15	.30	.60	1.25

KM#	Date	Mintage	Fine	VF	XF	Unc
28	1973	.291	.15	.30	.60	1.25
36	1974	.276	.15	.30	.60	1.25
46	1975	.821	.15	.30	.60	1.25
57	1976	1.853	.15	.30	.60	1.25
69	1977	.565	.15	.30	.60	1.25
70	1977	.565	.15	.30	.60	1.25

F.A.O. Issue

KM#	Date	Mintage	Fine	VF	XF	Unc
82	1978	.875	.15	.30	.60	1.25

KM#	Date	Mintage	Fine	VF	XF	Unc
95	1979	.665	.15	.30	.60	1.25

1980 Olympics - Archery

KM#	Date	Mintage	Fine	VF	XF	Unc
108	1980	.350	.25	.50	1.00	2.00
122	1981	.512	.15	.30	.60	1.25

Social Conquests

KM#	Date	Mintage	Fine	VF	XF	Unc
137	1982	.178	.15	.30	.60	1.25

Nuclear War Threat - Beast Above Man and Woman

KM#	Date	Mintage	Fine	VF	XF	Unc
151	1983	.172	.15	.30	.60	1.25

Guglielmo Marconi

KM#	Date	Mintage	Fine	VF	XF	Unc
165	1984	.165	.15	.30	.60	1.25

War on Drugs - 3 Figures in Discussion

KM#	Date	Mintage	Fine	VF	XF	Unc
179	1985	.210	—	—	.25	1.00

Revolution of Technology

KM#	Date	Mintage	Fine	VF	XF	Unc
193	1986	.150	—	—	.25	1.00

15th Anniversary - Resumption of Coinage

KM#	Date	Mintage	Fine	VF	XF	Unc
207	1987	.143	—	—	.25	1.00

Fortifications - Gate Tower

KM#	Date	Mintage	Fine	VF	XF	Unc
224	1988	.038	—	—	.25	1.00

History - Teacher and Student

KM#	Date	Mintage	Fine	VF	XF	Unc
237	1989	.037	—	—	.25	1.00

1600 Years of History - Balance Scale

KM#	Date	Mintage	Fine	VF	XF	Unc
254	1990	1.086	—	—	.25	1.00

Clasped Hands

KM#	Date	Mintage	Fine	VF	XF	Unc
267	1991	—	—	—	.25	1.00

Columbus - Sailing Ship

KM#	Date	Mintage	Fine	VF	XF	Unc
284	1992	—	—	—	.25	1.00

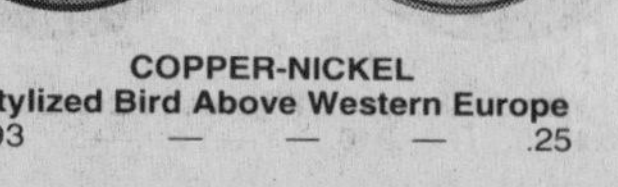

COPPER-NICKEL

Stylized Bird Above Western Europe

KM#	Date	Mintage	Fine	VF	XF	Unc
299	1993	—	—	—	.25	1.00

Two Stonecutters

KM#	Date	Mintage	Fine	VF	XF	Unc
312	1994	.040	—	—	.25	1.00

200 LIRE

ALUMINUM-BRONZE

KM#	Date	Mintage	VF	XF	Unc
83	1978	.530	.25	.75	1.50

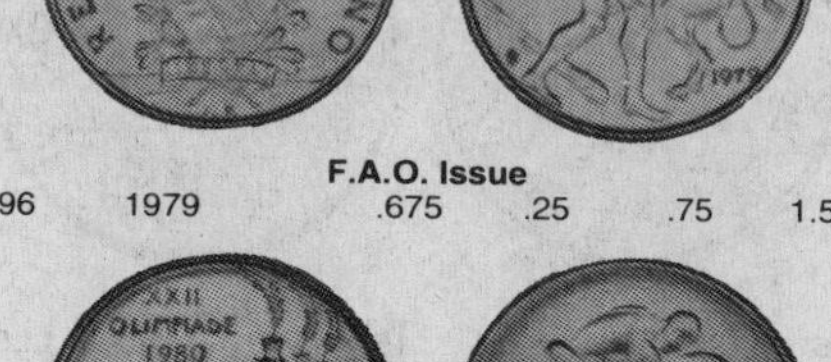

F.A.O. Issue

KM#	Date	Mintage	VF	XF	Unc
96	1979	.675	.25	.75	1.50

1980 Olympics - Wrestling

KM#	Date	Mintage	VF	XF	Unc
109	1980	.675	.50	1.00	2.50

F.A.O. Issue

KM#	Date	Mintage	VF	XF	Unc
123	1981	.700	.25	.75	1.50

Social Conquests

KM#	Date	Mintage	VF	XF	Unc
138	1982	.178	.25	.75	1.50

Nuclear War Threat - Rider Spearing Victim

KM#	Date	Mintage	VF	XF	Unc
152	1983	.172	.25	.75	1.50

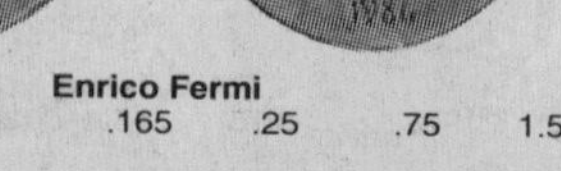

Enrico Fermi

KM#	Date	Mintage	VF	XF	Unc
166	1984	.165	.25	.75	1.50

War on Drugs - Family Group

KM#	Date	Mintage	VF	XF	Unc
180	1985	.210	—	.25	1.25

Revolution of Technology

KM#	Date	Mintage	VF	XF	Unc
194	1986	.150	—	.25	1.25

15th Anniversary - Resumption of Coinage

KM#	Date	Mintage	VF	XF	Unc
208	1987	.143	—	.25	1.25

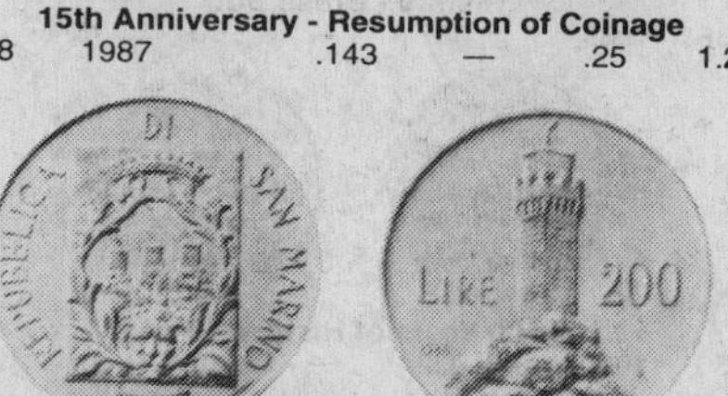

Fortifications - Tower

KM#	Date	Mintage	VF	XF	Unc
225	1988	.038	—	.25	1.25

History - Stylized View of San Marino

KM#	Date	Mintage	VF	XF	Unc
238	1989	1.037	—	.25	1.25

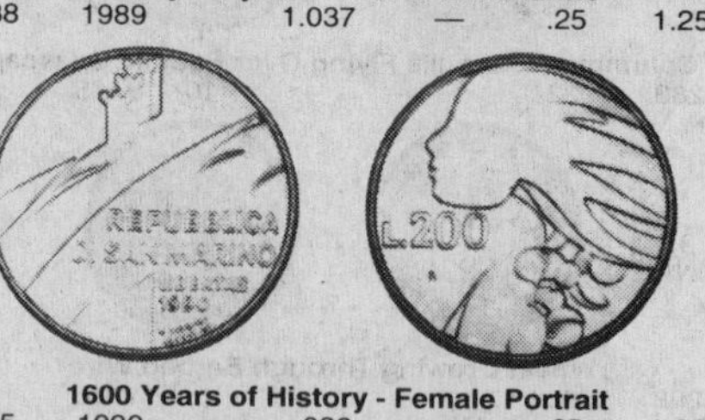

1600 Years of History - Female Portrait

KM#	Date	Mintage	VF	XF	Unc
255	1990	.036	—	.25	1.25

Hand Holding Coin Die

KM#	Date	Mintage	VF	XF	Unc
268	1991	—	—	.25	1.25

Columbus Navigating By the Stars

KM#	Date	Mintage	VF	XF	Unc
285	1992	—	—	.25	1.25

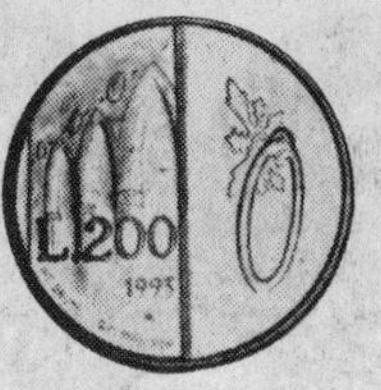

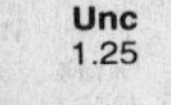

Door and Arches

KM#	Date	Mintage	VF	XF	Unc
300	1993	—	—	.25	1.25

Man and Tame Bear

KM#	Date	Mintage	VF	XF	Unc
313	1994	.040	—	.25	1.25

500 LIRE

11.0000 g, .835 SILVER, .2953 oz ASW

KM#	Date	Mintage	VF	XF	Unc
21	1972	.291	—	6.00	10.00

NOTE: 22,374 coins remelted at the mint.

KM#	Date	Mintage	VF	XF	Unc
29	1973	.291	—	6.00	10.00

NOTE: 6,544 coins remelted at the mint.

KM#	Date	Mintage	VF	XF	Unc
37	1974	.276	—	6.00	10.00

NOTE: 56,295 coins remelted at the mint.

KM#	Date	Mintage	VF	XF	Unc
47	1975	.291	—	6.00	10.00

NOTE: 119,743 coins remelted at the mint.

Numismatic Agency Opening

KM#	Date	Mintage	VF	XF	Unc
48	1975	.200	—	6.00	10.00

NOTE: 47,495 coins remelted at the mint.

KM#	Date	Mintage	VF	XF	Unc
58	1976	.195	—	6.00	10.00

NOTE: 40,509 coins remelted at the mint.

Social Security

KM#	Date	Mintage	VF	XF	Unc
59	1976	.195	—	6.00	10.00

NOTE: 106,604 coins remelted at the mint.

KM#	Date	Mintage	VF	XF	Unc
71	1977	.180	—	6.00	10.00

NOTE: 45,483 coins remelted at the mint.

KM#	Date	Mintage	VF	XF	Unc
84	1978	.130	—	6.00	10.00

NOTE: 16,297 coins remelted at the mint.

KM#	Date	Mintage	VF	XF	Unc
97	1979	.125	—	8.00	12.50

NOTE: 33,278 coins remelted at the mint.

1980 Olympics

KM#	Date	Mintage	VF	XF	Unc
110	1980	.125	—	8.00	12.50

NOTE: 47,724 coins remelted at the mint.

2000th Anniversary of Virgil's Death

KM#	Date	Mintage	VF	XF	Unc
124	1981	.075	—	8.00	12.50

NOTE: 9,122 coins remelted at the mint.

2000th Anniversary of Virgil's Death

KM#	Date	Mintage	VF	XF	Unc
125	1981	.075	—	8.00	12.50

NOTE: 9,122 coins remelted at the mint.

KM#	Date	Mintage	VF	XF	Unc
126	1981	.100	—	8.00	12.50

NOTE: 21,124 coins remelted at the mint.

Centennial of Death of Garibaldi

KM#	Date	Mintage	VF	XF	Unc
139	1982	.048	—	8.00	12.50
	1982	.013	—	Proof	22.50

NOTE: 112 uncirculated and 369 proof coins remelted at the mint.

ALUMINUM-BRONZE CENTER, STEEL RING
Social Conquests

KM#	Date	Mintage	VF	XF	Unc
140	1982	1.900	—	.50	1.50

Nuclear War Threat - 3 Horses Above 2 People

KM#	Date	Mintage	VF	XF	Unc
153	1983	1.922	—	.50	1.50

11.0000 g, .835 SILVER, .2953 oz ASW
500th Anniversary - Birth of Raphael the Artist

KM#	Date	Mintage	VF	XF	Unc
154	1983	.042	—	8.00	12.50
	1983	.012	—	Proof	22.50

NOTE: 80 uncirculated and 1,939 proof coins remelted at the mint.

ALUMINUM-BRONZE CENTER, STEEL RING
Albert Einstein

KM#	Date	Mintage	VF	XF	Unc
167	1984	2.633	—	.50	1.25

11.0000 g, .835 SILVER, .2953 oz ASW
1984 Summer Olympics

KM#	Date	Mintage	VF	XF	Unc
168	1984	.052	—	6.00	10.00
	1984	.015	—	Proof	20.00

NOTE: 2,920 uncirculated and 20 proof coins remelted at the mint.

ALUMINUM-BRONZE CENTER, STEEL RING
War on Drugs - Cured Addict

KM#	Date	Mintage	VF	XF	Unc
181	1985	2.647	—	.50	1.25

11.0000 g, .835 SILVER, .2953 oz ASW
European Music Year

KM#	Date	Mintage	VF	XF	Unc
182	1985	.040	—	6.00	10.00
	1985	.012	—	Proof	15.00

NOTE: 6,704 uncirculated and 122 proof coins remelted at the mint.

ALUMINUM-BRONZE CENTER, STEEL RING
Revolution of Technology

KM#	Date	Mintage	VF	XF	Unc
195	1986	3.111	—	.50	1.25

11.0000 g, .835 SILVER, .2953 oz ASW
Soccer - Field

KM#	Date	Mintage	VF	XF	Unc
196	1986	.045	—	—	10.00
	1986	.012	—	Proof	15.00

NOTE: 5,212 uncirculated and 60 proof coins remelted at the mint.

ALUMINUM-BRONZE CENTER, STEEL RING
15th Anniversary of Resumption of Coinage

KM#	Date	Mintage	VF	XF	Unc
209	1987	3.063	—	.50	1.50

11.0000 g, .835 SILVER, .2953 oz ASW
Zagreb University Games - Runner

KM#	Date	Mintage	VF	XF	Unc
213	1987	.035	—	—	10.00
	1987	.010	—	Proof	15.00

NOTE: 9,208 uncirculated and 1,206 proof coins remelted at the mint.

Winter Olympics - Downhill Skier

KM#	Date	Mintage	VF	XF	Unc
216	1988	.032	—	—	10.00
	1988	9,600	—	Proof	15.00

NOTE: 146 uncirculated and 3 proof coins remelted at the mint.

ALUMINUM-BRONZE CENTER, STEEL RING
Fortifications - Hilltop Fortification

KM#	Date	Mintage	VF	XF	Unc
226	1988	3.526	—	.50	1.50

History - Stone Carver

KM#	Date	Mintage	VF	XF	Unc
239	1989	3.145	—	.50	1.50

11.0000 g, .835 SILVER, .2953 oz ASW
San Marino Grand Prix

KM#	Date	Mintage	VF	XF	Unc
243	1989	.030	—	—	10.00
	1989	8,000	—	Proof	25.00

NOTE: 5,180 coins remelted at the mint.

World Cup Soccer Championship Game

KM#	Date	Mintage	VF	XF	Unc
246	1990	.040	—	—	10.00
	1990	.019	—	Proof	25.00

ALUMINUM-BRONZE CENTER, STEEL RING
1600 Years of History - Birds and Stamp

KM#	Date	Mintage	VF	XF	Unc
256	1990	*.060	—	.50	1.50

Hand Holding Flowers

KM#	Date	Mintage	VF	XF	Unc
269	1991	—	—	.50	1.50

11.0000 g, .835 SILVER, .2953 oz ASW
Barcelona Olympics - Priestess Lighting Fire With Sun Beam

KM#	Date	Mintage	VF	XF	Unc
271	1991	*.060	—	—	10.00
	1991	*8,000	—	Proof	25.00

Olympics - Chariot

KM#	Date	Mintage	VF	XF	Unc
276	1992	*.070	—	—	12.50
	1992	—	—	Proof	25.00

ALUMINUM-BRONZE CENTER, STEEL RING
Columbus - Winds Blowing Ship

KM#	Date	Mintage	VF	XF	Unc
286	1992	—	—	—	1.50

11.0000 g, .835 SILVER, .2953 oz ASW
Wildlife Protection - 2 European Polecats

KM#	Date	Mintage	VF	XF	Unc
291	1993	*.035	—	—	10.00
	1993	—	—	Proof	25.00

ALUMINUM-BRONZE CENTER, STEEL RING
Growth From a Tree Stump

KM#	Date	Mintage	VF	XF	Unc
01	1993	—	—	—	1.50

Saint Marino Receiving Mt. Titano

KM#	Date	Mintage	VF	XF	Unc
14	1994	.040	—	—	1.50

1000 LIRE

14.6000 g, .835 SILVER, .3919 oz ASW
600th Anniversary - Birth of Brunelleschi

KM#	Date	Mintage	VF	XF	Unc
72	1977	.180	—	—	15.00

NOTE: 38,145 coins remelted at the mint.

150th Anniversary - Birth of Tolstoy

KM#	Date	Mintage	VF	XF	Unc
85	1978	.130	—	—	15.00

NOTE: 17,892 coins remelted at the mint.

European Unity

KM#	Date	Mintage	VF	XF	Unc
98	1979	.125	—	—	15.00

NOTE: 14,945 coins remelted at the mint.

1500th Anniversary - Birth of St. Benedict

KM#	Date	Mintage	VF	XF	Unc
112	1980	.125	—	—	15.00

NOTE: 49,095 coins remelted at the mint.

2000th Anniversary of Virgil's Death

KM#	Date	Mintage	VF	XF	Unc
127	1981	.075	—	—	15.00

NOTE: 9,122 coins remelted at the mint.

Centennial - Death of Garibaldi

KM#	Date	Mintage	VF	XF	Unc
141	1982	.048	—	—	15.00
	1982	.013	—	Proof	25.00

NOTE: 112 uncirculated and 369 proof coins remelted at the mint.

500th Anniversary - Birth of Raphael the Artist

KM#	Date	Mintage	VF	XF	Unc
155	1983	.042	—	—	15.00
	1983	.012	—	Proof	25.00

NOTE: 80 uncirculated and 1,939 proof coins remelted at the mint.

1984 Summer Olympiad

KM#	Date	Mintage	VF	XF	Unc
169	1984	.052	—	—	15.00
	1984	.015	—	Proof	27.50

NOTE: 2,920 uncirculated and 20 proof coins remelted at the mint.

European Music Year - J.S. Bach

KM#	Date	Mintage	VF	XF	Unc
183	1985	.040	—	—	12.00
	1985	.012	—	Proof	25.00

NOTE: 6,704 uncirculated and 122 proof coins remelted at the mint.

Soccer - Flags

KM#	Date	Mintage	VF	XF	Unc
197	1986	.045	—	—	18.00
	1986	.012	—	Proof	30.00

NOTE: 5,212 uncirculated and 60 proof coins remelted at the mint.

15th Anniversary - Resumption of Coinage

KM#	Date	Mintage	VF	XF	Unc
210	1987	.043	—	—	18.00

NOTE: 13 coins remelted at the mint.

Zagreb University Games - Pole Vaulter

KM#	Date	Mintage	VF	XF	Unc
214	1987	.035	—	—	18.00
	1987	.010	—	Proof	30.00

NOTE: 9,207 uncirculated and 1,206 proof coins remelted at the mint.

Summer Olympics - Diver

KM#	Date	Mintage	VF	XF	Unc
217	1988	.032	—	—	20.00
	1988	9,600	—	Proof	32.50

NOTE: 146 uncirculated and 3 proof coins remelted at the mint.

Fortifications - Walls and Towers

KM#	Date	Mintage	VF	XF	Unc
227	1988	.038	—	—	20.00

History - 2 Men in Boat

KM#	Date	Mintage	VF	XF	Unc
240	1989	.032	—	—	20.00

San Marino Grand Prix

KM#	Date	Mintage	VF	XF	Unc
244	1989	.030	—	—	20.00
	1989	8,000	—	Proof	35.00

NOTE: 5,180 coins remelted at the mint.

World Cup Soccer Championship Games

KM#	Date	Mintage	VF	XF	Unc
247	1990	.040	—	—	20.00
	1990	.019	—	Proof	35.00

1600 Years of History - Hand and 2 Figures

KM#	Date	Mintage	VF	XF	Unc
257	1990	.036	—	—	20.00

Hand Holding Dove

KM#	Date	Mintage	VF	XF	Unc
270	1991	—	—	—	20.00

Barcelona Olympics

KM#	Date	Mintage	VF	XF	Unc
272	1991	*.060	—	—	22.50
	1991	*8,000	—	Proof	37.50

Olympics - 3 Athletes

KM#	Date	Mintage	VF	XF	Unc
277	1992	*.070	—	—	27.50
	1992	—	—	Proof	45.00

Columbus Studying Chart

KM#	Date	Mintage	VF	XF	Unc
287	1991	—	—	—	20.00

Wildlife Protection - Falcon and Woodpecker

KM#	Date	Mintage	VF	XF	Unc
292	1993	*.035	—	—	20.00
	1993	—	—	Proof	35.00

Wing Above Globe

KM#	Date	Mintage	VF	XF	Unc
302	1993	—	—	—	20.00

Founder Building First San Marino Church

KM#	Date	Mintage	VF	XF	Unc
315	1994	.040	—	—	20.00

Olympics - Ski Jumper

KM#	Date	Mintage	VF	XF	Unc
316	1994	—	—	Proof	28.00

SCUDO

3.0000 g, .917 GOLD, .0883 oz AGW

KM#	Date	Mintage	VF	XF	Unc
38	1974	.087	—	—	65.00

NOTE: 2,491 coins remelted at the mint.

KM#	Date	Mintage	VF	XF	Unc
49	1975	.090	—	—	65.00

NOTE: 37,668 coins remelted at the mint.

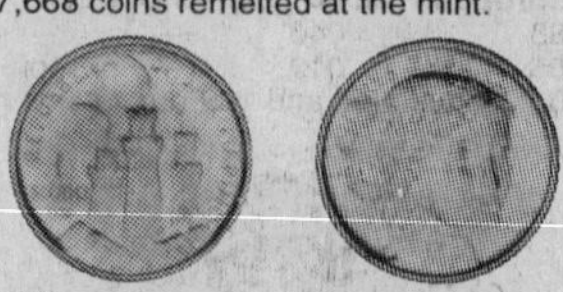

KM#	Date	Mintage	VF	XF	Unc
60	1976	.065	—	—	65.00

NOTE: 30,026 coins remelted at the mint.

Democrazia

KM#	Date	Mintage	VF	XF	Unc
73	1977	.035	—	—	65.00

NOTE: 1,839 coins remelted at the mint.

Miss Liberta

KM#	Date	Mintage	VF	XF	Unc
86	1978	.038	—	—	65.00

NOTE: 9,021 coins remelted at the mint.

Peace

KM#	Date	Mintage	VF	XF	Unc
99	1979	.038	—	—	65.00

NOTE: 4,152 coins remelted at the mint.

KM#	Date	Mintage	VF	XF	Unc
113	1980	.038	—	—	65.00

NOTE: 10,309 coins remelted at the mint.

World Food Day

KM#	Date	Mintage	VF	XF	Unc
128	1981	.031	—	—	65.00

NOTE: 196 coins remelted at the mint.

KM#	Date	Mintage	VF	XF	Unc
142	1982	.017	—	—	65.00

NOTE: 1,192 coins remelted at the mint.

2.0000 g, .917 GOLD, .0590 oz AGW
Perpetual Liberty

KM#	Date	Mintage	VF	XF	Unc
156	1983	.014	—	—	65.00

NOTE: 917 coins remelted at the mint.

Peace
Obv: Similar to 2 Scudi, KM#171.

KM#	Date	Mintage	VF	XF	Unc
170	1984	.011	—	—	65.00

NOTE: 979 coins remelted at the mint.

International Year For Youth

KM#	Date	Mintage	VF	XF	Unc
184	1985	.010	—	—	90.00

NOTE: 1,162 coins remelted at the mint.

3.3920 g, .917 GOLD, .1000 oz AGW
Insects at Work

KM#	Date	Mintage	VF	XF	Unc
198	1986	9,000	—	—	70.00

NOTE: 1,308 coins remelted at the mint.

European Year for Environment

KM#	Date	Mintage	VF	XF	Unc
211	1987	8,000	—	—	70.00

NOTE: 962 coins remelted at the mint.

Disarmament

KM#	Date	Mintage	VF	XF	Unc
28	1988	7,000	—	—	70.00

NOTE: 873 coins remelted at the mint.

3.2258 g, .900 GOLD, .0933 oz AGW
French Revolution

KM#	Date	Mintage	VF	XF	Unc
41	1989	7,500	—	—	65.00

NOTE: 731 coins remelted at the mint.

San Marino's Presidency of the European Council

KM#	Date	Mintage	VF	XF	Unc
58	1990	7,300	—	—	65.00

Peace - Child Fleeing

KM#	Date	Mintage	VF	XF	Unc
273	1991	*7,500	—	Proof	65.00

San Marino's Entry Into the UN

KM#	Date	Mintage	VF	XF	Unc
288	1992	8,500	—	Proof	65.00

International Monetary Fund - 3 Figures

KM#	Date	Mintage	VF	XF	Unc
303	1993	*8,502	—	—	60.00
	1993	—	—	Proof	70.00

2 SCUDI

6.0000 g, .917 GOLD, .1769 oz AGW

KM#	Date	Mintage	VF	XF	Unc
39	1974	.077	—	—	110.00

NOTE: 1,637 coins remelted at the mint.

KM#	Date	Mintage	VF	XF	Unc
50	1975	.080	—	—	110.00

NOTE: 33,373 coins remelted at the mint.

KM#	Date	Mintage	VF	XF	Unc
61	1976	.055	—	—	110.00

NOTE: 20,246 coins remelted at the mint.

Democrazia

KM#	Date	Mintage	VF	XF	Unc
74	1977	.034	—	—	110.00

NOTE: 912 coins remelted at the mint.

Miss Liberta

KM#	Date	Mintage	VF	XF	Unc
87	1978	.037	—	—	110.00

NOTE: 8,120 coins remelted at the mint.

Peace

KM#	Date	Mintage	VF	XF	Unc
100	1979	.037	—	—	110.00

NOTE: 3,238 coins remelted at the mint.

KM#	Date	Mintage	VF	XF	Unc
114	1980	.037	—	—	110.00

NOTE: 9,340 coins remelted at the mint.

World Food Day

KM#	Date	Mintage	VF	XF	Unc
129	1981	.030	—	—	110.00

NOTE: 196 coins remelted at the mint.

KM#	Date	Mintage	VF	XF	Unc
143	1982	.016	—	—	110.00

NOTE: 244 coins remelted at the mint.

4.0000 g, .917 GOLD, .1179 oz AGW
Perpetual Liberty

KM#	Date	Mintage	VF	XF	Unc
157	1983	.013	—	—	110.00

NOTE: 17 coins remelted at the mint.

Liberty

KM#	Date	Mintage	VF	XF	Unc
171	1984	.010	—	—	110.00

NOTE: 12 coins remelted at the mint.

International Year For Youth

KM#	Date	Mintage	VF	XF	Unc
185	1985	9,000	—	—	110.00

NOTE: 200 coins remelted at the mint.

6.7840 g, .917 GOLD, .2000 oz AGW
Insects at Work

KM#	Date	Mintage	VF	XF	Unc
199	1986	8,000	—	—	120.00

NOTE: 329 coins remelted at the mint.

European Year for Environment

KM#	Date	Mintage	VF	XF	Unc
212	1987	7,000	—	—	120.00

NOTE: 14 coins remelted at the mint.

Disarmament

KM#	Date	Mintage	VF	XF	Unc
229	1988	6,000	—	—	120.00

NOTE: 7 coins remelted at the mint.

6.4516 g, .900 GOLD, .1867 oz AGW
French Revolution

KM#	Date	Mintage	VF	XF	Unc
242	1989	6,500	—	—	110.00

San Marino's Presidency of the European Council

KM#	Date	Mintage	VF	XF	Unc
259	1990	6,800	—	—	110.00

Peace - New Shoots Growing From Stump

KM#	Date	Mintage	VF	XF	Unc
274	1991	*6,500	—	Proof	110.00

San Marino's Entry Into the UN

KM#	Date	Mintage	VF	XF	Unc
289	1992	7,500	—	Proof	110.00

International Monetary Fund - 2 Figures

KM#	Date	Mintage	VF	XF	Unc
304	1993	*7,500	—	—	100.00
	1993	—	—	Proof	120.00

5 SCUDI

15.0000 g, .917 GOLD, .4422 oz AGW

KM#	Date	Mintage	VF	XF	Unc
62	1976	8,000	—	—	625.00

NOTE: 25 coins remelted at the mint.

Democrazia

KM#	Date	Mintage	VF	XF	Unc
75	1977	.016	—	—	240.00

NOTE: 29 coins remelted at the mint.

Peace

KM#	Date	Mintage	VF	XF	Unc
101	1979	.024	—	—	240.00

NOTE: 161 coins remelted at the mint.

Justice

KM#	Date	Mintage	VF	XF	Unc
115	1980	.024	—	—	240.00

NOTE: 1,428 coins remelted at the mint.

World Food Day

KM#	Date	Mintage	VF	XF	Unc
130	1981	.024	—	—	240.00

NOTE: 33 coins remelted at the mint.

Defense of Liberty

KM#	Date	Mintage	VF	XF	Unc
144	1982	.015	—	—	240.00

NOTE: 19 coins remelted at the mint.

10.0000 g, .917 GOLD, .2949 oz AGW

Perpetual Liberty

KM#	Date	Mintage	VF	XF	Unc
158	1983	.011	—	—	250.00

NOTE: 25 coins remelted at the mint.

Justice

KM#	Date	Mintage	VF	XF	Unc
172	1984	9,000	—	—	300.00

NOTE: 28 coins remelted at the mint.

Libertas

KM#	Date	Mintage	VF	XF	Unc
186	1985	7,400	—	—	400.00

NOTE: 13 coins remelted at the mint.

16.9590 g, .917 GOLD, .5000 oz AGW

Work - Bees

KM#	Date	Mintage	VF	XF	Unc
200	1986	7,000	—	—	330.00

NOTE: 614 coins remelted at the mint.

United Nations

KM#	Date	Mintage	VF	XF	Unc
215	1987	6,000	—	—	330.00

NOTE: 49 coins remelted at the mint.

Human Rights

KM#	Date	Mintage	VF	XF	Unc
230	1988	5,000	—	—	330.00

NOTE: 11 coins remelted at the mint.

Entrance of San Marino in Common Market

KM#	Date	Mintage	VF	XF	Unc
245	1989	6,000	—	—	330.00

Founding of the Republic

KM#	Date	Mintage	VF	XF	Unc
260	1990	6,500	—	Proof	320.00

Peace and Freedom - Family

KM#	Date	Mintage	VF	XF	Unc
275	1991	7,000	—	Proof	320.00

Customer Agreement With E.E.C.

KM#	Date	Mintage	VF	XF	Unc
290	1992	*6,500	—	Proof	320.00

International Monetary Fund - Figure Holding Scale

KM#	Date	Mintage	VF	XF	Unc
305	1993	*7,000	—	Proof	320.00

10 SCUDI

30.0000 g, .917 GOLD, .8844 oz AGW

KM#	Date	Mintage	VF	XF	Unc
88	1978	.020	—	—	600.00

NOTE: 54 coins remelted at the mint.

MINT SETS (MS)

KM#	Date	Mintage	Identification	Issue Price	Mkt. Val.
MS1	1972(8)	—	KM14-21	5.00	12.50
MS2	1973(8)	—	KM22-29	6.00	12.50
MS3	1974(8)	60,000	KM30-37	9.00	12.50
MS4	1974(2)	60,000	KM38-39	—	175.00
MS5	1975(8)	—	KM40-47	6.50	12.50
MS6	1975(5)	—	KM40-44	—	—
MS7	1975(2)	90,000	KM49-50	—	175.00
MS8	1976(8)	—	KM51-58	6.00	12.50
MS9	1976(2)	40,000	KM60-61	—	175.00
MS10	1977(9)	—	KM63-71	—	15.00
MS11	1977(2)	30,000	KM73-74	—	175.00
MS12	1978(9)	—	KM76-84	—	15.00
MS13	1979(9)	—	KM89-98	—	15.00
MS14	1980(9)	—	KM102-110	—	15.00
MS15	1981(9)	—	KM116-123,126	—	15.00
MS16	1981(3)	—	KM124-125,127	—	—
MS17	1982(9)	—	KM131-138,140	6.00	8.50
MS18	1982(2)	—	KM139,141	—	27.50
MS19	1983(9)	—	KM145-153	5.50	8.50
MS20	1983(2)	—	KM154-155	—	27.50
MS21	1984(9)	—	KM159-167	—	—
MS22	1984(2)	—	KM168-169	—	22.00
MS23	1985(9)	—	KM173-181	—	8.50
MS24	1985(2)	—	KM182-183	—	22.00
MS25	1986(9)	—	KM187-195	7.00	8.50
MS26	1986(2)	—	KM196-197	—	30.00
MS27	1987(10)	43,000	KM201-210	—	25.00
MS28	1987(2)	—	KM213-214	—	30.00
MS29	1988(10)	*80,000	KM218-227	22.00	26.00
MS30	1988(2)	—	KM216-217	—	30.00
MS31	1989(10)	32,000	KM231-240	—	28.00
MS32	1989(2)	30,000	KM243-244	—	30.00
MS33	1989(2)	6,500	KM241-242	—	170.00
MS34	1990(10)	36,000	KM248-257	—	35.00
MS35	1990(2)	40,000	KM246-247	—	175.00
MS36	1990(2)	6,800	KM258-259	—	175.00
MS37	1991(10)	36,000	KM261-270	—	32.00
MS38	1991(2)	25,000	KM271-272	—	32.00
MS39	1992(10)	45,000	KM278-287	—	32.00
MS40	1992(2)	—	KM276-277	34.00	40.00
MS41	1994(10)	40,000	KM307-315	18.00	25.00

PROOF SETS

KM#	Date	Mintage	Identification	Issue Price	Mkt. Val.
PS1	1989(2)	8,000	KM243-244	55.00	60.00
PS2	1990(2)	18,800	KM246-247	55.00	60.00
PS3	1991(2)	8,000	KM271-272	55.00	60.00
PS4	1991(2)	6,800	KM273-274	—	175.00
PS5	1993(2)	—	KM303-304	158.00	160.00

Listings For

SARAWAK: refer to Malaysia

SAUDI ARABIA

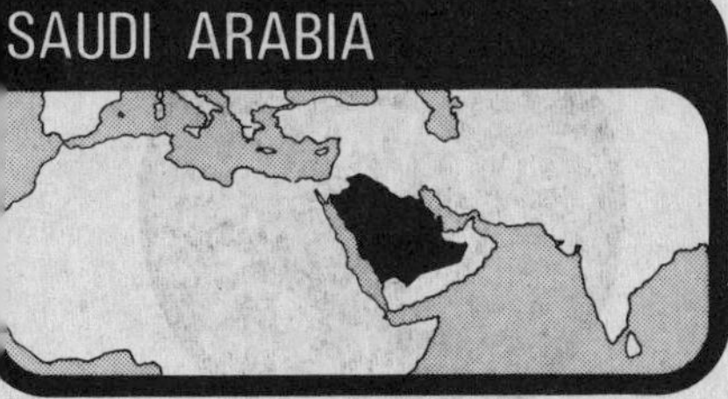

The Kingdom of Saudi Arabia, an independent and bsolute hereditary monarchy comprising the former sul-anate of Nejd, the old kingdom of Hejaz, Asir and Al Iasa, occupies four-fifths of the Arabian peninsula. The ingdom has an area of 830,000 sq. mi. (2,149,690 sq. m.) and a population of *16.1 million. Capital: Riyadh. he economy is based on oil, which provides 85 percent f Saudi Arabia's revenue.

Mohammed united the Arabs in the 7th century and his ollowers founded a great empire with its capital at Aedina. The Turks established nominal rule over much f Arabia in the 16th and 17th centuries, and in the 18th entury divided it into principalities.

The Kingdom of Saudi Arabia was created by King Abd l-Aziz Bin Saud (1882-1953), a descendant of earlier Vahhabi rulers of the Arabian peninsula. In 1901 he eized Riyadh, capital of the Sultanate of Nejd, and in 905 established himself as Sultan. In 1913 he captured he Turkish province of Al Hasa; took the Hejaz in 1925 nd by 1926 most of Asir. In 1932 he combined Nejd and Iejaz into the single kingdom of Saudi Arabia. Asir was ncorporated into the kingdom a year later.

The following areas of Saudi Arabia were coin-issuing entities of interest to numismatics.

TITLES

العربية السعودية

Al-Arabiyat as-Sa'udiyat

المملكة العربية السعودية

Al-Mamlaka(t) al-'Arabiya(t) as-Sa'udiya(t)

MECCA

Mecca, the metropolis of Islam and the capital of Hejaz, s located inland from the Red Sea due east of the port f Jidda. A center of non-political commercial, cultural and religious activities, Mecca remained virtually inde-pendent until 1259. Two centuries of Egyptian rule were ollowed by four centuries of Turkish rule which lasted until the Arab revolts which extinguished all Turkish pretensions to sovereignty over any part of the Arabian peninsula.

MINTNAME

مكة

Makkah, Mecca

RULERS

Sharifs of Mecca

Ghalib b. Ma'sud, AH1219-1229

Yahya b. Surer, AH1230-1240

Abdul Muttalib and Ibn Awn, AH1240-1248

ANONYMOUS WAHHABI ISSUES

1/2 MAHMUDI

COPPER
Mintname: *Mecca*

KM#	Date	Good	VG	Fine	VF
5	AH1240	250.00	450.00	600.00	800.00

MAHMUDI

COPPER
Mintname: *Mecca*

KM#	Date	Good	VG	Fine	VF
1	AH1219	100.00	150.00	300.00	400.00

KM#	Date	Good	VG	Fine	VF
2	AH1220	100.00	150.00	300.00	400.00
	1221	100.00	150.00	300.00	400.00
	1222	100.00	150.00	300.00	400.00

Mintname: *Mecca*
Obv: Bird. Rev: Fish.

KM#	Date	Good	VG	Fine	VF
3	AH1223	125.00	175.00	300.00	450.00

KM#	Date	Good	VG	Fine	VF
4	AH1230	125.00	175.00	300.00	450.00

HEJAZ

Hejaz, a province of Saudi Arabia and a former vilayet of the Ottoman empire, occupies an 800-mile long (1,287 km.) coastal strip between Nejd and the Red Sea. The province was a Turkish dependency until freed in World War I. Husain Ibn Ali, Amir of Mecca, opposed the Turkish control and, with the aid of Lawrence of Arabia, wrested much of Hejaz from the Turks and in 1916 assumed the title of King of Hejaz. Ibn Saud of Nejd conquered Hejaz in 1925, and in 1926 combined it and Nejd into a single kingdom.

TITLES

الحجاز

al-Hejaz

RULERS

al Husain Ibn Ali
AH1334-42/1916-24AD

Abd Al-Aziz Bin Sa'ud
AH1342/1924AD

MONETARY SYSTEM

40 Para = 1 Piastre (Ghirsh)
20 Piastres = 1 Riyal
100 Piastres = 1 Dinar

COUNTERMARKED COINAGE

Maria Theresa Thalers, as well as many Turkish and Egyptian coins, are found countermarked *al-Hijaz*. The countermark occurs in various sizes and styles of lettering. The mark may have been applied during 1916, and is reckoned by some authorities to have been used as late as 1923 although there is no evidence that it was ever applied officially. On Turkish and Egyptian coins the c/m is usually on the obverse trying to deface the Ottoman toughra.

NOTE: Caution should be excercised in the purchase of any of the Hejaz countermarked coins. The authenticity of most of the pieces on the market today is the subject of controversy, particularly pieces other than the Maria Theresa Thalers from the Vienna Mint, the Turkish 20 Piastres and 10 Piastres of AH1327, and the Turkish 20 and 40 Para nickel pieces (#'s 3, 4, 5, 6, 13, 14, 17 and 18 below). Also, the small 6mm size countermark is not believed to be original. Any coin dating after 1923 with the countermark is most doubtful. The following coins show the types which may be found with the countermark.

NOTE: Previously listed Turkish 10 and 20 Para with accession date AH1255 are considered a recent fabrication. Previously listed Turkish 10 Para with accession date AH1327 and w/*Hejaz* c/m KM#1 and 2 are now believed spurious by leading authorities.

20 PARA

NICKEL
Accession Date: AH1327
c/m: *Hejaz* on Turkey 20 Para, KM#761.

KM#	Year	Good	VG	Fine	VF
3	2	5.00	7.00	15.00	30.00
	3	4.00	6.00	12.00	25.00
	4	2.00	4.00	10.00	20.00
	5	2.00	4.00	10.00	20.00
	6	2.00	4.00	10.00	20.00

40 PARA

NICKEL
Accession Date: AH1327
c/m: *Hejaz* on Turkey 40 Para, KM#766.

KM#	Year	Good	VG	Fine	VF
4	3	4.00	6.00	15.00	30.00
	4	2.00	5.00	10.00	20.00
	5	2.00	5.00	10.00	20.00

COPPER-NICKEL
c/m: *Hejaz* on Turkey 40 Para, KM#779.

KM#	Year	Good	VG	Fine	VF
5	8	4.00	6.00	10.00	20.00
	9	6.00	10.00	25.00	60.00

Accession Date: AH1336
c/m: *Hejaz* on Turkey 40 Para, KM#828.

KM#	Year	Good	VG	Fine	VF
6	4	10.00	20.00	40.00	75.00

2 PIASTRES

SILVER
Accession Date: AH1327
c/m: *Hejaz* on Turkey 2 Kurush, KM#749.

KM#	Year	Good	VG	Fine	VF
7	1	12.50	20.00	40.00	75.00
	2	12.50	20.00	40.00	75.00
	3	12.50	20.00	40.00	75.00
	4	12.50	20.00	40.00	75.00
	5	12.50	20.00	40.00	75.00
	6	12.50	20.00	40.00	75.00

c/m: *Hejaz* on Turkey 2 Kurush, KM#770.

KM#	Year	Good	VG	Fine	VF
8	7	12.50	20.00	40.00	75.00
	8	12.50	20.00	40.00	75.00
	9	12.50	20.00	40.00	75.00

c/m: *Hejaz* on Egypt 2 Qirsh, KM#307.

KM#	Year	Good	VG	Fine	VF
9	2H	12.50	20.00	40.00	75.00
	3H	12.50	20.00	40.00	75.00

NOTE: The above coins are all controversial.

5 PIASTRES

SILVER
Accession Date: AH1327
c/m: *Hejaz* on Turkey 5 Kurush, KM#750.

KM#	Year	Good	VG	Fine	VF
10	1	12.50	20.00	40.00	75.00
	2	12.50	20.00	40.00	75.00
	3	12.50	20.00	40.00	75.00
	4	12.50	20.00	40.00	75.00
	5	12.50	20.00	40.00	75.00
	6	12.50	20.00	40.00	75.00
	7	12.50	20.00	40.00	75.00

c/m: *Hejaz* on Turkey 5 Kurush, KM#771.

KM#	Year	Good	VG	Fine	VF
11	7	12.50	20.00	40.00	75.00
	8	12.50	20.00	40.00	75.00
	9	12.50	20.00	40.00	75.00

c/m: *Hejaz* on Egypt 5 Qirsh, KM#308.

KM#	Year	Good	VG	Fine	VF
12	2H	12.50	20.00	40.00	75.00
	3H	12.50	20.00	40.00	75.00
	4H	12.50	20.00	40.00	75.00
	6H	12.50	20.00	40.00	75.00

10 PIASTRES

SILVER
Accession Date: AH1327
c/m: *Hejaz* on Turkey 10 Kurush, KM#751.

KM#	Year	Good	VG	Fine	VF
13	1	20.00	30.00	60.00	100.00

KM#	Year	Good	VG	Fine	VF
	2	20.00	30.00	60.00	100.00
	3	20.00	30.00	60.00	100.00
	4	20.00	30.00	60.00	100.00
	5	20.00	30.00	60.00	100.00
	6	20.00	30.00	60.00	100.00
	7	20.00	30.00	60.00	100.00

c/m: *Hejaz* on Turkey 10 Kurush, KM#772.

KM#	Year	Good	VG	Fine	VF
14	7	20.00	30.00	60.00	100.00
	8	20.00	30.00	60.00	100.00
	9	20.00	30.00	60.00	100.00
	10	20.00	30.00	60.00	100.00

c/m: *Hejaz* on Egypt 10 Qirsh, KM#309.

KM#	Year	Good	VG	Fine	VF
15	2H	20.00	30.00	60.00	100.00
	3H	20.00	30.00	60.00	100.00
	4H	20.00	30.00	60.00	100.00
	6H	20.00	30.00	60.00	100.00

20 PIASTRES

SILVER
Accession Date: AH1327
c/m: *Hejaz* on Egypt 20 Qirsh, KM#310.

KM#	Year	Good	VG	Fine	VF
16	2H	35.00	60.00	100.00	150.00
	3H	35.00	60.00	100.00	150.00
	4H	35.00	60.00	100.00	150.00
	6H	35.00	60.00	100.00	150.00

c/m: *Hejaz* on Turkey 20 Kurush, KM#780.

KM#	Year	Good	VG	Fine	VF
17	8	35.00	60.00	100.00	150.00
	9	35.00	60.00	100.00	150.00
	10	35.00	60.00	100.00	150.00

c/m: *Hejaz* on Austria M.T. Thaler, KM#T1.

KM#	Year	Good	VG	Fine	VF
18	1780 (restrike)	15.00	30.00	60.00	125.00

REGULAR COINAGE

NOTE: All the regular coins of Hejaz bear the accessional date AH1334 of Al-Husain Ibn Ali, plus the regnal year. Many of the bronze coins occur with a light silver wash mostly on thicker specimens. A variety of planchet thickness exist.

1/8 PIASTRE

BRONZE

KM#	Date	Year	VG	Fine	VF	XF
21	AH1334	5	15.00	25.00	50.00	75.00

NOTE: Reeded and plain edge varieties exist.

1/4 PIASTRE

BRONZE, 1.14 g

KM#	Date	Year	VG	Fine	VF	XF
22	AH1334	5	4.00	8.00	20.00	35.00
	1334	6/5	75.00	150.00	300.00	600.00
	1334	6	100.00	200.00	400.00	700.00

NOTE: Reeded and plain edge varieties exist.

KM#	Date	Year	VG	Fine	VF	XF
25	AH1334	8	5.00	10.00	20.00	35.00

1/2 PIASTRE

BRONZE

KM#	Date	Year	VG	Fine	VF	XF
23	AH1334	5	3.00	7.50	20.00	35.00

NOTE: Reeded and plain edge varieties exist.

Similar to 1/4 Piastre, KM#25.

KM#	Date	Year	VG	Fine	VF	XF
26	AH1334	8	—	—	Rare	—

NOTE: All known specimens are overstruck by Nejd KM#1.

PIASTRE

BRONZE

KM#	Date	Year	VG	Fine	VF	XF
24	AH1334	5	6.00	10.00	20.00	35.00
		6/5	100.00	200.00	400.00	600.00

KM#	Date	Year	VG	Fine	VF	XF
27	AH1334	8	6.00	10.00	25.00	50.00

5 PIASTRES

6.1000 g, .917 SILVER, .1798 oz ASW

KM#	Date	Year	VG	Fine	VF	XF
28	AH1334	8	15.00	40.00	75.00	150.00

10 PIASTRES

12.0500 g, .917 SILVER, .3552 oz ASW

KM#	Date	Year	VG	Fine	VF	XF
29	AH1334	8	100.00	170.00	400.00	800.00

20 PIASTRES

(1 Ryal)

24.1000 g, .917 SILVER, .7105 oz ASW

KM#	Date	Year	VG	Fine	VF	XF
30	AH1334	8	20.00	40.00	70.00	85.00
		9	30.00	50.00	90.00	125.00

DINAR HASHIMI

GOLD

KM#	Date	Year	Fine	VF	XF	Unc
31	AH1334	8	125.00	200.00	300.00	450.00

NEJD

Nejd, a province of Saudi Arabia which may be described as an open steppe, occupies the core of the Arabian peninsula. The province became a nominal dependency of the Turkish empire in 1871 and a sultanate of King Ibn-Saud in 1906.

TITLES

Nejd نجد

RULERS

Abd Al-Aziz Bin Sa'ud
AH1322-1373/1905-1953AD
(Over all of Hejaz after 1926, and then in all Saudi Arabia after 1932).

MONETARY SYSTEM

40 Para = 1 Piastre (Ghirsh)
20 Piastres = 1 Riyal
100 Piastres = 1 Dinar

COUNTERMARKED COINAGE

Maria Theresa Thalers were countermarked *Nejd* between 1916-1923 and after 1935.

NOTE: Other Turkish and Egyptian coins are reported with the Nejd cmk., but their legitimacy remains a matter of controversy. They are listed here, but should be regarded with caution. Only the large countermark is currently considered to be authentic. Indian Rupees cmk.'d *Nejd* are rather dubious. Coins bearing both the Nejd and Hejaz countermarks are of very questionable legitimacy as are all countermarked modern Maria Theresa Thalers from mints other than the Vienna Mint.

NOTE: Previously listed Turkish 10 and 20 Para w/*Nejd* are considered a recent fabrication.

5 PIASTRES

SILVER
Accession Date: AH1327
c/m: *Nejd* on Egypt 5 Qirsh, KM#308.

KM#	Year	Good	VG	Fine	VF
1	2H	25.00	50.00	100.00	150.00
	3H	25.00	50.00	100.00	150.00
	4H	25.00	50.00	100.00	150.00
	6H	25.00	50.00	100.00	150.00

c/m: *Nejd* on Egypt 5 Piastre, KM#318.

KM#	Date	Year	Good	VG	Fine	VF
2	AH1335	1916	25.00	50.00	100.00	150.00

KM#	Date	Year	Good	VG	Fine	VF
		1917	25.00	50.00	100.00	150.00
		1917H	25.00	50.00	100.00	150.00

Accession Date: AH1327
c/m: *Nejd* on Turkey 5 Kurush, KM#750.

KM#	Year	Good	VG	Fine	VF
	1	25.00	50.00	100.00	150.00
	2	25.00	50.00	100.00	150.00
	3	25.00	50.00	100.00	150.00
	4	25.00	50.00	100.00	150.00
	5	25.00	50.00	100.00	150.00
	6	25.00	50.00	100.00	150.00
	7	25.00	50.00	100.00	150.00

c/m: *Nejd* on Turkey 5 Kurush, KM#771.

KM#	Year	Good	VG	Fine	VF
	7	25.00	50.00	100.00	150.00
	8	25.00	50.00	100.00	150.00
	9	25.00	50.00	100.00	150.00

RUPEE

SILVER
c/m: *Nejd* on India Rupee, KM#450.

KM#	Date	Year	Good	VG	Fine	VF
	1835	—	25.00	50.00	100.00	150.00

c/m: *Nejd* on India Rupee, KM#457.

KM#	Date	Year	Good	VG	Fine	VF
	1840	—	25.00	50.00	125.00	275.00

c/m: *Nejd* on India Rupee, KM#458.

KM#	Date	Year	Good	VG	Fine	VF
	1840	—	25.00	50.00	125.00	225.00

c/m: *Nejd* on India Rupee, KM#473.

KM#	Date	Year	Good	VG	Fine	VF
	1862-76	—	25.00	50.00	100.00	150.00

c/m: *Nejd* on Indian Rupee, KM#492.

KM#	Date	Year	Good	VG	Fine	VF
A9	1877-1901	—	25.00	50.00	100.00	150.00

10 PIASTRES

SILVER
Accession Date: AH1293
c/m: *Nejd* on Egypt 10 Qirsh, KM#295.

KM#	Year	Good	VG	Fine	VF
9	10W	50.00	70.00	125.00	200.00
	11W	50.00	70.00	125.00	200.00
	12W	50.00	70.00	125.00	200.00
	13W	50.00	70.00	125.00	200.00
	14W	50.00	70.00	125.00	200.00
	15W	50.00	70.00	125.00	200.00
	16W	50.00	70.00	125.00	200.00
	17W	50.00	70.00	125.00	200.00
	18W	50.00	70.00	125.00	200.00
	19W	50.00	70.00	125.00	200.00
	20W	50.00	70.00	125.00	200.00
	21W	50.00	70.00	125.00	200.00
	22W	50.00	70.00	125.00	200.00
	23W	50.00	70.00	125.00	200.00
	24W	50.00	70.00	125.00	200.00
	25W	50.00	70.00	125.00	200.00
	26W	50.00	70.00	125.00	200.00
	27W	50.00	70.00	125.00	200.00
	29W	50.00	70.00	125.00	200.00
	29H	50.00	70.00	125.00	200.00
	30H	50.00	70.00	125.00	200.00
	31H	50.00	70.00	125.00	200.00
	32H	50.00	70.00	125.00	200.00
	33H	50.00	70.00	125.00	200.00

Accession Date: AH1327
c/m: *Nejd* on Turkey 10 Kurush, KM#751.

KM#	Year	Good	VG	Fine	VF
10	1	50.00	70.00	125.00	200.00
	2	50.00	70.00	125.00	200.00
	3	50.00	70.00	125.00	200.00
	4	50.00	70.00	125.00	200.00
	5	50.00	70.00	125.00	200.00
	6	50.00	70.00	125.00	200.00
	7	50.00	70.00	125.00	200.00

c/m: *Nejd* on Turkey 10 Kurush, KM#772.

KM#	Year	Good	VG	Fine	VF
11	7	50.00	70.00	125.00	200.00
	8	50.00	70.00	125.00	200.00
	9	50.00	70.00	125.00	200.00
	10	50.00	70.00	125.00	200.00

20 PIASTRES

SILVER
Accession Date: AH1255
c/m: *Nejd* on Turkey 20 Kurush, KM#675.

KM#	Year	Good	VG	Fine	VF
B12	6-23	75.00	125.00	200.00	350.00

Accession Date: AH1277
c/m: *Nejd* on Turkey 20 Kurush, KM#693.

KM#	Year	Good	VG	Fine	VF
C12	1-15	75.00	125.00	200.00	350.00

Accession Date: AH1293
c/m: *Nejd* on Turkey 20 Kurush, KM#722.

KM#	Year	Good	VG	Fine	VF
A12	1	75.00	125.00	200.00	350.00
	2	75.00	125.00	200.00	350.00
	3	75.00	125.00	200.00	350.00

Accession Date: AH1327
c/m: *Nejd* on Egypt 20 Qirsh, KM#310.

KM#	Year	Good	VG	Fine	VF
12	2H	75.00	125.00	200.00	350.00
	3H	75.00	125.00	200.00	350.00
	4H	75.00	125.00	200.00	350.00
	6H	75.00	125.00	200.00	300.00

c/m: *Nejd* on Egypt 20 Piastre, KM#321.

KM#	Year	Good	VG	Fine	VF
A13	1916	75.00	125.00	200.00	350.00
	1917	75.00	125.00	200.00	350.00
	1917H	75.00	125.00	200.00	350.00

c/m: *Nejd* on Turkey 20 Kurush, KM#780.

KM#	Year	Good	VG	Fine	VF
13	8	75.00	125.00	200.00	350.00
	9	75.00	125.00	200.00	350.00
	10	75.00	125.00	200.00	350.00

c/m: *Nejd* on Austria M.T. Thaler, KM#T1.

KM#	Date	Year	Good	VG	Fine	VF
14	1780	—	40.00	80.00	200.00	425.00

REGULAR COINAGE

Struck at occupied Mecca, Hejaz Mint by Ibn Sa'ud while establishing his kingdom.

1/4 GHIRSH

COPPER

KM#	Date	Mintage	VG	Fine	VF	XF
1	AH1343	—	15.00	25.00	50.00	75.00

NOTE: Several varieties exist as well as reeded and plain edges. Some specimens struck over Hejaz KM#23 and KM#26.

1/2 GHIRSH

COPPER
Obv. leg. right of toughra: *Al-Faisal al Saud*

KM#	Date	Mintage	VG	Fine	VF	XF
2.1	AH1343	—	6.00	12.50	25.00	45.00

Obv. leg. right of toughra: *al-Faisal.*

KM#	Date	Mintage	VG	Fine	VF	XF
2.2	AH1343	—	7.00	15.00	30.00	55.00

NOTE: Varieties exist. Some specimens struck over Hejaz KM#23 and KM#26.

KM#	Date	Mintage	VG	Fine	VF	XF
3	AH1344, yr. 2	—	3.00	8.00	20.00	30.00

HEJAZ and NEJD

ROYAL TITLES

Appearing on Coins

AH1344 (1926AD)
King of Hejaz and Sultan of Nejd

1/4 GHIRSH

COPPER-NICKEL

KM#	Date	Mintage	VG	Fine	VF	XF
4	AH1344	—	1.25	2.00	4.00	15.00
	1344	—	—	—	Proof	—

1/2 GHIRSH

COPPER-NICKEL

KM#	Date	Mintage	VG	Fine	VF	XF
5	AH1344	—	2.50	4.00	12.00	18.00
	1344	—	—	—	Proof	—

GHIRSH

COPPER-NICKEL

KM#	Date	Mintage	VG	Fine	VF	XF
6	AH1344	—	2.00	3.00	7.00	15.00
	1344	—	—	—	Proof	—

HEJAZ and NEJD and DEPENDENCIES

ROYAL TITLES

Appearing on Coins

AH1346-1348 (1928-1930AD)
King of Hejaz and Nejd and Dependencies

1/4 GHIRSH

COPPER-NICKEL

KM#	Date	Mintage	VG	Fine	VF	XF
7	AH1346	3.000	3.00	5.00	8.00	20.00

KM#	Date	Mintage	VG	Fine	VF	XF
13	AH1348	—	3.00	5.00	8.00	20.00
	1348	—	—	—	Proof	—

1/2 GHIRSH

COPPER-NICKEL

KM#	Date	Mintage	VG	Fine	VF	XF
8	AH1346	3.000	3.00	5.00	10.00	30.00

KM#	Date	Mintage	VG	Fine	VF	XF
14	AH1348	—	3.00	5.00	8.00	25.00
	1348	—	—	—	Proof	—

GHIRSH

COPPER-NICKEL

KM#	Date	Mintage	VG	Fine	VF	XF
9	AH1346	3.000	3.00	5.00	10.00	35.00

KM#	Date	Mintage	VG	Fine	VF	XF
15	AH1348	—	3.00	5.00	8.50	25.00
	1348	—	—	—	Proof	—

1/4 RIYAL

6.0500 g, .917 SILVER, .1783 oz ASW

KM#	Date	Mintage	VG	Fine	VF	XF
10	AH1346	.400	12.50	20.00	45.00	75.00
	1346	—	—	—	Proof	—
	1348	.200	17.50	30.00	60.00	100.00
	1348	—	—	—	Proof	—

1/2 RIYAL

12.1000 g, .917 SILVER, .3567 oz ASW

KM#	Date	Mintage	VG	Fine	VF	XF
11	AH1346	.200	55.00	100.00	165.00	300.00
	1346	—	—	—	Proof	200.00
	1348	.100	55.00	100.00	165.00	300.00
	1348	—	—	—	Proof	—

RIYAL

24.1000 g, .917 SILVER, .7105 oz ASW

KM#	Date	Mintage	VG	Fine	VF	XF
12	AH1346	.800	15.00	25.00	50.00	80.00
	1346	—	—	—	Proof	350.00
	1348	.400	20.00	30.00	85.00	120.00
	1348	—	—	—	Proof	—

SAUDI ARABIA

RULERS

Abd Al-Aziz Bin Sa'ud
AH1344-1373/1926-1953AD
Sa'ud Bin Abd Al-Aziz
AH1373-1383/1953-1964AD
Faisal Bin Abd Al-Aziz
AH1383-1395/1964-1975AD
Khalid Bin Abd Al-Aziz
AH1395-1403/1975-1982AD
Fahad Bin Abd Al-Aziz, AH1403-/1982-AD

MONETARY SYSTEM

Until 1960

22 Ghirsh = 1 Riyal
40 Riyals = 1 Guinea
20 Ghirsh = 1 Riyal

NOTE: Copper-nickel, reeded-edge coins dated AH1356 and silver coins dated AH1354 were struck at Philadelphia between 1944-1949.

ROYAL TITLES

Appearing on coins

AH1356 (1937AD) and later
King of the Kingdom of Saudi Arabia

1/4 GHIRSH

COPPER-NICKEL
Plain edge

KM#	Date	Mintage	VG	Fine	VF	XF
19.1	AH1356	1.000	1.00	2.00	6.00	15.00

Reeded edge

KM#	Date	Mintage	VG	Fine	VF	XF
19.2	AH1356	21.500	.25	.50	1.00	2.50

NOTE: Struck in 1947 (AH1366-67) at Philadelphia.

1/2 GHIRSH

COPPER-NICKEL
Plain edge

KM#	Date	Mintage	VG	Fine	VF	XF
20.1	AH1356	1.000	1.25	2.00	6.00	15.00

Reeded edge

KM#	Date	Mintage	VG	Fine	VF	XF
20.2	AH1356	10.850	.15	.25	1.00	3.00

NOTE: Struck in 1947 (AH1366-67) at Philadelphia.

GHIRSH

COPPER-NICKEL
Plain edge

KM#	Date	Mintage	VG	Fine	VF	XF
21.1	AH1356	4.000	1.00	2.00	6.00	12.00

Reeded edge

KM#	Date	Mintage	VG	Fine	VF	XF
21.2	AH1356	7.150	.50	1.00	2.50	5.00

NOTE: Struck in 1947 (AH1366-67) at Philadelphia.

KM#	Date	Mintage	Fine	VF	XF	Unc
40	AH1376	10.000	.15	.25	.50	1.00
	1378	50.000	.15	.25	.50	1.00

2 GHIRSH

COPPER-NICKEL

KM#	Date	Mintage	Fine	VF	XF	Unc
41	AH1376	50.000	.10	.35	.75	2.00
	1379	28.110	.10	.35	.70	1.50

4 GHIRSH

COPPER-NICKEL

KM#	Date	Mintage	Fine	VF	XF	Unc
42	AH1376	49.100	.25	.50	1.00	4.00
	1378	10.000	.25	.50	1.00	4.00

1/4 RIYAL

3.1000 g, .917 SILVER, .0913 oz ASW

KM#	Date	Mintage	Fine	VF	XF	Unc
16	AH1354	.900	1.75	2.50	3.00	5.00
	1354	—	—	—	Proof	150.00

2.9500 g, .917 SILVER, .0869 oz ASW

KM#	Date	Mintage	Fine	VF	XF	Unc
37	AH1374	4.000	BV	1.00	3.00	5.00

1/2 RIYAL

5.8500 g, .917 SILVER, .1724 oz ASW

KM#	Date	Mintage	Fine	VF	XF	Unc
17	AH1354	.950	2.50	4.00	6.00	8.00

5.9500 g, .917 SILVER, .1754 oz ASW

KM#	Date	Mintage	Fine	VF	XF	Unc
38	AH1374	2.000	2.50	3.00	4.50	6.50

RIYAL

11.6000 g, .917 SILVER, .3419 oz ASW

KM#	Date	Mintage	Fine	VF	XF	Unc
18	AH1354	60.000	BV	3.00	5.00	9.00
	1354	20.000	—	—	Proof	—
	1367	Inc. Ab.	BV	3.00	5.00	9.00
	1370	—	BV	3.00	5.00	9.00

KM#	Date	Mintage	Fine	VF	XF	Unc
39	AH1374	48.000	BV	3.00	6.00	12.00

COUNTERMARKED COINAGE

70 = '65'/COUNTERMARK

The following pieces are countermarked examples of earlier types bearing the Arabic numerals "65". They were countermarked in a move to break money changers' monopoly on small coins in AH1365 (1946AD). These countermarks vary and are found with the Arabic numbers raised in a circle. Incuse countermarks are considered a recent fabrication.

1/4 GHIRSH

c/m: '65' on 1/4 Ghirsh, KM#4.

KM#	Date	Mintage	Good	VG	Fine	VF
22	AH1344	—	2.50	4.00	10.00	20.00

c/m: '65' on 1/4 Ghirsh, KM#7.

KM#	Date	Mintage	Good	VG	Fine	VF
23	AH1346	—	2.50	4.00	10.00	20.00

c/m: '65' on 1/4 Ghirsh, KM#13.

KM#	Date	Mintage	Good	VG	Fine	VF
24	AH1348	—	2.50	4.00	10.00	20.00

Plain edge
c/m: '65' on 1/4 Ghirsh, KM#19.

KM#	Date	Mintage	Good	VG	Fine	VF
25	AH1356	—	2.50	4.00	8.00	15.00

1/2 GHIRSH

c/m: '65' on 1/2 Ghirsh, KM#5.

KM#	Date	Mintage	Good	VG	Fine	VF
26	AH1344	—	2.50	4.00	7.50	25.00

c/m: '65' on 1/2 Ghirsh, KM#8.

KM#	Date	Mintage	Good	VG	Fine	VF
27	AH1346	—	2.50	4.00	7.50	25.00

c/m: '65' on 1/2 Ghirsh, KM#14.

KM#	Date	Mintage	Good	VG	Fine	VF
28	AH1348	—	2.50	4.00	7.50	25.00

Plain edge
c/m: '65' on 1/2 Ghirsh, KM#20.1.

KM#	Date	Mintage	Good	VG	Fine	VF
29	AH1356	—	1.25	2.25	5.00	12.00

GHIRSH

c/m: '65' on 1 Ghirsh, KM#6.

KM#	Date	Mintage	Good	VG	Fine	VF
30	AH1344	—	2.50	4.00	20.00	38.00

c/m: '65' on 1 Ghirsh, KM#9.

KM#	Date	Mintage	Good	VG	Fine	VF
31	AH1346	—	2.50	4.00	10.00	25.00

c/m: '65' on 1 Ghirsh, KM#15.

KM#	Date	Mintage	Good	VG	Fine	VF
32	AH1348	—	5.00	10.00	30.00	40.00

Plain edge
c/m: '65' on 1 Ghirsh, KM#21.

KM#	Date	Mintage	Good	VG	Fine	VF
33	AH1356	—	2.00	3.00	8.00	20.00

MONETARY REFORM

5 Halala = 1 Ghirsh

HALALA

BRONZE

KM#	Date	Mintage	Fine	VF	XF	Unc
44	AH1383	5.000	.50	.60	.75	1.00

Obv: Different inscription.
Rev: Arabic *H* for Hegira left of curved year.

KM#	Date	Mintage	Fine	VF	XF	Unc
60	AH1397	—	—	—	Rare	—

NOTE: Not released for circulation.

5 HALALA

(1 Ghirsh)

COPPER-NICKEL

KM#	Date	Mintage	Fine	VF	XF	Unc
45	AH1392	130.000	.10	.15	.30	.50

KM#	Date	Mintage	Fine	VF	XF	Unc
53	AH1397	20.000	.15	.25	.50	1.75
	1400	—	.15	.25	.50	1.50

F.A.O. Issue

KM#	Date	Year	Mintage	VF	XF	Unc
57	AH1398	1978	1.500	.30	.50	1.00

KM#	Date	Mintage	Fine	VF	XF	Unc
61	AH1408	80.000	—	.30	.50	1.00
	1408	5,000	—	—	Proof	5.00

10 HALALA

COPPER-NICKEL

KM#	Date	Mintage	Fine	VF	XF	Unc
46	AH1392	55.000	.10	.20	.35	.50

KM#	Date	Mintage	Fine	VF	XF	Unc
54	AH1397	50.000	.15	.25	1.00	2.50
	1400	29.500	.25	.75	1.00	3.00

F.A.O. Issue

KM#	Date	Year	Mintage	VF	XF	Unc
58	AH1398	1978	1.000	.25	.50	1.00

KM#	Date	Mintage	Fine	VF	XF	Unc
62	AH1408	100.000	—	.30	.60	1.25
	1408	5,000	—	—	Proof	6.00

25 HALALA

COPPER-NICKEL
Error. Denomination in masculine gender.

KM#	Date	Mintage	Fine	VF	XF	Unc
47	AH1392	48.465	.75	1.50	4.50	12.00

Denomination in feminine gender

KM#	Date	Mintage	Fine	VF	XF	Unc
48	AH1392	Inc. Ab.	.25	.50	1.00	2.00

F.A.O. Issue

KM#	Date	Year	Mintage	VF	XF	Unc
49	AH1392	1973	.200	.20	.50	1.00

KM#	Date	Mintage	Fine	VF	XF	Unc
55	AH1397	20.000	.10	.35	.50	1.00
	1400	57.000	.35	.50	.75	1.50

KM#	Date	Mintage	Fine	VF	XF	Unc
63	AH1408	100.000	—	.40	.70	1.50
	1408	5,000	—	—	Proof	7.50

50 HALALA

COPPER-NICKEL
F.A.O. Issue

KM#	Date	Year	Mintage	VF	XF	Unc
50	AH1392	1972	.500	.30	.60	1.00

KM#	Date	Mintage	Fine	VF	XF	Unc
51	AH1392	16.000	.20	.35	.60	1.25

KM#	Date	Mintage	Fine	VF	XF	Unc
56	AH1397	20.000	.50	.75	1.00	3.00
	1400	21.600	.75	1.00	1.50	3.50

KM#	Date	Mintage	Fine	VF	XF	Unc
64	AH1408	70.000	.20	.50	2.25	3.50
	1408	5,000	—	—	Proof	15.00

100 HALALA

COPPER-NICKEL

KM#	Date	Year	Mintage	VF	XF	Unc
52	AH1396	(1976)	10.000	.65	1.00	3.00
	1400	(1980)	4.950	1.75	3.00	5.00

F.A.O. Issue

KM#	Date	Year	Mintage	VF	XF	Unc
59	AH1397	1977	—	—	60.00	100.00
	1398	1978	.250	.75	1.50	2.50

NOTE: AH1397 date struck as samples for the Saudi-Arabia government by the British Royal Mint.

KM#	Date	Mintage	Fine	VF	XF	Unc
65	AH1408	40.000	—	1.00	2.00	3.00
	1408	5,000	—	—	Proof	22.00

TRADE COINAGE

GUINEA

7.9881 g, .917 GOLD, .2354 oz AGW

36 AH1370 2.000 — BV 100.00 125.00

KM#	Date	Mintage	Fine	VF	XF	Unc
43	AH1377	1.579	—	BV	120.00	145.00

MINT SETS (MS)

KM#	Date	Mintage	Identification	Issue Price	Mkt. Val.
MS1	AH1408(1988)(5)	—	KM61-65	20.00	25.00

PROOF SETS (PS)

KM#	Date	Mintage	Identification	Issue Price	Mkt. Val.
PS1	AH1408(1987/8)(5)	5,000	KM61-65	40.00	55.00

SENEGAL

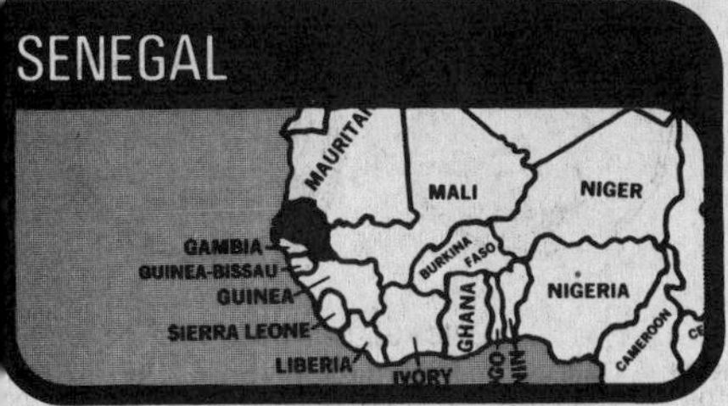

The Republic of Senegal, located on the bulge of West frica between Mauritania and Guinea-Bissau, has an rea of 75,750 sq. mi. (196,190 sq. km.) and a popula-on of *7.5 million. Capital: Dakar. The economy is pri-narily agricultural. Peanuts and products, phosphates, nd canned fish are exported.

An abundance of megalithic remains indicates that enegal was inhabited in prehistoric times. The Portu-uese had some trading stations on the banks of the enegal River in the 15th century. French commercial stablishments date from the 17th century. The French radually acquired control over the interior regions, vhich were administered as a protectorate until 1920, nd as a colony thereafter. After the 1958 French consti-utional referendum, Senegal became a member of the rench Community with virtual autonomy. In 1959 enegal and the French Soudan merged to form the Mali ederation, which became fully independent on June 20, 960. (April 4, the date the transfer of power agreement vas signed with France, is celebrated as Senegal's inde-endence day). The Federation broke up on Aug. 20, 960, when Senegal seceded and proclaimed the Republic of Senegal. Soudan became the Republic of Mali a month later.

Senegal is a member of a monetary union of autono-nous republics called the Monetary Union of West frican States (Union Monetaire Ouest-Africaine). The ther members are Ivory Coast, Benin, Burkina Faso Upper Volta), Niger, Mauritania and Togo. Mali was a nember, but seceded in 1962. Some of the member countries have issued coinage in addition to the common currency issued by the Monetary Union of West African States.

10 FRANCS

3.2000 g, .900 GOLD, .0926 oz AGW
8th Anniversary of Independence

KM#	Date	Mintage	VF	XF	Unc
	1968	—	—	Proof	65.00

25 FRANCS

8.0000 g, .900 GOLD, .2315 oz AGW
8th Anniversary of Independence

KM#	Date	Mintage	VF	XF	Unc
2	1968	—	—	Proof	125.00

50 FRANCS

16.0000 g, .900 GOLD, .4630 oz AGW
8th Anniversary of Independence

KM#	Date	Mintage	VF	XF	Unc
3	1968	—	—	Proof	250.00

28.2800 g, .925 SILVER, .8411 oz ASW
25th Anniversary of Eurafrique Program

KM#	Date	Mintage	VF	XF	Unc
5	1975	1,968	—	—	85.00
	1975	.010	—	Proof	100.00

100 FRANCS

32.0000 g, .900 GOLD, .9260 oz AGW
8th Anniversary of Independence

KM#	Date	Mintage	VF	XF	Unc
4	1968	—	—	Proof	450.00

150 FRANCS

79.9400 g, .925 SILVER, 2.3776 oz ASW
25th Anniversary of Eurafrique Program
Rev: Similar to 50 Francs, KM#5.

KM#	Date	Mintage	VF	XF	Unc
6	1975	1,075	—	—	130.00
	1975	.010	—	Proof	150.00

250 FRANCS

3.9800 g, .917 GOLD, .1172 oz AGW
25th Anniversary of Eurafrique Program

KM#	Date	Mintage	VF	XF	Unc
7	1975	1,000	—	—	75.00
	1975	1,250	—	Proof	75.00

500 FRANCS

7.9600 g, .917 GOLD, .2344 oz AGW
25th Anniversary of Eurafrique Program

KM#	Date	Mintage	VF	XF	Unc
8	1975	500 pcs.	—	—	125.00
	1975	1,250	—	Proof	125.00

1000 FRANCS

15.9500 g, .916 GOLD, .4697 oz AGW
25th Anniversary of Eurafrique Program

KM#	Date	Mintage	VF	XF	Unc
9	1975	217 pcs.	—	—	275.00
	1975	1,250	—	Proof	250.00

2500 FRANCS

39.9300 g, .916 GOLD, 1.1760 oz AGW
25th Anniversary of Eurafrique Program

KM#	Date	Mintage	VF	XF	Unc
10	1975	195 pcs.	—	—	675.00
	1975	1,250	—	Proof	650.00

MINT SETS (MS)

KM#	Date	Mintage	Identification	Issue Price	Mkt. Val.
MS1	1975(4)	195	KM7-10	—	1150.

PROOF SETS (PS)

KM#	Date	Mintage	Identification	Issue Price	Mkt. Val.
PS1	1968(4)	—	KM1-4	—	900.00
PS2	1975(2)	—	KM5-6	—	250.00

Listings For

SERBIA: refer to Yugoslavia

SEYCHELLES

The Republic of Seychelles, an archipelago of 85 granite and coral islands situated in the Indian Ocean 600 miles (965 km.) northeast of Madagascar, has an area of 156 sq. mi. (455 sq. km.) and a population of *70,000. Among these islands are the Aldabra Islands, the Farquhar Group, and Ile Desroches, which the United Kingdom ceded to the Seychelles upon its independence. Capital: Victoria, on Mahe. The economy is based on fishing, a plantation system of agriculture, and tourism. Copra, cinnamon and vanilla are exported.

Although the Seychelles are marked on Portuguese charts of the early 16th century, the first recorded visit to the islands, by an English ship, occurred in 1609. The Seychelles were annexed to France by Captain Lazare Picault in 1743 and permanently settled in 1768, with the intention of establishing spice plantations to compete with the Dutch monopoly of the spice trade. British troops seized the islands in 1810, during the Napoleonic Wars; they were formally ceded to Britain by the Treaty of Paris, 1814. The Seychelles were a dependency of Mauritius until Aug. 31, 1903, when they became a separate British Crown Colony. The colony was granted limited internal self-government in 1970, and attained independence on June 28, 1976, becoming Britain's last African possession to do so. Seychelles is a member of the Commonwealth of Nations. The president is the Head of State and of Govern- ment.

RULERS

British, until 1976

MINT MARKS

PM - Pobjoy Mint

None - British Royal Mint

MONETARY SYSTEM

100 Cents = 1 Rupee

CENT

BRONZE

KM#	Date	Mintage	VF	XF	Unc
5	1948	.300	.25	.50	1.25
	1948	—	—	Proof	50.00

KM#	Date	Mintage	VF	XF	Unc
14	1959	.030	.75	1.50	3.00
	1959	—	—	Proof	—
	1961	.030	.50	1.00	2.25
	1961	—	—	Proof	—
	1963	.040	.50	1.00	1.50
	1963	—	—	Proof	—
	1965	.020	2.00	3.00	5.00
	1969	*5,000	15.00	25.00	60.00
	1969	—	—	Proof	5.00

*Latest reports indicate only 5,000 circulation strikes have been released to date in addition to proof issues.

ALUMINUM
F.A.O. Issue - Cow

KM#	Date	Mintage	VF	XF	Unc
17	1972	2.350	—	.10	.25

2 CENTS

BRONZE

KM#	Date	Mintage	VF	XF	Unc
6	1948	.350	.35	.60	1.50
	1948	—	—	Proof	75.00

KM#	Date	Mintage	VF	XF	Unc
15	1959	.030	.50	1.00	2.50
	1959	—	—	Proof	—
	1961	.030	.50	1.00	2.75
	1961	—	—	Proof	—
	1963	.040	.75	1.25	2.50
	1963	—	—	Proof	—
	1965	.020	2.00	3.00	4.00
	1968	.020	2.00	3.00	5.50
	1969	5,000	—	Proof	4.00

5 CENTS

BRONZE

KM#	Date	Mintage	VF	XF	Unc
7	1948	.300	.40	.80	2.00
	1948	—	—	Proof	100.00

KM#	Date	Mintage	VF	XF	Unc
16	1964	.020	1.00	1.75	4.50
	1964	—	—	Proof	—
	1965	.040	1.50	2.50	5.50
	1967	.020	1.50	3.00	6.00
	1968	.040	1.00	2.00	7.00
	1969	.100	.50	1.00	5.00
	1969	—	—	Proof	4.00
	1971	.025	.50	1.50	2.50

ALUMINUM
F.A.O. Issue - Cabbage

KM#	Date	Mintage	VF	XF	Unc
18	1972	2.200	—	.10	.25
	1975	1.200	—	.10	.25

10 CENTS

COPPER-NICKEL

KM#	Date	Mintage	VF	XF	Unc
1	1939	.036	8.00	20.00	70.00
	1939	—	—	Proof	150.00
	1943	.036	4.00	10.00	45.00
	1944	.036	4.00	10.00	45.00
	1944	—	—	Proof	175.00

KM#	Date	Mintage	VF	XF	Unc
8	1951	.036	2.00	5.00	9.00
	1951	—	—	Proof	135.00

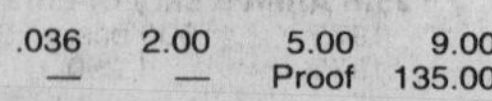

NICKEL-BRASS

KM#	Date	Mintage	VF	XF	Unc
10	1953	.130	.50	1.00	2.00
	1953	—	—	Proof	100.00
	1965	.040	1.00	1.50	6.00
	1967	.020	4.00	7.50	15.00
	1968	.050	1.00	4.00	12.50
	1969	.060	1.00	2.00	8.00
	1969	—	—	Proof	2.00
	1970	.075	.50	1.00	4.50
	1971	.100	.50	1.00	1.75
	1972	.120	.30	.50	1.00
	1973	.100	.15	.25	1.00
	1974	.100	.15	.25	.75

25 CENTS

2.9200 g, .500 SILVER .0469 oz ASW

KM#	Date	Mintage	VF	XF	Unc
2	1939	.036	7.50	35.00	125.00
	1939	—	—	Proof	200.00
	1943	.036	5.00	25.00	100.00
	1944	.036	3.50	20.00	85.00
	1944	—	—	Proof	300.00

COPPER-NICKEL

KM#	Date	Mintage	VF	XF	Unc
9	1951	.036	2.00	7.50	28.00
	1951	—	—	Proof	160.00

KM#	Date	Mintage	VF	XF	Unc
11	1954	.124	.75	1.00	2.00
	1954	—	—	Proof	120.00
	1960	.040	.75	1.25	2.00
	1960	—	—	Proof	—
	1964	.040	1.00	2.00	5.00
	1965	.040	1.00	2.00	5.00
	1966	.010	3.50	10.00	22.50
	1967	.020	2.50	4.00	15.00
	1968	.020	2.50	4.00	15.00
	1969	.100	1.00	2.00	4.00
	1969	—	—	Proof	2.00
	1970	.040	1.50	3.00	10.00
	1972	.120	.50	.75	1.00
	1973	.100	.50	.75	1.00
	1974	.100	.50	.75	1.00

1/2 RUPEE

5.8300 g, .500 SILVER, .0937 oz ASW

KM#	Date	Mintage	VF	XF	Unc
3	1939	.036	10.00	35.00	150.00
	1939	—	—	Proof	250.00

COPPER-NICKEL

KM#	Date	Mintage	VF	XF	Unc
12	1954	.072	.50	1.25	3.75
	1954	—	—	Proof	150.00
	1960	.060	.50	1.00	3.00
	1960	—	—	Proof	150.00
	1966	.015	1.50	5.00	17.50

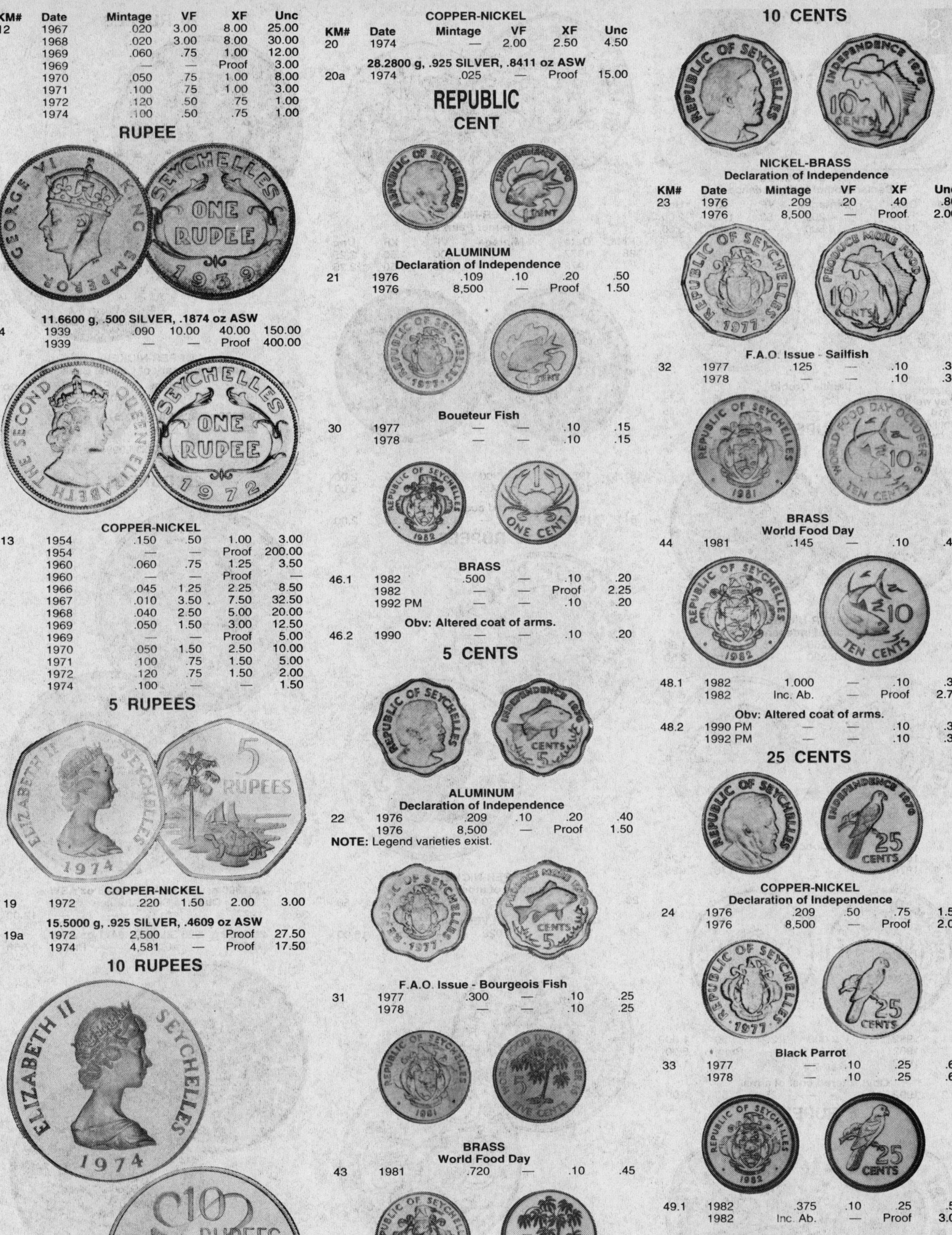

KM#	Date	Mintage	VF	XF	Unc
12	1967	.020	3.00	8.00	25.00
	1968	.020	3.00	8.00	30.00
	1969	.060	.75	1.00	12.00
	1969	—	—	Proof	3.00
	1970	.050	.75	1.00	8.00
	1971	.100	.75	1.00	3.00
	1972	.120	.50	.75	1.00
	1974	.100	.50	.75	1.00

RUPEE

11.6600 g, .500 SILVER, .1874 oz ASW

KM#	Date	Mintage	VF	XF	Unc
4	1939	.090	10.00	40.00	150.00
	1939	—	—	Proof	400.00

COPPER-NICKEL

KM#	Date	Mintage	VF	XF	Unc
13	1954	.150	.50	1.00	3.00
	1954	—	—	Proof	200.00
	1960	.060	.75	1.25	3.50
	1960	—	—	Proof	—
	1966	.045	1.25	2.25	8.50
	1967	.010	3.50	7.50	32.50
	1968	.040	2.50	5.00	20.00
	1969	.050	1.50	3.00	12.50
	1969	—	—	Proof	5.00
	1970	.050	1.50	2.50	10.00
	1971	.100	.75	1.50	5.00
	1972	.120	.75	1.50	2.00
	1974	.100	—	—	1.50

5 RUPEES

COPPER-NICKEL

KM#	Date	Mintage	VF	XF	Unc
19	1972	.220	1.50	2.00	3.00

15.5000 g, .925 SILVER, .4609 oz ASW

KM#	Date	Mintage	VF	XF	Unc
19a	1972	2,500	—	Proof	27.50
	1974	4,581	—	Proof	17.50

10 RUPEES

COPPER-NICKEL

KM#	Date	Mintage	VF	XF	Unc
20	1974	—	2.00	2.50	4.50

28.2800 g, .925 SILVER, .8411 oz ASW

KM#	Date	Mintage	VF	XF	Unc
20a	1974	.025	—	Proof	15.00

REPUBLIC

CENT

ALUMINUM
Declaration of Independence

KM#	Date	Mintage	VF	XF	Unc
21	1976	.109	.10	.20	.50
	1976	8,500	—	Proof	1.50

Boueteur Fish

KM#	Date	Mintage	VF	XF	Unc
30	1977	—	—	.10	.15
	1978	—	—	.10	.15

BRASS

KM#	Date	Mintage	VF	XF	Unc
46.1	1982	.500	—	.10	.20
	1982	—	—	Proof	2.25
	1992 PM	—	—	.10	.20

Obv: Altered coat of arms.

KM#	Date	Mintage	VF	XF	Unc
46.2	1990	—	—	.10	.20

5 CENTS

ALUMINUM
Declaration of Independence

KM#	Date	Mintage	VF	XF	Unc
22	1976	.209	.10	.20	.40
	1976	8,500	—	Proof	1.50

NOTE: Legend varieties exist.

F.A.O. Issue - Bourgeois Fish

KM#	Date	Mintage	VF	XF	Unc
31	1977	.300	—	.10	.25
	1978	—	—	.10	.25

BRASS
World Food Day

KM#	Date	Mintage	VF	XF	Unc
43	1981	.720	—	.10	.45

KM#	Date	Mintage	VF	XF	Unc
47.1	1982	1.500	—	.10	.25
	1982	Inc. Ab.	—	Proof	2.50

Obv: Altered coat of arms.

KM#	Date	Mintage	VF	XF	Unc
47.2	1990 PM	—	—	.10	.25
	1992 PM	—	—	.10	.25

10 CENTS

NICKEL-BRASS
Declaration of Independence

KM#	Date	Mintage	VF	XF	Unc
23	1976	.209	.20	.40	.80
	1976	8,500	—	Proof	2.00

F.A.O. Issue - Sailfish

KM#	Date	Mintage	VF	XF	Unc
32	1977	.125	—	.10	.30
	1978	—	—	.10	.30

BRASS
World Food Day

KM#	Date	Mintage	VF	XF	Unc
44	1981	.145	—	.10	.45

KM#	Date	Mintage	VF	XF	Unc
48.1	1982	1.000	—	.10	.30
	1982	Inc. Ab.	—	Proof	2.75

Obv: Altered coat of arms.

KM#	Date	Mintage	VF	XF	Unc
48.2	1990 PM	—	—	.10	.30
	1992 PM	—	—	.10	.30

25 CENTS

COPPER-NICKEL
Declaration of Independence

KM#	Date	Mintage	VF	XF	Unc
24	1976	.209	.50	.75	1.50
	1976	8,500	—	Proof	2.00

Black Parrot

KM#	Date	Mintage	VF	XF	Unc
33	1977	—	.10	.25	.65
	1978	—	.10	.25	.65

KM#	Date	Mintage	VF	XF	Unc
49.1	1982	.375	.10	.25	.50
	1982	Inc. Ab.	—	Proof	3.00

Obv: Altered coat of arms.

KM#	Date	Mintage	VF	XF	Unc
49.2	1989 PM	1.500	—	—	1.25

50 CENTS

COPPER-NICKEL
Declaration of Independence

KM#	Date	Mintage	VF	XF	Unc
25	1976	.209	.50	1.00	2.00
	1976	8,500	—	Proof	3.00

Vanilla Orchid

KM#	Date	Mintage	VF	XF	Unc
34	1977	—	.15	.35	.75
	1978	—	.15	.35	.75

RUPEE

COPPER-NICKEL
Declaration of Independence

KM#	Date	Mintage	VF	XF	Unc
26	1976	.259	.75	1.00	1.50
	1976	8,500	—	Proof	2.50

Triton Conch Shell

KM#	Date	Mintage	VF	XF	Unc
35	1977	—	.50	.75	1.25
	1978	—	.50	.75	1.25

KM#	Date	Mintage	VF	XF	Unc
50.1	1982	2.000	.25	.50	1.00
	1982	Inc. Ab.	—	Proof	5.00
	1983	—	.25	.50	1.00

Obv: Altered coat of arms.

KM#	Date	Mintage	VF	XF	Unc
50.2	1992 PM	—	.25	.50	1.00

5 RUPEES

COPPER-NICKEL
Declaration of Independence

KM#	Date	Mintage	VF	XF	Unc
27	1976	.050	1.25	1.75	3.00

15.5000 g, .925 SILVER, .4609 oz ASW

KM#	Date	Mintage	VF	XF	Unc
27a	1976	8,500	—	Proof	15.00

COPPER-NICKEL
Coco-de-mer Palm Tree

KM#	Date	Mintage	VF	XF	Unc
36	1977	—	1.00	1.50	2.25
	1978	—	1.00	1.50	2.25

KM#	Date	Mintage	VF	XF	Unc
51.1	1982	.300	1.00	1.50	2.00
	1982	Inc. Ab.	—	Proof	5.00

Obv: Altered coat of arms.

KM#	Date	Mintage	VF	XF	Unc
51.2	1992 PM	—	1.00	1.50	2.00

10 RUPEES

COPPER-NICKEL
Declaration of Independence

KM#	Date	Mintage	VF	XF	Unc
28	1976	.050	2.00	2.50	4.50

28.2800 g, .925 SILVER, .8411 oz ASW

KM#	Date	Mintage	VF	XF	Unc
28a	1976	.029	—	Proof	15.00

COPPER-NICKEL
F.A.O. Issue - Turtle

KM#	Date	Mintage	VF	XF	Unc
37	1977	—	2.00	2.50	3.50
	1977	—	—	Proof	5.00
	1978	—	2.00	2.50	3.50

10.0000 g, .925 SILVER, .2974 oz ASW
Endangered Wildlife - Magpie Robin
Similar to 25 Rupees, KM#65.

KM#	Date	Mintage	VF	XF	Unc
64	1993	*.020	—	Proof	12.50

20 RUPEES

COPPER-NICKEL
5th Anniversary of Central Bank

KM#	Date	Mintage	VF	XF	Unc
52	1983	—	4.00	5.00	6.00

19.4400 g, .925 SILVER, .5781 oz ASW

KM#	Date	Mintage	VF	XF	Unc
52a	1983	5,000	—	Proof	50.00

33.9000 g, .917 GOLD, .9994 oz AGW

KM#	Date	Mintage	VF	XF	Unc
52b	1983	50 pcs.	—	Proof	1500.

25 RUPEES

28.2800 g, .500 SILVER, .4546 oz ASW
Queen's Silver Jubilee

KM#	Date	Mintage	VF	XF	Unc
38	1977	.017	—	—	12.00

28.2800 g, .925 SILVER, .8411 oz ASW

KM#	Date	Mintage	VF	XF	Unc
38a	1977	.015	—	Proof	17.50

COPPER-NICKEL
World Fisheries Conference

KM#	Date	Mintage	VF	XF	Unc
53	1983	.100	5.00	5.25	6.00

28.2800 g, .925 SILVER, .8411 oz ASW

KM#	Date	Mintage	VF	XF	Unc
53a	1983	.020	—	Proof	25.00

47.5400 g, .917 GOLD, 1.4015 oz AGW

KM#	Date	Mintage	VF	XF	Unc
53b	1983	100 pcs.	—	Proof	1500.

31.4700 g, .925 SILVER, .9359 oz ASW
40th Anniversary of Queen Elizabeth's Coronation

KM#	Date	Mintage	VF	XF	Unc
63	1993	*.010	—	Proof	45.00

28.2800 g, .925 SILVER, .8411 oz ASW
Endangered Wildlife - Magpie Robin

KM#	Date	Mintage	VF	XF	Unc
65	1993	*.020	—	Proof	30.00

31.4600 g, .925 SILVER, .9359 oz ASW
World Cup Soccer - Goalie at Net

KM#	Date	Mintage	VF	XF	Unc
67	1993	*.015	—	Proof	40.00

Space Shuttle
Obv: Coat of arms. Rev: Space shuttle.

KM#	Date	Mintage	VF	XF	Unc
68	1993	*.010	—	Proof	40.00

First French Landing

KM#	Date	Mintage	VF	XF	Unc
69	1993	*.010	—	Proof	40.00

1992 Olympics - Balance Beam Gymnasts

KM#	Date	Mintage	VF	XF	Unc
70	1993	*.040	—	Proof	40.00

Protect Our World - Fish and Coral

KM#	Date	Mintage	VF	XF	Unc
71	1993	*.010	—	Proof	40.00

19.4400 g, .925 SILVER, .5782 oz ASW
Central Banking

KM#	Date	Mintage	VF	XF	Unc
72	1993	*1,000	—	Proof	40.00

50 RUPEES

28.2800 g, .925 SILVER, .8411 oz ASW
Conservation - Squirrel Fish

KM#	Date	Mintage	VF	XF	Unc
39	1978	4,453	—	—	22.50
	1978	4,281	—	Proof	30.00

19.4400 g, .925 SILVER, .5781 oz ASW
UNICEF and International Year of the Child

KM#	Date	Mintage	VF	XF	Unc
42	1980	.010	—	Proof	17.50

Decade For Women

KM#	Date	Mintage	VF	XF	Unc
54	1985	500 pcs.	—	Proof	45.00

100 RUPEES

31.6500 g, .925 SILVER, .9413 oz ASW
Conservation - White-tailed Tropicbird

KM#	Date	Mintage	VF	XF	Unc
40	1978	4,453	—	—	30.00
	1978	4,075	—	Proof	35.00

World Food Day

KM#	Date	Mintage	VF	XF	Unc
45	1981	6,000	—	—	25.00
	1981	5,000	—	Proof	30.00

35.0000 g, .500 SILVER, .5627 oz ASW

KM#	Date	Mintage	VF	XF	Unc
45a	1981	.010	—	Proof	27.50

19.4400 g, .925 SILVER, .5781 oz ASW
10th Anniversary of Independence

KM#	Date	Mintage	VF	XF	Unc
55	1986	1,000	—	Proof	35.00

10th Anniversary of Liberation

KM#	Date	Mintage	VF	XF	Unc
57	1987 PM	1,000	—	Proof	35.00

19.4000 g, .917 SILVER, .5720 oz ASW
10th Anniversary of Central Bank

KM#	Date	Mintage	VF	XF	Unc
59	1988 PM	—	—	Proof	25.00

1.7000 g, .917 GOLD, .0501 oz AGW
10th Anniversary of Central Bank
Similar to KM#59.

KM#	Date	Mintage	VF	XF	Unc
60	1988 PM	—	—	Proof	45.00

250 RUPEES

6.2200 g, .999 GOLD, .0500 oz AGW
Endangered Wildlife - Magpie Robin
Similar to 25 Rupees, KM#65.

KM#	Date	Mintage	VF	XF	Unc
66	1993	—	—	Proof	—

500 RUPEES

7.1300 g, .900 GOLD, .2036 oz AGW
Decade For Women

KM#	Date	Mintage	VF	XF	Unc
62	1985	500 pcs.	—	Proof	200.00

1000 RUPEES

15.9800 g, .917 GOLD, .4707 oz AGW
Declaration of Independence
Obv: President Mancham. Rev: Tortoise, date, value.

KM#	Date	Mintage	VF	XF	Unc
29	1976	5,000	—	—	225.00
	1976	1,000	—	Proof	325.00

10th Anniversary of Independence

KM#	Date	Mintage	VF	XF	Unc
56	1986	100 pcs.	—	Proof	500.00

10th Anniversary of Liberation

KM#	Date	Mintage	VF	XF	Unc
58	1987 PM	100 pcs.	—	Proof	450.00

15.9400 g, .917 GOLD, .4698 oz AGW
10th Anniversary of Central Bank
Similar to 100 Rupees, KM#59.

KM#	Date	Mintage	VF	XF	Unc
61	1988 PM	*5,000	—	Proof	250.00

15.9800 g, .917 GOLD, .4710 oz AGW
Central Banking

KM#	Date	Mintage	VF	XF	Unc
73	1993	*200 pcs.	—	Proof	350.00

1500 RUPEES

33.4370 g, .900 GOLD, .9676 oz AGW
Conservation - Black Paradise Flycatcher

KM#	Date	Mintage	VF	XF	Unc
41	1978	683 pcs.	—	—	450.00
	1978	201 pcs.	—	Proof	850.00

MINT SETS (MS)

KM#	Date	Mintage	Identification	Issue Price	Mkt. Val.
MS1	1972(7)	—	KM10-13,17-19	—	8.50
MS2	1974(5)	—	KM10-13,20	—	8.50
MS3	1976(8)	—	KM21-28	—	16.00
MS4	1982(6)	—	KM46-51	—	5.00
MS5	1992(6)	—	KM46-48,49.2,50-51	12.00	12.00

PROOF SETS (PS)

KM#	Date	Mintage	Identification	Issue Price	Mkt. Val.
PS1	1939(4)	—	KM1-4	—	1000.
PS2	1969(7)	5,000	KM10-16	8.40	25.00
PS3	1974(2)	5,000	KM19a,20a	37.00	35.00
PS4	1976(9)	1,000	KM21-26,27a,28a,29	375.00	375.00
PS5	1976(8)	7,500	KM21-26,27a,28a	42.50	45.00
PS6	1982(6)	5,000	KM46-51	29.95	20.00

Listings For

SHARJAH: refer to United Arab Emirates

SHRI (SRI) LANKA

The Democratic Socialist Republic of Shri (Sri) Lanka (formerly Ceylon) situated in the Indian Ocean 18 miles (29 km.) southeast of India, has an area of 25,332 sq. mi. (65,610 sq. km.) and a population of *16.9 million. Capital: Colombo. The economy is chiefly agricultural. Tea, coconut products and rubber are exported.

The earliest known inhabitants of Ceylon, the Veddahs, were subjugated by the Sinhalese from northern India in the 6th century B.C. Sinhalese rule was maintained until 1408, after which the island was controlled by China for 30 years. The Portuguese came to Ceylon in 1505 and maintained control of the coastal area for 150 years. They were supplanted by the Dutch in 1658, who were in turn supplanted by the British who seized the Dutch colonies in 1796, and made them a Crown Colony in 1802. In 1815, the British conquered the independent Kingdom of Kandy in the central part of the island. Constitutional changes in 1931 and 1946 granted the Ceylonese a measure of autonomy and a parliamentary form of government. Britain granted Ceylon independence as a self-governing republic within the British Commonwealth on Feb. 4, 1948. On May 22, 1972, the Ceylonese adopted a new Constitution which declared Ceylon to be the Republic of Shri Lanka - 'Resplendent Island'. Shri Lanka is a member of the Commonwealth of Nations. The president is Chief of State. The prime minister is Head of Government.

RULERS

British, 1796-1972

CEYLON

British Colonial Coinage

MINT MARKS

H - Heaton, Birmingham
B - Bombay

MONETARY SYSTEM

4 Pies = 1 Stiver
4 Stivers = 1 Fanam
12 Fanams = 1 Rixdollar = 1 Rupee = 1-1/2 Shillings
2 Rupees = 3 Shillings

DUMP COINAGE

1/4 PICE

(1/256 Rixdaler)

COPPER, dump
Obv: C.G., date. Rev: Value.

KM#	Date	Mintage	Good	VG	Fine	VF
72	1813	—	—	—	Rare	—

1/48 RIXDOLLAR

COPPER, dump
Rev: Elephant faces left.

KM#	Date	Mintage	Good	VG	Fine	VF
63	1801	—	5.00	10.00	17.50	25.00
	1802	—	5.00	10.00	17.50	25.00
	1803	—	5.00	10.00	17.50	25.00
	1811	—	6.50	12.00	22.50	35.00
	1812	—	6.50	12.00	20.00	30.00
	1813	—	8.50	15.00	22.50	35.00
	1814	—	8.50	15.00	22.50	35.00
	1815	—	8.50	15.00	22.50	35.00
	1816	—	75.00	125.00	175.00	225.00

Obv: 2 parallel lines under 48.

KM#	Date	Mintage	Good	VG	Fine	VF
66	1802	—	15.00	20.00	30.00	60.00

Rev: Elephant faces right.

KM#	Date	Mintage	Good	VG	Fine	VF
69	1803	—	—	—	Unique	—

1/24 RIXDOLLAR

COPPER, dump

KM#	Date	Mintage	Good	VG	Fine	VF
64	1801	—	10.00	22.50	35.00	50.00

M#	Date	Mintage	Good	VG	Fine	VF
4	1802	—	7.00	18.50	40.00	50.00
	1803	—	6.00	17.50	30.00	40.00
	1805	—	10.00	18.50	45.00	55.00
	1811	—	7.00	16.50	30.00	40.00
	1812	—	7.00	18.50	30.00	40.00
	1813	—	7.00	18.50	35.00	45.00
	1814	—	12.50	23.50	32.50	45.00
	1815	—	12.50	21.50	45.00	55.00
	1816	—	20.00	55.00	85.00	110.00
	Obv: 2 parallel lines under 24.					
7	1802	—	55.00	120.00	300.00	350.00
	Rev: Elephant faces right.					
0	1803	—	50.00	125.00	175.00	250.00
	1805	—	50.00	125.00	175.00	250.00

1/12 RIXDOLLAR

COPPER, dump

Rev: Elephant faces left.

KM#	Date	Mintage	Good	VG	Fine	VF
5	1801	—	10.00	25.00	32.50	45.00
	1802	—	8.00	16.50	25.00	35.00
	1803	—	8.00	16.50	25.00	35.00
	1804	—	12.50	25.00	35.00	55.00
	1805	—	12.50	25.00	35.00	55.00
	1811	—	9.00	22.50	35.00	45.00
	1812	—	9.00	22.50	35.00	45.00
	1813	—	9.00	30.00	45.00	60.00
	1814	—	9.00	27.50	45.00	60.00
	1815	—	9.00	22.50	35.00	55.00
	Obv: 2 parallel lines under 12.					
8	1802	3 known	—	—	Rare	—
	Rev: Elephant faces right.					
1	1803	—	85.00	170.00	300.00	400.00

24 STIVERS

.892 SILVER

KM#	Date	Mintage	VG	Fine	VF	XF
6	1803	—	17.50	35.00	65.00	100.00
	1804	—	20.00	40.00	70.00	100.00
	1805	—	35.00	70.00	120.00	150.00
	1808	—	25.00	55.00	100.00	150.00
	1809	—	35.00	70.00	115.00	150.00

48 STIVERS

.892 SILVER

KM#	Date	Mintage	VG	Fine	VF	XF
77	1803	—	30.00	60.00	125.00	150.00
	1804	—	30.00	60.00	125.00	150.00
	1805	—	30.00	60.00	125.00	150.00
	1808	—	30.00	60.00	125.00	150.00
	1809	—	25.00	50.00	100.00	125.00
	Rev: Elephant faces right.					
78	1803	—	75.00	125.00	175.00	225.00

96 STIVERS

.833 SILVER

KM#	Date	Mintage	VG	Fine	VF	XF
79	1803	—	—	—	—	—
	1808	—	40.00	80.00	125.00	175.00
	1809	—	45.00	90.00	150.00	200.00

MILLED COINAGE

1/2 STIVER

COPPER

KM#	Date	Mintage	Fine	VF	XF	Unc
80	1815	2.400	4.00	12.00	30.00	125.00
	1815	—	—	—	Proof	300.00

STIVER

COPPER

KM#	Date	Mintage	Fine	VF	XF	Unc
81	1815	2.800	3.50	10.00	30.00	125.00
	1815	—	—	—	Proof	350.00

2 STIVERS

COPPER

Obv: W/o rose below bust.

KM#	Date	Mintage	Fine	VF	XF	Unc
82.1	1815	1.920	5.00	15.00	50.00	200.00
	1815	—	—	—	Proof	500.00
	Obv: Rose below bust.					
82.2	1815	—	—	—	Proof	900.00

1/192 RIXDOLLAR

COPPER

KM#	Date	Mintage	Fine	VF	XF	Unc
73	1802	3.600	2.50	7.50	20.00	60.00
	1802	—	—	—	Proof	100.00
	1802	—	—		Gilt Proof	85.00
	1804	—	—	—	Proof	175.00
	1804	—	—		Gilt Proof	175.00

1/96 RIXDOLLAR

COPPER

KM#	Date	Mintage	Fine	VF	XF	Unc
74	1802	1.800	4.00	8.00	22.50	75.00
	1802	—	—	—	Proof	125.00
	1802	—	—		Gilt Proof	100.00

1/48 RIXDOLLAR

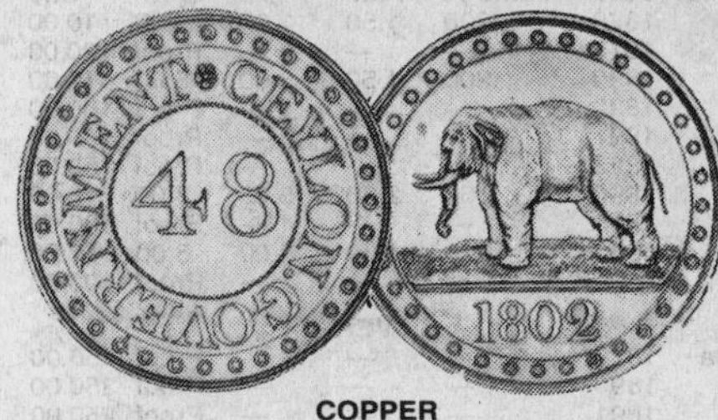

COPPER

KM#	Date	Mintage	Fine	VF	XF	Unc
75	1802	2.700	5.00	10.00	25.00	80.00
	1802	—	—	—	Proof	150.00
	1802	—	—		Gilt Proof	120.00
	1804	—	—	—	Proof	225.00
	1804	—	—		Gilt Proof	225.00

RIX DOLLAR

.892 SILVER

KM#	Date	Mintage	Fine	VF	XF	Unc
84	1821	.400	12.00	28.00	80.00	220.00
	1821	—	—	—	Proof	250.00

COUNTERMARKED COINAGE

1/3 RIXDOLLAR

SILVER, dump

c/m: Crown on Madras Arcot 1/4 Rupee.

KM#	Date	Mintage	VG	Fine	VF	XF
85	ND(1823)	.260	22.50	50.00	90.00	150.00

1-1/3 RIXDOLLAR

(16 Fanams)

SILVER, dump

c/m: Crown on Madras Arcot Rupee.

KM#	Date	Mintage	VG	Fine	VF	XF
86	ND(1823)	.282	80.00	160.00	240.00	360.00

HOMELAND COINAGE

4 Farthings = 1 Penny

1/4 FARTHING

COPPER and BRONZE

NOTE: From 1839 through 1868 homeland type 1/4 Farthings were issued by Great Britain for circulation in Ceylon. These are listed under Great Britain.

1/2 FARTHING

COPPER and BRONZE

NOTE: From 1828 through 1868 homeland type 1/2 Farthings were issued by Great Britain for circulation in Ceylon. These are listed under Great Britain.

1-1/2 PENCE

SILVER

NOTE: From 1834 through 1870 homeland type 1 1/2 Pence were issued by Great Britain for circulation in Ceylon and Jamaica. These are listed under Great Britain.

DECIMAL COINAGE

100 Cents = 1 Rupee

1/4 CENT

COPPER

KM#	Date	Mintage	Fine	VF	XF	Unc
90	1870	.200	1.50	3.00	5.00	10.00
	1870	—	—	—	Proof	100.00
	1890	.200	1.50	3.00	5.00	10.00
	1890	—	—	—	Proof	100.00
	1891	—	—	—	Proof	150.00
	1892	—	—	—	Proof	150.00
	1898	.160	2.50	5.00	8.00	15.00
	1898	—	—	—	Proof	100.00
	1901	.216	1.50	3.00	5.00	10.00
	1901	—	—	—	Proof	100.00

SILVER

KM#	Date	Mintage	Fine	VF	XF	Unc
90a	1870	—	—	—	Proof	250.00
	1890	—	—	—	Proof	250.00
	1891	—	—	—	Proof	250.00
	1898	—	—	—	Proof	250.00

GOLD

KM#	Date	Mintage	Fine	VF	XF	Unc
90b	1870	—	—	—	Proof	1000.
	1891	—	—	—	Proof	1000.
	1891	—	—	—	Proof	1000.

COPPER

KM#	Date	Mintage	Fine	VF	XF	Unc
100	1904	.103	2.50	5.00	10.00	20.00
	1904	—	—	—	Proof	150.00

1/2 CENT

COPPER

KM#	Date	Mintage	Fine	VF	XF	Unc
91	1870	3.040	1.00	1.50	3.00	8.00
	1870	—	—	—	Proof	120.00
	1890	.400	1.50	3.50	8.00	16.00
	1890	—	—	—	Proof	125.00
	1891	1.000	1.25	2.75	4.00	12.00
	1891	—	—	—	Proof	125.00
	1892	—	—	—	Proof	225.00
	1895	4.040	1.00	1.75	3.00	8.00
	1895	—	—	—	Proof	120.00
	1898	4.000	1.25	2.50	4.00	10.00
	1898	—	—	—	Proof	120.00
	1901	2.020	1.25	2.50	4.00	10.00

SILVER

KM#	Date	Mintage	Fine	VF	XF	Unc
91a	1870	—	—	—	Proof	300.00
	1890	—	—	—	Proof	300.00
	1891	—	—	—	Proof	300.00
	1895	—	—	—	Proof	300.00
	1898	—	—	—	Proof	300.00

GOLD

KM#	Date	Mintage	Fine	VF	XF	Unc
91b	1870	—	—	—	Proof	1100.
	1891	—	—	—	Proof	1100.
	1895	—	—	—	Proof	1100.

COPPER

KM#	Date	Mintage	Fine	VF	XF	Unc
101	1904	2.012	1.00	2.00	5.00	12.00
	1904	—	—	—	Proof	120.00
	1905	1.000	1.50	3.00	6.00	15.00
	1905	—	—	—	Proof	120.00
	1906	3.056	1.00	2.00	5.00	12.00
	1906	—	—	—	Proof	120.00
	1908	1.000	1.50	3.00	6.00	15.00
	1908	—	—	—	Proof	200.00
	1909	3.000	1.00	2.00	5.00	12.00
	1909	—	—	—	Proof	120.00

KM#	Date	Mintage	Fine	VF	XF	Unc
106	1912	5.008	1.25	2.75	4.00	10.00
	1912	—	—	—	Proof	120.00
	1914	2.000	1.25	2.75	6.00	12.00
	1914	—	—	—	Proof	120.00
	1917	2.000	1.50	3.00	6.00	12.00
	1917	—	—	—	Proof	120.00
	1926	5.000	.50	1.00	2.00	5.00
	1926	—	—	—	Proof	120.00

KM#	Date	Mintage	Fine	VF	XF	Unc
110	1937	3.026	.30	.85	1.50	3.50
	1937	—	—	—	Proof	175.00
	1940	5.080	.25	.65	1.25	3.00

CENT

COPPER

KM#	Date	Mintage	Fine	VF	XF	Unc
92	1870	7.055	1.50	3.00	6.00	15.00
	1870	—	—	—	Proof	125.00
	1890	4.940	1.50	3.00	5.00	12.00
	1890	—	—	—	Proof	125.00
	1891	1.328	2.00	4.00	8.00	20.00
	1891	—	—	—	Proof	125.00
	1892	5.000	1.50	3.00	6.00	15.00
	1892	—	—	—	Proof	125.00
	1900	1.000	2.50	5.00	10.00	20.00
	1900	—	—	—	Proof	175.00
	1901	1.014	2.50	5.00	10.00	20.00

SILVER

KM#	Date	Mintage	Fine	VF	XF	Unc
92a	1870	—	—	—	Proof	425.00
	1891	—	—	—	Proof	425.00
	1892	—	—	—	Proof	425.00

GOLD

KM#	Date	Mintage	Fine	VF	XF	Unc
92b	1870	—	—	—	Proof	1150.
	1891	—	—	—	Proof	1150.

COPPER

KM#	Date	Mintage	Fine	VF	XF	Unc
102	1904	2.529	1.00	2.00	4.00	8.00
	1904	—	—	—	Proof	125.00
	1905	1.509	1.25	2.25	5.00	10.00
	1905	—	—	—	Proof	125.00
	1906	1.751	1.25	2.25	5.00	10.00
	1906	—	—	—	Proof	125.00
	1908	—	1.00	2.00	4.00	8.00
	1908	—	—	—	Proof	225.00
	1909	2.500	1.00	2.00	4.00	8.00
	1909	—	—	—	Proof	125.00
	1910	8.236	.50	1.00	2.50	5.00
	1910	—	—	—	Proof	125.00

KM#	Date	Mintage	Fine	VF	XF	Unc
107	1912	5.855	.50	1.00	2.00	4.00
	1912	—	—	—	Proof	115.00
	1914	6.000	.50	1.00	2.25	5.00
	1914	—	—	—	Proof	115.00
	1917	1.000	1.00	1.75	3.00	8.00
	1917	—	—	—	Proof	115.00
	1920	2.000	.50	1.00	2.25	5.00
	1920	—	—	—	Proof	115.00
	1922	2.930	.50	1.00	2.25	5.00
	1922	—	—	—	Proof	115.00
	1923	2.500	.50	1.00	2.25	5.00
	1923	—	—	—	Proof	115.00
	1925	7.490	.35	.75	1.50	3.50
	1925	—	—	—	Proof	115.00
	1926	3.750	.35	.75	1.50	3.50
	1926	—	—	—	Proof	115.00
	1928	2.500	.35	.75	1.50	4.00
	1928	—	—	—	Proof	115.00
	1929	5.000	.35	.75	1.50	3.50
	1929	—	—	—	Proof	115.00

KM#	Date	Mintage	Fine	VF	XF	Unc
111	1937	4.538	.25	.50	1.25	3.00
	1937	—	—	—	Proof	100.00
	1940	10.190	.15	.30	1.00	2.00
	1940	—	—	—	Proof	75.00
	1942	20.780	.15	.30	1.00	2.00

BRONZE

KM#	Date	Mintage	Fine	VF	XF	Unc
111a	1942	Inc. Ab.	.15	.30	.75	1.75
	1942	—	—	—	Proof	75.00
	1943	43.705	.15	.30	.50	1.00
	1945	34.100	.15	.35	.60	1.20
	1945*	—	—	—	Proof	20.00

***NOTE:** These were restruck in quantity.

2 CENTS

NICKEL-BRASS

KM#	Date	Mintage	Fine	VF	XF	Unc
117	1944	30.165	.10	.25	.50	1.00

BRASS

KM#	Date	Mintage	Fine	VF	XF	Unc
117a	1944	—	—	—	Proof	—

Obv. leg: W/o EMPEROR OF INDIA.

KM#	Date	Mintage	Fine	VF	XF	Unc
119	1951	15.000	.10	.25	.75	1.50
	1951	—	—	—	Proof	20.00

KM#	Date	Mintage	Fine	VF	XF	Unc
124	1955	37.131	.10	.15	.25	.50
	1957	38.200	.10	.15	.25	.50
	1957	—	—	—	Proof	75.00

5 CENTS

COPPER

KM#	Date	Mintage	Fine	VF	XF	Unc
93	1870	7.009	5.00	10.00	30.00	80.00
	1870	—	—	—	Proof	175.00
	1890	1.001	7.50	20.00	50.00	110.00
	1890	—	—	—	Proof	200.00
	1891	—	—	—	Proof	350.00
	1892	1.000	7.50	20.00	50.00	110.00
	1892	—	—	—	Proof	200.00

SILVER

KM#	Date	Mintage	Fine	VF	XF	Unc
93a	1890	—	—	—	Proof	500.00
	1891	—	—	—	Proof	500.00
	1892	—	—	—	Proof	500.00

GOLD

M#	Date	Mintage	Fine	VF	XF	Unc
3b	1891	—	—	—	Proof	1200.

COPPER-NICKEL

M#	Date	Mintage	Fine	VF	XF	Unc
03	1909	2.000	1.50	3.00	5.00	15.00
	1910	4.000	1.00	2.00	3.50	10.00

M#	Date	Mintage	Fine	VF	XF	Unc
08	1912H	4.000	.75	1.50	3.00	8.00
	1920	6.000	.50	1.00	2.00	6.00
	1926	3.000	.75	1.50	4.00	10.00

NICKEL-BRASS

M#	Date	Mintage	Fine	VF	XF	Unc
13.1	1942	12.752	.35	.75	1.50	4.00
	1942	—	—	—	Proof	50.00
	1943	Inc. Ab.	.35	.75	1.50	4.00
	1943	—	—	—	Proof	50.00

Thin Planchet

M#	Date	Mintage	Fine	VF	XF	Unc
13.2	1944	18.064	.20	.35	.70	1.75
	1945	31.192	.15	.30	.60	1.50
	1945	—	—	—	Proof	60.00

IOTE: Varieties exist in bust, denomination and legend lacement for 1945.

Obv. leg: W/o EMPEROR OF INDIA.

M#	Date	Mintage	Fine	VF	XF	Unc
20	1951	—	—	—	Proof	20.00

10 CENTS

1.1664 g, .800 SILVER, .0300 oz ASW

M#	Date	Mintage	Fine	VF	XF	Unc
4	1892	2.500	1.50	3.50	7.00	15.00
	1892	—	—	—	Proof	150.00
	1893	2.500	1.50	3.50	7.00	15.00
	1893	—	—	—	Proof	150.00
	1894	3.000	1.50	3.50	7.00	15.00
	1894	—	—	—	Proof	150.00
	1897	1.500	1.50	3.50	9.00	20.00
	1899	1.000	1.75	4.00	10.00	25.00
	1900	1.000	1.75	4.00	10.00	25.00

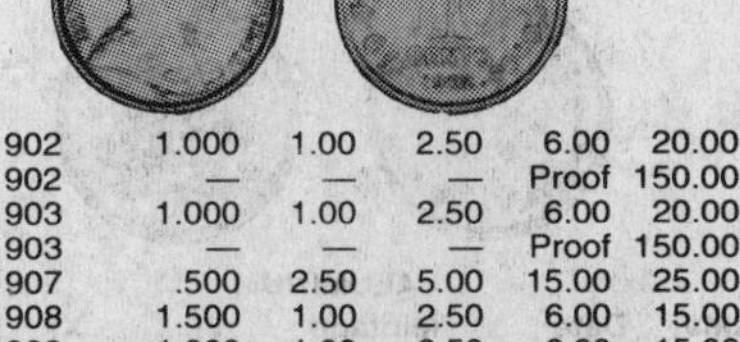

M#	Date	Mintage	Fine	VF	XF	Unc
7	1902	1.000	1.00	2.50	6.00	20.00
	1902	—	—	—	Proof	150.00
	1903	1.000	1.00	2.50	6.00	20.00
	1903	—	—	—	Proof	150.00
	1907	.500	2.50	5.00	15.00	25.00
	1908	1.500	1.00	2.50	6.00	15.00
	1909	1.000	1.00	2.50	6.00	15.00
	1910	2.000	1.00	2.50	6.00	15.00
04	1911	1.000	1.00	1.75	5.00	12.00
	1912	1.000	1.25	2.00	6.00	15.00
	1913	2.000	1.00	1.50	4.00	10.00
	1914	2.000	1.00	1.50	4.00	10.00
	1914	—	—	—	Proof	150.00
	1917	.879	1.00	2.50	7.50	17.50
	1917	—	—	—	Proof	150.00

1.1664 g, .550 SILVER, .0206 oz ASW

M#	Date	Mintage	Fine	VF	XF	Unc
04a	1919B	.750	1.50	3.50	10.00	20.00
	1919B	—	—	—	Proof	150.00
	1920B	3.059	1.00	2.50	6.00	15.00
	1920B	—	—	—	Proof	150.00

KM#	Date	Mintage	Fine	VF	XF	Unc
104a	1921B	1.583	.75	1.75	5.00	10.00
	1921B	—	—	—	Proof	150.00
	1922	.282	1.75	3.50	10.00	25.00
	1922	—	—	—	Proof	150.00
	1924	1.508	.75	1.75	4.00	10.00
	1924	—	—	—	Proof	150.00
	1925	1.500	.75	1.75	4.00	10.00
	1925	—	—	—	Proof	150.00
	1926	1.500	.75	1.75	4.00	10.00
	1926	—	—	—	Proof	150.00
	1927	1.500	.75	1.75	4.00	10.00
	1927	—	—	—	Proof	150.00
	1928	1.500	.75	1.75	4.00	10.00
	1928	—	—	—	Proof	150.00

1.1664 g, .800 SILVER, .0300 oz ASW

KM#	Date	Mintage	Fine	VF	XF	Unc
112	1941	16.271	.65	1.00	2.50	6.00

NICKEL-BRASS

KM#	Date	Mintage	Fine	VF	XF	Unc
118	1944	30.500	.25	.50	1.00	2.00
	1944	—	—	—	Proof	—

Obv. leg: W/o EMPEROR OF INDIA.

KM#	Date	Mintage	Fine	VF	XF	Unc
121	1951	34.760	.10	.20	.40	1.00
	1951	—	—	—	Proof	15.00
	1951	*3.000	—		Proof restrike	4.00

***NOTE:** Restrikes differ in the formation of native characters.

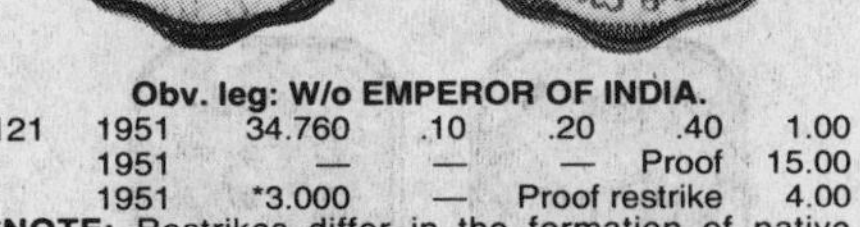

25 CENTS

2.9160 g, .800 SILVER, .0750 oz ASW

KM#	Date	Mintage	Fine	VF	XF	Unc
95	1892	.500	5.00	10.00	22.00	50.00
	1892	—	—	—	Proof	150.00
	1893	1.500	3.00	7.00	15.00	35.00
	1893	—	—	—	Proof	150.00
	1895	1.200	3.00	7.00	15.00	35.00
	1899	.600	5.00	10.00	22.00	50.00
	1900	.400	6.00	12.00	25.00	60.00

KM#	Date	Mintage	Fine	VF	XF	Unc
98	1902	.400	4.00	8.00	20.00	40.00
	1902	—	—	—	Proof	150.00
	1903	.400	4.00	8.00	20.00	40.00
	1903	—	—	—	Proof	150.00
	1907	.120	7.50	20.00	30.00	50.00
	1908	.400	4.00	8.00	15.00	35.00
	1909	.400	4.00	8.00	15.00	35.00
	1910	.800	2.00	5.00	10.00	20.00
105	1911	.400	3.00	6.00	12.00	30.00
	1911	—	—	—	Proof	175.00
	1913	1.200	1.50	2.50	7.50	17.50
	1913	—	—	—	Proof	175.00
	1914	.400	3.00	6.00	12.00	25.00
	1914	—	—	—	Proof	175.00
	1917	.300	4.00	8.00	15.00	35.00
	1917	—	—	—	Proof	175.00

2.9160 g, .550 SILVER, .0516 oz ASW

KM#	Date	Mintage	Fine	VF	XF	Unc
105a	1919B	1.400	1.25	3.00	7.50	15.00
	1919B	—	—	—	Proof	150.00
	1920B	1.600	1.25	3.00	7.50	15.00
	1920B	—	—	—	Proof	150.00
	1921B	.600	3.50	7.50	15.00	30.00
	1921B	—	—	—	Proof	150.00
	1922	1.211	1.25	3.25	7.50	15.00
	1922	—	—	—	Proof	150.00
	1925	1.004	1.25	3.50	7.50	15.00
	1925	—	—	—	Proof	150.00
	1926	1.000	1.25	3.50	7.50	15.00
	1926	—	—	—	Proof	150.00

NICKEL-BRASS

KM#	Date	Mintage	Fine	VF	XF	Unc
115	1943	13.920	.25	.50	1.00	2.00

Obv. leg: W/o EMPEROR OF INDIA.

KM#	Date	Mintage	Fine	VF	XF	Unc
122	1951	25.940	.10	.30	.60	1.50
	1951	—	—	—	Proof	20.00
	1951	*2.500	—		Proof restrike	4.00

***NOTE:** Numerals 9 and 5 differ on restrikes.

50 CENTS

5.8319 g, .800 SILVER, .1500 oz ASW

KM#	Date	Mintage	Fine	VF	XF	Unc
96	1892	.250	10.00	20.00	40.00	80.00
	1892	—	—	—	Proof	200.00
	1893	.750	6.00	12.00	27.50	45.00
	1893	—	—	—	Proof	175.00
	1895	.450	5.00	8.00	30.00	60.00
	1899	.100	12.50	30.00	50.00	100.00
	1900	.200	5.00	10.00	30.00	70.00

KM#	Date	Mintage	Fine	VF	XF	Unc
99	1902	.200	5.00	10.00	30.00	70.00
	1902	—	—	—	Proof	175.00
	1903	.800	3.00	8.00	18.00	35.00
	1903	—	—	—	Proof	175.00
	1910	.200	7.00	13.00	30.00	60.00
109	1913	.400	7.00	13.00	30.00	60.00
	1913	—	—	—	Proof	175.00
	1914	.200	5.00	15.00	30.00	60.00
	1914	—	—	—	Proof	175.00
	1917	1.073	2.50	5.00	10.00	20.00
	1917	—	—	—	Proof	175.00

5.8319 g, .550 SILVER, .1031 oz ASW

KM#	Date	Mintage	Fine	VF	XF	Unc
109a	1919B	.750	1.00	3.00	7.00	16.00
	1919B	—	—	—	Proof	120.00
	1920B	.800	1.00	3.00	7.00	16.00
	1920B	—	—	—	Proof	120.00
	1921B	.800	1.00	3.00	7.00	16.00
	1921B	—	—	—	Proof	120.00
	1922	1.040	1.00	3.00	7.00	16.00
	1922	—	—	—	Proof	120.00
	1924	1.010	1.00	3.00	7.00	16.00
	1924	—	—	—	Proof	120.00
	1925	.500	2.00	5.00	10.00	20.00
	1925	—	—	—	Proof	120.00
	1926	.500	2.00	5.00	10.00	20.00
	1926	—	—	—	Proof	120.00
	1927	.500	2.00	5.00	10.00	20.00
	1927	—	—	—	Proof	120.00
	1928	.500	2.00	5.00	10.00	20.00

KM#	Date	Mintage	Fine	VF	XF	Unc
109a	1928	—	—	—	Proof	120.00
	1929	.500	2.00	5.00	10.00	20.00
	1929	—	—	—	Proof	120.00

5.8319 g, .800 SILVER, .1500 oz ASW

KM#	Date	Mintage	Fine	VF	XF	Unc
114	1942	.662	2.00	4.00	8.00	17.50

BRASS

KM#	Date	Mintage	Fine	VF	XF	Unc
114a	1943	6 known	—	—	Proof	500.00

NICKEL-BRASS

KM#	Date	Mintage	Fine	VF	XF	Unc
116	1943	8.600	.35	.75	1.50	3.00

Obv. leg: W/o EMPEROR OF INDIA.

KM#	Date	Mintage	Fine	VF	XF	Unc
123	1951	19.980	.20	.35	.75	1.50
	1951	—	—	—	Proof	20.00
	1951	*1.500	—	Proof restrike		5.00

***NOTE:** Restrikes differ slightly in the formation of native inscriptions.

RUPEE

COPPER-NICKEL
2500 Years of Buddhism

KM#	Date	Mintage	Fine	VF	XF	Unc
125	1957	2.000	.50	1.00	2.00	3.00
	1957	1,800	—	—	Proof	12.00

5 RUPEES

28.2757 g, .925 SILVER, .8409 oz ASW
2500 Years of Buddhism

KM#	Date	Mintage	Fine	VF	XF	Unc
126	1957	.500	8.00	12.50	17.50	30.00
	1957	1,800	—	—	Proof	65.00

REPUBLIC

CENT

ALUMINUM

KM#	Date	Mintage	Fine	VF	XF	Unc
127	1963	33.000	—	—	—	.10
	1963	—	—	—	Proof	—
	1965	12.000	—	—	.10	.15
	1967	10.000	—	—	.10	.15
	1968	22.505	—	—	—	.10
	1969	10.000	—	—	—	.10
	1970	15.000	—	—	—	.10
	1971	55.000	—	—	—	.10
	1971	—	—	—	Proof	.50

2 CENTS

ALUMINUM

KM#	Date	Mintage	Fine	VF	XF	Unc
128	1963	26.000	—	—	.10	.15
	1963	—	—	—	Proof	—
	1965	7.000	—	—	.10	.15
	1967	15.000	—	—	.10	.15
	1968	15.000	—	—	.10	.15
	1969	—	—	—	.10	.15
	1970	13.000	—	—	.10	.15
	1971	45.000	—	—	.10	.15
	1971	—	—	—	Proof	1.00

5 CENTS

NICKEL-BRASS

KM#	Date	Mintage	Fine	VF	XF	Unc
129	1963	16.000	—	.10	.15	.25
	1963	—	—	—	Proof	—
	1965	9.000	—	.10	.15	.25
	1968	12.000	—	.10	.15	.25
	1968	—	—	—	Proof	3.00
	1969	2.500	—	.10	.20	.40
	1970	7.000	—	.10	.15	.25
	1971	32.000	—	.10	.15	.25
	1971	—	—	—	Proof	1.50

10 CENTS

NICKEL-BRASS

KM#	Date	Mintage	Fine	VF	XF	Unc
130	1963	14.000	—	.10	.15	.25
	1963	—	—	—	Proof	—
	1965	3.000	—	.10	.15	.35
	1969	6.000	—	.10	.15	.25
	1970	—	—	.10	.15	.25
	1971	29.000	—	.10	.15	.20
	1971	—	—	—	Proof	1.25

25 CENTS

COPPER-NICKEL

KM#	Date	Mintage	Fine	VF	XF	Unc
131	1963	30.000	—	.10	.20	.40
	1963	—	—	—	Proof	—
	1965	8.000	—	.10	.25	.50
	1968	—	—	.10	.25	.50
	1969	—	—	.10	.25	.50
	1970	—	—	.10	.25	.50
	1971	24.000	—	.10	.15	.30
	1971	—	—	—	Proof	1.50

50 CENTS

COPPER-NICKEL

KM#	Date	Mintage	Fine	VF	XF	Unc
132	1963	15.000	.10	.20	.35	.75
	1963	—	—	—	Proof	—
	1965	7.000	.10	.20	.35	.75
	1968	—	.10	.20	.35	.75
	1969	—	.10	.20	.35	.75
	1970	—	.10	.20	.35	.75
	1971	4.000	.25	.50	.75	1.50
	1971	—	—	—	Proof	2.00
	1972	8.000	.10	.20	.35	.75

RUPEE

COPPER-NICKEL

KM#	Date	Mintage	Fine	VF	XF	Unc
133	1963	20.000	.10	.20	.40	1.00
	1963	—	—	—	Proof	—
	1965	5.000	.15	.25	.50	1.00
	1969	2.500	.15	.25	.50	1.50
	1970	—	.15	.25	.50	1.50
	1971	5.000	.15	.25	.50	1.25
	1971	—	—	—	Proof	3.00
	1972	7.000	.15	.25	.50	1.00

2 RUPEES

COPPER-NICKEL
F.A.O. Issue

KM#	Date	Mintage	Fine	VF	XF	Unc
134	1968	.500	.50	1.50	2.25	3.00

PROOF SETS (PS)

KM#	Date	Mintage	Identification	Issue Price	Mkt. Val.
PS1	1951(6)	150*	KM111a,119-123	—	40.00

***NOTE:** Restrikes exist.

KM#	Date	Mintage	Identification	Issue Price	Mkt. Val.
PS2	1957(2)	400	KM125-126	—	90.00
PS3	1957(4)	700	KM125-126 (2 each)	—	160.00
PS4	1971(7)	20,000	KM127-133	—	10.00

SHRI (SRI) LANKA

100 Cents = 1 Rupee

CENT

ALUMINUM

KM#	Date	Mintage	VF	XF	Unc
137	1975	52.778	—	.10	.25
	1975	1,431	—	Proof	2.00
	1978	34.006	—	.10	.25
	1978	Inc. Ab.	—	Proof	2.00
	1989	—	—	.10	.25

2 CENTS

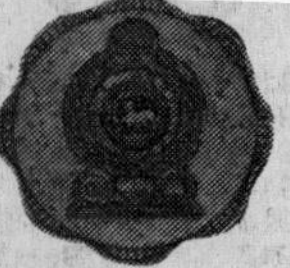

ALUMINUM

KM#	Date	Mintage	VF	XF	Unc
138	1975	62.503	—	.10	.25
	1975	1,431	—	Proof	2.50
	1977	2.500	—	.10	.25
	1978	23.425	—	.10	.25
	1978	Inc. Ab.	—	Proof	3.00

5 CENTS

NICKEL-BRASS

KM#	Date	Mintage	VF	XF	Unc
139	1975	19.584	—	.10	.25
	1975	1,431	—	Proof	2.50

ALUMINUM

KM#	Date	Mintage	VF	XF	Unc
139a	1978	272.308	—	.10	.25
	1978	Inc. Ab.	—	Proof	3.00
	1988	40.000	—	.10	.25
	1991	—	—	.10	.25

10 CENTS

NICKEL-BRASS

KM#	Date	Mintage	VF	XF	Unc
140	1975	10.800	—	.10	.25
	1975	1,431	—	Proof	4.25

ALUMINUM

KM#	Date	Mintage	VF	XF	Unc
140a	1978	188.820	—	.10	.25
	1978	Inc. Ab.	—	Proof	3.00
	1988	40.000	—	.10	.25
	1991	—	—	.10	.25

25 CENTS

COPPER-NICKEL
Security edge

KM#	Date	Mintage	VF	XF	Unc
141.1	1975	39.600	—	.10	.25
	1975	1,431	—	Proof	3.00
	1978	65.009	—	.10	.25
	1978	Inc. Ab.	—	Proof	3.00

Reeded edge

KM#	Date	Mintage	VF	XF	Unc
141.2	1982	90.000	—	.10	.25
	1982	Inc. Ab.	—	Proof	3.00
	1989	—	—	.10	.25
	1991	—	—	.10	.25

50 CENTS

COPPER-NICKEL
Security edge

KM#	Date	Mintage	VF	XF	Unc
135.1	1972	11.000	.15	.30	.60
	1975	34.000	.15	.30	.60
	1975	1,431	—	Proof	4.00
	1978	66.010	.15	.30	.60
	1978	Inc. Ab.	—	Proof	4.00

Reeded edge

KM#	Date	Mintage	VF	XF	Unc
135.2	1982	65.000	.10	.20	.50
	1982	Inc. Ab.	—	Proof	4.00
	1991	—	.10	.20	.50

RUPEE

COPPER-NICKEL
Security edge

KM#	Date	Mintage	VF	XF	Unc
136.1	1972	5.000	.30	.60	1.25
	1975	31.500	.25	.50	1.00
	1975	1,431	—	Proof	6.50
	1978	37.018	.25	.50	1.00
	1978	Inc. Ab.	—	Proof	6.50

Reeded edge

KM#	Date	Mintage	VF	XF	Unc
136.2	1982	75.000	.25	.50	1.00
	1982	Inc. Ab.	—	Proof	5.00

Inauguration of President Jayawardene

KM#	Date	Mintage	VF	XF	Unc
144	1978	1.997	.30	.60	1.25
	1978	2,600	—	Proof	8.00

3rd Anniversary of Induction of President
Obv: 2 lions above flag. Rev: Portrait of President Premadasa in circle of swans.

KM#	Date	Mintage	VF	XF	Unc
151	1992	—	—	—	1.25
	1992	—	—	Proof	8.00

2 RUPEES

COPPER-NICKEL
Non-Aligned Nations Conference

KM#	Date	Mintage	VF	XF	Unc
142	1976	2.000	.50	1.00	1.50
	1976	1,000	—	Proof	6.00

Mahaweli Dam

KM#	Date	Mintage	VF	XF	Unc
145	1981	5.000	.25	.50	1.25

KM#	Date	Mintage	VF	XF	Unc
147	1984	25.000	.25	.50	1.00

5 RUPEES

NICKEL
Non-Aligned Nations Conference

KM#	Date	Mintage	VF	XF	Unc
143	1976	1.000	.75	1.25	2.50
	1976	1,000	—	Proof	8.00

COPPER-NICKEL
50th Anniversary of Universal Adult Franchise

KM#	Date	Mintage	VF	XF	Unc
146	1981	2.000	.50	1.00	2.25

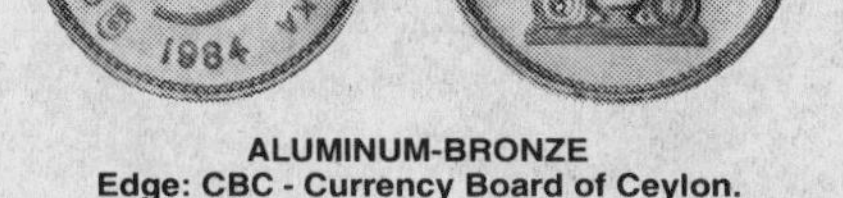

ALUMINUM-BRONZE
Edge: CBC - Currency Board of Ceylon.

KM#	Date	Mintage	VF	XF	Unc
148.1	1984	25.000	.35	.75	2.25

Edge: CBSL - Currency Board of Shri Lanka.

KM#	Date	Mintage	VF	XF	Unc
148.2	1986	—	.35	.75	2.25
	1991	—	.35	.75	2.25

NOTE: Varieties in edge inscriptions exist.

10 RUPEES

COPPER-NICKEL
I.Y.S.H.

KM#	Date	Mintage	VF	XF	Unc
149	1987	2.000	—	—	3.00

100 RUPEES

10.2000 g, .925 SILVER, .3033 oz ASW
Fifth SAF Games

KM#	Date	Mintage	VF	XF	Unc
152	1991	—	—	Proof	30.00

500 RUPEES

28.2800 g, .925 SILVER, .8411 oz ASW
40th Anniversary of Central Bank

KM#	Date	Mintage	VF	XF	Unc
150	1990	5,000	—	Proof	55.00

1.6000 g, .500 GOLD, .0257 oz AGW
Fifth SAF Games

KM#	Date	Mintage	VF	XF	Unc
153	1991	—	—	Proof	20.00

PROOF SETS (PS)

KM#	Date	Mintage	Identification	Issue Price	Mkt. Val.
PS1	1978 (7)	20,000	KM135-138,139a-140a,141	26.00	25.00

SIERRA LEONE

The Republic of Sierra Leone, a British Commonwealth nation located in western Africa between Guinea and Liberia, has an area of 27,699 sq. mi. (71,740 sq. km.) and a population of *4.1 million. Capital: Freetown. The economy is predominantly agricultural but mining contributes significantly to export revenues. Diamonds, iron ore, palm kernels, cocoa, and coffee are exported.

The coast of Sierra Leone was first visited by Portuguese and British slavers in the 15th and 16th centuries. The first settlement, at Freetown, 1787, was established as a refuge for freed slaves within the British Empire, runaway slaves from the United States and Negroes discharged from the British armed forces. The first settlers were virtually wiped out by tribal attacks and disease. The colony was re-established under the auspices of the Sierra Leone Company and transferred to the British Crown in 1807. The interior region was secured and established as a protectorate in 1896. Sierra Leone became independent within the Commonwealth on April 27, 1961, and adopted a republican constitution ten years later. It is a member of the Commonwealth of Nations. The president is Chief of State and Head of Government.

For similar coinage refer to British West Africa.

RULERS

British, until 1971

MONETARY SYSTEM

Until 1906
100 Cents = 50 Pence = 1 Dollar
Until 1964
12 Pence = 1 Shilling
Commencing 1964
100 Cents = 1 Leone

SIERRA LEONE COMPANY

10 CENTS

.902 SILVER
Obv: Lion. Rev: Clasped hands.

KM#	Date	Mintage	Fine	VF	XF	Unc
3	1805	6,100	35.00	80.00	150.00	275.00

NOTE: Earlier dates (1791-1796) exist for this type.

COUNTERMARKED COINAGE

1/4 DOLLAR

.903 SILVER
c/m: Crowned WR on 1/4 cut of a Spanish or Colonial 8 Reales.

KM#	Date	Mintage	VG	Fine	VF	XF
10	ND(1832)	—	250.00	450.00	800.00	1150.

1/2 DOLLAR

.903 SILVER
c/m: Crowned WR on Spanish or Spanish Colonial 4 Reales.

KM#	Date	Mintage	VG	Fine	VF	XF
13	ND(1832)	—	200.00	350.00	600.00	900.00

1/2 CENT

BRONZE
Bonga Fish

KM#	Date	Mintage	VF	XF	Unc
16	1964	.600	—	.15	.25
	1964	.010	—	Proof	.50
	2.8300 g, .925 SILVER, .0841 oz ASW				
16a	1964	22 pcs.	—	Proof	650.00

BRONZE

KM#	Date	Mintage	VF	XF	Unc
31	1980	—	—	.10	.20
	1980	.010	—	Proof	1.50

CENT

BRONZE
Palm Branches and Fruit Stalks

KM#	Date	Mintage	VF	XF	Unc
17	1964	35.000	—	.15	.25
	1964	.010	—	Proof	.75
	5.6700 g, .925 SILVER, .1686 oz ASW				
17a	1964	22 pcs.	—	Proof	650.00

BRONZE

KM#	Date	Mintage	VF	XF	Unc
32	1980	—	.10	.15	.25
	1980	.010	—	Proof	1.50

5 CENTS

COPPER-NICKEL
Kapok Tree

KM#	Date	Mintage	VF	XF	Unc
18	1964	.900	.15	.25	.50
	1964	.010	—	Proof	.75
	2.4900 g, .925 SILVER, .0740 oz ASW				
18a	1964	22 pcs.	—	Proof	650.00

COPPER-NICKEL

KM#	Date	Mintage	VF	XF	Unc
33	1980	—	.10	.25	.40
	1980	.010	—	Proof	2.50
	1984	—	.10	.25	.40

10 CENTS

COPPER-NICKEL
Cocoa Beans

KM#	Date	Mintage	VF	XF	Unc
9	1964	24.000	.25	.40	.65
	1964	.010	—	Proof	1.00

4.9200 g, .925 SILVER, .1463 oz ASW

KM#	Date	Mintage	VF	XF	Unc
9a	1964	22 pcs.	—	Proof	650.00

COPPER-NICKEL

KM#	Date	Mintage	VF	XF	Unc
4	1978	.200	.25	.40	.70
	1980	—	.20	.35	.60
	1980	.010	—	Proof	5.00
	1984	—	.20	.35	.60

20 CENTS

COPPER-NICKEL

KM#	Date	Mintage	VF	XF	Unc
0	1964	11.000	.35	.60	1.00
	1964	.010	—	Proof	1.00

8.2200 g, .925 SILVER, .2444 oz ASW

KM#	Date	Mintage	VF	XF	Unc
0a	1964	22 pcs.	—	Proof	650.00

COPPER-NICKEL

KM#	Date	Mintage	VF	XF	Unc
0	1978	2.375	.35	.60	1.00
	1980	—	.35	.50	.85
	1980	.010	—	Proof	7.00
	1984	—	.35	.60	.85

50 CENTS

COPPER-NICKEL

KM#	Date	Mintage	VF	XF	Unc
5	1972	1.000	1.00	1.50	2.50
	1972	2,000	—	Proof	5.00
	1980	—	1.00	1.25	2.25
	1980	.010	—	Proof	10.00
	1984	—	1.00	1.25	2.25

LEONE

COPPER-NICKEL
Sir Milton Marcai

KM#	Date	Mintage	VF	XF	Unc
21	1964	.010	—	Proof	10.00

22.6220 g, .925 SILVER, .6738 oz ASW

KM#	Date	Mintage	VF	XF	Unc
21a	1964	12 pcs.	—	Proof	1000.
	1976	962 pcs.	—	Proof	100.00

.917 GOLD

KM#	Date	Mintage	VF	XF	Unc
21b	1964	10 pcs.	—	Proof	2500.

COPPER-NICKEL
10th Anniversary of Bank

KM#	Date	Mintage	VF	XF	Unc
26	1974	.103	1.00	1.50	3.00

28.2800 g, .925 SILVER, .8411 oz ASW

KM#	Date	Mintage	VF	XF	Unc
26a	1974	.022	—	Proof	15.00

GOLD

KM#	Date	Mintage	VF	XF	Unc
26b	1974	100 pcs.	—	—	1200.

28.2800 g, .925 SILVER, .8411 oz ASW
70th Birthday of Dr. Siaka Stevens

KM#	Date	Mintage	VF	XF	Unc
27	1975	.140	—	—	12.50
	1975	.041	—	Proof	15.00

57.6050 g, .917 GOLD, 1.6985 oz AGW

KM#	Date	Mintage	VF	XF	Unc
27a	1975	100 pcs.	—	Proof	1200.

COPPER-NICKEL
O.A.U. Summit Conference

KM#	Date	Mintage	VF	XF	Unc
36	1980	.075	1.00	2.00	3.00

28.2800 g, .925 SILVER, .8411 oz ASW

KM#	Date	Mintage	VF	XF	Unc
36a	1980	.015	—	Proof	30.00

9.5000 g, .925 SILVER, .2825 oz ASW
Freetown Bicentennial

KM#	Date	Mintage	VF	XF	Unc
40	1987	3,000	—	Proof	25.00

16.0000 g, .917 GOLD, .4716 oz AGW

KM#	Date	Mintage	VF	XF	Unc
40a	1987	1,250	—	Proof	275.00

NICKEL-BRONZE

KM#	Date	Mintage	VF	XF	Unc
43	1987	—	.50	.75	1.50
	1988	—	.50	.75	1.50

2 LEONES

COPPER-NICKEL
F.A.O. Regional Conference for Africa

KM#	Date	Mintage	VF	XF	Unc
29	1976	.020	1.00	2.00	4.50

10 LEONES

28.2800 g, .925 SILVER, .8411 oz ASW
Year of the Scout

KM#	Date	Mintage	VF	XF	Unc
38	1983	.010	—	—	25.00
	1983	.010	—	Proof	32.50

World Wildlife Fund - Pygmy Hippopotamus

KM#	Date	Mintage	VF	XF	Unc
41	1987	.025	—	Proof	35.00

100 LEONES

15.9800 g, .917 GOLD, .4711 oz AGW
Year of the Scout

KM#	Date	Mintage	VF	XF	Unc
39	1983	2,000	—	—	350.00
	1983	2,000	—	Proof	450.00

1/4 GOLDE

13.6360 g, .900 GOLD, .3946 oz AGW
5th Anniversary of Independence

KM#	Date	Mintage	VF	XF	Unc
22	1966	5,000	—	—	200.00

15.0000 g, .916 GOLD, .4418 oz AGW

KM#	Date	Mintage	VF	XF	Unc
22a	1966	600 pcs.	—	Proof	300.00

10.3150 g, PALLADIUM

KM#	Date	Mintage	VF	XF	Unc
22b	1966	100 pcs.	—	Proof	125.00

1/2 GOLDE

27.2730 g, .900 GOLD, .7891 oz AGW
5th Anniversary of Independence

KM#	Date	Mintage	VF	XF	Unc
23	1966	2,500	—	—	350.00

30.0000 g, .916 GOLD, .8836 oz AGW

KM#	Date	Mintage	VF	XF	Unc
23a	1966	600 pcs.	—	Proof	450.00

20.6290 g, PALLADIUM

KM#	Date	Mintage	VF	XF	Unc
23b	1966	100 pcs.	—	Proof	200.00

GOLDE

54.5450 g, .900 GOLD, 1.5783 oz AGW
5th Anniversary of Independence

KM#	Date	Mintage	VF	XF	Unc
24	1966	1,500	—	—	800.00

60.0000 g, .916 GOLD, 1.7672 oz AGW

KM#	Date	Mintage	VF	XF	Unc
24a	1966	400 pcs.	—	Proof	1000.

41.2590 g, PALLADIUM

KM#	Date	Mintage	VF	XF	Unc
24b	1966	100 pcs.	—	Proof	400.00

41.2590 g, PLATINUM

KM#	Date	Mintage	VF	XF	Unc
24c	1966	—	—	Proof	1000.

5 GOLDE

15.9800 g, .917 GOLD, .4711 oz AGW
O.A.U. Summit Conference

KM#	Date	Mintage	VF	XF	Unc
37	1980	457 pcs.	—	—	250.00
	1980	325 pcs.	—	Proof	300.00

World Wildlife Fund - Duiker Zebra

KM#	Date	Mintage	VF	XF	Unc
42	1987	5,000	—	Proof	350.00

10 GOLDE

57.6000 g, .916 GOLD, 1.6965 oz AGW
70th Birthday Dr. Siaka Stevens

KM#	Date	Mintage	VF	XF	Unc
28	1975	727 pcs.	—	—	850.00
	1975	307 pcs.	—	Proof	1000.

MINT SETS (MS)

KM#	Date	Mintage	Identification	Issue Price	Mkt. Val.
MS1	1966(3)	—	KM22-24	—	1400.

PROOF SETS (PS)

KM#	Date	Mintage	Identification	Issue Price	Mkt. Val.
PS1	1964(6)	10,000	KM16-21	—	12.50
PS2	1964(6)	12	KM16a-20a,21b	—	5750.
PS3	1964(6)	10	KM16a-21a	—	4250.
PS4	1966(3)	400	KM22a-24a	—	1750.
PS5	1972(2)	1,000	KM25 (2 pcs. with 50 cent bank note (0 serial#) in plush case	—	15.00
PS6	1980(6)	10,000	KM30-35	34.00	30.00

SINGAPORE

The Republic of Singapore, a British Commonwealth nation situated at the southern tip of the Malay peninsula, has an area of 224 sq. mi. (633 sq. km.) and a population of *2.7 million. Capital: Singapore. The economy is based on entrepot trade, manufacturing and oil. Rubber, petroleum products, machinery and spices are exported.

Singapore's modern history - it was an important shipping center in the 14th century before the rise of Malacca and Penang - began in 1819 when Sir Thomas Stamford Raffles, an agent for the British East India Company, founded the town of Singapore. By 1825 its trade exceeded that of Malacca and Penang combined. The opening of the Suez Canal (1869) and the demand for rubber and tin created by the automobile and packaging industries combined to make Singapore one of the major ports of the world. In 1826 Singapore, Penang and Malacca were combined to form the Straits Settlements, which was made a Crown Colony in 1867. Singapore became a separate Crown Colony in 1946 when the Straits Settlements was dissolved. It joined in the formation of Malaysia in 1963, but brok away on Aug. 9, 1965, to become an independent republic. Singapore is a member of the Commonwealth of Nations. The president is Chief of State. The prime minister is Head of Government.

For earlier coinage see Straits Settlements, Malaya, Malaya and British Borneo, and Malaysia.

MINT MARKS

sm Singapore Mint monogram

MONETARY SYSTEM

100 Cents = 1 Dollar

CENT

BRONZE
Apartment Building

KM#	Date	Mintage	VF	XF	Unc
1	1967	7.500	—	.20	.40
	1967	2,000	—	Proof	2.25
	1968	2.696	—	.25	.50
	1968	5,000	—	Proof	2.00
	1969	7.220	—	.20	.30
	1969	3,000	—	Proof	10.00
	1970	1.402	—	.40	.80
	1971	9.731	—	.20	.25
	1972	1.655	—	.20	.70
	1972	749 pcs.	—	Proof	40.00
	1973	6.377	—	.10	.20
	1973	1,000	—	Proof	5.00
	1974	9.421	—	—	.20
	1974	1,500	—	Proof	4.00
	1975	24.226	—	—	.20
	1975	3,000	—	Proof	1.50
	1976	2.500	—	.10	.60
	1976 *sm*	3,500	—	Proof	1.25
	1977 *sm*	3,500	—	Proof	1.25
	1978 *sm*	4,000	—	Proof	1.25
	1979 *sm*	3,500	—	Proof	1.25
	1980 *sm*	.014	—	Proof	1.00
	1982 *sm*	.020	—	Proof	1.00
	1983 *sm*	.015	—	Proof	1.00
	1984 *sm*	.015	—	Proof	1.00

COPPER-CLAD STEEL

KM#	Date	Mintage	VF	XF	Unc
1a	1976	13.665	—	—	.25
	1977	13.940	—	—	.25
	1978	5.931	—	—	.25
	1979	11.986	—	—	.15
	1980	19.922	—	—	.15
	1981	38.084	—	—	.10
	1982	24.105	—	—	.10
	1983	2.204	—	—	.10
	1984	5.695	—	—	.10
	1985	.148	—	.15	.35

2.9200 g, .925 SILVER, .0869 oz ASW

KM#	Date	Mintage	VF	XF	Unc
1b	1981 *sm*	.030	—	Proof	5.00

BRONZE
Vanda Miss Joaquim Plants

KM#	Date	Mintage	VF	XF	Unc
49	1986	.120	—	—	.10
	1987	.120	—	—	.10
	1988	—	—	—	.10

KM#	Date	Mintage	VF	XF	Unc
9	1989	.070	—	—	.10
	1990	—	—	—	.10

1.8100 g, .925 SILVER, .0538 oz ASW

KM#	Date	Mintage	VF	XF	Unc
9a	1985 *sm*	.020	—	Proof	2.25
	1986 *sm*	.015	—	Proof	2.25
	1987	.015	—	Proof	2.25
	1988	.015	—	Proof	2.25
	1989	.015	—	Proof	2.25

COPPER CLAD STEEL
Similar to KM#49 but motto ribbon on arms curves down at center.

KM#	Date	Mintage	VF	XF	Unc
8	1992	—	—	—	.10

.925 SILVER

KM#	Date	Mintage	VF	XF	Unc
8a	1992	—	—	Proof	2.25

5 CENTS

COPPER-NICKEL
Great White Egret

KM#	Date	Mintage	VF	XF	Unc
	1967	28.000	—	.15	.30
	1967	2,000	—	Proof	3.25
	1968	4.217	—	.20	.40
	1968	5,000	—	Proof	3.00
	1969	14.778	—	.10	.30
	1969	3,000	—	Proof	15.00
	1970	3.065	—	.20	.40
	1971	13.202	—	.10	.20
	1972	9.817	—	.10	.20
	1972	749 pcs.	—	Proof	50.00
	1973	2.980	—	.30	.50
	1973	1,000	—	Proof	7.50
	1974	10.868	—	.10	.20
	1974	1,500	—	Proof	6.50
	1975	1.729	—	.40	1.00
	1975	3,000	—	Proof	2.50
	1976	15.541	—	.10	.15
	1976 *sm*	3,500	—	Proof	2.25
	1977	9.957	—	.10	.15
	1977 *sm*	3,500	—	Proof	2.25
	1978	5.956	—	.10	.20
	1978 *sm*	4,000	—	Proof	2.25
	1979	9.974	—	—	.10
	1979 *sm*	3,500	—	Proof	2.25
	1980	20.534	—	—	.15
	1980 *sm*	.014	—	Proof	2.00
	1981	.110	—	—	.10
	1982	.160	—	—	.10
	1982 *sm*	.020	—	Proof	2.00
	1983	.040	—	—	.10
	1983 *sm*	.015	—	Proof	2.00
	1984	18.880	—	—	.10
	1984 *sm*	.015	—	Proof	2.00
	1985	.148	—	—	.10

ALUMINUM
F.A.O. Issue

KM#	Date	Mintage	VF	XF	Unc
	1971	3.049	—	.10	.35

COPPER-NICKEL CLAD STEEL

KM#	Date	Mintage	VF	XF	Unc
2a	1980	12.001	—	—	.10
	1981	23.866	—	—	.10
	1982	24.413	—	—	.10
	1983	4.016	—	—	.10
	1984	3.200	—	—	.10

1.6500 g, .925 SILVER, .0491 oz ASW

KM#	Date	Mintage	VF	XF	Unc
2b	1981 *sm*	.030	—	Proof	5.00

ALUMINUM-BRONZE
Fruit Salad Plant

KM#	Date	Mintage	VF	XF	Unc
50	1985	14.840	—	—	.10
	1986	33.520	—	—	.10
	1987	37.480	—	—	.10
	1988	26.680	—	—	.10
	1989	—	—	—	.10
	1990	—	—	—	.10

2.0000 g, .925 SILVER, .0595 oz ASW

KM#	Date	Mintage	VF	XF	Unc
50a	1985 *sm*	.020	—	Proof	2.50
	1986 *sm*	.015	—	Proof	2.50
	1987	.015	—	Proof	2.50
	1988	.015	—	Proof	2.50
	1989	.015	—	Proof	2.50

ALUMINUM-BRONZE
Similar to KM#50 but motto ribbon on arms curves down at center.

KM#	Date	Mintage	VF	XF	Unc
99	1992	—	—	—	.10

.925 SILVER

KM#	Date	Mintage	VF	XF	Unc
99a	1992	—	—	Proof	2.50

10 CENTS

COPPER-NICKEL
Stylized Great Crowned Seahorse

KM#	Date	Mintage	VF	XF	Unc
3	1967	40.000	—	.15	.30
	1967	2,000	—	Proof	4.50
	1968	36.261	—	.20	.40
	1968	5,000	—	Proof	4.25
	1969	25.000	—	.10	.50
	1969	3,000	—	Proof	20.00
	1970	21.304	—	.20	.50
	1971	33.041	—	.10	.30
	1972	2.675	—	.10	.35
	1972	749 pcs.	—	Proof	60.00
	1973	14.290	—	.10	.25
	1973	1,000	—	Proof	10.00
	1974	13.450	—	.10	.25
	1974	1,500	—	Proof	7.50
	1975	.828	.10	.60	1.25
	1975	3,000	—	Proof	4.00
	1976	29.718	—	.10	.25
	1976 *sm*	3,500	—	Proof	3.50
	1977	11.776	—	.10	.20
	1977 *sm*	3,500	—	Proof	3.50
	1978	5.936	—	.10	.30
	1978 *sm*	4,000	—	Proof	3.50
	1979	12.001	—	.10	.20
	1979 *sm*	3,500	—	Proof	3.50
	1980	40.299	—	.10	.20
	1980 *sm*	.014	—	Proof	3.00
	1981	58.600	—	.10	.20
	1982	48.514	—	.10	.20
	1982 *sm*	.020	—	Proof	3.00
	1983	10.415	—	.10	.20
	1983 *sm*	.015	—	Proof	3.00
	1984	29.700	—	.10	.20
	1984 *sm*	.015	—	Proof	3.00
	1985	.148	—	.10	.20

3.3500 g, .925 SILVER, .0996 oz ASW

KM#	Date	Mintage	VF	XF	Unc
3a	1981 *sm*	.030	—	Proof	7.50

COPPER-NICKEL
Star Jasmine Plant

KM#	Date	Mintage	VF	XF	Unc
51	1985	34.200	—	—	.20
	1986	172.920	—	—	.20
	1987	106.920	—	—	.20
	1988	54.455	—	—	.20
	1989	—	—	—	.20
	1990	—	—	—	.20
	1991	—	—	—	.20

3.0500 g, .925 SILVER, .0907 oz ASW

KM#	Date	Mintage	VF	XF	Unc
51a	1985 *sm*	.020	—	Proof	4.00
	1986 *sm*	.015	—	Proof	4.00
	1987	.015	—	Proof	4.00
	1988	.015	—	Proof	4.00
	1989	.015	—	Proof	4.00

COPPER-NICKEL
Similar to KM#51 but motto ribbon on arms curves down at center.

KM#	Date	Mintage	VF	XF	Unc
100	1992	—	—	—	.20

.925 SILVER

KM#	Date	Mintage	VF	XF	Unc
100a	1992	—	—	Proof	4.00

20 CENTS

COPPER-NICKEL
Swordfish

KM#	Date	Mintage	VF	XF	Unc
4	1967	36.500	.15	.30	.60
	1967	2,000	—	Proof	7.00
	1968	10.934	.15	.30	.60
	1968	5,000	—	Proof	6.00
	1969	8.460	.15	.30	.60
	1969	3,000	—	Proof	30.00
	1970	3.250	.15	.30	.60
	1971	1.732	.15	.70	2.00
	1972	9.107	.15	.30	.60
	1972	749 pcs.	—	Proof	70.00
	1973	8.838	.15	.30	.60
	1973	1,000	—	Proof	17.50
	1974	4.567	.15	.30	.60
	1974	1,500	—	Proof	12.50
	1975	1.546	.15	.50	1.00
	1975	3,000	—	Proof	6.50
	1976	19.760	.15	.25	.50
	1976 *sm*	3,500	—	Proof	6.00
	1977	7.074	.15	.30	.60
	1977 *sm*	3,500	—	Proof	6.00
	1978	4.450	.15	.30	.60
	1978 *sm*	4,000	—	Proof	6.00
	1979	14.865	—	.15	.30
	1979 *sm*	3,500	—	Proof	6.00
	1980	27.903	—	.15	.30
	1980 *sm*	.014	—	Proof	5.00
	1981	46.997	—	.15	.30
	1982	25.234	—	.15	.30
	1982 *sm*	.020	—	Proof	4.00
	1983	6.424	—	.15	.30
	1983 *sm*	.015	—	Proof	4.00
	1984	9.290	—	.15	.30
	1984 *sm*	.015	—	Proof	4.00
	1985	.148	—	.15	.30

6.5100 g, .925 SILVER, .1936 oz ASW

KM#	Date	Mintage	VF	XF	Unc
4a	1981 *sm*	.030	—	Proof	12.50

COPPER-NICKEL
Powder-puff Plant

KM#	Date	Mintage	VF	XF	Unc
52	1985	22.020	—	.15	.30
	1986	90.480	—	.15	.30
	1987	80.050	—	.15	.30
	1988	27.000	—	.15	.30
	1989	—	—	.15	.30
	1990	—	—	.15	.30

5.2400 g, .925 SILVER, .1559 oz ASW

KM#	Date	Mintage	VF	XF	Unc
52a	1985 *sm*	.020	—	Proof	6.50
	1986 *sm*	.015	—	Proof	6.50
	1987	.015	—	Proof	6.50
	1988	.015	—	Proof	6.50
	1989	.015	—	Proof	6.50

COPPER-NICKEL
Similar to KM#51 but motto ribbon on arms curves down at center.

KM#	Date	Mintage	VF	XF	Unc
101	1992	—	—	—	.30

.925 SILVER

KM#	Date	Mintage	VF	XF	Unc
101a	1992	—	—	Proof	6.50

50 CENTS

COPPER-NICKEL
Zebra Fish

KM#	Date	Mintage	VF	XF	Unc
5	1967	11.000	.30	.40	.80
	1967	2,000	—	Proof	10.00
	1968	3.189	.30	.60	1.50
	1968	5,000	—	Proof	8.50
	1969	2.008	.30	.60	1.50
	1969	3,000	—	Proof	35.00
	1970	3.102	.30	.60	1.50
	1971	3.933	.30	.60	1.50
	1972	5.427	.30	.50	.90
	1972	749 pcs.	—	Proof	90.00
	1973	4.474	.30	.50	.90
	1973	1,000	—	Proof	30.00
	1974	11.550	—	.40	.75
	1974	1,500	—	Proof	22.50
	1975	1.432	.35	.75	2.00
	1975	3,000	—	Proof	10.00
	1976	5.728	.30	.50	.90
	1976 *sm*	3,500	—	Proof	8.50
	1977	6.953	—	.40	.75
	1977 *sm*	3,500	—	Proof	8.50
	1978	3.934	—	.40	.75
	1978 *sm*	4,000	—	Proof	8.50
	1979	8.461	—	.40	.75
	1979 *sm*	3,500	—	Proof	8.50
	1980	14.717	—	.35	.60
	1980 *sm*	.014	—	Proof	7.00
	1981	29.542	—	.35	.60
	1982	13.756	—	.35	.60
	1982 *sm*	.020	—	Proof	5.00
	1983	4.482	—	.35	.60
	1983 *sm*	.015	—	Proof	5.00
	1984	4.210	—	.35	.60
	1984 *sm*	.015	—	Proof	5.00
	1985	.148	—	.35	.60

10.8200 g, .925 SILVER, .3218 oz ASW

KM#	Date	Mintage	VF	XF	Unc
5a	1981 *sm*	.030	—	Proof	15.00

COPPER-NICKEL
Yellow Allamanda Plant
Reeded edge.

KM#	Date	Mintage	VF	XF	Unc
53.1	1985	11.384	—	.35	.60
	1986	26.126	—	.35	.60
	1987	33.472	—	.35	.60
	1988	25.000	—	.35	.60

Lettered edge.

KM#	Date	Mintage	VF	XF	Unc
53.2	1989	—	—	.35	.60
	1990	—	—	.35	.60

8.5600 g, .925 SILVER, .2546 oz ASW

KM#	Date	Mintage	VF	XF	Unc
53.1a	1985 *sm*	.020	—	Proof	12.00
	1986 *sm*	.015	—	Proof	12.00
	1987	.015	—	Proof	12.00
	1988	.015	—	Proof	12.00
53.2a	1989	.015	—	Proof	12.00

COPPER-NICKEL
Similar to KM#53 but motto ribbon on arms curves down at center.

KM#	Date	Mintage	VF	XF	Unc
102	1992	—	—	—	.60

.925 SILVER

KM#	Date	Mintage	VF	XF	Unc
102a	1992	—	—	Proof	12.00

DOLLAR

COPPER-NICKEL

KM#	Date	Mintage	VF	XF	Unc
6	1967	3.000	.65	1.00	2.00
	1967	2,000	—	Proof	22.50
	1968	2.194	.65	1.00	2.00
	1968	5,000	—	Proof	20.00
	1969	1.871	.65	1.00	2.00
	1969	3,000	—	Proof	75.00
	1970	.560	.65	1.25	2.50
	1971	.900	.65	1.00	2.00
	1972	.458	.75	2.00	4.00
	1972	749 pcs.	—	Proof	150.00
	1973	.341	.75	1.50	3.00
	1973	1,000	—	Proof	50.00
	1974	.352	.75	1.50	3.00
	1974	1,500	—	Proof	40.00
	1975	.430	.75	1.50	3.00
	1975	3,000	—	Proof	20.00
	1976	.150	.75	2.00	4.00
	1976 *sm*	3,500	—	Proof	15.00
	1977	.132	.75	3.00	6.00
	1977 *sm*	3,500	—	Proof	15.00
	1978	.037	1.00	6.00	12.00
	1978 *sm*	4,000	—	Proof	15.00
	1979	.168	—	2.00	4.00
	1979 *sm*	3,500	—	Proof	15.00
	1980	.166	—	2.00	4.00
	1980 *sm*	.014	—	Proof	10.00
	1981	1.230	—	1.00	2.00
	1982	1.080	—	1.00	2.00
	1983	.101	—	1.25	3.00
	1984	.170	—	1.00	2.00
	1985	.148	—	.65	1.25

18.0500 g, .925 SILVER, .5368 oz ASW

KM#	Date	Mintage	VF	XF	Unc
6a	1975	3,000	—	Proof	50.00
	1976 *sm*	.010	—	Proof	17.50
	1977 *sm*	.010	—	Proof	17.50
	1978 *sm*	.010	—	Proof	20.00
	1979 *sm*	8,000	—	Proof	20.00
	1980 *sm*	.015	—	Proof	17.50
	1981 *sm*	.030	—	Proof	12.50
	1982 *sm*	.020	—	Proof	15.00
	1983 *sm*	.015	—	Proof	12.50
	1984 *sm*	.015	—	Proof	12.50

COPPER-NICKEL
Periwinkle

KM#	Date	Mintage	VF	XF	Unc
54	1985	.120	—	—	1.75
	1986	.120	—	—	1.75

9.9700 g, .925 SILVER, .2965 oz ASW

KM#	Date	Mintage	VF	XF	Unc
54a	1985 *sm*	.020	—	Proof	15.00
	1986 *sm*	.015	—	Proof	15.00

ALUMINUM-BRONZE

KM#	Date	Mintage	VF	XF	Unc
54b	1987	16.544	—	.75	1.50
	1988	64.560	—	.75	1.50
	1989	—	—	.75	1.50
	1990	—	—	.75	1.50

8.4273 g, .925 SILVER, .2507 oz ASW

KM#	Date	Mintage	VF	XF	Unc
54c	1987	.015	—	Proof	15.00
	1988	.015	—	Proof	15.00
	1989	—	—	Proof	15.00

ALUMINUM-BRONZE
Similar to KM#54 but motto ribbon on arms curves down at center.

KM#	Date	Mintage	VF	XF	Unc
103	1992	—	—	—	1.50

.925 SILVER

KM#	Date	Mintage	VF	XF	Unc
103a	1992	—	—	Proof	15.00

5 DOLLARS

25.0000 g, .500 SILVER, .4019 oz ASW
7th South East Asia Peninsular Games

KM#	Date	Mintage	VF	XF	Unc
10	1973	.250	—	—	10.00
	1973	5,000	—	Proof	60.00

NOTE: 10,000 PNC were issued. Current retail is $20.00.

COPPER-NICKEL
Changi Airport

KM#	Date	Mintage	VF	XF	Unc
19	1981	.220	—	3.50	6.00

18.0500 g, .925 SILVER, .5368 oz ASW

KM#	Date	Mintage	VF	XF	Unc
19a	1981 *sm*	.020	—	Proof	22.50

COPPER-NICKEL
Benjamin Shears Bridge

KM#	Date	Mintage	VF	XF	Unc
22	1982	.260	—	3.50	6.00

18.0500 g, .925 SILVER, .5368 oz ASW

KM#	Date	Mintage	VF	XF	Unc
22a	1982 *sm*	.020	—	Proof	22.50

COPPER-NICKEL
12th SEA Games

KM#	Date	Mintage	VF	XF	Unc
25	1983	.270	—	3.50	6.00

20.0000 g, .925 SILVER, .5949 oz ASW

KM#	Date	Mintage	VF	XF	Unc
25a	1983 *sm*	.020	—	Proof	25.00

COPPER-NICKEL
25 Years of Nation Building

KM#	Date	Mintage	VF	XF	Unc
32	1984	.270	—	3.50	6.00

20.0000 g, .925 SILVER, .5949 oz ASW

KM#	Date	Mintage	VF	XF	Unc
32a	1984 *sm*	.020	—	Proof	20.00

COPPER-NICKEL

25 Years of Public Housing
Obv: Coat of arms & legend.

M#	Date	Mintage	VF	XF	Unc
8	1985	.117	—	3.50	6.00
	20.0000 g, .925 SILVER, .5949 oz ASW				
8a	1985 *sm*	.020	—	Proof	20.00

COPPER-NICKEL
100th Anniversary of National Museum

8	1987	.070	—	—	6.00
	20.0000 g, .925 SILVER, .5949 oz ASW				
8a	1987 *sm*	.025	—	Proof	17.50

COPPER-NICKEL
100th Anniversary of Singapore Fire Brigade

0	1988	.050	—	—	8.00
	20.0000 g, .925 SILVER, .5949 oz ASW				
0a	1988 *sm*	.025	—	Proof	20.00

COPPER-NICKEL
Rapid Transit System

4	1989	.060	—	—	8.00
	20.0000 g, .925 SILVER, .5949 oz ASW				
4a	1989	.030	—	Proof	20.00

Save the Children Fund

7	1989	*.020	—	Proof	50.00

COPPER-ALUMINUM-NICKEL
25th Anniversary of Independence

KM#	Date	Mintage	VF	XF	Unc
94	1990	1.000	—	—	8.00

COPPER-NICKEL
Civil Defense

86	1991	.055	—	—	8.00
	1991	5,000	—	Proof	16.50
	20.0000 g, .925 SILVER, .4949 oz ASW				
86a	1991	.015	—	Proof	25.00

ALUMINUM-BRONZE CENTER, COPPER-NICKEL RING
Vanda Miss Joaquim

104	1992	—	—	—	6.00
	.925 SILVER				
104a	1992	—	—	Proof	25.00

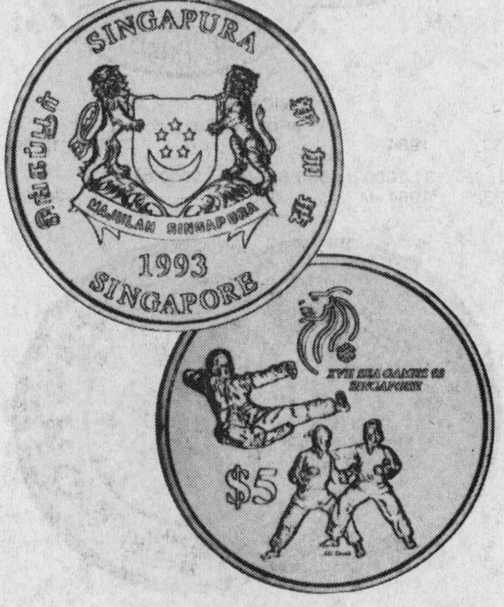

COPPER-NICKEL
XVII Sea Games - Martial Arts

115	1993	.023	—	—	8.00
	1993	2,000	—	Proof	17.50
	20.0000 g, .9255 SILVER, .5949 oz ASW				
115a	1993	.012	—	Proof	30.00

10 DOLLARS

31.1000 g, .900 SILVER, .8999 oz ASW
Obv. leg: SINGAPORE inverted.

KM#	Date	Mintage	VF	XF	Unc
9.1	1972	.080	—	—	20.00
	1972	3,000	—	Proof	85.00

9.2	1973	.080	—	—	17.50
	1973	5,000	—	Proof	60.00
	31.1000 g, .500 SILVER, .5000 oz ASW				
9.2a	1974	.100	—	—	10.00
	1974	6,000	—	Proof	40.00

10th Anniversary of Independence

11	1975	.200	—	—	6.50
	1975	.010	—	Proof	25.00

KM#	Date	Mintage	VF	XF	Unc
15	1976	.150	—	—	6.50
	1976 *sm*	.010	—	Proof	25.00
	1977	.150	—	—	6.50
	1977 *sm*	.010	—	Proof	25.00

ASEAN 10th Anniversary

KM#	Date	Mintage	VF	XF	Unc
16	1977	.200	—	—	6.50
	1977 *sm*	.010	—	Proof	30.00

Communications Satellites

KM#	Date	Mintage	VF	XF	Unc
17.1	1978	.167	—	—	6.00
	1978 *sm*	.010	—	Proof	30.00
	1979	.168	—	—	6.00
	1979 *sm*	9,000	—	Proof	30.00
	1980 *sm*	.014	—	Proof	17.50

NICKEL

KM#	Date	Mintage	VF	XF	Unc
17.1a	1980	.120	—	7.50	8.50

Obv: Raised stars and moon in arms.

KM#	Date	Mintage	VF	XF	Unc
17.2	1980 *sm*	.015	—	Proof	15.00

Year of the Rooster

KM#	Date	Mintage	VF	XF	Unc
20	1981	.180	—	12.00	20.00

31.1000 g, .500 SILVER, .5000 oz ASW

KM#	Date	Mintage	VF	XF	Unc
20a	1981 *sm*	.020	—	Proof	70.00

NICKEL
Year of the Dog

KM#	Date	Mintage	VF	XF	Unc
23	1982	.210	—	9.00	16.50

31.1000 g, .500 SILVER, .5000 oz ASW

KM#	Date	Mintage	VF	XF	Unc
23a	1982 *sm*	.020	—	Proof	45.00

NICKEL
Year of the Pig

KM#	Date	Mintage	VF	XF	Unc
26	1983	.307	—	7.50	12.50

31.1000 g, .500 SILVER, .5000 oz ASW

KM#	Date	Mintage	VF	XF	Unc
26a	1983 *sm*	.020	—	Proof	35.00

NICKEL
Year of the Rat

KM#	Date	Mintage	VF	XF	Unc
33	1984	.300	—	7.50	12.50

31.1000 g, .500 SILVER, .5000 oz ASW

KM#	Date	Mintage	VF	XF	Unc
33a	1984 *sm*	.020	—	Proof	35.00

NICKEL
Year of the Ox

KM#	Date	Mintage	VF	XF	Unc
44	1985	.307	—	7.50	12.50

31.1000 g, .500 SILVER, .5000 oz ASW

KM#	Date	Mintage	VF	XF	Unc
44a	1985 *sm*	.020	—	Proof	55.00

NICKEL
Year of the Tiger

KM#	Date	Mintage	VF	XF	Unc
59	1986	.300	—	8.00	16.00

31.1000 g, .500 SILVER, .5000 oz ASW

KM#	Date	Mintage	VF	XF	Unc
59a	1986	.020	—	Proof	45.00

NICKEL
Year of the Rabbit

KM#	Date	Mintage	VF	XF	Unc
66	1987	.300	—	7.50	12.50

31.1000 g, .500 SILVER, .5000 oz ASW

KM#	Date	Mintage	VF	XF	Unc
66a	1987 *sm*	.025	—	Proof	20.00

COPPER-NICKEL
Association of South East Asian Nations
Obv: Coat of arms above 1967-1987.
Rev: ASEAN logo within legend, value below.

KM#	Date	Mintage	VF	XF	Unc
67	1987	.080	—	6.50	8.50

31.1030 g, .500 SILVER, .5000 oz ASW

KM#	Date	Mintage	VF	XF	Unc
67a	1987 *sm*	.025	—	Proof	20.00

NICKEL
Year of the Dragon

KM#	Date	Mintage	VF	XF	Unc
69	1988	.300	—	12.00	17.50

31.1030 g, .500 SILVER, .5000 oz ASW

KM#	Date	Mintage	VF	XF	Unc
69a	1988	.025	—	Proof	35.00

NICKEL
Year of the Snake

KM#	Date	Mintage	VF	XF	Unc
71	1989	.250	—	8.00	16.00

31.1030 g, .925 SILVER, .9250 oz ASW

KM#	Date	Mintage	VF	XF	Unc
71a	1989	.025	—	Proof	35.00

NICKEL
Year of the Horse

KM#	Date	Mintage	VF	XF	Unc
'5	1990	.330	—	—	15.00

31.1030 g, .925 SILVER, .9250 oz ASW

'5a	1990 *sm*	.030	—	Proof	30.00

25th Anniversary of Independence
Similar to 5 Dollars, KM#94.

5	1990	.050	—	Proof	25.00

NICKEL
Year of the Goat

4	1991 *sm*	.300	—	—	15.00

31.1030 g, .925 SILVER, .9250 oz ASW

4a	1991 *sm*	.030	—	Proof	30.00

NICKEL
Year of the Monkey
Similar to 500 Dollars, KM#93.

2	1992	.300	—	—	15.00

31.1030 g, .925 SILVER, .9250 oz ASW

2a	1992	*.030	—	Proof	30.00

.925 SILVER, 1.8500 oz ASW
25th Anniversary - Board of Commissioners of Currency

05	1992	*.015	—	Proof	65.00

COPPER-NICKEL
Year of the Rooster
Obv: Similar to 250 Dollars, KM#114.

13	1993	.209	—	P/L	17.50

62.2070 g, .999 SILVER, 2.0000 oz ASW

13a	1993	.040	—	Proof	45.00

50 DOLLARS

31.1000 g, .500 SILVER, .5000 oz ASW
International Financial Center

KM#	Date	Mintage	VF	XF	Unc
18	1980	.025	—	—	35.00
	1980 *sm*	.015	—	Proof	45.00
	1981	.050	—	—	32.50
	1981 *sm*	.020	—	Proof	40.00

10.0000 g, .917 GOLD, .2945 oz AGW
Save the Children Fund

78	1989	*3,000	—	Proof	250.00

100 DOLLARS

6.9119 g, .900 GOLD, .2000 oz AGW
10th Anniversary of Independence

12	1975	.100	—	—	120.00
	1975	3,000	—	Proof	200.00

31.1035 g, .999 GOLD, 1.0000 oz AGW
25th Anniversary - Board of Commissioners of Currency
Obv: Coat of arms.
Rev: Logo, legend and denomination.

106	1992	*1,000	—	Proof	615.00

150 DOLLARS

150th Anniversary of Founding of Singapore
24.8830 g, .920 GOLD, .7360 oz AGW

7	1969	.198	—	—	400.00
	1969	500 pcs.	—	Proof	2000.

200 DOLLARS

31.1035 g, .999 PLATINUM, 1.0000 oz APW
25th Anniversary - Board of Commissioners of Currency
Obv: Coat of arms.
Rev: Logo, legend and denomination.

107	1992	500 pcs.	—	Proof	800.00

250 DOLLARS

17.2797 g, .900 GOLD, .5000 oz AGW
10th Anniversary of Independence

KM#	Date	Mintage	VF	XF	Unc
13	1975	.030	—	—	250.00
	1975	2,000	—	Proof	500.00

31.1040 g, .999 GOLD, 1.0000 oz AGW
25th Anniversary of Independence

96	1990	6,000	—	Proof	675.00

31.1035 g, .999 GOLD, 1.0000 oz AGW
Year of the Rooster

114	1993	8,900	—	Proof	600.00

500 DOLLARS

34.5594 g, .900 GOLD, 1.0000 oz AGW
10th Anniversary of Independence

14	1975	.030	—	—	550.00
	1975	2,000	—	Proof	1000.

16.9650 g, .917 GOLD, .5000 oz AGW
Year of the Rooster

21	1981 *sm*	.012	—	Proof	550.00

Year of the Dog

24	1982 *sm*	5,500	—	Proof	600.00

Year of the Pig

KM#	Date	Mintage	VF	XF	Unc
27	1983 *sm*	5,000	—	Proof	600.00

Year of the Rat

KM#	Date	Mintage	VF	XF	Unc
34	1984 *sm*	4,000	—	Proof	650.00

Year of the Ox

KM#	Date	Mintage	VF	XF	Unc
45	1985 *sm*	4,000	—	Proof	700.00

Year of the Tiger

KM#	Date	Mintage	VF	XF	Unc
60	1986 *sm*	3,000	—	Proof	900.00

Year of the Rabbit

KM#	Date	Mintage	VF	XF	Unc
64 (67)	1987 *sm*	2,400	—	Proof	1250.

Year of the Dragon

KM#	Date	Mintage	VF	XF	Unc
73	1988 *sm*	4,000	—	Proof	800.00

Year of the Snake

KM#	Date	Mintage	VF	XF	Unc
72	1989 *sm*	2,500	—	Proof	1100.

Year of the Horse

KM#	Date	Mintage	VF	XF	Unc
76	1990 *sm*	5,000	—	Proof	600.00

31.1040 g, .999 PLATINUM, 1.0000 oz APW
25th Anniversary of Independence

KM#	Date	Mintage	VF	XF	Unc
97	1990	1,000	—	Proof	1000.

16.9650 g, .917 GOLD, .5000 oz AGW
Year of the Goat

KM#	Date	Mintage	VF	XF	Unc
85	1991 *sm*	5,000	—	Proof	500.00

Year of the Monkey

KM#	Date	Mintage	VF	XF	Unc
93	1992 *sm*	5,000	—	Proof	500.00

GOLD BULLION ISSUES

1 DOLLAR

(1/10 Ounce)

3.1100 g, .999 GOLD, .1000 oz AGW
Rev: Carp and lotus flower.

KM#	Date	Mintage	VF	XF	Unc
28	1983	.020	—		*BV + 15%*
	1984	.010	—		*BV + 15%*

2 DOLLARS

(1/4 Ounce)

7.7750 g, .999 GOLD, .2500 oz AGW
Rev: Qilin.

KM#	Date	Mintage	VF	XF	Unc
29	1983	.020	—		*BV + 12%*
	1984	.010	—		*BV + 12%*

5 DOLLARS

(1/2 Ounce)

15.5500 g, .999 GOLD, .5000 oz AGW
Rev: Phoenix.

KM#	Date	Mintage	VF	XF	Unc
30	1983	.010	—		*BV + 9%*
	1984	.010	—		*BV + 9%*

(1/20 Ounce)

1.5550 g, .999 GOLD, .0500 oz AGW

KM#	Date	Mintage	VF	XF	Unc
79	1990	8,000	—	—	45.00
	1990	*2,000	—	Proof	90.00

Rev: Year of the Goat privy mark.

KM#	Date	Mintage	VF	XF	Unc
87	1991	8,000	—	—	45.00
	1991	2,500	—	Proof	90.00

Rev: Similar to KM#87 but w/Year of the Rooster privy mark.

KM#	Date	Mintage	VF	XF	Unc
108	1992	—	—	—	45.00
	1992	—	—	Proof	90.00
	1993	—	—	—	45.00
	1993	*1,500	—	Proof	90.00

10 DOLLARS

(1 Ounce)

31.1000 g, .999 GOLD, 1.0000 oz AGW
Rev: Dragon.

KM#	Date	Mintage	VF	XF	Unc
31	1983	.010	—		*BV + 7%*
	1984	.010	—	Proof	*BV + 7%*

(1/10 Ounce)

3.1103 g, .999 GOLD, .1000 oz AGW

KM#	Date	Mintage	VF	XF	Unc
80	1990	*5,000	—	—	75.00
	1990	*2,000	—	Proof	140.00

Rev: Year of the Goat privy mark.

KM#	Date	Mintage	VF	XF	Unc
88	1991	5,500	—	—	75.00
	1991	2,500	—	Proof	140.00

Rev: Similar to KM#88 but w/Year of the Rooster privy mark.

KM#	Date	Mintage	VF	XF	Unc
109	1992	—	—	—	75.00
	1992	—	—	Proof	140.00
	1993	—	—	—	75.00
	1993	*1,500	—	Proof	140.00

25 DOLLARS

(1/4 Ounce)

7.7757 g, .999 GOLD, .2500 oz AGW

KM#	Date	Mintage	VF	XF	Unc
1	1990	*5,000	—	—	125.00
	1990	*2,000	—	Proof	220.00

Rev: Year of the Goat privy mark.

KM#	Date	Mintage	VF	XF	Unc
9	1991	5,500	—	—	125.00
	1991	2,500	—	Proof	220.00

Rev: Similar to KM#89 but w/Year of the Rooster privy mark.

KM#	Date	Mintage	VF	XF	Unc
10	1992	—	—	—	125.00
	1992	—	—	Proof	220.00
	1993	—	—	—	125.00
	1993	*1,500	—	Proof	220.00

50 DOLLARS

(1/2 Ounce)

15.5500 g, .999 GOLD, .5000 oz AGW

KM#	Date	Mintage	VF	XF	Unc
2	1990	*5,000	—	—	250.00
	1990	*2,000	—	Proof	400.00

Rev: Year of the Goat privy mark.

KM#	Date	Mintage	VF	XF	Unc
0	1991	5,500	—	—	250.00
	1991	2,500	—	Proof	400.00

Rev: Similar to KM#90 but w/Year of the Rooster privy mark.

KM#	Date	Mintage	VF	XF	Unc
11	1992	—	—	—	250.00
	1992	—	—	Proof	400.00
	1993	—	—	—	250.00
	1993	*1,500	—	Proof	400.00

100 DOLLARS

(1 Ounce)

31.1000 g, .999 GOLD, 1.0000 oz AGW

KM#	Date	Mintage	VF	XF	Unc
3	1990	*5,000	—	—	500.00
	1990	*2,000	—	Proof	650.00

Rev: Year of the Goat privy mark.

KM#	Date	Mintage	VF	XF	Unc
1	1991	.013	—	—	500.00
	1991	2,500	—	Proof	650.00

Rev: Similar to KM#91 but w/Year of the Rooster privy mark.

KM#	Date	Mintage	VF	XF	Unc
12	1992	—	—	—	500.00
	1992	—	—	Proof	650.00
	1993	—	—	—	500.00
	1993	*1,500	—	Proof	650.00

MINT SETS (MS)

KM#	Date	Mintage	Identification	Issue Price	Mkt. Val.
MS1	1967(6)	8,000	KM1-6	1.50	20.00
MS2	1968(6)	16,000	KM1-6	1.50	20.00
MS3	1969(6)	14,000	KM1-6	1.50	25.00
MS4	1970(6)	13,000	KM1-6	1.50	60.00
MS5	1970(6)*	27,000	KM1-6	1.75	60.00
MS7	1972(6)	13,000	KM1-6	3.00	35.00
MS8	1973(6)	15,000	KM1-6	2.00	18.00
MS9	1974(6)	20,000	KM1-6	2.00	15.00
MS10	1975(6)	30,000	KM1-6	*12.00	15.00
MS11	1975(3)	30,000	KM12-14	—	875.00
MS12	1976(6)	35,000	KM1-6	2.00	12.00
MS13	1977(6)	40,000	KM1a,2-6	2.00	12.00
MS14	1978(6)	55,000	KM1a,2-6	—	25.00
MS15	1979(6)	65,000	KM1a,2-6	—	10.00
MS16	1980(6)	70,000	KM1a,2-6	—	8.00
MS17	1981(6)	110,000	KM1a,2-6	5.00	6.50
MS18	1982(6)	160,000	KM1a,2-6	5.00	6.50
MS19	1983(6)	40,000	KM1a,2-6 w/medallion, I.A.P.N.	—	9.00
MS20	1983(6)	150,000	KM1a,2-6	5.00	8.00
MS21	1984(6)	160,000	KM1a,2-6	3.75	7.50
MS22	1985(6)	148,424	KM1a,2-6	—	15.00
MS23	1986(6)	120,000	KM49-54	—	7.00
MS24	1987(6)	120,000	KM49-54	—	7.00
MS25	1988(6)	120,000	KM49-53,54b	—	5.50
MS26	1989(6)	100,000	KM49,50-53,54b	—	5.50
MS27	1990(6)	100,000	KM49b,50-53,54b	—	5.50
MS28	1990(5)	5,000	KM79-83	—	1000.
MS29	1992(7)	*55,000	KM98-104	—	9.00

***NOTE:** Issued only in package of 3 sets plus KM#11, each set in plastic wallet for Expo '70 Osaka Japan.

PROOF SETS (PS)

KM#	Date	Mintage	Identification	Issue Price	Mkt. Val.
PS1	1967(6)	2,000	KM1-6	25.00	60.00
PS2	1968(6)	5,000	KM1-6	25.00	55.00
PS3	1969(6)	3,000	KM1-6	25.00	275.00
PS4	1972(6)	749	KM1-6	25.00	475.00
PS5	1973(6)	1,000	KM1-6	32.00	175.00
PS6	1974(6)	1,500	KM1-6	34.00	130.00
PS7	1975(6)	3,000	KM1-6	35.00	60.00
PS8	1975(3)	2,000	KM12-14	—	2680.
PS9	1976(6)	3,500	KM1-6	37.00	50.00
PS10	1977(6)	3,500	KM1-6	—	50.00
PS11	1978(6)	4,000	KM1-6	—	60.00
PS12	1979(7)	3,500	KM1-6,17.1	—	120.00
PS13	1980(7)	14,000	KM1-6,17.1	64.00	90.00
PS14	1981(6)	30,000	KM1b-2b,3a-6a, .925 Silver	82.00	100.00
PS15	1982(6)	20,000	KM1-5,6a	52.00	50.00
PS16	1983(6)	15,000	KM1-5,6a	52.00	50.00
PS17	1984(6)	15,000	KM1-5,6a	52.00	50.00
PS18	1985(6)	20,000	KM49a-54a	40.00	50.00
PS19	1986(6)	15,000	KM49a-54a	—	48.00
PS20	1987(6)	15,000	KM49a-53a,54c	42.00	48.00
PS22	1988(6)	15,000	KM49a-53a,54c	—	45.00
PS24	1989(6)	15,000	KM49a-53a,54c	—	45.00
PS25	1989(5)	200	KMMB51-55	—	1975.
PS26	1990(6)	15,000	KM49a-53a,54c	—	45.00
PS27	1990(5)	2,000	KM79-83	—	1500.
PS28	1991(5)	2,500	KM87-91	—	1500.
PS29	1991(2)	5,000	KM86,86a	—	40.00
PS30	1992(7)	*15,000	KM98a-104a	—	72.50
PS31	1992(5)	—	KM108-112, ingot	—	1500.
PS32	1992(3)	*200	KM105-107	—	1490.
PS33	1993(5)	*1,500	KM108-112, ingot	—	1500.
PS34	1993(2)	—	KM115,115a	—	50.00

SLOVAKIA

The Republic of Slovakia, formerly the "Slovak Socialist Republic", which was united with the Czech Republic has an area of 18,923 sq. mi. (49,035 sq. km.) and a population of 4.9 million. Capital: Bratislava. Textiles, steel, and wood products are exported.

The Slovak lands were united with the Czechs and the Czechoslovak State came into existence on Oct. 28, 1918 upon the dissolution of AustriaHungary. This territory was broken up for the benefit of Germany, Poland, and Hungary by the Munich agreement signed by the United Kingdom, France, Germany, and Italy on Sept. 29, 1938. In March 1939, the German-influenced Slovak government proclaimed Slovakia independent and Germany incorporated the Czech lands into The Third Reich as the "Protectorate of Bohemia and Moravia". A government-in-exile was set up in London in July 1940. The Soviets and USA forces liberated the area by May, 1945. Communist influence increased steadily while pressure for liberalization culminated in the overthrow of the Stalinist leader Antonin Novotn'y and his associates in 1968. The Communist Party then introduced far reaching reforms which received warnings from Moscow, followed by occcupation by Warsaw Pact forces resulting in stationing of Soviet forces. Mass demonstrations for reform began in Nov. 1989 and the Federal Assembly abolished the Communist Party's sole right to govern. New governments followed on Dec. 3 and Dec. 10. The Movement for Democratic Slovakia was apparent in the June 1992 elections with the Slovak National Council adopting a declaration of sovereignty, later a constitution for an independent Slovakia with the Federal Assembly voting for the dissolution of the Czech and Slovak Federal Republic, to come into effect on Dec. 31, 1992 and both new republics came into being on Jan. 1, 1993.

MONETARY SYSTEM

100 Halierov = 1 Koruna

AUTONOMOUS REPUBLIC

5 HALIEROV

ZINC

KM#	Date	Mintage	Fine	VF	XF	Unc
8	1942	1.000	1.50	2.50	4.50	8.00

10 HALIEROV

BRONZE

KM#	Date	Mintage	Fine	VF	XF	Unc
1	1939	15.000	1.50	2.00	4.00	8.00
	1942	7.000	1.50	2.00	4.00	8.00

20 HALIEROV

BRONZE

KM#	Date	Mintage	Fine	VF	XF	Unc
4	1940	10.972	1.25	2.00	3.00	6.00
	1941	4.028	1.25	2.00	3.00	6.00
	1942	6.474	1.25	3.00	5.00	9.00

ALUMINUM

KM#	Date	Mintage	Fine	VF	XF	Unc
4a	1942	Inc. Ab.	1.00	1.50	2.00	4.50
	1943	15.000	1.00	1.50	2.00	4.50

50 HALIEROV

COPPER-NICKEL

KM#	Date	Mintage	Fine	VF	XF	Unc
5	1940	—	30.00	45.00	60.00	125.00
	1941	8.000	1.00	2.00	3.00	6.00

ALUMINUM

KM#	Date	Mintage	Fine	VF	XF	Unc
5a	1943	4.400	1.00	1.50	2.50	5.00
	1944	2.621	1.25	2.00	4.00	7.00

KORUNA

COPPER-NICKEL

KM#	Date	Mintage	Fine	VF	XF	Unc
6	1940	2.350	.75	1.25	2.25	6.00
	1941	11.650	.50	1.00	2.00	5.00
	1942	6.000	.50	1.00	2.00	5.00
	1944	.884	1.50	2.50	4.50	10.00
	1945	3.321	.75	1.25	2.25	6.00

5 KORUN

NICKEL

KM#	Date	Mintage	Fine	VF	XF	Unc
2	1939	5.101	1.50	2.00	3.50	12.50

Approximately 2,000,000 pieces were melted down by the Czechoslovak National Bank in 1947.

10 KORUN

7.0000 g, .500 SILVER, .1125 oz ASW.
Pribina
Rev: Variety 1 - Cross atop church held by left figure.

KM#	Date	Mintage	Fine	VF	XF	Unc
9.1	1944	1.071	2.00	4.00	5.00	8.00

Rev: Variety 2 - W/o cross.

KM#	Date	Mintage	Fine	VF	XF	Unc
9.2	1944	Inc. Ab.	2.50	5.00	7.00	10.00

20 KORUN

15.0000 g, .500 SILVER, .2411 oz ASW
Dr. Joseph Tiso

KM#	Date	Mintage	Fine	VF	XF	Unc
3	1939	.200	5.00	10.00	15.00	40.00

St. Kyrill and St. Methodius
Rev: Variety 1 - Single bar cross in church at lower right.

KM#	Date	Mintage	Fine	VF	XF	Unc
7.1	1941	2.500	2.00	3.50	5.00	10.00

Rev: Variety 2 - Double bar cross.

KM#	Date	Mintage	Fine	VF	XF	Unc
7.2	1941	Inc. Ab.	4.00	6.50	9.00	15.00

50 KORUN

16.5000 g, .700 SILVER, .3713 oz ASW
5th Anniversary of Independence

KM#	Date	Mintage	Fine	VF	XF	Unc
10	1944	2.000	3.00	5.00	7.50	12.50

REPUBLIC

10 HALERU

ALUMINUM

KM#	Date	Mintage	VF	XF	Unc
17	1993	—	—	—	.30

20 HALERU

ALUMINUM

KM#	Date	Mintage	VF	XF	Unc
18	1993	—	—	—	.40

50 HALERU

ALUMINUM

KM#	Date	Mintage	VF	XF	Unc
15	1993	—	—	—	.50

KORUNA

ALUMINUM - BRONZE

KM#	Date	Mintage	VF	XF	Unc
12	1993	—	—	—	.65

2 KORUNY

NICKEL CLAD STEEL

KM#	Date	Mintage	VF	XF	Unc
13	1993	—	—	—	.75

5 KORUNY

NICKEL CLAD STEEL

KM#	Date	Mintage	VF	XF	Un
14	1993	—	—	—	1.2

10 KORUNY

BRASS

KM#	Date	Mintage	VF	XF	Unc
11	1993	—	—	—	2.5

100 KORUNY

12.9300 g, .700 SILVER, .2910 oz ASW
National Independence

KM#	Date	Mintage	VF	XF	Unc
16	1993	—	—	—	9.0

200 KORUNY

19.9700 g, .750 SILVER, .4816 oz ASW
150th Anniversary of Slovak Language

KM#	Date	Mintage	VF	XF	Unc
19	1993	—	—	—	16.5

Jan Kollar

KM#	Date	Mintage	VF	XF	Unc
20	1993	—	—	—	16.5

SLOVENIA

The Republic of Slovenia is located northwest of Yugoslavia in the valleys of the Danube River. It has an area of 7,819 sq. mi. and a population of *1.9 million. Capital: Ljubljana. Agriculture is the main industry with large amounts of hops and fodder crops grown as well as many varieties of fruit trees. Sheep raising, timber production and the mining of mercury from one of the country's oldest mines are also very important to their economy.

Slovenia was important as a land route between Europe and the eastern Mediterranean region. The Roman Catholic Austro-Hungarian Empire gained control of the area during the 14th century and retained its dominance until World War I. The United Kingdom of the Serbs, Croats and Slovenes was founded in 1918 and consisted of various groups of South Slavs.

In 1929, King Alexander declared his assumption of power temporarily, however he was assassinated in 1934. His son Peter's regent, Prince Paul tried to settle internal problems, however, the Slovenes denounced the agreement he made. He resigned in 1941 and Peter assumed the throne. He was forced to flee when the invaders entered Yugoslavia. Slovenia was divided between Germany and Italy. Even though Yugoslavia attempted to remain neutral, the Nazis occupied the country and were resisted by guerilla armies, most notably Marshal Josif Broz Tito.

Under Marshal Tito, the Constitution of 1946 established 6 constitutent republics which made up Yugoslavia. Each republic was permitted to fly their own flag, use their own language, control their judiciary system under supervision of the Communist Party and handle their local administration through its representative Peoples Assembly.

A legal opposition group, the Slovene League of Social Democrats, was formed in Jan. 1989. In Oct. 1989 the Slovene Assembly voted a constitutional amendment giving it the right secede from Yugoslavia. On July 2, 1990 the Assembly adopted a "declaration of sovereignty" and in Sept. proclaimed its control over the territorial defence force on its soil. A referendum on Dec. 23 resulted in a majority vote for independence, which was formally declared on Dec. 26.

In Feb. 1991 parliament ruled that henceforth Slovenian law took precedence over federal. On June 25 Slovenia declared independence, but agreed to suspend this for 3 months at peace talks sponsored by the EC. Federal troops moved into Slovenia on June 27 to secure Yugoslavia's external borders, but after some fighting finally withdrew by the end of July. The 3-month moratorium agreed at the EC having expired, Slovenia (and Croatia) declared their complete independence of the Yugoslav federation on Oct. 8, 1991.

The Republic of Slovenia declared their independence Currency was introduced on Oct. 12, 1991.

MONETARY SYSTEM

100 Stotinov = 1 Tolar

10 STOTINOV

ALUMINUM
Salamandar - Larval Stage

KM#	Date	Mintage	VF	XF	Unc
7	1992	.500	—	—	.25
	1992	—	—	Proof	1.50
	1993	.500	—	—	.25
	1993	—	—	Proof	1.50

20 STOTINOV

ALUMINUM
Obv: Similar to 10 Stotinov, KM#7. Rev: Owl.

KM#	Date	Mintage	VF	XF	Unc
8	1992	.500	—	—	.25
	1992	—	—	Proof	2.00
	1993	.500	—	—	.25
	1993	—	—	Proof	2.00

50 STOTINOV

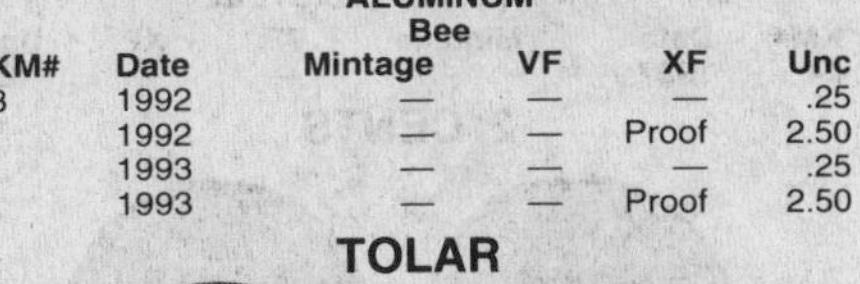

ALUMINUM
Bee

KM#	Date	Mintage	VF	XF	Unc
3	1992	—	—	—	.25
	1992	—	—	Proof	2.50
	1993	—	—	—	.25
	1993	—	—	Proof	2.50

TOLAR

BRASS
3 Fish

KM#	Date	Mintage	VF	XF	Unc
4	1992	—	—	—	.65
	1992	—	—	Proof	3.00
	1993	—	—	—	.65
	1993	—	—	Proof	3.00
	1994	—	—	—	.50

2 TOLARJA

BRASS
Bird in Flight

KM#	Date	Mintage	VF	XF	Unc
5	1992	—	—	—	1.00
	1992	—	—	Proof	3.50
	1993	—	—	—	1.00
	1993	—	—	Proof	3.50
	1994	—	—	—	.75

5 TOLARJEV

BRASS
Head and Horns of Ibex

KM#	Date	Mintage	VF	XF	Unc
6	1992	—	—	—	1.50
	1992	—	—	Proof	4.50
	1993	—	—	—	1.50
	1993	—	—	Proof	4.50
	1994	—	—	—	1.25

Battle of Sisek

KM#	Date	Mintage	VF	XF	Unc
9	1993	.100	—	—	1.75

Operosorum Labacensium Academy

KM#	Date	Mintage	VF	XF	Unc
12	1993	.100	—	—	1.75

500 TOLARJEV

15.0000 g, .925 SILVER, .4461 oz ASW
1st Anniversary of Independence

KM#	Date	Mintage	VF	XF	Unc
1	1991	.050	—	Proof	35.00

Battle of Sisek

KM#	Date	Mintage	VF	XF	Unc
10	1993	*5,000	—	Proof	28.00

Operosorum Labacensium Academy

KM#	Date	Mintage	VF	XF	Unc
13	1993	.010	—	Proof	28.00

5000 TOLARJEV

7.0000 g, .900 GOLD, .2025 oz AGW
1st Anniversary of Independence

KM#	Date	Mintage	VF	XF	Unc
2.1	1991	4,000	—	Proof	250.00

Rev: Bird's beak lower than center of spiral.

KM#	Date	Mintage	VF	XF	Unc
2.2	1991	Inc. Ab.	—	Proof	260.00

Battle of Sisek

KM#	Date	Mintage	VF	XF	Unc
11	1993	*2,000	—	Proof	275.00

Operosorum Labacensium Academy

KM#	Date	Mintage	VF	XF	Unc
14	1993	4,000	—	Proof	250.00

MINT SETS (MS)

KM#	Date	Mintage	Identification	Issue Price	Mkt. Val.
MS1	1992(6)	—	KM3-8	—	8.00
MS2	1992(5)	15,000	KM4-8	—	7.00
MS3	1993(6)	—	KM3-8	—	8.00
MS4	1993(5)	15,000	KM4-8	—	7.00

PROOF SETS (PS)

KM#	Date	Mintage	Identification	Issue Price	Mkt. Val.
PS1	1991(2)	—	KM1, 2.2	—	300.00
PS2	1992(6)	1,000	KM3-8	—	18.50
PS3	1992(5)	1,000	KM4-8	—	16.50
PS4	1993(6)	1,000	KM3-8	—	18.50
PS5	1993(5)	1,000	KM4-8	—	16.50

SOLOMON ISLANDS

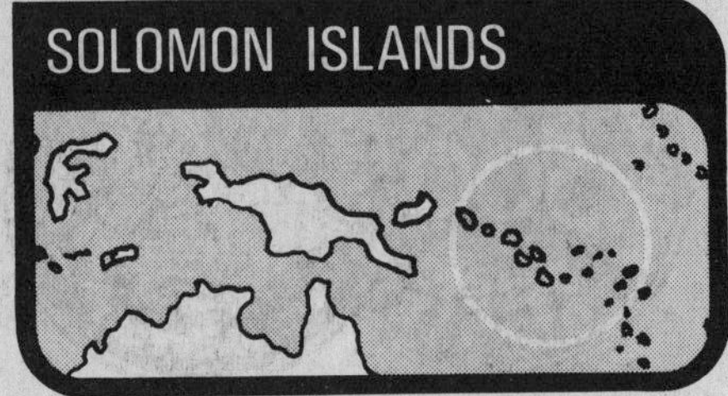

The Solomon Islands, located in the southwest Pacific east of Papua New Guinea, has an area of 10,983 sq. mi. (28,450 sq. km.) and a population of *324,000. Capital: Honiara. The most important islands of the Solomon chain are Guadalcanal (scene of some of the fiercest fighting of World War II), Malaitia, New Georgia, Florida, Vella Lavella, Choiseul, Rendova, San Cristobal, the Lord Howe group, the Santa Cruz islands, and the Duff group. Copra is the only important cash crop but it is hoped that timber will become an economic factor.

The Solomon Islands were discovered by Spanish navigator Alvaro de Mendana in 1567, and in 1569 he made an unsuccessful attempt to colonize them. European knowledge of the group would not be completed until the end of the 18th century. Germany declared a protectorate over the northern Solomons in 1885. The British protectorate over the southern Solomons was established in 1893. In 1899 Germany transferred its claim to all Solomon Islands except Buka and Bougainville to Great Britain in exchange for recognition of German claims in Western Samoa. Australia occupied the two German islands in 1914, and administered them after 1920.

The Japanese invaded the Solomons during 1942-43, but were driven out by an American counteroffensive after a series of bloody clashes.

Following World War II, the islands returned to the status of a British protectorate. In 1976 the protectorate was abolished, and the Solomons became a self-governing dependency. Full independence was achieved on July 7, 1978. Solomon Islands is a member of the Commonwealth of Nations. The Queen of England is Chief of State.

RULERS

British

MINT MARKS

FM - Franklin Mint, U.S.A.*

NOTE: From 1977 the Franklin Mint has produced coinage in up to 3 different qualities. Qualities of issue are designated in ( ) after each date and are defined as follows:

(M) MATTE - Normal circulation strike or a dull finish produced by sandblasting special uncirculated (polish finish) or proof quality dies.

(U) - SPECIAL UNCIRCULATED - Polished or proof-like in appearance without any frosted features.

(P) PROOF - The highest quality obtainable having mirror-like fields and frosted features.

MONETARY SYSTEM

100 Cents = 1 Dollar

CENT

BRONZE
F.A.O. Issue - Food Bowl

KM#	Date	Mintage	VF	XF	Unc
1	1977	1.828	—	.10	.20
	1977FM(M)	6,000	—	—	.50
	1977FM(U)	—	—	—	2.00
	1977FM(P)	.014	—	Proof	1.00
	1978FM(M)	6,000	—	—	.50
	1978FM(U)	544 pcs.	—	—	2.00
	1978FM(P)	5,122	—	Proof	1.00
	1979FM(M)	6,000	—	—	.50
	1979FM(U)	677 pcs.	—	—	2.00
	1979FM(P)	2,845	—	Proof	1.50
	1980FM(M)	6,000	—	—	.50
	1980FM(U)	624 pcs.	—	—	2.00
	1980FM(P)	1,031	—	Proof	1.50
	1981	—	—	—	.50
	1981FM(M)	6,000	—	—	.50
	1981FM(U)	212 pcs.	—	—	2.00
	1981FM(P)	448 pcs.	—	Proof	1.50
	1982FM(U)	—	—	—	2.00
	1982FM(P)	—	—	Proof	1.50
	1983FM(M)	—	—	—	.50
	1983FM(U)	200 pcs.	—	—	3.00
	1983FM(P)	—	—	Proof	1.50

BRONZE PLATED STEEL

KM#	Date	Mintage	VF	XF	Unc
1a	1985	—	—	—	.20

BRONZE PLATED STEEL

KM#	Date	Mintage	VF	XF	Unc
24	1987	—	—	—	.25

2 CENTS

BRONZE
Eagle Spirit of Malaita

KM#	Date	Mintage	VF	XF	Unc
2	1977	2.400	—	.10	.25
	1977FM(M)	6,000	—	—	.75
	1977FM(U)	—	—	—	3.00
	1977FM(P)	.014	—	Proof	1.50
	1978FM(M)	6,000	—	—	.75
	1978FM(U)	544 pcs.	—	—	3.00
	1978FM(P)	5,122	—	Proof	1.50
	1979FM(M)	6,000	—	—	.75
	1979FM(U)	677 pcs.	—	—	3.00
	1979FM(P)	2,845	—	Proof	2.00
	1980FM(M)	6,000	—	—	.75
	1980FM(U)	624 pcs.	—	—	3.00
	1980FM(P)	1,031	—	Proof	2.00
	1981FM(M)	6,000	—	—	.75
	1981FM(U)	212 pcs.	—	—	3.00
	1981FM(P)	448 pcs.	—	Proof	2.00
	1982FM(U)	—	—	—	3.00
	1982FM(P)	—	—	Proof	2.00
	1983FM(M)	—	—	—	.75
	1983FM(U)	200 pcs.	—	—	3.00
	1983FM(P)	—	—	Proof	2.00

BRONZE PLATED STEEL

KM#	Date	Mintage	VF	XF	Unc
2a	1985	—	—	—	.25

BRONZE PLATED STEEL
Obv: Similar to 1 Cent, KM#24.

KM#	Date	Mintage	VF	XF	Unc
25	1987	—	—	—	.25

5 CENTS

COPPER-NICKEL
Santa Ysabel - Native Mask

KM#	Date	Mintage	VF	XF	Unc
3	1977	1.200	.10	.20	.40
	1977FM(U)	—	—	—	3.00
	1977FM(M)	6,000	—	—	1.50
	1977FM(P)	.014	—	Proof	2.00
	1978FM(M)	6,000	—	—	1.50
	1978FM(U)	544 pcs.	—	—	3.00
	1978FM(P)	5,122	—	Proof	2.00
	1979FM(M)	6,000	—	—	1.50
	1979FM(U)	677 pcs.	—	—	3.00
	1979FM(P)	2,845	—	Proof	2.50
	1980FM(M)	6,000	—	—	1.50
	1980FM(U)	624 pcs.	—	—	3.00
	1980FM(P)	1,031	—	Proof	2.50
	1981	—	—	—	—
	1981FM(M)	6,000	—	—	1.50
	1981FM(U)	212 pcs.	—	—	3.00
	1981FM(P)	448 pcs.	—	Proof	2.50
	1982FM(U)	—	—	—	3.00
	1982FM(P)	—	—	Proof	2.50
	1983FM(M)	—	—	—	1.50
	1983FM(U)	200 pcs.	—	—	4.00
	1983FM(P)	—	—	Proof	2.50
	1985	—	—	—	.30

Obv: Similar to 1 Cent, KM#24.

KM#	Date	Mintage	VF	XF	Unc
26	1988	—	—	—	.30

10 CENTS

COPPER-NICKEL
Ngorieru - Sea Spirit

KM#	Date	Mintage	VF	XF	Unc
4	1977	3.600	.15	.25	.50
	1977FM(M)	6,000	—	—	2.00
	1977FM(U)	—	—	—	5.00
	1977FM(P)	.014	—	Proof	3.00
	1978FM(M)	6,000	—	—	2.00
	1978FM(U)	544 pcs.	—	—	5.00
	1978FM(P)	5,122	—	Proof	3.00
	1979FM(M)	6,000	—	—	2.00
	1979FM(U)	677 pcs.	—	—	5.00
	1979FM(P)	2,845	—	Proof	4.00
	1980FM(M)	6,000	—	—	2.00
	1980FM(U)	624 pcs.	—	—	5.00

KM#	Date	Mintage	VF	XF	Unc
4	1980FM(P)	1,031	—	Proof	4.00
	1981FM(M)	6,000	—	—	2.00
	1981FM(U)	212 pcs.	—	—	5.00
	1981FM(P)	448 pcs.	—	Proof	4.00
	1982FM(U)	—	—	—	5.00
	1982FM(P)	—	—	Proof	4.00
	1983FM(M)	—	—	—	2.00
	1983FM(U)	200 pcs.	—	—	6.00
	1983FM(P)	—	—	Proof	4.00

KM#	Date	Mintage	VF	XF	Unc
27	1988	—	—	—	.50

NICKEL CLAD STEEL

KM#	Date	Mintage	VF	XF	Unc
27a	1988	—	—	—	.50
	1990	—	—	—	.50

20 CENTS

COPPER-NICKEL
Malaita Pendant Design

KM#	Date	Mintage	VF	XF	Unc
5	1977	3.000	.20	.35	.80
	1977FM(M)	5,000	—	—	3.00
	1977FM(P)	.014	—	Proof	4.00
	1978	.293	.25	.50	1.00
	1978FM(M)	5,000	—	—	3.00
	1978FM(U)	544 pcs.	—	—	6.00
	1978FM(P)	5,122	—	Proof	4.00
	1979FM(M)	5,000	—	—	3.00
	1979FM(U)	677 pcs.	—	—	6.00
	1979FM(P)	2,845	—	Proof	4.00
	1980FM(M)	5,000	—	—	3.00
	1980FM(U)	624 pcs.	—	—	6.00
	1980FM(P)	1,031	—	Proof	4.00
	1981FM(M)	5,000	—	—	3.00
	1981FM(U)	212 pcs.	—	—	6.00
	1981FM(P)	448 pcs.	—	Proof	4.00
	1982FM(U)	—	—	—	6.00
	1982FM(P)	—	—	Proof	4.00
	1983FM(M)	—	—	—	3.00
	1983FM(U)	200 pcs.	—	—	7.00
	1983FM(P)	—	—	Proof	4.00

NICKEL CLAD STEEL

KM#	Date	Mintage	VF	XF	Unc
28	1989	—	—	—	.75

50 CENTS

COPPER-NICKEL
10th Anniversary of Independence

KM#	Date	Mintage	VF	XF	Unc
23	1988	—	—	—	2.5

Circulation Type

KM#	Date	Mintage	VF	XF	Unc
29	1990	—	—	—	2.50

DOLLAR

COPPER-NICKEL
Nusu-Nusu Head - Sea Spirit

KM#	Date	Mintage	VF	XF	Unc
6	1977	1.500	1.00	1.50	2.50
	1977FM(M)	3,000	—	—	5.00
	1977FM(P)	.014	—	Proof	6.00
	1978FM(M)	3,000	—	—	5.00
	1978FM(U)	544 pcs.	—	—	10.00
	1978FM(P)	5,122	—	Proof	6.00
	1979FM(M)	3,000	—	—	5.00
	1979FM(U)	677 pcs.	—	—	10.00
	1979FM(P)	2,845	—	Proof	7.00
	1980FM(M)	3,000	—	—	5.00
	1980FM(U)	624 pcs.	—	—	10.00
	1980FM(P)	1,031	—	Proof	8.00
	1981FM(M)	3,000	—	—	5.00
	1981FM(U)	212 pcs.	—	—	10.00
	1981FM(P)	448 pcs.	—	Proof	8.00
	1982FM(U)	—	—	—	10.00
	1982FM(P)	—	—	Proof	8.00
	1983FM(M)	—	—	—	5.00
	1983FM(U)	200 pcs.	—	—	12.00
	1983FM(P)	—	—	Proof	8.00

1984 Olympics - Runners

KM#	Date	Mintage	VF	XF	Unc
19	1984	5,000	—	—	5.00

50th Anniversary of Pearl Harbor

KM#	Date	Mintage	VF	XF	Unc
30	1991	—	—	—	7.50

28.2800 g, .925 SILVER, .8411 oz ASW

KM#	Date	Mintage	VF	XF	Unc
30a	1991	*.025	—	Proof	60.00

COPPER-NICKEL
50th Anniversary of Battle of the Coral Sea

KM#	Date	Mintage	VF	XF	Unc
35	1992	—	—	—	7.00

28.2800 g, .925 SILVER, .8411 oz ASW

KM#	Date	Mintage	VF	XF	Unc
35a	1992	*.025	—	Proof	45.00

COPPER-NICKEL
50th Anniversary of Battle of Guadalcanal
Rev: Marines landing on beach.

KM#	Date	Mintage	VF	XF	Unc
41	1992	—	—	—	6.50

28.2800 g, .925 SILVER, .8411 oz ASW

KM#	Date	Mintage	VF	XF	Unc
41a	1992	*.025	—	Proof	45.00

5 DOLLARS

28.2800 g, .925 SILVER, .8411 oz ASW
Bokolo - Fossilized Clam Shell

KM#	Date	Mintage	VF	XF	Unc
7	1977FM(U)	200 pcs.	—	—	65.00
	1977FM(P)	.015	—	Proof	12.50
	1978FM(P)	5,148	—	Proof	15.00
	1979FM(P)	2,845	—	Proof	20.00
	1980FM(P)	1,031	—	Proof	25.00
	1981FM(P)	448 pcs.	—	Proof	35.00
	1983FM(P)	339 pcs.	—	Proof	35.00

COPPER-NICKEL

KM#	Date	Mintage	VF	XF	Unc
7a	1978FM(M)	200 pcs.	—	—	40.00
	1978FM(U)	544 pcs.	—	—	18.00
	1979FM(M)	200 pcs.	—	—	40.00
	1979FM(U)	677 pcs.	—	—	18.00
	1980FM(M)	200 pcs.	—	—	40.00
	1980FM(U)	624 pcs.	—	—	18.00
	1981FM(M)	200 pcs.	—	—	40.00
	1981FM(U)	212 pcs.	—	—	35.00
	1983FM(U)	202 pcs.	—	—	35.00

28.2800 g, .925 SILVER, .8411 oz ASW
Coronation Jubilee
Obv: Similar to 20 Cents, KM#5.

KM#	Date	Mintage	VF	XF	Unc
8	1978FM(P)	8,886	—	Proof	16.50

COPPER-NICKEL
Battle of Guadalcanal
Obv: Similar to 20 Cents, KM#5.

KM#	Date	Mintage	VF	XF	Unc
13	1982FM(U)	—	—	—	25.00

28.2800 g, .925 SILVER, .8411 oz ASW

KM#	Date	Mintage	VF	XF	Unc
13a	1982FM(P)	1,368	—	Proof	45.00

30.2800 g, .500 SILVER, .4868 oz ASW
30th Anniversary of Coronation

KM#	Date	Mintage	VF	XF	Unc
15	1983FM(P)	2,944	—	Proof	25.00

28.2800 g, .925 SILVER, .8411 oz ASW
International Year of the Child

KM#	Date	Mintage	VF	XF	Unc
16	1983	5,775	—	Proof	25.00

28.8800 g, .925 SILVER, .8589 oz ASW
Decade For Women

KM#	Date	Mintage	VF	XF	Unc
22	1985	1,050	—	Proof	30.00

10 DOLLARS

COPPER-NICKEL
Frigate Bird
Obv: Similar to 20 Cents, KM#5.

KM#	Date	Mintage	VF	XF	Unc
10	1979FM(M)	100 pcs.	—	—	65.00
	1979FM(U)	777 pcs.	—	—	20.00
	1980FM(M)	100 pcs.	—	—	65.00
	1980FM(U)	624 pcs.	—	—	20.00
	1981FM(M)	100 pcs.	—	—	65.00
	1981FM(U)	212 pcs.	—	—	25.00
	1982FM(U)	—	—	—	20.00

42.2700 g, .925 SILVER, 1.2571 oz ASW

KM#	Date	Mintage	VF	XF	Unc
10a	1979FM(P)	4,670	—	Proof	27.50
	1980FM(P)	1,569	—	Proof	30.00
	1981FM(P)	593 pcs.	—	Proof	40.00
	1982FM(P)	579 pcs.	—	Proof	40.00

COPPER-NICKEL
5th Anniversary of Independence

KM#	Date	Mintage	VF	XF	Unc
17	1983FM(U)	202 pcs.	—	—	22.50

40.5000 g, .925 SILVER, 1.2045 oz ASW

KM#	Date	Mintage	VF	XF	Unc
17a	1983FM(P)	425 pcs.	—	Proof	55.00

33.4400 g, .925 SILVER, .9946 oz ASW
1984 Olympics - Runners

KM#	Date	Mintage	VF	XF	Unc
20	1984	2,500	—	Proof	37.50

31.8000 g, .925 SILVER, .9457 oz ASW
Alvardo de Neyra

KM#	Date	Mintage	VF	XF	Unc
47	1991	—	—	Proof	40.00

31.4200 g, .925 SILVER, .9359 oz ASW
1992 Olympics - Runner

KM#	Date	Mintage	VF	XF	Unc
48	1991	—	—	Proof	40.00

3.1300 g, .999 GOLD, .1006 oz AGW
50th Anniversary of Pearl Harbor

KM#	Date	Mintage	VF	XF	Unc
31	1991	*500 pcs.	—	Proof	90.00

50th Anniversary of Battle of the Coral Sea

KM#	Date	Mintage	VF	XF	Unc
36	1992	500 pcs.	—	Proof	90.00

31.4700 g, .925 SILVER, .9359 oz ASW
First Lunar Vehicle

KM#	Date	Mintage	VF	XF	Unc
40	1992	—	—	Proof	40.00

3.1300 g, .999 GOLD, .1006 oz AGW
50th Anniversary of Battle of Guadalcanal

KM#	Date	Mintage	VF	XF	Unc
42	1992	500 pcs.	—	Proof	90.00

31.4700 g, .925 SILVER, .9359 oz ASW
40th Anniversary of Coronation of Queen Elizabeth

KM#	Date	Mintage	VF	XF	Unc
46	1992	—	—	Proof	35.00

28.2800 g, .925 SILVER, .8411 oz ASW
100 Years as British Protectorate

KM#	Date	Mintage	VF	XF	Unc
49	1993	5,000	—	Proof	45.00

25 DOLLARS

7.8100 g, .999 GOLD, .2514 oz AGW
50th Anniversary of Pearl Harbor

KM#	Date	Mintage	VF	XF	Unc
32	1991	*3,000	—	Proof	275.00

50th Anniversary of Battle of the Coral Sea

KM#	Date	Mintage	VF	XF	Unc
37	1992	*3,000	—	Proof	275.00

50th Anniversary Battle of Guadalcanal

KM#	Date	Mintage	VF	XF	Unc
43	1992	*3,000	—	Proof	275.00

50 DOLLARS

15.6000 g, .999 GOLD, .5016 oz AGW
50th Anniversary of Pearl Harbor

KM#	Date	Mintage	VF	XF	Unc
33	1991	*500 pcs.	—	Proof	450.00

50th Anniversary of Battle of the Coral Sea

KM#	Date	Mintage	VF	XF	Unc
38	1992	*500 pcs.	—	Proof	450.00

50th Anniversary of Battle of Guadalcanal

KM#	Date	Mintage	VF	XF	Unc
44	1992	*500 pcs.	—	Proof	450.00

100 DOLLARS

9.3700 g, .900 GOLD, .2711 oz AGW
Attainment of Sovereignty

KM#	Date	Mintage	VF	XF	Unc
9	1978FM(M)	50 pcs.	—	—	275.00
	1978FM(U)	213pcs.	—	—	225.00
	1978FM(P)	3,159	—	Proof	200.00

7.6400 g, .500 GOLD, .1228 oz AGW
Native Art

KM#	Date	Mintage	VF	XF	Unc
11	1980FM(U)	50 pcs.	—	—	200.00
	1980FM(P)	7,500	—	Proof	100.00

Shark

KM#	Date	Mintage	VF	XF	Unc
12	1981FM(P)	675 pcs.	—	Proof	250.00

9.3700 g, .900 GOLD, .2711 oz AGW
Battle of Guadalcanal

KM#	Date	Mintage	VF	XF	Unc
14	1982FM(P)	311 pcs.	—	Proof	350.00

5th Anniversary of Independence

KM#	Date	Mintage	VF	XF	Unc
18	1983FM(P)	268 pcs.	—	Proof	275.00

7.5000 g, .917 GOLD, .2211 oz AGW
1984 Olympics - Weight Lifter

KM#	Date	Mintage	VF	XF	Unc
21	1984	500 pcs.	—	Proof	250.00

31.2100 g, .999 GOLD, 1.0035 oz AGW
50th Anniversary of Pearl Harbor

KM#	Date	Mintage	VF	XF	Unc
34	1991	*500 pcs.	—	Proof	900.00

50th Anniversary of Battle of Coral Sea

KM#	Date	Mintage	VF	XF	Unc
39	1992	*500 pcs.	—	Proof	875.00

50th Anniversary of Battle of Guadalcanal

KM#	Date	Mintage	VF	XF	Unc
45	1992	*500 pcs.	—	Proof	875.00

MINT SETS (MS)

KM#	Date	Mintage	Identification	Issue Price	Mkt. Val.
MS1	1978(7)	544	KM1-6,7a	22.00	35.00
MS2	1979(8)	677	KM1-6,7a,10	31.00	45.00
MS3	1980(8)	624	KM1-6,7a,10	35.00	55.00
MS4	1981(8)	212	KM1-6,7a,10	36.00	60.00
MS5	1982(8)	—	KM1-6,10,13	36.00	60.00
MS6	1983(8)	192	KM1-6,7a,17	36.00	70.00

PROOF SETS (PS)

KM#	Date	Mintage	Identification	Issue Price	Mkt. Val.
PS1	1977(7)	72,748	KM1-7	40.00	20.00
PS2	1978(7)	5,122	KM1-7	45.00	35.00
PS3	1979(8)	2,845	KM1-7,10a	77.00	70.00
PS4	1980(8)	1,031	KM1-7,10a	135.00	80.00
PS5	1981(8)	448	KM1-7,10a	137.00	100.00
PS6	1982(8)	—	KM1-6,10a,13a	87.00	110.00
PS7	1983(8)	334	KM1-7,17a	137.00	90.00
PS8	1991(4)	500	KM31-34	1650.	1700.
PS9	1992(4)	*500	KM42-45	1595.	—

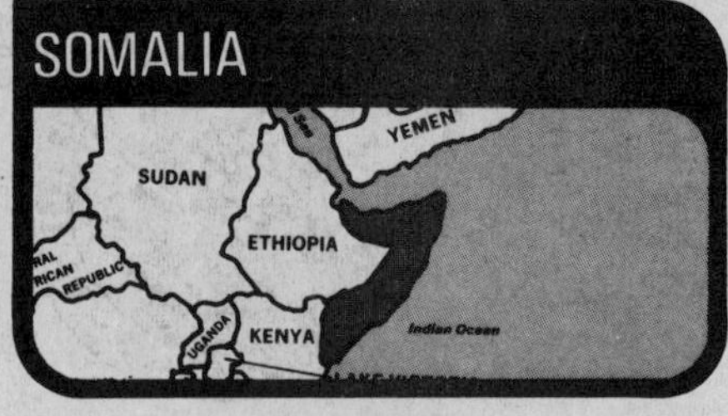

The Somali Democratic Republic, comprising the former British Somaliland Protectorate and Italian Somaliland, is located on the coast of the eastern projection of the African continent commonly referred to as the Horn. It has an area of 246,201 sq. mi. (637,660 sq. km.) and a population of *8.2 million. Capital: Mogadishu. The economy is pastoral and agricultural. Livestock, bananas and hides are exported.

The area of the British Somaliland Protectorate was known to the Egyptains at least 1,500 years B.C., and was occupied by the Arabs and Portuguese before British sea captains obtained trading and anchorage rights in 1827. The land of sandy clay and sporadic rainfall acquired a strategic importance with the opening of the Suez Canal in 1869. After negotiating treaties with the tribes, Britain declared the area a protectorate in 1888. Italy acquired Italian Somaliland in 1895 by purchase from the Sultan of Zanzibar. Britain occupied Italian Somaliland in 1941 and administered it until April 1, 1950, when it was returned to Italy as a U.N. trusteeship. The British Somaliland protectorate became independent on July 1, 1960. Five days later it joined with Italian Somaliland to form the Somali Republic. The country is presently under a revolutionary military regime installed Oct. 21, 1969. In January 1991, President Muhammad Siad Barre was ousted in a popular uprising. In the north, the Somali National Movement proclaimed the independence of the Somaliland Republic on May 18, 1991.

RULERS

Italian, until 1941
British, until 1950

MINT MARKS

Az - Arezzo (Italy)
R - Rome

ITALIAN SOMALILAND

TITLES

الصومال الايطليانية

Al-Somal Al-Italiyaniya(t)
Al-Jumhuriya(t) ad -
Dimiqratiya(t) as-Somaliya(t)
Jumhuriya(t) as - Somal ad - dimiqratiya(t)

MONETARY SYSTEM

100 Bese=1 Rupia

BESA

BRONZE

KM#	Date	Mintage	Fine	VF	XF	Unc
1	1909R	2.000	10.00	17.50	30.00	100.00
	1910R	.500	10.00	17.50	30.00	100.00
	1913R	.200	12.50	20.00	35.00	160.00
	1921R	.500	12.50	20.00	35.00	160.00

2 BESE

BRONZE

KM#	Date	Mintage	Fine	VF	XF	Unc
2	1909R	.500	12.50	20.00	37.50	130.00
	1910R	.250	12.50	20.00	37.50	130.00
	1913R	.300	12.50	20.00	47.50	145.00
	1921R	.600	12.50	20.00	47.50	145.00
	1923R	1.500	12.50	20.00	47.50	145.00
	1924R	Inc. Ab.	12.50	20.00	47.50	145.00

4 BESE

BRONZE

KM#	Date	Mintage	Fine	VF	XF	Unc
3	1909R	.250	18.00	35.00	75.00	150.00
	1910R	.250	18.00	35.00	75.00	150.00
	1913R	.050	25.00	60.00	125.00	200.00
	1921R	.200	18.00	35.00	75.00	150.00
	1923R	1.000	18.00	35.00	75.00	150.00
	1924R	Inc. Ab.	18.00	50.00	100.00	175.00

1/4 RUPIA

2.9160 g, .917 SILVER, .0859 oz ASW

KM#	Date	Mintage	Fine	VF	XF	Unc
4	1910R	.400	12.50	25.00	60.00	120.00
	1913R	.100	30.00	50.00	120.00	225.00

1/2 RUPIA

5.8319 g, .917 SILVER, .1719 oz ASW

KM#	Date	Mintage	Fine	VF	XF	Unc
5	1910R	.400	20.00	37.50	70.00	125.00
	1912R	.100	20.00	40.00	75.00	135.00
	1913R	.100	20.00	40.00	75.00	135.00
	1915R	.050	25.00	50.00	120.00	235.00
	1919R	.200	20.00	37.50	70.00	125.00

RUPIA

11.6638 g, .917 SILVER, .3437 oz ASW

KM#	Date	Mintage	Fine	VF	XF	Unc
6	1910R	.300	25.00	50.00	90.00	150.00
	1912R	.600	25.00	50.00	90.00	150.00
	1913R	.300	25.00	50.00	90.00	150.00
	1914R	.300	25.00	50.00	90.00	150.00
	1915R	.250	25.00	50.00	90.00	150.00
	1919R	.400	25.00	50.00	90.00	150.00
	1920R	1.300	500.00	900.00	2000.	3250.
	1921R	.940	950.00	2150.	3350.	5500.

MONETARY REFORM

100 Centesimi = 1 Lira

5 LIRE

6.0000 g, .835 SILVER, .1611 oz ASW

KM#	Date	Mintage	Fine	VF	XF	Unc
7	1925R	.400	50.00	100.00	175.00	275.00

10 LIRE

12.0000 g, .835 SILVER, .3221 oz ASW

KM#	Date	Mintage	Fine	VF	XF	Un
8	1925R	.100	75.00	150.00	250.00	375.0

SOMALIA

MONETARY SYSTEM

100 Centesimi = 1 Somalo

CENTESIMO

COPPER

KM#	Date	Year	Mintage	VF	XF	Un
1	AH1369	1950	4.000	.15	.25	.7

5 CENTESIMI

COPPER

KM#	Date	Year	Mintage	VF	XF	Un
2	AH1369	1950	6.800	.20	.50	1.0

10 CENTESIMI

COPPER

KM#	Date	Year	Mintage	VF	XF	Un
3	AH1369	1950	7.400	.30	.75	1.5

50 CENTESIMI

3.8000 g, .250 SILVER, .0305 oz ASW

KM#	Date	Year	Mintage	VF	XF	Un
4	AH1369	1950	1.800	1.00	3.50	8.5

SOMALO

7.6000 g, .250 SILVER, .0610 oz ASW

KM#	Date	Year	Mintage	VF	XF	Un
5	AH1369	1950	11.480	2.00	4.50	10.0C

SOMALI REPUBLIC

MONETARY SYSTEM

100 Centesimi = 1 Somalo =
1 Scellino = 1 Shilling

5 CENTESIMI

BRASS

KM#	Date	Mintage	VF	XF	Unc
6	1967	10.000	—	.15	.35

10 CENTESIMI

BRASS

KM#	Date	Mintage	VF	XF	Unc
7	1967	15.000	.10	.20	.50

50 CENTESIMI

COPPER-NICKEL

KM#	Date	Mintage	VF	XF	Unc
8	1967	5.100	.50	.75	2.50

SCELLINO

(Schilling)

COPPER-NICKEL

KM#	Date	Mintage	VF	XF	Unc
9	1967	8.150	1.00	3.00	6.00

20 SHILLINGS

2.8000 g, .900 GOLD, .0810 oz AGW
5th Anniversary of Independence

KM#	Date	Mintage	VF	XF	Unc
10	1965Az	6,325	—	Proof	60.00
	1966Az	—	—	Proof	60.00

50 SHILLINGS

7.0000 g, .900 GOLD, .2025 oz AGW
5th Anniversary of Independence

KM#	Date	Mintage	VF	XF	Unc
11	1965Az	6,325	—	Proof	120.00
	1966Az	—	—	Proof	120.00

100 SHILLINGS

14.0000 g, .900 GOLD, .4051 oz AGW
5th Anniversary of Independence

KM#	Date	Mintage	VF	XF	Unc
12	1965Az	6,325	—	Proof	225.00
	1966Az	—	—	Proof	225.00

200 SHILLINGS

28.0000 g, .900 GOLD, .8102 oz AGW
5th Anniversary of Independence

KM#	Date	Mintage	VF	XF	Unc
13	1965Az	6,325	—	Proof	425.00
	1966Az	—	—	Proof	425.00

500 SHILLINGS

70.0000 g, .900 GOLD, 2.0257 oz AGW
5th Anniversary of Independence
Obv: Similar to 20 Shillings, KM#10.

KM#	Date	Mintage	VF	XF	Unc
14	1965Az	6,325	—	Proof	925.00
	1966Az	—	—	Proof	925.00

DEMOCRATIC REPUBLIC

5 SHILLINGS

COPPER-NICKEL
2nd F.A.O. Conference

KM#	Date	Mintage	VF	XF	Unc
15	1970	.100	1.50	2.00	3.50
	1970	1,000	—	Proof	22.50

20 SHILLINGS

2.8000 g, .900 GOLD, .0810 oz AGW
10th Anniversary of Independence

KM#	Date	Mintage	VF	XF	Unc
16	1970	8,000	—	Proof	75.00

50 SHILLINGS

7.0000 g, .900 GOLD, .2025 oz AGW
10th Anniversary of Independence

KM#	Date	Mintage	VF	XF	Unc
17	1970	8,000	—	Proof	165.00

1st Anniversary of the 1969 Revolution

KM#	Date	Mintage	VF	XF	Unc
18	1970	—	—	Proof	165.00

100 SHILLINGS

14.0000 g, .900 GOLD, .4051 oz AGW
10th Anniversary of Independence

KM#	Date	Mintage	VF	XF	Unc
19	1970	8,000	—	Proof	325.00

1st Anniversary of the 1969 Revolution

KM#	Date	Mintage	VF	XF	Unc
20	1970	—	—	Proof	325.00

200 SHILLINGS

28.0000 g, .900 GOLD, .8102 oz AGW
10th Anniversary of Independence

KM#	Date	Mintage	VF	XF	Unc
21	1970	8,000	—	Proof	600.00

1st Anniversary of the 1969 Revolution

KM#	Date	Mintage	VF	XF	Unc
22	1970	—	—	Proof	550.00

500 SHILLINGS

70.0000 g, .900 GOLD, 2.0257 oz AGW
10th Anniversary of Independence
Obv: Similar to 200 Shillings, KM#22.

KM#	Date	Mintage	VF	XF	Unc
23	1970	8,000	—	Proof	1150.

MONETARY REFORM

100 Senti = 1 Shilling

5 SENTI

ALUMINUM
F.A.O. Issue

KM#	Date	Mintage	VF	XF	Unc
A24	1976	—	—	—	120.00

F.A.O. Issue

KM#	Date	Mintage	VF	XF	Unc
24	1976	18.500	.10	.15	.25

10 SENTI

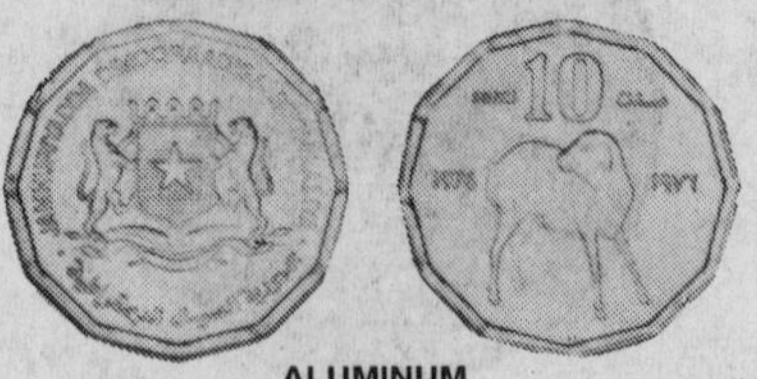

ALUMINUM
F.A.O. Issue

KM#	Date	Mintage	VF	XF	Unc
25	1976	40.500	.10	.15	.35

50 SENTI

COPPER-NICKEL
F.A.O. Issue

KM#	Date	Mintage	VF	XF	Unc
26	1976	10.080	.15	.25	.75
		NICKEL PLATED STEEL			
26a	1984	—	.25	.50	1.50

SHILLING

COPPER-NICKEL
F.A.O. Issue

KM#	Date	Mintage	VF	XF	Unc
27	1976	20.040	.25	.50	2.00
		NICKEL PLATED STEEL			
27a	1984	—	.35	.75	3.00

10 SHILLINGS

COPPER-NICKEL
10th Anniversary of Republic - Workers

KM#	Date	Mintage	VF	XF	Unc
28	1979	—	—	2.00	5.00
		28.2800 g, .925 SILVER, .8411 oz ASW			
28a	1979	*5,000	—	Proof	30.00

COPPER-NICKEL
10th Anniversary of Republic
People Kneeling

KM#	Date	Mintage	VF	XF	Unc
29	1979	—	—	2.00	5.00
		28.2800 g, .925 SILVER, .8411 oz ASW			
29a	1979	*5,000	—	Proof	30.00

COPPER-NICKEL
10th Anniversary of Republic - Lab Workers

KM#	Date	Mintage	VF	XF	Unc
30	1979	—	—	2.00	5.00
		28.2800 g, .925 SILVER, .8411 oz ASW			
30a	1979	*5,000	—	Proof	30.00

COPPER-NICKEL
10th Anniversary of Republic - Dancers

KM#	Date	Mintage	VF	XF	Unc
31	1979	—	—	2.00	5.00
		28.2800 g, .925 SILVER, .8411 oz ASW			
31a	1979	*5,000	—	Proof	30.00

COPPER-NICKEL
10th Anniversary of Republic -
Man and Woman

KM#	Date	Mintage	VF	XF	Unc
32	1979	—	—	2.00	5.00
		28.2800 g, .925 SILVER, .8411 oz ASW			
32a	1979	*5,000	—	Proof	30.00

25 SHILLINGS

COPPER-NICKEL
World Fisheries Conference

KM#	Date	Mintage	VF	XF	Unc
40	ND(1984)	.100	—	2.50	6.00
		28.2800 g, .925 SILVER, .8411 oz ASW			
40a	ND(1984)	.020	—	Proof	50.00
		47.5400 g, .917 GOLD, 1.4011 oz AGW			
40b	ND(1984)	200 pcs.	—	Proof	1250.

150 SHILLINGS

28.2800 g, .925 SILVER, .8411 oz ASW
International Year of Disabled Persons
Obv: Coat of arms, date.

KM#	Date	Mintage	VF	XF	Unc
8	1983	5,500	—	—	25.00
	1983	5,500	—	Proof	35.00

1500 SHILLINGS

15.9800 g, .917 GOLD, .4711 oz AGW
10th Anniversary of Republic
Obv: Similar to KM#35.

KM#	Date	Mintage	VF	XF	Unc
33	1979	500 pcs.	—	—	225.00
	1979	500 pcs.	—	Proof	245.00

10th Anniversary of Republic
Obv: Similar to KM#35.

KM#	Date	Mintage	VF	XF	Unc
34	1979	500 pcs.	—	—	225.00
	1979	500 pcs.	—	Proof	245.00

10th Anniversary of Republic

KM#	Date	Mintage	VF	XF	Unc
35	1979	500 pcs.	—	—	225.00
	1979	500 pcs.	—	Proof	245.00

10th Anniversary of Republic

KM#	Date	Mintage	VF	XF	Unc
36	1979	500 pcs.	—	—	225.00
	1979	500 pcs.	—	Proof	245.00

10th Anniversary of Republic
Obv: Similar to KM#35.

KM#	Date	Mintage	VF	XF	Unc
37	1979	500 pcs.	—	—	225.00
	1979	500 pcs.	—	Proof	245.00

International Year of Disabled Persons

KM#	Date	Mintage	VF	XF	Unc
39	1983	—	—	—	300.00
	1983	—	—	Proof	350.00

MINT SETS (MS)

KM#	Date	Mintage	Identification	Issue Price	Mkt. Val.
MS1	1979(5)	—	KM33-37	2375.	1125.

PROOF SETS (PS)

KM#	Date	Mintage	Identification	Issue Price	Mkt. Val.
PS1	1965(5)	6,325	KM10-14	—	1750.
PS2	1965(5)	—	KM10-14, Gilt Copper Nickel	—	—
PS3	1970(5)	8,000	KM16-17,19,21,23	334.95	2325.
PS4	1970(3)	14,500	KM18,20,22	—	850.00
PS5	1979(5)	5,000	KM28a-32a	325.00	150.00
PS6	1979(5)	—	KM33-37	3125.	1225.

Listings For
SOMALILAND: refer to Djibouti

SOUTH AFRICA

The Republic of South Africa, located at the southern tip of Africa, has an area, including the enclave of Walvis Bay, of 472,359 sq. mi. (1,221,040 sq. km.) and a population of *38.5 million. Capitals: Administrative, Pretoria; Legislative, Cape Town; Judicial, Bloemfontein. Manufacturing, mining and agriculture are the principal industries. Exports include wool, diamonds, gold, and metallic ores.

Portuguese navigator Bartholomew Diaz became the first European to sight the region of South Africa when he rounded the Cape of Good Hope in 1488, but throughout the 16th century the only white men to come ashore were the survivors of ships wrecked while attempting the stormy Cape passage. The first permanent settlement was established by Jan van Riebeeck of the Dutch East India Company in 1652. In subsequent decades additional Dutch and Germans and Huguenot refugees from France settled in the Cape area to form the Afrikaner segment of today's population.

Great Britain captured the Cape colony in 1795, and again in 1806, receiving permanent title in 1814. To escape British political rule and cultural dominance, many Afrikaner farmers (Boers) migrated northward (the Great Trek) beginning in 1836, and established the independent Boer Republics of the Transvaal (the South African Republic, Zuid Afrikaansche Republic) in 1852, and the Orange Free State in 1854. British political intrigues against the two republics, coupled with the discovery of diamonds and gold in the Boer-settled regions, led to the bitter Boer Wars (1880-81, 1899-1902) and the incorporation of the Boer republics into the British Empire.

On May 31, 1910, the two former Boer Republics (Transvaal and Orange Free State) were joined with the British colonies of Cape of Good Hope and Natal to form the Union of South Africa, a dominion of the British Empire. In 1934 the Union achieved status as a sovereign state within the British Empire.

Political integration of the various colonies did not still the conflict between the Afrikaners and the Englishspeaking groups, which continued to have a significant impact on political developments. A resurgence of Afrikaner nationalism in the 1940's and 1950's led to a referendum in the white community authorizing the relinquishment of dominion status and the establishment of a republic. The decision took effect on May 31, 1961. The Republic of South Africa withdrew from the British Commonwealth in Oct. 1961.

South African coins and currency bear inscriptions in both Afrikaans and English.

RULERS

British until 1961

MONETARY SYSTEM

Until 1961

12 Pence = 1 Shilling
2 Shillings = 1 Florin
20 Shillings = 1 Pound

Commencing 1961

100 Cents = 1 Rand

ZUID-AFRIKAANSCHE REPUBLICK

MONETARY SYSTEM

12 Pence = 1 Shilling
20 Shillings = 1 Pond

PENNY

BRONZE

KM#	Date	Mintage	Fine	VF	XF	Unc
2	1892	.028	3.00	6.00	18.00	40.00
	1892	*8-10 pcs.	—	—	Proof	4000.
	1893	.055	30.00	45.00	110.00	200.00
	1894	.011	5.00	10.00	30.00	120.00
	1898	.263	1.00	2.00	5.00	15.00
	1895	.182	10.00	50.00	250.00	700.00

3 PENCE

1.4138 g, .925 SILVER, .0420 oz ASW

KM#	Date	Mintage	Fine	VF	XF	Unc
3	1892	.024	3.00	6.00	20.00	90.00
	1892	*35-40 pcs.	—	—	Proof	1150.
	1893	.135	3.00	10.00	75.00	125.00
	1894	.104	4.00	12.50	65.00	175.00
	1895	.113	3.00	20.00	100.00	200.00
	1896	.166	2.00	4.00	8.00	40.00
	1897	.201	2.00	4.00	8.00	35.00

6 PENCE

2.8276 g, .925 SILVER, .0841 oz ASW

KM#	Date	Mintage	Fine	VF	XF	Unc
4	1892	.028	4.00	7.50	45.00	100.00
	1892	*40-50 pcs.	—	—	Proof	600.00
	1893	.096	3.00	6.00	90.00	180.00
	1894	.168	3.00	6.00	65.00	200.00
	1895	.179	3.00	6.00	65.00	200.00
	1896	.205	2.00	4.00	8.00	30.00
	1896	1 known	—	—	Proof	—
	1897	.220	1.50	3.00	6.00	35.00
	1897	1 known	—	—	Proof	—

SHILLING

5.6555 g, .925 SILVER, .1682 oz ASW

KM#	Date	Mintage	Fine	VF	XF	Unc
5	1892	.130	7.50	15.00	55.00	120.00
	1892	*40-50 pcs.	—	—	Proof	650.00
	1893	.137	10.00	50.00	250.00	700.00
	1894	.366	4.00	6.00	150.00	350.00
	1895	.327	4.00	10.00	250.00	500.00
	1896	.437	4.00	10.00	75.00	150.00
	1897	.397	2.00	4.00	10.00	30.00

2 SHILLINGS

11.3100 g, .925 SILVER, .3364 oz ASW

KM#	Date	Mintage	Fine	VF	XF	Unc
6	1892	.055	10.00	25.00	75.00	150.00
	1892	*50-60 pcs.	—	—	Proof	600.00
	1893	.107	15.00	50.00	300.00	650.00
	1894	.173	5.00	25.00	275.00	600.00
	1895	.150	7.50	35.00	300.00	850.00
	1896	.353	4.00	8.00	25.00	50.00
	1897	.148	3.00	6.00	20.00	50.00

2-1/2 SHILLINGS

14.1380 g, .925 SILVER, .4205 oz ASW

KM#	Date	Mintage	Fine	VF	XF	Unc
7	1892	.016	15.00	30.00	100.00	220.00
	1892	*50-60 pcs.	—	—	Proof	500.00
	1893	.135	20.00	80.00	400.00	700.00
	1894	.135	10.00	30.00	250.00	600.00
	1895	.182	10.00	40.00	350.00	700.00
	1896	.285	5.00	10.00	30.00	70.00
	1897	.149	5.00	10.00	30.00	70.00

5 SHILLINGS

28.2759 g, .925 SILVER, .8410 oz ASW
Single shaft wagon tongue.

KM#	Date	Mintage	Fine	VF	XF	Unc
8.1	1892	.014	60.00	120.00	250.00	500.00

Double shaft wagon tongue

KM#	Date	Mintage	Fine	VF	XF	Unc
8.2	1892	4,327	75.00	150.00	350.00	750.00
	1892	*25-30 pcs.	—	—	Proof	3250.

Beware of counterfeit double shafts. Aside from there being two shafts on the wagon in the coat of arms (reverse), the two wheels of the wagon must be the same size. On single shaft crowns, the rear wheel is noticeably larger than the front wheel.

Single shaft wagon tongue

Double shaft wagon tongue

1/2 POND

3.9940 g, .916 GOLD, .1176 oz AGW
Rev: Double shaft wagon tongue

KM#	Date	Mintage	Fine	VF	XF	Unc
9.1	1892	.010	100.00	150.00	200.00	350.00
	1892	*20-25 pcs.	—	—	Proof	6000.

Rev: Single shaft wagon tongue

KM#	Date	Mintage	Fine	VF	XF	Unc
9.2	1892	—	—	—	Unique	—
	1893	—	500.00	1000.	2000.	3000.
	1894	.039	75.00	90.00	200.00	600.00
	1895	.135	75.00	90.00	150.00	400.00
	1896	.104	75.00	90.00	150.00	400.00
	1897	.075	75.00	90.00	150.00	400.00

EEN (1) POND

7.9880 g, .916 GOLD, .2353 oz AGW
Coarse beard

KM#	Date	Mintage	Fine	VF	XF	Unc
1.1	1874	142 pcs.	2250.	3000.	4000.	9000.

Fine beard

KM#	Date	Mintage	Fine	VF	XF	Unc
1.2	1874	695 pcs.	1500.	2000.	3000.	650

Rev: Double shaft wagon tongue

KM#	Date	Mintage	Fine	VF	XF	Unc
10.1	1892	.016	120.00	150.00	250.00	400.
	1892	*12-15 pcs.	—	—	Proof	900

Rev: Single shaft wagon tongue

KM#	Date	Mintage	Fine	VF	XF	Unc
10.2	1892	—	300.00	500.00	1750.	450
	1893	.062	120.00	150.00	300.00	650.0
	1894	.318	120.00	150.00	350.00	700.0
	1895	.336	120.00	150.00	350.00	700.0
	1896	.235	120.00	135.00	250.00	600.0
	1897	.311	120.00	135.00	175.00	375.0
	1898	.137	120.00	135.00	150.00	275.0
	1898/stamped 99	130 pcs.	2500.	3000.	5000.	750
	1898/stamped 9	Unique	—	—	—	—
	1900	.788	120.00	135.00	175.00	300.0

.999 GOLD
Veld Boer War Siege Issue

KM#	Date	Mintage	Fine	VF	XF	Unc
11	1902	986 pcs.	550.00	1100.	2000.	3500

PROOF SETS (PS)

KM# Date	Mintage	Identification	Issue Price	Mkt. Val
PS1011892(9)	—	KM2-10	—	25,750

UNION

MONETARY SYSTEM
12 Pence = 1 Shilling
2 Shillings = 1 Florin
20 Shillings = 1 Pound

1/4 PENNY FARTHING

BRONZE
Rev. denomination: 1/4 PENNY 1/4

KM#	Date	Mintage	Fine	VF	XF	Unc
12.1	1923	.033	2.00	5.00	10.00	20.00
	1923	1,402	—	—	Proof	30.00
	1924	.095	1.50	2.50	5.00	10.00

Rev. denomination: 1/4 PENNY

KM#	Date	Mintage	Fine	VF	XF	Unc
12.2	1926	16 pcs.	—	—	Proof	6000.
	1928	.064	1.50	3.00	5.00	12.50
	1930	6,560	30.00	60.00	120.00	200.00
	1930	14 pcs.	—	—	Proof	1200.
	1931	.154	1.00	1.50	4.00	6.00

Rev. denomination: 1/4 D

KM#	Date	Mintage	Fine	VF	XF	Unc
12.3	1931	Inc. Ab.	5.00	10.00	15.00	35.00
	1931	62 pcs.	—	—	Proof	200.00
	1932	.105	1.00	1.50	3.50	7.00
	1932	12 pcs.	—	—	Proof	375.00
	1933	76 pcs.	750.00	1450.	2200.	3250.
	1933	20 pcs.	—	—	Proof	4000.
	1934	52 pcs.	750.00	1450.	2200.	3250.

KM#	Date	Mintage	Fine	VF	XF	Unc
12.3	1934	24 pcs.	—	—	Proof	3750.
	1935	.061	1.00	1.50	3.50	8.00
	1935	20 pcs.	—	—	Proof	3000.
	1936	43 pcs.	350.00	750.00	1100.	2000.
	1936	40 pcs.	—	—	Proof	3000.

KM#	Date	Mintage	Fine	VF	XF	Unc
23	1937	.038	1.50	3.00	6.00	12.50
	1937	116 pcs.	—	—	Proof	40.00
	1938	.051	1.00	2.00	4.00	8.00
	1938	44 pcs.	—	—	Proof	100.00
	1939	.102	.50	1.50	3.00	7.50
	1939	30 pcs.	—	—	Proof	125.00
	1941	.091	.50	1.50	3.00	7.50
	1942	3.756	.25	.50	1.00	2.00
	1943	9.918	.25	.50	.75	1.50
	1943	104 pcs.	—	—	Proof	50.00
	1944	4.468	.25	.50	.75	2.00
	1944	150 pcs.	—	—	Proof	35.00
	1945	5.297	.25	.50	1.50	3.00
	1945	150 pcs.	—	—	Proof	35.00
	1946	4.378	.25	.50	1.50	4.00
	1946	150 pcs.	—	—	Proof	35.00
	1947	3.895	.25	.50	1.50	4.00
	1947	2,600	—	—	Proof	4.00

KM#	Date	Mintage	Fine	VF	XF	Unc
32.1	1948	2.415	.25	.50	1.00	2.00
	1948	1,120	—	—	Proof	3.00
	1949	3.568	.25	.50	1.00	2.50
	1949	800 pcs.	—	—	Proof	5.00
	1950	8.694	.25	.50	.75	1.50
	1950	500 pcs.	—	—	Proof	8.00

Rev. leg. reversed: SUID AFRIKA-SOUTH AFRICA

KM#	Date	Mintage	Fine	VF	XF	Unc
32.2	1951	3.511	.15	.35	.75	2.50
	1951	2,000	—	—	Proof	2.00
	1952	2.805	.15	.35	.75	2.00
	1952	.016	—	—	Proof	2.00

KM#	Date	Mintage	Fine	VF	XF	Unc
44	1953	7.193	.15	.25	.50	1.50
	1953	5,000	—	—	Proof	2.00
	1954	6.568	.15	.25	.50	1.50
	1954	3,150	—	—	Proof	2.00
	1955	11.798	.15	.25	.50	1.50
	1955	2,850	—	—	Proof	2.00
	1956	1.287	.15	.25	.50	2.50
	1956	1,700	—	—	Proof	3.00
	1957	3.065	.15	.25	.50	1.50
	1957	1,130	—	—	Proof	4.00
	1958	5.452	.15	.25	.50	1.50
	1958	985 pcs.	—	—	Proof	5.00
	1959	1.567	.15	.25	.50	1.50
	1959	900 pcs.	—	—	Proof	6.00
	1960	1.023	.15	.25	.50	2.00
	1960	3,360	—	—	Proof	1.50

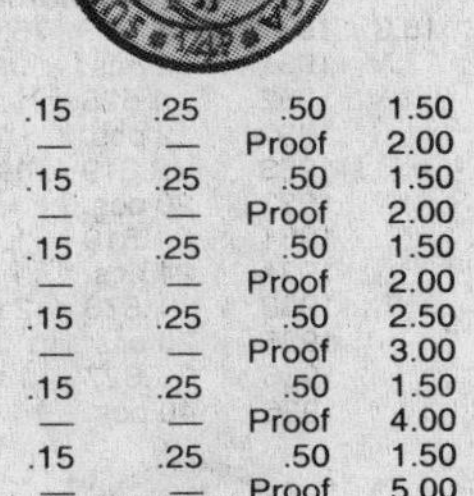

1/2 PENNY

BRONZE
Rev. denomination: 1/2 PENNY 1/2

KM#	Date	Mintage	Fine	VF	XF	Unc
13.1	1923	.012	25.00	40.00	70.00	100.00
	1923	1,402	—	—	Proof	100.00
	1924	.064	7.50	12.50	30.00	60.00
	1925	.069	7.50	12.50	30.00	80.00
	1926	.065	10.00	15.00	35.00	100.00

Rev. denomination: 1/2 PENNY

KM#	Date	Mintage	Fine	VF	XF	Unc
13.2	1928	.105	5.00	12.50	35.00	75.00
	1929	.272	2.50	5.00	15.00	35.00
	1930	.147	3.50	7.00	20.00	40.00
	1930	14 pcs.	—	—	Proof	400.00
	1930 w/o star after date					
		Inc. Ab.	4.00	8.00	25.00	50.00
	1931	.145	3.50	7.00	25.00	50.00

Rev. denomination: 1/2 D

KM#	Date	Mintage	Fine	VF	XF	Unc
13.3	1931	62 pcs.	—	—	Proof	1000.
	1932	.106	5.00	10.00	30.00	75.00
	1932	12 pcs.	—	—	Proof	1000.
	1933	.063	8.00	25.00	55.00	100.00
	1933	20 pcs.	—	—	Proof	500.00
	1934	.326	1.50	5.00	15.00	45.00
	1934	24 pcs.	—	—	Proof	500.00
	1935	.405	1.50	5.00	15.00	40.00
	1935	20 pcs.	—	—	Proof	500.00
	1936	.407	1.50	5.00	15.00	30.00
	1936	40 pcs.	—	—	Proof	200.00

KM#	Date	Mintage	Fine	VF	XF	Unc
24	1937	.638	1.00	2.00	9.00	15.00
	1937	116 pcs.	—	—	Proof	50.00
	1938	.560	1.00	2.00	6.00	15.00
	1938	44 pcs.	—	—	Proof	125.00
	1939	.271	2.50	5.00	10.00	20.00
	1939	30 pcs.	—	—	Proof	175.00
	1940	1.535	.30	.75	3.00	8.00
	1941	2.053	.30	.75	3.00	8.00
	1942	8.382	.25	.60	2.00	6.00
	1943	5.135	.25	.60	2.00	6.00
	1943	104 pcs.	—	—	Proof	60.00
	1944	3.920	.25	.75	3.00	8.00
	1944	150 pcs.	—	—	Proof	35.00
	1945	2.357	.25	.60	2.50	7.00
	1945	150 pcs.	—	—	Proof	35.00
	1946	1.022	.25	.75	3.00	9.00
	1946	150 pcs.	—	—	Proof	35.00
	1947	.258	1.00	3.00	6.00	17.50
	1947	2,600	—	—	Proof	10.00

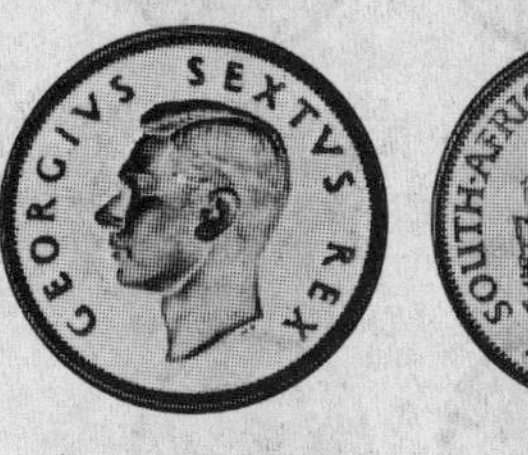

KM#	Date	Mintage	Fine	VF	XF	Unc
33	1948	.685	.50	1.00	4.00	9.00
	1948	1,120	—	—	Proof	15.00
	1949	1.850	.25	.50	1.75	4.00
	1949	800 pcs.	—	—	Proof	15.00
	1950	2.186	.25	.50	1.50	3.00
	1950	500 pcs.	—	—	Proof	6.00
	1951	3.746	.25	.50	1.25	3.00
	1951	2,000	—	—	Proof	5.00
	1952	4.174	.25	.50	1.00	2.50
	1952	1,550	—	—	Proof	4.00

KM#	Date	Mintage	Fine	VF	XF	Unc
45	1953	5.572	.15	.35	1.00	3.00
	1953	5,000	—	—	Proof	4.00
	1954	.101	2.00	4.00	7.50	12.50
	1954	3,150	—	—	Proof	15.00
	1955	3.774	.15	.35	1.00	3.00
	1955	2,850	—	—	Proof	4.00
	1956	1.305	.15	.35	1.00	3.00
	1956	1,700	—	—	Proof	4.00
	1957	2.025	.15	.35	1.00	3.00
	1957	1,130	—	—	Proof	4.00
	1958	2.171	.15	.35	1.00	2.50
	1958	985 pcs.	—	—	Proof	5.00
	1959	2.397	.15	.25	.75	2.00
	1959	900 pcs.	—	—	Proof	6.00
	1960	2.552	.15	.25	.75	2.00
	1960	3,360	—	—	Proof	1.50

PENNY

BRONZE
Rev. denomination: 1 PENNY 1

KM#	Date	Mintage	Fine	VF	XF	Unc
14.1	1923	.091	3.00	7.00	17.50	35.00
	1923	1,402	—	—	Proof	50.00
	1924	.134	4.00	10.00	25.00	50.00

Rev. denomination: PENNY

KM#	Date	Mintage	Fine	VF	XF	Unc
14.2	1926	.393	3.00	10.00	40.00	100.00
	1926	16 pcs.	—	—	Proof	600.00
	1927	.285	3.00	10.00	40.00	90.00
	1928	.386	3.00	10.00	40.00	90.00
	1929	1.093	1.00	5.00	15.00	35.00
	1930	.754	1.00	5.00	20.00	40.00
	1930	14 pcs.	—	—	Proof	600.00

Rev. denomination: 1 D.

KM#	Date	Mintage	Fine	VF	XF	Unc
14.3	1931	.284	1.00	5.00	17.50	40.00
	1931	62 pcs.	—	—	Proof	400.00
	1932	.260	1.00	5.00	20.00	50.00
	1932	12 pcs.	—	—	Proof	800.00
	1933	.225	2.00	10.00	30.00	45.00
	1933	20 pcs.	—	—	Proof	500.00
	1933 w/o star after date					
		Inc. Ab.	4.00	10.00	30.00	50.00
	1934	2.090	.50	1.50	8.00	22.50
	1934	24 pcs.	—	—	Proof	600.00
	1935	2.295	.50	1.50	8.00	22.50
	1935	20 pcs.	—	—	Proof	600.00
	1936	1.819	.35	1.00	5.00	20.00
	1936	40 pcs.	—	—	Proof	300.00

KM#	Date	Mintage	Fine	VF	XF	Unc
25	1937	3.281	.50	1.50	10.00	25.00
	1937	116 pcs.	—	—	Proof	75.00
	1938	1.840	.50	1.50	8.00	30.00
	1938	44 pcs.	—	—	Proof	100.00
	1939	1.506	.50	1.50	10.00	25.00
	1939	30 pcs.	—	—	Proof	175.00
	1940	3.592	.35	1.00	4.00	10.00
	1940 w/o star after date					
		Inc. Ab.	1.50	3.00	6.00	15.00
	1941	7.871	.25	.75	2.50	7.00
	1942	14.428	.25	.75	2.00	6.00
	1942 w/o star after date					
		Inc. Ab.	3.00	6.00	12.50	30.00
	1943	4.010	.25	.75	2.50	6.00
	1943	104 pcs.	—	—	Proof	70.00
	1944	6.425	.25	.75	2.50	7.00
	1944	150 pcs.	—	—	Proof	45.00
	1945	4.810	.25	.75	2.50	7.00
	1945	150 pcs.	—	—	Proof	45.00
	1946	2.605	.25	.75	3.00	8.00
	1946	150 pcs.	—	—	Proof	45.00
	1947	.135	2.50	4.00	7.50	17.50
	1947	2,600	—	—	Proof	7.00

KM#	Date	Mintage	Fine	VF	XF	Unc
34.1	1948	2.398	.25	.75	2.50	6.00
	1948	1,120	—	—	Proof	5.00
	1948 w/o star after date					
		Inc. Ab.	1.00	2.00	5.00	10.00
	1949	3.634	.25	.75	2.00	6.00
	1949	800 pcs.	—	—	Proof	12.00
	1950	4.890	.25	.75	2.00	5.00
	1950	500 pcs.	—	—	Proof	10.00

Rev. leg: SUID AFRIKA-SOUTH AFRICA

KM#	Date	Mintage	Fine	VF	XF	Unc
34.2	1951	3.787	.25	.75	1.50	4.00
	1951	2,000	—	—	Proof	5.00
	1952	12.674	.25	.50	1.00	2.50
	1952	.016	—	—	Proof	4.00

KM#	Date	Mintage	Fine	VF	XF	Unc
46	1953	5.491	.20	.35	.75	2.00
	1953	5,000	—	—	Proof	2.00
	1954	6.665	1.00	2.00	5.00	10.00
	1954	3,150	—	—	Proof	15.00
	1955	6.508	.20	.35	.75	3.00
	1955	2,850	—	—	Proof	2.00
	1956	4.390	.20	.35	1.00	4.00
	1956	1,700	—	—	Proof	3.00
	1957	3.973	.20	.35	.75	3.00
	1957	1,130	—	—	Proof	5.00
	1958	5.311	.20	.35	.75	3.00
	1958	985 pcs.	—	—	Proof	6.00
	1959	5.066	.20	.35	.75	2.00
	1959	900 pcs.	—	—	Proof	7.00
	1960	5.106	.20	.35	.75	2.00
	1960	3,360	—	—	Proof	2.00

3 PENCE

1.4100 g, .800 SILVER, .0362 oz ASW

KM#	Date	Mintage	Fine	VF	XF	Unc
15.1	1923	.302	4.00	8.00	20.00	45.00
	1923	1,402	—	—	Proof	50.00
	1924	.501	4.00	10.00	25.00	50.00
	1925	Inc. Bl	10.00	35.00	200.00	475.00

Rev. denomination: 3 PENCE

KM#	Date	Mintage	Fine	VF	XF	Unc
15.2	1925	.358	5.00	25.00	90.00	175.00
	1926	1.572	1.00	3.50	20.00	50.00
	1926	16 pcs.	—	—	Proof	2000.
	1927	2.285	1.00	2.50	15.00	45.00
	1928	.919	1.50	3.50	20.00	50.00
	1929	1.948	1.00	2.50	15.00	45.00
	1930	.981	1.00	3.50	20.00	50.00
	1930	14 pcs.	—	—	Proof	800.00

Rev. denomination: 3D

KM#	Date	Mintage	Fine	VF	XF	Unc
15.3	1931	66 pcs.	750.00	1000.	1750.	3500.
	1931	62 pcs.	—	—	Proof	3500.
	1932	2.622	1.00	2.50	15.00	30.00
	1932	12 pcs.	—	—	Proof	1000.
	1933	5.135	1.00	2.50	15.00	30.00
	1933	20 pcs.	—	—	Proof	1000.
	1934	2.357	1.00	2.50	15.00	30.00
	1934	24 pcs.	—	—	Proof	1000.
	1935	1.655	1.00	2.50	15.00	30.00
	1935	20 pcs.	—	—	Proof	1000.
	1936	1.095	1.00	2.50	15.00	35.00
	1936	40 pcs.	—	—	Proof	250.00

KM#	Date	Mintage	Fine	VF	XF	Unc
26	1937	3.576	.50	1.00	3.00	10.00
	1937	116 pcs.	—	—	Proof	80.00
	1938	2.394	.50	1.50	7.00	20.00
	1938	44 pcs.	—	—	Proof	100.00
	1939	3.224	.50	1.50	5.00	12.50
	1939	30 pcs.	—	—	Proof	250.00
	1940	4.887	.50	1.00	3.00	12.50
	1941	8.968	.50	1.00	3.00	9.00
	1942	8.056	.50	1.00	3.00	9.00
	1943	14.827	.50	1.00	2.50	6.00
	1943	104 pcs.	—	—	Proof	80.00
	1944	3.331	.50	1.00	3.00	9.00
	1944	150 pcs.	—	—	Proof	60.00
	1945/3	4.094	1.00	3.00	10.00	20.00
	1945	Inc. Ab.	.50	1.00	3.00	9.00
	1945	150 pcs.	—	—	Proof	60.00
	1946	2.219	.50	1.00	3.00	10.00
	1946	150 pcs.	—	—	Proof	65.00
	1947	1.127	.50	1.00	2.50	8.00
	1947	2,600	—	—	Proof	8.00

KM#	Date	Mintage	Fine	VF	XF	Unc
35.1	1948	2.720	.50	1.00	3.00	7.00
	1948	1,120	—	—	Proof	5.00
	1949	1.904	.50	1.00	3.00	7.00
	1949	800 pcs.	—	—	Proof	5.00
	1950	4.096	.50	1.00	2.50	5.00
	1950	500 pcs.	—	—	Proof	7.00

1.4100 g, .500 SILVER, .0226 oz ASW
Rev: Modified design.

KM#	Date	Mintage	Fine	VF	XF	Unc
35.2	1951	6.323	.25	.50	1.00	3.00
	1951	2,000	—	—	Proof	4.00
	1952	13.057	.25	.50	1.00	2.00
	1952	.016	—	—	Proof	2.00

NOTE: Many varieties exist of George VI 3 Pence.

KM#	Date	Mintage	Fine	VF	XF	Unc
47	1953	5.483	.25	.50	1.00	3.00
	1953	5,000	—	—	Proof	3.00
	1954	3.898	.25	.50	1.00	3.50
	1954	3,150	—	—	Proof	4.00
	1955	4.720	.25	.50	1.00	3.00
	1955	2,850	—	—	Proof	3.00
	1956	6.189	.25	.50	1.00	3.00
	1956	1,700	—	—	Proof	4.00
	1957	1.893	.25	.50	1.00	3.00
	1957	1,130	—	—	Proof	5.00
	1958	3.227	.25	.50	1.00	3.00
	1958	985 pcs.	—	—	Proof	6.00
	1959	2.552	.25	.50	1.00	2.00
	1959 no K-G on reverse					
		Inc. Ab.	2.00	3.00	5.00	10.00
	1959	900 pcs.	—	—	Proof	7.00
	1960	.018	1.00	2.50	4.00	7.00
	1960	3,360	—	—	Proof	3.00

6 PENCE

2.8300 g, .800 SILVER, .0727 oz ASW

KM#	Date	Mintage	Fine	VF	XF	Unc
16.1	1923	.208	4.00	15.00	35.00	80.00
	1923	1,402	—	—	Proof	80.00
	1924	.326	3.50	12.50	30.00	70.00

Rev. denomination: 6 PENCE

KM#	Date	Mintage	Fine	VF	XF	Unc
16.2	1925	.079	5.00	20.00	60.00	125.00
	1926	.722	2.00	10.00	45.00	100.00
	1926	16 pcs.	—	—	Proof	3000.
	1927	1.548	1.50	4.00	25.00	50.00
	1929	.784	2.00	8.00	30.00	60.00
	1930	.448	2.00	8.00	35.00	70.00
	1930	14 pcs.	—	—	Proof	1000.

Rev. denomination: 6 D

KM#	Date	Mintage	Fine	VF	XF	Unc
16.3	1931	4,743	75.00	150.00	250.00	550.00
	1931	62 pcs.	—	—	Proof	1000.
	1932	1.525	1.00	5.00	17.50	35.00
	1932	12 pcs.	—	—	Proof	1200.
	1933	2.819	1.00	5.00	17.50	35.00
	1933	20 pcs.	—	—	Proof	1200.
	1934	1.519	1.00	7.00	20.00	40.00
	1934	24 pcs.	—	—	Proof	1200.
	1935	.573	2.00	8.00	30.00	100.00
	1935	20 pcs.	—	—	Proof	1200.
	1936	.627	1.00	7.00	20.00	40.00
	1936	40 pcs.	—	—	Proof	275.00

KM#	Date	Mintage	Fine	VF	XF	Unc
27	1937	1.696	1.00	2.00	7.00	17.50
	1937	116 pcs.	—	—	Proof	90.00
	1938	1.725	1.00	2.00	7.00	17.50
	1938	44 pcs.	—	—	Proof	125.00
	1939	30 pcs.	—	—	Proof	3750.
	1940	1.629	1.00	1.50	5.00	10.00
	1941	2.263	1.00	1.50	5.00	10.00
	1942	4.936	.75	1.25	3.00	8.00
	1943	3.776	.75	1.25	3.00	8.00
	1943	104 pcs.	—	—	Proof	90.00
	1944	.228	2.00	7.00	15.00	30.00
	1944	150 pcs.	—	—	Proof	75.00
	1945	.420	1.00	5.00	15.00	35.00
	1945	150 pcs.	—	—	Proof	75.00
	1946	.290	1.00	6.00	15.00	30.00
	1946	150 pcs.	—	—	Proof	80.00
	1947	.577	1.00	1.50	5.00	10.00
	1947	2,600	—	—	Proof	10.00

KM#	Date	Mintage	Fine	VF	XF	Unc
36.1	1948	2.266	.75	1.25	2.50	6.00
	1948	1,120	—	—	Proof	10.00
	1949	.196	3.00	7.50	15.00	30.00
	1949	800 pcs.	—	—	Proof	15.00
	1950	2.122	.75	1.00	2.00	5.00
	1950	500 pcs.	—	—	Proof	15.00

2.8300 g, .500 SILVER, .0454 oz ASW

KM#	Date	Mintage	Fine	VF	XF	Unc
36.2	1951	2.602	.50	1.00	2.00	4.00
	1951	2,000	—	—	Proof	4.00
	1952	4.265	.50	.75	1.25	3.00
	1952	.016	—	—	Proof	2.00

KM#	Date	Mintage	Fine	VF	XF	Unc
48	1953	2.496	.50	.75	1.75	4.50
	1953	5,000	—	—	Proof	3.00
	1954	2.196	.50	1.00	2.00	4.50
	1954	3,150	—	—	Proof	4.00
	1955	1.969	.50	1.00	2.00	4.50
	1955	2,850	—	—	Proof	3.00
	1956	1.772	.50	1.00	2.00	5.00
	1956	1,700	—	—	Proof	4.00
	1957	3.288	.50	.75	1.75	4.50
	1957	1,130	—	—	Proof	6.00
	1958	1.172	.50	1.00	2.00	4.50
	1958	985 pcs.	—	—	Proof	6.00
	1959	.261	1.00	2.00	4.00	12.00
	1959	900 pcs.	—	—	Proof	8.00
	1960	1.587	.50	.75	1.25	2.50
	1960	3,360	—	—	Proof	2.50

SHILLING

5.6600 g, .800 SILVER, .1455 oz ASW
Rev. denomination: 1 SHILLING 1

KM#	Date	Mintage	Fine	VF	XF	Unc
17.1	1923	.808	4.00	15.00	35.00	75.00
	1923	1,402	—	—	Proof	80.00
	1924	1.269	3.50	12.50	30.00	75.00

Rev. denomination: SHILLING

KM#	Date	Mintage	Fine	VF	XF	Unc
17.2	1926	.238	15.00	75.00	400.00	1150.
	1926	16 pcs.	—	—	Proof	3000.
	1927	.488	10.00	25.00	150.00	375.00
	1928	.889	8.00	25.00	100.00	250.00
	1929	.926	5.00	10.00	30.00	175.00
	1930	.422	6.00	15.00	60.00	150.00
	1930	14 pcs.	—	—	Proof	1000.

KM#	Date	Mintage	Fine	VF	XF	Unc
17.3	1931	6,541	80.00	165.00	375.00	600.00
	1931	62 pcs.	—	—	Proof	1200.
	1932	2.537	2.50	5.00	15.00	30.00
	1932	12 pcs.	—	—	Proof	1400.
	1933	1.463	3.50	7.00	30.00	70.00
17.3	1933	20 pcs.	—	—	Proof	1400.
	1934	.821	3.50	7.00	35.00	80.00
	1934	24 pcs.	—	—	Proof	1400.
	1935	.685	4.00	8.50	45.00	90.00
	1935	20 pcs.	—	—	Proof	1400.
	1936	.693	3.50	7.00	25.00	60.00
	1936	40 pcs.	—	—	Proof	500.00

KM#	Date	Mintage	Fine	VF	XF	Unc
28	1937	1.194	1.50	3.00	10.00	25.00
	1937	116 pcs.	—	—	Proof	120.00
	1938	1.160	1.50	3.00	10.00	25.00
	1938	44 pcs.	—	—	Proof	250.00
	1939	30 pcs.	—	—	Proof	4000.
	1940	1.365	1.50	2.50	7.50	17.50
	1941	1.826	1.50	2.50	7.50	17.50
	1942	3.867	1.50	2.50	7.50	17.50
	1943	4.188	1.00	2.00	5.00	10.00
	1943	104 pcs.	—	—	Proof	175.00
	1944	.048	8.00	20.00	45.00	80.00
	1944	160 pcs.	—	—	Proof	150.00
	1945	.054	8.00	20.00	45.00	80.00
	1945	150 pcs.	—	—	Proof	150.00
	1946	.027	10.00	30.00	60.00	120.00
	1946	150 pcs.	—	—	Proof	200.00
	1947	7,184	10.00	20.00	40.00	70.00
	1947	2,600	—	—	Proof	125.00

KM#	Date	Mintage	Fine	VF	XF	Unc
37.1	1948	4,974	10.00	20.00	40.00	70.00
	1948	1,120	—	—	Proof	125.00
	1949	800 pcs.	—	—	Proof	225.00
	1950	1.704	1.50	2.50	4.00	8.00
	1950	500 pcs.	—	—	Proof	125.00

5.6600 g, .500 SILVER, .0909 oz ASW
Rev. denomination: 1 S.

KM#	Date	Mintage	Fine	VF	XF	Unc
37.2	1951	2.405	1.00	1.50	4.00	8.00
	1951	2,000	—	—	Proof	4.00
	1952	1.934	1.00	1.50	3.50	7.00
	1952	1,550	—	—	Proof	3.00

KM#	Date	Mintage	Fine	VF	XF	Unc
49	1953	2.672	.75	1.25	2.50	5.50
	1953	5,000	—	—	Proof	4.00
	1954	3.576	.75	1.25	2.00	5.50
	1954	3,150	—	—	Proof	4.00
	1955	2.206	.75	1.25	2.50	5.50
	1955	2,850	—	—	Proof	5.50
	1956	2.142	.75	1.25	2.50	6.00
	1956	1,700	—	—	Proof	6.00
	1957	.791	1.00	2.00	5.00	10.00
	1957	1,130	—	—	Proof	6.00
	1958	4.067	.75	1.25	2.00	5.50
	1958	985 pcs.	—	—	Proof	8.00
	1959	.205	1.50	3.00	5.00	10.00
	1959	900 pcs.	—	—	Proof	10.00
	1960	2.187	.75	1.25	2.00	5.50
	1960	3,360	—	—	Proof	3.00

FLORIN

11.3100 g, .800 SILVER, .2909 oz ASW

KM#	Date	Mintage	Fine	VF	XF	Unc
18	1923	.695	5.00	20.00	40.00	80.00
	1923	1,402	—	—	Proof	125.00
	1924	1.513	4.00	15.00	40.00	150.00
	1925	.050	200.00	400.00	1500.	2500.
	1926	.324	7.50	40.00	250.00	650.00
	1927	.399	7.50	35.00	200.00	600.00
	1928	1.092	4.00	10.00	100.00	200.00
	1929	.648	5.00	15.00	120.00	225.00
	1930	.267	5.00	15.00	75.00	150.00
	1930	14 pcs.	—	—	Proof	1200.

2 SHILLINGS

11.3100 g, .800 SILVER, .2909 oz ASW
Rev. denomination: 2 SHILLINGS

KM#	Date	Mintage	Fine	VF	XF	Unc
22	1931	383 pcs.	175.00	275.00	600.00	950.00
	1931	62 pcs.	—	—	Proof	1800.
	1932	1.315	3.00	6.00	18.00	45.00
	1932	12 pcs.	—	—	Proof	2000.
	1933	.891	4.00	8.00	25.00	60.00
	1933	20 pcs.	—	—	Proof	2000.
	1934	.559	4.00	8.00	25.00	60.00
	1934	24 pcs.	—	—	Proof	1650.
	1935	.554	5.00	9.00	25.00	70.00
	1935	20 pcs.	—	—	Proof	1650.
	1936	.669	4.00	8.00	25.00	60.00
	1936	40 pcs.	—	—	Proof	650.00

KM#	Date	Mintage	Fine	VF	XF	Unc
29	1937	1.495	2.50	5.00	10.00	30.00
	1937	116 pcs.	—	—	Proof	150.00
	1938	.214	5.00	10.00	20.00	50.00
	1938	44 pcs.	—	—	Proof	325.00
	1939	.279	5.00	10.00	20.00	50.00
	1939	30 pcs.	—	—	Proof	1000.
	1940	2.600	2.50	3.50	8.00	20.00
	1941	1.764	2.50	3.50	8.00	20.00
	1942	2.847	2.00	3.00	5.00	10.00
	1943	3.125	2.00	3.00	5.00	10.00
	1943	104 pcs.	—	—	Proof	150.00
	1944	.225	3.50	7.00	17.50	40.00
	1945	.473	3.00	6.00	15.00	35.00
	1945	150 pcs.	—	—	Proof	120.00
	1946	.014	7.50	20.00	40.00	90.00
	1946	150 pcs.	—	—	Proof	200.00
	1947	2,892	15.00	25.00	40.00	75.00
	1947	2,600	—	—	Proof	125.00

KM#	Date	Mintage	Fine	VF	XF	Unc
38.1	1948	6,773	15.00	20.00	40.00	70.00
	1948	1,120	—	—	Proof	125.00
	1949	.203	5.00	10.00	15.00	35.00
	1949	800 pcs.	—	—	Proof	125.00
	1950	4,945	20.00	40.00	80.00	150.00
	1950	500 pcs.	—	—	Proof	175.00

11.3100 g, .500 SILVER, .1818 oz ASW
Rev. denomination: 2 S

KM#	Date	Mintage	Fine	VF	XF	Unc
38.2	1951	.730	2.00	3.00	5.00	10.00
	1951	2,000	—	—	Proof	15.00
	1952	3.570	1.50	2.00	3.00	6.50
	1952	.016	—	—	Proof	8.00

KM#	Date	Mintage	Fine	VF	XF	Unc
50	1953	3.274	1.50	2.25	4.00	8.50
	1953	5,000	—	—	Proof	9.00
	1954	5.866	1.50	2.25	3.00	7.00
	1954	3,150	—	—	Proof	8.00
	1955	3.745	1.50	2.25	3.00	7.50
	1955	2,850	—	—	Proof	8.00
	1956	2.549	1.50	2.25	4.00	9.00
	1956	1,700	—	—	Proof	10.00
	1957	2.507	1.50	2.25	4.00	10.00
	1957	1,130	—	—	Proof	11.00
	1958	2.821	1.50	2.25	4.00	10.00
	1958	985 pcs.	—	—	Proof	11.00
	1959	1.219	1.50	2.25	4.00	10.00
	1959	900 pcs.	—	—	Proof	14.00
	1960	1.951	1.50	2.25	3.00	5.00
	1960	3,360	—	—	Proof	4.00

2-1/2 SHILLINGS

14.1400 g, .800 SILVER, .3637 oz ASW
Rev. leg: ZUID-AFRICA,
denomination: 2-1/2 SHILLINGS 2-1/2

KM#	Date	Mintage	Fine	VF	XF	Unc
19.1	1923	1.227	4.00	15.00	35.00	70.00
	1923	1,402	—	—	Proof	125.00
	1924	2.556	3.50	10.00	50.00	120.00
	1925	.460	8.00	30.00	180.00	600.00

Rev. denomination: 2-1/2 SHILLINGS

KM#	Date	Mintage	Fine	VF	XF	Unc
19.2	1926	.205	10.00	40.00	250.00	650.00
	1926	16 pcs.	—	—	Proof	4000.
	1927	.194	10.00	40.00	350.00	850.00
	1928	.984	5.00	25.00	125.00	325.00
	1929	.617	5.00	25.00	175.00	350.00
	1930	.324	5.00	15.00	100.00	250.00
	1930	14 pcs.	—	—	Proof	1650.

Rev. leg: SUID. AFRICA

KM#	Date	Mintage	Fine	VF	XF	Unc
19.3	1931	790 pcs.	200.00	350.00	700.00	1300.
	1931	62 pcs.	—	—	Proof	2200.
	1932	1.029	4.00	6.00	22.50	40.00
	1932	12 pcs.	—	—	Proof	2400.
	1933	.136	8.00	40.00	185.00	300.00
	1933	20 pcs.	—	—	Proof	2400.
	1934	.416	4.00	8.00	30.00	100.00
	1934	24 pcs.	—	—	Proof	1650.
	1935	.345	5.00	12.50	32.50	100.00
	1935	20 pcs.	—	—	Proof	1650.
	1936	.553	4.00	8.00	25.00	70.00
	1936	40 pcs.	—	—	Proof	800.00

KM#	Date	Mintage	Fine	VF	XF	Unc
30	1937	1.154	3.00	5.00	15.00	32.50
	1937	116 pcs.	—	—	Proof	175.00
	1938	.534	4.00	8.00	20.00	60.00
	1938	44 pcs.	—	—	Proof	400.00
	1939	.133	6.00	15.00	40.00	80.00
	1939	30 pcs.	—	—	Proof	800.00
	1940	2.976	3.00	4.50	8.00	20.00
	1941	1.988	3.00	4.50	8.00	20.00
	1942	3.180	3.00	4.50	8.00	20.00
	1943	2.098	3.00	4.50	8.00	20.00
	1943	104 pcs.	—	—	Proof	175.00
	1944	1.360	3.00	5.00	10.00	25.00
	1944	150 pcs.	—	—	Proof	130.00
	1945	.183	3.50	7.00	25.00	60.00
	1945	150 pcs.	—	—	Proof	130.00
	1946	.011	15.00	30.00	50.00	90.00
	1946	150 pcs.	—	—	Proof	180.00
	1947	3,582	20.00	35.00	60.00	100.00
	1947	2,600	—	—	Proof	150.00

KM#	Date	Mintage	Fine	VF	XF	Unc
39.1	1948	1,600	30.00	50.00	80.00	120.00
	1948	1,120	—	—	Proof	150.00
	1949	1,891	30.00	50.00	80.00	120.00
	1949	800 pcs.	—	—	Proof	175.00
	1950	5,076	30.00	50.00	80.00	125.00
	1950	500 pcs.	—	—	Proof	200.00

14.1400 g, .500 SILVER, .2273 oz ASW
Rev. denomination: 2-1/2 S

KM#	Date	Mintage	Fine	VF	XF	Unc
39.2	1951	.783	3.00	4.50	6.00	15.00
	1951	2,000	—	—	Proof	9.00
	1952	1.996	2.00	3.00	4.00	8.50
	1952	.016	—	—	Proof	5.00

KM#	Date	Mintage	Fine	VF	XF	Unc
51	1953	2.513	2.00	3.00	4.00	8.50
	1953	6,000	—	—	Proof	6.00
	1954	4.249	2.00	3.00	4.00	8.50
	1954	3,150	—	—	Proof	9.00
	1955	3.863	2.00	3.00	4.00	8.50
	1955	2,850	—	—	Proof	8.00
	1956	2.437	2.00	3.00	4.00	8.50
	1956	1,700	—	—	Proof	13.00
	1957	2.137	2.00	3.00	4.00	8.50

KM#	Date	Mintage	Fine	VF	XF	Un
51	1957	1,130	—	—	Proof	14.0
	1958	2.260	2.00	3.00	4.50	9.0
	1958	985 pcs.	—	—	Proof	14.0
	1959	.046	2.50	4.00	6.00	12.0
	1959	900 pcs.	—	—	Proof	18.0
	1960	.012	3.00	5.00	7.50	12.5
	1960	3,360	—	—	Proof	5.0

5 SHILLINGS

28.2800 g, .800 SILVER, .7274 oz ASW
Royal Visit

KM#	Date	Mintage	Fine	VF	XF	Unc
31	1947	.300	BV	7.00	7.50	10.00
	1947	5,600	—	—	Proof	30.00

KM#	Date	Mintage	Fine	VF	XF	Unc
40.1	1948	.780	BV	6.00	7.50	10.00
	1948	1,000	—	—	P/L	20.00
	1948	1,120	—	—	Proof	20.00
	1949	.535	BV	6.00	7.50	10.00
	1949	2,000	—	—	P/L	40.00
	1949	800 pcs.	—	—	Proof	50.00
	1950	.083	BV	10.00	12.50	25.00
	1950	1,200	—	—	P/L	70.00
	1950	500 pcs.	—	—	Proof	80.00

28.2800 g, .500 SILVER, .4546 oz ASW
Rev. denomination: 5 S.

KM#	Date	Mintage	Fine	VF	XF	Unc
40.2	1951	.363	BV	5.00	7.00	10.00
	1951	1,483	—	—	P/L	40.00
	1951	2,000	—	—	Proof	22.00

300th Anniversary Founding of Capetown

KM#	Date	Mintage	Fine	VF	XF	Unc
41	1952	1.698	BV	4.50	5.50	7.50
	1952	.012	—	—	P/L	12.50
	1952	.016	—	—	Proof	13.00

KM#	Date	Mintage	Fine	VF	XF	Unc
52	1953	.250	BV	5.00	7.00	10.00
	1953	8,000	—	—	P/L	15.00
	1953	5,000	—	—	Proof	16.00
	1953	—	—		Matte Proof	700.00
	1954	.010	BV	10.00	15.00	30.00
	1954	3,890	—	—	P/L	40.00
	1954	3,150	—	—	Proof	50.00
	1955	.040	BV	7.50	10.00	15.00
	1955	2,230	—	—	P/L	22.50
	1955	2,850	—	—	Proof	20.00
	1956	.100	BV	5.00	7.00	10.00
	1956	2,200	—	—	P/L	22.50
	1956	1,700	—	—	Proof	25.00
	1957	.154	BV	5.00	7.00	10.00
	1957	1,600	—	—	P/L	30.00
	1957	1,130	—	—	Proof	30.00
	1958	.233	BV	5.00	7.00	10.00
	1958	1,500	—	—	P/L	30.00
	1958	985 pcs.	—	—	Proof	35.00
	1959	2,989	35.00	65.00	125.00	175.00
	1959	2,200	—	—	P/L	225.00
	1959	950 pcs.	—	—	Proof	250.00

50th Anniversary of South African Union

KM#	Date	Mintage	Fine	VF	XF	Unc
55	1960	.396	BV	4.50	5.50	6.50
	1960	.022	—	—	P/L	10.00
	1960	3,360	—	—	Proof	12.50

NOTE: Many varieties exist of letters HM below building.

1/2 SOVEREIGN

3.9940 g, .917 GOLD, .1177 oz AGW
British type w/Pretoria mint mark: SA

KM#	Date	Mintage	Fine	VF	XF	Unc
20	1923	655 pcs.	—	—	Proof	450.00
	1925	.947	55.00	70.00	80.00	100.00
	1926	.809	55.00	70.00	80.00	100.00

1/2 POUND

3.9940 g, .917 GOLD, .1177 oz AGW
Similar to 1 Pound, KM#43.

KM#	Date	Mintage	Fine	VF	XF	Unc
42	1952	4,002	—	—	—	65.00
	1952	.012	—	—	Proof	70.00

KM#	Date	Mintage	Fine	VF	XF	Unc
53	1953	4,000	—	—	Proof	75.00
	1954	1,275	—	—	Proof	85.00
	1955	900 pcs.	—	—	Proof	100.00
	1956	508 pcs.	—	—	Proof	200.00
	1957	560 pcs.	—	—	Proof	160.00
	1958	515 pcs.	—	—	Proof	175.00
	1959	500 pcs.	—	—	—	90.00
	1959	630 pcs.	—	—	Proof	150.00
	1960	1,052	—	—	—	65.00
	1960	1,950	—	—	Proof	75.00

SOVEREIGN

7.9881 g, .917 GOLD, .2354 oz AGW
British type w/Pretoria mint mark: SA

KM#	Date	Mintage	Fine	VF	XF	Unc
21	1923	64 pcs.	200.00	300.00	400.00	500.00
	1923	655 pcs.	—	—	Proof	550.00
	1924	3,184	800.00	1750.	3000.	4250.
	1925	6.086	—	BV	110.00	125.00
	1926	11.108	—	BV	110.00	125.00
	1927	16.380	—	BV	110.00	125.00
	1928	18.235	—	BV	110.00	125.00
		Obv: Modified effigy, slightly smaller bust.				
A22	1929	12.024	—	BV	110.00	125.00
	1930	10.028	—	BV	110.00	125.00
	1931	8.512	—	BV	110.00	125.00
	1932	1.067	—	BV	110.00	145.00

POUND

7.9881 g, .917 GOLD, .2354 oz AGW

KM#	Date	Mintage	Fine	VF	XF	Unc
43	1952	4,508	—	—	—	125.00
	1952	.012	—	—	Proof	135.00

KM#	Date	Mintage	Fine	VF	XF	Unc
54	1953	4,000	—	—	Proof	135.00
	1954	1,275	—	—	Proof	150.00
	1955	900 pcs.	—	—	Proof	170.00
	1956	508 pcs.	—	—	Proof	275.00
	1957	560 pcs.	—	—	Proof	265.00
	1958	515 pcs.	—	—	Proof	275.00
	1959	502 pcs.	—	—	—	175.00
	1959	630 pcs.	—	—	Proof	225.00
	1960	1,161	—	—	—	125.00
	1960	1,950	—	—	Proof	135.00

REPUBLIC

MONETARY SYSTEM
100 Cents = 1 Rand

1/2 CENT

BRASS

KM#	Date	Mintage	VF	XF	Unc
56	1961	39.189	.15	.25	1.00
	1961	7,530	—	Proof	.50
	1962	17.895	.15	.25	1.00
	1962	3,844	—	Proof	.75
	1963	11.611	.15	.25	2.00
	1963	4,025	—	Proof	.50
	1964	9.258	.15	.25	1.00
	1964	.016	—	Proof	.50

BRONZE
Bilingual
Sparrows

KM#	Date	Mintage	VF	XF	Unc
81	1970	*57.721	.10	.25	.50
	1970	.010	—	Proof	2.50
	1971	8,000	—	—	2.50
	1971	.012	—	Proof	2.50
	1972	8,000	—	—	2.50
	1972	.012	—	Proof	2.50
	1973	.020	.10	.20	2.50
	1973	.011	—	Proof	2.50
	1974	.020	.20	.40	2.50
	1974	.015	—	Proof	2.50
	1975	.020	.10	.20	2.50
	1975	.018	—	Proof	2.50
	1977	.020	.10	.20	2.50
	1977	.019	—	Proof	2.50
	1978	.018	.10	.20	2.50
	1978	.019	—	Proof	2.50
	1980	.015	—	Proof	2.50
	1981	.010	—	Proof	2.50
	1983	.014	—	Proof	2.50

***NOTE:** Coins dated 1970 were also struck for circulation in 1971, 1972 and 1973.

President Fouche
Similar to 1 Cent, KM#91.

KM#	Date	Mintage	VF	XF	Unc
90	1976	.020	—	—	1.00
	1976	.021	—	Proof	1.50

President Diederichs

KM#	Date	Mintage	VF	XF	Unc
97	1979	.018	—	—	1.00
	1979	.017	—	Proof	1.50

President Vorster

KM#	Date	Mintage	VF	XF	Unc
108	1982	.012	—	Proof	1.50

CENT

BRASS

KM#	Date	Mintage	VF	XF	Unc
57	1961	52.266	.15	.40	1.50
	1961	7,530	—	Proof	.75
	1962	21.929	.15	.40	1.50
	1962	3,844	—	Proof	1.00
	1963	9.081	.15	.50	3.00
	1963	4,025	—	Proof	1.00
	1964	14.265	.15	.40	1.50
	1964	.016	—	Proof	2.00

BRONZE
English legend
Sparrows

KM#	Date	Mintage	VF	XF	Unc
65.1	1965	1,180	—	—	4.00
	1965	.025	—	Proof	2.50
	1966	50.157	—	.10	.50
	1967	21.114	—	.10	.50
	1969	10.196	—	.10	.50

Afrikaans legend

KM#	Date	Mintage	VF	XF	Unc
65.2	1965	846 pcs.	100.00	200.00	300.00
	1965	185 pcs.	—	Proof	350.00
	1966	50.157	—	.10	.50
	1966	.025	—	Proof	1.00
	1967	21.114	—	.10	.50
	1967	.025	—	Proof	1.00
	1969	10.196	—	.10	.50
	1969	.012	—	Proof	1.50

President Charles Swart
English legend

KM#	Date	Mintage	VF	XF	Unc
74.1	1968	6.000	—	.10	.30
	1968	.025	—	Proof	1.00

Afrikaans legend

KM#	Date	Mintage	VF	XF	Unc
74.2	1968	6.000	—	.10	.30

Bilingual

KM#	Date	Mintage	VF	XF	Unc
82	1970	37.072	—	—	.30
	1970	.010	—	Proof	1.00
	1971	34.053	—	—	.30
	1971	.012	—	Proof	1.00
	1972	35.662	—	—	.30
	1972	.010	—	Proof	1.00
	1973	35.898	.10	.20	.40
	1973	.011	—	Proof	1.00
	1974	54.940	—	—	.25
	1974	.015	—	Proof	1.00
	1975	62.982	—	—	.25
	1975	.018	—	Proof	1.00
	1977	72.444	—	—	.25
	1977	.019	—	Proof	1.00
	1978	70.152	—	—	.20
	1978	.017	—	Proof	.50
	1980	63.432	—	—	.20
	1980	.015	—	Proof	.50
	1981	63.444	—	—	.20
	1981	.010	—	Proof	.50
	1983	182.131	—	—	.20
	1983	.014	—	Proof	.50
	1984	107.155	—	—	.20
	1984	.011	—	Proof	.50
	1985	186.042	—	—	.20
	1985	9,859	—	Proof	.50
	1986	169.734	—	—	.20
	1986	7,000	—	Proof	.50
	1987	120.674	—	—	.20
	1987	6,781	—	Proof	.50
	1988	240.272	—	—	.20
	1988	7,250	—	Proof	.50
	1989	—	—	—	.20
	1989	—	—	Proof	.50

President Fouche

KM#	Date	Mintage	VF	XF	Unc
91	1976	91.860	—	.30	.50
	1976	.021	—	Proof	.75

President Diederichs

KM#	Date	Mintage	VF	XF	Unc
98	1979	63.432	—	.30	.50
	1979	.015	—	Proof	.75

President Vorster

KM#	Date	Mintage	VF	XF	Unc
109	1982	145.954	—	.30	.50
	1982	.012	—	Proof	.75

COPPER PLATED STEEL

KM#	Date	Mintage	VF	XF	Unc
132	1990	—	—	—	.20
	1990	—	—	Proof	.50
	1991	—	—	—	.20
	1991	—	—	Proof	.50
	1992	—	—	—	.20
	1993	—	—	—	.20

2 CENTS

BRONZE
English legend
White-tailed Gnu

KM#	Date	Mintage	VF	XF	Unc
66.1	1965	29.887	—	.10	.30
	1966	9.267	—	.10	.35
	1966	.025	—	Proof	.50
	1967	11.862	—	.10	.30
	1967	.025	—	Proof	.50
	1969	5.817	—	.10	.40
	1969	.012	—	Proof	.50

Afrikaans legend

KM#	Date	Mintage	VF	XF	Unc
66.2	1965	29.887	—	.10	.30
	1965	.025	—	Proof	.50
	1966	9.267	—	.10	.30
	1967	11.862	—	.10	.30
	1969	5.817	—	.10	.35

President Charles Swart
English legend

KM#	Date	Mintage	VF	XF	Unc
75.1	1968	5.500	—	.20	.50

Afrikaans legend

KM#	Date	Mintage	VF	XF	Unc
75.2	1968	5.525	—	.20	.5
	1968	.025	—	Proof	1.0

Bilingual

KM#	Date	Mintage	VF	XF	Unc
83	1970	35.217	—	—	.25
	1970	.010	—	Proof	.50
	1971	24.093	—	—	.25
	1971	.012	—	Proof	.50
	1972	7.304	—	—	.30
	1972	.010	—	Proof	.50
	1973	18.685	—	—	.25
	1973	.011	—	Proof	.50
	1974	25.301	—	—	.25
	1974	.015	—	Proof	.50
	1975	24.982	—	—	.25
	1975	.018	—	Proof	.50
	1977	45.116	—	—	.25
	1977	.019	—	Proof	.50
	1978	50.527	—	—	.25
	1978	.017	—	Proof	.50
	1980	37.795	—	—	.25
	1980	.015	—	Proof	.50
	1981	79.350	—	—	.25
	1981	.010	—	Proof	.50
	1983	112.575	—	—	.25
	1983	.014	—	Proof	.50
	1984	101.497	—	—	.25
	1984	.011	—	Proof	.50
	1985	102.708	—	—	.25
	1985	9,859	—	Proof	.50
	1986	683.294	—	—	.25
	1986	7,100	—	Proof	.50
	1987	104.981	—	—	.25
	1987	6,781	—	Proof	.50
	1988	182.036	—	—	.25
	1988	7,250	—	Proof	.50
	1989	—	—	—	.25
	1989	—	—	Proof	.50
	1990	—	—	—	.25
	1990	—	—	Proof	.50

President Fouche

KM#	Date	Mintage	VF	XF	Unc
92	1976	51.474	—	.25	.50
	1976	.021	—	Proof	.75

President Diederichs

KM#	Date	Mintage	VF	XF	Unc
99	1979	40.043	—	.25	.50
	1979	.015	—	Proof	.75

President Vorster

KM#	Date	Mintage	VF	XF	Unc
110	1982	53.962	—	.25	.50
	1982	.012	—	Proof	.75

COPPER PLATED STEEL

KM#	Date	Mintage	VF	XF	Unc
133	1990	—	—	—	1.50
	1990	—	—	Proof	2.00
	1991	—	—	—	1.50
	1992	—	—	—	.25
	1992	—	—	Proof	2.00
	1993	—	—	—	.25

2-1/2 CENTS

1.4100 g, .500 SILVER, .0226 oz ASW

KM#	Date	Mintage	VF	XF	Unc
58	1961	.292	.50	1.00	2.00
	1961	7,530	—	Proof	4.00
	1962	8,745	2.00	4.00	8.00
	1962	3,844	—	Proof	8.00
	1963	.033	1.50	2.50	4.00
	1963	4,025	—	Proof	6.00
	1964	.014	2.00	4.00	6.00
	1964	.016	—	Proof	4.00

5 CENTS

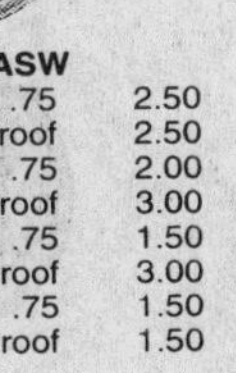

2.8300 g, .500 SILVER, .0454 oz ASW

KM#	Date	Mintage	VF	XF	Unc
59	1961	1.479	.50	.75	2.50
	1961	7,530	—	Proof	2.50
	1962	4.188	.50	.75	2.00
	1962	3,844	—	Proof	3.00
	1963	8.054	.50	.75	1.50
	1963	4,025	—	Proof	3.00
	1964	3.567	.50	.75	1.50
	1964	.016	—	Proof	1.50

NICKEL
English legend
Blue Crane

KM#	Date	Mintage	VF	XF	Unc
67.1	1965	32.690	—	.10	.35
	1965	.025	—	Proof	.60
	1966	4.101	—	.10	.45
	1967	4.590	—	.10	.45
	1969	5.020	—	.10	.45

Afrikaans legend

KM#	Date	Mintage	VF	XF	Unc
67.2	1965	32.690	—	.10	.35
	1966	4.101	—	.10	.45
	1966	.025	—	Proof	.60
	1967	4.590	—	.10	.45
	1967	.025	—	Proof	.60
	1969	5.020	—	.10	.45
	1969	.012	—	Proof	.60

President Charles Swart
English legend

KM#	Date	Mintage	VF	XF	Unc
76.1	1968	6.000	—	.10	.60
	1968	.025	—	Proof	.60

Afrikaans legend

KM#	Date	Mintage	VF	XF	Unc
76.2	1968	6.000	—	.10	.60

Bilingual

KM#	Date	Mintage	VF	XF	Unc
84	1970	6.652	—	.10	.35
	1970	.010	—	Proof	.60
	1971	20.329	—	.10	.35
	1971	.012	—	Proof	.60
	1972	3.117	—	.10	.40
	1972	9,000	—	Proof	.60
	1973	17.092	—	.10	.35
	1973	.011	—	Proof	.60
	1974	19.978	—	.10	.35
	1974	.015	—	Proof	.60
	1975	21.982	—	.10	.30
	1975	.018	—	Proof	.60
	1977	51.729	—	.10	.30
	1977	.019	—	Proof	.60
	1978	30.050	—	.10	.30
	1978	.019	—	Proof	.60
	1980	46.665	—	.10	.30
	1980	.015	—	Proof	.60
	1981	40.351	—	.10	.30
	1981	.010	—	Proof	.60
	1983	57.487	—	.10	.30
	1983	.014	—	Proof	.60
	1984	67.345	—	.10	.30
	1984	.011	—	Proof	.60
	1985	57.167	—	.10	.30
	1985	9,859	—	Proof	.60
	1986	54.226	—	.10	.30
	1986	7,100	—	Proof	.60
	1987	42.786	—	.10	.30
	1987	5,297	—	Proof	.60
	1988	110.164	—	.10	.30
	1988	7,250	—	Proof	.60
	1989	35.540	—	.20	5.00
	1989	Inc. Ab.	—	Proof	6.00

President Fouche

KM#	Date	Mintage	VF	XF	Unc
93	1976	48.972	—	.30	.75
	1976	.019	—	Proof	1.50

President Diederichs

KM#	Date	Mintage	VF	XF	Unc
100	1979	17.533	—	.30	.75
	1979	.017	—	Proof	1.50

President Vorster

KM#	Date	Mintage	VF	XF	Unc
111	1982	47.236	—	.30	.75
	1982	.012	—	Proof	1.50

COPPER PLATED STEEL

KM#	Date	Mintage	VF	XF	Unc
134	1990	—	—	—	.30
	1990	—	—	Proof	.60
	1991	—	—	—	.30
	1992	—	—	—	.30
	1992	—	—	Proof	.60
	1993	—	—	—	.30

10 CENTS

5.6600 g, .500 SILVER, .0909 oz ASW

KM#	Date	Mintage	VF	XF	Unc
60	1961	1.136	.75	1.25	2.50
	1961	7,530	—	Proof	2.50
	1962	2.447	.75	1.25	2.50
	1962	3,844	—	Proof	3.50
	1963	3.327	.75	1.25	2.50
	1963	4,025	—	Proof	3.50
	1964	4.153	.75	1.25	2.00
	1964	.016	—	Proof	2.50

NICKEL
English legend
Aloe Plant

KM#	Date	Mintage	VF	XF	Unc
68.1	1965	29.210	—	.10	.35
	1966	3.685	—	.10	.45
	1966	.025	—	Proof	.60
	1967	.050	—	—	1.00
	1967	.025	—	Proof	.60
	1969	.558	—	.10	.50
	1969	.012	—	Proof	1.00

Afrikaans legend

KM#	Date	Mintage	VF	XF	Unc
68.2	1965	29.210	—	.10	.35
	1965	.025	—	Proof	.60
	1966	3.685	—	.10	.45
	1967	.050	—	—	1.00
	1969	.558	.10	.20	2.50

President Charles Swart
English legend

KM#	Date	Mintage	VF	XF	Unc
77.1	1968	.050	—	—	2.00

Afrikaans legend

KM#	Date	Mintage	VF	XF	Unc
77.2	1968	.050	—	—	1.50
	1968	.025	—	Proof	.60

Bilingual

KM#	Date	Mintage	VF	XF	Unc
85	1970	7.598	—	.10	.35
	1970	.010	—	Proof	.60
	1971	6.440	—	.10	.35
	1971	.012	—	Proof	.60
	1972	10.028	—	.10	.35
	1972	.010	—	Proof	.60
	1973	1.760	—	.10	.35
	1973	.011	—	Proof	.60
	1974	9.897	—	.10	.35
	1974	.015	—	Proof	.60
	1975	12.982	—	.10	.35
	1975	.018	—	Proof	.60
	1977	28.851	—	.10	.35
	1977	.019	—	Proof	.60
	1978	25.008	—	.10	.35
	1978	.019	—	Proof	.60
	1980	5.040	—	.10	.35
	1980	.015	—	Proof	.60
	1981	9.604	—	.10	.35
	1981	.010	—	Proof	.60
	1983	26.495	—	.10	.35
	1983	.014	—	Proof	.60
	1984	35.465	—	.10	.35
	1984	.011	—	Proof	.60
	1985	29.270	—	.10	.35
	1985	9,859	—	Proof	.60
	1986	24.480	—	.10	.35
	1986	7,100	—	Proof	.60
	1987	43.234	—	.10	.35

KM#	Date	Mintage	VF	XF	Unc
85	1987	6,781	—	Proof	.60
	1988	48.267	—	.10	.35
	1988	7,250	—	Proof	.60
	1989	—	—	—	.35
	1989	—	—	Proof	.60

President Fouche

KM#	Date	Mintage	VF	XF	Unc
94	1976	30.986	—	.40	1.00
	1976	.021	—	Proof	1.50

President Diederichs

KM#	Date	Mintage	VF	XF	Unc
101	1979	5.042	—	.40	1.00
	1979	.017	—	Proof	1.50

President Vorster

KM#	Date	Mintage	VF	XF	Unc
112	1982	15.806	—	.40	1.00
	1982	.012	—	Proof	1.50

BRASS PLATED STEEL

KM#	Date	Mintage	VF	XF	Unc
135	1990	—	—	—	.40
	1990	—	—	Proof	.60
	1991	—	—	—	.40
	1992	—	—	—	.40
	1992	—	—	Proof	.60
	1993	—	—	—	.40

20 CENTS

11.3100 g, .500 SILVER, .1818 oz ASW

KM#	Date	Mintage	VF	XF	Unc
61	1961	2.954	1.00	1.50	3.00
	1961	7,530	—	Proof	3.50
	1962 sm.2	3.568	1.00	1.50	3.00
	1962 lg.2	I.A.	—	—	—
	1962	3,844	—	Proof	4.00
	1963	4.380	1.00	1.50	3.00
	1963	4,025	—	Proof	4.00
	1964	4.335	1.00	1.50	3.00
	1964	.016	—	Proof	2.50

NICKEL
English legend
Protea Cynaroides and Protea Repens

KM#	Date	Mintage	VF	XF	Unc
69.1	1965	29.210	.15	.20	.40
	1965	.025	—	Proof	.60
	1966	4.049	.15	.20	.50
	1967	.058	—	—	1.00
	1969	9,952	—	—	10.00

Afrikaans legend

KM#	Date	Mintage	VF	XF	Unc
69.2	1965	29.210	.15	.20	.40
	1966	4.049	.15	.20	.50
	1966	.025	—	Proof	.60
	1967	.058	—	—	1.00
	1967	.025	—	Proof	.60
	1969	9,952	—	—	6.00
	1969	.012	—	Proof	4.00

President Charles Swart
English legend

KM#	Date	Mintage	VF	XF	Unc
78.1	1968	.050	—	—	3.00
	1968	.025	—	Proof	.60

Afrikaans legend

KM#	Date	Mintage	VF	XF	Unc
78.2	1968	.050	—	—	3.50

Bilingual

KM#	Date	Mintage	VF	XF	Unc
86	1970	.014	—	—	10.00
	1970	.010	—	Proof	1.50
	1971	5.893	.15	.25	.60
	1971	.012	—	Proof	1.50
	1972	9.069	.15	.25	.60
	1972	.010	—	Proof	1.50
	1973	.020	—	—	5.00
	1973	.011	—	Proof	1.50
	1974	2.436	.15	.35	.75
	1974	.015	—	Proof	1.50
	1975	12.982	—	.20	.60
	1975	.018	—	Proof	1.00
	1977	30.650	—	.20	.60
	1977	.019	—	Proof	.75
	1978	10.049	—	.20	.60
	1978	.019	—	Proof	.75
	1980	13.335	—	.20	.60
	1980	.015	—	Proof	.75
	1981	8.534	—	.20	.60
	1981	.010	—	Proof	.75
	1983	25.667	—	.20	.60
	1983	.014	—	Proof	.75
	1984	31.607	—	.20	.60
	1984	.011	—	Proof	.75
	1985	29.329	—	.20	.60
	1985	9,859	—	Proof	.75
	1986	11.408	—	.20	.60
	1986	7,100	—	Proof	.75
	1987	36.904	—	.20	.60
	1987	6,781	—	Proof	.75
	1988	43.115	—	.20	.60
	1988	7,250	—	Proof	.75
	1989	—	—	.20	.60
	1989	—	—	Proof	.75
	1990	—	—	.20	.60
	1990	—	—	Proof	.75

NOTE: Varieties exist.

President Fouche

KM#	Date	Mintage	VF	XF	Unc
95	1976	18.826	—	.70	1.50
	1976	.021	—	Proof	2.50

President Diederichs

KM#	Date	Mintage	VF	XF	Unc
102	1979	5.032	—	.70	1.50
	1979	.015	—	Proof	2.50

President Vorster

KM#	Date	Mintage	VF	XF	Unc
113	1982	18.083	—	.70	1.50
	1982	.012	—	Proof	2.50

BRASS PLATED STEEL

KM#	Date	Mintage	VF	XF	Unc
136	1990	—	—	—	4.00
	1990	—	—	Proof	8.00
	1991	—	—	—	4.00
	1992	—	—	—	.50
	1992	—	—	Proof	8.00
	1993	—	—	—	.50

50 CENTS

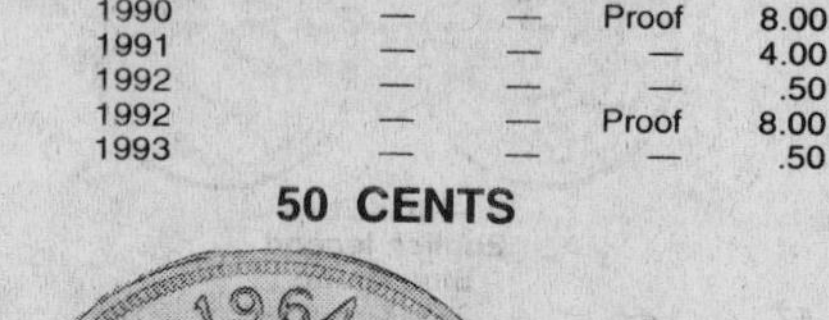

28.2800 g, .500 SILVER, .4546 oz ASW

KM#	Date	Mintage	VF	XF	Unc
62	1961	.026	BV	12.00	15.00
	1961	.020	—	P/L	15.00
	1961	8,530	—	Proof	25.00
	1962	.015	BV	12.00	15.00
	1962	6,024	—	P/L	22.00
	1962	3,844	—	Proof	40.00
	1963*	.143	BV	7.00	12.00
	1963	.010	—	P/L	17.50
	1963	4,025	—	Proof	30.00
	1964	.086	BV	7.50	12.50
	1964	.025	—	P/L	15.00
	1964	.016	—	Proof	15.00

NOTE: Varieties exist w/narrow, high relief and wide, low letters.

NICKEL
English legend
Zantedeschia Elliottiana

KM#	Date	Mintage	VF	XF	Unc
70.1	1965	30 to 50 pcs.	—	Proof	3500.
	1966	8.056	—	.50	2.50
	1966	.025	—	Proof	4.00
	1967	.052	In sets only		1.50
	1967	.025	—	Proof	4.00
	1969	7,968	In sets only		10.00
	1969	.012	—	Proof	10.00

Afrikaans legend

KM#	Date	Mintage	VF	XF	Unc
70.2	1965	.028	—	—	6.00
	1965	.025	—	Proof	6.00
	1966	8.056	—	.50	2.50
	1967	.052	In sets only		3.50
	1969	7,968	In sets only		15.00

President Charles Swart
English legend

KM#	Date	Mintage	VF	XF	Unc
79.1	1968	.750	—	.50	1.50

Afrikaans legend

KM#	Date	Mintage	VF	XF	Unc
79.2	1968	.750	—	.50	2.00
	1968	.025	—	Proof	3.50

Bilingual

KM#	Date	Mintage	VF	XF	Unc
87	1970	4.098	—	.50	1.50
	1970	.010	—	Proof	2.00
	1971	5.062	—	.50	1.50
	1971	.012	—	Proof	2.00
	1972	.771	—	.50	1.50
	1972	.010	—	Proof	2.00
	1973	1.043	—	.50	1.50
	1973	.011	—	Proof	2.00
	1974	1.942	—	.50	1.50
	1974	.015	—	Proof	2.00
	1975	4.888	—	.50	1.50
	1975	.018	—	Proof	2.00
	1977	10.196	—	.50	1.50
	1977	.019	—	Proof	2.00
	1978	5.071	—	.50	1.50
	1978	.017	—	Proof	2.00
	1980	4.268	—	.50	1.50
	1980	.015	—	Proof	2.00
	1981	5.681	—	.50	1.50
	1981	.010	—	Proof	2.00
87	1983	5.150	—	.40	1.00
	1983	.014	—	Proof	1.50
	1984	9.687	—	.40	1.00
	1984	.011	—	Proof	1.50
	1985	13.339	—	.40	1.00
	1985	9,859	—	Proof	1.50
	1986	2.294	—	.40	1.00
	1986	7,100	—	Proof	1.50
	1987	19.071	—	.40	1.00
	1987	6,781	—	Proof	1.50
	1988	27.698	—	.40	1.00
	1988	7,250	—	Proof	1.50
	1989	—	—	.40	1.00
	1989	—	—	Proof	1.50
	1990	—	—	.40	1.00
	1990	—	—	Proof	1.50

NOTE: Varieties exist.

President Fouche

KM#	Date	Mintage	VF	XF	Unc
96	1976	9.632	.75	1.50	3.00
	1976	.021	—	Proof	5.00

President Diederichs

KM#	Date	Mintage	VF	XF	Unc
103	1979	5.051	.75	1.50	3.50
	1979	.015	—	Proof	5.00

President Vorster

KM#	Date	Mintage	VF	XF	Unc
114	1982	2.070	.75	1.50	3.50
	1982	.012	—	Proof	5.00

BRASS PLATED STEEL

KM#	Date	Mintage	VF	XF	Unc
137	1990	—	—	—	5.00
	1990	—	—	Proof	10.00
	1991	—	—	—	5.00
	1992	—	—	—	1.00
	1992	—	—	Proof	10.00
	1993	—	—	—	1.00

RAND

3.9940 g, .917 GOLD, .1177 oz AGW

KM#	Date	Mintage	VF	XF	Unc
63	1961	4,246	—		*BV + 15%*
	1961	4,932	Proof		*BV + 20%*
	1962	3,955	—		*BV + 15%*
	1962	2,344	Proof		*BV + 20%*
	1963	4,023	—		*BV + 15%*
	1963	2,508	Proof		*BV + 20%*
	1964	5,866	—		*BV + 15%*
	1964	4,000	Proof		*BV + 20%*
	1965	.010	—		*BV + 15%*
	1965	6,024	Proof		*BV + 20%*
	1966	.010	—		*BV + 15%*
	1966	.011	Proof		*BV + 20%*
	1967	.010	—		*BV + 15%*
	1967	.011	Proof		*BV + 20%*
63	1968	.010	—		*BV + 15%*
	1968	.011	Proof		*BV + 20%*
	1969	.010	—		*BV + 15%*
	1969	8,000	Proof		*BV + 20%*
	1970	.010	—		*BV + 15%*
	1970	7,000	Proof		*BV + 20%*
	1971	.010	—		*BV + 15%*
	1971	7,650	Proof		*BV + 20%*
	1972	.012	—		*BV + 15%*
	1972	7,500	Proof		*BV + 20%*
	1973	.015	—		*BV + 15%*
	1973	.012	Proof		*BV + 20%*
	1974	.023	—		*BV + 15%*
	1974	.017	Proof		*BV + 20%*
	1975	.012	—		*BV + 15%*
	1975	.018	Proof		*BV + 20%*
	1976	.012	—		*BV + 15%*
	1976	.021	Proof		*BV + 20%*
	1977	.027	—		*BV + 15%*
	1977	.020	Proof		*BV + 20%*
	1978	.013	—		*BV + 15%*
	1978	.019	Proof		*BV + 20%*
	1979	.017	—		*BV + 15%*
	1979	.017	Proof		*BV + 20%*
	1980	.014	—		*BV + 15%*
	1980	.018	Proof		*BV + 20%*
	1981	9,274	—		*BV + 15%*
	1981	.010	Proof		*BV + 20%*
	1982	.014	—		*BV + 20%*
	1983	.015	—		*BV + 20%*

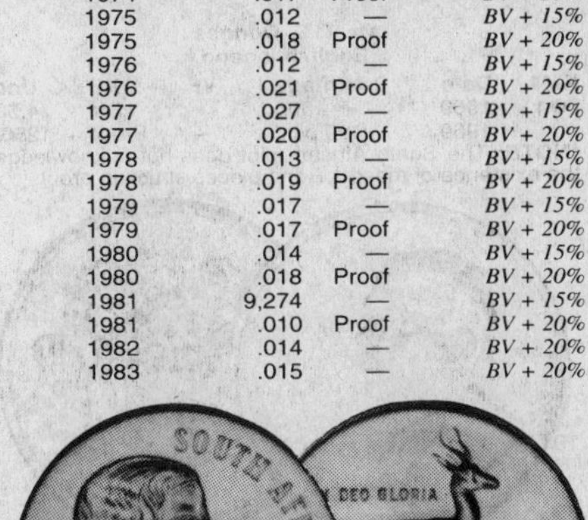

15.0000 g, .800 SILVER, .3858 oz ASW
English legend

KM#	Date	Mintage	VF	XF	Unc
71.1	1965	—	—	—	—
	1965	.025	—	Proof	20.00
	1966	1.434	—	BV	5.00
	1966	20 pcs.	—	Proof	1250.
	1968	.050	In sets only		7.50
	1968	.025	—	Proof	6.00

Afrikaans legend

KM#	Date	Mintage	VF	XF	Unc
71.2	1965	85 to 120 pcs.	V.I.P. Proof		1000.
	1966	1.434	—	BV	4.50
	1966	.025	—	Proof	6.00
	1968	.050	In sets only		7.50
	1968	*20 pcs.	—	Proof	1250.

1st Anniversary of Death of Dr. Verwoerd
English legend

KM#	Date	Mintage	VF	XF	Unc
72.1	1967	1.544	—	BV	4.00
	1967	*20 pcs.	—	Proof	1250.

Afrikaans legend

KM#	Date	Mintage	VF	XF	Unc
72.2	1967	1.544	—	BV	4.00
	1967	.025	—	Proof	6.00

Dr. T. E. Donges
English legend

KM#	Date	Mintage	VF	XF	Unc
80.1	1969	.506	—	BV	4.50
	1969	*20 pcs.	—	Proof	1250.

***NOTE:** The South African mint does not acknowledge the existence of these 1 Rand pieces struck in proof.

Afrikaans legend

KM#	Date	Mintage	VF	XF	Unc
80.2	1969	.506	—	BV	4.50
	1969	.012	—	Proof	6.00

Bilingual

KM#	Date	Mintage	VF	XF	Unc
88	1970	.014	—	BV	6.00
	1970	.010	—	Proof	8.00
	1971	.020	—	BV	6.00
	1971	.012	—	Proof	8.00
	1972	.020	—	BV	6.00
	1972	.010	—	Proof	8.00
	1973	.020	—	BV	6.00
	1973	.011	—	Proof	8.00
	1975	.020	—	BV	6.00
	1975	.018	—	Proof	8.00
	1976	.020	—	BV	6.00
	1976	.021	—	Proof	8.00
	1977	.019	—	Proof	9.00
	1978	.017	—	Proof	9.00
	1979	.015	—	Proof	9.00
	1980	.015	—	Proof	9.00
	1981	.012	—	Proof	12.50
	1982	.010	—	Proof	12.50
	1983	.014	—	Proof	12.50
	1984	.011	—	Proof	12.50
	1987	4,526	—	BV	15.00
	1987	.013	—	Proof	17.50
	1988	21 pcs.	—	—	—
	1988	7,250	—	Proof	15.00
	1989	3,684	—	BV	15.00
	1989	.015	—	Proof	17.50
	1990	—	—	BV	10.00

NICKEL

KM#	Date	Mintage	VF	XF	Unc
88a	1977	29.871	—	.75	2.00
	1977	10 pcs.	—	Proof	1500.
	1978	12.021	—	.75	2.00
	1978	10 pcs.	—	Proof	1500.
	1980	2.690	—	.75	2.00
	1981	2.035	—	.75	2.00
	1983	7.182	—	.75	2.00
	1983	10 pcs.	—	Proof	1500.
	1984	5.736	—	.75	2.00
	1984	.011	—	Proof	5.00
	1986	1.570	—	.75	2.00
	1986	7,000	—	Proof	5.00

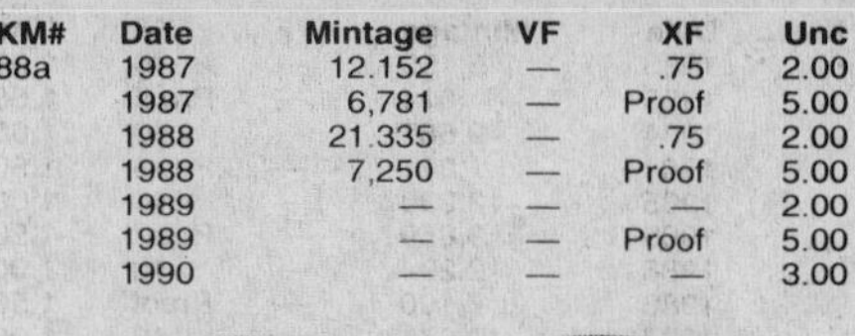

KM#	Date	Mintage	VF	XF	Unc
88a	1987	12.152	—	.75	2.00
	1987	6,781	—	Proof	5.00
	1988	21.335	—	.75	2.00
	1988	7,250	—	Proof	5.00
	1989	—	—	—	2.00
	1989	—	—	Proof	5.00
	1990	—	—	—	3.00

15.0000 g, .800 SILVER, .3858 oz ASW
50th Anniversary of Pretoria Mint

KM#	Date	Mintage	VF	XF	Unc
89	1974	.020	—	—	12.50
	1974	.015	—	Proof	15.00

NICKEL
President Diederichs

KM#	Date	Mintage	VF	XF	Unc
104	1979	13.466	2.00	4.00	10.00
	1979	5 pcs.	—	Proof	2000.

President Vorster

KM#	Date	Mintage	VF	XF	Unc
115	1982	7.685	2.50	5.00	10.00
	1982	15 pcs.	—	Proof	1500.

15.0000 g, .800 SILVER, .3858 oz ASW
75th Anniversary of Parliament

KM#	Date	Mintage	VF	XF	Unc
116	1985	8,731	—	—	12.50
	1985	.026	—	Proof	20.00

NICKEL
President Marais Viljoen

KM#	Date	Mintage	VF	XF	Unc
117	1985	3.983	2.50	5.00	10.00
	1985	9,859	—	Proof	5.00

15.0000 g, .800 SILVER, .3858 oz ASW
100th Anniversary of Johannesburg

KM#	Date	Mintage	VF	XF	Unc
119	1986	7,501	—	—	12.50
	1986	5,683	—	Proof	25.00

Year of the Disabled
Obv: Similar to KM#119.

KM#	Date	Mintage	VF	XF	Unc
120	1986	1,005	—	—	40.00
	1986	5,150	—	Proof	60.00

Bartolomeu Dias

KM#	Date	Mintage	VF	XF	Unc
122	1988	7,091	—	—	12.50
	1988	9,640	—	Proof	22.50

Huguenots

KM#	Date	Mintage	VF	XF	Unc
125	1988	5,497	—	—	12.50
	1988	9,028	—	Proof	22.50

The Great Trek

KM#	Date	Mintage	VF	XF	Unc
128	1988	6,555	—	—	12.50
	1988	7,941	—	Proof	22.50

NICKEL PLATED COPPER

KM#	Date	Mintage	VF	XF	Unc
138	1991	—	—	—	2.50
	1992	—	—	—	1.75
	1992	—	—	Proof	20.00
	1993	—	—	—	1.75

NICKEL
President Botha

KM#	Date	Mintage	VF	XF	Unc
141	1990	—	—	1.75	3.50
	1990	—	—	Proof	10.00

NICKEL PLATED COPPER

KM#	Date	Mintage	VF	XF	Unc
148	1990	—	—	—	10.00
	1990	—	—	Proof	20.00

14.9700 g, .925 SILVER, .4452 oz ASW
South African Nursing Schools

KM#	Date	Mintage	VF	XF	Unc
142	1991	—	—	—	12.50
	1991	—	—	Proof	17.50

Coinage Centennial

KM#	Date	Mintage	VF	XF	Unc
143	1992	—	—	—	15.00
	1992	—	—	Proof	20.00

2 RAND

7.9881 g, .917 GOLD, .2354 oz AGW

KM#	Date	Mintage	VF	XF	Unc
64	1961	3,014	—		*BV + 10%*
	1961	3,932	Proof		*BV + 15%*
	1962	.010	—		*BV + 10%*
	1962	2,344	Proof		*BV + 15%*
	1963	3,179	—		*BV + 10%*
	1963	2,508	Proof		*BV + 15%*
	1964	3,994	—		*BV + 10%*
	1964	4,000	Proof		*BV + 15%*
	1965	.010	—		*BV + 10%*
	1965	6,024	Proof		*BV + 15%*
	1966	.010	—		*BV + 10%*
	1966	.011	Proof		*BV + 15%*
	1967	.010	—		*BV + 10%*
	1967	.011	Proof		*BV + 15%*
	1968	.010	—		*BV + 10%*
	1968	.011	Proof		*BV + 15%*
	1969	.010	—		*BV + 10%*
	1969	8,000	Proof		*BV + 15%*
	1970	.010	—		*BV + 10%*
	1970	7,000	Proof		*BV + 15%*
	1971	.010	—		*BV + 10%*
	1971	7,650	Proof		*BV + 15%*
	1972	.018	—		*BV + 10%*
	1972	7,500	Proof		*BV + 15%*
	1973	.014	—		*BV + 10%*
	1973	.013	Proof		*BV + 15%*
	1974	.013	—		*BV + 10%*
	1974	.017	Proof		*BV + 15%*
	1975	.012	—		*BV + 10%*
64	1975	.018	Proof		*BV + 15%*
	1976	.012	—		*BV + 10%*
	1976	.021	Proof		*BV + 15%*
	1977	.012	—		*BV + 10%*
	1977	.020	Proof		*BV + 15%*
	1978	.011	—		*BV + 10%*
	1978	.019	Proof		*BV + 15%*
	1979	.012	—		*BV + 10%*
	1979	.020	Proof		*BV + 15%*
	1980	.012	—		*BV + 10%*
	1980	.018	Proof		*BV + 15%*
	1981	8,538	—		*BV + 10%*
	1981	.010	Proof		*BV + 15%*
	1982	2,030	—		*BV + 10%*
	1982	.012	Proof		*BV + 15%*
	1983	.015	—		*BV + 15%*

NICKEL PLATED COPPER

KM#	Date	Mintage	VF	XF	Unc
139	1989	—	—	—	2.00
	1990	—	—	—	2.00
	1990	—	—	Proof	7.50
	1991	—	—	—	2.00
	1992	—	—	Proof	7.50
	1993	—	—	—	2.00

33.4700 g, .925 SILVER, .9954 oz ASW
Coin Minting

KM#	Date	Mintage	VF	XF	Unc
145	1992	—	—	Proof	40.00

Barcelona Olympics - 3 Event Athletes

KM#	Date	Mintage	VF	XF	Unc
147	1992	—	—	Proof	50.00

BULLION ISSUES

Mint Marks

GRC - Gold Reef City

1/10 KRUGERRAND

3.3900 g, .917 GOLD, .1000 oz AGW

KM#	Date	Mintage	VF	XF	Unc
105	1980	.857	—		*BV + 15%*
	1980	60 pcs.	—	Proof	2500.
	1981	1.321	—		*BV + 15%*
	1981	7,500	—	Proof	90.00
	1982	1.065	—		*BV + 15%*
	1982	.011	—	Proof	90.00
	1983	.508	—		*BV + 15%*
	1983	.012	—	Proof	90.00
	1984	.898	—		*BV + 15%*
	1984	.013	—	Proof	90.00
	1985	.282	—		*BV + 15%*
	1985	6,700	—	Proof	90.00
	1986	.087	—		*BV + 15%*
	1986	8,001	—	Proof	90.00
	1987	.053	—		*BV + 15%*
	1987	6,065	—	Proof	90.00
	1987 GRC	1,126	—	Proof	400.00
	1988	.087	—		*BV + 15%*
	1988	2,056	—	Proof	90.00
	1988 GRC	949 pcs.	—	Proof	400.00
	1989	—	—		*BV + 15%*
	1989	3,316	—	Proof	90.00
	1989 GRC	377 pcs.	—	Proof	1000.
	1990	—	—		*BV + 15%*
	1990	3,459	—	Proof	90.00
	1990 GRC	1,096	—	Proof	275.00
	1991	3,524	—	Proof	90.00
	1991 GRC	426 pcs.	—	Proof	275.00
	1992	1,789	—	Proof	90.00

1/4 KRUGERRAND

8.4800 g, .917 GOLD, .2500 oz AGW

KM#	Date	Mintage	VF	XF	Unc
106	1980	.534	—		*BV + 10%*
	1980	60 pcs.	—	Proof	3000.
	1981	.726	—		*BV + 10%*
	1981	7,500	—	Proof	175.00
	1982	1.269	—		*BV + 10%*
	1982	.011	—	Proof	175.00
	1983	.064	—		*BV + 10%*
	1983	.012	—	Proof	175.00
	1984	.503	—		*BV + 10%*
	1984	.013	—	Proof	175.00
	1985	.594	—		*BV + 10%*
	1985	6,700	—	Proof	175.00
	1986	8,001	—	Proof	175.00
	1987	6,050	—	Proof	175.00
	1987 GRC	1,121	—	Proof	500.00
	1988	5,946	—		*BV + 10%*
	1988	2,056	—	Proof	175.00
	1988 GRC	835 pcs.	—	Proof	500.00
	1989	—	—		*BV + 10%*
	1989	3,316	—	Proof	175.00
	1989 GRC	318 pcs.	—	Proof	1400.
	1990	—	—		*BV + 10%*
	1990	2,750	—	Proof	175.00
	1990 GRC	1,066	—	Proof	400.00
	1991	1,626	—	Proof	175.00
	1991 GRC	426 pcs.	—	Proof	400.00
	1992	1,629	—	Proof	175.00

1/2 KRUGERRAND

16.9700 g, .917 GOLD, .5000 oz AGW

KM#	Date	Mintage	VF	XF	Unc
107	1980	.374	—		*BV + 8%*
	1980	60 pcs.	—	Proof	3500.
	1981	.178	—		*BV + 8%*
	1981	9,000	—	Proof	300.00
	1982	.429	—		*BV + 8%*
	1982	.013	—	Proof	300.00
	1983	.060	—		*BV + 8%*
	1983	.014	—	Proof	300.00
	1984	.187	—		*BV + 8%*
	1984	9,900	—	Proof	300.00
	1985	.104	—		*BV + 8%*
	1985	5,945	—	Proof	300.00
	1986	8,002	—	Proof	300.00
	1987	5,389	—	Proof	300.00
	1987 GRC	1,186	—	Proof	800.00
	1988	5,454	—		*BV + 8%*
	1988	2,282	—	Proof	300.00
	1988 GRC	1,026	—	Proof	800.00
	1989	—	—		*BV + 8%*
	1989	3,727	—	Proof	300.00
	1989 GRC	399 pcs.	—	Proof	1500.
	1990	—	—		*BV + 8%*
	1990	2,850	—	Proof	300.00

KM#	Date	Mintage	VF	XF	Unc
107	1990 GRC	1,066	—	Proof	500.00
	1991	3,459	—	Proof	300.00
	1991 GRC	426 pcs.	—	Proof	500.00
	1992	1,501	—	Proof	300.00

KRUGERRAND

33.9305 g, .917 GOLD, 1.0000 oz AGW

KM#	Date	Mintage	VF	XF	Unc
73	1967	.040	—		*BV + 5%*
	1967	.010	—	Proof	525.00
	1968	.020	—		*BV + 5%*
	1968 frosted bust and frosted reverse				
		*5,000	—	Proof	1000.
	1968	8,956	—	Proof	550.00
	1969	.020	—		*BV + 5%*
	1969	.010	—	Proof	525.00

***NOTE:** In 1967-1969 superior quality specimens exhibiting proof-like surfaces are known. In addition, the following varieties are known: 1968 with normal mirror like obverse and reverse; 1968 with mirror like obverse and frosted reverse; 1969 with normal mirror like obverse and reverse; and 1969 with frosted bust and reverse frosted.

KM#	Date	Mintage	VF	XF	Unc
	1970	.211	—		*BV + 5%*
	1970	.010	—	Proof	500.00
	1971	.550	—		*BV + 5%*
	1971	6,000	—	Proof	500.00
	1972	.544	—		*BV + 5%*
	1972	6,625	—	Proof	500.00
	1973	.859	—		*BV + 5%*
	1973	.010	—	Proof	500.00
	1974	3.204	—		*BV + 5%*
	1974	6,352	—	Proof	500.00
	1975	4.804	—		*BV + 5%*
	1975	5,600	—	Proof	500.00
	1976	3.005	—		*BV + 5%*
	1976	6,600	—	Proof	500.00
	1977 188 serrations on edge				
		3.331	—		*BV + 5%*
	1977 188 serrations on edge				
		8,500	—	Proof	500.00
	1977 220 serrations on edge				
		Inc. Ab.	—		*BV + 5%*
	1977 220 serrations on edge				
		Inc. Ab.	—	Proof	500.00
	1978	6.012	—		*BV + 5%*
	1978	.010	—	Proof	500.00
	1979	4.941	—		*BV + 5%*
	1979	.012	—	Proof	500.00
	1980	3.143	—		*BV + 5%*
	1980	.012	—	Proof	500.00
	1981	3.560	—		*BV + 5%*
	1981	.013	—	Proof	500.00
	1982	2.566	—		*BV + 5%*
	1982	.017	—	Proof	500.00
	1983	3.368	—		*BV + 5%*
	1983	.019	—	Proof	500.00
	1984	2.070	—		*BV + 5%*
	1984	.014	—	Proof	500.00
	1985	.875	—		*BV + 5%*
	1985	.010	—	Proof	500.00
	1986	.020	—	Proof	500.00
	1987	.011	—		*BV + 5%*
	1987	.011	—	Proof	500.00
	1987 GRC	1,160	—	Proof	1200.
	1988	.615	—		*BV + 5%*
	1988	4,268	—	Proof	500.00
	1988 GRC	1,220	—	Proof	1200.
	1989	—	—		*BV + 5%*
	1989	5,070	—	Proof	500.00
	1989 GRC	987 pcs.	—	Proof	1600.
	1990	—	—		*BV + 5%*
	1990	3,032	—	Proof	500.00
	1990 GRC	1,066	—	Proof	1600.
	1991	2,181	—	Proof	500.00
	1991 GRC	426 pcs.	—	Proof	1600.
	1992	2,067	—	Proof	500.00

OUNCE

33.9305 g, .917 GOLD, 1.0000 oz AGW
75th Anniversary of Parliament

KM#	Date	Mintage	VF	XF	Unc
118	1985	3,019	—	Proof	1600.

1/10 PROTEA

3.3900 g, .917 GOLD, .1000 oz AGW
100th Anniversary of Johannesburg

KM#	Date	Mintage	VF	XF	Unc
131	1986	5,212	—	Proof	120.00

Bartolomew Dias

KM#	Date	Mintage	VF	XF	Unc
123	1988	2,199	—	Proof	120.00

Huguenots

KM#	Date	Mintage	VF	XF	Unc
126	1988	2,060	—	Proof	120.00

The Great Trek

KM#	Date	Mintage	VF	XF	Unc
129	1988	2,999	—	Proof	120.00

Coinage Centennial

KM#	Date	Mintage	VF	XF	Unc
144	1992	—	—	Proof	120.00

PROTEA

33.9300 g, .917 GOLD, 1.0000 oz AGW
100th Anniversary of Johannesburg

KM#	Date	Mintage	VF	XF	Unc
121	1986	4,701	—	Proof	900.00

Bartolomeu Dias

KM#	Date	Mintage	VF	XF	Unc
124	1988	3,776	—	Proof	925.00

Huguenots

KM#	Date	Mintage	VF	XF	Unc
127	1988	3,391	—	Proof	925.00

The Great Trek

KM#	Date	Mintage	VF	XF	Unc
130	1988	2,956	—	Proof	925.00

Coinage Centennial

KM#	Date	Mintage	VF	XF	Unc
146	1992	—	—	Proof	925.00

MINT SETS (MS)

KM#	Date	Mintage	Identification	Issue Price	Mkt. Val.
MS1	1967(7)	50,000	KM65.1-70.1,72.1	7.50	12.00
MS2	1967(7)	50,000	KM65.2-70.2,72.2	7.50	12.00
MS3	1968(7)	50,000	KM71.1,74.1-79.1	7.50	15.00
MS4	1968(7)	50,000	KM71.2,74.2-79.2	7.50	15.00
MS5	1969(7)	7,500	KM65.1-70.1,80.1	7.50	50.00
MS6	1969(7)	7,500	KM65.2-70.2,80.2	7.50	50.00
MS7	1970(8)	16,000	KM81-88	7.50	15.00
MS8	1971(8)	20,000	KM81-88	7.50	10.00
MS9	1972(8)	20,000	KM81-88	7.50	10.00
MS10	1973(8)	20,000	KM81-88	7.50	10.00
MS11	1974(8)	20,000	KM81-87,89	7.50	17.50
MS12	1975(8)	20,000	KM81-88	7.50	10.00
MS13	1976(8)	20,000	KM88,90-96	5.65	10.00
MS14	1977(8)	20,000	KM81-87,88a	—	10.00
MS15	1978(8)	20,000	KM81-87,88a	—	10.00
MS16	1979(8)	20,000	KM97-103,104	—	25.00
MS17	1980(7)	20,000	KM82-87,88a	—	10.00
MS18	1981(7)	10,000	KM82-87,88a	—	10.00
MS19	1982(7)	10,000	KM82-87,115	—	25.00
MS20	1983(7)	23,000	KM82-87,88a	—	10.00
MS21	1984(7)	13,875	KM82-87,88a	—	10.00
MS22	1985(7)	10,200	KM82-87,117	—	15.00
MS23	1986(7)	9,100	KM82-87,88a	—	12.00
MS24	1987(7)	7,642	KM82-87,88a	—	12.00
MS25	1988(7)	6,250	KM82-87,88a	—	25.00
MS26	1989(7)	—	KM82-87,88a	—	15.00
MS27	1990(8)	—	KM137,139,148	—	25.00
MS28	1991(8)	—	KM132-139	—	25.00
MS29	1993(8)	—	KM132-139	—	25.00

PROOF SETS (PS)

KM#	Date	Mintage	Identification	Issue Price	Mkt. Val.
PS1	1923(10)	655	KM12.1-17.1,18,19.1,20-21	—	1450.
PS2	1923(8)	747	KM12.1-17.1,18,19.1	—	500.00
PS3	1926(6)	3 known	KM12.2,14.2-17.2,19.2	—	20,000.
PS4	1930(8)	14	KM12.2-17.2,18,19.2	—	12,000.
PS5	1930(8)	Inc. Ab.	KM12.2(dated 1928), 13.2-17.2,18,19.2	—	20,000.
PS6	1931(8)	62	KM12.3-17.3,19.3,22	—	13,500.
PS7	1932(8)	12	KM12.3-17.3,19.3,22	—	13,500.
PS8	1933(8)	20	KM12.3-17.3,19.3,22	—	9000.
PS9	1934(8)	24	KM12.3-17.3,19.3,22	—	9000.
PS10	1935(8)	20	KM12.3-17.3,19.3,22	—	9000.
PS11	1936(8)	40	KM12.3-17.3,19.3,22	—	7250.
PS12	1937(8)	116	KM23-30	—	800.00
PS13	1938(8)	44	KM23-30	—	1500.
PS14	1939(8)	30	KM23-30	—	12,000.
PS15	1943(8)	104	KM23-30	—	7000.
PS16	1944(8)	150	KM23-30	—	600.00
PS17	1945(8)	150	KM23-30	—	600.00
PS18	1946(8)	150	KM23-30	—	700.00
PS19	1947(8)	2,600	KM23-30	—	200.00
PS20	1948(9)	1,120	KM32.1,33,34.1-40.1	—	280.00
PS21	1949(9)	800	KM32.1,33,34.1-40.1	—	450.00
PS22	1950(9)	500	KM32.1,33,34.1-40.1	—	475.00
PS23	1951(9)	2,000	KM32.2,33,34.2-40.2	—	75.00
PS24	1952(11)	12,000	KM32.2,33,34.2-39.2, 41-43	—	180.00
PS25	1952(9)	3,500	KM32.2,33,34.2-39.2, 41	—	35.00
PS26	1953(11)	3,000	KM44-54	29.40	220.00
PS27	1953(9)	2,000	KM44-52	4.35	50.00
PS28	1953(2)	1,000	KM53-54	25.20	200.00
PS29	1954(11)	875	KM44-54	29.40	300.00
PS30	1954(9)	2,275	KM44-52	4.35	75.00
PS31	1954(2)	350	KM53-54	25.20	235.00

KM#	Date	Mintage	Identification	Issue Price	Mkt. Val.
PS32	1955(11)	600	KM44-54	29.40	320.00
PS33	1955(9)	2,250	KM44-52	4.35	60.00
PS34	1955(2)	300	KM53-54	25.20	260.00
PS35	1956(11)	350	KM44-54	29.40	480.00
PS36	1956(9)	1,350	KM44-52	4.35	70.00
PS37	1956(2)	158	KM53-54	25.20	410.00
PS38	1957(11)	380	KM44-54	29.40	480.00
PS39	1957(9)	750	KM44-52	4.35	80.00
PS40	1957(2)	180	KM53-54	25.20	400.00
PS41	1958(11)	360	KM44-54	29.40	600.00
PS42	1958(9)	625	KM44-52	4.35	100.00
PS43	1958(2)	155	KM53-54	25.20	500.00
PS44	1959(11)	390	KM44-54	29.40	675.00
PS45	1959(9)	560	KM44-52	4.35	350.00
PS46	1959(2)	240	KM53-54	25.20	320.00
PS47	1960(11)	1,500	KM44-51,53-55	29.40	230.00
PS48	1960(9)	1,860	KM44-51,55	4.35	50.00
PS49	1960(2)	450	KM53-54	25.20	180.00
PS50	1961(9)	3,139	KM56-64	—	200.00
PS51	1961(7)	4,391	KM56-62	—	40.00
PS52	1961(2)	793	KM63-64		*BV + 20%*
PS53	1962(9)	1,544	KM56-64	—	210.00
PS54	1962(7)	2,300	KM56-62	—	50.00
PS55	1962(2)	800	KM63-64		*BV + 20%*
PS56	1963(9)	1,500	KM56-64	—	200.00
PS57	1963(7)	2,525	KM56-62	—	40.00
PS58	1963(2)	1,008	KM63-64		*BV + 20%*
PS59	1964(9)	3,000	KM56-64	—	190.00
PS60	1964(7)	13,000	KM56-62	—	30.00
PS61	1964(2)	1,000	KM63-64		*BV + 20%*
PS62	1965(9)	5,099	KM63-64,65.1,66.2,67.1, 68.2,69.1,70.2,71.1	23.50	185.00
PS63	1965(9)	85	KM63-64,65.1-66.2,67.1, 68.2,69.1,70.2,71.2 V.I.P.	—	1200.
PS64	1965(7)	19,889	KM65.1,66.2,67.1,68.2, 69.1,70.2,71.1	5.00	50.00
PS65	1965(2)	925	KM63-64	18.15	*BV + 20%*
PS66	1966(9)	10,000	KM63-64,65.2,66.1,67.2, 68.1,69.2,70.1,71.2	24.10	185.00
PS67	1966(7)	15,000	KM65.2,66.1,67.2,68.1, 69.2,70.1,71.2	5.00	15.00
PS68	1966(2)	1,000	KM63-64	18.15	*BV + 20%*
PS69	1967(9)	10,000	KM63-64,65.2,66.1,67.2, 68.1,69.2,70.1,72.2	24.10	185.00
PS70	1967(7)	15,000	KM65.2,66.1,67.2,68.1, 69.2,70.1,72.2	5.00	15.00
PS71	1967(2)	1,000	KM63-64	18.15	*BV + 20%*
PS72	1968(9)	10,000	KM63-64,71.1,74.1,75.2, 76.1,77.2,78.1,79.2	35.00	185.00
PS73	1968(7)	15,000	KM71.1,74.1,75.2,76.1, 77.2,78.1,79.2	16.00	15.00
PS74	1968(2)	1,000	KM63-64	28.00	*BV + 20%*
PS75	1969(9)	7,000	KM63-64,65.2,66.1,67.2, 68.1,69.2,70.1,80.2	34.85	185.00
PS76	1969(7)	5,000	KM65.2,66.1,67.2,68.1, 69.2,70.1,80.2	13.95	10.00
PS77	1969(2)	1,000	KM63-64	27.85	*BV + 20%*
PS78	1970(10)	6,000	KM63-64,81-88	35.05	185.00
PS79	1970(8)	4,000	KM81-88	14.00	15.00
PS80	1970(2)	1,000	KM63-64	28.05	*BV + 20%*
PS81	1971(10)	7,000	KM63-64,81-88	35.00	185.00
PS82	1971(8)	5,000	KM81-88	14.00	15.00
PS83	1971(2)	650	KM63-64	28.00	*BV + 20%*
PS84	1972(10)	6,000	KM63-64,81-88	32.80	185.00
PS85	1972(8)	4,000	KM81-88	13.10	15.00
PS86	1972(2)	1,500	KM63-64	26.25	*BV + 20%*
PS87	1973(10)	6,850	KM63-64,81-88	32.00	185.00
PS88	1973(8)	4,000	KM81-88	12.80	15.00
PS89	1973(2)	6,088	KM63-64	25.60	*BV + 20%*
PS90	1974(10)	11,000	KM63-64,81-87,89	52.50	185.00
PS91	1974(8)	4,000	KM81-87,89	15.00	15.00
PS92	1974(2)	5,600	KM63-64	45.00	*BV + 20%*
PS93	1975(10)	12,500	KM63-64,81-87,89	116.40	185.00
PS94	1975(8)	5,500	KM81-88	14.55	15.00
PS95	1975(2)	7,000	KM63-64	101.85	*BV + 20%*
PS96	1976(10)	14,000	KM63-64,88,90-96	92.00	185.00
PS97	1976(8)	7,000	KM88,90-96	11.50	18.50
PS98	1976(2)	8,000	KM63-64	80.50	*BV + 20%*
PS99	1977(10)	12,000	KM63-64,81-88	92.00	185.00
PS100	1977(8)	7,000	KM81-88	11.50	20.00
PS101	1977(2)	8,000	KM63-64	80.50	*BV + 20%*
PS102	1978(10)	10,000	KM63-64,81-88	—	185.00
PS103	1978(8)	7,000	KM81-88	—	20.00
PS104	1978(2)	9,000	KM63-64		*BV + 20%*
PS105	1979(10)	10,000	KM63-64,97-103,104a	—	185.00
PS106	1979(8)	5,000	KM88,97-103	—	25.00
PS107	1979(2)	10,000	KM63-64		*BV + 20%*
PS108	1980(10)	10,000	KM63-64,81-88	—	185.00
PS109	1980(8)	5,000	KM81-88	—	25.00
PS110	1980(2)	8,000	KM63-64		*BV + 20%*
PS111	1980(2)	8,000	KM63-64	—	—
PS112	1981(10)	6,000	KM63-64,81-88	—	185.00
PS113	1981(8)	4,900	KM81-88	—	25.00
PS114	1981(2)	6,238	KM63-64		*BV + 20%*
PS115	1982(10)	7,100	KM63-64,108-115	—	190.00
PS116	1982(8)	4,900	KM88,108-114	—	25.00
PS117	1982(2)	6,930	KM63-64		*BV + 20%*
PS118	1983(10)	7,300	KM63-64,81-88	—	185.00
PS119	1983(8)	6,835	KM81-88	—	25.00
PS120	1983(2)	7,300	KM63-64		*BV + 20%*
PS121	1984(8)	11,250	KM82-88,88a	—	17.50
PS122	1985(8)	9,859	KM82-87,116,117	—	30.00
PS123	1986(8)	7,000	KM82-87,88a,119	—	30.00
PS124	1986(2)	428	KM73,121	—	1400.
PS125	1987(8)	6,781	KM82-88,88a	—	30.00
PS126	1987(4)	750	KM73,105-107	—	1075.
PS127	1988(8)	7,250	KM82-88,88a	—	50.00
PS128	1988(4)	806	KM73,105-107	—	1075.
PS129	1988(3)	3,388	KM122,125,128	—	70.00
PS130	1988(3)	600	KM124,127,130	—	2750.
PS131	1989(8)	9,571	KM82-88,88a	—	50.00
PS132	1989(4)	—	KM73,105-107	—	1075.
PS133	1990(8)	—	KM137,139,148	—	50.00
PS134	1990(4)	—	KM73,105-107	—	1075
PS135	1992(8)	—	KM132-139	—	50.00

Listings For

SOUTH ARABIA: refer to Yemen Republic

SOUTH KOREA: refer to Korea/South

SOUTH VIETNAM: refer to Vietnam/South

SOUTHERN RHODESIA: refer to Zimbabwe

SPAIN

The Spanish State, forming the greater part of the Iberian Peninsula of southwest Europe, has an area of 195,988 sq. mi. (504,714 sq. km.) and a population of 39.4 million including the Balearic and the Canary Islands. Capital: Madrid. The economy is based on agriculture, industry and tourism. Machinery, fruit, vegetables and chemicals are exported.

It isn't known when man first came to the Iberian Peninsula - the Altamira caves off the Cantabrian coast approximately 50 miles west of Santander were fashioned in Palaeolithic times. Spain was a battleground for centuries before it became a united nation, fought for by Phoenicians, Carthaginians, Greeks, Celts, Romans, Vandals, Visigoths and Moors. Ferdinand and Isabella destroyed the last Moorish stronghold in 1492, freeing the national energy and resources for the era of discovery and colonization that would make Spain the most powerful country in Europe during the 16th century. After the destruction of the Spanish Armada, 1588, Spain never again played a major role in European politics. Forcing Ferdinand to give up his throne and placing him under military guard at Valencay in 1808, Napoleonic France ruled Spain until 1814. When the monarchy was restored in 1814 it continued, only interrupted by the short-lived republic of 1873-74, until the exile of Alfonso XIII in 1931 when the Second Republic was established.

Discontent against the mother country increased after 1808 as colonists faced new imperialist policies from Napoleon or Spanish liberals. The revolutionary movement was established which resulted in the eventual independence of the Vice-royalties of New Spain, New Granada and Rio de la Plata within 2 decades.

The doomed republic was trapped in a tug-of-war between the right and left wing forces inevitably resulting in the Spanish Civil War of 1936-38. The leftist Republicans were supported by the USSR and the International Brigade was of mainly communist volunteers from all over the western world. The right wing Nationalists were supported by the Fascist governments of Italy and Germany. Under the leadership of Gen. Francisco Franco, the Nationalists emerged victorious and immediately embarked on a program of reconstruction and neutrality as dictated by the new "Caudillo" (leader) Franco.

The monarchy was reconstituted in 1947 under the regency of General Francisco Franco; the king designate to be crowned after Franco's death. Franco died on Nov. 20, 1975. Two days after his passing, Juan Carlos de Borbon, the grandson of Alfonso XIII, was proclaimed King of Spain.

RULERS

Carlos IV, 1788-1808
Jose Napoleon, 1808-1813
Ferdinand VII, 1808-1833 (in exile until 1814)
Isabel II, 1833-1868
Carlos IV, 1833-1840 (pretender)
Provisional Government, 1868-1871
Amadeo I, 1871-1873
1st Republic, 1873-1874
Carlos VII, 1872-1875 (pretender)
Alfonso XII, 1874-1885
Regency, 1885-1886
Alfonso XIII, 1886-1931
2nd Republic and Civil War, 1931-1939
Francisco Franco, caudillo, 1939-1947
Caudillo and regent, 1947-1975
Juan Carlos I, 1975

NOTE: From 1868 to 1982, two dates may be found on most Spanish coinage. The larger date is the year of authorization and the smaller date incused on the two six pointed-stars found on most types is the year of issue. The latter appears in parentheses in these listings.

HOMELAND MINT MARKS

Until 1851

(b) Brussels, privy marks only
B - Burgos
B, BA - Barcelona
BGA - Berga
Bo - Bilbao
C - Catalonia

NOTE: The Catalonia Mint was located at Reus between February 1-25, 1809 and March 31, 1809 to May 20, 1810 and again from April 14 to August 15, 1810. It was then temporarily located at Tarragonia until May 9, 1811 and finally located at Palma de Mallorca from June 2, 1811 to June 20, 1814.

CA - Cuenca
G, Flower over G - Granada
J, JA - Jubia
M, MD - Madrid
P,p.P., P.L., PA - Pamplona
S, S/L - Seville
Sr - Santander
T, To, Tole - Toledo
V, VA, VAL - Valencia
Crowned C - Cadiz
Crowned M - Madrid

Aqueduct - Segovia, until 1864

After 1848

OM - Oeschger Mesdach & Co.
3-Pointed star - Segovia after 1868
4-Pointed star - Jubia
6-Pointed star - Madrid
7-Pointed star - Seville
8-Pointed star - Barcelona
Other letters after date are initials of mint officials.

After 1982

Crowned M - Madrid

COLONIAL MINT MARKS

Many Spanish Colonial mints struck coins similar to regular Spanish issues until the 1820's. These issues are easily distinguished from regular Spanish issues by the following mint marks.

C, CH, Ch - Chihuahua, Mexico
D, DO, Do - Durango, Mexico
Ga - Guadalajara, Mexico
G, GG - Guatemala
G, Go - Guanajuato, Mexico
L, LIMAE, LIMA - Lima, Peru
M, MA - Manila, Philippines
M, Mo - Mexico City, Mexico
NG - Nueva Grenada, Guatemala
NR - Nueva Reino, Colombia
PDV - Valladolid Michoacan, Mexico
P, PN, Pn - Popayan, Colombia
P, POTOSI - Potosi, Bolivia
So - Santiago, Chile
Z, Zs - Zacatecas, Mexico
5-pointed Star - Manila, Philippines

MINTMASTERS INITIALS

BARCELONA MINT

Letter	Date	Name
CC	1842-1843	
PS	1836-1841,1843-1848	Francisco Paradaltas and Simeon Sola y Roca
SM	1850	Simeon Sola y Roca and Francisco Miro
SP	1822-1823	Pablo Sala and Francisco Paradaltas

MADRID MINT

Letter	Date	Name
AF	1808	Antonio de Goycoechea
AI	1807-1808	Antonio de Goycoechea and Ildefonso de Urquiza
AI	1808-1812	Antonio Rafael Narvaez and Isidoro Ramos del Manzano
FA	1799-1808	Francisco Herrera and Antonio Goicoechea
FM	1801	Francisco Herrera and Manuel de Lamas
IA	1808	Ildefonso de Urquiza and Antonio Goycoechea
IA	1810	Isidoro Ramos del Manzano and Antonio Rafael Narvaez
IG	1808-1810	Ildefonso de Urquiza and Gregorio Lazaro Labrandero
MF	1788-1802	Manuel de Lamas and Francisco Herrera
RN	1812-1813	Antonio Rafael Narvaez
RS	1810-1812	Antonio Rafael Narvaez and Jose Sanchez Delgado

SEVILLE MINT

Letter	Date	Name
C	1790-1791,1801-1808	Carlos Tiburcio de Roxas
CJ	1815-1821	Carlos Tiburcio de Roxas and Joaquin Delgado Diaz
CN	1791-1810,1812	Carlos Tiburcio de Roxas and Nicolas Lamas
DR	1835-1838	Joaquin Delgado Diaz and Benito de Roxas
J	1823	Jose Sanchez Delgado o Joaquin Delgado
JB	1824-1833	Joaquin Delgado Diaz and Benito de Roxas
LA	1810,1812	Leonardo Carrero and Antonio de Larra
RD	1821-1823	Carlos Tiburcio de Roxas and Joaquin Delgado Diaz
RD	1835	Benito de Roxas and Joaquin Delgado Diaz
RD	1838-1852	Benito de Roxas and Vicente Delgado

VALENCIA MINT

Letter	Date	Name
GS	1811	Gregorio Lazaro Labrandero and Sixto Giber Polo
R	1821	
SG	1809-1814	Sixto Giber Polo

MONETARY SYSTEM

34 Maravedi = 1 Real (of Silver)
16 Reales = 1 Escudo

NOTE: The early coinage of Spain is listed by denomination based on a system of 16 Reales de Plata (silver) = 1 Escudo (gold). However, in the Constitutional period from 1808-1850, a concurrent system was introduced in which 20 Reales de Vellon (billon) = 8 Reales de Plata. This system does not necessarily refer to the composition of the coin itself. To avoid confusion we have listed the coins using the value as it appears on each coin, ignoring the monetary base.

KINGDOM

MARAVEDI

COPPER
Mint mark: Aqueduct
Similar to 4 Maravedis, C#61.

C#	Date	Mintage	VG	Fine	VF	XF
59	1802	—	15.00	30.00	50.00	70.00

NOTE: Earlier dates (1791-1799) exist for this type.

Mint mark: J, JA
Obv: Head of Ferdinand right.
Rev: Arms in angles of cross.

C#	Date	Mintage	VG	Fine	VF	XF
112	1824	—	15.00	20.00	45.00	90.00

C#	Date	Mintage	VG	Fine	VF	XF
167.1	1842	—	15.00	25.00	50.00	125.00
	1843	—	75.00	150.00	300.00	425.00

Mint mark: Crowned M

C#	Date	Mintage	VG	Fine	VF	XF
167.2	1842 DG	—	100.00	200.00	300.00	400.00

Mint mark: Aqueduct

C#	Date	Mintage	VG	Fine	VF	XF
167.3	1842	—	15.00	25.00	50.00	95.00

2 MARAVEDIS

COPPER
Mint mark: Aqueduct
Similar to 4 Maravedis, C#61.

C#	Date	Mintage	VG	Fine	VF	XF
60	1801	—	3.00	6.00	10.00	20.00
	1802	—	3.00	7.00	12.00	24.00
	1803	—	3.00	6.00	10.00	20.00
	1804	—	6.00	12.50	20.00	35.00
	1805	—	3.00	6.00	10.00	20.00
	1806	—	6.00	12.50	22.50	37.00
	1807	—	3.00	6.00	10.00	20.00
	1808	—	3.00	6.00	10.00	20.00

NOTE: Earlier dates (1788-1800) exist for this type.

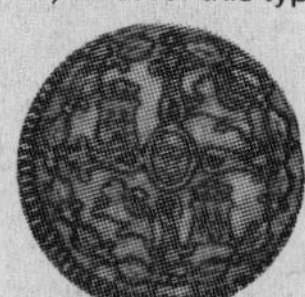

Mint mark: J, JA

C#	Date	Mintage	VG	Fine	VF	XF
106	1812	—	10.00	15.00	30.00	45.00
	1813	—	5.00	11.00	20.00	30.00
	1814	—	5.00	11.00	20.00	28.00
	1815	—	5.00	11.00	20.00	28.00
	1816	—	5.00	10.00	18.00	22.00
	1817	—	5.00	11.00	20.00	35.00

Mint mark: Aqueduct

C#	Date	Mintage	VG	Fine	VF	XF
116	1816	—	4.00	8.00	12.00	25.00
	1817	—	3.00	6.00	10.00	15.00
	1818	—	3.00	6.00	10.00	15.00
	1819	—	3.00	6.00	10.00	15.00
	1820	—	3.00	6.00	10.00	15.00
	1824	—	2.00	4.00	6.00	12.00
	1825	—	2.00	4.00	6.00	12.00
	1826	—	2.00	4.00	6.00	12.00
	1827	—	2.00	4.00	6.00	12.00
	1828	—	2.00	4.00	6.00	12.00
	1829	—	2.00	4.00	6.00	12.00
	1830	—	2.00	4.00	6.00	12.00
	1831	—	2.00	4.00	6.00	12.00
	1832	—	2.00	4.00	6.00	12.00
	1833	—	2.00	4.00	6.00	12.00

Obv. leg: FERDIN. IIV. (error).

C#	Date	Mintage	VG	Fine	VF	XF
116a	1832	—	20.00	35.00	65.00	125.00

Mint mark: J, JA
Thin laureate bust

C#	Date	Mintage	VG	Fine	VF	XF
109	1817	—	4.00	8.00	18.00	30.00
	1818	—	4.00	7.00	15.00	28.00
	1819	—	4.00	7.00	15.00	28.00
	1820	—	4.00	7.00	15.00	28.00
	1821	—	18.00	35.00	65.00	95.00

Large bare head

C#	Date	Mintage	VG	Fine	VF	XF
113	1824	—	5.00	12.00	20.00	30.00
	1826	—	4.00	10.00	18.00	28.00
	1827	—	6.00	15.00	23.00	35.00

Mint mark: B, BA

C#	Date	Mintage	VG	Fine	VF	XF
168.1	1855	—	15.00	25.00	50.00	100.00
	1858	—	12.50	20.00	40.00	75.00

Mint mark: J, JA

C#	Date	Mintage	VG	Fine	VF	XF
168.2	1838	—	15.00	35.00	70.00	100.00
	1840	—	40.00	80.00	150.00	225.00
	1841	—	45.00	110.00	200.00	275.00
	1842	—	45.00	110.00	200.00	300.00
	1844	—	40.00	80.00	175.00	250.00
	1848	—	7.00	15.00	25.00	50.00
	1849	—	7.00	15.00	25.00	50.00

Mint mark: Crowned M

C#	Date	Mintage	VG	Fine	VF	XF
168.3	1837 DG	—	75.00	150.00	275.00	500.00

Mint mark: Aqueduct

C#	Date	Mintage	VG	Fine	VF	XF
168.4	1836	—	12.00	30.00	75.00	125.00
	1837	—	12.00	25.00	70.00	110.00
	1838	—	5.00	7.50	15.00	22.50
	1839	—	5.00	7.50	15.00	22.50
	1840	—	5.00	7.50	15.00	22.50
	1841	—	5.00	7.50	15.00	22.50
	1842	—	5.00	7.50	15.00	22.50
	1843	—	5.00	7.50	15.00	22.50
	1844	—	5.00	7.50	15.00	22.50
	1845	—	5.00	7.50	15.00	22.50
	1846	—	5.00	7.50	15.00	22.50
	1847	—	5.00	7.50	15.00	22.50
	1848	—	5.00	7.50	15.00	22.50
	1849	—	5.00	7.50	15.00	22.50
	1850	—	5.00	7.50	15.00	22.50

4 MARAVEDIS

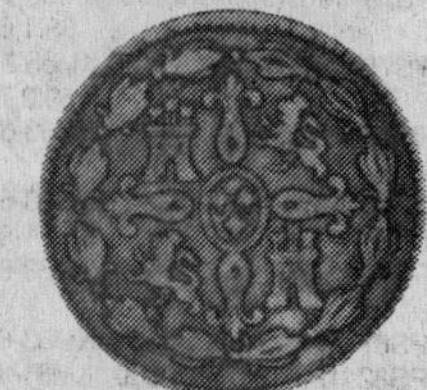

COPPER
Mint mark: Aqueduct

C#	Date	Mintage	VG	Fine	VF	XF
61	1801	—	3.00	6.00	8.00	12.50
	1802	—	3.00	6.00	8.00	12.50
	1803	—	3.00	6.00	8.00	12.50
	1804	—	5.00	10.00	14.00	25.00
	1805	—	5.00	10.00	14.00	25.00
	1806	—	5.00	10.00	14.00	25.00
	1807	—	5.00	9.00	12.50	20.00
	1808	—	3.00	6.00	8.00	12.50

NOTE: Earlier dates (1788-1800) exist for this type.

Mint mark: J, JA
Similar to 2 Maravedis, C#106.

C#	Date	Mintage	VG	Fine	VF	XF
107	1812	—	4.50	11.00	25.00	35.00
	1813	—	4.50	11.00	20.00	30.00
	1814	—	4.00	10.00	20.00	30.00
	1815	—	4.50	11.00	20.00	30.00
	1816	—	4.00	10.00	20.00	30.00
117.1	1817	—	4.50	11.00	20.00	35.00
	1818	—	8.00	16.00	22.50	40.00

Mint mark: Aqueduct

C#	Date	Mintage	VG	Fine	VF	XF
117.2	1816	—	4.00	7.00	10.00	20.00
	1818	—	5.00	10.00	16.00	30.00
	1819	—	4.00	7.00	14.00	25.00
	1820	—	4.00	7.00	10.00	20.00
	1823	—	3.00	6.00	10.00	19.00
	1824	—	3.00	6.00	10.00	17.00
	1825	—	3.00	6.00	10.00	19.00
	1826	—	3.00	6.00	10.00	19.00

C#	Date	Mintage	VG	Fine	VF	XF
117.2	1827	—	3.00	6.00	10.00	19.00
	1828	—	3.00	6.00	9.00	18.00
	1829	—	3.00	6.00	9.00	16.00
	1830	—	3.00	6.00	8.00	15.00
	1831	—	3.00	6.00	9.00	16.00
	1832	—	3.00	6.00	10.00	17.00
	1833	—	3.00	6.00	9.00	16.00

Mint mark: J, JA
Small head
Similar to 2 Maravedis, C#106 but w/thin laureate bust.

C#	Date	Mintage	VG	Fine	VF	XF
110.1	1817	—	5.00	9.00	14.00	25.00
	1818	—	5.00	9.00	17.50	27.50
	1819	—	5.00	10.00	18.00	28.00
	1820	—	5.00	9.00	14.00	30.00

Mint mark: Aqueduct

C#	Date	Mintage	VG	Fine	VF	XF
110.2	1817	—	5.00	9.00	14.00	30.00

Mint mark: J, JA
Large head

C#	Date	Mintage	VG	Fine	VF	XF
114	1824	—	4.00	8.00	12.00	25.00
	1825	—	6.00	12.00	30.00	55.00
	1826	—	4.00	8.00	12.00	20.00
	1827	—	5.00	10.00	14.00	18.00
161.1	1835	—	10.00	17.50	30.00	65.00
	1836	—	7.50	12.50	25.00	50.00

Mint mark: Crowned M

C#	Date	Mintage	VG	Fine	VF	XF
161.2	1836 DG	—	125.00	225.00	375.00	500.00

Mint mark: Aqueduct

C#	Date	Mintage	VG	Fine	VF	XF
161.3	1835	—	12.50	25.00	50.00	75.00
	1836	—	7.50	15.00	35.00	50.00

Mint mark: B, BA

C#	Date	Mintage	VG	Fine	VF	XF
169.1	1853	—	50.00	100.00	200.00	275.00
	1855	—	10.00	15.00	25.00	65.00

Mint mark: J, JA

C#	Date	Mintage	VG	Fine	VF	XF
169.2	1837	—	7.00	14.00	30.00	45.00
	1840	—	30.00	50.00	125.00	180.00
	1841	—	7.00	14.00	40.00	50.00
	1842	—	7.00	14.00	65.00	90.00
	1843	—	7.00	14.00	60.00	85.00
	1844	—	7.00	14.00	75.00	125.00
	1845	—	7.00	13.00	25.00	35.00
	1846	—	7.00	14.00	60.00	80.00
	1847	—	5.00	10.00	18.00	25.00
	1848	—	7.00	13.00	25.00	35.00
	1849	—	7.00	14.00	35.00	50.00
	1850	—	5.00	10.00	18.00	25.00

Mint mark: Aqueduct

C#	Date	Mintage	VG	Fine	VF	XF
169.3	1837	—	5.00	9.00	20.00	30.00
	1838	—	5.00	9.00	20.00	30.00
	1839	—	10.00	20.00	35.00	50.00
	1840	—	5.00	9.00	25.00	35.00
	1841	—	5.00	9.00	18.00	30.00
	1842	—	5.00	9.00	15.00	25.00
	1843	—	8.00	15.00	35.00	55.00
	1844	—	5.00	9.00	18.00	30.00
	1845	—	5.00	9.00	18.00	30.00
	1846	—	5.00	9.00	18.00	35.00
	1847	—	5.00	10.00	15.00	30.00
	1848	—	5.00	9.00	20.00	30.00
	1849	—	4.00	8.00	20.00	30.00
	1850	—	8.00	15.00	35.00	50.00

8 MARAVEDIS

COPPER
Mint mark: Aqueduct

C#	Date	Mintage	VG	Fine	VF	XF
62	1801	—	4.00	8.00	12.00	18.50
	1802	—	4.00	8.00	12.00	18.50
	1803	—	4.00	8.00	12.00	18.50
62	1804	—	5.00	9.00	14.00	20.00
	1805	—	4.00	8.00	12.00	18.50
	1806	—	5.00	9.00	14.00	20.00
	1807	—	4.00	8.00	12.00	18.50
	1808	—	3.00	7.00	9.00	15.00

NOTE: Earlier dates (1788-1800) exist for this type.

C#	Date	Mintage	VG	Fine	VF	XF
82	1809	—	25.00	50.00	75.00	100.00
	1810	—	20.00	40.00	65.00	80.00
	1811	—	14.00	28.00	45.00	55.00
	1812	—	10.00	20.00	35.00	40.00
	1813	—	16.00	32.50	50.00	60.00

Mint mark: J, JA

C#	Date	Mintage	VG	Fine	VF	XF
108	1811	—	20.00	40.00	85.00	125.00
	1812	—	15.00	35.00	65.00	80.00
	1813	—	7.00	14.00	30.00	40.00
	1814	—	7.00	14.00	30.00	40.00
	1815	—	7.00	14.00	30.00	40.00
	1816	—	5.00	10.00	25.00	35.00
	1817	—	6.00	12.00	20.00	30.00

Mint mark: Aqueduct

C#	Date	Mintage	VG	Fine	VF	XF
118	1815	—	9.00	18.00	30.00	45.00
	1816	—	5.00	10.00	25.00	30.00
	1817	—	5.00	10.00	20.00	30.00
	1818	—	5.00	10.00	20.00	30.00
	1819	—	6.00	12.00	12.50	25.00
	1820	—	5.00	10.00	20.00	25.00
	1821	—	10.00	25.00	40.00	55.00
	1822	—	9.00	18.00	40.00	55.00
	1823	—	5.00	10.00	20.00	25.00
	1824	—	5.00	9.00	15.00	17.50
	1825	—	5.00	9.00	15.00	17.50
	1826	—	5.00	9.00	15.00	17.50
	1827	—	5.00	10.00	17.00	18.50
	1828	—	8.00	15.00	25.00	40.00
	1829	—	4.00	7.00	10.00	15.00
	1830	—	5.00	10.00	12.00	15.00
	1831	—	4.00	7.00	9.00	12.50
	1832	—	4.00	7.00	9.00	11.50
	1833	—	4.00	7.00	9.00	11.50

Mint mark: J, JA

C#	Date	Mintage	VG	Fine	VF	XF
111	1817	—	4.00	8.00	10.00	25.00
	1818	—	4.00	7.00	10.00	15.00
	1819	—	4.00	7.00	10.00	15.00
	1820	—	4.00	7.00	10.00	15.00
	1821	—	3.00	6.00	10.00	15.00

Obv: Bust, leg: FERN 7o POR LA. . . .

C#	Date	Mintage	VG	Fine	VF	XF
115	1822	—	6.00	12.00	20.00	35.00
	1823	—	5.00	10.00	17.50	30.00

Obv: Value omitted.

C#	Date	Mintage	VG	Fine	VF	XF
115a	1823	—	6.00	12.00	20.00	35.00

Obv: Bust, leg: FERDIN.VII D.G.HISP.REX.

C#	Date	Mintage	VG	Fine	VF	XF
114.5	1823	—	6.00	11.00	18.00	30.00
	1824	—	6.00	11.00	18.00	25.00
	1825	—	6.00	11.00	18.00	25.00
	1826	—	5.00	9.00	15.00	20.00
	1827	—	5.00	9.00	16.00	22.50

Mint mark: Aqueduct

C#	Date	Mintage	VG	Fine	VF	XF
114.7	1823	—	5.00	9.00	15.00	25.00

Mint mark: P, P.P., P.L., PA
Obv: Bust, leg: FERDIN.VII.D.G. HISP.REX.

C#	Date	Mintage	VG	Fine	VF	XF
118a	1823	—	12.00	25.00	45.00	65.00

Mint mark: J, JA

C#	Date	Mintage	VG	Fine	VF	XF
162.1	1835	—	10.00	17.50	35.00	60.00
	1836	—	10.00	20.00	45.00	75.00

Mint mark: Crowned M

C#	Date	Mintage	VG	Fine	VF	XF
162.2	1835 DG	—	125.00	225.00	300.00	400.00

Mint mark: Aqueduct

C#	Date	Mintage	VG	Fine	VF	XF
162.3	1835	—	4.00	10.00	20.00	35.00
	1836	—	3.00	8.00	16.00	30.00

Charles V - Pretender Issue

C#	Date	Mintage	VG	Fine	VF	XF
154	1837	—	175.00	300.00	475.00	600.00

CAST BELL METAL
Mint mark: P, P.P., P.L., PA

C#	Date	Mintage	Good	VG	Fine	VF
170a.1	1837	—	50.00	75.00	100.00	175.00

Mint mark within oval

C#	Date	Mintage	Good	VG	Fine	VF
170a.2	1837	—	50.00	75.00	100.00	175.00

COPPER
Mint mark: B, BA

C#	Date	Mintage	VG	Fine	VF	XF
170.1	1853	—	25.00	45.00	65.00	115.00
	1854	*	—	—	—	—
	1855	—	40.00	60.00	90.00	125.00
	1858	—	20.00	40.00	60.00	100.00

*NOTE: Only counterfeits seen.

Mint mark: J, JA

C#	Date	Mintage	VG	Fine	VF	XF
170.2	1837	—	5.00	10.00	22.00	30.00
	1838	—	6.00	12.00	25.00	35.00
	1839	—	10.00	25.00	55.00	70.00
	1840	—	12.00	20.00	32.50	40.00
	1841	—	6.00	12.00	20.00	30.00
	1842	—	5.00	10.00	18.00	25.00
	1843	—	5.00	10.00	18.00	25.00
	1844	—	5.00	12.00	20.00	32.50
	1845	—	5.00	10.00	15.00	20.00
	1846	—	5.00	10.00	18.00	25.00
	1847	—	5.00	10.00	18.00	25.00
	1848	—	5.00	10.00	15.00	20.00
	1849	—	10.00	15.00	20.00	30.00
	1850	—	5.00	10.00	18.00	25.00

Mint mark: Aqueduct

C#	Date	Mintage	VG	Fine	VF	XF
170.3	1837	—	5.00	10.00	20.00	35.00
	1838	—	5.00	10.00	20.00	30.00
	1839	—	5.00	9.00	17.00	25.00
	1840	—	5.00	9.00	20.00	27.50
	1841	—	5.00	9.00	17.00	25.00
	1842	—	5.00	9.00	17.00	25.00
	1843	—	5.00	9.00	17.00	25.00
	1844	—	4.00	8.00	13.00	17.50
	1845	—	4.00	8.00	15.00	22.50
	1846	—	5.00	9.00	17.00	25.00
	1847	—	5.00	11.00	17.50	25.00
	1848	—	6.00	12.50	18.50	25.00
	1849	—	5.00	10.00	12.50	25.00
	1850	—	7.00	15.00	30.00	40.00

1/2 REAL

1.6900 g, .903 SILVER, .0490 oz ASW
Mint mark: Crowned M
Obv: Bust of Charles IV right.
Rev: Crowned arms.

C#	Date	Mintage	VG	Fine	VF	XF
66.1	1802 FA	—	8.00	15.00	27.50	35.00
	1803 FA	—	5.00	10.00	18.50	30.00
	1804 FA	—	7.00	13.00	22.50	30.00
	1808 AI	—	7.00	14.00	25.00	35.00
	1808 FA	—	8.00	16.00	27.50	40.00

NOTE: Earlier dates (1789-1800) exist for this type.

Mint mark: S, S/L

C#	Date	Mintage	VG	Fine	VF	XF
66.2	1802 CN	—	8.00	16.00	32.50	40.00
	1805 CN	—	8.00	16.00	32.50	40.00
	1807 CN	—	7.00	13.00	25.00	30.00

NOTE: Earlier dates (1793-1800) exist for this type.

Mint mark: Crowned C
Obv: Laureate bust right. Rev: Crowned arms.

C#	Date	Mintage	VG	Fine	VF	XF
132.1	1814 CI	—	5.00	10.00	22.50	35.00
	1814 CJ	—	5.00	10.00	25.00	40.00

Mint mark: Crowned M

C#	Date	Mintage	VG	Fine	VF	XF
132.2	1815 GJ	—	6.00	12.50	27.50	40.00
	1816 GJ	—	6.00	12.00	18.00	30.00
	1817 GJ	—	6.00	12.00	18.00	35.00
	1818 GJ	—	6.00	12.00	16.00	30.00
	1819 GJ	—	6.00	12.00	18.00	35.00
	1820 GJ	—	6.00	12.50	18.00	30.00
	1824 AJ	—	8.00	15.00	25.00	35.00
	1826 AJ	—	6.00	12.50	25.00	30.00
	1828 AJ	—	8.00	15.00	25.00	30.00
	1830 AJ	—	6.00	12.00	17.50	35.00
	1831 AJ	—	9.00	17.50	25.00	35.00
	1832 AJ	—	6.00	12.00	20.00	30.00
	1833 AJ	—	6.00	12.00	25.00	35.00
	1833 JI	—	11.00	22.00	40.00	65.00

Mint mark: S, S/L

C#	Date	Mintage	VG	Fine	VF	XF
132.3	1825 JB	—	4.00	7.00	15.00	25.00
	1831 JB	—	4.00	7.00	15.00	25.00
	1832 JB	—	6.00	12.00	20.00	35.00
	1833 JB	—	7.00	13.00	20.00	35.00

Mint mark: C
Obv: Small draped bust.

C#	Date	Mintage	VG	Fine	VF	XF
132a.1	1812 SF	—	15.00	30.00	50.00	70.00
	1813 SF	—	15.00	30.00	50.00	70.00
	1814 SF	—	20.00	35.00	55.00	75.00

Mint mark: Crowned M

C#	Date	Mintage	VG	Fine	VF	XF
132a.2	1813 IJ	—	9.00	18.00	30.00	45.00
	1813 GJ	—	7.50	15.00	25.00	35.00
	1814 GJ	—	10.00	20.00	35.00	50.00

REAL

3.3800 g, .917 SILVER, .0995 oz ASW
Mint mark: Crowned M
Obv: Bust of Charles IV right.
Rev: Crowned arms.

C#	Date	Mintage	VG	Fine	VF	XF
68.1	1801 FA	—	5.00	10.00	16.00	25.00
	1802 FA	—	5.00	10.00	20.00	35.00
	1803 FA	—	6.00	12.00	18.00	25.00
	1805 FA	—	6.00	12.00	19.00	30.00
	1807 FA	—	6.00	12.00	18.00	25.00
	1807 AI	—	7.00	14.00	20.00	40.00
	1808 AI	—	7.00	14.00	19.00	30.00

NOTE: Earlier dates (1788-1800) exist for this type.

Mint mark: S, S/L

C#	Date	Mintage	VG	Fine	VF	XF
68.2	1802 CN	—	10.00	20.00	45.00	65.00
	1807 CN	—	9.00	18.00	35.00	50.00

NOTE: Earlier dates (1793-1800) exist for this type.

Mint mark: C
Obv: Large laureate bust.
Rev: Crowned arms.

C#	Date	Mintage	VG	Fine	VF	XF
133.1	1811 SF	—	12.50	22.50	40.00	55.00

Mint mark: Crowned C

C#	Date	Mintage	VG	Fine	VF	XF
133.2	1813 CJ	—	10.00	20.00	30.00	45.00

Mint mark: Crowned M

C#	Date	Mintage	VG	Fine	VF	XF
133.3	1815 GJ	—	8.00	16.50	32.50	50.00
	1816 GJ	—	8.00	16.50	30.00	50.00
	1817 GJ	—	8.00	16.50	25.00	45.00
	1819 GJ	—	10.00	20.00	27.50	45.00
	1820 GJ	—	9.00	18.50	25.00	55.00
	1824 AJ	—	15.00	30.00	55.00	80.00
	1826 AJ	—	10.00	20.00	40.00	60.00
	1828 AJ	—	10.00	20.00	40.00	60.00
	1830 AJ	—	7.00	15.00	22.00	35.00
	1831 AJ	—	8.00	17.00	30.00	45.00
	1832 AJ	—	7.00	15.00	20.00	40.00
	1833 AJ	—	10.00	20.00	30.00	50.00
	1833 JI	—	11.00	22.50	38.50	60.00
	1833 JJ	—	9.00	18.00	30.00	40.00

Mint mark: S, S/L

C#	Date	Mintage	VG	Fine	VF	XF
133.4	1830 JB	—	10.00	19.00	32.00	50.00
	1831 JB	—	6.00	12.00	25.00	35.00
	1832 JB	—	7.00	14.00	25.00	35.00
	1833 JB	—	7.00	14.00	20.00	30.00

Mint mark: C
Obv: Small draped bust.

C#	Date	Mintage	VG	Fine	VF	XF
133a.1	1811 SF	—	13.50	25.00	45.00	65.00
	1814 SF	—	22.50	40.00	80.00	130.00

Mint mark: Crowned M

C#	Date	Mintage	VG	Fine	VF	XF
133a.2	1813 IJ	—	22.50	40.00	60.00	85.00
	1814 IJ	—	15.00	30.00	45.00	75.00
	1814 GJ	—	9.00	18.50	30.00	50.00

C#	Date	Mintage	VG	Fine	VF	XF
171.1	1837 CL	—	30.00	60.00	110.00	150.00
	1838 CL	—	9.00	18.00	22.00	30.00
	1838 DG	—	50.00	90.00	170.00	230.00
	1839 CL	—	8.00	16.50	35.00	65.00
	1840 CL	—	15.00	30.00	60.00	115.00
	1841 CL	—	30.00	60.00	115.00	225.00
	1842 CL	—	35.00	70.00	140.00	180.00
	1843 CL	—	16.00	32.50	60.00	115.00
	1844 CL	—	7.00	15.00	30.00	60.00
	1845 CL	—	4.00	8.00	15.00	25.00
	1847 CL	—	4.00	8.00	15.00	25.00
	1848 CL	—	4.00	8.00	15.00	25.00
	1849 CL	—	4.00	8.00	15.00	25.00

Mint mark: S, S/L

C#	Date	Mintage	VG	Fine	VF	XF
171.2	1840 RD	—	20.00	45.00	100.00	130.00
	1844 RD	—	10.00	20.00	45.00	70.00
	1845 RD	—	15.00	30.00	70.00	100.00
	1850 RD	—	7.00	14.00	25.00	40.00
	1851 RD	—	7.00	14.00	25.00	40.00
	1852 RD	—	6.00	12.00	20.00	30.00

2 REALES

6.7700 g, .903 SILVER, .1965 oz ASW
Mint mark: Crowned M
Obv: Bust of Charles IV right.

C#	Date	Mintage	VG	Fine	VF	XF
69.1	1801 FA	—	7.00	15.00	22.00	35.00
	1802 FA	—	7.00	15.00	22.00	35.00
	1803 FA	—	7.00	15.00	22.00	35.00
	1804 FA	—	7.00	15.00	22.00	35.00
	1805 FA	—	7.00	15.00	22.00	35.00
	1806 FA	—	7.00	15.00	22.00	35.00
	1807 FA	—	7.00	15.00	22.00	35.00
	1807 AI	—	8.00	17.00	30.00	50.00
	1808 FA	—	7.00	15.00	22.00	35.00
	1808 IG	—	8.00	17.00	30.00	50.00
	1808 AI	—	7.00	15.00	25.00	40.00

NOTE: Earlier dates (1788-1800) exist for this type.

Mint mark: S, S/L

C#	Date	Mintage	VG	Fine	VF	XF
69.2	1801 CN	—	8.00	16.00	25.00	40.00
	1802 CN	—	8.00	16.00	25.00	40.00
	1803 CN	—	8.00	16.00	25.00	40.00
	1804 CN	—	8.00	16.00	25.00	40.00
	1805 CN	—	8.00	16.00	25.00	40.00
	1806 CN	—	8.00	16.00	25.00	40.00
	1807 CN	—	8.00	16.00	25.00	40.00
	1808 CN	—	8.00	16.00	25.00	40.00

NOTE: Earlier dates (1793-1800) exist for this type.

Mint mark: C

C#	Date	Mintage	VG	Fine	VF	XF
134.1	1811 SF	—	8.00	17.00	30.00	50.00
	1812 SF	—	40.00	70.00	125.00	175.00
	1813 SF	—	8.00	17.00	30.00	50.00
	1814 SF	—	14.00	27.50	35.00	55.00

Mint mark: Crowned C

C#	Date	Mintage	VG	Fine	VF	XF
134.2	1810 CI	—	9.00	18.00	25.00	40.00
	1810 CI w/small crowned C					
		—	11.00	21.00	35.00	60.00
	1811 CI	—	9.00	18.00	25.00	40.00
	1812 CI	—	9.00	18.00	25.00	40.00

Mint mark: Crowned M

C#	Date	Mintage	VG	Fine	VF	XF
134.3	1814 GJ	—	8.00	16.00	23.00	35.00
	1815 GJ	—	8.00	16.00	23.00	35.00
	1816 GJ	—	8.00	16.00	25.00	40.00
	1817 GJ	—	8.00	16.00	23.00	35.00
	1818 GJ	—	9.00	19.00	25.00	40.00
	1819 GJ	—	9.00	19.00	25.00	45.00
	1820 GJ	—	8.00	16.00	23.00	35.00
	1821 AJ	—	7.00	15.00	30.00	50.00
	1822 AJ	—	16.00	32.50	40.00	65.00
	1823 AJ	—	8.00	16.00	25.00	40.00
	1824 AJ	—	8.00	16.00	25.00	40.00
	1825 AJ	—	8.00	16.00	25.00	40.00
	1826 AJ	—	8.00	16.00	23.00	35.00
	1827 AJ	—	8.00	16.00	25.00	40.00
	1828 AJ	—	8.00	16.00	23.00	35.00
	1829 AJ	—	8.00	16.00	23.00	35.00
	1830 AJ	—	8.00	16.00	23.00	30.00
	1831 AJ	—	8.00	16.00	25.00	40.00
	1832 AJ	—	8.00	16.00	23.00	35.00
	1833 AJ	—	9.00	18.00	25.00	40.00

Mint mark: S, S/L

C#	Date	Mintage	VG	Fine	VF	XF
134.4	1815 CJ	—	10.00	20.00	30.00	50.00
	1820 CJ	—	8.00	16.00	25.00	40.00
	1821 CJ	—	7.00	14.00	20.00	30.00
	1823 CJ	—	8.00	16.00	25.00	40.00
	1824 J	—	15.00	30.00	40.00	65.00
	1824 JB	—	8.00	16.00	25.00	40.00
	1825 JB	—	8.00	16.00	25.00	40.00
	1826 JB	—	8.00	16.00	25.00	40.00
	1827 JB	—	8.00	16.00	25.00	40.00
	1828 JB	—	8.00	16.00	25.00	40.00
	1829 JB	—	8.00	16.00	25.00	40.00
	1830 JB	—	8.00	16.00	25.00	40.00
	1831 JB	—	8.00	16.00	25.00	40.00
	1832 JB	—	8.00	16.00	25.00	45.00
	1833 JB	—	9.00	18.00	27.00	50.00

Mint mark: B, BA
Obv: Bare head of Ferdinand right.
Rev: Crowned arms.

C#	Date	Mintage	VG	Fine	VF	XF
134a.1	1812 SF	—	80.00	150.00	275.00	400.00

Mint mark: C

C#	Date	Mintage	VG	Fine	VF	XF
134a.2	1810 FS	—	14.00	27.50	45.00	60.00
	1810 SF	—	30.00	55.00	80.00	140.00
	1811 SF	—	11.00	22.50	35.00	50.00
	1811 FS	—	15.00	30.00	45.00	60.00

Mint mark: Crowned M

C#	Date	Mintage	VG	Fine	VF	XF
134a.3	1812 IJ	—	9.00	17.50	25.00	40.00
	1813 IJ	—	7.00	15.00	20.00	30.00
	1813 IG	—	12.00	25.00	40.00	60.00
	1813 GJ	—	7.00	15.00	20.00	30.00
	1814 GJ	—	12.00	25.00	40.00	60.00

Mint mark: V, VAL.

C#	Date	Mintage	VG	Fine	VF	XF
134a.4	1811 GS	—	70.00	140.00	200.00	250.00
	1812 GS	—	65.00	125.00	160.00	200.00

Mint mark: Crowned M
Obv: Young head of Isabella right.
Rev: Crowned arms in collar of The Golden Fleece.

C#	Date	Mintage	VG	Fine	VF	XF
63.1	1836 CR	—	20.00	40.00	80.00	110.00
	1836 DG	—	55.00	110.00	225.00	300.00
	1837 CR	—	60.00	125.00	250.00	350.00
	1838 CR	—	60.00	115.00	230.00	300.00
	1839 CL	—	45.00	90.00	200.00	300.00
	1841 CL	—	15.00	30.00	45.00	75.00
	1842 CL	—	45.00	90.00	200.00	325.00
	1843 CL	—	17.50	35.00	75.00	110.00

Mint mark: S, S/L

C#	Date	Mintage	VG	Fine	VF	XF
63.2	1836 DR	—	20.00	40.00	95.00	150.00
	1839 RD	—	17.00	35.00	60.00	100.00
	1840 RD	—	22.00	45.00	90.00	140.00

Charles V - Pretender Issue

C#	Date	Mintage	Good	VG	Fine	VF
156	1838	—	225.00	375.00	450.00	600.00

6.7700 g, .903 SILVER, .1965 oz ASW
Mint mark: Crowned M

C#	Date	Mintage	VG	Fine	VF	XF
172.1	1844 CL	—	11.00	22.50	35.00	60.00
	1845 CL	—	11.00	22.50	35.00	50.00
	1847 CL	—	10.00	20.00	30.00	45.00
	1848 CL	—	11.00	22.50	35.00	55.00
	1849 CL	—	10.00	20.00	30.00	40.00

Mint mark: S, S/L

C#	Date	Mintage	VG	Fine	VF	XF
172.2	1845 RD	—	22.00	45.00	100.00	165.00
	1848 RD	—	17.00	35.00	65.00	80.00
	1850/45 RD	—	30.00	60.00	100.00	150.00
	1850 RD	—	20.00	40.00	70.00	100.00
	1851 RD	—	10.00	20.00	30.00	40.00

4 REALES

13.5400 g, .917 SILVER, .3931 oz ASW
Mint mark: Crowned M
Similar to 2 Reales, C#69.2.

C#	Date	Mintage	VG	Fine	VF	XF
70.1	1804 FA	—	20.00	30.00	55.00	80.00
	1805 FA	—	20.00	30.00	55.00	70.00
	1806 FA	—	25.00	40.00	80.00	125.00
	1808 AI	—	30.00	50.00	70.00	100.00
	1808 FA	—	30.00	50.00	70.00	100.00

NOTE: Earlier dates (1788-1797) exist for this type.

Mint mark: S, S/L

C#	Date	Mintage	VG	Fine	VF	XF
70.2	1803 CN	—	20.00	40.00	60.00	85.00
	1807 CN	—	22.00	45.00	65.00	100.00

Mint mark: C

C#	Date	Mintage	VG	Fine	VF	XF
135a.1	1809 MP	—	65.00	125.00	225.00	600.00
	1809 SF	—	75.00	150.00	250.00	650.00
	1810 SF	—	100.00	200.00	325.00	775.00
	1814 SF	—	175.00	325.00	525.00	850.00

Mint mark: V, VAL.

C#	Date	Mintage	VG	Fine	VF	XF
135a.2	1809 SG	—	90.00	175.00	240.00	300.00
	1810 SG	—	35.00	65.00	110.00	150.00
	1811 SG	—	40.00	70.00	130.00	175.00

Mint mark: C
Obv: Armored bust.

C#	Date	Mintage	VG	Fine	VF	XF
135c	1811 SF	—	60.00	150.00	300.00	425.00

Obv: Laureate bust.

C#	Date	Mintage	VG	Fine	VF	XF
135.1	1812 SF	—	100.00	225.00	450.00	600.00
	1813 SF	—	275.00	550.00	800.00	1000.

Mint mark: Crowned C

C#	Date	Mintage	VG	Fine	VF	XF
135.2	1812 CJ	—	25.00	45.00	70.00	100.00
	1812 CI	—	35.00	65.00	100.00	150.00

Mint mark: Crowned M

C#	Date	Mintage	VG	Fine	VF	XF
135.3	1814 GJ	—	90.00	175.00	300.00	400.00
	1815 GJ	—	12.00	25.00	40.00	65.00
	1816 GJ	—	20.00	40.00	65.00	100.00
	1817 GJ	—	18.00	35.00	60.00	90.00
	1818 GJ	—	18.00	35.00	60.00	100.00
	1819 GJ	—	70.00	125.00	200.00	300.00
	1822 SR	—	30.00	55.00	90.00	160.00
	1824 AJ	—	16.00	32.50	40.00	70.00
	1830 AJ	—	15.00	30.00	40.00	70.00

Mint mark: S, S/L

C#	Date	Mintage	VG	Fine	VF	XF
135.4	1818 CJ	—	20.00	40.00	65.00	100.00
	1818 J	—	25.00	45.00	85.00	140.00
	1819 CJ	—	20.00	40.00	55.00	80.00
	1820 CJ	—	20.00	40.00	60.00	90.00
	1824 J	—	20.00	40.00	90.00	150.00
	1824 JB	—	20.00	40.00	45.00	70.00
	1825 JB	—	15.00	30.00	50.00	80.00
	1826 JB	—	20.00	35.00	55.00	90.00
	1828 JB	—	20.00	40.00	75.00	120.00
	1830 JB	—	15.00	30.00	50.00	80.00
	1832 JB	—	15.00	30.00	45.00	70.00
	1833 JB	—	20.00	35.00	55.00	90.00

Mint mark: Crowned M
Obv. leg: FERDINANDUS

C#	Date	Mintage	VG	Fine	VF	XF
135b	1813 IJ	—	75.00	150.00	300.00	400.00
	1813 GJ	—	90.00	175.00	350.00	500.00
	1814 GJ	—	90.00	175.00	350.00	500.00
164.1	1834 CR	—	60.00	125.00	210.00	350.00
	1834 DG	—	110.00	300.00	550.00	850.00
	1835 CR	—	20.00	35.00	70.00	100.00
	1836 CR	—	20.00	40.00	80.00	125.00

Mint mark: S, S/L

C#	Date	Mintage	VG	Fine	VF	XF
164.2	1835 DR	—	20.00	35.00	75.00	110.00
	1836 DR	—	20.00	35.00	75.00	110.00

Mint mark: B, BA

C#	Date	Mintage	VG	Fine	VF	XF
173a	1836 PS	—	35.00	65.00	155.00	225.00
	1837 PS	—	35.00	70.00	130.00	175.00
	1837 RS	—	20.00	40.00	85.00	125.00

C#	Date	Mintage	VG	Fine	VF	XF
173.1	1837 PJ	—	15.00	30.00	50.00	70.00
	1838 PS	—	25.00	50.00	80.00	110.00
	1839 PS	—	80.00	175.00	375.00	525.00
	1840 PS	—	25.00	50.00	85.00	120.00
	1841 PS	—	15.00	30.00	50.00	65.00
	1842 CC	—	20.00	40.00	60.00	85.00
	1843 CC	—	75.00	150.00	350.00	425.00
	1843 PS	—	75.00	150.00	350.00	450.00
	1844 PS	—	20.00	40.00	70.00	100.00
	1845 PS	—	35.00	70.00	135.00	200.00
	1846 PS	—	80.00	175.00	300.00	450.00
	1847 PS	—	35.00	70.00	120.00	175.00

Mint mark: Crowned M

C#	Date	Mintage	VG	Fine	VF	XF
173.2	1837 CR	—	25.00	45.00	65.00	90.00
	1838 CL	—	45.00	90.00	150.00	225.00
	1839 CL	—	25.00	60.00	100.00	150.00
	1840 CL	—	20.00	35.00	70.00	100.00
	1841 CL	—	20.00	35.00	70.00	100.00
	1842 CL	—	40.00	80.00	140.00	250.00
	1843 CL	—	40.00	80.00	140.00	200.00
	1844 CL	—	45.00	90.00	175.00	275.00
	1845 CL	—	40.00	80.00	160.00	250.00
	1846 CL	—	35.00	65.00	110.00	175.00
	1847 CL	—	25.00	65.00	110.00	175.00
	1848 CL	—	15.00	30.00	35.00	45.00
	1848 DG	—	125.00	200.00	475.00	750.00
	1849 CL	—	15.00	30.00	35.00	45.00

Mint mark: S, S/L

C#	Date	Mintage	VG	Fine	VF	XF
173.3	1837 DR	—	20.00	40.00	70.00	100.00
	1838 DR	—	25.00	50.00	100.00	200.00
	1838 RD	—	25.00	45.00	85.00	160.00
	1839 DR	—	35.00	70.00	180.00	300.00
	1839 RD	—	35.00	70.00	140.00	250.00
	1840 RD	—	50.00	100.00	210.00	400.00
	1841 RD	—	20.00	40.00	75.00	150.00
	1842 RD	—	20.00	40.00	70.00	150.00
	1843 RD	—	15.00	30.00	50.00	80.00
	1844 RD	—	40.00	80.00	185.00	375.00
	1845 RD	—	40.00	80.00	160.00	350.00

8 REALES

27.0700 g, .903 SILVER, .7859 oz ASW
Mint mark: Crowned M
Similar to 2 Reales, C#69.2.

C#	Date	Mintage	VG	Fine	VF	XF
71.1	1802 MF	—	200.00	375.00	500.00	700.00
	1802 FA	—	100.00	200.00	275.00	400.00
	1803 FA	—	150.00	300.00	450.00	550.00
	1805 FA	—	100.00	210.00	275.00	350.00
	1808 FA	—	150.00	300.00	500.00	600.00
	1808 AI	—	140.00	280.00	425.00	650.00
	1808 IG	—	200.00	375.00	475.00	750.00

NOTE: Earlier dates (1788-1797) exist for this type.

Mint mark: S, S/L

C#	Date	Mintage	VG	Fine	VF	XF
71.2	1802 CN	—	125.00	250.00	375.00	500.00
	1803 CN	—	150.00	300.00	500.00	650.00

NOTE: Earlier dates (1788-1800) exist for this type.

Mint mark: Crowned M

C#	Date	Mintage	VG	Fine	VF	XF
93	1809 IG	—	40.00	80.00	200.00	350.00
	1810 JG	—	550.00	1100.	2500.	3250.

Mint mark: S, S/L

C#	Date	Mintage	VG	Fine	VF	XF
136b	1808 CN	—	50.00	100.00	185.00	275.00
	1809 CN	—	50.00	100.00	185.00	275.00

Mint mark: Crowned M

C#	Date	Mintage	VG	Fine	VF	XF
136c	1812 IJ	—	225.00	450.00	600.00	800.00
	1813 IJ	—	200.00	400.00	550.00	750.00
	1813 IG	—	225.00	450.00	600.00	800.00
	1813 GJ	—	250.00	500.00	700.00	900.00

Mint mark: C

C#	Date	Mintage	VG	Fine	VF	XF
136a.1	1809 MP	—	450.00	875.00	1200.	1500.
	1809 SF	—	400.00	800.00	1100.	1300.
	1810 SF	—	425.00	850.00	1200.	1500.

Mint mark: V, VAL

C#	Date	Mintage	VG	Fine	VF	XF
136a.2	1811 GS	—	350.00	700.00	1100.	1500.
	1811 SG	—	300.00	600.00	1000.	1200.

Mint mark: C

C#	Date	Mintage	VG	Fine	VF	XF
136.1	1811 SF	—	625.00	1250.	—	—
	1812 SF	—	475.00	950.00	1800.	—
	1813 SF	—	475.00	950.00	1650.	1950.
	1814 SF	—	625.00	1250.	—	—

Mint mark: Crowned C

C#	Date	Mintage	VG	Fine	VF	XF
136.2	1810 CI	—	300.00	600.00	900.00	1300.
	1811 CI	—	175.00	325.00	575.00	850.00
	1811 CJ	—	190.00	425.00	700.00	950.00
	1812 CJ	—	175.00	400.00	650.00	900.00
	1813 CJ	—	75.00	125.00	200.00	300.00
	1814 CJ	—	75.00	125.00	200.00	300.00
	1815 CJ	—	500.00	1000.	1900.	2600.

Mint mark: Crowned M

C#	Date	Mintage	VG	Fine	VF	XF
136.3	1814 GJ	—	50.00	100.00	150.00	250.00
	1815 GJ	—	50.00	100.00	150.00	250.00
	1816 GJ	—	50.00	100.00	150.00	200.00
	1817 GJ	—	65.00	125.00	200.00	300.00
	1818 GJ	—	50.00	100.00	175.00	300.00
	1823 AJ	—	425.00	850.00	1400.	1700.
	1824 AJ	—	275.00	550.00	900.00	1250.
	1825 AJ	—	300.00	600.00	1100.	1600.
	1830 AJ	—	400.00	800.00	1600.	2000.

Mint mark: S, S/L

C#	Date	Mintage	VG	Fine	VF	XF
136.4	1809 CN	—	75.00	125.00	200.00	350.00
	1810 CN	—	450.00	900.00	1350.	2000.
	1812 CN	—	825.00	1650.	2400.	3600.
	1814 CJ	—	250.00	500.00	1150.	1600.
	1815 CJ	—	65.00	125.00	175.00	250.00
	1816 CJ	—	50.00	100.00	150.00	200.00
	1817 CJ	—	50.00	100.00	150.00	200.00
	1818 CJ	—	50.00	100.00	150.00	200.00
	1819 CJ	—	65.00	125.00	200.00	300.00
	1820 CJ	—	50.00	100.00	150.00	200.00

1/2 ESCUDO

1.6900 g, .875 GOLD, .0475 oz AGW
Obv: Laureate head of Ferdinand right.
Rev: Crowned oval arms.

C#	Date	Mintage	VG	Fine	VF	XF
141	1817 GJ	—	50.00	90.00	150.00	175.00

ESCUDO

3.3800 g, .875 GOLD, .0951 oz AGW
Mint mark: Crowned M
Obv: Bust of Charles IV right.
Rev: Crowned shield in order chain.

C#	Date	Mintage	VG	Fine	VF	XF
73	1801 FA	—	65.00	80.00	100.00	150.00
	1807 FA	—	65.00	80.00	100.00	150.00

NOTE: Earlier dates (1788-1799) exist for this type.

Similar to 1/2 Escudo, C#141.

C#	Date	Mintage	VG	Fine	VF	XF
142	1817 GJ	—	150.00	300.00	500.00	800.00

2 ESCUDOS

6.7700 g, .875 GOLD, .1905 oz AGW

Mint mark: Crowned M

C#	Date	Mintage	VG	Fine	VF	X
74.1	1801 MF	—	125.00	150.00	175.00	225.0
	1801 FM	—	150.00	200.00	350.00	500.0
	1801 FA/MF	—	125.00	150.00	175.00	225.0
	1801 FA	—	125.00	150.00	175.00	225.0
	1802 FA	—	125.00	150.00	175.00	225.0
	1803 FA	—	125.00	150.00	175.00	225.0
	1804 FA	—	125.00	150.00	175.00	225.0
	1805 FA	—	125.00	150.00	175.00	225.0
	1806 FA	—	125.00	150.00	175.00	225.0
	1807 FA	—	125.00	150.00	175.00	225.0
	1807 AI	—	125.00	150.00	175.00	225.0
	1808 AI	—	125.00	150.00	175.00	225.0
	1808 FA	—	300.00	600.00	1000.	1500

NOTE: Earlier dates (1788-1800) exist for this type.

Mint mark: S, S/L

C#	Date	Mintage	VG	Fine	VF	XF
74.2	1801 CN	—	125.00	150.00	175.00	250.0
	1802 CN	—	125.00	150.00	175.00	250.00
	1803 CN	—	125.00	150.00	175.00	250.00
	1804 CN	—	125.00	150.00	175.00	250.00
	1805 CN	—	150.00	200.00	350.00	500.00
	1806 CN	—	125.00	150.00	175.00	250.00
	1807 CN	—	125.00	150.00	175.00	250.00
	1808 CN	—	125.00	150.00	175.00	250.00

NOTE: Earlier dates (1790-1800) exist for this type.

Mint mark: S
Obv: Wide armored, bare head of Ferdinand right.

C#	Date	Mintage	VG	Fine	VF	XF
143a	1808 CN	—	125.00	150.00	200.00	300.00
	1809 CN	—	135.00	175.00	250.00	350.00

Mint mark: S
Obv: Draped bust, bare head of Ferdinand right.

C#	Date	Mintage	VG	Fine	VF	XF
143b.1	1809 CN	—	150.00	250.00	400.00	650.00

Mint mark: Crowned C
Obv: Draped bust, bare head of Ferdinand right.

C#	Date	Mintage	VG	Fine	VF	XF
143b.2	1811 CI	—	250.00	450.00	750.00	1250.

Mint mark: Crowned C
Obv: Laureate armored bust of Ferdinand right.
Rev: Crowned arms in collar of The Golden Fleece.

C#	Date	Mintage	VG	Fine	VF	XF
143c	1811 CI	—	125.00	200.00	300.00	500.00

Mint mark: Crowned M
Obv: Large laureate military bust of Ferdinand right.

C#	Date	Mintage	VG	Fine	VF	XF
143d	1812 IJ	—	175.00	350.00	600.00	950.00

Obv: Small laureate military bust of Ferdinand right.

C#	Date	Mintage	VG	Fine	VF	XF
143e	1813 IG	—	250.00	500.00	900.00	1400.
	1813 IJ	—	150.00	275.00	400.00	600.00
	1813 GJ	—	125.00	175.00	300.00	450.00
	1814 GJ	—	125.00	225.00	350.00	500.00

Mint mark: Crowned C
Obv: Laureate bust of Ferdinand right.

C#	Date	Mintage	VG	Fine	VF	XF
143f.1	1811 CI	—	125.00	150.00	225.00	350.00
	1812 CI	—	125.00	150.00	225.00	350.00
	1813 CI	—	150.00	175.00	275.00	450.00
	1813 CJ	—	125.00	150.00	225.00	350.00
	1814 CJ	—	125.00	150.00	225.00	350.00

NOTE: Large and small varieties of the crowned C mint mark exist.

Mint mark: C
Obv: Laureate head of Ferdinand right.

C#	Date	Mintage	VG	Fine	VF	XF
143f.2	1811 SF	—	500.00	1000.	1750.	2500.
	1812 SF	—	450.00	900.00	1400.	2000.
	1813 SF	—	350.00	750.00	1200.	1750.

NOTE: Varieties in the bust design exist.

Mint mark: Crowned M

C#	Date	Mintage	VG	Fine	VF	XF
143f.3	1814 GJ	—	125.00	175.00	225.00	300.00
	1815 GJ	—	135.00	225.00	350.00	500.00
	1816 GJ	—	150.00	275.00	475.00	600.00
	1817 GJ	—	150.00	275.00	475.00	600.00
	1818 GJ	—	125.00	150.00	200.00	300.00
	1819 GJ	—	125.00	150.00	200.00	300.00
	1820 GJ	—	125.00	125.00	175.00	250.00
	1822 AJ	—	150.00	275.00	475.00	600.00
	1823 AJ	—	150.00	300.00	500.00	750.00
	1824 AJ	—	125.00	125.00	175.00	250.00
	1825 AJ	—	125.00	125.00	175.00	250.00
	1826 AJ	—	135.00	175.00	250.00	350.00
	1827 AJ	—	135.00	200.00	300.00	450.00
	1828 AJ	—	135.00	225.00	350.00	500.00
	1829 AJ	—	125.00	125.00	175.00	250.00
	1830 AJ	—	125.00	125.00	175.00	250.00
	1831 AJ	—	125.00	125.00	175.00	250.00
	1832 AJ	—	125.00	125.00	175.00	250.00
	1833 AJ	—	125.00	125.00	175.00	250.00

Mint mark: S, S/L

C#	Date	Mintage	VG	Fine	VF	XF
143f.4	1815 CJ	—	125.00	125.00	175.00	225.00
	1816 CJ	—	125.00	125.00	175.00	225.00
	1817 CJ	—	135.00	175.00	250.00	350.00
	1818 CJ	—	125.00	125.00	175.00	225.00
	1819 CJ	—	125.00	125.00	175.00	225.00
	1820 CJ	—	125.00	125.00	175.00	225.00
	1821 CJ	—	125.00	150.00	200.00	300.00
	1824 J	—	500.00	1000.	1750.	2500.
	1824 JB	—	135.00	175.00	275.00	400.00
	1825 JB	—	125.00	125.00	175.00	225.00
	1826 JB	—	125.00	125.00	175.00	225.00
	1827 JB	—	125.00	125.00	175.00	225.00
	1828 JB	—	135.00	175.00	275.00	400.00
	1829 JB	—	135.00	175.00	275.00	400.00
	1830 JB	—	135.00	225.00	350.00	500.00
	1831 JB	—	125.00	125.00	175.00	225.00
	1832 JB	—	125.00	125.00	175.00	225.00
	1833 JB	—	125.00	125.00	175.00	225.00

4 ESCUDOS

13.5400 g, .875 GOLD, .3809 oz AGW
Mint mark: Crowned M
Obv: Bust of Charles IV right.
Rev: Crowned arms in collar of The Golden Fleece.

C#	Date	Mintage	VG	Fine	VF	XF
75.1	1801 MF	—	300.00	600.00	850.00	1250.
	1801 FA	—	200.00	250.00	350.00	500.00
	1803 FA	—	225.00	300.00	425.00	600.00

NOTE: Earlier dates (1788-1796) exist for this type.

Mint mark: S, S/L

C#	Date	Mintage	VG	Fine	VF	XF
75.2	1801 C	—	1000.	2200.	3000.	4500.
	1808 C	—	1000.	2200.	3000.	4500.

Mint mark: Crowned M

C#	Date	Mintage	VG	Fine	VF	XF
144	1814 GJ	—	225.00	400.00	550.00	800.00
	1815 GJ	—	225.00	350.00	500.00	700.00
	1816 GJ	—	300.00	600.00	800.00	1200.
	1818 GJ	—	225.00	400.00	550.00	800.00
	1819 GJ	—	225.00	350.00	500.00	700.00
	1820 GJ	—	200.00	250.00	350.00	500.00
	1824 AI	—	750.00	1500.	2100.	3000.

8 ESCUDOS

27.0700 g, .875 GOLD, .7616 oz AGW
Mint mark: Crowned M
Obv: Bust of Charles IV right.

C#	Date	Mintage	VG	Fine	VF	XF
76.1	1802 FA	—	450.00	700.00	1100.	1700.
	1803 FA	—	900.00	1700.	2500.	4000.
	1805 FA	—	550.00	1100.	1600.	2600.

NOTE: Earlier dates (1788-1790) exist for this type.

Mint mark: Crowned C
Obv: Laureate uniformed bust of Ferdinand right.
Rev: Crowned arms.

C#	Date	Mintage	VG	Fine	VF	XF
145	1811 CI	—	750.00	1250.	3600.	6000.

Mint mark: C
Obv: Laureate head.

C#	Date	Mintage	VG	Fine	VF	XF
145a.1	1813 SF	—	3000.	7000.	10,000.	15,000.
	1814 SF	—	4000.	8000.	11,500.	*16,500.

***NOTE:** Stack's CICF Sale 4-89, XF realized $16,500.

Mint mark: Crowned M

C#	Date	Mintage	VG	Fine	VF	XF
145a.2	1814 GJ	—	1000.	2000.	2800.	4000.
	1816 GJ	—	1500.	3000.	4200.	6000.
	1817 GJ	—	1100.	2250.	3100.	4500.
	1819 GJ	—	1800.	3500.	5000.	7500.
	1820 GJ	—	450.00	750.00	1540.	1870.

DE VELLON COINAGE

REAL

1.3540 g, .903 SILVER, .0393 oz ASW
Mint mark: Crowned M

C#	Date	Mintage	VG	Fine	VF	XF
88	1812 AI	—	17.50	45.00	95.00	145.00
	1813 RN	—	25.00	60.00	120.00	180.00

2 REALES

2.7080 g, .903 SILVER, .0786 oz ASW
Mint mark: Crowned M

C#	Date	Mintage	VG	Fine	VF	XF
89	1811 AI	—	40.00	100.00	200.00	300.00
	1812 AI	—	35.00	80.00	160.00	240.00
	1812 RN	—	25.00	60.00	120.00	180.00
	1813 RN	—	60.00	150.00	300.00	450.00

4 REALES

5.4160 g, .903 SILVER, .1572 oz ASW
Mint mark: Crowned M

C#	Date	Mintage	VG	Fine	VF	XF
90.1	1808 AI	—	25.00	65.00	130.00	200.00
	1809 AI	—	10.00	17.50	30.00	45.00
	1810 AI	—	7.50	12.50	22.50	35.00
	1811 AI	—	6.50	10.00	20.00	30.00
	1811 RS	—	20.00	50.00	100.00	150.00

C#	Date	Mintage	VG	Fine	VF	XF
90.1	1812 AI	—	10.00	17.50	30.00	45.00
	1812 RS	—	25.00	40.00	80.00	120.00
	1812 RN	—	10.00	17.50	30.00	45.00
	1813 RN	—	12.50	25.00	47.50	70.00

Mint mark: S, S/L

C#	Date	Mintage	VG	Fine	VF	XF
90.2	1810 LA	—	30.00	70.00	140.00	210.00
	1812 LA	—	12.50	30.00	60.00	90.00

Mint mark: B, BA

C#	Date	Mintage	VG	Fine	VF	XF
137.5	1822 SP	—	10.00	20.00	32.50	50.00
	1823 SP	—	12.50	30.00	60.00	90.00

Mint mark: Crowned M

C#	Date	Mintage	VG	Fine	VF	XF
137.6	1822 SR	—	12.50	27.50	55.00	85.00
	1823 SR	—	15.00	35.00	65.00	100.00

Mint mark: S, S/L

C#	Date	Mintage	VG	Fine	VF	XF
137.7	1823 RD	—	12.50	27.50	55.00	85.00

Mint mark: V, VAL.
Obv: Small bare head bust of Ferdinand right.

C#	Date	Mintage	VG	Fine	VF	XF
137.1	1823 R Spanish arms	—	10.00	20.00	35.00	55.00

10 REALES

13.5400 g, .903 SILVER, .3931 oz ASW
Mint mark: Crowned M

C#	Date	Mintage	VG	Fine	VF	XF
91	1809 AI	—	200.00	500.00	1000.	1500.
	1810 AI	—	120.00	300.00	600.00	900.00
	1811 AI	.058	60.00	150.00	300.00	475.00
	1812 AI	.490	35.00	80.00	160.00	250.00
	1812 RN	I.A.	35.00	80.00	160.00	250.00
	1813 RN	.135	70.00	175.00	350.00	525.00

Mint mark: Bo

C#	Date	Mintage	VG	Fine	VF	XF
138.1	1821 UG	—	15.00	35.00	70.00	100.00

Mint mark: Crowned M

C#	Date	Mintage	VG	Fine	VF	XF
138.2	1821 SR	—	10.00	17.50	30.00	45.00

Mint mark: Sr

C#	Date	Mintage	VG	Fine	VF	XF
138.3	1821 LT	—	15.00	35.00	70.00	100.00

Mint mark: S, S/L

C#	Date	Mintage	VG	Fine	VF	XF
138.4	1821 RD	—	17.50	40.00	80.00	125.00

Mint mark: Crowned M

C#	Date	Mintage	VG	Fine	VF	XF
174.1	1840 CL	—	70.00	175.00	350.00	525.00
	1840 DG	—	225.00	600.00	1200.	1800.
	1841 CL	—	65.00	165.00	325.00	500.00
	1842 CL	—	70.00	175.00	350.00	525.00
	1843 CL	—	55.00	140.00	275.00	425.00
	1844 CL	—	70.00	175.00	350.00	525.00
	1845 CL	—	100.00	250.00	500.00	750.00

Mint mark: S, S/L

C#	Date	Mintage	VG	Fine	VF	XF
174.2	1841 RD	—	75.00	150.00	300.00	600.00
	1842 RD	—	75.00	150.00	300.00	600.00
	1843 RD	—	75.00	150.00	300.00	600.00

20 REALES

27.0800 g, .903 SILVER, .7863 oz ASW
Mint mark: B, BA

C#	Date	Mintage	VG	Fine	VF	XF
92.1	1811	—	75.00	180.00	360.00	550.00
	1812	—	110.00	275.00	550.00	850.00

Mint mark: Crowned M

C#	Date	Mintage	VG	Fine	VF	XF
92.2	1808 AI	.017	100.00	250.00	500.00	750.00
	1809 AI	.700	35.00	80.00	160.00	250.00
	1810 IA	.993	400.00	1000.	2000.	3000.
	1810 AI	Inc. Ab.	30.00	75.00	150.00	225.00
	1811 AI	.460	30.00	75.00	150.00	225.00
	1812 AI	.250	65.00	140.00	275.00	425.00
	1813 RN	.068	100.00	240.00	480.00	725.00

Mint mark: S, S/L

C#	Date	Mintage	VG	Fine	VF	XF
92.3	1812 LA	.013	120.00	300.00	600.00	900.00

Mint mark: B, BA

C#	Date	Mintage	VG	Fine	VF	XF
139.1	1822 SP	—	120.00	300.00	1150.	1750.
	1823 SP	—	40.00	80.00	150.00	300.00

Mint mark: S, S/L

C#	Date	Mintage	VG	Fine	VF	XF
139.2	1822 RD	—	40.00	100.00	150.00	300.00
	1823 RD	—	50.00	125.00	225.00	400.00

Mint mark: Crowned M
Smaller letters.

C#	Date	Mintage	VG	Fine	VF	XF
139a	1821 SR	—	400.00	1000.	2000.	3000.
	1822 SR	—	25.00	50.00	100.00	175.00
	1823 SR	—	60.00	125.00	200.00	300.00

C#	Date	Mintage	VG	Fine	VF	XF
140	1833 DG	—	400.00	1000.	2000.	3000.

Obv. leg. ends: DIOS
Rev: Similar to C#175.1.

C#	Date	Mintage	VG	Fine	VF	XF
165	1834 DG	—	325.00	825.00	1650.	2500.
	1834 NC	4,769	200.00	500.00	1000.	1500.
	1835 CR	.013	160.00	400.00	800.00	1200.
	1836 CR	.048	125.00	325.00	650.00	1000.

C#	Date	Mintage	VG	Fine	VF	XF
175.1	1837 CR	.115	70.00	175.00	350.00	525.00
	1838 CL	.231	65.00	165.00	325.00	500.00
	1839 CL	.074	400.00	1000.	2000.	3000.
	1840 CL	6,012	650.00	1625.	3250.	5000.
	1847 DG	—	500.00	1250.	2500.	3750.
	1848 CL	.067	50.00	125.00	250.00	400.00
	1849 CL	.120	70.00	175.00	350.00	525.00
	1850 DG	—	500.00	1250.	2500.	3750.

Mint mark: S, S/L

C#	Date	Mintage	VG	Fine	VF	XF
175.2	1842 RD	.012	225.00	500.00	1000.	1500.

80 REALES

6.7700 g, .875 GOLD, .1905 oz AGW
Mint mark: Crowned M

C#	Date	Mintage	VG	Fine	VF	XF
94	1809 AI	—	100.00	150.00	250.00	375.00
	1810 AI	—	200.00	500.00	1000.	1500.

C#	Date	Mintage	VG	Fine	VF	XF
94a	1811 AI	.440	100.00	150.00	275.00	450.00
	1812/1 AI	—	100.00	200.00	400.00	650.00
	1812 AI	.238	100.00	200.00	400.00	650.00
	1813 RN	.161	125.00	250.00	450.00	750.00

Mint mark: B, BA

C#	Date	Mintage	VG	Fine	VF	XF
146.1	1822 SP	—	125.00	250.00	500.00	800.00
	1823 SP	—	100.00	125.00	200.00	300.00

Mint mark: Crowned M

C#	Date	Mintage	VG	Fine	VF	XF
146.2	1822 SR	—	100.00	125.00	160.00	225.00
	1823 SR	—	100.00	135.00	225.00	350.00

Mint mark: S, S/L

C#	Date	Mintage	VG	Fine	VF	XF
146.3	1823 RD	—	140.00	300.00	600.00	900.00

Mint mark: B, BA
Obv. leg. ends: DIOS

C#	Date	Mintage	VG	Fine	VF	XF
166.1	1836 PS	—	400.00	1000.	2000.	3000.

Mint mark: Crowned M

C#	Date	Mintage	VG	Fine	VF	XF
166.2	1834 CR	—	100.00	125.00	175.00	275.00
	1835 CR	—	100.00	125.00	160.00	250.00
	1836 CL	—	100.00	125.00	200.00	325.00
	1836 CR	—	110.00	200.00	400.00	600.00

Mint mark: S, S/L

C#	Date	Mintage	VG	Fine	VF	XF
166.3	1835 DR	—	125.00	215.00	425.00	650.00
	1835 RD	—	110.00	175.00	350.00	525.00
	1836 DR	—	110.00	175.00	350.00	525.00
	1837 DR	—	110.00	175.00	350.00	525.00

Mint mark: B, BA

C#	Date	Mintage	VG	Fine	VF	XF
176.1	1836 PS	—	400.00	1000.	2000.	3000.
	1838 PS CONSTITUCION	—	100.00	125.00	225.00	350.00
	1838 PS CONST	—	110.00	200.00	400.00	600.00
	1839 PS CONSTITUCION	—	170.00	400.00	800.00	1200.
	1839 PS CONST	—	100.00	125.00	225.00	350.00
	1840 PS	—	100.00	125.00	150.00	225.00
	1841 PS	—	100.00	125.00	150.00	225.00
	1842 CC	—	100.00	125.00	200.00	300.00
	1842 PS	—	600.00	1500.	3000.	4500.
	1843 CC	—	450.00	1000.	2100.	3250.
	1843 PS	—	325.00	800.00	1600.	2400.
	1844 PS	—	100.00	125.00	200.00	300.00
	1845 PS	—	100.00	125.00	200.00	300.00
	1846 PS	—	100.00	125.00	180.00	275.00
	1847 PS	—	100.00	125.00	210.00	325.00
	1848 PS	—	150.00	325.00	625.00	950.00

Mint mark: Crowned M

C#	Date	Mintage	VG	Fine	VF	XF
176.2	1834 CR	—	100.00	125.00	180.00	275.00
	1835 CR	—	100.00	125.00	160.00	250.00
	1836 CL	—	100.00	125.00	250.00	400.00
	1836 CR	—	120.00	265.00	525.00	800.00
	1837 CR	—	135.00	320.00	625.00	950.00
	1838 CL	—	130.00	300.00	600.00	900.00
	1839 CL	—	135.00	325.00	650.00	1000.
	1840 CL	—	110.00	200.00	400.00	600.00
	1841 CL	—	100.00	165.00	325.00	500.00
	1842 CL	—	175.00	400.00	800.00	1200.
	1843 CL	—	100.00	125.00	180.00	275.00
	1844 CL	—	100.00	125.00	200.00	300.00
	1845 CL	—	100.00	125.00	160.00	250.00
	1846 CL	—	100.00	150.00	300.00	450.00
	1847 CL	—	110.00	200.00	400.00	600.00
	1848 CL	—	100.00	150.00	300.00	450.00
	1849 CL	—	200.00	500.00	1000.	1500.

Mint mark: S, S/L

C#	Date	Mintage	VG	Fine	VF	XF
176.3	1835 DR	—	110.00	220.00	425.00	650.00
	1835 RD	—	100.00	125.00	250.00	375.00
	1836 DR	—	100.00	175.00	350.00	525.00
	1837 DR	—	100.00	170.00	375.00	550.00
	1838 DR	—	130.00	300.00	600.00	900.00
	1838 RD	—	165.00	400.00	800.00	1200.
	1839 RD	—	100.00	150.00	300.00	475.00
	1840 RD	—	100.00	140.00	275.00	425.00
	1841 RD	—	100.00	150.00	300.00	450.00
	1842 RD	—	100.00	140.00	275.00	425.00
	1843 RD	—	100.00	150.00	300.00	450.00
	1844 RD	—	100.00	150.00	300.00	450.00
	1845 RD	—	100.00	125.00	225.00	350.00
	1846 RD	—	100.00	175.00	350.00	525.00
	1847 RD	—	100.00	165.00	325.00	500.00
	1848 RD	—	200.00	500.00	1000.	1600.

Mint mark: B, BA
Obv. leg. ends: CONSTITUCION

C#	Date	Mintage	VG	Fine	VF	XF
176a	1837 PS	—	110.00	250.00	500.00	750.00
	1838 PS	—	100.00	125.00	225.00	350.00

160 REALES

13.5400 g, .875 GOLD, .3809 oz AGW
Mint mark: Crowned M

C#	Date	Mintage	VG	Fine	VF	XF
147	1822 SR	—	250.00	400.00	650.00	1000.

320 REALES

27.0700 g, .875 GOLD, .7616 oz AGW
Mint mark: Crowned M

C#	Date	Mintage	VG	Fine	VF	XF
95	1810 AI	.064	1500.	3250.	6500.	10,000.
	1810 RS	I.A.	1750.	4500.	9000.	13,750.
	1812 RS	.060	1500.	3000.	6500.	9500.

C#	Date	Mintage	VG	Fine	VF	XF
148	1822 SR	—	600.00	1300.	2750.	4250.
	1823 SR	—	1100.	2400.	5000.	7500.

DECIMAL COINAGE

10 Decimos = 1 Real
100 Centimos = 1 Real

1/20 REAL

COPPER
Mint mark: Aqueduct

Y#	Date	Mintage	VG	Fine	VF	XF
15	1852	—	5.00	12.50	22.50	35.00
	1853	—	2.50	5.00	10.00	20.00

5 CENTIMOS

COPPER
Mint mark: Aqueduct

Y#	Date	Mintage	VG	Fine	VF	XF
24	1854	—	90.00	225.00	400.00	650.00
	1855	—	5.00	12.50	22.50	35.00
	1856	—	2.00	4.50	7.50	12.50
	1857	—	2.25	5.50	9.00	15.00
	1858	—	10.00	25.00	40.00	70.00
	1859	—	2.00	4.50	7.50	12.50
	1860	—	2.50	6.50	11.00	18.00
	1861	—	3.50	9.00	15.00	25.00
	1862	—	3.50	9.00	15.00	25.00
	1863	—	2.50	6.50	11.00	18.00
	1864	—	5.00	12.50	22.50	35.00

1/10 REAL

COPPER
Mint mark: Aqueduct

Y#	Date	Mintage	VG	Fine	VF	XF
16	1850	—	3.00	7.50	12.50	25.00
	1851	—	10.00	22.50	40.00	65.00
	1852	—	3.00	7.50	12.50	25.00
	1853	—	2.50	5.00	10.00	20.00

10 CENTIMOS

COPPER
Mint mark: Aqueduct

Y#	Date	Mintage	VG	Fine	VF	XF
25	1854	—	100.00	250.00	450.00	750.00
	1855	—	5.00	12.50	21.00	35.00
	1856	—	2.75	7.00	12.00	20.00
	1857	—	2.00	4.50	7.50	12.50
	1858	—	5.00	12.50	21.00	35.00
	1859	—	2.00	4.50	7.50	12.50
	1860	—	2.00	4.50	7.50	12.50
	1861	—	2.50	6.50	11.00	18.00
	1862	—	2.75	7.00	12.00	20.00
	1863	—	3.50	9.00	15.00	25.00
	1864	—	8.50	21.00	35.00	60.00

1/5 REAL

COPPER
Mint mark: Aqueduct

Y#	Date	Mintage	VG	Fine	VF	XF
17	1853	—	10.00	22.50	35.00	60.00

25 CENTIMOS

COPPER
Mint mark: 8-pointed star

Y#	Date	Mintage	VG	Fine	VF	XF
26.1	1863	—	50.00	125.00	200.00	350.00
	1864	—	17.50	40.00	70.00	120.00

Mint mark: Aqueduct

Y#	Date	Mintage	VG	Fine	VF	XF
26.2	1854	—	2.75	7.00	12.00	20.00
	1855	—	2.00	4.50	7.50	12.50
	1856	—	2.00	4.50	7.50	12.50
	1857	—	2.25	5.50	9.00	15.00
	1858	—	2.00	4.50	7.50	12.50
	1859	—	2.00	4.50	7.50	12.50
	1860	—	2.00	4.50	7.50	12.50
	1861	—	2.00	4.50	7.50	12.50
	1862	—	2.00	4.50	7.50	12.50
	1863	—	2.00	4.50	7.50	12.50
	1864	—	2.50	6.50	11.00	18.00

1/2 REAL

COPPER
Mint mark: 4-pointed star
Similar to 1/5 Real, Y#17.

Y#	Date	Mintage	VG	Fine	VF	XF
18.1	1850	—	17.50	40.00	70.00	120.00

Mint mark: 6-pointed star

Y#	Date	Mintage	VG	Fine	VF	XF
18.2	1848 DG	—	50.00	125.00	225.00	400.00
	1848	—	5.00	10.00	20.00	45.00

Mint mark: Aqueduct

Y#	Date	Mintage	VG	Fine	VF	XF
18.3	1848	—	35.00	90.00	150.00	250.00
	1849	—	25.00	70.00	120.00	200.00
	1850	—	5.00	10.00	20.00	40.00
	1851	—	5.00	10.00	20.00	40.00
	1852	—	5.00	10.00	20.00	40.00
	1853	—	5.00	10.00	20.00	40.00

REAL

1.3146 g, .900 SILVER, .0380 oz ASW
Mint mark: 8-pointed star

Y#	Date	Mintage	VG	Fine	VF	XF
19.1	1852	—	7.00	16.00	27.50	40.00
	1853	—	3.00	7.50	12.50	18.00
	1854	—	5.00	12.50	21.00	30.00
	1855	—	4.25	10.00	17.50	25.00

Mint mark: 6-pointed star

Y#	Date	Mintage	VG	Fine	VF	XF
19.2	1852	—	2.00	5.00	8.00	14.00
	1853	—	5.00	12.50	21.00	30.00
	1854	—	14.00	35.00	60.00	85.00
	1855	—	14.00	35.00	60.00	85.00

Mint mark: 7-pointed star

Y#	Date	Mintage	VG	Fine	VF	XF
19.3	1850	—	5.00	12.50	21.00	30.00
	1851	—	32.50	85.00	140.00	200.00
	1852	—	2.00	5.25	8.75	12.50
	1853	—	2.50	6.25	10.00	15.00
	1854	—	7.00	16.00	27.50	40.00
	1855	—	5.00	12.50	21.00	30.00

Mint mark: 8-pointed star

Y#	Date	Mintage	VG	Fine	VF	XF
27.1	1857	—	4.25	10.00	17.50	25.00
	1858	—	5.00	12.50	21.00	30.00
	1859	—	10.00	25.00	40.00	60.00
	1860/59	—	3.25	8.50	14.00	20.00
	1860	—	3.25	8.50	14.00	20.00
	1861	—	3.25	8.50	14.00	20.00
	1862	—	6.00	15.00	25.00	35.00
	1863	—	7.00	16.00	27.50	40.00
	1864	—	10.00	25.00	40.00	60.00

Mint mark: 6-pointed star

Y#	Date	Mintage	VG	Fine	VF	XF
27.2	1857	—	4.25	10.00	17.50	25.00
	1858	—	9.25	22.50	37.50	55.00
	1859	—	3.00	6.00	10.00	18.00
	1860	—	3.25	8.50	14.00	20.00
	1861	—	9.25	22.50	37.50	55.00
	1862	—	4.00	8.00	15.00	30.00
	1863	—	5.00	12.50	20.00	30.00
	1864	—	7.00	16.00	27.50	40.00

Mint mark: 7-pointed star

Y#	Date	Mintage	VG	Fine	VF	XF
27.3	1857	—	20.00	50.00	85.00	120.00
	1858	—	7.50	19.00	30.00	45.00
	1859	—	10.00	25.00	40.00	60.00
	1860	—	3.25	8.50	14.00	22.50
	1861	—	18.00	45.00	75.00	110.00
	1862	—	9.25	22.50	37.50	55.00
	1863	—	3.25	8.50	14.00	22.50
	1864	—	7.00	16.00	27.50	40.00

2 REALES

2.6291 g, .900 SILVER, .0761 oz ASW
Mint mark: 8-pointed star

Y#	Date	Mintage	VG	Fine	VF	XF
20.1	1852	—	12.50	21.00	35.00	50.00
	1853	—	5.00	12.50	17.50	30.00
	1854	—	18.00	45.00	75.00	110.00
	1855	—	12.50	21.00	35.00	50.00

Mint mark: 6-pointed star

Y#	Date	Mintage	VG	Fine	VF	XF
20.2	1851	—	50.00	125.00	200.00	300.00
	1852	—	10.00	25.00	40.00	60.00
	1853	—	6.00	15.00	25.00	35.00
	1854	—	6.00	15.00	25.00	35.00
	1855	—	5.00	12.50	21.00	30.00

Mint mark: 7-pointed star

Y#	Date	Mintage	VG	Fine	VF	XF
20.3	1850	—	12.50	30.00	50.00	75.00
	1851	—	55.00	135.00	225.00	325.00
	1852	—	5.00	12.50	21.00	30.00
	1853	—	3.00	7.50	12.50	18.00
	1854	—	5.00	12.50	21.00	30.00
	1855	—	5.00	12.50	21.00	30.00

Mint mark: 8-pointed star

Y#	Date	Mintage	VG	Fine	VF	XF
28.1	1857	—	4.25	10.00	17.50	25.00
	1858	—	10.00	25.00	60.00	120.00
	1860/59	—	—	—	—	—
	1860	—	7.50	19.00	30.00	45.00
	1861	—	7.50	19.00	30.00	45.00
	1862	—	22.50	55.00	95.00	140.00
	1863	—	40.00	100.00	175.00	250.00
	1864	—	65.00	165.00	275.00	400.00

Mint mark: 6-pointed star

Y#	Date	Mintage	VG	Fine	VF	XF
28.2	1857	—	10.00	25.00	40.00	60.00
	1859	—	4.50	8.50	14.00	20.00
	1860	—	16.00	40.00	70.00	100.00
	1861	—	4.25	10.00	17.50	25.00
	1862	—	4.50	8.50	14.00	20.00
	1863	—	16.00	40.00	70.00	100.00
	1864	—	30.00	70.00	120.00	175.00

Mint mark: 7-pointed star

Y#	Date	Mintage	VG	Fine	VF	XF
28.3	1857	—	20.00	40.00	80.00	120.00
	1858	—	13.00	32.50	55.00	80.00
	1859	—	15.00	37.50	60.00	90.00
	1860	—	7.50	19.00	30.00	45.00
	1861	—	5.00	12.50	21.00	30.00
	1862	—	12.50	21.00	35.00	50.00
	1863	—	5.00	12.50	21.00	30.00
	1864	—	10.00	25.00	40.00	60.00

4 REALES

5.2582 g, .900 SILVER, .1521 oz ASW
Mint mark: 8-pointed star

Y#	Date	Mintage	VG	Fine	VF	XF
21.1	1852	—	7.50	15.00	35.00	55.00
	1853	—	10.00	25.00	40.00	60.00
	1854	—	9.25	22.50	37.50	55.00
	1855	—	60.00	150.00	250.00	350.00

Mint mark: 6-pointed star

Y#	Date	Mintage	VG	Fine	VF	XF
21.2	1852	—	5.00	10.00	20.00	30.00
	1853	—	16.00	40.00	65.00	95.00
	1854	—	7.50	19.00	30.00	45.00
	1855	—	15.00	37.50	60.00	90.00

Mint mark: 7-pointed star

Y#	Date	Mintage	VG	Fine	VF	XF
21.3	1852	—	5.00	12.50	21.00	30.00
	1853	—	5.00	12.50	21.00	30.00
	1854	—	4.25	10.00	17.50	25.00
	1855	—	12.50	21.00	35.00	50.00

Mint mark: 8-pointed star

Y#	Date	Mintage	VG	Fine	VF	XF
29.1	1857	—	65.00	160.00	275.00	400.00
	1858	—	15.00	37.50	60.00	90.00
	1859	—	10.00	25.00	40.00	60.00
	1860	—	10.00	25.00	40.00	60.00
	1861	—	7.50	15.00	30.00	50.00
	1862	—	60.00	150.00	250.00	350.00
	1864	—	65.00	155.00	260.00	375.00

Mint mark: 6-pointed star

Y#	Date	Mintage	VG	Fine	VF	XF
29.2	1856	—	12.50	25.00	50.00	75.00
	1857	—	7.50	15.00	30.00	45.00
	1858	—	6.00	12.50	25.00	35.00
	1859	—	5.00	10.00	21.00	30.00
	1860	—	32.50	85.00	140.00	200.00
	1861	—	7.50	15.00	30.00	45.00
	1862	—	5.00	10.00	20.00	30.00
	1863	—	5.00	10.00	20.00	30.00
	1864	—	20.00	50.00	85.00	120.00

Mint mark: 7-pointed star

Y#	Date	Mintage	VG	Fine	VF	XF
29.3	1857	—	30.00	70.00	120.00	175.00
	1858	—	40.00	100.00	175.00	250.00
	1859	—	30.00	70.00	120.00	175.00
	1860	—	10.00	25.00	40.00	60.00
	1861	—	12.50	30.00	50.00	75.00
	1862	—	15.00	37.50	60.00	90.00
	1863	—	12.50	21.00	35.00	50.00
	1864	—	10.00	25.00	40.00	60.00

10 REALES

13.1455 g, .900 SILVER, .3804 oz ASW
Mint mark: 8-pointed star
Similar to 4 Reales, Y#21.

Y#	Date	Mintage	VG	Fine	VF	XF
22.1	1851	—	150.00	375.00	625.00	900.00
	1852	—	25.00	60.00	100.00	150.00
	1853	—	10.00	25.00	40.00	60.00
	1854	—	15.00	37.50	60.00	90.00
	1855	—	30.00	70.00	120.00	175.00

Mint mark: 6-pointed star

Y#	Date	Mintage	VG	Fine	VF	XF
22.2	1851	—	25.00	60.00	100.00	150.00
	1852	—	10.00	20.00	40.00	60.00
	1853	—	10.00	20.00	40.00	60.00
	1854	—	14.00	35.00	60.00	85.00
	1855	—	50.00	125.00	200.00	300.00

Mint mark: 7-pointed star

Y#	Date	Mintage	VG	Fine	VF	XF
22.3	1851	—	75.00	180.00	300.00	450.00
	1852	—	7.50	20.00	35.00	50.00
	1853	—	10.00	25.00	40.00	60.00
	1854	—	10.00	25.00	40.00	60.00
	1855	—	16.00	40.00	70.00	100.00
	1856	—	150.00	400.00	700.00	1000.

Mint mark: 8-pointed star

Y#	Date	Mintage	VG	Fine	VF	XF
30.1	1859	—	60.00	150.00	250.00	350.00
	1860	—	60.00	150.00	250.00	350.00
	1861	—	37.50	90.00	150.00	225.00
	1862	—	50.00	125.00	200.00	300.00
	1863	—	100.00	275.00	450.00	650.00
	1864	—	55.00	135.00	225.00	325.00

Mint mark: 6-pointed star

Y#	Date	Mintage	VG	Fine	VF	XF
30.2	1857	—	32.50	85.00	140.00	200.00
	1858	—	20.00	50.00	85.00	120.00
	1859	—	20.00	50.00	85.00	120.00
	1860	—	15.00	30.00	45.00	90.00
	1861	—	20.00	50.00	85.00	120.00
	1862	—	12.50	21.00	35.00	50.00
	1863	—	7.50	15.00	25.00	45.00
	1864	—	20.00	50.00	85.00	120.00
	1865	—	45.00	115.00	190.00	275.00

Mint mark: 7-pointed star

Y#	Date	Mintage	VG	Fine	VF	XF
30.3	1857	—	65.00	165.00	275.00	400.00
	1858	—	55.00	135.00	225.00	325.00
	1859	—	60.00	150.00	250.00	350.00
	1860	—	100.00	250.00	425.00	600.00
	1861	—	25.00	60.00	100.00	150.00
	1863	—	40.00	100.00	175.00	250.00
	1864	—	125.00	325.00	550.00	800.00

20 REALES

26.2910 g, .900 SILVER, .7607 oz ASW
Mint mark: Crowned M
Rev: Similar to C#140.

Y#	Date	Mintage	VG	Fine	VF	XF
13.1	1850 CL	.126	35.00	65.00	95.00	135.00
	1850 DG	—	400.00	1000.	1750.	2500.

Mint mark: 7-pointed star

Y#	Date	Mintage	VG	Fine	VF	XF
13.2	1850 RD	—	200.00	500.00	750.00	1000.

Mint mark: 8-pointed star

Y#	Date	Mintage	VG	Fine	VF	XF
23.1	1850	—	325.00	850.00	1400.	2000.
	1851	1.055	150.00	300.00	400.00	600.00
	1852	1.053	250.00	625.00	1000.	1500.

Mint mark: 6-pointed star

Y#	Date	Mintage	VG	Fine	VF	XF
23.2	1850	.500	20.00	40.00	70.00	115.00
	1851	Inc. Ab.	15.00	30.00	50.00	80.00
	1852	Inc. Ab.	30.00	70.00	110.00	165.00
	1854	1.355	17.50	35.00	65.00	100.00
	1855	1.229	17.50	35.00	65.00	100.00

Mint mark: 7-pointed star

Y#	Date	Mintage	VG	Fine	VF	XF
23.3	1850	—	325.00	850.00	1400.	2000.
	1851	Inc. Ab.	25.00	60.00	100.00	150.00
	1852	Inc. Ab.	25.00	60.00	100.00	150.00
	1853	—	400.00	1000.	1900.	2750.
	1854	Inc. Ab.	20.00	40.00	80.00	120.00
	1855	Inc. Ab.	20.00	40.00	90.00	150.00

Mint mark: 8-pointed star

Y#	Date	Mintage	VG	Fine	VF	XF
31.1	1857	.713	200.00	475.00	850.00	1250.
	1859	.880	240.00	600.00	1000.	1450.
	1862	1.594	400.00	1000.	1750.	2500.
	1863	.520	400.00	1000.	1750.	2500.

Mint mark: 6-pointed star

Y#	Date	Mintage	VG	Fine	VF	XF
31.2	1856	1.021	15.00	25.00	40.00	60.00
	1857	Inc. Ab.	12.50	20.00	40.00	60.00
	1858	1.626	15.00	30.00	50.00	75.00
	1859	Inc. Ab.	17.50	37.50	60.00	90.00
	1860	.941	17.50	40.00	70.00	100.00
	1861	1.352	12.50	20.00	40.00	60.00
	1862	Inc. Ab.	25.00	60.00	100.00	150.00
	1863	Inc. Ab.	60.00	140.00	250.00	350.00
	1864	2.776	20.00	50.00	85.00	120.00

Mint mark: 7-pointed star

Y#	Date	Mintage	VG	Fine	VF	XF
31.3	1856	Inc. Ab.	70.00	175.00	300.00	425.00
	1857	Inc. Ab.	30.00	70.00	120.00	175.00
	1858	Inc. Ab.	30.00	70.00	120.00	175.00
	1859	Inc. Ab.	70.00	175.00	300.00	425.00
	1860	Inc. Ab.	45.00	115.00	190.00	275.00
	1861	Inc. Ab.	75.00	190.00	300.00	450.00
	1862	Inc. Ab.	85.00	200.00	350.00	500.00
	1863	Inc. Ab.	85.00	200.00	325.00	475.00

1.6674 g, .900 GOLD, .0482 oz AGW
Mint mark: 6-pointed star

Y#	Date	Mintage	VG	Fine	VF	XF
32	1857	—	200.00	500.00	825.00	1200.
	1861	—	40.00	85.00	140.00	200.00
	1862	—	175.00	400.00	700.00	1000.
	1863	—	425.00	1000.	1750.	2500.

40 REALES

3.3349 g, .900 GOLD, .0965 oz AGW
Mint mark: 8-pointed star

Y#	Date	Mintage	VG	Fine	VF	XF
33.1	1863	—	60.00	75.00	100.00	150.00
	1864	—	400.00	900.00	1500.	2200.

Mint mark: 6-pointed star

Y#	Date	Mintage	VG	Fine	VF	XF
33.2	1861	—	100.00	225.00	400.00	600.00
	1862	—	55.00	65.00	100.00	150.00
	1863	—	55.00	65.00	80.00	120.00

Obv: Draped bust of Isabel II left.
Rev: Crowned draped arms.

Y#	Date	Mintage	VG	Fine	VF	XF
A35.1	1864	—	55.00	65.00	75.00	120.00

Mint mark: 7-pointed star

Y#	Date	Mintage	VG	Fine	VF	XF
A35.2	1864	—	175.00	375.00	625.00	900.00

100 REALES

8.3371 g, .900 GOLD, .2412 oz AGW
Mint mark: 8-pointed star

Y#	Date	Mintage	VG	Fine	VF	XF
A23.1	1850 SM	—	400.00	850.00	1400.	2100.

Mint mark: 6-pointed star

Y#	Date	Mintage	VG	Fine	VF	XF
A23.2	1850 CL	—	125.00	150.00	200.00	300.00
	1850 DG	—	1500.	4000.	7000.	10,000
	1851 CL	—	200.00	500.00	825.00	1200.

Mint mark: 7-pointed star

Y#	Date	Mintage	VG	Fine	VF	XF
A23.3	1850 RD	—	400.00	900.00	1500.	2200.

Mint mark: 8-pointed star

Y#	Date	Mintage	VG	Fine	VF	XF
B23.1	1851	—	700.00	1500.	2750.	4000.
	1854	—	125.00	175.00	250.00	350.00
	1855	—	125.00	150.00	200.00	300.00

Mint mark: 6-pointed star

Y#	Date	Mintage	VG	Fine	VF	XF
B23.2	1851	—	700.00	1500.	2500.	3750.
	1852	—	550.00	1200.	2000.	3000.
	1854	—	125.00	150.00	250.00	375.00
	1855	—	125.00	150.00	175.00	275.00

Mint mark: 7-pointed star

Y#	Date	Mintage	VG	Fine	VF	XF
B23.3	1851	—	1250.	3000.	5000.	7500.
	1852	—	600.00	1400.	2500.	3500.
	1854	—	125.00	150.00	200.00	300.00
	1855	—	125.00	140.00	160.00	225.00

Mint mark: 8-pointed star
Similar to 2 Reales, C#33.

Y#	Date	Mintage	VG	Fine	VF	XF
35.1	1856	—	250.00	600.00	1100.	1650.
	1857	—	125.00	145.00	175.00	275.00
	1858	—	125.00	165.00	275.00	400.00
	1859	—	125.00	140.00	150.00	200.00
	1860	—	125.00	140.00	150.00	200.00
	1861	—	250.00	525.00	900.00	1350.
	1862	—	175.00	350.00	475.00	350.00

Mint mark: 6-pointed star

Y#	Date	Mintage	VG	Fine	VF	XF
35.2	1856	—	125.00	140.00	150.00	175.00
	1857	—	175.00	400.00	650.00	950.00
	1858	—	125.00	175.00	300.00	450.00
	1859	—	125.00	140.00	160.00	225.00
	1860	—	125.00	135.00	145.00	175.00
	1861	—	125.00	135.00	145.00	175.00
	1862	—	125.00	135.00	145.00	175.00

Mint mark: 7-pointed star

Y#	Date	Mintage	VG	Fine	VF	XF
35.3	1856	—	250.00	600.00	1100.	1650.
	1857	—	125.00	135.00	150.00	225.00
	1858	—	125.00	150.00	250.00	375.00
	1859	—	125.00	135.00	150.00	200.00
	1860	—	125.00	135.00	150.00	200.00
	1861	—	125.00	135.00	150.00	175.00
	1862	—	125.00	135.00	150.00	175.00

Mint mark: 6-pointed star
Rev: Crowned and mantled rectangluar arms.

Y#	Date	Mintage	VG	Fine	VF	XF
B35.1	1863	—	125.00	135.00	160.00	200.00
	1864	—	125.00	135.00	145.00	175.00

Mint mark: 7-pointed star

Y#	Date	Mintage	VG	Fine	VF	XF
B35.2	1863	—	175.00	375.00	625.00	900.00
	1864	—	175.00	400.00	700.00	1000.

SECOND DECIMAL COINAGE

100 Centimos = 1 Escudo

NOTE: For similar coins, with denominations expressed Cs. de Peso, see Philippines.

1/2 CENTIMO

COPPER
Mint mark: 8-pointed star

Y#	Date	Mintage	VG	Fine	VF	XF
36.1	1866 OM	—	5.00	12.50	21.00	35.00
	1867 OM	—	2.25	5.50	9.00	15.00
	1868 OM	—	2.25	5.50	9.00	15.00

Mint mark: 4-pointed star

Y#	Date	Mintage	VG	Fine	VF	XF
36.2	1866 OM	—	3.50	9.00	15.00	25.00
	1867 OM	—	2.25	5.50	9.00	15.00
	1868 OM	—	1.50	3.50	6.00	10.00

Mint mark: 6-pointed star

Y#	Date	Mintage	VG	Fine	VF	XF
36.3	1865	—	45.00	115.00	200.00	325.00
	1867 OM	—	18.00	45.00	75.00	125.00

Mint mark: 3-pointed star

Y#	Date	Mintage	VG	Fine	VF	XF
36.4	1866 OM	—	2.25	5.50	9.00	15.00
	1867 OM	—	2.00	4.00	7.00	12.50
	1868 OM	—	4.00	9.00	12.50	20.00

Mint mark: 7-pointed star

Y#	Date	Mintage	VG	Fine	VF	XF
36.5	1867 OM	—	6.00	14.00	25.00	40.00
	1868 OM	—	3.50	9.00	15.00	25.00

CENTIMO

COPPER
Mint mark: 8-pointed star

Y#	Date	Mintage	VG	Fine	VF	XF
37.1	1866	—	6.00	14.00	25.00	40.00
	1866 OM	—	3.50	7.00	10.00	15.00
	1867 OM	—	3.50	7.00	10.00	15.00
	1868 OM	—	2.00	4.00	7.00	12.50

Mint mark: 4-pointed star

Y#	Date	Mintage	VG	Fine	VF	XF
37.2	1866	—	8.50	21.00	35.00	60.00
	1866 OM	—	6.00	14.00	25.00	40.00
	1867 OM	—	4.50	11.00	18.00	30.00
	1868 OM	—	1.50	3.50	6.00	10.00

Mint mark: 6-pointed star

Y#	Date	Mintage	VG	Fine	VF	XF
37.3	1865	—	55.00	150.00	250.00	400.00

Mint mark: 3-pointed star

Y#	Date	Mintage	VG	Fine	VF	XF
37.4	1866	—	6.00	14.00	25.00	40.00
	1866 OM	—	4.00	8.00	16.00	30.00
	1867	—	20.00	50.00	90.00	150.00
	1867 OM	—	2.25	5.50	9.00	15.00
	1868 OM	—	2.25	5.50	9.00	15.00

Mint mark: 7-pointed star

Y#	Date	Mintage	VG	Fine	VF	XF
37.5	1867 OM	—	2.00	5.00	9.00	15.00
	1868 OM	—	2.00	5.00	9.00	15.00

2-1/2 CENTIMOS

COPPER
Mint mark: 8-pointed star

Y#	Date	Mintage	VG	Fine	VF	XF
38.1	1866	—	2.75	7.00	12.00	20.00
	1866 OM	—	2.75	7.00	12.00	20.00
	1867 OM	—	2.00	5.00	8.00	12.50
	1868 OM	—	2.00	5.00	8.00	12.50

Mint mark: 4-pointed star

Y#	Date	Mintage	VG	Fine	VF	XF
38.2	1866 OM	—	10.00	25.00	45.00	75.00
	1867 OM	—	2.00	4.50	7.50	12.50
	1868 OM	—	2.00	4.50	7.50	12.50

Mint mark: 6-pointed star

Y#	Date	Mintage	VG	Fine	VF	XF
38.3	1865	—	65.00	175.00	275.00	475.00
	1867 OM	—	17.50	40.00	70.00	120.00

Mint mark: 3-pointed star

Y#	Date	Mintage	VG	Fine	VF	XF
38.4	1866 OM	—	25.00	60.00	100.00	175.00
	1867 OM	—	2.50	6.50	11.00	18.00
	1868 OM	—	2.00	4.50	7.50	12.50

Mint mark: 7-pointed star

Y#	Date	Mintage	VG	Fine	VF	XF
38.5	1867 OM	—	2.00	4.50	7.50	12.50
	1868 OM	—	2.75	7.00	12.00	20.00

5 CENTIMOS

COPPER
Mint mark: 8-pointed star

Y#	Date	Mintage	VG	Fine	VF	XF
39.1	1866	—	10.00	25.00	40.00	70.00
	1866 OM	—	7.00	18.00	30.00	50.00
	1867	—	75.00	175.00	300.00	525.00
	1867 OM	—	2.00	4.50	7.50	12.50
	1868 OM	—	2.00	4.50	7.50	12.50

Mint mark: 4-pointed star

Y#	Date	Mintage	VG	Fine	VF	XF
39.2	1866	—	8.50	21.00	35.00	60.00
	1867 OM	—	2.00	4.50	7.50	12.50
	1868 OM	—	3.50	9.00	15.00	25.00

Mint mark: 6-pointed star

Y#	Date	Mintage	VG	Fine	VF	XF
39.3	1865	—	80.00	200.00	325.00	550.00

Mint mark: 3-pointed star

Y#	Date	Mintage	VG	Fine	VF	XF
39.4	1866 OM	—	3.50	9.00	15.00	25.00
	1867 OM	—	3.50	9.00	15.00	25.00
	1868 OM	—	2.50	6.50	11.00	18.00

Mint mark: 7-pointed star

Y#	Date	Mintage	VG	Fine	VF	XF
39.5	1867 OM	—	4.50	11.00	18.00	30.00
	1868 OM	—	2.00	4.50	7.50	12.50

10 CENTIMOS

1.2980 g, .810 SILVER, .0338 oz ASW
Mint mark: 6-pointed star
Similar to 20 Centimos, Y#41.

Y#	Date	Mintage	VG	Fine	VF	XF
40.1	1865	—	5.00	12.50	21.00	30.00
	1866	—	12.00	30.00	50.00	70.00
	1867	—	100.00	250.00	425.00	600.00
	1868 (68)	—	5.00	12.50	21.00	30.00

Mint mark: 7-pointed star

Y#	Date	Mintage	VG	Fine	VF	XF
40.2	1864	—	16.00	40.00	65.00	95.00
	1865	—	5.00	12.50	20.00	30.00
	1866	—	12.50	21.00	35.00	50.00
	1868	—	60.00	150.00	275.00	400.00

20 CENTIMOS

2.5960 g, .810 SILVER, .0676 oz ASW
Mint mark: 6-pointed star

Y#	Date	Mintage	VG	Fine	VF	XF
41.1	1864	—	25.00	60.00	100.00	150.00
	1865	—	7.00	16.00	27.50	40.00
	1866	—	50.00	125.00	200.00	300.00
	1867	—	75.00	175.00	300.00	450.00
	1868 (68)	—	3.50	8.50	14.00	20.00

Mint mark: 7-pointed star

Y#	Date	Mintage	VG	Fine	VF	XF
41.2	1864	—	9.00	22.50	37.50	55.00
	1865	—	10.00	25.00	40.00	60.00
	1866	—	12.00	30.00	50.00	70.00

40 CENTIMOS

5.1920 g, .810 SILVER, .1352 oz ASW
Mint mark: 8-pointed star

Y#	Date	Mintage	VG	Fine	VF	XF
42.1	1865	—	80.00	200.00	350.00	500.00

Mint mark: 6-pointed star

Y#	Date	Mintage	VG	Fine	VF	XF
42.2	1864	—	12.50	21.00	35.00	50.00
	1865	—	5.00	10.00	12.50	25.00
	1866	—	3.50	7.50	12.50	25.00
	1867	—	3.50	7.50	12.50	20.00
	1868 (68)	—	3.50	7.50	12.50	20.00

Mint mark: 7-pointed star

Y#	Date	Mintage	VG	Fine	VF	XF
42.3	1864	—	60.00	150.00	250.00	350.00
	1865	—	7.50	19.00	30.00	45.00
	1866	—	6.00	12.50	22.50	35.00

ESCUDO

12.9800 g, .900 SILVER, .3756 oz ASW
Mint mark: 6-pointed star

Y#	Date	Mintage	VG	Fine	VF	XF
43.1	1864	—	20.00	50.00	85.00	120.00
	1865	—	16.00	40.00	65.00	95.00
	1866	—	16.00	40.00	65.00	95.00
	1867	—	6.50	12.50	22.50	35.00
	1868 (68)	—	6.00	10.00	15.00	25.00

Mint mark: 7-pointed star

Y#	Date	Mintage	VG	Fine	VF	XF
43.2	1864	—	100.00	250.00	425.00	600.00
	1866	—	75.00	175.00	300.00	450.00

2 ESCUDOS

25.9600 g, .900 SILVER, .7512 oz ASW
Mint mark: 6-pointed star
Obv: Head of Isabel II right.
Rev: Crowned arms between pillars.

Y#	Date	Mintage	VG	Fine	VF	XF
44	1865	—	800.00	2000.	3750.	5500.
	1866	—	1000.	2250.	4000.	6000.
	1867	4.234	12.50	25.00	40.00	70.00
	1868(68)	2.225	25.00	60.00	100.00	150.00

1.6774 g, .900 GOLD, .0485 oz AGW

Y#	Date	Mintage	Fine	VF	XF	Unc
45	1865	—	35.00	60.00	100.00	175.00
	1867	—	400.00	800.00	1350.	2000.
	1868 (68)	—	300.00	600.00	1000.	1500.

4 ESCUDOS

3.3548 g, .900 GOLD, .0971 oz AGW
Mint mark: 6-pointed star

Y#	Date	Mintage	Fine	VF	XF	Unc
46.1	1865	—	55.00	70.00	90.00	140.00
	1866	—	55.00	70.00	90.00	140.00
	1867	—	55.00	65.00	80.00	120.00
	1868 (68)	—	75.00	100.00	140.00	225.00

Mint mark: 7-pointed star

Y#	Date	Mintage	Fine	VF	XF	Unc
46.2	1865	—	275.00	550.00	950.00	1300.
	1866	—	250.00	500.00	900.00	1200.

10 ESCUDOS

8.3870 g, .900 GOLD, .2427 oz AGW
Mint mark: 6-pointed star

Y#	Date	Mintage	Fine	VF	XF	Unc
47.1	1866	—	250.00	400.00	650.00	950.00
	1867	—	125.00	200.00	325.00	450.00
	1868 (68)	—	125.00	150.00	175.00	250.00

Mint mark: 7-pointed star

Y#	Date	Mintage	Fine	VF	XF	Unc
47.2	1865	—	1500.	3500.	6000.	8500.

Mint mark: 6-pointed star

Y#	Date	Mintage	Fine	VF	XF	Unc
47.3	1868 (73)	—	125.00	160.00	200.00	300.00

NOTE: This coin issued during the First Republic.

PROVISIONAL COINAGE

25 MILESIMAS DE ESCUDO

BRONZE
Battle of Alcolea Bridge
Mint mark: 3-pointed star

Y#	Date	Mintage	Fine	VF	XF	Unc
A50	1868	.010	60.00	120.00	250.00	500.00

THIRD DECIMAL COINAGE

10 Milesimas = 1 Centimo
100 Centimos = 1 Peseta

CENTIMO

COPPER
Mint mark: 8-pointed star

Y#	Date	Mintage	Fine	VF	XF	Unc
51	1870OM	169.891	.50	1.00	3.00	15.00

BRONZE
Mint mark: 6-pointed star

Y#	Date	Mintage	Fine	VF	XF	Unc
96	1906(6) SL-V	7.500	.35	.75	1.50	4.00
	1906(6) SM-V	Inc. Ab.	100.00	200.00	350.00	700.00

Y#	Date	Mintage	Fine	VF	XF	Unc
98	1911(1) PC-V	1.462	3.50	7.00	20.00	50.00
	1912(2) PC-V	2.109	.75	1.00	2.00	7.50
	1913(3) PC-V	1.429	1.00	1.75	4.00	12.00

2 CENTIMOS

COPPER
Mint mark: 8-pointed star

Y#	Date	Mintage	Fine	VF	XF	Unc
52	1870OM	115.869	.50	1.00	3.50	15.00

BRONZE
Mint mark: 6-pointed star

Y#	Date	Mintage	Fine	VF	XF	Unc
97	1904(04) SM-V	10.000	.35	.75	2.50	10.00
	1905(05) SM-V	5.000	.35	.75	2.50	10.00

Y#	Date	Mintage	Fine	VF	XF	Unc
99	1911(11) PC-V	2.284	.35	.75	2.50	10.00
	1912(12) PC-V	5.216	.35	.75	3.00	12.00

5 CENTIMOS

COPPER
Mint mark: 8-pointed star

Y#	Date	Mintage	Fine	VF	XF	Unc
53	1870OM	287.381	2.00	7.50	15.00	75.00

Charles VII - Pretender Issue

Y#	Date	Mintage	Fine	VF	XF	Unc
66	1875(b)	.050	18.00	30.00	50.00	75.00

BRONZE

Y#	Date	Mintage	Fine	VF	XF	Unc
69	1877OM	34.376	.50	3.50	12.00	60.00
	1878OM	67.954	.50	3.50	12.00	60.00
	1879OM	54.994	.50	3.50	12.00	60.00

10 CENTIMOS

COPPER
Mint mark: 8-pointed star

Y#	Date	Mintage	Fine	VF	XF	Unc
54.1	1869OM	—	—	—	Rare	—

Rev: W/o mint mark.

Y#	Date	Mintage	Fine	VF	XF	Unc
54.2	1870OM	170.088	2.00	7.50	20.00	100.00

Charles VII - Pretender Issue

Y#	Date	Mintage	Fine	VF	XF	Unc
67	1875(b)	.100	15.00	25.00	50.00	75.00

BRONZE

Y#	Date	Mintage	Fine	VF	XF	Unc
70	1877OM	29.567	.35	3.50	17.50	75.00
	1878OM	68.740	.35	3.50	17.50	70.00
	1879OM	56.313	.35	5.00	25.00	95.00

20 CENTIMOS

1.0000 g, .835 SILVER, .0268 oz ASW
Mint mark: 6-pointed star

Y#	Date	Mintage	Fine	VF	XF	Unc
55	1869(69) SN-M	91 pcs.	1100.	1800.	2750.	6000.
	1870(70) SN-M	5,000	150.00	225.00	400.00	1000.

25 CENTIMOS

COPPER-NICKEL

Y#	Date	Mintage	Fine	VF	XF	Unc
100	1925 PC-S	8.001	.35	.75	2.50	12.50
	1925	—	3.00	6.00	20.00	50.00

Y#	Date	Mintage	Fine	VF	XF	Unc
101	1927 PC-S	12.000	.35	1.00	2.00	7.50

50 CENTIMOS

2.5000 g, .835 SILVER, .0671 oz ASW
Mintmark: 6-pointed star

Y#	Date	Mintage	Fine	VF	XF	Unc
56	1869(69) SN-M	.453	10.00	20.00	100.00	325.00
	1870(70) SN-M	.540	20.00	40.00	250.00	900.00

Y#	Date	Mintage	Fine	VF	XF	Unc
A76	1880(80) MS-M	2.787	1.50	3.00	20.00	95.00
	1881(81) MS-M	5.647	1.50	3.00	25.00	115.00
	1885(85) MS-M	—	Reported, not confirmed			
	1885/1(86) MS-M	1.468	6.00	12.00	35.00	175.00
	1885(86) MS-M	Inc. Ab.	1.50	4.00	27.50	125.00

Y#	Date	Mintage	Fine	VF	XF	Unc
79	1889(89) MP-M	.537	5.00	10.00	35.00	140.00
	1892/89(92) PG-M	3.954	4.00	8.00	25.00	120.00
	1892(92) PG-M	Inc. Ab.	1.00	2.50	10.00	40.00
	1892(22) PG-M	—	8.00	17.50	35.00	130.00
	1892/82(82) PG-M	—	10.00	20.00	50.00	120.00
	1892(82) PG-M	—	10.00	20.00	50.00	120.00
	1892(G2) PG-M	—	15.00	27.50	65.00	150.00
	1892(62) PG-M	—	17.50	35.00	100.00	200.00
	1892(62) PG-M/MP-M	—	—	—	—	—

NOTE: Varieties exist.

Y#	Date	Mintage	Fine	VF	XF	Unc
83	1894(94) PG-V	1.109	3.00	9.00	35.00	110.00

Y#	Date	Mintage	Fine	VF	XF	Unc
87	1896(96) PG-V	.297	15.00	32.50	100.00	250.00
	1900(00) SM-V	2.128	1.00	3.00	10.00	35.00

Y#	Date	Mintage	Fine	VF	XF	Unc
92	1904(04) SM-V	4.851	.75	2.25	5.00	20.00
	1904(10) PC-V	1.303	.75	2.25	5.00	25.00

Y#	Date	Mintage	Fine	VF	XF	Unc
93	1910(10) PC-V	4.526	.75	2.25	5.00	25.00

Y#	Date	Mintage	Fine	VF	XF	Unc
102	1926 PC-S	4.000	.75	2.25	5.00	15.00

PESETA

5.0000 g, .835 SILVER, .1342 oz ASW
Mint mark: 6-pointed star
Obv. leg: GOBIERNO PROVISIONAL

Y#	Date	Mintage	Fine	VF	XF	Unc
A55	1869(69) SN-M	7.000	3.50	15.00	90.00	300.00

Obv. leg: ESPANA

Y#	Date	Mintage	Fine	VF	XF	Unc
58	1869(69) SN-M	.367	30.00	220.00	850.00	2250.
	1870(70) SN-M	3.865	7.50	30.00	160.00	450.00
	1870(73) DE-M	5.165	4.00	25.00	145.00	350.00

Y#	Date	Mintage	Fine	VF	XF	Unc
B75	1876(76) DE-M	4.427	3.50	30.00	160.00	450.00

Y#	Date	Mintage	Fine	VF	XF	Unc
B76	1881(81) MS-M	.799	18.00	100.00	525.00	1250.
	1882/81(82) MS-M	—	10.00	75.00	325.00	750.00
	1882(82) MS-M	3.506	3.50	15.00	185.00	500.00
	1883(83) MS-M	8.440	3.00	15.00	120.00	350.00
	1884/3(84) MS-M	5,839	250.00	525.00	1650.	4500.
	1885(85) MS-M	3.336	3.50	15.00	185.00	500.00
	1885(86) MS-M	3.954	3.50	12.50	145.00	450.00

Y#	Date	Mintage	Fine	VF	XF	Unc
80	1889(89) MP-M	.760	35.00	85.00	265.00	1250.
	1891(91) PG-M	4.948	3.00	15.00	60.00	250.00

Y#	Date	Mintage	Fine	VF	XF	Unc
84	1893(93) PG-L	1.958	5.50	18.00	145.00	450.00
	1894(94) PG-V	1.044	18.00	65.00	200.00	800.00

Y#	Date	Mintage	Fine	VF	XF	Unc
88	1896(96) PG-V	6.412	2.50	7.00	20.00	90.00
	1899(99) SG-V	7.472	2.50	7.00	20.00	80.00
	1900(00) SM-V	18.650	2.00	5.00	15.00	70.00
	1901(01) SM-V	8.449	2.00	6.00	20.00	80.00
	1902(02) SM-V	2.599	7.50	15.00	40.00	150.00

Y#	Date	Mintage	Fine	VF	XF	Unc
94	1903(03) SM-V	10.602	2.00	5.50	20.00	65.00
	1904(04) SM-V	5.294	2.00	6.00	30.00	90.00
	1905(05) SM-V	.492	30.00	70.00	280.00	800.00

2 PESETAS

10.0000 g, .835 SILVER, .2685 oz ASW
Mint mark: 6-pointed star

Y#	Date	Mintage	Fine	VF	XF	Unc
59	1869(68) SN-M	—	17.50	50.00	165.00	600.00
	1869(69) SN-M	3.270	5.00	10.00	30.00	250.00
	1870(70) SN-M	1.504	6.50	12.50	65.00	300.00
	1870(73) DE-M	11.880	5.00	8.00	27.50	200.00
	1870(74) DE-M	14.893	5.00	8.00	27.50	175.00
	1870(75) DE-M	4.997	7.00	10.00	40.00	275.00

Y#	Date	Mintage	Fine	VF	XF	Unc
C76	1879(79) EM-M	5.578	5.50	9.00	32.50	250.00
	1881(81) MS-M	3.639	5.50	9.00	32.50	250.00
	1882/1(82) MS-M	20.343	4.50	7.50	25.00	200.00
	1882(82) MS-M	Inc. Ab.	4.50	7.50	25.00	175.00
	1883(83) MS-M	3.318	5.00	9.00	28.00	200.00
	1884(84) MS-M	2.839	5.50	10.00	30.00	225.00

Y#	Date	Mintage	Fine	VF	XF	Unc
81	1889(89) MP-M	.559	15.00	30.00	125.00	350.00
	1891(91) PG-M	.093	75.00	150.00	475.00	1200.

Y#	Date	Mintage	Fine	VF	XF	Un
81	1892(92) PG-M	1.379	7.00	15.00	50.00	175.0

Y#	Date	Mintage	Fine	VF	XF	Unc
85	1894(94) PG-V	.279	35.00	125.00	365.00	1000

Y#	Date	Mintage	Fine	VF	XF	Unc
95	1905(05) SM-V	3.589	4.50	8.00	16.00	30.0

5 PESETAS

25.0000 g, .900 SILVER, .7234 oz ASW
Mint mark: 6-pointed star

Y#	Date	Mintage	Fine	VF	XF	Unc
60	1869(69) SN-M	100 pcs.	3500.	5500.	7500.	12,000.
	1870(70) SN-M	5.923	10.00	20.00	45.00	250.00

Y#	Date	Mintage	Fine	VF	XF	Unc
61	1871(71) SD-M	13.641	10.00	20.00	45.00	200.00
	1871(73) SD-M	Inc. Ab.	20.00	40.00	135.00	250.00
	1871(73) DE-M	2.870	100.00	225.00	550.00	1500.
	1871(74) DE-M	5.075	10.00	20.00	80.00	200.00
	1871(75) DE-M	3.000	10.00	20.00	80.00	175.00

Mint mark: 6-pointed star

Y#	Date	Mintage	Fine	VF	XF	Unc
74	1875(75) DE-M	8.641	10.00	20.00	65.00	175.00
	1876(76) DE-M	8.548	10.00	20.00	65.00	225.00

Y#	Date	Mintage	Fine	VF	XF	Unc
75	1877(77) DE-M	6.987	10.00	20.00	65.00	225.00
	1878(78) DE-M	5.000	10.00	20.00	65.00	225.00
	1878(78) EM-M	4.147	10.00	20.00	75.00	250.00
	1879(79) EM-M	1.634	15.00	35.00	140.00	300.00
	1881(81) MS-M	.699	25.00	75.00	280.00	600.00

Y#	Date	Mintage	Fine	VF	XF	Unc
76	1882/1 MS-M	—	30.00	60.00	250.00	800.00
	1882(81) MS-M	—	10.00	22.00	100.00	350.00
	1882(82) MS-M	1.662	10.00	22.00	90.00	225.00
	1883(83) MS-M	5.507	8.00	12.00	45.00	150.00
	1884(84) MS-M	5.848	8.00	12.00	45.00	150.00
	1885(85) MS-M	3.144	8.00	12.00	45.00	150.00
	1885(86) MS-M	1.951	10.00	20.00	160.00	300.00
	1885(87) MS-M	9.000	8.00	12.00	45.00	150.00
	1885(87) MP-M	2.803	15.00	25.00	135.00	275.00

Y#	Date	Mintage	Fine	VF	XF	Unc
82	1888(88) MS-M	—	165.00	350.00	725.00	1600.
	1888(88) MP-M	10.644	8.00	12.00	45.00	150.00
	1889(89) MP-M	4.681	10.00	15.00	60.00	175.00
	1890(90) MP-M	4.275	10.00	15.00	60.00	175.00
	1890(90) PG-M	3.000	10.00	15.00	60.00	175.00
	1891(91) PG-M	11.660	8.00	12.00	45.00	150.00
	1892(92) PG-M	1.294	12.50	20.00	85.00	250.00

Y#	Date	Mintage	Fine	VF	XF	Unc
86	1892(92) PG-M	7.000	10.00	20.00	65.00	250.00
	1893(93) PG-L	2.500	12.00	20.00	75.00	325.00
	1893(93) PG-V	.518	25.00	75.00	275.00	600.00
	1894(94) PG-V	3.871	12.00	20.00	75.00	300.00

Y#	Date	Mintage	Fine	VF	XF	Unc
89	1896(96) PG-V	4.272	10.00	15.00	55.00	125.00
	1897(97) SG-V	6.733	8.00	12.00	45.00	100.00
	1898(98) SG-V	39.977	8.00	15.00	30.00	70.00
	1899(99) SG-V	13.930	30.00	60.00	150.00	250.00

NOTE: All other date and mintmasters or assayers initial combinations on crowns of this era are contemporary counterfeits.

10 PESETAS

3.2258 g, .900 GOLD, .0933 oz AGW
Mint mark: 6-pointed star

Y#	Date	Mintage	Fine	VF	XF	Unc
77	1878(78) EM-M	.091	125.00	200.00	300.00	400.00
	1879(79) EM-M	.033	400.00	800.00	1250.	1750.
	1878(61) DE-M	496 pcs.	—	—	750.00	1000.
	1878(62) DE-M	.018	—	—	75.00	85.00

NOTE: The above 2 coins were restruck by the Spanish Mint from original dies in 1961 and 1962 and are considered official restrike issues.

20 PESETAS

6.4516 g, .900 GOLD, .1867 oz AGW
Mint mark: 6-pointed star

Y#	Date	Mintage	Fine	VF	XF	Unc
A82	1889(89) MP-M	.875	125.00	200.00	300.00	425.00
	1890(90) MP-M	2.344	100.00	115.00	150.00	250.00
	1887(61) PG-V	800 pcs.	—	—	550.00	850.00
	1887(62) PG-V	.011	—	—	100.00	150.00

NOTE: For above two coins dated (61) & (62) see note after 10 Pesetas, Y#77.

Y#	Date	Mintage	Fine	VF	XF	Unc
A86	1892(92) PG-M	2.430	800.00	1400.	2000.	2750.

Y#	Date	Mintage	Fine	VF	XF	Unc
A89	1899(99) SM-V	2.086	125.00	175.00	250.00	350.00
	1896(61) MP-M	900 pcs.	—	—	600.00	750.00
	1896(62) MP-M	.012	—	—	110.00	160.00

NOTE: For above 2 coins dated (61) & (62) see note after 10 Pesetas, Y#77.

Y#	Date	Mintage	Fine	VF	XF	Unc
91	1904(04) SM-V	3,814	1000.	2200.	3250.	4500.

25 PESETAS

8.0645 g, .900 GOLD, .2333 oz AGW
Mint mark: 6-pointed star

Y#	Date	Mintage	Fine	VF	XF	Unc
A62	1871(75) SD-M	25 pcs.	—	—	Rare	—

Y#	Date	Mintage	Fine	VF	XF	Unc
78	1876(76) DE-M	1.281	120.00	135.00	150.00	200.00
	1877(77) DE-M	10.048	120.00	135.00	150.00	200.00
	1878(78) DE-M	5.192	120.00	135.00	150.00	200.00
	1878(78) EM-M	3.000	120.00	135.00	150.00	200.00
	1879(79) EM-M	3.478	120.00	135.00	150.00	200.00
	1880(80) MS-M	6.863	120.00	135.00	150.00	200.00
	1876(61) DE-M	300 pcs.	—	—	1800.	2500.
	1876(62) DE-M	6,000	—	—	300.00	400.00

NOTE: For above 2 coins dated (61) & (62) see note after 10 Pesetas, Y#77.

Y#	Date	Mintage	Fine	VF	XF	Unc
A78	1881(81) MS-M	4.366	120.00	135.00	150.00	200.00
	1882(82) MS-M	.414	200.00	400.00	600.00	800.00

Y#	Date	Mintage	Fine	VF	XF	Unc
A78	1883(83) MS-M	.669	200.00	425.00	650.00	900.00
	1884(84) MS-M	1.033	150.00	250.00	450.00	600.00
	1885(85) MS-M	.503	500.00	900.00	1200.	1600.
	1885(86) MS-M	.491	750.00	1500.	2000.	2500.

100 PESETAS

32.2581 g, .900 GOLD, .9334 oz AGW
Mint mark: 6-pointed star
Provisional Government

Y#	Date	Mintage	Fine	VF	XF	Unc
B62	1870(70) SD-M	12 pcs.	—	—	Rare	—

.900 YELLOW GOLD

Y#	Date	Mintage	Fine	VF	XF	Unc
C62	1871(71) SD-M	25 pcs.	—	—	Rare	—

.900 RED GOLD

Y#	Date	Mintage	Fine	VF	XF	Unc
C62a	1871(71) SD-M	50 pcs.	—	—	Rare	—

Y#	Date	Mintage	Fine	VF	XF	Unc
90	1897(97) SG-V	.150	600.00	900.00	1250.	2000.
	1897(61) SG-V	810 pcs.	—	—	1500.	2000.
	1897(62) SG-V	6,000	—	—	550.00	750.00

NOTE: The above 2 coins were restruck by the Spanish Mint from original dies in 1961 and 1962 and are considered official restrike issues.

REVOLUTIONARY COINAGE

NOTE: Former Y#62, 2 Pesetas, 1873 Cartagena Mint, Cantonal issue similar to Y#64, 10 Reales and Y#63, 5 Pesetas are all considered fantasies struck later for collectors. Refer to *Unusual World Coins*, 3rd edition.

DIEZ (10) REALES

(2-1/2 Pesetas)

13.5000 g, .900 SILVER, .3907 oz ASW
Mint: Cartagena

Y#	Date	Mintage	Fine	VF	XF	Unc
64	1873	—	150.00	350.00	650.00	1200.

CINCO (5) PESETAS

(20 Reales)

25.0000 g, .900 SILVER, .7234 oz ASW
Mint: Cartagena

Y#	Date	Mintage	Fine	VF	XF	Unc
63	1873	—	100.00	175.00	250.00	450.00

NOTE: Several varieties exist.

REPUBLIC

1931-1939

5 CENTIMOS

IRON
Mint mark: 6-pointed star

Y#	Date	Mintage	Fine	VF	XF	Unc
103	1937	10.000	.35	1.00	3.00	25.00

10 CENTIMOS

IRON

Y#	Date	Mintage	Fine	VF	XF	Unc
A103	1938	1,000	350.00	550.00	800.00	2000.

25 CENTIMOS

COPPER-NICKEL

Y#	Date	Mintage	Fine	VF	XF	Unc
107	1934	12.272	.20	.50	1.75	5.50

Mint: Vienna

Y#	Date	Mintage	Fine	VF	XF	Unc
109	1937	42.000	.20	.40	1.25	4.50

NOTE: This coin was issued by way of decree April 5, 1938, by Franco and the Nationalist forces that controlled the majority of Spain by this point in time.

COPPER

Y#	Date	Mintage	Fine	VF	XF	Unc
104	1938	45.500	.75	2.00	4.00	15.00

50 CENTIMOS

COPPER
Mint mark: 6-pointed star

Y#	Date	Mintage	Fine	VF	XF	Unc
105	1937(34)	50.000	.35	1.00	2.00	7.50
	1937(36)	1.000	.35	1.50	3.50	10.00
	1937 w/o dates in stars	Inc. Ab.	5.00	10.00	20.00	50.00
	1937 w/o stars	Inc. Ab.	2.00	3.50	7.50	20.00

NOTE: Several varieties exist.

PESETA

5.0000 g, .835 SILVER, .1342 oz ASW
Mint mark: 6-pointed star

Y#	Date	Mintage	Fine	VF	XF	Unc
108	1933(3-4)	2.000	2.00	3.50	7.50	20.00

NOTE: Several varieties exist.

BRASS

Y#	Date	Mintage	Fine	VF	XF	Unc
106	1937	50.000	.50	1.00	2.00	5.00

NATIONALIST GOVERNMENT

1939-1947

5 CENTIMOS

ALUMINUM
Mint mark: 6-pointed star

Y#	Date	Mintage	Fine	VF	XF	Unc
110	1940	175.000	.10	.15	.75	10.00
	1941	202.107	.10	.15	.25	7.50
	1945	221.500	.10	.15	.25	3.00
	1953	31.573	.15	.25	.90	12.50

10 CENTIMOS

ALUMINUM
Mint mark: 6-pointed star

Y#	Date	Mintage	Fine	VF	XF	Unc
111	1940	225.000	.15	.50	1.00	12.50
	1941	247.981	.10	.20	.75	7.00
	1945	250.000	.10	.40	.90	4.00
	1953	865.850	.10	.40	.90	3.00

NOTE: Varieties exist.

PESETA

ALUMINUM-BRONZE
Mint mark: 6-pointed star

Y#	Date	Mintage	Fine	VF	XF	Unc
112	1944	150.000	.15	.65	2.00	10.00
	1946(48)	—	50.00	75.00	165.00	350.00

KINGDOM

1949-

NOTE: The Madrid Mint has produced coinage in different qualities. Qualities of issue are designated in ( ) after each date as follows:

(M) MATTE - Normal circulation strike or a dull finish.

(U) SPECIAL UNCIRCULATED - Polished or proof-like in appearance without any frosted features.

10 CENTIMOS

ALUMINUM
Mint mark: 6-pointed star

Y#	Date	Mintage	Fine	VF	XF	Unc
121	1959	900.000	—	—	—	.10
	1959	.101	—	—	Proof	1.50

50 CENTIMOS

NOTE: All 50 Centimos listed here are no longer legal tender.

COPPER-NICKEL
Mint mark: 6-pointed star
Rev: Arrows pointing down.

Y#	Date	Mintage	Fine	VF	XF	Unc
115	1949(51)	.990	1.00	2.00	3.00	12.50

Rev: Arrows pointing up.

Y#	Date	Mintage	Fine	VF	XF	Unc
116	1949(51)	8.010	.10	.25	1.00	5.00
	1949(E51)	*5,000	75.00	150.00	325.00	700.00
	1949(52)	18.567	.10	.15	1.00	5.00
	1949(53)	17.500	.10	.15	1.00	5.00
	1949(54)	37.000	.10	.15	.75	4.00
	1949(56)	38.000	.10	.15	.75	4.00
	1949(62)	31.000	—	.15	.50	1.00
	1963(63)	4.000	.10	.15	1.50	6.00
	1963(64)	20.000	—	.10	.15	.50
	1963(65)	14.000	—	.10	.15	.50

***NOTE:** Issued to commemorate a numismatic exposition December 2, 1951. An E replaces the 19 on the lower star.

ALUMINUM

Y#	Date	Mintage	Fine	VF	XF	Unc
124	1966(67)	80.000	—	—	.10	.50
	1966(68)	100.000	—	—	.10	.50
	1966(69)	50.000	—	—	.10	.50
	1966(70)	.023	—	—	6.00	14.00
	1966(71)	99.000	—	—	.10	.50
	1966(72)	2.283	—	—	.10	1.00
	1966(72)	.023	—	—	Proof	4.00
	1966(73)	10.000	—	—	.10	.50
	1966(73)	.028	—	—	Proof	5.00
	1966(74)	—	—	—	.10	.50
	1966(74)	.025	—	—	Proof	6.50
	1966(75)	.075	—	—	Proof	2.00

Y#	Date	Mintage	Fine	VF	XF	Unc
126	1975(76)	4.060	—	—	.10	.50
	1975(76)	—	—	—	Proof	2.00

World Cup Soccer Games

Y#	Date	Mintage	Fine	VF	XF	Unc
132	1980(80)	15.000	—	—	.10	.50

PESETA

ALUMINUM-BRONZE
Mint mark: 6-pointed star

Y#	Date	Mintage	Fine	VF	XF	Unc
113	1947(48)	15.000	.15	.50	2.00	12.50
	1947(49)	27.600	.15	.40	1.00	15.00
	1947(50)	4.000	.25	1.00	4.00	25.00
	1947(51)	9.185	.15	.75	3.00	10.00
	1947(E51)	*5,000	75.00	150.00	325.00	700.00
	1947(52)	19.195	.10	.20	.50	4.00
	1947(53)	34.000	.10	.20	.50	4.00
	1947(54)	50.000	.10	.20	.50	4.00
	1947(56)	—	1.50	4.50	12.50	100.00
	1953(54)	40.272	.10	.20	.50	4.00
	1953(56)	118.000	—	.10	.25	2.00
	1953(60)	45.160	—	.10	.20	4.00
	1953(61)	25.830	—	.10	.25	3.00
	1953(62)	66.252	—	.10	.20	1.50
	1953(63)	37.000	—	.10	.25	3.00
	1963(63)	36.000	—	.10	.25	1.50
	1963(64)	80.000	—	.10	.20	.75
	1963(65)	70.000	—	.10	.35	.75
	1963(66)	63.000	—	.10	.20	.75
	1963(67)	11.300	—	.10	.25	6.00

***NOTE:** Issued to commemorate a numismatic exposition December 2, 1951. An E replaces 19 on the lower star.

Y#	Date	Mintage	Fine	VF	XF	Unc
125	1966(67)	59.000	—	.10	.20	.50
	1966(68)	120.000	—	.10	.20	.50
	1966(69)	120.000	—	.10	.20	.50
	1966(70)	75.000	—	.10	.20	.50
	1966(71)	115.270	—	.10	.20	.50
	1966(72)	106.000	—	.10	.20	.50
	1966(72)	.023	—	—	Proof	6.00
	1966(73)	152.000	—	.10	.20	.50
	1966(73)	.028	—	—	Proof	7.00
	1966(74)	181.000	—	—	.10	.20
	1966(74)	.025	—	—	Proof	8.50
	1966(75)	227.580	—	—	.10	.20
	1966(75)	.025	—	—	Proof	2.50

Y#	Date	Mintage	Fine	VF	XF	Unc
127	1975(76)	170.380	—	—	.10	.25
	1975(76)	—	—	—	Proof	2.00
	1975(77)	247.370	—	—	.10	.25
	1975(77)	Inc. Ab.	—	—	Proof	2.00
	1975(78)	*604.000	—	—	.10	.25
	1975(79)	507.000	—	—	.10	.25
	1975(79)	—	—	—	Proof	1.00
	1975(80)	545.000	—	—	.10	.25

***NOTE:** Two varieties exist of this date.

World Cup Soccer Games

Y#	Date	Mintage	Fine	VF	XF	Unc
133	1980(80)	200.000	—	—	.10	.25
	1980(81)	200.000	—	—	.10	.25
	1980(82)	333.000	—	—	.10	.25

ALUMINUM
Mint mark: Crowned M

Y#	Date	Mintage	Fine	VF	XF	Unc
140.1	1982	Inc. KM133	—	—	.10	.20
	1983	200.000	—	—	.10	.20
	1984	161.000	—	—	.10	.20
	1985	219.000	—	—	.10	.15
	1986	301.000	—	—	—	.15
	1987	300.000	—	—	—	.15
	1988	225.000	—	—	—	.15
	1989	—	—	—	—	.15

Madrid Numismatic Exposition

Y#	Date	Mintage	Fine	VF	XF	Unc
140.2	1987//E-87	.060	—	—	Proof	15.00

Y#	Date	Mintage	Fine	VF	XF	Unc
165	1989	—	—	—	—	.15
	1990	—	—	—	—	.15
	1991	—	—	—	—	.15
	1993	—	—	—	—	.15

2 PESETAS

ALUMINUM
Mint mark: Crowned M

Y#	Date	Mintage	Fine	VF	XF	Unc
141	1982	—	—	—	.10	.15
	1984	47.000	—	—	.10	.15

2-1/2 PESETAS

ALUMINUM-BRONZE
Mint mark: 6-pointed star

Y#	Date	Mintage	Fine	VF	XF	Unc
114	1953(54)	22.729	.10	.25	1.25	2.00
	1953(56)	30.322	.10	.25	1.00	1.50
	1953(68)	1,000	—	—	350.00	600.00
	1953(69)	2,000	—	—	400.00	700.00
	1953(70)	6,800	—	—	65.00	125.00
	1953(71)	10,000	—	—	45.00	100.00

5 PESETAS

NICKEL
Mint mark: 6-pointed star

Y#	Date	Mintage	Fine	VF	XF	Unc
117	1949(49)	.612	.50	1.00	2.00	6.00
	1949(50)	21.000	.25	.50	1.00	3.00
	1949(51)	.145	45.00	120.00	225.00	500.00
	1949(E51)	*6,000	175.00	450.00	725.00	1250.

***NOTE:** Issued to commemorate a numismatic exposition December 2, 1951. An E replaces the 19 on the lower star.

COPPER-NICKEL

Y#	Date	Mintage	Fine	VF	XF	Unc
118	1957(58)	13.000	.10	.20	.50	5.00
	1957(BA)	*.043	15.00	35.00	75.00	125.00
	1957(59)	107.000	—	.10	.20	1.00
	1957(60)	26.000	—	.10	.25	2.00
	1957(61)	78.992	—	.10	.25	4.00
	1957(62)	40.963	—	.10	.25	1.50
	1957(63)	50.000	—	.50	2.00	20.00
	1957(64)	51.000	—	.10	.25	1.50
	1957(65)	25.000	—	.10	.25	1.50
	1957(66)	28.000	—	.10	.25	2.50
	1957(67)	30.000	—	.10	.25	1.50
	1957(68)	60.000	—	.10	.25	1.00
	1957(69)	40.000	—	.10	.25	1.25
	1957(70)	43.000	—	.10	.25	1.25
	1957(71)	77.000	—	.10	.25	1.50
	1957(72)	70.000	—	—	.10	.50
	1957(72)	.023	—	—	Proof	7.00
	1957(73)	78.000	—	—	.10	1.50
	1957(73)	.028	—	—	Proof	9.00
	1957(74)	100.000	—	—	.10	.25
	1957(74)	.025	—	—	Proof	11.00
	1957(75)	139.047	—	—	.10	.25
	1957(75)	.025	—	—	Proof	3.50

***NOTE:** Issued to commemorate the 1958 Barcelona Exposition w/BA replacing the star on left side of rev.

Y#	Date	Mintage	Fine	VF	XF	Unc
128	1975(76)	156.658	—	—	.10	.50
	1975(76)	—	—	—	Proof	2.50
	1975(77)	154.327	—	—	.10	.50
	1975(77)	Inc. Ab.	—	—	Proof	2.00
	1975(78)	414.000	—	—	.10	.25
	1975(79)	436.000	—	—	.10	.25
	1975(79)	—	—	—	Proof	1.75
	1975(80)	298.000	—	—	.10	.25

World Cup Soccer Games

Y#	Date	Mintage	Fine	VF	XF	Unc
134	1980(80)	75.000	—	—	.10	.25
	1980(81)	200.000	—	—	.10	.25
	1980(82)	291.000	—	—	.10	.25

Mule. Obv: Y#128. Rev: Y#134 w/(80) star.

Y#	Date	Mintage	Fine	VF	XF	Unc
138	1975(80)	.030	—	—	40.00	60.00

Mint mark: Crowned M

Y#	Date	Mintage	Fine	VF	XF	Unc
128a	1982	Inc. KM134	—	—	.10	.25
	1983	149.000	—	—	.10	.25
	1984	66.000	—	—	.10	.25
	1989	—	—	—	.10	.25

ALUMINUM-BRONZE

Y#	Date	Mintage	Fine	VF	XF	Unc
166	1989	—	—	—	—	.20
	1990	—	—	—	—	.20
	1991	—	—	—	—	.20
	1992	—	—	—	—	.20

NICKEL-BRASS
Jacobeo

Y#	Date	Mintage	Fine	VF	XF	Unc
233	1993	—	—	—	—	.50

10 PESETAS

COPPER-NICKEL
Mint mark: Crowned M

Y#	Date	Mintage	Fine	VF	XF	Unc
143	1983	—	—	.10	.20	.50
	1984	—	—	.10	.20	.50
	1985	45.750	—	.10	.20	.50

Y#	Date	Mintage	Fine	VF	XF	Unc
235	1992	—	—	.15	.25	.65

Joan Miro

Y#	Date	Mintage	Fine	VF	XF	Unc
234	1993	—	—	—	—	.80

25 PESETAS

COPPER-NICKEL
Mint mark: 6-pointed star

Y#	Date	Mintage	Fine	VF	XF	Unc
119	1957(58)	8.635	—	.20	.50	8.00
	1957(BA)	*.043	15.00	35.00	70.00	125.00
	1957(59)	42.185	—	.20	.40	2.00
	1957(61)	24.120	—	8.00	20.00	50.00
	1957(64)	42.200	—	.20	.30	1.25
	1957(65)	20.000	—	.20	.30	1.50
	1957(66)	15.000	—	.20	.30	1.75
	1957(67)	20.000	—	.20	.30	1.50
	1957(68)	30.000	—	.20	.30	1.25
	1957(69)	24.000	—	.20	.30	1.25
	1957(70)	25.000	—	.20	.30	.75
	1957(71)	7.800	—	1.00	5.00	20.00
	1957(72)	4.733	—	.20	.30	1.75
	1957(72)	.023	—	—	Proof	10.00
	1957(73)	.028	—	—	Proof	15.00
	1957(74)	5.000	—	.20	.30	.75
	1957(74)	.025	—	—	Proof	15.00
	1957(75)	10.270	—	.20	.30	.75
	1957(75)	.025	—	—	Proof	5.00

***NOTE:** Issued to commemorate the 1958 Barcelona Exposition w/BA replacing the star on left side of rev.

Y#	Date	Mintage	Fine	VF	XF	Unc
129	1975(76)	35.333	—	.20	.25	1.00
	1975(76)	—	—	—	Proof	2.00
	1975(77)	44.990	—	.20	.25	1.00
	1975(77)	Inc. Ab.	—	—	Proof	2.00
	1975(78)	98.000	—	.20	.25	.50
	1975(79)	172.000	—	.20	.25	.50
	1975(79)	—	—	—	Proof	2.00
	1975(80)	136.000	—	.20	.25	.50

World Cup Soccer Games

Y#	Date	Mintage	Fine	VF	XF	Unc
135	1980(80)	35.000	—	.20	.30	.60
	1980(81)	80.000	—	.20	.30	.60
	1980(82)	246.000	—	.20	.30	.60

Mint mark: Crowned M

Y#	Date	Mintage	Fine	VF	XF	Unc
129a	1982	Inc. Ab.	—	.20	.25	.50
	1983	278.000	—	.20	.25	.50
	1984	242.000	—	.20	.25	.50

NICKEL-BRONZE
1992 Olympics - Discus Thrower

Y#	Date	Mintage	Fine	VF	XF	Unc
170	1990	—	—	.20	.25	.50
	1991	—	—	.20	.25	.50

1992 Olympics - High Jumper

Y#	Date	Mintage	Fine	VF	XF	Unc
173	1990	—	—	—	—	1.50
	1991	—	—	—	—	1.50

Sevilla - Tower

Y#	Date	Mintage	Fine	VF	XF	Unc
230	1992	—	—	—	—	1.50

BRASS
Tower of Seville

Y#	Date	Mintage	Fine	VF	XF	Unc
231	1992	—	—	—	—	1.50

NICKEL-BRONZE
Pais Vasco

Y#	Date	Mintage	Fine	VF	XF	Unc
238	1993	—	—	—	—	1.50

50 PESETAS

COPPER-NICKEL
Mint mark: 6-pointed star

Y#	Date	Mintage	Fine	VF	XF	Unc
120	1957(58)	21.471	—	.50	1.00	3.00
	1957(BA)	*.043	15.00	35.00	70.00	125.00
	1957(59)	28.000	—	.50	1.00	3.00
	1957(60)	24.800	—	.50	1.00	3.00
	1957(67)	.850	.50	1.00	2.00	5.00
	1957(68)	1,000	—	—	425.00	650.00
	1957(69)	1,200	—	—	350.00	500.00
	1957(70)	.019	—	—	55.00	125.00
	1957(71)	4.400	—	.50	.75	3.00
	1957(72)	.023	—	—	Proof	14.00
	1957(73)	.028	—	—	Proof	17.50
	1957(74)	.025	—	—	Proof	21.00
	1957(75)	.025	—	—	Proof	7.00

***NOTE:** Issued to commemorate the 1958 Barcelona Exposition w/BA replacing the star on left side of rev.
NOTE: Edge varieties exist.

Y#	Date	Mintage	Fine	VF	XF	Unc
130	1975(76)	4.000	—	.50	.60	1.50
	1975(76)	—	—	—	Proof	3.00
	1975(78)	17.000	—	.50	.60	1.25
	1975(79)	33.000	—	.50	.60	1.00
	1975(79)	—	—	—	Proof	3.00
	1975(80)	30.000	—	.50	.60	1.00

World Cup Soccer Games

Y#	Date	Mintage	Fine	VF	XF	Unc
136	1980(80)	15.000	—	.50	.60	1.00
	1980(81)	20.000	—	.50	.60	1.00
	1980(82)	57.950	—	.50	.60	1.00

Mint mark: Crowned M

Y#	Date	Mintage	Fine	VF	XF	Unc
130a	1982	Inc. Ab.	—	.50	.60	.80
	1983	93.000	—	.50	.60	.80
	1984	17.500	—	.50	.60	.80
	1985	—	—	.50	.60	.80

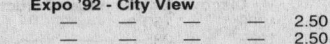

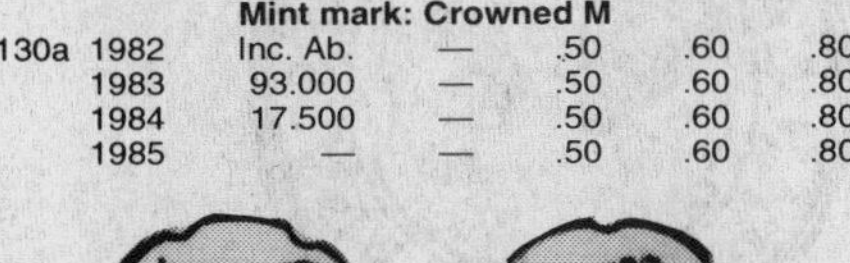

Expo '92 - Juan Carlos I

Y#	Date	Mintage	Fine	VF	XF	Unc
171	1990	—	—	—	—	2.25

Expo '92 - City View

Y#	Date	Mintage	Fine	VF	XF	Unc
174	1990	—	—	—	—	2.50
	1991	—	—	—	—	2.50

1992 Olympics - Logo

Y#	Date	Mintage	Fine	VF	XF	Unc
232	1992	—	—	—	—	2.75

Extremadura

Y#	Date	Mintage	Fine	VF	XF	Unc
239	1993	—	—	—	—	2.75

100 PESETAS

19.0000 g, .800 SILVER, .4887 oz ASW
Mint mark: 6-pointed star

Y#	Date	Mintage	Fine	VF	XF	Unc
122	1966(66)	35.000	—	BV	4.00	6.00
	1966(67)	15.000	—	BV	4.00	8.00
	1966(68)	24.000	—	BV	4.00	8.00
	1966(69) 69 w/straight 9 in star					
		1.000	—	—	60.00	120.00
	1966(69) 69 w/curved 9 in star					
		Inc. Ab.	—	—	50.00	100.00
	1966(70)	.995	BV	6.00	8.00	12.00

NOTE: 1966(69) coins heavily altered. Authentication recommended.

COPPER-NICKEL

Y#	Date	Mintage	Fine	VF	XF	Unc
131	1975(76)	4.000	—	1.00	1.75	3.00
	1975(76)	—	—	—	Proof	5.00

World Cup Soccer Games

Y#	Date	Mintage	Fine	VF	XF	Unc
137	1980(80)	20.000	—	1.00	1.75	3.00

ALUMINUM-BRONZE

Y#	Date	Mintage	Fine	VF	XF	Unc
139	1982	117.600	—	1.00	1.50	2.75
	1982	—	—	—	Proof	10.00
	1983	—	—	1.00	1.50	2.75
	1983 inverted fleur de lis in center of arms					
		—	—	1.50	2.00	3.50
	1984	208.000	—	1.00	1.50	2.75
	1985	118.000	—	1.00	1.50	2.75
	1986	160.000	—	1.00	1.50	2.75
	1987	—	—	1.00	1.50	2.75
	1988	125.000	—	1.00	1.50	2.75
	1989	—	—	1.00	1.50	2.75
	1990	—	—	1.00	1.50	2.75
	1992	—	—	1.50	2.00	3.50

NOTE: Varieties exist.

1.6800 g, .925 SILVER, .0500 oz ASW
Discovery of America - Mayan Pyramid

Y#	Date	Mintage	Fine	VF	XF	Unc
153	1989	*.150	—	—	—	5.00
	1989	*.085	—	—	Proof	8.00

Brother Juniper Serra
Rev: Mission ruins within legend.

Y#	Date	Mintage	Fine	VF	XF	Unc
197	1990(M)	*.090	—	—	—	7.00
	1990(U)	*.050	—	—	—	5.00

Celestino Mutis
Rev: Flower plant within legend.

Y#	Date	Mintage	Fine	VF	XF	Unc
209	1991(M)	*.060	—	—	—	7.00
	1991(U)	*.030	—	—	—	5.00
	1991(P)		—	—	Proof	10.00

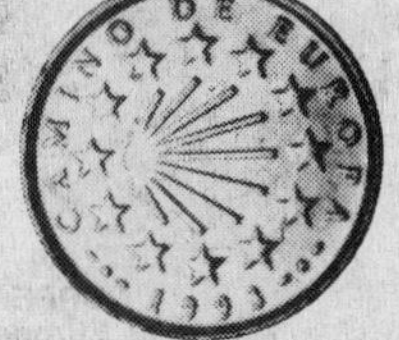

NICKEL-BRASS
European Unity

Y#	Date	Mintage	Fine	VF	XF	Unc
236	1993	—	—	—	—	3.50

200 PESETAS

COPPER-NICKEL

Y#	Date	Mintage	Fine	VF	XF	Unc
146.1	1986	43.000	—	2.00	2.50	3.50
	1987	67.000	—	2.00	2.50	3.50
	1988	37.000	—	2.00	2.50	3.50

Madrid Numismatic Exposition

Y#	Date	Mintage	Fine	VF	XF	Unc
146.2	1987	.060	—	—	Proof	25.00

3.3700 g, .925 SILVER, .1000 oz ASW
Discovery of America - Astrolobe

Y#	Date	Mintage	Fine	VF	XF	Unc
154	1989	*.150	—	—	—	7.00
	1989	*.085	—	—	Proof	12.00

COPPER-NICKEL

Y#	Date	Mintage	Fine	VF	XF	Unc
172	1990	—	—	—	—	4.50
	1991	—	—	—	—	4.50

3.3700 g, .925 SILVER, .1000 oz ASW
Alonso de Frcilla
Rev: Hand writing in a book within legend.

Y#	Date	Mintage	Fine	VF	XF	Unc
198	1990(M)	*.090	—	—	—	10.00
	1990(U)	*.050	—	—	—	8.00

Las Casas
Rev: 3 indian figures within legend.

Y#	Date	Mintage	Fine	VF	XF	Unc
210	1991(M)	*.060	—	—	—	10.00
	1991(U)	*.030	—	—	—	8.00
	1991(P)	—	—	—	Proof	15.00

COPPER-NICKEL
Madrid as European Culture Capital

Y#	Date	Mintage	Fine	VF	XF	Unc
228	1992	—	—	—	—	6.50

12.2500 g, .925 SILVER, .3643 oz ASW

Y#	Date	Mintage	Fine	VF	XF	Unc
228a	1992	*1.000	—	—	—	28.00

COPPER-NICKEL
Juan Luis Vives

Y#	Date	Mintage	Fine	VF	XF	Unc
237	1993	—	—	—	—	7.00

500 PESETAS

COPPER-ALUMINUM-NICKEL
Wedding Anniversary of Juan Carlos and Sofia

Y#	Date	Mintage	Fine	VF	XF	Unc
147	1987	10.000	—	—	5.50	8.00
	1987	81.400	—	—	Proof	—
	1988	Inc. Ab.	—	—	5.50	8.00
	1989	—	—	—	5.50	8.00
	1990	—	—	—	5.50	8.00

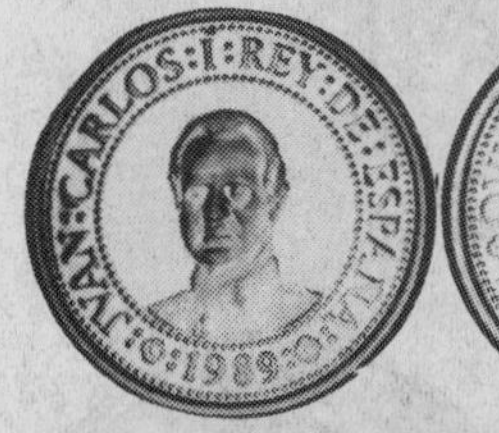

6.7500 g, .925 SILVER, .2008 oz ASW
Discovery of America - Juego De Pelota Game

Y#	Date	Mintage	Fine	VF	XF	Unc
155	1989	*.150	—	—	—	10.00
	1989	*.085	—	—	Proof	15.00

Juan de la Cosa
Rev: Ocean navigation map within legend.

Y#	Date	Mintage	Fine	VF	XF	Unc
199	1990(M)	*.090	—	—	—	12.00
	1990(U)	*.050	—	—	—	10.00

Jorge Juan
Rev: World globe map within legend.

Y#	Date	Mintage	Fine	VF	XF	Unc
211	1991(M)	*.060	—	—	—	12.00
	1991(U)	*.030	—	—	—	10.00
	1991(P)	—	—	—	Proof	17.50

1000 PESETAS

13.5000 g, .925 SILVER, .4015 oz ASW
Discovery of America - Capture of Granada

Y#	Date	Mintage	Fine	VF	XF	Unc
156	1989	*.150	—	—	—	17.00
	1989	*.085	—	—	Proof	22.00

Magallanes and Elcano
Rev: Primitive global world map within legend.

Y#	Date	Mintage	Fine	VF	XF	Unc
200	1990(M)	*.090	—	—	—	20.00
	1990(U)	*.050	—	—	—	18.00

Simon Bolivar and San Martin
Rev: Portrait within legend.

Y#	Date	Mintage	Fine	VF	XF	Unc
212	1991(M)	*.060	—	—	—	20.00
	1991(U)	*.030	—	—	—	18.00
	1991(P)	—	—	—	Proof	25.00

2000 PESETAS

27.0000 g, .925 SILVER, .8031 oz ASW
Discovery of America - Columbus

Y#	Date	Mintage	Fine	VF	XF	Unc
157	1989	*.150	—	—	—	30.00
	1989	*.085	—	—	Proof	35.00

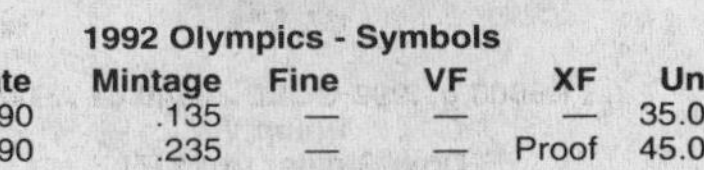

1992 Olympics - Symbols

Y#	Date	Mintage	Fine	VF	XF	Unc
167	1990	.135	—	—	—	35.00
	1990	.235	—	—	Proof	45.00

1992 Olympics - Archer
Obv: Similar to Y#167.

Y#	Date	Mintage	Fine	VF	XF	Unc
168	1990	.135	—	—	—	35.00
	1990	.235	—	—	Proof	45.00

1992 Olympics - Soccer Player

Y#	Date	Mintage	Fine	VF	XF	Unc
175	1990	*.135	—	—	—	35.00
	1990	*.235	—	—	Proof	45.00

1992 Olympics - Human Pyramid

Y#	Date	Mintage	Fine	VF	XF	Unc
176	1990	*.135	—	—	—	35.00
	1990	*.235	—	—	Proof	45.00

1992 Olympics - Greek Runner
Obv: Similar to Y#167.

Y#	Date	Mintage	Fine	VF	XF	Unc
179	1990	*.080	—	—	—	40.00
	1990	*.180	—	—	Proof	50.00

1992 Olympics - Ancient Boat
Obv: Similar to Y#167.

Y#	Date	Mintage	Fine	VF	XF	Unc
180	1990	*.080	—	—	—	40.00
	1990	*.180	—	—	Proof	50.00

1992 Olympics - Basketball Players
Obv: Similar to Y#167.

Y#	Date	Mintage	Fine	VF	XF	Unc
181	1990	*.080	—	—	—	40.00
	1990	*.180	—	—	Proof	50.00

1992 Olympics - Pelota Player
Obv: Similar to Y#167.

Y#	Date	Mintage	Fine	VF	XF	Unc
182	1990	*.080	—	—	—	40.00
	1990	*.180	—	—	Proof	50.00

Hidalgo, Morelos and Juarez
Rev: Aztec pictorial design within legend.

Y#	Date	Mintage	Fine	VF	XF	Unc
201	1990(M)	*.090	—	—	—	35.00
	1990(U)	*.050	—	—	—	30.00

Olympics - Torch and Flag

Y#	Date	Mintage	Fine	VF	XF	Unc
186	1991	*.072	—	—	—	40.00
	1991	*.180	—	—	—	45.00

Olympics - Tennis Player
Obv: Similar to Y#186.

Y#	Date	Mintage	Fine	VF	XF	Unc
187	1991	*.072	—	—	—	40.00
	1991	*.180	—	—	Proof	45.00

Medal rotation.

Olympics - Medieval Rider
Obv: Similar to Y#186.

Y#	Date	Mintage	Fine	VF	XF	Unc
188	1991	*.072	—	—	—	40.00
	1991	*.180	—	—	Proof	45.00

Medal rotation.

Olympics Bowling
Obv: Similar to Y#186.

Y#	Date	Mintage	Fine	VF	XF	Unc
189	1991	*.072	—	—	—	40.00
	1991	*.180	—	—	Proof	45.00

Medal rotation.

Ibero - American Series

Y#	Date	Mintage	Fine	VF	XF	Unc
193	1991	*.050	—	—	Proof	45.00

Federman, Quesada and Benalcazar

Y#	Date	Mintage	Fine	VF	XF	Unc
213	1991(M)	*.060	—	—	—	35.00
	1991(U)	*.030	—	—	—	30.00
	1991(P)	—	—	—	Proof	50.00

Olympics - Tug-of-War

Y#	Date	Mintage	Fine	VF	XF	Unc
221	1992	*.072	—	—	—	40.00
	1992	*.180	—	—	Proof	45.00

Olympics - Wheelchair Basketball

Y#	Date	Mintage	Fine	VF	XF	Unc
222	1992	*.072	—	—	—	40.00
	1992	*.180	—	—	Proof	45.00

Olympics - Sprinters

Y#	Date	Mintage	Fine	VF	XF	Unc
223	1992	*.072	—	—	—	40.00
	1992	*.180	—	—	Proof	45.00

Olympics - Chariot Racing

Y#	Date	Mintage	Fine	VF	XF	Unc
224	1992	*.072	—	—	—	40.00
	1992	*.180	—	—	Proof	45.00

5000 PESETAS

54.0000 g, .925 SILVER, 1.6061 oz ASW
Discovery of America - Santa Maria

Y#	Date	Mintage	Fine	VF	XF	Unc
158	1989	*.150	—	—	—	100.00
	1989	*.150	—	—	Proof	120.00

1.6800 g, .999 GOLD, .0540 oz AGW
Discovery of America - Compass Face

Y#	Date	Mintage	Fine	VF	XF	Unc
159	1989	*.032	—	—	—	100.00
	1989	*.075	—	—	Proof	125.00

54.0000 g, .925 SILVER, 1.6061 oz ASW
Cortes, Montezuma and Marina
Rev: Scene from Aztec mythology within legend.

Y#	Date	Mintage	Fine	VF	XF	Unc
202	1990	*.065	—	—	—	90.00
	1990	*.065	—	—	Proof	100.00

1.6800 g, .999 GOLD, .0540 oz AGW
Philip V
Obv: Similar to Y#159.

Y#	Date	Mintage	Fine	VF	XF	Unc
204	1990	*.015	—	—	—	100.00
	1990	*.032	—	—	Proof	125.00

54.0000 g, .925 SILVER, 1.6061 oz ASW
Pizarro and Atahualpa
Rev: Incan ruins in mountains within legend.

Y#	Date	Mintage	Fine	VF	XF	Unc
214	1991	*.030	—	—	—	90.00
	1991	*.050	—	—	Proof	100.00

1.6800 g, .999 GOLD, .0540 oz AGW
Fernando VI
Obv: Similar to Y#159.

Y#	Date	Mintage	Fine	VF	XF	Unc
216	1991	*6,000	—	—	—	100.00
	1991	*.021	—	—	Proof	125.00

10,000 PESETAS

168.7500 g, .925 SILVER, 5.0191 oz ASW
Illustration reduced. Actual size: 73mm
Regional Automony - Crowned Provincial Arms

Y#	Date	Mintage	Fine	VF	XF	Unc
160	1989	*.060	—	—	—	175.00
	1989	—	—	—	Proof	200.00

3.3700 g, .999 GOLD, .1084 oz AGW
Discovery of America - Armillary Sphere

Y#	Date	Mintage	Fine	VF	XF	Unc
161	1989	*.017	—	—	—	200.00
	1989	*.060	—	—	Proof	225.00

1992 Olympics - Stylized Field Hockey Player

Y#	Date	Mintage	Fine	VF	XF	Unc
177	1990	*.080	—	—	—	225.00
	1990	*.045	—	—	Proof	250.00

1992 Olympics - Stylized Gymnast

Y#	Date	Mintage	Fine	VF	XF	Unc
183	1990	*.020	—	—	—	225.00
	1990	*.050	—	—	Proof	250.00

168.7500 g, .925 SILVER, 5.0191 oz ASW
Illustration reduced. Actual size: 73mm.
Spanish Royal Family
Rev: Similar to Y#215.

Y#	Date	Mintage	Fine	VF	XF	Unc
203	1990	*.040	—	—	—	175.00

3.3700 g, .999 GOLD, .1084 oz AGW
Quauchtemoc
Obv: Similar to 5,000 Pesetas, Y#159.

Y#	Date	Mintage	Fine	VF	XF	Unc
205	1990	*9,000	—	—	—	200.00
	1990	*.026	—	—	Proof	235.00

Olympics - Karate Participant

Y#	Date	Mintage	Fine	VF	XF	Unc
190	1991	*.018	—	—	—	225.00
	1991	*.045	—	—	Proof	250.00

168.7500 g, .925 SILVER, 5.0191 oz ASW
Illustration reduced. Actual size: 73mm.
Discoverers and Liberators
Obv: Similar to Y#203.

Y#	Date	Mintage	Fine	VF	XF	Unc
215	1991	*.035	—	—	—	175.00
	1991	—	—	—	Proof	200.00

3.3700 g, .999 GOLD, .1084 oz AGW
Tupac Amaru II
Obv: Similar to Y#161.

Y#	Date	Mintage	Fine	VF	XF	Unc
217	1991	*6,000	—	—	—	200.00
	1991	*.021	—	—	Proof	235.00

Olympics - Baseball Player

Y#	Date	Mintage	Fine	VF	XF	Unc
225	1992	*.018	—	—	—	200.00
	1992	*.045	—	—	Proof	235.00

20,000 PESETAS

6.7500 g, .999 GOLD, .2170 oz AGW
Discovery of America - Pinzon Brother

Y#	Date	Mintage	Fine	VF	XF	Unc
162	1989	*.015	—	—	—	350.00
	1989	*.058	—	—	Proof	400.00

1992 Olympics - La Sagrada Familia
Cathedral Towers

Y#	Date	Mintage	Fine	VF	XF	Unc
178	1990	*.042	—	—	—	400.00
	1990	*.037	—	—	Proof	450.00

1992 Olympics - Ruins of Empuries

Y#	Date	Mintage	Fine	VF	XF	Unc
184	1990	*.015	—	—	—	400.00
	1990	*.035	—	—	Proof	450.00

Tupac Amaru I
Obv: Similar to Y#162.

Y#	Date	Mintage	Fine	VF	XF	Unc
206	1990	*8,000	—	—	—	350.00
	1990	*.024	—	—	Proof	420.00

Olympics - Montjuic Stadium

Y#	Date	Mintage	Fine	VF	XF	Unc
191	1991	*.013	—	—	—	375.00
	1991	*.032	—	—	Proof	400.00

Huascar
Obv: Portrait of Juan Carlos.

Y#	Date	Mintage	Fine	VF	XF	Unc
218	1991	*6,000	—	—	—	350.00
	1991	*.021	—	—	Proof	420.00

Olympics - Dome Building

Y#	Date	Mintage	Fine	VF	XF	Unc
226	1992	*.013	—	—	—	350.00
	1992	*.032	—	—	Proof	420.00

40,000 PESETAS

13.5000 g, .999 GOLD, .4341 oz AGW
Discovery of America - Sea Monster Attacking Ship

Y#	Date	Mintage	Fine	VF	XF	Unc
163	1989	*.012	—	—	—	675.00
	1989	*.037	—	—	Proof	750.00

Juan Carlos
Obv: Similar to Y#163.

Y#	Date	Mintage	Fine	VF	XF	Unc
207	1990	*6,000	—	—	—	675.00
	1990	*.011	—	—	Proof	775.00

Imperial Double Eagle
Obv: Similar to Y#163.

Y#	Date	Mintage	Fine	VF	XF	Unc
219	1991	*5,000	—	—	—	675.00
	1991	*9,000	—	—	Proof	775.00

80,000 PESETAS

27.0000 g, .999 GOLD, .8682 oz AGW
Discovery of America - Ferdinand and Isabella

164	1989	*8,000	—	—	—	1250.
	1989	*.013	—	—	Proof	1400.

1992 Olympics - Discus Thrower

169	1990	.025	—	—	—	1300.
	1990	.030	—	—	Proof	1450.

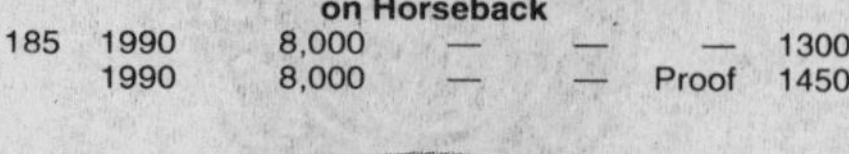

1992 Olympics - Prince Balthasar Carlos on Horseback

185	1990	8,000	—	—	—	1300.
	1990	8,000	—	—	Proof	1450.

Carlos V
Obv: Similar to Y#164.

208	1990	*6,000	—	—	—	1250.
	1990	*7,000	—	—	Proof	1450.

Olympics - Women Tossing Man

Y#	Date	Mintage	Fine	VF	XF	Unc
192	1991	*7,000	—	—	—	1300.
	1991	*7,000	—	—	Proof	1450.

Carlos III
Obv: Similar to Y#164.

220	1991	*5,000	—	—	—	1250.
	1991	*6,000	—	—	Proof	1450.

Olympics - 2 Children Playing

227	1992	*7,000	—	—	—	1325.
	1992	*7,000	—	—	Proof	1500.

MINT SETS (MS)

KM#	Date	Mintage	Identification	Issue Price	Mkt. Val.
MS1	1949(E51)(3)	5,000	Y113,116,117	—	2500.
MS2	1958Ba(3)	—	Y118-120	—	375.00

NOTE: The following sets contain 10 Centimos, Y121 dated 1959. Other denominations have the date in the stars.

KM#	Date	Mintage	Identification	Issue Price	Mkt. Val.
MS3	1966(8)	—	Y113,114,116,118-122	—	—
MS4	1968(8)	1,000	Y114,118-122,124,125	3.60	1250.
MS5	1969(8)	1,200	Y114,118-122,124,125	3.60	1250.
MS6	1970(8)	6,000	Y114,118-122,124,125	3.60	250.00
MS7	1971(8)	10,000	Y114,118-122,124,125 (100 Peseta coin has star date of 70).	3.60	125.00
MS8	1980(80)(6)	—	Y132-137	—	10.00
MS9	1990(M)(5)	—	Y197-201	—	85.00
MS10	1990(U)(5)	—	Y197-201	—	70.00
MS11	1991(M)(5)	—	Y209-213	—	85.00
MS12	1991(U)(5)	—	Y209-213	—	70.00
MS13	Mixed dates(10)	—	Y143(84),Y139(88),Y147 (89),Y171,174(90),Y165,170, 172-173(91),Y166(92)	—	—

PROOF SETS (PS)

KM#	Date	Mintage	Identification	Issue Price	Mkt. Val.
PS1	1972(6)	30,000	Y118-121,124,125	10.00	25.00
PS2	1973(6)	25,000	Y118-121,124,125	10.00	45.00
PS3	1974(6)	23,000	Y118-121,124,125	10.00	25.00
PS4	1975(6)	75,000	Y118-121,124,125	10.00	17.50
PS5	1976(6)	.400	Y126-131	7.50	10.00
PS6	1977(3)	.300	Y127-129	—	5.00
PS7	1979(4)	.300	Y127-130	—	7.50
PS8	1987(6)	—	Y147,Pn4,4a,5-6, Mint Medal	55.00	55.00
PS9	1987(2)	—	Y140.2,146.2	—	40.00
PS10	1989(7)	—	KM153-158,160	—	425.00
PS12	1989(5)	—	Y159,161-164	3177.	2900.
PS13	1991(7)	—	KM209-215	—	525.00

SPAIN-Local

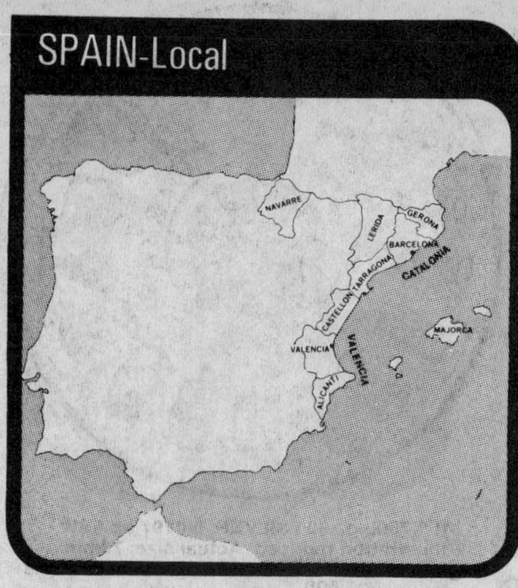

The following cities and provinces of Spain were coin-issuing entities.

BALEARIC ISLANDS

(Yslas Baleares)

Majorca

The Balearic Islands, an archipelago located in the Mediterranean Sea off the east coast of Spain including Majorca, Minorca, Cabrera, Ibiza, Formentera and a number of islets.

Majorca, largest of the Balearic Islands is famous for its 1,000-year-old olive trees.

RULERS

Ferdinand (Fernando) VII, 1808-1833

MONETARY SYSTEM

12 Dineros = 6 Doblers = 1 Sueldo (Sou)
30 Sueldos = 1 Duro

12 DINEROS

COPPER

C#	Date	Mintage	VG	Fine	VF	XF
L51	1811	—	40.00	75.00	125.00	275.00
	1812 DEI GRATIA, small date	—	5.00	8.00	15.00	35.00
	1812 DEI GRATIA, large date	—	5.00	8.00	15.00	35.00
	1812 DEI GRAT	—	12.50	20.00	35.00	85.00

30 SUELDOS

(Sous)

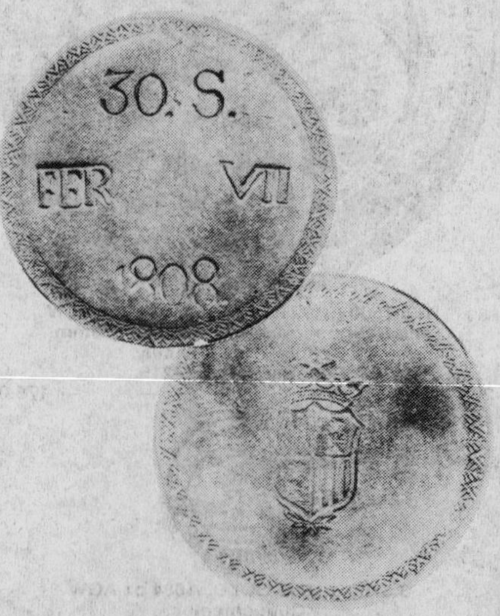

SILVER
Obv. and rev: Ornate rim.

L7.1	1808	—	50.00	90.00	130.00	250.00

Obv: FER.VII, value and date in depression.

C#	Date	Mintage	VG	Fine	VF	XF
L7.2	1808	—	40.00	80.00	120.00	200.00

Rev: Similar to C#L52.2.

C#	Date	Mintage	VG	Fine	VF	XF
L52.1	1808 FER. VII		100.00	175.00	250.00	350.00

Obv: W/o FER VII.

C#	Date	Mintage	VG	Fine	VF	XF
L52.2	1808	—	150.00	300.00	700.00	1250.

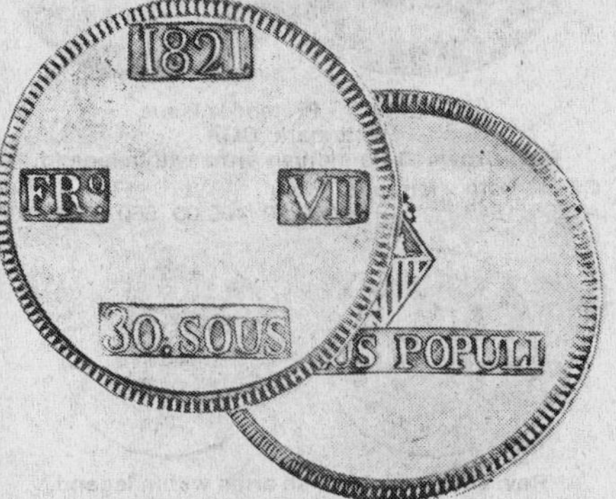

C#	Date	Mintage	VG	Fine	VF	XF
L53.1	1821 FRo. VII		40.00	75.00	125.00	200.00

Obv: (error) FRo.VII inverted.

C#	Date	Mintage	VG	Fine	VF	XF
L53.2	1821 FRo. VII		300.00	600.00	1000.	1500.

5 PESETAS

SILVER

Obv. leg. ends: . . . . .CONST.

C#	Date	Mintage	VG	Fine	VF	XF
L9.1	1823	—	40.00	75.00	125.00	200.00

Obv. leg. ends: . . . . .EYND.

C#	Date	Mintage	VG	Fine	VF	XF
L9.2	1823	—	80.00	120.00	180.00	275.00

BARCELONA

Barcelona was a maritime province located in north-east Spain. The city was the provincial capital of Barcelona. Barçelona is a major port and commercial center.

RULERS

Joseph (Jose) Napoleon, 1808-1814
Ferdinand (Fernando) VII, restored 1814-1833

MINT MARKS

Ba - Barcelona

MONETARY SYSTEM

4 Quartos = 1 Sueldo
6 Sueldos = 1 Peseta

1/2 QUARTO

COPPER

Similar to 4 Quartos, C#L14.

C#	Date	Mintage	Good	VG	Fine	VF
L11	ND(1811)	—	20.00	40.00	60.00	80.00

QUARTO

COPPER

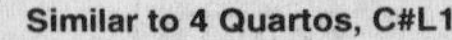

Similar to 4 Quartos, C#L14.

C#	Date	Mintage	Good	VG	Fine	VF
L12	1808	—	17.50	35.00	70.00	100.00
	1809	—	10.00	20.00	35.00	50.00
	1810	—	10.00	20.00	35.00	50.00
	1811	—	20.00	40.00	80.00	120.00
	1812	—	10.00	20.00	35.00	50.00
	1813	—	20.00	40.00	75.00	150.00

2 QUARTOS

COPPER

Similar to 4 Quartos, C#L14.

C#	Date	Mintage	Good	VG	Fine	VF
L13	1808	—	10.00	25.00	50.00	80.00
	1809	—	10.00	20.00	30.00	40.00
	1810	—	20.00	40.00	80.00	125.00
	1813	—	10.00	25.00	50.00	70.00
	1814	—	20.00	60.00	125.00	200.00

3 QUARTOS

COPPER

C#	Date	Mintage	Good	VG	Fine	VF
L21	1823	—	2.00	5.00	15.00	20.00

4 QUARTOS

COPPER

C#	Date	Mintage	Good	VG	Fine	VF
L14	1808	—	10.00	30.00	60.00	90.00
	1809	—	5.00	10.00	20.00	30.00
	1810	—	3.00	10.00	15.00	20.00
	1811	—	4.00	10.00	15.00	20.00
	1812	—	3.00	10.00	15.00	20.00
	Obv. leg: Widely spaced.					
L14b	1813	—	5.00	12.50	25.00	30.00
	1814	—	7.50	15.00	30.00	40.00
	CAST COPPER					
L14a	1808	—	5.00	11.50	15.00	20.00
	1809	—	3.00	9.50	15.00	20.00
	1810	—	2.00	9.50	15.00	20.00
	1811	—	4.00	10.00	15.00	25.00
	1812	—	3.00	9.50	15.00	20.00
L14c	1813	—	5.00	11.50	15.00	20.00
	1814	—	5.00	11.50	15.00	20.00

6 QUARTOS

COPPER

C#	Date	Mintage	Good	VG	Fine	VF
L22	1823	—	10.00	20.00	30.00	40.00

PESETA

SILVER

C#	Date	Mintage	VG	Fine	VF	XF
L15	1809	—	20.00	40.00	55.00	80.00
	1810	—	15.00	25.00	30.00	40.00
	1811	—	15.00	25.00	30.00	40.00
	1812	—	18.00	35.00	45.00	65.00
	1813	—	20.00	40.00	50.00	70.00
	1814	—	35.00	60.00	85.00	120.00

2-1/2 PESETAS

SILVER

C#	Date	Mintage	VG	Fine	VF	XF
L16	1808	—	150.00	275.00	325.00	400.00
	1809	—	125.00	200.00	250.00	300.00
	1810	—	200.00	400.00	500.00	650.00
	1814	—	300.00	575.00	725.00	975.00

5 PESETAS

SILVER

C#	Date	Mintage	VG	Fine	VF	XF
L17	1808	—	125.00	250.00	400.00	600.00
	1809	—	125.00	250.00	400.00	600.00
	1810	—	125.00	250.00	400.00	600.00
	1811	—	125.00	250.00	325.00	450.00
	1812	—	125.00	250.00	400.00	700.00
	1813	—	300.00	600.00	900.00	1250.
	1814	—	1000.	2100.	2800.	3500.

20 PESETAS

GOLD

C#	Date	Mintage	VG	Fine	VF	XF
L18	1812Ba	—	250.00	600.00	850.00	1100.
	1813Ba	—	350.00	750.00	1100.	1450.
	1814Ba	—	1000.	2500.	3500.	5000.

CATALONIA

Catalonia, a triangular territory forming the northeast corner of the Iberian Peninsula, was formerly a province of Spain and also formerly a principality of Aragon. In 1833 the region was divided into four provinces, Barcelona, Gerona, Lerida and Tarragona.

RULERS

Ferdinand (Fernando) VII, 1808-1833
Isabel II, 1833-1868

MINT MARKS

C - Catalonia

MONETARY SYSTEM

12 Ardites (Dineros) = 8 Ochavos =
4 Quartos = 1 Sueldo
6 Sueldos = 1 Peseta
5 Pesetas = 1 Duro

OCHAVO

COPPER

C#	Date	Mintage	Good	VG	Fine	VF
L34	1813	—	10.00	20.00	30.00	40.00

QUARTO

COPPER

Obv: Crowned spade Catalonian arms.
Rev: Crowned Spanish arms.

C#	Date	Mintage	Good	VG	Fine	VF
L35	1813	—	10.00	15.00	25.00	35.00

QUARTO/Y MEDIO

(1-1/2 Quartos)

COPPER

Obv: Crowned round Catalonian arms.
Rev: Crowned oval Spanish arms.

C#	Date	Mintage	Good	VG	Fine	VF
L36	1811	—	10.00	20.00	40.00	65.00
	1812	—	25.00	65.00	100.00	125.00
	1813	—	10.00	20.00	27.50	35.00

II QUARTOS

COPPER

Obv: Crowned lozenge Catalonian arms in branches. Rev: Crowned Spanish arms.

C#	Date	Mintage	Good	VG	Fine	VF
L37	1813	—	7.50	15.00	25.00	35.00
	1814	—	10.00	22.50	32.50	40.00

III QUARTOS

COPPER

C#	Date	Mintage	Good	VG	Fine	VF
L38	1810	—	9.00	17.50	22.50	35.00
	1811	—	7.00	12.50	17.50	25.00
	1812	—	5.00	7.50	10.00	20.00
	1813	—	5.00	7.50	10.00	20.00
	1814	—	5.00	7.50	10.00	20.00

C#	Date	Mintage	VG	Fine	VF	XF
L40	1836 CATHAL	—	50.00	125.00	225.00	300.00
	1836 CATALUNA	—	40.00	80.00	120.00	150.00

C#	Date	Mintage	VG	Fine	VF	XF
L40a	1836	—	12.50	25.00	32.50	40.00
	1837	—	5.00	7.50	12.50	25.00
	1838	—	6.00	10.00	15.00	30.00
	1839	—	6.00	10.00	15.00	30.00
	1840	—	12.00	25.00	40.00	65.00
	1841	—	5.00	7.50	12.50	25.00
	1842	—	20.00	40.00	80.00	110.00
	1843	—	22.00	45.00	65.00	80.00
	1844	—	10.00	15.00	20.00	30.00
	1845	—	20.00	40.00	75.00	100.00
	1846	—	10.00	20.00	25.00	35.00

VI QUARTOS

COPPER

C#	Date	Mintage	Good	VG	Fine	VF
L39	1810	—	10.00	20.00	30.00	50.00
	1811/0	—	12.00	25.00	40.00	60.00
	1811	—	10.00	20.00	30.00	50.00
	1812	—	7.50	12.50	20.00	35.00
	1813	—	7.50	12.50	20.00	35.00
	1814	—	12.00	25.00	40.00	60.00

C#	Date	Mintage	VG	Fine	VF	XF
L40.3	1836	—	110.00	250.00	400.00	500.00

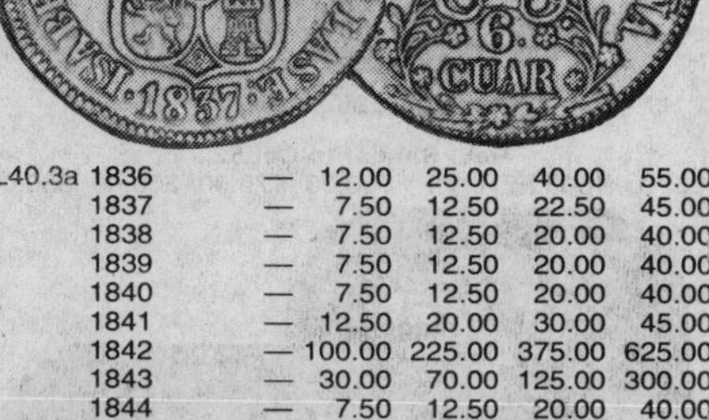

C#	Date	Mintage	VG	Fine	VF	XF
L40.3a	1836	—	12.00	25.00	40.00	55.00
	1837	—	7.50	12.50	22.50	45.00
	1838	—	7.50	12.50	20.00	40.00
	1839	—	7.50	12.50	20.00	40.00
	1840	—	7.50	12.50	20.00	40.00
	1841	—	12.50	20.00	30.00	45.00
	1842	—	100.00	225.00	375.00	625.00
	1843	—	30.00	70.00	125.00	300.00
	1844	—	7.50	12.50	20.00	40.00
	1845	—	7.50	12.50	20.00	40.00
	1846	—	7.50	12.50	20.00	40.00
	1847	—	45.00	125.00	200.00	250.00
	1848	—	45.00	125.00	200.00	250.00

Charles V - Pretender Issue
Mint mark: BGA
Rev: Crowned Catalonian arms within legend.

C#	Date	Mintage	Good	VG	Fine	VF
A155	1840	—	250.00	400.00	550.00	600.00

Rev: Crowned Spanish arms within legend.

C#	Date	Mintage	Good	VG	Fine	VF
155	1840	—	300.00	500.00	575.00	650.00

PESETA

SILVER
Mint mark: B

C#	Date	Mintage	VG	Fine	VF	XF
L40.7	1836 PS	—	20.00	50.00	80.00	125.00
	1837 PS	—	25.00	65.00	110.00	140.00

GERONA

Gerona, a maritime frontier province in the extreme north-east corner of Spain and the provincial capital city of Gerona. The city of Gerona is the ancient city of Gerunda where St. Paul and St. James known as Santiago, patron saint of Spain and one of the twelve apostles, first rested when they came to Spain.

RULERS

Ferdinand (Fernando) VII, 1808-1833

MONETARY SYSTEM

12 Ardites (Dineros) = 8 Ochavos =
4 Quartos = 1 Sueldo
6 Sueldos = 1 Peseta
5 Pesetas = 1 Duro

DURO

SILVER

C#	Date	Mintage	VG	Fine	VF	XF
L41	1808	—	50.00	80.00	125.00	200.00

COPPER

C#	Date	Mintage	VG	Fine	VF	XF
L41a	1809	—	60.00	90.00	150.00	200.00

NOTE: Rim reading on the Duro is hand cut making each example unique.

5 PESETAS

SILVER

Rev. leg: GERONA. . . . . .

C#	Date	Mintage	VG	Fine	VF	XF
L42	1809	—	1250.	2300.	3800.	4500.

LERIDA

Lerida, a frontier province of northern Spain and the provincial capital city of Lerida. The province is bounded on the north by France and on the east by Barcelona and Gerona.

RULERS

Ferdinand VII, 1808-1833

MONETARY SYSTEM

12 Ardites (Dineros) = 8 Ochavos =
4 Quartos = 1 Sueldo
6 Sueldos = 1 Peseta
5 Pesetas = 1 Duro

5 PESETAS

SILVER

C#	Date	Mintage	VG	Fine	VF	XF
L45	1809	—	1800.	2500.	4000.	5000.

Rev. leg: LERIDA. . . . .

C#	Date	Mintage	VG	Fine	VF	XF
L46	1809	—	1500.	2300.	3750.	4500.

NAVARRE

Navarre, a frontier province of northern Spain and a former kingdom which included part of the south-west corner of France. The Kingdom of Navarre was ultimately divided and absorbed by France and Spain.

RULERS

Carlos VII (IV in Spain),
1788-1808
Ferdinand (Fernando) III
(VII in Spain), 1808-1833

1/2 MARAVEDI

COPPER

Similar to 6 Maravedi, C#L92.

C#	Date	Mintage	VG	Fine	VF	XF
L81	1818PP	—	15.00	27.50	35.00	40.00
	1819PP	—	20.00	40.00	50.00	60.00

C#	Date	Mintage	VG	Fine	VF	XF
L82	1831PP	—	12.00	25.00	35.00	45.00
	1381PP (error)		90.00	165.00	200.00	250.00
	1832PP	—	90.00	165.00	200.00	250.00

MARAVEDI

COPPER

C#	Date	Mintage	VG	Fine	VF	XF
L83	1818PP	—	10.00	20.00	30.00	40.00
	1824Ja	—	10.00	20.00	27.50	35.00
	1825PP	—	8.00	12.50	22.50	30.00
	1826PP	—	8.00	12.50	22.50	30.00

Obv: Laureate bust. Rev: Arms.

C#	Date	Mintage	VG	Fine	VF	XF
L83a	1818PP	—	9.00	17.50	22.50	30.00
	1819PP	—	9.00	17.50	22.50	30.00
	1820PP	—	10.00	20.00	27.50	35.00

Similar to 1/2 Maravedi, C#L82.

C#	Date	Mintage	VG	Fine	VF	XF
L84	1829PP	—	7.50	15.00	20.00	25.00
	1830/20PP	—	7.50	15.00	20.00	25.00
	1830PP	—	7.50	15.00	20.00	25.00
	1831PP	—	9.00	17.50	22.50	30.00
	1832PP	—	9.00	17.50	22.50	30.00
	1833PP	—	15.00	30.00	45.00	50.00

3 MARAVEDIS

COPPER

Similar to 6 Maravedi, C#L92a.

C#	Date	Mintage	VG	Fine	VF	XF
L89	1818PP	—	25.00	45.00	65.00	85.00
	1819PP	—	20.00	35.00	55.00	70.00
	1820PP	—	20.00	35.00	55.00	70.00
	1825PP	—	20.00	35.00	55.00	70.00
	1826PP	—	20.00	35.00	55.00	70.00

Similar to 6 Maravedi, C#L92a, but leg: FERDIN. III. . . . .

C#	Date	Mintage	VG	Fine	VF	XF
L89a	1818PP	—	15.00	30.00	45.00	65.00
	1819PP	—	15.00	30.00	45.00	65.00

Similar to 1/2 Maravedi, C#L82.

C#	Date	Mintage	VG	Fine	VF	XF
L90	1829PP	—	12.50	25.00	40.00	60.00
	1830PP	—	10.00	15.00	20.00	40.00
	1831PP	—	15.00	30.00	45.00	65.00
	1832PP	—	12.50	25.00	40.00	60.00
	1833PP	—	12.50	25.00	40.00	60.00

6 MARAVEDIS

COPPER

Obv: Young bust, bare head. Rev: Arms.

C#	Date	Mintage	VG	Fine	VF	XF
L92	1818PP	—	25.00	50.00	80.00	100.00

Obv: Laureate bust.

C#	Date	Mintage	VG	Fine	VF	XF
L92a	1818PP	—	35.00	70.00	120.00	150.00
	1819PP	—	25.00	50.00	80.00	100.00
	1820PP	—	30.00	55.00	90.00	125.00

TARRAGONA

Tarragona, a maritime province in north east Spain, south of Barcelona and Lerida, and the provincial capital city of Tarragona. The province produces excellent wines; the city is a flourishing seaport.

RULERS

Ferdinand (Fernando) III,
(VII in Spain) 1808-1833

5 PESETAS

SILVER

Obv. leg: FER/ VII/ (raised periods).
Rev: Curved base crown/shield.

C#	Date	Mintage	VG	Fine	VF	XF
L96.1	1809. small 0	—	60.00	90.00	140.00	200.00

Obv. leg: FER/ VII/ (raised periods).
Rev: Curved base crown/shield.

C#	Date	Mintage	VG	Fine	VF	XF
L96.2	1809. large 0	—	60.00	90.00	140.00	200.00

Obv. leg: FER VII.
Rev: Straight base crown/shield.

C#	Date	Mintage	VG	Fine	VF	XF
L96.3	1809. small 0	—	60.00	90.00	140.00	200.00

Obv. leg: FER VII. Rev: Similar to C#L96.1.

C#	Date	Mintage	VG	Fine	VF	XF
L96.4	1809. small 0	—	60.00	90.00	140.00	200.00

Obv. leg: FER VII.
Rev: Similar to C#L96.3.

C#	Date	Mintage	VG	Fine	VF	XF
L96.5	1809. small 0, lazy 9	—	60.00	90.00	140.00	200.00

Obv. leg: FER//F.o.

C#	Date	Mintage	VG	Fine	VF	XF
L96.6	1809.	—	—	—	Rare	—

TORTOSA

Tortosa, a fortified city of Spain, is in Tarragona province.

RULERS

Fernando VII, 1808-1833

DURO

(5 Pesetas)

SILVER, uniface
4 c/m: Tower, 1, DURO & TOR. raised R • SA.

C#	Date	Mintage	VG	Fine	VF	XF
L100	ND (1808-9)	—	350.00	750.00	1250.	2000.

VALENCIA

Valencia, a maritime province of eastern Spain and the capital city of Valencia. Once a former kingdom, Valencia included the present provinces of Castellon de la Plana and Alicante.

RULERS

Ferdinand (Fernando) VII, 1808-1833

2 REALES DE VELLON

(1 Real)

SILVER

C#	Date	Mintage	VG	Fine	VF	XF
L103	1809LL	—	17.50	32.50	55.00	90.00

4 REALES DE VELLON

(2 Reales)

SILVER

C#	Date	Mintage	VG	Fine	VF	XF
L106	1823LL	—	12.50	22.50	37.50	65.00

NOTE: The 4 Reales de Vellon circulated as a regular issue 2 Reales while the 2 Reales de Vellon circulated as a regular 1 Real.

SPAIN-Civil War

Gijon, Santandier, Bilbao, ASTURIAS, Vitoria, Leon, REPUBLICAN ZONE, CASTILE-LEON, FRANCE, CATALONIA, Tarragona, PORTUGAL, Madrid, Barcelona, BALEARIC ISLANDS, MINORCA, MAJORCA, Alicante, NATIONALIST ZONE, Seville, MOROCCO, ALGERIA

With the loss of her American empire, Spain drifted into chaotic times. Stung by their defeats in Cuba, the army blamed the Socialists for what they considered to be mismanagement at home. Additional political complications were derived from the successful Russian Revolution which gave impetus to an already thriving Socialist party and trade union movement. Finally, King Alphonso XIII committed the fatal mistake of encouraging a reckless general to start a campaign in Morocco that ended in the virtual extermination of the Spanish army. Fearing that the inevitable parliamentary investigation would incriminate the crown, he offered no objection when General Primo de Rivera seized the government and established himself as dictator in 1926. Rivera fell from power in 1930, and the government was taken over by an alliance of Liberals and Socialists who tried to separate the Church and State, take the army out of politics, and introduce effective labor and agrarian reforms despite numerous strikes and street riots. The election of 1936 brought to power a coalition of Socialists, Liberals and Communists, to the dismay of the traditionalists and landowners.

A number of right-wing generals, including the young and clever Francisco Franco, began preparations for a military coup which erupted into a civil war in July of 1936. The destructive conflict, in which more than a million died, lasted three years. During the struggle, areas under control of both the Nationalist (rebels) and the Republican (Loyalists) issued coinages that circulated to whatever extent the political and military situation permitted. The war ended defeat for the Loyalists when Madrid fell to Franco on March 28, 1939.

During the Spanish Civil War (1936-1939) a great many coins and tokens were minted in the provincial districts. The coins are grouped here under the heading of the district in which they most commonly circulated.

REPUBLICAN ZONE

ARENYS DE MAR

A resort village on the Mediterranean shore that is 20 miles north of Barcelona. One of the villages in the area of operations of General Mola at the beginning of the war.

50 CENTIMOS

ALUMINUM, uniface

KM#	Date	Mintage	Fine	VF	XF
1	ND(1937)	6,000	50.00	70.00	95.00

PESETA

ALUMINUM, uniface

KM#	Date	Mintage	Fine	VF	XF
2	ND(1937)	3,500	70.00	95.00	125.00

ASTURIAS AND LEON

Asturias is a province on the northern coast of Spain with the province of Leon just to its south. The councils of these adjoining provinces decided to mint coins in 1937 for use in the area due to lack of other circulating coins in the north.

50 CENTIMOS

COPPER-NICKEL
Mint: Gijon

KM#	Date	Mintage	Fine	VF	XF	Unc
1	1937	.200	15.00	20.00	25.00	35.00

PESETA

COPPER
Mint: Guernica

KM#	Date	Mintage	Fine	VF	XF	Unc
2	1937	.100	10.00	12.50	15.00	30.00

2 PESETAS

COPPER-NICKEL
Mint: Gijon

KM#	Date	Mintage	Fine	VF	XF	Unc
3	1937	.400	5.00	7.50	10.00	20.00

NOTE: Varieties exist with differences in the leaves.

EUZKADI

Viscayan Republic

Euzkadi or the Viscayan Republic was located in north central Spain adjoining the southeast corner of France. It was made up of 4 provinces - Bilbao, Guipuzcoa, Navarre, and Victoria. These Basque provinces declared autonomy on October 8, 1936. The 2 nickel coins were made in Brussels, Belgium and saw some circulation before the end of the Republic on June 18, 1937.

PESETA

NICKEL
Mint: Brussels

KM#	Date	Mintage	Fine	VF	XF	Unc
1	1937	7.000	2.50	4.50	6.50	10.00

2 PESETAS

NICKEL
Mint: Brussels

KM#	Date	Mintage	Fine	VF	XF	Unc
2	1937	6.000	3.00	5.00	7.00	12.50

IBI

A village north and west of Alicante on the east coast of Spain. The isolation of the area in comparison with other contending areas made the maintaining of this area during the war very difficult.

25 CENTIMOS

COPPER

KM#	Date	Mintage	Fine	VF	XF	Unc
1.1	1937	.030	10.00	20.00	25.00	40.00

NOTE: Varieties exist.

Obv: Map in field.

KM#	Date	Mintage	Fine	VF	XF	Unc
1.2	1937	7,000	40.00	50.00	70.00	115.00

PESETA

NICKEL-BRASS

KM#	Date	Mintage	Fine	VF	XF	Unc
2	1937	5,000	25.00	35.00	50.00	80.00

L'AMETLLA DEL VALLES

A town in the province of Tarragona in northeastern Spain. The town adopted the name L'Ametlla del Valles in 1933. Before that the name was La Ametlla.

25 CENTIMOS

BRASS

KM#	Date	Mintage	Fine	VF	XF	Unc
1	ND(1937)	.050	10.00	20.00	30.00	45.00

50 CENTIMOS

ALUMINUM

KM#	Date	Mintage	Fine	VF	XF	Unc
2.1	ND(1937)	3,000	30.00	40.00	70.00	100.00

Obv: W/o legend.

KM#	Date	Mintage	Fine	VF	XF	Unc
2.2	ND(1937)	.030	10.00	15.00	30.00	50.00

PESETA

ALUMINUM

KM#	Date	Mintage	Fine	VF	XF	Unc
3.1	ND(1937)	3,000	25.00	45.00	60.00	90.00

Obv: W/o legend.

KM#	Date	Mintage	Fine	VF	XF	Unc
3.2	ND(1937)	.030	10.00	15.00	25.00	50.00

MENORCA

Menorca is the smaller of the 2 major islands in the Balearic Islands. A serious coin and supply shortage developed during the war because of the isolation of the island from the mainland.

5 CENTIMOS

BRASS

KM#	Date	Mintage	Fine	VF	XF	Unc
1	1937	.042	—	15.00	20.00	25.00

NOTE: Varieties exist.

10 CENTIMOS

BRASS

KM#	Date	Mintage	Fine	VF	XF	Unc
2	1937	.032	—	15.00	20.00	30.00

NOTE: Varieties exist.

25 CENTIMOS

BRASS

KM#	Date	Mintage	Fine	VF	XF	Unc
3	1937	.038	—	15.00	20.00	30.00

PESETA

BRASS

KM#	Date	Mintage	Fine	VF	XF	Unc
4	1937	.037	—	15.00	20.00	30.00

2-1/2 PESETAS

BRASS

KM#	Date	Mintage	Fine	VF	XF	Unc
5	1937	.024	—	20.00	30.00	35.00

NULLES

Nulles is a mountain village in the province of Tarragona. The mountainous terrain of the area isolated the village from friendly forces and normal commerce. Therefore, in 1937, an undated series of 5 denominations were issued.

5 CENTIMOS

ZINC, octagonal, 23mm
Uniface, similar to 10 Centimos, KM#2.

KM#	Date	Mintage	Fine	VF	XF
1	ND(1937)	5,000	45.00	75.00	110.00

10 CENTIMOS

ZINC, uniface

KM#	Date	Mintage	Fine	VF	XF
2	ND(1937)	3,000	80.00	130.00	165.00

25 CENTIMOS

BRASS, square, 20mm
Uniface, similar to 10 Centimos, KM#2.

KM#	Date	Mintage	Fine	VF	XF
3	ND(1937)	5,000	70.00	95.00	110.00

50 CENTIMOS

BRASS, octagonal, 22mm
Uniface, similar to 10 Centimos, KM#2.

KM#	Date	Mintage	Fine	VF	XF
4	ND(1937)	1,000	70.00	115.00	140.00

PESETA

BRASS, uniface

KM#	Date	Mintage	Fine	VF	XF
5	ND(1937)	5,000	75.00	95.00	110.00

OLOT

A village in the province of Gerona in northeastern Spain near the French border. The village council authorized 2 denominations of coins on September 24, 1937.

10 CENTIMOS

IRON

KM#	Date	Mintage	Good	VG	Fine	VF
1	1937	.025	80.00	90.00	100.00	160.00

15 CENTIMOS

IRON

KM#	Date	Mintage	Good	VG	Fine	VF
2	1937	100 pcs.	1000.	1500.	2000.	Rare

NOTE: The above is considered a pattern.

SANTANDER, PALENCIA & BURGOS

Three provinces in northern Spain with Santander being the northern-most on the Spanish coast. The three provinces met in council and issued two denominations of coins for use in the provinces.

50 CENTIMOS

COPPER-NICKEL, 20mm

KM#	Date	Mintage	Fine	VF	XF	Unc
1.1	1937	.100	—	8.00	12.00	25.00
	Rev: Letters PR or PJR below CTS.					
1.2	1937	.010	12.00	20.00	30.00	45.00

PESETA

COPPER-NICKEL

KM#	Date	Mintage	Fine	VF	XF	Unc
2	1937	.300	—	7.50	10.00	25.00

SEGARRA DE GAIA

A village in the southern part of the province of Tarragona. A single denomination of coin was authorized in 1937.

PESETA

COPPER-NICKEL, uniface.
Value over bars of Aragon in circle.

KM#	Date	Mintage	Fine	VF	XF	Unc
1	ND(1937)	5,000	15.00	25.00	40.00	65.00
	COPPER, 23mm Uniface					
1a	ND(1937)	.020	15.00	25.00	40.00	50.00

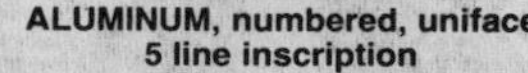

ALUMINUM, numbered, uniface
5 line inscription

KM#	Date	Mintage	Fine	VF	XF	Unc
2	ND(1937)	.030	Reported, not confirmed			
	BRASS					
2a	ND(1937)	—	30.00	40.00	70.00	85.00

NATIONALIST ZONE

CAZALLA DE SIERRA

A town 43 miles north of Seville that issued a 10 Centimos in brass in 1936 (undated).

10 CENTIMOS

BRASS

KM#	Date	Mintage	Fine	VF	XF	Unc
1	ND(1936)	.010	22.00	30.00	40.00	—

EL ARAHAL

A town 30 miles east of Seville. Issued 3 undated types of coins in 1936.

50 CENTIMOS

BRASS, uniface

KM#	Date	Mintage	Fine	VF	XF	Unc
1	ND(1936)	3,000	25.00	40.00	50.00	70.00

PESETA

BRASS, uniface

KM#	Date	Mintage	Fine	VF	XF	Unc
2	ND(1936)	.010	20.00	30.00	45.00	65.00

2 PESETAS

BRASS, uniface

KM#	Date	Mintage	Fine	VF	XF	Unc
3	ND(1936)	.010	20.00	30.00	45.00	65.00

LORA DEL RIO

A town 35 miles northeast of Seville. Issued an undated 25 Centimos in 1936.

25 CENTIMOS

BRASS
Obv: 5 line inscription, wheat ear to right.
Rev: Crowned arms of Lora del Rio on cross.

KM#	Date	Mintage	Fine	VF	XF	Unc
1	ND(1936)	1,500	80.00	110.00	160.00	215.00

MARCHENA

A village 30 miles east of Seville. It was the last issue in Seville province. Two varieties of undated coins were produced in 1936.

25 CENTIMOS

BRASS, Uniface

KM#	Date	Mintage	Fine	VF	XF	Unc
1.1	ND(1936)	5,000	30.00	75.00	100.00	—

Value as 0.25C, uniface.

KM#	Date	Mintage	Fine	VF	XF	Unc
1.2	ND(1936)	500 pcs.	75.00	100.00	200.00	—

NOTE: Countermarked varieties exist.

LA PUEBLA DE CAZALLA

A village only a few miles east of El Arahal and some 40 miles from Sevilla. Undated coins of 2 values were issued in 1936.

10 CENTIMOS

BRASS, 23mm

KM#	Date	Mintage	Fine	VF	XF	Unc
1	ND(1936)	1,500	35.00	65.00	90.00	150.00

NOTE: Counterstamped varieties exist.

25 CENTIMOS

BRASS, 25mm

KM#	Date	Mintage	Fine	VF	XF	Unc
2	ND(1936)	5,000	30.00	60.00	85.00	140.00

NOTE: Counterstamped varieties exist.

Listings For

STRAITS SETTLEMENTS: refer to Malaysia

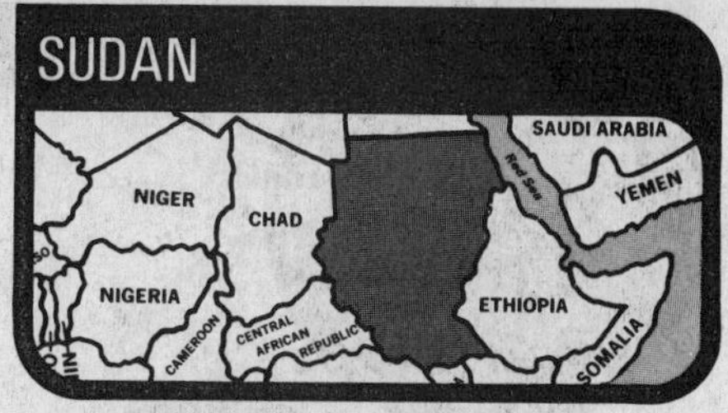

The Democratic Republic of the Sudan, located in northeast Africa on the Red Sea between Egypt and Ethiopia, has an area of 967,500 sq. mi. (2,505,810 sq. km.) and a population of *24.5 million. Capital: Khartoum. Agriculture and livestock raising are the chief occupations. Cotton, gum arabic and peanuts are exported.

The Sudan, site of the powerful Nubian kingdom of Roman times, was a collection of small independent states from the 14th century until 1820-22 when it was conquered and united by Mohammed Ali, Pasha of Egypt. Egyptian forces were driven from the area during the Mahdist revolt, 1881-98, but the Sudan was retaken by Anglo-Egyptian expeditions, 1896-98, and established as an Anglo-Egyptian condominium in 1899. Britain supplied the administrative apparatus and personnel, but the appearance of joint Anglo-Egyptian administration was continued until Jan. 9, 1954, when the first Sudanese self-government parliament was inaugurated. The Sudan achieved independence on Jan. 1, 1956 with the consent of the British and Egyptian government.

TITLES

جمهورية السودان

Jumhuriya(t) as-Sudan

الجمهورية توركية السودان
الرميقراطية

Al-Jumhuriya(t) as-Sudan ad-Dimiqratiya(t)

MINTNAME

Omdurman ام درمان

RULERS

Mohammed Ahmed (the Mahdi), AH1298-1302/1881-1885AD

Abdullah Ibn Mohammed (the Khalifa) AH1302-1316/1885-1898AD

MONETARY SYSTEM

40 Para = 1 Ghirsh = Piastre

MOHAMMED AHMED

(the Mahdi)

Khartoum Mint

Translation of Arabic legends on Mahdi coinage:

بامر المهدى =By order of the Mahdi (in Tughra)

= 5 (Regnal Year)

ضرب =Struck (Duriba)

فى = In (Fi)

الهجرة = Hejira

١٣٠٢ =1302

سنة =Sanat (year)

10 PIASTRES

SILVER

KM#	Date	Year	VG	Fine	VF	XF
1	AH1302	5	—	—	Rare	—

20 PIASTRES

SILVER

KM#	Date	Year	VG	Fine	VF	XF
2	AH1302	5	225.00	325.00	500.00	700.00

100 PIASTRES

GOLD

KM#	Date	Year	VG	Fine	VF	XF
3	AH1255	2	—	—	Rare	—

NOTE: Struck by the Mahdi which is a copy of Egyptian coin under Turkish Sultan. This issue is more crude than the Egyptian type and has crude edge milling. Reverse Arabic legend "Struck in Misr" (Egypt); however they were struck in the Sudan about AH1302.

ABDULLAH IBN MOHAMMED

(the Khalifa)

Omdurman Mint

مقبول = Accepted (money) i.e., legal (Tughra) - 'Maqbul'

سنة ٥ = Sanat (year) 5

سنة ٤ = Sanat (year) 4

سنة ١١ = Sanat (year) 11

ضرب = Struck - 'Duriba'

فى = In (Fi)

ام درمان = Omdurman

١٣٠٤ = 1304(A.H.)

١٣٠٩ = 1309(A.H.)

٢٠ = 20

قرش - ش = Qirsh = Piastres

عملة جديدة = New coinage (in tughra) - 'Umla Jadida'

جيد = Good - 'Jayyid'

عز نصره = May his victory be glorified 'Azza Nasruhu'

ش ٢٠ = 20 Piastres

NOTE: The coins of the Khalifa have been rearranged in this edition by KM#'s rather than by metallic composition. Except for the 10 Para (KM#8), which is of copper (more or less pure), the remaining coins (KM#4-26) show the following progressive debasement:

AH Year Metallic Composition
1304 - Silver
1309 - Debased Silver
1310 - Debased Silver, Silver Washed Copper, Billon
1311 - Billon, Silver-Washed Copper, Copper
1312 - Billon, Silver-Washed Copper, Copper
1315 - Copper, Sometimes Silver-Washed

NOTE: The metal is not indicated beneath the photos, as usual, because each type occurs in a range of debasements. Different degrees of debasement do not constitute definable subtypes.

10 PARA

25mm

KM#	Date	Year	VG	Fine	VF	XF
8	AH1308	6	—	—	—	—

NOTE: Probably a pattern.

PIASTRE

(Ghirsh)

Plain borders, 18mm

KM#	Date	Year	VG	Fine	VF	XF
4	AH1304	1	60.00	100.00	150.00	250.00
	1311	9	40.00	65.00	100.00	175.00
	1311	11	40.00	65.00	100.00	175.00

2 PIASTRES

Plain borders, 18mm

KM#	Date	Year	VG	Fine	VF	XF
9	AH1310	8	65.00	100.00	250.00	325.00
	1311	9	65.00	100.00	250.00	325.00
	1311	11	65.00	100.00	250.00	325.00

Wreath borders

KM#	Date	Year	VG	Fine	VF	XF
18	AH1311	8	20.00	35.00	75.00	100.00
	1311	11	20.00	35.00	75.00	100.00

Borders of small crescents and few stars.

KM#	Date	Year	VG	Fine	VF	XF
22.1	AH1311	—	25.00	40.00	125.00	160.00

Borders of crescents, stars and roses.

KM#	Date	Year	VG	Fine	VF	XF
22.2	AH1312	—	25.00	40.00	125.00	160.00

2-1/2 PIASTRES

Obv: *Umla Jadida* below toughra.
Border of crescents, stars, roses.

KM#	Date	Year	VG	Fine	VF	XF
23.1	AH1312	—	20.00	50.00	140.00	175.00

NOTE: KM#23.1 differs from KM#22 by the presence of the *Shadda* which looks like the letter W, after the numeral "2" on the reverse.

Obv: *Maqbul* below toughra.

KM#	Date	Year	VG	Fine	VF	XF
23.2	AH1312	—	30.00	85.00	275.00	350.00

Border of crescents only.

KM#	Date	Year	VG	Fine	VF	XF
24	AH1312	—	25.00	75.00	250.00	325.00

4 PIASTRES

Plain borders, 25mm

KM#	Date	Year	VG	Fine	VF	XF
10	AH1310	8	175.00	250.00	450.00	625.00

5 PIASTRES

Border of double crescents.

KM#	Date	Year	VG	Fine	VF	XF
5.1	AH1304	4	35.00	55.00	150.00	200.00
	1304	5	20.00	40.00	125.00	160.00
	1311	11	15.00	27.50	75.00	100.00

NOTE: Coins of AH1304/yr. 4 come in two varieties, one with numeral 1 at top on reverse and one with 4.

Obv: Denomination below toughra.

KM#	Date	Year	VG	Fine	VF	XF
5.2	AH1311	11	15.00	27.50	75.00	100.00

Plain borders, 21-22mm

KM#	Date	Year	VG	Fine	VF	XF
11	AH1310	8	45.00	75.00	250.00	300.00

Borders of crescents and stars.

KM#	Date	Year	VG	Fine	VF	XF
19	AH1311	—	20.00	40.00	80.00	100.00

Borders of crescents only

KM#	Date	Year	VG	Fine	VF	XF
20	AH1311	—	40.00	60.00	100.00	175.00

10 PIASTRES

Borders of double crescents.

KM#	Date	Year	VG	Fine	VF	XF
6	AH1304	4	75.00	150.00	250.00	350.00
	1311	11	50.00	100.00	200.00	300.00

NOTE: Edge varieties exist.

Plain borders

KM#	Date	Year	VG	Fine	VF	XF
12	AH1310	8	100.00	350.00	600.00	850.00

Wreath borders

KM#	Date	Year	VG	Fine	VF	XF
13	AH1310	8	300.00	600.00	900.00	1150.

20 PIASTRES

Borders of double crescents.

KM#	Date	Year	VG	Fine	VF	XF
7	AH1304	4	20.00	37.50	60.00	100.00
	1304 on obv. w/1 on rev.					
		5	20.00	37.50	60.00	100.00
	1306	5	40.00	60.00	90.00	200.00
	1309 on obv. w/1 on rev., normal date					
		5	20.00	37.50	60.00	100.00
	1309 on obv. w/1 on rev., 9 of date retrograde					
		5	20.00	37.50	60.00	100.00
	1309 on obv. w/o 1 on rev., normal date					
		5	40.00	60.00	90.00	200.00

Borders of crescents, stars and roses.
Rev: *Azza Nasruhu.*

KM#	Date	Year	VG	Fine	VF	XF
14	AH1310	10	10.00	15.00	25.00	40.00
	1311	—	10.00	15.00	25.00	40.00
	1311	9	10.00	15.00	25.00	40.00
	1311	11	10.00	15.00	25.00	40.00
	1312	11	10.00	15.00	25.00	40.00
	1312	12	10.00	15.00	25.00	40.00
	1312	—	10.00	15.00	25.00	40.00

Borders of crescents only.
Rev: W/o *Azza Nasruhu.*

KM#	Date	Year	VG	Fine	VF	XF
21	AH1302	9	15.00	65.00	125.00	175.00
	1311	11	12.50	25.00	40.00	75.00
	1312	12	12.50	25.00	40.00	75.00

NOTE: The date 1302 on the year 9 is in error for 1312, and is not to be confused with the Mahdi crown, KM#2.
NOTE: Varieties exist.

Rev: W/ *Azza Nasruhu.*

KM#	Date	Year	VG	Fine	VF	XF
25	AH1311	11	10.00	20.00	30.00	55.00
	1312	12	10.00	20.00	30.00	55.00

AH1315, R.Y. 8

AH1312, R.Y. 12
Rev: Wreath borders w/spears below.

KM#	Date	Year	VG	Fine	VF	XF
15	AH1310	8	10.00	17.50	27.50	55.00
	1311	11	12.00	25.00	40.00	75.00
	1312	12	7.00	12.50	20.00	40.00
	1315	8	6.00	11.50	18.50	35.00

NOTE: Many die varieties of this type exist.

Obv. and rev: Wreath w/spears below.

KM#	Date	Year	VG	Fine	VF	XF
16	AH1310	8	20.00	50.00	100.00	150.00
	1311	12	20.00	50.00	100.00	150.00

Wreath borders. W/o spears on either side.

KM#	Date	Year	VG	Fine	VF	XF
17	AH1310	8	8.00	15.00	25.00	40.00
	1315	12	8.00	15.00	25.00	40.00

AH1312, R.Y. 12
Wreath borders. Obv: Spears below.

KM#	Date	Year	VG	Fine	VF	XF
26	AH1312	12	4.00	6.50	10.00	20.00
	1313	13	7.00	14.00	20.00	35.00
	1315	8	7.00	12.50	17.50	30.00
	1315	12	7.00	12.50	17.50	30.00

NOTE: Many die varieties of this type exist.

REPUBLIC

10 Millim (Milliemes) = 1 Ghirsh (Piastre)
100 Ghirsh (Piastre) = 1 Pound

MILLIM

BRONZE
Obv: Large legend and denomination.

KM#	Date	Year	Mintage	VF	XF	Unc
29.1	AH1376	1956	5.000	—	.10	.20
	1379	1960	1.300	—	.10	.25
	1386	1966	—	—	Proof	—
	1387	1967	—	—	.10	.20
	1388	1968	—	—	.10	.20
	1389	1969	—	—	.10	.20

Small legend and denomination.

KM#	Date	Year	Mintage	VF	XF	Unc
29.2	AH1387	1967	7,834	—	Proof	.25
	1388	1968	5,251	—	Proof	.50
	1389	1969	2,149	—	Proof	.75

NOTE: Except for the proof sets, mintage figures have not generally been made available since 1967.

Obv: New Arabic legend.

KM#	Date	Year	Mintage	VF	XF	Unc
39	AH1390	1970	1,646	—	Proof	1.00
	1391	1971	1,772	—	Proof	1.00

NOTE: Existence of circulation strikes of KM#39, 40 and 44 1970 or 1971 is uncertain.

2 MILLIM

BRONZE
Obv: Large denomination.

KM#	Date	Year	Mintage	VF	XF	Unc
30.1	AH1376	1956	5.000	—	.10	.35
	1386	1966	—	—	Proof	—
	1387	1967	—	—	.10	.20
	1388	1968	—	—	.10	.20
	1389	1969	—	—	.10	.20

Obv: Small denomination.

KM#	Date	Year	Mintage	VF	XF	Unc
30.2	AH1387	1967	7,834	—	Proof	.50
	1388	1968	5,251	—	Proof	.75
	1389	1969	2,149	—	Proof	1.00

Obv: New Arabic legend.

KM#	Date	Year	Mintage	VF	XF	Unc
40	AH1390	1970	1,646	—	Proof	1.25
	1391	1971	1,772	—	Proof	1.25

5 MILLIM

BRONZE
Obv: Thin legend and large denomination.

KM#	Date	Year	Mintage	VF	XF	Unc
31.1	AH1376	1956	30.000	.10	.20	.40
	1382	1962	6.000	.10	.20	.40
	1386	1966	4.000	.10	.15	.30
	1386	1966	—	—	Proof	—
	1387	1967	4.000	.10	.15	.30
	1388	1968	—	.10	.15	.30
	1389	1969	—	.10	.15	.30

NOTE: Varieties of size of camel and rider exist.

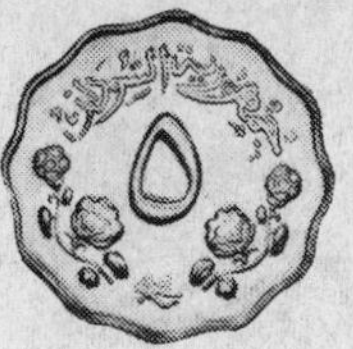

Obv: Thick legend and small denomination.

KM#	Date	Year	Mintage	VF	XF	Unc
31.2	AH1387	1967	7,834	—	Proof	.75
	1388	1968	5,251	—	Proof	1.00
	1389	1969	2,149	—	Proof	1.25

Obv: New large Arabic legend and denomination.

KM#	Date	Year	Mintage	VF	XF	Unc
41.1	AH1390	1970	—	.20	.40	.80
	1391	1971	3.000	.20	.40	.80

Obv: Small legend and denomination.

KM#	Date	Year	Mintage	VF	XF	Unc
41.2	AH1390	1970	1,646	—	Proof	1.25
	1391	1971	1,772	—	Proof	1.25

2nd Anniversary of Revolution

KM#	Date	Year	Mintage	VF	XF	Unc
47	AH1391	1971	.500	.10	.15	.35

F.A.O. Issue

KM#	Date	Year	Mintage	VF	XF	Unc
53	AH1392	1972	6.000	—	.10	.20
	1393	1973	9.000	—	.10	.15

Similar to 10 Millim, KM#55 but round.

KM#	Date	Year	Mintage	VF	XF	Unc
54	AH1392	1972	—	—	.10	.30

BRASS
Obv: Thick legend and denomination.
Rev: Ribbon w/3 equal sections.

KM#	Date	Year	Mintage	VF	XF	Unc
54a.1	AH1395	1975	4.132	—	.10	.25
	1398	1978	—	—	.10	.25

Rev: Ribbon w/long center section.

KM#	Date	Year	Mintage	VF	XF	Unc
54a.2	AH1398	1978	—	—	.10	.25

Obv: Thin legend and denomination, different style.
Rev: Ribbon w/3 equal sections.

KM#	Date	Year	Mintage	VF	XF	Unc
54a.3	AH1400	1980	—	—	Proof	1.00

F.A.O. Issue

KM#	Date	Year	Mintage	VF	XF	Unc
60	AH1396	1976	7.868	—	.10	.20
	1398	1978	7.000	—	.10	.20

20th Anniversary of Independence

KM#	Date	Year	Mintage	VF	XF	Unc
94	AH1396	1976	—	.15	.20	.25

10 MILLIM

BRONZE
Obv: Large denomination.

KM#	Date	Year	Mintage	VF	XF	Unc
32.1	AH1376	1956	15.00	.10	.20	.40
	1380	1960	12.250	.10	.15	.30
	1381	1962	high date —	.10	.15	.30
	1381	1962	low date —	.10	.15	.30
	1386	1966	1.000	.10	.15	.40
	1386	1966	—	—	Proof	—
	1387	1967	1.000	.10	.15	.30
	1388	1968	—	.10	.15	.30
	1389	1969	—	.10	.15	.30

NOTE: Varieties in style and size of camel and rider exist.

Obv: Small legend and denomination.

KM#	Date	Year	Mintage	VF	XF	Unc
32.2	AH1387	1967	7,834	—	Proof	1.00
	1388	1968	5,251	—	Proof	1.25
	1389	1969	2,149	—	Proof	1.50

Obv: New large Arabic legend and denomination.

KM#	Date	Year	Mintage	VF	XF	Unc
42.1	AH1390	1970	—	.20	.40	.90
	1391	1971	3.000	.20	.40	.90

Obv: Small legend and denomination.

KM#	Date	Year	Mintage	VF	XF	Unc
42.2	AH1390	1970	1,646	—	Proof	1.25
	1391	1971	1,772	—	Proof	1.25

2nd Anniversary of Revolution

KM#	Date	Year	Mintage	VF	XF	Unc
48	AH1391	1971	.500	10.00	15.00	25.00

KM#	Date	Year	Mintage	VF	XF	Unc
55	AH1392	1972	6.500	.10	.15	.40

BRASS
Obv: Thick legend and denomination.
Rev: Ribbon w/3 equal sections.

KM#	Date	Year	Mintage	VF	XF	Unc
55a.1	AH1395	1975	12.000	.10	.15	.35
	1398	1978	9.410	.10	.20	.45

Similar to KM#111.

KM#	Date	Year	Mintage	VF	XF	Unc
55a.2	AH1398	1978	—	.50	1.00	2.50

Obv: Thin legend and denomination, different style.
Rev: Ribbon w/3 equal sections.

KM#	Date	Year	Mintage	VF	XF	Unc
55a.3	AH1400	1980	2.490	.10	.20	.45
	1400	1980	—	—	Proof	1.50

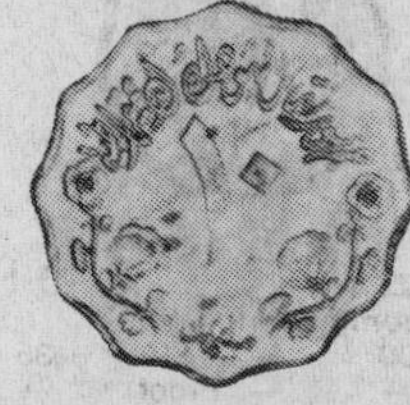

F.A.O. Issue

KM#	Date	Year	Mintage	VF	XF	Unc
61	AH1396	1976	3.000	.10	.15	.25
	1398	1978	—	.10	.15	.25

20th Anniversary of Independence

KM#	Date	Year	Mintage	VF	XF	Unc
62	AH1396	1976	3.610	.10	.15	.35

Rev: Ribbon w/long center section.

KM#	Date	Year	Mintage	VF	XF	Unc
111	AH1400	1980	—	.50	2.00	4.00

GHIRSH

BRASS
Rev: Ribbon above bird w/3 equal sections.

KM#	Date	Year	Mintage	VF	XF	Unc
97	AH1403	1983	1.140	.10	.15	.25

ALUMINUM-BRONZE

KM#	Date	Year	Mintage	VF	XF	Unc
99	AH1408	1987	—	.10	.15	.25

2 GHIRSH

COPPER-NICKEL

KM#	Date	Year	Mintage	VF	XF	Unc
33	AH1376	1956	5.000	.15	35	.50
	1381	1962	—	.15	35	.50

KM#	Date	Year	Mintage	VF	XF	Unc
36	AH1382	1963	1.250	.15	.35	.75
	1386	1966	—	—	Proof	—
	1387	1967	—	.15	.35	.75
	1387	1967	7,834	—	Proof	1.25
	1388	1968	—	.15	.35	.75
	1388	1968	5,251	—	Proof	1.50
	1389	1969	—	.15	.35	.75
	1389	1969	2,149	—	Proof	1.75

Obv: New large Arabic legend and denomination.

KM#	Date	Year	Mintage	VF	XF	Unc
43.1	AH1390	1970	—	.30	.60	1.25

Obv: Small legend and denomination.

KM#	Date	Year	Mintage	VF	XF	Unc
43.2	AH1390	1970	1,646	—	Proof	1.25
	1391	1971	1,772	—	Proof	1.25

2nd Anniversary of Revolution

KM#	Date	Year	Mintage	VF	XF	Unc
49	AH1391	1971	.500	.15	.30	.50

Obv: Thick legend and denomination.
Rev: Ribbon w/3 equal sections.

KM#	Date	Year	Mintage	VF	XF	Unc
57.1	AH1395	1975	1.000	.10	.20	.40
	1398	1978	1.250	.10	.20	.40

Obv: Legend different style.
Rev: Ribbon w/long center section.

KM#	Date	Year	Mintage	VF	XF	Unc
57.2	AH1398	1978	—	.10	.20	.40
	1400	1980	—	.10	.20	.40

BRASS

KM#	Date	Year	Mintage	VF	XF	Unc
57.2a	1403	1983	.100	.50	1.00	2.25

COPPER - NICKEL

Obv: Thin legend and denomination.
Rev: Ribbon w/3 equal sections.

KM#	Date	Year	Mintage	VF	XF	Unc
57.3	AH1399	1979	2.000	.10	.20	.40
	1400	1980	6.825	.10	.20	.40
	1400	1980	Inc. Ab.	—	Proof	2.00

COPPER-NICKEL
F.A.O. Issue
Obv: Thick denomination.

KM#	Date	Year	Mintage	VF	XF	Unc
63.1	AH1396	1976	.500	.10	.20	.40
	1398	1978	Inc. Ab.	.10	.20	.40

Obv: Thin denomination.

KM#	Date	Year	Mintage	VF	XF	Unc
63.2	AH1398	1978	Inc. Ab.	5.00	7.00	10.00

20th Anniversary of Independence

KM#	Date	Year	Mintage	VF	XF	Unc
64	AH1396	1976	1.750	.10	.20	.50

5 GHIRSH

COPPER-NICKEL
Obv: Large denomination.

KM#	Date	Year	Mintage	VF	XF	Unc
34.1	AH1376	1956	40.000	.15	.30	.75
	1387	1967	—	.20	.30	.60
	1388	1968	—	.20	.30	.60
	1389	1969	—	.20	.30	.60

Obv: Small denomination.

KM#	Date	Year	Mintage	VF	XF	Unc
34.2	AH1386	1966	—	—	Proof	1.50
	1387	1967	7,834	—	Proof	1.50
	1388	1968	5,251	—	Proof	1.75
	1389	1969	2,149	—	Proof	2.00

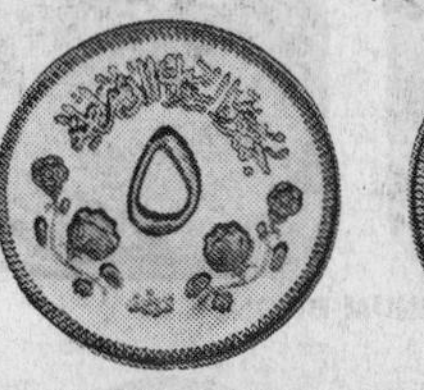

KM#	Date	Year	Mintage	VF	XF	Unc
44	AH1390	1970	1,646	—	Proof	2.00
	1391	1971	1,772	—	Proof	2.00

2nd Anniversary of Revolution

KM#	Date	Year	Mintage	VF	XF	Unc
51	AH1391	1971	.500	.20	.30	.75

Obv: Large legend and denomination.
Rev: Ribbon above bird w/3 equal sections.

KM#	Date	Year	Mintage	VF	XF	Unc
58.1	AH1395	1975	1.600	.20	.30	.65

Obv: Small legend, different style.

KM#	Date	Year	Mintage	VF	XF	Unc
58.3	AH1397	1977	2.000	.20	.30	.65
	1398	1978	1.000	.20	.30	.65
	1400	1980	1.000	.20	.30	.65
	1400	1980	Inc. Ab.	—	Proof	3.00

Obv: Large legend style changed, small denomination.
Rev: Ribbon w/long center section.

KM#	Date	Year	Mintage	VF	XF	Unc
58.2	AH1400	1980	Inc. KM58.1	.20	.30	.65

NOTE: Edge varieties exist.

Obv: Large legend and denomination.

KM#	Date	Year	Mintage	VF	XF	Unc
58.4	AH1400	1980	Inc. KM58.1	.20	.30	.65

NOTE: Edge varieties exist.

F.A.O. Issue

KM#	Date	Year	Mintage	VF	XF	Unc
65	AH1396	1976	.500	.20	.30	.65
	1398	1978	—	.20	.30	.65

20th Anniversary of Independence

KM#	Date	Year	Mintage	VF	XF	Unc
66	AH1396	1976	3.940	.25	.50	1.00

Council of Arab Economic Unity

KM#	Date	Year	Mintage	VF	XF	Unc
74	AH1398	1978	5.040	.15	.25	.50

NOTE: Edge varieties exist.

F.A.O. Issue

KM#	Date	Year	Mintage	VF	XF	Unc
84	AH1401	1981	1.000	.20	.40	.75

NOTE: Edge varieties exist.

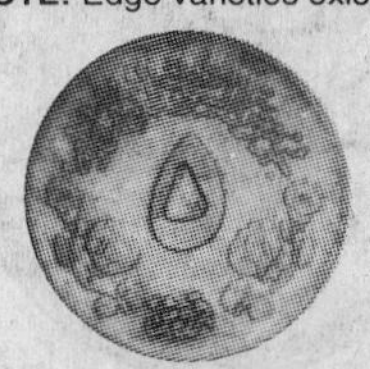

BRASS
Obv: Large denomination.
Rev: Ribbon w/3 equal sections.

KM#	Date	Year	Mintage	VF	XF	Unc
110.1	AH1403	1983	—	.15	.25	.50

Obv: Small denomination, legend different style.

KM#	Date	Year	Mintage	VF	XF	Unc
110.3	AH1403	1983	—	5.00	7.00	10.00

Rev: Ribbon w/long center section.

KM#	Date	Year	Mintage	VF	XF	Unc
110.2	AH1403	1983	—	.20	.50	1.00

Obv: Large denomination, legend similar to KM#110.1.

KM#	Date	Year	Mintage	VF	XF	Unc
110.4	AH1403	1983	—	.50	3.00	5.00

ALUMINUM-BRONZE

KM#	Date	Year	Mintage	VF	XF	Unc
100	AH1408	1987	—	.15	.25	.50

10 GHIRSH

COPPER-NICKEL
Obv: Large denomination.

KM#	Date	Year	Mintage	VF	XF	Unc
35.1	AH1376	1956	15.000	.35	.75	2.00
	1386	1966	—	—	Proof	—
	1387	1967	—	.30	.60	1.50
	1388	1968	—	.30	.60	1.50
	1389	1969	—	.30	.60	1.50

Obv: Small denomination.

KM#	Date	Year	Mintage	VF	XF	Unc
35.2	AH1387	1967	7,834	—	Proof	1.75
	1388	1968	5,251	—	Proof	2.00
	1389	1969	2,149	—	Proof	2.25

Obv: New large Arabic legend and denomination.

KM#	Date	Year	Mintage	VF	XF	Unc
45.1	AH1390	1970	—	.60	1.25	2.50
	1391	1971	.385	.60	1.25	2.50

Obv: Small legend and denomination.

KM#	Date	Year	Mintage	VF	XF	Unc
45.2	AH1390	1970	1,646	—	Proof	3.00
	1391	1971	1,772	—	Proof	3.00

2nd Anniversary of Revolution

KM#	Date	Year	Mintage	VF	XF	Unc
52	AH1391	1971	.500	.40	.75	2.00

Obv: Thick legend.
Rev: Ribbon w/3 equal sections.

KM#	Date	Year	Mintage	VF	XF	Unc
59.1	AH1395	1975	1.000	.35	.75	2.00

Obv: Thin legend, different style.

KM#	Date	Year	Mintage	VF	XF	Unc
59.5	AH1397	1977	1.000	.35	.75	2.00
	1400	1980	2.965	.35	.75	2.00
	1400	1980	—	—	Proof	4.50

Rev: Ribbon w/long center section.

KM#	Date	Year	Mintage	VF	XF	Unc
59.2	AH1400	1980	—	.35	.75	2.00

NOTE: Edge varieties exist.

Reduced size.

KM#	Date	Year	Mintage	VF	XF	Unc
59.3	AH1403	1983	—	.35	.75	2.00

NOTE: Edge varieties exist.

Obv: Similar to KM#59.3.
Rev: Ribbon w/3 equal sections.

KM#	Date	Year	Mintage	VF	XF	Unc
59.4	AH1403	1983	1.100	7.00	10.00	20.00

F.A.O. Issue

KM#	Date	Year	Mintage	VF	XF	Unc
67	AH1396	1976	.500	.30	.60	1.25
	1398	1978	—	.30	.60	1.25

20th Anniversary of Independence

KM#	Date	Year	Mintage	VF	XF	Unc
68	AH1396	1976	5.540	.25	.50	1.00

NOTE: Edge varieties exist.

Council of Arab Economic Unity

KM#	Date	Year	Mintage	VF	XF	Unc
95	AH1398	1978	1.000	.40	.80	1.50

NOTE: Edge varieties exist.

F.A.O. Issue

KM#	Date	Year	Mintage	VF	XF	Unc
85	AH1401	1981	1.000	.40	.80	1.50

NOTE: Edge varieties exist.

ALUMINUM-BRONZE

KM#	Date	Year	Mintage	VF	XF	Unc
107	AH1408	1987	—	.40	.80	1.50

20 GHIRSH

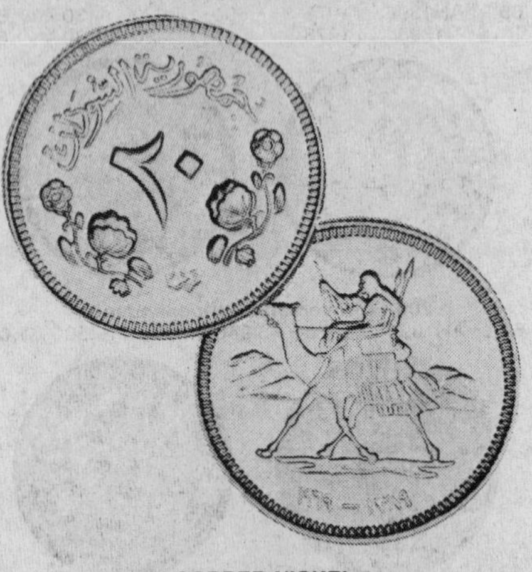

COPPER-NICKEL

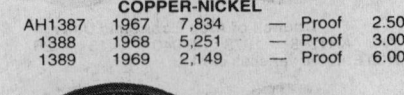

KM#	Date	Year	Mintage	VF	XF	Unc
37	AH1387	1967	7,834	—	Proof	2.50
	1388	1968	5,251	—	Proof	3.00
	1389	1969	2,149	—	Proof	6.00

Obv: New Arabic legend.

KM#	Date	Year	Mintage	VF	XF	Unc
46	AH1390	1970	1,646	—	Proof	8.00
	1391	1971	1,772	—	Proof	8.00

KM#	Date	Year	Mintage	VF	XF	Unc
98	AH1403	1983	.072	—	—	4.00

F.A.O. Issue

KM#	Date	Year	Mintage	VF	XF	Unc
96	AH1405	1985	—	—	—	3.00

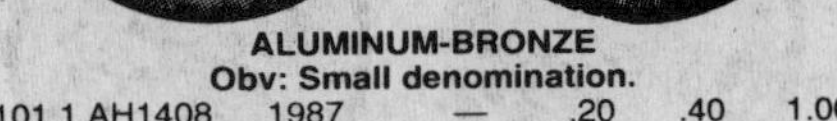

ALUMINUM-BRONZE
Obv: Small denomination.

KM#	Date	Year	Mintage	VF	XF	Unc
101.1	AH1408	1987	—	.20	.40	1.00

Obv: Large denomination.

KM#	Date	Year	Mintage	VF	XF	Unc
101.2	AH1408	1987	—	.20	.40	1.00

25 GHIRSH

COPPER-NICKEL
F.A.O. Issue

KM#	Date	Year	Mintage	VF	XF	Unc
38	AH1388	1968	.224	—	P/L	14.50

ALUMINUM-BRONZE

KM#	Date	Year	Mintage	VF	XF	Unc
102	AH1408	1987	—	.35	.75	2.00

STAINLESS STEEL

KM#	Date	Year	Mintage	VF	XF	Unc
108	AH1409	1989	—	.35	.75	2.00

50 GHIRSH

COPPER-NICKEL
F.A.O. Issue
Rev: Large design.

KM#	Date	Year	Mintage	VF	XF	Unc
56.1	AH1392	1972	1.000	1.00	2.00	4.00
	Rev: Small design.					
56.2	AH1392	1972	30,000	5.00	10.00	20.00

NOTE: Struck in 1976.

Establishment of Arab Cooperative
F.A.O. Issue

KM#	Date	Year	Mintage	VF	XF	Unc
69	AH1396	1976	—	1.00	2.00	4.00

8th Anniversary of 1969 Revolt

KM#	Date	Year	Mintage	VF	XF	Unc
73	AH1397	1977	.100	1.00	2.00	4.00

ALUMINUM-BRONZE

KM#	Date	Year	Mintage	VF	XF	Unc
103	AH1408	1987	—	.50	1.00	2.50

33rd Anniversary of Independence

KM#	Date	Year	Mintage	VF	XF	Unc
105	AH1409	1989	—	1.00	2.00	3.50

STAINLESS STEEL

KM#	Date	Year	Mintage	VF	XF	Unc
109	AH1409	1989	—	.50	1.00	2.50

POUND

COPPER-NICKEL
Rural Women and F.A.O. Issue

KM#	Date	Year	Mintage	VF	XF	Unc
75	AH1398	1978	.456	2.00	3.00	5.00

ALUMINUM-BRONZE

KM#	Date	Year	Mintage	VF	XF	Unc
104	AH1408	1987	—	1.00	2.00	4.00

STAINLESS STEEL

KM#	Date	Year	Mintage	VF	XF	Unc
106	AH1409	1989	—	.75	1.50	3.50

2-1/2 POUNDS

28.2800 g, .925 SILVER, .8410 oz ASW
Conservation - Shoebill Stork

KM#	Date	Year	Mintage	VF	XF	Unc
70	AH1396	1976	5,183	—	—	18.00
	1396	1976	5,590	—	Proof	22.00

5 POUNDS

35.0000 g, .925 SILVER, 1.0409 oz ASW
Conservation - Hippopotamus

KM#	Date	Year	Mintage	VF	XF	Unc
71	AH1396	1976	5,087	—	—	25.00
	1396	1976	5,393	—	Proof	30.00

17.5000 g, .925 SILVER, .5205 oz ASW
Khartoum Meeting of O.A.U.

KM#	Date	Year	Mintage	VF	XF	Unc
76	AH1398	1978	21 pcs.	—	—	—
	1398	1978	1,423	—	Proof	22.00
	1398*	1978	2,000	—	Proof	17.00

***NOTE:** With counterstamp between dates.

1400th Anniversary of Islam

KM#	Date	Year	Mintage	VF	XF	Unc
80	AH1400	1980	7,500	—	—	20.00
	1400	1980	5,500	—	Proof	25.00

28.2800 g, .925 SILVER, .8410 oz ASW
25th Anniversary of Independence

KM#	Date	Year	Mintage	VF	XF	Unc
86	AH1401	1981	.020	—	—	35.00
	AH1401	1981	.020	—	Proof	45.00

19.4400 g, .925 SILVER, .5781 oz ASW
UNICEF and I.Y.C.

KM#	Date	Year	Mintage	VF	XF	Unc
87	AH1401	1981	.035	—	Proof	16.50

Decade For Women

KM#	Date	Year	Mintage	VF	XF	Unc
92	AH1404	1984	.020	—	Proof	18.00

10 POUNDS

35.0000 g, .925 SILVER, 1.0409 oz ASW
Khartoum Meeting of O.A.U.

KM#	Date	Year	Mintage	VF	XF	Unc
77	AH1398	1978	21 pcs.	—	—	—
	1398	1978	1,417	—	Proof	35.00
	1398*	1978	2,000	—	Proof	30.00

***NOTE:** With counterstamp between dates.

1400th Anniversary of Islam

KM#	Date	Year	Mintage	VF	XF	Unc
81	AH1400	1980	3,000	—	—	25.00
	1400	1980	2,000	—	Proof	35.00

28.2800 g, .925 SILVER, .8411 oz ASW
Year of the Disabled Persons

KM#	Date	Year	Mintage	VF	XF	Unc
88	AH1401	1981	.010	—	—	20.00
	1401	1981	.010	—	Proof	30.00

25 POUNDS

8.2500 g, .917 GOLD, .2432 oz AGW
Khartoum Meeting of O.A.U.

KM#	Date	Year	Mintage	VF	XF	Unc
78	AH1398	1978	15 pcs.	—	—	600.00
	1398	1978	467 pcs.	—	Proof	225.00
	1398*	1978	350 pcs.	—	Proof	175.00

***NOTE:** CS with counterstamp between dates.

1400th Anniversary of Islam

KM#	Date	Year	Mintage	VF	XF	Unc
82	AH1400	1980	7,500	—	—	120.00
	1400	1980	5,500	—	Proof	135.00

50 POUNDS

17.5000 g, .917 GOLD, .5160 oz AGW
Khartoum Meeting of O.A.U.

KM#	Date	Year	Mintage	VF	XF	Unc
79	AH1398	1978	11 pcs.	—	—	1500.
	1398	1978	211 pcs.	—	Proof	325.00
	1398*	1978	350 pcs.	—	Proof	275.00

***NOTE:** With counterstamp between dates.

1400th Anniversary of Islam

KM#	Date	Year	Mintage	VF	XF	Unc
83	AH1400	1980	3,000	—	—	250.00
	1400	1980	2,000	—	Proof	275.00

7.9900 g, .917 GOLD, .2353 oz AGW
25th Anniversary of Independence

KM#	Date	Year	Mintage	VF	XF	Unc
89	AH1401	1981	5,000	—	—	120.00
	AH1401	1981	5,000	—	Proof	130.00

100 POUNDS

33.4370 g, .900 GOLD, .9676 oz AGW
Conservation - Scimitar-horned Oryx

KM#	Date	Year	Mintage	VF	XF	Un
72	AH1396	1976	872 pcs.	—	—	450.0
	1396	1976	251 pcs.	—	Proof	750.0

15.9800 g, .917 GOLD, .4706 oz AGW
25th Anniversary of Independence

KM#	Date	Year	Mintage	VF	XF	Un
90	AH1401	1981	2,500	—	—	225.0
	AH1401	1981	2,500	—	Proof	250.0

Year of the Disabled Persons

KM#	Date	Year	Mintage	VF	XF	Un
91	AH1401	1981	2,000	—	—	350.0
	1401	1981	2,000	—	Proof	450.0

8.1000 g, .917 GOLD, .2388 oz AGW
Decade For Women

KM#	Date	Year	Mintage	VF	XF	Un
93	AH1404	1984	513 pcs.	—	Proof	275.0

MINT SETS (MS)

KM#	Date	Mintage	Identification	Issue Price	Mkt. Va
MS1	1976(2)	—	KM70-71	—	60.C

PROOF SETS (PS)

KM#	Date	Mintage	Identification	Issue Price	Mkt. Va
PS1	1967(8)	7,834	KM29-32,34-37	15.25	6.C
PS2	1968(8)	5,251	KM29-32,34-37	15.25	7.C
PS3	1969(8)	2,149	KM29-32,34-37	15.25	9.0
PS4	1970(8)	1,646	KM39-46	15.25	15.0
PS5	1971(8)	1,772	KM39-46	15.25	15.C
PS6	1976(2)	—	KM70a-71a	—	60.C
PS7	1978(4)	—	KM76-79	—	600.C
PS8	1980(5)	—	KM54,55a,57-59	—	12.C
PS9	1980(4)	—	KM80-83	—	535.C

DARFUR

The province of Darfur makes up most of the wester border of the Republic of Sudan. Darfur had been a independent kingdom until taken over by Egypt in 1874 While the British were involved in subduing the easter Sudan, Ali Dinar established the sultanate of Darfur. H coins copied the type of 20 Para of Mohammed II c Egypt. The mint was located at Al Fasher (the capitol c the province) and was active from 1908 to 1914 wit most of the coins bearing a 1327 (1909AD) date.

TITLES

al-Fasher الفشير

RULERS

Ali Dinar, 1896-1916

PIASTRE

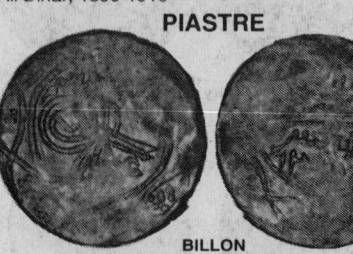

BILLON
Mint: Al-Fasher

KM#	Date	Good	VG	Fine	V
1	AH1327	15.00	30.00	45.00	60.0

NOTE: Very crudely struck, flan size varies.

SURINAM

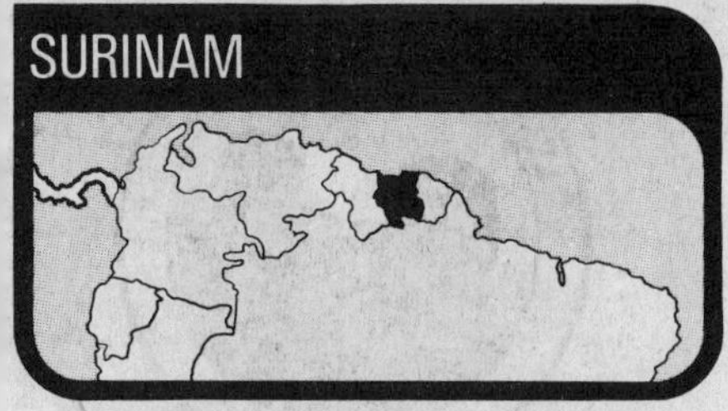

The Republic of Surinam also known as Dutch Guiana, located on the north central coast of South America between Guyana and French Guiana has an area of 63,037 sq. mi. (163,270 sq. km.) and a population of *401,000. Capital: Paramaribo. The country is rich in minerals and forests, and self-sufficient in rice, the staple food crop. The mining, processing and exporting of bauxite is the principal economic activity.

Lieutenants of Amerigo Vespucci sighted the Guiana coast in 1499. Spanish explorers of the 16th century, disappointed at finding no gold, departed leaving the area to be settled by the British in 1652. The colony prospered and the Netherlands acquired it in 1667 in exchange for the Dutch rights in Nieuw Nederland (state of New York). During the European wars of the 18th and 19th centuries, which were fought in part in the new world, Surinam was occupied by the British from 1781-1784 and 1796-1814. Surinam became an autonomous part of the Kingdom of the Netherlands on Dec. 15, 1954. Full independence was achieved on Nov. 25, 1975. In 1980, a revolution installed a military government.

RULERS

Dutch, until 1975

MINT MARKS

FM - Franklin Mint, U.S.A.**
P - Philadelphia, U.S.A.
S - Sydney
(u) - Utrecht (privy marks only)

****NOTE:** From 1975 the Franklin Mint has produced coinage in up to 3 different qualities. Qualities of issue are designated in ( ) after each date and are defined as follows:

(M) MATTE - Normal circulation strike or a dull finish produced by sandblasting special uncirculated (polish finish) or proof quality dies.

(U) SPECIAL UNCIRCULATED - Polished or proof-like in appearance without any frosted features.

(P) PROOF - The highest quality obtainable having mirror-like fields and frosted features.

MONETARY SYSTEM

100 Cents = 1 Gulden (Guilders)

World War II Coinage

The 1942-43 issues following are homeland coinage types of the Netherlands - KM#152, KM#163 and KM#164 - were executed expressly for use in Surinam. Related issues produced for use in both Curacao and Surinam are listed under Curacao. They are distinguished by the presence of a palm tree (acorn on Homeland issues) and a mint mark (P-Philadelphia, D-Denver, S-San Francisco) flanking the date. Also see the Netherlands for similar issues.

CENT

KM#	Date	Mintage	Fine	VF	XF	Unc
	BRASS					
2	1943P palm	4.000	1.50	3.00	7.00	17.50
	BRONZE					
2a	1957(u)	1.200	1.00	1.50	2.50	4.50
	1957(u)	—	—	—	Proof	22.50
	1959(u)	1.800	1.00	1.50	2.50	4.50
	1959(u)	—	—	—	Proof	22.50
	1960(u)	1.200	1.00	1.50	2.50	4.50
	1960(u)	—	—	—	Proof	22.50

NOTE: For similar coins dated 1942P see Netherlands Antilles (Curacao).

MODERN COINAGE

CENT

KM#	Date	Mintage	Fine	VF	XF	Unc
3	1962(u) fish	6.000	—	.15	.35	1.00
3	1962(u)S	650 pcs.	—	—	Proof	25.00
	1966(u)	9.500	—	.15	.35	1.00
	1966(u)	—	—	—	Proof	50.00
	1970(u) cock	5.000	—	.15	.30	.65
	1972(u)	6.000	—	.15	.30	.65
	ALUMINUM					
3a	1974(u)	1.000	—	.10	.25	.50
	1975(u)	1.000	—	.10	.25	.50
	1976(u)	3.000	—	.10	.25	.50
	1977(u)	10.000	—	—	.10	.25
	1978(u)	6.000	—	—	.10	.25
	1979(u)	10.000	—	—	.10	.25
	1980(u) cock and star privy marks	8.000	—	—	.10	.25
	1982(u) anvil	8.000	—	—	.10	.25
	1984	5.000	—	—	.10	.25
	1985	2.000	—	—	.10	.25
	1986	3.000	—	—	.10	.25
	COPPER PLATED STEEL					
3b	1987	—	—	—	—	.10
	1988	*1,500	—	—	Proof	2.00
	1989	—	—	—	—	.10

5 CENT

For a 5 cent coin dated 1943 see Netherlands Antilles (Curacao).

KM#	Date	Mintage	Fine	VF	XF	Unc
	NICKEL-BRASS					
4.1	1962(u) fish	2.200	.25	.50	1.00	2.00
	1962(u)S	650 pcs.	—	—	Proof	20.00
	1966(u) privy marks	1.800	.25	.50	1.00	2.00
	1966(u)	—	—	—	Proof	50.00
	1966 w/o privy marks	.400	.50	1.00	2.50	5.00
	1971(u) cock	.500	.30	.60	1.25	2.50
	1972(u)	1.500	.25	.50	1.00	2.00
	Medal struck					
4.2	1966(u)	—	3.50	7.00	11.50	20.00
	ALUMINUM					
4.1a	1976(u)	5.500	—	.15	.25	.55
	1978(u)	3.000	—	.15	.25	.55
	1979(u)	2.000	—	.15	.25	.55
	1980(u) cock and star privy marks	1.000	—	.15	.25	.55
	1982(u) anvil	1.000	—	.15	.25	.55
	1985(u)	1.000	—	.15	.25	.55
	1986(u)	1.500	—	.15	.25	.55
	COPPER PLATED STEEL					
4.1b	1987	—	—	—	—	.10
	1988	*1,500	—	—	Proof	2.00
	1989	—	—	—	—	.10

10 CENT

KM#	Date	Mintage	Fine	VF	XF	Unc
	1.4000 g, .640 SILVER, .0288 oz ASW					
1	1942P palm	1.500	5.00	10.00	20.00	35.00

NOTE: For similar coins dated 1941P and 1943P see Netherlands Antilles (Curacao).

KM#	Date	Mintage	Fine	VF	XF	Unc
	COPPER-NICKEL					
5	1962(u) fish	3.000	—	.25	1.00	1.75
	1962(u)S	650 pcs.	—	—	Proof	18.50
	1966(u)	2.500	—	.25	1.00	2.00
	1966(u)	—	—	—	Proof	60.00
	1971(u) cock	.500	—	1.00	3.00	6.50
	1972(u)	1.500	—	.20	.50	1.00
	1974(u)	1.500	—	.20	.50	1.00
	1976(u)	5.000	—	.10	.25	.50
	1978(u)	2.000	—	.10	.25	.50
	1979(u)	2.000	—	.10	.25	.50
	1982(u) anvil	1.000	—	.10	.25	.50
	1985(u)	1.000	—	.10	.25	.50
	NICKEL PLATED STEEL					
5a	1986(u)	1.500	—	.10	.25	.50
	1987	—	—	.10	.25	.50
	1988	*1,500	—	—	Proof	3.00
	1989	—	—	.10	.25	.50

25 CENT

KM#	Date	Mintage	Fine	VF	XF	Unc
	COPPER-NICKEL					
6	1962(u) fish	2.300	.25	.50	1.00	1.75
	1962(u)S	650 pcs.	—	—	Proof	20.00
	1966(u)	2.300	.25	.50	1.00	2.25
	1966(u)	—	—	—	Proof	60.00
	1972(u) cock	1.800	.25	.50	1.00	2.25
	1974(u)	1.500	.25	.50	1.00	2.25
	1976(u)	5.000	—	.20	.30	.60
	1979(u)	2.000	—	.20	.30	.60
	1982(u) anvil	2.000	—	.20	.30	.60
	1985(u)	1.000	—	.20	.30	.60
	1986(u)	1.500	—	.20	.30	.60
	NICKEL PLATED STEEL					
6a	1987	—	—	.20	.30	.60
	1988	*1,500	—	—	Proof	5.00
	1989	—	—	.20	.30	.60

100 CENT

KM#	Date	Mintage	Fine	VF	XF	Unc
	COPPER-NICKEL					
15	1987	—	—	—	—	1.75
	1988	—	—	—	—	1.75
	1988	*1,500	—	—	Proof	12.00
	1989	—	—	—	—	1.75

250 CENT

KM#	Date	Mintage	Fine	VF	XF	Unc
	COPPER-NICKEL					
16	1987	—	—	—	—	3.50
	1988	*1,500	—	—	Proof	17.50
	1989	—	—	—	—	3.50

GULDEN

KM#	Date	Mintage	Fine	VF	XF	Unc
	10.0000 g, .720 SILVER, .2315 oz ASW					
7	1962(u)	.150	—	3.00	5.00	10.00
	1962(u)S	650 pcs.	—	—	Proof	40.00
	1966(u)	*.100	10.00	30.00	70.00	125.00
	1966(u)	—	—	—	Proof	175.00

***NOTE:** Never officially released to circulation.

KM#	Date	Mintage	Fine	VF	XF	Unc
	NICKEL COATED BRONZE					
7a	1962	—	—	—	Proof	4000.

10 GULDEN

15.9500 g, .925 SILVER, .4743 oz ASW
1st Anniversary of Independence

KM#	Date	Mintage	Fine	VF	XF	Unc
8	1976(u)	.100	—	—	8.00	15.00
	1976(u)	5,711	—	—	Proof	25.00

25 GULDEN

25.8500 g, .925 SILVER, .7687 oz ASW
1st Anniversary of Independence

KM#	Date	Mintage	Fine	VF	XF	Unc
9	1976(u)	.075	—	—	20.00	25.00
	1976(u)F	5,503	—	—	Proof	38.00

15.5000 g, .925 SILVER, .4610 oz ASW
1st Anniversary of Revolution

KM#	Date	Mintage	Fine	VF	XF	Unc
11	1981FM(U)	.010	—	—	18.00	32.50
	1981FM(P)	800 pcs.	—	—	Proof	70.00

25.1000 g, .925 SILVER, .7435 oz ASW
5th Anniversary of Revolution

KM#	Date	Mintage	Fine	VF	XF	Unc
13	1985(u)	4,800	—	—	—	40.00
	1985(u)	200 pcs.	—	—	Proof	80.00

25 GUILDERS

28.2800 g, .925 SILVER, .8411 oz ASW
World Cup Soccer

KM#	Date	Mintage	Fine	VF	XF	Unc
24	1990	.050	—	—	Proof	45.00

Save The Children

KM#	Date	Mintage	Fine	VF	XF	Unc
28	1991	.030	—	—	Proof	55.00

30 GULDEN

14.0200 g, .925 SILVER, .4170 oz ASW
30th Anniversary of Central Bank

KM#	Date	Mintage	Fine	VF	XF	Unc
19	1987(u)	7,000	—	—	30.00	40.00

50 GUILDERS

28.2800 g, .925 SILVER, .8411 oz ASW
Seoul Olympics - Swimming

KM#	Date	Mintage	Fine	VF	XF	Unc
20	1988	*.025	—	—	Proof	55.0

125th Anniversary of the Surinam Bank

KM#	Date	Mintage	Fine	VF	XF	Unc
22	1990	*7,500	—	—	Proof	65.0

26.0000 g, .925 SILVER, .7733 oz ASW
15th Anniversary of Independence
Similar to 500 Guilders, KM#27.

KM#	Date	Mintage	Fine	VF	XF	Unc
26	1990	*5,000	—	—	Proof	50.0

35th Anniversary of Central Bank

KM#	Date	Mintage	Fine	VF	XF	Unc
30	1992	*1,500	—	—	Proof	55.0

100 GULDEN

6.7200 g, .900 GOLD, .1945 oz ASW
1st Anniversary of Independence

KM#	Date	Mintage	Fine	VF	XF	Unc
10	1976(u)	.020	—	—	—	100.0
	1976(u)	4,749	—	—	Proof	150.0

NOTE: 900 Unc. pieces have been reported struck i 'rose' gold. They are valued between $200. and $225.

100 GUILDERS

20.1200 g, .999 SILVER, .6468 oz ASW
Barcelona Olympics - Basketball

KM#	Date	Mintage	Fine	VF	XF	Unc
32	1992	—	—	—	Proof	50.00

Barcelona Olympics - Cyclists

KM#	Date	Mintage	Fine	VF	XF	Unc
33	1992	—	—	—	Proof	50.00

200 GULDEN

7.1200 g, .500 GOLD, .1144 oz AGW
1st Anniversary of Revolution

KM#	Date	Mintage	VF	XF	Unc
2	1981FM(U)	.011	—	—	— 100.00
	1981FM(P)	1,363	—	—	Proof 175.00

250 GUILDERS

6.7200 g, .900 GOLD, .1944 oz AGW
5th Anniversary of Revolution
Similar to 25 Gulden, KM#13.

KM#	Date	Mintage	VF	XF	Unc
4	1985(u)	5,000	—	—	— 145.00
	1985(u)	200 pcs.	—	—	Proof 225.00

7.9800 g, .917 GOLD, .2354 oz AGW
World Cup Soccer

KM#	Date	Mintage	VF	XF	Unc
25	1990	—	—	—	Proof 200.00

Save The Children

KM#	Date	Mintage	VF	XF	Unc
29	1991	3,000	—	—	— 185.00

500 GUILDERS

7.9800 g, .917 GOLD, .2354 oz AGW
40th Anniversary of Military Sports Organization
Obv: Similar to 1,000 Guilders, KM#18.

KM#	Date	Mintage	VF	XF	Unc
7	1988	2,500	—	—	Proof 215.00

Seoul Olympics - Swimming

KM#	Date	Mintage	Fine	VF	XF	Unc
21	1988	*2,000	—	—	Proof	250.00

125th Anniversary of the Surinam Bank
Similar to 50 Guilders, KM#22.

KM#	Date	Mintage	Fine	VF	XF	Unc
23	1990	*2,000	—	—	Proof	300.00

15th Anniversary of Independence

KM#	Date	Mintage	Fine	VF	XF	Unc
27	1990	*1,250	—	—	Proof	325.00

35th Anniversary of Central Bank
Similar to 50 Guilders, KM#30.

KM#	Date	Mintage	Fine	VF	XF	Unc
31	1992	*300 pcs.	—	—	Proof	300.00

1000 GUILDERS

15.9800 g, .917 GOLD, .4708 oz AGW
40th Anniversary of Military Sports Organization

KM#	Date	Mintage	Fine	VF	XF	Unc
18	1988	1,250	—	—	Proof	400.00

PROOF SETS (PS)

KM#	Date	Mintage	Identification	Issue Price	Mkt. Val.
PS1	1962(5)	650	KM3-7	—	100.00
PS2	1966(5)	—	KM3-7	—	400.00
PS3	1976(3)	—	KM8-10	145.00	215.00
PS4	1976(2)	—	KM8-9	50.00	70.00
PS5	1988(6)	*1,500	KM3b,4.1b,5-6,15-16	42.00	42.00

SWAZILAND

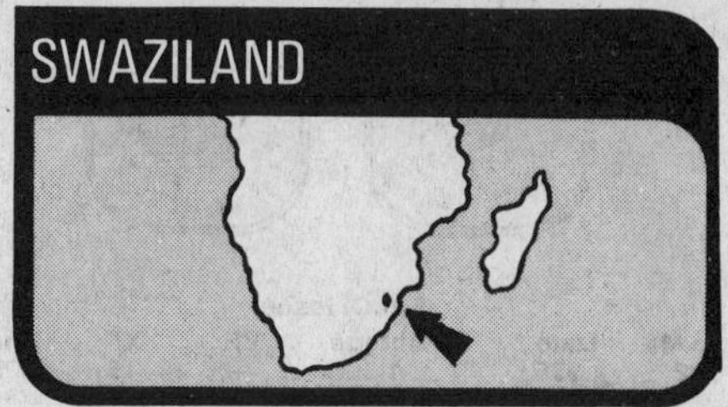

The Kingdom of Swaziland, located in south-eastern Africa, has an area of 6,704 sq. mi. (17,360 sq. km.) and a population of *756,000. Capital: Mbabane (administrative); Lobamba (legislative). The diversified economy includes mining, agriculture, and light industry. Asbestos, iron ore, wood pulp, and sugar are exported.

The people of the present Swazi nation established themselves in an area including what is now Swaziland in the early 1800s. The first Swazi contact with the British came early in the reign of the extremely able Swazi leader Mswati when he asked the British for aid against Zulu raids into Swaziland. The British and Transvaal responded by guaranteeing the independence of Swaziland, 1881. South Africa assumed the power of protection and adminstration in 1894 and Swaziland continued under this administration until the conquest of the Transvaal during the Anglo-Boer War, when administration was transferred to the British government. After World War II, Britain began to prepare Swaziland for independence, which was achieved on Sept. 6, 1968. The Kingdom is a member of the Commonwealth of Nations. The king of Swaziland is normally Chief of State. The prime minister is Head of Government.

RULERS

Sobhuza II, 1968-1982
Queen Ntombi, Regent for
Prince Makhosetive, 1982-1986
King Makhosetive, 1986

MONETARY SYSTEM

100 Cents = 1 Luhlanga
25 Luhlanga = 1 Lilangeni
(plural - Emalangeni)

CENT

BRONZE
Ananas

KM#	Date	Mintage	VF	XF	Unc
7	1974	6.002	—	—	.10
	1974	.013	—	Proof	.75
	1975	—	—	.10	.15
	1979	.500	—	.10	.15
	1979	.010	—	Proof	.75
	1982	—	—	.10	.15
	1983	1.100	—	.10	.15

F.A.O. Issue

KM#	Date	Mintage	VF	XF	Unc
21	1975	2.500	—	.10	.15

COPPER PLATED STEEL

KM#	Date	Mintage	VF	XF	Unc
39	1986	2.000	—	—	.15
	1987	10.000	—	—	.15

2 CENTS

BRONZE

KM#	Date	Mintage	VF	XF	Unc
8	1974	2.252	—	.15	.25
	1974	.013	—	Proof	.75
	1975	—	—	.15	.25
	1979	1.000	—	.15	.25
	1979	.010	—	Proof	1.00
	1982	.500	—	.15	.25

F.A.O. Issue

KM#	Date	Mintage	VF	XF	Unc
22	1975	1.500	—	.15	.25

5 CENTS

2.7500 g, .800 SILVER, .0707 oz ASW
Independence Commemorative

KM#	Date	Mintage	VF	XF	Unc
1	1968	.010	—	Proof	4.00

COPPER-NICKEL
Arum Lily

KM#	Date	Mintage	VF	XF	Unc
9	1974	1.252	.10	.20	.40
	1974	.013	—	Proof	1.00
	1975	1.500	.10	.20	.40
	1979	1.680	.10	.20	.40
	1979	.010	—	Proof	1.75

KM#	Date	Mintage	VF	XF	Unc
40	1986	—	.15	.25	.50

10 CENTS

4.3800 g, .800 SILVER, .1126 oz ASW
Independence Commemorative

KM#	Date	Mintage	VF	XF	Unc
2	1968	.010	—	Proof	6.00

COPPER-NICKEL
Sugar Cane

KM#	Date	Mintage	VF	XF	Unc
10	1974	.752	.15	.25	.50
	1974	.013	—	Proof	1.00
	1979	.500	.15	.25	.50
	1979	4,231	—	Proof	2.50

F.A.O. Issue

KM#	Date	Mintage	VF	XF	Unc
23	1975	1.500	.15	.25	.50

KM#	Date	Mintage	VF	XF	Unc
41	1986	—	—	—	.50

20 CENTS

6.6300 g, .800 SILVER, .1705 oz ASW
Independence Commemorative

KM#	Date	Mintage	VF	XF	Unc
3	1968	.010	—	Proof	7.00

COPPER-NICKEL

KM#	Date	Mintage	VF	XF	Unc
11	1974	.502	.35	.75	1.50
	1974	.013	—	Proof	1.50
	1975	1.000	.35	.75	1.50
	1979	—	.35	.75	1.50
	1979	.010	—	Proof	3.00
	1984	—	.35	.75	1.50

F.A.O. Issue

KM#	Date	Mintage	VF	XF	Unc
31	1981	.150	.25	.50	1.75

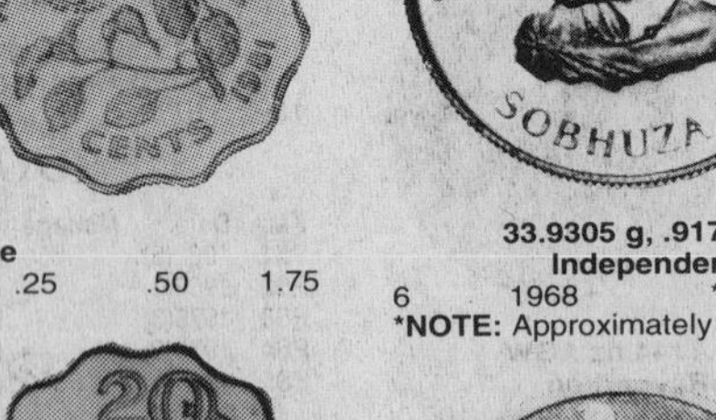

KM#	Date	Mintage	VF	XF	Unc
42	1986	—	.35	.75	1.50

50 CENTS

10.3900 g, .800 SILVER, .2672 oz ASW
Independence Commemorative

KM#	Date	Mintage	VF	XF	Unc
4	1968	.010	—	Proof	8.00

COPPER-NICKEL

KM#	Date	Mintage	VF	XF	Unc
12	1974	.252	1.00	1.50	2.50
	1974	.013	—	Proof	3.00
	1975	.500	1.00	1.50	2.50
	1979	—	.50	1.00	2.00
	1979	.010	—	Proof	5.00
	1981	1.150	.50	1.00	2.50

KM#	Date	Mintage	VF	XF	Unc
43	1986	1.000	.40	.80	1.75

LUHLANGA

15.0000 g, .800 SILVER .3858 oz ASW
Independence Commemorative

KM#	Date	Mintage	VF	XF	Unc
5	1968	.010	—	Proof	10.00

LILANGENI

33.9305 g, .917 GOLD, 1.0000 oz AGW
Independence Commemorative

KM#	Date	Mintage	VF	XF	Unc
6	1968	*2,000	—	Proof	650.00

*NOTE: Approximately 1,450 melted.

COPPER-NICKEL

KM#	Date	Mintage	VF	XF	Unc
13	1974	.127	1.50	2.50	4.00
	1974	.013	—	Proof	5.00
	1979	—	1.00	2.00	4.00
	1979	.110	—	Proof	6.00

F.A.O. Issue And International Women's Year

KM#	Date	Mintage	VF	XF	Unc
24	1975	.100	1.50	2.50	4.50

F.A.O. Issue

KM#	Date	Mintage	VF	XF	Unc
28	1976	.100	1.50	2.50	4.50

15.5500 g, .999 GOLD, .5000 oz AGW
80th Anniversary of Birth of King Sobhuza II
Rev: Dates 1921-1979.

M#	Date	Mintage	VF	XF	Unc
9.1	1979	1,250	—	—	250.00
	1979	Inc. Ab.	—	Proof	275.00

Rev: Dates 1923-1979.

9.2	1979	—	—	—	300.00

COPPER-NICKEL
F.A.O. Issue

2	1981	.871	1.50	3.00	7.00

11.6600 g, .925 SILVER, .3468 oz ASW

2a	1981	5,000	—	—	15.00
	1981	5,000	—	Proof	20.00

NICKEL-BRASS

	1986	1.025	—	—	4.00
	1992	—	—	—	2.50

2 EMALANGENI

17.0000 g, .925 SILVER, .5056 oz ASW
Diamond Jubilee of King Sobhuza II

	1981	—	—	Proof	10.00

COPPER-NICKEL

a	1981	.050	2.00	4.00	6.00

5 EMALANGENI

10.3000 g, .925 SILVER, .3063 oz ASW
75th Anniversary of Birth of King Sobhuza II

	1974	—	—	Proof	17.50

5.5600 g, .900 GOLD, .1609 oz AGW
75th Anniversary of Birth of King Sobhuza II

KM#	Date	Mintage	VF	XF	Unc
15	1974	.060	—	Proof	100.00

7-1/2 EMALANGENI

16.2000 g, .925 SILVER, .4818 oz ASW
75th Anniversary of Birth of King Sobhuza II

16	1974	—	—	Proof	55.00

10 EMALANGENI

11.1200 g, .900 GOLD, .3218 oz AGW
75th Anniversary of Birth of King Sobhuza II

17	1974	.040	—	Proof	275.00

25.5000 g, .925 SILVER, .7584 oz ASW
75th Anniversary of Birth of King Sobhuza II

25	1975	*1,000	—	—	40.00
	1975	*1,500	—	Proof	55.00

15 EMALANGENI

32.6000 g, .925 SILVER, .9696 oz ASW
75th Anniversary of Birth of King Sobhuza II
Obv: Similar to 25 Emalangeni, KM#20.

KM#	Date	Mintage	VF	XF	Unc
18	1974	—	—	Proof	55.00

NOTE: Stamped serial number of issue on reverse.

20 EMALANGENI

22.2300 g, .900 GOLD, .6433 oz AGW
75th Anniversary of Birth of King Sobhuza II

19	1974	*.025	—	Proof	320.00

25 EMALANGENI

27.7800 g, .900 GOLD, .8039 oz AGW
75th Anniversary of Birth of King Sobhuza II

20	1974	*.015	—	—	425.00

28.2800 g, .925 SILVER, .8411 oz ASW

Diamond Jubilee of King Sobhuza II

KM#	Date	Mintage	VF	XF	Unc
34	1981	*.010	—	—	35.00
	1981	*.010	—	Proof	50.00

Accession of King Makhosetive
Similar to 250 Emalangeni, KM#38.

KM#	Date	Mintage	VF	XF	Unc
37	1986	*2,500	—	Proof	45.00

50 EMALANGENI

4.3100 g, .900 GOLD, .1247 oz AGW
75th Anniversary of Birth of King Sobhuza II

KM#	Date	Mintage	VF	XF	Unc
26	1975	3,510	—	—	70.00
	1975	3,262	—	Proof	85.00

100 EMALANGENI

8.6400 g, .900 GOLD, .2500 oz AGW
75th Anniversary of Birth of King Sobhuza II

KM#	Date	Mintage	VF	XF	Unc
27	1975	1,000	—	—	150.00
	1975	1,000	—	Proof	235.00

250 EMALANGENI

15.9800 g, .917 GOLD, .4711 oz AGW
Diamond Jubilee of King Sobhuza II

KM#	Date	Mintage	VF	XF	Unc
35	1981	2,000	—	—	225.00
	1981	2,000	—	Proof	350.00

Accession of King Makhosetive

KM#	Date	Mintage	VF	XF	Unc
38	1986	250 pcs.	—	—	275.00
	1986	250 pcs.	—	Proof	375.00

GOLD BULLION ISSUES

2 EMALANGENI

31.1000 g, .999 GOLD, 1.0000 oz AGW
80th Anniversary of Birth of King Sobhuza II

KM#	Date	Mintage	VF	XF	Unc
30	1979	1,250	—	—	450.00
	1979	Inc. Ab.	—	Proof	550.00

5 EMALANGENI

31.1000 g, .999 GOLD, 1.0000 oz AGW
Queen Elizabeth II Silver Jubilee

KM#	Date	Mintage	VF	XF	Unc
36	1978	—	—	Proof	550.00

MINT SETS (MS)

KM#	Date	Mintage	Identification	Issue Price	Mkt. Val.
MS1	1974(7)	—	KM7-13	10.00	9.00
MS2	1975(3)	1,000	KM25-27	—	260.00
MS3	1986(6)	—	KM39-44	—	8.00

PROOF SETS (PS)

KM#	Date	Mintage	Identification	Issue Price	Mkt. Val.
PS1	1968(5)	10,000	KM1-5	25.80	35.00
PS2	1974(7)	20,000	KM7-13	18.00	13.00
PS3	1974(4)	—	KM15,17,19,20	745.00	1000.
PS4	1974(3)	—	KM14,16,17	70.00	350.00
PS5	1975(3)	1,000	KM25-27	—	375.00
PS6	1975(2)	25,000	KM26-27	252.00	320.00
PS7	1979(7)	3,231	KM7-13	34.00	20.00
PS8	1979(2)	—	KM29.1,30	1172.	825.00

SWEDEN

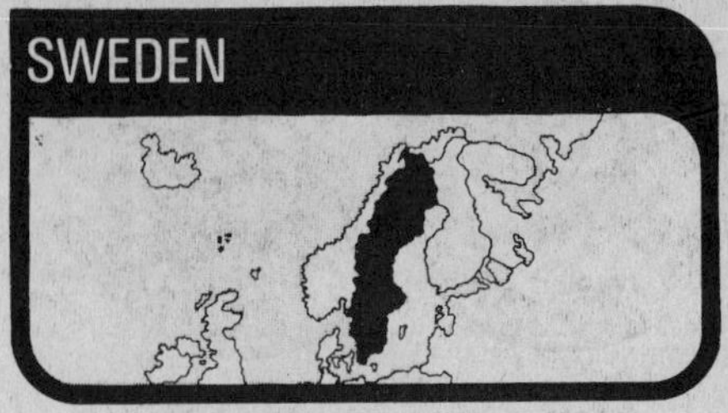

The Kingdom of Sweden, a limited constitutional monarchy located in northern Europe between Norway and Finland, has an area of 173,732 sq. mi. (449,960 sq. km.) and a population of *8.5 million. Capital: Stockholm. Mining, lumbering and a specialized machine industry dominate the economy. Machinery, paper, iron and steel, motor vehicles and wood pulp are exported.

Sweden was founded as a Christian stronghold by Olaf Skottkonung late in the 10th century. After conquering Finland late in the 13th century, Sweden, together with Norway, came under the rule of Denmark, 1397-1523, in an association known as the Union of Kalmar. Modern Sweden had its beginning in 1523 when Gustavus Vasa drove the Danes out of Sweden and was himself chosen king. Under Gustavus Adolphus II and Charles XII, Sweden was one of the great powers of 17th century Europe - until Charles invaded Russia in 1708, and was defeated at the Battle of Pultowa in June, 1709. Early in the 18th century, a coalition of Russia, Poland and Denmark took away Sweden's Baltic empire and in 1809 Sweden was forced to cede Finland to Russia. Norway was ceded to Sweden by the Treaty of Kiel in January, 1814. The Norwegians resisted for a time but later signed the Act of Union at the Convention of Moss in August, 1814. The Union was dissolved in 1905 and Norway became independent. A new constitution which took effect on Jan. 1, 1975, restricts the function of the king largely to a ceremonial role.

RULERS

Gustavus IV Adolph, 1792-1809
Charles XIII, 1809-1818
Charles XIV Johan, 1818-1844
Oscar I, 1844-1859
Charles XV, 1859-1872
Oscar II, 1872-1907
Gustavus V, 1907-1950
Gustavus VI, 1950-1973
Charles XVI Gustav, 1973 -

MINTMASTERS INITIALS

Letter	Date	Name
AG,G	1838-1855	Alexander Grandinson
AL	1898-1916	Adolf Lindberg, engraver
CB	1821-1837	Christopher Borg
D	1986	Bengt Dennis
EB	1876-1908	Emil Brusewitz
EL	1916-1944	Erik Lindberg, engraver
G	1799-1830	Lars Grandel, engraver
G	1927-1945	Alf Grabe
LA	1854-1897	Lea Ahlborn, engraver
LB	1819-1821	Lars Bergencreutz
LH	1944-1974	Leo Holmberg, engraver
OL	1773-1819	Olof Lidijn
ST,T	1855-1876	Sebastian Tham
TS	1945-1961	Torsten Swensson
U	1961-1986	Benkt Ulvfot
W	1908-1927	Karl-August Wallroth

MONETARY SYSTEM

1798-1830

48 Skilling = 1 Riksdaler Species
2 Riksdaler (Speciesdaler) = 1 Ducat

1830-1855

32 Skilling Banco = 1 Riksdaler Riksgalds
12 Riksdaler Riksgalds = 3 Riksdaler Species

1855-1873

100 Ore = 4 Riksdaler Riksmynt
4 Riksdaler Riksmynt = 1 Riksdaler Species

Commencing 1873

100 Ore = 1 Riksdaler Riksmynt = 1 Krona

1/12 SKILLING

COPPER

KM#	Date	Mintage	VG	Fine	VF	X
388	1802	2.039	.50	1.00	2.00	6.0
	1803	1.008	.75	1.50	3.00	9.0
	1805	2.526	.50	1.00	2.00	6.0
	1808	3.476	.50	1.00	2.00	6.0

KM#	Date	Mintage	VG	Fine	VF	XF
99	1812	2.880	.75	2.00	6.00	12.00

KM#	Date	Mintage	VG	Fine	VF	XF
17	1825 reeded edge					
		.576	1.50	3.00	7.00	15.00
	1825 plain edge					
		—	4.00	8.00	15.00	35.00

1/6 SKILLING

COPPER

KM#	Date	Mintage	VG	Fine	VF	XF
25	1830 reeded edge					
		2.544	.50	1.50	4.00	10.00
	1830 plain edge					
		Inc. Ab.	1.00	3.00	7.00	15.00
	1831	Inc. Ab.	2.50	5.00	10.00	20.00

Draped bust w/pearl border.

KM#	Date	Mintage	VG	Fine	VF	XF
33.1	1832	.912	6.50	12.50	25.00	50.00

Plain border

KM#	Date	Mintage	VG	Fine	VF	XF
33.2	1832	Inc. Ab.	1.50	3.00	6.00	12.00

Obv: Naked bust w/pearl border.

KM#	Date	Mintage	VG	Fine	VF	XF
34	1832	Inc. Ab.	5.00	10.00	20.00	40.00

KM#	Date	Mintage	VG	Fine	VF	XF
38	1835	.538	.50	1.00	3.00	8.00
	1836/5	1.498	.50	1.00	2.50	7.50
	1836	Inc. Ab.	.50	1.00	2.50	7.50
	1838	.427	1.25	3.50	6.00	17.50
	1839	.827	.50	1.00	3.00	8.00
	1840/35	.860	.60	1.30	4.00	10.00
	1840	Inc. Ab.	.50	1.00	3.00	8.00
	1843/35	.865	1.75	3.50	8.50	21.50
	1843	Inc. Ab.	1.25	2.50	6.00	15.00
	1844	.071	30.00	60.00	120.00	180.00

KM#	Date	Mintage	VG	Fine	VF	XF
51	1844/35	.291	5.00	10.00	20.00	40.00
	1844	Inc. Ab.	.50	1.25	3.00	9.00
	1845	.092	2.00	4.00	10.00	30.00
	1846	.067	2.00	4.00	10.00	30.00
	1847	.823	.50	1.00	2.50	7.50
	1849	.537	.50	1.00	2.50	7.50
	1850	.407	1.00	2.00	5.00	15.00
	1851	.486	.50	1.00	2.50	7.50
	1852	.462	.50	1.00	2.50	7.50
	1853	.126	1.50	3.00	7.50	22.50
	1854	.422	.50	1.00	2.50	7.50
	1855	.311	.50	1.00	2.50	7.50

1/4 SKILLING

COPPER

KM#	Date	Mintage	VG	Fine	VF	XF
389	1802	3.383	.75	1.50	4.00	12.00
	1803	3.217	.75	1.50	4.00	12.00
	1805	5.189	.75	1.50	4.00	12.00
	1806	8.141	.75	1.50	4.00	12.00
	1807	.641	1.00	2.00	5.50	17.50
	1808 narrow crown					
		7.480	1.00	2.00	5.00	15.00
	1808 wider crown					
		Inc. Ab.	.75	1.50	4.00	12.00

KM#	Date	Mintage	VG	Fine	VF	XF
407	1817	1.152	10.00	25.00	50.00	100.00

KM#	Date	Mintage	VG	Fine	VF	XF
410	1819	2.450	.50	1.50	5.00	25.00
	1820	2.610	.50	1.50	5.00	25.00
	1821	2.208	.50	1.50	5.00	25.00
	1824 space between crown & monogram					
		.768	1.00	3.00	10.00	40.00
	1824 crown touches monogram					
		Inc. Ab.	1.00	3.00	10.00	40.00
	1825 open 4 in denomination					
		2.496	.50	1.50	5.00	25.00
	1825 closed 4 in denomination					
		Inc. Ab.	.50	1.50	5.00	25.00
	1827 open 4 in denomination					
		3.200	.50	1.50	5.00	25.00
	1827 closed 4 in denomination					
		Inc. Ab.	.50	1.50	5.00	25.00
	1828	4.320	.50	1.50	5.00	25.00
	1829	4.896	.50	1.50	5.00	25.00
	1830	.256	1.00	3.00	10.00	40.00

KM#	Date	Mintage	VG	Fine	VF	XF
435	1832	.160	5.00	10.00	35.00	70.00
	1833/2	.096	3.50	7.00	20.00	40.00

1/3 SKILLING

COPPER

KM#	Date	Mintage	VG	Fine	VF	XF
439	1835	.483	2.50	5.00	15.00	35.00
	1836	.985	1.00	2.00	6.00	17.50
	1837	1.096	1.00	2.00	6.00	17.50
	1839/37	.921	3.00	6.00	18.00	40.00
	1839	Inc. Ab.	1.00	2.00	6.00	17.50
	1840/37	.692	4.00	8.00	22.00	50.00
	1840	Inc. Ab.	1.00	2.00	6.00	17.50
	1841	.013	25.00	50.00	100.00	150.00
	1842	.612	1.00	2.00	6.00	17.50
	1843	.593	1.00	2.00	6.00	17.50

KM#	Date	Mintage	VG	Fine	VF	XF
452	1844	.226	1.00	2.00	5.00	15.00
	1845	.192	1.00	2.00	5.00	15.00
	1846	.079	2.50	5.00	10.00	30.00
	1847	.783	1.00	2.00	5.00	15.00
	1848/7	.933	1.50	2.75	7.00	21.50
	1848	Inc. Ab.	1.00	2.00	5.00	15.00
	1850 BANCO					
		.537	1.00	2.00	5.00	15.00
	1850 BANCO w/2 dots above A (error)					
		Inc. Ab.	4.00	8.00	20.00	60.00
	1851	.538	1.00	2.00	5.00	15.00
	1852	.489	1.00	2.00	5.00	15.00
	1853	.070	2.50	5.00	10.00	30.00
	1854	.495	1.00	2.00	5.00	15.00
	1855	.377	1.00	2.00	5.00	15.00

1/2 SKILLING

COPPER

Obv: 3 crowns on orb. Rev: Value, date.

KM#	Date	Mintage	VG	Fine	VF	XF
379	1801	3.203	1.00	2.50	5.00	20.00
	1802	1.188	1.00	2.50	5.00	20.00

NOTE: Earlier dates (1799-1800) exist for this type.

KM#	Date	Mintage	VG	Fine	VF	XF
390	1802	*2.340	1.00	3.00	7.00	20.00
	1803	*5.048	1.00	3.00	7.00	20.00
	1804	(.595)	35.00	100.00	225.00	500.00
	1805	*.173	1.25	3.00	7.00	20.00
	1807	1.950	1.25	4.00	8.00	25.00
	1809	4.845	1.25	4.00	8.00	25.00

***NOTE:** Struck over 18th century 1 ore - worth 50 per cent to 100 per cent more if earlier date visible.

KM#	Date	Mintage	VG	Fine	VF	XF
404	1815	1.421	2.00	6.00	15.00	30.00
	1816	.566	2.50	9.00	18.00	37.50
	1817	Inc. Ab.	3.00	12.50	25.00	50.00

KM#	Date	Mintage	VG	Fine	VF	XF
411	1819	1.264	1.00	2.50	7.50	30.00
	1820	1.296	1.00	2.50	7.50	30.00
	1821	1.840	1.00	2.50	7.50	30.00
	1822	.944	1.00	2.50	7.50	30.00
	1822 L & S reversed					
		Inc. Ab.	31.00	64.00	145.00	409.00
	1824	.640	1.00	2.50	7.50	30.00
	1825	.816	2.00	4.00	15.00	60.00
	1827 SKIL-LING					
		.800	1.00	2.50	7.50	30.00
	1827 SKIL LING					
		Inc. Ab.	5.00	10.00	25.00	75.00
	1828	1.872	1.00	2.50	7.50	30.00
	1829	2.560	1.00	2.50	7.50	30.00
	1830	.588	1.50	3.50	10.00	35.00

KM#	Date	Mintage	VG	Fine	VF	XF
436	1832	.288	3.50	7.00	20.00	40.00
	1833	3 pcs.	—	—	Rare	—

2/3 SKILLING

COPPER

KM#	Date	Mintage	VG	Fine	VF	XF
440	1835	.198	3.00	6.00	20.00	60.00
	1836	.928	1.50	3.00	10.00	30.00
	1837	1.026	1.50	3.00	10.00	35.00
	1839	.654	1.50	3.00	10.00	35.00
	1840	.646	1.50	3.00	10.00	35.00
	1842	.526	1.50	3.00	10.00	35.00
	1843	.626	1.50	3.00	10.00	35.00

KM#	Date	Mintage	VG	Fine	VF	XF
453	1844	.266	3.50	7.00	20.00	60.00
	1845/4	.495	4.00	8.50	25.00	70.00
	1845	Inc. Ab.	3.50	7.00	20.00	60.00

Redesigned smaller head

KM#	Date	Mintage	VG	Fine	VF	XF
458	1845/4	Inc. KM453	3.00	6.50	18.50	55.00
	1845	Inc. KM453	2.50	5.00	15.00	45.00
	1846/4	.123	1.90	3.75	12.50	37.50
	1846	Inc. Ab.	1.50	3.00	10.00	30.00
	1847	.089	1.50	3.00	10.00	30.00
	1849/4	.219	2.00	4.00	13.50	40.00
	1849	Inc. Ab.	1.50	3.00	10.00	30.00
	1850	.329	1.50	3.00	10.00	30.00
	1851	.467	1.50	3.00	10.00	30.00
	1852	.297	1.50	3.00	10.00	30.00
	1853	.052	4.00	8.00	25.00	75.00
	1854	.408	1.50	3.00	10.00	30.00
	1855	.506	1.50	3.00	10.00	30.00

SKILLING

COPPER

KM#	Date	Mintage	VG	Fine	VF	XF
391	1802	—	3.00	7.00	15.00	60.00
	1803	—	6.00	14.00	30.00	100.00
	1805	—	3.00	7.00	15.00	60.00

NOTE: Struck over 18th century 2 Ore - worth 50 percent to 100 percent more if earlier date visible.

KM#	Date	Mintage	VG	Fine	VF	XF
400	1812	.480	4.00	10.00	27.50	55.00
	1814	.730	4.00	12.00	30.00	60.00
	1815	Inc. Ab.	4.00	10.00	27.50	55.00
	1816	.230	4.00	10.00	27.50	55.00
	1817	.202	6.00	15.00	35.00	75.00

KM#	Date	Mintage	VG	Fine	VF	XF
412	1819	1.176	1.50	5.00	15.00	60.00
	1820 oblique milling	1.376	1.50	5.00	15.00	60.00
	1820 square milling	Inc. Ab.	6.00	12.50	40.00	100.00
	1821	.704	1.50	5.00	15.00	60.00
	1822	.520	2.00	6.00	17.50	70.00
	1825	.472	1.50	5.00	15.00	50.00
	1827	.504	1.50	5.00	15.00	60.00
	1828	.664	1.50	5.00	15.00	60.00
	1829	.344	1.50	4.00	15.00	60.00
	1830	.312	2.50	6.00	17.50	70.00

KM#	Date	Mintage	VG	Fine	VF	XF
437	1832	8,000	50.00	100.00	250.00	450.00

KM#	Date	Mintage	VG	Fine	VF	XF
441	1835 wide wreath	.186	50.00	100.00	250.00	500.00
	1835 narrow wreath	Inc. Ab.	3.00	6.00	15.00	45.00
	1836/5	.651	4.00	8.00	20.00	60.00
	1836	Inc. Ab.	3.00	6.00	15.00	45.00
	1837	.628	5.00	10.00	25.00	60.00
	1838	.140	5.00	10.00	25.00	60.00
	1839	.360	5.00	10.00	25.00	60.00
	1840	.278	5.00	10.00	25.00	60.00
	1842	.499	5.00	10.00	25.00	60.00
	1843	.361	5.00	10.00	25.00	60.00

Large head of Oscar I.

KM#	Date	Mintage	VG	Fine	VF	XF
454	1844	.093	6.00	12.00	30.00	90.00
	1845/4	.097	6.00	12.00	30.00	90.00

Redesigned, smaller head.

KM#	Date	Mintage	VG	Fine	VF	XF
466	1847	.150	3.00	6.00	15.00	45.00
	1849	.306	3.00	6.00	15.00	45.00
	1850	.137	3.00	6.00	15.00	45.00
	1851	.151	3.00	6.00	15.00	45.00
	1852	.154	3.00	6.00	15.00	45.00
	1853	.031	6.00	12.00	30.00	90.00
	1854	.064	3.00	6.00	15.00	45.00
	1855	.040	5.00	10.00	25.00	75.00

2 SKILLING

COPPER

KM#	Date	Mintage	VG	Fine	VF	XF
442	1835	.079	10.00	20.00	60.00	200.00
	1836 wide wreath	.583	120.00	250.00	500.00	1000.
	1836 narrow wreath	Inc. Ab.	3.50	7.50	22.50	75.00
	1837	.388	4.00	8.00	25.00	80.00
	1839	.270	4.00	8.00	25.00	80.00
	1840	.069	5.00	10.00	30.00	90.00
	1841	.093	5.00	10.00	30.00	90.00
	1842	.123	5.00	10.00	30.00	90.00
	1843	.162	5.00	10.00	30.00	100.00

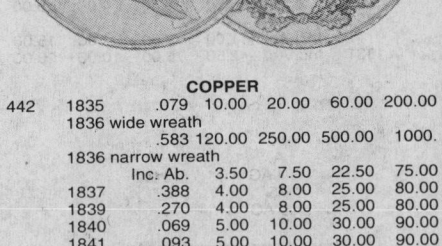

KM#	Date	Mintage	VG	Fine	VF	XF
455	1844	.089	7.50	15.00	50.00	150.00
	1845	.120	7.50	15.00	50.00	150.00

Obv: Smaller head. Rev: Similar to KM#442.

KM#	Date	Mintage	VG	Fine	VF	XF
459	1845	Inc. Ab.	7.50	15.00	45.00	135.00
	1846	.056	6.00	12.00	35.00	100.00
	1847	.115	5.00	12.00	35.00	100.00
	1849	.138	5.00	12.00	35.00	100.00
	1850	.081	5.00	12.00	35.00	100.00
	1851	.083	5.00	12.00	35.00	100.00
	1852	.061	5.00	12.00	35.00	100.00
	1853	.023	8.00	15.00	50.00	150.00
	1854	.038	5.00	12.00	35.00	100.00
	1855	.011	8.00	15.00	50.00	150.00

4 SKILLING

COPPER

M#	Date	Mintage	VG	Fine	VF	XF
67	1849	.444	4.00	8.00	30.00	90.00
	1850	.170	6.00	12.00	40.00	120.00
	1851	.038	7.50	15.00	50.00	150.00
	1852	.038	7.50	15.00	50.00	150.00
	1855	.074	6.00	12.00	40.00	120.00
	1855 denomination and BANCO larger	Inc. Ab.	10.00	20.00	70.00	200.00

1/32 RIKSDALER

1.0600 g, .750 SILVER, .0255 oz ASW

KM#	Date	Mintage	VG	Fine	VF	XF
71	1851 AG	—	—	—	Rare	—
	1852/1 AG	.480	1.50	3.50	7.00	25.00
	1852 AG	I.A.	1.00	2.50	5.00	15.00
	1853 AG small AG	.775	1.00	2.50	5.00	15.00
	1853 AG large AG	Inc. Ab.	1.00	2.50	5.00	15.00

1/24 RIKSDALER

.382 SILVER

KM#	Date	Mintage	VG	Fine	VF	XF
95	1810 OL	.742	3.50	7.00	20.00	60.00
	1811 OL	.378	4.00	8.00	20.00	60.00
	1812 OL	.537	4.00	8.00	20.00	60.00
	1813 OL	.444	4.00	8.00	20.00	60.00
	1814 OL	.101	5.00	10.00	30.00	75.00
	1816 OL	.160	5.00	10.00	30.00	75.00

1/16 RIKSDALER

2.1300 g, .750 SILVER, .0513 oz ASW

KM#	Date	Mintage	VG	Fine	VF	XF
43	1835 CB	.433	4.00	8.00	15.00	40.00
	1836/5 CB	.088	6.00	15.00	25.00	60.00

KM#	Date	Mintage	VG	Fine	VF	XF
60	1845 AG	4,185	12.50	25.00	50.00	100.00
	1846/5 AG	.034	11.50	22.50	45.00	90.00
	1846 AG	I.A.	10.00	20.00	40.00	80.00
	1848/5 AG	4.173	—	—	—	—
	1848 AG	I.A.	1.50	4.00	8.00	25.00
	1849 AG	—	—	—	Rare	—
	1850 AG	1.006	2.00	5.00	10.00	30.00
	1851 AG	.847	2.00	5.00	10.00	30.00
	1852 AG	.934	2.00	5.00	10.00	30.00
	1855 AG	.830	2.00	5.00	10.00	30.00

1/12 RIKSDALER

.507 SILVER

KM#	Date	Mintage	VG	Fine	VF	XF
398	1811 OL	.735	12.00	30.00	65.00	150.00

2.8300 g, .750 SILVER, .0682 oz ASW

KM#	Date	Mintage	VG	Fine	VF	XF
430	1831 CB	.212	6.50	12.00	25.00	50.00
	1832/1 CB	1.463	6.50	13.50	25.00	40.00
	1832 CB	I.A.	5.00	10.00	20.00	40.00
	1833/1 CB	.157	7.50	15.00	32.50	60.00
	1833 CB	I.A.	6.00	12.00	25.00	50.00

1/8 RIKSDALER

4.2500 g, .750 SILVER, .1024 oz ASW

KM#	Date	Mintage	VG	Fine	VF	XF
426	1830 CB reeded edge	1.796	12.50	25.00	50.00	100.00
	1830 CB stars & flowers on edge	Inc. Ab.	37.50	75.00	150.00	300.00
	1831 CB	1.470	3.50	7.00	15.00	40.00
	1832 CB	2.829	3.00	6.00	12.00	35.00
	1833 CB	1.032	3.50	7.00	15.00	40.00
	1834 CB	.103	6.00	12.00	25.00	60.00
	1835 CB	.103	6.00	12.00	25.00	60.00
	1836 CB	9.024	15.00	30.00	60.00	100.00
	1837 CB	4,818	17.50	35.00	70.00	120.00

KM#	Date	Mintage	VG	Fine	VF	XF
472	1852 AG	.046	40.00	80.00	175.00	350.00

1/6 RIKSDALER

6.2500 g, .691 SILVER, .1388 oz ASW

KM#	Date	Mintage	VG	Fine	VF	XF
385	1801 OL	.420	10.00	25.00	50.00	100.00
	1802 OL	1.254	7.00	17.50	40.00	75.00
	1803 OL	2.341	7.00	17.50	40.00	75.00
	1804 OL	2.156	7.00	17.50	40.00	75.00
	1805 OL	.978	7.00	17.50	40.00	75.00
	1806 OL	.341	8.00	20.00	45.00	85.00
	1807 OL	.909	7.00	17.50	40.00	75.00
	1808 OL	.943	7.00	17.50	40.00	75.00
	1809 OL	.707	8.00	20.00	45.00	85.00

NOTE: Earlier date (1800) exists for this type.

KM#	Date	Mintage	VG	Fine	VF	XF
393	1809 OL	—	50.00	120.00	225.00	450.00
	1810 OL	.297	15.00	30.00	80.00	225.00
	1814/0 OL	.199	20.00	45.00	90.00	225.00
	1814 OL	I.A.	20.00	45.00	90.00	225.00

Obv: NORR in legends.

KM#	Date	Mintage	VG	Fine	VF	XF
405	1815 OL	.059	60.00	135.00	300.00	550.00
	1817 OL	.091	60.00	125.00	275.00	500.00

KM#	Date	Mintage	VG	Fine	VF	XF
413	1819 OL	.052	30.00	60.00	125.00	300.00
	1826 CB	1,974	45.00	90.00	180.00	400.00

6.1900 g, .691 SILVER, .1375 oz ASW

KM#	Date	Mintage	VG	Fine	VF	XF
421	1828 CB edge inscription	1,974	—	—	Rare	—
	1828 CB w/o edge inscription	1,024	—	—	Rare	—
	1829 CB	2,039	20.00	40.00	80.00	175.00

1/4 RIKSDALER

8.5000 g, .750 SILVER, .2049 oz ASW

KM#	Date	Mintage	VG	Fine	VF	XF
427	1830 CB	.704	10.00	25.00	50.00	100.00
	1831 CB	2.470	8.00	20.00	40.00	90.00
	1832 CB	.522	10.00	25.00	50.00	100.00
	1833 CB	.063	18.00	35.00	75.00	150.00
	1834/3 CB	.953	9.00	20.00	45.00	95.00
	1834 CB	I.A.	8.00	20.00	40.00	90.00
	1836 CB	2,766	50.00	100.00	225.00	450.00

NOTE: Previously listed 1830 plain edge variety is normal but a weakly struck example.

KM#	Date	Mintage	VG	Fine	VF	XF
464	1846/4 AG	.221	20.00	45.00	90.00	200.00
	1848/4 AG	.130	20.00	45.00	90.00	200.00
	1852/44 AG	—	—	—	Rare	—
	1852 AG	—	—	—	Rare	—

1/3 RIKSDALER

.878 SILVER

KM#	Date	Mintage	VG	Fine	VF	XF
402	1813 OL	.063	115.00	235.00	400.00	800.00
	1814 OL	.033	135.00	275.00	500.00	950.00

9.7500 g, .878 SILVER, .2752 oz ASW

KM#	Date	Mintage	VG	Fine	VF	XF
418	1827 CB	—	—	—	Rare	—
	1828 CB	.061	50.00	100.00	200.00	400.00
	1829 CB	.109	50.00	100.00	200.00	425.00

NOTE: Previously listed 1828 and 1829 plain edge varieties are normal but weakly struck examples.

1/2 RIKSDALER

17.0000 g, .750 SILVER, .4099 oz ASW

KM#	Date	Mintage	VG	Fine	VF	XF
431	1831 CB	.270	45.00	90.00	150.00	335.00
	1832 CB	.142	80.00	150.00	275.00	550.00
	1833/1 CB	.191	70.00	140.00	225.00	450.00
	1833 CB	I.A.	70.00	140.00	225.00	450.00
	1836/1 CB	2,482	130.00	235.00	425.00	850.00
	1836 CB	I.A.	125.00	225.00	400.00	800.00
	1838 CB	4 pcs.	—	—	Rare	—

NOTE: Previously listed 1831 plain edge variety is normal but a weakly struck example.

KM#	Date	Mintage	VG	Fine	VF	XF
461	1845 AG	.022	90.00	180.00	360.00	725.00
	1846/5 AG	.082	85.00	175.00	345.00	685.00
	1846 AG	I.A.	75.00	145.00	285.00	600.00
	1848/7 AG	.074	60.00	125.00	275.00	650.00
	1848/5 AG	I.A.	60.00	125.00	275.00	650.00
	1848 AG	I.A.	50.00	100.00	220.00	500.00
	1852/45 AG	1,104	1000.	1500.	2650.	4600.
	1852 AG	I.A.	1000.	1500.	2650.	4500.

RIKSDALER

29.3600 g, .878 SILVER, .8287 oz ASW

KM#	Date	Mintage	VG	Fine	VF	XF
386	1801 OL	.091	80.00	175.00	360.00	725.00
	1805 OL	.150	80.00	175.00	350.00	650.00
	1806 OL	.205	70.00	150.00	300.00	550.00
	1807 OL	.037	80.00	175.00	350.00	650.00

KM#	Date	Mintage	VG	Fine	VF	XF
401	1812 OL	.043	100.00	200.00	400.00	800.00
	1814/2 OL	Inc. Ab.	125.00	250.00	450.00	900.00
	1814 OL	6,600	125.00	250.00	450.00	900.00

Obv: NORR added to legend

KM#	Date	Mintage	VG	Fine	VF	XF
403	1814 OL	I.A.	250.00	600.00	1200.	2200.
	1815 OL	.066	100.00	200.00	350.00	750.00
	1816/5 OL	.012	100.00	200.00	400.00	800.00
	1816 OL	I.A.	100.00	200.00	400.00	800.00
	1817 OL	9,895	125.00	250.00	500.00	1000.
	1818 OL	.015	165.00	325.00	650.00	1250.

29.2500 g, .878 SILVER, .8256 oz ASW

KM#	Date	Mintage	VG	Fine	VF	XF
408	1818 OL	Inc. KM403	65.00	125.00	325.00	750.00
	1819 OL	.014	100.00	200.00	450.00	950.00
	1819 LB	I.A.	75.00	175.00	400.00	900.00
	1820 LB large bust	.011	150.00	250.00	500.00	1000.
	1820 LB small bust	Inc. Ab.	150.00	250.00	500.00	1000.
	1820 LB bust of Charles XIII	Inc. Ab.	—	—	Rare	—
	1821 LB	.029	50.00	100.00	300.00	550.00

KM#	Date	Mintage	VG	Fine	VF	XF
408	1822 CB	.034	40.00	80.00	200.00	500.00
	1823 CB large bust	.026	40.00	80.00	200.00	500.00
	1823 CB small bust	Inc. Ab.	40.00	80.00	200.00	500.00
	1824 CB	.053	40.00	80.00	200.00	500.00
	1825 CB	.020	40.00	80.00	200.00	500.00
	1826 CB	7,538	75.00	150.00	350.00	750.00
	1827 CB	.017	40.00	80.00	200.00	500.00

300 Years of Political and Religious Freedom

KM#	Date	Mintage	VG	Fine	VF	XF
415	1821 CB	7,339	60.00	125.00	250.00	450.00

Obv: Similar to KM#420.
Rev: 7 angel heads around arms.

KM#	Date	Mintage	VG	Fine	VF	XF
419	1827 CB	610 pcs.	250.00	500.00	1000.	1500

Rev: 9 angel heads around arms.

KM#	Date	Mintage	VG	Fine	VF	XF
420	1827 CB	I.A.	350.00	750.00	1500.	3000
	1829 CB	409 pcs.	400.00	800.00	1650.	3500

34.0000 g, .750 SILVER, .8198 oz ASW

KM#	Date	Mintage	VG	Fine	VF	XF
432	1831 CB	.047	35.00	70.00	175.00	350.00
	1832/1 CB	2,100	175.00	350.00	750.00	1350.
	1832 CB	I.A.	150.00	300.00	650.00	1100.
	1833/1 CB	.039	40.00	80.00	200.00	400.00
	1833 CB	I.A.	35.00	70.00	175.00	350.00
	1834/1 CB	.068	30.00	60.00	150.00	325.00
	1834 CB	I.A.	30.00	60.00	150.00	300.00
	1835 CB	.331	30.00	60.00	150.00	300.00
	1836 CB	.093	35.00	70.00	175.00	350.00
	1837 CB	.177	30.00	60.00	150.00	300.00
	1837 CB-G	I.A.	60.00	125.00	300.00	600.00
	1838 AG	.834	30.00	60.00	150.00	300.00
	1838 AG-G	I.A.	70.00	150.00	350.00	700.00
	1839 AG	.212	30.00	60.00	150.00	300.00
	1840 AG	.068	45.00	90.00	225.00	500.00
	1841 AG	.549	30.00	60.00	150.00	300.00
	1842 AG	.288	35.00	70.00	175.00	350.00

NOTE: Previously listed 1834 plain edge variety is normal but a weakly struck example.

Rev: Arms w/3 crowns.

KM#	Date	Mintage	VG	Fine	VF	XF
450	1842 AG	I.A.	35.00	70.00	175.00	350.00
	1843/2AG	3 pcs.	—	—	Rare	—

KM#	Date	Mintage	Fine	VF	XF	Unc
456	1844 AG	.088	60.00	125.00	350.00	500.00
	1845 AG large head	.043	65.00	130.00	400.00	650.00

KM#	Date	Mintage	Fine	VF	XF	Unc
462	1845 AG small head	Inc. KM456	75.00	150.00	400.00	700.00
	1846 AG obv. GOTH.	.111	45.00	100.00	300.00	500.00
	1846 AG obv. GOTH w/o period	Inc. Ab.	45.00	100.00	300.00	550.00
	1847 AG	.060	60.00	125.00	350.00	750.00
	1848 AG	.185	45.00	90.00	275.00	500.00
	1850 AG	.070	50.00	100.00	325.00	550.00
	1851 AG	.122	45.00	90.00	275.00	500.00
	1852 AG	.054	60.00	125.00	350.00	700.00
	1853AG GOTH, small date	.109	45.00	90.00	275.00	500.00
	1853 AG GOTH w/o period, small date	Inc. Ab.	45.00	90.00	275.00	500.00
	1853 large date	Inc. Ab.	50.00	100.00	300.00	575.00
	1854 AG	.034	60.00	125.00	350.00	650.00
	1855 AG small date	.161	45.00	90.00	275.00	500.00
	1855 AG large date	Inc. Ab.	60.00	125.00	350.00	650.00

MONETARY REFORM

100 Ore = 1 Riksdaler Riksmynt
4 Riksdaler Riksmynt = 1 Riksdaler Specie

1/2 ORE

BRONZE

KM#	Date	Mintage	VG	Fine	VF	XF
476	1856	.026	15.00	30.00	60.00	125.00
	1857	1.312	.50	1.00	1.50	5.00
	1858/7	1.849	.75	1.50	3.00	10.00
	1858	Inc. Ab.	.50	1.00	1.50	5.00

KM#	Date	Mintage	VG	Fine	VF	XF
500	1867 lg.dt.	.064	2.50	5.00	10.00	20.00
	1867 small date	Inc. Ab.	4.00	8.00	15.00	30.00

ORE

BRONZE

KM#	Date	Mintage	Fine	VF	XF	Unc
477	1856	.024	35.00	70.00	140.00	300.00
	1857	1.596	1.50	3.00	9.00	20.00
	1858/7	6.290	2.50	5.00	15.00	30.00
	1858 L.A.	I.A.	1.00	2.50	7.50	17.50
	1858 L.A	I.A.	1.00	2.50	7.50	17.50
	1858 LA	I.A.	1.00	2.50	7.50	17.50

KM#	Date	Mintage	Fine	VF	XF	Unc
490	1860/57	.046	15.00	30.00	60.00	125.00
	1860	I.A.	15.00	30.00	60.00	125.00
	1861	.300	3.00	8.00	15.00	30.00
	1862	.079	5.00	12.00	25.00	50.00
	1863	.450	5.00	12.00	25.00	50.00
	1864 L.A.	1.848	1.25	3.00	6.00	15.00
	1864 LA	I.A.	1.25	3.00	6.00	15.00
	1865/2	.561	7.00	15.00	30.00	60.00
	1865/4	I.A.	7.00	15.00	30.00	60.00
	1865	I.A.	2.50	6.00	12.00	27.50
	1866	.327	1.25	3.00	6.00	15.00
	1867	.956	1.25	3.00	6.00	15.00
	1870	1.079	1.25	3.00	6.00	15.00
	1871/61	1.063	2.50	6.00	12.00	25.00
	1871 L.A.	I.A.	1.25	3.00	6.00	15.00
	1871 LA	I.A.	1.25	3.00	6.00	15.00
	1872 L.A.	1.897	1.00	3.00	6.00	12.00
	1872 LA.	I.A.	1.00	3.00	6.00	12.00
	1872 LA	I.A.	1.00	2.50	5.00	10.00

KM#	Date	Mintage	Fine	VF	XF	Unc
508	1873 LA	1.867	3.00	6.00	12.00	25.00
	1873 L.A.	I.A.	3.00	6.00	12.00	25.00
	1873 LA.	I.A.	3.00	6.00	12.00	25.00
	1873 SVFRIGES (error)	I.A.	20.00	40.00	60.00	125.00

2 ORE

BRONZE

KM#	Date	Mintage	Fine	VF	XF	Unc
478	1856	.022	40.00	80.00	150.00	350.00
	1857 long beard	1.143	3.00	7.50	20.00	45.00
	1857 short beard	Inc. Ab.	3.00	7.50	20.00	45.00
	1858/7	2.831	5.00	10.00	30.00	60.00
	1858	Inc. Ab.	3.00	7.50	20.00	40.00

KM#	Date	Mintage	Fine	VF	XF	Unc
491	1860/57	.197	10.00	25.00	50.00	100.00
	1860	Inc. Ab.	10.00	25.00	50.00	100.00
	1861	1.626	2.50	6.00	12.00	25.00
	1862	.213	6.00	15.00	30.00	60.00
	1863/2	1.621	3.00	7.50	15.00	35.00
	1863	Inc. Ab.	2.50	6.00	12.00	25.00
	1864	.600	2.50	6.00	12.00	25.00
	1865	.629	4.00	10.00	20.00	40.00
	1866/5	.400	6.00	15.00	30.00	60.00
	1866	Inc. Ab.	3.00	7.50	15.00	30.00
	1867 L.A.	.428	2.50	6.00	12.00	25.00
	1867 LA	Inc. Ab.	2.50	6.00	12.00	25.00
	1871/61	.718	3.00	7.00	13.50	25.00
	1871	Inc. Ab.	2.50	6.00	12.00	25.00
	1872/1	1.646	5.00	12.00	25.00	50.00
	1872	Inc. Ab.	2.00	5.00	10.00	20.00

KM#	Date	Mintage	Fine	VF	XF	Unc
509	1873	1.294	7.50	15.00	30.00	60.00

NOTE: Previously dated 1873 w/o dots above "O" in GOTH is a weakly struck example.

5 ORE

BRONZE

KM#	Date	Mintage	Fine	VF	XF	Unc
480	1857 small L.A					
		.731	4.00	10.00	35.00	70.00
	1857 large L.A					
		Inc. Ab.	4.00	10.00	35.00	70.00
	1857 curved top 5					
		Inc. Ab.	20.00	60.00	125.00	250.00
	1858/7	1.193	4.00	10.00	35.00	75.00
	1858	Inc. Ab.	10.00	20.00	60.00	125.00

KM#	Date	Mintage	Fine	VF	XF	Unc
492	1860/57	.068	25.00	60.00	120.00	250.00
	1860	Inc. Ab.	20.00	50.00	100.00	200.00
	1861/57	.343	8.00	25.00	50.00	100.00
	1861	Inc. Ab.	6.00	15.00	30.00	60.00
	1862 star	.136	7.00	17.50	35.00	75.00
	1862 rose	I.A.	30.00	75.00	150.00	300.00
	1863/2	.633	6.50	16.50	32.50	85.00
	1863	Inc. Ab.	6.00	15.00	30.00	75.00
	1864/2	.264	6.50	16.50	32.50	85.00
	1864	Inc. Ab.	6.00	15.00	30.00	75.00
	1865	.104	7.00	17.50	35.00	75.00
	1866/5	.120	20.00	50.00	100.00	200.00
	1866	Inc. Ab.	7.00	17.50	35.00	75.00
	1867/6	.741	3.50	11.00	27.50	55.00
	1867	Inc. Ab.	3.00	10.00	25.00	50.00
	1872/66	.620	8.00	20.00	50.00	100.00
	1872	Inc. Ab.	3.00	10.00	25.00	50.00

KM#	Date	Mintage	Fine	VF	XF	Unc
510	1873/2	.783	25.00	40.00	75.00	150.00

NOTE: Previously dated 1873 w/o dots above "O" in GOTH is a weakly struck example.

10 ORE

.8500 g, .750 SILVER, .0204 oz ASW

KM#	Date	Mintage	Fine	VF	XF	Unc
473	1855 AG small AG					
		1.359	15.00	30.00	75.00	165.00
	1855 AG larger AG					
		Inc. Ab.	15.00	30.00	75.00	165.00
	1855 G long beard					
		Inc. Ab.	3.00	7.50	20.00	45.00
	1855 G shorter beard					
		Inc. Ab.	3.00	7.50	20.00	45.00
	1855 T	Inc. Ab.	3.00	7.50	20.00	45.00
	1857 ST	1.007	3.00	7.50	20.00	45.00
	1858/7 ST	.354	5.00	12.00	30.00	65.00
	1858 ST	I.A.	4.00	10.00	25.00	50.00
	1859/7 ST					
		1.684	4.00	10.00	25.00	50.00
	1859/8 ST	I.A.	4.00	10.00	25.00	50.00
	1859 ST	I.A.	3.00	7.50	20.00	45.00

KM#	Date	Mintage	Fine	VF	XF	Unc
495	1861 ST	.579	4.00	10.00	25.00	55.00
	1862 ST	I.A.	300.00	600.00	900.00	1900.
	1863 ST	.449	6.00	15.00	35.00	75.00
	1864 ST	I.A.	4.00	10.00	25.00	50.00
	1865 ST	.560	4.00	10.00	25.00	50.00
	1867 ST	.609	4.00	10.00	25.00	50.00

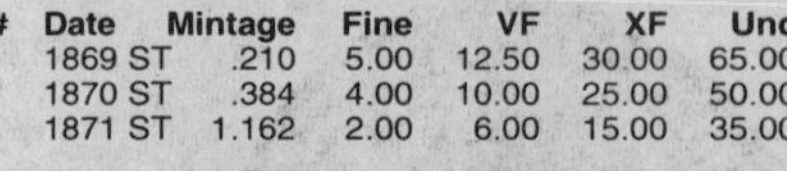

KM#	Date	Mintage	Fine	VF	XF	Unc
495	1869 ST	.210	5.00	12.50	30.00	65.00
	1870 ST	.384	4.00	10.00	25.00	50.00
	1871 ST	1.162	2.00	6.00	15.00	35.00

KM#	Date	Mintage	Fine	VF	XF	Unc
507	1872 ST	.120	60.00	90.00	150.00	225.00
	1873 ST	.635	50.00	75.00	100.00	175.00
	1873 ST inverted A in SVERIGE (error)					
		Inc. Ab.	65.00	130.00	200.00	350.00
	1873 ST SVF.RIGES (error)					
		Inc. Ab.	50.00	100.00	200.00	450.00

25 ORE

2.1300 g, .750 SILVER, .0513 oz ASW

KM#	Date	Mintage	Fine	VF	XF	Unc
474	1855 ST	.437	6.00	15.00	40.00	80.00
	1856 ST	1.763	5.00	12.00	30.00	65.00
	1857/6 ST	.434	12.00	30.00	70.00	140.00
	1857 ST	I.A.	10.00	25.00	65.00	125.00
	1858/7 ST					
		1.183	10.00	25.00	65.00	140.00
	1858 ST	I.A.	10.00	25.00	65.00	140.00
	1859/7 ST	—	6.50	16.50	45.00	90.00
	1859/8 ST	—	6.50	16.50	45.00	90.00
	1859 ST	—	6.00	15.00	40.00	80.00

KM#	Date	Mintage	Fine	VF	XF	Unc
497	1862 ST	1,740	450.00	800.00	1200.	3000.
	1864/2 ST	.266	16.50	32.50	65.00	140.00
	1864 ST	I.A.	15.00	30.00	60.00	125.00
	1865 ST	.400	15.00	30.00	60.00	125.00
	1866 ST	.039	17.50	35.00	70.00	140.00
	1867/6 ST	.198	18.00	37.50	75.00	150.00
	1867 ST	I.A.	15.00	35.00	70.00	125.00
	1871/61 ST					
		.660	12.00	22.50	50.00	100.00
	1871 ST	I.A.	11.00	20.00	45.00	90.00

50 ORE

4.2500 g, .750 SILVER, .1024 oz ASW

KM#	Date	Mintage	Fine	VF	XF	Unc
481	1857 ST	.492	50.00	100.00	200.00	400.00

KM#	Date	Mintage	Fine	VF	XF	Unc
498	1862 ST	2,319	500.00	800.00	1250.	3000.

RIKSDALER RIKSMYNT

8.5000 g, .750 SILVER, .2049 oz ASW
Obv: Short goatee.

KM#	Date	Mintage	Fine	VF	XF	Unc
482	1857 ST	.645	50.00	90.00	180.00	550.00

Obv: Long goatee.

KM#	Date	Mintage	Fine	VF	XF	Unc
483	1857 ST	Inc. Ab.	40.00	80.00	160.00	500.00

KM#	Date	Mintage	Fine	VF	XF	Unc
493	1860 ST	.125	50.00	90.00	180.00	550.00
	1861/0 ST	.158	60.00	100.00	200.00	600.00
	1861 ST	Inc. Ab.	50.00	90.00	180.00	550.00
	1862 ST	—	850.00	1250.	2000.	4500.
	1864 ST	.085	60.00	100.00	200.00	600.00
	1865 ST	.059	100.00	200.00	400.00	900.00
	1867/6 ST	.106	60.00	100.00	225.00	650.00
	1867 ST	Inc. Ab.	50.00	90.00	180.00	550.00
	1871/61 ST					
		.208	60.00	100.00	225.00	650.00
	1871 ST	Inc. Ab.	40.00	80.00	160.00	500.00

NOTE: Previously listed 1864 w/o edge lettering variety is a weakly struck example.

Obv: Deepened hairlines.

KM#	Date	Mintage	Fine	VF	XF	Unc
511	1873 ST	166	350.00	600.00	1000.	1750.

2 RIKSDALER RIKSMYNT

17.0000 g, .750 SILVER, .4099 oz ASW

KM#	Date	Mintage	Fine	VF	XF	Unc
484	1857 ST	.288	120.00	250.00	450.00	950.00

KM#	Date	Mintage	Fine	VF	XF	Unc
499	1862 ST					
		640 pcs.	550.00	1200.	2000.	3500.
	1864/2 ST	.038	200.00	400.00	650.00	1500.
	1864 ST	Inc. Ab.	200.00	400.00	650.00	1500.
	1871 ST small date and large head					
		.019	220.00	425.00	700.00	1600.

Obv: Small head. Rev: Large date.

KM#	Date	Mintage	Fine	VF	XF	Unc
505	1871 ST	Inc. Ab.	150.00	300.00	550.00	1250.

RIKSDALER SPECIE

(4 Riksdaler Riksmynt)

34.0000 g, .750 SILVER, .8198 oz ASW
Obv: Bust right w/short goatee. Rev: Crowned, supported arms, small mintmasters initials.

KM#	Date	Mintage	Fine	VF	XF	Unc
475	1855 ST	2,117	—	—	Rare	—
	1856/5 ST	.776	250.00	500.00	750.00	1500.
	1856 ST	Inc. Ab.	100.00	200.00	400.00	1000.

Obv: Long goatee. Rev: Large mintmasters initials.

KM#	Date	Mintage	Fine	VF	XF	Unc
479	1856 ST	Inc. Ab.	60.00	120.00	300.00	600.00
	1857 ST	.483	60.00	120.00	350.00	700.00
	1859 ST	.101	65.00	135.00	375.00	800.00

KM#	Date	Mintage	Fine	VF	XF	Unc
496	1861 ST	.207	65.00	125.00	275.00	550.00
	1862/1 ST	.943	45.00	90.00	275.00	550.00
	1862 ST L.A., edge lettering large and small					
		Inc. Ab.	45.00	90.00	275.00	550.00
	1862 ST L A					
		Inc. Ab.	45.00	90.00	275.00	550.00
	1862 ST w/o engravers initials					
		Inc. Ab.	90.00	165.00	375.00	750.00
	1862 ST w/o edge lettering					
		Inc. Ab.	140.00	275.00	550.00	1250.
	1863 ST	.268	65.00	135.00	325.00	650.00
	1864 ST	.535	45.00	90.00	275.00	550.00
	1865 ST	.107	65.00	135.00	325.00	650.00
	1866/5 ST	.041	85.00	160.00	375.00	800.00
	1866 ST	Inc. Ab.	80.00	150.00	350.00	700.00
	1867 ST	.064	65.00	135.00	325.00	650.00
	1868 ST	.120	65.00	135.00	325.00	650.00
	1869 ST	.314	40.00	80.00	225.00	450.00
	1870 ST	.161	65.00	135.00	325.00	650.00

NOTE: Previously listed 1862 and 1866 w/o edge lettering varieties are normal but weakly struck examples.

Obv: Larger head.

KM#	Date	Mintage	Fine	VF	XF	Unc
506	1871 ST	.260	40.00	80.00	250.00	500.00

MONETARY REFORM

100 Ore = 1 Krona

DATE VARIETIES

1916 short tailed 6

1936 long tailed 6

ORE

BRONZE

Obv: Small lettering.

KM#	Date	Mintage	Fine	VF	XF	Unc
514	1874	2.370	4.00	9.00	17.50	35.00
	1875/4	2.829	35.00	50.00	85.00	160.00
	1875	Inc. Ab.	4.00	9.00	17.50	35.00
	1876	1.889	17.50	25.00	40.00	85.00
	1877	1.590	9.00	17.50	30.00	65.00

Obv: Large lettering.

KM#	Date	Mintage	Fine	VF	XF	Unc
523	1877	Inc. Ab.	9.00	17.50	30.00	65.00
	1878	1.570	10.00	20.00	30.00	75.00
	1879	1.630	6.00	12.50	25.00	50.00
	1880	1.713	140.00	200.00	375.00	600.00

Obv: Legend lengthened.

KM#	Date	Mintage	Fine	VF	XF	Unc
528	1879	Inc. Ab.	125.00	180.00	325.00	500.00
	1880	Inc. Ab.	12.50	20.00	35.00	70.00
	1881	1.984	5.00	10.00	20.00	40.00
	1882	2.587	3.00	6.00	12.00	25.00
	1883	2.587	3.00	6.00	12.00	25.00
	1884	2.626	3.00	6.00	12.00	25.00
	1885	2.464	3.00	6.00	12.00	25.00
	1886	1.234	4.00	8.00	15.00	35.00
	1888	1.738	4.00	8.00	15.00	35.00
	1889	1.189	4.00	8.00	15.00	35.00
	1890	1.949	2.00	5.00	12.00	25.00
	1891	2.723	2.00	5.00	12.00	25.00
	1892	Inc. Ab.	45.00	65.00	110.00	225.00
	1893	2.145	2.00	5.00	12.00	25.00
	1894	.590	20.00	30.00	45.00	100.00
	1895/3	2.012	8.00	15.00	25.00	60.00
	1895	Inc. Ab.	1.00	3.00	7.00	15.00
	1896	1.463	1.00	3.00	7.00	15.00
	1897	2.544	.50	2.00	4.00	10.00
	1898	2.959	.50	2.00	4.00	10.00
	1899	2.821	.50	2.00	4.00	10.00
	1900	2.929	.50	2.00	4.00	10.00
	1901	3.075	.50	2.00	4.00	10.00
	1902	2.685	.50	2.00	4.00	10.00
	1903	2.696	.50	2.00	4.00	10.00
	1904	2.033	.50	1.00	4.00	10.00
	1905	3.556	.50	1.00	3.00	8.00

KM#	Date	Mintage	Fine	VF	XF	Unc
543	1906	1.783	4.00	10.00	20.00	40.00
	1907	8.251	.20	.75	3.00	6.00

Obv: Small cross.

KM#	Date	Mintage	Fine	VF	XF	Unc
552.1	1909	3.810	7.50	12.50	25.00	120.00

Obv: Large cross.

KM#	Date	Mintage	Fine	VF	XF	Unc
552.2	1909	Inc. Ab.	2.50	5.00	10.00	40.00
	1910	1.583	4.00	9.00	15.00	60.00
	1911	3.150	1.00	2.50	5.00	20.00
	1912/1	3.170	10.00	25.00	50.00	200.00
	1912	Inc. Ab.	1.00	2.50	5.00	20.00
	1913/12	3.197	5.00	15.00	25.00	100.00
	1913	Inc. Ab.	1.00	2.50	5.00	20.00
	1914 open 4					
		2.214	45.00	75.00	150.00	350.00
	1914 closed 4					
		Inc. Ab.	.75	2.50	9.00	40.00
552.2	1915/3	4.471	3.00	7.00	12.00	50.00
	1915	Inc. Ab.	.25	.75	2.00	8.00
	1916 short 6					
		7.620	.25	.75	2.00	7.50
	1916 long 6					
		Inc. Ab.	.30	1.00	2.50	12.00
	1920	5.548	.25	.50	1.25	5.00
	1921	7.442	.25	.50	1.25	5.00
	1922	1.166	2.50	5.00	7.50	30.00
	1923	4.512	.35	1.00	2.00	8.00
	1924	2.579	.25	1.00	2.00	9.00
	1925	4.715	.20	.50	1.00	5.00
	1926	6.739	.20	.50	1.00	5.00
	1927	3.601	.20	.50	1.00	5.00
	1928	2.381	.50	1.00	3.00	12.00
	1929 curved 2					
		6.091	.20	.50	1.00	5.00
	1929 straight 2					
		Inc. Ab.	.50	1.00	3.00	12.00
	1930	5.477	.20	.50	1.00	5.00
	1931	5.680	.20	.50	1.00	5.00
	1932	3.339	.30	.75	2.00	8.00
	1933	3.427	.30	.75	1.25	6.00
	1934	6.121	.20	.40	.75	4.00
	1935	4.600	.20	.40	.75	4.00

KM#	Date	Mintage	Fine	VF	XF	Unc
	1936 long 6					
		6.116	.30	.75	1.50	5.00

KM#	Date	Mintage	Fine	VF	XF	Unc
	1936 short 6					
		Inc. Ab.	.20	.40	.75	4.00
	1937	7.738	.20	.30	.75	3.00
	1938	6.993	.20	.30	.75	3.00
	1939	6.562	.20	.30	.75	3.00
	1940	4.060	.20	.30	.50	2.00
	1941	11.599	.20	.30	.50	2.00
	1942	3.992	.20	.30	.75	3.00
	1950	22.421	—	.20	.40	2.00

IRON

World War I Issues

KM#	Date	Mintage	Fine	VF	XF	Unc
560	1917	8.128	1.50	3.00	6.00	12.00
	1918	9.706	2.00	4.00	8.00	16.00
	1919	7.170	2.50	5.00	10.00	20.00

World War II Issues

Similar to KM#552.

KM#	Date	Mintage	Fine	VF	XF	Unc
572	1942	10.053	.20	.40	1.00	4.00
	1943	10.714	.20	.40	1.25	6.00
	1944	8.699	.20	.40	1.00	6.00
	1945	9.527	.20	.40	1.00	6.00
	1945 serif 4					
		Inc. Ab.	5.00	10.00	17.00	35.00
	1946	6.611	.20	.50	2.00	8.00
	1947	14.245	.20	.30	.75	3.00
	1948	15.442	.20	.30	.75	3.00
	1949	11.779	.20	.30	.75	3.00
	1950	14.432	.20	.30	.75	3.00

BRONZE

KM#	Date	Mintage	Fine	VF	XF	Unc
580	1952 TS	3.819	.20	.40	1.00	5.00
	1953 TS	22.636	—	.10	.50	3.00

KM#	Date	Mintage	Fine	VF	XF	Unc
580	1954 TS	15.492	—	.10	.50	3.00
	1955 TS	24.008	—	.10	.50	3.00
	1956 TS	20.792	—	.10	.50	3.00
	1957 TS	21.019	—	.10	.50	3.00
	1958 TS	20.220	—	.10	.50	3.00
	1959 TS	14.028	—	.10	.50	3.00
	1960 TS	21.840	—	.10	.40	2.00
	1961 TS	11.458	—	.10	.60	3.00
	1961 U	4.928	.20	.40	1.00	5.00
	1962 U	19.698	—	.10	.50	3.00
	1963 U	26.070	—	.10	.20	.60
	1964 U	19.290	—	.10	.20	.60
	1965 U	22.335	—	.10	.20	.60
	1966 U	24.093	—	—	.10	.40
	1967 U	30.420	—	—	.10	.40
	1968 U	20.760	—	—	.10	.40
	1969 U	20.198	—	—	.10	.40
	1970 U	44.400	—	—	.10	.40
	1971 U	16.490	—	—	.10	.40

NOTE: Varieties exist.

2 ORE

BRONZE
Obv: Small lettering

KM#	Date	Mintage	Fine	VF	XF	Unc
515	1874	1.914	2.00	7.00	20.00	60.00
	1875/74	2.441	30.00	55.00	100.00	225.00
	1875	Inc. Ab.	1.00	7.00	25.00	60.00
	1876/5	1.402	30.00	60.00	120.00	225.00
	1876	Inc. Ab.	3.00	12.50	35.00	90.00
	1877	1.015	3.00	12.50	35.00	90.00
	1878	.865	75.00	135.00	275.00	600.00

Obv: Large lettering

KM#	Date	Mintage	Fine	VF	XF	Unc
524	1877	Inc. Ab.	3.00	12.50	40.00	120.00
	1878	Inc. Ab.	4.00	15.00	50.00	150.00
	1879	.935	2.00	10.00	35.00	100.00
	1880	.825	3.00	15.00	50.00	140.00
	1881	1.244	1.00	4.00	12.50	60.00
	1882	1.777	1.00	4.00	12.50	60.00
	1883	1.483	1.00	4.00	12.50	60.00
	1884 open 4	1.316	1.00	4.00	12.50	60.00
	1884 closed 4	Inc. Ab.	20.00	45.00	100.00	300.00
	1885	.615	2.00	7.00	20.00	60.00
	1886	1.241	1.00	4.00	12.00	55.00
	1888	.865	1.00	4.00	12.00	55.00
	1889	.589	1.00	4.00	12.00	55.00
	1890/89	.912	40.00	80.00	250.00	500.00
	1890	Inc. Ab.	.75	2.00	7.50	30.00
	1891	.942	.75	2.00	7.50	30.00
	1892	.688	.75	2.00	7.50	35.00
	1893	.558	.75	2.00	7.50	35.00
	1894 open 4	.586	1.50	3.00	15.00	60.00
	1894 closed 4	Inc. Ab.	20.00	40.00	120.00	250.00
	1895	.781	.75	2.00	8.00	35.00
	1896	.908	.75	2.00	8.00	30.00
	1897	1.300	.50	2.00	8.00	30.00
	1898	1.527	.50	2.00	8.00	30.00
	1899	2.172	.50	2.00	8.00	30.00
	1900 oval OO	.688	2.00	5.00	20.00	70.00
	1900 round OO	Inc. Ab.	40.00	80.00	250.00	500.00
	1901	1.420	.50	2.00	6.00	25.00
	1902	2.040	.50	2.00	6.00	25.00
	1904	.698	.50	2.00	8.00	30.00
	1905	1.430	.50	2.00	6.00	25.00

KM#	Date	Mintage	Fine	VF	XF	Unc
544	1906/5	.994	150.00	250.00	500.00	1000.
	1906	Inc. Ab.	5.00	12.00	30.00	90.00
	1907	3.810	.25	1.00	4.00	20.00

KM#	Date	Mintage	Fine	VF	XF	Unc
553	1909	1.580	.75	3.00	12.50	50.00
	1910	.809	4.00	12.00	40.00	100.00
	1912	.446	6.00	18.00	50.00	130.00
	1913	.806	.50	3.00	17.50	60.00
	1914	1.200	.50	3.00	17.50	60.00
	1915/4	.814	6.00	18.00	50.00	130.00
	1915	Inc. Ab.	.50	3.00	17.50	60.00
	1916/5	2.820	4.00	12.00	40.00	100.00
	1916 short 6	Inc. Ab.	.25	1.00	8.00	35.00
	1916 long 6	Inc. Ab.	.25	1.00	8.00	35.00
	1919	1.203	.25	1.00	7.00	30.00
	1920	3.465	.30	.75	3.00	15.00
	1921	2.958	.30	.75	3.00	15.00
	1922	.932	1.00	3.00	10.00	45.00
	1923	.769	2.00	4.00	12.00	55.00
	1924	1.283	.50	1.25	7.00	35.00
	1925	3.903	.20	.75	3.00	15.00
	1926	3.579	.20	.75	3.00	15.00
	1927	2.190	.20	.75	3.00	15.00
	1928	.832	.50	1.50	8.00	35.00
	1929	2.384	.20	.60	3.00	14.00
	1930	2.590	.20	.60	3.00	14.00
	1931	2.296	.20	.60	3.00	14.00
	1932	1.179	.50	1.25	8.00	35.00
	1933	1.721	.20	.75	3.00	14.00
	1934	1.795	.20	.75	3.00	14.00
	1935	3.678	.20	.40	1.50	8.00
	1936 short 6	2.244	.10	.40	1.50	10.00
	1936 long 6	Inc. Ab.	1.00	1.50	5.00	20.00
	1937	2.981	.15	.40	1.50	8.00
	1938	3.225	.15	.40	1.50	8.00
	1939	4.014	.10	.40	1.00	7.50
	1940	3.305	.10	.40	1.00	7.50
	1941	7.337	.10	.40	1.00	7.50
	1942	1.614	.50	1.00	2.00	15.00
	1950	5.823	.10	.25	.75	5.00

IRON
World War I Issues
Similar to KM#553.

KM#	Date	Mintage	Fine	VF	XF	Unc
561	1917	4.576	2.50	4.50	10.00	20.00
	1918	4.982	4.00	9.00	18.00	35.00
	1919	2.923	7.00	15.00	30.00	65.00
	1920	1 pc.	—	—	—	—

World War II Issues
Similar to KM#553.

KM#	Date	Mintage	Fine	VF	XF	Unc
573	1942	9.344	.15	.30	3.00	12.00
	1943	6.999	.15	.30	3.00	12.00
	1944	6.126	.15	.30	3.00	12.00
	1945	4.773	.20	.40	3.50	15.00
	1946	5.854	.15	.30	3.00	12.00
	1947	9.536	.15	.30	2.00	8.00
	1948	11.424	.15	.30	2.00	8.00
	1949 long 9	10.600	.15	.30	2.00	8.00
	1949 short 9	I.A.	.15	.30	2.00	8.00
	1950	13.323	.15	.30	2.00	8.00

BRONZE

KM#	Date	Mintage	Fine	VF	XF	Unc
581	1952 TS	3.011	.20	.50	1.50	7.50
	1953 TS	15.620	.10	.20	1.00	5.00
	1954 TS	10.086	.10	.20	1.00	5.00
	1955 TS	12.963	.10	.20	1.00	5.00
	1956 TS	13.890	.10	.20	1.00	5.00
	1957 TS	9.997	.10	.20	1.00	5.00
	1958 TS	10.106	.10	.20	1.00	5.00
	1959 TS	11.572	.10	.20	1.00	5.00
	1960 TS	11.093	.10	.20	1.00	5.00
	1961 TS	9.673	.10	.20	1.00	5.00
	1961 U	1.075	1.50	3.00	5.00	17.50
	1962 U	9.569	—	.10	.50	2.50
	1963 U	13.338	—	.10	.50	2.50
	1964 U	19.346	—	.10	.20	1.00
	1965 U	23.356	—	.10	.20	1.00
	1966 U	18.278	—	.10	.20	1.00
	1967 U	23.931	—	—	.10	.50
	1968 U	26.238	—	—	.10	.50
	1969 U	16.843	—	—	.10	.50
	1970 U	31.254	—	—	.10	.50
	1971 U	19.179	—	—	.10	.50

NOTE: Varieties exist.

5 ORE

BRONZE
Obv: Small lettering.

KM#	Date	Mintage	Fine	VF	XF	Unc
516	1874	.866	5.00	25.00	60.00	125.00
	1875/4	1.234	6.00	30.00	75.00	150.00
	1875	Inc. Ab.	4.00	20.00	50.00	100.00
	1876	.609	4.00	20.00	50.00	100.00
	1877	.514	15.00	60.00	150.00	300.00
	1878	.364	4.00	20.00	50.00	100.00
	1879	.350	20.00	75.00	150.00	300.00
	1880/70	.403	15.00	50.00	125.00	250.00
	1880	Inc. Ab.	15.00	50.00	125.00	250.00
	1881	.625	4.00	20.00	50.00	100.00
	1882/1	.825	15.00	60.00	120.00	240.00
	1882	Inc. Ab.	4.00	20.00	60.00	120.00
	1883	.578	4.00	20.00	50.00	100.00
	1884	.784	4.00	20.00	50.00	100.00
	1885	.282	4.00	20.00	50.00	100.00
	1886	.269	4.50	20.00	60.00	120.00
	1887	.251	5.00	25.00	70.00	140.00
	1888	.214	5.00	25.00	70.00	140.00
	1889	.220	3.00	15.00	45.00	90.00

Obv: Large lettering.

KM#	Date	Mintage	Fine	VF	XF	Unc
533	1888	Inc. Ab.	75.00	120.00	175.00	400.00
	1889	Inc. Ab.	3.00	15.00	45.00	90.00
	1890	.339	3.00	15.00	60.00	120.00
	1891/81	.374	2.00	10.00	35.00	100.00
	1891	Inc. Ab.	2.00	10.00	35.00	100.00
	1892	.586	1.00	7.00	30.00	80.00
	1895	.529	1.00	7.00	30.00	80.00
	1896	.309	2.00	10.00	35.00	95.00
	1897	.570	1.00	6.00	20.00	60.00
	1898	.721	1.00	6.00	20.00	60.00
	1899*	1.225	1.00	6.00	20.00	60.00
	1900	.365	1.00	6.00	20.00	60.00
	1901	.442	1.00	6.00	20.00	60.00
	1902	.652	1.00	6.00	20.00	60.00
	1903	.243	2.00	9.00	30.00	80.00
	1904	.414	1.00	6.00	20.00	50.00
	1905	.545	1.00	6.00	25.00	55.00

***NOTE:** Varieties exist.

KM#	Date	Mintage	Fine	VF	XF	Unc
545	1906	.565	.75	5.00	20.00	50.00
	1907	1.953	.50	2.00	10.00	30.00

Obv: Small cross.

KM#	Date	Mintage	Fine	VF	XF	Unc
554.1	1909	.917	2.00	12.00	60.00	200.00

Obv: Large cross.

KM#	Date	Mintage	Fine	VF	XF	Unc
554.2	1909	Inc. Ab.	10.00	65.00	350.00	1150.
	1910	.031	175.00	350.00	700.00	1500.
	1911	.778	1.00	5.00	40.00	140.00
	1912	.547	1.50	6.00	50.00	190.00
	1913	.762	1.00	4.00	40.00	135.00
	1914	.400	3.00	9.00	60.00	225.00
	1915	1.222	.50	4.00	20.00	70.00
	1916/5	.955	15.00	30.00	60.00	175.00
	1916 short 6					
		Inc. Ab.	.50	4.00	20.00	70.00
	1916 long 6					
		Inc. Ab.	.50	4.00	20.00	70.00
	1917	1 pc.	—	—	—	—
	1919	1.129	.50	2.00	12.00	50.00
	1920	2.361	.50	2.00	8.00	30.00
	1921	1.879	.30	1.00	10.00	40.00
	1922	.763	.50	5.00	25.00	95.00
	1923	.506	2.00	9.00	60.00	195.00
	1924	.900	.40	3.00	17.50	70.00
	1925	1.944	.30	1.50	9.00	40.00
	1926	1.742	.30	1.50	9.00	40.00
	1927	.036	125.00	225.00	600.00	1250.
	1928	.987	.30	2.00	10.00	50.00
	1929	1.670	.30	1.00	9.00	40.00
	1930	1.716	.30	1.00	9.00	40.00
	1931	1.131	.20	1.00	9.00	40.00
	1932	1.165	.20	1.00	9.00	40.00
	1933	.574	2.00	5.00	25.00	100.00
	1934	1.710	.20	.75	5.00	30.00
	1935	1.682	.20	.75	5.00	30.00
	1936 short 6					
		1.626	.20	.75	6.00	30.00
	1936 long 6					
		Inc. Ab.	.40	1.00	7.00	35.00
	1937	2.637	.20	.50	4.00	20.00
	1938	2.354	.20	.50	4.00	20.00
	1939	2.592	.20	.75	6.00	25.00
	1940	2.730	.20	.50	3.00	15.00
	1940 serif 4					
		Inc. Ab.	.20	.50	3.00	15.00
	1941	2.055	.20	.50	3.00	15.00
	1942	.395	2.50	6.00	25.00	95.00
	1950	12.559	.10	.20	.75	5.00

NOTE: Varieties exist.

IRON
World War I Issues
Similar to KM#554.

KM#	Date	Mintage	Fine	VF	XF	Unc
562	1917	2.953	7.00	15.00	30.00	60.00
	1918	2.458	15.00	30.00	60.00	100.00
	1919	2.302	15.00	30.00	50.00	80.00

World War II Issues

KM#	Date	Mintage	Fine	VF	XF	Unc
574	1942	4.343	.20	.75	8.00	30.00
	1943	5.570	.20	.75	8.00	30.00
	1944	4.562	.20	.75	8.00	30.00
	1945	3.771	.20	.75	8.00	30.00
	1946	2.375	—	.50	5.00	20.00
	1947	6.035	—	.50	5.00	20.00
	1948	6.250	—	.50	5.00	20.00
	1949	7.840	—	.50	4.00	17.50
	1950	5.290	—	.50	4.00	17.50

BRONZE

KM#	Date	Mintage	Fine	VF	XF	Unc
582	1952 TS	3.065	.20	.50	2.50	12.00
	1953 TS	12.329	.20	.50	2.50	12.00
	1954 TS	7.232	.20	.50	2.50	12.00
	1955 TS	8.465	.20	.50	2.50	12.00
	1956 TS	7.997	.20	.50	2.50	12.00
	1957 TS	6.276	.20	.50	2.50	12.00
	1958 TS	9.498	.20	.50	2.50	12.00
	1959 TS	8.370	.20	.50	2.50	12.00

KM#	Date	Mintage	Fine	VF	XF	Unc
582	1960 TS	10.542	.20	.40	2.00	10.00
	1961 TS	3.909	.20	.40	2.00	10.00
	1961 U	2.452	.20	.50	2.50	12.00
	1962 U	22.306	—	.10	.50	3.00
	1963 U	17.156	—	.10	.50	3.00
	1964 U	10.923	—	.10	.75	7.00
	1964 U 50 in crown					
		Inc. Ab.	2.50	5.00	10.00	25.00
	1965 U	22.635	—	.10	.20	1.00
	1966 U	18.213	—	.10	.20	1.00
	1967 U	20.776	—	.10	.20	1.00
	1968 U	27.094	—	.10	.20	1.00
	1969 U	26.887	—	.10	.20	1.00
	1970 U	29.420	—	.10	.20	1.00
	1971 U	15.749	—	.10	.20	1.00

KM#	Date	Mintage	Fine	VF	XF	Unc
596	1972 U	107.894	—	—	.10	.20
	1973 U	193.038	—	—	.10	.20

COPPER-TIN-ZINC

KM#	Date	Mintage	Fine	VF	XF	Unc
600	1976 U	4.672	—	—	.10	.35
	1977 U	31.037	—	—	.10	.25
	1978 U	46.022	—	—	.10	.25
	1979 U	65.833	—	—	.10	.25
	1980 U	60.997	—	—	.10	.20
	1981 U	19.791	—	—	.10	.20

COPPER-ZINC

KM#	Date	Mintage	Fine	VF	XF	Unc
600a	1981 U	35.170	—	—	.10	.15
	1982 U	40.471	—	—	.10	.15
	1983 U	36.471	—	—	.10	.15
	1984 U	13.455	—	—	.10	.15

10 ORE

1.4500 g, .400 SILVER, .0186 oz ASW
Obv: Small lettering.

KM#	Date	Mintage	Fine	VF	XF	Unc
517	1874 ST	2.875	12.00	20.00	45.00	100.00
	1875/4 ST					
		1.503	60.00	90.00	150.00	300.00
	1875 ST	Inc. Ab.	50.00	80.00	130.00	270.00
	1876/5 ST					
		1.814	15.00	30.00	60.00	120.00
	1876 ST	Inc. Ab.	12.50	25.00	50.00	100.00

Obv: Large lettering.

KM#	Date	Mintage	Fine	VF	XF	Unc
530	1880 EB	.851	30.00	45.00	65.00	130.00
	1881 EB	.763	30.00	45.00	65.00	130.00
	1882/1 EB	.735	65.00	100.00	150.00	300.00
	1882 EB	I.A.	30.00	45.00	65.00	130.00
	1883 EB	.694	20.00	35.00	55.00	100.00
	1884 EB	1.560	12.00	25.00	50.00	100.00
	1887 EB	1.513	12.00	25.00	50.00	100.00
	1890 EB	.922	12.00	25.00	50.00	100.00
	1891 EB	.827	12.00	25.00	50.00	100.00
	1892 EB	1.215	4.00	10.00	35.00	70.00
	1894 EB	1.733	2.50	7.50	25.00	45.00
	1896 EB	2.084	2.00	6.00	20.00	35.00
	1897 EB	.819	2.50	7.50	25.00	45.00
	1898 EB	2.087	1.00	4.50	20.00	35.00
	1899 EB	2.041	1.00	4.50	20.00	35.00
	1900 EB	1.173	1.50	6.00	20.00	35.00
	1902 EB	1.946	1.00	4.50	20.00	35.00
	1903 EB	1.509	1.00	4.50	20.00	35.00
	1904 EB	3.280	.75	2.50	12.50	25.00

NOTE: Varieties exist.

KM#	Date	Mintage	Fine	VF	XF	Unc
549	1907 EB	7.320	.60	2.00	9.00	17.50

KM#	Date	Mintage	Fine	VF	XF	Unc
555	1909 W	1.610	2.50	7.00	22.50	65.00
	1911 W	3.180	.75	3.00	10.00	30.00
	1913 W	1.581	1.50	5.00	17.50	50.00
	1914 W	1.571	1.00	3.50	10.00	30.00
	1914 serif 4					
		Inc. Ab.	1.50	5.00	17.50	50.00
	1915 W	1.547	1.00	5.00	15.00	45.00
	1916/5 W	3.035	5.00	10.00	30.00	100.00
	1916 W	Inc. Ab.	1.00	3.00	10.00	30.00
	1917 W	4.996	.75	1.50	5.00	17.50
	1918 W	4.114	.75	1.50	5.00	17.50
	1919 W	5.740	.75	1.50	5.00	17.50
	1927 W	2.510	.40	1.00	5.00	20.00
	1928 G	2.901	.40	1.00	5.00	20.00
	1929 G	5.505	.40	1.00	3.00	15.00
	1930 G	3.223	.40	1.00	3.00	15.00
	1931 G	4.272	.40	1.00	3.00	15.00
	1933 G	1.948	1.00	2.00	7.00	25.00
	1934 G	4.059	.40	.60	1.25	7.50
	1935 G	2.426	.40	.60	1.25	7.50
	1936 G short 6					
		5.097	2.50	7.00	20.00	60.00
	1936 G long 6					
		Inc. Ab.	.30	.50	1.50	7.50
	1937 G	5.117	.30	.40	1.00	6.00
	1938 G	7.428	.30	.40	1.00	6.00
	1938 G	—	—	—	Proof	15.00
	1939/29 G					
		2.021	5.00	10.00	20.00	50.00
	1939 G	Inc. Ab.	.30	.75	2.50	12.00
	1939 G	—	—	—	Proof	20.00
	1940 G	3.017	.30	.50	1.00	6.00
	1941 G	9.106	.30	.60	1.00	6.00
	1942 G	3.692	.30	.60	1.00	6.00

NICKEL-BRONZE

KM#	Date	Mintage	Fine	VF	XF	Unc
563	1920 W	3.612	.50	2.00	9.00	40.00
	1920 lg. W	I.A.	20.00	40.00	80.00	275.00
	1921 W	2.270	.50	2.00	9.00	40.00
	1923 W	2.144	.50	2.00	10.00	50.00
	1924 W	1.600	.75	3.00	15.00	65.00
	1925 W	1.472	1.00	5.00	25.00	90.00
	1940 G	3.374	.20	.50	3.00	17.50
	1941	.816	.75	2.00	7.50	30.00
	1946 TS	4.117	.10	.30	1.50	8.00
	1947 TS	4.133	.10	.30	1.50	8.00

1.4400 g, .400 SILVER, .0185 oz ASW

KM#	Date	Mintage	Fine	VF	XF	Unc
575	1942 G	1.600	.30	.50	1.50	8.00
	1942 G	—	—	—	Proof	35.00
	1943 G	7.661	.30	.50	1.50	8.00
	1944 G	12.277	.30	.40	1.00	5.00
	1945 G	11.703	.30	.40	1.00	5.00
	1945 TS	Inc. Ab.	.30	.60	1.50	8.00
	1945 TS/G	I.A.	.50	.75	2.50	10.00
	1946/5 TS open 6					
		3.576	10.00	20.00	40.00	90.00
	1946 TS open 6					
		Inc. Ab.	.50	1.50	4.50	30.00
	1946 TS closed 6					
		Inc. Ab.	.30	.75	4.00	15.00
	1947 TS	7.293	.20	.40	1.00	5.00
	1948 TS	10.419	.20	.40	.75	5.00
	1949 TS	12.044	.20	.30	.75	5.00
	1950 TS	31.824	.20	.30	.75	4.00

NOTE: Varieties exist.

KM#	Date	Mintage	Fine	VF	XF	Unc
583	1952 TS	4.660	BV	.40	1.00	5.00
	1953 TS	28.484	BV	.30	.75	4.00
	1954 TS	15.913	BV	.30	.75	4.00
	1955 TS	16.687	BV	.30	.75	4.00
	1956 TS	21.986	BV	.25	.50	3.00
	1957 TS	21.294	BV	.25	.50	3.00
	1958 TS	19.605	BV	.25	.50	3.00
	1959 TS	18.523	BV	.25	.50	3.00
	1960 TS	16.605	BV	.25	.50	3.00
	1961 TS	8.284	BV	.25	.50	3.00
	1961 U	7.843	BV	.25	.50	3.00
	1962 U	8.619	BV	.25	.50	3.00

COPPER-NICKEL

KM#	Date	Mintage	Fine	VF	XF	Unc
591	1962 U	8.814	.10	.25	.50	3.00
	1963 U	28.170	—	—	.10	.50
	1964 U	36.895	—	—	.10	.50

KM#	Date	Mintage	Fine	VF	XF	Unc
591	1965 U	29.870	—	—	.10	.50
	1966 U	20.435	—	—	.10	.50
	1967 U	18.245	—	—	.10	.50
	1968 U	51.490	—	—	.10	.40
	1969 U	55.880	—	—	.10	.40
	1970 U	60.910	—	—	.10	.40
	1971 U	27.075	—	—	.10	.40
	1972 U	36.750	—	—	.10	.20
	1973 U	160.740	—	—	.10	.20

KM#	Date	Mintage	Fine	VF	XF	Unc
601	1976 U	4.173	—	—	.10	.40
	1977 U	44.517	—	—	.10	.30
	1978 U	74.342	—	—	.10	.30
	1979 U	75.306	—	—	.10	.20
	1980 U	108.294	—	—	.10	.15
	1981 U	102.454	—	—	.10	.15
	1982 U	103.906	—	—	.10	.15
	1983 U	77.315	—	—	.10	.15
	1984 U	122.100	—	—	.10	.15
	1985 U	74.222	—	—	.10	.15
	1986 U	83.193	—	—	.10	.15
	1986 D	17.205	—	—	.10	.15
	1987 D	146.877	—	—	.10	.15
	1988 D	194.986	—	—	.10	.15
	1989 D	245.181	—	—	.10	.15
	1990 D	139.238	—	—	.10	.15
	1991 D	5.177	—	—	.10	.15

25 ORE

2.4200 g, .600 SILVER, .0467 oz ASW
Obv: Small lettering

KM#	Date	Mintage	Fine	VF	XF	Unc
518	1874 ST	2.100	12.00	25.00	60.00	150.00
	1875/4 ST	1.131	50.00	95.00	180.00	350.00
	1875 ST	Inc. Ab.	40.00	75.00	140.00	275.00
	1876/5 ST	2.225	15.00	30.00	75.00	175.00
	1876 ST	Inc. Ab.	12.00	25.00	60.00	150.00
	1877 EB	.894	15.00	30.00	75.00	175.00
	1878/7 EB	.859	70.00	150.00	300.00	700.00
	1878 EB	Inc. Ab.	60.00	125.00	250.00	650.00

Obv: Large lettering

KM#	Date	Mintage	Fine	VF	XF	Unc
531	1874 ST	Inc. Ab.	6.00	17.50	50.00	150.00
	1880 EB	1.180	6.00	17.50	50.00	150.00
	1881 EB	1.392	5.00	15.00	40.00	120.00
	1883 EB	1.100	3.00	10.00	30.00	90.00
	1885 EB	1.168	4.50	12.00	37.50	110.00
	1889 EB	.422	4.50	12.00	37.50	110.00
	1890 EB	.469	3.00	10.00	30.00	90.00
	1896 EB	.794	2.50	8.00	25.00	80.00
	1897 EB	1.097	1.50	6.00	20.00	75.00
	1898 EB	1.458	1.50	6.00	20.00	75.00
	1899 EB	1.458	1.50	6.00	20.00	75.00
	1902 EB	1.259	1.50	6.00	20.00	75.00
	1904 EB	.692	1.50	6.00	20.00	75.00
	1905 EB	.732	1.50	6.00	20.00	75.00

KM#	Date	Mintage	Fine	VF	XF	Unc
550	1907 EB	3.223	1.00	3.50	15.00	40.00

KM#	Date	Mintage	Fine	VF	XF	Unc
556	1910 W large cross	2.044	1.00	4.00	10.00	50.00
	1910 W small cross	Inc. Ab.	10.00	40.00	100.00	400.00
	1912 W	1.014	1.00	4.00	20.00	60.00
	1914 W	3.719	1.00	2.50	10.00	35.00
	1916 W	1.270	1.00	4.00	20.00	55.00
	1917 W	1.657	1.00	2.00	10.00	35.00
	1918 W small 8	2.365	1.00	3.00	12.00	45.00
	1918 W wide 8	Inc. Ab.	1.50	3.50	15.00	50.00
	1919 W	3.205	1.00	2.00	8.00	30.00
	1927 W	1.688	1.00	2.50	8.00	30.00
	1928 G	.837	1.50	3.50	15.00	50.00
	1929 G	1.125	1.00	2.50	10.00	35.00
	1930 G	3.490	.75	1.50	4.00	15.00
	1931 G	1.392	.75	1.50	4.00	15.00
	1932 G	1.133	.75	1.50	4.00	15.00
	1933 G	.964	.75	2.00	10.00	30.00
	1934 G	1.404	.75	1.50	2.50	10.00
	1936 G	1.852	.75	1.50	2.50	10.00
	1937 G small G					
	1937 G	—	—	—	Proof	20.00
	1937 G lg. G	I.A.	1.00	2.00	4.50	15.00
	1938 G	3.679	.50	1.00	2.00	6.00
	1939 G	2.137	.50	1.00	2.00	6.00
	1940 G	2.302	.50	1.00	2.00	6.00
	1941 G	1.960	.50	1.00	2.00	6.00

NICKEL-BRONZE

KM#	Date	Mintage	Fine	VF	XF	Unc
566	1921 W	1.355	2.50	6.00	25.00	100.00
	1940 G	2.333	.25	1.00	5.00	20.00
	1941 G	1.057	.25	1.00	5.00	25.00
	1946 TS	2.066	.20	.40	2.00	10.00
	1947 TS	1.594	.20	.50	2.00	10.00

2.3200 g, .400 SILVER, .0298 oz ASW

KM#	Date	Mintage	Fine	VF	XF	Unc
578	1943 G	9.855	BV	.75	2.00	10.00
	1944 G	9.532	BV	.75	2.00	10.00
	1945 G	5.363	BV	.75	2.00	10.00
	1945 TS	I.A.	.50	1.50	3.00	15.00
	1945 G/TS	I.A.	BV	1.00	5.00	20.00
	1946 TS	2.250	BV	.60	3.00	15.00
	1947 TS	5.633	BV	.50	1.50	6.00
	1948 TS	3.191	BV	.60	1.50	6.00
	1949 TS	5.812	BV	.60	1.50	6.00
	1950 TS	12.059	BV	.60	1.00	4.00

KM#	Date	Mintage	Fine	VF	XF	Unc
584	1952 TS	2.114	BV	.50	1.50	7.50
	1953 TS	18.177	BV	.50	1.25	6.50
	1954 TS	9.492	BV	.50	1.25	6.50
	1955 TS	7.663	BV	.50	1.50	7.50
	1956 TS	10.931	BV	.50	1.00	5.00
	1957 TS	12.498	BV	.50	1.00	5.00
	1958 TS	6.884	BV	.50	1.00	5.00
	1959 TS	4.772	BV	.50	1.00	5.00
	1960 TS	4.374	BV	1.00	3.00	15.00
	1961 TS	8.380	BV	.50	1.00	5.00

COPPER-NICKEL

KM#	Date	Mintage	Fine	VF	XF	Unc
592	1962 U	4.426	.10	.30	1.00	5.00
	1963 U	26.710	.10	.20	.40	2.00
	1964 U	17.300	.10	.20	.40	2.00
	1965 U	6.884	.10	.20	.40	2.00
	1966 U	12.932	—	.10	.20	1.00
	1967 U	28.038	—	—	.10	.50
	1968 U	14.366	—	—	.10	.50
	1969 U	20.214	—	—	.10	.50
	1970 U	23.780	—	—	.10	.50
	1971 U	8.606	—	—	.10	.50
	1972 U	13.270	—	—	.10	.50
	1973 U	76.993	—	—	.10	.30

KM#	Date	Mintage	Fine	VF	XF	Unc
602	1976 U	2.815	—	—	.10	.50
	1977 U	5.509	—	—	.10	.40
	1978 U	54.593	—	—	.10	.25
	1979 U	48.423	—	—	.10	.25
	1980 U	38.889	—	—	.10	.25
	1981 U	46.371	—	—	.10	.25
	1982 U	43.218	—	—	.10	.25
	1983 U	28.954	—	—	.10	.25
	1984 U	7.302	—	—	.10	.25

50 ORE

5.0000 g, .600 SILVER, .0965 oz ASW

KM#	Date	Mintage	Fine	VF	XF	Unc
519	1875 ST	1.908	7.50	35.00	120.00	325.00
	1877 EB	.149	60.00	120.00	300.00	800.00
	1878 EB	.319	10.00	50.00	150.00	450.00
	1880 EB	.188	20.00	60.00	175.00	500.00
	1881 EB	.268	15.00	50.00	150.00	450.00
	1883 EB	.770	6.00	30.00	100.00	250.00
	1898 EB	.505	6.00	30.00	100.00	250.00
	1899 EB	.720	6.00	30.00	100.00	250.00

KM#	Date	Mintage	Fine	VF	XF	Unc
546	1906 EB	.319	3.00	15.00	60.00	175.00
	1907 EB	.803	2.50	10.00	50.00	125.00

KM#	Date	Mintage	Fine	VF	XF	Unc
559	1911 W	.472	4.00	15.00	45.00	150.00
	1912 W	.482	5.00	17.00	50.00	170.00
	1914 W	.378	5.00	17.00	50.00	170.00
	1916/5 W	.537	5.00	18.50	50.00	180.00
	1916 W	I.A.	4.00	15.00	40.00	150.00
	1919 W	.458	4.00	15.00	45.00	125.00
	1927 W	.672	2.00	6.00	25.00	75.00
	1928 G	1.135	1.50	4.00	12.00	50.00
	1929 G	.471	2.00	6.00	25.00	75.00
	1930 G	.548	2.00	6.00	25.00	70.00
	1931 G	.671	1.50	4.00	20.00	55.00
	1933 G	.548	1.50	4.00	20.00	55.00
	1934 G	.613	1.50	4.00	12.00	45.00
	1935 G	.691	1.50	4.00	12.00	45.00
	1936 G short 6	.823	1.50	4.00	12.00	45.00
	1936 G long 6	Inc. Ab.	2.00	7.00	20.00	65.00
	1938 G	.442	1.00	2.50	7.50	25.00
	1939 G	.922	1.00	2.00	5.00	15.00
	1939 G	—	—	—	Proof	50.00

NICKEL-BRONZE

KM#	Date	Mintage	Fine	VF	XF	Unc
564	1920 W	.480	2.00	8.00	40.00	175.00
	1921 W	.215	5.00	20.00	70.00	300.00
	1924 W	.645	2.00	8.00	60.00	225.00
	1940 G	1.341	.50	1.50	7.50	30.00
	1946 TS	1.426	.50	1.50	5.00	20.00
	1947 TS	1.032	.50	1.00	5.00	20.00

NOTE: Varieties exist.

4.8000 g, .400 SILVER, .0617 oz ASW

KM#	Date	Mintage	Fine	VF	XF	Unc
579	1943 G	.785	2.00	5.00	15.00	60.00
	1944 G	1.540	.75	1.50	4.00	15.00
	1945 G	2.585	.75	1.50	4.00	15.00
	1946 TS	1.091	.75	1.50	4.00	15.00
	1947 TS	1.771	.75	1.50	4.00	15.00
	1948 TS	1.731	.75	1.50	4.00	15.00
	1949 TS	1.883	.75	1.50	4.00	15.00
	1950 TS	3.354	.65	1.00	3.00	12.00

KM#	Date	Mintage	Fine	VF	XF	Unc
585	1952 TS	1.198	.75	1.50	6.00	25.00
	1953 TS	4.396	.65	1.25	5.00	22.50
	1954 TS	5.779	.65	1.25	5.00	22.50
	1955 TS	2.700	1.00	2.00	7.50	27.50
	1956 TS	7.057	.50	1.00	4.00	15.00
	1957 TS	2.405	.65	1.25	5.00	20.00
	1958 TS	1.660	.65	1.25	5.00	20.00
	1961 TS	2.775	.50	1.00	4.50	17.50

COPPER-NICKEL

KM#	Date	Mintage	Fine	VF	XF	Unc
593	1962 U	1.400	.50	1.00	5.00	25.00
	1963 U	5.808	.15	.25	1.00	10.00
	1964 U	5.325	.15	.25	1.00	10.00
	1965 U	6.453	.15	.25	.50	6.00
	1966 U	6.309	.15	.25	.40	5.00
	1967 U	7.890	.15	.25	.40	5.00
	1968 U	9.198	—	.15	.25	1.00
	1969 U	7.265	—	.15	.25	1.00
	1970 U	9.426	—	.15	.25	1.00
	1971 U	7.218	—	.15	.25	1.00
	1972 U	7.388	—	.15	.25	1.00
	1973 U	52.467	—	.15	.20	.60

KM#	Date	Mintage	Fine	VF	XF	Unc
603	1976 U	2.589	—	.15	.25	.70
	1977 U	10.360	—	—	.15	.30
	1978 U	33.282	—	—	.15	.30
	1979 U	30.274	—	—	.15	.30
	1980 U	28.666	—	—	.15	.30
	1981 U	15.516	—	—	.15	.30
	1982 U	14.778	—	—	.15	.30
	1983 U	17.530	—	—	.15	.30
	1984 U	27.541	—	—	.15	.30
	1985 U	14.062	—	—	.15	.30
	1986 U	.937	—	—	.15	.30
	1987 D	1.077	—	—	.15	.30
	1988 D	.532	—	—	.15	.30
	1989 D	.606	—	—	.15	.30
	1990 D	31.935	—	—	.15	.30
	1991 D	16.315	—	—	.15	.30

BRONZE

KM#	Date	Mintage	Fine	VF	XF	Unc
625	1992	39.531	—	—	.15	.30
	1993	—	—	—	.15	.30

KRONA

7.5000 g, .800 SILVER, .1929 oz ASW

KM#	Date	Mintage	Fine	VF	XF	Unc
520	1875 ST	3.531	15.00	60.00	200.00	600.00
	1876/5 ST	2.510	20.00	75.00	225.00	800.00
	1876 ST	Inc. Ab.	15.00	65.00	215.00	675.00

Obv: OCH replaces O in royal title.

KM#	Date	Mintage	Fine	VF	XF	Unc
525	1877 EB	.554	20.00	85.00	300.00	950.00
	1879 EB	.077	55.00	135.00	450.00	1400.
	1880 EB	.177	17.50	75.00	275.00	900.00
	1881 EB	.619	20.00	85.00	300.00	950.00
	1883 EB	.205	25.00	100.00	350.00	1000.
	1884 EB	.382	17.50	75.00	275.00	900.00
	1887 EB	.058	50.00	130.00	450.00	1500.
	1888 EB	.062	50.00	130.00	450.00	1500.
	1889 EB	.425	17.50	70.00	250.00	775.00
	1889 EB lock of hair below NO in NORGES	Inc. Ab.	125.00	450.00	1000.	3000.

Obv: W/o initials below bust.

KM#	Date	Mintage	Fine	VF	XF	Unc
535	1890 EB	.594	15.00	60.00	200.00	625.00
	1897 EB	.735	10.00	40.00	125.00	400.00
	1898 EB	1.860	6.50	30.00	100.00	325.00
	1901/898 EB	.271	15.00	60.00	200.00	625.00
	1901 EB	Inc. Ab.	10.00	50.00	170.00	500.00
	1903 EB	.473	9.00	45.00	125.00	425.00
	1904 EB	.564	8.00	35.00	120.00	420.00

KM#	Date	Mintage	Fine	VF	XF	Unc
547	1906 EB	.427	6.50	30.00	100.00	325.00
	1907 EB	1.058	5.00	20.00	80.00	275.00

Obv: W/dots in date.

KM#	Date	Mintage	Fine	VF	XF	Unc
557.1	1.9.1.0 W	.643	4.00	20.00	60.00	200.00
	1.9.1.2 W	.303	10.00	40.00	150.00	450.00
	1.9.1.3 W	.353	5.00	20.00	65.00	200.00
	1.9.1.4 W	.622	4.00	20.00	60.00	200.00
	1.9.1.5. W	1.416	4.00	15.00	45.00	150.00
	1.9.1.6/5. W	1.139	6.00	25.00	75.00	225.00
	1.9.1.6 W	I.A.	4.00	20.00	60.00	200.00
	1.9.1.8 W	.258	4.00	8.00	45.00	225.00
	1.9.2.3 W	.746	3.00	12.00	40.00	150.00
	1.9.2.4 W	2.066	2.50	10.00	30.00	100.00

Obv: W/o dots in date.

KM#	Date	Mintage	Fine	VF	XF	Unc
557.2	1924 W	Inc. Ab.	3.00	12.50	35.00	125.00
	1925 W	.370	4.00	17.50	70.00	220.00
	1926 W	.465	3.00	15.00	45.00	150.00
	1927 G	.401	4.00	17.50	60.00	200.00
	1928 G	.739	3.00	10.00	35.00	125.00
	1929 G	1.346	2.50	6.00	20.00	60.00
	1930 G	1.744	2.50	5.00	12.00	45.00
	1931 G	1.008	2.50	5.00	12.00	45.00
	1932 G	1.036	2.50	5.00	12.00	45.00
	1933 G	1.045	2.50	5.00	12.00	45.00
	1934 G	.586	2.50	5.00	20.00	60.00
	1935 G	1.604	2.00	3.00	5.00	15.00
	1936/5 G	3.223	1.50	2.00	3.50	12.50
	1936 G	Inc. Ab.	1.50	2.00	3.00	10.00
	1937 G	2.667	1.50	2.00	3.00	10.00
	1938 G	1.911	1.50	2.00	3.00	10.00
	1938 G	—	—	—	Proof	30.00
	1939 G	7.589	1.50	2.00	3.00	5.00
	1940 G	6.917	1.50	2.00	3.00	5.00
	1941/4 G	2.183	5.00	10.00	20.00	50.00
	1941 G	Inc. Ab.	1.50	2.00	3.50	10.00
	1942 G	.240	50.00	100.00	200.00	550.00

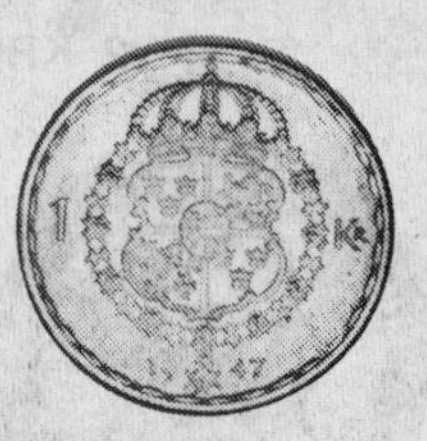

7.0000 g .400 SILVER, .0900 oz ASW

KM#	Date	Mintage	Fine	VF	XF	Unc
576	1942 G	5.650	1.00	1.50	5.00	20.00
	1943 G plain 4	7.916	1.00	1.50	5.00	20.00
	1943 G crosslet 4	Inc. Ab.	1.00	1.50	5.00	20.00
	1944 G	7.423	1.00	1.50	3.00	12.00
	1945 G	7.359	1.00	1.50	3.00	12.00
	1945 TS	Inc. Ab.	1.50	2.00	4.50	17.50
	1945 TS/G	I.A.	2.00	3.00	6.00	25.00
	1946 TS	19.170	1.00	1.50	2.00	9.00
	1947 TS	9.124	1.00	1.50	2.00	9.00
	1948 TS	10.447	1.00	1.50	2.00	9.00
	1949 TS	7.981	1.00	1.50	2.00	9.00
	1950 TS	5.310	1.00	1.50	3.00	12.00

KM#	Date	Mintage	Fine	VF	XF	Unc
586	1952 TS	1.102	BV	1.50	5.00	35.00
	1953/2 TS	I.A.	1.50	3.00	10.00	45.00
	1953 TS	3.306	BV	1.50	5.00	30.00
	1954 TS	6.461	BV	1.50	5.00	25.00
	1955 TS	4.141	BV	1.50	5.00	25.00
	1956 TS	6.227	BV	1.50	4.50	18.00
	1957 TS	3.544	BV	1.50	5.00	20.00
	1958 TS	1.439	1.00	2.50	7.50	35.00
	1959 TS	1.187	2.50	5.00	15.00	65.00
	1960 TS	4.085	BV	1.50	4.00	15.00
	1961 TS	4.283	BV	1.50	4.00	15.00
	1961 U	2.973	BV	2.00	6.00	30.00
	1962 U	6.839	BV	1.50	4.00	15.00
	1963 U	14.228	BV	1.00	2.00	7.00
	1964 U	15.973	BV	.75	1.50	5.00
	1965 U	18.639	BV	.75	1.50	5.00
	1966 U	22.396	BV	.75	1.50	4.00
	1967 U	17.235	BV	.75	1.50	4.00
	1968 U	12.326	BV	.75	1.50	4.00

COPPER-NICKEL CLAD COPPER

KM#	Date	Mintage	Fine	VF	XF	Unc
586a	1968 U	5.177	—	.25	1.00	4.00
	1969 U	30.856	—	.25	.30	1.50
	1970 U	25.315	—	.25	.30	1.50
	1971 U	18.342	—	.25	.30	1.50
	1972 U	21.941	—	.25	.30	1.50
	1973 U	142.000	—	.25	.30	1.00

KM#	Date	Mintage	Fine	VF	XF	Unc
604	1976 U	4.321	—	.25	.40	1.25
	1977 U	80.478	—	.25	.30	.50
	1978 U	81.408	—	.25	.30	.50
	1979 U	47.450	—	.25	.30	.40
	1980 U	51.694	—	.25	.30	.40
	1981 U	62.079	—	.25	.30	.40

COPPER-NICKEL

KM#	Date	Mintage	Fine	VF	XF	Unc
604a	1982 U	24.837	—	—	.25	.40
	1983 U	23.530	—	—	.25	.40
	1984 U	37.805	—	—	.25	.40
	1985 U	4.893	—	—	.25	.40
	1986 U	.901	—	—	.25	.40
	1987 D	21.543	—	—	.25	.40
	1988 D	30.342	—	—	.25	.40
	1989 D	55.963	—	—	.25	.40
	1990 D	54.470	—	—	.25	.40
	1991 D	34.250	—	—	.25	.40
	1992D	16.771	—	—	.25	.40
	1993D	—	—	—	.25	.40

2 KRONOR

15.0000 g, .800 SILVER, .3858 oz ASW

KM#	Date	Mintage	Fine	VF	XF	Unc
521	1876 EB wide date, 6mm wide, large E.B.					
		.370	700.00	1600.	3200.	—
	1876 EB wide date, small E.B.					
		Inc. Ab.	225.00	500.00	1400.	3500.
	1876 EB smaller date, 5mm wide					
		Inc. Ab.	20.00	100.00	450.00	1000.
	1877 EB	.168	25.00	125.00	475.00	1250.
	1878 EB	.193	20.00	100.00	450.00	1150.
	1880/76 EB					
		.128	50.00	200.00	750.00	2000.
	1880 EB	Inc. Ab.	40.00	150.00	700.00	1850.

Obv: OCH replaces O in royal title.

KM#	Date	Mintage	Fine	VF	XF	Unc
527	1878 EB	Inc. Ab.	550.00	950.00	2000.	4000.
	1880 EB	Inc. Ab.	40.00	190.00	725.00	2000.

Obv: W/o initials below bust.

KM#	Date	Mintage	Fine	VF	XF	Unc
536	1890 EB	.072	40.00	150.00	475.00	1250.
	1892 EB	.087	35.00	150.00	500.00	1300.
	1893 EB	.049	45.00	175.00	550.00	1350.
	1897 EB	.207	15.00	50.00	225.00	525.00
	1898 EB	.141	15.00	50.00	250.00	550.00
	1900 EB	.131	15.00	55.00	265.00	625.00
	1903 EB	.064	40.00	120.00	400.00	1000.
	1904 EB	.175	15.00	45.00	200.00	500.00

Silver Jubilee

KM#	Date	Mintage	Fine	VF	XF	Unc
537	1897 EB	.246	6.00	8.00	10.00	20.00

KM#	Date	Mintage	Fine	VF	XF	Unc
548	1906 EB	.112	10.00	30.00	95.00	375.00
	1907 EB	.301	7.50	20.00	75.00	350.00

Golden Wedding Anniversary

KM#	Date	Mintage	Fine	VF	XF	Unc
551	1907 EB	.251	7.00	9.00	11.00	22.00

KM#	Date	Mintage	Fine	VF	XF	Unc
558	1910 W	.375	7.50	22.50	75.00	200.00
	1910 W mintmasters initial further away from date	Inc. Ab.	45.00	125.00	375.00	850.00
	1912 W	.157	10.00	35.00	120.00	300.00
	1913 W	.305	6.00	20.00	70.00	200.00
	1914 W	.192	6.00	22.50	85.00	225.00
	1915 W	.156	9.00	30.00	95.00	250.00
	1922 W	.202	6.00	12.50	40.00	125.00
	1924 W	.199	6.00	15.00	50.00	150.00
	1926 W	.222	6.00	10.00	35.00	120.00
	1928 G	.160	6.00	12.50	55.00	175.00
	1929 G	.184	6.00	10.00	35.00	125.00
	1930 G	.178	6.00	9.00	30.00	100.00
	1931 G	.211	5.00	6.50	20.00	50.00
	1934 G	.273	4.50	6.00	12.50	40.00
	1935 G	.211	4.50	6.00	15.00	45.00
	1936 G	.491	4.50	6.00	9.00	25.00
	1937 G	.130	6.00	10.00	25.00	75.00
	1937 G	—	—	—	Proof	250.00
	1938 G	.639	4.50	6.00	7.50	20.00
	1938 G	—	—	—	Proof	40.00
	1939 G	1.200	4.50	6.00	7.00	15.00
	1939 G	—	—	—	Proof	40.00
	1940 G	.518	4.50	6.00	7.00	15.00
	1940 G serif 4					
		Inc. Ab.	5.00	7.00	12.50	30.00

400th Anniversary of Political Liberty

KM#	Date	Mintage	Fine	VF	XF	Unc
567	1921 W	.265	4.00	6.00	8.00	15.00

300th Anniversary Death of Gustaf II Adolf

KM#	Date	Mintage	Fine	VF	XF	Unc
569	1932 G	.254	5.00	7.50	10.00	16.00

300th Anniversary Settlement of Delaware

KM#	Date	Mintage	Fine	VF	XF	Unc
571	1938 G	.509	4.00	5.00	6.50	10.00

14.0000 g, .400 SILVER, .1800 oz ASW

KM#	Date	Mintage	Fine	VF	XF	Unc
577	1942 G	.200	2.50	4.50	8.00	35.00
	1943 G	.272	5.00	10.00	20.00	70.00
	1944 G	.627	1.50	2.50	5.00	20.00
	1945 G	.970	1.50	2.50	4.50	17.50
	1945 G w/o dots in motto					
		Inc. Ab.	10.00	20.00	40.00	80.00
	1945 TS	Inc. Ab.	1.50	3.50	6.50	25.00
	1945 TS/G	I.A.	3.00	5.00	9.00	35.00
	1946 TS	.978	1.50	2.00	3.50	17.50
	1947 TS	1.466	1.50	2.00	3.00	15.00
	1948 TS	.282	1.50	3.50	7.50	30.00
	1949 TS	.332	1.50	3.50	6.50	25.00
	1950/1 TS					
		3.727	1.50	2.00	5.00	15.00
	1950 TS	Inc. Ab.	1.50	2.00	4.00	8.50

KM#	Date	Mintage	Fine	VF	XF	Unc
587	1952 TS	.315	2.00	4.00	8.00	25.00
	1953 TS	1.009	1.25	1.75	2.50	10.00
	1954 TS	2.301	1.25	1.75	2.50	8.50
	1955 TS	1.138	1.25	1.75	2.50	10.00
	1956 TS	1.709	1.25	1.75	2.50	10.00
	1957 TS	.689	1.50	2.00	6.50	20.00
	1958 TS	1.104	1.25	1.75	2.50	10.00
	1959 TS	.581	1.50	2.00	6.50	20.00
	1961 TS	.534	1.50	2.00	4.50	15.00
	1963 U	1.469	1.25	1.75	2.50	6.50
	1964 U	1.213	1.25	1.75	2.50	5.00
	1965 U	1.190	1.25	1.75	2.50	5.00
	1966 U	.989	1.25	1.75	2.50	6.00

COPPER-NICKEL

KM#	Date	Mintage	Fine	VF	XF	Unc
587a	1968 U	1.171	.45	.65	1.75	4.00
	1969 U	1.148	.45	.65	1.00	2.50
	1970 U	1.159	.45	.65	1.00	2.50
	1971 U	1.213	.45	.65	1.50	3.00

5 KRONOR

2.2402 g, .900 GOLD, .0648 oz AGW

KM#	Date	Mintage	Fine	VF	XF	Unc
532	1881 EB	.065	40.00	60.00	90.00	145.00
	1882 EB	.030	50.00	70.00	100.00	225.00
	1883 EB	.028	60.00	90.00	120.00	250.00
	1886/3 EB	.042	40.00	60.00	90.00	135.00
	1886 EB	Inc. Ab.	40.00	60.00	90.00	135.00
	1894 EB	.051	40.00	60.00	90.00	135.00
	1899 EB	.104	40.00	50.00	70.00	100.00

KM#	Date	Mintage	Fine	VF	XF	Unc
541	1901 EB	.109	40.00	50.00	70.00	100.00

KM#	Date	Mintage	Fine	VF	XF	Unc
565	1920 W	.103	40.00	50.00	70.00	100.00

25.0000 g, .900 SILVER, .7234 oz ASW
500th Anniversary of Riksdag

KM#	Date	Mintage	Fine	VF	XF	Unc
570	1935 G	.664	7.50	10.00	12.50	22.00

22.7000 g, .400 SILVER, .2920 oz ASW
70th Birthday of Gustav VI Adolf

KM#	Date	Mintage	Fine	VF	XF	Unc
588	1952 TS	.219	7.50	12.50	17.50	30.00

18.0000 g, .400 SILVER, .2315 oz ASW
Regular Issue

KM#	Date	Mintage	Fine	VF	XF	Unc
589	1954 TS	1.510	—	BV	4.00	10.00
	1955 TS	3.569	—	BV	3.50	7.50
	1971 U	.713	—	BV	3.50	5.50

Constitution Sesquincentennial

KM#	Date	Mintage	Fine	VF	XF	Unc
590	1959 TS	.504	—	BV	5.00	10.00

80th Birthday of Gustav VI Adolf

KM#	Date	Mintage	Fine	VF	XF	Unc
594	1962 U	.256	—	10.00	17.50	32.50

100th Anniversary of Constitution Reform

KM#	Date	Mintage	Fine	VF	XF	Unc
595	1966 U	1.024	—	BV	3.50	5.00

COPPER-NICKEL CLAD NICKEL

KM#	Date	Mintage	Fine	VF	XF	Unc
597	1972 U	21.736	—	1.00	1.25	2.00
	1973 U	1.139	—	1.00	2.00	4.00

COPPER-NICKEL

KM#	Date	Mintage	Fine	VF	XF	Unc
605	1976 U	2.253	—	—	1.00	2.00
	1977 U	3.985	—	—	1.00	2.00
	1978 U	3.952	—	—	1.00	2.00
	1979 U	3.164	—	—	1.00	2.00
	1980 U	2.222	—	—	1.00	2.00
	1981 U	5.507	—	—	1.00	1.25
	1982 U	36.604	—	—	1.00	1.25
	1983 U	31.364	—	—	1.00	1.25
	1984 U	27.687	—	—	1.00	1.25
	1985 U	10.375	—	—	1.00	1.25
	1986 U	.714	—	—	1.00	1.25
	1987 D	15.117	—	—	1.00	1.25
	1988 D	18.644	—	—	1.00	1.25
	1989 D	.961	—	—	1.00	1.25
	1990 D	10.558	—	—	1.00	1.25
	1991 D	15.793	—	—	1.00	1.25
	1992 D	5.351	—	—	1.00	1.25

COPPER-NICKEL CLAD NICKEL

KM#	Date	Mintage	Fine	VF	XF	Unc
605a	1993	—	—	—	1.00	1.25

10 KRONOR

4.4803 g, .900 GOLD, .1296 oz AGW

KM#	Date	Mintage	Fine	VF	XF	Unc
512.1	1873 ST	.200	70.00	85.00	125.00	250.00
	1874/3 ST	.461	70.00	85.00	110.00	160.00
	1874 ST	Inc. Ab.	70.00	85.00	100.00	140.00
	1874 ST	—	—	—	Proof	1300.
	1876 ST	.133	70.00	85.00	110.00	160.00

Obv: OCH substituted for O. in royal title.

KM#	Date	Mintage	Fine	VF	XF	Unc
512.2	1876 EB	.037	70.00	90.00	175.00	300.00
	1877 EB	.055	75.00	150.00	250.00	375.00
	1880 EB	.027	75.00	150.00	250.00	375.00
	1880 EB L.A.	Inc. Ab.	75.00	150.00	250.00	375.00
	1883 EB L.A.	.149	70.00	85.00	100.00	155.00
	1883 LA	Inc. Ab.	70.00	85.00	100.00	155.00
	1883 L.A. larger L.A.	Inc. Ab.	70.00	85.00	100.00	155.00
	1894 EB	.036	70.00	85.00	120.00	200.00
	1895 EB	.065	70.00	85.00	120.00	200.00

Obv: Larger head.

KM#	Date	Mintage	Fine	VF	XF	Unc
542	1901 EB	.213	65.00	80.00	95.00	135.00
	1901 EB	Inc. Ab.	—	—	Proof	525.00

18.0000 g, .830 SILVER, .4803 oz ASW
90th Birthday of Gustav VI Adolf

KM#	Date	Mintage	Fine	VF	XF	Unc
598	1972 U	2.000	—	3.00	6.00	9.00

COPPER-ALUMINUM-ZINC

KM#	Date	Mintage	Fine	VF	XF	Unc
620	1991	106.548	—	—	—	3.00
	1992	42.507	—	—	—	3.00
	1993	—	—	—	—	3.00

20 KRONOR

8.9606 g, .900 GOLD, .2593 oz AGW

KM#	Date	Mintage	Fine	VF	XF	Unc
513	1873 ST	.115	150.00	200.00	300.00	500.00
	1874 ST	.240	150.00	200.00	300.00	400.00
	1875 ST	.359	150.00	200.00	300.00	400.00
	1876/5 ST	.240	200.00	350.00	600.00	1200.
	1876 ST	Inc. Ab.	200.00	350.00	600.00	1200.

Rev: Arms wider

KM#	Date	Mintage	Fine	VF	XF	Unc
522	1876 EB	Inc. Ab.	150.00	200.00	300.00	400.00
	1877 EB	.103	150.00	200.00	300.00	400.00

Obv: OCH substituted for O. in royal title.

KM#	Date	Mintage	Fine	VF	XF	Unc
526	1877 EB	Inc. Ab.	150.00	200.00	275.00	375.00
	1878/7 EB	.245	150.00	200.00	275.00	375.00
	1878 EB	Inc. Ab.	150.00	200.00	275.00	375.00
	1879 EB	.075	150.00	200.00	400.00	600.00
	1879 EB	Unique	—	—	Proof	10,000.
	1880 EB	.127	150.00	200.00	275.00	375.00
	1881 EB	.047	175.00	350.00	600.00	1000.
	1884 EB	.191	150.00	200.00	250.00	350.00
	1885 EB	6,250	400.00	800.00	1700.	2500.
	1886 EB	.173	150.00	200.00	250.00	350.00
	1887 EB	.059	175.00	350.00	600.00	1000.
	1889 EB	.202	150.00	200.00	250.00	350.00
	1890 EB	.155	150.00	200.00	250.00	350.00
	1895 EB	.135	150.00	200.00	250.00	350.00
	1898 EB	.313	150.00	200.00	250.00	325.00
	1899 EB	.261	150.00	200.00	250.00	325.00

Obv: Larger head.

KM#	Date	Mintage	Fine	VF	XF	Unc
540	1900 EB	.104	140.00	200.00	350.00	550.00
	1901 EB	.227	140.00	160.00	250.00	350.00
	1902 EB	.114	140.00	160.00	300.00	400.00

KM#	Date	Mintage	Fine	VF	XF	Unc
568	1925 W	.387	150.00	300.00	400.00	600.00

50 KRONOR

27.0000 g, .925 SILVER, .8029 oz ASW
Constitutional Reform

KM#	Date	Mintage	Fine	VF	XF	Unc
599	1975 U	.500	—	—	—	16.50

Wedding of King Carl XVI Gustav and Queen Silvia

KM#	Date	Mintage	Fine	VF	XF	Unc
606	1976 U	2.000	—	—	—	12.50

100 KRONOR

16.0000 g, .925 SILVER, .4759 oz ASW
Parliament

KM#	Date	Mintage	Fine	VF	XF	Unc
608	1983	.400	—	—	—	22.50

Stockholm Conference

KM#	Date	Mintage	Fine	VF	XF	Unc
610	1984	.300	—	—	—	22.50

International Youth Year

KM#	Date	Mintage	Fine	VF	XF	Unc
611	1985	.120	—	—	—	25.00

European Music Year

KM#	Date	Mintage	Fine	VF	XF	Unc
612	1985	.120	—	—	—	25.00

International Year of the Forest

KM#	Date	Mintage	Fine	VF	XF	Unc
613	1985	.120	—	—	—	25.00

350th Anniversary of Swedish Colony in Delaware
Obv: Large head.

KM#	Date	Mintage	Fine	VF	XF	Unc
614.1	1988	.032	—	—	—	27.50

Obv: Small head.

KM#	Date	Mintage	Fine	VF	XF	Unc
614.2	1988	.118	—	—	—	25.00

200 KRONOR

27.0000 g, .925 SILVER, .8029 oz ASW
Swedish Royal Succession Law

KM#	Date	Mintage	Fine	VF	XF	Unc
607	1980 U	.500	—	—	P/L	45.00

10th Anniversary of Reign

KM#	Date	Mintage	Fine	VF	XF	Unc
609	1983	.100	—	—	—	55.00

Ice Hockey

KM#	Date	Mintage	Fine	VF	XF	Unc
616	1989	*.080	—	—	—	55.00

War Ship - Vasa

KM#	Date	Mintage	Fine	VF	XF	Unc
618	1990	.050	—	—	—	60.00

200th Anniversary of Death of Gustav III

KM#	Date	Mintage	Fine	VF	XF	Unc
621	1992	.050	—	—	—	55.00

20th Anniversary of Reign

KM#	Date	Mintage	Fine	VF	XF	Unc
623	1993	.450	—	—	—	60.00

50th Birthday of Queen Silvia

KM#	Date	Mintage	Fine	VF	XF	Unc
626	1993	.050	—	—	—	48.00

1000 KRONOR

5.8000 g, .900 GOLD, .1678 oz AGW
350th Anniversary of Swedish Colony in Delaware

KM#	Date	Mintage	Fine	VF	XF	Unc
615	1988	.010	—	—	—	450.00

Ice Hockey

KM#	Date	Mintage	Fine	VF	XF	Unc
617	1989	.020	—	—	—	225.00

The Vasa - Arms

KM#	Date	Mintage	Fine	VF	XF	Unc
619	1990	.015	—	—	—	285.00

200th Anniversary of Death of Gustav III

KM#	Date	Mintage	Fine	VF	XF	Unc
622	1992	.015	—	—	—	285.00

20th Anniversary of Reign
Obv: Portrait of King.

KM#	Date	Mintage	Fine	VF	XF	Unc
624	1993	.015	—	—	—	285.00

50th Birthday of Queen Silvia

KM#	Date	Mintage	Fine	VF	XF	Unc
627	1993	.015	—	—	—	250.00

TRADE COINAGE

DUCAT

3.5000 g, .976 GOLD, .1098 oz AGW

KM#	Date	Mintage	VG	Fine	VF	XF
380	1801 OL	3,100	225.00	550.00	1100.	1800.
	1802 OL	4,827	175.00	375.00	750.00	1500.
	1803 OL	7,300	150.00	350.00	700.00	1200.
	1804 OL	8,700	175.00	375.00	750.00	1500.
	1805 OL	.013	150.00	350.00	700.00	1200.
	1806 OL	.014	150.00	350.00	700.00	1200.
	1807 OL	.011	150.00	350.00	700.00	1200.
	1808 OL	.033	150.00	350.00	700.00	1200.
	1809 OL	.021	150.00	350.00	700.00	1200.

NOTE: Earlier dates (1793-1800) exist for this type.

KM#	Date	Mintage	VG	Fine	VF	XF
387	1801 OL	900 pcs.	500.00	1100.	2250.	3750.

KM#	Date	Mintage	VG	Fine	VF	XF
392	1804 OL	1,254	400.00	900.00	1800.	3000.

KM#	Date	Mintage	VG	Fine	VF	XF
396	1810 OL	.014	150.00	350.00	700.00	1200.
	1811 OL	9,750	175.00	400.00	800.00	1300.
	1812 OL	.016	150.00	350.00	700.00	1200.
	1813 OL	.026	150.00	350.00	700.00	1200.
	1814 OL	.022	150.00	350.00	700.00	1200.

KM#	Date	Mintage	VG	Fine	VF	XF
406	1815 OL	8,060	185.00	400.00	800.00	1300.
	1816 OL	6,130	200.00	450.00	900.00	1400.
	1817 OL	5,673	225.00	450.00	1000.	1500.

Dalarna Mines Commemorative

KM#	Date	Mintage	VG	Fine	VF	XF
397	1810 OL	1,322	250.00	550.00	1100.	1800.

KM#	Date	Mintage	VG	Fine	VF	XF
409	1818 OL	6,389	100.00	225.00	450.00	800.00
	1819 OL	1,828	—	—	Rare	—
	1820 LB	7,248	110.00	250.00	500.00	900.00

Obv: Bust right. Rev: Shield.

KM#	Date	Mintage	VG	Fine	VF	XF
416	1821 LB	.019	100.00	225.00	450.00	800.00
	1822 CB	5,222	100.00	225.00	500.00	900.00
	1823 AG	3,155	100.00	225.00	500.00	900.00
	1824 CB	3,370	100.00	225.00	500.00	900.00
	1825 CB	8,127	100.00	225.00	450.00	800.00
	1826 CB	4,126	100.00	225.00	450.00	800.00
	1827/6 CB	4,579	110.00	250.00	500.00	875.00
	1827 CB	I.A.	100.00	225.00	450.00	800.00
	1828 CB	5,150	100.00	225.00	450.00	800.00
	1829 CB	5,642	100.00	225.00	450.00	800.00

KM#	Date	Mintage	VG	Fine	VF	XF
428	1830 CB	5,269	85.00	200.00	375.00	750.00
	1831 CB	3,917	85.00	200.00	375.00	750.00
	1832 CB	2,082	85.00	200.00	375.00	750.00
	1833 CB	2,310	85.00	200.00	375.00	750.00
	1834 CB	3,142	85.00	200.00	375.00	750.00
	1835 CB	7,622	85.00	200.00	375.00	750.00
	1836 CB	1,947	—	—	Rare	—
	1837 CB	.013	75.00	175.00	350.00	700.00
	1838 AG	.015	75.00	175.00	350.00	700.00
	1839 AG	.010	75.00	175.00	350.00	700.00
	1840 AG	1,840	125.00	300.00	600.00	1200.
	1841 AG	.013	75.00	175.00	350.00	700.00
	1842 AG	.030	75.00	175.00	350.00	700.00
	1843 AG	.074	70.00	160.00	325.00	650.00

Obv: Large head of Oscar I right.

KM#	Date	Mintage	VG	Fine	VF	XF
457	1844 AG	946 pcs.	—	—	Rare	—
	1845/4 AG	.046	125.00	300.00	600.00	900.00

Obv: Smaller head.

KM#	Date	Mintage	VG	Fine	VF	XF
463	1845/4 AG	I.A.	75.00	165.00	325.00	650.00
	1845 AG	I.A.	65.00	150.00	300.00	600.00
	1846 AG	.022	65.00	150.00	300.00	600.00
	1847/4 AG	.018	75.00	165.00	350.00	675.00
	1847 AG	I.A.	65.00	150.00	300.00	600.00
	1848 AG	.037	65.00	150.00	300.00	600.00
	1849/4 AG	.014	75.00	165.00	350.00	675.00
	1849 AG	I.A.	65.00	150.00	300.00	600.00
	1850 AG	.020	65.00	150.00	300.00	600.00
	1851 AG	.016	65.00	150.00	300.00	600.00
	1852 AG	.027	65.00	150.00	300.00	600.00
	1853 AG	.013	65.00	150.00	300.00	600.00

KM#	Date	Mintage	VG	Fine	VF	XF
463	1854 AG small AG	.020	65.00	150.00	300.00	600.00
	1854 AG large AG	Inc. Ab.	65.00	150.00	300.00	600.00
	1855 AG	.018	65.00	150.00	300.00	600.00
	1856 ST	.012	65.00	150.00	300.00	600.00
	1857 ST small ST	.027	65.00	150.00	300.00	600.00
	1857 ST large ST	Inc. Ab.	65.00	150.00	300.00	600.00
	1858 ST	.041	65.00	150.00	300.00	600.00
	1859 ST	.031	65.00	150.00	300.00	600.00

KM#	Date	Mintage	VG	Fine	VF	XF
494	1860 ST	.058	60.00	125.00	275.00	550.00
	1861/0 ST	.038	70.00	140.00	325.00	625.00
	1861 ST	I.A.	60.00	125.00	275.00	550.00
	1862 ST	.042	60.00	125.00	275.00	550.00
	1863 ST	.037	50.00	100.00	250.00	450.00
	1864/3 ST	.038	70.00	140.00	325.00	625.00
	1864 ST small L.A.	Inc. Ab.	60.00	125.00	275.00	550.00
	1864 ST larger L.A.	Inc. Ab.	60.00	125.00	275.00	550.00
	1865 ST large year and ST	.039	60.00	125.00	275.00	550.00
	1865 ST smaller year and ST	Inc. Ab.	60.00	125.00	275.00	550.00
	1866 ST large ST	.032	60.00	125.00	275.00	550.00
	1866 ST smaller ST	Inc. Ab.	60.00	125.00	275.00	550.00
	1867 ST	.011	60.00	125.00	275.00	550.00
	1867 TS	I.A.	125.00	300.00	600.00	1000.
	1868 ST small ST	9,398	65.00	150.00	300.00	600.00
	1868 ST larger ST	Inc. Ab.	65.00	150.00	300.00	600.00

2 DUCAT

7.0000 g, .986 GOLD, .2219 oz AGW

KM#	Date	Mintage	VG	Fine	VF	XF
429	1830 CB	2 pcs.	—	—	Rare	—
	1836 CB	1,500	250.00	650.00	1300.	2000.
	1837 CB	1,989	250.00	650.00	1300.	2000.
	1838 AG	1,000	300.00	700.00	1500.	2400.
	1839 AG	2,200	250.00	650.00	1300.	2000.
	1842 AG	1,546	300.00	700.00	1500.	2400.
	1843 AG	2,159	250.00	650.00	1300.	2000.

KM#	Date	Mintage	VG	Fine	VF	XF
470	1850 AG	819 pcs.	400.00	900.00	1900.	2800.
	1852 AG	386 pcs.	—	—	Rare	—
	1857 ST	763 pcs.	350.00	800.00	1600.	2500.

4 DUCAT

14.0000 g, .976 GOLD, .4394 oz AGW

KM#	Date	Mintage	VG	Fine	VF	XF
444	1837 CB	1,625	400.00	900.00	1900.	2800.
	1838 AG	625 pcs.	450.00	1000.	2000.	3000.
	1839 AG	2,000	400.00	900.00	1900.	2800.
	1841 AG	2,084	450.00	1000.	2100.	3300.
	1843 AG	4,405	350.00	800.00	1600.	2500.

KM#	Date	Mintage	VG	Fine	VF	XF
465	1846 AG	400 pcs.	600.00	1300.	2600.	3800.
	1850 AG	507 pcs.	500.00	1000.	2100.	3200.
	1852 AG	2 pcs.	—	—	Rare	—

CAROLIN-10 FRANCS

3.2258 g, .900 GOLD, .0933 oz AGW

KM#	Date	Mintage	Fine	VF	XF	Unc
501	1868	.033	75.00	150.00	300.00	500.00
	1869	.031	75.00	150.00	300.00	550.00
	1871	5,153	125.00	250.00	500.00	800.00
	1871 larger ear	Inc. Ab.	175.00	350.00	700.00	1000.
	1872	.012	125.00	250.00	500.00	750.00
	1872 larger ear	Inc. Ab.	275.00	550.00	800.00	1250.

MINT SETS (MS)

KM#	Date	Mintage	Identification	Issue Price	Mkt. Val.
MS1	1973(6)	20,000	KM586a,591-593,596-597	5.00	27.00
MS2	1976(6)	61,234	KM600-605, Swedish, spc	5.00	18.00
MS3	1976(6)	10,000	KM600-605, English, spc	5.00	18.00
MS4	1977(6)	43,346	KM600-605, Swedish, spc	5.00	17.00
MS5	1977(6)	5,800	KM600-605, English, spc	5.00	27.00
MS6	1978(6)	20,115	KM600-605, Swedish, spc	5.00	18.00
MS7	1978(6)	1,500	KM600-605, English, spc	5.00	45.00
MS8	1978(6)	31,245	KM600-605, Swedish, hpc	5.00	18.00
MS9	1979(6)	10,200	KM600-605, Swedish, spc	5.00	14.00
MS10	1979(6)	1,900	KM600-605, English, spc	5.00	35.00
MS11	1979(6)	38,957	KM600-605, Swedish, hpc	5.00	14.00
MS12	1979(6)	9,871	KM600-605, English, hpc	5.00	27.00
MS13	1980(6)	10,140	KM600-605, Swedish, spc	5.00	10.00
MS14	1980(6)	2,000	KM600-605, English, spc	5.00	35.00
MS15	1980(6)	45,495	KM600-605, Swedish, hpc	5.50	10.00
MS16	1980(6)	9,880	KM600-605, English, hpc	5.50	27.00
MS17	1981(6)	11,927	KM600a,601-605, Swedish, spc	5.50	8.00
MS18	1981(6)	2,000	KM600a,601-605, English, spc	5.50	35.00
MS19	1981(6)	65,338	KM600a,601-605, Swedish, hpc	5.50	8.00
MS20	1981(6)	5,000	KM600a,601-605, English, hpc	5.50	35.00
MS21	1982(6)	9,463	KM600a,601-603,604a, 605, Swedish, spc	5.50	8.00
MS22	1982(6)	2,300	KM600a,601-603,604a, 605, English, spc	5.50	27.00
MS23	1982(6)	58,772	KM600a,601-603,604a, 605, Swedish, hpc	5.50	8.00
MS24	1982(6)	4,978	KM600a,601-603,604a, 605, English, hpc	5.50	35.00
MS25	1983(6)	10,300	KM600a,601-603,604a, 605, Swedish, spc	6.00	8.00
MS26	1983(6)	2,750	KM600a,601-603,604a, 605, English, spc	6.00	27.00
MS27	1983(6)	57,205	KM600a,601-603,604a, 605, Swedish, hpc	6.00	8.00
MS28	1983(6)	5,017	KM600a,601-603,604a, 605, English, hpc	6.00	35.00
MS29	1984(6)	10,100	KM600a,601-603,604a, 605, Swedish, spc	6.00	8.00
MS30	1984(6)	1,600	KM600a,601-603,604a, 605, English, spc	6.00	45.00
MS31	1984(6)	70,849	KM600a,601-603,604a, 605, Swedish, hpc	6.00	8.00
MS32	1984(6)	4,271	KM600a,601-603,604a, 605, English, hpc	6.00	40.00
MS33	1985(4)	8,000	KM601,603,604a,605, Swedish, spc	6.50	8.00
MS34	1985(4)	1,445	KM601,603,604a,605, English, spc	6.50	45.00
MS35	1985(4)	52,462	KM601,603,604a,605, Swedish, hpc	6.50	8.00
MS36	1985(4)	2,717	KM601,603,604a,605, English, hpc	6.50	50.00
MS37	1986(4)	16,265	KM601,603,604a,605, Swedish, spc	6.50	22.00
MS38	1986(4)	1,880	KM601,603,604a,605, English, spc	6.50	35.00
MS39	1986(4)	54,890	KM601,603,604a,605, Swedish, hpc	6.50	22.00
MS40	1986(4)	967	KM601,603,604a,605, English, hpc	6.50	110.00
MS41	1987(4)	5,600	KM601,603,604a,605, Swedish, spc	6.50	7.50
MS42	1987(4)	1,100	KM601,603,604a,605, English, spc	6.50	45.00
MS43	1987(4)	70,060	KM601,603,604a,605,		

KM#	Date	Mintage	Identification	Issue Price	Mkt. Val.
MS43			Swedish, hpc	6.50	7.50
MS44	1987(4)	557	KM601,603,604a,605, Swedish and English, hpc	6.50	275.00
MS45	1988(4)	4,815	KM601,603,604a,605, Swedish, spc	6.50	7.50
MS46	1988(4)	2,456	KM601,603,604a,605, English, spc	6.50	27.00
MS47	1988(4)	56,753	KM601,603,604a,605, Swedish, hpc	6.50	7.50
MS48	1988(4)	1,777	KM601,603,604a,605, English, hpc	6.50	60.00
MS49	1989(4)	7,170	KM601,603,604a,605, spc	6.50	7.50
MS50	1989(4)	56,895	KM601,603,604a,605, hpc	6.50	7.50
MS51	1990(4)	6,503	KM601,603,604a,605, spc	10.00	10.00
MS52	1990(4)	55,265	KM601,603,604a,605, hpc	12.00	12.00
MS53	1991(5)	9,759	KM601,603,604a,605,620 Swedish spc	—	14.00
MS54	1991(5)	1,680	KM601,603,604a,605,620 English spc	—	14.00
MS55	1991(5)	65,401	KM601,603,604a,605,620 Swedish hpc	—	16.50
MS56	1991(5)	2,884	KM601,603,604a,605,620 English hpc	—	17.50
MS57	1991(5)	5,000	KM601(3),603(2), medal	—	8.50
MS58	1992(4)	61,183	KM604a,605,620,625 Swedish, spc	6.50	9.00
MS59	1992(4)	1,840	KM604a,605,620,625 English, spc	6.50	9.00
MS60	1992(4)	5,600	KM604a,605,620,625 Swedish, hpc	6.50	15.00
MS61	1992(4)	2,187	KM604a,605,620,625 English, hpc	6.50	20.00
MS62	1993(4)	—	KM604a-605a,620,625 Swedish, spc	6.50	8.50
MS63	1993(4)	—	KM604a-605a,620,625 English, spc	6.50	8.50
MS64	1993(4)	—	KM604a-605a,620,625 Swedish, hpc	6.50	10.00
MS65	1993(4)	—	KM604a-605a,620,625 English, hpc	6.50	18.00

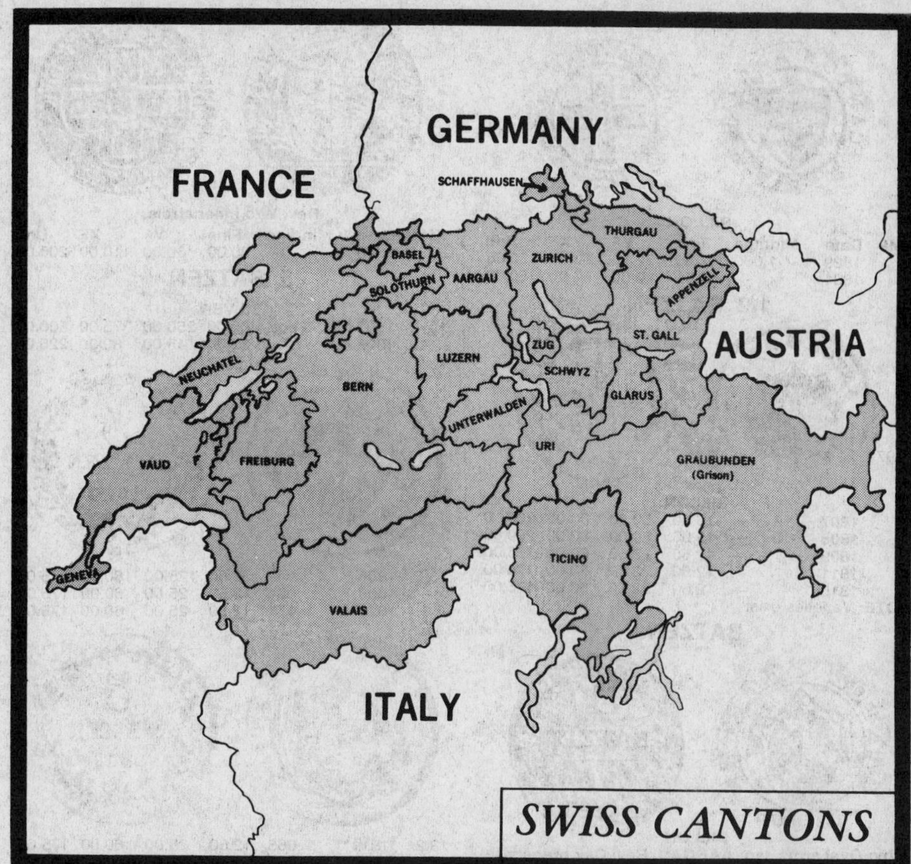

In Switzerland, canton is the name given to each of the 23 states comprising the Swiss Federation. The origin of the cantons is rooted in the liberty-loving instincts of the peasants of Helvetia.

After the Romans departed Switzerland to defend Rome against the barbarians, Switzerland became, in the Middle Ages, a federation of fiefs of the Holy Roman Empire. In 888 it was again united by Rudolf of Burgundy, a minor despot, and for 150 years Switzerland had a king. Upon the death of the last Burgundian king, the kingdom crumbled into a loose collection of feudal fiefs ruled by bishops and ducal families who made their own laws and levied their own taxes. Eventually this division of rule by arbitrary despots became more than the freedom-loving and resourceful peasants could bear. The citizens living in the remote valleys of Uri, Schwyz (from which Switzerland received its name) and Unterwalden decided to liberate themselves from all feudal obligations and become free men.

On Aug. 1, 1291, the elders of these three small states met on a tiny heath known as the Rutli on the shores of the Lake of Lucerne and negotiated an 'eternal pact' which recognized their right to local self-government, and pledged one another assistance against any encroachment upon these rights. The pact was the beginning of the 'Everlasting League' and the foundation of the Swiss Confederation.

CANTONAL MINT MARKS OF SWITZERLAND

Mint mark	Canton	Mint
A.-B.	Geneva	Geneva 1847 (Auguste Bovet)
A.B.	Graubunden	Geneva 1842 (Antoine Bovy)
A-B	Graubunden	Private coiner 1836 (Antoine Bovy)
A-B	Graubunden	Geneva 1842 (Antoine Bovy)
B	Basel	Basel 1826 (Bel-Bessiere)
B	Freiburg	Freiburg 1830 (Bel-Bessiere)
B	Glarus	Unknown site 1806-1814
B	Graubunden	Bern 1820
B	Graubunden	Private coiner 1826
B	Luzern	Luzern 1807-1814 (Bruppacher)
B	Schwyz	Schwyz or Aargau 1810
B	Zurich	Zurich 1806-1813 (Bruckmann)
BEL	Basel	Basel 1826 (Bel-Bessiere)
BEL	Freiburg	Freiburg 1830-1846 (Bel-Bessiere)
BEL	Vaud	Lausanne 1826-1834 (Bel-Bessiere)
D	Zurich	Stuttgart 1842-1848
DB	Schwyz	Schwyz 1843-1846
F	Glarus	Unknown site 1806-1807
G	Geneva	Geneva An 8-13
H	Geneva	Geneva 1817 (Hoyer)
H	Schwyz	Schwyz or Aargau 1810-1811
HB	Graubunden	Private coiner 1836 (Bruppacher)
K	St. Gall	St. Gall 1807-1817 (Kukler)
M	Aargau	Aargau 1807-1808 (Meyer)
M	Schwyz	Aargau or Schwyz 1844
N	Graubunden	Bern 1825 (Nett)
SIBER	Vaud	Lausanne 1845 (Siber)
Star	Ticino	Luzern 1813

AARGAU

Argau, Argovie

Located in north central Switzerland. Was named after the river Aar. Was admitted to the Swiss Confederation in 1803.

MONETARY SYSTEM

10 Rappen = 4 Kreuzer = 1 Batzen

10 Batzen = 1 Frank

RAPPEN

BILLON

KM#	Date	Mintage	Fine	VF	XF	Unc
15	1809	.044	25.00	45.00	80.00	175.00
	1811	.039	10.00	17.50	25.00	60.00
	1816	—	10.00	17.50	25.00	60.00

Rev: Wreath of stars and flowers.

KM#	Date	Mintage	Fine	VF	XF	Unc
18	1810	.020	25.00	45.00	80.00	175.00

2 RAPPEN

BILLON

KM#	Date	Mintage	Fine	VF	XF	Unc
11	1808	.092	6.00	12.50	17.50	35.00
	1811	—	15.00	30.00	40.00	75.00
	1812	—	6.00	12.50	20.00	50.00
	1813	—	6.00	12.50	20.00	50.00
	1814	—	6.00	12.50	20.00	50.00
	1816	—	6.00	12.50	20.00	50.00

2-1/2 RAPPEN

(Ein (1) Kreuzer)

BILLON

KM#	Date	Mintage	Fine	VF	XF	Unc
25	1831	—	8.00	17.50	30.00	75.00

5 RAPPEN

BILLON

KM#	Date	Mintage	Fine	VF	XF	Unc
24	1829	1,000	12.50	22.50	60.00	150.00
	1831	—	12.50	22.50	60.00	150.00

1/2 BATZEN

BILLON

KM#	Date	Mintage	Fine	VF	XF	Unc
8	1807	—	15.00	50.00	80.00	200.00
	1808	—	15.00	50.00	80.00	200.00
	1809	—	12.50	22.50	60.00	175.00
	1811	—	12.50	22.50	60.00	175.00
	1815	—	12.50	22.50	60.00	175.00

NOTE: Varieties exist.

BATZEN

BILLON

Obv: Oval arms, leg: AARGAU. Rev: Oak branches.

KM#	Date	Mintage	Fine	VF	XF	Unc
5	1805	1,000	45.00	90.00	150.00	350.00

Obv. leg: ARGAU.

KM#	Date	Mintage	Fine	VF	XF	Unc
6	1806	—	45.00	125.00	180.00	450.00

Obv: Pointed arms w/garlands.

KM#	Date	Mintage	Fine	VF	XF	Unc
7	1806	—	45.00	125.00	180.00	400.00

KM#	Date	Mintage	Fine	VF	XF	Unc
9	1807	.132	15.00	27.50	50.00	150.00
	1808	.184	15.00	27.50	50.00	150.00
	1809	.350	15.00	27.50	50.00	150.00
	1810	.215	15.00	27.50	50.00	150.00
	1811	.060	15.00	27.50	50.00	150.00
	1816	—	20.00	45.00	125.00	275.00

NOTE: Varieties exist.

Obv. leg: ARGAU. Rev: Palm branches.

KM#	Date	Mintage	Fine	VF	XF	Unc
12	1808	—	80.00	110.00	160.00	500.00

Rev: Beaded inner circle

KM#	Date	Mintage	Fine	VF	XF	Unc
21	1826	—	10.00	25.00	37.50	100.00

Rev: W/o inner circle.

KM#	Date	Mintage	Fine	VF	XF	Unc
22	1826	—	30.00	60.00	110.00	200.00

5 BATZEN

SILVER

KM#	Date	Mintage	Fine	VF	XF	Unc
10	1807 M	250 pcs.	200.00	250.00	375.00	800.00
	1808 M	.114	25.00	45.00	80.00	225.00

KM#	Date	Mintage	Fine	VF	XF	Unc
13.1	1808	—	60.00	125.00	180.00	375.00
	1809	.084	12.50	25.00	60.00	175.00
	1810	.171	12.50	25.00	60.00	175.00

KM#	Date	Mintage	Fine	VF	XF	Unc
13.2	*1811*	.065	12.50	25.00	60.00	175.00

KM#	Date	Mintage	Fine	VF	XF	Unc
13.3	1812	.073	70.00	150.00	300.00	750.00
	1814	—	70.00	150.00	300.00	750.00
	1815	—	12.50	25.00	60.00	175.00

KM#	Date	Mintage	Fine	VF	XF	Unc
23	1826	.508	10.00	20.00	45.00	150.00

10 BATZEN

SILVER

Obv: Palm and laurel wreath flanking arms.

KM#	Date	Mintage	Fine	VF	XF	Unc
14	1808	3,884	55.00	120.00	175.00	650.00
	1809	9,842	40.00	90.00	150.00	650.00
	1818	3,223	50.00	100.00	200.00	700.00

Obv: Laurel branches both sides of arms.

KM#	Date	Mintage	Fine	VF	XF	Unc
16	1809	Inc. Ab.	50.00	100.00	200.00	750.00

20 BATZEN

SILVER

KM#	Date	Mintage	Fine	VF	XF	Unc
17	1809	.014	60.00	125.00	200.00	700.00

4 FRANK

SILVER

KM#	Date	Mintage	Fine	VF	XF	Unc
20	1812	2,527	250.00	400.00	600.00	1850.

APPENZELL

Located in northeast Switzerland, completely surrounded by the canton of St. Gall. The name was derived from "Abbot's Cell". Achieved independence from the abbots of St. Gall in the period 1377/1411. Divided by religious differences into two half cantons, Ausser-Rhoden (Protestant) and Inner-Rhoden (Catholic). Both were joined to the Canton to Santis 1797-1803, but regained their independent status in 1803.

MONETARY SYSTEM

4 Pfenning = 1 Kreuzer
10 Rappen = 4 Kreuzer = 1 Batzen
10 Batzen = 1 Franken

AUSSER RHODEN

PFENNIG

COPPER

KM#	Date	Mintage	Fine	VF	XF	Unc
11	1816	.066	90.00	150.00	210.00	350.00

KREUZER

BILLON

KM#	Date	Mintage	Fine	VF	XF	Unc
10	1813	.086	22.50	30.00	50.00	125.00

1/2 BATZEN

BILLON

KM#	Date	Mintage	Fine	VF	XF	Unc
	1808	.073	25.00	70.00	110.00	250.00
	1809	.060	17.50	30.00	60.00	125.00
	1816	.081	20.00	45.00	110.00	150.00

BATZEN

BILLON

KM#	Date	Mintage	Fine	VF	XF	Unc
6	1808	.266	20.00	45.00	110.00	250.00
	1816	.203	20.00	45.00	110.00	250.00

1/2 FRANKEN

SILVER

KM#	Date	Mintage	Fine	VF	XF	Unc
7	1809	6,534	90.00	200.00	275.00	850.00

2 FRANKEN

SILVER

KM#	Date	Mintage	Fine	VF	XF	Unc
8	1812	1,861	180.00	265.00	550.00	1200.

4 FRANKEN

SILVER

KM#	Date	Mintage	Fine	VF	XF	Unc
9	1812	2,357	250.00	400.00	750.00	1800.

KM#	Date	Mintage	Fine	VF	XF	Unc
12	1816	1,850	275.00	475.00	900.00	2000.

BASEL

Basilea

A bishopric in northwest Switzerland, founded in the 5th century. The first coinage was c.1000AD. During the Reformation Basel became Protestant and the bishop resided henceforth in the town of Porrentruy. The Congress of Vienna gave the territories of the Bishopric to Bern. Today they form the Canton Jura and the French speaking part of Bern.

CANTON

MONETARY SYSTEM

After 1803

10 Rappen = 1 Batzen
10 Batzen = 1 Frank

RAPPEN

BILLON

KM#	Date	Mintage	Fine	VF	XF	Unc
201	1810	—	6.00	10.00	25.00	45.00
	1818	—	6.00	10.00	25.00	45.00

2 RAPPEN

BILLON

KM#	Date	Mintage	Fine	VF	XF	Unc
202	1810	—	6.00	10.00	25.00	50.00
	1818	—	6.00	10.00	25.00	50.00

5 RAPPEN

BILLON

KM#	Date	Mintage	Fine	VF	XF	Unc
204	1826B	—	10.00	15.00	40.00	90.00

KM#	Date	Mintage	Fine	VF	XF	Unc
205	1826	—	50.00	125.00	240.00	450.00

Obv: Value in exergue.

KM#	Date	Mintage	Fine	VF	XF	Unc
206	1826	—	50.00	100.00	220.00	400.00

1/2 BATZEN

BILLON

KM#	Date	Mintage	Fine	VF	XF	Unc
197	1809	—	12.50	20.00	60.00	100.00

BATZEN

BILLON
Under the Republic

KM#	Date	Mintage	Fine	VF	XF	Unc
195	1805	—	30.00	55.00	85.00	200.00

As a Canton

KM#	Date	Mintage	Fine	VF	XF	Unc
196	1805	—	37.50	80.00	125.00	275.00
	1806	—	17.50	40.00	85.00	200.00
	1809	—	9.00	17.50	40.00	125.00
	1810	—	12.00	25.00	35.00	125.00

KM#	Date	Mintage	Fine	VF	XF	Unc
207	1826	—	50.00	120.00	225.00	350.00

KM#	Date	Mintage	Fine	VF	XF	Unc
208	1826B	—	5.00	18.00	35.00	85.00

3 BATZEN

SILVER

KM#	Date	Mintage	Fine	VF	XF	Unc
198	1809	—	10.00	25.00	50.00	125.00
	1810	—	15.00	40.00	65.00	150.00

5 BATZEN

SILVER

KM#	Date	Mintage	Fine	VF	XF	Unc
199	1809	—	20.00	40.00	85.00	300.00
	1810	—	12.50	25.00	65.00	275.00

Obv: BATZEN

KM#	Date	Mintage	Fine	VF	XF	Unc
209	1826	—	12.50	25.00	45.00	225.00

Obv: BATZn

KM#	Date	Mintage	Fine	VF	XF	Unc
210	1826	—	25.00	85.00	200.00	500.00

BERN

A city and canton in west central Switzerland. It was founded as a military post in 1191 and became an imperial city with the mint right in 1218. It was admitted to the Swiss Confederation as a canton in 1353.

MINTMASTERS INITIALS

D-B - J. De Beyer

DUPLONE

7.6400 g, .900 GOLD, .2210 oz AGW
Obv: Crowned pointed shield. Rev: Standing Swiss.

KM#	Date	Mintage	VG	Fine	VF	XF
163	1819	—	250.00	500.00	1000.	2000.
	1829	—	300.00	600.00	1200.	2200.

NOTE: Earlier date (1797) exists for this type.

MONETARY REFORM

MONETARY SYSTEM
Commencing 1803
10 Rappen = 1 Batzen
10 Batzen = 1 Frank

RAPPEN

BILLON
Obv. leg: CANTON BERN

KM#	Date	Mintage	Fine	VF	XF	Unc
172	1811	—	6.00	12.50	18.00	45.00
	1829	—	12.50	22.50	37.50	80.00

Obv. leg: REPUBL. BERN

KM#	Date	Mintage	Fine	VF	XF	Unc
175	1818	—	6.00	12.50	18.00	45.00
	1819	—	6.00	12.50	18.00	45.00
	1836	—	6.00	12.50	18.00	45.00

2 RAPPEN

BILLON

KM#	Date	Mintage	Fine	VF	XF	Unc
171	1809	—	10.00	20.00	50.00	125.00

2-1/2 RAPPEN

BILLON

KM#	Date	Mintage	Fine	VF	XF	Unc
173	1811	.114	7.00	15.00	20.00	50.00
	1829	—	7.00	15.00	20.00	50.00

5 RAPPEN

BILLON
Rev: W/inner beaded circle.

KM#	Date	Mintage	Fine	VF	XF	Unc
192	1826	—	3.00	10.00	20.00	65.00

Rev: W/o inner beaded circle.

KM#	Date	Mintage	Fine	VF	XF	Unc
193	1826	—	6.00	20.00	30.00	90.00

1/2 BATZEN

BILLON

KM#	Date	Mintage	Fine	VF	XF	Unc
176	1818	—	5.00	15.00	30.00	110.00
	1824	—	5.00	15.00	30.00	110.00

BATZEN

BILLON

KM#	Date	Mintage	Fine	VF	XF	Unc
177	1818	—	5.00	12.50	30.00	90.00
	1824	—	5.00	12.50	30.00	90.00

Obv. denomination: BATZ

KM#	Date	Mintage	Fine	VF	XF	Unc
194.1	1826	—	2.50	10.00	20.00	60.00

Obv. denomination: BAZ

KM#	Date	Mintage	Fine	VF	XF	Unc
194.2	1826	—	5.00	12.50	30.00	75.00

NOTE: These are found overstruck on 1 Batzen, KM#87.

2-1/2 BATZEN

SILVER
Obv. denomination: BATZ

KM#	Date	Mintage	Fine	VF	XF	Unc
195.1	1826	—	10.00	25.00	50.00	125.00

Obv. denomination: BAZ

KM#	Date	Mintage	Fine	VF	XF	Unc
195.2	1826	—	20.00	40.00	60.00	175.00

5 BATZEN

SILVER

KM#	Date	Mintage	Fine	VF	XF	Unc
170	1808	—	17.50	40.00	60.00	200.00
	1810	—	17.50	40.00	60.00	200.00
	1811	—	80.00	110.00	275.00	750.00
	1818	—	40.00	65.00	140.00	250.00

Obv. denomination: BATZ

KM#	Date	Mintage	Fine	VF	XF	Unc
196.1	1826	—	12.50	25.00	35.00	120.00

Obv. denomination: BAZ

KM#	Date	Mintage	Fine	VF	XF	Unc
196.2	1826	—	17.50	40.00	65.00	175.00

Obv: Denomination in exergue.

KM#	Date	Mintage	Fine	VF	XF	Unc
196.3	1826	—	20.00	50.00	100.00	225.00

FRANK

SILVER

KM#	Date	Mintage	Fine	VF	XF	Unc
174	1811	.011	37.50	110.00	240.00	600.00

2 FRANKEN

SILVER

KM#	Date	Mintage	Fine	VF	XF	Unc
198	1835	—	90.00	150.00	320.00	900.00

4 FRANKEN

SILVER

KM#	Date	Mintage	Fine	VF	XF	Unc
190	1823	—	200.00	450.00	900.00	2500.

KM#	Date	Mintage	Fine	VF	XF	Unc
199	1835	—	150.00	300.00	600.00	2000.

COUNTERSTAMPED COINAGE

40 BATZEN (BZ)

During the period 1816-1819 an estimated 660,000 French Ecus of Louis XV and Louis XVI 1726-1793 and 6 Livres dated 1793-1794 along with 40 Batzen and 4 Franken of the Helvetian Republic were counterstamped with a bear and 40 BZ. on shields.

Approximately ninety percent of the counterstamped pieces were melted by 1851. It is estimated some 5,000 pieces or less still exist.

SILVER

c/s: On France Louis XV Ecu, C#42.

KM#	Date	Year	VG	Fine	VF	XF
178	ND	(1726-41)	200.00	250.00	350.00	750.00

c/s: On France Louis XV Ecu, C#47.

KM#	Date	Year	VG	Fine	VF	XF
179	ND	(1740-71)	200.00	250.00	350.00	750.00

c/s: On France Louis XV Ecu, C#47a.

KM#	Date	Year	VG	Fine	VF	XF
180	ND	(1770-74)	175.00	225.00	300.00	700.00

c/s: On France Louis XVI Ecu, C#78.

KM#	Date	Year	VG	Fine	VF	XF
181	ND	(1774-92)	175.00	225.00	300.00	700.00

c/s: On France Louis XVI Constitutional Ecu, C#93.

KM#	Date	Year	VG	Fine	VF	XF
182	ND	(1792-93)	225.00	300.00	500.00	1000.

c/s: On France 6 Livres, C#123.

KM#	Date	Year	VG	Fine	VF	XF
183	ND	(1793-94)	400.00	650.00	925.00	1500.

c/s: On Helvetia 40 Batzen, KM#4.1.

184 ND (1798) — Reported, not confirmed

c/s: On Helvetia 40 Batzen, KM#4.2.

185 ND (1798) — Reported, not confirmed

c/s: On Helvetia 4 Franken, KM#10.

186 ND (1799-1801) — Reported, not confirmed

TRADE COINAGE

4 DUCAT

14.0000 g, .986 GOLD, .4438 oz AGW
Obv: Crowned supported arms.
Rev: Small denomination and date.

KM#	Date	Mintage	VG	Fine	VF	XF
155.1	1825	—	—	—	Rare	—

FREIBURG

Friburg, Fribourg, Freyburg

A canton and city located in western Switzerland. The city was founded in 1178 and obtained the mint right in 1422. It joined the Swiss Confederation in 1481. During the Helvetian Republic period it was known as Sarine Et Broye but changed the name back to Freiburg in 1803.

MONETARY SYSTEM

10 Rappen = 1 Batzen
10 Batzen = 1 Frank

2-1/2 RAPPEN

BILLON
Obv: Arms, value below.

KM#	Date	Mintage	Fine	VF	XF	Unc
81	1827	—	6.00	9.00	16.00	50.00

Obv: Pointed arms.

KM#	Date	Mintage	Fine	VF	XF	Unc
91	1846BEL	—	6.00	9.00	16.00	50.00

5 RAPPEN

BILLON

KM#	Date	Mintage	Fine	VF	XF	Unc
70	1806	—	15.00	25.00	35.00	150.00

Obv: Date.

KM#	Date	Mintage	Fine	VF	XF	Unc
82	1827	—	15.00	22.50	32.50	125.00
	1828	—	12.50	20.00	25.00	100.00

Rev: Date.

KM#	Date	Mintage	Fine	VF	XF	Unc
87	1830BEL	—	5.00	10.00	15.00	50.00
	1831BEL	—	4.00	9.00	12.00	48.00

1/2 BATZEN

BILLON

KM#	Date	Mintage	Fine	VF	XF	Unc
73	1810	—	12.50	20.00	27.50	125.00
	1811	—	8.00	17.50	25.00	125.00

BATZEN

BILLON

KM#	Date	Mintage	Fine	VF	XF	Unc
71	1806	—	12.00	18.00	65.00	250.00

KM#	Date	Mintage	Fine	VF	XF	Unc
74	1810	—	12.00	18.00	65.00	250.00

KM#	Date	Mintage	Fine	VF	XF	Unc
75	1811	—	8.00	14.00	27.50	75.00

Obv. value: BAZ

KM#	Date	Mintage	Fine	VF	XF	Unc
83	1827	—	8.00	14.00	27.50	75.00
	1828	—	8.00	14.00	27.50	75.00

Obv. value: BATZ.

KM#	Date	Mintage	Fine	VF	XF	Unc
85	1829	—	8.00	14.00	27.50	75.00

KM#	Date	Mintage	Fine	VF	XF	Unc
88	1830B	—	8.00	14.00	27.50	75.00

5 BATZEN

SILVER

KM#	Date	Mintage	Fine	VF	XF	Unc
76	1811	—	15.00	35.00	50.00	235.00
	1814	—	15.00	35.00	50.00	235.00

KM#	Date	Mintage	Fine	VF	XF	Unc
84	1827	—	15.00	35.00	50.00	235.00
	1828	—	15.00	35.00	60.00	265.00
	1829	—	12.50	25.00	55.00	265.00

KM#	Date	Mintage	Fine	VF	XF	Unc
89	1830	—	12.50	25.00	55.00	265.00

10 BATZEN

SILVER

KM#	Date	Mintage	Fine	VF	XF	Unc
77	1811	4,907	70.00	125.00	275.00	1250.

KM#	Date	Mintage	Fine	VF	XF	Unc
78	1812	Inc. Ab.	70.00	125.00	275.00	1250.

4 FRANKEN

SILVER

KM#	Date	Mintage	Fine	VF	XF	Unc
79	1813	2,429	225.00	425.00	700.00	1600.

GENEVA

A canton and city in southwestern Switzerland. The city became a bishopric c.400 AD and was part of the Burgundian Kingdom for 500 years. They became completely independent in 1530. In 1798 they were occupied by France but became independent again in 1813. They joined the Swiss Confederation in 1815.

MONETARY SYSTEM

1814-1838

12 Deniers = 4 Quarts = 1 Sol
12 Sols = 1 Florin
12 Florins, 9 Sols = 1 Thaler
35 Florins = 1 Pistole

6 DENIERS

KM#	Date	Mintage	Fine	VF	XF	Unc
			BILLON			
115	1817	—	2.50	5.00	14.00	30.00
			SILVER			
115a	1817	—	—	—	100.00	150.00

KM#	Date	Mintage	Fine	VF	XF	Unc
			BILLON			
118	1819	—	2.50	5.00	14.00	30.00
	1825	—	4.00	7.00	17.50	35.00
	1833	—	2.50	5.00	14.00	30.00
			SILVER			
118a	1819	—	—	—	100.00	150.00
	1825	—	—	—	115.00	175.00
	1833	—	—	—	100.00	150.00

SOL

KM#	Date	Mintage	Fine	VF	XF	Unc
			BILLON			
116	1817 H	—	2.00	5.00	10.00	27.50
			SILVER			
116a	1817 H	—	—	—	85.00	135.00

KM#	Date	Mintage	Fine	VF	XF	Unc
			BILLON			
119	1819	—	2.00	5.00	10.00	27.50
			SILVER			
119a	1819	—	—	—	85.00	135.00

KM#	Date	Mintage	Fine	VF	XF	Unc
			BILLON			
120	1825	—	2.00	5.00	10.00	27.50
	1833	—	2.00	5.00	10.00	27.50
			SILVER			
120a	1825	—	—	—	85.00	135.00
	1833	—	—	—	85.00	135.00

1-1/2 SOL

KM#	Date	Mintage	Fine	VF	XF	Unc
			BILLON			
117	1817 H	—	2.50	9.00	20.00	40.00

KM#	Date	Mintage	Fine	VF	XF	Unc
121	1825	—	2.50	9.00	20.00	40.00

SILVER

KM#	Date	Mintage	Fine	VF	XF	Unc
121a	1825	—	—	—	130.00	200.00

NOTE: Types KM#115a, 118a, 116a, 120, 120a and 121a struck in fine silver are presentation pieces.

DECIMAL COINAGE

100 Centimes = 1 Franc

CENTIME

BILLON

KM#	Date	Mintage	Fine	VF	XF	Unc
125	1839	.325	2.50	4.50	9.00	25.00

SILVER

KM#	Date	Mintage	Fine	VF	XF	Unc
125a	1839	—	—	—	80.00	125.00

COPPER

KM#	Date	Mintage	Fine	VF	XF	Unc
130	1840	—	2.50	4.50	9.00	25.00
	1844	—	2.50	4.50	9.00	25.00
	1846	—	3.50	6.00	9.00	25.00

KM#	Date	Mintage	Fine	VF	XF	Unc
132	1847	—	2.50	4.50	9.00	25.00

SILVER

KM#	Date	Mintage	Fine	VF	XF	Unc
132a	1847	—	—	—	80.00	125.00

2 CENTIMES

BILLON

KM#	Date	Mintage	Fine	VF	XF	Unc
126	1839	.078	4.00	8.00	25.00	60.00

SILVER

KM#	Date	Mintage	Fine	VF	XF	Unc
126a	1839	—	—	—	200.00	300.00

4 CENTIMES

BILLON

KM#	Date	Mintage	Fine	VF	XF	Unc
127	1839	.331	3.75	8.00	17.50	35.00

SILVER

KM#	Date	Mintage	Fine	VF	XF	Unc
127a	1839	—	—	—	115.00	175.00

5 CENTIMES

BILLON

KM#	Date	Mintage	Fine	VF	XF	Unc
131	1840	.699	3.00	8.00	9.00	15.00

SILVER

KM#	Date	Mintage	Fine	VF	XF	Unc
131a	1840	—	—	—	45.00	75.00

BILLON

Rev: Arms on shield.

KM#	Date	Mintage	Fine	VF	XF	Unc
133	1847 A.-B.	I.A.	3.00	8.00	17.50	40.00

SILVER

KM#	Date	Mintage	Fine	VF	XF	Unc
133a	1847	—	—	—	130.00	200.00

10 CENTIMES

BILLON

KM#	Date	Mintage	Fine	VF	XF	Unc
128	1839	—	3.00	8.00	17.50	35.00
	1844	—	3.00	7.00	12.50	27.50

SILVER

KM#	Date	Mintage	Fine	VF	XF	Unc
128a	1839	—	—	—	115.00	175.00

BILLON

KM#	Date	Mintage	Fine	VF	XF	Unc
134	1847 A.-B.	—	3.00	7.00	12.50	27.50

SILVER

KM#	Date	Mintage	Fine	VF	XF	Unc
134a	1847	—	—	—	85.00	135.00

25 CENTIMES

BILLON

KM#	Date	Mintage	Fine	VF	XF	Unc
129	1839	—	2.50	8.00	17.50	35.00
	1844	—	2.50	8.00	17.50	35.00

SILVER

KM#	Date	Mintage	Fine	VF	XF	Unc
129a	1839	—	—	—	115.00	175.00

BILLON

KM#	Date	Mintage	Fine	VF	XF	Unc
135	1847 A.-B.	—	3.75	8.00	17.50	35.00

SILVER

KM#	Date	Mintage	Fine	VF	XF	Unc
136	1847	—	—	—	115.00	175.00

NOTE: Types KM#125a-129a, 131a-134a and 136 struck in fine silver are presentation pieces.

5 FRANCS

SILVER

KM#	Date	Mintage	Fine	VF	XF	Unc
137	1848	1,176	150.00	210.00	275.00	600.00

10 FRANCS

SILVER

Obv: Similar to 5 Francs, KM#137.

KM#	Date	Mintage	Fine	VF	XF	Unc
138	1848	385 pcs.	125.00	275.00	500.00	1250.
	1851	678 pcs.	100.00	250.00	425.00	900.00

3.8000 g, .750 GOLD, .0916 oz AGW

KM#	Date	Mintage	Fine	VF	XF	Unc
139	1848	336 pcs.	600.00	1250.	1750.	2500.

20 FRANCS

7.6000 g, .750 GOLD, .1833 oz AGW

KM#	Date	Mintage	Fine	VF	XF	Unc
140	1848	3,421	300.00	650.00	1100.	1650.

GLARUS

A canton in eastern Switzerland. Independence was gained in c.1390 but from 1798-1803 it was occupied by the French. They rejoined the Swiss Confederation in 1803.

MONETARY SYSTEM

3 Rappen = 1 Schilling
100 Rappen = 1 Frank

SCHILLING

BILLON

KM#	Date	Mintage	Fine	VF	XF	Unc
10	1806 F	—	15.00	30.00	100.00	500.00
	1807 F	—	20.00	40.00	80.00	500.00

Obv: Shield w/garlands.

KM#	Date	Mintage	Fine	VF	XF	Unc
13	1808	—	20.00	45.00	80.00	500.00
	1809	—	15.00	40.00	100.00	500.00
	1811	—	15.00	40.00	90.00	500.00
	1812	—	15.00	40.00	90.00	500.00
	1813	—	15.00	40.00	90.00	500.00

Obv: Shield in branches.

KM#	Date	Mintage	Fine	VF	XF	Unc
15	1809	—	15.00	30.00	80.00	500.00
	1810	—	250.00	500.00	1000.	500.00

3 SCHILLING

BILLON

KM#	Date	Mintage	Fine	VF	XF	Unc
11	1806	.134	70.00	125.00	260.00	1250.

KM#	Date	Mintage	Fine	VF	XF	Unc
14	1808	—	70.00	125.00	260.00	1250.
	1812	—	70.00	125.00	260.00	1250.

KM#	Date	Mintage	Fine	VF	XF	Unc
16	1809	—	70.00	125.00	260.00	1250.
	1810	—	70.00	125.00	260.00	1250.
	1814	—	70.00	125.00	260.00	1250.

15 SCHILLING

SILVER

KM#	Date	Mintage	Fine	VF	XF	Unc
12	1806 B	7,067	125.00	250.00	600.00	3000.
	1807 B	Inc. Ab.	125.00	250.00	600.00	3000.
	1811 B	Inc. Ab.	180.00	325.00	1000.	4500.
	1813 B	Inc. Ab.	125.00	250.00	600.00	3000.
	1814 B	Inc. Ab.	180.00	375.00	900.00	4000.

40 BATZEN

.900 SILVER
Glarus Shooting Festival

KM#	Date	Mintage	VF	XF	Unc	BU
20	1847	3,200	1500.	2000.	3750.	5500.

GRAUBUNDEN

The largest and most easterly of the Swiss cantons. The district was set up in the reign of Roman Emperor Augustus and was one of the various factions sparring for power in the 14th and 15th centuries. The name is derived from "Grey League". The first coins were issued in c. 1600. They joined the Swiss Confederation in 1803.

MINTMASTERS INITIALS

A-B - Bouey
H.B. - Bruppacher

MONETARY SYSTEM

15 Rappen = 6 Bluzger = 1 Schweizer Batzen
10 Schweizer Batzen = 1 Frank
16 Franken = 1 Duplone

1/6 BATZEN

BILLON
Rev. value: 1/6 BATZEN

KM#	Date	Mintage	Fine	VF	XF	Unc
5	1807	.058	7.50	15.00	30.00	90.00
	1820	.480	20.00	32.50	55.00	150.00

Rev. value: 1/6 BAZEN

KM#	Date	Mintage	Fine	VF	XF	Unc
16	1842 A.B.	.172	6.00	12.50	30.00	90.00

1/2 BATZEN

BILLON

KM#	Date	Mintage	Fine	VF	XF	Unc
6	1807	.075	25.00	50.00	100.00	275.00
	1820 B	.060	17.50	40.00	80.00	200.00

KM#	Date	Mintage	Fine	VF	XF	Unc
9	1812	.100	30.00	75.00	200.00	500.00

KM#	Date	Mintage	Fine	VF	XF	Unc
13	1836 A-B	.212	15.00	30.00	60.00	150.00
	1842 A-B	.162	10.00	25.00	40.00	135.00

BATZEN

BILLON

KM#	Date	Mintage	Fine	VF	XF	Unc
7	1807	.056	10.00	30.00	60.00	225.00

KM#	Date	Mintage	Fine	VF	XF	Unc
11	1820 B	.050	10.00	30.00	60.00	225.00
	1826 B	.050	15.00	37.50	90.00	250.00

Rev: Value w/short "1".

KM#	Date	Mintage	Fine	VF	XF	Unc
14	1836 HB	Inc. Ab.	60.00	125.00	275.00	750.00

Rev: Value w/tall "1".

KM#	Date	Mintage	Fine	VF	XF	Unc
15	1836	.099	15.00	25.00	50.00	200.00
	1842 A-B	.100	10.00	22.50	40.00	175.00

5 BATZEN

SILVER

KM#	Date	Mintage	Fine	VF	XF	Unc
8	1807	6,398	50.00	100.00	150.00	450.00
	1820	.016	50.00	100.00	150.00	450.00
	1826	—	80.00	170.00	210.00	525.00

10 BATZEN

SILVER

KM#	Date	Mintage	Fine	VF	XF	Unc
12	1825N	2,000	200.00	320.00	600.00	1250.

4 FRANCS

.880 SILVER
Chur in Graubunden Shooting Festival

KM#	Date	Mintage	VF	XF	Unc	BU
17	1842	6,000	500.00	700.00	1500.	2400.

16 FRANKEN

7.6400 g, .900 GOLD, .2211 oz AGW

KM#	Date	Mintage	Fine	VF	XF	Unc
10	1813	100 pcs.	2500.	4000.	7500.	12,500.

LUZERN

Lucerne

A canton and city in central Switzerland. The city grew around the Benedictine Monastery which was founded in 750. They joined the Swiss Confederation as the 4th member in 1332. Few coins were issued before the 1500s.

MINTMASTERS INITIALS

B, Br Bruppacher
HL - Hedlinger
M - Meyer

ANGSTER

COPPER
Similar to 1 Rappen, KM#96.

KM#	Date	Mintage	Fine	VF	XF	Unc
76	1804	—	12.50	25.00	50.00	150.00
	1811	—	10.00	20.00	30.00	75.00
	1823	—	5.00	10.00	15.00	30.00
	1832	—	5.00	10.00	15.00	30.00
	1834	—	5.00	10.00	15.00	30.00

NOTE: Earlier dates (1775-1791) exist for this type.

Obv. leg: CANTON LUZERN

KM#	Date	Mintage	Fine	VF	XF	Unc
117	1839	—	5.00	10.00	15.00	30.00
	1843	—	5.00	10.00	15.00	30.00

RAPPEN

COPPER
Similar to KM#96.

KM#	Date	Mintage	Fine	VF	XF	Unc
75	1804	—	5.00	10.00	15.00	40.00

NOTE: Earlier dates (1774-1796) exist for this type.

KM#	Date	Mintage	Fine	VF	XF	Unc
96	1804	—	5.00	7.50	12.50	35.00

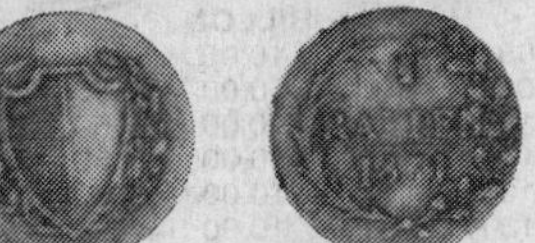

Rev. value: 1 RAPPEN or RAPEN

KM#	Date	Mintage	Fine	VF	XF	Unc
115	1831	—	5.00	7.50	12.50	35.00
116	1834	—	5.00	7.50	12.50	35.00

Obv. leg: CANTON LUZERN, oak circle.

KM#	Date	Mintage	Fine	VF	XF	Unc
118	1839	—	5.00	7.50	12.50	35.00

Obv. leg: CANTON LUZERN, oak wreath.

KM#	Date	Mintage	Fine	VF	XF	Unc
119	1839	—	5.00	7.50	12.50	35.00
	1843	—	5.00	7.50	12.50	35.00
	1844	—	5.00	7.50	12.50	35.00
	1845	—	5.00	7.50	12.50	35.00
	1846	—	5.00	7.50	12.50	35.00

1/2 BATZEN - 5 RAPPEN

BILLON

KM#	Date	Mintage	Fine	VF	XF	Unc
106	1813	—	10.00	27.50	50.00	125.00

BATZEN - 10 RAPPEN

BILLON
Obv. value: 1 BAZ. Rev: X RAPPEN.

KM#	Date	Mintage	Fine	VF	XF	Unc
95	1803	—	15.00	35.00	50.00	200.00

KM#	Date	Mintage	Fine	VF	XF	Unc
97	1804	—	9.00	15.00	25.00	125.00
	1805	—	—	—	—	—
	1806	—	17.50	37.50	65.00	220.00

Obv. leg: MONETA REIPUB.LUCERNENCIS

KM#	Date	Mintage	Fine	VF	XF	Unc
99	1805	—	12.50	20.00	30.00	135.00

KM#	Date	Mintage	Fine	VF	XF	Unc
101	1807	—	6.00	12.50	25.00	125.00
	1808	—	6.00	12.50	25.00	125.00
	1809	—	6.00	12.50	25.00	125.00
	1810	—	6.00	12.50	25.00	125.00
	1811	—	6.00	12.50	25.00	125.00

KM#	Date	Mintage	Fine	VF	XF	Unc
107	1813	—	6.00	12.50	25.00	125.00

2-1/2 BATZEN

SILVER
Obv: Date (Republica).

KM#	Date	Mintage	Fine	VF	XF	Unc
110	1815	—	30.00	60.00	90.00	225.00

Rev: Date (Canton).

KM#	Date	Mintage	Fine	VF	XF	Unc
111	1815	—	12.50	20.00	30.00	135.00

5 BATZEN

SILVER

KM#	Date	Mintage	Fine	VF	XF	Unc
100	1806	—	30.00	60.00	90.00	300.00

KM#	Date	Mintage	Fine	VF	XF	Unc
104	1810	—	25.00	45.00	80.00	275.00

KM#	Date	Mintage	Fine	VF	XF	Unc
108	1813	—	25.00	45.00	80.00	275.00
	1814	—	25.00	45.00	80.00	275.00

KM#	Date	Mintage	Fine	VF	XF	Unc
112	1815	—	25.00	45.00	80.00	275.00
	1816	—	25.00	45.00	80.00	275.00

10 BATZEN

SILVER

KM#	Date	Mintage	Fine	VF	XF	Unc
105	1811	—	225.00	425.00	650.00	2500.
	1812	—	50.00	120.00	200.00	1250.

40 BATZEN

SILVER

KM#	Date	Mintage	Fine	VF	XF	Unc
113	1816	3,107	350.00	500.00	950.00	1750.
	1817	3,989	400.00	550.00	1100.	2000.

4 FRANKEN

SILVER

KM#	Date	Mintage	Fine	VF	XF	Unc
109	1813	—	200.00	300.00	550.00	1200.
	1814	.044	90.00	140.00	300.00	1000.

10 FRANKS

3.2258 g, .900 GOLD, .0933 oz AGW

KM#	Date	Mintage	Fine	VF	XF	Unc
98	1804	—	600.00	1100.	1500.	3300.

20 FRANKS

6.4516 g, .900 GOLD, .1867 oz AGW

KM#	Date	Mintage	Fine	VF	XF	Unc
102	1807 B	—	1400.	2500.	4250.	8000.

NEUCHATEL

A canton on the west central border of Switzerland. The first coins (bracteates) were struck in the 11th century. They were under Prussian rule from 1707 to 1806. France occupied the canton from 1806-1815. They reverted to Prussia until 1857, when they became a full member of the Swiss Confederation.

RULERS

Friedrich Wilhelm III, of Prussia, 1797-1806
Alexandre Berthier, Prince, 1806-1814
Friedrich Wilhelm III, 1814-1840

MONETARY SYSTEM

4 Kreuzer = 1 Batzen
7 Kreuzer = 1 Piecette
21 Batzen = 1 Gulden
2 Gulden = 1 Thaler

1/2 KREUZER

BILLON

KM#	Date	Mintage	Fine	VF	XF	Unc
64	1802	—	30.00	70.00	100.00	250.00
	1803	—	—	—	—	—

KREUZER

BILLON

KM#	Date	Mintage	Fine	VF	XF	Unc
62	1802	—	7.50	15.00	40.00	150.00
	1803	—	5.00	9.00	15.00	50.00

NOTE: Earlier date (1800) exists for this type.

KM#	Date	Mintage	Fine	VF	XF	Unc
66	1807	—	5.00	9.00	18.00	55.00
	1808	—	5.00	9.00	18.00	55.00

KM#	Date	Mintage	Fine	VF	XF	Unc
71	1817	.303	5.00	9.00	15.00	50.00
	1818	Inc. Ab.	7.50	10.00	15.00	60.00

1/2 BATZEN

BILLON

Obv: Crowned arms, leg: F.G.BOR.REX.PR. . . . . .
Rev: Cross.

KM#	Date	Mintage	Fine	VF	XF	Unc
55	1803	—	5.00	9.00	18.00	55.00

NOTE: Earlier dates (1798-1799) exist for this type.

Obv. leg: F.W.III.BOR.REX.P. . . . . .,

KM#	Date	Mintage	Fine	VF	XF	Unc
57	1803	—	5.00	9.00	18.00	55.00

NOTE: Earlier dates (1799-1800) exist for this type.

Rev. value: DEMI BATZ

KM#	Date	Mintage	Fine	VF	XF	Unc
67	1807	—	9.00	12.50	22.50	60.00

Rev. value: 1/2 BATZ

KM#	Date	Mintage	Fine	VF	XF	Unc
68.1	1807	—	4.50	7.50	15.00	50.00
	1808	—	4.50	7.50	20.00	65.00
	1809	—	6.00	10.00	22.50	65.00

Rev. value: 2/1 BATZ

KM#	Date	Mintage	VG	Fine	VF	XF
68.2	1807	—	—	—	—	—

BATZEN

BILLON

KM#	Date	Mintage	Fine	VF	XF	Unc
65	1806	—	15.00	22.50	32.50	125.00
	1807	—	5.00	8.00	15.00	50.00
	1808	—	5.00	8.00	15.00	50.00
	1809	—	7.50	10.00	25.00	60.00
	1810	—	10.00	18.00	35.00	75.00

KM#	Date	Mintage	Fine	VF	XF	Unc
69	1807	—	5.00	7.50	15.00	50.00
	1808	—	5.00	7.50	15.00	50.00

ST. GALL

St. Gallen

A canton in northeast Switzerland which completely surrounds the canton of Appenzell. It joined the Swiss Confederation in 1803.

PFENNIG

BILLON

Uniface, arms on concave planchet.

KM#	Date	Mintage	Fine	VF	XF	Unc
100	ND	.151	5.00	8.00	15.00	75.00

2 PFENNIG

BILLON

KM#	Date	Mintage	Fine	VF	XF	Unc
108	1808	—	100.00	180.00	230.00	600.00

1/2 KREUZER

BILLON

KM#	Date	Mintage	Fine	VF	XF	Unc
109	1808 K	.111	10.00	17.50	27.50	80.00
	1809 K	.118	10.00	17.50	27.50	80.00
	1810 K	.101	10.00	17.50	27.50	80.00
	1811 K	.099	10.00	17.50	27.50	80.00
	1812 K	.175	10.00	17.50	27.50	80.00
	1813 K	.149	10.00	17.50	27.50	80.00
	1814 K	.114	10.00	17.50	27.50	80.00
	1815 K	.136	10.00	17.50	27.50	80.00
	1816 K	.238	10.00	17.50	27.50	80.00
	1817 K	—	10.00	17.50	27.50	80.00

KREUZER

BILLON

KM#	Date	Mintage	Fine	VF	XF	Unc
01	1807 K	.162	10.00	20.00	45.00	150.00
	1808 K	.202	10.00	20.00	45.00	150.00

KM#	Date	Mintage	Fine	VF	XF	Unc
02	1807	Inc. KM101	100.00	180.00	230.00	500.00
	1809 K	.160	6.00	9.00	15.00	50.00
	1810 K	.146	6.00	9.00	15.00	50.00
	1811 K	.106	6.00	9.00	15.00	50.00
	1812 K	.135	6.00	9.00	15.00	50.00
	1813 K	.102	6.00	9.00	15.00	50.00
	1815 K	1.116	6.00	9.00	15.00	50.00
	1816 K	.135	6.00	9.00	15.00	50.00

1/2 BATZEN

BILLON

KM#	Date	Mintage	Fine	VF	XF	Unc
103	1807	.110	10.00	15.00	30.00	100.00
	1808 K	.209	5.00	10.00	25.00	70.00
	1809 K	.267	5.00	10.00	25.00	70.00
	1810 K	.290	5.00	10.00	27.50	75.00
	1811 K	.349	5.00	10.00	45.00	150.00
	1812 K	.252	5.00	10.00	45.00	150.00
	1813 K	.154	5.00	10.00	45.00	150.00
	1814 K	.140	5.00	10.00	45.00	150.00
	1815 K	.181	5.00	10.00	45.00	150.00
	1816 K	.134	5.00	10.00	45.00	150.00
	1817 K	—	15.00	22.50	60.00	225.00

KM#	Date	Mintage	Fine	VF	XF	Unc
104	1807 K					—
		Inc. KM103	10.00	15.00	30.00	100.00
	1808 K					—
		Inc. KM103	5.00	10.00	25.00	90.00
	1809 K					—
		Inc. KM103	5.00	10.00	25.00	90.00
	1810 K					—
		Inc. KM103	10.00	15.00	30.00	100.00

NOTE: Some varieties of KM#104 do not have the K mint mark.

BATZEN

BILLON

KM#	Date	Mintage	Fine	VF	XF	Unc
105	1807 K	.063	12.50	20.00	45.00	200.00
	1808 K	.133	6.00	10.00	25.00	150.00
	1809 K	.187	10.00	20.00	40.00	150.00

KM#	Date	Mintage	Fine	VF	XF	Unc
106	1807	Inc. KM105	15.00	27.50	45.00	200.00

Obv: Date. Rev. value: 1 BATZEN.

KM#	Date	Mintage	Fine	VF	XF	Unc
110	1810 K	.259	5.00	12.50	40.00	125.00
	1811 K	.319	5.00	12.50	40.00	125.00
	1812 K	.341	5.00	12.50	40.00	125.00
	1813 K	—	5.00	12.50	40.00	125.00
	1814 K	.229	5.00	12.50	40.00	125.00
	1815 K	1.008	5.00	12.50	40.00	125.00
	1816 K	.068	5.00	12.50	40.00	125.00
	1817 K	—	15.00	22.50	70.00	250.00

NOTE: Many varieties of KM#110 are known, including some w/o the K mint mark.

6 KREUZER

BILLON
Obv: Arms in oak branches.
Rev: Value and date in oak branches.

KM#	Date	Mintage	Fine	VF	XF	Unc
107	1807	4,510	55.00	80.00	150.00	600.00

5 BATZEN

SILVER
Obv: Date in exergue.

KM#	Date	Mintage	Fine	VF	XF	Unc
111	1810 K	—	27.50	40.00	65.00	300.00
	1811 K	—	40.00	60.00	90.00	350.00
	1812 K	—	55.00	120.00	160.00	400.00
	1813 K	—	35.00	55.00	90.00	350.00

KM#	Date	Mintage	Fine	VF	XF	Unc
113	1813 K	—	27.50	50.00	80.00	300.00
	1814 K	—	27.50	50.00	80.00	300.00
	1817 K	—	40.00	60.00	90.00	350.00

KM#	Date	Mintage	Fine	VF	XF	Unc
114	1817 K	—	40.00	60.00	90.00	350.00

1/2 FRANKEN

SILVER

KM#	Date	Mintage	Fine	VF	XF	Unc
112	1810 K	759 pcs.	300.00	725.00	1200.	3000.

SCHAFFHAUSEN

A canton located on the north central border of Switzerland. The first coins, which were issued in the 13th century were known as "Ram Bracteates". It joined the Swiss Confederation in 1501.

MONETARY SYSTEM

4 Kreuzer = 1 Batzen

KREUZER

BILLON

KM#	Date	Mintage	Fine	VF	XF	Unc
65	1808	.216	40.00	80.00	120.00	300.00

1/2 BATZEN

BILLON

KM#	Date	Mintage	Fine	VF	XF	Unc
66	1808	.080	20.00	30.00	55.00	300.00

KM#	Date	Mintage	Fine	VF	XF	Unc
68	1809	.030	22.00	35.00	65.00	325.00

BATZEN

BILLON

KM#	Date	Mintage	Fine	VF	XF	Unc
67	1808	.064	55.00	80.00	150.00	300.00

Rev. value: 1 BATZEN

KM#	Date	Mintage	Fine	VF	XF	Unc
69	1809	.015	27.50	45.00	90.00	275.00

SCHWYZ

Schwytz, Suitensis

A canton in central Switzerland. In 1291 it became one of the three cantons that would ultimately become the Swiss Confederation and were known as the "Everlasting League". The first coinage was issued in 1624.

MINTMASTERS INITIALS

S - Stedelin

MONETARY SYSTEM

2 Angster = 1 Rappen
10 Rappen = 1 Batzen
10 Batzen = 1 Frank
4 Franken = 1 Thaler

ANGSTER

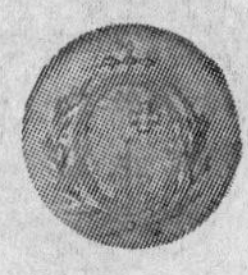

COPPER

55	1810	—	5.00	9.00	18.00	30.00
	1811	—	5.00	9.00	18.00	30.00
	1812	—	5.00	9.00	18.00	30.00
	1813	—	12.50	20.00	30.00	75.00
	1814	—	7.50	15.00	25.00	50.00
	1815	—	12.50	20.00	30.00	75.00
	1816	—	5.00	9.00	18.00	30.00
	1821	—	12.50	20.00	30.00	75.00
	1827	—	12.50	20.00	30.00	75.00
	1838	—	12.50	20.00	30.00	75.00
	1843	—	5.00	9.00	15.00	30.00
	1845	—	5.00	9.00	15.00	30.00
	1846	—	5.00	9.00	15.00	30.00

RAPPEN

COPPER

59	1811	—	5.00	12.50	20.00	35.00
	1812	—	3.50	7.50	10.00	25.00
	1815	—	3.50	7.50	10.00	25.00
	1845	—	3.75	5.00	8.00	20.00
	1846	—	6.00	12.00	18.00	30.00

NOTE: Many varieties exist, including some w/value 1 RAPEN and mint mark B.

KM#	Date	Mintage	Fine	VF	XF	Unc
60	1811	—	5.00	12.00	18.00	30.00
	1812	—	3.00	7.00	9.00	25.00

KM#	Date	Mintage	Fine	VF	XF	Unc
65	1815	—	3.00	7.00	9.00	25.00
	1816	—	7.50	12.00	18.00	30.00
	1843	—	3.75	5.00	9.00	25.00
	1844	—	7.50	12.00	18.00	30.00
	1845	—	3.00	5.00	9.00	25.00
	1846	—	6.00	12.00	18.00	30.00

2 RAPPEN

BILLON

KM#	Date	Mintage	Fine	VF	XF	Unc
61	1811	—	6.00	10.00	16.00	40.00
	1812	—	6.00	10.00	16.00	40.00
	1813	—	6.00	10.00	16.00	40.00

NOTE: Varieties of these coins are known with value as 2 RAPEN.

KM#	Date	Mintage	Fine	VF	XF	Unc
62	1811	—	6.00	12.00	18.00	40.00
	1812	—	3.75	7.50	12.50	35.00
	1813	—	5.00	12.00	18.00	40.00
	1814	—	3.75	7.50	12.50	35.00
	1815	—	3.75	7.50	12.50	35.00
	1842	—	15.00	30.00	40.00	80.00
	1843	—	3.75	7.50	12.50	35.00
	1843 DB	—	3.75	7.50	12.50	35.00
	1844 DB	—	10.00	15.00	27.50	60.00
	1845 DB	—	3.75	7.50	12.50	35.00
	1846 DB	—	3.75	7.50	12.50	35.00

NOTE: Many varieties exist, including some w/value 2 RAPEN and mint mark B.

2/3 BATZEN

BILLON

KM#	Date	Mintage	Fine	VF	XF	Unc
56	1810	—	15.00	37.50	60.00	150.00
	1811	—	15.00	37.50	60.00	150.00

Rev. value: 2/3 BATZEN

KM#	Date	Mintage	Fine	VF	XF	Unc
63	1812	—	55.00	90.00	130.00	300.00

Rev. value: 2/3 BATZ

KM#	Date	Mintage	Fine	VF	XF	Unc
64	1812	—	60.00	150.00	180.00	400.00

2 BATZEN

BILLON

KM#	Date	Mintage	Fine	VF	XF	Unc
57	1810B	—	60.00	130.00	210.00	700.00

4 BATZEN

SILVER
Obv: Arms in laurel branches.
Rev: Value and date in wreath, leg. around border.

KM#	Date	Mintage	Fine	VF	XF	Unc
58	1810 H	—	200.00	350.00	450.00	1500.
	1811 H	—	80.00	150.00	275.00	1200.

NOTE: Varieties exist with value 4 BATZ.

TRADE COINAGE

DUCAT

3.5000 g, .986 GOLD, .1109 oz AGW

KM#	Date	Mintage	VG	Fine	VF	XF
66	1844 M	50 pcs.	2000.	4000.	7000.	9000.

SOLOTHURN

Solodornensis, Soleure

A canton in northwest Switzerland. Bracteates were struck in the 1300s even though the mint right was not officially granted until 1381. They joined the Swiss Confederation in 1481.

MONETARY SYSTEM

Commencing 1804
10 Rappen = 4 Kreuzer = 1 Batzen
10 Batzen = 1 Frank

RAPPEN

BILLON

KM#	Date	Mintage	Fine	VF	XF	Unc
71	1813	—	18.00	30.00	50.00	125.00

2-1/2 RAPPEN

BILLON

KM#	Date	Mintage	Fine	VF	XF	Unc
85	1830	—	5.00	10.00	25.00	60.00

5 RAPPEN

BILLON

KM#	Date	Mintage	Fine	VF	XF	Unc
78	1826	—	20.00	35.00	60.00	150.00

KREUZER

BILLON

KM#	Date	Mintage	Fine	VF	XF	Unc
72	1813	—	10.00	15.00	30.00	75.00

BATZEN - 10 RAPPEN

BILLON

KM#	Date	Mintage	Fine	VF	XF	Unc
65	1805	—	15.00	30.00	50.00	150.00

KM#	Date	Mintage	Fine	VF	XF	Unc
66	1807	—	60.00	100.00	200.00	500.00
	1808	—	15.00	30.00	50.00	150.00
	1809	—	15.00	30.00	50.00	150.00

KM#	Date	Mintage	Fine	VF	XF	Unc
67	1809	—	15.00	30.00	50.00	150.00
	1810	—	6.00	12.50	30.00	80.00
	1811	—	6.00	12.50	30.00	80.00

KM#	Date	Mintage	Fine	VF	XF	Unc
79	1826	—	12.00	18.00	37.50	100.00

KM#	Date	Mintage	Fine	VF	XF	Unc
80	1826	—	6.00	12.50	27.50	95.00

2-1/2 BATZEN

SILVER
Obv: Crowned oval arms in laurel branches.
Rev: Cross in quatrefoil.

KM#	Date	Mintage	Fine	VF	XF	Unc
81	1826	—	20.00	40.00	80.00	175.00

5 BATZEN

SILVER

KM#	Date	Mintage	Fine	VF	XF	Unc
68	1809	—	90.00	200.00	300.00	750.00
	1811	—	40.00	80.00	135.00	400.00

Obv. value: 5 BATZ

KM#	Date	Mintage	Fine	VF	XF	Unc
82	1826	—	30.00	50.00	90.00	250.00

Obv. value: 5 BAZ.

KM#	Date	Mintage	Fine	VF	XF	Unc
83	1826	—	37.50	75.00	125.00	275.00

FRANK

SILVER

KM#	Date	Mintage	Fine	VF	XF	Unc
70	1812	2,000	200.00	450.00	600.00	1250.

4 FRANKEN

SILVER

KM#	Date	Mintage	Fine	VF	XF	Unc
73	1813	250 pcs.	400.00	550.00	1000.	2000.

8 FRANKEN

3.8200 g, .900 GOLD, .1105 oz AGW

KM#	Date	Mintage	Fine	VF	XF	Unc
74	1813	106 pcs.	2750.	5000.	8250.	—

16 FRANKEN

7.6400 g, .900 GOLD, .2211 oz AGW

KM#	Date	Mintage	Fine	VF	XF	Unc
75	1813	150 pcs.	2750.	5000.	8250.	—

32 FRANKEN

15.2800 g, .900 GOLD, .4421 oz AGW
Obv: Crowned oval arms on spade shield in branches, date below.
Rev: Standing knight holding shield, value below.

KM#	Date	Mintage	Fine	VF	XF	Unc
76	1813	—	—	—	Rare	—

THURGAU

Thurgovie

A canton in northeast Switzerland. They were ruled by the Swiss Confederates beginning c. 1460 until 1798. In 1803 they joined the Swiss Confederation.

MONETARY SYSTEM

4 Kreuzer = 1 Schweizer Batzen
10 Batzen = 1 Frank

1/2 KREUZER

BILLON

KM#	Date	Mintage	Fine	VF	XF	Unc
1	1808	.100	90.00	180.00	240.00	600.00

KREUZER

BILLON

KM#	Date	Mintage	Fine	VF	XF	Unc
2	1808	.099	17.50	37.50	55.00	125.00

1/2 BATZEN

BILLON

KM#	Date	Mintage	Fine	VF	XF	Unc
3	1808	.149	22.50	45.00	80.00	200.00

BATZEN

BILLON

KM#	Date	Mintage	Fine	VF	XF	Unc
4	1808	.232	25.00	40.00	95.00	350.00
	1809	Inc. Ab.	25.00	40.00	95.00	350.00

5 BATZEN

SILVER

KM#	Date	Mintage	Fine	VF	XF	Unc
5	1808	2,580	275.00	450.00	600.00	2250.

TICINO

Tessin

A canton in southeast Switzerland. They were previously known as the Lombard vassal state of Bellinzona. They joined the Swiss Confederation in 1803.

MONETARY SYSTEM

12 Denari = 1 Soldo
20 Soldi = 1 Franco

TRE (3) DENARI

COPPER
Obv: Arms. Rev: Value above branches.

KM#	Date	Mintage	Fine	VF	XF	Unc
5	1814	.417	9.00	15.00	27.50	125.00
	1835	.598	9.00	15.00	27.50	125.00

KM#	Date	Mintage	Fine	VF	XF	Unc
9	1841	.322	9.00	15.00	27.50	125.00

SEI (6) DENARI

COPPER
Obv: Arms. Rev: Value and date within wreath.

KM#	Date	Mintage	Fine	VF	XF	Unc
1	1813	.280	9.00	15.00	32.50	130.00
	1835	.364	15.00	27.50	40.00	140.00
	1841	.241	9.00	15.00	32.50	130.00

TRE (3) SOLDI

BILLON

KM#	Date	Mintage	Fine	VF	XF	Unc
2	1813 star	1.405	15.00	35.00	60.00	200.00
	1813 w/o star	Inc. Ab.	15.00	30.00	45.00	185.00
	1835	.323	7.00	15.00	30.00	150.00
	1838	.514	7.00	15.00	30.00	150.00
	1841	.243	7.00	15.00	30.00	150.00

1/4 FRANCO

SILVER

KM#	Date	Mintage	Fine	VF	XF	Unc
7	1835	.058	20.00	40.00	60.00	350.00

1/2 FRANCO

SILVER

KM#	Date	Mintage	Fine	VF	XF	Unc
8	1835	.044	20.00	45.00	80.00	400.00

FRANCO

SILVER

KM#	Date	Mintage	Fine	VF	XF	Unc
3	1813 star	5,920	95.00	200.00	275.00	1250.
	1813 w/o star	Inc. Ab.	70.00	150.00	225.00	1100.

2 FRANCHI

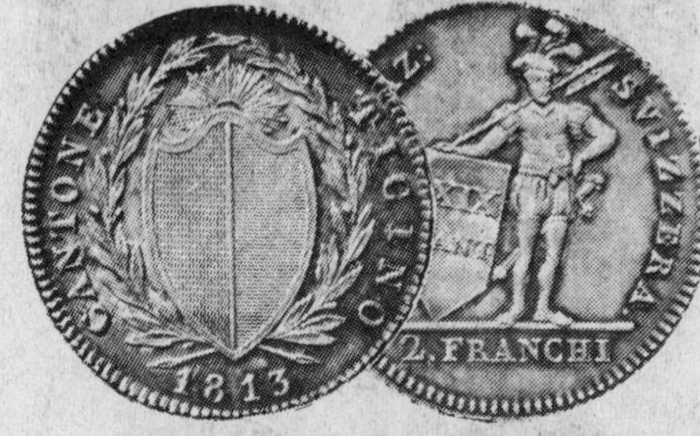

SILVER

KM#	Date	Mintage	Fine	VF	XF	Unc
4	1813 star	4,150	140.00	300.00	550.00	2000.
	1813 w/o star	Inc. Ab.	120.00	250.00	450.00	1750.

4 FRANCHI

SILVER

KM#	Date	Mintage	Fine	VF	XF	Unc
6	1814 star	7,921	250.00	575.00	850.00	4000.
	1814 w/o star	Inc. Ab.	250.00	475.00	750.00	3000.

NOTE: Coins of 3 Soldi, Franco, 2 Franchi and 4 Franchi with star mint mark were struck at Luzern. Those without star were coined at Bern.

UNTERWALDEN

Subsilvania

A canton in central Switzerland which was one of the three original cantons which became the Swiss Confederation in 1291. It is made up of two half cantons - Nidwalden and Obwalden. They had their own coinage beginning in the 1500s.

MINTMASTERS INITIALS

S - Samson

MONETARY SYSTEM

4 Kreuzer = 1 Batzen
10 Batzen = 1 Frank

NIDWALDEN

1/2 BATZEN

BILLON

KM#	Date	Mintage	Fine	VF	XF	Unc
11	1811	.012	40.00	80.00	125.00	300.00

BATZEN - 10 RAPPEN

BILLON

KM#	Date	Mintage	Fine	VF	XF	Unc
12	1811	.012	40.00	80.00	125.00	300.00

5 BATZEN

SILVER

KM#	Date	Mintage	Fine	VF	XF	Unc
13	1811	3,600	150.00	300.00	450.00	1750.

OBWALDEN

1/2 BATZEN

BILLON

KM#	Date	Mintage	Fine	VF	XF	Unc
51	1812	—	30.00	70.00	110.00	350.00

BATZEN

BILLON

KM#	Date	Mintage	Fine	VF	XF	Unc
52	1812	—	30.00	70.00	110.00	350.00

5 BATZEN

SILVER

KM#	Date	Mintage	Fine	VF	XF	Unc
53	1812	—	100.00	250.00	400.00	1000.

URI

Uranie

A canton in central Switzerland. It is one of the three original cantons which became the Swiss Confederation in 1291. They had their own coinage from the early 1600s until 1811.

MONETARY SYSTEM

10 Rappen = 1 Batzen
10 Batzen = 1 Frank

RAPPEN

BILLON

KM#	Date	Mintage	Fine	VF	XF	Unc
40	1811	.019	100.00	175.00	210.00	400.00

1/2 BATZEN

BILLON

KM#	Date	Mintage	Fine	VF	XF	Unc
41	1811	.015	60.00	95.00	200.00	400.00

BATZEN - 10 RAPPEN

BILLON

KM#	Date	Mintage	Fine	VF	XF	Unc
42	1811	.020	60.00	95.00	200.00	400.00

2 BATZEN

SILVER

KM#	Date	Mintage	Fine	VF	XF	Unc
43	1811	4,995	120.00	180.00	300.00	750.00

4 BATZEN

SILVER

KM#	Date	Mintage	Fine	VF	XF	Unc
44	1811	3,510	150.00	275.00	450.00	1500.

VAUD

Waadt

A canton in southwest Switzerland. They had possession of Bern from 1536 until 1798. They joined the Swiss Confederation in 1803.

MINTMASTERS INITIALS

BEL - Bel Bessiere

MONETARY SYSTEM

10 Rappen = 1 Batz
10 Batz = 1 Franc
4 Francs = 1 Thaler

RAPPEN

BILLON

KM#	Date	Mintage	Fine	VF	XF	Unc
5	1804	.211	30.00	80.00	150.00	250.00

KM#	Date	Mintage	Fine	VF	XF	Unc
12	1807	Inc. Ab.	20.00	60.00	100.00	200.00

2-1/2 RAPPEN

BILLON

KM#	Date	Mintage	Fine	VF	XF	Unc
14	1809	.230	10.00	15.00	27.50	60.00

KM#	Date	Mintage	Fine	VF	XF	Unc
18	1816	—	10.00	15.00	27.50	60.00

1/2 BATZEN - 5 RAPPEN

BILLON

KM#	Date	Mintage	Fine	VF	XF	Unc
6	1804	2.962	6.00	10.00	15.00	40.00
	1805	Inc. Ab.	10.00	15.00	35.00	120.00
	1806	Inc. Ab.	10.00	15.00	35.00	120.00
	1807	Inc. Ab.	5.00	8.00	12.50	50.00
	1808	Inc. Ab.	10.00	15.00	35.00	75.00
	1809	—	5.00	8.00	12.50	50.00
	1810	—	5.00	8.00	12.50	50.00
	1811	—	5.00	8.00	12.50	50.00
	1813	—	5.00	8.00	12.50	50.00
	1814	—	5.00	8.00	12.50	50.00
	1816	—	5.00	8.00	12.50	50.00
	1817	—	9.00	15.00	25.00	60.00
	1818	—	4.00	7.50	12.50	35.00
	1819	—	5.00	8.00	12.50	30.00

BATZEN - 10 RAPPEN

BILLON

Obv: W/o branches around shield.

KM#	Date	Mintage	Fine	VF	XF	Unc
7	1804	—	45.00	100.00	180.00	400.00

KM#	Date	Mintage	Fine	VF	XF	Unc
8	1804	—	8.00	27.50	40.00	120.00
	1805	—	5.50	10.00	30.00	100.00
	1806	—	6.00	12.50	25.00	90.00
	1807	—	6.00	12.50	25.00	90.00
	1808	—	400.00	600.00	1000.	—
	1809	—	15.00	25.00	40.00	100.00
	1810	—	5.00	10.00	20.00	45.00
	1811	—	5.00	10.00	20.00	45.00
	1812	—	5.00	10.00	20.00	45.00
	1813	—	5.00	10.00	20.00	45.00
	1814	—	5.00	10.00	20.00	45.00
	1815	—	5.00	10.00	20.00	45.00
	1816	—	5.00	10.00	20.00	45.00
	1817	—	5.00	10.00	20.00	45.00
	1818	—	4.00	8.00	15.00	35.00
	1819	—	5.00	8.00	15.00	35.00
	1820	—	6.00	12.50	25.00	75.00

KM#	Date	Mintage	Fine	VF	XF	Unc
20	1826	—	27.50	60.00	100.00	225.00
	1827 BEL	—	5.50	10.00	17.00	40.00
	1828 BEL	—	5.50	8.00	15.00	40.00
	1829 BEL	—	5.50	8.00	15.00	40.00
	1830 BEL	—	5.50	8.00	15.00	40.00
	1831	—	5.50	8.00	15.00	40.00
	1832 BEL	—	6.00	12.00	17.50	40.00
	1834 BEL	—	12.50	37.50	60.00	150.00

5 BATZEN

SILVER

KM#	Date	Mintage	Fine	VF	XF	Unc
9	1804	1,692	150.00	350.00	500.00	1200.

KM#	Date	Mintage	Fine	VF	XF	Unc
11	1805	—	90.00	200.00	260.00	600.00
	1806	—	90.00	200.00	260.00	600.00

KM#	Date	Mintage	Fine	VF	XF	Unc
13	1807	—	27.50	80.00	100.00	325.00
	1810	—	27.50	80.00	100.00	325.00
	1811	—	27.50	80.00	100.00	325.00
	1812	—	27.50	70.00	95.00	275.00
	1813	—	27.50	70.00	95.00	275.00
	1814	—	30.00	90.00	135.00	350.00

KM#	Date	Mintage	Fine	VF	XF	Unc
21.1	1826	—	12.50	27.50	80.00	200.00
	1827 BEL	—	10.00	20.00	45.00	150.00
	1828 BEL	—	10.00	20.00	45.00	150.00
	1829 BEL	—	12.50	27.50	80.00	200.00
	1830 BEL	—	10.00	20.00	45.00	150.00
	1831 BEL	—	10.00	20.00	45.00	150.00

Rev: Plumes in quatre foil.

KM#	Date	Mintage	Fine	VF	XF	Unc
21.2	1827 BEL	—	10.00	30.00	45.00	150.00

10 BATZEN

SILVER

KM#	Date	Mintage	Fine	VF	XF	Unc
10	1804	1,234	150.00	300.00	600.00	2500.

KM#	Date	Mintage	Fine	VF	XF	Unc
15	1810	1,234	45.00	100.00	160.00	600.00
	1811	2,963	45.00	100.00	160.00	600.00

KM#	Date	Mintage	Fine	VF	XF	Unc
19	1823	6,198	45.00	100.00	160.00	600.00

20 BATZEN

SILVER

KM#	Date	Mintage	Fine	VF	XF	Unc
16	1810	6,590	35.00	85.00	220.00	800.00
	1811	Inc. Ab.	35.00	85.00	220.00	800.00

40 BATZEN

SILVER

KM#	Date	Mintage	Fine	VF	XF	Unc
17	1812	2,485	225.00	475.00	800.00	1750.

NOTE: 616 pieces were melted in 1851.

FRANC

SILVER

KM#	Date	Mintage	Fine	VF	XF	Unc
22	1845	8,626	20.00	40.00	85.00	200.00

NOTE: This coin was struck to commemorate a Shooting Festival held on August 10, 1845. It had legal tender status.

COUNTERSTAMPED COINAGE

39 BATZEN (BZ)

As in the canton of Bern, French Ecus dated 1726 to 1793 along with 6 Livres dated 1793-1794 were counterstamped from 1816-1819 and freely circulated. In Vaud, the counterstamp consisted of the arms of Vaud on one side and the new value 39 BZ on the other.

SILVER

c/s: On France Louis XV Ecu, C#42.

KM#	Date	Year	VG	Fine	VF	XF
23	ND	(1726-41)	600.00	1000.	1500.	2000.

KM#	Date	Year	VG	Fine	VF	XF
	c/s: On France Louis XV Ecu, C#47.					
24	ND	(1740-71)	600.00	1000.	1500.	2000.
	c/s: On France Louis XV Ecu, C#47a.					
25	ND	(1770-74)	600.00	1000.	1500.	2000.
	c/s: On France Louis XVI Ecu, C#78.					
26	ND	(1774-92)	600.00	1000.	1500.	2000.
	c/s: On France Louis XVI Constitutional Ecu, C#93.					
27	ND	(1792-93)	750.00	1600.	2400.	3200.
	c/s: On France 6 Livres, C#123.					
28	ND	(1793-94)	900.00	2000.	2750.	3750.

ZUG

Tugium, Tugiensis

A canton in central Switzerland. They joined the Swiss Confederation in 1352 and had their own coinage from 1564 to 1805.

MONETARY SYSTEM

6 Angster = 3 Rappen
= 1 Schilling = 1 Assis

ANGSTER

COPPER

Obv: Arms in branches.
Rev: Date, value in cartouche.

KM#	Date	Mintage	VG	Fine	VF	XF
61	1804	—	20.00	40.00	60.00	120.00

NOTE: Earlier dates (1778-1796) exist for this type.

RAPPEN

COPPER

Obv: Arms in branches.
Rev: Date, value in cartouche.

KM#	Date	Mintage	VG	Fine	VF	XF
63	1805	—	3.75	7.50	10.00	18.00

NOTE: Earlier dates (1782-1794) exist for this type.

ZURICH

Thicurinae, Thuricensis, Ticurinae, Turicensis

A canton in north central Switzerland. It was the mint for the dukes of Swabia in the 10th and 11th centuries. The mint right was obtained in 1238. The first coinage struck were bracteates and the last coins were struck in 1848. It joined the Swiss Confederation in 1351.

MINTMASTERS INITIALS

B - Bruckmann
V - Vorster

MONETARY SYSTEM

Commencing 1803
3 Haller = 1 Rappen
4 Rappen = 1 Schilling
10 Schilling = 4 Batzen
160 Batzen = 1 Ducat

3 HALLER

BILLON

KM#	Date	Mintage	Fine	VF	XF	Unc
180	ND	3.518	4.50	6.00	10.00	25.00
		Error: HALER				
181	ND	Inc. Ab.	9.00	15.00	25.00	55.00

NOTE: These were struck from 1827-1841.

RAPPEN

BILLON

KM#	Date	Mintage	Fine	VF	XF	Unc
194	1842	—	4.50	9.00	20.00	45.00
	1844	—	12.00	20.00	30.00	60.00
	1845	—	4.50	9.00	16.00	30.00
	1846	—	40.00	100.00	250.00	400.00
	1848	—	4.50	9.00	16.00	35.00

2 RAPPEN

BILLON

KM#	Date	Mintage	Fine	VF	XF	Unc
195	1842D	.460	9.00	15.00	22.50	45.00

10 SCHILLING

SILVER

KM#	Date	Mintage	Fine	VF	XF	Unc
182	ND(1806)	—	15.00	37.50	60.00	150.00
	1807 B	—	27.50	45.00	80.00	200.00
	1808 B	—	12.50	27.50	50.00	125.00
	1809 B	—	12.50	27.50	50.00	125.00
	1810 B	—	12.50	27.50	50.00	125.00
	1811 B	—	12.50	27.50	50.00	125.00

8 BATZEN

SILVER

KM#	Date	Mintage	Fine	VF	XF	Unc
184	1810 B	.108	40.00	60.00	125.00	300.00
	1814 B	Inc. Ab.	50.00	90.00	150.00	400.00

10 BATZEN

SILVER

KM#	Date	Mintage	Fine	VF	XF	Unc
185	1812 B	.028	60.00	90.00	150.00	400.00

20 BATZEN

SILVER

Rev: Large date, thick stems.

KM#	Date	Mintage	Fine	VF	XF	Unc
186	1813 B	—	90.00	165.00	270.00	400.00

Rev: Small date, thin stems.

KM#	Date	Mintage	Fine	VF	XF	Unc
187	1813	—	90.00	165.00	270.00	400.00

Obv: Longer garlands. Rev: Small date, thin stems.

KM#	Date	Mintage	Fine	VF	XF	Unc
188	1813	—	100.00	175.00	280.00	420.00

KM#	Date	Mintage	Fine	VF	XF	Unc
192	1826	—	120.00	200.00	350.00	750.00

40 BATZEN

SILVER

Obv: Shield 18mm wide, short right hand garland.
Rev: Large date.

KM#	Date	Mintage	Fine	VF	XF	Unc
189	1813	—	80.00	120.00	250.00	500.00

Obv: Shield 19mm wide, long right hand garland.
Rev: Small date.

KM#	Date	Mintage	Fine	VF	XF	Unc
190	1813 B	—	80.00	120.00	250.00	500.00

Obv: Shield 18mm wide, short right hand garland, small wreath. Rev: Small date.

KM#	Date	Mintage	Fine	VF	XF	Unc
191	1813 B	—	80.00	120.00	250.00	500.00

TRADE COINAGE

DUCAT

3.5000 g, .986 GOLD, .1109 oz AGW

KM#	Date	Mintage	Fine	VF	XF	Unc
185	1810 B	—	600.00	900.00	1250.	3000.

SWITZERLAND

The Swiss Confederation, located in central Europe north of Italy and south of Germany, has an area of 15,941 sq. mi. (41,290 sq. km.) and a population of *6.6 million. Capital: Bern. The economy centers about a welldeveloped manufacturing industry. Machinery, chemicals, watches and clocks, and textiles are exported.

Switzerland, the habitat of lake dwellers in prehistoric times, was peopled by the Celtic Helvetians when Julius Caesar made it a part of the Roman Empire in 58 B.C. After the decline of Rome, Switzerland was invaded by Teutonic tribes, who established small temporal holdings which in the Middle Ages, became a federation of fiefs of the Holy Roman Empire. As a nation, Switzerland originated in 1291 when the districts of Nidwalden, Schwyz and Uri united to defeat Austria and attain independence as the Swiss Confederation. After acquiring new cantons in the 14th century, Switzerland was made independent from the Holy Roman Empire by the 1648 Treaty of Westphalia. The revolutionary armies of Napoleonic France occupied Switzerland and set up the Helvetian Republic, 1798-1803. After the fall of Napoleon, the Congress of Vienna, 1815, recognized the independence of Switzerland and guaranteed its neutrality. The Swiss Constitutions of 1848 and 1874 established a union modeled upon that of the United States.

MINT MARKS

A - Paris
AB - Strasbourg
B - Bern
B. - Brussels 1874
BA - Basel
BB - Strasbourg
S - Solothurn

NOTE: The coinage of Switzerland has been struck at the Bern Mint since 1853 with but a few exceptions. All coins minted there carry a 'B' mint mark through 1969, except for the 2-Centime and 2-Franc values where the mint mark was discontinued after 1968. In 1968 and 1969 some issues were struck at both Bern (B) and in London (no mint mark).

Up through 1981 all circulation coinage was atruck with normal coin die alignment. Commencing with 1982 all pieces are struck with medallic die alignment.

MONETARY SYSTEM

10 Rappen = 1 Batzen
10 Batzen = 1 Franc
16 Franken = 1 Duplone

HELVETIAN REPUBLIC

RAPPEN

BILLON

Obv: Fasces in branches. Rev: Value in wreath.

KM#	Date	Mintage	Fine	VF	XF	Unc
11	1801	—	5.00	10.00	20.00	70.00
	1802	—	7.50	15.00	25.00	75.00

NOTE: Earlier date (1800) exists for this type.

1/2 BATZEN

BILLON

KM#	Date	Mintage	Fine	VF	XF	Unc
6	1802	—	10.00	16.00	28.00	120.00
	1803	—	12.50	25.00	45.00	140.00

NOTE: Earlier dates (1799-1800) exist for this type.

BATZEN

BILLON

Obv: HELVET.REPUBL. in wreath.
Rev: Similar to 1 Rappen, KM#11.

KM#	Date	Mintage	Fine	VF	XF	Unc
8	1801B	—	12.50	22.50	37.50	125.00
	1802B	—	12.50	22.50	37.50	125.00
	1803B	—	12.50	22.50	37.50	125.00

NOTE: Earlier dates (1799-1800) exist for this type.

5 BATZEN

SILVER

Obv: Standing Swiss holding flag.
Rev: Value within wreath.

KM#	Date	Mintage	Fine	VF	XF	Unc
9	1802B	—	200.00	275.00	425.00	750.00

NOTE: Earlier dates (1799-1800) exist for this type.

10 BATZEN

SILVER

Obv: Standing Swiss holding flag.
Rev: Value within wreath.

KM#	Date	Mintage	Fine	VF	XF	Unc
1	1801B	—	75.00	160.00	300.00	600.00

NOTE: Earlier dates (1798-1799) exist for this type.

4 FRANKEN

SILVER

KM#	Date	Mintage	Fine	VF	XF	Unc
10	1801B	—	375.00	650.00	1000.	2250.

NOTE: Earlier date (1799) exists for this type.

SWITZERLAND

Confoederatio Helvetica

MONETARY SYSTEM

100 Rappen (Centimes) = 1 Franc

RAPPEN

BRONZE

KM#	Date	Mintage	Fine	VF	XF	Unc
3	1850A	2.270	28.00	50.00	80.00	175.00
	1851A	2.730	10.00	20.00	45.00	100.00
	1853B thick cross	2.008	17.00	25.00	60.00	165.00
	1853B thin cross	Inc. Ab.	750.00	1500.	2500.	3500.
	1855B	.500	250.00	350.00	500.00	1000.
	1856B	2.500	15.00	20.00	45.00	125.00
	1857B	1.587	25.00	35.00	50.00	100.00
	1863B	.501	120.00	160.00	225.00	475.00
	1864B	.501	125.00	180.00	250.00	550.00
	1866B	1.000	50.00	75.00	100.00	265.00
	1868B	2.000	10.00	20.00	30.00	70.00
	1870B	.500	50.00	75.00	160.00	380.00
	1872B	2.080	10.00	15.00	25.00	60.00
	1875B	.975	20.00	25.00	35.00	75.00
	1876B	1.000	20.00	25.00	35.00	75.00
	1877B	.923	20.00	25.00	35.00	75.00
	1878B	.981	20.00	25.00	35.00	75.00
	1879B	.998	20.00	25.00	35.00	75.00
	1880B	.992	20.00	25.00	35.00	75.00
	1882B	1.000	10.00	15.00	20.00	55.00
	1883B	1.000	10.00	15.00	20.00	55.00
	1884B	1.000	10.00	15.00	20.00	55.00
	1887B	1.504	7.00	10.00	15.00	35.00
	1889B	.500	20.00	35.00	55.00	190.00
	1890B	1.000	8.00	13.00	16.00	35.00
	1891B thick cross	2.000	8.00	13.00	16.00	35.00
	1891B thin cross	Inc. Ab.	8.00	13.00	16.00	35.00
	1892B	1.000	8.00	13.00	16.00	35.00
	1894B	1.000	8.00	13.00	16.00	45.00
	1895B	2.000	2.00	3.50	5.00	15.00
	1896B	36 pcs.	—	—	Rare	—
	1897B	.500	12.00	20.00	25.00	65.00
	1898B	1.500	3.00	4.50	7.00	20.00
	1899B	1.500	3.00	4.50	7.00	20.00
	1900B	2.000	2.00	4.00	6.00	20.00
	1902B	.950	30.00	45.00	60.00	200.00
	1903B	1.000	15.00	20.00	25.00	60.00
	1904B	1.000	15.00	20.00	25.00	50.00
	1905B	2.000	4.00	6.00	8.00	20.00
	1906B	1.000	7.00	9.00	20.00	60.00
	1907B	2.000	4.00	6.50	9.00	22.50
3	1908B	3.000	1.00	2.00	3.50	12.00
	1909B	1.000	9.00	12.00	15.00	32.50
	1910B	.500	3.00	5.00	7.00	20.00
	1911B	.500	3.00	5.00	7.00	20.00
	1912B	2.000	.25	1.00	2.50	12.00
	1913B	3.000	.25	.50	1.00	6.00
	1914B	3.500	.25	.75	1.50	9.00
	1915B	3.000	.25	.75	1.50	9.00
	1917B	2.000	.25	1.00	2.50	15.00
	1918B	3.000	.25	.75	1.50	6.00
	1919B	3.000	.25	.75	1.50	6.00
	1920B	1.000	.25	1.00	2.50	12.00
	1921B	3.000	.25	.75	1.50	7.00
	1924B	2.000	.25	.75	1.50	9.00
	1925/4B	2.500	.25	1.00	3.00	12.00
	1925B	Inc. Ab.	.25	1.00	3.00	12.00
	1926B	2.000	.25	1.00	3.00	12.00
	1927B	1.500	.25	1.00	3.00	12.00
	1928B	2.000	.25	.75	1.50	9.00
	1929B	4.000	.25	.50	1.00	6.00
	1930B	2.500	.25	.50	1.00	7.00
	1931B	5.000	.25	.50	1.00	3.50
	1932B	5.000	.25	.50	1.00	5.00
	1933B	3.000	.25	.75	1.50	9.00
	1934B	3.000	.25	.50	1.00	5.00
	1936B	2.000	.25	.50	1.00	9.00
	1937B	2.400	.25	.50	1.00	5.00
	1938B	5.300	.25	.50	1.00	5.00
	1939B	.010	15.00	18.00	25.00	45.00
	1940B	3.027	.25	.50	1.00	6.00
	1941B	12.794	.20	.30	.50	4.00

ZINC

KM#	Date	Mintage	Fine	VF	XF	Unc
3a	1942B	17.969	.25	.50	1.00	5.25
	1943B	8.647	.25	.50	1.00	7.25
	1944B	11.825	.25	.50	1.00	5.25
	1945B	2.800	2.00	3.00	4.50	20.00
	1946B	12.063	.25	.50	1.00	5.25

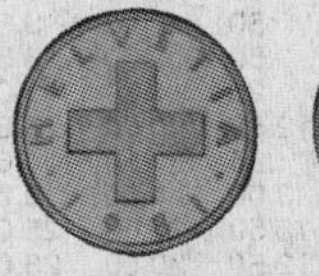

BRONZE

KM#	Date	Mintage	Fine	VF	XF	Unc
46	1948B	10.500	—	.10	.50	1.25
	1949B	11.100	—	.10	.50	1.25
	1950B	3.610	.10	.25	1.00	4.25
	1951B	22.624	—	.10	.50	1.25
	1952B	11.520	—	.10	.30	1.25
	1953B	5.947	—	.10	.50	1.75
	1954B	5.175	—	.10	.50	1.75
	1955B	5.282	—	.10	.60	2.50
	1956B	4.960	—	.10	.50	1.75
	1957B	15.226	—	.10	.20	.60
	1958B	20.142	—	.10	.20	.60
	1959B	5.582	—	.10	.25	1.25
	1962B	5.010	—	.10	.25	1.25
	1963B	15.920	—	—	.10	.35
	1966B	5.030	—	—	.10	.35
	1967B	3.020	—	—	.10	.35
	1968B	4.920	—	—	.10	.35
	1969B	4.810	—	—	.10	.35
	1970	7.810	—	—	.10	.35
	1971	5.030	—	—	.10	.35
	1973	3.000	—	—	.10	.35
	1974	3.007	—	—	.10	.25
	1974	2,400	—	—	Proof	10.00
	1975	3.010	—	—	.10	.25
	1975	.010	—	—	Proof	1.00
	1976	3.005	—	—	.10	.25
	1976	5,130	—	—	Proof	1.50
	1977	2.007	—	—	.10	.25
	1977	7,030	—	—	Proof	1.00
	1978	2.010	—	—	.10	.25
	1978	.010	—	—	Proof	1.00
	1979	1.030	—	—	.10	.25
	1979	.010	—	—	Proof	1.00
	1980	1.030	—	—	.10	.25
	1980	.010	—	—	Proof	1.00
	1981	4.935	—	—	.10	.15
	1981	.010	—	—	Proof	1.00
	1982	6.655	—	—	.10	.15
	1982	.010	—	—	Proof	1.00
	1983	4.031	—	—	.10	.15
	1983	.011	—	—	Proof	1.00
	1984	3.995	—	—	.10	.15
	1984	.014	—	—	Proof	1.00
	1985	3.027	—	—	.10	.15
	1985	.012	—	—	Proof	1.00
	1986B	2.031	—	—	.10	.15
	1986B	.010	—	—	Proof	1.00
	1987B	1.028	—	—	.10	.15
	1987B	8,800	—	—	Proof	1.00
	1988B	2.029	—	—	.10	.15
	1988B	9,000	—	—	Proof	1.00
	1989B	2.032	—	—	.10	.15
	1989B	8,800	—	—	Proof	1.00
	1990B	1.032	—	—	.10	.15
	1990B	8,900	—	—	Proof	1.00
	1991B	.536	—	—	.10	.15
	1991B	9,900	—	—	Proof	1.00
	1992B	.527	—	—	.10	.15
	1992B	7,450	—	—	Proof	1.00
	1993B	.522	—	—	.10	.15
	1993B	6,200	—	—	Proof	1.00

2 RAPPEN

BRONZE

KM#	Date	Mintage	Fine	VF	XF	Unc
4	1850A	7.290	1.00	2.50	5.00	35.00
	1851A	3.720	1.00	2.50	5.00	35.00
	1866B	1.000	5.50	9.00	16.00	45.00
	1870B	.540	20.00	30.00	45.00	120.00
	1875B	.984	3.00	6.00	12.00	35.00
	1879B	.990	3.00	6.00	12.00	35.00
	1883B	1.000	2.00	3.00	5.00	20.00
	1886B	1.000	2.00	3.00	5.00	20.00
	1888B	.500	15.00	20.00	30.00	110.00
	1890B	1.000	1.00	2.00	4.00	20.00
	1893B	2.000	1.00	2.00	3.00	15.00
	1896B	20 pcs.	—	—	Rare	—
	1897B	.487	10.00	15.00	22.00	60.00
	1898B	.500	10.00	15.00	22.00	60.00
	1899B	1.000	2.50	3.50	5.00	20.00
	1900B	1.000	2.50	3.50	5.00	20.00
	1902B	.500	12.50	22.50	28.00	75.00
	1903B	.500	12.50	22.50	28.00	60.00
	1904B	.500	12.50	22.50	28.00	60.00
	1906B	.500	12.50	22.50	28.00	60.00
	1907B	1.000	1.00	2.00	4.00	20.00
	1908B	1.000	1.00	2.00	3.00	17.00
	1909B	1.000	1.00	2.00	3.00	17.00
	1910B	.500	6.00	8.00	12.00	60.00
	1912B	1.000	.50	2.00	3.50	12.00
	1913B	1.000	.50	2.00	3.50	18.00
	1914B	1.000	.50	2.00	3.50	15.00
	1915B	1.000	.50	2.00	3.50	15.00
	1918B	1.000	.50	2.00	3.50	15.00
	1919B	2.000	.25	.50	1.00	6.00
	1920B	.500	12.50	20.00	25.00	70.00
	1925B	1.250	.25	.50	1.00	9.00
	1926B	.750	3.00	4.50	8.00	37.50
	1927B	.500	12.50	20.00	25.00	65.00
	1928B	.500	12.50	20.00	25.00	65.00
	1929B	.750	1.00	3.00	7.00	22.00
	1930B	1.000	.25	.50	1.00	10.00
	1931B	1.288	.25	.50	1.00	10.00
	1932B	1.500	.25	.50	1.00	7.50
	1933B	1.000	.25	.50	1.00	10.00
	1934B	.500	3.00	5.00	10.00	35.00
	1936B	.500	2.50	4.00	6.00	25.00
	1937B	1.200	.25	.50	.85	6.00
	1938B	1.369	.25	.50	.85	9.50
	1941B	3.448	.25	.50	.85	3.75

ZINC

KM#	Date	Mintage	Fine	VF	XF	Unc
4a	1942B	8.954	.25	.50	.85	6.00
	1943B	4.499	.25	.50	.85	8.00
	1944B	8.086	.25	.50	.85	6.00
	1945B	3.640	.50	1.00	2.50	12.00
	1946B	1.393	2.50	5.50	7.50	35.00

BRONZE

KM#	Date	Mintage	Fine	VF	XF	Unc
47	1948B	10.197	.10	.25	.50	3.00
	1951B	9.622	.10	.25	.50	3.00
	1952B	1.915	.10	.25	.75	3.00
	1953B	2.006	.10	.25	.75	3.00
	1954B	2.539	.10	.15	.50	2.50
	1955B	2.493	.10	.15	.50	2.50
	1957B	8.099	.10	.15	.50	1.75
	1958B	6.078	.10	.15	.50	1.75
	1963B	10.065	—	.10	.15	.60
	1966B	2.510	—	.10	.20	.60
	1967B	1.510	—	.10	.25	.60
	1968B	2.860	—	.10	.15	.45
	1969	6.200	—	.10	.15	.35
	1970	3.115	—	.10	.15	.30
	1974	3.540	—	.10	.15	.30
	1974	2,400	—	—	Proof	20.00

5 RAPPEN

BILLON

KM#	Date	Mintage	Fine	VF	XF	Unc
5	1850BB	7.970	3.00	8.00	20.00	90.00
	1850AB	Inc. Ab.	40.00	70.00	425.00	950.00
	1850	Inc. Ab.	300.00	500.00	1250.	2100.
	1851BB	12.042	200.00	400.00	850.00	1750.
	1872B	1.213	14.00	20.00	30.00	90.00
	1873B	1.622	14.00	20.00	30.00	90.00
	1874B	1.700	12.00	20.00	28.00	90.00
	1876B	.989	20.00	35.00	55.00	120.00
	1877B	.978	20.00	35.00	60.00	130.00

COPPER-NICKEL

KM#	Date	Mintage	Fine	VF	XF	Unc
26	1879B	1.000	5.00	12.00	35.00	150.00
	1880B	2.000	1.00	2.50	11.50	65.00
	1881B	2.000	1.00	2.50	11.50	60.00
	1882B	3.000	.65	1.50	10.00	45.00
	1883B	3.000	.65	1.50	10.00	45.00
	1884B	2.000	1.00	2.50	11.50	70.00
	1885B	3.000	.65	1.50	10.00	45.00
	1887B	.500	22.00	45.00	90.00	335.00
	1888B	1.500	1.00	2.50	10.00	55.00
	1889B	.500	22.00	45.00	90.00	320.00
	1890B	1.000	5.00	8.00	28.00	90.00
	1891B	1.000	5.00	8.00	28.00	100.00
	1892B	1.000	5.00	8.00	28.00	100.00
	1893B	2.000	.65	1.50	8.00	35.00
	1894B	2.000	.65	1.50	8.00	35.00
	1895B	2.000	.65	1.50	8.00	35.00
	1896B	16 pcs.	—	—	Rare	—
	1897B	.500	5.00	10.00	25.00	120.00
	1898B	2.500	.35	.75	6.00	35.00
	1899B	1.500	.65	1.50	15.00	75.00
	1900B	2.000	.35	.75	7.00	40.00
	1901B	3.000	.35	.75	7.00	40.00
	1902B	1.000	5.00	10.00	30.00	120.00
	1903B	2.000	.35	.75	10.00	60.00
	1904B	1.000	5.00	10.00	30.00	120.00
	1905B	1.000	3.00	7.00	20.00	80.00
	1906B	3.000	.35	.75	3.00	30.00
	1907B	5.000	.35	.75	3.00	18.50
	1908B	3.000	.35	.75	3.00	25.00
	1909B	2.000	.35	.75	3.00	30.00
	1910B	1.000	1.50	3.00	5.00	60.00
	1911B	2.000	.35	.75	2.00	18.00
	1912B	3.000	.35	.75	2.00	18.00
	1913B	3.000	.35	.75	2.00	18.00
	1914B	3.000	.35	.75	2.00	45.00
	1915B	3.000	.35	.75	2.00	70.00
	1917B	1.000	1.00	2.00	3.00	50.00
	1919B	6.000	.15	.50	2.00	18.00
	1920B	5.000	.15	.50	2.00	22.00
	1921B	3.000	.15	.50	2.00	20.00
	1922B	4.000	.15	.50	1.00	18.00
	1925B	3.000	.15	.50	1.00	20.00
	1926B	3.000	.15	.50	1.00	20.00
	1927B	2.000	.15	.50	1.25	25.00
	1928B	2.000	.15	.50	1.25	25.00
	1929B	2.000	.15	.30	.80	17.50
	1930B	3.000	.15	.30	.80	17.50
	1931B	5.037	.15	.30	.80	11.00
	1940B	1.416	.20	.35	2.50	40.00
	1942B	5.078	.15	.30	.90	18.00
	1943B	6.591	.15	.30	.90	18.00
	1944B	9.981	.15	.30	.90	18.00
	1945B	.985	.25	.50	3.50	45.00
	1946B	6.179	.10	.15	.60	7.25
	1947B	5.125	.10	.15	.60	9.50
	1948B	4.710	.10	.15	.60	5.00
	1949B	4.589	.10	.15	.60	5.00
	1950B	.920	.25	.50	1.75	5.00
	1951B	2.141	.10	.25	1.75	20.00
	1952B	4.690	—	.10	.30	3.50
	1953B	9.131	—	.10	.30	3.00
	1954B	8.038	—	.10	.30	3.00
	1955B	19.943	—	.10	.20	1.75
	1957B	10.147	—	.10	.20	1.75
	1958B	10.217	—	.10	.20	1.75
	1959B	11.086	—	.10	.20	1.75
	1962B	23.840	—	.10	.15	.60
	1963B	29.730	—	.10	.15	.50
	1964B	17.080	—	.10	.15	.50
	1965B	1.430	.10	.30	.90	1.25
	1966B	10.010	—	.10	.15	.35
	1967B	13.010	—	.10	.25	.90
	1968B	10.020	—	.10	.15	.35
	1969B	32.990	—	—	.10	.25
	1970	34.800	—	—	.10	.25
	1971	40.020	—	—	.10	.25
	1974	30.002	—	—	.10	.25
	1974	2,400	—	—	Proof	15.00
	1975	34.005	—	—	.10	.25
	1975	.010	—	—	Proof	1.25
	1976	12.005	—	—	.10	.25
	1976	5,130	—	—	Proof	2.25
	1977	14.012	—	—	.10	.20
	1977	7,030	—	—	Proof	1.25
	1978	16.415	—	—	.10	.20
	1978	.010	—	—	Proof	1.00
	1979	27.010	—	—	.10	.20
	1979	.010	—	—	Proof	1.00
	1980	15.500	—	—	.10	.20
	1980	.010	—	—	Proof	1.00

BRASS

KM#	Date	Mintage	Fine	VF	XF	Unc
26a	1918B	6.000	10.00	15.00	25.00	40.00

NICKEL

KM#	Date	Mintage	Fine	VF	XF	Unc
26b	1932B	6.000	.15	.25	.60	5.50
	1933B	3.000	.15	.25	.60	7.25
	1934B	4.000	.15	.25	.60	5.50
	1936B	1.000	.15	.25	.75	8.50
	1937B	2.000	.15	.25	.60	9.50
	1938B	1.000	.15	.25	.75	7.25
26b	1939B	10.048	.15	.25	.60	5.50
	1941B	3.030	.50	1.00	2.00	20.00

ALUMINUM-BRASS

KM#	Date	Mintage	Fine	VF	XF	Unc
26c	1981	79.020	—	—	.10	.20
	1981	.010	—	—	Proof	1.00
	1982	75.340	—	—	.10	.20
	1982	.010	—	—	Proof	1.00
	1983	92.746	—	—	.10	.20
	1983	.011	—	—	Proof	1.00
	1984	69.960	—	—	.10	.20
	1984	.014	—	—	Proof	1.00
	1985	60.032	—	—	.10	.20
	1985	.012	—	—	Proof	1.00
	1986B	55.041	—	—	.10	.20
	1986B	.010	—	—	Proof	1.00
	1987B	39.828	—	—	.10	.20
	1987B	8,800	—	—	Proof	1.00
	1988B	5.044	—	—	.10	.20
	1988B	9,000	—	—	Proof	1.00
	1989B	45.031	—	—	.10	.20
	1989B	8,800	—	—	Proof	1.00
	1990B	16.042	—	—	.10	.20
	1990B	8,900	—	—	Proof	1.00
	1991B	35.036	—	—	.10	.20
	1991B	9,900	—	—	Proof	1.00
	1992B	35.027	—	—	.10	.20
	1992B	7,450	—	—	Proof	1.00
	1993B	38.022	—	—	.10	.20
	1993B	6,200	—	—	Proof	1.00

10 RAPPEN

BILLON

KM#	Date	Mintage	Fine	VF	XF	Unc
6	1850BB	8.780	3.00	12.00	25.00	120.00
	1851BB	4.530	22.50	50.00	120.00	275.00
	1871B	.844	18.00	25.00	40.00	120.00
	1873B	1.398	12.00	20.00	30.00	80.00
	1875B	.174	275.00	520.00	650.00	1200.
	1876B	1.962	12.00	20.00	30.00	70.00

COPPER-NICKEL

KM#	Date	Mintage	Fine	VF	XF	Unc
27	1879B	1.000	3.00	10.00	25.00	140.00
	1880B	2.000	.50	1.00	9.00	65.00
	1881B	3.000	.50	1.00	9.00	60.00
	1882B	3.000	.50	1.00	9.00	60.00
	1883B	2.000	.50	1.00	9.00	65.00
	1884B	3.000	.50	1.00	9.00	50.00
	1885B	3.000	.50	1.00	9.00	50.00
	1894B	1.000	1.00	2.00	15.00	75.00
	1895B	2.000	.50	1.00	9.00	50.00
	1896B	16 pcs.	—	—	Rare	—
	1897B	.500	2.00	5.00	20.00	90.00
	1898B	1.000	7.50	15.00	25.00	150.00
	1899B	.500	7.50	15.00	25.00	150.00
	1900B	1.500	1.00	2.50	9.00	55.00
	1901B	1.000	1.00	2.50	9.00	55.00
	1902B	1.000	1.00	2.50	9.00	60.00
	1903B	1.000	1.00	2.50	9.00	60.00
	1904B	1.000	1.00	2.50	9.00	60.00
	1906B	1.000	1.00	2.50	9.00	50.00
	1907B	2.000	.25	.50	4.00	30.00
	1908B	2.000	.25	.50	4.00	30.00
	1909B	2.000	.25	.50	4.00	30.00
	1911B	1.000	1.00	2.50	6.00	45.00
	1912B	1.500	.25	.50	4.00	40.00
	1913B	2.000	.25	.50	4.00	40.00
	1914B	2.000	.25	.50	4.00	55.00
	1915B	1.200	1.00	3.00	10.00	130.00
	1919B	3.000	.15	.25	1.00	18.50
	1920B	3.500	.15	.25	1.00	18.50
	1921B	3.000	.15	.25	1.00	18.50
	1922B	2.000	.20	.50	1.50	30.00
	1924B	2.000	.20	.50	1.50	25.00
	1925B	3.000	.15	.25	1.00	18.50
	1926B	3.000	.15	.25	1.00	18.50
	1927B	2.000	.15	.25	1.00	18.50
	1928B	2.000	.15	.25	1.00	18.50
	1929B	2.000	.15	.25	1.00	18.50
	1930B	2.000	.20	.50	2.00	35.00
	1931B	2.244	.20	.50	2.00	35.00
	1940B	2.000	.20	.50	2.00	35.00
	1942B	2.110	.20	.50	2.00	35.00
	1943B	3.176	.20	.50	2.00	30.00
	1944B	6.133	.10	.20	.50	8.50
	1945B	.993	.20	.50	2.50	50.00
	1946B	4.010	.10	.20	.50	30.00
	1947B	3.152	.10	.20	.50	30.00
	1948B	1.000	.20	.50	1.00	35.00
	1949B	2.269	.15	.25	.50	30.00
	1950B	3.200	.10	.15	.30	3.50
	1951B	3.430	.10	.15	.30	6.00
	1952B	4.452	.10	.15	.30	6.00
	1953B	6.149	.10	.15	.30	6.00

KM#	Date	Mintage	Fine	VF	XF	Unc
27	1954B	3.200	.10	.15	.30	11.00
	1955B	11.795	.10	.15	.30	3.50
	1957B	10.092	.10	.15	.30	3.50
	1958B	10.040	.10	.15	.30	3.50
	1959B	13.053	.10	.15	.30	3.50
	1960B	4.040	.10	.15	.30	3.50
	1961B	7.949	—	.10	.25	1.25
	1962B	34.965	—	.10	.25	.90
	1964B	16.340	—	.10	.25	.90
	1965B	14.190	—	.10	.25	.90
	1966B	4.025	—	.10	.25	.90
	1967B	10.000	—	.10	.25	.90
	1968B	14.065	—	.10	.15	.35
	1969B	28.855	—	.10	.15	.35
	1970	40.020	—	.10	.15	.35
	1972	7.877	—	.10	.15	.35
	1973	30.350	—	.10	.15	.35
	1974	30.007	—	—	.10	.30
	1974	2,400	—	—	Proof	15.00
	1975	25.003	—	—	.10	.30
	1975	.010	—	—	Proof	1.75
	1976	19.013	—	—	.10	.30
	1976	5,130	—	—	Proof	3.00
	1977	10.007	—	—	.10	.30
	1977	7,030	—	—	Proof	1.75
	1978	19.958	—	—	.10	.30
	1978	.010	—	—	Proof	1.75
	1979	18.010	—	—	.10	.30
	1979	.010	—	—	Proof	1.50
	1980	18.005	—	—	.10	.30
	1980	.010	—	—	Proof	1.50
	1981	30.140	—	—	.10	.30
	1981	.010	—	—	Proof	1.50
	1982	50.110	—	—	.10	.30
	1982	.010	—	—	Proof	1.50
	1983	40.033	—	—	.10	.30
	1983	.011	—	—	Proof	1.50
	1984	22.022	—	—	.10	.30
	1984	.014	—	—	Proof	1.50
	1985	3.032	—	—	.10	.30
	1985	.012	—	—	Proof	1.50
	1986B	2.324	—	—	.10	.30
	1986B	.010	—	—	Proof	1.50
	1987B	5.028	—	—	.10	.30
	1987B	8,800	—	—	Proof	1.50
	1988B	5.029	—	—	.10	.30
	1988B	9,000	—	—	Proof	1.50
	1989B	41.031	—	—	.10	.30
	1989B	8,800	—	—	Proof	1.50
	1990B	40.032	—	—	.10	.30
	1990B	8,900	—	—	Proof	1.50
	1991B	35.046	—	—	.10	.30
	1991B	9,900	—	—	Proof	1.50
	1992B	18.027	—	—	.10	.30
	1992B	7,450	—	—	Proof	1.50
	1993B	27.022	—	—	.10	.30
	1993B	6,200	—	—	Proof	1.50
			BRASS			
27a	1918B	6.000	15.00	17.50	30.00	60.00
	1919B	3.000	50.00	70.00	85.00	150.00
			NICKEL			
27b	1932B	3.500	.10	.25	.75	11.50
	1933B	2.000	.10	.25	.75	12.00
	1934B	3.000	.10	.25	.75	11.50
	1936B	1.500	.15	.30	.90	12.00
	1937B	1.000	.15	.30	.90	11.50
	1938B	1.000	.15	.30	.90	11.50
	1939B	10.022	.15	.30	.90	11.50

20 RAPPEN

BILLON

KM#	Date	Mintage	Fine	VF	XF	Unc
7	1850BB	5.390	4.00	12.00	30.00	130.00
	1851BB	6.160	50.00	150.00	375.00	850.00
	1858B	1.548	10.00	18.00	35.00	150.00
	1859B	2.776	5.00	8.00	25.00	80.00

NICKEL

KM#	Date	Mintage	Fine	VF	XF	Unc
29	1881B	1.000	.75	1.50	10.00	60.00
	1883B	2.500	.50	1.00	6.00	40.00
	1884B	4.000	.50	1.00	6.00	30.00
	1885B	3.000	.50	1.00	6.00	35.00
	1887B	.500	3.00	5.00	25.00	145.00
	1891B	1.000	.50	1.00	10.00	45.00
	1893B	1.000	.50	1.00	10.00	45.00
	1894B	1.000	.50	1.00	10.00	45.00
	1896B	1.000	.50	1.00	10.00	45.00
	1897B	.500	1.00	3.00	12.00	160.00
	1898B	.500	1.00	3.00	12.00	140.00
	1899B	.500	1.00	3.00	12.00	140.00
	1900B	1.000	.50	1.00	6.00	45.00

KM#	Date	Mintage	Fine	VF	XF	Unc
29	1901B	1.000	.50	1.00	6.00	45.00
	1902B	1.000	.50	1.00	6.00	45.00
	1903B	1.000	.50	1.00	6.00	45.00
	1906B	1.000	.50	1.00	6.00	45.00
	1907B	1.000	.50	1.00	4.00	35.00
	1908B	1.500	.25	.50	4.00	32.00
	1909B	2.000	.25	.50	4.00	30.00
	1911B	1.000	.25	.50	4.00	35.00
	1912B	2.000	.25	.50	4.00	30.00
	1913B	1.500	.25	.50	4.00	30.00
	1919B	1.500	.25	.50	4.00	30.00
	1920B	3.100	.25	.50	4.00	15.00
	1921B	2.500	.25	.50	4.00	15.00
	1924B	1.100	.25	.50	4.00	20.00
	1925B	1.500	.25	.50	4.00	15.00
	1926B	1.500	.25	.50	4.00	15.00
	1927B	.500	1.00	2.50	10.00	150.00
	1929B	2.000	.20	.30	.90	12.50
	1930B	2.000	.20	.30	.90	12.50
	1931B	2.250	.20	.30	.90	12.00
	1932B	2.000	.20	.30	.90	12.00
	1933B	1.500	.20	.30	.90	12.00
	1934B	2.000	.20	.30	.90	12.00
	1936B	1.000	.20	.30	.90	15.00
	1938B	2.805	.20	.30	.90	12.00
			COPPER-NICKEL			
29a	1939B	8.100	—	.20	.60	35.00
	1943B	10.173	—	.20	.40	25.00
	1944B	7.139	—	.20	.40	10.00
	1945B	1.992	.20	.50	1.75	38.00
	1947B	5.131	—	.20	.40	12.00
	1950B	5.970	—	.20	.40	5.00
	1951B	3.640	—	.20	.40	8.00
	1952B	3.070	—	.20	.40	8.00
	1953B	6.958	—	.20	.40	5.00
	1954B	1.504	.20	.30	.90	17.00
	1955B	9.104	—	.20	.40	6.00
	1956B	5.111	—	.20	.40	7.00
	1957B	2.535	—	.20	.40	15.00
	1958B	5.037	—	.20	.40	6.00
	1959B	10.136	—	.20	.35	3.00
	1960B	15.467	—	.20	.35	3.00
	1961B	8.234	—	.20	.35	3.00
	1962B	30.145	—	.20	.35	2.00
	1963B	9.020	—	.20	.35	2.00
	1964B	14.370	—	—	.20	1.50
	1965B	15.005	—	—	.20	1.50
	1966B	10.785	—	—	.20	.60
	1967B	8.995	—	—	.20	.60
	1968B	10.540	—	—	.20	.50
	1969B	39.875	—	—	.20	.50
	1970	45.605	—	—	.20	.50
	1971	25.160	—	—	.20	.50
	1974	30.025	—	—	.20	.40
	1974	2,400	—	—	Proof	25.00
	1975	50.060	—	—	.20	.40
	1975	.010	—	—	Proof	2.25
	1976	23.150	—	—	.20	.40
	1976	5,130	—	—	Proof	3.75
	1977	14.012	—	—	.20	.40
	1977	7,030	—	—	Proof	2.25
	1978	14.815	—	—	.20	.40
	1978	.010	—	—	Proof	2.00
	1979	18.380	—	—	.20	.40
	1979	.010	—	—	Proof	2.00
	1980	24.560	—	—	.20	.40
	1980	.010	—	—	Proof	2.00
	1981	22.020	—	—	.20	.40
	1981	.010	—	—	Proof	2.00
	1982	25.035	—	—	.20	.40
	1982	.010	—	—	Proof	2.00
	1983	10.026	—	—	.20	.40
	1983	.011	—	—	Proof	2.00
	1984	22.055	—	—	.20	.40
	1984	.014	—	—	Proof	2.00
	1985	40.027	—	—	.20	.40
	1985	.012	—	—	Proof	2.00
	1986B	10.299	—	—	.20	.40
	1986B	.010	—	—	Proof	2.00
	1987B	10.028	—	—	.20	.40
	1987B	8,800	—	—	Proof	2.00
	1988B	25.029	—	—	.20	.40
	1988B	9,000	—	—	Proof	2.00
	1989B	20.031	—	—	.20	.40
	1989B	8,800	—	—	Proof	2.00
	1990B	6.534	—	—	.20	.40
	1990B	8,900	—	—	Proof	2.00
	1991B	48.076	—	—	.20	.40
	1991B	9,900	—	—	Proof	2.00
	1992B	12.627	—	—	.20	.40
	1992B	7,450	—	—	Proof	2.00
	1993B	32.522	—	—	.20	.40
	1993B	6,200	—	—	Proof	2.00

1/2 FRANC

2.5000 g, .900 SILVER, .0723 oz ASW

KM#	Date	Mintage	Fine	VF	XF	Unc
8	1850A	4.500	75.00	150.00	325.00	900.00
	1851A	Inc. Ab.	75.00	150.00	300.00	850.00

2.5000 g, .835 SILVER, .0671 oz ASW

KM#	Date	Mintage	Fine	VF	XF	Unc
23	1875B	1.000	20.00	40.00	150.00	650.00
	1877B	1.000	35.00	100.00	325.00	975.00
	1878B	1.000	35.00	100.00	350.00	1000.
	1879B	1.000	10.00	20.00	75.00	400.00
	1881B	1.000	5.00	10.00	60.00	350.00
	1882B	1.000	5.00	10.00	75.00	400.00
	1894A	.800	15.00	40.00	125.00	350.00
	1896B	28 pcs.	—	—	Rare	—
	1898B	1.600	2.00	4.00	15.00	100.00
	1899B	.400	5.00	8.00	75.00	350.00
	1900B	.400	5.00	8.00	75.00	350.00
	1901B	.200	30.00	125.00	500.00	1350.
	1903B	.800	2.00	4.00	20.00	120.00
	1904B	.400	6.00	12.00	225.00	1250.
	1905B	.600	2.00	5.00	25.00	190.00
	1906B	1.000	1.00	3.00	25.00	210.00
	1907B	1.200	1.00	2.50	25.00	190.00
	1908B	.800	1.50	2.50	16.50	125.00
	1909B	1.000	1.00	2.00	15.00	110.00
	1910B	1.000	1.00	2.00	15.00	110.00
	1913B	.800	1.50	2.50	15.00	95.00
	1914B	2.000	1.00	1.50	5.00	45.00
	1916B	.800	1.50	2.50	10.00	100.00
	1920B	5.400	1.00	1.50	4.00	25.00
	1921B	6.000	1.00	1.50	4.00	27.50
	1928B	1.000	1.00	2.00	9.00	90.00
	1929B	2.000	1.00	1.50	4.00	30.00
	1931B	1.000	1.00	1.50	5.00	45.00
	1932B	1.000	1.00	1.50	5.00	30.00
	1934B	2.000	1.00	2.00	9.00	25.00
	1936B	.400	1.50	3.00	6.00	40.00
	1937B	1.000	1.00	1.50	3.50	18.00
	1939B	1.001	1.00	1.50	3.50	22.00
	1940B	2.002	1.00	1.50	3.50	18.00
	1941B	.200	1.50	2.50	3.50	25.00
	1942B	2.969	1.00	1.50	3.00	10.00
	1943B	4.572	1.00	1.50	3.00	10.00
	1944B	7.456	1.00	1.50	3.00	10.00
	1945B	4.928	1.00	1.50	2.50	6.00
	1946B	6.817	1.00	1.50	2.50	6.00
	1948B	6.113	1.00	1.50	2.50	6.00
	1950B	7.148	1.00	1.50	2.50	6.00
	1951B	8.530	BV	1.00	1.50	5.00
	1952B	14.023	BV	1.00	1.50	3.75
	1953B	3.567	BV	1.00	1.50	6.00
	1955B	1.320	BV	1.00	2.00	12.00
	1956B	4.250	BV	1.00	1.50	5.00
	1957B	12.085	BV	1.00	1.50	3.50
	1958B	11.558	BV	1.00	1.50	3.50
	1959B	12.581	BV	1.00	1.50	3.50
	1960B	14.528	BV	1.00	1.50	3.50
	1961B	6.906	BV	1.00	1.50	3.50
	1962B	18.272	BV	1.00	1.50	3.50
	1963B	25.168	BV	1.00	1.50	3.50
	1964B	22.720	BV	1.00	1.50	3.50
	1965B	17.920	BV	1.00	1.50	3.50
	1966B	10.008	BV	1.00	1.50	3.50
	1967B	16.096	BV	1.00	1.50	3.50
			COPPER-NICKEL			
23a.1	1968	20.000	—	—	.40	.65
	1968B	44.920	—	—	.40	.65
	1969	31.400	—	—	.40	.65
	1969B	51.704	—	—	.40	.65
	1970	52.620	—	—	.40	.65
	1971	34.472	—	—	.40	.65
	1972	9.996	—	—	.40	.65
	1973	5.000	—	—	.40	.65
	1974	45.006	—	—	.40	.65
	1974	2,400	—	—	Proof	35.00
	1975	27.234	—	—	.40	.65
	1975	.010	—	—	Proof	3.25
	1976	10.009	—	—	.40	.65
	1976	5,130	—	—	Proof	5.00
	1977	19.011	—	—	.40	.65
	1977	7,030	—	—	Proof	3.25
	1978	20.818	—	—	.40	.65
	1978	.010	—	—	Proof	2.50
	1979	27.010	—	—	.40	.65
	1979	.010	—	—	Proof	2.50
	1980	31.064	—	—	.40	.65
	1980	.010	—	—	Proof	2.50
	1981	30.155	—	—	.40	.65
	1981	.010	—	—	Proof	2.50
		Obv. and rev: Medallic alignment. Obv: 22 stars.				
23a.2	1982	30.151	—	—	.40	.65
	1982	.010	—	—	Proof	8.50
		Obv: 23 stars.				
23a.3	1983	22.020	—	—	.40	.65
	1983	.011	—	—	Proof	2.50
	1984	22.036	—	—	.40	.65
	1984	.014	—	—	Proof	2.50
	1985	6.026	—	—	.40	.70
	1985	.012	—	—	Proof	2.50
	1986B	5.031	—	—	.40	.70
	1986B	.010	—	—	Proof	2.50
	1987B	10.028	—	—	.40	.65
	1987B	8,800	—	—	Proof	2.50
	1988B	5.029	—	—	.40	.70

KM#	Date	Mintage	Fine	VF	XF	Unc
23a.3	1988B	9,000	—	—	Proof	2.50
	1989B	10.031	—	—	.40	.65
	1989B	8,800	—	—	Proof	2.50
	1990B	20.032	—	—	.40	.65
	1990B	8,900	—	—	Proof	2.50
	1991B	10.036	—	—	.40	.65
	1991B	9,900	—	—	Proof	2.50
	1992B	30.027	—	—	.45	.75
	1992B	7,450	—	—	Proof	2.50
	1993B	13.022	—	—	.45	.75
	1993B	6,200	—	—	Proof	2.50

FRANC

5.0000 g, .900 SILVER, .1447 oz ASW

KM#	Date	Mintage	Fine	VF	XF	Unc
9	1850A	5.750	100.00	175.00	300.00	900.00
	1851A	Inc. Ab.	100.00	175.00	325.00	1050.
	1857B	526 pcs.	3000.	5500.	9000.	14,500.

5.0000 g, .800 SILVER, .1286 oz ASW

KM#	Date	Mintage	Fine	VF	XF	Unc
9a	1860B	.515	210.00	400.00	1350.	3000.
	1861B	3.002	20.00	60.00	150.00	750.00

5.0000 g, .835 SILVER, .1342 oz ASW

KM#	Date	Mintage	Fine	VF	XF	Unc
24	1875B	1.036	20.00	100.00	400.00	1250.
	1876B	2.500	5.00	10.00	100.00	450.00
	1877B	2.520	5.00	10.00	125.00	550.00
	1880B	.944	15.00	100.00	450.00	1950.
	1886B	1.000	4.00	10.00	75.00	350.00
	1887B	1.000	4.00	10.00	75.00	350.00
	1894A	1.200	4.00	10.00	75.00	350.00
	1896B	28 pcs.	—	—	Rare	—
	1898B	.400	4.00	10.00	75.00	350.00
	1899B	.400	4.00	10.00	75.00	350.00
	1900B	.400	4.00	10.00	85.00	550.00
	1901B	.400	5.00	20.00	150.00	900.00
	1903B	1.000	3.00	5.00	30.00	250.00
	1904B	.400	8.00	20.00	450.00	2000.
	1905B	.700	3.00	5.00	30.00	300.00
	1906B	.700	3.00	5.00	40.00	500.00
	1907B	.800	3.00	5.00	40.00	450.00
	1908B	1.200	3.00	5.00	25.00	250.00
	1909B	.900	3.00	5.00	25.00	210.00
	1910B	1.000	3.00	5.00	15.00	180.00
	1911B	1.200	3.00	4.00	15.00	150.00
	1912B	1.200	3.00	4.00	15.00	150.00
	1913B	1.200	3.00	4.00	15.00	120.00
	1914B	4.200	3.00	4.00	15.00	100.00
	1916B	1.000	3.00	4.00	15.00	125.00
	1920B	3.300	3.00	4.00	5.00	35.00
	1920B	—	—	—	Proof	150.00
	1921B	3.800	3.00	4.00	5.00	35.00
	1928B	1.500	3.00	4.00	5.00	27.50
	1931B	1.000	3.00	4.00	5.00	40.00
	1932B	.500	3.00	4.00	10.00	100.00
	1934B	.500	3.00	4.00	10.00	90.00
	1936B	.500	3.00	4.00	10.00	75.00
	1937B	1.000	1.50	2.50	4.50	35.00
	1939B	2.106	1.50	2.50	4.00	18.00
	1940B	2.003	1.50	2.50	4.00	15.00
	1943B	3.526	1.50	2.00	3.75	11.00
	1943B	—	—	—	Proof	150.00
	1944B	6.225	1.50	2.00	3.75	11.00
	1945B	7.794	1.50	2.00	3.00	9.00
	1946B	2.539	1.50	2.00	3.00	12.00
	1947B	.624	2.00	2.50	3.00	15.00
	1952B	2.853	1.50	2.00	3.00	7.00
	1953B	.786	1.50	2.50	4.50	30.00
	1955B	.194	2.50	5.00	11.00	30.00
	1956B	2.500	1.50	2.00	3.00	8.00
	1957B	6.420	1.50	2.00	3.00	6.00
	1958B	3.580	1.50	2.00	3.00	7.00
	1959B	1.859	1.50	2.00	3.00	7.00
	1960B	3.523	BV	2.00	3.00	7.00
	1961B	6.549	BV	2.00	3.00	7.00
	1962B	6.220	BV	2.00	3.00	7.00
	1963B	13.476	BV	2.00	3.00	5.00
	1964B	12.560	BV	2.00	3.00	5.00
	1965B	5.032	BV	2.00	3.00	7.00
	1966B	3.032	BV	2.00	3.00	7.00
	1967B	2.088	BV	2.00	3.00	8.00

COPPER-NICKEL

KM#	Date	Mintage	Fine	VF	XF	Unc
24a.1	1968	15.000	—	—	.85	1.25
	1968B	40.864	—	—	.85	1.25
	1969B	37.598	—	—	.85	1.25
	1970	24.240	—	—	.85	1.25
	1971	11.496	—	—	.85	1.25
	1973	5.000	—	—	.85	1.75
	1974	15.012	—	—	.85	1.25
	1974	2,400	—	—	Proof	50.00
24a.1	1975	13.012	—	—	.85	1.25
	1975	.010	—	—	Proof	4.50
	1976	5.009	—	—	.85	1.25
	1976	5,130	—	—	Proof	7.50
	1977	6.019	—	—	.85	1.25
	1977	7,030	—	—	Proof	4.50
	1978	13.548	—	—	.85	1.25
	1978	.010	—	—	Proof	3.50
	1979	10.800	—	—	.85	1.25
	1979	.010	—	—	Proof	3.50
	1980	11.002	—	—	.85	1.25
	1980	.010	—	—	Proof	4.00
	1981	18.013	—	—	.85	1.25
	1981	.010	—	—	Proof	4.00

Obv. and rev: Medallic alignment. Obv: 22 stars.

KM#	Date	Mintage	Fine	VF	XF	Unc
24a.2	1982	15.039	—	—	.80	1.00
	1982	.010	—	—	Proof	12.00

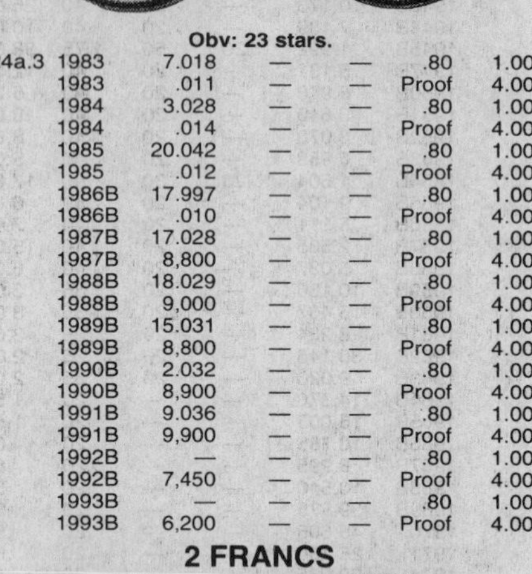

Obv: 23 stars.

KM#	Date	Mintage	Fine	VF	XF	Unc
24a.3	1983	7.018	—	—	.80	1.00
	1983	.011	—	—	Proof	4.00
	1984	3.028	—	—	.80	1.00
	1984	.014	—	—	Proof	4.00
	1985	20.042	—	—	.80	1.00
	1985	.012	—	—	Proof	4.00
	1986B	17.997	—	—	.80	1.00
	1986B	.010	—	—	Proof	4.00
	1987B	17.028	—	—	.80	1.00
	1987B	8,800	—	—	Proof	4.00
	1988B	18.029	—	—	.80	1.00
	1988B	9,000	—	—	Proof	4.00
	1989B	15.031	—	—	.80	1.00
	1989B	8,800	—	—	Proof	4.00
	1990B	2.032	—	—	.80	1.00
	1990B	8,900	—	—	Proof	4.00
	1991B	9.036	—	—	.80	1.00
	1991B	9,900	—	—	Proof	4.00
	1992B	—	—	—	.80	1.00
	1992B	7,450	—	—	Proof	4.00
	1993B	—	—	—	.80	1.00
	1993B	6,200	—	—	Proof	4.00

2 FRANCS

10.0000 g, .900 SILVER, .2894 oz ASW

KM#	Date	Mintage	Fine	VF	XF	Unc
10	1850A	2.500	200.00	400.00	725.00	1700.
	1857B	622 pcs.	3000.	7200.	10,500.	16,500.

10.0000 g, .800 SILVER, .2572 oz ASW

KM#	Date	Mintage	Fine	VF	XF	Unc
10a	1860B	2.001	50.00	100.00	300.00	1400.
	1862B	1.000	60.00	110.00	400.00	1650.
	1863B	.500	175.00	300.00	1000.	3250.

10.0000 g, .835 SILVER, .2685 oz ASW

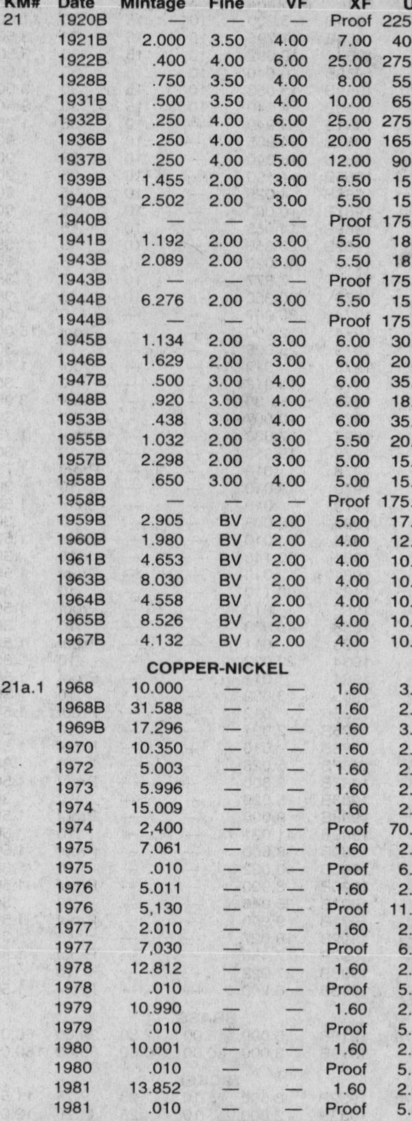

KM#	Date	Mintage	Fine	VF	XF	Unc
21	1874B	1.000	10.00	20.00	200.00	1100.
	1875B	.982	12.50	25.00	300.00	1300.
	1878B	1.500	8.00	15.00	150.00	725.00
	1879B	.518	17.50	35.00	400.00	2700.
	1886B	1.000	5.00	8.00	100.00	475.00
	1894A	.700	6.00	10.00	125.00	725.00
	1896B	20 pcs.	—	—	Rare	—
	1901B	.050	125.00	175.00	1250.	6000.
	1903B	.300	4.00	10.00	100.00	575.00
	1904B	.200	6.00	20.00	275.00	1200.
	1905B	.300	4.00	8.00	100.00	600.00
	1906B	.400	4.00	8.00	110.00	725.00
	1907B	.300	4.00	8.00	125.00	850.00
	1908B	.200	6.00	20.00	275.00	1200.
	1909B	.300	4.00	8.00	75.00	375.00
	1910B	.250	5.00	10.00	150.00	900.00
	1911B	.400	4.00	6.00	40.00	275.00
	1912B	.400	4.00	6.00	40.00	275.00
	1913B	.300	4.00	6.00	40.00	275.00
	1914B	1.000	4.00	5.00	15.00	145.00
	1916B	.250	5.00	8.00	75.00	600.00
	1920B	2.300	3.50	4.00	7.00	40.00
21	1920B	—	—	—	Proof	225.00
	1921B	2.000	3.50	4.00	7.00	40.00
	1922B	.400	4.00	6.00	25.00	275.00
	1928B	.750	3.50	4.00	8.00	55.00
	1931B	.500	3.50	4.00	10.00	65.00
	1932B	.250	4.00	6.00	25.00	275.00
	1936B	.250	4.00	5.00	20.00	165.00
	1937B	.250	4.00	5.00	12.00	90.00
	1939B	1.455	2.00	3.00	5.50	15.00
	1940B	2.502	2.00	3.00	5.50	15.00
	1940B	—	—	—	Proof	175.00
	1941B	1.192	2.00	3.00	5.50	18.00
	1943B	2.089	2.00	3.00	5.50	18.00
	1943B	—	—	—	Proof	175.00
	1944B	6.276	2.00	3.00	5.50	15.00
	1944B	—	—	—	Proof	175.00
	1945B	1.134	2.00	3.00	6.00	30.00
	1946B	1.629	2.00	3.00	6.00	20.00
	1947B	.500	3.00	4.00	6.00	35.00
	1948B	.920	3.00	4.00	6.00	18.00
	1953B	.438	3.00	4.00	6.00	35.00
	1955B	1.032	2.00	3.00	5.50	20.00
	1957B	2.298	2.00	3.00	5.00	15.00
	1958B	.650	3.00	4.00	5.00	15.00
	1958B	—	—	—	Proof	175.00
	1959B	2.905	BV	2.00	5.00	17.00
	1960B	1.980	BV	2.00	4.00	12.00
	1961B	4.653	BV	2.00	4.00	10.00
	1963B	8.030	BV	2.00	4.00	10.00
	1964B	4.558	BV	2.00	4.00	10.00
	1965B	8.526	BV	2.00	4.00	10.00
	1967B	4.132	BV	2.00	4.00	10.00

COPPER-NICKEL

KM#	Date	Mintage	Fine	VF	XF	Unc
21a.1	1968	10.000	—	—	1.60	3.50
	1968B	31.588	—	—	1.60	2.75
	1969B	17.296	—	—	1.60	3.00
	1970	10.350	—	—	1.60	2.75
	1972	5.003	—	—	1.60	2.75
	1973	5.996	—	—	1.60	2.75
	1974	15.009	—	—	1.60	2.25
	1974	2,400	—	—	Proof	70.00
	1975	7.061	—	—	1.60	2.25
	1975	.010	—	—	Proof	6.00
	1976	5.011	—	—	1.60	2.25
	1976	5,130	—	—	Proof	11.00
	1977	2.010	—	—	1.60	2.25
	1977	7,030	—	—	Proof	6.00
	1978	12.812	—	—	1.60	2.25
	1978	.010	—	—	Proof	5.00
	1979	10.990	—	—	1.60	2.00
	1979	.010	—	—	Proof	5.00
	1980	10.001	—	—	1.60	2.00
	1980	.010	—	—	Proof	5.50
	1981	13.852	—	—	1.60	2.00
	1981	.010	—	—	Proof	5.50

Obv. and rev: Medallic alignment. Obv: 22 stars.

KM#	Date	Mintage	Fine	VF	XF	Unc
21a.2	1982	5.912	—	—	1.60	2.25
	1982	.010	—	—	Proof	14.00

Obv: 23 stars.

KM#	Date	Mintage	Fine	VF	XF	Unc
21a.3	1983	3.023	—	—	1.60	2.25
	1983	.011	—	—	Proof	5.50
	1984	2.029	—	—	1.60	2.25
	1984	.014	—	—	Proof	5.50
	1985	3.022	—	—	1.60	2.25
	1985	.012	—	—	Proof	5.50
	1986B	3.032	—	—	1.60	2.25
	1986B	.010	—	—	Proof	5.50
	1987B	8.028	—	—	1.60	2.00
	1987B	8,800	—	—	Proof	5.50
	1988B	10.029	—	—	1.60	2.00
	1988B	9,000	—	—	Proof	5.50
	1989B	8.031	—	—	1.60	2.00
	1989B	8,800	—	—	Proof	5.50
	1990B	5.045	—	—	1.60	2.25
	1990B	8,900	—	—	Proof	5.50
	1991B	12.036	—	—	1.60	2.00
	1991B	9,900	—	—	Proof	5.50
	1992B	10.027	—	—	1.60	2.00
	1992B	7,450	—	—	Proof	5.50
	1993B	13.049	—	—	1.60	2.00
	1993B	6,200	—	—	Proof	5.50

5 FRANCS

25.0000 g, .900 SILVER, .7234 oz ASW

KM#	Date	Mintage	Fine	VF	XF	Unc
11	1850A	.140	225.00	375.00	725.00	1850.
	1851A	.360	200.00	325.00	550.00	1450.
	1873B	.030	1100.	1700.	2850.	6250.
	1874B.	1.400	150.00	225.00	475.00	1450.
	1874B	.196	200.00	275.00	625.00	1550.

NOTE: The dot after the B is for Brussels. For coins dated 1855 see Shooting Talers.

KM#	Date	Mintage	Fine	VF	XF	Unc
34	1888B	.025	300.00	450.00	1350.	5000.
	1889B	.225	100.00	175.00	400.00	2000.
	1890B	.305	100.00	175.00	400.00	1700.
	1891B	.150	100.00	175.00	420.00	2250.
	1892B	.190	100.00	175.00	400.00	1700.
	1894B	.034	450.00	1200.	2500.	8000.
	1895B	.046	325.00	600.00	2000.	6500.
	1896B	2,000	—	—	Rare	62,500.
	1900B	.033	425.00	725.00	1600.	5000.
	1904B	.040	360.00	600.00	1350.	4250.
	1907B	.277	110.00	175.00	300.00	1600.
	1908B	.200	120.00	185.00	350.00	1600.
	1909B	.120	125.00	200.00	400.00	2000.
	1912B	.011	1800.	3500.	5500.	10,500.
	1916B	.022	650.00	1350.	2450.	4500.

KM#	Date	Mintage	Fine	VF	XF	Unc
37	1922B	2.400	50.00	70.00	125.00	425.00
	1923B	11.300	40.00	50.00	90.00	250.00
	1923B	—	—	—	Proof	900.00

KM#	Date	Mintage	Fine	VF	XF	Unc
38	1924B	.182	200.00	400.00	625.00	1450.
	1925B	2.830	50.00	90.00	170.00	375.00
	1926B	2.000	50.00	90.00	190.00	420.00
	1928B	.024	3000.	8000.	13,000.	20,000.

15.0000 g, .835 SILVER, .4027 oz ASW

NOTE: The several varieties of number KM#40, the 1931 and 1967 5 Francs, are distinguished by the relation of the edge lettering to the head of William Tell and in the amount of rotation of the reverse in relation to the obverse. Beginning above the head the normal sequence is:

a) PROVIDEBIT ******** *** DOMINUS**

A fairly common variety shows the lettering:

b) ******** *** DOMINUS PROVIDEBIT**

A somewhat rarer variety shows:

c) ******** PROVIDEBIT *** DOMINUS**

The reverse of the regular issue is upset 180 degrees. There are varieties with:

d) The reverse rotated about 15 degrees to the left of the normal upset position.

e) The reverse rotated about 15 degrees to the right of the normal position.

Raised edge lettering.

KM#	Date	Mintage	Fine	VF	XF	Unc
40	1931B(a)	3.520	4.50	6.00	20.00	85.00
	1931B(b)	I.A.	15.00	30.00	75.00	250.00
	1931B(c)	I.A.	200.00	450.00	675.00	1250.
	1932B	10.580	4.00	5.50	8.00	25.00
	1933B	5.900	4.00	5.50	8.00	25.00
	1935B	3.000	4.00	5.50	8.00	32.50
	1937B	.645	4.50	6.50	10.00	55.00
	1939B	2.197	4.00	5.50	10.00	30.00
	1940B	1.601	4.00	5.50	10.00	32.50
	1948B	.416	4.50	6.50	10.00	55.00
	1949B	.407	4.50	6.50	10.00	60.00
	1950B	.482	4.50	6.50	10.00	50.00
	1951B	1.196	4.00	5.50	10.00	30.00
	1951B	—	—	—	Proof	250.00
	1952B	.155	30.00	70.00	100.00	280.00
	1953B	3.403	BV	5.00	10.00	18.00
	1954B	6.600	BV	5.00	10.00	16.00
	1965B	5.021	BV	5.00	9.00	12.00
	1966B	9.016	BV	5.00	9.00	12.00
	1967B (a)	13.817	BV	5.00	9.00	12.00
	1967B (b)	—	15.00	30.00	60.00	150.00
	1967B (c)	—	50.00	250.00	550.00	1000.
	1969B	8.637	BV	5.00	9.00	12.00

NOTE: A few examples of the 1968B were struck in error on silver flans.

COPPER-NICKEL

KM#	Date	Mintage	Fine	VF	XF	Unc
40a.1	1968B	33.871	—	—	3.75	6.50
	1970	6.306	—	—	3.75	6.50
	1973	5.002	—	—	3.75	4.50
	1974	6.007	—	—	3.75	4.50
	1974	2,400	—	—	Proof	110.00
	1975	2.500	—	—	3.75	4.50

KM#	Date	Mintage	Fine	VF	XF	Unc
40a.1	1975	.010	—	—	Proof	10.00
	1976	1.500	—	—	3.75	4.50
	1976	5,130	—	—	Proof	16.00
	1977	—	—	—	3.75	4.50
	1977	7,030	—	—	Proof	10.00
	1978	.900	—	—	3.75	4.50
	1978	.010	—	—	Proof	8.50
	1979	—	—	—	3.75	4.50
	1979	.010	—	—	Proof	8.50
	1980	4.016	—	—	3.75	4.50
	1980	.010	—	—	Proof	10.00
	1981	6.008	—	—	3.75	4.50
	1981	.010	—	—	Proof	10.00

Obv. and rev: Medallic alignment.

KM#	Date	Mintage	Fine	VF	XF	Unc
40a.2	1982	5.040	—	—	3.75	4.50
	1982	.010	—	—	Proof	20.00
	1983	4.022	—	—	3.75	4.50
	1983	.011	—	—	Proof	10.00
	1984	3.939	—	—	3.75	4.50
	1984	.014	—	—	Proof	10.00

Incuse edge lettering.

KM#	Date	Mintage	Fine	VF	XF	Unc
40a.3	1985	4.038	—	—	3.75	4.50
	1985	.012	—	—	Proof	10.00
	1986B	7.083	—	—	3.75	4.50
	1986B	.010	—	—	Proof	10.00
	1987B	7.028	—	—	3.75	4.50
	1987B	8,800	—	—	Proof	10.00
	1988B	7.029	—	—	3.75	4.50
	1988B	9,000	—	—	Proof	10.00
	1989B	5.031	—	—	3.75	4.50
	1989B	8,800	—	—	Proof	10.00
	1990B	1.049	—	—	4.00	6.00
	1990B	8,900	—	—	Proof	10.00
	1991B	.544	—	—	5.00	25.00
	1991B	9,900	—	—	Proof	50.00
	1992B	5.034	—	—	3.75	4.50
	1992B	7,450	—	—	Proof	10.00
	1993B	5.022	—	—	3.75	4.50
	1993B	6,200	—	—	Proof	10.00

COMMEMORATIVE COINAGE

5 FRANCS

15.0000 g, .835 SILVER, .4027 oz ASW
Confederation Armament Fund

KM#	Date	Mintage	VF	XF	Unc	BU
41	1936B	.200	20.00	45.00	60.00	90.00

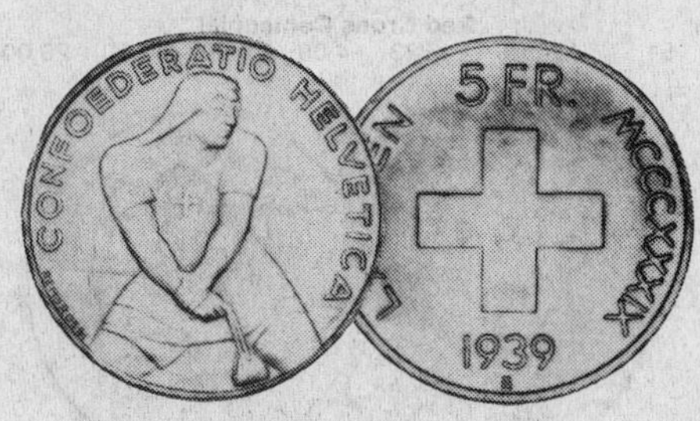

600th Anniversary Battle of Laupen

KM#	Date	Mintage	VF	XF	Unc	BU
42	1939B	.031	550.00	800.00	1000.	1250.

Zurich Exposition

KM#	Date	Mintage	VF	XF	Unc	BU
43	1939*	.060	75.00	125.00	175.00	300.00
	1939	—	—	Matte Proof		1000.

*Minted at Huguenin, Le Locle.

650th Anniversary of Confederation

KM#	Date	Mintage	VF	XF	Unc	BU
44	1941B	.100	50.00	120.00	150.00	200.00

500th Anniversary Battle of St. Jakob An Der Birs

KM#	Date	Mintage	VF	XF	Unc	BU
45	1944B	.102	35.00	90.00	115.00	165.00

Swiss Constitution Centennial

KM#	Date	Mintage	VF	XF	Unc	BU
48	1948B	.500	10.00	12.50	20.00	30.00

Red Cross Centennial

KM#	Date	Mintage	VF	XF	Unc	BU
51	1963B	.623	4.00	6.00	12.50	20.00

COPPER-NICKEL

100th Anniversary of Revision of Constitution

KM#	Date	Mintage	Fine	VF	XF	Unc
52	1974	3.700	—	—	4.00	5.50
	1974	.130	—	—	Proof	15.00

European Monument Protection Year

KM#	Date	Mintage	Fine	VF	XF	Unc
53	1975	2.500	—	—	4.00	6.00
	1975	.060	—	—	Proof	22.50

500th Anniversary of Battle of Murten

KM#	Date	Mintage	Fine	VF	XF	Unc
54	1976	1.500	—	—	4.00	6.00
	1976	.100	—	—	Proof	15.00

150th Anniversary of Death of Johann Pestalozzi

KM#	Date	Mintage	Fine	VF	XF	Unc
55	1977	.800	—	—	5.00	9.00
	1977	.050	—	—	Proof	35.00

150th Anniversary of Birth of Henry Dunant

KM#	Date	Mintage	Fine	VF	XF	Unc
56	1978	.900	—	—	4.00	6.50
	1978	.060	—	—	Proof	15.00

Centennial of Birth of Albert Einstein

KM#	Date	Mintage	Fine	VF	XF	Unc
57	1979	.900	—	—	5.00	9.00
	1979	.035	—	—	Proof	125.00

Centennial of Birth of Albert Einstein

KM#	Date	Mintage	Fine	VF	XF	Unc
58	1979	.900	—	—	4.00	6.00
	1979	.035	—	—	Proof	65.00

Ferdinand Hodler - Painter

KM#	Date	Mintage	Fine	VF	XF	Unc
59	1980	.950	—	—	4.00	6.00
	1980	.050	—	—	Proof	20.00

500th Anniversary of Stans Convention of 1481

KM#	Date	Mintage	Fine	VF	XF	Ur
60	1981	.900	—	—	4.00	6.(
	1981	.050	—	—	Proof	16.(

100th Anniversary of Gotthard Railway

KM#	Date	Mintage	Fine	VF	XF	Unc
61	1982	1.100	—	—	4.00	7.(
	1982	.065	—	—	Proof	30.(

100th Anniversary of Birth of Ernest Ansermet

KM#	Date	Mintage	Fine	VF	XF	Unc
62	1983	.951	—	—	4.00	6.5
	1983	.060	—	—	Proof	25.(

Centennial of Birth of Auguste Piccard

KM#	Date	Mintage	Fine	VF	XF	Unc
63	1984	1.000	—	—	4.00	5.5
	1984	.075	—	—	Proof	22.5

European Year of Music

KM#	Date	Mintage	Fine	VF	XF	Unc
64	1985	1.156	—	—	4.00	5.5
	1985	.084	—	—	Proof	15.0

500th Anniversary of the Battle of Sempach

KM#	Date	Mintage	Fine	VF	XF	Unc
65	1986B	1.080	—	—	4.00	5.5
	1986B	.076	—	—	Proof	17.5

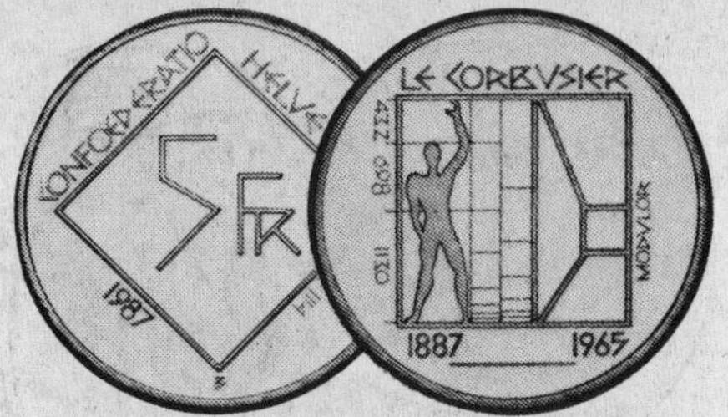

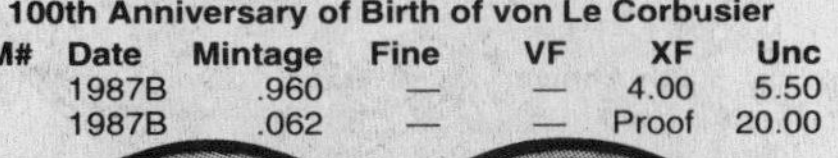

100th Anniversary of Birth of von Le Corbusier

KM#	Date	Mintage	Fine	VF	XF	Unc
66	1987B	.960	—	—	4.00	5.50
	1987B	.062	—	—	Proof	20.00

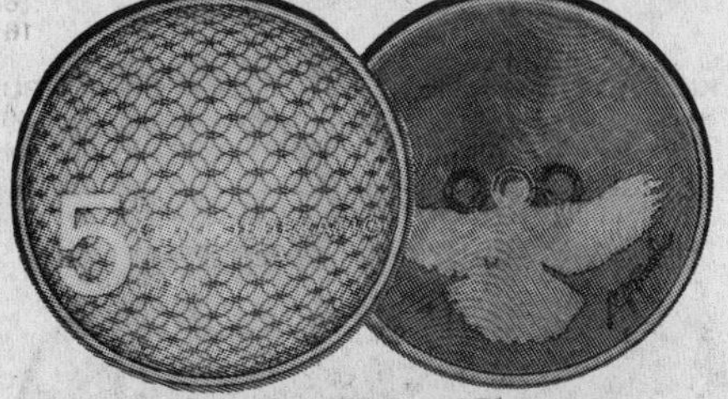

Olympics - Dove and Rings

KM#	Date	Mintage	Fine	VF	XF	Unc
67	1988B	1.026	—	—	4.00	5.50
	1988B	.069	—	—	Proof	20.00

General Guisan - 1939 Mobilization

KM#	Date	Mintage	Fine	VF	XF	Unc
68	1989B	1.270	—	—	4.00	5.50
	1989B	.069	—	—	Proof	22.00

Gottfried Keller

KM#	Date	Mintage	Fine	VF	XF	Unc
69	1990B	1.100	—	—	—	5.50
	1990B	.069	—	—	Proof	22.00

10 FRANCS

3.2258 g, .900 GOLD, .0933 oz AGW

KM#	Date	Mintage	Fine	VF	XF	Unc
36	1911B	.100	75.00	150.00	250.00	425.00
	1912B	.200	60.00	100.00	125.00	175.00
	1913B	.600	60.00	100.00	125.00	175.00
	1914B	.200	60.00	100.00	125.00	175.00
	1915B	.400	60.00	100.00	125.00	175.00
	1916B	.130	60.00	100.00	125.00	175.00
	1922B	1.020	60.00	100.00	125.00	165.00

20 FRANCS

6.4516 g, .900 GOLD, .1867 oz AGW
Reeded edge.

KM#	Date	Mintage	Fine	VF	XF	Unc
31.1	1883	.250	75.00	80.00	90.00	135.00

Edge: DOMINUS XXX PROVIDEBIT XXXXXXXXXX

KM#	Date	Mintage	Fine	VF	XF	Unc
31.3	1886	.250	75.00	80.00	90.00	135.00
	1887B	176 pcs.	—	15,000.	17,500.	20,000.
	1888B	4,224	4000.	5000.	7000.	11,000.
	1889B	.100	75.00	80.00	90.00	150.00
	1890B	.125	75.00	80.00	90.00	135.00
	1891B	.100	75.00	80.00	90.00	140.00
	1892B	.100	75.00	80.00	90.00	135.00
31.3	1893B	.100	75.00	80.00	90.00	135.00
	1893B*	25 pcs.	—	—	Rare	—
	1894B	.121	75.00	80.00	90.00	135.00
	1895B	.200	75.00	80.00	90.00	135.00
	1895B*	19 pcs.	—	—	Rare	—
	1896B	.400	75.00	80.00	90.00	135.00

***NOTE:** Struck of bright Valaisan gold from Gondo with a small cross punched in the center of the Swiss cross.

Edge: DOMINUS XXX/XXXXXXXXXX PROVIDEBIT

KM#	Date	Mintage	Fine	VF	XF	Unc
31.2	1896B	Inc. Ab.	Reported, not confirmed			

KM#	Date	Mintage	Fine	VF	XF	Unc
35.1	1897B	.400	BV	75.00	80.00	100.00
	1897B*	29 pcs.	—	—	Rare	—
	1898B	.400	BV	75.00	80.00	100.00
	1899B	.300	BV	75.00	80.00	100.00
	1900B	.400	BV	75.00	80.00	100.00
	1901B	.500	BV	75.00	80.00	100.00
	1902B	.600	BV	75.00	80.00	100.00
	1903B	.200	BV	75.00	80.00	120.00
	1904B	.100	BV	75.00	80.00	135.00
	1905B	.100	BV	75.00	80.00	135.00
	1906B	.100	BV	75.00	80.00	120.00
	1907B	.150	BV	75.00	80.00	100.00
	1908B	.355	BV	75.00	80.00	100.00
	1909B	.400	BV	75.00	80.00	100.00
	1910B	.375	BV	75.00	80.00	100.00
	1911B	.350	BV	75.00	80.00	100.00
	1912B	.450	BV	75.00	80.00	100.00
	1913B	.700	BV	75.00	80.00	100.00
	1914B	.700	BV	75.00	80.00	100.00
	1915B	.750	BV	75.00	80.00	100.00
	1916B	.300	BV	75.00	80.00	100.00
	1922B	2.784	BV	75.00	80.00	100.00
	1925B	.400	BV	75.00	80.00	100.00
	1926B	.050	120.00	150.00	175.00	250.00
	1927B	5.015	BV	75.00	80.00	100.00
	1930B	3.372	BV	75.00	80.00	100.00
	1935B	.175	BV	75.00	80.00	100.00
	1935L-B**	20.009	BV	75.00	80.00	100.00

***NOTE:** Struck of bright Valaisan gold from Gondo with a small cross punched in the center of the Swiss cross.

****NOTE:** The 1935L-B issue was struck in 1945, 1946 and 1947.

Edge: AD LEGEM ANNI MCMXXXI

KM#	Date	Mintage	Fine	VF	XF	Unc
35.2	1947B	9.200	BV	75.00	80.00	100.00
	1949B	10.000	BV	75.00	80.00	100.00

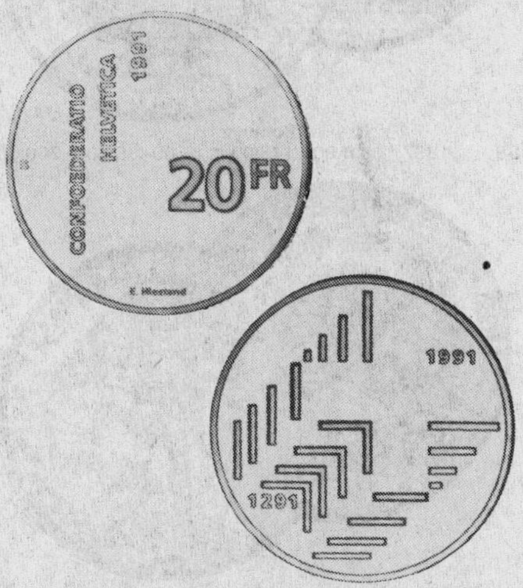

20.0000 g, .835 SILVER, .5369 oz ASW
700 Years of Confederation

KM#	Date	Mintage	Fine	VF	XF	Unc
70	1991B	2.440	—	—	—	15.00
	1991B	.100	—	—	Proof	35.00

Gertrud Kurz

KM#	Date	Mintage	Fine	VF	XF	Unc
72	1992B	.325	—	—	—	20.00
	1992B	.036	—	—	Proof	40.00

500th Anniversary of Birth of Paracelsus

KM#	Date	Mintage	Fine	VF	XF	Unc
73	1993B	.260	—	—	—	20.00
	1993B	.030	—	—	Proof	40.00

25 FRANCS

5.6450 g, .900 GOLD, .1634 oz AGW

KM#	Date	Mintage	Fine	VF	XF	Unc
49	1955B	5.000	—	—	—	—
	1958B	5.000	—	—	—	—
	1959B	5.000	—	—	—	—

50 FRANCS

11.2900 g, .900 GOLD, .3267 oz AGW

KM#	Date	Mintage	Fine	VF	XF	Unc
50	1955B	2.000	—	—	—	—
	1958B	2.000	—	—	—	—
	1959B	2.000	—	—	—	—

NOTE: KM#49 and 50 are not available in commercial channels.

100 FRANCS

32.2581 g, .900 GOLD, .9334 oz AGW

KM#	Date	Mintage	Fine	VF	XF	Unc
39	1925B	5,000	—	6000.	7500.	10,000.

250 FRANCS

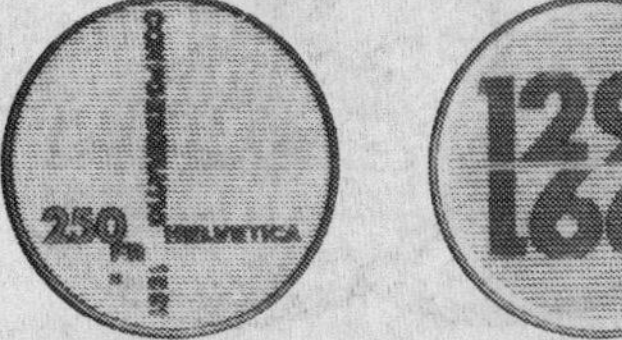

8.0000 g, .900 GOLD, .2315 oz AGW

700 Years of Confederation
Edge: Plus sign between dates.

KM#	Date	Mintage	Fine	VF	XF	Unc
71.1	1991B	.800	—	—	—	200.00

NOTE: 200,000 recalled and melted due to poor quality.

Edge: Elongated plus sign between dates.

KM#	Date	Mintage	Fine	VF	XF	Unc
71.2	1991B	.200	—	—	—	200.00

SHOOTING FESTIVAL COMMEMORATIVES

The listings which follow have traditionally been categorized as "Swiss Shooting Thalers" in many catalogs. Technically, all are medallic issues, rather than "coins", excepting the Solothurn issue of 1855, which according to the Swiss Federal Finance Department was "legally equal" to the then current silver 5 Francs issue to which it was identical in design, aside from bearing an edge inscription which read, EIDGEN FREISCHIESSEN SOLOTHURN (National Shooting Fest (in) Solothurn). For subsequent issues, denominations have been indicated "with government consent (though they) were not given legal tender status". The presence of the denomination was intended to indicate these "talers were of the same weight and fineness as (prescribed for) legal tender coins". Two generally associated "Shooting Festival" coins of earlier dates - 1842 Graubunden and 1847 Glarus -will be found incorporated in the listings for these cantons, as they were issued prior to the Swiss confederation of 1848.

5 FRANCS

.835 SILVER
Solothurn
Similar to KM#11 but edge is lettered:
EIDGEN FREISCHIESEN SOLOTHURN 1855*

KM#	Date	Mintage	VF	XF	Unc	BU
S3	1855	3,000	1000.	2000.	4500.	7000.

Bern

KM#	Date	Mintage	VF	XF	Unc	BU
S4	1857	5,195	300.00	425.00	850.00	1600.

Zurich

KM#	Date	Mintage	VF	XF	Unc	BU
S5	1859	6,000	175.00	275.00	550.00	950.00

Stans in Nidwalden

KM#	Date	Mintage	VF	XF	Unc	BU
S6	1861	6,000	175.00	275.00	600.00	1000.

La Chaux-De-Fonds in Neuchatel

KM#	Date	Mintage	VF	XF	Unc	BU
S7	1863	6,000	175.00	275.00	600.00	1150.

Schaffhausen

KM#	Date	Mintage	VF	XF	Unc	BU
S8	1865	.010	115.00	185.00	300.00	600.00

Schwyz

KM#	Date	Mintage	VF	XF	Unc	BU
S9	1867	8,000	145.00	215.00	350.00	700.00

Zug

KM#	Date	Mintage	VF	XF	Unc	BU
S10	1869	6,000	145.00	235.00	375.00	800.00

Zurich

KM#	Date	Mintage	VF	XF	Unc	BU
S11	1872	.010	100.00	145.00	255.00	450.00

St. Gallen

KM#	Date	Mintage	VF	XF	Unc	BU
S12	1874	.015	75.00	110.00	200.00	325.00

Lausanne

KM#	Date	Mintage	VF	XF	Unc	BU
S13	1876	.020	75.00	100.00	200.00	325.00

Basel

KM#	Date	Mintage	VF	XF	Unc	BU
S14	1879	.030	50.00	75.00	165.00	300.00

Fribourg

KM#	Date	Mintage	VF	XF	Unc	BU
S15	1881	.030	50.00	75.00	165.00	300.00

Lugano

KM#	Date	Mintage	VF	XF	Unc	BU
S16	1883	.030	50.00	75.00	165.00	300.00

Bern

KM#	Date	Mintage	VF	XF	Unc	BU
S17	1885	.025	50.00	75.00	165.00	300.00

Fribourg

KM#	Date	Mintage	VF	XF	Unc	BU
S18	1934B	.040	25.00	40.00	75.00	100.00
	1934B	—	—	Matte Proof		650.00

Lucerne

KM#	Date	Mintage	VF	XF	Unc	BU
S20	1939B	.040	25.00	40.00	75.00	100.00
	1939B	—	—	Matte Proof		1150.

100 FRANCS

25.9000 g, .900 GOLD, .7494 oz AGW
Fribourg

KM#	Date	Mintage	VF	XF	Unc	BU
S19	1934B	2,000	1800.	2200.	3000.	3650.

17.5000 g, .900 GOLD, .5064 oz AGW
Lucerne

KM#	Date	Mintage	VF	XF	Unc	BU
S21	1939B	6,000	500.00	625.00	850.00	1000.

MINT SETS (MS)

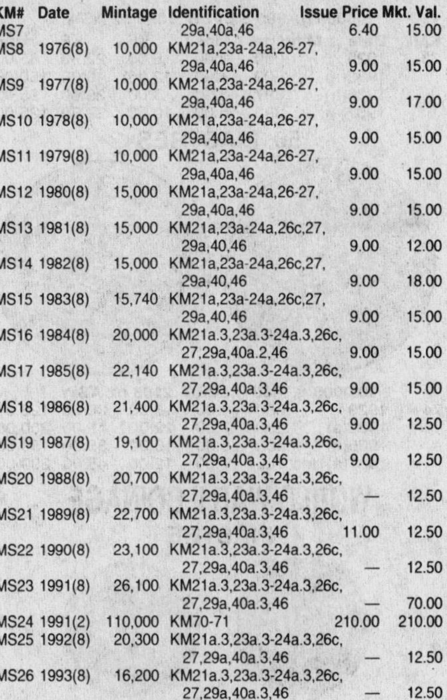

KM#	Date	Mintage	Identification	Issue Price	Mkt. Val.
MS1	1896(9)	—	KM3-4,21,23-24,26-27, 29,34	—	Rare
MS2	1970(9)	10,000	KM21a,23a-24a,26-27, 29a,40a,46-47	6.40	15.00
MS3	1971(5)	5,000	KM23a-24a,26,29a,46	2.40	18.00
MS4	1972(3)	5,000	KM21a,23a,27	2.40	12.00
MS5	1973(6)	10,000	KM21a,23a-24a,27,40a, 46	6.40	13.00
MS6	1974(9)	10,000	KM21a,23a-24a,26-27, 29a,40a,46-47	6.40	15.00
MS7	1975(8)	10,000	KM21a,23a-24a,26-27, 29a,40a,46	6.40	15.00
MS8	1976(8)	10,000	KM21a,23a-24a,26-27, 29a,40a,46	9.00	15.00
MS9	1977(8)	10,000	KM21a,23a-24a,26-27, 29a,40a,46	9.00	17.00
MS10	1978(8)	10,000	KM21a,23a-24a,26-27, 29a,40a,46	9.00	15.00
MS11	1979(8)	10,000	KM21a,23a-24a,26-27, 29a,40a,46	9.00	15.00
MS12	1980(8)	15,000	KM21a,23a-24a,26-27, 29a,40a,46	9.00	15.00
MS13	1981(8)	15,000	KM21a,23a-24a,26c,27, 29a,40,46	9.00	12.00
MS14	1982(8)	15,000	KM21a,23a-24a,26c,27, 29a,40,46	9.00	18.00
MS15	1983(8)	15,740	KM21a,23a-24a,26c,27, 29a,40,46	9.00	15.00
MS16	1984(8)	20,000	KM21a.3,23a.3-24a.3,26c, 27,29a,40a.2,46	9.00	15.00
MS17	1985(8)	22,140	KM21a.3,23a.3-24a.3,26c, 27,29a,40a.3,46	9.00	15.00
MS18	1986(8)	21,400	KM21a.3,23a.3-24a.3,26c, 27,29a,40a.3,46	9.00	12.50
MS19	1987(8)	19,100	KM21a.3,23a.3-24a.3,26c, 27,29a,40a.3,46	9.00	12.50
MS20	1988(8)	20,700	KM21a.3,23a.3-24a.3,26c, 27,29a,40a.3,46	—	12.50
MS21	1989(8)	22,700	KM21a.3,23a.3-24a.3,26c, 27,29a,40a.3,46	11.00	12.50
MS22	1990(8)	23,100	KM21a.3,23a.3-24a.3,26c, 27,29a,40a.3,46	—	12.50
MS23	1991(8)	26,100	KM21a.3,23a.3-24a.3,26c, 27,29a,40a.3,46	—	70.00
MS24	1991(2)	110,000	KM70-71	210.00	210.00
MS25	1992(8)	20,300	KM21a.3,23a.3-24a.3,26c, 27,29a,40a.3,46	—	12.50
MS26	1993(8)	16,200	KM21a.3,23a.3-24a.3,26c, 27,29a,40a.3,46	—	12.50

PROOF SETS (PS)

KM#	Date	Mintage	Identification	Issue Price	Mkt. Val.
PS1	1974(9)	2,400	KM21a,23a-24a,26-27, 29a,40a,46-47	12.80	465.00
PS2	1975(8)	10,000	KM21a,23a-24a,26-27, 29a,40a,46	16.75	37.50
PS3	1976(8)	5,130	KM21a,23a-24a,26-27, 29a,40a,46	16.75	75.00
PS4	1977(8)	7,030	KM21a,23a-24a,26-27, 29a,40a,46	16.75	35.00
PS5	1978(8)	10,090	KM21a,23a-24a,26-27, 29a,40a,46	28.00	30.00
PS6	1979(8)	10,150	KM21a,23a-24a,26-27, 29a,40a,46	28.00	30.00
PS7	1980(8)	10,010	KM21a,23a-24a,26-27, 29a,40a,46	30.00	40.00
PS8	1981(8)	10,280	KM21b,23b-24a,26a,27, 29a,40,46	30.00	35.00
PS9	1982(8)	10,090	KM21b,23b-24a,26a,27, 29a,40,46	30.00	100.00
PS10	1983(8)	11,390	KM21b,23b-24a,26a-27a, 29a,40,46	30.00	35.00
PS11	1984(8)	14,100	KM21b,23b,24a,26a-27a, 29a,40,46	30.00	40.00
PS12	1985(8)	12,060	KM21a.3,23a.3-24a.3, 26c,27,29a,40a.3,46	30.00	37.50
PS13	1986(8)	10,000	KM21a.3,23a.3-24a.3, 26c,27,29a,40a.3,46	30.00	35.00
PS14	1987(8)	8,800	KM21a.3,23a.3-24a.3, 26c,27,29a,40a.3,46	30.00	35.00
PS15	1988(8)	9,150	KM21a.3,23a.3-24a.3, 26c,27,29a,40a.3,46	—	35.00
PS16	1989(8)	8,800	KM21a.3,23a.3-24a.3, 26c,27,29a,40a.3,46	36.50	40.00
PS17	1990(8)	8,900	KM21a.3,23a.3-24a.3, 26c,27,29a,40a.3,46	—	40.00
PS18	1991(8)	9,900	KM21a.3,23a.3-24a.3, 26c,27,29a,40a.3,46	—	120.00
PS19	1992(8)	7,450	KM21a.3,23a.3-24a.3, 26c,27,29a,40a.3,46	—	40.00
PS20	1993(8)	6,200	KM21a.3,23a.3-24a.3, 26c,27,29a,40a.3,46	—	40.00

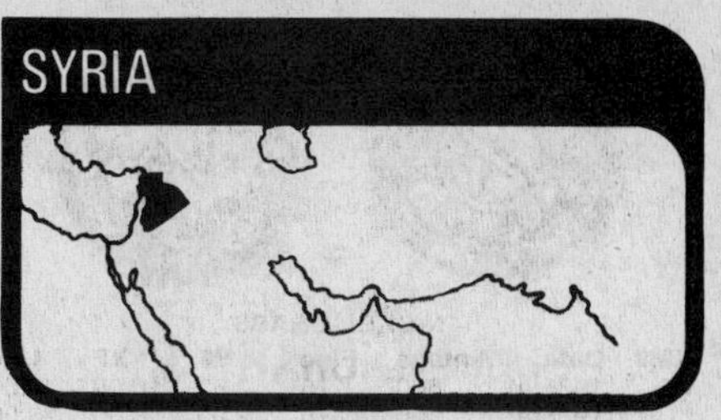

The Syrian Arab Republic, located in the Near East at the eastern end of the Mediterranean Sea, has an area of 71,498 sq. mi. (185,180 sq. km.) and a population of *12 million. Capital: Greater Damascus. Agriculture and animal breeding are the chief industries. Cotton, crude oil and livestock are exported.

Ancient Syria, a land bridge connecting Europe, Africa and Asia, has spent much of its history in thrall to the conqueror's whim. Its subjection by Egypt about 1500 B.C. was followed by successive conquests by the Hebrews, Phoenicians, Babylonians, Assyrians, Persians, Macedonians, Romans, Byzantines and finally, in 636 A.D., by the Moslems. The Arabs made Damascus, one of the oldest continuously inhabited cities of the world, the trade center and capital of an empire stretching from India to Spain. In 1516, following the total destruction of Damascus by the Mongols of Tamerlane, Syria fell to the Ottoman Turks and remained a part of Turkey until the end of World War I. The Leage of Nations gave France a mandate to the Levant states of Syria and Lebanon in 1920. In 1930, following a series of uprisings, France recognized Syria as an independent republic, but still subject to the mandate. Lebanon became fully independent on Nov. 22, 1943, and Syria on Jan. 1, 1944.

TITLES

الجمهورية السورية

al-Jumhuriya(t) al-Suriya(t)

الجمهورية لعربية السورية

al-Jumhuriya(t) al-Arabiya(t) as-Suriya(t)
Haleb (Aleppa)

RULERS

Ottoman, until 1918
Faysal, 1918-1920

MINT MARKS

(a) - Paris, privy marks only

MINTNAME

Damascus د مشق

Haleb حلب

MONETARY SYSTEM

100 Piastres (Qirsh) = 1 Pound (Lira)

KINGDOM

DINAR

GOLD, 6.70 g

KM#	Date	Mintage	VG	Fine	VF	XF
67	AH1338	12 pcs.	—	—	—	8250.

FRENCH PROTECTORATE

1/2 PIASTRE

COPPER-NICKEL

KM#	Date	Mintage	Fine	VF	XF	Unc
68	1921(a)	4.000	.25	1.00	3.50	15.00

NICKEL-BRASS

KM#	Date	Mintage	Fine	VF	XF	Unc
75	1935(a)	.600	.75	2.50	10.00	40.00
	1936(a)	.800	.75	2.00	8.00	25.00

PIASTRE

NICKEL-BRASS

KM#	Date	Mintage	Fine	VF	XF	Unc
71	1929(a)	.750	.50	2.00	7.00	32.50
	1933(a)	.600	1.00	3.00	10.00	40.00
	1935(a)	1.950	.35	1.00	3.50	22.50
	1936(a)	1.400	.50	1.25	5.00	25.00

ZINC

KM#	Date	Mintage	Fine	VF	XF	Unc
71a	1940(a)	2.060	1.00	3.00	15.00	65.00

2 PIASTRES

ALUMINUM-BRONZE

KM#	Date	Mintage	Fine	VF	XF	Unc
69	1926(a)	.600	5.00	10.00	25.00	80.00
	1926 w/o privy marks	—	—	—	—	—

2-1/2 PIASTRES

ALUMINUM-BRONZE

KM#	Date	Mintage	Fine	VF	XF	Unc
76	1940(a)	2.000	1.25	2.50	6.00	15.00

5 PIASTRES

ALUMINUM-BRONZE

KM#	Date	Mintage	Fine	VF	XF	Unc
70	1926(a)	.300	.75	2.00	8.00	25.00
	1926 w/o privy marks	.400	.75	3.00	12.00	35.00
	1933(a)	1.200	.40	2.00	12.50	40.00
	1935(a)	2.000	.30	1.50	8.00	25.00
	1936(a)	.900	.50	2.00	10.00	30.00
	1940(a)	.500	.50	1.50	4.00	15.00

10 PIASTRES

2.0000 g, .680 SILVER .0437 oz ASW

KM#	Date	Mintage	Fine	VF	XF	Unc
72	1929	1.000	3.00	7.50	25.00	75.00

25 PIASTRES

5.0000 g, .680 SILVER .1093 oz ASW

KM#	Date	Mintage	Fine	VF	XF	Unc
73	1929	1.000	3.00	5.00	22.50	85.00
	1933(a)	.500	4.00	12.00	40.00	150.00
	1936(a)	.897	3.50	7.00	25.00	95.00
	1937(a)	.393	5.00	10.00	32.50	125.00

50 PIASTRES

10.0000 g, .680 SILVER .2186 oz ASW

KM#	Date	Mintage	Fine	VF	XF	Unc
74	1929	.880	4.00	8.00	30.00	125.00
	1933(a)	.250	7.00	12.00	45.00	200.00
	1936(a)	.400	5.00	10.00	35.00	150.00
	1937(a)	Inc. Ab.	7.00	12.00	45.00	200.00

WORLD WAR II COINAGE

PIASTRE

BRASS

KM#	Date	Mintage	Fine	VF	XF	Unc
77	ND	—	.75	1.00	3.00	6.00

2-1/2 PIASTRES

ALUMINUM

KM#	Date	Mintage	Fine	VF	XF	Unc
78	ND	—	10.00	15.00	25.00	50.00

REPUBLIC

1944-1958

2-1/2 PIASTRES

COPPER-NICKEL

KM#	Date	Year	Mintage	VF	XF	Unc
81	AH1367	1948	2.500	.30	.50	2.00
	1375	1956	5.000	.25	.40	.75

5 PIASTRES

COPPER-NICKEL

KM#	Date	Year	Mintage	VF	XF	Unc
82	AH1367	1948	8.000	.50	1.00	2.50
	1375	1956	4.000	.35	.60	1.00

10 PIASTRES

COPPER-NICKEL

KM#	Date	Year	Mintage	VF	XF	Unc
83	AH1367	1948	—	.60	1.00	2.50
	1375	1956	4.000	.40	.85	1.50

25 PIASTRES

2.5000 g, .600 SILVER .0482 oz ASW

KM#	Date	Year	Mintage	VF	XF	Unc
79	AH1366	1947	6.300	2.50	5.00	17.50

50 PIASTRES

5.0000 g, .600 SILVER .0965 oz ASW

KM#	Date	Year	Mintage	VF	XF	Unc
80	AH1366	1947	4.500	3.50	7.00	20.00

1/2 POUND

3.3793 g, .900 GOLD, .0978 oz AGW

KM#	Date	Year	Mintage	VF	XF	Unc
84	AH1369	1950	.100	60.00	65.00	100.00

LIRA

10.0000 g, .680 SILVER, .2186 oz ASW

KM#	Date	Year	Mintage	VF	XF	Unc
85	AH1369	1950	7.000	5.00	7.50	15.00

POUND

6.7586 g, .900 GOLD .1956 oz AGW

KM#	Date	Year	Mintage	VF	XF	Unc
86	AH1369	1950	.250	100.00	110.00	150.00

UNITED ARAB REPUBLIC

1958-1961

2-1/2 PIASTRES

ALUMINUM-BRONZE

KM#	Date	Year	Mintage	VF	XF	Unc
90	AH1380	1960	1.100	.10	.15	.50

5 PIASTRES

ALUMINUM-BRONZE

KM#	Date	Year	Mintage	VF	XF	Unc
91	AH1380	1960	4.240	.10	.15	.40

10 PIASTRES

ALUMINUM-BRONZE

KM#	Date	Year	Mintage	VF	XF	Unc
92	AH1380	1960	2.800	.10	.20	.65

25 PIASTRES

2.5000 g, .600 SILVER, .0482 oz ASW

KM#	Date	Year	Mintage	VF	XF	Unc
87	AH1377	1958	2.300	1.50	2.00	6.00

50 PIASTRES

5.000 g, .600 SILVER, .0965 oz ASW

88	AH1377	1958	.120	3.00	6.50	15.00

1st Anniversary of Founding of United Arab Republic

89	AH1378	1959	1.500	3.00	4.50	9.00

SYRIAN ARAB REPUBLIC

1961—

2-1/2 PIASTRES

ALUMINUM-BRONZE

93	AH1382	1962	8.000	.10	.20	.50
	1385	1965	8.000	.10	.20	.50

104	AH1393	1973	10.000	.10	.15	.25

5 PIASTRES

ALUMINUM-BRONZE

94	AH1382	1962	7.000	.10	.15	.30
	1385	1965	18.000	.10	.15	.30

F.A.O. Issue

100	AH1391	1971	15.000	.10	.15	.25

105	AH1394	1974	—	.10	.15	.25

F.A.O. Issue

KM#	Date	Year	Mintage	VF	XF	Unc
110	AH1396	1976	2.000	.10	.15	.25

Similar to KM#94 but heavier neck feathers.

116	AH1399	1979	—	.10	.15	.25

10 PIASTRES

ALUMINUM-BRONZE

95	AH1382	1962	6.000	.10	.15	.40
	1385	1965	22.000	.10	.15	.40

106	AH1394	1974	—	.10	.15	.30

BRASS
F.A.O. Issue
Similar to 5 Piastres, KM#110.

111	AH1396	1976	.500	.10	.15	.25

ALUMINUM-BRONZE

117	AH1399	1979	—	.10	.15	.30

25 PIASTRES

NICKEL

96	AH1387	1968	15.000	.20	.30	.60

25th Anniversary Al-Ba'ath Party

101	AH1392	1972	—	.15	.25	.60

107	AH1394	1974	—	.10	.25	.50

F.A.O. Issue

112	AH1396	1976	1.000	.10	.25	.50

COPPER-NICKEL

KM#	Date	Year	Mintage	VF	XF	Unc
118	AH1399	1979	—	.10	.25	.50

50 PIASTRES

NICKEL

97	AH1387	1968	10.000	.25	.50	.85

25th Anniversary Al-Ba'ath Party

102	AH1392	1972	—	.20	.30	.75

108	AH1394	1974	—	.20	.30	.75

F.A.O. Issue

113	AH1396	1976	1.000	.10	.20	.40

COPPER-NICKEL

119	AH1399	1979	—	.20	.30	.75

POUND

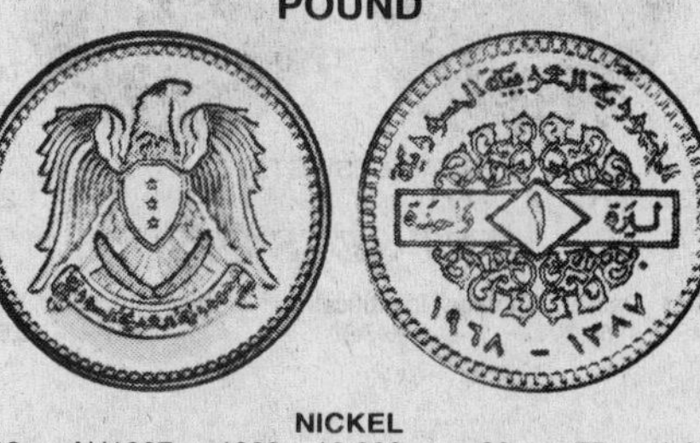

NICKEL

98	AH1387	1968	10.000	.30	.75	1.25
	1391	1971	10.000	.30	.75	1.25

F.A.O. Issue

KM#	Date	Year	Mintage	VF	XF	Unc
99	AH1388	1968	.500	.40	.85	1.50

25th Anniversary Al-Ba'ath Party

KM#	Date	Year	Mintage	VF	XF	Unc
103	AH1392	1972	10.000	.30	.75	1.25
109	AH1394	1974	—	.30	.70	1.25

F.A.O. Issue

KM#	Date	Year	Mintage	VF	XF	Unc
114	AH1396	1976	.500	.30	.70	1.25

Re-Election of President

KM#	Date	Year	Mintage	VF	XF	Unc
115	AH1398	1978	—	.65	1.25	3.00

COPPER-NICKEL

KM#	Date	Year	Mintage	VF	XF	Unc
120.1	AH1399	1979	—	.30	.70	1.25

STAINLESS STEEL

KM#	Date	Year	Mintage	VF	XF	Unc
120.2	AH1412	1991	—	.30	.70	1.25

MINT SETS (MS)

KM#	Date	Mintage	Identification	Issue Price	Mkt. Val.
MS1	1968(3)	—	KM96-98	—	5.50

Listings For

TANNA-TUVA: refer to Russia

TANZANIA

The United Republic of Tanzania, located on the east coast of Africa between Kenya and Mozambique, consists of Tanganyika and the islands of Zanzibar and Pemba. It has an area of 364,900 sq. mi. (945,090 sq. km.) and a population of *25.2 million. Capital: Dar es Salaam (Haven of Peace). The chief exports are cotton, coffee, diamonds, sisal, cloves, petroleum products, and cashew nuts.

Tanzania is a member of the Commonwealth of Nations. The President is Chief of State.

GERMAN EAST AFRICA

German East Africa (Tanganyika), located on the coast of east-central Africa between British East Africa (now Kenya) and Portuguese East Africa (now Mozambique), had an area of 362,284 sq. mi. (938,216 sq. km.) and a population of about 6 million. Capital: Dar es Salaam. Chief products prior to German control were ivory and slaves; after German control, sisal, coffee, and rubber. Germany acquired control of the area by treaties with coastal chiefs in 1884, established it as a protectorate in 1891, and proclaimed it the Colony of German East Africa in 1897. After World War I, Tanganyika was entrusted to Great Britain as a League of Nations mandate, and after World War II as a United Nations trust territory. Tanganyika became an independent nation within the British Commonwealth on Dec. 9, 1961.

TITLES

شراكتة المانيا

Sharaka(t) Almaniya

RULERS

Wilhelm II, 1888-1918

MINT MARKS

A - Berlin
J - Hamburg
T - Tabora

MONETARY SYSTEM

Until 1904

64 Pesa = 1 Rupie

Commencing 1904

100 Heller = 1 Rupie

PESA

COPPER

KM#	Date	Mintage	Fine	VF	XF	Unc
1	1890	1.000	.75	3.00	6.00	18.00
	1890	—	—	—	Proof	110.00
	1891	12.551	1.00	3.75	7.50	20.00
	1892	27.541	1.00	3.75	7.50	20.00

1/2 HELLER

BRONZE

KM#	Date	Mintage	Fine	VF	XF	Unc
6	1904A	1.201	1.25	3.50	6.50	28.00
	1905A	7.192	2.25	5.25	9.00	32.50
	1905J	4.000	2.25	5.25	9.00	32.50
	1906J	6.000	1.25	3.50	6.50	28.00
	1906J	—	—	—	Proof	150.00

HELLER

BRONZE

KM#	Date	Mintage	Fine	VF	XF	Unc
7	1904A	10.256	.75	2.25	4.00	18.50
	1904A	—	—	—	Proof	65.00
	1904J	2.500	.75	2.25	7.00	25.00
	1905A	3.760	.75	2.25	7.00	25.00
	1905A	—	—	—	Proof	65.00
	1905J	7.556	.75	2.25	4.00	18.50
	1906A	3.004	.75	2.25	7.00	25.00
	1906A	—	—	—	Proof	65.00
	1906J	1.962	.75	2.25	7.00	25.00
	1907J	17.790	.75	1.50	4.00	18.50
	1908J	12.205	.75	1.50	4.00	18.50
	1908J	—	—	—	Proof	85.00
	1909J	1.698	2.50	7.50	15.00	35.00
	1909J	—	—	—	Proof	85.00
	1910J	5.096	.75	1.50	4.00	18.50
	1910J	—	—	—	Proof	75.00
	1911J	6.420	.75	1.50	4.00	18.50
	1911J	—	—	—	Proof	75.00
	1912J	7.012	.75	1.50	4.00	18.50
	1912J	—	—	—	Proof	75.00
	1913A	—	.75	1.50	4.00	18.50
	1913A	—	—	—	Proof	75.00
	1913J	5.186	.75	1.50	4.00	18.50
	1913J	—	—	—	Proof	115.00

5 HELLER

BRONZE

KM#	Date	Mintage	Fine	VF	XF	Unc
11	1908J	.600	10.00	20.00	60.00	300.00
	1908J	—	—	—	Proof	975.00
	1909J	.756	10.00	20.00	60.00	300.00
	1909J	60 pcs.	—	—	Proof	975.00

COPPER-NICKEL

KM#	Date	Mintage	Fine	VF	XF	Unc
13	1913A	1.000	5.00	10.00	15.00	50.00
	1913A	—	—	—	Proof	110.00
	1913J	1.000	5.00	10.00	15.00	45.00
	1913J	—	—	—	Proof	110.00
	1914J	1.000	4.00	8.00	12.00	45.00
	1914J	—	—	—	Proof	110.00

BRASS, 1 1/2-2mm thick
Obv: Oval base on crown.

KM#	Date	Mintage	Fine	VF	XF	Unc
14.1	1916T	.030	3.50	7.00	15.00	45.00

Obv: Flat base on crown, 1mm or less thick.

KM#	Date	Mintage	Fine	VF	XF	Unc
14.2	1916T	Inc. Ab.	3.50	6.00	10.00	35.00

10 HELLER

COPPER-NICKEL

KM#	Date	Mintage	Fine	VF	XF	Unc
12	1908J	—	3.00	10.00	20.00	60.00
	1908J	—	—	—	Proof	170.00
	1909J	1.990	3.00	10.00	20.00	60.00
	1909J	—	—	—	Proof	140.00
	1910J	.500	• 3.00	10.00	20.00	60.00
	1910J	—	—	—	Proof	140.00
	1911A	.500	5.00	15.00	35.00	90.00
	1911A	—	—	—	Proof	150.00
	1914J	.200	5.00	15.00	35.00	90.00
	1914J	—	—	—	Proof	170.00

20 HELLER

Obverse A
Large Crown

Obverse B
Small Crown

Reverse A
Curled Tip On Second L

Reverse B
Pointed Tips On L's

Reverse C
Curled Tips On L's

COPPER

KM#	Date	Mintage	Good	VG	Fine	VF
15	1916T obv. A & rev. A					
		.300	2.00	4.00	6.00	10.00
	1916T obv. A & rev. B					
		Inc. Ab.	40.00	70.00	125.00	200.00
	1916T obv. B & rev. A					
		Inc. Ab.	18.00	40.00	60.00	85.00
	1916T obv. B & rev. B					
		Inc. Ab.	2.00	4.00	6.00	10.00
	1916T obv. A & rev. C					
		Inc. Ab.	—	—	Rare	—
	1916T obv. B & rev. C					
		Inc. Ab.	—	—	Rare	—

BRASS

KM#	Date	Mintage	Good	VG	Fine	VF
15a	1916T obv. A & rev. A					
		1.600	2.00	4.00	6.00	10.00
	1916T obv. A & rev. B					
		Inc. Ab.	2.00	4.00	7.00	12.50
	1916T obv. B & rev. A					
		Inc. Ab.	2.00	4.00	7.00	12.50
	1916T obv. B & rev. B					
		Inc. Ab.	2.00	4.00	6.00	10.00
	1916T obv. A & rev. C					
		Inc. Ab.	2.50	5.00	10.00	30.00
	1916T obv. B & rev. C					
		Inc. Ab.	3.00	6.00	12.00	35.00

1/4 RUPIE

2.9160 g, .917 SILVER, .0859 oz ASW

KM#	Date	Mintage	Fine	VF	XF	Unc
3	1891	.077	5.00	12.00	35.00	85.00
	1891	—	—	—	Proof	175.00
	1898	.100	6.00	18.00	50.00	135.00
	1901	.350	5.00	12.00	35.00	85.00

KM#	Date	Mintage	Fine	VF	XF	Unc
8	1904A	.300	5.00	12.00	35.00	110.00
	1904A	—	—	—	Proof	175.00
	1906A	.300	5.00	12.00	35.00	110.00
	1906A	—	—	—	Proof	175.00
	1906J	.100	8.00	20.00	55.00	140.00
	1907J	.200	7.00	18.00	50.00	135.00
	1907J	—	—	—	Proof	300.00
	1909A	.300	6.00	13.50	37.50	120.00
	1910J	.600	5.00	12.00	35.00	110.00
	1910J	—	—	—	Proof	175.00
	1912J	.400	6.00	13.50	37.50	120.00
	1912J	—	—	—	Proof	175.00
	1913A	.200	6.00	13.50	37.50	120.00
	1913A	—	—	—	Proof	175.00
	1913J	.400	5.00	12.00	35.00	110.00
	1913J	—	—	—	Proof	175.00
	1914J	.200	6.00	13.50	37.50	120.00
	1914J	—	—	—	Proof	175.00

1/2 RUPIE

5.8319 g, .917 SILVER, .1719 oz ASW

KM#	Date	Mintage	Fine	VF	XF	Unc
4	1891	.068	12.50	25.00	60.00	120.00
	1891	—	—	—	Proof	175.00
	1897	.075	14.00	30.00	75.00	170.00
	1901	.215	12.50	25.00	60.00	145.00

KM#	Date	Mintage	Fine	VF	XF	Unc
9	1904A	.400	12.50	25.00	60.00	165.00
	1904A	—	—	—	Proof	225.00
	1906A	.050	25.00	90.00	175.00	300.00
	1906A	—	—	—	Proof	250.00
	1906J	.050	25.00	90.00	175.00	300.00
	1907J	.140	14.00	40.00	85.00	165.00
	1907J	—	—	—	Proof	225.00
	1909A	.100	14.00	35.00	75.00	165.00
	1910J	.300	14.00	35.00	75.00	165.00
	1910J	—	—	—	Proof	300.00
	1912J	.200	12.50	25.00	70.00	165.00
	1913A	.100	12.50	25.00	70.00	165.00
	1913J	.200	14.00	35.00	75.00	165.00
	1914J	.100	14.00	35.00	80.00	165.00

RUPIE

11.6638 g, .917 SILVER, .3437 oz ASW

KM#	Date	Mintage	Fine	VF	XF	Unc
2	1890	.154	10.00	18.00	35.00	80.00
	1890	—	—	—	Proof	300.00
	1891	.126	10.00	18.00	40.00	90.00
	1891	—	—	—	Proof	300.00
	1892	.360	10.00	18.00	35.00	80.00
	1892	—	—	—	Proof	300.00
	1893	.142	12.50	27.50	60.00	200.00
	1894	.048	20.00	125.00	250.00	400.00
	1897	.244	12.50	27.50	60.00	180.00
	1898	.357	12.50	27.50	60.00	180.00
	1899	.227	15.00	32.50	75.00	225.00
	1900	.209	12.50	27.50	60.00	180.00
	1901	.319	12.50	25.00	55.00	170.00
	1902	.151	15.00	35.00	80.00	240.00

KM#	Date	Mintage	Fine	VF	XF	Unc
10	1904A	1.000	11.50	22.50	45.00	120.00
	1904A	—	—	—	Proof	200.00
	1905A	.300	15.00	27.50	60.00	135.00
	1905A	—	—	—	Proof	200.00
	1905J	1.000	11.50	22.50	45.00	120.00
	1905J	—	—	—	Proof	200.00
	1906A	.950	11.50	22.50	45.00	120.00
	1906J	.700	15.00	27.50	65.00	140.00
	1907J	.880	9.00	15.00	35.00	115.00
	1908J	.500	12.50	25.00	50.00	125.00
	1908J	—	—	—	Proof	200.00
	1909A	.200	15.00	27.50	60.00	135.00
	1910J	.270	9.00	15.00	35.00	115.00
	1911A	.300	12.50	25.00	50.00	125.00
	1911A	—	—	—	Proof	200.00
	1911J	1.400	9.00	15.00	35.00	115.00
	1911J	—	—	—	Proof	250.00
	1912J	.300	12.50	25.00	50.00	125.00
	1912J	—	—	—	Proof	200.00
	1913A	.400	12.50	25.00	50.00	125.00
	1913J	1.400	9.00	15.00	35.00	115.00
	1913J	—	—	—	Proof	250.00
	1914J	.500	11.50	22.50	45.00	120.00

2 RUPIEN

23.3200 g, .917 SILVER, .6872 oz ASW

KM#	Date	Mintage	Fine	VF	XF	Unc
5	1893	.033	120.00	200.00	475.00	1000.
	1893	—	—	—	Proof	2400.
	1894	.018	160.00	250.00	625.00	1200.

15 RUPIEN

7.1680 g, .750 GOLD, .1728 oz AGW
Obv: Right arabesque ends below T of OSTAFRIKA.

KM#	Date	Mintage	Fine	VF	XF	Unc
16.1	1916T	9,803	375.00	650.00	900.00	1100.

Obv: Right arabesque ends below first A of OSTAFRIKA.

KM#	Date	Mintage	Fine	VF	XF	Unc
16.2	1916T	6,395	375.00	675.00	925.00	1150.

ZANZIBAR

The British protectorate of Zanzibar and adjacent small islands, located in the Indian Ocean 22 miles (35 km.) off the coast of Tanganyika, comprised a portion of British East Africa. Zanzibar was also the name of a sultanate which included the Zanzibar and Kenya protectorates. Zanzibar has an area of 637 sq. mi. (1,651 sq. km.). Chief city: Zanzibar. The islands are noted for their cloves, of which Zanzibar is the world's foremost producer.

Zanzibar came under Portuguese control in 1503, was conquered by the Omani Arabs in 1698, became independent of Oman in 1860, and (with Pemba) came under British control in 1890. Britain granted the protectorate self-government in 1961, and independence within the British Commonwealth on Dec. 19, 1963. On April 26, 1964, Tanganyika and Zanzibar (with Pemba) united to form the United Republic of Tanganyika and Zanzibar. The name of the country, which remained within the British Commonwealth was changed to Tanzania on Oct. 29, 1964.

TITLES

Zanjibara زنجباراه

RULERS

Sultan Barghash Ibn Sa' Id,
1870-1888AD
Sultan Ali Bin Hamud, 1902-1911AD

MONETARY SYSTEM

64 Pysa (Pice) = 1 Rupee
136 Pysa = 1 Ryal (to 1908)
100 Cents = 1 Rupee (to 1909)

PYSA

COPPER

KM#	Date	Mintage	Fine	VF	XF	Unc
1	AH1299	4.640	1.00	1.50	3.00	25.00
	1299	—	—	—	Proof	150.00
7	AH1304	18.680	1.25	1.75	4.00	35.00
	1304	—	—	—	Proof	175.00

1/4 RYAL

SILVER

KM#	Date	Mintage	Fine	VF	XF	Unc
2	AH1299	—	—	—	Rare	—

1/2 RYAL

SILVER

KM#	Date	Mintage	Fine	VF	XF	Unc
3	AH1299	—	—	—	Rare	—

RYAL

SILVER

KM#	Date	Mintage	Fine	VF	XF	Unc
4	AH1299	.060	125.00	175.00	275.00	500.00

21/2 RYALS

GOLD

KM#	Date	Mintage	Fine	VF	XF	Unc
5	AH1299	—	—	—	—	17,000.

5 RYALS

GOLD

KM#	Date	Mintage	Fine	VF	XF	Unc
6	AH1299	2,000	—	—	—	11,000.

DECIMAL COINAGE

100 Cents = 1 Rupee

CENT

BRONZE

KM#	Date	Mintage	Fine	VF	XF	Unc
8	1908	1.000	40.00	80.00	150.00	350.00

10 CENTS

BRONZE

KM#	Date	Mintage	Fine	VF	XF	Unc
9	1908	.100	75.00	125.00	200.00	475.00

20 CENTS

NICKEL

KM#	Date	Mintage	Fine	VF	XF	Unc
10	1908	.100	100.00	200.00	350.00	700.00

TANZANIA

MONETARY SYSTEM

100 Senti = 1 Shilingi

5 SENTI

BRONZE

KM#	Date	Mintage	VF	XF	Unc
1	1966	55.250	.10	.20	.40
	1966	5,500	—	Proof	1.00
	1971	5.000	.10	.20	.35
	1972	—	.10	.20	.35
	1973	20.000	.10	.20	.35
	1974	12.500	.10	.20	.35
	1975	—	.10	.20	.35
	1976	37.500	.10	.20	.35
	1977	10.000	.10	.20	.35
	1979	7.200	.10	.20	.35
	1980	10.000	.10	.20	.35
	1981	13.650	.10	.20	.35
	1982	—	.10	.20	.35
1	1983	.018	.10	.20	.35
	1984	—	.10	.20	.35

10 SENTI

NICKEL-BRASS

KM#	Date	Mintage	VF	XF	Unc
11	1977	19.505	3.00	6.00	12.50
	1979	8.000	3.00	6.00	12.50
	1980	10.000	3.00	6.00	12.50
	1981	10.000	3.00	6.00	12.50
	1984	—	3.00	6.00	12.50

20 SENTI

NICKEL-BRASS

KM#	Date	Mintage	VF	XF	Unc
2	1966	26.500	.15	.30	.75
	1966	5,500	—	Proof	1.50
	1970	5.000	.15	.30	.75
	1973	20.100	.15	.30	.75
	1975	—	.15	.30	.75
	1976	10.000	.15	.30	.75
	1977	10.000	.15	.30	.75
	1979	10.000	.15	.30	.75
	1980	10.000	.15	.30	.75
	1981	10.000	.15	.30	.75
	1982	—	.15	.30	.75
	1983	.050	.15	.30	.75
	1984	—	.15	.30	.75

50 SENTI

COPPER-NICKEL

KM#	Date	Mintage	VF	XF	Unc
3	1966	6.250	.20	.40	1.00
	1966	5,500	—	Proof	2.00
	1970	10.000	.20	.40	1.00
	1973	10.000	.25	.50	1.25
	1980	10.000	.25	.50	1.25
	1981	—	.25	.50	1.25
	1982	10.000	.25	.50	1.25
	1983	—	.25	.50	1.25
	1984	10.000	.25	.50	1.25

NICKEL CLAD STEEL

Obv: Portrait right, country name, date.
Rev: Rabbit, denomination, legend.

KM#	Date	Mintage	VF	XF	Unc
26	1988	10.000	.20	.40	1.00
	1989	—	.20	.40	1.00

SHILINGI

COPPER-NICKEL

KM#	Date	Mintage	VF	XF	Unc
4	1966	48.000	.25	.50	1.25
	1966	5,500	—	Proof	3.00
	1972	10.000	.25	.50	1.25
	1974	15.000	.30	.60	1.50
	1975	—	.30	.60	1.50
	1977	5.000	.30	.60	1.50
	1980	10.000	.25	.50	1.25
	1981	—	.30	.60	1.50
	1982	10.000	.30	.60	1.50
	1983	10.000	.30	.60	1.50
	1984	10.000	.30	.60	1.50

NICKEL CLAD STEEL

KM#	Date	Mintage	VF	XF	Unc
22	1987	5.000	.25	.50	1.25
	1988	10.000	.25	.50	1.25
	1989	—	.25	.50	1.25
	1990	—	.25	.50	1.25

5 SHILINGI

COPPER-NICKEL
F.A.O. Issue
10th Anniversary of Independence

KM#	Date	Mintage	VF	XF	Unc
5	1971	1.000	1.00	1.50	2.25

F.A.O. Issue

KM#	Date	Mintage	VF	XF	Unc
6	1972	8.000	1.00	1.50	2.25
	1973	5.000	1.00	1.50	2.25
	1980	5.000	1.00	1.50	2.25

10th Anniversary Bank of Tanzania

KM#	Date	Mintage	VF	XF	Unc
10	1976	1.000	1.00	1.50	3.50
	1976	200 pcs.	—	Proof	40.00

F.A.O. Regional Conference for Africa

KM#	Date	Mintage	VF	XF	Unc
12	1978	.050	1.00	1.50	2.00
	1978	2,000	—	Proof	12.50

KM#	Date	Mintage	VF	XF	Unc
23	1987	5.000	1.00	1.50	3.50
	1988	10.000	1.00	1.50	3.00
	1989	—	1.00	1.50	3.50

NICKEL CLAD STEEL

KM#	Date	Mintage	VF	XF	Unc
23a	1990	—	1.00	1.50	3.50
	1991	—	1.00	1.50	3.50

10 SHILINGI

COPPER-NICKEL

KM#	Date	Mintage	VF	XF	Unc
20	1987	10.000	1.00	1.50	2.50
	1988	10.000	1.00	1.50	2.50
	1989	—	1.00	1.50	2.50

NICKEL CLAD STEEL

KM#	Date	Mintage	VF	XF	Unc
20a	1990	—	1.00	1.50	2.50
	1991	—	1.00	1.50	2.50
	1992	—	1.00	1.50	2.50

20 SHILINGI

COPPER-NICKEL
20th Anniversary of Independence

KM#	Date	Mintage	VF	XF	Unc
13	1981	.997	3.00	5.00	10.00

16.0000 g, .925 SILVER, .4759 oz ASW

KM#	Date	Mintage	VF	XF	Unc
13a	1981	.020	—	Proof	35.00

COPPER-NICKEL
20th Anniversary of Central Bank

KM#	Date	Mintage	VF	XF	Unc
21	1986	—	3.50	6.00	12.00

16.0000 g, .925 SILVER, .4759 oz ASW

KM#	Date	Mintage	VF	XF	Unc
21a	1986	—	—	Proof	125.00

NICKEL BONDED STEEL
Obv: Portrait right. Rev: Elephants.

KM#	Date	Mintage	VF	XF	Unc
27	1990	—	—	—	3.00
	1991	—	—	—	3.00
	1992	—	—	—	3.00

25 SHILINGI

25.4000 g, .500 SILVER, .4083 oz ASW
Conservation - Southern Giraffe
Obv: Similar to 1500 Shilingi, KM#9.

KM#	Date	Mintage	VF	XF	Unc
7	1974	8,848	—	—	22.00

28.2800 g, .925 SILVER, .8411 oz ASW

KM#	Date	Mintage	VF	XF	Unc
7a	1974	.013	—	Proof	30.00

COPPER-NICKEL
25 Years of Independence

KM#	Date	Mintage	VF	XF	Unc
30	1985	—	—	Proof	100.00

NICKEL BONDED STEEL
25th Anniversary of Central Bank

KM#	Date	Mintage	VF	XF	Unc
28	1991	—	—	—	3.00

13.0400 g, .925 SILVER, .3878 oz ASW

KM#	Date	Mintage	VF	XF	Unc
28a	1991	*2,000	—	Proof	90.00

50 SHILINGI

31.8500 g, .500 SILVER, .5120 oz ASW
Conservation - Black Rhinoceros
Obv: Similar to 1500 Shilingi, KM#9.

KM#	Date	Mintage	VF	XF	Unc
8	1974	8,826	—	—	24.00

35.0000 g, .925 SILVER, 1.0409 oz ASW

KM#	Date	Mintage	VF	XF	Unc
8a	1974	.012	—	Proof	32.50

100 SHILINGI

23.3300 g, .925 SILVER, .6938 oz ASW
Decade For Women

KM#	Date	Mintage	VF	XF	Unc
16	1984	1,000	—	Proof	40.00

COPPER-NICKEL
Wildlife - Elephant Mother and Calf

KM#	Date	Mintage	VF	XF	Unc
18	1986	—	—	—	7.00

19.4400 g, .925 SILVER, .5782 oz ASW

KM#	Date	Mintage	VF	XF	Unc
18a	1986	.025	—	Proof	40.00

Save The Children Fund

Obv: Male potrait.

KM#	Date	Mintage	VF	XF	Unc
24	1990	*.020	—	Proof	50.00

200 SHILINGI

28.2800 g, .925 SILVER, .8411 oz ASW
20th Anniversary of Independence
Obv: Similar to 20 Shilingi, KM#13.

KM#	Date	Mintage	VF	XF	Unc
14	1981	110 pcs.	—	—	100.00
	1981	Inc. Ab.	—	Proof	125.00

250 SHILINGI

28.1600 g, .925 SILVER, .8374 oz ASW
24th Anniversary of Independence

KM#	Date	Mintage	VF	XF	Unc
29	1985	—	—	Proof	250.00

1000 SHILINGI

8.1000 g, .900 GOLD, .2344 oz AGW
Decade For Women

KM#	Date	Mintage	VF	XF	Unc
17	1984	500 pcs.	—	Proof	225.00

1500 SHILINGI

33.4370 g, .900 GOLD, .9676 oz AGW
Conservation - Cheetah

KM#	Date	Mintage	VF	XF	Unc
9	1974	2,779	—	—	425.00
	1974	866 pcs.	—	Proof	625.00

2000 SHILINGI

15.9800 g, .917 GOLD, .4712 oz AGW

20th Anniversary of Independence
Rev: Similar to 20 Shilingi, KM#13.

KM#	Date	Mintage	VF	XF	Unc
15	1981	110 pcs.	—	—	450.00
	1981	Inc. Ab.	—	Proof	500.00

Wildlife - Banded Green Sunbird

KM#	Date	Mintage	VF	XF	Unc
19	1986	5,000	—	Proof	350.00

10.0000 g, .917 GOLD, .2948 oz AGW
Save the Children Fund

KM#	Date	Mintage	VF	XF	Unc
25	1990	*3,000	—	Proof	275.00

2500 SHILINGI

46.8500 g, .917 GOLD, 1.3808 oz ASW
25 Years of Independence

KM#	Date	Mintage	VF	XF	Unc
31	1985	—	—	Proof	850.00

PROOF SETS (PS)

KM#	Date	Mintage	Identification	Issue Price	Mkt. Val.
PS1	1966(4)	5,500	KM1-4	10.50	7.50
PS2	1974(2)	30,000	KM7a-8a	50.00	62.50
PS3	1985(3)	—	KM29-31	—	1200.

Listings For

TARIM: refer to Yemen Democratic Republic

TCHAD: refer to Chad

THAILAND

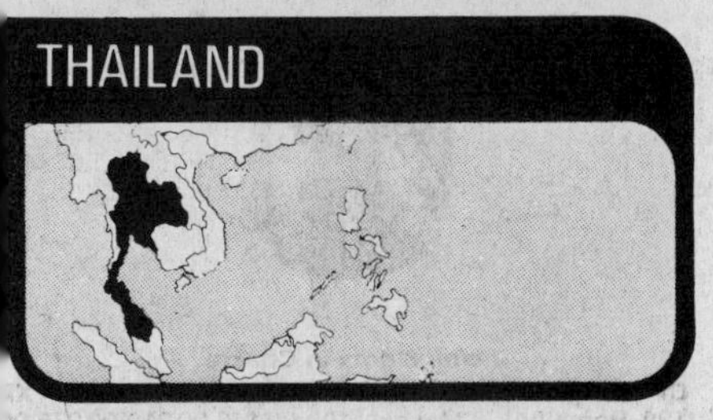

The Kingdom of Thailand (formerly Siam), a constitutional monarchy located in the center of mainland southeast Asia between Burma and Laos, has an area of 198,457 mi. (514,000 sq. km.) and a population of *55.5 million. Capital: Bangkok. The economy is based on agriculture and mining. Rubber, rice, teakwood, tin and tungsten are exported.

The history of The Kingdom of Siam, the only country in south and southeast Asia that was never colonized by an European power, dates from the 6th century A.D. when tribes of the Thai stock migrated into the area from the Asiatic continent, a process that accelerated with the Mongol invasion of China in the 13th century. After 400 years of sporadic warfare with the neighboring Burmese, King Taskin won the last battle in 1767. He founded a new capital, Dhonburi, on the west bank of the Chao Praya River. King Rama I moved the capital to Bangkok in 1782, thus initiating the so-called Bangkok Period of Siamese coinage characterized by Pot Duang money (bullet coins) stamped with regal symbols.

The Thai were introduced to the Western world by the Portuguese, who were followed by the Dutch, British and French. Rama III of the present ruling dynasty negotiated a treaty of friendship and commerce with Britain in 1826, and in 1896 the independence of the kingdom was guaranteed by an Anglo-French accord.

In 1909 Siam ceded to Great Britain its suzerain rights over the dependencies of Kedah, Kelantan, Trengganu and Perlis, Malay states situated in southern Siam just north of British Malaya which eliminated any British jurisdiction in Siam proper.

The absolute monarchy was changed into a constitutional monarchy in 1932.

On Dec. 8, 1941, after five hours of fighting, Thailand agreed to permit Japanese troops passage through the country to invade Northern British Malaysia. This eventually led to increased Japanese intervention and finally occupation of the country. On Jan. 25, 1942, Thailand declared war on Great Britain and the United State. A free Thai guerilla movement was soon organized to counteract the Japanese. In July 1943 Japan transferred the four northern Malay States back to Thailand. These were returned to Great Britain after peace treaties were signed in 1946.

RULERS

Rama I (Phra Buddha Yodfa Chulalok), 1782-1809
Rama II (Phra Buddha Lert La Nabhalai), 1809-1824
Rama III (Phra Nang Klao), 1824-1851
Rama IV (Phra Chom Klao 'Mongkut'), 1851-1868
Rama V (Phra Maha Chulalongkorn), 1868-1910
Rama VI (Phra Maha Vajiravudh), 1910-1925
Rama VII (Phra Maha Prajadhipok), 1925-1935
Rama VIII (Phra Maha Ananda Mahidol), 1935-1946
Rama IX (Phra Maha Bhumifhol Adulyadej), 1946

MONETARY SYSTEM

Old currency system

2 Solos = 1 Att
2 Att = 1 Sio (Pai)
2 Sio = 1 Sik
2 Sik = 1 Fuang
2 Fuang = 1 Salung (not Sal'ung)
4 Salung = 1 Baht
4 Baht = 1 Tamlung
20 Tamlung = 1 Chang

UNITS OF OLD THAI CURRENCY

Chang -	ชั่ง	Sik -	ซีก
Tamlung -	ตำลึง	Sio (Pai) -	เสี้ยว
Baht -	บาท	Att -	อัฐ
Salung -	สลึง	Solos -	โสพส
Fuang -	เฟื้อง		

MINT MARKS

H-Heaton Birmingham

DATING

Typical BE Dating

Typical CS Dating

NOTE: Sometimes the era designator *BE* or *CS* will actually appear on the coin itself.

Denomination

2-1/2 (Satang) RS Dating

DATE CONVERSION TABLES

B.E. date - 543 = A.D. date
Ex: 2516 - 543 = 1973

R.S. date + 1781 = A.D. date
Ex: 127 + 1781 = 1908

C.S. date + 638 = A.D. date
Ex 1238 + 638 = 1876

Primary denominations used were 1 Baht, 1/4 and 1/8 Baht up to the reign of Rama IV. Other denominations are much scarcer.

BULLET COINAGE

Gold and silver "bullet" coins have been a medium of exchange since medieval times. Interesting enough is the fact that a 1 Baht bullet made of gold will weigh the same as a 1 Baht bullet in silver. The reason for this is that Baht originally was a weight not a denomination. It was a coinage weight only until the time of Rama VII, (1925-1935) and now it is a weight and also a denomination (as far as standard weight coins are concerned). Usually 1 gold Baht was equal to 16 silver Baht on an exchange basis.

Bullet Weights

Grams

BAHT	1/2 BAHT	1/4 BAHT	1/8 BAHT
15.40	7.70	3.85	1.92

1/16 BAHT	1/32 BAHT	1/64 BAHT
0.96	0.48	0.24

Chopmarks exist on bullet coins as they do on many other coins that have traveled on their way through the Orient. One must be careful not to mistake a money changers chopmark for the regular dynastic marks on the bullet. Some chopmarks are rather simple in design while others appear to be rather elaborate.

DYNASTIC MARKS

Chakra

The Chakra, symbol of the God Vishnu, is the mark of the Bangkok Dynasty. It varies slightly in design between issues, being very ornate on ceremonial issues.

RAMA I

1782-1809

Tri

Unalom

The trident, the symbol of the Hindu God, Siva, used as the first mark of Rama I. The unalom is an ornamented conch shell, used as the second mark of Rama I.

RAMA II

1809-1824

Krut

A facing Krut, half man - half bird, used as the mark of Rama II.

RAMA III

1824-1851

Krut Sio

Prasat

Dok Mai

The Krut bird to left, used as the first mark of Rama III. The Prasat, the palace used as second mark of Rama III. The Dok Mai was a flower used as third mark of Rama III.

Bai Matum

Ruang Puang

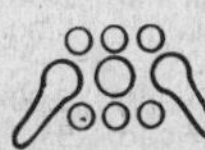

Arrow Head

The Bai Matum is a bale-fruit tree used as the fourth mark of Rama III. The Ruang Puang is a beehive used as the fifth mark of Rama III. Very similar to Dok Mai, having only 1 dot below the point used as the sixth mark of Rama III.

Chaleo

A symbol of varied meanings. In this instance it is believed to represent a charm to ward off evil spirits, found as a seventh mark on bullet coinage of Rama III.

RAMA IV

1851-1868

P'ra Tao Mongkut

The P'ra Tao or royal water pot was used as the first mark of Rama IV. The Royal Siamese Crown was used as the second mark of Rama IV.

RAMA V

1868-1910

P'ra Kieo 1876 Cho Rampeuy 1880

The Royal Coronet worn on the top knot of the Royal Princess on ceremonial occasions. First used on the occasion of the funeral of Princess Charoenkamol Suksawadi who died in 1874. The Thai flower was on a ceremonial issue along with an ornate crown of 2 vessels in memory of Somdet Pira Deb Sirindhra, the mother of Rama V and commemorating his age, dated CS1242.

MARKET VALUATIONS

Market valuations are primarily based on the quality and condition of the countermarks found on bullet coinage.

SILVER POT DUANG

(Bullet Coins)

1/128 BAHT

SILVER, 0.12 g

C#	King	Mark	VG	Fine	VF	XF
120	Rama IV	P'ra Tao	—	—	—	—

ATT

(1/64 Baht)

SILVER, 0.24 g

C#	King	Mark	VG	Fine	VF	XF
121	Rama IV	P'ra Tao	20.00	30.00	45.00	75.00

SIO

(Pai) (1/32 Baht)

SILVER, 0.48 g

C#	King	Mark	VG	Fine	VF	XF
1	Rama I	Tri	10.00	15.00	22.00	32.00
8	Rama I	Unalom	10.00	15.00	22.00	32.00
42	Rama III	Prasat	10.00	15.00	22.00	32.00
51	Rama III	Dok Mai	10.00	15.00	22.00	32.00
61	Rama III	Bai Matum	10.00	15.00	22.00	32.00
71	Rama III	Ruang Puang	10.00	15.00	22.00	32.00
81	Rama III	Arrow Head	10.00	15.00	22.00	32.00
122	Rama IV	P'ra Tao	10.00	15.00	20.00	30.00

SIK

(1/16 Baht)

SILVER, 0.96 g

C#	King	Mark	VG	Fine	VF	XF
2	Rama I	Tri	12.00	20.00	30.00	50.00
9	Rama I	Unalom	16.00	27.00	40.00	65.00
16	Rama II	Krut	20.00	35.00	50.00	85.00
43	Rama III	Prasat	6.00	10.00	15.00	25.00
52	Rama III	Dok Mai	5.00	6.00	10.00	16.00
62	Rama III	Bai Matum	5.00	8.00	12.00	20.00
72	Rama III	Ruang Puang	5.00	8.00	12.00	20.00
82	Rama III	Arrow Head	5.00	8.00	12.00	20.00
123	Rama IV	P'ra Tao	3.00	5.00	8.50	12.50
133	Rama IV	Mongkut	6.00	10.00	14.00	20.00

FUANG

(1/8 Baht)

SILVER, 1.92 g

C#	King	Mark	VG	Fine	VF	XF
3	Rama I	Tri	15.00	25.00	37.00	62.00
10	Rama I	Unalom	15.00	25.00	37.00	62.00
17	Rama II	Krut	20.00	35.00	50.00	85.00
44	Rama III	Prasat	6.00	10.00	15.00	25.00
44.1	Rama III	Prasat and Unalom	25.00	40.00	60.00	100.00
44.2	Rama III	Prasat and Krut	25.00	40.00	60.00	100.00
53	Rama III	Dok Mai	5.00	8.00	12.00	20.00
63	Rama III	Bai Matum	4.00	7.00	10.00	16.00
73	Rama III	Ruang Puang	4.00	7.00	10.00	16.00
83	Rama III	Arrow Head	4.00	7.00	11.00	17.00
124	Rama IV	P'ra Tao	3.00	5.00	8.00	13.00
134	Rama IV	Mongkut	3.00	5.00	8.00	13.00

SALU'NG

(1/4 Baht)

SILVER, 3.85 g

C#	King	Mark	VG	Fine	VF	XF
4	Rama I	Tri	11.00	18.00	27.00	45.00
11	Rama I	Unalom	15.00	25.00	37.00	65.00
18	Rama II	Krut	20.00	25.00	40.00	70.00
45	Rama III	Prasat	6.00	10.00	15.00	25.00
54	Rama III	Dok Mai	6.00	10.00	15.00	25.00
64	Rama III	Bai Matum	5.00	8.00	12.00	20.00
74	Rama III	Ruang Puang	5.00	9.00	13.00	22000
84	Rama III	Arrow Head	5.00	9.00	13.00	22.00
125	Rama IV	P'ra Tao	5.00	8.00	12.00	20.00
135	Rama IV	Mongkut	5.00	8.00	12.00	20.00

2 SALU'NG

(1/2 Baht)

SILVER, 7.70 g

C#	King	Mark	VG	Fine	VF	XF
5	Rama I	Tri	12.00	22.00	35.00	60.00
12	Rama I	Unalom	15.00	25.00	37.50	65.00
19	Rama II	Krut	25.00	35.00	50.00	85.00
46	Rama III	Prasat	7.00	12.00	18.00	30.00
55	Rama III	Dok Mai	18.00	30.00	45.00	75.00
65	Rama III	Bai Matum	12.00	20.00	30.00	50.00

C#	King	Mark	VG	Fine	VF	XF
136	Rama IV	Mongkut	7.00	12.00	20.00	32.00
136.1	Rama IV	Mongkut and Prasat	20.00	35.00	50.00	75.00

BAHT

SILVER, 15.40 g

C#	King	Mark	VG	Fine	VF	XF
1	Rama I	Tri	15.00	20.00	25.00	40.00

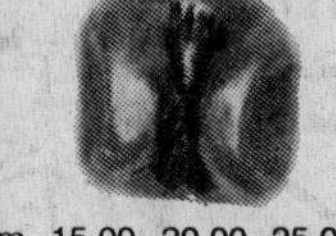

C#	King	Mark	VG	Fine	VF	XF
13	Rama I	Unalom	15.00	20.00	25.00	40.00

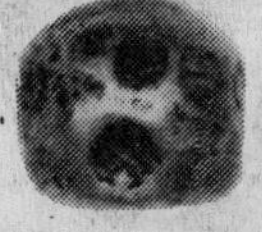
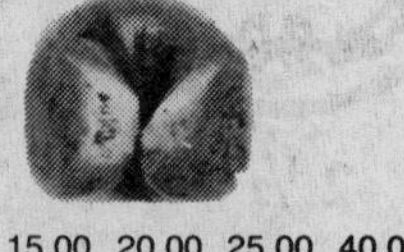

C#	King	Mark	VG	Fine	VF	XF
20	Rama II	Krut	15.00	20.00	25.00	40.00
39	Rama III	Chaleo	—	—	Rare	—
47	Rama III	Prasat	15.00	20.00	25.00	40.00
56	Rama III	Dok Mai	30.00	50.00	75.00	125.00
66	Rama III	Bai Matum	27.00	45.00	65.00	110.00
127	Rama IV	P'ra Tao	Reported, not confirmed			

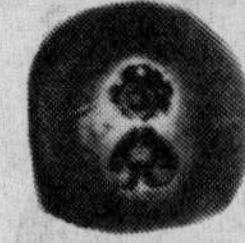

C#	King	Mark	VG	Fine	VF	XF
137.1	Rama IV	Mongkut	15.00	25.00	35.00	60.00
137.2	Rama IV	Mongkut and Prasat	42.50	70.00	100.00	160.00

Death of Princess Charoenkamol Suksawadi

C#	King	Mark	VG	Fine	VF	XF
177	Rama V	P'ra Kieo	—	—	Rare	—

1-1/2 BAHT

SILVER, 23.10 g

C#	King	Mark	VG	Fine	VF	XF
48	Rama III	Prasat	—	—	Rare	—

2 BAHT

SILVER, 30.80 g

C#	King	Mark	VG	Fine	VF	XF
14	Rama I	Unalom	—	—	Rare	—
21	Rama II	Krut	—	—	Rare	—
49	Rama III	Prasat	—	—	Rare	—

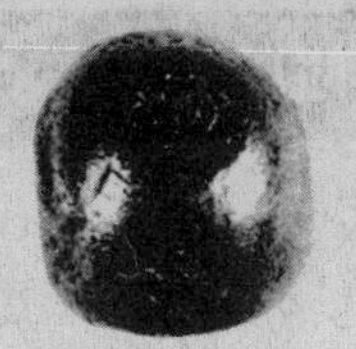

c/m: 8 dots in Chakra

C#	King	Mark	VG	Fine	VF	XF
138	Rama IV	Mongkut	100.00	140.00	210.00	375.00

c/m: 6 blades in Chakra

C#	King	Mark	VG	Fine	VF	XF
138.1	Rama IV	Mongkut	200.00	300.00	420.00	700.00

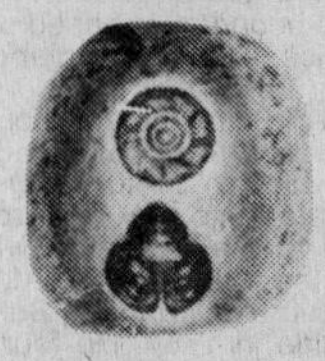

c/m: 8 blades in Chakra, elaborate design.

C#	King	Mark	VG	Fine	VF	XF
138.2	Rama IV	Mongkut	100.00	150.00	225.00	425.00

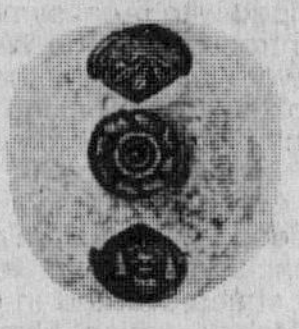

Somdet P'ra Deb Sirindhra

C#	King	Mark	VG	Fine	VF	XF
188	Rama V	Cho Rampeuy	225.00	335.00	450.00	750.00

2-1/2 BAHT

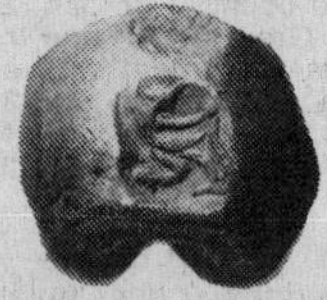

SILVER, 38.50 g

C#	King	Mark	VG	Fine	VF	XF
31	Rama III	Krut Sio	250.00	365.00	525.00	800.00

NOTE: Three varieties exist.

TAMLUNG

(4 Baht)

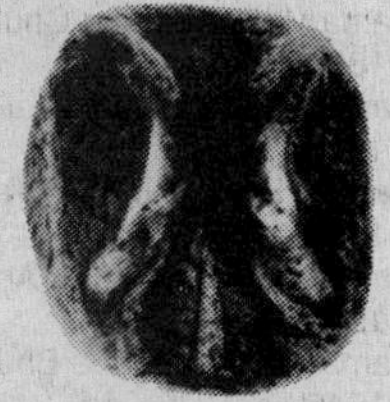

SILVER, 61.60 g

c/m: 8 dots in Chakra

C#	King	Mark	VG	Fine	VF	XF
139.1	Rama IV	Mongkut	225.00	350.00	450.00	800.00

c/m: 7 dots in Chakra

C#	King	Mark	VG	Fine	VF	XF
139.2	Rama IV	Mongkut	200.00	300.00	420.00	750.00

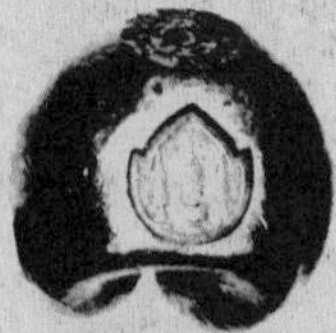

Cremation of Somdet P'ra Deb Sirindhra

C#	King	Mark	VG	Fine	VF	XF
189	Rama V	Cho Rampeuy	250.00	365.00	525.00	850.00

4-1/2 BAHT

SILVER

C#	King	Mark	VG	Fine	VF	XF
32	Rama III	Krut Sio	600.00	750.00	950.00	1200.

8 BAHT

SILVER, 123.20 g

C#	King	Mark	VG	Fine	VF	XF
33	Rama III	Krut Sio	625.00	800.00	1000.	1250.

2-1/2 TAMLUNG

(10 Baht)

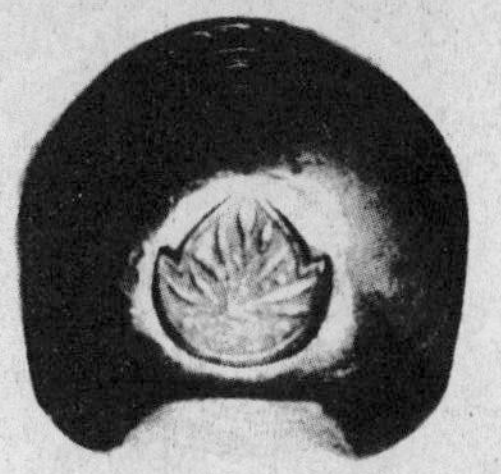

SILVER, 154.00 g
Cremation of Somdet P'ra Deb Sirindhra

C#	King	Mark	VG	Fine	VF	XF
190	Rama V	Cho Rampeuy	500.00	650.00	800.00	1000.

5 TAMLUNG

(20 Baht)

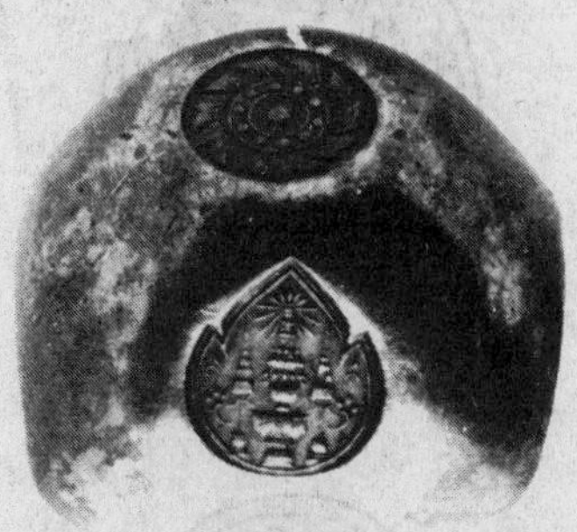

SILVER, 308.00 g
Cremation of Somdet P'ra Deb Sirindhra

C#	King	Mark	VG	Fine	VF	XF
191	Rama V	Cho Rampeuy	1200.	1500.	1850.	2250.

10 TAMLUNG

(40 Baht)

SILVER, 616.00 g
Cremation of Somdet P'ra Deb Sirindhra

C#	King	Mark	VG	Fine	VF	XF
192	Rama V	Cho Rampeuy	2250.	3000.	3750.	4500.

20 TAMLUNG

(80 Baht)

SILVER, 1185.-1232. g
Cremation of Somdet P'ra Deb Sirindhra

C#	King	Mark	VG	Fine	VF	XF
193	Rama V	Cho Rampeuy	4500.	6000.	7500.	9000.

Chakra-wheel engraved turning counterclockwise.

C#	King	Mark	VG	Fine	VF	XF
140.1	Rama IV	Mongkut	4500.	6000.	7500.	9000.

Illustration reduced. Actual size: 65mm
Chakra-wheel engraved turning clockwise.

C#	King	Mark	VG	Fine	VF	XF
140.2	Rama IV	Mongkut	4500.	6000.	7500.	9000.

GOLD POT DUANG

(Bullet Coins)

1/32 GOLD BAHT

GOLD, 0.48 g

C#	King	Mark	VG	Fine	VF	XF
152	Rama IV	P'ra Tao	60.00	90.00	115.00	175.00
162	Rama IV	Mongkut	—	—	—	—

1/16 GOLD BAHT

GOLD, 0.96 g

C#	King	Mark	VG	Fine	VF	XF
92	Rama III	Prasat	75.00	120.00	150.00	250.00
153	Rama IV	P'ra Tao	100.00	150.00	200.00	300.00
163	Rama IV	Mongkut	70.00	100.00	125.00	225.00

1/8 GOLD BAHT

GOLD, 1.96 g

C#	King	Mark	VG	Fine	VF	XF
93	Rama III	Prasat	125.00	175.00	250.00	350.00
103	Rama III	Dok Mai	150.00	200.00	300.00	400.00
113	Rama III	Bai Matum	150.00	200.00	300.00	400.00
154	Rama IV	P'ra Tao	100.00	150.00	200.00	275.00

1/4 GOLD BAHT

GOLD, 3.85 g

C#	King	Mark	VG	Fine	VF	XF
155	Rama IV	P'ra Tao	200.00	300.00	400.00	750.00
165	Rama IV	Mongkut	250.00	325.00	425.00	800.00

1/2 GOLD BAHT

GOLD, 7.70 g

C#	King	Mark	VG	Fine	VF	XF
105	Rama III	Dok Mai	—	—	Rare	—
166	Rama IV	Mongkut	200.00	350.00	600.00	1650.

GOLD BAHT

GOLD, 15.40 g

C#	King	Mark	VG	Fine	VF	XF
96	Rama III	Prasat	900.00	1750.	3250.	5500.
167	Rama IV	Mongkut	800.00	1650.	3000.	5000.

1-1/2 GOLD BAHT

(Met Kanoon)

GOLD, 23.10 g

C#	King	Mark	VG	Fine	VF	XF
167.5	Rama IV	Mongkut	—	—	Rare	—

NOTE: Unlike other bullet coins this does not have its ends hammered into the normal bullet configuration.

2 GOLD BAHT

GOLD, 30.80 g

C#	King	Mark	VG	Fine	VF	XF
168	Rama IV	Mongkut	—	—	Rare	—

4 GOLD BAHT

GOLD, 61.60 g

C#	King	Mark	VG	Fine	VF	XF
169	Rama IV	Mongkut	—	—	Rare	—

TRANSITIONAL COINAGE

A series of hammered flat coinage ordered by Rama IV to alleviate a shortage in small bullet coinage while awaiting arrival of the modern coinage presses from England.

FUANG

SILVER, 1.85 g, uniface
Obv: Chakra above Royal Crown and P'ra Tao at left and right.

C#	Date	Mintage	VG	Fine	VF	XF
170	ND(c.1856)	—	250.00	425.00	600.00	850.00

2.00 g, 15mm
Obv: Royal Crown.
Rev. leg: *Krungthep* (Bangkok).

C#	Date	Mintage	VG	Fine	VF	XF
173	ND(c.1856)	—	—	—	—	—

SALUNG

SILVER, 3.70 g, uniface
Obv: Chakra above Royal Crown and P'ra Tao at left and right.

C#	Date	Mintage	VG	Fine	VF	XF
171	ND(c.1856)	—	275.00	450.00	625.00	900.00

Obv: Royal Crown.
Rev. leg: *Krungthep* (Bangkok).

C#	Date	Mintage	VG	Fine	VF	XF
174	ND(c.1856)	—	—	—	—	—

GOLD 1/2 FUANG

GOLD, 1.00 g, uniface
Obv: Chakra above Royal Crown and P'ra Tao at left and right.

C#	Date	Mintage	VG	Fine	VF	XF
172	ND(c.1856)	—	—	—	—	—

GOLD FUANG

GOLD, 1.80 g
Obv: Royal Crown.
Rev. leg: *Krungthep* (Bangkok).

C#	Date	Mintage	VG	Fine	VF	XF
175	ND(c.1856)	—	—	—	—	—

GOLD SALUNG

GOLD, 3.80 g
Obv: Royal Crown.
Rev. leg: *Krungthep* (Bangkok).

C#	Date	Mintage	VG	Fine	VF	XF
176	ND(c.1856)	—	—	—	—	—

COUNTERMARKED TRADE COINAGE

Foreign trade brought in quantities of Latin American silver 8 reales which were not widely accepted by the public. As a result many were then officially countermarked with the royal marks "Chakra and "Mongkut" in the period 1858-1860 to guarantee their current exchange value.

DOLLAR

.903 SILVER
c/m: Chakra and Mongkut on Mexico-Chihuahua 8 Reales, KM#377.2.

C#	Date	Year	Good	VG	Fine	VF
141.1	ND	(1831-57)	350.00	600.00	1000.	1500.

c/m: Chakra and Mongkut on Mexico-Durango 8 Reales, KM#377.4.

C#	Date	Year	Good	VG	Fine	VF
141.4	ND	(1825-57)	400.00	700.00	1150.	1650.

c/m: Chakra and Mongkut on Mexico-Guanajanto 8 Reales, KM#377.8.

C#	Date	Year	Good	VG	Fine	VF
141.6	ND	(1825-57)	300.00	550.00	950.00	1450.

c/m: Chakra and Mongkut on Mexico City 8 Reales, KM#377.10.

C#	Date	Year	Good	VG	Fine	VF
141.8	ND	(1824-57)	300.00	550.00	950.00	1450.

c/m: Chakra and Mongkut on Mexico-Zacatecas 8 Reales, KM#377.13.

C#	Date	Year	Good	VG	Fine	VF
141.11	ND	(1825-57)	400.00	700.00	1150.	1650.

c/m: Chakra and Mongkut on Peru-Cuzco 8 Reales, KM#142.4.

C#	Date	Year	Good	VG	Fine	VF
141.14	ND	(1830-34)	450.00	800.00	1250.	1750.

c/m: Chakra and Mongkut on Peru-Lima 8 Reales, KM#142.10.

C#	Date	Year	Good	VG	Fine	VF
141.17	ND	(1841-55)	450.00	800.00	1250.	1750.

c/m: Chakra and Mongkut on Philippines countermarked 8 Reales, KM#129.

C#	Date	Year	Good	VG	Fine	VF
141.20	ND	(1825-57)	600.00	1000.	1750.	2500.

LOCAL COINAGE

The following tin coins were struck in 5 of the 7 districts formerly comprising the Kingdom of Patani, during the period of Thai Suzerainty (1832-1902).

JARING

(Jering)

All coins of Jaring are uniface

One of the 7 provinces cut out of Patani State after the uprising of 1830/31. It lies on the east coast of the Malay peninsula. The uniface tin coins were made from 1845 to 1894.

TITLES

Jering جريج

PITIS

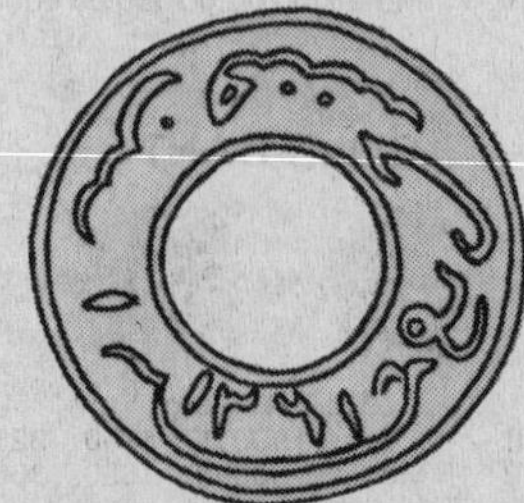

TIN
Arabic leg: *Ini Pitis Jering Sanat 1261*

KM#	Date	Good	VG	Fine	VF
1	AH1261	10.00	15.00	30.00	65.00

Arabic leg: *Ini Pitis Balad Jarin Sanat 1297*

KM#	Date	Good	VG	Fine	VF
2	AH1297	10.00	15.00	30.00	65.00

Arabic leg: *Hadha al-Diwan al-Raj al-Adil Fi Balad al-Jarin 1302*

KM#	Date	Good	VG	Fine	VF
3	AH1302	11.50	17.50	35.00	70.00
	1312	11.50	17.50	35.00	70.00

Crude imitation of KM#3

KM#	Date	Good	VG	Fine	VF
3a	ND	6.00	10.00	15.00	30.00

LEGEH

Ligeh, Ligor, Langkat

One of the inland provinces cut out of Patani State. Coins attributable to Legeh run from 1840 to 1893. Siam again assumed control in 1902.

TITLES

Dar es-Salam دار السلام

Negri Ligkeh نكري لغكه

PITIS

TIN
Obv. leg: Arabic *Pitis Negeri Langkat Dar al-Salam.* Rev. leg: Arabic *Malik al Adil Khalifat al-Mu'minin.*

KM#	Date	Good	VG	Fine	VF
1	ND	13.50	20.00	40.00	70.00

NOTE: For a piece dated 1256, sometimes attributed to Legeh, see KM#4 of Kelantan (Malaysia).

Obv. leg: Arabic *Al-Sultan al-Muzaffar Daulat Langkat Khalifat.* Rev. leg: Arabic *Al-Shamar Wal-Qamar Fi Rabi al-Awal Sanat 1307*

KM#	Date	Good	VG	Fine	VF
2	AH1307	7.50	15.00	30.00	55.00
	1313	— Reported, not confirmed			

PATANI

Pattani

Patani (Pattani), a former Malay state in the Malay peninsula, is a small province or 'changwat' of Thailand (Siam) on the eastern side of peninsula Thailand near the border of Malaya, has an area of 777 sq. mi. (2,012 sq. km.) and a population of about 275,000. After the 1830/31 uprising it was one of 7 provinces administered by Siam through Malayan governors. Patani was the most prolific coin issuer of the Siamese period having made coins periodically from 1845 to 1891. Formerly ruled by a Moslem Rajah subject to Siam.

TITLES

Khalifat al-Karam خليفة الكرم

al-Patani الفطاني

PITIS

TIN

Obv. leg: Arabic *Ini Pitis Belanja Raja Patani.* Rev. leg: Arabic *Khalifat al-Mu'minin Sanat 1261.*

KM#	Date	Good	VG	Fine	VF
1	AH1261	7.50	12.50	17.50	25.00

Obv. leg: Arabic *al-Sultan al-Azam Wa Khalifat al-Karam.* Rev. leg: Arabic *Al-Malik al-Balad al-Patani al-Imami 1284*

KM#	Date	Good	VG	Fine	VF
2	AH1284	7.50	12.50	17.50	25.00

Obv. leg: Arabic *al-Sultan al-Patani Sanat 1297.* Rev. leg: Arabic *Wa Khalifat al-Karam.*

KM#	Date	Good	VG	Fine	VF
3	AH1297	7.50	12.50	17.50	25.00

Obv. leg: Arabic *al-Matsaraf Fi Balad al-Patania Sanat 1301.* Rev. leg: Arabic *Zarb FI Harat al-Daulat Azza Nasrahu*

KM#	Date	Good	VG	Fine	VF
4	AH1301	12.50	17.50	25.00	35.00

Obv. leg: Arabic *al-Matsaraf Fi Balad al-Patani Sanat 1309.* Rev. leg: Arabic *Ini Pitis Belanja di-Dalam Negri Patani*

KM#	Date	Good	VG	Fine	VF
5	AH1309	7.50	12.50	17.50	25.00

KUPANG

GOLD

Obv: Bull standing to left. Rev. leg: Arabic *Malik al-Adil* in 2 lines.

KM#	Date	Year	Fine	VF	XF	Unc
50	ND	(1800-50)	45.00	50.00	60.00	80.00

Obv: Bull standing to left. Rev. leg: Arabic *al-Adil*

KM#	Date	Year	Fine	VF	XF	Unc
51	ND	(1800-50)	45.00	50.00	60.00	80.00

Obv: Bull standing to left. Rev. leg: Arabic *Malik al-Adil* in 3 lines.

KM#	Date	Year	Fine	VF	XF	Unc
52	ND	(1800-50)	45.00	50.00	60.00	80.00

Obv: Bull standing to left. Rev. leg: Arabic *Asma Adil.*

KM#	Date	Year	Fine	VF	XF	Unc
53	ND	(1800-50)	45.00	50.00	60.00	80.00

Obv: Bull standing to right. Rev. leg: Arabic *Malik al-Adil* in 2 lines.

KM#	Date	Year	Fine	VF	XF	Unc
54	ND	(1800-50)	60.00	85.00	110.00	140.00

Obv: 8-pointed star. Rev. leg: Arabic *Malik al-Adil.*

KM#	Date	Year	Fine	VF	XF	Unc
55	ND	(1800-50)	50.00	60.00	75.00	100.00

Obv: 6-pointed star. Rev. leg: Arabic *Malik al-Adil.*

KM#	Date	Year	Fine	VF	XF	Unc
56	ND	(1800-50)	45.00	50.00	60.00	80.00

Obv: 4-petalled flower. Rev. leg: Arabic *Malik al-Adil.*

KM#	Date	Year	Fine	VF	XF	Unc
57	ND	(1800-50)	50.00	60.00	70.00	90.00

Obv. leg: Arabic *Dama Shah.* Rev. leg: Arabic *Binaqdi Sahibi.*

KM#	Date	Year	Fine	VF	XF	Unc
58	ND	(1800-50)	50.00	60.00	70.00	90.00

Obv. leg: Arabic *Shah Adil.* Rev. leg: Arabic *Malik al-Adil.*

KM#	Date	Year	Fine	VF	XF	Unc
59	ND	(1800-50)	50.00	60.00	70.00	90.00

Obv. leg: Arabic *al-Julus Kelantan.* Rev. leg: Arabic *al-Mutawakkilu Ala Liah.*

KM#	Date	Year	Fine	VF	XF	Unc
60	ND	(1800-50)	50.00	60.00	70.00	90.00

Obv. leg: Arabic *Aqam'u'd-Din.* Rev. leg: Arabic *Malik al-Adil.*

KM#	Date	Year	Fine	VF	XF	Unc
61	ND	(1800-50)	50.00	60.00	70.00	90.00

Obv. leg: Arabic *Shah Alam.* Rev. leg: Arabic *Malik al-Adil.*

KM#	Date	Year	Fine	VF	XF	Unc
62	ND	(1800-50)	50.00	60.00	70.00	90.00

Obv. leg: Arabic *Sultan.* Rev. leg: Arabic *Mu'azzam Shah.*

KM#	Date	Year	Fine	VF	XF	Unc
63	ND	(1800-50)	60.00	70.00	85.00	110.00

Obv. leg: Arabic *Sultan Muhammad.* Rev. leg: Arabic *Mu'azzam Shah.*

KM#	Date	Year	Fine	VF	XF	Unc
64	ND	(1800-50)	60.00	70.00	85.00	110.00

Obv. leg: Arabic *al-Julus Kelantan.* Rev. leg: Arabic *Khalifata'r-Rahman.*

KM#	Date	Year	Fine	VF	XF	Unc
65	ND(1800-50)	—	40.00	50.00	60.00	90.00

REMAN

Rhaman

Another of the inland provinces cut from Patani State. Only a single type tin coin is presently known from Reman. This piece was minted about 1890.

TITLES

Rehman رحمن

PITIS

TIN

Uniface. Retrograde Arabic leg: *Ini Pitis Rahman Raja Melayu*

KM#	Date	Good	VG	Fine	VF
1	ND	12.50	20.00	40.00	70.00

SAI

Saiburi, Teluban

Sai is one of the provinces on the east coast of Malaya cut from the state of Patani. The tin Pitis of this province were made from c.1870 to 1891 and are distinctive in that they have a reverse that bears no legend. It carries only a decorative motif.

TITLES

al-Saiwi السيوي

PITIS

TIN

Obv. leg: Arabic *Malik al-Adil Fi Balad al-Saiwi 1290*

KM#	Date	Good	VG	Fine	VF
1	AH1290	12.50	17.50	25.00	50.00

Obv. leg: Arabic *al-Dawlat al-Khairiyat Fi Balad al-Saiwi 1307*

KM#	Date	Good	VG	Fine	VF
2	AH1307	12.50	17.50	25.00	50.00

NOTE: A number of Chinese token issues are tentatively assigned to the Patani state of Jala (Jalor).

THAILAND

REGULAR COINAGE

1/16 FUANG

(1 Solot)

TIN

Dark color and crude rims. Usually plain edge.

Y#	Date	Year	VG	Fine	VF	XF
5	ND	(1862)	1.00	2.50	6.00	12.00

NOTE: Rotated dies are common.

Y#	Date	Year	VG	Fine	VF	XF
16	ND	(1868)	5.00	10.00	20.00	50.00

1/2 ATT

(1 Solot)

COPPER

Y#	Date	Mintage	Fine	VF	XF	Unc
17	CS1236(1874)	—	1.00	2.00	10.00	50.00
	1244(1882)	2.560	1.00	2.00	10.00	50.00

COPPER-NICKEL

Y#	Date	Mintage	Fine	VF	XF	Unc
17a	CS1244(1882)	—	75.00	150.00	300.00	1150.

BRONZE

Y#	Date	Mintage	Fine	VF	XF	Unc
21	CS1249(1887)	—	2.00	4.00	12.50	150.00
	RS109(1890)	10.240	1.00	2.00	10.00	100.00
	118(1899)	—	1.00	2.00	10.00	100.00
	118(1899)	—	—	—	Proof	1500.
	124(1905)	—	1.00	2.00	10.00	100.00

NOTE: These coins were also minted in RS114, RS115, RS121, and RS122. The last year had a mintage of 5,120,000. Coins with these dates have not been observed and were probably additional mintings of coins dated RS109 and RS118. A nickel pattern dated RS114 does exist. Varieties in numeral size and rotated dies exist.

1/8 FUANG

(1 Att)

TIN
Dark color, reeded edge.
Obv: Large elephant. Rev: Lower row of jewels in crown between lines.

Y#	Date	Year	VG	Fine	VF	XF
6.1	ND	(1862)	1.50	3.50	7.00	18.00

Rev: Lower row of jewels in crown enclosed.

Y#	Date	Year	VG	Fine	VF	XF
6.2	ND	(1862)	1.50	3.50	9.00	18.00

Obv: Small elephant. Rev: Lower row of jewels in crown between lines.

Y#	Date	Year	VG	Fine	VF	XF
6.3	ND	(1862)	1.50	3.50	9.00	18.00

Rev: Lower row of jewels in crown enclosed.

Y#	Date	Year	VG	Fine	VF	XF
6.4	ND	(1862)	5.00	10.00	20.00	50.00

ATT

(1/64 Baht)

COPPER

Y#	Date	Mintage	Fine	VF	XF	Unc
18	CS1236(1874)	—	1.50	2.50	10.00	100.00
	1238(1876)	—	1.50	2.50	10.00	100.00
	CS1244(1882)	15.300	1.50	2.50	10.00	100.00

BRONZE

Y#	Date	Mintage	Fine	VF	XF	Unc
22	CS1249(1887)	—	2.00	4.00	15.00	150.00
	RS109(1890)	10.240	1.50	2.50	10.00	125.00
	114*(1895)	5.120	1.50	2.50	10.00	125.00
	115(1896)	—	1.50	2.50	10.00	125.00
	118(1899)	—	1.50	2.50	10.00	125.00
	118(1899)	—	—	—	Proof	1000.
	121(1902)	11.251	1.50	2.50	10.00	125.00
	122*(1903)	4.109	1.50	2.50	10.00	125.00
	124(1905)	—	1.50	2.50	10.00	125.00

***NOTE:** RS114 and RS122 exist with large and small numerals.

1/4 FUANG

(1/32 Baht = 1 Sio)

COPPER
Thick (2.5mm) planchet, crude with plain edge.

Y#	Date	Year	VG	Fine	VF	XF
1	ND	(1865)	15.00	35.00	65.00	125.00

BRASS

Y#	Date	Year	VG	Fine	VF	XF
1a	ND	(1865)	15.00	40.00	80.00	150.00

COPPER
Thin (1.5mm) planchet

Y#	Date	Year	VG	Fine	VF	XF
3	ND	(1865)	15.00	35.00	65.00	125.00

BRASS

Y#	Date	Year	VG	Fine	VF	XF
3a	ND	(1865)	—	—	—	—

NOTE: Rotated dies are common.

2 ATT

(1/32 Baht = 1 Sio)

COPPER

Y#	Date	Mintage	Fine	VF	XF	Unc
19	CS1236(1874)	—	2.00	4.00	15.00	200.00
	1238(1876)	—	2.00	4.00	15.00	200.00
	1244(1882)	10.200	2.00	4.00	15.00	200.00

BRONZE

Y#	Date	Mintage	Fine	VF	XF	Unc
23	CS1249(1887)	—	3.50	7.00	25.00	275.00
	RS109(1890)	5.120	1.50	3.00	12.00	125.00
	114(1895)	—	1.50	3.00	12.00	125.00
	115(1896)	—	1.50	3.00	12.00	125.00
	118(1899)	—	1.50	3.00	12.00	125.00
	119(1900)	.735	2.50	5.00	20.00	165.00
	121(1902)	2.797	1.50	3.00	12.00	125.00
	122(1903)	2.323	1.50	3.00	12.00	125.00
	124(1905)	—	1.50	3.00	12.00	125.00

NOTE: Varieties in numeral size and rotated dies exist.

1/2 FUANG

(1/16 Baht = 1 Sik)

COPPER
Thick (3mm) planchet. Crude, plain edges.

Y#	Date	Year	VG	Fine	VF	XF
2	ND	(1865)	10.00	20.00	50.00	100.00

BRASS

Y#	Date	Year	VG	Fine	VF	XF
2a	ND	(1865)	12.00	25.00	60.00	125.00

COPPER
Thin (1.5mm) planchet.

Y#	Date	Year	VG	Fine	VF	XF
4	ND	(1865)	12.00	25.00	80.00	200.00

BRASS

Y#	Date	Year	VG	Fine	VF	XF
4a	ND	(1865)	15.00	30.00	90.00	225.00

NOTE: Rotated dies are common.

1/16 BAHT

(1 Sik)

SILVER, 1.00 g
Thick Flan

Y#	Date	Mintage	Fine	VF	XF	Unc
7.1 (Y7)	ND(1860)	—	20.00	30.00	150.00	400.00

Obv: Smaller crown, Rev: Larger elephant.

Y#	Date	Mintage	Fine	VF	XF	Unc
7.2 (Y7.1)	ND(1860)	—	40.00	60.00	250.00	600.00

.900 GOLD, 1.00 g
Reeded edge. Thin flan.

Y#	Date	Mintage	Fine	VF	XF	Unc
7a	ND(1864)	—	—	—	—	—

4 ATT

(1/16 Baht = 1 Sik)

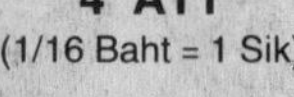

COPPER

Y#	Date	Mintage	Fine	VF	XF	Unc
20	CS1238(1876)	—	20.00	60.00	180.00	550.00

NOTE: Frequently counterfeited.

FUANG

(1/8 Baht)

SILVER, 1.94 g
Thick flan
Denomination indicated by number of stars outside chakra; 1 star = 1/8 Baht.

Y#	Date	Mintage	Fine	VF	XF	Unc
8	ND(1860)	—	5.00	10.00	40.00	150.00

.900 GOLD, 1.94 g
Reeded edge. Thin flan.

Y#	Date	Mintage	Fine	VF	XF	Unc
8a	ND (1864)	—	1200.	2200.	4000.	6000.

SILVER, 1.89 g

Y#	Date	Mintage	Fine	VF	XF	Unc
28	ND(1868)	—	3.00	7.00	40.00	150.00

Y#	Date	Mintage	Fine	VF	XF	Unc
32	ND(1876-1900)	—	2.50	6.50	20.00	80.00
	ND(1876-1900)	—	—	—	Proof	3000.

GOLD

Y#	Date	Mintage	Fine	VF	XF	Unc
32b	ND(1876)	—	1000.	2250.	4500.	7500.

SILVER

Y#	Date	Mintage	Fine	VF	XF	Unc
32a	RS120(1901)	—	3.00	6.00	18.00	140.00
	121(1902)	.380	3.00	6.00	18.00	140.00
	122(1903)	.460	3.00	6.00	18.00	140.00
	123(1904)	.310	3.00	6.00	18.00	140.00
	124(1905)	.410	3.00	6.00	18.00	140.00
	125(1906)	—	3.00	6.00	18.00	140.00
	126(1907)	—	3.00	6.00	18.00	140.00
	127(1908)	.480	3.00	6.00	18.00	140.00

GOLD

Y#	Date	Mintage	Fine	VF	XF	Unc
32c	RS122(1903)	—	400.00	800.00	1500.	3250.
	123(1904)	—	400.00	800.00	1500.	3250.
	124(1905)	—	400.00	800.00	1500.	3250.
	125(1906)	—	400.00	800.00	1500.	3250.
	126(1907)	—	400.00	800.00	1500.	3250.
	127(1908)	—	400.00	800.00	1500.	3250.
	128(1909)	—	400.00	800.00	1500.	3250.
	129(1910)	—	400.00	800.00	1500.	3250.

SALUNG

(1/4 Baht)

SILVER, 3.71 g
Denomination indicated by number of stars outside chakra; 2 stars = 1/4 Baht.

Y#	Date	Mintage	Fine	VF	XF	Unc
9	ND(1860)	—	15.00	30.00	150.00	350.00

GOLD, 3.71 g

Y#	Date	Mintage	Fine	VF	XF	Unc
9a	ND(1864)	—	—	—	—	—

SILVER, 3.82 g

Y#	Date	Mintage	Fine	VF	XF	Unc
29	ND(1868)	—	7.50	15.00	75.00	225.00

Y#	Date	Mintage	Fine	VF	XF	Unc
33	ND(1876-1900)	—	5.00	12.00	35.00	165.00
	ND(1876-1900)	—	—	—	Proof	3000.

Y#	Date	Mintage	Fine	VF	XF	Unc
33a	RS120(1901)	—	4.50	10.00	30.00	250.00
	121(1902)	.560	3.00	8.00	25.00	200.00
	122(1903)	.340	3.00	8.00	25.00	200.00
	123(1904)	.190	3.00	8.00	25.00	200.00
	125(1906)	—	3.00	8.00	25.00	200.00
	126(1907)	—	3.00	8.00	25.00	200.00
	127(1908)	.270	3.00	8.00	25.00	200.00

2 SALUNG

(1/2 Baht)

SILVER, 7.54 g
Thick flan
Denomination indicated by number of stars outside chakra; 4 stars = 1/2 Baht.

Y#	Date	Mintage	Fine	VF	XF	Unc
10.1	ND(1860)	—	30.00	175.00	500.00	1200.

Thin flan

Y#	Date	Mintage	Fine	VF	XF	Unc
10.2	ND(1864)	—	—	Reported, not confirmed		

GOLD, 7.55 g

Y#	Date	Mintage	Fine	VF	XF	Unc
10.2a	ND(1864)	—	—	—	*Rare	—

***NOTE:** Spink-Taisei Auction #15, 9-93 Unc. realized $23,000.

Reeded edge.

Y#	Date	Mintage	Fine	VF	XF	Unc
15.5	ND(1895)	—	—	—	—	—

BAHT

15.4500 g, .900 SILVER, .4470 oz ASW
Denomination indicated by number of stars outside chakra; 8 stars = 1 Baht.

Y#	Date	Mintage	Fine	VF	XF	Unc
11	ND(1860)	—	12.00	20.00	150.00	350.00

GOLD, 15.25 g

Y#	Date	Mintage	Fine	VF	XF	Unc
11a	ND(1864)	—	—	—	*Rare	—

***NOTE:** Spink-Taisei Auction #15, 9-93 Unc. realized $34,000.

SILVER

Y#	Date	Mintage	Fine	VF	XF	Unc
31	ND(1868)	—	12.00	20.00	150.00	650.00

Y#	Date	Mintage	Fine	VF	XF	Unc
34	ND(1876-1900)	—	5.00	15.00	45.00	200.00
	ND(1876-1900)	—	—	—	Proof	8500.

Queen's Royal Mint Visit
Obv. leg: *Rong Krasab* (Royal Mint) and RS date 116 added in field.

Y#	Date	Mintage	Fine	VF	XF	Unc
B34	RS116(1897)	—	—	—	6500.	8500.

Y#	Date	Mintage	Fine	VF	XF	Unc
34a	RS120(1901)	—	150.00	250.00	750.00	2250.
	121(1902)	*4.070	7.00	30.00	90.00	400.00
	122(1903)	19.150	6.00	25.00	75.00	300.00
	123(1904)	4.790	6.00	25.00	60.00	300.00
	124(1905)	6.770	6.00	25.00	60.00	300.00
	125(1906)	—	6.00	25.00	60.00	300.00
	126(1907)	—	15.00	40.00	120.00	450.00

***NOTE:** Because of a faulty die used the second 1 appears to be a 0 in some examples of this date.

2 BAHT

30.2000 g, .900 SILVER, .8738 oz ASW
Denomination indicated by number of stars outside chakra; 16 stars = 2 Baht.

Y#	Date	Mintage	Fine	VF	XF	Unc
12	ND(c.1863)	—	200.00	400.00	850.00	1500.

GOLD, 30.30 g

Y#	Date	Mintage	Fine	VF	XF	Unc
12a	ND(1864)	—	—	—	*Rare	—

***NOTE:** Spink-Taisei Auction #15, 9-93 Unc. realized $44,000.

PAT DUENG

(2-1/2 BAHT)

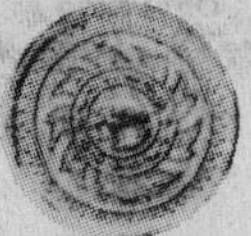

***.997 GOLD, 2.20 g**
Rev: Crude elephant.

Y#	Date	Mintage	Fine	VF	XF	Unc
13	ND(1863)	—	1200.	2000.	3000.	4500.

GOLD, 1.90-2.00 g

Y#	Date	Mintage	Fine	VF	XF	Unc
13.1	ND(1895)	—	1000.	1750.	2500.	3000.

Rev: Refined elephant.

Y#	Date	Mintage	Fine	VF	XF	Unc
13.5	ND(1895)	—	1000.	1500.	2200.	2750.

TAMLUNG

(4 Baht)

60.4000 g, .900 SILVER, 1.7477 oz ASW
Plain edge
60th Birthday of Rama IV

Y#	Date	Mintage	Fine	VF	XF	Unc
A12	ND(1864)	—	—	—	*Rare	—

***NOTE:** Spink-Taisei Auction #15, 9-93 Unc. realized $16,000.

.997 GOLD, 60.77 g

Y#	Date	Mintage	Fine	VF	XF	Unc
A12a	ND(1864)	—	—	—	Rare	—

NOTE: Spink-Taisei Auction #4, 2-88, XF specimen realized $74,800.

PIT

(4 Baht)

Reeded edge, 3.40 g.
Rev: Crude elephant.

Y#	Date	Mintage	Fine	VF	XF	Unc
14	ND(1863)	—	1000.	1500.	2300.	4000.

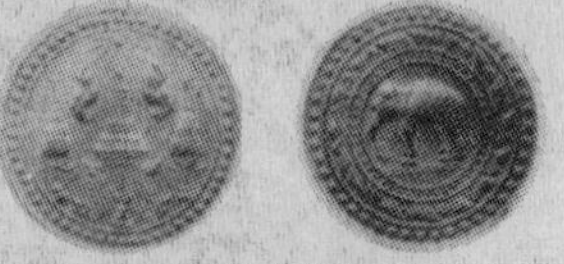

3.65-4.00 g
Rev: Refined elephant.

Y#	Date	Mintage	Fine	VF	XF	Unc
14.5	ND(1895)	—	1000.	1600.	2500.	3500.

TOT

(8 Baht)

.997 GOLD, 6.80 g
Reeded edge.

Rev: Crude elephant.

Y#	Date	Mintage	Fine	VF	XF	Unc
15	ND(1863)	—	1750.	3250.	6500.	20,000.

GOLD, 7.30-8.00 g

Y#	Date	Mintage	Fine	VF	XF	Unc
15.1	ND(1895)	—	1500.	2500.	3500.	8000.

Rev: Refined elephant.

Y#	Date	
15.6	ND(1895)	Reported, not confirmed

PRESENTATION COINAGE

Bannakin (Royal Gift) Coins

FUANG

(1/8 Baht)

SILVER, 2.00 g, plain edge
Similar to 1/8 Baht, Y#8.
Obv: Larger crown.

KM#	Date	Year	Mintage	VF	XF	Unc
11	ND	(1857-58)	—	1000.	1650.	2800.

SALUNG

(1/4 Baht)

SILVER, 3.90 g
Plain edge

KM#	Date	Year	Mintage	VF	XF	Unc
12	ND	(1857-58)	—	1500.	2500.	3500.

1/2 BAHT

SILVER
Plain edge

KM#	Date	Year	Mintage	VF	XF	Unc
13	ND	(1857-58)	—	—	Rare	—

NOTE: The total mintage for KM#11-13 equalled 840 Baht.

1 BAHT

SILVER, 15.50 g
Milled edge

KM#	Date	Year	Mintage	VF	XF	Unc
14	ND	(1857-58)	2,400	1500.	2500.	3500.
	ND	(c.1868)	—	—	Rare	—

NOTE: Spink-Taisei Auction #4, Feb. 1988, realized $20,125.

PAT DUENG

(2-1/2 Baht)

GOLD, 2.15 g

KM#	Date	Year	Mintage	VF	XF	Unc
10	ND	(1857-58)	—	—	Rare	—

DECIMAL COINAGE

100 Satang = 1 Baht
25 Satang = 1 Salung

1/2 SATANG

BRONZE

Y#	Date	Year	Mintage	VF	XF	Unc
50	(BE)2480	(1937)	—	.50	1.50	2.50

BRONZE

Y#	Date	Year	Mintage	VF	XF	Unc
35	RS127	(1908)	17.000	2.50	5.00	18.00
	128	(1909)	.150	3.50	7.00	25.00
	129	(1910)	9.000	1.50	3.50	18.00
	130	(1911)	30.000	1.50	3.50	12.50
	132	(1913)	—	—	60.00	100.00
	BE2456	(1913)	10.000	1.00	1.50	4.00
	2457	(1914)	1.000	2.00	4.00	12.50
	2458	(1915)	5.000	.75	1.00	2.75
	2461	(1918)	18.880	.65	1.25	3.00
	2462	(1919)	6.400	.65	1.50	2.75
	2463	(1920)	17.240	1.00	1.50	3.50
	2464	(1921)	6.360	15.00	25.00	45.00
	2466	(1923)	14.000	.75	1.00	2.75
	2467	(1924)	Inc. Ab.	1.00	1.50	3.50
	2469	(1926)	20.000	.50	.75	2.50
	2470	(1927)	—	.50	.75	2.50
	2472	(1929)	—	.50	1.00	2.75
	2478	(1935)	—	.50	.70	2.00
	2480	(1937)	—	.50	.70	2.00

NOTE: Variations in lettering exist.

BRONZE

Y#	Date	Year	Mintage	VF	XF	Unc
51	BE2482	(1939)	24.400	1.50	3.00	6.00

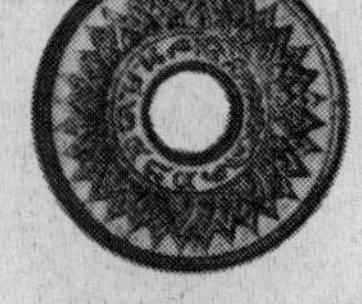

Y#	Date	Year	Mintage	VF	XF	Unc
54	BE2484	(1941)	—	.50	1.50	3.00

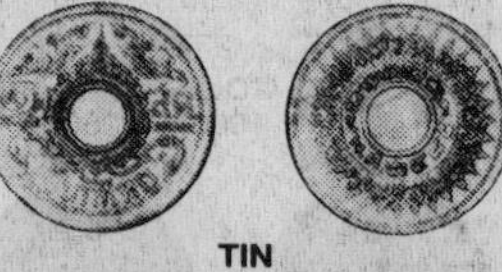

TIN
BE date & denomination in Thai numerals, w/o hole.

Y#	Date	Year	Mintage	VF	XF	Unc
57	BE2485	(1942)	20.700	.30	.50	1.00

NOTE: Approximately 790,000 coins were restruck for circulation 1967-73.

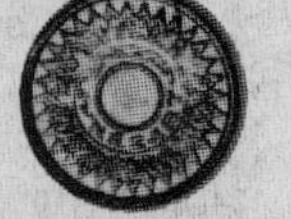

BE date and denomination in Western numerals, w/o hole.

Y#	Date	Year	Mintage	VF	XF	Unc
60	BE2487	—	.500	.10	.20	.50

ALUMINUM

Y#	Date	Year	Mintage	VF	XF	Unc
186	BE2530	(1987)	.093	—	—	.10
	2531	(1988)	.200	—	—	.10
	2533	(1990)	—	—	—	.10
	2534	(1991)	—	—	—	.10
	2535	(1992)	—	—	—	.10

2-1/2 SATANG

COPPER-NICKEL

Y#	Date	Year	Mintage	VF	XF	Unc
24	RS116H	(1897)	5.080	3.00	5.00	12.00
	116H	(1897)	—	—	Proof	25.00

NOTE: Issued in 1898 although dated RS116 (1897).

5 SATANG

COPPER-NICKEL

Y#	Date	Year	Mintage	VF	XF	Unc
25	RS116H	(1897)	5.080	10.00	15.00	40.00
	116H	(1897)	—	—	Proof	65.00

NOTE: Issued in 1898 although dated RS116 (1897).

NICKEL

Y#	Date	Year	Mintage	VF	XF	Unc
36	RS127	(1908)	7.000	3.00	4.00	8.00
	128	(1909)	4.000	3.50	4.50	10.00
	129	(1910)	4.000	1.50	2.00	7.00
	131	(1912)	2.000	1.50	2.50	8.00
	132	(1913)	—	—	90.00	150.00
	BE2456	(1913)	2.000	1.50	2.50	6.00
	2457	(1914)	2.000	1.50	2.50	6.00
	2461	(1918)	2.000	1.50	2.50	6.00
	2462	(1919)	2.000	1.00	2.00	6.00
	2463	(1920)	9.900	1.00	1.50	4.50
	2464	(1921)	13.000	.60	1.25	3.00
	2469	(1926)	20.000	.60	1.25	3.00
	2478	(1935)	10.000	.60	1.25	3.00
	2480	(1937)	20.000	.60	1.25	3.00
	2482	(1939)	—Reported, not confirmed			

NOTE: Variations in lettering exist.

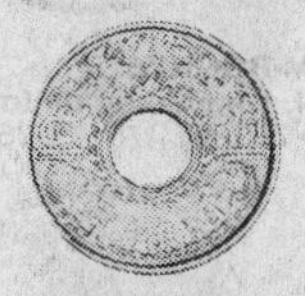

1.5000 g, .650 SILVER, .0313 oz ASW

Y#	Date	Year	Mintage	VF	XF	Unc
55	BE2484	(1941)	—	1.50	3.00	4.50

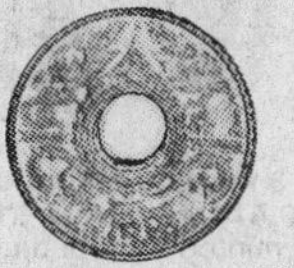
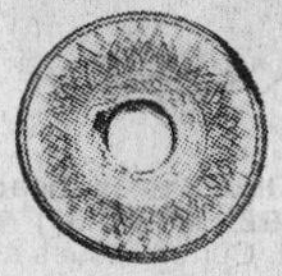

TIN
BE date and denomination in Thai numerals.

Y#	Date	Year	Mintage	VF	XF	Unc
58	BE2485	(1942)	—	.50	1.50	3.00

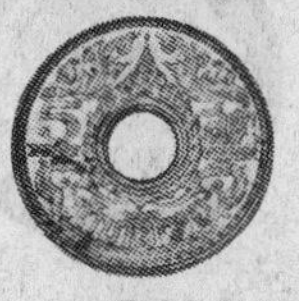

Thick (2.2mm) planchet.
BE date and denomination in Western numerals.

Y#	Date	Year	Mintage	VF	XF	Unc
61	BE2487	(1944)	—	.50	1.25	3.00
	2488	(1945)	—	.50	1.25	3.00

Medium planchet

Y#	Date	Year	Mintage	VF	XF	Unc
61b	BE2488	(1945)	—	.50	1.25	3.00

Thin (2.0mm) planchet.

Y#	Date	Year	Mintage	VF	XF	Unc
61a	BE2488	(1945)	—	.50	1.25	3.00

Obv: King Ananda, child head.

Y#	Date	Year	Mintage	VF	XF	Unc
64	BE2489	(1946)	—	.50	1.00	2.00

Obv: King Ananda, youth head.

Y#	Date	Year	Mintage	VF	XF	Unc
68	BE2489	(1946)	24.480	.15	.50	1.00

Obv: King Bhumiphol, 1 medal on uniform.

Y#	Date	Year	Mintage	VF	XF	Unc
72	BE2493	(1950)	*6.480	.50	.75	1.25

***NOTE:** Coins bearing this date were also struck in 1954, 58, 59, and 73. Mintages are included here.

ALUMINUM-BRONZE

Y#	Date	Year	Mintage	VF	XF	Unc
72a	BE2493	(1950)	15.500	.25	1.00	2.00

Obv: Smaller head, 3 medals on uniform.

Y#	Date	Year	Mintage	VF	XF	Unc
78	BE2500	(1957)	*46.440	—	.10	.25

***NOTE:** Current issues are minted without date change.

BRONZE

Y#	Date	Year	Mintage	VF	XF	Unc
78a	BE2500	(1957)	*6.240	.50	1.50	2.00

TIN

Y#	Date	Year	Mintage	VF	XF	Unc
78b	BE2500	(1957)	—	1.75	3.00	5.00

NOTE: The above coins were struck to replace Y#72 in mint sets.

ALUMINUM

Y#	Date	Year	Mintage	VF	XF	Unc
208	BE2530	(1987)	—	—	—	20.00
	2531	(1988)	.704	—	—	.10
	2533	(1990)	—	—	—	.10
	2534	(1991)	—	—	—	.10
	2535	(1992)	—	—	—	.10

10 SATANG

COPPER-NICKEL

Y#	Date	Year	Mintage	VF	XF	Unc
26	RS116H	(1897)	3.810	20.00	50.00	160.00
	116H	(1897)	—	—	Proof	185.00

NICKEL

Y#	Date	Year	Mintage	VF	XF	Unc
37	RS127	(1908)	7.000	1.50	3.00	8.50
	129	(1910)	5.000	1.50	3.00	8.50
	130	(1911)	.500	2.00	5.00	12.00
	131	(1912)	1.500	1.50	3.00	10.00
	BE2456	(1913)	1.000	1.25	2.00	6.00
	2457	(1914)	1.000	1.25	2.00	6.00
	2461	(1918)	.770	2.50	3.50	9.00
	2462	(1919)	.774	1.25	1.50	3.50
	2463	(1920)	Inc. Ab.	1.25	1.50	3.50
	2464	(1921)	21.727	1.00	1.25	3.00
	2478	(1935)	5.000	1.00	1.25	3.00
	2480	(1937)	5.000	.75	1.00	2.50
	2482	(1939)	Reported, not confirmed			

NOTE: Variations in lettering exist.

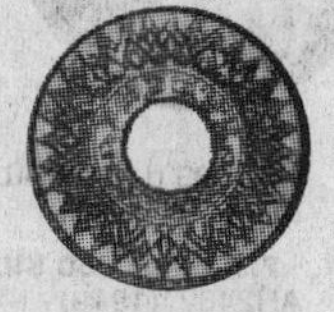

2.5000 g, .650 SILVER, .0522 oz ASW

Y#	Date	Year	Mintage	VF	XF	Unc
56	BE2484	(1941)	—	2.00	4.00	8.00

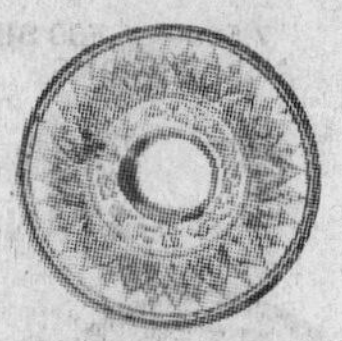

TIN
BE date and denomination in Thai numerals.

Y#	Date	Year	Mintage	VF	XF	Unc
59	BE2485	(1942)	.230	1.00	2.00	3.50

Thick (2.5mm) planchet.
BE date and denomination in Western numerals.

Y#	Date	Year	Mintage	VF	XF	Unc
62	BE2487	(1944)	—	1.00	2.00	3.50
	2488	(1945)	—	3.50	7.00	15.00

Thin (2.0mm) planchet.

Y#	Date	Year	Mintage	VF	XF	Unc
62a	BE2488	(1945)	—	1.00	2.50	4.00

Obv: King Ananda, child head.

Y#	Date	Year	Mintage	VF	XF	Unc
65	BE2489	(1946)	—	.50	1.25	2.25

Obv: Youth head.

Y#	Date	Year	Mintage	VF	XF	Unc
69	BE2489	(1946)	40.470	.50	1.25	2.00

Obv: King Bhumiphol, 1 medal on uniform.

Y#	Date	Year	Mintage	VF	XF	Unc
73	BE2493	(1950)	*139.695	.40	1.00	1.50

***NOTE:** These coins were also struck in 1954-1973 and the mintages are also included here.

ALUMINUM-BRONZE

Y#	Date	Year	Mintage	VF	XF	Unc
73a	BE2493	(1950)	4.060	.75	1.50	2.50

Obv: Smaller head. 3 medals on uniform.
Rev. leg: Thin style.

Y#	Date	Year	Mintage	VF	XF	Unc
79	BE2500	(1957)	*55.410	.10	.25	.50

***NOTE:** Current issues are minted without date change.

Rev. leg: Thick style.

Y#	Date	Year	Mintage	VF	XF	Unc
79d	BE2500	(1957)	—	.10	.25	.50

BRONZE
Rev. leg: Thick style.

Y#	Date	Year	Mintage	VF	XF	Unc
79a	BE2500	(1957)	*13.365	.25	.75	1.25
	2501	(1958)	—	.25	.75	1.25

Rev. leg: Thin style.

Y#	Date	Year	Mintage	VF	XF	Unc
79c	BE2500	(1957)	Inc. Ab.	2.50	5.00	10.00

TIN

Y#	Date	Year	Mintage	VF	XF	Unc
79b	BE2500	(1957)	—	15.00	25.00	70.00

ALUMINUM

Y#	Date	Year	Mintage	VF	XF	Unc
209	BE2530	(1987)	—	—	—	20.00
	2531	(1988)	.900	—	—	.10
	2533	(1990)	—	—	—	.10
	2534	(1991)	—	—	—	.10
	2535	(1992)	—	—	—	.10

20 SATANG

COPPER-NICKEL

Y#	Date	Year	Mintage	VF	XF	Unc
27	RS116H	(1897)	3.126	12.00	25.00	60.00

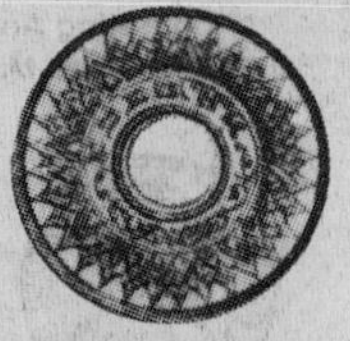

3.0000 g, .650 SILVER, .0627 oz ASW
BE date and denomination in Thai numerals.

Y#	Date	Year	Mintage	VF	XF	Unc
A56	BE2485	(1942)	—	3.00	6.00	12.00

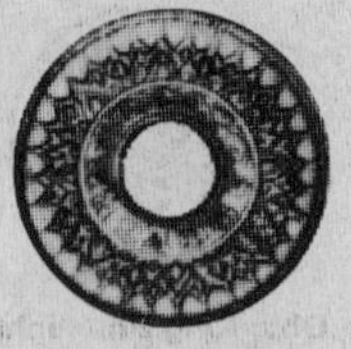

TIN
BE date and denomination in Western numerals.

Y#	Date	Year	Mintage	VF	XF	Unc
63	BE2488	(1945)	—	1.00	2.50	4.00

SALUNG = 1/4 BAHT

Y#	Date	Year	Mintage	VF	XF	Unc
	3.7500 g, .800 SILVER, .0965 oz ASW					
43	BE2458	(1915)	2.040	5.00	10.00	20.00
	3.7500 g, .650 SILVER, .0784 oz ASW					
43a	BE2460	(1917)	1.100	3.50	7.00	15.00
	2461	(1918)	2.170	3.50	7.00	15.00
	2462	(1919)	7.860	2.50	5.00	10.00
	2467	(1924)	2.100	3.50	7.00	18.00
	2468	(1925)	—	3.50	7.00	18.00
	3.7500 g, .500 SILVER, .0603 oz ASW					
43b	BE2462	(1919)	dot after legend Inc. Ab.	40.00	55.00	75.00

25 SATANG = 1/4 BAHT

3.7500 g, .650 SILVER, .0784 oz ASW

Y#	Date	Year	Mintage	VF	XF	Unc
48	BE2472	(1929)	—	3.00	7.00	18.00

TIN
Obv: King Ananda, child head.

Y#	Date	Year	Mintage	VF	XF	Unc
66	BE2489	(1946)	—	2.50	4.00	6.00

Obv: Youth head.

Y#	Date	Year	Mintage	VF	XF	Unc
70	BE2489	(1946)	dot *226.348	.20	.40	.75
	BE2489	(1946)	w/o dot Inc. Ab.	.20	.40	.75

***NOTE:** These coins were also struck 1954-64 and mintage figure is a total.

ALUMINUM-BRONZE
Obv: King Bhumiphol, 1 medal on uniform.

Y#	Date	Year	Mintage	VF	XF	Unc
76	BE2493	(1950)	23.170	.75	1.75	3.00

Obv: Smaller head; 3 medals on uniform.

Y#	Date	Year	Mintage	VF	XF	Unc
80	BE2500	(1957)	dot *620.480	.10	.15	.25
	BE2500	(1957)	w/o dot Inc. Ab.	Reported, not confirmed		

***NOTE:** Current issues are minted without date change and with and without reeded edges.

BRASS

Y#	Date	Year	Mintage	VF	XF	Unc
109	BE2520	(1977)	183.356	—	.10	.15

NOTE: Date varieties exist.

ALUMINUM-BRONZE

Y#	Date	Year	Mintage	VF	XF	Unc
187	BE2530	(1987)	5.108	—	—	.10
	2531	(1988)	42.096	—	—	.10
	2532	(1989)	—	—	—	.10
	2533	(1990)	—	—	—	.10
	2534	(1991)	—	—	—	.10
	2535	(1992)	—	—	—	.10
	2536	(1993)	—	—	—	.10

2 SALUNG = 1/2 BAHT

Y#	Date	Year	Mintage	VF	XF	Unc
	7.5000 g, .800 SILVER, .1929 oz ASW					
44	BE2458	(1915)	2.740	5.00	10.00	20.00
	7.5000 g, .650 SILVER, .1568 oz ASW					
44a	AH2462	(1919)	3.230	5.00	10.00	20.00
	2463	(1920)	4.970	5.00	10.00	20.00
	2464	(1921)	—	5.00	10.00	20.00
	7.5000 g, .500 SILVER, .1206 oz ASW					
44b	AH2462	(1919)	large dot after legend Inc. Ab.	6.50	12.50	25.00
	2462	(1919)	small dot after legend Inc. Ab.	6.50	12.50	25.00

50 SATANG = 1/2 BAHT

7.5000 g, .650 SILVER, .1567 oz ASW

Y#	Date	Year	Mintage	VF	XF	Unc
49	BE2472	(1929)	17.008	6.00	12.50	25.00

TIN
Obv: King Ananda, child head.

Y#	Date	Year	Mintage	VF	XF	Unc
67	BE2489	(1946)	—	15.00	30.00	90.00

Obv: Youth head.

Y#	Date	Year	Mintage	VF	XF	Unc
71	BE2489	(1946)	*17.008	.75	1.00	1.5

***NOTE:** These coins were minted from 1954-57 and mintage figure is a total.

ALUMINUM-BRONZE
Obv: King Bhumiphol, 1 medal on uniform.

Y#	Date	Year	Mintage	VF	XF	Unc
77	BE2493	(1950)	20.710	.75	1.75	3.5

Obv: Smaller head; 3 medals on uniform.

Y#	Date	Year	Mintage	VF	XF	Unc
81	BE2500	(1957)	*439.874	.10	.15	.2

***NOTE:** Current issues are minted without date change

Y#	Date	Year	Mintage	VF	XF	Unc
168	BE2523	(1980)	122.260	.10	.15	.2

BRASS

Y#	Date	Year	Mintage	VF	XF	Unc
203	BE2531	(1988)	23.776	—	—	.1
	2532	(1989)	—	—	—	.1
	2533	(1990)	—	—	—	.1
	2534	(1991)	—	—	—	.1
	2535	(1992)	—	—	—	.1

BAHT

15.0000 g, .900 SILVER, .4340 oz ASW

Y#	Date	Year	Mintage	VF	XF	Unc
39	RS127	(1908)	1.037	2500.	3500.	750

Y#	Date	Year	Mintage	VF	XF	Unc
45	BE2456	(1913)	2.690	10.00	15.00	25.0
	2457	(1914)	.490	12.50	20.00	35.0
	2458	(1915)	5.000	10.00	15.00	25.0
	2459	(1916)	9.080	10.00	15.00	25.0
	2460,	(1917)	14.340	10.00	15.00	25.0
	2461	(1918)	3.840	10.00	15.00	25.0

NOTE: BE2456 is often found weakly struck so it doe appear similar to a counterfeit.

COPPER-NICKEL-SILVER-ZINC

Y#	Date	Year	Mintage	VF	XF	Unc
82	BE2500	(1957)	*3.143	.75	1.50	3.00

***NOTE:** These coins were minted from 1958-60 and mintage figure is a total.

SILVER

Y#	Date	Year	Mintage	VF	XF	Unc
82a	BE2500	(1957)	—	—	—	30.00

COPPER-NICKEL
King Bhumiphol & Queen Sirikit

Y#	Date	Year	Mintage	VF	XF	Unc
83	BE2504	(1961)	4.430	.40	.75	1.50

Y#	Date	Year	Mintage	VF	XF	Unc
84	BE2505	(1962)	*883.086	.10	.15	.30

***NOTE:** These coins were minted from 1962-82 and mintage figure is a total.

King's 36th Birthday

Y#	Date	Year	Mintage	VF	XF	Unc
85	ND	(1963)	3.000	.25	.75	1.50

5th Asian Games

Y#	Date	Year	Mintage	VF	XF	Unc
87	BE2509	1966	9.000	.25	.75	1.50

6th Asian Games

Y#	Date	Year	Mintage	VF	XF	Unc
91	BE2513	1970	9.000	.25	.75	1.50

F.A.O. Issue

Y#	Date	Year	Mintage	VF	XF	Unc
96	BE2515	(1972)	9.000	.10	.25	.75

Prince Vajiralongkorn Investiture

Y#	Date	Year	Mintage	VF	XF	Unc
97	BE2515	(1972)	9.000	.15	.40	1.00

25th Anniversary World Health Organization

Y#	Date	Year	Mintage	VF	XF	Unc
99	BE2516	1973	1.000	.25	.65	1.25

Y#	Date	Year	Mintage	VF	XF	Unc
100	BE2517	(1974)	248.978	.15	.40	1.00

8th SEAP Games

Y#	Date	Year	Mintage	VF	XF	Unc
105	BE2518	1975	3.000	.25	.65	1.25

75th Birthday of Princess Mother

Y#	Date	Year	Mintage	VF	XF	Unc
107	BE2518	(1975)	9.000	.15	.40	1.00

Y#	Date	Year	Mintage	VF	XF	Unc
110	BE2520	(1977)	506.460	.10	.20	.50

F.A.O. Issue

Y#	Date	Year	Mintage	VF	XF	Unc
112	BE2520	(1977)	2.000	.15	.40	1.00

Graduation of Princess Sirindhorn

Y#	Date	Year	Mintage	VF	XF	Unc
114	BE2520	(1977)	8.998	.15	.40	1.00

BRONZE

Y#	Date	Year	Mintage	VF	XF	Unc
114a	BE2520	(1977)	—	—	—	—

Investiture of Princess Sirindhorn

Y#	Date	Year	Mintage	VF	XF	Unc
124	BE2520	(1977)	5.000	.15	.40	1.00

Graduation of Crown Prince Vijiralongkorn

Y#	Date	Year	Mintage	VF	XF	Unc
127	BE2521	(1978)	5.000	.10	.20	.50

8th Asian Games

Y#	Date	Year	Mintage	VF	XF	Unc
130	BE2521	1978	5.000	.10	.20	.50

World Food Day

Y#	Date	Year	Mintage	VF	XF	Unc
157	BE2525	(1982)	1.500	.10	.20	.50

Obv: Large portrait w/collar touching hairline.

Y#	Date	Year	Mintage	VF	XF	Unc
159.1	BE2525	(1982)	123.585	.10	.20	.50
	2527	(1984)	—	.10	.20	.50
	2528	(1985)	—	.10	.20	.50

Obv: Small portrait w/space between collar and lower hairline.

Y#	Date	Year	Mintage	VF	XF	Unc
159.2	BE2525	(1982)	Inc. Ab.	2.50	5.00	10.00

Circulation Coinage

Y#	Date	Year	Mintage	VF	XF	Unc
183	BE2529	(1986)	—	—	—	.10
	2530	(1987)	325.271	—	—	.10
	2531	(1988)	391.442	—	—	.10
	2532	(1989)	—	—	—	.10
	2533	(1990)	—	—	—	.10
	2534	(1991)	—	—	—	.10
	2535	(1992)	—	—	—	.10

2 BAHT

COPPER-NICKEL
Graduation of Princess Chulabhorn

Y#	Date	Year	Mintage	VF	XF	Unc
134	BE2522	(1979)	5.000	.20	.40	1.00

COPPER-NICKEL CLAD COPPER
International Youth Year

Y#	Date	Year	Mintage	VF	XF	Unc
176	BE2528	1985	5.000	.20	.40	1.00

XIII SEA Games

Y#	Date	Year	Mintage	VF	XF	Unc
177	BE2528	1985	5.000	.20	.40	1.00

National Years of the Trees

Y#	Date	Year	Mintage	VF	XF	Unc
178	ND	(1986)	3.000	.50	1.00	3.50

Year of Peace

Y#	Date	Year	Mintage	VF	XF	Unc
180	BE2529	1986	5.000	—	—	.50

Chulachomklao Royal Military Academy

Y#	Date	Year	Mintage	VF	XF	Unc
188	BE2530	(1987)	—	—	—	.50

Princess Chulabhorn Awarded Einstein Medal

Y#	Date	Year	Mintage	VF	XF	Unc
191	BE2529	(1986)	—	—	—	.50

King's 60th Birthday

Y#	Date	Year	Mintage	VF	XF	Unc
194	BE2530	(1987)	—	—	—	.50

72nd Anniversary of Thai Cooperatives

Y#	Date	Year	Mintage	VF	XF	Unc
204	BE2531	(1988)	—	—	—	.50

42nd Year of Reign of King Bhumifhol

Y#	Date	Year	Mintage	VF	XF	Unc
210	BE2531	(1988)	—	—	—	.50

100th Anniversary of Siriraj Hospital

Y#	Date	Year	Mintage	VF	XF	Unc
220	BE2531	(1988)	—	—	—	.50

Crown Prince's Birthday

Y#	Date	Year	Mintage	VF	XF	Unc
222	BE2531	(1988)	—	—	—	.50

72nd Anniversary of Chulalongkorn University

Y#	Date	Year	Mintage	VF	XF	Unc
225	BE2532	(1989)	3.000	—	—	.50

Centennial of First Medical College

Y#	Date	Year	Mintage	VF	XF	Unc
230	BE2533	(1990)	3.412	—	—	.50

90th Birthday of Queen Mother

Y#	Date	Year	Mintage	VF	XF	Unc
232	BE2533	(1990)	2.000	—	—	.50

100th Anniversary - Office of
the Comptroller General

Y#	Date	Year	Mintage	VF	XF	Unc
235	BE2533	(1990)	1.000	—	—	.50

36th Birthday of Princess Sirindhorn

Y#	Date	Year	Mintage	VF	XF	Unc
237	BE2534	(1991)	2.300	—	—	.50

80th Anniversary of Thai Boy Scouts

Y#	Date	Year	Mintage	VF	XF	Unc
240	BE2534	(1991)	2.000	—	—	1.50

World Health Organization

Y#	Date	Year	Mintage	VF	XF	Unc
243	BE2534	(1991)	—	—	—	1.00

Centenary Celebration of King's Father

Y#	Date	Year	Mintage	VF	XF	Unc
248	BE2535	(1992)	—	—	—	.50

Ministry of Justice Centennial

Y#	Date	Year	Mintage	VF	XF	Unc
251	1992		—	—	—	.50

Ministry of Interior Centennial

Y#	Date	Year	Mintage	VF	XF	Unc
253	1992		—	—	—	.50

Princess Sirindhorn's Magsaysay Foundation Award

Y#	Date	Year	Mintage	VF	XF	Unc
255	1992		—	—	—	.50

Queen's 60th Birthday

Y#	Date	Year	Mintage	VF	XF	Unc
259	BE2535	(1992)	—	—	—	.50

60th Anniversary of the National Assembly -
Anatasamakhom Throne Hall

Y#	Date	Year	Mintage	VF	XF	Unc
268	BE2535	(1992)	—	—	—	.50

Ministry of Agriculture

Y#	Date	Year	Mintage	VF	XF	Unc
270	BE2535	(1992)	—	—	—	.5

King's 64th Birthday

Y#	Date	Year	Mintage	VF	XF	Unc
272	BE2535	(1992)	—	—	—	.50

Centennial of Thai Teacher Training - Emblem

276	BE2535	(1992)	—	—	—	.50

Centennial of Thai National Bank - Seated Figure

277	BE2535	(1992)	—	—	—	.50

Centennial of Attorney General's Office - Scale

278	BE2536	(1993)	—	—	—	.50

Centennial of Thai Red Cross - Symbols

279	BE2536	(1993)	—	—	—	.50

Treasury Department

282	BE2536	(1993)	—	—	—	.50

100th Anniversary of Rama VII

288	BE2536	(1993)	—	—	—	.50

5 BAHT

COPPER-NICKEL

98	BE2515	(1972)	30.016	.30	.60	1.20

COPPER-NICKEL CLAD COPPER

111	BE2520	(1977)	27.257	.30	.60	1.20
	2522	(1979)	72.740	.30	.60	1.20

King's 50th Birthday
Obv. leg: *Prathet Thai.*

Y#	Date	Year	Mintage	VF	XF	Unc
120	BE2520	(1977)	5.000	.35	.75	1.50

Error: Obv. leg. *Siam Minta.*

121	BE2520	(1977)	—	1.00	2.00	4.50

8th Asian Games

131	BE2521	1978	.500	.35	.75	1.50

Royal Cradle Ceremony

132	BE2522	(1979)	1.000	.35	.75	1.50

Queen's Anniversary and F.A.O. Ceres Medal

137	BE2523	(1980)	9.000	.25	.50	1.25

80th Birthday of King's Mother

140	BE2523	(1980)	3.504	.25	.50	1.25

Rama VII Constitutional Monarchy

Y#	Date	Year	Mintage	VF	XF	Unc
144	BE2523	(1980)	2.113	.25	.50	1.25

King Rama VI Birth Centennial

142	BE2524	(1981)	2.222	.25	.50	1.25

Bicentennial of Bangkok

149	BE2525	(1982)	5.000	.25	.50	1.25

World Food Day

158	BE2525	(1982)	.400	.35	.75	1.50

160	BE2525	(1982)	.200	.50	1.00	1.75
	2528	(1985)	—	.50	1.00	1.75
	2529	(1986)	—	.50	1.00	1.75

75th Anniversary of Boy Scouts

161	BE2525	(1982)	.200	.50	1.00	1.75

84th Birthday of Princess Mother

Y#	Date	Year	Mintage	VF	XF	Unc
171	BE2527	(1984)	.480	.35	.75	1.50

200th Anniversary - Birth of Rama III

Y#	Date	Year	Mintage	VF	XF	Unc
184	BE2530	(1987)	—	—	—	.75

Circulation Coinage

Y#	Date	Year	Mintage	VF	XF	Unc
185	BE2530	(1987)	14.000	—	—	.75
	2531	(1988)	—	—	—	.75

King's 60th Birthday

Y#	Date	Year	Mintage	VF	XF	Unc
195	BE2530	(1987)	—	—	—	1.00

42nd Year - Reign of King Bhumifhol

Y#	Date	Year	Mintage	VF	XF	Unc
211	BE2531	(1988)	—	—	—	1.00

Circulation Coinage

Y#	Date	Year	Mintage	VF	XF	Unc
219	BE2531	(1988)	—	—	—	.50
	2532	(1989)	—	—	—	.50
	2533	(1990)	—	—	—	.50
	2534	(1991)	—	—	—	.50
	2535	(1992)	—	—	—	.50

Queen's 60th Birthday

Y#	Date	Year	Mintage	VF	XF	Unc
260	BE2535	(1992)	—	—	—	1.25

10 BAHT

5.0000 g, .800 SILVER, .1286 oz ASW
King Bhumiphol 25th Anniversary of Reign

Y#	Date	Year	Mintage	VF	XF	Unc
92	BE2514	(1971)	2.000	BV	1.50	2.50

NICKEL
Crown Prince Vajiralongkorn and Princess Soamsawali Wedding

Y#	Date	Year	Mintage	VF	XF	Unc
117	BE2520	(1977)	1.890	.50	1.00	2.00

Graduation of Princess Sirindhorn

Y#	Date	Year	Mintage	VF	XF	Unc
115	BE2520	(1977)	2.095	.50	1.00	2.00

BRONZE

Y#	Date	Year	Mintage	VF	XF	Unc
115a	BE2520	(1977)	—	—	—	20.00

NICKEL
Graduation of Princess Chulabhorn

Y#	Date	Year	Mintage	VF	XF	Unc
135	BE2522	(1979)	1.196	.50	1.00	2.00

80th Birthday of King's Mother

Y#	Date	Year	Mintage	VF	XF	Unc
141	BE2523	(1980)	1.288	.50	1.00	2.00

30th Anniversary of Buddhist Fellowship

Y#	Date	Year	Mintage	VF	XF	Unc
145	BE2523	(1980)	1.035	.50	1.00	2.00

King Rama IX Anniversary of Reign

Y#	Date	Year	Mintage	VF	XF	Unc
146	BE2524	(1981)	2.039	.50	1.00	2.00

50th Birthday of Queen Sirikit

Y#	Date	Year	Mintage	VF	XF	Unc
154	BE2525	(1982)	.500	.75	1.25	2.25
	2525	(1982)	9,999	—	Proof	15.00

75th Anniversary of Boy Scouts
Similar to 5 Baht, Y#161.

Y#	Date	Year	Mintage	VF	XF	Unc
162	BE2525	(1982)	.100	1.00	1.50	2.50
	2525	(1982)	1,500	—	Proof	25.00

100th Anniversary of Postal Service

Y#	Date	Year	Mintage	VF	XF	Unc
163	BE2526	(1983)	.300	.50	1.00	2.00
	2526	(1983)	5,000	—	Proof	17.50

700th Anniversary of Thai Alphabet

Y#	Date	Year	Mintage	VF	XF	Unc
165	BE2526	(1983)	.500	.50	1.00	2.00
	2526	(1983)	4,667	—	Proof	17.50

84th Birthday of Princess Mother
Similar to 5 Baht, Y#171.

Y#	Date	Year	Mintage	VF	XF	Unc
172	BE2527	(1984)	.180	.75	1.25	2.25
	2527	(1984)	3,192	—	Proof	20.00

72nd Anniversary of Government Savings Bank

Y#	Date	Year	Mintage	VF	XF	Unc
175	BE2528	(1985)	.500	.50	1.00	2.0
	2528	(1985)	2,600	—	Proof	20.0

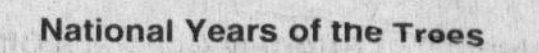

National Years of the Trees

Y#	Date	Year	Mintage	VF	XF	Unc
79	ND	(1986)	.100	.75	1.50	4.00
	ND	(1986)	5,000	—	Proof	17.50

6th ASEAN Orchid Congress

Y#	Date	Year	Mintage	VF	XF	Unc
81	BE2529	1986	—	—	—	2.00
	2529	1986	—	—	Proof	17.50

Chulachomklao Royal Military Academy

Y#	Date	Year	Mintage	VF	XF	Unc
89	BE2530	(1987)	—	—	—	2.00

Asian Institute of Technology

Y#	Date	Year	Mintage	VF	XF	Unc
90	BE2530	(1987)	—	—	—	2.00
	2530	(1987)	—	—	Proof	17.50

Princess Chulabhorn Awarded Einstein Medal

Y#	Date	Year	Mintage	VF	XF	Unc
92	BE2529	(1986)	—	—	—	2.00
	2529	(1986)	—	—	Proof	17.50

King's 60th Birthday

Y#	Date	Year	Mintage	VF	XF	Unc
96	BE2530	(1987)	—	—	—	2.00
	2530	(1987)	—	—	Proof	17.50

72nd Anniversary of Thai Cooperatives

Y#	Date	Year	Mintage	VF	XF	Unc
205	BE2531	(1988)	—	—	—	2.00
	2530	(1988)	—	—	Proof	17.50

42nd Year - Reign of King Bhumifhol

Y#	Date	Year	Mintage	VF	XF	Unc
212	BE2531	(1988)	—	—	—	2.00
	2531	(1988)	—	—	Proof	17.50

100th Anniversary of Siriraj Hospital

Y#	Date	Year	Mintage	VF	XF	Unc
221	BE2531	(1988)	—	—	—	2.00
	2531	(1988)	—	—	Proof	17.50

Crown Prince's Birthday

Y#	Date	Year	Mintage	VF	XF	Unc
223	BE2531	(1988)	—	—	—	2.00
	2531	(1988)	—	—	Proof	17.50

STAINLESS STEEL RING, ALUMINUM-BRONZE CORE

Y#	Date	Year	Mintage	VF	XF	Unc
227	BE2531	(1988)	.100	—	—	2.00
	2532	(1989)	200.000	—	—	2.00
	2534	(1991)	—	—	—	2.00
	2535	(1992)	—	—	—	2.00
	2536	(1993)	—	—	—	2.00

NICKEL
Chulalongkorn University

Y#	Date	Year	Mintage	VF	XF	Unc
228	BE2532	(1989)	.500	—	—	2.00

COPPER-NICKEL
Centennial of First Medical College

Y#	Date	Year	Mintage	VF	XF	Unc
231	BE2533	(1990)	.290	—	—	2.00
	2533	(1990)	5,000	—	Proof	17.50

90th Birthday of the Princess Mother

Y#	Date	Year	Mintage	VF	XF	Unc
233	BE2533	(1990)	.500	—	—	2.50
	2533	(1990)	3,200	—	Proof	17.50

100th Anniversary - Office of Comptroller General

Y#	Date	Year	Mintage	VF	XF	Unc
236	BE2533	(1990)	.300	—	—	2.50

36th Birthday of Princess Sirindhorn

Y#	Date	Year	Mintage	VF	XF	Unc
238	BE2534	(1991)	1.000	—	—	2.50
	2534	(1991)	1,000	—	Proof	20.00

80th Anniversary of Thai Boy Scouts

Y#	Date	Year	Mintage	VF	XF	Unc
241	BE2534	(1991)	1.000	—	—	3.00

World Health Organization

Y#	Date	Year	Mintage	VF	XF	Unc
244	BE2534	(1991)	—	—	—	3.00
	2534	(1991)	—	—	Proof	17.50

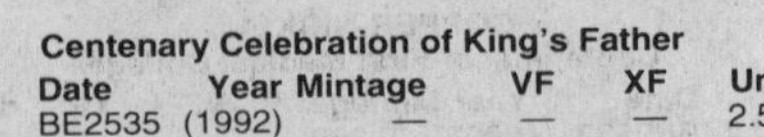

Centenary Celebration of King's Father

Y#	Date	Year	Mintage	VF	XF	Unc
249	BE2535	(1992)	—	—	—	2.50
	2535	(1992)	—	—	Proof	17.50

Ministry of Justice Centennial

Y#	Date	Year	Mintage	VF	XF	Unc
252	BE2535	(1992)	—	—	—	2.50
	2535	(1992)	—	—	Proof	17.50

Ministry of Interior Centennial

Y#	Date	Year	Mintage	VF	XF	Unc
254	BE2535	(1992)	—	—	—	2.50
	2535	(1992)	—	—	Proof	17.50

Princess Sirindhorn's Magsaysay Foundation Award

Y#	Date	Year	Mintage	VF	XF	Unc
256	BE2535	(1992)	—	—	—	2.50
	2535	(1992)	—	—	Proof	17.50

Queen's 60th Birthday

Y#	Date	Year	Mintage	VF	XF	Unc
261	BE2535	(1992)	—	—	—	2.50

60th Anniversary of National Assembly

Y#	Date	Year	Mintage	VF	XF	Unc
269	BE2535	(1992)	—	—	—	2.50

Ministry of Agriculture

Y#	Date	Year	Mintage	VF	XF	Unc
271	BE2535	(1992)	—	—	—	2.50
	2535	(1992)	—	—	Proof	17.50

King's 64th Birthday

Y#	Date	Year	Mintage	VF	XF	Unc
273	BE2535	(1992)	—	—	—	2.50

Centennial of Thai Teacher Training - Emblem

Y#	Date	Year	Mintage	VF	XF	Unc
284	BE2535	(1992)	—	—	—	2.50

Centennial of Thai National Bank - Seated Figure

Y#	Date	Year	Mintage	VF	XF	Unc
285	BE2535	(1992)	—	—	—	2.50

Centennial of Thai Red Cross - Symbols

Y#	Date	Year	Mintage	VF	XF	Unc
280	BE2536	(1993)	—	—	—	2.50

Treasury Department

Y#	Date	Year	Mintage	VF	XF	Unc
283	BE2536	(1993)	—	—	—	2.50

Centennial of Attorney General's Office

Y#	Date	Year	Mintage	VF	XF	Unc
286	BE2536	(1993)	—	—	—	2.50

100th Anniversary of Rama VII

Y#	Date	Year	Mintage	VF	XF	Unc
289	BE2536	(1993)	—	—	—	2.50

20 BAHT

19.6000 g, .750 SILVER, .4726 oz ASW
King Bhumiphol 36th Birthday

Y#	Date	Year	Mintage	VF	XF	Unc
86	ND	(1963)	1.000	—	5.00	8.50

50 BAHT

24.7000 g, .900 SILVER, .7147 oz ASW
20th Year Buddhist Fellowship

Y#	Date	Year	Mintage	VF	XF	Unc
95	BE2514	(1971)	.200	—	9.00	15.00
	2514	(1971)	.060	—	P/L	18.00

24.8500 g, .400 SILVER, .3195 oz ASW
National Museum Centennial

Y#	Date	Year	Mintage	VF	XF	Unc
101	BE2517	(1974)	.200	—	7.00	14.00

25.5500 g, .500 SILVER, .4173 oz ASW
Conservation - Sumatran Rhinoceros

Y#	Date	Year	Mintage	VF	XF	Unc
102	BE2517	(1974)	.020	—	—	20.00

28.2800 g, .925 SILVER, .8411 oz ASW

Y#	Date	Year	Mintage	VF	XF	Unc
102a	BE2517	(1974)	9,885	—	Proof	40.00

100 BAHT

31.9000 g, .500 SILVER, .5128 oz ASW
Conservation - Brown-antlered Deer

Y#	Date	Year	Mintage	VF	XF	Unc
103	BE2517	(1974)	.020	—	—	25.00

35.0000 g, .925 SILVER, 1.0409 oz ASW

Y#	Date	Year	Mintage	VF	XF	Unc
103a	BE2517	(1974)	9,294	—	Proof	50.00

25.0000 g, .900 SILVER, .7234 oz AGW
100th Anniversary - Ministry of Finance

Y#	Date	Year	Mintage	VF	XF	Unc
106	BE2518	(1975)	.030	—	8.00	12.50

COPPER-NICKEL
International Monetary Fund

Y#	Date	Year	Mintage	VF	XF	Unc
242	BE2534	1991	.500	—	—	10.00
	2534	1991	.060	—	Proof	40.00

King and Prince in Scouting - Emblem

Y#	Date	Year	Mintage	VF	XF	Unc
287	SE2536	(1993)	—	—	—	10.00

150 BAHT

3.7500 g, .900 GOLD, .1085 oz AGW

Queen Sirikit 36th Birthday

Y#	Date	Year	Mintage	VF	XF	Unc
88	BE2511	(1968)	.200	—	—	50.00

22.0000 g, .925 SILVER, .6543 oz ASW
75th Birthday of Princess Mother

Y#	Date	Year	Mintage	VF	XF	Unc
108	BE2518	(1975)	.200	—	10.00	18.00

F.A.O. Issue

Y#	Date	Year	Mintage	VF	XF	Unc
113	BE2520	(1977)	.050	—	10.00	20.00

Crown Prince Vajiralongkorn and
Princess Soamsawali Wedding

Y#	Date	Year	Mintage	VF	XF	Unc
118	BE2520	(1977)	.200	—	10.00	18.00

Graduation of Princess Sirindhorn

Y#	Date	Year	Mintage	VF	XF	Unc
116	BE2520	(1977)	.100	—	10.00	18.00

Investiture of Princess Sirindhorn

Y#	Date	Year	Mintage	VF	XF	Unc
125	BE2520	(1977)	.050	—	10.00	20.00

9th World Orchid Conference

Y#	Date	Year	Mintage	VF	XF	Unc
123	BE2521	1978	.030	—	10.00	22.50

Graduation of Crown Prince Vijiralongkorn

Y#	Date	Year	Mintage	VF	XF	Unc
128	BE2521	(1978)	.050	—	10.00	20.00

7.5000 g, .925 SILVER, .2230 oz ASW
King's 60th Birthday
Similar to 6000 Baht, Y#202.

Y#	Date	Year	Mintage	VF	XF	Unc
197	BE2530	(1987)	—	—	—	20.00
	2530	(1987)	—	—	Proof	120.00

42nd Year of Reign of King Bhumifhol
Similar to 10 Baht, Y#212.

Y#	Date	Year	Mintage	VF	XF	Unc
213	BE2531	(1988)	—	—	—	22.50
	2531	(1988)	—	—	Proof	135.00

Queen's 60th Birthday
Similar to 10 Baht, Y#261.

Y#	Date	Year	Mintage	VF	XF	Unc
262	BE2535	(1992)	—	—	—	20.00

200 BAHT

22.0000 g, .925 SILVER, .6544 oz ASW
Royal Cradle Ceremony

Y#	Date	Year	Mintage	VF	XF	Unc
133	BE2522	(1979)	.050	—	10.00	20.00

23.3200 g, .925 SILVER, .6935 oz ASW
International Year of the Child

Y#	Date	Year	Mintage	VF	XF	Unc
152	BE2524	1981	9,525	—	Proof	60.00

23.1800 g, .925 SILVER, .6894 oz ASW
25th Anniversary of World Wildlife Fund
Siamese Fireback Pheasant

Y#	Date	Year	Mintage	VF	XF	Unc
206	BE2530	1987	*.025	—	Proof	50.00

250 BAHT

28.2800 g, .925 SILVER, .8411 oz ASW
International Year of Disabled Persons

Y#	Date	Year	Mintage	VF	XF	Unc
169	BE2526	1983	307 pcs.	—	—	200.00
	2526	1983	233 pcs.	—	Proof	475.00

300 BAHT

7.5000 g, .900 GOLD, .2170 oz AGW
Queen Sirikit 36th Birthday

Y#	Date	Year	Mintage	VF	XF	Unc
89	BE2511	(1968)	.101	—	—	100.00

22.0000 g, .925 SILVER, .6543 oz ASW
Graduation of Princess Chulabhorn

Y#	Date	Year	Mintage	VF	XF	Unc
136	BE2522	(1979)	.020	—	15.00	20.00

15.0000 g, .925 SILVER, .4461 oz ASW
King's 60th Birthday
Similar to 6000 Baht, Y#202.

Y#	Date	Year	Mintage	VF	XF	Unc
198	BE2530	(1987)	—	—	—	18.00
	2530	(1987)	—	—	Proof	25.00

42nd Year of Reign of King Bhumifhol
Similar to 10 Baht, Y#212.

Y#	Date	Year	Mintage	VF	XF	Unc
214	BE2531	(1988)	—	—	—	20.00
	2531	(1988)	—	—	Proof	35.00

Queen's 60th Birthday
Similar to 10 Baht, Y#261.

Y#	Date	Year	Mintage	VF	XF	Unc
263	BE2535	(1992)	—	—	—	17.50

400 BAHT

10.0000 g, .900 GOLD, .2893 oz AGW
King Bhumiphol 25th Anniversary of Reign

Y#	Date	Year	Mintage	VF	XF	Unc
93	BE2514	(1971)	.047	—	—	130.00

600 BAHT

15.0000 g, .900 GOLD, .4340 oz AGW
Queen Sirikit 36th Birthday

Y#	Date	Year	Mintage	VF	XF	Unc
90	BE2511	(1968)	.046	—	—	190.00

14.9000 g, .925 SILVER, .4432 oz ASW
Queen's Anniversary and F.A.O. Ceres Medal

Y#	Date	Year	Mintage	VF	XF	Unc
138	BE2523	(1980)	.023	—	28.00	38.00

Rama VI Birth Centennial

Y#	Date	Year	Mintage	VF	XF	Unc
143	BE2524	(1981)	.019	—	28.00	38.00

King Rama IX Anniversary of Reign

Y#	Date	Year	Mintage	VF	XF	Unc
147	BE2524	(1981)	.015	—	28.00	38.00

Bicentennial of Bangkok

Y#	Date	Year	Mintage	VF	XF	Unc
150	BE2525	(1982)	.015	—	28.00	38.00

22.0000 g, .925 SILVER, .6543 oz ASW
50th Birthday of Queen Sirikit

Y#	Date	Year	Mintage	VF	XF	Unc
155	BE2525	(1982)	3,895	—	28.00	55.00
	2525	(1982)	1,011	—	Proof	250.00

100th Anniversary of Postage Stamps

Y#	Date	Year	Mintage	VF	XF	Unc
164	BE2526	1983	5,000	—	28.00	55.00
	2526	1983	1,400	—	Proof	225.00

700th Anniversary of Thai Alphabet

Y#	Date	Year	Mintage	VF	XF	Unc
166	BE2526	(1983)	4,300	—	28.00	55.00
	2526	(1983)	780 pcs.	—	Proof	235.00

84th Birthday of Princess Mother

Y#	Date	Year	Mintage	VF	XF	Unc
173	BE2527	(1984)	3,530	—	28.00	45.00
	2527	(1984)	497 pcs.	—	Proof	285.00

6th ASEAN Orchid Congress
Similar to 10 Baht, Y#181.

Y#	Date	Year	Mintage	VF	XF	Unc
182	BE2529	1986	—	—	—	40.00
	2529	1986	—	—	Proof	190.00

Princess Chulabhorn Awarded Einstein Medal
Similar to 10 Baht, Y#192.

Y#	Date	Year	Mintage	VF	XF	Unc
193	BE2529	(1986)	—	—	—	50.00
	2529	(1986)	—	—	Proof	175.00

30.0000 g, .925 SILVER, .8922 oz ASW

King's 60th Birthday
Similar to 6000 Baht, Y#202.

Y#	Date	Year	Mintage	VF	XF	Unc
199	BE2530	(1987)	—	—	—	100.00
	2530	(1987)	—	—	Proof	350.00

Asian Institute of Technology
Similar to 10 Baht, Y#190.

Y#	Date	Year	Mintage	VF	XF	Unc
229	BE2530	(1987)	—	—	—	40.00
	2530	(1987)	—	—	Proof	125.00

42nd Year of Reign of King Bhumifhol
Similar to 10 Baht, Y#212.

Y#	Date	Year	Mintage	VF	XF	Unc
215	BE2531	(1988)	—	—	—	45.00
	2531	(1988)	—	—	Proof	175.00

Crown Prince's Birthday

Y#	Date	Year	Mintage	VF	XF	Unc
224	BE2531	(1988)	—	—	—	45.00
	2531	(1988)	—	—	Proof	225.00

30.0000 g, .900 SILVER, .8682 oz ASW
72nd Anniversary of Chulalongkorn University

Y#	Date	Year	Mintage	VF	XF	Unc
226	BE2532	(1989)	.010	—	—	50.00

30.0000 g, .925 SILVER, .8922 oz ASW
90th Birthday of Princess Mother

Y#	Date	Year	Mintage	VF	XF	Unc
234	BE2533	(1990)	.020	—	—	45.00
	2533	(1990)	2,000	—	Proof	150.00

30.0000 g, .900 SILVER, .8682 oz ASW
36th Birthday of Princess Sirindhorn

Y#	Date	Year	Mintage	VF	XF	Unc
239	BE2534	(1991)	.030	—	—	45.00
	2534	(1991)	250 pcs.	—	Proof	375.00

30.0000 g, .925 SILVER, .8922 oz ASW
World Health Organization
Similar to 10 Baht, Y#244.

Y#	Date	Year	Mintage	VF	XF	Unc
245	BE2534	(1991)	—	—	—	45.00
	2534	(1991)	—	—	Proof	145.00

Centenary Celebration of King's Father
Similar to 10 Baht, Y#249.

Y#	Date	Year	Mintage	VF	XF	Unc
250	BE2535	(1992)	—	—	—	45.00
	2535	(1992)	—	—	Proof	250.00

Princess Sirindhorn's Magsaysay Foundation Award

Y#	Date	Year	Mintage	VF	XF	Unc
257	BE2535	(1992)	—	—	—	40.00
	2535	(1992)	—	—	Proof	250.00

Queen's 60th Birthday
Similar to 10 Baht, Y#261.

Y#	Date	Year	Mintage	VF	XF	Unc
264	BE2535	(1992)	—	—	—	40.00
	2535	(1992)	—	—	Proof	300.00

King's 64th Birthday
Similar to 10 Baht, Y#273.

Y#	Date	Year	Mintage	VF	XF	Unc
274	BE2535	(1992)	—	—	—	40.00
	2535	(1992)	—	—	Proof	300.00

Centennial of Thai Red Cross Emblems

Y#	Date	Year	Mintage	VF	XF	Unc
281	BE2536	(1993)	—	—	—	40.00

100th Anniversary of Rama VII
Similar to 10 Baht, Y#289.

Y#	Date	Year	Mintage	VF	XF	Unc
290	BE2536	(1993)	—	—	—	30.00

800 BAHT

20.0000 g, .900 GOLD, .5787 oz AGW
King Bhumiphol 25th Anniversary of Reign

Y#	Date	Year	Mintage	VF	XF	Unc
94	BE2514	(1971)	.022	—	—	250.00

1500 BAHT

3.7500 g, .900 GOLD, .1085 oz AGW
King's 60th Birthday

Y#	Date	Year	Mintage	VF	XF	Unc
200	BE2530	(1987)	—	—	—	80.00
	2530	(1987)	—	—	Proof	120.00

42nd Year - Reign of King Bhumifhol

Y#	Date	Year	Mintage	VF	XF	Unc
216	BE2531	(1988)	—	—	—	75.00
	2531	(1988)	—	—	Proof	150.00

Queen's 60th Birthday
Similar to 10 Baht, Y#261.

Y#	Date	Year	Mintage	VF	XF	Unc
265	BE2535	(1992)	.010	—	—	75.00

2500 BAHT

15.0000 g, .900 GOLD, .4340 oz AGW
Crown Prince Vajiralongkorn and
Princess Soamsawali Wedding

Y#	Date	Year	Mintage	VF	XF	Unc
119	BE2520	(1977)	.020	—	—	225.00

Investiture of Princess Sirindhorn

Y#	Date	Year	Mintage	VF	XF	Unc
126	BE2520	(1977)	5,000	—	—	325.00

International Year of Disabled Persons

Y#	Date	Year	Mintage	VF	XF	Unc
170	BE2526	(1983)	92 pcs.	—	—	650.00
	2526	(1983)	793 pcs.	—	Proof	750.00

15.9800 g, .900 GOLD, .4625 oz AGW
25th Anniversary of World Wildlife Fund
Asian Elephant

Y#	Date	Year	Mintage	VF	XF	Unc
207	BE2530	1987	*5,000	—	Proof	400.00

3000 BAHT

15.0000 g, .900 GOLD, .4340 oz AGW
Graduation of Crown Prince Vijiralongkorn

Y#	Date	Year	Mintage	VF	XF	Unc
129	BE2521	(1978)	.010	—	—	200.00

7.5000 g, .900 GOLD, .2170 oz AGW
King's 60th Birthday

Y#	Date	Year	Mintage	VF	XF	Unc
201	BE2530	(1987)	—	—	—	150.00
	2530	(1987)	—	—	Proof	240.00

42nd Year - Reign of King Bhumifhol

Y#	Date	Year	Mintage	VF	XF	Unc
217	BE2531	(1988)	—	—	—	150.00
	2531	(1988)	—	—	Proof	300.00

Queen's 60th Birthday
Similar to 10 Baht, Y#261.

Y#	Date	Year	Mintage	VF	XF	Unc
266	BE2535	(1992)	.010	—	—	150.00

4000 BAHT

17.1700 g, .900 GOLD, .4969 oz AGW
International Year of the Child

Y#	Date	Year	Mintage	VF	XF	Unc
153	BE2524	(1981)	3,963	—	Proof	400.00

5000 BAHT

33.4370 g, .900 GOLD, .9676 oz AGW
Conservation - White-Eyed River Martin

Y#	Date	Year	Mintage	VF	XF	Unc
104	BE2517	(1974)	2,602	—	—	650.00
	BE2517	(1974)	623 pcs.	—	Proof	1850.

30.0000 g, .900 GOLD, .8681 oz AGW
King's 50th Birthday

Y#	Date	Year	Mintage	VF	XF	Unc
122	BE2520	(1977)	6,400	—	—	425.00

6000 BAHT

15.0000 g, .900 GOLD, .4341 oz AGW
50th Birthday of Queen Sirikit

Y#	Date	Year	Mintage	VF	XF	Unc
156	BE2525	(1982)	1,471	—	—	350.00
	2525	(1982)	99 pcs.	—	Proof	2600.

700th Anniversary of Thai Alphabet

Y#	Date	Year	Mintage	VF	XF	Unc
167	BE2526	(1983)	700 pcs.	—	—	350.00
	2526	(1983)	235 pcs.	—	Proof	600.00

84th Birthday of Princess Mother

Y#	Date	Year	Mintage	VF	XF	Unc
174	BE2527	(1984)	835 pcs.	—	—	350.00
	2527	(1984)	246 pcs.	—	Proof	600.00

King's 60th Birthday

Y#	Date	Year	Mintage	VF	XF	Unc
202	BE2530	(1987)	—	—	—	275.00
	2530	(1987)	—	—	Proof	425.00

Asian Institute of Technology

Y#	Date	Year	Mintage	VF	XF	Unc
247	BE2530	(1987)	—	—	—	350.00

42nd Year of Reign of King Bhumifhol

Y#	Date	Year	Mintage	VF	XF	Unc
218	BE2531	(1988)	—	—	—	300.00
	2531	(1988)	—	—	Proof	500.00

World Health Organization

Y#	Date	Year	Mintage	VF	XF	Unc
246	BE2534	(1991)	—	—	—	300.00
	2534	(1991)	—	—	Proof	600.00

Princess Sirindhorn's Magsaysay Foundation Award
Obv: Princess seated w/children. Rev: Obverse
of medal above larger reverse w/inscription.

Y#	Date	Year	Mintage	VF	XF	Unc
258	BE2535	(1992)	—	—	—	300.00
	2535	(1992)	—	—	Proof	600.00

Queen's 60th Birthday
Similar to 10 Baht, Y#261.

Y#	Date	Year	Mintage	VF	XF	Unc
267	BE2535	(1992)	.010	—	—	300.00

King's 64th Birthday
Similar to 10 Baht, Y#273.

Y#	Date	Year	Mintage	VF	XF	Unc
275	BE2535	(1992)	—	—	—	300.00

100th Anniversary of Rama VII
Obv: Portrait left.
Rev: Royal crown and accouterments.

Y#	Date	Year	Mintage	VF	XF	Unc
291	BE2536	(1993)	—	—	—	300.00

9000 BAHT

12.0000 g, .900 GOLD, .3472 oz AGW
Queen's Anniversary and F.A.O. Ceres Medal
Similar to 5 Baht, Y#137.

Y#	Date	Year	Mintage	VF	XF	Unc
139	BE2523	(1980)	3,900	—	—	400.00

King Rama VI Birth Centennial

Y#	Date	Year Mintage	VF	XF	Unc
A143	BE2524 (1981)	2,600	—	—	400.00

15.0000 g, .900 GOLD, .4340 oz AGW
King Rama IX Anniversary of Reign

Y#	Date	Year Mintage	VF	XF	Unc
148	BE2524 (1981)	4,000	—	—	400.00

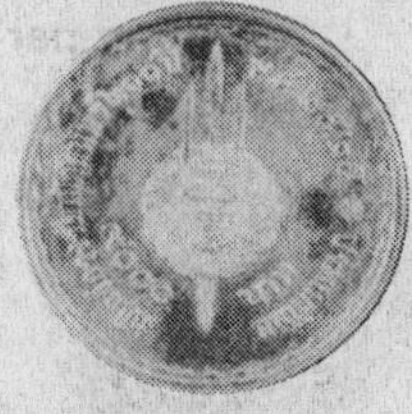

Bicentennial of Bangkok

Y#	Date	Year Mintage	VF	XF	Unc
151	BE2525 (1982)	3,290	—	—	400.00

OCCUPATION COINAGE

These coins were to be circulated in the 4 occupied provinces of Malaya during World War II. They were not put into circulation there but were later used in Japanese military service clubs in Bangkok before Japan's surrender in 1945.

SEN

TIN

KM#	Date	Mintage	VF	XF	Unc
5	BE2486	(1943)	—	—	—

5 SEN

TIN

KM#	Date	Mintage	VF	XF	Unc
10	BE2486	(1943)	—	—	—

10 SEN

TIN

KM#	Date	Mintage	VF	XF	Unc
15	BE2486	(1943)	—	350.00	500.00

BULLION ISSUES

In 1943, the government of Thailand made an internal loan by virtue of the Royal Act of Internal Loan related regulation of the Ministry of Finance, both dated 17th May, 1943.

Eight years later another Regulation of the Ministry of Finance dated 11th June, 1951 related to the actual redemption of the loan above mentioned was proclaimed with the following effect:

Bond holders have the choice to be paid either in gold coins or gold bars or in other forms, all of which should bear the Garuda emblem and the specific inscription as to its weight and gold purity.

50 BAHT

8.6930 g, .995 GOLD, .2781 oz AGW

KM#	Date	Mintage	VF	XF	Unc
1	ND(1951)	—	200.00	250.00	300.00

100 BAHT

17.3870 g, .995 GOLD, .5562 oz AGW

KM#	Date	Mintage	VF	XF	Unc
2	ND(1951)	—	450.00	500.00	600.00

1000 BAHT

173.8790 g, .995 GOLD, 5.5620 oz AGW

KM#	Date	Mintage	VF	XF	Unc
3	ND(1951)	—	4000.	5000.	6000.

MINT SETS (MS)

KM#	Date	Mintage	Identification	Issue Price	Mkt. Val.
MS1	ND(1895)(3)	—	Y13-15	—	—
MS2	Mixed(32)	—	Two each Y57,70,72,73 78a,78-87,91	22.00	60.00
MS3	Mixed(30)	—	Two each Y60,70,72,73, 78,78a,79,79a,80-86	—	30.00
MS4	Mixed(10)	—	Y70,72,73,78,78a,79, 79a,80-82	—	12.00
MS5	Mixed(8)	—	Y83,85-87,91,92,95,97	11.00	40.00
MS6	1975(2)	—	Y102-103	32.50	45.00
MS7	1988(7)	—	Y183,185-187,203, 208-209	—	3.50
MS8	1991(8)	—	Y183,186-187,203, 208-209,219,227	4.00	10.00
MS9	1992(8)	—	Y183,186-187,203, 208-209,219,227	—	10.00

PROOF SETS (PS)

KM#	Date	Mintage	Identification	Issue Price	Mkt. Val.
PS1	1975(2)	30,000	Y102a-103a	50.00	65.00

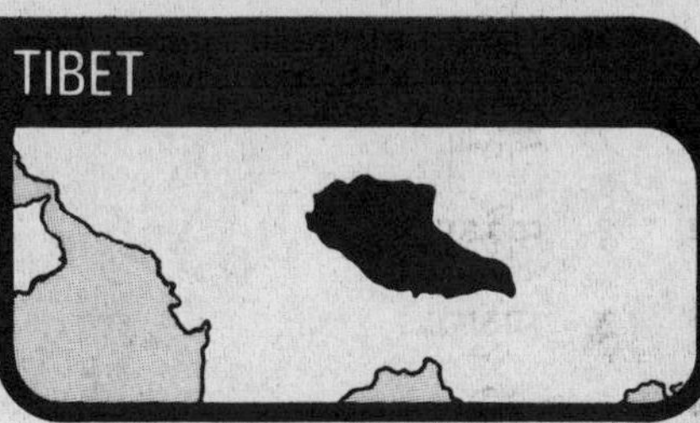

Tibet, an autonomous region of China located in central Asia between the Himalayan and Kunlun Mts. has an area of 471,660 sq. mi. (1,221,599 sq. km.) and a population of *1.9 million. Capital: Lhasa. The economy is based on agriculture and livestock raising. Wool, livestock, salt and hides are exported.

Lamaism, a form of Buddhism, developed in Tibet in the 8th century. From that time until the 1900s, the Dalai Lama virtually isolated the country from the outside world. The British in India achieved some influence in the early 20th century, and encouraged Tibet to declare its independence from China in 1913. The Communist revolution in China marked a new era in Tibetan history. Chinese Communist troops invaded Tibet in Oct., 1950. After a token resistance, Tibet signed an agreement with China in which China recognized the spiritual and temporal leadership of the Dalai Lama, and Tibet recognized the suzerainty of China. In 1959, a nationwide revolt triggered by Communist-initiated land reform broke out. The revolt was ruthlessly crushed. The Dalai Lama fled to India, and on Sept. 1, 1965, the Chinese made Tibet an autonomous region of China.

The first coins to circulate in Tibet were those of neighboring Nepal about 1570. Shortly after 1720, the Nepalese government began striking specific issues for use in Tibet; they were exchanged with the Tibetans for an equal weight in silver bullion. The first Tibetan government mint opened in 1791, but operations were suspended two years later. The Chinese opened a second mint in Lhasa in 1792. It produced a coinage until 1836. Shortly thereafter, the Tibetan mint was reopened and the government of Tibet continued to strike coins until 1953.

DATING

Based on the Tibetan calendar, Tibetan coins are dated by the cycle which contains 60 years. Example 15th cycle 25th year = 1891 AD.

13/40 = 1786	14/40 = 1846	15/40 = 1906
13/60 = 1806	14/60 = 1866	15/60 = 1926
14/20 = 1826	15/20 = 1886	16/20 = 1946

Certain Sino-Tibetan issues are dated in the year of reign of the Emperor of China.

MONETARY SYSTEM

15 Skar = 1-1/2 Sho = 1 Tangka
10 Sho = 1 Srang

TANGKA

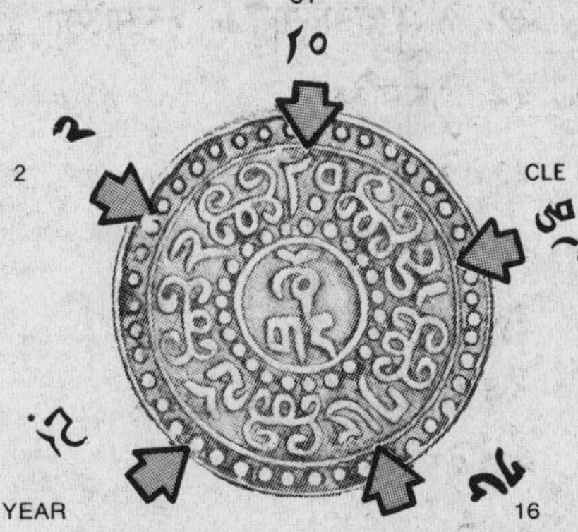

16(th)CYCLE 2(nd)YEAR = 1928AD

16(th) CYCLE 7(th) YEAR = 1933AD

16(th) CYCLE 7(th) YEAR = 1933AD

NUMERALS

1	༡	གཅིག		
2	༢	གཉིས		
3	༣	གསུམ		
4	༤	བཞི		
5	༥	ལྔ		
6	༦	དྲུག		
7	༧	བདུན		
8	༨	བརྒྱད		
9	༩	དགུ		
10	༡༠	བཅུ	or	བཅུ་ཐམ་པ
11	༡༡	བཅུག	or	བཅུ་གཅིག
12	༡༢	བཅུས	or	བཅུ་གཉིས
13	༡༣	བཅུ་ས	or	བཅུ་གསུམ
14	༡༤	བཅུ་བཞི		
15	༡༥	བཅོ་ལྔ		
16	༡༦	བཅུ་དྲུག		
17	༡༧	བཅུ་བདུན		
18	༡༨	བཅོ་བརྒྱད		
19	༡༩	བཅུ་དགུ		
20	༢༠	ཉི་ཤུ		
21	༢༡	ཉི་ཤུ་རྩ་གཅིག	or	ཉེར་གཅིག
22	༢༢	ཉེར་གཉིས		
23	༢༣	ཉེར་གསུམ		
24	༢༤	ཉེར་བཞི		
25	༢༥	ཉེར་ལྔ		
26	༢༦	ཉེར་དྲུག		
27	༢༧	ཉེར་བདུན		
28	༢༨	ཉེར་བརྒྱད		

SINO-TIBETAN COINAGE

RULERS

Chia Ch'ing, 1796-1820
Tao Kuang, 1820-1851
Hsuan T'ung, 1909-1911

Early Period: 1792-1836

SHO

SILVER, 3.40-3.80 g
25-29mm

C#	Date	Year	Good	VG	Fine	VF
83	8	(1803)	12.50	30.00	45.00	65.00
	9	(1804)	12.50	30.00	45.00	65.00
	24	(1819)	12.50	25.00	35.00	50.00
	25	(1820)	10.00	20.00	27.50	37.50

NOTE: Earlier dates (1-5) exist for this type.

One Miscal in Manchu script added, 30mm.

C#	Date	Year	Good	VG	Fine	VF
85	6	(1801)	—	—	Rare	—

26-28mm

C#	Date	Year	Good	VG	Fine	VF
93	1	(1821)	25.00	40.00	70.00	100.00
	2	(1822)	10.00	15.00	25.00	40.00
	3	(1823)	10.00	15.00	25.00	40.00
	4	(1824)	15.00	30.00	40.00	60.00
	15	(1835)	30.00	40.00	60.00	90.00
	16	(1836)	30.00	40.00	60.00	90.00

NOTE: Varieties of legend are reported but some authorities believe all of these are patterns.

In the name of Hsuan T'ung:

1/2 SKAR

COPPER, 3.10-3.60 g

Y#	Date	Mintage	Good	VG	Fine	VF
A4	(1910)	—	—	—	Rare	—

SKAR

COPPER, 5.40-6.60 g

Y#	Date	Mintage	Good	VG	Fine	VF
4	(1910)	—	40.00	50.00	80.00	160.00

SHO

SILVER, 3.30-4.10 g

Y#	Date	Mintage	Good	VG	Fine	VF
5	(1910)	—	20.00	30.00	40.00	60.00

NOTE: A variety exists, having the inner circle of dots, on the Chinese side, connected by lines.

2 SHO

SILVER, 5.20-8.40 g

Y#	Date	Mintage	Good	VG	Fine	VF
6	(1910)	—	25.00	40.00	80.00	150.00

NOTE: Varieties with different dragon claws exist.

TIBETAN COINAGE

'Kong-par' TANGKA

SILVER, 5.00-5.60 g
Rev: Sun and moon above date arch.

C#	Date	Year	Good	VG	Fine	VF
60.2	13-46	—	8.50	12.00	20.00	30.00

NOTE: It is believed that this type was struck in the 1820's.

4.20-5.60 g
Obv: Similar to C#60.1 but larger Buddhist characters.
Rev: Crescent and 3 dots above date arch.

C#	Date	Year	Good	VG	Fine	VF
60.3	13-46	—	3.00	4.50	7.00	10.00

NOTE: It is believed that this type was struck in the 1860's. Numerous minor varieties exist.

3.60-5.20 g
Mint: Giamda

C#	Date	Year	Good	VG	Fine	VF
A13.1	15-24	(1890)	3.00	4.00	6.00	9.00
	15-25	(1891)	4.00	5.50	9.00	14.00

Rev: 2 circles around lotus.

C#	Date	Year	Good	VG	Fine	VF
A13.2	15-24	(1890)	—	—	Rare	—

Miscellaneous TANGKAS

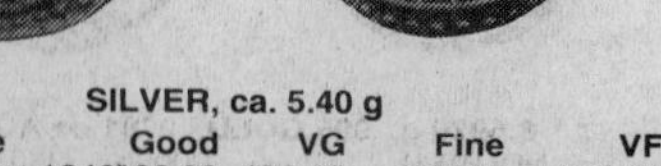

SILVER, ca. 5.40 g

C#	Date	Good	VG	Fine	VF
15	ND(ca.1840)	100.00	150.00	225.00	350.00

4.60-4.80 g

C#	Date	Year	Good	VG	Fine	VF
27	15-28	(1894)	4.00	8.00	13.00	20.00
	15-30	(1896)	15.00	23.00	30.00	40.00
	15-40	(1906)	4.00	8.00	13.00	20.00
	15-46	(1912)	25.00	35.00	45.00	60.00

NOTE: In addition to the above meaningful (probably) dates, the following meaningless ones exist: 13-16, 13-31, 13-92, 16-16, 16-61, 16-69, 16-92, 16-93, 92-39, 96-61 (sixes may be reversed threes and nines reversed ones). These are of billon, varying from 3.9 to 4.7 g.

NOTE: The legend appears to be in ornamental Lansa script and has yet to be deciphered. The type is a copy of the Nepalese issue: 'Cho-Tang'. Although struck unofficially, it was legal tender, due to an edict issued in 1881 ordering that no distinction be made between false and genuine coins!

NOTE: This type was cut to make change and the resulting fractions are occasionally encountered.

'Ga-den' TANGKA

SILVER, 5.00-5.50 g
Obv: 5 petals around lotus center.

Y#	Date	Mintage	Good	VG	Fine	VF
13	ND(ca.1850)	—	5.00	10.00	15.00	25.00

NOTE: Two major and numerous minor die varieties exist.

4.00-5.20 g
Dodpal Mint
Obv: 5 dots around lotus center, North symbol.

Y#	Date	Mintage	VG	Fine	VF	XF
13.1	ND(ca1875)	—	1.00	2.00	3.00	4.50

NOTE: Five major varieties exist.

Tip Arsenal Mint
3.90-5.20 g
Obv: 3 elongated dots on either side of lotus center and new arrangement of 8 symbols.

Y#	Date	Mintage	VG	Fine	VF	XF
13.2	ND(ca.1895-1901)		1.00	2.25	3.75	5.00

NOTE: Five major varieties exist.

BILLON, 4.70-5.30 g
Obv: 7 dots around lotus center, uniform edge and thickness.

Y#	Date	Mintage	VG	Fine	VF	XF
13.3	ND(ca.1900)	—	20.00	25.00	40.00	50.00

3.80-5.70 g
Similar to Y#13.3, but not uniform.

Y#	Date	Mintage	VG	Fine	VF	XF
13.4	ND(ca.1901-06)		1.00	2.00	3.00	4.50

NOTE: Eight major varieties exist, including an error having the 8 symbols rotated one position clockwise.

3.80 g
Obv: 8mm circle around lotus, North and West symbols are similar.

Y#	Date	Mintage	VG	Fine	VF	XF
13.5	ND(ca.1905)	—	20.00	25.00	40.00	50.00

3.00-5.60 g
Mint: Dode
Obv: 9 dots within lotus circle.

Y#	Date	Mintage	VG	Fine	VF	XF
13.6	ND(ca.1906-12)		1.00	2.00	3.00	4.50

NOTE: Eight major varieties exist. See Y#13.9, 13.10 and 13.11 for other types, having 9 dots within lotus circle.

SILVER, 2.70-5.00 g

Y#	Date	Mintage	VG	Fine	VF	XF
14	ND(ca.1909)	—	3.00	4.50	6.50	9.00

NOTE: Struck for presentation to monks.

BILLON, 3.30-5.88 g
Obv: 11 dots within lotus circle.

Y#	Date	Mintage	VG	Fine	VF	XF
13.7	ND(ca.1912-23)		1.00	2.00	3.00	4.50

NOTE: Four major varieties and numerous minor ones exist (40 to 78 dots compose outer circles).

Northeast symbol on obv:

3.00-5.00 g
Obv: 9 dots within lotus circle.

Y#	Date	Mintage	VG	Fine	VF	XF
13.8	ND(ca.1914-23)		1.00	2.00	2.75	3.50

NOTE: Five major and numerous minor varieties exist (35 to 68 dots compose outer circles).

Northeast symbol on obv:

Mint: Ser-Khang
3.30-4.60 g

Y#	Date	Mintage	VG	Fine	VF	XF
13.9	ND(ca.1920)	—	4.00	7.00	11.00	15.00

NOTE: Several other features are unique to this type.

Mint: Dode
3.80-4.30 g
Obv: 9 dots within lotus circle, uniform thickness (1.mm).

Y#	Date	Mintage	VG	Fine	VF	XF
13.10	1929-30	—	7.00	10.00	15.00	25.00

NOTE: Two minor die varieties exist.

SILVER, 3.10-5.30 g
Mint: Tapchi

Y#	Date	Mintage	VG	Fine	VF	XF
31	ND(1946-48)	—	3.00	4.00	6.00	10.00

NOTE: This type was struck for presentation to monks.

2 TANGKA

BILLON, 7.80-10.50 g
Mint: Dode

Y#	Date	Mintage	VG	Fine	VF	XF
15	ND(ca.1912)	—	100.00	150.00	200.00	275.00

NOTE: Struck in a collar.

SHO-SRANG COINAGE

Size same as 'Kong-par' Tangka

1/8 SHO

COPPER
Mint: Dode

Y#	Date	Year	Good	VG	Fine	VF
A7	1	(1909)	35.00	50.00	80.00	125.00

NOTE: A silver striking of this type exists (rare).

1/4 SHO

COPPER

Y#	Date	Year	Good	VG	Fine	VF
B7	1	(1909)	35.00	50.00	80.00	125.00

NOTE: The above coin struck in silver is a forgery.

2 1/2 SKAR

COPPER
Mint: Dode

Y#	Date	Year	Good	VG	Fine	VF
10	15-43	(1909)	125.00	175.00	250.00	350.00

23.5mm, 3.69-6.09 g
Obv: Lion looking upwards.

Y#	Date	Year	Good	VG	Fine	VF
16	15-47	(1913)	4.00	8.00	15.00	25.00
	15-48	(1914)	4.00	8.00	15.00	25.00
	15-49	(1915)	10.00	20.00	25.00	35.00
	15-50	(1916)	8.00	15.00	20.00	30.00
	15-51	(1917)	6.00	12.00	17.50	27.50
	15-52	(1918)	4.00	8.00	15.00	25.00

Mint: Mekyi
Obv: Lion looking backwards.

Y#	Date	Year	Good	VG	Fine	VF
16.1	15-48	(1914)	4.00	10.00	16.50	25.00

Mint: Dode

Y#	Date	Year	Good	VG	Fine	VF
A19	15-52	(1918)	30.00	50.00	65.00	80.00
	15-53	(1919)	35.00	60.00	75.00	90.00
	15-55	(1921)	35.00	60.00	75.00	90.00

NOTE: Counterfeits dated 15-55 exist.

5 SKAR

COPPER
Mint: Dode

Y#	Date	Year	Good	VG	Fine	VF
A10	15-43	(1909)	125.00	175.00	250.00	350.00

27mm
Obv: Lion looking upwards.

Y#	Date	Year	Good	VG	Fine	VF
17	15-47	(1913)	2.00	4.00	8.00	25.00
	15-48	(1914)	1.00	2.00	4.00	12.00
	15-49	(1915)	1.00	2.00	4.00	12.00
	15-50	(1916)	1.00	2.00	4.00	12.00
	15-51	(1917)	1.00	2.00	4.00	12.00
	15-52	(1918)	2.00	4.00	8.00	25.00

Mint: Mekyi
Obv: Lion looking backwards.

Y#	Date	Year	Good	VG	Fine	VF
17.1	15-48	(1914)	.60	1.50	4.00	10.00
	15-49	(1915)	.40	1.00	3.50	8.00
	15-50	(1916)	.40	1.00	3.50	8.00
	15-51	(1917)	.40	1.00	3.50	8.00
	15-52	(1918)	.40	1.00	3.50	8.00

Obv: Lion looking backwards and upwards.

Y#	Date	Year	Good	VG	Fine	VF
17.2	15-48	(1914)	1.50	3.00	7.00	15.00

Rev: Flower w/8 petals rather than wheel w/8 spokes.

Y#	Date	Year	Good	VG	Fine	VF
17.3	15-48	(1914)	1.50	3.00	7.00	15.00

21mm
Mint: Lower Dode

Y#	Date	Year	Good	VG	Fine	VF
19	15-52	(1918)	.80	2.00	3.00	4.50
	15-53	(1919)	.60	1.50	2.50	4.00
	15-54	(1920)	.50	1.25	2.00	3.50
	15-55	(1921)	.50	1.25	2.00	3.50
	15-56	(1922)	.50	1.25	2.00	3.50
	56-15 (error)					
		(1922)	10.00	15.00	20.00	30.00

NOTE: Reverse inscription reads counterclockwise on error date coin.

Mint: Upper Dode
Rev: Dot added above center.

Y#	Date	Year	Good	VG	Fine	VF
19.1	15-55	(1921)	5.00	7.50	12.00	18.00
	15-56	(1922)	2.00	3.50	5.00	8.00

7 1/2 SKAR

COPPER
Mint: Dode

Y#	Date	Year	Good	VG	Fine	VF
11	15-43	(1909)	125.00	175.00	250.00	350.00

Y#	Date	Year	Good	VG	Fine	VF
20	15-52	(1918)	.60	1.50	2.50	4.50
	15-53	(1919)	.50	1.25	2.00	3.50
	15-54	(1920)	.50	1.25	2.00	3.50
	15-55	(1921)	.50	1.25	2.00	3.50
	15-56	(1922)	.50	1.25	2.00	3.50
	15-60	(1926)	10.00	15.00	20.00	30.00

NOTE: Some 15-52, 15-53 and 15-55 specimens have the reverse central 'whirlwind' in a counterclockwise direction.

SHO

COPPER, 25.6mm
Mint: Dode
Rev: Central leg. horizontal.

Y#	Date	Year	Good	VG	Fine	VF
21	15-52	(1918)	15.00	20.00	30.00	50.00

NOTE: Two varieties exist (lion's head).

Mint: Mekyi
24mm, 3.95-7.13 g
Obv: Lion looking up, w/o dot.

Y#	Date	Year	Good	VG	Fine	VF
21.1	15-52	(1918)	.50	1.25	1.75	4.00
	15-53	(1919)	.30	.75	1.25	3.00
	15-54	(1920)	.30	.75	1.25	3.00
	15-55	(1921)	.30	.75	1.25	3.00
	15-56	(1922)	.30	.75	1.25	3.00
	15-57	(1923)	.50	1.25	1.75	4.00
	15-58	(1924)	.30	.75	1.25	3.00
	15-59	(1925)	.30	.75	1.25	3.00
	15-60	(1926)	.30	.75	1.25	3.00
	16-1	(1927)	.30	.75	1.25	3.00
	16-2	(1928)	.30	.75	1.25	3.00

Mint: Ser-Khang
3.01-7.27 g
Obv: Lion looking up, w/dot.

Y#	Date	Year	Good	VG	Fine	VF
21.2	15-54	(1920)	.50	1.25	2.00	3.50
	54-15(error)					
		(1920)	15.00	20.00	30.00	45.00
	15/51-54(error)					
		(1920)	15.00	20.00	30.00	45.00
	15-55	(1921)	.40	1.00	1.50	3.00
	15-55 (error) 'year' and '55' transposed					
		(1921)	15.00	20.00	30.00	45.00

Obv: Lion looking diagonally upwards, w/dot.

Y#	Date	Year	Good	VG	Fine	VF
21.3	15-54	(1920)	2.00	3.00	5.00	8.00
	15-55	(1921)	.30	.75	1.25	2.50
	15-56	(1922)	.30	.75	1.25	2.50
	15-57	(1923)	.40	1.00	1.75	3.50
	15-58	(1924)	.30	.75	1.25	2.50
	15-59	(1925)	.30	.75	1.25	2.50
	15-60	(1926)	.30	.75	1.25	2.50
	16-1/15-60					
		(1927)	6.00	10.00	15.00	20.00
	16-1	(1927)	.30	.75	1.25	2.00
	16-2	(1928)	.30	.75	1.25	2.00

NOTE: Specimens dated 15-54 may all be contemporary forgeries.

Mint: Dode
24mm, 3.43-4.73 g
Rev: Central leg. vertical.

Y#	Date	Year	VG	Fine	VF	XF
21a	15-56	(1922)	5.00	7.00	10.00	17.50

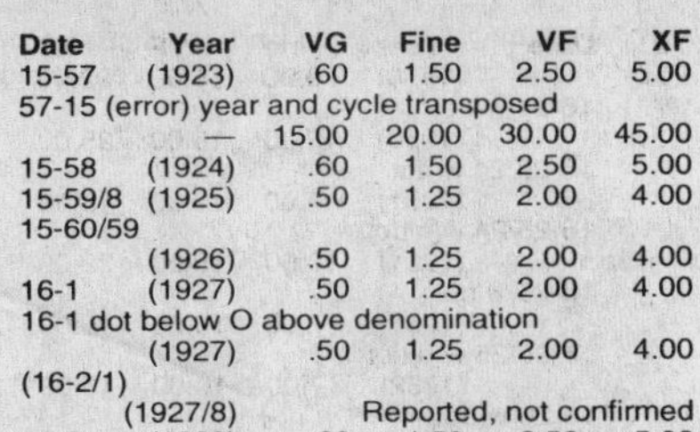

Y#	Date	Year	VG	Fine	VF	XF
21a	15-57	(1923)	.60	1.50	2.50	5.00
	57-15 (error) year and cycle transposed					
		—	15.00	20.00	30.00	45.00
	15-58	(1924)	.60	1.50	2.50	5.00
	15-59/8	(1925)	.50	1.25	2.00	4.00
	15-60/59					
		(1926)	.50	1.25	2.00	4.00
	16-1	(1927)	.50	1.25	2.00	4.00
	16-1 dot below O above denomination					
		(1927)	.50	1.25	2.00	4.00
	(16-2/1)					
		(1927/8)	Reported, not confirmed			
	16-2	(1928)	.60	1.50	2.50	5.00

NOTE: Two varieties (lion) exist for each of the following dates: 15-56, 15-57, 15-58 & 16-2.

Mint: Tapchi
24mm, 4.02-6.09 g
The following marks are located in the position indicated by the arrow:

a: ● b: ⬮ c: ✚ d: ↓ e: ⌄ f: ⌄̇ g: ▮

Y#	Date	Year	VG	Fine	VF	XF
23	16-6 (a)	(1932)	1.00	1.75	3.00	5.00
	16-7 (a)	(1933)	1.25	2.00	3.25	5.50
	16-8 (a)	(1934)	1.50	2.50	4.00	7.00
	16-9 (a)	(1935)	.75	1.50	2.50	4.00
	16-9 (b)	(1935)	.75	1.25	2.00	3.00
	16-10 (a)	(1936)	2.00	3.50	6.00	10.00
	16-10 (b)	(1936)	2.00	3.50	6.00	10.00
	16-10 (c)	(1936)	.75	1.25	2.00	3.00
	16-11 (a)	(1937)	1.50	2.50	4.00	7.00
	16-11 (b)	(1937)	2.00	3.50	6.00	10.00
	16-11 (c)	(1937)	1.50	2.50	4.00	7.00
	16-11 (d)	(1937)	1.50	2.50	4.00	7.00
	16-11 (e)	(1937)	.75	1.25	2.00	3.00
	16-11 (f)	(1937)	2.00	3.50	6.00	10.00
	16-11 (g)	(1937)	—	—	—	—
	16-12 (d)	(1938)	2.00	3.50	6.00	10.00
	16-12 (f)	(1938)	1.50	2.50	4.00	7.00
	16-12 (g)	(1938)	1.50	2.50	4.00	7.00

NOTE: Exist with thick and thin planchets and many obverse varieties.

3 SHO

COPPER
Single cloud line

Y#	Date	Year	VG	Fine	VF	XF
27	16-20	(1946)	5.00	10.00	15.00	25.00

NOTE: Three varieties of conch-shell on reverse.

Double cloud-line

Y#	Date	Year	VG	Fine	VF	XF
27.1	16-20	(1946)	10.00	20.00	35.00	50.00

5 SHO

SILVER

Y#	Date	Year	VG	Fine	VF	XF
8	1	(1909)	—	—	Rare	—

Mint: Dode
10.30 g
Obv: Lion looking upwards.

Y#	Date	Year	VG	Fine	VF	XF
18	15-47	(1913)	27.50	35.00	50.00	75.00
	15-48	(1914)	22.50	30.00	42.50	60.00
	15-49	(1915)	22.50	30.00	42.50	60.00
	15-50	(1916)	22.50	30.00	42.50	60.00
	15-58	(1924)	—	—	Rare	—
	15-59	(1925)	30.00	50.00	80.00	110.00
	15-60	(1926)	30.00	50.00	80.00	110.00

NOTE: Two 15-50 varieties exist; small and large lions, or 14mm vs. 15mm lion-circle.

Mint: Mekyi
Obv: Lion looking backwards.

Y#	Date	Year	VG	Fine	VF	XF
18.1	15-49	(1915)	22.50	30.00	40.00	55.00
	15-50	(1916)	22.50	30.00	42.50	60.00
	15-51	(1917)	22.50	30.00	42.50	60.00
	15-52	(1918)	22.50	30.00	42.50	60.00
	15-53	(1919)	30.00	50.00	80.00	110.00
	15-56	(1922)	30.00	50.00	80.00	110.00
	15-59	(1925)	50.00	80.00	110.00	150.00
	15-60	(1926)	50.00	80.00	110.00	150.00
	16-1	(1927)	30.00	50.00	80.00	110.00

COPPER

Y#	Date	Year	VG	Fine	VF	XF
18.1a	15-53	(1919)	—	—	Rare	—

SILVER
Mint: Dode

Y#	Date	Year	VG	Fine	VF	XF
18.2	15-52	(1918)	40.00	50.00	80.00	110.00

Y#	Date	Year	VG	Fine	VF	XF
32	ND	(1928-29)	—	—	Rare	—

COPPER, 29mm
Mint: Tapchi
Obv: 2 mountains w/two suns.

Y#	Date	Year	VG	Fine	VF	XF
28	16-21	(1947)	1.40	3.50	6.00	10.00

Obv: 3 mountains w/2 suns.

Y#	Date	Year	VG	Fine	VF	XF
28.1	16-21	(1947)	.80	2.00	2.75	4.00
	16-22 dot after "cycle"					
		(1948)	.40	1.00	1.75	3.00
	16-22 dot after 16 and after "cycle"					
		(1948)	1.00	2.50	3.50	5.00
	16-22 dot after 6					
		(1948)	1.00	2.50	3.50	5.00
	16-22	(1948)	.40	1.00	1.75	3.00
	16-23	(1949)	.40	1.00	1.75	3.00
	16-23 dot after 16					
		(1949)	1.00	2.50	3.50	5.00
	16-24	(1950)	3.25	8.00	13.00	20.00
	16-24/23					
		(1950)	3.25	8.00	13.00	20.00

NOTE: A modern medallic series dated 16-21 (1947) exists struck in copper, silver and gold which were authorized by the Dalai Lama while in exile. Refer to *Unusual World Coins,* 3rd edition, Krause Publications, 1992.

COPPER
Obv: Cloud above middle mountain missing.

Y#	Date	Year	VG	Fine	VF	XF
28.2	16-22	(1948)	4.00	10.00	15.00	25.00

Obv: Moon and sun above mountains.

Y#	Date	Year	VG	Fine	VF	XF
28a	16-23	(1949)	2.50	6.00	10.00	17.50
	16-24 cloud merged w/middle mountain					
			3.25	8.00	13.00	20.00
	16-24	(1950)	.40	1.00	2.25	4.00
	16-24 moon cut above sun					
			2.00	5.00	8.00	14.00
	16-25/24		.80	2.00	4.00	7.00
	16-25	(1951)	.40	1.00	2.25	4.00
	16-26	(1952)	1.20	3.00	5.00	9.00
	dot before 26		.70	1.75	3.50	6.00
	16-27	(1953)	.90	2.25	4.25	7.50
	16-27	(1953)				
	dots before 27 and after cycle					
			1.10	2.75	4.75	8.50
	16-27	(1953)				
	dot after cycle		1.10	2.75	4.75	8.50

NOTE: Edge varieties exist.

SRANG

SILVER, 18.50 g
Mint: Dode

Y#	Date	Year	VG	Fine	VF	XF
9	1	(1909)	100.00	175.00	250.00	350.00

NOTE: 8 obverse varieties exist.

Plain edge.

12	15-43	(1909)	100.00	150.00	275.00	375.00

NOTE: Varieties exist.

Obv: Lion looking upwards. reeded edge.

A18	15-48	(1914)	250.00	450.00	650.00	800.00

Obv: Lion looking backwards.

A18.1	15-52	(1918)	100.00	200.00	350.00	500.00
	15-53	(1919)	125.00	250.00	400.00	550.00

1 1/2 SRANG

SILVER, 5.00 g
Mint: Tapchi

24	16-10	(1936)	3.00	6.00	7.50	11.00
	16-11	(1937)	2.50	5.00	6.50	9.00
	16-12	(1938)	3.00	6.00	7.50	11.00
	16-20	(1946)	6.00	10.00	14.00	20.00

3 SRANG

SILVER, 11.30 g
Mint: Tapchi

Y#	Date	Year	Fine	VF	XF	Unc
25	16-7	(1933)	8.50	12.00	18.00	25.00
	16-8	(1934)	8.50	12.00	18.00	25.00

26	16-9	(1935)	5.00	10.00	15.00	20.00
	16-10	(1936)	5.00	8.00	12.00	17.50
	16-11	(1937)	5.00	8.00	12.00	17.50
	16-12	(1938)	5.00	8.00	12.00	17.50
	16-20	(1946)	8.50	11.00	16.00	22.00

NOTE: Dates for Y#25 and 26 are written in words, not numerals. Obverse varieties exist.

5 SRANG

No coins of this denomination are known to have been struck. Two Tanka types (Y#14 & 31, see under 'ga-den' Tangkas) circulated briefly with this value and later with a value of 10 Srang.

10 SRANG

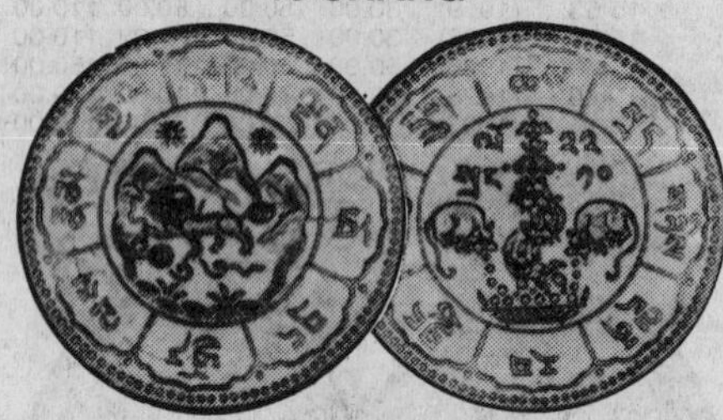

BILLON
Mint: Tapchi
Obv: 2 suns. Rev: Numerals for denomination.

29	16-22	(1948)	4.50	7.00	12.50	18.00

Rev: Word for denomination.

29.1	16-23/22					
		(1949)	12.00	16.00	25.00	35.00
	16-23 w/dot					
		(1949)	6.00	8.50	14.00	20.00
	16-23 w/o dot					
		(1949)	6.00	8.50	14.00	20.00

Obv: Moon and sun.

Y#	Date	Year	Fine	VF	XF	Unc
29a	16-23 w/dot					
		(1949)	20.00	30.00	45.00	65.00
	16-24/23 w/dot					
		(1950)	7.00	10.00	15.00	22.00
	16-24/22	(1950)	6.00	9.00	18.00	25.00
	16-24 moon cut above sun					
		(1950)	10.00	15.00	22.00	30.00
	16-24 w/dot					
		(1950)	12.00	16.00	25.00	35.00
	16-25/24 w/dot					
		(1951)	7.00	10.00	15.00	22.00
	16-25/24 w/o dot					
		(1951)	10.00	15.00	22.00	30.00
	16-25 w/dot					
		(1951)	7.00	10.00	15.00	22.00
	16-26/25 w/o dot					
		(1952)	7.00	10.00	15.00	22.00
	16-26 w/dot					
		(1952)	7.00	10.00	15.00	22.00

***NOTE:** The 'dot' is after the denomination. A modern medallic series dated 16-24 (1950) exist struck in copper-nickel, silver and gold which were authorized by the Dalai Lama while in exile. Refer to *Unusual World Coins*, 3rd edition, Krause Publications, 1992.

BILLON
Mint: Dogu

30	16-24	(1950)	5.00	8.00	14.00	20.00
	16-25	(1951)	5.00	8.00	14.00	20.00

20 SRANG

GOLD
Mint: Ser-Khang

22	15-52	(1918)	300.00	400.00	500.00	700.00
	15-53	(1919)	300.00	450.00	550.00	800.00
	15-54	(1920)	300.00	500.00	650.00	850.00
	15-55	(1921)	400.00	700.00	1000.	1500.

TRADE COINAGE

MONETARY SYSTEM
1 Rupee = 3 Tangka

1/4 RUPEE

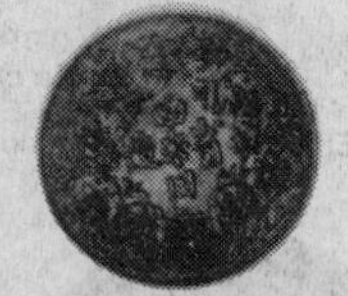

.935 SILVER, 2.80 g
Mint: Szechuan (China)

Y#	Date	Mintage	Fine	VF	XF	Unc
1	ND(1904-05,1912)					
		.120	30.00	50.00	75.00	150.00

NOTE: Varieties exist.

GOLD

1a	ND(1905)	—	—	—	Rare	—

1/2 RUPEE

.935 SILVER, 5.60 g

2	ND(1904,1907,1912)					
		.130	35.00	60.00	90.00	170.00

NOTE: Varieties exist.

GOLD

2a	ND(1905)	—	—	—	Rare	—

RUPEE

.935 SILVER, 11.40 g
Mint: Chengdu (Szechuan)
Obv: Small bust w/o collar. Rev: Vertical rosette.

Y#	Date	Mintage	Fine	VF	XF	Unc
3	ND(1903-05)	*14.127	15.00	22.50	32.50	65.00

NOTE: 2 reverse varieties exist.

Rev: Horizontal rosette.

Y#	Date	Mintage	Fine	VF	XF	Unc
3.1	ND(1903-05)	—	25.00	35.00	50.00	90.00

NOTE: 2 reverse varieties exist.

Obv: Small bust w/o collar. Rev: Vertical rosette.

Y#	Date	Mintage	Fine	VF	XF	Unc
3.2	ND(1905-12)	*14.127	8.00	14.00	28.00	50.00

NOTE: 2 reverse varieties exist.

GOLD

Y#	Date	Mintage	Fine	VF	XF	Unc
3b	ND(1905)	—	—	—	Rare	—

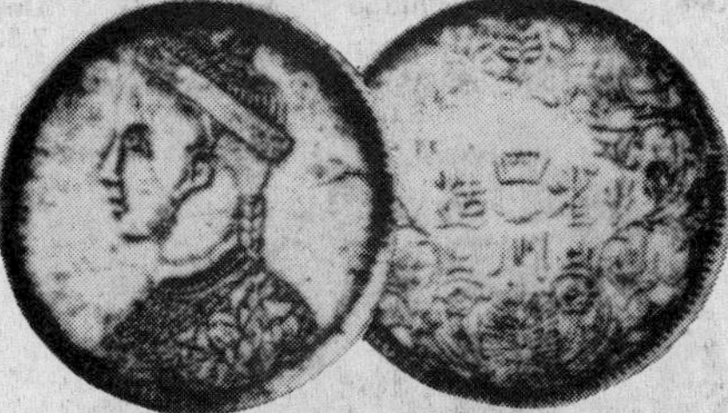

Obv: Small bust w/flat nose, w/collar.
Rev: Vertical rosette.

Y#	Date	Mintage	Fine	VF	XF	Unc
3.4	ND(1912-30)	—	15.00	22.50	32.50	65.00

Rev: Horizontal rosette.

Y#	Date	Mintage	Fine	VF	XF	Unc
3.5	ND(1912-30)	—	25.00	35.00	50.00	90.00

.500 SILVER
Mint: Kanting (Taschienlu)
Obv: Large bust.

Y#	Date	Mintage	Fine	VF	XF	Unc
3.3	ND(1930-42)	—	26.00	40.00	65.00	110.00

DEBASED SILVER/BILLON

Y#	Date	Mintage	Fine	VF	XF	Unc
3a	ND(1930-38)	—	6.50	13.00	25.00	50.00

NOTE: Coins w/copper base and silver wash exist.
***NOTE:** Mintage figures are for 1900-1928 and do not include pieces struck between 1929-1938. Total mintage of the 1 Rupee between 1902 and 1942 was between 25.5 and 27.5 million according to Chinese sources. In addition to the types illustrated above, large quantities of the following coins also circulated in Tibet; China Dollars, Y#318a, 329 and 345 plus Szechuan issues Y#449 and 459 and India Rupees, KM#473, 492 and 508. Similar crown size pieces struck in silver and gold are fantasies. Refer to *Unusual World Coins*, 3rd edition.
NOTE: Rupees, due to their inscriptions also called Szechuan Rupees, were cut in half and quarter. They were in use as smaller denominations until 1934.
NOTE: Rupees exist with local merchant countermarks in Chinese, Tibetan and other scripts.

Listings For

TIMOR: refer to Indonesia

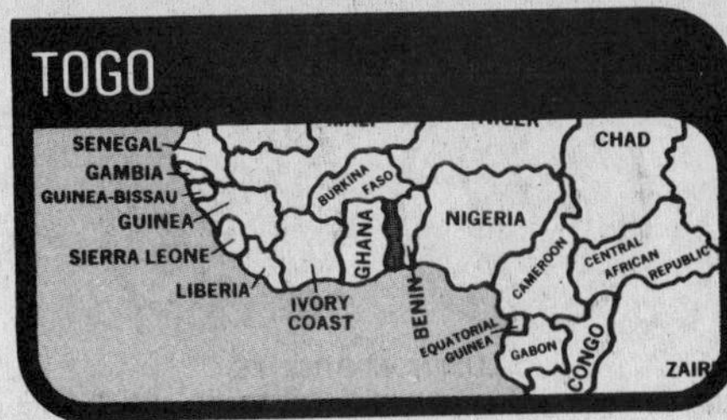

The Republic of Togo (formerly part of German Togoland), situated on the Gulf of Guinea in West Africa between Ghana and Dahomey, has an area of 21,622 sq. mi. (56,790 sq. km.) and a population of *3.4 million. Capital: Lome. Agriculture and herding, the production of dye-woods, and the mining of phosphates and iron ore are the chief industries. Copra, phosphates and coffee are exported.

Although Brazilians were the first traders to settle in Togo, Germany achieved possession, in 1884, by inducing coastal chiefs to place their territories under German protection. The German protectorate was extended international recognition at the Berlin conference of 1885 and its ultimate boundaries delimited by treaties with France in 1897 and with Britain in 1904. Togoland was occupied by Anglo-French forces in 1914, subsequently becoming a League of Nations mandate and a U.N. trusteeship divided, for administrative purpose, between Great Britain and France. The British portion voted in 1957 for incorporation with Ghana. The French portion became the independent Republic of Togo on April 27, 1960.

RULERS

German, 1884-1914
Anglo - French, 1914-1957
French, 1957-1960

MINT MARKS

(a) - Paris, privy marks only

MONETARY SYSTEM

100 Centimes = 1 Franc

50 CENTIMES

ALUMINUM-BRONZE

KM#	Date	Mintage	Fine	VF	XF	Unc
1	1924(a)	3.691	1.50	6.00	15.00	70.00
	1925(a)	2.064	2.00	7.00	20.00	90.00
	1926(a)	.445	5.00	15.00	65.00	200.00

FRANC

ALUMINUM-BRONZE

KM#	Date	Mintage	Fine	VF	XF	Unc
2	1924(a)	3.472	2.50	7.00	40.00	125.00
	1925(a)	2.768	3.00	8.00	45.00	140.00

ALUMINUM

KM#	Date	Mintage	Fine	VF	XF	Unc
4	1948(a)	5.000	2.00	6.00	20.00	50.00

2 FRANCS

ALUMINUM-BRONZE

KM#	Date	Mintage	Fine	VF	XF	Unc
3	1924(a)	.750	5.00	20.00	60.00	250.00
	1925(a)	.580	7.00	25.00	80.00	300.00

ALUMINUM
Similar to 1 Franc, KM#4.

KM#	Date	Mintage	Fine	VF	XF	Unc
5	1948(a)	5.000	3.00	8.00	25.00	60.00

5 FRANCS

ALUMINUM-BRONZE

KM#	Date	Mintage	Fine	VF	XF	Unc
6	1956(a)	10.000	1.50	3.00	6.00	12.50

REPUBLIC

2500 FRANCS

.925 SILVER
10th Year of General Eyadema as President
Similar to 5000 Francs, KM#8.

KM#	Date	
7	1977	Reported, not confirmed

5000 FRANCS

24.3600 g, .925 SILVER, .7245 oz ASW
10th Year of General Eyadema as President

KM#	Date	Mintage	Fine	VF	XF	Unc
8	1977	—	—	—	Proof	55.00

10000 FRANCS

49.3200 g, .925 SILVER, 1.4669 oz ASW
10th Year of General Eyadema as President

KM#	Date	Mintage	Fine	VF	XF	Unc
9	1977	—	—	—	Proof	85.00

15000 FRANCS

4.4800 g, .917 GOLD, .1320 oz AGW
10th Year of General Eyadema as President

KM#	Date	Mintage	Fine	VF	XF	Unc
10	1977	—	—	—	Proof	150.00

25000 FRANCS

9.0000 g, .917 GOLD, .2653 oz AGW
10th Year of General Eyadema as President

KM#	Date	Mintage	Fine	VF	XF	Unc
11	1977	—	—	—	Proof	250.00

50000 FRANCS

18.0000 g, .917 GOLD, .5306 oz AGW
10th Year of General Eyadema as President
Similar to 25,000 Francs, KM#11.

KM#	Date	Mintage	Fine	VF	XF	Unc
12	1977	—	—	—	Proof	450.00

TOKELAU ISLANDS

Tokelau or Union Islands, a New Zealand Territory located in the South Pacific 2,100 miles (3,379 km.) northeast of New Zealand and 300 miles (483 km.) north of Samoa, has an area of 4 sq. mi. (10 sq. km.) and a population of *2,000. Geographically, the group consists of four atolls - Atafu, Nukunono, Fakaofo and Swains - but the last belongs to American Samoa (and the United States claims the other three). The people are of Polynesian origin; Samoan is the official language. The islands are administered by the New Zealand Minister for Foreign Affairs; councils of family elders handle local government at the village level. The chief settlement is Fenuafala, on Fakaofo. It is connected by wireless with the offices of the New Zealand Administrative Center, located at Apia, Western Samoa. Subsistence farming and the production of copra for export are the main occupations. Revenue is also derived from the sale of postage stamps and, since 1978, coins.

Great Britain annexed the group of islands in 1889. They were added to the Gilbert and Ellice Islands colony in 1916. In 1926, they were brought under the jurisdiction of Western Samoa, which was held as a mandate of the League of Nations by New Zealand. They were declared a part of New Zealand in 1948.

Tokelau Islands issued its first coin in 1978, a "$1 Tahi Tala," Tokelauan for "One Dollar." The coin has a number of unusual features. The edge is inscribed, "Tokelau's First Coin." The obverse portrait of Queen Elizabeth II is identified by neither name nor title. The three dots of each such group comprising the obverse border symbolize the three principal atolls.

RULERS

British

TALA

COPPER-NICKEL

KM#	Date	Mintage	VF	XF	Unc
1	1978	.010	1.00	2.00	7.50
	27.2500 g, .925 SILVER, .8104 oz ASW				
1a	1978	5,000	—	Proof	22.50

COPPER-NICKEL

KM#	Date	Mintage	VF	XF	Unc
2	1979	.011	1.00	2.00	6.50
	27.2500 g, .925 SILVER, .8104 oz ASW				
2a	1979	—	—	Proof	22.50

COPPER-NICKEL
Coconut Crab

KM#	Date	Mintage	VF	XF	Unc
3	1980	.010	1.00	2.00	3.50

27.2500 g, .925 SILVER, .8104 oz ASW

KM#	Date	Mintage	VF	XF	Unc
3a	1980	6,004	—	Proof	20.00

COPPER-NICKEL
Frigate Bird

KM#	Date	Mintage	VF	XF	Unc
4	1981	6,500	1.00	2.00	3.50

27.2500 g, .925 SILVER, .8104 oz ASW

KM#	Date	Mintage	VF	XF	Unc
4a	1981	6,500	—	Proof	21.50

COPPER-NICKEL
Outrigger Canoe

KM#	Date	Mintage	VF	XF	Unc
5	1982	.010	1.00	2.00	3.50

27.2500 g, .925 SILVER, .8104 oz ASW

KM#	Date	Mintage	VF	XF	Unc
5a	1982	5,000	—	Proof	25.00

COPPER-NICKEL
Water Conservation

KM#	Date	Mintage	VF	XF	Unc
6	1983	2,000	1.00	2.50	6.00

5 TALA

28.2800 g, .925 SILVER, .8411 oz ASW

Water Conservation
Obv: Similar to 1 Tala, KM#6.

KM#	Date	Mintage	VF	XF	Unc
7	1983	1,000	—	Proof	45.00

27.0500 g, .925 SILVER, .8045 oz ASW
Fishermen in Sailboat
Plain edge.

KM#	Date	Mintage	VF	XF	Unc
8.1	1984	1,500	—	—	25.00

Reeded edge.

KM#	Date	Mintage	VF	XF	Unc
8.2	1984	500 pcs.	—	Proof	50.00

Olympics - Javelin Thrower

KM#	Date	Mintage	VF	XF	Unc
10	1988	—	—	—	25.00

27.2100 g, .925 SILVER, .8093 oz ASW
Capt. John Byron and HMS Dolphin
Plain edge

KM#	Date	Mintage	VF	XF	Unc
9.1	1989	1,500	—	—	25.00

Reeded edge

KM#	Date	Mintage	VF	XF	Unc
9.2	1989	500 pcs.	—	Proof	50.00

COPPER-NICKEL
50th Anniversary of Attack on Pearl Harbor

KM#	Date	Mintage	VF	XF	Unc
11	1991	—	—	P/L	8.50

Battle of Guadalcanal

KM#	Date	Mintage	VF	XF	Unc
13	1991	—	—	P/L	8.50

General Dwight Eisenhower

KM#	Date	Mintage	VF	XF	Unc
14	1991	—	—	P/L	8.50

Raising the Flag on Iwo Jima

KM#	Date	Mintage	VF	XF	Unc
15	1991	—	—	P/L	8.50

50 TALA

31.1030 g, .999 SILVER, 1.0000 oz ASW
50th Anniversary of Attack on Pearl Harbor
Similar to 5 Tala, KM#11.

KM#	Date	Mintage	VF	XF	Unc
12	1991	*.050	—	Proof	50.00

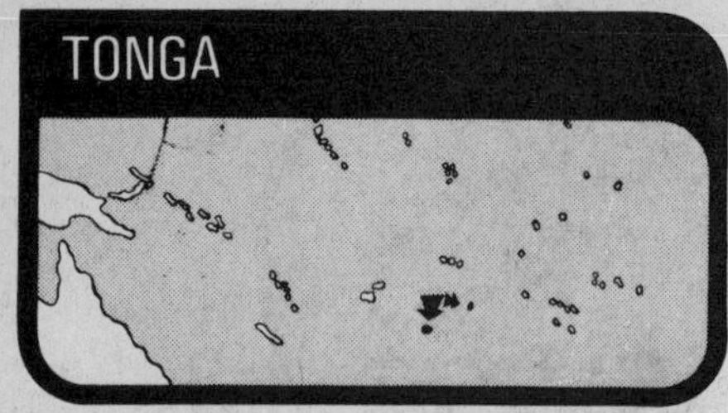

The Kingdom of Tonga (or Friendly Islands), a member of the British Commonwealth, is an archipelago situated in the southern Pacific Ocean south of Western Samoa and east of Fiji comprising 150 islands. Tonga has an area of 270 sq. mi. (748 sq. km.) and a population of *100,000. Capital: Nuku'alofa. Primarily agricultural, the kingdom exports bananas and copra.

Dutch navigators Willem Schouten and Jacob Lemaire were the first Europeans to visit Tonga in 1616. They were followed by the noted Dutch explorer Abel Tasman who visited the Tongatapu group in 1643. No further European contact was made until 1773 when British navigator Capt. James Cook arrived and, impressed by the peaceful deportment of the natives, named the islands the Friendly Islands. Within a few years of Cook's visit, Tonga was embroiled in a civil war that lasted until the great chief Tauffahau, who reigned as Siasoi Tupou I (1845-93), was converted to Christianity and brought unity and peace to the islands. Tonga became a self-governing protectorate of Great Britain in 1900 and a fully independent state on June 4, 1970. The monarchy is a member of the Commonwealth of Nations. The monarch is Chief of State and Head of Government.

RULERS

Queen Salote, 1918-1965
King Taufa'ahau, 1965

MONETARY SYSTEM

16 Pounds = 1 Koula

1/4 KOULA

8.1250 g, .916 GOLD, .2395 oz AGW

KM#	Date	Mintage	VF	XF	Unc
1	1962	—	—	—	115.00
	1962	6,300	—	Proof	135.00
	PLATINUM				
1a	1962	—	—	Proof	500.00

1/2 KOULA

16.2500 g, .916 GOLD, .4789 oz AGW

KM#	Date	Mintage	VF	XF	Unc
2	1962	—	—	—	220.00
	1962	3,000	—	Proof	260.00
	PLATINUM				
2a	1962	—	—	Proof	750.00

KOULA

32.5000 g, .916 GOLD, .9278 oz AGW

KM#	Date	Mintage	VF	XF	Unc
3	1962	—	—	—	450.00
	1962	—	—	Proof	600.00
	PLATINUM				
3a	1962	—	—	Proof	1000.

DECIMAL COINAGE

100 Seniti = 1 Pa'anga
100 Pa'anga = 1 Hau

SENITI

BRONZE
Giant Tortoise

KM#	Date	Mintage	VF	XF	Unc
4	1967	.500	.10	.15	1.00
	1967	—	—	Proof	2.00
27	1968	.500	.10	.15	1.00
	1968	—	—	Proof	2.00
	BRASS				
27a	1974	.500	.10	.15	1.00

BRONZE
F.A.O. Issue

KM#	Date	Mintage	VF	XF	Unc
42	1975	1.000	—	.10	.15
	1979	1.000	—	.10	.15

World Food Day

KM#	Date	Mintage	VF	XF	Unc
66	1981	1.544	—	.10	.15
	1990	—	—	.10	.15

2 SENITI

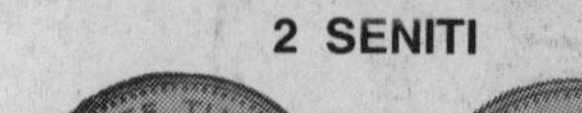

BRONZE
Giant Tortoise

KM#	Date	Mintage	VF	XF	Unc
5	1967	.500	—	.10	.75
	1967	—	—	Proof	2.00
28	1968	.200	—	.10	.75
	1968	—	—	Proof	2.00
	1974	.025	—	.10	.75

F.A.O. Issue

KM#	Date	Mintage	VF	XF	Unc
43	1975	.400	—	.10	.15
	1979	.500	—	.10	.20

World Food Day

KM#	Date	Mintage	VF	XF	Unc
67	1981	1.102	—	.10	.20
	1990	—	—	.10	.20

5 SENITI

COPPER-NICKEL

KM#	Date	Mintage	VF	XF	Unc
6	1967	.300	.10	.15	.40
	1967	—	—	Proof	2.50
29	1968	.100	.10	.15	.35
	1968	—	—	Proof	2.50
	1974	.075	.10	.15	.35

F.A.O. Issue

KM#	Date	Mintage	VF	XF	Unc
44	1975	.100	.10	.15	.40
	1977	.110	.10	.15	.40
	1979	.100	.10	.15	.40

World Food Day

KM#	Date	Mintage	VF	XF	Unc
68	1981	.941	.10	.15	.40
	1990	—	.10	.15	.40
	1991	—	.10	.15	.40

10 SENITI

COPPER-NICKEL

KM#	Date	Mintage	VF	XF	Unc
7	1967	.300	.20	.35	.75
	1967	—	—	Proof	3.00
30	1968	.100	.20	.40	.75

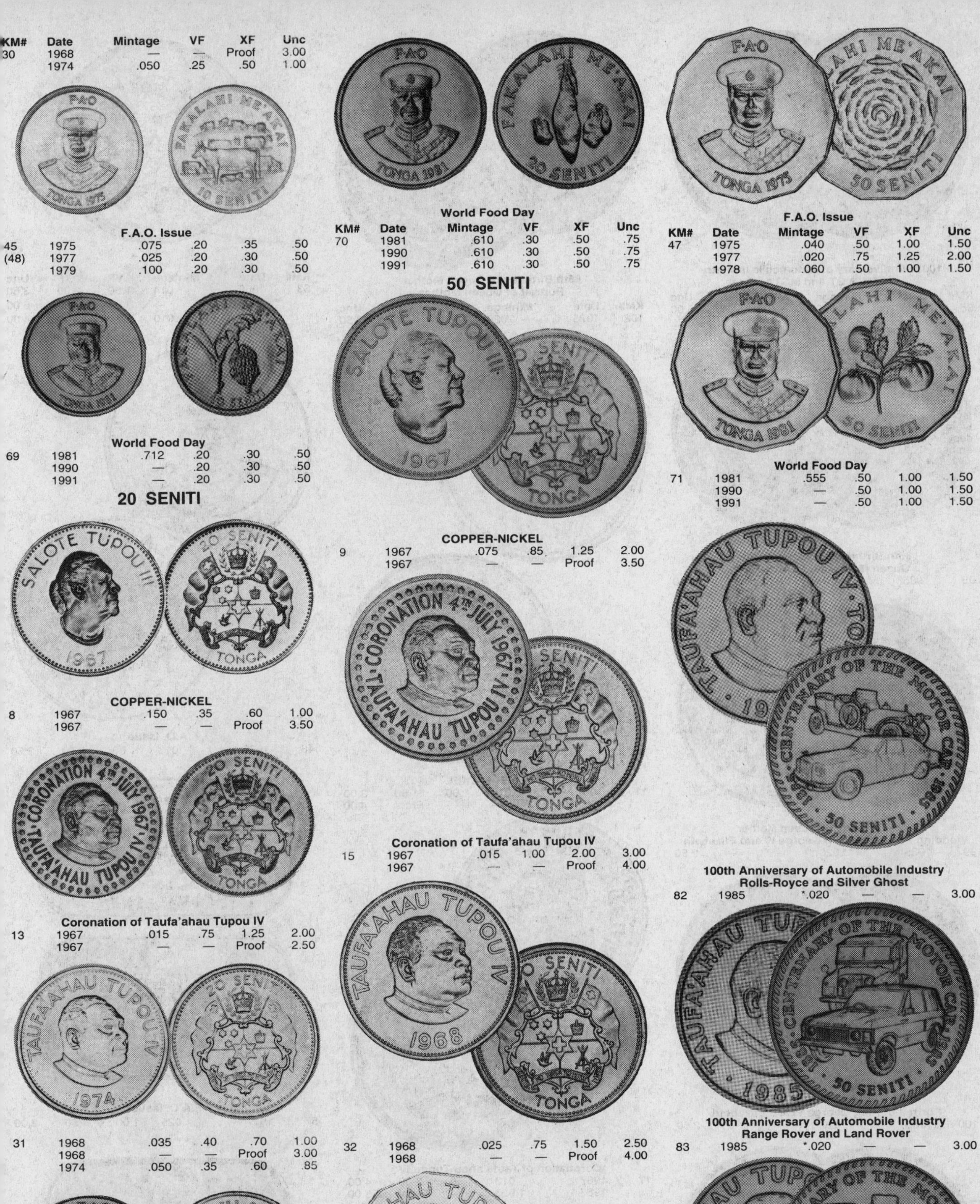

KM#	Date	Mintage	VF	XF	Unc
30	1968	—	—	Proof	3.00
	1974	.050	.25	.50	1.00

F.A.O. Issue

KM#	Date	Mintage	VF	XF	Unc
45	1975	.075	.20	.35	.50
(48)	1977	.025	.20	.30	.50
	1979	.100	.20	.30	.50

World Food Day

KM#	Date	Mintage	VF	XF	Unc
69	1981	.712	.20	.30	.50
	1990	—	.20	.30	.50
	1991	—	.20	.30	.50

20 SENITI

COPPER-NICKEL

KM#	Date	Mintage	VF	XF	Unc
8	1967	.150	.35	.60	1.00
	1967	—	—	Proof	3.50

Coronation of Taufa'ahau Tupou IV

KM#	Date	Mintage	VF	XF	Unc
13	1967	.015	.75	1.25	2.00
	1967	—	—	Proof	2.50

KM#	Date	Mintage	VF	XF	Unc
31	1968	.035	.40	.70	1.00
	1968	—	—	Proof	3.00
	1974	.050	.35	.60	.85

F.A.O. Issue

KM#	Date	Mintage	VF	XF	Unc
46	1975	.075	.35	.60	1.00
	1977	.025	.35	.60	1.00
	1979	.050	.35	.60	1.00

World Food Day

KM#	Date	Mintage	VF	XF	Unc
70	1981	.610	.30	.50	.75
	1990	.610	.30	.50	.75
	1991	.610	.30	.50	.75

50 SENITI

COPPER-NICKEL

KM#	Date	Mintage	VF	XF	Unc
9	1967	.075	.85	1.25	2.00
	1967	—	—	Proof	3.50

Coronation of Taufa'ahau Tupou IV

KM#	Date	Mintage	VF	XF	Unc
15	1967	.015	1.00	2.00	3.00
	1967	—	—	Proof	4.00

KM#	Date	Mintage	VF	XF	Unc
32	1968	.025	.75	1.50	2.50
	1968	—	—	Proof	4.00

KM#	Date	Mintage	VF	XF	Unc
41	1974	.050	.75	1.25	2.00

F.A.O. Issue

KM#	Date	Mintage	VF	XF	Unc
47	1975	.040	.50	1.00	1.50
	1977	.020	.75	1.25	2.00
	1978	.060	.50	1.00	1.50

World Food Day

KM#	Date	Mintage	VF	XF	Unc
71	1981	.555	.50	1.00	1.50
	1990	—	.50	1.00	1.50
	1991	—	.50	1.00	1.50

100th Anniversary of Automobile Industry
Rolls-Royce and Silver Ghost

KM#	Date	Mintage	VF	XF	Unc
82	1985	*.020	—	—	3.00

100th Anniversary of Automobile Industry
Range Rover and Land Rover

KM#	Date	Mintage	VF	XF	Unc
83	1985	*.020	—	—	3.00

100th Anniversary of Automobile Industry
Mini Morris Cowley and Touring Car

KM#	Date	Mintage	VF	XF	Unc
84	1985	*.020	—	—	3.00

100th Anniversary of Automobile Industry
MGB GT and MGTA

KM#	Date	Mintage	VF	XF	Unc
85	1985	*.020	—	—	3.00

85th Birthday of Queen Mother
Queen Mother as a Young Girl

KM#	Date	Mintage	VF	XF	Unc
98	1985	*.020	—	—	2.50

85th Birthday of Queen Mother
Wedding Portrait of King George VI and Elizabeth

KM#	Date	Mintage	VF	XF	Unc
99	1985	*.020	—	—	2.50

85th Birthday of Queen Mother
Portrait of King George VI and Elizabeth

KM#	Date	Mintage	VF	XF	Unc
100	1985	*.020	—	—	2.50

85th Birthday of Queen Mother
Queen Mother holding Queen Elizabeth II

KM#	Date	Mintage	VF	XF	Unc
101	1985	*.020	—	—	2.50

85th Birthday of Queen Mother
Portrait of Queen Mother

KM#	Date	Mintage	VF	XF	Unc
102	1985	*.020	—	—	2.50

PA'ANGA

COPPER-NICKEL

KM#	Date	Mintage	VF	XF	Unc
11	1967	.078	1.00	1.50	3.00
	1967	—	—	Proof	4.00

Coronation of Taufa'ahau Tupou IV

KM#	Date	Mintage	VF	XF	Unc
17	1967	.013	1.50	2.00	4.00
	1967	1,923	—	Proof	5.00

KM#	Date	Mintage	VF	XF	Unc
33	1968	.014	1.50	2.00	3.50
	1968	—	—	Proof	6.00
	1974	.010	1.50	2.00	4.00

F.A.O. Issue

KM#	Date	Mintage	VF	XF	Unc
48	1975	.013	1.00	2.00	3.50

F.A.O. Issue

KM#	Date	Mintage	VF	XF	Unc
57	1977	.025	1.00	1.50	3.00

60th Birthday and F.A.O. Issue
Rev: Similar to KM#57.

KM#	Date	Mintage	VF	XF	Unc
58	1978	.010	1.00	2.00	4.00

24.5000 g,.999 SILVER, .7869 oz ASW*

KM#	Date	Mintage	VF	XF	Unc
58a	1978	750 pcs.	—	Proof	42.50

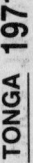

COPPER-NICKEL
F.A.O. Technical Cooperation Program

KM#	Date	Mintage	VF	XF	Unc
60	1979	.026	1.00	1.50	3.00

24.5000 g, .999 SILVER, .7869 oz ASW

KM#	Date	Mintage	VF	XF	Unc
60a	1979	850 pcs.	—	Proof	42.50

COPPER-NICKEL
F.A.O. and Rural Women's Advancement

KM#	Date	Mintage	VF	XF	Unc
62	1980	8,000	1.00	2.00	4.00

24.5000 g, .999 SILVER, .7869 oz ASW

KM#	Date	Mintage	VF	XF	Unc
62a	1980	2,200	—	Proof	40.00

COPPER-NICKEL
World Food Day
Obv: Similar to KM#57.

KM#	Date	Mintage	VF	XF	Unc
72	1981	.485	1.00	1.50	3.50

24.5000 g, .999 SILVER, .7869 oz ASW

KM#	Date	Mintage	VF	XF	Unc
72a	1981	3,500	—	Proof	35.00

COPPER-NICKEL
Christmas

KM#	Date	Mintage	VF	XF	Unc
77	1982	5,000	1.00	2.00	4.00
	1982	—	—	Proof	6.00

15.5000 g, .925 SILVER, .4610 oz ASW

KM#	Date	Mintage	VF	XF	Unc
77a	1982	2,500	—	Proof	17.50

26.0000 g, .917 GOLD, .7666 oz AGW

KM#	Date	Mintage	VF	XF	Unc
77b	1982	250 pcs.	—	Proof	500.00

30.4000 g, .950 PLATINUM, .9286 oz APW

KM#	Date	Mintage	VF	XF	Unc
77c	1982	25 pcs.	—	Proof	800.00

COPPER-NICKEL
Christmas

KM#	Date	Mintage	VF	XF	Unc
80	1983	5,000	1.00	1.50	3.50

15.5000 g, .925 SILVER, .4610 oz ASW

KM#	Date	Mintage	VF	XF	Unc
80a	1983	2,500	—	Proof	17.50

26.0000 g, .917 GOLD, .7666 oz AGW

KM#	Date	Mintage	VF	XF	Unc
80b	1983	250 pcs.	—	Proof	500.00

30.4000 g, .950 PLATINUM, .9286 oz APW

KM#	Date	Mintage	VF	XF	Unc
80c	1983	25 pcs.	—	Proof	800.00

COPPER-NICKEL
Christmas

KM#	Date	Mintage	VF	XF	Unc
81	1984	5,000	1.00	1.50	3.50

15.5000 g, .925 SILVER, .4610 oz ASW

KM#	Date	Mintage	VF	XF	Unc
81a	1984	2,500	—	Proof	17.50

26.0000 g, .917 GOLD, .7666 oz AGW

KM#	Date	Mintage	VF	XF	Unc
81b	1984	250 pcs.	—	Proof	500.00

30.4000 g, .950 PLATINUM, .9286 oz APW

KM#	Date	Mintage	VF	XF	Unc
81c	1984	25 pcs.	—	Proof	800.00

SILVER-CLAD COPPER-NICKEL
100th Anniversary of Automobile Industry
Rolls-Royce and Silver Ghost

KM#	Date	Mintage	VF	XF	Unc
86	1985	—	—	Proof	8.00

28.2800 g, .925 SILVER, .8411 oz ASW

KM#	Date	Mintage	VF	XF	Unc
86a	1985	5,000	—	Proof	30.00

SILVER-CLAD COPPER-NICKEL
100th Anniversary of Automobile Industry
Range Rover and Land Rover

KM#	Date	Mintage	VF	XF	Unc
87	1985	—	—	Proof	8.00

28.2800 g, .925 SILVER, .8411 oz ASW

KM#	Date	Mintage	VF	XF	Unc
87a	1985	5,000	—	Proof	30.00

SILVER-CLAD COPPER-NICKEL
100th Anniversary of Automobile Industry
Mini Morris Cowley and Touring Car

KM#	Date	Mintage	VF	XF	Unc
88	1985	—	—	Proof	8.00

28.2800 g, .925 SILVER, .8411 oz ASW

KM#	Date	Mintage	VF	XF	Unc
88a	1985	5,000	—	Proof	30.00

SILVER-CLAD COPPER-NICKEL
100th Anniversary of Automobile Industry
MGB GT and MG TA
Similar to 50 Seniti, KM#85.

KM#	Date	Mintage	VF	XF	Unc
89	1985	—	—	Proof	8.00

28.2800 g, .925 SILVER, .8411 oz ASW

KM#	Date	Mintage	VF	XF	Unc
89a	1985	5,000	—	Proof	30.00

SILVER-CLAD COPPER-NICKEL
85th Birthday of Queen Mother
Queen Mother as a Young Girl
Similar to 50 Seniti, KM#98.

KM#	Date	Mintage	VF	XF	Unc
103	1985	—	—	Proof	8.00

28.2800 g, .925 SILVER, .8411 oz ASW

KM#	Date	Mintage	VF	XF	Unc
103a	1985	5,000	—	Proof	30.00

SILVER-CLAD COPPER-NICKEL
85th Birthday of Queen Mother
Wedding Portrait of King George VI and Elizabeth
Similar to 50 Seniti, KM#99.

KM#	Date	Mintage	VF	XF	Unc
104	1985	—	—	Proof	8.00

28.2800 g, .925 SILVER, .8411 oz ASW

KM#	Date	Mintage	VF	XF	Unc
104a	1985	5,000	—	Proof	30.00

SILVER-CLAD COPPER-NICKEL
85th Birthday of Queen Mother
Portrait of King George VI and Elizabeth
Similar to 50 Seniti, KM#100.

KM#	Date	Mintage	VF	XF	Unc
105	1985	—	—	Proof	8.00

28.2800 g, .925 SILVER, .8411 oz ASW

KM#	Date	Mintage	VF	XF	Unc
105a	1985	5,000	—	Proof	30.00

SILVER-CLAD COPPER-NICKEL
85th Birthday of Queen Mother
Queen Mother holding Queen Elizabeth II
Similar to 50 Seniti, KM#101.

KM#	Date	Mintage	VF	XF	Unc
106	1985	—	—	Proof	8.00

28.2800 g, .925 SILVER, .8411 oz ASW

KM#	Date	Mintage	VF	XF	Unc
106a	1985	5,000	—	Proof	30.00

SILVER-CLAD COPPER-NICKEL
85th Birthday of Queen Mother
Portrait of Queen Mother
Similar to 50 Seniti, KM#102.

KM#	Date	Mintage	VF	XF	Unc
107	1985	—	—	Proof	8.00

28.2800 g, .925 SILVER, .8411 oz ASW

KM#	Date	Mintage	VF	XF	Unc
107a	1985	5,000	—	Proof	30.00

COPPER-NICKEL
Christmas

KM#	Date	Mintage	VF	XF	Unc
118	1985	—	1.00	1.50	3.50

15.5000 g, .925 SILVER, .4610 oz ASW

KM#	Date	Mintage	VF	XF	Unc
118a	1985	250 pcs.	—	Proof	50.00

26.0000 g, .917 GOLD, .7666 oz AGW

KM#	Date	Mintage	VF	XF	Unc
118b	1985	250 pcs.	—	Proof	500.00

30.4000 g, .950 PLATINUM, .9286 oz APW

KM#	Date	Mintage	VF	XF	Unc
118c	1985	—	—	Proof	800.00

COPPER-NICKEL
Christmas
Obv: Taufa'ahan Tupou IV. Rev: Three Wise Men.

KM#	Date	Mintage	VF	XF	Unc
123	1986	—	—	—	3.50

15.5000 g, .925 SILVER, .4610 oz ASW

KM#	Date	Mintage	VF	XF	Unc
123a	1986	—	—	—	50.00

26.0000 g, .917 GOLD, .7666 oz AGW

KM#	Date	Mintage	VF	XF	Unc
123b	1986	—	—	—	500.00

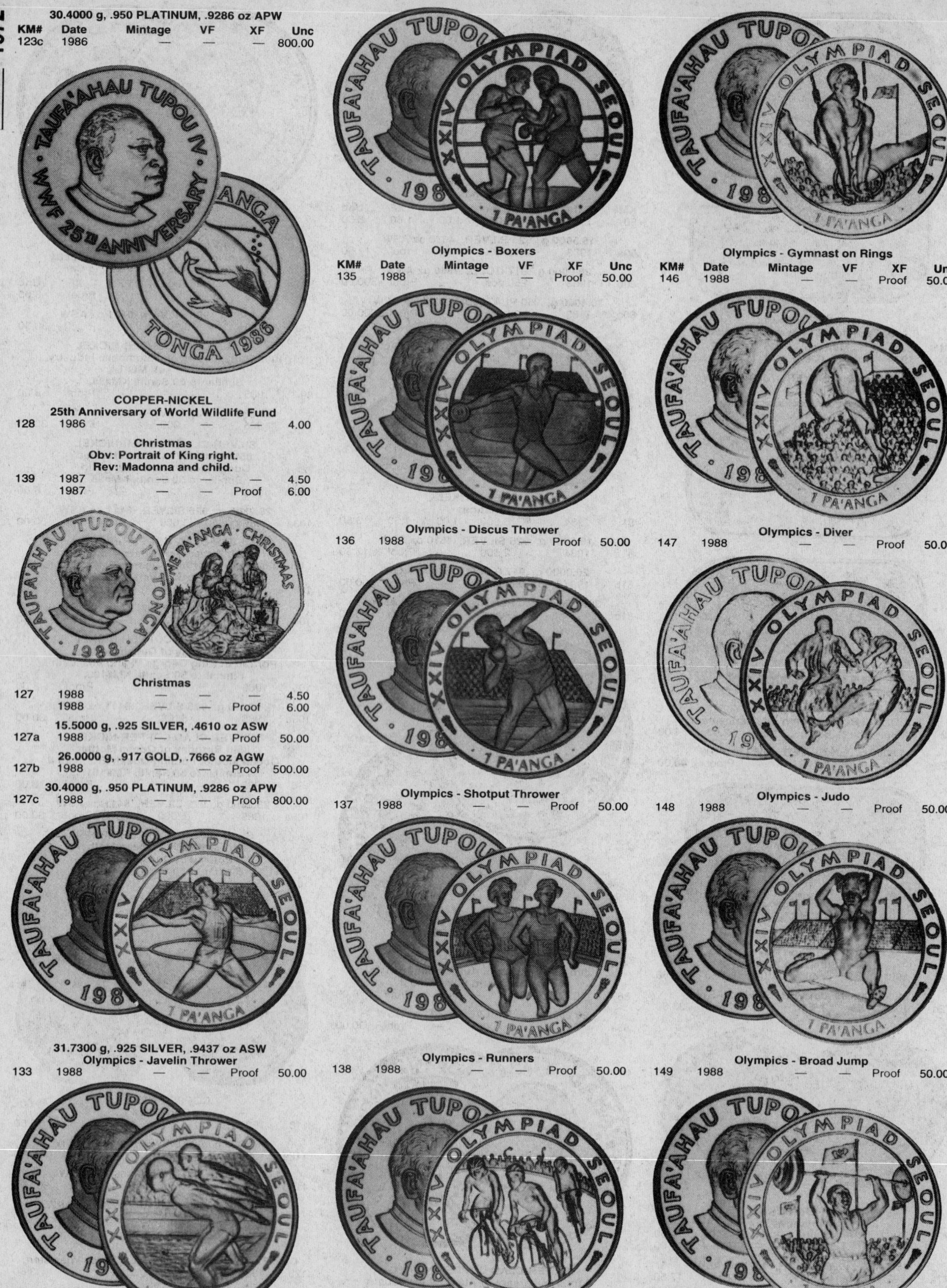

30.4000 g, .950 PLATINUM, .9286 oz APW

KM#	Date	Mintage	VF	XF	Unc
123c	1986	—	—	—	800.00

COPPER-NICKEL
25th Anniversary of World Wildlife Fund

KM#	Date	Mintage	VF	XF	Unc
128	1986	—	—	—	4.00

Christmas
Obv: Portrait of King right.
Rev: Madonna and child.

KM#	Date	Mintage	VF	XF	Unc
139	1987	—	—	—	4.50
	1987	—	—	Proof	6.00

Christmas

KM#	Date	Mintage	VF	XF	Unc
127	1988	—	—	—	4.50
	1988	—	—	Proof	6.00

15.5000 g, .925 SILVER, .4610 oz ASW

KM#	Date	Mintage	VF	XF	Unc
127a	1988	—	—	Proof	50.00

26.0000 g, .917 GOLD, .7666 oz AGW

KM#	Date	Mintage	VF	XF	Unc
127b	1988	—	—	Proof	500.00

30.4000 g, .950 PLATINUM, .9286 oz APW

KM#	Date	Mintage	VF	XF	Unc
127c	1988	—	—	Proof	800.00

31.7300 g, .925 SILVER, .9437 oz ASW
Olympics - Javelin Thrower

KM#	Date	Mintage	VF	XF	Unc
133	1988	—	—	Proof	50.00

Olympics - Swimmers

KM#	Date	Mintage	VF	XF	Unc
134	1988	—	—	Proof	50.00

Olympics - Boxers

KM#	Date	Mintage	VF	XF	Unc
135	1988	—	—	Proof	50.00

Olympics - Discus Thrower

KM#	Date	Mintage	VF	XF	Unc
136	1988	—	—	Proof	50.00

Olympics - Shotput Thrower

KM#	Date	Mintage	VF	XF	Unc
137	1988	—	—	Proof	50.00

Olympics - Runners

KM#	Date	Mintage	VF	XF	Unc
138	1988	—	—	Proof	50.00

Olympics - Bicycling

KM#	Date	Mintage	VF	XF	Unc
145	1988	—	—	Proof	50.00

Olympics - Gymnast on Rings

KM#	Date	Mintage	VF	XF	Unc
146	1988	—	—	Proof	50.00

Olympics - Diver

KM#	Date	Mintage	VF	XF	Unc
147	1988	—	—	Proof	50.00

Olympics - Judo

KM#	Date	Mintage	VF	XF	Unc
148	1988	—	—	Proof	50.00

Olympics - Broad Jump

KM#	Date	Mintage	VF	XF	Unc
149	1988	—	—	Proof	50.00

Olympics - Weightlifter

KM#	Date	Mintage	VF	XF	Unc
150	1988	—	—	Proof	50.00

31.6000 g, .925 SILVER, .9398 oz ASW
Olympics - Diver

KM#	Date	Mintage	VF	XF	Unc
140	1991	—	—	Proof	50.00

Explorers - Schouten and LeMaire

KM#	Date	Mintage	VF	XF	Unc
141	1991	—	—	Proof	55.00

Endangered Wildlife - Birds

KM#	Date	Mintage	VF	XF	Unc
143	1991	—	—	Proof	60.00

31.4700 g, .925 SILVER, .9359 oz ASW
40th Anniversary of Queen Elizabeth's Coronation

KM#	Date	Mintage	VF	XF	Unc
144	1993	*.010	—	Proof	55.00

Herman Orbeth

KM#	Date	Mintage	VF	XF	Unc
151	1993	*.010	—	Proof	40.00

Johannes Gutenberg

KM#	Date	Mintage	VF	XF	Unc
152	1993	*.010	—	Proof	40.00

Protect Our World - Alexander von Humboldt

KM#	Date	Mintage	VF	XF	Unc
153	1993	*.010	—	Proof	40.00

Sailing Ship - La Princesa

KM#	Date	Mintage	VF	XF	Unc
154	1993	*.015	—	Proof	40.00

2 PA'ANGA

COPPER-NICKEL
Coronation of Taufa'ahau Tupou IV
Rev: Similar to KM#37.

KM#	Date	Mintage	VF	XF	Unc
19	1967	.010	2.00	3.00	5.00
	1967	—	—	Proof	8.00

Rev: Similar to KM#19.

KM#	Date	Mintage	VF	XF	Unc
37	1968	.014	2.00	3.00	5.00
	1968	—	—	Proof	8.00
	1974	.010	2.00	3.00	6.00

F.A.O. Issue

KM#	Date	Mintage	VF	XF	Unc
49	1975	.013	2.00	3.00	5.00
	1977	.012	2.00	3.00	5.00

60th Birthday and F.A.O. Issue
Rev: Similar to KM#49.

KM#	Date	Mintage	VF	XF	Unc
59	1978	.010	2.00	3.00	5.00

42.1000 g, .999 SILVER, 1.3523 oz ASW

KM#	Date	Mintage	VF	XF	Unc
59a	1978	750 pcs.	—	Proof	40.00

COPPER-NICKEL
F.A.O. - SEA Resource Management

KM#	Date	Mintage	VF	XF	Unc
61	1979	8,000	2.50	3.50	7.00
	42.1000 g, .999 SILVER, 1.3523 oz ASW				
61a	1979	850 pcs.	—	Proof	50.00

COPPER-NICKEL
F.A.O. and SEA Resource Management
Rev: Similar to KM#61.

KM#	Date	Mintage	VF	XF	Unc
63	1980	8,000	2.50	3.50	7.00
	42.1000 g, .999 SILVER, 1.3523 oz ASW				
63a	1980	2,200	—	Proof	45.00

COPPER-NICKEL
World Food Day
Obv: Similar to KM#63.

KM#	Date	Mintage	VF	XF	Unc
73	1981	.485	2.00	2.50	4.00
	42.1000 g, .999 SILVER, 1.3523 oz ASW				
73a	1981	3,500	—	Proof	37.50

28.2800 g, .500 SILVER, .4546 oz ASW
Commonwealth Games

KM#	Date	Mintage	VF	XF	Unc
120	1986	.050	2.00	4.00	8.00
	28.2800 g, .925 SILVER, .8411 oz ASW				
120a	1986	.020	—	Proof	32.50

Wildlife - Whales

KM#	Date	Mintage	VF	XF	Unc
121	1986	.025	—	Proof	40.00

155.5200 g, .999 SILVER, 5.0000 oz ASW
America's Cup
Illustration reduced. Actual size: 65mm.

KM#	Date	Mintage	VF	XF	Unc
124	1987	7,500	—	Proof	140.00

Olympics - Swimmers
Illustration reduced. Actual size: 65mm
Obv: Similar to 10 Pa'anga, KM#130.

KM#	Date	Mintage	VF	XF	Unc
129	1988	2,000	—	Proof	120.00

5 PA'ANGA

31.0000 g, .999 SILVER, .9957 oz ASW
Constitution Centennial

KM#	Date	Mintage	VF	XF	Unc
50	1975	2,118	—	—	25.00
	1975	418 pcs.	—	Proof	35.00

10 PA'ANGA

62.0000 g, .999 SILVER, 1.9915 oz ASW
Constitution Centennial
Rev: Similar to 5 Pa'anga, KM#50.

KM#	Date	Mintage	VF	XF	Unc
51	1975	1,116	—	—	45.00
	1975	420 pcs.	—	Proof	55.00

0.4000 g, .917 GOLD, .0117 oz AGW
F.A.O. and Rural Women's Advancement
Obv: Queen Salote. Rev: Female symbol on dove.

KM#	Date	Mintage	VF	XF	Unc
64	1980	750 pcs.	—	—	25.00
	1980	2,000	—	Proof	25.00

28.2800 g, .925 SILVER, .8411 oz ASW
Commonwealth Games

KM#	Date	Mintage	VF	XF	Unc
78	1982	500 pcs.	—	—	30.00
	1982	1,000	—	Proof	30.00

5.1000 g, .375 GOLD, .0615 oz AGW
100th Anniversary of Automobile Industry
Rolls-Royce and Silver Ghost
Similar to 50 Seniti, KM#82.

KM#	Date	Mintage	VF	XF	Unc
90	1985	1,000	—	Proof	50.00
	7.9600 g, .917 GOLD, .2347 oz AGW				
90a	1985	500 pcs.	—	Proof	150.00

5.1000 g, .375 GOLD, .0615 oz AGW
100th Anniversary of Automobile Industry
Range Rover and Land Rover
Similar to 50 Seniti, KM#83.

KM#	Date	Mintage	VF	XF	Unc
91	1985	1,000	—	Proof	50.00
	7.9600 g, .917 GOLD, .2347 oz AGW				
91a	1985	500 pcs.	—	Proof	150.00

5.1000 g, .375 GOLD, .0615 oz AGW
100th Anniversary of Automobile Industry

Mini Morris Cowley and Touring Car
Similar to 50 Seniti, KM#84.

KM#	Date	Mintage	VF	XF	Unc
92	1985	1,000	—	Proof	50.00

7.9600 g, .917 GOLD, .2347 oz AGW

KM#	Date	Mintage	VF	XF	Unc
92a	1985	500 pcs.	—	Proof	150.00

5.1000 g, .375 GOLD, .0615 oz AGW
100th Anniversary of Automobile Industry
MGB GT and MG TA
Similar to 50 Seniti, KM#85.

KM#	Date	Mintage	VF	XF	Unc
93	1985	1,000	—	Proof	50.00

7.9600 g, .917 GOLD, .2347 oz AGW

KM#	Date	Mintage	VF	XF	Unc
93a	1985	500 pcs.	—	Proof	150.00

5.1000 g, .375 GOLD, .0615 oz AGW
85th Birthday of Queen Mother
Queen Mother as a Young Girl
Similar to 50 Seniti, KM#98.

KM#	Date	Mintage	VF	XF	Unc
108	1985	1,000	—	Proof	50.00

7.9600 g, .917 GOLD, .2347 oz AGW

KM#	Date	Mintage	VF	XF	Unc
108a	1985	500 pcs.	—	Proof	150.00

5.1000 g, .375 GOLD, .0615 oz AGW
85th Birthday of Queen Mother
Wedding Portrait of King George VI and Elizabeth
Similar to 50 Seniti, KM#99.

KM#	Date	Mintage	VF	XF	Unc
109	1985	1,000	—	Proof	50.00

7.9600 g, .917 GOLD, .2347 oz AGW

KM#	Date	Mintage	VF	XF	Unc
109a	1985	500 pcs.	—	Proof	150.00

5.1000 g, .375 GOLD, .0615 oz AGW
85th Birthday of Queen Mother
Portrait of King George VI and Elizabeth
Similar to 50 Seniti, KM#100.

KM#	Date	Mintage	VF	XF	Unc
110	1985	1,000	—	Proof	50.00

7.9600 g, .917 GOLD, .2347 oz AGW

KM#	Date	Mintage	VF	XF	Unc
110a	1985	500 pcs.	—	Proof	150.00

5.1000 g, .375 GOLD, .0615 oz AGW
85th Birthday of Queen Mother
Queen Mother holding Queen Elizabeth II
Similar to 50 Seniti, KM#101.

KM#	Date	Mintage	VF	XF	Unc
111	1985	1,000	—	Proof	50.00

7.9600 g, .917 GOLD, .2347 oz AGW

KM#	Date	Mintage	VF	XF	Unc
111a	1985	500 pcs.	—	Proof	150.00

5.1000 g, .375 GOLD, .0615 oz AGW
85th Birthday of Queen Mother
Portrait of Queen Mother
Similar to 50 Seniti, KM#102.

KM#	Date	Mintage	VF	XF	Unc
112	1985	1,000	—	Proof	50.00

7.9600 g, .917 GOLD, .2347 oz AGW

KM#	Date	Mintage	VF	XF	Unc
112a	1985	500 pcs.	—	Proof	150.00

COPPER-NICKEL
America's Cup - National Flags
Obv: Taufa'ahau Tupou IV.

KM#	Date	Mintage	VF	XF	Unc
126	1987	—	—	—	7.00

31.1030 g, .999 PALLADIUM, 1.0000 oz APW

KM#	Date	Mintage	VF	XF	Unc
126a	1987	.025	—	Proof	175.00

311.0400 g, .999 SILVER, 10.0000 oz ASW
America's Cup - Sailboat and Map
Reduced. Actual size: 75mm

Obv: Taufa'ahau Tupou IV.

KM#	Date	Mintage	VF	XF	Unc
125	1987	5,000	—	Proof	250.00

15.5500 g, .999 GOLD, .5000 oz AGW
Summer Olympics - Boxing

KM#	Date	Mintage	VF	XF	Unc
130	1988	*2,000	—	Proof	225.00

31.1000 g, .999 PALLADIUM, 1.0000 oz APW
Summer Olympics - Shot Putter

KM#	Date	Mintage	VF	XF	Unc
131	1988	*2,000	—	Proof	145.00

15.6300 g, .950 PLATINUM, .5000 oz APW
Summer Olympics - Discus Thrower

KM#	Date	Mintage	VF	XF	Unc
132	1988	*2,000	—	Proof	250.00

20 PA'ANGA

140.0000 g, .999 SILVER, 4.4971 oz ASW
Constitution Centennial
Rev: Similar to 5 Pa'anga, KM#50.

KM#	Date	Mintage	VF	XF	Unc
52	1975	1,170	—	—	85.00
	1975	800 pcs.	—	Proof	125.00

0.8000 g, .917 GOLD, .0235 oz AGW
F.A.O. and Rural Women's Advancement
Obv: Queen Salote. Rev: Female symbol on dove.

KM#	Date	Mintage	VF	XF	Unc
65	1980	750 pcs.	—	—	35.00
	1980	2,000	—	Proof	35.00

25 PA'ANGA

5.0000 .g, .917 GOLD, .1474 .oz AGW
Constitution Centennial
Obv: King George Tupou I. Rev: Arms.

KM#	Date	Mintage	VF	XF	Unc
53	1975	405 pcs.	—	—	85.00
	1975	105 pcs.	—	Proof	135.00

50 PA'ANGA

10.0000 g, .917 GOLD, .2948 oz AGW
Constitution Centennial
Obv: King George Tupou II. Rev: Arms.

KM#	Date	Mintage	VF	XF	Unc
54	1975	205 pcs.	—	—	180.00
	1975	105 pcs.	—	Proof	225.00

75 PA'ANGA

15.0000 g, .917 GOLD, .4423 oz AGW
Constitution Centennial
Obv: Queen Salote Tupou III. Rev: Arms.

KM#	Date	Mintage	VF	XF	Unc
55	1975	204 pcs.	—	—	250.00
	1975	105 pcs.	—	Proof	350.00

100 PA'ANGA

20.0000 g, .917 GOLD, .5897 oz AGW
Constitution Centennial

KM#	Date	Mintage	VF	XF	Unc
56	1975	205 pcs.	—	—	350.00
	1975	105 pcs.	—	Proof	400.00

7.7760 g. .5833 GOLD, .1458 oz AGW
Olympics - Gymnast on Rings

KM#	Date	Mintage	VF	XF	Unc
155	1993	3,000	—	Proof	125.00

1/4 HAU

16.0000 g, .980 PALLADIUM, .5041 oz APW
Coronation of Taufa'ahau Tupou IV

KM#	Date	Mintage	VF	XF	Unc
21	1967	1,700	—	—	75.00

1/2 HAU

32.0000 g, .980 PALLADIUM, 1.0082 oz APW
Coronation of Taufa'ahau Tupou IV

KM#	Date	Mintage	VF	XF	Unc
23	1967	1,650	—	—	125.00

28.2800 g, .925 SILVER, .8411 oz ASW
Wedding and Treaty of Friendship

KM#	Date	Mintage	VF	XF	Unc
74	1981	1,000	—	—	30.00
	1981	.015	—	Proof	25.00

10.0000 g, .917 GOLD, .2948 oz AGW
Wildlife - Ground Dwelling Birds

KM#	Date	Mintage	VF	XF	Unc
122	1986	5,000	—	Proof	200.00

HAU

64.0000 g, .980 PALLADIUM, 2.0164 oz APW
Coronation of Taufa'ahau Tupou IV

KM#	Date	Mintage	VF	XF	Unc
25	1967	1,500	—	—	225.00

7.9900 g, .917 GOLD, .2356 oz AGW
Wedding and Treaty of Friendship

KM#	Date	Mintage	VF	XF	Unc
75	1981	500 pcs.	—	—	150.00
	1981	2,500	—	Proof	150.00

Commonwealth Games
Obv: Similar to 10 Pa'anga, KM#78.

KM#	Date	Mintage	VF	XF	Unc
79	1982	500 pcs.	—	—	150.00
	1982	500 pcs.	—	Proof	150.00

52.0000 g, .950 PLATINUM, 1.5884 oz APW
100th Anniversary of Automobile Industry
Rolls Royce and Silver Ghost
Similar to 50 Seniti, KM#82.

KM#	Date	Mintage	VF	XF	Unc
94	1985	—	—	Proof	*BV + 15%*

100th Anniversary of Automobile Industry
Range Rover and Land Rover
Similar to 50 Seniti, KM#83.

KM#	Date	Mintage	VF	XF	Unc
95	1985	—	—	Proof	*BV + 15%*

100th Anniversary of Automobile Industry
Mini Morris Cowley and Touring Car
Similar to 50 Seniti, KM#84.

KM#	Date	Mintage	VF	XF	Unc
96	1985	—	—	Proof	*BV + 15%*

100th Anniversary of Automobile Industry
MGA GT and MG TA
Similar to 50 Seniti, KM#85.

KM#	Date	Mintage	VF	XF	Unc
97	1985	—	—	Proof	*BV + 15%*

85th Birthday of Queen Mother
Queen Mother as a Young Girl
Similar to 50 Seniti, KM#98.

KM#	Date	Mintage	VF	XF	Unc
113	1985	—	—	Proof	*BV + 15%*

85th Birthday of Queen Mother
Wedding Portrait of King George VI and Elizabeth
Similar to 50 Seniti, KM#99.

KM#	Date	Mintage	VF	XF	Unc
114	1985	—	—	Proof	*BV + 15%*

85th Birthday of Queen Mother
Portrait of King George VI and Elizabeth
Similar to 50 Seniti, KM#100.

KM#	Date	Mintage	VF	XF	Unc
115	1985	—	—	Proof	*BV + 15%*

85th Birthday of Queen Mother
Queen Mother holding Queen Elizabeth II
Similar to 50 Seniti, KM#101.

KM#	Date	Mintage	VF	XF	Unc
116	1985	—	—	Proof	*BV + 15%*

85th Birthday of Queen Mother
Portrait of Queen Mother
Similar to 50 Seniti, KM#102.

KM#	Date	Mintage	VF	XF	Unc
117	1985	—	—	Proof	*BV + 15%*

5 HAU

15.9800 g, .917 GOLD, .4711 oz AGW
Wedding and Treaty of Friendship

KM#	Date	Mintage	VF	XF	Unc
76	1981	250 pcs.	—	—	275.00
	1981	1,000	—	Proof	275.00

COUNTERMARKED COINAGE

20 SENITI

COPPER-NICKEL
c/m: 1918/TTIV/1968 on KM#13.

KM#	Date	Mintage	VF	XF	Unc
14	1967	1,577	—	Proof	4.00

50 SENITI

GILT COPPER-NICKEL
c/m: IN MEMORIAM/1965-1970 on KM#9.

KM#	Date	Mintage	VF	XF	Unc
10	1967	Inc. Ab.	—	—	2.00

COPPER-NICKEL
c/m: 1918/TTIV/1968 on KM#15.

KM#	Date	Mintage	VF	XF	Unc
16	1967	1,577	—	Proof	5.00

PA'ANGA

GILT COPPER-NICKEL
c/m: IN MEMORIAM/1965-1970 on KM#11.

KM#	Date	Mintage	VF	XF	Unc
12	1967	Inc. Ab.	—	—	4.00

COPPER-NICKEL
c/m: 1918/TTIV/1968 on KM#17.

KM#	Date	Mintage	VF	XF	Unc
18	1967	1,577	—	Proof	5.00

GILT COPPER-NICKEL
c/m: Oil Rig 1969 OIL SEARCH on KM#17.

KM#	Date	Mintage	VF	XF	Unc
34	1968	5,017	1.25	2.50	3.50

c/m: COMMONWEALTH MEMBER/1970 on KM#17.

KM#	Date	Mintage	VF	XF	Unc
35	1968	3,000	2.00	3.00	4.00

c/m: INVESTITURE/1971 on KM#17.

KM#	Date	Mintage	VF	XF	Unc
36	1968	3,000	2.00	3.00	4.00
	1968	1,000	—	Proof	6.00

2 PA'ANGA

COPPER-NICKEL
c/m: 1918/TTIV/1968 on KM#19.

KM#	Date	Mintage	VF	XF	Unc
20	1967	1,577	—	Proof	8.00

GILT COPPER-NICKEL
c/m: Oil Rig 1969 OIL SEARCH on KM#37.

KM#	Date	Mintage	VF	XF	Unc
38	1968	5,039	2.00	4.00	6.00

c/m: COMMONWEALTH MEMBER/1970 on KM#37.

KM#	Date	Mintage	VF	XF	Unc
39	1968	3,006	3.00	5.00	8.00

c/m: INVESTITURE/1971 on KM#37.

KM#	Date	Mintage	VF	XF	Unc
40	1968	3,000	3.00	5.00	8.00
	1968	1,000	—	Proof	9.00

1/4 HAU

16.0000 g, .980 PALLADIUM, .5040 oz APW
c/m: 1918/TTIV/1968 on Y#15.

KM#	Date	Mintage	VF	XF	Unc
22	1967	400 pcs.	—	—	100.00

1/2 HAU

32.0000 g, .980 PALLADIUM, 1.0082 oz APW
c/m: 1918/TTIV/1968 on Y#16a.

M#	Date	Mintage	VF	XF	Unc
4	1967	513 pcs.	—	—	200.00

HAU

64.0000 g, .980 PALLADIUM, 2.0164 oz APW
c/m: 1918/TTIV/1968 on Y#17.

M#	Date	Mintage	VF	XF	Unc
5	1967	400 pcs.	—	—	350.00

MINT SETS (MS)

M#	Date	Mintage	Identification	Issue Price	Mkt. Val.
S1	1962(3)	—	KM1-3	—	800.00
S2	1967(3)	1,500	KM21,23,25	207.00	450.00
S3	1968(3)	400	KM22,24,26	—	650.00
S4	1970(2)	10,000	KM10,12	2.30	8.00
S5	1969(2)	10,000	KM34,38	13.68	12.00
S6	1970(2)	3,000	KM35,39	13.68	15.00
S7	1971(2)	3,000	KM36,40	4.80	15.00
S8	1974(8)	10,000	KM27-33,37	7.60	15.00
S9	1975(8)	—	KM42-49	7.75	12.00
S10	1975(4)	—	KM53-56	384.50	850.00
S11	1975(3)	—	KM50-52	59.60	170.00
S12	1977(5)	—	KM44-47	.85	4.00
S13	1977(2)	—	KM49,57	3.00	8.00
S14	1978(2)	—	KM58-59	3.00	9.00
S15	1978(5)	—	KM42-46	—	2.00
S16	1979(2)	8,008	KM60-61	3.00	10.00
S17	1980(2)	8,000	KM62-63	3.00	12.00
S18	1980(2)	750	KM64-65, Gold	30.00	60.00
S19	1981(8)	15,000	KM66-73	5.38	10.00
S20	1985(5)	*20,000	KM98-102	26.25	15.00
S21	1985(4)	*20,000	KM82-85, auto industry	21.00	12.00

PROOF SETS (PS)

PS#	Date	Mintage	Identification	Issue Price	Mkt. Val.
S1	1962(3)	250	KM1-3	—	975.00
S2	1962(3)	25	KM1a-3a, Platinum	—	2250.
S3	1967(7)	5,000	KM4-9,11	15.00	12.00
S4	1967(4)	1,923	KM13,15,17,19	17.25	20.00
S5	1968(8)	2,500	KM27-33,37	22.50	25.00
S6	1968(4)	1,577	KM14,16,18,20	22.80	25.00
S8	1971(2)	1,000	KM36,40	13.40	20.00
S9	1975(3)	418	KM50-52	82.00	225.00
S10	1975(4)	105	KM53-56	538.00	1100.
S11	1978(2)	750	KM58a-59a	—	75.00
PS12	1979(2)	854	KM60a-61a	45.00	90.00
S13	1980(2)	400	KM62a-63a	80.00	75.00
S14	1980(2)	200	KM64-65	60.00	60.00
S-A15	1981(3)	—	KM74-76	—	475.00
S15	1981(2)	3,500	KM72a-73a	88.00	60.00
S16	1985(5)	*20,000	KM98-102, Copper-Nickel	26.25	20.00
PS17	1985(5)	*10,000	KM103-107, Silver-clad Copper-Nickel	55.00	40.00
PS18	1985(5)	*5,000	KM103a-107a, .925 Silver	180.00	150.00
PS19	1985(5)	*1,000	KM108-112, .374 Gold	315.00	250.00
PS20	1985(5)	*500	KM108a-112a, .917 Gold	775.00	750.00
PS21	1985(5)	*50	KM113-117, .950 Platinum	5850.	*BV + 15%*
PS22	1985(4)	*10,000	KM86-89	44.00	32.50
PS23	1985(4)	*5,000	KM86a-89a, .925 Silver	144.00	120.00
PS24	1985(4)	*1,000	KM90-93, .374 Gold	252.00	200.00
PS25	1985(4)	*500	KM90a-93a, .917 Gold	620.00	600.00
PS26	1985(4)	*50	KM94-97, .950 Platinum	4680.	*BV + 15%*
PS28	1988(4)	2,000	KM129-132	—	750.00

Listings For

TONKIN: refer to Vietnam

TRINIDAD & TOBAGO

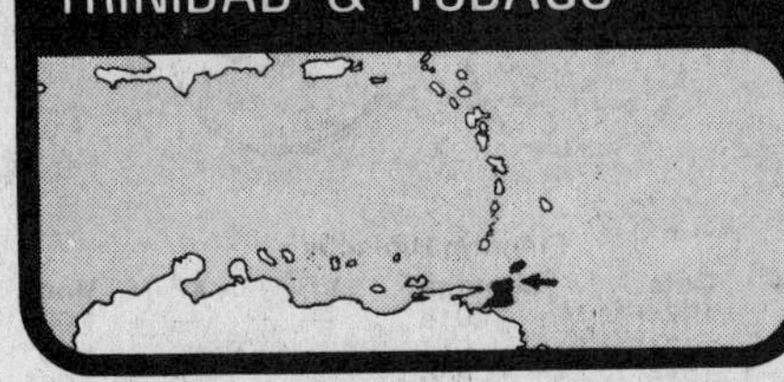

The Republic of Trinidad and Tobago, a member of the British Commonwealth situated 7 miles (11 km.) off the coast of Venezuela, has an area of 1,981 sq. mi. (5,130 sq. km.) and a population of *1.2 million. Capital: Port-of-Spain. The island of Trinidad contains the world's largest natural asphalt bog. Birds of Paradise live on little Tobago, the only place outside of their native New Guinea where they can be found in a wild state. Petroleum and petroleum products are the mainstay of the economy. Petroleum products, crude oil and sugar are exported.

Trinidad and Tobago were discovered by Columbus in 1498. Trinidad remained under Spanish rule from the time of its settlement in 1592 until its capture by the British in 1797. It was ceded to the British in 1802. Tobago was occupied at various times by the French, Dutch and English before being ceded to Britain in 1814. Trinidad and Tobago were merged into a single colony in 1888. The colony was part of the Federation of the West Indies until Aug. 31, 1962, when it became an independent member of the Commonwealth of Nations. A new constitution establishing a republican form of government was adopted on Aug. 1, 1976. Trinidad and Tobago is a member of the Commonwealth of Nations. The President is Chief of State. The Prime Minister is Head of Government.

RULERS

British, until 1976

TRINIDAD

Trinidad was discovered by Columbus in 1498. It remained under Spanish rule from the time of its settlement in 1592 until its capture by the British in 1797. It was ceded to the British in 1802.

MONETARY SYSTEM

9 Bits or Shillings = 8 Reales

CUT & COUNTERMARKED COINAGE

3 PENCE

SILVER
Cut quarter segment from Spanish Colonial 1 Real.

Kann#	Date	Mintage	Good	VG	Fine	VF
3	ND(1804)	—	18.00	25.00	50.00	75.00

6 PENCE

SILVER
Cut half segment from Spanish Colonial 1 Real.

Kann#	Date	Mintage	Good	VG	Fine	VF
6	ND(1804)	—	18.00	25.00	50.00	75.00

SHILLING

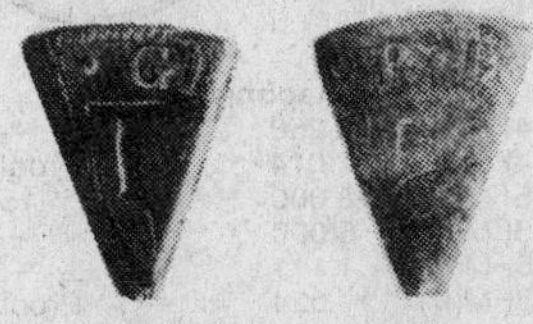

SILVER, 3.00-3.31 g
c/m: T on 1/8 or 1/9 cut of Spanish or Spanish Colonial 8 Reales

Kann#	Date	Mintage	Good	VG	Fine	VF
9	ND(1798-1801)	—	400.00	500.00	800.00	1200.

NOTE: The attribution of this type has been questioned.

2.98 g
c/m: T on center plug cut from Spanish or Spanish Colonial 8 Reales, C#26.

Kann#	Date	Mintage	Good	VG	Fine	VF
10	ND(1811)	.025	120.00	150.00	260.00	400.00

9 SHILLINGS

SILVER
c/m: T on holed Spanish or Spanish Colonial 8 Reales

Kann#	Date	Mintage	Good	VG	Fine	VF
13	ND(1811)	.025	400.00	500.00	700.00	900.00

Similar to KM#13 but w/o T c/m.

Kann#	Date	Mintage	Good	VG	Fine	VF
14	ND(1811)	I.A.	300.00	400.00	600.00	800.00

TRINIDAD AND TOBAGO

MINT MARKS

FM - Franklin Mint, U.S.A.*

***NOTE:** From 1975 the Franklin Mint has produced coinage in up to 3 different qualities. Qualities of issue are designated in ( ) after each date and are defined as follows:

(M) MATTE - Normal circulation strike or a dull finish produced by sandblasting special uncirculated (polish finish) or proof quality dies.

(U) SPECIAL UNCIRCULATED - Polished or proof-like in appearance without any frosted features.

(P) PROOF - The highest quality obtainable having mirror-like fields and frosted features.

MONETARY SYSTEM

100 Cents = 1 Dollar

CENT

BRONZE

KM#	Date	Mintage	VF	XF	Unc
1	1966	24.500	—	—	.15
	1966	8,000	—	Proof	1.00
	1967	4.000	—	—	.15
	1968	5.000	—	—	.15
	1970	5.000	—	—	.15
	1970	2,104	—	Proof	1.50
	1971	10.600	—	—	.15
	1971FM(M)	.286	—	—	.20
	1971FM(P)	.012	—	Proof	.50
	1972	16.500	—	—	.15
	1973	10.000	—	—	.15

10th Anniversary of Independence

KM#	Date	Mintage	VF	XF	Unc
9	1972	5.000	—	.10	.15
	1972FM(M)	.125	—	—	.25
	1972FM(P)	.016	—	Proof	.50

KM#	Date	Mintage	VF	XF	Unc
17	1973FM(M)	.127	—	—	.50
	1973FM(P)	.020	—	Proof	.75

Balisier Hummingbird

KM#	Date	Mintage	VF	XF	Unc
25	1974FM(M)	.128	—	—	.25
	1974FM(P)	.014	—	Proof	.50
	1975	10.000	—	—	.15
	1975FM(M)	.125	—	—	.15
	1975FM(U)	1,111	—	—	1.25

KM#	Date	Mintage	VF	XF	Unc
25	1975FM(P)	.024	—	Proof	.50
	1976	15.050	—	—	.15

5 CENTS

BRONZE

KM#	Date	Mintage	VF	XF	Unc
2	1966	7.500	—	.10	.25
	1966	8,000	—	Proof	1.25
	1967	3.000	—	.10	.25
	1970	2,104	—	Proof	1.75
	1971	2.400	—	.10	.25
	1971FM(M)	.057	—	—	.15
	1971FM(P)	.012	—	Proof	.75
	1972	2.250	—	.10	.20

10th Anniversary of Independence

KM#	Date	Mintage	VF	XF	Unc
10	1972	.015	—	—	.35
	1972FM(M)	.025	—	—	.25
	1972FM(P)	.016	—	Proof	.75

KM#	Date	Mintage	VF	XF	Unc
57	1973FM(M)	.027	—	—	.50
	1973FM(P)	.020	—	Proof	.75

Bird of Paradise

KM#	Date	Mintage	VF	XF	Unc
26	1974FM(M)	.028	—	—	.50
	1974FM(P)	.014	—	Proof	.75
	1975	1.500	—	.10	.20
	1975FM(M)	.025	—	—	.20
	1975FM(U)	1,111	—	—	1.50
	1975FM(P)	.024	—	Proof	.75
	1976	7.500	—	.10	.20

10 CENTS

COPPER-NICKEL

KM#	Date	Mintage	VF	XF	Unc
3	1966	7.800	—	.10	.30
	1966	8,000	—	Proof	1.50
	1967	4.000	—	.10	.30
	1970	2,104	—	Proof	2.00
	1971	—	—	.10	.30
	1971FM(M)	.029	—	—	.35
	1971FM(P)	.012	—	Proof	1.00
	1972	4.000	—	.10	.30

10th Anniversary of Independence

KM#	Date	Mintage	VF	XF	Unc
11	1972	.041	—	—	.40
	1972FM(M)	.013	—	—	.60
	1972FM(P)	.016	—	Proof	1.00

KM#	Date	Mintage	VF	XF	Unc
58	1973FM(M)	.014	—	—	1.00
	1973FM(P)	.020	—	Proof	1.00

Flaming Hibiscus

KM#	Date	Mintage	VF	XF	Unc
27	1974FM(M)	.016	—	—	1.00
	1974FM(P)	.014	—	Proof	1.00
	1975	4.000	—	.10	.25
	1975FM(M)	.013	—	—	.50
	1975FM(U)	1,111	—	—	1.75
	1975FM(P)	.024	—	Proof	1.00
	1976	14.720	—	.10	.20

25 CENTS

COPPER-NICKEL

KM#	Date	Mintage	VF	XF	Unc
4	1966	7.200	.10	.15	.35
	1966	8,000	—	Proof	1.75
	1967	1.800	.10	.15	.50
	1970	2,014	—	Proof	2.25
	1971	1.500	.10	.15	.50
	1971FM(M)	.011	—	—	.65
	1971FM(P)	.012	—	Proof	1.25
	1972	3.000	.10	.15	.35

10th Anniversary of Independence

KM#	Date	Mintage	VF	XF	Unc
12	1972	.014	—	—	.60
	1972FM(M)	5,000	—	—	1.50
	1972FM(P)	.016	—	Proof	1.25

KM#	Date	Mintage	VF	XF	Unc
59	1973FM(M)	6,575	—	—	2.25
	1973FM(P)	.020	—	Proof	1.25

Chaconia

KM#	Date	Mintage	VF	XF	Unc
28	1974FM(M)	8,258	—	—	1.75
	1974FM(P)	.014	—	Proof	1.25
	1975	3.000	.10	.15	.30
	1975FM(M)	5,000	—	—	1.50
	1975FM(U)	1,111	—	—	2.00
	1975FM(P)	.024	—	Proof	1.25
	1976	9.000	.10	.15	.30

50 CENTS

COPPER-NICKEL

KM#	Date	Mintage	VF	XF	Unc
5	1966	.975	.25	.50	1.25
	1966	8,000	—	Proof	2.00
	1967	.750	.25	.50	1.25
	1970	2,104	—	Proof	2.50
	1971FM(M)	5,714	—	—	2.00
	1971FM(P)	.012	—	Proof	1.50

10th Anniversary of Independence

KM#	Date	Mintage	VF	XF	Unc
13	1972	.375	.50	.75	1.50
	1972FM(M)	2,500	—	—	5.00
	1972FM(P)	.016	—	Proof	1.50

Steel Band

KM#	Date	Mintage	VF	XF	Unc
22	1973FM(M)	4,075	—	—	2.50
	1973FM(P)	.020	—	Proof	1.50
	1974FM(M)	5,758	—	—	2.00
	1974FM(P)	.014	—	Proof	1.50
	1975FM(M)	2,500	—	—	3.75
	1975FM(U)	1,111	—	—	2.25
	1975FM(P)	.024	—	Proof	1.50
	1976	.750	.50	.75	1.50

DOLLAR

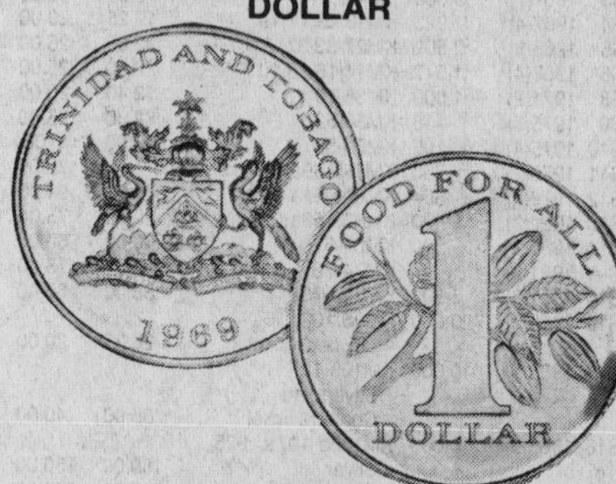

NICKEL
F.A.O. Issue

KM#	Date	Mintage	VF	XF	Unc
6	1969	.250	.50	1.00	2.00

KM#	Date	Mintage	VF	XF	Unc
7	1970	2,014	—	Proof	5.00

COPPER-NICKEL

KM#	Date	Mintage	VF	XF	Unc
7a	1971FM(M)	2,857	—	—	4.00
	1971FM(P)	.012	—	Proof	2.00

10th Anniversary of Independence

KM#	Date	Mintage	VF	XF	Unc
14	1972	9,700	—	—	4.00
	1972FM(M)	1,250	—	—	12.50
	1972FM(P)	.016	—	Proof	2.00

Coerico

KM#	Date	Mintage	VF	XF	Unc
23	1973FM(M)	2,825	—	—	3.00
	1973FM(P)	.020	—	Proof	2.00
	1974FM(M)	4,508	—	—	3.00
	1974FM(P)	.014	—	Proof	2.00
	1975FM(M)	1,250	—	—	5.00
	1975FM(U)	1,111	—	—	3.00
	1975FM(P)	.024	—	Proof	2.00

5 DOLLARS

29.7000 g, .925 SILVER, .8833 oz ASW
Scarlet Ibis

KM#	Date	Mintage	VF	XF	Unc
8	1971FM(M)	571 pcs.	—	—	25.00
	1971FM(P)	.011	—	Proof	10.00
	1973FM(M)	1,825	—	—	15.00
	1973FM(P)	.025	—	Proof	10.00
	1974FM(P)	.016	—	Proof	10.00
	1975FM(P)	.026	—	Proof	10.00

COPPER-NICKEL

KM#	Date	Mintage	VF	XF	Unc
8a	1974FM(M)	3,508	—	—	4.00
	1975FM(M)	250 pcs.	—	—	15.00
	1975FM(U)	1,111	—	—	6.00

29.7000 g, .925 SILVER, .8833 oz ASW

10th Anniversary of Independence

KM#	Date	Mintage	VF	XF	Unc
15	1972	.010	—	—	10.00
	1972FM	250 pcs.	—	—	40.00
	1972FM	.019	—	Proof	10.00

10 DOLLARS

35.0000 g, .925 SILVER, 1.0409 oz ASW
10th Anniversary of Independence

KM#	Date	Mintage	VF	XF	Unc
16	1972	—	—	—	15.00
	1972FM(M)	125 pcs.	—	—	125.00
	1972FM(P)	.026	—	Proof	12.50

Antique Mariners Map

KM#	Date	Mintage	VF	XF	Unc
24	1973FM(M)	1,700	—	—	15.00
	1973FM(P)	.024	—	Proof	12.50
	1974FM(P)	.021	—	Proof	12.50
	1975FM(P)	.028	—	Proof	15.00

COPPER-NICKEL

KM#	Date	Mintage	VF	XF	Unc
24a	1974FM(M)	3,632	—	—	7.50
	1975FM(M)	125 pcs.	—	—	50.00
	1975FM(U)	1,111	—	—	10.00

REPUBLIC

CENT

BRONZE

KM#	Date	Mintage	VF	XF	Unc
29	1976FM(M)	.150	—	—	.15
	1976FM(U)	582 pcs.	—	—	1.50
	1976FM(P)	.010	—	Proof	.50
	1977	25.000	—	—	.15
	1977FM(M)	.150	—	—	.15
	1977FM(U)	633 pcs.	—	—	1.50
	1977FM(P)	5,337	—	Proof	.50
	1978	12.500	—	—	.15
	1978FM(M)	.150	—	—	.15
	1978FM(U)	472 pcs.	—	—	1.50
	1978FM(P)	4,845	—	Proof	1.00
	1979	30.200	—	—	.15

KM#	Date	Mintage	VF	XF	Unc
29	1979FM(M)	.150	—	—	.15
	1979FM(U)	518 pcs.	—	—	1.50
	1979FM(P)	3,270	—	Proof	.15
	1980	12.500	—	—	.10
	1980FM(M)	.075	—	—	.15
	1980FM(U)	796 pcs.	—	—	1.50
	1980FM(P)	2,393	—	Proof	1.00
	1981	—	—	—	.15
	1981FM(M)	—	—	—	.15
	1981FM(U)	—	—	—	1.50
	1981FM(P)	—	—	Proof	1.00
	1982	—	—	—	.15
	1983	—	—	—	.15
	1984	—	—	—	.15
	1985	25.400	—	—	.15
	1986	10.000	—	—	.15
	1987	10.000	—	—	.15
	1988	5.000	—	—	.15
	1989	—	—	—	.15
	1990	—	—	—	.15
	1991	—	—	—	.15

2.0000 g, .925 SILVER, .0594 oz ASW

KM#	Date	Mintage	VF	XF	Unc
29a	1981FM(P)	898 pcs.	—	Proof	7.50

BRONZE
20th Anniversary of Independence
Obv: Coat of Arms.

KM#	Date	Mintage	VF	XF	Unc
42	1982FM(M)	—	—	—	.15
	1982FM(U)	—	—	—	1.50
	1982FM(P)	—	—	Proof	1.00

2.0000 g, .925 SILVER, .0594 oz ASW

KM#	Date	Mintage	VF	XF	Unc
42a	1982FM(P)	699 pcs.	—	Proof	7.50

BRONZE

KM#	Date	Mintage	VF	XF	Unc
51	1983FM(M)	—	—	—	.15
	1983FM(P)	—	—	Proof	1.00
	1984FM(P)	—	—	Proof	1.00

2.0000 g, .925 SILVER, .0594 oz ASW

KM#	Date	Mintage	VF	XF	Unc
51a	1983FM(P)	1,344	—	Proof	7.50
	1984FM(P)	—	—	Proof	7.50

5 CENTS

BRONZE

KM#	Date	Mintage	VF	XF	Unc
30	1976FM(M)	.030	—	—	.20
	1976FM(U)	582 pcs.	—	—	1.75
	1976FM(P)	.010	—	Proof	.75
	1977	12.000	—	.10	.20
	1977FM(M)	.030	—	—	.20
	1977FM(U)	633 pcs.	—	—	1.75
	1977FM(P)	5,337	—	Proof	.75
	1978	1.500	—	.10	.20
	1978FM(M)	.030	—	—	.20
	1978FM(U)	472 pcs.	—	—	1.75
	1978FM(P)	4,845	—	Proof	1.25
	1979	—	—	.10	.20
	1979FM(M)	.030	—	—	.20
	1979FM(U)	518 pcs.	—	—	1.75
	1979FM(P)	3,270	—	Proof	1.25
	1980	15.000	—	.10	.20
	1980FM(M)	.015	—	—	.20
	1980FM(U)	796 pcs.	—	—	1.75
	1980FM(P)	2,393	—	Proof	1.25
	1981	—	—	.10	.20
	1981FM(M)	—	—	—	.20
	1981FM(U)	—	—	—	1.75
	1981FM(P)	—	—	Proof	1.25
	1983	—	—	.10	.20
	1984	4.095	—	.10	.20
	1988	20.000	—	.10	.20
	1990	—	—	.10	.20

3.5000 g, .925 SILVER, .1040 oz ASW

KM#	Date	Mintage	VF	XF	Unc
30a	1981FM(P)	898 pcs.	—	Proof	10.00

BRONZE

20th Anniversary of Independence
Obv: Coat of Arms.

KM#	Date	Mintage	VF	XF	Unc
43	1982FM(M)	—	—	—	.20
	1982FM(U)	—	—	—	1.75
	1982FM(P)	—	—	Proof	1.25
	3.5000 g, .925 SILVER, .1040 oz ASW				
43a	1982FM(P)	699 pcs.	—	Proof	10.00

BRONZE
Obv: Coat of arms.

KM#	Date	Mintage	VF	XF	Unc
52	1983FM(M)	—	—	—	.20
	1983FM(P)	—	—	Proof	1.25
	1984FM(P)	—	—	Proof	1.25
	3.5000 g, .925 SILVER, .1040 oz ASW				
52a	1983FM(P)	1,324	—	Proof	10.00
	1984FM(P)	—	—	Proof	10.00

10 CENTS

COPPER-NICKEL

KM#	Date	Mintage	VF	XF	Unc
31	1976FM(M)	.015	—	—	.50
	1976FM(U)	582 pcs.	—	—	2.00
	1976FM(P)	.010	—	Proof	1.00
	1977	17.280	—	.10	.20
	1977FM(M)	.015	—	—	.50
	1977FM(U)	633 pcs.	—	—	2.00
	1977FM(P)	5,337	—	Proof	1.00
	1978	10.000	—	.10	.20
	1978FM(M)	.015	—	—	.50
	1978FM(U)	472 pcs.	—	—	2.00
	1978FM(P)	4,845	—	Proof	1.50
	1979	1.970	—	.10	.30
	1979FM(M)	.015	—	—	.50
	1979FM(U)	518 pcs.	—	—	2.00
	1979FM(P)	3,270	—	Proof	1.50
	1980	20.000	—	.10	.30
	1980FM(M)	7,500	—	—	.50
	1980FM(U)	796 pcs.	—	—	2.00
	1980FM(P)	2,393	—	Proof	1.50
	1981	—	—	.10	.30
	1981FM(M)	—	—	—	.50
	1981FM(U)	—	—	—	2.00
	1981FM(P)	—	—	Proof	1.50
	1990	—	—	.10	.30
	1.5000 g, .925 SILVER, .0446 oz ASW				
31a	1981FM(P)	898 pcs.	—	Proof	10.00

COPPER-NICKEL
20th Anniversary of Independence
Obv: Coat of Arms.

KM#	Date	Mintage	VF	XF	Unc
44	1982FM(M)	—	—	—	.50
	1982FM(U)	—	—	—	2.00
	1982FM(P)	—	—	Proof	1.50
	1.5000 g, .925 SILVER, .0446 oz ASW				
44a	1982FM(P)	699 pcs.	—	Proof	10.00

COPPER-NICKEL
Obv: Coat of arms.

KM#	Date	Mintage	VF	XF	Unc
53	1983FM(M)	—	—	—	.50
	1983FM(P)	—	—	Proof	1.50
	1984FM(P)	—	—	Proof	1.50
	1.5000 g, .925 SILVER, .0446 oz ASW				
53a	1983FM(P)	—	—	Proof	10.00
	1984FM(P)	—	—	Proof	10.00

25 CENTS

COPPER-NICKEL

KM#	Date	Mintage	VF	XF	Unc
32	1976FM(M)	6,000	—	—	1.00
32	1976FM(U)	582 pcs.	—	—	2.25
	1976FM(P)	.010	—	Proof	1.25
	1977	9.000	.10	.15	.30
	1977FM(M)	6,000	—	—	1.00
	1977FM(U)	633 pcs.	—	—	2.25
	1977FM(P)	5,337	—	Proof	1.25
	1978	5.470	.10	.15	.30
	1978FM(M)	6,000	—	—	1.00
	1978FM(U)	472 pcs.	—	—	2.25
	1978FM(P)	4,845	—	Proof	1.75
	1979	—	.10	.15	.40
	1979FM(M)	6,000	—	—	1.00
	1979FM(U)	518 pcs.	—	—	2.25
	1979FM(P)	3,270	—	Proof	1.75
	1980	15.000	.10	.15	.40
	1980FM(M)	3,000	—	—	1.00
	1980FM(U)	796 pcs.	—	—	2.25
	1980FM(P)	2,393	—	Proof	1.75
	1981	—	.10	.15	.40
	1981FM(M)	—	—	—	1.00
	1981FM(U)	—	—	—	2.25
	1981FM(P)	—	—	Proof	1.75
	1983	—	.10	.15	.40
	1983FM(M)	—	—	—	1.00
	1983FM(P)	—	—	Proof	1.75
	1984	—	—	Proof	1.75
	3.6000 g, .925 SILVER, .1070 oz ASW				
32a	1981FM(P)	898 pcs.	—	Proof	10.00
	1983FM(P)	—	—	Proof	10.00
	1984FM(P)	—	—	Proof	10.00

COPPER-NICKEL
20th Anniversary of Independence
Obv: Coat of Arms.

KM#	Date	Mintage	VF	XF	Unc
45	1982FM(M)	—	—	—	1.00
	1982FM(U)	—	—	—	2.25
	1982FM(P)	—	—	Proof	1.75
	3.6000 g, .925 SILVER, .1070 oz ASW				
45a	1982FM(P)	699 pcs.	—	Proof	10.00

50 CENTS

COPPER-NICKEL

KM#	Date	Mintage	VF	XF	Unc
33	1976FM(M)	3,000	—	—	3.25
	1976FM(U)	582 pcs.	—	—	2.50
	1976FM(P)	.010	—	Proof	1.50
	1977	1.500	.25	.50	1.00
	1977FM(M)	3,000	—	—	3.00
	1977FM(U)	633 pcs.	—	—	2.50
	1977FM(P)	5,337	—	Proof	1.50
	1978	.563	.50	.75	1.50
	1978FM(M)	3,000	—	—	3.00
	1978FM(U)	472 pcs.	—	—	2.50
	1978FM(P)	4,845	—	Proof	2.00
	1979	.750	.50	.75	1.50
	1979FM(M)	3,000	—	—	3.25
	1979FM(U)	518 pcs.	—	—	2.50
	1979FM(P)	3,270	—	Proof	2.00
	1980	3.750	.25	.50	1.00
	1980FM(M)	1,500	—	—	3.00
	1980FM(U)	796 pcs.	—	—	2.50
	1980FM(P)	2,393	—	Proof	2.00
	1981FM(M)	—	—	—	3.00
	1981FM(U)	—	—	—	2.50
	1981FM(P)	—	—	Proof	2.00
	7.2500 g, .925 SILVER, .2156 oz ASW				
33a	1981FM(P)	898 pcs.	—	Proof	12.50

COPPER-NICKEL
20th Anniversary of Independence
Obv: Coat of Arms.

KM#	Date	Mintage	VF	XF	Unc
46	1982FM(M)	—	—	—	3.00
	1982FM(U)	—	—	—	2.50
	1982FM(P)	—	—	Proof	2.00
	7.2500 g, .925 SILVER, .2156 oz ASW				
46a	1982FM(P)	699 pcs.	—	Proof	12.50

COPPER-NICKEL
Obv: Coat of arms.

KM#	Date	Mintage	VF	XF	Unc
54	1983FM(M)	—	—	—	3.00
	1983FM(P)	—	—	Proof	2.00
	1984FM(P)	—	—	Proof	2.00
	7.2500 g, .925 SILVER, .2156 oz ASW				
54a	1983FM(P)	1,325	—	Proof	12.50
	1984FM(P)	—	—	Proof	12.50

DOLLAR

COPPER-NICKEL

KM#	Date	Mintage	VF	XF	Unc
34	1976FM(M)	1,500	—	—	5.00
	1976FM(U)	582 pcs.	—	—	3.00
	1976FM(P)	.010	—	Proof	2.00
	1977FM(M)	1,500	—	—	5.00
	1977FM(U)	633 pcs.	—	—	3.00
	1977FM(P)	5,337	—	Proof	2.00
	1978FM(M)	1,500	—	—	3.75
	1978FM(U)	472 pcs.	—	—	3.00
	1978FM(P)	4,845	—	Proof	2.50
	1979FM(M)	1,500	—	—	3.75
	1979FM(U)	518 pcs.	—	—	3.00
	1979FM(P)	3,270	—	Proof	2.50
	1980FM(M)	750 pcs.	—	—	5.00
	1980FM(U)	796 pcs.	—	—	3.00
	1980FM(P)	2,393	—	Proof	2.50
	1981FM(M)	—	—	—	5.00
	1981FM(U)	—	—	—	3.00
	1981FM(P)	—	—	Proof	2.50
	1983FM(M)	—	—	—	5.00
	1983FM(P)	—	—	Proof	2.50
	1984FM(P)	—	—	Proof	2.50
	18.6000 g, .925 SILVER, .5532 oz ASW				
34a	1981FM(P)	898 pcs.	—	Proof	15.00
	1983FM(P)	2,544	—	Proof	15.00
	1984FM(P)	—	—	Proof	15.00

F.A.O. Issue

KM#	Date	Mintage	VF	XF	Unc
38	1979	—	.50	1.25	2.75

COPPER-NICKEL
20th Anniversary of Independence
Obv: Coat of Arms.

KM#	Date	Mintage	VF	XF	Unc
47	1982FM(M)	—	—	—	5.00
	1982FM(U)	—	—	—	3.00
	1982FM(P)	—	—	Proof	2.50
	18.6000 g, .925 SILVER, .5532 oz ASW				
47a	1982FM(P) 699 pcs.		—	Proof	20.00

5 DOLLARS

29.7000 g, .925 SILVER, .8833 oz ASW

KM#	Date	Mintage	VF	XF	Unc
35	1976FM(P)	.011	—	Proof	10.00
	1977FM(P)	6,107	—	Proof	10.00
	1978FM(P)	5,460	—	Proof	10.00
	1979FM(P)	3,755	—	Proof	15.00
	1980FM(P)	2,393	—	Proof	20.00
	1981FM(P)	—	—	Proof	25.00
	1983FM(P)	—	—	Proof	25.00
	1984FM(P)	—	—	Proof	25.00
	COPPER-NICKEL				
35a	1976FM(M) 300 pcs.		—	—	17.50
	1976FM(U) 582 pcs.		—	—	12.50
	1977FM(M) 300 pcs.		—	—	17.50
	1977FM(U) 633 pcs.		—	—	12.50
	1978FM(M) 300 pcs.		—	—	17.50
	1978FM(U) 472 pcs.		—	—	12.50
	1979FM(M) 300 pcs.		—	—	17.50
	1979FM(U) 518 pcs.		—	—	12.50
	1980FM(M) 150 pcs.		—	—	17.50
	1980FM(U) 796 pcs.		—	—	12.50
	1981FM(M)	—	—	—	17.50
	1981FM(U)	—	—	—	12.50
	1981FM(P)	—	—	Proof	12.50
	1983FM(U)	—	—	—	17.50
	1983FM(P)	1,312	—	Proof	12.50
	1984FM(P)	—	—	Proof	12.50

20th Anniversary of Independence

KM#	Date	Mintage	VF	XF	Unc
48	1982FM(M)	—	—	—	17.50
	1982FM(U)	—	—	—	12.50
	1982FM(P)	—	—	Proof	15.00
	30.0000 g, .925 SILVER, .8922 oz ASW				
48a	1982FM(P) 699 pcs.		—	Proof	30.00

10 DOLLARS

35.0000 g, .925 SILVER, 1.0409 oz ASW
Rev: Similar to KM#16.

KM#	Date	Mintage	VF	XF	Unc
36	1976FM(P)	.013	—	Proof	10.00
	1977FM(P)	6,643	—	Proof	12.00
	1978FM(P)	7,449	—	Proof	12.00
	1979FM(P)	4,994	—	Proof	17.50
	1980FM(P)	3,726	—	Proof	17.50
	COPPER-NICKEL				
36a	1976FM(M) 150 pcs.		—	—	40.00
	1976FM(U) 582 pcs.		—	—	12.50
	1977FM(M) 150 pcs.		—	—	40.00
	1977FM(U) 633 pcs.		—	—	12.50
	1978FM(M) 150 pcs.		—	—	40.00
	1978FM(U) 472 pcs.		—	—	12.50
	1979FM(M) 150 pcs.		—	—	40.00
	1979FM(U) 796 pcs.		—	—	12.50
	1980FM(M)	—	—	—	40.00
	1980FM(U)	—	—	—	12.50

5th Anniversary of the Republic
Obv: Coat of arms.

KM#	Date	Mintage	VF	XF	Unc
40	1981FM(U)	—	—	—	15.00
	35.0000 g, .925 SILVER, 1.0409 oz ASW				
40a	1981FM(P)	2,374	—	Proof	27.50

COPPER-NICKEL
20th Anniversary of Independence
Obv: Coat of Arms.

KM#	Date	Mintage	VF	XF	Unc
49	1982FM(M)	—	—	—	15.00
	1982FM(U)	—	—	—	20.00
	1982FM(P)	—	—	Proof	22.50

35.0000 g, .925 SILVER, 1.0409 oz ASW

KM#	Date	Mintage	VF	XF	Unc
49a	1982FM(P)	1,682	—	Proof	25.00

COPPER-NICKEL
Obv: Coat of arms.

KM#	Date	Mintage	VF	XF	Unc
55	1983FM(U) 288 pcs.		—	—	20.00
	35.0000 g, .925 SILVER, 1.0409 oz ASW				
55a	1983FM(P)	1,565	—	Proof	30.00
	1984FM(P)	—	—	Proof	30.00

25 DOLLARS

30.2800 g, .500 SILVER, .4868 oz ASW
10th Anniversary of Caribbean Development Bank

KM#	Date	Mintage	VF	XF	Unc
39	1980FM(P)	3,039	—	Proof	20.00

100 DOLLARS

6.2100 g, .500 GOLD, .0998 oz AGW

KM#	Date	Mintage	VF	XF	Unc
37	1976FM(M) 200 pcs.		—	—	85.00
	1976FM(P)	.029	—	Proof	60.00

5th Anniversary of the Republic

KM#	Date	Mintage	VF	XF	Unc
41	1981FM(U) 100 pcs.		—	—	175.00
	1981FM(P) 400 pcs.		—	Proof	150.00

20th Anniversary of Independence

KM#	Date	Mintage	VF	XF	Unc
50	1982FM(P)	1,380	—	Proof	100.00

200 DOLLARS

11.1700 g, .500 GOLD, .1796 oz AGW
20th Anniversary of Central Bank

KM#	Date	Mintage	VF	XF	Unc
56	1984FM(P)	1,200	—	Proof	125.00

MINT SETS (MS)

KM#	Date	Mintage	Identification	Issue Price	Mkt. Val.
MS1	1973(8)	1,575	KM8,18-24	24.00	22.00
MS2	1974(8)	3,258	KM8a,22-23,24a,25-28	25.00	15.00
MS3	1975(8)	1,111	KM8a,22-23,24a,25-28	27.50	20.00
MS4	1976(8)	582	KM29-34,35a-36a	27.50	30.00
MS5	1977(8)	632	KM29-34,35a-36a	27.50	30.00
MS6	1978(8)	472	KM29-34,35a-36a	27.50	30.00
MS7	1979(8)	518	KM29-34,35a-36a	28.50	30.00
MS8	1980(8)	796	KM29-34,35a-36a	28.50	30.00
MS9	1981(8)	—	KM29-34,35a,40	28.50	45.50
MS10	1982(8)	—	KM42-49	28.50	45.50
MS11	1983(8)	281	KM32,34,35a,51-55	37.00	45.50

PROOF SETS (PS)

KM#	Date	Mintage	Identification	Issue Price	Mkt. Val.
PS1	1966(5)	8,000	KM1-5	12.50	7.50
PS2	1970(6)	2,104	KM1-5,7	15.25	12.50
PS3	1971(7)	11,039	KM1-5,7a,8	21.00	15.00
PS4	1971(6)	488	KM1-5,6	15.00	12.50
PS5	1972(8)	13,874	KM9-16	35.00	22.00
PS6	1972(7)	15,957	KM9-15	22.00	15.00
PS7	1973(8)	14,615	KM8,17,19-24	35.00	22.00
PS8	1973(7)	5,050	KM,8,17,19-23	22.00	15.00
PS9	1974(8)	13,991	KM8,22-28	50.00	22.00
PS10	1975(8)	24,472	KM8,22-28	55.00	22.00
PS11	1976(8)	10,099	KM29-36	55.00	25.00
PS12	1977(8)	5,337	KM29-36	55.00	35.00
PS13	1978(8)	4,845	KM29-36	55.00	35.00
PS14	1979(8)	3,270	KM29-36	57.00	45.00
PS15	1980(8)	2,393	KM29-36	66.00	50.00
PS16	1981(8)	—	KM29-34,35a,40a	87.00	52.50
PS17	1981(8)	—	KM29a-34a,35,40a	222.00	115.00
PS18	1982(8)	—	KM42-49	87.00	60.00
PS19	1982(8)	—	KM42a-49a	222.00	125.00
PS20	1983(8)	461	KM32,34,35a,51-54,55a	87.00	60.00
PS21	1983(8)	753	KM32a,34a,35,51a-55a	197.00	115.00
PS22	1984(8)	—	KM32,34,35a,51-54,55a	87.00	60.00
PS23	1984(8)	—	KM32a,34a,35,51a-55a	197.00	115.00

TRISTAN DA CUNHA

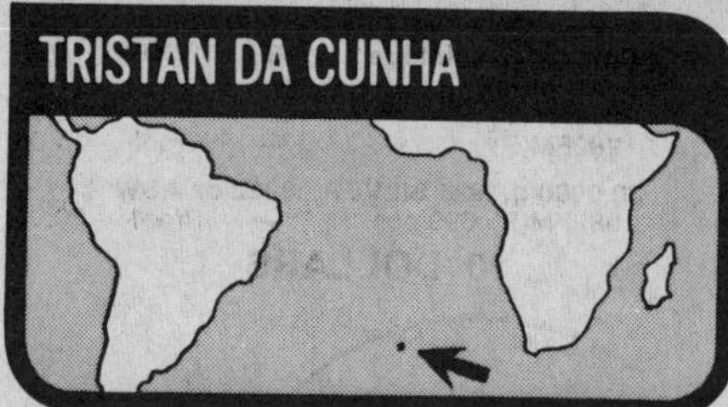

Tristan da Cunha is the principal island and group name of a small cluster of volcanic islands located in the South Atlantic midway between the Cape of Good Hope and South America, and 1,500 miles (2,414 km.) southsouthwest of the British colony of St. Helena. The other islands are Inaccessible, Gough, and the three Nightingale Islands. The group, which comprises a dependency of St. Helena, has a total area of 40 sq. mi. (104 sq. km.) and a population of less than 300. There is a village of 60 houses called Edinburgh. Potatoes are the staple subsistence crop.

Tristan da Cunha was discovered in 1506 by Portuguese admiral Tristao da Cunha. Unsuccessful attempts to colonize the islands were made by the Dutch in 1656, but the first permanent inhabitant didn't arrive until 1810. During the exile of Napoleon on St. Helena, Britain placed a temporary garrison on Tristan da Cunha to prevent any attempt to rescue Napoleon from his island prison. The islands were formally annexed to Britain in 1816 and became a dependency of St. Helena in 1938.

RULERS

British

MINT MARKS

PM - Pobjoy Mint

MONETARY SYSTEM

25 Pence = 1 Crown
4 Crowns = 1 Pound

25 PENCE

COPPER-NICKEL
Queen's Silver Jubilee

KM#	Date	Mintage	Fine	VF	XF	Unc
1	1977	.050	—	1.00	1.75	3.00
		28.2800 g, .925 SILVER, .8411 oz ASW				
1a	1977	.025	—	—	Proof	20.00

COPPER-NICKEL
80th Birthday of Queen Mother

KM#	Date	Mintage	Fine	VF	XF	Unc
3	1980	.065	—	1.00	1.75	3.00
		28.2800 g, .925 SILVER, .8411 oz ASW (OMS)				
3a	1980	.025	—	—	Proof	20.00

COPPER-NICKEL
Wedding of Prince Charles and Lady Diana

KM#	Date	Mintage	Fine	VF	XF	Unc
4	1981PM	—	—	1.00	1.75	3.00
		28.2800 g, .925 SILVER, .8411 oz ASW				
4a	1981PM	.030	—	—	Proof	20.00

50 PENCE

28.2800 g, .925 SILVER, .8411 oz ASW
40th Wedding Anniversary of Queen Elizabeth and Prince Philip

KM#	Date	Mintage	Fine	VF	XF	Unc
7	1987	2,000	—	—	Proof	35.00
		47.5400 g, .917 GOLD, 1.4001 oz AGW				
7a	1987	75 pcs.	—	—	Proof	1250.
		COPPER-NICKEL				
7b	1987	—	—	—	—	4.50

CROWN

COPPER-NICKEL
25th Anniversary of Coronation

KM#	Date	Mintage	Fine	VF	XF	Unc
2	1978PM	—	—	1.00	1.75	3.00

28.2800 g, .925 SILVER, .8411 oz ASW

KM#	Date	Mintage	Fine	VF	XF	Unc
2a	1978PM	.070	—	—	—	15.00
	1978PM	.025	—	—	Proof	20.00

International Year of the Scout
Obv: Portrait of Queen Elizabeth II.

KM#	Date	Mintage	Fine	VF	XF	Unc
5	1983	.010	—	—	—	17.50
	1983	.010	—	—	Proof	25.00

2 POUNDS

15.9800 g, .917 GOLD, .4712 oz AGW
International Year of the Scout
Obv: Portrait of Queen Elizabeth II.
Rev: Sail boat.

KM#	Date	Mintage	Fine	VF	XF	Unc
6	1983	2,000	—	—	—	350.00
	1983	2,000	—	—	Proof	500.00

COPPER-NICKEL
90th Anniversary of Queen Mother

KM#	Date	Mintage	Fine	VF	XF	Unc
8	1990	—	—	—	—	12.00

28.2800 g, .925 SILVER, .8411 oz ASW

KM#	Date	Mintage	Fine	VF	XF	Unc
8a	1990	*.010	—	—	Proof	55.00

TUNISIA

The Republic of Tunisia, located on the northern coast of Africa between Algeria and Libya, has an area of 63,170 sq. mi. (163,610 sq. km.) and a population of *7.9 million. Capital: Tunis. Agriculture is the backbone of the economy. Crude oil, phosphates, olive oil, and wine are exported.

Tunisia, settled by the Phoenicians in the 12th century B.C., was the center of the seafaring Carthaginian empire. After the total destruction of Carthage, Tunisia became part of Rome's African province. It remained a part of the Roman Empire (except for the 439-533 interval of Vandal conquest) until taken by the Arabs, 648, who administered it until the Turkish invasion of 1570. Under Turkish control, the public revenue was heavily dependent upon the piracy of Mediterranean shipping, an endeavor that wasn't abandoned until 1819 when a coalition of powers threatened appropriate reprisal. Deprived of its major source of income, Tunisia underwent a financial regression that ended in bankruptcy, enabling France to establish a protectorate over the country in 1881. National agitation and guerrilla fighting forced France to grant Tunisian internal autonomy in 1955 and to recognize Tunisian independence on March 20, 1956. Tunisia abolished the monarchy and established a republic on July 25, 1957.

TITLES

المملكة التونسية

al-Mamlaka(t) at-Tunisiya(t)

الجمهورية التونسية

al-Jumhuriya(t) a-Tunisiya(t)

MINT MARKS

A - Paris, AH1308/1891-AH1348/1928
(a) - Paris, privy marks, AH1349/1929-AH1376/1957
FM - Franklin Mint, Franklin Center, PA
- Numismatic Italiana, Arezzo, Italy

TUNIS

Tunis, the capital and major seaport of Tunisia, existed in the Carthaginian era, but its importance dates only from the Moslem conquest, following which it became a major center of Arab power and prosperity. Spain seized it in 1535, lost it in 1564, retook it in 1573 and ceded it to the Turks in 1574. Thereafter the history of Tunis merged with that of Tunisia.

RULERS

Ottoman, until 1881

LOCAL RULERS

Hammuda Pasha II
AH1196-1229/1782-1813AD
'Uthman
AH1229-1230/1813-1814AD
Mahmud Pasha
AH1230-1239/1814-1824AD
Husayn II
AH1239-1251/1824-1835AD
Mustapha
AH1251-1253/1835-1837AD
Ahmad I Pasha
AH1253-1271/1837-1855AD
Muhammad Bey
AH1271-1276/1855-1859AD
Muhammad Al-Sadiq Bey
AH1276-1299/1859-1882AD
Ali Bey
AH1299-1320/1882-1902AD
Muhammad Al-Hadi Bey
AH1320-1324/1902-1906AD
Muhammad Al-Nasir Bey
AH1324-1340/1906-1922AD
Muhammad Al-Habib Bey
AH1340-1348/1922-1929AD
Ahmad Pasha Bey
AH1348-1361/1929-1942AD
Muhammad Al-Munsif Bey
AH1361-1362/1942-1943AD
Muhammad Al-Amin Bey
AH1362-1376/1943-1957AD

NOTE: All coins struck until AH1298/1881AD bear the name of the Ottoman Sultan; the name of the Bey of Tunis was added in AH1272/1855AD. After AH1298, when the French established their protectorate, only the Bey's name appears on the coin until AH1376/1956AD.

MINT

تونس

TUNIS

With exceptions noted in their proper place, all coins were struck at Tunis prior to AH1308/1891AD. Thereafter, all coins were struck at Paris with mint mark A until 1928, symbols of the mint from 1929-1957.

MONETARY SYSTEM

Until 1891

6 Burben (Bourbine) = 1 Burbe (Bourbe)
2 Burbe (Bourbe) = 1 Nasri
13 Burbe = 1 Kharub (Caroub)
16 Kharub (Caroub) = 1 Piastre (Rial Sebili)

Arabic name	French name	Value
Qafsi of Falls Raqiq	Bourbine	1/12 Nasri
Fals	Bourbe	6 Qafsi or 1/2 Nasri
Nasri	Asper	1/52 Riyal
Kharub	Caroub	1/16 Riyal
1/8 Riyal	1/8 Piastre	1 Kharub
1/4 Riyal	1/4 Piastre	4 Kharub
1/2 Riyal	1/2 Piastre	8 Kharub
Riyal	Piastre	16 Kharub

OTTOMAN ISSUES

SELIM III

AH1203-1222/1789-1807AD

NASRI

(Asper)

BILLON, 9x9mm, square
Obv. leg: *Sultan Selim.* Rev: Date and mint.

KM#	Date	Mintage	Good	VG	Fine	VF
75	AH1216	—	30.00	60.00	100.00	150.00

4 KHARUB

BILLON, 21mm, 4.00 g

KM#	Date	Mintage	Good	VG	Fine	VF
74	AH1216	—	50.00	100.00	150.00	250.00
	1217	—	50.00	100.00	150.00	250.00

NOTE: Earlier date (AH1215) exists for this type.

8 KHARUB

BILLON, 27-28mm, 7.10-7.70 g
Similar to 1 Piastre, KM#72.

KM#	Date	Mintage	Good	VG	Fine	VF
73	AH1216	—	15.00	25.00	40.00	75.00
	1217	—	15.00	25.00	40.00	75.00
	1218	—	15.00	25.00	40.00	75.00
	1219	—	15.00	25.00	40.00	75.00
	1220	—	15.00	25.00	40.00	75.00
	1221	—	15.00	25.00	40.00	75.00
	1222	—	15.00	25.00	40.00	75.00

NOTE: Varieties of ornamentation exist.
NOTE: Earlier dates (AH1206-1215) exist for this type.

PIASTRE

BILLON, 14.90-16.00 g

KM#	Date	Mintage	Good	VG	Fine	VF
72.2	AH1216	—	18.00	30.00	50.00	85.00
	1217	—	18.00	30.00	50.00	85.00
	1218	—	18.00	30.00	50.00	85.00
	1219	—	18.00	30.00	50.00	85.00
	1220	—	18.00	30.00	50.00	85.00
	1221	—	18.00	30.00	50.00	85.00
	1222	—	18.00	30.00	50.00	85.00

NOTE: Varieties of ornamentation exist.
NOTE: Earlier dates (AH1206-1215) exist for this type.

MUSTAFA IV

AH1222-1223/1807-1808AD

4 KHARUB

BILLON, 21mm, 3.50 g
Similar To 1 Piastre, KM#72.

KM#	Date	Mintage	Good	VG	Fine	VF
78	AH1223	—	100.00	150.00	300.00	400.00

8 KHARUB

BILLON, 27mm, 7.50 g

KM#	Date	Mintage	Good	VG	Fine	VF
76	AH1222	—	125.00	200.00	350.00	600.00
	1223	—	125.00	200.00	350.00	600.00

PIASTRE

BILLON, 35mm, 16.00 g

KM#	Date	Mintage	Good	VG	Fine	VF
77	AH1222	—	100.00	175.00	300.00	500.00
	1223	—	100.00	175.00	300.00	500.00

MAHMUD II

AH1223-1255/1808-1839AD

BURBEN

COPPER, 0.80 g

KM#	Date	Mintage	Good	VG	Fine	VF
85	AH1230	—	15.00	27.50	50.00	80.00
	1231	—	15.00	27.50	50.00	80.00
	1232	—	15.00	27.50	50.00	80.00

NASRI

(Asper)

BILLON, 8mm square, 0.20 g

KM#	Date	Mintage	Good	VG	Fine	VF
83	AH1228	—	—	—	—	—
	1229	—	—	—	—	—

KHARUB

BILLON, 0.60-0.70 g

KM#	Date	Mintage	Good	VG	Fine	VF
91	AH1229	—	—	—	—	—
	1241	—	6.00	10.00	17.50	30.00
	1242	—	6.00	10.00	17.50	30.00
	1249	—	3.00	5.00	10.00	20.00
	1250	—	3.00	5.00	10.00	20.00
	1251	—	3.00	5.00	10.00	20.00
	1252	—	3.00	5.00	10.00	20.00
	1253	—	3.00	5.00	10.00	20.00
	1254	—	3.00	5.00	10.00	20.00
	1255	—	3.00	5.00	10.00	20.00

2 KHARUB

BILLON, 16mm, 1.30 g

KM#	Date	Mintage	Good	VG	Fine	VF
92	AH1243	—	9.00	15.00	35.00	60.00
	1244	—	9.00	15.00	35.00	60.00

4 KHARUB

BILLON, 21mm, 3.50 g

KM#	Date	Mintage	Good	VG	Fine	VF
81	AH1223	—	30.00	60.00	100.00	150.00
	1228	—	30.00	60.00	100.00	150.00
	1231	—	30.00	60.00	100.00	150.00

20mm, 2.50 g

KM#	Date	Mintage	Good	VG	Fine	VF
88	AH1240	—	6.00	10.00	30.00	60.00
	1241	—	6.00	10.00	30.00	60.00
	1242	—	6.00	10.00	30.00	60.00
	1243	—	6.00	10.00	30.00	60.00
	1245	—	6.00	10.00	30.00	60.00
	1246	—	6.00	10.00	30.00	60.00
	1249	—	6.00	10.00	30.00	60.00
	1250	—	6.00	10.00	30.00	60.00
	1252	—	6.00	10.00	30.00	60.00
	1253	—	6.00	10.00	30.00	60.00
	1254	—	6.00	10.00	30.00	60.00
	1255	—	6.00	10.00	30.00	60.00

8 KHARUB

BILLON, 27mm, 7.50 g

KM#	Date	Mintage	Good	VG	Fine	VF
84	AH1228	—	30.00	60.00	100.00	150.00
	1229	—	30.00	60.00	100.00	150.00
	1230	—	30.00	60.00	100.00	150.00
	1231	—	30.00	60.00	100.00	150.00
	1232	—	30.00	60.00	100.00	150.00
	1233	—	30.00	60.00	100.00	150.00

26mm, 5.00 g

KM#	Date	Mintage	Good	VG	Fine	VF
89	AH1240	—	6.00	10.00	20.00	40.00
	1241	—	6.00	10.00	20.00	40.00
	1242	—	6.00	10.00	20.00	40.00
	1243	—	6.00	10.00	20.00	40.00
	1244	—	6.00	10.00	20.00	40.00
	1245	—	6.00	10.00	20.00	40.00
	1246	—	6.00	10.00	20.00	40.00
	1247	—	6.00	10.00	20.00	40.00
	1248	—	6.00	10.00	20.00	40.00
	1251	—	8.00	12.00	30.00	60.00
	1252	—	6.00	10.00	20.00	40.00
	1253	—	6.00	10.00	20.00	40.00
	1254	—	6.00	10.00	20.00	40.00

PIASTRE

BILLON, 16.00 g

KM#	Date	Mintage	Good	VG	Fine	VF
82	AH1225	—	20.00	40.00	70.00	125.00
	1226	—	20.00	40.00	70.00	125.00
	1227	—	20.00	40.00	70.00	125.00
	1228	—	20.00	40.00	70.00	125.00
	1229	—	20.00	40.00	70.00	125.00
	1230	—	20.00	40.00	70.00	125.00
	1231	—	20.00	40.00	70.00	125.00
	1232	—	20.00	40.00	70.00	125.00
	1233	—	25.00	50.00	80.00	150.00
	1234	—	40.00	75.00	125.00	200.00

11.00-11.50 g

KM#	Date	Mintage	Good	VG	Fine	VF
90	AH1240	—	5.50	9.00	15.00	30.00
	1241	—	5.50	9.00	15.00	30.00
	1242	—	5.50	9.00	15.00	30.00
	1243	—	5.50	9.00	15.00	30.00
	1244	—	5.50	9.00	15.00	30.00
	1245	—	5.50	9.00	15.00	30.00
	1246	—	5.50	9.00	15.00	30.00
	1247	—	5.50	9.00	15.00	30.00
	1248	—	5.50	9.00	15.00	30.00
	1249	—	5.50	9.00	15.00	30.00
	1250	—	5.50	9.00	15.00	30.00
	1251	—	5.50	9.00	15.00	30.00
	1252	—	5.50	9.00	15.00	30.00
	1253	—	5.50	9.00	15.00	30.00
	1254	—	5.50	9.00	15.00	30.00
	1255	—	5.50	9.00	15.00	30.00

2 PIASTRES

BILLON, 39mm, 27.40 g

KM#	Date	Mintage	Good	VG	Fine	VF
86	AH1232	—	Reported, not confirmed			

38mm, 23.00 g

KM#	Date	Mintage	Good	VG	Fine	VF
93	AH1244	—	35.00	60.00	100.00	150.00
	1245	—	35.00	60.00	100.00	150.00
	1246	—	35.00	60.00	125.00	175.00
	1248	—	75.00	125.00	175.00	350.00

SULTANI

.986 GOLD, 20mm, 2.50-3.20 g

KM#	Date	Mintage	Fine	VF	XF	Unc
87	AH1236	—	200.00	300.00	400.00	550.00

SULTAN ABDUL MEJID

AH1255-1277/1839-1861AD

Without the name of the Bey of Tunis

PRE-REFORM COINAGE

4 KHARUB

BILLON, 20mm, 2.77 g

KM#	Date	Mintage	Good	VG	Fine	VF
97	AH1256	—	35.00	65.00	125.00	200.00

8 KHARUB

BILLON, 26mm, 5.00 g

KM#	Date	Mintage	Good	VG	Fine	VF
98	AH1256	—	35.00	65.00	130.00	225.00

PIASTRE

BILLON, 32mm, 11.00 g

KM#	Date	Mintage	Good	VG	Fine	VF
96	AH1255	—	35.00	60.00	100.00	150.00

REFORM COINAGE

After AH1263/1847AD

BURBE

COPPER, 1.00 g

KM#	Date	Mintage	Good	VG	Fine	VF
101	AH1263	—	2.00	4.00	10.00	20.00
	1264	—	2.00	4.00	10.00	20.00
	1265	—	2.00	4.00	10.00	20.00
	1266	—	2.00	4.00	10.00	20.00
	1267	—	2.00	4.00	10.00	20.00

NASRI

(Asper)

COPPER, 2.00 g

KM#	Date	Mintage	Good	VG	Fine	VF
102	AH1263	—	2.00	4.00	7.00	15.00
	1264	—	2.00	4.00	7.00	15.00
	1265	—	2.00	4.00	7.00	15.00
	1266	—	2.00	4.00	7.00	15.00
	1267	—	2.00	4.00	7.00	15.00

1/2 KHARUB

(3-1/4 Nasri)

COPPER, 5.50 g
Reeded edge.

KM#	Date	Mintage	Good	VG	Fine	VF
103.1	AH1263	—	4.00	8.00	15.00	30.00

Plain edge.

KM#	Date	Mintage	Good	VG	Fine	VF
103.2	AH1264	—	2.50	4.00	7.50	15.00
	1265	—	2.50	4.00	7.50	15.00
	1266	—	2.50	4.00	7.50	15.00
	1267	—	2.50	4.00	7.50	15.00
	1268	—	2.50	4.00	7.50	15.00
	1269	—	2.50	4.00	7.50	15.00

KHARUB

COPPER, 11.50 g
Reeded edge.

KM#	Date	Mintage	Good	VG	Fine	VF
104.1	AH1263	—	8.00	15.00	35.00	50.00

Plain edge.

KM#	Date	Mintage	Good	VG	Fine	VF
104.2	AH1263	—	4.00	8.00	15.00	25.00
	1264	—	2.00	4.00	10.00	15.00
	1265	—	2.00	4.00	10.00	15.00
	1266	—	2.00	4.00	10.00	15.00
	1267	—	2.00	4.00	10.00	15.00
	1268	—	2.00	4.00	10.00	15.00
	1269	—	1.00	2.00	5.00	10.00
	1270	—	6.00	10.00	20.00	30.00
	1271	—	6.00	10.00	20.00	30.00

c/m: Arabic '1' on KM#104.

KM#	Date	Mintage	Good	VG	Fine	VF
105	AH1263-71	—	3.00	6.00	12.00	25.00

2 PIASTRES

SILVER, 28mm, 6.50 g

KM#	Date	Mintage	Good	VG	Fine	VF
106	AH1263	—	15.00	22.00	60.00	135.00
	1264	—	15.00	22.00	60.00	135.00

Modified design

KM#	Date	Mintage	Good	VG	Fine	VF
109	AH1267	—	15.00	22.00	60.00	135.00

5 PIASTRES

SILVER, 33mm, 16.00 g

KM#	Date	Mintage	Good	VG	Fine	VF
107	AH1263	—	75.00	150.00	300.00	600.00
	1264	—	75.00	150.00	300.00	600.00

Modified design

KM#	Date	Mintage	Good	VG	Fine	VF
108	AH1265	—	35.00	60.00	125.00	200.00
	1266	—	11.00	18.00	35.00	65.00
	1267	—	11.00	18.00	35.00	65.00
	1268	—	11.00	18.00	35.00	65.00
	1269	—	11.00	18.00	35.00	65.00
	1270	—	11.00	18.00	35.00	65.00
	1271	—	11.00	18.00	35.00	65.00

SULTAN ABDUL MEJID

With Muhammad Bey
AH1272-1276/1856-1859AD

The copper coins of this series exhibit two major varieties of calligraphy, the first having thin, crude lettering, the second having thicker, more elegant lettering.

3 NASRI

(3 Asper)

COPPER, 5.80 g

KM#	Date	Mintage	Good	VG	Fine	VF
112.1	AH1272	—	4.50	7.50	15.00	30.00
	1273	—	4.50	7.50	15.00	30.00

Thick legend.

KM#	Date	Mintage	Good	VG	Fine	VF
112.2	AH1272	—	4.50	7.50	15.00	30.00
	1274	—	4.50	7.50	15.00	30.00

6 NASRI

(6 Asper)

COPPER, 11.60 g

KM#	Date	Mintage	Good	VG	Fine	VF
113.1	AH1272	—	2.75	4.50	10.00	20.00
	1273	—	2.75	4.50	10.00	20.00

Thick legend.

KM#	Date	Mintage	Good	VG	Fine	VF
113.2	AH1272	—	2.75	4.50	10.00	20.00
	1273	—	2.75	4.50	10.00	20.00
	1274	—	2.75	4.50	10.00	20.00

KHARUB

COPPER
c/m: Arabic '1' on 6 Nasri, KM#113.1 and 113.2.

KM#	Date	Mintage	Good	VG	Fine	VF
114	AH1272-4	—	3.00	6.00	12.00	25.00

13 NASRI

(13 Asper)

COPPER, 23.00 g

KM#	Date	Mintage	Good	VG	Fine	VF
115.1	AH1272	—	5.00	8.50	12.50	25.00
	1273	—	5.00	8.50	12.50	25.00

Thick legend.

KM#	Date	Mintage	Good	VG	Fine	VF
115.2	AH1273	—	5.00	8.50	12.50	25.00
	1274	—	5.00	8.50	12.50	25.00
	1275	—	6.00	10.00	15.00	30.00

2 KHARUB

COPPER
c/m: Arabic '2' on 13 Nasri, KM#115.1.

KM#	Date	Mintage	Good	VG	Fine	VF
116	AH1272	—	3.50	6.00	10.00	25.00
	1273	—	3.50	6.00	10.00	25.00

c/m: Arabic '2' on 13 Nasri, KM#115.2.

KM#	Date	Mintage	Good	VG	Fine	VF
131	AH1273	—	3.50	6.00	10.00	25.00
	1274	—	3.50	6.00	10.00	25.00
	1275	—	3.50	6.00	10.00	25.00

Thick legend. 23.00 g

KM#	Date	Mintage	Good	VG	Fine	VF
134.1	AH1273	—	6.00	10.00	20.00	40.00
	1274	—	6.00	10.00	20.00	40.00
	1275	—	3.00	6.00	12.00	25.00
	1276	—	5.00	8.00	15.00	30.00
	Thin legend.					
134.2	AH1276	—	12.00	18.00	28.00	45.00

SILVER, 0.40 g

KM#	Date	Mintage	Good	VG	Fine	VF
132	AH1273	—	5.00	12.00	25.00	40.00
	1274	—	5.00	12.00	25.00	40.00
	1275	—	5.00	12.00	25.00	40.00
	1276	—	5.00	12.00	30.00	50.00

4 KHARUB

SILVER, 0.80 g

KM#	Date	Mintage	VG	Fine	VF	XF
135	AH1274	—	15.00	30.00	70.00	125.00
	1275	—	15.00	30.00	70.00	125.00

8 KHARUB

SILVER, 1.60 g

KM#	Date	Mintage	VG	Fine	VF	XF
136	AH1274	—	15.00	40.00	75.00	150.00
	1275	—	15.00	40.00	75.00	150.00

PIASTRE

SILVER, 3.20 g
Thick legend.

KM#	Date	Mintage	VG	Fine	VF	XF
117.1	AH1272	—	15.00	30.00	70.00	135.00
	1273	—	15.00	30.00	70.00	135.00
	Thin legend.					
117.2	AH1272	—	20.00	35.00	65.00	125.00

2 PIASTRES

SILVER, 6.40 g
Thick legend.

KM#	Date	Mintage	VG	Fine	VF	XF
118.1	AH1272	—	20.00	50.00	100.00	180.00
	Thin legend.					
118.2	AH1272	—	25.00	55.00	110.00	190.00

3 PIASTRES

SILVER, 9.60 g

KM#	Date	Mintage	VG	Fine	VF	XF
119	AH1272	—	50.00	125.00	200.00	300.00

4 PIASTRES

SILVER, 31mm, 12.80 g

KM#	Date	Mintage	VG	Fine	VF	XF
120	AH1272	—	75.00	150.00	300.00	400.00

5 PIASTRES

SILVER, 33mm, 16.00 g

KM#	Date	Mintage	VG	Fine	VF	XF
121	AH1272	—	150.00	300.00	600.00	1000.
	1273	—	150.00	300.00	600.00	1000.
	1274	—	150.00	300.00	600.00	1000.

.9800 g, .900 GOLD, 12mm, .0284 oz AGW

KM#	Date	Mintage	VG	Fine	VF	XF
122	AH1272	—	22.50	30.00	75.00	130.00
	1273	—	22.50	30.00	75.00	130.00
	1274	—	22.50	30.00	75.00	130.00
	1275	—	22.50	30.00	75.00	130.00

10 PIASTRES

1.7700 g, 1.000 GOLD, .0569 oz AGW

KM#	Date	Mintage	VG	Fine	VF	XF
123	AH1272	—	40.00	60.00	100.00	160.00

1.9700 g, .900 GOLD, .0570 oz AGW

KM#	Date	Mintage	VG	Fine	VF	XF
124	AH1272	—	40.00	60.00	100.00	160.00
	1274	—	40.00	60.00	100.00	160.00

20 PIASTRES

3.5500 g, 1.000 GOLD, 21mm, .1141 oz AGW

KM#	Date	Mintage	VG	Fine	VF	XF
125	AH1272	—	100.00	125.00	200.00	425.00

25 PIASTRES

4.9200 g, .900 GOLD, 20mm, .1424 oz AGW

KM#	Date	Mintage	VG	Fine	VF	XF
133	AH1273	—	125.00	150.00	250.00	425.00
	1274	—	125.00	150.00	250.00	425.00
	1275	—	125.00	150.00	250.00	425.00

40 PIASTRES

7.1000 g, 1.000 GOLD, 26mm, .2283 oz AGW

KM#	Date	Mintage	VG	Fine	VF	XF
126	AH1272	—	135.00	175.00	300.00	550.00

50 PIASTRES

9.8400 g, .900 GOLD, .2847 oz AGW

KM#	Date	Mintage	VG	Fine	VF	XF
127	AH1272	—	175.00	200.00	300.00	500.00
	1273	—	175.00	200.00	300.00	500.00
127	1274	—	175.00	200.00	300.00	500.00
	1275	—	175.00	200.00	300.00	500.00

80 PIASTRES

14.2100 g, 1.000 GOLD, 31mm, .4569 oz AGW

KM#	Date	Mintage	VG	Fine	VF	XF
128	AH1272	—	325.00	450.00	800.00	1100.

100 PIASTRES

17.7100 g, 1.000 GOLD, 33mm, .5694 oz AGW

KM#	Date	Mintage	VG	Fine	VF	XF
129	AH1272	—	400.00	600.00	800.00	1250.

19.6800 g, .900 GOLD, .5695 oz AGW

KM#	Date	Mintage	VG	Fine	VF	XF
130	AH1272	—	375.00	500.00	750.00	1250.
	1273	—	375.00	500.00	750.00	1250.
	1274	—	375.00	500.00	750.00	1250.

SULTAN ABDUL MEJID

With Muhammad al-Sadiq Bey
AH1276-1277/1859-1860AD

2 KHARUB

COPPER, 23.00 g
Thin legend.

KM#	Date	Mintage	VG	Fine	VF	XF
137.1	AH1276	—	10.00	20.00	35.00	80.00
	Thick legend.					
137.2	AH1276	—	10.00	20.00	35.00	80.00

8 KHARUB

SILVER, 18mm, 1.60 g

KM#	Date	Mintage	VG	Fine	VF	XF
142	AH1276	—	60.00	100.00	250.00	450.00
	1277	—	60.00	100.00	250.00	450.00

PIASTRE

SILVER, 22mm, 3.20 g

KM#	Date	Mintage	VG	Fine	VF	XF
143	AH1278 (sic)	—	75.00	150.00	300.00	500.00

2 PIASTRES

SILVER, 6.40 g

KM#	Date	Mintage	VG	Fine	VF	XF
138	AH1276	—	—	—	Rare	—

25 PIASTRES

GOLD, 20mm, 4.90 g

KM#	Date	Mintage	VG	Fine	VF	XF
139	AH1276	—	125.00	200.00	325.00	650.00

50 PIASTRES

GOLD, 26mm, 9.80 g

KM#	Date	Mintage	VG	Fine	VF	XF
140	AH1276	—	150.00	300.00	500.00	750.00

100 PIASTRES

GOLD, 33mm, 19.70 g

KM#	Date	Mintage	VG	Fine	VF	XF
141	AH1276	—	1000.	1250.	1500.	2000.

SULTAN ABDUL AZIZ

With Muhammad al-Sadiq Bey
AH1277-1293/1860-1876AD

1/4 KHARUB

COPPER, 1.00 g

KM#	Date	Mintage	VG	Fine	VF	XF
153	AH1281	3.200	2.00	3.00	5.00	12.00

1.50 g

KM#	Date	Mintage	VG	Fine	VF	XF
171	AH1289	—	4.50	7.50	20.00	45.00

1/2 KHARUB

COPPER, 1.80 g

KM#	Date	Mintage	VG	Fine	VF	XF
154	AH1281	3.200	.60	1.00	2.00	7.00

3.20 g

KM#	Date	Mintage	VG	Fine	VF	XF
172	AH1289	—	2.50	8.00	20.00	40.00

KHARUB

COPPER, 3.50 g

KM#	Date	Mintage	VG	Fine	VF	XF
155	AH1281	5.600	.60	1.00	3.00	8.00

6.20 g

KM#	Date	Mintage	VG	Fine	VF	XF
173	AH1289	—	1.50	2.25	8.00	20.00
	1290	—	2.25	3.50	10.00	25.00

2 KHARUB

COPPER, 7.50 g

KM#	Date	Mintage	VG	Fine	VF	XF
156	AH1281	12.000	.75	1.25	4.00	12.00

NOTE: Thick and thin planchets exist.

12.90 g

KM#	Date	Mintage	VG	Fine	VF	XF
157	AH1281	—	10.00	15.00	20.00	40.00
	1283	—	2.50	6.00	15.00	25.00
	1284	—	2.50	6.00	15.00	25.00

NOTE: 3 varieties of inscription exist for AH1283. Slightly thinner planchets exist.

12.00-12.50 g

KM#	Date	Mintage	VG	Fine	VF	XF
174	AH1289	—	1.75	3.00	6.00	12.50
	1290	—	3.50	6.00	12.50	30.00

4 KHARUB

COPPER, 15.00 g

KM#	Date	Mintage	VG	Fine	VF	XF
158	AH1281	12.000	1.50	2.50	6.00	10.00
	1283	—	25.00	40.00	60.00	125.00

8 KHARUB

COPPER, 30.00 g

KM#	Date	Mintage	VG	Fine	VF	XF
159	AH1281	10.000	2.00	5.00	10.00	20.00

NOTE: KM#153-156, 158 and 159 were struck at the Heaton Mint, Birmingham, and are relatively common in higher grades.

SILVER, 1.80 g

KM#	Date	Mintage	VG	Fine	VF	XF
160	AH1281	—	30.00	50.00	100.00	150.00
	1282	—	30.00	50.00	100.00	150.00
	1283	—	30.00	50.00	100.00	150.00
	1284	—	30.00	50.00	100.00	150.00
	1285	—	30.00	50.00	100.00	150.00
	1286	—	30.00	50.00	100.00	150.00
	1287	—	30.00	50.00	100.00	150.00
	1288	—	30.00	50.00	100.00	150.00
	1289	—	15.00	25.00	50.00	100.00
	1290	—	30.00	50.00	100.00	150.00
	1291	—	30.00	50.00	100.00	150.00
	1292	—	30.00	50.00	100.00	150.00
	1293	—	30.00	50.00	100.00	150.00

PIASTRE

SILVER, 3.20 g

KM#	Date	Mintage	VG	Fine	VF	XF
145	AH1279	—	20.00	35.00	60.00	100.00
	1280	—	20.00	35.00	60.00	100.00
	1281	—	20.00	35.00	60.00	100.00
	1282	—	20.00	35.00	60.00	100.00
	1284	—	20.00	35.00	60.00	100.00
	1287	—	20.00	35.00	60.00	100.00
	1288	—	20.00	35.00	60.00	100.00
	1289	—	5.00	9.00	20.00	50.00
	1290	—	6.00	10.00	25.00	60.00
	1291	—	20.00	35.00	60.00	100.00
	1292	—	20.00	35.00	60.00	100.00
	1293	—	20.00	35.00	60.00	100.00

c/m: Star on Piastre, KM#145.

KM#	Date	Mintage	VG	Fine	VF	XF
146	AH1279-93	—	6.00	10.00	20.00	45.00

2 PIASTRES

SILVER, 6.27 g

KM#	Date	Mintage				
161	AH1281 Paris	—			Proof	350.00

NOTE: Without name of the Bey of Tunis - possibly a pattern.

6.40 g

KM#	Date	Mintage	VG	Fine	VF	XF
147	AH1279	—	30.00	60.00	100.00	150.00
	1280	—	30.00	60.00	100.00	150.00
	1282	—	30.00	60.00	100.00	150.00
	1283	—	30.00	60.00	100.00	150.00
	1284	—	30.00	60.00	100.00	150.00
	1287	—	30.00	60.00	100.00	150.00
	1288	—	30.00	60.00	100.00	150.00
	1289	—	10.00	15.00	30.00	60.00
	1290	—	10.00	15.00	30.00	60.00
	1291	—	30.00	60.00	100.00	150.00
	1292	—	30.00	60.00	100.00	150.00
	1293	—	30.00	60.00	100.00	150.00

c/m: Star on 2 Piastres, KM#147.

KM#	Date	Mintage	VG	Fine	VF	XF
165	AH1287-93	—	6.00	10.00	25.00	55.00

3 PIASTRES

SILVER, 30mm, 9.60 g

KM#	Date	Mintage	VG	Fine	VF	XF
166	AH1288	—	100.00	150.00	250.00	400.00

4 PIASTRES

SILVER, 12.80 g

KM#	Date	Mintage	VG	Fine	VF	XF
167	AH1288	—	20.00	40.00	95.00	180.00
	1290	—	12.00	25.00	50.00	100.00
	1291	—	12.00	25.00	50.00	100.00
	1292	—	15.00	30.00	80.00	150.00
	1293	—	15.00	30.00	80.00	150.00

c/m: Star on KM#167.

KM#	Date	Mintage	VG	Fine	VF	XF
168	AH1288-93	—	15.00	40.00	80.00	110.00

Mule. Obv: KM#186. Rev: KM#167.

KM#	Date	Mintage	VG	Fine	VF	XF
175	AH1292	—	35.00	50.00	100.00	210.00

5 PIASTRES

.9800 g, .900 GOLD, .0284 oz AGW

KM#	Date	Mintage	VG	Fine	VF	XF
162	AH1281	—	20.00	30.00	50.00	110.00
	1281	—	—	—	Proof	150.00

c/m: Star on KM#162.

KM#	Date	Mintage	VG	Fine	VF	XF
163	AH1281	—	20.00	30.00	50.00	110.00

KM#	Date	Mintage	VG	Fine	VF	XF
169	AH1288	—	20.00	30.00	50.00	100.00
	1289	—	20.00	30.00	50.00	100.00
	1290	—	20.00	30.00	50.00	100.00
	1291	—	20.00	30.00	50.00	100.00
	1292	—	25.00	40.00	60.00	110.00

NOTE: Varieties exist for AH1290 dated coins.

c/m: Star on KM#169.

KM#	Date	Mintage	VG	Fine	VF	XF
170	AH1288	—	20.00	35.00	60.00	100.00
	1289	—	20.00	35.00	60.00	100.00
	1290	—	20.00	35.00	60.00	100.00
	1291	—	20.00	35.00	60.00	100.00
	1292	—	20.00	35.00	60.00	100.00

16.0000 g, .900 SILVER, 33mm, .4630 oz ASW

KM#	Date	Mintage	VG	Fine	VF	XF
164	AH1281	—	100.00	150.00	250.00	350.00
	1282	—	100.00	150.00	250.00	350.00
	1288	—	100.00	150.00	250.00	350.00
	1290	—	100.00	150.00	250.00	350.00
	1291	—	100.00	150.00	250.00	350.00
	1293	—	100.00	150.00	250.00	350.00

10 PIASTRES

1.9700 g, .900 GOLD, .0570 oz AGW

KM#	Date	Mintage	VG	Fine	VF	XF
150	AH1280	—	40.00	60.00	80.00	180.00
	1281	—	40.00	60.00	80.00	180.00
	1281	—	—	—	Proof	275.00
	1284	—	40.00	60.00	80.00	180.00
	1287	—	40.00	60.00	80.00	180.00
	1288	—	40.00	60.00	80.00	180.00

c/m: Star on KM#150.

KM#	Date	Mintage	VG	Fine	VF	XF
151	AH1280-8	—	45.00	70.00	85.00	135.00

25 PIASTRES

4.9200 g, .900 GOLD, .1424 oz AGW

KM#	Date	Mintage	VG	Fine	VF	XF
148	AH1278	—	100.00	150.00	225.00	300.00
	1279	—	100.00	150.00	225.00	300.00
	1280	—	100.00	150.00	225.00	300.00
	1281	—	100.00	150.00	225.00	300.00
	1281	—	—	—	Proof	400.00
	1282	—	100.00	150.00	225.00	300.00
	1283	—	100.00	150.00	225.00	300.00
	1284	—	100.00	150.00	225.00	300.00
	1285	—	100.00	150.00	225.00	300.00
	1286	—	100.00	150.00	225.00	300.00
	1287	—	100.00	150.00	225.00	300.00
	1288	—	100.00	150.00	225.00	300.00
	1289	—	100.00	125.00	165.00	250.00
	1290	—	100.00	125.00	165.00	250.00
	1291	—	100.00	125.00	165.00	250.00

50 PIASTRES

9.8400 g., .900 GOLD, .2847 oz AGW

KM#	Date	Mintage	VG	Fine	VF	XF
152	AH1280	—	200.00	225.00	285.00	500.00
	1281	—	200.00	225.00	275.00	350.00
	1281	—	—	—	Proof	550.00
	1286	—	200.00	225.00	275.00	350.00
	1288	—	200.00	225.00	275.00	350.00
	1293	—	250.00	275.00	350.00	450.00

100 PIASTRES

19.6800 g, .900 GOLD, .5695 oz AGW

KM#	Date	Mintage	VG	Fine	VF	XF
149	AH1279	—	375.00	575.00	950.00	2000.
	1280	—	375.00	575.00	950.00	2000.
	1281	—	375.00	575.00	950.00	2000.
	1281	—	—	—	Proof	3000.
	1283	—	375.00	575.00	950.00	2000.
	1285	—	375.00	575.00	950.00	2000.
	1286	—	375.00	575.00	950.00	2000.

NOTE: KM#148-150, 152, 161, 162, 164 and 166, dated AH1281, were all struck at Tunis, from dies produced at the Heaton Mint in Birmingham, hence their obvious superiority.

SULTAN MURAD V

With Muhammad al-Sadiq Bey
AH1293/1876AD

4 PIASTRES

SILVER, 12.80 g

KM#	Date	Mintage	VG	Fine	VF	XF
176	AH1293	—	—	—	Rare	—

25 PIASTRES

4.9200 g, .900 GOLD, 20mm, .1424 oz AGW

KM#	Date	Mintage	VG	Fine	VF	XF
177	AH1293	—	300.00	500.00	750.00	1500.

SULTAN ABDUL HAMID II

With Muhammad al-Sadiq Bey
AH1293-1299/1876-1882AD

2 KHARUB

COPPER, 31mm, 12.50 g

KM#	Date	Mintage	VG	Fine	VF	XF
180	AH1293	—	12.50	20.00	45.00	85.00

8 KHARUB

SILVER, 1.50 g

Obv: *al-Ghazi*

KM#	Date	Mintage	VG	Fine	VF	XF
181	AH1294	—	37.50	75.00	150.00	275.00
	1295	—	30.00	60.00	125.00	225.00
	1296	—	37.50	75.00	150.00	275.00
	1297	—	37.50	75.00	150.00	275.00
	1298	—	37.50	75.00	150.00	275.00

Obv: W/o *al-Ghazi*

KM#	Date	Mintage	VG	Fine	VF	XF
188	AH1293	—	60.00	125.00	250.00	400.00
	1294	—	60.00	125.00	250.00	400.00

PIASTRE

SILVER, 22.5mm, 3.20 g
Obv: W/o *al-Ghazi*

KM#	Date	Mintage	VG	Fine	VF	XF
182	AH1293	—	35.00	75.00	150.00	300.00
	1294	—	35.00	75.00	150.00	300.00

Obv: *al-Ghazi* added.

KM#	Date	Mintage	VG	Fine	VF	XF
189	AH1294	—	35.00	75.00	150.00	300.00
	1295	—	35.00	75.00	150.00	300.00
	1296	—	35.00	75.00	150.00	300.00
	1297	—	35.00	75.00	150.00	300.00
	1298	—	35.00	75.00	150.00	300.00

c/m: Star on KM#182.

KM#	Date	Mintage	VG	Fine	VF	XF
183	AH1293-4	—	35.00	60.00	100.00	150.00

c/m: Star on KM#189.

KM#	Date	Mintage	VG	Fine	VF	XF
190	AH1294-8	—	35.00	60.00	100.00	150.00

2 PIASTRES

SILVER, 26.5mm, 6.40 g

KM#	Date	Mintage	VG	Fine	VF	XF
184	AH1293	—	40.00	70.00	150.00	300.00
	1294	—	40.00	70.00	150.00	300.00

Obv: *al-Ghazi* added.

KM#	Date	Mintage	VG	Fine	VF	XF
191	AH1294	—	40.00	70.00	150.00	300.00
	1297	—	60.00	100.00	175.00	350.00

c/m: Star on KM#184.

KM#	Date	Mintage	VG	Fine	VF	XF
185	AH1293	—	35.00	75.00	150.00	300.00
	1294	—	35.00	75.00	150.00	300.00

c/m: Star on KM#191.

KM#	Date	Mintage	VG	Fine	VF	XF
192	AH1294	—	35.00	75.00	150.00	300.00

4 PIASTRES

SILVER, 12.8 g, 31mm
Obv: W/o *al-Ghazi*

KM#	Date	Mintage	VG	Fine	VF	XF
186	AH1293	—	20.00	60.00	125.00	250.00
	1294	—	20.00	60.00	125.00	250.00

Obv: *al-Ghazi* added.

KM#	Date	Mintage	VG	Fine	VF	XF
193	AH1294	—	20.00	60.00	125.00	250.00
	1295	—	20.00	60.00	125.00	250.00
	1296	—	20.00	60.00	125.00	250.00
	1297	—	20.00	60.00	125.00	250.00

c/m: Star on KM#186.

KM#	Date	Mintage	VG	Fine	VF	XF
187	AH1293	—	20.00	35.00	75.00	150.00
	1294	—	20.00	35.00	75.00	150.00

c/m: Star on KM#193.

KM#	Date	Mintage	VG	Fine	VF	XF
194	AH1294	—	20.00	35.00	75.00	150.00
	1295	—	20.00	35.00	75.00	150.00
	1296	—	20.00	35.00	75.00	150.00
	1297	—	20.00	35.00	75.00	150.00

5 PIASTRES

0.9800 g, .900 GOLD, 12.5mm, .0284 oz AGW

KM#	Date	Mintage	VG	Fine	VF	XF
195	AH1294	—	40.00	75.00	150.00	250.00

10 PIASTRES

1.9700 g, .900 GOLD, .5700 oz AGW

KM#	Date	Mintage	VG	Fine	VF	XF
199	AH1295	—	—	—	—	—

25 PIASTRES

4.9200 g, .900 GOLD, .1424 oz AGW

KM#	Date	Mintage	VG	Fine	VF	XF
196	AH1294	—	85.00	110.00	175.00	250.00
	1295	—	85.00	110.00	175.00	250.00
	1296	—	85.00	110.00	175.00	250.00
	1297	—	85.00	110.00	175.00	250.00
	1298	—	—	—	Rare	—

50 PIASTRES

9.8400 g, .900 GOLD, 26mm, .2847 oz AGW

Obv: W/o *al-Ghazi.*

KM#	Date	Mintage	VG	Fine	VF	XF
197	AH1294	—	—	—	Rare	—

Obv: *al-Ghazi* added.

KM#	Date	Mintage	VG	Fine	VF	XF
198	AH1295	—	—	—	Rare	—
	1297	—	150.00	200.00	250.00	350.00

PROOF SETS (PS)

KM#	Date	Mintage	Identification	Issue Price	Mkt. Val.
PS1	1864(AH1281) (5)	—	KM148-150,152,162	—	4375.

TUNISIA

FRENCH PROTECTORATE

MUHAMMAD AL-SADIQ BEY

Alone: AH1298-1299/1881-1882AD

8 KHARUB

SILVER, 18.5mm, 1.60 g

KM#	Date	Mintage	Fine	VF	XF	Unc
201	AH1299	—	200.00	400.00	750.00	1250.

PIASTRE

SILVER, 3.20 g

KM#	Date	Mintage	Fine	VF	XF	Unc
202	AH1299	—	200.00	400.00	750.00	1250.

2 PIASTRES

SILVER, 26.5mm, 6.40 g

KM#	Date	Mintage	Fine	VF	XF	Unc
203	AH1299	—	200.00	400.00	750.00	1250.

25 PIASTRES

4.9200 g, .900 GOLD, 20mm, .1424 oz AGW

KM#	Date	Mintage	Fine	VF	XF	Unc
200	AH1298	—	100.00	250.00	500.00	750.00
	1300	—	100.00	250.00	500.00	750.00

50 PIASTRES

9.8400 g, .900 GOLD, 26mm, .2847 oz AGW

KM#	Date	Mintage	Fine	VF	XF	Unc
204	AH1299	—	300.00	400.00	650.00	1000.

ALI BEY

AH1299-1320/AD1882-1902

8 KHARUB

SILVER, 1.60 g

KM#	Date	Mintage	Fine	VF	XF	Unc
205	AH1300	—	15.00	25.00	55.00	115.00
	1301	—	15.00	25.00	55.00	115.00
	1302	—	15.00	25.00	55.00	115.00
	1303	—	15.00	25.00	55.00	115.00
	1304	—	15.00	25.00	55.00	115.00
	1305	—	15.00	25.00	55.00	115.00
	1306	—	15.00	25.00	55.00	115.00
	1307	—	15.00	25.00	55.00	115.00
	1308	—	15.00	25.00	55.00	115.00

PIASTRE

SILVER, 3.20 g

KM#	Date	Mintage	Fine	VF	XF	Unc
206	AH1300	—	18.00	30.00	75.00	155.00
	1301	—	18.00	30.00	75.00	155.00
	1302	—	18.00	30.00	75.00	155.00
	1303	—	18.00	30.00	75.00	155.00
	1304	—	18.00	30.00	75.00	155.00
	1305	—	18.00	30.00	75.00	155.00
	1306	—	18.00	30.00	75.00	155.00
	1307	—	18.00	30.00	75.00	155.00
	1308	—	18.00	30.00	75.00	155.00

Modified design.

KM#	Date	Mintage	Fine	VF	XF	Unc
215	AH1308	—	20.00	35.00	75.00	150.00

2 PIASTRES

SILVER, 6.40 g

KM#	Date	Mintage	Fine	VF	XF	Unc
207	AH1300	—	30.00	50.00	125.00	275.00
	1301	—	30.00	50.00	125.00	275.00
	1302	—	30.00	50.00	125.00	275.00
	1303	—	30.00	50.00	125.00	275.00
	1304	—	30.00	50.00	125.00	275.00
	1305	—	30.00	50.00	125.00	275.00
	1306	—	30.00	50.00	125.00	275.00
	1307	—	30.00	50.00	125.00	275.00
	1308	—	30.00	50.00	125.00	275.00

Modified design.

KM#	Date	Mintage	Fine	VF	XF	Unc
210	AH1308	—	40.00	70.00	125.00	275.00

4 PIASTRES

SILVER, 12.80 g

KM#	Date	Mintage	Fine	VF	XF	Unc
208	AH1300	—	30.00	50.00	150.00	325.00
	1301	—	30.00	50.00	150.00	325.00
	1302	—	30.00	50.00	150.00	325.00
	1303	—	30.00	50.00	150.00	325.00
	1304	—	30.00	50.00	150.00	325.00
	1305	—	30.00	50.00	150.00	325.00
	1306	—	30.00	50.00	150.00	325.00
	1307	—	30.00	50.00	150.00	325.00
	1308	—	30.00	50.00	150.00	325.00

Modified design.

KM#	Date	Mintage	Fine	VF	XF	Unc
216	AH1308	—	40.00	70.00	180.00	350.00

25 PIASTRES

4.9200 g, .900 GOLD, .1424 oz AGW

KM#	Date	Mintage	Fine	VF	XF	Unc
209	AH1300	—	85.00	110.00	150.00	250.00
	1302	—	85.00	110.00	150.00	250.00

25 PIASTRES-15 FRANCS

4.8730 g, .900 GOLD, .1410 oz AGW

KM#	Date	Mintage	Fine	VF	XF	Unc
212	AH1304	.080	85.00	110.00	175.00	300.00
	1308	Inc. Ab.	85.00	110.00	175.00	300.00

Rev: Modified design.

KM#	Date	Mintage	Fine	VF	XF	Unc
214	AH1307A	.052	85.00	110.00	175.00	300.00
	1308A	.120	85.00	110.00	175.00	300.00
	1308A	—	—	—	Proof	2000.

50 PIASTRES

4.8730 g, .900 GOLD, .1410 oz AGW

KM#	Date	Mintage	Fine	VF	XF	Unc
213	AH1304	—	200.00	350.00	500.00	750.00

100 PIASTRES

9.7460 g, .900 GOLD, .2820 oz AGW

KM#	Date	Mintage	Fine	VF	XF	Unc
211	AH1303	—	300.00	600.00	1000.	1500.

DECIMAL SYSTEM

100 Centimes = 1 Franc

NOTE: The following coins all bear French inscriptions on one side, Arabic on the other, and usually have both AH and AD dates. They are struck in the name of the Tunisian Bey.

CENTIME

BRONZE

Obv. leg: *Ali.*

KM#	Date	Year	Mintage	VF	XF	Unc
219	AH1308	1891A	.500	6.00	10.00	23.00

2 CENTIMES

BRONZE

Obv. leg: *Ali.*

KM#	Date	Year	Mintage	VF	XF	Unc
220	AH1308	1891A	1.000	2.25	5.00	15.00

5 CENTIMES

BRONZE

Obv. leg: *Ali.*

KM#	Date	Year	Mintage	VF	XF	Unc
221	AH1308	1891A	4.300	2.00	7.00	23.00
	1308	1891A	—	—	Proof	50.00
	1309	1892A	1.192	2.50	8.00	23.00
	1310	1893A	1.008	3.00	10.00	25.00

Obv. leg: *Muhammad al-Hadi.*

KM#	Date	Year	Mintage	VF	XF	Unc
228	AH1321	1903A	.500	6.00	10.00	25.00
	1322	1904A	1.000	5.50	8.00	20.00

Obv. leg: *Muhammad al-Nasir.*

KM#	Date	Year	Mintage	VF	XF	Unc
235	AH1325	1907A	1.000	2.00	4.00	17.00
	1326	1908A	1.000	2.00	4.00	17.00
	1330	1912A	1.000	2.00	4.00	17.00
	1332	1914A	1.000	2.00	4.00	17.00
	1334	1916A	2.000	1.50	3.00	12.00
	1336	1917A	2.021	1.50	3.00	12.00

NICKEL BRONZE

Obv. leg: *Mohammed al-Nasir.*

KM#	Date	Year	Mintage	VF	XF	Unc
242	AH1337	1918(a)	1.549	1.00	2.50	12.00
	1337	1919(a)	4.451	.75	2.00	12.00
	1338/7	1920(a)	2.206	3.00	7.50	25.00
	1338	1920(a)	Inc. Ab.	2.00	5.00	20.00
	1339	1920(a)	Inc. Ab.	1.00	2.50	12.00

Reduced Size

KM#	Date	Year	Mintage	VF	XF	Unc
245	AH1339	1920(a)	1.794	10.00	20.00	40.00

Obv. leg: *Ahmad.*

KM#	Date	Year	Mintage	VF	XF	Unc
258	AH1350	1931(a)	2.000	3.00	10.00	20.00
	1352	1933(a)	1.000	3.00	12.00	25.00
	1357	1938(a)	1.200	1.00	3.00	6.00

10 CENTIMES

BRONZE

Obv. leg: *Ali.*

KM#	Date	Year	Mintage	VF	XF	Unc
222	AH1308	1891A	2.600	4.00	8.00	22.00
	1309	1892A	1.374	4.00	10.00	25.00
	1310	1892A	—	75.00	125.00	200.00
	1310	1893A	.026	75.00	125.00	200.00

Obv. leg: *Muhammad al-Hadi.*

KM#	Date	Year	Mintage	VF	XF	Unc
229	AH1321	1903A	.250	6.00	15.00	30.00
	1322	1904A	.500	6.00	12.00	20.00

Obv. leg: *Muhammad al-Nasir.*

KM#	Date	Year	Mintage	VF	XF	Unc
236	AH1325	1907A	.500	3.00	6.00	20.00
	1326	1908A	.500	3.00	6.00	20.00
	1329	1911A	.500	3.00	6.00	20.00
	1330	1912A	.500	3.00	6.00	20.00
	1332	1914A	.500	3.00	6.00	20.00
	1334	1916A	1.000	3.00	6.00	20.00
	1336	1917A	1.050	3.00	6.00	20.00

NICKEL-BRONZE

Obv. leg: *Muhammed al-Nasir.*

KM#	Date	Year	Mintage	VF	XF	Unc
243	AH1337	1918(a)	1.288	2.00	4.00	12.00
	1337	1919(a)	2.712	1.25	3.00	10.00
	1338	1920(a)	3.000	1.25	3.00	10.00

Obv. leg: *Muhammad al-Habib.*

KM#	Date	Year	Mintage	VF	XF	Unc
254	AH1345	1926(a)	1.000	10.00	20.00	100.00

Obv. leg: *Ahmad.*

KM#	Date	Year	Mintage	VF	XF	Unc
259	AH1350	1931(a)	.750	4.00	12.00	30.00
	1352	1933(a)	1.000	4.00	12.00	30.00
	1357	1938(a)	1.200	1.50	4.00	10.00

ZINC

Obv. leg: *Ahmad.*

KM#	Date	Year	Mintage	VF	XF	Unc
267	AH1360	1941(a)	5.000	2.50	6.00	25.00
	1361	1942(a)	10.000	1.50	4.00	20.00

Obv. leg: *Muhammad al Amin.*

KM#	Date	Year	Mintage	VF	XF	Unc
271	AH1364	1945(a)	10.000	20.00	40.00	70.00

NOTE: Most were probably melted.

20 CENTIMES

ZINC

Obv. leg: *Ahmad.*

KM#	Date	Year	Mintage	VF	XF	Unc
268	AH1361	1942(a)	5.000	8.00	20.00	35.00

Obv. leg: *Muhammad al-Amin.*

KM#	Date	Year	Mintage	VF	XF	Unc
272	AH1364	1945(a)	5.205	30.00	60.00	90.00

NOTE: A large quantity was remelted.

25 CENTIMES

NICKEL-BRONZE

Obv. leg: *Muhammad al-Nasir.*

KM#	Date	Year	Mintage	VF	XF	Unc
244	AH1337	1918(a)	—	3.50	8.50	25.00
	1337	1919(a)	2.000	2.00	5.00	20.00
	1338	1920(a)	2.000	2.00	5.00	20.00

Obv. leg: *Ahmad.*

KM#	Date	Year	Mintage	VF	XF	Unc
260	AH1350	1931(a)	.300	5.00	12.00	30.00
	1352	1933(a)	.400	5.00	12.00	30.00
	1357	1938(a)	.480	3.00	7.50	15.00

50 CENTIMES

2.5000 g, .835 SILVER, .0671 oz ASW

Obv. leg: *Ali.*

KM#	Date	Year	Mintage	VF	XF	Unc
223	AH1308	1891A	1.470	8.00	18.00	35.00
	1309	1892A	1,000	—	100.00	175.00
	1310	1893A	1,000	—	100.00	175.00
	1311	1893A	—	—	100.00	175.00
	1311	1894A	1,000	—	100.00	175.00
	1313	1895A	1,000	—	100.00	175.00
	1314	1896A	1,000	—	100.00	175.00
	1315	1897A	1,000	—	100.00	175.00
	1316	1898A	1,000	—	100.00	175.00
	1317	1899A	1,000	—	100.00	175.00
	1318	1900A	1,000	—	100.00	175.00
	1319	1901A	1,000	—	100.00	175.00
	1320	1902A	1,000	—	100.00	175.00

Obv. leg: *Muhammad al-Hadi.*

KM#	Date	Year	Mintage	VF	XF	Unc
230	AH1321	1903A	1,003	—	100.00	175.00
	1322	1904A	1,003	—	100.00	175.00
	1323	1905A	1,003	—	100.00	175.00
	1324	1906A	1,003	—	100.00	175.00

Obv. leg: *Muhammad al-Nasir.*

KM#	Date	Year	Mintage	VF	XF	Unc
237	AH1325	1907A	.201	4.00	10.00	40.00
	1326	1908A	2,006	—	75.00	135.00
	1327	1909A	1,003	—	100.00	175.00
	1328	1910A	1,003	—	100.00	175.00
	1329	1911A	1,003	—	100.00	175.00
	1330	1912A	.201	4.00	10.00	35.00
	1331	1913A	1,003	—	100.00	175.00
	1332	1914A	.201	4.00	10.00	35.00
	1334	1915A	.707	2.00	6.00	18.00
	1334	1916A	3.614	1.50	4.00	15.00
	1335	1916A	Inc. Ab.	1.50	4.00	15.00
	1335	1917A	2.139	1.50	4.00	15.00
	1336	1917A	Inc. Ab.	1.50	4.00	15.00
	1337	1918A	1,003	—	100.00	175.00
	1338	1919A	1,003	—	100.00	175.00
	1339	1920A	1,003	—	100.00	175.00
	1340	1921A	1,003	—	100.00	175.00

ALUMINUM-BRONZE

KM#	Date	Year	Mintage	VF	XF	Unc
246	AH1340	1921(a)	4.000	.50	1.50	15.00
	1345	1926(a)	1.000	1.00	2.50	25.00
	1352	1933(a)	.500	2.00	5.00	40.00
	1360	1941(a)	4.646	.35	1.25	10.00
	1364	1945(a)	11.180	.20	.60	10.00

2.5000 g, .835 SILVER, .0671 oz ASW
Obv. leg: ***Muhammad al-Habib.***

KM#	Date	Year	Mintage	VF	XF	Unc
249	AH1341	1922A	1,003	—	100.00	200.00
	1342	1923A	2,009	—	100.00	200.00
	1343	1924A	1,003	—	100.00	200.00
	1344	1925A	1,003	—	100.00	200.00
	1345	1926A	1,003	—	100.00	200.00
	1346	1927A	1,003	—	100.00	200.00
	1347	1928A	1,003	—	100.00	200.00

FRANC

5.0000 g, .835 SILVER, .1342 oz ASW
Obv. leg: ***Ali.***

KM#	Date	Year	Mintage	VF	XF	Unc
224	AH1308	1891A	1.575	10.00	20.00	40.00
	1309	1892A	1.575	10.00	20.00	40.00
	1310	1893A	703 pcs.	—	135.00	225.00
	1311	1894A	703 pcs.	—	135.00	225.00
	1313	1895A	703 pcs.	—	135.00	225.00
	1314	1896A	703 pcs.	—	135.00	225.00
	1315	1897A	703 pcs.	—	135.00	225.00
	1316	1898A	703 pcs.	—	135.00	225.00
	1317	1899A	703 pcs.	—	135.00	225.00
	1318	1900A	703 pcs.	—	135.00	225.00
	1319	1901A	700 pcs.	—	135.00	225.00
	1320	1902A	703 pcs.	—	135.00	225.00

Obv. leg: ***Muhammad al-Hadi.***

KM#	Date	Year	Mintage	VF	XF	Unc
231	AH1321	1903A	703 pcs.	—	135.00	225.00
	1322	1904A	.500	30.00	50.00	110.00
	1323	1905A	703 pcs.	—	135.00	225.00
	1324	1906A	703 pcs.	—	135.00	225.00

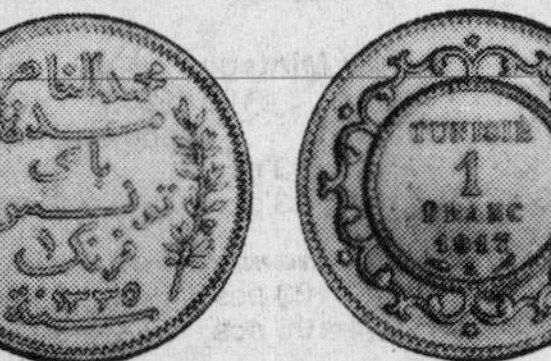

Obv. leg: ***Muhammad al-Nasir.***

KM#	Date	Year	Mintage	VF	XF	Unc
238	AH1325	1907A	.301	4.00	10.00	35.00
	1326	1908A	.401	4.00	8.00	35.00
	1327	1909A	703 pcs.	—	135.00	225.00
	1328	1910A	703 pcs.	—	135.00	225.00
	1329	1911A	1.051	2.75	6.50	30.00
	1330	1912A	.501	3.25	8.00	30.00
	1331	1913A	703 pcs.	—	135.00	225.00
	1332	1914A	.201	3.50	9.00	30.00
	1333	1914A	I.A.	3.50	9.00	30.00
	1334	1915A	1.060	2.00	5.00	12.00
	1334	1916A	3.270	1.50	4.00	10.00
	1335	1916A	Inc. Ab.	1.50	4.00	10.00
	1335	1917A	1.628	2.00	5.00	12.00
	1336	1918A	.804	1.75	4.50	15.00
	1337	1918A	Inc. Ab.	1.75	4.50	15.00
	1338	1919A	703 pcs.	—	135.00	225.00
	1339	1920A	703 pcs.	—	135.00	225.00
	1340	1921A	703 pcs.	—	135.00	225.00

ALUMINUM-BRONZE

KM#	Date	Year	Mintage	VF	XF	Unc
247	AH1340	1921(a)	5.000	1.00	2.50	15.00
	1344	1926(a)	1.000	1.50	4.00	25.00
	1345	1926(a)	1.000	1.50	4.00	25.00
	1360	1941(a)	6.612	.50	1.50	10.00
	1364	1945(a)	10.699	.35	1.00	10.00

5.0000 g, .835 SILVER, .1342 oz ASW
Obv. leg: ***Muhammad al-Habib.***

KM#	Date	Year	Mintage	VF	XF	Unc
250	AH1341	1922A	703 pcs.	—	135.00	275.00
	1342	1923A	1,409	—	100.00	250.00
	1343	1924A	703 pcs.	—	135.00	275.00
	1344	1925A	703 pcs.	—	135.00	275.00
	1345	1926A	703 pcs.	—	135.00	275.00
	1346	1927A	703 pcs.	—	135.00	275.00

5.5000 g, .835 SILVER, .1476 oz ASW

KM#	Date	Year	Mintage	VF	XF	Unc
250a	AH1347	1928A	703 pcs.	—	135.00	275.00

2 FRANCS

10.0000 g, .835 SILVER, .2685 oz ASW
Obv. leg: ***Ali.***

KM#	Date	Year	Mintage	VF	XF	Unc
225	AH1308	1891A	.595	12.00	25.00	60.00
	1309	1892A	.432	12.00	25.00	60.00
	1310	1893A	300 pcs.	—	150.00	250.00
	1311	1893A	—	—	150.00	250.00
	1311	1894A	300 pcs.	—	150.00	250.00
	1313	1895A	300 pcs.	—	150.00	250.00
	1314	1896A	300 pcs.	—	150.00	250.00
	1315	1897A	300 pcs.	—	150.00	250.00
	1316	1898A	300 pcs.	—	150.00	250.00
	1317	1899A	300 pcs.	—	150.00	250.00
	1318	1900A	300 pcs.	—	150.00	250.00
	1319	1901A	300 pcs.	—	150.00	250.00
	1320	1902A	300 pcs.	—	150.00	250.00

Obv. leg: ***Muhammad al-Hadi.***

KM#	Date	Year	Mintage	VF	XF	Unc
232	AH1321	1903A	303 pcs.	—	150.00	250.00
	1322	1904A	.150	40.00	75.00	200.00
	1323	1905A	303 pcs.	—	150.00	250.00
	1324	1906A	303 pcs.	—	150.00	250.00

Obv. leg: ***Muhammad al-Nasir.***

KM#	Date	Year	Mintage	VF	XF	Unc
239	AH1325	1907A	306 pcs.	—	150.00	250.00
	1326	1908A	.101	20.00	40.00	85.00
	1327	1909A	303 pcs.	—	150.00	250.00
	1328	1910A	303 pcs.	—	150.00	250.00
	1329	1911A	.475	7.50	15.00	40.00
	1330	1912A	.200	10.00	20.00	45.00
	1331	1913A	303 pcs.	—	150.00	250.00
	1332	1914A	.100	8.50	15.00	25.00
	1333	1914A	I.A.	8.50	15.00	25.00
	1334	1915A	.408	8.50	15.00	25.00
	1334	1916A	1.000	8.50	12.50	20.00
	1335	1916A	Inc. Ab.	8.50	15.00	35.00
	1336	1917A	303 pcs.	—	150.00	250.00
	1337	1918A	303 pcs.	—	150.00	250.00
	1338	1919A	303 pcs.	—	150.00	250.00
	1339	1920A	303 pcs.	—	150.00	250.00
	1340	1921A	303 pcs.	—	150.00	250.00

ALUMINUM-BRONZE

KM#	Date	Year	Mintage	VF	XF	Unc
248	AH1340	1921(a)	1.500	2.00	5.00	25.00
	1343	1924(a)	.500	3.50	8.50	40.00
	1345	1926(a)	.500	3.50	8.50	40.00
	1360	1941(a)	1.976	1.50	4.00	15.00
	1364	1945(a)	6.464	.75	2.00	15.00

10.0000 g, .835 SILVER, .2685 oz ASW
Obv. leg: ***Muhammad al-Habib.***

KM#	Date	Year	Mintage	VF	XF	Unc
251	AH1341	1922A	303 pcs.	—	150.00	325.00
	1342	1923A	690 pcs.	—	135.00	275.00
	1343	1924A	303 pcs.	—	150.00	325.00
	1344	1925A	303 pcs.	—	150.00	325.00
	1345	1926A	303 pcs.	—	150.00	325.00
	1346	1927A	303 pcs.	—	150.00	325.00
	1347	1928A	303 pcs.	—	150.00	325.00

5 FRANCS

5.0000 g, .680 SILVER, .1093 oz ASW
Obv. leg: ***Ahmad.***

Y#	Date	Mintage	VF	XF	Unc
261	AH1353(a)	2.000	3.50	5.00	17.50
	1355(a)	2.000	3.50	5.00	17.50

KM#	Date	Year	Mintage	VF	XF	Unc
264	AH1358(a)	1939	1.600	3.00	6.00	15.00

ALUMINUM-BRONZE
Obv. leg: ***Muhammad al-Amin.***

KM#	Date	Year	Mintage	VF	XF	Unc
273	AH1365(a)	1946	10.000	1.50	10.00	10.00

COPPER-NICKEL

KM#	Date	Year	Mintage	VF	XF	Unc
277	AH1373(a)	1954	18.000	.20	1.00	3.00
	1376(a)	1957	4.000	.50	1.00	2.50

10 FRANCS

3.2258 g, .900 GOLD, .0933 oz AGW
Obv. leg: ***Ali.***

KM#	Date	Year	Mintage	VF	XF	Unc
226	AH1308	1891A	.400	50.00	70.00	100.00
	1308	1891A	—	—	Proof	1250.
	1309	1892A	83 pcs.	—	450.00	850.00
	1310	1893A	83 pcs.	—	450.00	850.00
	1311	1894A	83 pcs.	—	450.00	850.00
	1313	1895A	83 pcs.	—	450.00	850.00
	1314	1896A	83 pcs.	—	450.00	850.00
	1315	1897A	83 pcs.	—	450.00	850.00
	1316	1898A	83 pcs.	—	450.00	850.00
	1317	1899A	83 pcs.	—	450.00	850.00
	1318	1900A	83 pcs.	—	450.00	850.00
	1319	1901A	80 pcs.	—	450.00	850.00
	1320	1902A	83 pcs.	—	450.00	850.00

Obv. leg: ***Muhammad al-Hadi.***

KM#	Date	Year	Mintage	VF	XF	Unc
233	AH1321	1903A	83 pcs.	—	450.00	900.00
	1322	1904A	83 pcs.	—	450.00	900.00
	1323	1905A	83 pcs.	—	450.00	900.00
	1324	1906A	83 pcs.	—	450.00	900.00

Obv. leg: ***Muhammad al-Nasir.***

KM#	Date	Year	Mintage	VF	XF	Unc
240	AH1325	1907A	36 pcs.	—	500.00	900.00
	1326	1908A	166 pcs.	—	300.00	500.00
	1327	1909A	83 pcs.	—	450.00	850.00
	1328	1910A	83 pcs.	—	450.00	850.00
	1329	1911A	83 pcs.	—	450.00	850.00
	1330	1912A	83 pcs.	—	450.00	850.00
	1331	1913A	83 pcs.	—	450.00	850.00
	1332	1914A	83 pcs.	—	450.00	850.00
	1334	1915A	83 pcs.	—	450.00	850.00
	1334	1916A	83 pcs.	—	450.00	850.00
	1336	1917A	83 pcs.	—	450.00	850.00
	1337	1918A	83 pcs.	—	450.00	850.00
	1338	1919A	83 pcs.	—	450.00	850.00
	1339	1920A	83 pcs.	—	450.00	850.00
	1340	1921A	83 pcs.	—	450.00	850.00

Obv. leg: ***Muhammad al-Habib Bey.***

KM#	Date	Year	Mintage	VF	XF	Unc
252	AH1341	1922A	83 pcs.	—	450.00	850.00
	1342	1923A	169 pcs.	—	300.00	500.00
	1343	1924A	83 pcs.	—	450.00	850.00
	1344	1925A	83 pcs.	—	450.00	850.00
	1345	1926A	83 pcs.	—	450.00	850.00
	1346	1927A	83 pcs.	—	450.00	850.00
	1347	1928A	83 pcs.	—	450.00	850.00

10.0000 g, .680 SILVER, .2186 oz ASW
Obv. leg: *Ahmad.*

KM#	Date	Year	Mintage	VF	XF	Unc
255	AH1349	1930(a)	.060	35.00	60.00	110.00
	1350	1931(a)	1,103	150.00	250.00	350.00
	1351	1932(a)	.060	35.00	60.00	110.00
	1352	1933(a)	1,103	150.00	250.00	350.00
	1353	1934(a)	.030	30.00	50.00	90.00

KM#	Date	Mintage	VF	XF	Unc
262	AH1353(a)	1.501	4.50	9.00	15.00
	1354(a)	1,103	—	150.00	250.00
	1355(a)	2,006	—	135.00	225.00
	1356(a)	1,103	—	150.00	250.00

KM#	Date	Year	Mintage	VF	XF	Unc
265	AH1358	1939(a)	.501	6.00	15.00	35.00
	1359	1940(a)	—			
	1360	1941(a)	1,103	—	135.00	225.00
	1361	1942(a)	1,103	—	135.00	225.00

Obv. leg: *Muhammad al-Amin.*

KM#	Date	Year	Mintage	VF	XF	Unc
269	AH1363(a)	1943	1,503	—	225.00	350.00
	1364(a)	1944	2,206	—	200.00	300.00

20 FRANCS

6.4516 g, .900 GOLD, .1867 oz AGW
Obv. leg: *Ali.*

KM#	Date	Year	Mintage	VF	XF	Unc
227	AH1308	1891A	.400	BV	80.00	100.00
	1308	1891	—	—	Proof	1500.
	1309	1892A	.937	BV	80.00	100.00
	1310	1892A	Inc. Ab.	BV	80.00	100.00
	1310	1893A	.035	BV	80.00	100.00
	1311	1894A	20 pcs.	—	550.00	1000.
	1313	1895A	20 pcs.	—	550.00	1000.
	1314	1896A	20 pcs.	—	550.00	1000.
	1315	1897A	.164	BV	80.00	100.00
	1316	1898A	.150	BV	80.00	100.00
	1316	1899A	.150	BV	80.00	100.00
	1318	1900A	.150	BV	80.00	100.00
	1319	1901A	.150	BV	80.00	100.00
	1320	1902A	20 pcs.	—	550.00	1000.

Obv. leg: *Muhammad al-Hadi.*

KM#	Date	Year	Mintage	VF	XF	Unc
234	AH1321	1903A	.300	BV	85.00	110.00
	1321	1904A	.600	BV	85.00	110.00
	1322	1904A	Inc. Ab.	BV	85.00	110.00
	1323	1905A	23 pcs.	—	550.00	1000.
	1324	1906A	23 pcs.	—	550.00	1000.

Obv. leg: *Muhammad al-Nasir.*

KM#	Date	Year	Mintage	VF	XF	Unc
241	AH1325	1907A	26 pcs.	—	550.00	1000.
	1326	1908A	46 pcs.	—	450.00	850.00
	1327	1909A	23 pcs.	—	550.00	1000.
	1328	1910A	23 pcs.	—	550.00	1000.
	1329	1911A	23 pcs.	—	550.00	1000.
	1330	1912A	23 pcs.	—	550.00	1000.
	1331	1913A	23 pcs.	—	550.00	1000.
	1332	1914A	23 pcs.	—	550.00	1000.
	1334	1915A	23 pcs.	—	550.00	1000.
	1334	1916A	23 pcs.	—	550.00	1000.
	1336	1917A	23 pcs.	—	550.00	1000.
	1337	1918A	23 pcs.	—	550.00	1000.
	1338	1919A	23 pcs.	—	550.00	1000.
	1339	1920A	23 pcs.	—	550.00	1000.
	1340	1921A	23 pcs.	—	550.00	1000.

Obv. leg: *Muhammad al-Habib.*

KM#	Date	Year	Mintage	VF	XF	Unc
253	AH1341	1922A	23 pcs.	—	550.00	1000.
	1342	1923A	49 pcs.	—	450.00	850.00
	1343	1924A	23 pcs.	—	550.00	1000.
	1344	1925A	23 pcs.	—	550.00	1000.
	1345	1926A	23 pcs.	—	550.00	1000.
	1346	1927A	23 pcs.	—	550.00	1000.
	1347	1928A	23 pcs.	—	550.00	1000.

20.0000 g, .680 SILVER, .4372 oz ASW
Obv. leg: *Ahmad.*

KM#	Date	Year	Mintage	VF	XF	Unc
256	AH1349	1930(a)	.020	60.00	100.00	170.00
	1350	1931(a)	53 pcs.	200.00	300.00	500.00
	1351	1932(a)	.020	75.00	125.00	185.00
	1352	1933(a)	53 pcs.	200.00	300.00	500.00
	1353	1934(a)	9,500	60.00	100.00	170.00

NOTE: It is believed that an additional number of coins dated AH1353/1934(a) were struck and included in mintage figures of KM#263 of the same date.

KM#	Date	Mintage	VF	XF	Unc
263	AH1353(a)	1.250	10.00	20.00	55.00
	1354(a)	53 pcs.	—	275.00	450.00
	1355(a)	106 pcs.	—	225.00	375.00
	1356(a)	53 pcs.	—	275.00	450.00

KM#	Date	Year	Mintage	VF	XF	Unc
266	AH1358	1939(a)	.100	20.00	40.00	90.00
	1359	1940(a)	Reported, not confirmed			
	1360	1941(a)	53 pcs.	—	275.00	450.00
	1361	1942(a)	53 pcs.	—	275.00	450.00

Obv. leg: *Muhammad al-Amin.*

KM#	Date	Year	Mintage	VF	XF	Unc
270	AH1363(a)	1943	103 pcs.	—	300.00	500.00
	1364(a)	1944	106 pcs.	—	300.00	500.00

COPPER-NICKEL

KM#	Date	Year	Mintage	VF	XF	Unc
274	AH1370	1950(a)	10.000	.50	2.00	6.00
	1376	1957(a)	4.000	.35	1.00	4.00

50 FRANCS

COPPER-NICKEL
Obv. leg: *Muhammad al-Amin.*

KM#	Date	Year	Mintage	VF	XF	Unc
275	AH1370	1950(a)	5.000	.50	2.00	6.00
	1376	1957(a)	.600	1.00	2.50	5.00

100 FRANCS

6.5500 g, .900 GOLD, .1895 oz AGW
Obv. leg: *Ahmad.*

KM#	Date	Year	Mintage	VF	XF	Unc
257	AH1349	1930(a)	3,000	90.00	110.00	135.00
	1350	1931(a)	33 pcs.	—	500.00	900.00
	1351	1932(a)	3,000	90.00	110.00	135.00

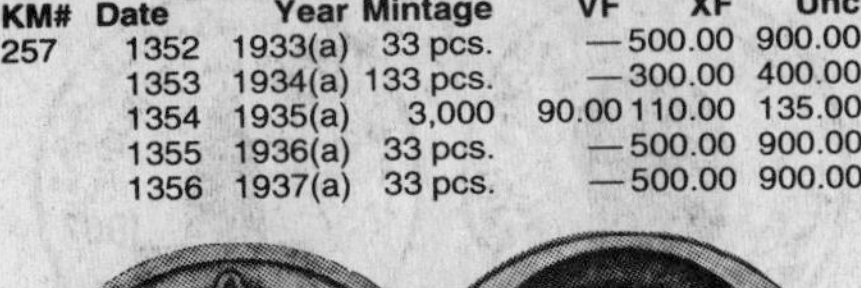

KM#	Date	Year	Mintage	VF	XF	Unc
257	1352	1933(a)	33 pcs.	—	500.00	900.00
	1353	1934(a)	133 pcs.	—	300.00	400.00
	1354	1935(a)	3,000	90.00	110.00	135.00
	1355	1936(a)	33 pcs.	—	500.00	900.00
	1356	1937(a)	33 pcs.	—	500.00	900.00

COPPER-NICKEL
Obv. leg: *Muhammad al-Amin.*

KM#	Date	Year	Mintage	VF	XF	Unc
276	AH1370	1950(a)	8.000	2.00	5.00	10.00
	1376	1957(a)	1.000	2.00	4.00	8.00

REPUBLIC

1000 Millim = 1 Dinar

MILLIM

ALUMINUM

KM#	Date	Mintage	VF	XF	Unc
280	1960	—	—	.10	.25
	1983	—	—	.10	.25

2 MILLIM

ALUMINUM

KM#	Date	Mintage	VF	XF	Unc
281	1960	—	—	.10	.25
	1983	—	—	.10	.25

5 MILLIM

ALUMINUM

KM#	Date	Mintage	VF	XF	Unc
282	1960	—	—	.10	.25
	1983	—	—	.10	.25

10 MILLIM

BRASS

KM#	Date	Year	Mintage	VF	XF	Unc
306	AH1380	1960	—	.15	.25	.50
	1403	1983	—	.15	.25	.50
	1414	1993	—	.15	.25	.50

20 MILLIM

BRASS

KM#	Date	Year	Mintage	VF	XF	Unc
307	AH1380	1960	—	.30	.50	.80
	1403	1983	—	.30	.50	.80
	1414	1993	—	.30	.50	.80

50 MILLIM

BRASS

KM#	Date	Year	Mintage	VF	XF	Unc
308	AH1380	1960	—	.65	.85	1.25
	1403	1983	—	.65	.85	1.25
	1414	1993	—	.65	.85	1.25

100 MILLIM

BRASS

KM#	Date	Year	Mintage	VF	XF	Unc
309	AH1380	1960	—	1.25	1.50	2.00
	1403	1983	—	1.25	1.50	2.00
	1414	1993	—	1.25	1.50	2.00

1/2 DINAR

NICKEL

KM#	Date	Mintage	VF	XF	Unc
291	1968(a)	.500	1.00	2.00	4.00

COPPER-NICKEL
F.A.O. Issue

KM#	Date	Mintage	VF	XF	Unc
303	1976	—	1.50	3.50	7.50
	1983	—	1.50	3.50	7.50

F.A.O. Issue

KM#	Date	Mintage	VF	XF	Unc
318	1988	—	1.50	3.50	7.50
	1990	—	1.50	3.50	7.50

DINAR

20.0000 g, .925 SILVER, .5949 oz ASW
Hannibal

KM#	Date	Mintage	VF	XF	Unc
292	1969FM-NI	.015	—	Proof	13.50
	1969NI	5,000	—	Proof	32.00

Masinissa
Obv: Similar to KM#292.

KM#	Date	Mintage	VF	XF	Unc
293	1969FM-NI	.015	—	Proof	30.00
	1969NI	5,000	—	Proof	40.00

Jugurtha
Obv: Similar to KM#292.

KM#	Date	Mintage	VF	XF	Unc
294	1969FM-NI	.015	—	Proof	12.50
	1969NI	5,000	—	Proof	30.00

Virgil
Obv: Similar to KM#292.

KM#	Date	Mintage	VF	XF	Unc
295	1969FM-NI	.015	—	Proof	12.50
	1969NI	5,000	—	Proof	30.00

St. Augustine
Obv: Similar to KM#292.

KM#	Date	Mintage	VF	XF	Unc
296	1969FM-NI	.015	—	Proof	12.50
	1969NI	5,000	—	Proof	30.00

Phoenician Ship
Obv: Similar to KM#292.

KM#	Date	Mintage	VF	XF	Unc
297	1969FM-NI	.015	—	Proof	32.50
	1969NI	5,000	—	Proof	80.00

Neptune
Obv: Similar to KM#292.

KM#	Date	Mintage	VF	XF	Unc
298	1969FM-NI	.015	—	Proof	13.50
	1969NI	5,000	—	Proof	32.00

Venus
Obv: Similar to KM#292.

KM#	Date	Mintage	VF	XF	Unc
299	1969FM-NI	.015	—	Proof	20.00
	1969NI	5,000	—	Proof	45.00

Thysdrus-El Djem
Obv: Similar to KM#292.

KM#	Date	Mintage	VF	XF	Unc
300	1969FM-NI	.015	—	Proof	12.50
	1969NI	5,000	—	Proof	30.00

21.1840 g, .925 SILVER, .6300 oz ASW
Sbeitla-Sufetula
Obv: Similar to KM#292.

KM#	Date	Mintage	VF	XF	Unc
301	1969FM-NI	.015	—	Proof	13.50
	1969NI	5,000	—	Proof	32.00

18.0000 g, .680 SILVER, .3935 oz ASW
F.A.O. Issue

KM#	Date	Mintage	VF	XF	Unc
302	1970(a)	.100	—	5.00	10.00
	1970(a)	1,250	—	Proof	40.00

COPPER-NICKEL
F.A.O. Issue

KM#	Date	Mintage	VF	XF	Unc
304	1976	—	2.00	4.00	8.00
	1983	—	2.00	4.00	8.00

NOTE: Coins dated 1976 exist w/or w/o dots below *Tunisiye.*

F.A.O. Issue

KM#	Date	Mintage	VF	XF	Unc
319	1988	—	2.00	4.00	8.00
	1989	—	2.00	4.00	8.00
	1990	—	2.00	4.00	8.00

2 DINARS

3.8000 g, .900 GOLD, .1099 oz AGW
10th Anniversary of Republic

KM#	Date	Mintage	VF	XF	Unc
286	1967NI	7,259	—	Proof	65.00

5 DINARS

11.7900 g, .900 GOLD, .3412 oz AGW
Obv. and rev: French legends.

KM#	Date	Mintage	VF	XF	Unc
283	1962	—	—	Proof	550.00

Obv. and rev: Arabic legends.

KM#	Date	Mintage	VF	XF	Unc
320	1962	—	—	Proof	550.00

Obv. and rev: French legends.

KM#	Date	Mintage	VF	XF	Unc
284	1963	—	—	Proof	550.00

9.3600 g, .900 GOLD, .2708 oz AGW

KM#	Date	Mintage	VF	XF	Unc
284a	1976	—	—	Proof	500.00

Obv. and rev: Arabic legends.

KM#	Date	Mintage	VF	XF	Unc
321	1963	—	—	Proof	550.00

9.5000 g, .900 GOLD, .2749 oz AGW
10th Anniversary of Republic

KM#	Date	Mintage	VF	XF	Unc
287	1967NI	7,259	—	Proof	125.00

24.0000 g, .680 SILVER, .5247 oz ASW
20th Anniversary of Independence

KM#	Date	Mintage	VF	XF	Unc
305	1976	.201	—	—	15.00
	1976	—	—	Proof	30.00

9.4120 g, .900 GOLD, .2723 oz AGW
Obv: Habib Bourguiba. Rev: President's return.

KM#	Date	Mintage	VF	XF	Unc
310	1981	1,450	—	Proof	170.00

27.2200 g, .925 SILVER, .8096 oz ASW
International Year of the Child
Obv: Similar to 1 Dinar, KM#302.

KM#	Date	Mintage	VF	XF	Unc
313	1982	7,575	—	—	16.50
	1982	1,108	—	Proof	30.00

9.4120 g, .900 GOLD, .2723 oz AGW
Obv: Presidential portrait. Rev: Coat of arms.
French legend.

KM#	Date	Mintage	VF	XF	Unc
325	1982	725 pcs.	—	Proof	220.00

Rev: Arabic legend.

KM#	Date	Mintage	VF	XF	Unc
326	AH1402	725 pcs.	—	Proof	220.00

25th Anniversary of Republic
French legends.

KM#	Date	Mintage	VF	XF	Unc
327	1983-85	—	—	Proof	220.00

Arabic legends.

KM#	Date	Mintage	VF	XF	Unc
328	AH1403-05(1983-85)	—	—	Proof	220.00

Obv: Map. Rev: Allegorical design.
French legends.

KM#	Date	Mintage	VF	XF	Unc
329	1988	375 pcs.	—	—	250.00
	1989	Inc. Ab.	—	—	250.00

Arabic legends.

KM#	Date	Mintage	VF	XF	Unc
330	AH1408	375 pcs.	—	—	250.00
	1409	Inc. Ab.	—	—	250.00

10 DINARS

23.4800 g, .900 GOLD, .6795 oz AGW
Obv. and rev: French legends.

KM#	Date	Mintage	VF	XF	Unc
322	1962	—	—	Proof	1000.

Obv. and rev: Arabic legends.

KM#	Date	Year	Mintage	VF	XF	Unc
285	AH1382	1962	—	—	Proof	1000.
	1384	1964	—	—	Proof	1000.

19.0000 g, .900 GOLD, .5498 oz AGW
10th Anniversary of Republic

KM#	Date	Mintage	VF	XF	Unc
288	1967NI	6,480	—	Proof	250.00

.900 GOLD
20th Anniversary of Independence

KM#	Date	Mintage	VF	XF	Unc
324	1976	*2,000	—	—	600.00

18.7700g, .900 GOLD, .5431 oz AGW
Obv. and rev: French legends.

KM#	Date	Mintage	VF	XF	Unc
342	1979	—	—	—	900.00

Obv. and rev: Arabic legends.

KM#	Date	Year	Mintage	VF	XF	Unc
343	AH1399	1979	—	—	—	900.00

18.8240 g, .900 GOLD, .5447 oz AGW
Obv: Habib Bourguiba. Rev: President's return.

KM#	Date	Mintage	VF	XF	Unc
311	1981	2,000	—	Proof	320.00

18.8080 g, .900 GOLD, .5442 oz AGW
25th Anniversary of Independence
Obv: Habib Bourguiba. Rev: Silhouette of girl.

KM#	Date	Mintage	VF	XF	Unc
312	1981	2,000	—	Proof	320.00

38.0000 g, .900 SILVER, 1.0995 oz ASW
Gabes Bank

KM#	Date	Mintage	VF	XF	Unc
314	1982	2,500	—	Proof	30.00

Central Bank at Nabeul

KM#	Date	Mintage	VF	XF	Unc
315	1982	1,000	—	Proof	40.00

Sfax Branch Office

KM#	Date	Mintage	VF	XF	Unc
316	1982	1,000	—	Proof	40.00

Obv: President's portrait. Rev: Coat of Arms,
French legend.

KM#	Date	Mintage	VF	XF	Unc
331	1982	700 pcs.	—	Proof	50.00

Arabic legend.

KM#	Date	Mintage	VF	XF	Unc
332	AH1402	700 pcs.	—	Proof	50.00

Tunisian girl.

KM#	Date	Mintage	VF	XF	Unc
333	1982	2,000	—	Proof	35.00

25th Anniversary of Republic
French legend.

KM#	Date	Mintage	VF	XF	Unc
334	1983-85	—	—	Proof	40.00

Arabic legend.

KM#	Date	Mintage	VF	XF	Unc
335	AH1403-05(1983-85)	—	—	Proof	40.00

50th Anniversary of the Socialist Party

KM#	Date	Mintage	VF	XF	Unc
336	1984	—	—	Proof	40.00

18.8080 g, .900 GOLD, .5442 oz AGW
Obv: Portrait left. Rev: Statue of Burgiba.

KM#	Date	Year	Mintage	VF	XF	Unc
323	AH1405	1985	2,000	—	Proof	550.00

30th Anniversary of Independence

KM#	Date	Mintage	VF	XF	Unc
337	1986	—	—	Proof	550.00

30th Anniversary of Republic

KM#	Date	Mintage	VF	XF	Unc
338	1987	2,000	—	Proof	550.00

38.0000 g, .900 SILVER, 1.0995 oz ASW

KM#	Date	Mintage	VF	XF	Unc
339	1988	4,000	—	Proof	30.00

18.8080 g, .900 GOLD, .5442 oz AGW
Obv: Map. Rev: Allegorical design.
French legend

KM#	Date	Mintage	VF	XF	Unc
340	1988	375 pcs.	—	—	650.00
	1989	Inc. Ab.	—	—	650.00

Arabic legend.

KM#	Date	Mintage	VF	XF	Unc
341	AH1408	375 pcs.	—	—	650.00
	1409	Inc. Ab.	—	—	650.00

20 DINARS

38.0000 g, .900 GOLD, 1.0996 oz AGW
10th Anniversary of Republic

KM#	Date	Mintage	VF	XF	Unc
289	1967NI	3,536	—	—	500.00

40 DINARS

76.0000 g, .900 GOLD, 2.1991 oz AGW
10th Anniversary of Republic
Obv: Similar to 10 Dinars, KM#288.

KM#	Date	Mintage	VF	XF	Unc
290	1967NI	3,031	—	Proof	1000.

75 DINARS

15.5500 g, .900 GOLD, .4500 oz AGW
International Year of the Child

KM#	Date	Mintage	VF	XF	Unc
317	1982	4,518	—	Proof	225.00

MINT SETS (MS)

KM#	Date	Mintage	Identification	Issue Price	Mkt. Val.
MS1	1960(7)	—	KM280-282,306-309	—	5.50

PROOF SETS (PS)

KM#	Date	Mintage	Identification	Issue Price	Mkt. Val.
PS2	1967(5)	3,031	KM286-290	—	1950.
PS3	1969FM-NI(10)	*15,202	KM292-301	77.00	150.00
PS4	1969NI(10)	5,000	KM292-301	—	365.00

***NOTE:** Many sets were ruined while in storage.

TURKEY

a map of The Mints of the Ottoman Empire

The Republic of Turkey, a parliamentary democracy of the Near East located partially in Europe and partially in Asia between the Black and the Mediterranean Seas, has an area of 301,382 sq. mi. (780,580 sq. km.) and a population of *55.4 million. Capital: Ankara. Turkey exports cotton, hazelnuts, and tobacco, and enjoys a virtual monopoly in meerschaum.

The Ottoman Turks, a tribe from Central Asia, first appeared in the early 13th century, and by the 17th century had established the Ottoman Empire which stretched from the Persian Gulf to the southern frontier of Poland, and from the Caspian Sea to the Algerian plateau. The defeat of the Turkish navy by the Holy League in 1571, and of the Turkish forces besieging Vienna in 1683, began the steady decline of the Ottoman Empire which, accelerated by the rise of nationalism, contracted its European border, and by the end of World War I deprived it of its Arab lands. The present Turkish boundaries were largely fixed by the Treaty of Lausanne in 1923. The sultanate and caliphate, the political and spiritual ruling institutions of the old empire, were separated and the sultanate abolished in 1922. On Oct. 29, 1923, Turkey formally became a republic.

RULERS

Selim III, AH1203-1222/ 1789-1807AD
Mustafa IV, AH1222-1223/ 1807-1808AD
Mahmud II, AH1223-1255/ 1808-1839AD
Abdul Mejid, AH1255-1277/ 1839-1861AD
Abdul Aziz, AH1277-1293/ 1861-1876AD
Murad V, AH1293/1876AD
Abdul Hamid II, AH1293-1327/ 1876-1909AD
Muhammad V, AH1327-1336/ 1909-1918AD
Muhammad VI, AH1336-1341/ 1918-1923AD
Republic, AH1341/AD1923

MINTNAMES

Baghdad بغداد
See Iraq-Mesopotamia

Bursa بروسة
(Brusah)

Constantine (Constaniyah, Qusantinah) See Algeria-Algiers قسطنتنيه

Constantinople قسطنطنية
(Qustantiniyah)

Damascus دمشق
(Damask) See Syria

Dimishk د مشق
(Sham)

Edirne ادرنة
(Adrianople)

Haleb حلب
(Aleppo)
See Syria

Islambul اسلامبول or اسلامبول
Istanbul

Jaza'Ir جزاير
(See Algeria-Algiers)

Kara Amid
(Amid)

Kosova قوصوه

Manistir مناستر

al-Mascara المعسكر
See Algeria-Algiers

Medea مديه
See Algeria-Algiers

Mecca مكه
See Saudi Arabia

Misr مصر
See Egypt

Revan روان
(Erevan, now Yerevan)
See Russian Caucasia-Armenia

Salonika سلانيك
(Selanik, Saloniki)

Taqidemt تاقدمت
See Algeria-Algiers

Tarabalus طرابلس
See Libya-Tripoli

Tarabalus Gharb طرابلس غرب
See Libya-Tripoli

Tiflis تفليس
See Russian Caucasia-Georgia

Tunis تونس
See Tunisia-Tunis

Van وان
(Wan) - Until AH1032. AH1133-34
See Russian Caucasia - Armenia

MONETARY EQUIVALENTS

3 Akche = 1 Para
5 Para = Beshlik (Beshparalik)
10 Para = Onluk
20 Para = Yirmilik
30 Para = Zolota
40 Para = Kurush (Piastre)
1-1/2 Kurush (Piastres) = Altmishlik

MONETARY SYSTEM

Silver Coinage

40 Para = 1 Kurush (Piastre)
2 Kurush (Piastres) = 1 Ikilik
2-1/2 Kurush (Piastres) = Yuzluk
3 Kurush (Piastres) = Uechlik
5 Kurush (Piastres) = Beshlik
6 Kurush (Piastres) = Altilik

Gold Coinage

100 Kurush (Piastres) = 1 Turkish Pound (Lira)

This system has remained essentially unchanged since its introduction by Ahmad III in 1688, except that the Asper and Para have long since ceased to be coined. The Piastre, established as a crown-sized silver coin approximately equal to the French Ecu of Louis XIV, has shrunk to a tiny copper coin, worth about 1/15 of a U.S. cent. Since the establishment of the Republic in 1923, the Turkish terms, Kurus and Lira, have replaced the European names Piastres and Turkish Pounds.

MINT VISIT ISSUES

From time to time, certain cities of the Ottoman Empire, such as Bursa, Edirne, Kosova, Manistir and Salonika were honored by having special coins struck at Istanbul, but with inscriptions stating that they were struck in the city of honor. These were produced on the occasion of the Sultan's visit to that city. The coins were struck in limited, but not small quantities, and were probably intended for distribution to the notables of the city and the Sultan's own followers. Because they were of the same size and type as the regular circulation issues struck at Istanbul, many specimens found their way into circulation and worn or mounted specimens are found today, although some have been preserved in XF or better condition. Mintage statistics are not known.

MONNAIE DE LUXE

In the 23rd year of the reign of Abdul Hamid II, two parallel series of gold coins were produced, regular mint issues and 'monnaies de luxe', which were intended primarily for presentation and jewelry purposes. The 'Monnaie de Luxe' were struck to a slightly less weight and the same fineness as regular issues, but were broader and thinner, and from more ornate dies.

Coins are listed by type, followed by a list of reported years. Most of the reported years have never been confirmed and other years may also exist. Mintage figures are known for the AH1293 and 1327 series, but are unreliable and of little utility.

Although some years are undoubtedly much rarer than others, there is at present no date collecting of Ottoman gold and therefore little justification for higher prices for rare dates.

There is no change in design in the regular series. Only the toughra, accessional date and regnal year vary. The deluxe series show ornamental changes. The standard coins generally do not bear the denomination.

HONORIFIC TITLES

El Ghazi

Reshat

The first coinage of Abdul Hamid II has a flower right of the toughra while the second coinage has *el Ghazi* (The Victorious). The first coinage of Mohammad Reshat V has *Reshat* right of the toughra while his second coinage has *el Ghazi*.

SELIM III

AH1203-1222/1789-1807AD

THIRD COINAGE

Light coinage based on a Piastre weighing approximately 12.80 g with second toughra.

PARA

.465 SILVER, 0.32 g
Mintname: *Islambul*

KM#	Date	Year	VG	Fine	VF	XF
486	AH1203	14	.75	1.25	6.00	12.00
		15	.75	1.25	6.00	12.00
		16	.75	1.25	6.00	12.00
		17	.75	1.25	6.00	12.00
		18	.75	1.25	6.00	12.00
		19	2.00	4.00	12.00	30.00

NOTE: Earlier dates (Yr. 1-13) exist for this type.

5 PARA

.465 SILVER, 1.60 g
Mintname: *Islambul*

KM#	Date	Year	VG	Fine	VF	XF
489	AH1203	14	6.50	10.00	25.00	40.00
		15	6.50	10.00	25.00	40.00
		16	6.50	10.00	25.00	40.00
		17	6.50	10.00	25.00	40.00
		18	6.50	10.00	25.00	40.00
		19	10.00	15.00	35.00	75.00

NOTE: Earlier dates (Yr. 1-13) exist for this type.

10 PARA

.465 SILVER, 3.05 g
Mintname: *Islambul*

KM#	Date	Year	VG	Fine	VF	XF
492	AH1203	14	4.00	8.00	17.50	35.00
		15	4.00	8.00	17.50	35.00
		16	4.00	8.00	17.50	35.00
		17	4.00	8.00	17.50	35.00

KM#	Date	Year	VG	Fine	VF	XF
492		18	4.00	8.00	17.50	35.00
		19	8.00	15.00	25.00	55.00

NOTE: Earlier dates (Yr. 1-13) exist for this type.

20 PARA

.465 SILVER, 6.45 g
Mintname: *Islambul*

KM#	Date	Year	VG	Fine	VF	XF
495	AH1203	15	50.00	100.00	190.00	350.00
		16	50.00	100.00	190.00	350.00
		19	—	—	Rare	—

NOTE: Earlier dates (Yr. 1-13) exist for this type.

PIASTRE

.465 SILVER, 12.62 g
Mintname: *Islambul*

KM#	Date	Year	VG	Fine	VF	XF
498	AH1203	14	20.00	30.00	60.00	125.00
		15	25.00	35.00	70.00	150.00
		16	25.00	35.00	70.00	150.00
		17	25.00	35.00	70.00	150.00
		18	25.00	35.00	70.00	150.00
		19	150.00	250.00	400.00	750.00

NOTE: Earlier dates (Yr. 1-13) exist for this type.

2 PIASTRES

.465 SILVER, 25.60 g
Mintname: *Islambul*

KM#	Date	Year	VG	Fine	VF	XF
504	AH1203	14	10.00	12.00	30.00	45.00
		15	10.00	12.00	30.00	45.00
		16	10.00	12.00	30.00	45.00
		17	10.00	12.00	30.00	45.00
		18	30.00	75.00	100.00	200.00
		19	75.00	150.00	250.00	400.00

NOTE: Earlier dates (Yr. 1-13) exist for this type.

YUZLUK

.465 SILVER, 32.00 g
Mintname: *Islambul*

KM#	Date	Year	VG	Fine	VF	XF
507	AH1203	14	10.00	12.00	25.00	40.00
		15	10.00	12.00	25.00	50.00
		16	10.00	12.00	25.00	55.00
		17	10.00	12.00	25.00	70.00
		18	30.00	40.00	60.00	110.00
		19	50.00	75.00	150.00	350.00

NOTE: Earlier dates (Yr. 1-13) exist for this type.

1/4 ZERI MAHBUB

GOLD, 0.60 g
Mintname: *Islambul*

KM#	Date	Year	VG	Fine	VF	XF
510	AH1203	14	22.50	35.00	50.00	75.00
		15	22.50	35.00	50.00	75.00
		16	22.50	35.00	50.00	75.00
		17	22.50	35.00	50.00	75.00

NOTE: Earlier dates (Yr. 7-13) exist for this type.
NOTE: With *Azza Nasara*.

1/4 ALTIN

(Findik)

GOLD, 15mm, 0.90 g
Mintname: *Islambul*
Plain borders

KM#	Date	Year	VG	Fine	VF	XF
514	AH1203	14	22.50	35.00	50.00	70.00
		15	22.50	35.00	50.00	70.00
		16	22.50	35.00	50.00	70.00
		17	22.50	35.00	50.00	70.00
		18	22.50	35.00	50.00	70.00
		19	30.00	50.00	75.00	125.00

NOTE: Earlier dates (Yr. 1-13) exist for this type.

1/2 ZERI MAHBUB

GOLD, 1.10-1.20 g
Mintname: *Islambul*

KM#	Date	Year	VG	Fine	VF	XF
517	AH1203	14	40.00	65.00	80.00	100.00
		15	40.00	65.00	80.00	100.00
		16	40.00	65.00	80.00	100.00
		17	40.00	65.00	80.00	100.00
		18	50.00	80.00	120.00	180.00
		19	100.00	200.00	300.00	400.00

NOTE: Earlier dates (Yr. 1-12) exist for this type.

1/2 ALTIN

GOLD, 1.65 g
Mintname: *Islambul*

KM#	Date	Year	VG	Fine	VF	XF
520	AH1203	18	60.00	90.00	135.00	185.00

NOTE: Earlier dates (Yr. 1-13) exist for this type.

ZERI MAHBUB

GOLD
Mintname: *Islambul*

KM#	Date	Year	VG	Fine	VF	XF
523	AH1203	14	35.00	50.00	90.00	120.00
		15	35.00	50.00	90.00	120.00
		16	35.00	50.00	90.00	120.00
		17	35.00	50.00	90.00	120.00
		18	35.00	50.00	90.00	120.00
		19	35.00	50.00	90.00	120.00

NOTE: Earlier dates (Yr. 10-13) exist for this type.

ALTIN

GOLD, 3.45 g
Mintname: *Islambul*

KM#	Date	Year	VG	Fine	VF	XF
527	AH1203	17	60.00	85.00	135.00	185.00
		18	60.00	85.00	135.00	185.00
		19	60.00	85.00	135.00	185.00

MUSTAFA IV

AH1222-1223/1807-1808AD

MANGHIR

COPPER
Mintname: *Qustantiniyah*

KM#	Date	Year	VG	Fine	VF	XF
534	AH1222	1	—	—	—	—

AKCE

.465 SILVER, 12mm, 0.12 g
Mintname: *Qustantiniyah*
Similar to Para, KM#536.

KM#	Date	Year	
535	AH1222	1	Reported, not confirmed
		2	Reported, not confirmed

PARA

.465 SILVER, 0.40 g
Mintname: *Qustantiniyah*

KM#	Date	Year	VG	Fine	VF	XF
536	AH1222	1	15.00	17.50	35.00	50.00
		2	20.00	40.00	50.00	75.00

5 PARA

.465 SILVER, 1.50 g
Mintname: *Qustantiniyah*

KM#	Date	Year	VG	Fine	VF	XF
537	AH1222	1	50.00	55.00	150.00	250.00
		2	60.00	110.00	250.00	325.00

10 PARA

.465 SILVER, 3.14 g
Mintname: *Qustantiniyah*

KM#	Date	Year	VG	Fine	VF	XF
538	AH1222	1	40.00	50.00	125.00	200.00
		2	50.00	70.00	250.00	350.00

PIASTRE

.465 SILVER, 12.95 g
Mintname: *Qustantiniyah*

KM#	Date	Year	VG	Fine	VF	XF
539	AH1222	1	250.00	450.00	650.00	850.00
		2	300.00	500.00	850.00	1200.

2 ZOLOTA

.465 SILVER, 19.45 g
Mintname: *Qustantiniyah*

KM#	Date	Year	VG	Fine	VF	XF
540.1	AH1222	1	600.00	1000.	2000.	3000.

Obv: Regnal year between ornaments.

KM#	Date	Year	VG	Fine	VF	XF
540.2	AH1222	1	—	—	—	—

2 PIASTRES

.465 SILVER, 26.10 g
Mintname: *Qustantiniyah*

KM#	Date	Year	VG	Fine	VF	XF
541	AH1222	1	500.00	850.00	1750.	2500.

21/2 PIASTRES

.465 SILVER, 42mm, 32.80 g
Mintname: *Qustantiniyah*

KM#	Date	Year	VG	Fine	VF	XF
542	AH1222	1	650.00	1100.	1750.	2500.

1/4 ALTIN

GOLD, 0.77 g
Mintname: *Qustantiniyah*

KM#	Date	Year	VG	Fine	VF	XF
543	AH1222	1	40.00	60.00	100.00	150.00
		2	45.00	65.00	120.00	175.00

1/2 ZERI MAHBUB

GOLD, 1.20 g
Mintname: *Qustantiniyah*

KM#	Date	Year	VG	Fine	VF	XF
544	AH1222	1	60.00	90.00	135.00	200.00
		2	60.00	90.00	135.00	200.00

ZERI MAHBUB

GOLD, 2.35 g
Mintname: *Qustantiniyah*

KM#	Date	Year	VG	Fine	VF	XF
545	AH1222	1	90.00	150.00	250.00	350.00
		2	125.00	200.00	300.00	450.00

ALTIN

GOLD, 3.20 g
Mintname: *Qustantiniyah*

KM#	Date	Year	VG	Fine	VF	XF
546	AH1222	1	70.00	100.00	120.00	170.00
		2	90.00	120.00	140.00	200.00

MAHMUD II

AH1223-1255/1808-1839AD

Silver Coinage

The silver currency of the reign of Mahmud II is characterized by frequent change of standard, so that the Piastre (Kurus), which began with 5.90 g of pure silver, had dropped to only 0.56 g in the lower denominations (token currency), and 0.94 g in the higher (actual currency). From time to time, the fineness, diameter, weight and type of the coins were changed, with the result that it is difficult, and not very meaningful, to attempt to trace individual denominations through the 32 years of his reign. For that reason, following Craig and others, the coins are grouped by standards of weight, fineness, or size. Changes in fineness, weight, and size are regularly indicated, as are distinguishing features whenever necessary for the proper identification of coins. The tolerance on Mahmud's silver coinage was considerable, particularly on the smaller denominations, and the weights listed are approximate. During the 15th-16th years of his reign, Mahmud II obtained the title *ADLI* = "Just" which was inscribed right of his toughra.

First Series

Years 1-2

AKCE

.465 SILVER, 9mm, 0.10-0.16 g
Mintname: *Qustantiniyah*

KM#	Date	Year	VG	Fine	VF	XF
550	AH1223	1	6.00	15.00	35.00	70.00
		2	6.00	15.00	35.00	70.00

PARA

.465 SILVER, 0.32 g
Mintname: *Qustantiniyah*

KM#	Date	Year	VG	Fine	VF	XF
551	AH1223	1	4.00	10.00	16.00	30.00
		2	4.00	10.00	16.00	30.00

5 PARA

.465 SILVER, 1.50-1.60 g
Mintname: *Qustantiniyah*

KM#	Date	Year	VG	Fine	VF	XF
552	AH1223	1	8.00	20.00	45.00	80.00
		2	8.00	20.00	45.00	80.00

10 PARA

.465 SILVER, 2.80-3.20 g
Mintname: *Qustantiniyah*

KM#	Date	Year	VG	Fine	VF	XF
553	AH1223	*1	10.00	20.00	45.00	90.00
		2	12.00	25.00	55.00	100.00

***NOTE:** Two obverse varieties exist.

30 PARA

SILVER, 9.53 g
Mintname: *Qustantiniyah*

KM#	Date	Year	VG	Fine	VF	XF
549	AH1223	1 Unique	—	—	—	—

PIASTRE

.465 SILVER, 12.00-13.18 g
Mintname: *Qustantiniyah*

KM#	Date	Year	VG	Fine	VF	XF
554	AH1223	1	100.00	300.00	550.00	800.00
		2	150.00	350.00	650.00	850.00

Second Series

Years 2-14

AKCE

.465 SILVER, 11mm, 0.10-0.12 g
Mintname: *Qustantiniyah*

KM#	Date	Year	VG	Fine	VF	XF
556	AH1223	5	2.50	10.00	30.00	50.00
		12	2.50	10.00	30.00	50.00

PARA

.465 SILVER, 0.18-0.26 g
Mintname: *Qustantiniyah*

KM#	Date	Year	VG	Fine	VF	XF
557	AH1223	3	1.00	3.00	4.00	10.00
		4	1.00	3.00	4.00	10.00
		5	1.00	3.00	4.00	10.00
		6	1.00	3.00	4.00	10.00
		7	1.00	3.00	4.00	10.00
		8	1.00	3.00	4.00	10.00
		9	1.00	3.00	4.00	10.00
		10	1.00	3.00	4.00	10.00
		11	1.00	3.00	4.00	10.00
		12	1.00	3.00	4.00	10.00
		13	1.00	3.00	4.00	10.00
		14	1.00	3.00	4.00	10.00

5 PARA

.465 SILVER, 1.01-1.20 g
Mintname: *Qustantiniyah*

KM#	Date	Year	VG	Fine	VF	XF
558	AH1223	3	3.00	6.00	20.00	35.00
		4	3.00	6.00	20.00	35.00
		5	3.00	6.00	20.00	35.00
		6	3.00	6.00	20.00	35.00
		7	3.00	6.00	20.00	35.00
		8	3.00	6.00	20.00	35.00
		9	3.00	6.00	20.00	35.00
		10	3.00	6.00	20.00	35.00
		11	3.00	6.00	20.00	35.00
		12	3.00	6.00	20.00	35.00
		13	3.00	6.00	20.00	35.00
		14	3.00	6.00	20.00	35.00

10 PARA

.465 SILVER, 2.10-2.50 g
Mintname: *Qustantiniyah*

KM#	Date	Year	VG	Fine	VF	XF
559	AH1223	3	2.00	5.00	15.00	30.00
		4	2.00	5.00	15.00	30.00
		5	2.00	5.00	15.00	30.00
		6	2.00	5.00	15.00	30.00
		7	2.00	5.00	15.00	30.00
		8	2.00	5.00	15.00	30.00
		9	2.00	5.00	15.00	30.00
		10	2.00	5.00	15.00	30.00
		11	2.00	5.00	15.00	30.00
		12	2.00	5.00	15.00	30.00
		13	2.00	5.00	15.00	30.00
		14	2.00	5.00	15.00	30.00

PIASTRE

.465 SILVER, 33mm, 9.60 g
Mintname: *Qustantiniyah*

KM#	Date	Year	VG	Fine	VF	XF
560	AH1223	3	12.00	18.00	32.00	100.00
		4	12.00	18.00	32.00	100.00
		5	12.00	18.00	32.00	100.00
		6	12.00	18.00	32.00	100.00
		7	12.00	18.00	32.00	100.00
		8	12.00	18.00	32.00	100.00
		9	12.00	18.00	32.00	100.00
		10	12.00	18.00	32.00	100.00
		11	12.00	18.00	32.00	100.00
		12	12.00	18.00	32.00	100.00
		13	12.00	18.00	32.00	100.00

Third Series - Cihadiye

(Jyhadiye)

Years 3-11

PIASTRE

.730 SILVER, 4.60-5.20 g
Mintname: *Qustantiniyah*

KM#	Date	Year	VG	Fine	VF	XF
562	AH1223	3	175.00	300.00	500.00	850.00

100 PARA

(2-1/2 Piastres)

.730 SILVER, 12.50-13.20 g
Mintname: *Qustantiniyah*

KM#	Date	Year	VG	Fine	VF	XF
563	AH1223	2	— Reported, not confirmed			
		3	100.00	175.00	350.00	600.00
		4	100.00	175.00	350.00	600.00
		5	100.00	175.00	350.00	600.00
		6	100.00	175.00	350.00	600.00
		7	100.00	175.00	350.00	600.00
		8	100.00	175.00	350.00	600.00
		9	100.00	175.00	350.00	600.00
		10	175.00	300.00	550.00	800.00
		11	350.00	600.00	850.00	1250.

5 PIASTRES

.730 SILVER, 24.00-26.00 g
Mintname: *Qustantiniyah*

KM#	Date	Year	VG	Fine	VF	XF
564	AH1223	3	20.00	30.00	55.00	90.00
		4	20.00	30.00	50.00	85.00
		5	20.00	30.00	50.00	85.00
		6	20.00	30.00	50.00	85.00
		7	20.00	30.00	50.00	85.00
		8	20.00	30.00	75.00	110.00
		9	20.00	30.00	75.00	110.00
		10	100.00	150.00	225.00	350.00
		11	275.00	400.00	650.00	1000.

Fourth Series

Years 14-15

PARA

.465 SILVER, 0.15 g
Mintname: *Qustantiniyah*

KM#	Date	Year	VG	Fine	VF	XF
566	AH1223	14	1.25	2.50	6.00	12.00
		15	1.25	2.50	6.00	12.00

5 PARA

.465 SILVER, 18mm, 0.85 g
Mintname: *Qustantiniyah*

KM#	Date	Year	VG	Fine	VF	XF
567	AH1223	14	7.00	15.00	50.00	80.00

10 PARA

.465 SILVER, 22mm, 1.60-1.80 g
Mintname: *Qustantiniyah*

KM#	Date	Year	VG	Fine	VF	XF
568	AH1223	14	5.00	10.00	35.00	60.00
		15	10.00	20.00	50.00	100.00

PIASTRE

.465 SILVER, 32mm, 5.50 g
Mintname: *Qustantiniyah*

KM#	Date	Year	VG	Fine	VF	XF
569	AH1223	14	25.00	35.00	75.00	150.00
		15	45.00	60.00	100.00	175.00

2 PIASTRES

.465 SILVER, 11.50-13.40 g
Mintname: *Qustantiniyah*

KM#	Date	Year	VG	Fine	VF	XF
570	AH1223	14	25.00	50.00	100.00	200.00
		15	30.00	60.00	120.00	225.00

NOTE: Some coins have stars above and below regnal year box.

Fifth Series

Years 15-16
Reeded edge on all but Para

PARA

.730 SILVER, 0.14-0.17 g
Mintname: *Qustantiniyah*

KM#	Date	Year	VG	Fine	VF	XF
572	AH1223	15	1.50	3.00	6.00	15.00
		16	1.50	3.00	6.00	15.00

5 PARA

.730 SILVER, 0.80 g
Mintname: *Qustantiniyah*

KM#	Date	Year	VG	Fine	VF	XF
573	AH1223	15	8.00	17.50	40.00	60.00
		16	7.50	15.00	35.00	50.00

10 PARA

.730 SILVER, 1.60 g
Mintname: *Qustantiniyah*

KM#	Date	Year	VG	Fine	VF	XF
574	AH1223	15	7.50	15.00	20.00	35.00
		16	7.50	15.00	20.00	35.00

PIASTRE

.730 SILVER, 6.15 g
Mintname: *Qustantiniyah*

KM#	Date	Year	VG	Fine	VF	XF
575	AH1223	15	20.00	30.00	50.00	100.00
		16	20.00	30.00	50.00	100.00

2 PIASTRES

.730 SILVER, 12.00-13.00 g
Mintname: *Qustantiniyah*

KM#	Date	Year	VG	Fine	VF	XF
576	AH1223	15	10.00	18.00	40.00	70.00
		16	10.00	20.00	45.00	80.00

Sixth Series

Years 16-21

PARA

.600 SILVER, 12mm, 0.15-0.20 g
Mintname: *Qustantiniyah*

KM#	Date	Year	VG	Fine	VF	XF
578	AH1223	17	1.50	3.00	10.00	17.50
		18	1.50	3.00	10.00	17.50
		19	1.50	3.00	10.00	17.50
		20	1.50	3.00	10.00	17.50
		21	1.50	3.00	10.00	17.50

ZOLOTA

SILVER, 2.98 g
Mintname: *Qustantiniyah*

KM#	Date	Year	VG	Fine	VF	XF
581	AH1223	16	—	—	Unique	—

30 PARA

.600 SILVER, 3.00-3.40 g
Mintname: *Qustantiniyah*

KM#	Date	Year	VG	Fine	VF	XF
579	AH1223	17	4.00	6.00	15.00	30.00
		18	4.00	6.00	15.00	30.00
		19	4.00	6.00	15.00	30.00
		20	4.00	6.00	15.00	30.00
		21	4.00	6.00	15.00	35.00

NOTE: This coin occurs frequently in high grade.

60 PARA

.600 SILVER, 5.60-6.25 g
Mintname: *Qustantiniyah*

KM#	Date	Year	VG	Fine	VF	XF
580	AH1223	16	8.00	12.00	25.00	40.00
		17	5.00	8.00	16.00	25.00
		18	5.00	8.00	16.00	25.00
		19	5.00	8.00	16.00	25.00
		20	5.00	8.00	16.00	25.00
		21	5.00	8.00	16.00	25.00

NOTE: This coin occurs frequently in high grade.

Seventh Series

Years 21-22
Wavy borders

NOTE: A Para was struck in this series, in low grade silver .460, in the year 22, but is not distinguishable from yr. 22 pieces of the eighth series KM#586.

AKCE

SILVER
Mintname: *Qustantiniyah*

KM#	Date	Year	VG	Fine	VF	XF
582	AH1223	21	3.00	5.00	7.00	15.00

20 PARA

.833 SILVER, 0.80 g
Mintname: *Qustantiniyah*

KM#	Date	Year	VG	Fine	VF	XF
583	AH1223	21	4.00	6.00	9.00	15.00
		22	20.00	35.00	60.00	100.00

NOTE: This coin occurs frequently in high grade, also with open and closed rosettes on obverse and reverse.

PIASTRE

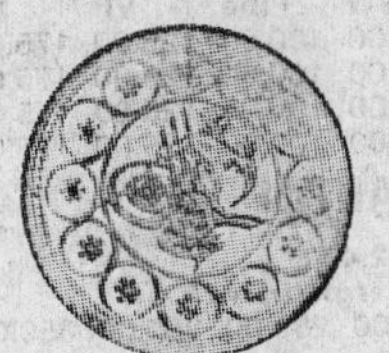
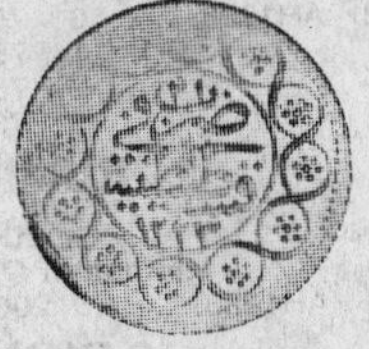

.833 SILVER, 1.40-1.60 g
Mintname: *Qustantiniyah*

KM#	Date	Year	VG	Fine	VF	XF
584	AH1223	21	5.00	6.50	11.00	20.00
		22	25.00	35.00	60.00	100.00

NOTE: This coin occurs frequently in high grade, also with open and closed rosettes on obverse and reverse.

10 PIASTRES

Two different designs exist dated year 22 and are both considered patterns.

Eighth Series - Cedid

(Jadid)

Years 22-25

NOTE: Coins of the eighth series are readily distinguished from the ninth series, as they lack the large dot below the inner wreath that appears on the ninth series. In the eighth and ninth series, with the exception of the Para, all coins have the word *Adli* (the Just) right of the toughra, sometimes with vertical mark below. The Para is distinguished only by date, however. Many coins are debased with a silver wash.

PARA

.220 SILVER, 0.10 g
Mintname: *Qustantiniyah*

KM#	Date	Year	VG	Fine	VF	XF
586	AH1223	22	.65	1.60	2.50	8.00
		23	.65	1.60	2.50	8.00
		24	.65	1.60	2.50	8.00
		25	.90	2.00	3.50	8.00

10 PARA

.220 SILVER, 17mm, 0.80 g
Mintname: *Qustantiniyah*

KM#	Date	Year	VG	Fine	VF	XF
587	AH1223	22	2.00	6.00	15.00	35.00
		23	2.00	6.00	15.00	35.00
		24	2.00	6.00	15.00	35.00
		25	2.00	6.00	15.00	35.00

20 PARA

.220 SILVER, 1.40-1.80 g
Mintname: *Qustantiniyah*

KM#	Date	Year	VG	Fine	VF	XF
588	AH1223	21	—	—	Rare	—
		22	1.00	2.00	5.00	12.00
		23	1.00	2.00	5.00	12.00
		24	1.00	2.00	5.00	12.00
		25	1.00	2.00	5.00	12.00

PIASTRE

.220 SILVER, 2.60-3.00 g
Mintname: *Qustantiniyah*

KM#	Date	Year	VG	Fine	VF	XF
589	AH1223	22	2.75	3.00	6.25	15.00
		23	2.75	3.00	6.25	15.00
		24	2.75	3.00	6.25	15.00
		25	2.75	3.00	6.25	15.00

100 PARA

(2-1/2 Piastres)

.220 SILVER, 7.20-7.80 g
Mintname: *Qustantiniyah*

KM#	Date	Year	VG	Fine	VF	XF
590	AH1223	22	4.75	7.50	11.00	25.00
		23	3.50	5.00	8.00	15.00
		24	3.50	5.00	8.00	15.00
		25	3.50	5.00	8.00	15.00

5 PIASTRES

.220 SILVER, 15.00-16.00 g
Mintname: *Qustantiniyah*

KM#	Date	Year	VG	Fine	VF	XF
591	AH1223	22	3.00	5.00	12.50	25.00
		23	3.00	5.00	12.50	25.00
		24	3.00	5.00	12.50	25.00
		25	3.00	5.00	15.00	30.00

Ninth Series

Years 25-32

Rosette or dot added beneath inner wreath on obverse and reverse except on 1 Akce and 1 Para.

AKCE

.170 SILVER, 0.04-0.07 g
Mintname: *Qustantiniyah*

KM#	Date	Year	VG	Fine	VF	XF
593	AH1223	25	5.00	10.00	25.00	55.00
		26	2.50	4.00	15.00	40.00
		27	2.50	4.00	15.00	40.00

PARA

.170 SILVER, 0.08-0.15 g
Mintname: *Qustantiniyah*

KM#	Date	Year	VG	Fine	VF	XF
594	AH1223	26	1.00	1.50	2.75	7.00
		27	.75	1.25	2.00	5.00
		28	.75	1.25	2.00	5.00
		29	.75	1.25	2.00	5.00
		30	.75	1.25	2.00	5.00
		31	.75	1.25	2.00	5.00
		32	.75	1.25	2.00	5.00

10 PARA

.170 SILVER, 0.50-0.75 g
Mintname: *Qustantiniyah*

KM#	Date	Year	VG	Fine	VF	XF
595	AH1223	25	2.00	3.00	5.00	12.50
		26	5.00	7.50	10.00	18.50
		27	2.00	3.00	5.00	12.50
		28	2.00	3.00	5.00	12.50
		29	2.00	3.00	5.00	12.50
		30	2.00	3.00	5.00	12.50
		31	2.00	3.00	5.00	12.50
		32	2.00	3.00	5.00	12.50

20 PARA

.170 SILVER, 1.35-1.60 g
Mintname: *Qustantiniyah*

KM#	Date	Year	VG	Fine	VF	XF
596	AH1223	25	2.00	2.50	4.00	10.00
		26	2.00	2.50	4.00	10.00
		27	2.00	2.50	4.00	10.00
		28	2.00	2.50	4.00	10.00
		29	2.00	2.50	4.00	10.00
		30	2.00	2.50	4.00	10.00
		31	2.00	2.50	4.00	10.00
		32	2.00	2.50	4.00	10.00

NOTE: Years 26 and 31 are easily confused.

PIASTRE

.170 SILVER, 2.60-3.00 g
Mintname: *Qustantiniyah*

KM#	Date	Year	VG	Fine	VF	XF
597	AH1223	25	3.50	5.00	8.00	17.50
		26	3.50	5.00	8.00	17.50

100 PARA

(2-1/2 Piastres)

.170 SILVER, 6.40-7.80 g
Mintname: *Qustantiniyah*

KM#	Date	Year	VG	Fine	VF	XF
598	AH1223	25	3.00	4.50	9.00	18.50
		26	3.00	4.50	9.00	18.50

5 PIASTRES

.170 SILVER, 13.00-16.00 g
Mintname: *Qustantiniyah*

KM#	Date	Year	VG	Fine	VF	XF
599	AH1223	25	4.00	7.00	12.50	25.00
		26	4.00	7.00	12.50	25.00

Tenth Series

Years 26-32

1-1/2 PIASTRE

.435 SILVER, 2.60-3.00 g

Mintname: *Qustantiniyah*

KM#	Date	Year	VG	Fine	VF	XF
601	AH1223	26	4.00	6.00	12.00	25.00
		27	3.50	5.00	10.00	20.00
		28	3.50	5.00	10.00	20.00
		29	3.50	5.00	10.00	20.00
		30	3.50	5.00	10.00	20.00
		31	3.50	5.00	10.00	20.00
		32	3.50	5.00	10.00	20.00

3 PIASTRES

.435 SILVER, 5.60-6.20 g
Mintname: *Qustantiniyah*

KM#	Date	Year	VG	Fine	VF	XF
602	AH1223	26	5.00	7.50	12.00	25.00
		27	4.50	6.00	10.00	20.00
		28	4.50	6.00	10.00	20.00
		29	4.50	6.00	10.00	20.00
		30	4.50	6.00	10.00	20.00
		31	4.50	6.00	10.00	20.00
		32	4.50	6.00	10.00	20.00

6 PIASTRES

.435 SILVER, 11.00-13.00 g
Mintname: *Qustantiniyah*

KM#	Date	Year	VG	Fine	VF	XF
603	AH1223	26	6.00	8.00	15.00	40.00
		27	6.00	8.00	15.00	30.00
		28	6.00	8.00	15.00	30.00
		29	6.00	8.00	15.00	30.00
		30	6.00	8.00	15.00	30.00
		31	6.00	8.00	15.00	30.00
		32	6.50	9.00	17.50	32.50

Gold Coinage

The gold emissions of Mahmud II are characterized by several simultaneous series, each with its characteristic name. They are distinguished by weight and by special symbols, such as the ornament right of the toughra, the border, and variations in design. These are indicated for each series, along with the weights and diameters of each denomination. Each series comprises several denominations, with the basic unit known as the Altin (Gold Coin) or Tak (Single); other denominations include the Double (Clifte), Half (Yarim, or Nisfiye), and Quarter (Ceyrek, or Rubiye). Not all denominations were struck in every series. Some series can be divided into several subvarieties, which are listed separately below. Finally, a few coins were struck that do not fit into any of the series.

Zeri Mahbub Series

"Beloved Gold Series"

The obverse of all denominations consists of a toughra, with mint name and date below on the 1 and 1/2 Zeri Mahbub only. The reverse of the 1 and 1/2 bears a four-line inscription; the reverse of the 1/4, the mint and date.

FIRST TYPE

Lily on 1 and 1/2 Zeri Mahbub, branch with one rose on the 1/4 Zeri Mahbub.

1/4 ZERI MAHBUB

GOLD, 0.70-0.80 g
Mintname: *Qustantiniyah*

KM#	Date	Year	VG	Fine	VF	XF
605	AH1223	1	15.00	20.00	30.00	40.00
		2	15.00	20.00	30.00	40.00
		3	15.00	25.00	40.00	60.00
		4	15.00	20.00	30.00	40.00
		5	15.00	20.00	30.00	40.00

1/2 ZERI MAHBUB

GOLD, 1.10-1.20 g
Mintname: *Qustantiniyah*

KM#	Date	Year	VG	Fine	VF	XF
606	AH1223	1	35.00	50.00	70.00	90.00
		2	35.00	50.00	70.00	90.00
		3	35.00	50.00	70.00	90.00
		4	35.00	50.00	70.00	90.00
		5	35.00	50.00	70.00	90.00

ZERI MAHBUB

GOLD, 2.30-2.40 g
Mintname: *Qustantiniyah*

KM#	Date	Year	VG	Fine	VF	XF
607	AH1223	1	50.00	75.00	100.00	150.00
		2	50.00	75.00	100.00	150.00
		3	— Reported, not confirmed			
		4	— Reported, not confirmed			
		5	150.00	275.00	400.00	750.00

SECOND TYPE

Rose replaces lily on 1 and 1/2 Zeri Mahbub, branch with 2 roses replaces branch with 1 rose on the 1/4 Zeri Mahbub.

1/4 ZERI MAHBUB

GOLD, 0.75-0.79 g
Mintname: *Qustantiniyah*

KM#	Date	Year	VG	Fine	VF	XF
608	AH1223	6	15.00	20.00	30.00	45.00
		7	15.00	20.00	30.00	45.00
		8	15.00	20.00	30.00	45.00
		9	15.00	20.00	30.00	45.00
		10	15.00	20.00	30.00	45.00
		11	15.00	20.00	35.00	50.00
		12	15.00	20.00	35.00	50.00
		13	15.00	20.00	35.00	50.00
		14	15.00	20.00	35.00	50.00

1/2 ZERI MAHBUB

GOLD, 18mm, 1.10-1.20 g
Mintname: *Qustantiniyah*

KM#	Date	Year	VG	Fine	VF	XF
609	AH1223	6	Reported, not confirmed			
		7	Reported, not confirmed			
		8	40.00	60.00	80.00	100.00
		9	Reported, not confirmed			
		10	Reported, not confirmed			
		11	Reported, not confirmed			
		12	40.00	60.00	80.00	100.00

ZERI MAHBUB

GOLD, 2.30-2.40 g
Mintname: *Qustantiniyah*

KM#	Date	Year	VG	Fine	VF	XF
610	AH1223	6	40.00	75.00	85.00	125.00
		7	40.00	75.00	85.00	125.00
		8	40.00	75.00	85.00	125.00
		9	40.00	75.00	85.00	125.00
		10	40.00	75.00	85.00	125.00
		11	40.00	75.00	85.00	125.00
		12	40.00	75.00	85.00	125.00
		13	Reported, not confirmed			
		14	40.00	75.00	85.00	125.00
		15	40.00	75.00	85.00	125.00

Rumi Series

Characterized by a flower right of toughra and an ornamental border, consisting of a wavy line hexagon, on both sides.

1/2 RUMI ALTIN

GOLD, 1.20 g
Mintname: *Qustantiniyah*

KM#	Date	Year	VG	Fine	VF	XF
612	AH1223	10	75.00	100.00	125.00	175.00
		11	75.00	100.00	125.00	175.00
		12	75.00	100.00	125.00	175.00
		13	75.00	100.00	125.00	175.00

RUMI ALTIN

GOLD, 2.40 g
Mintname: *Qustantiniyah*

KM#	Date	Year	VG	Fine	VF	XF
613	AH1223	10	200.00	250.00	300.00	350.00

2 RUMI ALTIN

GOLD, 4.70-4.80 g
Mintname: *Qustantiniyah*

KM#	Date	Year	VG	Fine	VF	XF
614	AH1223	8	80.00	100.00	125.00	200.00
		9	80.00	100.00	125.00	200.00
		10	80.00	100.00	125.00	200.00
		11	80.00	100.00	125.00	200.00
		12	80.00	100.00	125.00	200.00
		13	80.00	100.00	125.00	200.00
		22	80.00	125.00	150.00	225.00

New Rumi Series

Similar to the Rumi series, except that the wavy borders are replaced by an inscription containing the name and titles of Mahmud II.

RUMI ALTIN

GOLD, 23mm, 2.40 g
Mintname: *Qustantiniyah*

KM#	Date	Year	VG	Fine	VF	XF
616	AH1223	9	Reported, not confirmed			
		10	40.00	50.00	90.00	120.00
		11	40.00	50.00	90.00	120.00
		12	40.00	50.00	90.00	120.00
		13	40.00	50.00	90.00	120.00
		14	40.00	50.00	90.00	120.00
		15	40.00	50.00	90.00	120.00

2 RUMI ALTIN

GOLD, 4.70-4.80 g
Mintname: *Qustantiniyah*

KM#	Date	Year	VG	Fine	VF	XF
617	AH1223	9	100.00	125.00	150.00	200.00
		10	100.00	125.00	150.00	200.00
		11	100.00	125.00	150.00	200.00
		12	100.00	125.00	150.00	200.00

Surre Series

'Surre' means a purse. the amount sent by the Sultan annually to the Hejaz for the holy cities. They were used by pilgrims to Mecca. They bear the mint name *Darulhilafe* in place of *Constantinople*, with either of 2 epithets, *El-Aliye* (the Lofty) or *Es-Seniye* (the Sublime) and are therefore known as Elaliye and Esseniye Altins, respectively.

El-Aliye Surre Series

1/4 SURRE ALTIN

GOLD, 0.48 g
Mintname: *Darulhilafe*

KM#	Date	Year	VG	Fine	VF	XF
619	AH1223	15	30.00	50.00	100.00	150.00
		16	30.00	50.00	100.00	150.00

1/2 SURRE ALTIN

GOLD, 15-16mm, 0.78 g
Mintname: ***Darulhilafe***

KM#	Date	Year	VG	Fine	VF	XF
620	AH1223	15	40.00	60.00	150.00	250.00
		16	40.00	60.00	150.00	250.00

SURRE ALTIN

GOLD, 1.56 g
Mintname: ***Darulhilafe***

KM#	Date	Year	VG	Fine	VF	XF
621	AH1223	15	60.00	85.00	110.00	150.00
		16	60.00	85.00	110.00	150.00

Esseniye Surre Series

1/4 SURRE ALTIN

GOLD, 0.48 g
Mintname: ***Darulhilafe***

KM#	Date	Year	VG	Fine	VF	XF
623	AH1223	15	30.00	45.00	100.00	150.00

1/2 SURRE ALTIN

GOLD, 0.78 g
Mintname: ***Darulhilafe***

KM#	Date	Year	VG	Fine	VF	XF
624	AH1223	15	50.00	75.00	200.00	300.00

SURRE ALTIN

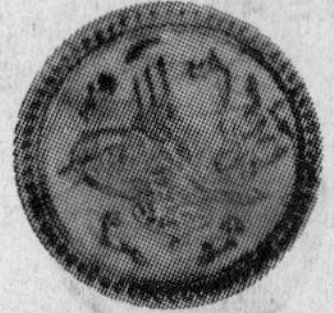

GOLD, 1.50 g
Mintname: ***Darulhilafe***

KM#	Date	Year	VG	Fine	VF	XF
625	AH1223	15	60.00	90.00	150.00	225.00

Additional Series

The following type does not fit into any of the recognized series.

1/4 ALTIN

GOLD, 14mm, 0.58 g
Considered a 1/4 Zeri Mahbub.
***Azze Nasaru* above mintname:**
Qustantiniyah

KM#	Date	Year	VG	Fine	VF	XF
627	AH1223	13	15.00	20.00	40.00	60.00
		14	15.00	20.00	40.00	60.00
		15	15.00	20.00	40.00	60.00

Adli Series

Types as the Zeri Mahbub series, except that the word *Adli* replaces the flower right of toughra.

1/4 ADLI ALTIN

GOLD, 0.40-0.45 g
Mintname: ***Qustantiniyah***

KM#	Date	Year	VG	Fine	VF	XF
629	AH1223	16	20.00	30.00	75.00	125.00
		17	20.00	30.00	75.00	125.00

1/2 ADLI ALTIN

GOLD, 0.75-0.85 g
Mintname: ***Qustantiniyah***

KM#	Date	Year	VG	Fine	VF	XF
630	AH1223	15	45.00	60.00	75.00	90.00
		16	Reported, not confirmed			
		17	45.00	60.00	75.00	90.00
		18	45.00	60.00	75.00	90.00
		19	45.00	60.00	75.00	90.00
		20	45.00	60.00	75.00	90.00
		21	45.00	60.00	75.00	90.00
		22	45.00	60.00	75.00	90.00
		23	45.00	60.00	75.00	90.00
		24	Reported, not confirmed			
		25	45.00	60.00	75.00	90.00
		26	Reported, not confirmed			
		27	45.00	60.00	75.00	90.00
		28	Reported, not confirmed			
		29	45.00	60.00	75.00	90.00
		30	45.00	60.00	75.00	90.00
		31	45.00	60.00	75.00	90.00
		32	45.00	60.00	75.00	90.00

ADLI ALTIN

GOLD, 1.50-1.60 g
Mintname: ***Qustantiniyah***

KM#	Date	Year	VG	Fine	VF	XF
631	AH1223	15	30.00	40.00	100.00	130.00
		17	30.00	40.00	100.00	130.00
		18	30.00	40.00	100.00	130.00
		19	30.00	40.00	100.00	130.00
		20	30.00	40.00	100.00	130.00

New Adli Series

Toughra on obverse, mint and date on reverse. Additional legends around, obverse and reverse. Mintname Qustantiniyah has epithet ***Al-Mahrusa*** added.

1/4 NEW ADLI ALTIN

GOLD, 0.38-0.43 g
Mintname: ***Qustantiniyah***

KM#	Date	Year	VG	Fine	VF	XF
633	AH1223	15	10.00	20.00	30.00	45.00
		17	10.00	20.00	30.00	45.00
		18	10.00	20.00	30.00	45.00
		19	10.00	20.00	30.00	45.00
		20	10.00	20.00	30.00	45.00
		21	10.00	20.00	30.00	45.00
		22	10.00	20.00	30.00	45.00
		23	10.00	20.00	30.00	45.00
		24	10.00	20.00	40.00	55.00

1/2 NEW ADLI ALTIN

GOLD, 0.78 g
Mintname: ***Qustantiniyah***

KM#	Date	Year	VG	Fine	VF	XF
634	AH1223	16	30.00	40.00	50.00	75.00
		17	30.00	40.00	50.00	75.00
		18	30.00	40.00	50.00	75.00
		19	30.00	40.00	50.00	75.00
		20	30.00	40.00	50.00	75.00
		21	Reported, not confirmed			

NEW ADLI ALTIN

GOLD, 1.58 g
Mintname: ***Qustantiniyah***

KM#	Date	Year	VG	Fine	VF	XF
635	AH1223	16	27.50	40.00	60.00	80.00
		17	27.50	40.00	60.00	80.00
		18	27.50	40.00	60.00	80.00
		19	27.50	40.00	60.00	80.00
		20	27.50	40.00	60.00	80.00
		21	Reported, not confirmed			
		22	Reported, not confirmed			

Hayriye Series

Similar to the New Adli, but in place of the ring of legend around the edge, there are alternating ovals of inscription and branches.

1/2 HAYRIYE ALTIN

GOLD, 0.86 g
Mintname: ***Qustantiniyah***

KM#	Date	Year	VG	Fine	VF	XF
637	AH1223	21	25.00	35.00	45.00	65.00
		22	25.00	35.00	45.00	65.00
		23	25.00	35.00	45.00	65.00
		24	25.00	35.00	45.00	65.00
		25	25.00	35.00	45.00	65.00
		26	25.00	35.00	45.00	65.00

HAYRIYE ALTIN

GOLD, 1.73 g
Mintname: ***Qustantiniyah***

KM#	Date	Year	VG	Fine	VF	XF
638	AH1223	21	30.00	35.00	45.00	90.00
		22	30.00	35.00	45.00	90.00
		23	30.00	35.00	45.00	90.00
		24	30.00	35.00	45.00	90.00
		25	30.00	35.00	45.00	90.00
		26	Reported, not confirmed			

2 HAYRIYE ALTIN

GOLD, 3.55 g
Mintname: ***Qustantiniyah***

KM#	Date	Year	VG	Fine	VF	XF
639	AH1223	21	100.00	125.00	150.00	200.00

New (Yeni) Series

The Yeni or new series comprises but 1 denomination, distinguished by starlike wavy pattern around edge.

1/4 NEW ALTIN

Yeni Rubiye

GOLD, 12mm, 0.26-0.31 g
Mintname: ***Qustantiniyah***

KM#	Date	Year	VG	Fine	VF	XF
641	AH1223	24	15.00	25.00	40.00	55.00
		25	15.00	25.00	40.00	55.00
		26	15.00	25.00	40.00	55.00
		27	15.00	25.00	40.00	55.00
		28	15.00	25.00	40.00	55.00
		29	Reported, not confirmed			
		30	17.50	22.50	25.00	30.00

Cedid Mahmudiye Series

Like the Hayriye, but ovals of inscription and branches replaced by a wreath design.

1/4 CEDID MAHMUDIYE

GOLD, 0.38-0.40 g
Mintname: ***Qustantiniyah***

KM#	Date	Year	VG	Fine	VF	XF
643	AH1223	26	15.00	25.00	35.00	45.00
		27	15.00	25.00	35.00	45.00
		28	15.00	25.00	35.00	45.00
		29	15.00	25.00	35.00	45.00
		30	15.00	25.00	35.00	45.00
		31	15.00	25.00	35.00	45.00
		32	15.00	25.00	35.00	45.00

1/2 CEDID MAHMUDIYE

GOLD, 0.76-0.80 g
Mintname: *Qustantiniyah*

KM#	Date	Year	VG	Fine	VF	XF
644	AH1223	26	20.00	30.00	45.00	65.00
		27	20.00	30.00	45.00	65.00
		28	20.00	30.00	45.00	65.00
		29	20.00	30.00	45.00	65.00
		30	20.00	30.00	45.00	65.00
		31	20.00	30.00	45.00	65.00
		32	20.00	30.00	45.00	65.00

CEDID MAHMUDIYE

GOLD, 1.58-1.60 g
Mintname: *Qustantiniyah*

KM#	Date	Year	VG	Fine	VF	XF
645	AH1223	26	30.00	40.00	55.00	75.00
		27	30.00	40.00	55.00	75.00
		28	30.00	40.00	55.00	75.00
		29	30.00	40.00	55.00	75.00
		30	30.00	40.00	55.00	75.00
		31	30.00	40.00	55.00	75.00
		32	30.00	40.00	55.00	75.00

Mint Visit Coinage

Mahmud II's visit to Edirne.

ادرنة

Edirne Mint mark:

1/2 HAYRIYE ALTIN

GOLD, 0.88 g
Mintname: *Edirne*

KM#	Date	Year	VG	Fine	VF	XF
647	AH1223	24	60.00	100.00	150.00	250.00

1 HAYRIYE ALTIN

GOLD, 1.80 g
Mintname: *Edirne*

KM#	Date	Year	VG	Fine	VF	XF
648	AH1223	24	100.00	120.00	150.00	200.00

2 HAYRIYE ALTIN

GOLD, 3.55 g
Mintname: *Edirne*

KM#	Date	Year	VG	Fine	VF	XF
649	AH1223	24	175.00	225.00	275.00	350.00

ABDUL MEJID

AH1255-1277/1839-1861AD

Standard, fineness, and denominations of the silver coinage similar to the ninth (for the 1, 10, and 20 Para) and tenth (for the 1-1/2, 3, and 6 Piastres) series of Mahmud II (C#202-204, 206-208).

Pre-Reform Coinage

PARA

BILLON, 0.14-0.20 g
Mintname: *Qustantiniyah*

KM#	Date	Year	VG	Fine	VF	XF
651	AH1255	1	1.50	2.25	3.00	5.00
		2	1.50	2.25	3.00	5.00
		3	2.50	4.00	5.00	7.50
		4	1.50	2.25	3.00	5.00
		5	1.50	2.25	3.00	5.00
		6	7.50	10.00	15.00	20.00

10 PARA

BILLON, 0.60-0.80 g
Mintname: *Qustantiniyah*

KM#	Date	Year	VG	Fine	VF	XF
652	AH1255	1	2.00	3.00	4.00	7.50
		2	2.00	3.00	4.00	7.50
		3	3.00	4.00	5.00	8.00
		4	2.00	3.00	4.00	7.50
		5	2.00	3.00	4.00	7.50

20 PARA

BILLON, 1.35-1.60 g
Mintname: *Qustantiniyah*

KM#	Date	Year	VG	Fine	VF	XF
653	AH1255	1	.50	1.00	2.50	4.00
		2	1.50	2.50	4.00	7.50
		3	1.50	2.50	4.00	7.50
		4	1.00	2.00	3.50	5.00
		5	2.00	3.00	5.00	9.00

1-1/2 PIASTRES

SILVER, 2.60-3.00 g
Mintname: *Qustantiniyah*

KM#	Date	Year	VG	Fine	VF	XF
654	AH1255	1	6.00	8.50	13.00	19.00
		2	5.00	6.50	12.00	18.00
		3	7.00	9.00	14.00	20.00
		4	5.00	6.50	12.00	18.00
		5	5.00	6.50	12.00	18.00

3 PIASTRES

SILVER, 5.60-6.20 g
Mintname: *Qustantiniyah*

KM#	Date	Year	VG	Fine	VF	XF
655	AH1255	1	20.00	40.00	100.00	150.00
		2	45.00	75.00	150.00	200.00
		3	100.00	200.00	275.00	350.00
		4	100.00	200.00	275.00	350.00

6 PIASTRES

SILVER, 12.42-13.00 g
Mintname: *Qustantiniyah*

KM#	Date	Year	VG	Fine	VF	XF
656	AH1255	1	40.00	50.00	75.00	150.00
		2	80.00	120.00	200.00	325.00
		4	—	—	Rare	—

1/4 MEMDUHIYE ALTIN

GOLD, 0.38-0.40 g
Mintname: *Qustantiniyah*

KM#	Date	Year	VG	Fine	VF	XF
657	AH1255	1	17.50	25.00	35.00	55.00
		2	17.50	25.00	35.00	55.00
		3	17.50	25.00	35.00	55.00
		4	17.50	25.00	35.00	55.00
		5	17.50	25.00	35.00	55.00

1/2 MEMDUHIYE ALTIN

GOLD, 0.78-0.80 g
Mintname: *Qustantiniyah*

KM#	Date	Year	VG	Fine	VF	XF
658	AH1255	1	40.00	50.00	60.00	80.00
		2	40.00	50.00	60.00	80.00
		3	40.00	50.00	60.00	80.00
		4	40.00	50.00	60.00	80.00
		5	40.00	50.00	60.00	80.00

MEMDUHIYE ALTIN

GOLD, 1.58-1.60 g
Mintname: *Qustantiniyah*

KM#	Date	Year	VG	Fine	VF	XF
659	AH1255	1	45.00	55.00	75.00	150.00
		2	45.00	55.00	75.00	150.00
		3	45.00	55.00	75.00	150.00
		4	45.00	55.00	75.00	150.00
		5	45.00	55.00	75.00	150.00

NOTE: The Memduhiye issue of Abdul Mejid was of the same fineness, weight and diameter as the Mahmudiye issue of Mahmud II. Although officially valued at 20 Piastres, the actual value of the Memduhiye Altin varied with the relative prices of gold and silver.

1/2 ZERI MAHBUB

GOLD, 0.80 g
Rev: 4-line inscription, mintname: *Qustantiniyah.*

KM#	Date	Year	VG	Fine	VF	XF
660	AH1255	1	45.00	60.00	75.00	100.00
		2	45.00	60.00	75.00	100.00
		3	45.00	60.00	75.00	100.00
		4	45.00	60.00	75.00	100.00
		5	45.00	60.00	75.00	100.00
		6	75.00	100.00	120.00	200.00

Modern Coinage

MONETARY SYSTEM

1844-1923

40 Para = 1 Kurush (Piastre)
100 Kurush (Piastre) = 1 Lira

NOTE: The 20 Kurush coin was known as a Mecidi, after the name of Abdul Mejid, who established the currency reform in 1844. The entire series is sometimes called Mejidiye coinage.

PARA

COPPER
Accession date: AH1255
Mintname: *Qustantiniyah*
Thick planchet, 1.00-1.10 g

KM#	Year	Mintage	VG	Fine	VF	XF
665.1	8	1.000	2.00	4.00	10.00	20.00
	9	.375	5.00	10.00	30.00	50.00
	10	1.250	3.00	5.00	12.00	25.00
	11	.165	2.00	4.00	8.00	15.00
	12	1.600	2.00	4.00	8.00	15.00
	13	.800	2.00	3.00	6.00	12.00
	14	.300	4.00	6.00	15.00	25.00
	15	.700	3.00	6.00	12.00	20.00
	16	3.400	3.00	6.00	12.00	20.00
	Medium planchet, 0.80-0.90 g					
665.2	16	Inc. Ab.	.50	1.00	1.75	5.00
	17	.800	1.00	3.00	6.00	10.00
	18	4.500	.75	1.50	2.50	5.00
	Thin planchet, 0.50-0.60 g					
665.3	18	Inc. Ab.	.50	1.00	2.50	5.00
	19	2.500	.25	.50	1.25	2.50
	21	2.000	10.00	20.00	45.00	70.00

NOTE: The thin planchet coin of "year 16" is actually year 19 with broken 9.

5 PARA

COPPER
Accession date: AH1255
Mintname: *Qustantiniyah*
Thick planchet, 4.90-6.80 g

KM#	Year	Mintage	VG	Fine	VF	XF
666.1	7	—	7.50	15.00	20.00	50.00
	8	1.000	1.00	2.00	7.50	15.00
	9	.300	10.00	20.00	50.00	100.00
	10	.800	1.50	3.00	6.00	15.00
	11	2.542	1.50	3.00	6.00	15.00
	12	3.680	.75	1.25	5.00	15.00
	13	4.640	.75	1.25	5.00	15.00
	14	3.400	.75	1.25	8.00	25.00
	15	5.060	.75	1.25	8.00	25.00
	Medium planchet, 3.70-4.20 g					
666.2	15	Inc. Ab.	2.00	4.00	20.00	40.00
	16	6.300	.50	1.00	2.00	10.00
	17	6.500	.50	1.00	2.00	10.00
	Thin planchet, 2.50-3.30 g					
666.3	18	2.000	1.25	2.75	15.00	25.00
	19	9.300	.50	1.00	2.00	10.00
	20	10.060	.50	1.00	2.00	10.00
	21	6.200	.50	1.00	2.00	10.00

10 PARA

COPPER
Accession date: AH1255
Mintname: *Qustantiniyah*
Thick planchet, 9.00-12.80 g

KM#	Year	Mintage	VG	Fine	VF	XF
667.1	15	.750	5.00	15.00	30.00	75.00
	Medium planchet, 7.50-8.20 g					
667.2	16	9.120	.75	1.50	3.75	12.00
	17	9.110	.75	1.50	3.75	12.00
	18	1.900	1.25	2.50	5.00	15.00
	Thin planchet, 4.90-5.70 g					
667.3	17	Inc. Ab.	2.50	5.00	6.50	15.00
	18	Inc. Ab.	1.25	2.50	5.00	15.00
	19	33.600	.35	.75	2.00	12.00
	20	20.800	.35	.75	2.00	12.00
	21	7.500	.35	.75	2.00	12.00

20 PARA

COPPER
Accession date: AH1255
Mintname: *Qustantiniyah*
Thick planchet, 14.00-16.00 g

KM#	Year	Mintage	VG	Fine	VF	XF
668.1	16	4.350	1.25	2.50	5.00	15.00
	17	2.050	2.00	4.00	7.50	20.00
	Thin planchet, 10.00-11.00 g					
668.2	17	Inc. Ab.	1.00	2.00	4.50	15.00
	19	1.200	1.00	2.00	4.50	15.00
	20	3.000	1.00	2.00	4.50	15.00
	21	8.400	.50	1.00	3.00	15.00

0.6013 g, .830 SILVER, .0160 oz ASW
Mintname: *Qustantiniyah*

KM#	Year	Mintage	VG	Fine	VF	XF
669	9	.400	3.00	6.00	25.00	60.00
	10	.910	2.50	5.00	15.00	25.00
	11	.390	2.00	4.00	15.00	25.00
	12	.270	3.75	7.50	20.00	35.00
	13	.230	4.50	9.00	40.00	75.00
	14	.180	3.75	7.50	15.00	25.00
	15	.240	4.00	8.00	30.00	50.00
	16	.270	2.50	5.00	15.00	25.00
	17	.170	5.00	10.00	40.00	75.00
	18	.260	2.00	4.00	20.00	35.00
	19	.900	2.00	4.25	20.00	35.00
	20	.150	2.00	4.25	15.00	25.00
	21	.250	4.25	8.50	15.00	25.00
	22	.190	4.25	8.50	15.00	25.00
	23	.620	50.00	150.00	300.00	500.00

40 PARA

COPPER
Accession date: AH1255
Mintname: *Qustantiniyah*

KM#	Year	Mintage	VG	Fine	VF	XF
670	17	1.450	2.50	5.00	7.50	30.00
	17		—	—	Proof	—
	18	3.950	1.50	3.25	8.00	30.00
	19	11.3000	1.25	2.50	6.50	30.00
	20	14.030	1.25	2.50	6.50	30.00
	21	9.300	1.25	2.50	6.50	30.00
	22	4.140	2.50	5.00	10.00	35.00
	23	—	50.00	75.00	100.00	150.00

KURUSH

1.2027 g, .830 SILVER, .0321 oz ASW
Accession date: AH1255
Mintname: *Qustantiniyah*

KM#	Year	Mintage	VG	Fine	VF	XF
671	6	—	20.00	30.00	50.00	100.00
	7	.650	1.00	2.00	6.00	12.00
	8	1.420	1.00	2.00	6.00	12.00
	9	.910	1.00	2.00	6.00	12.00
	10	.970	1.00	2.50	7.00	15.00
	11	1.040	1.00	2.50	7.00	15.00
	12	1.100	1.00	2.50	7.00	15.00
	13	.820	1.00	2.50	7.00	15.00
	14	.790	1.00	2.50	7.00	15.00
	15	.960	1.00	3.00	8.00	20.00
	16	1.220	1.00	2.50	7.00	15.00
	17	.810	7.00	15.00	30.00	75.00
	18	.720	1.50	4.00	10.00	25.00
	19	2.270	1.00	3.00	8.00	20.00
	20	1.165	1.00	3.00	8.00	20.00
	21	1.405	1.00	2.50	7.00	15.00
	22	.825	1.00	3.00	8.00	20.00
	23	.755	5.00	10.00	20.00	50.00

2 KURUSH

2.4055 g, .830 SILVER, .0642 oz ASW
Accession date: AH1255
Mintname: *Qustantiniyah*

KM#	Year	Mintage	VG	Fine	VF	XF
672	7	1.035	1.00	2.00	6.00	12.00
	8	1.150	1.00	2.00	6.00	12.00
	9	.530	1.00	3.00	8.00	20.00
	10	.543	1.50	4.00	10.00	25.00
	11	.695	1.50	4.00	10.00	20.00
	12	.685	1.50	5.00	12.00	25.00
	13	.540	1.50	5.00	12.00	25.00
	14	.280	5.00	10.00	25.00	50.00
	15	.300	1.50	5.00	12.00	25.00
	16	.510	1.50	5.00	12.00	25.00
	19	.275	20.00	40.00	65.00	135.00
	20	.105	15.00	30.00	50.00	115.00
	21	—	—	—	Rare	—

5 KURUSH

6.0130 g, .830 SILVER, .1605 oz ASW
Accession date: AH1255
Mintname: *Qustantiniyah*

KM#	Year	Mintage	VG	Fine	VF	XF
673	6	1.347	2.00	4.00	10.00	22.50
	7	2.612	2.00	4.00	10.00	22.50
	8	.362	2.00	4.00	10.00	22.50
	9	.240	2.50	5.00	12.00	30.00
	10	.252	3.00	6.00	15.00	40.00
	11	.314	2.50	4.50	17.00	35.00
	12	.452	2.50	4.50	15.00	35.00
	13	.498	2.50	4.50	15.00	35.00
	14	.354	2.50	4.50	15.00	35.00
	15	.680	2.00	4.00	10.00	22.50
	16	.972	2.00	4.00	10.00	22.50
	17	.206	2.50	4.50	15.00	35.00
	18	.218	2.50	4.50	15.00	35.00
	19	.384	2.50	4.50	15.00	35.00
	20	.310	2.50	4.50	15.00	35.00
	21	.324	2.50	4.50	15.00	35.00
	22	.214	2.50	4.50	15.00	35.00
	23	.120	5.00	10.00	22.50	50.00

10 KURUSH

12.0270 g, .830 SILVER, .3210 oz ASW
Accession date: AH1255
Mintname: *Qustantiniyah*

KM#	Year	Mintage	VG	Fine	VF	XF
674	6	.338	15.00	35.00	80.00	150.00
	7	.012	350.00	500.00	800.00	1100.
	9	—	—	—	Rare	—
	13	—	—	—	Rare	—

20 KURUSH

24.0550 g, .830 SILVER, .6419 oz ASW
Accession date: AH1255
Mintname: *Qustantiniyah*
Rev: Small inscription.

KM#	Year	Mintage	VG	Fine	VF	XF
675	6	2.013	6.00	12.00	20.00	45.00
	7	.740	6.00	12.00	20.00	45.00
	8	1.671	6.00	12.00	20.00	45.00
	9	3.125	6.00	10.00	18.00	40.00

KM#	Year	Mintage	VG	Fine	VF	XF
675	10	1.020	6.00	12.00	20.00	45.00
	11	.815	6.00	12.00	20.00	45.00
	12	.684	6.00	12.00	20.00	45.00
	13	.485	6.00	12.00	20.00	45.00
	14	.633	6.00	12.00	20.00	45.00
	15	.797	6.00	12.00	20.00	45.00

Rev: Large inscription.

KM#	Year	Mintage	VG	Fine	VF	XF
676	8	Inc. Ab.	—	—	—	—
	15	Inc. Ab.	6.00	12.00	20.00	45.00
	16	.320	6.00	12.00	20.00	45.00
	17	.410	8.00	15.00	30.00	55.00
	18	.340	10.00	20.00	35.00	70.00
	19	.201	40.00	75.00	125.00	200.00
	20	.103	10.00	20.00	35.00	75.00
	21	.513	8.00	15.00	30.00	60.00
	22	.624	8.00	15.00	30.00	60.00
	23	.317	25.00	40.00	80.00	150.00

25 KURUSH

1.8040 g, .917 GOLD, .0532 oz AGW
Accession date: AH1255
Mintname: *Qustantiniyah*

KM#	Year	Mintage	VG	Fine	VF	XF
677	17	—	25.00	35.00	70.00	110.00
	18	—	25.00	35.00	70.00	110.00
	19	—	25.00	35.00	70.00	110.00
	20	—	25.00	35.00	70.00	110.00
	21	—	25.00	35.00	70.00	110.00
	22	—	25.00	35.00	70.00	110.00
	23	—	25.00	35.00	70.00	110.00

50 KURUSH

3.6080 g, .917 GOLD, .1064 oz AGW
Accession date: AH1255
Mintname: *Qustantiniyah*

KM#	Year	Mintage	VG	Fine	VF	XF
678	6	—	BV	50.00	70.00	110.00
	7	—	BV	50.00	70.00	110.00
	8	—	BV	50.00	70.00	110.00
	9	—	BV	50.00	70.00	110.00
	10	—	BV	50.00	70.00	110.00
	11	—	BV	50.00	70.00	110.00
	12	—	BV	50.00	70.00	110.00
	13	—	BV	50.00	70.00	110.00
	15	—	BV	50.00	70.00	110.00
	16	—	BV•	50.00	70.00	110.00
	17	—	BV	50.00	70.00	110.00
	20	—	1750.	2500.	3500.	5000.
	22	—	1750.	2500.	3500.	5000.

100 KURUSH

7.2160 g, .917 GOLD, .2128 oz AGW
Accession date: AH1255
Mintname: *Qustantiniyah*

KM#	Year	Mintage	VG	Fine	VF	XF
679	5	—	—	BV	100.00	115.00
	6	—	—	BV	100.00	115.00
	7	—	—	BV	100.00	115.00
	8	—	—	BV	100.00	115.00
	9	—	—	BV	100.00	115.00
	10	—	—	BV	100.00	115.00
	11	—	—	BV	100.00	115.00
	12	—	—	BV	100.00	115.00
	13	—	—	BV	100.00	115.00
	14	—	—	BV	100.00	115.00
	15	—	—	BV	100.00	115.00
	16	—	—	BV	100.00	115.00
	17	—	—	BV	100.00	115.00
	18	—	—	BV	100.00	115.00
	19	—	—	BV	100.00	115.00
	20	—	—	BV	100.00	115.00
	21	—	—	BV	100.00	115.00
	22	—	—	BV	100.00	115.00
	23	—	—	BV	100.00	115.00

250 KURUSH

18.0400 g, .917 GOLD, .5319 oz AGW
Accession date: AH1255
Mintname: *Qustantiniyah*

KM#	Year	Mintage	VG	Fine	VF	XF
680	7	—	250.00	275.00	450.00	650.00
	18	—	250.00	275.00	450.00	650.00
	22	—	2000.	3000.	4000.	6000.

NOTE: This is the first Ottoman coin to bear a numeral denomination, the 250 is at 6 o'clock on the obverse.

500 KURUSH

36.0800 g, .917 GOLD, 1.0638 oz AGW
Accession date: AH1255
Mintname: *Qustantiniyah*

KM#	Year	Mintage	VG	Fine	VF	XF
681	18	9,140	BV	525.00	750.00	1100.
	20	—	2000.	3000.	4000.	6000.
	22	—	2000.	3000.	4000.	6000.

Mint Visit Coinage

Abdul Mejid's visit to Edirne.

ادرنة

Edirne Mint mark

50 KURUSH

3.6080 g, .917 GOLD, .1064 oz AGW
Accession date: AH1255
Mintname: *Edirne*

KM#	Year	Mintage	Fine	VF	XF	Unc
682	8	.010	250.00	375.00	550.00	1150.

100 KURUSH

7.2160 g, .917 GOLD, .2128 oz AGW
Accession date: AH1255
Mintname: *Edirne*

KM#	Year	Mintage	Fine	VF	XF	Unc
683	8	.010	300.00	525.00	700.00	1400.

ABDUL AZIZ

AH1277-1293/1861-1876AD

5 PARA

COPPER
Accession date: AH1277
Mintname: *Qustantiniyah*

KM#	Year	Mintage	VG	Fine	VF	XF
685	1	—	2.25	5.00	12.50	20.00

KM#	Year	Mintage	Fine	VF	XF	Unc
699	4	16.000	1.00	3.00	5.00	10.00

10 PARA

COPPER
Accession date: AH1277
Mintname: *Qustantiniyah*

KM#	Year	Mintage	VG	Fine	VF	XF
686	1	—	3.00	4.00	10.00	20.00

KM#	Year	Mintage	Fine	VF	XF	Unc
700	4	8.000	1.00	3.00	5.00	10.00
	4	—	—	—	Proof	125.00

20 PARA

COPPER
Accession date: AH1277
Mintname: *Qustantiniyah*

KM#	Year	Mintage	VG	Fine	VF	XF
687	1	—	4.00	5.00	12.50	25.00

KM#	Year	Mintage	Fine	VF	XF	Unc
701	4	4.000	1.00	2.50	6.00	12.00
	4	—	—	—	Proof	175.00

0.6013 g, .830 SILVER, .0160 oz ASW

KM#	Year	Mintage	VG	Fine	VF	XF
688	1	.420	3.50	6.00	12.00	25.00
	2	.850	3.50	6.00	12.00	25.00
	3	1.570	3.50	6.00	12.00	25.00
	4	.930	25.00	50.00	100.00	150.00
	5	.740	3.50	6.00	12.00	25.00
	6	.520	5.00	10.00	17.50	40.00
	7	.350	7.50	15.00	30.00	60.00

40 PARA

COPPER
Accession date: AH1277
Mintname: *Qustantiniyah*

KM#	Year	Mintage	Fine	VF	XF	Unc
702	4	2.000	3.00	9.00	15.00	30.00

KURUSH

1.2027 g, .830 SILVER, .0321 oz ASW
Accession date: AH1277
Mintname: *Qustantiniyah*

KM#	Year	Mintage	VG	Fine	VF	XF
689	1	.545	2.00	3.00	10.00	25.00
	2	2.245	2.00	3.00	7.50	20.00
	3	1.370	2.00	3.00	7.50	20.00
	4	.900	2.00	3.00	7.50	20.00
	5	.685	2.00	3.00	7.50	20.00
	7	.535	35.00	75.00	100.00	200.00

2 KURUSH

2.4055 g, .830 SILVER, .0642 oz ASW
Accession date: AH1277
Mintname: *Qustantiniyah*

KM#	Year	Mintage	VG	Fine	VF	XF
690	1	.055	25.00	50.00	100.00	200.00
	2	.065	45.00	90.00	200.00	400.00
	3	.235	20.00	35.00	75.00	125.00
	5	.135	40.00	75.00	125.00	250.00
	5	—	—	—	Proof	1500.

5 KURUSH

6.0130 g, .830 SILVER, .1605 oz ASW
Accession date: AH1277
Mintname: *Qustantiniyah*

KM#	Year	Mintage	VG	Fine	VF	XF
691	1	.016	2.50	4.00	8.50	20.00
	2	.280	5.00	10.00	17.50	35.00
	3	.288	2.50	4.00	8.50	20.00
	4	.280	2.50	4.00	8.50	20.00
	5	.242	2.50	4.00	8.50	20.00
	6	.342	2.50	4.00	8.50	20.00
	7	.248	2.50	4.00	8.50	20.00
	8	.020	70.00	130.00	225.00	350.00
	9	.050	2.50	4.00	8.50	20.00
	10	.230	2.50	4.00	8.50	20.00
	11	.126	2.50	4.00	8.50	20.00
	12	.186	2.50	4.00	8.50	20.00
	13	.284	2.50	4.00	8.50	20.00
	14	.202	5.00	10.00	17.50	35.00
	15	.154	10.00	20.00	35.00	70.00

10 KURUSH

12.0270 g, .830 SILVER, .3210 oz ASW
Accession date: AH1277
Mintname: *Qustantiniyah*

KM#	Year	Mintage	VG	Fine	VF	XF
692	1	—	20.00	50.00	100.00	200.00
	2	.280	50.00	100.00	200.00	350.00
	5	—	—	—	Proof	6000.

20 KURUSH

24.0550 g, .830 SILVER, .6419 oz ASW
Accession date: AH1277
Mintname: *Qustantiniyah*
Rev: Similar to Y#22.

KM#	Year	Mintage	VG	Fine	VF	XF
693	1	1.055	6.00	10.00	20.00	40.00
	2	3.106	6.00	10.00	20.00	40.00
	3	.257	10.00	20.00	35.00	70.00
	4	.234	12.00	25.00	50.00	100.00
	5	.387	8.00	12.50	25.00	50.00
	6	.314	6.00	10.00	20.00	40.00
	7	.640	6.00	10.00	20.00	40.00
	8	1.457	6.00	10.00	20.00	40.00
	9	.859	6.00	10.00	20.00	40.00
	10	.528	6.00	10.00	20.00	40.00
	11	.530	6.00	10.00	20.00	40.00
	12	.233	6.00	10.00	20.00	40.00
	12	—	—	—	Proof	1000.
	13	.514	6.00	10.00	20.00	40.00
	14	.584	6.00	10.00	20.00	40.00
	15	4.034	6.00	10.00	20.00	40.00

25 KURUSH

1.8040 g, .917 GOLD, .0532 oz AGW
Accession date: AH1277
Mintname: *Qustantiniyah*

KM#	Year	Mintage	VG	Fine	VF	XF
694	1	.052	27.50	32.50	40.00	60.00
	2	.086	27.50	32.50	40.00	60.00
	3	.089	27.50	32.50	40.00	60.00
	4	.069	27.50	32.50	40.00	60.00
	5	.067	27.50	32.50	40.00	60.00
	6	.073	27.50	32.50	40.00	60.00
	7	.116	27.50	32.50	40.00	60.00

KM#	Year	Mintage	VG	Fine	VF	XF
694	9	.177	27.50	32.50	40.00	60.00
	11	.065	27.50	32.50	40.00	60.00
	12	.122	27.50	32.50	40.00	60.00
	13	.152	27.50	32.50	40.00	60.00
	15	.017	32.50	45.00	60.00	100.00

50 KURUSH

3.6080 g, .917 GOLD, .1064 oz AGW
Accession date: AH1277
Mintname: *Qustantiniyah*

KM#	Year	Mintage	VG	Fine	VF	XF
695	1	5,800	65.00	125.00	250.00	350.00
	2	—	65.00	125.00	250.00	350.00
	3	—	1750.	2500.	3500.	5000.
	7	2,000	60.00	85.00	150.00	250.00
	8	2,000	Reported, not confirmed			
	9	.025	60.00	85.00	150.00	250.00

100 KURUSH

7.2160 g, .917 GOLD, .2128 oz AGW
Accession date: AH1277
Mintname: *Qustantiniyah*

KM#	Year	Mintage	VG	Fine	VF	XF
696	1	2.347	—	BV	100.00	115.00
	2	3.129	—	BV	100.00	115.00
	3	.478	—	BV	100.00	115.00
	4	.628	—	BV	100.00	115.00
	5	.561	—	BV	100.00	115.00
	6	.330	—	BV	100.00	115.00
	7	1.491	—	BV	100.00	115.00
	8	.495	—	BV	100.00	115.00
	9	1.570	—	BV	100.00	115.00
	10	.304	—	BV	100.00	115.00
	11	.866	—	BV	100.00	115.00
	12	.372	—	BV	100.00	115.00
	13	.246	—	BV	100.00	115.00
	14	.286	—	BV	100.00	115.00
	15	3,600	110.00	120.00	160.00	200.00

250 KURUSH

18.0400 g, .917 GOLD, .5319 oz AGW
Accession date: AH1277
Mintname: *Qustantiniyah*

KM#	Year	Mintage	VG	Fine	VF	XF
697	1	3,880	325.00	425.00	800.00	1250.
	5	—	375.00	525.00	900.00	1550.
	7	2,800	300.00	400.00	600.00	1000.
	8	.030	250.00	325.00	450.00	650.00
	9	8,000	250.00	350.00	500.00	700.00

500 KURUSH

36.0800 g, .917 GOLD, 1.0638 oz AGW
Accession date: AH1277
Mintname: *Qustantiniyah*

KM#	Year	Mintage	VG	Fine	VF	XF
698	1	3,180	525.00	700.00	1000.	1400.
	3	1,580	600.00	800.00	1250.	1750.
	5	—	800.00	1000.	1750.	2500.
	7	.021	BV	525.00	650.00	950.00
	8	.071	BV	525.00	650.00	950.00
	9	.074	BV	525.00	650.00	950.00
	10	.030	BV	525.00	650.00	950.00
	11	.036	BV	525.00	650.00	950.00
	13	.059	BV	525.00	650.00	950.00

Mint Visit Coinage

Abdul Aziz's visit to Bursa.

بروسة

Bursa Mint mark

KURUSH

1.2027 g, .830 SILVER, .0321 oz ASW
Accession date: AH1277
Mintname: *Bursa*

KM#	Year	Mintage	Fine	VF	XF	Unc
703	1	.040	200.00	300.00	500.00	1000.

2 KURUSH

2.4055 g, .830 SILVER, .0642 oz ASW
Accession date: AH1277
Mintname: *Bursa*

KM#	Year	Mintage	Fine	VF	XF	Unc
704	1	.040	150.00	225.00	400.00	800.00

5 KURUSH

6.0130 g, .830 SILVER, .1605 oz ASW
Accession date: AH1277
Mintname: *Bursa*

KM#	Year	Mintage	Fine	VF	XF	Unc
705	1	.018	125.00	200.00	350.00	550.00

25 KURUSH

1.8040 g, .917 GOLD, .0532 oz AGW
Accession date: AH1277
Mintname: *Bursa*

KM#	Year	Mintage	Fine	VF	XF	Unc
706	1	4,800	150.00	300.00	450.00	650.00

50 KURUSH

3.6080 g, .917 GOLD, .1064 oz AGW
Accession date: AH1277
Mintname: *Bursa*

KM#	Year	Mintage	Fine	VF	XF	Unc
707	1	2,476	200.00	400.00	650.00	1000.

100 KURUSH

7.2160 g, .917 GOLD, .2128 oz AGW
Accession date: AH1277
Mintname: *Bursa*

KM#	Year	Mintage	Fine	VF	XF	Unc
708	1	9,737	400.00	650.00	1000.	1600.

MURAD V

AH1293/1876AD

KURUSH

1.2027 g, .830 SILVER, .0321 oz ASW
Accession date: AH1293
Mintname: *Qustantiniyah*
Obv: W/o flower right of toughra.

KM#	Year	Mintage	VG	Fine	VF	XF
710	1	.280	75.00	125.00	175.00	300.00

5 KURUSH

6.0130 g, .830 SILVER, .1605 oz ASW
Accession date: AH1293
Mintname: *Qustantiniyah*
Obv: W/o flower right of toughra.

KM#	Year	Mintage	VG	Fine	VF	XF
711	1	.020	100.00	150.00	250.00	400.00

20 KURUSH

24.0550 g, .830 SILVER, .6419 oz ASW
Accession date: AH1293
Mintname: *Qustantiniyah*
Obv: W/o flower right of toughra.

KM#	Year	Mintage	VG	Fine	VF	XF
712	1	.128	25.00	45.00	60.00	100.00

NOTE: Beware of specimens of KM#722 altered to appear as a piece of Murad. The toughra is very different.

25 KURUSH

1.8040 g, .917 GOLD, .0532 oz AGW
Accession date: AH1293
Mintname: *Qustantiniyah*
Obv: Crescent above toughra.

KM#	Year	Mintage	VG	Fine	VF	XF
713	1	.014	100.00	175.00	300.00	450.00

50 KURUSH

3.6080 g, .917 GOLD, .1064 oz AGW
Accession date: AH1293
Mintname: *Qustantiniyah*
Obv: Crescent above toughra.

KM#	Year	Mintage	VG	Fine	VF	XF
714	1	4,500	300.00	500.00	750.00	1250.

100 KURUSH

7.2160 g, .917 GOLD, .2128 oz AGW
Accession date: AH1293
Mintname: *Qustantiniyah*
Obv: Crescent above toughra.

KM#	Year	Mintage	VG	Fine	VF	XF
715	1	7,700	BV	110.00	175.00	250.00

ABDUL HAMID II

AH1293-1327/1876-1909AD

5 PARA

COPPER
Accession date: AH1293
Mintname: *Qustantiniyah*

KM#	Year	Mintage	VG	Fine	VF	XF
728	2	—	—	—	Rare	—
	3	—	.25	.50	3.00	10.00
	4	—	.25	.50	3.00	10.00

1.0023 g, .100 SILVER, .0032 oz ASW

KM#	Year	Mintage	VG	Fine	VF	XF
743	25	3.336	.25	.50	1.25	4.00
	26	—	.25	.50	1.25	4.00
	27	—	.25	.50	1.25	4.00
	28	—	.50	1.00	3.00	12.00
	30	—	6.00	12.00	20.00	40.00

10 PARA

2.0046 g, .100 SILVER, .0064 oz ASW
Accession date: AH1293
Mintname: *Qustantiniyah*

KM#	Year	Mintage	VG	Fine	VF	XF
744	25	3.492	.15	.25	1.00	4.00
	26	—	.15	.25	1.00	4.00
	27	—	.15	.25	1.00	4.00
	28	—	.15	.25	1.50	6.00
	30	—	1.00	2.00	5.00	15.00

NOTE: Varieties exist.

20 PARA

0.6013 g, .830 SILVER, .0160 oz ASW
Mintname: *Qustantiniyah*
Accession date: AH1293
Obv: Flower right of toughra.

KM#	Year	Mintage	VG	Fine	VF	XF
717	1	.110	25.00	50.00	100.00	175.00
	4	.050	40.00	100.00	200.00	300.00

Obv: *el-Ghazi* right of toughra.

KM#	Year	Mintage	VG	Fine	VF	XF
734	8	.350	5.00	7.50	15.00	35.00

KURUSH

1.2027 g, .830 SILVER, .0321 oz ASW
Accession date: AH1293
Mintname: *Qustantiniyah*
Obv: Flower right of toughra.

KM#	Year	Mintage	VG	Fine	VF	XF
718	1	.345	40.00	75.00	150.00	250.00
	2	.020	50.00	100.00	175.00	300.00
	4	.045	40.00	75.00	150.00	250.00

Obv: *el-Ghazi* right of toughra.

KM#	Year	Mintage	VG	Fine	VF	XF
735	8	.210	1.00	1.75	3.50	7.00
	9	.600	.65	1.25	2.50	5.00
	11	8.830	.65	1.25	2.50	5.00
	13	.130	4.00	10.00	20.00	35.00
	16	4.000	.65	1.25	2.50	5.00
	17	6.440	.65	1.25	2.50	5.00
	18	.040	5.00	15.00	30.00	50.00
	19	3.070	.65	1.25	2.50	5.00
	20	4.122	.65	1.25	2.50	5.00
	21	.040	3.00	7.50	15.00	30.00
	22	3.979	.65	1.25	2.50	5.00
	23	3.760	.65	1.25	2.50	5.00
	24	2.041	.65	1.25	2.50	5.00
	25	.084	3.00	7.50	15.00	30.00
	26	.055	3.00	7.50	15.00	30.00
	27	9.945	.65	1.25	2.50	5.00
	28	16.139	.65	1.25	2.50	5.00
	29	7.076	.65	1.25	2.50	5.00
	30	.707	.65	1.25	2.50	5.00
	31	1.366	.65	1.25	2.50	5.00
	32	1.140	.65	1.25	2.50	5.00
	33	1.700	.65	1.25	2.50	5.00
	34	—	40.00	60.00	115.00	225.00

NOTE: Varieties exist.

2 KURUSH

2.4055 g, .830 SILVER, .0642 oz ASW
Accession date: AH1293
Mintname: *Qustantiniyah*
Obv: Flower right of toughra.

KM#	Year	Mintage	VG	Fine	VF	XF
719	1	.010	250.00	500.00	800.00	1500.

Obv: *el-Ghazi* right of toughra.

KM#	Year	Mintage	VG	Fine	VF	XF
736	8	.103	2.00	2.50	5.00	10.00
	9	.605	1.75	2.75	4.50	8.00
	11	5.115	1.50	2.00	4.00	7.00
	12	.325	1.75	2.75	4.50	8.00
	13	.030	15.00	22.50	35.00	75.00
	16	.980	1.50	2.00	4.00	7.00
	17	3.736	1.50	2.00	4.00	7.00
	18	.023	15.00	25.00	35.00	75.00
	19	3.507	1.50	2.00	4.00	7.00
	20	3.370	1.50	2.00	4.00	7.00
	21	.021	15.00	25.00	35.00	75.00
	22	2.980	1.50	2.00	4.00	7.00
	23	3.139	1.50	2.00	4.00	7.00
	24	1.490	1.75	2.25	4.50	8.00
	25	.014	15.00	25.00	35.00	75.00
	26	.017	15.00	25.00	35.00	75.00
	27	4.689	1.50	2.00	4.00	7.00
	28	7.567	1.50	2.00	4.00	7.00
	29	7.775	1.50	2.00	4.00	7.00
	30	1.366	1.50	2.00	4.00	7.00
	31	3.014	1.50	2.00	4.00	7.00
	32	1.625	1.50	2.00	4.00	7.00
	33	2.173	1.50	2.00	4.00	7.00
	34	—	45.00	90.00	140.00	200.00

NOTE: Varieties exist.

5 KURUSH

6.0130 g, .830 SILVER, .1605 oz ASW
Accession date: AH1293
Mintname: *Qustantiniyah*
Obv: Flower right of toughra.

KM#	Year	Mintage	VG	Fine	VF	XF
720	1	.042	50.00	100.00	150.00	250.00
	2	.014	30.00	60.00	100.00	200.00
	3	.016	10.00	20.00	35.00	75.00
	4	.269	7.50	15.00	30.00	60.00

Obv: *el-Ghazi* right of toughra.

KM#	Year	Mintage	VG	Fine	VF	XF
737	8	.082	4.00	8.00	11.00	17.50
	9	.614	BV	3.50	5.00	9.50
	11	1.788	BV	3.50	5.00	9.50
	12	1.880	BV	3.50	5.00	9.50
	13	2.182	BV	3.50	5.00	9.50
	14	.380	BV	3.50	5.00	9.50
	15	.194	BV	4.00	6.00	12.00
	16	.914	BV	3.50	5.00	9.50
	17	1.337	BV	3.50	5.00	9.50
	18	.012	20.00	35.00	55.00	85.00
	19	.031	10.00	20.00	35.00	60.00
	20	.162	4.00	7.50	12.00	20.00
	21	.018	15.00	30.00	45.00	75.00
	22	.008	15.00	30.00	45.00	75.00
	23	.007	15.00	30.00	45.00	75.00
	24	.126	BV	3.75	6.50	10.00
	25	.013	15.00	30.00	45.00	75.00
	26	.008	15.00	30.00	45.00	75.00
	27	.016	15.00	30.00	45.00	75.00
	28	.006	15.00	30.00	45.00	75.00
	29	.007	15.00	30.00	45.00	75.00
	30	.038	5.00	10.00	15.00	30.00
	31/30	3.175	6.00	13.00	25.00	35.00
	31	Inc. Ab.	3.50	4.50	7.00	15.00
	32	3.334	BV	3.25	4.50	9.50
	33	.907	BV	3.50	6.00	11.50
	34	—	50.00	80.00	110.00	200.00

NOTE: Varieties exist.

10 KURUSH

12.0270 g, .830 SILVER, .3210 oz ASW
Accession date: AH1293
Mintname: *Qustantiniyah*

KM#	Year	Mintage	VG	Fine	VF	XF
721	1	.004	125.00	200.00	300.00	500.00
	3	.005	12.50	25.00	50.00	100.00

Obv: *el-Ghazi* right of toughra.

KM#	Year	Mintage	VG	Fine	VF	XF
738	12	—	25.00	50.00	100.00	175.00
	13	.161	5.00	10.00	20.00	45.00
	20	.034	25.00	50.00	100.00	175.00
	31	.051	20.00	40.00	75.00	125.00
	32	.575	7.50	12.50	15.00	25.00
	33	.273	6.00	10.00	12.50	20.00

121/2 KURUSH

0.8770 g, .917 GOLD, .0258 oz AGW
Accession date: AH1293
Mintname: *Qustantiniyah*
Monnaie de Luxe

KM#	Year	Mintage	VG	Fine	VF	XF
745	25	720 pcs.	40.00	70.00	100.00	125.00
	28	800 pcs.	40.00	70.00	100.00	125.00
	29	.012	20.00	30.00	45.00	75.00
	30	.013	20.00	30.00	45.00	75.00
	31	.024	20.00	30.00	45.00	75.00
	32	.014	20.00	30.00	45.00	75.00
	33	.013	20.00	30.00	45.00	75.00
	34	—	20.00	30.00	45.00	75.00

20 KURUSH

24.0550 g, .830 SILVER, .6419 oz ASW
Accession date: AH1293
Mintname: *Qustantiniyah*
Obv: Flower right of toughra.
Rev: Similar to KM#712.

KM#	Year	Mintage	VG	Fine	VF	XF
722	1	1.402	BV	12.00	25.00	40.00
	2	1.357	BV	12.00	20.00	35.00
	3	5.940	BV	12.00	20.00	35.00

25 KURUSH

1.8040 g, .917 GOLD, .0532 oz AGW
Accession date: AH1293
Mintname: *Qustantiniyah*
Obv: Flower right of toughra.

KM#	Year	Mintage	VG	Fine	VF	XF
723	1	—	—	—	Rare	—
	2	—	—	—	Rare	—
	3	5,000	50.00	100.00	150.00	200.00
	4	3,600	50.00	100.00	150.00	200.00
	5	—	50.00	100.00	125.00	175.00
	6	—	50.00	100.00	125.00	175.00

Obv: *el-Ghazi* right of toughra.

KM#	Year	Mintage	VG	Fine	VF	XF
729	6	—	—	—	Rare	—
	7	—	BV	25.00	32.00	45.00
	8	—	BV	25.00	32.00	45.00
	9	—	BV	25.00	32.00	45.00
	10	—	BV	25.00	32.00	45.00
	11	—	BV	25.00	32.00	45.00
	12	—	BV	25.00	32.00	45.00
	13	—	BV	25.00	32.00	45.00
	14	—	BV	25.00	32.00	45.00
	15	—	BV	25.00	32.00	45.00
	16	—	BV	25.00	32.00	45.00
	17	—	BV	25.00	32.00	45.00
	18	—	BV	25.00	32.00	45.00
	19	—	BV	25.00	32.00	45.00
	20	—	BV	25.00	32.00	45.00
	21	—	BV	25.00	32.00	45.00
	22	—	BV	25.00	32.00	45.00
	23	—	BV	25.00	32.00	45.00
	24	—	BV	25.00	32.00	45.00
	25	.057	BV	25.00	32.00	45.00
	26	—	BV	25.00	32.00	45.00
	27	—	BV	25.00	32.00	45.00
	28	—	BV	25.00	32.00	45.00
	29	—	BV	25.00	32.00	45.00
	30	—	BV	25.00	32.00	45.00
729	31	—	BV	25.00	32.00	45.00
	32	—	BV	25.00	32.00	45.00
	33	—	BV	25.00	32.00	45.00
	34	—	BV	25.00	32.00	45.00

1.7540 g, .917 GOLD, .0517 oz AGW
Monnaie de Luxe

KM#	Year	Mintage	VG	Fine	VF	XF
739	18	—	—	—	Rare	—
	23	—	50.00	65.00	75.00	95.00
	24	—	50.00	65.00	75.00	95.00
	25	—	50.00	65.00	75.00	95.00
	26	—	50.00	65.00	75.00	95.00
	27	—	50.00	65.00	75.00	95.00
	28	—	50.00	65.00	75.00	95.00
	29	—	50.00	65.00	75.00	95.00
	30	—	50.00	65.00	75.00	95.00
	31	—	50.00	65.00	75.00	95.00
	32	—	50.00	65.00	75.00	95.00
	33	—	50.00	65.00	75.00	95.00
	34	—	50.00	65.00	75.00	95.00

50 KURUSH

3.6080 g, .917 GOLD, .1064 oz AGW
Accession date: AH1293
Mintname: *Qustantiniyah*
Obv: Flower right of toughra.

KM#	Year	Mintage	VG	Fine	VF	XF
724	1	—	75.00	100.00	150.00	300.00
	3	—	75.00	100.00	150.00	300.00
	6	—	100.00	200.00	350.00	750.00

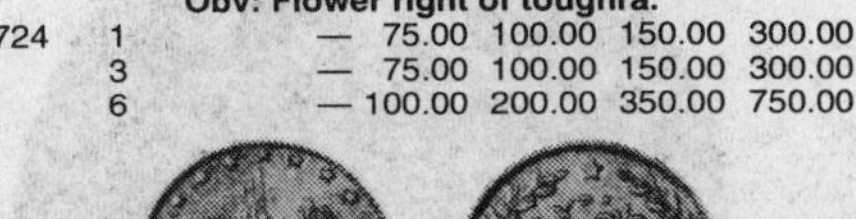

Obv: *el-Ghazi* right of toughra.

KM#	Year	Mintage	VG	Fine	VF	XF
731	7	—	BV	50.00	60.00	90.00
	8	—	BV	50.00	60.00	90.00
	9	—	BV	50.00	60.00	90.00
	10	—	BV	50.00	60.00	90.00
	11	—	BV	50.00	60.00	90.00
	12	—	BV	50.00	60.00	90.00
	13	—	BV	50.00	60.00	90.00
	14	—	BV	50.00	60.00	90.00
	15	—	BV	50.00	60.00	90.00
	16	—	BV	50.00	60.00	90.00
	17	—	BV	50.00	60.00	90.00
	18	—	BV	50.00	60.00	90.00
	19	—	BV	50.00	60.00	90.00
	20	—	BV	50.00	60.00	90.00
	21	—	BV	50.00	60.00	90.00
	22	—	BV	50.00	60.00	90.00
	23	—	BV	50.00	60.00	90.00
	24	—	BV	50.00	60.00	90.00
	25	.013	BV	50.00	60.00	90.00
	26	—	BV	50.00	60.00	90.00
	27	—	BV	50.00	60.00	90.00
	28	—	BV	50.00	60.00	90.00
	29	—	BV	50.00	60.00	90.00
	30	—	BV	50.00	60.00	90.00
	31	—	BV	50.00	60.00	90.00
	32	—	BV	50.00	60.00	90.00
	33	—	BV	50.00	60.00	90.00
	34	—	BV	50.00	60.00	90.00

3.5080 g, .917 GOLD, .1034 oz AGW
Monnaie de Luxe

KM#	Year	Mintage	VG	Fine	VF	XF
740	18	—	—	—	Rare	—
	23	—	50.00	75.00	90.00	140.00
	24	—	50.00	75.00	90.00	140.00
	25	—	50.00	75.00	90.00	140.00
	26	—	50.00	75.00	90.00	140.00
	27	—	50.00	75.00	90.00	140.00
	28	—	50.00	75.00	90.00	140.00
	29	—	50.00	75.00	90.00	140.00
	30	—	50.00	75.00	90.00	140.00
	31	—	50.00	75.00	90.00	140.00
	32	—	50.00	75.00	90.00	140.00
740	33	—	50.00	75.00	90.00	140.00
	34	—	50.00	75.00	90.00	140.00

100 KURUSH

7.2160 g, .917 GOLD, .2128 oz AGW
Accession date: AH1293
Mintname: *Qustantiniyah*
Obv: Flower right of toughra.

KM#	Year	Mintage	VG	Fine	VF	XF
725	1	—	110.00	150.00	200.00	275.00
	2	—	110.00	150.00	200.00	275.00
	3	—	110.00	150.00	200.00	275.00
	4	—	150.00	200.00	300.00	400.00
	6	—	110.00	150.00	200.00	275.00

Obv: *el-Ghazi* right of toughra.

KM#	Year	Mintage	VG	Fine	VF	XF
730	6	—	—	BV	100.00	115.00
	7	—	—	BV	100.00	115.00
	8	—	—	BV	100.00	115.00
	9	—	—	BV	100.00	115.00
	10	—	—	BV	100.00	115.00
	11	—	—	BV	100.00	115.00
	12	—	—	BV	100.00	115.00
	13	—	—	BV	100.00	115.00
	14	—	—	BV	100.00	115.00
	15	—	—	BV	100.00	115.00
	16	—	—	BV	100.00	115.00
	17	—	—	BV	100.00	115.00
	18	—	—	BV	100.00	115.00
	19	—	—	BV	100.00	115.00
	20	—	—	BV	100.00	115.00
	21	—	—	BV	100.00	115.00
	22	—	—	BV	100.00	115.00
	23	—	—	BV	100.00	115.00
	24	—	—	BV	100.00	115.00
	25	3,000	—	BV	100.00	115.00
	26	—	—	BV	100.00	115.00
	27	—	—	BV	100.00	115.00
	28	—	—	BV	100.00	115.00
	29	—	—	BV	100.00	115.00
	30	—	—	BV	100.00	115.00
	31	—	—	BV	100.00	115.00
	32	—	—	BV	100.00	115.00
	33	—	—	BV	100.00	115.00
	34	—	—	BV	100.00	115.00

7.0160 g, .917 GOLD, .2068 oz AGW
Monnaie de Luxe

KM#	Year	Mintage	VG	Fine	VF	XF
741	18	—	—	—	Rare	—
	23	—	BV	100.00	135.00	190.00
	24	—	BV	100.00	135.00	190.00
	25	—	BV	100.00	135.00	190.00
	26	—	BV	100.00	135.00	190.00
	27	—	BV	100.00	135.00	190.00
	28	—	BV	100.00	135.00	190.00
	29	—	BV	100.00	135.00	190.00
	30	—	BV	100.00	135.00	190.00
	31	—	BV	100.00	135.00	190.00
	32	—	BV	100.00	135.00	190.00
	33	—	BV	100.00	135.00	190.00
	34	—	BV	100.00	135.00	190.00

250 KURUSH

18.0400 g, .917 GOLD, .5319 oz AGW
Accession date: AH1293
Mintname: *Qustantiniyah*
Obv: Flower right of toughra.

KM#	Year	Mintage	VG	Fine	VF	XF
726	1	120 pcs.	600.00	1000.	1600.	2000.

Obv: *El Ghazi* right of toughra.

KM#	Year	Mintage	VG	Fine	VF	XF
732	11	—	BV	250.00	300.00	450.00
	12	—	BV	250.00	300.00	450.00
	13	—	BV	250.00	300.00	450.00
	14	—	BV	250.00	300.00	450.00
	15	—	BV	250.00	300.00	450.00
	16	—	BV	250.00	300.00	450.00
	17	—	BV	250.00	300.00	450.00
	18	—	BV	250.00	300.00	450.00
	19	—	BV	250.00	300.00	450.00
	20	—	BV	250.00	300.00	450.00
	21	—	BV	250.00	300.00	450.00
	22	—	BV	250.00	300.00	450.00
	23	—	BV	250.00	300.00	450.00
	24	—	BV	250.00	300.00	450.00
	25	400 pcs.	BV	250.00	300.00	450.00
	26	—	BV	250.00	300.00	450.00
	27	—	BV	250.00	300.00	450.00
	28	—	BV	250.00	300.00	450.00
	29	—	BV	250.00	300.00	450.00
	30	—	BV	250.00	300.00	450.00
	31	—	BV	250.00	300.00	450.00
	32	—	BV	250.00	300.00	450.00
	33	—	BV	250.00	300.00	450.00
	43	—	BV	250.00	300.00	450.00

17.5400 g, .917 GOLD, .5169 oz AGW
Monnaie de Luxe

KM#	Year	Mintage	VG	Fine	VF	XF
742	24	—	BV	275.00	400.00	600.00
	25	—	BV	275.00	400.00	600.00
	26	—	BV	275.00	400.00	600.00
	27	—	BV	275.00	400.00	600.00
	28	—	BV	275.00	400.00	600.00
	29	—	BV	275.00	400.00	600.00
	30	—	BV	275.00	400.00	600.00
	31	—	BV	275.00	400.00	600.00
	32	—	BV	275.00	400.00	600.00
	33	—	BV	275.00	400.00	600.00
	34	—	—	—	Rare	—

500 KURUSH

36.0800 g, .917 GOLD, 1.0638 oz AGW
Accession date: AH1293
Mintname: *Qustantiniyah*
Obv: Flower right of toughra.

KM#	Year	Mintage	VG	Fine	VF	XF
727	1	—	BV	500.00	650.00	900.00
	2	—	BV	500.00	650.00	900.00
	3	—	BV	500.00	650.00	900.00
	4	—	BV	500.00	650.00	900.00
	6	—	BV	500.00	650.00	900.00

Obv: *El Ghazi* right of toughra.

KM#	Year	Mintage	VG	Fine	VF	XF
733	11	—	BV	500.00	550.00	750.00
	12	—	BV	500.00	550.00	750.00
733	13	—	BV	500.00	550.00	750.00
	14	—	BV	500.00	550.00	750.00
	15	—	BV	500.00	550.00	750.00
	16	—	BV	500.00	550.00	750.00
	17	—	BV	500.00	550.00	750.00
	18	—	BV	500.00	550.00	750.00
	19	—	BV	500.00	550.00	750.00
	20	—	BV	500.00	550.00	750.00
	21	—	BV	500.00	550.00	750.00
	22	—	BV	500.00	550.00	750.00
	23	—	BV	500.00	550.00	750.00
	24	—	BV	500.00	550.00	750.00
	25	.011	BV	500.00	550.00	750.00
	26	—	BV	500.00	550.00	750.00
	27	—	BV	500.00	550.00	750.00
	28	—	BV	500.00	550.00	750.00
	29	—	BV	500.00	550.00	750.00
	30	—	BV	500.00	550.00	750.00
	31	—	BV	500.00	550.00	750.00
	32	—	BV	500.00	550.00	750.00
	33	—	BV	500.00	550.00	750.00
	34	—	BV	500.00	550.00	750.00

35.0800 g, .917 GOLD, 1.0338 oz AGW
Monnaie de Luxe

KM#	Year	Mintage	VG	Fine	VF	XF
746	26	—	600.00	750.00	900.00	1200.
	27	—	600.00	750.00	900.00	1200.
	28	—	600.00	750.00	900.00	1200.
	29	—	600.00	750.00	900.00	1200.
	30	—	600.00	750.00	900.00	1200.
	31	—	600.00	750.00	900.00	1200.
	32	—	600.00	750.00	900.00	1200.
	33	—	600.00	750.00	900.00	1200.
	34	—	600.00	750.00	900.00	1200.

MUHAMMAD V

AH1327-1336/1909-1918AD

5 PARA

NICKEL
Accession date: AH1327
Mintname: *Qustantiniyah*
Obv: *Reshat* right of toughra.

KM#	Year	Mintage	VG	Fine	VF	XF
759	2	1.664	1.00	2.00	4.00	8.00
	3	21.760	.50	1.00	2.00	4.00
	4	21.392	.50	1.00	2.00	4.00
	5	30.579	.50	1.00	2.00	4.00
	6	15.751	.50	1.00	2.00	4.00
	7	2.512	15.00	35.00	60.00	100.00

Obv: *el-Ghazi* right of toughra.

KM#	Year	Mintage	VG	Fine	VF	XF
767	7	.740	15.00	30.00	45.00	70.00

10 PARA

NICKEL
Accession date: AH1327
Mintname: *Qustantiniyah*
Obv: *Reshat* right of toughra.

KM#	Year	Mintage	VG	Fine	VF	XF
760	2	2.576	.25	.50	2.00	5.00
	3	18.992	.15	.25	.50	2.00
	4	18.576	.15	.25	.50	2.00
	5	31.799	.15	.25	.50	2.00
	6	17.024	.15	.25	.50	2.00
	7	21.680	.30	.65	1.50	4.00

Obv: *el-Ghazi* right of toughra.

KM#	Year	Mintage	VG	Fine	VF	XF
768	7	Inc. KM760	.30	.60	1.50	4.00
	8	7.590	.50	1.00	4.00	10.00

20 PARA

NICKEL
Accession date: AH1327
Mintname: *Qustantiniyah*
Obv: *Reshat* right of toughra.

KM#	Year	Mintage	VG	Fine	VF	XF
761	2	1.524	.25	.50	2.00	8.00
	3	11.418	.15	.35	1.50	6.00
	4	10.848	.15	.25	1.00	5.00
	5	24.350	.15	.25	1.00	5.00
	6	20.663	.15	.25	1.00	5.00
	7	—	—	—	Rare	—
	W/o R.Y.	—	5.00	8.50	15.00	25.00

Obv: *el-Ghazi* at right of toughra.

KM#	Year	Mintage	VG	Fine	VF	XF
769	7	—	—	—	Rare	—

40 PARA

NICKEL
Accession date: AH1327
Mintname: *Qustantiniyah*
Obv: *Reshat* right of toughra.

KM#	Year	Mintage	VG	Fine	VF	XF
766	3	1.992	.50	1.00	3.00	10.00
	4	8.716	.15	.30	1.00	5.00
	5	9.248	.15	.30	1.00	5.00

COPPER-NICKEL
Obv: *el-Ghazi* right of toughra.

KM#	Year	Mintage	VG	Fine	VF	XF
779	8	16.339	.15	.30	1.00	5.00
	9	3.034	1.00	2.00	6.00	15.00

KURUSH

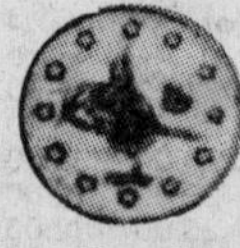
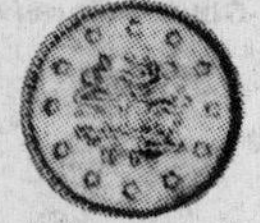

1.2027 g, .830 SILVER, .0321 oz ASW
Accession date: AH1327
Mintname: *Qustantiniyah*

KM#	Year	Mintage	VG	Fine	VF	XF
748	1	1.270	.75	1.50	3.00	6.00
	2	8.770	.65	1.25	2.50	5.00
	3	.840	1.50	3.00	6.00	12.50

2 KURUSH

2.4055 g, .830 SILVER, .0642 oz ASW
Accession date: AH1327

Mintname: ***Qustantiniyah***
Obv: ***Reshat*** right of toughra.

KM#	Year	Mintage	VG	Fine	VF	XF
749	1	5.157	1.75	2.25	3.50	7.50
	2	11.120	1.50	2.00	3.00	6.50
	3	6.110	1.50	2.00	3.00	6.50
	4	4.031	1.50	2.00	3.00	6.50
	5	.301	2.50	5.00	10.00	20.00
	6	1.884	2.00	2.50	4.00	8.00

NOTE: Varieties exist.

Obv: *el-Ghazi* right of toughra.

KM#	Year	Mintage	VG	Fine	VF	XF
770	7	.017	12.50	25.00	40.00	75.00
	8	.398	20.00	30.00	50.00	100.00
	9	.008	60.00	100.00	200.00	350.00

5 KURUSH

6.0130 g, .830 SILVER, .1605 oz ASW
Accession date: AH1327
Mintname: *Qustantiniyah*
Obv: *Reshat* right of toughra.

KM#	Year	Mintage	VG	Fine	VF	XF
750	1	1.558	BV	3.50	6.00	10.00
	2	1.886	BV	3.50	6.00	10.00
	3	1.273	BV	3.50	6.00	10.00
	4	1.635	BV	3.50	6.00	10.00
	5	.194	6.00	9.00	15.00	28.00
	6	.664	3.25	3.50	5.00	9.00
	7	.834	3.25	3.50	5.00	9.00

Obv: *el-Ghazi* right of toughra.

KM#	Year	Mintage	VG	Fine	VF	XF
771	7	Inc. KM750	3.50	4.50	7.00	10.00
	8	.648	4.00	7.00	10.00	20.00
	9	3,938	50.00	100.00	200.00	350.00

10 KURUSH

12.0270 g, .830 SILVER, .3210 oz ASW
Accession date: AH1327
Mintname: *Qustantiniyah*
Obv: *Reshat* right of toughra.

KM#	Year	Mintage	VG	Fine	VF	XF
751	1	.110	12.50	25.00	50.00	100.00
	2	Inc. Ab.	10.00	20.00	50.00	100.00
	3	8,000	150.00	250.00	500.00	1000.
	4	.096	3.50	7.50	15.00	25.00
	5	.034	10.00	20.00	50.00	100.00
	6	.081	7.50	12.50	17.50	30.00
	7	.582	5.00	10.00	16.50	32.00

Obv: *el-Ghazi* right of toughra.

KM#	Year	Mintage	VG	Fine	VF	XF
772	7	Inc. KM751	3.50	7.50	15.00	28.00
	8	.408	7.00	9.00	17.50	32.00
	9	.299	10.00	20.00	35.00	50.00
	10	.666	12.50	25.00	50.00	85.00

12-1/2 KURUSH

.9020 g, .917 GOLD, .0266 oz AGW
Accession date: AH1327
Mintname: *Qustantiniyah*
Monnaie de Luxe
Obv: *Reshat* right of toughra.

KM#	Year	Mintage	VG	Fine	VF	XF
762	2	—	20.00	30.00	50.00	90.00
	3	—	20.00	30.00	50.00	90.00
	4	—	20.00	30.00	50.00	90.00
	5	—	20.00	30.00	50.00	90.00
	6	—	20.00	30.00	50.00	90.00

20 KURUSH

24.0550 g, .830 SILVER, .6419 oz ASW
Accession date: AH1327
Mintname: *Qustantiniyah*
Rev: Similar to KM#712.

KM#	Year	Mintage	VG	Fine	VF	XF
780	8	.713	BV	12.00	20.00	35.00
	9	5.962	BV	10.00	15.00	30.00
	10	11.025	BV	12.00	20.00	35.00

25 KURUSH

1.8040 g, .917 GOLD, .0532 oz AGW
Accession date: AH1327
Mintname: *Qustantiniyah*
Obv: *Reshat* right of toughra.

KM#	Year	Mintage	VG	Fine	VF	XF
752	1	—	BV	30.00	40.00	50.00
	2	—	BV	30.00	40.00	50.00
	3	—	BV	30.00	40.00	50.00
	4	—	BV	30.00	40.00	50.00
	5	—	BV	30.00	40.00	50.00
	6	—	BV	30.00	40.00	50.00

1.7540 g, .917 GOLD, .0517 oz AGW
Monnaie de Luxe

KM#	Year	Mintage	VG	Fine	VF	XF
763	2	—	35.00	50.00	60.00	70.00
	3	—	35.00	50.00	60.00	70.00
	4	—	35.00	50.00	60.00	70.00
	5	—	50.00	60.00	75.00	100.00
	6	—	50.00	60.00	75.00	100.00

1.8040 g, .917 GOLD, .0532 oz AGW
Obv: *el-Ghazi* right of toughra.

KM#	Year	Mintage	VG	Fine	VF	XF
773	7	—	BV	35.00	45.00	55.00
	8	—	BV	35.00	45.00	55.00
	9	—	BV	35.00	45.00	55.00
	10	—	1000.	1500.	2000.	3000.

1.7540 g, .917 GOLD, .0517 oz AGW
Monnaie de Luxe

KM#	Year	Mintage	VG	Fine	VF	XF
774	8	—	1750.	2500.	3500.	5000.

50 KURUSH

3.6080 g, .917 GOLD, .1064 oz AGW
Accession date: AH1327
Mintname: *Qustantiniyah*
Obv: *Reshat* right of toughra.

KM#	Year	Mintage	VG	Fine	VF	XF
753	1	—	1000.	1500.	2000.	3000.
	2	—	BV	55.00	65.00	80.00
	3	—	BV	55.00	65.00	80.00
	4	—	BV	55.00	65.00	80.00
	5	—	BV	55.00	65.00	80.00
	6	—	BV	55.00	65.00	80.00

3.5080 g, .917 GOLD, .1034 oz AGW
Monnaie de Luxe

KM#	Year	Mintage	VG	Fine	VF	XF
764	2	—	60.00	70.00	100.00	120.00
	3	—	60.00	70.00	100.00	120.00
	4	—	60.00	70.00	100.00	120.00
	5	—	60.00	70.00	100.00	120.00
	6	—	60.00	70.00	100.00	120.00

3.6080 g, .917 GOLD, .1064 oz AGW
Obv: *el-Ghazi* right of toughra.

KM#	Year	Mintage	VG	Fine	VF	XF
775	7	—	60.00	75.00	150.00	250.00
	8	—	60.00	75.00	150.00	250.00
	9	—	60.00	75.00	150.00	250.00
	10	—	1000.	1500.	2000.	3000.

3.5080 g, .917 GOLD, .1034 oz AGW
Monnaie de Luxe

KM#	Year	Mintage	VG	Fine	VF	XF
781	8	—	250.00	400.00	600.00	1000.

100 KURUSH

7.2160 g, .917 GOLD, .2128 oz AGW
Accession date: AH1327
Mintname: *Qustantiniyah*
Obv: *Reshat* right of toughra.

KM#	Year	Mintage	VG	Fine	VF	XF
754	1	—	—	BV	100.00	135.00
	2	—	—	BV	100.00	135.00
	3	—	—	BV	100.00	135.00
	4	—	—	BV	100.00	135.00
	5	—	—	BV	100.00	135.00
	6	—	—	BV	100.00	135.00
	7	—	—	BV	100.00	135.00

7.0160 g, .917 GOLD, .2068 oz AGW
Monnaie de Luxe

KM#	Year	Mintage	VG	Fine	VF	XF
755	1	—	BV	100.00	135.00	200.00
	2	—	BV	100.00	135.00	200.00
	3	—	BV	100.00	135.00	200.00
	4	—	BV	100.00	135.00	200.00
	5	—	BV	100.00	135.00	200.00
	6	—	BV	100.00	135.00	200.00

7.2160 g, .917 GOLD, .2128 oz AGW
Obv: *el-Ghazi* right of toughra.

KM#	Year	Mintage	VG	Fine	VF	XF
776	7	—	—	BV	110.00	150.00
	8	—	—	BV	110.00	150.00
	9	—	—	BV	110.00	150.00
	10	—	—	BV	110.00	150.00

7.0160 g, .917 GOLD, .2068 oz AGW
Monnaie de Luxe

KM#	Year	Mintage	VG	Fine	VF	XF
782	8	—	250.00	400.00	600.00	1000.

250 KURUSH

18.0400 g, .917 GOLD, .5319 oz AGW
Accession date: AH1327
Mintname: *Qustantiniyah*
Obv: *Reshat* right of toughra.

KM#	Year	Mintage	VG	Fine	VF	XF
756	1	—	—	BV	350.00	425.00
	2	—	—	BV	350.00	425.00
	3	—	—	BV	350.00	425.00
	4	—	—	BV	350.00	425.00
	5	—	—	BV	350.00	425.00
	6	—	—	BV	350.00	425.00

17.5400 g, .917 GOLD, .5169 oz AGW
Monnaie de Luxe

KM#	Year	Mintage	VG	Fine	VF	XF
757	1	—	BV	350.00	450.00	625.00
	2	—	BV	350.00	450.00	625.00
	3	—	BV	350.00	450.00	625.00
	4	—	BV	350.00	450.00	625.00
	5	—	BV	350.00	450.00	625.00
	6	—	BV	350.00	450.00	625.00

18.0400 g, .917 GOLD, .5319 oz AGW
Obv: *el-Ghazi* right of toughra.

KM#	Year	Mintage	VG	Fine	VF	XF
777	7	30 pcs.	1250.	1750.	2800.	4000.
	8	21 pcs.	1750.	2500.	3500.	5000.
	9	28 pcs.	1750.	2500.	3500.	5000.

17.5400 g, .917 GOLD, .5169 oz AGW
Monnaie de Luxe

KM#	Year	Mintage	VG	Fine	VF	XF
783	8	—	1250.	1750.	2500.	3500.

500 KURUSH

36.0800 g, .917 GOLD, 1.0638 oz AGW
Ascession date: AH1327
Mintname: *Qustantiniyah*
Obv: *Reshat* right of toughra.

KM#	Year	Mintage	VG	Fine	VF	XF
758	1	—	—	BV	525.00	650.00
	2	—	—	BV	525.00	650.00
	3	—	—	BV	525.00	650.00
	4	—	—	BV	525.00	650.00
	5	—	—	BV	525.00	650.00
	6	—	—	BV	525.00	650.00

35.0800 g, .917 GOLD, 1.0338 oz AGW
Monnaie de Luxe

KM#	Year	Mintage	VG	Fine	VF	XF
765	2	—	600.00	750.00	900.00	1350.
	3	—	600.00	750.00	900.00	1350.
	4	—	600.00	750.00	900.00	1350.
	5	—	600.00	750.00	900.00	1350.
	6	—	600.00	750.00	900.00	1350.

36.0800 g, .917 GOLD, 1.0638 oz AGW
Obv: *el-Ghazi* right of toughra.

KM#	Year	Mintage	VG	Fine	VF	XF
784	7	484 pcs.	1750.	2500.	3500.	5000.
	8	19 pcs.	1750.	2500.	3500.	5000.
	9	22 pcs.	1750.	2500.	3500.	5000.
	10	—	1750.	2500.	3500.	5000.

35.0800 g, .917 GOLD, 1.0338 oz AGW
Monnaie de Luxe

KM#	Year	Mintage	VG	Fine	VF	XF
778	7	295 pcs.	1200.	1750.	2500.	3500.
	8	1,216	1000.	1500.	2200.	3000.

Mint Visit Coinage

Muhammad V's visit to Bursa

بروسة

Bursa Mint mark

2 KURUSH

2.4055 g, .830 SILVER, .0642 oz ASW
Accession date: AH1327
Mintname: *Bursa*

KM#	Year	Mintage	Fine	VF	XF	Unc
785	1	—	15.00	25.00	45.00	95.00

5 KURUSH

6.0130 g, .830 SILVER, .1605 oz ASW
Accession date: AH1327
Mintname: *Bursa*

KM#	Year	Mintage	Fine	VF	XF	Unc
786	1	—	20.00	35.00	60.00	115.00

25 KURUSH

1.8040 g, .917 GOLD, .0532 oz AGW
Accession date: AH1327
Mintname: *Bursa*

KM#	Year	Mintage	Fine	VF	XF	Unc
787	1	—	185.00	275.00	400.00	800.00

50 KURUSH

3.6080 g, .917 GOLD, .1064 oz AGW
Accession date: AH1327
Mintname: *Bursa*

KM#	Year	Mintage	Fine	VF	XF	Unc
788	1	—	165.00	275.00	350.00	650.00

100 KURUSH

7.2160 g, .917 GOLD, .2128 oz AGW
Accession date: AH1327
Mintname: *Bursa*

KM#	Year	Mintage	Fine	VF	XF	Unc
789	1	—	215.00	325.00	400.00	700.00

Muhammad V's visit to Edirne

ادرنة

Edirne Mint mark

2 KURUSH

2.4055 g, .830 SILVER, .0642 oz ASW
Accession date: AH1327
Mintname: *Edirne*

KM#	Year	Mintage	Fine	VF	XF	Unc
790	2	—	15.00	25.00	45.00	95.00

5 KURUSH

6.0130 g, .830 SILVER, .1605 oz ASW
Accession date: AH1327
Mintname: *Edirne*

KM#	Year	Mintage	Fine	VF	XF	Unc
791	2	—	20.00	35.00	60.00	115.00

10 KURUSH

12.0270 g, .830 SILVER, .3210 oz ASW
Accession date: AH1327
Mintname: *Edirne*

KM#	Year	Mintage	Fine	VF	XF	Unc
792	2	—	90.00	150.00	250.00	455.00

50 KURUSH

3.6080 g, .917 GOLD, .1064 oz AGW
Accession date: AH1327
Mintname: *Edirne*

KM#	Year	Mintage	Fine	VF	XF	Unc
793	2	—	200.00	275.00	350.00	600.00

100 KURUSH

7.2160 g, .917 GOLD, .2128 oz AGW
Accession date: AH1327
Mintname: *Edirne*

KM#	Year	Mintage	Fine	VF	XF	Unc
794	2	—	250.00	350.00	475.00	700.00

500 KURUSH

36.0800 g, .917 GOLD, 1.0638 oz AGW
Accession date: AH1327
Mintname: *Edirne*

KM#	Year	Mintage	Fine	VF	XF	Unc
795	2	—	1500.	2500.	3500.	4000.

Muhammad V's visit to Kosova

قوصوه

Kosova Mint mark

2 KURUSH

2.4055 g, .830 SILVER, .0642 oz ASW
Accession date: AH1327
Mintname: *Kosova*

KM#	Year	Mintage	Fine	VF	XF	Unc
796	3	.013	15.00	25.00	45.00	95.00

5 KURUSH

6.0130 g, .830 SILVER, .1605 oz ASW
Accession date: AH1327
Mintname: *Kosova*

KM#	Year	Mintage	Fine	VF	XF	Unc
797	3	3,000	20.00	35.00	60.00	115.00

10 KURUSH

12.0270 g, .830 SILVER, .3210 oz ASW
Accession date: AH1327
Mintname: *Kosova*

KM#	Year	Mintage	Fine	VF	XF	Unc
798	3	1,500	100.00	175.00	300.00	525.00

50 KURUSH

3.6080 g, .917 GOLD, .1064 oz AGW
Accession date: AH1327
Mintname: *Kosova*

KM#	Year	Mintage	Fine	VF	XF	Unc
799	3	1,200	225.00	275.00	400.00	700.00

100 KURUSH

7.2160 g, .917 GOLD, .2128 oz AGW
Accession date: AH1327
Mintname: *Kosova*

KM#	Year	Mintage	Fine	VF	XF	Unc
800	3	750 pcs.	250.00	300.00	450.00	750.00

500 KURUSH

36.0800 g, .917 GOLD, 1.0638 oz AGW
Accession date: AH1327
Mintname: *Kosova*

KM#	Year	Mintage	Fine	VF	XF	Unc
801	3	20 pcs.	3000.	4000.	5000.	6000.

Muhammad V's visit to Manastir

مناستر

Manastir Mint mark

2 KURUSH

2.4055 g, .830 SILVER, .0642 oz ASW
Accession date: AH1327
Mintname: *Manastir*

KM#	Year	Mintage	Fine	VF	XF	Unc
802	3	.013	15.00	25.00	45.00	95.00

5 KURUSH

6.0130 g, .830 SILVER, .1605 oz ASW
Accession date: AH1327
Mintname: *Manastir*

KM#	Year	Mintage	Fine	VF	XF	Unc
803	3	3,000	20.00	35.00	60.00	115.00

10 KURUSH

12.0270 g, .830 SILVER, .3210 oz ASW
Accession date: AH1327
Mintname: *Manastir*

KM#	Year	Mintage	Fine	VF	XF	Unc
804	3	1,500	100.00	175.00	275.00	525.00

50 KURUSH

3.6080 g, .917 GOLD, .1064 oz AGW
Accession date: AH1327
Mintname: *Manastir*

KM#	Year	Mintage	Fine	VF	XF	Unc
805	3	1,200	200.00	325.00	450.00	700.00

100 KURUSH

7.2160 g, .917 GOLD, .2128 oz AGW
Accession date: AH1327
Mintname: *Manastir*

KM#	Year	Mintage	Fine	VF	XF	Unc
806	3	750 pcs.	225.00	350.00	450.00	750.00

500 KURUSH

36.0800 g, .917 GOLD, 1.0638 oz AGW
Accession date: AH1327
Mintname: *Manastir*

KM#	Year	Mintage	Fine	VF	XF	Unc
807	3	20 pcs.	2500.	4000.	5000.	6250.

Muhammad V's visit to Salonika

Salonika Mint mark

2 KURUSH

2.4055 g, .830 SILVER, .0642 oz ASW
Accession date: AH1327
Mintname: *Salonika*

KM#	Year	Mintage	Fine	VF	XF	Unc
808	3	.013	15.00	25.00	45.00	95.00

5 KURUSH

6.0130 g, .830 SILVER, .1605 oz ASW
Accession date: AH1327
Mintname: *Salonika*

KM#	Year	Mintage	Fine	VF	XF	Unc
809	3	3,000	20.00	35.00	60.00	115.00

10 KURUSH

12.0270 g, .830 SILVER, .3210 oz ASW
Accession date: AH1327
Mintname: *Salonika*

KM#	Year	Mintage	Fine	VF	XF	Unc
810	3	1,500	100.00	175.00	275.00	525.00

50 KURUSH

3.6080 g, .917 GOLD, .1064 oz AGW
Accession date: AH1327
Mintname: *Salonika*

KM#	Year	Mintage	Fine	VF	XF	Unc
811	3	1,200	200.00	325.00	400.00	700.00

100 KURUSH

7.2160 g, .917 GOLD, .2128 oz AGW
Accession date: AH1327
Mintname: *Salonika*

KM#	Year	Mintage	Fine	VF	XF	Unc
812	3	750 pcs.	225.00	350.00	450.00	750.00

500 KURUSH

36.0800 g, .917 GOLD, 1.0638 oz AGW
Accession date: AH1327
Mintname: *Salonika*

KM#	Year	Mintage	Fine	VF	XF	Unc
813	3	20 pcs.	2500.	4000.	5250.	6750.

MUHAMMAD VI

AH1336-1341/1918-1923AD

40 PARA

COPPER-NICKEL
Accession date: AH1336
Mintname: *Qustantiniyah*

KM#	Year	Mintage	VG	Fine	VF	XF
828	4	6.520	1.75	2.50	4.00	10.00

2 KURUSH

2.4055 g, .830 SILVER, .0642 oz ASW
Accession date: AH1336
Mintname: *Qustantiniyah*

KM#	Year	Mintage	VG	Fine	VF	XF
815	1	.025	50.00	100.00	150.00	220.00
	2	.003	75.00	125.00	200.00	350.00

5 KURUSH

6.0130 g, .830 SILVER, .1605 oz ASW
Accession date: AH1336
Mintname: *Qustantiniyah*

KM#	Year	Mintage	VG	Fine	VF	XF
816	1	.010	50.00	125.00	175.00	265.00
	2	2,000	75.00	150.00	225.00	385.00

10 KURUSH

12.0270 g, .830 SILVER, .3210 oz ASW
Accession date: AH1336
Mintname: *Qustantiniyah*

KM#	Year	Mintage	VG	Fine	VF	XF
817	1	—	120.00	250.00	400.00	600.00
	2	1,000	200.00	400.00	600.00	1000.

20 KURUSH

24.0550 g, .830 SILVER, .6419 oz ASW
Accession date: AH1336
Mintname: *Qustantiniyah*

KM#	Year	Mintage	VG	Fine	VF	XF
818	1	—	30.00	60.00	125.00	185.00
	2	1,530	350.00	525.00	650.00	925.00

25 KURUSH

1.8040 g, .917 GOLD, .0532 oz AGW
Accession date: AH1336
Mintname: *Qustantiniyah*

KM#	Year	Mintage	VG	Fine	VF	XF
819	1	—	30.00	40.00	50.00	100.00
	2	—	30.00	40.00	50.00	100.00
	3	—	40.00	75.00	150.00	200.00
	4	—	50.00	90.00	200.00	300.00
	5	—	80.00	140.00	240.00	375.00

1.7540 g, .917 GOLD, .0517 oz AGW
Monnaie de Luxe

KM#	Year	Mintage	VG	Fine	VF	XF
825	2	—	60.00	80.00	100.00	150.00
	3	—	60.00	80.00	100.00	150.00

50 KURUSH

3.6080 g, .917 GOLD, .1064 oz AGW
Accession date: AH1336
Mintname: *Qustantiniyah*

KM#	Year	Mintage	VG	Fine	VF	XF
820	1	—	100.00	125.00	150.00	300.00
	2	—	100.00	125.00	150.00	300.00
	3	—	150.00	200.00	250.00	500.00
	4	—	250.00	450.00	750.00	1500.
	5	—	200.00	300.00	450.00	1000.

100 KURUSH

7.2160 g, .917 GOLD, .2128 oz AGW
Accession date: AH1336
Mintname: *Qustantiniyah*

KM#	Year	Mintage	VG	Fine	VF	XF
821	1	—	BV	110.00	140.00	180.00
	2	—	BV	110.00	140.00	180.00
	3	—	150.00	180.00	225.00	450.00
	4	—	Reported, not confirmed			
	5	—	400.00	600.00	800.00	1000.

7.0160 g, .917 GOLD, .2068 oz AGW
Monnaie de Luxe

KM#	Year	Mintage	VG	Fine	VF	XF
826	2	—	250.00	300.00	325.00	375.00
	3	—	250.00	300.00	325.00	375.00

250 KURUSH

18.0400 g, .917 GOLD, .5319 oz AGW
Accession date: AH1336
Mintname: *Qustantiniyah*

KM#	Year	Mintage	VG	Fine	VF	XF
822	1	—	1750.	3000.	4500.	6500.
	2	26 pcs.	1750.	3000.	4500.	6500.
	3	31 pcs.	1750.	3000.	4500.	6500.
	4	—	Reported, not confirmed			
	5	—	Reported, not confirmed			

17.5400 g, .917 GOLD, .5169 oz AGW
Monnaie de Luxe

KM#	Year	Mintage	VG	Fine	VF	XF
827	2	.019	300.00	500.00	700.00	900.00
	3	Inc. Ab.	250.00	425.00	600.00	800.00

500 KURUSH

36.0800 g, .917 GOLD, 1.0638 oz AGW
Accession date: AH1336
Mintname: *Qustantiniyah*

KM#	Year	Mintage	VG	Fine	VF	XF
823	1	—	1000.	1200.	1450.	1800.
	2	—	1000.	1200.	1450.	1800.

KM#	Year	Mintage	VG	Fine	VF	XF
823	3	—	1000.	1200.	1450.	1800.
	4	23 pcs.	2000.	4000.	6000.	8000.
	5	22 pcs.	2000.	4000.	6000.	8000.

35.0800 g, .917 GOLD, 1.0338 oz AGW
Monnaie de Luxe

KM#	Year	Mintage	VG	Fine	VF	XF
824	1	—	1000.	1250.	1750.	2400.
	2	5,207	600.00	750.00	950.00	1300.
	3	Inc. Ab.	600.00	750.00	950.00	1300.
	4	88 pcs.	1500.	2000.	2500.	3200.

REPUBLIC

OLD MONETARY SYSTEM

100 PARA

ALUMINUM-BRONZE

KM#	Date	Mintage	Fine	VF	XF	Unc
830	AH1340	1.798	3.00	5.00	10.00	60.00
	1341	5.583	1.00	2.50	5.00	30.00
834	1926	4.388	1.00	2.50	6.00	32.00
	1928	—	150.00	225.00	400.00	600.00

5 KURUS

ALUMINUM-BRONZE

KM#	Date	Mintage	Fine	VF	XF	Unc
831	AH1340	5.023	1.00	2.50	7.00	32.00
	1341	23.545	1.00	2.50	7.00	32.00

KM#	Date	Mintage	Fine	VF	XF	Unc
835	1926	.356	1.00	2.50	7.00	32.00
	1928	—	175.00	250.00	500.00	700.00

10 KURUS

ALUMINUM-BRONZE

KM#	Date	Mintage	Fine	VF	XF	Unc
832	AH1340	4.836	1.50	3.00	8.00	35.00
	1341	14.223	1.50	3.00	8.00	35.00

NOTE: Varieties exist.

KM#	Date	Mintage	Fine	VF	XF	Unc
836	1926	.856	1.50	3.00	8.00	35.00
	1928	—	125.00	200.00	375.00	575.00

25 KURUS

NICKEL

KM#	Date	Mintage	Fine	VF	XF	Unc
833	AH1341	4.973	2.00	4.00	10.00	30.00

KM#	Date	Mintage	Fine	VF	XF	Unc
837	1926	.027	175.00	275.00	475.00	675.00
	1928	5.794	1.50	3.00	8.00	30.00

NOTE: Varieties exist.

Gold Coinage

The gold coins continued to be struck to the weights and finenesses of the old Ottoman system, but were tariffed at the going price of gold. The same continues to hold true today. Both regular and the "Monnaie de Luxe" series were produced.

25 KURUSH

1.8040 g, .917 GOLD, .0532 oz AGW
Rev: AH Date: *23 Nisan 1336.*

KM#	Date	Mintage	Fine	VF	XF	Unc
840	1926	4,539	40.00	75.00	140.00	175.00
	1927	.014	40.00	75.00	120.00	150.00
	1928	8,424	40.00	75.00	130.00	165.00
	1929	—	40.00	75.00	120.00	150.00

1.7540 g, .917 GOLD, .0517 oz AGW
Monnaie de Luxe

KM#	Date	Mintage	Fine	VF	XF	Unc
844	1927	4,103	50.00	75.00	125.00	200.00
	1928	4,549	50.00	75.00	125.00	200.00

50 KURUSH

3.6080 g, .917 GOLD, .1064 oz AGW
Rev: AH Date: *23 Nisan 1336.*

KM#	Date	Mintage	Fine	VF	XF	Unc
841	1926	2,168	60.00	100.00	165.00	225.00
	1927	2,116	60.00	100.00	165.00	225.00
	1928	2,431	60.00	100.00	165.00	225.00
	1929	—	60.00	100.00	165.00	225.00

3.5080 g, .917 GOLD, .1034 oz AGW
Monnaie de Luxe

KM#	Date	Mintage	Fine	VF	XF	Unc
845	1927	3,903	75.00	150.00	250.00	375.00
	1928	3,620	75.00	150.00	250.00	375.00

100 KURUSH

7.2160 g, .917 GOLD, .2128 oz AGW
Rev: AH Date: *23 Nisan 1336.*

KM#	Date	Mintage	Fine	VF	XF	Unc
842	1926	1,073	110.00	130.00	250.00	350.00
	1927	—	110.00	130.00	250.00	350.00
	1928	920 pcs.	110.00	130.00	250.00	350.00
	1929	—	110.00	130.00	250.00	350.00

7.0160 g, .917 GOLD, .2069 oz AGW
Monnaie de Luxe

KM#	Date	Mintage	Fine	VF	XF	Unc
846	1927	8,676	125.00	150.00	250.00	350.00
	1928	6,092	125.00	150.00	250.00	350.00

250 KURUSH

18.0400 g, .917 GOLD, .5319 oz AGW
Rev: AH Date: *23 Nisan 1336.*

KM#	Date	Mintage	Fine	VF	XF	Unc
843	1926	604 pcs.	250.00	275.00	350.00	500.00
	1927	886 pcs.	250.00	275.00	350.00	500.00
	1928	110 pcs.	250.00	275.00	350.00	500.00
	1929	—	250.00	275.00	350.00	500.00

17.5400 g, .917 GOLD, .5169 oz AGW
Monnaie de Luxe

KM#	Date	Mintage	Fine	VF	XF	Unc
847	1927	7,411	BV	250.00	350.00	500.00
	1928	5,045	BV	250.00	350.00	500.00

500 KURUSH

36.0800 g, .917 GOLD, 1.0638 oz AGW
Rev: AH Date: *23 Nisan 1336.*

KM#	Date	Mintage	Fine	VF	XF	Unc
839	1925	226 pcs.	BV	500.00	550.00	750.00
	1926	2,268	BV	500.00	550.00	750.00
	1927	4,011	BV	500.00	550.00	750.00
	1928	375 pcs.	BV	500.00	550.00	750.00
	1929	—	BV	500.00	550.00	750.00

35.0800 g, .917 GOLD, 1.0344 oz AGW
Monnaie de Luxe

KM#	Date	Mintage	Fine	VF	XF	Unc
848	1927	5,097	BV	500.00	600.00	800.00
	1928	2,242	BV	500.00	600.00	800.00

DECIMAL COINAGE

Western numerals and Latin alphabet

40 Para = 1 Kurus
100 Kurus = 1 Lira

NOTE: Mintage figures of the 1930's and early 1940's may not be exact. It is suspected that in some cases, figures for a particular year may include quantities struck with the previous year's date.

10 PARA

(1/4 Kurus)

ALUMINUM-BRONZE

KM#	Date	Mintage	VG	Fine	VF	XF
868	1940	30.800	.25	.75	2.50	5.00
	1941	22.400	.25	.75	2.50	5.00
	1942	26.800	.25	.75	2.50	5.00

1/2 KURUS

(20 Para)

BRASS

KM#	Date	Mintage	Fine	VF	XF	Unc
884	1948	150 pcs.	—	—	300.00	550.00

NOTE: Not released to circulation.

KURUS

COPPER-NICKEL

KM#	Date	Mintage	VG	Fine	VF	XF
861	1935	.784	2.00	4.00	6.00	15.00
	1936	5.300	.25	1.00	2.50	7.00
	1937	4.500	.25	1.00	2.50	7.00

KM#	Date	Mintage	VG	Fine	VF	XF
867	1938	16.400	.25	.50	1.50	4.00
	1939	21.600	.25	.50	1.50	4.00
	1940	8.800	.50	1.00	2.00	8.00
	1941	6.700	.25	.75	1.75	5.00
	1942	10.800	.25	.50	1.50	4.00
	1943	4.000	.25	.75	1.75	5.00
	1944	6.000	.25	.75	1.75	5.00

BRASS

KM#	Date	Mintage	Fine	VF	XF	Unc
881	1947	.890	1.00	1.50	2.50	5.00
	1948	35.470	.15	.25	.50	1.50
	1949	29.530	.15	.25	.50	1.25
	1950	32.800	.15	.25	.50	1.25
	1951	6.310	.15	.30	.75	2.25

Olive Branch

KM#	Date	Mintage	Fine	VF	XF	Unc
895	1961	1.180	—	—	.10	.30
	1962	3.620	—	—	.10	.25
	1963	1.085	—	—	.10	.30

BRONZE

KM#	Date	Mintage	Fine	VF	XF	Unc
895a	1963	1.180	—	—	.10	.30
	1964	2.520	—	—	.10	.20
	1965	1.860	—	—	.10	.20
	1966	1.820	—	—	.10	.20
	1967	2.410	—	—	.10	.20
	1968	1.040	—	—	.10	.20
	1969	.900	—	—	.10	.20
	1970	1.960	—	—	.10	.20
	1971	2.940	—	—	.10	.20
	1972	.720	—	—	.10	.30
	1973	.540	—	—	.10	.30
	1974	.510	—	—	.10	.30

ALUMINUM

KM#	Date	Mintage	Fine	VF	XF	Unc
895b	1975	.690	—	.10	.25	1.00
	1976	.200	—	.10	.25	1.50
	1977	.108	—	.10	.25	1.75

BRONZE
F.A.O. Issue

KM#	Date	Mintage	Fine	VF	XF	Unc
924	1979	.015	—	.25	1.00	3.00

ALUMINUM

KM#	Date	Mintage	Fine	VF	XF	Unc
924a	1979	.015	—	.25	1.00	3.00

2-1/2 KURUS

BRASS

KM#	Date	Mintage	Fine	VF	XF	Unc
885	1948	24.720	.25	.50	1.00	3.00
	1949	23.720	.25	.50	1.00	3.00
	1950	11.560	.35	.65	1.25	4.00
	1951	2.000	2.00	5.00	12.00	40.00

5 KURUS

COPPER-NICKEL

KM#	Date	Mintage	VG	Fine	VF	XF
862	1935	.100	2.00	5.00	8.00	20.00
	1936	2.900	.50	1.00	2.00	8.00
	1937	4.060	.30	.75	1.50	8.00
	1938	13.380	.25	.50	1.00	5.00
	1939	12.520	.25	.50	1.00	5.00
	1940	4.340	.30	.75	1.50	5.00
	1942	10.160	.20	.40	1.00	5.00
	1943	15.360	.20	.40	1.00	5.00

BRASS

KM#	Date	Mintage	Fine	VF	XF	Unc
887	1949	4.500	.25	.50	1.00	4.00
	1950	45.900	.15	.35	.75	3.00
	1951	29.600	.15	.35	.75	3.00
	1955	15.300	.15	.35	.75	3.00
	1956	21.380	.15	.35	.75	3.00
	1957	3.320	.25	.50	1.00	4.00

BRONZE, 2.50 g

KM#	Date	Mintage	Fine	VF	XF	Unc
890.1	1958	25.870	.10	.25	.50	1.50
	1959	21.580	—	—	.10	.30
	1960	17.150	—	—	.10	.30
	1961	11.110	—	—	.10	.20
	1962	15.280	—	—	.10	.30
	1963	17.680	—	—	.10	.20
	1964	18.190	—	—	.10	.30
	1965	19.170	—	—	.10	.20
	1966	19.840	—	—	.10	.30
	1967	16.170	—	—	.10	.30
	1968	26.050	—	—	.10	.30

Reduced weight, 2.00 g

KM#	Date	Mintage	Fine	VF	XF	Unc
890.2	1969	33.630	—	—	.10	.30
	1970	29.360	—	—	.10	.30
	1971	17.440	—	—	.10	.30
	1972	22.670	—	—	.10	.20
	1973	17.370	—	—	.10	.20

1.35 g

KM#	Date	Mintage	Fine	VF	XF	Unc
890.3	1974	13.540	—	—	.10	.20

ALUMINUM

KM#	Date	Mintage	Fine	VF	XF	Unc
890a	1975	1.560	—	—	.10	.30
	1976	1.321	—	—	.10	.30
	1977	.190	—	.10	.20	1.00

F.A.O. Issue

KM#	Date	Mintage	Fine	VF	XF	Unc
906	1975	1.019	—	—	.50	1.50

F.A.O. Issue

KM#	Date	Mintage	Fine	VF	XF	Unc
907	1976	.017	—	.50	1.50	4.00

BRONZE
F.A.O. Issue

KM#	Date	Mintage	Fine	VF	XF	Unc
934	1980	.013	—	.25	.75	2.00

10 KURUS

COPPER-NICKEL

KM#	Date	Mintage	VG	Fine	VF	XF
863	1935	.060	2.00	5.00	8.00	20.00
	1936	3.580	.75	2.00	5.00	12.50
	1937	3.020	.50	1.00	4.00	8.00
	1938	6.610	.50	1.00	4.00	8.00
	1939	4.610	.50	1.00	2.50	5.00
	1940	6.960	.50	1.00	2.50	5.00

BRASS

KM#	Date	Mintage	Fine	VF	XF	Unc
888	1949	27.000	.10	.25	.75	3.00
	1951	6.200	.10	.25	.75	3.00
	1955	10.090	.10	.25	.75	3.00
	1956	9.910	.10	.25	.75	3.00

BRONZE, 4.00 g

KM#	Date	Mintage	Fine	VF	XF	Unc
891.1	1958	14.770	—	.10	.25	1.50
	1959	11.160	—	—	.10	.40
	1960	9.450	—	—	.10	.40
	1961	5.370	—	—	.10	.40
	1962	9.250	—	—	.10	.40
	1963	10.390	—	—	.10	.40
	1964	9.890	—	—	.10	.40
	1965	10.480	—	—	.10	.40
	1966	12.200	—	—	.10	.40
	1967	11.410	—	—	.10	.40
	1968	1.862	—	—	.10	.40

Reduced weight, 3.50 g

KM#	Date	Mintage	Fine	VF	XF	Unc
891.2	1969	21.190	—	—	.10	.20
	1970	19.930	—	—	.10	.20
	1971	14.780	—	—	.10	.20
	1972	17.960	—	—	.10	.20
	1973	11.930	—	—	.10	.20

2.50 g

KM#	Date	Mintage	Fine	VF	XF	Unc
891.3	1974	9.280	—	—	.10	.20

ALUMINUM

KM#	Date	Mintage	Fine	VF	XF	Unc
891a	1975	2.165	—	—	.10	.30
	1976	.559	—	.10	.20	.60
	1977	.106	—	.10	.50	1.00

BRONZE
F.A.O. Issue, 3.50 g

KM#	Date	Mintage	Fine	VF	XF	Unc
898.1	1971	.630	—	.10	.15	.75
	1972	.500	—	.10	.50	2.00
	1973	.010	—	4.00	10.00	30.00

2.50 g

KM#	Date	Mintage	Fine	VF	XF	Unc
898.2	1974	.605	—	.10	.50	1.00

ALUMINUM

KM#	Date	Mintage	Fine	VF	XF	Unc
898a	1975	.517	—	.10	.25	.75

F.A.O. Issue

KM#	Date	Mintage	Fine	VF	XF	Unc
908	1976	.017	—	.50	2.00	5.00

BRONZE
F.A.O. Issue

KM#	Date	Mintage	Fine	VF	XF	Unc
935	1980	.013	—	.25	1.00	2.50

25 KURUS

3.0000 g, .830 SILVER, .0801 oz ASW

KM#	Date	Mintage	VG	Fine	VF	XF
864	1935	.888	1.00	2.00	6.00	15.00
	1936	10.576	1.00	2.00	10.00	20.00
	1937	8.536	1.00	2.00	10.00	20.00

NICKEL-BRONZE

KM#	Date	Mintage	VG	Fine	VF	XF
880	1944	20.000	.25	.50	1.00	2.50
	1945	5.328	.50	1.00	1.50	3.00
	1946	2.672	.50	1.25	2.00	4.00

BRASS

KM#	Date	Mintage	Fine	VF	XF	Unc
886	1948	18.000	.10	.20	.40	1.25
	1949	21.000	.10	.20	.40	1.25
	1951	2.000	.25	.50	2.50	10.00
	1955	9.624	.10	.20	.40	1.25
	1956	14.376	.10	.20	.40	1.25

STAINLESS STEEL
Obv: Smooth ground under woman's feet.

KM#	Date	Mintage	Fine	VF	XF	Unc
892.1	1959	21.864	.10	.15	.30	.75

Obv: Rough ground under woman's feet.

KM#	Date	Mintage	Fine	VF	XF	Unc
892.2	1960	14.778	—	.10	.15	.70
	1961	7.248	—	.10	.15	1.00
	1962	10.722	—	.10	.15	.80
	1963	11.016	—	.10	.15	.80
	1964	13.962	—	.10	.15	.70
	1965	9.816	—	.10	.15	.70
	1966	2.424	—	.10	.15	.80

Reduced weight, 4.00 g

KM#	Date	Mintage	Fine	VF	XF	Unc
892.3	1966	7.596	—	—	.10	.50
	1967	17.022	—	—	.10	.25
	1968	31.482	—	—	.10	.25
	1969	34.566	—	—	.10	.25
	1970	32.960	—	—	.10	.25
	1973	20.496	—	—	.10	.25
	1974	16.602	—	—	.10	.25
	1977	10.204	—	—	.10	.25
	1978	.185	.35	.75	1.25	2.00

50 KURUS

6.0000 g, .830 SILVER, .1601 oz ASW

KM#	Date	Mintage	VG	Fine	VF	XF
865	1935	.630	3.00	6.00	10.00	25.00
	1936	5.082	2.00	5.00	8.00	17.00
	1937	4.270	12.00	30.00	50.00	100.00

4.0000 g, .600 SILVER, .0772 oz ASW

KM#	Date	Mintage	Fine	VF	XF	Unc
882	1947	9.296	1.00	2.50	3.50	6.00
	1948	12.704	1.00	2.50	3.50	6.00

NOTE: Edge varieties exist.

STAINLESS STEEL

KM#	Date	Mintage	Fine	VF	XF	Unc
899	1971	16.756	—	.10	.15	.25
	1972	22.152	—	.10	.15	.25
	1973	18.928	—	.10	.15	.25
	1974	14.480	—	.10	.15	.25
	1975	27.714	—	.10	.15	.25
	1976	27.476	—	.10	.15	.25
	1977	5.062	—	.10	.15	.30
	1979	3.714	—	.10	.15	.30

F.A.O. Issue

KM#	Date	Mintage	Fine	VF	XF	Unc
913	1978	.010	—	.20	.50	1.75

F.A.O. Issue

KM#	Date	Mintage	Fine	VF	XF	Unc
925	1979	.020	—	.20	.50	1.75

F.A.O. Issue

KM#	Date	Mintage	Fine	VF	XF	Unc
936	1980	.013	—	.10	.20	1.00

100 KURUS
(1 Lira)

12.0000 g, .830 SILVER, .3203 oz ASW
Obv: High star.

KM#	Date	Mintage	VG	Fine	VF	XF
860.1	1934	.718	15.00	30.00	40.00	70.00

Obv: Low star.

KM#	Date	Mintage	VG	Fine	VF	XF
860.2	1934	Inc. Ab.	10.00	20.00	30.00	40.00

1/2 LIRA

7.8600 g, .925 SILVER, .2337 oz ASW
100th Anniversary of Ataturk's Birth

KM#	Date	Mintage	Fine	VF	XF	Unc
941	1981	.025	—	—	—	12.50
		8.0000 g, .917 GOLD, .2358 oz AGW				
941a	1981	.025	—	—	—	125.00

LIRA

12.0000 g, .830 SILVER, .3203 oz ASW
Kemal Ataturk

KM#	Date	Mintage	VG	Fine	VF	XF
866	1937	1.624	5.00	10.00	15.00	30.00
	1938	8.282	25.00	50.00	75.00	150.00
	1939	.376	5.00	10.00	15.00	30.00

Ismet Inonu

KM#	Date	Mintage	VG	Fine	VF	XF
869	1940	.253	7.50	12.50	15.00	20.00
	1941	6.167	4.50	10.00	12.50	20.00

7.5000 g, .600 SILVER, .1447 oz ASW

KM#	Date	Mintage	Fine	VF	XF	Unc
883	1947	11.104	1.50	3.50	5.00	8.50
	1948	16.896	1.50	3.00	4.00	7.50

NOTE: Edge varieties exist.

COPPER-NICKEL

KM#	Date	Mintage	Fine	VF	XF	Unc
889	1957	25.000	.25	.50	1.00	2.50

STAINLESS STEEL

KM#	Date	Mintage	Fine	VF	XF	Unc
889a.1	1959	7.452	—	.10	.20	.50
	1960	11.436	—	.10	.20	.50
	1961	2.100	—	.10	.20	1.00
	1962	4.228	—	.10	.20	.50
	1963	4.316	—	.10	.20	.50
	1964	4.976	—	.10	.20	.50
	1965	5.348	—	.10	.20	.50
	1966	8.040	—	.10	.20	.50
	1977	—	—	.10	.20	.50
		Reduced weight, 7.00 g				
889a.2	1967	10.444	—	.10	.20	.50
	1968	12.728	—	.10	.20	.50
	1969	6.612	—	.10	.20	.50
	1970	8.652	—	.10	.20	.50
	1971	10.504	—	.10	.20	.50
	1972	26.512	—	.10	.20	.50
	1973	12.596	—	.10	.20	.50
	1974	11.596	—	.10	.20	.50
	1975	20.348	—	.10	.20	.50
	1976	23.144	—	.10	.20	.50
	1977	30.244	—	.10	.20	.50
	1978	22.156	—	.10	.20	.50
	1979	9.289	—	.10	.20	.50
	1980	3.585	—	.10	.20	.50

F.A.O. Issue

KM#	Date	Mintage	Fine	VF	XF	Unc
914	1978	.020	—	.50	1.00	2.00

F.A.O. Issue
Similar to 50 Kurus, KM#925.

KM#	Date	Mintage	Fine	VF	XF	Unc
926	1979	.020	—	.50	1.00	2.00

F.A.O. Issue

KM#	Date	Mintage	Fine	VF	XF	Unc
937	1980	.013	—	.40	.75	1.50

16.0000 g, .925 SILVER, .4758 oz ASW
100th Anniversary of Ataturk's Birth

KM#	Date	Mintage	Fine	VF	XF	Unc
942	1981	—	—	—	—	22.50
		16.0000 g, .917 GOLD, .4716 oz AGW				
942a	1981	.025	—	—	—	250.00

ALUMINUM

KM#	Date	Mintage	Fine	VF	XF	Unc
943	1981	.015	—	—	.10	.25
	1982	.017	—	—	.10	.25

Rev: Large (5mm) 1.

KM#	Date	Mintage	Fine	VF	XF	Unc
962.1	1983	.090	—	—	.10	.20
	1984	.024	—	—	.10	.20
		Rev: Small (3.5mm) 1.				
962.2	1985	.042	—	—	.10	.20
	1987	.520	—	—	.10	.20
	1988	.130	—	—	.10	.20
	1989	—	—	—	.10	.20

Obv: Similar to KM#943. Rev: Crescent opens right w/thin "1".

KM#	Date	Mintage	Fine	VF	XF	Unc
990	1982	—	—	—	—	—

2-1/2 LIRA

STAINLESS STEEL, 12.00 g

KM#	Date	Mintage	Fine	VF	XF	Unc
893.1	1960	4.015	—	.25	1.00	6.00
	1961	1.222	—	.25	1.00	9.00
	1962	3.636	—	.25	1.00	6.00
	1963	3.108	—	.25	1.00	6.00
	1964	2.710	—	.25	1.00	6.00
	1965	1.246	—	.25	1.00	7.00
	1966	1.788	—	.25	1.00	6.00
	1967	5.333	—	.25	1.00	5.00
	1968	2.707	—	.25	1.00	5.00
		Reduced weight, 9.00 g				
893.2	1969	1.378	—	.15	.75	3.50
	1970	3.777	—	.15	.75	3.50
	1971	2.170	—	.15	.75	3.50
	1972	9.147	—	.15	.50	3.50
	1973	4.348	—	.15	.50	4.00
	1974	3.816	—	.15	.50	4.00
	1975	9.811	—	.15	.50	3.00
	1976	3.952	—	.15	.50	3.00
	1977	21.473	—	.10	.25	.50
	1978	15.738	—	.10	.25	.50
	1979	6.074	—	.10	.25	.50
	1980	2.621	—	.10	.25	.75

F.A.O. Issue

KM#	Date	Mintage	Fine	VF	XF	Unc
896	1970	.200	—	.10	.25	.75

F.A.O. Issue

KM#	Date	Mintage	Fine	VF	XF	Unc
910	1977	.025	—	.25	.50	1.25

F.A.O. Issue

KM#	Date	Mintage	Fine	VF	XF	Unc
915	1978	.010	—	1.00	2.00	4.00

F.A.O. Issue

KM#	Date	Mintage	Fine	VF	XF	Unc
927	1979	.020	—	1.00	2.00	4.00

F.A.O. Issue

KM#	Date	Mintage	Fine	VF	XF	Unc
938	1980	.013	—	.50	1.50	3.00

5 LIRA

STAINLESS STEEL

KM#	Date	Mintage	Fine	VF	XF	Unc
905	1974	2.842	—	.15	.75	3.00
	1975	10.855	—	.15	.25	2.00
	1976	17.532	—	.15	.25	2.00
	1977	1.617	—	.15	.75	3.00
	1978	.076	1.50	2.50	3.50	6.00
	1979	6.074	—	.15	.30	1.00

International Women's Year and F.A.O. Issue

KM#	Date	Mintage	Fine	VF	XF	Unc
909	1976	.017	—	1.50	2.50	5.00

F.A.O. Issue

KM#	Date	Mintage	Fine	VF	XF	Unc
911	1977	.025	—	.75	1.50	2.00

F.A.O. Issue

KM#	Date	Mintage	Fine	VF	XF	Unc
916	1978	.010	—	1.25	3.00	4.00

F.A.O. Issue

KM#	Date	Mintage	Fine	VF	XF	Unc
928	1979	.020	—	1.25	3.00	4.00

F.A.O. Issue

KM#	Date	Mintage	Fine	VF	XF	Unc
939	1980	.013	—	1.00	2.00	3.00

ALUMINUM
Rev: Crescent opens left.

KM#	Date	Mintage	Fine	VF	XF	Unc
944	1981	62.355	—	—	.10	.30

Rev: Crescent opens right.

KM#	Date	Mintage	Fine	VF	XF	Unc
949.1	1982	69.975	—	—	.10	.30

Rev: Bolder, larger 5.

KM#	Date	Mintage	Fine	VF	XF	Unc
949.2	1983	—	—	—	.10	.30

KM#	Date	Mintage	Fine	VF	XF	Unc
963	1984	17.316	—	—	.10	.30
	1985	9.405	—	—	.10	.30
	1986	.010	—	—	.20	.50
	1987	2.145	—	—	.20	.50
	1988	.035	—	—	.20	.50
	1989	—	—	—	.20	.50

10 LIRA

15.0000 g, .830 SILVER, .4003 oz ASW

KM#	Date	Mintage	Fine	VF	XF	Unc
894	1960	8.000	—	4.50	6.00	9.00
	1960	—	—	—	P/L	15.00

ALUMINUM
Rev: Crescent opens left.

KM#	Date	Mintage	Fine	VF	XF	Unc
945	1981	25.520	—	.10	.25	.50

Rev: Crescent opens right.

KM#	Date	Mintage	Fine	VF	XF	Unc
950.1	1982	17.092	—	.10	.25	.50

KM#	Date	Mintage	Fine	VF	XF	Unc
950.2	1983	90.300	—	.10	.25	.60

KM#	Date	Mintage	Fine	VF	XF	Unc
964	1984	23.360	—	.10	.25	.50
	1985	41.736	—	—	.10	.25
	1986	79.780	—	—	.10	.25
	1987	61.060	—	—	.10	.25
	1988	13.312	—	—	.10	.25
	1989	—	—	—	.10	.25

20 LIRA

ALUMINUM
World Food Day

KM#	Date	Mintage	Fine	VF	XF	Unc
946	1981	.010	—	—	1.25	2.25

COPPER-NICKEL

KM#	Date	Mintage	Fine	VF	XF	Unc
965	1984	1.644	—	.10	.25	1.00

25 LIRA

14.6000 g, .830 SILVER, .3896 oz ASW

50th Anniversary of National Assembly

KM#	Date	Mintage	Fine	VF	XF	Unc
897	1970	.023	—	—	10.00	15.00
	1970	Inc. Ab.	—	—	Proof	35.00

ALUMINUM

KM#	Date	Mintage	Fine	VF	XF	Unc
975	1985	37.014	—	—	.10	.35
	1986	50.820	—	—	.10	.35
	1987	59.022	—	—	.10	.35
	1988	40.137	—	—	.10	.35
	1989	—	—	—	.10	.35

50 LIRA

19.0000 g, .830 SILVER, .5070 oz ASW
900th Anniversary - Battle of Malazgirt

KM#	Date	Mintage	Fine	VF	XF	Unc
900	1971	.033	—	—	12.00	22.50
	1971	Inc. Ab.	—	—	Proof	30.00

20.1000 g, .830 SILVER, .5363 oz ASW
50th Anniversary - Kemal Ataturk's Entry Into Smyrna

KM#	Date	Mintage	Fine	VF	XF	Unc
901	1972	.172	—	—	8.00	12.00
	1972	—	—	—	Proof	18.00

13.0000 g, .900 SILVER, .3761 oz ASW
50th Anniversary of Republic

KM#	Date	Mintage	Fine	VF	XF	Unc
902	1973	.070	—	—	6.00	9.00
	1973	Inc. Ab.	—	—	Proof	20.00

8.8500 g, .830 SILVER, .2361 oz ASW
F.A.O. Issue

KM#	Date	Mintage	Fine	VF	XF	Unc
912	1977	.025	—	—	7.00	10.00

COPPER-NICKEL-ZINC

KM#	Date	Mintage	Fine	VF	XF	Unc
966	1984	14.731	—	.10	.20	.50
	1985	52.658	—	.10	.20	.40
	1986	82.588	—	.10	.20	.40
	1987	41.918	—	.10	.20	.40

ALUMINUM-BRONZE

KM#	Date	Mintage	Fine	VF	XF	Unc
987	1988	3.236	—	—	—	.10
	1989	—	—	—	—	.10
	1990	—	—	—	—	.10

100 LIRA

22.0000 g, .900 SILVER, .6367 oz ASW
50th Anniversary of Republic

KM#	Date	Mintage	Fine	VF	XF	Unc
903	1973	.065	—	—	10.00	15.00

COPPER-NICKEL
World Championship Soccer - Madrid

KM#	Date	Mintage	Fine	VF	XF	Unc
951	1982	.100	.50	1.00	2.00	5.00

COPPER-NICKEL-ZINC

KM#	Date	Mintage	Fine	VF	XF	Unc
967	1984	.758	—	.15	.30	.75
	1985	.866	—	.15	.30	.75
	1986	12.064	—	.15	.30	.75
	1987	98.990	—	.10	.20	.60
	1988	28.204	—	.10	.20	.50

ALUMINUM-BRONZE

KM#	Date	Mintage	Fine	VF	XF	Unc
988	1988	16.145	—	—	—	.10
	1989	—	—	—	—	.10
	1990	—	—	—	—	.10
	1991	—	—	—	—	.10
	1992	—	—	—	—	.10

150 LIRA

9.0000 g, .800 SILVER, .2314 oz ASW
World Cup Soccer Championship

KM#	Date	Mintage	Fine	VF	XF	Unc
917	1978	5,000	—	—	—	25.00

F.A.O. Issue
Reeded edge

KM#	Date	Mintage	Fine	VF	XF	Unc
918.1	1978	.010	—	—	—	12.50

Lettered edge

KM#	Date	Mintage	Fine	VF	XF	Unc
918.2	1978	2,500	—	—	Proof	22.50

F.A.O. Issue
Reeded edge

KM#	Date	Mintage	Fine	VF	XF	Unc
929.1	1979	.010	—	—	—	12.50

Lettered edge

KM#	Date	Mintage	Fine	VF	XF	Unc
929.2	1979	2,500	—	—	Proof	22.50

200 LIRA

9.0000 g, .830 SILVER, .2402 oz ASW

705th Anniversary - Death of Mevlana

KM#	Date	Mintage	Fine	VF	XF	Unc
919	1978	.010	—	—	—	20.00
	1978	1,000	—	—	Proof	35.00

500 LIRA

6.0000 g, .917 GOLD, .1769 oz AGW
50th Anniversary of Republic

KM#	Date	Mintage	Fine	VF	XF	Unc
904	1973	.030	—	—	—	100.00

8.0000 g, .917 GOLD, .2358 oz AGW
F.A.O. Issue

KM#	Date	Mintage	Fine	VF	XF	Unc
920	1978	650 pcs.	—	—	Proof	175.00

705th Anniversary - Death of Jalaladdin Rumi

KM#	Date	Mintage	Fine	VF	XF	Unc
921	1978	900 pcs.	—	—	Proof	175.00

F.A.O. Issue

KM#	Date	Mintage	Fine	VF	XF	Unc
930	1979	783 pcs.	—	—	Proof	175.00

23.3300 g, .925 SILVER, .6938 oz ASW
UNICEF and I.Y.C.

KM#	Date	Mintage	Fine	VF	XF	Unc
931	1979(1981)	.010	—	—	—	20.00

9.0000 g, .900 SILVER, .2604 oz ASW
F.A.O. Issue
Reeded edge

KM#	Date	Mintage	Fine	VF	XF	Unc
940.1	1980	.013	—	—	—	12.50

Lettered edge

KM#	Date	Mintage	Fine	VF	XF	Unc
940.2	1980	4,000	—	—	Proof	25.00

23.3300 g, .925 SILVER, .6938 oz ASW
World Championship Soccer - Madrid

KM#	Date	Mintage	Fine	VF	XF	Unc
952	1982	.012	—	—	Proof	22.50

World Championship Soccer - Madrid

KM#	Date	Mintage	Fine	VF	XF	Unc
953	1982	.012	—	—	Proof	22.50

COPPER-NICKEL
Lydia - First Coin in the World

KM#	Date	Mintage	Fine	VF	XF	Unc
957	1983	3,542	—	—	3.50	7.50

World Fisheries Conference

KM#	Date	Mintage	Fine	VF	XF	Unc
968	ND(1984)	3,000	—	—	2.50	6.00

28.2800 g, .925 SILVER, .8411 oz ASW

KM#	Date	Mintage	Fine	VF	XF	Unc
968a	ND(1984)	.763	—	—	Proof	45.00

47.5400 g, .917 GOLD, 1.4009 oz AGW

KM#	Date	Mintage	Fine	VF	XF	Unc
968b	ND(1984)					
		74 pcs.	—	—	Proof	1550.

COPPER-NICKEL
40th Anniversary of F.A.O.

KM#	Date	Mintage	Fine	VF	XF	Unc
979	ND(1986)	3,000	—	—	Proof	10.00

ALUMINUM-BRONZE

KM#	Date	Mintage	Fine	VF	XF	Unc
989	1988	6.992	—	—	—	.40
	1989	—	—	—	—	.40
	1990	—	—	—	—	.40
	1991	—	—	—	—	.40

1000 LIRA

16.0000 g, .917 GOLD, .4717 oz AGW
F.A.O Issue

KM#	Date	Mintage	Fine	VF	XF	Unc
922	1978	650 pcs.	—	—	Proof	375.00

705th Anniversary - Death of Mevlana

KM#	Date	Mintage	Fine	VF	XF	Unc
923	1978	450 pcs.	—	—	Proof	375.00

F.A.O. Issue

KM#	Date	Mintage	Fine	VF	XF	Unc
932	1979	900 pcs.	—	—	Proof	375.00

COPPER-NICKEL
Shelter For The Homeless

KM#	Date	Mintage	Fine	VF	XF	Unc
980	ND(1987)	—	—	—	Proof	6.00

NICKEL-BRONZE
Peace

KM#	Date	Mintage	Fine	VF	XF	Unc
985	1986	—	—	—	Proof	6.00

COPPER-NICKEL
400th Anniversary - Death of Architect Sinan

KM#	Date	Mintage	Fine	VF	XF	Unc
991	1988	—	—	—	Proof	8.00

Environmental Protection

KM#	Date	Mintage	Fine	VF	XF	Unc
996	1990	.500	—	—	—	12.00

COPPER-ZINC-NICKEL

KM#	Date	Mintage	Fine	VF	XF	Unc
997	1990	—	—	—	—	3.00
	1991	—	—	—	—	3.00

1500 LIRA

16.0000 g, .925 SILVER, .4758 oz ASW
F.A.O. Issue

KM#	Date	Mintage	Fine	VF	XF	Unc
947	1981	6,000	—	—	—	20.00
	1982	500 pcs.	—	—	—	35.00

World Food Day

KM#	Date	Mintage	Fine	VF	XF	Unc
958	1983	1,552	—	—	Proof	37.50

2500 LIRA

NICKEL-BRONZE

KM#	Date	Mintage	Fine	VF	XF	Unc
1015	1991	—	—	—	—	5.00
	1992	—	—	—	—	5.00

3000 LIRA

28.2800 g, .925 SILVER, .8411 oz ASW
International Year of Disabled Persons

KM#	Date	Mintage	Fine	VF	XF	Unc
948	1981	.014	—	—	—	25.00
	1981	.016	—	—	Proof	35.00

International Year of the Scout

KM#	Date	Mintage	Fine	VF	XF	Unc
959	1982	.012	—	—	—	25.00
	1982	.014	—	—	Proof	35.00

16.0000 g, .925 SILVER, .4758 oz ASW
60th Anniversary of the Republic

KM#	Date	Mintage	Fine	VF	XF	Unc
960	1983	4,000	—	—	Proof	30.00

5000 LIRA

7.1300 g, .500 GOLD, .1146 oz AGW
World Championship Soccer - Madrid

KM#	Date	Mintage	Fine	VF	XF	Unc
954	1982	2,400	—	—	Proof	125.00

23.3300 g, .925 SILVER, .6939 oz ASW
Decade for Women

KM#	Date	Mintage	Fine	VF	XF	Unc
969	1984	.020	—	—	Proof	20.00

1984 Summer Olympics

KM#	Date	Mintage	Fine	VF	XF	Unc
970	ND(1984)	1760	—	—	Proof	40.00

Winter Olympics

KM#	Date	Mintage	Fine	VF	XF	Unc
971	1984	510 pcs.	—	—	Proof	75.00

50th Anniversary of Womans Suffrage

KM#	Date	Mintage	Fine	VF	XF	Unc
972	1984	1,000	—	—	Proof	50.00

500th Anniversary of Turkish Navy

M#	Date	Mintage	Fine	VF	XF	Unc
76	1985	1,000	—	—	Proof	50.00

Forestry

77	1985	2,000	—	—	Proof	40.00

Youth Year

78	1985	2,000	—	—	Proof	40.00

Architect - Sinan

011	1988	—	—	—	Proof	35.00

COPPER-NICKEL
Yunus Emre Sevgi Yili

005	1991	—	—	—	Proof	7.00

Turkish Jews

018	1992	—	—	—	Proof	7.00

NICKEL-BRONZE

025	1992	—	—	—	Proof	3.00

10000 LIRA

17.1700 g, .900 GOLD, .4900 oz AGW
UNICEF and I.Y.C.
Similar to 500 Lira, KM#931.

KM#	Date	Mintage	Fine	VF	XF	Unc
933	1979(1981)	4,450	—	—	Proof	225.00

23.3300 g, .925 SILVER, .6939 oz ASW
Soccer

986	1986	5,000	—	—	Proof	30.00

Soccer - Cactus

1009	1986	—	—	—	Proof	40.00

A. Ersoy - Poet

1010	1986	—	—	—	Proof	40.00

World Peace

1022	1986	*1,200	—	—	Proof	65.00

22.9700 g, .925 SILVER, .6832 oz ASW
Shelter For The Homeless

981	ND(1987)	—	—	—	Proof	45.00

130 Years of Turkish Forestry

982	1987	5,000	—	—	Proof	50.00

23.3300 g, .925 SILVER, .6939 oz ASW
Winter Olympics - Bear Holding Torch

KM#	Date	Mintage	Fine	VF	XF	Unc
983	1988	*.010	—	—	Proof	35.00

Summer Olympics - Torch

984	1988	1,000	—	—	—	150.00
	1988	*.010	—	—	Proof	35.00

20000 LIRA

23.3200 g, .925 SILVER, .6938 oz ASW
Environmental Protection

998	1988	5,000	—	—	Proof	45.00

400th Anniversary - Death of Architect Sinan
Similar to 1000 Lira, KM#991.

1001	1988	*5,000	—	—	Proof	40.00

Golden Horn

1012	1988	400 pcs.	—	—	Proof	100.00

Teacher's Day
Similar to 200,000 Lire, KM#1004.

1003	1989	1,013	—	—	Proof	35.00

Istanbul Metro

1013	1989	—	—	—	Proof	110.00

Soccer

992	1990	*5,000	—	—	Proof	40.00

75th Anniversary - Battle of Gallipoli

KM#	Date	Mintage	Fine	VF	XF	Unc
993	1990	*5,000	—	—	Proof	35.00

Soccer

KM#	Date	Mintage	Fine	VF	XF	Unc
995	1990	*5,000	—	—	Proof	35.00

70th Anniversary of Parliament

KM#	Date	Mintage	Fine	VF	XF	Unc
1014	1990	*5,000	—	—	Proof	35.00

28.2800 g, .925 SILVER, .8411 oz ASW
Winter Olympics - Speed Skater

KM#	Date	Mintage	Fine	VF	XF	Unc
999	ND(1990)	.015	—	—	Proof	40.00

Summer Olympics - Bicyclist

KM#	Date	Mintage	Fine	VF	XF	Unc
1000	ND(1990)	.015	—	—	Proof	40.00

30000 LIRA

15.9800 g, .917 GOLD, .4712 oz AGW
International Year of Disabled Persons

KM#	Date	Mintage	Fine	VF	XF	Unc
955	1981	4,000	—	—	—	400.00
	1981	3,000	—	—	Proof	450.00

International Year of the Scout
Obv: Denomination within sprays.

KM#	Date	Mintage	Fine	VF	XF	Unc
961	1983	2,000	—	—	—	450.00
	1983	2,000	—	—	Proof	500.00

50000 LIRA

7.1300 g, .900 GOLD, .2063 oz AGW
Decade for Women

KM#	Date	Mintage	Fine	VF	XF	Unc
973	1984	800 pcs.	—	—	Proof	250.00

22.8700 g, .925 SILVER, .6801 oz ASW
Yunus Emre Sevgi Yili

KM#	Date	Mintage	Fine	VF	XF	Unc
1006	1991	5,000	—	—	Proof	35.00

Mozart Opera

KM#	Date	Mintage	Fine	VF	XF	Unc
1007	1991	5,000	—	—	Proof	35.00

22.7700 g, .925 SILVER, .6772 oz ASW
Hmet Adnan Saygun - Musician

KM#	Date	Mintage	Fine	VF	XF	Unc
1019	ND(1991)	—	—	—	Proof	35.00

23.3300 g, .925 SILVER, .6858 oz ASW
Turkish Jews

KM#	Date	Mintage	Fine	VF	XF	Unc
1016	1992	*5,000	—	—	Proof	30.0

23.0800 g, .925 SILVER, .6184 oz ASW
200th Birthday of Rossini

KM#	Date	Mintage	Fine	VF	XF	Unc
1023	1992	—	—	—	Proof	35.0

1994 World Cup Soccer - Torch With Ball

KM#	Date	Mintage	Fine	VF	XF	Unc
1020	ND(1993)	*.020	—	—	Proof	50.0

1994 World Cup Soccer - Bridge Behind Player

KM#	Date	Mintage	Fine	VF	XF	Unc
1021	ND(1993)	*.020	—	—	Proof	50.0

25th Anniversary of Turkish Red Crescent

KM#	Date	Mintage	Fine	VF	XF	Unc
1024	1993	—	—	—	Proof	35.0

100000 LIRA

33.8200 g, .917 GOLD, .9972 oz AGW
Islamic World 15th Century

KM#	Date	Mintage	Fine	VF	XF	Unc
956	1982	.012	—	—	Proof	750.00

200000 LIRA

33.8200 g, .917 GOLD, .9972 oz AGW
50th Anniversary of Womans Suffrage

KM#	Date	Mintage	Fine	VF	XF	Unc
974	1984	58 pcs.	—	—	Proof	1850.

7.2160 g, .917 GOLD, .2126 oz AGW
400th Anniversary - Death of Architect Sinan
Similar to 1000 Lira, KM#991.

KM#	Date	Mintage	Fine	VF	XF	Unc
1002	1988	500 pcs.	—	—	Proof	250.00

Teacher's Day

KM#	Date	Mintage	Fine	VF	XF	Unc
1004	1989	197 pcs.	—	—	Proof	250.00

75th Anniversary of Battle of Gallipoli

KM#	Date	Mintage	Fine	VF	XF	Unc
994	1990	*500 pcs.	—	—	Proof	200.00

500000 LIRA

7.1300 g, .900 GOLD, .2063 oz AGW
Yunus Emre

KM#	Date	Mintage	Fine	VF	XF	Unc
1008	1991	500 pcs.	—	—	Proof	220.00

7.1400 g, .900 GOLD, .2066 oz AGW
Turkish Jews

KM#	Date	Mintage	Fine	VF	XF	Unc
1017	1992	—	—	—	Proof	220.00

BULLION ISSUES

Since 1943, the Turkish government has issued regular and deluxe gold coins in five denominations corresponding to the old traditional 25, 50, 100, 250, and 500 Kurush of the Ottoman period. The regular coins are all dated 1923, plus the year of the republic (e.g. 1923/40 = 1963), de Luxe coins bear actual AD dates. For a few years, 1944-1950, the bust of Ismet Inonu replaced that of Kemal Ataturk.

25 KURUSH

1.8041 g, .917 GOLD, .0532 oz AGW
Ismet Inonu

KM#	Date	Mintage	Fine	VF	XF	Unc
850	1923/20	—	BV	50.00	65.00	90.00
	1923/22	3,228	BV	50.00	75.00	120.00
	1923/23	2,757	BV	50.00	75.00	120.00
	1923/24	.046	BV	50.00	65.00	90.00
	1923/25	.020	BV	50.00	70.00	110.00
	1923/26	.011	BV	50.00	70.00	110.00

Kemal Ataturk

KM#	Date	Mintage	Fine	VF	XF	Unc
851	1923/20	.014	BV	25.00	30.00	45.00
	1923/27	.018	BV	25.00	30.00	45.00
	1923/28	.015	BV	25.00	30.00	45.00
	1923/29	.015	BV	25.00	30.00	45.00
	1923/30	.017	BV	25.00	30.00	45.00
	1923/31	.019	BV	25.00	30.00	45.00
	1923/32	5,455	BV	25.00	30.00	45.00
851	1923/33	.011	BV	25.00	30.00	45.00
	1923/34	.020	BV	25.00	30.00	45.00
	1923/35	.025	BV	25.00	30.00	45.00
	1923/36	.034	BV	25.00	30.00	45.00
	1923/37	.031	BV	25.00	30.00	45.00
	1923/38	.035	BV	25.00	30.00	45.00
	1923/39	.046	BV	25.00	30.00	45.00
	1923/40	.049	BV	25.00	30.00	45.00
	1923/41	.059	BV	25.00	30.00	45.00
	1923/42	.074	BV	25.00	30.00	45.00
	1923/43	.090	BV	25.00	30.00	45.00
	1923/44	.085	BV	25.00	30.00	45.00
	1923/45	.073	BV	25.00	30.00	45.00
	1923/46	.089	BV	25.00	30.00	45.00
	1923/47	.119	BV	25.00	30.00	45.00
	1923/48	.112	BV	25.00	30.00	45.00
	1923/49	.112	BV	25.00	30.00	45.00
	1923/50	.067	BV	25.00	30.00	45.00
	1923/51	.040	BV	25.00	30.00	45.00
	1923/52	.071	BV	25.00	30.00	45.00
	1923/53	.124	BV	25.00	30.00	45.00
	1923/54	196	BV	25.00	30.00	45.00
	1923/55	.112	BV	25.00	30.00	45.00
	1923/56	—	BV	25.00	30.00	45.00
	1923/57	—	BV	25.00	30.00	45.00

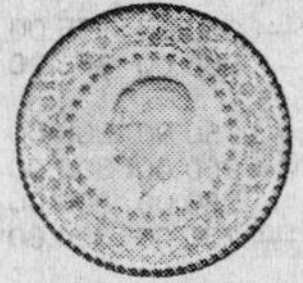
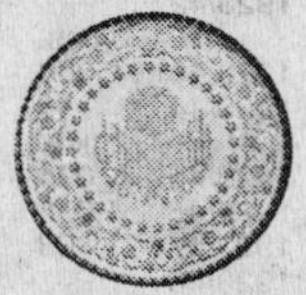

1.7540 g, .917 GOLD, .0517 oz AGW
Monnaie de Luxe
Kemal Ataturk

KM#	Date	Mintage	Fine	VF	XF	Unc
870	1942	138 pcs.	—	50.00	75.00	150.00
	1943	386 pcs.	—	50.00	75.00	125.00
	1944	811 pcs.	—	50.00	75.00	125.00
	1946	235 pcs.	—	50.00	75.00	150.00
	1950	2,053	—	30.00	40.00	60.00
	1951	2,035	—	30.00	40.00	60.00
	1952	3,374	—	30.00	40.00	60.00
	1953	1,944	—	30.00	40.00	60.00
	1954	2,244	—	30.00	40.00	60.00
	1955	2,573	—	30.00	40.00	60.00
	1956	4,004	—	30.00	40.00	60.00
	1957	8,842	—	30.00	40.00	60.00
	1958	9,546	—	30.00	40.00	60.00
	1959	.017	—	25.00	35.00	50.00
	1960	.019	—	25.00	35.00	50.00
	1961	.035	—	25.00	35.00	50.00
	1962	.031	—	25.00	35.00	50.00
	1963	.047	—	25.00	35.00	50.00
	1964	.057	—	25.00	35.00	50.00
	1965	.078	—	25.00	35.00	50.00
	1966	.106	—	25.00	35.00	50.00
	1967	.114	—	25.00	35.00	50.00
	1968	.152	—	25.00	35.00	50.00
	1969	.163	—	25.00	35.00	50.00
	1970	.224	—	25.00	35.00	50.00
	1971	.306	—	25.00	35.00	50.00
	1972	.271	—	25.00	35.00	50.00
	1973	.162	—	25.00	35.00	50.00
	1974	.141	—	25.00	35.00	50.00
	1975	.202	—	25.00	35.00	50.00
	1976	.583	—	25.00	35.00	50.00
	1977	1.089	—	25.00	35.00	50.00
	1978	.238	—	25.00	35.00	50.00
	1980	—	—	25.00	35.00	50.00

Monnaie de Luxe
Ismet Inonu

KM#	Date	Mintage	Fine	VF	XF	Unc
875	1943	Inc. KM870	80.00	100.00	150.00	200.00
	1944	Inc. KM870	80.00	100.00	150.00	200.00
	1945	592 pcs.	80.00	100.00	150.00	200.00
	1946	Inc. KM870	80.00	100.00	150.00	200.00
	1947	3,443	80.00	100.00	125.00	200.00
	1948	714 pcs.	80.00	100.00	150.00	200.00
	1949	552 pcs.	80.00	100.00	150.00	200.00

50 KURUSH

3.6083 g, .917 GOLD, .1064 oz AGW
Ismet Inonu

KM#	Date	Mintage	Fine	VF	XF	Unc
852	1923/20	—	60.00	100.00	125.00	175.00
	1923/22	1,093	60.00	100.00	125.00	175.00
	1923/23	897 pcs.	60.00	125.00	150.00	200.00
	1923/24	.011	60.00	100.00	125.00	175.00
	1923/25	3,004	60.00	100.00	125.00	175.00
	1923/26	817 pcs.	60.00	125.00	150.00	200.00
	1923/27	5,228	60.00	100.00	125.00	175.00

Kemal Ataturk

KM#	Date	Mintage	Fine	VF	XF	Unc
853	1923/20	.012	BV	50.00	60.00	75.00
	1923/27	I.A.	BV	50.00	60.00	75.00
	1923/28	3,300	BV	50.00	60.00	75.00
	1923/29	6,384	BV	50.00	60.00	75.00
853	1923/30	4,590	BV	50.00	60.00	75.00
	1923/31	9,068	BV	50.00	60.00	75.00
	1923/32	4,344	BV	50.00	60.00	75.00
	1923/33	3,958	BV	50.00	60.00	75.00
	1923/34	9,499	BV	50.00	60.00	75.00
	1923/35	9,307	BV	50.00	60.00	75.00
	1923/36	.012	BV	50.00	60.00	75.00
	1923/37	9,049	BV	50.00	60.00	75.00
	1923/38	9,854	BV	50.00	60.00	75.00
	1923/39	.011	BV	50.00	60.00	75.00
	1923/40	.013	BV	50.00	60.00	75.00
	1923/41	.013	BV	50.00	60.00	75.00
	1923/42	.018	BV	50.00	60.00	75.00
	1923/43	.026	BV	50.00	60.00	75.00
	1923/44	.026	BV	50.00	60.00	75.00
	1923/45	.025	BV	50.00	60.00	75.00
	1923/46	.028	BV	50.00	60.00	75.00
	1923/47	.038	BV	50.00	60.00	75.00
	1923/48	.035	BV	50.00	60.00	75.00
	1923/49	.028	BV	50.00	60.00	75.00
	1923/50	.016	BV	50.00	60.00	75.00
	1923/51	.008	BV	50.00	60.00	75.00
	1923/52	.014	BV	50.00	60.00	75.00
	1923/53	.028	BV	50.00	60.00	75.00
	1923/54	.054	BV	50.00	60.00	75.00
	1923/55	.016	BV	50.00	60.00	75.00
	1923/57	—	BV	50.00	60.00	75.00

3.5080 g, .917 GOLD, .1034 oz AGW
Monnaie de Luxe
Kemal Ataturk

KM#	Date	Mintage	Fine	VF	XF	Unc
871	1942	115 pcs.	100.00	150.00	200.00	250.00
	1943	91 pcs.	100.00	150.00	200.00	250.00
	1944	950 pcs.	80.00	125.00	150.00	175.00
	1946	565 pcs.	80.00	125.00	150.00	175.00
	1950	1,971	—	50.00	80.00	150.00
	1951	1,780	—	50.00	80.00	150.00
	1952	2,557	—	50.00	80.00	150.00
	1953	2,392	—	50.00	80.00	150.00
	1954	1,714	—	50.00	80.00	150.00
	1955	4,143	—	50.00	70.00	125.00
	1956	2,956	—	50.00	70.00	125.00
	1957	6,855	—	50.00	70.00	125.00
	1958	6,381	—	50.00	70.00	125.00
	1959	.012	—	50.00	60.00	75.00
	1960	.012	—	50.00	60.00	75.00
	1961	.015	—	50.00	60.00	75.00
	1962	.022	—	50.00	60.00	75.00
	1963	.029	—	50.00	60.00	75.00
	1964	.034	—	50.00	60.00	75.00
	1965	.044	—	50.00	60.00	75.00
	1966	.058	—	50.00	60.00	75.00
	1967	.064	—	50.00	60.00	75.00
	1968	.082	—	50.00	60.00	75.00
	1969	.079	—	50.00	60.00	75.00
	1970	.109	—	50.00	60.00	75.00
	1971	.154	—	50.00	60.00	75.00
	1972	.110	—	50.00	60.00	75.00
	1973	.073	—	50.00	60.00	75.00
	1974	.045	—	50.00	60.00	75.00
	1975	.072	—	50.00	60.00	75.00
	1976	.196	—	50.00	60.00	75.00
	1977	.361	—	50.00	60.00	75.00
	1978	.161	—	50.00	60.00	75.00
	1980	—	—	50.00	60.00	75.00

Monnaie de Luxe
Ismet Inonu

KM#	Date	Mintage	Fine	VF	XF	Unc
876	1943	Inc. KM871	—	150.00	200.00	250.00
	1944	Inc. KM871	—	125.00	175.00	225.00
	1945	515 pcs.	—	125.00	175.00	225.00
	1946	Inc. KM871	—	100.00	150.00	200.00
	1947	3,481	—	100.00	150.00	200.00
	1948	773 pcs.	—	100.00	150.00	200.00
	1949	582 pcs.	—	100.00	150.00	200.00

100 KURUSH

7.2160 g, .917 GOLD, .2126 oz AGW
Ismet Inonu

KM#	Date	Mintage	Fine	VF	XF	Unc
854	1923/20	—	—	BV	100.00	150.00
	1923/22	3 pcs.	—	—	Rare	—
	1923/23	.381	—	BV	100.00	150.00
	1923/24	2,274	—	BV	100.00	160.00
	1923/25	.028	—	BV	100.00	160.00
	1923/26	2,097	—	BV	100.00	160.00
	1923/27	.017	—	BV	100.00	160.00

Kemal Ataturk

KM#	Date	Mintage	Fine	VF	XF	Unc
855	1923/20	.029	—	BV	100.00	120.00
	1923/27	I.A.	—	BV	100.00	120.00
	1923/28	3 pcs.	—	—	Rare	—
	1923/29	2,111	—	BV	100.00	120.00
	1923/30	.013	—	BV	100.00	120.00
	1923/31	.109	—	BV	100.00	120.00
	1923/32	.134	—	BV	100.00	120.00
	1923/33	.216	—	BV	100.00	120.00
	1923/34	.463	—	BV	100.00	120.00
	1923/35	.405	—	BV	100.00	120.00
	1923/36	.025	—	BV	100.00	120.00
	1923/37	.131	—	BV	100.00	120.00
	1923/38	.159	—	BV	100.00	120.00
	1923/39	.085	—	BV	100.00	120.00
	1923/40	.010	—	BV	100.00	120.00
	1923/41	.164	—	BV	100.00	120.00
	1923/42	.063	—	BV	100.00	120.00
	1923/43	.056	—	BV	100.00	120.00
	1923/44	.198	—	BV	100.00	120.00
	1923/45	.176	—	BV	100.00	120.00
	1923/46	1.290	—	BV	100.00	120.00
	1923/47	.513	—	BV	100.00	120.00
	1923/48	600 pcs.	100.00	125.00	150.00	200.00
	1923/49	1,300	—	100.00	120.00	150.00
	1923/50	.047	—	BV	100.00	120.00
	1923/51	.240	—	BV	100.00	120.00
	1923/52	1.047	—	BV	100.00	120.00
	1923/53	.550	—	BV	100.00	120.00
	1923/54	.018	—	BV	100.00	120.00
	1923/55	.309	—	BV	100.00	120.00
	1923/57	—	—	BV	100.00	120.00
	1923/58	—	—	BV	100.00	120.00

7.0160 g, .917 GOLD, .2069 oz AGW
Monnaie de Luxe
Kemal Ataturk

KM#	Date	Mintage	Fine	VF	XF	Unc
872	1942	8,659	—	125.00	150.00	225.00
	1943	6,594	—	125.00	150.00	225.00
	1944	7,160	—	125.00	150.00	225.00
	1948	.014	—	125.00	150.00	200.00
	1950	.025	—	125.00	150.00	200.00
	1951	.035	—	125.00	150.00	175.00
	1952	.041	—	125.00	150.00	175.00
	1953	.032	—	125.00	150.00	175.00
	1954	.024	—	125.00	150.00	175.00
	1955	4,881	—	125.00	150.00	200.00
	1956	.011	—	100.00	120.00	145.00
	1957	.049	—	100.00	120.00	145.00
	1958	.067	—	100.00	120.00	145.00
	1959	.089	—	100.00	120.00	145.00
	1960	.057	—	100.00	120.00	145.00
	1961	.077	—	100.00	120.00	145.00
	1962	.108	—	100.00	120.00	145.00
	1963	.146	—	100.00	120.00	145.00
	1964	.128	—	100.00	120.00	145.00
	1965	.157	—	100.00	120.00	145.00
	1966	.190	—	100.00	120.00	145.00
	1967	.177	—	100.00	120.00	145.00
	1968	.143	—	100.00	120.00	145.00
	1969	.206	—	100.00	120.00	145.00
	1970	.253	—	100.00	120.00	145.00
	1971	.293	—	100.00	120.00	145.00
	1972	.222	—	100.00	120.00	145.00
	1973	.140	—	100.00	120.00	145.00
	1974	.082	—	100.00	120.00	145.00
	1975	.142	—	100.00	120.00	145.00
	1976	.265	—	100.00	120.00	145.00
	1977	.277	—	100.00	120.00	145.00
	1978	.086	—	100.00	120.00	145.00
	1980	—	—	100.00	120.00	145.00

Monnaie de Luxe
Ismet Inonu

KM#	Date	Mintage	Fine	VF	XF	Unc
877	1943	Inc. KM872	150.00	200.00	275.00	325.00
	1944	Inc. KM872	150.00	200.00	275.00	375.00
	1945	2,202	150.00	200.00	275.00	400.00
	1946	8,863	150.00	200.00	275.00	325.00
	1947	.028	150.00	200.00	275.00	325.00
	1948	Inc. KM872	150.00	200.00	275.00	325.00
	1949	6,578	150.00	200.00	275.00	325.00
877	1950	Inc. KM872	150.00	200.00	275.00	325.00

250 KURUSH

18.0400 g, .917 GOLD, .5319 oz AGW
Ismet Inonu

KM#	Date	Mintage	Fine	VF	XF	Unc
856	1923/20	—	—	250.00	300.00	400.00
	1923/23	.014	—	250.00	300.00	400.00
	1923/24	60 pcs.	—	300.00	400.00	500.00

Kemal Ataturk

KM#	Date	Mintage	Fine	VF	XF	Unc
857	1923/20	.010	—	BV	300.00	350.00
	1923/29	3 pcs.	—	—	Rare	—
	1923/30	130 pcs.	—	500.00	700.00	900.00
	1923/31	—	—	500.00	700.00	900.00
	1923/38	245 pcs.	—	350.00	375.00	600.00
	1923/39	389 pcs.	—	350.00	375.00	600.00
	1923/40	435 pcs.	—	350.00	375.00	600.00
	1923/41	349 pcs.	—	350.00	375.00	600.00
	1923/42	460 pcs.	—	350.00	375.00	600.00
	1923/43	1,008	—	250.00	300.00	400.00
	1923/44	712 pcs.	—	250.00	300.00	400.00
	1923/45	1,034	—	250.00	300.00	400.00
	1923/46	1,035	—	250.00	300.00	400.00
	1923/47	1,408	—	250.00	300.00	400.00
	1923/48	904 pcs.	—	250.00	300.00	400.00
	1923/49	1,066	—	250.00	300.00	400.00
	1923/50	975 pcs.	—	250.00	300.00	400.00
	1923/51	298 pcs.	—	250.00	300.00	400.00
	1923/52	610 pcs.	—	250.00	300.00	400.00
	1923/53	586 pcs.	—	250.00	300.00	400.00
	1923/54	289 pcs.	—	250.00	300.00	400.00
	1923/55	267 pcs.	—	250.00	300.00	400.00
	1923/57	—	—	250.00	300.00	400.00

17.5400 g, .917 GOLD, .5169 oz AGW
Monnaie de Luxe
Kemal Ataturk

KM#	Date	Mintage	Fine	VF	XF	Unc
873	1942	.010	—	300.00	425.00	600.00
	1943	.011	—	300.00	425.00	600.00
	1944	.015	—	350.00	700.00	900.00
	1946	.016	—	350.00	700.00	900.00
	1947	.042	—	300.00	425.00	600.00
	1948	.013	—	300.00	425.00	600.00
	1950	.045	—	300.00	425.00	600.00
	1951	.041	—	250.00	300.00	400.00
	1952	.059	—	250.00	300.00	400.00
	1953	.045	—	250.00	300.00	400.00
	1954	.040	—	250.00	300.00	400.00
	1955	7,067	—	250.00	300.00	400.00
	1956	.014	—	250.00	300.00	400.00
	1957	.047	—	250.00	300.00	400.00
	1958	.075	—	250.00	300.00	400.00
	1959	.093	—	250.00	300.00	400.00
	1960	.050	—	250.00	300.00	400.00
	1961	.065	—	250.00	300.00	400.00
	1962	.099	—	250.00	300.00	400.00
	1963	.137	—	250.00	300.00	400.00
	1964	.152	—	250.00	300.00	400.00
	1965	.194	—	250.00	300.00	400.00
	1966	.218	—	250.00	300.00	400.00
	1967	.201	—	250.00	300.00	400.00
	1968	.150	—	250.00	300.00	400.00
	1969	.262	—	250.00	300.00	400.00
873	1970	.301	—	250.00	300.00	400.00
	1971	.356	—	250.00	300.00	400.00
	1972	.305	—	250.00	300.00	400.00
	1973	.198	—	250.00	300.00	400.00
	1974	.142	—	250.00	300.00	400.00
	1975	.223	—	250.00	300.00	400.00
	1976	.345	—	250.00	300.00	400.00
	1977	.227	—	250.00	300.00	400.00
	1978	.311	—	250.00	300.00	400.00
	1980	—	—	250.00	300.00	400.00

Monnaie de Luxe
Ismet Inonu

KM#	Date	Mintage	Fine	VF	XF	Unc
878	1943	Inc. KM873	—	250.00	300.00	425.00
	1944	Inc. KM873	—	250.00	300.00	425.00
	1945	4,135	—	300.00	400.00	550.00
	1946	Inc. KM873	—	250.00	300.00	425.00
	1947	Inc. KM873	—	250.00	300.00	425.00
	1948	Inc. KM873	—	250.00	300.00	425.00
	1949	.011	—	250.00	300.00	425.00
	1950	Inc. KM873	—	250.00	300.00	425.00

500 KURUSH

36.0800 g, .917 GOLD, 1.0638 oz AGW
Ismet Inonu
Similar to 100 Kurush, KM#855.

KM#	Date	Mintage	Fine	VF	XF	Unc
858	1923/20	—	—	BV	550.00	700.00
	1923/23	9,006	—	BV	550.00	700.00
	1923/24	7,923	—	650.00	800.00	900.00
	1923/25	272 pcs.	—	750.00	900.00	1000.

Kemal Ataturk

KM#	Date	Mintage	Fine	VF	XF	Unc
859	1923/20	.012	—	BV	550.00	700.00
	1923/27	615 pcs.	—	650.00	800.00	1000.
	1923/28	34 pcs.	—	650.00	800.00	1000.
	1923/29	137 pcs.	—	575.00	700.00	900.00
	1923/30	45 pcs.	—	575.00	700.00	900.00
	1923/31	100 pcs.	—	575.00	700.00	900.00
	1923/32	74 pcs.	—	575.00	700.00	900.00
	1923/33	268 pcs.	—	550.00	650.00	800.00
	1923/34	758 pcs.	—	550.00	650.00	800.00
	1923/35	1,586	—	BV	500.00	530.00
	1923/36	765 pcs.	—	BV	500.00	530.00
	1923/37	983 pcs.	—	BV	500.00	530.00
	1923/38	1,738	—	BV	500.00	530.00
	1923/39	2,629	—	BV	500.00	530.00
	1923/40	2,763	—	BV	500.00	530.00
	1923/41	3,440	—	BV	500.00	530.00
	1923/42	3,335	—	BV	500.00	530.00
	1923/43	4,914	—	BV	500.00	530.00
	1923/44	4,308	—	BV	500.00	530.00
	1923/45	3,488	—	BV	500.00	530.00
	1923/46	5,636	—	BV	500.00	530.00
	1923/47	7,588	—	BV	500.00	530.00
	1923/48	6,060	—	BV	500.00	530.00
	1923/49	4,235	—	BV	500.00	530.00

KM#	Date	Mintage	Fine	VF	XF	Unc
859	1923/50	4,733	—	BV	500.00	530.00
	1923/51	2,757	—	BV	500.00	530.00
	1923/52	2,041	—	BV	500.00	530.00
	1923/53	4,819	—	BV	500.00	530.00
	1923/54	1,401	—	BV	500.00	530.00
	1923/55	1,484	—	BV	500.00	530.00
	1923/57	—	—	BV	500.00	530.00

35.0800 g, .917 GOLD, 1.0338 oz AGW
Monnaie de Luxe
Kemal Ataturk

KM#	Date	Mintage	Fine	VF	XF	Unc
874	1942	2,949	—	500.00	530.00	575.00
	1943	1,210	—	500.00	530.00	575.00
	1944	1,254	—	500.00	530.00	575.00
	1947	3,699	—	500.00	530.00	575.00
	1950	59 pcs.	—	500.00	530.00	575.00
	1951	21 pcs.	—	500.00	530.00	575.00
	1952	26 pcs.	—	500.00	530.00	575.00
	1953	35 pcs.	—	500.00	530.00	575.00
	1954	182 pcs.	—	500.00	530.00	575.00
	1955	14 pcs.	—	500.00	530.00	575.00
	1956	13 pcs.	—	500.00	530.00	575.00
	1957	68 pcs.	—	500.00	530.00	575.00
	1958	121 pcs.	—	500.00	530.00	575.00
	1959	294 pcs.	—	550.00	700.00	900.00
	1960	208 pcs.	—	550.00	700.00	900.00
	1961	619 pcs.	—	550.00	700.00	900.00
	1962	1,228	—	500.00	530.00	575.00
	1963	1,985	—	500.00	530.00	575.00
	1964	2,787	—	500.00	530.00	575.00
	1965	4,631	—	500.00	530.00	575.00
	1966	5,572	—	500.00	530.00	575.00
	1967	6,637	—	500.00	530.00	575.00
	1968	5,983	—	500.00	530.00	575.00
	1969	7,152	—	500.00	530.00	575.00
	1970	.011	—	500.00	530.00	575.00
	1971	.015	—	500.00	530.00	575.00
	1972	.015	—	500.00	530.00	575.00
	1973	7,939	—	500.00	530.00	575.00
	1974	5,412	—	500.00	530.00	575.00
	1975	6,205	—	500.00	530.00	575.00
	1976	.011	—	500.00	530.00	575.00
	1977	6,931	—	500.00	530.00	575.00
	1978	5,740	—	500.00	530.00	575.00
	1980	—	—	500.00	530.00	575.00

Monnaie de Luxe
Ismet Inonu

KM#	Date	Mintage	Fine	VF	XF	Unc
879	1943	Inc. KM874	—	500.00	530.00	575.00
	1944	Inc. KM874	—	500.00	530.00	575.00
	1945	115 pcs.	—	500.00	530.00	575.00
	1946	298 pcs.	—	500.00	530.00	575.00
	1947	Inc. KM874	—	500.00	530.00	575.00
	1948	40 pcs.	—	500.00	530.00	575.00

MINT SETS (MS)

KM#	Date	Mintage	Identification	Issue Price	Mkt. Val.
MS1	1962(6)	—	KM889a.1,890.1-891.1, 892.2,893.1,894	—	Rare
MS2	1964(6)	—	KM889a.1,890.1-891.1, 892.2,893.1,895a	—	7.50
MS3	1965(6)	—	KM889a.1,890.1-891.1, 892.2,893.1,895a	—	7.50
MS4	1966(6)	—	KM889a.1,890.1-891.1, 892.2,893.1,895a	—	7.50
MS5	1968(6)	—	KM889a.2,890.1-891.1, 892.3,893.1,895a	—	7.50
MS6	1969(6)	—	KM889a.2,890.2-891.2, 892.3,893.2,895a	—	6.00
MS7	1970(6)	—	KM889a.2,890.2-891.2, 892.3,893.2,895a	—	6.00
MS8	1971(6)	—	KM889a.2,890.2-891.2, 892.2,895a,899	—	6.00
MS9	1972(6)	—	KM889a.2,890.2-891.2, 892.2,895a,899	—	4.00
MS10	1973(7)	—	KM889a.2,890.2-891.2, 892.3,893.2,895a,899	—	4.00
MS11	1974(7)	—	KM889a.2,890.3-892.3, 893.2,895a,899	—	4.00
MS12	1975(7)	—	KM889a.2,890a-891a, 893.2,895c,899,905	—	4.00
MS13	1976(7)	—	KM889a.2,890a-891a, 893.2,895c,899,905	—	4.00
MS14	1977(8)	—	KM889a.2,890a-891a, 892.3,893.2,895c, 899,905	—	3.50
MS15	1978(4)	—	KM889a.2,892.3,893.2, 905	—	3.00
MS16	1979(4)	—	KM889a.2,893.2,899,905	—	3.00
MS17	1980(2)	—	KM889a.2,893.2	—	2.00
MS18	1981(3)	—	KM943-945	—	3.00
MS19	1982(3)	—	KM943,949,950	—	3.00
MS20	1983(2)	—	KM949,950	—	3.00
MS21	1984(6)	—	KM962-967	—	5.50
MS22	1985(6)	—	KM962-964,966,967.975	—	5.00
MS23	1986(5)	—	KM963-967	—	4.00
MS24	1989(7)	—	KM962-964,975,987-988	2.00	2.00
MS25	1990(5)	—	KM987-989,996-997	4.00	8.50

TURKMENISTAN

The Turkmenistan Republic (formerly the Turkmen Soviet Socialist Republic) covers the territory of the Trans-Caspian Region of Turkestan, the Charjiui Vilayet of Bukhara and the part of Khiva located on the right bank of the Oxus. Bordered on the north by the Autonomous Kara-Kalpak Republic (a constituent of Uzbekistan), by Iran and Afghanistan on the south, by the Usbek Republic on the east and the Caspian Sea on the west. It has an area of 186,400 sq. mi. (488,100 sq. km.) and a population of 3.5 million. Capital: Ashkhabad (formerly Poltoratsk). Main occupation is agricultural products including cotton and maize. It is rich in minerals, oil, coal, sulphur and salt and is also famous for its carpets, Turkoman horses and Karakui sheep.

The Turkomans arrived in Trancaspia as nomadic Seluk Turks in the 11th century. It often became subjected to one of the neighboring states. Late in the 19th century the Czarist Russians invaded with their first victory at Kyzyl Arvat in 1877, arriving in Ashkhabad in 1882 resulting in submission of the Turkmen tribes. By Mar. 18, 1884 the Transcaspian province of Russian Turkestan was formed. During WW I the Czarist government tried to conscript the Turkmen; this led to a revolt in Oct. 1916 under the leadership of Aziz Chapykov. In 1918 the Turks captured Baku from the Red army and the British sent a constingent to Merv to prevent a German-Turkish offensive toward Afghanistan and India. In mid-1919 a Bureau of Turkistan Moslem Communist Organization was formed in Moscow hoping to develop one large republic including all surrounding Turkic areas within a Soviet federation. A Turkistan Autonomous Soviet Socialist Republic was formed and plans to partition Turkistan into five republics according to the principle of nationalities was quickly implemented by Joseph Stalin. On Oct. 27, 1924 Turkmenistan became a Soviet Socialist Republic and was accepted as a member of the U.S.S.R. on Jan. 29, 1925. The Bureau of T.M.C.O. was disbanded in 1934. In Aug. 1990 the Turkmen Supreme Soviet adopted a declaration of sovereignty followed by a declaration of independence in Oct. 1991 joining the Commonwealth of Independent States in Dec. A new constitution was adopted in 1992 providing for an executive presidency.

TENNESI

COPPER PLATED STEEL
President Saparmyrat Nyyazow

KM#	Date	Mintage	VF	XF	Unc
1	1993	—	—	—	.20

5 TENNESI

COPPER PLATED STEEL
President Saparmyrat Nyyazow

KM#	Date	Mintage	VF	XF	Unc
2	1993	—	—	—	.40

10 TENNESI

COPPER PLATED STEEL
President Saparmyrat Nyyazow

KM#	Date	Mintage	VF	XF	Unc
3	1993	—	—	—	.65

20 TENNESI

NICKEL PLATED STEEL
President Saparmyrat Nyyazow

KM#	Date	Mintage	VF	XF	Unc
4	1993	—	—	—	1.25

50 TENNESI

NICKEL PLATED STEEL
President Saparmyrat Nyyazow

KM#	Date	Mintage	VF	XF	Unc
5	1993	—	—	—	3.00

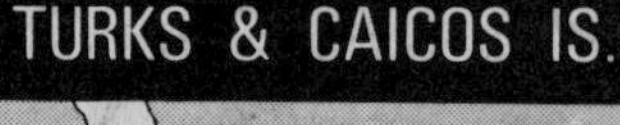

TURKS & CAICOS IS.

The Colony of the Turks and Caicos Islands, a British colony situated in the West Indies at the eastern end of the Bahama Islands, has an area of 166 sq. mi. (430 sq. km.) and a population of *10,000. Capital: Cockburn Town, on Grand Turk. The principal industry of the colony is the production of salt, which is gathered by raking. Salt, crayfish, and conch shells are exported.

The Turks and Caicos Islands were discovered by Juan Ponce de Leon in 1512, but were not settled until 1678 when Bermudians arrived to rake salt from the salt ponds. The British settlers were driven from the island by the Spanish in 1710, during the long War of the Spanish Succession. They returned and throughout the remaining years of the war repulsed repeated attacks by France and Spain. In 1799 the islands were granted representation in the Bahamian assembly, but in 1848, on petition of the inhabitants, they were made a separate colony under Jamaica. They were annexed by Jamaica in 1873 and remained a dependency until 1959 when they became a unit territory of the Federation of the West Indies. When the Federation was dissolved in 1962, the Turks and Caicos Islands became a separate Crown Colony.

RULERS

British

MONETARY SYSTEM

1 Crown = 1 Dollar U.S.A.

1/4 CROWN

COPPER-NICKEL

KM#	Date	Mintage	Fine	VF	XF	Unc
51	1981	—	—	—	—	.75

1/2 CROWN

COPPER-NICKEL

KM#	Date	Mintage	Fine	VF	XF	Unc
52	1981	—	—	—	—	1.50

CROWN

COPPER-NICKEL

KM#	Date	Mintage	Fine	VF	XF	Unc
1	1969	.050	—	—	2.00	4.00
	1969	6,000	—	—	Proof	5.00

KM#	Date	Mintage	Fine	VF	XF	Unc
5	1975	590 pcs.	—	—	Matte	10.00
	1975	1,370	—	—	Proof	7.50
	1976	1,960	—	—	—	6.00
	1976	2,270	—	—	Proof	7.50
	1977	1,420	—	—	Proof	6.00

Prince Andrew's Marriage

KM#	Date	Mintage	Fine	VF	XF	Unc
60	1986	.020	—	—	—	4.00

28.2800 g, .925 SILVER, .8411 oz ASW

KM#	Date	Mintage	Fine	VF	XF	Unc
60a	1986	5,000	—	—	Proof	15.00

COPPER-NICKEL

KM#	Date	Mintage	Fine	VF	XF	Unc
122	1986	—	—	—	—	4.00

World Wildlife Fund - Iguana

KM#	Date	Mintage	Fine	VF	XF	Unc
64	1988	—	—	—	—	4.50

28.2800 g, .925 SILVER, .8411 oz ASW

KM#	Date	Mintage	Fine	VF	XF	Unc
64a	1988	*.025	—	—	Proof	30.00

5 CROWNS

COPPER-NICKEL
Queen Mothers 90th Birthday

KM#	Date	Mintage	Fine	VF	XF	Unc
66	1990	—	—	—	—	5.00
	28.2800 g, .925 SILVER, .8411 oz ASW					
66a	1990	*.010	—	—	Proof	50.00

COPPER-NICKEL
Royal Birthdays

74	1991	—	—	—	—	7.50

10th Wedding Anniversary of the Prince and Princess of Wales

76	1991	—	—	—	—	7.50

10th Wedding Anniversary of the Prince and Princess of Wales - Prince Charles

121	1991	—	—	—	—	7.50

24.2400 g, .500 SILVER, .3897 oz ASW

KM#	Date	Mintage	Fine	VF	XF	Unc
6	1975	440 pcs.	—	—	Matte	18.00
	1975	1,320	—	—	Proof	15.00
	1976	1,760	—	—	—	12.50
	1976	2,220	—	—	Proof	12.50
	1977	1,370	—	—	Proof	15.00

14.5800 g, .500 SILVER, .2344 oz ASW
Lord Mountbatten
Obv: Similar to 10 Crowns, KM#45.

47	1980	—	—	—	Proof	8.00

COPPER-NICKEL
Discovery of America - Columbus Before Ferdinand and Isabella

75	1991	—	—	—	—	7.50

Olympics - Equestrian and 3 Events

KM#	Date	Mintage	Fine	VF	XF	Unc
68	1992	—	—	—	—	6.50

Olympics - Gymnast on Rings and 5 Events

69	1992	—	—	—	—	6.50

Olympics - Weightlifting and 3 Events

70	1992	—	—	—	—	6.50

Olympics - Rifle Shooting and 3 Events

71	1992	—	—	—	—	6.50

Olympics - Sail Boarding and 3 Events

KM#	Date	Mintage	Fine	VF	XF	Unc
72	1992	—	—	—	—	6.50

Olympics - Ski Jumper and 4 Events

KM#	Date	Mintage	Fine	VF	XF	Unc
73	1992	—	—	—	—	6.50

40th Anniversary - Reign of Elizabeth II

KM#	Date	Mintage	Fine	VF	XF	Unc
77	1992	—	—	—	—	7.50

28.0400g, .925 SILVER, .8339 oz ASW

KM#	Date	Mintage	Fine	VF	XF	Unc
77a	1992	—	—	—	Proof	40.00

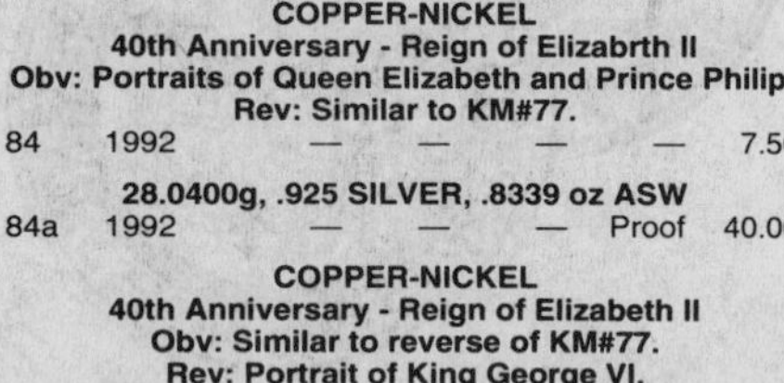

COPPER-NICKEL

40th Anniversary - Reign of Elizabrth II

Obv: Portraits of Queen Elizabeth and Prince Philip.

Rev: Similar to KM#77.

KM#	Date	Mintage	Fine	VF	XF	Unc
84	1992	—	—	—	—	7.50

28.0400g, .925 SILVER, .8339 oz ASW

KM#	Date	Mintage	Fine	VF	XF	Unc
84a	1992	—	—	—	Proof	40.00

COPPER-NICKEL

40th Anniversary - Reign of Elizabeth II

Obv: Similar to reverse of KM#77.

Rev: Portrait of King George VI.

KM#	Date	Mintage	Fine	VF	XF	Unc
85	1992	—	—	—	—	7.50

28.0400 g, .925 SILVER, .8339 oz ASW

KM#	Date	Mintage	Fine	VF	XF	Unc
85a	1992	—	—	—	Proof	40.00

COPPER-NICKEL

40th Anniversary - Reign of Elizabeth II - Windsor Castle.

Obv: Similar to reverse of KM#77. Rev: Castle.

KM#	Date	Mintage	Fine	VF	XF	Unc
86	1992	—	—	—	—	7.50

28.0400 g, .925 SILVER, .8339 oz ASW

KM#	Date	Mintage	Fine	VF	XF	Unc
86a	1992	—	—	—	Proof	40.00

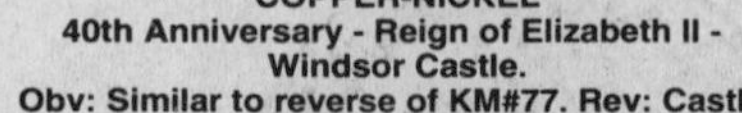

COPPER-NICKEL

World Cup '94 - Jules Rimet and Trophy

KM#	Date	Mintage	Fine	VF	XF	Unc
87	ND(1993)	—	—	—	—	9.00

World Cup '94 - Uruguay Winners - 2 Players

KM#	Date	Mintage	Fine	VF	XF	Unc
88	ND(1993)	—	—	—	—	9.00

World Cup '94 - Italy Winners - Dino Zoff

KM#	Date	Mintage	Fine	VF	XF	Unc
89	ND(1993)	—	—	—	—	9.00

World Cup '94 - West Germany Winners - Franz Beckenbauer

KM#	Date	Mintage	Fine	VF	XF	Unc
90	ND(1993)	—	—	—	—	9.00

World Cup '94 - Brazil Winners - Pele

KM#	Date	Mintage	Fine	VF	XF	Unc
91	ND(1993)	—	—	—	—	9.00

World Cup '94 - England Winners - Bobby Moore

KM#	Date	Mintage	Fine	VF	XF	Unc
92	ND(1993)	—	—	—	—	9.00

World Cup '94 - Argentina Winners - Mario Kempes

KM#	Date	Mintage	Fine	VF	XF	Unc
93	ND(1993)	—	—	—	—	9.00

World Cup '94 - USA Host - Trophy and Flag

KM#	Date	Mintage	Fine	VF	XF	Unc
94	ND(1993)	—	—	—	—	9.00

40th Anniversary of Coronation - Westminster Abbey

KM#	Date	Mintage	Fine	VF	XF	Unc
103	ND(1993)	—	—	—	—	8.50

40th Anniversary of Coronation - Crown Jewels

KM#	Date	Mintage	Fine	VF	XF	Unc
104	ND(1993)	—	—	—	—	8.50

40th Anniversary of Coronation - Queen, Clergy and Maids of Honor

KM#	Date	Mintage	Fine	VF	XF	Unc
105	ND(1993)	—	—	—	—	8.50

40th Anniversary of Coronation - Consort's Homage

KM#	Date	Mintage	Fine	VF	XF	Unc
106	ND(1993)	—	—	—	—	8.50

40th Anniversary of Coronation - Queen on Throne

KM#	Date	Mintage	Fine	VF	XF	Unc
107	ND(1993)	—	—	—	—	8.50

40th Anniversary of Coronation - Queen in Coach

KM#	Date	Mintage	Fine	VF	XF	Unc
108	ND(1993)	—	—	—	—	8.50

10 CROWNS

29.9800 g, .925 SILVER, .8916 oz ASW
Age of Exploration - Spacecrafts

KM#	Date	Mintage	Fine	VF	XF	Unc
7	1975	1,250	—	—	Matte	20.00
	1975	2,935	—	—	Proof	20.00

Obv: Similar to KM#7.

KM#	Date	Mintage	Fine	VF	XF	Unc
12	1976	4,185	—	—	—	17.50
	1976	2,220	—	—	Proof	22.50
	1977	1,370	—	—	Proof	27.50

29.7000 g, .925 SILVER, .8832 oz ASW
10th Anniversary of Prince Charles' Investiture

KM#	Date	Mintage	Fine	VF	XF	Unc
45	1979	.025	—	—	Proof	16.50

23.3300 g, .500 SILVER, .3750 oz ASW
Lord Mountbatten
Obv: Similar to KM#45.

KM#	Date	Mintage	Fine	VF	XF	Unc
48	1980	—	—	—	Proof	15.00

29.7000 g, .925 SILVER, .8832 oz ASW
Wedding of Prince Charles and Lady Diana
Similar to 100 Crowns, KM#54.

KM#	Date	Mintage	Fine	VF	XF	Unc
53	1981	.040	—	—	Proof	25.00

23.2800 g, .925 SILVER, .6923 oz ASW
International Year of the Child

KM#	Date	Mintage	Fine	VF	XF	Unc
55	1982	7,928	—	—	Proof	27.50

World Football Championship - 1 Player

KM#	Date	Mintage	Fine	VF	XF	Unc
56	1982	7,865	—	—	Proof	27.50

World Football Championship - 2 Players

KM#	Date	Mintage	Fine	VF	XF	Unc
57	1982	7,165	—	—	Proof	27.50

Summer Olympics - Javelin Thrower

KM#	Date	Mintage	Fine	VF	XF	Unc
58	1984	2,160	—	—	Proof	37.50

Decade For Women

KM#	Date	Mintage	Fine	VF	XF	Unc
63	1985	1,001	—	—	Proof	40.00

20 CROWNS

38.7000 g, .925 SILVER, 1.1509 oz ASW
Birth of Churchill Centenary

KM#	Date	Mintage	Fine	VF	XF	Unc
2	1974	.268	—	—	Matte	20.00
	1974	8,400*	—	—	Proof	25.00

NOTE: 4,100 issued individually while 4,300 were issued in binational sets along with Cayman Islands 25 Dollars, KM#10.

Age of Exploration - Christopher Columbus
Obv: Similar to 10 Crowns, KM#7.

KM#	Date	Mintage	Fine	VF	XF	Unc
8	1975	1,037	—	—	Matte	27.50
	1975	2,769	—	—	Proof	32.50

U.S. Bicentennial

Obv: Similar to 10 Crowns, KM#7.

KM#	Date	Mintage	Fine	VF	XF	Unc
13	1976	5,022	—	—	Matte	22.50
	1976	4,474	—	—	Proof	27.50

Victoria Portraits
Obv: Similar to 10 Crowns, KM#7.

KM#	Date	Mintage	Fine	VF	XF	Unc
14	1976	.025	—	—	—	20.00
	1976	.022	—	—	Proof	25.00
	1977	1,934	—	—	Proof	40.00

George III Portraits
Obv: Similar to 1/2 Crown, KM#52.

KM#	Date	Mintage	Fine	VF	XF	Unc
18	1977	—	—	—	—	40.00
	1977	1,973	—	—	Proof	50.00

XI Commonwealth Games
Obv: Similar to 10 Crowns, KM#55.

KM#	Date	Mintage	Fine	VF	XF	Unc
23	1978	.010	—	—	Proof	27.50

29.8100 g, .500 SILVER, .4792 oz ASW
Lord Mountbatten
Obv: Similar to 10 Crowns, KM#45.

KM#	Date	Mintage	Fine	VF	XF	Unc
49	1980	—	—	—	Proof	22.50

28.0400 g, .925 SILVER, .8339 oz ASW
Discovery of America - Santa Maria

KM#	Date	Mintage	Fine	VF	XF	Unc
67	1991	—	—	—	Proof	20.00

Discovery of America - The Nina

KM#	Date	Mintage	Fine	VF	XF	Unc
115	1991	—	—	—	Proof	20.00

Discovery of America - The Pinta

KM#	Date	Mintage	Fine	VF	XF	Unc
116	1991	—	—	—	Proof	20.00

Discovery of America - Ships Set Sail

KM#	Date	Mintage	Fine	VF	XF	Unc
117	1991	—	—	—	Proof	20.00

Discovery of America - Ships Crossing the Atlantic

KM#	Date	Mintage	Fine	VF	XF	Unc
118	1991	—	—	—	Proof	20.00

Discovery of America - Sighting Land

KM#	Date	Mintage	Fine	VF	XF	Unc
119	1991	—	—	—	Proof	20.00

Discovery of America - Columbus Explores the Caribbean

KM#	Date	Mintage	Fine	VF	XF	Unc
120	1991	—	—	—	Proof	20.00

31.1000 g, .999 SILVER,1.000 oz ASW
Olympics - Equestrian and 3 Events
Obv: Similar to KM#2 reverse.

KM#	Date	Mintage	Fine	VF	XF	Unc
78	1992	.020	—	—	Proof	35.00

Olympics - Gymnast on Rings and 5 Events

KM#	Date	Mintage	Fine	VF	XF	Unc
79	1992	*.020	—	—	Proof	35.00

Olympics - Weightlifting and 3 Events

KM#	Date	Mintage	Fine	VF	XF	Unc
80	1992	*.020	—	—	Proof	35.00

Olympics - Rifle Shooting and 3 Events

KM#	Date	Mintage	Fine	VF	XF	Unc
81	1992	*.020	—	—	Proof	35.00

1992 Olympics - Sail Boarding and 3 Events

KM#	Date	Mintage	Fine	VF	XF	Unc
82	1992	*.020	—	—	Proof	35.00

1992 Olympics - Ski Jumper and 4 Events

KM#	Date	Mintage	Fine	VF	XF	Unc
83	1992	*.020	—	—	Proof	35.00

World Cup '94 - Jules Rimet
Similar to 5 Crowns, KM#87.

KM#	Date	Mintage	Fine	VF	XF	Unc
95	ND(1993)	*.010	—	—	Proof	45.00

World Cup '94 - Uruguay Winners - 2 Players
Similar to 5 Crowns, KM#88.

KM#	Date	Mintage	Fine	VF	XF	Unc
96	ND(1993)	*.010	—	—	Proof	45.00

World Cup '94 - Italy Winners - Dino Zoff
Similar to 5 Crowns, KM#89.

KM#	Date	Mintage	Fine	VF	XF	Unc
97	ND(1993)	*.010	—	—	Proof	45.00

World Cup '94 - West Germany Winners - Franz Breckenbauer
Similar to 5 Crowns, KM#90.

KM#	Date	Mintage	Fine	VF	XF	Unc
98	ND(1993)	*.010	—	—	Proof	45.00

World Cup '94 - Brazil Winners - Pele
Similar to 5 Crowns, KM#91.

KM#	Date	Mintage	Fine	VF	XF	Unc
99	ND(1993)	*.010	—	—	Proof	45.00

World Cup '94 - England Winners - Bobby Moore
Similar to 5 Crowns, KM#92.

KM#	Date	Mintage	Fine	VF	XF	Unc
100	ND(1993)	*.010	—	—	Proof	45.00

World Cup '94 - Argentina Winners - Mario Kempes
Similar to 5 Crowns, KM#93.

KM#	Date	Mintage	Fine	VF	XF	Unc
101	ND(1993)	*.010	—	—	Proof	45.00

World Cup '94 - USA Host - Trophy and Flag

KM#	Date	Mintage	Fine	VF	XF	Unc
102	ND(1993)	*.010	—	—	Proof	45.00

40th Anniversary of Coronation - Westminster Abbey
Similar to 5 Crowns, KM#103.

KM#	Date	Mintage	Fine	VF	XF	Unc
109	ND(1993)	*.010	—	—	Proof	42.50

40th Anniversary of Coronation - Crown Jewels
Similar to 5 Crowns, KM#104.

KM#	Date	Mintage	Fine	VF	XF	Unc
110	ND(1993)	*.010	—	—	Proof	42.50

40th Anniversary of Coronation - Queen, Clergy, and Maids of Honor
Similar to 5 Crowns, KM#105.

KM#	Date	Mintage	Fine	VF	XF	Unc
111	ND(1993)	*.010	—	—	Proof	42.50

40th Anniversary of Coronation - Consort's Homage
Similar to 5 Crowns, KM#106.

KM#	Date	Mintage	Fine	VF	XF	Unc
112	ND(1993)	*.010	—	—	Proof	42.50

40th Anniversary of Coronation - Queen on Throne
Similar to 5 Crowns, KM#107.

KM#	Date	Mintage	Fine	VF	XF	Unc
113	ND(1993)	*.010	—	—	Proof	42.50

40th Anniversary of Coronation - Queen in Coach
Similar to 5 Crowns, KM#108.

KM#	Date	Mintage	Fine	VF	XF	Unc
114	ND(1993)	*.010	—	—	Proof	42.50

25 CROWNS

4.5000 g, .500 GOLD, .0723 oz AGW

KM#	Date	Mintage	Fine	VF	XF	Unc
9.1	1975	1,272	—	—	—	45.00
	1975	2,096	—	—	Proof	45.00

19mm

KM#	Date	Mintage	Fine	VF	XF	Unc
9.2	1976	—	—	—	—	45.00
	1976	2,185	—	—	Proof	45.00
	1977	2,125	—	—	Proof	45.00

43.7500 g, .925 SILVER, 1.3012 oz ASW
Queen's Silver Jubilee
Obv: Similar to 10 Crowns, KM#7.

KM#	Date	Mintage	Fine	VF	XF	Unc
19	1977	—	—	—	Matte	25.00
	1977	.013	—	—	Proof	30.00

25th Anniversary of Coronation
Lion of England
Obv: Similar to 50 Crowns, KM#39.

KM#	Date	Mintage	Fine	VF	XF	Unc
24	1978	—	—	—	Proof	45.00

Griffin of Edward III
Obv: Similar to 50 Crowns, KM#39.

KM#	Date	Mintage	Fine	VF	XF	Unc
25	1978	—	—	—	Proof	45.00

Red Dragon of Wales
Obv: Similar to 50 Crowns, KM#39.

KM#	Date	Mintage	Fine	VF	XF	Unc
26	1978	—	—	—	Proof	45.00

White Greyhound of Richmond
Obv: Similar to 50 Crowns, KM#39.

KM#	Date	Mintage	Fine	VF	XF	Unc
27	1978	—	—	—	Proof	45.00

Unicorn of Scotland
Obv: Similar to 50 Crowns, KM#39.

KM#	Date	Mintage	Fine	VF	XF	Unc
28	1978	—	—	—	Proof	65.00

White Horse of Hannover
Similar to 50 Crowns, KM#39.

KM#	Date	Mintage	Fine	VF	XF	Unc
29	1978	—	—	—	Proof	45.00

Black Bull of Clarence
Obv: Similar to 50 Crowns, KM#39.

KM#	Date	Mintage	Fine	VF	XF	Unc
30	1978	—	—	—	Proof	45.00

Yale of Beaufort
Obv: Similar to 50 Crowns, KM#41.

KM#	Date	Mintage	Fine	VF	XF	Unc
31	1978	—	—	—	Proof	45.00

Falcon of the Plantaganets
Similar to 50 Crowns, KM#42.

KM#	Date	Mintage	Fine	VF	XF	Unc
32	1978	—	—	—	Proof	45.00

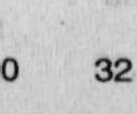

White Lion of Mortimer
Similar to 50 Crowns, KM#43.

KM#	Date	Mintage	Fine	VF	XF	Unc
33	1978	—	—	—	Proof	45.00

50 CROWNS

9.0000 g, .500 GOLD, .1447 oz AGW
Birth of Churchill Centenary

KM#	Date	Mintage	Fine	VF	XF	Unc
3	1974	.030	—	—	Matte	75.00
	1974	4,000	—	—	Proof	85.00

6.2200 g, .500 GOLD, .1000 oz AGW
Age of Exploration - Christopher Columbus

KM#	Date	Mintage	Fine	VF	XF	Unc
10	1975	2,863	—	—	—	90.00
	1975	1,577	—	—	Proof	100.00

U.S. Bicentennial

KM#	Date	Mintage	Fine	VF	XF	Unc
15	1976	905 pcs.	—	—	—	100.00
	1976	2,421	—	—	Proof	90.00

55.1800 g, .925 SILVER, 1.6412 oz ASW
Victoria Portraits
Similar to 100 Crowns, KM#17.

KM#	Date	Mintage	Fine	VF	XF	Unc
16	1976	3,500	—	—	Matte	50.00
	1976	2,908	—	—	Proof	55.00
	1977	940 pcs.	—	—	Proof	70.00

9.0000 g, .500 GOLD, .1447 oz AGW
Queen's Silver Jubilee

KM#	Date	Mintage	Fine	VF	XF	Unc
20	1977	—	—	—	—	70.00
	1977	2,903	—	—	Proof	90.00

55.1800 g, .925 SILVER, 1.6412 oz ASW
George III Portraits
Similar to 100 Crowns, KM#22.

KM#	Date	Mintage	Fine	VF	XF	Unc
21	1977	—	—	—	—	60.00
	1977	958 pcs.	—	—	Proof	90.00

9.0000 g, .500 GOLD, .1447 oz AGW

25th Anniversary of Coronation
Lion of England

KM#	Date	Mintage	Fine	VF	XF	Unc
34	1978	261 pcs.	—	—	Proof	175.00

Griffin of Edward III

KM#	Date	Mintage	Fine	VF	XF	Unc
35	1978	266 pcs.	—	—	Proof	175.00

Red Dragon of Wales

KM#	Date	Mintage	Fine	VF	XF	Unc
36	1978	266 pcs.	—	—	Proof	175.00

White Greyhound of Richmond

KM#	Date	Mintage	Fine	VF	XF	Unc
37	1978	270 pcs.	—	—	Proof	175.00

Unicorn of Scotland

KM#	Date	Mintage	Fine	VF	XF	Unc
38	1978	268 pcs.	—	—	Proof	175.00

White Horse of Hannover

KM#	Date	Mintage	Fine	VF	XF	Unc
39	1978	266 pcs.	—	—	Proof	175.00

Black Bull of Clarence

KM#	Date	Mintage	Fine	VF	XF	Unc
40	1978	269 pcs.	—	—	Proof	175.00

Yale of Beaufort

KM#	Date	Mintage	Fine	VF	XF	Unc
41	1978	254 pcs.	—	—	Proof	175.00

Falcon of the Plantagenets

KM#	Date	Mintage	Fine	VF	XF	Unc
42	1978	265 pcs.	—	—	Proof	175.00

White Lion of Mortimer

KM#	Date	Mintage	Fine	VF	XF	Unc
43	1978	265 pcs.	—	—	Proof	175.00

136.0800 g, .925 SILVER, 4.0699 oz ASW
Illustration reduced. Actual size: 63mm.
Columbus Proposes Atlantic Voyage
to Ferdinand and Isabella

KM#	Date	Mintage	Fine	VF	XF	Unc
61	1986	.020	—	—	Proof	90.00

100 CROWNS

18.0150 g, .500 GOLD, .2896 oz AGW
Birth of Churchill Centenary

KM#	Date	Mintage	VF	XF	Unc
4	1974	4,500	—	—	150.00
	1974	5,100	—	Proof	150.00

12.4400 g, .500 GOLD, .2000 oz AGW
Age of Exploration - Spacecrafts

KM#	Date	Mintage	VF	XF	Unc
11	1975	756 pcs.	—	—	125.00
	1975	1,508	—	Proof	125.00

18.0150 g, .500 GOLD, .2896 oz AGW
Victoria Portraits

KM#	Date	Mintage	VF	XF	Unc
17	1976	250 pcs.	—	—	170.00
	1976	350 pcs.	—	Proof	220.00
	1977	1,655	—	—	165.00
	1977	2,648	—	Proof	190.00

George III Portraits

KM#	Date	Mintage	VF	XF	Unc
22	1977	—	—	—	175.00
	1977	844 pcs.	—	Proof	215.00

XI Commonwealth Games

KM#	Date	Mintage	VF	XF	Unc
44	1978	540 pcs.	—	Proof	250.00

10th Anniversary of Prince Charles' Investiture

KM#	Date	Mintage	VF	XF	Unc
46	1979	.010	—	—	150.00

12.9600 g, .500 GOLD, .2083 oz AGW
Lord Mountbatten
Obv: Similar to 10 Crowns, KM#45.

KM#	Date	Mintage	VF	XF	Unc
50	1980	—	—	Proof	150.00

6.4800 g, .900 GOLD, .1875 oz AGW
Wedding of Prince Charles and Lady Diana

KM#	Date	Mintage	VF	XF	Unc
54	1981	1,205	—	Proof	125.00

World Football Championship - 2 Players

KM#	Date	Mintage	VF	XF	Unc
59	1982	565 pcs.	—	Proof	225.00

7.1300 g, .900 GOLD, .2063 oz AGW
Decade For Women

KM#	Date	Mintage	VF	XF	Unc
62	1985	313 pcs.	—	Proof	275.00

10.0000 g, .917 GOLD, .2949 oz AGW
World Wildlife Fund - Jumbo Shrimp

KM#	Date	Mintage	VF	XF	Unc
65	1988	*5,000	—	Proof	250.00

MINT SETS (MS)

KM#	Date	Mintage	Identification	Issue Price	Mkt. Val.
MS1	1975(7)	440	KM5-11	214.00	350.00

PROOF SETS (PS)

KM#	Date	Mintage	Identification	Issue Price	Mkt. Val.
PS1	1974(2)	1,600	KM2,4	—	170.00
PS2	1975(7)	1,270	KM5-8,9.1,10-11	313.00	385.00
PS3	1976(4)	2,185	KM5,6,9.2,12	78.00	85.00
PS4	1976(3)	—	KM14,16,17	280.00	280.00
PS5	1976(2)	1,951	KM13,15	108.00	115.00
PS6	1977(4)	1,370	KM5,6,9.2,12	87.50	100.00
PS7	1977(3)	—	KM18,21,22	280.00	380.00
PS8	1977(2)	—	KM14,18	62.00	115.00
PS9	1978(10)	—	KM24-33	560.00	470.00
PS10	1978(10)	—	KM34-43	1120.	1750.
PS11	1979(2)	—	KM45,46	227.50	170.00
PS12	1980(4)	—	KM47-50	457.50	195.00
PS13	1980(3)	—	KM47-49	107.50	45.00
PS14	ND(1993)(8)	—	KM87-94	67.20	70.00
PS15	ND(1993)(8)	—	KM95-102	319.68	325.00
PS16	ND(1993)(6)	—	KM103-108	49.95	50.00
PS17	ND(1993)(6)	—	KM109-114	234.00	240.00

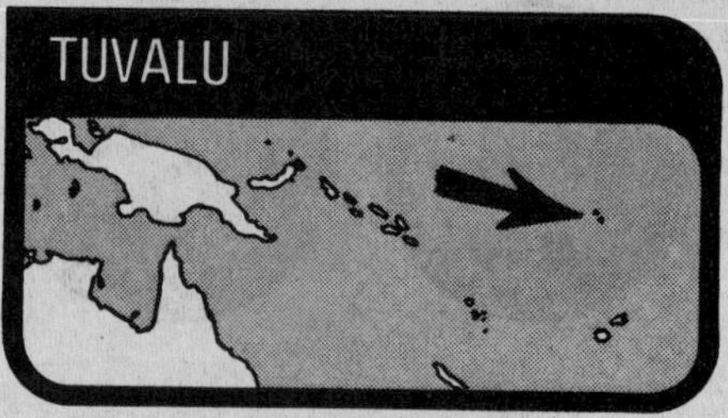

Tuvalu (formerly the Ellice or Lagoon Islands of the Gilbert and Ellice Islands), located in the South Pacific north of the Fiji Islands, has an area of 10 sq. mi. (26 sq. km.) and a population of *9,000. Capital: Funafuti. The independent state includes the islands of Nanumanga, Nanumea, Nui, Niutao, Viatupa, Funafuti, Nukufetau, Nukulailai and Nurakita. The latter four islands were claimed by the United States until relinquished by the Feb. 7, 1979, Treaty of Friendship signed by the United States and Tuvalu. The principal industries are copra production and phosphate mining.

The islands were discovered in 1764 by John Byron, a British navigator, and annexed by Britain in 1892. In 1915 they became part of the crown colony of the Gilbert and Ellice Islands. In 1974 the islanders voted to separate from the Gilberts, becoming on Jan. 1, 1976, the separate constitutional dependency of Tuvalu. Full independence was attained on Oct. 1, 1978. Tuvalu is a member of the Commonwealth of Nations. The Queen of England is Head of State.

RULERS

British

MONETARY SYSTEM

100 Cents = 1 Dollar

CENT

BRONZE

KM#	Date	Mintage	Fine	VF	XF	Unc
1	1976	.093	—	—	.10	.20
	1976	.020	—	—	Proof	1.00
	1981	—	—	—	.10	.20
	1981	—	—	—	Proof	1.00
	1985	—	—	—	.10	.20

2 CENTS

BRONZE

KM#	Date	Mintage	Fine	VF	XF	Unc
2	1976	.051	—	.10	.15	.30
	1976	.020	—	—	Proof	1.00
	1981	—	—	.10	.15	.30
	1981	—	—	—	Proof	1.00
	1985	—	—	.10	.15	.30

5 CENTS

COPPER-NICKEL

KM#	Date	Mintage	Fine	VF	XF	Unc
3	1976	.026	—	.10	.20	.40
	1976	.020	—	—	Proof	1.00
	1981	—	—	.10	.20	.40
	1981	—	—	—	Proof	1.00
	1985	—	—	.10	.20	.40

10 CENTS

COPPER-NICKEL
Crab

KM#	Date	Mintage	Fine	VF	XF	Unc
4	1976	.026	.15	.20	.30	.60
	1976	.020	—	—	Proof	2.00
	1981	—	.15	.20	.30	.60
4	1981	—	—	—	Proof	2.00
	1985	—	.15	.20	.30	.60

20 CENTS

COPPER-NICKEL
Flying Fish

KM#	Date	Mintage	Fine	VF	XF	Unc
5	1976	.036	.30	.40	.50	1.00
	1976	.020	—	—	Proof	2.50
	1981	—	.30	.40	.50	1.00
	1981	—	—	—	Proof	2.50
	1985	—	.30	.40	.50	1.00

50 CENTS

COPPER-NICKEL
Octopus

KM#	Date	Mintage	Fine	VF	XF	Unc
6	1976	.019	.50	.75	1.00	2.00
	1976	.020	—	—	Proof	3.00
	1981	—	.50	.75	1.00	2.00
	1981	—	—	—	Proof	3.00
	1985	—	.50	.75	1.00	2.00

DOLLAR

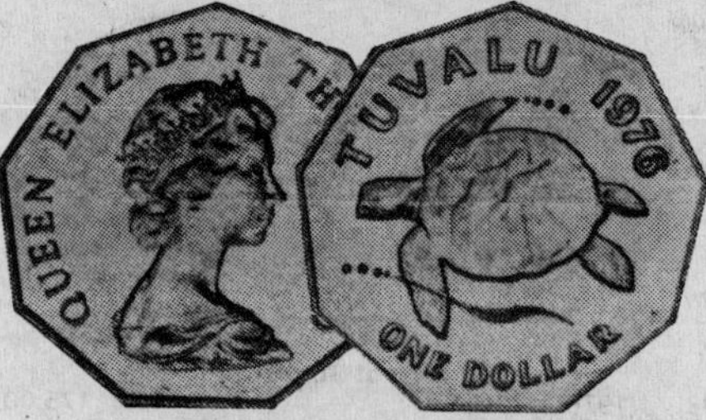

COPPER-NICKEL
Sea Turtle

KM#	Date	Mintage	Fine	VF	XF	Unc
7	1976	.021	1.00	1.50	2.00	4.00
	1976	.020	—	—	Proof	4.50
	1981	—	1.00	1.50	2.00	4.00
	1981	—	—	—	Proof	4.50
	1985	—	1.00	1.50	2.00	4.00

5 DOLLARS

28.2800 g, .925 SILVER, .8411 oz ASW
Outrigger Canoe

KM#	Date	Mintage	VF	XF	Unc
8	1976	.020	—	Proof	18.00

COPPER-NICKEL
Wedding of Prince Charles and Lady Diana

KM#	Date	Mintage	VF	XF	Unc
12	1981	—	—	—	7.50
	28.2800 g, .925 SILVER, .8411 oz ASW				
12a	1981	.035	—	Proof	35.00

10 DOLLARS

35.0000 g, .500 SILVER, .5627 oz ASW
1st Anniversary of Independence - Ship
Obv: Similar to 5 Dollars, KM#8.

KM#	Date	Mintage	VF	XF	Unc
10	1979	5,000	—	—	17.50
	35.0000 g, .925 SILVER, 1.0409 oz ASW				
10a	1979	2,500	—	Proof	40.00

35.0000 g, .500 SILVER, .5627 oz ASW
80th Birthday of Queen Mother
Obv: Similar to 5 Dollars, KM#8.

KM#	Date	Mintage	VF	XF	Unc
11	1980	—	—	—	17.50
	35.0000 g, .925 SILVER, 1.0409 oz ASW				
11a	1980	—	—	Proof	40.00

35.0000 g, .500 SILVER, .5627 oz ASW
Duke of Edinburgh Award
Obv: Similar to 5 Dollars, KM#8.

KM#	Date	Mintage	VF	XF	Unc
13	1981	5,000	—	—	15.00

35.0000 g, .925 SILVER, 1.0409 oz ASW

KM#	Date	Mintage	VF	XF	Unc
13a	1981	3,000	—	Proof	25.00

35.0000 g, .500 SILVER, .5627 oz ASW
Royal Visit
Obv: Similar to 5 Dollars, KM#8.

KM#	Date	Mintage	VF	XF	Unc
15	1982	2,500	—	—	22.50
	35.0000 g, .925 SILVER, 1.0409 oz ASW				
15a	1982	2,500	—	Proof	35.00

20 DOLLARS

31.4700 g, .925 SILVER, .9359 oz ASW
40th Anniversary of Coronation

KM#	Date	Mintage	Fine	VF	XF	Unc
16	1993	*.010	—	—	Proof	47.50
		Sir Isaac Newton				
17	1993	*.010	—	—	Proof	42.50
		HMS Royalist				
18	1993	*.015	—	—	Proof	42.50
		Leatherback Turtle				
19	1993	*.010	—	—	Proof	42.50
		Dugong - Manatee-like Animal				
20	1991	*.010	—	—	Proof	42.50

50 DOLLARS

15.9800 g, .917 GOLD, .4710 oz AGW
Native Meeting Hut

KM#	Date	Mintage	VF	XF	Unc
9	1976	2,074	—	Proof	275.00

Wedding of Prince Charles and Lady Diana

KM#	Date	Mintage	VF	XF	Unc
14	1981	5,000	—	Proof	250.00

100 DOLLARS

7.7760 g, .5833 GOLD, .1458 oz AGW
Todos Los Santos

KM#	Date	Mintage	Fine	VF	XF	Unc
21	1994	3,000	—	—	Proof	125.00

MINT SETS (MS)

KM#	Date	Mintage	Identification	Issue Price	Mkt. Val.
MS1	1985(7)	—	KM1-7	10.00	10.00

PROOF SETS (PS)

KM#	Date	Mintage	Identification	Issue Price	Mkt. Val.
PS1	1976(7)	20,000	KM1-7	13.00	15.00
PS2	1981(7)	—	KM1-7	—	15.00

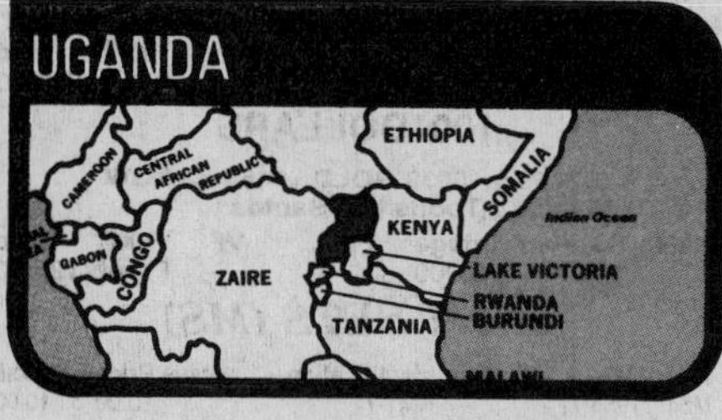

The Republic of Uganda, a former British protectorate located astride the equator in east-central Africa, has an area of 91,134 sq. mi. (236,040 sq. km.) and a population of *17 million. Capital: Kampala. Agriculture, including livestock, is the basis of the economy; there is some mining of copper, tin, gold and lead. Coffee, cotton, copper and tea are exported.

Uganda was first visited by Arab slavers in the 1830s. They were followed in the 1860s by British explorers searching for the headwaters of the Nile. The explorers, and the missionaries who followed them into the Lake Victoria region of south-central Africa in 1877-79, found well-developed African kingdoms dating back several centuries. In 1894 the local native Kingdom of Buganda was established as a British protectorate that was extended in 1896 to encompass an area substantially the same as the present Republic of Uganda. The protectorate was given a ministerial form of government in 1955, full internal self-government on March 1, 1962, and complete independence on Oct. 9, 1962. Uganda is a member of the Commonwealth of Nations. The president is Chief of State and Head of Government.

For earlier coinage refer to East Africa.

RULERS

British until 1962

MONETARY SYSTEM

100 Cents = 1 Shilling

5 CENTS

KM#	Date	Mintage	VF	XF	Unc
	BRONZE				
1	1966	41.000	.10	.15	.30
	1966	—	—	Proof	1.00
	1974	10.000	.15	.25	.50
	1975	14.784	.15	.25	.50
	COPPER PLATED STEEL				
1a	1976	10.000	.15	.25	.50

10 CENTS

KM#	Date	Mintage	VF	XF	Unc
	BRONZE				
2	1966	19.100	.10	.15	.35
	1966	—	—	Proof	1.00
	1968	20.000	.10	.15	.35
	1970	6.000	.15	.25	.50
	1972	5.000	.15	.25	.50
	1974	5.000	.15	.25	.50
	1975	14.110	.15	.25	.50
	COPPER PLATED STEEL				
2a	1976	10.000	.15	.25	.50

20 CENTS

KM#	Date	Mintage	VF	XF	Unc
	BRONZE				
3	1966	7.000	.30	.70	1.65
	1966	—	—	Proof	2.00
	1974	2.000	.25	.50	1.25

50 CENTS

KM#	Date	Mintage	VF	XF	Unc
	COPPER-NICKEL				
4	1966	16.000	.20	.40	1.00
	1966	—	—	Proof	1.25
	1970	3.000	.20	.40	1.25
	1974	10.000	.20	.40	1.00
	NICKEL PLATED STEEL				
4a	1976	10.000	.20	.40	1.00

SHILLING

KM#	Date	Mintage	VF	XF	Unc
	COPPER-NICKEL				
5	1966	24.500	.25	.50	1.25
	1966	—	—	Proof	2.50
	1968	10.000	.30	.70	1.65
	1972	—	.30	.70	1.65
	1975	15.540	.30	.70	1.65
	COPPER-NICKEL PLATED STEEL				
5a	1976	10.000	.30	.70	1.65
	1978	—	.30	.70	1.65
	NICKEL PLATED STEEL				
5b	1986	—	.30	.70	1.65

KM#	Date	Mintage	VF	XF	Unc
	COPPER PLATED STEEL				
27	1987	—	—	—	.25
	1987	—	—	Proof	2.00

2 SHILLINGS

KM#	Date	Mintage	VF	XF	Unc
	COPPER-NICKEL				
6	1966	4.000	1.00	2.00	4.00
	1966	—	—	Proof	5.00

4.0000 g, .999 SILVER, .1284 oz ASW
Visit of Pope Paul VI

KM#	Date	Mintage	VF	XF	Unc
8	1969	8,170	—	Proof	6.50
	1970	Inc. Ab.	—	Proof	6.50

KM#	Date	Mintage	VF	XF	Unc
	COPPER PLATED STEEL				
28	1987	—	—	—	.50
	1987	—	—	Proof	4.00

5 SHILLINGS

COPPER-NICKEL
F.A.O. Issue

KM#	Date	Mintage	VF	XF	Unc
7	1968	.100	2.00	3.00	5.00
	1968	5,000	—	Proof	7.00

10.0000 g, .999 SILVER, .3212 oz ASW
Visit of Pope Paul VI - Crested Cranes

KM#	Date	Mintage	VF	XF	Unc
9	1969	7,670	—	Proof	12.00
	1970	Inc. Ab.	—	Proof	12.00

KM#	Date	Mintage	VF	XF	Unc
	COPPER-NICKEL				
18	1972	*8.000	55.00	75.00	135.00

NOTE: Withdrawn from circulation. Almost entire mintage was melted.

KM#	Date	Mintage	VF	XF	Unc
	STAINLESS STEEL				
29	1987	—	—	—	1.50
	1987	—	—	Proof	6.00

10 SHILLINGS

20.0000 g, .999 SILVER, .6424 oz ASW
Visit of Pope Paul VI - Martyrs' Shrine

KM#	Date	Mintage	VF	XF	Unc
10	1969	6,720	—	Proof	17.50
	1970	Inc. Ab.	—	Proof	17.50

COPPER-NICKEL
Wedding of Prince Charles and Lady Diana

KM#	Date	Mintage	VF	XF	Unc
21	1981	.010	—	—	7.50

STAINLESS STEEL

KM#	Date	Mintage	VF	XF	Unc
30	1987	—	—	—	2.50
	1987	—	—	Proof	12.00

20 SHILLINGS

40.0000 g, .999 SILVER, 1.2848 oz ASW
Visit of Pope Paul VI - Map
Obv: Arms.

KM#	Date	Mintage	VF	XF	Unc
11	1969	6,670	—	Proof	25.00
	1970	Inc. Ab.	—	Proof	30.00

25 SHILLINGS

50.0000 g, .999 SILVER, 1.6061 oz ASW
Visit of Pope Paul VI - Globe
Obv: Arms.

KM#	Date	Mintage	VF	XF	Unc
12	1969	6,070	—	Proof	35.00
	1970	Inc. Ab.	—	Proof	40.00

30 SHILLINGS

60.0000 g, .999 SILVER, 1.9273 oz ASW
Illustration reduced. Actual size: 60mm.
Visit of Pope Paul VI
Obv: Arms.

KM#	Date	Mintage	VF	XF	Unc
13	1969	6,720	—	Proof	45.00
	1970	Inc. Ab.	—	Proof	50.00

50 SHILLINGS

6.9100 g, .900 GOLD, .1999 oz AGW
Visit of Pope Paul VI - Martyrs' Shrine

KM#	Date	Mintage	VF	XF	Unc
14	1969	4,390	—	Proof	125.00
	1970	Inc. Ab.	—	Proof	125.00

100 SHILLINGS

13.8200 g, .900 GOLD, .3999 oz AGW
Visit of Pope Paul VI - Map

KM#	Date	Mintage	VF	XF	Unc
15	1969	4,190	—	Proof	225.00
	1970	Inc. Ab.	—	Proof	225.00

31.4700 g, .925 SILVER, .9360 oz ASW
Wedding of Prince Charles and Lady Diana

KM#	Date	Mintage	VF	XF	Unc
22	1981	5,000	—	Proof	27.50

200 SHILLINGS

28.2800 g, .925 SILVER, .8411 oz ASW
International Year of Disabled Persons

KM#	Date	Mintage	VF	XF	Unc
26	1981	.010	—	—	25.00
	1981	.010	—	Proof	35.00

500 SHILLINGS

69.1200 g, .900 GOLD, 2.0002 oz AGW
Visit of Pope Paul VI - Globe
Obv: Arms.

KM#	Date	Mintage	VF	XF	Unc
16	1969	1,680	—	Proof	1000.
	1970	Inc. Ab.	—	Proof	1000.

136.0000 g, .500 SILVER, 2.1864 oz ASW
Wildlife - Elephants

KM#	Date	Mintage	VF	XF	Unc
23	1981	700 pcs.	—	—	150.00

136.0000 g, .925 SILVER, 4.0450 oz ASW

KM#	Date	Mintage	VF	XF	Unc
23a	1981	700 pcs.	—	Proof	225.00

1000 SHILLINGS

138.2400 g, .900 GOLD, 4.0005 oz AGW
Visit of Pope Paul VI

KM#	Date	Mintage	VF	XF	Unc
17	1969	1,390	—	Proof	2100.
	1970	Inc. Ab.	—	Proof	2100.

10.0000 g, .500 GOLD, .1607 oz AGW
Wedding of Prince Charles and Lady Diana
Rev: Busts of Charles and Diana right.

KM#	Date	Mintage	VF	XF	Unc
24	1981	1,500	—	Proof	125.00

COPPER-NICKEL
Matterhorn Mountain in Switzerland
Rev: Multi-color plastic applique.

KM#	Date	Mintage	VF	XF	Unc
35	1993	.015	—	Proof	25.00

2000 SHILLINGS

15.9800 g, .917 GOLD, .4710 oz AGW
International Year of Disabled Persons

KM#	Date	Mintage	VF	XF	Unc
31	1981	2,005	—	—	600.00
	1981	2,005	—	Proof	750.00

5000 SHILLINGS

33.9300 g, .917 GOLD, 1.0000 oz AGW
Wildlife - Crested Crane
Rev: Facing portrait of Dr. Milton Obote.

KM#	Date	Mintage	VF	XF	Unc
25	1981	100 pcs.	—	—	700.00
	1981	100 pcs.	—	Proof	750.00

12.0000 g, .999 SILVER, .3858 oz ASW
Soccer - Ball and Net

KM#	Date	Mintage	VF	XF	Unc
32	1992	*.010	—	—	30.00

10,000 SHILLING

20.0000 g, .999 SILVER, .6430 oz ASW
Soccer - Mount Rushmore Behind 2 Players

KM#	Date	Mintage	VF	XF	Unc
33	ND(1992)	*.010	—	Proof	45.00

Papal Visit

KM#	Date	Mintage	VF	XF	Unc
34	1993	—	—	Proof	40.00

POUND

7.9800 g, .917 GOLD, .2353 oz AGW
O.A.U. Conference Kampala 1975

KM#	Date	Mintage	VF	XF	Unc
20	1975	2,000	—	Proof	1000.

MINT SETS (MS)

KM#	Date	Mintage	Identification	Issue Price	Mkt. Val.
MS1	1987(4)	—	KM27-30	10.50	12.50

PROOF SETS (PS)

KM#	Date	Mintage	Identification	Issue Price	Mkt. Val.
PS1	1966(6)	8,250	KM1-6	7.75	12.50
PS2	1969(10)	1,390	KM8-17	790.00	3600.
PS3	1969(6)	6,070	KM8-13	78.50	140.00
PS4	1970(10)	Inc. KM-PS2	KM8-17	790.00	3600.
PS5	1970(6)	Inc. KM-PS3	KM8-13	78.50	155.00
PS6	1987(4)	2,500	KM27-30	25.00	25.00

Listings For

UMM AL QAIWAIN: refer to United Arab Emirates

UKRAINE

Ukraine (formerly the Ukrainian Soviet Socialist Republic) is bordered by Russia to the east, Russia and Belarus to the north, Poland, Slovakia and Hungary to the west, Romania and Moldova to the southwest and in the south by the Black Sea and the Sea of Azov. It has an area of 233,088 sq. mi. (603,700 sq. km.) and a population of 51.9 million. Capital: Kyiv (Kiev). Ukraine was the site of the Chernobyl nuclear power station disaster in 1986. Coal, grain, vegetables and heavy industrial machinery are major exports.

The territory of Ukraine has been inhabited for over 30,000 years. As the result of its location, Ukraine has served as the gateway to Europe for millennia and its early history has been recorded by Arabic, Greek, Roman, as well as Ukrainian historians.

Ukraine, which was known as *Rus'* until the sixteenth century (and from which the name Russia was derived in the 17th century). became the major political and cultural center of Eastern Europe in the 9th century. The Rus' Kingdom, under a dynasty of Varangian origin, due to its posistion on the intersection of the north-south Scandinavia to Byzantium and the east-west Orient to Europe trade routes, became a focal point of world trade. At its apex Rus' stretched from the Baltic to the Black Sea and from the upper Volga River in the east, almost to the Vistula River in the west. It has family ties to many European dynasties. In 988 knyaz (king) Volodymyr adopted Christianity from Byzantium. With it came church books written in the Cyrillic alphabet, which originated in Bulgaria. The Mongol invasion in 1240 brought an end to the might of the Rus' Kingdom.

In the seventeenth century, after almost four hundred years of Mongol, Lithuanian, Polish, and Turkish domination, the Cosack State under Hetman Bohdan Khmelnytsky regained Ukrainian independence. The Hetman State lasted until the mid-eighteenth century and was followed by a period of foreign rule. Eastern Ukraine was controlled by Russia, which enforced russification through introduction of the Russian language and prohibiting the use of the Ukrainian language in schools, books and public life. Western Ukraine came under relatively benign Austro-Hungarian rule.

With the disintegration of the Russian and Austro-Hungarian Empires in 1917 and 1918. Eastern Ukraine declared its full independence on January 22, 1918 and Western Ukraine followed suit on November 1 of that year. On January 22, 1919 both parts united into one state that had to defend itself on three fronts: from the "Red Bolsheviks" and their puppet Ukrainian Soviet Republic formed in Kharkiv, from the "White" czarist Russian forces, and from Poland. Ukraine lost the war. In 1920 Eastern Ukraine was occupied by the Bolsheviks and in 1922 was incorporated into the Soviet union. There followed a brief resurgence of Ukrainian language and culture until Stalin suppressed it in 1928. The artificial famine-genocide of 1932-33 killed 7-10 million Ukrainians, and Stalinist purges in the mid-1930s took a heavy toll. Western Ukraine was partitioned between Poland, Romania, Hungary and Czechoslovakia.

On August 24, 1991 Ukraine once again declared its independence. On December 1, 1991 over 90% of Ukraine's electorate approved full independence from the Soviet Union. On December 5, 1991 the Ukrainian Parliament abrogated the 1922 treaty which incorporated Ukraine into the Soviet Union. Later, Leonid Kravchuk was elected president by a 65% majority.

Ukraine is a charter member of the United Nations and has inherited the third largest nuclear arsenal in the world, which by recent agreement with the USA will be dismantled within the next decade. Ukrainians in the homeland and the diaspora make up 1% of the world's population.

Rulers

Russian, 1793-1917

MINT

w/o mm - Lugansk

MONETARY SYSTEM

(2) Kopijk КОПiЙКН
(5 and up) Kopijok КОПiЙОК
100 Kopijok (Kopiyok) КОПiЙОК = 1 Karbovanets КАРБОВАНЕЦЬ

2 KOPIJK

ALUMINUM

KM#	Date	Mintage	VF	XF	Unc
4	1993	—	—	—	15.00

10 KOPIJOK

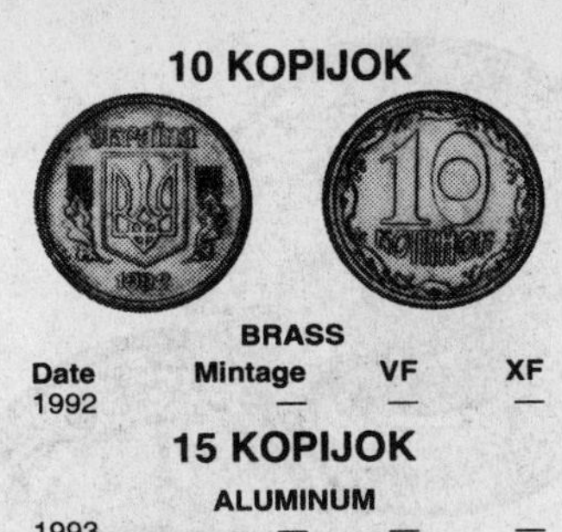

BRASS

KM#	Date	Mintage	VF	XF	Unc
1	1992	—	—	—	10.00

15 KOPIJOK

ALUMINUM

KM#	Date	Mintage	VF	XF	Unc
5	1993	—	—	—	30.00

25 KOPIJOK

BRASS

KM#	Date	Mintage	VF	XF	Unc
2	1992	—	—	—	15.00

50 KOPIJOK

BRASS

KM#	Date	Mintage	VF	XF	Unc
3	1992	—	—	—	20.00

UNITED ARAB EMIRATES

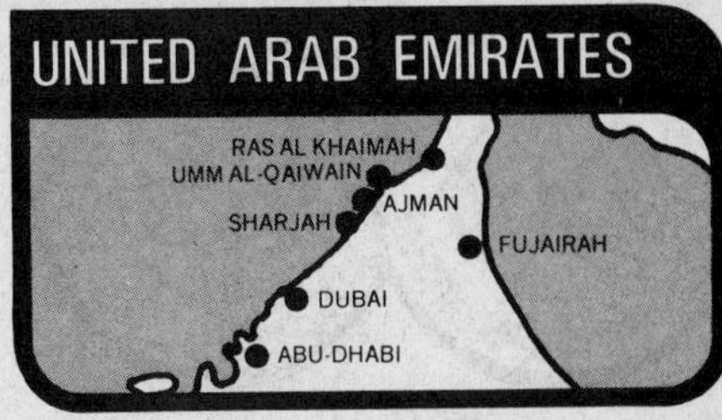

Five of the former Trucial States which comprise The United Arab Emirates, and which were formerly British treaty protectorates located along the southern shore of the Arabian Peninsula, have issued Non-Circulating Legal Tender Coins (NCLT). They are Ajman, Fujairah, Ras al Khaimah, Sharjah and Umm al-Qaiwain. These coins have been declared legal tender by the issuing states but are not intended to circulate. No circulation strikes were minted, and none of the coins were available at face value.

AJMAN

Ajman is the smallest and poorest of the emirates in the United Arab Emirates. It has an estimated area of 100 sq. mi. (250 sq. km.) and a population of 6,000. Ajman's first act as an autonomous entity was a treaty with Great Britain in 1820. On December 2, 1971 Ajman became one of the 6 original members of the United Arab Emirates.

TITLES

اجمان

Ajman

RULERS

Rashid III, 1928-1981

MONETARY SYSTEM

100 Dirhams = 1 Ryal

RIYAL

3.9500 g, .640 SILVER, .0812 oz ASW
Rev: 2 dates.

KM#	Date	Year	Mintage	VF	XF	Unc
1.1	AH1389	1969	.020	—	—	5.00
	1389	1969	1,200	—	Proof	10.00

Rev: 3 dates.

KM#	Date	Year	Mintage	VF	XF	Unc
1.2	AH1390	1970	—	—	—	20.00

2 RIYALS

6.4500 g, .835 SILVER, .1731 oz ASW
Rev: 2 dates.

KM#	Date	Year	Mintage	VF	XF	Unc
2.1	AH1389	1969	.020	—	—	10.00
	1389	1969	1,200	—	Proof	20.00

Rev: 3 dates.

KM#	Date	Year	Mintage	VF	XF	Unc
2.2	AH1390	1970	—	—	—	30.00

5 RIYALS

15.0000 g, .835 SILVER, .4027 oz ASW
Rev: 2 dates.

KM#	Date	Year	Mintage	VF	XF	Unc
3.1	AH1389	1969	.010	—	—	17.50
	1389	1969	1,200	—	Proof	35.00

Rev: 3 dates.

KM#	Date	Year	Mintage	VF	XF	Unc
3.2	AH1390	1970	—	—	—	50.00
	1390	1970	—	—	Proof	90.00

15.0000 g, .925 SILVER, .4460 oz ASW
Death of Gamal Abdel Nassar

KM#	Date	Year	Mintage	VF	XF	Unc
12	AH1390	1970	5,000	—	Proof	15.00

Rev: Dag Hammarskjold

KM#	Date	Year	Mintage	VF	XF	Unc
17	ND	(1970)	1,175	—	Proof	50.00

Rev: Mahatma Gandhi

KM#	Date	Year	Mintage	VF	XF	Unc
18	ND	(1970)	1,175	—	Proof	50.00

Rev: Martin Luther King

KM#	Date	Year	Mintage	VF	XF	Unc
19	ND	(1970)	1,175	—	Proof	50.00

Rev: George C. Marshall

KM#	Date	Year	Mintage	VF	XF	Unc
20	ND	(1970)	1,175	—	Proof	50.00

Rev: Bertrand A. Russell

KM#	Date	Year	Mintage	VF	XF	Unc
21	ND	(1970)	1,175	—	Proof	50.00

Rev: Albert Schweitzer

KM#	Date	Year	Mintage	VF	XF	Unc
22	ND	(1970)	1,175	—	Proof	50.00

Rev: Jan Palac

KM#	Date	Year	Mintage	VF	XF	Unc
23	ND	(1970)	1,175	—	Proof	50.00

Rev: Albert J. Luthuli

KM#	Date	Year	Mintage	VF	XF	Unc
24	ND	(1970)	1,175	—	Proof	50.00

F.A.O. Issue

KM#	Date	Year	Mintage	VF	XF	Unc
26	AH1390	1970	2,000	—	Proof	40.00

NOTE: This issue is not recognized by the FAO.

Save Venice

KM#	Date	Year	Mintage	VF	XF	Unc
27	ND	(1971)	4,800	—	Proof	30.00

71/2 RIYALS

23.0000 g, .925 SILVER, .6840 oz ASW
Rashid bin Humaid al-Na'ini
Rev: Bonefish

KM#	Date	Year	Mintage	VF	XF	Unc
5	AH1389	1970	4,350	—	—	35.00
	1389	1970	650 pcs.	—	Proof	75.00

Rev: Barbary Falcon

KM#	Date	Year	Mintage	VF	XF	Unc
6	AH1389	1970	4,350	—	—	35.00
	1389	1970	650 pcs.	—	Proof	75.00

Rev: Gazelle

KM#	Date	Year	Mintage	VF	XF	Unc
7	AH1389	1970	4,350	—	—	35.00
	1389	1970	650 pcs.	—	Proof	75.00

23.0000 g, .835 SILVER, .6175 oz ASW
Death of Gamal Abdel Nassar

KM#	Date	Year	Mintage	VF	XF	Unc
13	AH1390	1970	6,000	—	Proof	30.00

10 RIYALS

30.0000 g, .925 SILVER, .8923 oz ASW
Rev: Vladimir Lenin

KM#	Date	Year	Mintage	VF	XF	Unc
9.1	ND	(1970)	—	—	Proof	55.00
	ND	(1970)	—		Matte Proof	—

Obv: PROOF added.

KM#	Date	Year	Mintage	VF	XF	Unc
9.2	ND	(1970)	3,200	—	Proof	45.00

25 RIYALS

5.1750 g, .900 GOLD, .1497 oz AGW
Death of Gamal Abdel Nassar

KM#	Date	Year	Mintage	VF	XF	Unc
15	AH1390	1970	1,100	—	Proof	125.00

NOTE: Some of these coins have a serial number on the obverse below the bust.

Rev: Dag Hammarskjold

KM#	Date	Year	Mintage	VF	XF	Unc
28	ND	(1970)	—	—	Proof	125.00

Rev: Mahatma Gandhi

KM#	Date	Year	Mintage	VF	XF	Unc
29	ND	(1970)	—	—	Proof	125.00

Rev: Martin Luther King

KM#	Date	Year	Mintage	VF	XF	Unc
30	ND	(1970)	—	—	Proof	125.00

Rev: George C. Marshall

KM#	Date	Year	Mintage	VF	XF	Unc
31	ND	(1970)	—	—	Proof	125.00

Rev: Bertrand A. Russell

KM#	Date	Year	Mintage	VF	XF	Unc
32	ND	(1970)	—	—	Proof	125.00

Rev: Albert Schweitzer

KM#	Date	Year	Mintage	VF	XF	Unc
33	ND	(1970)	—	—	Proof	125.00

Rev: Jan Palac

KM#	Date	Year	Mintage	VF	XF	Unc
34	ND	(1970)	—	—	Proof	125.00

Rev: Albert J. Luthuli

KM#	Date	Year	Mintage	VF	XF	Unc
35	ND	(1970)	—	—	Proof	125.00

Save Venice
Rev. leg: Save Venice.

KM#	Date	Year	Mintage	VF	XF	Unc
36	ND	(1971)	—	—	Proof	125.00

50 RIYALS

10.3500 g, .900 GOLD, .2995 oz AGW
Death of Gamal Abdel Nassar
Similar to 7.5 Riyals, KM#13.

KM#	Date	Year	Mintage	VF	XF	Unc
16	AH1390	1970	700 pcs.	—	Proof	225.00

NOTE: Some of these coins have a serial number below the bust on the obverse.

Save Venice

KM#	Date	Year	Mintage	VF	XF	Unc
39	ND	(1971)	—	—	Proof	225.00

75 RIYALS

15.5300 g, .900 GOLD, .4494 oz AGW
F.A.O. Issue
Obv: Fish

KM#	Date	Year	Mintage	VF	XF	Unc
41	AH1389	1970	—	—	Proof	350.00

100 RIYALS

20.7000 g, .900 GOLD, .5990 oz AGW
Rev: Vladimir Lenin

KM#	Date	Year	Mintage	VF	XF	Unc
10	ND	(1970)	1,000	—	Proof	375.00

Save Venice

KM#	Date	Year	Mintage	VF	XF	Unc
40	ND	(1971)	—	—	Proof	375.00

MINT SETS (MS)

KM#	Date	Mintage	Identification	Issue Price	Mkt. Val.
MS1	1969(3)	—	KM1-3	—	32.50
MS2	1970(3)	4,350	KM5-7	—	100.00

PROOF SETS (PS)

KM#	Date	Mintage	Identification	Issue Price	Mkt. Val.
PS1	1969(3)	1,200	KM1-3	11.22	65.00
PS2	1970(8)	1,175	KM17-24	—	400.00
PS3	1970(8)	—	KM28-35	—	1000.
PS4	1970(4)	—	KM12,13,15,16	—	400.00
PS5	1970(3)	100	KME4-6	—	190.00
PS6	1970(3)	650	KM5-7	19.50	225.00
PS7	1970(3)	—	KME9,E7,10	—	475.00
PS8	1970(2)	800	KME7,10	—	415.00
PS9	1970(2)	5,000	KM12,13	9.50	45.00
PS10	1970(3)	—	KM12,13,15	—	170.00
PS11	1970(3)	—	KM9.1-9.2,10	—	475.00
PS12	1971(4)	—	KM27,36,39,40	—	760.00

FUJAIRAH

Fujairah is the only emirate of the United Arab Emirates that does not have territory on the Persian Gulf. It is on the eastern side of the "horn" of Oman. It has an estimated area of 450 sq. mi. (1200 sq. km.) and a population of 27,000. Fujairah has been, historically a frequent rival of Sharjah. As recently as 1952 Great Britain recognized Fujairah as an autonomous state. An original member of the United Arab Emirates.

TITLES

Fujairah(t) الفجيرة

RULERS

Mohamad bin Hamad al-Sharqi, 1952-74
Hamad, 1974

RIYAL

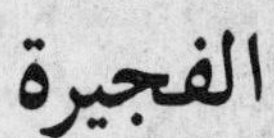

3.0000 g, 1.0000 SILVER, .0964 oz ASW
Desert Fort
Obv: Similar to KM#2.

KM#	Date	Year	Mintage	VF	XF	Unc
1	AH1388	1969	4,050	—	Proof	15.00
	1389	1970	Inc. Ab.	—	Proof	15.00

2 RIYALS

6.0000 g, 1.0000 SILVER, .1928 oz ASW
President Richard Nixon

KM#	Date	Year	Mintage	VF	XF	Unc
2	AH1388	1969	6,250	—	Proof	25.00
	1389	1970	Inc. Ab.	—	Proof	25.00

5 RIYALS

15.0000 g, 1.0000 SILVER, .4823 oz ASW
1972 Munich Olympics
Obv: Similar to KM#2.

KM#	Date	Year	Mintage	VF	XF	Unc
3	AH1388	1969	3,550	—	Proof	45.00
	1389	1970	1,300	—	Proof	45.00

10 RIYALS

30.0000 g, 1.0000 SILVER, .9645 oz ASW
Apollo XI
Obv: Fineness in oval at lower left, mintage figure stamped at lower right.

KM#	Date	Year	Mintage	VF	XF	Unc
4.1	AH1388	1969	.014	—	Proof	45.00

Obv: Mintage figure stamped at lower left, fineness in oval at lower right.

KM#	Date	Year	Mintage	VF	XF	Unc
4.2	AH1389	1970	—	—	Proof	45.00

Apollo XII

KM#	Date	Year	Mintage	VF	XF	Unc
5	AH1388	1969	.015	—	Proof	45.00
	1389	1970	.015	—	Proof	45.00

Apollo XIII

KM#	Date	Year	Mintage	VF	XF	Unc
19	AH1389	1970	.015	—	Proof	45.00

Visit of Pope Paul VI to Philippines
Obv: Similar to KM#4.

KM#	Date	Year	Mintage	VF	XF	Unc
20	AH1389	1970	300 pcs.	—	Proof	50.00

Visit of Pope Paul VI to Australia
Obv: Similar to KM#4.

KM#	Date	Year	Mintage	VF	XF	Unc
21	AH1389	1970	.012	—	Proof	50.00

Apollo XIV
Obv: Similar to KM#4.

KM#	Date	Year	Mintage	VF	XF	Unc
22	AH1389	1970	.014	—	Proof	50.00

25 RIYALS

5.1800 g, .900 GOLD, .1499 oz AGW
U.S. President Nixon

KM#	Date	Year	Mintage	VF	XF	Unc
7	AH1388	1969	3,280	—	Proof	115.00
	1389	1970	Inc. Ab.	—	Proof	115.00

NOTE: The 1969 issue has the fineness incuse, the 1970 issue has the fineness both raised and incuse.

50 RIYALS

10.3600 g, .900 GOLD,.2998 oz AGW
1972 Munich Olympics

KM#	Date	Year	Mintage	VF	XF	Unc
8	AH1388	1969	1,230	—	Proof	225.00
	1389	1970	400 pcs.	—	Proof	225.00

100 RIYALS

20.7300 g, .900 GOLD, .5999 oz AGW
Apollo XI
Obv: Similar to KM#24.

KM#	Date	Year	Mintage	VF	XF	Unc
9	AH1388	1969	2,140	—	Proof	350.00

Apollo XII

KM#	Date	Year	Mintage	VF	XF	Unc
10	AH1388	1969	3,040	—	Proof	350.00
	1389	1970	—	—	Proof	350.00

Apollo XIII
Obv: Similar to KM#24.
Rev: Similar to 10 Riyals, KM#19.

KM#	Date	Year	Mintage	VF	XF	Unc
23	AH1389	1970	600 pcs.	—	Proof	375.00

Visit of Pope Paul VI to Philippines

KM#	Date	Year	Mintage	VF	XF	Unc
24	AH1389	1970	290 pcs.	—	Proof	500.00

Visit of Pope Paul VI to Australia
Obv: Similar to KM#24.
Rev: Similar to 10 Riyals, KM#21.

KM#	Date	Year	Mintage	VF	XF	Unc
26	AH1389	1970	250 pcs.	—	Proof	500.00

Apollo XIV
Obv: Similar to KM#24.

KM#	Date	Year	Mintage	VF	XF	Unc
25	AH1389	1971	550 pcs.	—	Proof	375.00

200 RIYALS

41.4600 g, .900 GOLD, 1.1998 oz AGW
Mohamad bin Hamad al-Sharqi
Obv: Arms.

KM#	Date	Year	Mintage	VF	XF	Unc
11	AH1388	1969	680 pcs.	—	Proof	675.00

NOTE: The above pieces are serially numbered on the obverse.

PROOF SETS (PS)

KM#	Date	Mintage	Identification	Issue Price	Mkt. Val.
PS1	Mixed 1969-71(18)		—	—	—
PS2	Mixed 1969-71(9)		KM1-5,19-22	—	375.00
PS3	Mixed 1969-71(8)		KM4,5,19,22,9,10,23,25	—	1650.
PS4	1969(8)	—	KM1-4,7-9,11	—	1450.
PS5	1969(5)	2,550	KM1-5	40.00	175.00
PS6	1969(5)	5,000	KM7-11	280.00	1700.
PS7	1969(4)	—	KM1-4	—	130.00
PS8	1970(5)	200	KM1-5	40.00	185.00

RAS AL-KHAIMA

Ras al Khaima is only one of the coin issuing emirates that was not one of the original members of the United Arab Emirates. It was a part of Sharjah. It has an estimated area of 650 sq. mi. (1700 sq. km.) and a population of 30,000. Ras al Khaima is the only member of the United Arab Emirates that has agriculture as its principal industry.

TITLES

راس الخيمة

Ras al Khaima(t)

RULERS

Saqr, 1948

MONETARY SYSTEM

100 Dirhams = 1 Riyal

50 DIRHAMS

COPPER-NICKEL
Barbary Falcon

KM#	Date	Year	Mintage	VF	XF	Unc
28	AH1390	1970	—	—	—	7.50

RIYAL

3.9500 g, .640 SILVER, .0812 oz ASW

KM#	Date	Year	Mintage	VF	XF	Unc
1	AH1389	1969	—	—	—	10.00
	1389	1969	1,500	—	Proof	15.00

2 RIYALS

6.4500 g, .835 SILVER, .1731 oz ASW

KM#	Date	Year	Mintage	VF	XF	Unc
2	AH1389	1969	—	—	—	15.00
	1389	1969	1,500	—	Proof	25.00

2 1/2 RIYALS

7.5000 g. .925 SILVER, .2231 oz ASW
Barbary Falcon

KM#	Date	Year	Mintage	VF	XF	Unc
29	AH1390	1970	—	—	—	17.50

5 RIYALS

15.0000 g, .835 SILVER, .4027 oz ASW

KM#	Date	Year	Mintage	VF	XF	Unc
3	AH1389	1969	—	—	—	20.00
	1389	1969	1,500	—	Proof	30.00

7 1/2 RIYALS

22.5000 g, .925 SILVER, .6692 oz ASW
Barbary Falcon

KM#	Date	Year	Mintage	VF	XF	Unc
30	AH1390	1970	—	—	—	30.00

Giacomo Agostini

KM#	Date	Year	Mintage	VF	XF	Unc
5	ND	(1970)	*2,000	—	Proof	550.00

Centennial of Rome - Man Plowing

KM#	Date	Mintage	VF	XF	Unc
17	1970	*2,000	—	Proof	125.00

World Championship Football - Jules Rimet Cup
Rev: Jules Rimet cup.
Similar to 10 Riyals, KM#6.

KM#	Date	Mintage	VF	XF	Unc
32	1970	*2,000	—	Proof	250.00

10 RIYALS

30.0000 g, .925 SILVER, .8921 oz ASW
1st Anniversary of Death of Dwight Eisenhower

KM#	Date	Mintage	VF	XF	Unc
31	1970	4,500	—	—	15.00
	1970	1,400	—	Proof	22.50

World Championship Football - Jules Rimet Cup
Obv: Similar to KM#18.

6	1970	*2,000	—	Proof	450.00

Felice Gimondi
Obv: Similar to KM#18.

KM#	Date	Year	Mintage	VF	XF	Unc
7	ND	(1970)	*2,000	—	Proof	650.00

Centennial of Rome - Emperor

KM#	Date	Mintage	VF	XF	Unc
18	1970	*2,000	—	Proof	200.00

15 RIYALS

45.0000 g, .925 SILVER, 1.3384 oz ASW
Champions of Sport
Obv: Denomination.

8	ND	*2,000	—	Proof	750.00

Centennial of Rome - Founders

19	1970	*2,000	—	Proof	225.00

World Championship Football - Jules Rimet Cup

33	1970	—	—	Proof	600.00

50 RIYALS

10.3500 g, .900 GOLD, .2995 oz AGW
Gigi Riva

KM#	Date	Year	Mintage	VF	XF	Unc
10	ND	(1970)	*2,000	—	Proof	375.00

Centennial of Rome - Vittorio Emanuele II

KM#	Date	Mintage	VF	XF	Unc
21	1970	*2,000	—	Proof	300.00

75 RIYALS

15.5300 g, .900 GOLD, .4494 oz AGW
Gianni Rivera

KM#	Date	Year	Mintage	VF	XF	Unc
11	ND	(1970)	*2,000	—	Proof	450.00

Centennial of Rome - Capitol

KM#	Date	Mintage	VF	XF	Unc
22	1970	*2,000	—	Proof	400.00

100 RIYALS

20.7000 g, .900 GOLD, .5990 oz AGW
World Championship Football - Jules Rimet Cup

12	1970	*2,000	—	Proof	650.00

Centennial of Rome - WW I Victory

23	1970	*2,000	—	Proof	500.00

150 RIYALS

31.0500 g, .900 GOLD, .8985 oz AGW
1972 Munich Olympics

KM#	Date	Year	Mintage	VF	XF	Unc
13	ND	(1970)	3,060	—	Proof	1450.

Centennial of Rome - Standing Liberty

KM#	Date	Mintage	VF	XF	Unc
24	1970	*2,000	—	Proof	800.00

200 RIYALS

41.4000 g, .900 GOLD, 1.1980 oz AGW
Champions of Sport

KM#	Date	Year	Mintage	VF	XF	Unc
14	ND	(1970)	*2,000	—	Proof	1250.

Centennial of Rome - Romulus and Remus

KM#	Date	Mintage	VF	XF	Unc
25	1970	*2,000	—	Proof	1000.

MINT SETS (MS)

KM#	Date	Mintage	Identification	Issue Price	Mkt. Val.
MS1	1969(3)	—	KM1-3	—	45.00

PROOF SETS (PS)

KM#	Date	Mintage	Identification	Issue Price	Mkt. Val.
PS1	1969(3)	1,500	KM1-3	10.80	70.00
PS2	(1970) (9)	—	KM5-8,10-14	—	4600.
PS3	1970(8)	—	KM17-19,21-25	—	2560.
PS4	(1970) (5)	—	KM10-14	—	2600.
PS5	1970(5)	—	KM21-25	—	2400.
PS6	(1970) (4)	—	KM5-8	41.50	2000.
PS7	1970(3)	—	KM17-19	—	160.00
PS8	1970(4)	—	KM6,10-12	—	2000.

SHARJAH

Sharjah is the only one of the emirates that shares boundaries with all of the others plus Oman. It has an area of 1,000 sq. mi. (2,600 sq. km.) and a population of 40,000. Sharjah was an important pirate base in the 18th and early 19th centuries. Most of the treaties and diplomatic relations were with Great Britain.

TITLES

Ash-Sharqa(t) الشارجة

RULERS

Saqr III, 1951-1965
Khalid III, 1965-1972

5 RUPEES

25.0000 g, .720 SILVER, .5787 oz ASW
President John F. Kennedy Memorial

KM#	Date	Mintage	VF	XF	Unc
1	1964	—	—	—	12.50
	1964 PROOF below flags on obv.				
		—	—	Proof	20.00

NOTE: KM#1 was ordered by the Sheik, who according to the British had no authority to issue it.

RIYAL

3.0000 g, .999 SILVER, .0963 oz ASW
Mona Lisa

KM#	Date	Year	Mintage	VF	XF	Unc
2	AH1389	1970	3,850	—	Proof	12.50

2 RIYALS

6.0000 g, .999 SILVER, .1927 oz ASW
Mexico World Soccer Cup

KM#	Date	Year	Mintage	VF	XF	Unc
3	AH1389	1970	4,500	—	Proof	22.50

5 RIYALS

15.0000 g, .999 SILVER, .4818 oz ASW
Napoleon

KM#	Date	Year	Mintage	VF	XF	Unc
4	AH1389	1970	2,500	—	Proof	37.50

10 RIYALS

30.0000 g, .999 SILVER, .9636 oz ASW
Bolivar
Obv: Similar to 1 Riyal, KM#2.

KM#	Date	Year	Mintage	VF	XF	Unc
5	AH1389	1970	3,200	—	Proof	45.00

25 RIYALS

5.1800 g, .900 GOLD, .1499 oz AGW
Mona Lisa

KM#	Date	Year	Mintage	VF	XF	Unc
7	AH1389	1970	6,775	—	Proof	160.00

50 RIYALS

10.3600 g, .900 GOLD, .2998 oz AGW
Mexico World Soccer Cup
Obv: Similar to 25 Riyals, KM#7.

KM#	Date	Year	Mintage	VF	XF	Unc
8	AH1389	1970	1,815	—	Proof	225.00

100 RIYALS

20.7300 g, .900 GOLD, .5999 oz AGW
Napoleon

KM#	Date	Year	Mintage	VF	XF	Unc
9	AH1389	1970	—	—	Proof	450.00

Bolivar

KM#	Date	Year	Mintage	VF	XF	Unc
10	AH1389	1970	—	—	Proof	375.00

200 RIYALS

41.4600 g, .900 GOLD, 1.1998 oz AGW
Khalid III
Obv: Similar to 25 Riyals, KM#7.

KM#	Date	Year	Mintage	VF	XF	Unc
11	AH1389	1970	435 pcs.	—	Proof	700.00

PROOF SETS (PS)

KM#	Date	Mintage	Identification	Issue Price	Mkt. Val.
PS1	1970(9)	—	KM2-5,7-11	—	2025.
PS2	1970(5)	—	KM7-11	—	1900.
PS3	1970(4)	2,500	KM2-5	25.30	120.00

UMM AL-QAIWAIN

This emirate is the second smallest, least developed and smallest in population. The area is 300 sq. mi. (800 sq. km.) and the population is 5,000. The first recognition by the West was in 1820. Most of the emirate is uninhabited desert. Native boat building is an important activity. One of the original members of the United Arab Emirates.

TITLES

ام القيوين

Umm al-Qaiwain

RULERS

Ahmed II, 1929

RIYAL

3.0000 g, .999 SILVER, .0963 oz ASW
Old Cannon

KM#	Date	Year	Mintage	VF	XF	Unc
1	AH1389	1970	2,050	—	Proof	10.00

2 RIYALS

6.0000 g, .999 SILVER, .1927 oz ASW
Fort of the 19th Century

KM#	Date	Year	Mintage	VF	XF	Unc
2	AH1389	1970	2,050	—	Proof	17.50

5 RIYALS

15.0000 g, .999 SILVER, .4818 oz ASW
Gazelle

KM#	Date	Year	Mintage	VF	XF	Unc
3	AH1389	1970	2,100	—	Proof	32.50

10 RIYALS

30.0000 g, .999 SILVER, .9636 oz ASW
Facade of the Great Rock Temple
Obv: Similar to 5 Riyals, KM#3.

KM#	Date	Year	Mintage	VF	XF	Unc
4	AH1389	1970	2,000	—	Proof	40.00

25 RIYALS

5.1800 g, .900 GOLD, .1499 oz AGW
Old Cannon

KM#	Date	Year	Mintage	VF	XF	Unc
6	AH1389	1970	500 pcs.	—	Proof	135.00

50 RIYALS

10.3600 g, .900 GOLD, .2998 oz AGW
Fort of the 19th Century

KM#	Date	Year	Mintage	VF	XF	Unc
7	AH1389	1970	420 pcs.	—	Proof	250.00

100 RIYALS

20.7300 g, .900 GOLD, .5999 oz AGW
Gazelle

KM#	Date	Year	Mintage	VF	XF	Unc
8	AH1389	1970	300 pcs.	—	Proof	425.00

200 RIYALS

41.4600 g, .900 GOLD, 1.1998 oz AGW
Sheik Ahmed Ben Rashid al Maalla
Obv: Similar to 25 Riyals, KM#6.

KM#	Date	Year	Mintage	VF	XF	Unc
9	AH1389	1970	230 pcs.	—	Proof	690.00

PROOF SETS (PS)

KM#	Date	Mintage	Identification	Issue Price	Mkt. Val.
PS1	1970(4)	2,000	KM1-4	26.30	100.00
PS2	1970(4)	230	KM6-9	—	1500.
PS3	1970(8)	—	KM1-4,6-9	—	1700.

UNITED ARAB EMIRATES

The seven United Arab Emirates (formerly known as the Trucial Sheikhdoms or States), located along the southern shore of the Persian Gulf, are comprised of the Sheikhdoms of Abu Dhabi, Dubai, al-Sharjah, Ajman, Umm al-Qaiwain, Ras al-Khaimah and al-Fujairah. They have a combined area of about 32,000 sq. mi. (83,600 sq. km.) and a population of *2.1 million. Capital: Abu Zaby (Abu Dhabi). Since the oil strikes of 1958-60, the economy has centered about petroleum.

The Trucial States came under direct British influence in 1892 when the Maritime Truce Treaty enacted after the supression of pirate activity along the Trucial Coast was enlarged to enjoin the states from disposing of any territory, or entering into any foreign agreements, without British consent in return for British protection from external aggression. In March of 1971 Britain reaffirmed its decision to terminate its treaty relationships with the Trucial Sheikhdoms, whereupon the seven states joined with Bahrain and Qatar in an effort to form a union of Arab Emirates under British protection. When the prospective members failed to agree on terms of union, Bahrain and Qatar declared their respective independence, Aug. and Sept. of 1971. Six of the sheikhdoms united to form the United Arab Emirates on Dec. 2, 1971. Ras al Khaimah joined a few weeks later.

TITLES

الامارات العربية المتحدة

al-Imara(t) al-Arabiya(t) al-Muttahidah

MONETARY SYSTEM

فلسا فلس فلوس

Falus, Fulus   *Fals, Fils*   *Falsan*

100 Fils = 1 Dirham

FIL

BRONZE
F.A.O. Issue - Date Palms

KM#	Date	Year	Mintage	VF	XF	Unc
1	AH1393	1973	4.000	.10	.15	.20
	1395	1975	—	.10	.15	.20

5 FILS

BRONZE
F.A.O. Issue - Mata Hari Fish

KM#	Date	Year	Mintage	VF	XF	Unc
2	AH1393	1973	11.400	.10	.15	.25
	1402	1982	—	.10	.15	.25
	1407	1987	—	.10	.15	.25
	1408	1988	—	.10	.15	.25

10 FILS

BRONZE
Arab Dhow

KM#	Date	Year	Mintage	VF	XF	Unc
3	AH1393	1973	6.400	.15	.35	.75
	1402	1982	—	.15	.35	.75
	1404	1984	—	.15	.35	.75
	1407	1987	—	.15	.35	.75
	1408	1988	—	.15	.35	.75

25 FILS

COPPER-NICKEL
Arab Dune Gazelle

KM#	Date	Year	Mintage	VF	XF	Unc
4	AH1393	1973	10.400	.25	.35	.50
	1402	1982	—	.25	.35	.50
	1403	1983	—	.25	.35	.50
	1404	1984	—	.25	.35	.50
	1406	1986	—	.25	.35	.50
	1407	1987	—	.25	.35	.50
	1408	1988	—	.25	.35	.50
	1409	1989	—	.25	.35	.50

50 FILS

COPPER-NICKEL
Oil Derricks

KM#	Date	Year	Mintage	VF	XF	Unc
5	AH1393	1973	8.400	.35	.50	1.50
	1402	1982	—	.35	.50	1.50

KM#	Date	Year	Mintage	VF	XF	Unc
5	1404	1984	—	.35	.50	1.50
	1407	1987	—	.35	.50	1.50
	1408	1988	—	.35	.50	1.50
	1409	1989	—	.35	.50	1.50

DIRHAM

COPPER-NICKEL
Jug

KM#	Date	Year	Mintage	VF	XF	Unc
6	AH1393	1973	13.000	.50	.75	2.00
	1402	1982	—	.50	.75	2.00
	1404	1984	—	.50	.75	2.00
	1406	1986	—	.50	.75	2.00
	1407	1987	—	.50	.75	2.00
	1408	1988	—	.50	.75	2.00
	1409	1989	—	.50	.75	2.00

27th Chess Olympiad in Dubai

KM#	Date	Mintage	VF	XF	Unc
10	1986	—	—	—	10.00

25th Anniversary of Off Shore Oil Drilling

KM#	Date	Mintage	VF	XF	Unc
11	1987	—	—	—	10.00

10th Anniversary of al-Ain University

KM#	Date	Mintage	VF	XF	Unc
14	ND(1987)	—	—	—	8.00

Soccer

KM#	Date	Mintage	VF	XF	Unc
15	ND(1990)	—	—	—	6.50

5 DIRHAMS

COPPER-NICKEL
1500th Anniversary of al-Hegira

KM#	Date	Year	Mintage	VF	XF	Unc
9	AH1401	1981	—	—	—	6.00

50 DIRHAMS

27.2200 g, .925 SILVER, .8095 oz ASW
IYC and UNICEF

KM#	Date	Year	Mintage	VF	XF	Unc
7	AH1400	1980	8,031	—	Proof	20.00

500 DIRHAMS

19.9700 g, .917 GOLD, .5886 oz AGW
5th Anniversary of United Arab Emirates

KM#	Date	Mintage	VF	XF	Unc
12	1976	.011	—	Proof	275.00

750 DIRHAMS

17.1700 g, .900 GOLD, .4969 oz AGW
IYC and UNICEF

KM#	Date	Year	Mintage	VF	XF	Unc
8	AH1400	1980	3,063	—	Proof	245.00

1000 DIRHAMS

39.9400 g, .917 GOLD, 1.1771 oz AGW
5th Anniversary of United Arab Emirates

KM#	Date	Mintage	VF	XF	Unc
13	1976	.010	—	Proof	600.00

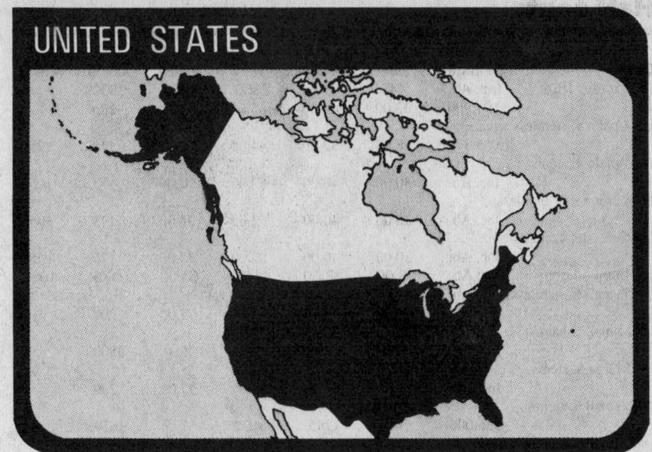

The United States of America as politcally organized under the Articles of Confederation consisted of the 13 original British-American colonies — New Hampshire, Massachusetts, Rhode Island, Connecticut, New York, New Jersey, Pennsylvania, Delaware, Virginia, North Carolina, South Carolina, Georgia and Maryland — clustered along the eastern seaboard of North America between the forests of Maine and the marshes of Georgia. Under the Articles of Confederation, the United States had no national capital; Philadelphia, where the "United States in Congress Assembled" met, was the "seat of government." The population during this political phase of America's history (1781-1789) was about 3 million, most of whom lived on self-sufficient family farms. Fishing, lumbering and the production of grains for export were major economic endeavors. Rapid strides were also being made in industry and manufacturing; by 1775, the (then) colonies were acccounting for one-seventh of the world's production of raw iron.

On the basis of the voyage of John Cabot to the North American mainland in 1497, England claimed the entire continent. The first permanent English settlement was established at Jamestown, Virginia, in 1607. France and Spain also claimed extensive territory in North America. At the end of the French and Indian Wars (1763), England acquired all of the territory east of the Mississippi River, including East and West Florida. From 1776 to 1781, the States were governed by the Continental Congress. From 1781 to 1789, they were organized under the Articles of Confederation, during which period the individual States had the right to issue money. Independence from Great Britain was attained by the American Revolution in 1776. The Constitution which organized and governs the present United States was ratified on Nov. 21, 1788.

U.S. MINT ISSUES OF 1792

The better part of a year passed between the establishment of the United States Mint and the introduction of regular half-cent and cent coinage in 1793. During this time several pattern issues, including a substantial issue of about 1500 half-dismes, were executed under the supervision of David Rittenhouse who was appointed as Mint Director by President Washington on April 14, 1792, just twelve days after the law establishing the Mint was enacted.

Rittenhouse did not actually accept the appointment until July 1, and sometime during the two weeks following the first U.S. coins — the 1792 half-dismes — were apparently struck. The dies for this coin were prepared by Robert Birch (the similar disme obverse, and apparently the reverse was executed by Adam Eckfeldt), and the actual striking did not take place in the first mint building, but in the cellar of a building where the mint's early equipment acquisitions were being stored, as its construction did not commence until July 31.

Those first half-dismes, which are reputed to carry a portrait of Martha Washington, were struck at the request of President Washington from silver which he presented for their execution, the popular opinion being that it was taken from his silver service.

Construction of the Mint building progressed rapidly, so that all was in readiness for the installation of two coining presses purchased abroad which arrived on September 21. In his annual address to Congress on November 6, President Washington remarked on the "small beginning" which had been made in the production of coins. The first coins actually struck at the Mint, however, were probably silver center cent patterns produced on December 17 from dies prepared by Henry Voight. These coins carried a silver plug worth three-quarters of a cent in the center of a copper planchet valued at one-quarter of a cent, while similar pieces were also prepared without the silver plug.

Three other patterns of 1792 exist. Chronologically the first was probably a cent created by Robert Birch which carries an obverse bust similar to that on the half-disme and bears the abbreviation "G.W.Pt." (George Washington President) at the base of the reverse. The second is a similar cent which has Birch's name signed to the bust and a reverse similar to that adopted in 1793, with the fraction 1/100 at the base. The final pattern was apparently intended for a quarter and engraved by Joseph Wright.

HALF DISME

KM#	Date	Good	Fine	VF
75	1792	1,000.	3,000.	5,000.
75a	1792 Copper (unique)	2,000.	3,500.	6,000.

DISME

KM#	Date	
76	1792 Silver (3 known)	
76a	1792 Copper (2 reeded edge, about 10 plain edge)	Garrett 54,000.

SILVER CENTER CENT

KM#	Date	
77	1792 Silver Center (about 8 known)	Norweb MS-60 143,000
77a	1792 No Silver Center (copper or billon, 4 known)	Norweb EF-40 35,200

BIRCH CENT

KM#	Date	
78	1792 Copper (known with plain and two types of lettered edges, about 15 known combined.)	Garrett 200,000.
78a	1792 "G.W. Pt." on reverse below wreath tie, White Metal (unique)	Garrett 90,000.

WRIGHT QUARTER

KM#	Date	
79	1792 Copper, Reeded Edge (2 known)	
79b	1792 White Metal Die-Trial	Garrett 12,000.

Half cents

Liberty Cap

Head facing left

Designer: Adam Eckfeldt. **Size:** 22 millimeters. **Weight:** 6.74 grams. **Composition:** 100% copper.

Date	Mintage	G-4	VG-8	F-12	VF-20	XF-40	MS-60
1793	35,334	1600.	2250.	4500.	6500.	11,000.	—

Head facing right

Designers: Robert Scot (1794) and John Smith Gardner (1795). **Size:** 23.5 millimeters. **Weight:** 6.74 grams (1794-1795) and 5.44 grams (1795-1797). **Composition:** 100% copper. **Notes:** The "lettered edge" varieties have "Two Hundred for a Dollar" inscribed around the edge. The "pole" varieties have a pole, upon which the cap is hanging, resting on Liberty's shoulder. The "punctuated date" varieties have a comma after the 1 in the date. The 1797 "1 above 1" variety has a second 1 above the 1 in the date.

Date	Mintage	G-4	VG-8	F-12	VF-20	XF-40	MS-60
1794	81,600	265.	375.	750.	1400.	2450.	—
1795 lettered edge, pole	25,600	245.	350.	550.	1000.	1900.	—
1795 plain edge, no pole	109,000	225.	285.	540.	915.	1700.	—
1795 lettered edge, punctuated date	Inc. Ab.	245.	350.	550.	1000.	2100.	—
1795 plain edge, punctuated date	Inc. Ab.	240.	335.	535.	900.	1800.	—
1796 pole	5,090	5500.	6900.	9500.	12,500.	20,000.	—
1796 no pole	1,390	—	—	—	Rare	—	—
1797 pl. edge	119,215	265.	375.	575.	1000.	1900.	—
1797 let. edge	Inc. Ab.	1000.	1600.	2500.	5000.	—	—
1797 1 above 1	Inc. Ab.	225.	285.	540.	915.	1700.	—

Draped Bust

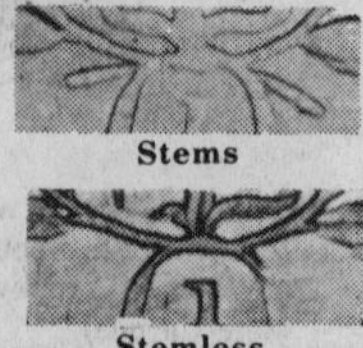
Stems

Stemless

Designer: Robert Scot. **Size:** 23.5 millimeters. **Weight:** 5.44 grams. **Composition:** 100% copper. **Notes:** The wreath on the reverse was redesigned slightly in 1802, resulting in "reverse of 1800" and "reverse of 1802" varieties. The "stems" varieties have stems extending from the wreath above and on both sides of the fraction on the reverse. On the "crosslet 4" variety, a serif appears at the far right of the crossbar on the 4 in the date. The "spiked chin" variety appears to have a spike extending from Liberty's chin, the result of a damaged die. Varieties of the 1805 strikes are distinguished by the size of the 5 in the date. Varieties of the 1806 strikes are distinguished by the size of the 6 in the date.

Date	Mintage	G-4	VG-8	F-12	VF-20	XF-40	MS-60
1800	211,530	30.00	42.50	65.00	150.	325.	—
1802/0 rev. 1800	14,366	5000.	8500.	12,000.	—	—	—
1802/0 rev. 1802	Inc. Ab.	440.	975.	2350.	4000.	9800.	—
1803	97,900	33.00	44.00	65.00	125.	325.	—
1804 plain 4, stemless wreath	1,055,312	28.00	32.00	44.00	63.00	140.	1050.
1804 plain 4, stems	Inc. Ab.	30.00	40.00	52.00	75.00	175.	1050.
1804 crosslet 4, stemless	Inc. Ab.	30.00	40.00	52.00	75.00	175.	1050.
1804 crosslet 4, stems	Inc. Ab.	30.00	40.00	52.00	75.00	175.	1050.
1804 spiked chin	Inc.Ab.	28.00	32.00	44.00	63.00	175.	1050.
1805 small 5, stemless	814,464	29.00	37.00	50.00	77.00	200.	—
1805 small 5, stems	Inc. Ab.	475.	995.	2250.	3000.	3800.	—
1805 large 5, stems	Inc. Ab.	29.00	37.00	50.00	77.00	200.	—
1806 small 6, stems	356,000	185.	295.	450.	775.	1650.	—
1806 small 6, stemless	Inc. Ab.	28.00	32.00	44.00	63.00	185.	1040.
1806 large 6, stems	Inc. Ab.	28.00	32.00	44.00	63.00	185.	—
1807	476,000	28.00	32.00	50.00	77.00	325.	1500.
1808/7	400,000	60.00	105.	200.	625.	—	—
1808	Inc. Ab.	29.00	37.00	50.00	77.00	330.	1050.

Classic Head

Designer: John Reich. **Size:** 23.5 millimeters. **Weight:** 5.44 grams. **Composition:** 100% copper. **Notes:** Restrikes listed were produced privately in the mid-1800s. The 1831 restrikes have two varieties with different-size berries in the wreath on the reverse. The 1828 strikes have either 12 or 13 stars on the obverse.

Date	Mintage	G-4	VG-8	F-12	VF-20	XF-40	MS-60
1809/6	1,154,572	26.00	32.00	36.00	56.00	80.00	500.
1809	Inc. Ab.	21.00	30.00	36.00	53.00	75.00	475.
1810	215,000	31.00	36.00	45.00	105.	200.	1750.
1811	63,140	80.00	175.	550.	1100.	1950.	—
1811 restrike, reverse of 1802, uncirculated						—	6500.
1825	63,000	33.00	39.00	47.00	67.00	225.	1000.
1826	234,000	28.00	35.00	40.00	56.00	110.	675.
1828 13 stars	606,000	21.00	30.00	35.00	44.00	57.00	220.
1828 12 stars	Inc. Ab.	25.00	35.00	40.00	56.00	80.00	500.
1829	487,000	25.00	32.00	35.00	46.00	69.00	600.
1831 original	2,200	—	—	—	4000.	5000.	7500.
1831 restrike, lg. berries, reverse of 1836, proof						—	6000.
1831 restrike, sm. berries, reverse of 1852, proof						—	7000.
1832	154,000	21.00	30.00	35.00	44.00	57.00	220.
1833	120,000	21.00	30.00	35.00	44.00	57.00	220.
1834	141,000	21.00	30.00	35.00	44.00	57.00	220.
1835	398,000	21.00	30.00	35.00	44.00	57.00	350.
1836 original	—	—		Proof only	—	—	6500.
1836 restrike, reverse of 1852, proof only						—	6500.

Braided Hair

Designer: Christian Gobrecht. **Size:** 23 millimeters. **Weight:** 5.44 grams. **Composition:** 100% copper. **Notes:** 1840-1848 strikes, both originals and restrikes, are known in proof only; mintages are unknown. The small-date varieties of the 1849, both originals and restrikes, are known in proof only. Restrikes were produced clandestinely by Philadelphia Mint personnel in the mid-1800s.

Date	Mintage	G-4	VG-8	F-12	VF-20	XF-40	MS-60	Prf-60
1840 original	—	—	—	Proof only		—	—	3800.
1840 restrike	—	—	—	Proof only		—	—	3200.

Date	Mintage	G-4	VG-8	F-12	VF-20	XF-40	MS-60	Prf-60
1841 original	—	—	—		Proof only	—	—	3800.
1841 restrike	—	—	—		Proof only	—	—	3000.
1842 original	—	—	—		Proof only	—	—	3800.
1842 restrike	—	—	—		Proof only	—	—	3200.
1843 original	—	—	—		Proof only	—	—	3800.
1843 restrike	—	—	—		Proof only	—	—	3200.
1844 original	—	—	—		Proof only	—	—	3800.
1844 restrike	—	—	—		Proof only	—	—	3200.
1845 original	—	—	—		Proof only	—	—	3800.
1845 restrike	—	—	—		Proof only	—	—	3200.
1846 original	—	—	—		Proof only	—	—	3800.
1846 restrike	—	—	—		Proof only	—	—	3200.
1847 original	—	—	—		Proof only	—	—	3800.
1847 restrike	—	—	—		Proof only	—	—	3200.
1848 original	—	—	—		Proof only	—	—	3800.
1848 restrike	—	—	—		Proof only	—	—	3200.
1849 original, small date			—		Proof only	—	—	3800.
1849 restrike small date			—		Proof only	—	—	3200.

Date	Mintage	G-4	VG-8	F-12	VF-20	XF-40	MS-60
1849 lg. date	39,864	39.00	43.00	50.00	58.00	80.00	400.
1850	39,812	36.00	40.00	48.00	55.00	80.00	400.
1851	147,672	27.00	34.00	43.00	50.00	63.00	185.
1852	—	—	—		Proof only	—	4250.
1853	129,694	27.00	34.00	43.00	50.00	63.00	170.
1854	55,358	29.00	37.00	44.00	52.00	75.00	175.
1855	56,500	29.00	37.00	44.00	52.00	75.00	170.
1856	40,430	35.00	39.00	50.00	60.00	85.00	275.
1857	35,180	50.00	55.00	65.00	80.00	110.	275.

Large cents

Flowing Hair

Chain reverse

Designer: Henry Voigt. **Size:** 26-27 millimeters. **Weight:** 13.48 grams. **Composition:** 100% copper.

Date	Mintage	G-4	VG-8	F-12	VF-20	XF-40	MS-60
1793 chain	36,103	2500.	4850.	6650.	9750.	25,000	—

Wreath reverse

Designer: Adam Eckfeldt. **Size:** 26-28 millimeters. **Weight:** 13.48 grams. **Composition:** 100% copper.

Date	Mintage	G-4	VG-8	F-12	VF-20	XF-40	MS-60
1793 wreath	63,353	975.	1450.	1950.	3750.	6950.	—

Liberty Cap

Designers: Joseph Wright (1793-1795) and John Smith Gardner (1795-1796). **Size:** 29 millimeters. **Weight:** 13.48 grams (1793-1795) and 10.89 grams (1795-1796). **Notes:** The heavier pieces were struck on a thicker planchet. The Liberty design on the obverse was revised slightly in 1794, but the 1793 design was used on some 1794 strikes. The 1795 "lettered edge" variety has "One Hundred for a Dollar" and a leaf inscribed on the edge.

Date	Mintage	G-4	VG-8	F-12	VF-20	XF-40	MS-60
1793 cap	11,056	1850.	2800.	4500.	6000.	—	—
1794	918,521	165.	250.	440.	825.	1450.	—
1794 head '93	Inc. Ab.	325.	500.	1100.	2000.	—	—
1795	501,500	160.	200.	415.	725.	1400.	—
1795 lettered edge, "One Cent" high in wreath	37,000	180.	275.	450.	750.	1375.	—
1796 Lib. Cap	109,825	175.	260.	415.	900.	1650.	—

Draped Bust

Stems

Stemless

Designer: Robert Scot. **Size:** 29 millimeters. **Weight:** 10.98 grams. **Composition:** 100% copper. **Notes:** The "stemless" variety does not have stems extending from the wreath above and on both sides of the fraction on the reverse. The 1801 "3 errors" variety has the fraction on the reverse reading "1/000", has only one stem extending from the wreath above and on both sides of the fraction on the reverse, and "United" in "United States of America" appears as "Iinited."

Date	Mintage	G-4	VG-8	F-12	VF-20	XF-40	MS-60
1796	363,375	70.00	90.00	165.	335.	750.	—
1797	897,510	40.00	60.00	125.	325.	750.	—
1797 stemless	Inc. Ab.	60.00	100.	200.	1500.	2250.	—
1798	1,841,745	30.00	50.00	125.	325.	700.	—
1798/97	Inc. Ab.	70.00	115.	185.	450.	800.	—
1799	42,540	900.	1650.	4000.	5900.	—	—
1800	2,822,175	37.00	45.00	110.	425.	700.	—
1801	1,362,837	37.00	45.00	110.	375.	690.	—
1801 3 errors	Inc. Ab.	37.00	65.00	170.	425.	700.	—
1802	3,435,100	35.00	42.00	95.00	285.	700.	2000.
1803	2,471,353	35.00	42.00	95.00	285.	665.	2000.
1804	756,838	600.	1000.	1800.	3250.	5000.	—
1805	941,116	35.00	42.00	100.	290.	665.	—
1806	348,000	40.00	65.00	125.	475.	750.	—
1807	727,221	30.00	42.00	120.	350.	665.	—

Classic Head

Designer: John Reich. **Size:** 29 millimeters. **Weight:** 10.89 grams. **Composition:** 100% copper.

Date	Mintage	G-4	VG-8	F-12	VF-20	XF-40	MS-60
1808	1,109,000	33.00	65.00	195.	510.	1075.	3150.
1809	222,867	70.00	135.	250.	800.	1500.	—
1810	1,458,500	32.00	65.00	190.	500.	1075.	3150.
1811	218,025	65.00	105.	250.	695.	1070.	—
1812	1,075,500	33.00	65.00	190.	510.	1075.	3150.

Large cents

Date	Mintage	G-4	VG-8	F-12	VF-20	XF-40	MS-60
1813	418,000	45.00	72.00	200.	600.	1200.	—
1814	357,830	32.00	65.00	190.	530.	1100.	3150.

Coronet

Designer: Robert Scot. **Size:** 28-29 millimeters. **Weight:** 10.89 grams. **Composition:** 100% copper. **Notes:** The 1817 strikes have either 13 or 15 stars on the obverse.

Date	Mintage	G-4	VG-8	F-12	VF-20	XF-40	MS-60
1816	2,820,982	12.50	17.00	30.00	70.00	120.	300.
1817 13 stars	3,948,400	11.00	13.00	21.00	40.00	100.	225.
1817 15 stars	Inc. Ab.	12.00	20.00	30.00	60.00	155.	450.
1818	3,167,000	10.00	13.00	21.00	40.00	100.	350.
1819	2,671,000	11.00	13.00	21.00	40.00	100.	315.
1820	4,407,550	11.00	13.00	21.00	40.00	100.	225.
1821	389,000	17.50	30.00	45.00	100.	250.	—
1822	2,072,339	11.00	15.00	24.00	46.00	135.	350.
1823	Inc. 1824	30.00	55.00	90.00	235.	650.	—
1823/22	Inc. 1824	27.00	45.00	65.00	175.	350.	1750.
1824	1,262,000	11.50	16.00	28.00	60.00	80.00	575.
1824/22	Inc. Ab.	20.00	95.00	220.	295.	—	1500.
1825	1,461,100	10.50	14.00	24.00	55.00	150.	350.
1826	1,517,425	10.50	14.00	24.00	50.00	130.	600.
1826/25	Inc. Ab.	18.00	30.00	60.00	115.	250.	800.
1827	2,357,732	10.50	12.50	20.00	45.00	115.	600.
1828	2,260,624	10.00	12.50	20.00	50.00	115.	300.
1829	1,414,500	11.00	13.00	21.00	45.00	120.	350.
1830	1,711,500	11.00	13.00	20.00	40.00	110.	325.
1831	3,359,260	10.00	11.00	20.00	35.00	100.	325.
1832	2,362,000	10.00	11.00	20.00	40.00	100.	325.
1833	2,739,000	10.00	11.00	20.00	35.00	100.	325.
1834	1,855,100	10.00	11.00	20.00	40.00	100.	350.
1835	3,878,400	10.00	11.00	20.00	40.00	100.	325.
1836	2,111,000	10.00	11.00	20.00	40.00	95.00	300.

Braided Hair

Slanting 5s

Upright 5s

Designer: Christian Gobrecht. **Size:** 27.5 millimeters. **Weight:** 10.89 grams. **Composition:** 100% copper. **Notes:** 1840 and 1842 strikes are known with both small and large dates, with little difference in value. 1855 and 1856 strikes are known with both slanting and upright 5s in the date, with little difference in value. A slightly larger Liberty head and larger reverse lettering were used beginning in 1843. One 1843 variety uses the old obverse with the new reverse.

Date	Mintage	G-4	VG-8	F-12	VF-20	XF-40	MS-60
1837	5,558,300	9.50	10.50	16.50	33.00	90.00	300.
1838	6,370,200	9.50	10.50	16.50	33.00	80.00	225.
1839	3,128,661	9.50	10.50	16.50	42.00	100.	350.
1839/36	Inc. Ab.	175.	350.	750.	1500.	—	—
1840	2,462,700	9.50	10.50	11.50	19.00	58.00	265.
1841	1,597,367	10.00	12.00	15.00	23.00	68.00	300.
1842	2,383,390	9.50	10.50	11.50	18.00	55.00	265.
1843	2,425,342	9.50	10.50	17.00	25.00	65.00	225.
1843 obverse 1842 with reverse of 1844							
	Inc. Ab.	10.00	13.00	19.00	38.00	80.00	350.
1844	2,398,752	9.75	10.50	12.00	17.00	49.00	160.
1844/81	Inc. Ab.	12.00	20.00	28.00	60.00	130.	450.
1845	3,894,804	9.50	10.50	12.00	14.00	40.00	160.
1846	4,120,800	9.50	10.50	12.00	14.00	40.00	160.
1847	6,183,669	9.50	10.50	12.00	14.00	40.00	160.
1848	6,415,799	9.50	10.50	12.00	14.00	40.00	160.

Large cents

Date	Mintage	G-4	VG-8	F-12	VF-20	XF-40	MS-60
1849	4,178,500	9.50	10.50	12.00	14.00	40.00	160.
1850	4,426,844	9.50	10.50	12.00	14.00	40.00	160.
1851	9,889,707	9.50	10.50	12.00	14.00	40.00	160.
1851/81	Inc. Ab.	10.00	12.50	18.00	35.00	95.00	400.
1852	5,063,094	9.50	10.50	12.00	14.00	40.00	160.
1853	6,641,131	9.50	10.50	12.00	14.00	40.00	160.
1854	4,236,156	9.50	10.50	12.00	14.00	40.00	160.
1855	1,574,829	9.75	11.00	14.00	17.00	45.00	170.
1856	2,690,463	9.50	10.50	12.00	14.00	40.00	160.
1857	333,456	25.00	28.00	35.00	55.00	85.00	300.

Small cents

Flying Eagle

Large letters; "AM" connected

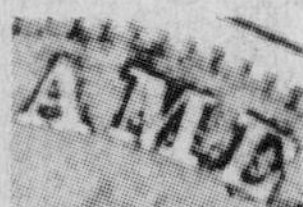

Small letters; "AM" separated

Designer: James B. Longacre. **Size:** 19 millimeters. **Weight:** 4.67 grams. **Composition:** 88% copper, 12% nickel. **Notes:** On the large-letter variety of 1858, the "A" and "M" in "America" are connected at their bases; on the small-letter variety, the two letters are separated.

Date	Mintage	G-4	VG-8	F-12	VF-20	XF-40	AU-50	MS-60	MS-65	Prf-65
1856	Est. 1,000	3500.	3900.	4500.	5100.	5400.	5600.	6300.	20,000.	21,000.
1857	17,450,000	16.50	19.00	24.00	36.00	88.00	165.	225.	2500.	16,750.
1858 LL	24,600,000	17.50	20.00	25.00	40.00	105.	165.	265.	2500.	15,000.
1858 SL	Inc. Ab.	17.50	20.00	25.00	40.00	105.	165.	265.	2500.	13,000.

Indian Head

1859

1860-1909

1864 "L"

Copper-nickel composition

Designer: James B. Longacre. **Size:** 19 millimeters. **Weight:** 4.67 grams. **Composition:** 88% copper, 12% nickel.

Date	Mintage	G-4	VG-8	F-12	VF-20	XF-40	AU-50	MS-60	MS-65	Prf-65
1859	36,400,000	7.50	8.00	11.00	31.00	75.00	160.	180.	2350.	4900.
1860	20,566,000	5.00	7.00	9.50	15.00	42.00	75.00	140.	1000.	2400.
1861	10,100,000	16.00	20.00	24.00	38.00	75.00	155.	200.	1000.	2400.
1862	28,075,000	3.75	5.00	5.50	11.00	25.00	49.00	100.	1000.	1750.
1863	49,840,000	3.00	4.00	5.50	11.00	22.00	45.00	55.00	750.	1750.
1864	13,740,000	15.00	18.00	21.00	26.00	42.00	77.00	140.	1000.	2300.

Bronze composition

Weight: 3.11 grams. **Composition:** 95% copper, 5% tin and zinc. **Notes:** The 1864 "L" variety has the designer's initial in Liberty's hair to the right of her neck.

Date	Mintage	G-4	VG-8	F-12	VF-20	XF-40	AU-50	MS-60	MS-65	Prf-65
1864	39,233,714	5.50	6.50	10.00	22.00	37.00	50.00	77.00	450.	2800.
1864 L	Inc. Ab.	35.00	48.00	70.00	115.	190.	225.	315.	1150.	44,000.
1865	35,429,286	5.25	7.00	9.50	19.50	30.00	42.00	77.00	400.	900.
1866	9,826,500	29.00	33.00	45.00	77.00	135.	180.	240.	840.	725.
1867	9,821,000	29.00	33.00	45.00	94.00	135.	195.	250.	945.	850.
1868	10,266,500	29.00	33.00	45.00	77.00	125.	175.	240.	850.	675.
1869/8	6,420,000	110.	160.	195.	310.	400.	525.	625.	2400.	—
1869	Inc. Ab.	40.00	65.00	160.	235.	275.	350.	420.	1100.	875.
1870	5,275,000	34.00	40.00	140.	220.	295.	350.	470.	1100.	875.
1871	3,929,500	38.00	70.00	170.	280.	310.	385.	455.	1200.	1050.
1872	4,042,000	56.00	95.00	225.	280.	350.	420.	525.	1675.	1400.
1873	11,676,500	12.00	15.50	30.00	39.00	91.00	120.	170.	595.	610.
1874	14,187,500	12.00	15.50	25.00	39.00	85.00	120.	170.	500.	550.
1875	13,528,000	12.00	15.50	23.00	39.00	77.00	115.	170.	595.	700.
1876	7,944,000	23.00	30.00	37.00	55.00	105.	135.	190.	630.	560.

Date	Mintage	G-4	VG-8	F-12	VF-20	XF-40	AU-50	MS-60	MS-65	Prf-65
1877	852,500	310.	345.	490.	675.	1350.	1900.	2200.	4900.	4150.
1878	5,799,850	23.00	30.00	35.00	55.00	95.00	125.	190.	595.	525.
1879	16,231,200	4.50	5.00	7.00	14.00	30.00	40.00	63.00	385.	525.
1880	38,964,955	2.75	3.50	5.50	7.50	20.00	30.00	63.00	350.	500.
1881	39,211,575	2.75	3.75	5.50	7.50	18.50	25.00	35.00	280.	500.
1882	38,581,100	2.75	3.75	5.50	7.50	16.00	25.00	39.00	280.	500.
1883	45,589,109	2.00	3.75	5.50	7.50	16.00	25.00	35.00	280.	525.
1884	23,261,742	2.75	4.00	6.00	10.00	20.00	30.00	50.00	335.	500.
1885	11,765,384	3.95	6.50	9.75	19.50	48.00	65.00	100.	490.	500.
1886	17,654,290	3.00	5.00	10.00	27.00	58.00	75.00	105.	490.	500.
1887	45,226,483	1.30	1.80	3.00	4.95	13.50	25.00	35.00	245.	500.
1888	37,494,414	1.30	1.80	3.00	4.95	13.50	25.00	35.00	350.	500.
1889	48,869,361	1.30	1.65	2.75	4.50	12.00	25.00	35.00	250.	520.
1890	57,182,854	1.30	1.65	2.50	4.50	10.00	23.00	35.00	250.	520.
1891	47,072,350	1.30	1.65	2.50	4.50	10.00	23.00	35.00	250.	500.
1892	37,649,832	1.30	1.65	2.50	4.50	10.00	23.00	35.00	250.	530.
1893	46,642,195	1.30	1.65	2.50	4.50	10.00	23.00	35.00	250.	650.
1894	16,752,132	1.75	3.00	6.50	10.00	18.00	32.00	49.00	375.	650.
1895	38,343,636	1.25	1.75	2.50	4.00	10.00	19.00	30.00	165.	530.
1896	39,057,293	1.20	1.75	2.50	4.00	10.00	17.00	30.00	160.	540.
1897	50,466,330	1.20	1.75	2.50	4.00	10.00	17.00	30.00	160.	475.
1898	49,823,079	1.20	1.75	2.50	4.00	10.00	17.00	30.00	160.	475.
1899	53,600,031	1.20	1.30	2.00	3.50	9.50	17.00	30.00	160.	475.
1900	66,833,764	1.20	1.30	2.25	3.50	9.50	15.00	22.00	145.	330.
1901	79,611,143	1.05	1.20	1.75	2.75	7.50	15.00	22.00	145.	330.
1902	87,376,722	1.05	1.20	1.75	2.75	7.50	15.00	22.00	145.	330.
1903	85,094,493	1.05	1.20	1.75	2.75	7.50	15.00	22.00	145.	330.
1904	61,328,015	1.05	1.20	1.75	2.75	7.50	15.00	22.00	145.	330.
1905	80,719,163	1.05	1.20	1.75	2.75	7.50	15.00	22.00	145.	330.
1906	96,022,255	1.05	1.20	1.75	2.75	7.50	15.00	22.00	145.	330.
1907	108,138,618	1.05	1.20	1.75	2.75	7.50	15.00	22.00	145.	330.
1908	32,327,987	1.05	1.20	2.00	3.00	7.50	15.00	22.00	145.	330.
1908S	1,115,000	25.00	28.00	30.00	40.00	84.00	135.	225.	595.	—
1909	14,370,645	1.60	2.00	2.65	4.50	9.00	19.00	31.00	145.	450.
1909S	309,000	195.	215.	230.	245.	325.	390.	500.	975.	—

Lincoln

Wheat reverse

"VDB"

Memorial reverse

Wheat reverse, bronze composition

Designer: Victor D. Brenner. **Size:** 19 millimeters. **Weight:** 3.11 grams. **Composition:** 95% copper, 5% tin and zinc. **Notes:** The 1909 "VDB" varieties have the designer's initials inscribed at the 6 o'clock position on the reverse. The initials were removed until 1918, when they were restored on the obverse.

Date	Mintage	G-4	VG-8	F-12	VF-20	XF-40	AU-50	MS-60	MS-65	Prf-65
1909	72,702,618	.50	.55	.85	1.35	2.25	5.50	15.00	80.00	460.
1909VDB	27,995,000	2.10	2.30	2.40	2.75	3.00	6.00	10.00	45.00	2800.
1909S	1,825,000	42.00	46.00	53.00	63.00	95.00	120.	155.	250.	—
1909SVDB	484,000	350.	400.	475.	520.	575.	615.	715.	1900.	—
1910	146,801,218	.15	.20	.25	.60	63.00	4.75	14.00	63.00	450.
1910S	6,045,000	7.00	7.75	8.50	12.00	23.00	49.00	75.00	195.	—
1911	101,177,787	.25	.30	.50	1.95	5.25	7.00	18.00	135.	450.
1911D	12,672,000	4.25	5.50	6.75	11.50	32.00	50.00	77.00	700.	—
1911S	4,026,000	17.00	20.00	22.00	24.00	43.00	65.00	120.	800.	—
1912	68,153,060	.65	.85	1.85	3.90	12.00	18.00	25.00	160.	450.
1912D	10,411,000	770.	5.00	6.00	15.00	39.50	54.00	120.	840.	—
1912S	4,431,000	12.00	12.75	14.25	17.25	40.00	52.00	90.00	975.	—
1913	76,532,352	.45	.50	1.25	3.50	9.50	11.00	23.00	220.	450.
1913D	15,804,000	2.00	2.50	3.00	7.00	24.00	40.00	84.00	745.	—
1913S	6,101,000	5.75	6.25	7.75	12.00	30.00	51.00	110.	1250.	—
1914	75,238,432	.35	.40	1.50	3.75	10.00	18.50	40.00	155.	450.
1914D	1,193,000	84.00	91.00	110.	175.	420.	595.	840.	4300.	—
1914S	4,137,000	9.75	10.75	12.00	19.75	40.00	63.00	175.	3900.	—
1915	29,092,120	1.10	1.35	3.90	10.75	41.00	60.00	84.00	365.	450.
1915D	22,050,000	1.00	1.25	2.20	3.50	10.00	22.00	49.00	390.	—
1915S	4,833,000	7.00	8.50	9.00	11.50	31.00	46.00	105.	1550.	—
1916	131,833,677	.15	.20	.45	1.50	4.50	5.00	11.00	85.00	665.
1916D	35,956,000	.25	.35	1.25	2.50	9.50	16.00	53.00	980.	—
1916S	22,510,000	.60	1.00	1.50	2.50	9.00	17.00	60.00	3650.	—
1917	196,429,785	.10	.15	.35	.75	2.75	5.00	11.00	120.	—
1917D	55,120,000	.30	.40	1.00	2.20	7.50	13.50	56.00	560.	—
1917S	32,620,000	.45	.55	.80	2.20	6.75	15.00	58.00	1325.	—
1918	288,104,634	.10	.15	.35	.60	2.50	4.50	11.00	100.	—
1918D	47,830,000	.30	.35	1.00	2.00	7.00	13.00	53.00	800.	—
1918S	34,680,000	.45	.50	.80	2.00	6.50	16.00	59.00	2800.	—
1919	392,021,000	.10	.15	.20	.50	2.00	5.00	8.50	56.00	—
1919D	57,154,000	.20	.30	.60	2.20	7.50	11.00	45.00	560.	—

Date	Mintage	G-4	VG-8	F-12	VF-20	XF-40	AU-50	MS-60	MS-65	Prf-65
1919S	139,760,000	.10	.25	.50	.85	2.00	6.00	30.00	910.	—
1920	310,165,000	.10	.15	.20	.45	2.50	4.00	9.75	63.00	—
1920D	49,280,000	.20	.35	.75	2.00	8.00	11.00	53.00	595.	—
1920S	46,220,000	.20	.30	.40	1.25	4.00	14.00	85.00	2800.	—
1921	39,157,000	.25	.35	.60	2.00	5.75	10.00	39.00	125.	—
1921S	15,274,000	.75	.85	1.50	3.50	12.00	50.00	100.	2500.	—
1922D	7,160,000	5.85	6.75	8.00	9.50	17.00	42.00	70.00	490.	—
1922	Inc. Ab.	265.	275.	370.	575.	2100.	3200.	5600.	23,500.	—
1923	74,723,000	.20	.30	.35	1.80	6.00	7.00	9.75	140.	—
1923S	8,700,000	1.70	1.90	3.00	5.00	20.00	70.00	190.	2450.	—
1924	75,178,000	.20	.25	.30	1.50	5.75	7.00	22.00	155.	—
1924D	2,520,000	9.25	10.50	11.50	19.00	48.00	100.	235.	2800.	—
1924S	11,696,000	.75	1.10	1.50	3.75	16.00	28.00	120.	2500.	—
1925	139,949,000	.10	.15	.20	.85	2.50	4.50	8.50	59.00	—
1925D	22,580,000	.40	.45	.70	2.90	7.50	12.00	47.00	775.	—
1925S	26,380,000	.30	.35	.45	1.25	6.75	14.00	61.00	2500.	—
1926	157,088,000	.10	.15	.20	.85	2.00	3.50	7.00	35.00	—
1926D	28,020,000	.30	.35	.65	1.75	4.00	10.00	45.00	1050.	—
1926S	4,550,000	3.50	3.75	4.00	4.75	11.00	50.00	100.	3000.	—
1927	144,440,000	.10	.15	.25	.85	2.00	3.75	7.25	70.00	—
1927D	27,170,000	.25	.30	.45	1.00	3.25	9.50	35.00	800.	—
1927S	14,276,000	.60	.70	1.60	3.00	9.50	16.00	65.00	1200.	—
1928	134,116,000	.10	.15	.20	.80	2.00	3.75	7.00	56.00	—
1928D	31,170,000	.25	.30	.35	.75	2.25	6.00	20.00	295.	—
1928S	17,266,000	.45	.50	.70	1.75	3.50	10.00	48.00	630.	—
1929	185,262,000	.15	.20	.25	.80	1.50	3.75	5.50	70.00	—
1929D	41,730,000	.15	.20	.25	.45	2.00	5.00	16.00	115.	—
1929S	50,148,000	.15	.20	.25	1.00	2.25	3.75	7.75	140.	—
1930	157,415,000	.15	.20	.30	.45	1.50	2.50	4.25	23.00	—
1930D	40,100,000	.15	.20	.30	.50	1.75	5.75	12.00	67.00	—
1930S	24,286,000	.20	.25	.35	.70	1.60	3.00	6.00	49.00	—
1931	19,396,000	.40	.50	.65	1.00	2.50	6.00	16.50	91.00	—
1931D	4,480,000	2.85	2.95	3.50	4.00	7.00	28.00	45.00	330.	—
1931S	866,000	34.00	34.50	37.00	39.00	42.00	49.00	59.00	245.	—
1932	9,062,000	1.95	2.10	2.15	2.25	3.50	9.00	19.00	53.00	—
1932D	10,500,000	.90	1.00	1.10	1.35	3.75	8.00	14.00	53.00	—
1933	14,360,000	1.15	1.25	1.50	1.80	3.75	8.00	16.00	59.00	—
1933D	6,200,000	2.00	2.10	2.25	2.50	4.50	11.00	17.00	35.00	—
1934	219,080,000	—	.10	.15	.20	.75	1.50	3.00	15.00	—
1934D	28,446,000	.10	.15	.20	.25	2.00	6.50	18.00	35.00	—
1935	245,338,000	—	.10	.15	.20	.75	1.00	1.50	7.75	—
1935D	47,000,000	—	.10	.15	.20	.75	3.00	4.50	15.00	—
1935S	38,702,000	—	.20	.25	.30	2.25	5.00	10.00	42.00	—
1936	309,637,569	—	.10	.15	.20	.75	1.00	1.50	6.25	800.
1936D	40,620,000	—	.10	.15	.25	.75	1.50	1.75	9.00	—
1936S	29,130,000	.10	.15	.25	.30	.75	1.75	2.25	10.00	—
1937	309,179,320	—	.10	.15	.20	.70	.90	1.00	6.25	190.
1937D	50,430,000	—	.10	.15	.25	.70	1.00	1.90	7.70	—
1937S	34,500,000	—	.10	.15	.25	.60	1.50	1.75	10.50	—
1938	156,696,734	—	.10	.15	.20	.50	1.00	1.60	7.00	140.
1938D	20,010,000	.15	.15	.25	.30	.75	1.50	2.00	9.00	—
1938S	15,180,000	.30	.35	.45	.60	.80	1.25	1.80	11.00	—
1939	316,479,520	—	.10	.15	.20	.25	.40	.65	4.25	110.
1939D	15,160,000	.35	.40	.50	.60	.85	1.90	2.25	12.50	—
1939S	52,070,000	—	.15	.20	.25	.45	.90	1.15	15.00	—
1940	586,825,872	—	—	.15	.20	.25	.40	.85	4.25	125.
1940D	81,390,000	—	.10	.15	.20	.25	.50	.90	5.25	—
1940S	112,940,000	—	.10	.15	.20	.25	.75	1.00	7.00	—
1941	887,039,100	—	—	—	—	.15	.30	.85	4.25	115.
1941D	128,700,000	—	—	—	.10	.15	1.00	1.75	8.50	—
1941S	92,360,000	—	—	—	.10	.15	1.25	2.00	9.00	—
1942	657,828,600	—	—	—	—	.15	.25	.50	2.75	140.
1942D	206,698,000	—	—	—	.10	.15	.25	.50	4.25	—
1942S	85,590,000	—	—	—	.15	.25	1.50	4.00	24.00	—

Steel composition

Weight: 2.7 grams. **Composition:** steel coated with zinc.

Date	Mintage	G-4	VG-8	F-12	VF-20	XF-40	AU-50	MS-60	MS-65	Prf-65
1943	684,628,670	—	—	—	—	.40	.60	.70	2.80	—
1943D	217,660,000	—	—	—	—	.45	.65	1.00	5.00	—
1943S	191,550,000	—	—	—	—	.45	.70	1.50	8.50	—

Copper-zinc composition

Weight: 3.11 grams. **Composition:** 95% copper, 5% zinc. **Notes:** The 1955 "doubled die" has distinct doubling of the date and lettering on the obverse.

Date	Mintage	XF-40	MS-60	Prf-65	Date	Mintage	XF-40	MS-60	Prf-65
1944	1,435,400,000	.10	.40	—	1946S	198,100,000	.15	.50	—
1944D	430,578,000	.10	.45	—	1947	190,555,000	.15	1.00	—
1944D/S	—	150.	375.	—	1947D	194,750,000	.10	.40	—
1944S	282,760,000	.15	.45	—	1947S	99,000,000	.15	.45	—
1945	1,040,515,000	.10	.50	—	1948	317,570,000	.10	.50	—
1945D	226,268,000	.10	.70	—	1948D	172,637,000	.10	.45	—
1945S	181,770,000	.15	.45	—	1948S	81,735,000	.15	.50	—
1946	991,655,000	.10	.30	—	1949	217,775,000	.10	.40	—
1946D	315,690,000	.10	.45	—	1949D	153,132,000	.10	.40	—

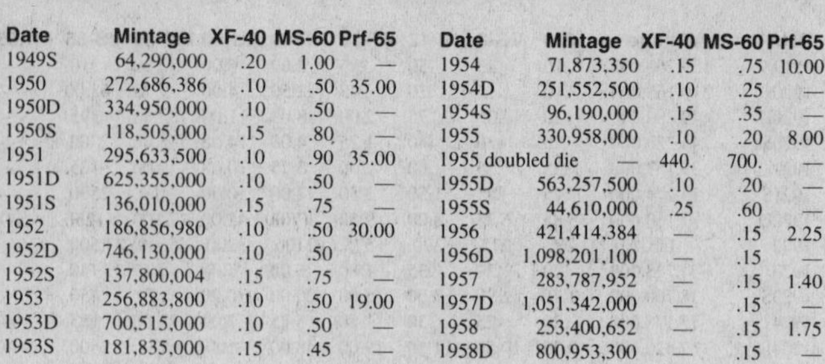

Date	Mintage	XF-40	MS-60	Prf-65
1949S	64,290,000	.20	1.00	—
1950	272,686,386	.10	.50	35.00
1950D	334,950,000	.10	.50	—
1950S	118,505,000	.15	.80	—
1951	295,633,500	.10	.90	35.00
1951D	625,355,000	.10	.50	—
1951S	136,010,000	.15	.75	—
1952	186,856,980	.10	.50	30.00
1952D	746,130,000	.10	.50	—
1952S	137,800,004	.15	.75	—
1953	256,883,800	.10	.50	19.00
1953D	700,515,000	.10	.50	—
1953S	181,835,000	.15	.45	—
1954	71,873,350	.15	.75	10.00
1954D	251,552,500	.10	.25	—
1954S	96,190,000	.15	.35	—
1955	330,958,000	.10	.20	8.00
1955 doubled die	—	440.	700.	—
1955D	563,257,500	.10	.20	—
1955S	44,610,000	.25	.60	—
1956	421,414,384	—	.15	2.25
1956D	1,098,201,100	—	.15	—
1957	283,787,952	—	.15	1.40
1957D	1,051,342,000	—	.15	—
1958	253,400,652	—	.15	1.75
1958D	800,953,300	—	.15	—

Lincoln Memorial reverse

Reverse designer: Frank Gasparro. **Weight:** 3.11 grams (1959-82) and 2.5 grams (1982-present). **Composition:** 95% copper, 5% tin and zinc (1959-62); 95% copper, 5% zinc (1962-82); 97.6% zinc, 2.4% copper (1982-present). **Notes:** The dates were modified in 1960, 1970 and 1982, resulting in large-date and small-date varieties for those years. The 1972 "doubled die" shows doubling of "In God We Trust." The 1979-S Type II proof has a clearer mintmark than the Type I proof. Some 1982 cents have the predominantly copper composition; others have the predominantly zinc composition. They can be distinguished by weight. The 1983 "doubled die reverse" shows doubling of "United States of America." The 1984 "doubled die" shows doubling of Lincoln's ear on the obverse.

Date	Mintage	XF-40	MS-65	Prf-65
1959	610,864,291	—	.20	1.00
1959D	1,279,760,000	—	.20	—
1960 small date	588,096,602	1.50	4.50	15.00
1960 large date	Inc. Ab.	—	.15	.95
1960D small date	1,580,884,000	—	.25	—
1960D large date	Inc. Ab.	—	.15	—
1961	756,373,244	—	.15	.40
1961D	1,753,266,700	—	.15	—
1962	609,263,019	—	.15	.40
1962D	1,793,148,400	—	.15	—
1963	757,185,645	—	.15	.40
1963D	1,774,020,400	—	.15	—
1964	2,652,525,762	—	.15	.40
1964D	3,799,071,500	—	.15	—
1965	1,497,224,900	—	.15	—
1966	2,188,147,783	—	.15	—
1967	3,048,667,100	—	.15	—
1968	1,707,880,970	—	.15	—
1968D	2,886,269,600	—	.15	—
1968S	261,311,510	—	.15	.85
1969	1,136,910,000	—	.25	—
1969D	4,002,832,200	—	.15	—
1969S	547,309,631	—	.15	.85
1970	1,898,315,000	—	.15	—
1970D	2,891,438,900	—	.15	—
1970S	693,192,814	—	.15	.85
1970S small date	—	—	45.00	.80
1971	1,919,490,000	—	.25	—
1971D	2,911,045,600	—	.25	—

1955 doubled die

1972 doubled die

1983 doubled die

Small date

Large date

Large date

Small date

Large date

Small date

Date	Mintage	XF-40	MS-65	Prf-65
1971S	528,354,192	—	.15	.85
1972	2,933,255,000	—	.15	—
1972 doubled die	—	120.	300.	—
1972D	2,665,071,400	—	.15	—
1972S	380,200,104	—	.15	.90
1973	3,728,245,000	—	.10	—
1973D	3,549,576,588	—	.10	—
1973S	319,937,634	—	.15	.80
1974	4,232,140,523	—	.10	—
1974D	4,235,098,000	—	.10	—
1974S	412,039,228	—	.15	.80
1975	5,451,476,142	—	.10	—
1975D	4,505,245,300	—	.10	—
1975S	(2,845,450)	—	—	4.50
1976	4,674,292,426	—	.10	—
1976D	4,221,592,455	—	.10	—
1976S	(4,149,730)	—	—	3.00
1977	4,469,930,000	—	.10	—
1977D	4,149,062,300	—	.10	—
1977S	(3,251,152)	—	—	1.95
1978	5,558,605,000	—	.10	—
1978D	4,280,233,400	—	.10	—
1978S	(3,127,781)	—	—	1.90
1979	6,018,515,000	—	.10	—
1979D	4,139,357,254	—	.10	—
1979S T-I	(3,677,175)	—	—	2.00
1979S T-II	(Inc. Ab.)	—	—	2.20
1980	7,414,705,000	—	.10	—
1980D	5,140,098,660	—	.10	—
1980S	(3,554,806)	—	—	1.35
1981	7,491,750,000	—	.10	—
1981D	5,373,235,677	—	.10	—
1981S T-I	(4,063,083)	—	—	1.00
1981S T-II	(Inc. Ab.)	—	—	28.00
1982 copper large date	10,712,525,000	—	.10	—
1982 copper small date		—	.15	—
1982 zinc large date		—	.35	—
1982 zinc small date		—	.75	—
1982D copper large date	6,012,979,368	—	.10	—
1982D zinc large date		—	.20	—
1982D zinc small date		—	.10	—
1982S	(3,857,479)	—	.10	2.25
1983	7,752,355,000	—	.10	—
1983 doubled die rev.		—	195.	—
1983D	6,467,199,428	—	.10	—
1983S	(3,279,126)	—	—	3.50
1984	8,151,079,000	—	.10	—
1984 doubled die	—	—	130.	—
1984D	5,569,238,906	—	.25	—
1984S	(3,065,110)	—	—	4.50
1985	5,648,489,887	—	.10	—
1985D	5,287,399,926	—	.10	—
1985S	(3,362,821)	—	—	3.00
1986	4,491,395,493	—	.15	—
1986D	4,442,866,698	—	.10	—
1986S	(3,010,497)	—	—	8.00
1987	4,682,466,931	—	.10	—
1987D	4,879,389,514	—	.10	—
1987S	(4,227,728)	—	—	3.95
1988	6,092,810,000	—	.10	—
1988D	5,253,740,443	—	.10	—
1988S	(3,262,948)	—	—	4.50
1989	7,261,535,000	—	.10	—
1989D	5,345,467,111	—	.10	—
1989S	(3,220,194)	—	—	4.50
1990	6,851,765,000	—	.10	—
1990D	4,922,894,533	—	.10	—
1990S	Proof only	—	—	8.00
1990 no S	—	—	—	2100.
1991	—	—	.10	—
1991D	—	—	.10	—
1991S	Proof only	—	—	9.00
1992	—	—	.10	—
1992D	—	—	.10	—
1992S	Proof only	—	—	7.00
1993	—	—	—	—
1993D	—	—	—	—
1993S	Proof only	—	—	6.00
1994	—	—	.10	—
1994D	—	—	.10	—
1994S	Proof only	—	—	7.00

Two-cent

Small motto

Large motto

Designer: James B. Longacre. **Size:** 23 millimeters. **Weight:** 6.22 grams. **Composition:** 95% copper, 5% tin and zinc. **Notes:** The motto "In God We Trust" was modified in 1864, resulting in small-motto and large-motto varieties for that year.

Date	Mintage	G-4	VG-8	F-12	VF-20	XF-40	AU-50	MS-60	MS-65	Prf-65
1864 SM	19,847,500.	60.00	75.00	100.	135.	230.	325.	550.	1700.	30,000.
1864 LM	Inc. Ab.	7.00	11.00	19.50	21.00	27.00	45.00	100.	400.	1000.
1865	13,640,000	7.00	11.00	19.50	21.00	27.00	45.00	100.	400.	1000.
1866	3,177,000	7.00	11.00	19.50	21.00	27.00	45.00	100.	510.	1000.
1867	2,938,750	7.00	11.00	19.50	21.00	27.00	60.00	110.	450.	1000.
1868	2,803,750	7.00	11.00	19.50	24.00	33.00	65.00	145.	450.	1000.
1869	1,546,000	8.50	11.00	19.50	22.00	36.00	75.00	135.	465.	1000.
1870	861,250	8.00	12.00	18.50	32.50	57.00	90.00	210.	630.	1000.
1871	721,250	10.00	15.00	22.00	40.00	75.00	120.	235.	690.	1000.
1872	65,000	75.00	120.	170.	250.	375.	490.	775.	2750.	1000.
1873	Est. 1100	—	—	Proof only		—	—	—	—	2000.
		Impaired proof		900.	930.	960.	990.	—	—	—

Silver three-cent

Type I

Designer: James B. Longacre. **Size:** 14 millimeters. **Weight:** .8 grams. **Composition:** 75% silver (.0193 ounces), 25% copper. **Notes:** The Type I design has no outlines in the star.

Date	Mintage	G-4	VG-8	F-12	VF-20	XF-40	AU-50	MS-60	MS-65	Prf-65
1851	5,447,400	13.50	15.00	20.00	25.00	65.00	120.	145.	1350.	—
1851O	720,000	18.00	22.00	35.00	54.00	130.	225.	375.	1850.	—
1852	18,663,500	13.50	15.00	20.00	25.00	60.00	120.	145.	1350.	—
1853	11,400,000	13.50	15.00	20.00	25.00	50.00	130.	145.	1350.	—

Type II

Weight: .75 grams. **Composition:** 90% silver (.0218 ounces), 10% copper. **Notes:** The Type II design has three lines outlining the star.

Date	Mintage	G-4	VG-8	F-12	VF-20	XF-40	AU-50	MS-60	MS-65	Prf-65
1854	671,000	13.50	17.00	25.00	38.00	110.	230.	280.	5500.	25,000.
1855	139,000	21.00	29.00	49.00	85.00	165.	250.	440.	12,000.	15,000.
1856	1,458,000	14.00	18.00	25.00	40.00	95.00	210.	230.	6700.	—
1857	1,042,000	13.50	17.00	22.00	35.00	85.00	225.	280.	5500.	9750.
1858	1,604,000	13.50	17.00	25.00	40.00	95.00	210.	230.	5500.	7000.

Type III

Notes: The Type III design has two lines outlining the star.

Date	Mintage	G-4	VG-8	F-12	VF-20	XF-40	AU-50	MS-60	MS-65	Prf-65
1859	365,000	13.50	17.00	22.00	32.00	55.00	125.	145.	1200.	2250.
1860	287,000	17.00	20.00	25.00	32.00	55.00	125.	145.	1200.	7500.
1861	498,000	14.00	18.00	24.00	32.00	68.00	125.	145.	1200.	2250.
1862	343,550	17.00	20.00	25.00	32.00	55.00	125.	145.	1200.	2500.
1863	21,460	200.	225.	280.	315.	350.	375.	565.	2750.	1500.
1864	12,470	250.	275.	325.	375.	425.	465.	565.	2150.	1500.
1865	8,500	260.	300.	350.	375.	400.	450.	565.	3125.	1500.
1866	22,725	225.	250.	280.	325.	375.	450.	600.	2650.	1500.
1867	4,625	285.	325.	350.	375.	400.	485.	625.	4100.	1500.
1868	4,100	285.	325.	350.	375.	400.	440.	625.	4800.	1500.
1869	5,100	285.	325.	350.	375.	460.	525.	625.	4550.	1500.
1870	4,000	285.	325.	350.	375.	400.	440.	625.	4600.	1625.
1871	4,360	285.	325.	350.	375.	400.	440.	565.	2150.	1500.
1872	1,950	325.	375.	450.	550.	650.	750.	950.	6400.	1500.
1873	600	—	—	Proof only		—	—	—	—	1750.
		Impaired proof		750.	850.	950.	1200.	—	—	—

Nickel three-cent

Designer: James B. Longacre. **Size:** 17.9 millimeters. **Weight:** 1.94 grams. **Composition:** 75% copper, 25% nickel.

Date	Mintage	G-4	VG-8	F-12	VF-20	XF-40	AU-50	MS-60	MS-65	Prf-65
1865	11,382,000	7.00	7.25	7.75	8.50	15.00	37.50	95.00	900.	1700.

Nickel three-cent

Date	Mintage	G-4	VG-8	F-12	VF-20	XF-40	AU-50	MS-60	MS-65	Prf-65
1866	4,801,000	7.00	7.25	7.75	8.50	15.00	37.50	95.00	900.	1250.
1867	3,915,000	7.00	7.25	7.75	8.50	15.00	37.50	95.00	900.	1025.
1868	3,252,000	7.00	7.25	7.75	8.50	15.00	37.50	95.00	900.	1025.
1869	1,604,000	7.00	7.25	7.75	8.50	15.00	40.00	95.00	900.	900.
1870	1,335,000	7.00	7.75	8.50	10.00	16.00	42.00	100.	900.	1000.
1871	604,000	7.00	7.75	8.75	11.00	18.00	45.00	100.	900.	500.
1872	862,000	7.00	7.50	8.50	10.00	17.00	43.00	100.	1250.	875.
1873	1,173,000	7.00	7.25	7.75	8.50	16.00	42.00	100.	2400.	900.
1874	790,000	7.00	7.50	8.50	10.00	17.00	43.00	110.	2000.	875.
1875	228,000	8.00	9.00	11.50	16.00	25.00	63.00	160.	900.	1300.
1876	162,000	11.00	14.00	17.00	24.00	38.00	100.	175.	2150.	500.
1877	Est. 900	—	—	Proof only		—	—	—	—	1400.
		Impaired proof		875.	900.	950.	975.	—	—	—
1878	2,350	—	—	Proof only		—	—	—	—	700.
		Impaired proof		375.	400.	425.	450.	—	—	—
1879	41,200	45.00	50.00	60.00	70.00	80.00	120.	240.	900.	650.
1880	24,955	63.00	70.00	90.00	105.	130.	150.	265.	900.	650.
1881	1,080,575	7.00	7.25	7.50	8.00	14.00	38.00	95.00	900.	600.
1882	25,300	63.00	70.00	84.00	95.00	110.	145.	250.	1000.	650.
1883	10,609	125.	145.	175.	200.	240.	270.	375.	2900.	650.
1884	5,642	290.	330.	350.	380.	425.	450.	550.	4800.	650.
1885	4,790	350.	380.	425.	460.	500.	600.	725.	1950.	675.
1886	4,290	—	—	Proof only		—	—	—	—	650.
		Impaired proof		—	—	—	—	—	—	—
1887/6	7,961	—	—	Proof only		—	—	—	—	625.
		Impaired proof		—	—	—	—	—	—	—
1887	Inc. Ab.	240.	250.	275.	300.	325.	425.	500.	1175.	700.
1888	41,083	35.00	40.00	45.00	50.00	70.00	110.	270.	900.	650.
1889	21,561	63.00	70.00	90.00	105.	125.	150.	260.	900.	650.

Half dimes

Flowing Hair

Designer: Robert Scot. **Size:** 16.5 millimeters. **Weight:** 1.35 grams. **Composition:** 89.24% silver (.0388 ounces), 10.76% copper.

Date	Mintage	G-4	VG-8	F-12	VF-20	XF-40	MS-60
1794	86,416	850.	1050.	1450.	2000.	3450.	8500.
1795	Inc. Ab.	600.	750.	1000.	1400.	2650.	5050.

Draped Bust

Small eagle

Heraldic eagle

"Libekty"

Small-eagle reverse

Designer: Robert Scot. **Size:** 16.5 millimeters. **Weight:** 1.35 grams. **Composition:** 89.24% silver (.0388 ounces), 10.76% copper. **Notes:** Some 1796 strikes have "Liberty" spelled as "Libekty." The 1797 strikes have either 13, 15 or 16 stars on the obverse.

Date	Mintage	G-4	VG-8	F-12	VF-20	XF-40	MS-60
1796	10,230	825.	1150	1550.	2600.	4150.	5650.
1796 "Likerty"	Inc. Ab.	825.	1150.	1550.	2600.	4150.	—
1796/5	Inc. Ab.	1025.	1750.	2000.	3350.	5450.	9000.
1797 13 stars	44,527	1100.	1425.	1850.	3100.	5150.	11,500.
1797 15 stars	Inc. Ab.	775.	950.	1250.	2000.	3650.	5650.
1797 16 stars	Inc. Ab.	800.	1000.	1300.	2150.	3350.	5650.

Heraldic-eagle reverse

Notes: Some 1800 strikes have "Liberty" spelled as "Libekty."

Date	Mintage	G-4	VG-8	F-12	VF-20	XF-40	MS-60
1800	24,000	500.	625.	800.	1250.	2450.	5050.
1800 "Libekty"	Inc. Ab.	550.	675.	875.	1375.	2575.	5050.

Date	Mintage	G-4	VG-8	F-12	VF-20	XF-40	MS-60
1801	33,910	575.	700.	925.	1500.	2650.	10,000.
1802	13,010	9500.	13,500.	20,000.	35,000.	60,000.	—
1803	37,850	500.	625.	800.	1250.	2450.	5050.
1805	15,600	600.	750.	975.	1550.	2750.	—

Liberty Cap

Designer: William Kneass. **Size:** 15.5 millimeters. **Weight:** 1.35 grams. **Composition:** 89.24% silver (.0388 ounces), 10.76% copper. **Notes:** Design modifications in 1835, 1836 and 1837 resulted in variety combinations with large and small dates, and large and small "5C." inscriptions on the reverse.

Date	Mintage	G-4	VG-8	F-12	VF-20	XF-40	AU-50	MS-60	MS-65
1829	1,230,000	12.00	18.00	25.00	60.00	125.	225.	290.	3000.
1830	1,240,000	12.00	18.00	25.00	60.00	125.	225.	290.	3000.
1831	1,242,700	12.00	18.00	25.00	60.00	125.	225.	290.	3000.
1832	965,000	12.00	18.00	25.00	60.00	125.	300.	450.	7000.
1833	1,370,000	12.00	18.00	25.00	60.00	125.	230.	325.	3500.
1834	1,480,000	12.00	18.00	25.00	60.00	125.	230.	290.	3000.
1835 large date, large "5C."	2,760,000	12.00	18.00	25.00	60.00	110.	250.	290.	3000.
1835 large date, small "5C."	Inc. Ab.	12.00	18.00	25.00	60.00	125.	230.	290.	3000.
1835 small date, large "5C."	Inc. Ab.	12.00	18.00	25.00	60.00	125.	225.	290.	3000.
1835 small date, small "5C."	Inc. Ab.	12.00	18.00	25.00	60.00	125.	225.	290.	3000.
1836 large "5C."	1,900,000	12.00	18.00	25.00	60.00	125.	225.	290.	3000.
1836 small "5C."	Inc. Ab.	12.00	18.00	25.00	60.00	125.	225.	290.	3000.
1837 large "5C."	2,276,000	12.00	18.00	25.00	60.00	125.	225.	290.	3000.
1837 small "5C."	Inc. Ab.	25.00	40.00	60.00	105.	150.	350.	1250.	8500.

Seated Liberty

No stars

1837-1859

Stars

Obverse legend

1860-1873

No stars around rim

Designer: Christian Gobrecht. **Size:** 15.5 millimeters. **Weight:** 1.34 grams. **Composition:** 90% silver (.0388 ounces), 10% copper. **Notes:** A design modification in 1837 resulted in small-date and large-date varieties for that year.

Date	Mintage	G-4	VG-8	F-12	VF-20	XF-40	AU-50	MS-60	MS-65
1837 sm. date	Inc. Ab.	25.00	35.00	53.00	100.	210.	375.	590.	4500.
1837 lg. date	Inc. Ab.	25.00	35.00	53.00	100.	210.	375.	590.	4500.
1838O	70,000	70.00	110.	225.	400.	750.	2500.	—	—

Stars around rim

Notes: The two varieties of 1838 are distinguished by the size of the stars on the obverse. The 1839-O with reverse of 1838-O was struck from rusted reverse dies. The result is a bumpy surface on this variety's reverse.

Date	Mintage	G-4	VG-8	F-12	VF-20	XF-40	AU-50	MS-60	MS-65
1838 lg.stars	2,255,000	5.00	6.25	10.00	25.00	65.00	135.	250.	2100.
1838 sm.stars	Inc. Ab.	20.00	30.00	50.00	125.	225.	285.	750.	10,500.
1839	1,069,150	8.00	10.00	13.00	29.00	70.00	170.	250.	2100.
1839O	1,034,039	9.00	12.00	16.00	31.00	75.00	200.	400.	2100.
1839O rev. 1838O	—	375.	575.	750.	1200.	2250.	3500.	—	—
1840	1,344,085	5.00	6.25	13.00	21.00	65.00	135.	450.	2100.
1840O	935,000	10.00	13.00	18.00	35.00	85.00	200.	600.	10,500.

Drapery added to Liberty

Notes: In 1840 drapery was added to Liberty's left elbow. Varieties for the 1848 Philadelphia strikes are distinguished by the size of the numerals in the date.

Date	Mintage	G-4	VG-8	F-12	VF-20	XF-40	AU-50	MS-60	MS-65
1840	Inc. Ab.	20.00	32.50	50.00	75.00	150.	250.	700.	6500.
1840O	Inc. Ab.	30.00	50.00	80.00	125.	325.	950.	—	—
1841	1,150,000	5.00	6.25	8.75	22.00	55.00	95.00	160.	1750.
1841O	815,000	10.00	15.00	22.50	40.00	85.00	200.	650.	—
1842	815,000	5.00	6.25	8.75	22.00	55.00	95.00	160.	1750.
1842O	350,000	28.00	40.00	65.00	225.	700.	1800.	—	—
1843	1,165,000	5.00	6.25	8.75	18.00	41.00	95.00	160.	1750.
1844	430,000	6.50	8.50	11.00	24.00	60.00	110.	225.	2450.
1844O	220,000	60.00	85.00	195.	350.	950.	2800.	—	15,000.
1845	1,564,000	5.00	6.25	8.75	22.00	44.00	95.00	160.	1750.
1845/1845	Inc. Ab.	8.00	11.00	15.00	30.00	75.00	200.	225.	5000.
1846	27,000	150.	200.	350.	550.	1200.	2850.	—	—
1847	1,274,000	6.00	7.00	8.00	18.00	55.00	95.00	225.	2450.
1848 med. date	668,000	7.00	8.50	11.00	32.00	60.00	125.	225.	2450.
1848 lg. date	Inc. Ab.	15.00	20.00	30.00	50.00	125.	300.	425.	2450.
1848O	600,000	12.00	17.50	25.00	42.50	90.00	225.	600.	5000.
1849/8	1,309,000	12.00	17.50	25.00	45.00	100.	180.	500.	5000.
1849/6	Inc. Ab.	10.00	14.00	20.00	35.00	75.00	175.	425.	5000.
1849	Inc. Ab.	6.00	8.00	11.00	18.00	45.00	95.00	600.	5000.
1849O	140,000	22.00	40.00	75.00	200.	450.	800.	1200.	16,000.
1850	955,000	5.00	6.25	8.75	18.00	41.00	175.	250.	2750.
1850O	690,000	11.00	16.00	22.50	50.00	100.	350.	800.	4000.
1851	781,000	5.00	6.25	8.75	18.00	50.00	115.	300.	2450.
1851O	860,000	10.00	15.00	25.00	35.00	75.00	165.	800.	2450.
1852	1,000,500	6.00	7.00	12.50	18.00	41.00	115.	160.	1750.
1852O	260,000	30.00	48.00	70.00	125.	265.	800.	—	11,000.
1853	135,000	25.00	38.00	55.00	85.00	185.	350.	500.	8500.
1853O	160,000	135.	190.	275.	450.	1000.	3000.	—	—

Arrows at date

Weight: 1.24 grams. **Composition:** 90% silver (.0362 ounces), 10% copper.

Date	Mintage	G-4	VG-8	F-12	VF-20	XF-40	AU-50	MS-60	MS-65	Prf-65
1853	13,210,020	5.00	6.25	8.75	17.00	50.00	100.	160.	2450.	20,000.
1853O	2,200,000	6.00	8.00	11.00	24.00	60.00	125.	325.	—	—
1854	5,740,000	5.00	6.50	8.75	17.00	50.00	135.	250.	4550.	20,000.
1854O	1,560,000	7.00	9.00	12.00	20.00	55.00	175.	700.	—	—
1855	1,750,000	5.50	7.00	12.00	20.00	55.00	135.	250.	5000.	20,000.
1855O	600,000	12.00	17.00	25.00	55.00	125.	275.	1000.	—	—

Arrows at date removed

Notes: On the 1858 inverted date variety, the date was engraved into the die upside down and then re-engraved right side up. Another 1858 variety has the date doubled.

Date	Mintage	G-4	VG-8	F-12	VF-20	XF-40	AU-50	MS-60	MS-65	Prf-65
1856	4,880,000	5.00	6.25	9.00	18.00	41.00	95.00	225.	1750.	22,500.
1856O	1,100,000	8.00	10.00	12.00	27.00	70.00	200.	600.	—	—
1857	7,280,000	5.00	6.25	8.75	15.00	45.00	95.00	225.	1750.	5000.
1857O	1,380,000	7.00	9.00	11.00	25.00	65.00	200.	450.	—	—
1858	3,500,000	5.00	6.25	8.75	18.00	45.00	85.00	160.	1750.	9000.
1858 inverted date	Inc. Ab.	30.00	40.00	65.00	115.	200.	350.	700.	—	—
1858 doubled date	Inc. Ab.	35.00	50.00	90.00	140.	240.	500.	1200.	—	—
1858O	1,660,000	7.00	9.00	12.00	26.00	65.00	190.	265.	—	—
1859	340,000	9.00	12.00	15.00	33.00	85.00	175.	250.	3000.	5000.
1859O	560,000	8.00	10.00	13.00	30.00	80.00	175.	350.	—	—

Transitional patterns

Notes: These non-circulation pieces were struck as experiments in transferring the legend "United States of America" from the reverse to the obverse.

Date	Mintage	G-4	VG-8	F-12	VF-20	XF-40	AU-50	MS-60	MS-65	Prf-65
1859 obverse of 1859, reverse 1860						—	—	—	—	17,500.
1860 obverse of 1859, reverse 1860						—	—	4000.	8500.	—

Obverse legend

Notes: In 1860 the legend "United States of America" replaced the stars on the obverse.

Date	Mintage	G-4	VG-8	F-12	VF-20	XF-40	AU-50	MS-60	MS-65	Prf-65
1860	799,000	6.00	7.50	12.50	25.00	40.00	70.00	140.	1300.	2150.
1860O	1,060,000	8.00	10.00	15.00	25.00	40.00	85.00	350.	3550.	—
1861	3,361,000	5.00	6.25	8.00	14.00	28.00	57.00	140.	1300.	1850.
1861/0	Inc. Ab.	20.00	30.00	50.00	90.00	150.	500.	800.	—	—
1862	1,492,550	5.00	6.25	8.00	16.00	30.00	57.00	140.	1300.	1850.
1863	18,460	135.	165.	200.	260.	375.	500.	800.	3250.	3500.
1863S	100,000	15.00	23.00	35.00	65.00	125.	250.	900.	—	—
1864	48,470	225.	290.	350.	450.	625.	700.	950.	4500.	3500.
1864S	90,000	22.50	34.00	50.00	80.00	200.	425.	1000.	—	—
1865	13,500	200.	250.	325.	425.	500.	800.	1300.	4700.	3500.
1865S	120,000	12.50	18.00	25.00	50.00	100.	300.	975.	—	—
1866	10,725	185.	225.	285.	375.	475.	600.	1000.	4700.	3500.
1866S	120,000	12.50	18.00	25.00	50.00	100.	300.	950.	6000.	—

Half dimes

Date	Mintage	G-4	VG-8	F-12	VF-20	XF-40	AU-50	MS-60	MS-65	Prf-65
1867	8,625	350.	400.	475.	550.	625.	800.	1300.	4700.	3500.
1867S	120,000	12.50	18.00	25.00	55.00	100.	300.	900.	—	—
1868	89,200	30.00	60.00	95.00	135.	195.	300.	600.	5000.	3500.
1868S	280,000	10.00	14.00	20.00	33.00	60.00	150.	325.	—	—
1869	208,600	6.50	8.00	20.00	30.00	50.00	175.	475.	4900.	3500.
1869S	230,000	10.00	14.00	20.00	33.00	60.00	150.	500.	—	—
1870	536,600	6.00	7.50	9.00	17.00	35.00	125.	275.	4400.	1850.
1870S		Unique, Superior Galleries, July 1986, B.U., $253,000.								
1871	1,873,960	5.00	6.25	8.00	14.00	28.00	65.00	160.	4400.	1850.
1871S	161,000	16.00	22.00	30.00	45.00	85.00	135.	350.	3800.	—
1872	2,947,950	5.00	6.25	8.00	13.00	25.00	65.00	160.	4400.	1850.
1872S mint mark in wreath										
	837,000	5.00	6.50	8.00	15.00	30.00	65.00	165.	4400.	—
1872S mint mark below wreath										
	Inc. Ab.	5.00	6.50	8.00	15.00	30.00	65.00	160.	2400.	—
1873	712,600	8.00	10.00	12.50	18.00	32.00	85.00	200.	4450.	3500.
1873S	324,000	8.00	10.00	14.00	22.00	45.00	65.00	200.	[illegible]00.	—

Nickel five-cent

Shield

With rays

Without rays

Designer: James B. Longacre. **Size:** 20.5 millimeters. **Weight:** 5 grams. **Composition:** 75% copper, 25% nickel. **Notes:** In 1867 the rays between the stars on the reverse were eliminated, resulting in varieties with and without rays for that year.

Date	Mintage	G-4	VG-8	F-12	VF-20	XF-40	AU-50	MS-60	MS-65	Prf-65
1866	14,742,500	11.00	13.00	20.00	31.00	95.00	140.	200.	3600.	3450.
1867 with rays										
	2,019,000	13.00	16.00	25.00	50.00	125.	250.	290.	4200.	37,500.
1867 without rays										
	28,890,500	7.00	9.50	10.00	14.00	26.00	56.00	100.	700.	1200.
1868	28,817,000	7.00	9.50	10.00	14.00	26.00	50.00	100.	700.	1150.
1869	16,395,000	7.00	9.50	10.00	14.00	31.00	52.00	100.	700.	940.
1870	4,806,000	9.50	10.00	11.00	17.50	45.00	56.00	100.	1050.	1200.
1871	561,000	25.00	30.00	45.00	75.00	95.00	160.	270.	1550.	1000.
1872	6,036,000	9.50	10.00	11.00	17.50	40.00	70.00	115.	780.	825.
1873	4,550,000	9.50	10.00	12.00	19.00	34.00	65.00	125.	780.	1000.
1874	3,538,000	10.00	11.50	12.50	19.00	38.00	70.00	125.	1100.	650.
1875	2,097,000	10.00	12.50	17.50	40.00	65.00	85.00	150.	2600.	1125.
1876	2,530,000	10.00	12.00	16.50	32.00	55.00	90.00	125.	1250.	1000.
1877	Est. 900	—	—	Proof only		—	—	—	—	1875.
	Impaired proof			—	1000.	1050.	1100.	—	—	—
1878	2,350	—	—	Proof only		—	—	—	—	1000.
	Impaired proof			550.	600.	650.	675.	—	—	—
1879	29,100	240.	280.	330.	415.	480.	550.	625.	2000.	825.
1880	19,995	265.	325.	350.	400.	550.	600.	650.	4000.	1000.
1881	72,375	150.	180.	250.	300.	400.	430.	530.	1250.	650.
1882	11,476,600	8.75	9.50	11.00	16.00	30.00	50.00	100.	700.	650.
1883	1,456,919	12.00	14.00	17.50	22.50	32.50	60.00	100.	700.	650.
1883/2	—	—	50.00	75.00	180.	225.	275.	325.	3000.	—

Liberty

With "Cents"

Without "Cents"

Altered

Authentic

Nickel five-cent

Designer: Charles E. Barber. **Size:** 21.2 millimeters. **Weight:** 5 grams. **Composition:** 75% copper, 25% nickel. **Notes:** In 1883 "Cents" was added to the reverse, resulting in varieties with "Cents" and without "Cents" for that year.

Date	Mintage	G-4	VG-8	F-12	VF-20	XF-40	AU-50	MS-60	MS-65	Prf-65
1883 NC	5,479,519	2.60	3.25	3.60	5.00	6.75	11.50	32.00	400.	800.
1883 WC	16,032,983	5.00	7.00	12.00	20.00	36.00	68.00	94.00	600.	550.
1884	11,273,942	7.00	9.00	13.00	22.00	42.00	68.00	120.	775.	500.
1885	1,476,490	180.	250.	315.	390.	600.	650.	850.	1800.	875.
1886	3,330,290	44.00	56.00	115.	175.	220.	325.	470.	1900.	700.
1887	15,263,652	5.40	6.25	11.00	14.00	29.00	60.00	90.00	700.	500.
1888	10,720,483	7.50	9.00	14.00	23.00	40.00	80.00	115.	675.	500.
1889	15,881,361	3.75	5.00	9.25	13.50	29.00	60.00	94.00	650.	500.
1890	16,259,272	4.25	5.50	11.00	17.00	31.00	66.00	100.	825.	500.
1891	16,834,350	3.50	4.50	9.50	13.00	28.00	60.00	94.00	800.	500.
1892	11,699,642	3.50	4.00	9.50	14.50	31.00	66.00	100.	690.	500.
1893	13,370,195	3.50	4.00	10.00	14.50	28.00	60.00	95.00	775.	500.
1894	5,413,132	5.25	7.00	26.00	56.00	120.	150.	170.	1100.	500.
1895	9,979,884	2.25	2.75	7.00	12.00	28.00	60.00	87.00	1075.	780.
1896	8,842,920	3.00	4.00	9.50	15.00	32.00	69.00	94.00	1075.	500.
1897	20,428,735	1.50	2.00	3.75	6.50	19.00	55.00	80.00	950.	500.
1898	12,532,087	1.50	2.00	4.50	6.50	20.00	57.00	80.00	600.	500.
1899	26,029,031	.80	1.10	4.00	5.50	16.00	50.00	80.00	600.	500.
1900	27,255,995	.80	1.00	3.75	5.00	15.00	41.00	70.00	550.	500.
1901	26,480,213	.80	1.00	3.75	5.00	15.00	41.00	70.00	550.	500.
1902	31,480,579	.80	1.00	3.75	5.00	15.00	41.00	70.00	550.	500.
1903	28,006,725	.80	1.00	3.75	5.00	15.00	41.00	70.00	550.	500.
1904	21,404,984	.80	1.00	3.75	5.00	15.00	41.00	70.00	550.	725.
1905	29,827,276	.80	1.00	3.75	5.00	15.00	41.00	70.00	550.	500.
1906	38,613,725	.80	1.00	3.75	5.00	15.00	41.00	70.00	550.	500.
1907	39,214,800	.80	1.00	3.75	5.00	15.00	41.00	70.00	550.	500.
1908	22,686,177	.80	1.00	3.75	5.00	15.00	41.00	70.00	775.	500.
1909	11,590,526	1.00	1.30	5.00	6.00	17.00	60.00	80.00	725.	500.
1910	30,169,353	.80	1.00	3.75	5.00	15.00	41.00	70.00	550.	500.
1911	39,559,372	.80	1.00	3.75	5.00	15.00	41.00	70.00	550.	500.
1912	26,236,714	.80	1.00	3.75	5.00	15.00	41.00	70.00	550.	500.
1912D	8,474,000	.80	1.10	4.25	7.50	36.00	95.00	145.	800.	—
1912S	238,000	38.00	41.00	65.00	220.	400.	530.	595.	2300.	—
1913	Only 5 known, Hawn Sale, Oct. 1993, Prf, $962,500.									

Buffalo

Mound type

Line type

1918/17D

Mound type

Designer: James Earle Fraser. **Size:** 21.2 millimeters. **Weight:** 5 grams. **Composition:** 75% copper, 25% nickel.

Date	Mintage	G-4	VG-8	F-12	VF-20	XF-40	AU-50	MS-60	MS-65	Prf-65
1913	30,993,520	5.00	5.75	6.00	8.00	12.00	21.00	32.00	105.	2200.
1913D	5,337,000	8.00	9.50	11.00	14.00	25.00	41.00	56.00	295.	—
1913S	2,105,000	11.00	12.50	17.00	25.00	41.00	53.00	63.00	825.	—

Line type

Notes: In 1913 the reverse design was modified so the ground under the buffalo was represented as a line rather than a mound. On the 1937-D 3-legged variety, the buffalo's right front leg is missing, the result of a damaged die.

Date	Mintage	G-4	VG-8	F-12	VF-20	XF-40	AU-50	MS-60	MS-65	Prf-65
1913	29,858,700	5.00	5.75	7.00	9.00	13.50	20.00	29.00	400.	1350.
1913D	4,156,000	34.00	40.00	50.00	62.00	70.00	115.	170.	975.	—
1913S	1,209,000	84.00	100.	140.	160.	195.	280.	335.	2800.	—
1914	20,665,738	5.60	6.30	7.50	9.50	17.00	27.00	45.00	390.	1100.
1914D	3,912,000	32.00	42.00	50.00	67.00	105.	140.	210.	1295.	—
1914S	3,470,000	6.00	7.00	11.00	18.00	35.00	50.00	110.	2400.	—
1915	20,987,270	3.15	3.50	5.60	7.50	13.50	26.00	45.00	325.	1100.
1915D	7,569,500	7.50	11.50	20.00	38.00	55.00	75.00	170.	2725.	—
1915S	1,505,000	12.00	18.00	29.00	63.00	125.	210.	420.	2700.	—
1916	63,498,066	1.25	1.75	2.50	3.75	4.90	15.00	38.00	295.	2000.
1916/16	Inc. Ab.	1500.	3350.	5300.	8400.	11,000.	14,000.	16,000.	63,000.	—
1916D	13,333,000	6.00	8.50	11.50	25.00	50.00	75.00	140.	3150.	—
1916S	11,860,000	4.00	5.50	9.00	19.00	48.00	74.00	155.	2675.	—
1917	51,424,029	1.25	2.00	3.00	6.00	11.00	26.00	42.00	520.	—
1917D	9,910,800	6.00	9.00	18.00	45.00	90.00	120.	275.	2950.	—
1917S	4,193,000	5.25	8.75	18.00	45.00	105.	195.	280.	2800.	—
1918	32,086,314	1.50	2.25	3.50	5.60	18.00	35.00	56.00	1395.	—

Nickel five-cent

Date	Mintage	G-4	VG-8	F-12	VF-20	XF-40	AU-50	MS-60	MS-65	Prf-65
1918/17D	8,362,314	385.	500.	800.	2275.	4000.	5950.	12,000.	84,000.	—
1918D	Inc. Ab.	5.00	7.00	16.00	67.00	160.	245.	330.	3425.	—
1918S	4,882,000	4.00	5.25	13.00	59.00	160.	210.	280.	8400.	—
1919	60,868,000	1.25	1.60	2.00	4.00	10.00	22.00	42.00	435.	—
1919D	8,006,000	6.50	11.00	22.00	75.00	170.	265.	420.	3700.	—
1919S	7,521,000	4.50	7.00	15.00	65.00	160.	250.	435.	7150.	—
1920	63,093,000	1.15	1.50	2.00	3.00	10.00	24.00	45.00	700.	—
1920D	9,418,000	5.00	7.00	14.00	70.00	210.	280.	420.	5000.	—
1920S	9,689,000	2.75	4.75	9.00	49.00	150.	195.	335.	13,500.	—
1921	10,663,000	1.75	2.50	3.50	6.00	20.00	42.00	84.00	580.	—
1921S	1,557,000	17.50	25.00	48.00	315.	700.	875.	1050.	4400.	—
1923	35,715,000	1.15	1.50	2.00	4.00	6.75	17.00	35.00	500.	—
1923S	6,142,000	2.50	4.00	10.00	85.00	190.	230.	295.	550.	—
1924	21,620,000	1.15	1.50	2.00	5.50	8.75	28.00	49.00	500.	—
1924D	5,258,000	3.00	4.75	9.50	57.00	150.	220.	280.	2950.	—
1924S	1,437,000	6.50	9.50	38.00	425.	1075.	1250.	1675.	4600.	—
1925	35,565,100	.90	1.35	2.00	4.00	7.00	21.00	31.00	320.	—
1925D	4,450,000	5.50	7.50	19.50	60.00	165.	200.	350.	3775.	—
1925S	6,256,000	2.50	4.50	11.50	53.00	140.	225.	390.	25,000.	—
1926	44,693,000	.70	.95	1.50	2.50	7.00	17.00	28.00	175.	—
1926D	5,638,000	4.00	7.50	20.00	63.00	120.	160.	210.	2500.	—
1926S	970,000	7.25	10.00	27.00	300.	850.	1085.	2250.	21,000.	—
1927	37,981,000	.70	.95	1.50	2.50	7.00	18.00	25.00	245.	—
1927D	5,730,000	1.75	2.75	6.00	11.00	39.00	65.00	125.	2550.	—
1927S	3,430,000	1.25	2.00	3.75	18.00	65.00	105.	385.	14,000.	—
1928	23,411,000	.65	.90	1.50	2.50	5.50	18.00	27.00	365.	—
1928D	6,436,000	1.50	2.00	2.75	4.50	14.00	25.00	31.00	980.	—
1928S	6,936,000	.85	1.35	2.25	3.15	10.00	30.00	175.	3850.	—
1929	36,446,000	.65	.90	1.50	2.50	8.00	15.00	25.00	300.	—
1929D	8,370,000	1.25	1.75	2.50	6.00	12.50	28.00	42.00	1125.	—
1929S	7,754,000	.70	.95	1.50	2.75	10.00	21.00	36.00	420.	—
1930	22,849,000	.60	.80	1.25	2.25	6.00	15.00	23.00	120.	—
1930S	5,435,000	.65	.85	1.25	2.75	9.50	25.00	34.00	530.	—
1931S	1,200,000	3.75	4.25	4.75	5.50	12.50	28.00	38.00	280.	—
1934	20,213,003	.60	.70	.85	1.40	6.00	13.00	21.00	315.	—
1934D	7,480,000	.65	.95	1.50	3.50	5.50	18.00	36.00	1365.	—
1935	58,264,000	.50	.55	.65	1.25	4.00	8.50	18.00	94.00	—
1935D	12,092,000	.60	.90	1.45	3.50	8.50	21.00	27.00	450.	—
1935S	10,300,000	.50	.55	.65	1.75	5.50	13.00	24.00	220.	—
1936	119,001,420	.50	.55	.65	1.25	3.50	7.50	14.00	75.00	950.
1936D	24,814,000	.50	.55	.75	1.95	4.00	10.50	17.50	92.00	—
1936S	14,930,000	.50	.55	.65	1.40	4.00	12.00	16.00	80.00	—
1937	79,485,769	.50	.55	.65	1.25	3.50	7.00	13.00	42.00	950.
1937D	17,826,000	.50	.55	.65	1.40	4.00	9.00	14.00	52.00	—
1937D 3 Leg.	Inc. Ab.	150.	225.	295.	325.	490.	750.	1375.	13,000.	—

1937D three-legged

Date	Mintage	G-4	VG-8	F-12	VF-20	XF-40	AU-50	MS-60	MS-65	Prf-65
1937S	5,635,000	.50	.55	.65	1.40	4.00	9.00	14.00	65.00	—
1938D	7,020,000	.50	.55	.65	1.50	4.00	8.50	13.00	41.00	—
1938 D/D	—	2.25	4.25	5.75	8.00	11.00	13.50	16.00	90.00	—
1938D/S	Inc. Ab.	6.00	7.50	9.00	11.00	15.00	21.00	35.00	170.	—

Jefferson

Wartime
(note mintmark)

Pre-war composition

Designer: Felix Schlag. **Size:** 21.2 millimeters. **Weight:** 5 grams. **Composition:** 75% copper, 25% nickel. **Notes:** Some 1939 strikes have doubling of the word "Monticello" on the reverse.

Nickel five-cent

Date	Mintage	G-4	VG-8	F-12	VF-20	XF-40	MS-60	MS-65	Prf-65
1938	19,515,365	—	.40	.50	1.00	1.50	3.50	7.00	45.00
1938D	5,376,000	.60	.90	1.00	1.25	1.75	4.25	7.50	—
1938S	4,105,000	1.25	1.50	1.75	2.00	2.50	5.00	8.00	—
1939	120,627,535	—	—	.15	.25	.30	1.75	2.00	40.00
Doubled Monticello			7.50	10.00	25.00	50.00	200.	—	—
1939D	3,514,000	2.50	3.00	3.50	4.50	6.75	40.00	50.00	—
1939S	6,630,000	.40	.45	.60	1.00	3.25	17.00	30.00	—
1940	176,499,158	—	—	—	—	.25	1.00	1.25	45.00
1940D	43,540,000	—	—	.15	.30	.40	2.50	2.75	—
1940S	39,690,000	—	—	.15	.20	.50	2.75	3.50	—
1941	203,283,720	—	—	—	—	.20	.85	1.10	35.00
1941D	53,432,000	—	—	.15	.25	.35	2.50	4.00	—
1941S	43,445,000	—	—	.15	.25	.40	3.75	5.75	—
1942	49,818,600	—	—	—	—	.40	3.75	6.00	25.00
1942D	13,938,000	—	.30	.40	.60	2.00	19.00	35.00	—

Wartime composition

Composition: 56% copper, 35% silver (.0563 ounces), 9% manganese.

Date	Mintage	G-4	VG-8	F-12	VF-20	XF-40	MS-60	MS-65	Prf-65
1942P	57,900,600	.40	.65	.85	1.00	1.75	8.00	20.00	110.
1942S	32,900,000	.40	.70	1.00	1.10	1.75	9.00	15.00	—
1943P	271,165,000	.30	.50	.85	1.00	1.50	4.00	6.50	—
1943/2P	Inc. Ab.	20.00	30.00	45.00	70.00	110.	250.	600.	—
1943D	15,294,000	.55	.90	1.10	1.50	1.75	2.75	5.50	—
1943S	104,060,000	.40	.65	.85	1.00	1.50	3.50	5.75	—
1944P	119,150,000	.30	.50	.85	1.00	1.50	3.50	6.00	—
1944D	32,309,000	.40	.65	.85	1.00	1.75	9.00	12.00	—
1944S	21,640,000	.45	.85	.95	1.25	2.00	5.50	15.00	—
1945P	119,408,100	.30	.50	.85	1.00	1.75	4.00	7.50	—
1945D	37,158,000	.40	.65	.85	1.00	1.25	3.25	6.50	—
1945S	58,939,000	.30	.50	.70	.80	.90	2.25	7.50	—

Pre-war composition resumed

Notes: The 1979-S Type II proof has a clearer mintmark than the Type I.

Date	Mintage	G-4	VG-8	F-12	VF-20	XF-40	MS-60	MS-65	Prf-65
1946	161,116,000	—	—	—	.15	.20	.40	.60	—
1946D	45,292,200	—	—	—	.25	.35	.75	.95	—
1946S	13,560,000	—	—	—	.30	.40	.60	.70	—
1947	95,000,000	—	—	—	.15	.20	.40	.55	—
1947D	37,822,000	—	—	—	.20	.30	.65	.75	—
1947S	24,720,000	—	—	—	.15	.20	.55	.65	—
1948	89,348,000	—	—	—	.15	.20	.35	.55	—
1948D	44,734,000	—	—	—	.25	.35	1.00	1.25	—
1948S	11,300,000	—	—	—	.25	.50	1.00	1.25	—
1949	60,652,000	—	—	—	.20	.25	.75	1.25	—
1949D	36,498,000	—	—	—	.30	.40	1.00	1.25	—
1949D/S	Inc. Ab.	—	—	20.00	40.00	75.00	175.	350.	—
1949S	9,716,000	—	.25	.35	.45	1.50	2.00	2.50	—
1950	9,847,386	—	.25	.45	.50	.75	1.90	2.25	42.00
1950D	2,630,030	—	5.00	5.00	5.25	5.50	6.50	9.00	—
1951	28,609,500	—	—	—	.40	.50	1.00	1.50	32.00
1951D	20,460,000	—	.25	.30	.40	.50	1.25	1.50	—
1951S	7,776,000	—	.30	.40	.50	.75	1.75	4.00	—
1952	64,069,980	—	—	—	.15	.20	.85	1.25	26.00
1952D	30,638,000	—	—	—	.20	.35	1.00	1.75	—
1952S	20,572,000	—	—	—	.15	.20	.65	.90	—
1953	46,772,800	—	—	—	.15	.25	.35	.45	25.00
1953D	59,878,600	—	—	—	.15	.20	.30	.40	—
1953S	19,210,900	—	—	—	.15	.20	.40	.50	—
1954	47,917,350	—	—	—	—	—	.20	.30	18.00
1954D	117,136,560	—	—	—	—	—	.30	.40	—
1954S	29,384,000	—	—	—	—	.15	.35	.45	—
1954S/D	Inc. Ab.	—	—	3.50	7.00	11.00	25.00	40.00	—
1955	8,266,200	—	.25	.35	.40	.45	.75	1.25	10.00
1955D	74,464,100	—	—	—	—	—	.20	.30	—
1955D/S	Inc. Ab.	—	—	3.00	7.00	12.00	45.00	63.00	—
1956	35,885,384	—	—	—	—	—	.25	.35	2.50
1956D	67,222,940	—	—	—	—	—	.20	.35	—
1957	39,655,952	—	—	—	—	—	.25	.35	1.25
1957D	136,828,900	—	—	—	—	—	.20	.40	—
1958	17,963,652	—	—	—	.15	.20	.30	.55	2.00
1958D	168,249,120	—	—	—	—	—	.20	.35	—

Date	Mintage	MS-65	Prf-65
1959	28,397,291	.35	.80
1959D	160,738,240	.25	—
1960	57,107,602	.25	.60
1960D	192,582,180	.25	—
1961	76,668,244	.25	.40
1961D	229,342,760	.25	—
1962	100,602,019	.25	.40
1962D	280,195,720	.25	—
1963	178,851,645	.25	.40
1963D	276,829,460	.25	—
1964	1,028,622,762	.25	.40
1964D	1,787,297,160	.25	—
1965	136,131,380	.25	—
1966	156,208,283	.25	—
1967	107,325,800	.25	—
1968	None minted	—	—

Date	Mintage	MS-65	Prf-65
1968D	91,227,880	.25	—
1968S	103,437,510	.25	.50
1969	None minted	—	—
1969D	202,807,500	.25	—
1969S	123,099,631	.25	.50
1970	None minted	—	—
1970D	515,485,380	.25	—
1970S	241,464,814	.25	.50
1971	106,884,000	.60	—
1971D	316,144,800	.25	—
1971S	Proof only	—	1.25
1972	202,036,000	.25	—
1972D	351,694,600	.20	—
1972S	Proof only	—	1.10
1973	384,396,000	.15	—
1973D	261,405,000	.15	—

Nickel five-cent

Date	Mintage	MS-65	Prf-65	Date	Mintage	MS-65	Prf-65
1973S	Proof only	—	1.00	1984P	746,769,000	.20	—
1974	601,752,000	.15	—	1984D	517,675,146	.20	—
1974D	277,373,000	.20	—	1984S	Proof only	—	2.50
1974S	Proof only	—	1.00	1985P	647,114,962	.20	—
1975	181,772,000	.35	—	1985D	459,747,446	.20	—
1975D	401,875,300	.15	—	1985S	Proof only	—	1.75
1975S	Proof only	—	1.00	1986P	536,883,483	.25	—
1976	367,124,000	.15	—	1986D	361,819,140	.80	—
1976D	563,964,147	.15	—	1986S	Proof only	—	4.50
1976S	Proof only	—	1.00	1987P	371,499,481	.15	—
1977	585,376,000	.15	—	1987D	410,590,604	.15	—
1977D	297,313,460	.35	—	1987S	Proof only	—	1.50
1977S	Proof only	—	.55	1988P	771,360,000	.15	—
1978	391,308,000	.15	—	1988D	663,771,652	.15	—
1978D	313,092,780	.15	—	1988S	Proof only	—	2.50
1978S	Proof only	—	.55	1989P	898,812,000	.15	—
1979	463,188,000	.15	—	1989D	570,842,474	.15	—
1979D	325,867,672	.15	—	1989S	Proof only	—	2.00
1979S T-I	Proof only	—	.75	1990P	661,636,000	.15	—
1979S T-II	Proof only	—	1.45	1990D	663,938,503	.15	—
1980P	593,004,000	.15	—	1990S	Proof only	—	3.50
1980D	502,323,448	.15	—	1991P	—	.15	—
1980S	Proof only	—	.65	1991D	—	.15	—
1981P	657,504,000	.15	—	1991S	Proof only	—	3.00
1981D	364,801,843	.15	—	1992P	—	.15	—
1981S T-I	Proof only	—	.65	1992D	—	.15	—
1981S T-II	Proof only	—	1.75	1992S	Proof only	—	2.50
1982P	292,355,000	.55	—	1993P	—	.15	—
1982D	373,726,544	1.75	—	1993D	—	.15	—
1982S	Proof only	—	1.25	1993S	Proof only	—	2.00
1983P	561,615,000	.70	—	1994P	—	.15	—
1983D	536,726,276	.75	—	1994D	—	.15	—
1983S	Proof only	—	1.50	1994S	Proof only	—	3.50

Dimes

Draped Bust

Small eagle

Heraldic eagle

Small-eagle reverse

Designer: Robert Scot. **Size:** 19 millimeters. **Weight:** 2.7 grams. **Composition:** 89.24% silver (.0775 ounces), 10.76% copper. **Notes:** The 1797 strikes have either 13 or 16 stars on the obverse.

Date	Mintage	G-4	VG-8	F-12	VF-20	XF-40	MS-60
1796	22,135	1050.	1600.	1900.	3100.	5000.	7000.
1797 13 stars	25,261	1150.	1750.	2100.	3450.	5500.	7500.
1797 16 stars	Inc. Ab.	1050.	1600.	1900.	3250.	5250.	7000.

Heraldic-eagle reverse

Notes: The 1798 overdates have either 13 or 16 stars on the obverse. Varieties of the regular 1798 strikes are distinguished by the size of the 8 in the date. The 1804 strikes have either 13 or 14 stars on the obverse. The 1805 strikes have either 4 or 5 berries on the olive branch held by the eagle.

Date	Mintage	G-4	VG-8	F-12	VF-20	XF-40	MS-60
1798	27,550	450.	560.	750.	1125.	1975.	6000.
1798/97 13 stars	Inc. Ab.	1650.	2600.	4100.	6100.	7500.	—
1798/97 16 stars	Inc. Ab.	475.	650.	950.	1800.	2775.	6000.
1798 small 8	Inc. Ab.	850.	1200.	1650.	2800.	4400.	—
1800	21,760	450.	560.	750.	1125.	1975.	5400.
1801	34,640	450.	560.	750.	1150.	2100.	—
1802	10,975	660.	975.	1400.	2650.	4850.	—
1803	33,040	450.	560.	750.	1125.	1975.	5500.
1804 13 stars	8,265	925.	1275.	2100.	4400.	7500.	—
1804 14 stars	Inc. Ab.	1200.	1700.	2350.	4750.	8000.	—
1805 4 berries	120,780	425.	525.	725.	950.	1800.	4050.
1805 5 berries	Inc. Ab.	550.	650.	975.	1200.	1850.	4200.
1807	165,000	425.	525.	725.	975.	1800.	4050.

Liberty Cap

Designer: John Reich. **Size:** 18.8 millimeters. **Weight:** 2.7 grams. **Composition:** 89.24% silver (.0775 ounces), 10.76% copper. **Notes:** Varieties of the 1814, 1821, and 1828 strikes are distinguished by the size of the numerals in the dates. The 1820 varieties are distinguished by the size of the 0 in the date. The 1823 overdates have either large "E's" or small "E's" in "United States of America" on the reverse.

Date	Mintage	G-4	VG-8	F-12	VF-20	XF-40	AU-50	MS-60	MS-65
1809	51,065	100.	200.	375.	585.	875.	1250.	4200.	22,500.
1811/9	65,180	55.00	90.00	165.	275.	575.	1050.	4000.	22,500.
1814 sm. dt.	421,500	40.00	60.00	90.00	185.	450.	700.	800.	11,500.
1814 lg. dt.	Inc.Ab.	17.50	26.00	44.00	115.	350.	625.	800.	11,500.
1820 lg. O	942,587	17.00	24.00	35.00	105.	330.	625.	800.	11,500.
1820 sm. O	Inc.Ab.	17.00	24.00	35.00	105.	330.	625.	800.	11,500.
1821 lg. dt.	1,186,512	16.00	23.00	38.00	105.	330.	625.	800.	11,500.
1821 sm. dt.	Inc.Ab.	18.50	25.00	45.00	125.	370.	625.	800.	11,500.
1822	100,000	300.	450.	800.	1250.	2500.	4450.	6000.	—
1823/22 lg.E's	440,000	15.00	20.00	33.00	95.00	300.	625.	800.	11,500.
1823/22 sm.E's	Inc.Ab.	17.50	25.00	45.00	125.	380.	625.	800.	11,500.
1824/22	Undetermined	30.00	40.00	60.00	165.	450.	1100.	2500.	—
1825	510,000	15.00	22.00	35.00	95.00	300.	775.	1000.	11,500.
1827	1,215,000	15.00	22.00	35.00	95.00	300.	775.	1000.	11,500.
1828 lg.dt.	125,000	30.00	40.00	60.00	165.	500.	875.	2200.	—

Reduced size

Size: 18.5 millimeters. **Notes:** The three varieties of 1829 strikes and two varieties of 1830 strikes are distinguished by the size of "10C." on the reverse. On the 1833 "high 3" variety, the last 3 in the date is higher than the first 3. The two varieties of the 1834 strikes are distinguished by the size of the 4 in the date.

Date	Mintage	G-4	VG-8	F-12	VF-20	XF-40	AU-50	MS-60	MS-65
1828 sm.dt.	Inc. Ab.	20.00	35.00	50.00	125.	325.	515.	1400.	—
1829 lg.10C.	770,000	20.00	28.00	38.00	75.00	275.	475.	625.	8000.
1829 med.10C.	Inc. Ab.	17.50	25.00	35.00	85.00	265.	425.	625.	8000.
1829 sm.10C.	Inc. Ab.	14.00	17.00	22.00	60.00	185.	415.	625.	8000.
1830 lg.10C.	510,000	14.00	17.00	22.00	60.00	185.	415.	625.	8000.
1830 sm.10C.	Inc. Ab.	15.00	19.00	25.00	63.00	200.	415.	625.	8000.
1830/29	Inc. Ab.	20.00	33.00	50.00	90.00	260.	550.	1040.	—
1831	771,350	14.00	17.00	22.00	60.00	185.	350.	600.	7000.
1832	522,500	14.00	17.00	22.00	60.00	185.	350.	600.	7000.
1833	485,000	14.00	17.00	22.00	60.00	185.	350.	600.	7000.
1834 lg. 4	635,000	14.00	17.00	22.00	60.00	185.	350.	600.	7000.
1835	1,410,000	14.00	17.00	22.00	60.00	185.	350.	600.	9100.
1836	1,190,000	14.00	17.00	22.00	60.00	185.	350.	600.	7000.
1837	1,042,000	14.00	17.00	22.00	60.00	185.	350.	625.	7000.

Seated Liberty

No stars

Stars

Drapery

Arrows at date

Obverse legend

No stars

Designer: Christian Gobrecht. **Size:** 17.9 millimeters. **Weight:** 2.67 grams. **Composition:** 90% silver (.0773 ounces), 10% copper. **Notes:** The two 1837 varieties are distinguished by the size of the numerals in the date.

Dimes

Date	Mintage	G-4	VG-8	F-12	VF-20	XF-40	AU-50	MS-60	MS-65
1837 sm.date	Inc. Ab.	29.00	40.00	75.00	275.	550.	750.	1100.	6500.
1837 lg.date	Inc. Ab.	29.00	40.00	75.00	275.	550.	850.	1100.	6500.
1838O	406,034	40.00	55.00	90.00	325.	650.	1000.	3500.	21,000.

Stars around rim

Notes: The two 1838 varieties are distinguished by the size of the stars on the obverse. The 1838 "partial drapery" variety has drapery on Liberty's left elbow. The 1839-O with reverse of 1838-O variety was struck from rusted dies. This variety has a bumpy surface on the reverse.

Date	Mintage	G-4	VG-8	F-12	VF-20	XF-40	AU-50	MS-60	MS-65
1838 sm.stars	1,992,500	20.00	30.00	45.00	75.00	175.	425.	1400.	—
1838 lg.stars	Inc. Ab.	9.00	11.00	15.00	25.00	60.00	170.	575.	8500.
1838 partial drapery									
	Inc. Ab.	20.00	25.00	45.00	85.00	175.	300.	1200.	—
1839	1,053,115	8.00	11.00	15.00	35.00	70.00	170.	265.	3000.
1839O	1,323,000	7.00	12.00	20.00	40.00	85.00	300.	950.	—
1839O rev. 1838O	—	125.	185.	275.	475.	625.	—	—	—
1840	1,358,580	8.00	11.00	15.00	25.00	60.00	170.	265.	3000.
1840O	1,175,000	8.00	15.00	20.00	40.00	85.00	250.	1500.	—

Drapery added to Liberty

Notes: In 1840 drapery was added to Liberty's left elbow.

Date	Mintage	G-4	VG-8	F-12	VF-20	XF-40	AU-50	MS-60	MS-65
1840	Inc. Ab.	25.00	45.00	85.00	135.	275.	1000.	—	—
1841	1,622,500	6.00	7.50	10.00	17.00	45.00	175.	260.	2500.
1841O	2,007,500	8.00	11.00	15.00	28.00	60.00	250.	1500.	—
1841O lg. O	Inc. Ab.	600.	900.	1200.	2500.	—	—	—	—
1842	1,887,500	6.00	7.50	10.00	17.00	45.00	175.	260.	2500.
1842O	2,020,000	8.00	11.00	15.00	40.00	120.	750.	2300.	—
1843	1,370,000	6.00	8.00	10.00	17.00	45.00	175.	260.	2500.
1843/1843	—	15.00	20.00	30.00	70.00	125.	200.	400.	—
1843O	150,000	35.00	65.00	125.	275.	700.	2000.	—	—
1844	72,500	125.	175.	225.	400.	900.	1850.	3000.	—
1845	1,755,000	6.00	7.50	10.00	19.00	45.00	120.	260.	2500.
1845/1845	Inc. Ab.	10.00	15.00	25.00	45.00	135.	—	—	—
1845O	230,000	19.00	35.00	60.00	165.	475.	1200.	—	—
1846	31,300	95.00	125.	150.	300.	850.	2000.	—	—
1847	245,000	13.50	20.00	30.00	60.00	125.	350.	950.	—
1848	451,500	9.00	12.00	17.00	30.00	65.00	165.	750.	7050.
1849	839,000	7.00	9.50	11.00	18.00	50.00	125.	500.	7050.
1849O	300,000	10.00	18.00	30.00	85.00	175.	1200.	—	—
1850	1,931,500	6.00	7.00	9.00	25.00	60.00	120.	260.	2500.
1850O	510,000	10.00	14.00	28.00	60.00	135.	400.	1250.	—
1851	1,026,500	6.00	7.00	9.00	19.00	60.00	120.	325.	—
1851O	400,000	10.00	15.00	30.00	75.00	150.	450.	1500.	—
1852	1,535,500	6.00	7.00	9.00	15.00	50.00	120.	290.	2500.
1852O	430,000	14.00	22.00	30.00	85.00	175.	425.	1800.	—
1853	95,000	65.00	85.00	100.	180.	300.	450.	800.	—

Arrows at date

Weight: 2.49 grams. **Composition:** 90% silver (.0721 ounces), 10% copper.

Date	Mintage	G-4	VG-8	F-12	VF-20	XF-40	AU-50	MS-60	MS-65	Prf-65
1853	108850.	5.40	6.25	7.50	14.00	45.00	125.	330.	3800.	38,000.
1853O	1,100,000	6.00	7.00	10.00	40.00	110.	400.	900.	—	—
1854	4,470,000	5.75	6.25	7.50	14.00	45.00	125.	330.	3800.	38,000.
1854O	1,770,000	5.50	6.50	9.00	25.00	75.00	175.	600.	—	—
1855	2,075,000	5.40	6.25	7.50	15.00	48.00	170.	350.	3800.	38,000.

Arrows at date removed

Notes: The two 1856 varieties are distinguished by the size of the numerals in the date.

Date	Mintage	G-4	VG-8	F-12	VF-20	XF-40	AU-50	MS-60	MS-65	Prf-65
1856 small date										
	5,780,000	5.40	6.50	8.25	12.50	32.00	115.	250.	7050.	38,000.
1856 large date										
	Inc. Ab.	10.00	12.00	15.00	25.00	65.00	175.	475.	—	—
1856O	1,180,000	7.00	9.00	12.00	25.00	70.00	200.	500.	—	—
1856S	70,000	100.	165.	225.	425.	800.	1500.	—	—	—
1857	5,580,000	5.40	6.25	8.25	12.50	32.00	100.	260.	2500.	4000.
1857O	1,540,000	6.00	7.25	9.00	18.00	50.00	200.	350.	—	—
1858	1,540,000	5.40	6.25	8.25	17.50	40.00	115.	260.	2500.	4000.
1858O	290,000	15.00	19.00	35.00	60.00	125.	275.	800.	—	—
1858S	60,000	80.00	125.	175.	290.	600.	1100.	1800.	—	—
1859	430,000	6.00	7.00	12.00	25.00	50.00	140.	350.	—	4000.
1859O	480,000	7.50	9.50	12.50	25.00	70.00	225.	550.	—	—
1859S	60,000	100.	130.	225.	400.	900.	2000.	—	—	—
1860S	140,000	28.00	36.00	48.00	100.	225.	800.	—	—	—

Dimes

Transitional pattern

Notes: This non-circulation strike was an experiment in transferring the legend "United States of America" from the reverse to the obverse.

Date	Mintage	G-4	VG-8	F-12	VF-20	XF-40	AU-50	MS-60	MS-65	Prf-65
1859 obverse of 1859, reverse of 1860					—	—	—	—	—	25,000.

Obverse legend

Notes: In 1860 the legend "United States of America" replaced the stars on the obverse. The 1873 "closed-3" and "open-3" varieties are distinguished by the amount of space between the upper left and lower left serifs of the 3 in the date.

Date	Mintage	G-4	VG-8	F-12	VF-20	XF-40	AU-50	MS-60	MS-65	Prf-65
1860	607,000	6.00	7.50	12.00	18.00	40.00	85.00	200.	—	1400.
1860O	40,000	300.	475.	800.	1350.	2500.	4200.	6000.	—	—
1861	1,884,000	4.50	5.50	7.00	12.00	28.00	65.00	125.	—	1400.
1861S	172,500	35.00	70.00	125.	225.	375.	900.	—	—	—
1862	847,550	5.50	7.00	8.50	14.00	35.00	65.00	150.	—	1400.
1862S	180,750	30.00	52.00	85.00	140.	300.	700.	—	—	—
1863	14,460	250.	375.	500.	600.	750.	900.	1200.	—	1400.
1863S	157,500	30.00	35.00	55.00	90.00	200.	400.	1200.	—	—
1864	11,470	250.	325.	400.	500.	600.	775.	1650.	—	1400.
1864S	230,000	19.00	27.00	37.00	80.00	140.	325.	1200.	—	—
1865	10,500	275.	350.	450.	550.	675.	1050.	1250.	—	1400.
1865S	175,000	22.00	29.00	47.00	85.00	185.	700.	—	—	—
1866	8,725	300.	375.	575.	675.	800.	1200.	1800.	—	4400.
1866S	135,000	35.00	45.00	75.00	110.	200.	400.	1500.	—	—
1867	6,625	350.	450.	600.	700.	850.	1350.	1800.	—	4400.
1867S	140,000	30.00	40.00	70.00	95.00	195.	385.	1200.	—	—
1868	464,000	10.00	12.00	20.00	31.00	70.00	175.	300.	—	1400.
1868S	260,000	12.00	17.00	27.00	55.00	115.	285.	600.	—	—
1869	256,600	12.00	16.00	30.00	55.00	115.	200.	600.	—	1400.
1869S	450,000	12.00	14.00	18.00	38.00	85.00	150.	400.	—	—
1870	471,000	9.75	11.00	15.00	32.00	70.00	135.	300.	—	1400.
1870S	50,000	215.	280.	375.	450.	575.	850.	2000.	—	—
1871	907,710	7.75	9.00	11.00	21.00	42.00	130.	300.	—	1400.
1871CC	20,100	675.	850.	1300.	2000.	3200.	5000.	—	—	—
1871S	320,000	13.00	20.00	30.00	75.00	135.	350.	900.	—	—
1872	2,396,450	6.50	8.00	10.00	18.00	31.00	95.00	175.	—	1400.
1872CC	35,480	350.	500.	850.	1200.	2500.	4000.	—	—	—
1872S	190,000	29.00	45.00	70.00	125.	215.	450.	1100.	—	—
1873 closed 3										
	1,568,600	7.00	8.50	10.00	18.00	50.00	100.	200.	—	1400.
1873 open 3										
	Inc. Ab.	15.00	18.00	30.00	48.00	100.	225.	650.	—	—
1873CC	12,400	—	—			Unique	—	—	—	—

Arrows at date

Weight: 2.5 grams. **Composition:** 90% silver (.0724 ounces), 10% copper.

Date	Mintage	G-4	VG-8	F-12	VF-20	XF-40	AU-50	MS-60	MS-65	Prf-65
1873	2,378,500	8.00	13.00	25.00	50.00	150.	350.	500.	6000.	6000.
1873CC	18,791	650.	850.	1300.	2500.	3500.	6000.	—	—	—
1873S	455,000	10.00	16.00	17.00	60.00	180.	320.	1500.	—	—
1874	2,940,700	8.00	13.00	17.50	50.00	150.	315.	500.	6000.	6000.
1874CC	10,817	1500.	2200.	3500.	5500.	11,000.	—	—	—	—
1874S	240,000	20.00	30.00	55.00	100.	250.	450.	1500.	—	—

Arrows at date removed

Notes: On the 1876-CC doubled-obverse variety, doubling appears in the words "of America" in the legend.

Date	Mintage	G-4	VG-8	F-12	VF-20	XF-40	AU-50	MS-60	MS-65	Prf-65
1875	10,350,700	5.50	6.50	7.50	11.00	22.00	60.00	125.	2250.	4600.
1875CC mint mark in wreath										
	4,645,000	6.50	8.00	11.00	18.00	30.00	90.00	160.	2700.	—
1875CC mint mark under wreath										
	Inc. Ab.	7.00	9.00	13.00	25.00	50.00	165.	235.	3000.	—
1875S mint mark in wreath										
	9,070,000	8.00	12.00	17.00	25.00	45.00	125.	225.	3100.	—
1875S mint mark under wreath										
	Inc. Ab.	5.50	6.25	7.50	11.50	22.00	60.00	110.	1150.	—
1876	11,461,150	5.50	6.25	7.50	11.00	24.00	60.00	110.	1150.	1200.
1876CC	8,270,000	5.50	6.50	7.50	18.00	30.00	60.00	175.	—	—
1876CC (doubled obverse)										
	Inc. Ab.	15.00	25.00	40.00	125.	250.	400.	700.	—	—
1876S	10,420,000	5.50	6.50	12.50	20.00	35.00	60.00	110.	1150.	—
1877	7,310,510	5.50	6.25	8.50	13.00	23.00	60.00	110.	1150.	1200.
1877CC	7,700,000	5.50	6.50	9.00	18.00	30.00	75.00	175.	—	—
1877S	2,340,000	7.75	9.00	12.00	20.00	39.00	90.00	150.	—	—
1878	1,678,800	5.50	6.50	10.00	18.00	30.00	60.00	110.	1150.	1200.
1878CC	200,000	40.00	55.00	90.00	145.	250.	450.	775.	3900.	—
1879	15,100	165.	200.	250.	275.	350.	400	600.	4300.	4400.

Date	Mintage	G-4	VG-8	F-12	VF-20	XF-40	AU-50	MS-60	MS-65	Prf-65
1880	37,335	100.	125.	165.	210.	250.	325.	450.	4300.	4400.
1881	24,975	125.	150.	180.	230.	325.	425.	650.	4300.	4400.
1882	3,911,100	5.40	6.25	7.50	11.00	22.00	60.00	110.	1150.	1200.
1883	7,675,712	5.50	6.25	7.50	11.00	24.00	60.00	110.	1150.	1200.
1884	3,366,380	5.50	6.25	7.50	11.00	22.00	60.00	110.	1150.	1200.
1884S	564,969	14.00	17.00	29.00	43.00	80.00	175.	500.	—	—
1885	2,533,427	5.50	6.25	7.50	11.00	22.00	60.00	110.	1150.	1200.
1885S	43,690	300.	450.	600.	1100.	1500.	2500.	3000.	—	—
1886	6,377,570	5.50	6.25	7.50	11.00	22.00	60.00	110.	1150.	1200.
1886S	206,524	30.00	40.00	57.00	80.00	115.	225.	600.	—	—
1887	11,283,939	5.50	6.25	7.50	11.00	22.00	60.00	110.	1150.	1200.
1887S	4,454,450	5.50	6.25	7.50	11.00	22.00	60.00	110.	1150.	—
1888	5,496,487	5.50	6.25	7.50	11.00	22.00	60.00	110.	1150.	1200.
1888S	1,720,000	6.00	6.75	9.50	14.00	35.00	95.00	200.	—	—
1889	7,380,711	5.50	6.25	7.50	11.00	22.00	60.00	110.	1150.	1200.
1889S	972,678	14.00	17.00	23.00	40.00	75.00	150.	475.	4500.	—
1890	9,911,541	5.50	6.25	7.50	11.00	22.00	60.00	110.	1150.	1200.
1890S	1,423,076	8.00	10.00	18.00	32.00	70.00	135.	400.	4900.	—
1890S/S	Inc. Ab.	100.	120.	150.	185.	275.	450.	—	—	—
1891	15,310,600	5.50	6.25	7.50	11.00	22.00	60.00	110.	1150.	1200.
1891O	4,540,000	5.50	6.50	7.75	11.50	22.00	70.00	475.	2250.	—
1891O/horz. O	Inc. Ab.	100.	120.	150.	185.	275.	400.	—	—	—
1891S	3,196,116	5.50	6.25	7.50	12.00	28.00	70.00	500.	4400.	—

Barber

Designer: Charles E. Barber. **Size:** 17.9 millimeters. **Weight:** 2.5 grams. **Composition:** 90% silver (.0724 ounces), 10% copper.

Date	Mintage	G-4	VG-8	F-12	VF-20	XF-40	AU-50	MS-60	MS-65	Prf-65
1892	12,121,245	2.60	4.25	12.25	15.50	25.00	60.00	100.	750.	1450.
1892O	3,841,700	4.00	6.00	19.50	27.00	31.00	59.00	145.	2050.	—
1892S	990,710	33.00	42.00	105.	155.	190.	225.	325.	4550.	—
1893	3,340,792	4.00	6.00	14.00	20.00	40.00	65.00	165.	925.	1450.
1893O	1,760,000	14.00	25.00	95.00	105.	115.	135.	260.	2600.	—
1893S	2,491,401	6.50	11.50	21.00	30.00	39.00	110.	230.	2400.	—
1894	1,330,972	7.00	14.00	85.00	105.	115.	130.	250.	1175.	1450.
1894O	720,000	32.00	52.00	160.	195.	290.	600.	945.	8300.	—
1894S	24	Stacks Sale. Jan. 1990, Ch. Proof $275,000.							—	—
1895	690,880	65.00	77.00	260.	345.	365.	410.	610.	1925.	2000.
1895O	440,000	160.	260.	625.	900.	1375.	1950.	2200.	10,000.	—
1895S	1,120,000	15.00	24.00	93.00	115.	125.	180.	390.	6200.	—
1896	2,000,762	5.85	11.75	35.00	45.00	52.00	85.00	165.	1560.	1450.
1896O	610,000	41.00	62.00	155.	260.	350.	550.	725.	6300.	—
1896S	575,056	41.00	52.00	155.	215.	240.	410.	585.	4440.	—
1897	10,869,264	1.30	2.25	5.85	8.50	23.00	68.00	100.	750.	1450.
1897O	666,000	36.00	47.00	195.	255.	325.	520.	725.	6600.	—
1897S	1,342,844	8.00	14.00	55.00	71.00	78.00	195.	325.	4550.	—
1898	16,320,735	1.30	1.45	6.00	11.00	28.00	60.00	100.	750.	1450.
1898O	2,130,000	11.00	42.00	75.00	95.00	125.	165.	390.	4100.	—
1898S	1,702,507	3.90	6.20	18.00	27.00	35.00	95.00	250.	5700.	—
1899	19,580,846	1.30	1.45	4.50	7.00	20.00	60.00	100.	750.	1450.
1899O	2,650,000	8.00	30.00	60.00	80.00	110.	200.	325.	5750.	—
1899S	1,867,493	2.90	6.50	11.00	18.00	32.00	85.00	275.	4300.	—
1900	17,600,912	1.35	2.50	6.00	12.50	28.00	60.00	90.00	1080.	1450.
1900O	2,010,000	4.90	8.45	68.00	94.00	155.	270.	565.	6000.	—
1900S	5,168,270	2.25	2.90	8.00	19.00	33.00	75.00	155.	1920.	—
1901	18,860,478	1.30	1.45	4.50	7.00	22.00	60.00	115.	1170.	1450.
1901O	5,620,000	2.25	3.25	9.75	15.50	42.00	115.	295.	2600.	—
1901S	593,022	35.00	45.00	200.	260.	370.	585.	775.	4750.	—
1902	21,380,777	1.30	1.45	3.90	6.75	21.00	60.00	120.	750.	1450.
1902O	4,500,000	2.20	3.90	11.00	20.00	35.00	105.	300.	3350.	—
1902S	2,070,000	3.90	6.50	29.00	40.00	71.00	130.	295.	4080.	—
1903	19,500,755	1.30	1.45	3.90	6.75	21.00	60.00	120.	1100.	1450.
1903O	8,180,000	2.00	2.75	7.00	11.00	26.00	91.00	250.	7500.	—
1903S	613,300	30.00	39.00	260.	450.	700.	750.	775.	4550.	—
1904	14,601,027	1.30	1.45	5.25	8.50	20.00	60.00	100.	3250.	1450.
1904S	800,000	19.00	29.00	100.	130.	230.	420.	525.	4400.	—
1905	14,552,350	1.30	1.45	3.90	6.50	21.00	60.00	100.	750.	1450.
1905O	3,400,000	2.25	4.25	19.50	30.00	45.00	105.	215.	4200.	—
1905S	6,855,199	2.10	3.00	6.50	17.00	33.00	75.00	200.	1250.	—
1906	19,958,406	1.30	1.45	3.00	6.50	21.00	60.00	100.	750.	1450.
1906D	4,060,000	2.10	3.00	6.50	11.00	32.00	80.00	150.	2650.	—
1906O	2,610,000	3.50	7.50	35.00	45.00	49.00	120.	210.	1250.	—
1906S	3,136,640	1.60	3.50	11.00	23.00	40.00	91.00	215.	1350.	—
1907	22,220,575	1.30	1.45	3.00	6.50	21.00	46.00	100.	750.	1450.
1907D	4,080,000	1.45	2.60	7.50	10.00	40.00	105.	225.	4800.	—
1907O	5,058,000	1.45	2.60	18.00	28.00	32.00	72.00	165.	1750.	—
1907S	3,178,470	1.90	3.90	7.75	13.00	35.00	100.	275.	3100.	—

Date	Mintage	G-4	VG-8	F-12	VF-20	XF-40	AU-50	MS-60	MS-65	Prf-65
1908	10,600,545	1.30	1.45	3.00	6.50	21.00	60.00	100.	750.	1450.
1908D	7,490,000	1.30	1.80	5.50	9.50	25.00	55.00	140.	1800.	—
1908O	1,789,000	2.30	4.50	36.00	49.00	57.00	125.	250.	2100.	—
1908S	3,220,000	1.65	2.60	7.50	12.00	34.00	91.00	195.	2900.	—
1909	10,240,650	1.30	1.45	3.00	6.50	21.00	60.00	100.	750.	1700.
1909D	954,000	2.95	6.75	49.00	60.00	78.00	150.	335.	3000.	—
1909O	2,287,000	1.65	3.40	7.80	15.00	27.00	91.00	165.	1400.	—
1909S	1,000,000	3.00	6.50	64.00	74.00	135.	325.	450.	3400.	—
1910	11,520,551	1.30	1.45	4.50	7.50	22.00	46.00	100.	750.	1450.
1910D	3,490,000	1.40	3.25	7.50	11.00	37.00	91.00	175.	2700.	—
1910S	1,240,000	1.50	4.50	31.00	44.00	52.00	150.	350.	1800.	—
1911	18,870,543	1.30	1.45	3.00	6.50	19.50	80.00	100.	750.	1700.
1911D	11,209,000	1.30	1.45	3.90	7.00	21.50	60.00	100.	750.	—
1911S	3,520,000	1.30	3.00	7.00	15.00	35.00	85.00	145.	1000.	—
1912	19,350,700	1.30	1.45	3.00	6.50	21.00	55.00	100.	750.	1700.
1912D	11,760,000	1.30	1.45	4.00	6.75	21.00	55.00	100.	750.	—
1912S	3,420,000	1.30	1.80	5.25	7.50	23.00	72.00	160.	1200.	—
1913	19,760,622	1.30	1.45	2.80	6.50	21.00	55.00	110.	960.	1450.
1913S	510,000	8.00	11.50	61.00	110.	175.	295.	360.	1325.	—
1914	17,360,655	1.30	1.45	2.80	6.50	21.00	55.00	100.	750.	1700.
1914D	11,908,000	1.30	1.45	4.00	6.75	21.00	55.00	100.	750.	—
1914S	2,100,000	1.60	2.25	5.00	10.00	26.00	72.00	160.	1200.	—
1915	5,620,450	1.30	1.45	3.00	6.50	21.00	55.00	115.	750.	2000.
1915S	960,000	1.75	3.50	22.00	31.00	43.00	150.	225.	2500.	—
1916	18,490,000	1.30	1.45	5.00	6.75	25.00	55.00	120.	750.	—
1916S	5,820,000	1.30	1.45	4.00	6.50	25.00	55.00	100.	750.	—

Mercury

Designer: Adolph A. Weinman. **Size:** 17.9 millimeters. **Weight:** 2.5 grams. **Composition:** 90% silver (.0724 ounces), 10% copper. **Notes:** "MS-65FSB" values are for coins with fully split and rounded horizontal bands around the fasces on the reverse. The 1945-S "micro" variety has a smaller mintmark than the normal variety.

Date	Mintage	G-4	VG-8	F-12	VF-20	XF-40	MS-60	MS-65	65FSB	Prf-65
1916	22,180,080	2.25	3.50	4.75	7.25	11.00	25.00	100.	140.	—
1916D	264,000	435.	665.	1100.	1900.	2450.	4050.	11,750.	15,500.	—
1916S	10,450,000	3.50	4.50	5.75	9.75	16.50	34.00	195.	490.	—
1917	55,230,000	1.00	2.10	2.75	5.50	8.00	28.00	150.	350.	—
1917D	9,402,000	3.50	5.25	8.00	16.00	38.00	125.	1825.	5650.	—
1917S	27,330,000	1.25	2.35	3.25	6.00	9.50	49.00	775.	1690.	—
1918	26,680,000	1.25	3.00	4.25	11.00	25.00	70.00	390.	675.	—
1918D	22,674,800	2.25	3.00	4.00	9.50	23.00	105.	875.	11,000.	—
1918S	19,300,000	2.00	2.50	3.50	6.50	14.00	85.00	1100.	5300.	—
1919	35,740,000	1.00	2.25	3.25	5.50	8.00	35.00	360.	550.	—
1919D	9,939,000	3.00	4.25	6.00	15.00	39.00	140.	1800.	5500.	—
1919S	8,850,000	2.50	3.60	5.00	13.00	29.00	175.	1225.	4350.	—
1920	59,030,000	1.00	2.10	2.75	5.00	7.00	27.00	230.	410.	—
1920D	19,171,000	2.25	3.25	4.25	7.00	15.00	100.	1250.	3050.	—
1920S	13,820,000	2.00	2.80	4.00	6.50	13.50	70.00	1175.	4875.	—
1921	1,230,000	19.50	30.00	70.00	175.	425.	1050.	2900.	4000.	—
1921D	1,080,000	30.00	41.00	110.	220.	500.	1150.	2850.	4000.	—
1923	50,130,000	1.00	2.10	2.75	4.25	7.00	25.00	115.	210.	—
1923S	6,440,000	2.25	3.50	4.25	9.50	29.00	135.	1500.	3800.	—
1924	24,010,000	1.00	2.10	2.75	5.00	9.00	38.00	170.	550.	—
1924D	6,810,000	2.25	3.25	5.50	10.00	29.00	155.	1275.	3300.	—
1924S	7,120,000	2.00	3.00	4.00	8.00	29.00	155.	1550.	6000.	—
1925	25,610,000	1.00	2.10	2.75	4.25	7.50	28.00	210.	535.	
1925D	5,117,000	4.00	5.75	8.50	25.00	85.00	260.	1700.	5200.	—
1925S	5,850,000	2.00	2.80	4.00	8.00	30.00	140.	2200.	4250.	—
1926	32,160,000	1.00	1.85	2.25	4.25	6.50	28.00	235.	540.	
1926D	6,828,000	1.95	3.00	4.00	7.50	15.00	70.00	550.	2500.	—
1926S	1,520,000	5.50	9.50	15.00	34.00	190.	770.	3000.	4950.	—
1927	28,080,000	1.00	1.80	2.25	4.25	6.50	21.00	180.	360.	—
1927D	4,812,000	2.75	3.75	5.00	12.00	42.00	175.	1525.	4750.	—
1927S	4,770,000	1.90	2.65	3.75	5.50	11.00	125.	1050.	4550.	—
1928	19,480,000	1.00	1.80	2.25	4.25	6.50	21.00	115.	260.	—
1928D	4,161,000	3.00	4.25	6.00	15.00	30.00	135.	975.	2500.	—
1928S	7,400,000	1.75	2.35	3.25	5.00	12.00	70.00	495.	1550.	—
1929	25,970,000	1.00	1.80	2.35	3.75	5.00	19.50	58.00	175.	—
1929D	5,034,000	2.65	3.60	5.00	8.00	12.00	28.00	100.	150.	—
1929S	4,730,000	1.65	1.90	2.25	4.25	5.50	34.00	155.	340.	—
1930	6,770,000	1.50	1.80	2.25	4.25	5.50	22.00	155.	290.	—
1930S	1,843,000	3.50	4.25	5.00	7.50	13.00	70.00	135.	260.	—
1931	3,150,000	2.00	2.75	3.50	5.00	11.00	35.00	155.	420.	—
1931D	1,260,000	5.50	7.50	11.00	18.00	30.00	77.00	210.	340.	—
1931S	1,800,000	3.50	4.00	5.00	7.50	13.00	63.00	210.	1300.	—
1934	24,080,000	1.00	1.45	1.75	3.00	5.00	15.00	32.00	52.00	—
1934D	6,772,000	1.80	2.10	2.75	4.00	8.00	32.00	84.00	210.	—

Fully split bands

1942/41

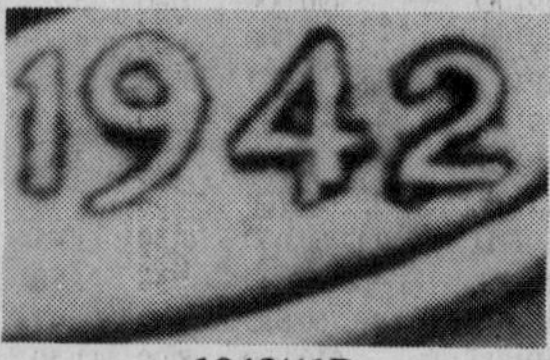
1942/41D

Date	Mintage	G-4	VG-8	F-12	VF-20	XF-40	MS-60	MS-65	65FSB	Prf-65
1935	58,830,000	1.00	1.20	1.50	2.15	4.25	11.00	27.00	36.00	—
1935D	10,477,000	1.75	2.00	3.00	4.75	9.25	32.00	58.00	390.	—
1935S	15,840,000	1.35	1.50	1.75	3.00	5.50	24.00	35.00	145.	—
1936	87,504,130	1.00	1.25	1.50	2.25	3.50	8.50	24.00	36.00	1100.
1936D	16,132,000	1.25	1.50	2.00	3.25	6.75	22.00	42.00	115.	—
1936S	9,210,000	1.25	1.50	1.75	2.75	4.75	17.00	28.00	36.00	—
1937	56,865,756	1.00	1.25	1.50	2.00	3.25	10.00	24.00	36.00	350.
1937D	14,146,000	1.25	1.50	1.90	3.00	5.50	21.00	41.00	60.00	—
1937S	9,740,000	1.25	1.50	1.90	3.00	5.50	18.00	31.00	110.	—
1938	22,198,728	1.00	1.25	1.50	2.25	3.50	14.00	23.00	36.00	280.
1938D	5,537,000	1.75	2.00	2.25	3.75	6.00	15.00	26.00	36.00	—
1938S	8,090,000	1.35	1.55	1.85	2.35	3.75	15.00	29.00	42.00	—
1939	67,749,321	1.00	1.25	1.50	2.00	3.25	10.00	19.00	78.00	265.
1939D	24,394,000	1.25	1.45	1.75	2.25	3.50	12.50	20.00	36.00	—
1939S	10,540,000	1.55	1.75	2.00	2.50	4.25	24.00	40.00	340.	—
1940	65,361,827	.60	.70	.80	1.00	2.50	6.50	19.00	36.00	240.
1940D	21,198,000	.60	.70	.80	1.00	1.50	8.50	20.00	36.00	—
1940S	21,560,000	.60	.70	.80	1.00	1.50	8.50	20.00	49.00	—
1941	175,106,557	.60	.70	.80	1.00	1.50	5.50	19.00	36.00	190.
1941D	45,634,000	.60	.70	.80	1.00	1.50	8.00	21.00	36.00	—
1941S	43,090,000	.60	.70	.80	1.00	1.50	10.00	19.00	36.00	—
1942	205,432,329	.60	.70	.80	1.00	1.50	5.50	20.00	36.00	190.
1942/41	Inc. Ab.	155.	180.	230.	250.	310.	1600.	6500.	9200.	—
1942D	60,740,000	.60	.70	.80	1.00	1.50	8.50	20.00	36.00	—
1942/41D	Inc. Ab.	165.	190.	240.	260.	400.	1400.	5000.	7150.	—
1942S	49,300,000	.60	.70	.80	1.00	1.50	10.00	20.00	61.00	—
1943	191,710,000	.60	.70	.80	1.00	1.50	6.50	19.00	36.00	—
1943D	71,949,000	.60	.70	.80	1.00	1.50	8.50	24.00	36.00	—
1943S	60,400,000	.60	.70	.80	1.00	1.50	10.00	20.00	49.00	—
1944	231,410,000	.60	.70	.80	1.00	1.50	5.50	20.00	62.00	—
1944D	62,224,000	.60	.70	.80	1.00	1.50	8.50	20.00	36.00	—
1944S	49,490,000	.60	.70	.80	1.00	1.50	10.00	20.00	36.00	—
1945	159,130,000	.60	.70	.80	1.00	1.50	5.50	22.00	3125.	—
1945D	40,245,000	.60	.70	.80	1.00	1.50	8.00	20.00	36.00	—
1945S	41,920,000	.60	.70	.80	1.00	1.50	8.50	20.00	78.00	—
1945S micro	Inc. Ab.	1.50	1.65	1.85	3.00	4.25	17.00	52.00	450.	—

Roosevelt

Reverse mintmark (1946-64)

Obverse mintmark (1968-present)

Silver composition

Designer: John R. Sinnock. **Size:** 17.9 millimeters. **Weight:** 2.5 grams. **Composition:** 90% silver (.0724 ounces), 10% copper.

Date	Mintage	G-4	VG-8	F-12	VF-20	XF-40	AU-50	MS-60	MS-65	Prf-65
1946	225,250,000	—	—	—	.45	.80	.95	1.05	2.50	—
1946D	61,043,500	—	—	—	.45	.80	1.10	1.25	4.50	—
1946S	27,900,000	—	—	—	.45	.80	1.10	2.00	5.25	—
1947	121,520,000	—	—	—	.45	.80	.95	1.00	4.75	—
1947D	46,835,000	—	—	—	.45	.95	1.20	1.40	10.00	—
1947S	34,840,000	—	—	—	.45	.95	1.10	1.35	5.50	—
1948	74,950,000	—	—	—	.45	.95	1.10	1.75	11.00	—
1948D	52,841,000	—	—	—	.45	1.20	1.50	2.00	10.00	—
1948S	35,520,000	—	—	—	.45	.95	1.10	1.35	9.00	—
1949	30,940,000	—	—	—	1.00	1.50	4.50	6.00	29.00	—
1949D	26,034,000	—	—	.60	.80	1.25	2.00	3.50	12.50	—
1949S	13,510,000	—	1.00	1.25	1.50	2.75	7.50	9.00	55.00	—

Dimes

Date	Mintage	G-4	VG-8	F-12	VF-20	XF-40	AU-50	MS-60	MS-65	Prf-65
1950	50,181,500	—	—	—	.45	.95	1.10	1.35	4.60	30.00
1950D	46,803,000	—	—	—	.45	.80	.95	1.00	4.60	—
1950S	20,440,000	—	.85	1.00	1.10	1.25	5.00	7.00	35.00	—
1951	102,937,602	—	—	—	.45	.85	1.00	1.10	3.30	26.00
1951D	56,529,000	—	—	—	.40	.80	.95	1.00	3.50	—
1951S	31,630,000	—	—	.95	1.00	1.05	2.75	3.25	24.00	—
1952	99,122,073	—	—	—	.45	.95	1.10	1.20	3.30	25.00
1952D	122,100,000	—	—	—	.45	.80	.95	1.00	3.80	—
1952S	44,419,500	—	—	.95	1.00	1.05	1.10	1.35	7.00	—
1953	53,618,920	—	—	—	.45	.90	1.00	1.10	3.60	20.00
1953D	136,433,000	—	—	—	.45	.80	.95	1.00	3.50	—
1953S	39,180,000	—	—	—	.45	.95	1.10	1.35	2.25	—
1954	114,243,503	—	—	—	.45	.75	.90	.95	2.15	10.00
1954D	106,397,000	—	—	—	.45	.80	.95	1.00	2.15	—
1954S	22,860,000	—	—	—	.45	.60	.65	.75	2.20	—
1955	12,828,381	—	—	—	.45	.60	.80	.90	3.00	9.00
1955D	13,959,000	—	—	—	.45	.60	.80	.90	2.25	—
1955S	18,510,000	—	—	—	.45	.60	.80	.90	2.00	—
1956	109,309,384	—	—	—	.40	.50	.60	.80	2.00	2.50
1956D	108,015,100	—	—	—	.40	.50	.60	.80	1.65	—
1957	161,407,952	—	—	—	.40	.50	.60	.80	1.60	1.50
1957D	113,354,330	—	—	—	.40	.50	.60	.80	3.00	—
1958	32,785,652	—	—	—	.40	.50	.60	.80	1.80	2.00
1958D	136,564,600	—	—	—	.40	.50	.60	.80	1.50	—
1959	86,929,291	—	—	—	.40	.50	.60	.80	1.50	1.50
1959D	164,919,790	—	—	—	.40	.50	.60	.80	1.35	—
1960	72,081,602	—	—	—	.40	.50	.60	.80	1.40	1.40
1960D	200,160,400	—	—	—	.40	.50	.60	.80	1.35	—
1961	96,758,244	—	—	—	.40	.50	.60	.80	1.35	1.10
1961D	209,146,550	—	—	—	.40	.50	.60	.80	1.35	—
1962	75,668,019	—	—	—	.40	.50	.60	.80	1.35	1.10
1962D	334,948,380	—	—	—	.40	.50	.60	.80	1.35	—
1963	126,725,645	—	—	—	.40	.50	.60	.80	1.35	1.10
1963D	421,476,530	—	—	—	.40	.50	.60	.80	1.35	—
1964	933,310,762	—	—	—	.40	.50	.60	.80	1.35	1.00
1964D	1,357,517,180	—	—	—	.40	.50	.60	.80	1.35	—

Clad composition

Weight: 2.27 grams. **Composition:** clad layers of 75% copper and 25% nickel, bonded to a pure-copper core. **Notes:** The 1979-S Type II proof has a clearer mintmark than the Type I. On the 1982 no-mintmark variety, the mintmark was inadvertently left off.

Date	Mintage	G-4	VG-8	F-12	VF-20	XF-40	AU-50	MS-60	MS-65	Prf-65
1965	1,652,140,570	—	—	—	—	—	—	—	.40	—
1966	1,382,734,540	—	—	—	—	—	—	—	.30	—
1967	2,244,007,320	—	—	—	—	—	—	—	.30	—
1968	424,470,000	—	—	—	—	—	—	—	.25	—
1968D	480,748,280	—	—	—	—	—	—	—	.25	—
1968S	Proof only	—	—	—	—	—	—	—	—	.65
1969	145,790,000	—	—	—	—	—	—	—	.45	—
1969D	563,323,870	—	—	—	—	—	—	—	.40	—
1969S	Proof only	—	—	—	—	—	—	—	—	.65
1970	345,570,000	—	—	—	—	—	—	—	.30	—
1970D	754,942,100	—	—	—	—	—	—	—	.30	—
1970S	Proof only	—	—	—	—	—	—	—	—	.65
1971	162,690,000	—	—	—	—	—	—	—	.35	—
1971D	377,914,240	—	—	—	—	—	—	—	.35	—
1971S	Proof only	—	—	—	—	—	—	—	—	.80
1972	431,540,000	—	—	—	—	—	—	—	.30	—
1972D	330,290,000	—	—	—	—	—	—	—	.25	—
1972S	Proof only	—	—	—	—	—	—	—	—	.80
1973	315,670,000	—	—	—	—	—	—	—	.25	—
1973D	455,032,426	—	—	—	—	—	—	—	.20	—
1973S	Proof only	—	—	—	—	—	—	—	—	.60
1974	470,248,000	—	—	—	—	—	—	—	.20	—
1974D	571,083,000	—	—	—	—	—	—	—	.20	—
1974S	Proof only	—	—	—	—	—	—	—	—	.75
1975	585,673,900	—	—	—	—	—	—	—	.30	—
1975D	313,705,300	—	—	—	—	—	—	—	.25	—
1975S	Proof only	—	—	—	—	—	—	—	—	.60
1976	568,760,000	—	—	—	—	—	—	—	.35	—
1976D	695,222,774	—	—	—	—	—	—	—	.35	—
1976S	Proof only	—	—	—	—	—	—	—	—	.75
1977	796,930,000	—	—	—	—	—	—	—	.20	—
1977D	376,607,228	—	—	—	—	—	—	—	.25	—
1977S	Proof only	—	—	—	—	—	—	—	—	.60
1978	663,980,000	—	—	—	—	—	—	—	.20	—
1978D	282,847,540	—	—	—	—	—	—	—	.20	—
1978S	Proof only	—	—	—	—	—	—	—	—	.60
1979	315,440,000	—	—	—	—	—	—	—	.20	—
1979D	390,921,184	—	—	—	—	—	—	—	.20	—
1979S T-I	Proof only	—	—	—	—	—	—	—	—	.55
1979S T-II	Proof only	—	—	—	—	—	—	—	—	1.25
1980P	735,170,000	—	—	—	—	—	—	—	.20	—
1980D	719,354,321	—	—	—	—	—	—	—	.20	—
1980S	Proof only	—	—	—	—	—	—	—	—	.50
1981P	676,650,000	—	—	—	—	—	—	—	.20	—
1981D	712,284,143	—	—	—	—	—	—	—	.20	—
1981S T-I	Proof only	—	—	—	—	—	—	—	—	.50
1981S T-II	Proof only	—	—	—	—	—	—	—	—	4.00
1982P	519,475,000	—	—	—	—	—	—	—	1.10	—
1982 no mint mark				—	—	—	100.	125.	190.	—
1982D	542,713,584	—	—	—	—	—	—	—	.30	—
1982S	Proof only	—	—	—	—	—	—	—	—	.65
1983P	647,025,000	—	—	—	—	—	—	—	.75	—

Dimes

Date	Mintage	G-4	VG-8	F-12	VF-20	XF-40	AU-50	MS-60	MS-65	Prf-65
1983D	730,129,224	—	—	—	—	—	—	—	.70	—
1983S	Proof only	—	—	—	—	—	—	—	—	1.10
1984P	856,669,000	—	—	—	—	—	—	—	.25	—
1984D	704,803,976	—	—	—	—	—	—	—	.35	—
1984S	Proof only	—	—	—	—	—	—	—	—	1.60
1985P	705,200,962	—	—	—	—	—	—	—	.35	—
1985D	587,979,970	—	—	—	—	—	—	—	.30	—
1985S	Proof only	—	—	—	—	—	—	—	—	1.10
1986P	682,649,693	—	—	—	—	—	—	—	.35	—
1986D	473,326,970	—	—	—	—	—	—	—	.35	—
1986S	Proof only	—	—	—	—	—	—	—	—	2.00
1987P	762,709,481	—	—	—	—	—	—	—	.20	—
1987D	653,203,402	—	—	—	—	—	—	—	.20	—
1987S	Proof only	—	—	—	—	—	—	—	—	1.25
1988P	1,030,550,000	—	—	—	—	—	—	—	.20	—
1988D	962,385,488	—	—	—	—	—	—	—	.20	—
1988S	Proof only	—	—	—	—	—	—	—	—	1.50
1989P	1,298,400,000	—	—	—	—	—	—	—	.20	—
1989D	896,535,597	—	—	—	—	—	—	—	.20	—
1989S	Proof only	—	—	—	—	—	—	—	—	1.45
1990P	1,034,340,000	—	—	—	—	—	—	—	.20	—
1990D	839,995,824	—	—	—	—	—	—	—	.20	—
1990S	Proof only	—	—	—	—	—	—	—	—	2.50
1991P	—	—	—	—	—	—	—	—	.20	—
1991D	—	—	—	—	—	—	—	—	.20	—
1991S	Proof only	—	—	—	—	—	—	—	—	2.75
1992P	—	—	—	—	—	—	—	—	.20	—
1992D	—	—	—	—	—	—	—	—	.20	—
1992S	Proof only	—	—	—	—	—	—	—	—	1.80
1993P	—	—	—	—	—	—	—	—	.20	—
1993D	—	—	—	—	—	—	—	—	.20	—
1993S	Proof only	—	—	—	—	—	—	—	—	1.80
1994P	—	—	—	—	—	—	—	—	.20	—
1994D	—	—	—	—	—	—	—	—	.20	—
1994S	Proof only	—	—	—	—	—	—	—	—	3.50

20-cent

Mintmark

Designer: William Barber. **Size:** 22 millimeters. **Weight:** 5 grams. **Composition:** 90% silver (.1447 ounces), 10% copper.

Date	Mintage	G-4	VG-8	F-12	VF-20	XF-40	AU-50	MS-60	MS-65	Prf-65
1875	39,700	60.00	70.00	90.00	145.	240.	400.	1300.	8400.	9500.
1875S	1,155,000	50.00	55.00	75.00	115.	170.	380.	500.	5500.	—
1875CC	133,290	60.00	70.00	90.00	155.	275.	525.	1450.	9500.	—
1876	15,900	100.	120.	150.	215.	350.	600.	1500.	9500.	6000.
1876CC	10,000	Norweb Sale, Oct. 1987, MS-64, $69,300.							—	—
1877	510	—	Proof only		—	—	—	—	—	23,000.
Impaired proof				—	1850.	2100.	2450.	—	—	—
1878	600	—	Proof only		—	—	—	—	—	23,000.
Impaired proof				—	1175.	1575.	2000.	—	—	—

Quarters

Draped Bust

Small eagle

Heraldic eagle

Small-eagle reverse

Designer: Robert Scot. **Size:** 27.5 millimeters. **Weight:** 6.74 grams. **Composition:** 89.24% silver (.1935 ounces), 10.76% copper.

Date	Mintage	G-4	VG-8	F-12	VF-20	XF-40	AU-50	MS-60	MS-65
1796	6,146	4350.	6000.	9150.	14,000.	17,000.	19,000.	28,000.	125,000.

Quarters

Heraldic-eagle reverse

Date	Mintage	G-4	VG-8	F-12	VF-20	XF-40	AU-50	MS-60	MS-65
1804	6,738	1000.	1475.	2350.	4000.	8250.	16,500.	22,000.	116,000.
1805	121,394	210.	300.	450.	850.	2200.	4150.	4400.	56,500.
1806	206,124	225.	285.	425.	800.	2150.	4150.	4400.	56,500.
1806/5	Inc. Ab.	225.	315.	465.	875.	2250.	4150.	4400.	56,500.
1807	220,643	210.	300.	450.	850.	2200.	4150.	5650.	56,500.

Liberty Cap

Motto

No motto

Designer: John Reich. **Size:** 27 millimeters. **Weight:** 6.74 grams. **Composition:** 89.24% silver (.1935 ounces), 10.76% copper. **Notes:** Varieties of the 1819 strikes are distinguished by the size of the 9 in the date. Varieties of the 1820 strikes are distinguished by the size of the 0 in the date. One 1822 variety and one 1828 variety have "25" engraved over "50" in the denomination. The 1827 restrikes were produced privately using dies sold as scrap by the U.S. Mint.

Date	Mintage	G-4	VG-8	F-12	VF-20	XF-40	AU-50	MS-60	MS-65
1815	89,235	60.00	80.00	110.	335.	850.	2000.	3100.	22,000.
1818	361,174	39.00	50.00	90.00	275.	725.	1300.	1550.	13,000.
1818/15	Inc. Ab.	65.00	80.00	110.	315.	800.	2000.	3100.	22,000.
1819 sm.9	144,000	55.00	70.00	100.	300.	775.	1350.	1550.	13,000.
1819 lg.9	Inc. Ab.	55.00	70.00	100.	300.	775.	1350.	1550.	13,000.
1820 sm.O	127,444	60.00	75.00	110.	315.	800.	1500.	3000.	13,000.
1820 lg.O	Inc. Ab.	50.00	65.00	100.	275.	725.	1300.	1550.	13,000.
1821	216,851	50.00	65.00	100.	275.	725.	1300.	1550.	13,000.
1822	64,080	75.00	90.00	130.	400.	975.	1400.	1550.	13,000.
1822 25/50C.	I.A.	2500.	3500.	4750.	6500.	8750.	10,000.	15,000.	25,000.
1823/22	17,800	8250.	12,000.	17,500.	24,500.	31,500.	—	—	—
		Superior, Aug. 1990, proof, $62,500.					—	—	—
1824/2	Unrecorded	100.	140.	200.	575.	1250.	1400.	1800.	13,000.
1825/22	168,000	100.	140.	200.	575.	1250.	1500.	1900.	13,000.
1825/23	Inc. Ab.	50.00	65.00	100.	275.	725.	1500.	1900.	13,000.
1825/24	Inc. Ab.	50.00	65.00	100.	275.	725.	1500.	1900.	13,000.
1827 original	4,000	Superior, Aug. 1990, proof, $42,000.							—
1827 restrike	I.A.	Superior, Aug. 1990, proof, $23,000.						—	—
1828	102,000	50.00	65.00	95.00	275.	775.	1500.	1900.	13,000.
1828 25/50C.	I.A.	150.	200.	300.	650.	1350.	2000.	3100.	—

No motto

Designer: William Kneass. **Size:** 24.3 millimeters. **Notes:** In 1831 the motto "E Pluribus Unum" was removed from the reverse. Varieties of the 1831 strikes are distinguished by the size of the lettering on the reverse.

Date	Mintage	G-4	VG-8	F-12	VF-20	XF-40	AU-50	MS-60	MS-65
1831 small letters	398,000	45.00	50.00	60.00	90.00	240.	750.	900.	13,000.
1831 lg.let.	Inc. Ab.	45.00	50.00	60.00	90.00	240.	750.	900.	13,000.
1832	320,000	45.00	50.00	60.00	90.00	240.	750.	900.	13,000.
1833	156,000	48.00	54.00	65.00	100.	265.	800.	1000.	17,000.
1834	286,000	45.00	50.00	60.00	90.00	240.	750.	900.	13,000.
1835	1,952,000	45.00	50.00	60.00	90.00	240.	750.	900.	13,000.
1836	472,000	45.00	50.00	60.00	90.00	240.	750.	900.	13,000.
1837	252,400	45.00	50.00	60.00	90.00	240.	750.	900.	13,000.
1838	832,000	45.00	50.00	60.00	90.00	240.	750.	900.	13,000.

Seated Liberty

No drapery

Designer: Christian Gobrecht. **Size:** 24.3 millimeters. **Weight:** 6.68 grams. **Composition:** 90% silver (.1934 ounces), 10% copper.

Date	Mintage	G-4	VG-8	F-12	VF-20	XF-40	AU-50	MS-60	MS-65
1838	Inc. Ab.	11.00	15.00	26.00	55.00	195.	475.	900.	—
1839	491,146	9.50	15.00	24.00	52.00	195.	450.	900.	25,000.
1840O	425,200	9.50	15.00	28.00	60.00	300.	400.	900.	25,000.

Without drapery

Arrows at date

1853 reverse rays

Motto above eagle

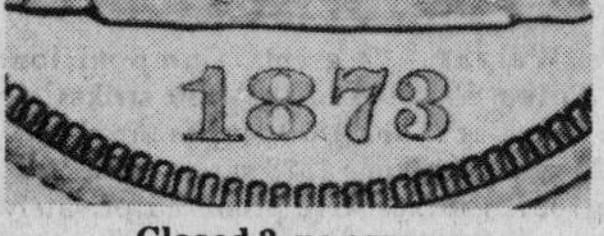

Closed 3, no arrows

Open 3, arrows

Drapery added to Liberty

Notes: In 1840 drapery was added to Liberty's left elbow. Two varieties for 1842 and 1842-O are distinguished by the size of the numerals in the date. 1852 obverse dies were used to strike the 1853 no-arrows variety, with the 2 being recut to form a 3.

Date	Mintage	G-4	VG-8	F-12	VF-20	XF-40	AU-50	MS-60	MS-65
1840	188,127	28.00	35.00	50.00	75.00	180.	350.	750.	—
1840O	Inc. Ab.	20.00	30.00	50.00	110.	185.	500.	1150.	—
1841	120,000	45.00	60.00	80.00	120.	225.	—	800.	—
1841O	452,000	12.50	24.00	40.00	70.00	150.	—	800.	—
1842 sm. dt.	88,000				Stacks, Jan. 1989, proof, $22,000.				—
1842 lg. dt.	Inc. Ab.	85.00	115.	150.	225.	425.	875.	2700.	—
1842O sm. dt.	769,000	375.	500.	850.	1550.	3250.	—	—	—
1842O lg. dt.	Inc. Ab.	10.00	16.00	30.00	60.00	165.	650.	—	—
1843	645,600	9.50	15.00	18.00	40.00	80.00	—	290.	3500.
1843O	968,000	15.00	27.00	45.00	100.	200.	—	—	—
1844	421,200	12.50	16.00	20.00	43.00	80.00	185.	290.	3500.
1844O	740,000	12.50	21.00	38.00	55.00	125.	375.	1200.	—
1845	922,000	9.50	15.00	25.00	40.00	75.00	185.	450.	3500.
1846	510,000	12.50	20.00	35.00	65.00	115.	245.	485.	3500.
1847	734,000	9.50	12.50	25.00	45.00	75.00	190.	425.	3500.
1847O	368,000	22.00	40.00	80.00	110.	225.	675.	725.	—
1848	146,000	30.00	42.00	70.00	130.	210.	425.	1175.	—
1849	340,000	12.00	20.00	40.00	70.00	100.	375.	1000.	—
1849O	Unrecorded	350.	545.	900.	1500.	3000.	7000.	—	—
1850	190,800	23.00	45.00	55.00	85.00	150.	325.	1000.	—
1850O	412,000	17.50	30.00	40.00	80.00	175.	585.	1100.	—
1851	160,000	30.00	50.00	75.00	135.	225.	400.	1000.	—
1851O	88,000	175.	265.	325.	575.	1000.	2600.	—	—
1852	177,060	35.00	45.00	75.00	110.	185.	400.	900.	—
1852O	96,000	165.	255.	300.	550.	900.	2500.	—	—
1853 recut date	44,200	225.	275.	375.	525.	750.	1500.	3250.	—

Arrows at date, reverse rays

Weight: 6.68 grams. **Composition:** 90% silver (.18 ounces), 10% copper.

Date	Mintage	G-4	VG-8	F-12	VF-20	XF-40	AU-50	MS-60	MS-65	Prf-65
1853 rays										
	15,210,020	7.25	14.00	20.00	40.00	165.	350.	900.	17,500.	—
1853/4	Inc. Ab.	30.00	65.00	100.	165.	300.	800.	2000.	—	—
1853O rays										
	1,332,000	10.00	26.00	30.00	75.00	250.	1250.	3000.	—	—

Reverse rays removed

Notes: The 1854-O "huge O" variety has an oversized mintmark.

Date	Mintage	G-4	VG-8	F-12	VF-20	XF-40	AU-50	MS-60	MS-65	Prf-65
1854	12,380,000	7.50	14.00	21.00	32.00	165.	285.	410.	8500.	15,000.
1854O	1,484,000	9.00	17.00	28.00	45.00	145.	325.	1500.	—	—
1854O huge O										
	Inc. Ab.	90.00	145.	200.	275.	475.	—	—	—	—

Quarters

Date	Mintage	G-4	VG-8	F-12	VF-20	XF-40	AU-50	MS-60	MS-65	Prf-65
1855	2,857,000	7.50	12.50	18.00	24.00	65.00	285.	410.	8500.	15,000.
1855O	176,000	30.00	45.00	90.00	245.	500.	—	1850.	—	—
1855S	396,400	25.00	45.00	65.00	145.	325.	—	1750.	—	—

Arrows at date removed

Date	Mintage	G-4	VG-8	F-12	VF-20	XF-40	AU-50	MS-60	MS-65	Prf-65
1856	7,264,000	7.50	12.50	23.00	32.00	58.00	145.	325.	3500.	15,000.
1856O	968,000	12.00	16.00	26.00	40.00	110.	375.	850.	—	—
1856S	286,000	35.00	55.00	75.00	175.	425.	1050.	—	—	—
1856S/S	Inc. Ab.	45.00	70.00	125.	265.	750.	—	—	—	—
1857	9,644,000	7.50	12.50	17.50	28.00	50.00	145.	290.	3500.	15,000.
1857O	1,180,000	13.00	17.00	27.00	40.00	80.00	275.	900.	—	—
1857S	82,000	75.00	100.	140.	235.	450.	975.	—	—	—
1858	7,368,000	7.50	12.50	21.00	28.00	50.00	190.	290.	3500.	11,500.
1858O	520,000	10.00	17.00	30.00	45.00	85.00	300.	900.	—	—
1858S	121,000	45.00	70.00	120.	200.	475.	1650.	—	—	—
1859	1,344,000	11.00	15.00	23.00	30.00	63.00	190.	700.	—	7000.
1859O	260,000	18.00	25.00	35.00	50.00	90.00	450.	900.	—	—
1859S	80,000	90.00	125.	175.	275.	575.	7000.	—	—	—
1860	805,400	9.50	13.00	23.00	30.00	64.00	155.	900.	11,500.	4000.
1860O	388,000	11.00	19.00	35.00	50.00	95.00	225.	925.	—	—
1860S	56,000	145.	225.	350.	625.	2750.	9000.	—	—	—
1861	4,854,600	7.50	12.50	17.50	28.00	45.00	190.	290.	3500.	4000.
1861S	96,000	60.00	80.00	135.	240.	500.	3750.	—	—	—
1862	932,550	8.00	12.50	18.00	35.00	60.00	175.	290.	3500.	4000.
1862S	67,000	55.00	70.00	125.	225.	450.	1250.	2750.	—	—
1863	192,060	25.00	35.00	50.00	75.00	150.	300.	750.	—	7000.
1864	94,070	50.00	60.00	90.00	125.	245.	400.	900.	11,500.	7000.
1864S	20,000	185.	325.	425.	850.	1700.	3000.	—	—	—
1865	59,300	55.00	70.00	95.00	120.	250.	375.	875.	11,500.	7000.
1865S	41,000	70.00	100.	135.	225.	450.	1250.	2000.	—	—
1866	—		Unique	—	—	—	—	—	—	—

Motto above eagle

Notes: In 1866 the motto "In God We Trust" was added to the reverse. The 1873 closed-3 and open-3 varieties are distinguished by the amount of space between the upper left and lower left serifs in the 3.

Date	Mintage	G-4	VG-8	F-12	VF-20	XF-40	AU-50	MS-60	MS-65	Prf-65
1866	17,525	225.	285.	375.	425.	615.	1100.	2000.	—	6750.
1866S	28,000	185.	260.	400.	650.	1250.	1800.	—	—	—
1867	20,625	175.	200.	240.	325.	475.	—	1300.	—	6750.
1867S	48,000	145.	200.	275.	375.	625.	1750.	3000.	—	—
1868	30,000	105.	155.	200.	255.	375.	525.	1200.	—	6750.
1868S	96,000	50.00	70.00	110.	195.	425.	1100.	2300.	—	—
1869	16,600	200.	260.	325.	425.	550.	950.	1400.	—	6750.
1869S	76,000	60.00	95.00	150.	240.	400.	1275.	—	—	—
1870	87,400	40.00	48.00	80.00	135.	250.	325.	1000.	—	6550.
1870CC	8,340	1500.	3250.	4750.	8000.	12,500.	—	—	—	—
1871	119,160	30.00	40.00	55.00	115.	185.	—	1000.	—	6550.
1871CC	10,890	1250.	2250.	3250.	5250.	8000.	15,000.	—	—	—
1871S	30,900	240.	300.	400.	575.	825.	—	3000.	—	—
1872	182,950	30.00	40.00	50.00	100.	155.	—	1000.	—	4050.
1872CC	22,850	375.	525.	900.	1750.	3000.	4000.	—	—	—
1872S	83,000	400.	525.	1050.	1700.	2850.	—	4700.	—	—
1873 clsd.3	212,600	140.	200.	300.	425.	625.	750.	—	—	8000.
1873 open 3	Inc. Ab.	30.00	35.00	50.00	90.00	145.	325.	750.	—	—
1873CC	4,000				RARCOA, Aug. 1990, MS-65, $310,000.				—	—

Arrows at date

Date	Mintage	G-4	VG-8	F-12	VF-20	XF-40	AU-50	MS-60	MS-65	Prf-65
1873	1,271,700	10.00	15.00	28.00	50.00	190.	380.	650.	4500.	5500.
1873CC	12,462	1350.	2350.	3450.	6500.	9500.	—	—	—	—
1873S	156,000	25.00	35.00	70.00	145.	275.	600.	1100.	—	—
1874	471,900	17.50	30.00	45.00	75.00	200.	400.	750.	4500.	5500.
1874S	392,000	18.50	28.00	40.00	110.	195.	400.	700.	—	—

Arrows at date removed

Notes: The 1876-CC fine-reeding variety has a more finely reeded edge.

Date	Mintage	G-4	VG-8	F-12	VF-20	XF-40	AU-50	MS-60	MS-65	Prf-65
1875	4,293,500	7.50	12.50	19.50	28.00	60.00	115.	350.	4100.	2100.
1875CC	140,000	50.00	80.00	145.	250.	400.	700.	1400.	—	—
1875S	680,000	22.00	30.00	50.00	80.00	165.	300.	575.	—	—
1876	17,817,150	7.50	12.50	19.50	28.00	55.00	115.	350.	4100.	2100.
1876CC	4,944,000	9.00	15.00	22.50	35.00	70.00	200.	350.	3900.	—
1876CC fine reeding										
	Inc. Ab.	9.00	15.00	22.00	35.00	70.00	210.	375.	—	—
1876S	8,596,000	7.50	12.50	19.50	28.00	70.00	115.	220.	1950.	—
1877	10,911,710	7.50	12.50	19.50	28.00	55.00	115.	220.	1950.	2100.
1877CC	4,192,000	7.50	15.00	25.00	35.00	70.00	200.	375.	—	—
1877S	8,996,000	6.75	12.00	19.50	28.00	55.00	115.	220.	1950.	—

Date	Mintage	G-4	VG-8	F-12	VF-20	XF-40	AU-50	MS-60	MS-65	Prf-65
1877S/horizontal S										
	Inc. Ab.	25.00	48.00	65.00	100.	225.	375.	650.	—	—
1878	2,260,800	9.00	14.00	25.00	40.00	65.00	165.	360.	4100.	2100.
1878CC	996,000	16.00	25.00	38.00	55.00	100.	215.	425.	4100.	—
1878S	140,000	75.00	140.	185.	250.	425.	800.	1500.	—	—
1879	14,700	135.	160.	200.	250.	325.	400.	525.	—	2100.
1880	14,955	145.	160.	200.	250.	325.	400.	525.	—	2100.
1881	12,975	135.	160.	200.	250.	325.	400.	525.	—	2100.
1882	16,300	150.	175.	210.	265.	335.	450.	600.	—	2100.
1883	15,439	155.	180.	210.	265.	335.	450.	600.	—	2100.
1884	8,875	180.	220.	270.	350.	425.	475.	650.	—	2100.
1885	14,530	145.	170.	200.	250.	325.	400.	600.	—	2100.
1886	5,886	300.	345.	400.	540.	675.	850.	1000.	—	2100.
1887	10,710	210.	220.	250.	315.	400.	475.	650.	—	2100.
1888	10,833	150.	180.	210.	260.	325.	475.	600.	—	2100.
1888S	1,216,000	8.00	14.00	22.00	30.00	65.00	135.	220.	1950.	2100.
1889	12,711	160.	190.	220.	275.	340.	450.	600.	—	2100.
1890	80,590	50.00	55.00	80.00	110.	185.	275.	400.	—	2100.
1891	3,920,600	6.75	12.50	20.00	30.00	55.00	150.	220.	1950.	2100.
1891O	68,000	125.	165.	225.	425.	600.	—	—	—	—
1891S	2,216,000	6.75	12.00	20.00	33.00	60.00	135.	350.	4400.	—

Barber

Mintmark

Designer: Charles E. Barber. **Size:** 24.3 millimeters. **Weight:** 6.25 grams. **Composition:** 90% silver (.1809 ounces), 10% copper.

Date	Mintage	G-4	VG-8	F-12	VF-20	XF-40	AU-50	MS-60	MS-65	Prf-65
1892	8,237,245	2.50	4.00	14.00	35.00	72.00	120.	205.	1900.	1850.
1892O	2,640,000	4.00	7.50	15.00	47.00	85.00	155.	250.	2100.	—
1892S	964,079	18.00	26.00	33.00	49.00	110.	285.	375.	7500.	—
1893	5,484,838	3.00	4.00	14.00	30.00	75.00	130.	205.	1900.	1850.
1893O	3,396,000	3.50	5.50	22.00	50.00	85.00	160.	245.	2900.	—
1893S	1,454,535	5.00	9.00	28.00	40.00	90.00	245.	380.	6700.	—
1894	3,432,972	2.75	5.50	22.00	35.00	78.00	125.	205.	2050.	1850.
1894O	2,852,000	4.00	10.00	30.00	42.00	72.00	180.	325.	6300.	—
1894S	2,648,821	4.00	10.00	30.00	48.00	90.00	175.	325.	6700.	—
1895	4,440,880	2.75	6.00	20.00	35.00	75.00	125.	205.	4900.	1850.
1895O	2,816,000	3.75	5.75	17.00	32.00	80.00	200.	340.	3100.	—
1895S	1,764,681	4.00	9.00	24.00	38.00	80.00	210.	345.	6000.	—
1896	3,874,762	2.75	4.00	14.00	26.00	75.00	125.	210.	2650.	1850.
1896O	1,484,000	3.75	8.75	38.00	180.	320.	580.	800.	8500.	—
1896S	188,039	210.	375.	600.	825.	1600.	2600.	3250.	24,500.	—
1897	8,140,731	3.50	6.00	22.00	35.00	72.00	125.	205.	2100.	1850.
1897O	1,414,800	9.50	15.00	70.00	165.	310.	550.	725.	5100.	—
1897S	542,229	11.00	22.00	60.00	135.	235.	525.	660.	6800.	—
1898	11,100,735	2.00	7.75	19.00	35.00	72.00	125.	225.	2050.	1850.
1898O	1,868,000	4.00	15.00	35.00	60.00	135.	350.	460.	7900.	—
1898S	1,020,592	3.75	7.75	19.00	35.00	89.00	165.	345.	3700.	—
1899	12,624,846	2.00	7.75	13.00	26.00	74.00	125.	205.	2000.	2200.
1899O	2,644,000	5.00	14.00	30.00	52.00	100.	265.	350.	6300.	—
1899S	708,000	6.75	15.00	35.00	80.00	105.	180.	345.	3600.	—
1900	10,016,912	2.10	5.50	18.00	35.00	70.00	125.	205.	2000.	2200.
1900O	3,416,000	4.50	8.00	34.00	60.00	110.	225.	375.	4100.	—
1900S	1,858,585	4.25	6.50	16.00	39.00	77.00	150.	300.	5600.	—
1901	8,892,813	2.75	3.10	14.00	35.00	73.00	125.	205.	2300.	1900.
1901O	1,612,000	14.00	34.00	60.00	150.	260.	560.	700.	7400.	—
1901S	72,664	1250.	2100.	3000.	4500.	5700.	7100.	9000.	48,000.	—
1902	12,197,744	2.00	2.75	14.00	26.00	72.00	125.	190.	2000.	2275.
1902O	4,748,000	3.75	5.00	20.00	52.00	86.00	180.	360.	5800.	—
1902S	1,524,612	6.00	11.50	21.00	57.00	115.	190.	375.	4400.	—
1903	9,670,064	2.20	3.00	14.00	35.00	74.00	125.	205.	2500.	1850.
1903O	3,500,000	3.75	12.00	29.00	52.00	97.00	200.	275.	7500.	—
1903S	1,036,000	7.00	11.50	23.00	42.00	85.00	220.	340.	3400.	—
1904	9,588,813	2.20	3.00	18.00	35.00	72.00	125.	205.	2400.	1850.
1904O	2,456,000	4.50	6.75	30.00	67.00	160.	325.	650.	3250.	—
1905	4,968,250	2.75	3.25	17.00	34.00	72.00	125.	205.	2200.	1850.
1905O	1,230,000	4.50	7.00	25.00	52.00	125.	275.	360.	6100.	—
1905S	1,884,000	4.50	7.00	15.00	44.00	95.00	185.	280.	6700.	—
1906	3,656,435	2.75	3.50	15.00	35.00	72.00	130.	205.	1700.	1850.
1906D	3,280,000	2.60	4.50	23.00	39.00	75.00	150.	210.	5400.	—
1906O	2,056,000	2.75	4.50	29.00	47.00	80.00	180.	250.	2000.	—
1907	7,192,575	2.10	2.75	14.00	34.00	72.00	125.	205.	2000.	1850.
1907D	2,484,000	2.60	4.00	16.00	40.00	82.00	170.	275.	4100.	—
1907O	4,560,000	2.40	3.25	14.00	39.00	77.00	140.	225.	4000.	—
1907S	1,360,000	3.50	4.50	28.00	60.00	100.	200.	340.	5600.	—

Date	Mintage	G-4	VG-8	F-12	VF-20	XF-40	AU-50	MS-60	MS-65	Prf-65
1908	4,232,545	2.20	3.00	14.00	26.00	72.00	125.	205.	2150.	4050.
1908D	5,788,000	2.50	3.25	14.00	26.00	72.00	130.	225.	2400.	—
1908O	6,244,000	2.50	3.25	19.00	32.00	85.00	130.	205.	2100.	—
1908S	784,000	7.00	11.50	48.00	120.	215.	365.	625.	8000.	—
1909	9,268,650	2.00	2.75	13.00	32.00	72.00	125.	205.	1900.	1850.
1909D	5,114,000	2.50	3.00	13.50	32.00	72.00	155.	225.	2450.	—
1909O	712,000	7.00	13.00	38.00	88.00	180.	335.	625.	12,500.	—
1909S	1,348,000	2.60	4.25	15.00	28.00	72.00	170.	260.	2500.	—
1910	2,244,551	2.60	3.00	17.00	30.00	72.00	130.	200.	2050.	1850.
1910D	1,500,000	2.75	4.00	16.00	33.00	80.00	160.	265.	3000.	—
1911	3,720,543	2.10	3.00	14.00	26.00	72.00	125.	205.	1900.	1850.
1911D	933,600	3.00	11.00	70.00	175.	260.	425.	550.	7200.	—
1911S	988,000	2.75	3.75	16.50	30.00	88.00	195.	280.	1600.	—
1912	4,400,700	2.10	2.75	13.00	25.00	72.00	125.	205.	1900.	1850.
1912S	708,000	3.00	4.00	19.00	33.00	72.00	190.	325.	2450.	—
1913	484,613	8.00	20.00	45.00	110.	400.	600.	1000.	5500.	2500.
1913D	1,450,800	2.75	4.00	15.00	30.00	82.00	150.	260.	2300.	—
1913S	40,000	325.	475.	1400.	2450.	3000.	3500.	4300.	10,000.	—
1914	6,244,610	2.00	2.10	13.00	25.00	72.00	125.	205.	1900.	2200.
1914D	3,046,000	2.00	3.00	14.00	26.00	72.00	125.	205.	1900.	—
1914S	264,000	55.00	90.00	135.	180.	325.	535.	800.	4700.	—
1915	3,480,450	2.10	3.00	14.50	27.00	72.00	125.	205.	2000.	2500.
1915D	3,694,000	2.10	2.75	13.50	26.00	72.00	125.	205.	1900.	—
1915S	704,000	4.00	5.00	17.00	35.00	80.00	190.	285.	2300.	—
1916	1,788,000	2.10	3.00	14.50	27.00	72.00	125.	205.	1900.	—
1916D	6,540,800	2.00	2.60	13.00	25.00	72.00	125.	205.	1900.	—

Standing Liberty

Type I

Type II

Type I

Type II

Mintmark

1918/17S

Type I

Designer: Hermon A. MacNeil. **Size:** 24.3 millimeters. **Weight:** 6.25 grams. **Composition:** 90% silver (.1809 ounces), 10% copper. **Notes:** "MS-65FH" values are for coins that have full detail on Liberty's head.

Date	Mintage	G-4	VG-8	F-12	VF-20	XF-40	AU-50	MS-60	MS-65	-65FH
1916	52,000	900.	1250.	1500.	2150.	2700.	3300.	4250.	13,500.	21,000.
1917	8,792,000	8.00	10.00	14.00	32.00	62.00	110.	160.	750.	950.
1917D	1,509,200	12.00	14.00	25.00	60.00	90.00	120.	215.	1170.	1875.
1917S	1,952,000	12.00	14.50	20.00	65.00	130.	195.	200.	1425.	2200.

Type II

Notes: In 1917 the obverse design was modified to cover Liberty's bare right breast.

Date	Mintage	G-4	VG-8	F-12	VF-20	XF-40	AU-50	MS-60	MS-65	-65FH
1917	13,880,000	11.00	13.00	16.00	22.00	48.00	80.00	125.	475.	1050.
1917D	6,224,400	16.00	21.00	49.00	65.00	95.00	110.	175.	1300.	4000.
1917S	5,522,000	15.00	20.00	35.00	70.00	80.00	115.	160.	1100.	3350.
1918	14,240,000	12.00	15.00	21.00	33.00	53.00	73.00	125.	500.	1250.
1918D	7,380,000	19.00	25.00	44.00	60.00	90.00	140.	180.	1550.	5600.
1918S	11,072,000	13.00	16.00	24.00	30.00	45.00	85.00	165.	1700.	15,000.
1918/17S	Inc.Ab.	950.	1200.	1625.	2200.	4000.	8100.	9400.	52,000.	78,000.
1919	11,324,000	22.00	29.00	45.00	55.00	70.00	90.00	135.	490.	1000.
1919D	1,944,000	40.00	63.00	115.	175.	250.	330.	425.	2600.	19,500.
1919S	1,836,000	38.00	58.00	95.00	200.	375.	525.	650.	3500.	17,000.
1920	27,860,000	13.00	15.00	19.00	24.00	35.00	60.00	125.	500.	1300.
1920D	3,586,400	20.00	30.00	60.00	80.00	100.	150.	200.	2000.	6250.
1920S	6,380,000	14.00	17.00	25.00	35.00	55.00	80.00	180.	2600.	18,000.
1921	1,916,000	60.00	80.00	110.	185.	230.	315.	400.	1975.	3500.
1923	9,716,000	12.00	14.00	22.00	26.00	33.00	60.00	125.	400.	1575.

Quarters

Date	Mintage	G-4	VG-8	F-12	VF-20	XF-40	AU-50	MS-60	MS-65	-65FH
1923S	1,360,000	85.00	140.	175.	295.	375.	450.	550.	1875.	3900.
1924	10,920,000	13.00	15.00	19.00	23.00	45.00	60.00	125.	470.	1200.
1924D	3,112,000	21.00	30.00	50.00	68.00	95.00	120.	150.	470.	6250.
1924S	2,860,000	15.00	18.00	21.00	27.00	77.00	165.	220.	1950.	5200.
1925	12,280,000	2.25	3.00	5.00	14.00	25.00	50.00	125.	495.	950.
1926	11,316,000	2.25	3.00	5.00	14.00	32.00	65.00	125.	495.	1375.
1926D	1,716,000	5.50	7.00	11.00	18.50	40.00	72.00	125.	495.	12,250.
1926S	2,700,000	3.50	4.25	10.00	19.00	90.00	200.	300.	2500.	12,500.
1927	11,912,000	2.25	3.00	5.00	14.00	25.00	60.00	125.	475.	1100.
1927D	976,400	5.50	7.00	15.00	40.00	72.00	120.	135.	500.	3500.
1927S	396,000	7.00	10.00	55.00	150.	1050.	2400.	3450.	10,000.	20,000.
1928	6,336,000	2.25	3.00	5.00	14.00	25.00	50.00	125.	525.	1250.
1928D	1,627,600	4.00	5.00	8.00	18.00	34.00	63.00	135.	475.	4350.
1928S	2,644,000	2.50	3.25	5.50	16.00	33.00	68.00	135.	450.	700.
1929	11,140,000	2.25	3.00	4.50	13.00	30.00	50.00	125.	475.	700.
1929D	1,358,000	4.00	5.00	6.50	18.00	30.00	70.00	135.	475.	4700.
1929S	1,764,000	2.40	2.75	5.25	13.50	32.00	52.00	130.	450.	700.
1930	5,632,000	2.25	2.75	5.00	13.00	30.00	60.00	125.	475.	700.
1930S	1,556,000	2.40	3.25	5.25	13.50	26.00	53.00	130.	475.	700.

Washington

Reverse mintmark (1932-64)

Bicentennial reverse

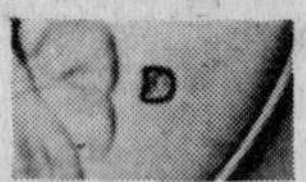

Obverse mintmark (1968-present)

Silver composition

Designer: John Flanagan. **Size:** 24.3 millimeters. **Weight:** 6.25 grams. **Composition:** 90% silver (.1809 ounces), 10% copper.

Date	Mintage	G-4	VG-8	F-12	VF-20	XF-40	AU-50	MS-60	MS-65	Prf-65
1932	5,404,000	3.00	3.25	4.50	6.75	9.00	14.00	28.00	185.	—
1932D	436,800	34.00	38.00	45.00	65.00	150.	265.	400.	5000.	—
1932S	408,000	28.00	30.00	35.00	45.00	60.00	95.00	260.	3600.	—
1934	31,912,052	2.00	3.00	3.75	4.50	5.75	11.00	21.00	91.00	—
1934D	3,527,200	3.25	4.00	6.00	7.00	10.00	33.00	100.	960.	—
1935	32,484,000	2.00	3.00	3.75	4.50	5.75	11.00	20.00	84.00	—
1935D	5,780,000	2.40	4.00	6.00	7.00	10.00	39.00	112.	310.	—
1935S	5,660,000	2.40	3.00	4.50	5.00	7.50	18.00	53.00	190.	—
1936	41,303,837	2.00	3.00	4.00	4.50	6.00	11.00	17.00	74.00	950.
1936D	5,374,000	2.80	3.50	4.00	14.00	30.00	93.00	310.	910.	—
1936S	3,828,000	2.80	3.00	4.00	7.00	10.00	24.00	56.00	110.	—
1937	19,701,542	2.00	3.00	4.00	5.75	7.50	11.75	23.00	85.00	340.
1937D	7,189,600	2.75	3.00	4.00	7.00	9.00	14.00	38.00	105.	—
1937S	1,652,000	3.50	4.00	4.50	12.00	20.00	46.00	95.00	175.	—
1938	9,480,045	2.80	3.00	4.50	7.50	12.00	24.00	49.00	100.	275.
1938S	2,832,000	2.80	3.00	4.50	7.50	11.00	22.00	51.00	125.	—
1939	33,548,795	2.00	3.00	3.75	4.25	5.50	10.50	14.00	49.00.	250.
1939D	7,092,000	2.40	3.00	3.75	4.50	7.50	13.00	29.00	77.00	—
1939S	2,628,000	3.00	3.50	5.00	6.00	10.00	26.00	59.00	130.	—
1940	35,715,246	2.00	3.00	3.75	4.00	4.50	8.25	10.00	42.00	190.
1940D	2,797,600	3.25	3.50	7.00	10.00	15.50	28.00	62.00	110.	—
1940S	8,244,000	2.40	3.00	3.75	4.25	5.50	9.00	16.00	35.00	—
1941	79,047,287	—	—	1.50	2.00	3.25	4.50	7.50	23.00	135.
1941D	16,714,800	—	—	1.50	2.00	3.25	6.50	18.00	34.00	—
1941S	16,080,000	—	—	1.50	2.00	3.25	6.50	15.00	70.00	—
1942	102,117,123	—	—	1.50	2.00	3.25	4.00	6.50	23.00	135.
1942D	17,487,200	—	—	1.50	2.00	3.25	5.00	10.00	29.00	—
1942S	19,384,000	—	—	1.50	2.00	4.50	14.00	50.00	125.	—
1943	99,700,000	—	—	1.50	2.00	2.25	2.75	5.00	23.00	—
1943D	16,095,600	—	—	1.50	2.00	3.25	7.50	14.00	30.00	—
1943S	21,700,000	—	—	1.50	2.00	5.50	11.50	29.00	39.00	—
1944	104,956,000	—	—	1.50	2.00	3.25	3.75	4.50	16.00	—
1944D	14,600,800	—	—	1.50	2.00	3.25	5.00	9.00	21.00	—

Quarters

Date	Mintage	G-4	VG-8	F-12	VF-20	XF-40	AU-50	MS-60	MS-65	Prf-65
1944S	12,560,000	—	—	1.50	2.00	3.25	5.50	9.00	26.00	—
1945	74,372,000	—	—	1.50	2.00	3.25	4.00	5.00	14.00	—
1945D	12,341,600	—	—	1.50	2.00	3.25	5.00	7.50	22.00	—
1945S	17,004,001	—	—	1.50	2.00	3.25	4.50	6.00	18.00	—
1946	53,436,000	—	—	1.50	2.00	2.25	2.50	4.75	15.00	—
1946D	9,072,800	—	—	1.50	2.00	2.25	2.75	4.00	12.00	—
1946S	4,204,000	—	—	1.50	2.00	2.25	2.50	4.00	19.00	—
1947	22,556,000	—	—	1.50	2.00	3.00	3.75	6.50	12.00	—
1947D	15,338,400	—	—	1.50	2.00	3.00	4.25	5.50	14.00	—
1947S	5,532,000	—	—	1.50	2.00	2.25	2.50	5.00	16.50	—
1948	35,196,000	—	—	1.50	2.00	2.25	2.50	4.00	10.00	—
1948D	16,766,800	—	—	1.50	2.00	2.25	2.50	5.00	12.00	—
1948S	15,960,000	—	—	1.50	2.00	3.25	3.60	5.00	12.50	—
1949	9,312,000	—	—	1.50	2.00	3.50	9.00	19.00	25.00	—
1949D	10,068,400	—	—	1.50	2.50	4.00	7.00	8.75	20.00	—
1950	24,971,512	—	—	1.50	2.50	3.00	3.75	5.00	8.00	55.00
1950D	21,075,600	—	—	1.50	2.50	2.75	3.00	4.50	8.00	—
1950D/S	Inc. Ab.	21.00	25.00	30.00	60.00	140.	215.	260.	515.	—
1950S	10,284,004	—	—	1.50	3.00	3.25	5.75	7.25	13.50	—
1950S/D	Inc. Ab.	21.00	25.00	30.00	60.00	170.	315.	460.	625.	—
1951	43,505,602	—	—	1.00	1.75	2.00	2.25	4.75	6.00	38.00
1951D	35,354,800	—	—	1.00	1.75	2.00	2.25	3.25	5.50	—
1951S	9,048,000	—	—	1.00	1.75	4.25	8.25	12.75	18.50	—
1952	38,862,073	—	—	1.00	1.75	2.00	2.25	3.00	5.50	30.00
1952D	49,795,200	—	—	1.00	1.75	2.00	1.95	3.25	6.00	—
1952S	13,707,800	—	—	1.00	2.00	2.50	5.25	8.50	11.50	—
1953	18,664,920	—	—	1.00	1.75	2.00	2.50	3.25	5.25	20.00
1953D	56,112,400	—	—	—	—	1.50	1.75	2.25	5.25	—
1953S	14,016,000	—	—	1.00	1.75	2.25	2.75	4.00	6.50	—
1954	54,645,503	—	—	—	—	—	1.50	2.00	4.75	12.00
1954D	42,305,500	—	—	—	1.25	1.50	1.75	2.00	4.50	—
1954S	11,834,722	—	—	—	1.25	1.50	1.75	2.00	5.25	—
1955	18,558,381	—	—	—	1.25	1.50	1.75	2.00	6.00	12.00
1955D	3,182,400	—	—	—	1.50	1.75	2.00	2.25	7.50	—
1956	44,813,384	—	—	—	1.00	1.50	1.75	2.00	4.00	7.00
1956D	32,334,500	—	—	—	1.00	1.75	2.25	2.75	4.00	—
1957	47,779,952	—	—	—	—	1.00	1.75	2.75	6.50	3.50
1957D	77,924,160	—	—	—	—	1.00	1.75	2.00	4.50	—
1958	7,235,652	—	—	—	—	1.00	2.00	2.50	6.50	6.00
1958D	78,124,900	—	—	—	—	1.00	1.75	2.00	4.50	—
1959	25,533,291	—	—	—	—	1.00	1.75	2.00	4.00	4.25
1959D	62,054,232	—	—	—	—	1.00	1.75	2.00	4.00	—
1960	30,855,602	—	—	—	—	1.00	1.75	2.75	5.00	3.75
1960D	63,000,324	—	—	—	—	1.00	1.75	2.00	4.00	—
1961	40,064,244	—	—	—	—	1.00	1.25	1.50	4.00	3.50
1961D	83,656,928	—	—	—	—	1.00	1.25	1.50	4.00	—
1962	39,374,019	—	—	—	—	1.00	1.25	1.50	4.00	3.50
1962D	127,554,756	—	—	—	—	1.00	1.25	1.50	4.00	—
1963	77,391,645	—	—	—	—	1.00	1.25	1.50	3.75	3.50
1963D	135,288,184	—	—	—	—	1.00	1.25	1.50	3.75	—
1964	564,341,347	—	—	—	—	1.00	1.25	1.50	3.75	3.50
1964D	704,135,528	—	—	—	—	1.00	1.25	1.50	3.75	—

Clad composition

Weight: 5.67 grams. **Composition:** clad layers of 75% copper and 25% nickel bonded to a pure-copper core.

Date	Mintage	MS-65	Prf-65	Date	Mintage	MS-65	Prf-65
1965	1,819,717,540	.80	—	1971	109,284,000	.50	—
1966	821,101,500	.80	—	1971D	258,634,428	.50	—
1967	1,524,031,848	1.00	—	1971S	Proof only	—	.95
1968	220,731,500	.80	—	1972	215,048,000	.40	—
1968D	101,534,000	1.00	—	1972D	311,067,732	.40	—
1968S	Proof only	—	1.25	1972S	Proof only	—	.95
1969	176,212,000	1.00	—	1973	346,924,000	.40	—
1969D	114,372,000	1.25	—	1973D	232,977,400	.40	—
1969S	Proof only	—	1.00	1973S	Proof only	—	.95
1970	136,420,000	.50	—	1974	801,456,000	.40	—
1970D	417,341,364	.50	—	1974D	353,160,300	.40	—
1970S	Proof only	—	.95	1974S	Proof only	—	.95

Bicentennial reverse

Reverse designer: Jack L. Ahr.

Date	Mintage	G-4	VG-8	F-12	VF-20	XF-40	MS-60	MS-65	Prf-65
1976	809,784,016	—	—	—	—	—	—	.60	—
1976D	860,118,839	—	—	—	—	—	—	.60	—
1976S	—	—	—	—	—	—	—	—	.90

Bicentennial reverse, silver composition

Weight: 5.75 grams. **Composition:** clad layers of 80% copper and 20% silver bonded to a core of 79.1% copper and 20.9% silver (.074 total ounces of silver).

Date	Mintage	G-4	VG-8	F-12	VF-20	XF-40	MS-60	MS-65	Prf-65
1976S silver	11,000,000	—	—	—	—	—	—	1.10	1.95

Regular design resumed, clad composition

Notes: The 1979-S Type II proof has a clearer mintmark than the Type I.

Date	Mintage	MS-65	Prf-65
1977	468,556,000	.40	—
1977D	258,898,212	.45	—
1977S	Proof only	—	.95
1978	521,452,000	.40	—
1978D	287,373,152	.40	—
1978S	Proof only	—	.95
1979	515,708,000	.50	—
1979D	489,789,780	.50	—
1979S T-I	Proof only	—	.95
1979S T-II	Proof only	—	1.45
1980P	635,832,000	.50	—
1980D	518,327,487	.50	—
1980S	Proof only	—	.95
1981P	601,716,000	.50	—
1981D	575,722,833	.50	—
1981S T-I	Proof only	—	.95
1981S T-II	Proof only	—	3.00
1982P	500,931,000	5.25	—
1982D	480,042,788	1.00	—
1982S	Proof only	—	2.25
1983P	673,535,000	5.75	—
1983D	617,806,446	6.00	—
1983S	Proof only	—	1.75
1984P	676,545,000	.85	—
1984D	546,483,064	2.00	—
1984S	Proof only	—	1.60
1985P	775,818,962	2.50	—
1985D	519,962,888	3.25	—
1985S	Proof only	—	1.25
1986P	551,199,333	4.00	—
1986D	504,298,660	2.75	—
1986S	Proof only	—	2.00
1987P	582,499,481	.50	—
1987D	655,594,696	.50	—
1987S	Proof only	—	1.10
1988P	562,052,000	1.50	—
1988D	596,810,688	.60	—
1988S	Proof only	—	1.25
1989P	512,868,000	.50	—
1989D	896,535,597	.50	—
1989S	Proof only	—	1.35
1990P	613,792,000	.50	—
1990D	927,638,181	.50	—
1990S	Proof only	—	2.75
1991P	—	.50	—
1991D	—	.50	—
1991S	Proof only	—	2.95
1992P	—	.50	—
1992D	—	.50	—
1992S	Proof only	—	2.40
1993P	—	.50	—
1993D	—	.50	—
1993S	Proof only	—	1.75
1994P	—	.50	—
1994D	—	.50	—
1994S	Proof only	—	3.50

Half dollars

Flowing Hair

Designer: Robert Scot. **Size:** 32.5 millimeters. **Weight:** 13.48 grams. **Composition:** 89.24% silver (.3869 ounces), 10.76% copper. **Notes:** The 1795 "recut date" variety had the date cut into the dies twice, so both sets of numbers are visible on the coin. The 1795 "3 leaves" variety has three leaves under each of the eagle's wings on the reverse.

Date	Mintage	G-4	VG-8	F-12	VF-20	XF-40	MS-60
1794	23,464	1150.	1950.	2950.	4000.	9500.	—
1795	299,680	450.	625.	950.	2150.	5500.	9500.
1795 recut date	Inc. Ab.	500.	700.	1000.	2275.	7000.	9500.
1795 3 leaves	Inc. Ab.	1850.	2500.	3300.	5850.	9500.	—

Draped Bust

Small-eagle reverse

Designer: Robert Scot. **Size:** 32.5 millimeters. **Weight:** 13.48 grams. **Composition:** 89.24% silver (.3869 ounces), 10.76% copper. **Notes:** The 1796 strikes have either 15 or 16 stars on the obverse.

Date	Mintage	G-4	VG-8	F-12	VF-20	XF-40	MS-60
1796 15 stars	3,918	10,000.	12,000.	15,000.	27,000.	39,000.	—
1796 16 stars	Inc. Ab.	10,000.	12,000.	15,000.	27,000.	39,000.	—
1797	Inc. Ab.	10,000.	12,000.	15,000.	27,000.	39,000.	—

Small eagle

Heraldic eagle

Heraldic-eagle reverse

Notes: The two varieties of the 1803 strikes are distinguished by the size of the 3 in the date. The several varieties of the 1806 strikes are distinguished by the style of 6 in the date, size of the stars on the obverse, and whether the stem of the olive branch held by the reverse eagle extends through the claw.

Date	Mintage	G-4	VG-8	F-12	VF-20	XF-40	MS-60
1801	30,289	190.	285.	500.	800.	1850.	9500.
1802	29,890	175.	240.	440.	750.	1575.	8750.
1803 sm. 3	188,234	150.	170.	285.	450.	1000.	6300.
1803 lg. 3	Inc. Ab.	140.	150.	225.	380.	750.	5700.
1805	211,722	140.	150.	225.	350.	800.	5700.
1805/4	Inc. Ab.	150.	250.	475.	600.	1200.	8750.
1806 round top 6, large stars	839,576	125.	150.	210.	325.	625.	5400.
1806 round top 6, small stars	Inc. Ab.	125.	150.	210.	325.	625.	5400.
1806 pointed top 6, stem not through claw	Inc. Ab.	125.	150.	210.	325.	625.	5400.
1806 pointed top 6, stem through claw	Inc. Ab.	125.	150.	210.	325.	625.	5400.
1806/5	Inc. Ab.	125.	150.	210.	450.	775.	5400.
1806/inverted 6	Inc. Ab.	175.	225.	535.	875.	1175.	9250.
1807	301,076	125.	150.	210.	285.	625.	5400.

Liberty Cap

Designer: John Reich. **Size:** 32.5 millimeters. **Weight:** 13.48 grams. **Composition:** 89.24% silver (.3869 ounces), 10.76% copper. **Notes:** There are three varieties of the 1807 strikes. Two are distinguished by the size of the stars on the obverse. The third was struck from a reverse die that had a 5 cut over a 2 in the "50C." denomination. Two varieties of the 1811 are distinguished by the size of the 8 in the date. A third has a period between the 8 and second 1 in the date. One variety of the 1817 has a period between the 1 and 7 in the date. Two varieties of the 1819/18 overdate are distinguished by the size of the 9 in the date. Two varieties of the 1820 are distinguished by the size of the date. On the 1823 varieties, the "broken 3" appears to be almost separated in the middle of the 3 in the date; the "patched 3" has the error repaired; the "ugly 3" has portions of its detail missing. The 1827 "curled-2" and "square-2" varieties are distinguished by the numeral's base — either curled or square. Among the 1828 varieties, "knobbed 2" and "no knob" refers to whether the upper left serif of the digit is rounded. The 1830 varieties are distinguished by the size of the 0 in the date. The four 1834 varieties are distinguished by the sizes of the stars, date and letters in the inscriptions. The 1836 "50/00" variety was struck from a reverse die that had "50" recut over "00" in the denomination.

Date	Mintage	G-4	VG-8	F-12	VF-20	XF-40	AU-50	MS-60	MS-65
1807 sm. stars	750,500	55.00	100.	175.	300.	625.	2000.	3200.	—
1807 lg. stars	Inc. Ab.	50.00	65.00	150.	285.	625.	2000.	3200.	—
1807 50/20 C.	Inc. Ab.	45.00	60.00	75.00	140.	350.	1500.	2900.	—
1808	1,368,600	37.50	42.50	53.00	90.00	185.	450.	1000.	—
1808/7	Inc. Ab.	40.00	50.00	60.00	125.	200.	500.	1500.	—
1809	1,405,810	36.00	42.50	55.00	100.	440.	600.	1000.	—
1810	1,276,276	34.50	38.00	46.00	100.	225.	500.	1000.	—
1811 sm. 8	1,203,644	32.00	37.50	45.00	70.00	145.	450.	750.	—
1811 lg. 8	Inc. Ab.	32.50	37.00	50.00	85.00	165.	450.	750.	—
1811 dt. 18.11	Inc. Ab.	35.00	40.00	60.00	95.00	185.	500.	1400.	—

"50 Cents" reverse

"Half Dol." reverse

Date	Mintage	G-4	VG-8	F-12	VF-20	XF-40	AU-50	MS-60	MS-65
1812	1,628,059	32.50	37.50	45.00	100.	180.	325.	700.	—
1812/11	Inc. Ab.	42.50	50.00	80.00	115.	225.	700.	2150.	—
1813	1,241,903	32.50	37.50	45.00	95.00	225.	350.	875.	—
1814	1,039,075	34.50	38.00	47.00	70.00	145.	500.	1800.	—
1814/13	Inc. Ab.	42.50	52.50	69.00	100.	200.	350.	900.	—
1815/12	47,150	750.	1000.	1350.	1875.	2800.	3600.	4500.	—
1817	1,215,567	31.50	33.00	40.00	65.00	135.	250.	700.	—
1817/13	Inc. Ab.	80.00	135.	185.	325.	500.	975.	1100.	—
1817/14					5 pieces known		—		—
1817 dt. 181.7	Inc. Ab.	37.00	47.00	70.00	115.	195.	395.	700.	—
1818	1,960,322	31.50	33.00	40.00	70.00	135.	250.	700.	—
1818/17	Inc. Ab.	31.50	33.00	40.00	70.00	135.	250.	700.	—
1819	2,208,000	31.50	33.00	40.00	70.00	135.	250.	700.	—
1819/18 sm. 9	Inc. Ab.	31.50	33.00	40.00	70.00	135.	250.	700.	—
1819/18 lg. 9	Inc. Ab.	31.50	33.00	40.00	70.00	135.	250.	700.	—
1820 sm. dt.	751,122	39.00	49.00	67.00	135.	210.	300.	700.	—
1820 lg. dt.	Inc. Ab.	39.00	50.00	67.00	135.	210.	300.	700.	—
1820/19	Inc. Ab.	37.00	49.00	75.00	130.	225.	275.	700.	—
1821	1,305,797	33.00	35.00	40.00	70.00	135.	250.	700.	—
1822	1,559,573	32.00	34.00	40.00	65.00	135.	250.	700.	—
1822/1	Inc. Ab.	50.00	69.00	110.	185.	300.	475.	1100.	—
1823	1,694,200	31.50	33.00	40.00	65.00	135.	250.	700.	—
1823 broken 3	Inc. Ab.	37.00	52.00	84.00	115.	220.	400.	700.	—
1823 patched 3	Inc. Ab.	37.00	50.00	75.00	95.00	195.	325.	700.	—
1823 ugly 3	Inc. Ab.	35.00	40.00	65.00	95.00	185.	265.	700.	—
1824	3,504,954	31.00	33.00	40.00	50.00	95.00	250.	700.	—
1824/21	Inc. Ab.	35.00	40.00	58.00	95.00	185.	250.	700.	—
1824/various dates									
	Inc. Ab.	31.50	33.00	40.00	65.00	145.	250.	700.	—
1825	2,943,166	31.50	33.00	40.00	50.00	95.00	250.	700.	—
1826	4,004,180	31.50	33.00	40.00	50.00	95.00	250.	700.	—
1827 curled 2	5,493,400	33.00	36.00	42.50	85.00	150.	250.	700.	—
1827 square 2	Inc. Ab.	31.50	33.00	40.00	50.00	95.00	250.	700.	—
1827/6	Inc. Ab.	35.00	40.00	60.00	90.00	145.	265.	1100.	—
1828 curled base 2, no knob									
	3,075,200	30.00	33.00	37.50	50.00	95.00	250.	700.	6000.
1828 curled base 2, knobbed 2									
	Inc. Ab.	35.00	45.00	60.00	85.00	150.	350.	750.	—
1828 small 8s, square base 2, large letters									
	Inc. Ab.	27.50	32.00	34.00	43.00	90.00	250.	700.	15,500.
1828 small 8s, square base 2, small letters									
	Inc. Ab.	27.50	32.00	65.00	125.	250.	350.	750.	—
1828 large 8s, square base 2									
	Inc. Ab.	27.50	32.00	34.00	43.00	90.00	250.	700.	—
1829	3,712,156	27.50	32.00	34.00	43.00	90.00	250.	700.	—
1829/27	Inc. Ab.	35.00	40.00	60.00	85.00	165.	250.	800.	—
1830 small 0 in date									
	4,764,800	27.50	32.00	34.00	43.00	89.00	250.	700.	6000.
1830 large 0 in date									
	Inc. Ab.	27.50	32.00	34.00	43.00	89.00	250.	700.	6000.
1831	5,873,660	27.50	32.00	34.00	43.00	89.00	250.	700.	6000.
1832 sm. lt.	4,797,000	27.50	32.00	34.00	43.00	89.00	250.	700.	6000.
1832 lg. let.	Inc. Ab.	30.00	38.00	45.00	65.00	195.	495.	1250.	8500.
1833	5,206,000	27.50	32.00	34.00	43.00	89.00	250.	700.	6000.
1834 small date, large stars, small letters									
	6,412,004	27.50	32.00	34.00	43.00	89.00	250.	700.	6000.
1834 small date, small stars, small letters									
	Inc. Ab.	27.50	32.00	34.00	43.00	89.00	250.	700.	6000.
1834 large date, small letters									
	Inc. Ab.	27.50	32.00	34.00	43.00	89.00	250.	700.	6000.

Half dollars

Date	Mintage	G-4	VG-8	F-12	VF-20	XF-40	AU-50	MS-60	MS-65
1834 large date, large letters									
	Inc. Ab.	27.50	32.00	34.00	43.00	89.00	250.	700.	6000.
1835	5,352,006	27.50	32.00	34.00	43.00	89.00	250.	700.	6000.
1836	6,545,000	27.50	32.00	34.00	43.00	89.00	250.	700.	6000.
1836 50/00	Inc. Ab.	50.00	60.00	80.00	160.	225.	475.	1100.	—

Reeded edge, "50 Cents" on reverse

Designer: Christian Gobrecht. **Size:** 30 millimeters. **Weight:** 13.36 grams. **Composition:** 90% silver (.3867 ounces), 10% copper.

Date	Mintage	G-4	VG-8	F-12	VF-20	XF-40	AU-50	MS-60	MS-65
1836	1,200	750.	900.	1150.	1275.	1750.	3000.	5000.	—
1837	3,629,820	32.00	40.00	50.00	85.00	150.	365.	750.	13,500.

"Half Dol." on reverse

Date	Mintage	G-4	VG-8	F-12	VF-20	XF-40	AU-50	MS-60	MS-65
1838	3,546,000	32.00	38.00	41.00	60.00	125.	475.	1200.	8500.
1838O	Est. 20				Auction '82, MS-63, $47,000.				—
1839	3,334,560	32.00	38.00	41.00	60.00	125.	365.	750.	8500.
1839O	178,976	105.	140.	185.	300.	500.	—	3250.	—

Seated Liberty

Mintmark

Designer: Christian Gobrecht. **Size:** 30.6 millimeters. **Weight:** 13.36 grams. **Composition:** 90% silver (.3867 ounces), 10% copper. **Notes:** The 1839 varieties are distinguished by whether there's drapery extending from Liberty's left elbow. One variety of the 1840 strikes has smaller lettering; another used the old reverse of 1838. Varieties of 1842 and 1846 are distinguished by the size of the numerals in the date.

Date	Mintage	G-4	VG-8	F-12	VF-20	XF-40	AU-50	MS-60	MS-65
1839 no drapery from elbow									
	Inc. Ab.	38.00	65.00	110.	250.	725.	1500.	2350.	107 K
1839 drapery	Inc. Ab.	20.00	28.00	40.00	70.00	115.	265.	450.	—
1840 sm. let.	1,435,008	16.50	20.00	30.00	60.00	110.	350.	575.	8250.
1840 rev. 1838	Inc. Ab.	105.	130.	215.	300.	500.	1200.	2500.	—
1840O	855,100	17.00	23.00	34.00	70.00	125.	300.	585.	—
1841	310,000	35.00	45.00	80.00	140.	265.	425.	1300.	—
1841O	401,000	17.00	25.00	45.00	85.00	150.	240.	875.	—
1842 sm. date	2,012,764	27.00	32.00	40.00	75.00	125.	325.	1300.	12,000.
1842 lg. date	Inc. Ab.	16.00	21.00	33.00	50.00	75.00	120.	1250.	12,000.
1842O sm. date	957,000	500.	800.	1400.	2250.	4000.	—	—	—
1842O lg. date	Inc. Ab.	17.00	23.00	34.00	65.00	135.	285.	500.	—
1843	3,844,000	16.00	21.00	30.00	50.00	80.00	180.	410.	5500.
1843O	2,268,000	16.00	21.00	30.00	55.00	90.00	250.	550.	—
1844	1,766,000	16.00	21.00	30.00	50.00	85.00	180.	410.	5500.
1844O	2,005,000	16.00	21.00	36.00	55.00	80.00	195.	525.	—
1844/1844O	Inc. Ab.	350.	650.	975.	1375.	2700.	—	—	—
1845	589,000	30.00	40.00	50.00	90.00	170.	340.	900.	—
1845O	2,094,000	16.00	21.00	30.00	42.00	100.	240.	550.	—
1845O no drapery									
	Inc. Ab.	25.00	30.00	50.00	90.00	150.	375.	750.	—
1846 med. dt.	2,210,000	16.00	20.00	28.00	40.00	70.00	175.	500.	9000.
1846 tall dt.	Inc. Ab.	22.00	30.00	60.00	80.00	125.	250.	650.	12,000.
1846/horizontal 6									
	Inc. Ab.	140.	185.	250.	375.	550.	1000.	2500.	—
1846O med.dt.	2,304,000	16.00	18.00	28.00	38.00	100.	225.	550.	12,000.
1846O tall dt.	Inc. Ab.	125.	245.	325.	500.	950.	2000.	3600.	—
1847/1846	1,156,000	1900.	2900.	3200.	4250.	5750.	—	—	—
•1847	Inc. Ab.	20.00	30.00	45.00	60.00	90.00	190.	480.	9000.
1847O	2,584,000	15.00	25.00	35.00	50.00	95.00	250.	640.	7000.
1848	580,000	30.00	50.00	75.00	135.	240.	475.	1400.	9000.
1848O	3,180,000	18.00	25.00	40.00	50.00	95.00	285.	750.	9000.
1849	1,252,000	22.00	35.00	50.00	85.00	150.	365.	1250.	9000.
1849O	2,310,000	15.00	25.00	40.00	60.00	115.	250.	650.	9000.
1850	227,000	200.	250.	340.	375.	500.	875.	1500.	—
1850O	2,456,000	15.00	25.00	40.00	55.00	115.	250.	650.	9000.
1851	200,750	250.	300.	375.	465.	600.	800.	1800.	—
1851O	402,000	37.00	45.00	57.00	90.00	175.	300.	610.	9000.
1852	77,130	300.	350.	425.	525.	650.	800.	1450.	—
1852O	144,000	50.00	80.00	125.	250.	425.	800.	1850.	—
1853O	Unrecorded			Garrett Sale, 1979, VF, $40,000.					

Arrows at date, reverse rays

Weight: 12.44 grams. **Composition:** 90% silver (.36 ounces), 10% copper.

Date	Mintage	G-4	VG-8	F-12	VF-20	XF-40	AU-50	MS-60	MS-65	Prf-65
1853 rays on reverse	3,532,708	16.50	30.00	45.50	90.00	250.	505.	1700.	21,500.	—
1853O rays on reverse	1,328,000	19.00	30.00	45.50	100.	290.	700.	2100.	21,500.	—

Reverse rays removed

Date	Mintage	G-4	VG-8	F-12	VF-20	XF-40	AU-50	MS-60	MS-65	Prf-65
1854	2,982,000	15.00	20.00	29.00	50.00	100.	270.	675.	10,000.	—
1854O	5,240,000	15.00	20.00	29.00	50.00	100.	265.	500.	10,000.	—
1855	759,500	23.00	30.00	40.00	60.00	150.	325.	1200.	10,000.	22,500.
1855/4	Inc. Ab.	35.00	60.00	80.00	125.	225.	400.	1500.	—	—
1855O	3,688,000	15.00	20.00	29.00	50.00	100.	270.	650.	10,000.	—
1855S	129,950	300.	425.	650.	1300.	2650.	6000.	—	—	—

Arrows at date removed

Date	Mintage	G-4	VG-8	F-12	VF-20	XF-40	AU-50	MS-60	MS-65	Prf-65
1856	938,000	18.00	25.00	32.00	47.50	90.00	150.	410.	6500.	12,500.
1856O	2,658,000	15.00	21.00	28.00	45.00	82.00	150.	450.	12,500.	—
1856S	211,000	40.00	50.00	95.00	200.	375.	1250.	2500.	19,000.	—
1857	1,988,000	15.00	18.00	28.00	45.00	82.00	150.	410.	5500.	12,500.
1857O	818,000	18.00	21.00	25.00	55.00	100.	250.	850.	12,500.	—
1857S	158,000	50.00	65.00	110.	225.	450.	800.	2400.	19,000.	—
1858	4,226,000	15.00	18.00	35.00	60.00	80.00	150.	410.	6500.	12,500.
1858O	7,294,000	14.00	17.00	35.00	45.00	70.00	150.	450.	12,500.	—
1858S	476,000	20.00	30.00	48.00	90.00	175.	400.	950.	12,500.	—
1859	748,000	16.50	27.00	42.00	55.00	90.00	200.	650.	6600.	5500.
1859O	2,834,000	15.00	25.00	40.00	50.00	85.00	150.	450.	6500.	—
1859S	566,000	20.00	28.00	45.00	70.00	150.	200.	750.	12,500.	—
1860	303,700	18.00	21.00	35.00	70.00	120.	350.	1000.	6500.	5500.
1860O	1,290,000	15.00	18.00	35.00	45.00	63.00	150.	450.	5500.	—
1860S	472,000	18.00	30.00	50.00	70.00	130.	175.	850.	12,500.	—
1861	2,888,400	15.00	25.00	35.00	45.00	70.00	150.	410.	5500.	5500.
1861O	2,532,633	15.00	25.00	40.00	50.00	70.00	150.	450.	5500.	—
1861S	939,500	17.00	20.00	35.00	45.00	70.00	150.	975.	9500.	—
1862	253,550	24.00	32.00	50.00	80.00	150.	225.	750.	5500.	5500.
1862S	1,352,000	16.00	27.00	35.00	60.00	90.00	175.	450.	9000.	—
1863	503,660	18.00	25.00	40.00	70.00	130.	250.	750.	5500.	5500.
1863S	916,000	16.00	25.00	35.00	45.00	80.00	150.	410.	9000.	—
1864	379,570	24.00	32.00	55.00	85.00	160.	200.	750.	5500.	5500.
1864S	658,000	16.50	20.00	40.00	50.00	85.00	165.	450.	9000.	—
1865	511,900	18.00	23.00	40.00	60.00	110.	240.	750.	4200.	5500.
1865S	675,000	17.00	21.00	30.00	50.00	75.00	160.	450.	9000.	—
1866	—	—	—	—	Proof, unique		—	—	—	
1866S	60,000	75.00	110.	165.	275.	475.	1500.	5000.	—	—

Motto above eagle

Notes: In 1866 the motto "E Pluribus Unum" was added to the reverse. The "closed-3" and "open-3" varieties are distinguished by the amount of space between the upper left and lower left serifs of the 3.

Date	Mintage	G-4	VG-8	F-12	VF-20	XF-40	AU-50	MS-60	MS-65	Prf-65
1866	745,625	15.00	24.00	29.00	40.00	80.00	145.	350.	4800.	3750.
1866S	994,000	15.00	24.00	29.00	39.00	75.00	145.	350.	5000.	—

Date	Mintage	G-4	VG-8	F-12	VF-20	XF-40	AU-50	MS-60	MS-65	Prf-65
1867	449,925	16.00	27.00	45.00	80.00	145.	240.	350.	4800.	3750.
1867S	1,196,000	15.00	24.00	29.00	39.00	75.00	145.	350.	7000.	—
1868	418,200	30.00	40.00	55.00	120.	200.	300.	525.	7100.	3750.
1868S	1,160,000	15.00	24.00	29.00	39.00	95.00	165.	350.	7000.	—
1869	795,900	15.00	24.00	29.00	39.00	80.00	160.	385.	4600.	3750.
1869S	656,000	15.00	27.00	35.00	50.00	80.00	160.	600.	7000.	—
1870	634,900	17.00	27.00	35.00	60.00	95.00	160.	475.	7000.	3750.
1870CC	54,617	500.	850.	1300.	2350.	4200.	—	—	—	—
1870S	1,004,000	15.00	24.00	40.00	60.00	110.	275.	575.	7000.	—
1871	1,204,560	16.00	24.00	29.00	39.00	70.00	145.	350.	7000.	3750.
1871CC	153,950	135.	180.	295.	425.	875.	2000.	3500.	9150.	—
1871S	2,178,000	15.00	24.00	29.00	39.00	63.00	145.	400.	7000.	—
1872	881,550	15.00	24.00	29.00	39.00	63.00	145.	430.	4500.	3750.
1872CC	272,000	70.00	110.	150.	300.	650.	1700.	2500.	8800.	—
1872S	580,000	23.00	28.00	55.00	85.00	170.	375.	975.	7000.	—
1873 closed 3	801,800	15.00	24.00	38.00	70.00	100.	235.	500.	4500.	3750.
1873 open 3	Inc. Ab.	2650.	3350.	4750.	6500.	9250.	—	—	—	—
1873CC	122,500	110.	130.	240.	400.	800.	1300.	4100.	9000.	3750.

1873S no arrows, 5,000 minted, no specimens known to survive.

Arrows at date

Weight: 12.5 grams. **Composition:** 90% silver (.3618 ounces), 10% copper.

Date	Mintage	G-4	VG-8	F-12	VF-20	XF-40	AU-50	MS-60	MS-65	Prf-65
1873	1,815,700	16.50	25.00	36.00	80.00	225.	535.	950.	21,500.	9000.
1873CC	214,560	100.	120.	225.	400.	800.	1250.	4500.	—	—
1873S	233,000	45.00	60.00	90.00	195.	400.	725.	1600.	21,500.	—
1874	2,360,300	16.50	25.00	36.00	80.00	225.	535.	950.	21,500.	9000.
1874CC	59,000	200.	300.	450.	750.	1150.	2300.	4500.	21,500.	—
1874S	394,000	25.00	30.00	55.00	125.	275.	575.	1700.	21,500.	—

Arrows at date removed

Date	Mintage	G-4	VG-8	F-12	VF-20	XF-40	AU-50	MS-60	MS-65	Prf-65
1875	6,027,500	15.00	24.00	29.00	37.00	60.00	120.	425.	3500.	2550.
1875CC	1,008,000	17.00	33.00	40.00	60.00	120.	300.	540.	5450.	—
1875S	3,200,000	15.00	24.00	29.00	37.00	60.00	120.	340.	2900.	—
1876	8,419,150	15.00	24.00	32.00	40.00	60.00	135.	340.	5300.	3750.
1876CC	1,956,000	17.00	30.00	35.00	55.00	100.	275.	560.	4200.	—
1876S	4,528,000	15.00	24.00	32.00	40.00	63.00	145.	340.	2900.	—
1877	8,304,510	15.00	24.00	29.00	45.00	63.00	145.	340.	2900.	3750.
1877CC	1,420,000	17.00	33.00	35.00	60.00	95.00	275.	630.	3250.	—
1877S	5,356,000	15.00	24.00	29.00	37.00	65.00	145.	340.	2900.	—
1878	1,378,400	20.00	28.00	36.00	50.00	115.	170.	425.	3650.	2550.
1878CC	62,000	250.	300.	425.	800.	1350.	2300.	4000.	—	—
1878S	12,000	6750.	8000.	10,000.	13,000.	17,500.	20,000.	25,000.	—	—
1879	5,900	200.	220.	290.	350.	400.	475.	700.	2900.	2550.
1880	9,755	190.	210.	240.	310.	375.	475.	700.	2900.	2550.
1881	10,975	170.	195.	240.	300.	365.	465.	700.	2900.	2550.
1882	5,500	210.	230.	290.	365.	440.	500.	800.	3600.	2550.
1883	9,039	180.	210.	240.	290.	375.	475.	750.	2900.	2550.
1884	5,275	225.	285.	330.	395.	450.	550.	800.	2900.	2550.
1885	6,130	215.	235.	300.	360.	435.	525.	800.	2900.	2550.
1886	5,886	260.	325.	410.	450.	495.	600.	850.	4800.	2550.
1887	5,710	325.	385.	450.	550.	650.	750.	900.	2900.	2550.
1888	12,833	175.	200.	235.	300.	375.	425.	700.	2900.	2550.
1889	12,711	175.	200.	235.	300.	375.	425.	700.	2900.	2550.
1890	12,590	175.	200.	235.	300.	375.	425.	700.	3250.	2550.
1891	200,600	40.00	50.00	60.00	90.00	140.	290.	500.	3250.	2550.

Barber

Mintmark

Designer: Charles E. Barber. **Size:** 30.6 millimeters. **Weight:** 12.5 grams. **Composition:** 90% silver (.3618 ounces), 10% copper.

Date	Mintage	G-4	VG-8	F-12	VF-20	XF-40	AU-50	MS-60	MS-65	Prf-65
1892	935,245	18.00	23.00	39.00	75.00	180.	310.	420.	3100.	2500.
1892O	390,000	75.00	130.	180.	285.	415.	475.	975.	5900.	—
1892S	1,029,028	100.	130.	175.	275.	390.	585.	850.	5900.	—
1893	1,826,792	13.00	17.00	39.00	65.00	150.	340.	500.	3500.	2500.

Half dollars

Date	Mintage	G-4	VG-8	F-12	VF-20	XF-40	AU-50	MS-60	MS-65	Prf-65
1893O	1,389,000	15.00	26.00	45.00	115.	260.	370.	550.	10,500.	—
1893S	740,000	50.00	67.00	120.	250.	370.	520.	1100.	10,500.	—
1894	1,148,972	13.00	23.00	48.00	82.00	195.	350.	520.	3500.	2500.
1894O	2,138,000	9.00	13.00	47.00	91.00	235.	370.	500.	5400.	—
1894S	4,048,690	7.50	12.00	40.00	60.00	190.	340.	440.	9600.	—
1895	1,835,218	7.50	12.00	39.00	78.00	165.	325.	535.	3400.	2500.
1895O	1,766,000	8.00	17.00	43.00	85.00	220.	360.	535.	6000.	—
1895S	1,108,086	14.00	23.00	49.00	100.	250.	360.	500.	7800.	—
1896	950,762	11.00	17.00	39.00	80.00	190.	325.	500.	6600.	3400.
1896O	924,000	16.00	20.00	72.00	145.	345.	620.	1100.	12,500.	—
1896S	1,140,948	52.00	65.00	100.	180.	350.	550.	1100.	10,250.	—
1897	2,480,731	6.50	7.50	25.00	58.00	135.	310.	425.	3125.	2500.
1897O	632,000	45.00	58.00	260.	490.	845.	1175.	1500.	5400.	—
1897S	933,900	82.00	100.	250.	410.	650.	975.	1200.	9000.	—
1898	2,956,735	6.50	7.50	25.00	57.00	135.	300.	425.	3100.	2500.
1898O	874,000	13.00	21.00	72.00	160.	350.	495.	715.	7550.	—
1898S	2,358,550	7.75	14.00	34.00	73.00	200.	350.	600.	10,000.	—
1899	5,538,846	4.75	7.50	25.00	57.00	135.	300.	425.	3100.	3900.
1899O	1,724,000	7.25	10.50	39.00	85.00	210.	360.	550.	6000.	—
1899S	1,686,411	6.75	12.00	38.00	78.00	180.	340.	535.	6000.	—
1900	4,762,912	4.75	7.50	25.00	58.00	135.	300.	425.	3100.	2500.
1900O	2,744,000	7.00	10.00	37.00	82.00	240.	360.	685.	14,500.	—
1900S	2,560,322	7.00	10.00	31.00	86.00	180.	325.	520.	9600.	—
1901	4,268,813	4.75	7.50	25.00	58.00	135.	300.	425.	4200.	3250.
1901O	1,124,000	7.00	11.50	43.00	105.	270.	450.	1250.	20,000.	—
1901S	847,044	12.00	17.00	91.00	195.	500.	880.	1400.	12,500.	—
1902	4,922,777	4.75	7.50	25.00	57.00	135.	300.	425.	3100.	2900.
1902O	2,526,000	6.00	10.00	35.00	72.00	180.	350.	650.	11,000.	—
1902S	1,460,670	6.50	10.00	39.00	80.00	200.	360.	540.	5150.	—
1903	2,278,755	8.00	12.00	30.00	62.00	130.	325.	480.	7500.	3125.
1903O	2,100,000	5.50	10.00	38.00	72.00	180.	350.	570.	9000.	—
1903S	1,920,772	6.00	10.00	37.00	74.00	210.	365.	540.	9000.	—
1904	2,992,670	5.00	7.50	25.00	58.00	135.	300.	425.	4550.	3400.
1904O	1,117,600	8.00	12.00	47.00	110.	300.	500.	1000.	9600.	—
1904S	553,038	10.50	18.00	100.	280.	560.	910.	1525.	13,750.	—
1905	662,727	8.50	10.50	43.00	72.00	215.	375.	540.	5400.	3125.
1905O	505,000	9.50	15.00	52.00	125.	225.	415.	680.	6000.	—
1905S	2,494,000	5.25	8.00	32.00	72.00	190.	345.	515.	9600.	—
1906	2,638,675	4.75	7.00	25.00	62.00	130.	300.	425.	3100.	2500.
1906D	4,028,000	4.75	7.50	25.00	59.00	140.	350.	425.	3950.	—
1906O	2,446,000	5.25	8.00	39.00	66.00	190.	300.	540.	6000.	—
1906S	1,740,154	5.50	11.00	40.00	63.00	180.	300.	525.	6000.	—
1907	2,598,575	4.75	7.50	25.00	57.00	135.	300.	425.	3100.	3250.
1907D	3,856,000	4.75	7.50	25.00	58.00	150.	300.	425.	3100.	—
1907O	3,946,000	4.75	7.50	25.00	58.00	145.	300.	490.	3300.	—
1907S	1,250,000	6.50	11.00	52.00	91.00	290.	450.	775.	12,000.	—
1908	1,354,545	6.00	8.50	29.00	65.00	150.	310.	425.	3100.	3250.
1908D	3,280,000	4.75	7.50	25.00	60.00	145.	310.	480.	3100.	—
1908O	5,360,000	4.75	7.50	25.00	57.00	140.	310.	480.	3250.	—
1908S	1,644,828	5.50	10.50	36.00	72.00	180.	340.	680.	6000.	—
1909	2,368,650	4.75	7.00	22.00	56.00	135.	300.	425.	3100.	3200.
1909O	925,400	6.00	10.00	39.00	77.00	260.	475.	700.	5000.	—
1909S	1,764,000	4.75	7.50	25.00	71.00	165.	330.	520.	3250.	—
1910	418,551	8.00	12.00	55.00	110.	260.	415.	585.	4400.	3450.
1910S	1,948,000	4.75	7.50	25.00	66.00	165.	325.	585.	4200.	—
1911	1,406,543	5.25	8.00	25.00	62.00	140.	300.	425.	3100.	2500.
1911D	695,080	6.00	10.00	32.00	80.00	175.	310.	500.	3100.	—
1911S	1,272,000	5.25	8.00	28.00	66.00	165.	320.	550.	6600.	—
1912	1,550,700	4.75	7.50	25.00	58.00	150.	320.	440.	3600.	3200.
1912D	2,300,800	4.75	7.50	25.00	57.00	135.	300.	425.	3100.	—
1912S	1,370,000	4.75	7.50	25.00	60.00	155.	320.	500.	5000.	—
1913	188,627	15.00	21.00	80.00	175.	325.	650.	910.	3500.	3000.
1913D	534,000	6.00	9.00	31.00	66.00	175.	320.	495.	6000.	—
1913S	604,000	6.50	10.00	39.00	78.00	190.	370.	585.	3850.	—
1914	124,610	18.00	27.00	150.	295.	450.	750.	950.	11,000.	3575.
1914S	992,000	6.00	9.00	30.00	65.00	175.	345.	500.	3700.	—
1915	138,450	16.00	22.00	80.00	200.	350.	685.	975.	4600.	3250.
1915D	1,170,400	4.75	7.50	25.00	57.00	135.	300.	425.	3100.	—
1915S	1,604,000	4.75	7.50	25.00	58.00	135.	300.	490.	3100.	—

Walking Liberty

Mintmark on obverse

Designer: Adolph A. Weinman. **Size:** 30.6 millimeters. **Weight:** 12.5 grams. **Composition:** 90% silver (.3618 ounces), 10% copper.

Date	Mintage	G-4	VG-8	F-12	VF-20	XF-40	AU-50	MS-60	MS-65	Prf-65
1916	608,000	19.00	25.00	55.00	120.	160.	210.	275.	1400.	—
1916D	1,014,400	11.00	17.00	30.00	70.00	135.	175.	260.	1950.	—
1916S	508,000	55.00	68.00	115.	280.	510.	645.	800.	5100.	—
1917D	765,400	11.50	15.00	30.00	84.00	150.	210.	430.	6300.	—
1917S	952,000	12.50	20.00	48.00	235.	595.	975.	1750.	11,000.	—

Mintmark on reverse

Date	Mintage	G-4	VG-8	F-12	VF-20	XF-40	AU-50	MS-60	MS-65	Prf-65
1917	12,292,000	4.00	8.00	10.50	20.00	35.00	63.00	85.00	950.	—
1917D	1,940,000	8.50	11.00	19.00	50.00	140.	310.	675.	15,500.	—
1917S	5,554,000	5.00	8.00	13.50	25.00	48.00	105.	280.	11,300.	—
1918	6,634,000	4.00	9.00	17.00	45.00	130.	250.	410.	3500.	—
1918D	3,853,040	6.00	9.50	18.00	51.00	140.	315.	750.	22,750.	—

Half dollars

Date	Mintage	G-4	VG-8	F-12	VF-20	XF-40	AU-50	MS-60	MS-65	Prf-65
1918S	10,282,000	4.00	8.00	14.00	27.00	49.00	120.	330.	12,500.	—
1919	962,000	10.50	14.00	30.00	140.	375.	560.	915.	4800.	—
1919D	1,165,000	9.50	12.00	32.00	165.	450.	900.	2300.	40,000.	—
1919S	1,552,000	10.00	13.50	25.00	135.	600.	1100.	1700.	9750.	—
1920	6,372,000	4.00	8.00	13.00	23.00	53.00	91.00	220.	6750.	—
1920D	1,551,000	8.50	10.00	25.00	125.	315.	600.	1040.	9000.	—
1920S	4,624,000	6.00	8.00	14.00	42.00	150.	350.	590.	7800.	—
1921	246,000	50.00	80.00	180.	525.	1350.	1950.	2250.	11,000.	—
1921D	208,000	77.00	100.	240.	650.	1900.	2500.	2650.	11,000.	—
1921S	548,000	19.00	24.00	60.00	525.	3900.	6700.	8100.	32,500.	—
1923S	2,178,000	7.00	10.00	18.00	65.00	250.	490.	1050.	12,250.	—
1927S	2,392,000	4.00	7.00	11.00	35.00	95.00	245.	610.	8850.	—
1928S	1,940,000	4.00	7.00	12.50	42.00	115.	290.	620.	4950.	—
1929D	1,001,200	6.25	7.50	10.50	19.00	70.00	155.	245.	2200.	—
1929S	1,902,000	4.00	6.75	10.00	16.00	64.00	155.	300.	2300.	—
1933S	1,786,000	5.50	8.50	10.00	11.50	45.00	155.	450.	3350.	—
1934	6,964,000	2.50	2.75	3.50	4.50	11.00	26.50	48.00	410.	—
1934D	2,361,400	3.25	4.00	5.50	7.50	25.00	56.00	97.00	1235.	—
1934S	3,652,000	3.00	3.50	4.50	6.00	25.00	70.00	215.	2600.	—
1935	9,162,000	2.50	2.75	3.50	4.50	9.00	19.50	44.00	290.	—
1935D	3,003,800	3.25	4.00	5.50	7.50	25.00	56.00	105.	1235.	—
1935S	3,854,000	3.10	3.50	4.50	5.50	25.00	68.00	110.	1950.	—
1936	12,617,901	2.50	2.75	3.50	4.50	9.00	19.50	39.00	145.	2500.
1936D	4,252,400	2.95	3.50	4.50	5.50	17.00	47.00	85.00	325.	—
1936S	3,884,000	3.00	3.50	4.50	5.50	17.00	45.00	110.	535.	—
1937	9,527,728	2.50	2.75	3.50	4.50	9.00	19.50	36.00	175.	1175.
1937D	1,676,000	6.00	7.00	8.75	10.50	28.00	155.	170.	490.	—
1937S	2,090,000	5.00	6.00	7.25	8.00	16.50	56.00	110.	535.	—
1938	4,118,152	3.00	3.50	4.50	6.50	11.00	42.00	65.00	220.	720.
1938D	491,600	18.00	20.00	28.00	45.00	110.	260.	365.	950.	—
1939	6,820,808	2.50	2.75	3.50	4.50	10.00	22.00	40.00	150.	665.
1939D	4,267,800	3.00	3.50	4.50	5.50	10.50	24.00	39.00	145.	—
1939S	2,552,000	4.50	4.75	6.00	8.75	12.50	39.00	91.00	260.	—
1940	9,167,279	2.45	3.50	4.00	5.50	9.00	14.00	24.00	115.	550.
1940S	4,550,000	2.45	3.50	4.00	5.50	10.00	21.00	28.00	390.	—
1941	24,207,412	2.45	2.65	3.50	4.50	7.00	7.75	26.00	110.	500.
1941D	11,248,400	2.45	2.65	3.50	4.50	6.00	12.50	32.00	125.	—
1941S	8,098,000	2.60	2.80	3.75	4.75	7.00	28.00	84.00	1125.	—
1942	47,839,120	2.45	2.65	3.50	4.50	5.50	7.75	26.00	110.	500.
1942D	10,973,800	2.45	2.65	3.50	4.50	6.00	16.00	31.00	245.	—
1942S	12,708,000	2.45	2.65	3.50	4.75	7.00	21.00	32.00	425.	—
1943	53,190,000	2.45	2.65	3.50	4.50	5.50	7.75	26.00	110.	—
1943D	11,346,000	2.45	2.65	3.50	4.50	6.00	20.00	39.00	200.	—
1943S	13,450,000	2.45	2.65	3.75	4.75	6.00	21.00	33.00	435.	—
1944	28,206,000	2.45	2.65	3.50	4.50	5.50	7.75	26.00	125.	—
1944D	9,769,000	2.45	2.65	3.50	4.50	6.00	18.00	34.00	125.	—
1944S	8,904,000	2.45	2.65	3.50	4.75	6.25	20.00	34.00	700.	—
1945	31,502,000	2.45	2.65	3.50	4.50	5.50	7.75	26.00	110.	—
1945D	9,966,800	2.45	2.65	3.50	4.50	6.00	14.00	30.00	120.	—
1945S	10,156,000	2.45	2.65	3.50	4.75	6.00	17.00	32.00	185.	—
1946	12,118,000	2.45	2.65	3.50	4.50	5.50	12.50	26.00	135.	—
1946D	2,151,000	4.50	4.75	6.00	8.75	9.50	17.00	29.00	120.	—
1946S	3,724,000	2.60	2.80	3.50	5.00	5.50	14.00	29.00	110.	—
1947	4,094,000	2.60	2.80	3.50	5.00	7.00	17.00	30.00	130.	—
1947D	3,900,600	2.60	2.80	3.50	5.00	7.00	17.00	31.00	120.	—

Franklin

Designer: John R. Sinnock. **Size:** 30.6 millimeters. **Weight:** 12.5 grams. **Composition:** 90% silver (.3618 ounces), 10% copper. **Notes:** "MS-65FBL" values are for coins with full lines across the bell on the reverse.

Date	Mintage	G-4	VG-8	F-12	VF-20	XF-40	AU-50	MS-60	MS-65	-65FBL	Prf-65
1948	3,006,814	—	3.50	4.00	4.50	9.00	10.00	19.50	63.00	—	—
1948D	4,028,600	—	3.50	4.00	4.50	8.00	9.00	10.00	200.	—	—
1949	5,614,000	—	3.50	4.00	6.00	11.00	15.00	49.00	90.00	250.	—
1949D	4,120,600	—	3.50	4.00	6.00	12.00	19.00	43.00	825.	—	—
1949S	3,744,000	—	3.75	4.75	6.00	10.00	30.00	60.00	140.	450.	—
1950	7,793,509	—	—	4.00	4.50	9.00	12.00	37.50	95.00	—	350.
1950D	8,031,600	—	—	4.00	4.50	9.00	10.00	25.00	485.	—	—
1951	16,859,602	—	—	4.00	4.50	7.00	8.00	14.00	80.00	—	250.
1951D	9,475,200	—	—	3.50	4.25	5.00	12.50	35.00	195.	—	—
1951S	13,696,000	—	—	3.50	4.25	5.00	20.00	31.00	72.00	360.	—
1952	21,274,073	—	—	3.50	4.25	5.00	6.00	9.50	65.00	—	135.
1952D	25,395,600	—	—	3.00	3.50	4.50	5.00	8.50	190.	—	—
1952S	5,526,000	—	—	3.50	4.25	4.75	12.00	37.50	56.00	400.	—
1953	2,796,920	3.75	4.00	4.25	5.00	6.00	10.00	21.00	135.	—	70.00
1953D	20,900,400	—	—	3.00	3.50	4.00	8.00	8.75	215.	—	—

Mintmark

Date	Mintage	G-4	VG-8	F-12	VF-20	XF-40	AU-50	MS-60	MS-65	65FBL	Prf-65
1953S	4,148,000	—	—	3.50	4.25	4.75	10.00	18.00	51.00	700.	—
1954	13,421,503	—	—	3.00	3.50	4.75	5.50	6.00	64.00	—	55.00
1954D	25,445,580	—	—	3.00	3.00	4.00	5.00	5.75	165.	—	—
1954S	4,993,400	—	—	3.50	4.25	4.75	6.50	7.50	50.00	165.	—
1955	2,876,381	4.50	5.00	6.50	7.00	7.50	8.00	8.50	50.00	—	40.00
1956	4,701,384	—	—	3.50	4.00	4.50	5.50	7.25	44.00	—	22.00
1957	6,361,952	—	—	3.50	4.00	4.50	5.00	7.25	44.00	—	13.00
1957D	19,966,850	—	—	—	—	2.75	3.00	6.25	45.00	—	—
1958	4,917,652	—	—	2.75	3.00	3.50	3.75	5.00	44.00	—	13.00
1958D	23,962,412	—	—	—	2.00	2.50	3.00	4.00	44.00	—	—
1959	4,917,652	—	—	—	2.00	2.50	3.00	5.00	160.	—	12.00
1959D	13,053,750	—	—	—	2.00	2.50	3.00	5.50	180.	—	—
1960	7,715,602	—	—	—	2.00	2.50	3.00	4.50	165.	—	12.00
1960D	18,215,812	—	—	—	2.00	2.50	3.00	4.50	500.	—	—
1961	11,318,244	—	—	—	2.00	2.50	3.00	4.50	250.	—	8.50
1961D	20,276,442	—	—	—	2.00	2.50	3.00	4.50	525.	—	—
1962	12,932,019	—	—	—	2.00	2.50	2.50	4.50	215.	—	8.50
1962D	35,473,281	—	—	—	2.00	2.50	3.00	4.50	475.	—	—
1963	25,239,645	—	—	—	2.00	2.50	2.65	2.75	90.00	—	8.50
1963D	67,069,292	—	—	—	2.00	2.10	2.25	2.50	90.00	—	—

Kennedy

Reverse mintmark (1964)

Bicentennial reverse

Obverse mintmark (1968-present)

90% silver composition

Designers: Gilroy Roberts and Frank Gasparro. **Size:** 30.6 millimeters. **Weight:** 12.5 grams. **Composition:** 90% silver (.3618 ounces), 10% copper.

Date	Mintage	G-4	VG-8	F-12	VF-20	XF-40	MS-60	MS-65	Prf-65
1964	277,254,766	—	—	—	—	—	2.25	3.50	8.00
1964D	156,205,446	—	—	—	—	—	2.25	3.50	—

40% silver composition

Weight: 11.5 grams. **Composition:** clad layers of 80% copper and 20% silver bonded to a core of 79.1% copper and 20.9% silver (.148 total ounces of silver).

Date	Mintage	G-4	VG-8	F-12	VF-20	XF-40	MS-60	MS-65	Prf-65
1965	65,879,366	—	—	—	—	—	1.25	2.50	—
1966	108,984,932	—	—	—	—	—	1.20	2.40	—
1967	295,046,978	—	—	—	—	—	1.00	2.25	—
1968D	246,951,930	—	—	—	—	—	1.00	2.25	—
1968S	3,041,506	—	—	—	—	Proof only		—	3.50
1969D	129,881,800	—	—	—	—	—	1.00	2.00	—
1969S	2,934,631	—	—	—	—	—	—	—	3.50
1970D	2,150,000	—	—	—	—	—	12.00	15.00	—
1970S	2,632,810	—	—	—	—	Proof only		—	7.50

Clad composition

Weight: 11.34 grams. **Composition:** clad layers of 75% copper and 25% nickel bonded to a pure-copper core.

Date	Mintage	G-4	VG-8	F-12	VF-20	XF-40	MS-60	MS-65	Prf-65
1971	155,640,000	—	—	—	—	—	1.50	2.50	—
1971D	302,097,424	—	—	—	—	—	1.00	1.50	—
1971S	3,244,183	—	—	—	—	Proof only		—	2.75
1972	153,180,000	—	—	—	—	—	2.00	2.50	—
1972D	141,890,000	—	—	—	—	—	2.00	2.50	—
1972S	3,267,667	—	—	—	—	Proof only		—	2.50
1972S	3,267,667	—	—	—	—	Proof only		—	2.50
1973	64,964,000	—	—	—	—	—	1.35	2.50	—
1973D	83,171,400	—	—	—	—	—	—	2.50	—
1973S	Proof only	—	—	—	—	—	—	—	1.75
1974	201,596,000	—	—	—	—	—	1.00	2.00	—
1974D	79,066,300	—	—	—	—	—	1.20	2.00	—
1974S	Proof only	—	—	—	—	—	—	—	1.75

Bicentennial design, clad composition

Reverse designer: Seth Huntington.

Date	Mintage	G-4	VG-8	F-12	VF-20	XF-40	MS-60	MS-65	Prf-65
1976	234,308,000	—	—	—	—	—	1.00	1.50	—
1976D	287,565,248	—	—	—	—	—	1.00	1.50	—
1976S		—	—	—	—	—	—	—	1.25

Bicentennial design, silver composition

Weight: 11.5 grams. **Composition:** 40% silver (.148 ounces), 60% copper.

Date	Mintage	G-4	VG-8	F-12	VF-20	XF-40	MS-60	MS-65	Prf-65
1976S silver	11,000,000	—	—	—	—	—	—	6.00	5.75

Regular design resumed, clad composition

Notes: 1979-S Type II proof has a clearer mintmark than the Type I.

Date	Mintage	G-4	VG-8	F-12	VF-20	XF-40	MS-60	MS-65	Prf-65
1977	43,598,000	—	—	—	—	—	2.60	2.50	—
1977D	31,449,106	—	—	—	—	—	2.60	2.50	—
1977S	Proof only	—	—	—	—	—	—	—	1.75
1978	14,350,000	—	—	—	—	—	1.25	2.50	—
1978D	13,765,799	—	—	—	—	—	1.00	2.50	—
1978S	Proof only	—	—	—	—	—	—	—	1.75
1979	68,312,000	—	—	—	—	—	—	1.50	—
1979D	15,815,422	—	—	—	—	—	—	1.25	—
1979S T-I	Proof only	—	—	—	—	—	—	—	2.00
1979S T-II	Proof only	—	—	—	—	—	—	—	14.00
1980P	44,134,000	—	—	—	—	—	—	1.75	—
1980D	33,456,449	—	—	—	—	—	—	2.00	—
1980S	Proof only	—	—	—	—	—	—	—	1.25
1981P	29,544,000	—	—	—	—	—	—	2.00	—
1981D	27,839,533	—	—	—	—	—	—	2.00	—
1981S T-I	Proof only	—	—	—	—	—	—	—	1.25
1981S T-II	Proof only	—	—	—	—	—	—	—	14.50
1982P	10,819,000	—	—	—	—	—	—	1.50	—
1982D	13,140,102	—	—	—	—	—	—	1.50	—
1982S	Proof only	—	—	—	—	—	—	—	3.50
1983P	34,139,000	—	—	—	—	—	—	1.50	—
1983D	32,472,244	—	—	—	—	—	—	1.50	—
1983S	Proof only	—	—	—	—	—	—	—	3.00
1984P	26,029,000	—	—	—	—	—	—	1.50	—
1984D	26,262,158	—	—	—	—	—	—	1.50	—
1984S	Proof only	—	—	—	—	—	—	—	6.50
1985P	18,706,962	—	—	—	—	—	—	1.50	—
1985D	19,814,034	—	—	—	—	—	—	1.25	—
1985S	Proof only	—	—	—	—	—	—	—	4.50
1986P	13,107,633	—	—	—	—	—	—	2.00	—
1986D	15,336,145	—	—	—	—	—	—	1.50	—
1986S	Proof only	—	—	—	—	—	—	—	15.00
1987P	2,890,758	—	—	—	—	—	—	3.00	—
1987D	2,890,758	—	—	—	—	—	—	3.00	—
1987S	Proof only	—	—	—	—	—	—	—	3.50
1988P	13,626,000	—	—	—	—	—	—	2.50	—
1988D	12,000,096	—	—	—	—	—	—	2.50	—
1988S	Proof only	—	—	—	—	—	—	—	7.25
1989P	24,542,000	—	—	—	—	—	—	2.50	—
1989D	23,000,216	—	—	—	—	—	—	2.50	—
1989S	Proof only	—	—	—	—	—	—	—	3.50
1990P	22,780,000	—	—	—	—	—	—	1.50	—
1990D	20,096,242	—	—	—	—	—	—	1.50	—
1990S	Proof only	—	—	—	—	—	—	—	6.50
1991P	—	—	—	—	—	—	—	1.50	—
1991D	—	—	—	—	—	—	—	1.50	—
1991S	Proof only	—	—	—	—	—	—	—	8.50
1992P	—	—	—	—	—	—	—	1.00	—
1992D	—	—	—	—	—	—	—	1.00	—
1992S	Proof only	—	—	—	—	—	—	—	7.00
1993P	—	—	—	—	—	—	—	1.00	—
1993D	—	—	—	—	—	—	—	1.00	—
1993S	Proof only	—	—	—	—	—	—	—	6.00
1994P	—	—	—	—	—	—	—	1.00	—
1994D	—	—	—	—	—	—	—	1.00	—
1994S	Proof only	—	—	—	—	—	—	—	7.00

Silver dollars

Flowing Hair

Designer: Robert Scot. **Size:** 39-40 millimeters. **Weight:** 26.96 grams. **Composition:** 89.24% silver (.7737 ounces), 10.76% copper. **Notes:** The two 1795 varieties have either two or three leaves under each of the eagle's wings on the reverse.

Date	Mintage	G-4	VG-8	F-12	VF-20	XF-40	MS-60
1794	1,758	10,000.	13,500.	18,500.	27,500.	42,500.	—
1795 2 leaves	203,033	800.	900.	1500.	2300.	4950.	40,000.
1795 3 leaves	Inc. Ab.	800.	900.	1500.	2300.	4950.	40,000.

Draped Bust

Small eagle

Designer: Robert Scot. **Size:** 39-40 millimeters. **Weight:** 26.96 grams. **Composition:** 89.24% silver (.7737 ounces), 10.76% copper. **Notes:** The 1796 varieties are distinguished by the size of the numerals in the date and letters in "United States of America." The 1797 varieties are distinguished by the number of stars to the left and right of the word "Liberty" and by the size of the letters in "United States of America." The 1798 varieties have either 13 or 15 stars on the obverse.

Date	Mintage	G-4	VG-8	F-12	VF-20	XF-40	MS-60
1795	Inc. Ab.	600.	800.	1070.	1825.	3750.	17,000.
1796 small date, small letters	72,920	625.	800.	1150.	1950.	3650.	15,500.
1796 small date, large letters	Inc. Ab.	625.	775.	1070.	1825.	3550.	15,500.
1796 large date, small letters	Inc. Ab.	575.	765.	1070.	1825.	3550.	15,500.
1797 9 stars left, 7 stars right, small letters	7,776	1500.	2000.	2750.	4500.	8450.	22,000.
1797 9 stars left, 7 stars right, large letters	Inc. Ab.	585.	775.	1070.	1825.	3550.	15,500.
1797 10 stars left, 6 stars right	Inc. Ab.	585.	775.	1070.	1825.	3550.	15,500.
1798 13 stars	327,536	900.	1150.	1450.	2400.	4500.	18,000.
1798 15 stars	Inc. Ab.	1100.	1600.	2100.	3150.	6900.	18,000.

Heraldic eagle

Notes: The 1798 "knob 9" variety has a serif on the lower left of the 9 in the date. The 1798 varieties are distinguished by the number of arrows held by the eagle on the reverse and the number of berries on the olive branch. On the 1798 "high 8" variety, the 8 in the date is higher than the other numerals. The 1799 varieties are distinguished by the number and positioning of the stars on the obverse and by the size of the berries in the olive branch on the reverse. On the 1799 "irregular date" variety, the first 9 in the date is smaller than the other numerals. Some varieties of the 1800 strikes had letters in the legend cut twice into the dies; as the dies became worn, the letters were touched up. On the 1800 "very wide date, low 8" variety, the spacing between the numerals in the date are wider than other varieties and the 8 is lower than the other numerals. The 1800 "small berries" variety refers to the size of the berries in the olive branch on the reverse. The

1800 "12 arrows" and "10 arrows" varieties refer to the number of arrows held by the eagle. The 1800 "Americai" variety appears to have the faint outline of an "I" after "America" in the reverse legend. The "close" and "wide" varieties of 1802 refer to the amount of space between the numerals in the date. For the 1802 "perfect date" varieties, all numerals in the date are of the same size. The 1803 large-3 and small-3 varieties are distinguished by the size of the 3 in the date.

Date	Mintage	G-4	VG-8	F-12	VF-20	XF-40	MS-60
1798 knob 9	Inc. Ab.	375.	450.	575.	850.	1675.	9000.
1798 10 arrows	Inc. Ab.	355.	415.	525.	700.	1300.	9000.
1798 4 berries	Inc. Ab.	355.	415.	525.	700.	1300.	9000.
1798 5 berries, 12 arrows	Inc. Ab.	355.	415.	525.	700.	1300.	9000.
1798 high 8	Inc. Ab.	355.	415.	525.	700.	1300.	9000.
1798 13 arrows	Inc. Ab.	355.	415.	525.	700.	1300.	9000.
1799/98 13 star reverse	423,515	355.	415.	525.	700.	1300.	15,000.
1799/98 15 star reverse	Inc. Ab.	400.	500.	850.	1150.	2000.	15,000.
1799 irregular date, 13 star reverse	Inc. Ab.	355.	415.	525.	690.	1250.	9000.
1799 irregular date, 15 star reverse	Inc. Ab.	355.	415.	525.	690.	1250.	9000.
1799 perfect date, 7 and 6 star obverse, no berries	Inc. Ab.	355.	415.	525.	690.	1250.	9000.
1799 perfect date, 7 and 6 star obverse, small berries	Inc. Ab.	355.	415.	525.	690.	1250.	9000.
1799 perfect date, 7 and 6 star obverse, medium large berries	Inc. Ab.	355.	415.	525.	690.	1250.	9000.
1799 perfect date, 7 and 6 star obverse, extra large berries	Inc. Ab.	355.	415.	525.	690.	1250.	9000.
1799 8 stars left, 5 stars right on obverse	Inc. Ab.	425.	500.	800.	1100.	2000.	9000.
1800 "R" in "Liberty" double cut	220,920	355.	415.	525.	690.	1300.	9000.
1800 first "T" in "States" double cut	Inc. Ab.	355.	415.	525.	690.	1300.	9000.
1800 both letters double cut	Inc. Ab.	355.	415.	525.	690.	1300.	9000.
1800 "T" in "United" double cut	Inc. Ab.	355.	415.	525.	690.	1300.	9000.
1800 very wide date, low 8	Inc. Ab.	355.	415.	525.	690.	1300.	9000.
1800 sm. berries	Inc. Ab.	355.	415.	525.	690.	1300.	9000.
1800 dot date	Inc. Ab.	355.	415.	525.	690.	1300.	9000.
1800 12 arrows	Inc. Ab.	355.	415.	525.	690.	1300.	9000.
1800 10 arrows	Inc. Ab.	355.	415.	525.	690.	1300.	9000.
1800 "Americai"	Inc. Ab.	360.	415.	525.	800.	1500.	9000.
1801	54,454	375.	450.	600.	850.	1900.	9000.
1801	Unrecorded		Proof restrike, rare				
1802/1 close	Inc. Ab.	360.	425.	550.	850.	1600.	9000.
1802/1 wide	Inc. Ab.	360.	425.	550.	850.	1600.	9000.
1802 close, perfect date	Inc. Ab.	375.	450.	600.	875.	1650.	9000.
1802 wide, perfect date	Inc. Ab.	375.	450.	600.	875.	1650.	9000.
1802	Unrecorded		Proof restrike, rare				
1803 lg. 3	85,634	360.	425.	600.	850.	1575.	9000.
1803 sm. 3	Inc. Ab.	375.	450.	650.	900.	1700.	9000.
1803	Unrecorded		Proof restrike, rare				
1804	15 known		3 varieties Hawn Sale, Oct. 1993, AU-55, $522,500.				—

Gobrecht

Designer: Christian Gobrecht. **Size:** 38.1 millimeters. **Weight:** 26.73 grams. **Composition:** 90% silver (.7736 ounces), 10% copper. **Notes:** Several obverse and reverse combinations exist, as described. Restrikes were produced by the U.S. Mint between 1855 and 1860.

Date	Mintage	VF-20	XF-40	AU-50	Prf-60
1836 "C. Gobrecht F." below base. Rev: eagle flying left amid stars. Plain edge.	—	—	—	—	—
1836 Obv: same as above. Rev: eagle flying in plain field. Plain edge.	—	—	—	—	—

Obverse stars

Reverse stars

Date	Mintage	VF-20	XF-40	AU-50	Prf-60
1836 "C. Gobrecht F." on base. Rev: eagle flying left amid stars. Plain edge.	—	2500.	3750.	4750.	7500.
1836 Same as above, reeded edge.	—	—	—	—	—
1836 Obv: same as above. Rev: eagle flying in plain field. Plain edge.	—	—	—	—	10,000.
1838 Similar obv., designer's name omitted, stars added around border. Rev: eagle flying left in plain field. Reeded edge.	—	3000.	4500.	—	7500.
1838 Same as above. Plain edge. Restrikes only.	3 known	—	—	—	—
1838 Obv: same as above. Rev: eagle flying left amid stars. Plain edge. Restrikes only.	2 known	—	—	—	—
1839 Obv: same as above. Rev: eagle in plain field. Reeded edge. Also known with plain edge and plain edge with eagle amid stars.	—	—	3750.	—	15,000.

Seated Liberty

No motto

Designer: Christian Gobrecht. **Size:** 38.1 millimeters. **Weight:** 26.73 grams. **Composition:** 90% silver (.7736 ounces), 10% copper.

Date	Mintage	G-4	VG-8	F-12	VF-20	XF-40	AU-50	MS-60	MS-65	Prf-65
1840	61,005	130.	160.	225.	300.	475.	750.	1600.	—	—
1841	173,000	100.	130.	180.	220.	375.	575.	1300.	24,000.	—
1842	184,618	90.00	120.	160.	200.	300.	550.	1100.	24,000.	—
1843	165,100	90.00	120.	160.	200.	300.	550.	1400.	24,000.	—
1844	20,000	200.	250.	300.	425.	575.	800.	2000.	—	—
1845	24,500	150.	200.	250.	350.	500.	750.	3000.	—	—
1846	110,600	90.00	120.	160.	200.	275.	500.	1400.	24,000.	—
1846O	59,000	110.	140.	190.	325.	700.	2000.	4000.	—	—
1847	140,750	90.00	120.	160.	200.	300.	650.	850.	24,000.	—
1848	15,000	225.	250.	400.	550.	800.	1400.	2050.	—	—
1849	62,600	110.	140.	190.	240.	350.	700.	1600.	—	—
1850	7,500	400.	450.	600.	800.	1300.	2600.	3500.	—	—
1850O	40,000	200.	260.	350.	650.	1400.	3200.	5000.	—	—
1851	1,300	—	—	8000.	9500.	13,500.	16,500.	—	—	—
1852	1,100	—	—	6000.	7500.	11,500.	15,000.	—	—	—
1853	46,110	160.	190.	240.	375.	575.	800.	1300.	—	—
1854	33,140	900.	1200.	1500.	2000.	3000.	4200.	7000.	—	—
1855	26,000	750.	1000.	1300.	1900.	2650.	4500.	9000.	—	—
1856	63,500	250.	350.	450.	600.	800.	1300.	2000.	—	—
1857	94,000	250.	350.	450.	650.	900.	1400.	1800.	—	—
1858	Est. 200	—	—	—	Proof only		—	—	—	—
	Impaired Proof		—	—	4200.	5500.	6250.	—	—	—
1859	256,500	200.	250.	350.	450.	700.	1000.	2500.	24,000.	13,500.
1859O	360,000	85.00	100.	155.	195.	275.	500.	850.	24,000.	—
1859S	20,000	200.	275.	385.	600.	1350.	3000.	—	—	—
1860	218,930	140.	180.	230.	300.	475.	925.	1300.	24,000.	13,500.

Silver dollars

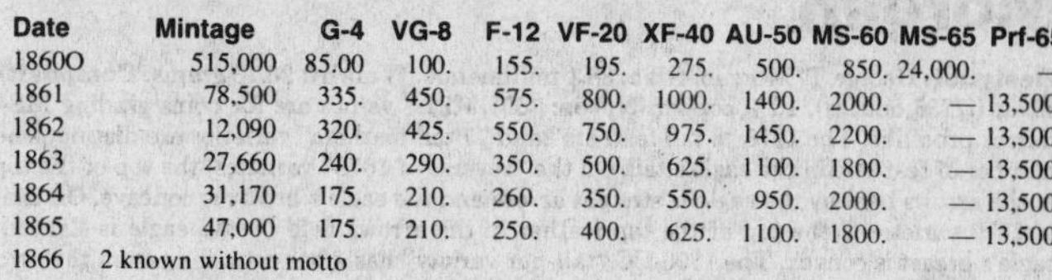

Date	Mintage	G-4	VG-8	F-12	VF-20	XF-40	AU-50	MS-60	MS-65	Prf-65
1860O	515,000	85.00	100.	155.	195.	275.	500.	850.	24,000.	—
1861	78,500	335.	450.	575.	800.	1000.	1400.	2000.	—	13,500.
1862	12,090	320.	425.	550.	750.	975.	1450.	2200.	—	13,500.
1863	27,660	240.	290.	350.	500.	625.	1100.	1800.	—	13,500.
1864	31,170	175.	210.	260.	350.	550.	950.	2000.	—	13,500.
1865	47,000	175.	210.	250.	400.	625.	1100.	1800.	—	13,500.
1866	2 known without motto									

Motto added on reverse

Notes: In 1866 the motto "In God We Trust" was added to the reverse above the eagle.

Date	Mintage	G-4	VG-8	F-12	VF-20	XF-40	AU-50	MS-60	MS-65	Prf-65
1866	49,625	150.	200.	250.	350.	550.	900.	1600.	28,500.	12,000.
1867	47,525	170.	250.	300.	450.	675.	1000.	1800.	28,500.	12,000.
1868	162,700	140.	190.	225.	350.	525.	900.	2000.	28,500.	12,000.
1869	424,300	115.	150.	200.	325.	500.	800.	2000.	28,500.	12,000.
1870	416,000	100.	135.	175.	225.	325.	600.	1500.	28,500.	12,000.
1870CC	12,462	200.	245.	325.	500.	975.	2250.	4250.	—	—
1870S	Unrecorded				Stacks, Nov. 1989, VF, $77,000.				—	—
1871	1,074,760	85.00	95.00	165.	200.	315.	550.	1150.	28,500.	12,000.
1871CC	1,376	1650.	2350.	3200.	5000.	8500.	15,000.	—	—	—
1872	1,106,450	85.00	95.00	165.	200.	315.	550.	1250.	28,500.	12,000.
1872CC	3,150	900.	1250.	1600.	2150.	3750.	6500.	15,000.	—	—
1872S	9,000	150.	225.	400.	575.	1100.	3000.	10,000.	—	—
1873	293,600	130.	150.	200.	250.	350.	600.	1350.	28,500.	12,000.
1873CC	2,300	2450.	3500.	5000.	8500.	14,000.	25,000.	40,000.	—	—
1873S	700		None known to exist				—		—	—

Trade

Designer: William Barber. **Size:** 38.1 millimeters. **Weight:** 27.22 grams. **Composition:** 90% silver (.7878 ounces), 10% copper.

Date	Mintage	G-4	VG-8	F-12	VF-20	XF-40	AU-50	MS-60	MS-65	Prf-65
1873	397,500	90.00	105.	125.	165.	250.	325.	1000.	19,000.	12,000.
1873CC	124,500	150.	175.	225.	275.	425.	675.	1500.	19,000.	—
1873S	703,000	130.	145.	160.	180.	260.	350.	1200.	12,000.	—
1874	987,800	80.00	90.00	125.	165.	225.	325.	700.	7500.	12,000.
1874CC	1,373,200	80.00	90.00	105.	165.	240.	350.	1000.	17,000.	—
1874S	2,549,000	70.00	80.00	95.00	120.	165.	250.	675.	7500.	—
1875	218,900	200.	225.	290.	365.	550.	800.	1850.	19,000.	6000.
1875CC	1,573,700	80.00	90.00	105.	130.	200.	375.	900.	18,500.	—
1875S	4,487,000	60.00	70.00	85.00	100.	120.	210.	500.	7500.	—
1875S/CC	Inc.Ab.	275.	325.	400.	500.	750.	1000.	1500.	—	—
1876	456,150	70.00	80.00	100.	125.	165.	400.	675.	7500.	6000.
1876CC	509,000	110.00	125.00	150.	200.	325.	400.	900.	13,000.	—
1876S	5,227,000	60.00	70.00	85.00	100.	120.	210.	480.	7500.	—
1877	3,039,710	60.00	70.00	85.00	105.	130.	210.	525.	7500.	19,000.
1877CC	534,000	110.	125.	150.	200.	325.	500.	1200.	13,000.	—
1877S	9,519,000	60.00	70.00	85.00	100.	120.	210.	480.	7500.	—
1878	900		Proof only				—		—	22,000.
	Impaired Proof		—	—	1000.	1150.	1500.	—	—	—
1878CC	97,000	425.	525.	675.	850.	1350.	2100.	5500.	—	—
1878S	4,162,000	60.00	70.00	85.00	100.	120.	210.	480.	7500.	—
1879	1,541		Proof only				—		—	22,000.
	Impaired Proof		—	—	900.	950.	1100.	—	—	—
1880	1,987		Proof only				—		—	19,500.
	Impaired Proof		—	—	900.	950.	1100.	—	—	—
1881	960		Proof only				—		—	20,000.
	Impaired Proof		—	—	950.	1000.	1250.	—	—	—
1882	1,097		Proof only				—		—	20,000.
	Impaired Proof		—	—	950.	1000.	1250.	—	—	—
1883	979		Proof only				—		—	20,000.
	Impaired Proof		—	—	950.	1000.	1250.	—	—	—
1884	10		Proof only			Superior, Aug. 1990, $75,000.				—
1885	5			Proof only, Stack's, Jan. 1989, $104,500.						—

Morgan

Designer: George T. Morgan. **Size:** 38.1 millimeters. **Weight:** 26.73 grams. **Composition:** 90% silver (.7736 ounces), 10% copper. **Notes:** "65DMPL" values are for coins grading MS-65 deep-mirror prooflike. The 1878 "8 tail feathers" and "7 tail feathers" varieties are distinguished by the number of feathers in the eagle's tail. On the "reverse of 1878" varieties, the top of the top feather in the arrows held by the eagle is straight across and the eagle's breast is concave. On the "reverse of 1879 varieties," the top of the top feather in the arrows held by the eagle is slanted and the eagle's breast is convex. The 1890-CC "tail-bar variety" has a bar extending from the arrow feathers to the wreath on the reverse, the result of a die gouge.

Reverse of 1879

7 over 8 tail feathers

Date	Mintage	G-4	VG-8	F-12	VF-20	XF-40	AU-50	MS-60	MS-63	MS-64	MS-65	65DMPL	Prf-60	Prf-65
1878 8 tail feathers	750,000	7.00	10.00	12.50	14.00	18.00	29.00	43.00	63.00	195.	900.	7450.	925.	5850.
1878 7 tail feathers, reverse of 1878	Inc. Ab.	7.00	9.50	10.00	11.50	12.50	19.00	25.00	45.00	125.	750.	5550.	—	7800.
1878 7 tail feathers, reverse of 1879	Inc. Ab.	7.00	11.00	12.50	15.00	17.50	28.00	31.00	125.	315.	1650.	10,500.	—	—
1878 7 over 8 tail feathers	9,759,550	7.00	12.50	15.00	19.00	28.00	42.00	63.00	135.	350.	1750.	10,500.	—	—
1878CC	2,212,000	12.50	19.00	23.00	27.00	33.00	46.00	70.00	100.	150.	900.	2750.	—	—
1878S	9,744,000	7.00	9.00	9.50	11.50	12.50	15.00	18.00	31.00	48.00	250.	2150.	—	—
1879	14,807,100	7.00	9.00	9.50	10.00	11.00	14.00	24.00	42.00	100.	650.	8800.	850.	4000.
1879CC	756,000	17.00	32.00	48.00	100.	275.	700.	1300.	2200.	3800.	14,000.	—	—	—
1879O	2,887,000	7.00	9.00	9.50	10.00	11.50	17.50	39.00	160.	500.	2650.	15,500.	—	—
1879S reverse of 1878	9,110,000	7.00	11.50	12.50	15.00	19.00	30.00	91.00	280.	1100.	5000.	—	—	—
1879S reverse of 1879	9,110,000	7.00	9.00	10.00	11.00	12.00	14.00	20.00	31.00	43.00	130.	400.	—	—
1880	12,601,335	7.00	9.00	9.50	10.00	11.00	12.50	25.00	38.00	110.	800.	3500.	850.	4000.
1880CC reverse of 1878	591,000	25.00	33.00	53.00	60.00	91.00	125.	145.	240.	490.	1250.	14,500.	—	—
1880CC reverse of 1879	591,000	25.00	33.00	53.00	60.00	88.00	120.	140.	170.	270.	550.	4000.	—	—
1880O	5,305,000	7.00	9.00	9.50	10.00	11.00	22.00	38.00	350.	1350.	16,500.	82,000.	—	—
1880S	8,900,000	7.00	9.00	9.50	10.00	11.00	14.00	20.00	28.00	42.00	130.	350.	—	—
1881	9,163,975	7.00	8.50	9.50	10.00	11.00	14.00	24.00	35.00	95.00	750.	—	850.	4000.
1881CC	296,000	50.00	72.00	100.	125.	130.	140.	170.	180.	220.	400.	1400.	—	—
1881O	5,708,000	7.00	9.00	9.50	10.00	11.00	12.50	20.00	42.00	130.	1150.	—	—	—
1881S	12,760,000	7.00	9.00	10.00	11.00	12.00	13.00	20.00	31.00	43.00	110.	350.	—	—
1882	11,101,100	7.00	9.00	9.50	10.00	11.00	12.50	24.00	38.00	55.00	500.	3800.	850.	4000.
1882CC	1,133,000	14.00	26.00	30.00	36.00	44.00	51.00	60.00	65.00	90.00	200.	600.	—	—
1882O	6,090,000	7.00	9.00	9.50	10.00	11.50	12.50	22.00	45.00	80.00	800.	4500.	—	—
1882S	9,250,000	7.00	9.00	10.00	11.00	12.00	15.00	21.00	31.00	45.00	130.	800.	—	—
1883	12,291,039	7.00	9.00	9.50	10.00	11.00	12.50	22.00	38.00	48.00	140.	1000.	850.	4000.
1883CC	1,204,000	14.00	26.00	29.00	36.00	44.00	50.00	57.00	63.00	75.00	180.	500.	—	—
1883O	8,725,000	7.00	9.00	9.50	10.00	11.00	12.00	17.00	34.00	46.00	120.	750.	—	—
1883S	6,250,000	7.00	10.00	11.50	14.00	19.00	95.00	315.	1200.	3000.	20,000.	—	—	—
1884	14,070,875	7.00	9.00	9.50	10.00	11.00	14.00	20.00	38.00	49.00	250.	2650.	850.	4000.
1884CC	1,136,000	38.00	48.00	52.00	53.00	54.00	55.00	57.00	65.00	80.00	200.	500.	—	—
1884O	9,730,000	7.00	8.50	9.50	10.00	11.00	12.00	20.00	31.00	41.00	120.	450.	—	—
1884S	3,200,000	7.50	10.00	11.50	14.00	28.00	220.	3900.	19,000.	47,000.	107,000.	—	—	—
1885	17,787,767	7.00	9.00	9.50	10.00	11.00	12.00	17.00	32.00	43.00	120.	400.	850.	4000.
1885CC	228,000	150.	165.	175.	185.	190.	200.	210.	215.	270.	450.	950.	—	—
1885O	9,185,000	7.00	9.00	9.50	10.00	11.00	12.00	20.00	31.00	41.00	110.	350.	—	—
1885S	1,497,000	7.50	10.00	14.00	16.50	20.00	44.00	88.00	180.	430.	1300.	9000.	—	—
1886	19,963,886	7.00	9.00	9.50	10.00	11.00	12.00	17.00	31.00	43.00	120.	500.	850.	4000.
1886O	10,710,000	7.00	9.50	11.50	12.50	16.50	49.00	205.	1800.	4550.	38,000.	—	—	—
1886S	750,000	11.00	12.50	15.00	20.00	45.00	50.00	105.	260.	600.	2250.	6500.	—	—
1887	20,290,710	7.00	9.00	9.50	10.00	11.00	12.00	17.00	31.00	43.00	120.	400.	850.	4000.
1887O	11,550,000	7.00	9.00	9.50	10.00	12.50	20.00	34.00	105.	450.	4300.	16,500.	—	—
1887S	1,771,000	7.00	10.00	12.50	14.00	17.50	31.00	60.00	160.	550.	3350.	—	—	—
1888	19,183,833	7.00	9.00	9.50	10.00	11.00	12.00	17.00	35.00	48.00	250.	1500.	850.	4400.
1888O	12,150,000	7.00	9.00	9.50	10.00	11.50	14.00	20.00	36.00	63.00	500.	1650.	—	—
1888S	657,000	8.50	12.50	20.00	24.00	30.00	50.00	100.	245.	600.	2100.	15,000.	—	—
1889	21,726,811	7.00	9.00	9.00	9.50	10.00	11.50	17.00	35.00	45.00	400.	4500.	850.	4000.
1889CC	350,000	95.00	150.	175.	285.	725.	3100.	6600.	11,500.	24,000.	94,500.	—	—	—
1889O	11,875,000	7.00	9.00	10.00	11.00	15.00	30.00	70.00	230.	550.	3650.	19,000.	—	—
1889S	700,000	11.00	12.50	20.00	22.00	25.00	48.00	83.00	180.	330.	1050.	—	—	—
1890	16,802,590	7.00	9.00	9.50	10.00	11.50	12.50	21.00	38.00	200.	3000.	13,000.	850.	4000.
1890CC	2,309,041	12.50	19.00	23.00	29.00	40.00	82.00	205.	380.	700.	4000.	9500.	—	—
1890CC tail bar	Inc. Ab.	12.50	19.00	23.00	29.00	40.00	82.00	205.	380.	700.	4000.	—	—	—
1890O	10,701,000	7.00	9.00	9.50	10.00	12.50	20.00	31.00	69.00	200.	1750.	10,500.	—	—
1890S	8,230,373	7.00	9.00	9.50	11.00	13.00	22.00	38.00	56.00	200.	700.	5000.	—	—
1891	8,694,206	7.00	9.00	10.00	12.00	14.00	22.00	38.00	140.	650.	4500.	—	850.	4000.
1891CC	1,618,000	15.00	22.00	27.00	32.00	40.00	82.00	120.	285.	600.	2150.	15,500.	—	—
1891O	7,954,529	8.50	9.00	10.00	12.50	17.50	30.00	70.00	240.	900.	5500.	25,000.	—	—
1891S	5,296,000	8.50	9.00	9.50	11.00	12.50	21.00	38.00	57.00	220.	900.	7500.	—	—

Silver dollars

Date	Mintage	G-4	VG-8	F-12	VF-20	XF-40	AU-50	MS-60	MS-63	MS-64	MS-65	65DMPL	Prf-60	Prf-65
1892	1,037,245	8.00	12.50	13.50	15.00	17.50	50.00	91.00	315.	600.	2350.	9500.	850.	4000.
1892CC	1,352,000	18.00	26.00	39.00	45.00	82.00	175.	300.	700.	1100.	3400.	—	—	—
1892O	2,744,000	7.00	11.50	12.50	15.00	16.50	44.00	83.00	225.	500.	4500.	23,500.	—	—
1892S	1,200,000	12.00	13.00	16.00	34.00	105.	2450.	10,000.	19,000.	28,500.	50,000.	—	—	—
1893	378,792	29.00	44.00	48.00	54.00	68.00	145.	280.	650.	1200.	5000.	—	850.	4000.
1893CC	677,000	30.00	48.00	72.00	115.	410.	725.	1070.	2750.	5400.	33,000.	—	—	—
1893O	300,000	55.00	78.00	83.00	90.00	150.	365.	1250.	3950.	16,500.	82,000.	—	—	—
1893S	100,000	380.	610.	875.	1100.	3000.	12,500.	27,500.	44,000.	63,000.	138,500.	—	—	—
1894	110,972	135.	185.	225.	250.	290.	515.	800.	2400.	3800.	10,500.	—	1050.	4100.
1894O	1,723,000	8.00	15.00	19.00	24.00	27.00	115.	600.	2300.	4400.	24,000.	—	—	—
1894S	1,260,000	11.50	15.00	22.00	33.00	77.00	155.	300.	690.	1100.	3400.	14,000.	—	—
1895	12,880	Proof only		6250.	9500.	12,000.	13,000.	—	—	—	—	—	14,000.	26,000.
1895O	450,000	46.00	91.00	95.00	105.	165.	695.	6950.	14,500.	21,000.	33,000.	—	—	—
1895S	400,000	90.00	115.	145.	190.	360.	565.	1100.	2750.	3750.	17,500.	—	—	—
1896	9,967,762	7.00	9.00	9.50	10.00	11.00	12.50	20.00	31.00	48.00	200.	950.	850.	4000.
1896O	4,900,000	7.00	9.00	11.00	12.00	15.00	88.00	720.	5550.	19,500.	35,500.	—	—	—
1896S	5,000,000	8.00	10.00	17.50	35.00	115.	300.	640.	1150.	2150.	5500.	—	—	—
1897	2,822,731	7.00	9.00	9.50	10.00	11.00	12.50	17.00	38.00	46.00	300.	2150.	850.	4800.
1897O	4,004,000	7.00	9.00	10.00	11.50	15.00	70.00	600.	2550.	12,000.	23,500.	—	—	—
1897S	5,825,000	7.00	9.00	10.00	11.00	13.00	20.00	35.00	46.00	100.	500.	1650.	—	—
1898	5,884,735	7.00	9.00	9.50	10.00	11.00	12.00	17.00	36.00	50.00	250.	1650.	850.	4000.
1898O	4,440,000	8.00	10.00	11.00	12.00	13.00	14.00	17.00	32.00	43.00	120.	700.	—	—
1898S	4,102,000	7.00	11.50	12.50	16.50	24.00	50.00	110.	240.	450.	1050.	7500.	—	—
1899	330,846	15.00	19.00	26.00	30.00	40.00	56.00	76.00	100.	180.	600.	2250.	850.	5850.
1899O	12,290,000	7.00	9.00	9.50	10.00	11.00	12.00	17.00	45.00	56.00	120.	700.	—	—
1899S	2,562,000	7.00	11.50	12.50	17.50	25.00	56.00	105.	230.	500.	1050.	7050.	—	—
1900	8,880,938	7.00	8.50	9.00	9.50	10.00	11.50	20.00	35.00	48.00	200.	6500.	850.	4000.
1900O	12,590,000	7.00	8.00	9.00	10.00	12.00	13.00	20.00	38.00	46.00	130.	2250.	—	—
1900O/CC	1490.	11.00	16.50	19.00	22.00	27.00	75.00	170.	300.	490.	1300.	—	—	—
1900S	3,540,000	7.00	10.00	12.50	16.50	25.00	44.00	91.00	175.	350.	1400.	6300.	—	—
1901	6,962,813	8.00	14.00	16.50	25.00	38.00	155.	1350.	7000.	25,000.	126,000.	—	910.	5850.
1901O	13,320,000	7.00	9.00	9.50	10.00	11.00	12.50	21.00	35.00	48.00	200.	3000.	—	—
1901S	2,284,000	7.50	12.50	15.00	21.00	38.00	95.00	215.	390.	700.	2500.	—	—	—
1902	7,994,777	7.00	9.50	10.00	11.00	12.00	22.00	36.00	55.00	110.	550.	—	850.	4000.
1902O	8,636,000	7.00	9.00	9.50	10.00	11.00	12.00	17.00	34.00	48.00	150.	3500.	—	—
1902S	1,530,000	13.00	17.00	30.00	44.00	57.00	88.00	140.	250.	500.	2300.	—	—	—
1903	4,652,755	7.00	12.50	14.00	15.00	16.50	19.00	29.00	42.00	57.00	200.	8450.	850.	4000.
1903O	4,450,000	100.	110.	120.	125.	130.	135.	145.	160.	200.	350.	4150.	—	—
1903S	1,241,000	10.00	15.00	19.00	56.00	215.	785.	1900.	3450.	3900.	5300.	—	—	—
1904	2,788,650	7.00	9.50	10.00	11.50	15.00	30.00	57.00	140.	500.	2600.	—	850.	4000.
1904O	3,720,000	7.00	9.50	10.00	11.00	12.00	13.00	17.00	31.00	43.00	130.	600.	—	—
1904S	2,304,000	9.00	12.50	16.50	32.00	150.	480.	800.	1500.	2250.	5000.	—	—	—
1921	44,690,000	6.50	7.00	7.50	8.00	9.00	9.50	13.00	25.00	32.00	150.	—	—	—
1921D	20,345,000	6.50	7.00	7.50	8.00	9.00	11.00	25.00	31.00	62.00	350.	6000.	—	—
1921S	21,695,000	6.50	7.00	7.50	8.00	9.00	11.00	25.00	38.00	140.	1150.	—	—	—

Peace

Designer: Anthony DeFrancisci. **Size:** 38.1 millimeters. **Weight:** 26.73 grams. **Composition:** 90% silver (.7736 ounces), 10% copper.

Mintmark

Date	Mintage	G-4	VG-8	F-12	VF-20	XF-40	AU-50	MS-60	MS-63	MS-64	MS-65
1921	1,006,473	15.00	20.00	25.00	34.00	41.00	75.00	120.	225.	400.	1750.
1922	51,737,000	6.50	7.00	7.50	8.00	9.00	10.00	11.00	20.00	40.00	200.
1922D	15,063,000	6.50	7.00	7.50	8.00	9.00	10.00	17.00	30.00	70.00	400.
1922S	17,475,000	6.50	7.00	7.50	8.00	9.00	10.00	20.00	40.00	285.	2000.
1923	30,800,000	6.50	7.00	7.50	8.00	9.00	10.00	11.00	20.00	40.00	200.
1923D	6,811,000	6.50	7.00	7.50	8.00	9.00	14.00	25.00	65.00	200.	1650.
1923S	19,020,000	6.50	7.00	7.50	8.00	9.00	10.00	20.00	75.00	350.	4500.
1924	11,811,000	6.50	7.00	7.50	8.00	9.00	10.00	11.00	20.00	40.00	300.
1924S	1,728,000	7.00	8.50	9.50	11.50	15.00	47.00	125.	390.	1000.	4000.
1925	10,198,000	6.50	7.00	7.50	8.00	9.00	10.00	11.00	20.00	40.00	200.
1925S	1,610,000	6.50	7.00	7.50	10.00	12.50	26.00	50.00	110.	550.	6500.
1926	1,939,000	6.50	7.00	7.50	9.00	11.00	15.00	20.00	25.00	50.00	450.
1926D	2,348,700	6.50	7.00	7.50	9.00	11.50	25.00	45.00	100.	210.	700.
1926S	6,980,000	6.50	7.00	7.50	9.00	11.50	16.00	27.00	50.00	190.	1100.
1927	848,000	8.00	12.50	14.00	16.50	21.00	30.00	45.00	85.00	300.	2150.
1927D	1,268,900	7.50	11.50	12.50	14.00	20.00	69.00	110.	200.	550.	3600.
1927S	866,000	9.00	11.50	12.50	14.00	19.00	55.00	85.00	155.	650.	4000.
1928	360,649	65.00	90.00	95.00	100.	110.	140.	160.	250.	500.	2250.
1928S	1,632,000	6.50	10.00	11.50	12.50	15.00	38.00	70.00	280.	1000.	10,000.
1934	954,057	8.00	12.50	14.00	15.00	20.00	32.00	55.00	100.	200.	1050.
1934D	1,569,500	6.50	11.50	12.50	14.00	17.50	32.00	75.00	155.	500.	1750.
1934S	1,011,000	8.00	11.50	14.00	38.00	150.	440.	1000.	2250.	3150.	5000.
1935	1,576,000	6.50	9.00	10.00	11.50	15.00	22.00	41.00	75.00	200.	600.
1935S	1,964,000	6.50	9.00	10.00	12.50	16.50	60.00	105.	250.	300.	800.

Clad dollars

Eisenhower

Designer: Frank Gasparro. **Size:** 38.1 millimeters. **Weight:** 24.59 grams (silver issues) and 22.58 grams (copper-nickel issues). **Clad composition:** 75% copper and 25% nickel bonded to a pure copper core. **Silver clad composition:** clad layers of 80% copper and 20% silver bonded to a core of 79.1% copper and 20.9% silver (.3163 total ounces of silver).

Date	Mintage	(Proof)	MS-65	Prf-65
1971	47,799,000	—	2.80	—
1971D	68,587,424	—	1.70	—
1971S silver	6,868,530	(4,265,234)	3.80	4.10
1972	75,890,000	—	1.60	—
1972D	92,548,511	—	1.60	—
1972S silver	2,193,056	(1,811,631)	4.00	4.50
1973	2,000,056	—	3.80	—
1973D	2,000,000	—	3.80	—
1973S silver	1,833,140	(1,005,617)	3.90	24.00
1973S clad	—	2,769,624	—	4.75
1974	27,366,000	—	1.60	—
1974D	35,466,000	—	1.70	—
1974S silver	1,720,000	(1,306,579)	3.90	7.00
1974S clad	—	(2,617,350)	—	4.00

Type I Bicentennial reverse

Type II Bicentennial reverse

Bicentennial design

Reverse designer: Dennis R. Williams. **Silver composition:** 40% silver (.3163 ounces), 60% copper. **Notes:** In 1976 the lettering on the reverse was changed to thinner letters, resulting in Type I and Type II varieties for that year.

Date	Mintage	(Proof)	MS-65	Prf-65
1976 Type I	117,337,000	—	2.50	—
1976 Type II	Inc. Ab.	—	1.60	—
1976D Type I	103,228,274	—	1.80	—
1976D Type II	Inc. Ab.	—	1.60	—
1976S cld Type I	—	(2,909,369)	—	4.00
1976S cld Type II	—	(4,149,730)	—	3.80
1976S silver	11,000,000	(4,000,000)	6.00	7.60

Regular design resumed

Date	Mintage	(Proof)	MS-65	Prf-65
1977	12,596,000	—	1.60	—
1977D	32,983,006	—	1.60	—
1977S clad	—	(3,251,152)	—	3.50
1978	25,702,000	—	1.70	—
1978D	33,012,890	—	1.60	—
1978S clad	—	(3,127,788)	—	3.30

Anthony

Designer: Frank Gasparro. **Size:** 26.5 millimeters. **Weight:** 8.1 grams. **Composition:** clad layers of 75% copper and 25% nickel bonded to a pure copper core. **Notes:** The 1979-S and 1981-S Type II coins have a clearer mintmark than the Type I varieties for those years.

Date	Mintage	MS-65	Date	Mintage	MS-65
1979P	360,222,000	1.45	1979S Prf. Type II	—	63.00
1979D	288,015,744	1.40	1980P	27,610,000	1.45
1979S	109,576,000	1.55	1980D	41,628,708	1.45
1979S Prf. Type I	3,677,175	3.80	1980S	20,422,000	1.45

Clad dollars

Mintmark

Date	Mintage	MS-65	Date	Mintage	MS-65
1980S Prf.	3,547,030	4.00	1981S	3,492,000	2.40
1981P	3,000,000	2.50	1981S Prf.Type I	4,063,083	5.75
1981D	3,250,000	2.50	1981S Prf. Type II	—	86.00

Type coins

Description	MS-64	Proof-64
Draped Bust half cents (red & brown)	4150.	—
Classic Head half cents (red & brown)	650.	—
Braided Hair half cents (red & brown)	650.	—
Draped Bust large cents (red & brown)	9500.	—
Classic Head large cents (red & brown)	11,500.	—
Coronet large cents (red & brown)	950.	—
Braided Hair large cents (red & brown)	350.	—
Flying Eagle cents	750.	4550.
Indian Head cents, 1859 copper-nickel	650.	2350.
Indian Head cents, 1860-1864 copper-nickel	250.	900.
Indian Head cents, bronze (red & brown)	55.00	175.
Two-cent (red & brown)	180.	550.
Nickel three-cent	290.	400.
Silver three-cent, Type I	600.	—
Silver three-cent, Type II	1950.	3500.
Silver three-cent, Type III	500.	650.
Flowing Hair half dimes	14,500.	—
Draped Bust half dimes, small eagle	22,500.	—
Draped Bust half dimes, heraldic eagle	16,500.	—
Liberty Cap half dimes	1050.	—
Seated Liberty half dimes, no stars	1800.	—
Seated Liberty half dimes, no drapery	700.	—
Seated Liberty half dimes, stars around rim	650.	2350.
Seated Liberty half dimes, with arrows	1200.	—
Seated Liberty half dimes, obverse legend	700.	750.
Shield nickels, with rays	650.	2350.
Shield nickels, no rays	300.	400.
Liberty nickels, no "Cents"	90.00	400.
Liberty nickels, with "Cents"	190.	250.
Buffalo nickels, Type I	70.00	1250.
Buffalo nickels, Type II	—	900.
Jefferson nickels, wartime	—	100.
Draped Bust dimes, small eagle	16,500.	—
Draped Bust dimes, heraldic eagle	16,500.	—
Liberty Cap dimes, 1809-1827 (large size)	5000.	—
Liberty Cap dimes, 1828-1837 (reduced size)	2250.	—
Seated Liberty dimes, no stars	3300.	—
Seated Liberty dimes, no drapery	1250.	—
Seated Liberty dimes, stars around rim	1150.	2000.
Seated Liberty dimes, 1853-1855 with arrows	1650.	19,000.
Seated Liberty dimes, obverse legend	350.	700.
Seated Liberty dimes, 1873-1874 with arrows	2900.	1700.
Barber dimes	300.	1000.
Mercury dimes	—	175.
Twenty-cent	2250.	3000.
Draped Bust quarters, heraldic eagle	25,000.	—
Liberty Cap quarters, 1815-1828 (large size)	5000.	—
Liberty Cap quarters, 1831-1838 (reduced size)	3900.	—
Seated Liberty quarters, no drapery	7000.	—
Seated Liberty quarters, no motto	1300.	2000.
Seated Liberty quarters, arrows and rays	5000.	—
Seated Liberty quarters, 1854-1855, with arrows	4050.	—
Seated Liberty quarters, with motto	900.	1050.
Seated Liberty quarters, 1873-1874, with arrows	2250.	2900.
Barber quarters	600.	1250.
Standing Liberty quarters, Type I, full head	380.	—
Standing Liberty quarters, Type II	210.	—
Standing Liberty quarters, Type II, full head	350.	—
Flowing Hair half dollars	94,500.	—
Draped Bust half dollars, heraldic eagle	22,500.	—
Liberty Cap half dollars	2750.	—
Liberty Cap half dollars, reeded edge	4500.	—
Seated Liberty half dollars, no drapery	44,000.	—
Seated Liberty half dollars, no motto	2100.	1900.
Seated Liberty half dollars, arrows and rays	8000.	—
Seated Liberty half dollars, 1854-1855, with arrows	2750.	—
Seated Liberty half dollars, with motto	1300.	1250.
Seated Liberty half dollars, 1873-1874, with arrows	5000.	3150.
Barber half dollars	1300.	1650.
Walking Liberty half dollars	—	380.
Draped Bust dollars, small eagle	88,000.	—
Draped Bust dollars, heraldic eagle	27,500.	—
Seated Liberty dollars, no motto	6000.	6500.
Seated Liberty dollars, with motto	6000.	5500.
Morgan dollars	—	2350.
Trade dollars	2750.	3100.

Gold dollars

Liberty Head

Mintmark

Designer: James B. Longacre. **Size:** 13 millimeters. **Weight:** 1.672 grams. **Composition:** 90% gold (.0484 ounces), 10% copper. **Notes:** On the "closed wreath" varieties of 1849, the wreath on the reverse extends closer to the numeral 1.

Date	Mintage	F-12	VF-20	XF-40	AU-50	MS-60
1849 open wreath	688,567	120.	145.	160.	200.	500.
1849 closed wreath	Inc. Ab.	120.	145.	160.	200.	500.
1849C closed wreath	11,634	285.	475.	875.	2200.	4200.
1849C open wreath	Inc. Ab.			Extremely Rare		—
1849D open wreath	21,588	285.	410.	750.	1250.	2900.
1849O open wreath	215,000	135.	165.	210.	440.	910.
1850	481,953	115.	150.	170.	190.	420.
1850C	6,966	390.	585.	975.	2200.	6200.
1850D	8,382	350.	550.	1150.	1950.	6000.
1850O	14,000	195.	260.	370.	775.	2700.
1851	3,317,671	115.	150.	170.	190.	420.
1851C	41,267	275.	450.	650.	1150.	2300.
1851D	9,882	275.	425.	775.	1500.	3800.
1851O	290,000	150.	175.	195.	250.	690.
1852	2,045,351	115.	150.	170.	190.	420.
1852C	9,434	275.	390.	775.	1300.	3200.
1852D	6,360	325.	700.	1375.	2000.	5700.
1852O	140,000	140.	165.	195.	300.	1050.
1853	4,076,051	115.	150.	170.	190.	420.
1853C	11,515	240.	490.	1000.	1650.	5200.
1853D	6,583	340.	700.	1075.	2300.	6500.
1853O	290,000	140.	160.	195.	220.	585.
1854	736,709	115.	150.	170.	190.	420.
1854D	2,935	550.	890.	1850.	6500.	14,500.
1854S	14,632	260.	315.	440.	725.	1800.

Small Indian Head

Designer: James B. Longacre. **Size:** 15 millimeters. **Weight:** 1.672 grams. **Composition:** 90% gold (.0484 ounces), 10% copper.

Date	Mintage	F-12	VF-20	XF-40	AU-50	MS-60
1854	902,736	210.	290.	520.	750.	3000.
1855	758,269	210.	290.	520.	750.	3000.
1855C	9,803	675.	975.	2350.	5150.	10,000.
1855D	1,811	1400.	2300.	4700.	9500.	19,500.
1855O	55,000	370.	575.	800.	1500.	7700.
1856S	24,600	390.	650.	1250.	2500.	8000.

Large Indian Head

Designer: James B. Longacre. **Size:** 15 millimeters. **Weight:** 1.672 grams. **Composition:** 90% gold (.0484 ounces), 10% copper. **Notes:** The 1856 varieties are distinguished by whether the 5 in the date is slanted or upright. The 1873 varieties are distinguished by the amount of space between the upper left and lower left serifs in the 3.

Date	Mintage	F-12	VF-20	XF-40	AU-50	MS-60	Prf-65
1856 upright 5	1,762,936	130.	160.	180.	325.	585.	—
1856 slanted 5	Inc. Ab.	120.	140.	170.	190.	370.	—
1856D	1,460	2600.	3900.	7000.	12,250.	22,500.	—
1857	774,789	120.	140.	170.	190.	375.	—
1857C	13,280	350.	575.	1150.	2850.	9750.	—
1857D	3,533	285.	850.	1800.	3800.	11,000.	—
1857S	10,000	285.	525.	750.	1950.	8550.	—
1858	117,995	120.	140.	170.	190.	375.	19,000.
1858D	3,477	390.	775.	1300.	2600.	7500.	—
1858S	10,000	300.	400.	625.	1800.	6500.	—
1859	168,244	120.	140.	160.	190.	425.	12,000.
1859C	5,235	300.	490.	1250.	2600.	10,500.	—
1859D	4,952	475.	875.	1400.	2700.	7500.	—
1859S	15,000	260.	310.	550.	1950.	7000.	—
1860	36,668	120.	140.	170.	190.	375.	12,000.
1860D	1,566	2300.	2750.	4700.	7700.	25,000.	—
1860S	13,000	200.	325.	400.	800.	2850.	—
1861	527,499	120.	140.	170.	190.	375.	18,000.
1861D	Unrecorded	4900.	6800.	13,500.	19,500.	39,500.	—
1862	1,361,390	120.	140.	170.	190.	375.	12,000.
1863	6,250	360.	450.	875.	1900.	4400.	12,000.
1864	5,950	285.	370.	475.	750.	1500.	12,000.
1865	3,725	285.	370.	585.	850.	1600.	12,000.
1866	7,130	290.	380.	450.	700.	1200.	12,000.
1867	5,250	345.	440.	550.	750.	1200.	12,000.
1868	10,525	260.	295.	400.	585.	1200.	12,000.
1869	5,925	325.	360.	520.	800.	1300.	12,000.
1870	6,335	260.	285.	425.	520.	1050.	12,000.
1870S	3,000	350.	475.	800.	1400.	3000.	—
1871	3,930	260.	285.	440.	525.	750.	18,000.
1872	3,530	285.	315.	480.	575.	900.	18,000.
1873 closed 3	125,125	325.	425.	850.	1200.	3250.	18,000.
1873 open 3	Inc. Ab.	120.	140.	170.	190.	425.	—
1874	198,820	120.	140.	170.	190.	425.	19,000.
1875	420	1800.	2500.	4200.	5900.	9100.	45,000.
1876	3,245	220.	250.	360.	475.	890.	12,000.
1877	3,920	150.	175.	350.	480.	760.	24,000.
1878	3,020	180.	215.	365.	470.	795.	12,000.
1879	3,030	165.	190.	300.	400.	550.	12,000.
1880	1,636	145.	160.	200.	235.	450.	12,000.
1881	7,707	145.	160.	200.	235.	450.	12,000.
1882	5,125	160.	175.	210.	235.	450.	12,000.
1883	11,007	145.	165.	200.	235.	450.	12,000.
1884	6,236	140.	160.	190.	230.	450.	12,000.
1885	12,261	145.	160.	200.	235.	450.	12,000.
1886	6,016	145.	165.	200.	235.	450.	12,000.
1887	8,543	145.	165.	200.	235.	450.	12,000.
1888	16,580	145.	165.	200.	235.	450.	12,000.
1889	30,729	145.	165.	200.	235.	365.	12,000.

Gold $2.50 (Quarter eagle)

Liberty Cap

Designer: Robert Scot. **Size:** 20 millimeters. **Weight:** 4.37 grams. **Composition:** 91.67% gold (.1289 ounces), 8.33% copper. **Notes:** The 1796 "no-stars" variety does not have stars on the obverse. The 1804 varieties are distinguished by the number of stars on the obverse.

Date	Mintage	F-12	VF-20	XF-40	MS-60
1796 no stars	963	9500.	21,000.	31,000.	100,000.
1796 stars	432	7500.	9000.	14,000.	85,000.
1797	427	7500.	9500.	14,500.	52,000.
1798	1,094	2800.	4000.	6250.	28,000.
1802/1	3,035	2800.	3750.	5000.	14,500.
1804 13-star reverse	3,327	13,000.	18,500.	30,000.	—
1804 14-star reverse	Inc. Ab.	2800.	3750.	5750.	16,000.
1805	1,781	2800.	3750.	5400.	18,500.
1806/4	1,616	2800.	3750.	5000.	14,500.
1806/5	Inc. Ab.	4750.	6500.	12,500.	—
1807	6,812	2800.	3500.	4500.	14,500.

Turban Head

Designer: John Reich. **Sizes:** 20 millimeters (1808), 18.5 millimeters (1821-1827), and 18.2 millimeters (1829-1834). **Weight:** 4.37 grams. **Composition:** 91.67% gold (.1289 ounces), 8.33% copper.

Date	Mintage	F-12	VF-20	XF-40	MS-60
1808	2,710	9000.	12,500.	22,000.	45,000.
1821	6,448	3250.	4000.	5750.	14,000.
1824/21	2,600	3250.	4000.	5000.	10,500.

Gold $2.50

Date	Mintage	F-12	VF-20	XF-40	MS-60
1825	4,434	3250.	4000.	5750.	10,500.
1826/25	760	3500.	5500.	7500.	19,000.
1827	2,800	3250.	4000.	6300.	14,000.
1829	3,403	3250.	3750.	4500.	8500.
1830	4,540	3250.	3750.	4500.	8500.
1831	4,520	3250.	3750.	4500.	8500.
1832	4,400	3250.	3750.	4500.	8500.
1833	4,160	3250.	3750.	4500.	8500.
1834	4,000	6750.	10,000.	16,500.	37,000.

Liberty Without Turban

Mintmark

Designer: William Kneass. **Size:** 18.2 millimeters. **Weight:** 4.18 grams. **Composition:** 89.92% gold (.1209 ounces), 10.08% copper.

Date	Mintage	VF-20	XF-40	AU-50	MS-60	MS-65
1834	112,234	300.	550.	1100.	3000.	37,000.
1835	131,402	265.	500.	900.	2850.	37,000.
1836	547,986	255.	500.	900.	2850.	37,000.
1837	45,080	265.	500.	900.	2850.	37,000.
1838	47,030	265.	500.	900.	2850.	37,000.
1838C	7,880	1000.	2300.	5200.	19,500.	—
1839	27,021	265.	500.	1800.	6000.	37,000.
1839C	18,140	550.	1800.	3500.	13,600.	—
1839D	13,674	950.	2750.	5750.	18,000.	—
1839O	17,781	500.	1250.	2600.	6500.	55,000.

Coronet Head

1848 "Cal."

Designer: Christian Gobrecht. **Size:** 18 millimeters. **Weight:** 4.18 grams. **Composition:** 90% gold (.121 ounces), 10% copper. **Notes:** Varieties for 1843 are distinguished by the size of the numerals in the date. One 1848 variety has "Cal." inscribed on the reverse, indicating it was made from California gold. The 1873 "closed-3" and "open-3" varieties are distinguished by the amount of space between the upper left and lower left serifs in the 3 in the date.

Date	Mintage	F-12	VF-20	XF-40	AU-50	MS-60	Prf-65
1840	18,859	180.	245.	700.	1625.	3600.	—
1840C	12,822	325.	600.	1250.	4000.	12,000.	—
1840D	3,532	500.	2000.	4100.	9500.	—	—
1840O	33,580	225.	250.	900.	1800.	7500.	—
1841	—	—	—	30,000.	85,000.	—	—
1841C	10,281	275.	475.	1150.	3250.	16,000.	—
1841D	4,164	800.	1375.	2900.	7500.	15,500.	—
1842	2,823	350.	850.	3000.	6250.	14,500.	—
1842C	6,729	525.	1200.	2600.	5000.	14,500.	—
1842D	4,643	800.	1500.	2900.	9500.	16,000.	—
1842O	19,800	375.	375.	1125.	2900.	12,000.	—
1843	100,546	200.	225.	250.	375.	750.	—
1843C sm. dt.	26,064	750.	2500.	4900.	10,000.	24,000.	—
1843C lg. dt.	Inc. Ab.	300.	525.	900.	2850.	8000.	—
1843D	36,209	300.	650.	1100.	2500.	7500.	—
1843O sm. dt.	288,002	200.	225.	325.	450.	1150.	—
1843O lg. dt.	76,000	250.	350.	450.	1000.	2000.	—
1844	6,784	200.	400.	850.	2500.	8000.	—
1844C	11,622	325.	675.	1550.	6500.	16,000.	—
1844D	17,332	325.	625.	1200.	2700.	6500.	—
1845	91,051	200.	275.	325.	500.	1100.	—
1845D	19,460	325.	650.	1700.	2500.	8500.	—
1845O	4,000	750.	1500.	2400.	6000.	14,000.	—

Date	Mintage	F-12	VF-20	XF-40	AU-50	MS-60	Prf-65
1846	21,598	300.	400.	725.	2400.	7250.	—
1846C	4,808	275.	1000.	2000.	5000.	14,000.	—
1846D	19,303	350.	750.	1200.	2600.	7750.	—
1846O	66,000	200.	300.	525.	1600.	5000.	—
1847	29,814	200.	275.	400.	1100.	3800.	—
1847C	23,226	300.	600.	1150.	2300.	7450.	—
1847D	15,784	300.	600.	1250.	2750.	7500.	—
1847O	124,000	200.	275.	425.	1150.	3500.	
1848	7,497	350.	625.	1000.	3500.	8200.	—
1848 "Cal."	1,389	5000.	8000.	14,000.	17,000.	30,000.	—
1848C	16,788	300.	750.	1500.	3200.	9000.	—
1848D	13,771	350.	600.	1325.	2350.	8000.	—
1849	23,294	300.	500.	650.	1400.	3600.	—
1849C	10,220	325.	600.	1400.	4750.	19,000.	—
1849D	10,945	400.	700.	1550.	3150.	13,000.	—
1850	252,923	175.	200.	225.	300.	900.	—
1850C	9,148	275.	600.	1400.	3250.	14,000.	—
1850D	12,148	275.	700.	1200.	2850.	14,000.	—
1850O	84,000	200.	300.	575.	1400.	4400.	—
1851	1,372,748	135.	150.	185.	235.	300.	—
1851C	14,923	375.	675.	1400.	3650.	12,500.	—
1851D	11,264	275.	650.	1300.	3450.	12,000.	—
1851O	148,000	200.	250.	350.	1200.	4750.	—
1852	1,159,681	135.	150.	185.	235.	350.	—
1852C	9,772	350.	625.	1550.	4000.	17,000.	—
1852D	4,078	450.	850.	2400.	6500.	18,000.	—
1852O	140,000	200.	250.	300.	975.	1700.	—
1853	1,404,668	175.	185.	210.	250.	450.	—
1853D	3,178	500.	1350.	2650.	5000.	16,000.	—
1854	596,258	175.	185.	210.	250.	425.	—
1854C	7,295	250.	625.	1650.	4100.	14,000.	—
1854D	1,760	1400.	2700.	5000.	8000.	18,000.	—
1854O	153,000	200.	250.	300.	650.	1700.	—
1854S	246	18,000.	40,000.	65,000.	95,000.	—	—
1855	235,480	175.	185.	210.	275.	600.	—
1855C	3,677	500.	1300.	2850.	4800.	17,000.	—
1855D	1,123	2500.	3750.	7500.	14,000.	23,000.	—
1856	384,240	175.	185.	200.	225.	275.	32,000.
1856C	7,913	500.	850.	2000.	4500.	13,500.	—
1856D	874	4500.	7250.	13,000.	23,000.	45,000.	—
1856O	21,100	200.	250.	715.	2250.	7000.	—
1856S	71,120	200.	250.	435.	1050.	7000.	—
1857	214,130	175.	185.	210.	250.	390.	—
1857D	2,364	565.	1500.	3000.	4000.	10,000.	—
1857O	34,000	200.	250.	350.	1650.	6000.	—
1857S	69,200	200.	325.	500.	1600.	5000.	—
1858	47,377	200.	250.	300.	400.	2000.	20,000.
1858C	9,056	265.	600.	1300.	3000.	9000.	—
1859	39,444	200.	250.	300.	720.	1350.	20,000.
1859D	2,244	600.	1350.	2300.	7000.	23,000.	—
1859S	15,200	200.	300.	1200.	4000.	6250.	—
1860	22,675	200.	250.	300.	600.	1250.	20,000
1860C	7,469	350.	750.	2250.	6000.	19,500.	—
1860S	35,600	200.	250.	700.	1800.	5000.	—
1861	1,283,878	150.	175.	200.	225.	350.	20,000.
1861S	24,000	200.	400.	1700.	3400.	5500.	—
1862	98,543	200.	250.	300.	550.	1450.	20,000.
1862/1	Inc. Ab.	—	850.	1900.	5750.	13,500.	—
1862S	8,000	650.	950.	2500.	5950.	15,500.	—
1863	30			RARCOA, Aug. 1990, proof only, $80,000.			
1863S	10,800	300.	465.	1700.	3000.	6600.	—
1864	2,874	2000.	5400.	11,500.	24,000.	42,000.	20,000.
1865	1,545	1550.	4325.	9600.	17,000.	32,000.	37,500.
1865S	23,376	200.	225.	630.	2000.	4500.	—
1866	3,110	550.	1200.	5000.	11,000.	20,000.	20,000.
1866S	38,960	200.	300.	975.	2600.	8400.	—
1867	3,250	225.	360.	840.	1700.	5500.	20,000.
1867S	28,000	200.	250.	875.	2400.	5000.	—
1868	3,625	200.	300.	500.	1000.	3000.	20,000
1868S	34,000	200.	250.	500.	1500.	5000.	—
1869	4,345	200.	250.	500.	850.	4800.	20,000.
1869S	29,500	200.	250.	600.	1200.	4500.	—
1870	4,555	210.	275.	550.	1000.	3800.	20,000.
1870S	16,000	200.	285.	350.	1300.	5500.	—
1871	5,350	210.	275.	350.	900.	2400.	20,000.
1871S	22,000	225.	285.	350.	800.	3000.	—
1872	3,030	225.	360.	825.	2000.	8000.	20,000.
1872S	18,000	225.	285.	500.	1375.	4300.	—
1873 closed 3	178,025	200.	250.	300.	475.	1300.	20,000.
1873 open 3	Inc. Ab.	175.	200.	225.	250.	325.	—
1873S	27,000	200.	250.	575.	1100.	4000.	—
1874	3,940	200.	250.	500.	1000.	3700.	20,000.
1875	420	1500.	3600.	5250.	9000.	16,000.	32,000.
1875S	11,600	200.	250.	400.	800.	4500.	—
1876	4,221	210.	300.	750.	1600.	6500.	20,000.
1876S	5,000	210.	250.	800.	1800.	6000.	—
1877	1,652	325.	450.	800.	1700.	3500.	48,000.
1877S	35,400	125.	180.	210.	250.	850.	—
1878	286,260	125.	150.	160.	180.	245.	18,000.
1878S	178,000	125.	150.	160.	210.	425.	—
1879	88,990	125.	150.	160.	180.	270.	18,000.
1879S	43,500	125.	150.	160.	1000.	2500.	—
1880	2,996	215.	250.	350.	600.	1500.	20,000.
1881	691	700.	1350.	4500.	7500.	14,500.	20,000
1882	4,067	125.	225.	300.	350.	1200.	18,000
1883	2,002	125.	225.	400.	1000.	2700.	20,000
1884	2,023	125.	225.	400.	500.	2000.	32,000
1885	887	500.	800.	1700.	3000.	7500.	32,000
1886	4,088	125.	210.	300.	550.	1400.	18,000
1887	6,282	125.	190.	225.	500.	1300.	18,000
1888	16,098	125.	190.	225.	300.	525.	18,000

Gold $2.50

Date	Mintage	F-12	VF-20	XF-40	AU-50	MS-60	Prf-65
1889	17,648	125.	190.	250.	275.	450.	18,000.
1890	8,813	125.	190.	280.	295.	475.	18,000.
1891	11,040	125.	190.	250.	275.	450.	18,000.
1892	2,545	135.	195.	200.	325.	950.	18,000.
1893	30,106	125.	150.	200.	260.	300.	18,000.
1894	4,122	125.	150.	200.	325.	850.	18,000.
1895	6,199	125.	150.	200.	270.	425.	18,000.
1896	19,202	125.	150.	160.	180.	245.	18,000.
1897	29,904	125.	150.	160.	180.	245.	18,000.
1898	24,165	125.	150.	160.	180.	245.	18,000.
1899	27,350	125.	150.	160.	180.	245.	18,000.
1900	67,205	125.	150.	160.	180.	245.	18,000.
1901	91,322	125.	150.	160.	180.	245.	18,000.
1902	133,733	125.	150.	160.	180.	245.	16,000.
1903	201,257	125.	150.	160.	180.	245.	16,000.
1904	160,960	125.	150.	160.	180.	245.	16,000.
1905	217,944	125.	150.	160.	180.	245.	16,000.
1906	176,490	125.	150.	160.	180.	245.	16,000.
1907	336,448	125.	150.	160.	180.	245.	16,000.

Indian Head

Mintmark

Designer: Bela Lyon Pratt. **Size:** 18 millimeters. **Weight:** 4.18 grams. **Composition:** 90% gold (.121 ounces), 10% copper.

Date	Mintage	VF-20	XF-40	AU-50	MS-60	MS-63	MS-65	Prf-65
1908	565,057	135.	155.	175.	260.	1050.	6000.	14,400.
1909	441,899	135.	155.	175.	310.	1150.	6600.	19,000.
1910	492,682	135.	155.	175.	295.	1250.	8400.	15,000.
1911	704,191	135.	155.	175.	290.	1150.	9100.	14,400.
1911D	55,680	700.	950.	1150.	2700.	6400.	30,000.	—
1912	616,197	135.	160.	180.	300.	1200.	12,250.	15,000.
1913	722,165	135.	155.	175.	265.	1200.	10,250.	14,400.
1914	240,117	140.	160.	190.	550.	2800.	19,000.	15,500.
1914D	448,000	135.	155.	175.	350.	1900.	19,000.	—
1915	606,100	135.	155.	175.	265.	1200.	6000.	15,000
1925D	578,000	135.	155.	175.	220.	1050.	6350.	—
1926	446,000	135.	155.	175.	220.	1050.	6000.	—
1927	388,000	135.	155.	175.	220.	1050.	6500.	—
1928	416,000	135.	155.	175.	220.	1050.	6700.	—
1929	532,000	135.	155.	175.	220.	1050.	9250.	—

Gold $3

Designer: James B. Longacre. **Size:** 20.5 millimeters. **Weight:** 5.015 grams. **Composition:** 90% gold (.1452 ounces), 10% copper. **Notes:** The 1873 "closed-3" and "open-3" varieties are distinguished by the amount of space between the upper left and lower left serifs of the 3 in the date.

Date	Mintage	F-12	VF-20	XF-40	AU-50	MS-60	Prf-65
1854	138,618	365.	505.	650.	850.	2050.	35,000.
1854D	1,120	—	6500.	12,000.	23,500.	60,000.	—
1854O	24,000	365.	600.	950.	3000.	8200.	—
1855	50,555	365.	505.	650.	850.	2500.	—
1855S	6,600	550.	900.	2000.	5000.	12,750.	—
1856	26,010	365.	535.	690.	1200.	2700.	—
1856S	34,500	500.	760.	1200.	2000.	7000.	—
1857	20,891	365.	535.	690.	1100.	3000.	35,000.
1857S	14,000	510.	760.	1800.	4000.	10,000.	—
1858	2,133	550.	800.	1450.	2300.	5000.	35,000.
1859	15,638	365.	505.	725.	1150.	2700.	35,000.
1860	7,155	550.	760.	850.	1200.	2900.	35,000.
1860S	7,000	525.	760.	2500.	5500.	12,500.	—
1861	6,072	550.	760.	1100.	2100.	4000.	35,000.
1862	5,785	525.	760.	1100.	2100.	4000.	35,000.
1863	5,039	600.	760.	1125.	2400.	4000.	35,000.
1864	2,680	600.	760.	1150.	2400.	4000.	35,000.

Gold $3

Date	Mintage	F-12	VF-20	XF-40	AU-50	MS-60	Prf-65
1865	1,165	700.	800.	1600.	6000.	14,000.	35,000.
1866	4,030	525.	760.	1500.	2400.	4200.	35,000.
1867	2,650	575.	800.	1150.	2400.	4200.	35,000.
1868	4,875	525.	760.	1100.	2400.	3900.	35,000.
1869	2,525	575.	760.	1100.	2500.	4200.	35,000.
1870	3,535	525.	760.	1100.	2400.	4200.	35,000.
1870S	Unique	Private Sale. 1992 XF-40 $1,500,000.					
1871	1,330	550.	880.	1200.	2600.	3900.	35,000.
1872	2,030	525.	800.	1200.	2200.	3500.	35,000.
1873 open 3	25			Proof only	—		—
1873 closed 3	Unknown	—	4000.	6500.	10,000.	23,000.	—
1874	41,820	365.	525.	800.	1300.	3000.	35,000.
1875	20			Proof only			
		RARCOA. Aug. 1990. proof. $159,000.					—
1876	45			14,000.	18,000.		90,000.
1877	1,488	600.	900.	3000.	5000.	6700.	35,000.
1878	82,324	365.	500.	1000.	1300.	3000.	30,000.
1879	3,030	550.	800.	1400.	2400.	3900.	30,000.
1880	1,036	550.	900.	1400.	2600.	3900.	30,000.
1881	554	900.	1600.	2500.	3900.	5500.	32,000.
1882	1,576	550.	1000.	1500.	2500.	4000.	30,000.
1883	989	550.	1000.	1500.	2600.	4400.	32,000.
1884	1,106	550.	1000.	2000.	3000.	4000.	30,000.
1885	910	550.	1000.	1700.	2700.	4000.	32,000.
1886	1,142	550.	1000.	1600.	3000.	4400.	30,000.
1887	6,160	525.	800.	1200.	2100.	3100.	30,000.
1888	5,291	525.	800.	1200.	2100.	3100.	30,000.
1889	2,429	525.	800.	1200.	2100.	3100.	30,000.

Gold $4 (Stella)

Flowing Hair

Coiled Hair

Designers: Charles E. Barber (Flowing Hair type) and George T. Morgan (Coiled Hair type). **Notes:** These are patterns, rather than coins struck for circulation. Examples in other metals also exist; values listed here are only for those struck in gold.

Date	Type	Mintage	VF-20	XF-40	AU-50	Prf-65
1879	Flowing Hair	415	—	—	—	90,000.
Impaired Proofs		—	10,000.	13,500.	33,000.	—
1879	Coiled Hair	10	—	—	—	500,000.
1880	Flowing Hair	15	—	—	—	225,000.
1880	Coiled Hair	10	—	—	—	500,000.

Gold $5 (Half eagle)

Liberty Cap

Small eagle

Heraldic eagle

Designer: Robert Scot. **Size:** 25 millimeters. **Weight:** 8.75 grams. **Composition:** 91.67% gold (.258 ounces), 8.33% copper. **Notes:** From 1795 through 1798, varieties exist with either a "small eagle" or a "large (heraldic) eagle" on the reverse. After 1798, only the heraldic eagle was used. Two 1797 varieties are distinguished by the number of stars on the obverse. 1798 varieties are distinguished by the size of the 8 in the date and the number of stars on the reverse. 1804 varieties are distinguished by the size of the 8 in the date. 1806 varieties are distinguished by whether the top of the 6 has a serif.

Date	Mintage	F-12	VF-20	XF-40	MS-60
1795 sm. eagle	8,707	5250.	7250.	9250.	31,500.
1795 lg. eagle	Inc. Ab.	6900.	10,000.	15,000.	48,000.
1796/95 small eagle	6,196	6000.	9100.	14,000.	—
1797/95 large eagle	3,609	5000.	7000.	9600.	30,000.

Date	Mintage	F-12	VF-20	XF-40	MS-60
1797 15 stars, small eagle	Inc. Ab.	7500.	10.000.	18.500.	45.000.
1797 16 stars, small eagle	Inc. Ab.	7000.	9000.	17.500.	55.000.
1798 sm.eagle	7 known	—	—	45.000.	—
1798 large eagle, small 8	24.867	1500.	1850.	3700.	10.500.
1798 large eagle, large 8, 13-star reverse	Inc. Ab.	1200.	1850.	3000.	7300.
1798 large eagle, large 8, 14-star reverse	Inc. Ab.	1600.	2300.	4300.	24.000.
1799	7.451	1300.	1600.	3000.	12.500.
1800	37.628	1150.	1550.	2150.	6000.
1802/1	53.176	1150.	1550.	2000.	6000.
1803/2	33.506	1150.	1550.	2000.	6000.
1804 sm. 8	30.475	1150.	1550.	2000.	6000.
1804 lg. 8	Inc. Ab.	1150.	1550.	2000.	6000.
1805	33.183	1150.	1550.	2000.	6000.
1806 pointed 6	64.093	1150.	1550.	2200.	10.000.
1806 round 6	Inc. Ab.	1150.	1550.	2000.	6000.
1807	32.488	1150.	1550.	2000.	6000.

Turban Head

Capped draped bust Capped head

Capped draped bust

Designer: John Reich. **Size:** 25 millimeters. **Weight:** 8.75 grams. **Composition:** 91.67% gold (.258 ounces), 8.33% copper. **Notes:** The 1810 varieties are distinguished by the size of the numerals in the date and the size of the 5 in the "5D." on the reverse. The 1811 varieties are distinguished by the size of the 5 in the "5D." on the reverse.

Date	Mintage	F-12	VF-20	XF-40	MS-60
1807	51.605	1250.	1650.	2150.	6000.
1808	55.578	1250.	1650.	2150.	6000.
1808/7	Inc. Ab.	1400.	1550.	2400.	9500.
1809/8	33.875	1250.	1500.	2150.	6000.
1810 small date, small 5	100.287		6500.	12.000.	—
1810 small date, large 5	Inc. Ab.	1300.	1650.	2400.	6000.
1810 large date, small 5	Inc. Ab.	3750.	4750.	7500.	24.000.
1810 large date, large 5	Inc. Ab.	1250.	1400.	2000.	6000.
1811 small 5	99.581	1250.	1400.	2000.	5500.
1811 large 5	Inc. Ab.	1150.	1350.	2000.	6500.
1812	58.087	1000.	1350.	2000.	6250.

Capped head

Notes: 1820 varieties are distinguished by whether the 2 in the date has a curved base or square base, and by the size of the letters in the reverse inscriptions. 1832 varieties are distinguished by whether the 2 in the date has a curved base or square base and by the number of stars on the reverse. 1834 varieties are distinguished by whether the 4 has a serif at its far right.

Date	Mintage	F-12	VF-20	XF-40	MS-60
1813	95.428	1300.	1500.	2250.	6600.
1814/13	15.454	1600.	2000.	4000.	10.000.
1815	635	Private sale Jan. 1994, MS-61, $150.000.			
1818	48.588	1500.	1900.	2850.	8500.
1819	51.723	—	—	40.000.	—
1820 curved base 2, small letters	263.806	1500.	1900.	4500.	16.000.
1820 curved base 2, large letters	Inc. Ab.	1500.	1900.	4500.	40.000.
1820 sq. base 2	Inc. Ab.	1500.	1900.	3100.	8500.
1821	34.641	2200.	3850.	7300.	23.000.
1822	(3 known) 17.796	Private Sale 1993, VF-30, $1.000.000.			
1823	14.485	1600.	2000.	3700.	14.500.
1824	17.340	2200.	3500.	8800.	—
1825/21	29.060	3250.	5000.	6500.	20.000.
1825/24	Inc. Ab.	Bowers & Merena, Mar. 1989, XF, $148.500.			
1826	18.069	2750.	6000.	7100.	25.000.
1827	24.913	—	—	—	32.500.
1828/7	28.029	Bowers & Merena, Jun. 1989, XF, $20.900.			
1828	Inc. Ab.	—	—	30.000.	—
1829 lg. dt.	57.442	Superior, July 1985, MS-65, $104.500.			
1829 sm. dt.	Inc. Ab.	Private Sale, 1992 (XF-45), $89.000.			
1830 sm. "5D."	126.351	3500.	5000.	6500.	15.000.
1830 lg. "5D."	Inc. Ab.	3500.	5000.	7000.	16.500.
1831	140.594	3500.	5100.	6500.	16.500.
1832 curved base 2, 12-stars	157.487	—	Rare	—	—
1832 square base 2, 13 stars	Inc. Ab.	4000.	6500.	8750.	21.000.
1833	193.630	3500.	5000.	6250.	15.500.
1834 plain 4	50.141	3500.	5000.	6250.	16.000.
1834 crosslet 4	Inc. Ab.	4000.	6000.	8250.	26.500.

Gold $5

Liberty Without Turban

Designer: William Kneass. **Size:** 22.5 millimeters. **Weight:** 8.36 millimeters. **Composition:** 89.92% gold (.2418 ounces), 10.08% copper. **Notes:** 1834 varieties are distinguished by whether the 4 has a serif at its far right.

Date	Mintage	VF-20	XF-40	AU-50	MS-60	MS-65
1834 plain 4	658.028	300.	500.	850.	2950.	90.000.
1834 crosslet 4	Inc. Ab.	1150.	2375.	5250.	15.000.	—
1835	371.534	300.	500.	900.	2900.	62.000.
1836	553.147	300.	500.	850.	2900.	62.000.
1837	207.121	325.	525.	925.	3500.	62.000.
1838	286.588	300.	500.	900.	3250.	62.000.
1838C	17.179	1550.	4250.	9500.	20.000.	—
1838D	20.583	1450.	3500.	7000.	15.000.	—

Coronet Head

No motto

Designer: Christian Gobrecht. **Size:** 21.6 millimeters. **Weight:** 8.359 grams. **Composition:** 90% gold (.242 ounces), 10% copper. **Notes:** Varieties for the 1842 Philadelphia strikes are distinguished by the size of the letters in the reverse inscriptions. Varieties for the 1842-C and -D strikes are distinguished by the size of the numerals in the date. Varieties for the 1843-O strikes are distinguished by the size of the letters in the reverse inscriptions.

Date	Mintage	F-12	VF-20	XF-40	MS-60	Prf-65
1839	118.143	200.	250.	435.	3500.	—
1839/8 curved date	Inc. Ab.	200.	300.	600.	1750.	—
1839C	17.205	450.	950.	2000.	20.000.	—
1839D	18.939	400.	800.	1700.	11.000.	—
1840	137.382	190.	225.	350.	4100.	—
1840C	18.992	400.	700.	1650.	15.500.	—
1840D	22.896	400.	700.	1500.	11.000.	—
1840O	40.120	200.	325.	700.	7500.	—
1841	15.833	200.	375.	1200.	7500.	—
1841C	21.467	300.	675.	1450.	12.000.	—
1841D	30.495	325.	600.	1250.	12.000.	—
1841O	50		2 known	—		—
1842 sm. let.	27.578	150.	300.	1300.	10.000.	—
1842 lg. let.	Inc. Ab.	350.	700.	2000.	11.500.	—
1842C sm. dt.	28.184	1750.	3500.	12.250.	—	—
1842C lg. dt.	Inc. Ab.	350.	750.	1500.	17.500.	—
1842D sm. dt.	59.608	350.	650.	1250.	12.000.	—
1842D lg. dt.	Inc. Ab.	1250.	2250.	6000.	18.000.	—
1842O	16.400	350.	1000.	5000.	24.000.	—
1843	611.205	150.	180.	210.	2200.	—
1843C	44.201	350.	600.	1400.	13.000.	—
1843D	98.452	350.	550.	1000.	8000.	—
1843O sm. let.	19.075	325.	550.	1400.	11.000.	—
1843O lg. let.	82.000	200.	325.	900.	15.000.	—
1844	340.330	150.	180.	250.	2100.	—
1844C	23.631	300.	725.	2700.	13.500.	—
1844D	88.982	375.	550.	1050.	10.000.	—
1844O	364.600	200.	225.	600.	5000.	—
1845	417.099	150.	180.	210.	2750.	—
1845D	90.629	360.	850.	1850.	11.000.	—
1845O	41.000	200.	350.	1100.	9500.	—
1846	395.942	150.	180.	210.	3000.	—
1846C	12.995	425.	900.	2500.	17.500.	—
1846D	80.294	400.	550.	1350.	9250.	—
1846O	58.000	200.	350.	1450.	12.750.	—
1847	915.981	150.	180.	210.	1550.	—
1847C	84.151	375.	575.	1450.	16.500.	—
1847D	64.405	400.	500.	1100.	9000.	—
1847O	12.000	475.	2300.	10.500.	29.000.	—
1848	260.775	150.	180.	250.	2500.	—
1848C	64.472	400.	650.	1600.	15.000.	—
1848D	47.465	400.	500.	1500.	13.000.	—
1849	133.070	150.	180.	300.	2700.	—
1849C	64.823	350.	500.	1100.	11.500.	—
1849D	39.036	350.	700.	1350.	11.500.	—
1850	64.491	200.	350.	875.	5700.	—
1850C	63.591	325.	550.	1100.	13.000.	—
1850D	43.984	350.	500.	1500.	18.000.	—
1851	377.505	150.	180.	265.	2800.	—
1851C	49.176	325.	600.	1100.	11.000.	—
1851D	62.710	350.	525.	1375.	11.500.	—
1851O	41.000	325.	650.	1500.	—	—
1852	573.901	150.	180.	210.	1850.	—

Date	Mintage	F-12	VF-20	XF-40	MS-60	Prf-65
1852C	72.574	350.	550.	1100.	11.750.	—
1852D	91.584	350.	500.	1000.	9000.	—
1853	305.770	150.	180.	210.	2250.	—
1853C	65.571	350.	525.	1000	12.000.	—
1853D	89.678	350.	500.	900.	9000.	—
1854	160.675	160.	200.	500.	3000.	—
1854C	39.283	400.	600.	1600.	14.500.	—
1854D	56.413	350.	500.	1000.	9250.	—
1854O	46.000	250.	300.	500.	6800.	—
1854S	268	Bowers & Ruddy. Oct. 1982. AU-55. $170.000.				—
1855	117.098	160.	200.	250.	2400.	—
1855C	39.788	350.	625.	1750.	13.500.	—
1855D	22.432	400.	600.	1500.	16.000.	—
1855O	11.100	350.	700.	2900.	16.500.	—
1855S	61.000	200.	425.	1100.	10.000.	—
1856	197.990	175.	310.	340.	3500.	—
1856C	28.457	350.	600.	1300.	12.000.	—
1856D	19.786	400.	600.	1300.	7800.	—
1856O	10.000	400.	800.	2800.	—	—
1856S	105.100	190.	300.	800.	—	—
1857	98.188	160.	200.	250.	3000.	—
1857C	31.360	300.	600.	1300.	8000.	—
1857D	17.046	300.	600.	1250.	8000.	—
1857O	13.000	300.	700.	2000.	—	—
1857S	87.000	200.	300.	700.	7000.	—
1858	15.136	200.	275.	800.	5250.	70.000.
1858C	38.856	375.	800.	1250.	11.000.	—
1858D	15.362	300.	600.	1200.	12.000.	—
1858S	18.600	350.	650.	2600.	—	—
1859	16.814	200.	275.	600.	6500.	—
1859C	31.847	300.	525.	1400.	13.000.	—
1859D	10.366	400.	725.	2000.	11.500.	—
1859S	13.220	450.	1250.	4750.	—	—
1860	19.825	200.	300.	600.	6500.	—
1860C	14.813	350.	800.	2000.	11.500.	—
1860D	14.635	300.	800.	1800.	13.500.	—
1860S	21.200	450.	1200.	2800.	18.500.	—
1861	688.150	150.	175.	210.	1900.	—
1861C	6.879	700.	1500.	3400.	25.000.	—
1861D	1.597	2500.	4000.	7000.	—	—
1861S	18.000	450.	1100.	4500.	—	—
1862	4.465	450.	750.	2500.	—	—
1862S	9.500	1400.	4500.	10.500.	—	—
1863	2.472	500.	1150.	3450.	—	—
1863S	17.000	425.	1200.	4750.	—	—
1864	4.220	400.	600.	2100.	11.500.	—
1864S	3.888	2200.	6750.	15.000.	—	—
1865	1.295	600.	1200.	3150.	—	—
1865S	27.612	425.	1200.	3600.	—	—
1866S	9.000	600.	1600.	6000.	—	—

Mintmark

With motto

Notes: In 1866 the motto "In God We Trust" was added above the eagle on the reverse. The 1873 "closed-3" and "open-3" varieties are distinguished by the amount of space between the upper left and lower left serifs of the 3 in the date.

Date	Mintage	VF-20	XF-40	AU-50	MS-60	MS-65	Prf-65
1866	6,730	725.	1800.	4400.	12,500.	—	35,000.
1866S	34,920	1350.	4500.	8500.	18,500.	—	—
1867	6,920	550.	2500.	4000.	8000.	—	35,000.
1867S	29,000	1600.	5000.	10,000.	—	—	—
1868	5,725	650.	1800.	4000.	10,000.	—	35,000.
1868S	52,000	500.	2400.	7200.	—	—	—
1869	1,785	875.	2300.	5000.	—	—	35,000.
1869S	31,000	375.	2400.	9750.	—	—	—
1870	4,035	700.	2800.	4500.	—	—	35,000.
1870CC	7,675	4400.	9500.	20,000.	—	—	—
1870S	17,000	1200.	4000.	11,500.	—	—	—
1871	3,230	875.	2150.	6500.	—	—	35,000.
1871CC	20,770	975.	3000.	13,000.	—	—	—
1871S	25,000	550.	2000.	6000.	17,500.	—	—
1872	1,690	750.	2000.	4700.	15,000.	—	35,000.
1872CC	16,980	850.	3500.	14,000.	—	—	—
1872S	36,400	525.	1850.	7000.	—	—	—
1873 closed 3	49,305	225.	250.	625.	2800.	—	35,000.
1873 open 3	63,200	225.	250.	625.	2800.	—	—
1873CC	7,416	2200.	6500.	15,500.	—	—	—
1873S	31,000	875.	2700.	—	—	—	—
1874	3,508	625.	2200.	5000.	—	—	35,000.
1874CC	21,198	675.	1750.	5500.	12,000.	—	—
1874S	16,000	725.	3750.	9000.	—	—	—
1875	220	45,000.	55,000.	96,000.	—	—	110,000.
1875CC	11,828	1500.	5400.	13,000.	—	—	—
1875S	9,000	950.	3300.	—	—	—	—
1876	1,477	1000.	2600.	5300.	15,500.	—	35,000.
1876CC	6,887	1500.	5750.	9500.	—	—	—
1876S	4,000	1700.	5000.	12,750.	—	—	—
1877	1,152	800.	2400.	4500.	12,000.	—	35,000.
1877CC	8,680	1000.	3300.	8000.	—	—	—

Date	Mintage		F-12	VF-20	XF-40	MS-60	Prf-65
1877S	26.700	325.	900.	3600.	—	—	—
1878	131.740	120.	225.	250.	1000.	—	35.000.
1878CC	9.054	3500.	9000.	20.000.	—	—	—
1878S	144.700	175.	275.	475.	1200.	—	—
1879	301.950	120.	175.	250.	525.	—	20.000.
1879CC	17.281	350.	1300.	3000.	—	—	—
1879S	426.200	200.	275.	325.	975.	—	—
1880	3,166.436	120.	145.	175.	250.	—	20.000.
1880CC	51.017	350.	875.	2000.	7500.	—	—
1880S	1,348.900	120.	145.	175.	190.	—	—
1881	5.708.802	120.	145.	175.	195.	7000.	20.000.
1881/80	Inc. Ab.	350.	700.	1800.	4050.	—	—
1881CC	13.886	500.	1500.	4150.	9000.	—	—
1881S	969.000	120.	145.	175.	190.	—	—
1882	2,514.568	120.	175.	195.	250.	7000.	20.000.
1882CC	82.817	375.	650.	1500.	5000.	—	—
1882S	969.000	120.	145.	175.	190.	—	—
1883	233.461	120.	175.	200.	550.	7000.	20.000.
1883CC	12.958	375.	800.	3500.	12.000.	—	—
1883S	83.200	195.	225.	330.	1150.	—	—
1884	191.078	150.	175.	260.	1250.	—	20.000.
1884CC	16.402	450.	825.	4250.	—	—	—
1884S	177.000	200.	275.	325.	775.	—	—
1885	601.506	120.	145.	160.	190.	—	20.000.
1885S	1.211.500	120.	175.	190.	225.	7000.	—
1886	388.432	150.	185.	225.	375.	—	20.000.
1886S	3.268.000	120.	165.	175.	225.	—	—
1887	87	Proof only		—	—	—	100.000.
1887S	1.912.000	120.	175.	185.	240.	—	—
1888	18.296	175.	250.	300.	2000.	—	20.000.
1888S	293.900	190.	275.	800.	2800.	—	—
1889	7.565	400.	700.	1500.	—	—	20.000.
1890	4.328	250.	400.	1500.	3500.	—	20.000.
1890CC	53.800	300.	400.	550.	1250.	—	—
1891	61.413	120.	235.	250.	775.	7500.	20.000.
1891CC	208.000	250.	375.	500.	850.	—	—
1892	753.572	120.	145.	180.	220.	—	20.000.
1892CC	82.968	300.	600.	700.	1550.	—	—
1892O	10.000	600.	1250.	2250.	4700.	—	—
1892S	298.400	175.	225.	325.	2500.	—	—
1893	1.528.197	120.	175.	195.	225.	5000.	20.000.
1893CC	60.000	300.	400.	625.	2000.	—	—
1893O	110.000	200.	300.	400.	2000.	—	—
1893S	224.000	175.	200.	325.	600.	7500.	—
1894	957.955	120.	175.	195.	300.	5000.	20.000.
1894O	16.600	195.	350.	475.	2000.	—	—
1894S	55.900	275.	350.	850.	3750.	7500.	—
1895	1.345.936	120.	145.	160.	190.	5000.	20.000.
1895S	112.000	250.	375.	1000.	5000.	26.000.	—
1896	59.063	160.	185.	225.	350.	7500.	20.000.
1896S	155.400	225.	275.	600.	2100.	—	—
1897	867.883	120.	145.	160.	190.	5000.	20.000.
1897S	354.000	165.	250.	525.	1800.	—	—
1898	633.495	120.	145.	160.	190.	5000.	20.000.
1898S	1.397.400	120.	145.	175.	300.	5000.	—
1899	1.710.729	120.	145.	160.	190.	5000.	20.000.
1899S	1.545.000	120.	145.	160.	190.	5000.	—
1900	1.405.730	120.	145.	160.	190.	5000.	20.000.
1900S	329.000	165.	200.	300.	700.	5000.	—
1901	616.040	120.	145.	160.	190.	5000.	12.500.
1901S	3.648.000	120.	145.	160.	190.	5000.	—
1902	172.562	120.	145.	160.	190.	5000.	12.500.
1902S	939.000	120.	145.	160.	190.	5000.	—
1903	227.024	120.	145.	160.	190.	5000.	15.000.
1903S	1.855.000	120.	145.	160.	190.	5000.	—
1904	392.136	120.	145.	160.	190.	5000.	12.500.
1904S	97.000	180.	225.	300.	800.	11.000.	—
1905	302.308	120.	145.	160.	190.	7200.	12.500.
1905S	880.700	120.	175.	260.	900.	5000.	—
1906	348.820	120.	145.	160.	190.	5000.	12.500.
1906D	320.000	120.	145.	160.	190.	5000.	—
1906S	598.000	120.	145.	185.	275.	5000.	—
1907	626.192	120.	145.	160.	190.	5000.	20.000.
1907D	888.000	120.	145.	160.	190.	5000.	—
1908	421.874	120.	145.	160.	190.	5000.	—

Indian Head

Designer: Bela Lyon Pratt. **Size:** 21.6 millimeters. **Weight:** 8.359 grams. **Composition:** 90% gold (.242 ounces), 10% copper.

Date	Mintage	VF-20	XF-40	AU-50	MS-60	MS-63	MS-65	Prf-65
1908	578.012	195.	225.	240.	300.	2500.	14.500.	22.000.
1908D	148.000	195.	225.	240.	300.	3400.	26.500.	—
1908S	82.000	225.	450.	540.	1850.	3700.	20.000.	—
1909	627.138	195.	225.	240.	445.	3400.	19.500.	26.500.
1909D	3.423.560	195.	225.	240.	300.	2500.	20.500.	—
1909O	34.200	600.	900.	1600.	6900.	30.000.	120.000.	—

Gold $5

Date	Mintage	VF-20	XF-40	AU-50	MS-60	MS-63	MS-65	Prf-65
1909S	297,200	215.	230.	275.	1175.	6600.	42,000.	—
1910	604,250	195.	225.	240.	300.	3700.	30,000.	24,000.
1910D	193,600	195.	225.	240.	510.	4800.	36,000.	—
1910S	770,200	195.	225.	240.	1800.	7200.	42,000.	—
1911	915,139	195.	225.	240.	300.	3400.	24,000.	25,000.
1911D	72,500	350.	500.	600.	5600.	19,000.	68,500.	—
1911S	1,416,000	195.	235.	250.	840.	6000.	42,000.	—
1912	790,144	195.	225.	240.	300.	3400.	21,500.	24,000.
1912S	392,000	215.	235.	250.	1550.	8500.	42,000.	—
1913	916,099	195.	225.	240.	300.	3400.	21,000.	25,000.
1913S	408,000	250.	300.	350.	2650.	15,000.	66,000.	—
1914	247,125	195.	225.	240.	300.	3400.	23,500.	25,000.
1914D	247,000	195.	225.	240.	300.	3700.	48,000.	—
1914S	263,000	215.	230.	255.	1050.	7550.	47,000.	—
1915	588,075	195.	225.	240.	300.	3400.	23,500.	33,000.
1915S	164,000	300.	325.	425.	2650.	8700.	66,000.	—
1916S	240,000	195.	225.	265.	660.	4700.	30,000.	—
1929	662,000	2000.	3500.	4850.	6000.	9250.	45,500.	—

Gold $10 (Eagle)

Liberty Cap

Small eagle

Small eagle

Designer: Robert Scot. **Size:** 33 millimeters. **Weight:** 17.5 grams. **Composition:** 91.67% gold (.5159 ounces), 8.33% copper.

Date	Mintage	F-12	VF-20	XF-40	MS-60
1795 13 leaves	5,583	6000.	8500.	11,000.	39,500.
1795 9 leaves	Inc. Ab.	17,000.	30,000.	50,000.	—
1796	4,146	6000.	8500.	11,000.	50,000.
1797 sm. eagle	3,615	6000.	10,250.	35,000.	—

Heraldic eagle

Heraldic eagle

Notes: The 1798/97 varieties are distinguished by the positioning of the stars on the obverse.

Date	Mintage	F-12	VF-20	XF-40	MS-60
1797 lg. eagle	10,940	2500.	3500.	5000.	14,000.
1798/97, 9 stars left, 4 right	900	4500.	8000.	20,000.	70,000.
1798/97, 7 stars left, 6 right	842	15,000.	27,500.	57,500.	—
1799	37,449	2400.	3000.	4500.	11,000.
1800	5,999	2400.	3250.	5000.	13,750.
1801	44,344	2400.	3000.	4000.	11,000.
1803	15,017	2600.	3250.	4000.	11,000.
1804	3,757	3750.	4200.	8500.	32,500.

Coronet Head

Old-style head

New-style head

Gold $10

Old-style head, no motto

Designer: Christian Gobrecht. **Size:** 27 millimeters. **Weight:** 16.718 grams. **Composition:** 90% gold (.4839 ounces), 10% copper.

Date	Mintage	F-12	VF-20	XF-40	MS-60	Prf-65
1838	7,200	350.	900.	2750.	26,000.	—
1839 lg. lts.	38,248	450.	800.	1700.	16,000.	—

New-style head, no motto

Notes: The 1842 varieties are distinguished by the size of the numerals in the date.

Date	Mintage	F-12	VF-20	XF-40	MS-60	Prf-65
1839 sm. lts.	Inc. Ab.	700.	1600.	4000.	—	—
1840	47,338	380.	425.	750.	13,000.	—
1841	63,131	380.	415.	650.	14,000.	—
1841O	2,500	850.	2000.	7000.	—	—
1842 sm. dt.	81,507	380.	425.	700.	—	—
1842 lg. dt.	Inc. Ab.	380.	415.	750.	13,500.	—
1842O	27,400	250.	285.	700.	12,500.	—
1843	75,462	380.	415.	700.	7500.	—
1843O	175,162	380.	415.	600.	7750.	—
1844	6,361	475.	1300.	3600.	—	—
1844O	118,700	380.	425.	600.	11,000.	—
1845	26,153	380.	750.	2100.	—	—
1845O	47,500	350.	425.	800.	12,500.	—
1846	20,095	500.	900.	2850.	—	—
1846O	81,780	350.	600.	1400.	—	—
1847	862,258	240.	265.	325.	5250.	—
1847O	571,500	250.	290.	400.	5000.	—
1848	145,484	300.	350.	400.	5500.	—
1848O	38,850	400.	600.	1400.	—	—
1849	653,618	240.	265.	300.	3850.	—
1849O	23,900	500.	800.	3600.	—	—
1850	291,451	240.	265.	300.	3850.	—
1850O	57,500	350.	400.	600.	—	—
1851	176,328	300.	325.	525.	9500.	—
1851O	263,000	280.	300.	550.	—	—
1852	263,106	330.	425.	525.	3850.	—
1852O	18,000	500.	700.	2600.	—	—
1853	201,253	240.	265.	300.	3850.	—
1853O	51,000	350.	400.	575.	—	—
1854	54,250	350.	400.	700.	—	—
1854O sm. dt.	52,500	225.	400.	1250.	12,000.	—
1854O lg. dt.	Inc. Ab.	375.	600.	2250.	—	—
1854S	123,826	280.	300.	575.	11,000.	—
1855	121,701	240.	265.	300.	3850.	—
1855O	18,000	350.	600.	2000.	—	—
1855S	9,000	850.	1900.	4250.	—	—
1856	60,490	300.	330.	360.	4800.	—
1856O	14,500	400.	600.	2900.	—	—
1856S	68,000	330.	380.	625.	10,000.	—
1857	16,606	330.	380.	1000.	—	—
1857O	5,500	700.	1000.	3000.	—	—
1857S	26,000	380.	525.	800.	7750.	—
1858	2,521	2500.	5000.	11,000.	—	—
1858O	20,000	330.	380.	850.	12,000.	—
1858S	11,800	750.	2150.	7000.	—	—
1859	16,093	330.	380.	1000.	—	—
1859O	2,300	1275.	3500.	9000.	—	—
1859S	7,000	900.	2500.	7400.	—	—
1860	15,105	330.	380.	1000.	12,500.	—
1860O	11,100	400.	575.	2100.	17,000.	—
1860S	5,000	750.	2700.	9000.	—	—
1861	113,233	280.	325.	375.	8000.	—
1861S	15,500	675.	1900.	4750.	—	—
1862	10,995	350.	475.	1350.	—	—
1862S	12,500	700.	1950.	5000.	—	—
1863	1,248	2000.	3650.	11,000.	50,000.	—
1863S	10,000	725.	1700.	6500.	—	—
1864	3,580	800.	1900.	4900.	—	—
1864S	2,500	2750.	5800.	11,500.	—	—
1865	4,005	750.	2150.	5250.	—	—
1865S	16,700	1450.	5000.	20,000.	—	—
1865S/inverted 186	—	—	2500.	7500.	—	—
1866S	8,500	1300.	3000.	6500.	—	—

Reverse motto

New-style head, with motto

Notes: In 1866 the motto "In God We Trust" was added above the eagle on the reverse. The 1873 "closed-3" and "open-3" varieties are distinguished by the amount of space between the upper left and lower left serifs of the 3 in the date.

Date	Mintage	VF-20	XF-40	AU-50	MS-60	MS-65	Prf-65
1866	3,780	750.	3000.	6750.	—	—	60,000.
1866S	11,500	1750.	3900.	9500.	—	—	—
1867	3,140	1750.	4500.	10,500.	—	—	60,000.
1867S	9,000	2600.	8500.	20,000.	—	—	—
1868	10,655	600.	1800.	5750.	15,000.	—	60,000.
1868S	13,500	1600.	5000.	20,000.	—	—	—
1869	1,855	1750.	5000.	11,500.	—	—	65,000.
1869S	6,430	1800.	5000.	11,500.	—	—	—
1870	4,025	750.	1450.	5000.	—	—	60,000.
1870CC	5,908	7000.	19,000.	32,500.	—	—	—
1870S	8,000	2000.	7500.	14,000.	—	—	—

Date	Mintage	VF-20	XF-40	AU-50	MS-60	MS-65	Prf-65
1871	1,820	1600.	4000.	8750.	3500.	—	60,000.
1871CC	8,085	2250.	6000.	15,000.	—	—	—
1871S	16,500	1750.	4700.	8000.	—	—	—
1872	1,650	3000.	8000.	18,000.	—	—	60,000.
1872CC	4,600	2500.	10,000.	25,000.	—	—	—
1872S	17,300	900.	2000.	8500.	—	—	—
1873 closed 3	825	4200.	14,000.	28,000.	—	—	60,000.
1873CC	4,543	2700.	12,000.	27,000.	—	—	—
1873S	12,000	1600.	5000.	9000.	—	—	—
1874	53,160	300.	350.	550.	2450.	—	60,000.
1874CC	16,767	875.	5000.	10,500.	—	—	—
1874S	10,000	1700.	5000.	14,250.	—	—	—
1875	120		Akers, Aug. 1990, proof, $115,000.				—
1875CC	7,715	2500.	15,000.	35,000.	—	—	—
1876	732	3000.	11,000.	20,000.	—	—	50,000.
1876CC	4,696	3000.	10,000.	19,000.	—	—	—
1876S	5,000	2100.	4000.	12,000.	—	—	—
1877	817	3500.	9000.	16,000.	—	—	40,000.
1877CC	3,332	2400.	6000.	13,000.	—	—	—
1877S	17,000	600.	2200.	7500.	—	—	—
1878	73,800	290.	350.	450.	2550.	—	50,000.
1878CC	3,244	3500.	11,750.	27,000.	—	—	—
1878S	26,100	650.	2000.	10,000.	—	—	—
1879	384,770	285.	300.	375.	850.	—	40,000.
1879CC	1,762	5000.	12,500.	26,000.	—	—	—
1879O	1,500	2200.	7700.	17,000.	—	—	—
1879S	224,000	310.	360.	425.	1700.	—	—
1880	1,644,876	265.	280.	285.	400.	—	40,000.
1880CC	11,190	425.	675.	2200.	8500.	—	—
1880O	9,200	400.	950.	3000.	7500.	—	—
1880S	506,250	265.	285.	325.	600.	—	—
1881	3,877,260	265.	285.	310.	350.	—	40,000.
1881CC	24,015	400.	550.	1300.	7500.	—	—
1881O	8,350	400.	875.	3000.	8000.	—	—
1881S	970,000	265.	280.	300.	450.	6500.	—
1882	2,324,480	265.	280.	285.	325.	6500.	40,000.
1882CC	6,764	475.	1800.	5250.	10,000.	—	—
1882O	10,820	400.	850.	2500.	5000.	—	—
1882S	132,000	265.	280.	300.	1100.	13,500.	—
1883	208,740	275.	285.	325.	450.	6500.	40,000.
1883CC	12,000	400.	850.	3000.	9250.	—	—
1883O	800	3200.	8500.	17,000.	37,500.	—	—
1883S	38,000	295.	375.	450.	1350.	13,500.	—
1884	76,905	265.	285.	400.	1850.	13,500.	86,000.
1884CC	9,925	525.	1300.	4000.	10,000.	—	—
1884S	124,250	265.	280.	400.	1300.	6500.	—
1885	253,527	265.	280.	300.	775.	6500.	40,000.
1885S	228,000	265.	280.	360.	600.	6500.	—
1886	236,160	280.	300.	400.	1100.	6500.	40,000.
1886S	826,000	265.	280.	295.	340.	6500.	—
1887	53,680	310.	300.	475.	1800.	50,000.	40,000.
1887S	817,000	265.	280.	300.	425.	6500.	—
1888	132,996	300.	325.	365.	1500.	50,000.	40,000.
1888O	21,335	265.	285.	350.	750.	—	—
1888S	648,700	265.	285.	300.	500.	6500.	—
1889	4,485	400.	500.	1000.	3750.	—	40,000.
1889S	425,400	265.	280.	285.	375.	6500.	—
1890	58,043	300.	315.	425.	2250.	13,500.	40,000.
1890CC	17,500	375.	450.	600.	2000.	—	—
1891	91,868	265.	280.	300.	450.	13,500.	40,000.
1891CC	103,732	300.	350.	550.	1000.	—	—
1892	797,552	285.	280.	295.	325.	6500.	40,000.
1892CC	40,000	375.	550.	1000.	4000.	—	—
1892O	28,688	285.	300.	325.	600.	—	—
1892S	115,500	300.	310.	350.	750.	13,500.	—
1893	1,840,895	265.	280.	300.	350.	5000.	40,000.
1893CC	14,000	380.	600.	1075.	2700.	—	—
1893O	17,000	265.	280.	350.	675.	—	—
1893S	141,350	300.	310.	350.	800.	13,500.	—
1894	2,470,778	265.	280.	295.	360.	5000.	40,000.
1894O	107,500	265.	280.	375.	2000.	13,500.	—
1894S	25,000	300.	475.	1200.	4500.	13,500.	—
1895	567,826	265.	280.	295.	325.	6500.	40,000.
1895O	98,000	265.	300.	325.	650.	13,500.	—
1895S	49,000	265.	400.	1250.	4000.	40,000.	—
1896	76,348	265.	280.	295.	350.	6500.	40,000.
1896S	123,750	265.	350.	1000.	6750.	—	—
1897	1,000,159	265.	280.	295.	325.	5000.	40,000.
1897O	42,500	265.	300.	375.	850.	11,000.	—
1897S	234,750	265.	325.	500.	2000.	6500.	—
1898	812,197	265.	280.	295.	325.	6500.	40,000.
1898S	473,600	265.	280.	350.	525.	6500.	—
1899	1,262,305	265.	280.	295.	325.	5000.	40,000.
1899O	37,047	300.	315.	375.	950.	13,500.	—
1899S	841,000	265.	300.	325.	475.	6500.	—
1900	293,960	265.	280.	295.	325.	6500.	40,000.
1900S	81,000	300.	330.	400.	1600.	12,500.	—
1901	1,718,825	265.	280.	295.	325.	4500.	40,000.
1901O	72,041	300.	325.	350.	675.	13,500.	—
1901S	2,812,750	265.	280.	295.	300.	4500.	—
1902	82,513	265.	280.	295.	350.	12,500.	40,000.
1902S	469,500	265.	280.	295.	350.	6500.	—
1903	125,926	265.	280.	295.	350.	6500.	40,000.
1903O	112,771	265.	290.	325.	565.	6500.	—
1903S	538,000	265.	300.	340.	375.	6500.	—
1904	162,038	265.	280.	295.	325.	6500.	40,000.
1904O	108,950	265.	300.	350.	575.	6500.	—
1905	201,078	265.	280.	295.	325.	6500.	40,000.
1905S	369,250	265.	350.	425.	4000.	6500.	—
1906	165,497	265.	280.	295.	325.	6500.	40,000.
1906D	981,000	265.	280.	295.	325.	6500.	—
1906O	86,895	265.	310.	350.	750.	13,500.	—
1906S	457,000	280.	300.	325.	675.	6500.	—

Date	Mintage	VF-20	XF-40	AU-50	MS-60	MS-65	Prf-65
1907	1,203,973	265.	280.	295.	325.	5000.	40,000.
1907D	1,030,000	265.	280.	295.	325.	5000.	—
1907S	210,500	275.	325.	400.	1000.	6500.	—

Indian Head

Reverse motto

No motto

Designer: Augustus Saint-Gaudens. **Size:** 27 millimeters. **Weight:** 16.718 grams. **Composition:** 90% gold (.4839 ounces), 10% copper. **Notes:** 1907 varieties are distinguished by whether the edge is rolled or wired, and whether the legend "E Pluribus Unum" has periods between each word.

Date	Mintage	VF-20	XF-40	AU-50	MS-60	MS-63	MS-65	Prf-65
1907 wire edge, periods before & after leg.	500	—	4500.	—	7800.	12,000.	39,000.	60,000.
1907 same, without stars on edge		—	Unique	—	—	—	—	—
1907 rolled edge, periods	42	—	—	—	21,500.	34,000.	60,000.	—
1907 without periods	239,406	425.	450.	500.	625.	2200.	9000.	—
1908 without motto	33,500	535.	585.	600.	900.	3350.	12,000.	—
1908D without motto	210,000	400.	425.	500.	720.	4100.	36,000.	—

With motto

Notes: In 1908 the motto "In God We Trust" was added on the reverse to the left of the eagle.

Date	Mintage	VF-20	XF-40	AU-50	MS-60	MS-63	MS-65	Prf-65
1908	341,486	375.	390.	400.	420.	1700.	7550.	35,000.
1908D	836,500	375.	400.	525.	710.	3500.	24,000.	—
1908S	59,850	400.	535.	700.	2500.	6600.	34,000.	—
1909	184,863	360.	390.	400.	480.	2450.	15,500.	39,000.
1909D	121,540	400.	440.	500.	975.	11,000.	42,000.	—
1909S	292,350	375.	425.	475.	840.	2650.	14,500.	—
1910	318,704	380.	390.	400.	430.	1600.	7550.	35,000.
1910D	2,356,640	360.	390.	400.	445.	1600.	7800.	—
1910S	811,000	475.	500.	550.	1050.	4100.	48,000.	—
1911	505,595	360.	375.	400.	430.	2300.	7200.	35,000.
1911D	30,100	400.	550.	750.	4800.	12,500.	90,000.	—
1911S	51,000	350.	450.	600.	1500.	3250.	9100.	—
1912	405,083	350.	390.	400.	435.	1600.	8400.	35,000.
1912S	300,000	350.	400.	510.	900.	2500.	46,000.	—
1913	442,071	350.	375.	400.	430.	1100.	8400.	35,000.
1913S	66,000	550.	650.	780.	5150.	25,000.	162,000.	—
1914	151,050	320.	350.	360.	395.	1800.	10,500.	35,000.
1914D	343,500	320.	360.	370.	400.	1700.	10,500.	—
1914S	208,000	350.	375.	500.	635.	3700.	39,500.	—
1915	351,075	320.	360.	380.	480.	1700.	7450.	42,000.
1915S	59,000	350.	500.	575.	2700.	8800.	73,000.	—
1916S	138,500	375.	475.	535.	725.	3500.	18,500.	—
1920S	126,500	6500.	7500.	8000.	15,000.	33,000.	120,000.	—
1926	1,014,000	380.	390.	400.	445.	1600.	6700.	—
1930S	96,000	3500.	5000.	7500.	8300.	12,500.	51,000.	—
1932	4,463,000	380.	390.	400.	445.	1600.	6000.	—
1933	312,500	—	—	—	57,000.	87,000.	450,000.	—

Gold $20 (Double eagle)

Coronet Head

"Twenty D.," no motto

Gold $20

Reverse motto

1861 Paquet reverse

"Twenty D.," no motto

Designer: James B. Longacre. **Size:** 34 millimeters. **Weight:** 33.436 grams. **Composition:** 90% gold (.9677 ounces), 10% copper. **Notes:** In 1861 the reverse was redesigned by Anthony C. Paquet, but it was withdrawn soon after its release. The letters in the inscriptions on the Paquet-reverse variety are taller than on the regular reverse.

Date	Mintage	VF-20	XF-40	AU-50	MS-60	MS-65	Prf-65
1849	1	Unique, in Smithsonion collection				—	—
1850	1,170,261	530.	625.	1000.	4100.	—	—
1850O	141,000	600.	1100.	3000.	7500.	—	—
1851	2,087,155	490.	525.	650.	2750.	—	—
1851O	315,000	600.	750.	1700.	11,500.	—	—
1852	2,053,026	500.	525.	675.	2200.	—	—
1852O	190,000	600.	750.	2400.	12,000.	—	—
1853	1,261,326	490.	600.	800.	5500.	—	—
1853O	71,000	625.	1000.	3400.	7500.	—	—
1854	757,899	500.	625.	950.	6500.	—	—
1854O	3,250	13,500.	30,000.	60,000.	—	—	—
1854S	141,468	550.	650.	1000.	4750.	28,000.	—
1855	364,666	550.	575.	1000.	9000.	28,000.	—
1855O	8,000	3000.	6000.	14,750.	—	—	—
1855S	879,675	500.	575.	1200.	8750.	—	—
1856	329,878	500.	575.	1000.	8750.	—	—
1856O	2,250	15,000.	30,000.	60,000.	—	—	—
1856S	1,189,750	500.	575.	850.	5800.	—	—
1857	439,375	500.	565.	825.	5000.	—	—
1857O	30,000	800.	1600.	4500.	—	—	—
1857S	970,500	500.	575.	850.	6000.	—	—
1858	211,714	550.	700.	1850.	6500.	—	—
1858O	35,250	1000.	1750.	6000.	8000.	—	—
1858S	846,710	500.	575.	925.	8500.	—	—
1859	43,597	900.	2250.	8000.	30,000.	—	—
1859O	9,100	2750.	6750.	15,000.	—	—	—
1859S	636,445	500.	600.	1000.	6750.	—	—
1860	577,670	500.	600.	800.	6500.	—	—
1860O	6,600	3000.	6250.	14,000.	—	—	—
1860S	544,950	500.	600.	1450.	7250.	—	—
1861	2,976,453	500.	520.	700.	2750.	—	—
1861 Paquet rev.	Inc. Ab.	Bowers & Merena, Nov. 1988, MS-67, $660,000.					—
1861O	17,741	1750.	3750.	7000.	—	—	—
1861S	768,000	550.	650.	1500.	7500.	—	—
1861S Paquet rev.	Inc. Ab.	4500.	9750.	20,000.	—	—	—
1862	92,133	725.	1600.	3750.	14,750.	—	—
1862S	854,173	550.	775.	1700.	8000.	—	—
1863	142,790	550.	900.	1800.	12,500.	—	—
1863S	966,570	490.	600.	1400.	6750.	—	—
1864	204,285	550.	700.	2000.	10,500.	—	—
1864S	793,660	550.	825.	2800.	10,000.	—	—
1865	351,200	475.	600.	1050.	7000.	—	—
1865S	1,042,500	490.	545.	1400.	8000.	—	—
1866S	Inc. Below	1350.	3750.	7750.	—	—	—

"Twenty D.," with motto

Notes: In 1866 the motto "In God We Trust" was added to the reverse above the eagle. The 1873 "closed-3" and "open-3" varieties are distinguished by the amount of space between the upper left and lower left serif in the 3 in the date.

Date	Mintage	VF-20	XF-40	AU-50	MS-60	MS-65	Prf-65
1866	698,775	485.	625.	1500.	8000.	—	—
1866S	842,250	500.	800.	2600.	—	—	—
1867	251,065	485.	500.	750.	1500.	—	—
1867S	920,750	485.	625.	1675.	13,250.	—	—
1868	98,600	550.	900.	2450.	7500.	—	—
1868S	837,500	485.	725.	1900.	10,250.	—	—
1869	175,155	485.	750.	2200.	6000.	44,000.	—
1869S	686,750	485.	600.	1750.	6250.	—	—
1870	155,185	500.	1000.	2700.	—	—	—
1870CC	3,789	35,000.	65,000.	80,000.	125,000.	—	—
1870S	982,000	485.	550.	775.	6000.	—	—
1871	80,150	700.	1100.	2250.	6500.	—	—
1871CC	17,387	1850.	4500.	10,500.	35,000.	—	—
1871S	928,000	485.	550.	850.	5500.	—	—
1872	251,880	485.	500.	700.	4000.	—	—
1872CC	26,900	1100.	1650.	6100.	14,000.	—	—
1872S	780,000	485.	525.	675.	2500.	—	—
1873 closed 3	Est. 208,925	600.	825.	1700.	15,000.	—	—
1873 open 3	Est. 1,500,900	480.	490.	515.	625.	—	—
1873CC	22,410	950.	1600.	4500.	16,000.	—	—
1873S	1,040,600	485.	525.	575.	1950.	—	—
1874	366,800	475.	550.	825.	1900.	—	—
1874CC	115,085	550.	700.	2350.	11,500.	—	—

Gold $20

Date	Mintage	VF-20	XF-40	AU-50	MS-60	MS-65	Prf-65
1874S	1,214,000	485.	500.	650.	2200.	—	—
1875	295,740	490.	525.	550.	975.	—	—
1875CC	111,151	525.	650.	750.	2400.	—	—
1875S	1,230,000	485.	490.	550.	1100.	—	—
1876	583,905	485.	490.	525.	950.	—	—
1876CC	138,441	525.	725.	1150.	7500.	—	—
1876S	1,597,000	485.	490.	515.	1100.	—	—

"Twenty Dollars"

Notes: In 1877 the denomination on the reverse was changed to read "Twenty Dollars" instead of "Twenty D."

Date	Mintage	VF-20	XF-40	AU-50	MS-60	MS-65	Prf-65
1877	397,670	485.	510.	550.	875.	—	—
1877CC	42,565	600.	850.	1800.	—	—	—
1877S	1,735,000	480.	500.	575.	1000.	—	—
1878	543,645	480.	500.	550.	750.	—	—
1878CC	13,180	750.	2000.	5250.	18,000.	—	—
1878S	1,739,000	480.	500.	525.	1500.	—	—
1879	207,630	500.	525.	575.	1650.	—	—
1879CC	10,708	850.	2500.	6500.	—	—	—
1879O	2,325	3250.	4250.	14,500.	45,000.	—	—
1879S	1,223,800	480.	490.	550.	1650.	—	—
1880	51,456	485.	510.	850.	—	—	—
1880S	836,000	500.	575.	750.	—	—	—
1881	2,260	3500.	7500.	16,500.	45,000.	—	—
1881S	727,000	480.	550.	700.	—	—	—
1882	630	8000.	15,000.	30,000.	50,000.	—	—
1882CC	39,140	675.	775.	1150.	4400.	—	—
1882S	1,125,000	480.	490.	510.	1000.	—	—
1883	92	—	—	—	—	—	—
1883CC	59,962	600.	625.	1000.	4700.	—	—
1883S	1,189,000	480.	490.	505.	725.	—	—
1884	71	Stacks, Nov. 1989, proof, $71,500.					—
1884CC	81,139	525.	800.	950.	2900.	—	—
1884S	916,000	480.	490.	505.	600.	—	—
1885	828	6500.	8750.	18,500.	42,500.	—	—
1885CC	9,450	1000.	1800.	4000.	12,000.	—	—
1885S	683,500	480.	525.	550.	650.	—	—
1886	1,106	8000.	12,500.	25,000.	32,000.	—	—
1887	121	—	—	—	—	—	65,000.
1887S	283,000	500.	525.	550.	1000.	—	—
1888	226,266	480.	525.	550.	1100.	—	—
1888S	859,600	485.	525.	550.	650.	—	—
1889	44,111	650.	700.	750.	1175.	—	—
1889CC	30,945	650.	700.	1200.	3500.	—	—
1889S	774,700	480.	525.	550.	700.	—	—
1890	75,995	600.	675.	700.	1000.	—	—
1890CC	91,209	675.	725.	950.	4250.	—	—
1890S	802,750	480.	525.	550.	1400.	—	—
1891	1,442	3100.	4250.	8250.	27,000.	—	—
1891CC	5,000	1900.	2900.	5500.	18,000.	—	—
1891S	1,288,125	480.	490.	505.	600.	—	—
1892	4,523	1200.	1750.	2750.	7000.	—	—
1892CC	27,265	675.	850.	1550.	5750.	—	—
1892S	930,150	480.	490.	505.	565.	—	—
1893	344,339	480.	500.	525.	600.	—	—
1893CC	18,402	675.	925.	1300.	2800.	—	—
1893S	996,175	480.	490.	525.	590.	—	—
1894	1,368,990	480.	490.	505.	565.	—	—
1894S	1,048,550	480.	490.	525.	600.	—	—
1895	1,114,656	480.	490.	505.	520.	—	—
1895S	1,143,500	440.	445.	525.	600.	7200.	—
1896	792,663	480.	490.	505.	565.	—	—
1896S	1,403,925	480.	490.	505.	565.	—	—
1897	1,383,261	480.	490.	505.	565.	—	—
1897S	1,470,250	480.	500.	525.	565.	—	—
1898	170,470	480.	490.	505.	800.	—	—
1898S	2,575,175	480.	490.	505.	565.	7100.	—
1899	1,669,384	480.	490.	505.	565.	7100.	—
1899S	2,010,300	480.	490.	505.	580.	—	—
1900	1,874,584	480.	490.	505.	565.	7100.	—
1900S	2,459,500	480.	490.	505.	600.	7200.	—
1901	111,526	480.	490.	505.	600.	7000.	—
1901S	1,596,000	480.	490.	505.	565.	—	—
1902	31,254	550.	600.	700.	1025.	7200.	—
1902S	1,753,625	480.	490.	505.	565.	—	—
1903	287,428	480.	490.	505.	565.	7000.	—
1903S	954,000	480.	490.	505.	565.	7200.	—
1904	6,256,797	480.	490.	505.	565.	4000.	—
1904S	5,134,175	480.	490.	505.	565.	7000.	—
1905	59,011	525.	550.	575.	1475.	—	—
1905S	1,813,000	480.	490.	505.	565.	—	—
1906	69,690	600.	640.	800.	1000.	7000.	—
1906D	620,250	480.	490.	505.	565.	—	—
1906S	2,065,750	480.	490.	505.	565.	—	—
1907	1,451,864	480.	490.	505.	565.	7200.	—
1907D	842,250	480.	490.	505.	565.	7000.	—
1907S	2,165,800	480.	490.	505.	565.	—	—

Saint-Gaudens

No motto

Designer: Augustus Saint-Gaudens. **Size:** 34 millimeters. **Weight:** 33.436 grams. **Composition:** 90% gold (.9677 ounces), 10% copper. **Notes:** The "Roman numerals" varieties for 1907 use Roman numerals for the date instead of Arabic numerals. The lettered-edge varieties have "E Pluribus Unum" on the edge, with stars between the words.

Roman numerals

No motto

Reverse motto

Arabic numerals

Date	Mintage	VF-20	XF-40	AU-50	MS-60	MS-63	MS-65	Prf-65
1907 extremely high relief, plain edge								
	—		Unique	—		—	—	—
1907 extremely high relief, lettered edge								
	Unrecorded		Prf-68 Private sale 1990 $1,500,000.				—	—
1907 high relief, Roman numerals, plain edge								
			Unique - AU-55 $150,000.			—	—	—
1907 high relief, Roman numerals, wire rim								
	11,250	2500.	3600.	4000.	6400.	11,000.	30,000.	—
1907 high relief, Roman numerals, flat rim								
	Inc. Ab.	3000.	4000.	4500.	6500.	12,500.	35,000.	—
1907 large letters on edge						Unique	—	—
1907 small letters on edge								
	361,667	495.	515.	535.	610.	950.	4550.	—
1908	4,271,551	495.	505.	525.	585.	700.	1650.	—
1908D	663,750	495.	505.	520.	600.	1100.	10,750.	—

With motto

Notes: In 1908 the motto "In God We Trust" was added at the bottom of the reverse.

Date	Mintage	VF-20	XF-40	AU-50	MS-60	MS-63	MS-65	Prf-65
1908	156,359	495.	505.	550.	600.	1800.	13,250.	41,000.
1908D	349,500	495.	505.	550.	585.	1125.	3650.	—
1908S	22,000	800.	1150.	1350.	3000.	9600.	27,500.	—
1909/8	161,282	500.	465.	600.	2000.	6850.	48,000.	—
1909	Inc. Ab.	495.	505.	550.	875.	10,000.	38,500.	45,000.
1909D	52,500	575.	600.	650.	1325.	3250.	36,000.	—
1909S	2,774,925	495.	505.	510.	585.	645.	4800.	—
1910	482,167	495.	505.	520.	585.	880.	7900.	50,000.
1910D	429,000	495.	505.	520.	575.	870.	4550.	—
1910S	2,128,250	495.	505.	520.	575.	1100.	14,000.	—
1911	197,350	495.	505.	520.	585.	2300.	11,000.	41,000.
1911D	846,500	495.	505.	520.	575.	645.	2050.	—
1911S	775,750	495.	505.	520.	595.	875.	7200.	—
1912	149,824	495.	505.	520.	600.	2750.	13,250.	41,000.
1913	168,838	495.	515.	525.	600.	4150.	18,000.	41,000.
1913D	393,500	495.	505.	520.	595.	1000.	6000.	—
1913S	34,000	495.	520.	560.	1150.	5600.	27,500.	—
1914	95,320	500.	525.	550.	680.	2700.	11,000.	41,000.
1914D	453,000	495.	505.	520.	575.	800.	3750.	—
1914S	1,498,000	495.	505.	520.	575.	800.	3500.	—
1915	152,050	495.	505.	530.	630.	2700.	14,000.	56,000.
1915S	567,500	495.	505.	520.	575.	800.	2150.	—
1916S	796,000	495.	505.	525.	625.	800.	2050.	—
1920	228,250	495.	505.	520.	575.	1400.	15,500.	—
1920S	558,000	4500.	6000.	7200.	18,000.	39,500.	96,000.	—
1921	528,500	7200.	9550.	15,000.	30,000.	60,000.	144,000.	—
1922	1,375,500	495.	505.	520.	575.	800.	6000.	—
1922S	2,658,000	500.	525.	600.	740.	1825.	24,000.	—
1923	566,000	495.	505.	520.	575.	800.	7200.	—
1923D	1,702,250	495.	505.	520.	575.	800.	1700.	—
1924	4,323,500	495.	505.	520.	575.	775.	1550.	—
1924D	3,049,500	700.	1150.	1350.	2100.	5200.	48,000.	—
1924S	2,927,500	700.	800.	975.	1700.	4350.	42,000.	—
1925	2,831,750	495.	505.	520.	575.	645.	1250.	—
1925D	2,938,500	875.	1100.	1300.	2250.	6500.	45,000.	—
1925S	3,776,500	875.	950.	1200.	4700.	24,000.	60,000.	—
1926	816,750	495.	505.	520.	575.	800.	1750.	—
1926D	481,000	1800.	2500.	4500.	8500.	35,000.	60,000.	—
1926S	2,041,500	700.	950.	1100.	1900.	3500.	38,000.	—
1927	2,946,750	495.	505.	520.	575.	645.	1250.	—
1927D	180,000	—	—	150,000.	265,000.	—	522,500.	—
1927S	3,107,000	2000.	4500.	5500.	10,500.	26,000.	100,000.	—
1928	8,816,000	495.	505.	520.	575.	645.	1250.	—
1929	1,779,750	4000.	7000.	10,000.	15,000.	19,000.	57,000.	—
1930S	74,000	6000.	9000.	13,000.	22,500.	36,000.	72,000.	—
1931	2,938,250	4250.	8500.	10,000.	15,000.	24,000.	66,000.	—
1931D	106,500	5500.	7500.	9500.	15,000.	21,500.	60,000.	—
1932	1,101,750	7000.	9500.	12,000.	14,500.	20,000.	54,000.	—
1933	445,500				None placed in circulation		—	—

Proof sets

Notes: Proof coins are produced through a special process involving specially selected and highly polished planchets and dies. They usually receive two strikings from the coin press at increased pressure. The result is a coin with mirrorlike surfaces and, in recent years, a cameo effect on its raised design surfaces. Proof sets have been sold off and on by the U.S. Mint since 1858. Listings here are for sets from what is commonly called the modern era, since 1936. Values for earlier proofs are included in the regular date listings. Sets were not offered in years not listed. Since 1968, proof coins have been produced at the San Francisco Mint; before that they were produced at the Philadelphia Mint. In 1942 the five-cent coin was struck in two compositions. Some proof sets for that year contain only one type (five-coin set); others contain both types. Two types of packaging were used in 1955: a box and a flat, plastic holder. The 1960 large-date and small-date sets are distinguished by the size of the date on the cent. Some 1968 sets are missing the mintmark on the dime, the result of an error in the preparation of an obverse die. The 1970 large-date and small-date sets are distinguished by the size of the date on the cent. Some 1970 sets are missing the mintmark on the dime, the result of an error in the preparation of an obverse die. Some 1971 sets are missing the mintmark on the five-cent piece, the result of an error in the preparation of an obverse die. The 1976 three-piece set contains the quarter, half dollar and dollar with the Bicentennial designs. The 1979 and 1981 Type II sets have clearer mintmarks than the Type I sets for those years. Some 1983 sets are missing the mintmark on the dime, the result of an error in the preparation of an obverse die. Prestige sets contain the five regular-issue coins plus a commemorative silver dollar from that year: 1983, Olympics; 1984, Olympics; 1986, Statue of Liberty; 1987, Constitution Bicentennial; and 1988, Olympics.

Date	Sets Sold	Issue Price	Value
1936	3,837	1.89	3350.
1937	5,542	1.89	2100.
1938	8,045	1.89	1000.
1939	8,795	1.89	970.
1940	11,246	1.89	760.
1941	15,287	1.89	620.
1942 6 coins	21,120	1.89	620.
1942 5 coins	Inc. Ab.	1.89	600.
1950	51,386	2.10	400.
1951	57,500	2.10	285.
1952	81,980	2.10	160.
1953	128,800	2.10	115.
1954	233,300	2.10	70.00
1955 box	378,200	2.10	60.00
1955 flat pack	Inc. Ab.	2.10	57.00
1956	669,384	2.10	27.00
1957	1,247,952	2.10	13.00
1958	875,652	2.10	19.00
1959	1,149,291	2.10	15.00
1960 large date	1,691,602	2.10	9.00
1960 small date	Inc. Ab.	2.10	19.00
1961	3,028,244	2.10	7.50
1962	3,218,019	2.10	7.50
1963	3,075,645	2.10	7.50
1964	3,950,762	2.10	7.50
1968S	3,041,509	5.00	4.00
1968 S no mint mark dime	—	5.00	7950.
1969S	2,934,631	5.00	4.00
1970S large date	2,632,810	5.00	7.50
1970S small date	Inc. Ab.	5.00	84.00
1970S no mint mark dime			
	Est. 2,200	5.00	620.
1971S	3,224,138	5.00	3.60
1971S no mint mark nickel			
	Est. 1,655	5.00	850.
1972S	3,267,667	5.00	3.90
1973S	2,769,624	7.00	5.00
1974S	2,617,350	7.00	5.00
1975S	2,909,369	7.00	7.00
1976S 3 coins	3,998,621	12.00	11.00
1976S	4,149,730	7.00	8.00
1977S	3,251,152	9.00	5.30
1978S	3,127,788	9.00	6.00
1979S Type I	3,677,175	9.00	6.50
1979S Type II	Inc.Ab.	9.00	67.00
1980S	3,547,030	10.00	6.65
1981S Type I	4,063,083	11.00	7.50
1981S Type II	—	11.00	165.
1982S	3,857,479	11.00	4.50
1983S Prestige set	140,361	59.00	110.
1983S	3,138,765	11.00	5.50
1983S no mint mark dime	—	11.00	470.
1984S Prestige set	316,680	59.00	28.00
1984S	2,748,430	11.00	10.00
1985S	3,362,821	11.00	6.00
1986S Prestige set	599,317	48.50	24.00
1986S	2,411,180	11.00	16.50
1987S	3,972,233	11.00	5.00
1987S Prestige set	435,495	45.00	20.00
1988S	3,031,287	11.00	9.50
1988S Prestige set	231,661	45.00	24.00
1989S	3,009,107	11.00	8.50
1989S Prestige set	211,087	45.00	32.00
1990S	2,793,433	11.00	21.00
1990S no S 1¢	3,555	11.00	1850.
1990S Prestige set	506,126	45.00	27.00
1990S no S 1¢ Prestige set	—	45.00	1850.
1991S	2,610,833	11.00	22.00
1991S Prestige set	256,954	59.00	70.00
1992S	2,675,618	12.50	20.00
1992S Prestige set	183,285	59.00	59.00
1992S Silver	1,009,585	21.00	24.00
1992S Silver premier	308,055	37.00	32.00
1993S	—	12.50	17.00
1993S Prestige set	—	57.00	60.00
1993S Silver	—	21.00	20.00
1993S Silver premier	—	37.00	27.00

Mint sets

Notes: Mint, or uncirculated, sets contain one uncirculated coin of each denomination from each mint produced for circulation that year. Values listed here are only for those sets sold by the U.S. Mint. Sets were not offered in years not listed. In years when the Mint did not offer the sets, some private companies compiled and marketed uncirculated sets. Mint sets from 1947 through 1958 contained two examples of each coin mounted in cardboard holders, which caused the coins to tarnish. Beginning in 1959, the sets have been packaged in sealed Pliofilm packets and include only one specimen of each coin struck for that year. Listings for 1965, 1966 and 1967 are for "special mint sets," which were of higher quality than regular mint sets and were prooflike. They were packaged in plastic cases. The 1970 large-date and small-date varieties are distinguished by the size of the date on the cent. The 1976 three-piece set contains the quarter, half dollar and dollar with the Bicentennial design. The 1971 and 1972 sets do not include a dollar coin; the 1979 set does not include an S-mintmarked dollar.

Date	Sets Sold	Issue Price	Value
1947	Est. 5,000	4.87	630.
1948	Est. 6,000	4.92	225.
1949	Est. 5,200	5.45	540.
1950	None issued	—	—
1951	8,654	6.75	390.
1952	11,499	6.14	280.
1953	15,538	6.14	225.
1954	25,599	6.19	110.
1955	49,656	3.57	69.00
1956	45,475	3.34	57.00
1957	32,324	4.40	95.00
1958	50,314	4.43	90.00
1959	187,000	2.40	15.00
1960	260,485	2.40	14.00
1961	223,704	2.40	14.00
1962	385,285	2.40	10.50
1963	606,612	2.40	9.00
1964	1,008,108	2.40	9.00
Date	**Sets Sold**	**Issue Price**	**Value**
1965 SMS*	2,360,000	4.00	3.65
1966 SMS*	2,261,583	4.00	4.35
1967 SMS*	1,863,344	4.00	6.00
1968	2,105,128	2.50	3.10
1969	1,817,392	2.50	3.20
1970 large date	2,038,134	2.50	10.50
1970 small date	Inc. Ab.	2.50	39.00
1971	2,193,396	3.50	2.95
1972	2,750,000	3.50	2.80
1973	1,767,691	6.00	7.50
1974	1,975,981	6.00	5.75
1975	1,921,488	6.00	6.15
1976 3 coins	4,908,319	9.00	9.00
1976	1,892,513	6.00	6.45
1977	2,006,869	7.00	5.60
1978	2,162,609	7.00	5.60
1979	2,526,000	8.00	5.35
1980	2,815,066	9.00	6.75
1981	2,908,145	11.00	7.50
1982 & 1983	None issued	—	—
1984	1,832,857	7.00	4.50
1985	1,710,571	7.00	5.00
1986	1,153,536	7.00	18.50
1987	2,890,758	7.00	4.60
1988	1,646,204	7.00	3.35
1989	1,987,915	7.00	3.10
1990	1,809,184	7.00	5.20
1991	—	7.00	6.60
1992	—	7.00	9.10
1993	1,500,098	7.00	10.00

Uncirculated rolls

Notes: Listings are for rolls containing uncirculated coins. Large-date and small-date varieties for 1960 and 1970 apply to the one-cent coins.

Date	Cents	Nickels	Dimes	Quarters	Halves
1934	230.	1765.	1250.	1100.	1550.
1934D	900.	3400.	3400.	5550.	—
1934S	—	—	—	—	—
1935	100.	1000.	850.	855.	1200.
1935D	210.	2150.	3300.	5650.	4050.
1935S	500.	1450.	1650.	4550.	6300.
1936	78.00	750.	650.	750.	1135.
1936D	155.	900.	2000.	—	2250.
1936S	125.	1000.	1150.	3650.	3300.
1937	53.00	500.	650.	750.	1200.
1937D	85.00	750.	1250.	1500.	4150.
1937S	105.	750.	1325.	5400.	3150.
1938	69.00	100.	1010.	2140.	1900.
1938D	105.	125.	1050.	—	—
1938D Buffalo	—	500.	—	—	—
1938S	65.00	125.	1400.	2455.	—
1939	38.00	57.00	700.	565.	1250.
1939D	110.	1610.	550.	1050.	1300.
1939S	67.00	695.	1550.	2585.	2500.
1940	38.00	26.00	380.	455.	950.
1940D	32.00	76.00	650.	2250.	—
1940S	32.00	105.	600.	600.	1200.
1941	57.00	31.00	350.	225.	850.
1941D	120.	95.00	650.	800.	1150.
1941S	120.	145.	400.	950.	3500.

Uncirculated rolls

Date	Cents	Nickels	Dimes	Quarters	Halves
1942	22.50	150.	250.	210.	800.
1942P	—	295.	—	—	—
1942D	15.50	755.	550.	500.	1250.
1942S	180.	275.	750.	3000.	1650.
1943	30.00	145.	300.	140.	850.
1943D	43.00	105.	450.	600.	1650.
1943S	90.00	145.	750.	1200.	1400.
1944	14.00	140.	250.	100.	850.
1944D	20.00	355.	400.	285.	1100.
1944S	9.00	160.	415.	285.	1200.
1945	27.00	160.	240.	85.00	850.
1945D	9.00	125.	300.	290.	1000.
1945S	6.50	90.00	300.	180.	1150.
1946	11.50	22.50	30.00	160.	1000.
1946D	9.00	17.50	35.00	105.	800.
1946S	10.00	11.50	55.00	100.	1000.
1947	43.00	33.00	55.00	205.	1050.
1947D	8.25	21.50	100.	145.	900.
1947S	27.50	15.50	85.00	100.	—
1948	20.00	15.00	175.	110.	365.
1948D	10.50	54.00	155.	125.	285.
1948S	21.00	19.00	90.00	155.	—
1949	19.00	20.00	550.	750.	950.
1949D	19.00	27.50	215.	270.	800.
1949S	44.00	39.00	915.	—	1150.
1950	29.50	24.00	90.00	90.00	550.
1950D	30.00	195.	65.00	105.	530.
1950S	29.00	—	485.	240.	—
1951	25.00	41.00	55.00	105.	315.
1951D	10.50	31.00	60.00	100.	750.
1951S	28.00	69.00	245.	600.	550.
1952	17.50	33.00	70.00	90.00	265.
1952D	7.60	39.00	35.00	90.00	170.
1952S	73.00	19.00	225.	330.	835.
1953	3.80	6.00	55.00	75.00	280.
1953D	3.80	6.30	25.00	50.00	160.
1953S	11.00	15.00	25.00	85.00	280.
1954	6.00	5.00	24.00	50.00	120.
1954D	3.80	6.30	25.00	50.00	120.
1954S	3.00	5.50	25.00	50.00	135.
1955	4.15	10.50	25.00	55.00	135.
1955D	2.80	6.30	25.00	55.00	—
1955S	12.00	—	27.00	—	—
1956	2.50	3.50	24.00	50.00	100.
1956D	2.00	3.15	24.00	55.00	—
1957	1.55	4.25	24.00	50.00	120.
1957D	1.45	3.00	25.00	50.00	110.
1958	1.55	3.15	24.00	50.00	85.00
1958D	1.10	3.15	24.00	50.00	85.00
1959	1.00	2.85	24.00	50.00	105.
1959D	.75	2.65	24.00	50.00	120.
1960 lg. dt.	.70	2.85	24.00	48.00	85.00
1960 sm. dt.	56.00	—	—	—	—
1960D lg. dt.	.85	2.85	24.00	48.00	110.
1960D sm. dt.	.85	—	—	—	—
1961	.90	3.15	24.00	48.00	90.00
1961D	.85	3.00	24.00	48.00	90.00
1962	.90	2.85	24.00	48.00	70.00
1962D	.75	3.45	24.00	48.00	70.00
1963	.75	2.80	24.00	48.00	55.00
1963D	.75	2.80	24.00	48.00	55.00
1964	.90	4.40	24.00	48.00	48.00
1964D	.90	4.40	24.00	48.00	48.00
1965	1.05	2.85	7.50	17.50	19.50
1966	1.90	2.85	8.00	19.00	19.50
1967	.90	4.40	7.50	24.00	19.50
1968	1.70	—	7.90	22.50	—
1968D	1.55	3.50	7.60	28.00	19.50
1968S	.70	3.80	—	—	—
1969	4.50	—	19.00	25.00	—
1969D	1.00	5.00	11.50	25.00	19.50
1969S	1.25	5.00	—	—	—
1970	3.50	—	9.00	19.00	—
1970D	1.00	3.50	9.00	17.50	195.
1970S	1.10	3.50	—	—	—
1970S sm. dt.	1510.	—	—	—	—
1971	7.50	14.00	11.50	26.50	15.50
1971D	5.50	4.75	9.00	35.00	14.00
1971S	4.15	—	—	—	—
1972	1.00	4.15	8.50	14.00	19.00
1972D	1.00	5.00	9.00	19.50	17.50
1972S	.85	—	—	—	—
1973	1.10	3.80	8.00	19.50	19.50
1973D	.90	3.50	8.50	19.50	16.00
1973S	1.00	—	—	—	—
1974	.70	3.80	9.00	16.00	16.00
1974D	.85	5.40	8.00	22.50	16.00
1974S	1.25	—	—	—	—
1975	1.00	10.00	10.50	—	—
1975D	1.00	6.30	8.50	—	—
1976	1.00	11.50	15.00	19.00	16.00
1976D	3.15	9.50	14.00	19.00	16.00
1977	.90	3.80	7.50	15.50	20.00
1977D	.90	5.65	7.90	15.50	20.00
1978	1.05	3.55	8.50	19.50	20.00
1978D	1.05	4.15	9.00	15.50	19.50
1979	1.25	3.45	7.90	19.00	17.50
1979D	.85	4.90	7.90	19.00	17.50
1980	1.00	4.00	7.50	14.00	16.00
1980D	1.00	3.30	7.50	14.00	16.00
1981	.85	3.50	7.50	15.50	21.00
1981D	.90	3.50	7.00	15.50	24.00
1982	.85	20.00	55.00	170.	24.00
1982D	.90	57.00	12.50	30.00	24.00
1983	1.25	26.00	31.50	210.	19.50
1983D	1.40	29.00	31.50	225.	19.00
1984	1.75	5.00	12.50	30.00	19.50
1984D	9.00	5.65	14.50	70.00	17.50
1985	2.40	6.65	13.00	90.00	23.00
1985D	1.90	6.50	10.00	110.	19.50
1986	4.75	6.00	14.50	150.	26.00

Date	Cents	Nickels	Dimes	Quarters	Halves
1986D	2.00	29.00	14.50	105.	23.00
1987	3.15	4.00	7.50	16.00	55.00
1987D	1.75	4.00	7.50	15.50	55.00
1988	1.50	3.45	9.00	59.00	16.00
1988D	1.50	3.80	8.00	17.50	17.50
1989	.90	3.15	7.00	19.50	17.50
1990	.95	3.15	7.20	17.00	14.00
1990D	.95	3.50	7.20	14.00	15.50
1991	.95	3.50	7.90	14.00	15.50
1991D	.75	3.50	7.90	14.00	15.50
1992	1.00	4.00	7.50	19.50	14.00
1992D	.75	3.50	7.50	15.50	15.50
1993	1.00	4.00	7.50	19.50	14.00
1993D	.55	3.50	7.50	15.50	15.50
1994	1.00	4.15	7.50	19.50	14.00
1994D	.75	3.50	7.50	15.50	15.50

Commemoratives 1893-1954

Quarters

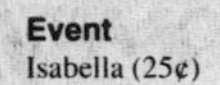

Date	Event	Mintage	AU-50	MS-60	MS-63	MS-64	MS-65
1893	Isabella (25¢)	24,214	215.	325.	600.	950.	2000.

Half dollars

Notes: Values for "PDS sets" contain one example each from the Philadelphia, Denver and San Francisco mints. "Type coin" prices are for the most inexpensive single coin available from the date and mintmark combinations listed. The Alabama half-dollar varieties are distinguished by whether a "2x2" appears on the obverse behind the head. The Grant half-dollar varieties are distinguished by whether a star appears above the word "Grant" on the obverse. The Missouri half-dollar varieties are distinguished by whether a "2 ★ 4" appears on the obverse to the left of the head.

2x2

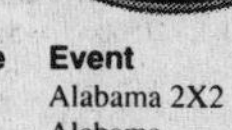

Date	Event	Mintage	AU-50	MS-60	MS-63	MS-64	MS-65
1921	Alabama 2X2	6,006	140.	275.	630.	1100.	3400.
1921	Alabama	59,038	60.00	195.	580.	900.	3400.

Date	Event	Mintage	AU-50	MS-60	MS-63	MS-64	MS-65
1936	Albany	17,671	195.	215.	235.	315.	655.

Date	Event	Mintage	AU-50	MS-60	MS-63	MS-64	MS-65
1937	Antietam	18,028	400.	410.	445.	485.	660.

Date	Event	Mintage	AU-50	MS-60	MS-63	MS-64	MS-65
1935	Arkansas PDS set	5,505	—	245.	255.	330.	1300.
1936	Arkansas PDS set	9,660	—	245.	255.	330.	1450.
1937	Arkansas PDS set	5,505	—	245.	290.	345.	1650.
1938	Arkansas PDS set	3,155	—	365.	425.	670.	2300.
1939	Arkansas PDS set	2,104	—	730.	800.	1100.	2800.
	Arkansas type coin	—	73.00	80.00	85.00	110.	380.

See also Robinson-Arkansas

Date	Event	Mintage	AU-50	MS-60	MS-63	MS-64	MS-65
1936	Bay Bridge	71,424	90.00	95.00	120.	175.	400.

"1934" added to 1935-38 issues

Date	Event	Mintage	AU-50	MS-60	MS-63	MS-64	MS-65
1934	Boone	10,007	92.00	97.00	105.	115.	180.
1935	Boone PDS set w/1934	5,005	—	545.	970.	1200.	1800.
1935	Boone PDS set	2,003	—	255.	275.	330.	545.
1936	Boone PDS set	5,005	—	255.	275.	330.	545.
1937	Boone PDS set	2,506	—	580.	655.	750.	1150.
1938	Boone PDS set	2,100	—	825.	910.	1050.	2050.
	Boone type coin	—	73.00	85.00	90.00	110.	180.

Date	Event	Mintage	AU-50	MS-60	MS-63	MS-64	MS-65
1936	Bridgeport	25,015	95.00	105.	115.	155.	425.

Date	Event	Mintage	AU-50	MS-60	MS-63	MS-64	MS-65
1925S	California Jubilee	86,594	85.00	110.	235.	385.	900.

Commemoratives, 1893-1954

Date	Event	Mintage	AU-50	MS-60	MS-63	MS-64	MS-65
1936	Cincinnati PDS set	5,005	—	765.	835.	1000.	2650.
1936	Cincinnati type coin	—	215.	255.	275.	340.	750.

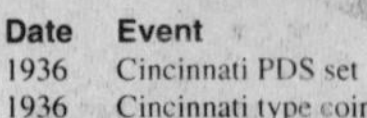

Date	Event	Mintage	AU-50	MS-60	MS-63	MS-64	MS-65
1936	Cleveland - Great Lakes	50,030	55.00	61.00	66.00	100.	285.

Date	Event	Mintage	AU-50	MS-60	MS-63	MS-64	MS-65
1936	Columbia PDS set	9,007	—	560.	620.	675.	835.
1936	Columbia type coin	—	175.	195.	210.	225.	275.

Date	Event	Mintage	AU-50	MS-60	MS-63	MS-64	MS-65
1892	Columbian Expo	950,000	11.00	36.00	110.	265.	700.
1893	Columbian Expo	1,550,405	11.00	36.00	95.00	255.	800.

Date	Event	Mintage	AU-50	MS-60	MS-63	MS-64	MS-65
1935	Connecticut	25,018	160.	195.	215.	330.	650.

Date	Event	Mintage	AU-50	MS-60	MS-63	MS-64	MS-65
1936	Delaware	20,993	190.	215.	245.	290.	600.

Date	Event	Mintage	AU-50	MS-60	MS-63	MS-64	MS-65
1936	Elgin	20,015	180.	205.	215.	235.	330.

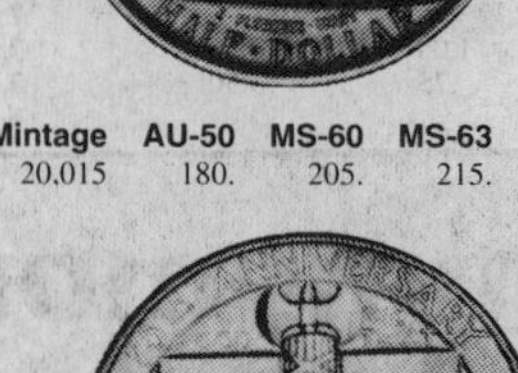

Date	Event	Mintage	AU-50	MS-60	MS-63	MS-64	MS-65
1936	Gettysburg	26,928	210.	225.	265.	345.	650.

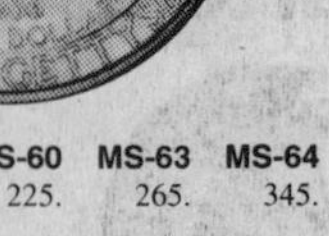

Star added

Date	Event	Mintage	AU-50	MS-60	MS-63	MS-64	MS-65
1922	Grant with star	4,256	535.	885.	2250.	3150.	8500.
1922	Grant	67,405	68.00	80.00	215.	400.	950.

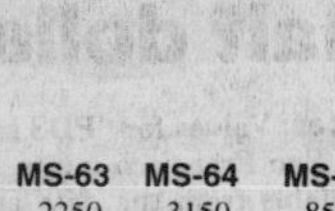

Date	Event	Mintage	AU-50	MS-60	MS-63	MS-64	MS-65
1928	Hawaiian	10,008	825.	1095.	1750.	2500.	5200.

Date	Event	Mintage	AU-50	MS-60	MS-63	MS-64	MS-65
1935	Hudson	10,008	410.	465.	610.	730.	1450.

Date	Event	Mintage	AU-50	MS-60	MS-63	MS-64	MS-65
1924	Huguenot-Walloon	142,080	63.00	85.00	100.	195.	750.

Commemoratives, 1893-1954

Date	Event	Mintage	AU-50	MS-60	MS-63	MS-64	MS-65
1918	Lincoln-Illinois	100,058	68.00	80.00	95.00	210.	600.

Date	Event	Mintage	AU-50	MS-60	MS-63	MS-64	MS-65
1946	Iowa	100,057	68.00	73.00	80.00	90.00	100.

Date	Event	Mintage	AU-50	MS-60	MS-63	MS-64	MS-65
1925	Lexington-Concord	162,013	58.00	68.00	95.00	195.	1100.

Date	Event	Mintage	AU-50	MS-60	MS-63	MS-64	MS-65
1936	Long Island	81,826	61.00	68.00	73.00	120.	440.

Date	Event	Mintage	AU-50	MS-60	MS-63	MS-64	MS-65
1936	Lynchburg	20,013	140.	155.	180.	270.	410.

Date	Event	Mintage	AU-50	MS-60	MS-63	MS-64	MS-65
1920	Maine	50,028	61.00	85.00	170.	315.	750.

Date	Event	Mintage	AU-50	MS-60	MS-63	MS-64	MS-65
1934	Maryland	25,015	120.	140.	150.	205.	425.

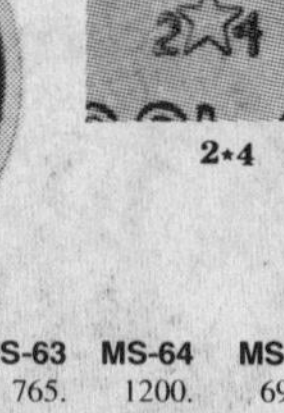

2★4

Date	Event	Mintage	AU-50	MS-60	MS-63	MS-64	MS-65
1921	Missouri 2★4	5,000	245.	380.	765.	1200.	6950.
1921	Missouri	15,428	180.	310.	675.	1100.	6950.

Date	Event	Mintage	AU-50	MS-60	MS-63	MS-64	MS-65
1923S	Monroe	274,077	38.00	43.00	95.00	390.	2750.

Date	Event	Mintage	AU-50	MS-60	MS-63	MS-64	MS-65
1938	New Rochelle	15,266	275.	295.	330.	350.	485.

Date	Event	Mintage	AU-50	MS-60	MS-63	MS-64	MS-65
1936	Norfolk	16,936	385.	400.	420.	450.	465.

Date	Event	Mintage	AU-50	MS-60	MS-63	MS-64	MS-65
1926	Oregon	47,955	85.00	92.00	135.	180.	255.
1926S	Oregon	83,055	85.00	92.00	135.	205.	255.
1928	Oregon	6,028	165.	175.	190.	275.	450.
1933D	Oregon	5,008	290.	305.	325.	380.	465.
1934D	Oregon	7,006	195.	210.	225.	270.	410.
1936	Oregon	10,006	120.	150.	155.	225.	305.
1936S	Oregon	5,006	130.	170.	195.	235.	365.

Commemoratives, 1893-1954

Date	Event	Mintage	AU-50	MS-60	MS-63	MS-64	MS-65
1937D	Oregon	12,008	110.	130.	155.	205.	305.
1938	Oregon PDS set	6,005	—	670.	680.	730.	900.
1939	Oregon PDS set	3,004	—	970.	1300.	1650.	2050.
	Oregon type coin	—	92.00	97.00	135.	180.	255.

Date	Event	Mintage	AU-50	MS-60	MS-63	MS-64	MS-65
1915S	Panama - Pacific	27,134	195.	295.	695.	1250.	2700.

1921 version

Date	Event	Mintage	AU-50	MS-60	MS-63	MS-64	MS-65
1920	Pilgrim	152,112	68.00	73.00	85.00	170.	750.
1921	Pilgrim	20,053	81.00	97.00	170.	290.	1000.

Date	Event	Mintage	AU-50	MS-60	MS-63	MS-64	MS-65
1936	Rhode Island PDS set	15,010	—	215.	235.	385.	1200.
1936	Rhode Island type coin	—	68.00	73.00	80.00	130.	390.

Date	Event	Mintage	AU-50	MS-60	MS-63	MS-64	MS-65
1937	Roanoke	29,030	175.	190.	210.	225.	265.

Date	Event	Mintage	AU-50	MS-60	MS-63	MS-64	MS-65
1936	Robinson-Arkansas	25,265	68.00	80.00	85.00	140.	420.
		(See also Arkansas)					

Date	Event	Mintage	AU-50	MS-60	MS-63	MS-64	MS-65
1935S	San Diego	70,132	61.00	68.00	73.00	80.00	95.00
1936D	San Diego	30,092	61.00	68.00	76.00	80.00	120.

Date	Event	Mintage	AU-50	MS-60	MS-63	MS-64	MS-65
1926	Sesquicentennial	141,120	68.00	73.00	160.	500.	5500.

Date	Event	Mintage	AU-50	MS-60	MS-63	MS-64	MS-65
1935	Spanish Trail	10,008	670.	790.	825.	865.	1050.

Date	Event	Mintage	AU-50	MS-60	MS-63	MS-64	MS-65
1925	Stone Mountain	1,314,709	34.00	41.00	51.00	75.00	195.

Date	Event	Mintage	AU-50	MS-60	MS-63	MS-64	MS-65
1934	Texas	61,463	80.00	95.00	100.	110.	160.
1935	Texas PDS set	9,994	—	290.	310.	330.	475.
1936	Texas PDS set	8,911	—	290.	310.	330.	475.
1937	Texas PDS set	6,571	—	330.	365.	425.	475.
1938	Texas PDS set	3,775	—	545.	850.	890.	1300.
	Texas type coins	—	80.00	95.00	100.	110.	160.

Date	Event	Mintage	AU-50	MS-60	MS-63	MS-64	MS-65
1925	Fort Vancouver	14,994	205.	275.	400.	545.	1150.

Date	Event	Mintage	AU-50	MS-60	MS-63	MS-64	MS-65
1927	Vermont	28,142	120.	155.	210.	380.	1050.

Date	Event	Mintage	AU-50	MS-60	MS-63	MS-64	MS-65
1946	B.T. Washington PDS set	200,113	—	36.00	49.00	61.00	150.
1947	B.T. Washington PDS set	100,017	—	45.00	73.00	105.	275.
1948	B.T. Washington PDS set	8,005	—	92.00	105.	160.	180.
1949	B.T. Washington PDS set	6,004	—	205.	215.	230.	270.
1950	B.T. Washington PDS set	6,004	—	95.00	110.	150.	160.
1951	B.T. Washington PDS set	7,004	—	120.	135.	150.	160.
	B.T. Washington type coin	—	10.00	12.00	16.00	23.00	40.00

Date	Event	Mintage	AU-50	MS-60	MS-63	MS-64	MS-65
1951	Washington-Carver PDS set	10,004	—	68.00	85.00	110.	495.
1952	Washington-Carver PDS set	8,006	—	73.00	110.	120.	275.
1953	Washington-Carver PDS set	8,003	—	68.00	80.00	130.	485.
1954	Washington-Carver PDS set	12,006	—	61.00	80.00	92.00	440.
	Washington-Carver type coin	—	10.00	12.00	20.00	23.00	60.00

Date	Event	Mintage	AU-50	MS-60	MS-63	MS-64	MS-65
1936	Wisconsin	25,015	170.	175.	190.	205.	245.

Date	Event	Mintage	AU-50	MS-60	MS-63	MS-64	MS-65
1936	York County	25,015	155.	170.	180.	190.	230.

Silver dollars

Date	Event	Mintage	AU-50	MS-60	MS-63	MS-64	MS-65
1900	Lafayette ($1)	36,026	275.	545.	1750.	3200.	8500.

Commemoratives, 1893-1954

Gold dollars

Notes: The Grant gold-dollar varieties are distinguished by whether a star appears on the obverse above the word "Grant."

Jefferson **McKinley**

Date	Event	Mintage	AU-50	MS-60	MS-63	MS-64	MS-65
1903	Louisiana, Jefferson	17,500	280.	405.	1200.	1950.	2750.
1903	Louisiana, McKinley	17,500	330.	410.	1150.	1900.	2850.

Date	Event	Mintage	AU-50	MS-60	MS-63	MS-64	MS-65
1904	Lewis and Clark Expo	10,025	395.	800.	2900.	4450.	6500.
1905	Lewis and Clark Expo	10,041	495.	850.	3600.	6200.	16,000.

Date	Event	Mintage	AU-50	MS-60	MS-63	MS-64	MS-65
1915S	Panama-Pacific Expo	15,000	320.	435.	1150.	1800.	2600.

Date	Event	Mintage	AU-50	MS-60	MS-63	MS-64	MS-65
1916	McKinley Memorial	9,977	320.	435.	1050.	1550.	2700.
1917	McKinley Memorial	10,000	325.	440.	1500.	2300.	3650.

With star

Date	Event	Mintage	AU-50	MS-60	MS-63	MS-64	MS-65
1922	Grant Memorial w/o star	5,016	950.	1400.	1950.	2350.	3050.
1922	Grant Memorial w/star	5,000	1100.	1550.	1950.	2450.	3200.

Gold $2.50

Date	Event	Mintage	AU-50	MS-60	MS-63	MS-64	MS-65
1915S	Panama Pacific Expo.	6,749	1025.	1350.	2700.	3750.	4750.

Date	Event	Mintage	AU-50	MS-60	MS-63	MS-64	MS-65
1926	Philadelphia Sesquicentennial	46,019	295.	350.	830.	1550.	8000.

Gold $50

Date	Event	Mintage	AU-50	MS-60	MS-63	MS-64	MS-65
1915S	Panama-Pacific Expo. round	483	21,000.	23,500.	35,000.	44,500.	99,500.
1915S	Panama-Pacific Expo. octagon	645	18,500.	21,000.	28,500.	44,500.	88,000.

Commemoratives 1982-present

Half dollars

Date	Mintage	(Proof)	MS-65	Prf-65
1982D Geo. Washington	2,210,458	—	3.90	—
1982S Geo. Washington	—	(4,894,044)	—	3.90

Date	Mintage	(Proof)	MS-65	Prf-65
1986D Statue of Liberty	928,008	—	3.50	—
1986S Statue of Liberty	—	(6,925,627)	—	3.40

Date	Mintage	(Proof)	MS-65	Prf-65
1989D Congress	163,753	—	13.00	—
1989S Congress	767,897	—	—	7.00

Date	Mintage	(Proof)	MS-65	Prf-65
1991D Mt. Rushmore	172,754	—	11.00	—
1991S Mt. Rushmore	753,257	—	—	11.00

Date	Mintage	(Proof)	MS-65	Prf-65
1992P Olympic	161,607	—	6.25	—
1992S Olympic	—	(519,645)	—	9.00

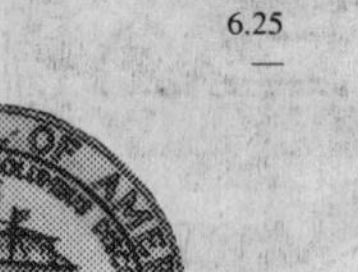

Date	Mintage	(Proof)	MS-65	Prf-65
1992D Columbus	135,702	—	10.00	—
1992S Columbus	—	(390,154)	—	10.00

Date	Mintage	(Proof)	MS-65	Prf-65
1993W Madison/Bill of Rights	—	—	14.00	—
1993S Madison/Bill of Rights	—	—	—	13.00

Date	Mintage	(Proof)	MS-65	Prf-65
1993P World War II	—	—	10.00	10.00

Commemoratives, 1982-present

Date	Mintage	(Proof)	MS-65	Prf-65
1994 World Cup Soccer	—	—	—	—
1994 World Cup Soccer	—	—	—	—

Silver dollars

Date	Mintage	(Proof)	MS-65	Prf-65
1983P Olympic	294,543	—	10.00	—
1983D Olympic	174,014	—	24.00	—
1983S Olympic	174,014	(1,577,025)	21.00	9.00

Date	Mintage	(Proof)	MS-65	Prf-65
1984P Olympic	217,954	—	15.00	—
1984D Olympic	116,675	—	40.00	—
1984S Olympic	116,675	(1,801,210)	42.00	11.00

Date	Mintage	(Proof)	MS-65	Prf-65
1986P Statue of Liberty	723,635	—	9.00	—
1986S Statue of Liberty	—	(6,414,638)	—	8.00

Date	Mintage	(Proof)	MS-65	Prf-65
1987P Constitution	451,629	—	9.00	—
1987S Constitution	—	(2,747,116)	—	9.00

Date	Mintage	(Proof)	MS-65	Prf-65
1988D Olympic	191,368	—	20.00	—
1988S Olympic	—	(1,359,366)	—	8.00

Date	Mintage	(Proof)	MS-65	Prf-65
1989D Congress	135,203	—	20.00	—
1989S Congress	—	(762,198)	—	15.00

Date	Mintage	(Proof)	MS-65	Prf-65
1990W Eisenhower	241,669	—	20.00	—
1990P Eisenhower	—	(638,335)	—	11.00

Date	Mintage	(Proof)	MS-65	Prf-65
1991P Mt. Rushmore	133,139	—	29.00	—
1991S Mt. Rushmore	—	(738,419)	—	25.00

Date	Mintage	(Proof)	MS-65	Prf-65
1991D Korean War	213,049	—	17.00	—
1991P Korean War	—	(618,488)	—	16.00

Commemoratives, 1982-present

Date	Mintage	(Proof)	MS-65	Prf-65
1991D USO	124,958	—	42.00	—
1991S USO	—	(321,275)	—	28.00

Date	Mintage	(Proof)	MS-65	Prf-65
1992D Olympic	187,552	—	23.00	—
1992S Olympic	—	(504,505)	—	26.00

Date	Mintage	(Proof)	MS-65	Prf-65
1992D White House	123,803	—	65.00	—
1992W White House	—	(375,851)	—	69.00

Date	Mintage	(Proof)	MS-65	Prf-65
1992D Columbus	106,949	—	31.00	—
1992P Columbus	—	(385,241)	—	31.00

Date	Mintage	(Proof)	MS-65	Prf-65
1993D Madison/Bill of Rights	—	—	28.00	—
1993S Madison/Bill of Rights	—	—	—	26.00

Date	Mintage	(Proof)	MS-65	Prf-65
1993D World War II	—	—	31.00	—
1993W World War II	—	—	—	37.00

Date	Mintage	(Proof)	MS-65	Prf-65
1994 World Cup Soccer	—	—	—	—
1994 World Cup Soccer	—	—	—	—

Gold $5

Date	Mintage	(Proof)	MS-65	Prf-65
1986W Statue of Liberty	95,248	(404,013)	125.	125.

Date	Mintage	(Proof)	MS-65	Prf-65
1987W Constitution	214,225	(651,659)	117.	117.

Date	Mintage	(Proof)	MS-65	Prf-65
1988W Olympic	62,913	(281,456)	117.	117.

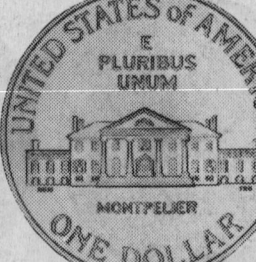

Date	Mintage	(Proof)	MS-65	Prf-65
1989W Congress	46,899	(164,690)	115.	115.

Date	Mintage	(Proof)	MS-65	Prf-65
1991W Mt. Rushmore	31,959	(111,991)	125.	125.

Date	Mintage	(Proof)	MS-65	Prf-65
1992W Olympic	27,732	(77,313)	145.	145.

Date	Mintage	(Proof)	MS-65	Prf-65
1992W Columbus	24,329	(79,730)	195.	210.

Date	Mintage	(Proof)	MS-65	Prf-65
1993W Madison/Bill of Rights	—	—	175.	180.

Date	Mintage	(Proof)	MS-65	Prf-65
1993W World War II	—	—	155.	155.

Date	Mintage	(Proof)	MS-65	Prf-65
1994 World Cup Soccer	—	—	—	—

Gold $10

Date	Mintage	(Proof)	MS-65	Prf-65
1984W Olympic	75,886	(381,085)	235.	235.
1984P Olympic	33,309	—	—	265.
1984D Olympic	34,533	—	—	250.
1984S Olympic	48,551	—	—	240.

COIN SETS

Olympic

Date	Price
1983 & 1984 proof dollars.	18.00

Date	Price
1983 collectors set1983 PDS uncirculated dollars.	32.00
1984 collectors set1984 PDS uncirculated dollars.	55.00
1983 & 1984 gold and silver uncirculated set. One 1983 and one 1984 uncirculated dollar and one 1984 uncirculated gold $10.	245.
1983 & 1984 gold and silver proof set. One 1983 and one 1984 proof dollar and one 1984 proof gold $10.	245.
1983 & 1984 6 coin set. One 1983 and one 1984 uncirculated and proof dollar. One uncirculated and one proof gold $10.	490.
1988 2 coin set: uncirculated silver dollar and gold $5.	130.
1988 2 coin set: proof silver dollar and gold $5.	120.
1988 4 coin set: 1 each of proof and uncirculated issues.	230.
1992 2 coin set: uncirculated half dollar and silver dollar.	24.00
1992 2 coin set: proof half dollar and silver dollar.	35.00
1992 3 coin set: uncirculated half dollar, silver dollar and gold $5.	165.
1992 3 coin set: proof half dollar, silver dollar and gold $5.	165.
1992 6 coin set: 1 each of proof and uncirculated issues.	330.

Statue of Liberty

Date	Price
1986 2 coin set: proof silver dollar and clad half dollar.	11.00
1986 2 coin set: uncirculated silver dollar and clad half dollar.	12.00
1986 3 coin set: uncirculated silver dollar, clad half dollar and gold $5.	130.
1986 3 coin set: proof silver dollar, clad half dollar and gold $5.	130.
1986 6 coin set: 1 each of the proof and uncirculated issues.	280.

Constitution

Date	Price
1987 2 coin set: uncirculated silver dollar and gold $5.	125.
1987 2 coin set: proof silver dollar and gold $5.	125.
1987 4 coin set: 1 each of the proof and uncirculated issues.	240.

Congress

Date	Price
1989 2 coin set: uncirculated silver dollar and clad half dollar.	38.00
1989 2 coin set: proof silver dollar and clad half dollar.	23.00
1989 3 coin set: uncirculated silver dollar, clad half and gold $5.	140.
1989 3 coin set: proof silver dollar, clad half and gold $5.	135.
1989 6 coin set: 1 each of the proof and uncirculated issues.	250.

Mt. Rushmore

Date	Price
1991 2 coin set: uncirculated half dollar and silver dollar.	35.00
1991 2 coin set: proof half dollar and silver dollar.	35.00
1991 3 coin set: uncirculated half dollar, silver dollar and gold $5.	160.
1991 3 coin set: proof half dollar, silver dollar and gold $5.	150.
1991 6 coin set: 1 each of proof and uncirculated issues.	295.

Columbus Quincentenary

Date	Price
1992 2 coin set: uncirculated half dollar and silver dollar.	35.00
1992 2 coin set: proof half dollar and silver dollar.	35.00
1992 3 coin set: uncirculated half dollar, silver dollar and gold $5.	235.
1992 3 coin set: proof half dollar, silver dollar and gold $5.	235.
1992 6 coin set: 1 each of proof and uncirculated issues.	445.

Madison/Bill of Rights

Date	Price
1993 2 coin set: uncirculated half dollar and silver dollar.	30.00
1993 2 coin set: proof half dollar and silver dollar.	30.00
1993 3 coin set: uncirculated half dollar, silver dollar and gold $5.	205.
1993 3 coin set: proof half dollar, silver dollar and gold $5.	205.
1993 6 coin set: 1 each of proof and uncirculated issues.	400.

World War II

Date	Price
1993 2 coin set: uncirculated half dollar and silver dollar.	30.00
1993 2 coin set: proof half dollar and silver dollar.	35.00
1993 3 coin set: uncirculated half dollar, silver dollar and gold $5.	195.
1993 3 coin set: proof half dollar, silver dollar and gold $5.	200.
1993 6 coin set: 1 each of proof and uncirculated issues.	410.

American Eagle bullion coins

Notes: American Eagle bullion coins are traded for their precious-metal content and compete with similar coins from other countries.

Silver

Prices based on $5.12 spot silver.

One-ounce

Designers: Adolph A. Weinman (obverse) and John Mercanti (reverse). **Size:** 40.6 millimeters. **Weight:** 31.101 grams. **Composition:** 99.93% silver (1 ounce), .07% copper.

Date	Mintage	Unc	Prf.
1986	5.393.005	11.25	—
1986S	1.446.778	—	20.00
1987	11.442.335	7.60	—
1987S	904.732	—	20.00
1988	5.004.500	7.90	—
1988S	557.370	—	74.00
1989	5.203.327	7.90	—
1989S	617.694	—	21.00
1990	5.840.210	7.60	—
1990S	695.510	—	28.00
1991	7.191.066	7.60	—
1991S	511.924	—	22.00
1992	5.540.068	7.60	—
1992S	498.552	—	22.00
1993	—	7.60	—
1993P	—	—	31.00

Gold

Prices based on $373.40 spot gold.

Tenth-ounce

Designers: Augustus Saint-Gaudens (obverse) and Miley Busiek (reverse). **Size:** 16.5 millimeters. **Weight:** 3.393 grams. **Composition:** 91.67% gold (.1 ounce), 5.33% copper, 3% silver.

Date	Mintage	Unc	Prf.
1986	912.609	50.00	—
1987	580.266	50.00	—
1988	159.500	65.00	—
1988P	143.881	—	64.00
1989	264.790	54.00	—
1989P	82.924	—	60.00
1990	210.210	50.00	—
1990P	99.349	—	62.00
1991	165.200	50.00	—
1991P	70.344	—	62.00
1992	209.300	50.00	—
1992P	64.902	—	75.00
1993	—	50.00	—
1993P	—	—	888.

Quarter-ounce

Size: 22 millimeters. **Weight:** 8.483 grams. **Composition:** 91.67% gold (.25 ounces), 5.33% copper, 3% silver.

Date	Mintage	Unc	Prf.
1986	726.031	106.	—
1987	269.255	106.	—
1988	49.000	106.	—
1988P	98.028	—	129.
1989	81.789	130.	—
1989P	53.593	—	129.
1990	41.000	106.	—
1990P	62.674	—	135.
1991	36.100	150.	—
1991P	50.839	—	135.
1992P	46.290	—	120.
1993	—	106.	—
1993P	—	—	160.

Half-ounce

Size: 27 millimeters. **Weight:** 16.966 grams. **Composition:** 91.67% gold (.5 ounces), 5.33% copper, 3% silver.

Date	Mintage	Unc	Prf.
1986	599.566	216.	—
1987	131.255	216.	—
1987P	143.398	—	250.
1988	45.000	216.	—
1988P	76.528	—	260.
1989	44.829	216.	—
1989P	44.264	—	260.
1990	31.000	600.	—
1990P	51.636	—	295.
1991	24.100	425.	—
1991P	53.125	—	250.
1992	54.404	290.	—
1992P	40.982	—	250.
1993	—	216.	—
1993P	—	—	320.

One-ounce

Size: 32.7 millimeters. **Weight:** 33.931 grams. **Composition:** 91.67% gold (1 ounce), 5.33% copper, 3% silver.

Date	Mintage	Unc	Prf.
1986	1,362.650	396.	—
1986W	446.290	—	490.
1987	1,045.500	396.	—
1987W	147.498	—	495.
1988	465.000	396.	—
1988W	87.133	—	510.
1989	415.790	396.	—
1989W	53.960	—	510.
1990	373.210	396.	—
1990W	62.401	—	510.
1991	243.100	396.	—
1991W	50.411	—	510.
1992	275.000	396.	—
1992W	44.835	—	570.
1993	—	396.	—
1993W	—	—	620.

TERRITORIAL GOLD

Territorial gold pieces (also referred to as "Private" and "Pioneer" gold) are those struck outside the U.S. Mint and not recognized as official issues by the federal government. The pieces so identified are of various shapes, denominations, and degrees of intrinsic value, and were locally required because of the remoteness of the early gold fields from a federal mint and/or an insufficient quantity of official coinage in frontier areas.

The legality of these privately issued pieces derives from the fact that federal law prior to 1864 prohibited a state from coining money, but did not specifically deny that right to an individual, providing that the privately issued coins did not closely resemble those of the United States.

In addition to coin-like gold pieces, the private minters of the gold rush days also issued gold in ingot and bar form. Ingots were intended for circulation and were cast in regular values and generally in large denominations. Bars represent a miner's deposit after it had been assayed, refined, cast into convenient form (generally rectangular), and stamped with the appropriate weight, fineness, and value. Although occasionally cast in even values for the convenience of banks, bars were more often of odd denomination, and when circulated were rounded off to the nearest figure. Ingots and bars are omitted from this listing.

Georgia and North Carolina

The first territorial gold pieces were struck in 1830 by **Templeton Reid**, a goldsmith and assayer who established a private mint at Gainesville, Georgia, at the time gold was being mined on a relatively large scale in Georgia and North Carolina. Reid's pieces were issued in denominations of $2.50, $5, and $10. Except for an undated variety of the $10 piece, all are dated 1830.

The southern Appalachians were also the scene of a private gold minting operation conducted by Christopher Bechtler Sr., his son August, and nephew Christopher Jr. The Bechtlers, a family of German metallurgists, established a mint at Rutherfordton, North Carolina, which produced territorial gold coins for a longer period than any other private mint in American history. Christopher Bechtler Sr. ran the Bechtler mint from July 1831 until his death in 1842, after which the mint was taken over by his son August who ran it until 1852.

The Bechtler coinage includes but 3 denominations -$1, $2.50, and $5 -but they were issued in a wide variety of weights and sizes. The coinage is undated, except for 3 varieties of the $5 piece which carry the inscription "Aug. 1, 1834" to indicate that they conform to the new weight standard adopted by the U.S. Treasury for official gold coins. **Christopher Bechtler Sr.** produced $2.50 and $5 gold coins for Georgia, and $1, $2.50, and $5 coins for North Carolina. The dollar coins have the distinction of being the first gold coins of that denomination to be produced in the United States. While under the supervision of **August Bechtler**, the Bechtler mint issued $1 and $5 coins for North Carolina.

California

Norris, Grieg & Norris produced the first territorial gold coin struck in California, a $5 piece struck in 1849 at Benicia City, though it bears the imprint of San Francisco. The coining facility was owned by Thomas H. Norris, Charles Greig, and Hiram A. Norris, members of a New York engineering firm. A unique 1850 variety of this coin has the name STOCKTON beneath the date, instead of SAN FRANCISCO.

Early in 1849, John Little Moffat, a New York assayer, established an assay office at San Francisco in association with Joseph R. Curtis, Philo H. Perry, and Samuel Ward. The first issues of the **Moffat & Co.** assay office consisted of rectangular $16 ingots and assay bars of various and irregular denominations. In early August, the firm began striking $5 and $10 gold coins which resemble those of the U.S. Mint in design, but carry the legend S.M.V. (Standard Mint Value) CALIFORNIA GOLD on the reverse. Five-dollar pieces of the same design were also issued in 1850.

On Sept. 30, 1850, Congress directed the Secretary of the Treasury to establish an official Assay Office in California. Moffat & Co. obtained a contract to perform the duties of the U.S. Assay Office. **Augustus Humbert**, a New York watchcase maker, was appointed U.S. Assayer of Gold in California. Humbert stamped the first octagonal coin-ingots of the Provisional Government Mint on Jan. 31, 1851. The $50 pieces were accepted at par with standard U.S. gold coins, but were not officially recognized as coins. Officially, they were designated as "ingots." Colloquially, they were known as slugs, quintuple eagles, or 5-eagle pieces.

The $50 ingots failed to alleviate the need of California for gold coins. The banks regarded them as disadvantageous to their interests and utilized them only when compelled to do so by public need or convenience. Being of sound value, the ingots drove the overvalued $5, $10, and $20 territorial gold coins from circulation, bringing about a return to the use of gold dust for everyday transactions. Eventually, the slugs became so great a nuisance that they were discounted 3 percent when accepted. This unexpected turn of events forced Moffat & Co. to resume the issuing of $10 and $20 gold coins in 1852. The $10 piece was first issued with the Moffat & Co. imprint on Liberty's coronet, and later with the official imprint of Augustus Humbert on reverse. The $20 piece was issued with the Humbert imprint.

On Feb. 14, 1852, John L. Moffat withdrew from Moffat & Co. to enter the diving bell business, and Moffat & Co. was reorganized as the **United States Assay Office of Gold**, composed of Joseph R. Curtis, Philo H. Perry, and Samuel Ward. The U.S. Assay Office of Gold issued gold coins in denominations of $50 and $10 in 1852, and $20 and $10 in 1853. With the exception of the $50 slugs, they carry the imprint of the Assay Office on reverse. The .900 fine issues of this facility reflect an attempt to bring the issues of the U.S. Assay Office into conformity with the U.S. Mint standard.

The last territorial gold coins to bear the imprint of Moffat & Co. are $20 pieces issued in 1853, after the retirement of John L. Moffat. These coins do not carry a mark of fineness, and generally assay below the U.S. Mint standard.

Templeton Reid, previously mentioned in connection with the private gold issues of Georgia, moved his coining equipment to California when gold was discovered there, and in 1849 issued $10 and $25 gold pieces. No specimens are available to present-day collectors. The only known $10 piece is in the Smithsonian Collection. The only known specimen of the $25 piece was stolen from the U.S. Mint Cabinet Collection in 1858 and was never recovered.

Little is known of the origin and location of the **Cincinnati Mining & Trading Co.** It is believed that the firm was organized in the East and was forced to abandon most of its equipment while enroute to California. A few $5 and $10 gold coins were struck in 1849. Base metal counterfeits exist.

The **Massachusetts & California Co.** was organized in Northampton, Mass., in May 1849 by Josiah Hayden, S. S. Wells, Miles G. Moies, and others. Coining equipment was taken to San Francisco where $5 gold pieces were struck in 1849. The few pieces extant are heavily alloyed with copper.

Wright & Co., a brokerage firm located in Portsmouth Square, San Francisco, issued an undated $10 gold piece in the autumn of 1849 under the name of **Miners' Bank**. Unlike most territorial gold pieces, the Miners' Bank eagle was alloyed with copper. The coinage proved to be unpopular because of its copper-induced color and low intrinsic value. The firm was dissolved on Jan. 14, 1850.

In 1849, Dr. **J. S. Ormsby** and Major William M. Ormsby struck gold coins of $5 and $10 denominations at Sacramento under the name of Ormsby & Co. The coinage, which is identified by the initials J. S. O., is undated. Ormsby & Co. coinage was greatly over-valued, the eagle assaying at as little as $9.37.

The **Pacific Co.** of San Francisco issued $5 and $10 gold coins in 1849. The clouded story of this coinage is based on conjecture. It is believed that the well-struck pattern coins of this type were struck in the East by the Pacific Co. that organized in Boston and set sail for California on Feb. 20, 1849, and that the crudely hand-struck pieces were made by the jewelry firm of Broderick and Kohler after the dies passed into their possession. In any event, the intrinsic value of the initial coinage exceeded face value, but by the end of 1849, when they passed out of favor, the coins had been debased so flagrantly that the eagles assayed for as little as $7.86.

Dubosq & Co., a Philadelphia jewelry firm owned by Theodore Dubosq Sr. and Jr. and Henry Dubosq, took melting and coining equipment to San Francisco in 1849, and in 1850 issued $5 and $10 gold coins struck with dies allegedly made by U.S. Mint Engraver James B. Longacre. Dubosq & Co. coinage was immensely popular with the forty-niners because its intrinsic worth was in excess of face value.

The minting equipment of David C. Broderick and Frederick D. Kohler (see Pacific Co.) was acquired in May 1850 by San Francisco jewelers George C. Baldwin and Thomas S. Holman, who organized a private minting venture under the name of **Baldwin & Co.** The firm produced a $5 piece of Liberty Head design and a $10 piece with Horseman device in 1850. Liberty Head $10 and $20 pieces were coined in 1851. Baldwin & Co. produced the first $20 piece issued in California.

Schultz & Co. of San Francisco, a brass foundry located in the rear of the Baldwin & Co. establishment, and operated by Judge G. W. Schultz and William T. Garratt, issued $5 gold coins from early 1851 until April of that year. The inscription "SHULTS & CO." is a misspelling of SCHULTZ & CO.

Dunbar & Co. of San Francisco issued a $5 gold piece in 1851, after Edward E. Dunbar, owner of the California Bank in San Francisco, purchased the coining equipment of the defunct Baldwin & Co.

The San Francisco-based firm of **Wass, Molitor & Co.** was owned by 2 Hungarian exiles, Count S. C. Wass and A. P. Molitor, who initially founded the firm as a gold smelting and assaying plant. In response to a plea from the commercial community for small gold coins, Wass, Molitor & Co. issued $5 and $10 gold coins in 1852. The $5 piece was coined with small head and large head varieties, and the $10 piece with small head, large head, and small close-date varieties. The firm produced a second issue of gold coins in 1855, in denominations of $10, $20, and $50.

The U.S. Assay Office in California closed its doors on Dec. 14, 1853, to make way for the newly established San Francisco Branch Mint. The Mint, however, was unable to start immediate quantity production due to the lack of refining acids. During the interim, John G. Kellogg, a former employee of Moffat & Co., and John Glover Richter, a former assayer in the U.S. Assay Office, formed **Kellogg & Co.** for the purpose of supplying businessmen with urgently needed coinage. The firm produced $20 coins dated 1854 and 1855, after which Augustus Humbert replaced Richter and the enterprise reorganized as Kellogg & Humbert Melters, Assayers & Coiners. Kellogg & Humbert endured until 1860, but issued coins, $20 pieces, only in 1855.

Oregon

The Oregon Exchange Co., a private mint located at Oregon City, Oregon Territory, issued $5 and $10 pieces of local gold in 1849. The initials K., M., T., A., W. R. C. (G on the $5 piece), and S. on the obverse represent the eight founders of the **Oregon Exchange Co.** : William Kilborne, Theophilus Magruder, James Taylor, George Abernathy, William Willson, William Rector, John Campbell, and Noyes Smith. Campbell is erroneously represented by a G on the $5 coin. For unknown reasons, the initials A and W are omitted from the $10 piece. O.T. (Oregon Territory) is erroneously presented as T.O. on the $5 coin.

Utah

In 1849, the **Mormons** settled in the Great Salt Lake Valley of Utah and established the Deseret Mint in a small adobe building in Salt Lake City. Operating under the direct supervision of Brigham Young, the Deseret Mint issued $2.50, $5, $10, and $20 gold coins in 1849. Additional $5 pieces were struck in 1850 and 1860, the latter in a temporary mint set up in Barlow's jewelry shop. The Mormon $20 piece was the first of that denomination to be struck in the United States. The initials G.S.L.C.P.G. on Mormon coins denotes "Great Salt Lake City Pure Gold." It was later determined that the coinage was grossly deficient in value, mainly because no attempt was made to assay or refine the gold.

Colorado

The discovery of gold in Colorado Territory was accompanied by the inevitable need for coined money. Austin M. Clark, Milton E. Clark, and Emanuel H. Gruber, bankers of Leavenworth, Kansas, moved to Denver where they established a bank and issued $2.50, $5, $10, and $20 gold coins in 1860 and 1861. To protect the holder from loss by abrasion, **Clark, Gruber & Co.** made their coins slightly heavier than full value required. The 1860 issues carry the inscription PIKE'S PEAK GOLD on reverse. CLARK, GRUBER & CO. appears on the reverse of the 1861 issues, and PIKE'S PEAK on the coronet of Liberty. The government purchased the plant of Clark, Gruber & Co. in 1863 and operated it as a federal Assay Office until 1906.

In the summer of 1861, **John Parsons**, an assayer whose place of business was located in South Park at the Tarryall Mines, Colorado, issued undated gold coins in the denominations of $2.50 and $5. They, too, carry the inscription PIKE'S PEAK GOLD on reverse.

J. J. Conway & Co., bankers of Georgia Gulch, Colorado operated the Conway Mint for a short period in 1861. Undated gold coins in the denominations of $2.50, $5, and $10 were issued. A variety of the $5 coin does not carry the numeral 5 on reverse. The issues of the Conway Mint were highly regarded for their scrupulously maintained value.

NOTE: The above introduction is organized chronologically by geographical region. However, for ease of use the following listings appear alphabetically by state and issuer, except for small California gold.

Small California Gold

During the California gold rush, a wide variety of U.S. and foreign coins was used for small change, but their number was extremely limited. More common was the use of gold dust, though this offered the miner relatively low value for his gold.

By 1852 California jewelers had begun to manufacture 25¢, 50¢ and $1 gold pieces in round and octagonal shapes. Makers included Antonio Louis Nouizillet, Isadore Routhier, Robert B. Gray, Pierre Frontier, Eugene Diviercy, Herman J. Brand, Herman and Jacob Levison, Reuben N. Hershfield and Noah Mitchell. M. Deriberpie was an engraver who cut dies for Nouizillet. Only two or three of these companies were in production at any one time. Many varieties bear the maker's initials. In general, the large Liberty Head types, Eagle reverses and Washington Head types were made by Frontier and his partners. The small Liberty Head types were generally made by Nouizillet and later by Gray and then the Levison brothers and the California Jewelry Co. Coins initialed "G.G." are apparently patterns made by Frontier and Diviercy for the New York firm of Gaime, Guillemot & Co., that never went into production.

The gold rush era coins were generally struck from unrefined native gold-silver alloy. Some were hand struck from hand engraved dies. Others were pressed from high quality hubbed dies into reeded collars. After establishment of the San Francisco Mint in 1854, private coinage gradually died out. By 1857-1858, almost no private gold coins were being made. Production resumed, however, in 1859 as the small denomination gold pieces proved popular as souvenirs and for use in jewelry. By then intrinsic value was generally ignored. Planchets were thinner and were often low-grade surfaced with pure gold. New designs such as the Indian Heads were introduced and the use of polished dies to impart proof-like surfaces became common.

Though all private coinage was outlawed by the Private Coinages Act of 1864, this law was unenforced in California and production of small denominated gold continued through 1882. In the spring of 1883, Col. Henry Finnegass of the U.S. Secret Service halted production of the private gold pieces. Undenominated tokens (lacking DOLLARS, CENTS or the equivalent on reverse) were also made during this latter period, sometimes by the same manufacturing jeweler using the same obverse die as the small denomination gold coins.

Approximately 15,000 pieces of California small denomination gold are estimated to exist, in a total of 500 varieties. A few varieties are undated, mostly gold rush era pieces; and a few are back-dated. Major varieties are listed here. Individual listings may consist of several varieties; prices quoted are for the most common variety. True MS-65 coins are rare and bring substantial premiums. Walter Breen has established that Period One pieces (1852-1856) were "circulating issues", unlike those made 1859-1882 or later which were souvenirs or jewelry pieces. Public awareness to these differences will no doubt eventually place premium values on Period One coins. For further information consult W. Breen and R.J. Gillio CALIFORNIA PIONEER FRACTIONAL GOLD, 1983.

1/4 DOLLAR - OCTAGONAL

Obv: Large Liberty head.
Rev: Value and date within beaded circle.

KM#	Date	VF	XF	AU	Unc
1.1	1853	150.00	200.00	350.00	525.00
	1854	150.00	200.00	350.00	525.00
	1855	150.00	200.00	350.00	450.00
	1856	150.00	200.00	250.00	400.00

Rev: Value and date within wreath.

KM#	Date	VF	XF	AU	Unc
1.2	1859	75.00	125.00	195.00	290.00
	1864	120.00	150.00	230.00	390.00
	1866	120.00	150.00	230.00	390.00
	1867	75.00	110.00	195.00	290.00
	1868	90.00	135.00	230.00	390.00
	1869	90.00	135.00	230.00	390.00
	1870	75.00	110.00	195.00	290.00
	1871	75.00	110.00	195.00	290.00

Obv: Large Liberty head above date.
Rev: Value and CAL within wreath.

KM#	Date	VF	XF	AU	Unc
1.3	1872	75.00	110.00	180.00	320.00
	1873	65.00	90.00	155.00	240.00

Obv: Small Liberty head.
Rev: Value and date within beaded circle.

KM#	Date	VF	XF	AU	Unc
1.4	1853	150.00	200.00	300.00	450.00

Obv: Small Liberty head above date.
Rev: Value within wreath.

KM#	Date	VF	XF	AU	Unc
1.5	1854	100.00	150.00	200.00	325.00

Obv: Small Liberty head.
Rev: Value and date within wreath.

KM#	Date	VF	XF	AU	Unc
1.6	1855	150.00	200.00	250.00	400.00
	1856	150.00	200.00	250.00	400.00
	1857*	75.00	110.00	155.00	265.00
	1860	90.00	120.00	180.00	315.00
	1870	100.00	150.00	210.00	345.00

*Modern restrikes exist.

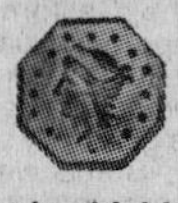 

Rev: Value in shield and date within wreath.

KM#	Date	VF	XF	AU	Unc
1.7	1863	100.00	150.00	230.00	345.00
	1864	90.00	135.00	195.00	345.00
	1865/4	100.00	200.00	335.00	525.00
	1866	100.00	200.00	310.00	500.00
	1867	100.00	160.00	255.00	415.00
	1868	100.00	160.00	255.00	415.00
	1869	100.00	160.00	255.00	415.00
	1870	100.00	160.00	280.00	450.00

Obv: Small Liberty head above date.
Rev: Value and CAL within wreath.

KM#	Date	VF	XF	AU	Unc
1.8	1870	85.00	110.00	155.00	265.00
	1871	85.00	110.00	155.00	265.00
	1873	125.00	175.00	280.00	415.00
	1874	90.00	135.00	230.00	320.00
	1875/3	150.00	195.00	255.00	415.00
	1876	80.00	120.00	200.00	320.00

Obv: Goofy Liberty head.
Rev: Value and date within wreath.

KM#	Date	VF	XF	AU	Unc
1.9	1870	90.00	135.00	255.00	450.00

Obv: Oriental Liberty head above date.
Rev: 1/4 CALDOLL within wreath.

KM#	Date	VF	XF	AU	Unc
1.10	1881	200.00	400.00	725.00	1100.

Obv: Large Liberty head above 1872.
Rev: Value and 1871 within wreath.

KM#	Date	VF	XF	AU	Unc
1.11	1872-71	425.00	900.00	1400.	2150.

Obv: Large Indian head above date.
Rev: Value within wreath.

KM#	Date	VF	XF	AU	Unc
2.1	1852	120.00	200.00	300.00	500.00
	1868	130.00	225.00	360.00	600.00
	1874	120.00	200.00	335.00	550.00
	1876	100.00	150.00	280.00	475.00
	1880	85.00	125.00	200.00	310.00
	1881	85.00	125.00	200.00	310.00

Rev: Value and CAL within wreath.

KM#	Date	VF	XF	AU	Unc
2.2	1872	75.00	110.00	180.00	265.00
	1873	130.00	200.00	310.00	420.00
	1874	75.00	110.00	180.00	265.00
	1875	75.00	110.00	180.00	265.00
	1876	75.00	110.00	180.00	265.00

Obv: Small Indian head above date.

KM#	Date	VF	XF	AU	Unc
2.3	1875	95.00	175.00	300.00	475.00
	1876	95.00	175.00	300.00	475.00
	1881	95.00	175.00	300.00	475.00

Obv: Aztec Indian head above date.

KM#	Date	VF	XF	AU	Unc
2.4	1880	90.00	150.00	255.00	450.00

Obv: Dumb Indian head above date.
Rev: Value and CAL within wreath.

KM#	Date	VF	XF	AU	Unc
2.6	1881	350.00	750.00	1275.	2150.

Obv: Young Indian head above date.
Rev: Value within wreath.

KM#	Date	VF	XF	AU	Unc
2.7	1881	250.00	500.00	775.00	1350.

Rev: Value and CAL within wreath.

KM#	Date	VF	XF	AU	Unc
2.8	1882	250.00	500.00	775.00	1350.

Obv: Washington head above date.

KM#	Date	VF	XF	AU	Unc
3	1872	200.00	300.00	525.00	1100.

1/4 DOLLAR - ROUND

Obv: Defiant eagle above date.
Rev: 25¢ within wreath.

KM#	Date	VF	XF	AU	Unc
4	1854	10,000.	20,000.	25,000.	30,000.

Superior Sale Sept. 1988 Gem Unc $44,000.

Obv: Large Liberty head.
Rev: Value and date within wreath.

KM#	Date	VF	XF	AU	Unc
5.1	1853	—	—	400.00	575.00
	1854	450.00	650.00	875.00	1450.
	1859	90.00	110.00	180.00	290.00
	1865	90.00	175.00	230.00	365.00
	1866	90.00	135.00	230.00	365.00
	1867	60.00	90.00	155.00	240.00
	1868	60.00	90.00	155.00	240.00
	1870	60.00	90.00	155.00	240.00
	1871	60.00	90.00	155.00	240.00

Obv: Large Liberty head above date.
Rev: Value and CAL within wreath.

KM#	Date	VF	XF	AU	Unc
5.2	1871	75.00	110.00	155.00	240.00
	1872	90.00	150.00	210.00	365.00
	1873	75.00	110.00	155.00	240.00

Obv: Small Liberty head.
Rev: 25¢ in wreath.

KM#	Date	VF	XF	AU	Unc
5.3	ND	750.00	1000.	1550.	2200.

Rev: 1/4 DOLL. or DOLLAR and date in wreath.

KM#	Date	VF	XF	AU	Unc
5.4	ND	275.00	400.00	900.00	1300.
	1853	350.00	600.00	875.00	1350.
	1855	150.00	200.00	250.00	400.00
	1856	150.00	200.00	300.00	450.00
	1860	90.00	110.00	155.00	290.00
	1863/1860	250.00	500.00	775.00	1000.
	1864	90.00	135.00	230.00	380.00
	1865	90.00	110.00	155.00	290.00
	1866	120.00	195.00	360.00	550.00
	1867	90.00	110.00	155.00	290.00
	1869	90.00	110.00	155.00	290.00
	1870	120.00	195.00	360.00	550.00

Rev: Value in shield and date within wreath.

KM#	Date	VF	XF	AU	Unc
5.5	1863	150.00	225.00	400.00	575.00

Obv: Small Liberty head above date.
Rev: Value and CAL within wreath.

KM#	Date	VF	XF	AU	Unc
5.6	ND	120.00	175.00	310.00	550.00
	1870	90.00	110.00	155.00	240.00
	1871	90.00	110.00	155.00	240.00
	1873	120.00	225.00	360.00	530.00
	1874	120.00	200.00	310.00	425.00
	1875	120.00	175.00	310.00	550.00
	1876	95.00	120.00	200.00	345.00

Obv: Goofy Liberty head.
Rev: Value and date within wreath.

KM#	Date	VF	XF	AU	Unc
5.7	1870	90.00	135.00	230.00	370.00

Obv: Liberty head with H and date below.
Rev: Value and CAL in wreath.

KM#	Date	VF	XF	AU	Unc
5.8	1871	80.00	120.00	200.00	345.00

Obv: Large Indian head above date.
Rev: Value within wreath.

KM#	Date	VF	XF	AU	Unc
6.1	1852	100.00	150.00	260.00	450.00
	1868	125.00	200.00	335.00	500.00
	1874	125.00	200.00	335.00	500.00
	1876	75.00	120.00	180.00	290.00
	1880	75.00	120.00	180.00	290.00
	1881	75.00	120.00	180.00	290.00

Rev: Value and CAL within wreath.

KM#	Date	VF	XF	AU	Unc
6.2	1872	90.00	120.00	180.00	310.00
	1873	100.00	150.00	260.00	420.00
	1874	90.00	120.00	180.00	310.00
	1875	75.00	115.00	170.00	265.00
	1876	90.00	120.00	180.00	310.00

Obv: Small Indian head above date.

KM#	Date	VF	XF	AU	Unc
6.3	1875	85.00	115.00	200.00	310.00
	1876	100.00	150.00	260.00	450.00

Obv: Young Indian head above date.

KM#	Date	VF	XF	AU	Unc
6.4	1882	500.00	750.00	1000.	1600.

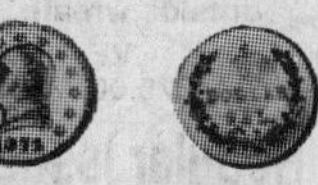

Obv: Washington head above date.

KM#	Date	VF	XF	AU	Unc
7	1872	200.00	300.00	525.00	1100.

1/2 DOLLAR - OCTAGONAL

 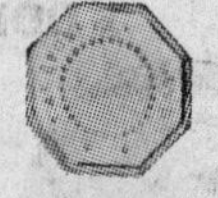

Obv: Liberty head above date.
Rev: 1/2 DOLLAR in beaded circle. CALIFORNIA GOLD around circle.

KM#	Date	VF	XF	AU	Unc
8.1	1853	200.00	300.00	400.00	550.00
	1854	200.00	300.00	400.00	550.00
	1856	300.00	325.00	550.00	750.00

Rev: Small eagle with rays ("peacock").

KM#	Date	VF	XF	AU	Unc
8.2	1853	750.00	1000.	1500.	2500.

Obv: Large Liberty head.
Rev: Large eagle with date.

KM#	Date	VF	XF	AU	Unc
8.3	1853	750.00	1250.	2350.	3700.

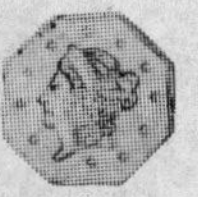 

Rev: Value and date within wreath.

KM#	Date	VF	XF	AU	Unc
8.4	1859	100.00	150.00	270.00	420.00
	1866	125.00	200.00	300.00	475.00
	1867	125.00	200.00	300.00	475.00
	1868	125.00	200.00	300.00	475.00
	1869	125.00	200.00	300.00	475.00
	1870	125.00	200.00	300.00	475.00
	1871	85.00	115.00	200.00	345.00

Obv: Large Liberty head above date.
Rev: Value and CAL within wreath.

KM#	Date	VF	XF	AU	Unc
8.5	1872	75.00	115.00	180.00	290.00
	1873	75.00	115.00	180.00	290.00

Obv: Liberty head.
Rev: Date in wreath, HALF DOL. CALIFORNIA GOLD around wreath.

KM#	Date	VF	XF	AU	Unc
8.6	1854	200.00	275.00	460.00	600.00
	1855	200.00	250.00	460.00	600.00
	1856	200.00	250.00	460.00	600.00
	1868	75.00	100.00	180.00	290.00

Obv: Small Liberty head.
Rev: HALF DOLLAR and date in wreath.

KM#	Date	VF	XF	AU	Unc
8.7	1864	75.00	110.00	180.00	290.00
	1870	95.00	175.00	300.00	500.00

Rev: CAL.GOLD HALF DOL and date in wreath.

KM#	Date	VF	XF	AU	Unc
8.8	1869	85.00	110.00	180.00	290.00
	1870	85.00	110.00	180.00	290.00

 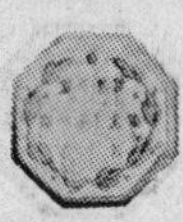

Obv: Small Liberty head above date.
Rev: Value and CAL in wreath.

KM#	Date	VF	XF	AU	Unc
8.9	1870	75.00	95.00	155.00	290.00
	1871	75.00	95.00	155.00	290.00
	1873	125.00	200.00	360.00	500.00
	1874	125.00	200.00	360.00	500.00
	1875	400.00	500.00	775.00	1100.
	1876	130.00	200.00	360.00	580.00

Obv: Goofy Liberty head.
Rev: Value and date within wreath.

KM#	Date	VF	XF	AU	Unc
8.10	1870	85.00	130.00	255.00	500.00

Obv: Oriental Liberty head above date.
Rev: 1/2 CALDOLL within wreath.

KM#	Date	VF	XF	AU	Unc
8.11	1881	250.00	350.00	625.00	1100.

Obv: Large Indian head above date.
Rev: Value within wreath.

KM#	Date	VF	XF	AU	Unc
9.1	1852	300.00	400.00	560.00	925.00
	1868	200.00	350.00	515.00	850.00
	1874	200.00	350.00	515.00	850.00
	1876	200.00	250.00	460.00	795.00
	1880	125.00	150.00	260.00	420.00
	1881	200.00	350.00	515.00	850.00

Rev: Value and CAL within wreath.

KM#	Date	VF	XF	AU	Unc
9.2	1852	175.00	225.00	400.00	610.00
	1868	175.00	225.00	400.00	610.00
	1872	100.00	125.00	230.00	475.00
	1873	150.00	200.00	350.00	500.00
	1874/3	100.00	125.00	230.00	475.00
	1874	150.00	185.00	335.00	530.00
	1875	90.00	110.00	210.00	470.00
	1876	100.00	125.00	230.00	475.00
	1878	150.00	200.00	335.00	530.00
	1880	150.00	200.00	335.00	530.00
	1881	150.00	200.00	335.00	530.00

Obv: Small Indian head above date.

KM#	Date	VF	XF	AU	Unc
9.3	1875	125.00	225.00	350.00	610.00
	1876	125.00	225.00	350.00	610.00

Obv: Young Indian head above date.

KM#	Date	VF	XF	AU	Unc
9.4	1881	200.00	250.00	415.00	725.00
	1882	250.00	400.00	565.00	875.00

1/2 DOLLAR - ROUND

Obv: Arms of California and date.
Rev: Eagle and legends.

KM#	Date	VF	XF	AU	Unc
10	1853	2000.	3000.	5000.	7500.

Obv: Liberty head.
Rev: Large eagle and legends.

KM#	Date	VF	XF	AU	Unc
11.1	1854	1500.	2000.	3000.	5500.

Obv: Liberty head and date.
Rev: HALF DOL. CALIFORNIA GOLD around wreath.

KM#	Date	VF	XF	AU	Unc
11.2	1854	200.00	300.00	525.00	800.00

 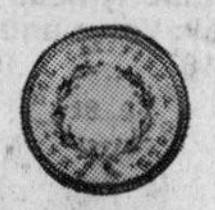

Obv: Liberty head.
Rev: Date in wreath. Value and CALIFORNIA GOLD around wreath.

KM#	Date	VF	XF	AU	Unc
11.3	1852	175.00	250.00	500.00	700.00
	1853	175.00	250.00	500.00	700.00
	1854*	100.00	200.00	350.00	500.00
	1855	300.00	450.00	750.00	1000.
	1856	200.00	275.00	450.00	750.00
	1860	85.00	150.00	250.00	425.00

*Beware of Kroll type counterfeits.

Rev: Small eagle and legends.

KM#	Date	VF	XF	AU	Unc
11.4	1853	2000.	4000.	7000.	10,500.

Rev: Value in wreath. CALIFORNIA GOLD and date around wreath.

KM#	Date	VF	XF	AU	Unc
11.5	1853	200.00	300.00	525.00	850.00

Rev: Value and date within wreath.

KM#	Date	VF	XF	AU	Unc
11.6	1854	1000.	1500.	2250.	2900.
	1855	275.00	325.00	585.00	925.00
	1859	85.00	125.00	180.00	290.00
	1865	130.00	200.00	300.00	610.00
	1866	130.00	200.00	300.00	610.00
	1867	100.00	150.00	260.00	450.00
	1868	100.00	150.00	260.00	450.00
	1869	130.00	200.00	300.00	610.00
	1870	85.00	125.00	180.00	290.00
	1871	85.00	125.00	180.00	290.00
	1873	130.00	200.00	300.00	610.00

Obv: Liberty head above date.
Rev: Value and CAL within wreath.

KM#	Date	VF	XF	AU	Unc
11.7	1870	85.00	125.00	180.00	265.00
	1871	85.00	125.00	180.00	265.00
	1872	130.00	200.00	360.00	620.00
	1873	150.00	200.00	300.00	500.00
	1874	125.00	200.00	300.00	450.00
	1875	125.00	200.00	300.00	450.00
	1876	125.00	200.00	300.00	450.00

Obv: Liberty head.
Rev: Value and date within wreath. CALIFORNIA GOLD outside.

KM#	Date	VF	XF	AU	Unc
11.8	1863	200.00	300.00	465.00	800.00

Obv: Liberty head.
Rev: HALF DOLLAR and date in wreath.

KM#	Date	VF	XF	AU	Unc
11.9	1864	85.00	100.00	180.00	290.00
	1866	—	—	Rare	—
	Superior Sale Sept. 1988 Unique Unc$2860.				
	1867	85.00	125.00	200.00	345.00
	1868	85.00	125.00	200.00	345.00
	1869	85.00	125.00	200.00	345.00
	1870	150.00	200.00	235.00	480.00

Obv: Goofy Liberty head.
Rev: Value and date within wreath.

KM#	Date	VF	XF	AU	Unc
11.11	1870	100.00	150.00	260.00	500.00

Obv: Liberty head with H and date below.
Rev: Value and CAL within wreath.

KM#	Date	VF	XF	AU	Unc
11.12	1871	100.00	150.00	285.00	500.00

Obv: Large Indian head above date.
Rev: Value within wreath.

KM#	Date	VF	XF	AU	Unc
12.1	1852	200.00	250.00	435.00	700.00
	1868	200.00	250.00	435.00	700.00
	1874	200.00	250.00	435.00	700.00
	1876	125.00	175.00	310.00	530.00
	1878/6	250.00	500.00	765.00	1200.
	1880	125.00	175.00	285.00	450.00
	1881	125.00	175.00	285.00	450.00

Rev: Value and CAL within wreath.

KM#	Date	VF	XF	AU	Unc
12.2	1872	125.00	175.00	310.00	500.00
	1873	125.00	175.00	310.00	500.00
	1874/3	150.00	195.00	360.00	600.00
	1874	125.00	175.00	310.00	500.00
	1875/3	125.00	175.00	335.00	550.00
	1875	150.00	195.00	360.00	600.00
	1876/5/3	125.00	175.00	335.00	550.00
	1876	200.00	250.00	490.00	800.00

Obv: Small Indian head above date.

KM#	Date	VF	XF	AU	Unc
12.3	1875	140.00	175.00	335.00	450.00
	1876	150.00	185.00	360.00	600.00

Obv: Young Indian head above date.

KM#	Date	VF	XF	AU	Unc
12.4	1882	350.00	500.00	775.00	1150.

DOLLAR - OCTAGONAL

Obv: Liberty head.
Rev: Large eagle and legends.

KM#	Date	VF	XF	AU	Unc
13.1	ND	1200.	1750.	2550.	3700.
	1853	2000.	3000.	3600.	5250.
	1854	1200.	1750.	2550.	3700.

Rev: Value and date in beaded circle. CALIFORNIA GOLD initials around circle.

KM#	Date	VF	XF	AU	Unc
13.2	1853 DERI	300.00	400.00	565.00	850.00
	1853 FD	250.00	350.00	460.00	700.00
	1853 N	300.00	400.00	615.00	950.00
	1854 DERI	400.00	600.00	925.00	1250.
	1854 FD	250.00	350.00	460.00	700.00
	1855 FD	250.00	350.00	460.00	700.00
	1856	1500.	2000.	3100.	4750.
	1863*	95.00	150.00	230.00	345.00

*Modern restrikes exist.

Rev: Value and date inside wreath. Legends outside wreath.

KM#	Date	VF	XF	AU	Unc
13.3	1854	250.00	350.00	515.00	800.00
	1855 NR	250.00	350.00	515.00	800.00
	1858 K	120.00	175.00	260.00	370.00
	1859 FD	825.00	1100.	1700.	2700.
	1860	135.00	190.00	280.00	420.00
	1868 G	185.00	260.00	380.00	560.00
	1869 G	135.00	190.00	280.00	420.00
	1870 G	275.00	350.00	465.00	700.00
	1871	275.00	350.00	465.00	700.00

Obv: Goofy Liberty head.
Rev: Value and date inside wreath.

KM#	Date	VF	XF	AU	Unc
13.4	1870	135.00	190.00	280.00	475.00

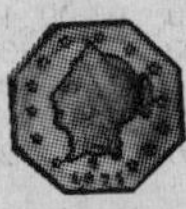

Obv: Liberty head above date.
Rev: Value and date within wreath. CALIFORNIA GOLD around wreath.

KM#	Date	VF	XF	AU	Unc
13.5	1871 G	135.00	190.00	255.00	370.00
	1874	600.00	850.00	1450.	2250.
	1875	600.00	850.00	1450.	2250.
	1876	600.00	850.00	1450.	2250.

Obv: Large Indian head above date.
Rev: 1 DOLLAR inside wreath. CALIFORNIA GOLD around wreath.

KM#	Date	VF	XF	AU	Unc
14.1	1872	500.00	750.00	1285.	1850.
	1873/2	600.00	850.00	1450.	2250.
	1873	350.00	500.00	775.00	1250.
	1874	275.00	350.00	465.00	800.00
	1875	275.00	350.00	465.00	800.00
	1876	275.00	350.00	465.00	800.00

Obv: Small Indian head above date.
Rev: 1 DOLLAR CAL inside wreath.

KM#	Date	VF	XF	AU	Unc
14.2	1875	525.00	750.00	1150.	1600.
	1876	600.00	850.00	1250.	1750.

Rev: 1 DOLLAR inside wreath. CALIFORNIA GOLD around wreath.

KM#	Date	VF	XF	AU	Unc
14.3	1876	500.00	800.00	1275.	2150.

DOLLAR - ROUND

Obv: Liberty head.
Rev: Large eagle and legends.

KM#	Date	VF	XF	AU	Unc
15.1	1853	—	—	Rare	—

Superior Sale Sept. 1987 MS63 $35,200.

Rev: Value and date inside wreath. CALIFORNIA GOLD around wreath.

KM#	Date	VF	XF	AU	Unc
15.2	1854 GL	2000.	3000.	4150.	6200.
	1854 FD	3500.	4000.	5150.	7500.
	1854	—	—	Rare	—
	Superior Sale Sept. 1988 Fine $13,200.				
	1857	—	—	Rare	—
	1870 G	700.00	900.00	1550.	2150.
	1871	750.00	1000.	1650.	2700.

Obv: Liberty head above date. Rev: Value inside wreath. CALIFORNIA GOLD around wreath.

KM#	Date	VF	XF	AU	Unc
15.3	1870 G	600.00	800.00	1400.	1900.
	1871 G	750.00	1000.	1650.	2700.

Obv: Goofy Liberty head.
Rev: Value and date inside wreath. CALIFORNIA GOLD around wreath.

KM#	Date	VF	XF	AU	Unc
15.4	1870	500.00	750.00	1100.	1600.

Obv: Large Indian head above date.
Rev: Value inside wreath. CALIFORNIA GOLD outside wreath.

KM#	Date	VF	XF	AU	Unc
16	1872	575.00	750.00	1450.	2150.

Regular Issues

CALIFORNIA

Baldwin & Company

5 DOLLARS

KM#	Date	Fine	VF	XF	Unc
17	1850	3500.	5500.	8500.	17,500.

10 DOLLARS

KM#	Date	Fine	VF	XF	Unc
18	1850 Horseman	15,000.	27,500.	35,000.	55,000.

KM#	Date	Fine	VF	XF	Unc
19	1851	9500.	14,000.	28,000.	—

20 DOLLARS

KM#	Date	Fine	VF	XF	Unc
20	1851	—	—	—	—

Stack's-Superior Sale Dec.1988, XF-40 $52,800.

NOTE: Beware of copies cast in base metals.

Blake & Company

20 DOLLARS

KM#	Date	Fine	VF	XF	Unc
21	1855	—	—	—	—

NOTE: Many modern copies exist.

J. H. Bowie

5 DOLLARS

KM#	Date	Fine	VF	XF	Unc
22	1849	—	—	—	—

Cincinnati Mining and Trading Company

5 DOLLARS

KM#	Date	Fine	VF	XF	Unc
23	1849	—	—	Rare	—

10 DOLLARS

KM#	Date	Fine	VF	XF	Unc
24	1849	—	—	Rare	—

Brand Sale 1984, XF $104,500.

Dubosq & Company

5 DOLLARS

KM#	Date	Fine	VF	XF	Unc
26	1850	25,000.	42,500.	Rare	—

10 DOLLARS

KM#	Date	Fine	VF	XF	Unc
27	1850	25,000.	45,000.	Rare	—

Dunbar & Company

5 DOLLARS

KM#	Date	Fine	VF	XF	Unc
28	1851	22,500.	32,500.	52,500.	—

Spink & Son Sale 1988, AU $62,000.

Augustus Humbert United States Assayer

10 DOLLARS

AUGUSTUS HUMBERT imprint

KM#	Date	Fine	VF	XF	Unc
29.1	1852/1	2000.	3500.	5500.	15,000.
	1852	1500.	2500.	4750.	11,500.

Error: IINITED.

KM#	Date	Fine	VF	XF	Unc
29.2	1852/1	—	—	Rare	—
	1852	—	—	Rare	—

20 DOLLARS

KM#	Date	Fine	VF	XF	Unc
30	1852/1	4500.	6000.	9500.	—

Garrett Sale Mar.1980, Humberts Proof $325,000.
Private Sale May 1989, Humberts Proof (PCGS Pr-65) $1,350,000.

50 DOLLARS

Obv: 50 D C 880 THOUS, eagle. Edge: Lettered. Rev: 50 in center.

KM#	Date	Fine	VF	XF	Unc
31.1	1851	9500.	12,000.	22,000.	—

Obv: 887 THOUS.

KM#	Date	Fine	VF	XF	Unc
31.1a	1851	6000.	9,000.	16,000.	30,000.

Obv: 880 THOUS. Rev: Without 50.

KM#	Date	Fine	VF	XF	Unc
31.2	1851	4500.	8500.	17,500.	35,000.

Obv: 887 THOUS.

KM#	Date	Fine	VF	XF	Unc
31.2a	1851	—	12,500.	22,500.	—

ASSAYER inverted

KM#	Date	Fine	VF	XF	Unc
31.3	1851	—	—	Unique	—

Obv: 880 THOUS. Rev: Rays from central star.

KM#	Date	Fine	VF	XF	Unc
31.4	1851	—	—	Unique	—

Obv: 880 THOUS. Rev: "Target".

KM#	Date	Fine	VF	XF	Unc
32.1	1851	6500.	9500.	17,000.	35,000.

Obv: 887 THOUS.

KM#	Date	Fine	VF	XF	Unc
32.1a	1851	6500.	9500.	17,000.	35,000.

Garrett Sale March 1980, Humberts Proof $500,000.

Rev: Small design.

KM#	Date	Fine	VF	XF	Unc
32.2	1851	6500.	9500.	16,000.	—
	1852	4500.	8500.	19,500.	39,500.

Kellogg & Company

20 DOLLARS

Obv: Thick date. Rev: Short arrows.

KM#	Date	Fine	VF	XF	Unc
33.1	1854	2000.	3000.	5500.	11,750.

Obv: Medium date.

KM#	Date	Fine	VF	XF	Unc
33.2	1854	2000.	3000.	5500.	11,750.

Obv: Thin date.

KM#	Date	Fine	VF	XF	Unc
33.3	1854	2000.	3000.	4500.	11,500.

Rev: Long arrows.

KM#	Date	Fine	VF	XF	Unc
33.4	1854	2000.	3000.	4500.	11,500.
	1855	2500.	3500.	5500.	13,500.

Garrett Sale March 1980, Proof $230,000.

Rev: Medium arrows.

KM#	Date	Fine	VF	XF	Unc
33.5	1855	2500.	3500.	4500.	13,500.

Rev: Short arrows.

KM#	Date	Fine	VF	XF	Unc
33.6	1855	2500.	3500.	4500.	13,500.

50 DOLLARS

KM#	Date	Fine	VF	XF	Unc
34	1855	—	—	—	—

Bowers & Merena Sale Sept. 1984, Proof $165,000.

Massachusetts and California Company

5 DOLLARS

KM#	Date	Fine	VF	XF	Unc
35	1849	35,000.	55,000.	Rare	—

Proof 110,000.

Miners Bank
10 DOLLARS

RED GOLD

KM#	Date	Fine	VF	XF	Unc
36	ND(1849)	—	7500.	12,500.	35,000.

Garrett Sale March 1980, MS-65 $135,000.

YELLOW GOLD

KM#	Date	Fine	VF	XF	Unc
36a	ND(1849)	—	—	—	—

Rare as most specimens have heavy copper alloy.

Moffat & Co.
5 DOLLARS

KM#	Date	Fine	VF	XF	Unc
37.1	1849	800.00	1200.	2500.	6500.

Rev: Die break at DOL.

KM#	Date	Fine	VF	XF	Unc
37.2	1849	800.00	1200.	2500.	6000.

Rev: Die break on sheild.

KM#	Date	Fine	VF	XF	Unc
37.3	1849	800.00	1200.	2500.	6000.

Rev: Small letters.

KM#	Date	Fine	VF	XF	Unc
37.4	1850	800.00	1500.	4000.	8500.

Rev: Large letters.

KM#	Date	Fine	VF	XF	Unc
37.5	1850	800.00	1500.	3500.	9000.

Garrett Sale March 1980, MS-60 $21,000.

10 DOLLARS

Rev. val: TEN DOL., arrow below period.

KM#	Date	Fine	VF	XF	Unc
38.1	1849	1800.	3500.	6000.	9750.

Rev: Arrow above period.

KM#	Date	Fine	VF	XF	Unc
38.2	1849	1800.	3500.	6000.	9750.

Rev. val: TEN D., large letters.

KM#	Date	Fine	VF	XF	Unc
38.3	1849	2250.	5000.	7500.	12,500.

Rev: Small letters.

KM#	Date	Fine	VF	XF	Unc
38.4	1849	2250.	5000.	7500.	12,500.

MOFFAT & CO. imprint, wide date.

KM#	Date	Fine	VF	XF	Unc
39.1	1852	2000.	4250.	8500.	13,500.

Close date

KM#	Date	Fine	VF	XF	Unc
39.2	1852	1800.	4000.	8500.	13,500.

NOTE: Struck by Augustus Humbert.

20 DOLLARS

KM#	Date	Fine	VF	XF	Unc
40	1853	2250.	4000.	6500.	11,500.

NOTE: Struck by Curtis, Perry & Ward.

Norris, Greig & Norris
HALF EAGLE

Obv: Period after ALLOY. Plain edge.

KM#	Date	Fine	VF	XF	Unc
41.1	1849	2200.	3750.	8500.	17,500.

Obv: W/o period after ALLOY.

KM#	Date	Fine	VF	XF	Unc
41.2	1849	2200.	3750.	8500.	17,500.

Obv: Period after ALLOY. Reeded edge.

KM#	Date	Fine	VF	XF	Unc
41.3	1849	1950.	3500.	9000.	22,500.

Obv: W/o period after ALLOY.

KM#	Date	Fine	VF	XF	Unc
41.4	1849	1950.	3500.	9000.	22,500.

Rev: STOCKTON beneath date.

KM#	Date	Fine	VF	XF	Unc
42	1850	—	—	Unique	—

J.S. Ormsby
5 DOLLARS

Plain edge

KM#	Date	Fine	VF	XF	Unc
43.1	ND(1849)	—	—	Unique	—

Reeded edge

KM#	Date	Fine	VF	XF	Unc
43.2	ND(1849)	—	—	Unique	—

Superior Auction 1989, VF $137,500.

10 DOLLARS

KM#	Date	Fine	VF	XF	Unc
44	ND(1849)	—	—	—	—

Garrett Sale March 1980, F-12 $100,000.

Pacific Company
5 DOLLARS

KM#	Date	Fine	VF	XF	Unc
45	1849	—	—	—	—

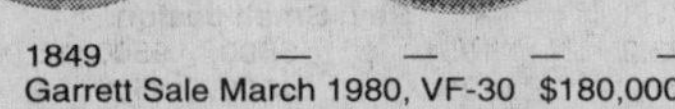

Garrett Sale March 1980, VF-30 $180,000.

10 DOLLARS

Plain edge

KM#	Date	Fine	VF	XF	Unc
46.1	1849	—	—	Rare	—

Waldorf Sale 1964, $24,000.

Reeded edge

KM#	Date	Fine	VF	XF	Unc
46.2	1849	—	—	Rare	—

Templeton Reid
10 DOLLARS

KM#	Date	Fine	VF	XF	Unc
47	1849	—	—	Unique	—

20 DOLLARS

KM#	Date	Fine	VF	XF	Unc
48	1849	—	—	Unknown	—

NOTE: Only known specimen of above stolen from U.S. Mint in 1858 and never recovered. Also see listings under Georgia.

Schultz & Company
5 DOLLARS

KM#	Date	Fine	VF	XF	Unc
49	1851	—	—	45,000.	—

Stacks Sale July 1984, EF $36,300.

United States Assay Office of Gold
10 DOLLARS

Obv: TEN DOLS 884 THOUS.
Rev: O of OFFICE below I of UNITED.

KM#	Date	Fine	VF	XF	Unc
50.1	1852	1750.	2500.	3750.	9250.

Garrett Sale March 1980, MS-60 $18,000.

Rev: O below N, strong beads.

KM#	Date	Fine	VF	XF	Unc
51.2	1852	1750.	2500.	3750.	9250.

Rev: Weak beads.

KM#	Date	Fine	VF	XF	Unc
51.3	1852	1750.	2500.	3750.	9250.

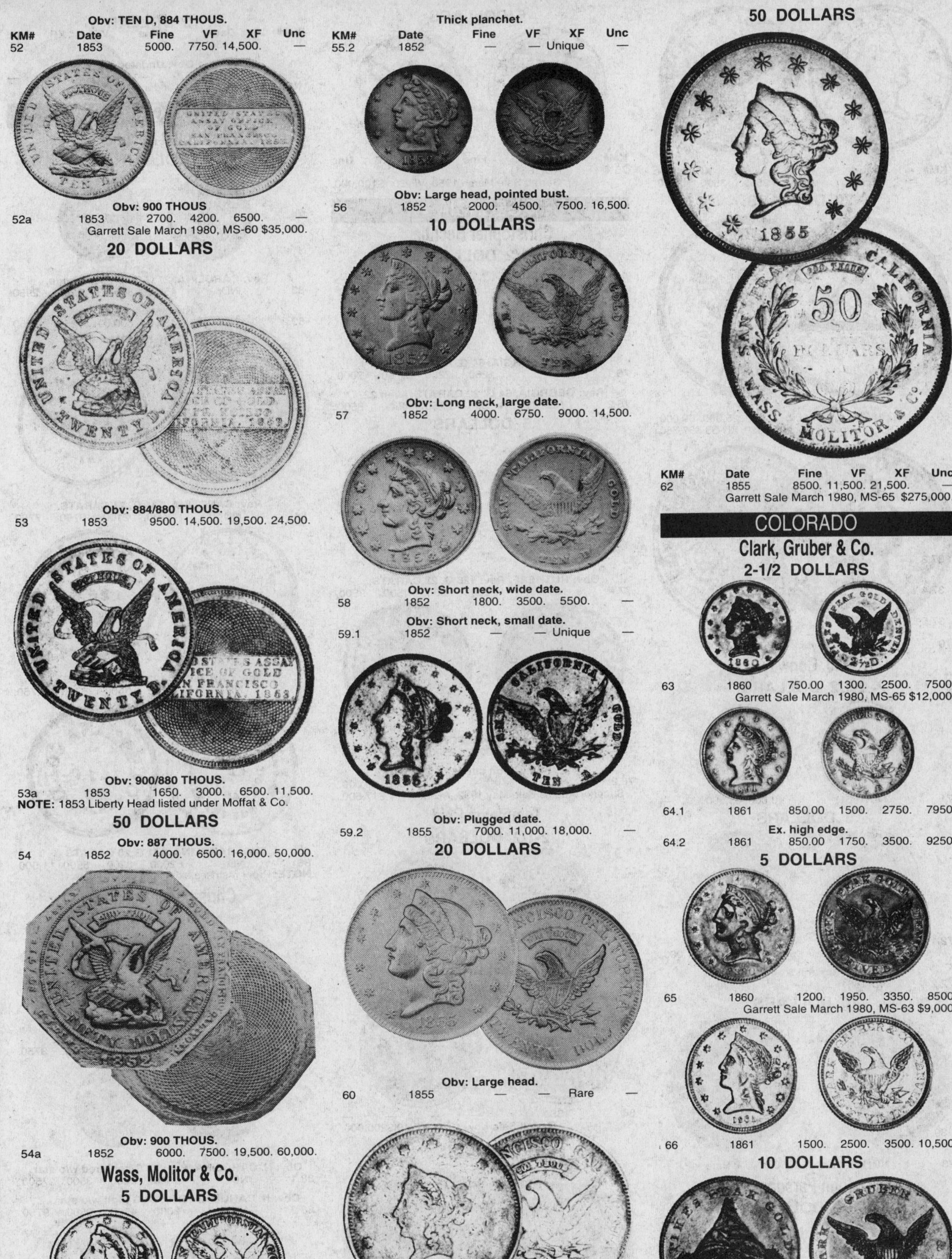

Obv: TEN D, 884 THOUS.

KM#	Date	Fine	VF	XF	Unc
52	1853	5000.	7750.	14,500.	—

Obv: 900 THOUS

KM#	Date	Fine	VF	XF	Unc
52a	1853	2700.	4200.	6500.	—

Garrett Sale March 1980, MS-60 $35,000.

20 DOLLARS

Obv: 884/880 THOUS.

KM#	Date	Fine	VF	XF	Unc
53	1853	9500.	14,500.	19,500.	24,500.

Obv: 900/880 THOUS.

KM#	Date	Fine	VF	XF	Unc
53a	1853	1650.	3000.	6500.	11,500.

NOTE: 1853 Liberty Head listed under Moffat & Co.

50 DOLLARS

Obv: 887 THOUS.

KM#	Date	Fine	VF	XF	Unc
54	1852	4000.	6500.	16,000.	50,000.

Obv: 900 THOUS.

KM#	Date	Fine	VF	XF	Unc
54a	1852	6000.	7500.	19,500.	60,000.

Wass, Molitor & Co.

5 DOLLARS

Obv: Small head, rounded bust.

KM#	Date	Fine	VF	XF	Unc
55.1	1852	2500.	5000.	7500.	16,500.

Thick planchet.

KM#	Date	Fine	VF	XF	Unc
55.2	1852	—	—	Unique	—

Obv: Large head, pointed bust.

KM#	Date	Fine	VF	XF	Unc
56	1852	2000.	4500.	7500.	16,500.

10 DOLLARS

Obv: Long neck, large date.

KM#	Date	Fine	VF	XF	Unc
57	1852	4000.	6750.	9000.	14,500.

Obv: Short neck, wide date.

KM#	Date	Fine	VF	XF	Unc
58	1852	1800.	3500.	5500.	—

Obv: Short neck, small date.

KM#	Date	Fine	VF	XF	Unc
59.1	1852	—	—	Unique	—

Obv: Plugged date.

KM#	Date	Fine	VF	XF	Unc
59.2	1855	7000.	11,000.	18,000.	—

20 DOLLARS

Obv: Large head.

KM#	Date	Fine	VF	XF	Unc
60	1855	—	—	Rare	—

Obv: Small head.

KM#	Date	Fine	VF	XF	Unc
61	1855	5000.	9500.	16,000.	—

50 DOLLARS

KM#	Date	Fine	VF	XF	Unc
62	1855	8500.	11,500.	21,500.	—

Garrett Sale March 1980, MS-65 $275,000.

COLORADO

Clark, Gruber & Co.

2-1/2 DOLLARS

KM#	Date	Fine	VF	XF	Unc
63	1860	750.00	1300.	2500.	7500.

Garrett Sale March 1980, MS-65 $12,000.

KM#	Date	Fine	VF	XF	Unc
64.1	1861	850.00	1500.	2750.	7950.

Ex. high edge.

KM#	Date	Fine	VF	XF	Unc
64.2	1861	850.00	1750.	3500.	9250.

5 DOLLARS

KM#	Date	Fine	VF	XF	Unc
65	1860	1200.	1950.	3350.	8500.

Garrett Sale March 1980, MS-63 $9,000.

KM#	Date	Fine	VF	XF	Unc
66	1861	1500.	2500.	3500.	10,500.

10 DOLLARS

KM#	Date	Fine	VF	XF	Unc
67	1860	2750.	3950.	7500.	16,500.

KM#	Date	Fine	VF	XF	Unc
68	1861	1500.	2500.	3500.	10,500.

20 DOLLARS

KM#	Date	Fine	VF	XF	Unc
69	1860	12,000.	17,000.	25,000.	60,000.

Superior Auction 1989, AU-55 $57,750.

KM#	Date	Fine	VF	XF	Unc
70	1861	4000.	6000.	12,000.	—

J.J. Conway

2-1/2 DOLLARS

KM#	Date	Fine	VF	XF	Unc
71	ND(1861)	—	40,000.	65,000.	—

5 DOLLARS

KM#	Date	Fine	VF	XF	Unc
72.1	ND(1861)	—	—	—	—

Brand Sale June 1984, XF-40 $44,000.

Rev: Numeral 5 omitted.

KM#	Date	Fine	VF	XF	Unc
72.2	ND(1861)	—	—	Unique	—

10 DOLLARS

KM#	Date	Fine	VF	XF	Unc
73	ND(1861)	—	50,000.	Rare	—

John Parsons

2-1/2 DOLLARS

KM#	Date	Fine	VF	XF	Unc
74	ND(1861)	—	—	—	—

Garrett Sale March 1980, VF-20 $85,000.

5 DOLLARS

KM#	Date	Fine	VF	XF	Unc
75	ND(1861)	—	—	—	—

Garrett Sale March 1980, VF-20 $100,000.

GEORGIA

Christopher Bechtler

2-1/2 DOLLARS

Rev: GEORGIA, 64 G, 22 CARATS

KM#	Date	Fine	VF	XF	Unc
76.1	ND	1250.	2250.	3750.	7000.

Rev: GEORGIA, 64 G, 22 CARATS, even 22.

KM#	Date	Fine	VF	XF	Unc
76.2	ND	1800.	2750.	4500.	8500.

5 DOLLARS

Obv: RUTHERF. Rev: 128 G, 22 CARATS.

KM#	Date	Fine	VF	XF	Unc
77	ND	2200.	2900.	4500.	9500.

Obv: RUTHERFORD.

KM#	Date	Fine	VF	XF	Unc
78.1	ND	2000.	2900.	4750.	12,500.

Rev: Colon after 128 G:

KM#	Date	Fine	VF	XF	Unc
78.2	ND	—	—	10,000.	20,000.

Superior Adams Sale May 1992, AU-50 $17,600.

Templeton Reid

2-1/2 DOLLARS

KM#	Date	Fine	VF	XF	Unc
79	1830	15,000.	39,500.	52,500.	—

5 DOLLARS

KM#	Date	Fine	VF	XF	Unc
80	1830	—	—	—	—

Garrett Sale Nov. 1979, XF-40 $200,000.

10 DOLLARS

Obv: With date.

KM#	Date	Fine	VF	XF	Unc
81	1830	—	—		47,500.

Obv: Undated.

KM#	Date	Fine	VF	XF	Unc
82	ND(1830)	—	—	—	—

NOTE: Also see listings under California.

NORTH CAROLINA

August Bechtler

DOLLAR

Rev: CAROLINA, 27 G. 21C., plain edge.

KM#	Date	Fine	VF	XF	Unc
83.1	ND	450.00	800.00	1250.	2950.

Reeded edge

KM#	Date	Fine	VF	XF	Unc
83.2	ND	450.00	800.00	1250.	2950.

5 DOLLARS

Rev: CAROLINA, 134 G. 21 CARATS.

KM#	Date	Fine	VF	XF	Unc
84	ND	1200.	2100.	3750.	7750.

Rev: CAROLINA, 128 G. 22 CARATS.

KM#	Date	Fine	VF	XF	Unc
85	ND	2200.	3500.	5750.	11,750.

Rev: CAROLINA, 141 G:20 CARATS.

KM#	Date	Fine	VF	XF	Unc
86	ND	2000.	3200.	5500.	11,500.

NOTE: Proof restrikes exist from original dies.

Christopher Bechtler

DOLLAR

Obv: CAROLINA, N reversed. Rev: 28 G.

KM#	Date	Fine	VF	XF	Unc
87	ND	900.00	1200.	1700.	3750.

Obv: N. CAROLINA. Rev: 28 G centered w/o star.

KM#	Date	Fine	VF	XF	Unc
88.1	ND	1500.	2200.	3500.	7500.

Obv: N. CAROLINA. Rev: 28 G high w/o star. . . .

KM#	Date	Fine	VF	XF	Unc
88.2	ND	3000.	4500.	6500.	9750.

Obv: N CAROLINA. Rev: 30 G.

KM#	Date	Fine	VF	XF	Unc
89	ND	850.00	1100.	1800.	3700.

2-1/2 DOLLARS

Rev: CAROLINA, 67 G. 21 CARATS.

KM#	Date	Fine	VF	XF	Unc
90.1	ND	1200.	1750.	3300.	6500.

Rev: 64 G 22 CARATS, uneven 22.

KM#	Date	Fine	VF	XF	Unc
90.2	ND	1300.	1850.	3750.	7500.

Rev: Even 22.

KM#	Date	Fine	VF	XF	Unc
90.3	ND	1450.	2000.	4250.	7950.

Rev: CAROLINA, 70 G. 20 CARATS.

KM#	Date	Fine	VF	XF	Unc
91	ND	1500.	2000.	3750.	7500.

Obv: NORTH CAROLINA, 20 C.75 G. Rev: RUTHERFORD in a circle. Border of large beads.

KM#	Date	Fine	VF	XF	Unc
92.1	ND	—	4500.	6750.	11,500.

Obv: NORTH CAROLINA, w/o 75 G, wide 20 C.

KM#	Date	Fine	VF	XF	Unc
92.2	ND	2800.	4500.	6500.	11,250.

Obv: Narrow 20 C.

KM#	Date	Fine	VF	XF	Unc
92.3	ND	2800.	4500.	6500.	11,250.

Obv: NORTH CAROLINA w/o 75 G, CAROLINA above 250 instead of GOLD.

KM#	Date	Fine	VF	XF	Unc
93.1	ND	—	—	Unique	—

Obv: NORTH CAROLINA, 20 C. Rev: 75 G. Border finely serrated.

KM#	Date	Fine	VF	XF	Unc
93.2	ND	3000.	4500.	7250.	—

5 DOLLARS

Rev: CAROLINA, 134 G. star 21 CARATS.

KM#	Date	Fine	VF	XF	Unc
94	ND	1750.	2950.	4500.	8500.

Rev: 21 above CARATS, w/o star.

KM#	Date	Fine	VF	XF	Unc
95	ND	1750.	2950.	4500.	8500.

Obv: RUTHERFORD. Rev: CAROLINA, 140 G. 20 CARATS. Plain edge.

KM#	Date	Fine	VF	XF	Unc
96.1	1834	1550.	2950.	4250.	7950.

Reeded edge

KM#	Date	Fine	VF	XF	Unc
96.2	1834	1750.	3150.	4750.	8750.

Obv: RUTHERF. Rev: CAROLINA. 140 G. 20 CARATS. 20 close to CARATS.

KM#	Date	Fine	VF	XF	Unc
97.1	1834	1800.	3150.	5250.	9000.

Rev: 20 away from CARATS.

KM#	Date	Fine	VF	XF	Unc
97.2	1834	1800.	3150.	5250.	9000.

Obv: RUTHERF. Rev: CAROLINA, 141 G, 20 CARATS.

KM#	Date	Fine	VF	XF	Unc
98	ND	—	Proof restrike		—

Rev: NORTH CAROLINA, 150 G, below 20 CARATS.

KM#	Date	Fine	VF	XF	Unc
99.1	ND	2500.	3500.	6500.	15,000.

Rev: Without 150 G.

KM#	Date	Fine	VF	XF	Unc
99.2	ND	2800.	4500.	7950.	16,500.

OREGON

Oregon Exchange Co.

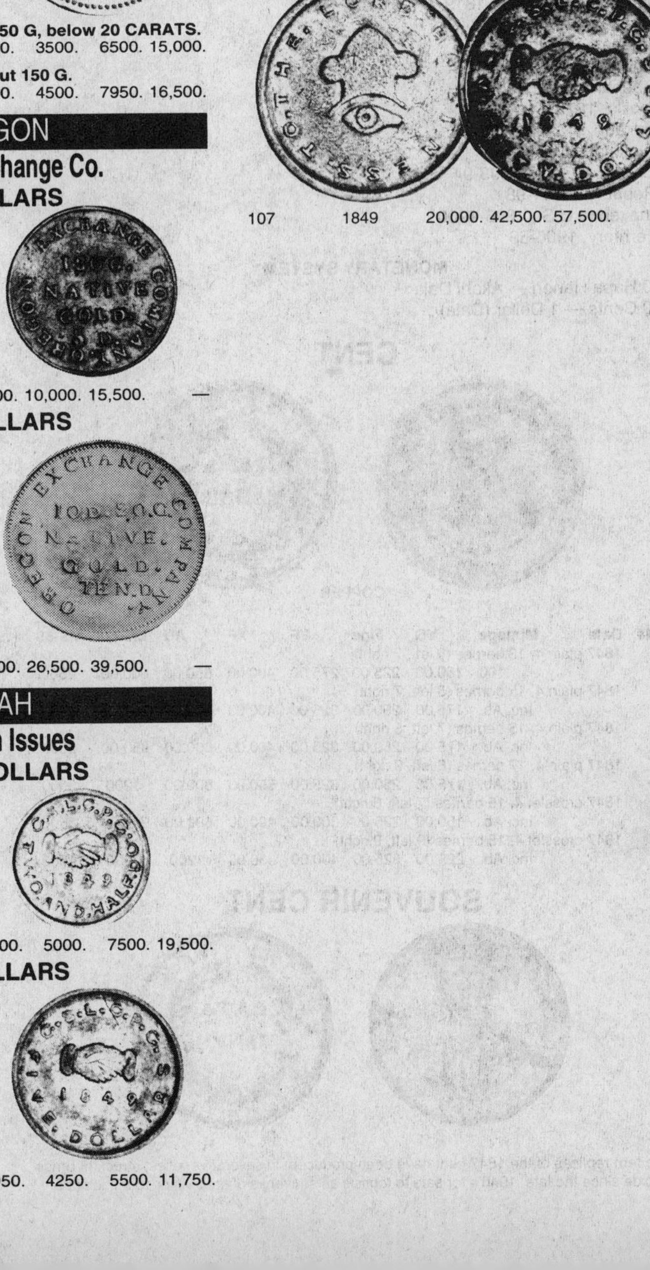

5 DOLLARS

KM#	Date	Fine	VF	XF	Unc
100	1849	6000.	10,000.	15,500.	—

10 DOLLARS

KM#	Date	Fine	VF	XF	Unc
101	1849	17,500.	26,500.	39,500.	—

UTAH

Mormon Issues

2-1/2 DOLLARS

KM#	Date	Fine	VF	XF	Unc
102	1849	3500.	5000.	7500.	19,500.

5 DOLLARS

KM#	Date	Fine	VF	XF	Unc
103	1849	2950.	4250.	5500.	11,750.
104	1850	3000.	4500.	6500.	—
105	1860	5500.	9000.	14,000.	25,500.

10 DOLLARS

KM#	Date	Fine	VF	XF	Unc
106	1849	—	—	Rare	—

Heritage ANA Sale July 1988, AU $93,000.

20 DOLLARS

KM#	Date	Fine	VF	XF	Unc
107	1849	20,000.	42,500.	57,500.	—

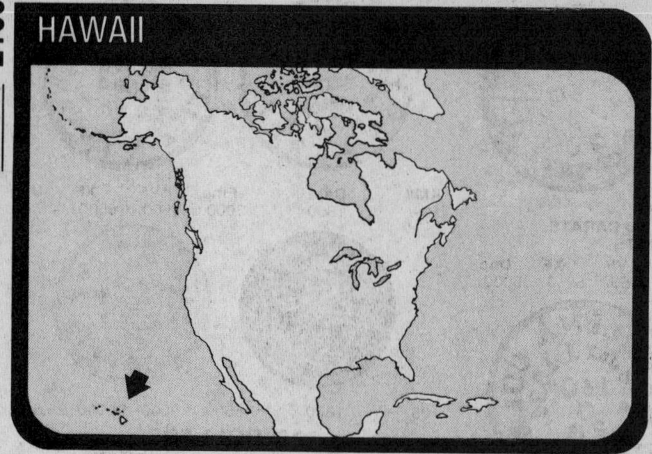

The 50th state of Hawaii, called the 'Aloha State', consists of eight main islands and numerous smaller islets of coral and volcanic origin. Situated in the central Pacific Ocean 2,400 miles from San Francisco, the Hawaiian archipelago has an area of 6,450 sq. mi. and a population of 1,083,000. Capitol: Honolulu. The principal sources of income are, in order: tourism, defense, and agriculture. The main exports are sugar cane and pineapple.

The islands, originally populated by Polynesians from the Society Islands, were rediscovered by British navigator Capt. James Cook in 1778. He named them the Sandwich Islands. King Kamehameha I (the Great) united the islands under one kingdom which endured until 1893, when Queen Liliuokalani was deposed and a provisional government established. This was followed in 1894 by a republic which governed Hawaii until 1898, when the islands were ceded to the United States. Hawaii was organized as a territory in 1900, and attained statehood on August 21, 1959.

RULERS

Kamehameha I, 1795-1819
Kamehameha II, 1819-24
Kamehameha III, 1825-54
Kamehameha IV, 1854-63
Kamehameha V, 1863-72
Lunalilo, 1873-74
Kalakaua, 1874-91
Liliuokalani, 1891-93
Provisional Govt., 1893-94
  Republic, 1894-98
Annexed to U.S., 1898-1900
  Territory, 1900-59

MONETARY SYSTEM

100 Hapa Haneri — Akahi Dala
100 Cents — 1 Dollar (Dala)

CENT

COPPER

KM#	Date	Mintage	VG	Fine	VF	XF	AU	MS-60	MS-65
1a	1847 plain 4, 13 berries (6 left, 7 right)								
		.100	150.00	225.00	275.00	400.00	550.00	800.00	2500.
1b	1847 plain 4, 15 berries (8 left, 7 right)								
		Inc. Ab.	175.00	250.00	325.00	400.00	600.00	950.00	2500.
1f	1847 plain 4, 15 berries (7 left, 8 right)								
		Inc. Ab.	175.00	250.00	325.00	400.00	600.00	950.00	2500.
1c	1847 plain 4, 17 berries (8 left, 9 right)								
		Inc. Ab.	175.00	250.00	325.00	550.00	800.00	1200.	3000.
1d	1847 crosslet 4, 15 berries (7 left, 8 right)								
		Inc. Ab.	150.00	225.00	300.00	400.00	600.00	900.00	2500.
1e	1847 crosslet 4, 18 berries (9 left, 9 right)								
		Inc. Ab.	225.00	325.00	400.00	650.00	1200.	2000.	4500.

SOUVENIR CENT

Modern replicas of the 1847 cent have been produced in several varieties, struck of brass oroide since the late 1940's for sale to tourists as souvenirs of their visits to the islands.

10 CENTS (UMI KENETA)

2.5000 g, .900 SILVER, .0724 oz ASW

KM#	Date	Mintage	VG	Fine	VF	XF	AU	MS-60	MS-65
3	1883	.250	30.00	40.00	80.00	250.00	550.00	1000.	3000.
	1883	26 pcs.	—	—	—	—	Proof	6500.	13,500.

1/4 DOLLAR (HAPAHA)

6.2200 g, .900 SILVER, .1800 oz ASW

KM#	Date	Mintage	VG	Fine	VF	XF	AU	MS-60	MS-65
5	1883	.500	35.00	45.00	60.00	90.00	150.00	225.00	650.00
	1883/1383								
		Inc. Ab.	40.00	50.00	60.00	100.00	175.00	250.00	750.00
	1883	26 pcs.	—	—	—	—	Proof	6000.	12,500.

COPPER

KM#	Date	Mintage	VG	Fine	VF	XF	AU	MS-60	MS-65
5a	1883	18 pcs.	—	—	—	—	Proof	4500.	9000.

1/2 DOLLAR (HAPALUA)

12.5000 g, .900 SILVER, .3618 oz ASW

KM#	Date	Mintage	VG	Fine	VF	XF	AU	MS-60	MS-65
6	1883	.700	50.00	65.00	90.00	250.00	500.00	900.00	3500.
	1883	26 pcs.	—	—	—	—	Proof	7000.	15,000.

COPPER

KM#	Date	Mintage	VG	Fine	VF	XF	AU	MS-60	MS-65
6a	1883	18 pcs.	—	—	—	—	Proof	5000.	10,000.

DOLLAR (AKAHI DALA)

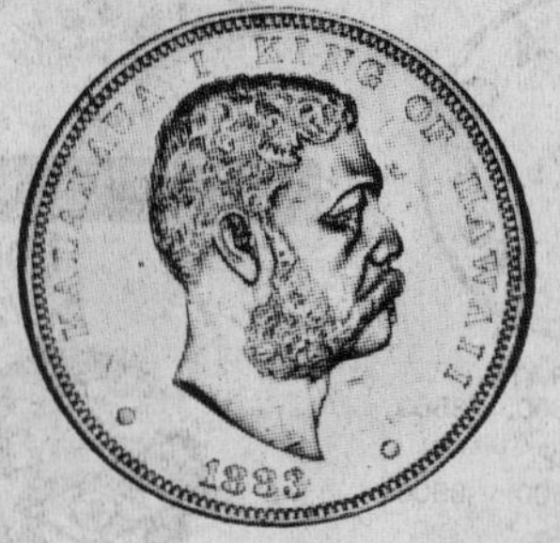

26.7300 g, .900 SILVER, .7736 oz ASW

KM#	Date	Mintage	VG	Fine	VF	XF	AU	MS-60	MS-65
7	1883	.500	170.00	200.00	275.00	600.00	1500.	5000.	13,500.
	1883	26 pcs.	—	—	—	—	Proof	9000.	30,000.

COPPER

KM#	Date	Mintage	VG	Fine	VF	XF	AU	MS-60	MS-65
7a	1883	18 pcs.	—	—	—	—	Proof	8000.	15,000.

NOTE: Official records indicate the following quantities of the above issues were redeemed and melted: KM#1, 88,305; KM#3, 79; KM#5, 257,400; KM#6, 612,245; KM#7, 453,652. That leaves approximate net mintages of: KM#1, 11,600; KM#3, 250,000; KM#5, (regular date) 202,600, (overdate) 40,000; KM#6, 87,700; KM#7, 46,300.

URUGUAY

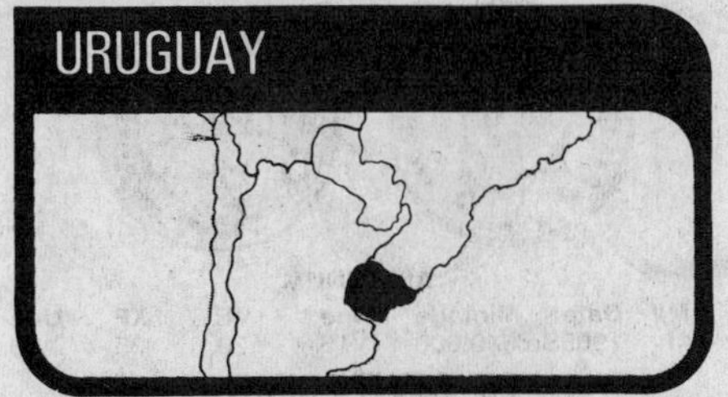

The Oriental Republic of Uruguay (so called because of its location on the east bank of the Uruguay River) is situated on the Atlantic coast of South America between Argentina and Brazil. This most advanced of South American countries has an area of 68,536 sq. mi. (176,220 sq. km.) and a population of *3 million. Capital: Montevideo. Uruguay's chief economic asset is its rich, rolling grassy plains. Meat, wool, hides and skins are exported.

Uruguay was discovered in 1516 by Juan Diaz de Solis, a Spaniard, but settled by the Portuguese who founded Colonia in 1680. Spain contested Portuguese possession and, after a long struggle, gained control of the country in 1778. During the general South American struggle for independence, Uruguay cast off the Spanish bond, only to be reconquered by the Portuguese from Brazil in the struggle of 1816-20. Revolt flared anew in 1825 and independence was reasserted in 1828 with the help of Argentina. The Uruguayan Republic was established in 1830.

MINT MARKS

A - Paris, Berlin, Vienna
(a) Paris, privy marks only
D - Lyon (France)
H - Birmingham
Mo - Mexico City
(p) Poissy, France
So - Santiago (Small O above S)
(u) - Utrecht

MONETARY SYSTEM

100 Centesimo = 1 Peso
1975-1993
1000 Old Pesos = 1 Nue (New) Peso
Commencing 1994
1000 Nuevos Pesos = 1 Peso Uruguayo

CENTESIMO

BRONZE, 5.00 g

KM#	Date	Mintage	Fine	VF	XF	Unc
11	1869A	1.000	1.00	2.00	12.00	40.00
	1869H	1.000	1.00	2.00	12.00	40.00

COPPER-NICKEL, 2.00 g

KM#	Date	Mintage	Fine	VF	XF	Unc
19	1901A	6.000	.45	.75	4.00	20.00
	1901A	—	—	—	Proof	225.00
	1909A	5.000	.45	.75	3.00	10.00
	1924(p)	3.000	.45	.75	2.50	10.00
	1936A	2.000	.50	1.00	3.00	12.00

1.50 g

KM#	Date	Mintage	Fine	VF	XF	Unc
32	1953	5.000	.15	.30	.50	1.00
	1953	—	—	—	Proof	60.00

2 CENTESIMOS

BRONZE, 10.00 g

KM#	Date	Mintage	Fine	VF	XF	Unc
12	1869A	3.000	1.00	2.50	15.00	45.00
	1869H	2.000	1.00	2.50	15.00	45.00

COPPER-NICKEL, 3.50 g

KM#	Date	Mintage	Fine	VF	XF	Unc
20	1901A	7.500	.50	1.25	3.50	16.00
	1909A	10.000	.50	1.00	2.00	8.00
	1924(p)	11.000	.50	1.00	2.75	8.00
	1936A	6.500	.50	1.25	3.50	10.00
	1941So	10.000	.50	1.00	2.75	8.00

COPPER, 3.50 g

KM#	Date	Mintage	Fine	VF	XF	Unc
20a	1943So	5.000	.25	.50	2.00	6.00
	1944So	3.500	.25	.50	2.00	6.00
	1945So	2.500	.25	.50	2.00	7.00
	1946So	2.500	.25	.50	2.50	7.50
	1947So	5.000	.25	.50	1.50	5.00
	1948So	7.500	.25	.50	1.00	4.00
	1949So	7.400	.25	.50	1.00	4.00
	1951So	12.500	.25	.50	1.00	3.00

COPPER-NICKEL, 2.50 g

KM#	Date	Mintage	Fine	VF	XF	Unc
33	1953	50.000	.15	.30	.50	1.25
	1953	—	—	—	Proof	65.00

NICKEL-BRASS, 2.00 g

KM#	Date	Mintage	Fine	VF	XF	Unc
37	1960	17.500	—	.15	.25	.50
	1960	—	—	—	Proof	40.00

4 CENTESIMOS

BRONZE, 20.00 g

KM#	Date	Mintage	Fine	VF	XF	Unc
13	1869A	2.000	2.50	6.00	18.00	75.00
	1869H	6.250	2.50	6.00	18.00	60.00

5 CENTESIMOS

COPPER, 4.25 g

KM#	Date	Mintage	VG	Fine	VF	XF
1	1840	1,500	125.00	250.00	400.00	650.00
	1844/0	—	95.00	190.00	325.00	475.00
	1854/40	—	20.00	30.00	50.00	100.00

4.35 g

KM#	Date	Mintage	VG	Fine	VF	XF
6	1855	—	75.00	125.00	225.00	500.00

KM#	Date	Mintage	Fine	VF	XF	Unc
8	1857D	—	6.00	12.00	28.00	65.00

COPPER-NICKEL, 5.00 g

KM#	Date	Mintage	Fine	VF	XF	Unc
21	1901A	6.000	.25	.75	2.50	15.00
	1901A	—	—	—	Proof	325.00
	1909A	5.000	.25	.75	2.00	10.00
	1909A	—	—	—	Proof	125.00
	1924(p)	5.000	.35	1.00	3.50	8.00
	1936A	3.000	.35	1.00	3.00	8.00
	1941So	2.400	.25	.75	2.00	6.00
	1941S(O)	—	—	—	Proof	200.00

COPPER, 5.00 g

KM#	Date	Mintage	Fine	VF	XF	Unc
21a	1944So	4.000	.20	.65	1.50	7.00
	1946So	2.000	.20	.50	2.00	8.00
	1947So	2.000	.20	.50	2.00	8.00
	1948So	3.000	.20	.50	1.50	7.00
	1949So	2.800	.20	.50	1.50	7.00
	1951So	15.000	.20	.50	1.50	5.00

COPPER-NICKEL, 3.50 g

KM#	Date	Mintage	Fine	VF	XF	Unc
34	1953	17.500	.20	.30	.50	1.00
	1953	—	—	—	Proof	75.00

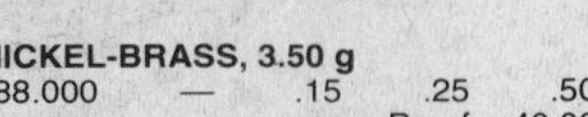

NICKEL-BRASS, 3.50 g

KM#	Date	Mintage	Fine	VF	XF	Unc
38	1960	88.000	—	.15	.25	.50
	1960	—	—	—	Proof	40.00

10 CENTESIMOS

2.5000 g, .900 SILVER, .0723 oz ASW

14 1877A privy mark anchor points left

KM#	Date	Mintage	Fine	VF	XF	Unc
14	1877A privy mark anchor points left	3.000	3.50	6.00	10.00	35.00
	1877A privy mark anchor points right	Inc. Ab.	50.00	75.00	150.00	400.00
	1893/77So	—	—	—	—	—
	1893 w/o mm	—	50.00	70.00	110.00	250.00
	1893So	1.000	2.50	7.00	15.00	50.00

ALUMINUM-BRONZE, 8.00 g
Constitution Centennial
Obv: MORLON behind neck.

KM#	Date	Mintage	Fine	VF	XF	Unc
25	1930(a)	5.000	1.00	2.50	7.50	22.50

6.00 g

KM#	Date	Mintage	Fine	VF	XF	Unc
28	1936A	2.000	1.50	3.50	8.50	25.00

COPPER-NICKEL, 4.50 g

KM#	Date	Mintage	Fine	VF	XF	Unc
35	1953	28.250	.15	.20	.30	.75
	1953	—	—	—	Proof	75.00
	1959	10.000	.20	.30	.50	1.50

NICKEL-BRASS, 4.50 g

KM#	Date	Mintage	Fine	VF	XF	Unc
39	1960	72.500	.15	.20	.30	.75

20 CENTESIMOS

COPPER
28.00 g, 2.75mm thick
Rev: Small design.

KM#	Date	Mintage	VG	Fine	VF	XF
2.1	1840	2,125	20.00	60.00	100.00	200.00

Reduced weight 21.00 g, 1.75mm thick.

KM#	Date	Mintage	VG	Fine	VF	XF
2.2	1843/40	—	25.00	70.00	120.00	225.00
	1844	—	35.00	85.00	150.00	325.00

Rev: Small design.

KM#	Date	Mintage	VG	Fine	VF	XF
2.3	1854	—	20.00	40.00	80.00	150.00

Rev: Large design.

KM#	Date	Mintage	VG	Fine	VF	XF
7	1854	—	22.00	50.00	100.00	250.00
	1855	—	20.00	45.00	85.00	210.00

21.30 g

KM#	Date	Mintage	Fine	VF	XF	Unc
9	1857D	—	5.00	10.00	25.00	75.00

5.0000 g, .900 SILVER, .1446 oz ASW

KM#	Date	Mintage	Fine	VF	XF	Unc
15	1877A	1.500	3.00	5.00	12.00	45.00
	1893/73So	.750	5.00	7.50	15.00	65.00

5.0000 g, .800 SILVER, .1286 oz ASW

KM#	Date	Mintage	Fine	VF	XF	Unc
24	1920	2.500	2.00	3.50	8.00	25.00

Constitution Centennial
Obv: P. TURIN left of date.

KM#	Date	Mintage	Fine	VF	XF	Unc
26	1930(a)	2.500	2.00	3.50	8.00	25.00

3.0000 g, .720 SILVER, .0694 oz ASW

KM#	Date	Mintage	Fine	VF	XF	Unc
29	1942So	18.000	1.00	2.00	3.50	5.00

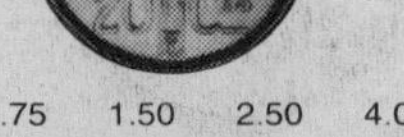

KM#	Date	Mintage	Fine	VF	XF	Unc
36	1954(u)	10.000	.75	1.50	2.50	4.00

ALUMINUM

KM#	Date	Mintage	Fine	VF	XF	Unc
44	1965So	40.000	.15	.20	.35	.60

25 CENTESIMOS

COPPER-NICKEL
Obv: HP below bust.

KM#	Date	Mintage	Fine	VF	XF	Unc
40	1960	48.000	.20	.35	.50	1.00
	1960	—	—	—	Proof	60.00

40 CENTESIMOS

COPPER
Obv: Male sunface.

KM#	Date	Mintage	VG	Fine	VF	XF
3	1844	—	40.00	80.00	150.00	275.00

Obv: Female sunface.

KM#	Date	Mintage	VG	Fine	VF	XF
4	1844	50 est.	175.00	375.00	750.00	1250.

NOTE: There are at least 12 different obverse and reverse die varieties known for the 40 Centesimos dated 1844.

KM#	Date	Mintage	Fine	VF	XF	Unc
10	1857D	—	5.00	10.00	45.00	120.00

50 CENTESIMOS

12.5000 g, .900 SILVER, .3617 oz ASW

KM#	Date	Mintage	Fine	VF	XF	Unc
16	1877A	.400	6.00	8.00	20.00	90.00
	1893/73So	.500	6.00	8.00	20.00	90.00
	1894	.800	6.00	8.00	20.00	90.00

NOTE: 1894 has larger letters.

KM#	Date	Mintage	Fine	VF	XF	Unc
22	1916	.400	4.00	8.00	20.00	75.00
	1917	5.600	3.00	5.00	17.50	60.00

7.0000 g, .720 SILVER, .1620 oz ASW

KM#	Date	Mintage	Fine	VF	XF	Unc
31	1943So	10.800	BV	2.00	3.00	9.00

COPPER-NICKEL
Obv: HP below bust.

KM#	Date	Mintage	Fine	VF	XF	Unc
41	1960	18.000	.20	.40	.60	1.00
	1960	—	—	—	Proof	60.00

ALUMINUM

KM#	Date	Mintage	Fine	VF	XF	Unc
45	1965So	50.000	.15	.25	.40	.70

PESO

27.0000 g, .875 SILVER, .7596 oz ASW

KM#	Date	Mintage	Fine	VF	XF	Unc
5	1844	1,500	200.00	350.00	700.00	1850.

NOTE: KM#5 exists both with coin and medal reverse alignments.

25.5000 g, .917 SILVER, .7518 oz ASW

KM#	Date	Mintage	Fine	VF	XF	Unc
17	1877A	.300	25.00	45.00	100.00	400.00
	1877A	—	—	—	Proof	1000.

25.0000 g, .900 SILVER, .7235 oz ASW

KM#	Date	Mintage	Fine	VF	XF	Unc
17a	1878A	*.100	125.00	350.00	800.00	1500.
	1893/73So	.500	25.00	50.00	100.00	425.00
	1893So	Inc. Ab.	20.00	35.00	85.00	400.00
	1893	.600	20.00	35.00	75.00	350.00
	1895	1.000	15.00	25.00	65.00	300.00

***NOTE:** 43,200 melted after they were recovered from salt water.

KM#	Date	Mintage	Fine	VF	XF	Unc
23	1917	2.000	10.00	20.00	50.00	250.00

9.0000 g, .720 SILVER, .2083 oz ASW

KM#	Date	Mintage	Fine	VF	XF	Unc
30	1942So	9.000	BV	2.25	4.50	12.50

COPPER-NICKEL
Obv: HP below bust.

KM#	Date	Mintage	Fine	VF	XF	Unc
42	1960	8.000	.25	.50	.75	1.25
	1960	—	—	—	Proof	75.00

ALUMINUM-BRONZE

KM#	Date	Mintage	Fine	VF	XF	Unc
46	1965So	60.000	—	.15	.35	.60
	1965So	25 pcs.	—	—	Proof	65.00

NICKEL-BRASS
Ceibo - National Flower

KM#	Date	Mintage	Fine	VF	XF	Unc
49	1968So	103.200	—	—	.15	.30
	1968So	50 pcs.	—	—	Proof	50.00

ALUMINUM-BRONZE

KM#	Date	Mintage	Fine	VF	XF	Unc
52	1969So	51.800	—	—	.15	.30

5 PESOS

8.4850 g, .917 GOLD, .2501 oz AGW
Constitution Centennial
Obv: L. BAZOR behind neck.

KM#	Date	Mintage	Fine	VF	XF	Unc
27	1930(a)	*.100	120.00	140.00	160.00	225.00

NOTE: Only 14,415 were released. Remainder withheld.

ALUMINUM-BRONZE

KM#	Date	Mintage	Fine	VF	XF	Unc
47	1965So	18.000	.20	.30	.50	1.00
	1965So	25 pcs.	—	—	Proof	75.00

NICKEL-BRASS
Ceibo - National Flower

KM#	Date	Mintage	Fine	VF	XF	Unc
50	1968So	42.680	.10	.20	.30	.40
	1968So	50 pcs.	—	—	Proof	65.00

ALUMINUM-BRONZE

KM#	Date	Mintage	Fine	VF	XF	Unc
53	1969So	42.320	—	—	.10	.30

10 PESOS

12.5000 g, .900 SILVER, .3617 oz ASW
Sesquicentennial of Revolution Against Spain

KM#	Date	Mintage	Fine	VF	XF	Unc
43	1961	3.000	—	BV	3.50	7.50
	1961	—	—	—	Proof	600.00

ALUMINUM-BRONZE

KM#	Date	Mintage	Fine	VF	XF	Unc
48	1965So	18.000	.15	.20	.35	1.00

NICKEL-BRASS
Ceibo - National Flower

KM#	Date	Mintage	Fine	VF	XF	Unc
51	1968So	90.000	.15	.20	.35	.65
	1968So	50 pcs.	—	—	Proof	80.00

ALUMINUM-BRONZE

KM#	Date	Mintage	Fine	VF	XF	Unc
54	1969So	10.000	.15	.20	.35	.65

20 PESOS

COPPER-NICKEL
Spears of Wheat

KM#	Date	Mintage	Fine	VF	XF	Unc
56	1970So	50.000	.15	.25	.40	.75
	1970So	—	—	—	Proof	80.00

50 PESOS

COPPER-NICKEL
Spears of Wheat

KM#	Date	Mintage	Fine	VF	XF	Unc
57	1970So	20.000	.20	.40	.60	1.50
	1970So	—	—	—	Proof	80.00

NICKEL-BRASS
Centennial of Birth of Rodo

KM#	Date	Mintage	Fine	VF	XF	Unc
58	1971So	15.000	.20	.50	1.00	2.00

6.0200 g, .900 SILVER, .1742 oz ASW

KM#	Date	Mintage	Fine	VF	XF	Unc
58a	1971So	1,000	—	—	Proof	17.50

GOLD

KM#	Date	Mintage	Fine	VF	XF	Unc
58b	1971So	100 pcs.	—	—	Proof	350.00

100 PESOS

COPPER-NICKEL

KM#	Date	Mintage	Fine	VF	XF	Unc
59	1973Mx	20.000	.25	.50	1.00	2.50

1000 PESOS

25.0000 g, .900 SILVER, .7234 oz ASW
F.A.O. Issue

KM#	Date	Mintage	Fine	VF	XF	Unc
55	1969So	.500	—	BV	8.00	12.50
	1969So	350 pcs.	—	—	Proof	150.00

BRONZE

KM#	Date	Mintage	Fine	VF	XF	Unc
55a	1969So	.011	—	—	25.00	40.00

GOLD

KM#	Date	Mintage	Fine	VF	XF	Unc
55b	1969So	450 pcs.	—	—	—	725.00

COUNTERSTAMPED COINAGE

PESO

SILVER

KM#	Date	Mintage	Fine	VF	XF	Unc
18	1895	—	75.00	125.00	200.00	—

NOTE: Dies were made in the Paysandu area of Uruguay, and Brazil 2,000 reis were overstruck to create an 1895 1 peso coin. These coins are considered by some to be a contemporary counterfeit and probably have no official standing.

MONETARY REFORM

1000 Old Pesos = 1 Nuevo (New) Peso

CENTESIMO

ALUMINUM

KM#	Date	Mintage	Fine	VF	XF	Unc
71	1977So	10.000	—	—	.15	.25

3.7000 g, .900 SILVER, .1071 oz ASW

KM#	Date	Mintage	Fine	VF	XF	Unc
71a	1979So	202 pcs.	—	—	Proof	15.00

6.2600 g, .900 GOLD, .1811 oz AGW

KM#	Date	Mintage	Fine	VF	XF	Unc
71b	1979So	50 pcs.	—	—	Proof	175.00

2 CENTESIMOS

ALUMINUM

KM#	Date	Mintage	Fine	VF	XF	Unc
72	1977So	17.000	—	—	.15	.25
	1978So	3.000	—	—	.15	.25

5.2000 g, .900 SILVER, .1505 oz ASW

KM#	Date	Mintage	Fine	VF	XF	Unc
72a	1979So	202 pcs.	—	—	Proof	20.00

9.2500 g, .900 GOLD, .2676 oz AGW

KM#	Date	Mintage	Fine	VF	XF	Unc
72b	1979So	52 pcs.	—	—	Proof	275.00

5 CENTESIMOS

ALUMINUM

KM#	Date	Mintage	Fine	VF	XF	Unc
73	1977So	11.000	—	—	.15	.25
	1978So	19.000	—	—	.15	.25

7.4000 g, .900 SILVER, .2141 oz ASW

KM#	Date	Mintage	Fine	VF	XF	Unc
73a	1979So	202 pcs.	—	—	Proof	20.00

12.5500 g, .900 GOLD, .3631 oz AGW

KM#	Date	Mintage	Fine	VF	XF	Unc
73b	1979So	52 pcs.	—	—	Proof	350.00

10 CENTESIMOS

ALUMINUM-BRONZE

KM#	Date	Mintage	Fine	VF	XF	Unc
66	1976So	127.400	—	—	.15	.35
	1977So	12.700	—	—	.20	.40
	1978So	19.900	—	—	.20	.40
	1981So	—	—	—	.20	.40

3.8000 g, .900 SILVER, .1100 oz ASW

KM#	Date	Mintage	Fine	VF	XF	Unc
66a	1976So	200 pcs.	—	—	Proof	20.00
	1977So	200 pcs.	—	—	Proof	20.00

6.0000 g. .900 GOLD, .1736 oz AGW

KM#	Date	Mintage	Fine	VF	XF	Unc
66b	1976So	50 pcs.	—	—	Proof	175.00

20 CENTESIMOS

ALUMINUM-BRONZE

KM#	Date	Mintage	Fine	VF	XF	Unc
67	1976So	40.000	—	—	.20	.45
	1977So	4.700	—	—	.20	.60
	1978So	15.300	—	—	.20	.45
	1981So	—	—	—	.20	.45
	6.4000 g, .900 SILVER, .1852 oz ASW					
67a	1976So	200 pcs.	—	—	Proof	22.50
	1977So	200 pcs.	—	—	Proof	22.50
	10.5000 g, .900 GOLD, .3038 oz AGW					
67b	1976So	50 pcs.	—	—	Proof	350.00

50 CENTESIMOS

ALUMINUM-BRONZE

KM#	Date	Mintage	Fine	VF	XF	Unc
68	1976So	30.000	—	—	.20	.50
	1977So	9.800	—	—	.20	.50
	1978So	.200	—	—	.20	.55
	1981So	—	—	—	.20	.50
	9.0000 g, .900 SILVER, .2604 oz ASW					
68a	1976So	200 pcs.	—	—	Proof	35.00
	1977So	200 pcs.	—	—	Proof	35.00
	15.0000 g, .900 GOLD, .4340 oz AGW					
68b	1976So	50 pcs.	—	—	Proof	500.00

NEW PESO

ALUMINUM-BRONZE

KM#	Date	Mintage	Fine	VF	XF	Unc
69	1976So	65.540	—	—	.30	.60
	1977So	7.360	—	—	.30	.65
	1978So	27.100	—	—	.30	.65
	13.5000 g, .900 SILVER, .3906 oz ASW					
69a	1976So	200 pcs.	—	—	Proof	40.00
	23.0000 g, .900 GOLD, .6655 oz AGW					
69b	1976So	50 pcs.	—	—	Proof	600.00

COPPER-NICKEL

KM#	Date	Mintage	Fine	VF	XF	Unc
74	1980So	50.000	—	.20	.35	.65
	1981So	—	—	.20	.35	.65
	7.0000 g, .900 SILVER, .2026 oz ASW					
74a	1980So	300 pcs.	—	—	Proof	25.00
	11.6500 g, .900 GOLD, .3371 oz AGW					
74b	1980So	100 pcs.	—	—	Proof	300.00
	6.9400 g, .900 SILVER, .2008 oz ASW					
	Obv: National flag.					
76	1981	100 pcs.	—	—	Proof	30.00

STAINLESS STEEL

KM#	Date	Mintage	Fine	VF	XF	Unc
95	1989	—	—	—	—	.10
	1990	—	—	—	—	.10

2 NEW PESOS

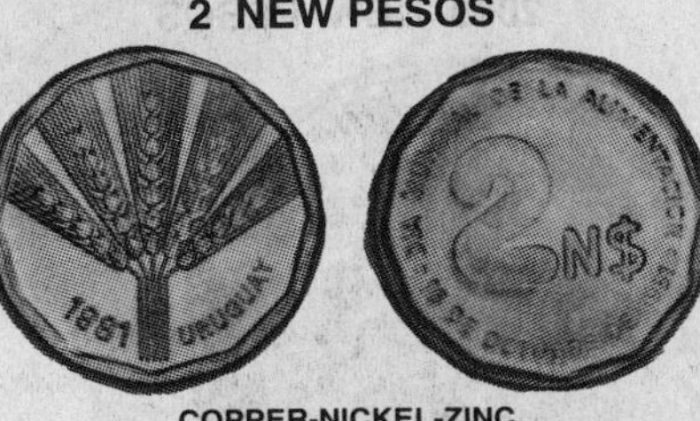

COPPER-NICKEL-ZINC
World Food Day

KM#	Date	Mintage	Fine	VF	XF	Unc
77	1981	95.000	—	.20	.35	.85
	14.5300 g, .900 GOLD, .4204 oz AGW					
77a	1981	100 pcs.	—	—	Proof	400.00

5 NEW PESOS

COPPER-NICKEL-ALUMINUM
150th Anniversary of Revolutionary Movement

KM#	Date	Mintage	Fine	VF	XF	Unc
65	ND(1975)So					
		3.000	.50	.75	1.25	3.00
	18.4300 g, .900 SILVER, .5332 oz ASW					
65a	ND(1975)So					
		2,000	—	—	Proof	15.00
	GOLD					
65b	ND(1975)So					
		1,000	—	—	Proof	500.00

NOTE: 50 pieces each in aluminum, alpaca and copper are reported to have been struck.

COPPER-ALUMINUM
250th Anniversary Founding of Montevideo

KM#	Date	Mintage	Fine	VF	XF	Unc
70	1976So	.300	.75	1.00	1.50	4.00
	SILVER					
70b	1976So	—	—	—	—	175.00
	30.0000 g, .900 GOLD, .8681 oz AGW					
70a	1976So	100 pcs.	—	—	Proof	725.00

COPPER-NICKEL

KM#	Date	Mintage	Fine	VF	XF	Unc
75	1980So	50.000	—	.20	.40	1.50
	1981So	—	—	.20	.40	1.50
	9.3000 g, .900 SILVER, .2691 oz ASW					
75a	1980So	300 pcs.	—	—	Proof	30.00
	15.6000 g, .900 GOLD, .4514 oz AGW					
75b	1980So	100 pcs.	—	—	Proof	450.00
	9.3000 g, .900 SILVER, .2691 oz ASW					
	Obv: Coat of arms.					
78	1981	100 pcs.	—	—	Proof	30.00

STAINLESS STEEL

KM#	Date	Mintage	Fine	VF	XF	Unc
92	1989	65.000	—	—	—	.10

10 NEW PESOS

COPPER-NICKEL

KM#	Date	Mintage	Fine	VF	XF	Unc
79	1981So	—	—	.20	.50	1.75
	11.6300 g, .900 SILVER, .3365 oz ASW					
79a	1981So	100 pcs.	—	—	Proof	35.00
	19.4800 g, .900 GOLD, .5637 oz AGW					
79b	1981So	100 pcs.	—	—	Proof	500.00

STAINLESS STEEL

KM#	Date	Mintage	Fine	VF	XF	Unc
93	1989	79.000	—	—	—	.20

20 NEW PESOS

COPPER-NICKEL
World Fisheries Conference

KM#	Date	Mintage	Fine	VF	XF	Unc
86	1984	3,771	—	—	—	12.50
	11.6600 g, .925 SILVER, .3468 oz ASW					
86a	1984	.025	—	—	Proof	20.00
	19.6000 g, .917 GOLD, .5776 oz AGW					
86b	1984	100 pcs.	—	—	Proof	600.00

50 NEW PESOS

STAINLESS STEEL

KM#	Date	Mintage	Fine	VF	XF	Unc
94	1989	—	—	—	—	.30
	1990	—	—	—	—	.30

100 NEW PESOS

12.0000 g, .900 SILVER, .3472 oz ASW

Hydroelectric Dam

KM#	Date	Mintage	Fine	VF	XF	Unc
80	1981So	.025	—	—	—	7.50

20.0000 g, .900 GOLD, .5787 oz AGW

KM#	Date	Mintage	Fine	VF	XF	Unc
80a	1981So	300 pcs.	—	—	Proof	375.00

STAINLESS STEEL
Portrait of a Gaucho

KM#	Date	Mintage	Fine	VF	XF	Unc
96	1989	—	—	—	—	.50
	1990	—	—	—	—	.50

200 NEW PESOS

COPPER-NICKEL
Unchained Liberty

KM#	Date	Mintage	Fine	VF	XF	Unc
97	1989	—	—	—	—	1.00
	1990	—	—	—	—	1.00

500 NEW PESOS

12.0000 g, .900 SILVER, .3472 oz ASW
Hydroelectric Dam

KM#	Date	Mintage	Fine	VF	XF	Unc
82	1983So	.015	—	—	—	7.50

20.0000 g, .900 GOLD, .5787 oz AGW

KM#	Date	Mintage	Fine	VF	XF	Unc
82a	1983So	100 pcs.	—	—	Proof	500.00

12.0000 g, .900 SILVER, .3473 oz ASW
General Leandro Gomez

KM#	Date	Mintage	Fine	VF	XF	Unc
90	1986Mo	6,000	—	—	Proof	25.00

COPPER-NICKEL
Artigas

KM#	Date	Mintage	Fine	VF	XF	Unc
98	1989	—	—	—	—	2.00
	1990	—	—	—	—	2.00

2000 NEW PESOS

25.0000 g, .900 SILVER, .7235 oz ASW
140th Anniversary of Silver Coinage and
25th Meeting of Interamerican Bank Governors

KM#	Date	Mintage	Fine	VF	XF	Unc
87	1984	.015	—	—	Proof	22.50

25th Meeting of Interamerican Bank Governors

KM#	Date	Mintage	Fine	VF	XF	Unc
88	1984	.015	—	—	Proof	22.50

5000 NEW PESOS

12.0000 g, .900 SILVER, .3472 oz ASW
Hydroelectric Dam

KM#	Date	Mintage	Fine	VF	XF	Unc
81	1981So	.015	—	—	Proof	20.00

20.0000 g, .900 GOLD, .5787 oz AGW

KM#	Date	Mintage	Fine	VF	XF	Unc
81a	1981So	3,000	—	—	Proof	325.00

35.0000 g, .900 SILVER, .7235 oz ASW
20th Anniversary of Central Bank

KM#	Date	Mintage	Fine	VF	XF	Unc
91	1987So	.010	—	—	Proof	20.00

Latin America Presidents Assembly

KM#	Date	Mintage	Fine	VF	XF	Unc
99	1988	—	—	—	Proof	20.00

20,000 NEW PESOS

20.0000 g, .900 GOLD, .5787 oz AGW
Hydroelectric Dam

KM#	Date	Mintage	Fine	VF	XF	Unc
85	1983So	2,500	—	—	Proof	375.00

130th Anniversary of Gold Coinage and
25th Meeting of Interamerican Bank Governors

KM#	Date	Mintage	Fine	VF	XF	Unc
89	1984	1,500	—	—	Proof	375.00

25,000 PESOS

12.5000 g, .900 SILVER, .3617 oz ASW
25th Anniversary of Central Bank

KM#	Date	Mintage	Fine	VF	XF	Unc
101	1992	—	—	—	—	15.00

50,000 NEW PESOS

27.0000 g, .925 SILVER, .8029 oz ASW
Ibero - American Series

KM#	Date	Mintage	Fine	VF	XF	Unc
100	1991	.070	—	—	Proof	42.50

MINT SETS (MS)

KM#	Date	Mintage	Identification	Issue Price	Mkt. Val.
MS1	1969/70(5)	—	KM52-54,56-57	—	3.50
MS2	1969/70(5)	—	KM52-54,56-57	—	3.50

NOTE: KM#MS1 was issued under the law no. 13,637 of Dec. 21, 1967 while MS2 was issued for the 11th Assembly of the Interamerica Bank.

KM#	Date	Mintage	Identification	Issue Price	Mkt. Val.
MS3	1976(4)	—	KM66-69	—	2.50

PROOF SETS (PS)

KM#	Date	Mintage	Identification	Issue Price	Mkt. Val.
PS1	1953(4)	100	KM32-35	—	275.00
PS3	1968(3)	50	KM49-51	—	200.00

VANUATU

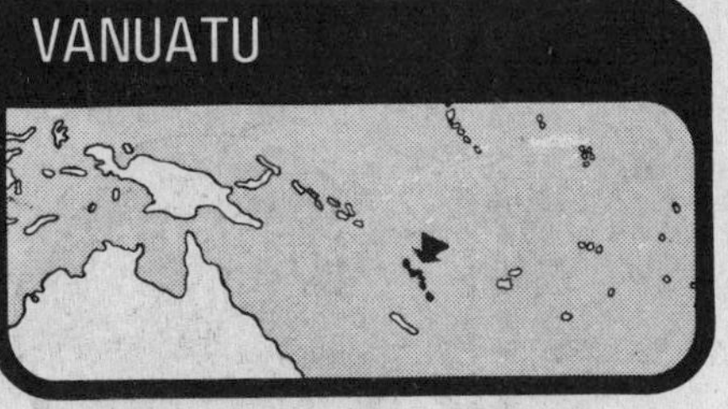

The Republic of Vanuatu, formerly New Hebrides Condominium, a group of islands located in the South Pacific 500 miles (800 km.) west of Fiji, are under the joint sovereignty of Great Britain and France. The islands have an area of 5,700 sq. mi. (14,760 sq. km.) and a population of *160,000, mainly Melanesians of mixed blood. Capital: Port-Vila. The volcanic and coral islands, while malarial and subject to frequent earthquakes, are extremely fertile, and produce copra, coffee, tropical fruits and timber for export.

The New Hebrides were discovered by Portuguese navigator Pedro de Quiros in 1606, visited by French explorer Bougainville in 1768, and named by British navigator Capt. James Cook in 1774. Ships of all nations converged on the islands to trade for sandalwood, prompting France and Britain to relinquish their individual claims and declare the islands a neutral zone in 1878. The New Hebrides were placed under the control of a mixed Anglo-French commission of naval officers during the native uprisings of 1887, and established as a condominium under the joint sovereignty of France and Great Britain in 1906.

MINT MARKS

(a) - Paris, privy marks only

MONETARY SYSTEM

100 Centimes = 1 Franc

NEW HEBRIDES

FRANC

NICKEL-BRASS

KM#	Date	Mintage	VF	XF	Unc
4.1	1970(a)	.435	.25	.50	.75

Obv. leg: I.E.O.M. added.

KM#	Date	Mintage	VF	XF	Unc
4.2	1975(a)	.350	.20	.40	.60
	1978(a)	.200	.20	.40	.60
	1979(a)	—	.20	.40	.60
	1982(a)	—	.20	.40	.60

2 FRANCS

NICKEL-BRASS

KM#	Date	Mintage	VF	XF	Unc
5.1	1970(a)	.264	.60	1.25	2.00

Obv. leg: I.E.O.M. added.

KM#	Date	Mintage	VF	XF	Unc
5.2	1973(a)	.200	.20	.40	.60
	1975(a)	.300	.20	.40	.60
	1978(a)	.150	.20	.40	.60
	1979(a)	—	.20	.40	.60
	1982(a)	—	.20	.40	.60

5 FRANCS

NICKEL-BRASS

KM#	Date	Mintage	VF	XF	Unc
6.1	1970(a)	.375	.50	.75	1.50

Obv. leg: I.E.O.M. added.

KM#	Date	Mintage	VF	XF	Unc
6.2	1975(a)	.350	.30	.60	1.00
	1979(a)	—	.30	.60	1.00
	1982(a)	—	.30	.60	1.00

10 FRANCS

NICKEL

KM#	Date	Mintage	VF	XF	Unc
2.1	1967(a)	.250	.30	.60	1.25
	1970(a)	.400	.30	.60	1.25

Obv. leg: I.E.O.M. added.

KM#	Date	Mintage	VF	XF	Unc
2.2	1973(a)	.200	.30	.60	1.25
	1975(a)	.300	.30	.60	1.25
	1977(a)	—	.30	.60	1.25
	1979(a)	—	.30	.60	1.25
	1982(a)	—	.30	.60	1.25

20 FRANCS

NICKEL

KM#	Date	Mintage	VF	XF	Unc
3.1	1967(a)	.250	.60	1.00	2.00
	1970(a)	.300	.60	1.00	2.00

Obv. leg: I.E.O.M. added.

KM#	Date	Mintage	VF	XF	Unc
3.2	1973(a)	.200	.60	1.00	2.00
	1975(a)	.150	.60	1.00	2.00
	1977(a)	—	.60	1.00	2.00
	1979(a)	—	.60	1.00	2.00
	1982(a)	—	.60	1.00	2.00

50 FRANCS

NICKEL

KM#	Date	Mintage	VF	XF	Unc
7	1972(a)	.200	1.50	2.50	3.50
	1979(a)	—	1.50	2.50	3.50

100 FRANCS

25.0000 g, .835 SILVER, .6712 oz ASW

KM#	Date	Mintage	VF	XF	Unc
1	1966(a)	.200	—	—	15.00
	1979(a)	—	—	—	20.00

FLEUR DE COIN SETS (SS)

KM#	Date	Mintage	Identification	Issue Price	Mkt. Val.
SS1	1966-7(3)	2,200	KM1,2.1,3.1	10.00	10.00

NOTE: These sets were issued with New Caledonia and French Polynesia 1967 sets.

VANUATU

VATU

NICKEL-BRASS

KM#	Date	Mintage	VF	XF	Unc
3	1983	—	—	.10	.35
	1983	—	—	Proof	1.50
	1990	—	—	.10	.35

2 VATU

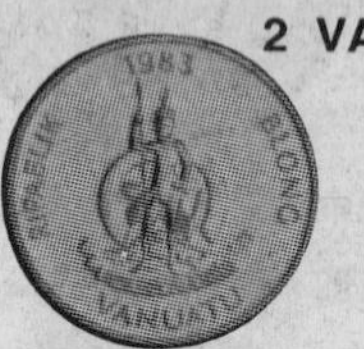

NICKEL-BRASS

KM#	Date	Mintage	VF	XF	Unc
4	1983	—	—	.10	.45
	1983	—	—	Proof	2.00
	1990	—	—	.10	.45

5 VATU

NICKEL-BRASS

KM#	Date	Mintage	VF	XF	Unc
5	1983	—	—	.15	.60
	1983	—	—	Proof	2.50
	1990	—	—	.15	.60

10 VATU

COPPER-NICKEL
F.A.O. Issue

KM#	Date	Mintage	VF	XF	Unc
6	1983	—	—	.15	.75
	1983	—	—	Proof	3.00
	1990	—	—	.15	.75

20 VATU

COPPER-NICKEL
F.A.O. Issue

KM#	Date	Mintage	VF	XF	Unc
7	1983	—	—	.30	1.25
	1983	—	—	Proof	4.00
	1990	—	—	.30	1.25

50 VATU

NICKEL
1st Anniversary of Independence

KM#	Date	Mintage	VF	XF	Unc
1	1981	—	—	1.00	2.50

15.0000 g, .925 SILVER, .4461 oz ASW

KM#	Date	Mintage	VF	XF	Unc
1a	1981	846 pcs.	—	Proof	50.00

COPPER-NICKEL
F.A.O. Issue

KM#	Date	Mintage	VF	XF	Unc
8	1983	—	—	1.00	2.50
	1983	—	—	Proof	7.00
	1990	—	—	1.00	2.50

34.0000 g, .925 SILVER, 1.0111 oz ASW
Seoul Olympics - Boxing

KM#	Date	Mintage	VF	XF	Unc
10	1988	—	—	Proof	80.00

31.4700 g, .925 SILVER, .9359 oz ASW
Voyager I

KM#	Date	Mintage	VF	XF	Unc
11	1992	—	—	Proof	50.00

Pedro Fernandez De Quiros

KM#	Date	Mintage	VF	XF	Unc
12	1992	—	—	Proof	50.00

Endangered Wild Life - Earth Pigeons

KM#	Date	Mintage	VF	XF	Unc
13	1992	—	—	Proof	50.00

Olympics - Canoes

KM#	Date	Mintage	VF	XF	Unc
14	1992	—	—	Proof	45.00

40th Anniversary of Coronation

KM#	Date	Mintage	VF	XF	Unc
15	1993	*.010	—	Proof	50.00

The Boudeuse

KM#	Date	Mintage	VF	XF	Unc
16	1993	*.015	—	Proof	45.00

100 VATU

NICKEL-BRASS

KM#	Date	Mintage	VF	XF	Unc
9	1988	—	—	—	3.75

10,000 VATU

15.9800 g, .917 GOLD, .4712 oz AGW
1st Anniversary of Independence

KM#	Date	Mintage	VF	XF	Unc
2	1981	538 pcs.	—	—	325.00
	1981	1,054	—	Proof	350.00

PROOF SETS (PS)

KM#	Date	Mintage	Identification	Issue Price	Mkt. Val.
PS1	1983(6)	—	KM3-8	—	20.00

VATICAN-PAPAL STATES

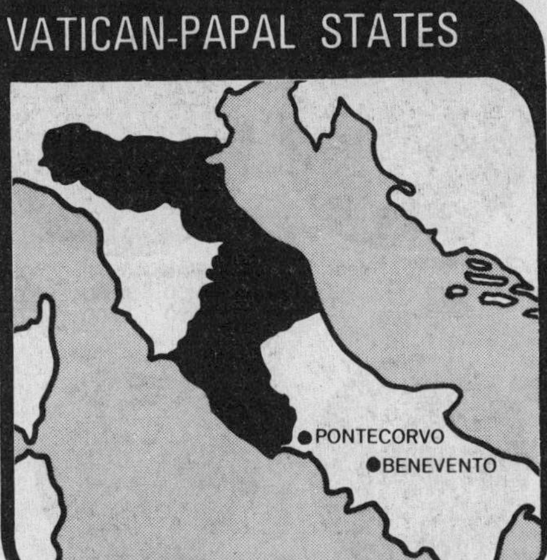

During many centuries prior to the formation of the unified Kingdom of Italy, when Italy was divided into numerous independent papal and ducal states, the Popes held temporal sovereignty over an area in central Italy comprising some 17,000 sq. mi. (44,030 sq. km.) including the city of Rome. At the time of the general unification of Italy under the Kingdom of Sardinia, 1861, the papal dominions beyond Rome were acquired by that kingdom diminishing the Pope's sovereignty to Rome and its environs. In 1870, while France's opposition to papal dispossession was neutralized by its war with Prussia, the Italian army seized weakly defended Rome and made it the capital of Italy, thereby abrogating the last vestige of papal temporal power. In 1871, the Italian Parliament enacted the Law of Guarantees, which guaranteed a special status for the Vatican area, and spiritual freedom and a generous income for the Pope. Pope Pius IX and his successors adamantly refused to acknowledge the validity of these laws and voluntarily "imprisoned" themselves in the Vatican. The impasse between State and Church lasted until the signing of the Lateran Treaty, Feb. 11, 1929, by which Italy recognized the sovereignty and independence of the new Vatican City state.

PONTIFFS

Pius VII, 1800-1823
  Sede Vacante, Aug. 20-Sept. 28, 1823
Leo XII, 1823-1829
  Sede Vacante, Feb. 10-Mar. 31, 1829
Pius VIII, 1829-1830
  Sede Vacante, Nov. 30, 1830-Feb. 2, 1831
Gregory XVI, 1831-1846
  Sede Vacante, June 1-16, 1846
Pius IX, 1846-1878
Leo XIII, 1878-1903
St. Pius X, 1903-1914
Benedict XV, 1914-1922

MINT MARKS

B - Bologna
R - Rome

MONETARY SYSTEM
(Until 1860)

150 Quattrini = 30 Baiocchi =
6 Grossi = 4 Carlini = 3 Giulio =
3 Paoli = 1 Testone.
100 Baiocchi = 1 Scudo
30 Paoli = Doppia

QUATTRINO

COPPER

C#	Date	Year	VG	Fine	VF	XF
106	1801R	—	6.00	12.00	25.00	45.00

C#	Date	Year	VG	Fine	VF	XF
107	1802R	II	4.00	7.50	12.50	25.00

Obv. value: QVATTRINO.

C#	Date	Year	VG	Fine	VF	XF
107a	1816B	XVI	4.00	7.50	12.50	25.00
	1816R	XVI	4.00	7.50	12.50	25.00
	1816R	XVII	4.00	7.50	12.50	25.00
	1821B	XXII	5.00	8.50	14.00	28.00
	1821R	XXII	4.00	7.50	12.50	25.00
	1822B	XXII	4.00	7.50	12.50	25.00

Obv. value: VN QVATTRINO.

C#	Date	Year	VG	Fine	VF	XF
107.5	1816B	XVI	15.00	25.00	40.00	70.00

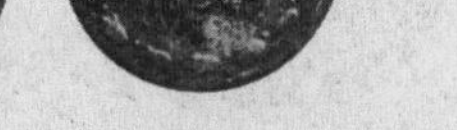

C#	Date	Year	VG	Fine	VF	XF
125.5	1824(B)	I	4.00	8.00	12.50	25.00

C#	Date	Year	VG	Fine	VF	XF
126	1824R	I	3.00	6.00	12.00	25.00
	1825R	II	3.00	6.00	12.00	25.00

C#	Date	Year	VG	Fine	VF	XF
126a	1826R	IV	3.00	6.00	12.00	25.00

C#	Date	Year	VG	Fine	VF	XF
135	1829R	I	4.00	9.00	15.00	35.00

C#	Date	Year	VG	Fine	VF	XF
144	1831R	I	2.00	4.00	7.50	15.00

NOTE: Retrograde 1's in date.

C#	Date	Year	VG	Fine	VF	XF
144a	1835R	V	2.00	4.00	7.50	20.00
	1836B	VI	2.00	4.00	7.50	20.00
	1838R	VIII	2.00	4.00	7.50	20.00
	1839B	IX	4.00	7.50	12.50	25.00
	1839R	IX	2.00	4.00	7.50	20.00
	1840B	X	4.00	7.50	12.50	25.00
	1841R	X	3.00	5.00	8.50	20.00
	1841R	XI	2.00	4.00	7.50	20.00
	1843B	XIII	2.00	4.00	7.50	20.00
	1843R	XIII	2.00	4.00	7.50	20.00
	1844B	XIV	2.00	4.00	7.50	20.00
	1844R	XIV	2.00	4.00	7.50	20.00

C#	Date	Mintage	VG	Fine	VF	XF
164	1851R yr.VI	.090	3.00	5.00	8.50	18.00
	1854B yr.IX	.173	3.00	5.00	8.50	18.00

MEZZO (1/2) BAIOCCO

COPPER

C#	Date	Year	VG	Fine	VF	XF
108	1801R	—	5.00	8.50	14.00	28.00

NOTE: Varieties exist.

C#	Date	Year	VG	Fine	VF	XF
109	1802R	II	3.00	5.00	8.50	15.00

C#	Date	Year	VG	Fine	VF	XF
109a	1816R	XVI	5.00	10.00	17.50	30.00
	1816R	XVII	5.00	10.00	17.50	30.00

C#	Date	Year	VG	Fine	VF	XF
109a.1	1816B	XVI	3.00	5.00	8.50	15.00
	1816B	XVII	3.00	5.00	8.50	15.00
	1822B	XXII	5.00	8.50	14.00	28.00
	1822R	XXII	5.00	8.50	14.00	28.00

C#	Date	Year	VG	Fine	VF	XF
109a.2	1822R	XXII	10.00	20.00	35.00	50.00

C#	Date	Year	VG	Fine	VF	XF
127	1824B	I	6.00	12.50	20.00	35.00

C#	Date	Year	VG	Fine	VF	XF
127a	1825R	II	4.00	9.00	18.00	30.00
	1826R	III	4.00	9.00	18.00	30.00

C#	Date	Year	VG	Fine	VF	XF
136	1829B	I	6.00	15.00	30.00	55.00
	1829R	I	6.00	15.00	30.00	55.00

C#	Date	Year	VG	Fine	VF	XF
145	1831R	I	2.00	4.00	7.50	22.00
	1832B	II	4.00	7.50	15.00	30.00
	1832B	III	3.50	6.50	12.50	25.00
	1833B	III	2.00	4.00	7.50	22.00
	1834B	IV	2.00	4.00	7.50	22.00

C#	Date	Year	VG	Fine	VF	XF
145a	1835B	V	2.00	4.00	7.50	15.00
	1835R	V	2.00	4.00	7.50	15.00
	1836B	VI	2.00	4.00	7.50	15.00
	1836R	VI	2.00	4.00	7.50	15.00
	1837B	VII	2.00	4.00	7.50	15.00
	1837R	VII	3.50	6.50	12.50	17.50
	1838B	VIII	2.00	4.00	7.50	15.00
	1838R	VIII	3.50	6.50	12.50	17.50
	1839B	IX	2.00	4.00	7.50	15.00
	1839R	IX	3.50	6.50	12.50	17.50
	1840R	IX	3.50	6.50	12.50	17.50
	1840B	X	3.00	5.00	8.50	15.00
	1840R	X	2.00	4.00	7.50	15.00
	1841B	X	3.00	6.00	9.00	17.50
	1841R	XI	2.00	4.00	7.50	15.00
	1842B	XI	2.00	4.00	7.50	15.00
	1842B	XII	2.00	4.00	7.50	15.00
	1842R	XII	2.00	4.00	7.50	15.00
	1843B	XII	2.00	4.00	7.50	15.00
	1843B	XIII	2.00	4.00	7.50	15.00
	1843R	XIII	2.00	4.00	7.50	15.00
	1844B	XIII	2.00	4.00	7.50	15.00
	1844B	XIV	2.00	4.00	7.50	15.00
	1844R	XIV	2.00	4.00	7.50	15.00
	1845B	XV	2.00	4.00	7.50	15.00
	1845R	XV	2.00	4.00	7.50	15.00

C#	Date	Mintage	VG	Fine	VF	XF
165	1847B yr.II	.074	2.00	4.00	7.50	20.00
	1847R yr.II	9,000	3.50	6.50	12.50	25.00
	1848/7B yr.II	.049	2.50	5.00	8.00	22.50
	1848B yr.II	I.A.	3.50	6.50	12.50	25.00
	1848R yr.II	.644	2.00	4.00	7.50	22.50
	1848R yr.III	I.A.	2.00	4.00	7.50	22.50
	1848R yr.IIII	Inc. Ab.	3.50	6.50	12.50	25.00
	1849B yr.III	.104	2.00	4.00	7.00	22.50
	1849B yr.IV	I.A.	2.00	4.00	7.50	22.50
	1849R yr.IIII	1.921	2.00	4.00	7.50	22.50
	1849R yr.IV	Inc. Ab.	2.00	4.00	7.00	22.50

C#	Date	Mintage	VG	Fine	VF	XF
166	1850B yr.IV	.176	2.00	4.00	7.50	15.00
	1850R yr.IV	5.552	2.00	4.00	7.50	15.00
	1850B yr.V	Inc. Ab.	2.00	4.00	7.50	15.00
	1850R yr.V	Inc. Ab.	2.00	4.00	7.50	15.00
	1851B yr.V	1.257	2.00	4.00	7.50	15.00
	1851R yr.V	4.001	2.00	4.00	7.50	15.00
	1851B yr.VI	Inc. Ab.	2.00	4.00	7.50	15.00
	1851R yr.VI	Inc. Ab.	2.00	4.00	7.50	15.00
	1852B yr.VI	.706	2.00	4.00	7.50	15.00

BAIOCCO

COPPER

C#	Date	Year	VG	Fine	VF	XF
110	1801R	I	20.00	35.00	50.00	75.00

NOTE: Earlier date (1800) exists for this type.

C#	Date	Year	VG	Fine	VF	XF
111	1801R	—	5.00	12.00	20.00	35.00

C#	Date	Year	VG	Fine	VF	XF
111.1	1801R	—	5.00	12.00	20.00	35.00

Rev: G. PASINATES S. C. below date

C#	Date	Year	VG	Fine	VF	XF
111.2	1801R	—	15.00	30.00	50.00	85.00

C#	Date	Year	VG	Fine	VF	XF
112	1802R	II	5.00	12.00	20.00	32.00
	1815B	XVI	5.00	12.00	20.00	32.00

C#	Date	Year	VG	Fine	VF	XF
112.1	1816B	XVI	5.00	12.00	20.00	32.00
	1816R	XVI	5.00	12.00	20.00	32.00

C#	Date	Year	VG	Fine	VF	XF
112.1	1816B	XVII	5.00	12.00	20.00	32.00
	1816R	XVII	10.00	22.50	38.00	65.00

C#	Date	Year	VG	Fine	VF	XF
137	1829R	I	7.50	18.00	30.00	45.00

NOTE: Two varieties of edge inscription exist.

C#	Date	Year	VG	Fine	VF	XF
146	1831R	I	5.00	10.00	15.00	25.00
	1832R	I	15.00	25.00	45.00	70.00
	1832R	II	7.50	12.50	25.00	45.00

C#	Date	Year	VG	Fine	VF	XF
146a	1835B	V	2.00	5.00	10.00	25.00
	1835R	V	2.00	5.00	10.00	25.00
	1836B	VI	2.00	5.00	10.00	25.00
	1836R	VI	2.00	5.00	10.00	25.00
	1837B	VII	2.00	5.00	10.00	25.00
	1837R	VII	2.00	5.00	10.00	25.00
	1838B	VIII	10.00	20.00	35.00	50.00
	1838R	VIII	5.00	10.00	15.00	25.00
	1839R	VIII	7.50	12.50	20.00	35.00
	1839B	IX	2.00	5.00	10.00	25.00
	1839R	IX	5.00	10.00	15.00	25.00
	1840B	X	2.00	5.00	10.00	25.00
	1840R	X	2.00	5.00	10.00	25.00
	1841B	X	5.00	10.00	15.00	25.00
	1841B	XI	10.00	20.00	35.00	50.00
	1841R	XI	3.50	6.50	12.50	17.50
	1842R	XI	3.50	6.50	12.50	17.50
	1842B	XII	2.00	5.00	10.00	25.00
	1842R	XII	3.50	6.50	12.50	17.50
	1843R	XII	3.50	6.50	12.50	17.50
	1843B	XIII	3.50	6.50	12.50	17.50
	1843R	XIII	3.50	6.50	12.50	17.50
	1844B	XIII	2.00	5.00	10.00	25.00
	1844B	XIV	2.00	5.00	10.00	25.00
	1844R	XIV	2.00	5.00	10.00	25.00
	1845B	XV	2.00	5.00	10.00	25.00
	1845R	XV	3.50	6.50	12.50	17.50

C#	Date	Mintage	VG	Fine	VF	XF
167	1846B yr.I	—	6.00	10.00	17.50	30.00
	1846R yr.I	7,500	4.00	7.50	12.50	25.00
	1847B yr.I	.058	4.00	7.50	12.50	25.00
	1847R yr.I	.014	7.50	12.50	20.00	35.00
	1847R yr.II	I.A.	4.00	7.50	12.50	25.00
	1848R yr.II	.494	3.50	6.50	12.50	17.50
	1848R yr.III	I.A.	2.00	4.00	7.50	15.00
	1848R yr.IV	I.A.	2.00	4.00	7.50	15.00

NOTE: Varieties of date wording exist.

C#	Date	Mintage	VG	Fine	VF	XF
167.1	1849R yr.IV	1.080	2.00	4.00	7.50	15.00

C#	Date	Mintage	VG	Fine	VF	XF
168	1849B yr.IV	.061	6.00	10.00	17.50	30.00
	1850B yr.IV	.402	2.00	7.00	12.50	25.00
	1850R yr.IV	4.681	2.00	6.00	9.00	17.50
	1850B yr.V	Inc. Ab.	2.00	7.00	12.50	25.00
	1850R yr.V	Inc. Ab.	2.00	6.00	9.00	17.50
	1851B yr.V	.899	2.00	6.00	9.00	17.50
	1851R yr.V	5.706	2.00	7.00	12.50	25.00
	1851B yr.VI	Inc. Ab.	2.00	4.00	7.50	15.00
	1851R yr.VI	Inc. Ab.	2.00	7.00	12.50	25.00
	1852B yr.VI	.655	2.00	4.00	7.50	15.00
	1852R yr.VI	1.211	7.50	15.00	20.00	35.00
	1853R yr.VII	.035	7.50	15.00	20.00	35.00

2 BAIOCCHI

COPPER

C#	Date	Mintage	VG	Fine	VF	XF
169	1848B yr.III	.644	3.00	8.00	12.00	20.00
	1848R yr.III	.227	3.00	8.00	12.00	20.00
	1849R yr.IV	1.117	3.00	8.00	12.00	20.00
	1849B yr.III	—	3.00	8.00	12.00	20.00
	1849B yr.IV	—	3.00	8.00	12.00	20.00

C#	Date	Mintage	VG	Fine	VF	XF
169a	1850B yr.IV	—	3.00	8.00	12.00	20.00
	1850R yr.IV	3.784	3.00	8.00	12.00	20.00
	1850B yr.V	—	7.50	12.50	20.00	35.00
	1850R yr.V	I.A.	2.00	7.00	12.00	20.00
	1851B yr.V	—	2.00	7.00	12.00	20.00
	1851R yr.V	2.557	2.00	7.00	12.00	20.00
	1851B yr.VI	—	2.00	7.00	12.00	20.00
	1851R yr.VI	I.A.	2.00	7.00	12.00	20.00
	1852B yr.V	—	5.00	10.00	17.50	30.00
	1852R yr.V	1.727	4.00	9.00	15.00	25.00
	1852B yr.VI	—	2.00	7.00	12.00	20.00
	1852R yr.VI	I.A.	2.00	7.00	12.00	20.00
	1852R yr.VII	I.A.	4.00	9.00	15.00	30.00
	1853R yr.VI	1.460	4.00	9.00	15.00	30.00
	1853B yr.VII	—	3.50	8.00	12.50	22.50
	1853R yr.VII	I.A.	2.00	7.00	12.00	20.00
	1853R yr.VIII	I.A.	2.00	7.00	12.00	20.00
	1854R yr.VIII	5,000	35.00	75.00	100.00	140.00

GROSSO

1.3210 g, .917 SILVER, .0389 oz ASW

C#	Date	Year	VG	Fine	VF	XF
113	1815R	XVI	7.50	15.00	22.50	40.00
	1816B	XVI	15.00	25.00	40.00	70.00
	1816B	XVII	7.50	15.00	22.50	40.00
	1817B	XVII	7.50	15.00	22.50	40.00

5 BAIOCCHI

1.3430 g, .900 SILVER, .0388 oz ASW

C#	Date	Year	VG	Fine	VF	XF
147	1835R	V	3.00	7.50	15.00	30.00
	1836B	VI	3.00	7.50	15.00	30.00
	1839R	IX	5.00	10.00	17.50	35.00
	1840B	X	3.00	7.50	15.00	30.00
	1841R	X	10.00	20.00	35.00	50.00
	1841B	XI	3.00	7.50	15.00	30.00
	1841R	XI	15.00	25.00	40.00	70.00
	1842B	XI	3.00	7.50	15.00	30.00
	1842R	XI	15.00	25.00	40.00	70.00
	1842B	XII	3.00	7.50	15.00	30.00
	1842R	XII	3.00	7.50	15.00	30.00
	1843B	XIII	3.00	7.50	15.00	30.00
	1843R	XIII	3.00	7.50	15.00	30.00
	1844B	XIII	3.00	7.50	15.00	30.00
	1844B	XIV	3.00	7.50	15.00	30.00
	1844/3R	—	3.50	8.00	17.50	32.50
	1844R	XIV	3.00	7.50	15.00	30.00
	1845B	XV	3.00	7.50	15.00	30.00
	1845R	XV	3.00	7.50	15.00	30.00
	1846R	XVI	3.00	7.50	15.00	30.00

C#	Date	Mintage	VG	Fine	VF	XF
171	1847B yr.I	2.387	3.00	7.50	15.00	30.00
	1847R yr.II	1.191	3.00	7.50	15.00	30.00
	1848R yr.II	2,122	18.00	40.00	75.00	125.00
	1849R yr.IV	.021	3.00	7.50	15.00	30.00
	1850R yr.V	.010	3.00	7.50	15.00	30.00
	1851R yr.V	.011	3.00	7.50	15.00	30.00
	1851R yr.VI	Inc. Ab.	3.00	7.50	15.00	30.00
	1852R yr.VII	.020	3.00	7.50	15.00	30.00
	1853R yr.VII	.014	3.00	7.50	15.00	30.00
	1855R yr.IX	9,200	18.00	40.00	75.00	120.00
	1855R yr.X	I.A.	18.00	40.00	75.00	120.00

1.4280 g, .800 SILVER, .0367 oz ASW

C#	Date	Mintage	VG	Fine	VF	XF
171a	1856R yr.X	3,440	18.00	40.00	75.00	120.00
	1857R yr.XI	.023	3.00	7.50	15.00	30.00
	1858R yr.XII	1.573	3.00	7.50	15.00	30.00
	1858B yr.XIII	.224	10.00	25.00	40.00	75.00
	1858R yr.XIII	Inc. Ab.	3.00	7.50	15.00	30.00
	1859B yr.XIII	.173	10.00	25.00	40.00	75.00
	1859R yr.XIII	.083	3.00	7.50	15.00	30.00
	1860R yr.XV	.169	3.00	7.50	15.00	30.00
	1861R yr.XVI	.147	3.00	7.50	15.00	30.00
	1862R yr.XVII	.135	3.00	7.50	15.00	30.00
	1863R yr.XVIII	.044	3.00	7.50	15.00	30.00
	1864R yr.XIX	.101	3.00	7.50	15.00	30.00

1.3330 g, .835 SILVER, .0357 oz ASW

C#	Date	Mintage	VG	Fine	VF	XF
171b	1865R yr.XIX	.106	9.00	15.00	25.00	45.00
	1865R yr.XX	Inc. Ab.	3.00	7.50	15.00	30.00
	1866R yr.XX	.040	5.00	10.00	17.50	35.00

COPPER

C#	Date	Mintage	VG	Fine	VF	XF
170	1849B yr.IV	—	5.00	12.00	22.50	37.50
	1849R yr.IV	.938	5.00	12.00	22.50	37.50
	1850B yr.IV	—	5.00	12.00	22.50	37.50
	1850R yr.IV	10.164	5.00	12.00	22.50	37.50
	1850B yr.V	—	5.00	12.00	22.50	37.50
	1850R yr.V	I.A.	5.00	12.00	22.50	37.50

Rev: Similar to C#170.

C#	Date	Mintage	VG	Fine	VF	XF
170a	1850B yr.V	—	5.00	12.00	22.50	37.50
	1850R yr.V	I.A.	5.00	12.00	22.50	37.50
	1851B yr.V	—	5.00	12.00	22.50	37.50
	1851R yr.V	7.949	5.00	12.00	22.50	37.50
	1851B yr.VI	—	4.00	10.00	22.50	37.50
	1851R yr.VI	I.A.	4.00	10.00	22.50	37.50
	1852B yr.VI	—	4.00	10.00	22.50	37.50
	1852R yr.VI	9.746	4.00	10.00	22.50	37.50
	1852B yr.VII	—	4.00	10.00	22.50	37.50
	1852R yr.VII	Inc. Ab.	4.00	10.00	22.50	37.50
	1853B yr.VII	—	4.00	10.00	22.50	37.50
	1853R yr.VII	8.428	4.00	10.00	22.50	37.50
	1853B yr.VIII	—	4.00	10.00	22.50	37.50
	1853R yr.VIII	Inc. Ab.	4.00	10.00	22.50	37.50
	1854B yr.VIII					
	1854R yr.VIII	1.977	9.00	17.50	25.00	45.00
	1854B yr.IX	—	4.00	10.00	22.50	37.50
	1854R yr.IX	I.A.	9.00	17.50	25.00	45.00

GIULIO

2.6420 g, .917 SILVER, .0779 oz ASW

C#	Date	Year	VG	Fine	VF	XF
114	1817/6B	XVIII	18.00	38.00	55.00	100.00
	1817B	XVIII	15.00	35.00	45.00	100.00

10 BAIOCCHI

2.6870 g, .900 SILVER, .0777 oz ASW

C#	Date	Year	VG	Fine	VF	XF
148	1836B	VI	12.50	25.00	40.00	75.00
	1836R	VI	5.00	15.00	17.50	40.00
	1839B	IX	5.00	15.00	17.50	40.00
	1839R	IX	5.00	15.00	17.50	40.00
	1841B	XI	5.00	10.00	17.50	35.00
	1841R	XI	10.00	20.00	35.00	50.00
	1842B	XI	5.00	15.00	17.50	40.00
	1842B	XII	5.00	10.00	17.50	35.00
	1842R	XII	12.50	25.00	40.00	75.00
	1843B	XIII	5.00	15.00	17.50	40.00
	1844B	XIV	5.00	15.00	17.50	40.00
	1846R	XVI	10.00	20.00	35.00	50.00

C#	Date	Mintage	VG	Fine	VF	XF
172	1847B yr.I	.011	12.50	25.00	40.00	75.00
	1847B yr.II	I.A.	12.50	25.00	40.00	75.00
	1847R yr.II	.012	5.00	10.00	15.00	30.00
	1848/7R yr.III	.033	5.00	10.00	15.00	30.00
	1848B yr.II	.017	12.50	25.00	40.00	75.00
	1848R yr.II	I.A.	5.00	10.00	15.00	30.00
	1848B yr.III	I.A.	12.50	25.00	40.00	75.00
	1848R yr.III	I.A.	5.00	10.00	15.00	30.00
	1849R yr.IIII	1,274	25.00	45.00	75.00	125.00
	1850R yr.IIII	.089	5.00	10.00	15.00	30.00
	1850R yr.V	I.A.	5.00	10.00	15.00	30.00
	1852R yr.VII	.033	5.00	10.00	15.00	30.00
	1853R yr.VII	.041	5.00	10.00	15.00	30.00
	1854R yr.VIII	5,570	35.00	75.00	100.00	175.00
	1855R yr.IX	4,400	35.00	75.00	100.00	175.00
	1856R yr.X	1,140	45.00	80.00	100.00	175.00

2.8570 g, .800 SILVER, .0734 oz ASW

C#	Date	Mintage	VG	Fine	VF	XF
172a	1858R yr.XII	2.548	3.50	7.50	15.00	25.00
	1858R yr.XIII		4.00	7.50	15.00	25.00
	1858B yr. XIII	Inc. Ab.	10.00	25.00	40.00	75.00
	1859R yr.XIII	.088	10.00	20.00	35.00	50.00
	1860R yr.XIV	.150	10.00	20.00	35.00	50.00
	1861R yr.XVI	.327	4.00	7.50	15.00	25.00
	1862R yr.XVI	7.417	3.00	7.50	15.00	25.00
	1862R yr.XVII	Inc. Ab.	3.00	7.50	15.00	25.00
	1863R yr.XVI	—	65.00	125.00	175.00	225.00
	1863R yr.XVII	1.084	4.00	7.50	15.00	25.00
	1863R yr.XVIII	Inc. Ab.	4.00	7.50	15.00	25.00
	1864R yr.XVIII	1.147	10.00	20.00	35.00	50.00
	1864R yr.XIX	Inc. Ab.	10.00	20.00	35.00	50.00

2.6660 g, .835 SILVER, .0715 oz ASW

C#	Date	Mintage	VG	Fine	VF	XF
172b	1865R yr.XIX	.409	8.00	15.00	22.50	40.00
	1865R yr.XX	Inc. Ab.	8.00	15.00	22.50	40.00

DOPPIO (2) GIULIO

(1/5 Scudo)

5.2850 g, .917 SILVER, .1558 oz ASW

C#	Date	Year	VG	Fine	VF	XF
115	1816B	XVII	20.00	40.00	75.00	100.00
	1816B	XVIII	20.00	40.00	75.00	100.00
	1818B	XVII	10.00	20.00	35.00	50.00
	1818B	XVIII	10.00	20.00	35.00	50.00

Sede Vacante

C#	Date	Year	VG	Fine	VF	XF
122	1823B	—	36.00	75.00	100.00	175.00

20 BAIOCCHI

5.2850 g, .917 SILVER, .1558 oz ASW

C#	Date	Year	VG	Fine	VF	XF
149	1834R	IV	10.00	20.00	35.00	50.00

5.3740 g, .900 SILVER, .1555 oz ASW

C#	Date	Year	VG	Fine	VF	XF
150	1835B	V	8.00	15.00	22.50	40.00
	1835R	V	10.00	20.00	35.00	50.00
	1836R	V	80.00	125.00	200.00	350.00
	1836B	VI	8.00	15.00	22.50	40.00
	1836R	VI	40.00	75.00	100.00	175.00
	1837R	VII	20.00	40.00	75.00	120.00
	1838B	VIII	8.00	15.00	22.50	40.00
	1838R	VIII	10.00	20.00	35.00	50.00
	1839R	IX	10.00	20.00	35.00	50.00
	1840B	X	8.00	15.00	22.50	40.00
	1841B	XI	8.00	15.00	22.50	40.00
	1841R	XI	10.00	20.00	35.00	50.00
	1842B	XII	25.00	45.00	75.00	125.00
	1842R	XII	10.00	20.00	35.00	50.00
	1844B	XIII	8.00	15.00	22.50	40.00
	1844R	XIII	100.00	200.00	350.00	650.00
	1844B	XIV	8.00	15.00	22.50	40.00
	1845B	XV	8.00	15.00	22.50	40.00
	1846R	XVI	10.00	20.00	35.00	50.00

C#	Date	Mintage	VG	Fine	VF	XF
173	1848R yr. II	—	8.00	20.00	35.00	50.00
	1848R yr. III	—	8.00	20.00	35.00	50.00
	1849B yr.III	—	10.00	25.00	40.00	75.00
	1849B yr.IV	—	15.00	25.00	40.00	75.00
	1849R yr.IV	—	8.00	20.00	35.00	50.00
	1850B yr.IV	—	15.00	25.00	40.00	75.00
	1850R yr.IV	—	8.00	15.00	22.50	40.00
	1850R yr.V	—	8.00	15.00	22.50	40.00
	1851B yr.V	—	15.00	25.00	40.00	75.00
	1852B yr.VII	—	30.00	60.00	90.00	125.00
	1852R yr.VII	.010	15.00	25.00	40.00	75.00
	1853R yr.VII	.126	10.00	25.00	40.00	75.00
	1854R yr.VIII	—	8.00	20.00	35.00	50.00
	1856R yr.X	—	10.00	25.00	40.00	75.00

NOTE: Two varieties of ANNO III exist.

5.7140 g, .800 SILVER, .1469 oz ASW

C#	Date	Mintage	VG	Fine	VF	XF
173a	1858B yr.XII	—	10.00	25.00	40.00	75.00
	1858R yr.XII	—	6.00	15.00	22.50	40.00
	1858B yr.XIII	—	10.00	20.00	35.00	60.00
	1858R yr.XIII	—	5.00	10.00	15.00	30.00
	1859B yr.XIII	.604	8.00	20.00	35.00	60.00
	1859R yr.XIII	1.104	5.00	12.00	20.00	35.00
	1859R yr.XIV	Inc. Ab.	5.00	12.00	20.00	35.00
	1860/50R	—	5.00	10.00	15.00	30.00
	1860R yr.XIV	3.656	5.00	10.00	15.00	30.00
	1860R yr.XV	Inc. Ab.	5.00	10.00	15.00	30.00
	1861R yr.XV	2.987	5.00	12.00	20.00	35.00
	1861R yr.XVI	Inc. Ab.	5.00	12.00	20.00	35.00
	1862R yr.XVI	1.150	5.00	12.00	20.00	35.00
	1862R yr.XVII	Inc. Ab.	5.00	12.00	20.00	35.00
	1863R yr.XVII	3.155	5.00	12.00	20.00	35.00
	1863R yr.XVIII	Inc. Ab.	5.00	12.00	20.00	35.00
	1864R yr.XVIII	2.100	5.00	12.00	20.00	35.00
	1864R yr.XIX	Inc. Ab.	10.00	20.00	35.00	60.00
	1865R yr.XIX	7.346	5.00	10.00	15.00	30.00
	1865R yr.XX	Inc. Ab.	5.00	10.00	15.00	30.00
	1866R yr.XX	5.600	5.00	10.00	15.00	30.00

30 BAIOCCHI

(Testone)

7.9280 g, .917 SILVER, .2337 oz ASW

C#	Date	Year	VG	Fine	VF	XF
116	1802R	III	17.50	35.00	60.00	100.00
	1803R	III	17.50	35.00	60.00	100.00

C#	Date	Year	VG	Fine	VF	XF
138	1830R	II	17.50	35.00	90.00	135.00

Sede Vacante

C#	Date	Year	VG	Fine	VF	XF
141	1830B	—	20.00	42.50	90.00	125.00
	1830R	—	20.00	42.50	90.00	125.00

C#	Date	Year	VG	Fine	VF	XF
151	1834R	IV	15.00	35.00	75.00	100.00

8.0610 g, .900 SILVER, .2332 oz ASW

C#	Date	Year	VG	Fine	VF	XF
152	1836B	VI	25.00	40.00	75.00	100.00
	1836R	VI	25.00	65.00	125.00	200.00
	1837B	VII	25.00	40.00	75.00	100.00
	1837R	VII	25.00	65.00	125.00	200.00
	1838R	VIII	25.00	40.00	75.00	100.00
	1846R	XVI	25.00	40.00	75.00	100.00

50 BAIOCCHI

13.2140 g, .917 SILVER, .3896 oz ASW

C#	Date	Year	VG	Fine	VF	XF
153	1832B	II	20.00	40.00	85.00	125.00
	1832R	II	25.00	45.00	85.00	125.00
	1834R	IV	25.00	45.00	85.00	125.00

NOTE: Two varieties of 1832B exist.

13.4350 g, .900 SILVER, .3887 oz ASW

C#	Date	Year	VG	Fine	VF	XF
154	1835R	V	22.50	40.00	75.00	100.00
	1836B	VI	22.50	40.00	75.00	100.00
	1836R	VI	45.00	65.00	110.00	175.00
	1837B	VII	22.50	40.00	75.00	100.00
	1840B	X	45.00	65.00	110.00	175.00
	1841B	XI	22.50	40.00	75.00	100.00
	1842R	XII	45.00	65.00	110.00	175.00
	1843R	XIII	22.50	40.00	75.00	125.00
	1845R	XV	22.50	40.00	75.00	125.00
	1846R	XVI	22.50	40.00	75.00	125.00

C#	Date	Mintage	VG	Fine	VF	XF
174	1850R yr.IV	.104	25.00	45.00	75.00	100.00
	1850R yr.V	I.A.	25.00	45.00	75.00	100.00
	1853R yr.VII	.684	50.00	75.00	110.00	175.00
	1853R yr.VIII	Inc. Ab.	25.00	45.00	75.00	100.00
	1854B yr.IX	2,718	25.00	45.00	75.00	100.00
	1856B yr.X	4,226	25.00	45.00	75.00	100.00
	1857B yr.XII	8,711	50.00	75.00	110.00	175.00

1/2 SCUDO

13.2500 g, .917 SILVER, .3907 oz ASW

C#	Date	Year	VG	Fine	VF	XF
117	1802R	II	30.00	70.00	100.00	140.00
	1802R	III	30.00	70.00	100.00	140.00
	1803R	III	30.00	70.00	100.00	140.00
	1816B	XVII	30.00	70.00	100.00	140.00

NOTE: Earlier date (1800) exists for this type.

Sede Vacante

C#	Date	Year	VG	Fine	VF	XF
123	1823B	—	40.00	75.00	125.00	175.00

Sede Vacante

C#	Date	Year	VG	Fine	VF	XF
132	1829B	—	35.00	70.00	120.00	165.00
	1829R	—	35.00	70.00	120.00	165.00

2 ZECCHINI

6.9040 g, .998 GOLD, .2215 oz AGW

C#	Date	Year	Fine	VF	XF	Unc
130	1825R	III	500.00	900.00	1500.	3000.

C#	Date	Year	Fine	VF	XF	Unc
131	1828R	V	500.00	900.00	1500.	3000.

SCUDO

26.2500 g, .917 SILVER, .7739 oz ASW

C#	Date	Year	VG	Fine	VF	XF
119	1802R	II	40.00	85.00	120.00	225.00
	1802R	III	45.00	100.00	140.00	250.00
	1802R	IV	40.00	85.00	120.00	225.00
	1803R	IV	70.00	125.00	175.00	300.00
	1805R	VI	40.00	85.00	120.00	225.00
	1807R	VIII	40.00	85.00	125.00	235.00

26.4280 g, .917 SILVER, .7792 oz ASW
Rev: Similar to C#120.

C#	Date	Year	VG	Fine	VF	XF
119.1	1815R	XVI	40.00	85.00	125.00	225.00
	1816B	XVII	40.00	75.00	125.00	225.00
	1817B	XVII	50.00	100.00	150.00	235.00
	1818B	XVIII	40.00	85.00	125.00	225.00

C#	Date	Year	VG	Fine	VF	XF
120	1816R	XVII	—	—	Rare	—

Sede Vacante

C#	Date	Year	VG	Fine	VF	XF
124	1823B	—	100.00	150.00	300.00	500.00

Sede Vacante

C#	Date	Year	VG	Fine	VF	XF
124.1	1823R	—	300.00	475.00	850.00	1500.

Obv: Large bust.

C#	Date	Year	VG	Fine	VF	XF
128.1	1825B	III	75.00	125.00	175.00	300.00

Obv: Small bust.

C#	Date	Year	VG	Fine	VF	XF
128.2	1825R	II	90.00	150.00	225.00	325.00
	1826R	III	90.00	150.00	225.00	325.00

Rev: Large rays above.

C#	Date	Year	VG	Fine	VF	XF
128.3	1826R	III	90.00	150.00	225.00	325.00

Sede Vacante

C#	Date	Year	VG	Fine	VF	XF
133	1829B	—	75.00	150.00	250.00	325.00
	1829R	—	125.00	200.00	275.00	400.00

C#	Date	Year	VG	Fine	VF	XF
139	1830B	I	85.00	150.00	185.00	300.00
	1830ROMA	I	65.00	125.00	175.00	250.00

Sede Vacante

C#	Date	Year	VG	Fine	VF	XF
142	1830B	—	65.00	125.00	175.00	250.00
	1830ROMA	—	85.00	150.00	200.00	300.00

C#	Date	Year	VG	Fine	VF	XF
155	1831B	AN. I	50.00	85.00	135.00	185.00
	1831R	AN. I	50.00	75.00	125.00	185.00
	1833B	AN. III	90.00	150.00	225.00	325.00
	1833R	AN. III	50.00	85.00	135.00	185.00
	1833R	A. III	90.00	150.00	225.00	350.00
	1834R	AN. IV	50.00	75.00	125.00	185.00
	1834R	A. IV	90.00	150.00	225.00	325.00

26.8710 g, .900 SILVER, .7776 oz ASW

C#	Date	Year	VG	Fine	VF	XF
156	1835B	V	50.00	75.00	110.00	175.00
	1835R	V	65.00	110.00	165.00	225.00
	1836R	VI	65.00	110.00	165.00	225.00
	1837R	VII	50.00	75.00	110.00	175.00
	1838B	VIII	65.00	110.00	165.00	225.00
	1838R	VIII	65.00	110.00	165.00	225.00
	1839R	VIII	65.00	110.00	165.00	225.00
	1839R	IX	65.00	110.00	165.00	225.00
	1840R	X	60.00	100.00	150.00	200.00
	1841R	XI	65.00	110.00	165.00	225.00
	1842R	XI	75.00	175.00	250.00	350.00
	1842R	XII	110.00	300.00	500.00	1000.
	1843R	XIII	50.00	75.00	110.00	175.00
	1844R	XIV	65.00	110.00	165.00	225.00
	1845R	XV	45.00	75.00	100.00	175.00
	1846R	XVI	45.00	75.00	100.00	175.00

Sede Vacante

C#	Date	Year	VG	Fine	VF	XF
162	1846R	—	90.00	175.00	250.00	350.00

Obv: NIC. CER. BARA below bust.

C#	Date	Mintage	VG	Fine	VF	XF
175	1846B yr.I	2,073	75.00	125.00	175.00	225.00
	1846R yr.I	1,820	125.00	200.00	275.00	400.00
	1847B yr.II	.020	60.00	100.00	150.00	200.00
	1847R yr.II	.012	75.00	125.00	175.00	225.00
	1848R yr.II	.029	60.00	100.00	150.00	200.00
	1848R yr.III	I.A.	75.00	125.00	175.00	225.00

Obv: W/o NIC. CER. BARA below bust.

C#	Date	Mintage	VG	Fine	VF	XF
175.1	1850R yr.IV	9,222	35.00	65.00	125.00	155.00
	1853R yr.VII	.527	35.00	65.00	125.00	155.00
	1853B yr.VIII	2,310	100.00	200.00	300.00	500.00
	1853R yr.VIII	Inc. Ab.	35.00	65.00	125.00	155.00
	1854B yr.IX	3,715	100.00	200.00	300.00	500.00
	1854R yr.IX	.146	35.00	65.00	125.00	155.00
	1856R yr.XI	1,050	100.00	200.00	300.00	500.00

1.7330 g, .900 GOLD, .0501 oz AGW, 14.4mm

C#	Date	Mintage	Fine	VF	XF	Unc
176	1853B yr.VIII	3,306	75.00	150.00	200.00	500.00
	1853R yr.VIII	.209	60.00	120.00	150.00	200.00
	1854B yr.VIII	5,539	75.00	150.00	200.00	500.00
	1854R yr.VIII	.097	60.00	120.00	150.00	200.00
	1854R yr.IX	Inc. Ab.	60.00	120.00	150.00	200.00
	1857R yr.XII	.016	75.00	125.00	175.00	300.00

16.3mm

C#	Date	Mintage	Fine	VF	XF	Unc
176a	1858R yr.XII	.359	60.00	120.00	150.00	200.00
	1858R yr.XIII	Inc. Ab.	60.00	120.00	150.00	200.00
	1859R yr.XIII	.103	60.00	120.00	150.00	200.00
	1861R yr.XV	.084	60.00	120.00	150.00	200.00
	1861R yr.XVI	Inc. Ab.	60.00	120.00	150.00	200.00
	1862R yr.XVI	.226	60.00	120.00	150.00	200.00
	1862R yr.XVII	Inc. Ab.	60.00	120.00	150.00	200.00
	1863R yr.XVII	.149	60.00	120.00	150.00	200.00
	1863R yr.XVIII	Inc. Ab.	60.00	120.00	150.00	200.00
	1864R yr.XIX	5,735	70.00	135.00	175.00	300.00
	1865R yr.XIX	.021	60.00	120.00	150.00	200.00

2-1/2 SCUDI

4.3340 g, .900 GOLD, .1254 oz AGW

C#	Date	Year	Fine	VF	XF	Unc
158	1835B	V	150.00	250.00	350.00	450.00
	1835R	V	150.00	250.00	350.00	450.00
	1836B	V	150.00	250.00	350.00	450.00
	1836B	VI	100.00	200.00	250.00	325.00
	1836R	VI	100.00	200.00	250.00	325.00
	1837R	VII	150.00	250.00	350.00	450.00
	1839R	IX	150.00	250.00	350.00	450.00
	1840B	X	100.00	200.00	250.00	325.00
	1841R	XI	150.00	250.00	350.00	500.00
	1842B	XII	100.00	200.00	250.00	325.00
	1842R	XII	175.00	275.00	400.00	600.00
	1843B	XIII	100.00	200.00	250.00	325.00
	1844B	XIII	150.00	250.00	350.00	450.00
	1845B	XV	175.00	275.00	400.00	600.00
	1845R	XV	150.00	250.00	350.00	500.00
	1846B	XVI	100.00	200.00	250.00	325.00

C#	Date	Mintage	Fine	VF	XF	Unc
177	1848R yr.II	3,197	175.00	275.00	375.00	500.00
	1853R yr.VII	.117	100.00	175.00	250.00	325.00
	1853R yr.VIII	Inc. Ab.	100.00	160.00	225.00	325.00
	1854R yr.VIII	.276	80.00	150.00	175.00	225.00
	1854B yr.IX	.032	80.00	150.00	175.00	275.00
	1854R yr.IX	Inc. Ab.	80.00	150.00	175.00	225.00
	1855R yr.IX	.059	80.00	150.00	175.00	225.00
	1855R yr.X	Inc. Ab.	80.00	150.00	175.00	225.00
	1856B yr.X	8,040	100.00	175.00	250.00	350.00
	1856R yr.X	.104	85.00	150.00	175.00	225.00
	1856R yr.XI	Inc. Ab.	85.00	150.00	175.00	225.00
	1857R yr.X	—	100.00	160.00	225.00	325.00
	1857R yr.XI	—	175.00	275.00	375.00	500.00
	1857B yr.XII	6,284	150.00	250.00	325.00	400.00
	1857R yr.XII	—	90.00	150.00	175.00	275.00
	1858R yr.XII	—	100.00	160.00	225.00	325.00
	1858B yr.XIII	2,787	175.00	275.00	375.00	500.00
	1858R yr.XIII	—	90.00	150.00	175.00	275.00
	1859B yr.XIII	.066	100.00	160.00	225.00	325.00
	1859R yr.XIII	—	80.00	150.00	175.00	250.00
	1859R yr.XIV	—	80.00	150.00	175.00	250.00
	1860R yr.XIV	—	80.00	150.00	175.00	250.00
	1860R yr.XV	—	80.00	150.00	175.00	250.00
	1861R yr.XV	—	80.00	150.00	175.00	250.00
	1861R yr.XVI	—	80.00	150.00	175.00	250.00
	1862R yr.XVI	—	80.00	150.00	175.00	250.00
	1862R yr.XVII	—	80.00	150.00	175.00	250.00
	1863R yr.XVII	—	80.00	150.00	175.00	250.00

5 SCUDI

8.6680 g, .900 GOLD, .2508 oz AGW

C#	Date	Year	Fine	VF	XF	Unc
159	1834R	IV	—	—	*Rare	—

***NOTE:** Bowers and Merena Guia sale 3-88 XF (cleaned) realized $12,650.

C#	Date	Year	Fine	VF	XF	Unc
160	1835B	V	275.00	550.00	700.00	1000.

C#	Date	Year	Fine	VF	XF	Unc
160	1835R	V	275.00	550.00	700.00	1000.
	1836R	VI	275.00	550.00	700.00	1000.
	1837R	VI	400.00	800.00	1200.	1800.
	1837R	VII	275.00	550.00	700.00	1000.
	1838R	VII	275.00	550.00	700.00	1000.
	1838R	VIII	275.00	550.00	700.00	1000.
	1839R	VIII	350.00	725.00	1000.	1500.
	1839R	IX	350.00	725.00	1000.	1500.
	1840R	IX	350.00	725.00	1000.	1500.
	1841B	XI	400.00	650.00	950.00	1750.
	1841R	XI	275.00	550.00	700.00	1000.
	1842B	XII	275.00	550.00	700.00	1000.
	1842R	XII	275.00	550.00	700.00	1000.
	1843B	XIII	400.00	650.00	950.00	1750.
	1843R	XIII	275.00	550.00	700.00	1000.
	1845R	XV	275.00	550.00	700.00	1000.
	1846R	XVI	275.00	550.00	700.00	1000.

Sede Vacante

C#	Date	Year	Fine	VF	XF	Unc
163	1846R	—	725.00	1200.	1600.	2500.

C#	Date	Mintage	Fine	VF	XF	Unc
178	1846B yr.I	.011	275.00	550.00	725.00	1000.
	1846R yr.I	5,755	325.00	575.00	900.00	1300.
	1847R yr.II	1,399	400.00	725.00	1000.	1400.
	1848R yr.III	1,633	325.00	575.00	800.00	1200.
	1850R yr.IV	6,473	350.00	725.00	1000.	1400.
	1854R yr.IX	.104	250.00	500.00	650.00	900.00

10 SCUDI

17.3360 g, .900 GOLD, .5016 oz AGW

C#	Date	Year	Fine	VF	XF	Unc
161	1835B	V	400.00	725.00	1000.	1350.
	1835R	V	300.00	600.00	800.00	1100.
	1836R	V	300.00	600.00	800.00	1100.
	1836B	V	300.00	600.00	800.00	1100.
	1836R	VI	350.00	725.00	1000.	1400.
	1837R	VI	350.00	725.00	1000.	1400.
	1837R	VII	300.00	600.00	800.00	1100.
	1838R	VII	300.00	600.00	800.00	1250.
	1838R	VIII	300.00	600.00	800.00	1250.
	1839R	VIII	300.00	600.00	800.00	1250.
	1839R	IX	350.00	725.00	1000.	1400.
	1840B	X	350.00	725.00	1000.	1400.
	1840R	X	300.00	600.00	800.00	1250.
	1841R	X	300.00	600.00	800.00	1250.
	1841B	XI	300.00	600.00	800.00	1250.
	1841R	XI	300.00	600.00	800.00	1250.
	1842R	XI	300.00	600.00	800.00	1250.
	1842B	XII	300.00	600.00	800.00	1250.
	1842R	XII	300.00	600.00	800.00	1250.
	1843R	XIII	350.00	725.00	1000.	1400.
	1844R	XIV	350.00	725.00	1000.	1400.
	1845B	XV	300.00	600.00	800.00	1250.
	1845R	XV	350.00	725.00	1000.	1400.

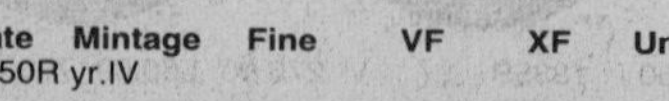

C#	Date	Mintage	Fine	VF	XF	Unc
179	1850R yr.IV	5,875	650.00	1250.	1750.	2750.
	1850R yr.V	I.A.	450.00	1000.	1500.	2000.
	1856R yr.XI	2,483	650.00	1000.	1500.	2500.

DOPPIA

5.4690 g, .917 GOLD, .1612 oz AGW
Mint: Rome

C#	Date	Year	Fine	VF	XF	Unc
121	(1800-01)	I	125.00	200.00	275.00	475.00
	(1801-02)	II	125.00	200.00	275.00	475.00
	(1802-03)	III	125.00	200.00	275.00	475.00
	(1803-04)	IV	125.00	200.00	275.00	475.00
	(1804-05)	V	125.00	200.00	275.00	475.00
	(1807-08)	VIII	125.00	200.00	275.00	475.00
	(1809-10)	X	125.00	200.00	275.00	475.00

Modified design

C#	Date	Year	Fine	VF	XF	Unc
121.1	(1815-16)	XVI	125.00	200.00	275.00	475.00
	(1817-18)	XVIII	150.00	200.00	300.00	500.00
	(1823-24)	XXIV	125.00	200.00	275.00	475.00

Mint: Bologna

C#	Date	Year	Fine	VF	XF	Unc
121.2	(1815-16)B	XVI	200.00	300.00	500.00	900.00
	(1816-17)B	XVII	175.00	275.00	450.00	800.00
	(1820-21)B	XXI	175.00	275.00	450.00	800.00
	(1821-22)B	XXII	175.00	275.00	450.00	800.00

Sede Vacante

C#	Date	Year	Fine	VF	XF	Unc
125	1823B	—	175.00	275.00	400.00	750.00
	1823R	—	175.00	275.00	400.00	750.00

C#	Date	Year	Fine	VF	XF	Unc
129	(1823-24)R	I	150.00	250.00	350.00	700.00
	(1824-25)B	II	150.00	250.00	350.00	700.00
	(1824-25)R	II	150.00	250.00	350.00	700.00

Sede Vacante

C#	Date	Year	Fine	VF	XF	Unc
134	1829B	—	300.00	450.00	850.00	1400.
	1829R	—	300.00	450.00	850.00	1400.

Sede Vacante

C#	Date	Year	Fine	VF	XF	Unc
143	1830R	—	325.00	650.00	1000.	1650.

5.4500 g, .917 GOLD, .1606 oz AGW

C#	Date	Year	Fine	VF	XF	Unc
157	1833R	III	300.00	500.00	900.00	1500.
	1834B	III	275.00	450.00	700.00	1150.

DECIMAL COINAGE

5 Centesimi = 1 Soldi
20 Soldi = 1 Lira

CENTESIMO

COPPER

C#	Date	Mintage	Fine	VF	XF	Unc
180	1866R yr.XXI	.500	5.00	10.00	20.00	55.00
	1867R yr.XXII	2.900	3.00	6.00	9.00	20.00
	1868R yr.XXII	1.950	8.00	20.00	30.00	55.00

1/2 SOLDO

(2-1/2 Centesimi)

COPPER

C#	Date	Mintage	Fine	VF	XF	Unc
181	1866R yr.XXI	.200	5.00	10.00	20.00	35.00
	1867R yr.XXI	2.890	2.00	5.00	12.00	25.00
	1867R yr.XXII	2.890	2.00	5.00	12.00	25.00

SOLDO

(5 Centesimi)

COPPER
Obv: Small bust.

C#	Date	Mintage	Fine	VF	XF	Unc
182	1866R yr.XXI	1.300	2.50	6.00	15.00	35.00

Obv: Large bust.

C#	Date	Mintage	Fine	VF	XF	Unc
182a	1866R yr.XXI lg. date	2.850	7.00	20.00	40.00	100.00
	1866R yr. XXI sm. date	Inc. Ab.	1.75	4.00	8.00	20.00
	1867R yr.XXI lg. date	6.500	3.50	10.00	20.00	50.00

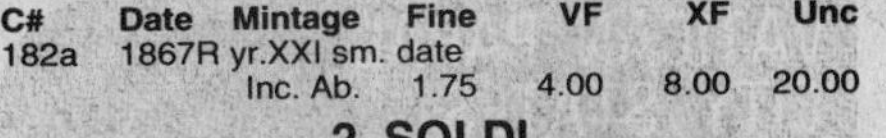

C#	Date	Mintage	Fine	VF	XF	Unc
182a	1867R yr.XXI sm. date	Inc. Ab.	1.75	4.00	8.00	20.00

2 SOLDI
(10 Centesimi)

COPPER

C#	Date	Mintage	Fine	VF	XF	Unc
183	1866R yr.XXI	3.500	3.50	8.00	17.50	50.00
	1867R yr.XXI	3.500	3.50	8.00	17.50	50.00

4 SOLDI
(20 Centesimi)

COPPER

C#	Date	Mintage	Fine	VF	XF	Unc
184	1866R yr.XXI	2.470	6.00	12.00	20.00	55.00
	1867R yr.XXI	2.100	6.00	12.00	20.00	55.00
	1867R yr.XXII	2.876	6.00	12.00	20.00	55.00
	1868R yr.XXII	4.987	6.00	12.00	20.00	47.50
	1868R yr.XXIII	4.876	6.00	12.00	20.00	47.50
	1869R yr.XXIII	2.767	6.00	12.00	20.00	55.00
	1869R yr.XXIV	3.150	6.00	12.00	20.00	50.00

5 SOLDI
(25 Centesimi)

1.2500 g, .835 SILVER, .0335 oz ASW

C#	Date	Mintage	Fine	VF	XF	Unc
186	1866R yr.XXI	.100	4.00	10.00	20.00	30.00
	1867R yr.XXI	.915	3.00	9.00	15.00	25.00
	1867R yr.XXII	1.124	3.00	9.00	15.00	25.00

10 SOLDI
(50 Centesimi)

2.5000 g, .835 SILVER, .0671 oz ASW
Obv. leg: PIUS IX PON. MAX. A. . . . .

C#	Date	Mintage	Fine	VF	XF	Unc
187	1866R yr.XXI	.290	15.00	22.50	40.00	60.00
	1867R yr.XXI	3.950	2.50	5.00	9.00	20.00
	1867R yr.XXII	3.950	2.50	5.00	9.00	20.00
187	1868R yr.XXII	8.200	2.50	5.00	9.00	18.00

Obv. leg: PIUS IX P.M.A. . . . .

C#	Date	Mintage	Fine	VF	XF	Unc
187a	1868R yr.XXIII	4.765	2.50	5.00	9.00	20.00
	1869R yr.XXIII	4.435	2.50	5.00	9.00	20.00
	1869R yr.XXIV	2.765	3.00	7.00	12.50	25.00

LIRA

5.0000 g, .835 SILVER, .1342 oz ASW
Obv: Small bust w/o ornament below.

C#	Date	Mintage	Fine	VF	XF	Unc
188	1866R yr.XX	100 pcs.	300.00	500.00	800.00	1400.

Obv: Ornament below bust.

C#	Date	Mintage	Fine	VF	XF	Unc
188b	1866R yr.XXI	1.765	15.00	25.00	35.00	85.00

Obv: Medium bust.

C#	Date	Mintage	Fine	VF	XF	Unc
188d	1866R yr.XXI	.275	30.00	100.00	135.00	200.00

Obv: Large bust, PIUS IX PON. MAX. AN. . .

C#	Date	Mintage	Fine	VF	XF	Unc
188a	1866R yr.XXI	1.675	4.00	10.00	25.00	50.00
	1867R yr.XXI	3.876	4.00	8.00	20.00	40.00
	1867R yr.XXII	3.987	4.00	8.00	20.00	40.00
	1868R yr.XXII	2.050	4.00	10.00	25.00	50.00

Obv. leg: PIUS IX PON.M.A. . . .

C#	Date	Mintage	Fine	VF	XF	Unc
188c	1868R yr.XXIII	3.877	4.00	8.00	20.00	40.00
	1869R yr.XXIII	1.145	7.50	12.50	27.50	55.00
	1869R yr.XXIV	.346	35.00	75.00	125.00	200.00

2 LIRE

10.0000 g, .835 SILVER, .2684 oz ASW
Obv: Small small bust w/o ornament.
Leg: PIUS IX PON MAX.A. . . .

C#	Date	Mintage	Fine	VF	XF	Unc
189	1866R yr.XX	610 pcs.	750.00	1500.	3000.	4500.

Obv: Ornament below large bust.

C#	Date	Mintage	Fine	VF	XF	Unc
189a (C189)	1866R yr.XXI	.987	12.50	20.00	40.00	85.00
	1867R yr.XXI	.224	75.00	150.00	250.00	500.00
	1867R yr.XXII	1.220	12.50	20.00	40.00	85.00
	1868R yr.XXII	.530	50.00	120.00	175.00	350.00

Obv. leg: PIUS IX PON.M.A. . . .

C#	Date	Mintage	Fine	VF	XF	Unc
189b (C189a)	1868R yr.XXIII	.978	12.50	20.00	40.00	85.00
	1869R yr.XXIV	.810	12.50	20.00	40.00	85.00
	1870R yr.XXIV	.179	40.00	100.00	150.00	275.00

2-1/2 LIRE

12.5000 g, .900 SILVER, .3617 oz ASW

C#	Date	Mintage	Fine	VF	XF	Unc
190	1867R yr.XXI	.257	35.00	75.00	125.00	220.00

5 LIRE

1.6120 g, .900 GOLD, .0466 oz AGW

C#	Date	Mintage	Fine	VF	XF	Unc
192	1866R yr.XXI	3,230	225.00	375.00	500.00	850.00
	1867R yr.XXII	3,787	175.00	350.00	500.00	800.00

25.0000 g, .900 SILVER, .7234 oz ASW

C#	Date	Mintage	Fine	VF	XF	Unc
191	1867R yr.XXI	5,800	100.00	200.00	350.00	550.00
	1870R yr.XXIV	.099	60.00	90.00	200.00	350.00
	1870R yr.XXV	.115	50.00	80.00	175.00	325.00

10 LIRE

3.2250 g, .900 GOLD, .0933 oz AGW

Obv. leg: PIUS IX PONT. MAX.A. . . .

C#	Date	Mintage	Fine	VF	XF	Unc
193	1866R yr.XXI	8,579	150.00	300.00	400.00	600.00
	1867R yr.XXI	8,580	150.00	300.00	400.00	600.00

Obv. leg: PIUS IX PON. MAX. A. . . . .

C#	Date	Mintage	Fine	VF	XF	Unc
193b	1867R yr.XXII	9,176	150.00	250.00	350.00	500.00

Obv. leg: PIUS IX P.M.A. . . . .

C#	Date	Mintage	Fine	VF	XF	Unc
193a	1869R yr.XXIV	5,944	175.00	350.00	550.00	850.00

20 LIRE

6.4510 g, .900 GOLD, .1866 oz AGW
Plain edge, small bust

C#	Date	Mintage	Fine	VF	XF	Unc
194	1866R yr.XX	945 pcs.	900.00	1500.	2500.	5500.

Reeded edge

C#	Date	Mintage	Fine	VF	XF	Unc
194.1	1866R yr.XX	.022	350.00	700.00	950.00	1450.
	1866R yr.XXI	.102	125.00	175.00	275.00	350.00
	1867R yr.XXI	.044	150.00	225.00	350.00	550.00

Obv: Medium bust.

C#	Date	Mintage	Fine	VF	XF	Unc
194.2	1867R yr.XXII	.057	125.00	175.00	275.00	350.00
	1868R yr.XXII	.038	150.00	225.00	350.00	550.00
	1868R yr.XXIII	Inc. Ab.	350.00	700.00	950.00	1450.

Obv: Large bust.

C#	Date	Mintage	Fine	VF	XF	Unc
194.3	1868R yr.XXIII	.112	125.00	175.00	250.00	300.00
	1869R yr.XXIII	.054	125.00	175.00	275.00	350.00
	1869R yr.XXIV	.076	125.00	175.00	250.00	300.00
	1870R yr.XXIV	.024	200.00	275.00	350.00	550.00
	1870R yr.XXV	.027	150.00	225.00	300.00	425.00

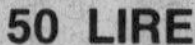

50 LIRE

16.1290 g, .900 GOLD, .4667 oz AGW

C#	Date	Mintage	Fine	VF	XF	Unc
195	1868R yr.XXII	1,172	850.00	950.00	1850.	4500.
	1868R yr.XXIII	257 pcs.	2750.	4000.	6000.	8500.
	1870R yr.XXIV	1,460	850.00	950.00	1750.	4000.

100 LIRE

32.2580 g, .900 GOLD, .9335 oz AGW

C#	Date	Mintage	Fine	VF	XF	Unc
196	1866R yr.XXI	1,117	900.00	1000.	2500.	4750.
	1868R yr.XXIII	545 pcs.	2250.	3000.	5000.	7000.
	1869R yr.XXIII	625 pcs.	2000.	2750.	4500.	6500.
	1869R yr.XXIV	450 pcs.	2500.	4250.	6000.	8500.

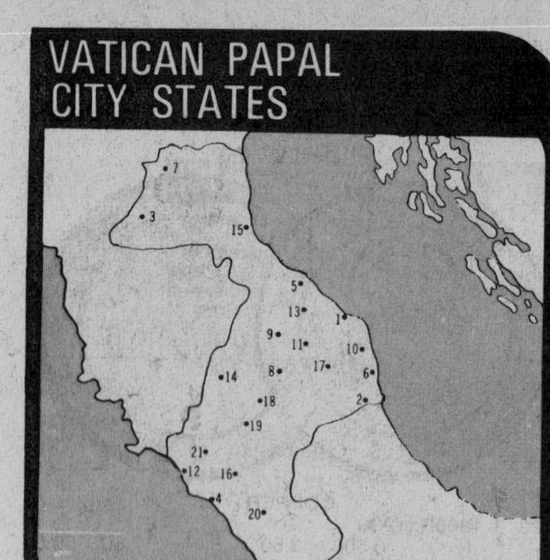

The 21 Papal City States spanned the Papal states from one end to the other. Most of the cities had been the holy see for hundreds of years. Many of them housed religious architecture and relics that were a veritable history of the church. Many had strong local families that helped administrate the city and occasionally opposed the Papal authority. Most of these cities stayed in the Papal states until 1860 when Papal territories began to crumble due to the move for unification of all Italy.

MINTS

17 of the mints functioned only during the Napoleonic period.

1 - Ancona
2 - Ascoli
3 - Bologna
4 - Civitavecchia
5 - Fano
6 - Fermo
7 - Ferrara
8 - Foligno
9 - Gubbio
10 - Macerata
11 - Matelica
12 - Montalto
13 - Pergola
14 - Perugia
15 - Ravenna
16 - Ronciglione
17 - San Severino
18 - Spoleto
19 - Terni
20 - Tivoli
21 - Viterbo

EXTRINSIC MINT

Avignon (Southern France)

PONTIFFS

Refer to Papal States.

MONETARY SYSTEM

6 Quattrini = 1 Bolognino or Baiocco
5 Baiocchi = 1 Grossi
2 Grossi = 1 Giuli = 1 Paoli
3 Giuli = 3 Paoli = 1 Testone
10 Giuli = 10 Paoli = 1 Scudo
3 Scudi = 1 Doppia

ANCONA

Anconna

A city in the Marches, was founded by Syracusan refugees about 390 B.C. It became a semi-independent republic under papal protection in the 14th century, and a papal state in 1532. From 1797 until the formation of the United Kingdom of Italy it was part of the Roman Republic (1798-99), a papal state (1799-1808), part of the Italian Kingdom of Napoleon (1808-14), a papal state (1814-48), a part of the Roman Republic (1848-49), and a papal state (1849-60).

MINT MARKS

A - Ancona

MONETARY SYSTEM

100 Baiocchi = 1 Scudo

ROMAN REPUBLIC

1798-1799, 1848-1849

BAIOCCO

CAST COPPER
Rev: A below date.

C#	Date	Year	VG	Fine	VF	XF
12	1849A	—	7.50	15.00	25.00	50.00

3 BAIOCCHI

CAST COPPER
Obv: Fasces, leg: REPUBBLICA ROMANA.

Rev: Value, date, mm.

C#	Date	Year	VG	Fine	VF	XF
13	1848A	—	45.00	90.00	150.00	250.00

NOTE: Some authorities consider this a contemporary counterfeit.

ROMAN REPUBLIC

Repubblica Romana

A short-lived Republican movement fostered by the French Revolution, submerged the Papal States in 1798-99. They reappeared in 1814, and except for the Republican movement of 1848-49, maintained their authority until 1860.

MINT MARKS

B - Bologna
R - Rome

1848-1849

1/2 BAIOCCO

COPPER

C#	Date	Year	Fine	VF	XF	Unc
21	1849R	—	5.00	10.00	15.00	30.00

BAIOCCO

COPPER

C#	Date	Year	Fine	VF	XF	Unc
22	1849R	—	7.50	15.00	30.00	50.00

3 BAIOCCHI

COPPER
Obv: Round 3.

C#	Date	Year	Fine	VF	XF	Unc
23.1	1849R	—	15.00	20.00	40.00	60.00

Obv: Flat topped 3.

C#	Date	Year	Fine	VF	XF	Unc
23.2	1849B	—	20.00	30.00	55.00	90.00
	1849R	—	15.00	20.00	40.00	60.00

Obv: Small round 3.

C#	Date	Year	Fine	VF	XF	Unc
23.3	1849R	—	12.50	25.00	45.00	80.00

4 BAIOCCHI

1.9500 g, .200 SILVER, .0125 oz ASW

C#	Date	Year	Fine	VF	XF	Unc
24	1849B	—	6.00	12.00	25.00	60.00
	1849R	—	5.00	10.00	20.00	40.00

8 BAIOCCHI

3.9000 g, .200 SILVER, .0251 oz ASW

C#	Date	Year	Fine	VF	XF	Unc
25	1849R	—	15.00	20.00	40.00	60.00

16 BAIOCCHI

7.8000 g, .200 SILVER, .0502 oz ASW

C#	Date	Year	Fine	VF	XF	Unc
26	1849R	—	20.00	35.00	55.00	90.00

40 BAIOCCHI

20.0000 g, .200 SILVER, .1286 oz ASW

C#	Date	Year	Fine	VF	XF	Unc
27	1849R	—	40.00	80.00	150.00	250.00

VATICAN CITY

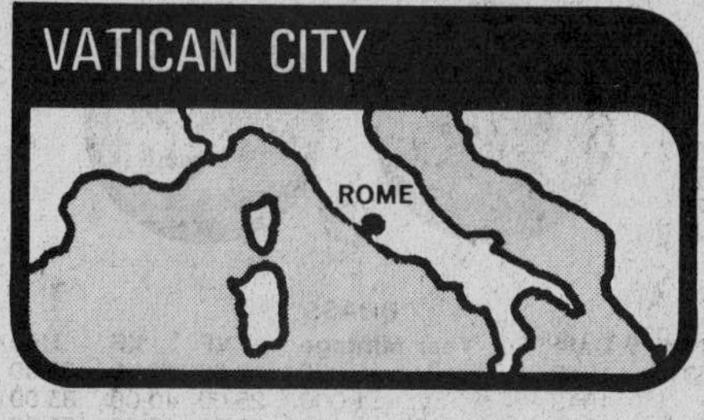

The State of the Vatican City, a papal state on the right bank of the Tiber River within the boundaries of Rome, has an area of 0.17 sq. mi. (0.44 sq. km.) and a population of *775. Capital: Vatican City.

Vatican City State, comprising the Vatican, St. Peter's and extraterritorial right to Castel Gandolfo and 13 buildings in Rome, is all that remains of the extensive papal states over which the Pope exercised temporal power in central Italy. During the struggle for Italian unification, the papal states, including Rome, were forcibly incorporated into the Kingdom of Italy in 1870. The resultant confrontation of crozier and sword remained unresolved until the signing of the Lateran Treaty, Feb. 11, 1929, between the Vatican and the Kingdom of Italy which recognized the independence and sovereignty of the State of the Vatican City, defined the relationship between the government and the church within Italy, and financially compensated the Holy See for its territorial losses in 1870.

Today the Pope exercises supreme legislative, executive and judicial power within the Vatican City, and the State of the Vatican City is recognized by many nations as an independent sovereign state under the temporal jurisdiction of the Pope, even to the extent of ambassadorial exchange.

PONTIFFS

Pius XI, 1922-1939
Sede Vacante, Feb. 10 - Mar. 2, 1939
Pius XII, 1939-1958
Sede Vacante, Oct. 9 -28, 1958
John XXIII, 1958-1963
Sede Vacante, June 3 - 21,1963
Paul VI, 1963-1978
Sede Vacante, Aug. 6 - 26, 1978
John Paul I, Aug. 26 - Sept. 28, 1978
Sede Vacante, Sept. 28 - Oct. 16, 1978
John Paul II, 1978

MONETARY SYSTEM

100 Centesimi = 1 Lira

5 CENTESIMI

COPPER

Y#	Date	Year	Mintage	VF	XF	Unc
1	1929	VIII	.010	5.00	7.50	16.00
	1930	IX	.100	2.50	4.00	6.00
	1931	X	.100	2.50	4.00	6.00
	1932	XI	.100	2.50	4.00	6.00
	1934	XIII	.100	2.50	4.00	6.00
	1935	XIV	.044	5.00	10.00	20.00
	1936	XV	.062	2.50	4.00	6.00
	1937	XVI	.062	2.50	4.00	6.00
	1938	XVII	—	—	Rare	—

Jubilee

Y#	Date	Year	Mintage	VF	XF	Unc
11	1933-34	—	.100	5.00	10.00	20.00

ALUMINUM-BRONZE

Y#	Date	Year	Mintage	VF	XF	Unc
22	1939	I	.062	2.50	4.00	7.50
	1940	II	.062	2.50	4.00	7.50
	1941	III	5,000	7.50	15.00	25.00

BRASS

Y#	Date	Year	Mintage	VF	XF	Unc
31	1942	IV	5,000	10.00	17.50	35.00
	1943	V	1,000	25.00	40.00	85.00
	1944	VI	1,000	25.00	40.00	85.00
	1945	VII	1,000	25.00	40.00	85.00
	1946	VIII	1,000	25.00	40.00	85.00

10 CENTESIMI

COPPER

Y#	Date	Year	Mintage	VF	XF	Unc
2	1929	VIII	.010	5.00	7.50	18.00
	1930	IX	.090	2.00	4.00	6.00
	1931	X	.090	2.00	4.00	6.00
	1932	XI	.090	2.00	4.00	6.00
	1934	XIII	.090	2.00	4.00	6.00
	1935	XIV	.090	2.00	4.00	6.00
	1936	XV	.081	2.00	4.00	8.00
	1937	XVI	.081	2.00	4.00	8.00
	1938	XVII	—	—	Rare	—

Jubilee

Y#	Date	Year	Mintage	VF	XF	Unc
12	1933-34	—	.090	5.00	10.00	20.00

ALUMINUM-BRONZE

Y#	Date	Year	Mintage	VF	XF	Unc
23	1939	I	.081	2.50	5.00	10.00
	1940	II	.081	2.50	5.00	10.00
	1941	III	7,500	7.50	15.00	25.00

BRASS

Y#	Date	Year	Mintage	VF	XF	Unc
32	1942	IV	7,500	7.50	15.00	25.00
	1943	V	1,000	40.00	60.00	85.00
	1944	VI	1,000	40.00	60.00	85.00
	1945	VII	1,000	40.00	60.00	85.00
	1946	VIII	1,000	40.00	60.00	85.00

20 CENTESIMI

NICKEL

Y#	Date	Year	Mintage	VF	XF	Unc
3	1929	VIII	.010	5.00	10.00	18.00
	1930	IX	.080	2.00	4.00	6.00
	1931	X	.080	2.00	4.00	6.00
	1932	XI	.080	2.00	4.00	6.00
	1934	XIII	.080	2.00	4.00	6.00
	1935	XIV	.011	25.00	50.00	75.00
	1936	XV	.064	2.00	4.00	6.00
	1937	XVI	.064	2.00	4.00	6.00

Jubilee

Y#	Date	Year	Mintage	VF	XF	Unc
13	1933-34	—	.080	5.00	10.00	20.00

Y#	Date	Year	Mintage	VF	XF	Unc
24	1939	I	.064	2.00	4.00	6.00

STAINLESS STEEL

Y#	Date	Year	Mintage	VF	XF	Unc
24a	1940	II	.064	2.00	4.00	5.50
	1941	III	.125	2.00	4.00	5.50

Y#	Date	Year	Mintage	VF	XF	Unc
33	1942	IV	.125	2.00	4.00	5.50
	1943	V	1,000	40.00	60.00	85.00
	1944	VI	1,000	40.00	60.00	85.00
	1945	VII	1,000	40.00	60.00	85.00
	1946	VIII	1,000	40.00	60.00	85.00

50 CENTESIMI

NICKEL

Y#	Date	Year	Mintage	VF	XF	Unc
4	1929	VIII	.010	5.00	10.00	18.00
	1930	IX	.080	2.00	4.00	6.00
	1931	X	.080	2.00	4.00	6.00
	1932	XI	.080	2.00	4.00	6.00
	1934	XIII	.080	2.00	4.00	6.00
	1935	XIV	.014	6.00	12.00	25.00
	1936	XV	.052	2.00	4.00	6.00
	1937	XVI	.052	2.00	4.00	6.00

Jubilee

Y#	Date	Year	Mintage	VF	XF	Unc
14	1933-34	—	.080	4.00	8.00	16.00

Y#	Date	Year	Mintage	VF	XF	Unc
25	1939	I	.052	2.00	4.00	6.00

STAINLESS STEEL

Y#	Date	Year	Mintage	VF	XF	Unc
25a	1940	II	.052	2.00	4.00	5.50
	1941	III	.180	2.00	4.00	5.50

Y#	Date	Year	Mintage	VF	XF	Unc
34	1942	IV	.180	2.00	4.00	5.50
	1943	V	1,000	40.00	60.00	85.00
	1944	VI	1,000	40.00	60.00	85.00
	1945	VII	1,000	40.00	60.00	85.00
	1946	VIII	1,000	40.00	60.00	85.00

LIRA

NICKEL

Y#	Date	Year	Mintage	VF	XF	Unc
5	1929	VIII	.010	5.00	10.00	18.00
	1930	IX	.080	2.00	4.00	6.00
	1931	X	.080	2.00	4.00	6.00
	1932	XI	.080	2.00	4.00	6.00
	1934	XIII	.080	2.00	4.00	6.00
	1935	XIV	.040	2.00	4.00	6.00
	1936	XV	.040	2.00	4.00	6.00
	1937	XVI	.070	2.00	4.00	6.00

Jubilee, enlargement of date area

Y#	Date	Year	Mintage	VF	XF	Unc
15	1933-34	—	.080	5.00	10.00	20.00

Y#	Date	Year	Mintage	VF	XF	Unc
26	1939	I	.070	3.00	5.00	10.00

STAINLESS STEEL

Y#	Date	Year	Mintage	VF	XF	Unc
26a	1940	II	.070	3.00	5.00	7.50
	1941	III	.284	1.00	2.00	4.00

Y#	Date	Year	Mintage	VF	XF	Unc
35	1942	IV	.284	1.00	2.00	4.00
	1943	V	1,000	40.00	60.00	85.00
	1944	VI	1,000	40.00	60.00	85.00
	1945	VII	1,000	40.00	60.00	85.00
	1946	VIII	1,000	40.00	60.00	85.00

ALUMINUM

Y#	Date	Year	Mintage	VF	XF	Unc
40	1947	IX	.120	1.00	2.00	4.00
	1948	X	.010	2.00	4.00	7.00
	1949	XI	.010	2.00	4.00	7.00

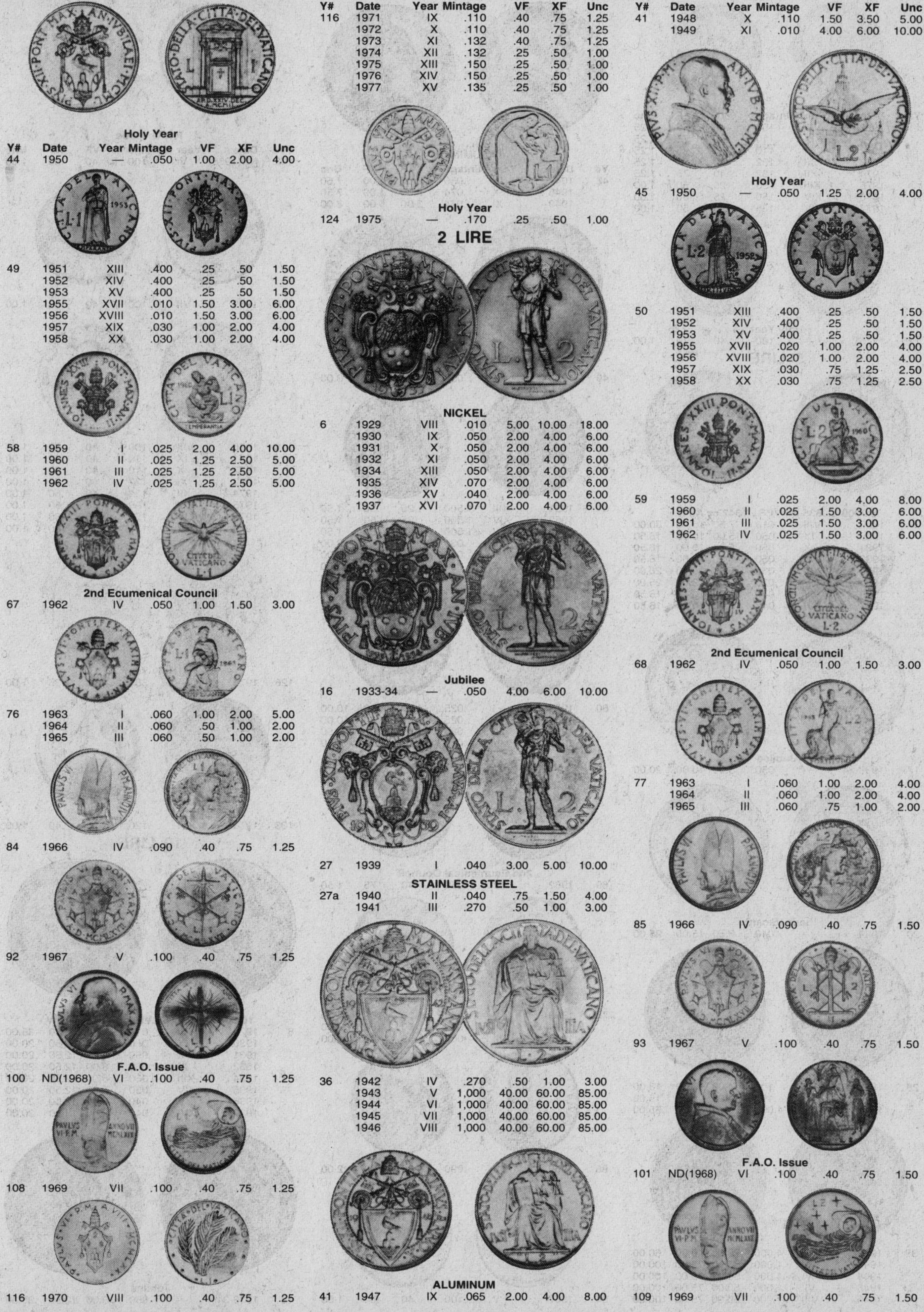

Holy Year

Y#	Date	Year	Mintage	VF	XF	Unc
44	1950	—	.050	1.00	2.00	4.00

Y#	Date	Year	Mintage	VF	XF	Unc
49	1951	XIII	.400	.25	.50	1.50
	1952	XIV	.400	.25	.50	1.50
	1953	XV	.400	.25	.50	1.50
	1955	XVII	.010	1.50	3.00	6.00
	1956	XVIII	.010	1.50	3.00	6.00
	1957	XIX	.030	1.00	2.00	4.00
	1958	XX	.030	1.00	2.00	4.00
58	1959	I	.025	2.00	4.00	10.00
	1960	II	.025	1.25	2.50	5.00
	1961	III	.025	1.25	2.50	5.00
	1962	IV	.025	1.25	2.50	5.00

2nd Ecumenical Council

Y#	Date	Year	Mintage	VF	XF	Unc
67	1962	IV	.050	1.00	1.50	3.00
76	1963	I	.060	1.00	2.00	5.00
	1964	II	.060	.50	1.00	2.00
	1965	III	.060	.50	1.00	2.00
84	1966	IV	.090	.40	.75	1.25
92	1967	V	.100	.40	.75	1.25

F.A.O. Issue

Y#	Date	Year	Mintage	VF	XF	Unc
100	ND(1968)	VI	.100	.40	.75	1.25
108	1969	VII	.100	.40	.75	1.25
116	1970	VIII	.100	.40	.75	1.25

Y#	Date	Year	Mintage	VF	XF	Unc
116	1971	IX	.110	.40	.75	1.25
	1972	X	.110	.40	.75	1.25
	1973	XI	.132	.40	.75	1.25
	1974	XII	.132	.25	.50	1.00
	1975	XIII	.150	.25	.50	1.00
	1976	XIV	.150	.25	.50	1.00
	1977	XV	.135	.25	.50	1.00

Holy Year

Y#	Date	Year	Mintage	VF	XF	Unc
124	1975	—	.170	.25	.50	1.00

2 LIRE

NICKEL

Y#	Date	Year	Mintage	VF	XF	Unc
6	1929	VIII	.010	5.00	10.00	18.00
	1930	IX	.050	2.00	4.00	6.00
	1931	X	.050	2.00	4.00	6.00
	1932	XI	.050	2.00	4.00	6.00
	1934	XIII	.050	2.00	4.00	6.00
	1935	XIV	.070	2.00	4.00	6.00
	1936	XV	.040	2.00	4.00	6.00
	1937	XVI	.070	2.00	4.00	6.00

Jubilee

Y#	Date	Year	Mintage	VF	XF	Unc
16	1933-34	—	.050	4.00	6.00	10.00
27	1939	I	.040	3.00	5.00	10.00

STAINLESS STEEL

Y#	Date	Year	Mintage	VF	XF	Unc
27a	1940	II	.040	.75	1.50	4.00
	1941	III	.270	.50	1.00	3.00
36	1942	IV	.270	.50	1.00	3.00
	1943	V	1,000	40.00	60.00	85.00
	1944	VI	1,000	40.00	60.00	85.00
	1945	VII	1,000	40.00	60.00	85.00
	1946	VIII	1,000	40.00	60.00	85.00

ALUMINUM

Y#	Date	Year	Mintage	VF	XF	Unc
41	1947	IX	.065	2.00	4.00	8.00
41	1948	X	.110	1.50	3.50	5.00
	1949	XI	.010	4.00	6.00	10.00

Holy Year

Y#	Date	Year	Mintage	VF	XF	Unc
45	1950	—	.050	1.25	2.00	4.00

Y#	Date	Year	Mintage	VF	XF	Unc
50	1951	XIII	.400	.25	.50	1.50
	1952	XIV	.400	.25	.50	1.50
	1953	XV	.400	.25	.50	1.50
	1955	XVII	.020	1.00	2.00	4.00
	1956	XVIII	.020	1.00	2.00	4.00
	1957	XIX	.030	.75	1.25	2.50
	1958	XX	.030	.75	1.25	2.50
59	1959	I	.025	2.00	4.00	8.00
	1960	II	.025	1.50	3.00	6.00
	1961	III	.025	1.50	3.00	6.00
	1962	IV	.025	1.50	3.00	6.00

2nd Ecumenical Council

Y#	Date	Year	Mintage	VF	XF	Unc
68	1962	IV	.050	1.00	1.50	3.00
77	1963	I	.060	1.00	2.00	4.00
	1964	II	.060	1.00	2.00	4.00
	1965	III	.060	.75	1.00	2.00
85	1966	IV	.090	.40	.75	1.50
93	1967	V	.100	.40	.75	1.50

F.A.O. Issue

Y#	Date	Year	Mintage	VF	XF	Unc
101	ND(1968)	VI	.100	.40	.75	1.50
109	1969	VII	.100	.40	.75	1.50

Y#	Date	Year	Mintage	VF	XF	Unc
117	1970	VIII	.100	.40	.75	1.25
	1971	IX	.110	.40	.75	1.25
	1972	X	.110	.40	.75	1.25
	1973	XI	.132	.40	.75	1.25
	1974	XII	.132	.40	.75	1.25
	1975	XIII	.150	.25	.50	1.00
	1976	XIV	.150	.25	.50	1.00
	1977	XV	.135	.25	.50	1.00

Holy Year

Y#	Date	Year	Mintage	VF	XF	Unc
125	1975	—	.180	.40	.70	1.00

5 LIRE

5.0000 g, .835 SILVER, .1342 oz ASW

Y#	Date	Year	Mintage	VF	XF	Unc
7	1929	VIII	.010	7.50	15.00	30.00
	1930	IX	.050	5.00	10.00	16.50
	1931	X	.050	5.00	10.00	16.50
	1932	XI	.050	5.00	10.00	16.50
	1934	XIII	.030	5.00	10.00	20.00
	1935	XIV	.020	6.00	12.00	25.00
	1936	XV	.040	5.00	10.00	16.50
	1937	XVI	.040	5.00	10.00	16.50

Jubilee

Y#	Date	Year	Mintage	VF	XF	Unc
17	1933-34	—	.050	5.00	10.00	20.00

Sede Vacante

Y#	Date	Year	Mintage	VF	XF	Unc
20	1939	—	.040	7.50	15.00	25.00
28	1939	I	.100	4.00	10.00	18.00
	1940	II	.100	4.00	8.00	15.00
	1941	III	4,000	25.00	35.00	55.00
37	1942	IV	4,000	25.00	40.00	60.00
	1943	V	1,000	50.00	75.00	100.00
	1944	VI	1,000	50.00	75.00	100.00
	1945	VII	1,000	50.00	75.00	100.00
	1946	VIII	1,000	50.00	75.00	100.00

ALUMINUM

Y#	Date	Year	Mintage	VF	XF	Unc
42	1947	IX	.050	2.00	4.00	7.50
	1948	X	.074	2.00	4.00	7.50
	1949	XI	.074	3.00	5.00	8.00

Holy Year

Y#	Date	Year	Mintage	VF	XF	Unc
46	1950	—	.050	3.00	5.00	8.00
51	1951	XIII	1.500	.25	.50	1.50
	1952	XIV	1.500	.25	.50	1.50
	1953	XV	1.500	.25	.50	1.50
	1955	XVII	.030	.50	.75	2.00
	1956	XVIII	.030	.50	.75	2.00
	1957	XIX	.030	.50	.75	2.00
	1958	XX	.030	.50	.75	2.00
60	1959	I	.025	4.00	6.00	10.00
	1960	II	.025	4.00	6.00	10.00
	1961	III	.025	1.50	3.00	4.50
	1962	IV	.025	.50	1.00	2.50

2nd Ecumenical Council

Y#	Date	Year	Mintage	VF	XF	Unc
69	1962	IV	.050	.40	.75	1.50
78	1963	I	.060	1.00	2.00	4.00
	1964	II	.060	.50	1.00	2.00
	1965	III	.060	.50	1.00	2.00
86	1966	IV	.090	.50	1.00	2.00
94	1967	V	.100	.40	.60	1.00

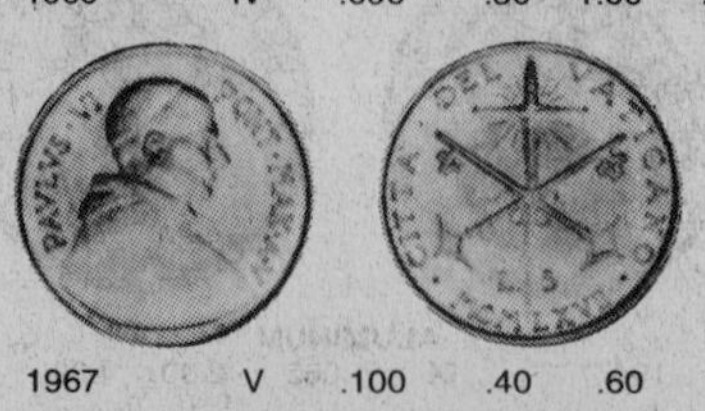

F.A.O. Issue

Y#	Date	Year	Mintage	VF	XF	Unc
102	ND(1968)	VI	.100	.40	.60	1.00
110	1969	VII	.100	.40	.60	1.00
118	1970	VIII	.100	.40	.60	1.00
	1971	IX	.110	.40	.60	1.00
	1972	X	.110	.40	.60	1.00
	1973	XI	.132	.40	.60	1.00
	1974	XII	.132	.40	.60	1.00
	1975	XIII	.150	.40	.60	1.00
	1976	XIV	.150	.40	.60	1.00
	1977	XV	.135	.40	.60	1.00

Holy Year

Y#	Date	Year	Mintage	VF	XF	Unc
126	1975	—	.380	.25	.35	1.00
133	1978	XVI	.120	.25	.40	1.00

10 LIRE

10.0000 g, .835 SILVER, .2684 oz ASW

Y#	Date	Year	Mintage	VF	XF	Unc
8	1929	VIII	.010	7.50	17.50	35.00
	1930	IX	.050	8.00	12.50	20.00
	1931	X	.050	8.00	12.50	20.00
	1932	XI	.050	8.00	12.50	20.00
	1934	XIII	.060	8.00	12.50	20.00
	1935	XIV	.050	8.00	12.50	20.00
	1936	XV	.040	8.00	12.50	20.00
	1937	XVI	.040	8.00	12.50	20.00

Jubilee

Y#	Date	Year	Mintage	VF	XF	Unc
18	1933-34	—	.050	8.00	12.50	20.00

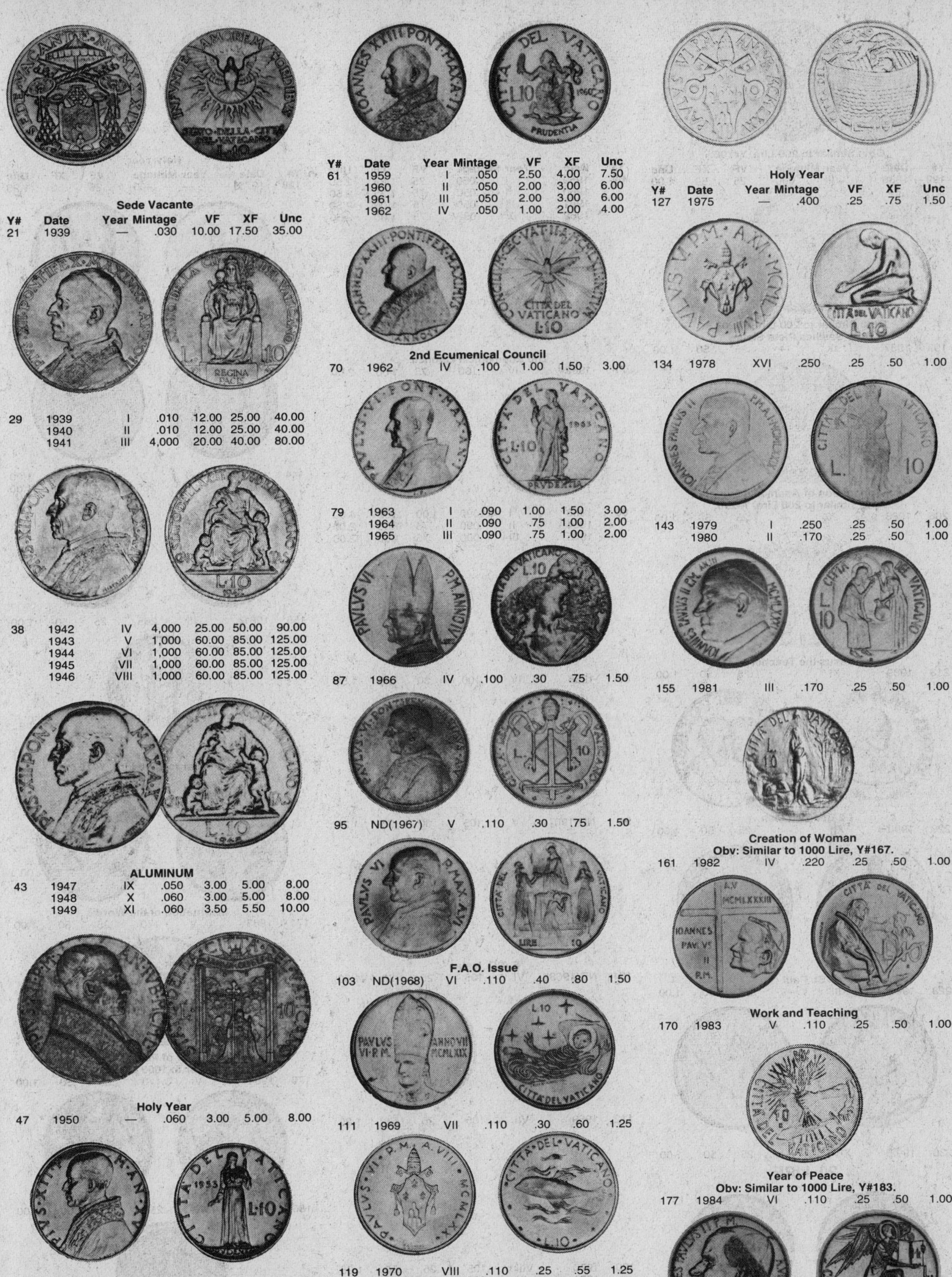

Sede Vacante

Y#	Date	Year	Mintage	VF	XF	Unc
21	1939	—	.030	10.00	17.50	35.00
29	1939	I	.010	12.00	25.00	40.00
	1940	II	.010	12.00	25.00	40.00
	1941	III	4,000	20.00	40.00	80.00
38	1942	IV	4,000	25.00	50.00	90.00
	1943	V	1,000	60.00	85.00	125.00
	1944	VI	1,000	60.00	85.00	125.00
	1945	VII	1,000	60.00	85.00	125.00
	1946	VIII	1,000	60.00	85.00	125.00

ALUMINUM

Y#	Date	Year	Mintage	VF	XF	Unc
43	1947	IX	.050	3.00	5.00	8.00
	1948	X	.060	3.00	5.00	8.00
	1949	XI	.060	3.50	5.50	10.00

Holy Year

Y#	Date	Year	Mintage	VF	XF	Unc
47	1950	—	.060	3.00	5.00	8.00
52	1951	XIII	1.130	.50	.75	1.50
	1952	XIV	1.130	.50	.75	1.50
	1953	XV	1.130	.50	.75	1.50
	1955	XVII	.080	.75	1.50	3.50
	1956	XVIII	.080	.75	1.50	3.50
	1957	XIX	.036	.75	1.50	3.50
	1958	XX	.030	.75	1.50	3.50

Y#	Date	Year	Mintage	VF	XF	Unc
61	1959	I	.050	2.50	4.00	7.50
	1960	II	.050	2.00	3.00	6.00
	1961	III	.050	2.00	3.00	6.00
	1962	IV	.050	1.00	2.00	4.00

2nd Ecumenical Council

Y#	Date	Year	Mintage	VF	XF	Unc
70	1962	IV	.100	1.00	1.50	3.00
79	1963	I	.090	1.00	1.50	3.00
	1964	II	.090	.75	1.00	2.00
	1965	III	.090	.75	1.00	2.00
87	1966	IV	.100	.30	.75	1.50
95	ND(1967)	V	.110	.30	.75	1.50

F.A.O. Issue

Y#	Date	Year	Mintage	VF	XF	Unc
103	ND(1968)	VI	.110	.40	.80	1.50
111	1969	VII	.110	.30	.60	1.25
119	1970	VIII	.110	.25	.55	1.25
	1971	IX	.160	.25	.50	1.00
	1972	X	.160	.25	.50	1.00
	1973	XI	.170	.25	.50	1.00
	1974	XII	.170	.25	.50	1.00
	1975	XIII	.200	.25	.50	1.00
	1976	XIV	.200	.25	.50	1.00
	1977	XV	.200	.25	.50	1.00

Holy Year

Y#	Date	Year	Mintage	VF	XF	Unc
127	1975	—	.400	.25	.75	1.50
134	1978	XVI	.250	.25	.50	1.00
143	1979	I	.250	.25	.50	1.00
	1980	II	.170	.25	.50	1.00
155	1981	III	.170	.25	.50	1.00

Creation of Woman
Obv: Similar to 1000 Lire, Y#167.

Y#	Date	Year	Mintage	VF	XF	Unc
161	1982	IV	.220	.25	.50	1.00

Work and Teaching

Y#	Date	Year	Mintage	VF	XF	Unc
170	1983	V	.110	.25	.50	1.00

Year of Peace
Obv: Similar to 1000 Lire, Y#183.

Y#	Date	Year	Mintage	VF	XF	Unc
177	1984	VI	.110	.25	.50	1.00
185	1985	VII	.090	.25	.50	1.00

Obv: Similar to 200 Lire, Y#196.

Y#	Date	Year	Mintage	VF	XF	Unc
192	1986	VIII	.090	.25	.50	1.00

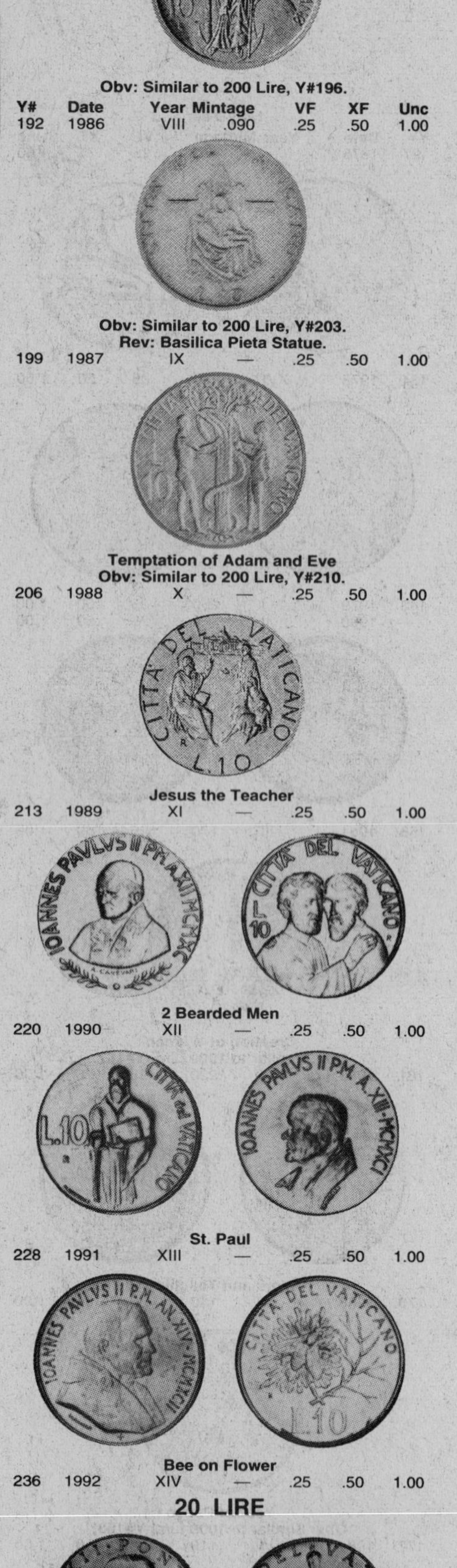

Obv: Similar to 200 Lire, Y#203.
Rev: Basilica Pieta Statue.

Y#	Date	Year	Mintage	VF	XF	Unc
199	1987	IX	—	.25	.50	1.00

Temptation of Adam and Eve
Obv: Similar to 200 Lire, Y#210.

Y#	Date	Year	Mintage	VF	XF	Unc
206	1988	X	—	.25	.50	1.00

Jesus the Teacher

Y#	Date	Year	Mintage	VF	XF	Unc
213	1989	XI	—	.25	.50	1.00

2 Bearded Men

Y#	Date	Year	Mintage	VF	XF	Unc
220	1990	XII	—	.25	.50	1.00

St. Paul

Y#	Date	Year	Mintage	VF	XF	Unc
228	1991	XIII	—	.25	.50	1.00

Bee on Flower

Y#	Date	Year	Mintage	VF	XF	Unc
236	1992	XIV	—	.25	.50	1.00

20 LIRE

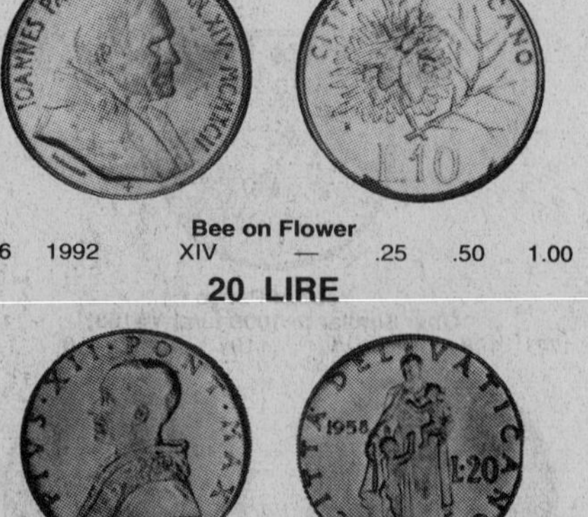

ALUMINUM-BRONZE

Y#	Date	Year	Mintage	VF	XF	Unc
A52	1957	XIX	.020	.75	1.25	2.50
	1958	XX	.060	.75	1.25	2.50

Y#	Date	Year	Mintage	VF	XF	Unc
62	1959	I	.050	.75	1.25	2.50
	1960	II	.050	.75	1.25	2.50
	1961	III	.050	.75	1.00	2.50
	1962	IV	.050	.75	1.00	2.50

2nd Ecumenical Council

Y#	Date	Year	Mintage	VF	XF	Unc
71	1962	IV	.100	.75	1.00	2.00

Y#	Date	Year	Mintage	VF	XF	Unc
80	1963	I	.090	1.00	2.00	4.00
	1964	II	.090	.75	1.00	2.00
	1965	III	.090	.75	1.00	2.00

Y#	Date	Year	Mintage	VF	XF	Unc
88	1966	IV	.100	.30	.75	1.50

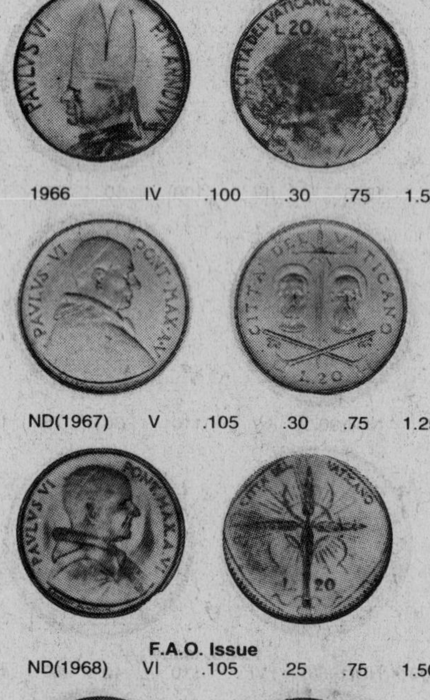

Y#	Date	Year	Mintage	VF	XF	Unc
96	ND(1967)	V	.105	.30	.75	1.25

F.A.O. Issue

Y#	Date	Year	Mintage	VF	XF	Unc
104	ND(1968)	VI	.105	.25	.75	1.50

Y#	Date	Year	Mintage	VF	XF	Unc
112	1969	VII	.105	.25	.60	1.25

Y#	Date	Year	Mintage	VF	XF	Unc
120	1970	VIII	.105	.25	.50	1.25
	1971	IX	.170	.25	.50	1.25
	1972	X	.170	.25	.50	1.00
	1973	XI	—	.25	.50	1.00
	1974	XII	—	.25	.50	1.00
	1975	XIII	.250	.25	.50	1.00
	1976	XIV	.250	.25	.50	1.00
	1977	XV	.250	.25	.50	1.00

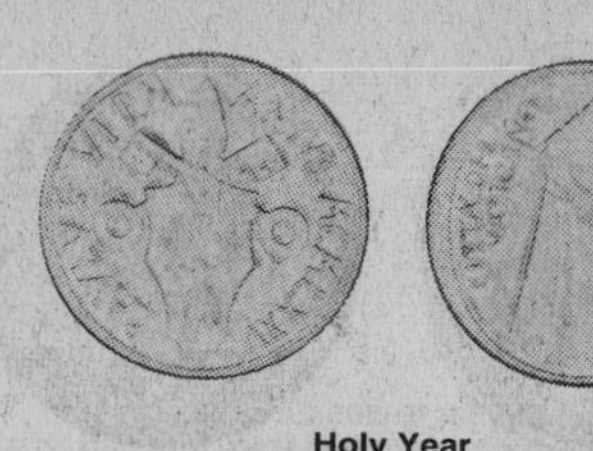

Holy Year

Y#	Date	Year	Mintage	VF	XF	Unc
128	1975	—	.400	.25	.50	1.25

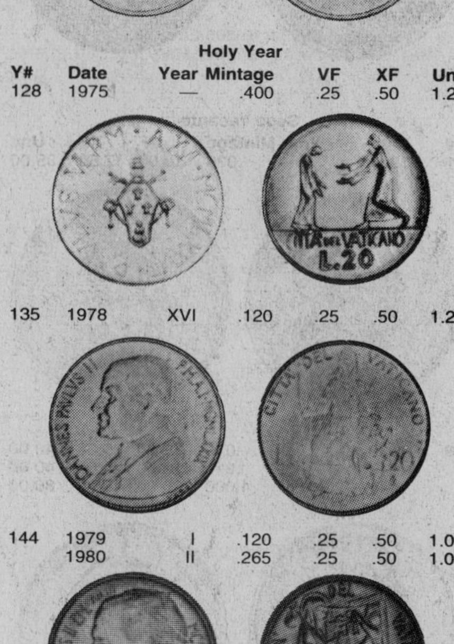

Y#	Date	Year	Mintage	VF	XF	Unc
135	1978	XVI	.120	.25	.50	1.25

Y#	Date	Year	Mintage	VF	XF	Unc
144	1979	I	.120	.25	.50	1.00
	1980	II	.265	.25	.50	1.00

Y#	Date	Year	Mintage	VF	XF	Unc
156	1981	III	.265	.25	.50	1.00

Marriage
Obv: Similar to 1000 Lire, Y#167.

Y#	Date	Year	Mintage	VF	XF	Unc
162	1982	IV	.360	.25	.50	1.00

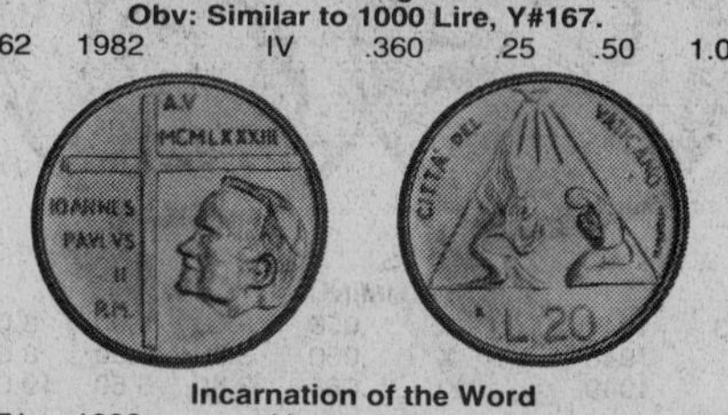

Incarnation of the Word

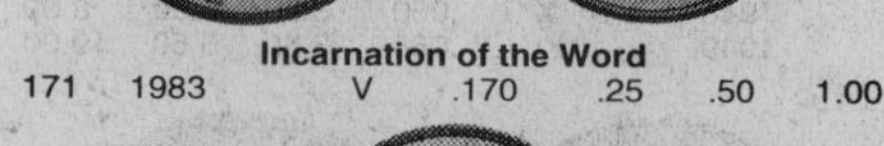

Y#	Date	Year	Mintage	VF	XF	Unc
171	1983	V	.170	.25	.50	1.00

Year of Peace
Obv: Similar to 1000 Lire, Y#183.

Y#	Date	Year	Mintage	VF	XF	Unc
178	1984	VI	.170	.25	.50	1.00

Y#	Date	Year	Mintage	VF	XF	Unc
186	1985	VII	.255	.25	.50	1.00

Obv: Similar to 200 Lire, Y#196.

Y#	Date	Year	Mintage	VF	XF	Unc
193	1986	VIII	.100	.25	.50	1.00

Obv: Similar to 200 Lire, Y#203.
Rev: Assumption of Mother Mary into Heaven.

Y#	Date	Year	Mintage	VF	XF	Unc
200	1987	IX	—	.25	.50	1.00

Forbidding of the Fruit to Adam and Eve
Similar to 200 Lire, Y#210.

Y#	Date	Year	Mintage	VF	XF	Unc
207	1988	X	—	.25	.50	1.00

The Harvest

Y#	Date	Year	Mintage	VF	XF	Unc
214	1989	XI	—	.25	.50	1.00

Pope and King

Y#	Date	Year	Mintage	VF	XF	Unc
221	1990	XII	—	.25	.50	1.00

Crane and Buildings

Y#	Date	Year	Mintage	VF	XF	Unc
229	1991	XIII	—	.25	.50	1.00

3 Children

Y#	Date	Year	Mintage	VF	XF	Unc
237	1992	XIV	—	.25	.50	1.00

50 LIRE

STAINLESS STEEL

Y#	Date	Year	Mintage	VF	XF	Unc
54	1955	XVII	.180	1.00	1.50	3.00
	1956	XVIII	.180	1.00	1.50	3.00
	1957	XIX	.180	1.00	1.50	3.00
	1958	XX	.060	1.00	1.50	3.00

Obv: Continuous leg.

Y#	Date	Year	Mintage	VF	XF	Unc
63	1959	I	.100	1.00	2.50	7.00

Y#	Date	Year	Mintage	VF	XF	Unc
63.1	1960	II	.100	1.00	2.50	7.50
	1961	III	.100	1.00	2.00	3.50
	1962	IV	.100	1.00	2.00	3.50

2nd Ecumenical Council

Y#	Date	Year	Mintage	VF	XF	Unc
72	1962	IV	.200	.50	1.25	2.50

Y#	Date	Year	Mintage	VF	XF	Unc
81	1963	I	.120	1.00	2.00	4.00
	1964	II	.120	.75	1.50	3.00
	1965	III	.120	.50	1.00	2.00
89	1966	IV	.150	.50	1.00	2.00
97	1967	V	.190	.50	1.00	2.00

F.A.O. Issue

Y#	Date	Year	Mintage	VF	XF	Unc
105	ND(1968)	VI	.190	.50	1.00	2.00
113	1969	VII	.190	.50	1.00	2.00
121	1970	VIII	.190	.30	.75	1.50

Y#	Date	Year	Mintage	VF	XF	Unc
121	1971	IX	.700	.30	.75	1.50
	1972	X	.700	.30	.75	1.25
	1973	XI	.750	.30	.75	1.25
	1974	XII	.750	.30	.75	1.25
	1975	XIII	.600	.30	.75	1.25
	1976	XIV	.600	.30	.75	1.25

Holy Year

Y#	Date	Year	Mintage	VF	XF	Unc
129	1975	—	.500	.40	.75	1.25
A121	1977	XV	.600	.20	.35	1.00

16th Year

Y#	Date	Year	Mintage	VF	XF	Unc
136	1978	XVI	.223	.25	.50	1.00
145	1979	I	.223	.25	.50	1.00
	1980	II	.250	.25	.50	1.00
157	1981	III	.240	.25	.50	1.00

Maternity
Obv: Similar to 1000 Lire, Y#167.

Y#	Date	Year	Mintage	VF	XF	Unc
163	1982	IV	.400	.25	.50	.75

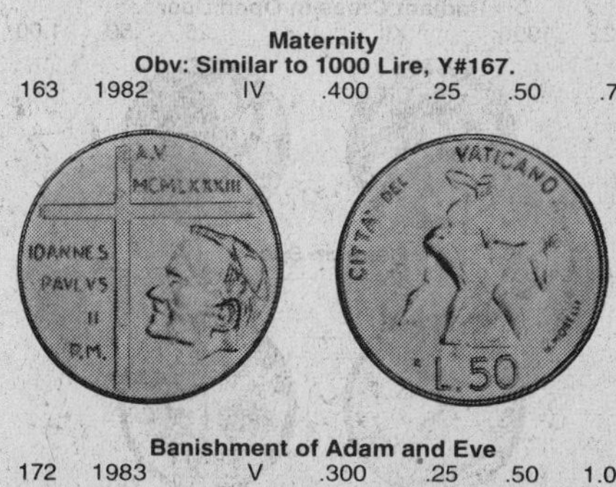

Banishment of Adam and Eve

Y#	Date	Year	Mintage	VF	XF	Unc
172	1983	V	.300	.25	.50	1.00

Year of Peace
Obv: Similar to 1000 Lire, Y#183.

Y#	Date	Year	Mintage	VF	XF	Unc
179	1984	VI	.300	.25	.50	1.00

Y#	Date	Year	Mintage	VF	XF	Unc
187	1985	VII	.360	.25	.50	1.00

Obv: Similar to 200 Lire, Y#196.

Y#	Date	Year	Mintage	VF	XF	Unc
194	1986	VIII	.100	.25	.50	1.00

Obv: Similar to 200 Lire, Y#203.
Rev: Mother Mary protecting kneeling sinners.

Y#	Date	Year	Mintage	VF	XF	Unc
201	1987	IX	—	.25	.50	1.00

Creation of Eve From Adam's Rib
Obv: Similar to 200 Lire, Y#210.

Y#	Date	Year	Mintage	VF	XF	Unc
208	1988	X	—	.25	.50	1.00

Human Solidarity

Y#	Date	Year	Mintage	VF	XF	Unc
215	1989	XI	—	.25	.50	1.00

Radiant Cross in Open Door

Y#	Date	Year	Mintage	VF	XF	Unc
222	1990	XII	—	.25	.50	1.00

Baptism Scene

Y#	Date	Year	Mintage	VF	XF	Unc
230	1991	XIII	—	.25	.50	1.00

Cross as Balance Scale Between
Agriculture and Industry

Y#	Date	Year	Mintage	VF	XF	Unc
238	1992	XIV	—	.25	.50	1.00

100 LIRE

8.8000 g, .900 GOLD, .2546 oz AGW

Y#	Date	Year	Mintage	VF	XF	Unc
9	1929	VIII	10,000	150.00	200.00	325.00
	1930	IX	2,621	300.00	700.00	1200.
	1931	X	3,343	200.00	350.00	600.00
	1932	XI	5,073	200.00	325.00	550.00
	1934	XIII	2,533	250.00	350.00	600.00
	1935	XIV	2,015	250.00	350.00	600.00

Jubilee

Y#	Date	Year	Mintage	VF	XF	Unc
19	1933-34	—	.023	125.00	175.00	245.00

5.1900 g, .900 GOLD, .1501 oz AGW

Y#	Date	Year	Mintage	VF	XF	Unc
10	1936	XV	8,239	175.00	225.00	300.00
	1937	XVI	2,000	1000.	2000.	3000.
	1938		6 pcs.	Rare	—	

Y#	Date	Year	Mintage	VF	XF	Unc
30	1939	I	2,700	175.00	250.00	400.00
	1940	II	2,000	175.00	250.00	400.00
	1941	III	2,000	175.00	250.00	400.00

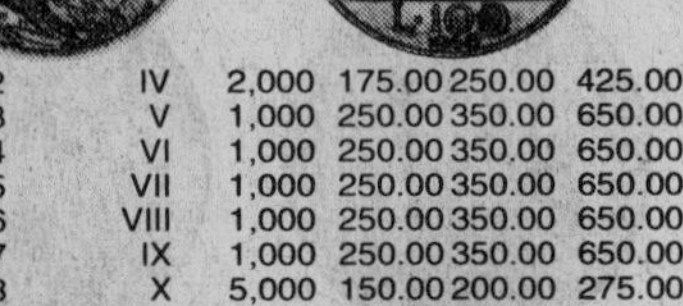

Y#	Date	Year	Mintage	VF	XF	Unc
39	1942	IV	2,000	175.00	250.00	425.00
	1943	V	1,000	250.00	350.00	650.00
	1944	VI	1,000	250.00	350.00	650.00
	1945	VII	1,000	250.00	350.00	650.00
	1946	VIII	1,000	250.00	350.00	650.00
	1947	IX	1,000	250.00	350.00	650.00
	1948	X	5,000	150.00	200.00	275.00
	1949	XI	1,000	250.00	350.00	650.00

Holy Year

Y#	Date	Year	Mintage	VF	XF	Unc
48	1950	—	.020	150.00	200.00	275.00

Y#	Date	Year	Mintage	VF	XF	Unc
53	1951	XIII	1,000	250.00	350.00	650.00
	1952	XIV	1,000	250.00	350.00	650.00
	1953	XV	1,000	250.00	350.00	650.00
	1954	XVI	1,000	250.00	350.00	650.00
	1955	XVII	1,000	250.00	350.00	650.00
	1956	XVIII	1,000	250.00	350.00	650.00

STAINLESS STEEL

Y#	Date	Year	Mintage	VF	XF	Unc
55	1955	XVII	1,300	.50	1.00	2.00
	1956	XVIII	1,400	.50	1.00	2.00
	1957	XIX	.900	.50	1.00	2.00
	1958	XX	.852	.50	1.00	2.00

5.1900 g, .900 GOLD, .1501 oz AGW

Y#	Date	Year	Mintage	VF	XF	Unc
A53	1957	XIX	2,000	200.00	250.00	350.00
	1958	XX	3,000	200.00	250.00	350.00

Y#	Date	Year	Mintage	VF	XF	Unc
66	1959	I	3,000	500.00	750.00	1250.

STAINLESS STEEL
Obv: Continuous legend.

Y#	Date	Year	Mintage	VF	XF	Unc
64	1959	I	.783	1.25	2.00	4.00

Y#	Date	Year	Mintage	VF	XF	Unc
64.1	1960	II	.783	1.75	3.00	7.50
	1961	III	.783	.75	1.00	2.50
	1962	IV	.783	.75	1.00	2.00

2nd Ecumenical Council

Y#	Date	Year	Mintage	VF	XF	Unc
73	1962	IV	1.566	.40	.75	1.50

Y#	Date	Year	Mintage	VF	XF	Unc
82	1963	I	.558	1.00	2.00	4.00
	1964	II	.558	.50	1.00	2.00
	1965	III	.558	.50	1.00	2.00

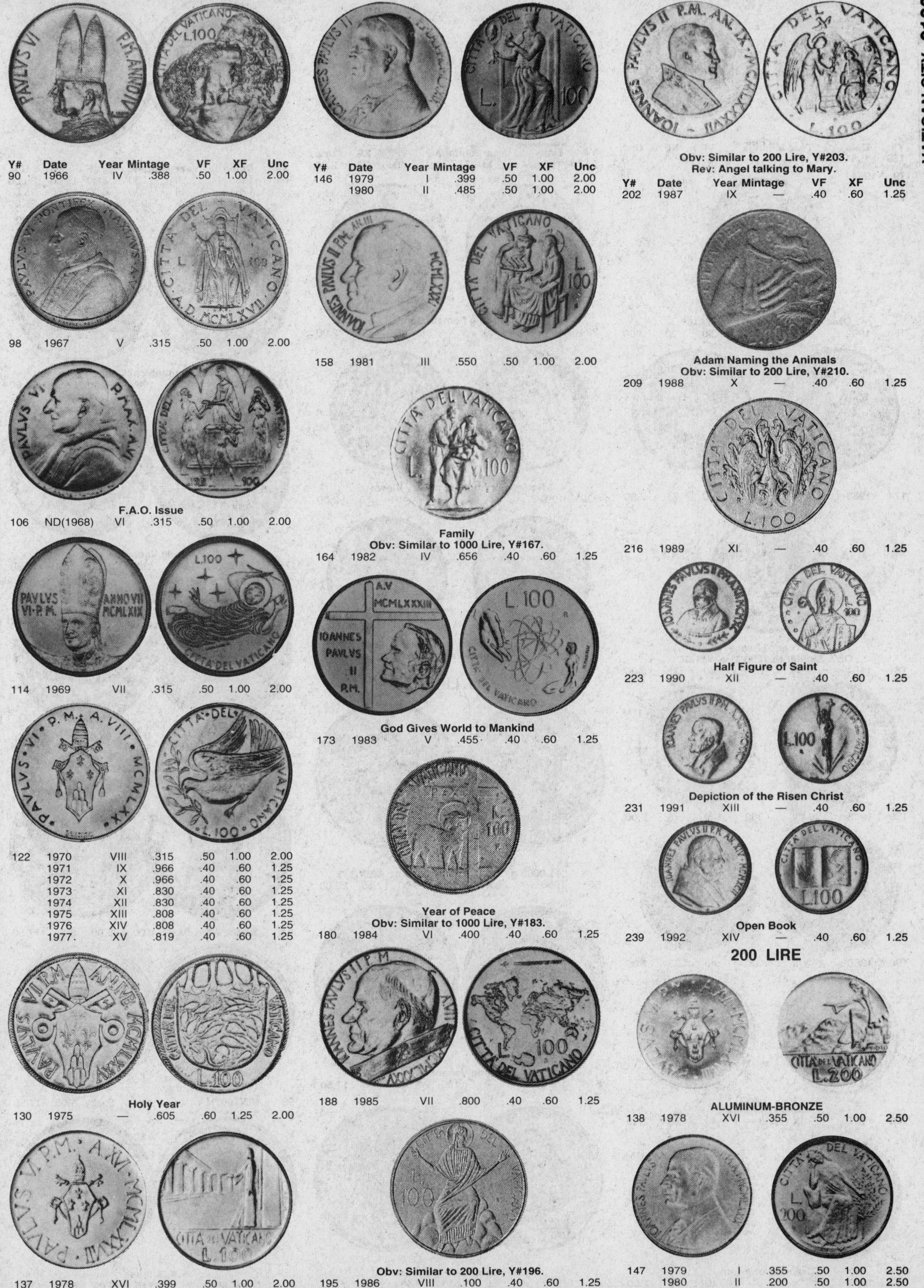

Y#	Date	Year	Mintage	VF	XF	Unc
90	1966	IV	.388	.50	1.00	2.00
98	1967	V	.315	.50	1.00	2.00

F.A.O. Issue

Y#	Date	Year	Mintage	VF	XF	Unc
106	ND(1968)	VI	.315	.50	1.00	2.00
114	1969	VII	.315	.50	1.00	2.00
122	1970	VIII	.315	.50	1.00	2.00
	1971	IX	.966	.40	.60	1.25
	1972	X	.966	.40	.60	1.25
	1973	XI	.830	.40	.60	1.25
	1974	XII	.830	.40	.60	1.25
	1975	XIII	.808	.40	.60	1.25
	1976	XIV	.808	.40	.60	1.25
	1977.	XV	.819	.40	.60	1.25

Holy Year

Y#	Date	Year	Mintage	VF	XF	Unc
130	1975	—	.605	.60	1.25	2.00
137	1978	XVI	.399	.50	1.00	2.00

Y#	Date	Year	Mintage	VF	XF	Unc
146	1979	I	.399	.50	1.00	2.00
	1980	II	.485	.50	1.00	2.00
158	1981	III	.550	.50	1.00	2.00

Family
Obv: Similar to 1000 Lire, Y#167.

Y#	Date	Year	Mintage	VF	XF	Unc
164	1982	IV	.656	.40	.60	1.25

God Gives World to Mankind

Y#	Date	Year	Mintage	VF	XF	Unc
173	1983	V	.455	.40	.60	1.25

Year of Peace
Obv: Similar to 1000 Lire, Y#183.

Y#	Date	Year	Mintage	VF	XF	Unc
180	1984	VI	.400	.40	.60	1.25
188	1985	VII	.800	.40	.60	1.25

Obv: Similar to 200 Lire, Y#196.

Y#	Date	Year	Mintage	VF	XF	Unc
195	1986	VIII	.100	.40	.60	1.25

Obv: Similar to 200 Lire, Y#203.
Rev: Angel talking to Mary.

Y#	Date	Year	Mintage	VF	XF	Unc
202	1987	IX	—	.40	.60	1.25

Adam Naming the Animals
Obv: Similar to 200 Lire, Y#210.

Y#	Date	Year	Mintage	VF	XF	Unc
209	1988	X	—	.40	.60	1.25
216	1989	XI	—	.40	.60	1.25

Half Figure of Saint

Y#	Date	Year	Mintage	VF	XF	Unc
223	1990	XII	—	.40	.60	1.25

Depiction of the Risen Christ

Y#	Date	Year	Mintage	VF	XF	Unc
231	1991	XIII	—	.40	.60	1.25

Open Book

Y#	Date	Year	Mintage	VF	XF	Unc
239	1992	XIV	—	.40	.60	1.25

200 LIRE

ALUMINUM-BRONZE

Y#	Date	Year	Mintage	VF	XF	Unc
138	1978	XVI	.355	.50	1.00	2.50
147	1979	I	.355	.50	1.00	2.50
	1980	II	.200	.50	1.00	2.50

Y#	Date	Year	Mintage	VF	XF	Unc
159	1981	III	.170	.50	1.00	2.50

Labor
Obv: Similar to 1000 Lire, Y#167.

Y#	Date	Year	Mintage	VF	XF	Unc
165	1982	IV	.500	.50	1.00	2.50

Creation of Man

Y#	Date	Year	Mintage	VF	XF	Unc
174	1983	V	.300	.40	.75	2.00

Year of Peace
Obv: Similar to 1000 Lire, Y#183.

Y#	Date	Year	Mintage	VF	XF	Unc
181	1984	VI	.250	.40	.75	2.00
189	1985	VII	.300	.40	.75	2.00
196	1986	VIII	.100	.40	.75	2.00

Queen of Peace

Y#	Date	Year	Mintage	VF	XF	Unc
203	1987	IX	—	.40	.75	2.00

Creation of Adam

Y#	Date	Year	Mintage	VF	XF	Unc
210	1988	X	—	.40	.75	2.00

Y#	Date	Year	Mintage	VF	XF	Unc
217	1989	XI	—	.40	.75	2.00

Standing Female Saint

Y#	Date	Year	Mintage	VF	XF	Unc
224	1990	XII	—	.40	.75	2.00

Redeemer Looking at City Views

Y#	Date	Year	Mintage	VF	XF	Unc
232	1991	XIII	—	.40	.75	2.00

Mother Nursing Child

Y#	Date	Year	Mintage	VF	XF	Unc
240	1992	XIV	—	.40	.75	2.00

500 LIRE

11.0000 g, .835 SILVER, .2953 oz ASW

Y#	Date	Year	Mintage	VF	XF	Unc
56	1958	XX	.020	6.00	12.50	25.00

Sede Vacante

Y#	Date	Year	Mintage	VF	XF	Unc
57	1958	—	.100	5.00	8.00	17.50

Obv: Continuous legend.

Y#	Date	Year	Mintage	VF	XF	Unc
65	1959	I	.030	6.00	12.50	25.00

Y#	Date	Year	Mintage	VF	XF	Unc
65.1	1960	II	.030	7.00	15.00	30.00
	1961	III	.030	6.00	12.50	25.00
	1962	IV	.030	6.00	12.50	25.00

2nd Ecumenical Council

Y#	Date	Year	Mintage	VF	XF	Unc
74	1962	IV	.060	6.00	12.50	25.00

Sede Vacante

Y#	Date	Year	Mintage	VF	XF	Unc
75	1963	—	.200	5.00	8.00	17.50
83	1963	I	.070	8.00	17.50	40.00
	1964	II	.070	7.00	15.00	30.00
	1965	III	.070	6.00	9.00	20.00
91	1966	IV	.100	5.00	8.00	17.50
99	ND(1967)	V	.110	5.00	8.00	17.50

F.A.O. Issue

Y#	Date	Year	Mintage	VF	XF	Unc
107	ND(1968)	VI	.110	5.00	8.00	17.50

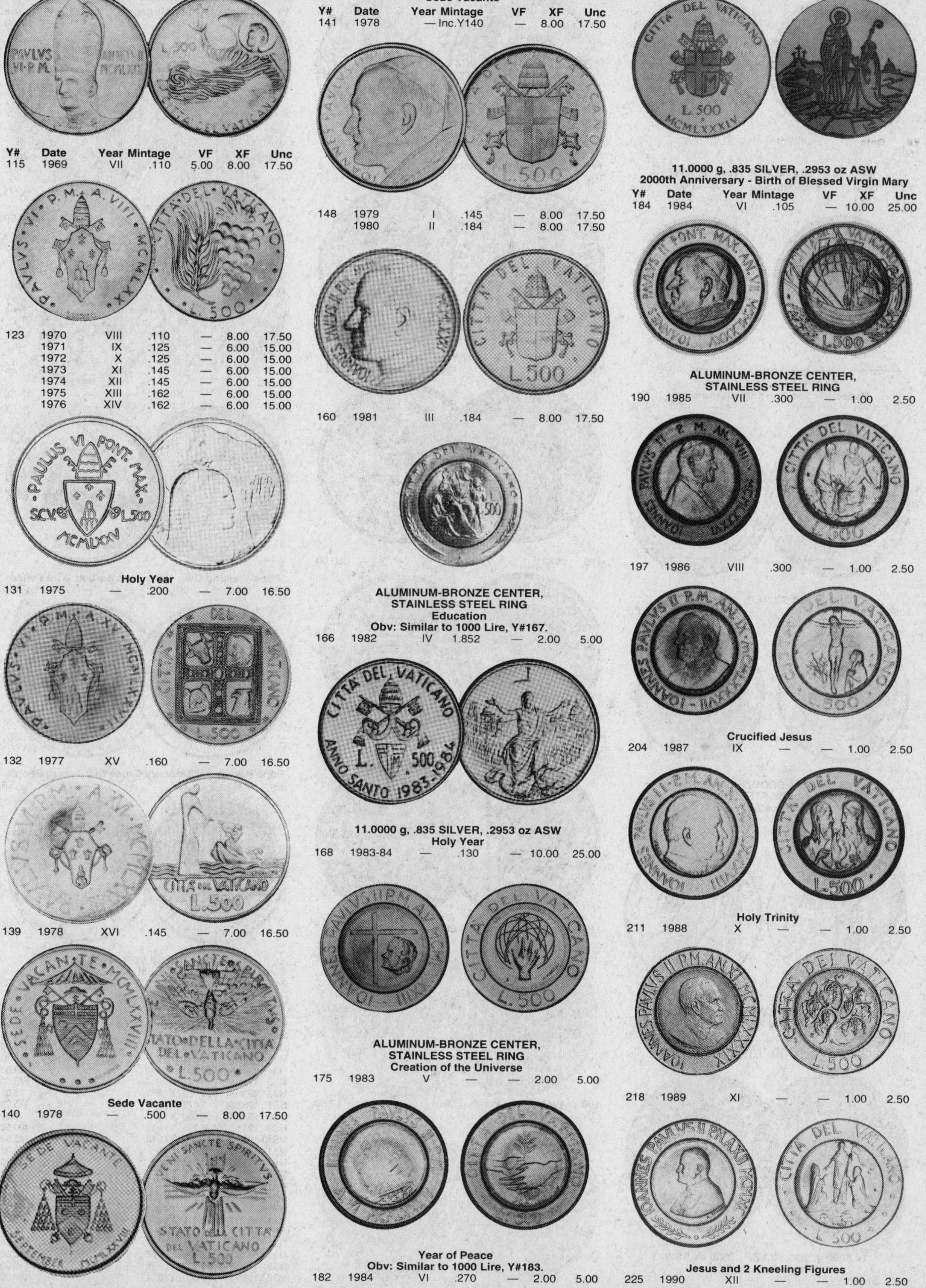

Y#	Date	Year	Mintage	VF	XF	Unc
115	1969	VII	.110	5.00	8.00	17.50
123	1970	VIII	.110	—	8.00	17.50
	1971	IX	.125	—	6.00	15.00
	1972	X	.125	—	6.00	15.00
	1973	XI	.145	—	6.00	15.00
	1974	XII	.145	—	6.00	15.00
	1975	XIII	.162	—	6.00	15.00
	1976	XIV	.162	—	6.00	15.00

Holy Year

Y#	Date	Year	Mintage	VF	XF	Unc
131	1975	—	.200	—	7.00	16.50
132	1977	XV	.160	—	7.00	16.50
139	1978	XVI	.145	—	7.00	16.50

Sede Vacante

Y#	Date	Year	Mintage	VF	XF	Unc
140	1978	—	.500	—	8.00	17.50

Sede Vacante

Y#	Date	Year	Mintage	VF	XF	Unc
141	1978	—	Inc.Y140	—	8.00	17.50
148	1979	I	.145	—	8.00	17.50
	1980	II	.184	—	8.00	17.50
160	1981	III	.184	—	8.00	17.50

ALUMINUM-BRONZE CENTER, STAINLESS STEEL RING
Education
Obv: Similar to 1000 Lire, Y#167.

Y#	Date	Year	Mintage	VF	XF	Unc
166	1982	IV	1.852	—	2.00	5.00

11.0000 g, .835 SILVER, .2953 oz ASW
Holy Year

Y#	Date	Year	Mintage	VF	XF	Unc
168	1983-84	—	.130	—	10.00	25.00

ALUMINUM-BRONZE CENTER, STAINLESS STEEL RING
Creation of the Universe

Y#	Date	Year	Mintage	VF	XF	Unc
175	1983	V	—	—	2.00	5.00

Year of Peace
Obv: Similar to 1000 Lire, Y#183.

Y#	Date	Year	Mintage	VF	XF	Unc
182	1984	VI	.270	—	2.00	5.00

11.0000 g, .835 SILVER, .2953 oz ASW
2000th Anniversary - Birth of Blessed Virgin Mary

Y#	Date	Year	Mintage	VF	XF	Unc
184	1984	VI	.105	—	10.00	25.00

ALUMINUM-BRONZE CENTER, STAINLESS STEEL RING

Y#	Date	Year	Mintage	VF	XF	Unc
190	1985	VII	.300	—	1.00	2.50
197	1986	VIII	.300	—	1.00	2.50

Crucified Jesus

Y#	Date	Year	Mintage	VF	XF	Unc
204	1987	IX	—	—	1.00	2.50

Holy Trinity

Y#	Date	Year	Mintage	VF	XF	Unc
211	1988	X	—	—	1.00	2.50
218	1989	XI	—	—	1.00	2.50

Jesus and 2 Kneeling Figures

Y#	Date	Year	Mintage	VF	XF	Unc
225	1990	XII	—	—	1.00	2.50

11.0000 g, .835 SILVER, .2953 oz ASW

Y#	Date	Year	Mintage	VF	XF	Unc
227	1991	—	—	—	—	27.50

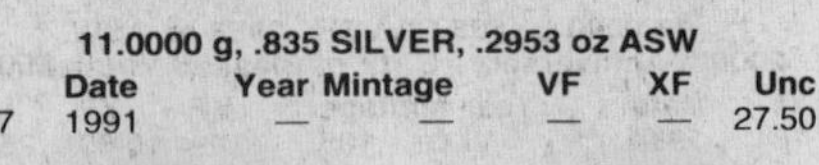

ALUMINUM-BRONZE CENTER, STAINLESS STEEL RING
Redeemer Sending Out Missionaries

Y#	Date	Year	Mintage	VF	XF	Unc
233	1991	XIII	—	—	1.00	2.50

11.0000 g, .835 SILVER, .2953 oz ASW

Y#	Date	Year	Mintage	VF	XF	Unc
235	1992	XIV	—	—	—	25.00

ALUMINUM-BRONZE CENTER, STAINLESS STEEL RING
Hands Holding Food

Y#	Date	Year	Mintage	VF	XF	Unc
241	1992	XIV	—	—	1.00	2.50

11.0000 g, .835 SILVER, .2953 oz ASW
World Peace

Y#	Date	Year	Mintage	VF	XF	Unc
243	1993	XV	—	—	—	25.00

1000 LIRE

14.6000 g, .835 SILVER, .3920 oz ASW
Pope John Paul I

Y#	Date	Year	Mintage	VF	XF	Unc
142	1978	—	—	—	—	25.00

Y#	Date	Year	Mintage	VF	XF	Unc
167	1982	IV	.210	—	—	17.50

Holy Year

Y#	Date	Year	Mintage	VF	XF	Unc
169	1983-84	—	.130	—	—	17.50

Prayer

Y#	Date	Year	Mintage	VF	XF	Unc
176	1983	V	.110	—	—	20.00

Year of Peace

Y#	Date	Year	Mintage	VF	XF	Unc
183	1984	VI	.105	—	—	20.00

Y#	Date	Year	Mintage	VF	XF	Unc
191	1985	VII	.086	—	—	22.50
198	1986	VIII	.080	—	—	17.50

Pope In Prayer

Y#	Date	Year	Mintage	VF	XF	Unc
205	1987	IX	—	—	—	17.50

Pope at Desk

Y#	Date	Year	Mintage	VF	XF	Unc
212	1988	X	—	—	—	17.50
219	1989	XI	—	—	—	17.50

Pope Walking Over Destroyed Barbed Wire Fence

Y#	Date	Year	Mintage	VF	XF	Unc
226	1990	XII	—	—	—	17.50

Pope Handing Missionary Cross to 2 Young People

Y#	Date	Year	Mintage	VF	XF	Unc
234	1991	XIII	—	—	—	17.50

11.0000 g, .835 SILVER, .2953 oz ASW
Pope's Personal Coat of Arms

Y#	Date	Year	Mintage	VF	XF	Unc
242	1992	XIV	—	—	—	17.50

MINT SETS (MS)

KM#	Date	Mintage	Identification	Issue Price	Mkt. Val.
MS1	1929(9)	10,000	Y1-9	—	470.00
MS2	1929(8)	10,000	Y1-8	—	170.00
MS3	1930(9)	2,621	Y1-9	—	825.00
MS4	1930(8)	50,000	Y1-8	—	75.00
MS5	1931(9)	3,343	Y1-9	—	575.00
MS6	1931(8)	50,000	Y1-8	—	75.00
MS7	1932(9)	5,073	Y1-9	—	475.00
MS8	1932(8)	50,000	Y1-8	—	75.00
MS9	1933-34(9)	23,235	Y11-19	—	400.00
MS10	1933-34(8)	50,000	Y11-18	—	125.00
MS11	1934(9)	2,533	Y1-9	—	575.00
MS12	1934(8)	30,000	Y1-8	—	75.00
MS13	1935(9)	2,015	Y1-9	—	685.00
MS14	1935(8)	9,000	Y1-8	—	250.00
MS15	1936(9)	8,239	Y1-8,10	—	350.00
MS16	1936(8)	40,000	Y1-8	—	75.00
MS17	1937(9)	2,000	Y1-8,10	—	3075.
MS18	1937(8)	20,000	Y1-8	—	75.00
MS19	1938(3)	—	Y1-2,10	—	Rare
MS20	1939(9)	2,700	Y22-30	—	435.00
MS21	1939(8)	10,000	Y22-29	—	110.00
MS22	1939(2)	30,000	Y20,21	—	60.00

KM#	Date	Mintage	Identification	Issue Price	Mkt. Val.
MS23	1940(9)	2,000	Y22,23,24a-27a,28-30	—	470.00
MS24	1940(8)	10,000	Y22,23,24a-27a,28-29	—	100.00
MS25	1941(9)	2,000	Y22,23,24a-27a,28-30	—	580.00
MS26	1941(8)	4,000	Y22,23,24a-27a,28-29	—	200.00
MS27	1942(9)	2,000	Y31-39	—	630.00
MS28	1942(8)	4,000	Y31-38	—	230.00
MS29	1943(9)	1,000	Y31-39	—	820.00
MS30	1943(8)	1,000	Y31-38	—	320.00
MS31	1944(9)	1,000	Y31-39	—	820.00
MS32	1944(8)	1,000	Y31-38	—	320.00
MS33	1945(9)	1,000	Y31-39	—	820.00
MS34	1945(8)	1,000	Y31-38	—	320.00
MS35	1946(9)	1,000	Y31-39	—	820.00
MS36	1946(8)	1,000	Y31-38	—	320.00
MS37	1947(5)	1,000	Y39-43	—	530.00
MS38	1947(4)	50,000	Y40-43	—	28.00
MS39	1947(2)	—	Y42-43	—	16.00
MS40	1948(5)	5,000	Y39-43	—	280.00
MS41	1948(4)	10,000	Y40-43	—	28.00
MS42	1949(5)	1,000	Y39-43	—	535.00
MS43	1949(4)	10,000	Y40-43	—	35.00
MS44	1950(5)	20,000	Y44-48	—	275.00
MS45	1950(4)	50,000	Y44-47	—	25.00
MS46	1951(5)	1,000	Y49-52,53	—	600.00
MS47	1951(4)	400,000	Y49-52	—	6.00
MS48	1952(5)	1,000	Y49-52,53	—	600.00
MS49	1952(4)	400,000	Y49-52	—	6.00
MS50	1953(5)	1,000	Y49-52,53	—	600.00
MS51	1953(4)	400,000	Y49-52	—	6.00
MS52	1955(7)	1,000	Y49-55	—	620.00
MS53	1955(6)	10,000	Y49-52,54,55	—	20.00
MS54	1956(7)	1,000	Y49-55	—	620.00
MS55	1956(6)	10,000	Y49-52,54,55	—	20.00
MS56	1957(8)	2,000	Y49-A52,A53,54,55	—	315.00
MS57	1957(7)	20,000	Y49-A52,54,55	—	15.00
MS58	1958(8)	3,000	Y49-A52,A53-56	—	340.00
MS59	1958(7)	20,000	Y49-A52,54-56	—	40.00
MS60	1959(9)	3,000	Y58-66	—	1075.
MS61	1959(8)	25,000	Y58-65	—	75.00
MS62	1960(8)	25,000	Y58-62,63.1-65.1	—	75.00
MS63	1961(8)	25,000	Y58-62,63.1-65.1	—	55.00
MS64	1962(8)	25,000	Y58-62,63.1-65.1	—	50.00
MS65	1962(8)	50,000	Y67-74	—	42.50
MS66	1963(8)	60,000	Y76-83	—	70.00
MS68	1964(8)	60,000	Y76-83	—	50.00
MS69	1965(8)	60,000	Y76-83	—	35.00
MS70	1966(8)	90,000	Y84-91	—	28.00
MS71	1967(8)	100,000	Y92-99	3.25	28.00
MS72	1968(8)	100,000	Y100-107	4.20	28.00
MS73	1969(8)	100,000	Y108-115	4.20	28.00
MS74	1970(8)	100,000	Y116-123	5.00	25.00
MS75	1971(8)	110,000	Y116-123	—	22.00
MS76	1972(8)	110,000	Y116-123	6.00	22.00
MS77	1973(8)	120,000	Y116-123	6.75	22.00
MS78	1974(8)	120,000	Y116-123	7.25	22.00
MS79	1975(8)	132,000	Y116-123	9.00	22.00
MS80	1975(8)	170,000	Y124-131	—	25.00
MS81	1976(8)	180,000	Y116-123	—	22.00
MS82	1977(8)	180,000	Y116-122,132	—	25.00
MS83	1978(7)	180,000	Y133-139	—	25.00
MS84	1979(6)	156,000	Y143-148	—	25.00
MS85	1980(6)	—	Y143-148	18.00	25.00
MS86	1981(6)	—	Y155-160	—	25.00
MS87	1982(7)	120,000	Y161-167	—	30.00
MS88	1983(7)	120,000	Y170-176	—	32.00
MS93	1983/84(2)	130,000	Y168-169	—	42.50
MS89	1984(7)	—	Y177-183	—	32.00
MS90	1985(7)	—	Y185-191	—	35.00
MS91	1986(7)	—	Y192-198	23.50	30.00
MS92	1987(7)	—	Y199-205	27.00	27.00
MS93	1987(5)	—	Y200-204	—	10.00
MS94	1988(7)	—	Y206-212	—	27.00
MS95	1989(7)	—	Y213-219	30.00	30.00
MS96	1990(7)	—	Y220-226	33.00	33.00
MS97	1991(7)	—	Y228-234	25.00	25.00
MS98	1992(7)	—	Y236-242	25.00	25.00

The Republic of Venezuela ("Little Venice"), located on the northern coast of South America between Colombia and Guyana, has an area of 352,145 sq. mi. (912,050 sq. km.) and a population of 20 million. Capital: Caracas. Petroleum and mining provide 70 percent of Venezuela's exports although they employ less than 2 percent of the work force. Coffee, grown on 60,000 plantations, is the chief crop.

Columbus discovered Venezuela on his third voyage in 1498. Initial exploration did not reveal Venezuela to be a land of great wealth. An active pearl trade operated on the off-shore islands and slavers raided the interior in search of Indians to be sold into slavery, but no significant mainland settlements were made before 1567 when Caracas was founded. Venezuela, the home of Bolivar, was among the first South American colonies to rebel against Spain in 1810. Independence was attained in 1821 but not recognized by Spain until 1845. Together with Ecuador, Panama and Colombia, Venezuela was part of "Gran Colombia" until 1830, when it became a sovereign and independent state.

RULERS

Spanish, until 1821

MINT MARKS

A - Paris
(a) - Paris, privy marks only
(aa) - Altona
(b) - Berlin
(bb) - Brussels
(c) - Caracas (1886-89 only)
(d) - Denver
H - Heaton, Birmingham
(l) - London
(p) - Philadelphia
(s) - San Francisco

MONETARY SYSTEM

16 Reales = 1 Escudo

PROVINCE OF BARINAS

This province, in west central Venezuela on the Apure plain, was occupied by rebel General Jose Antonio Paez in 1817. With the city of Barinas overrun with refugees, Paez called for all hoarded silver to be turned in to be recoined to facilitate trade. The coins were produced by Juan de Anzola, a local silversmith. When silver supplies became exhausted additional coins were produced by overstriking the earlier Republican copper issues of Cartagena. These coins found disfavor with Simon Bolivar who decreed that they should not circulate outside Barinas province and would be redeemed by the central government.

REPUBLICAN COINAGE

1/2 REAL

COPPER
Overstruck on Colombia Cartagena 1/2 Real, KM#2.
Obv: Small monogram.

KM#	Date	Mintage	Good	VG	Fine	VF
1.1	(1)800(1817)	—	75.00	150.00	250.00	400.00

Obv: Large monogram.

KM#	Date	Mintage	Good	VG	Fine	VF
1.2	(1)800(1817)	—	75.00	150.00	250.00	400.00

SILVER

KM#	Date	Mintage	Good	VG	Fine	VF
3	(1)800(1817) 1 known		—	—	—	1500.

2 REALES

SILVER

KM#	Date	Mintage	Good	VG	Fine	VF
2	(1)800(1817)	2 known	—	300.00	500.00	850.00

COPPER
Overstruck on Columbia Cartagena 2 Reales, KM#1.

KM#	Date	Mintage	Good	VG	Fine	VF
2a	(1)800(817)	—	60.00	120.00	200.00	350.00
	(1)880(817)	—	75.00	150.00	250.00	400.00

PROVINCE OF CARACAS

This province surrounds the national capital, also named Caracas, Spain opened the first mint in Venezuela in that city in November 1802. Coins were made initially from 1802 to 1805. Caracas rebelled on April 19, 1810, and the Spanish retreated, but retook the city in July, 1812 and Royalist coinage resumed. Copper and silver coins were struck through 1821, when Bolivar's troops defeated the Spanish.

ROYALIST COINAGE

1/8 REAL

COPPER

C#	Date	Mintage	Good	VG	Fine	VF
1	1802	.059	200.00	400.00	550.00	900.00
	1804	.019	500.00	800.00	1200.	1700.
	1805	.100	250.00	450.00	650.00	950.00
	1814	.012	200.00	375.00	550.00	850.00
	1817	4,500	800.00	1200.	1700.	2500.
	1818	.094	75.00	100.00	175.00	250.00

1/4 REAL

COPPER

C#	Date	Mintage	Good	VG	Fine	VF
2	1802	.014	500.00	700.00	1100.	1700.
	1804	6,589	1100.	1600.	2500.	4000.
	1805	.070	400.00	600.00	1000.	1500.
	1813	.010	11.50	25.00	45.00	75.00
	1814/3	.040	8.00	20.00	35.00	50.00
	1814	Inc. Ab.	8.00	15.00	30.00	45.00
	1816	.750	4.00	8.00	25.00	35.00

Small date **Large date**

C#	Date	Mintage	Good	VG	Fine	VF
	1817 large date	.490	2.00	4.00	10.00	20.00
	1817 small date	1.640	1.75	3.75	9.00	17.50
	1818	2.240	1.75	3.75	9.00	17.50
	1821	.650	2.50	5.00	15.00	30.00

REAL

SILVER, 2.45-3.25 g

C#	Date	Mintage	Good	VG	Fine	VF
5	1817 BS	6,500	700.00	1200.	1800.	3500.
	1818 BS	.014	250.00	450.00	550.00	900.00
	1820 BS	.011	400.00	500.00	800.00	1500.
	1821 BS	8,000	500.00	600.00	1000.	2500.

2 REALES

SILVER, 23-25mm,4.3-5.3 g

C#	Date	Mintage	Good	VG	Fine	VF
6.1	1817 BS	.076	40.00	70.00	130.00	200.00
	1818 BS	.777	6.75	13.50	22.50	37.50
	1819/8 BS	1.450	6.75	13.50	22.50	32.50
	1819 BS	I.A.	6.75	13.50	22.50	32.50
	1820 BS	.755	8.50	17.50	35.00	70.00
	1821 BS	.110	13.50	27.50	55.00	90.00

NOTE: Beware of contemporary counterfeits struck in German silver, (copper-nickel-zinc alloy).

4 REALES

SILVER, 9.50-10.30 g

C#	Date	Mintage	Good	VG	Fine	VF
7	1819 BS	.018	350.00	600.00	1000.	1650.
	1820 BS	.029	350.00	600.00	1000.	1650.

NOTE: Die varieties exist.

ROYALIST and/or REPUBLICAN COINAGE

REAL

SILVER, 2.4-3.0 g
Resembles Lima cob of 18th century.
Obv: L-M. Rev: M-L.

C#	Date	Good	VG	Fine	VF
12	(1810-21) LM*	25.00	50.00	90.00	150.00

2 REALES

SILVER
Obv: L-M. Rev: M-L.

C#	Date	Good	VG	Fine	VF
13	(1810-21) LM	13.50	22.00	37.50	65.00

NOTE: Of the many actual, false and blundered dates, the following have been noted: 184, 231, 816, 471, 817, 814, 751, 142, 182, 1816, 1817, 931, 781, 172, 174 and 718.

REPUBLICAN COINAGE

1812

19 refers to 19 April 1810, date of the Declaration of Independence.

1/8 REAL

COPPER
Caracas Mint

C#	Date	Mintage	Good	VG	Fine	VF
21	1812	7,000	150.00	225.00	500.00	800.00

1/4 REAL

COPPER, 26-30mm

C#	Date	Mintage	Good	VG	Fine	VF
22	1812	.030	35.00	65.00	90.00	150.00

1/2 REAL

SILVER
Obv: Large "1/2".

C#	Date	Mintage	Good	VG	Fine	VF
25.1	Ano 2(1812)	.016	550.00	700.00	1000.	1600.

Obv: Small "1/2" over "D - R".

C#	Date	Mintage	Good	VG	Fine	VF
25.2	Ano 2(1812) 2 pcs. known	—	—	Rare	—	

REAL

SILVER

C#	Date	Mintage	Good	VG	Fine	VF
26	Ano 2(1812)	.020	350.00	550.00	800.00	1500.

Under Gran Colombia

1/4 REAL

SILVER

C#	Date	Mintage	Good	VG	Fine	VF
31	1821	.090	100.00	175.00	400.00	700.00
	1822	.540	55.00	85.00	200.00	400.00

C#	Date	Mintage	Good	VG	Fine	VF
34	1829	.750	9.00	18.50	33.00	75.00
	1830	.650	12.50	22.50	37.50	85.00

1/2 REAL

SILVER

C#	Date	Mintage	Good	VG	Fine	VF
35	1829 O1 known	—	—	—	—	

PROVINCE OF GUAYANA

Coinage for this province in eastern Venezuela was authorized by an act of October 26, 1813. This was to alleviate the coin shortage caused by the isolation of the province from other Spanish forces. Around 1900, it was incorporated into British Guiana.

ROYALIST COINAGE

1/4 REAL

COPPER

C#	Date	Mintage	Good	VG	Fine	VF
40	1813	—	500.00	800.00	1200.	1600.
	1815	—	Reported, not confirmed			

1/2 REAL

COPPER

C#	Date	Mintage	Good	VG	Fine	VF
41	1813	—	22.50	40.00	100.00	200.00
	1814	—	3.50	9.00	25.00	60.00
	1815	—	3.50	9.00	25.00	60.00
	1816	—	7.00	13.50	27.50	65.00
	1817	—	3.50	9.00	25.00	60.00

NOTE: These types generally have only partial dates visible, examples with full clear dates command a premium.

PROVINCE OF MARACAIBO

A province in northwestern Venezuela includes the city of Maracaibo, situated on the channel between Lake Maracaibo and the Caribbean. This crude coinage was presumably necessary because of the temporary isolation of local Royalist forces from the main Spanish armies.

ROYALIST COINAGE

1/4 REAL

COPPER

KM#	Date	Mintage	Good	VG	Fine	VF
1	ND	—	25.00	55.00	90.00	150.00

1/2 REAL

COPPER

C#	Date	Mintage	Good	VG	Fine	VF
10	1813	—	135.00	250.00	385.00	550.00

2/4 REAL

COPPER

KM#	Date	Mintage	Good	VG	Fine	VF
3	ND	—	35.00	60.00	120.00	200.00

NOTE: Varieties exist.

REPUBLIC OF VENEZUELA

MONETARY SYSTEM

10 Centavos = 1 Real
10 Reales = 1 Peso

1/4 CENTAVO

COPPER, 2.9-3.0 g

Y#	Date	Mintage	VG	Fine	VF	XF
1	1843WW	3.840	2.00	7.50	22.50	55.00
	1852H	2.000	2.25	8.50	40.00	120.00

2.7 g

4	1852	4.000	2.00	7.50	22.50	55.00

1/2 CENTAVO

COPPER, 24mm, 5.7-6.0 g

2	1843WW	.960	2.75	9.50	25.00	70.00
	1843WW	—	—	—	Proof	300.00
	1852H	.500	4.50	13.50	40.00	150.00

22mm, 5.4 g

5	1852	1.000	2.75	9.50	25.00	70.00

CENTAVO

COPPER, 32mm, 11.4-12.1 g

3	1843WWYON	.480	13.50	32.50	70.00	150.00
	1852HEATON	.250	6.00	15.00	37.50	0.00

30mm, 10.9 g

6	1852	.500	4.00	9.50	27.50	75.00

Engrailed edge, thick planchet, 7.5 g.

7	1858 HEATON w/LIBERTAD incuse	1.000	2.00	6.00	15.00	40.00
	1858 HEATON w/LIBERTAD in relief	1.000	2.00	6.00	15.00	40.00
	1862HEATON	1.500	1.75	5.00	13.50	35.00
	1863HEATON	.500	3.50	9.00	22.50	60.00

1/2 REAL

1.1500 g, .900 SILVER, .0333 oz ASW
Similar to 2 Reales, Y#10 but value shown as 1-1/2 Real, erroneously.

8	1858A	.040	80.00	175.00	450.00	900.00

REAL

2.3000 g, .900 SILVER, .0666 oz ASW
Similar to 2 Reales, Y#10.

Y#	Date	Mintage	VG	Fine	VF	XF
9	1858A	.042	60.00	150.00	300.00	700.00

2 REALES

SILVER
Rev: Cross between 2 rosettes.

C#	Date	Mintage	Good	VG	Fine	VF
36	1818(1830)BS	.268	12.50	18.50	35.00	60.00

4.6000 g, .900 SILVER, .1331 oz ASW

Y#	Date	Mintage	VG	Fine	VF	XF
10	1858A	.030	80.00	185.00	350.00	825.00

5 REALES

11.5000 g, .900 SILVER, .3328 oz ASW

11	1858A	.026	65.00	160.00	340.00	850.00

10 REALES

SILVER

Y#	Date	Mintage	Fine	VF	XF	Unc
A11	1863A	*.300	—	—	4000.	7000.

***NOTE:** Almost entire issue melted, estimated 200 pcs. survived.

MONETARY REFORM

(1871-79)
100 Centavos = 1 Venezolano

CENTAVO

COPPER-NICKEL

Y#	Date	Mintage	VG	Fine	VF	XF
25	1876(P)	8.000	3.50	5.00	12.50	40.00
	1877(P)	2.000	5.00	8.00	20.00	55.00

2-1/2 CENTAVOS

COPPER-NICKEL

Y#	Date	Mintage	VG	Fine	VF	XF
26	1876(P)	1.500	5.00	10.00	25.00	80.00
	1877(P)	.500	6.00	15.00	35.00	100.00

5 CENTAVOS

1.2500 g, .835 SILVER, .0336 oz ASW

12	1874A	.800	3.50	5.00	15.00	35.00
	1876A	.520	4.00	9.00	20.00	50.00

10 CENTAVOS

2.5000 g, .835 SILVER, .0671 oz ASW

13	1874A	.800	4.50	12.00	22.00	50.00
	1876A	.280	10.00	25.00	60.00	140.00

20 CENTAVOS

5.0000 g, .835 SILVER, .1342 oz ASW

14	1874A	.400	10.00	20.00	40.00	120.00
	1876A	.136	20.00	45.00	100.00	300.00

50 CENTAVOS

12.5000 g, .835 SILVER, .3356 oz ASW

15	1873A	.200	20.00	50.00	100.00	525.00
	1874A	.200	20.00	50.00	100.00	525.00
	1876A	.158	25.00	60.00	120.00	550.00

VENEZOLANO

25.0000 g, .900 SILVER, .7234 oz ASW

16	1876A	.035	45.00	100.00	200.00	1000.
	1876A	—	—	—	Proof	7500.

5 VENEZOLANOS

8.0645 g, .900 GOLD, .2333 oz AGW

Y#	Date	Mintage	Fine	VF	XF	Unc
17	1875A	.069	115.00	200.00	300.00	550.00

MONETARY REFORM

100 Centimos = 1 Bolivar

5 CENTIMOS

COPPER-NICKEL

Y#	Date	Mintage	Fine	VF	XF	Unc
27	1896(b)	4.000	.50	2.00	12.50	55.00
	1915(p)	2.000	1.00	4.00	35.00	135.00
	1921(p)	2.000	.50	2.00	15.00	80.00
	1925(p)	2.000	.30	1.00	6.00	15.00
	1927(p)	2.000	.30	1.00	6.00	15.00
	1929(p)	2.000	.25	1.00	6.00	15.00
	1936(p)	5.000	.15	.50	4.00	8.00
	1938(p)	6.000	.10	.20	3.00	5.00

BRASS

Y#	Date	Mintage	Fine	VF	XF	Unc
29	1944(d)	4.000	.50	1.00	3.50	10.00

COPPER-NICKEL

Y#	Date	Mintage	Fine	VF	XF	Unc
29a	1945(p)	12.000	.10	.20	.40	1.50
	1946(p)	12.000	.10	.20	.40	1.50
	1948(p)	18.000	.10	.20	.30	1.50

Y#	Date	Mintage	Fine	VF	XF	Unc
38	1958(p)	25.000	—	—	.10	.30
38.1	1964	40.000	—	—	.10	.20
	1965	60.000	—	—	.10	.20
38.2	1971	40.000	—	—	.10	.20

COPPER-CLAD STEEL

Y#	Date	Mintage	Fine	VF	XF	Unc
49	1974	200.000	—	—	—	.15
	1976	200.000	—	—	—	.15
	1977	600.000	—	—	—	.15

NICKEL-CLAD STEEL

Y#	Date	Mintage	Fine	VF	XF	Unc
49a	1982	600.000	—	—	—	.10
	1983	600.000	—	—	—	.10

COPPER-NICKEL CLAD STEEL

Y#	Date	Mintage	Fine	VF	XF	Unc
49b	1986	500.000	—	—	—	.10

10 CENTIMOS

COPPER-NICKEL

Y#	Date	Mintage	Fine	VF	XF	Unc
A40	1971	60.000	—	—	.10	.25

12-1/2 CENTIMOS

COPPER-NICKEL

Y#	Date	Mintage	Fine	VF	XF	Unc
28	1896(b)	6.000	1.00	4.00	20.00	100.00
	1925(p)	.800	2.00	6.00	45.00	150.00
	1927(p)	.800	1.00	2.00	18.00	60.00
	1929(p)	.800	.15	.50	7.50	35.00
	1936(p)	1.200	.15	.30	3.50	20.00
	1938(p)	1.600	.15	.30	1.50	10.00

NOTE: Varieties exist.

BRASS

Y#	Date	Mintage	Fine	VF	XF	Unc
30	1944(d)	.800	2.00	4.00	8.00	60.00

COPPER-NICKEL

Y#	Date	Mintage	Fine	VF	XF	Unc
30a	1945(p)	11.200	.10	.20	.35	2.00
	1946(p)	9.200	.10	.20	.35	3.00
	1948(s)	6.000	.10	.20	.35	2.00

Obv: Large date.

Y#	Date	Mintage	Fine	VF	XF	Unc
39	1958(p)	10.000	—	—	.10	.50

Obv: Small date.

Y#	Date	Mintage	Fine	VF	XF	Unc
39.1	1969	1.500	—	—	—	150.00

25 CENTIMOS

1.2500 g, .835 SILVER, .0336 oz ASW

Y#	Date	Mintage	Fine	VF	XF	Unc
35	1954(p)	36.000	—	—	BV	1.00

Y#	Date	Mintage	Fine	VF	XF	Unc
35a	1960(a)	48.000	—	—	BV	.75

NICKEL

Y#	Date	Mintage	Fine	VF	XF	Unc
40	1965(aa)	240.000	—	—	.10	.30

1.75 g, 1.18mm thick

Y#	Date	Mintage	Fine	VF	XF	Unc
50	1977	240.000	—	—	.10	.20

NICKEL-CLAD STEEL, 1.50 g

Y#	Date	Mintage	Fine	VF	XF	Unc
50a	1978	200.000	—	—	.10	.20
	1987	150.000	—	—	.10	.20
50a	1989	—	—	—	.10	.20
	1990	—	—	—	.10	.20

NOTE: Varieties exist.

50 CENTIMOS

2.5000 g, .835 SILVER, .0671 OZ ASW

Y#	Date	Mintage	Fine	VF	XF	Unc
36	1954(p)	15.000	—	—	BV	2.00

Y#	Date	Mintage	Fine	VF	XF	Unc
36a	1960(a)	20.000	—	—	BV	1.50

NICKEL

Y#	Date	Mintage	Fine	VF	XF	Unc
41	1965(l)	180.000	—	.10	.15	.25
	1985	50.000	—	.10	.15	.25

NICKEL CLAD STEEL

Y#	Date	Mintage	Fine	VF	XF	Unc
41a	1988	100.000	—	.10	.15	.25
	1989	—	—	.10	.15	.25
	1990	—	—	.10	.15	.25

1/5 BOLIVAR

1.0000 g, .835 SILVER, .0268 oz ASW

Y#	Date	Mintage	VG	Fine	VF	XF
19	1879(bb)	.125	100.00	150.00	250.00	600.00

NOTE: Coin recalled and many melted upon issuance of the 1/4 Bolivar in 1894.

1/4 BOLIVAR

1.2500 g, .835 SILVER, .0336 oz ASW

Y#	Date	Mintage	Fine	VF	XF	Unc
20	1894A	2.000	1.50	3.00	8.00	20.00
	1900(a)	.407	4.00	12.00	25.00	80.00
	1901(a)	.393	5.00	15.00	45.00	125.00
	1903(p)	.400	5.00	15.00	45.00	125.00
	1911(a)	.600	2.00	3.00	10.00	40.00
	1912(a)	.800	3.00	5.00	15.00	50.00
	1919(p)	.400	2.00	3.00	10.00	50.00
	1921(p)	.800	1.50	3.00	8.00	30.00
	1924(p)	.400	1.50	3.00	8.00	30.00
	1929(p)	1.200	—	BV	1.00	6.00
	1935(p)	3.400	—	BV	1.00	3.00
	1936(p)	2.800	—	BV	1.00	3.00
	1944(p)	1.800	—	BV	1.00	2.00
	1945(p)	8.000	—	—	BV	1.50
	1946(p)	8.000	—	—	BV	1.00
	1948(s)	8.638	—	—	BV	1.00

1/2 BOLIVAR

2.5000 g, .835 SILVER, .0671 oz ASW

Y#	Date	Mintage	Fine	VF	XF	Unc
21	1879(bb)	.200	35.00	85.00	250.00	650.00
	1886(c)	.300	18.00	35.00	100.00	250.00
	1887(c)	.310	50.00	100.00	250.00	650.00
	1888(c)	.230	350.00	550.00	950.00	1850.
	1889(c)	.080	2000.	—	—	—
	1893A	.500	12.50	25.00	100.00	250.00
	1900A	.600	15.00	35.00	150.00	300.00
	1900(a)	—	30.00	50.00	200.00	400.00
	1901(a)	.600	15.00	35.00	150.00	300.00
	1903(p)	.200	50.00	100.00	300.00	700.00
	1911(a)	.300	25.00	50.00	200.00	400.00
	1912(a)	1.920	4.00	8.00	35.00	120.00
	1919(p)	.400	5.00	10.00	50.00	150.00

Y#	Date	Mintage	Fine	VF	XF	Unc
21	1921(p)	.600	2.00	6.00	15.00	50.00
	1924(p)	.800	2.00	6.00	15.00	50.00
	1929(p)	.400	1.00	2.00	7.50	20.00
	1935(p)	1.000	—	BV	1.00	7.00
	1936(p)	.600	1.00	2.00	5.00	20.00

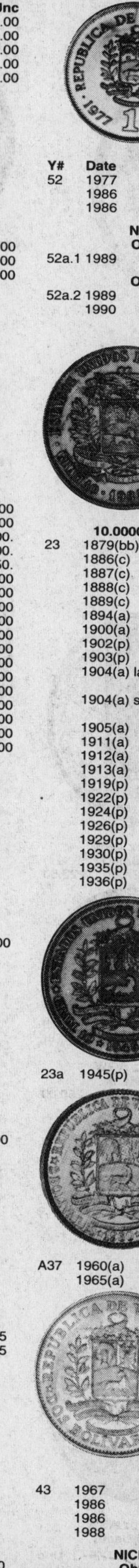

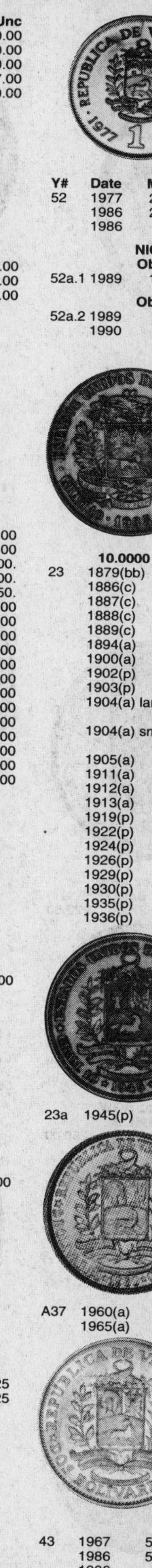

Y#	Date	Mintage	Fine	VF	XF	Unc
21a	1944(d)	.500	BV	1.00	3.00	6.00
	1945(p)	4.000	—	BV	1.00	4.00
	1946(p)	2.500	—	BV	1.00	4.00

BOLIVAR

5.0000 g, .835 SILVER, .1342 oz ASW

Y#	Date	Mintage	Fine	VF	XF	Unc
22	1879(bb)	.375	25.00	75.00	300.00	850.00
	1886(c)	.600	20.00	40.00	200.00	700.00
	1887(c)	.280	125.00	300.00	650.00	1200.
	1888(c)	.197	150.00	350.00	750.00	1400.
	1889(c)	.118	150.00	350.00	750.00	1450.
	1893(a)	.500	10.00	25.00	75.00	200.00
	1900(a)	.380	15.00	40.00	100.00	250.00
	1901(a)	.323	20.00	40.00	100.00	300.00
	1903(p)	.800	5.00	15.00	65.00	200.00
	1911(a)	1.500	3.00	5.00	25.00	100.00
	1912(a)	.820	5.00	15.00	70.00	250.00
	1919(p)	1.000	2.00	4.00	10.00	45.00
	1921(p)	1.000	2.00	4.00	10.00	40.00
	1924(p)	1.500	BV	1.50	5.00	30.00
	1926(p)	1.000	BV	1.50	5.00	30.00
	1929(p)	2.500	—	BV	1.50	7.00
	1935(p)	5.000	—	BV	1.50	4.00
	1936(p)	5.000	—	BV	1.50	4.00

Y#	Date	Mintage	Fine	VF	XF	Unc
22a	1945(p)	8.000	—	—	BV	3.00

Y#	Date	Mintage	Fine	VF	XF	Unc
37	1954(p)	13.500	—	—	BV	2.00

Y#	Date	Mintage	Fine	VF	XF	Unc
37a	1960(a)	30.000	—	—	BV	1.25
	1965(a)	20.000	—	—	BV	1.25

NICKEL

Y#	Date	Mintage	Fine	VF	XF	Unc
42	1967	180.000	—	.10	.15	.50

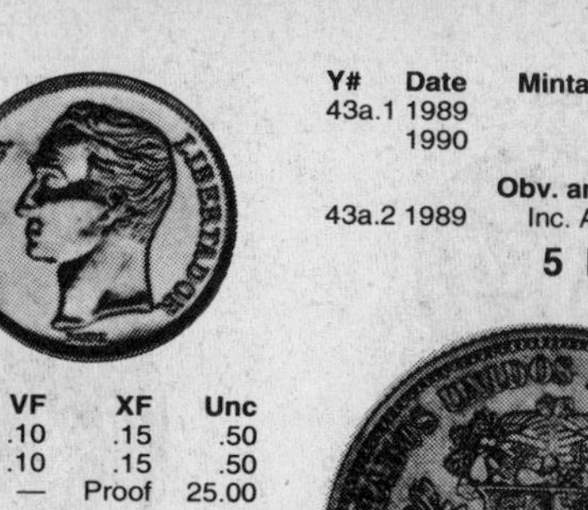

Y#	Date	Mintage	Fine	VF	XF	Unc
52	1977	200.000	—	.10	.15	.50
	1986	200.000	—	.10	.15	.50
	1986	50.000	—	—	Proof	25.00

NICKEL-CLAD STEEL, 4.2 g
Obv. and rev: Small letters.

Y#	Date	Mintage	Fine	VF	XF	Unc
52a.1	1989	100.000	—	.10	.15	.50

Obv. and rev: Large letters.

Y#	Date	Mintage	Fine	VF	XF	Unc
52a.2	1989	Inc. Ab.	—	.10	.15	.50
	1990	—	—	.10	.15	.50

2 BOLIVARES

10.0000 g, .835 SILVER, .2685 oz ASW

Y#	Date	Mintage	Fine	VF	XF	Unc
23	1879(bb)	.375	20.00	75.00	300.00	750.00
	1886(c)	.240	50.00	200.00	500.00	1200.
	1887(c)	.200	10.00	50.00	150.00	350.00
	1888(c)	.141	50.00	200.00	500.00	1200.
	1889(c)	.050	50.00	200.00	500.00	1200.
	1894(a)	.250	15.00	40.00	250.00	600.00
	1900(a)	.350	12.50	30.00	150.00	350.00
	1902(p)	.500	10.00	30.00	120.00	375.00
	1903(p)	.500	10.00	20.00	120.00	350.00
	1904(a) large 4	.500	5.00	15.00	100.00	400.00
	1904(a) small 4	.050	10.00	20.00	100.00	500.00
	1905(a)	.750	3.00	15.00	100.00	300.00
	1911(a)	.750	3.00	15.00	50.00	200.00
	1912(a)	.500	3.00	15.00	100.00	300.00
	1913(a)	.210	15.00	35.00	175.00	400.00
	1919(p)	1.000	BV	3.00	10.00	60.00
	1922(p)	1.000	BV	3.00	10.00	50.00
	1924(p)	1.250	BV	3.00	10.00	50.00
	1926(p)	1.000	BV	3.00	10.00	50.00
	1929(p)	1.500	BV	2.50	8.00	20.00
	1930(p)	.425	2.50	7.00	25.00	130.00
	1935(p)	3.000	BV	2.50	3.50	6.00
	1936(p)	2.500	BV	2.50	3.50	6.00

Y#	Date	Mintage	Fine	VF	XF	Unc
23a	1945(p)	3.000	—	BV	2.50	3.50

Y#	Date	Mintage	Fine	VF	XF	Unc
A37	1960(a)	4.000	—	—	BV	3.00
	1965(a)	7.170	—	—	BV	3.00

NICKEL

Y#	Date	Mintage	Fine	VF	XF	Unc
43	1967	50.000	—	.15	.25	1.00
	1986	50.000	—	.15	.25	1.00
	1986	—	—	—	Proof	—
	1988	80.000	—	.15	.25	1.00

NICKEL CLAD STEEL, 7.50 g
Obv. and rev: Small letters.

Y#	Date	Mintage	Fine	VF	XF	Unc
43a.1	1989	—	—	.15	.25	1.00
	1990	—	—	.15	.25	1.00

Obv. and rev: Large letters.

Y#	Date	Mintage	Fine	VF	XF	Unc
43a.2	1989	Inc. Ab.	—	.15	.25	1.00

5 BOLIVARES

25.0000 g, .900 SILVER, .7234 oz ASW

Y#	Date	Mintage	Fine	VF	XF	Unc
24	1879(bb)	.250	10.00	60.00	225.00	800.00
	1886(c)	.470	10.00	30.00	150.00	400.00
	1887(c)	.500	10.00	35.00	225.00	600.00
	1888(c)	.281	10.00	35.00	225.00	700.00
	1889(c)	.329	10.00	35.00	225.00	700.00
	1900(a)	.270	10.00	25.00	150.00	500.00
	1901(a)	.090	15.00	100.00	450.00	1100.
	1902(p)	.500	8.00	15.00	100.00	500.00
	1903(p)	.200	8.00	15.00	100.00	500.00
	1904(a)	.200	8.00	15.00	125.00	600.00
	1905(a)	.300	8.00	15.00	100.00	450.00
	1910(a)	.400	8.00	15.00	75.00	350.00
	1911(a)	1.104	6.00	12.00	40.00	225.00
	1912(a)	.696	6.00	12.00	40.00	225.00
	1919(p)	.400	6.00	12.00	25.00	175.00
	1921(p)	.500	6.00	12.00	20.00	100.00
	1924(p)	.500	6.00	12.00	20.00	100.00
	1926(p)	.800	6.00	12.00	20.00	80.00
	1929(p)	.800	6.00	12.00	20.00	60.00
	1935(p)	1.600	BV	10.00	15.00	35.00
	1936(p)	2.000	BV	10.00	15.00	35.00

NICKEL

Y#	Date	Mintage	Fine	VF	XF	Unc
44	1973	20.000	—	.50	.75	1.50

Y#	Date	Mintage	Fine	VF	XF	Unc
53	1977	60.000	—	.25	.50	1.00
	1987	25.000	—	.25	.50	1.00
	1987	—	—	—	Proof	30.00
	1988	20.000	—	.25	.50	1.00

NICKEL-CLAD STEEL, 13.3 g
Obv: Small letters. Rev: Large letters.

Y#	Date	Mintage	Fine	VF	XF	Unc
53a.1	1989	40.000	—	.25	.50	1.00
	1989	—	—	—	Proof	30.00

Obv: Large letters. Rev: Small letters.

Y#	Date	Mintage	Fine	VF	XF	Unc
53a.2	1989	—	—	.25	.50	1.00
	1990	—	—	.25	.50	1.00

10 BOLIVARES

3.2258 g, .900 GOLD, .0933 oz AGW

Y#	Date	Mintage	Fine	VF	XF	Unc
31	1930	*.500	BV	45.00	55.00	85.00

NOTE: Only 10% of the total mintage was released. The balance remaining as part of the nation's gold reserve.

30.0000 g, .900 SILVER, .8681 oz ASW
Centennial of Bolivar Portrait on Coinage

Y#	Date	Mintage	VF	XF	Unc	
45	1973	2.000	—	—	8.00	12.00

20 BOLIVARES

6.4516 g, .900 GOLD, .1867 oz AGW

Y#	Date	Mintage	Fine	VF	XF	Unc
32	1879	.041	BV	100.00	150.00	300.00
	1880	.084	BV	100.00	110.00	300.00
	1886	.023	BV	130.00	150.00	200.00
	1887	.132	115.00	160.00	220.00	500.00
	1888	.081	100.00	150.00	200.00	450.00
	1904(a)	.100	BV	90.00	100.00	125.00
	1905(a)	.100	BV	90.00	100.00	125.00
	1910(a)	.070	BV	90.00	100.00	125.00
	1911(a)	.080	BV	90.00	100.00	125.00
	1912(a)	.150	BV	90.00	100.00	125.00

25 BOLIVARES

28.2800 g, .925 SILVER, .8411 oz ASW
Conservation - Jaguar

Y#	Date	Mintage	VF	XF	Unc
46	1975	.200	—	—	20.00
	1975	.030	—	Proof	30.00

50 BOLIVARES

35.0000 g, .925 SILVER, 1.0409 oz ASW
Conservation - Giant Armadillo
Obv: Similar to 25 Bolivares, Y#46.

Y#	Date	Mintage	VF	XF	Unc
47	1975	.200	—	—	25.00
	1975	.030	—	Proof	30.00

31.1000 g, .900 SILVER, .9000 oz ASW
50th Anniversary of Central Bank

Y#	Date	Mintage	VF	XF	Unc
66	1990	—	—	Proof	22.50

15.5500 g, .900 GOLD, .4500 oz AGW
50th Anniversary of Central Bank

Y#	Date	Mintage	VF	XF	Unc
67	1990	—	—	Proof	250.00

75 BOLIVARES

17.0000 g, .900 SILVER, .4920 oz ASW
150th Anniversary of Sucre's Death

Y#	Date	Mintage	Fine	VF	XF	Unc
55	1980	.500	—	—	—	12.50

100 BOLIVARES

32.2580 g, .900 GOLD, .9334 oz AGW

Y#	Date	Mintage	Fine	VF	XF	Unc
34	1886	4,250	BV	600.00	700.00	1000.
	1887	.028	BV	600.00	700.00	1000.
	1888	.032	BV	600.00	700.00	1000.
	1889	.023	BV	600.00	700.00	1000.

22.0000 g, .900 SILVER, .6367 oz ASW
150th Anniversary of Bolivar's Death

Y#	Date	Mintage	Fine	VF	XF	Unc
56	1980	.500	—	—	—	18.00

27.0000 g, .835 SILVER, .7249 oz ASW
200th Anniversary of Birth of Andres Bello

Y#	Date	Mintage	VF	XF	Unc	
57	1981	.500	—	—	Proof	18.00

31.1000 g, .900 SILVER, .9000 oz ASW
200th Anniversary of Birth of Simon Bolivar

Y#	Date	Mintage	Fine	VF	XF	Unc
58	1983	.300	—	—	Proof	25.00

200th Anniversary of Birth of Jose M. Vargas

Y#	Date	Mintage	Fine	VF	XF	Unc
60	1986	.500	—	—	—	15.00
	1986	500 pcs.	—	—	Proof	200.00

500 BOLIVARES

18.0000 g, .900 GOLD, .5209 oz AGW
Nationalization of Oil Industry

Y#	Date	Mintage	VF	XF	Unc
54	1975	100 pcs.	—	—	9000.

31.1000 g, .900 SILVER, .9000 oz ASW
Jose Antonio Paez

Y#	Date	Mintage	VF	XF	Unc
64	1990	.030	—	Proof	25.00

Battle of Matasiete

Y#	Date	Mintage	VF	XF	Unc
69	1992	—	—	Proof	25.00

1000 BOLIVARES

33.4370 g, .900 GOLD, .9676 oz AGW
Conservation Series - Cock of the Rock

Y#	Date	Mintage	VF	XF	Unc
48	1975	*.010	—	—	450.00
	1975	*3,000	—	Proof	850.00

NOTE: An unknown quantity of proof coins was melted.

1100 BOLIVARES

27.0000 g, .925 SILVER, .8029 oz ASW
Ibero - American Series

Y#	Date	Mintage	VF	XF	Unc
68	1991	.060	—	Proof	45.00

3000 BOLIVARES

31.1000 g, .900 GOLD, .9000 oz AGW
200th Anniversary of Birth of Simon Bolivar

Y#	Date	Mintage	VF	XF	Unc
59	1983	.010	—	Proof	450.00

5000 BOLIVARES

15.5500 g, .900 GOLD, .4500 oz AGW
Rafael Urdaneta

Y#	Date	Mintage	VF	XF	Unc
62	1988	.025	—	Proof	250.00

Santiago Marino

Y#	Date	Mintage	VF	XF	Unc
63	1988	.025	—	Proof	250.00

Jose Antonio Paez

Y#	Date	Mintage	VF	XF	Unc
65	1990	.010	—	Proof	275.00

10,000 BOLIVARES

31.1000 g, .900 GOLD, .9000 oz AGW

Y#	Date	Mintage	VF	XF	Unc
61	1987	.050 .	—	Proof	450.00

MINT SETS (MS)

KM#	Date	Mintage	Identification	Issue Price	Mkt. Val.
MS1	1975(3)	—	Y46-48	250.00	500.00

PROOF SETS (PS)

KM#	Date	Mintage	Identification	Issue Price	Mkt. Val.
PS1	1975(3)	—	Y46-48	—	900.00

LEPROSARIUM COINAGE (L)

The Venezuelan Government maintained a large leper colony on Providencia Island, in Lake Maracaibo, where several hundred persons suffering from Hansen's disease were cared for. To provide for monetary transactions on the island, and to prevent ordinary coins from returning to general circulation after being handled by lepers, the Venezuelan Government formerly provided a distinctive currency. They had value only on the island until 30 years ago, when the illness was almost extinguished in South America and medical research revealed that little risk was involved in handling these coins.

MARACAIBO LAZARETO NACIONAL

5 CENTIMOS

BRASS

KM#	Date	Mintage	VG	Fine	VF	XF
L8	1913	—	—	—	—	—
	1916	—	4.50	8.00	15.00	28.00

1/8 BOLIVAR

BRASS

KM#	Date	Mintage	VG	Fine	VF	XF
L1	1913	—	5.00	10.00	20.00	35.00
	1916	—	—	—	—	—

COPPER-NICKEL

KM#	Date	Mintage	VG	Fine	VF	XF
L1a	1913	—	—	—	Rare	—

1/2 BOLIVAR

BRASS
Similar to 1/8 Bolivar, KM#L1.

KM#	Date	Mintage	VG	Fine	VF	XF
L2	1913	—	65.00	85.00	125.00	—
	1916	—	—	—	—	—

BOLIVAR

BRASS

Similar to 1/8 Bolivar, KM#L1.

KM#	Date	Mintage	VG	Fine	VF	XF
L3	1913	—	85.00	110.00	175.00	—
	1916	—	—	—	—	—

2 BOLIVARES

BRASS

Obv: Similar to 20 Bolivares, KM#L7.

KM#	Date	Mintage	VG	Fine	VF	XF
L4	1913	—	85.00	110.00	175.00	—
	1916	—	—	—	—	—

5 BOLIVARES

BRASS

Similar to 1/8 Bolivar, KM#L1.

KM#	Date	Mintage	VG	Fine	VF	XF
L5	1913	—	95.00	125.00	200.00	—
	1916	—	—	—	—	—

10 BOLIVARES

BRASS

Similar to 1/8 Bolivar, KM#L1.

KM#	Date	Mintage	VG	Fine	VF	XF
L6	1913	—	95.00	125.00	200.00	—
	1916	—	—	—	—	—

20 BOLIVARES

BRASS

Rev: Similar to 2 Bolivares, KM#L4.

KM#	Date	Mintage	VG	Fine	VF	XF
L7	1913	—	150.00	200.00	300.00	—
	1916	—	—	—	—	—

ISLA DE PROVIDENCIA

0.05 BOLIVAR

(5 Centimos)

BRASS

KM#	Date	Mintage	VG	Fine	VF	XF
L20	1939	—	3.00	6.00	10.00	20.00

0.12-1/2 BOLIVAR

(12-1/2 Centimos)

BRASS

KM#	Date	Mintage	VG	Fine	VF	XF
L21	1939	—	3.50	6.50	12.50	22.00

COPPER-NICKEL

KM#	Date	Mintage	VG	Fine	VF	XF
L21a	1939	—	—	—	Rare	—

0.50 BOLIVAR

(50 Centimos)

SILVER

KM#	Date	Mintage	VG	Fine	VF	XF
L22	1939	—	65.00	85.00	125.00	—

1 BOLIVAR

BRASS

KM#	Date	Mintage	VG	Fine	VF	XF
L23	1939	—	85.00	110.00	175.00	—

2 BOLIVARES

BRASS

KM#	Date	Mintage	VG	Fine	VF	XF
L24	1939	—	85.00	110.00	175.00	—

5 BOLIVARES

BRASS

KM#	Date	Mintage	VG	Fine	VF	XF
L25	1939	—	95.00	125.00	200.00	—

10 BOLIVARES

BRASS

KM#	Date	Mintage	VG	Fine	VF	XF
L26	1939	—	100.00	135.00	220.00	—

CABO BLANCO

A leper hospital located in Maiquetia near the capitol city of Caracas. Coins were struck in 1936 for this colony.

0.05 BOLIVAR

(5 Centimos)

BRASS

KM#	Date	Mintage	VG	Fine	VF	XF
L10	1936	—	—	—	—	—

0.12-1/2 BOLIVAR

(12-1/2 CENTIMOS)

BRASS

KM#	Date	Mintage	VG	Fine	VF	XF
L11	1936	—	75.00	100.00	150.00	—

0.50 BOLIVAR

(50 Centimos)

BRASS

KM#	Date	Mintage	VG	Fine	VF	XF
L12	1936	—	85.00	110.00	175.00	—

BOLIVAR

BRASS

KM#	Date	Mintage	VG	Fine	VF	XF
L13	1936	—	100.00	150.00	250.00	—

2 BOLIVARES

BRASS

KM#	Date	Mintage	VG	Fine	VF	XF
L14	1936	—	100.00	150.00	250.00	—

5 BOLIVARES

BRASS

KM#	Date	Mintage	VG	Fine	VF	XF
L15	1936	—	120.00	180.00	300.00	—

10 BOLIVARES

BRASS

KM#	Date	Mintage	VG	Fine	VF	XF
L16	1936	—	—	—	—	—

20 BOLIVARES

BRASS

KM#	Date	Mintage	VG	Fine	VF	XF
L17	1936	—	—	—	—	—

VIETNAM/ANNAM

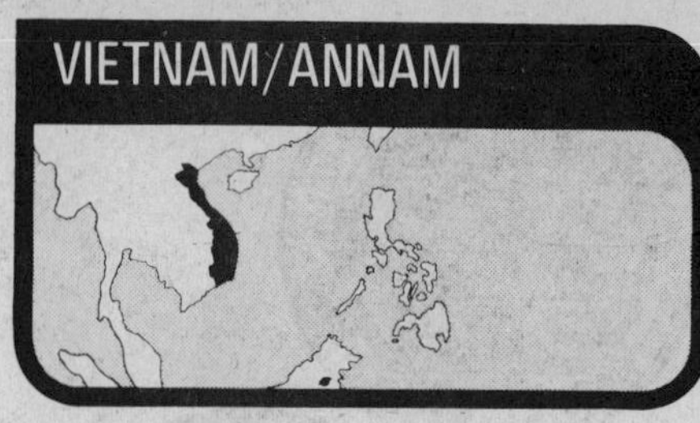

In 207 B.C. a Chinese general set up the Kingdom of Nam-Viet on the Red River. This kingdom was overthrown by the Chinese under the Han Dynasty in 111 B.C., whereupon the country became a Chinese province under the name of Giao-Chi, which was later changed to Annam or peaceful or pacified of the South. Chinese rule was maintained until 968, when the Vietnamese became independent until 1407 when China again invaded Vietnam. The Chinese were driven out in 1428 and the country became independent and named Dai-Viet. Gia Long renamed the country Dai Nam in 1802.

The former French Protectorate of Annam, now part of Vietnam, had an area of 57,840 sq. mi. (141,806 sq. km.) and supported a population of about 6 million. It was bounded on the North by Tonkin and on the South by Cochin China. Former capital: Hue. Chief products of the area are silk, cinnamon and rice. There are important mineral deposits in the mountainous inland.

United Dai Nam

EMPERORS

Gia Long, 1802-1820 嘉隆

Minh Mang, 1820-1841 明命

Thieu Tri, 1841-1847 紹治

Tu Duc, 1848-1883 嗣德

Kien Phuc, 1883-1884 建福

Ham Nghi, 1884-1885 咸宜

Protectorate of Annam

EMPERORS

Dong Khanh, 1885-1888 同慶

Thanh Thai, 1888-1907 成泰

Duy Tan, 1907-1916 維新

Khai Dinh, 1916-1925 啓定

Bao Dai, 1926-1945 保大

REBELS and INVADERS

Bao Hung, 1801-1802 寶興

Tri Nguyen, 1831-1834 治元

Nguyen Long, 1832-1833 元隆

IDENTIFICATION

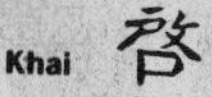

Khai 啓

寶 Bao　　通 Thong

Dinh 定

Khai Dinh Thong Bao

The square holed cash coins of Annam are easily identified by reading the characters top-bottom (emperor's name) and right-left ("Thong Bao" general currency). The character at right will change with some emperors.

CYCLICAL DATES

	庚	辛	壬	癸	甲	乙	丙	丁	戊	己
戌	1850 1910		1862 1922		1874 1934		1886 1946		1838 1898	
亥		1851 1911		1863 1923		1875 1935		1887 1947		1839 1899
子	1840 1900		1852 1912		1864 1924		1876 1936		1888 1948	
丑		1841 1901		1853 1913		1865 1925		1877 1937		1889 1949
寅	1830 1890		1842 1902		1854 1914		1866 1926		1878 1938	
卯		1831 1891		1843 1903		1855 1915		1867 1927		1879 1939
辰	1880 1940		1832 1892		1844 1904		1856 1916		1868 1928	
巳		1881 1941		1833 1893		1845 1905		1857 1917		1869 1929
午	1870 1930		1882 1942		1834 1894		1846 1906		1858 1918	
未		1871 1931		1883 1943		1835 1895		1847 1907		1859 1919
申	1860 1920		1872 1932		1884 1944		1836 1896		1848 1908	
酉		1861 1921		1873 1933		1885 1945		1837 1897		1849 1909

NOTE: This table has been adapted from *Chinese Bank Notes* by Ward Smith and Brian Matravers.

Cyclical dates consist of a pair of characters one of which indicates the animal associated with that year. Every 60 years, this pair of characters is repeated. The first character of a cyclical date corresponds to a character in the first row of the chart above. The second character is taken from the column at left. In this catalog where a cyclical date is used, the abbreviation CD appears before the A.D. date.

Annamese silver and gold coins were sometimes dated according to the year of the emperor's reign. In this case, simply add the year of reign to the year in which the reign simply add the year of reign to the year in which the reign would be 1849 (1847 plus 3 = 1850 -1 = 1849 or 1847 = 1; 1848 = 2; 1849 = 3). In this catalog the A.D. date appears in parenthesis followed by the year of reign.

NUMERALS

Column A, conventional; Column B, formal.

NUMBER	CONVENTIONAL	FORMAL	COMMERCIAL
1	一 元	壹 弌	〡
2	二	弍 貳	〢
3	三	叁 弎	〣
4	四	肆	〤
5	五	伍	〥
6	六	陸	〦
7	七	柒	〧
8	八	捌	〨
9	九	玖	〩
10	十	拾 什	十
20	十 二 or 廿	拾貳	〢十
25	五 十 二 or 五廿	伍拾貳	〢十〥
30	十 三 or 卅	拾叁	〣十
100	百 一	佰壹	〡百
1,000	千 一	仟壹	〡千
10,000	萬 一	萬壹	〡万
100,000	萬 十　億 一	萬拾　億壹	十万
1,000,000	萬百一	萬佰壹	〡百万

NOTE: This table has been adapted from *Chinese Bank Notes* by Ward Smith and Brian Matravers.

MONETARY SYSTEM

COPPER AND ZINC

10 Dong (zinc) = 1 Dong (copper)
600 Dong (zinc) = 1 Quan (string of cash)
Approx. 2600 Dong (zinc) = 1 Piastre

NOTE: Ratios between metals changed frequently, therefore the above is given as an approximate relationship.

SILVER AND GOLD

2-1/2 Quan = 1 Lang
10 Tien (Mace) = 1 Lang (Tael)
14 to 17 Piastres (silver) = 1 Piastre (gold)
14 to 17 Lang (silver) = 1 Lang (gold)

The real currency of Dai Nam and An Nam consisted of copper and zinc coins similar to Chinese cash-style coins and were called sapeques and dongs by the French.

The smaller gold pieces saw a limited circulation, mainly among the local merchants and foreign traders. The larger gold pieces were used mainly for hoarding, while most of these were intended as rewards and gifts. Many of these gold pieces appear to have been struck from silver coin dies or vice-versa.

The fineness of the gold and silver pieces varied considerably. The silver and gold dragon coins with the streaked edges were intended to be equivalant to the Mexican and Spanish Colonial 8 Reales (Dollar/Piastre) and 8 Escudos, and their minor denominations, but the silver normally exchanged for much less because their fineness usually ranged from .500 to .700 fine. The gold and silver coins with other designs and smooth edges are generally considered as presentation pieces but some did appear in circulation when their owners came upon hard times. Their fineness usually ranges from .500 to .999. Authentic gold of all designs are rarely found below .850 fine.

Only a few Vietnamese silver and gold pieces are inscribed with their weight and fineness and therefore must be weighed and tested. It should be remembered that Phan, Tien and Lang are weights and not denominations. The pieces inscribed with Van and Quan are money of account terms but could be considered the first Vietnamese denominations. The Vietnamese ignored these terms and exchanged them and all other metalic forms at the prevailing market value of their intrinsic weight and not their inscribed or total weight. Without testing devices or a specific gravity setup, you will only be able to determine the total weight of your piece. For the pieces described in this catalog without weights or terms inscribed on them, they are classified by their total weight. The following table will assist you to determine your pieces Phan, Tien or Lang weight:

PHAN SYSTEM

1 Phan	.3778 grams
5 Phan (or 1/2 Tien)	1.8892 grams
10 Phan (or 1 Tien)	3.7783 grams

TIEN SYSTEM

1/2 Tien (or 5 Phan)	1.8892 grams
1 Tien (or 10 Phan)	3.7783 grams
1/1/2 Tien	5.6675 grams
2 Tien	7.5566 grams
2-1/2 Tien (or 1/4 Lang)	9.4458 grams
3 Tien	11.3349 grams
4 Tien	15.1132 grams
5 Tien (or 1/2 Lang)	18.8915 grams
6 Tien	22.6698 grams
7 Tien	26.4481 grams
8 Tien	30.2264 grams
9 Tien	34.0047 grams
10 Tien (or 1 Lang)	37.7830 grams

NOTE: The Van and Quan pieces are denominations for fiat money. A 10 Van coin was officially worth 10 full weight 1 Tien coins of copper, but, of course, weighed less and less during the inflationary times of their period of issue. The 3 Quan silver bar was officially worth 3 full weight strings of copper coins. The weight of these Van and Quan coins and bars varied considerably and are specified at their listing. The heavier weight pieces are generally the earliest issues with the lighter ones the latest.

PALACE ISSUES

C#53 "1 Mach or 60 Dong"

There are many dollar size and larger copper and brass tokens with obverses similar to the small square holed cash coins listed here with eight, four, or two characters or dragon and fish on the reverse. These were believed to have been given as gifts or bestowed as rewards and circulated to some extent although they do not carry any designation of weight or denomination. The large 130135mm square holed copper pieces with the emperor's name on the obverse and an 8 character legend reverse were displayed in respect of the current emperor. They had a nominal 'trade value' of 600 sapeques as quoted by Bernard J. Permar in "Catalogue of Annam Coins, 9681955".

NOTE: Sch# are in reference to Albert Schroeder's "Annam, Etudes Numismatiques" or to the same numbering system used in "Gold and Silver Coins of Annam", by Bernard Permar and John Novak.

CHARACTER IDENTIFICATION

The Vietnamese used Chinese-style characters for official documents and coins and bars. Some were modified to their liking and will sometimes not match the Chinese character for the same word. The above identification and this table will translate most of the Vietnamese characters (Chinese-style) on their coins and bars described herein.

Chinese/French

Vietnamese/English

安南 An Nam = name of the French protectorate

大南 Dai Nam = name of the country under Gia Long's Nguyen dynasty

越南 Viet Nam = name used briefly during Minh Mang's reign and became the modern name of the country

河內 Ha Noi = city and province in north Dai Nam

內帑 Noi Thang = court treasury in the capital of Hue

年 Nien = year

造 Tao = made

銀 Ngan = silver

金 Kim = gold

錢 Tien = a weight of about 3.78 grams

兩 Lang = a weight of about 37.78 grams

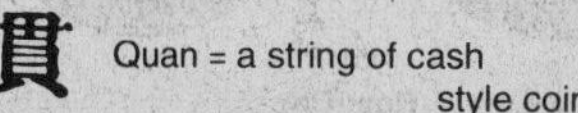

貫 Quan = a string of cash style coins

分 Phan = a weight of about .38 grams

文 Van = cash-style coins

中平 Trung Binh = a name of weight standard

PROVINCIAL DESIGNATORS

An Giang	江安
Bac Ninh	寧北
Binh Dinh	定平
Can Than	申庚
Dinh Tuong	商定
Gia Dinh	定嘉
Hung Yen	遠興
Lang Son	山諒
Nghe An	安清 or 安乂
Phu Yen	燕虎
Quang Nam	南廣
Quang Yen	義廣
Son Tay	西山
Thai Nguyen	原太

COPPER, BRASS and ZINC 'CASH' COINAGE

(1 Phan)

CAST BRASS
Rev: Plain.

C#	Date	Emperor	Good	VG	Fine	VF
57	(1801-02)	Bao Hung	—	—	Rare	—

COPPER ALLOYS, 24-25mm
Rev: Plain.

C#	Date	Emperor	Good	VG	Fine	VF
61.1	(1802-20)	Gia Long	1.25	2.00	3.50	6.00
22.6-24mm						
61.2	(1802-20)	Gia Long	.85	1.50	2.75	4.50

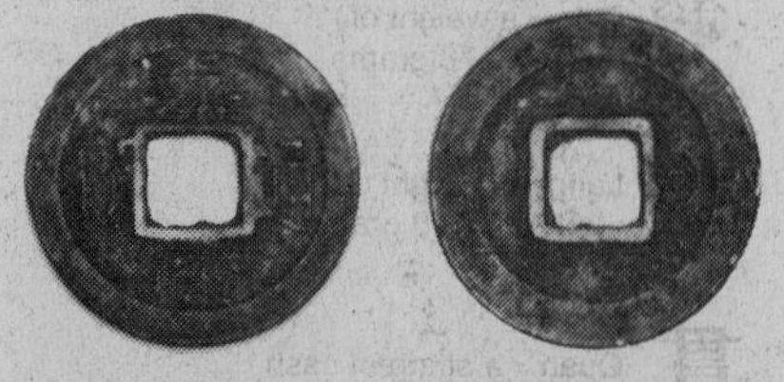

Rev: Dot.

C#	Date	Emperor	Good	VG	Fine	VF
61.3	(1802-20)	Gia Long	2.00	3.50	5.50	9.00
Rev: Circle.						
61.3a	(1802-20)	Gia Long	2.00	3.50	5.50	9.00
Obv: Double rim.						
61.3b	(1802-20)	Gia Long	2.00	3.50	5.50	9.00

C#	Date	Emperor	Good	VG	Fine	VF
Obv. & rev: Double rim.						
61.3c	(1802-20)	Gia Long	2.00	3.50	5.50	9.00
Rev: Crescent.						
61.4	(1802-20)	Gia Long	2.75	4.50	7.50	12.50

CAST ZINC
Rev: Plain.

C#	Date	Emperor	Good	VG	Fine	VF
73	(1802-20)	Gia Long	4.50	7.50	12.50	20.00

CAST COPPER ALLOYS, 24-25mm

C#	Date	Emperor	Good	VG	Fine	VF
81.1	(1820-41)	Minh Mang	1.00	1.75	2.75	4.50
22.7-24mm						
81.2	(1820-41)	Minh Mang	.75	1.25	2.00	3.50
21mm						
81.3	(1820-41)	Minh Mang	.75	1.25	2.00	3.50

CAST ZINC

C#	Date	Emperor	Good	VG	Fine	VF
79	(1820-41)	Minh Mang	1.25	2.00	3.50	8.00

CAST COPPER ALLOYS
Nguy Khoi Rebellion
Obv. leg: *Tri Nguyen Thong Bao.*

C#	Date	Emperor	Good	VG	Fine	VF
137	(1831-34)	Tri Nguyen	8.50	13.50	21.50	35.00

Nung Rebellion
Obv. leg: *Nguyen Long Thong Bao,* cursive *Nguyen.*

C#	Date	Emperor	Good	VG	Fine	VF
138.1	(1832-33)	Nguyen Long	8.50	13.50	21.50	35.00
Obv: Conventional *Nguyen.*						
138.2	(1823-33)	Nguyen Long	10.50	18.00	30.00	45.00
Obv: Cursive *Nguyen.* Rev: Double rim.						
139.1	(1832-33)	Nguygen Long	10.50	18.00	30.00	45.00

Rev: Character *Xuong.*

C#	Date	Emperor	Good	VG	Fine	VF
139.2	(1832-33)	Nguyen Long	10.50	18.00	30.00	45.00

 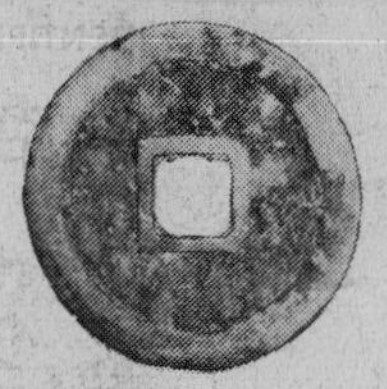

CAST COPPER ALLOYS, 24-25mm

C#	Date	Emperor	Good	VG	Fine	VF
141.1	(1841-47)	Thieu Tri	.60	1.00	1.75	3.00
23-24mm						
141.2	(1841-47)	Thieu Tri	.60	1.00	1.75	3.00
CAST ZINC						
140	(1841-47)	Thieu Tri	2.75	4.50	7.50	12.50

CAST COPPER ALLOYS, 24-25mm

C#	Date	Emperor	Good	VG	Fine	VF
201.1	(1848-83)	Tu Duc	1.25	2.00	3.50	6.00
22-24mm						
201.2	(1848-83)	Tu Duc	1.25	2.00	3.50	6.00

CAST ZINC
Obv: *Kien Phuc Thong Bao.*

C#	Date	Emperor	Good	VG	Fine	VF
271.1	(1883-84)	Kien Phuc	18.50	30.00	50.00	80.00

Obv: *Phuc* written differently.

C#	Date	Emperor	Good	VG	Fine	VF
271.2	(1883-84)	Kien Phuc	18.50	30.00	50.00	80.00

CAST COPPER ALLOYS
Obv: *Ham Nghi Thong Bao.*

C#	Date	Emperor	Good	VG	Fine	VF
281	(1884-85)	Ham Nghi	35.00	60.00	100.00	165.00

 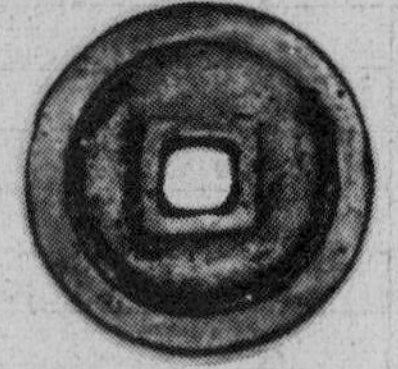

23-24mm

C#	Date	Emperor	Good	VG	Fine	VF
301.1	(1885-88)	Dong Khanh	2.75	4.50	7.50	12.50

26mm

C#	Date	Emperor	Good	VG	Fine	VF
301.2	(1885-88)	Dong Khanh	11.50	18.50	30.00	50.00

Rev: Blank.

Y#	Date	Emperor	Good	VG	Fine	VF
1	(1888-1907)	Than Thai	2.00	3.50	5.50	9.00

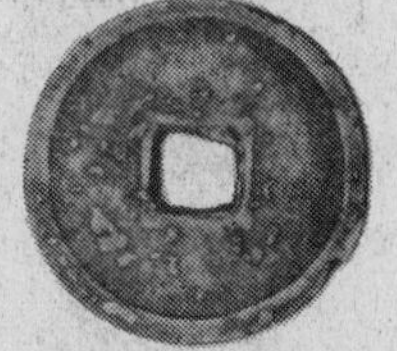

Similar to Y#5.1.

Y#	Date	Emperor	Good	VG	Fine	VF
4	(1916-25)	Khai Dinh	5.50	9.00	15.00	25.00

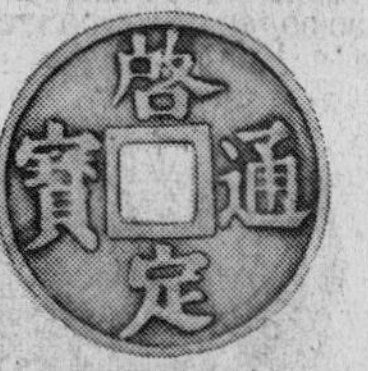
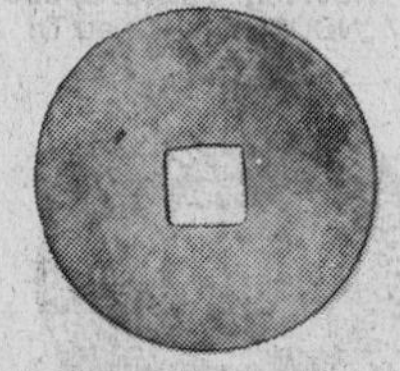

Struck, 22mm, uniface.

Y#	Date	Emperor	Good	VG	Fine	VF
5.1	(1916-25)	Khai Dinh	1.75	2.75	4.50	7.50

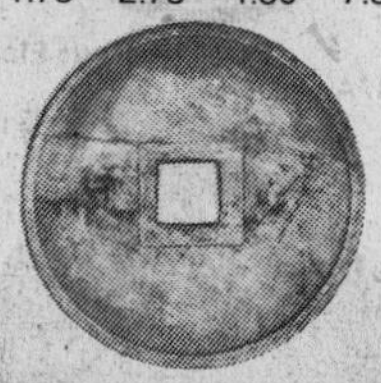

Larger size, characters slightly different.

Y#	Date	Emperor	Good	VG	Fine	VF
5.2	(1916-25)	Khai Dinh	2.00	3.50	6.00	10.00

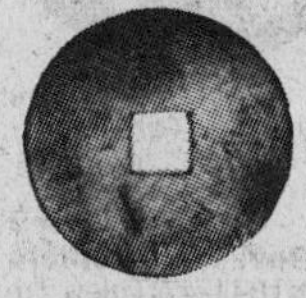

BRASS, struck 18mm

Y#	Date	Emperor	Good	VG	Fine	VF
6	(1926-45)	Bao Dai	4.50	7.50	12.50	20.00

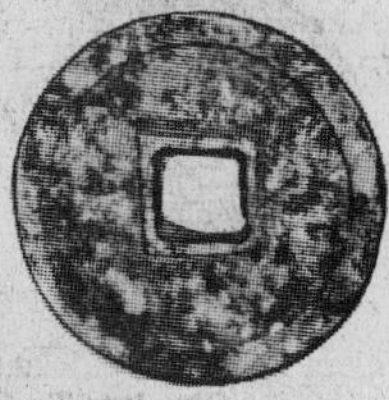

CAST BRASS, 24mm

Y#	Date	Emperor	Good	VG	Fine	VF
6a	(1926-45)	Bao Dai	4.50	7.50	12.50	20.00

CASH

(6 Phan)

CAST COPPER ALLOYS

Rev: *Luc Phan* in seal script.

C#	Date	Emperor	Good	VG	Fine	VF
62	(1802-20)	Gia Long	2.75	4.50	7.50	12.50

CASH

(7 Phan)

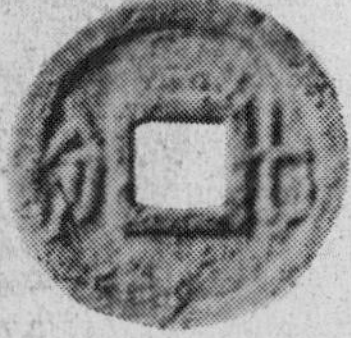

CAST ZINC

Rev: *That Phan.*

C#	Date	Emperor	Good	VG	Fine	VF
63	(1802-20)	Gia Long	5.50	9.00	15.00	25.00

6 VAN

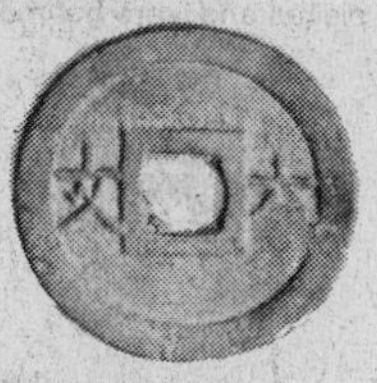

CAST COPPER ALLOYS, 24-26mm

Rev: *Luc Van.*

C#	Date	Emperor	Good	VG	Fine	VF
202	(1848-83)	Tu Duc	1.25	2.00	3.50	6.00

23mm

C#	Date	Emperor	Good	VG	Fine	VF
202.1	(1848-83)	Tu Duc	1.25	2.00	3.50	6.00

C#	Date	Emperor	Good	VG	Fine	VF
282	(1884-85)	Ham Nghi	35.00	60.00	100.00	165.00

Y#	Date	Emperor	Good	VG	Fine	VF
A2	(1888-1907)	Than Thoi	—	—	Rare	—

8 VAN

CAST ZINC

Rev: Plain.

C#	Date	Emperor	Good	VG	Fine	VF
191	(1848-83)	Tu Duc	2.00	3.50	5.50	9.00

Rev: *Ha Noi.*

C#	Date	Emperor	Good	VG	Fine	VF
192.1	(1848-83)	Tu Duc	5.00	8.50	13.50	21.50

Rev: *Son Tay.*

C#	Date	Emperor	Good	VG	Fine	VF
192.2	(1848-83)	Tu Duc	6.00	10.00	16.50	25.00

CAST COPPER ALLOYS

Obv: *Trung Bao* (heavy currency).

Rev: 7Bat Van and 7An Nam.

C#	Date	Emperor	Good	VG	Fine	VF
203	(1848-83)	Tu Duc	—	—	Rare	—

10 VAN

CAST COPPER ALLOYS

Rev: 4 Chinese characters *Tang* . . . . .*Shih Wen.*

C#	Date	Emperor	Good	VG	Fine	VF
65	(1802-20)	Gia Long	11.50	18.50	30.00	50.00

Rev: *Chuan Thap Van.*

C#	Date	Emperor	Good	VG	Fine	VF
204	(1848-83)	Tu Duc	11.50	18.50	30.00	50.00

Rev: *Chuan Nhat Thap Van.*

C#	Date	Emperor	Good	VG	Fine	VF
204a	(1848-83)	Tu Duc	11.50	18.50	30.00	50.00

Rev: *Thap Van.*

Y#	Date	Emperor	Good	VG	Fine	VF
2	(1888-1907)	Than Thoi	.50	.75	1.25	2.50

CAST BRASS

Y#	Date	Emperor	Good	VG	Fine	VF
3	(1907-16)	Duy Tan	.50	.75	1.25	2.50

Y#	Date	Emperor	Good	VG	Fine	VF
7	(1926-45)	Bao Dai	2.00	3.50	6.00	10.00

20 VAN

CAST COPPER or BRASS

Rev: *Chuan Nhi Thap Van.*

C#	Date	Emperor	Good	VG	Fine	VF
205	(1848-83)	Tu Duc	70.00	100.00	140.00	200.00

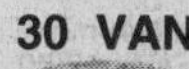

30 VAN

CAST COPPER or BRASS

Rev: *Chuan Tam Thap Van.*

C#	Date	Emperor	Good	VG	Fine	VF
205.5	(1848-83)	Tu Duc	85.00	120.00	170.00	240.00

40 VAN

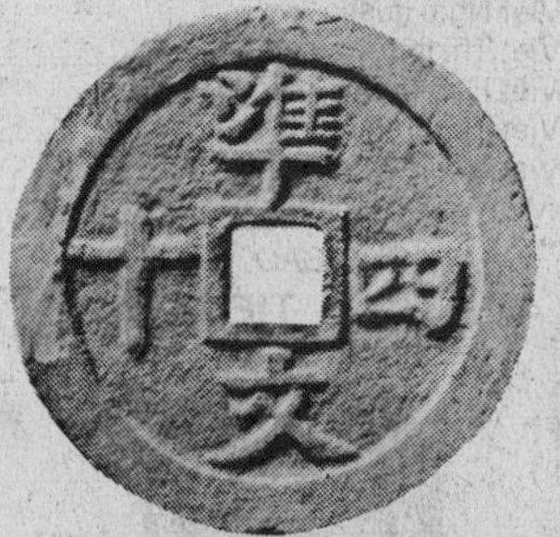

CAST COPPER or BRASS

Rev: *Chuan Tu Thap Van.*

C#	Date	Emperor	Good	VG	Fine	VF
206	(1848-83)	Tu Duc	85.00	120.00	170.00	240.00

50 VAN

CAST COPPER or BRASS
Rev: *Chuan Ngu Thap Van.*

C#	Date	Emperor	Good	VG	Fine	VF
206.5	(1848-83)	Tu Duc	70.00	100.00	140.00	200.00

60 VAN

CAST COPPER or BRASS, 43mm
Rev: *Chuan Luc Thap Van.*

207.1	(1848-83)	Tu Duc	42.50	60.00	85.00	120.00

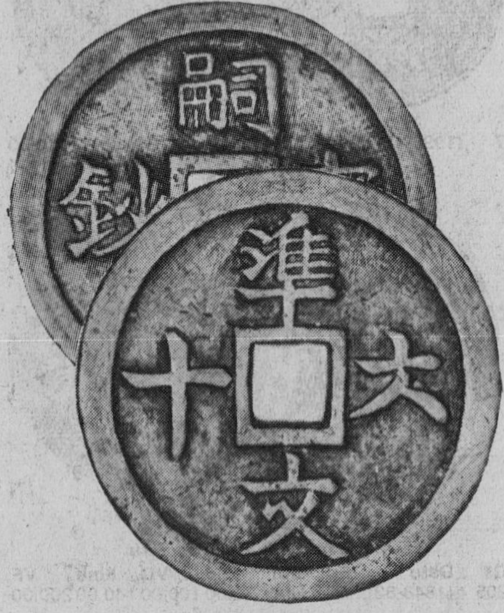

47-49mm

207.2	(1848-83)	Tu Duc	42.50	60.00	85.00	120.00

SILVER COINAGE

The silver dragon coins with crude oblique milled edges are considered to be those in imitation of the Mexican/Spanish Colonial 8 Reales (Dollar/Piastre) coins and its minor denominations. The smooth edge silver dragon coins and those with square center holes are considered presentation pieces. Each coin is compared to the Weight System table in the introduction and assigned the respective Tien or Lang designation corresponding to its actual weight in grams.

VIRTUES

Certain coins were issued in weights from 1 Tien through 1 Lang each with a different virtue.

1 Tien - Viet Tu (benignity)
2 Tien - Viet Hein (gratitude)
3 Tien - Viet Lang (kindness)
4 Tien - Viet De (respect)
5 Tien - Viet Ngai (justice)
6 Tien - Viet Thinh (obedience)
7 Tien - Viet Hue (benevolence)
8 Tien - Viet Thuan (submissiveness)
9 Tien - Viet Nhan (humanity)
1 Lang - Viet Trung (faithfulness)

"THONG BAO" SERIES

1/2 TIEN

SILVER, 1.80 g
Obv. leg: *Thieu Tri Thong Bao.* Rev: Blank.

Sch#	Date	Emperor	VG	Fine	VF	XF
257	ND(1841-47)	Thieu Tri	30.00	60.00	100.00	175.00

NOTE: Cash-style coins of silver were used as presentation pieces and were not meant for general circulation.

1.50 g
Obv. leg: *Tu Duc Thong Bao.*

367	ND(1848-83)	Tu Duc	27.50	55.00	90.00	160.00

Rev. leg: *Su Dan Phu Tho.*

367B	ND(1848-83)	Tu Duc	30.00	60.00	100.00	175.00

TIEN

SILVER, 4.50 g
Obv. leg: *Minh Mang Thong Bao.*

180	ND(1820-41) Minh Mang		30.00	60.00	100.00	175.00

NOTE: Cash-style coins of silver were used as presentation pieces and were not meant for general circulation.

3.60 g
Obv. leg: *Thieu Tri Thong Bao.*
Rev. leg: *Nhat Nguyen.*

250	ND(1841-47)	Thieu Tri	30.00	60.00	100.00	175.00

3.70-4.00 g
Rev: Sun, moon and 5 planets.

262	ND(1841-47)	Thieu Tri	27.50	55.00	90.00	160.00

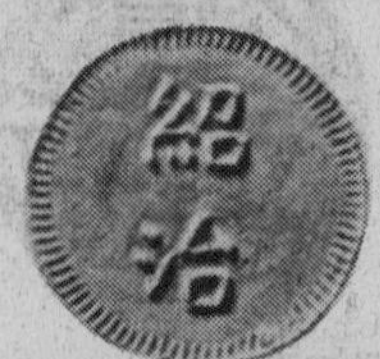

3.60-4.00 g
Obv. leg: *Thieu Tri.* Rev: Scepter and swastika.

264	ND(1841-47)	Thieu Tri	27.50	55.00	90.00	160.00

Rev: Mirror image of Sch#264.

265	ND(1841-47)	Thieu Tri	27.50	55.00	90.00	160.00

4.00 g
Obv. leg: *Thieu Tri.* Rev: Guitar.

Sch#	Date	Emperor	VG	Fine	VF	XF
266A	ND(1841-47) Thieu Tri		35.00	70.00	120.00	200.00

3.70 g
Rev. leg: *Tam Da,* above the Three Plenties.

267	ND(1841-47)	Thieu Tri	30.00	60.00	100.00	170.00

Rev: Flaming sun.

287A	ND(1841-47) Thieu Tri		21.50	42.50	70.00	125.00

Rev: Fan

291A	ND(1841-47) Thieu Tri		35.00	70.00	120.00	200.00

Obv. leg: *Thieu Tri Thong Bao.*
Rev: Two scepters and two swastikas.

256	ND(1841-47)	Thieu Tri	32.50	65.00	110.00	200.00

3.50 g
Obv. leg: *Tu Duc Thong Bao.*
Rev. leg: *Nhat Nguyen* cosmic evolution.

353	ND(1848-83)	Tu Duc	30.00	60.00	100.00	175.00

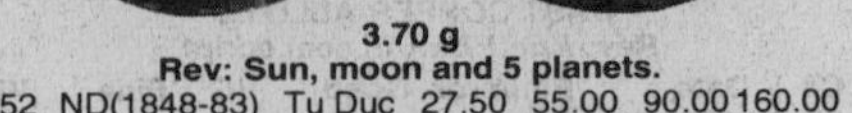

3.70 g
Rev: Sun, moon and 5 planets.

352	ND(1848-83)	Tu Duc	27.50	55.00	90.00	160.00

3.74 g
Rev. leg: *Nhat Duc* between 2 stylized fish.

354.1	ND(1848-83)	Tu Duc	27.50	55.00	90.00	160.00

Rev. leg: *Nhat Duc* between 2 goldfish.

Sch#	Date	Emperor	VG	Fine	VF	XF
354.2	ND(1848-83)	Tu Duc	27.50	55.00	90.00	160.00

3.80 g
Rev. leg: *Nhi Duc* between sun, moon and clouds.

355B	ND(1848-83)	Tu Duc	30.00	60.00	100.00	175.00

Rev. leg: *Tam Da*, above the Three Plenties.

357	ND(1848-83)	Tu Duc	35.50	70.00	120.00	200.00

3.60 g
Rev: 2 swastikas and 2 scepters which look like flowers.

361	ND(1848-83)	Tu Duc	32.50	65.00	130.00	225.00

3.70 g
Rev. leg: *Tu Bao*, between Four Precious Objects.

362	ND(1848-83)	Tu Duc	35.00	70.00	120.00	200.00

3.30 g
Rev: The Five Precious Objects.

363	ND(1848-83)	Tu Duc	30.00	60.00	100.00	175.00

3.50-3.70 g
Rev: Eight Precious Objects.

364	ND(1848-83)	Tu Duc	30.00	60.00	100.00	175.00

NOTE: There are three varieties of this coin based upon the placement of the symbols.

3.80 g
Rev. leg: *Nhat Tien Viet Tu* on dragon.

377	ND(1848-83)	Tu Duc	30.00	60.00	100.00	175.00

3.90 g
Rev: Sun, moon and 5 planets.

386	ND(1848-83)	Tu Duc	27.50	55.00	90.00	160.00

4.00 g
Rev. leg: *Tam Da*, above Three Plenties.

Sch#	Date	Emperor	VG	Fine	VF	XF
387	ND(1848-83)	Tu Duc	27.50	55.00	90.00	160.00

4.10 g
Rev: Scepter and Swastika.

388	ND(1848-83)	Tu Duc	35.00	70.00	120.00	200.00

3.80 g
Rev: Horn.

389	ND(1848-83)	Tu Duc	32.50	65.00	110.00	180.00

3.50 g
Rev: Five Precious Objects.

390	ND(1848-83)	Tu Duc	27.50	55.00	90.00	160.00

1-1/2 TIEN

SILVER, 5.00-6.00 g
Obv. leg: *Minh Mang*.

189	ND(1820-41)	Minh Mang	27.50	55.00	90.00	160.00

5.63 g
Obv. leg: *Thieu Tri*.

266B	ND(1841-47)	Thieu Tri	32.50	65.00	110.00	180.00

5.20 g
Obv. leg: *Tu Duc Thong Bao*.
Rev. leg: *Phu Tho Da Nam*.

358	ND(1848-83)	Tu Duc	35.00	70.00	120.00	200.00

5.30 g
Rev. leg: *Su Dan Phu Tho*.

Sch#	Date	Emperor	VG	Fine	VF	XF
351C	ND(1848-83)	Tu Duc	35.00	70.00	120.00	200.00

2 TIEN

SILVER, 7.60 g
Obv. leg: *Thieu Tri Thong Bao*.
Rev. leg: *Nhi Nghi*, between sun, moon and clouds.

251	ND(1841-47)	Thieu Tri	30.00	60.00	100.00	175.00

7.50 g
Rev: 2 facing dragons.

240	ND(1841-47)	Thieu Tri	45.00	90.00	150.00	250.00

7.60 g
Obv. leg: *Tu Duc Thong Bao*.
Rev. leg: *Su Dan Phu Tho*.

351B	ND(1848-83)	Tu Duc	30.00	60.00	100.00	175.00

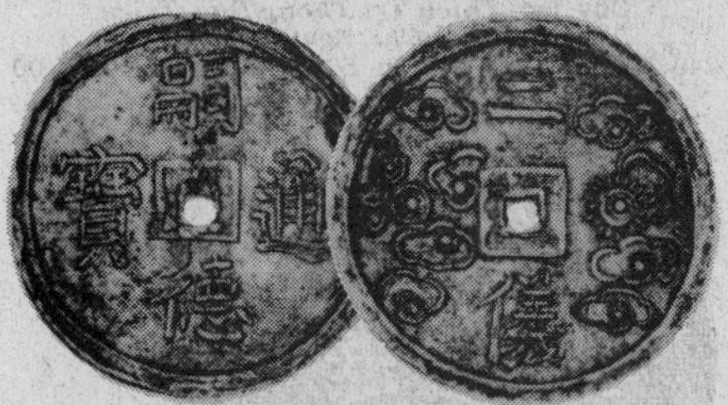

6.60 g
Obv. leg: *Tu Duc Thong Bao*.
Rev. leg: *Nhi Nghi* between sun, moon and clouds.

355	ND(1848-83)	Tu Duc	42.50	90.00	150.00	250.00

7.30 g
Rev. leg: *Nhi Tien Viet Hien* on dragon.

378	ND(1848-83)	Tu Duc	45.00	90.00	150.00	250.00

Rev: 2 facing dragons.

Sch#	Date	Emperor	VG	Fine	VF	XF
—	ND(1848-83)	Tu Duc	42.50	90.00	150.00	250.00

Obv. leg: ***Dong Khanh Thong Bao.***
Rev. leg: ***Su Dan Phu Tho.***

Sch#	Date	Emperor	VG	Fine	VF	XF
420	ND(1885-89)	Dong Khanh	45.00	90.00	150.00	250.00

Rev. leg: ***Nhi Nghi*** **between sun, moon and clouds.**

Sch#	Date	Emperor	VG	Fine	VF	XF
425A	ND(1885-89)	Dong Khanh	45.00	90.00	150.00	250.00

1/4 LANG

SILVER, 9.20 g
Obv. leg: ***Thieu Tri Thong Bao, Trieu Dan Lai Chi.*** **Rev: Dragon.**

Sch#	Date	Emperor	VG	Fine	VF	XF
249	ND(1841-47)	Thieu Tri	50.00	100.00	175.00	300.00

9.60 g
Obv. leg: ***Thieu Tri Thong Bao*** **around flaming sun.**
Rev. leg: ***Long Van Khe Hoi*** **around dragon.**

Sch#	Date	Emperor	VG	Fine	VF	XF
261	ND(1841-47)	Thieu Tri	62.50	125.00	200.00	350.00

9.40 g
Obv. leg: ***Tu Duc Thong Bao, Trieu Dan Lai Chi.*** **Rev: Simple dragon.**

Sch#	Date	Emperor	VG	Fine	VF	XF
350.1	ND(1848-83)	Tu Duc	50.00	100.00	175.00	300.00

Rev: Round faced dragon w/streamers.

Sch#	Date	Emperor	VG	Fine	VF	XF
350.2	ND(1848-83)	Tu Duc	50.00	100.00	175.00	300.00

Rev: Ornate dragon.

Sch#	Date	Emperor	VG	Fine	VF	XF
350.3	ND(1848-83)	Tu Duc	50.00	100.00	175.00	300.00

9.50-9.80 g
Obv. leg: ***Tu Duc Thong Bao*** **around flaming sun.**
Rev. leg: ***Long Van Khe Hoi*** **around dragon.**

Sch#	Date	Emperor	VG	Fine	VF	XF
375	ND(1848-83)	Tu Duc	62.50	125.00	200.00	350.00

8.80 g
Obv. leg: ***Dong Khanh Thong Bao*** **around flaming sun.**
Rev. leg: ***Long Van Khe Hoi*** **around dragon.**

Sch#	Date	Emperor	VG	Fine	VF	XF
422	ND(1885-88)	Dong Khanh	62.50	125.00	200.00	350.00

3 TIEN

SILVER, 13.30-13.70 g
Obv. leg: ***Minh Mang Thong Bao.***
Rev: Dragon.

Sch#	Date	Emperor	VG	Fine	VF	XF
184	ND(1820-41)	Minh Mang	67.50	135.00	225.00	375.00
185	(1833) Yr.14	Minh Mang	67.50	135.00	225.00	375.00

Sch#	Date	Emperor	VG	Fine	VF	XF
186	(1834) Yr.15	Minh Mang	67.50	135.00	225.00	375.00

13.30 g
Obv. leg: ***Thieu Tri Thong Bao.***
Rev: 2 facing dragons.

Sch#	Date	Emperor	VG	Fine	VF	XF
239	ND(1841-47)	Thieu Tri	70.00	140.00	240.00	400.00

13.50 g
Obv. leg: ***Thieu Tri Thong Bao.***
Rev: Small dragon.

Sch#	Date	Emperor	VG	Fine	VF	XF
260	ND(1841-47)	Thieu Tri	67.50	135.00	225.00	375.00

13.34 g
Rev: Large dragon.

Sch#	Date	Emperor	VG	Fine	VF	XF
259	ND(1841-47)	Thieu Tri	67.50	135.00	225.00	375.00

11.90 g

Rev. leg: ***Tam Tho*****, above Three Longevities.**

Sch#	Date	Emperor	VG	Fine	VF	XF
252	ND(1841-47)	Thieu Tri	67.50	135.00	225.00	375.00

Obv. leg: ***Tu Duc Thong Bao.***
Rev. leg: ***Long Van*** **on facing dragon.**
373 ND(1848-83) Tu Duc 70.00 140.00 240.00 400.00

11.30 g
Rev. leg: ***Tam Tien Viet Lang*** **on dragon.**
379 ND(1848-83) Tu Duc 70.00 140.00 240.00 400.00

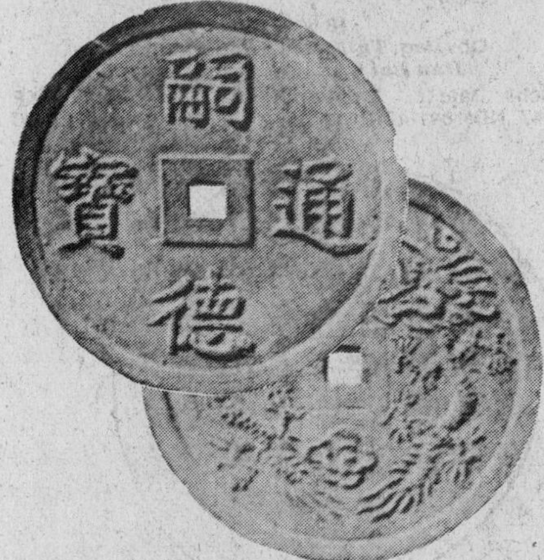

13.10 g
Rev: Flaming sun between 2 facing dragons w/long tails.
347.1 ND(1848-83)Tu Duc 70.00 140.00 240.00 400.00

Rev: 2 facing dragons w/short tails.
347.2 ND(1848-83)Tu Duc 70.00 140.00 240.00 400.00

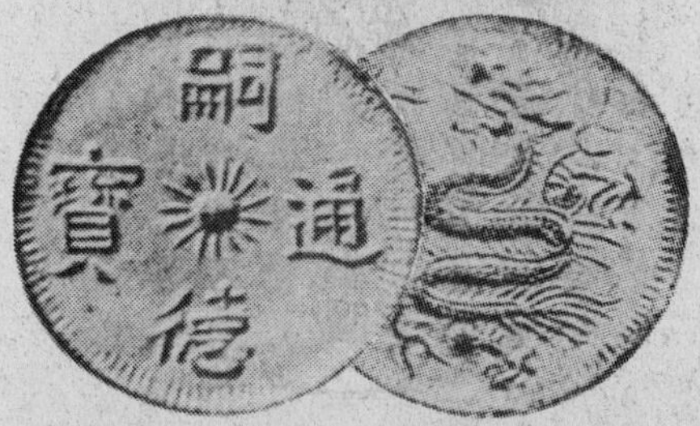

13.30 g

Sch#	Date	Emperor	VG	Fine	VF	XF
369	ND(1848-83)	Tu Duc	67.50	135.00	225.00	375.00

Plain edge, 32.2mm, 13.45 g
369A ND(1848-83)Tu Duc 45.00 90.00 150.00 250.00

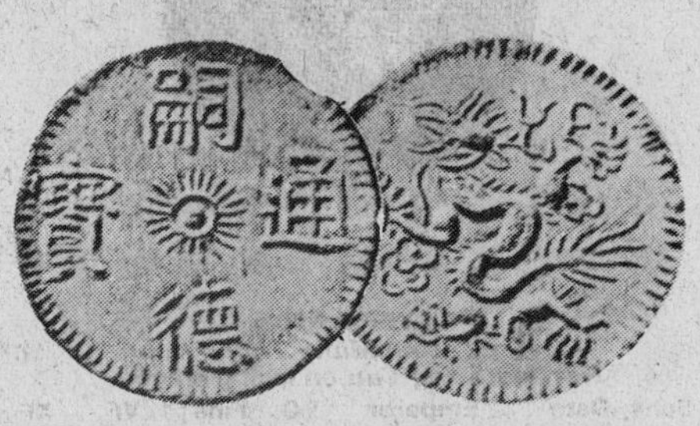

12.40 g
Obv: Dot in center of sun.
370 ND(1848-83) Tu Duc 45.00 90.00 150.00 250.00

Obv. leg: Large characters.
Rev. leg: ***Tam Tho*** **above the Three Longevities.**
407A ND(1848-83)Tu Duc 70.00 140.00 240.00 400.00

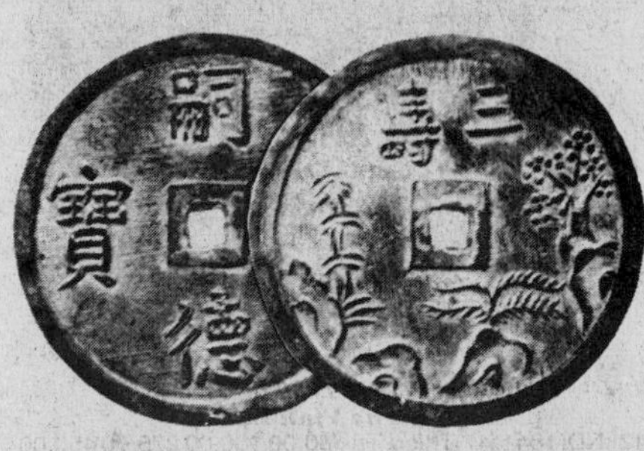

Obv. leg: Small characters. Rev: Finer style.
407B ND(1848-83)Tu Duc 70.00 140.00 240.00 400.00

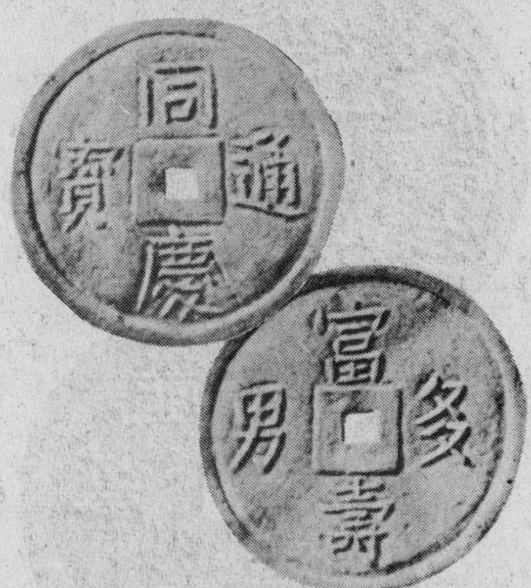

10.20 g
Obv. leg: ***Dong Khanh Thong Bao.***
Rev. leg: ***Su Dan Da Nam.***
421 ND(1885-88)
Dong Khanh 62.50 125.00 225.00 375.00

15.30 g
Obv. leg: ***Thanh Thai Thong Bao.***
Rev: Dragon.
428 ND(1888-1907)
Thanh Thai 70.00 140.00 240.00 400.00

4 TIEN

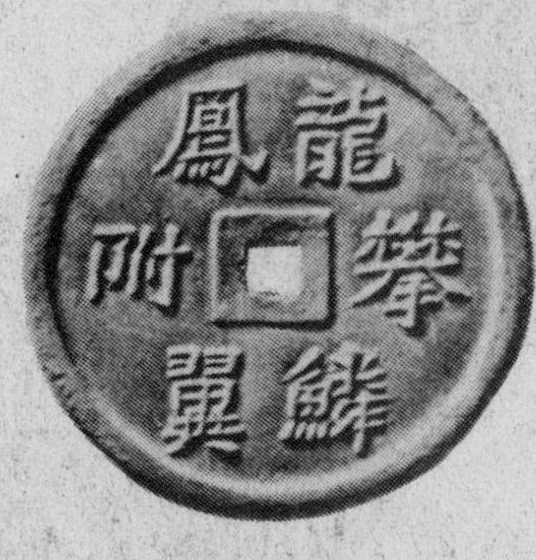

SILVER, 15.50 g
Obv. leg: ***Thieu Tri*** **between bird and dragon.**
Rev. leg: ***Phan Long Lau Phu Phung Duc.***

Sch#	Date	Emperor	VG	Fine	VF	XF
246	ND(1841-47)	Thieu Tri	70.00	140.00	240.00	400.00

Obv. leg: ***Thieu Tri Thong Bao.***
Rev. leg: ***Tu My*** **between Four Perfections.**
254 ND(1841-47)Thieu Tri 62.50 125.00 225.00 375.00

15.00-15.50 g
Obv. leg: ***Tu Duc Thong Bao.***
Rev. leg: ***Su Dan Phu Tho.***
351 ND(1848-83) Tu Duc 62.50 125.00 225.00 375.00

15.00 g
Rev. leg: ***Tu Tien Viet De*** **on dragon.**
380 ND(1848-83) Tu Duc 70.00 140.00 240.00 400.00

Rev. leg: *Tu My* between - Four Perfections.

Sch#	Date	Emperor	VG	Fine	VF	XF
—	ND(1848-83)	Tu Duc	70.00	140.00	240.00	400.00

Rev: Design finer style.

Sch#	Date	Emperor	VG	Fine	VF	XF
—	ND(1848-83)	Tu Duc	70.00	140.00	240.00	400.00

Obv. leg: *Dong Khanh Thong Bao.*
Rev. leg: *Tu My* between - Four Perfections.

Sch#	Date	Emperor	VG	Fine	VF	XF
—	ND(1885-88)	Dong Khanh	80.00	160.00	275.00	450.00

5 TIEN

SILVER, 19.00 g
Obv. leg: *Minh Mang Thong Bao.*
Rev. leg: *Long Van* on facing dragon.

Sch#	Date	Emperor	VG	Fine	VF	XF
188	ND(1820-41)	Minh Mang	70.00	140.00	240.00	400.00

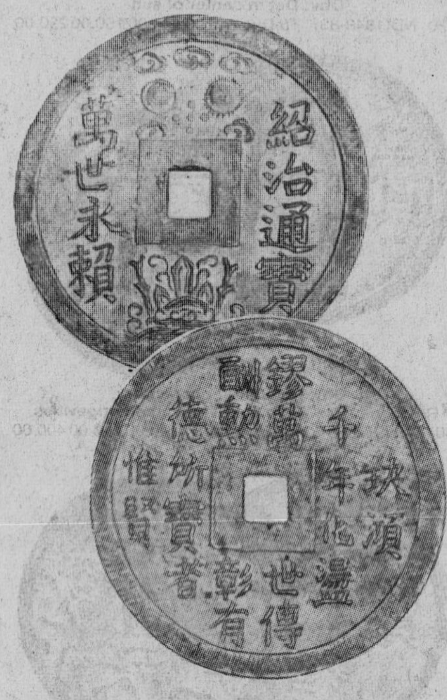

Obv. leg: *Thieu Tri Thong Bao, Van The Vinh Lai.*

Sch#	Date	Emperor	VG	Fine	VF	XF
242	ND(1841-47)	Thieu Tri	80.00	160.00	275.00	450.00

19.20 g
Obv. leg: *Thieu Tri* between bird and dragon.
Rev. leg: *Phan Long Lau Phu Phung Duc.*

Sch#	Date	Emperor	VG	Fine	VF	XF
243	ND(1841-47)	Thieu Tri	80.00	160.00	275.00	450.00

18.50-19.00 g
Obv. leg: *Thieu Tri Thong Bao, Trieu Dan Lai Chi.* Rev: Facing dragon.

Sch#	Date	Emperor	VG	Fine	VF	XF
247	ND(1841-47)	Thieu Tri	70.00	140.00	240.00	400.00

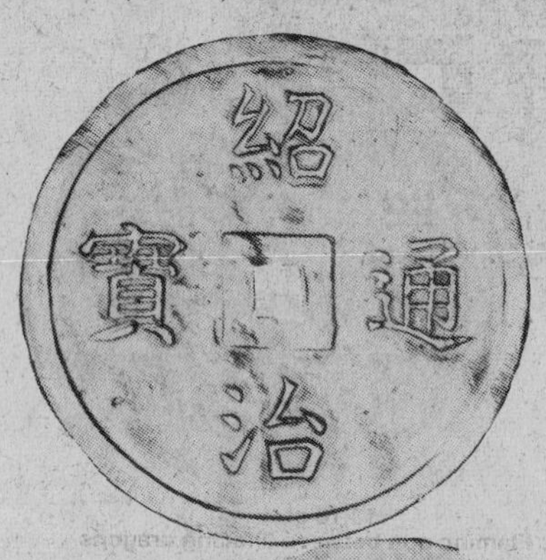

17.00-18.50 g
Obv. leg: *Thieu Tri Thong Bao.*
Rev. leg: *Phu Tho Da Nam.*

Sch#	Date	Emperor	VG	Fine	VF	XF
253	ND(1841-47)	Thieu Tri	70.00	140.00	240.00	400.00

Rev. leg: ***Ngu Phuc*** **between five bats.**

Sch#	Date	Emperor	VG	Fine	VF	XF
255	ND(1841-47)	Thieu Tri	80.00	160.00	275.00	450.00

19.00 g
Rev. leg: ***Long Van Khe Hoi*** **around facing dragon.**

Sch#	Date	Emperor	VG	Fine	VF	XF
261	ND(1841-47)	Thieu Tri	80.00	160.00	275.00	450.00

43mm, 26.60 g
Obv. leg: ***Tu Duc Thong Bao.***
Rev: 2 facing dragons.

Sch#	Date	Emperor	VG	Fine	VF	XF
347A	ND(1848-83)	Tu Duc	100.00	200.00	325.00	550.00

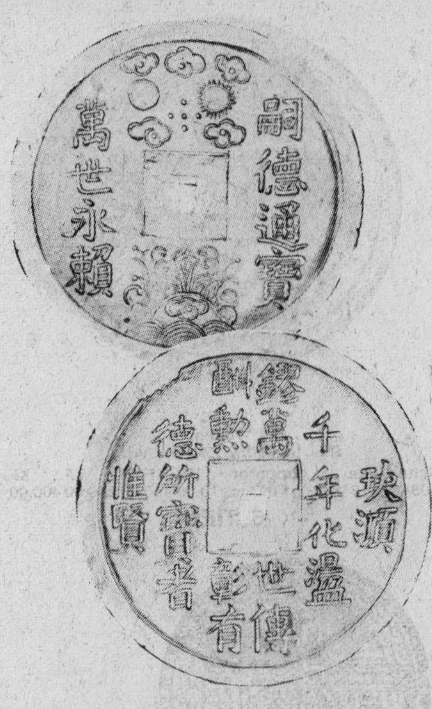

Obv. leg: ***Tu Duc Thong Bao, Van The Vinh Lai.***

Sch#	Date	Emperor	VG	Fine	VF	XF
348	ND(1848-83)	Tu Duc	80.00	160.00	275.00	450.00

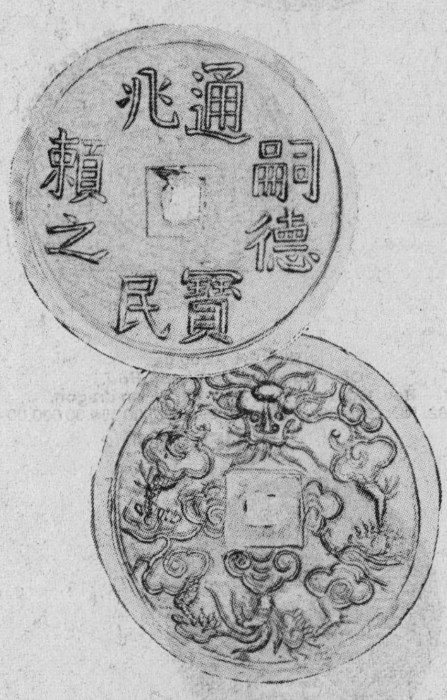

18.00 g
Obv. leg: ***Tu Duc Thong Bao, Trieu Dan Lai Chi.***

Sch#	Date	Emperor	VG	Fine	VF	XF
349.1	ND(1848-83)	Tu Duc	70.00	140.00	240.00	400.00

Rev: Round faced dragon.

Sch#	Date	Emperor	VG	Fine	VF	XF
349.2	ND(1848-83)	Tu Duc	70.00	140.00	240.00	400.00

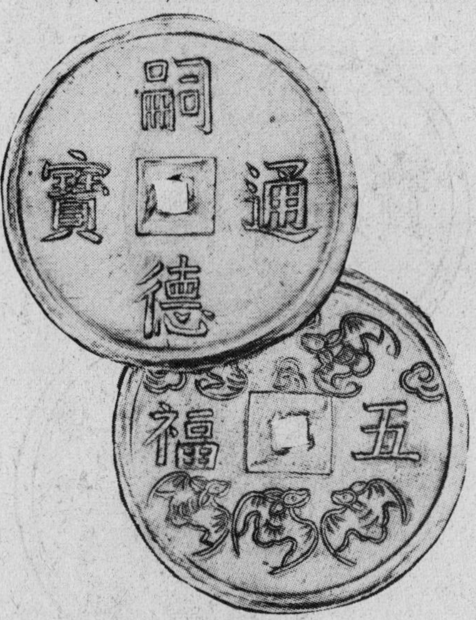

18.90 g
Obv. leg: ***Tu Duc Thong Bao.***
Rev. leg: ***Ngu Phuc*** **between five bats.**

Sch#	Date	Emperor	VG	Fine	VF	XF
359	ND(1848-83)	Tu Duc	80.00	160.00	275.00	450.00

18.50 g
Obv. & rev: Small sun at center.
Rev. leg: ***Long Van*** **on facing dragon.**

Sch#	Date	Emperor	VG	Fine	VF	XF
372.1	ND(1848-83)	Tu Duc	80.00	160.00	275.00	450.00

Obv. & rev: Large sun at center.

Sch#	Date	Emperor	VG	Fine	VF	XF
372.2	ND(1848-83)	Tu Duc	80.00	160.00	275.00	450.00

18.90-20.00 g
Obv: Flaming sun at center.
Rev. leg: *Long Van Khe Hoi* around facing dragon.

Sch#	Date	Emperor	VG	Fine	VF	XF
374	ND(1848-83)	Tu Duc	80.00	160.00	275.00	450.00

18.80 g
Rev. leg: *Ngu Tien Viet Ngai* on dragon.

Sch#	Date	Emperor	VG	Fine	VF	XF
381	ND(1848-83)	Tu Duc	80.00	160.00	275.00	450.00

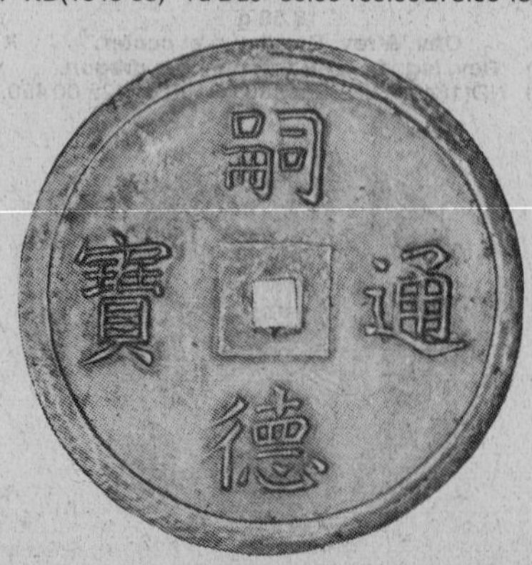

17.00 g
Rev. leg: *Phu Tho Da Nam.*

Sch#	Date	Emperor	VG	Fine	VF	XF
408A	ND(1848-83)	Tu Duc	70.00	140.00	240.00	400.00

6 TIEN

SILVER, 23.00 g
Obv. leg: *Tu Duc Thong Bao.*
Rev. leg: *Luc Tien Viet Thinh* on dragon.

Sch#	Date	Emperor	VG	Fine	VF	XF
382	ND(1848-83)	Tu Duc	100.00	200.00	350.00	600.00

7 TIEN

SILVER, 35mm, 26.30-26.70 g
Obv. leg: *Minh Mang Thong Bao*, around large sun. Rev: Small dragon.

Sch#	Date	Emperor	VG	Fine	VF	XF
181A	ND(1820-48)	Minh Mang	140.00	280.00	450.00	750.00

NOTE: Plain edge silver dragon coins are considered as medallic or presentation pieces while the crude oblique milled edge versions were meant for circulation for most Emperors.

40-42mm, 26.66-27.42 g
Obv: Large sun. Rev: Large dragon.

Sch#	Date	Emperor	VG	Fine	VF	XF
181B	ND(1820-48)	Minh Mang	140.00	280.00	450.00	600.00

Sch#	Date	Emperor	VG	Fine	VF	XF
181	(1832) Yr.13	Minh Mang	90.00	180.00	300.00	500.00

Obv: Small sun. Rev: Large dragon.

Sch#	Date	Emperor	VG	Fine	VF	XF
182	(1833) Yr.14	Minh Mang	70.00	140.00	240.00	400.00
183	(1834) Yr.15	Minh Mang	35.00	70.00	120.00	200.00

Sch#	Date	Emperor	VG	Fine	VF	XF
183A	(1835) Yr.16	Minh Mang	90.00	180.00	300.00	500.00

25.80-26.40 g
Obv. leg: *Thieu Tri Thong Bao.*
Rev: 2 facing dragons.

238	ND(1841-47)	Thieu Tri	175.00	350.00	600.00	1000.

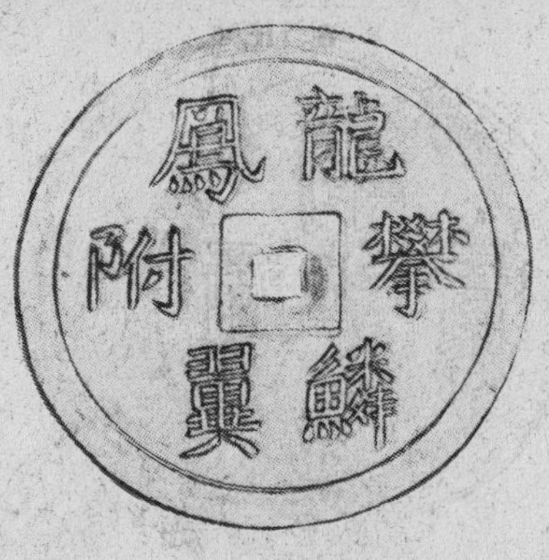

26.40-28.50 g
Obv. leg: *Thieu Tri* between bird and dragon.
Rev. leg: *Phan Long Lan Phu Phung Duc.*

Sch#	Date	Emperor	VG	Fine	VF	XF
244	ND(1841-47)	Thieu Tri	90.00	180.00	300.00	500.00

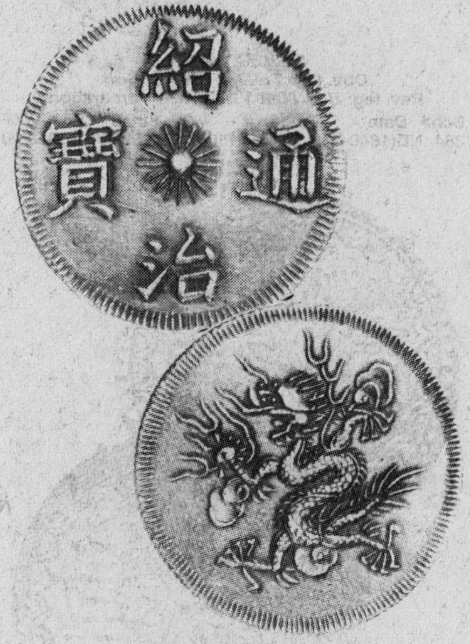

40.5mm, 26.50 g
Obv. large leg: *Thieu Tri Thong Bao.*
Rev: Small dragon left.

258.1	ND(1841-47)	Thieu Tri	70.00	140.00	240.00	400.00

Obv: Small leg.
Rev: Large dragon left.

258.2	ND(1841-47)	Thien Tri	90.00	180.00	300.00	500.00

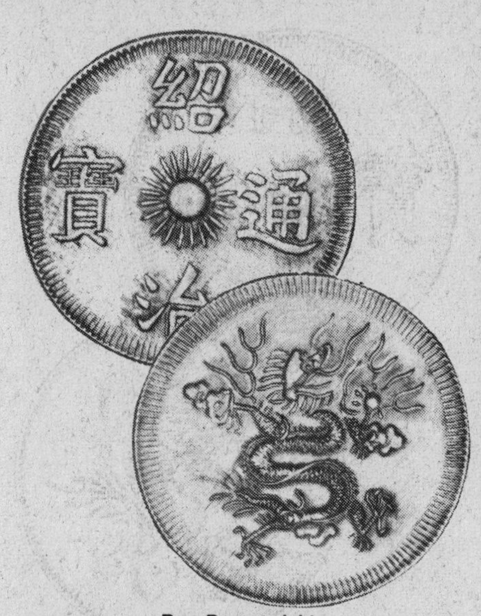

Rev: Dragon right.

Sch#	Date	Emperor	VG	Fine	VF	XF
258A	ND(1841-47)	Thieu Tri	100.00	200.00	350.00	600.00

51-53mm, 26.6 g
Obv. leg: *Tu Duc Thong Bao.*
Rev: Plain sun between 2 large facing dragons.

347B	ND(1848-83)	Tu Duc	150.00	300.00	500.00	850.00

Rev: Ornate sun between 2 small facing dragons.

347C	ND(1848-83)	Tu Duc	150.00	300.00	500.00	850.00

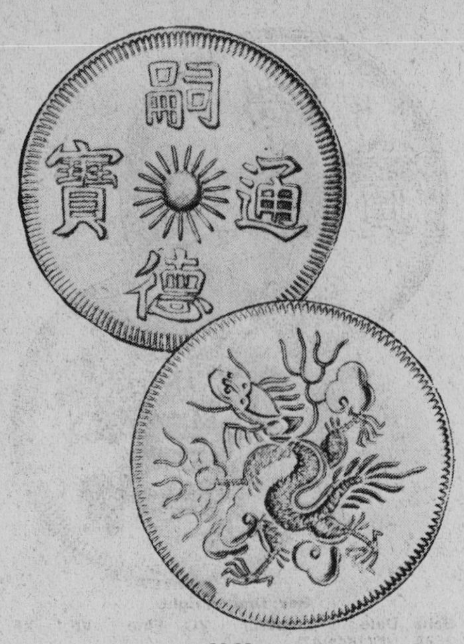

26.20 g
Rev: Dragon left.

Sch#	Date	Emperor	VG	Fine	VF	XF
368	ND(1848-83)	Tu Duc	70.00	140.00	240.00	400.00

26.50 g
Rev. leg: ***Long Van*** **on facing dragon.**

371	ND(1848-83)	Tu Duc	100.00	200.00	350.00	600.00

26.00 g
Rev. leg: ***That Tien Viet Hue*** **on dragon.**

383	ND(1848-83)	Tu Duc	150.00	300.00	500.00	850.00

7 TIEN 2 PHAN

(Dollar)

SILVER
Rev. leg: ***That Tien Nhi Phan.***

—	ND(1848-83)	Tu Duc	90.00	180.00	300.00	500.00

NOTE: Originally considered fantasies it has now been determined these were issued for payment of the war ransom to France in April 1865.

8 TIEN

SILVER, 30.50 g
Obv. leg: ***Tu Duc Thong Bao.***
Rev. leg: ***Bat Tien Viet Thuan*** **on dragon.**

Sch#	Date	Emperor	VG	Fine	VF	XF
384	ND(1848-83)	Tu Duc	150.00	300.00	500.00	850.00

9 TIEN

SILVER, 34.20 g
Obv. leg: ***Tu Duc Thong Bao.***
Rev. leg: ***Cuu Tien Viet Nhan*** **on dragon.**

385	ND(1848-83)	Tu Duc	175.00	350.00	600.00	1000.

LANG

SILVER, 38mm, 38.00 g
Obv. leg: ***Minh Mang Thong Bao*** **around small sun.**
Rev. leg: ***Long Van*** **on facing dragon.**

187	ND(1820-41) Minh Mang	120.00	240.00	400.00	650.00

40mm
Obv. & rev: Large sun at center.

Sch#	Date	Emperor	VG	Fine	VF	XF
187A	ND(1820-41)	Minh Mang	135.00	270.00	450.00	750.00

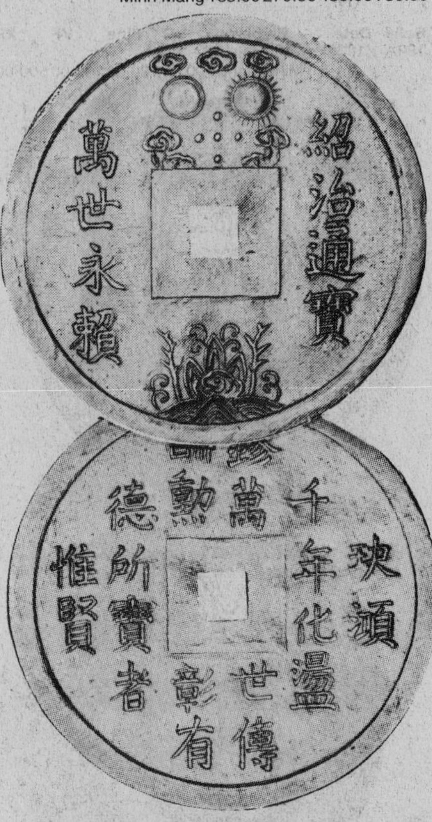

38-38.80 g
Illustration reduced, actual size 63mm
Obv. leg: ***Thieu Tri Thong Bao, Van The Vinh Lai.***

241	ND(1841-47)	Thieu Tri	175.00	350.00	600.00	1000.

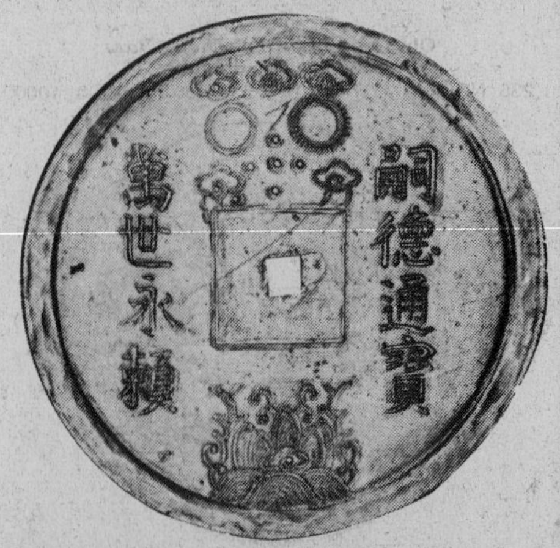

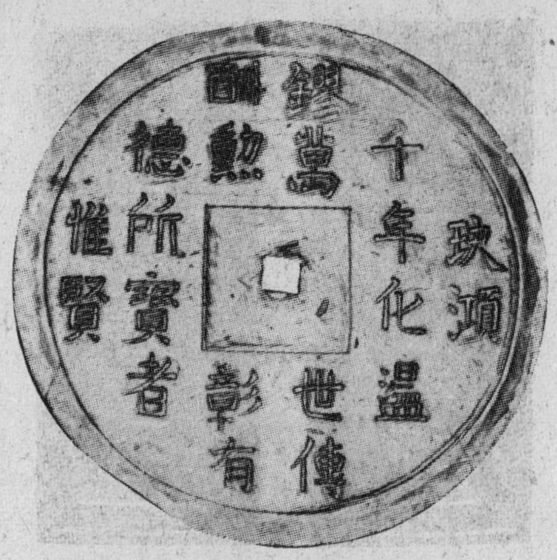

37.30 g
Illustration reduced, actual size 63mm
Obv. leg: *Tu Duc Thong Bao, Van The Vinh Lai.*

Sch#	Date	Emperor	VG	Fine	VF	XF
348	ND(1848-83)	Tu Duc	175.00	350.00	600.00	1000.

37.20 g
Obv. leg: *Tu Duc Thong Bao.*
Rev. leg: *Long Van* on facing dragon.

Sch#	Date	Emperor	VG	Fine	VF	XF
371	ND(1848-83)	Tu Duc	135.00	270.00	450.00	700.00

37.40 g
Rev. leg: *Nhat Lang Viet Trung* on dragon.

Sch#	Date	Emperor	VG	Fine	VF	XF
376	ND(1848-83)	Tu Duc	225.00	450.00	750.00	1250.

65mm, weight unknown.
Obv. leg: *Than Thai Thong Bao, Van The Vinh Lai.* Rev: Similar to Sch#241.

Sch#	Date	Emperor	VG	Fine	VF	XF
431	ND(1888-1907)	Thanh Thai	175.00	350.00	600.00	1000.

SILVER BARS

All of the bars described here are inscribed with their weight, except the 10 Lang "banana bars", and many contain a date or the name of the province in which they were made.

TIEN

SILVER, 3.80-3.90 g

Sch#	Date	Emperor	VG	Fine	VF	XF
174	ND(1820-41)	Minh Mang	45.00	75.00	100.00	150.00

4.20 g

Sch#	Date	Emperor	VG	Fine	VF	XF
175	ND(1820-41)	Minh Mang	45.00	75.00	100.00	150.00

1-1/2 TIEN

SILVER, 5.00-5.20 g

Sch#	Date	Emperor	VG	Fine	VF	XF
340	ND(1848-83)	Tu Duc	45.00	75.00	100.00	150.00

2 TIEN

SILVER, 8.00 g

Sch#	Date	Emperor	VG	Fine	VF	XF
176	ND(1820-41)	Minh Mang	50.00	85.00	120.00	175.00

7.00-7.50 g
Court Treasury. Rev: 5 characters.

Sch#	Date	Emperor	VG	Fine	VF	XF
331	ND(1848-83)	Tu Duc	50.00	85.00	120.00	175.00

7.90 g
Court Treasury. Rev: Error, third and fifth characters the same.

Sch#	Date	Emperor	VG	Fine	VF	XF
337	ND(1848-83)	Tu Duc	50.00	85.00	120.00	175.00

6.80 g
Rev: 4 characters.

Sch#	Date	Emperor	VG	Fine	VF	XF
335	ND(1848-83)	Tu Duc	50.00	85.00	120.00	175.00

3 TIEN

SILVER, 11.60 g

Sch#	Date	Emperor	VG	Fine	VF	XF
177	ND(1820-41)	Minh Mang	75.00	125.00	175.00	250.00

10.20 g
Court Treasury

Sch#	Date	Emperor	VG	Fine	VF	XF
332	ND(1848-83)	Tu Duc	75.00	125.00	175.00	250.00

4 TIEN

SILVER, 15.40 g

Sch#	Date	Emperor	VG	Fine	VF	XF
178	ND(1820-41)	Minh Mang	85.00	140.00	200.00	300.00

15.50 g
Court Treasury

Sch#	Date	Emperor	VG	Fine	VF	XF
236	ND(1841-47)	Thieu Tri	85.00	140.00	200.00	300.00

15.00 g
Court Treasury

Sch#	Date	Emperor	VG	Fine	VF	XF
333	ND(1848-83)	Tu Duc	85.00	140.00	200.00	300.00

5 TIEN

SILVER, weight unknown
Rev: *Trung Binh* at top.

Sch#	Date	Emperor	VG	Fine	VF	XF
122	ND(1802-20)	Gia Long	100.00	175.00	250.00	350.00

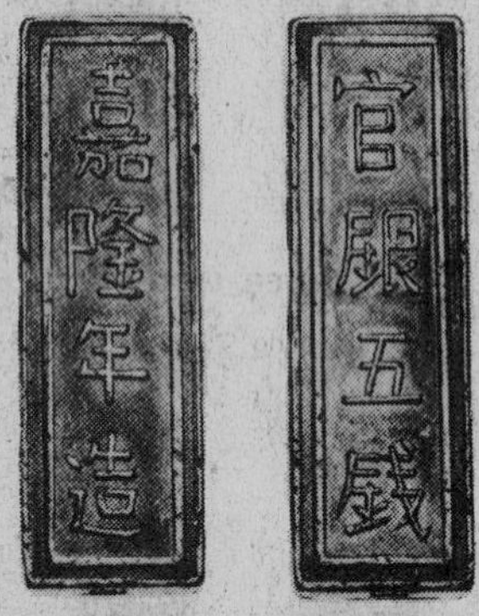

Rev: 4 characters.

Sch#	Date	Emperor	VG	Fine	VF	XF
122A	ND(1802-20)	Gia Long	100.00	175.00	250.00	350.00

SILVER, 19.00 g
Rev: 4 characters.

Sch#	Date	Emperor	VG	Fine	VF	XF
179	ND(1820-41)	Minh Mang	100.00	175.00	250.00	350.00

19.20 g
Court Treasury. Rev: 5 characters.

Sch#	Date	Emperor	VG	Fine	VF	XF
237	ND(1841-47)	Thieu Tri	100.00	175.00	250.00	350.00

19.00 g
Court Treasury

Sch#	Date	Emperor	VG	Fine	VF	XF
334	ND(1848-83)	Tu Duc	100.00	175.00	250.00	350.00

LANG

SILVER, 37.94 g
Large characters.

Sch#	Date	Emperor	VG	Fine	VF	XF
118	ND(1802-20)	Gia Long	25.00	40.00	55.00	80.00

NOTE: Produced as a common form of bullion into the 20th century.

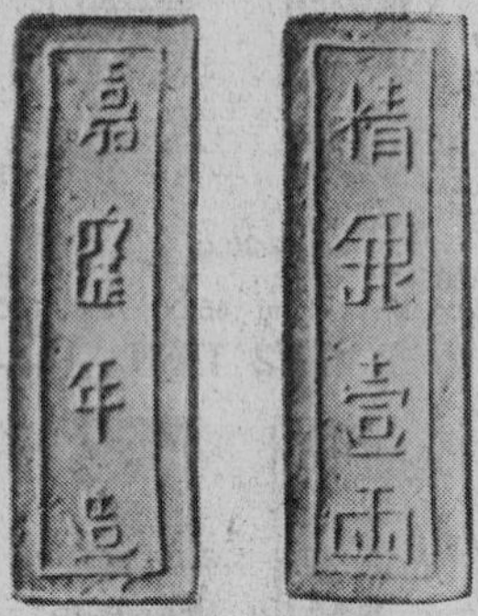

38.13-38.55 g
Small characters.

Sch#	Date	Emperor	VG	Fine	VF	XF
119	ND(1802-20)	Gia Long	60.00	100.00	140.00	200.00

NOTE: Varieties of edge inscriptions exist.

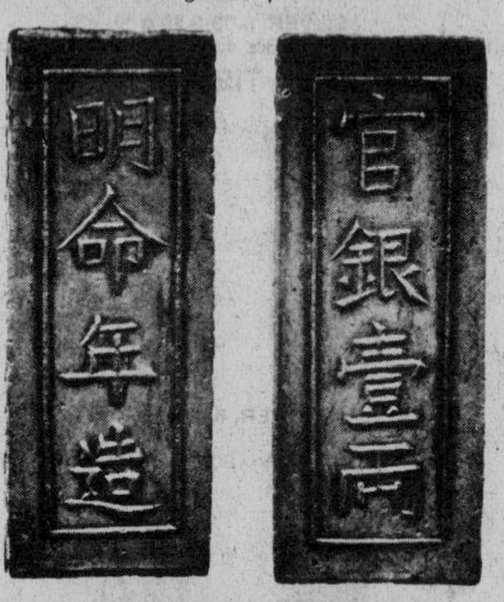

SILVER, 57.2-57.8mm, 38.16-38.57 g

Sch#	Date	Emperor	VG	Fine	VF	XF
169	ND(1820-41)	Minh Mang	75.00	125.00	175.00	250.00

41mm, weight unknown.

Sch#	Date	Emperor	VG	Fine	VF	XF
—	ND(1820-41)	Minh Mang	60.00	100.00	140.00	200.00

38.00 g
Court Treasury

Sch#	Date	Emperor	VG	Fine	VF	XF
219	ND(1841-47)	Thieu Tri	75.00	125.00	185.00	275.00

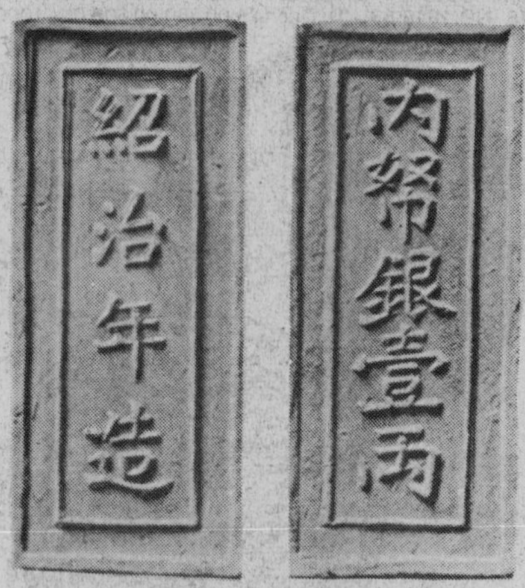

Rev: *Gia Dinh* at top.

Sch#	Date	Emperor	VG	Fine	VF	XF
—	CD1844	Thieu Tri	100.00	175.00	250.00	350.00

37.43-38.33 g
Court Treasury

Sch#	Date	Emperor	VG	Fine	VF	XF
324B	ND(1848-83)	Tu Duc	25.00	40.00	55.00	80.00

NOTE: Produced as a common form of bullion into the 20th century.

38.00 g
Binh Dinh on edge.

Sch#	Date	Emperor	VG	Fine	VF	XF
320A	ND(1848-83)	Tu Duc	60.00	100.00	140.00	200.00

Weight unknown
Dinh Tuong on edge.

Sch#	Date	Emperor	VG	Fine	VF	XF
320B	CD1859	Tu Duc	100.00	175.00	250.00	350.00

57mm, 38.29 g
***Phu Yen* on edge.**

Sch#	Date	Emperor	VG	Fine	VF	XF
320C	CD1859	Tu Duc	100.00	175.00	250.00	350.00
	Canh Than					
323	CD1860	Tu Duc	100.00	175.00	250.00	350.00

58mm, 38.69 g
Obv: Date. Rev: *Binh Dinh* at top.

Sch#	Date	Emperor	VG	Fine	VF	XF
321	CD1861	Tu Duc	100.00	175.00	250.00	350.00

Weight unknown
Rev. leg: *Phu Yen* at top.

Sch#	Date	Emperor	VG	Fine	VF	XF
322	CD1861	Tu Duc	100.00	175.00	250.00	350.00
	37.00 g					
	Obv: Date. Rev. leg: *An Giang*.					
324	CD1863	Tu Duc	150.00	250.00	350.00	500.00
	37.70 g					
	Court Treasury. Very crude.					
	Fineness (.700) inscribed on edge.					
423	ND(1885-88)	Dong Khanh	75.00	125.00	175.00	250.00
	Weight unknown					
	Date on edge					
—	CD1919	Khai Dinh	75.00	125.00	185.00	275.00
—	CD1922	Khai Dinh	75.00	125.00	185.00	275.00

5 LANG

SILVER, 181.00-191.00 g

Sch#	Date	Emperor	VG	Fine	VF	XF
170	ND(1820-41)	Minh Mang	200.00	350.00	500.00	700.00
	40x92mm, 186.00-191.00 g					
	Court Treasury					
220	ND(1841-47)	Thieu Tri	200.00	350.00	500.00	700.00

10 LANG

Curved Series

SILVER, about 385.00 g
Top: W/two 4-character rectangular markings.

Sch#	Date	Emperor	VG	Fine	VF	XF
—	ND(1802-19)	Gia Long	75.00	125.00	185.00	275.00

NOTE: Produced as a common form of bullion into the 20th century.

Sch#	Date	Emperor	VG	Fine	VF	XF
	Court Treasury. Similar to Sch#173.					
171	CD1832	Minh Mang	300.00	500.00	700.00	1000.
	***Quang An*. Similar to Sch#173.**					
—	CD1832	Minh Mang	300.00	500.00	700.00	1000.
	Court Treasury. Similar to Sch#173.					
172	CD1833	Minh Mang	300.00	500.00	700.00	1000.
	***Son Tay*. Similar to Sch#173.**					
—	CD1833	Minh Mang	300.00	500.00	700.00	1000.

***Son Tay*.**

Sch#	Date	Emperor	VG	Fine	VF	XF
173	CD1837	Minh Mang	300.00	500.00	700.00	1000.

383.00 g
***Son Tay*. Similar to Sch#173.**

Sch#	Date	Emperor	VG	Fine	VF	XF
330	CD1852	Tu Duc	Reported, not confirmed			
	***Thai Nguyen*. Similar to Sch#173.**					
325	CD1860	Tu Duc	275.00	450.00	625.00	900.00
	***Binh Dinh*. Similar to Sch#173.**					
326	CD1861	Tu Duc	275.00	450.00	625.00	900.00
	***Son Tay*. Similar to Sch#173.**					
327	CD1880	Tu Duc	275.00	450.00	625.00	900.00
	***Nghe An*. Similar to Sch#173.**					
328	CD1882	Tu Duc	275.00	450.00	625.00	900.00
	Top: W/two 4-character rectangular markings.					
—	ND(1848-83)	Tu Duc	75.00	125.00	185.00	275.00

NOTE: Produced as a common form of bullion into the 20th century.

NOTE: 10 Lang curved "banana bars" of these types without any characters on their top surfaces but with various markings on their ends and sides were also produced as a common form of bullion into the 20th century.

Flat Series

42x115mm
Court Treasury.

Sch#	Date	Emperor	VG	Fine	VF	XF
221	ND(1841-74)	Thieu Tri	250.00	425.00	600.00	850.00

NOTE: Illustration reduced 50% of actual size.

45x120mm. About 385.00 g
Rev. leg: *Hung Yen* at top.

Sch#	Date	Emperor	VG	Fine	VF	XF
222	CD1844	Thieu Tri	250.00	425.00	600.00	850.00
	Rev. leg: *Binh Dinh* at top.					
223	CD1844	Thieu Tri	250.00	425.00	600.00	850.00

***Quang Yen*.**

Sch#	Date	Emperor	VG	Fine	VF	XF
—	CD1844	Thieu Tri	250.00	425.00	600.00	850.00

NOTE: Illustration reduced 50% of actual size.

Sch#	Date	Emperor	VG	Fine	VF	XF
	Rev. leg: *Son Tay* at top.					
224	CD1845	Thieu Tri	250.00	425.00	600.00	850.00
	48x120mm, 385.00 g					
	Rev. leg: *Quang Nam* at top.					
225	CD1846	Thieu Tri	250.00	425.00	600.00	850.00
	Rev. leg: *Son Tay* at top.					
—	CD1846	Thieu Tri	250.00	425.00	600.00	850.00

Rev. leg: *Din Nam* at top.

Sch#	Date	Emperor	VG	Fine	VF	XF
—	CD1846	Thieu Tri	250.00	425.00	600.00	850.00

NOTE: Illustration reduced 50% of actual size.

46x120mm

Rev. leg: *Hung Yen* at top.

Sch#	Date	Emperor	VG	Fine	VF	XF
226	CD1847	Thieu Tri	250.00	425.00	600.00	850.00

Rev. leg: *Lang Son* at top.

Sch#	Date	Emperor	VG	Fine	VF	XF
227	CD1847	Thieu Tri	250.00	425.00	600.00	850.00

Rev. leg: *Bac Ninh* at top.

Sch#	Date	Emperor	VG	Fine	VF	XF
228	CD1847	Thieu Tri	250.00	425.00	600.00	850.00

Rev. leg: *Son Tay* at top.

Sch#	Date	Emperor	VG	Fine	VF	XF
229	CD1847	Thieu Tri	250.00	425.00	600.00	850.00

Rev. leg: *Gia Dinh* at top.

Sch#	Date	Emperor	VG	Fine	VF	XF
230	CD1847	Thieu Tri	250.00	425.00	600.00	850.00

Weight unknown

Rev. leg: *Hung Yen* at top.

Sch#	Date	Emperor	VG	Fine	VF	XF
—	CD1844	Thieu Tri	250.00	425.00	600.00	850.00

Rev. leg: *Son Tay* at top.

Sch#	Date	Emperor	VG	Fine	VF	XF
—	CD1844	Thieu Tri	250.00	425.00	600.00	850.00

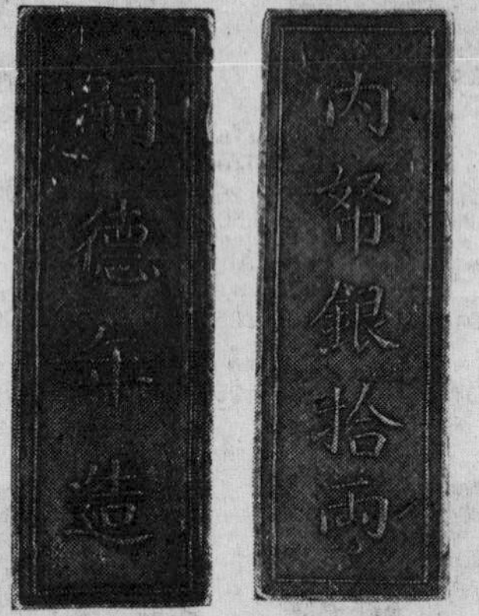

34x100mm, 382.50 g

Court Treasury

Sch#	Date	Emperor	VG	Fine	VF	XF
329	ND(1848-83)	Tu Duc	250.00	425.00	600.00	850.00

NOTE: Illustration reduced 50% of actual size.

20 LANG

SILVER, 49x122mm, 765.50 g

Court Treasury. Legends both sides framed within ornate border of dragons obv. and bats rev.

Sch#	Date	Emperor	VG	Fine	VF	XF
231	ND(1841-47)	Thieu Tri	—	—	Rare	—

30 LANG

SILVER, 55x127mm, 1149.00 g

Similar to 20 Lang, Sch #231.

Sch#	Date	Emperor	VG	Fine	VF	XF
232	ND(1841-47)	Thieu Tri		—	Rare	—

40 LANG

SILVER, 60x130mm, 1528.00 g

Similar to 20 Lang, Sch#231.

Sch#	Date	Emperor	VG	Fine	VF	XF
233	ND(1841-47)	Thieu Tri	—	—	Rare	—

50 LANG

SILVER, 65x140mm, 1915.00 g

Similar to 20 Lang, Sch#231.

Sch#	Date	Emperor	VG	Fine	VF	XF
234	ND(1841-47)	Thieu Tri	—	—	Rare	—

100 LANG

SILVER, 77x160mm, 3831.00 g

Similar to 20 Lang, Sch#231.

Sch#	Date	Emperor	VG	Fine	VF	XF
235	ND(1841-47)	Thieu Tri	—	—	Rare	—

QUAN SYSTEM

(Silver Bars Only)

1/2 QUAN

SILVER, weight unknown

Sch#	Date	Emperor	VG	Fine	VF	XF
338	ND(1848-83)	Tu Duc	42.50	70.00	100.00	150.00

7/10 QUAN

SILVER, 3.50 g

Sch#	Date	Emperor	VG	Fine	VF	XF
339	ND(1848-83)	Tu Duc	60.00	100.00	140.00	200.00

QUAN

SILVER, 5.00-5.28 g

Sch#	Date	Emperor	VG	Fine	VF	XF
340	ND(1848-83)	Tu Duc	50.00	85.00	120.00	175.00

1-1/2 QUAN

SILVER, 7.50-8.00 g

Sch#	Date	Emperor	VG	Fine	VF	XF
341	ND(1848-83)	Tu Duc	60.00	100.00	140.00	200.00

2 QUAN

SILVER, 10.50 g

Sch#	Date	Emperor	VG	Fine	VF	XF
342	ND(1848-83)	Tu Duc	65.00	110.00	160.00	225.00

10.30-10.50 g

Similar to Sch#342, but thinner characters.

Sch#	Date	Emperor	VG	Fine	VF	XF
345	ND(1848-83)	Tu Duc	75.00	125.00	175.00	250.00

2-1/2 QUAN

SILVER, 13.00-13.50 g

Sch#	Date	Emperor	VG	Fine	VF	XF
343	ND(1848-83)	Tu Duc	85.00	140.00	200.00	275.00

3 QUAN

SILVER, 15.92-16.20 g

Thick characters.

Sch#	Date	Emperor	VG	Fine	VF	XF
344	ND(1848-83)	Tu Duc	90.00	150.00	210.00	300.00

15.40 g

Thin characters.

Obv. & rev: Double borders.

Sch#	Date	Emperor	VG	Fine	VF	XF
346	ND(1848-83)	Tu Duc	90.00	150.00	210.00	300.00

GOLD COINAGE

1/2 TIEN

GOLD, 1.80 g

Obv. leg: *Thieu Tri Thong Bao*. Rev: Blank.

Sch#	Date	Emperor	VG	Fine	VF	XF
257	ND(1841-47)	Thieu Tri	150.00	275.00	450.00	700.00

Obv. leg: *Dong Khanh Thong Bao*. Rev: Blank.

Sch#	Date	Emperor	VG	Fine	VF	XF
424	ND(1885-88)	Dong Khanh	150.00	275.00	450.00	700.00

TIEN

GOLD, 3.65-4.00 g

Obv. leg: *Minh Mang Thong Bao*.

Rev: 5 planets.

Sch#	Date	Emperor	VG	Fine	VF	XF
209.1	ND(1820-41)	Minh Mang	300.00	600.00	900.00	1400.

Rev: Mirror image.

Sch#	Date	Emperor	VG	Fine	VF	XF
209.2	ND(1820-41)	Minh Mang	300.00	600.00	900.00	1400.

Obv. leg: *Thieu Tri Thong Bao*.

Rev. leg: *Nhat Nguyen*.

Sch#	Date	Emperor	VG	Fine	VF	XF
250B	ND(1841-47)	Thieu Tri	350.00	700.00	1150.	1800.

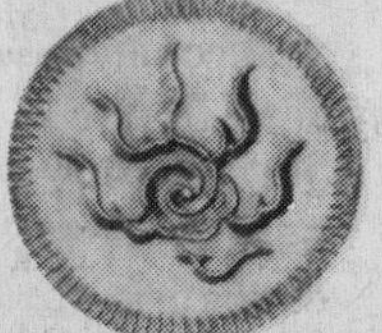

Rev: Flaming sun w/lower flames right.

Sch#	Date	Emperor	VG	Fine	VF	XF
287.1	ND(1841-47)	Thieu Tri	325.00	650.00	1000.	1500.

Rev: Flaming sun w/lower flames left.

287.2 ND(1841-47) Thieu Tri 325.00 650.00 1000. 1500.

3.80 g
Rev: Scepter and swastika.

288 ND(1841-47) Thieu Tri 325.00 650.00 1000. 1500.

4.00 g
Rev: Guitar.

289.1 ND(1841-47) Thieu Tri 325.00 650.00 1000. 1500.

Rev: Mirror image.

289.2 ND(1841-47) Thieu Tri — — — 1800.

Rev: Horn.

290 ND(1841-47) Thieu Tri 325.00 650.00 1000. 1500.

3.80 g
Rev: Fan.

291 ND(1841-47) Thieu Tri 325.00 650.00 1000. 1500.

4.00 g
Rev: Calabash.

292 ND(1841-47) Thieu Tri 325.00 650.00 1000. 1500.

4.20 g
Rev: Clappers.

Sch#	Date	Emperor	VG	Fine	VF	XF
293	ND(1841-47)	Thieu Tri	325.00	650.00	1000.	1500.

4.00 g
Rev: Books.

294 ND(1841-47) Thieu Tri 325.00 650.00 1000. 1500.

3.80 g
Rev: *Tam Da*, above the Three Plenties.

295 ND(1841-47) Thieu Tri 325.00 650.00 1000. 1500.

3.70 g
Rev. leg: *Nhat Nguyen*.

353B ND(1848-83) Tu Duc — — — 3000.

3.80 g
Rev: *Nhat Nguyen Tien Viet Tu* on dragon.

377 ND(1848-83) Tu Duc 325.00 650.00 1000. 1500.

Rev: Sun, moon and 5 planets.

386A ND(1848-83) Tu Duc 325.00 650.00 1000. 1500.

Rev: Scepter and swastika.

388B ND(1848-83) Tu Duc — — — 3000.

3.90 g
Obv. leg: *Thanh Thai Thong Bao*.
Rev: *Nhat Nguyen*.

432 ND(1888-1907) Thanh Thai 325.00 650.00 1000. 1500.

1-1/2 TIEN

GOLD, 5.40-6.50 g
Obv. leg: *Minh Mang*.
Rev: Five Precious symbols.

Sch#	Date	Emperor	VG	Fine	VF	XF
211	ND(1820-41)	Minh Mang	350.00	700.00	1100.	1650.

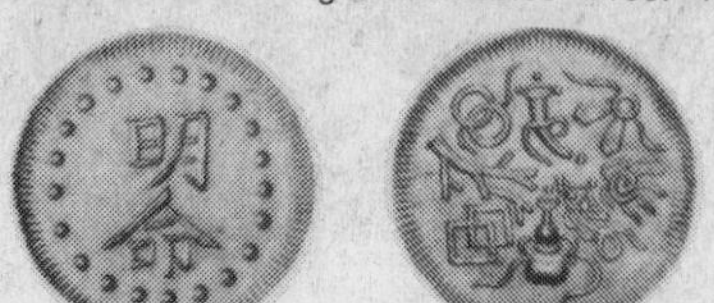

5.70 g
Rev: Eight Precious symbols.

212 ND(1820-41) Minh Mang 350.00 700.00 1100. 1650.

Rev: Mirror image.

213 ND(1820-41) Minh Mang 350.00 700.00 1100. 1650.

5.60 g
Obv. leg: *Tu Duc Thong Bao*.
Rev. leg: *Su Dan Phu Tho*.

406 ND(1848-83) Tu Duc 350.00 700.00 1000. 1500.

6.40-6.90 g
Obv. leg: *Dong Kanh Thong Bao*.
Rev. leg: *Nhi Nghi* between moon and sun.

425.1 ND(1885-88) Dong Khanh 240.00 480.00 800.00 1200.

Rev. leg: *Nhi Nghi* between sun and moon.

425.2 ND(1885-88) Dong Khanh 240.00 480.00 800.00 1200.

6.60 g
Obv. leg: *Thanh Thai Thong Bao*.
Rev. leg: *Nhi Nghi* between moon and sun.

435 ND(1888-1907) Thanh Thai 240.00 480.00 800.00 1200.

2 TIEN

GOLD, 7.80 g
Obv. leg: *Minh Mang*.
Rev. leg: *Tam Da* above the Three Plenties.

210 ND(1820-41) Minh Mang 350.00 700.00 1100. 1650.

Obv. leg: *Thieu Tri Thong Bao*.
Rev. leg: *Nhi Nghi* between moon and sun.

281 ND(1841-47) Thieu Tri 350.00 700.00 1100. 1650.

7.30 g
Obv. leg: *Tu Duc Thong Bao.*
Rev. leg: *Nhi Tien Viet Hien* on dragon.

Sch#	Date	Emperor	VG	Fine	VF	XF
378	ND(1848-83)	Tu Duc	350.00	700.00	1100.	1650.

Rev: Flaming sun between facing dragons.

402B	ND(1848-83)	Tu Duc	400.00	800.00	1200.	1800.

2-1/2 TIEN

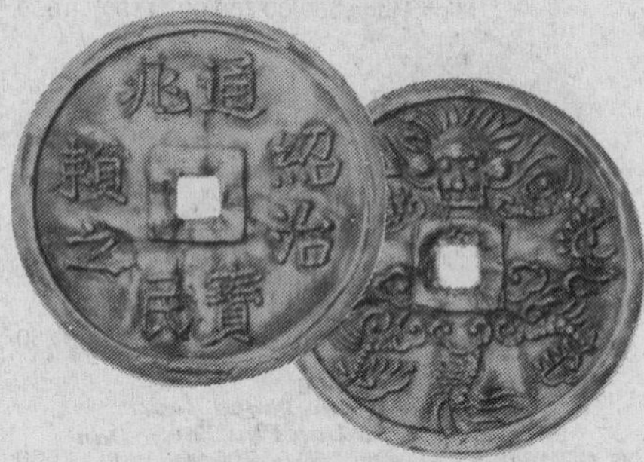

GOLD, 8.90 g
Obv. leg: *Thieu Tri Thong Bao.*
Rev: Facing dragon.

280B	ND(1841-47)	Thieu Tri	—	—	—	3250.

9.25-9.85 g
Obv. leg: *Thieu Tri Thong Bao, Trieu Dan Lai Chi.* Rev. leg: *Long Van Khe Hoi* around facing dragon.

375	ND(1848-83)	Tu Duc	400.00	750.00	1200.	1750.

3 TIEN

GOLD, 11.50-13.30 g
Obv. leg: *Minh Mang Thong Bao.*

207	ND (1820-40)	Minh Mang	550.00	1100.	1800.	2700.

Sch#	Date	Emperor	VG	Fine	VF	XF
208	(1833) Yr.14	Minh Mang	550.00	1100.	1800.	2700.

206C	(1834) Yr.15	Minh Mang	550.00	1100.	1800.	2700.

206D	(1835) Yr.16	Minh Mang	—	—	2000.	—

13.54 g
Obv. leg: *Thieu Tri Thong Bao.*
Rev: Large dragon.

285	ND(1841-47)	Thieu Tri	550.00	1100.	1800.	2700.

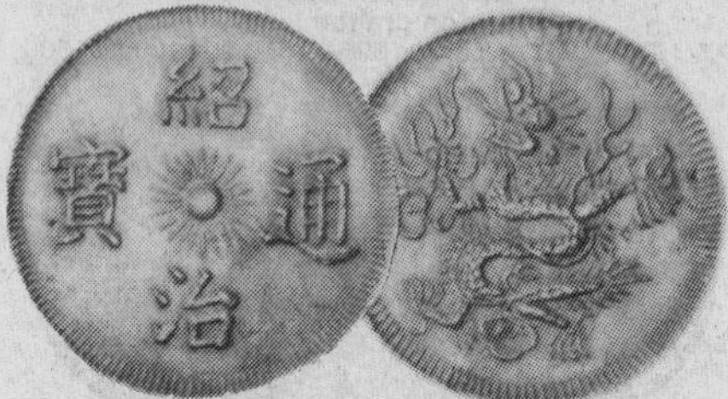

Rev: Small dragon.

286	ND(1841-47)	Thieu Tri	550.00	1100.	1800.	2700.

13.24 g
Obv. leg: *Tu Duc Thong Bao.*

413	ND(1848-83)	Tu Duc	550.00	1100.	1800.	2700.

11.00 g
Rev. leg: *Tam Thao* above Three Longevities.

Sch#	Date	Emperor	VG	Fine	VF	XF
407	ND(1848-83)	Tu Duc	600.00	1200.	2000.	3000.

11.20 g
Rev. leg: *Long Van* on facing dragon.

373B	ND(1848-83)	Tu Duc	600.00	1200.	2000.	3000.

11.30 g
Rev. leg: *Tam Tien Viet Lang* on dragon.

379B	ND(1848-83)	Tu Duc	550.00	1100.	1800.	2700.

10.50-12.40 g
Obv. leg: *Thanh Thai Thong Bao.*
Rev: Dragon.

433	ND(1888-1907)	Thanh Thai	1000.	2000.	3250.	5000.

10.00-10.50 g
Rev: *Tam Tho*, dragon above Three Longevities.

436	ND(1888-1907)	Thanh Thai	550.00	1100.	1800.	2700.

4 TIEN

GOLD, 14.70 g
Obv. leg: *Tu Duc Thong Bao.*
Rev. leg: *Su Dan Phu Tho.*

406	ND(1848-83)	Tu Duc	650.00	1300.	2200.	3300.

14.50-15.20 g
Rev. leg: *Tu My* between the Four Perfections.

409.1	ND(1848-83)	Tu Duc	650.00	1300.	2200.	3300.

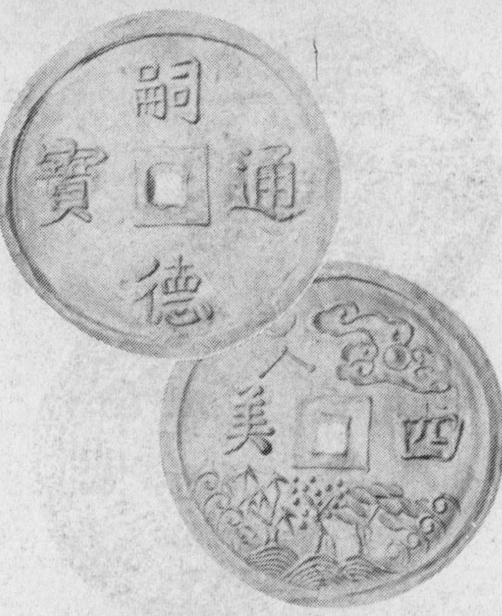

Rev: Finer style.

Sch#	Date	Emperor	VG	Fine	VF	XF
409.2	ND(1848-83)	Tu Duc	650.00	1300.	2200.	3300.

15.00 g
Rev. leg: *Tu Tien Viet De* on dragon.

380	ND(1848-83)	Tu Duc	650.00	1300.	2200.	3300.

13.16 g
Rev: Flaming sun between facing dragons.

402C	ND(1848-83)	Tu Duc	—	—	—	7000.

14.50 g
Obv. leg: *Thanh Thai Thong Bao.*
Rev. leg: *Tu My* between Four Perfections.

437	ND(1888-1907)	Thanh Thai	650.00	1300.	2200.	3300.

5 TIEN

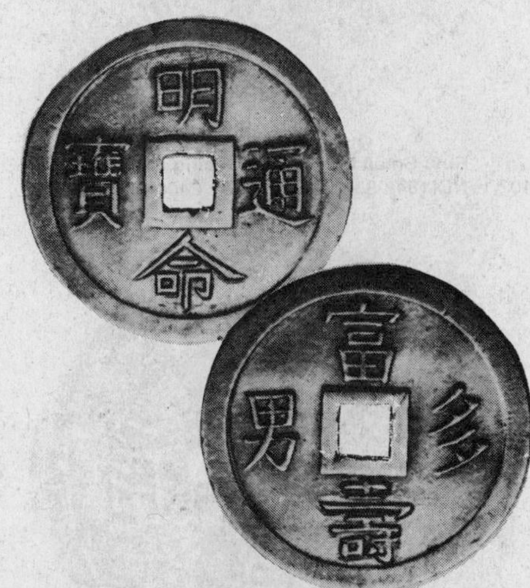

GOLD, 19.20 g
Obv. leg: *Minh Mang Thong Bao.*
Rev. leg: *Phu Tho Da Nam.*

205	ND(1820-41)	Minh Mang	1000.	2000.	3250.	5000.

17.61 g
Obv. leg: *Thieu Tri Thong Bao.*
Rev. leg: *Phu Tho Da Nam.*

Sch#	Date	Emperor	VG	Fine	VF	XF
253B	ND(1841-47)	Thieu Tri	1100.	2200.	3600.	5400.

19.50 g
Obv. leg: *Thieu Tri Thong Bao, Van The Vinh Lai.*

279	ND(1841-47)	Thieu Tri	1100.	2200.	3600.	5400.

18.00-20.00 g
Obv. leg: *Tu Duc Thong Bao.*
Rev. leg: *Long Van Khe Hoi* around dragon.

374B	ND(1848-83)	Tu Duc	1000.	2000.	3250.	5000.

18.90 g
Obv: Sun w/8 rays at center.
Rev. leg: *Long Van* on facing dragon.

414C	ND(1848-83)	Tu Duc	1000.	2000.	3250.	5000.

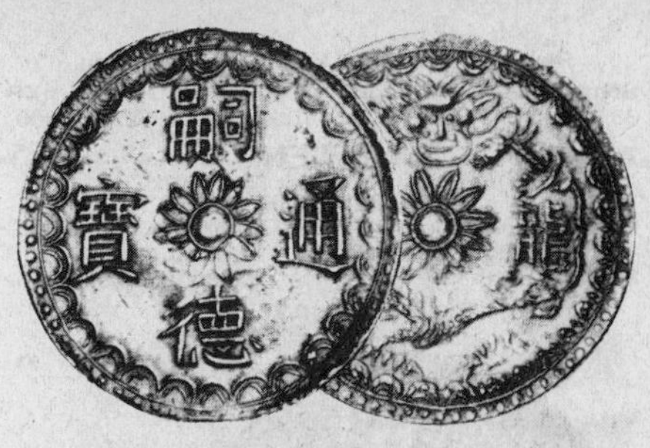

18.24 g
Obv: Sun w/12 rays at center.

Sch#	Date	Emperor	VG	Fine	VF	XF
414D	ND(1848-83)	Tu Duc	1000.	2000.	3250.	5000.

19.00 g
Obv. leg: *Tu Duc Thong Bao, Trieu Dan Lai Chi.* Rev: Facing dragon.

405	ND(1848-83)	Tu Duc	1000.	2000.	3250.	5000.

19.22 g
Obv. leg: *Tu Duc Thong Bao, Van The Vinh Lai.*

404	ND(1848-83)	Tu Duc	1200.	2400.	4000.	6000.

18.00 g
Obv. leg: *Tu Duc Thong Bao.*
Rev. leg: *Ngu Phuc* and 5 bats.

410	ND(1848-83)	Tu Duc	1000.	2000.	3250.	5000.

18.80 g

Rev. leg: *Ngu Tien Viet Ngai* on dragon.

Sch#	Date	Emperor	VG	Fine	VF	XF
381	ND(1848-83)	Tu Duc	1000.	2000.	3250.	5000.

6 TIEN

GOLD, 23.00 g
Obv. leg: *Tu Duc Thong Bao.*
Rev. leg: *Luc Tien Viet Thinh* on dragon.

Sch#	Date	Emperor	VG	Fine	VF	XF
382	ND(1848-83)	Tu Duc	1100.	2200.	3600.	5400.

7 TIEN

GOLD, 26.50-27.50 g
Obv. leg: *Minh Mang Thong Bao.*

Sch#	Date	Emperor	VG	Fine	VF	XF
—	ND(1820-40)	Minh Mang	1200.	2400.	4000.	6000.

Sch#	Date	Emperor	VG	Fine	VF	XF
—	(1832) Yr.13	Minh Mang	1200.	2400.	4000.	6000.
206	(1834) Yr.15	Minh Mang	1200.	2400.	4000.	6000.
206B	(1835) Yr.16	Minh Mang	1200.	2400.	4000.	6000.

26.60-27.00 g
Obv. leg: *Thieu Tri Thong Bao.*
Rev: Dragon left.

Sch#	Date	Emperor	VG	Fine	VF	XF
283	ND(1841-47)	Thieu Tri	1200.	2400.	4000.	6000.

28.15-28.20 g
Rev: Dragon right.

Sch#	Date	Emperor	VG	Fine	VF	XF
284	ND(1841-47)	Thieu Tri	1300.	2600.	4400.	6600.

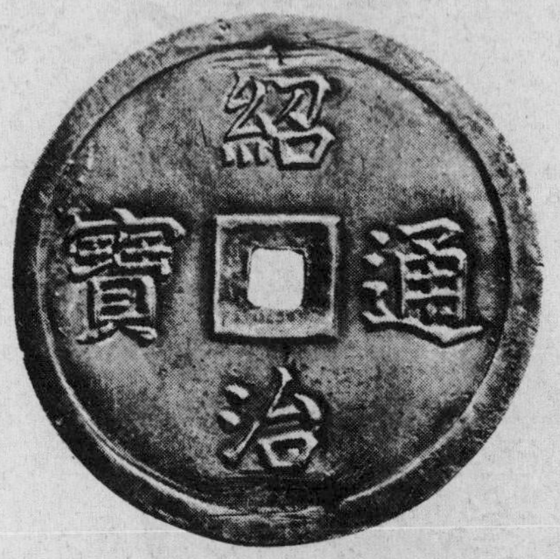

26.75 g
Rev: Flaming sun between facing dragons.

Sch#	Date	Emperor	VG	Fine	VF	XF
278	ND(1841-47)	Thieu Tri	1200.	2400.	4000.	6000.

Obv. leg: *Tu Duc Thong Bao.*
Obv. and rev: Dentilated borders.
Rev: Dragon left.

Sch#	Date	Emperor	VG	Fine	VF	XF
368B	ND(1848-83)	Tu Duc	1200.	2400.	4000.	6000.

26.80 g
Obv. and rev: Pearled borders.

Sch#	Date	Emperor	VG	Fine	VF	XF
411	ND(1848-83)	Tu Duc	1200	2400.	4000.	6000.

26.20 g
Rev. leg: *Long Van* on facing dragon.

Sch#	Date	Emperor	VG	Fine	VF	XF
414B	ND(1848-83)	Tu Duc	1200.	2400.	4000.	6000.

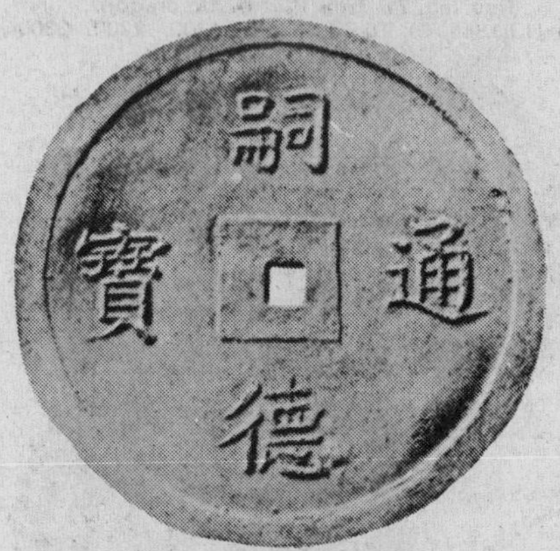

26.45-27.00 g
Obv: Small legends.
Rev: Small thin, curved facing dragons.

Sch#	Date	Emperor	VG	Fine	VF	XF
402.1	ND(1848-83)	Tu Duc	1200.	2400.	4000.	6000.

LANG

Obv: Large legends.
Rev: Large, thick facing dragons.

Sch#	Date	Emperor	VG	Fine	VF	XF
402.2	ND(1848-83)	Tu Duc	1200.	2400.	4000.	6000.

26.00 g
Rev. leg: *That Tien Viet Hue* on dragon.

383B	ND(1848-83)	Tu Duc	1200.	2400.	4000.	6000.

8 TIEN

GOLD, 30.50 g
Obv. leg: *Tu Duc Thong Bao.*
Rev. leg: *Bat Tien Viet Thuan* on dragon.

384B	ND(1848-83)	Tu Duc	1400.	2800.	4800.	7000.

9 TIEN

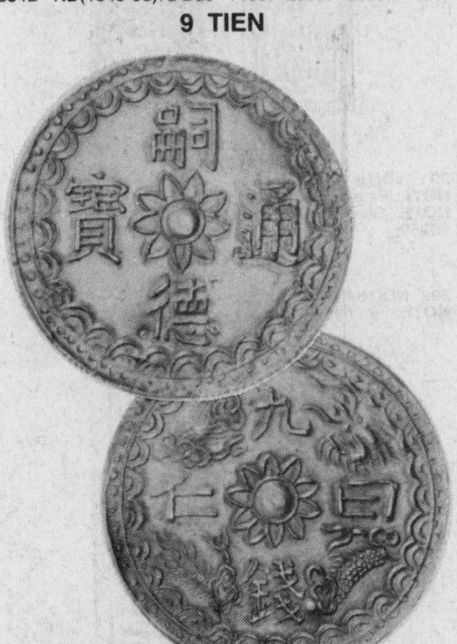

GOLD, 34.07-34.20 g
Obv. leg: *Tu Duc Thong Bao.*
Rev. leg: *Cuu Tien Viet Nhan* on dragon.

385B	ND(1848-83)	Tu Duc	1500.	3000.	5200.	8000.

GOLD, 37.70-38.00 g
Obv. leg: *Tu Duc Thong Bao, Van The Vinh Lai.*

Sch#	Date	Emperor	VG	Fine	VF	XF
403	ND(1848-83)	Tu Duc	2700.	5400.	9000.	14,500.

37.00-37.69 g
Obv. leg: *Tu Duc Thong Bao.*
Rev. leg: *Long Van* on facing dragon.

414	ND(1848-83)	Tu Duc	2500.	5000.	8000.	12,500.

37.40 g
Rev. leg: *Nhat Lang Viet Trung* on dragon.

376B	ND(1848-83)	Tu Duc	2700.	5400.	9000.	13,500.

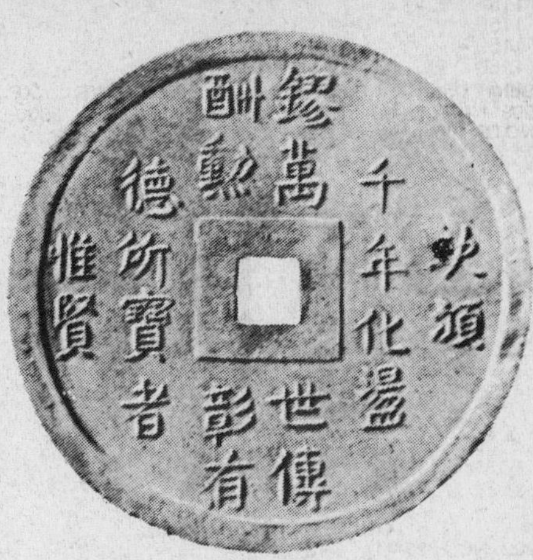

Weight unknown
Obv. leg: *Thanh Thai Thong Bao, Van The Vinh Lai.*

Sch#	Date	Emperor	VG	Fine	VF	XF
431	ND(1888-1907)	Thanh Thai	2700.	5400.	9000.	14,500.

GOLD BARS

TIEN

GOLD, weight unknown

200	ND(1820-41)	Minh Mang	325.00	650.00	1000.	1500.

.850 GOLD, 3.90 g
Court Treasury

273	ND(1841-47)	Thieu Tri	325.00	650.00	1000.	1500.

NOTE: Fineness on edge.

Weight unknown
Court Treasury

397	ND(1848-83)	Tu Duc	325.00	650.00	1000.	1500.

2 TIEN

GOLD, weight unknown

201	ND(1820-41)	Minh Mang	350.00	700.00	1100.	1650.

.850 GOLD, 7.50 g
Court Treasury

274	ND(1841-47)	Thieu Tri	360.00	720.00	1200.	2000.

NOTE: Fineness on edge.

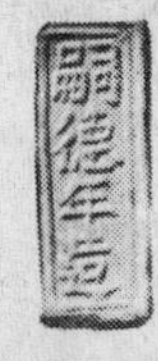

Weight unknown
Court Treasury

Sch#	Date	Emperor	VG	Fine	VF	XF
398	ND(1848-83)	Tu Duc	360.00	720.00	1200.	2000.

NOTE: Fineness on edge.

3 TIEN

GOLD, weight unknown

Sch#	Date	Emperor	VG	Fine	VF	XF
202	ND(1820-41)	Minh Mang	550.00	1100.	1800.	2700.

11.30 g

Sch#	Date	Emperor	VG	Fine	VF	XF
275	ND(1841-47)	Thieu Tri	550.00	1100.	1800.	2700.

Weight unknown
Court Treasury

Sch#	Date	Emperor	VG	Fine	VF	XF
399	ND(1848-83)	Tu Duc	550.00	1100.	1800.	2700.

4 TIEN

GOLD, weight unknown

Sch#	Date	Emperor	VG	Fine	VF	XF
203	ND(1820-41)	Minh Mang	—	—	Rare	—

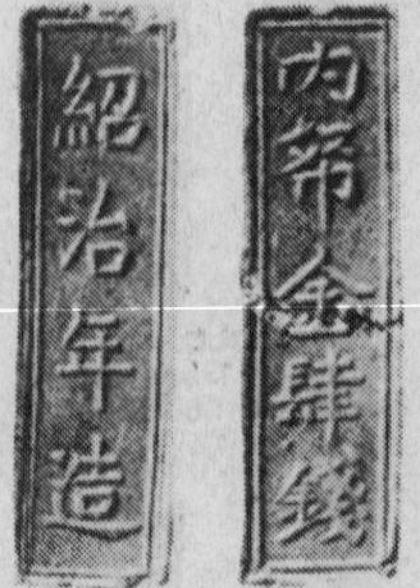

.850 GOLD, 15.25 g
Court Treasury

Sch#	Date	Emperor	VG	Fine	VF	XF
276	ND(1841-47)	Minh Mang	—	—	Rare	—

NOTE: Fineness on edge.

Weight unknown
Court Treasury

Sch#	Date	Emperor	VG	Fine	VF	XF
400	ND(1848-83)	Tu Duc	—	—	Rare	—

NOTE: Fineness on edge.

5 TIEN

GOLD, weight unknown

Sch#	Date	Emperor	VG	Fine	VF	XF
204	ND(1820-41)	Minh Mang	—	—	Rare	—

.850 GOLD, 18.85 g
Court Treasury

Sch#	Date	Emperor	VG	Fine	VF	XF
277	ND(1841-47)	Thieu Tri	—	—	Rare	—

NOTE: Fineness on edge.

Weight unknown
Court Treasury

Sch#	Date	Emperor	VG	Fine	VF	XF
401	ND(1848-83)	Tu Duc	—	—	Rare	—

NOTE: Fineness on edge.

LANG

.850 GOLD, weight unknown
Very crude.

Sch#	Date	Emperor	VG	Fine	VF	XF
190	ND(1820-41)	Minh Mang	—	—	Rare	—

NOTE: Fineness on edge.

Court Treasury

Sch#	Date	Emperor	VG	Fine	VF	XF
268	ND(1841-47)	Thieu Tri	—	—	Rare	—

Sch#	Date	Emperor	VG	Fine	VF	XF
269	CD1843	Thieu Tri	—	—	Rare	—

NOTE: Fineness on edge.

.950 GOLD, 37.40 g
Court Treasury

Sch#	Date	Emperor	VG	Fine	VF	XF
391	ND(1848-83)	Tu Duc	—	—	Rare	—

NOTE: Fineness on edge.
NOTE: Stack's NYINC sale 12-89 virtual Unc realized $8250.

.850 GOLD
Court Treasury

Sch#	Date	Emperor	VG	Fine	VF	XF
392	ND(1848-83)	Tu Duc	—	—	Rare	—

NOTE: Fineness on edge.

Court Treasury. Crude.

Sch#	Date	Emperor	VG	Fine	VF	XF
423	ND(1885-88)	Dong Khanh	—	—	Rare	—

36.10-36.70 g
Court Treasury

Sch#	Date	Emperor	VG	Fine	VF	XF
429	ND(1888-1907)	Thanh Thai	—	—	Rare	—

NOTE: Fineness on edge.

.800 GOLD
Court Treasury

Sch#	Date	Emperor	VG	Fine	VF	XF
430	ND(1888-1907)	Thanh Thai	—	—	Rare	—

NOTE: Fineness on edge.

5 LANG

.850 GOLD, weight unknown

Sch#	Date	Emperor	VG	Fine	VF	XF
191	ND(1820-41)	Minh Mang	—	—	Rare	—

NOTE: Fineness on edge.

190.25 g
Court Treasury

Sch#	Date	Emperor	VG	Fine	VF	XF
394	ND(1848-83)	Tu Duc	—	—	Rare	—

NOTE: Fineness on edge.

10 LANG

.850 GOLD, weight unknown
Similar to Silver 10 Lang, Sch#173.
Court Treasury

Sch#	Date	Emperor	VG	Fine	VF	XF
192	CD1837	Minh Mang	—	—	Rare	—

NOTE: Fineness on edge.

.750 GOLD, 382.40 g, 43x108mm
Court Treasury

Sch#	Date	Emperor	VG	Fine	VF	XF
270	ND(1841-47)	Thieu Tri	—	—	Rare	—

NOTE: Fineness on edge.

.900 GOLD, weight unknown. 30x100mm
Rev: 4 characters. All legends engraved.

Sch#	Date	Emperor	VG	Fine	VF	XF
396	ND(1848-83)	Tu Duc	—	—	Rare	—

NOTE: Fineness on edge.

Obv. leg: *Bac Ninh*.
Rev: 2 characters (engraved) plus hallmark.

Sch#	Date	Emperor	VG	Fine	VF	XF
395	CD1849	Tu Duc	—	—	Rare	—

30 LANG

.750 GOLD, weight unknown, 43x101mm
Obv. leg: *Dai Nam Nguyen Bao.*
Similar to 40 Lang, Sch#195.

Sch#	Date	Emperor	VG	Fine	VF	XF
193	Yr.21(1840)	Thieu Tri	—	—	Rare	—

NOTE: Fineness on edge.

40 LANG

.750 GOLD, weight unknown
Illustration reduced, actual size 43x107mm
Obv. leg: *Dai Nam Nguyen Bao.*

Sch#	Date	Emperor	VG	Fine	VF	XF
195	Yr.21(1840)	Minh Mang	—	—	Rare	—

NOTE: Fineness on edge.

.900 GOLD, 43x112mm
Obv. leg: *Viet Nam Nguyen Bao.*

Sch#	Date	Emperor	VG	Fine	VF	XF
194	ND(1820-41)	Minh Mang	—	—	Rare	—

NOTE: Fineness on edge.

50 LANG

.750 GOLD, weight unknown
48x118mm
Obv. leg: *Viet Nam Nguyen Bao.*

Sch#	Date	Emperor	VG	Fine	VF	XF
196	Yr.18(1837)	Minh Mang	—	—	Rare	—

NOTE: Fineness on edge.

.800 GOLD, 49x115mm
Obv. leg: *Dai Nam Nguyen Bao.*
Obv. and rev. leg. framed within ornate border.

Sch#	Date	Emperor	VG	Fine	VF	XF
197	Yr.19(1838)	Minh Mang	—	—	Rare	—

NOTE: Fineness on edge.

.700 GOLD, 1917.35 g
Court Treasury

Sch#	Date	Emperor	VG	Fine	VF	XF
271	CD1843	Thieu Tri	—	—	Rare	—

NOTE: Fineness on edge.

100 LANG

.850 GOLD, weight unknown, 59x138mm
Obv. leg: *Viet Nam Nguyen Bao*,
small characters.
Obv. and rev. leg. framed within ornate border.

Sch#	Date	Emperor	VG	Fine	VF	XF
198	Yr.14(1833)	Minh Mang	—	—	Rare	—

NOTE: Fineness on edge.

Similar to Sch#198 but large characters on obv.

Sch#	Date	Emperor	VG	Fine	VF	XF
199	Yr.14(1833)	Minh Mang	—	—	Rare	—

.700 GOLD, 3831.00 g
Illustration reduced. Actual size: 78 X 146mm.
Court Treasury
Obv. and rev. leg. framed within ornate border.

Sch#	Date	Emperor	VG	Fine	VF	XF
272	CD1843	Thieu Tri	—	—	Rare	—

NOTE: Fineness on edge.

VIETNAM/FRENCH COCHIN CHINA

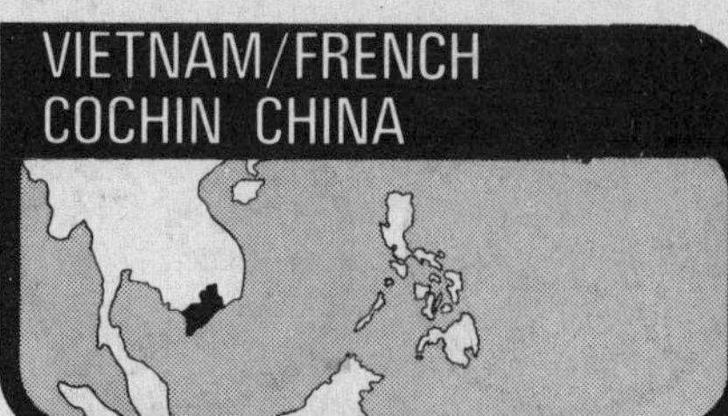

Cochin-China, a colony of France in Indo-China, now part of Vietnam, occupied an alluvial plain of the Mekong Delta along the South China Sea. In its colonial period, Cochin-China had an area of 24,981 sq. mi. (63,701 sq. km.) and a population of about 5 million. Capital: Saigon. The region was (and is) one of Asia's chief rice-growing areas. Fishing is also an important economic activity. French Cochin-China exported rice, fish and timber.

The region, inhabited mainly by Vietnamese, was formerly part of the ancient Khmer empire and later of the Empire of Dai Viet. It was brought under French control in 1862-67 and made a colony. The Japanese occupied the area before World War II to use as a base for the invasion of Malaya. When France regained power of the area following World War II, Cochin-China was included in the Federation of Indo-China as an autonomous republic. It was attached to Vietnam in 1949.

MINT MARKS

A - Paris
K - Bordeaux

MONETARY SYSTEM

5 Sapeques = 1 Cent
100 Cents = 1 Piastre

SAPEQUE

BRONZE
Center hole punched in France 1 Centime Y#41

KM#	Date	Mintage	Fine	VF	XF	Unc
1	1875K	1.000	6.00	12.00	25.00	75.00

KM#	Date	Mintage	Fine	VF	XF	Unc
2	1879A	20.000	3.00	6.00	12.50	35.00
	1885A	100 pcs.	—	—	Proof	400.00

NOTE: The above coin has 2/1000 on the reverse and thus is often mistaken for a 2 Sapeque.

CENT

BRONZE

KM#	Date	Mintage	Fine	VF	XF	Unc
3	1879A	.500	5.00	15.00	50.00	150.00
	1884A	.444	6.00	25.00	60.00	200.00
	1885A	.255	7.00	30.00	95.00	300.00
	1885A	100 pcs.	—	—	Proof	550.00

10 CENTS

2.7216 g, .900 SILVER, .0787 oz ASW

KM#	Date	Mintage	Fine	VF	XF	Unc
4	1879A	.400	20.00	35.00	90.00	275.00
	1884A	.510	25.00	60.00	125.00	350.00
	1885A	100 pcs.	—	—	Proof	750.00

20 CENTS

5.4431 g, .900 SILVER, .1575 oz ASW

KM#	Date	Mintage	Fine	VF	XF	Unc
5	1879A	.350	30.00	60.00	150.00	400.00
	1884A	.320	40.00	70.00	185.00	450.00
	1885A	100 pcs.	—	—	Proof	800.00

50 CENTS

13.6078 g, .900 SILVER, .3937 oz ASW

KM#	Date	Mintage	Fine	VF	XF	Unc
6	1879A	.180	90.00	150.00	300.00	750.00
	1884A	.010	400.00	600.00	800.00	2500.
	1885A	100 pcs.	—	—	Proof	1350.

PIASTRE

27.2156 g, .900 SILVER, .7875 oz ASW

KM#	Date	Mintage	Fine	VF	XF	Unc
7	1885A	100 pcs.	—	—	Proof	8000.

PROOF SETS (PS)

KM#	Date	Mintage	Identification	Issue Price	Mkt. Val.
PS1	1879A(5)	—	KM-E6-E10	—	2100.
PS2	1885A(5)	100	KM3-7	—	11,450.

VIETNAM-TONKIN

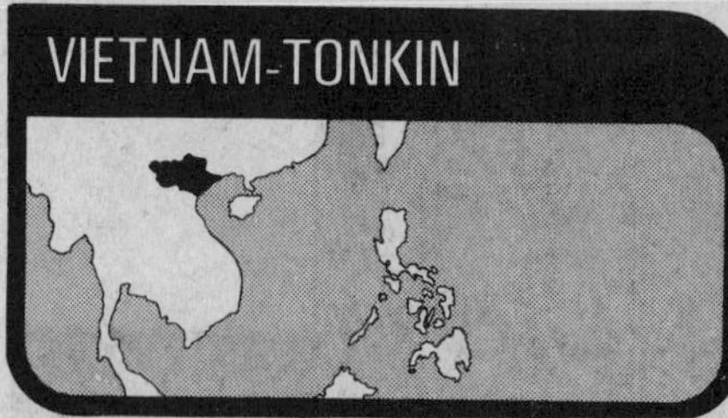

Tonkin, a former French protectorate in North IndoChina, comprises the greater part of present North Vietnam. It had an area of 44,672 sq. mi. (75,700 sq. km.) and a population of about 4 million. Capital: Hanoi. The initial value of Tonkin to France was contained in the access it afforded to the trade of China's Yunnan province.

France established a protectorate over Annam and Tonkin by the treaties of Tientsin and Hue negotiated in 1884. Tonkin was incorporated in the independent state of Vietnam (within the French Union) and upon the defeat of France by the Viet Minh became the body of North Vietnam.

MINT MARKS

(a) - Paris, privy marks only

1/600 PIASTRE

ZINC

KM#	Date	Mintage	Fine	VF	XF	Unc
1	1905(a)	60.000	3.00	7.00	15.00	35.00

NOTE: Previously it had been thought that genuine specimens of this coin were 1.5mm thick while thinner pieces were counterfeits. Recent evidence however indicates that the genuine coin is about 0.9 mm thick and weighs 2.14 grams while the 1.5 mm thick piece is a piefort weighing about 4.8 grams.

VIETNAM

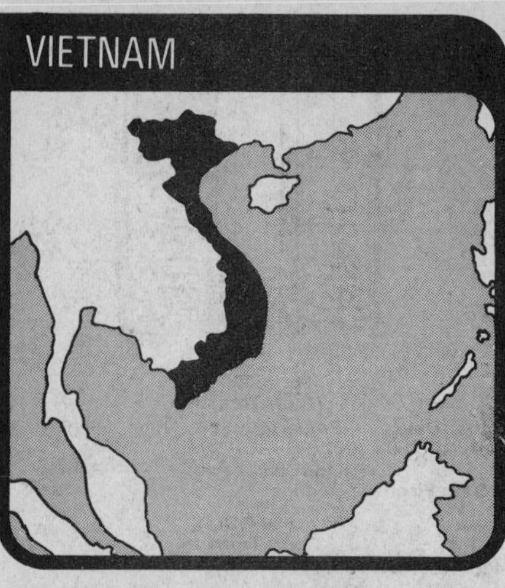

The Socialist Republic of Vietnam, located in Southeast Asia west of the South China Sea, has an area of 127,300 sq. mi. (329,560 sq. km.) and a population of *66.8 million. Capital: Hanoi. Agricultural products, coal, and mineral ores are exported.

At the start of World War II, Vietnamese Nationalists fled to China's Kwangsi provinces where Ho Chi Minh organized the Revolution to free Vietnam of French rule. The Japanese occupied Vietnam during World War II. As the end of the war drew near, they ousted the Vichy French administration and granted Vietnam independence under a puppet government headed by Bao Dai, emperor of Annam. The Bao Dai government collapsed at the end of the war, and on Sept. 2, 1945, Ho Chi Minh proclaimed the existence of an independent Vietnam consisting of Cochin-China, Annam, and Tonkin, and set up a Communist government. France recognized the new government as a free state, but reneged and in 1949 reinstalled Bao Dai as Ruler of Vietnam and extended the regime independence within the French Union. Ho Chi Minh led a guerrilla war, in the first Indochina war, against the French puppet state that raged on to the disastrous defeat of the French by the Viet Minh at Dien Bien Phu on May 7, 1954.

An agreement signed at Geneva on July 21, 1954, provided for a temporary division of Vietnam at the 17th parallel of latitude, between a Communist-dominated north and a U.S.-supported south. In Oct. 1955, South Vietnam deposed Bao Dai by referendum and authorized the establishment of a republic with Ngo Dinh Diem as president. The Republic of South Vietnam was proclaimed on Oct. 26, 1955, and was immediately recognized by some Western Powers.

The activities of Communists in South Vietnam led to U.S. intervention and the second Indochina war which came to a brief halt in 1973 (when a cease-fire was arranged and U.S. forces withdrawn), but didn't end until April 30, 1975 when South Vietnam surrendered unconditionally. The People's Revolutionary Party assumed power in the government of South Vietnam until July 2, 1976, when the two Vietnams were reunited as the Socialist Republic of Vietnam.

For earlier coinage refer to French Indo-China.

MONETARY SYSTEM

10 Xu = 1 Hao
10 Hao = 1 Dong

20 XU

ALUMINUM

KM#	Date	Mintage	Fine	VF	XF	Unc
1	1945	—	50.00	75.00	100.00	150.00

5 HAO

ALUMINUM
Value in incuse lettering

KM#	Date	Mintage	Fine	VF	XF	Unc
2.1	1946	—	30.00	50.00	75.00	125.00

NOTE: Commonly encountered with rotated dies.

Value in raised lettering

KM#	Date	Mintage	Fine	VF	XF	Unc
2.2	1946	—	5.00	8.00	12.50	25.00

DONG

ALUMINUM

KM#	Date	Mintage	Fine	VF	XF	Unc
3	1946	—	60.00	100.00	165.00	250.00

2 DONG

BRONZE

KM#	Date	Mintage	Fine	VF	XF	Unc
4	1946	—	20.00	35.00	60.00	100.00

NORTH VIETNAM

XU

ALUMINUM

KM#	Date	Mintage	Fine	VF	XF	Unc
5	1958	—	.75	1.50	2.50	5.00

2 XU

ALUMINUM

KM#	Date	Mintage	Fine	VF	XF	Unc
6	1958	—	.75	1.50	2.50	5.00

5 XU

ALUMINUM

KM#	Date	Mintage	Fine	VF	XF	Unc
7	1958	—	1.00	2.00	3.50	6.00

PROVISIONAL COINAGE

For use in occupied South Vietnam only.

XU

ALUMINUM

KM#	Date	Mintage	Fine	VF	XF	Unc
8	ND(1976)	—	.50	1.50	3.00	9.00

2 XU

ALUMINUM

KM#	Date	Mintage	Fine	VF	XF	Unc
9	1975	—	.50	1.50	3.00	9.00

5 XU

ALUMINUM

KM#	Date	Mintage	Fine	VF	XF	Unc
10	ND(1976)	—	.50	1.50	3.00	9.00

SOUTH VIETNAM

MINT MARKS

(a) - Paris, privy marks only

MONETARY SYSTEM

100 Xu (Su) = 1 Dong

10 SU

ALUMINUM
Rice Plant

KM#	Date	Mintage	Fine	VF	XF	Unc
1	1953(a)	20.000	.15	.25	.50	1.00

20 SU

ALUMINUM
Rice Plant

KM#	Date	Mintage	Fine	VF	XF	Unc
2	1953(a)	15.000	.30	.50	.85	1.75

50 XU

ALUMINUM

KM#	Date	Mintage	Fine	VF	XF	Unc
3	1953(a)	15.000	1.50	3.00	6.00	12.50

50 SU

ALUMINUM
Bamboo

KM#	Date	Mintage	Fine	VF	XF	Unc
4	1960	10.000	.25	.50	1.25	2.50
	1960	—	—	—	Proof	—

50 XU

ALUMINUM
Bamboo

KM#	Date	Mintage	Fine	VF	XF	Unc
6	1963	20.000	.20	.40	.75	1.50

DONG

COPPER-NICKEL
Bamboo

KM#	Date	Mintage	Fine	VF	XF	Unc
5	1960	105.000	.15	.25	.35	.75
	1960	—	—	—	Proof	—

Rice Plant

KM#	Date	Mintage	Fine	VF	XF	Unc
7	1964	44.000	.15	.25	.35	.75
	1964	—	—	—	Proof	—

NICKEL-CLAD STEEL

KM#	Date	Mintage	Fine	VF	XF	Unc
7a	1971	—	.10	.15	.25	.50

ALUMINUM
F.A.O. Issue

KM#	Date	Mintage	Fine	VF	XF	Unc
12	1971	30.000	.10	.15	.25	.50

5 DONG

COPPER-NICKEL
Rice Plant

KM#	Date	Mintage	Fine	VF	XF	Unc
9	1966	100.000	.10	.20	.40	.80

NICKEL-CLAD STEEL
F.A.O. Issue

KM#	Date	Mintage	Fine	VF	XF	Unc
9a	1971	15.000	.10	.25	.50	1.00

10 DONG

COPPER-NICKEL
Rice Plant

KM#	Date	Mintage	Fine	VF	XF	Unc
8	1964	15.000	.20	.40	.60	1.25

NICKEL-CLAD STEEL

KM#	Date	Mintage	Fine	VF	XF	Unc
8a	1968	30.000	.10	.15	.25	.60
	1970	50.000	.10	.15	.25	.60

BRASS-CLAD STEEL
F.A.O. Issue

KM#	Date	Mintage	Fine	VF	XF	Unc
13	1974	30.000	.10	.15	.30	.60

20 DONG

NICKEL-CLAD STEEL

KM#	Date	Mintage	Fine	VF	XF	Unc
10	1968	—	.25	.45	.85	1.85

F.A.O. Issue

KM#	Date	Mintage	Fine	VF	XF	Unc
11	1968	.500	.25	.50	1.00	2.00

50 DONG

NICKEL CLAD STEEL
F.A.O. Issue

KM#	Date	Mintage	Fine	VF	XF	Unc
14	1975	1.010	—	—	—	600.00

NOTE: It is reported that all but a few examples were "disposed of as scrap metal".

VIETNAM

MINT MARKS

(h) - Key - Havana, Cuba

HAO

ALUMINUM

KM#	Date	Mintage	Fine	VF	XF	Unc
11	1976	—	.50	1.00	2.50	5.00

2 HAO

ALUMINUM

KM#	Date	Mintage	Fine	VF	XF	Unc
12	1976	—	.75	1.50	3.00	6.00

5 HAO

ALUMINUM

KM#	Date	Mintage	Fine	VF	XF	Unc
13	1976	—	1.00	2.00	3.50	7.00

DONG

ALUMINUM

KM#	Date	Mintage	Fine	VF	XF	Unc
14	1976	—	6.00	12.00	25.00	50.00

5 DONG

BRASS
Mythological Bird - Phoenix

KM#	Date	Mintage	Fine	VF	XF	Unc
36	1989	—	—	—	Proof	5.00

8.7700 g, .900 SILVER, .2538 oz ASW

KM#	Date	Mintage	Fine	VF	XF	Unc
36a	1989	—	—	—	Proof	15.00

10 DONG

COPPER-NICKEL
Nature-Water Buffalo

KM#	Date	Mintage	Fine	VF	XF	Unc
15	1986(h)	5,000	—	—	—	12.00

Nature - Peacock

KM#	Date	Mintage	Fine	VF	XF	Unc
16	1986(h)	5,000	—	—	—	12.00

Nature - Elephant

KM#	Date	Mintage	Fine	VF	XF	Unc
17	1986(h)	5,000	—	—	—	12.00

Wildlife Preservation - Orangutan

KM#	Date	Mintage	Fine	VF	XF	Unc
28	1987(h)	.022	—	—	—	8.00

Dragon Ship

KM#	Date	Mintage	Fine	VF	XF	Unc
37	1988	—	—	—	—	8.00

Soccer - Italy

KM#	Date	Mintage	Fine	VF	XF	Unc
27	1989(h)	—	—	—	—	10.00

BRASS
Rev: Pillar top pagoda above water and legend.

KM#	Date	Mintage	Fine	VF	XF	Unc
38	1989	—	—	—	Proof	7.00

.900 SILVER

KM#	Date	Mintage	Fine	VF	XF	Unc
38a	1989	—	—	—	Proof	20.00

COPPER-NICKEL
Chimpanzees

KM#	Date	Mintage	Fine	VF	XF	Unc
33	1990(h)	.020	—	—	—	8.00

Steam and Sail Ship - Savannah

KM#	Date	Mintage	Fine	VF	XF	Unc
39	1991	—	—	—	—	8.00

20 DONG

BRASS
100th Anniversary of Birth of Ho Chi Minh

40 1989 — — — Proof 10.00

.900 SILVER

40a 1989 — — — Proof 35.00

100 DONG

12.0000 g, .999 SILVER, .3855 oz ASW
Junk Under Sail

18 1986 2,000 — — — 35.00

Wildlife - Water Buffalo

19 1986 5,000 — — — 45.00

Wildlife - Peacock

20 1986 5,000 — — — 45.00

Wildlife - Elephant

21 1986 5,000 — — — 45.00

100 Years of the Automobile

KM#	Date	Mintage	Fine	VF	XF	Unc
22	1986	2,000	—	—	—	22.50

6.0000 g, .999 SILVER, .1927 oz ASW
Calgary Olympics - Skier

23 1986 3,700 — — — 20.00

12.0000 g, .999 SILVER, .3855 oz ASW
Seoul Olympics - Fencer

24 1986 .010 — — — 20.00

Soccer - Mexico

29 1986(h) 2,000 — — — 50.00

15.9900 g, .980 SILVER, .5039 oz ASW

25 1988(h) 3,000 — — — 42.50

12.0000 g, .999 SILVER, .3855 oz ASW
Soccer - 1988

26 1988(h) — — — — 47.50

16.0000 g, .999 SILVER, .5145 oz ASW
Soccer - Italy

KM#	Date	Mintage	Fine	VF	XF	Unc
30	1989(h)	.010	—	—	Proof	45.00

Summer Olympics - Rowing

31 1989(h) — — — Proof 50.00

Winter Olympics - Hockey

32 1990(h) 5,000 — — Proof 50.00

12.0000 g, .999 SILVER, .3858 oz ASW
Soccer

34 1991(h) — — — — 30.00

16.0000 g, .999 SILVER, .5145 oz ASW
Steamship Savannah

35 1991(h) — — — Proof 55.00

Flying Dinosaur - Rhamphorhynchus

KM#	Date	Mintage	Fine	VF	XF	Unc
42	1993	—	—	—	Proof	45.00

Elephants

KM#	Date	Mintage	Fine	VF	XF	Unc
43	1993	—	—	—	Proof	45.00

500 DONG

GOLD, 3.103 g
100th Anniversary of Birth of Ho Chi Minh

KM#	Date	Mintage	Fine	VF	XF	Unc
41	1989	—	—	—	—	150.00

Listings For

VISCAYAN REPUBLIC: refer to Spain

WEST AFRICAN STATES

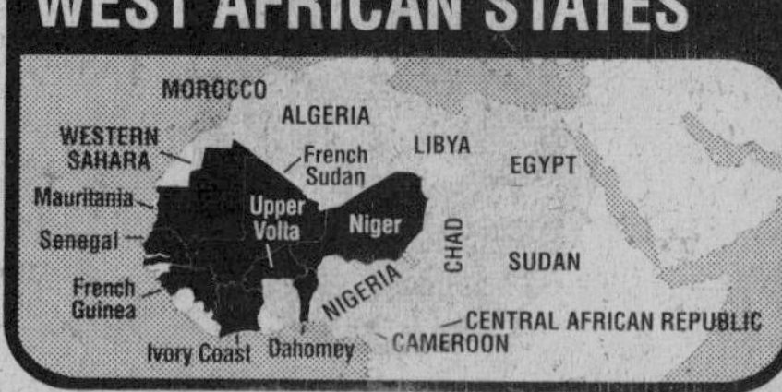

The West African States, a former federation of eight French colonial territories on the northwest coast of Africa, had area of 1,831,079 sq. mi. (4,742,495 sq. km.) and a population of about 17 million. Capital: Dakar. The constituent territories were Mauritania, Senegal, Dahomey, French Sudan, Ivory Coast, Upper Volta, Niger and French Guinea.

The members of the federation were overseas territories within the French Union until Sept. of 1958 when all but French Guinea approved the constitution of the Fifth French Republic, thereby electing to become autonomous members of the new French Community. French Guinea voted to become the fully independent Republic of Guinea. The other seven attained independence in 1960. The French West Africa territories were provided with a common currency, a practice which was continued as the monetary union of the West African States which provides a common currency to the autonomous republics of Dahomey (now Benin), Senegal, Upper Volta (now Burkina Faso), Ivory Coast, Mali, Togo and Niger.

For earlier coinage refer to Togo, and French West Africa.

MINT MARKS

(a) - Paris, privy marks only

MONETARY SYSTEM

100 Centimes = 1 Franc

FRANC

ALUMINUM

KM#	Date	Mintage	VF	XF	Unc
3	1961(a)	3.000	.15	.30	.60
	1962(a)	2.000	2.00	4.00	7.00
	1963(a)	4.500	1.50	3.50	6.00
	1964(a)	5.000	.15	.30	.60
	1965(a)	6.000	.15	.30	.60
	1967(a)	2.500	.15	.30	.60
	1970(a)	4.000	Reported, not confirmed		
	1971(a)	4.000	.15	.30	.60
	1972(a)	4.000	.15	.30	.60
	1973(a)	4.500	.15	.30	.60
	1974(a)	—	.15	.30	.60
	1975(a)	10.080	.15	.30	.60
	1976(a)	8.000	.15	.30	.60

NOTE: The 1962 and 1963 issue have the engraver general's name on the obverse.

STEEL

KM#	Date	Mintage	VF	XF	Unc
8	1976(a)	8.000	—	.10	.35
	1977(a)	14.700	—	.10	.35
	1978(a)	—	—	.10	.35
	1979(a)	—	—	.10	.35
	1980(a)	—	—	.10	.35
	1981(a)	—	—	.10	.35
	1982(a)	—	—	.10	.35
	1984(a)	—	—	.10	.35
	1985(a)	26.900	—	.10	.35
	1990(a)	—	—	.10	.35
	1991(a)	—	—	.10	.35
	1992(a)	—	—	.10	.35

5 FRANCS

ALUMINUM-BRONZE

KM#	Date	Mintage	VF	XF	Unc
2	1960(a)	5.000	.20	.40	.70
	1962(a)	5.000	—	—	—
	1963(a)	—	—	—	—
	1965(a)	6.510	.20	.40	.70
	1966(a)	6.000	Reported, not confirmed		
	1967(a)	6.010	.20	.40	.70
	1968(a)	6.000	.20	.45	.75
2	1969(a)	8.000	.20	.40	.70
	1970(a)	10.005	.20	.40	.70
	1971(a)	10.000	.20	.40	.70
	1972(a)	5.000	.20	.40	.70
	1973(a)	6.000	.20	.45	.75
	1974(a)	13.326	.10	.15	.30
	1975(a)	16.840	.20	.40	.70
	1976(a)	20.010	.20	.30	.60
	1977(a)	16.840	.20	.30	.60
	1978(a)	—	.20	.30	.60
	1979(a)	—	.10	.20	.40
	1980(a)	—	.10	.20	.40
	1981(a)	—	.10	.20	.40
	1982(a)	—	.10	.20	.40
	1984(a)	—	.10	.20	.40
	1985(a)	16.000	.10	.20	.40
	1986(a)	8.000	.10	.20	.40
	1987(a)	—	.10	.20	.40
	1988(a)	—	.10	.20	.40
	1989(a)	—	.10	.20	.40
	1990(a)	—	.10	.20	.40
	1991(a)	—	.10	.20	.40
	1992(a)	—	.10	.20	.40

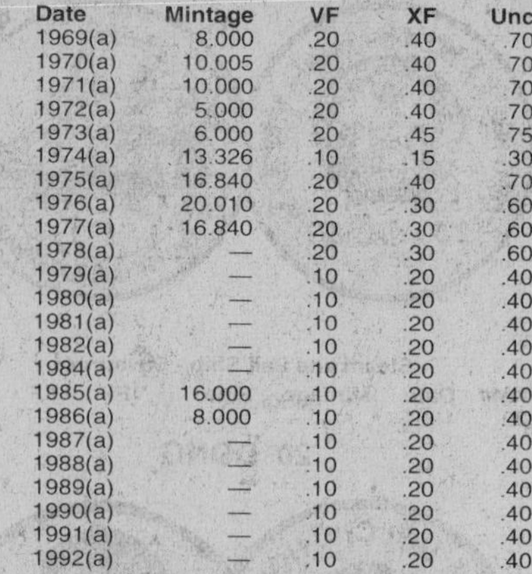

10 FRANCS

ALUMINUM-BRONZE

KM#	Date	Mintage	VF	XF	Unc
1	1959(a)	10.000	.15	.30	.60
	1961(a)	—	—	—	—
	1962(a)	—	—	—	—
	1964(a)	10.000	.20	.40	.70
	1965(a)	6.000	Reported, not confirmed		
	1966(a)	6.000	.20	.40	.70
	1967(a)	3.500	.25	.50	.90
	1968(a)	6.000	.20	.40	.70
	1969(a)	7.000	.25	.50	.90
	1970(a)	7.000	.15	.30	.60
	1971(a)	8.000	.15	.30	.60
	1972(a)	5.500	.20	.40	.70
	1973(a)	3.000	.20	.40	.70
	1974(a)	10.000	.15	.30	.60
	1975(a)	17.000	.15	.30	.60
	1976(a)	18.000	.15	.30	.60
	1977(a)	9.050	.15	.25	.50
	1978(a)	—	.15	.25	.50
	1979(a)	—	.15	.25	.50
	1980(a)	—	.15	.25	.50
	1981(a)	—	.15	.25	.50

BRASS
F.A.O. Issue

KM#	Date	Mintage	VF	XF	Unc
10	1981(a)	—	.25	.50	1.25
	1982(a)	—	.25	.50	1.25
	1983(a)	—	.25	.50	1.25
	1984(a)	—	.25	.50	1.25
	1985(a)	5.000	.25	.50	1.25
	1986(a)	7.500	.25	.50	1.25
	1987(a)	—	.25	.50	1.25
	1989(a)	—	.25	.50	1.25
	1990(a)	—	.25	.50	1.25
	1991(a)	—	.25	.50	1.25

25 FRANCS

ALUMINUM-BRONZE

KM#	Date	Mintage	VF	XF	Unc
5	1970(a)	7.000	.25	.45	.80
	1971(a)	7.000	.50	.75	1.25
	1972(a)	2.000	1.00	1.50	3.00
	1975(a)	5.035	.25	.45	.80
	1976(a)	3.365	.25	.45	.80
	1977(a)	3.288	.25	.45	.80
	1978(a)	—	.25	.45	.80
	1979(a)	—	.25	.45	.80

F.A.O. Issue

KM#	Date	Mintage	VF	XF	Unc
9	1980(a)	—	.25	1.00	2.25
	1981(a)	—	.25	1.00	2.25
	1982(a)	—	.25	1.00	2.25
	1984(a)	—	.25	1.00	2.25
	1985(a)	8.587	.25	1.00	2.25
	1987(a)	—	.25	1.00	2.25
	1989(a)	—	.25	1.00	2.25

50 FRANCS

COPPER-NICKEL
F.A.O. Issue

KM#	Date	Mintage	VF	XF	Unc
6	1972(a)	20.000	.35	.50	1.25
	1974(a)	3.000	.50	.75	1.50
	1975(a)	9.000	.25	.40	1.00
	1976(a)	6.002	.35	.50	1.25
	1977(a)	4.832	.35	.50	1.25
	1978(a)	—	.35	.50	1.25
	1979(a)	—	.35	.50	1.25
	1980(a)	—	.35	.50	1.25
	1981(a)	—	.35	.50	1.25
	1982(a)	—	.35	.50	1.25
	1984(a)	—	.35	.50	1.25
	1985(a)	4.120	.35	.50	1.25
	1986(a)	—	.35	.50	1.25
	1987(a)	—	.35	.50	1.25
	1989(a)	—	.35	.50	1.25
	1991(a)	—	.35	.50	1.25

100 FRANCS

NICKEL

KM#	Date	Mintage	VF	XF	Unc
4	1967(a)	—	.75	.90	2.00
	1968(a)	25.000	.75	.90	2.00
	1969(a)	25.000	.75	.90	2.00
	1970(a)	4.510	.80	.90	2.00
	1971(a)	12.000	.50	.75	1.75
	1972(a)	5.000	.60	.75	1.75
	1973(a)	5.000	.60	.75	1.75
	1974(a)	8.500	.60	.75	1.75
	1975(a)	16.000	.60	.75	1.75
	1976(a)	11.575	.60	.75	1.75
	1977(a)	9.355	.60	.75	1.75
	1978(a)	—	.60	.75	1.75
	1979(a)	—	.60	.75	1.75
	1980(a)	—	.60	.75	1.75
	1981(a)	—	.60	.75	1.75
	1982(a)	—	.60	.75	1.75
	1984(a)	—	.60	.75	1.75
	1985(a)	1.460	.60	.75	1.75
	1987(a)	—	.60	.75	1.75
	1991(a)	—	.60	.75	1.75
	1992(a)	—	.60	.75	1.75

250 FRANCS

BRASS CENTER, COPPER-NICKEL RING

KM#	Date	Mintage	VF	XF	Unc
13	1992	—	—	2.00	3.00

500 FRANCS

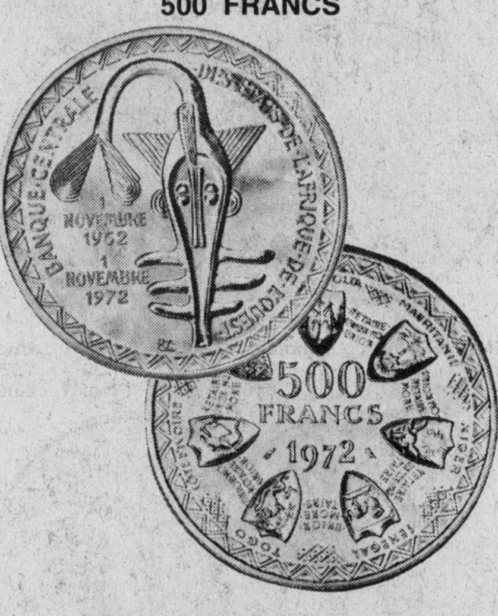

25.0000 g, .900 SILVER, .7234 oz ASW
10th Anniversary of Monetary Union

KM#	Date	Mintage	VF	XF	Unc
7	1972(a)	.100	—	22.00	35.00

5000 FRANCS

24.9500 g, .900 SILVER, .7220 oz ASW, 37mm
20th Anniversary of Monetary Union

KM#	Date	Mintage	VF	XF	Unc
11	1982(a)	.200	—	25.00	40.00

14.4900 g, .900 GOLD, .4193 oz AGW

KM#	Date	Mintage	VF	XF	Unc
12	1982(a)	—	—	—	450.00

FLEUR DE COIN SETS (SS)

KM#	Date	Mintage	Identification	Mkt.Val.
SS1	1968(a)	—	KM1-2,4	9.50

WESTERN SAMOA

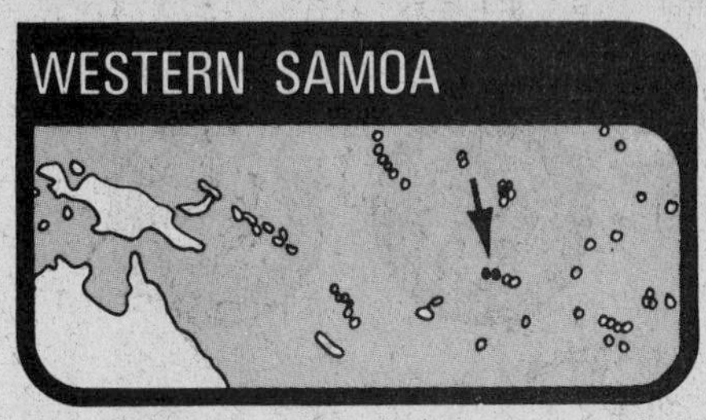

The Independent State of Western Samoa, located in the Pacific Ocean 1,600 miles (2,574 km.) northeast of New Zealand, has an area of 1,097 sq. mi. (2,860 sq. km.) and a population of *182,000. Capital: Apia. The economy is based on agriculture, fishing and tourism. Copra, cocoa and bananas are exported.

The first European to sight the Samoan group of islands was the Dutch navigator Jacob Roggeveen in 1772. Great Britain, the United States and Germany established consular representation at Apia in 1847, 1853 and 1861 respectively. The conflicting interests of the three powers produced the Berlin agreement of 1889 which declared Samoa neutral and had the effect of establishing a tripartite protectorate over the islands. A further agreement, 1899, recognized the rights of the United States in those islands east of 171 deg. west longitude (American Samoa) and of Germany in the other islands (Western Samoa). New Zealand occupied Western Samoa at the start of World War I and administered it as a League of Nations mandate and U. N. trusteeship until Jan. 1, 1962, when it became an independent state.

Western Samoa is a member of the Commonwealth of Nations. The Chief Executive is Chief of State. The prime minister is the Head of Government. The present Head of State, Malietoa Tanumafili II, holds his position for life. Future Heads of State will be elected by the Legislative Assembly for 5-year terms.

Western Samoa, which had used New Zealand coinage, converted to a decimal coinage in 1967.

RULERS

British, until 1962
Malietoa Tanumafili II, 1962 -

MONETARY SYSTEM

100 Sene = 1 Tala

SENE

BRONZE

KM#	Date	Mintage	VF	XF	Unc
1	1967	.915	.10	.15	.20
	1967	.015	—	Proof	.50
12	1974	3.380	—	.10	.15
	1987	—	—	.10	.15
	1988	—	—	.10	.15

1.9500 g, .925 SILVER, .0579 oz ASW

KM#	Date	Mintage	VF	XF	Unc
12a	1974	5,578	—	Proof	2.50

2 SENE

BRONZE

KM#	Date	Mintage	VF	XF	Unc
2	1967	.465	.10	.15	.25
	1967	.015	—	Proof	.50
13	1974	1.640	.10	.15	.20
	1988	—	.10	.15	.20

3.8000 g, .925 SILVER, .1130 oz ASW

KM#	Date	Mintage	VF	XF	Unc
13a	1974	5,578	—	Proof	3.00

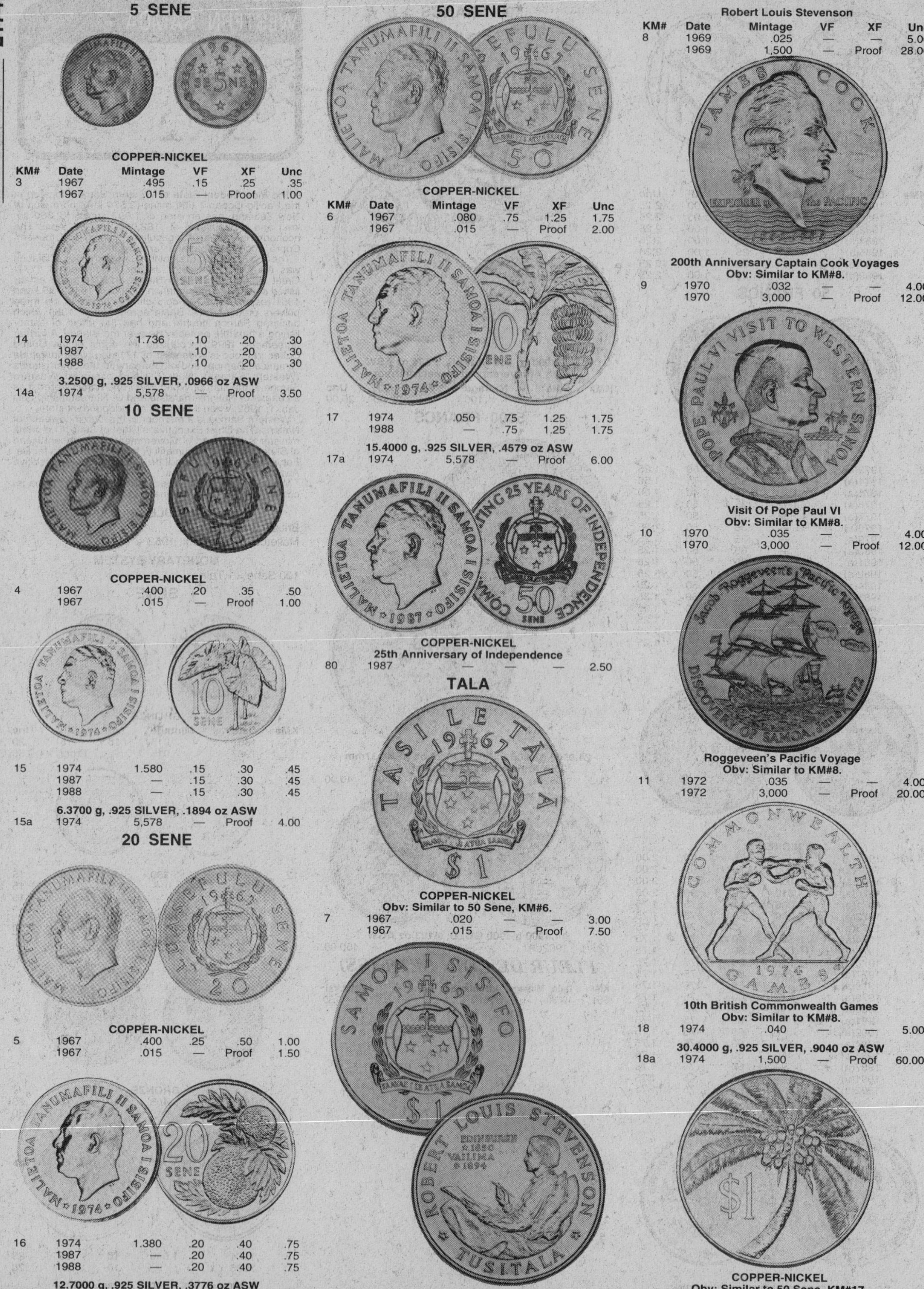

5 SENE

COPPER-NICKEL

KM#	Date	Mintage	VF	XF	Unc
3	1967	.495	.15	.25	.35
	1967	.015	—	Proof	1.00
14	1974	1.736	.10	.20	.30
	1987	—	.10	.20	.30
	1988	—	.10	.20	.30

3.2500 g, .925 SILVER, .0966 oz ASW

KM#	Date	Mintage	VF	XF	Unc
14a	1974	5,578	—	Proof	3.50

10 SENE

COPPER-NICKEL

KM#	Date	Mintage	VF	XF	Unc
4	1967	.400	.20	.35	.50
	1967	.015	—	Proof	1.00
15	1974	1.580	.15	.30	.45
	1987	—	.15	.30	.45
	1988	—	.15	.30	.45

6.3700 g, .925 SILVER, .1894 oz ASW

KM#	Date	Mintage	VF	XF	Unc
15a	1974	5,578	—	Proof	4.00

20 SENE

COPPER-NICKEL

KM#	Date	Mintage	VF	XF	Unc
5	1967	.400	.25	.50	1.00
	1967	.015	—	Proof	1.50
16	1974	1.380	.20	.40	.75
	1987	—	.20	.40	.75
	1988	—	.20	.40	.75

12.7000 g, .925 SILVER, .3776 oz ASW

KM#	Date	Mintage	VF	XF	Unc
16a	1974	5,578	—	Proof	5.00

50 SENE

COPPER-NICKEL

KM#	Date	Mintage	VF	XF	Unc
6	1967	.080	.75	1.25	1.75
	1967	.015	—	Proof	2.00
17	1974	.050	.75	1.25	1.75
	1988	—	.75	1.25	1.75

15.4000 g, .925 SILVER, .4579 oz ASW

KM#	Date	Mintage	VF	XF	Unc
17a	1974	5,578	—	Proof	6.00

COPPER-NICKEL
25th Anniversary of Independence

KM#	Date	Mintage	VF	XF	Unc
80	1987	—	—	—	2.50

TALA

COPPER-NICKEL
Obv: Similar to 50 Sene, KM#6.

KM#	Date	Mintage	VF	XF	Unc
7	1967	.020	—	—	3.00
	1967	.015	—	Proof	7.50

75th Anniversary - Death of
Robert Louis Stevenson

KM#	Date	Mintage	VF	XF	Unc
8	1969	.025	—	—	5.00
	1969	1,500	—	Proof	28.00

200th Anniversary Captain Cook Voyages
Obv: Similar to KM#8.

KM#	Date	Mintage	VF	XF	Unc
9	1970	.032	—	—	4.00
	1970	3,000	—	Proof	12.00

Visit Of Pope Paul VI
Obv: Similar to KM#8.

KM#	Date	Mintage	VF	XF	Unc
10	1970	.035	—	—	4.00
	1970	3,000	—	Proof	12.00

Roggeveen's Pacific Voyage
Obv: Similar to KM#8.

KM#	Date	Mintage	VF	XF	Unc
11	1972	.035	—	—	4.00
	1972	3,000	—	Proof	20.00

10th British Commonwealth Games
Obv: Similar to KM#8.

KM#	Date	Mintage	VF	XF	Unc
18	1974	.040	—	—	5.00

30.4000 g, .925 SILVER, .9040 oz ASW

KM#	Date	Mintage	VF	XF	Unc
18a	1974	1,500	—	Proof	60.00

COPPER-NICKEL
Obv: Similar to 50 Sene, KM#17.

KM#	Date	Mintage	VF	XF	Unc
19	1974	.024	—	—	4.00

31.1500 g, .925 SILVER, .9263 oz ASW

KM#	Date	Mintage	VF	XF	Unc
19a	1974	.011	—	Proof	10.00

COPPER-NICKEL
U.S. Bicentennial

KM#	Date	Mintage	VF	XF	Unc
20	1976	.040	—	—	3.50

30.4000 g, .925 SILVER, .9040 oz ASW

KM#	Date	Mintage	VF	XF	Unc
20a	1976	4,127	—	Proof	18.00

COPPER-NICKEL
Montreal Olympics - Weight Lifter
Obv: Similar to KM#8.

KM#	Date	Mintage	VF	XF	Unc
22	1976	.040	—	—	4.00

30.4000 g, .925 SILVER, .9040 oz ASW

KM#	Date	Mintage	VF	XF	Unc
22a	1976	6,000	—	Proof	17.50

COPPER-NICKEL
Queen's Silver Jubilee
Obv: Similar to KM#8.

KM#	Date	Mintage	VF	XF	Unc
24	1977	.027	—	—	3.50

30.4000 g, .925 SILVER, .9040 oz ASW

KM#	Date	Mintage	VF	XF	Unc
24a	1977	6,171	—	Proof	12.50

COPPER-NICKEL
Lindbergh's New York to Paris Flight
Obv: Similar to KM#8.

KM#	Date	Mintage	VF	XF	Unc
26	1977	.017	—	—	4.50

30.4000 g, .925 SILVER, .9040 oz ASW

KM#	Date	Mintage	VF	XF	Unc
26a	1977	4,522	—	Proof	17.50

COPPER-NICKEL
50th Anniversary First Transpacific Flight
Obv: Similar to KM#8.

KM#	Date	Mintage	VF	XF	Unc
28	1978	.020	—	—	3.50

30.4000 g, .925 SILVER, .9040 oz ASW

KM#	Date	Mintage	VF	XF	Unc
28a	1978	5,000	—	Proof	15.00

COPPER-NICKEL
XI Commonwealth Games
Obv: Similar to KM#8.

KM#	Date	Mintage	VF	XF	Unc
30	1978	7,710	—	—	6.00

30.4000 g, .925 SILVER, .9040 oz ASW

KM#	Date	Mintage	VF	XF	Unc
30a	1978	5,000	—	Proof	15.00

COPPER-NICKEL
Bicentenary of the Death of Captain James Cook
Obv: Similar to KM#8.

KM#	Date	Mintage	VF	XF	Unc
32	1979	5,000	—	—	4.00

1980 Olympics - Hurdles
Obv: Similar to KM#8.

KM#	Date	Mintage	VF	XF	Unc
35	1980	5,000	—	—	5.00

F.A.O. Issue
Obv: Similar to KM#8.

KM#	Date	Mintage	VF	XF	Unc
38	1980	.010	—	—	3.50

Governor Wilhelm Solf
Obv: Similar to KM#8.

KM#	Date	Mintage	VF	XF	Unc
40	1980	5,000	—	—	5.50

Wedding of Prince Charles and Lady Diana
Obv: Similar to KM#8.

KM#	Date	Mintage	VF	XF	Unc
43	1981	.012	—	—	5.00

IYDP - President Roosevelt
Obv: Similar to KM#8.

KM#	Date	Mintage	VF	XF	Unc
47	1981	8,000	—	—	3.00

Commonwealth Games - Javelin Thrower
Obv: Similar to KM#8.

KM#	Date	Mintage	VF	XF	Unc
50	1982	6,000	—	—	4.00

South Pacific Games - Runner
Obv: Similar to KM#8.

KM#	Date	Mintage	VF	XF	Unc
53	1983	8,000	—	—	3.00

ALUMINUM-BRONZE
Circulation Coinage

KM#	Date	Mintage	VF	XF	Unc
57	1984	1.000	.50	.75	1.00
		COPPER-NICKEL			
57a	1984	5,000	Reported, not confirmed		
		33.6300 g, .925 SILVER, 1.0000 oz ASW			
57b	1984	3,000	—	Proof	35.00

COPPER-NICKEL
Summer Olympics - Boxers

KM#	Date	Mintage	VF	XF	Unc
58	1984	5,000	—	—	5.00

Prince Andrew's Marriage

KM#	Date	Mintage	VF	XF	Unc
63	1986	.010	—	—	3.50

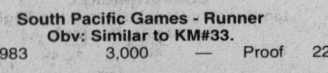

25th Anniversary of World Wildlife Fund

KM#	Date	Mintage	VF	XF	Unc
74	1986	—	—	—	3.50

40th Anniversary - Reign of Queen Elizabeth II

KM#	Date	Mintage	VF	XF	Unc
88	1992	—	—	—	4.50

10 TALA

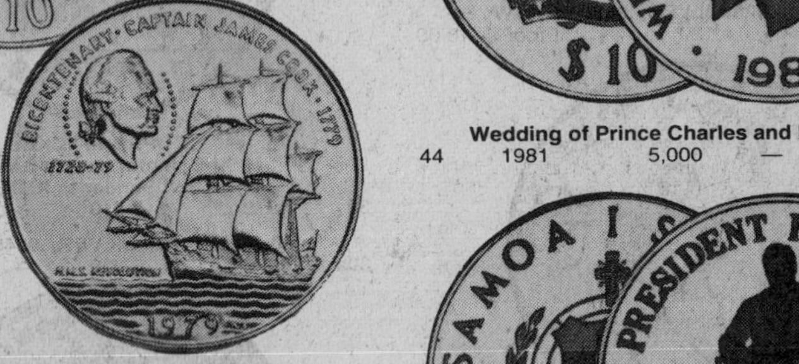

31.3300 g, .500 SILVER, .5036 oz ASW
Bicentenary - Death of Captain James Cook

KM#	Date	Mintage	VF	XF	Unc
33	1979	3,000	—	—	8.00
		31.4700 g, .925 SILVER, .9359 oz ASW			
33a	1979	5,000	—	Proof	17.50

31.3300 g, .500 SILVER, .5036 oz ASW
1980 Olympics - Hurdles
Obv: Similar to KM#33.

KM#	Date	Mintage	VF	XF	Unc
36	1980	3,000	—	—	8.50
		31.4700 g, .925 SILVER, .9359 oz ASW			
36a	1980	4,000	—	Proof	18.50

31.3300 g, .500 SILVER, .5036 oz ASW
F.A.O. Issue
Obv: Similar to KM#33.

KM#	Date	Mintage	VF	XF	Unc
39	1980	3,000	—	Proof	18.50

Governor Wilhelm Solf
Obv: Similar to KM#33.

KM#	Date	Mintage	VF	XF	Unc
41	1980	3,000	—	—	9.50
		31.4700 g, .925 SILVER, .9359 oz ASW			
41a	1980	4,000	—	Proof	18.50

Wedding of Prince Charles and Lady Diana

KM#	Date	Mintage	VF	XF	Unc
44	1981	5,000	—	Proof	17.50

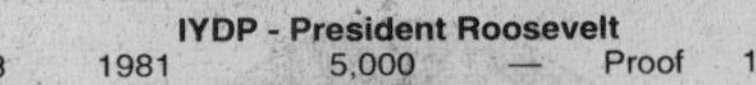

IYDP - President Roosevelt

KM#	Date	Mintage	VF	XF	Unc
48	1981	5,000	—	Proof	17.50

Commonwealth Games - Javelin Thrower
Obv: Similar to KM#33.

KM#	Date	Mintage	VF	XF	Unc
51	1982	4,000	—	Proof	20.00

South Pacific Games - Runner
Obv: Similar to KM#33.

KM#	Date	Mintage	VF	XF	Unc
54	1983	3,000	—	Proof	22.50

Summer Olympics - Boxers

KM#	Date	Mintage	VF	XF	Unc
59	1984	2,500	—	Proof	25.00

Prince Andrew's Marriage
Similar to 1 Tala, KM#63.

KM#	Date	Mintage	VF	XF	Unc
64	1986	2,500	—	Proof	20.00

31.1000 g, .999 SILVER, 1.0000 oz ASW
America's Cup Race

KM#	Date	Mintage	VF	XF	Unc
66	1987	*.050	—	Proof	20.00

31.4700 g, .925 SILVER, .9360 oz ASW
25th Anniversary of World Wildlife Fund

KM#	Date	Mintage	VF	XF	Unc
72	1986	*.025	—	Proof	35.00

1988 Olympics - 3 Torches & Athletes

KM#	Date	Mintage	VF	XF	Unc
70	1988	.020	—	—	40.00

31.1030 g, .999 SILVER, 1.0000 oz ASW
Kon-Tiki-Raft and Map

KM#	Date	Mintage	VF	XF	Unc
75	1988	*.020	—	Proof	45.00

31.4700 g, .925 SILVER, .9360 oz ASW
Save the Children Fund

KM#	Date	Mintage	VF	XF	Unc
79	1990	*.020	—	Proof	45.00

Summer Olympics - Shot Putter

KM#	Date	Mintage	VF	XF	Unc
82	1991	*.070	—	Proof	42.50

31.1030 g, .925 SILVER, .9250 oz ASW
RA Expeditions - RAI
Obv: Similar to KM#82.

KM#	Date	Mintage	VF	XF	Unc
83	1991	.015	—	Proof	45.00

31.4700 g, .925 SILVER, .9360 oz ASW
Olympics - Javelin Thrower

KM#	Date	Mintage	VF	XF	Unc
85	1991	*.070	—	Proof	45.00

Olympics - Hammer Thrower

KM#	Date	Mintage	VF	XF	Unc
86	1992	*.070	—	Proof	42.50

31.8600 g, .925 SILVER, .9476 oz ASW
World Cup Soccer - Arena

KM#	Date	Mintage	VF	XF	Unc
89	1992	*.020	—	Proof	45.00

25 TALA

155.5000 g, .999 SILVER, 5.0000 oz ASW
Kon-Tiki
Reduced size. Actual size: 65mm.

KM#	Date	Mintage	VF	XF	Unc
62	1986	*.025	—	Proof	60.00

America's Cup Race
Reduced size. Actual size: 65mm.

KM#	Date	Mintage	VF	XF	Unc
67	1987	*.035	—	Proof	55.00

50 TALA

31.1030 g, .999 PALLADIUM, 1.0000 oz APW
Kon-Tiki - Raft and Bamboo Poles

KM#	Date	Mintage	VF	XF	Unc
76	1988	*.010	—	Proof	175.00

7.7700 g, .999 GOLD, .2500 oz AGW
Trans-Antartica Expedition

KM#	Date	Mintage	VF	XF	Unc
78	1988	*.030	—	Proof	120.00

7.7760 g, .5833 GOLD, .1458 oz AGW
'96 Olympics - Discus Thrower

KM#	Date	Mintage	VF	XF	Unc
90	1993	7,500	—	Proof	125.00

100 TALA

15.5500 g, .917 GOLD, .4583 oz AGW
U.S. Bicentennial

KM#	Date	Mintage	VF	XF	Unc
21	1976	2,000	—	Proof	225.00

Montreal Olympics - Weight Lifter
Similar to 1 Tala, KM#22.

KM#	Date	Mintage	VF	XF	Unc
23	1976	2,500	—	Proof	225.00

Queen's Silver Jubilee

KM#	Date	Mintage	VF	XF	Unc
25	1977	2,500	—	Proof	225.00

Lindbergh's New York to Paris Flight

KM#	Date	Mintage	VF	XF	Unc
27	1977	660 pcs.	—	Proof	260.00

50th Anniversary Transpacific Flight
Similar to 1 Tala, KM#28.

KM#	Date	Mintage	VF	XF	Unc
29	1978	1,500	—	Proof	230.00

XI Commonwealth Games
Similar to 1 Tala, KM#30.

KM#	Date	Mintage	VF	XF	Unc
31	1978	1,000	—	Proof	235.00

12.5000 g, .917 GOLD, .3686 oz AGW
Bicentenary - Death of Captain James Cook
Similar to 10 Tala, KM#33.

KM#	Date	Mintage	VF	XF	Unc
34	1979	1,000	—	Proof	215.00

7.5000 g, .917 GOLD, .2211 oz AGW
1980 Olympics - Hurdles

KM#	Date	Mintage	VF	XF	Unc
37	1980	250 pcs.	—	—	120.00
	1980	1,000	—	Proof	130.00

Governor Wilhelm Solf

KM#	Date	Mintage	VF	XF	Unc
42	1980	250 pcs.	—	—	120.00
	1980	1,000	—	Proof	130.00

Wedding of Prince Charles and Lady Diana

KM#	Date	Mintage	VF	XF	Unc
45	1981	250 pcs.	—	—	115.00
	1981	1,500	—	Proof	125.00

IYDP - President Roosevelt
Similar to 1 Tala, KM#47.

KM#	Date	Mintage	VF	XF	Unc
49	1981	250 pcs.	—	—	115.00
	1981	1,500	—	Proof	125.00

Commonwealth Games - Javelin Thrower

KM#	Date	Mintage	VF	XF	Unc
52	1982	250 pcs.	—	—	120.00
	1982	1,000	—	Proof	140.00

South Pacific Games - Runner

KM#	Date	Mintage	VF	XF	Unc
55	1983	—	—	—	125.00
	1983	1,000	—	Proof	145.00

Summer Olympics - Boxers
Rev: Similar to 1 Tala, KM#58.

KM#	Date	Mintage	VF	XF	Unc
60	1984	200 pcs.	—	—	180.00
	1984	500 pcs.	—	Proof	200.00

7.5000 g, .900 GOLD, .2170 oz AGW
America's Cup Race

KM#	Date	Mintage	VF	XF	Unc
68	1987	*5,000	—	Proof	120.00

Kon-Tiki - Raft and Inscription

KM#	Date	Mintage	VF	XF	Unc
77	1988	*5,000	—	Proof	120.00

7.5000 g, .917 GOLD, .2211 oz AGW
Save The Children

KM#	Date	Mintage	VF	XF	Unc
81	1990	3,000	—	Proof	135.00

RA Expeditions - RA II
Obv: Similar to KM#81.

KM#	Date	Mintage	VF	XF	Unc
84	1991	5,000	—	Proof	140.00

7.5000 g, .900 GOLD, .2170 oz AGW
Olympics - Torch Runner

KM#	Date	Mintage	VF	XF	Unc
87	1991	*6,000	—	Proof	150.00

1000 TALA

33.9500 g, .917 GOLD, 1.0010 oz AGW
Wedding of Prince Charles and Lady Diana
Similar to 100 Tala, KM#45.

KM#	Date	Mintage	VF	XF	Unc
46	1981	100 pcs.	—	Proof	775.00

31.1000 g, .917 GOLD, .9170 oz AGW
South Pacific Games - Runner
Similar to 10 Tala, KM#54.

KM#	Date	Mintage	VF	XF	Unc
56	1983	100 pcs.	—	Proof	825.00

1984 Olympics - Boxers

KM#	Date	Mintage	VF	XF	Unc
61	1984	100 pcs.	—	Proof	825.00

33.9500 g, .917 GOLD, 1.0010 oz AGW
Prince Andrew's Marriage
Obv: Similar to 1 Tala, KM#8.
Rev: Similar to 1 Tala, KM#63.

KM#	Date	Mintage	VF	XF	Unc
65	1986	50 pcs.	—	Proof	875.

MINT SETS (MS)

KM#	Date	Mintage	Identification	Issue Price	Mkt. Val.
MS1	1967(6)	—	KM1-6	—	2.50
MS2	1974(7)	10,740	KM12-17,19	5.30	5.00

PROOF SETS (PS)

KM#	Date	Mintage	Identification	Issue Price	Mkt. Val.
PS1	1967(7)	15,000	KM1-7	10.00	7.00
PS2	1974(7)	5,578	KM12a-17a,19a	53.00	30.00
PS3	1988(3)	—	KM75-77	—	325.00
PS4	1991(2)	1,000	KM83-84	—	185.00

Listings For

WEST IRIAN: refer to Indonesia
WEST NEW GUINEA: refer to Indonesia

YEMEN REPUBLIC

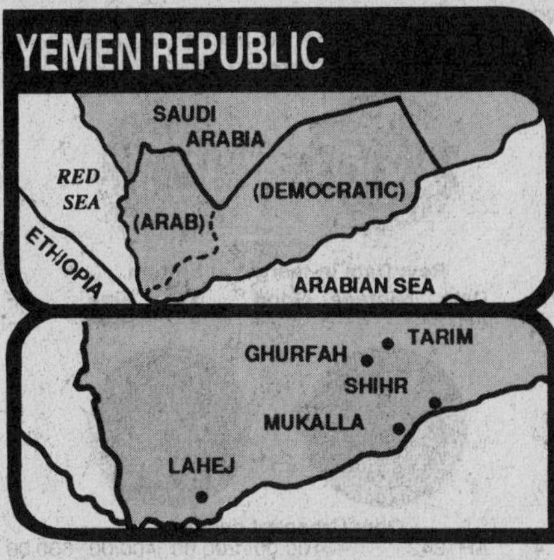

The Republic of Yemen, formerly Yemen Arab Republic and Peoples Republic of Yemen is located on the southern coast of the Arabian Peninsula. It has an area of 205,020 sq. mi. (531,000 sq. km.) and a population of 12 million. Capital: Sana'a. The port of Aden is the main commercial center and the area's most valuable natural resource. Recent oil and gas finds and a developing petroleum industry have improved their economic prospects. Agriculture and local handicrafts are the main industries. Cotton, fish, coffee, rock salt and hides are exported.

On May 22, 1990, the Yemen Arab Republic (North Yemen) and Peoples Democratic Republic of Yemen (South Yemen) merged into a unified Republic of Yemen.

TITLES

دار الخلافة

Dar al-Khilafa(t)

MUTAWWAKKILITE KINGDOM

One of the oldest centers of civilization in the Middle East, Yemen was once part of the Minaean Kingdom and of the ancient Kingdom of Sheba, after which it was captured successively by Egyptians, Ethiopians and Romans. It was converted to Islam in 628 A.D. and administered as a caliphate until 1538, when it came under Ottoman occupation which was maintained until 1918 when autonomy was achieved through revolution.

TITLES

المملكة المتوكلية اليمنية

al-Mamlaka(t) al-Mutawwakkiliya(t) al-Yemeniya(t)

RULERS

Imam Mansur, AH1307-1322/1890-1904AD
Imam Yahya, AH1322-1367/1904-1948AD
Imam Ahmad, AH1367-1382/1948-1962AD
Imam Badr, AH1382-1388/1962-1968AD (mostly in exile)

MINTNAME

سنة

Sana'a

MONETARY SYSTEM

2 Zalat = 1 Halala = 1/80 Riyal
2 Halala = 1 Buqsha = 1/40 Riyal
40 Buqsha = 1 Riyal

NOTE: The Riyal was called an IMADI RIYAL during the reign of Imam Yahya, and an AHMADI RIYAL during the reign of Imam Ahmad. Except for the 1 Zalat and Y#2.1, 2.6, B1, A3, A4 and all Imam Mansur issues which bear no indication of value, all of the Mutawwakkilite coins bear the denomination expressed as a fraction of the Riyal as follows:

BRONZE and ALUMINUM

Rub 1/160 Riyal = 1/4 Buqsha = 1 Zalat
Thumn ushr = 1/80 Riyal = 1/2 Buqsha = 1 Halala
Rub ushr = 1/40 Riyal = 1 Buqsha

SILVER

Nisf ushr = 1/20 Riyal = 2 Buqsha
Nisf thumn = 1/16 Riyal = 2-1/2 Buqsha
Ushr = 1/10 Riyal = 4 Buqsha
Thumn = 1/8 Riyal = 5 Buqsha
Rub = 1/4 Riyal = 10 Buqsha
Nisf = 1/2 Riyal = 20 Buqsha
1 Riyal = 40 Buqsha

DATING

All coins of Imam Yahya have accession date AH 1322 on obverse and actual date of issue on reverse. All coins of Imam Ahmad bear accession date AH1367 on obverse and actual date on reverse.

NOTE: Most coins struck for the Mutawakkilite kingdom, as well as the early issues of the Republic (Y#20 through Y#A25 and Y#32), were struck at the mint in Sana'a. The Sana'a Mint was essentially a medieval mint, using hand-cut dies and crudely machined blanks. There is a large amount of variation from one die to the next in arrangement of legends and ornaments, form of crescents, the number of stars, size of the circle, etc., and literally hundreds of subtypes could be identified. Types are divided only when there are changes in the inscriptions, or major variations in the basic type, such as the presence or absence of *Rabb al-Alamin* in the legend or the position of the word *Sana* (= year) in relation to the year.

IMAM MANSUR

AH1307-1322/1890-1904AD

It is thought that coins for this ruler were struck at Sa'da, Shahara or Qaflat Idhar.

1/4 BUQSHA

COPPER, 1.2-2.1 g, 17-18mm
Obv. leg: ***Billah/al-Mansur,/date/Sana.***
Rev. leg: ***Allah/Abd.***

KM#	Date	Mintage	Good	VG	Fine	VF
402.1	AH1312	—	—	—	—	—

1.30 g
Similar to KM#402.1 but w/o *Sana.*

KM#	Date	Mintage	Good	VG	Fine	VF
402.2	AH1313	—	—	—	—	—

Similar to 1 Buqsha, KM#410.

KM#	Date	Mintage	Good	VG	Fine	VF
403	AH1320	—	—	—	—	—

1/2 BUQSHA

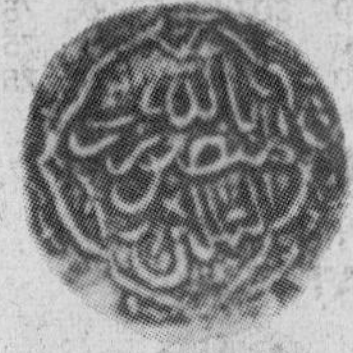

COPPER, 3.00 g, 23mm
Obv. leg: ***Billah/al-Mansur/Rabb al-Alamin.***
Rev. leg: ***Amir/sanat/al-mu'minin/1312.***

KM#	Date	Mintage	Good	VG	Fine	VF
405	AH1312	—	—	—	—	—

3.10 g, 24mm
Rev. leg: ***Allah/Abd/Amir al-mu'/minin/date/sana.***

KM#	Date	Mintage	Good	VG	Fine	VF
406	AH1313	—	—	—	—	—
	1314	—	—	—	—	—

BUQSHA

SILVER, 0.50 g, 16mm

KM#	Date	Mintage	Good	VG	Fine	VF
407.1	AH1311	—	—	—	—	—

0.60-0.70 g, 17mm
Rev: Date at bottom.

KM#	Date	Mintage	Good	VG	Fine	VF
407.2	AH1318	—	—	—	—	—

0.60-0.80 g, 15-16mm
Obv. leg: *Billah/al-Mansur*, ornament below.
Rev. leg: *Allah/Abd 1312/duriba*.

KM#	Date	Mintage	Good	VG	Fine	VF
408.1	AH1312	—	—	—	—	—

NOTE: Variety w/o duriba on reverse exists.

0.70-0.80 g
Obv: Year below legend.

KM#	Date	Mintage	Good	VG	Fine	VF
408.2	AH1312	—	—	—	—	—
	1314	—	—	—	—	—

NOTE: Variety w/o duriba on reverse exists.

SILVER, 0.40-0.80 g, 15-17mm
Obv: Different ornamentation below.

KM#	Date	Mintage	Good	VG	Fine	VF
408.3	AH1318	—	—	—	—	—

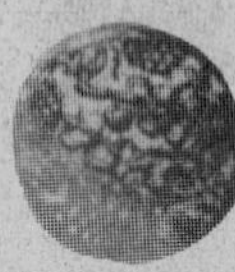

0.70-1.0g
Rev: Date above ornament at bottom.

KM#	Date	Mintage	Good	VG	Fine	VF
409	AH1315	—	—	—	—	—

0.60-1.10 g, 15-16mm
Rev: Date divided by ornament.

KM#	Date	Mintage	Good	VG	Fine	VF
410	AH1316	—	15.00	30.00	50.00	75.00
(Y-A1)	1320	—	15.00	30.00	50.00	75.00
	1321	—	15.00	30.00	50.00	75.00

NOTE: Varieties with 3 and 4 stars on reverse exist.

IMAM YAHYA

AH1322-1367/1904-1948AD

ZALAT

BRONZE
Accession Date: AH1322

Y#	Date	Mintage	Good	VG	Fine	VF
B1	ND	—	30.00	60.00	125.00	200.00

NOTE: Dated accessionally on obverse. Probably struck about 1925. Dies were reportedly prepared in Italy. See Y#A4.

0.90-1.60 g
Obv: Inscription in 3 lines above regnal year.

Y#	Date	Mintage	Good	VG	Fine	VF
1.1	AH1340	—	Reported, not confirmed			
	1341	—	15.00	30.00	100.00	160.00
	1342	—	5.00	12.00	30.00	50.00
	1343	—	4.00	10.00	20.00	40.00
	1344	—	5.00	12.00	30.00	50.00
	1345	—	10.00	25.00	75.00	125.00
	1346	—	4.00	10.00	20.00	40.00

NOTE: Obverse: Varieties w/2 stars. Reverse w/8 stars, 1343 also known w/7 stars. Edge plain but 1344 also exists w/traces of reeded edge. Size of inner circle varies.

Obv: Inscription in 2 lines above regnal year.

Y#	Date	Mintage	Good	VG	Fine	VF
1.2	AH1342	—	5.00	12.00	30.00	50.00

NOTE: Obv: Varieties w/1, 2 and 4 stars, and reverse w/8,11, 12, 13, 14, 15, 17, 20 and 22 stars exist. Some specimens show traces of reeded edge.

Rev: Date in margin at bottom.

Y#	Date	Mintage	Good	VG	Fine	VF
1.7	AH1342	—	—	—	Rare	—

Obv: Crescent design.

Y#	Date	Mintage	Good	VG	Fine	VF
1.4	AH1342	—	100.00	200.00	400.00	600.00

NOTE: Varieties exist w/11, 15, 16 and 17 stars on reverse and w/1 and 4 stars on obverse.

1/80 RIYAL

(1 Halala - 1/2 Buqsha)

BRONZE (Red or Yellow)
Accession Date: AH1322

Y#	Date	Mintage	Good	VG	Fine	VF
2.1	ND(AH1322) (accessional date only)	—	12.50	25.00	50.00	75.00

Thin flan, 1.50-3.00 g
Obv: *Rabb al-Alamin*.
Rev: Denomination added w/o mintname, *Sana* above date.

Y#	Date	Mintage	Good	VG	Fine	VF
2.2	AH1330	—	20.00	35.00	60.00	100.00
	1331	—	20.00	35.00	75.00	150.00
	1332	—	10.00	15.00	25.00	40.00
	1333	—	10.00	15.00	25.00	40.00
	1338	—	10.00	15.00	25.00	40.00
	1339	—	—	—	—	—
	ND Mule	—	20.00	30.00	60.00	100.00

NOTE: The number and arrangement of stars and the size of the circle on the reverse vary as well as the exact arrangement of the legends which sometimes vary within each year. The reverse exists w/10, 12, 14, 20, 22, 24 and 34 stars. The mule consists of 2 obverses. Probably struck at Shahara until 1333, later at Sana'a.

Thin flan, 3.00 g
Rev: *Sana* below date.

Y#	Date	Mintage	Good	VG	Fine	VF
2.6	AH1333	—	80.00	100.00	200.00	300.00

NOTE: 12 stars on reverse.

Rev: *Duriba Bi Sana'a* added.

Y#	Date	Mintage	Good	VG	Fine	VF
2.3	AH1339	—	—	Reported, not confirmed		
	1340	—	10.00	20.00	40.00	75.00
	1341	—	10.00	20.00	40.00	75.00

NOTE: AH1339 and1340 exist w/4 and 8 stars on reverse.

Obv: W/o *Rabb al-Alamin*.

Y#	Date	Mintage	Good	VG	Fine	VF
2.4	AH1341	—	12.00	25.00	50.00	85.00
	1342	—	12.00	25.00	50.00	85.00

NOTE: AH1342 coins exist w/4 and 6 stars and 1341 exists w/3 stars on reverse.

Obv: *Rabb al-Alamin*.
Rev: *Sana* above date.

Y#	Date	Mintage	Good	VG	Fine	VF
2.5	AH1341	—	7.00	12.00	25.00	40.00
	1342	—	2.00	5.00	12.00	20.00
	1343	—	2.00	5.00	12.00	20.00
	1344	—	2.00	5.00	12.00	20.00
	1345	—	1.50	4.00	8.00	15.00
	1346	—	1.50	3.00	6.00	12.00
	1347	—	1.50	4.00	8.00	15.00
	1348	—	1.50	4.00	8.00	15.00
	1349	—	1.50	4.00	8.00	15.00
	1350	—	1.50	4.00	8.00	15.00
	1351	—	2.00	6.00	12.00	20.00
	1352	—	2.00	6.00	12.00	20.00
	1353	—	2.00	6.00	12.00	20.00
	1358	—	Reported, not confirmed			
	1359	—	2.50	6.00	12.00	20.00
	1360	—	2.50	4.00	8.00	15.00
	1361	—	4.00	8.00	15.00	25.00

NOTE: Number and arrangement of stars on reverse (4, 5, 6, 7 or 8) as well as the size of the inner circle vary. Some examples of 1346 show the 6 reengraved over low 6. Varieties in the form of crescent and arrangement of legends exist.

1/40 RIYAL

(1 Buqsha)

SILVER, 0.77-1.25 g, 15-16mm

Y#	Date	Mintage	VG	Fine	VF	XF
A3	AH1322	—	—	—	—	—
	1323	—	Reported, not confirmed			

NOTE: Probably minted at Qaflat Idhar.

BRONZE (Red or Yellow)
Accession Date: AH1322
Obv: W/o *Rabb al-Alamin*, *Sana* below date.

Y#	Date	Mintage	Good	VG	Fine	VF
3.1	AH1341	—	10.00	20.00	40.00	80.00

NOTE: Varieties of borders and arrangement of legends exist.

Obv: *Rabb al-Alamin*.
Rev: *Sana* above date, small *Sana'a* in legend, leaf ornaments separate legend.

Y#	Date	Mintage	Good	VG	Fine	VF
3.2	AH1342	—	4.00	10.00	20.00	60.00
	1343	—	4.00	10.00	20.00	60.00
	1344	—	15.00	30.00	50.00	75.00
	13442 (error)	—	65.00	125.00	—	—
	1345	—	12.00	20.00	35.00	100.00

Rev: Large *Sana'a* in legend.

Y#	Date	Mintage	Good	VG	Fine	VF
3.3	AH1349	—	1.50	3.50	10.00	25.00
	1353	—	Reported, not confirmed			
	1358	—	2.00	4.00	10.00	25.00
	1359	—	2.00	4.00	10.00	25.00
	1360	—	2.00	4.00	10.00	25.00
	1361/0	—	10.00	20.00	50.00	75.00
	1362/0	—	2.50	5.00	10.00	35.00
	1362	—	1.50	3.50	10.00	30.00
	1363	—	1.50	5.00	12.00	35.00
	1364	—	1.50	5.00	12.00	35.00
	1365/4	—	2.25	5.00	12.00	35.00
	1365	—	2.50	5.00	12.00	35.00
	1366	—	1.50	3.50	12.00	30.00
	1367	—	10.00	20.00	50.00	75.00

NOTE: Varieties in arrangement of legends, ornaments, form of the crescent and size of the circle on reverse exist.

1/20 IMADI RIYAL

SILVER
Accession Date: AH1322

Y#	Date	Mintage	VG	Fine	VF	XF
A4	ND	—	60.00	120.00	250.00	400.00

NOTE: Dated accessionally on obverse. Probably struck about 1925. Dies were reportedly prepared in Italy. strikes in nickel reported. See Y#B1.

Obv: ***Rabb al-Alamin.*** **Rev: W/o** ***Sana.***

Y#	Date	Mintage	VG	Fine	VF	XF
B4	AH1337	—	—	—	Rare	—

NOTE: 3 stars on reverse.

Obv: W/o ***Rabb al-Alamin.***

Y#	Date	Mintage	VG	Fine	VF	XF
4.1	AH1337	—	40.00	80.00	150.00	250.00
	1338	—	—	—	Rare	—
	1339	—	40.00	80.00	150.00	250.00
	1340	—	20.00	30.00	60.00	100.00

NOTE: Varieties w/3 and 4 stars and size of circle on reverse exist.

Rev: Legend shifted to left.

Y#	Date	Mintage	VG	Fine	VF	XF
4.4	AH1340	—	—	—	Rare	—

NOTE: 3 stars on reverse.

Rev: ***Sana*** **below date, normal legend location.**

Y#	Date	Mintage	VG	Fine	VF	XF
4.2	AH1341	—	40.00	80.00	150.00	250.00
	x341	—	—	—	—	—

Rev: W/o ***Sana.***

Y#	Date	Mintage	VG	Fine	VF	XF
4.3	AH1342	—	5.00	12.00	30.00	60.00
	1343	—	4.00	10.00	25.00	50.00
	1344	—	4.00	10.00	25.00	50.00
	1345	—	4.00	10.00	25.00	50.00
	1347	—	5.00	12.00	30.00	60.00
	1348	—	4.00	10.00	25.00	50.00
	1349	—	4.00	10.00	25.00	50.00
	1350	—	4.00	12.00	30.00	60.00
	1351	—	5.00	15.00	35.00	75.00
	1352	—	4.00	12.00	30.00	60.00
	1353	—	4.00	12.00	30.00	60.00
	1358	—	3.00	8.00	20.00	40.00
	1359	—	3.00	8.00	20.00	40.00
	1362/59	—	5.00	15.00	30.00	60.00
	1363	—	4.00	10.00	30.00	60.00
	1364/4x	—	3.00	8.00	20.00	40.00
	1364	—	3.00	8.00	20.00	40.00
	1365	—	3.00	10.00	25.00	50.00
	1366/4	—	4.00	12.00	30.00	60.00
	1366	—	4.00	12.00	30.00	60.00

NOTE: Varieties in arrangement of legends exist.

NOTE: Recently reported variety of Y#5 dated w/2 digits AH(13)22 of the accessional year are considered contemporary counterfeits by leading authorities.

1/10 IMADI RIYAL

SILVER
Accession Date: AH1322
Obv: ***Rabb al-Alamin.***
Rev: W/o ***Sana.***

Y#	Date	Mintage	VG	Fine	VF	XF
5.1	AH1337	—	30.00	60.00	100.00	175.00

NOTE: Varieties w/3 and 5 stars, size of circle and form of crescent on reverse exist.

Obv: W/o ***Rabb al-Alamin.***

Y#	Date	Mintage	VG	Fine	VF	XF
5.2	AH1339	—	20.00	40.00	75.00	150.00
	1340	—	20.00	40.00	75.00	150.00
	1341	—	20.00	40.00	75.00	150.00

NOTE: AH1340 also exists w/3 stars, others w/6 stars on reverse.

Rev: ***Sana*** **below date.**

Y#	Date	Mintage	VG	Fine	VF	XF
5.3	AH1341	—	20.00	40.00	75.00	150.00
	1342	—	20.00	40.00	75.00	150.00

NOTE: Varieties w/3 and 6 stars on the reverse exist.

Obv: ***Rabb al-Alamin.***
Rev: ***Sana*** **above date.**

Y#	Date	Mintage	VG	Fine	VF	XF
5.4	AH1342	—	20.00	40.00	75.00	150.00

NOTE: Varieties w/8 and 9 stars on reverse exist.

Obv: W/o ***Rabb al-Alamin.***
Rev: ***Sana*** **above and below date.**

Y#	Date	Mintage	VG	Fine	VF	XF
5.6	AH1342	—	50.00	100.00	200.00	400.00

Rev: ***Sana*** **above date.**

Y#	Date	Mintage	VG	Fine	VF	XF
5.5	AH1342	—	4.00	10.00	25.00	50.00
	1343	—	4.00	10.00	25.00	50.00
	1344	—	3.00	8.00	20.00	40.00
	1345	—	3.00	8.00	20.00	40.00
	1347	—	3.00	8.00	20.00	40.00
	1348	—	3.00	8.00	20.00	35.00
	1349	—	3.00	6.00	15.00	30.00
	1350	—	—	Reported, not confirmed		
	1351	—	4.00	10.00	25.00	40.00
	1352	—	4.00	10.00	25.00	40.00
	1358/49	—	3.00	8.00	15.00	30.00
	1358	—	3.00	8.00	15.00	30.00
	1359/49	—	3.00	8.00	15.00	30.00
	1362/59	—	4.00	10.00	25.00	40.00
	1363	—	3.00	8.00	25.00	45.00
	1364/43	—	3.00	8.00	20.00	40.00
	1364	—	3.00	8.00	15.00	35.00
	1365	—	3.00	8.00	15.00	35.00
	1366/5	—	3.00	10.00	20.00	50.00

NOTE: Form of crescent, size of circle on reverse and arrangement of legends vary. Varieties with 6, 8, 9, 10 and 12 stars on reverse exist. Some earlier dates show traces of reeded edges.

Rev: W/o ***Sana.***

Y#	Date	Mintage	VG	Fine	VF	XF
5.7	AH1348	—	—	—	Rare	—

NOTE: 6 stars on reverse.

NOTE: Previously listed Y#5.8 dated AH(13)22 or (1)33(x) and (13)33 are considered contemporary counterfeits by leading authorities.

1/8 IMADI RIYAL

SILVER
Accession Date: AH1322
Rev: ***Thumn*** **in place of** ***Ushr*** **below date.**

Y#	Date	Mintage	VG	Fine	VF	XF
8	AH1339	—	300.00	500.00	1000.	1500.

1/4 IMADI RIYAL

SILVER
Accession Date: AH1322
Obv: W/o ***Rabb al-Alamin.***
Rev: ***Sana*** **below date.**

Y#	Date	Mintage	VG	Fine	VF	XF
6.1	AH1341	—	20.00	45.00	75.00	150.00
	1342	—	25.00	50.00	100.00	175.00

NOTE: AH1341 w/4 and 1342 w/6 stars on reverse.

Obv: ***Rabb al-Alamin.***
Rev: ***Sana*** **above date.**

Y#	Date	Mintage	VG	Fine	VF	XF
6.2	AH1342	—	30.00	50.00	100.00	175.00

Obv: Crescents and stars in border.

Y#	Date	Mintage	VG	Fine	VF	XF
6.3	AH1342	—	30.00	50.00	100.00	175.00

NOTE: Plain and traces of reeded edges known.

Obv: W/crescents only in border.

Y#	Date	Mintage	VG	Fine	VF	XF
6.4	AH1342	—	20.00	40.00	75.00	150.00
	1343	—	20.00	40.00	75.00	150.00

NOTE: Number and form of crescents on obverse vary, 14, 15 and 16 known. Plain and traces of reeded edges known.

Rev: Redesigned, date moved to margin.

Y#	Date	Mintage	VG	Fine	VF	XF
10	AH1343	—	20.00	60.00	100.00	175.00
	1344	—	4.25	10.00	25.00	75.00
	1345	—	4.25	10.00	25.00	60.00
	1349	—	—	Reported, not confirmed		
	1351	—	20.00	30.00	50.00	100.00
	1352	—	5.00	12.00	20.00	40.00
	1358	—	3.50	5.50	15.00	35.00
	1359	—	3.50	5.50	15.00	35.00
	1363	—	3.50	8.00	20.00	40.00
	1364/3	—	4.25	8.00	20.00	40.00
	1364	—	3.50	5.00	20.00	40.00
	1365/4	—	4.25	6.00	20.00	40.00
	1365	—	3.50	5.00	20.00	40.00
	1366	—	3.50	5.00	20.00	40.00

NOTE: The size of the reverse inner circle varies, the number of crescents on obverse from 12 to 16. Plain and traces of reeded edges are known.

IMADI RIYAL

SILVER, 28.07 g
Accession Date: AH1322

Y#	Date	Mintage	VG	Fine	VF	XF
7	AH1342	—		Reported, not confirmed		
	1344	—	7.00	12.00	18.00	30.00
	1365 (2 known)	—	—	—		1000.

NOTE: Several die varieties exist, possibly struck over a number of years with frozen date AH1344. Edge varieties exist.

GOLD, 35.50 g

Y#	Date	Mintage	VG	Fine	VF	XF
7a (Y-F10)	AH1344	—	—	—	Rare	—

NOTE: Probably a presentation issue.

PRESENTATION ISSUES

1/8 LIRA

(1/40 Riyal)

GOLD, 0.92 g
Accession Date: AH1322

Y#	Date	Mintage	VG	Fine	VF	XF
A10	AH(13)44	—	—	—	—	1350.

1/4 LIRA

(1/20 Riyal)

GOLD, 1.70 g
Accession Date: AH1322

Y#	Date	Mintage	VG	Fine	VF	XF
B10	AH(13)44	—	—	—	—	1500.

1/2 LIRA

(1/10 Riyal)

GOLD, 3.31 g
Accession Date: AH1322

Y#	Date	Mintage	VG	Fine	VF	XF
C10	AH(13)44	—	—	—	—	1650.

LIRA

(1/5 Riyal)

GOLD, 6.80 g
Accession Date: AH1322

Y#	Date	Mintage	VG	Fine	VF	XF
D10	AH(13)44	—	—	—	—	2000.

2-1/2 LIRA

(1/2 Riyal)

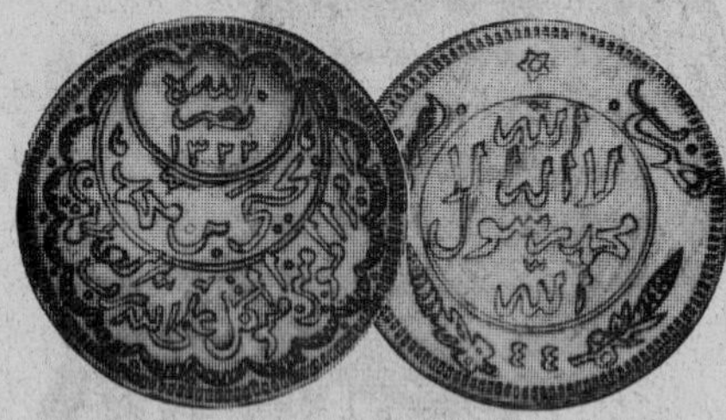

GOLD, 17.70 g
Accession Date: AH1322

Y#	Date	Mintage	VG	Fine	VF	XF
E10	AH(13)44	—	—	—	—	3500.

17.44-17.82 g

Y#	Date	Mintage	VG	Fine	VF	XF
K10	AH1352	—	—	—	—	2500.

10 LIRA

(2 Riyal)

GOLD, 69.83 g
Accession Date: AH1322
Obv: Similar to Gold 1/2 Riyal, Y#K10.

Y#	Date	Mintage	VG	Fine	VF	XF
M10	AH1352	—	—	—	—	6000.

Rev: 2 crossed flags in center, leg: *Duriba bi-dar al-khilafat al-mutawwakkiliyat bi Sana'a 'asimat al-Yaman Sana 1358.*

Y#	Date	Mintage	VG	Fine	VF	XF
N10	AH1358					
		2 known	—	—	—	—

IMAM AHMAD

AH1367-1382/1948-1962AD

1/80 RIYAL

(1 Halala = 1/2 Buqsha)

BRONZE
Accession Date: AH1367
Rev: *Sana* above date.

Y#	Date	Mintage	VG	Fine	VF	XF
11.1	AH1368	—	1.00	2.00	5.00	10.00
	1371	—	.30	1.00	3.00	8.00
	1372	—	.30	1.00	3.00	8.00
	1373	—	.30	.60	1.00	3.00
	1374	—	.30	1.00	3.00	8.00
	1275 (error for 1375)					
		—	1.00	2.00	6.00	12.00
	1375	—	—	—	—	—
	1376	—	—	—	—	—
	1376/86	—	1.00	2.00	4.00	8.00
	1278 (error for 1378)					
		—	1.00	2.00	6.00	12.00
	1378	—	.30	1.00	2.50	5.00
	1379	—	.50	1.00	2.50	5.00
	1380/79	—	.50	1.00	2.50	5.00
	1380/9	—	.50	1.00	2.50	5.00
	1380	—	—	—	—	—
	1381/80/78					
		—	.40	.85	1.50	2.50
	1381/79	—	.40	.85	1.50	2.50
	1381	—	.20	.40	.75	1.25
	1382	—	5.00	10.00	15.00	20.00

NOTE: There is a variation in the number of stars on reverse, as follows: AH1368 - 8 stars; AH1371-74 and some AH1381 (not overdate) - 7 stars; AH1375-1381 including some AH1381; and all AH1381 overdates - 8 stars. Varieties of arrangement of legends, form of crescent and size of circle on reverse exist.

Rev: W/o *Sana*.

Y#	Date	Mintage	VG	Fine	VF	XF
11.2	AH1373	—	—	—	Rare	—

Struck w/dies of 1/4 Ahmadi: Riyal, Y#15 on 1/80 Riyal planchet.

Y#	Date	Mintage	VG	Fine	VF	XF
11.3	AH(13)80	—	—	—	—	—

ALUMINUM
Rev: *Sana* above date.

Y#	Date	Mintage	VG	Fine	VF	XF
11a	AH1374	—	.25	1.00	2.50	5.00
	1375	—	.75	2.50	5.50	10.00
	1376	—	.25	1.50	4.00	8.00
	1377	—	.75	2.50	5.50	10.00
	1378	—	.25	1.00	2.50	5.00
	1379/5	—	.75	2.50	5.50	10.00
	1379/8	—	.75	2.50	5.50	10.00
	1379	—	.25	1.00	2.50	5.00
	1380	—	.25	1.00	2.50	5.00

NOTE: AH1374 and some 1380 have 7 stars, the rest have 8 stars on reverse. Dies of 1/80 Riyal, Y#11.1 were used.

Y#	Date	Mintage	VG	Fine	VF	XF
18	AH1367 (accessional year only)					
		—	.15	.25	.50	1.00

NOTE: Y#18 and 19 were struck privately in Lebanon in 1955 and 1956 and released into circulation in 1956.

1/40 RIYAL

(1 Buqsha)

BRONZE
Accession Date: AH1367
Rev: *Sana* above date, large *Sana'a* in legend.

Y#	Date	Mintage	VG	Fine	VF	XF
12.1	AH1368	—	.50	1.00	4.00	12.00
	1369	—	.75	1.25	5.00	15.00
	1370	—	.35	.75	3.00	6.00
	1371	—	.35	.75	3.00	6.00
	1372	—	.35	.75	2.00	4.00
	1373/1	—	—	—	—	—
	1373/2	—	.85	1,80	3.00	6.00
	1373	—	.35	.75	2.00	4.00
	1374	—	.35	.75	2.00	4.00
	1375/4	—	.50	1.00	3.00	6.00

NOTE: AH1368 also w/accession date 13677 (error) known.

Rev: Small *Sana'a* in legend.

Y#	Date	Mintage	VG	Fine	VF	XF
12.2	AH1371	—	.35	.75	3.00	6.00
	1375	—	.35	.75	2.00	4.00
	1376	—	.50	1.00	5.00	12.00
	1377/6	—	.85	1.75	4.00	8.00
	1378/5	—	—	—	—	—
	1379/7	—	.85	1.75	4.00	8.00
	1380/79	—	10.00	20.00	50.00	75.00
	1380	—	.85	1.75	4.00	8.00

NOTE: AH1376 and 1377/6 also exist w/accession date 1376 instead of 1367 on obverse. Varieties of arrangement of legends form of crescent and size of circle exist.

Rev: W/o *Sana.*

Y#	Date	Mintage	VG	Fine	VF	XF
12.3	AH1371	—	.50	1.00	4.00	12.00

ALUMINUM

Rev: *Sana* above date, large *Sana'a* in legend.

Y#	Date	Mintage	VG	Fine	VF	XF
12a.1	AH1371	—	.50	1.00	4.00	10.00
	1373	—	.50	1.00	4.00	10.00
	1374	—	.50	1.00	4.00	10.00
	1375	—	.50	1.00	4.00	10.00
	1377	—	15.00	30.00	50.00	90.00

Rev: Small *Sana'a* in legend.

Y#	Date	Mintage	VG	Fine	VF	XF
12a.2	AH1375	—	.50	1.00	4.00	10.00
	1376	—	.50	1.00	4.00	10.00
	1377/6	—	10.00	20.00	40.00	75.00
	1377	—	15.00	30.00	50.00	90.00

NOTE: AH1376 and 1377 plain dates also exists w/1376 instead of 1367 on obverse.

Y#	Date	Mintage	VG	Fine	VF	XF
19	AH1367 (accessional year only)	—	.15	.25	.35	.60

1/16 AHMADI RIYAL

SILVER
Accession Date: AH1367
Obv. leg: *Amir al-Mu'minin.*

Y#	Date	Mintage	VG	Fine	VF	XF
13	AH1367	—	.75	1.50	6.00	12.00
	1368	—	.75	1.50	5.00	10.00
	1371	—	.75	1.50	5.00	10.00
	1374	—	.75	1.50	4.00	8.00

NOTE: Arrangement of legends and size of inner circle on reverse vary.

Mule. Obv: 1/8 Ahmadi Riyal, Y#14. Rev: Y#13.

Y#	Date	Mintage	VG	Fine	VF	XF
13.1	AH1374	—	20.00	40.00	100.00	150.00

NOTE: Ends of crescents cut off on obverse.

1/10 AHMADI RIYAL

SILVER
Accession Date: AH1367

Y#	Date	Mintage	VG	Fine	VF	XF
A14	AH1370	—	400.00	750.00	1250.	1500.

1/8 AHMADI RIYAL

SILVER
Accession Date: AH1367
Pentagonal planchet

Y#	Date	Mintage	VG	Fine	VF	XF
14	AH1367	—	4.00	8.00	15.00	30.00
	1368	—	2.75	3.50	8.00	20.00
	1370	—	2.75	3.50	8.00	20.00
	1371	—	1.75	2.50	6.00	15.00
	1372	—	1.75	2.50	4.00	10.00
	1373	—	1.75	2.50	4.00	10.00
	1374	—	1.75	2.50	6.00	15.00
	1375/1	—	4.00	10.00	40.00	80.00
	1379/5	—	1.75	2.50	6.00	15.00
	1379	—	1.75	2.50	6.00	15.00
	1380	—	1.75	2.50	7.00	20.00

NOTE: Arrangement of legends and size of inner circle on reverse vary.

Hexagonal planchet

Y#	Date	Mintage	VG	Fine	VF	XF
14a	AH1368	—	250.00	500.00	1000.	1500.

1/4 AHMADI RIYAL

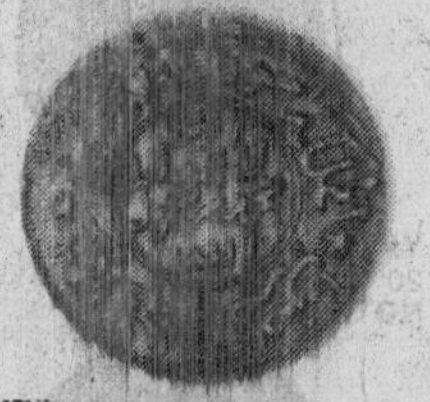

SILVER
Accession Date: AH1367

Y#	Date	Mintage	VG	Fine	VF	XF
15	AH(13)67	—	3.50	5.00	7.50	15.00
	(13)68	—	3.50	5.00	7.50	15.00
	(13)70	—	3.00	4.00	6.00	12.00
	(13)71/68	—	6.00	8.00	12.50	20.00
	(13)71/0	—	4.50	6.00	9.00	15.00
	(13)71	—	3.00	4.00	6.00	10.00
	(13)72	—	3.00	4.00	6.00	10.00
	(13)74	—	3.00	4.00	6.00	10.00
	(13)75/3	—	4.50	6.00	9.00	15.00
	(13)75	—	3.00	4.00	6.00	10.00
	(13)76	—	— Reported, not confirmed			
	(13)77/5	—	4.50	6.00	9.00	15.00
	(13)80	—	30.00	60.00	100.00	175.00

NOTE: The size of inner circle as well as the arrangement of legends on reverse vary. All dates have only the final 2 digits on the coin, reeded edge.

1/2 AHMADI RIYAL

SILVER
Accession Date: AH1367

Rev: Full dates. Denomination and mint name read inward.

Y#	Date	Mintage	VG	Fine	VF	XF
16.1	AH1367	—	6.00	10.00	16.00	35.00
	1368	—	6.00	10.00	15.00	35.00
	1369	—	5.00	8.00	12.50	20.00
	1370	—	7.50	12.50	20.00	40.00
	1371	—	7.50	12.50	20.00	40.00
	1372/68	—	6.00	10.00	15.00	30.00
	1373	—	9.00	15.00	25.00	45.00
	1377	—	—	—	—	—

NOTE: Size of circle on reverse varies. These coins were struck over blanks punched from Maria Theresa Thalers. The outer rings are reported to have circulated as currency, but this is doubtful, as they are found only counterstamped *Void* in Arabic. Refer to *Unusual World Coins*, 3rd edition, Krause Publications.

Similar to Y#16.1 but w/partial date; last 2 digits only.

Y#	Date	Mintage	VG	Fine	VF	XF
16.2	AH(13)75	—	6.00	10.00	15.00	22.50

Reeded edge.
Rev: Full date. Denomination and mint name read outward.

Y#	Date	Mintage	VG	Fine	VF	XF
16.3	AH1377	—	5.00	8.00	12.50	20.00
	1378	—	6.00	10.00	15.00	25.00
	1379	—	5.00	8.00	12.50	20.00
	1380	—	17.50	30.00	40.00	75.00
	1381	—	12.50	22.50	30.00	50.00
	1382	—	7.50	12.50	25.00	40.00

NOTE: Arrangement of legends and size of circles on reverse vary.

AHMADI RIYAL

SILVER
Accession Date: AH1367

Y#	Date	Mintage	Fine	VF	XF	Unc
17	AH1367	—	20.00	30.00	45.00	75.00
	1370	—	12.50	20.00	28.50	45.00
	1371	—	12.50	20.00	28.50	45.00
	1372/68	—	— Reported, not confirmed			
	1373	—	8.50	13.50	20.00	30.00
	1374	—	10.00	15.00	22.50	35.00
	1375	—	10.00	15.00	22.50	35.00
	1377	—	— Reported, not confirmed			
	1378	—	10.00	15.00	22.50	35.00
	1380	—	10.00	15.00	22.50	35.00
	1381	—	— Reported, not confirmed			

NOTE: These are usually found struck over Austrian Maria Theresa Talers and occasionally over other foreign crowns. Most AH1373 Riyals appear to be weakly struck from recut AH1372 dies, and the dates are easily confused. Varieties exist.

NOTE: Maria Theresa Talers and Eritrea Talleros exist c/s with obv. and rev. of the 1/16 Ahmadi Riyal (Y#13). Refer to "Unusual World Coins" 3rd edition.

GOLD 1/4 RIYAL

(Sovereign)

GOLD, 6.30-8.90 g
Accession Date: AH1367

Y#	Date	Mintage	Fine	VF	XF	Unc
G15	AH(13)71	—	—	350.00	550.00	850.00
	(13)75/3	—	—	350.00	550.00	850.00
	(13)75	—	—	350.00	550.00	850.00
	(13)77/5	—	—	350.00	550.00	850.00

NOTE: The above may be encountered with an additional c/m of an Arabic *1* indicating the equivalence to an English Sovereign. Dies of silver 1/4 Ahmadi Riyal, (Y#15) used.

GOLD 1/2 RIYAL

(2 Sovereigns)

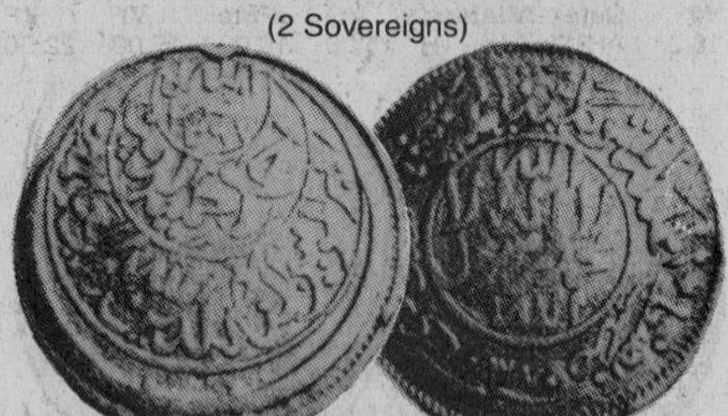

GOLD, 15.57-17.99 g
Accession Date: AH1367
Rev: Full dates. Denomination and mint name read inward.

Y#	Date	Mintage	Fine	VF	XF	Unc
G16.1	AH1370	—	450.00	650.00	900.00	1350.
	1371	—	450.00	650.00	900.00	1350.
	1377	—	450.00	650.00	900.00	1350.

Rev: Similar to Y#G16.1 but w/partial date, last 2 digits only.

Y#	Date	Mintage	Fine	VF	XF	Unc
G16.2	AH(13)75	—	450.00	650.00	900.00	1350.

Rev: Full date. Denomination and mint name read outward.

Y#	Date	Mintage	Fine	VF	XF	Unc
G16.3	AH1377	—	450.00	650.00	900.00	1350.
	1378	—	450.00	650.00	900.00	1350.
	1379	—	450.00	650.00	900.00	1350.
	1380	—	450.00	650.00	900.00	1350.
	1381	—	450.00	650.00	900.00	1350.

NOTE: The above may be encountered with an additional c/m of an Arabic *2* indicating the equivalence to 2 English Sovereigns. Dies of silver 1/2 Ahmadi Riyal, (Y#16) used.

GOLD RIYAL

(4 Sovereigns)

GOLD, 30.46-39.06 g
Accession Date: AH1367

Y#	Date	Mintage	Fine	VF	XF	Unc
G17	AH1371	—	—	—	Rare	—
	1372	—	—	—	Rare	—
	1373	—	—	700.00	900.00	1100.
	1374	—	—	700.00	900.00	1100.
	1375	—	—	700.00	900.00	1100.
	1377	—	—	700.00	900.00	1100.
	1378	—	—	700.00	900.00	1100.
	1381	—	—	700.00	900.00	1100.

NOTE: The above may be encountered with an additional c/m of an Arabic *4* indicating the equivalence to 4 English Sovereigns. Dies of silver Ahmadi Riyal, (Y#17) used.

ARAB REPUBLIC

1/80 RIYAL

(1/2 Buqsha)

BRONZE

Y#	Date	Mintage	VF	XF	Unc
20	AH1382	—	.50	2.00	5.00

NOTE: Varieties exist.

Rev: Full star.

Y#	Date	Mintage	VF	XF	Unc
21.1	AH1382	—	2.00	6.00	15.00

Rev: Outlined star.

Y#	Date	Mintage	VF	XF	Unc
21.2	AH1382	—	2.00	6.00	15.00
	13882 (error)	—	—	—	—

NOTE: Varieties exist.

1/2 BUQSHA

BRONZE

Y#	Date	Mintage	VF	XF	Unc
32	AH1382	—	3.00	5.00	8.50

NOTE: Varieties exist.

COPPER-ALUMINUM

Y#	Date	Year	Mintage	VF	XF	Unc
26	AH1382	1963	10.000	.15	.20	.30

NOTE: Y#26-31 were struck at Cairo.

1/40 RIYAL

(1 Buqsha)

BRASS or BRONZE

Y#	Date	Mintage	VF	XF	Unc
22	AH1382	—	.75	1.00	1.50
	1383/282	—	—	—	—
	1383	—	1.50	2.25	6.00
	1384/284	—	—	—	—
	1384/3	—	—	—	—
	1384	—	4.00	7.50	20.00

NOTE: Dated both sides; AH1382, AH1383 and AH1384/3 are dated AH1382 on obverse, actual date on reverse; AH1384 and AH1384/284 dated AH1384 on both sides. There are varieties of date size and design.

BUQSHA

COPPER-ALUMINUM

Y#	Date	Year	Mintage	VF	XF	Unc
27	AH1382	1963	10.377	.20	.30	.50

1/20 RIAL

(2 Buqsha)

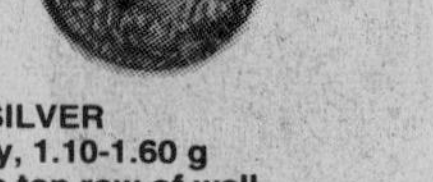

.720 SILVER
Thick variety, 1.10-1.60 g
Rev: 2 stones in top row of wall.

Y#	Date	Mintage	VF	XF	Unc
23.1	AH1382	—	6.00	10.00	30.00

Thin variety, 0.60-0.90 g
Rev: 3 stones in top row of wall.

Y#	Date	Mintage	VF	XF	Unc
23.2	AH1382	—	2.00	4.00	10.00

2 BUQSHA

COPPER-ALUMINUM

Y#	Date	Year	Mintage	VF	XF	Unc
A27	AH1382	1963	—	.25	.60	.75

1/10 RIYAL

(4 Buqsha)

.720 SILVER
Thick variety, 2.40-3.00 g
Rev: 3 stones in top row of wall.

Y#	Date	Mintage	VF	XF	Unc
24.1	AH1382	—	5.00	10.00	20.00

Thin variety, 1.40-1.80 g
Rev: 4 stones in top row of wall.

Y#	Date	Mintage	VF	XF	Unc
24.2	AH1382	—	2.00	4.00	10.00

5 BUQSHA

.720 SILVER

Y#	Date	Year	Mintage	VF	XF	Unc
28	AH1382	1963	1.600	1.25	1.50	2.00

2/10 RIYAL

(8 Buqsha)

.720 SILVER
Thick variety, 5.80-6.50 g

Y#	Date	Mintage	VF	XF	Unc
25.1	AH1382	—	8.00	15.00	25.00

Thin variety, 5.00-5.10 g

Y#	Date	Mintage	VF	XF	Unc
25.2	AH1382	—	60.00	100.00	150.00

1/4 RIAL
(10 Buqsha)

.720 SILVER
Thick variety, 6.00-7.00 g

A25.1	AH1382	—	40.00	65.00	150.00

Thin variety, 4.00-4.60 g

A25.2	AH1382	—	40.00	65.00	150.00

10 BUQSHA

5.0000 g, .720 SILVER, .1157 oz ASW

Y#	Date	Year	Mintage	VF	XF	Unc
29	AH1382	1963	1.024	2.00	2.25	2.75

20 BUQSHA

9.8500 g, .720 SILVER, .2280 oz ASW

30	AH1382	1963	1.016	4.00	5.00	6.50

RIAL

19.7500 g, .720 SILVER, .4571 oz ASW

31	AH1382	1963	4.614	5.00	6.00	8.00

DECIMAL COINAGE

فلسًا فلس فلوس

Falus, Fulus *Fals, Fils* *Falsan, Filsan*

100 Fils = 1 Riyal

FILS

ALUMINUM

33	AH1394	1974	*1.000	3.00	5.00	10.00

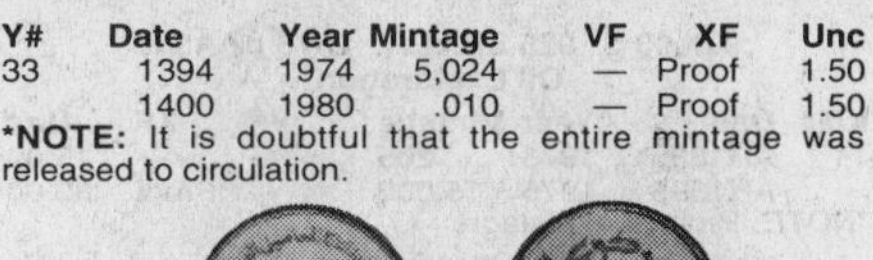

Y#	Date	Year	Mintage	VF	XF	Unc
33	1394	1974	5,024	—	Proof	1.50
	1400	1980	.010	—	Proof	1.50

***NOTE:** It is doubtful that the entire mintage was released to circulation.

F.A.O. Issue

43	AH1398	1978	7,050	—	1.25	3.00

5 FILS

BRASS

34	AH1394	1974	10.000	.50	1.00	2.50
	1394	1974	5,024	—	Proof	2.00
	1400	1980	.010	—	Proof	1.75

F.A.O. Issue

38	AH1394	1974	.500	—	.10	.25

10 FILS

BRASS

35	AH1394	1974	20.000	.50	1.00	2.50
	1394	1974	5,024	—	Proof	2.50
	1400	1980	.010	—	Proof	2.00

F.A.O. Issue

39	AH1394	1974	.200	—	.10	.25

25 FILS

COPPER-NICKEL

36	AH1394	1974	15.000	.25	.50	1.75
	1394	1974	5,024	—	Proof	3.00
	1399	1979	11.000	.25	.50	1.75
	1400	1980	.010	—	Proof	2.25

F.A.O. Issue

40	AH1394	1974	.040	.20	.40	1.00

50 FILS

COPPER-NICKEL

Y#	Date	Year	Mintage	VF	XF	Unc
37	AH1394	1974	10.000	.35	.75	2.50
	1394	1974	5,024	—	Proof	3.50
	1399	1979	4.000	.35	.75	2.50
	1400	1980	.010	—	Proof	2.50
	1405	1985	—	.35	.75	2.50

F.A.O. Issue

41	AH1394	1974	.025	.25	.50	1.25

RIYAL

12.0000 g, .925 SILVER, .3569 oz ASW
Qadhi Mohammed Mahmud Azzubairi Memorial

KM#	Date	Mintage	VF	XF	Unc
1	1969	3,200	—	Proof	15.00

20.4800 g, .900 GOLD, .5926 oz AGW

1a	1969	100 pcs.	—	Proof	475.00

COPPER-NICKEL

Y#	Date	Year	Mintage	VF	XF	Unc
42	AH1396	1976	7.800	.50	1.25	4.00
	1397	1977	—	.50	1.25	4.00
	1400	1980	—	—	Proof	5.00
	1405	1985	—	.50	1.25	4.00

F.A.O. Issue

44	AH1398	1978	7,050	—	2.00	5.00

2 RIYALS

25.0000 g, .925 SILVER, .7435 oz ASW
Apollo II - Cape Kennedy

Dentilated border.

KM#	Date	Mintage	VF	XF	Unc
2.1	1969	7,583	—	—	20.00
	1969	200 pcs.	—	Proof	40.00

Border of dots.

KM#	Date	Mintage	VF	XF	Unc
2.2	1969	1,000	—	Proof	35.00

Apollo II - Moon Landing
Dentilated border.

KM#	Date	Mintage	VF	XF	Unc
3.1	1969	7,583	—	—	20.00
	1969	200 pcs.	—	Proof	40.00

Border of dots.

KM#	Date	Mintage	VF	XF	Unc
3.2	1969	1,000	—	Proof	35.00

Qadhi Mohammed Mahmud Azzubairi Memorial

KM#	Date	Mintage	VF	XF	Unc
4	1969	4,200	—	Proof	35.00

42.2900 g, .900 GOLD, 1.2238 oz AGW

KM#	Date	Mintage	VF	XF	Unc
4a	1969	100 pcs.	—	Proof	1150.

2-1/2 RIYALS

9.0000 g, .925 SILVER, .2676 oz ASW
Oil Exploration

KM#	Date	Year	Mintage	VF	XF	Unc
14	AH1395	1975	*.205	—	—	15.00
	AH1395	1975	*5,000	—	Proof	35.00

***NOTE:** Projected mintage.

5 RIYALS

4.9000 g, .900 GOLD, .1418 oz AGW
Qadhi Mohammed Mahmud Azzubairi Memorial

KM#	Date	Mintage	VF	XF	Unc
6	1969	—	—	Proof	125.00

18.0000 g, .925 SILVER, .5353 oz ASW
Mona Lisa

KM#	Date	Year	Mintage	VF	XF	Unc
15	AH1395	1975	.235	—	—	20.00
	1395	1975	5,000	—	Proof	50.00

10 RIYALS

9.8000 g, .900 GOLD, .2836 oz AGW
Qadhi Mohammed Mahmud Azzubairi Memorial

KM#	Date	Mintage	VF	XF	Unc
7	1969	—	—	Proof	175.00

12.0800 g, .925 SILVER, .3569 oz ASW
Mule. Obv: KM#7. Rev: KM#1.

KM#	Date	Mintage	VF	XF	Unc
23	1969	—	—	Proof	40.00

36.0000 g, .925 SILVER, 1.0707 oz ASW

Montreal Olympics

KM#	Date	Year	Mintage	VF	XF	Unc
16	AH1395	1975	8,000	—	—	100.00
	1395	1975	4,000	—	Proof	150.00

15 RIYALS

54.0000 g, .925 SILVER, 1.6061 oz ASW
Jerusalem

KM#	Date	Year	Mintage	VF	XF	Unc
17	AH1395	1975	.070	—	—	40.00
	1395	1975	5,000	—	Proof	100.00

20 RIYALS

19.6000 g, .900 GOLD, .5672 oz AGW
Apollo II - Moon Landing

KM#	Date	Mintage	VF	XF	Unc
8	1969	—	—	Proof	450.00

Qadhi Mohammed Mahmud Azzubairi Memorial

KM#	Date	Mintage	VF	XF	Unc
9	1969	—	—	Proof	300.00

Albakiriah Mosque

KM#	Date	Year	Mintage	VF	XF	Unc
18	AH1395	1975	—	—	—	185.00
	1395	1975	3,500	—	Proof	225.00

25 RIYALS

.900 GOLD
Oil Exploration

KM#	Date	Year	Mintage	VF	XF	Unc
19	AH1395	1975	—	—	—	185.00
	1395	1975	3,500	—	Proof	225.00

28.2800 g, .925 SILVER, .8411 oz ASW
International Year of Disabled Persons

Y#	Date	Year	Mintage	VF	XF	Unc
46	AH1401	1981	.010	—	—	25.00
	1401	1981	.010	—	Proof	30.00
	20th Anniversary of Independence					
47	AH1402	1982	2,000	—	Proof	45.00

28.2500 g, .925 SILVER, .8402 oz ASW
International Year of the Child

Y#	Date	Year	Mintage	VF	XF	Unc
45	AH1403	1983	6,604	—	Proof	32.50

Decade for Women

Y#	Date	Year	Mintage	VF	XF	Unc
49	AH1405	1985	1,000	—	Proof	40.00

30 RIYALS

29.4000 g, .900 GOLD, .8508 oz AGW
Qadhi Mohammed Mahmud Azzubairi Memorial

KM#	Date	Mintage	VF	XF	Unc
10	1969	—	—	Proof	900.00

50 RIYALS

49.0000 g, .900 GOLD, 1.4180 oz AGW
Qadhi Mohammed Mahmud Azzubairi Memorial

KM#	Date	Mintage	VF	XF	Unc
11	1969	—	—	Proof	1000.
	SILVER, 49.97 g				
11a	1969	(restrike)	—	Proof	65.00

9.1000 g, .900 GOLD, .2633 oz AGW
Mona Lisa

KM#	Date	Year	Mintage	VF	XF	Unc
20	AH1395	1975	—	—	—	250.00
	1395	1975	3,500	—	Proof	350.00

75 RIYALS

13.6500 g, .900 GOLD, .3950 oz AGW
Montreal Olympics
Obv: Arms. Rev: XXI Olympiad.

KM#	Date	Year	Mintage	VF	XF	Unc
21	AH1395	1975	—	—	—	275.00
	1395	1975	3,500	—	Proof	375.00

100 RIYALS

18.2000 g, .900 GOLD, .5266 oz AGW

KM#	Date	Year	Mintage	VF	XF	Unc
22	AH1395	1975	—	—	—	350.00
	1395	1975	3,500	—	Proof	500.00

500 RIYALS

15.9800 g, .917 GOLD, .4711 oz AGW
International Year of the Disabled

KM#	Date	Year	Mintage	VF	XF	Unc
24	AH1401	1981	—	—	—	400.00
		1981	—	—	Proof	550.00

15.9000 g, .917 GOLD, .4686 oz AGW
20th Anniversary of Revolution

KM#	Date	Year	Mintage	VF	XF	Unc
48	AH1402	1982	1,000	—	Proof	350.00

MINT SETS (MS)

KM#	Date	Mintage	Identification	Issue Price	Mkt. Val.
MS1	1975(4)	—	KM14-17	50.00	175.00
MS2	1975(5)	—	KM18-22	360.00	1245.

PROOF SETS (PS)

KM#	Date	Mintage	Identification	Issue Price	Mkt. Val.
PS1	1969(7)	*2,000	KM1,4,6,7,9-11	375.00	2600.
PS2	1969(4)	1,500	KM1-4	—	130.00
PS4	1969(3)	—	KM2,3,6	78.00	220.00
PS5	1974(5)	5,024	Y33-37	15.00	12.50
PS6	1975(5)	3,500	KM18-22	485.00	1675.
PS7	1975(4)	5,000	KM14-17	75.00	325.00
PS8	1980(6)	10,000	Y33-37,42	31.00	15.00

EASTERN ADEN PROTECTORATE

Between 1200 B.C. and the 6th century A.D., what is now the Peoples Democratic Republic of Yemen was part of the Minaean kingdom. In subsequent years it was controlled by Persians, Egyptians and Turks. Aden, one of the cities mentioned in the Bible, had been a port for trade between the East and West for 2,000 years. British rule began in 1839 when the British East India Co. seized control to put an end to the piracy threatening trade with India. To protect their foothold in Aden, the British found it necessary to extend their control into the area known historically as the Hadhramaut, and to sign protection treaties with the shaiks of the hinterland.

QU'AITI STATE OF HADHRAMAUT

GHURFAH

A city sultanate of Eastern Aden Protectorate was an oasis settlement located in the Hadhramaut Wadi region of southern Arabia.

TITLES

al-Ghurfa(t) الغرفة

RULERS

Abdat Umar ibn Abdat
Ubayd ibn Saleh ibn Abdat
AH1358-1365/1939-1945AD

NOTE: The Arabic *129* in the obv. leg. is a chronogram for *Saleh*.

4 CHOMSIHS

.6500 g, .900 SILVER, .0188 oz ASW

KM#	Date	Mintage	Fine	VF	XF	Unc
1	AH1344	5,000	30.00	45.00	65.00	100.00

8 CHOMSIHS

1.1000 g, .900 SILVER, .0318 oz ASW

KM#	Date	Mintage	Fine	VF	XF	Unc
2	AH1344	5,000	27.50	37.50	55.00	85.00

15 CHOMSIHS

2.0000 g, .900 SILVER, .0578 oz ASW

KM#	Date	Mintage	Fine	VF	XF	Unc
3	AH1344	.010	10.00	15.00	22.50	35.00

30 CHOMSIHS

3.9500 g, .900 SILVER, .1142 oz ASW

KM#	Date	Mintage	Fine	VF	XF	Unc
4	AH1344	.010	15.00	22.50	32.50	50.00

45 CHOMSIHS

5.9000 g, .900 SILVER, .1707 oz ASW

KM#	Date	Mintage	Fine	VF	XF	Unc
5	AH1344	.010	175.00	275.00	425.00	600.00

60 CHOMSIHS

7.8000 g, .900 SILVER, .2257 oz ASW

KM#	Date	Mintage	Fine	VF	XF	Unc
6	AH1344	.010	37.50	55.00	80.00	125.00

QU'AITI STATE OF SHIHR AND MUKALLA

The Qu'aiti State of Shihr and Mukalla was comprised in Eastern Aden Protectorate located in southern Arabia.

KASADI of MUKALLA

A port, city sultanate and capital of the Qu'aiti state of Shihr and Mukalla in Eastern Aden Protectorate in southern Arabia, was a principal port servicing trade between the Middle East and India and Java.

TITLES

al-Mukala المكلا

RULERS

Salah ibn Muhammad,
AH12xx-1290/18xx-1873AD
Umar ibn Salah,
AH1290-1298/1873-1881AD

1/2 CHOMSIH

BRONZE

KM#	Date	Good	VG	Fine	VF
1	AH1276	25.00	45.00	75.00	120.00

CHOMSIH

BRONZE

KM#	Date	Good	VG	Fine	VF
2	AH1276	20.00	40.00	65.00	100.00

QU'AITI STATE

TITLES

Qaiti قيطي

RULERS

Munasir ibn Abdullah ibn Umar
AH1246-1283/1830-1866AD
Awadh ibn Umar
AH1283-1327/1866-1909AD

COUNTERMARKED COINAGE

1/12 ANNA

COPPER

c/m: Arabic in 10mm circle on India 1/12 Anna, KM#445.

KM#	Date	Year	Good	VG	Fine	VF
1	AH1307	(1835-48)	8.50	13.50	18.50	27.50

1/4 ANNA

COPPER

c/m: Arabic in 15mm circle on India-Bombay Presidency 1/4 Anna, KM#232.

KM#	Date	Year	Good	VG	Fine	VF
5	AH1307	(1833)	8.50	13.50	18.50	27.50

c/m: Arabic in 10mm circle on India-Bombay Presidency 1/4 Anna, KM#231.

KM#	Date	Year	Good	VG	Fine	VF
6	AH1307	(1830-32)	4.50	7.50	12.50	20.00

c/m: Arabic in 10mm circle on India 1/4 Anna, KM#446.

KM#	Date	Year	Good	VG	Fine	VF
7	AH1307	(1833-58)	4.50	7.50	12.50	20.00

c/m: Arabic in 15mm circle on India 1/4 Anna, KM#467.

KM#	Date	Year	Good	VG	Fine	VF
8	AH1307	(1862-76)	4.50	7.50	12.50	20.00

c/m: Arabic in 10mm circle on Mombasa 1/4 Anna, KM#1.

KM#	Date	Year	Good	VG	Fine	VF
9	AH1307	(1888)	7.50	12.50	17.50	25.00

c/m: Arabic in 10mm circle on Zanzibar Pysa, KM#1.

KM#	Date	Year	Good	VG	Fine	VF
10	AH1307	(AH1299)	7.50	12.50	17.50	25.00

1/2 ANNA

COPPER

c/m: Arabic in 15mm circle on India-Bombay Presidency 1/2 Anna, KM#251.

KM#	Date	Year	Good	VG	Fine	VF
15	AH1307	(1834)	8.50	13.50	18.50	27.50

c/m: Arabic in 15mm circle on India 1/2 Anna, KM#447.

KM#	Date	Year	Good	VG	Fine	VF
16	AH1307	(1835-45)	8.50	13.50	18.50	27.50

c/m: in 15mm circle on India 1/2 Anna, KM#468.

KM#	Date	Year	Good	VG	Fine	VF
17	AH1307	(1862-76)	8.50	13.50	18.50	27.50

1/4 RUPEE

SILVER

c/m: Arabic in 10mm circle on India-Bengal Presidency 1/4 Rupee, KM#96.

KM#	Date	Year	Good	VG	Fine	VF
20	(AH1307)	AH1204	8.50	13.50	18.50	27.50

1/2 RUPEE

SILVER

c/m: Arabic in 10mm circle on India 1/2 Rupee, KM#491.

KM#	Date	Year	Good	VG	Fine	VF
25	AH1307	(1877-99)	7.50	12.50	17.50	25.00

c/m: Arabic in 10mm circle on English 1 Shilling, KM#734.

KM#	Date	Year	Good	VG	Fine	VF
26	AH1307	(1838-87)	7.50	12.50	17.50	25.00

c/m: Arabic in 15mm circle on India 1/2 Rupee,

KM#491.

KM#	Date	Year	Good	VG	Fine	VF
27	AH1307	(1877-99)	10.00	15.00	22.50	30.00

c/m: Arabic in 15mm circle on Mexico 2 Reales, KM#88.

KM#	Date	Year	Good	VG	Fine	VF
28	AH1307	(1772-89)	10.00	15.00	22.50	30.00

c/m: Arabic in 15mm circle on India-Bengal Presidency 1/2 Rupee, KM#97.

KM#	Date	Year	Good	VG	Fine	VF
29	AH1307	(1793-1818,ND)	10.00	15.00	22.50	30.00

RUPEE

SILVER

c/m: Arabic in 10mm circle on India Rupee, KM#457.

KM#	Date	Year	Good	VG	Fine	VF
30	AH1307	(1840)	10.00	15.00	22.50	30.00

PRICES - Single c/m on coin. Add 15 percent for each additional c/m.

c/m: Arabic in 10mm circle on India Rupee, KM#458.

KM#	Date	Year	Good	VG	Fine	VF
32	AH1307	(1840)	10.00	15.00	22.50	30.00

c/m: Arabic in 15mm circle on India Rupee, KM#458.

KM#	Date	Year	Good	VG	Fine	VF
31	AH1307	(1840)	11.50	17.50	25.00	35.00

RYAL

SILVER

c/m: Arabic in 10mm circle on Austria MTT, KM#T1.

KM#	Date	Year	Good	VG	Fine	VF
35	AH1307	(1780)	25.00	35.00	45.00	55.00

c/m: Arabic in 15mm circle on Austria MTT, KM#T1.

KM#	Date	Year	Good	VG	Fine	VF
36	AH1307	(1780)	30.00	40.00	50.00	65.00

SOVEREIGN

GOLD

c/m: Arabic on English Sovereign, KM#767.

KM#	Date	Year	Good	VG	Fine	VF
40	AH1307	(1887-92)	—	—	Rare	—

REGULAR COINAGE

5 CHOMSIHS

COPPER and BRONZE

KM#	Date	Year	Good	VG	Fine	VF
45	AH1315	1897	4.50	7.50	15.00	25.00

KM#	Date	Year	Good	VG	Fine	VF
48	AH1318	1900	4.00	6.50	12.50	20.00

1/3 RYAL

SILVER

KM#	Date	Good	VG	Fine	VF
46	AH1315	150.00	250.00	350.00	500.00

1/2 RYAL

SILVER

KM#	Date	Good	VG	Fine	VF
47	AH1316	175.00	300.00	450.00	600.00

KATHIRI STATE OF SEIYUN & TARIM

Kathiri State of Seiyun and Tarim, a city sultanate in Eastern Aden Protectorate, was an important oasis settlement in the Hadhramaut Wadi region of southern Arabia. It became a British treaty protectorate in the 1880's.

TITLES

Tarim تريم

RULERS

Syed Hussein ibn Sahil, AH1258/1842AD

MINT MARKS

H - Heaton, Birmingham

MONETARY SYSTEM

120 Chomsihs = 1 Ryal

CHOMSIH

COPPER, thin

KM#	Date	Year	Mintage	VG	Fine	VF
5	AH1258	1842	—	10.00	17.50	27.50

3 CHOMSIHS

COPPER, thick

KM#	Date	Year	Mintage	VG	Fine	VF
6	AH1258	1842	—	15.00	25.00	45.00

4 CHOMSIHS

.8000 g, .900 SILVER, .0231 oz ASW

KM#	Date	Year	Mintage	Fine	VF	XF
10	AH1270	1853	—	55.00	85.00	125.00

6 CHOMSIHS

.9000 g, .900 SILVER, .0260 oz ASW

KM#	Date	Year	Mintage	Fine	VF	XF
15	AH1315H	1897	.335	3.00	6.50	12.50

8 CHOMSIHS

1.6500 g, .900 SILVER, .0477 oz ASW

KM#	Date	Year	Mintage	Fine	VF	XF
11	AH1270	1853	—	55.00	85.00	125.00

12 CHOMSIHS

1.5000 g, .900 SILVER, .0434 oz ASW

KM#	Date	Year	Mintage	Fine	VF	XF
16	AH1315H	1897	.167	6.00	10.00	15.00
	1315H	1897	—	—	Proof	75.00

16 CHOMSIHS

3.3500 g, .900 SILVER, .0969 oz ASW

KM#	Date	Year	Mintage	Fine	VF	XF
12	AH1270	1853	—	65.00	100.00	150.00

24 CHOMSIHS

3.1500 g, .900 SILVER, .0911 oz ASW

KM#	Date	Year	Mintage	Fine	VF	XF
17	AH1315H					
		1897	.083	5.00	10.00	15.00
	1315H	1897	—	—	Proof	125.00

30 CHOMSIHS

7.6500 g, .900 SILVER, .2213 oz ASW

KM#	Date	Year	Mintage	Fine	VF	XF
7	AH1258	1842	—	100.00	150.00	250.00

WESTERN ADEN PROTECTORATE

LAHEJ

A rather small partially independent sultanate situated north of the port city of Aden. Lahej had entered into a protective treaty relationship with Britain following Britain's capture of the port of Aden in 1839.

TITLES

لحج

Lahej

LOCAL RULERS

Ali ibn Mohasan
AH1265-1279/1849-1863AD
Fazal ibn Ali,
AH1291-1315/1874-1898AD

1/2 PESSA

COPPER

KM#	Date	Mintage	VG	Fine	VF	XF
1	ND(1860)	—	7.50	15.00	27.50	40.00

Accession date: AH1291

KM#	Date	Mintage	VG	Fine	VF	XF
2	ND(1896)	.678	10.00	17.50	35.00	50.00

SOUTH ARABIA

Fifteen of the sixteen Western Protectorate States, the Wahidi State of the Eastern Protectorate, and Aden Colony joined to form the Federation of South Arabia.

In 1959, Britain agreed to prepare South Arabia for full independence, which was achieved on Nov. 30, 1967, at which time South Arabia, including Aden, changed its name to the Peoples Republic of Southern Yemen. On Dec. 1, 1970, following the overthrow of the new government by the National Liberation Front, Southern Yemen changed its name to the Peoples Democratic Republic of Yemen.

TITLES

Al-Junubiya(t) al-'Arabiya(t)

MONETARY SYSTEM

1000 Fils = 1 Dinar

FILS

ALUMINUM

KM#	Date	Mintage	VF	XF	Unc
1	1964	10.000	—	.10	.15
	1964	—	—	Proof	1.25

5 FILS

BRONZE

KM#	Date	Mintage	VF	XF	Unc
2	1964	10.000	.15	.25	.50
	1964	—	—	Proof	1.50

25 FILS

COPPER-NICKEL

KM#	Date	Mintage	VF	XF	Unc
3	1964	4.000	.25	.45	.85
	1964	—	—	Proof	2.00

50 FILS

COPPER-NICKEL

KM#	Date	Mintage	VF	XF	Unc
4	1964	6.000	.45	.65	1.25
	1964	—	—	Proof	3.25

PROOF SETS (PS)

KM#	Date	Mintage	Identification	Issue Price	Mkt. Val.
PS1	1964(4)	10,500	KM1-4	9.90	8.00

PEOPLES DEMOCRATIC REPUBLIC OF YEMEN

TITLES

Al-Jumhuriya(t) al-Yamaniya(t)
ad-Dimiqratiya(t) ash-Sha'biya(t)

MONETARY SYSTEM

Falus, Fulus *Fals, Fils* *Falsan, Filsan*

1000 Fils = 1 Dinar

2-1/2 FILS

ALUMINUM

KM#	Date	Year	Mintage	VF	XF	Unc
3	AH1393	1973	20.000	.15	.25	.50

5 FILS

BRONZE

KM#	Date	Mintage	VF	XF	Unc
2	1971	2.000	.30	.60	1.00

ALUMINUM

KM#	Date	Year	Mintage	VF	XF	Unc
4	AH1393	1973	20.000	.15	.30	.50
	1404	1984	—	.15	.30	.50

10 FILS

ALUMINUM

KM#	Date	Mintage	VF	XF	Unc
9	1981	—	.35	.75	2.00

25 FILS

COPPER-NICKEL

KM#	Date	Mintage	VF	XF	Unc
5	1976	2.000	.25	.50	1.25
	1977	1.000	.25	.50	1.75
	1979	—	.25	.50	1.75
	1982	—	.25	.50	1.75
	1984	—	.25	.50	1.75

50 FILS

COPPER-NICKEL

KM#	Date	Mintage	VF	XF	Unc
6	1976	2.000	.35	.75	2.50
	1977	2.000	.35	.75	2.50
	1979	—	.35	.75	2.50
	1984	—	.35	.75	2.50

100 FILS

COPPER-NICKEL

KM#	Date	Mintage	VF	XF	Unc
10	1981	—	.50	1.00	3.00

250 FILS

COPPER-NICKEL
10th Anniversary of Independence

KM#	Date	Mintage	VF	XF	Unc
7	1977	.030	2.00	4.00	6.50

KM#	Date	Mintage	VF	XF	Unc
11	1981	—	1.50	3.00	5.00

2 DINARS

28.2800 g, .925 SILVER, .8411 oz ASW
IYDP - Abdulla Baradoni

KM#	Date	Mintage	VF	XF	Unc
12	1981	.010	—	—	25.00
	1981	.010	—	Proof	30.00

5 DINARS

12.5000 g, .925 SILVER, .3718 oz ASW
10th Anniversary of Independence

KM#	Date	Mintage	VF	XF	Unc
8	1977	6,000	—	Proof	40.00

50 DINARS

15.9800 g, .917 GOLD, .4712 oz AGW
International Year of Disabled Persons

KM#	Date	Mintage	VF	XF	Unc
13	1981	2,100	—	—	550.00
	1981	1,100	—	Proof	850.00

YUGOSLAVIA

The Federal Republic of Yugoslavia, a Balkan country located on the east shore of the Adriatic Sea, has an area of 39,450 sq. mi. (102,173 sq. km.) and a population of 10.5 million. Capital: Belgrade. The chief industries are agriculture, mining, manufacturing and tourism. Machinery, nonferrous metals, meat and fabrics are exported.

Yugoslavia was proclaimed on Dec. 1, 1918, after the union of the Kingdom of Serbia, Montenegro and the South Slav territories of Austria-Hungary; and changed its official name from the Kingdom of the Serbs, Croats and Slovenes to the Kingdom of Yugoslavia on Oct. 3, 1929. The republic was composed of six autonomous republics - Serbia, Croatia, Slovenia, Bosnia-Herzegovina, Macedonia and Montenegro - and two autonomous provinces within Serbia: Kosovo-Melohija and Vojvodina. The government of Yugoslavia attempted to remain neutral in World War II but, yielding to German pressure, aligned itself with the Axis powers in March of 1941; a few days later it was overthrown by revolutionary forces and its neutrality reasserted. The Nazis occupied the country on April 6, and throughout the remaining war years were resisted by a number of guerrilla armies, notably that of Marshal Josip Broz Tito. After the defeat of the Axis powers, a leftist coalition headed by Tito abolished the monarchy and, on Jan. 31, 1946, established a "People's Republic".

The collapse of the Federal Republic during 1991-1992 has resulted in the autonomous republics of Croatia, Slovenia, Bosnia-Herzegovina and Macedonia declaring their respective independence. Bosnia-Herzegovina is under military contest with the Serbian, Croat and Muslim populace opposing each other. Besides the remainder of the older Serbian sectors, a Serbian enclave in Knin located in southern Croatia has emerged called REPUBLIKE SRPSKE KRAJINE or Serbian Republic - Krajina whose capital is Knin and has also declared its independence in 1992.

The name Yugoslavia appears on the coinage in letters of the Cyrillic alphabet alone until formation of the Federated Peoples Republic of Yugoslavia in 1953, after which both the Cyrillic and Latin alphabets are employed. From 1965, the coin denomination appears in the 4 different languages of the federated republics in letters of both the Cyrillic and Latin alphabets.

Para ПАРА
Dinar ДИНАР, Dinara ДИНАРА
Dinari ДИНАРИ, Dinarjev

RULERS

Petar I, 1918-1921
Alexander I, 1921-1934
Petar II, 1934-1945

MINT MARKS

(a) - Paris, privy marks only
(b) - Brussels
(k) - КОВНИЦА, А.Д. = Kovnica,A.D. (Akcionarno Drustvo) Belgrade
(l) - London
(p) - Poissy (thunderbolt)
(v) - Vienna

MONETARY SYSTEM

100 Para = 1 Dinar

KINGDOM OF THE SERBS, CROATS AND SLOVENES

5 PARA

ZINC

KM#	Date	Mintage	Fine	VF	XF	Unc
1	1920(v)	3.826	3.00	7.50	15.00	40.00

10 PARA

ZINC

KM#	Date	Mintage	Fine	VF	XF	Unc
2	1920(v)	58.946	1.50	3.50	7.50	20.00

25 PARA

NICKEL-BRONZE

KM#	Date	Mintage	Fine	VF	XF	Unc
3	1920(v)	48.173	1.00	2.50	5.50	15.00

50 PARA

NICKEL-BRONZE

KM#	Date	Mintage	Fine	VF	XF	Unc
4	1925(b)	24.500	.50	1.00	2.00	6.00
	1925(p)	25.000	.50	1.50	3.00	7.00

DINAR

NICKEL-BRONZE

KM#	Date	Mintage	Fine	VF	XF	Unc
5	1925(b)	37.500	.50	1.00	2.00	6.00
	1925(p)	37.000	.75	1.50	3.00	7.00

2 DINARA

NICKEL-BRONZE

KM#	Date	Mintage	Fine	VF	XF	Unc
6	1925(b)	29.500	1.00	2.00	5.00	12.00
	1925(p)	25.004	1.00	2.50	5.50	14.00

20 DINARA

6.4516 g, .900 GOLD, .1867 oz AGW

KM#	Date	Mintage	Fine	VF	XF	Unc
7	1925(a)	1,000	125.00	150.00	200.00	250.00
	1925(a)	—	—	—	Proof	—

KINGDOM OF YUGOSLAVIA

25 PARA

BRONZE

KM#	Date	Mintage	Fine	VF	XF	Unc
17	1938	40.000	1.25	2.00	4.00	9.00
	1938	—	—	—	Proof	—

50 PARA

ALUMINUM-BRONZE

KM#	Date	Mintage	Fine	VF	XF	Unc
18	1938	100.000	.50	1.00	2.00	5.00

DINAR

ALUMINUM-BRONZE

KM#	Date	Mintage	Fine	VF	XF	Unc
19	1938	100.000	.50	.75	1.75	4.50
	1938	—	—	—	Proof	—

2 DINARA

ALUMINUM-BRONZE, 14mm crown

KM#	Date	Mintage	Fine	VF	XF	Unc
20	1938	74.250	.50	1.00	2.50	6.50
	1938	—	—	—	Proof	—

12mm crown

KM#	Date	Mintage	Fine	VF	XF	Unc
21	1938	.750	4.00	8.00	15.00	32.00
	1938	—	—	—	Proof	—

10 DINARA

7.0000 g, .500 SILVER, .1125 oz ASW

KM#	Date	Mintage	Fine	VF	XF	Unc
10	1931(l)	16.000	2.00	4.00	8.00	17.50
	1931(l)	—	—	—	Proof	—
	1931(a)	4.000	3.50	7.00	15.00	32.00
	1931(a)	—	—	—	Proof	—

NICKEL

KM#	Date	Mintage	Fine	VF	XF	Unc
22	1938	25.000	.50	1.00	2.50	5.00

20 DINARA

14.0000 g, .500 SILVER, .2250 oz ASW

KM#	Date	Mintage	Fine	VF	XF	Unc
11	1931	12.500	BV	6.00	12.00	32.00
	1931	—	—	—	Proof	—

9.0000 g, .750 SILVER, .2170 oz ASW

KM#	Date	Mintage	Fine	VF	XF	Unc
23	1938	15.000	BV	3.00	6.00	12.50

50 DINARA

23.3300 g, .750 SILVER, .5626 oz ASW

KM#	Date	Mintage	Fine	VF	XF	Unc
16	1932(k) signature at truncation					
		5.500	10.00	22.00	45.00	95.00
	1932(l) w/o signature at truncation					
		5.500	10.00	25.00	50.00	110.00
	1932(l)	—	—	—	Proof	—

15.0000 g, .750 SILVER, .3617 oz ASW

KM#	Date	Mintage	Fine	VF	XF	Unc
24	1938	10.000	4.00	6.00	10.00	16.50

COUNTERMARKED COINAGE

DUKAT

3.4900 g, .986 GOLD, .1106 oz AGW
c/m: Sword.
Obv. and rev: Small leg. w/ КОВНИЦА, А.Д. below head.

KM#	Date	Mintage	Fine	VF	XF	Unc
12.1	1931(k)	*.050	—	80.00	120.00	180.00
	1932(k)	Inc. Be.	—	—	Rare	—

c/m: Ear of corn.

KM#	Date	Mintage	Fine	VF	XF	Unc
12.2	1931(k)	*.150	—	70.00	110.00	170.00
	1932(k)	*.070	—	80.00	120.00	180.00
	1933(k)	*.040	—	150.00	200.00	300.00
	1934(k)					
		*2,000	—	500.00	800.00	1200.

c/m: Sword.
Obv. and rev: Large leg. w/o КОВНИЦА, А.Д. below head.

KM#	Date	Mintage	Fine	VF	XF	Unc
13	1931(v)	2,869	—	—	—	—

NOTE: Countermarks are a sword for Bosnia and an ear of corn for Serbia.

4 DUKATA

13.9600 g, .986 GOLD, .4425 oz AGW
c/m: Sword.
Obv. and rev: Small leg.

KM#	Date	Mintage	Fine	VF	XF	Unc
14.1	1931(k)	*.010	—	350.00	650.00	900.00
	1932(k)	Inc. Be.	—	—	Rare	—

c/m: Ear of corn.

KM#	Date	Mintage	Fine	VF	XF	Unc
14.2	1931(k)	*.015	—	350.00	650.00	900.00
	1932(k)	*.010	—	400.00	725.00	1000.
	1933(k)	*2,000	—	1000.	1600.	2500.
	1934(k)	—	—	1600.	2500.	3500.

Obv. and rev: W/o c/m.

KM#	Date	Mintage	Fine	VF	XF	Unc
14.3	1931(k)	—	—	—	—	—

Obv. and rev: Large leg. w/o КОВНИЦАаАаДа below busts.

KM#	Date	Mintage	Fine	VF	XF	Unc
A15.1	1931(v)	51 pcs.	—	—	Rare	—

c/m: Sword.

KM#	Date	Mintage	Fine	VF	XF	Unc
A15.2	1931(v)	Inc. Ab.	—	—	Rare	—

PEOPLES REPUBLIC

MONETARY SYSTEMS

100 Old Dinara = 1 New Dinar
Commencing 1990
10,000 Old Dinara = 1 New Dinar

5 PARA

COPPER-ZINC

KM#	Date	Mintage	Fine	VF	XF	Unc
42	1965	23.839	—	.10	.20	.40
43	1965	16.200	—	—	.10	.20
	1973	36.384	—	—	.10	.15
	1974	3.628	—	—	.10	.25
	1975	20.272	—	—	.10	.15
	1976	30.490	—	—	.10	.15
	1977	10.270	—	—	.10	.15
	1978	12.000	—	—	.10	.15
	1979	20.414	—	—	.10	.15
	1980	22.412	—	—	.10	.15
	1981	.630	—	.10	.25	.50

10 PARA

COPPER-ZINC

KM#	Date	Mintage	Fine	VF	XF	Unc
44	1965	15.400	—	—	.10	.20
	1973	16.647	—	—	.10	.20
	1974	60.139	—	—	.10	.20
	1975	36.954	—	—	.10	.15
	1976	36.111	—	—	.10	.15
	1977	40.451	—	—	.10	.15
	1978	50.129	—	—	.10	.15

KM#	Date	Mintage	Fine	VF	XF	Unc
44	1979	89.738	—	—	.10	.15
	1980	90.111	—	—	.10	.15
	1981	149.090	—	—	.10	.15
139	1990	174.028	—	—	.10	.15
	1991	60.828	—	—	.15	.35

20 PARA

COPPER-ZINC

KM#	Date	Mintage	Fine	VF	XF	Unc
45	1965	—	—	—	.10	.30
	1973	30.448	—	—	.10	.30
	1974	31.364	—	—	.10	.30
	1975	44.683	—	—	.10	.30
	1976	33.312	—	—	.10	.30
	1977	40.782	—	—	.10	.30
	1978	39.999	—	—	.10	.30
	1979	49.121	—	—	.10	.30
	1980	73.757	—	—	.10	.30
	1981	96.144	—	—	.10	.30
140	1990	41.353	—	.10	.20	.50
	1991	43.118	—	.10	.20	.50

25 PARA

BRONZE

KM#	Date	Mintage	Fine	VF	XF	Unc
84	1982	185.316	—	—	.10	.25
	1983	65.290	—	—	.15	.30

50 PARA

ZINC

KM#	Date	Mintage	Fine	VF	XF	Unc
25	1945	40.000	.50	1.00	2.50	9.00

ALUMINUM

KM#	Date	Mintage	Fine	VF	XF	Unc
29	1953	—	—	—	.10	.25

COPPER-ZINC
Rev: Narrow 0 in denomination.

KM#	Date	Mintage	Fine	VF	XF	Unc
46.1	1965	—	—	.10	.20	.65
	1973	23.739	—	.10	.20	.65
	1974	.033	1.00	1.50	2.50	5.00
	1975	10.220	—	.10	.20	.80
	1976	8.438	—	.10	.20	1.00
	1977	17.864	—	.10	.20	.75
	1978	40.177	—	.10	.20	.65
	1979	3.021	.50	1.00	2.00	5.00

Rev: Wide 0 in denomination.

KM#	Date	Mintage	Fine	VF	XF	Unc
46.2	1979	12.278	.20	.50	1.00	2.50
	1980	24.974	—	.10	.20	.65
	1981	40.319	—	.10	.20	.65

BRONZE

KM#	Date	Mintage	Fine	VF	XF	Unc
85	1982	79.584	—	—	.10	.20
	1983	72.100	—	—	.10	.20
	1984	59.642	.25	.50	1.00	1.50

COPPER-ZINC

KM#	Date	Mintage	Fine	VF	XF	Unc
141	1990	137.873	—	—	.10	.20
	1991	42.152	—	.20	.40	1.00

DINAR

ZINC

KM#	Date	Mintage	Fine	VF	XF	Unc
26	1945	90.000	.50	1.00	2.50	7.00

ALUMINUM

KM#	Date	Mintage	Fine	VF	XF	Unc
30	1953	—	—	.10	.15	.25
36	1963	—	—	—	.10	.15

COPPER-NICKEL

KM#	Date	Mintage	Fine	VF	XF	Unc
47	1965	75.822	.10	.15	.30	.60
48	1968	35.497	.10	.20	.40	.80

COPPER-NICKEL-ZINC

KM#	Date	Mintage	Fine	VF	XF	Unc
59	1973	18.974	—	.10	.15	.40
	1974	42.724	—	.10	.15	.35
	1975	30.260	—	.10	.15	.35
	1976	21.849	—	.10	.15	.35
	1977	30.468	—	.10	.15	.35
	1978	35.032	—	.10	.15	.35
	1979	39.848	—	.10	.15	.35
	1980	60.630	—	.10	.15	.35
	1981	56.650	—	.10	.15	.35

F.A.O. Issue

KM#	Date	Mintage	Fine	VF	XF	Unc
61	1976	.500	—	.10	.20	.50

NICKEL-BRASS

KM#	Date	Mintage	Fine	VF	XF	Unc
86	1982	70.105	—	—	.10	.30
	1983	114.180	—	—	.10	.20
	1984	172.185	—	—	.10	.20
	1985	64.436	—	—	.10	.25
	1986	122.643	—	—	.10	.20

COPPER-NICKEL-ZINC

KM#	Date	Mintage	Fine	VF	XF	Unc
142	1990	172.105	—	—	.10	.25
	1991	79.549	—	.15	.25	.75

2 DINARA

ZINC

KM#	Date	Mintage	Fine	VF	XF	Unc
27	1945	70.000	.50	1.25	3.00	9.00

ALUMINUM

KM#	Date	Mintage	Fine	VF	XF	Unc
31	1953	—	—	.10	.20	.30
37	1963	—	—	.10	.15	.25

COPPER-NICKEL-ZINC
F.A.O. Issue

KM#	Date	Mintage	Fine	VF	XF	Unc
55	1970	.500	—	.20	.40	1.00

KM#	Date	Mintage	Fine	VF	XF	Unc
57	1971	10.413	—	.10	.30	.70
	1972	18.440	—	.10	.20	.50
	1973	31.848	—	.10	.20	.45
	1974	10.989	—	.10	.20	.50
	1975	.092	2.00	4.00	7.50	15.00
	1976	6.092	—	.10	.20	.50
	1977	19.335	—	.10	.20	.50
	1978	13.035	—	.10	.20	.50
	1979	20.069	—	.10	.20	.45
	1980	36.088	—	.10	.20	.45
	1981	42.599	—	.10	.20	.45

NICKEL-BRASS

KM#	Date	Mintage	Fine	VF	XF	Unc
87	1982	40.632	—	.10	.15	.35
	1983	35.468	—	.10	.15	.35
	1984	51.500	—	.10	.15	.35
	1985	81.100	—	.10	.15	.35
	1986	50.453	—	.10	.15	.35

COPPER-NICKEL-ZINC

KM#	Date	Mintage	Fine	VF	XF	Unc
143	1990	15.936	.15	.30	.60	2.00
	1991	32.836	—	.20	.40	1.00
	1992	—	2.50	3.50	7.00	12.50

5 DINARA

ZINC

KM#	Date	Mintage	Fine	VF	XF	Unc
28	1945	50.000	.50	1.25	3.50	10.00

ALUMINUM

KM#	Date	Mintage	Fine	VF	XF	Unc
32	1953	—	.10	.25	.50	.75

KM#	Date	Mintage	Fine	VF	XF	Unc
38	1963	—	.10	.20	.35	.50

COPPER-NICKEL-ZINC
F.A.O. Issue

KM#	Date	Mintage	Fine	VF	XF	Unc
56	1970	.500	.20	.50	1.00	2.00

Regular Issue

KM#	Date	Mintage	Fine	VF	XF	Unc
58	1971	10.224	.20	.40	.60	1.00
	1972	27.974	.10	.20	.35	.60
	1973	12.705	.20	.40	.60	1.00
	1974	6.054	.25	.50	1.00	2.00
	1975	13.533	.10	.20	.35	.60
	1976	4.965	.10	.25	.40	.80
	1977	.922	.30	.60	1.20	2.50
	1978	1.000	.10	.25	.50	1.50
	1979	3.000	.10	.25	.40	.80
	1980	9.977	.10	.20	.35	.60
	1981	15.450	.10	.20	.35	.60

30th Anniversary of Nazi Defeat

KM#	Date	Mintage	Fine	VF	XF	Unc
60	1975	1.020	.25	.50	1.00	2.00

NICKEL-BRASS

KM#	Date	Mintage	Fine	VF	XF	Unc
88	1982	40.956	—	.10	.15	.50
	1983	40.156	—	.10	.15	.50
	1984	33.023	—	.10	.15	.50
	1985	94.422	—	.10	.15	.50
	1986	37.199	—	.10	.15	.50

COPPER-NICKEL-ZINC

KM#	Date	Mintage	Fine	VF	XF	Unc
144	1990	9.354	.25	.45	1.00	2.50
	1991	113.420	—	.25	.50	1.25
	1992	—	1.50	2.50	4.00	7.00

1990 Chess Olympiad - Logo

KM#	Date	Mintage	Fine	VF	XF	Unc
145	1990	.020	—	—	Proof	6.00

10 DINARA

ALUMINUM-BRONZE

KM#	Date	Mintage	Fine	VF	XF	Unc
33	1955	—	.15	.30	.75	1.50

KM#	Date	Mintage	Fine	VF	XF	Unc
39	1963	—	.15	.30	.75	1.25

COPPER-NICKEL

KM#	Date	Mintage	Fine	VF	XF	Unc
62	1976	10.550	.30	.60	.75	1.25
	1977	39.645	.30	.60	.75	1.00
	1978	29.834	.30	.60	.75	1.00
	1979	4.969	.30	.60	.75	1.00
	1980	10.139	.30	.60	.75	1.00
	1981	20.116	.30	.60	.75	1.00

COPPER-NICKEL-ZINC
F.A.O. Issue

KM#	Date	Mintage	Fine	VF	XF	Unc
63	1976	.500	.50	.75	1.00	2.50

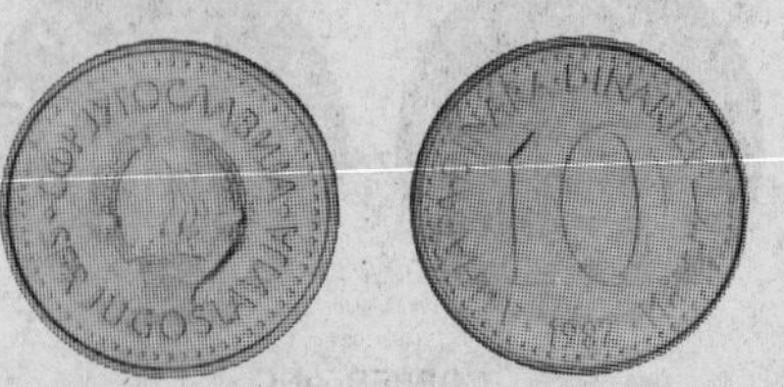

COPPER-NICKEL

KM#	Date	Mintage	Fine	VF	XF	Unc
89	1982	8.862	—	.10	.20	.80
	1983	42.400	—	.10	.20	.75
	1984	30.900	—	.10	.20	.75
	1985	31.647	—	.10	.20	.75
	1986	40.739	—	.10	.20	.75
	1987	104.988	—	.10	.20	.75
	1988	27.614	—	.10	.20	.75

40th Anniversary of Battle of Neretva River

KM#	Date	Mintage	Fine	VF	XF	Unc
96	1983	.900	—	1.00	1.50	3.00
	1983	.100	—	—	Proof	9.00

40th Anniversary of Battle of Sutjeska River

KM#	Date	Mintage	Fine	VF	XF	Unc
97.1	1983	.900	—	1.00	1.50	3.00
	1983	.100	—	—	Proof	9.00

Rev: W/o pathway in front of monument.

KM#	Date	Mintage	Fine	VF	XF	Unc
97.2	1983	—	—	3.00	6.00	10.00

BRASS

KM#	Date	Mintage	Fine	VF	XF	Unc
131	1988	35.992	—	—	.10	.25
	1989	75.000	—	—	.10	.25

20 DINARA

ALUMINUM-BRONZE

KM#	Date	Mintage	Fine	VF	XF	Unc
34	1955	—	.25	.50	.75	1.50

KM#	Date	Mintage	Fine	VF	XF	Unc
40	1963	—	.50	1.00	1.75	3.50

9.0000 g, .925 SILVER, .2676 oz ASW
25th Anniversary of Republic
Similar to 50 Dinara, KM#50.

KM#	Date	Mintage	Fine	VF	XF	Unc
49	1968	.010	—	—	Proof	25.00
	1968 NI	Inc. Ab.	—	—	Proof	25.00

COPPER-ZINC-NICKEL

KM#	Date	Mintage	Fine	VF	XF	Unc
112	1985	5.000	—	.10	.15	.50
	1986	20.932	—	.10	.15	.35
	1987	39.514	—	.10	.15	.35

BRASS

KM#	Date	Mintage	Fine	VF	XF	Unc
132	1988	29.775	—	—	.10	.25
	1989	12.994	—	—	.10	.25

50 DINARA

ALUMINUM-BRONZE

KM#	Date	Mintage	Fine	VF	XF	Unc
35	1955	—	.25	.50	1.00	2.00

KM#	Date	Mintage	Fine	VF	XF	Unc
41	1963	—	1.00	2.50	5.00	15.00

NOTE: Exists with filled letter in denomination.

20.0000 g, .925 SILVER, .5948 oz ASW
25th Anniversary of Republic

KM#	Date	Mintage	Fine	VF	XF	Unc
50	1968	.010	—	—	Proof	50.00
	1968 NI	Inc. Ab.	—	—	Proof	50.00

COPPER-ZINC-NICKEL

KM#	Date	Mintage	Fine	VF	XF	Unc
113	1985	25.488	—	.10	.25	.75
	1986	20.353	—	.10	.25	.75
	1987	21.792	—	.10	.25	.75
	1988	28.370	—	.10	.25	.75

BRASS

KM#	Date	Mintage	Fine	VF	XF	Unc
133	1988	46.973	—	—	.10	.25
	1989	*2.999	—	.50	1.00	2.00

*NOTE: Currently not issued.

100 DINARA

7.8200 g, .900 GOLD, .2263 oz AGW
25th Anniversary of Republic

KM#	Date	Mintage	VF	XF	Unc
51	1968	.010	—	Proof	125.00
	1968 NI	Inc. Ab.	—	Proof	125.00

10.0000 g, .925 SILVER, .2974 oz ASW
8th Mediterranean Games at Split

KM#	Date	Mintage	VF	XF	Unc
65	1978	.071	—	Proof	22.50

13.0000 g, .925 SILVER, .3867 oz ASW
1984 Winter Olympics - Ice Hockey

KM#	Date	Mintage	VF	XF	Unc
90	1982	.110	—	Proof	15.00

1984 Winter Olympics - Figure Skating

KM#	Date	Mintage	VF	XF	Unc
98	1983	.110	—	Proof	15.00

1984 Winter Olympics - Bobsledding

KM#	Date	Mintage	VF	XF	Unc
99	1983	.110	—	Proof	15.00

1984 Winter Olympics - Speed Skating

KM#	Date	Mintage	VF	XF	Unc
105	1984	.110	—	Proof	15.00

1984 Winter Olympics - Pairs Figure Skating

KM#	Date	Mintage	VF	XF	Unc
106	1984	.110	—	Proof	15.00

COPPER-ZINC-NICKEL

KM#	Date	Mintage	VF	XF	Unc
114	1985	18.684	.25	.65	1.50
	1986	17.905	.20	.50	1.00
	1987	94.069	—	.40	.80
	1988	50.294	—	.40	.80

COPPER-NICKEL-ZINC
40th Anniversary of Liberation from Fascism

115	1985	.200	—	Proof	4.00

COPPER-NICKEL
200th Anniversary of Birth of Karajich

127.1	1987	*.200	—	Proof	4.00

Obv: Similar to KM#115.

127.2	1987	Inc. Ab.	—	Proof	25.00

BRASS

134	1988	12.610	—	.15	.30
	1989	124.260	—	.15	.30

13.0000 g, .925 SILVER, .3867 oz ASW
1990 Chess Olympiad - Petrovaradin Clock Tower

146	1990	.010	—	Proof	35.00

150 DINARA

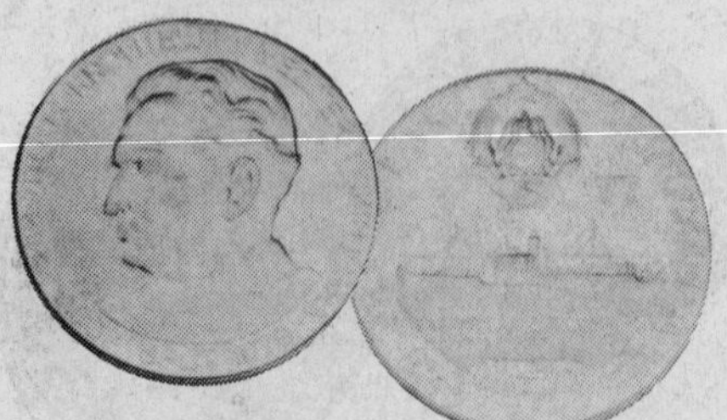

12.5000 g, .925 SILVER, .3717 oz ASW
8th Mediterranean Games at Split

66	1978	.070	—	Proof	22.50

17.0000 g, .925 SILVER, .5056 oz ASW
1990 Chess Olympiad - Globe

KM#	Date	Mintage	VF	XF	Unc
147	1990	.010	—	Proof	45.00

200 DINARA

15.6400 g, .900 GOLD, .4526 oz AGW
25th Anniversary of Republic

52	1968	.010	—	Proof	250.00
	1968 NI	Inc. Ab.	—	Proof	250.00

15.0000 g, .750 SILVER, .3617 oz ASW
85th Birthday of Tito

64	1977	.500	—	Proof	15.00

15.0000 g, .600 SILVER, .2701 oz ASW

64a	1977	.300	—	—	10.00

NOTE: Edge varieties exist w/inscription in cyrillic and western.

15.0000 g, .925 SILVER, .4461 oz ASW
8th Mediterranean Games at Split

KM#	Date	Mintage	VF	XF	Unc
67	1978	.058	—	Proof	25.00

250 DINARA

17.5000 g, .925 SILVER, .5204 oz ASW
8th Mediterranean Games at Split

68	1978	.048	—	Proof	30.00

17.0000 g, .925 SILVER, .5056 oz ASW
1984 Winter Olympics - Sarajevo View

91	1982	.110	—	Proof	20.00

1984 Winter Olympics - Artifact

100	1983	.110	—	Proof	20.00

1984 Winter Olympics - Radimlja Tombs

KM#	Date	Mintage	VF	XF	Unc
101	1983	.110	—	Proof	20.00

1984 Winter Olympics - Jajce Village

KM#	Date	Mintage	VF	XF	Unc
107	1984	.110	—	Proof	20.00

1984 Winter Olympics - Tito

KM#	Date	Mintage	VF	XF	Unc
108	1984	.110	—	Proof	20.00

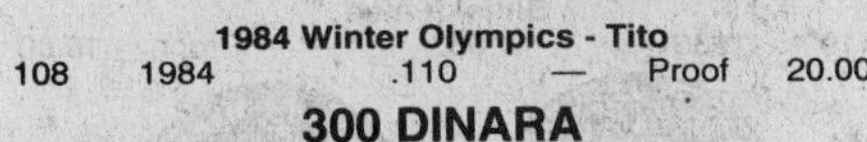

300 DINARA

20.0000 g, .925 SILVER, .5948 oz ASW
8th Mediterranean Games at Split

KM#	Date	Mintage	VF	XF	Unc
69	1978	.036	—	Proof	35.00

350 DINARA

22.5000 g, .925 SILVER, .6692 oz ASW
8th Mediterranean Games at Split

KM#	Date	Mintage	VF	XF	Unc
70	1978	.024	—	Proof	37.50

400 DINARA

25.0000 g, .925 SILVER, .7435 oz ASW
8th Mediterranean Games at Split

KM#	Date	Mintage	VF	XF	Unc
71	1978	.024	—	Proof	45.00

500 DINARA

39.1000 g, .900 GOLD, 1.1315 oz AGW
25th Anniversary of Republic

KM#	Date	Mintage	VF	XF	Unc
53	1968	.010	—	Proof	600.00
	1968 NI	Inc. Ab.	—	Proof	600.00

8.0000 g, .925 SILVER, .2379 oz ASW
Vukovar Congress

KM#	Date	Mintage	VF	XF	Unc
76	1980	.018	—	Proof	25.00

8.0000 g, .750 SILVER, .1865 oz ASW
World Table Tennis Championship Games

KM#	Date	Mintage	VF	XF	Unc
80	1981	.018	—	Proof	30.00

23.0000 g, .925 SILVER, .6841 oz ASW
1984 Winter Olympics - Downhill Skiing

KM#	Date	Mintage	VF	XF	Unc
92	1982	.110	—	Proof	25.00

1984 Winter Olympics - Ski Jumping

KM#	Date	Mintage	VF	XF	Unc
102	1983	.110	—	Proof	25.00

1984 Winter Olympics - Biathalon

KM#	Date	Mintage	VF	XF	Unc
103	1983	.110	—	Proof	25.00

1984 Winter Olympics - Cross Country Skiing

KM#	Date	Mintage	VF	XF	Unc
109	1984	.110	—	Proof	25.00

1984 Winter Olympics - Slalom

KM#	Date	Mintage	VF	XF	Unc
110	1984	.110	—	Proof	25.00

13.0000 g, .925 SILVER, .3867 oz ASW
Ski Jumping Championship - Herons
Obv: Similar to 10,000 Dinara, KM#123.

KM#	Date	Mintage	VF	XF	Unc
116	1985	.050	—	Proof	15.00

1000 DINARA

78.2000 g, .900 GOLD, 2.2630 oz AGW
25th Anniversary of Republic

KM#	Date	Mintage	VF	XF	Unc
54	1968	.010	—	Proof	1200.
	1968 NI	Inc. Ab.	—	Proof	1200.

14.0000 g, .925 SILVER, .4164 oz ASW
Vukovar Congress

KM#	Date	Mintage	VF	XF	Unc
77	1980	.016	—	Proof	35.00

25.9000 g, .750 SILVER, .6245 oz ASW
Tito's Death

KM#	Date	Mintage	VF	XF	Unc
78	1980	.800	—	—	32.00

NOTE: Eyes with and without pupils.

26.0000 g, .925 SILVER, .7733 oz ASW

KM#	Date	Mintage	VF	XF	Unc
78a	1980	.200	—	Proof	40.00
	1980 ZM	Inc. Ab.	—	Proof	60.00

14.0000 g, .750 SILVER, .4164 oz ASW
World Table Tennis Championship Games

KM#	Date	Mintage	VF	XF	Unc
81	1981	.016	—	Proof	35.00

40th Anniversary of Uprising and Revolution

KM#	Date	Mintage	VF	XF	Unc
82	1981	.100	—	Proof	20.00

18.0000 g, .925 SILVER, .5354 oz ASW
International Canoeing Championships - City View

KM#	Date	Mintage	VF	XF	Unc
93	1982	.046	—	Proof	30.00

23.0000 g, .925 SILVER, .6841 oz ASW
Ski Jumping Championship - Bloudek
Obv: Similar to 10,000 Dinara, KM#123.

KM#	Date	Mintage	VF	XF	Unc
117	1985	.020	—	Proof	30.00

Ski Jumping Championship - Slovenian Cradle
Obv: Similar to 10,000 Dinara, KM#123.

KM#	Date	Mintage	VF	XF	Unc
118	1985	.020	—	Proof	30.00

6.0000 g, .925 SILVER, .1784 oz ASW
Sinjska Alka

KM#	Date	Mintage	VF	XF	Unc
119	1985	.060	—	Proof	18.00

3.5000 g, .900 GOLD, .1013 oz AGW
1990 Chess Olympiad - Logo

KM#	Date	Mintage	VF	XF	Unc
148	1990	2,000	—	Proof	275.00

1500 DINARA

8.8000 g, .900 GOLD, .2546 oz AGW
8th Mediterranean Games at Split

KM#	Date	Mintage	VF	XF	Unc
72	1978	.035	—	Proof	175.00

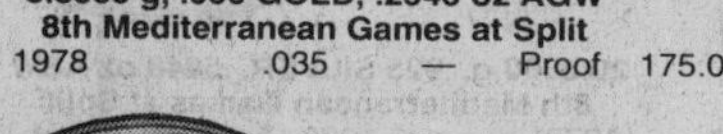

22.0000 g, .925 SILVER, .6542 oz ASW

Vukovar Congress

KM#	Date	Mintage	VF	XF	Unc
79	1980	.016	—	Proof	40.00

22.0000 g, .750 SILVER, .5329 oz ASW
World Table Tennis Championship Games

KM#	Date	Mintage	VF	XF	Unc
83	1981	.016	—	Proof	40.00

22.0000 g, .925 SILVER, .6542 oz ASW
International Canoeing Championships - Tito

KM#	Date	Mintage	VF	XF	Unc
94	1982	.036	—	Proof	30.00

2000 DINARA

11.8000 g, .900 GOLD, .3414 oz AGW
8th Mediterranean Games at Split

KM#	Date	Mintage	VF	XF	Unc
73	1978	.035	—	Proof	225.00

14.0000 g, .925 SILVER, .4164 oz ASW
Sinjska Alka

KM#	Date	Mintage	VF	XF	Unc
120	1985	.020	—	Proof	30.00

2500 DINARA

14.7000 g, .900 GOLD, .4254 oz AGW
8th Mediterranean Games at Split

KM#	Date	Mintage	VF	XF	Unc
74	1978	.035	—	Proof	275.00

3000 DINARA

26.0000 g, .925 SILVER, .7733 oz ASW
Sinjska Alka

KM#	Date	Mintage	VF	XF	Unc
121	1985	.020	—	Proof	40.00

13.0000 g, .925 SILVER, .3867 oz ASW
200th Anniversary - Birth of Karajich
Rev: Similar to 100 Dinara, KM#127.

KM#	Date	Mintage	VF	XF	Unc
128	1987	.*050	—	Proof	30.00

5000 DINARA

29.5000 g, .900 GOLD, .8536 oz AGW
8th Mediterranean Games at Split

KM#	Date	Mintage	VF	XF	Unc
75	1978	.012	—	Proof	450.00

8.0000 g, .900 GOLD, .2315 oz AGW
1984 Winter Olympics - Emblem

KM#	Date	Mintage	VF	XF	Unc
95	1982	.055	—	Proof	160.00

1984 Winter Olympics - Tito

KM#	Date	Mintage	VF	XF	Unc
104	1983	.055	—	Proof	150.00

1984 Winter Olympics - Flame

KM#	Date	Mintage	VF	XF	Unc
111	1984	.055	—	Proof	160.00

23.5000 g, .925 SILVER, .6989 oz ASW
40th Anniversary of Liberation from Fascism
Similar to 100 Dinara, KM#115.

KM#	Date	Mintage	VF	XF	Unc
122	1985	.100	—	Proof	40.00

17.0000 g, .925 SILVER, .5056 oz ASW
200th Anniversary - Birth of Karajich

KM#	Date	Mintage	VF	XF	Unc
129	1987	*.050	—	Proof	35.00

COPPER-ZINC-NICKEL
Non-aligned Summit - Symbol

KM#	Date	Mintage	VF	XF	Unc
135	1989	.050	—	Proof	4.50

10000 DINARA

8.0000 g, .900 GOLD, .2315 oz AGW
World Ski Jumping Championship

KM#	Date	Mintage	VF	XF	Unc
123	1985	.010	—	Proof	165.00

5.0000 g, .900 GOLD, .1447 oz AGW
Sinjska Alka

KM#	Date	Mintage	VF	XF	Unc
124	1985	.012	—	Proof	150.00

20000 DINARA

8.0000 g, .900 GOLD, .2315 oz AGW
Sinjska Alka

KM#	Date	Mintage	VF	XF	Unc
125	1985	8,000	—	Proof	250.00

40000 DINARA

14.0000 g, .900 GOLD, .4083 oz AGW
Sinjska Alka

KM#	Date	Mintage	VF	XF	Unc
126	1985	5,000	—	Proof	475.00

50000 DINARA

8.0000 g, .900 GOLD, .2315 oz AGW
200th Anniversary - Birth of Karajich
Similar to 5,000 Dinar, KM#129.

KM#	Date	Mintage	VF	XF	Unc
130	1987	*.010	—	Proof	175.00

13.0000 g, .925 SILVER, .3867 oz ASW
Non-aligned Summit - Standing Figure

KM#	Date	Mintage	VF	XF	Unc
136	1989	.015	—	Proof	25.00

100,000 DINARA

17.0000 g, .925 SILVER, .5056 oz ASW
Non-aligned Summit - Building

KM#	Date	Mintage	VF	XF	Unc
137	1989	.010	—	Proof	35.00

2,000,000 DINARA

8.0000 g, .900 GOLD, .2315 oz AGW
Non-aligned Summit - Symbol

KM#	Date	Mintage	VF	XF	Unc
138	1989	5,000	—	Proof	260.00

FEDERAL REPUBLIC

MONETARY SYSTEMS

1992-1993
10 Old Dinara = 1 New Dinar
1993
1 Million Old Dinara = 1 New Dinar
1.1.1994
1 Milliard Old Dinara = 1 New Dinar

DINAR

COPPER-ZINC

KM#	Date	Mintage	VF	XF	Unc
149	1992	49.269	.10	.30	.60

COPPER-ZINC-NICKEL

KM#	Date	Mintage	VF	XF	Unc
154	1993	—	.25	.50	1.00

BRASS

KM#	Date	Mintage	VF	XF	Unc
160	1994	—	—	—	1.25

2 DINARA

COPPER-ZINC

KM#	Date	Mintage	VF	XF	Unc
150	1992	10.571	.20	.40	1.00

COPPER-ZINC-NICKEL

KM#	Date	Mintage	VF	XF	Unc
155	1993	—	.10	.20	.50

5 DINARA

COPPER-ZINC

KM#	Date	Mintage	VF	XF	Unc
151	1992	26.658	.20	.40	1.00

COPPER-ZINC-NICKEL

KM#	Date	Mintage	VF	XF	Unc
156	1993	—	.10	.20	.50

10 DINARA

COPPER-ZINC-NICKEL

KM#	Date	Mintage	VF	XF	Unc
152	1992	76.607	.25	.50	1.00

KM#	Date	Mintage	VF	XF	Unc
157	1993	—	.20	.40	.80

50 DINARA

COPPER-ZINC-NICKEL

KM#	Date	Mintage	VF	XF	Unc
153	1992	50.571	.30	.70	1.50
158	1993	—	.30	.70	1.50

100 DINARA

BRASS

KM#	Date	Mintage	VF	XF	Unc
159	1993	—	.50	1.00	2.00

MINT SETS (MS)

KM#	Date	Mintage	Identification	Issue Price	Mkt. Val.
MS1	1953/55(7)	—	KM29-35	—	5.00
MS2	1963(6)	—	KM36-41	—	8.00
MS-A3	1965(5)	—	KM42,44-47	—	4.00
MS3	1965(5)	—	KM43-47	—	4.00
MS4	1982(6)	—	KM84-89	—	3.00
MS5	1983(6)	—	KM84-89	—	3.00
MS-A6	1983(2)	—	KM96-97 blue plastic wallet	—	6.50
MS6	1984(5)	—	KM85-89	—	3.00
MS7	1985(7)	—	KM86-89,112-114	—	3.00
MS8	1986(7)	—	KM86-89,112-114	—	3.00
MS9	1987(4)	—	KM89,112-114	—	3.00
MS10	1988(7)	—	KM89,113-114,131-134	—	3.00
MS11	1989(4)	—	KM131-134	—	6.50
MS12	1990(6)	—	KM139-144	—	4.50
MS13	1991(6)	—	KM139-144	—	4.00
MS14	1992(2)	—	KM143-144	—	35.00

PROOF SETS (PS)

KM#	Date	Mintage	Identification	Issue Price	Mkt. Val.
PS1	1968(6)	*10,000	KM49-54	—	2250.
PS2	1968(4)	*10,000	KM51-54	—	2125.
PS3	1968(2)	*10,000	KM49-50	15.00	75.00
PS4	1978(7)	6,000	KM65-71	—	185.00
PS5	1978(11)	12,000	KM65-75	—	1310.
PS6	1980(3)	—	KM76-77,79	—	90.00
PS7	1981(3)	—	KM80-81,83	—	95.00
PS8	1982(3)	—	KM90-92	—	60.00
PS9	1982(2)	—	KM93-94	—	50.00
PS10	1983(3)	—	KM98,100,102	—	60.00
PS11	1983(3)	—	KM99,101,103	—	60.00
PS-A12	1983(2)	.100	KM96-97	—	—
PS12	1984(3)	—	KM105,107,109	—	60.00
PS13	1984(3)	—	KM106,108,110	—	60.00
PS14	Mixed dates	—	KM95,104,111	—	470.00
PS15	1985(6)	—	KM119-121,124-126	—	1015.
PS16	1985(4)	—	KM116-118,123	—	250.00
PS17	1985(3)	—	KM116-118	—	75.00
PS18	1985(3)	—	KM119-121	—	85.00
PS19	1987(3)	—	KM128-130	—	240.00
PS20	1987(2)	—	KM128-129	—	65.00
PS21	1989(3)	—	KM136-138	—	320.00
PS22	1989(2)	—	KM136-137	—	60.00
PS23	1990(3)	—	KM146-148	—	380.00
PS24	1990(2)	.010	KM146-147	—	80.00

***NOTE**: Authorized mintages.

MONTENEGRO

The former independent kingdom of Montenegro, now one of the nominally autonomous federated units of Yugoslavia, was located in southeastern Europe north of Albania. As a kingdom, it had an area of 5,333 sq. mi. (13,812 sq. km.) and a population of about 250,000. Capital: Podgorica. The predominantly pastoral kingdom had few industries.

Montenegro became an independent state in 1355 following the break-up of the Serb empire. During the Turkish invasion of Albania and Herzegovina in the 15th century, the Montenegrins moved their capital to the remote mountain village of Cetinje where they maintained their independence through two centuries of intermittent attack, emerging as the only one of the Balkan states not subjugated by the Turks. When World War I began, Montenegro joined with Serbia and was subsequently invaded and occupied by the Austrians. Austria withdrew upon the defeat of the Central Powers, permitting the Serbians to move in and maintain the occupation. Montenegro then joined the kingdom of the Serbs, Croats and Slovenes, which later became Yugoslavia.

The coinage, issued under the autocratic rule of Prince Nicholas, is obsolete.

RULERS

Nicholas I, as Prince, 1860-1910
as King, 1910-1918

MINT MARKS

(a) - Paris, privy marks only

MONETARY SYSTEM

100 Para, ПАРА = 1 Perper, ПЕРПЕР

PARA

BRONZE

KM#	Date	Mintage	Fine	VF	XF	Unc
1	1906	.200	8.00	16.00	35.00	75.00

KM#	Date	Mintage	Fine	VF	XF	Unc
16	1913	.100	12.50	25.00	60.00	125.00
	1914	.200	6.00	12.00	25.00	70.00

2 PARE

BRONZE

KM#	Date	Mintage	Fine	VF	XF	Unc
2	1906	.600	4.00	8.00	18.00	35.00
	1908	.250	8.00	18.00	32.00	70.00

KM#	Date	Mintage	Fine	VF	XF	Unc
17	1913	.500	4.00	7.50	15.00	30.00
	1914	.400	4.50	9.00	18.00	45.00

10 PARA

NICKEL

KM#	Date	Mintage	Fine	VF	XF	Unc
3	1906	.750	2.50	5.00	12.00	25.00
	1908	.250	3.00	6.50	15.00	30.00

KM#	Date	Mintage	Fine	VF	XF	Unc
18	1913	.200	3.50	8.00	17.50	35.00
	1914	.800	2.50	5.00	12.00	25.00

20 PARA

NICKEL

KM#	Date	Mintage	Fine	VF	XF	Unc
4	1906	.600	3.00	6.00	12.00	25.00
	1908	.400	3.00	7.00	15.00	30.00

KM#	Date	Mintage	Fine	VF	XF	Unc
19	1913	.200	4.00	8.00	17.50	35.00
	1914	.800	3.00	6.00	12.00	25.00

PERPER

5.0000 g, .835 SILVER, .1342 oz ASW

KM#	Date	Mintage	Fine	VF	XF	Unc
5	1909(a)	*.500	8.50	17.50	35.00	90.00

***NOTE:** Approximately 30% melted.

KM#	Date	Mintage	Fine	VF	XF	Unc
14	1912	.520	8.00	14.00	30.00	80.00
	1914	.500	9.00	18.00	35.00	90.00

2 PERPERA

10.0000 g, .835 SILVER, .2685 oz ASW

KM#	Date	Mintage	Fine	VF	XF	Unc
7	1910	.300	15.00	30.00	65.00	160.00

KM#	Date	Mintage	Fine	VF	XF	Unc
20	1914	.200	15.00	35.00	75.00	170.00

5 PERPERA

24.0000 g, .900 SILVER, .6944 oz ASW

KM#	Date	Mintage	Fine	VF	XF	Unc
6	1909(a)	*.060	60.00	120.00	250.00	520.00

***NOTE:** Approximately 50% melted.

KM#	Date	Mintage	Fine	VF	XF	Unc
15	1912	.040	75.00	150.00	275.00	550.00
	1914	.020	85.00	160.00	300.00	620.00

10 PERPERA

3.3875 g, .900 GOLD, .0980 oz AGW

KM#	Date	Mintage	Fine	VF	XF	Unc
8	1910	.040	125.00	250.00	325.00	500.00

50th Year of Reign

KM#	Date	Mintage	Fine	VF	XF	Unc
9	1910	.035	125.00	250.00	325.00	500.00

20 PERPERA

6.7751 g, .900 GOLD, .1960 oz AGW

KM#	Date	Mintage	Fine	VF	XF	Unc
10	1910	.030	150.00	275.00	450.00	650.00

50th Year of Reign

KM#	Date	Mintage	Fine	VF	XF	Unc
11	1910	.030	150.00	275.00	450.00	650.00

100 PERPERA

33.8753 g, .900 GOLD, .9802 oz AGW

KM#	Date	Mintage	Fine	VF	XF	Unc
12	1910	300 pcs.	—	4500.	6500.	10,000.
	1910	25 pcs.	—	—		Proof 12,500.

50th Year of Reign

KM#	Date	Mintage	Fine	VF	XF	Unc
13	1910	500 pcs.	—	4500.	6500.	10,000.
	1910	Inc. Ab.	—	—		Proof 15,000.

CATTARO

A seaport of Montenegro, Yugoslavia, occupies a ledge between the Montenegrin mountains and an inlet of the Adriatic Sea which forms one of the finest natural harbors in the world. It has at various times been occupied by Turks, Venetians, Spaniards, French, English and Austrians. It became a part of Yugoslavia in 1918. Cattaro was united to the French Empire during the period of 1807-13. In 1813, while the city was besieged by Montenegrins and a British fleet, the French defenders issued an emergency cast silver coinage.

FRENCH SIEGE COINAGE

FRANC

CAST SILVER, 5.50-6.30 g

KM#	Date	Mintage	Good	VG	Fine	VF
1	1813	—	80.00	125.00	190.00	275.00

5 FRANCS

CAST SILVER, 28.00-30.00 g

KM#	Date	Mintage	Good	VG	Fine	VF
2	1813	—	300.00	500.00	800.00	1200.

10 FRANCS

CAST SILVER, 59.00-59.60 g

KM#	Date	Mintage	Good	VG	Fine	VF
3	1813	—	450.00	850.00	1250.	2000.

Serbia, a former inland Balkan kingdom has an area of 34,116 sq. mi. (88,361 sq. km.). Capital: Belgrade.

Serbia emerged as a separate kingdom in the 12th century and attained its greatest expansion and political influence in the mid-14th century. After the Battle of Kosovo, 1389, Serbia became a vassal principality of Turkey and remained under Turkish suzerainty until it was re-established as an independent kingdom by the 1887 Treaty of Berlin. Following World War I, which had its immediate cause in the assassination of Austrian Archduke Francis Ferdinand by a Serbian nationalist, Serbia joined with the Croats and Slovenes to form the new Kingdom of the South Slavs with Peter I of Serbia as king. The name of the kingdom was later changed to Yugoslavia. Invaded by Germany during World War II, Serbia emerged as a constituent republic of the Socialist Federal Republic of Yugoslavia.

RULERS

Michael, Obrenovich III
as Prince 1839-1842, 1860-1868
Milan, Obrenovich IV,
as Prince, 1868-1882
as King, 1882-1889
Alexander I, 1889-1902
Peter I, 1903-1918

MINT MARKS

A - Paris
(a) - Paris, privy mark only
(g) - Gorham Mfg. Co., Providence, R.I.
H - Birmingham
V - Vienna
БП (BP) Budapest

MONETARY SYSTEM

100 Para = 1 Dinara

DENOMINATIONS

ПАРА = Para
ПАРЕ = Pare
ДИНАР = Dinar
ДИНАРА = Dinara

KINGDOM

PARA

BRONZE

SERBIA spelled: СРБСКИ

KM#	Date	Mintage	Fine	VF	XF	Unc
1.1	1868	7.500	5.00	15.00	30.00	75.00
SERBIA spelled: СРЪСКИ						
1.2	1868	Inc. Ab.	6.00	17.00	35.00	90.00

2 PARE

BRONZE

KM#	Date	Mintage	Fine	VF	XF	Unc
23	1904	12.500	1.00	3.00	9.00	25.00

5 PARA

BRONZE

KM#	Date	Mintage	Fine	VF	XF	Unc
2	1868	7.420	4.00	12.00	35.00	85.00

KM#	Date	Mintage	Fine	VF	XF	Unc
7	1879	6.000	2.00	8.00	25.00	65.00
	1879	—	—	—	Proof	125.00

COPPER-NICKEL

KM#	Date	Mintage	Fine	VF	XF	Unc
18	1883	4.000	1.00	3.00	8.00	22.00
	1884H	3.000	1.00	3.00	8.00	25.00
	1884H	—	—	—	Proof	125.00
	1904*	8.000	1.00	2.50	5.00	12.00
	1904	Inc. Ab.	—	—	Proof	100.00
	1912*	10.000	.75	1.50	3.50	8.00
	1912	—	—	—	Proof	75.00
	1917(g)	5.000	5.00	10.00	20.00	32.00

***NOTE:** Medallic struck.

10 PARA

BRONZE

KM#	Date	Mintage	Fine	VF	XF	Unc
3	1868	6.590	5.00	16.00	35.00	85.00

KM#	Date	Mintage	Fine	VF	XF	Unc
8	1879	9.000	4.00	9.00	27.50	70.00
	1879	—	—	—	Proof	150.00

COPPER-NICKEL

KM#	Date	Mintage	Fine	VF	XF	Unc
19	1883	5.000	.75	1.75	5.00	15.00
	1884H	6.500	.75	1.75	4.50	12.00
	1884H	—	—	—	Proof	150.00
	1904	—	—	—	Proof	175.00
	1912*	7.700	.75	1.25	3.00	6.00
	1912	—	—	—	Proof	75.00
	1917(g)	5.000	1.00	2.50	7.00	22.00
	1917(g)	—	—	—	Proof	80.00

***NOTE:** Medallic struck.

20 PARA

COPPER-NICKEL

KM#	Date	Mintage	Fine	VF	XF	Unc
20	1883	2.500	1.00	3.50	12.00	25.00
	1884H	6.000	1.00	2.50	8.00	16.00
	1884H	—	—	—	Proof	150.00
	1904	—	—	—	Proof	175.00
	1912*	5.650	.75	1.50	4.00	8.00
	1912	—	—	—	Proof	100.00
	1917(g)	5.000	1.00	3.00	9.00	25.00

***NOTE:** Medallic struck.

50 PARA

2.5000 g, .835 SILVER, .0671 oz ASW

KM#	Date	Mintage	Fine	VF	XF	Unc
4	1875	2.000	8.00	18.00	55.00	150.00
	1875	—	—	—	Proof	300.00

KM#	Date	Mintage	Fine	VF	XF	Unc
9	1879	.600	5.00	15.00	30.00	95.00
	1879	—	—	—	Proof	250.00

Obv: Designers signature below neck.

KM#	Date	Mintage	Fine	VF	XF	Unc
24.1	1904*	1.400	2.00	5.00	12.00	25.00
	1912*	.800	2.50	6.00	15.00	30.00
	1915(a)	12.138	1.00	2.00	4.00	10.00

***NOTE:** Medallic struck.

Obv: W/o designers signature.

KM#	Date	Mintage	Fine	VF	XF	Unc
24.2	1915(a)	1.862	5.00	10.00	25.00	85.00

DINAR

5.0000 g, .835 SILVER, .1342 oz ASW

KM#	Date	Mintage	Fine	VF	XF	Unc
5	1875	3.000	15.00	30.00	90.00	275.00
	1875	—	—	—	Proof	450.00

KM#	Date	Mintage	Fine	VF	XF	Unc
10	1879	.800	6.00	15.00	45.00	125.00
	1879	—	—	—	Proof	250.00

KM#	Date	Mintage	Fine	VF	XF	Unc
21	1897	4.001	3.00	8.00	16.00	55.00

Obv: Designers signature below neck.

KM#	Date	Mintage	Fine	VF	XF	Unc
25.1	1904*	.994	4.50	12.00	25.00	65.00
	1912*	8.000	3.00	6.00	15.00	35.00
	1915(a)	10.688	2.00	4.00	8.00	17.50

***NOTE:** Medallic struck.

Obv: W/o designers signature.

KM#	Date	Mintage	Fine	VF	XF	Unc
25.2	1915(a)	2.322	4.50	12.00	25.00	65.00

2 DINARA

10.0000 g, .835 SILVER, .2684 oz ASW

KM#	Date	Mintage	Fine	VF	XF	Unc
6	1875	1.000	25.00	75.00	165.00	380.00
	1875	—	—	—	Proof	500.00

KM#	Date	Mintage	Fine	VF	XF	Unc
11	1879	.750	8.00	25.00	60.00	185.00
	1879	—	—	—	Proof	450.00

KM#	Date	Mintage	Fine	VF	XF	Unc
22	1897	1.000	6.00	15.00	35.00	85.00

Obv: Designers signature below neck.

KM#	Date	Mintage	Fine	VF	XF	Unc
26.1	1904*	1.150	7.50	15.00	32.00	80.00
	1912*	.800	8.00	16.00	35.00	85.00
	1915(a)	4.174	5.00	10.00	18.00	35.00

***NOTE:** Medallic struck.

Obv: W/o designers signature.

KM#	Date	Mintage	Fine	VF	XF	Unc
26.2	1915(a)	.826	5.00	15.00	35.00	85.00

5 DINARA

25.0000 g, .900 SILVER, .7234 oz ASW

Edge Type 1: БОГ*ЧУВА*СРБИЈУ***

KM#	Date	Mintage	Fine	VF	XF	Unc
12	1879	.200	30.00	65.00	140.00	320.00
	1879	—	—	—	Proof	600.00

Edge Type 2: БОГ*СРБИЈУ*ЧУВА***

KM#	Date	Mintage	Fine	VF	XF	Unc
13	1879	Inc. Ab.	40.00	80.00	175.00	450.00

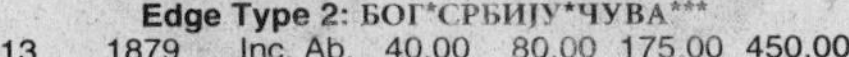

Karageorgevich Dynasty 100th Anniversary

Edge Type 1: БОГ*ЧУВА*СРБИЈУ***

KM#	Date	Mintage	Fine	VF	XF	Unc
27	1904	.200	35.00	75.00	160.00	420.00
	1904	—	—	—	Proof	650.00

Edge Type 2: БОГ*СРБИЈУ*ЧУВА***

KM#	Date	Mintage	Fine	VF	XF	Unc
28	1904	Inc. Ab.	—	—	—	—

10 DINARA

3.2258 g, .900 GOLD, .0933 oz AGW

KM#	Date	Mintage	Fine	VF	XF	Unc
16	1882V	.300	75.00	125.00	175.00	300.00

20 DINARA

6.4516 g, .900 GOLD, .1867 oz AGW
Obv. leg: Full title.

KM#	Date	Mintage	Fine	VF	XF	Unc
14	1879A	.050	125.00	160.00	300.00	550.00
	1879A	—	—	—	Proof	5000.

Obv. leg: Short title.

KM#	Date	Mintage	Fine	VF	XF	Unc
17	1882V	.300	100.00	120.00	180.00	325.00

GERMAN OCCUPATION WW II

50 PARA

ZINC

KM#	Date	Mintage	Fine	VF	XF	Unc
30	1942БП	—	2.00	4.50	10.00	20.00

DINAR

ZINC

KM#	Date	Mintage	Fine	VF	XF	Unc
31	1942БП	—	.50	1.50	6.00	12.00

2 DINARA

ZINC

KM#	Date	Mintage	Fine	VF	XF	Unc
32	1942БП	—	.50	1.50	6.50	15.00

10 DINARA

ZINC

KM#	Date	Mintage	Fine	VF	XF	Unc
33	1943БП	1.750	1.00	2.50	8.50	18.00

ZAIRE

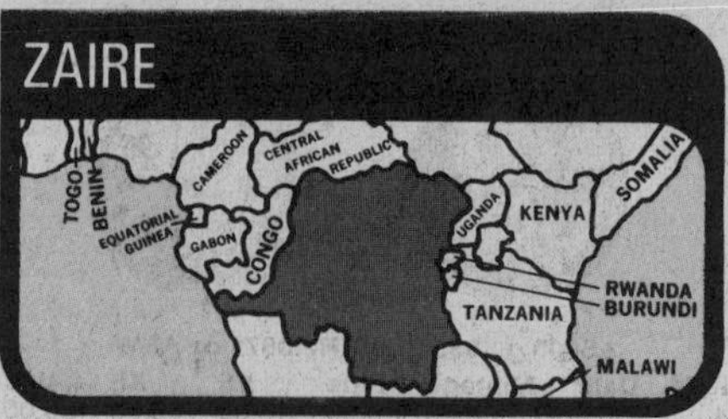

The Republic of Zaire (formerly the Belgian Congo), located in the south-central part of Africa, has an area of 905,568 sq. mi. (2,345,410 sq. km.) and a population of *34.3 million. Capital: Kinshasa. The mineral-rich country produces copper, tin, diamonds, gold, zinc, cobalt and uranium.

In ancient times the territory comprising Zaire was occupied by Negrito peoples (Pygmies) pushed into the mountains by Bantu and Nilotic invaders. The interior was first explored by the American correspondent Henry Stanley, who was subsequently commissioned by King Leopold II of Belgium to conclude development treaties with the local chiefs. The Berlin conference of 1885 awarded the area to Leopold, who administered and exploited it as his private property until it was annexed to Belgium in 1908. Following the eruption of bloody independence riots in 1959, Belgium granted the Belgian Congo independence as the Republic of the Congo on June 30, 1960. The nation officially changed its name to Zaire on Oct. 27, 1971.

CONGO FREE STATE

RULER

Leopold II

CENTIME

COPPER

KM#	Date	Mintage	Fine	VF	XF	Unc
1	1887	.180	1.50	3.00	6.00	18.00
	1888	Inc. Ab.	1.00	2.00	4.00	10.00

2 CENTIMES

COPPER

KM#	Date	Mintage	Fine	VF	XF	Unc
2	1887	.130	1.50	3.00	6.00	20.00
	1888	Inc. Ab.	1.00	2.00	4.00	10.00

5 CENTIMES

COPPER

KM#	Date	Mintage	Fine	VF	XF	Unc
3	1887	.180	2.00	4.00	8.00	20.00
	1888/7	Inc. Ab.	1.50	3.00	5.00	15.00
	1888	Inc. Ab.	1.50	3.00	6.00	20.00
	1894	.150	2.00	4.00	7.00	25.00

COPPER-NICKEL

KM#	Date	Mintage	Fine	VF	XF	Unc
9	1906	.100	5.00	10.00	18.00	40.00
	1908	.180	4.00	8.00	15.00	35.00

10 CENTIMES

COPPER

KM#	Date	Mintage	Fine	VF	XF	Unc
4	1887	.040	5.00	10.00	20.00	45.00
	1888	Inc. Ab.	2.00	3.50	8.00	25.00
	1889	.100	3.00	7.00	15.00	35.00
	1894	.150	2.50	5.00	10.00	30.00

COPPER-NICKEL

KM#	Date	Mintage	Fine	VF	XF	Unc
10	1906	.100	5.00	12.00	25.00	70.00
	1908	.800	3.00	8.00	22.00	60.00

20 CENTIMES

COPPER-NICKEL

KM#	Date	Mintage	Fine	VF	XF	Unc
11	1906	.100	5.00	12.00	25.00	60.00
	1908	.400	4.00	8.00	20.00	50.00

50 CENTIMES

2.5000 g .835 SILVER, .0671 oz ASW

KM#	Date	Mintage	Fine	VF	XF	Unc
5	1887	.020	7.00	15.00	30.00	70.00
	1887	—	—	—	Proof	225.00
	1891	.060	8.00	17.50	35.00	80.00
	1894	.040	8.00	20.00	40.00	100.00
	1896	.200	8.00	15.00	35.00	75.00

FRANC

5.0000 g, .835 SILVER, .1342 oz ASW

KM#	Date	Mintage	Fine	VF	XF	Unc
6	1887	.020	10.00	20.00	40.00	110.00
	1891	.070	10.00	22.00	45.00	120.00
	1894	.070	12.00	25.00	50.00	135.00
	1896	.160	9.00	18.00	35.00	100.00

2 FRANCS

10.0000 g, .835 SILVER, .2685 oz ASW

KM#	Date	Mintage	Fine	VF	XF	Unc
7	1887	.020	25.00	45.00	90.00	185.00
	1891	.030	30.00	50.00	125.00	275.00
	1894	.080	30.00	50.00	120.00	250.00
	1896	.100	30.00	50.00	100.00	200.00

5 FRANCS

25.0000 g, .900 SILVER, .7234 oz ASW
Obv. leg: LEOPOLD II R.D.BELGES. . . . .

KM#	Date	Mintage	Fine	VF	XF	Unc
8.1	1887	8,000	95.00	160.00	235.00	525.00
	1891	.030	100.00	175.00	250.00	550.00
	1894	.050	100.00	175.00	250.00	550.00
	1896	.110	90.00	150.00	225.00	500.00

Obv. leg: LEOPOLD II ROI DES BELGES. . . . .

KM#	Date	Mintage	Fine	VF	XF	Unc
8.2	1887	100 pcs.	1000.	2500.	4250.	6250.

BELGIAN CONGO

The Belgian Congo attained independence (as Republic of Zaire) with the distinction of being the most ill-prepared country to ever undertake self-government. Without a single doctor, lawyer or engineer, with no organized unit capable of maintaining law and order, independence disintegrated into an orgy of anarchy. Provinces seceded. Intertribal warfare erupted. Belgian troops intervened to protect Belgian citizens from retributive massacre. By 1961 four groups were fighting for political dominance. The most serious threat to the viability of the country was posed by the secession of mineral-rich Katanga province on July 11, 1960. After two and one-half years of sporadic warfare with a U.N. military force, Katanga's leaders capitulated, Jan. 14, 1963, and the rebellious province was partitioned into three provinces.

RULERS

Belgian, until 1960

MINT MARKS

H - Heaton, Birmingham

MONETARY SYSTEM

100 Centimes = 1 Franc

CENTIME

COPPER

KM#	Date	Mintage	Fine	VF	XF	Unc
15	1910	2.000	1.00	2.00	3.00	6.00
	1919	.500	1.00	2.00	3.00	7.00

2 CENTIMES

COPPER

KM#	Date	Mintage	Fine	VF	XF	Unc
16	1910	1.500	1.00	3.00	7.00	25.00
	1919	.500	1.50	3.50	10.00	30.00

5 CENTIMES

COPPER-NICKEL

KM#	Date	Mintage	Fine	VF	XF	Unc
12	1909	1.800	5.00	12.50	40.00	90.00

KM#	Date	Mintage	Fine	VF	XF	Unc
17	1910	6.000	.75	1.50	2.50	10.00
	1911	5.000	.75	1.50	2.50	10.00
	1917H	1.000	3.00	7.00	15.00	50.00
	1917H	—	—	—	Proof	150.00
	1919H	3.000	1.50	3.00	6.00	20.00
	1919	6.850	.50	1.00	2.00	9.00
	1920	2.740	.50	1.00	3.00	11.00
	1921	17.260	.25	.75	1.50	8.00
	1921H	3.000	1.00	2.00	5.00	15.00
	1925	11.000	.25	.75	2.00	8.00
	1926/5	5.770	2.25	4.50	—	—
	1926	Inc. Ab.	.25	1.00	2.00	8.00
	1927	2.000	.50	1.00	2.50	9.00
	1928/6	1.500	2.00	4.00	8.00	20.00
	1928	Inc. Ab.	.75	1.25	3.00	10.00

10 CENTIMES

COPPER-NICKEL

KM#	Date	Mintage	Fine	VF	XF	Unc
13	1909	1.500	8.00	20.00	50.00	125.00

KM#	Date	Mintage	Fine	VF	XF	Unc
18	1910	5.000	.50	1.00	3.00	10.00
	1911	5.000	.50	1.00	3.00	10.00
	1917H	.500	5.00	10.00	25.00	75.00
	1919	3.430	.50	1.00	3.50	11.00
	1919H	1.500	.75	1.25	4.00	12.00
	1920	1.510	.75	1.25	4.00	12.00
	1921	13.540	.25	.75	2.00	8.00
	1921H	3.000	.75	1.50	3.50	10.00
	1922	14.950	.25	1.00	2.50	8.00
	1924	3.600	.50	1.50	3.00	10.00
	1925/4	4.800	2.00	4.00	8.00	50.00
	1925	Inc. Ab.	.25	1.00	3.00	10.00
	1927	2.020	.25	1.00	3.00	8.00
	1928/7	5.600	1.00	3.00	8.00	40.00
	1928	Inc. Ab.	.25	1.00	3.00	8.00

20 CENTIMES

COPPER-NICKEL

KM#	Date	Mintage	Fine	VF	XF	Unc
14	1909	.300	10.00	25.00	65.00	175.00

KM#	Date	Mintage	Fine	VF	XF	Unc
19	1910	1.000	2.00	5.00	10.00	30.00
	1911	1.250	1.50	4.00	8.00	25.00

50 CENTIMES

COPPER-NICKEL
Rev: French leg. CONGO BELGE

KM#	Date	Mintage	Fine	VF	XF	Unc
22	1921	4.000	.60	2.00	8.00	27.50
	1922	6.000	.60	2.00	8.00	27.50
	1923	7.200	.60	2.00	8.00	27.50
	1924	1.096	.75	3.00	10.00	32.50
	1925	16.104	.60	2.00	7.00	22.50
	1926/5	16.000	1.00	4.00	12.00	45.00
	1926	Inc. Ab.	.60	2.00	8.00	22.00
	1927	10.000	.60	2.00	8.00	27.50
	1929/7	7.504	.60	2.00	9.00	32.00
	1929/8	Inc. Ab.	1.00	4.00	15.00	90.00
	1929	Inc. Ab.	.60	2.00	7.00	22.00

Rev: Flemish leg. BELGISCH CONGO

KM#	Date	Mintage	Fine	VF	XF	Unc
23	1921	4.000	.60	2.00	8.00	32.00
	1922	5.592	.60	2.00	7.00	27.50
	1923/1	7.208	1.00	5.00	16.50	70.00
	1923	Inc. Ab.	.60	2.00	7.00	22.00
	1924	7.000	.60	2.00	8.00	27.50
	1925/4	10.600	.75	5.00	17.50	80.00
	1925	Inc. Ab.	.60	2.00	7.00	27.50
	1926	25.200	.60	2.00	7.00	22.00
	1927	4.800	.60	2.00	8.00	27.50
	1928	7.484	.60	2.00	7.00	22.00
	1929/8	.116	25.00	50.00	75.00	120.00
	1929	Inc. Ab.	20.00	40.00	70.00	100.00

FRANC

COPPER-NICKEL
Rev: French leg. CONGO BELGE

KM#	Date	Mintage	Fine	VF	XF	Unc
20	1920	4.000	.85	2.75	10.00	37.50
	1922	5.000	.85	2.75	9.00	32.00
	1923/2	5.000	2.00	7.00	16.00	45.00
	1923	Inc. Ab.	.85	2.75	9.00	32.00
	1924	6.030	.85	2.75	9.00	35.00
	1925	10.470	.85	2.75	9.00	32.00
	1926/5	12.500	2.00	7.00	16.50	50.00
	1926	Inc. Ab.	.85	2.75	8.00	27.50
	1927	15.250	.85	2.75	8.00	27.50
	1929	5.763	.85	2.75	9.00	32.00
	1930	5.000	.85	2.75	10.00	40.00

Rev: Flemish leg. BELGISCH CONGO

KM#	Date	Mintage	Fine	VF	XF	Unc
21	1920	.475	2.00	5.00	16.50	50.00
	1921	3.525	.85	3.00	9.00	37.50
	1922	5.000	.85	3.00	9.00	37.50
	1923/2	7.362	2.00	5.00	17.00	55.00

KM#	Date	Mintage	Fine	VF	XF	Unc
21	1923	Inc. Ab.	.85	2.75	9.00	32.00
	1924	4.608	.85	3.00	10.00	37.50
	1925	9.530	.85	2.75	9.00	32.00
	1926/5	17.000	2.00	5.00	17.00	55.00
	1926	Inc. Ab.	.85	2.75	9.00	32.00
	1928	9.250	.85	2.75	9.00	32.00
	1929	4.250	.85	3.00	10.00	37.50

BRASS

KM#	Date	Mintage	Fine	VF	XF	Unc
26	1944	25.000	.25	.75	2.25	5.00
	1946	15.000	.50	1.00	2.50	6.00
	1949	15.000	.50	1.00	2.00	4.50

2 FRANCS

BRASS

KM#	Date	Mintage	Fine	VF	XF	Unc
25	1943	25.000	2.00	4.00	8.00	32.00

KM#	Date	Mintage	Fine	VF	XF	Unc
28	1946	13.000	.75	1.50	2.50	8.00
	1947	12.000	.75	1.50	3.00	10.00

5 FRANCS

NICKEL-BRONZE

KM#	Date	Mintage	Fine	VF	XF	Unc
24	1936	2.600	5.00	10.00	20.00	110.00
	1937	11.400	4.00	12.00	25.00	125.00

BRASS

KM#	Date	Mintage	Fine	VF	XF	Unc
29	1947	10.000	3.00	7.00	15.00	45.00

50 FRANCS

17.5000 g, .500 SILVER, .2814 oz ASW

KM#	Date	Mintage	Fine	VF	XF	Unc
27	1944	1.000	30.00	50.00	85.00	165.00

BELGIAN CONGO/ RUANDA-URUNDI

The Belgian Congo and Ruanda-Urundi were united administratively from 1925 to 1960. Ruanda-Urundi was made a U.N. Trust territory in 1946. Coins for these 2 areas were made jointly between 1952 and 1960. Ruanda-Urundi became the Republic of Rwanda on June 1, 1962.

For later coinage refer to Rwanda and Burundi, Rwanda, and Burundi.

MONETARY SYSTEM

100 Centimes = 1 Franc

50 CENTIMES

ALUMINUM

KM#	Date	Mintage	VF	XF	Unc
2	1954 DB	4.700	.35	.75	2.00
	1955 DB	20.300	.15	.60	1.50

FRANC

ALUMINUM

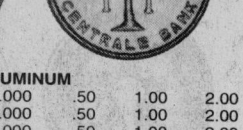

KM#	Date	Mintage	VF	XF	Unc
4	1957	10.000	.50	1.00	2.00
	1958	20.000	.50	1.00	2.00
	1959	20.000	.50	1.00	2.00
	1960	20.000	.50	1.00	2.00

5 FRANCS

BRASS

KM#	Date	Mintage	VF	XF	Unc
1	1952	10.000	2.50	5.00	10.00

ALUMINUM

KM#	Date	Mintage	VF	XF	Unc
3	1956 DB	10.000	1.00	2.00	3.75
	1958 DB	26.110	.75	1.75	3.00
	1959 DB	3.890	1.00	2.50	4.00

CONGO DEM REP.

Democratic Republic of the Congo achieved independence on June 30, 1960. It followed the same monetary system as when under the Belgians. Monetary Reform of 1967 introduced new denominations and coins. The name of the country was changed to Zaire in 1971.

MINT MARKS

(b) - Brussels, privy marks only

10 FRANCS

ALUMINUM

KM#	Date	Mintage	Fine	VF	XF	Unc
1	1965(b)	*100.000	.60	1.50	3.00	7.00

***NOTE:** Most recalled and melted down.

3.2260 g, .900 GOLD, .0934 oz AGW
5th Anniversary of Independence
Obv: Similar to 100 Francs, KM#6.

KM#	Date	Mintage				
2	1965	*3,000	—	—	Proof	80.00

***NOTE:** Approximately 70 per cent melted.

20 FRANCS

6.4520 g, .900 GOLD, .1867 oz AGW
5th Anniversary of Independence

KM#	Date	Mintage				
3	1965	*3,000	—	—	Proof	140.00

***NOTE:** Approximately 70 per cent melted.

25 FRANCS

8.0640 g, .900 GOLD, .2334 oz AGW
5th Anniversary of Independence

KM#	Date	Mintage				
4	1965	*3,000	—	—	Proof	170.00

***NOTE:** Approximately 70 per cent melted.

SILVER

KM#	Date	Mintage				
4a	1965	—	—	—	Proof	60.00

50 FRANCS

16.1290 g, .900 GOLD, .4668 oz AGW
5th Anniversary of Independence

KM#	Date	Mintage				
5	1965	*3,000	—	—	Proof	350.00

***NOTE:** Approximately 70 per cent melted.

100 FRANCS

32.2580 g, .900 GOLD, .9335 oz AGW
5th Anniversary of Independence
Rev: Similar to 50 Francs, KM#5.

KM#	Date	Mintage				
6	1965	*3,000	—	—	Proof	650.00

***NOTE:** Approximately 70 per cent melted.

SILVER

KM#	Date	Mintage	Fine	VF	XF	Unc
6a	1965	—	—	—	Proof	100.00

MONETARY REFORM

100 Sengis = 1 Likuta
100 Makuta (plural of Likuta) = 1 Zaire

10 SENGIS

ALUMINUM

7	1967	90.996	—	.15	.45	1.00

3.2000 g, .900 GOLD, .0926 oz AGW
5th Year of Presidency of Mobutu
Rev: Portrait of President Mobutu.

10	1970	1,000	—	—	—	85.00
	1970	1,000	—	—	Proof	100.00

LIKUTA

ALUMINUM

8	1967	49.180	—	.15	.50	1.25

5 MAKUTA

COPPER-NICKEL

9	1967	2.470	.25	.50	1.00	2.00

25 MAKUTAS

8.0000 g, .900 GOLD, .2315 oz AGW
5th Year of Presidency of Mobutu
Rev: Portrait of President Mobutu.

11	1970	1,000	—	—	—	150.00
	1970	1,000	—	—	Proof	170.00

50 MAKUTAS

16.0000 g, .900 GOLD, .4630 oz AGW
5th Year of Presidency of Mobutu
Rev: Portrait of President Mobutu.

12	1970	1,000	—	—	—	275.00
	1970	1,000	—	—	Proof	300.00

ZAIRE

32.0000 g, .900 GOLD, .9261 oz AGW
5th Year of Presidency of Mobutu

KM#	Date	Mintage	Fine	VF	XF	Unc
13	1970	1,000	—	—	—	500.00
	1970	1,000	—	—	Proof	550.00

MINT SETS (MS)

KM#	Date	Mintage	Identification	Issue Price	Mkt. Val.
MS1	1970(4)	1,000	KM10-13	1300.	1000.

PROOF SETS (PS)

PS1	1965(5)	*3,000	KM2-6	490.00	1290.
PS2	1970(4)	1,000	KM10-13	—	1120.

***NOTE:** Approximately 70 per cent melted.

KATANGA

Katanga, the southern province of the former Belgian Congo, had an area of 191,873 sq. mi. (496,951 sq. km.) and was noted for its mineral wealth.

MONETARY SYSTEM

100 Centimes = 1 Franc

FRANC

BRONZE

KM#	Date	Mintage	VF	XF	Unc
1	1961	—	1.00	1.50	2.50

5 FRANCS

BRONZE

2	1961	—	1.75	2.75	5.00

13.3300 g, .900 GOLD, .3857 oz AGW

2a	1961	.020	—	—	200.00

REPUBLIC OF ZAIRE

MONETARY SYSTEM

100 Makuta = 1 Zaire
1993 -
3,000,000 old Zaires = 1 Nouveau Zaire

5 MAKUTA

COPPER-NICKEL

12	1977	8.000	.50	1.00	3.00

10 MAKUTA

COPPER-NICKEL

KM#	Date	Mintage	VF	XF	Unc
7	1973	5.000	2.00	4.00	8.00
	1975	—	2.25	4.50	9.00
	1976	—	2.25	4.50	9.00
	1978	—	2.25	4.50	9.00

20 MAKUTA

COPPER-NICKEL

8	1973	—	3.00	5.00	10.00
	1976	—	3.50	6.00	12.00

ZAIRE

BRASS

13	1987	—	.50	1.00	2.00

2-1/2 ZAIRES

28.2800 g, .925 SILVER, .8411 oz ASW
Conservation - Mountain Gorillas

9	1975	5,735	—	—	35.00
	1975	6,629	—	Proof	40.00

5 ZAIRES

27.8400 g, .925 SILVER, .8280 oz ASW
Hotel Intercontinental

KM#	Date	Mintage	VF	XF	Unc
1	1971	—	—	Proof	30.00

35.0000 g, .925 SILVER, 1.0409 oz ASW
Conservation - Okapi
Obv: Similar to 2-1/2 Zaires, KM#9.

KM#	Date	Mintage	VF	XF	Unc
10	1975	5,734	—	—	30.00
	1975	6,431	—	Proof	35.00

BRASS

KM#	Date	Mintage	VF	XF	Unc
14	1987	—	.75	1.50	3.00

10 ZAIRES

9.9600 g, .900 GOLD, .2882 oz AGW
Hotel Intercontinental

KM#	Date	Mintage	VF	XF	Unc
2	1971	—	—	Proof	140.00

6.0400 g, .999 PLATINUM, .1940 oz APW

KM#	Date	Mintage	VF	XF	Unc
3	1971	—	—	Proof	150.00

BRASS

KM#	Date	Mintage	VF	XF	Unc
19	1988	—	1.50	3.00	6.00

20 ZAIRES

20.9000 g, .900 GOLD, .6048 oz AGW
Hotel Intercontinental

KM#	Date	Mintage	VF	XF	Unc
4	1971	—	—	Proof	300.00

3.8900 g, .999 PLATINUM, .1250 oz APW

KM#	Date	Mintage	VF	XF	Unc
5	1971	—	—	Proof	100.00

50 ZAIRES

46.9600 g, .900 GOLD, 1.3590 oz AGW
Hotel Intercontinental

KM#	Date	Mintage	VF	XF	Unc
6	1971	—	—	Proof	675.00

100 ZAIRES

33.4370 g, .900 GOLD, .9676 oz AGW
Conservation - Leopard

KM#	Date	Mintage	VF	XF	Unc
11	1975	1,415	—	—	500.00
	1975	279 pcs.	—	Proof	850.00

PROOF SETS (PS)

KM#	Date	Mintage	Identification	Issue Price	Mkt. Val.
PS1	1971(6)	—	KM1-6	—	1350.
PS2	1975(2)	500	KM9-10	60.00	75.00

ZAMBIA

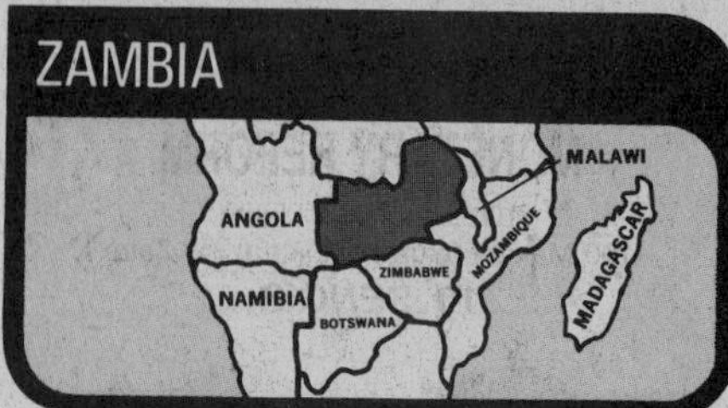

The Republic of Zambia (formerly Northern Rhodesia), a landlocked country in south-central Africa, has an area of 290,586 sq. mi. (752,610 sq. km.) and a population of *7.9 million. Capital: Lusaka. The economy of Zambia is based principally on copper, of which Zambia is the world's third largest producer. Copper, zinc, lead, cobalt and tobacco are exported.

The area that is now Zambia was brought within the British sphere of influence in 1888 by empire builder Cecil Rhodes, who obtained mining concessions in southcentral Africa from indigenous chiefs. The territory was ruled by the British South Africa Company, which Rhodes established, until 1924 when its administration was transferred to the British government as a protectorate. In 1953, Northern Rhodesia was joined with Nyasaland and the colony of Southern Rhodesia to form the Federation of Rhodesia and Nyasaland. Northern Rhodesia seceded from the Federation on Oct. 24, 1964, and became the independent Republic of Zambia. Zambia is a member of the Commonwealth of Nations. The president is Chief of State.

Zambia converted to a decimal coinage on January 16, 1969.

For earlier coinage refer to Rhodesia and Nyasaland.

RULERS

British, until 1964

MONETARY SYSTEM

12 Pence = 1 Shilling
20 Shillings = 1 Pound
100 Ngwee = 1 Kwacha

PENNY

BRONZE

KM#	Date	Mintage	Fine	VF	XF	Unc
5	1966	7.200	.15	.35	.80	2.00
	1966	60 pcs.	—	—	Proof	—

SIXPENCE

COPPER-NICKEL-ZINC
Morning Glory

KM#	Date	Mintage	Fine	VF	XF	Unc
1	1964	3.500	.15	.30	.60	1.20
	1964	5,000	—	—	Proof	1.50

KM#	Date	Mintage	Fine	VF	XF	Unc
6	1966	7.200	.25	.50	1.00	2.00
	1966	60 pcs.	—	—	Proof	—

SHILLING

COPPER-NICKEL
Crowned Hornbill

KM#	Date	Mintage	Fine	VF	XF	Unc
2	1964	3.510	.25	.50	1.00	2.00
	1964	5,000	—	—	Proof	2.50

KM#	Date	Mintage	Fine	VF	XF	Unc
7	1966	5.000	.35	.75	1.50	3.25
	1966	60 pcs.	—	—	Proof	—

2 SHILLINGS

COPPER-NICKEL
Bohor Reedbuck

KM#	Date	Mintage	Fine	VF	XF	Unc
3	1964	3.770	.35	.75	1.50	3.00
	1964	5,000	—	—	Proof	3.50

KM#	Date	Mintage	Fine	VF	XF	Unc
8	1966	5.000	.45	1.00	2.25	4.50
	1966	60 pcs.	—	—	Proof	—

5 SHILLINGS

COPPER-NICKEL
1st Anniversary of Independence

KM#	Date	Mintage	Fine	VF	XF	Unc
4	1965	.010	—	2.00	3.00	4.00
	1965	.020	—	—	Proof	5.50

DECIMAL COINAGE

100 Ngwee = 1 Kwacha

NGWEE

BRONZE
Aardvark

KM#	Date	Mintage	VF	XF	Unc
9	1968	8.000	.10	.15	.50
	1968	4,000	—	Proof	1.00
	1969	16.000	.10	.15	.40
	1972	21.000	.10	.15	.40
	1978	23.976	.10	.15	.40
	1978	.024	—	Proof	1.50

COPPER-CLAD-STEEL

KM#	Date	Mintage	VF	XF	Unc
9a	1982	10.000	.10	.20	.75
	1983	60.000	.10	.15	.40

2 NGWEE

BRONZE
Martial Eagle

KM#	Date	Mintage	VF	XF	Unc
10	1968	19.000	.10	.20	.75
	1968	4,000	—	Proof	1.25
	1978	—	.15	.25	.85
	1978	.024	—	Proof	1.75

COPPER-CLAD-STEEL

KM#	Date	Mintage	VF	XF	Unc
10a	1982	7.500	.10	.20	1.00
	1983	60.000	.10	.15	.50

5 NGWEE

COPPER-NICKEL
Morning Glory

KM#	Date	Mintage	VF	XF	Unc
11	1968	12.000	.20	.30	.60
	1968	4,000	—	Proof	1.50
	1972	9.000	.20	.30	.60
	1978	1.976	.20	.30	.60
	1978	.024	—	Proof	2.00
	1982	12.000	.20	.30	.60
	1987	10.000	.20	.30	.60

10 NGWEE

COPPER-NICKEL-ZINC
Crowned Hornbill

KM#	Date	Mintage	VF	XF	Unc
12	1968	1.000	.35	.75	1.50
	1968	4,000	—	Proof	1.75
	1972	1.000	.30	.50	1.00
	1978	1.976	.30	.50	1.00
	1978	.024	—	Proof	2.00
	1982	8.000	.30	.50	1.00
	1983	2,500	.30	.50	1.00
	1987	6.000	.30	.50	1.00

20 NGWEE

COPPER-NICKEL
Bohor Reedbuck

KM#	Date	Mintage	VF	XF	Unc
13	1968	1.500	1.00	2.00	3.00
	1968	4,000	—	Proof	2.50
	1972	7.500	.50	1.00	2.00
	1978	.024	—	Proof	3.00
	1983	.998	.75	1.50	2.50
	1987	—	.50	1.00	2.00
	1988	3.000	.50	1.00	2.00

World Food Day

KM#	Date	Mintage	VF	XF	Unc
22	1981	.970	.75	1.50	2.50

20th Anniversary - Bank of Zambia

KM#	Date	Mintage	VF	XF	Unc
23	1985	—	.50	1.00	1.50

11.3100 g, .925 SILVER, .3364 oz ASW

KM#	Date	Mintage	VF	XF	Unc
23a	1985	—	—	Proof	3.50

25 NGWEE

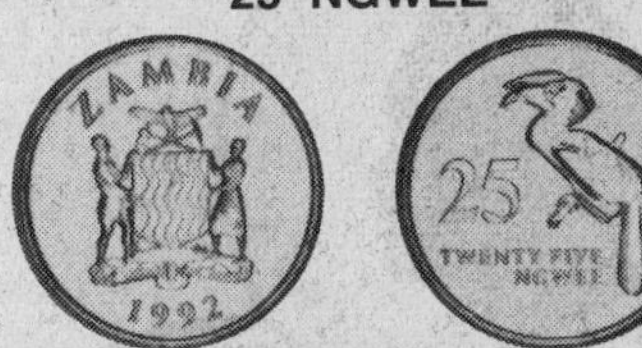

NICKEL PLATED STEEL
Crowned Hornbill

KM#	Date	Mintage	VF	XF	Unc
29	1992	—	—	—	1.00

50 NGWEE

COPPER-NICKEL
F.A.O. Issue

KM#	Date	Mintage	VF	XF	Unc
14	1969	.070	1.25	2.25	4.25

F.A.O. Issue

KM#	Date	Mintage	VF	XF	Unc
15	1972	.510	1.00	2.00	3.50

Second Republic 13th December 1972

KM#	Date	Mintage	VF	XF	Unc
16	1972	6.000	1.00	2.00	4.00
	1972	2,000	—	Proof	6.00
	1978	.024	—	Proof	5.00
	1983	.998	1.00	2.00	4.00

40th Anniversary of United Nations

KM#	Date	Mintage	VF	XF	Unc
24	1985	—	1.00	1.25	2.50

11.6600 g, .925 SILVER, .3468 oz ASW

KM#	Date	Mintage	VF	XF	Unc
24a	1985	—	—	Proof	5.00

NICKEL PLATED STEEL
Kafue Lechwe

KM#	Date	Mintage	VF	XF	Unc
30	1992	—	—	—	1.25

KWACHA

COPPER-NICKEL
10th Anniversary of Independence

KM#	Date	Mintage	VF	XF	Unc
17	1974	4,000	—	—	20.00
	1974	1,500	—	Proof	35.00

NICKEL-BRASS

KM#	Date	Mintage	VF	XF	Unc
26	1989	8.000	1.00	2.00	4.00

BRASS

KM#	Date	Mintage	VF	XF	Unc
38	1992	—	—	—	1.25

5 KWACHA

25.3100 g, .925 SILVER, .7527 oz ASW
Conservation - Kafue Lechwe

KM#	Date	Mintage	VF	XF	Unc
18	1979	3,250	—	—	22.50

28.2800 g, .925 SILVER, .8411 oz ASW

KM#	Date	Mintage	VF	XF	Unc
18a	1979	3,407	—	Proof	45.00

BRASS
Onyx

KM#	Date	Mintage	VF	XF	Unc
31	1992	—	—	—	1.50

10 KWACHA

31.6500 g, .925 SILVER, .9398 oz ASW
Conservation - Taita Falcon

KM#	Date	Mintage	VF	XF	Unc
19	1979	3,250	—	—	30.00

35.0000 g, .925 SILVER, 1.0409 oz ASW

KM#	Date	Mintage	VF	XF	Unc
19a	1979	3,256	—	Proof	50.00

27.2200 g, .925 SILVER, .8095 oz ASW
International year of the Child
Obv: Similar to 20 Ngwee, KM#13.

KM#	Date	Mintage	VF	XF	Unc
21	1980	.012	—	Proof	17.50

World Wildlife Fund Bird

KM#	Date	Mintage	VF	XF	Unc
25	1986	.025	—	Proof	50.00

70th Anniversary of Save the Children Fund

KM#	Date	Mintage	VF	XF	Unc
27	1989	*.020	—	Proof	50.00

BRASS
Rhinoceros

KM#	Date	Mintage	VF	XF	Unc
32	1992	—	—	—	2.00

20 KWACHA

10.1700 g, .999 SILVER, .3266 oz ASW
1994 Olympics - Slalom Skier

KM#	Date	Mintage	VF	XF	Unc
33	1994	—	—	Proof	25.00

100 KWACHA

28.2800 g, .925 SILVER, .8411 oz ASW
Barcelona Summer Olympics - Boxing

KM#	Date	Mintage	VF	XF	Unc
28	1991	*.050	—	Proof	60.00

200 KWACHA

33.4370 g, .900 GOLD, .9676 oz AGW
Conservation - African Wild Dog
Obv: Similar to 20 Ngwee, KM#13.

KM#	Date	Mintage	VF	XF	Unc
20	1979	455 pcs.	—	—	550.00
	1979	245 pcs.	—	Proof	850.00

250 KWACHA

136.0800 g, .925 SILVER, 4.0474 oz ASW
Illustration reduced. Actual size: 63mm
African Fish Eagle

KM#	Date	Mintage	VF	XF	Unc
34	1993	400 pcs.	—	—	220.00
	1993	5,000	—	Proof	165.00

Illustration reduced. Actual size: 63mm.
Saddle-Billed Stork

KM#	Date	Mintage	VF	XF	Unc
35	1993	400 pcs.	—	—	220.00
	1993	5,000	—	Proof	165.00

Illustration reduced. Actual size: 63mm.
Paradise Flycatcher

KM#	Date	Mintage	VF	XF	Unc
36	1993	400 pcs.	—	—	220.00
	1993	5,000	—	Proof	165.00

Illustration reduced. Actual size: 63mm.
Red-Breasted Swallow

KM#	Date	Mintage	VF	XF	Unc
37	1993	400 pcs.	—	—	220.00
	1993	5,000	—	Proof	165.00

MINT SETS (MS)

KM#	Date	Mintage	Identification	Issue Price	Mkt. Val.
MS1	1968(5)	—	KM9-13	2.00	6.00

PROOF SETS (PS)

KM#	Date	Mintage	Identification	Issue Price	Mkt. Val.
PS1	1964(3)	5,000	KM1-3	—	7.50
PS2	1965(2)	100	KM4 (2 pcs.)	—	12.00
PS3	1966(8)	30	KM5-8, double sets	—	—
PS4	1968(5)	4,000	KM9-13	10.00	8.00
PS5	1978(6)	20,000	KM9-13,16	21.00	16.50

Listings For

ZANZIBAR: refer to Tanzania

ZIMBABWE

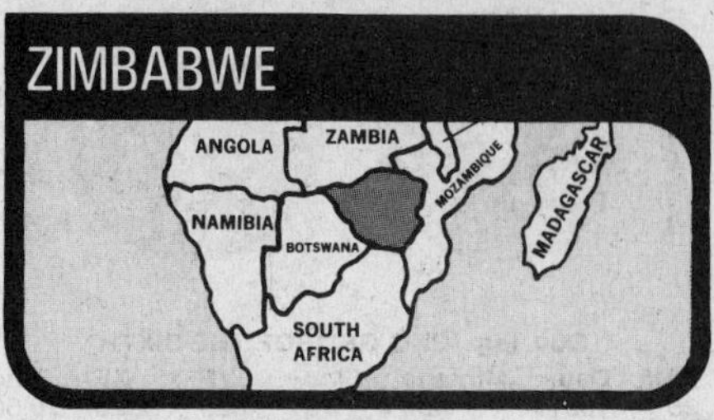

The Republic of Zimbabwe (formerly the Colony of Southern Rhodesia), located in the east-central part of southern Africa, has an area of 150,804 sq. mi. (390,580 sq. km.) and a population of *10.1 million. Capital: Harare (formerly Salisbury). The economy is based on agriculture and mining. Tobacco, sugar, asbestos, copper, chrome, ore and coal are exported.

The Rhodesian area, the habitat of paleolithic man, contains extensive evidence of earlier civilizations, notably the world-famous ruins of Zimbabwe, a gold-trading center that flourished about the 14th or 15th century A.D. The Portuguese of the 16th century were the first Europeans to attempt to develop south-central Africa, but it remained for Cecil Rhodes and the British South Africa Co. to open the hinterlands. Rhodes obtained a concession for mineral rights from local chiefs in 1888 and administered his African empire (named Southern Rhodesia in 1895) through the British South Africa Co. until 1923, when the British government annexed the area after the white settlers voted for existence as a separate entity, rather than for incorporation into the Union of South Africa. From Sept. of 1953 through 1963 Southern Rhodesia was joined with the British Protectorates of Northern Rhodesia and Nyasaland into a multiracial federation, known as the Federation of Rhodesia and Nyasaland. When the federation was dissolved at the end of 1963, Northern Rhodesia and Nyasaland became the independent states of Zambia and Malawi.

Britain was prepared to grant independence to Southern Rhodesia but declined to do so when the politically dominant white Rhodesians refused to give assurances of representative government. On Nov. 11, 1965, following two years of unsuccessful negotiation with the British government, Prime Minister Ian Smith issued an unilateral declaration of independence. Britain responded with economic sanctions supported by the United Nations. After further futile attempts to effect an accommodation, the Rhodesian Parliament severed all ties with Britain and on March 2, 1970, established the Republic of Rhodesia.

On March 3, 1978, Prime Minister Ian Smith and three moderate black nationalist leaders signed an agreement providing for black majority rule. The name of the country was changed to Zimbabwe Rhodesia. This arrangement was not accepted by Britain and following further negotiations, an acceptable form of independence was attained on April 18, 1980. The name of the country was changed to Zimbabwe which remains a member of the British Commonwealth of Nations.

SOUTHERN RHODESIA

RULERS

British until 1980

MONETARY SYSTEM

12 Pence = 1 Shilling
2 Shillings = 1 Florin
5 Shillings = 1 Crown
20 Shillings = 1 Pound

1/2 PENNY

COPPER-NICKEL

KM#	Date	Mintage	Fine	VF	XF	Unc
6	1934	.240	1.00	2.00	8.00	22.50
	1934	—	—	—	Proof	175.00
	1936	.240	4.00	8.00	25.00	125.00
	1936	—	—	—	Proof	—

KM#	Date	Mintage	Fine	VF	XF	Unc
14	1938	.240	.75	1.75	6.50	20.00
	1938	—	—	—	Proof	—
	1939	.480	1.00	2.00	9.00	60.00
	1939	—	—	—	Proof	—

BRONZE

KM#	Date	Mintage	Fine	VF	XF	Unc
14a	1942	.480	.60	1.50	3.50	18.50
	1942	—	—	—	Proof	—
	1943	.960	.35	.75	2.25	7.50
	1944	.960	.35	.75	2.50	9.00
	1944	—	—	—	Proof	—

Obv. leg: KING GEORGE THE SIXTH

KM#	Date	Mintage	Fine	VF	XF	Unc
26	1951	.480	.75	1.25	2.25	6.50
	1951	—	—	—	Proof	—
	1952	.480	.75	1.25	2.50	11.50
	1952	—	—	—	Proof	—

KM#	Date	Mintage	Fine	VF	XF	Unc
28	1954	.960	.75	2.00	10.00	75.00
	1954	20 pcs.	—	—	Proof	500.00

PENNY

COPPER-NICKEL

KM#	Date	Mintage	Fine	VF	XF	Unc
7	1934	.360	.75	1.50	3.50	30.00
	1934	—	—	—	Proof	175.00
	1935	.492	.75	2.50	12.00	125.00
	1935	—	—	—	Proof	—
	1936	1.044	.60	1.25	3.50	40.00
	1936	—	—	—	Proof	—

KM#	Date	Mintage	Fine	VF	XF	Unc
8	1937	.908	.60	1.25	3.50	25.00
	1937	—	—	—	Proof	500.00
	1938	.240	1.50	3.00	7.50	40.00
	1938	—	—	—	Proof	—
	1939	1.284	.45	1.00	3.50	40.00
	1939	—	—	—	Proof	—
	1940	1.080	.45	1.00	3.50	40.00
	1940	—	—	—	Proof	—
	1941	.720	.50	1.25	4.50	45.00
	1941	—	—	—	Proof	—
	1942	.960	.50	1.25	4.50	70.00
	1942	—	—	—	—	—

BRONZE

KM#	Date	Mintage	Fine	VF	XF	Unc
8a	1942	.480	4.00	6.50	22.50	100.00
	1942	—	—	—	Proof	500.00
	1943	3.120	.50	.80	2.50	15.00
	1944	2.400	.50	.80	2.50	20.00
	1944	—	—	—	Proof	—
	1947	3.600	.75	1.25	3.50	20.00
	1947	—	—	—	Proof	—

KM#	Date	Mintage	Fine	VF	XF	Unc
25	1949	1.440	.50	1.00	2.00	30.00
	1949	—	—	—	Proof	125.00
	1950	.720	1.00	1.75	5.00	45.00
	1950	—	—	—	Proof	125.00
	1951	4.896	.50	.75	1.25	10.00
	1951	—	—	—	Proof	125.00
	1952	2.400	.50	.75	1.75	15.00
	1952	—	—	—	Proof	—

KM#	Date	Mintage	Fine	VF	XF	Unc
29	1954	.960	4.00	8.00	25.00	175.00
	1954	20 pcs.	—	—	Proof	500.00

3 PENCE

1.4100 g, .925 SILVER, .0419 oz ASW

KM#	Date	Mintage	Fine	VF	XF	Unc
1	1932	.688	.75	1.50	6.50	35.00
	1932	—	—	—	Proof	60.00
	1934	.628	.75	2.00	10.00	70.00
	1934	—	—	—	Proof	—
	1935	.840	.75	2.00	7.00	55.00
	1935	—	—	—	Proof	—
	1936	1.052	.75	2.00	7.00	55.00
	1936	—	—	—	Proof	—

KM#	Date	Mintage	Fine	VF	XF	Unc
9	1937	1.228	.75	2.00	6.00	35.00
	1937	—	—	—	Proof	300.00

Obv: KING moved behind head.

KM#	Date	Mintage	Fine	VF	XF	Unc
16	1939	.160	6.00	10.00	22.00	150.00
	1939	—	—	—	Proof	300.00
	1940	1.200	.75	2.00	7.00	50.00
	1940	—	—	—	Proof	—
	1941	.600	2.50	5.00	10.00	60.00
	1941	—	—	—	Proof	—
	1942	2.000	.50	1.50	6.50	35.00
	1942	—	—	—	Proof	—

1.4100 g, .500 SILVER, .0226 oz ASW

KM#	Date	Mintage	Fine	VF	XF	Unc
16a	1944	1.600	.50	1.50	10.00	65.00
	1945	.800	1.00	3.00	12.00	70.00
	1945	—	—	—	Proof	—
	1946	2.400	.50	1.50	7.00	40.00
	1946	—	—	—	Proof	—

COPPER-NICKEL

KM#	Date	Mintage	Fine	VF	XF	Unc
16b	1947	8.000	.40	.80	2.50	20.00
	1947	—	—	—	Proof	250.00

KM#	Date	Mintage	Fine	VF	XF	Unc
20	1948	2.000	.40	.80	3.50	30.00
	1948	—	—	—	Proof	—
	1949	4.000	.40	.80	3.00	25.00
	1949	—	—	—	Proof	250.00
	1951	5.600	.40	.80	2.50	20.00
	1951	—	—	—	Proof	—
	1952	4.800	.40	.80	2.50	30.00
	1952	—	—	—	Proof	250.00

6 PENCE

2.8300 g, .925 SILVER, .0841 oz ASW

KM#	Date	Mintage	Fine	VF	XF	Unc
2	1932	.544	2.00	3.50	10.00	60.00
	1932	—	—	—	Proof	75.00
	1934	.214	3.00	7.00	30.00	100.00
	1935	.380	2.00	6.00	30.00	100.00
	1935	—	—	—	Proof	—
	1936	.675	1.50	3.50	15.00	65.00
	1936	—	—	—	Proof	—

KM#	Date	Mintage	Fine	VF	XF	Unc
10	1937	.823	2.50	5.00	15.00	60.00
	1937	—	—	—	Proof	300.00

Obv: KING moved behind head.

KM#	Date	Mintage	Fine	VF	XF	Unc
17	1939	.200	3.00	7.00	45.00	200.00
	1939	—	—	—	Proof	450.00
	1940	.600	1.50	3.00	20.00	75.00
	1940	—	—	—	Proof	—
	1941	.300	2.00	4.00	15.00	65.00
	1941	—	—	—	Proof	—
	1942	1.200	1.00	2.00	7.50	55.00
	1942	—	—	—	Proof	200.00

2.8300 g, .500 SILVER, .0454 oz ASW

KM#	Date	Mintage	Fine	VF	XF	Unc
17a	1944	.800	1.25	2.50	15.00	90.00
	1945	.400	15.00	25.00	45.00	150.00
	1945	—	—	—	Proof	—
	1946	1.600	1.25	2.50	15.00	60.00
	1946	—	—	—	Proof	—

COPPER-NICKEL

KM#	Date	Mintage	Fine	VF	XF	Unc
17b	1947	5.000	.50	1.00	4.00	20.00
	1947	—	—	—	Proof	250.00

KM#	Date	Mintage	Fine	VF	XF	Unc
21	1948	1.000	.50	1.25	4.50	27.50
	1948	—	—	—	Proof	—
	1949	2.000	.50	1.00	3.50	30.00
	1949	—	—	—	Proof	350.00
	1950	2.000	.50	1.00	4.50	45.00
	1950	—	—	—	Proof	350.00
	1951	2.800	.50	1.00	2.50	22.50
	1951	—	—	—	Proof	—
	1952	1.200	.50	1.50	3.50	45.00
	1952	—	—	—	Proof	—

SHILLING

5.6600 g, .925 SILVER, .1683 oz ASW
Bird Sculpture

KM#	Date	Mintage	Fine	VF	XF	Unc
3	1932	.896	2.00	4.00	12.00	100.00
	1932	—	—	—	Proof	120.00
	1934	.333	4.00	8.00	35.00	175.00
	1935	.830	2.00	4.00	12.00	125.00
	1935	—	—	—	Proof	220.00
	1936	1.663	1.50	3.50	10.00	125.00
	1936	—	—	—	Proof	—

KM#	Date	Mintage	Fine	VF	XF	Unc
11	1937	1.700	2.00	4.00	12.00	90.00
	1937	—	—	—	Proof	300.00

Obv: KING moved behind head.

KM#	Date	Mintage	Fine	VF	XF	Unc
18	1939	.420	7.00	15.00	70.00	300.00
	1939	—	—	—	Proof	500.00
	1940	.750	5.50	12.00	50.00	175.00

KM#	Date	Mintage	Fine	VF	XF	Unc
18	1940	—	—	—	Proof	—
	1941	.800	6.50	12.00	45.00	150.00
	1941	—	—	—	Proof	—
	1942	2.100	2.00	4.00	15.00	55.00
	1942	—	—	—	Proof	—

5.6600 g, .500 SILVER, .0909 oz ASW

KM#	Date	Mintage	Fine	VF	XF	Unc
18a	1944	1.600	2.00	4.00	12.50	80.00
	1946	1.700	3.50	8.00	50.00	120.00
	1946	—	—	—	Proof	—

COPPER-NICKEL

KM#	Date	Mintage	Fine	VF	XF	Unc
18b	1947	8.000	.75	1.50	4.50	40.00
	1947	—	—	—	Proof	300.00

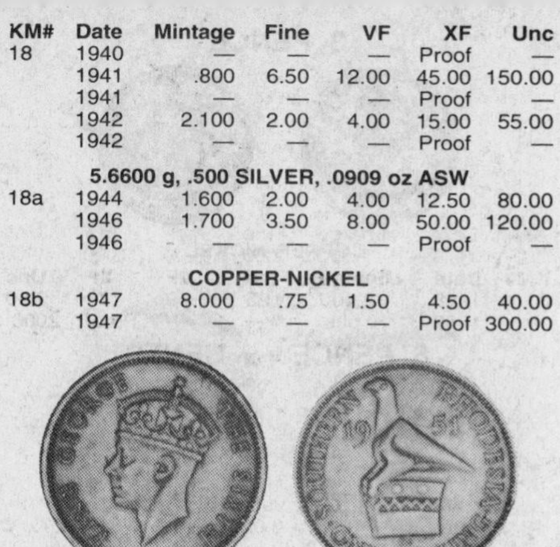

KM#	Date	Mintage	Fine	VF	XF	Unc
22	1948	1.500	.75	1.50	6.50	30.00
	1948	—	—	—	Proof	—
	1949	4.000	.75	1.25	4.50	35.00
	1949	—	—	—	Proof	300.00
	1950	2.000	1.00	3.00	10.00	55.00
	1950	—	—	—	Proof	225.00
	1951	3.000	.75	1.25	4.50	20.00
	1951	—	—	—	Proof	—
	1952	2.600	.75	1.50	4.50	55.00
	1952	—	—	—	Proof	—

2 SHILLINGS

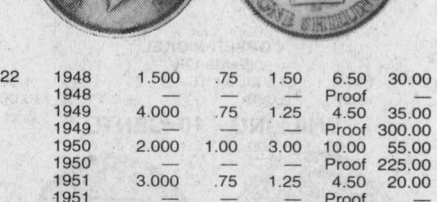

11.3100 g, .925 SILVER, .3363 oz ASW
Sable Antelope

KM#	Date	Mintage	Fine	VF	XF	Unc
4	1932	.498	4.00	10.00	30.00	110.00
	1932	—	—	—	Proof	125.00
	1934	.154	12.50	20.00	125.00	300.00
	1935	.365	5.00	10.00	40.00	125.00
	1935	—	—	—	Proof	—
	1936	.683	5.00	10.00	40.00	125.00
	1936	—	—	—	Proof	—

KM#	Date	Mintage	Fine	VF	XF	Unc
12	1937	.552	7.50	12.50	25.00	125.00
	1937	—	—	—	Proof	300.00

Obv: KING moved behind head.

KM#	Date	Mintage	Fine	VF	XF	Unc
19	1939	.120	35.00	75.00	250.00	450.00
	1939	—	—	—	Proof	650.00
	1940	.525	8.00	16.00	75.00	250.00
	1940	—	—	—	Proof	—
	1941	.400	8.00	16.00	100.00	300.00
	1941	—	—	—	Proof	—
	1942	.850	4.00	8.00	25.00	90.00

11.3100 g, .500 SILVER, .1818 oz ASW

KM#	Date	Mintage	Fine	VF	XF	Unc
19a	1944	1.300	6.00	12.00	35.00	135.00
	1946	.700	100.00	200.00	300.00	550.00
	1946	—	—	—	Proof	—

COPPER-NICKEL

KM#	Date	Mintage	Fine	VF	XF	Unc
19b	1947	3.750	1.75	4.00	12.50	55.00
	1947	—	—	—	Proof	300.00

KM#	Date	Mintage	Fine	VF	XF	Unc
23	1948	.750	1.00	3.00	10.00	40.00
	1948	—	—	—	Proof	—
	1949	2.000	1.00	3.00	10.00	50.00
	1949	—	—	—	Proof	350.00
	1950	1.000	1.00	4.00	15.00	75.00
	1950	—	—	—	Proof	350.00
	1951	2.600	1.00	3.00	6.00	27.50
	1951	—	—	—	Proof	—
	1952	1.800	1.00	3.00	10.00	75.00
	1952	—	—	—	Proof	—

KM#	Date	Mintage	Fine	VF	XF	Unc
30	1954	.300	30.00	75.00	225.00	850.00
	1954	20 pcs.	—	—	Proof	1750.

1/2 CROWN

14.1400 g, .925 SILVER, .4205 oz ASW

KM#	Date	Mintage	Fine	VF	XF	Unc
5	1932	.634	5.00	8.00	35.00	145.00
	1932	—	—	—	Proof	165.00
	1934	.419	6.00	10.00	45.00	250.00
	1934	—	—	—	Proof	—
	1935	.512	5.00	8.00	37.50	175.00
	1935	—	—	—	Proof	—
	1936	.518	5.00	8.00	37.50	175.00
	1936	—	—	—	Proof	—

KM#	Date	Mintage	Fine	VF	XF	Unc
13	1937	1.174	4.00	7.00	25.00	125.00
	1937	—	—	—	Proof	300.00

KM#	Date	Mintage	Fine	VF	XF	Unc
15	1938	.400	5.00	8.50	32.00	150.00
	1938	—	—	—	Proof	—
	1939	.224	10.00	20.00	65.00	300.00
	1939	—	—	—	Proof	600.00
	1940	.800	5.00	8.50	27.50	80.00
	1940	—	—	—	Proof	—
	1941	1.240	3.00	6.00	15.00	70.00
	1941	—	—	—	Proof	—
	1942	2.008	3.00	6.00	15.00	75.00
	1942	—	—	—	Proof	—

14.1400 g, .500 SILVER, .2273 oz ASW

KM#	Date	Mintage	Fine	VF	XF	Unc
15a	1944	.800	4.00	8.00	22.50	80.00
	1946	1.400	4.00	10.00	27.50	150.00
	1946	—	—	—	Proof	—

COPPER-NICKEL

KM#	Date	Mintage	Fine	VF	XF	Unc
15b	1947	6.000	1.00	2.00	4.00	18.00
	1947	—	—	—	Proof	400.00

KM#	Date	Mintage	Fine	VF	XF	Unc
24	1948	.800	1.00	2.00	10.00	50.00
	1948	—	—	—	Proof	—
	1949	1.600	1.00	2.00	8.00	50.00
	1949	—	—	—	Proof	600.00
	1950	1.200	1.00	2.00	10.00	75.00
	1950	—	—	—	Proof	550.00
	1951	3.200	1.00	2.00	6.00	25.00
	1951	—	—	—	Proof	500.00
	1952	2.800	1.00	2.00	6.00	75.00
	1952	—	—	—	Proof	500.00

KM#	Date	Mintage	Fine	VF	XF	Unc
31	1954	1.200	10.00	17.50	45.00	100.00
	1954	20 pcs.	—	—	Proof	1750.

CROWN

28.2800 g, .500 SILVER, .4546 oz ASW
Birth of Cecil Rhodes Centennial

KM#	Date	Mintage	Fine	VF	XF	Unc
27	1953	.124	4.00	6.00	9.00	15.00
	1953	1,500	—	—	Proof	120.00
	1953	—	—		Matte Proof	400.00

PROOF SETS (PS)

KM#	Date	Mintage	Identification	Issue Price	Mkt. Val.
PS1	1932(5)	496	KM1-5	—	550.00
PS2	1937(6)	40	KM8-13	—	2000.
PS3	1939(5)	10	KM15-19	—	2500.
PS6	1947(5)	10	KM15b-19b	—	1500.
PS4	1953(2)	3	KM27 double set	—	Rare
PS5	1954(4)	20	KM28-31	—	4500.

RHODESIA & NYASALAND

The Federation of Rhodesia and Nyasaland (or the Central African Federation), comprising the British protectorates of Northern Rhodesia and Nyasaland and the self-governing colony of Southern Rhodesia, was located in the east-central part of southern Africa. The multiracial federation had an area of about 487,000 sq. mi. (1,261,330 sq. km.) and a population of 6.8 million. Capital: Salisbury, in Southern Rhodesia.

The geographical unity of the three British possessions suggested the desirability of political and economic union as early as 1924. Despite objections by the African constituency of Northern Rhodesia and Nyasaland, who feared that African self-determination would be retarded by the dominant influence of prosperous and selfgoverning Southern Rhodesia, the Central African Federation was established in Sept. of 1953. As feared, the Federation was effectively and profitably dominated by the European constituency of Southern Rhodesia despite the fact that the three component countries largely retained their prefederation political structure. It was dissolved at the end of 1963, largely because of the effective opposition of the Nyasaland African Congress. Northern Rhodesia and Nyasaland became independent states in 1964. Southern Rhodesia unilaterally declared its independence the following year.

The coinage is obsolete.

For earlier coinage refer to Southern Rhodesia. For later coinage refer to Malawi, Zambia and Rhodesia.

RULERS

Elizabeth II, 1952-1964

MONETARY SYSTEM

12 Pence = 1 Shilling
5 Shillings = 1 Crown
20 Shillings = 1 Pound

1/2 PENNY

BRONZE
Giraffes

KM#	Date	Mintage	Fine	VF	XF	Unc
1	1955	.720	.15	.25	.50	2.50
	1955	2,010	—	—	Proof	5.00
	1956	.480	.20	.50	1.00	3.50
	1956	—	—	—	Proof	400.00
	1957	1.920	.10	.15	.25	2.50
	1957	—	—	—	Proof	400.00
	1958	2.400	.10	.15	.25	2.50
	1958	—	—	—	Proof	400.00
	1964	1.440	.10	.15	.25	1.00

PENNY

BRONZE
Elephants

KM#	Date	Mintage	Fine	VF	XF	Unc
2	1955	2.040	.15	.25	.75	3.50
	1955	2,010	—	—	Proof	5.00
	1956	4.800	.15	.25	.50	3.00
	1956	—	—	—	Proof	400.00
	1957	7.200	.10	.15	.25	2.50
	1957	—	—	—	Proof	—
	1958	2.880	.10	.15	.25	2.50
	1958	—	—	—	Proof	400.00
	1961	4.800	.10	.15	.25	1.50
	1961	—	—	—	Proof	—
	1962	6.000	.10	.15	.25	1.50
	1963	6.000	.10	.15	.25	1.50
	1963	—	—	—	Proof	400.00

3 PENCE

COPPER-NICKEL
Flame Lily

KM#	Date	Mintage	Fine	VF	XF	Unc
3	1955	1.200	.20	.50	1.00	4.00
	1955	10 pcs.	—	—	Proof	1200.
	1956	3.200	.50	1.00	2.50	20.00
	1956	—	—	—	Proof	600.00
	1957	6.000	.20	.50	.75	3.00
	1957	—	—	—	Proof	600.00
	1962	4.000	.20	.50	.75	3.00
	1962	—	—	—	Proof	—
	1963	2.000	.20	.50	.75	3.00
	1963	—	—	—	Proof	—
	1964	3.600	.15	.25	.50	1.50

1.4100 g, .500 SILVER, .0226 oz ASW

KM#	Date	Mintage	Fine	VF	XF	Unc
3a	1955	2,000	—	—	Proof	7.50

6 PENCE

COPPER-NICKEL
Lion

KM#	Date	Mintage	Fine	VF	XF	Unc
4	1955	.400	.50	1.00	2.50	7.50
4	1955	10 pcs.	—	—	Proof	1200.
	1956	.800	.75	2.00	7.00	40.00
	1956	—	—	—	Proof	—
	1957	4.000	.20	.50	1.00	3.00
	1957	—	—	—	Proof	—
	1962	2.800	.20	.50	1.00	2.50
	1962	—	—	—	Proof	—
	1963	.800	5.00	10.00	20.00	45.00
	1963	—	—	—	Proof	—

2.8300 g, .500 SILVER, .0454 oz ASW

KM#	Date	Mintage	Fine	VF	XF	Unc
4a	1955	2,000	—	—	Proof	10.00

SHILLING

COPPER-NICKEL
Antelope

KM#	Date	Mintage	Fine	VF	XF	Unc
5	1955	.200	1.50	2.50	6.50	15.00
	1955	10 pcs.	—	—	Proof	1200.
	1956	1.700	.75	1.50	3.50	30.00
	1956	—	—	—	Proof	—
	1957	3.500	.50	1.00	2.00	6.00
	1957	—	—	—	Proof	—

5.6600 g, .500 SILVER, .0909 oz ASW

KM#	Date	Mintage	Fine	VF	XF	Unc
5a	1955	2,000	—	—	Proof	12.50

2 SHILLINGS

COPPER-NICKEL
African Fish Eagle

KM#	Date	Mintage	Fine	VF	XF	Unc
6	1955	1.750	1.00	2.50	5.00	10.00
	1955	10 pcs.	—	—	Proof	1250.
	1956	1.850	1.00	2.50	4.00	10.00
	1956	—	—	—	Proof	—
	1957	1.500	1.00	2.50	4.00	10.00
	1957	—	—	—	Proof	—

11.3100 g, .500 SILVER, .1818 oz ASW

KM#	Date	Mintage	Fine	VF	XF	Unc
6a	1955	2,000	—	—	Proof	15.00

1/2 CROWN

COPPER-NICKEL

KM#	Date	Mintage	Fine	VF	XF	Unc
7	1955	1.600	1.00	2.50	4.00	12.50
	1955	10 pcs.	—	—	Proof	1350.
	1956	.160	7.50	15.00	35.00	250.00
	1956	—	—	—	Proof	—
	1957	2.400	7.50	15.00	35.00	100.00
	1957	—	—	—	Proof	—

14.1400 g, .500 SILVER, .2273 oz ASW

KM#	Date	Mintage	Fine	VF	XF	Unc
7a	1955	2,000	—	—	Proof	20.00

PROOF SETS (PS)

KM#	Date	Mintage	Identification	Issue Price	Mkt. Val.
PS1	1955(7)	10	KM1-7	—	6200.
PS2	1955(7)	2,000	KM1-2,3a-7a	—	75.00

RHODESIA

RULERS

British, until 1966

MONETARY SYSTEM

12 Pence = 1 Shilling = 10 Cents
10 Shillings = 1 Dollar
20 Shillings = 1 Pound

3 PENCE

COPPER-NICKEL

KM#	Date	Mintage	Fine	VF	XF	Unc
8	1968	2.400	.25	.50	.75	2.50
	1968	10 pcs.	—	—	Proof	2000.

6 PENCE = 5 CENTS

COPPER-NICKEL
Flame Lily

KM#	Date	Mintage	Fine	VF	XF	Unc
1	1964	13.500	.15	.25	.40	1.50
	1964	2,060	—	—	Proof	10.00

SHILLING = 10 CENTS

COPPER-NICKEL

KM#	Date	Mintage	Fine	VF	XF	Unc
2	1964	15.500	.15	.25	.75	1.75
	1964	2,060	—	—	Proof	10.00

2 SHILLINGS = 20 CENTS

COPPER-NICKEL
Bird Sculpture

KM#	Date	Mintage	Fine	VF	XF	Unc
3	1964	10.500	.25	.50	1.25	3.00
	1964	2,060	—	—	Proof	12.50

2-1/2 SHILLINGS = 25 CENTS

COPPER-NICKEL
Sable Antelope

KM#	Date	Mintage	Fine	VF	XF	Unc
4	1964	11.500	.50	.75	1.75	3.50
	1964	2,060	—	—	Proof	17.50

10 SHILLINGS

3.9940 g, .916 GOLD, .1177 oz AGW

KM#	Date	Mintage	Fine	VF	XF	Unc
5	1966	6,000	—	—	Proof	100.00

POUND

7.9881 g, .916 GOLD, .2354 oz AGW

KM#	Date	Mintage	Fine	VF	XF	Unc
6	1966	5,000	—	—	Proof	200.00

5 POUNDS

39.9403 g, .916 GOLD, 1.1772 oz AGW

KM#	Date	Mintage	Fine	VF	XF	Unc
7	1966	3,000	—	—	Proof	700.00

REPUBLIC

MONETARY SYSTEM

100 Cents = 1 Dollar

1/2 CENT

BRONZE

KM#	Date	Mintage	Fine	VF	XF	Unc
9	1970	10.000	—	.10	.20	.50
	1970	12 pcs.	—	—	Proof	1500.
	1971	2.000	—	.10	.25	1.00
	1972	2.000	—	.10	.25	1.00
	1972	12 pcs.	—	—	Proof	1500.
	1975	10.001	—	.10	.20	.50
	1975	10 pcs.	—	—	Proof	1500.
	1977	*—	—	—	800.00	1500.
	1977	10 pcs.	—	—	Proof	1500.

***NOTE:** Circulation mintage melted, less than 10 surviving specimens known.

CENT

BRONZE

KM#	Date	Mintage	Fine	VF	XF	Unc
10	1970	25.000	—	.10	.20	.50
	1970	12 pcs.	—	—	Proof	1500.
	1971	15.000	—	.10	.20	.50
	1972	10.000	—	.10	.20	.50
	1972	12 pcs.	—	—	Proof	1500.
	1973	5.000	—	.10	.20	.75
	1973	10 pcs.	—	—	Proof	1500.
	1974	—	—	.10	.20	.50
	1975	10.000	—	.10	.20	.50
	1975	10 pcs.	—	—	Proof	1500.
	1976	20.000	—	.10	.20	.50
	1976	10 pcs.	—	—	Proof	1500.
	1977	10.000	—	.10	.20	.50

2-1/2 CENTS

COPPER-NICKEL

KM#	Date	Mintage	Fine	VF	XF	Unc
11	1970	4.000	.15	.25	.40	1.00
	1970	12 pcs.	—	—	Proof	1500.

5 CENTS

COPPER-NICKEL

KM#	Date	Mintage	Fine	VF	XF	Unc
12	1973	—	.25	1.00	1.75	3.50
	1973	10 pcs.	—	—	Proof	1500.

KM#	Date	Mintage	Fine	VF	XF	Unc
13	1975	3.500	.15	.25	.40	.75
	1975	10 pcs.	—	—	Proof	1500.
	1976	8.038	.15	.25	.40	.75
	1977	3.015	.25	.75	1.50	3.00

10 CENTS

COPPER-NICKEL

KM#	Date	Mintage	Fine	VF	XF	Unc
14	1975	2.003	.15	.30	.60	1.50
	1975	10 pcs.	—	—	Proof	1500.

20 CENTS

COPPER-NICKEL

KM#	Date	Mintage	Fine	VF	XF	Unc
15	1975	1.937	.50	.75	1.00	3.00
	1975	10 pcs.	—	—	Proof	1650.
	1977	—	.75	1.00	1.75	4.00

25 CENTS

COPPER-NICKEL

KM#	Date	Mintage	Fine	VF	XF	Unc
16	1975	1.011	.50	1.00	1.75	4.00
	1975	10 pcs.	—	—	Proof	1750.

PROOF SETS (PS)

KM#	Date	Mintage	Identification	Issue Price	Mkt. Val.
PS1	1964(8)	10	KM1-4 double set	—	750.00
PS2	1964(4)	2,060	KM1-4	—	50.00
PS3	1966(3)	2,000	KM5-7	280.00	1000.
PS4	1968(2)	3	KM8 double set	—	4500.
PS5	1970(6)	3	KM9-11 double set	—	9000.
PS6	1973(2)	2	KM12 double set	—	3500.
PS7	1975(8)	1	KM13-16 double set	—	13,500.
PS8	1975(6)	4	KM9,10,13-16	—	10,000.
PS9	1975(4)	4	KM13-16	—	7000.

ZIMBABWE

MONETARY SYSTEM

100 Cents = 1 Dollar

CENT

BRONZE

KM#	Date	Mintage	VF	XF	Unc
1	1980	10.000	.10	.20	.40
	1980	.015	—	Proof	1.50
	1982	—	.10	.20	.40
	1983	—	.10	.20	.40
	1986	—	.10	.20	.40
	1988	—	.10	.20	.40

BRONZE PLATED STEEL

KM#	Date	Mintage	VF	XF	Unc
1a	1989	—	.10	.20	.40
	1991	—	.10	.20	.40

5 CENTS

COPPER-NICKEL

KM#	Date	Mintage	VF	XF	Unc
2	1980	—	.15	.30	.60
	1980	.015	—	Proof	1.50
	1982	—	.15	.30	.60
	1983	—	.15	.30	.60
	1988	—	.15	.30	.60
	1989	—	.15	.30	.60
	1990	—	.15	.30	.60

10 CENTS

COPPER-NICKEL

KM#	Date	Mintage	VF	XF	Unc
3	1980	—	.15	.30	1.00
	1980	.015	—	Proof	2.00
	1983	—	.15	.30	1.00
	1987	—	.15	.30	1.00
	1989	—	.15	.30	1.00
	1991	—	.15	.30	1.00

20 CENTS

COPPER-NICKEL

KM#	Date	Mintage	VF	XF	Unc
4	1980	—	.25	.50	1.50
	1980	.015	—	Proof	2.50
	1983	—	.25	.50	1.50
	1987	—	.20	.40	1.25
	1988	—	.20	.40	1.25
	1989	—	.20	.40	1.25
	1990	—	.20	.40	1.25
	1991	—	.20	.40	1.25

50 CENTS

COPPER-NICKEL

KM#	Date	Mintage	VF	XF	Unc
5	1980	—	.60	1.25	2.25
	1980	.015	—	Proof	4.00
	1988	—	.40	1.00	1.75
	1989	—	.40	1.00	1.75
	1990	—	.40	1.00	1.75

DOLLAR

COPPER-NICKEL

KM#	Date	Mintage	VF	XF	Unc
6	1980	—	1.00	1.50	3.00
	1980	.015	—	Proof	6.50

PROOF SETS (PS)

KM#	Date	Mintage	Identification	Issue Price	Mkt. Val.
PS1	1980	15,000	KM1-6	29.00	18.00

HEJIRA DATE CONVERSION CHART

HEJIRA (Hijra, Hegira), the name of the Mohammedan era (A.H. = Anno Hegirae) dates back to the Christian year 622 when Mohammed "fled" from Mecca, escaping to Medina to avoid persecution from the Koreish tribesmen. Based on a lunar year the Mohammedan year is 11 days shorter.

* = Leap Year (Christian Calendar)

AH Hejira	AD Christian Date
1102	1690, October 5
1103	1691, September 24
1104	1692, September 12*
1105	1693, September 2
1106	1694, August 22
1107	1695, August 12
1108	1696, July 31*
1109	1697, July 20
1110	1698, July 10
1111	1699, June 29
1112	1700, June 18
1113	1701, June 8
1114	1702, May 28
1115	1703, May 17
1116	1704, May 6*
1117	1705, April 25
1118	1706, April 15
1119	1707, April 4
1120	1708, March 23*
1121	1709, March 18
1122	1710, March 2
1123	1711, February 19
1124	1712, February 9*
1125	1713, January 28
1126	1714, January 17
1127	1715, January 7
1128	1715, December 27
1129	1716, December 16*
1130	1717, December 5
1131	1718, November 24
1132	1719, November 14
1133	1720, November 2*
1134	1721, October 22
1135	1722, October 12
1136	1723, October 1
1137	1724, September 29*
1138	1725, September 9
1139	1726, August 29
1140	1727, August 19
1141	1728, August 7*
1142	1729, July 27
1143	1730, July 17
1144	1731, July 6
1145	1732, June 24*
1146	1733, June 14
1147	1734, June 3
1148	1735, May 24
1149	1736, May 12*
1150	1737, May 1
1151	1738, April 21
1152	1739, April 10
1153	1740, March 29*
1154	1741, March 19
1155	1742, March 8
1156	1743, February 25
1157	1744, February 15*
1158	1745, February 3
1159	1746, January 24
1160	1747, January 13
1161	1748, January 2
1162	1748, December 22*
1163	1749, December 11
1164	1750, November 30
1165	1751, November 20
1166	1752, November 8*
1167	1753, October 29
1168	1754, October 18
1169	1755, October 7
1170	1756, September 26*
1171	1757, September 15
1172	1758, September 4
1173	1759, August 25
1174	1760, August 13*
1175	1761, August 2
1176	1762, July 28
1177	1763, July 12
1178	1764, July 1*
1179	1765, June 20
1180	1766, June 9
1181	1767, May 30
1182	1768, May 18*
1183	1769, May 7
1184	1770, April 27
1185	1771, April 16
1186	1772, April 4*
1187	1773, March 25
1188	1774, March 14
1189	1775, March 4
1190	1776, February 21*
1191	1777, February 9
1192	1778, January 30
1193	1779, January 19
1194	1780, January 8*
1195	1780, December 28*
1196	1781, December 17
1197	1782, December 7
1198	1783, November 26
1199	1784, November 14*
1200	1785, November 4

AH Hejira	AD Christian Date
1201	1786, October 24
1202	1787, October 13
1203	1788, October 2*
1204	1789, September 21
1205	1790, September 10
1206	1791, August 31
1207	1792, August 19*
1208	1793, August 9
1209	1794, July 29
1210	1795, July 18
1211	1796, July 7*
1212	1797, June 26
1213	1798, June 15
1214	1799, June 5
1215	1800, May 25
1216	1801, May 14
1217	1802, May 4
1218	1803, April 23
1219	1804, April 12*
1220	1805, April 1
1221	1806, March 21
1222	1807, March 11
1223	1808, February 28*
1224	1809, February 16
1225	1810, February 6
1226	1811, January 26
1227	1812, January 16*
1228	1813, January 4
1229	1813, December 24
1230	1814, December 14
1231	1815, December 3
1232	1816, November 21*
1233	1817, November 11
1234	1818, October 31
1235	1819, October 20
1236	1820, October 9*
1237	1821, September 28
1238	1822, September 18
1239	1823, September 7
1240	1824, August 26*
1241	1825, August 16
1242	1826, August 5
1243	1827, July 25
1244	1828, July 14*
1245	1829, July 3
1246	1830, June 22
1247	1831, June 12
1248	1832, May 31*
1249	1833, May 21
1250	1834, May 10
1251	1835, April 29
1252	1836, April 18*
1253	1837, April 7
1254	1838, March 27
1255	1839, March 17
1256	1840, March 5*
1257	1841, February 23
1258	1842, February 12
1259	1843, February 1
1260	1844, January 22*
1261	1845, January 10
1262	1845, December 30
1263	1846, December 20
1264	1847, December 9
1265	1848, November 27*
1266	1849, November 17
1267	1850, November 6
1268	1851, October 27
1269	1852, October 15*
1270	1853, October 4
1271	1854, September 24
1272	1855, September 13
1273	1856, September 1*
1274	1857, August 22
1275	1858, August 11
1276	1859, July 31
1277	1860, July 20*
1278	1861, July 9
1279	1862, June 29
1280	1863, June 18
1281	1864, June 6*
1282	1865, May 27
1283	1866, May 16
1284	1867, May 5
1285	1868, April 24*
1286	1869, April 13
1287	1870, April 3
1288	1871, March 23
1289	1872, March 11*
1290	1873, March 1
1291	1874, February 18
1292	1875, February 7
1293	1876, January 28*
1294	1877, January 16
1295	1878, January 5
1296	1878, December 26
1297	1879, December 15
1298	1880, December 4*
1299	1881, November 23
1300	1882, November 12
1301	1883, November 2
1302	1884, October 21*
1303	1885, October 10
1304	1886, September 30
1305	1887, September 19
1306	1888, September 7*
1307	1889, August 28
1308	1890, August 17
1309	1891, August 7
1310	1892, July 26*

AH Hejira	AD Christian Date
1311	1893, July 15
1312	1894, July 5
1313	1895, June 24
1314	1896, June 12*
1315	1897, June 2
1316	1898, May 22
1317	1899, May 12
1318	1900, May 1
1319	1901, April 20
1320	1902, April 10
1321	1903, March 30
1322	1904, March 18*
1323	1905, March 8
1324	1906, February 25
1325	1907, February 14
1326	1908, February 4*
1327	1909, January 23
1328	1910, January 13
1329	1911, January 2
1330	1911, December 22
1331	1912, December 11*
1332	1913, November 30
1333	1914, November 19
1334	1915, November 9
1335	1916, October 28*
1336	1917, October 17
1337	1918, October 7
1338	1919, September 26
1339	1920, September 15*
1340	1921, September 4
1341	1922, August 24
1342	1923, August 14
1343	1924, August 2*
1344	1925, July 22
1345	1926, July 12
1346	1927, July 1
1347	1928, June 20*
1348	1929, June 9
1349	1930, May 29
1350	1931, May 19
1351	1932, May 7*
1352	1933, April 26
1353	1934, April 16
1354	1935, April 5
1355	1936, March 24*
1356	1937, March 14
1357	1938, March 3
1358	1939, February 21
1359	1940, February 10*
1360	1941, January 29
1361	1942, January 19
1362	1943, January 8
1363	1943, December 28
1364	1944, December 17*
1365	1945, December 6
1366	1946, November 25
1367	1947, November 15
1368	1948, November 3*
1369	1949, October 24
1370	1950, October 13
1371	1951, October 2
1372	1952, September 21*
1373	1953, September 10
1374	1954, August 30
1375	1955, August 20
1376	1956, August 8*
1377	1957, July 29
1378	1958, July 18
1379	1959, July 7
1380	1960, June 25*
1381	1961, June 14
1382	1962, June 4
1383	1963, May 25
1384	1964, May 13*
1385	1965, May 2
1386	1966, April 22
1387	1967, April 11
1388	1968, March 31*
1389	1969, March 20
1390	1970, March 9
1391	1971, February 27
1392	1972, February 16*
1393	1973, February 4
1394	1974, January 25
1395	1975, January 14
1396	1976, January 3*
1397	1976, December 23*
1398	1977, December 12
1399	1978, December 2
1400	1979, November 21
1401	1980, November 9*
1402	1981, October 30
1403	1982, October 19
1404	1983, October 8
1405	1984, September 27*
1406	1985, September 16
1407	1986, September 6
1408	1987, August 26
1409	1988, August 14*
1410	1989, August 3
1411	1990, July 24
1412	1991, July 13
1413	1992, July 2*
1414	1993, June 21
1415	1994, June 10
1416	1995, May 31
1417	1996, May 19*
1418	1997, May 9
1419	1998, April 28
1420	1999, April 17
1421	2000, April 6*